# BIOGRAPHY AND GENEALOGY MASTER INDEX 1993

## The Gale Biographical Index Series

Biography and Genealogy Master Index
Second Edition, Supplements and Annual Volumes
*(GBIS Number 1)*

Children's Authors and Illustrators
Fourth Edition
*(GBIS Number 2)*

Author Biographies Master Index
Third Edition
*(GBIS Number 3)*

Journalist Biographies Master Index
*(GBIS Number 4)*

Performing Arts Biography Master Index
Second Edition
*(GBIS Number 5)*

Writers for Young Adults: Biographies Master Index
Third Edition
*(GBIS Number 6)*

Historical Biographical Dictionaries Master Index
*(GBIS Number 7)*

Twentieth-Century Author Biographies Master Index
*(GBIS Number 8)*

Artist Biographies Master Index
*(GBIS Number 9)*

Business Biography Master Index
*(GBIS Number 10)*

Abridged Biography and Genealogy Master Index
*(GBIS Number 11)*

ISSN 0730-1316

Gale Biographical Index Series
Number 1

# BIOGRAPHY AND GENEALOGY MASTER INDEX 1993

**A consolidated index to more than 450,000 biographical sketches in over 95 current and retrospective biographical dictionaries**

Barbara McNeil, Editor

*Senior Editor:* Peter M. Gareffa
*Editor:* Barbara McNeil
*Associate Editors:* Miranda Herbert Ferrara, Karen D. Kaus, Paula K. Woolverton

*Systems and Programming Supervisor:* Theresa Rocklin

*Data Entry Supervisor:* Benita Spight
*Data Entry Group Leader:* Gwendolyn Tucker
*Data Entry Associates:* Nancy S. Aiuto, Civie Ann Green, Arlene Kevonian

*Production Director:* Mary Beth Trimper
*Production Assistant:* Shanna Heilveil

*Art Director:* Cynthia Baldwin
*Keyliners:* C. J. Jonik, Nicholas Jakubiak



Library of Congress Catalog Number 82-15700
ISBN 0-8103-7605-9
ISSN 0730-1316

Printed in the United States of America

Published simultaneously in the United Kingdom
by Gale Research International Limited
(An affiliated company of Gale Research Inc.)

# Advisory Board
# For
# Biography and Genealogy Master Index

# Contents

# Introduction

*Biography and Genealogy Master Index 1993* is the twelfth in a series of annual updates to the *Biography and Genealogy Master Index (BGMI)* base volumes published in 1981. Containing more than 450,000 citations, *BGMI 1993* provides an index to 145 volumes and editions of over 95 biographical dictionaries, including new editions of sources previously indexed as well as new titles. With the publication of *BGMI 1993*, the total number of biographical sketches indexed by the *BGMI* base set and its twelve updates exceeds 8,832,000. The chart at the conclusion of this introduction provides further details on *BGMI* publications already available and those planned for the future.

## Concept and Scope

*BGMI* is a unique index that enables the user to determine which edition(s) of which publication to consult for biographical information. Almost as helpful, if there is no listing for a given individual in *BGMI* it reveals that there is no listing for that individual in any of the sources indexed. In cases where *BGMI* shows multiple listings for the same person, the user is able either to choose which source is the most convenient or to locate multiple sketches to compare and expand information furnished by a single listing.

Biographical sources indexed in *BGMI* are of several different types: 1) biographical dictionaries and who's whos, which supply information on a number of individuals; 2) subject encyclopedias, which include some biographical entries; 3) volumes of literary criticism, which may contain only a limited amount of biographical information but give critical surveys of a writer's works; and 4) indexes, which do not provide immediate information but refer the user to a body of information elsewhere. *BGMI* indexes only reference books containing multiple biographies; it does not index periodicals or books of biography about only one individual.

Sources indexed by *BGMI* cover both living and deceased persons from every field of activity and from all areas of the world. (Names from myth or legend and literary characters are not indexed.) The sources are predominantly current, readily available, "standard" reference books (for example, the Marquis Who's Who series); however, *BGMI* also includes important retrospective sources and general subject sources that cover both contemporary and noncontemporary people.

Although the majority of the sources indexed in *BGMI* covers individuals in the United States, this index also includes sources that cover individuals in foreign countries in such titles as *The Dictionary of National Biography* (Great Britain), *Dictionary of Canadian Biography*, and *Who's Who in the World*.

*BGMI 1993*, for example, indexes general works, both current and retrospective *(Current Biography Yearbook, Newsmakers)*. Also included are sources on special subject areas such as literature *(Benet's Reader's Encyclopedia of American Literature, Contemporary Authors, Contemporary Poets, The Writers Directory)*, law and politics *(The Almanac of American Politics, Who's Who in American Law, Who's Who in American Politics)*, entertainment *(International Motion Picture Almanac, Les Brown's Encylopedia of Television, Who's Who in Entertainment)*, religion *(Dictionary of the Ecumenical Movement, Religious Leaders in America, Who's Who in Religion)*, and art *(Dictionary of Design and Decoration, Twentieth Century Painters and Sculptors, World Artists)*. Other subject areas covered in *BGMI 1993* include business and finance, ethnic and special interest groups, history, music, psychology, sociology, and sports.

## How to Read a Citation

Each citation in *BGMI* gives the person's name followed by the years of birth and/or death as found in the source book. If a source has indicated that the dates may not be accurate, the questionable date(s) are followed by a question mark. If there is no year of birth, the death date is preceded by a lower case d. The codes for the books indexed follow the dates.

**Walsh**, William 1512?-1577 *DcNaB*

**Sokoine**, Edward d1984 *NewYTBS 84*

References to names that are identical in spelling and dates have been consolidated under a single name and date entry, as in the example below for *Bernard Goodwin*. When a name appears in more than one edition or volume of an indexed work, the title code for the book is given only once and is followed by the various codes for the editions in which the name appears.

**Goodwin**, Bernard 1907- *IntMPA 81, -82, -84, WhoAm 80, -82, -84, WhoWor 82*

Another feature of the *BGMI* updates is the portrait indicator. If the source has a portrait or photograph of the person, this is indicated by the abbreviation *[port]* after the source code.

**Daniel**, C William 1925- *WhoCan 84 [port]*

A list of the works indexed in *BGMI 1993*, and the codes used to refer to them, is printed on the endsheets. Complete bibliographic citations to the titles indexed follow this introduction.

## Editorial Practices

All names in an indexed work are included in *BGMI*. There is no need to consult the work itself if the name being researched is not found, since it is editorial policy to index every name in a particular book. Names that are not listed in the sources selected for indexing are not added to *BGMI*.

Many source books differ in their method of alphabetizing names; therefore, some names may have an alphabetic position in a source book different from their position in this index. Names are alphabetized in *BGMI* word-by-word, with the exception of prefixes (Del, Mc, Mac, O', Van, etc.) which are not treated as separate words.

**John**, Terry
**John-Sandy**, Rene Emanuel
**Johncock**, Gordon

**Delasa**, Jose M
**De las Heras**, Gonzalo
**Delavigne**, Casimir
**De La Warr**, Earl

Names appear in *BGMI* exactly as they are listed in the source books; no attempt has been made to determine whether names with similar spellings and dates refer to the same individual, or to add dates if they are known, but are not listed in the source. With a file consisting of millions of names, it is not possible to edit each name thoroughly and still publish on a timely basis. Therefore, several listings for the same individual may sometimes be found:

**Bellman**, Richard 1920- *ConAu 12NR*
**Bellman**, Richard 1920-1984 *ConAu 112*
**Bellman**, Richard E 1920- *WhoAm 84*
**Bellman**, Richard Ernest 1920- *WhoFrS 84*

Despite the variations in the form of the name, it is apparent that the same person is referred to in the above citations. The existence of such variations can be of importance to anyone attempting to determine biographical details about an individual.

In a very few cases, extremely long names have been shortened because of typesetting limitations. For example: Robertson, Alexander Thomas Parke Anthony Cecil would be shortened to:

**Robertson**, Alexander Thomas Parke A

It is believed that such editing will not affect the usefulness of individual entries.

## Research Aids

Researchers will need to look under all possible listings for a name, especially in the cases of:

1. Names with prefixes or suffixes:

   **Angeles**, Victoria De Los
   **De Los Angeles**, Victoria
   **Los Angeles**, Victoria De

2. Compound surnames which may be entered in sources under either part of the surname:

   **Garcia Lorca**, Federico
   **Lorca**, Federico Garcia

   **Benary-Isbert**, Margot
   **Isbert**, Margot Benary-

3. Chinese names which may be entered in sources in direct or inverted order:

   **Chiang**, Kai-Shek
   **Kai-Shek**, Chiang

   Or which may be listed by the Pinyin spelling:

   **Hsiang**, Chung-Hua
   **Xiang**, Zhonghua

4. Names transliterated in the sources from non-Roman alphabets:

   **Amelko**, Nikolai Nikolayevich
   **Amelko**, Nikolay Nikolayevich
   **Amel'ko**, Nikolay Nikolayevich

5. Pseudonyms, noms de plume, and stage names:

   **Clemens**, Samuel Langhorne
   **Twain**, Mark

   **Crosby**, Bing
   **Crosby**, Harry Lillis

6. Names which may be entered in the sources both under the full name and either initials or part of the name:

   **Eliot**, T S
   **Eliot**, Thomas Stearns

   **Welles**, George Orson
   **Welles**, Orson

All cross-references appearing in indexed publications have been retained in *BGMI*, but in the form of regular citations, e.g., *Morris, Julian SEE West, Morris* would appear in *BGMI* as *Morris, Julian* followed by the source code. No additional cross-references have been added.

## Suggestions Are Welcome

Additional sources will be indexed in future publications as their availability and usefulness become known. The editor welcomes suggestions for additional works which could be indexed, or any other comments and suggestions.

Please see the chart on the next page for publication information on *BGMI* in its hard
on-line, and CD-ROM formats.

## *BGMI* Corresponding Formats

The data base used to create *BGMI* and its updates is also available in a microfiche edition called *Bio-Base*, on-line through DIALOG Information Services, Inc. as *Biography Master Index (BMI)*, and on CD-ROM as *BGMI CD-ROM*. The chart below outlines the relationships, in existing and future publications, between the *BGMI* hardcover annual updates and cumulations, and the microfiche, on-line, and CD-ROM formats.

| YEAR OF PUBLICATION | HARDCOVER | | MICROFICHE | ELECTRONIC |
|---|---|---|---|---|
| 1980-81 | Biography and Genealogy Master Index, 2nd ed. | | Bio-Base, 2nd ed. (Superseded by 1984 Master Cumulation) | |
| 1982 | BGMI 1981-82 Supplement | | | |
| 1983 | BGMI 1983 Supplement | | Bio-Base 1983 Supplement (Superseded by 1984 Master Cumulation) | |
| 1984 | BGMI 1984 Supplement | | Bio-Base 1984 Master Cumulation | <u>ON-LINE</u><br>Entire data base is in DIALOG BMI File 287 (updated annually) |
| 1985 | BGMI 1985 | BGMI 1981-85 Cumulation | Bio-Base 1985 | |
| 1986 | BGMI 1986 | | Bio-Base 1985-86 | |
| 1987 | BGMI 1987 | | Bio-Base 1985-87 | |
| 1988 | BGMI 1988 | | Bio-Base 1985-88 | |
| 1989 | BGMI 1989 | | Bio-Base 1985-89 | |
| 1990 | BGMI 1990 | BGMI 1986-90 Cumulation | Bio-Base 1990 Master Cumulation (Supersedes all previous editions) | <u>CD-ROM</u><br>Entire data base is available as *BGMI CD-ROM* (updated annually) |
| 1991 | BGMI 1991 | | Bio-Base 1991 | |
| 1992 | BGMI 1992 | | Bio-Base 1991-92 | |
| 1993 | BG[illegible]3 | | Bio-Base 1991-93 | |
| 1994 | [illegible] | | Bio-Base 1991-94 | |
| 199[illegible] | [illegible] | BGMI 1991-95 Cumulation | Bio-Base 1995 Master Cumulation | |

# Bibliographic Key to Source Codes

| *Code* | *Book Indexed* |
|---|---|
| ***AfrAmW*** | *African American Writers.* Edited by Valerie Smith, Lea Baechler, and A. Walton Litz. New York: Charles Scribner's Sons, 1991. |
| ***AlmAP 92*** | *The Almanac of American Politics 1992.* The senators, the representatives and the governors: their records and election results, their states and districts. By Michael Barone and Grant Ujifusa. Washington, D.C.: National Journal, 1991. Use the Index to locate biographies. |
| ***AmMWSc 92*** | *American Men & Women of Science.* A biographical directory of today's leaders in physical, biological and related sciences. 18th edition, 1992-1993. New Providence, N.J.: R.R. Bowker, 1992. |
| ***AmPeW*** | *American Peace Writers, Editors, and Periodicals: A Dictionary.* By Nancy L. Roberts. New York: Greenwood Press, 1991. |
| ***AmPolLe*** | *American Political Leaders: From Colonial Times to the Present.* By Steven G. O'Brien. Santa Barbara, Calif.: ABC-Clio, 1991. |
| ***AnObit 1990*** | *The Annual Obituary, 1990.* Edited by Deborah Andrews. Chicago: St. James Press, 1991. Use the "Alphabetical Index of Entrants" to locate biographies. |
| ***Au&Arts*** | *Authors & Artists for Young Adults.* Detroit: Gale Research, 1991-1992.<br>***Au&Arts 7*** Volume 7, 1991<br>***Au&Arts 8*** Volume 8, 1992 |
| ***BenetAL 91*** | *Benet's Reader's Encyclopedia of American Literature.* First edition. Edited by George Perkins, Barbara Perkins, and Phillip Leininger. New York: HarperCollins Publishers, 1991. |
| ***BibAL 8*** | *Bibliography of American Literature.* Volume 8: Charles Warren Stoddard to Susan Bogert Warner. Compiled by Jacob Blanck. Edited and completed by Michael Winship. New Haven, Conn.: Yale University Press, 1990. |
| ***BiDBrF 2*** | *The Biographical Dictionary of British Feminists.* Volume two: A Supplement, 1900-1945. By Olive Banks. New York: New York University Press, 1990. |

***BiDExR*** *Biographical Dictionary of the Extreme Right since 1890.* By Philip Rees. New York: Simon & Schuster, 1990.

***BiInAmS*** *Biographical Index to American Science.* The seventeenth century to 1920. Compiled by Clark A. Elliott. Bibliographies and Indexes in American History, no. 16. New York: Greenwood Press, 1990.

***BlkLC*** *Black Literature Criticism.* Excerpts from criticism of the most significant works of Black authors over the past 200 years. Three volumes. Detroit: Gale Research, 1992.

***BlkOlyM*** *Black Olympian Medalists.* By James A. Page. Englewood, Col.: Libraries Unlimited, 1991.

***BlkwCEP*** *The Blackwell Companion to the Enlightenment.* By John W. Yolton, Roy Porter, Pat Rodgers, and Barbara Maria Stafford. Cambridge, Mass.: Basil Blackwell, 1991.

***BlkwEAR*** *The Blackwell Encyclopedia of the American Revolution.* Edited by Jack P. Greene and J.R. Pole. Cambridge, Mass.: Basil Blackwell, 1991.

Biographies begin on page 695.

***ChILR*** *Children's Literature Review.* Excerpts from reviews, criticism, and commentary on books for children and young people. Detroit: Gale Research, 1991-1992.

| | |
|---|---|
| ***ChILR 24*** | Volume 24, 1991 |
| ***ChILR 25*** | Volume 25, 1991 |
| ***ChILR 26*** | Volume 26, 1992 |

***ClMLC*** *Classical and Medieval Literature Criticism.* Excerpts from criticism of the works of world authors from classical antiquity through the fourteenth century, from the first appraisals to current evaluations. Detroit: Gale Research, 1991-1992.

| | |
|---|---|
| ***ClMLC 7*** | Volume 7, 1991 |
| ***ClMLC 8*** | Volume 8, 1992 |

***CnDBLB*** *Concise Dictionary of British Literary Biography.* Detroit: Gale Research, 1991-1992.

| | |
|---|---|
| ***CnDBLB 1*** | Volume 1: *Writers of the Middle Ages and Renaissance before 1660,* 1992. |
| ***CnDBLB 2*** | Volume 2: *Writers of the Restoration and Eighteenth Century, 1660-1789,* 1992. |
| ***CnDBLB 3*** | Volume 3: *Writers of the Romantic Period, 1789-1832,* 1992. |
| ***CnDBLB 4*** | Volume 4: *Victorian Writers, 1832-1890,* 1991. |
| ***CnDBLB 5*** | Volume 5: *Late Victorian and Edwardian Writers, 1890-1914,* 1991. |
| ***CnDBLB 6*** | Volume 6: *Modern Writers, 1914-1945,* 1991. |
| ***CnDBLB 7*** | Volume 7: *Writers after World War II, 1945-1960,* 1991. |
| ***CnDBLB 8*** | Volume 8: *Contemporary Writers, 1960 to the Present,* 1992. |

***ConAu*** *Contemporary Authors.* A bio-bibliographical guide to current writers in fiction, general nonfiction, poetry, journalism, drama, motion pictures, television, and other fields. Detroit: Gale Research, 1991-1992.

| | |
|---|---|
| ***ConAu 133*** | Volume 133, 1991 |
| ***ConAu 134*** | Volume 134, 1992 |
| ***ConAu 135*** | Volume 135, 1992 |

***ConAu AS*** *Contemporary Authors, Autobiography Series.* Detroit: Gale Research, 1991-1992.

| | |
|---|---|
| ***ConAu 14AS*** | Volume 14, 1991 |
| ***ConAu 15AS*** | Volume 15, 1992 |

***ConAu NR*** *Contemporary Authors, New Revision Series.* A bio-bibliographical guide to current writers in fiction, general nonfiction, poetry, journalism, drama, motion pictures, television, and other fields. Detroit: Gale Research, 1991-1992.

| | |
|---|---|
| ***ConAu 34NR*** | Volume 34, 1991 |
| ***ConAu 35NR*** | Volume 35, 1992 |
| ***ConAu 36NR*** | Volume 36, 1992 |

***ConBlB*** *Contemporary Black Biography: Profiles from the International Black Community.* Detroit: Gale Research, 1992.

| | |
|---|---|
| ***ConBlB 1*** | Volume 1, 1992 |
| ***ConBlB 2*** | Volume 2, 1992 |

***ConCom 92*** *Contemporary Composers.* Edited by Brian Morton and Pamela Collins. Chicago: St. James Press, 1992.

***ConLC*** *Contemporary Literary Criticism.* Excerpts from criticism of the works of today's novelists, poets, playwrights, short story writers, scriptwriters, and other creative writers. Detroit: Gale Research, 1991-1992.

| | |
|---|---|
| ***ConLC 65*** | Volume 65: Yearbook 1990; 1991 |
| ***ConLC 66*** | Volume 66, 1991 |
| ***ConLC 67*** | Volume 67, 1992 |
| ***ConLC 68*** | Volume 68, 1992 |
| ***ConLC 69*** | Volume 69, 1992 |

Use the "Cumulative Author Index" to locate entries in the Yearbook volume.

***ConMus*** *Contemporary Musicians: Profiles of the People in Music.* Detroit: Gale Research, 1992.

| | |
|---|---|
| ***ConMus 6*** | Volume 6, 1992 |
| ***ConMus 7*** | Volume 7, 1992 |

***ConNov 91*** *Contemporary Novelists.* Fifth edition. Edited by Lesley Henderson. Chicago: St. James Press, 1991.

***ConPo 91*** *Contemporary Poets.* Fifth edition. Edited by Tracy Chevalier. Chicago: St. James Press, 1991.

***ConSpAP*** *Contemporary Spanish American Poets: A Bibliography of Primary and Secondary Sources.* Compiled by Jacobo Sefami. Bibliographies and Indexes in World Literature, no. 33. New York: Greenwood Press, 1992.

***ConTFT 9*** *Contemporary Theatre, Film, and Television.* A biographical guide featuring performers, directors, writers, producers, designers, managers, choreographers, technicians, composers, executives, dancers, and critics in the United States and Great Britain. Volume 9. Detroit: Gale Research, 1992.

***CurBio 91*** *Current Biography Yearbook, 1991.* Edited by Charles Moritz. New York: H.W. Wilson Co., 1992.

The Obituaries section, indicated in this index by the code *N,* begins on page 629.

***DcAmImH*** *Dictionary of American Immigration History.* Edited by Francesco Cordasco. Metuchen, N.J.: Scarecrow Press, 1990.

***DcEcMov*** *Dictionary of the Ecumenical Movement.* Edited by Nicholas Lossky et al. Geneva: WCC Publications; Grand Rapids, Mich: William B. Eerdmans Publishing Co., 1991.

***DcLB*** *Dictionary of Literary Biography.* Detroit: Gale Research, 1991-1992.

***DcLB 106*** Volume 106: *British Literary Publishing Houses, 1820-1880.* Edited by Patricia J. Anderson and Jonathan Rose, 1991.

***DcLB 107*** Volume 107: *British Romantic Prose Writers, 1789-1832.* First Series. Edited by John R. Greenfield, 1991.

***DcLB 108*** Volume 108: *Twentieth-Century Spanish Poets.* First Series. Edited by Michael L. Perna, 1991.

***DcLB 109*** Volume 109: *Eighteenth-Century British Poets.* Second Series. Edited by John Sitter, 1991.

***DcLB 110*** Volume 110: *British Romantic Prose Writers, 1789-1832.* Second Series. Edited by John R. Greenfield, 1991.

***DcLB 111*** Volume 111: *American Literary Biographers.* Second Series. Edited by Steven Serafin, 1991.

***DcLB 112*** Volume 112: *British Literary Publishing Houses, 1881-1965.* Edited by Jonathan Rose and Patricia J. Anderson, 1991.

***DcLB 113*** Volume 113: *Modern Latin-American Fiction Writers.* First Series. Edited by William Luis, 1992.

***DcLB 114*** Volume 114: *Twentieth-Century Italian Poets.* First Series. Edited by Giovanna Wedel De Stasio, Glauco Cambon, and Antonio Illiano, 1992.

***DcLB 115*** Volume 115: *Medieval Philosophers.* Edited by Jeremiah Hackett, 1992.

***DcLB DS9*** *Dictionary of Literary Biography, Documentary Series: An Illustrated Chronicle.* Volume 9. Edited by Ronald Baughman. Detroit: Gale Research, 1991.

Use the "Cumulative Index" to locate entries.

***DcLB Y91*** *Dictionary of Literary Biography, Yearbook: 1991.* Edited by James W. Hipp. Detroit: Gale Research, 1992.

Use Table of Contents to locate entries. The Obituaries section, indicated in this index by the code *N,* begins on page 224.

***DcNCBi*** *Dictionary of North Carolina Biography.* Four volumes, A-O. Edited by William S. Powell. Chapel Hill, N.C.: University of North Carolina Press, 1979-1991.

***DcNCBi 1*** Volume 1, A-C, 1979.
***DcNCBi 2*** Volume 2, D-G, 1986.
***DcNCBi 3*** Volume 3, H-K, 1988.
***DcNCBi 4*** Volume 4, L-O, 1991.

***DcTwDes*** *Dictionary of Twentieth-Century Design.* By John Pile. New York: Facts on File, 1990.

***DrAPF 91*** *A Directory of American Poets and Fiction Writers.* 1991-1992 edition. New York: Poets & Writers, 1990.

***DramC*** *Drama Criticism.* Criticism of the most significant and widely studied dramatic works from all the world's literatures. Detroit: Gale Research, 1991-1992.

***DramC 1*** Volume 1, 1991
***DramC 2*** Volume 2, 1992

***EncAmaz 91*** *The Encyclopedia of Amazons.* Women warriors from antiquity to the modern era. First edition. By Jessica Amanda Salmonson. New York: Paragon House, 1991.

***EncEarC*** *Encyclopedia of Early Christianity.* Edited by Everett Ferguson. Garland reference library of the humanities, vol. 846. New York: Garland Publishing, 1990.

***EncTR 91*** *The Encyclopedia of the Third Reich.* Two volumes. Edited by Christian Zentner and Friedemann Bedurftig. Translation edited by Amy Hackett. New York: Macmillan Publishing Co., 1991.

***FacFETw*** *The Facts on File Encyclopedia of the Twentieth Century.* Edited by John Drexel New York: Facts on File, 1991.

***FrenWW*** *French Women Writers: A Bio-Bibliographical Source Book.* Edited by Eva Martin Sartori and Dorothy Wynne Zimmerman. New York: Greenwood Press, 1991.

***GuFrLit 1*** *Guide to French Literature: 1789 to the Present.* By Anthony Levi. Chicago: St. James Press, 1992.

***HanAmWH*** *Handbook of American Women's History.* Edited by Angela Howard Zophy. Garland Reference Library of the Humanities, vol. 696. New York: Garland Publishing, 1990.

***HisDSpE*** *Historical Dictionary of the Spanish Empire, 1402-1975.* Edited by James S. Olson et al. New York: Greenwood Press, 1992.

***IntAu&W 91*** *The International Authors and Writers Who's Who.* 12th edition, 1991-1992. Edited by Ernest Kay. Cambridge: International Biographical Centre, 1991.

The Pseudonyms of Authors Section, indicated in this index by the code *X*, begins on page 940.

***IntDcF 2-2*** *International Dictionary of Films and Filmmakers.* Second edition. Vol. 2. Edited by Nicholas Thomas. Chicago: St. James Press, 1991. Distributed by Gale Research, Detroit.

***IntMPA 92*** *International Motion Picture Almanac.* 1992 edition. Edited by Barry Monush. New York: Quigley Publishing Co, 1992.

Biographies are found in the "Who's Who in Motion Picture and Television" section. The listings are identical to those found in the *International Television Almanac.*

***IntWW 91*** *The International Who's Who.* 55th edition, 1991-1992. London: Europa Publications, 1991. Distributed by Gale Research, Detroit.

The Obituary section, indicated in this index by the code *N*, is located at the front of the volume.

***LesBEnT 92*** *Les Brown's Encyclopedia of Television.* Third edition. By Les Brown. Detroit: Gale Research, 1992.

***LiExTwC*** *Literary Exile in the Twentieth Century.* An analysis and biographical dictionary. Edited by Martin Tucker. New York: Greenwood Press, 1991.

Biographies begin on page 47.

***LitC*** *Literature Criticism from 1400 to 1800.* Excerpts from criticism of the works of fifteenth-, sixteenth-, seventeenth-, and eighteenth-century novelists, poets, playwrights, philosophers, and other creative writers, from the first published critical appraisals to current evaluations. Detroit: Gale Research, 1991-1992.

| | |
|---|---|
| ***LitC 16*** | Volume 16, 1991 |
| ***LitC 17*** | Volume 17, 1992 |
| ***LitC 18*** | Volume 18, 1992 |

***ModAWWr*** *Modern American Women Writers.* Edited by Elaine Showalter, Lea Baechler, and A. Walton Litz. New York: Charles Scribner's Sons, 1991.

***ModArCr 2*** *Modern Arts Criticism.* A biographical and critical guide to painters, sculptors, photographers, and architects from the beginning of the modern era to the present. Vol. 2. Detroit: Gale Research, 1992.

***NewAmDM*** *The New American Dictionary of Music.* By Philip D. Morehead with Anne MacNeil. New York: Dutton, 1991.

***NewYTBS 91*** *The New York Times Biographical Service, 1991.* A compilation of current biographical information of general interest. Volume 22, Numbers 1-12. Ann Arbor, Mich.: University Microfilms International, 1991.

Use the annual Index to locate biographies.

***News*** *Newsmakers: The People behind Today's Headlines.* Detroit: Gale Research, 1991-1992.

*News 91-3* — 1991, Issue 3; 1991
*News 91* — 1991 Cumulation; 1991
*News 92-1* — 1992, Issue 1; 1992
*News 92-2* — 1992, Issue 2; 1992

Use the "Cumulative Newsmaker Index" to locate entries in each quarterly edition. Biographies in each quarterly issue can also be located in the annual cumulation.

***NinCLC*** *Nineteenth-Century Literature Criticism.* Excerpts from criticism of the works of novelists, poets, playwrights, short story writers, philosophers, and other creative writers who died between 1800 and 1899, from the first published critical appraisals to current evaluations. Detroit: Gale Research, 1991-1992.

*NinCLC 31* — Volume 31, 1991
*NinCLC 33* — Volume 33, 1992
*NinCLC 34* — Volume 34, 1992

Volume 32 contains no biographies.

***NotBlAW 92*** *Notable Black American Women.* Edited by Jessie Carney Smith. Detroit: Gale Research, 1992.

***PoeCrit*** *Poetry Criticism.* Excerpts from criticism of the works of the most significant and widely studied poets of world literature. Detroit: Gale Research, 1991-1992.

*PoeCrit 3* — Volume 3, 1991
*PoeCrit 4* — Volume 4, 1992

***PorAmW*** *Portraits of American Women.* From settlement to the present. By G.J. Barker-Benfield and Catherine Clinton. New York: St. Martin's Press, 1991.

Use the Table of Contents to locate biographies.

***RComAH*** *The Reader's Companion to American History.* Edited by Eric Foner and John A. Garraty. Boston: Houghton Mifflin Co., 1991.

***ReelWom*** *Reel Women: Pioneers of the Cinema, 1896 to the Present.* By Ally Acker. New York: Continuum, 1991.

Use the Index to locate biographies.

***RfGEnL 91*** *Reference Guide to English Literature.* Second edition. Three volumes. Edited by D. L. Kirkpatrick. Chicago: St. James Press, 1991.

***RelLAm 91*** *Religious Leaders of America.* A biographical guide to founders and leaders of religious bodies, churches, and spiritual groups in North America. By J. Gordon Melton. Detroit: Gale Research, 1991.

***ScFEYrs*** *Science Fiction: The Early Years.* A full description of more than 3,000 science-fiction stories from earliest times to the appearance of the genre magazines in 1930. By Everett F. Bleiler. Kent, Ohio: Kent State University Press, 1990.

The first addenda, indicated in this index by the code *A,* begins on page 843. The second addenda, indicated in this index by the code *B,* begins on page 851.

***ShSCr*** *Short Story Criticism.* Excerpts from criticism of the works of short fiction writers. Detroit: Gale Research, 1991-1992.

***ShSCr 8*** Volume 8, 1991
***ShSCr 9*** Volume 9, 1992

***SmATA*** *Something about the Author.* Facts and pictures about authors and illustrators of books for young people. Detroit: Gale Research, 1991-1992.

***SmATA 65*** Volume 65, 1991
***SmATA 66*** Volume 66, 1991
***SmATA 67*** Volume 67, 1992
***SmATA 68*** Volume 68, 1992

***SmATA AS*** *Something about the Author, Autobiography Series.* Detroit: Gale Research, 1992.

***SmATA 13AS*** Volume 13, 1992
***SmATA 14AS*** Volume 14, 1992

***SourALJ*** *A Sourcebook of American Literary Journalism: Representative Writers in an Emerging Genre.* Edited by Thomas B. Connery. New York: Greenwood Press, 1992.

Use the Index to locate biographies.

***SovUnBD*** *The Soviet Union: A Biographical Dictionary.* Edited by Archie Brown. New York: Macmillan Publishing Co., 1990.

Appendix 5: New Politburo Members, indicated in this index by the code *A*, begins on page 488.

***SpAmWW*** *Spanish American Women Writers: A Bio-Bibliographical Source Book.* Edited by Diane E. Marting. New York: Greenwood Press, 1990.

***ThHEIm*** *The Thames and Hudson Encyclopaedia of Impressionism.* By Bernard Denvir. New York: Thames and Hudson, 1990.

***TwCLC*** *Twentieth-Century Literary Criticism.* Excerpts from criticism of the works of novelists, poets, playwrights, short story writers, and other creative writers who died between 1900 and 1960, from the first published critical appraisals to current evaluations. Detroit: Gale Research, 1991-1992.

***TwCLC 41*** Volume 41, 1991
***TwCLC 43*** Volume 43, 1992
***TwCLC 44*** Volume 44, 1992

Volume 42 contains entries on literary topics rather than on literary figures.

***TwCPaSc*** *Twentieth Century Painters and Sculptors.* By Frances Spalding. Dictionary of British Art, vol. 6. Suffolk, England: Antique Collectors' Club, 1990.

***TwCSFW*** *Twentieth-Century Science-Fiction Writers.* Third edition. Edited by Noelle Watson and Paul E. Schellinger. Twentieth-Century Writers Series. Chicago: St. James Press, 1991.

The "Foreign-Language Writers" section, indicated in this index by the code *A*, begins on page 913.

***TwCWW 91*** *Twentieth-Century Western Writers.* Second edition. Edited by Geoff Sadler. Twentieth-Century Writers Series. Chicago: St. James Press, 1991.

**Who 92** — *Who's Who, 1992.* An annual biographical dictionary. New York: St. Martin's Press, 1992.

| | |
|---|---|
| ***Who 92*** | Biographies |
| ***Who 92N*** | Obituary Section |
| ***Who 92R*** | "The Royal Family" section |

**WhoAmL 92** — *Who's Who in American Law.* Seventh edition, 1992-1993. Wilmette, Ill.: Marquis Who's Who, 1991.

**WhoAmP 91** — *Who's Who in American Politics, 1991-1992.* 13th edition. Two volumes. New Providence, N.J.: R.R. Bowker, 1991.

**WhoBlA 92** — *Who's Who among Black Americans, 1992/1993.* Seventh edition. Detroit: Gale Research, 1992.

The Obituaries section, indicated in this index by the code *N,* begins on page 1591.

**WhoEnt 92** — *Who's Who in Entertainment.* Second edition, 1992-1993. Wilmette, Ill.: Marquis Who's Who, 1992.

The Addendum, indicated in this index by code *A,* follows page 700.

**WhoFI 92** — *Who's Who in Finance and Industry.* 27th edition, 1992-1993. Wilmette, Ill.: Marquis Who's Who, 1991.

**WhoHisp 92** — *Who's Who among Hispanic Americans, 1992-1993.* Second edition. Detroit: Gale Research, 1992.

The Obituaries Section, indicated in this index by the code *N,* begins on page 743.

**WhoIns 92** — *Who's Who in Insurance, 1992.* Englewood, N.J.: Underwriter Printing and Publishing Co., 1992.

**WhoMW 92** — *Who's Who in the Midwest.* 23rd edition, 1992-1993. Wilmette, Ill.: Marquis Who's Who, 1992.

**WhoNob 90** — *The Who's Who of Nobel Prize Winners 1901-1990.* Second edition. Edited by Bernard S. Schlessinger and June H. Schlessinger. Phoenix, Ariz.: Oryx Press, 1991.

**WhoRel 92** — *Who's Who in Religion.* Fourth edition, 1992-1993. Wilmette, Ill.: Marquis Who's Who, 1992.

**WhoWest 92** — *Who's Who in the West.* 23rd edition, 1992-1993. Wilmette, Ill.: Marquis Who's Who, 1992.

**WomPsyc** — *Women in Psychology.* A bio-bibliographic sourcebook. Edited by Agnes N. O'Connell and Nancy Felipe Russo. New York: Greenwood Press, 1990.

**WomSoc** — *Women in Sociology.* A bio-bibliographical sourcebook. Edited by Mary Jo Deegan. New York: Greenwood Press, 1991.

***WorArt 1980*** *World Artists, 1980-1990.* An H.W. Wilson biographical dictionary. Edited by Claude Marks. New York: H.W. Wilson Co., 1991.

***WrDr 92*** *The Writers Directory 1992-1994.* Chicago: St. James Press, 1991. Distributed by Gale Research, Detroit.

# BIOGRAPHY AND GENEALOGY MASTER INDEX 1993

# A

**A B,** Orlando 1946- WhoHisp 92
**A. de Rosales,** Ramona WhoHisp 92
**Aaboe,** Asger 1922- AmMWSc 92
**Aadahl,** Jorg 1937- WhoFI 92, WhoWest 92
**Aadland,** Thomas Vernon 1950- WhoRel 92
**Aafedt,** Ole 1929- WhoAmP 91
**Aagaard,** George Nelson 1913- AmMWSc 92
**Aagaard,** James S 1930- AmMWSc 92
**Aagaard,** Knut 1939- AmMWSc 92
**Aagard,** Roger L 1931- AmMWSc 92
**Aagard,** Todd Allen 1961- WhoFI 92
**Aaker,** Thomas Nelson 1932- WhoEnt 92
**Aakvaag,** Torvild 1927- IntWW 91
**Aal,** Deborah Ruth Rosen 1948- WhoEnt 92
**Aal,** Katharyn Machan DrAPF 91
**Aalders,** Lewis Eldon 1933- AmMWSc 92
**Aalto,** Alvar 1898-1976 DcTwDes, FacFETw
**Aalund,** Ole 1930- AmMWSc 92
**Aames,** Willie 1960- IntMPA 92
**Aamodt,** Gary WhoAmP 91
**Aamodt,** Richard E 1936- AmMWSc 92
**Aamodt,** Roger Louis 1941- AmMWSc 92
**Aanenson,** Eric Evan 1944- WhoMW 92
**Aanerud,** Melvin Bernard 1943- WhoMW 92
**Aanestad,** Jonathan Robert 1954- WhoMW 92
**Aaraas,** Hans Tandberg 1919- IntWW 91
**Aardema,** Verna 1911- SmATA 68 [port], WrDr 92
**Aardema,** Verna Geneva 1911- IntAu&W 91
**Aarnes,** Asbjorn Sigurd 1923- IntWW 91
**Aarnio,** Eero 1932- DcTwDes, FacFETw
**Aaron,** Allen Harold 1932- WhoAmL 92
**Aaron,** Andrew Lewis 1953- WhoAmL 92
**Aaron,** Arthur Myron 1957- WhoAmL 92
**Aaron,** Barbara Diane 1957- WhoAmL 92
**Aaron,** Benjamin 1915- WhoAmL 92
**Aaron,** Bertram Donald 1922- WhoFI 92
**Aaron,** Betty WhoAmP 91
**Aaron,** Bud 1927- WhoWest 92
**Aaron,** Charles Sidney 1943- AmMWSc 92
**Aaron,** Chester 1923- WrDr 92
**Aaron,** David 1938- IntAu&W 91
**Aaron,** Frank W., Jr. 1942- WhoIns 92
**Aaron,** Henry J 1936- IntAu&W 91
**Aaron,** Henry Jacob 1936- WhoAmP 91, WhoFI 92
**Aaron,** Henry Louis 1934- FacFETw [port], WhoBlA 92
**Aaron,** Herbert Samuel 1929- AmMWSc 92
**Aaron,** Howard DrAPF 91
**Aaron,** Howard Berton 1939- AmMWSc 92
**Aaron,** James E. 1927- WrDr 92
**Aaron,** John A. d1972 LesBEnT 92
**Aaron,** Jonathan DrAPF 91
**Aaron,** Kenneth Ellyot 1948- WhoAmL 92
**Aaron,** M Robert 1922- AmMWSc 92
**Aaron,** Mark Lewis 1951- WhoFI 92
**Aaron,** Merik Roy 1947- WhoFI 92
**Aaron,** Michael 1959- WhoAmL 92
**Aaron,** Neal C. 1940- WhoIns 92
**Aaron,** Paul IntMPA 92, WhoEnt 92
**Aaron,** Ronald 1935- AmMWSc 92
**Aaron,** Roy H. 1929- IntMPA 92
**Aaron,** Roy Henry 1929- WhoWest 92
**Aaron,** Shirley Mae 1935- WhoWest 92
**Aaron,** Stephen WhoEnt 92
**Aaron,** Susan Sandra 1949- WhoFI 92
**Aaronoff,** Burton Robert 1935- AmMWSc 92
**Aaronovitch,** Sam 1919- WrDr 92
**Aarons,** Jules 1921- AmMWSc 92
**Aarons-Holder,** Charmaine Michele 1959- WhoAmL 92
**Aaronson,** Graham Raphael 1944- Who 92
**Aaronson,** Hubert Irving 1924- AmMWSc 92
**Aaronson,** Sheldon 1922- AmMWSc 92
**Aaronson,** Stuart Alan 1942- AmMWSc 92
**Aarrestad,** Ted Todd 1957- WhoEnt 92
**Aars,** Rallin James 1941- WhoFI 92
**Aarsvold,** Ole WhoAmP 91
**Aarvik,** Egil d1990 IntWW 91N
**Aarvold,** Carl Douglas d1991 Who 92N
**Aas,** Lynn W WhoAmP 91
**Aase,** Jan Kristian 1935- AmMWSc 92
**Aase,** Jon Morton 1936- WhoWest 92
**Aaseng,** Nate ConAu 36NR
**Aaseng,** Nathan 1953- ConAu 36NR
**Aaslestad,** Halvor Gunerius 1937- AmMWSc 92
**Aasved,** Craig Edward 1961- WhoWest 92
**Aba** EncAmaz 91
**Abad y Queipo,** Manuel 1751-1825 HisDSpE
**Abad y Sanchez,** Diego Jose 1727-1779 HisDSpE
**Abadi,** Djahanguir M 1929- AmMWSc 92
**Abadi,** Joseph 1938- WhoMW 92
**Abadie,** Robelynn Hood 1950- WhoFI 92
**Abadie,** Stanley Herbert 1925- AmMWSc 92
**Abadilla,** Joseph M. 1962- WhoEnt 92
**Abady,** Josephine Rose 1949- WhoEnt 92, WhoMW 92
**Abajian,** James deTarr 1914- WhoBlA 92
**Abajian,** Paul G 1941- AmMWSc 92
**Abajian,** Wendy Elisse 1955- WhoEnt 92
**Abakanowicz,** Magdalena 1930- IntWW 91
**Abalkhail,** Mohamed Ali 1935- IntWW 91
**Abalkin,** Leonid 1930- IntWW 91
**Abalkin,** Leonid Ivanovich 1930- SovUnBD
**Aballi,** Arturo Jose, Jr. 1944- WhoHisp 92
**Abalos,** Delma J. 1953- WhoHisp 92
**Abalos,** Robert Joseph 1960- WhoFI 92
**Abalos,** Ted Quinto 1930- WhoWest 92
**Abarbanel,** Henry D I 1943- AmMWSc 92
**Abarbanel,** Judith Edna 1956- WhoWest 92
**Abarbanel,** Sam X. 1914- IntMPA 92
**Abarbanel,** Stephen J. 1953- WhoAmL 92
**Abarca de Bolea,** Pedro Pablo HisDSpE
**Abare,** Marion Lavalette 1927- WhoMW 92
**Abarquez,** Josue Martinez 1938- WhoWest 92
**Abartis,** C. DrAPF 91
**Abasalo,** Mariano 1783-1816 HisDSpE
**Abascal,** Salvador 1910- BiDExR
**Abascal y Souza,** Jose Fernando 1748?-1821 HisDSpE
**Abashian,** Alexander 1930- AmMWSc 92
**Abashidze,** Grigor Grigorevich 1913- IntWW 91
**Abashidze,** Irakliy Vissarionovich 1909- IntWW 91
**Abasolo,** Santiago Domingo 1953- WhoFI 92
**Abata,** Russell James 1930- WhoRel 92
**Abate,** Catherine M 1947- WhoAmP 91
**Abate,** Ernest Nicholas 1943- WhoAmP 91
**Abate,** Frank J. 1928- WhoFI 92
**Abate,** Joseph Francis 1946- WhoAmP 91
**Abate,** Kenneth 1944- AmMWSc 92
**Abatemarco,** Michael J. 1947- WhoFI 92
**Abatie,** Rodger Paul 1951- WhoRel 92
**Abaunza,** Donald Richard 1945- WhoAmL 92
**Abaza,** Mohamed Maher O. 1930- IntWW 91
**Abazis,** Theodora Dimitrios 1950- WhoFI 92
**Abba** NewAmDM
**Abbado,** Claudio 1933- FacFETw, IntWW 91, NewAmDM, Who 92, WhoEnt 92
**Abbagnaro,** Louis Anthony 1942- WhoFI 92
**Abbas,** Ahmad 1914- ConNov 91, IntAu&W 91
**Abbas,** Daniel Cornelius 1947- AmMWSc 92
**Abbas,** Ferhat 1899-1985 FacFETw
**Abbas,** Khwaja Ahmad 1914- WrDr 92
**Abbas,** Mian Mohammad 1933- AmMWSc 92
**Abbas,** Sherkoh A. 1963- WhoMW 92
**Abbasabadi,** Alireza 1950- AmMWSc 92
**Abbaschian,** G J 1944- AmMWSc 92
**Abbasi,** Talat 1942- LiExTwC
**Abbasi,** Tariq Afzal 1946- WhoMW 92
**Abbate,** Carlos Alberto 1954- WhoEnt 92
**Abbate,** Fred John 1939- WhoFI 92
**Abbate,** Paul J 1919- WhoAmP 91
**Abbate,** Peter J, Jr 1949- WhoAmP 91
**Abbatiello,** Michael James 1921- AmMWSc 92
**Abbe,** Cleveland 1838-1916 BiInAmS
**Abbe,** Colman 1932- WhoFI 92
**Abbe,** Winfield Jonathan 1939- AmMWSc 92
**Abbensetts,** Michael 1938- IntAu&W 91, WrDr 92
**Abbey,** Chester Andrew 1928- WhoIns 92
**Abbey,** Edward 1927- IntAu&W 91
**Abbey,** Edward 1927-1989 BenetAL 91, TwCWW 91
**Abbey,** Edwin Austin 1852-1911 TwCPaSc
**Abbey,** George Marshall 1933- WhoAmL 92, WhoFI 92
**Abbey,** Helen 1920- AmMWSc 92
**Abbey,** Henry 1842-1911 BenetAL 91
**Abbey,** Joe Beverly 1935- WhoAmL 92
**Abbey,** John E. 1945- WhoEnt 92
**Abbey,** Kathleen Mary Kyburz 1950- AmMWSc 92
**Abbey,** Kirk J 1949- AmMWSc 92
**Abbey,** Merrill R. 1905- WrDr 92
**Abbey,** Merrill Ray 1905- WhoRel 92
**Abbey,** Paul Roger 1951- WhoMW 92
**Abbey,** Robert Fred, Jr 1947- AmMWSc 92
**Abbey,** W ScFEYrs
**Abbitt,** Jerry William 1947- WhoEnt 92
**Abbitt,** Watkins Moorman, Jr 1944- WhoAmP 91
**Abbot,** Edward Ambrose 1909- WhoFI 92
**Abbot,** Francis Ellingwood 1836-1903 RelLAm 91
**Abbot,** Henry 1740?-1791 DcNCBi 1
**Abbot,** Joel 1766-1826 BiInAmS
**Abbot,** John 1751-1840? BiInAmS
**Abbot,** Quincy Sewall 1932- WhoFI 92
**Abbot,** William Brimberry 1923- WhoRel 92
**Abbot,** Willis J. 1863-1934 BenetAL 91
**Abbot,** Willis John 1863-1934 AmPeW
**Abbott and Costello** FacFETw [port]
**Abbott,** Albert 1913- Who 92
**Abbott,** Alec B. 1956- WhoFI 92
**Abbott,** Alfreda Helen 1931- WhoAmP 91
**Abbott,** Alice WrDr 92
**Abbott,** Alvin Richard 1929- WhoRel 92
**Abbott,** Andrew Doyle 1913- AmMWSc 92
**Abbott,** Anthony Cecil 1923- Who 92
**Abbott,** Arthur Vaughan 1854-1906 BiInAmS
**Abbott,** Barbara S 1930- WhoAmP 91
**Abbott,** Barry A. 1950- WhoAmL 92
**Abbott,** Berenice 1898- DcTwDes, FacFETw, ModArCr 2 [port]
**Abbott,** Berenice 1898-1991 NewYTBS 91 [port]
**Abbott,** Bernard C 1920- AmMWSc 92
**Abbott,** Betty Jane 1931- AmMWSc 92
**Abbott,** Betty Lorraine 1923- WhoAmP 91
**Abbott,** Bryce Andrew 1958- WhoAmL 92
**Abbott,** Bud 1895-1974 FacFETw [port]
**Abbott,** Carl John 1944- WhoWest 92
**Abbott,** Charles Conrad 1843-1919 BiInAmS
**Abbott,** Charles Favour, Jr. 1937- WhoAmL 92, WhoFI 92, WhoWest 92
**Abbott,** Charlotte Tholen WhoEnt 92
**Abbott,** Craig Stephens 1941- WhoMW 92
**Abbott,** Cris Pye 1951- WhoFI 92
**Abbott,** Curtis Jeffrey, Jr. 1951- WhoAmL 92
**Abbott,** David Michael 1945- AmMWSc 92
**Abbott,** Dean William 1963- AmMWSc 92
**Abbott,** Diane Julie 1953- Who 92
**Abbott,** Donald Clayton 1923- AmMWSc 92
**Abbott,** Douglas E 1934- AmMWSc 92
**Abbott,** Dwayne Lamont 1959- WhoAmL 92
**Abbott,** Edith 1876-1957 DcAmImH, HanAmWH, WomSoc
**Abbott,** Edwin Abbott 1838-1926 ScFEYrs
**Abbott,** Edwin Hunt 1941- AmMWSc 92
**Abbott,** Eleanor Hallowell 1872-1958 BenetAL 91
**Abbott,** Emma 1850-1891 NewAmDM
**Abbott,** Frank Harry 1919- WhoAmL 92
**Abbott,** Gary Louis, Sr. 1947- WhoRel 92
**Abbott,** George 1887- BenetAL 91, IntAu&W 91, WhoEnt 92
**Abbott,** George Melvin 1959- WhoAmP 91
**Abbott,** Grace 1878-1939 AmPeW, DcAmImH, FacFETw, HanAmWH
**Abbott,** Greg Wayne 1957- WhoAmL 92
**Abbott,** Gregory WhoBlA 92
**Abbott,** Henry 1740?-1791 DcNCBi 1
**Abbott,** Herschel George 1921- AmMWSc 92
**Abbott,** Hirschel Theron, Jr. 1942- WhoAmL 92
**Abbott,** Isabella Aiona 1919- AmMWSc 92
**Abbott,** Jack Henry 1944- BenetAL 91
**Abbott,** Jacob 1803-1879 BenetAL 91
**Abbott,** James Alan 1928- Who 92

**Abbott,** James Ayre 1928- *WhoFI 92*
**Abbott,** James Edward 1959- *WhoAmL 92*
**Abbott,** James H 1924- *AmMWSc 92*
**Abbott,** James Samuel 1918- *WhoFI 92, WhoMW 92*
**Abbott,** James W *WhoAmP 91*
**Abbott,** Joan 1932- *AmMWSc 92*
**Abbott,** Joe Boone 1932- *WhoRel 92*
**Abbott,** John 1884-1956 *TwCPaSc*
**Abbott,** John 1948- *TwCPaSc*
**Abbott,** John B, Jr 1956- *IntAu&W 91*
**Abbott,** John D 1957- *WhoAmP 91*
**Abbott,** John David 1922- *WhoRel 92*
**Abbott,** John Patrick 1930- *WrDr 92*
**Abbott,** John Rodger 1933- *WhoWest 92*
**Abbott,** John S. 1805-1877 *BenetAL 91*
**Abbott,** John S 1952- *AmMWSc 92*
**Abbott,** John Sheldon 1926- *WhoAmL 92*
**Abbott,** Joseph Carter 1825-1881 *DcNCBi 1*
**Abbott,** Keith *DrAPF 91*
**Abbott,** Keith Eugene 1949- *WhoAmL 92*
**Abbott,** Kenneth Wayne 1944- *WhoAmL 92*
**Abbott,** Kevin Charles 1956- *WhoAmL 92*
**Abbott,** Laurence Frederick 1950- *AmMWSc 92*
**Abbott,** Lee K. *DrAPF 91*
**Abbott,** Loretta *WhoBlA 92*
**Abbott,** Lyman 1835-1922 *AmPeW, BenetAL 91, RelLAm 91*
**Abbott,** Lynn De Forrest, Jr 1913- *AmMWSc 92*
**Abbott,** Mabel Ernestine *ScFEYrs*
**Abbott,** Marlene Louise 1935- *WhoWest 92*
**Abbott,** Mary Elaine 1922- *WhoMW 92*
**Abbott,** Michael McFall 1938- *AmMWSc 92*
**Abbott,** Mitchel Theodore 1930- *AmMWSc 92*
**Abbott,** Morris Percy 1922- *Who 92*
**Abbott,** Norman John 1918- *AmMWSc 92*
**Abbott,** Pamela 1947- *ConAu 135*
**Abbott,** Patrick Leon 1940- *AmMWSc 92*
**Abbott,** Patti Marie 1942- *WhoWest 92*
**Abbott,** Peter Charles 1942- *Who 92*
**Abbott,** Philip *WhoEnt 92*
**Abbott,** R. Tucker 1919- *WrDr 92*
**Abbott,** Ralph Edwin 1940- *WhoFI 92*
**Abbott,** Richard Clark 1945- *WhoFI 92*
**Abbott,** Richard Newton, Jr 1949- *AmMWSc 92*
**Abbott,** Robert Carl 1955- *WhoWest 92*
**Abbott,** Robert Classie 1926- *AmMWSc 92*
**Abbott,** Robinson S, Jr 1926- *AmMWSc 92*
**Abbott,** Robinson Shewell 1926- *WhoMW 92*
**Abbott,** Roderick Evelyn 1938- *Who 92*
**Abbott,** Ronald William 1917- *Who 92*
**Abbott,** Rose Marie Savelkoul 1931- *AmMWSc 92*
**Abbott,** Russell J. 1942- *WhoWest 92*
**Abbott,** S L 1924- *WhoAmP 91*
**Abbott,** Samuel Warren 1837-1904 *BiInAmS*
**Abbott,** Seth R 1944- *AmMWSc 92*
**Abbott,** Stanley Evans 1939- *WhoEnt 92*
**Abbott,** Stephanie Lynn 1934- *WhoWest 92*
**Abbott,** Stephen *DrAPF 91*
**Abbott,** Stephen Dudley 1964- *AmMWSc 92*
**Abbott,** Steven Luse 1939- *WhoAmL 92*
**Abbott,** Thomas B 1921- *AmMWSc 92*
**Abbott,** Thomas Paul 1942- *AmMWSc 92, WhoMW 92*
**Abbott,** Ursula K 1927- *AmMWSc 92*
**Abbott,** William Ashton 1951- *AmMWSc 92*
**Abbott,** William H. *DrAPF 91*
**Abbott,** William Harold 1944- *AmMWSc 92*
**Abbott,** William M 1936- *AmMWSc 92*
**Abbott,** William Thomas 1938- *WhoFI 92*
**Abbott,** Wilton R 1916- *AmMWSc 92*
**Abbott,** Zane Allen, Jr. 1964- *WhoEnt 92*
**Abboud,** A. Robert 1929- *IntWW 91*
**Abboud,** Ann Creelman 1952- *WhoAmL 92*
**Abboud,** Christopher W 1956- *WhoAmP 91*
**Abboud,** Francois Mitry 1931- *AmMWSc 92*
**Abbrecht,** Peter H 1930- *AmMWSc 92*
**Abbruzzese,** Carlo Enrico 1923- *WhoWest 92*
**Abbruzzese,** Orlando Louis 1922- *WhoAmP 91*
**Abbundi,** Raymond Joseph 1949- *AmMWSc 92*
**Abd el-Krim** 1882-1963 *FacFETw*
**Abd,** Houshang S. 1950- *WhoWest 92*
**Abd Al-Wasi,** Abdul Wahhab Ahmad 1929- *IntWW 91*
**Abdali,** Syed Kamal 1940- *AmMWSc 92*
**Abdalla,** Sayed Abdel Rahman 1933- *IntWW 91*
**Abdallah,** Abdelwaheb 1940- *Who 92*
**Abdallah,** Abdulmuniem Husein 1929- *AmMWSc 92*
**Abdallah,** Ahmedou Ould 1940- *IntWW 91*
**Abdallah,** Bassam Joseph 1950- *WhoRel 92*
**Abdallah,** Mahmoud M. 1948- *WhoIns 92*
**Abdallah,** Michael Joseph 1952- *WhoIns 92*
**Abdeen,** Adnan Muhammad 1935- *WhoWest 92*
**Abdel Aziz Al-Sabilgi** 1911?- *WhoNob 90*
**Abdel-Baset,** Mahmoud B 1944- *AmMWSc 92*
**Abdel-Ghaffar,** Ahmed Mansour 1947- *AmMWSc 92*
**Abdel-Hady,** M A 1934- *AmMWSc 92*
**Abdel Halim Abu-Ghazala,** Mohamed 1930- *IntWW 91*
**Abdel-Khalik,** Said Ibrahim 1948- *AmMWSc 92*
**Abdel-Latif,** Ata A 1933- *AmMWSc 92*
**Abdel-Malek,** Anouar I. 1924- *IntWW 91*
**Abdel Meguid,** Abdel Razzaq 1931- *IntWW 91*
**Abdel Meguid,** Ahmed Esmat 1923- *IntWW 91*
**Abdel-Monem,** Mahmoud Mohamed 1938- *AmMWSc 92*
**Abdel-Rahman,** Aisha *IntWW 91*
**Abdel Wahab,** Mohamed Mahmoud F. 1932- *IntWW 91*
**Abdela,** Jack Samuel Ronald 1913- *Who 92*
**Abdellah,** Faye G *AmMWSc 92*
**Abdellah,** Faye Glenn *IntWW 91*
**Abdellaoui,** Aissa 1941- *IntWW 91*
**Abdelmalek,** Nabin N 1929- *AmMWSc 92*
**Abdelnoor,** Alexander Michael 1941- *AmMWSc 92*
**Abdelnour,** Ziad Khalil 1961- *WhoFI 92*
**Abdelrahman,** Talaat Ahmad Mohammad 1940- *WhoFI 92*
**Abdessalam,** Belaid 1928- *IntWW 91*
**Abdi,** Petrus Suhadi 1934- *WhoRel 92*
**Abdnor,** E James 1923- *WhoAmP 91*
**Abdnor,** James 1923- *IntWW 91*
**Abdo,** Nick 1950- *WhoEnt 92*
**Abdon,** Charles Cleveland 1952- *WhoEnt 92*
**Abdoo,** Frederick F. 1919- *WhoIns 92*
**Abdou,** Hamed M 1941- *AmMWSc 92, WhoFI 92*
**Abdou,** Nabih I 1934- *AmMWSc 92*
**Abdou-Sabet,** Sabet 1937- *WhoMW 92*
**Abdoun,** Amin Magzoub 1930- *IntWW 91*
**Abdrashitov,** Vadim 1945- *IntWW 91*
**Abdrashitov,** Vadim Yusupovich 1945- *SovUnBD*
**Abdul Hamid** 1842-1918 *FacFETw*
**Abdul Jamil Rais** 1912- *Who 92*
**Abdul Rahman Putra** d1990 *IntWW 91N*
**Abdul Rahman Putra,** Tunku d1990 *Who 92N*
**Abdul,** Corinna Gay 1961- *WhoWest 92*
**Abdul,** Paula *NewYTBS 91, WhoEnt 92*
**Abdul,** Paula 1962- *CurBio 91 [port]*
**Abdul,** Raoul 1929- *WhoBlA 92*
**Abdul Aziz,** Mahmood 1935- *Who 92*
**Abdu'l-Baha** 1844-1921 *RelLAm 91*
**Abdul-Ghani,** Abdulaziz 1939- *IntWW 91*
**Abdul-Hamid,** Ismail 1950- *WhoBlA 92*
**Abdul-Jabbar,** Kareem 1947- *FacFETw [port], WhoBlA 92, WhoWest 92*
**Abdul-Kabir,** Jamal 1941- *WhoBlA 92*
**Abdul Latif,** Java bin 1939- *IntWW 91*
**Abdul-Malik,** Ahmed H. 1927- *WhoBlA 92*
**Abdul-Malik,** Ibrahim *WhoBlA 92*
**Abdul-Rahman,** Tahira Sadiqa 1947- *WhoBlA 92*
**Abdulah,** Frank 1928- *IntWW 91*
**Abdulah,** Frank Owen 1928- *Who 92*
**Abdulai,** Yesufu Seyyid Momoh 1940- *IntWW 91*
**Abdulgani,** Roeslan 1914- *IntWW 91*
**Abdulla,** Riaz Fazal 1943- *AmMWSc 92*
**Abdulla Osman Daar,** Aden 1908- *IntWW 91*
**Abdullah Bin Ali** 1922- *IntWW 91, Who 92*
**Abdullah Bin Mohd Salleh** 1926- *IntWW 91*
**Abdullah Ibn Abdul Aziz,** Prince 1921- *IntWW 91*
**Abdullah ibn Hussein** 1882-1951 *FacFETw*
**Abdullah,** Al Munifi 1939- *IntWW 91*
**Abdullah,** Farooq 1937- *IntWW 91*
**Abdullah,** Larry Burley 1947- *WhoBlA 92*
**Abdullah,** Munir *AmMWSc 92*
**Abdullah,** Tariq Husam 1941- *WhoBlA 92*
**Abdullat,** Amjad 1960- *WhoWest 92*
**Abdulrahman,** Mustafa Salih 1930- *AmMWSc 92*
**Abdur-Razzaq,** Muhammad 1940- *WhoRel 92*
**Abdurazakov,** Bakhadyr Abbas 1927- *IntWW 91*
**Abdy,** Valentine 1937- *Who 92*
**Abe,** Benjamin Omara A. 1943- *WhoBlA 92*
**Abe,** Fumio *IntWW 91*
**Abe,** Gregory 1954- *WhoWest 92*
**Abe,** Isao 1914- *IntWW 91*
**Abe,** Kobo 1924- *FacFETw, IntWW 91, TwCSFW 91A*
**Abe,** Komi 1911- *ConCom 92*
**Abe,** Masao 1915- *WhoRel 92*
**Abe,** Ryo 1951- *AmMWSc 92*
**Abe,** Shintaro 1924- *IntWW 91*
**Abe,** Shintaro 1924-1991 *NewYTBS 91*
**a'Bear,** Howard *WrDr 92*
**Abebe,** Ruby 1949- *WhoBlA 92*
**Abebe,** Teshome 1949- *WhoBlA 92*
**Abec,** James Martin 1944- *WhoMW 92*
**Abed,** Eyad Husni 1959- *AmMWSc 92*
**Abedi,** Farrokh 1949- *AmMWSc 92*
**Abedin,** Zain-ul 1932- *AmMWSc 92*
**Abegg,** Carl F 1939- *AmMWSc 92*
**Abegg,** Carl Frank 1939- *WhoMW 92*
**Abegg,** Martin G. 1925- *WhoMW 92*
**Abegg,** Victor Paul 1945- *AmMWSc 92*
**Abejo,** Maria Rosalina 1922- *WhoRel 92, WhoWest 92*
**Abekawa,** Sumio 1947- *IntWW 91*
**Abel,** Alan Wilson 1939- *AmMWSc 92*
**Abel,** Arend Jesse 1960- *WhoAmL 92*
**Abel,** Brent Maxwell 1916- *WhoAmL 92*
**Abel,** Carl Friedrich 1723-1787 *NewAmDM*
**Abel,** Carlos Alberto 1930- *AmMWSc 92*
**Abel,** Charles Gerald 1920- *WhoFI 92*
**Abel,** Edward William 1931- *Who 92*
**Abel,** Elie *LesBEnT 92*
**Abel,** Elie 1920- *ConAu 36NR, WrDr 92*
**Abel,** Ernest Lawrence 1943- *AmMWSc 92, WhoMW 92*
**Abel,** Francis Lee 1931- *AmMWSc 92*
**Abel,** Gene Paul 1941- *WhoFI 92*
**Abel,** I W 1908-1987 *FacFETw*
**Abel,** Jacqueline S 1916- *WhoAmP 91*
**Abel,** James Wendell 1946- *WhoEnt 92*
**Abel,** John Fredrick 1940- *AmMWSc 92*
**Abel,** John H, Jr 1937- *AmMWSc 92*
**Abel,** John Jacob 1857-1938 *FacFETw*
**Abel,** Jonathan Stuart 1960- *WhoWest 92*
**Abel,** Kenneth Arthur 1926- *Who 92*
**Abel,** Larry Allen 1949- *AmMWSc 92*
**Abel,** Mark C 1950- *WhoAmP 91*
**Abel,** Mary *WhoAmP 91*
**Abel,** Paul Edward 1953- *WhoAmL 92*
**Abel,** Peter William 1949- *AmMWSc 92*
**Abel,** Renaul N. 1940- *WhoBlA 92*
**Abel,** Reuben 1911- *WrDr 92*
**Abel,** Richard Francis 1933- *WhoRel 92*
**Abel,** Richard Wayne 1941- *WhoWest 92*
**Abel,** Robert H. *DrAPF 91*
**Abel,** Robert Halsall 1941- *IntAu&W 91*
**Abel,** Wanda Jane 1958- *WhoAmL 92*
**Abel,** William T 1922- *AmMWSc 92*
**Abel,** Yves C. 1963- *WhoEnt 92*
**Abel Horowitz,** Michelle Susan 1950- *WhoMW 92*
**Abel-Smith,** Brian 1926- *Who 92, WrDr 92*
**Abel Smith,** Henriette Alice 1914- *Who 92*
**Abel Smith,** Henry 1900- *Who 92*
**Abela,** Wistin 1933- *IntWW 91*
**Abelard,** Peter 1079?-1142 *DcLB 115 [port], NewAmDM*
**Abele,** Lawrence Gordon 1946- *AmMWSc 92*
**Abele,** Robert Christopher 1958- *WhoAmL 92*
**Abeles,** Arthur 1914- *IntMPA 92*
**Abeles,** Benjamin 1925- *AmMWSc 92*
**Abeles,** Francine 1935- *AmMWSc 92*
**Abeles,** Jeanette 1933- *WhoEnt 92*
**Abeles,** Joseph Charles 1915- *WhoFI 92*
**Abeles,** Joseph Hy 1955- *AmMWSc 92*
**Abeles,** Kim Victoria 1952- *WhoWest 92*
**Abeles,** Peter 1924- *Who 92*
**Abeles,** Robert Heinz 1926- *AmMWSc 92*
**Abelev,** Garri Izrailevich 1928- *AmMWSc 92*
**Abelin,** Raymond Ferris 1955- *WhoEnt 92*
**Abeling,** Edwin John 1915- *AmMWSc 92*
**Abelite,** Jahnis John 1950- *WhoAmL 92*
**Abell,** Anthony 1906- *Who 92*
**Abell,** Charles 1910- *Who 92*
**Abell,** Creed Wills 1934- *AmMWSc 92*
**Abell,** David 1942- *Who 92*
**Abell,** George 1927-1983 *FacFETw*
**Abell,** James Logan 1951- *WhoWest 92*
**Abell,** Jared 1928- *AmMWSc 92*
**Abell,** John Norman 1931- *Who 92*
**Abell,** Kjeld 1901-1961 *FacFETw*
**Abell,** Lawrence Carlisle 1941- *WhoFI 92*
**Abell,** Liese Lewis 1909- *AmMWSc 92*
**Abell,** Murray Richardson 1920- *AmMWSc 92*
**Abell,** Paul Irving 1923- *AmMWSc 92*
**Abell,** Richard Bender 1943- *WhoAmL 92*
**Abell,** Roy 1931- *TwCPaSc*
**Abell,** William Shepherdson, Jr. 1943- *WhoAmL 92*
**Abella,** Alex 1950- *WhoHisp 92*
**Abella,** Isaac D 1934- *AmMWSc 92*
**Abella,** Marisela Carlota 1943- *WhoFI 92*
**Abella,** Olga 1958- *WhoHisp 92*
**Abelman,** Arthur Franklin 1933- *WhoAmL 92*
**Abelman,** Henry Moss 1953- *WhoAmL 92*
**Abelmann,** Walter H 1921- *AmMWSc 92*
**Abelov,** Stephen Lawrence 1923- *WhoFI 92, WhoMW 92*
**Abels,** Larry L 1937- *AmMWSc 92*
**Abels,** Robert Frederick 1926- *WhoWest 92*
**Abelson,** Alan 1925- *WhoFI 92*
**Abelson,** Elias 1932- *WhoAmL 92*
**Abelson,** John Norman 1938- *AmMWSc 92*
**Abelson,** Judith 1916- *IntAu&W 91*
**Abelson,** Lynn Alison 1959- *WhoWest 92*
**Abelson,** Philip Hauge 1913- *AmMWSc 92, FacFETw, IntWW 91*
**Abelson,** Raziel 1921- *WrDr 92*
**Abelson,** William Miles 1957- *WhoEnt 92*
**Abelt,** Ralph William 1929- *WhoFI 92*
**Abend,** Kenneth 1936- *AmMWSc 92*
**Abend,** Sheldon 1929- *IntMPA 92*
**Abendroth,** Reinhard P 1931- *AmMWSc 92*
**Abenes,** Fiorello Bigornia 1946- *AmMWSc 92*
**Aber,** Geoffrey Michael 1928- *Who 92*
**Aber,** James Sandusky 1952- *AmMWSc 92*
**Aber,** John Irwin 1951- *WhoMW 92*
**Aberbach,** David 1953- *ConAu 135, IntWW 91*
**Aberbach,** Joel David 1940- *WhoWest 92*
**Abercius** d200? *EncEarC*
**Aberconway,** Baron 1913- *IntWW 91, Who 92*
**Abercorn,** Duke of 1934- *Who 92*
**Abercrombie,** David 1909- *Who 92*
**Abercrombie,** Douglas 1934- *TwCPaSc*
**Abercrombie,** James 1707-1775 *DcNCBi 1*
**Abercrombie,** Lascalles 1881-1938 *FacFETw*
**Abercrombie,** Lascelles 1881-1938 *RfGEnL 91*
**Abercrombie,** Neil 1938- *AlmAP 92 [port], WhoAmP 91, WhoWest 92*
**Abercrombie,** Paul D *WhoAmP 91*
**Abercrombie,** Robert James 1898- *Who 92*
**Abercrombie,** Ronald Ford 1946- *AmMWSc 92*
**Abercrombie,** Virginia T. *DrAPF 91*
**Abercromby,** Ian George 1925- *Who 92*
**Abercromby,** James 1707-1775 *DcNCBi 1*
**Abercrumbie,** Paul Eric 1948- *WhoBlA 92*
**Aberdare,** Baron 1919- *Who 92*
**Aberdeen,** Bishop of 1934- *Who 92*
**Aberdeen,** Provost of *Who 92*
**Aberdeen And Orkney,** Bishop of 1927- *Who 92*
**Aberdeen And Orkney,** Dean of *Who 92*
**Aberdeen And Temair,** Marquess of 1920- *Who 92*
**Aberdeen And Temair,** J., Marchioness of *Who 92*
**Aberdour,** Lord 1952- *Who 92*
**Aberdour,** Master of 1986- *Who 92*
**Abere,** Andrew Evan 1961- *WhoFI 92*
**Abere,** Joseph Francis 1920- *AmMWSc 92, WhoMW 92*
**Abergavenny,** Marchioness of 1915- *Who 92*
**Abergavenny,** Marquess of 1914- *Who 92*
**Aberhart,** Donald John 1941- *AmMWSc 92*
**Aberhart,** William 1878-1943 *RelLAm 91*
**Aberkane,** Abdelhamid 1945- *IntWW 91*
**Aberle,** Elton D 1940- *AmMWSc 92*
**Aberle,** Sophie D 1899- *AmMWSc 92*
**Abernathy,** A Ray 1930- *AmMWSc 92*
**Abernathy,** Bobby F 1933- *AmMWSc 92*
**Abernathy,** Catherine Mary 1950- *WhoAmP 91*
**Abernathy,** Charles Owen 1941- *AmMWSc 92*
**Abernathy,** David Myles 1933- *WhoEnt 92*
**Abernathy,** Frederick Henry 1930- *AmMWSc 92*
**Abernathy,** George Henry 1929- *AmMWSc 92*
**Abernathy,** Harry Hoyle, Jr. 1925- *WhoAmL 92*
**Abernathy,** Henry Herman 1913- *AmMWSc 92*
**Abernathy,** James R., II *WhoBlA 92*
**Abernathy,** James Ralph 1926- *AmMWSc 92*
**Abernathy,** Lannie William 1964- *WhoEnt 92*
**Abernathy,** Nadine Coy 1949- *WhoMW 92*
**Abernathy,** Ralph 1926-1990 *AnObit 1990*
**Abernathy,** Ralph David *WhoAmP 91*
**Abernathy,** Ralph David 1926- *WhoRel 92*
**Abernathy,** Ralph David 1926-1990 *ConAu 133, ConBlB 1 [port], FacFETw, RelLAm 91, WhoBlA 92N*

**Abernathy**, Richard Paul 1932- *AmMWSc 92*
**Abernathy**, Robert O 1927- *AmMWSc 92*
**Abernathy**, Robert Shields 1923- *AmMWSc 92*
**Abernathy**, Ronald Lee 1950- *WhoBlA 92*
**Abernathy**, Wendy L. 1957- *WhoBlA 92*
**Abernethy**, Arthur Talmage 1872-1956 *DcNCBi 1*
**Abernethy**, Charles Laban 1872-1955 *DcNCBi 1*
**Abernethy**, David Ford 1958- *WhoAmL 92*
**Abernethy**, Donald Douglas 1931- *WhoAmP 91*
**Abernethy**, Jack Vernon 1945- *WhoAmP 91*
**Abernethy**, John Leo 1915- *AmMWSc 92*
**Abernethy**, Robert John 1940- *WhoWest 92*
**Abernethy**, Virginia Deane 1934- *AmMWSc 92*
**Abernethy**, William Leslie 1910- *Who 92*
**Abers**, Ernest S 1936- *AmMWSc 92*
**Abert**, John James 1788-1863 *BiInAmS*
**Abert**, Silvanus Thayer 1828-1903 *BiInAmS*
**Aberth**, Oliver George 1929- *AmMWSc 92*
**Aberth**, William H 1933- *AmMWSc 92*
**Abesamis**, Gil S. 1937- *WhoRel 92*
**Abeshouse**, Mark Alan 1956- *WhoFI 92*
**Abetti**, Pier Antonio 1921- *AmMWSc 92*
**Abety**, Modesto E. 1951- *WhoHisp 92*
**Abetz**, Otto 1903-1958 *BiDExR*, *EncTR 91 [port]*
**Abey**, Albert Edward 1935- *AmMWSc 92*
**Abeyta**, Frank *WhoHisp 92*
**Abeyta**, J. A., Jr. 1929- *WhoHisp 92*
**Abeyta**, Samuel James 1943- *WhoHisp 92*
**Abeyta**, Santiago Audoro Jim 1938- *WhoWest 92*
**Abgar** 179-216 *EncEarC*
**Abgar** V 9-46 *EncEarC*
**Abhari**, Bijan 1958- *WhoMW 92*
**Abhedananda**, Swami 1866-1939 *RelLAm 91*
**Abhyankar**, Shreeram 1930- *AmMWSc 92*
**Abhyankar**, Shreeram S. 1930- *WhoMW 92*
**Abi-Ali**, Ricky Salim 1940- *WhoFI 92*
**Abi-Nader**, Francis Joseph 1937- *WhoAmL 92*
**Abian**, Alexander 1925- *AmMWSc 92*
**Abiko**, Tokichi 1904- *IntWW 91*
**Abikoff**, William 1944- *AmMWSc 92*
**Abila**, Enedina Vejil 1939- *WhoHisp 92*
**Abildgaard**, Anette 1951- *WhoEnt 92*
**Abildgaard**, Charles Frederick 1930- *AmMWSc 92*, *WhoWest 92*
**Abildskov**, J A 1923- *AmMWSc 92*
**Abinader**, Elmaz *DrAPF 91*
**Abingdon**, Earl of *Who 92*
**Abinger**, Baron 1914- *Who 92*
**Abington**, James William 1933- *WhoRel 92*
**Abington**, Thomas d1707 *DcNCBi 1*
**Abirached**, Robert 1930- *IntWW 91*
**Abish**, Walter *DrAPF 91*
**Abish**, Walter 1931- *BenetAL 91*, *ConNov 91*, *LiExTwC*, *WrDr 92*
**Abisinito**, Kiatro Ottao *IntWW 91*
**Abitbol**, Carolyn Larkins 1946- *AmMWSc 92*
**Abkowitz**, Martin A 1918- *AmMWSc 92*
**Abkowitz**, Martin Arnold 1936- *AmMWSc 92*
**Abkowitz**, Stanley 1927- *AmMWSc 92*
**Ablad**, Bjorn Eric Bertil 1945- *WhoWest 92*
**Ablan**, Daniel Michael 1967- *WhoEnt 92*
**Ablard**, Charles David 1930- *WhoAmP 91*
**Able**, Kenneth Paul 1944- *AmMWSc 92*
**Able**, William F 1933- *WhoAmP 91*
**Ableman**, Paul 1927- *IntAu&W 91*, *WrDr 92*
**Abler**, David Gerard 1960- *WhoFI 92*
**Abler**, Ronald Francis 1939- *AmMWSc 92*
**Ables**, Charles Robert 1930- *WhoAmL 92*, *WhoAmP 91*
**Ables**, Ernest D 1934- *AmMWSc 92*
**Ables**, Harold Dwayne 1938- *AmMWSc 92*
**Ablete**, Thomas Robert d1945 *TwCPaSc*
**Ablin**, Joanne Marie 1931- *WhoAmP 91*
**Ablin**, Richard J 1940- *AmMWSc 92*
**Ablon**, Arnold Norman 1921- *WhoFI 92*
**Ablon**, Benjamin Manuel 1929- *WhoFI 92*
**Ablon**, Ralph E. 1916- *IntWW 91*
**Ablow**, Clarence Maurice 1919- *AmMWSc 92*
**Ablowitz**, Mark Jay 1945- *AmMWSc 92*
**Abney**, Armando J. 1953- *WhoHisp 92*
**Abney**, Joe L. 1941- *WhoAmL 92*
**Abney**, Richard John 1943- *WhoRel 92*
**Abney**, Robert 1949- *WhoBlA 92*
**Abney**, Thomas Scott 1938- *AmMWSc 92*
**Abney-Hastings** *Who 92*
**Aboff**, Sheldon Jay 1947- *WhoFI 92*
**Aboimov**, Ivan Pavlovich 1936- *IntWW 91*
**Abolhassni**, Mohsen 1947- *AmMWSc 92*
**Abolins**, Maris Arvids 1938- *AmMWSc 92*
**Abood**, Camille S. 1931- *WhoAmL 92*
**Abood**, Leo George 1922- *AmMWSc 92*
**Abood**, Mitchell E, Jr 1921- *WhoAmP 91*
**Abood**, Robert George 1961- *WhoAmL 92*
**Aborn**, Foster Litchfield 1934- *WhoFI 92*
**Abou-Donia**, Mohamed Bahie *AmMWSc 92*
**Abou-El-Seoud**, Mohamed Osman 1921- *AmMWSc 92*
**Abou-Gharbia**, Magid 1949- *AmMWSc 92*
**Abou-Khalil**, Samir 1943- *AmMWSc 92*
**Abou-Sabe**, Morad A 1937- *AmMWSc 92*
**Abou-Seeda**, Hassan A. H. 1930- *Who 92*
**Abouhalkah**, T A 1929- *AmMWSc 92*
**Aboul-Ela**, Mohamed Mohamed 1918- *AmMWSc 92*
**Abourezk**, James G 1931- *ConAu 135*, *IntWW 91*, *WhoAmP 91*
**Aboussie**, Marilyn 1948- *WhoAmL 92*
**About**, Edmond Francois Valentine 1828-1885 *ScFEYrs*
**Abouzeid**, George A. 1931- *WhoIns 92*
**Aboyade**, Ojetunji 1931- *Who 92*
**Aboyne**, Earl of 1973- *Who 92*
**Abplanalp**, Hans 1925- *AmMWSc 92*
**Abragam**, Anatole 1914- *IntWW 91*
**Abraham** *EncEarC [port]*
**Abraham**, Abram Kenneth 1951- *WhoRel 92*
**Abraham**, Albert David 1924- *WhoWest 92*
**Abraham**, Ann 1952- *Who 92*
**Abraham**, Bernard M 1918- *AmMWSc 92*
**Abraham**, Claude K. 1931- *ConAu 36NR*
**Abraham**, Claude Kurt 1931- *IntAu&W 91*, *WrDr 92*
**Abraham**, David 1955- *WhoFI 92*
**Abraham**, Donald Earl 1931- *WhoEnt 92*
**Abraham**, Donald James 1936- *AmMWSc 92*
**Abraham**, E Spencer 1952- *WhoAmP 91*
**Abraham**, Edathara Chacko *AmMWSc 92*
**Abraham**, Edward 1913- *Who 92*, *WrDr 92*
**Abraham**, Edward Penley 1913- *IntWW 91*
**Abraham**, F. Murray 1939- *CurBio 91 [port]*, *IntMPA 92*, *IntWW 91*, *WhoEnt 92*
**Abraham**, Farid Fadlow 1937- *AmMWSc 92*
**Abraham**, George 1918- *AmMWSc 92*
**Abraham**, George N *AmMWSc 92*
**Abraham**, Guy Emmanuel 1936- *WhoBlA 92*
**Abraham**, Henry J 1921- *IntAu&W 91*, *WrDr 92*
**Abraham**, Irene 1946- *AmMWSc 92*
**Abraham**, Jacob A 1948- *AmMWSc 92*
**Abraham**, James R *WhoAmP 91*
**Abraham**, Jerrold L 1944- *AmMWSc 92*
**Abraham**, John 1956- *AmMWSc 92*
**Abraham**, Katharine Gail 1954- *WhoFI 92*
**Abraham**, Kenneth Samuel 1946- *WhoAmL 92*
**Abraham**, L G, Jr 1926- *AmMWSc 92*
**Abraham**, Martin 1919- *Who 92*
**Abraham**, Marvin Meyer 1930- *AmMWSc 92*
**Abraham**, Mary Ann 1955- *WhoWest 92*
**Abraham**, Michael Lewis 1938- *WhoRel 92*
**Abraham**, Neal Broadus 1950- *AmMWSc 92*
**Abraham**, Nicholas Albert 1941- *WhoAmL 92*
**Abraham**, Phil 1959- *WhoEnt 92*
**Abraham**, Rajender 1932- *AmMWSc 92*
**Abraham**, Ralph Herman 1936- *AmMWSc 92*
**Abraham**, Reuben Israel 1951- *WhoRel 92*
**Abraham**, Richard Paul 1945- *WhoAmL 92*
**Abraham**, Robert Thomas 1952- *AmMWSc 92*
**Abraham**, Scott Jason 1965- *WhoEnt 92*
**Abraham**, Sinclair Reginald 1951- *WhoBlA 92*
**Abraham**, Spencer 1952- *News 91*
**Abraham**, Stephen Henry 1958- *WhoAmL 92*
**Abraham**, Victor Elias, Jr. 1935- *WhoHisp 92*
**Abraham**, W G 1921- *AmMWSc 92*
**Abraham**, Willard 1916- *WrDr 92*
**Abraham**, William H 1929- *AmMWSc 92*
**Abraham**, William Israel 1919- *WhoWest 92*
**Abraham**, William John, Jr. 1948- *WhoAmL 92*
**Abraham**, William Michael 1949- *AmMWSc 92*
**Abrahami**, Izzy *DrAPF 91*
**Abrahams**, Allan Rose 1908- *Who 92*
**Abrahams**, Andrew Wordsworth 1936- *WhoBlA 92*
**Abrahams**, Anthony Claud Walter 1923- *Who 92*
**Abrahams**, Athol Denis 1946- *AmMWSc 92*
**Abrahams**, Elihu 1927- *AmMWSc 92*
**Abrahams**, Frank *WhoEnt 92*
**Abrahams**, Gary *IntMPA 92*
**Abrahams**, Gerald Milton 1917- *Who 92*
**Abrahams**, Ivor 1935- *IntWW 91*, *TwCPaSc*, *Who 92*
**Abrahams**, Jim 1944- *IntMPA 92*
**Abrahams**, Johanna L 1913- *WhoAmP 91*
**Abrahams**, John Hambleton 1913- *WhoIns 92*
**Abrahams**, Joseph Isaac 1916- *WhoWest 92*
**Abrahams**, M S 1933- *AmMWSc 92*
**Abrahams**, Mort *IntMPA 92*, *LesBEnT 92*
**Abrahams**, Paul W 1935- *AmMWSc 92*
**Abrahams**, Peter 1919- *ConNov 91*, *FacFETw*, *IntAu&W 91*, *LiExTwC*, *RfGEnL 91*, *WrDr 92*
**Abrahams**, Roger D. 1933- *WrDr 92*
**Abrahams**, Roger David 1933- *IntAu&W 91*
**Abrahams**, Samuel 1923- *WhoAmL 92*
**Abrahams**, Sidney Cyril 1924- *AmMWSc 92*
**Abrahams**, Vivian Cecil 1927- *AmMWSc 92*
**Abrahams**, William *DrAPF 91*
**Abrahamsen**, Egil 1923- *Who 92*
**Abrahamsen**, Hans 1952- *ConCom 92*
**Abrahamsen**, Samuel 1917- *WhoRel 92*
**Abrahamson**, A. Craig 1954- *WhoAmL 92*
**Abrahamson**, Adolf Avraham 1920- *AmMWSc 92*
**Abrahamson**, Dale Raymond 1949- *AmMWSc 92*
**Abrahamson**, David 1947- *IntAu&W 91*
**Abrahamson**, Dean Edwin 1934- *AmMWSc 92*
**Abrahamson**, Earl Arthur 1924- *AmMWSc 92*
**Abrahamson**, Edwin William 1922- *AmMWSc 92*
**Abrahamson**, George R 1927- *AmMWSc 92*
**Abrahamson**, Harmon Bruce 1952- *AmMWSc 92*
**Abrahamson**, James A. 1933- *IntWW 91*
**Abrahamson**, Lark Anne 1952- *WhoWest 92*
**Abrahamson**, Lila 1927- *AmMWSc 92*
**Abrahamson**, Seymour 1927- *AmMWSc 92*
**Abrahamson**, Shirley Schlanger 1933- *WhoAmL 92*, *WhoAmP 91*, *WhoMW 92*
**Abrahamson**, Warren Gene, II 1947- *AmMWSc 92*
**Abrahamsson**, Bo Axel 1931- *IntWW 91*
**Abrahms**, Frederick Arthur 1931- *WhoMW 92*
**Abraira**, Carlos 1936- *AmMWSc 92*
**Abram**, James B. 1937- *WhoBlA 92*
**Abram**, James Baker, Jr 1937- *AmMWSc 92*
**Abram**, Marian Christine 1958- *WhoAmL 92*
**Abram**, Morris Berthold 1918- *WhoAmP 91*
**Abramoff**, Bonnie Marie 1960- *WhoAmL 92*
**Abramoff**, Peter 1927- *AmMWSc 92*
**Abramov**, Fedor Aleksandrovich 1920-1983 *SovUnBD*
**Abramov**, Fyodor Aleksandrovich 1920-1983 *ConAu 133*
**Abramov**, Grigoriy Grigoriyevich 1908- *IntWW 91*
**Abramov**, S. Zalman 1908- *ConAu 134*
**Abramovici**, Miron 1934- *AmMWSc 92*
**Abramovitch**, Rudolph Abraham Haim 1930- *AmMWSc 92*
**Abramovitz**, Max 1908- *IntWW 91*
**Abramovitz**, Michael John 1939- *WhoAmL 92*
**Abramovitz**, Moses 1912- *IntWW 91*
**Abramovsky**, Abraham 1946- *WhoAmL 92*
**Abramowicz**, Alfred L. 1919- *WhoMW 92*, *WhoRel 92*
**Abramowicz**, Daniel Albert 1957- *AmMWSc 92*
**Abramowitz**, Jerrold 1953- *WhoAmL 92*
**Abramowitz**, Jonathan 1947- *WhoEnt 92*
**Abramowitz**, Morton I 1933- *WhoAmP 91*
**Abramowitz**, Stanley 1936- *AmMWSc 92*
**Abrams**, Adolph 1919- *AmMWSc 92*
**Abrams**, Alan 1941- *WrDr 92*
**Abrams**, Albert 1921- *AmMWSc 92*
**Abrams**, Albert Maurice 1931- *AmMWSc 92*
**Abrams**, Arthur Jay 1934- *WhoRel 92*
**Abrams**, Burt Jay 1934- *WhoAmL 92*
**Abrams**, Cathi 1951- *WhoAmL 92*
**Abrams**, Charlie Frank, Jr 1944- *AmMWSc 92*
**Abrams**, Creighton Williams, Jr 1914-1974 *FacFETw*
**Abrams**, Dianne *IntMPA 92*
**Abrams**, Elliott *NewYTBS 91*
**Abrams**, Elliott 1948- *WhoAmP 91*
**Abrams**, Ellis 1917- *AmMWSc 92*
**Abrams**, Floyd *LesBEnT 92*
**Abrams**, Gerald David 1932- *AmMWSc 92*
**Abrams**, Gerald Stanley 1941- *AmMWSc 92*
**Abrams**, Harold Eugene 1933- *WhoAmL 92*
**Abrams**, Herbert L 1920- *AmMWSc 92*
**Abrams**, Herbert Leroy 1920- *IntWW 91*
**Abrams**, Holly *WhoAmP 91*
**Abrams**, Howard Charles 1954- *WhoWest 92*
**Abrams**, Hubert J 1925- *WhoAmP 91*
**Abrams**, Ira 1942- *WhoEnt 92*
**Abrams**, Irving M 1917- *AmMWSc 92*
**Abrams**, Israel Jacob 1926- *AmMWSc 92*
**Abrams**, James S., Jr. d1991 *NewYTBS 91*
**Abrams**, Jay Harrison 1948- *WhoFI 92*
**Abrams**, Jeanne Esther 1951- *WhoWest 92*
**Abrams**, Jerome Brian 1956- *WhoAmL 92*
**Abrams**, Joel Ivan 1928- *AmMWSc 92*
**Abrams**, Jonathan 1939- *AmMWSc 92*
**Abrams**, Karen 1960- *WhoAmL 92*
**Abrams**, Kenneth *WhoFI 92*
**Abrams**, Lee Norman 1935- *WhoAmL 92*
**Abrams**, Linsey *DrAPF 91*
**Abrams**, Linsey 1951- *IntAu&W 91*, *WrDr 92*
**Abrams**, Lloyd 1939- *AmMWSc 92*
**Abrams**, M. H. 1912- *WrDr 92*
**Abrams**, Mark 1906- *WrDr 92*
**Abrams**, Mark Alexander 1906- *Who 92*
**Abrams**, Marshall D 1940- *AmMWSc 92*
**Abrams**, Marvin Colin 1930- *AmMWSc 92*
**Abrams**, Michael Ellis 1932- *Who 92*
**Abrams**, Michael I 1947- *WhoAmP 91*
**Abrams**, Michael J 1948- *AmMWSc 92*
**Abrams**, Miriam Helen 1955- *WhoEnt 92*
**Abrams**, Muhal Richard 1930- *NewAmDM*
**Abrams**, Nancy 1954- *WhoAmL 92*
**Abrams**, Norman 1933- *WhoAmL 92*
**Abrams**, Philip 1939- *WhoAmP 91*
**Abrams**, Richard 1917- *AmMWSc 92*
**Abrams**, Richard Lee 1941- *AmMWSc 92*, *WhoWest 92*
**Abrams**, Richard M. 1932- *WrDr 92*
**Abrams**, Robert 1938- *WhoAmL 92*, *WhoAmP 91*
**Abrams**, Robert A 1939- *AmMWSc 92*
**Abrams**, Robert H. 1932- *WhoFI 92*
**Abrams**, Robert Jay 1938- *AmMWSc 92*
**Abrams**, Robert Marlow 1931- *AmMWSc 92*
**Abrams**, Roberta Busky 1937- *WhoFI 92*
**Abrams**, Roger Ian 1945- *WhoAmL 92*
**Abrams**, Ronald Bruce 1946- *WhoAmL 92*
**Abrams**, Ronald Lawrence 1952- *WhoAmP 91*
**Abrams**, Rosalie Silber *WhoAmP 91*
**Abrams**, Roslyn Maria 1948- *WhoBlA 92*
**Abrams**, Ruth I 1930- *WhoAmP 91*
**Abrams**, Ruth Ida 1930- *WhoAmL 92*
**Abrams**, Sam *DrAPF 91*
**Abrams**, Sol Bernard 1925- *WhoEnt 92*, *WhoFI 92*
**Abrams**, Stanley David 1940- *WhoAmL 92*
**Abrams**, Steve 1948- *WhoEnt 92*
**Abrams**, Steven Allen 1957- *AmMWSc 92*
**Abrams**, Steven Leon 1958- *WhoAmL 92*
**Abrams**, Suzanne Roberta 1947- *AmMWSc 92*
**Abrams**, Sylvia Fleck 1942- *WhoMW 92*, *WhoRel 92*
**Abrams**, William R 1945- *AmMWSc 92*
**Abramsky**, Jennifer 1946- *Who 92*
**Abramson**, Allan Lewis 1940- *AmMWSc 92*
**Abramson**, Ann 1925- *WhoAmP 91*
**Abramson**, Burton Ivan 1931- *WhoMW 92*
**Abramson**, Clarence Allen 1932- *WhoAmL 92*
**Abramson**, David C 1938- *AmMWSc 92*
**Abramson**, David Irvin 1905- *AmMWSc 92*
**Abramson**, Edward 1933- *AmMWSc 92*
**Abramson**, Edward E 1944- *AmMWSc 92*
**Abramson**, Elaine Sandra 1942- *WhoEnt 92*
**Abramson**, Frank 1947- *WhoAmL 92*
**Abramson**, Fred Paul 1941- *AmMWSc 92*
**Abramson**, Frederick Bruce 1935-1991 *WhoBlA 92N*
**Abramson**, Fredric David 1941- *AmMWSc 92*, *WhoAmL 92*
**Abramson**, H Norman 1926- *AmMWSc 92*
**Abramson**, Hanley N 1940- *AmMWSc 92*
**Abramson**, Harold Ira 1949- *WhoAmL 92*
**Abramson**, Herbert Francis 1930- *WhoMW 92*
**Abramson**, Herbert Wendell 1931- *WhoAmL 92*
**Abramson**, Honey 1927- *WhoMW 92*

**Abramson,** I Jerome 1935- *AmMWSc 92*
**Abramson,** Jerry Edwin 1946- *WhoAmP 91*
**Abramson,** Jon Stuart 1950- *AmMWSc 92*
**Abramson,** Jules 1936- *WhoEnt 92*
**Abramson,** Lee Richard 1933- *AmMWSc 92*
**Abramson,** Marc Laurence 1957- *WhoEnt 92*
**Abramson,** Mark Chad 1956- *WhoAmL 92*
**Abramson,** Mark Joseph 1949- *WhoWest 92*
**Abramson,** Martin 1919- *IntAu&W 91*
**Abramson,** Mason Harry 1916- *WhoWest 92*
**Abramson,** Michael A 1949- *WhoAmP 91*
**Abramson,** Morris Barnet 1910- *AmMWSc 92*
**Abramson,** N 1932- *AmMWSc 92*
**Abramson,** Neal *DrAPF 91*
**Abramson,** Norman Jay 1927- *AmMWSc 92*
**Abramson,** Paul Berrick 1939- *WhoAmL 92*
**Abramson,** Raymond Rue 1951- *WhoAmP 91*
**Abramson,** Robert M. *WhoEnt 92*
**Abramson,** Rochelle Susan 1953- *WhoEnt 92*
**Abramson,** Sidney 1921- *Who 92*
**Abramson,** Stanley L 1925- *AmMWSc 92*
**Abramson,** Stephan B 1945- *AmMWSc 92*
**Abramson,** Stephen Joseph 1949- *WhoEnt 92*
**Abrantes Fernandez,** Jose d1991 *NewYTBS 91*
**Abrash,** Henry I 1935- *AmMWSc 92*
**Abraszewski,** Andrzej 1938- *IntWW 91*
**Abravanel,** Allan Ray 1947- *WhoAmL 92, WhoWest 92*
**Abravanel,** Maurice 1903- *NewAmDM, WhoEnt 92*
**Abrecht,** Paul 1917- *DcEcMov*
**Abrell,** John William 1936- *AmMWSc 92*
**Abremski,** Kenneth Edward 1948- *AmMWSc 92*
**Abresch,** Donald Henry 1943- *WhoFI 92*
**Abreu,** John A. 1944- *WhoHisp 92*
**Abreu,** Jose Antonio 1939- *WhoEnt 92*
**Abreu,** Judith Ann *WhoEnt 92*
**Abreu,** Roberto Daniel 1937- *WhoHisp 92*
**Abreu,** Sergio Luis 1944- *AmMWSc 92*
**Abreu,** Zenaida *WhoHisp 92*
**Abrham,** Jaromir Vaclav 1931- *AmMWSc 92*
**Abrikosov,** Aleksey Alekseyevich 1928- *IntWW 91*
**Abril,** Jorge L. 1934- *WhoHisp 92*
**Abril,** Tony Rodriguez *WhoAmP 91*
**Abril Martoreli,** Fernando 1936- *IntWW 91*
**Abriola,** Linda Marie 1954- *AmMWSc 92*
**Abromson,** Irving Joel 1938- *WhoFI 92*
**Abromson-Leeman,** Sara R *AmMWSc 92*
**Abrons,** Richard S *DrAPF 91*
**Abrums,** John Denise 1923- *WhoWest 92*
**Abruna,** Hector D 1953- *AmMWSc 92*
**Abrunzo,** Victor Daniel, Jr. 1946- *WhoWest 92*
**Abrutyn,** Donald 1934- *AmMWSc 92*
**Abruzino,** Joseph Paul 1946- *WhoMW 92*
**Abruzzo,** John L 1931- *AmMWSc 92*
**Abs,** Hermann J. 1901- *IntWW 91*
**Abs,** Hermann Josef 1901- *EncTR 91 [port]*
**Absalom,** Roger Neil Lewis 1929- *WrDr 92*
**Abse,** Dannie *DrAPF 91*
**Abse,** Dannie 1923- *ConPo 91, IntAu&W 91, IntWW 91, Who 92, WrDr 92*
**Abse,** David Wilfred 1915- *AmMWSc 92*
**Abse,** Leo 1917- *Who 92*
**Absher,** Janet S. 1955- *WhoFI 92*
**Absher,** Thomas *DrAPF 91*
**Abshier,** Curtis Brent 1945- *AmMWSc 92*
**Abshire,** Brian Marshall 1954- *WhoRel 92*
**Abshire,** Claude James 1933- *AmMWSc 92*
**Abshire,** David Manker 1926- *IntAu&W 91, IntWW 91, WhoAmP 91, WrDr 92*
**Abshire,** Marc Eston 1960- *WhoWest 92*
**Absolon,** Karel B 1926- *AmMWSc 92*
**Abstein,** William Robert, II 1940- *WhoRel 92*
**Abston,** Nathaniel, Jr. 1952- *WhoBlA 92*
**Abt,** Evet Sue Loewen 1952- *WhoAmL 92*
**Abt,** Helmut Arthur 1925- *AmMWSc 92*
**Abt,** John J. 1904-1991 *NewYTBS 91 [port]*
**Abt,** Ralph Edwin 1960- *WhoAmL 92*
**Abt,** Richard Joel 1946- *WhoAmL 92*
**Abt,** Sylvia Hedy 1957- *WhoMW 92*
**Abu Nidal** 1937- *FacFETw*
**Abu Bakar,** Jamaluddin 1929- *Who 92*
**Abu Basha,** Hassan 1923- *IntWW 91*
**Abu-Ghazala,** Mohamed Abdel Halim *IntWW 91*
**Abu-Isa,** Ismat A. 1938- *WhoMW 92*
**Abu-Isa,** Ismat Ali 1938- *AmMWSc 92*
**Abu Mady,** Elias *DcAmImH*
**Abu-Shumays,** Ibrahim Khalil 1937- *AmMWSc 92*
**Abu Taleb,** Sufi Hassan 1925- *IntWW 91*
**Abuaf,** Niso 1951- *WhoFI 92*
**Abuba,** Ernest Hawkins 1947- *ConAu 133*
**Abubakar,** Iya 1934- *Who 92*
**Abudaber,** Mahmud Nuri 1953- *WhoEnt 92*
**Abugov,** Jeff 1959- *WhoEnt 92*
**Abuhoff,** Daniel Mark 1954- *WhoAmL 92*
**Abul-Haj,** Suleiman Kahil 1925- *WhoWest 92*
**Abul-Hajj,** Jusuf J 1940- *AmMWSc 92*
**Abul Nour,** Mohamed El Ahmadi 1932- *IntWW 91*
**Abuladze,** Tengiz 1933- *IntWW 91*
**Abuladze,** Tengiz Yevgen'evich 1924- *SovUnBD*
**Abulhassan,** Mohammad A. 1943- *IntWW 91*
**Abulizi,** Muhemaiti 1920- *IntWW 91*
**Aburdene,** Maurice Felix 1946- *AmMWSc 92*
**Aburdene,** Odeh Felix 1944- *WhoFI 92*
**Abushadi,** Mohamed Mahmoud 1913- *IntWW 91*
**Abushama,** Sayed El-Rashid Abushama Abdel 1937- *Who 92*
**Abushanab,** Elie 1936- *AmMWSc 92*
**Abuzzahab,** Faruk S, Sr 1932- *AmMWSc 92*
**Abzug,** Bella 1920- *FacFETw*
**Abzug,** Bella S 1920- *WhoAmP 91*
**Abzug,** Bella Savitsky 1920- *HanAmWH*
**Abzug,** Bella Savitzky 1920- *AmPolLe, IntWW 91*
**Abzug,** M J 1920- *AmMWSc 92*
**Abzug,** Robert Henry 1945- *WrDr 92*
**Acacius of Caesarea** d365 *EncEarC*
**Acacius of Constantinople** d489 *EncEarC*
**Acampora,** Ralph Joseph 1941- *WhoFI 92*
**Acara,** Margaret A 1934- *AmMWSc 92*
**Accardo,** Joseph, Jr 1938- *WhoAmP 91*
**Accardo,** Salvatore 1941- *IntWW 91, NewAmDM*
**Acciardo,** Gregory J 1957- *WhoAmP 91*
**Acciarri,** Jerry A 1932- *AmMWSc 92*
**Accinno,** Peter Clement 1950- *WhoFI 92*
**Acconci,** Vito 1940- *IntWW 91, WorArt 1980*
**Accordino,** Carmen Anthony 1929- *WhoAmL 92*
**Accordino,** Frank Joseph 1946- *WhoFI 92*
**Accornero,** Harry 1942- *WhoAmP 91*
**Accurso,** Catherine Josephine 1955- *WhoFI 92, WhoMW 92*
**Ace,** Goodman d1982 *LesBEnT 92*
**Ace,** Johnny 1929-1954 *NewAmDM*
**Acebo,** Alexander 1927- *WhoAmP 91*
**Acebo,** Kayla Kimberly 1965- *WhoMW 92*
**Acedo,** Gregoria N 1936- *AmMWSc 92*
**Acel,** Ervin 1935- *WhoEnt 92*
**Acerbo,** Giacomo 1888-1969 *BiDExR*
**Acerbo,** Samuel Nicholas 1929- *AmMWSc 92*
**Acerra,** Michele 1937- *WhoFI 92*
**Acerra,** Mike 1937- *WhoFI 92*
**Acers,** Maurice Wilson 1907- *WhoAmL 92*
**Aceto,** Mario Domenico 1930- *AmMWSc 92*
**Acevedo,** Eileen L. *WhoHisp 92*
**Acevedo,** Gary 1966- *WhoHisp 92*
**Acevedo,** George L. 1955- *WhoHisp 92*
**Acevedo,** Gerardo 1954- *WhoHisp 92*
**Acevedo,** Henry 1937- *WhoHisp 92*
**Acevedo,** Jorge Terrazas 1914- *WhoHisp 92*
**Acevedo,** Jose Enrique 1939- *WhoHisp 92*
**Acevedo,** Juan F. 1961- *WhoHisp 92*
**Acevedo,** Julio Eduardo 1931- *WhoHisp 92*
**Acevedo,** Luis 1947- *WhoAmP 91*
**Acevedo,** Martha Ophelia 1942- *WhoHisp 92*
**Acevedo,** Mary Ann 1943- *WhoHisp 92*
**Acevedo,** Nelson *WhoHisp 92*
**Acevedo,** Ralph Angel 1950- *WhoHisp 92*
**Acevedo-Vargas,** Luz Maria 1954- *WhoHisp 92*
**Acevedo y Torino,** Manuel Antonio 1770-1825 *HisDSpE*
**Aceves,** Jose *WhoHisp 92*
**Achampong,** Francis Kofi 1955- *WhoAmL 92*
**Achar,** B N Narahari 1939- *AmMWSc 92*
**Achari,** Raja Gopal 1943- *AmMWSc 92*
**Acharya,** Harsha 1944- *WhoIns 92*
**Acharya,** Seetharama A 1941- *AmMWSc 92*
**Achatz,** John 1948- *WhoAmL 92*
**Achbar,** Francine 1946- *WhoEnt 92*
**Achberger,** Charles William 1946- *WhoWest 92*
**Ache,** Hans Joachim 1931- *AmMWSc 92*
**Achebe,** Chinua 1930- *BlkLC [port], ConNov 91, ConPo 91, FacFETw, IntAu&W 91, IntWW 91, RfGEnL 91, Who 92, WrDr 92*
**Achen,** Dorothy Karen Thompson 1944- *WhoWest 92*
**Achenbach,** Jan Drewes 1935- *AmMWSc 92, WhoMW 92*
**Achenbaum,** Alvin Allen 1925- *WhoFI 92*
**Achenbaum,** W Andrew 1947- *ConAu 34NR*
**Acher,** Sylvain 1960- *WhoEnt 92*
**Acheson** *Who 92*
**Acheson,** Alice Brewen 1936- *WhoWest 92*
**Acheson,** Amy J. 1963- *WhoAmL 92*
**Acheson,** Anne 1882-1962 *TwCPaSc*
**Acheson,** Clint *WhoAmP 91*
**Acheson,** Dean 1893-1971 *FacFETw, RComAH*
**Acheson,** Dean Gooderham 1893-1971 *AmPolLe*
**Acheson,** Donald 1926- *Who 92*
**Acheson,** Donald Theodore 1935- *AmMWSc 92*
**Acheson,** Gilbert W. 1945- *WhoFI 92*
**Acheson,** James *WhoEnt 92*
**Acheson,** Louis Kruzan, Jr 1926- *AmMWSc 92*
**Acheson,** Roy Malcolm 1921- *Who 92*
**Acheson,** Willard Phillips 1927- *AmMWSc 92*
**Achey,** Frederick Augustus 1929- *AmMWSc 92*
**Achey,** Phillip M 1939- *AmMWSc 92*
**Achgill,** Ralph Kenneth 1938- *WhoMW 92*
**Achikzad,** Ghulam Faruq 1936- *WhoFI 92*
**Achille,** Jean-Claude 1926- *IntWW 91*
**Achilles,** Robert F 1924- *AmMWSc 92*
**Achillia and Amazon** *EncAmaz 91*
**Achkar,** Maria 1926- *WhoMW 92*
**Achmetov,** Nizametdin 1947- *LiExTwC*
**Achonry,** Bishop of 1931- *Who 92*
**Achor,** William Thomas 1929- *AmMWSc 92*
**Achorn,** Frank P 1923- *AmMWSc 92*
**Achour,** Habib 1913- *IntWW 91*
**Achram,** Denise Lynn 1954- *WhoFI 92*
**Achtel,** Robert Andrew 1941- *WhoWest 92*
**Achtenberg,** Anya *DrAPF 91*
**Achtenberg,** Benjamin Morris 1943- *WhoEnt 92*
**Achterberg,** Constance Margaret 1929- *WhoAmL 92*
**Achterman,** Janet Gibbs 1956- *WhoMW 92*
**Achugar,** Hugo J 1944- *IntAu&W 91*
**Acitelli,** Linda Katherine 1951- *WhoMW 92*
**Ackah,** Christian Abraham 1908- *WrDr 92*
**Ackal,** Elias, Jr 1934- *WhoAmP 91*
**Ackell,** Edmund Ferris 1925- *AmMWSc 92*
**Ackenhusen,** John Goodyear *AmMWSc 92*
**Acker,** Andrew French, III 1943- *AmMWSc 92*
**Acker,** Caren M.E. *DrAPF 91*
**Acker,** Charles Ernest 1868-1920 *BiInAmS*
**Acker,** Daniel R. 1910- *WhoBlA 92*
**Acker,** Duane *WhoAmP 91*
**Acker,** Duane Calvin 1931- *AmMWSc 92*
**Acker,** Frank Earl 1937- *AmMWSc 92*
**Acker,** Frederick George 1934- *WhoAmL 92*
**Acker,** Herbert William 1942- *WhoFI 92*
**Acker,** Iris Y. *WhoEnt 92*
**Acker,** Joan Elise 1924- *WhoWest 92*
**Acker,** Kathy 1948- *BenetAL 91, ConNov 91*
**Acker,** Lawrence Gene 1950- *WhoAmL 92*
**Acker,** Raymond Abijah 1932- *WhoRel 92*
**Acker,** Robert Harold 1928- *WhoAmP 91*
**Acker,** William Marsh, Jr. 1927- *WhoAmL 92, WhoAmP 91*
**Acker,** William Mitchell 1922- *WhoAmL 92*
**Ackerberg,** Robert C 1934- *AmMWSc 92*
**Ackeren,** Robert Van 1946- *IntWW 91*
**Ackerhalt,** Jay Richard 1947- *AmMWSc 92*
**Ackerknecht,** Lucy Kruger 1913- *WhoWest 92*
**Ackerley,** Barry *WhoEnt 92, WhoWest 92*
**Ackerlind,** E 1910- *AmMWSc 92*
**Ackerly,** Benjamin Clarkson 1942- *WhoAmL 92*
**Ackerman,** Anthony R. 1943- *WhoMW 92*
**Ackerman,** Bernice 1924- *AmMWSc 92*
**Ackerman,** Bettye 1928- *IntMPA 92*
**Ackerman,** Bruce Arnold 1943- *WhoAmL 92*
**Ackerman,** Bruce David 1934- *AmMWSc 92*
**Ackerman,** C D 1918- *AmMWSc 92*
**Ackerman,** David Paul 1949- *WhoAmL 92*
**Ackerman,** Diane *DrAPF 91*
**Ackerman,** Diane 1948- *IntAu&W 91, WrDr 92*
**Ackerman,** Elizabeth Davis 1940- *WhoRel 92*
**Ackerman,** Eric J 1954- *AmMWSc 92*
**Ackerman,** Eugene 1920- *AmMWSc 92*
**Ackerman,** F. Duane 1942- *WhoFI 92*
**Ackerman,** Gary Dean 1938- *WhoAmP 91*
**Ackerman,** Gary L. 1942- *AlmAP 92 [port], WhoAmP 91*
**Ackerman,** George Smith 1920- *WhoFI 92*
**Ackerman,** Grant Ross 1956- *WhoAmL 92*
**Ackerman,** Gustave Adolph, Jr *AmMWSc 92*
**Ackerman,** Harold A. 1928- *WhoAmL 92*
**Ackerman,** Harry *LesBEnT 92*
**Ackerman,** Harry S. d1991 *NewYTBS 91*
**Ackerman,** Hervey Winfield, Jr *AmMWSc 92*
**Ackerman,** Jack Lee 1959- *WhoMW 92*
**Ackerman,** James Howard 1928- *AmMWSc 92*
**Ackerman,** James L 1938- *AmMWSc 92*
**Ackerman,** James S. 1919- *WrDr 92*
**Ackerman,** Jerome Leonard 1950- *AmMWSc 92*
**Ackerman,** John C 1933- *WhoAmP 91*
**Ackerman,** John Cyril *WhoFI 92*
**Ackerman,** John Tryon 1941- *WhoWest 92*
**Ackerman,** Joseph John Henry 1949- *AmMWSc 92*
**Ackerman,** Kenneth Edward 1946- *WhoAmL 92*
**AcKerman,** Larry Joseph 1939- *AmMWSc 92*
**Ackerman,** Leopold, II 1921- *WhoFI 92*
**Ackerman,** Leslie *WhoEnt 92*
**Ackerman,** Linda Diane 1964- *WhoWest 92*
**Ackerman,** Mary Alice 1947- *WhoMW 92*
**Ackerman,** Mitchell 1949- *WhoEnt 92*
**Ackerman,** Norman Bernard 1930- *AmMWSc 92*
**Ackerman,** Patricia A. 1944- *WhoBlA 92*
**Ackerman,** Philip Charles 1944- *WhoAmL 92*
**Ackerman,** Philip John 1947- *IntWW 91*
**Ackerman,** Philip M 1940- *WhoAmP 91*
**Ackerman,** Ralph Austin 1945- *AmMWSc 92*
**Ackerman,** Richard C 1942- *WhoAmP 91*
**Ackerman,** Robert Adolph 1928- *WhoMW 92*
**Ackerman,** Robert Allan 1945- *ConTFT 9*
**Ackerman,** Robert Andrew 1956- *WhoEnt 92*
**Ackerman,** Robert Mitchell 1951- *WhoAmL 92*
**Ackerman,** Robert Wayne 1942- *WhoAmP 91*
**Ackerman,** Roy Alan 1951- *AmMWSc 92, WhoFI 92*
**Ackerman,** Sam 1934- *WhoAmP 91*
**Ackerman,** Scott Fulton 1944- *WhoRel 92*
**Ackerman,** Steven J 1951- *AmMWSc 92*
**Ackerman,** William 1949- *WhoEnt 92*
**Ackermann,** Georg K. *Who 92*
**Ackermann,** Gerald 1876-1960 *TwCPaSc*
**Ackermann,** Guenter Rolf 1924- *AmMWSc 92*
**Ackermann,** Hans Wolfgang 1936- *AmMWSc 92*
**Ackermann,** Martin Nicholas 1941- *AmMWSc 92*
**Ackermann,** Norbert Joseph, Jr 1942- *AmMWSc 92*
**Ackermann,** Philip Gulick 1909- *AmMWSc 92*
**Ackermann,** Russell Albert *WhoMW 92*
**Ackermann,** Uwe 1939- *AmMWSc 92*
**Ackers,** Gary K 1939- *AmMWSc 92*
**Ackers,** James George 1935- *Who 92*
**Ackerson,** Bruce J 1948- *AmMWSc 92*
**Ackerson,** Cathy *DrAPF 91*
**Ackerson,** Charles Stanley 1935- *WhoMW 92, WhoRel 92*
**Ackerson,** Duane *DrAPF 91*
**Ackerson,** Jon W 1943- *WhoAmP 91*
**Ackerson,** Nels John 1944- *WhoAmL 92*
**Ackerson,** Suzanne Stuesse 1958- *WhoMW 92*
**Ackhar,** Nabil Joseph 1947- *WhoFI 92*
**Ackhurst,** John 1816-1902 *BiInAmS*
**Ackland,** Joss 1928- *IntMPA 92, IntWW 91, Who 92*
**Ackland,** Rodney 1908- *IntAu&W 91, Who 92, WrDr 92*
**Ackles,** Janice Vogel *WhoWest 92*
**Ackles,** Kenneth Norman 1935- *AmMWSc 92*
**Ackley,** Everett Losey 1914- *WhoFI 92*
**Ackley,** Gardner 1915- *IntWW 91, WhoAmP 91*
**Ackley,** John Brian 1948- *WhoEnt 92*
**Ackley,** Marjorie Rose 1922- *WhoWest 92*
**Ackley,** Randall *DrAPF 91*
**Ackley,** Robert O. 1952- *WhoAmL 92*
**Ackley,** Stephen Fred 1944- *AmMWSc 92*
**Ackley,** William Benton 1918- *AmMWSc 92*
**Acklie,** Duane W 1931- *WhoAmP 91*
**Acklie,** Phyllis Ann 1933- *WhoMW 92*
**Acklin,** Thomas Patrick 1950- *WhoRel 92*
**Ackling,** Roger 1946- *TwCPaSc*
**Ackman,** Douglas Frederick 1935- *AmMWSc 92*
**Ackman,** Milton Roy 1932- *WhoAmL 92*

**Ackman**, Robert George 1927- *AmMWSc 92*
**Ackner** *Who 92*
**Ackner**, Baron 1920- *IntWW 91, Who 92*
**Ackord**, Marie M. 1939- *WhoBlA 92*
**Ackourey**, Paul Philip 1958- *WhoAmL 92*
**Ackrell**, Brian A C *AmMWSc 92*
**Ackridge**, Florence Gateward 1939- *WhoBlA 92*
**Ackrill**, John L. 1921- *WrDr 92*
**Ackrill**, John Lloyd 1921- *Who 92*
**Ackroyd**, David 1940- *WhoEnt 92*
**Ackroyd**, Jane 1957- *TwCPaSc*
**Ackroyd**, John 1932- *Who 92*
**Ackroyd**, Norman 1938- *IntWW 91, TwCPaSc, Who 92*
**Ackroyd**, Peter *NewYTBS 91 [port]*
**Ackroyd**, Peter 1917- *IntAu&W 91, WrDr 92*
**Ackroyd**, Peter 1949- *ConNov 91, IntAu&W 91, IntWW 91, Who 92, WrDr 92*
**Ackroyd**, Peter Runham 1917- *Who 92*
**Acland**, Alice 1912- *IntAu&W 91*
**Acland**, Antony 1930- *IntWW 91, Who 92*
**Acland**, Guy 1946- *Who 92*
**Acland**, John 1928- *Who 92*
**Acland**, John Dyke *Who 92*
**Acland**, Peter Bevil Edward 1902- *Who 92*
**Acland**, Richard 1906-1990 *AnObit 1990*
**Acland**, Richard Thomas Dyke d1990 *Who 92N*
**Acoba**, Simeon Rivera, Jr. 1944- *WhoAmL 92*
**Acobe**, Fernando 1941- *WhoHisp 92*
**Acon**, June Kay 1948- *WhoBlA 92*
**Acorace**, Joseph John 1935- *WhoAmP 91*
**Acorn**, Milton 1923- *BenetAL 91, WrDr 92*
**Acosta**, Able 1930- *WhoHisp 92*
**Acosta**, Adolovni Punsalan 1946- *WhoEnt 92*
**Acosta**, Alan T. 1952- *WhoHisp 92*
**Acosta**, Alirio 1933- *WhoHisp 92*
**Acosta**, Allan James 1924- *AmMWSc 92*
**Acosta**, Anibal A. 1929- *WhoHisp 92*
**Acosta**, Antonio A. 1929- *WhoHisp 92*
**Acosta**, Armando Joel 1956- *WhoHisp 92*
**Acosta**, Bert 1935- *WhoHisp 92*
**Acosta**, Carlos Alberto 1957- *WhoHisp 92*
**Acosta**, Carlos Julis 1939- *WhoHisp 92*
**Acosta**, Daniel, Jr 1945- *AmMWSc 92*
**Acosta**, Daniel G. 1956- *WhoAmL 92*
**Acosta**, Heriberto A. 1951- *WhoHisp 92*
**Acosta**, Ivan M. 1943- *WhoHisp 92*
**Acosta**, Ivonne *WhoHisp 92*
**Acosta**, Joel Eleno 1957- *WhoHisp 92*
**Acosta**, John *WhoHisp 92*
**Acosta**, Jose de 1540-1600 *HisDSpE*
**Acosta**, Joseph 1921- *WhoHisp 92*
**Acosta**, Juan M. 1961- *WhoHisp 92*
**Acosta**, Lucy 1960- *WhoHisp 92*
**Acosta**, Lucy G. 1926- *WhoHisp 92*
**Acosta**, Manuel Gregorio 1921- *WhoHisp 92*
**Acosta**, Nelia 1945- *WhoHisp 92*
**Acosta**, Norma A. 1958- *WhoHisp 92*
**Acosta**, Pamela Ann 1955- *WhoWest 92*
**Acosta**, Phyllis Brown 1933- *AmMWSc 92*
**Acosta**, Ralph 1934- *WhoAmP 91, WhoHisp 92*
**Acosta**, Raymond L. 1925- *WhoHisp 92*
**Acosta**, Raymond Luis 1925- *WhoAmL 92*
**Acosta**, Ricardo A. 1945- *WhoHisp 92*
**Acosta**, Ruth Ann *WhoHisp 92*
**Acosta**, Valentin 1933- *WhoHisp 92*
**Acosta-Colon**, Marie *WhoHisp 92*
**Acosta-Lespier**, Luis 1939- *WhoHisp 92*
**Acosta-Rubio**, Zelma Francisca 1965- *WhoAmL 92*
**Acquafresca**, Steve 1951- *WhoAmP 91*
**Acree**, Florence Hornbeck 1954- *WhoRel 92*
**Acree**, Terry Edward 1940- *AmMWSc 92*
**Acree**, William B, Jr 1944- *WhoAmP 91*
**Acres**, Douglas Ian 1924- *Who 92*
**Acres**, Robert Bruce 1951- *AmMWSc 92*
**Acret**, James Elvero 1930- *WhoAmL 92*
**Acrey**, Autry 1948- *WhoBlA 92*
**Acrivos**, Andreas 1928- *AmMWSc 92*
**Acrivos**, Juana Luisa Vivo 1928- *AmMWSc 92*
**Acruri**, James 1951- *IntMPA 92*
**Acs**, George 1923- *AmMWSc 92*
**Acton**, Baron 1941- *Who 92*
**Acton**, David Lawrence 1949- *WhoMW 92*
**Acton**, Donald Findlay 1934- *AmMWSc 92*
**Acton**, Edward McIntosh 1930- *AmMWSc 92*
**Acton**, Harold 1904- *IntAu&W 91, Who 92, WrDr 92*
**Acton**, Loren Wilber 1936- *AmMWSc 92*
**Acton**, Ronald Terry 1941- *AmMWSc 92*
**Acton**, Thomas Raymond 1953- *WhoRel 92*
**Acton**, William Antony 1904- *Who 92*
**Actor**, Paul 1933- *AmMWSc 92*
**Acuff**, Charles Davis 1934- *WhoMW 92*
**Acuff**, D Nicholas 1942- *WhoAmP 91*
**Acuff**, John Edgar 1940- *WhoAmL 92*
**Acuff**, Roy 1903- *NewAmDM*
**Acuff**, Roy Claxton 1903- *WhoEnt 92*
**Acuff**, Thomas Aldrich 1936- *WhoFI 92*
**Acuna**, Conrad Santos, Sr. 1946- *WhoHisp 92*
**Acuna**, Cristobal de 1597-1670 *HisDSpE*
**Acuna**, Mario Humberto 1940- *AmMWSc 92*
**Acuna**, Rodolfo 1932- *WhoHisp 92*
**Acworth**, Robert William 1938- *Who 92*
**Aczel**, Gyorgy 1917- *IntWW 91*
**Aczel**, Janos D 1924- *AmMWSc 92, IntWW 91*
**Aczel**, Tamas 1921- *IntAu&W 91, LiExTwC*
**Aczel**, Thomas 1930- *AmMWSc 92*
**Ada** *EncAmaz 91*
**Ada**, Gordon Leslie 1922- *IntWW 91*
**Ada**, Joseph Franklin 1943- *WhoAmP 91, WhoWest 92*
**Ada**, William C *WhoAmP 91*
**Adachi**, Kazuhiko *AmMWSc 92*
**Adachibara**, Akifumi 1924- *IntWW 91*
**Adade**, Anthony Kwasi 1957- *WhoFI 92*
**Adadimo** *EncAmaz 91*
**Adair**, Alvis V. 1940- *WhoBlA 92*
**Adair**, Andrew A. 1933- *WhoBlA 92*
**Adair**, Brian Campbell 1945- *Who 92*
**Adair**, Charles, Jr. 1950- *WhoBlA 92*
**Adair**, Charles Wallace, Jr 1914- *WhoAmP 91*
**Adair**, Dennis Wilton 1939- *AmMWSc 92*
**Adair**, Dianna Lynn 1950- *WhoWest 92*
**Adair**, Dwight Rial 1950- *WhoEnt 92*
**Adair**, Eleanor R 1926- *AmMWSc 92*
**Adair**, Evan Edward 1950- *WhoAmL 92*
**Adair**, Gerald Michael 1949- *AmMWSc 92*
**Adair**, Glenda R. 1962- *WhoFI 92*
**Adair**, Ian 1942- *IntAu&W 91*
**Adair**, James 1709?-1783? *BenetAL 91*
**Adair**, James Allen 1929- *WhoWest 92*
**Adair**, James E. *WhoBlA 92*
**Adair**, James Edwin 1935- *AmMWSc 92*
**Adair**, James R 1923- *IntAu&W 91, WrDr 92*
**Adair**, James Robert 1709?-1787? *DcNCBi 1*
**Adair**, James Robert, Jr. 1960- *WhoRel 92*
**Adair**, Jay Carlton 1946- *WhoEnt 92*
**Adair**, John 1732-1827 *DcNCBi 1*
**Adair**, John 1934- *WrDr 92*
**Adair**, Kenneth 1904- *WhoBlA 92*
**Adair**, Kent Thomas 1933- *AmMWSc 92*
**Adair**, Larry E 1946- *WhoAmP 91*
**Adair**, Red 1915- *IntWW 91*
**Adair**, Robert A. 1943- *WhoBlA 92*
**Adair**, Robert Kemp 1924- *AmMWSc 92, WrDr 92*
**Adair**, Sidney Arthur 1928- *WhoAmP 91*
**Adair**, Stephen Wood 1942- *WhoAmL 92*
**Adair**, Suzanne Frank 1941- *AmMWSc 92*
**Adair**, Thomas Weymon, III 1935- *AmMWSc 92*
**Adair**, Toby Warren, Jr. 1922- *WhoRel 92*
**Adair**, Wendell Hinton, Jr. 1944- *WhoAmL 92*
**Adair**, Wendy Hilty 1949- *WhoFI 92*
**Adair**, William Benjamin, Jr. 1951- *WhoAmL 92*
**Adair**, Winston Lee, Jr 1944- *AmMWSc 92*
**Adal** 1947- *WhoHisp 92*
**Adam** *EncEarC*
**Adam de la Halle** 1240?-1290? *NewAmDM*
**Adam**, Adolphe 1803-1856 *NewAmDM*
**Adam**, Alfredo Adam *WhoFI 92*
**Adam**, Carrolyne Lee 1944- *WhoMW 92*
**Adam**, Christopher Eric Forbes 1920- *Who 92*
**Adam**, David Peter 1941- *AmMWSc 92*
**Adam**, David Stuart Gordon 1927- *Who 92*
**Adam**, Encik Mohamed Adib Haji Mohamed 1941- *IntWW 91*
**Adam**, Gary Lee 1946- *WhoMW 92*
**Adam**, Gordon *Who 92*
**Adam**, Gordon Johnston 1934- *Who 92*
**Adam**, Helen *DrAPF 91*
**Adam**, Helen 1909- *ConPo 91, IntAu&W 91*
**Adam**, Joan *WhoAmP 91*
**Adam**, John Anthony 1949- *AmMWSc 92*
**Adam**, Karl 1876-1966 *EncTR 91*
**Adam**, Ken 1921- *IntMPA 92, IntWW 91*
**Adam**, Klaus 1943- *AmMWSc 92*
**Adam**, Madge Gertrude 1912- *Who 92*
**Adam**, Orval Michael 1930- *WhoFI 92*
**Adam**, Paul James 1934- *WhoFI 92*
**Adam**, Randall Edward 1943- *AmMWSc 92*
**Adam**, Robert 1728-1792 *BlkwCEP*
**Adam**, Robert Wilson 1923- *IntWW 91, Who 92*
**Adam**, Rodney Dean 1954- *WhoWest 92*
**Adam**, Theo 1926- *IntWW 91*
**Adam**, Wallace Burns 1933- *WhoWest 92*
**Adam Smith**, Janet 1905- *ConAu 35NR, Who 92*
**Adam-Smith**, Patsy 1924- *IntAu&W 91*
**Adam-Smith**, Patsy 1926- *WrDr 92*
**Adamantiades**, Achilles G 1934- *AmMWSc 92*
**Adamany**, David Walter 1936- *WhoMW 92*
**Adamcik**, Joe Alfred 1930- *AmMWSc 92*
**Adamczak**, Robert L 1927- *AmMWSc 92*
**Adamczyk**, Joseph Roger, Jr 1955- *WhoAmP 91*
**Adame**, Leonard 1947- *WhoHisp 92*
**Adamec**, Joseph Victor 1935- *WhoRel 92*
**Adamec**, Ladislav 1926- *IntWW 91*
**Adamec**, Ludwig W. 1924- *WrDr 92*
**Adamek**, Eduard Georg 1925- *AmMWSc 92*
**Adames**, Abdiel Jose 1938- *AmMWSc 92*
**Adames**, Fermin 1944- *WhoHisp 92*
**Adames**, Maria 1941- *WhoHisp 92*
**Adamez**, Alma Carrales 1958- *WhoHisp 92*
**Adami**, Edward F. *Who 92*
**Adami**, Franco 1933- *IntWW 91*
**Adami-Charney**, Anne Sybell 1949- *WhoEnt 92*
**Adamic**, Louis 1898-1951 *DcAmImH*
**Adamic**, Louis 1899-1951 *BenetAL 91*
**Adamishin**, Anatoliy Dmitrievich 1934- *IntWW 91*
**Adamkiewicz**, Vincent Witold 1924- *AmMWSc 92*
**Adamko**, Joseph Michael 1932- *WhoFI 92*
**Adamo**, Anthony Achille 1938- *WhoFI 92*
**Adamo**, David Tuesday 1949- *WhoBlA 92*
**Adamo**, Glenn Robert 1956- *WhoEnt 92*
**Adamo**, Joseph A *WhoAmP 91*
**Adamo**, Joseph Albert 1938- *AmMWSc 92*
**Adamo**, Ralph *DrAPF 91*
**Adamo**, Victor T. 1948- *WhoIns 92*
**Adamour**, Beth *DrAPF 91*
**Adamov**, Arthur 1908-1970 *GuFrLit 1*
**Adamovich**, Gregory V. 1894- *LiExTwC*
**Adams**, Abigail 1744-1818 *BenetAL 91, BlkwEAR [port], HanAmWH, RComAH*
**Adams**, Adrienne 1906- *ConAu 35NR*
**Adams**, Afesa M. 1936- *WhoBlA 92*
**Adams**, Aileen Kirkpatrick 1923- *Who 92*
**Adams**, Alan Leonard 1949- *WhoWest 92*
**Adams**, Alayne A 1938- *AmMWSc 92*
**Adams**, Albert James 1915- *Who 92*
**Adams**, Albert P *WhoAmP 91*
**Adams**, Albert W., Jr. 1948- *WhoBlA 92*
**Adams**, Albert Whitten 1927- *AmMWSc 92*
**Adams**, Alec Cecil Stanley 1909- *Who 92*
**Adams**, Alfred Thompson, Jr. 1927- *WhoAmL 92*
**Adams**, Alger LeRoy 1910- *WhoBlA 92*
**Adams**, Alice *DrAPF 91*
**Adams**, Alice 1926- *BenetAL 91, ConNov 91, IntAu&W 91, WrDr 92*
**Adams**, Alice Omega 1951- *WhoBlA 92*
**Adams**, Alicia Ann 1965- *WhoMW 92*
**Adams**, Alvin P, Jr *WhoAmP 91*
**Adams**, Andrew Martin 1943- *WhoWest 92*
**Adams**, Andy 1859-1935 *BenetAL 91, TwCWW 91*
**Adams**, Ann Louise 1934- *WhoWest 92*
**Adams**, Anna *DrAPF 91*
**Adams**, Anne Currin 1942- *WhoBlA 92*
**Adams**, Ansel 1902-1984 *DcTwDes, FacFETw [port]*
**Adams**, Anthony John 1953- *WhoAmL 92*
**Adams**, Anthony Patrick 1953- *WhoEnt 92, WhoWest 92*
**Adams**, Anthony Peter 1936- *Who 92*
**Adams**, Arlin Marvin 1921- *WhoAmL 92*
**Adams**, Arlon Taylor 1931- *AmMWSc 92*
**Adams**, Armenta Estella 1936- *WhoBlA 92*
**Adams**, Arnold Lucian 1952- *AmMWSc 92*
**Adams**, Arthur Clark 1948- *WhoWest 92*
**Adams**, Arthur Kinney 1883-1920 *BiInAmS*
**Adams**, Barbara *DrAPF 91*
**Adams**, Barnard Steeple 1917- *WhoWest 92*
**Adams**, Bart *IntAu&W 91X, TwCWW 91*
**Adams**, Beejay 1920- *WhoFI 92, WhoMW 92*
**Adams**, Beresford 1940- *WhoRel 92*
**Adams**, Bernard d1965 *TwCPaSc*
**Adams**, Bernard Charles 1915- *Who 92*
**Adams**, Betsy *DrAPF 91*
**Adams**, Bill 1879- *BenetAL 91*
**Adams**, Billie Morris Wright *WhoBlA 92*
**Adams**, Brent Larsen 1949- *AmMWSc 92*
**Adams**, Brent T 1948- *WhoAmP 91*
**Adams**, Brock 1927- *AlmAP 92 [port], WhoWest 92*
**Adams**, Brockman 1927- *IntWW 91, WhoAmP 91*
**Adams**, Brooke 1949- *IntMPA 92, WhoEnt 92*
**Adams**, Brooks 1848-1927 *BenetAL 91*
**Adams**, Buel Thomas 1933- *WhoFI 92*
**Adams**, C Howard 1917- *AmMWSc 92*
**Adams**, C. Lee 1940- *WhoFI 92*
**Adams**, Caren 1946- *ConAu 135*
**Adams**, Carl D 1934- *WhoAmP 91*
**Adams**, Carl Fillmore, Jr. 1950- *WhoFI 92*
**Adams**, Carl S *WhoAmP 91*
**Adams**, Carol Ann 1946- *WhoRel 92*
**Adams**, Carol J. 1951- *ConAu 134*
**Adams**, Carol Laurence 1944- *WhoBlA 92*
**Adams**, Carolyn Ethel 1943- *WhoEnt 92*
**Adams**, Carolyn Loraine 1957- *WhoAmL 92*
**Adams**, Catlin 1950- *IntMPA 92*
**Adams**, Cecil Ray 1948- *WhoBlA 92*
**Adams**, Celeste *WhoEnt 92*
**Adams**, Charles Baker 1814-1853 *BiInAmS*
**Adams**, Charles DeWitt, Jr. 1925- *WhoFI 92*
**Adams**, Charles Follen 1842-1918 *BenetAL 91*
**Adams**, Charles Francis 1807-1886 *AmPolLe, BenetAL 91*
**Adams**, Charles Francis 1854-1914 *BiInAmS*
**Adams**, Charles Francis 1910- *IntWW 91*
**Adams**, Charles Francis 1927- *WhoWest 92*
**Adams**, Charles Francis, Jr. 1835-1915 *BenetAL 91*
**Adams**, Charles Gilchrist 1936- *WhoBlA 92*
**Adams**, Charles Henry 1918- *AmMWSc 92*
**Adams**, Charles Hubert 1934- *WhoAmP 91*
**Adams**, Charles Jesse 1947- *WhoEnt 92*
**Adams**, Charles Joseph 1924- *WhoRel 92*
**Adams**, Charles Magee *ScFEYrs*
**Adams**, Charles Rex 1930- *AmMWSc 92*
**Adams**, Chelsea *DrAPF 91*
**Adams**, Christine 1947- *TwCPaSc*
**Adams**, Chuck *IntAu&W 91X, TwCWW 91, WrDr 92*
**Adams**, Cindy Heller *WhoEnt 92*
**Adams**, Clarence Lancelot, Jr. *WhoBlA 92*
**Adams**, Clark Edward 1942- *AmMWSc 92*
**Adams**, Claudette Coleman 1952- *WhoBlA 92*
**Adams**, Clifford Emerson *WhoWest 92*
**Adams**, Clifford Lowell 1915- *AmMWSc 92*
**Adams**, Clifton 1919- *IntAu&W 91*
**Adams**, Clifton 1919-1971 *TwCWW 91*
**Adams**, Corrine Brady 1941- *WhoAmL 92*
**Adams**, Curtis H 1917- *AmMWSc 92*
**Adams**, Curtis N. 1931- *WhoBlA 92*
**Adams**, Dale W 1934- *AmMWSc 92*
**Adams**, Daniel *WrDr 92*
**Adams**, Daniel 1773-1864 *BiInAmS*
**Adams**, Daniel Fenton 1922- *WhoAmL 92*
**Adams**, Daniel James 1963- *WhoEnt 92*
**Adams**, Daniel Otis 1918- *AmMWSc 92*
**Adams**, Danton F. 1904- *TwCPaSc*
**Adams**, Darius Mainard 1944- *AmMWSc 92*
**Adams**, David, Jr. 1927- *WhoBlA 92*
**Adams**, David B 1945- *AmMWSc 92*
**Adams**, David Bennion 1945- *WhoWest 92*
**Adams**, David C. *LesBEnT 92*
**Adams**, David Christopher 1967- *WhoWest 92*
**Adams**, David George 1936- *AmMWSc 92*
**Adams**, David Hardy 1950- *WhoMW 92*
**Adams**, David Huntington 1942- *WhoAmL 92*
**Adams**, David John 1949- *WhoWest 92*
**Adams**, David Lawrence 1945- *AmMWSc 92*
**Adams**, David M 1942- *WhoAmP 91*
**Adams**, David S *AmMWSc 92*
**Adams**, Dean 1957- *WhoEnt 92*
**Adams**, Deanna Sue Duncan 1942- *WhoWest 92*
**Adams**, Deborah *DrAPF 91*
**Adams**, Dennis Adams 1949- *WhoRel 92*
**Adams**, Dennis Ray 1949- *AmMWSc 92*
**Adams**, Dolly Desselle *WhoBlA 92*
**Adams**, Dolph Oliver 1939- *AmMWSc 92*
**Adams**, Don 1925- *WrDr 92*
**Adams**, Don 1926- *IntMPA 92*
**Adams**, Don 1940- *AmMWSc 92*
**Adams**, Don L. 1927- *WhoBlA 92*
**Adams**, Don M. *WhoAmL 92*
**Adams**, Don W 1935- *WhoAmP 91*
**Adams**, Donald E *AmMWSc 92*
**Adams**, Donald F 1935- *AmMWSc 92*
**Adams**, Donald Keith 1902-1971 *DcNCBi 1*
**Adams**, Donald Robert 1937- *AmMWSc 92*
**Adams**, Douglas 1952- *ConAu 34NR, IntAu&W 91, IntWW 91, TwCSFW 91, WrDr 92*
**Adams**, Douglas Glenn 1945- *WhoRel 92*
**Adams**, Douglas James 1946- *WhoAmL 92*
**Adams**, Douglas Noel 1952- *Who 92*
**Adams**, Earl Leonard, III 1953- *WhoBlA 92*

**Adams,** Earnest Dwight 1933- *AmMWSc 92*
**Adams,** Edie 1927- *IntMPA 92*
**Adams,** Edmund John 1938- *WhoAmL 92, WhoFI 92*
**Adams,** Edward B. 1939- *WhoBlA 92*
**Adams,** Edward Franklin 1936- *AmMWSc 92*
**Adams,** Edward John 1946- *WhoRel 92*
**Adams,** Elaine Parker 1940- *WhoBlA 92*
**Adams,** Elizabeth *DrAPF 91*
**Adams,** Emory Temple, Jr 1928- *AmMWSc 92*
**Adams,** Ernest Charles 1926- *WrDr 92*
**Adams,** Ernest Clarence 1925- *AmMWSc 92*
**Adams,** Ernest Victor 1920- *Who 92*
**Adams,** Eugene Bruce 1953- *WhoBlA 92*
**Adams,** Eugene William 1920- *WhoBlA 92*
**Adams,** Eva B. 1908-1991 *CurBio 91N*
**Adams,** Eva Bertrand d1991 *NewYTBS 91 [port]*
**Adams,** Eva Garza 1943- *WhoHisp 92*
**Adams,** Eva W. 1928- *WhoBlA 92*
**Adams,** Evelyn Eleanor 1925- *AmMWSc 92*
**Adams,** F. Gerard 1929- *WhoFI 92*
**Adams,** Forrest Hood 1919- *AmMWSc 92*
**Adams,** Francis 1862-1893 *NinCLC 33*
**Adams,** Francis L 1906- *AmMWSc 92*
**Adams,** Frank Alexander 1907- *Who 92*
**Adams,** Frank Clifton 1934- *WhoRel 92*
**Adams,** Frank R. 1883-1963 *BenetAL 91*
**Adams,** Frank Ramsay 1883-1963 *TwCWW 91*
**Adams,** Frank Robert 1947- *WhoMW 92*
**Adams,** Frank William 1925- *AmMWSc 92*
**Adams,** Franklin P. 1881-1960 *BenetAL 91*
**Adams,** Fred 1921- *AmMWSc 92*
**Adams,** Frederick Baldwin, Jr. 1910- *Who 92*
**Adams,** Frederick G. 1931- *WhoBlA 92*
**Adams,** Frocene Stathis 1938- *WhoWest 92*
**Adams,** Gabrielle H M 1939- *AmMWSc 92*
**Adams,** Gail Dayton 1918- *AmMWSc 92*
**Adams,** Gayle E 1927- *AmMWSc 92*
**Adams,** George Baker, Jr 1919- *AmMWSc 92*
**Adams,** George Bell 1930- *WhoAmL 92*
**Adams,** George Drayton 1915- *WhoAmP 91*
**Adams,** George Emery 1942- *WhoMW 92*
**Adams,** George G 1948- *AmMWSc 92*
**Adams,** George Matthew 1878-1962 *BenetAL 91*
**Adams,** George Wallace 1962- *WhoBlA 92*
**Adams,** George William 1948- *WhoEnt 92*
**Adams,** Gerald Drayson *IntMPA 92*
**Adams,** Gerald Edward 1930- *Who 92*
**Adams,** Gleason R. W. 1949- *WhoBlA 92*
**Adams,** Glen Cameron 1912- *WhoWest 92*
**Adams,** Glenda *DrAPF 91*
**Adams,** Glenda 1939- *WrDr 92*
**Adams,** Gregory Albert 1958- *WhoBlA 92*
**Adams,** Gregory Keith 1958- *WhoBlA 92*
**Adams,** Guy Randall 1955- *WhoEnt 92*
**Adams,** Hall, Jr. 1933- *WhoFI 92*
**Adams,** Hannah 1755-1831 *BenetAL 91*
**Adams,** Harold *DrAPF 91*
**Adams,** Harold B 1923- *IntAu&W 91*
**Adams,** Harold Elwood 1916- *AmMWSc 92*
**Adams,** Harrison *TwCWW 91*
**Adams,** Harroll 1925- *WhoAmP 91*
**Adams,** Harry 1924- *AmMWSc 92*
**Adams,** Harry William 1868-1947 *TwCPaSc*
**Adams,** Hazard 1926- *IntAu&W 91, WrDr 92*
**Adams,** Helen Elizabeth 1945- *AmMWSc 92*
**Adams,** Henrietta Faulconer 1939- *WhoBlA 92*
**Adams,** Henry 1838-1918 *BenetAL 91, ConAu 133, RComAH*
**Adams,** Henry Philip 1951- *WhoMW 92*
**Adams,** Henry Richard 1942- *AmMWSc 92*
**Adams,** Herbert C F 1953- *WhoAmP 91*
**Adams,** Herman Ray 1939- *AmMWSc 92*
**Adams,** Hervey 1903- *TwCPaSc*
**Adams,** Hervey Cadwallader 1903- *Who 92*
**Adams,** Hope Howlett 1942- *WhoRel 92*
**Adams,** Howard *WhoAmP 91*
**Adams,** Howard Glen 1940- *WhoBlA 92*
**Adams,** Iola 1910- *WhoAmP 91*
**Adams,** Irene *Who 92*
**Adams,** Isaac, Jr 1836-1911 *BiInAmS*
**Adams,** J Allen 1932- *WhoAmP 91*
**Adams,** J. Donald 1891-1968 *BenetAL 91*
**Adams,** J Mack 1933- *AmMWSc 92*
**Adams,** Jack *ScFEYrs*
**Adams,** Jack 1952- *WhoEnt 92, WhoFI 92, WhoWest 92*
**Adams,** Jack Donald 1919- *AmMWSc 92*
**Adams,** Jack H 1924- *AmMWSc 92*
**Adams,** Jackie W., Sr. 1927- *WhoBlA 92*
**Adams,** Jal Gustav 1914- *WhoWest 92*
**Adams,** James *Who 92*
**Adams,** James Alan 1936- *AmMWSc 92*
**Adams,** James F. 1927- *WrDr 92*
**Adams,** James Hall, Jr 1943- *AmMWSc 92*
**Adams,** James Homer 1939- *WhoRel 92*
**Adams,** James Jay 1955- *WhoRel 92, WhoWest 92*
**Adams,** James Kenneth 1953- *WhoRel 92*
**Adams,** James Luther 1901- *RelLAm 91, WhoRel 92*
**Adams,** James Malcolm 1954- *WhoBlA 92*
**Adams,** James Miller 1924- *AmMWSc 92*
**Adams,** James Mills 1936- *AmMWSc 92*
**Adams,** James Milton 1949- *AmMWSc 92*
**Adams,** James R. 1939- *WhoFI 92*
**Adams,** James Robert 1946- *WhoMW 92*
**Adams,** James Russell 1914- *AmMWSc 92*
**Adams,** James Russell 1945- *AmMWSc 92, WhoWest 92*
**Adams,** James Truslow 1878-1949 *BenetAL 91*
**Adams,** James W. 1949- *WhoEnt 92*
**Adams,** James William 1921- *AmMWSc 92*
**Adams,** James William Lemuel 1929- *WhoRel 92*
**Adams,** Jane N 1929- *AmMWSc 92*
**Adams,** Janet *WhoAmP 91*
**Adams,** Janice Lou 1939- *WhoMW 92*
**Adams,** Jason Hamilton 1964- *WhoEnt 92*
**Adams,** Jasper Emmett, Jr 1942- *AmMWSc 92*
**Adams,** Jean Ruth 1928- *AmMWSc 92*
**Adams,** Jean Tucker *WhoBlA 92*
**Adams,** Jeanette *DrAPF 91*
**Adams,** Jeffrey Karl 1950- *WhoWest 92*
**Adams,** Jeffry Dale 1952- *WhoMW 92*
**Adams,** Jennifer 1948- *Who 92*
**Adams,** Jill Elaine 1952- *WhoAmL 92*
**Adams,** Jo-Ann Marie 1949- *WhoWest 92*
**Adams,** Joanna Faucher 1944- *WhoWest 92*
**Adams,** Joe Dale 1946- *WhoRel 92*
**Adams,** Joe Greene 1955- *WhoAmL 92*
**Adams,** Joel Peter 1957- *WhoFI 92*
**Adams,** Joey 1911- *WhoEnt 92*
**Adams,** John *NewYTBS 91 [port], WhoEnt 92*
**Adams,** John 1704?-1740 *BenetAL 91*
**Adams,** John 1735-1826 *AmPolLe [port], BenetAL 91, BlkwEAR, RComAH*
**Adams,** John 1755-1826 *BlkwCEP*
**Adams,** John 1947- *ConCom 92, NewAmDM*
**Adams,** John Allan Stewart, Sr 1926- *AmMWSc 92*
**Adams,** John Anthony 1944- *ConAu 134, SmATA 67*
**Adams,** John Bertram *FacFETw*
**Adams,** John Brett 1940- *WhoFI 92*
**Adams,** John Buchanan, Jr. 1948- *WhoFI 92*
**Adams,** John Carter, Jr. 1936- *WhoFI 92*
**Adams,** John Clyde 1947- *AmMWSc 92*
**Adams,** John Collins 1938- *AmMWSc 92*
**Adams,** John Crawford *Who 92*
**Adams,** John David Vessot 1934- *WhoFI 92*
**Adams,** John Douglas Richard 1940- *Who 92*
**Adams,** John Edgar 1918- *AmMWSc 92*
**Adams,** John Edwin 1914- *AmMWSc 92*
**Adams,** John Evi 1937- *AmMWSc 92*
**Adams,** John George 1921- *AmMWSc 92*
**Adams,** John Hampton 1875-1935 *DcNCBi 1*
**Adams,** John Harold 1918- *Who 92*
**Adams,** John Howard 1939- *AmMWSc 92*
**Adams,** John Hurst 1929- *WhoBlA 92, WhoRel 92*
**Adams,** John Jillson 1934- *WhoAmL 92*
**Adams,** John Kendal 1933- *AmMWSc 92*
**Adams,** John Kenneth 1915- *IntAu&W 91, Who 92*
**Adams,** John Laurence 1943- *WhoFI 92*
**Adams,** John M. 1950- *WhoWest 92*
**Adams,** John Michael Geoffrey 1931-1985 *FacFETw*
**Adams,** John Nicholas William B. *Who 92*
**Adams,** John Oscar 1937- *WhoBlA 92*
**Adams,** John Phillips, Jr. 1920- *WhoWest 92*
**Adams,** John Pletch 1922- *AmMWSc 92*
**Adams,** John Powers 1938- *WhoAmL 92*
**Adams,** John Quincy 1767-1848 *AmPolLe [port], BenetAL 91, RComAH*
**Adams,** John R 1918- *AmMWSc 92*
**Adams,** John Roderick Seton 1936- *Who 92*
**Adams,** John Rodger 1937- *AmMWSc 92, WhoRel 92*
**Adams,** John Shepard 1961- *WhoWest 92*
**Adams,** John Turvill 1805-1882 *BenetAL 91*
**Adams,** John Wagstaff 1915- *AmMWSc 92*
**Adams,** John Wendell 1948- *WhoMW 92*
**Adams,** John Will 1954- *WhoEnt 92*
**Adams,** John William 1928- *AmMWSc 92*
**Adams,** Jonathan L. 1947- *WhoFI 92*
**Adams,** Joseph Lee, Jr 1944- *WhoAmP 91, WhoBlA 92*
**Adams,** Julia Davis 1900- *IntAu&W 91*
**Adams,** Julian 1919- *WrDr 92*
**Adams,** Julian Philip 1944- *AmMWSc 92*
**Adams,** Julie 1926- *IntMPA 92*
**Adams,** Junius Greene 1884-1962 *DcNCBi 1*
**Adams,** Junius Greene, III 1943- *AmMWSc 92*
**Adams,** Justin *WrDr 92*
**Adams,** Katharine Odell 1954- *WhoFI 92*
**Adams,** Katherine 1948- *Who 92*
**Adams,** Katherine 1952- *WhoBlA 92*
**Adams,** Kathryn Grace 1958- *WhoRel 92*
**Adams,** Kattie Johnson 1938- *WhoBlA 92*
**Adams,** Kenneth Allen Harry 1934- *AmMWSc 92*
**Adams,** Kenneth Francis 1946- *WhoFI 92*
**Adams,** Kenneth Galt 1920- *Who 92*
**Adams,** Kenneth H 1937- *AmMWSc 92*
**Adams,** Kenneth Howard 1906- *AmMWSc 92*
**Adams,** Kenneth Marvin 1958- *WhoAmL 92*
**Adams,** Kenneth Menzies 1922- *WrDr 92*
**Adams,** Kent J *WhoAmP 91*
**Adams,** Kevin C. *WhoWest 92*
**Adams,** Larry J 1949- *WhoAmP 91*
**Adams,** Laurence J *AmMWSc 92*
**Adams,** Laurie 1941- *WrDr 92*
**Adams,** Laurie Ann 1958- *WhoFI 92*
**Adams,** Lawrence Charles 1948- *WhoWest 92*
**Adams,** Lawrence Vaughan 1936- *WhoEnt 92*
**Adams,** Lehman D. 1925- *WhoBlA 92*
**Adams,** Leon Ashby, III 1951- *WhoWest 92*
**Adams,** Leon Milton 1913- *AmMWSc 92*
**Adams,** Leonard C 1921- *AmMWSc 92*
**Adams,** Leonard Joseph 1954- *WhoFI 92*
**Adams,** Leonie *IntWW 91N*
**Adams,** Leonie 1899- *BenetAL 91, IntAu&W 91*
**Adams,** Leslie *WrDr 92*
**Adams,** Leslie 1932- *WhoBlA 92*
**Adams,** Leslie Garry 1941- *AmMWSc 92*
**Adams,** Lillian Louise T. 1929- *WhoBlA 92*
**Adams,** Louis W, Jr 1951- *AmMWSc 92*
**Adams,** Lowell William 1946- *AmMWSc 92*
**Adams,** Lucretia McKey 1932- *WhoAmP 91*
**Adams,** M. Elizabeth 1906- *WhoBlA 92*
**Adams,** Marcus Webb, Jr. 1933- *WhoMW 92*
**Adams,** Mark Gordon *WhoWest 92*
**Adams,** Mark Kildee 1938- *WhoAmL 92*
**Adams,** Mark Lynn 1951- *WhoAmP 91*
**Adams,** Mark Reginald 1963- *WhoMW 92, WhoRel 92*
**Adams,** Martha Lovell 1925- *AmMWSc 92*
**Adams,** Martin P. 1956- *WhoBlA 92*
**Adams,** Marvin 1912- *WhoAmP 91*
**Adams,** Mary B *WhoAmP 91*
**Adams,** Mason 1919- *IntMPA 92, WhoEnt 92*
**Adams,** Maud 1945- *IntMPA 92*
**Adams,** Maude 1872-1953 *FacFETw*
**Adams,** Maurice Henry 1908- *Who 92*
**Adams,** Maurice Wayne 1918- *AmMWSc 92*
**Adams,** Max David 1941- *AmMWSc 92*
**Adams,** Max Dwain 1926- *AmMWSc 92*
**Adams,** Mendle Eugene 1938- *WhoRel 92*
**Adams,** Michael 1931-1967 *FacFETw*
**Adams,** Michael 1963- *WhoBlA 92*
**Adams,** Michael Evelyn 1920- *WrDr 92*
**Adams,** Michael F. 1948- *WhoFI 92*
**Adams,** Michael John 1945- *WhoMW 92*
**Adams,** Michael Keith 1934- *Who 92*
**Adams,** Michael Lee 1951- *WhoRel 92*
**Adams,** Michael Robert 1954- *WhoWest 92*
**Adams,** Michael Studebaker 1938- *AmMWSc 92*
**Adams,** Molly *WhoEnt 92*
**Adams,** Nelson Eddy 1945- *WhoBlA 92*
**Adams,** Nick Dwayne 1963- *WhoRel 92*
**Adams,** Noel Terry, Jr. 1959- *WhoAmL 92*
**Adams,** Norman 1927- *IntWW 91, TwCPaSc, Who 92*
**Adams,** Norman Joseph 1930- *WhoFI 92, WhoWest 92*
**Adams,** Norman Joseph 1933- *WhoFI 92*
**Adams,** Oscar Fay 1855-1919 *BenetAL 91*
**Adams,** Oscar W, Jr 1925- *WhoAmP 91, WhoBlA 92*
**Adams,** Oscar William, Jr. 1925- *WhoAmL 92*
**Adams,** Otto Eugene, Jr 1927- *AmMWSc 92*
**Adams,** P B 1929- *AmMWSc 92*
**Adams,** Paul Allison 1940- *AmMWSc 92*
**Adams,** Paul Ancil 1937- *WhoAmP 91*
**Adams,** Paul Brown 1929- *WhoBlA 92*
**Adams,** Paul Lieber 1924- *AmMWSc 92*
**Adams,** Paul Louis 1948- *AmMWSc 92*
**Adams,** Peggy Hoffman 1936- *WhoAmP 91*
**Adams,** Penny Sue 1953- *WhoRel 92*
**Adams,** Pepper 1930-1986 *NewAmDM*
**Adams,** Perseus 1933- *ConPo 91, LiExTwC*
**Adams,** Peter D 1937- *AmMWSc 92*
**Adams,** Peter Frederick Gordon 1936- *AmMWSc 92*
**Adams,** Phelps H. d1991 *NewYTBS 91*
**Adams,** Philip 1905 *WhoWest 92*
**Adams,** Philip 1915- *Who 92*
**Adams,** Philip George Doyne 1915- *IntWW 91*
**Adams,** Philip J *WhoAmP 91*
**Adams,** Philip James 1920- *WhoWest 92*
**Adams,** Phillip 1925- *AmMWSc 92*
**Adams,** Phillip A 1929- *AmMWSc 92*
**Adams,** Preston 1930- *AmMWSc 92*
**Adams,** Quinton Douglas 1919- *WhoBlA 92*
**Adams,** R.C. 1931- *WhoEnt 92*
**Adams,** R F and Tiffany, J A *ScFEYrs*
**Adams,** R. Kendal 1955- *WhoFI 92*
**Adams,** Ralph M 1933- *AmMWSc 92*
**Adams,** Ralph Melvin 1921- *AmMWSc 92*
**Adams,** Ralph Norman 1924- *AmMWSc 92*
**Adams,** Ralph Wyatt, Sr. 1915- *WhoAmL 92*
**Adams,** Ramon F. 1889-1976 *BenetAL 91*
**Adams,** Randall Henry 1939- *AmMWSc 92*
**Adams,** Raymond F 1924- *AmMWSc 92*
**Adams,** Raymond Kenneth 1928- *AmMWSc 92*
**Adams,** Rhonda Jean 1960- *WhoAmL 92*
**Adams,** Richard 1920- *ConAu 35NR, ConNov 91, WrDr 92*
**Adams,** Richard A *AmMWSc 92*
**Adams,** Richard Borlase 1921- *Who 92*
**Adams,** Richard Darwin 1947- *AmMWSc 92*
**Adams,** Richard E 1921- *AmMWSc 92*
**Adams,** Richard George 1920- *IntAu&W 91, IntWW 91, Who 92, WhoEnt 92*
**Adams,** Richard John Moreton G. *Who 92*
**Adams,** Richard Linwood 1928- *AmMWSc 92*
**Adams,** Richard Lynnden 1943- *WhoAmP 91*
**Adams,** Richard Maxwell 1938- *WhoWest 92*
**Adams,** Richard Melverne 1916- *AmMWSc 92*
**Adams,** Richard Melvin, Jr. 1951- *WhoBlA 92*
**Adams,** Richard Owen 1933- *AmMWSc 92*
**Adams,** Richard Sanford 1928- *AmMWSc 92*
**Adams,** Robert *WhoAmL 92*
**Adams,** Robert 1917-1984 *TwCPaSc*
**Adams,** Robert Allen 1945- *WhoIns 92*
**Adams,** Robert D 1926- *AmMWSc 92*
**Adams,** Robert Edward 1929- *AmMWSc 92*
**Adams,** Robert Granville 1927- *WhoWest 92*
**Adams,** Robert Henry 1937- *WhoMW 92*
**Adams,** Robert Hugo 1943- *WhoBlA 92, WhoFI 92*
**Adams,** Robert Joe 1935- *WhoMW 92*
**Adams,** Robert John 1915- *AmMWSc 92*
**Adams,** Robert Johnson 1950- *AmMWSc 92*
**Adams,** Robert Kenneth 1911- *WhoMW 92*
**Adams,** Robert Lazenby 1929- *WhoRel 92*
**Adams,** Robert Martin 1915- *IntAu&W 91, WrDr 92*
**Adams,** Robert McCormick, Jr. 1926- *IntWW 91, WrDr 92*
**Adams,** Robert Merrihew 1937- *ConAu 135, WhoRel 92*
**Adams,** Robert Milton, Jr. 1954- *WhoEnt 92*
**Adams,** Robert R 1917- *AmMWSc 92*
**Adams,** Robert Richard 1965- *WhoHisp 92*
**Adams,** Robert Scott 1949- *WhoWest 92*
**Adams,** Robert Thomas 1913- *WhoBlA 92*
**Adams,** Robert W 1934- *AmMWSc 92*
**Adams,** Robert Walker 1950- *WhoAmL 92*
**Adams,** Robert Walker, Jr 1920- *AmMWSc 92*
**Adams,** Rodney Franklin 1936- *WhoWest 92*
**Adams,** Rodney Kyle 1959- *WhoAmL 92*
**Adams,** Roger 1889-1971 *FacFETw*
**Adams,** Roger James 1936- *AmMWSc 92*
**Adams,** Roger Omar 1933- *AmMWSc 92*
**Adams,** Roger Sherrill 1936- *WhoMW 92*
**Adams,** Ronald, Jr. 1958- *WhoBlA 92*

**Adams,** Ronald John 1943- WhoWest 92
**Adams,** Roscoe H. 1941- WhoBlA 92
**Adams,** Roy Melville 1919- AmMWSc 92
**Adams,** Russell Francis 1955- WhoWest 92
**Adams,** Russell Lee 1930- WhoBlA 92
**Adams,** Russell S, Jr 1926- AmMWSc 92
**Adams,** Ruthie M 1934- WhoAmP 91
**Adams,** S Keith 1938- AmMWSc 92
**Adams,** Salvatore Charles 1934- WhoFI 92
**Adams,** Sam 1916- AmMWSc 92
**Adams,** Samuel 1722-1803 AmPolLe, BenetAL 91, BlkwEAR, RComAH
**Adams,** Samuel A 1934-1988 FacFETw
**Adams,** Samuel Clifford, Jr. 1920- WhoBlA 92
**Adams,** Samuel Franklin 1958- WhoAmL 92
**Adams,** Samuel Hopkins 1871-1958 BenetAL 91, ScFEYrs
**Adams,** Samuel Levi, Sr. 1926- WhoBlA 92
**Adams,** Samuel S 1937- AmMWSc 92
**Adams,** Sandra L. 1955- WhoRel 92
**Adams,** Sarah Virginia 1955- WhoWest 92
**Adams,** Scott Leslie 1955- WhoFI 92
**Adams,** Sheila Mary 1947- WhoBlA 92
**Adams,** Sheridan Dale 1967- WhoEnt 92
**Adams,** Sherman 1899-1986 AmPolLe, FacFETw [port]
**Adams,** Sid 1910- WhoAmP 91
**Adams,** Spencer Bell 1860-1943 DcNCBi 1
**Adams,** Stanley 1907- WhoEnt 92
**Adams,** Stanley 1927- ConAu 135
**Adams,** Stefon Lee 1963- WhoBlA 92
**Adams,** Stephen Shawn 1961- WhoWest 92
**Adams,** Steve 1951- WhoAmP 91
**Adams,** Steven Alva 1946- WhoWest 92
**Adams,** Steven Paul 1952- AmMWSc 92, WhoMW 92
**Adams,** Susan Virginia 1948- WhoFI 92
**Adams,** T Patton 1943- WhoAmP 91, WhoBlA 92
**Adams,** Taggart D. 1941- WhoAmL 92
**Adams,** Terrance Sturgis 1938- AmMWSc 92
**Adams,** Theodore Adolphus, Jr. 1929- WhoBlA 92
**Adams,** Theodore Floyd 1898-1980 RelLAm 91
**Adams,** Thomas 1930- AmMWSc 92
**Adams,** Thomas B 1910- WhoAmP 91
**Adams,** Thomas C 1918- AmMWSc 92
**Adams,** Thomas Edwards 1947- AmMWSc 92
**Adams,** Thomas Lawrence 1948- WhoAmL 92
**Adams,** Thomas Lynch, Jr. 1941- WhoAmL 92
**Adams,** Thomas Tilley 1929- WhoAmL 92
**Adams,** Thurman, Jr 1928- WhoAmP 91
**Adams,** Thurman Leon, Jr. 1945- WhoRel 92
**Adams,** Timothy Dow 1943- ConAu 133
**Adams,** Timothy Journay 1948- WhoEnt 92
**Adams,** Tony 1936- TwCPaSc
**Adams,** Tony 1953- IntMPA 92
**Adams,** Tucker Hart 1938- WhoFI 92
**Adams,** V. Toni 1946- WhoBlA 92
**Adams,** Verna May 1928- WhoBlA 92
**Adams,** Vernon Gerard 1959- WhoRel 92
**Adams,** Victorine Quille WhoBlA 92
**Adams,** Victorine Quille 1912- WhoAmP 91
**Adams,** Vivian Bliss 1906- WhoAmP 91
**Adams,** W. Dacres 1864-1951 TwCPaSc
**Adams,** Wade J 1940- AmMWSc 92
**Adams,** Walter 1922- WhoFI 92, WhoMW 92, WrDr 92
**Adams,** Walter C 1936- AmMWSc 92
**Adams,** Walter Hollis 1907- RelLAm 91
**Adams,** Walter Sydney 1876-1956 FacFETw
**Adams,** Warren Dale 1949- WhoWest 92
**Adams,** Weston 1938- WhoAmP 91
**Adams,** Wilhelmina F. 1901- WhoBlA 92
**Adams,** William Alfred 1941- AmMWSc 92
**Adams,** William Alfred 1960- WhoAmL 92
**Adams,** William C. 1948- WrDr 92
**Adams,** William Eugene 1930- AmMWSc 92
**Adams,** William Gillette 1939- WhoAmL 92
**Adams,** William Henry 1933- AmMWSc 92
**Adams,** William James 1932- IntWW 91, Who 92
**Adams,** William James, Jr. 1938- WhoRel 92
**Adams,** William Johnston 1934- WhoFI 92, WhoMW 92
**Adams,** William Lawreson 1932- AmMWSc 92
**Adams,** William Lee 1945- WhoWest 92
**Adams,** William LeRoy 1929- WhoFI 92
**Adams,** William Mansfield 1932- AmMWSc 92
**Adams,** William Richard 1923- WhoMW 92
**Adams,** William S 1919- AmMWSc 92
**Adams,** William Sanders 1934- AmMWSc 92
**Adams,** William Taylor 1822-1897 BenetAL 91
**Adams,** William Valere 1948- WhoAmL 92
**Adams,** William Walter, Jr 1929- WhoAmP 91
**Adams,** William Wells 1937- AmMWSc 92
**Adams-Dudley,** Lilly Annette 1950- WhoBlA 92
**Adams-Ender,** Clara Leach 1939- NotBlAW 92
**Adams-Esquivel,** Henry E. 1940- WhoHisp 92
**Adams-Schneider,** Lancelot 1919- Who 92
**Adams-Schneider,** Lancelot Raymond 1919- IntWW 91
**Adamshick,** Elizabeth Therese 1962- WhoRel 92
**Adamski,** George 1891-1965 RelLAm 91
**Adamski,** Richard J. WhoFI 92
**Adamski,** Robert J 1935- AmMWSc 92
**Adamson,** Albert S, Jr 1947- AmMWSc 92
**Adamson,** Arthur Wilson 1919- AmMWSc 92
**Adamson,** Campbell Who 92
**Adamson,** Campbell 1922- IntWW 91
**Adamson,** Crawfurd 1953- TwCPaSc
**Adamson,** David Jay 1957- WhoFI 92
**Adamson,** Donald 1939- IntAu&W 91, WrDr 92
**Adamson,** Douglas Hugo 1934- WhoAmL 92
**Adamson,** Geoffrey David 1946- WhoWest 92
**Adamson,** Gerald Edwin 1934- WhoWest 92
**Adamson,** Hamish Christopher 1935- Who 92
**Adamson,** Iain 1928- IntAu&W 91
**Adamson,** Ian Young Radcliffe 1941- AmMWSc 92
**Adamson,** James C. NewYTBS 91 [port]
**Adamson,** Janet Laurel 1882-1962 BiDBrF 2
**Adamson,** Jerome Eugene 1927- AmMWSc 92
**Adamson,** John Douglas 1932- AmMWSc 92
**Adamson,** Lucile Frances 1926- AmMWSc 92
**Adamson,** M. J. ConAu 134
**Adamson,** Mary Anne 1954- WhoWest 92
**Adamson,** Mary Jo 1935- ConAu 134
**Adamson,** Norman Joseph 1930- Who 92
**Adamson,** Randolph J. 1954- WhoRel 92, WhoWest 92
**Adamson,** Reggie D. 1951- WhoIns 92
**Adamson,** Richard H 1937- AmMWSc 92
**Adamson,** Robert 1943- ConPo 91, IntAu&W 91, WrDr 92
**Adamson,** S Lee 1954- AmMWSc 92
**Adamson,** Terrence Burdett 1946- WhoAmL 92
**Adamson,** Thomas 1901- Who 92
**Adamson,** Thomas C, Jr 1924- AmMWSc 92
**Adamson,** Thomas Charles, Jr. 1924- WhoMW 92
**Adamson,** William Owen Campbell 1922- Who 92
**Adamson,** William Robert 1927- WhoRel 92
**Adamson-Macedo,** Emeritus Colin 1922- Who 92
**Adamson-McMullen,** Tamela Jo 1959- WhoMW 92
**Adamsons,** Karlis, Jr 1926- AmMWSc 92
**Adamsson,** Slade DrAPF 91
**Adan,** Alvaro Jose 1949- WhoHisp 92
**Adang,** Peter J. 1940- WhoAmL 92
**Adanio,** Louis A. WhoIns 92
**Adaskaveg,** James Elliott 1960- AmMWSc 92
**Adaskin,** Eleanor Jean 1937- AmMWSc 92
**Adaskin,** Murray 1906- NewAmDM, WhoEnt 92
**Adato,** Perry Miller WhoEnt 92
**Adawi,** Ibrahim 1930- AmMWSc 92
**Aday,** Carla Renee 1963- WhoRel 92
**Adcock,** Betty DrAPF 91
**Adcock,** Fleur 1934- ConAu 34NR, ConPo 91, IntAu&W 91, WrDr 92
**Adcock,** James Luther 1943- AmMWSc 92
**Adcock,** James Michael 1949- WhoFI 92
**Adcock,** Louis Henry 1929- AmMWSc 92
**Adcock,** Robert Henry d1990 Who 92N
**Adcock,** Robert Wadsworth 1932- Who 92
**Adcock,** Willis Alfred 1922- AmMWSc 92
**Adda,** Lionel Paul 1922- AmMWSc 92
**Addamiano,** Arrigo 1923- AmMWSc 92
**Addams,** Charles 1912-1988 BenetAL 91, FacFETw
**Addams,** Jane 1860-1935 AmPeW, BenetAL 91, DcAmImH, FacFETw [port], HanAmWH, PorAmW [port], RComAH, WomSoc
**Addams,** Laura Jane 1860-1935 WhoNob 90
**Addams,** Robert Jean 1942- WhoWest 92
**Addanki,** Somasundaram 1932- AmMWSc 92
**Addei,** Arthella Harris 1943- WhoBlA 92
**Adderley** Who 92
**Adderley,** Cannonball 1928-1975 NewAmDM
**Adderley,** Herb Anthony 1939- WhoBlA 92
**Adderley,** Julian 1928-1975 FacFETw
**Adderley,** Nathaniel 1931- WhoBlA 92
**Adderly,** Alfonso Leo WhoBlA 92
**Adderly,** T. C., Jr. 1949- WhoBlA 92
**Addesso,** Dominic James 1953- WhoIns 92
**Addesso,** Patricia Joan 1955- WhoFI 92
**Addicks,** Mentor DrAPF 91
**Addicott,** Fredrick Taylor 1912- AmMWSc 92
**Addicott,** John Fredrick 1944- AmMWSc 92
**Addicott,** Warren O 1930- AmMWSc 92
**Addie,** Harvey Woodward 1930- WhoWest 92
**Addington** Who 92
**Addington,** Baron 1963- Who 92
**Addington,** Arnold Lee 1934- WhoMW 92
**Addington,** Arthur Charles 1939- IntAu&W 91, WrDr 92
**Addington,** Conley Richmond, Jr. 1945- WhoFI 92
**Addington,** Larry Holbrook 1932- IntAu&W 91, WrDr 92
**Addington,** Laurence Milton 1936- WhoAmL 92
**Addink,** Sylvan 1941- AmMWSc 92
**Addinsell,** Richard 1904-1977 NewAmDM
**Addis,** Laird Clark, Jr. 1937- WhoMW 92
**Addis,** Lonie R 1950- WhoAmP 91
**Addis,** Paul Bradley 1941- AmMWSc 92
**Addis,** Richard Barton 1929- WhoAmL 92, WhoWest 92
**Addis,** Sara Allen 1930- WhoFI 92
**Addis,** Thomas Homer, III 1945- WhoWest 92
**Addison** Who 92
**Addison,** Viscount 1914- Who 92
**Addison,** Adele 1925- NewAmDM, WhoBlA 92
**Addison,** Anne Simone Pomex 1927- WhoEnt 92
**Addison,** Anthony William 1946- AmMWSc 92
**Addison,** Carl Vernon, Jr. 1957- WhoRel 92
**Addison,** Caroline Elizabeth 1938- WhoBlA 92
**Addison,** Charles H. 1941- WhoIns 92
**Addison,** Cyril Clifford 1913- IntWW 91, Who 92
**Addison,** Duane Leroy 1930- WhoRel 92
**Addison,** Edward L. 1930- WhoFI 92
**Addison,** Herbert John 1932- WhoFI 92
**Addison,** Howard Alan 1950- WhoRel 92
**Addison,** Hugh 1881-1956 ScFEYrs
**Addison,** J. Bruce 1953- WhoWest 92
**Addison,** James Bruce 1953- WhoAmP 91
**Addison,** John 1920- ConTFT 9, IntMPA 92, IntWW 91
**Addison,** John Robert 1927- WhoWest 92
**Addison,** John West, Jr 1930- AmMWSc 92
**Addison,** Joseph 1672-1719 BlkwCEP, CnDBLB 2 [port], LitC 18, RfGEnL 91
**Addison,** Kenneth George 1923- Who 92
**Addison,** Leslie Wayne 1954- WhoRel 92
**Addison,** Linda Leuchter 1951- WhoAmL 92
**Addison,** Lloyd E. DrAPF 91
**Addison,** Michael Francis 1942- Who 92
**Addison,** Philip Harold 1909- Who 92
**Addison,** Randolph Dallas 1948- WhoAmL 92
**Addison,** Richard Frederick 1941- AmMWSc 92
**Addison,** Terry Hunter, Jr. 1950- WhoBlA 92
**Addison,** William 1905- IntAu&W 91, Who 92, WrDr 92
**Addiss,** Richard Robert, Jr 1929- AmMWSc 92
**Addiss,** Stephen 1935- WhoMW 92
**Addleton,** David Franklin 1954- WhoAmL 92
**Addor,** Roger Williams 1926- AmMWSc 92
**Adducci,** James Dominick 1951- WhoAmL 92
**Adducci,** Joseph Edward 1934- WhoMW 92
**Adduci,** Jerry M 1934- AmMWSc 92
**Addy,** Alva LeRoy 1936- AmMWSc 92
**Addy,** Frederick Seale 1932- WhoFI 92
**Addy,** John 1949- WhoAmP 91
**Addy,** John Keith 1937- AmMWSc 92
**Addy,** John Kelly 1949- WhoAmL 92
**Addy,** Lowell David 1951- WhoRel 92
**Addy,** Tralance Obuama 1944- AmMWSc 92, WhoBlA 92
**Addyman,** Peter Vincent 1939- Who 92
**Ade,** George d1944 SourALJ
**Ade,** George 1866-1944 BenetAL 91, FacFETw
**Ade,** Jerome C. 1950- WhoEnt 92
**Ade,** Ronald Charles 1929- WhoIns 92
**Adea** EncAmaz 91
**Adeane,** Edward 1939- Who 92
**Adebo,** Simeon Olaosebikan 1913- IntWW 91
**Adebo,** Simeon Olaosebikan, Chief 1913- Who 92
**Adedeji,** Adebayo 1930- IntWW 91
**Adegbile,** Gideon Sunday Adebisi 1941- WhoBlA 92
**Adegbola,** Sikiru Kolawole 1949- WhoFI 92, WhoWest 92
**Adekson,** Mary Olufunmilayo 1945- WhoMW 92
**Adel,** Arthur 1908- AmMWSc 92
**Adel,** Garry David 1956- WhoAmL 92
**Adelaide,** Archbishop of 1926- Who 92
**Adelaide,** Archbishop of 1934- Who 92
**Adelaide,** Dean of Who 92
**Adelaide of Susa** 931?-999 EncAmaz 91
**Adelberg,** Arnold M 1936- AmMWSc 92
**Adelberg,** Arnold Melvin 1936- WhoMW 92
**Adelberg,** Arthur William 1951- WhoAmL 92, WhoFI 92
**Adelberg,** Doris IntAu&W 91X, WrDr 92
**Adelberg,** Edward Allen 1920- AmMWSc 92
**Adelberg,** M. Bruce 1936- WhoFI 92
**Adelberger,** Eric George 1938- AmMWSc 92
**Adelberger,** Rexford E 1940- AmMWSc 92
**Adeler,** Max BenetAL 91
**Adeler,** Max 1847-1915 ScFEYrs
**Adeli,** Hojjat 1950- AmMWSc 92, WhoFI 92, WhoMW 92
**Adeli,** Muhammad Hossein 1952- IntWW 91
**Adelita** EncAmaz 91
**Adelman,** Albert H 1930- AmMWSc 92
**Adelman,** Barnet Reuben 1925- AmMWSc 92
**Adelman,** Bette Orovan 1936- WhoAmL 92
**Adelman,** Clifford 1942- WrDr 92
**Adelman,** Gary IntMPA 92
**Adelman,** Gary 1935- WhoMW 92
**Adelman,** Gerald S. 1942- WhoIns 92
**Adelman,** Ira Robert 1941- AmMWSc 92
**Adelman,** Irma Glicman 1930- IntWW 91, WrDr 92
**Adelman,** Jonathan Reuben 1948- WhoWest 92
**Adelman,** Joseph A. 1933- IntMPA 92
**Adelman,** Joseph Aaron 1933- WhoEnt 92
**Adelman,** Kenneth Lee 1946- IntWW 91
**Adelman,** Lucille Marie 1933- WhoRel 92
**Adelman,** Lynn S 1939- WhoAmP 91
**Adelman,** Mark Robert 1942- AmMWSc 92
**Adelman,** Pamela Bernice 1945- WhoMW 92
**Adelman,** Richard Charles 1940- AmMWSc 92
**Adelman,** Rick 1946- WhoWest 92
**Adelman,** Robert Leonard 1919- AmMWSc 92
**Adelman,** Saul Joseph 1944- AmMWSc 92
**Adelman,** Steven Allen 1945- WhoMW 92
**Adelman,** Steven Herbert 1945- WhoAmL 92
**Adelman,** William Joseph, Jr 1928- AmMWSc 92
**Adelmann,** Gerald William 1949- WhoMW 92
**Adelo,** A. Samuel 1923- WhoHisp 92
**Adels,** Robert Mitchell 1948- WhoEnt 92
**Adelsheim,** Mark Simon 1952- WhoEnt 92
**Adelsohn,** Ulf 1941- IntWW 91
**Adelson,** Bernard Henry 1920- AmMWSc 92
**Adelson,** Edward 1934- WhoMW 92
**Adelson,** Gary 1954- IntMPA 92
**Adelson,** Harold Ely 1931- AmMWSc 92
**Adelson,** Lawrence Seth 1950- WhoAmL 92
**Adelson,** Lester 1914- AmMWSc 92
**Adelson,** Mark Hirsch 1960- WhoAmL 92
**Adelson,** Maurice Bernard, IV 1952- WhoAmL 92
**Adelson,** Merv LesBEnT 92
**Adelson,** Merv 1929- IntMPA 92
**Adelson,** Mervyn Lee 1929- WhoWest 92
**Adelstein,** Abraham Manie 1916- Who 92
**Adelstein,** Peter Z 1924- AmMWSc 92
**Adelstein,** Robert Milton 1934- WhoWest 92
**Adelstein,** Robert Simon 1934- AmMWSc 92

**Adelstein**, Stanford M. 1931- *WhoMW 92*
**Adelstein**, Stanford Mark 1931- *WhoAmP 91*
**Adelstein**, Stanley James 1928- *AmMWSc 92*
**Adelstone**, Jeffrey Alan 1947- *WhoWest 92*
**Adem**, Alejandro 1961- *WhoMW 92*
**Ademola**, Adetokunbo 1906- *Who 92*
**Ademola**, Adetokunbo Adegboyega 1906- *IntWW 91*
**Aden**, David Paul 1946- *AmMWSc 92*
**Adenauer**, Konrad 1876-1967 *EncTR 91 [port], FacFETw [port]*
**Adeney**, Bernard 1878-1966 *TwCPaSc*
**Adeney**, Noel *TwCPaSc*
**Adent**, William A 1923- *AmMWSc 92*
**Ader**, David Lincoln 1943- *WhoAmL 92*
**Ader**, Joseph Daniel 1947- *WhoFI 92*
**Ader**, Robert 1932- *AmMWSc 92*
**Aderhold**, Freddie Gary 1939- *WhoFI 92*
**Aderholt**, Ben L. 1942- *WhoAmL 92*
**Aderman**, Morris 1927- *WhoMW 92*
**Aderson**, Sanford M. 1949- *WhoAmL 92*
**Aderton**, Jane Reynolds 1913- *WhoFI 92*
**Ades**, Dawn 1943- *IntAu&W 91, WrDr 92*
**Ades**, Diana Ruth 1962- *WhoFI 92*
**Ades**, Edwin W 1949- *AmMWSc 92*
**Ades**, Ibrahim Z 1946- *AmMWSc 92*
**Adesina**, Segun 1941- *IntWW 91*
**Adesiyan**, Hattie Rose Olagbegi *WhoMW 92*
**Adesnik**, Milton 1943- *AmMWSc 92*
**Adesuyi**, Sunday Adeniji 1948- *WhoBlA 92*
**Adetiloye**, Joseph Abiodun *Who 92*
**Adewoye**, Omoniyi 1939- *IntWW 91*
**Adewoyin**, Lawale Lanrewaju 1955- *WhoFI 92*
**Adey**, Christopher 1943- *IntWW 91*
**Adey**, W Ross 1922- *AmMWSc 92*
**Adey**, Walter Hamilton 1934- *AmMWSc 92*
**Adey**, William Ross 1922- *AmMWSc 92, WrDr 92*
**Adeyiga**, Adeyinka A. 1948- *WhoBlA 92*
**Adeyiga**, Olanrewaju Muniru 1949- *WhoBlA 92*
**Adgate**, Andrew 1762-1793 *NewAmDM*
**Adhav**, Ratnakar Shankar 1927- *AmMWSc 92*
**Adhikari**, P K 1928- *AmMWSc 92*
**Adhikari**, Santos Kumar 1923- *IntAu&W 91*
**Adhout**, Shahla Marvizi 1954- *AmMWSc 92*
**Adhya**, Sankar L 1937- *AmMWSc 92*
**Adiarte**, Arthur Lardizabal 1943- *AmMWSc 92*
**Adibhatla**, Sridhar 1955- *WhoMW 92*
**Adibi**, Siamak A 1932- *AmMWSc 92*
**Adickes**, H Wayne 1940- *AmMWSc 92*
**Adicoff**, Arnold 1923- *AmMWSc 92*
**Adicoff**, Arnold 1927- *WhoWest 92*
**Adie**, Jack Jesson 1913- *Who 92*
**Adie**, Kathryn 1945- *IntWW 91, Who 92*
**Adie**, Michael Edgar *Who 92*
**Adiele**, Moses Nkwachukwu 1951- *WhoBlA 92*
**Adin**, Anthony 1942- *AmMWSc 92*
**Adinoff**, Bernard 1919- *AmMWSc 92*
**Adinolfi**, Anthony M 1939- *AmMWSc 92*
**Adireksarn**, Pramara 1914- *IntWW 91*
**Adirim**, Aaron 1946- *WhoEnt 92*
**Adisa**, Opal Palmer *DrAPF 91*
**Adisesh**, Setty Ravanappa 1926- *AmMWSc 92*
**Adiseshiah**, Malcolm Sathianathan 1910- *IntWW 91, Who 92*
**Adisman**, I Kenneth 1919- *AmMWSc 92*
**Adivar**, Halide Ebib 1883-1964 *FacFETw*
**Adjani**, Isabelle 1955- *ConTFT 9, IntMPA 92, IntWW 91, News 91 [port]*
**Adjemian**, Haroutioon 1948- *AmMWSc 92*
**Adkins**, Arthur William Hope 1929- *IntAu&W 91, WrDr 92*
**Adkins**, Ben Frank 1938- *WhoWest 92*
**Adkins**, Betty A 1934- *WhoAmP 91*
**Adkins**, Cecelia 1923- *NotBlAW 92*
**Adkins**, Cecelia Nabrit 1923- *WhoBlA 92*
**Adkins**, Charles 1932- *BlkOlyM*
**Adkins**, Charles Eddington 1946- *WhoMW 92*
**Adkins**, David Jay 1961- *WhoAmL 92*
**Adkins**, Dean Aaron 1946- *AmMWSc 92*
**Adkins**, Dinah 1947- *WhoFI 92*
**Adkins**, Edward Cleland 1926- *WhoAmL 92*
**Adkins**, Edward James 1947- *WhoAmL 92*
**Adkins**, Elizabeth W. 1957- *WhoMW 92*
**Adkins**, George Young, Jr 1923- *WhoAmP 91*
**Adkins**, Iona W. 1925- *WhoBlA 92*
**Adkins**, James Calhoun 1915- *WhoAmP 91*
**Adkins**, James Scott *AmMWSc 92*
**Adkins**, Jeanne M 1949- *WhoAmP 91*
**Adkins**, John Earl, Jr 1937- *AmMWSc 92*
**Adkins**, Johnie Kemper 1961- *WhoRel 92*
**Adkins**, Joseph Wayne 1951- *WhoMW 92*
**Adkins**, Kenneth 1930- *WhoAmP 91*
**Adkins**, Patrick H 1948- *IntAu&W 91*
**Adkins**, Penny Lynn 1954- *WhoEnt 92*
**Adkins**, Rocky 1959- *WhoAmP 91*
**Adkins**, Ronald James 1932- *AmMWSc 92*
**Adkins**, Scott Allen 1967- *WhoMW 92*
**Adkins**, Sheila Alberta 1952- *WhoEnt 92*
**Adkins**, Steve B 1948- *WhoAmP 91*
**Adkins**, Theodore Roosevelt, Jr 1930- *AmMWSc 92*
**Adkins**, William Eugen 1948- *WhoMW 92*
**Adkins**, William H, II *WhoAmP 91*
**Adkins-Regan**, Elizabeth Kocher 1945- *AmMWSc 92*
**Adkinson**, Brian Lee 1959- *WhoFI 92*
**Adkinson**, Newton Franklin, Jr 1943- *AmMWSc 92*
**Adkison**, Claudia R 1941- *AmMWSc 92*
**Adkison**, Daniel Lee 1950- *AmMWSc 92*
**Adkisson**, Curtis Samuel 1942- *AmMWSc 92*
**Adkisson**, David C *WhoAmP 91*
**Adkisson**, Perry Lee 1929- *AmMWSc 92, IntWW 91*
**Adkisson**, Randall Lynn 1957- *WhoRel 92*
**Adkisson**, Richard Blanks 1932- *WhoAmL 92*
**Adkisson**, Tommy 1949- *WhoAmP 91*
**Adlai**, Richard Salvatore *WhoWest 92*
**Adlard**, Mark 1932- *TwCSFW 91, WrDr 92*
**Adldinger**, Hans Karl *AmMWSc 92*
**Adleman**, Robert H 1919- *IntAu&W 91*
**Adler**, Abraham 1952- *WhoEnt 92*
**Adler**, Alan David 1931- *AmMWSc 92*
**Adler**, Alexandra 1901- *AmMWSc 92*
**Adler**, Alfred 1870-1937 *FacFETw*
**Adler**, Alfred 1930- *AmMWSc 92*
**Adler**, Alice Joan 1935- *AmMWSc 92*
**Adler**, Allen 1946- *IntMPA 92*
**Adler**, Beatriz C 1929- *AmMWSc 92*
**Adler**, Beth Sharon 1960- *WhoAmL 92*
**Adler**, Betty Susan 1958- *WhoAmL 92*
**Adler**, C.S. *DrAPF 91*
**Adler**, C. S. 1932- *WrDr 92*
**Adler**, Carl George 1939- *AmMWSc 92*
**Adler**, Carol *DrAPF 91*
**Adler**, Cary Michael 1950- *WhoWest 92*
**Adler**, Charles David 1945- *WhoAmL 92*
**Adler**, Charles Francis, III 1957- *WhoAmL 92*
**Adler**, Charles Spencer 1941- *WhoWest 92*
**Adler**, Craig Richard 1959- *WhoFI 92*
**Adler**, Daniel Joseph 1954- *WhoAmL 92*
**Adler**, David Neil 1955- *WhoAmL 92*
**Adler**, Debra Ann Zei 1965- *WhoMW 92*
**Adler**, Donald James, Jr. 1958- *WhoWest 92*
**Adler**, Douglas B. 1952- *WhoAmL 92*
**Adler**, Dwain Robert 1955- *WhoEnt 92*
**Adler**, Earl 1932- *WhoIns 92*
**Adler**, Edward Andrew Koeppel 1948- *WhoAmL 92*
**Adler**, Edward Harold 1948- *WhoFI 92*
**Adler**, Eric 1937- *AmMWSc 92*
**Adler**, Eric L 1930- *AmMWSc 92*
**Adler**, Ernest E 1950- *WhoAmP 91*
**Adler**, Erwin Ellery 1941- *WhoAmL 92, WhoFI 92, WhoWest 92*
**Adler**, Felix 1851-1933 *BenetAL 91, RelLAm 91*
**Adler**, Fran *DrAPF 91*
**Adler**, Frank Leo 1922- *AmMWSc 92*
**Adler**, Frederick Richard 1925- *WhoAmL 92*
**Adler**, Friedrich 1879-1960 *EncTR 91*
**Adler**, George 1920- *AmMWSc 92*
**Adler**, George Fritz Werner 1926- *Who 92*
**Adler**, Helmut E. 1920- *WrDr 92*
**Adler**, Howard, Jr. 1925- *WhoAmL 92*
**Adler**, Howard Bruce 1951- *WhoAmL 92*
**Adler**, Howard Irving 1931- *AmMWSc 92*
**Adler**, Ilya 1945- *WhoHisp 92*
**Adler**, Ira Jay 1942- *WhoAmL 92*
**Adler**, Irene *ConAu 35NR*
**Adler**, Irving 1913- *IntAu&W 91*
**Adler**, Irving Larry 1943- *AmMWSc 92*
**Adler**, Irwin L 1928- *AmMWSc 92*
**Adler**, Isaac 1849-1918 *BiInAmS*
**Adler**, Jacob Henry 1919- *WrDr 92*
**Adler**, James R. 1950- *WhoEnt 92*
**Adler**, James Robert 1936- *WhoFI 92*
**Adler**, Jankel 1895-1949 *TwCPaSc*
**Adler**, John G 1935- *AmMWSc 92*
**Adler**, John Henry 1948- *AmMWSc 92*
**Adler**, John Stanley 1948- *WhoAmL 92*
**Adler**, John W., Jr. 1936- *WhoAmL 92*
**Adler**, Julius 1930- *AmMWSc 92, IntWW 91*
**Adler**, Kathleen Jo 1947- *WhoAmL 92*
**Adler**, Kenneth B 1945- *AmMWSc 92*
**Adler**, Kraig 1940- *AmMWSc 92*
**Adler**, Kurt Alfred 1905- *AmMWSc 92*
**Adler**, Kurt Herbert 1905-1987 *NewAmDM*
**Adler**, Larry 1914- *IntWW 91, NewAmDM, Who 92, WhoEnt 92*
**Adler**, Larry David 1944- *WhoFI 92*
**Adler**, Laszlo 1932- *AmMWSc 92*
**Adler**, Laurel Ann 1948- *WhoWest 92*
**Adler**, Lawrence 1923- *AmMWSc 92*
**Adler**, Lawrence H. 1960- *WhoAmL 92*
**Adler**, Lewis Gerard 1960- *WhoAmL 92*
**Adler**, Lou 1933- *WhoEnt 92*
**Adler**, Louis S. 1943- *WhoMW 92*
**Adler**, Louise Tale 1925- *AmMWSc 92*
**Adler**, Lucile *DrAPF 91*
**Adler**, Margot 1946- *RelLAm 91*
**Adler**, Margot Susanna 1946- *IntAu&W 91*
**Adler**, Marion Beth 1954- *WhoAmL 92*
**Adler**, Marnie *DrAPF 91*
**Adler**, Martin 1934- *WhoIns 92*
**Adler**, Martin E 1929- *AmMWSc 92*
**Adler**, Michael 1948- *AmMWSc 92*
**Adler**, Michael Lee 1947- *WhoMW 92*
**Adler**, Michael Stuart 1943- *AmMWSc 92*
**Adler**, Michael William 1939- *Who 92*
**Adler**, Milton Leon 1926- *WhoMW 92*
**Adler**, Mortimer J. 1902- *BenetAL 91, IntAu&W 91, WrDr 92*
**Adler**, Mortimer Jerome 1902- *FacFETw*
**Adler**, Norman 1928- *AmMWSc 92*
**Adler**, Patricia Ann 1951- *WhoWest 92*
**Adler**, Peggy 1942- *WhoEnt 92, WhoFI 92*
**Adler**, Peter Herman 1899-1990 *FacFETw, NewAmDM*
**Adler**, Philip N 1935- *AmMWSc 92*
**Adler**, Raffael *WhoEnt 92*
**Adler**, Ralph Peter Isaac 1937- *AmMWSc 92*
**Adler**, Renata *DrAPF 91*
**Adler**, Renata 1938- *BenetAL 91, ConNov 91, FacFETw, IntAu&W 91, WrDr 92*
**Adler**, Richard 1921- *NewAmDM, WhoEnt 92*
**Adler**, Richard 1948- *AmMWSc 92*
**Adler**, Richard Alan 1942- *WhoIns 92*
**Adler**, Richard B 1922- *AmMWSc 92*
**Adler**, Richard H 1922- *AmMWSc 92*
**Adler**, Richard John 1955- *AmMWSc 92*
**Adler**, Richard R *AmMWSc 92*
**Adler**, Robert 1913- *AmMWSc 92*
**Adler**, Robert Alan 1945- *AmMWSc 92*
**Adler**, Robert Frederick 1944- *AmMWSc 92*
**Adler**, Robert Garber 1929- *AmMWSc 92*
**Adler**, Robert J 1931- *AmMWSc 92*
**Adler**, Ronald John 1937- *AmMWSc 92*
**Adler**, Roy Lee 1931- *AmMWSc 92*
**Adler**, Ruben 1940- *AmMWSc 92*
**Adler**, Samuel 1898-1979 *FacFETw*
**Adler**, Samuel 1928- *NewAmDM*
**Adler**, Samuel Hans 1928- *WhoEnt 92*
**Adler**, Sanford Charles 1940- *AmMWSc 92*
**Adler**, Sara 1942- *WhoAmL 92*
**Adler**, Seymour Jack 1930- *WhoMW 92*
**Adler**, Seymour Jacob 1918- *AmMWSc 92*
**Adler**, Solomon Stanley 1945- *AmMWSc 92*
**Adler**, Stephen Fred 1930- *AmMWSc 92*
**Adler**, Stephen L 1939- *AmMWSc 92*
**Adler**, Thomas William 1940- *WhoMW 92*
**Adler**, Valerie *TwCPaSc*
**Adler**, Victor Eugene 1924- *AmMWSc 92*
**Adler**, Warren *NewYTBS 91 [port]*
**Adler**, Warren 1927- *IntAu&W 91, WhoEnt 92, WrDr 92*
**Adler**, William 1939- *AmMWSc 92*
**Adler**, William Fred 1937- *AmMWSc 92*
**Adlercreutz**, Herman 1932- *IntWW 91*
**Adlerstein**, Lee Alan 1947- *WhoAmL 92*
**Adlerstein**, Michael Gene *AmMWSc 92*
**Adlerz**, Warren Clifford 1928- *AmMWSc 92*
**Adley**, James Leonard 1931- *WhoMW 92*
**Adley**, Mark Atwood 1959- *WhoFI 92*
**Adley**, Robert 1947- *WhoAmP 91*
**Adley**, Robert James 1935- *Who 92*
**Adlof**, Richard Otto 1947- *AmMWSc 92*
**Adlon**, Percy 1935- *IntMPA 92*
**Adlum**, John 1759-1836 *BiInAmS*
**Adman**, Elinor Thomson 1941- *AmMWSc 92*
**Admani**, Karim 1937- *Who 92*
**Admire**, Ben H. 1949- *WhoAmL 92*
**Admire**, Rebecca Lynn 1960- *WhoFI 92*
**Adney**, Joseph Elliott, Jr 1923- *AmMWSc 92*
**Adney**, Robert William 1955- *WhoEnt 92*
**Adni**, Daniel 1951- *IntWW 91*
**Ado**, Andrey Dmitriyevich 1909- *IntWW 91*
**Adoff**, Arnold 1935- *IntAu&W 91, WrDr 92*
**Adolf**, Kathryn Ann 1957- *WhoWest 92*
**Adolf**, Ramond Romer 1932- *WhoFI 92*
**Adolfo** 1933- *IntWW 91, WhoHisp 92*
**Adolph**, Alan Robert 1932- *AmMWSc 92*
**Adolph**, Anne *ScFEYrs*
**Adolph**, Dale Dennis 1948- *WhoWest 92*
**Adolph**, Edward Frederick 1895- *AmMWSc 92*
**Adolph**, Gerald Stephen 1953- *WhoBlA 92*
**Adolph**, Horst Guenter 1932- *AmMWSc 92*
**Adolph**, Kenneth William 1944- *AmMWSc 92*
**Adolph**, Mary Rosenquist 1949- *WhoFI 92, WhoWest 92*
**Adolph**, Robert J 1927- *AmMWSc 92*
**Adolph**, William F, Jr 1949- *WhoAmP 91*
**Adolphe Legalite** *EncTR 91*
**Adolphe**, Bruce Mauri 1955- *WhoEnt 92*
**Adom**, Edwin Nii Amalai 1941- *WhoBlA 92*
**Adomian**, George *AmMWSc 92*
**Adomian**, Gerald E *AmMWSc 92*
**Adoor**, Gopalakrishnan 1941- *IntWW 91*
**Adorjan**, Carol 1934- *IntAu&W 91*
**Adorjan**, Carol M. *DrAPF 91*
**Adorjan**, Julius Joe 1938- *WhoFI 92*
**Adorney**, Charles Sam 1925- *WhoEnt 92*
**Adorno**, Theodor 1903-1969 *FacFETw*
**Adorno**, Theodore W. 1903-1969 *LiExTwC*
**Adouki**, Martin 1942- *IntWW 91*
**Adoula**, Cyrille 1921-1978 *FacFETw*
**Adoum**, Jorge Enrique 1923- *ConSpAP*
**Adoum**, Mahamat Ali 1947- *IntWW 91*
**Adragna**, Norma C *AmMWSc 92*
**Adragna**, Norma Cristina 1946- *WhoMW 92*
**Adrain**, Robert 1775-1843 *BiInAmS*
**Adrian** *Who 92*
**Adrian**, Baron 1927- *IntWW 91, Who 92*
**Adrian**, Alan Patrick 1916- *AmMWSc 92*
**Adrian**, Arthur Allen 1906- *IntAu&W 91, WrDr 92*
**Adrian**, Edgar Douglas 1889-1977 *FacFETw, WhoNob 90*
**Adrian**, Erle Keys, Jr 1936- *AmMWSc 92*
**Adrian**, Frances *SmATA 68, WrDr 92*
**Adrian**, Frank John 1929- *AmMWSc 92*
**Adrian**, Gary Alan 1951- *WhoEnt 92*
**Adrian**, Hal L. 1934- *WhoIns 92*
**Adrian**, Iris 1913- *IntMPA 92*
**Adrian**, Rhys 1928-1990 *AnObit 1990*
**Adrian**, Ronald John 1945- *AmMWSc 92*
**Adrian**, Thomas E 1950- *AmMWSc 92*
**Adrianopoli**, Barbara Catherine 1943- *WhoMW 92*
**Adrien**, J. F. M. L. *Who 92*
**Adrine**, Ronald Bruce 1947- *WhoBlA 92*
**Adrion**, William Richards 1943- *AmMWSc 92*
**Adrounie**, V Harry 1915- *AmMWSc 92, WhoMW 92*
**Adrouny**, George Adour 1916- *AmMWSc 92*
**Adshead**, Mary *Who 92*
**Adshead**, Mary 1904- *TwCPaSc*
**Adt**, Robert 1940- *AmMWSc 92*
**Adubato**, Michael F 1934- *WhoAmP 91*
**Aduddell**, J. Rucker 1944- *WhoEnt 92*
**Aduddle**, Larry Steven 1946- *WhoMW 92*
**Aduss**, Howard 1932- *AmMWSc 92*
**Advani**, Lal K. 1927- *IntWW 91*
**Advani**, Prem O. 1940- *WhoMW 92*
**Advani**, Suresh Gopaldas 1959- *AmMWSc 92*
**Advey**, Robert Joseph, Jr. 1946- *WhoMW 92*
**Ady**, Endre 1877-1919 *FacFETw*
**Ady**, Robert 1935- *WhoMW 92*
**Adyaa**, Gelegiyn 1934- *IntWW 91*
**Adye**, John Anthony 1939- *Who 92*
**Adyebo**, George *IntWW 91*
**Adyrkhayeva**, Svetlana Dzantemirovna 1938- *IntWW 91*
**Adzak**, Roy 1927- *TwCPaSc*
**Adzick**, Shirley Rae 1957- *WhoMW 92*
**AE** *RfGEnL 91*
**AE** 1867-1935 *FacFETw*
**Aebersold**, Ruedi H 1954- *AmMWSc 92*
**Aebi**, Charles Jerry 1931- *WhoRel 92*
**Aehegma**, Aelbert Clark *DrAPF 91*
**Aehrenthal**, Alois Lexa von 1854-1912 *FacFETw*
**Aein**, Joseph Morris 1936- *AmMWSc 92*
**Aelfric** 955?-1012? *RfGEnL 91*
**Aeneas of Gaza** d518 *EncEarC*
**Aepinus**, Franz Ulrich Theodosius 1724-1802 *BlkwCEP*
**Aeppli**, Alfred 1928- *AmMWSc 92*
**Aeppli**, Oswald 1916- *IntWW 91*
**Aermont**, Paul *ScFEYrs*
**Aerni**, Russell W 1929- *WhoAmP 91*
**Aerosmith** *NewAmDM*
**Aeschbacher**, Steven John 1960- *WhoAmL 92*
**Aeschliman**, Lea H 1943- *WhoAmP 91*
**Aesop**, G. Washington *BenetAL 91*
**Aethelburg** *EncAmaz 91*
**Aethelflaed** 870-918 *EncAmaz 91*
**Aetius** 300?-370 *EncEarC*
**Afanador**, Arthur Joseph 1942- *AmMWSc 92*
**Afanas'ev**, Viktor Grigor'evich 1922- *SovUnBD*
**Afanas'ev**, Yuriy Nikolaevich 1934- *SovUnBD*
**Afanasiyev**, Georgiy Dmitriyevich 1906- *IntWW 91*

**Afanasiyev,** Sergey Aleksandrovich 1918- *IntWW 91*
**Afanasiyev,** Viktor Grigorevich 1922- *IntWW 91*
**Afanasyevsky,** Nikolai Nikolayevich 1940- *IntWW 91*
**Affan,** Ali Osman 1934- *WhoFI 92*
**Affandi,** Achmad 1927- *IntWW 91*
**Affeldt,** John E *AmMWSc 92*
**Affeldt,** Thomas Michael 1946- *WhoAmL 92*
**Affens,** Steven Charles 1947- *WhoEnt 92*
**Affens,** Wilbur Allen 1918- *AmMWSc 92*
**Affirmed** 1975- *FacFETw*
**Affleck,** James G. 1923- *IntWW 91*
**Affleck,** Julie Karleen 1944- *WhoWest 92*
**Afflerbach,** Roy Carl, II 1945- *WhoAmP 91*
**Afflerback,** C. Vincent 1918- *WhoFI 92*
**Afflis,** Richard d1991 *NewYTBS 91*
**Affrime,** Marvin B. 1925- *DcTwDes*
**Affron,** Charles 1935- *WrDr 92*
**Affronti,** Lewis Francis 1928- *AmMWSc 92*
**Afghan,** Baderuddin Khan 1940- *AmMWSc 92*
**Afinogenov,** Aleksandr Nikolaevich 1904-1941 *SovUnBD*
**Afinogenov,** Alexander Nikolayevich 1904-1941 *FacFETw*
**Aflaq,** Michel 1910-1989 *FacFETw*
**Afnan,** Iraj Ruhi 1939- *AmMWSc 92*
**Afonin,** Venyamin Georgievich 1931- *IntWW 91*
**Afonso,** Adriano 1935- *AmMWSc 92*
**Afra' Bint Ghifar al-Humayriah** *EncAmaz 91*
**Afrah,** Hussein Kulmia 1920- *IntWW 91*
**Afremow,** Leonard Calvin 1933- *AmMWSc 92*
**Africa,** Thomas W. 1927- *WrDr 92*
**Africano,** Lillian 1935- *IntAu&W 91*
**Africanus,** Leo *HisDSpE*
**Afsar,** Mohammed Nurul *AmMWSc 92*
**Afsari,** Khosrow 1941- *WhoWest 92*
**Afsarmanesh,** Hamideh 1953- *WhoWest 92*
**Afsary,** Cyrus 1940- *WhoWest 92*
**Afshar,** Kamran 1948- *WhoFI 92*
**Afshar,** Siroos K 1949- *AmMWSc 92*
**Aft,** Harvey 1929- *AmMWSc 92*
**Aftanski,** J. Alan 1948- *WhoAmL 92*
**Aftel,** Mandy *DrAPF 91*
**Aftergood,** Lilla 1925- *AmMWSc 92*
**Aftergut,** Siegfried 1927- *AmMWSc 92*
**Afterman,** Allan B. 1944- *WhoMW 92*
**Afterman,** Allen 1941- *WrDr 92*
**Aftoora,** Patricia J. 1940- *WhoFI 92*
**Afzal,** Sayed Mohammad Javed 1952- *WhoWest 92*
**Aga KhanIII** 1877-1957 *FacFETw*
**Aga Khan,** Sadruddin, Prince 1933- *IntWW 91*
**Aga KhanIV,** Karim, Prince 1936- *IntWW 91*
**Aga Khan,** Karim, His Highness Prince 1936- *Who 92*
**Aga Khan,** Karim, IV 1936- *WhoRel 92*
**Aga Khan,** Sadruddin 1933- *Who 92*
**Agababian,** Haig Harold 1922- *WhoFI 92*
**Agabian,** Nina *AmMWSc 92*
**Agacinski,** Daniel Norman 1949- *WhoFI 92*
**Agacinski,** Juli Lynn 1963- *WhoEnt 92*
**Agadzhanova-Shutko,** Nina Ferdinandovna 1889-1974 *SovUnBD*
**Agalloco,** James Paul 1948- *AmMWSc 92*
**Agam,** Yaacov 1928- *IntWW 91*
**Agamanolis,** Dimitris 1938- *AmMWSc 92*
**Agamirzyan,** Ruben Sergeyevich 1922- *IntWW 91*
**Agan,** Diane W. 1944- *WhoMW 92*
**Agan,** Raymond John 1919- *AmMWSc 92*
**Agan,** Robert Bruce 1951- *WhoFI 92*
**Aganbegyan,** Abel 1932- *IntWW 91*
**Aganbegyan,** Abel Gazevich 1932- *SovUnBD*
**Agapetus I** *EncEarC*
**Agapos,** A. Michael 1932- *WhoFI 92*
**Agar** *Who 92*
**Agar,** Eileen 1900- *TwCPaSc*
**Agar,** G E 1931- *AmMWSc 92*
**Agar,** Herbert 1897-1980 *BenetAL 91*
**Agar,** John 1921- *IntMPA 92*
**Agar,** John George, Jr. 1921- *WhoEnt 92*
**Agard,** David Leon 1941- *WhoEnt 92*
**Agard,** Eugene Theodore 1932- *AmMWSc 92*
**Agard,** John *WrDr 92*
**Agardy,** Franklin J 1933- *AmMWSc 92*
**Agarwal,** Arun Kumar 1944- *AmMWSc 92*
**Agarwal,** Ashok Kumar 1950- *AmMWSc 92*
**Agarwal,** Avadhesh Kumar 1945- *WhoWest 92*
**Agarwal,** Dinesh 1955- *WhoAmL 92*
**Agarwal,** Girish Chandra 1930- *IntWW 91*
**Agarwal,** Gyan C 1940- *AmMWSc 92*
**Agarwal,** Jagdish Chandra 1926- *AmMWSc 92*
**Agarwal,** Jai Bhagwah 1938- *AmMWSc 92*
**Agarwal,** Kailash C *AmMWSc 92*
**Agarwal,** Kan L *AmMWSc 92*
**Agarwal,** Paul D 1924- *AmMWSc 92*
**Agarwal,** Rajiv Arishan 1959- *WhoWest 92*
**Agarwal,** Ramesh Chandra 1946- *AmMWSc 92*
**Agarwal,** Ramesh K 1947- *AmMWSc 92*
**Agarwal,** Shyam S 1941- *AmMWSc 92*
**Agarwal,** Som Prakash 1930- *AmMWSc 92*
**Agarwal,** Suresh Kumar 1932- *AmMWSc 92*
**Agarwal,** Vijendra Kumar 1948- *AmMWSc 92*
**Agarwal,** Vinod Kumar 1952- *AmMWSc 92*
**Agarwal,** Vipin K 1955- *AmMWSc 92*
**Agarwala,** Vinod Shanker 1939- *AmMWSc 92*
**Agarwalla,** Chaman Lall 1924- *WhoWest 92*
**Agassiz,** Alexander Emmanuel Rodolphe 1835-1910 *BiInAmS*
**Agassiz,** Elizabeth Cabot Cary 1822-1907 *BiInAmS*
**Agassiz,** Jean Louis Rodolphe 1807-1873 *BiInAmS*
**Agassiz,** Louis *BiInAmS*
**Agassiz,** Louis 1807-1873 *BenetAL 91*
**Agata,** Burton C. 1928- *WhoAmL 92*
**Agata,** Seth Hugh 1958- *WhoAmL 92*
**Agathos,** Spiros Nicholas 1950- *AmMWSc 92*
**Agatstein,** Richard 1952- *WhoIns 92*
**Agatston,** Robert Stephen 1923- *AmMWSc 92*
**Agawa,** Hiroyuki 1920- *ConAu 134*
**Agazzari,** Agostino 1578-1640 *NewAmDM*
**Agbabian,** Mihran S 1923- *AmMWSc 92*
**Agbeja,** Timothy Omolayo 1954- *WhoRel 92*
**Agbetsiafa,** Douglas Kofi *WhoMW 92*
**Agboruche,** William 1954- *WhoFI 92*
**Agee,** Bobby L. 1949- *WhoBlA 92*
**Agee,** Ernest M 1942- *AmMWSc 92*
**Agee,** George Steven 1952- *WhoAmP 91*
**Agee,** Herndon Royce 1933- *AmMWSc 92*
**Agee,** James *SourALJ*
**Agee,** James 1909-1955 *BenetAL 91, FacFETw*
**Agee,** James Kent 1945- *AmMWSc 92*
**Agee,** Joel *DrAPF 91*
**Agee,** Jonis *DrAPF 91*
**Agee,** Kevin Jerome 1960- *WhoRel 92*
**Agee,** Mark L. 1956- *WhoAmL 92*
**Agee,** Marvin H 1931- *AmMWSc 92*
**Agee,** Melinda Paige 1946- *WhoAmL 92*
**Agee,** Philip 1935- *ConAu 135*
**Agee,** Robert Edward 1935- *WhoBlA 92*
**Agee,** Robin Diane 1958- *WhoRel 92*
**Agee,** Steven Craig 1953- *WhoFI 92*
**Agee,** Thomas Lee 1964- *WhoBlA 92*
**Agee,** William J. 1938- *WhoFI 92, WhoWest 92*
**Agee,** William McReynolds 1938- *IntWW 91*
**Agema,** Gerald Walton 1947- *WhoMW 92*
**Agenbroad,** Larry Delmar 1933- *AmMWSc 92*
**Ager,** David John 1953- *AmMWSc 92*
**Ager,** Derek Victor 1923- *WrDr 92*
**Ager,** John Winfrid 1926- *AmMWSc 92*
**Ager,** Kenneth Gordon 1920- *Who 92*
**Ager,** Milton 1893-1979 *NewAmDM*
**Ager,** Thomas Alan 1946- *AmMWSc 92*
**Ager,** William Francis, Jr. 1921- *WhoAmL 92*
**Agerbek,** Sven 1926- *WhoFI 92, WhoWest 92*
**Agersborg,** Helmer Pareli K. 1928- *WhoFI 92*
**Agersborg,** Helmer Pareli Kjerschow, Jr 1928- *AmMWSc 92*
**Ageyev,** Geniy Yevgenevich 1929- *IntWW 91*
**Aggarwal,** Bharat Bhushan *AmMWSc 92*
**Aggarwal,** H R 1925- *AmMWSc 92*
**Aggarwal,** Ishwar D 1945- *AmMWSc 92*
**Aggarwal,** Jagdishkumar Keshoram 1936- *AmMWSc 92*
**Aggarwal,** Raj 1947- *WhoFI 92, WhoMW 92*
**Aggarwal,** Roshan Lal 1937- *AmMWSc 92*
**Aggarwal,** Shanti J 1933- *AmMWSc 92*
**Aggarwal,** Sundar Lal 1922- *AmMWSc 92, WhoFI 92*
**Aggarwal,** Surinder K 1938- *AmMWSc 92*
**Aggarwal,** Uma Nandan 1944- *WhoMW 92*
**Aggarwala,** Bhagwan D 1931- *AmMWSc 92*
**Aggeler,** Geoffrey Donovan 1939- *WhoEnt 92*
**Aggeler,** Judith 1944- *AmMWSc 92*
**Aggen,** George 1924- *AmMWSc 92*
**Agger,** Carolyn E. 1909- *WhoAmL 92*
**Agger,** James H. 1936- *WhoAmL 92, WhoFI 92*
**Aggrey,** Kwegyir d1986 *WhoBlA 92N*
**Aggrey,** O. Rudolph 1926- *WhoBlA 92*
**Aghajanian,** George Kevork 1932- *AmMWSc 92*
**Aghi,** Mukesh 1956- *WhoFI 92*
**Aghill,** Gordon *ConAu 36NR, TwCSFW 91*
**Aghion,** Victor 1956- *WhoAmL 92*
**Aghiorgoussis,** Maximos Demetrios 1935- *WhoRel 92*
**Agid,** Susan Randolph 1941- *WhoAmL 92*
**Agin,** Charles 1954- *WhoIns 92*
**Agin,** Daniel Pierre 1930- *AmMWSc 92*
**Agin,** Gary Paul 1940- *AmMWSc 92*
**Aginian,** Richard Dicran 1941- *WhoFI 92, WhoMW 92*
**Agins,** Barnett Robert 1922- *AmMWSc 92*
**Agius,** George 1924- *IntWW 91*
**Agle,** Dennis Eugene 1933- *WhoWest 92*
**Agle,** Nan Hayden 1905- *IntAu&W 91*
**Agler,** Larry E. 1947- *WhoIns 92*
**Agler,** Vickie 1946- *WhoAmP 91*
**Aglionby,** Francis John 1932- *Who 92*
**Agnelides,** Philip N *WhoAmP 91*
**Agnelli,** Giovanni 1921- *IntWW 91, Who 92*
**Agnelli,** Umberto 1934- *IntWW 91*
**Agnello,** Arthur Michael 1952- *AmMWSc 92*
**Agnello,** Eugene Joseph 1919- *AmMWSc 92*
**Agnello,** Vincent 1938- *AmMWSc 92*
**Agnew,** Allen Francis 1918- *AmMWSc 92*
**Agnew,** Anthony Stuart *Who 92*
**Agnew,** Charles William, Jr. 1933- *WhoMW 92*
**Agnew,** Christopher Mack 1944- *WhoRel 92*
**Agnew,** Cornelius Rea 1830-1888 *BiInAmS*
**Agnew,** Dan F. 1944- *WhoIns 92*
**Agnew,** Edward Charles, Jr. 1939- *WhoWest 92*
**Agnew,** Ewan *ScFEYrs*
**Agnew,** Franklin Ernest, III 1934- *WhoFI 92*
**Agnew,** Godfrey *Who 92*
**Agnew,** Harold Melvin 1921- *AmMWSc 92, IntWW 91*
**Agnew,** James Lambert 1944- *WhoMW 92*
**Agnew,** Jeanne Le Caine 1917- *AmMWSc 92*
**Agnew,** John Anthony Stuart 1914- *Who 92*
**Agnew,** Jonathan Geoffrey William 1941- *Who 92*
**Agnew,** Leslie Robert Corbet 1923- *AmMWSc 92*
**Agnew,** Lewis Edgar, Jr 1926- *AmMWSc 92*
**Agnew,** Peter Graeme 1914- *Who 92*
**Agnew,** Peter Tomlin 1948- *WhoFI 92*
**Agnew,** Robert A 1942- *AmMWSc 92*
**Agnew,** Robert A. 1952- *WhoEnt 92*
**Agnew,** Robert Morson 1932- *AmMWSc 92*
**Agnew,** Rudolph Ion Joseph 1934- *IntWW 91, Who 92*
**Agnew,** Spiro T 1918- *ConAu 135, FacFETw [port], IntAu&W 91, WrDr 92*
**Agnew,** Spiro Theodore 1918- *AmPolLe, IntWW 91, Who 92*
**Agnew,** Stanley Clarke 1926- *Who 92*
**Agnew,** Will Livingston *ScFEYrs*
**Agnew,** William Finley 1925- *AmMWSc 92*
**Agnew,** William G 1926- *AmMWSc 92*
**Agnew,** William Godfrey 1913- *Who 92*
**Agnew,** William Harold 1920- *WhoFI 92*
**Agnew-Marcelli,** G Marie 1927- *AmMWSc 92*
**Agnew of Lochnaw,** Crispin Hamlyn 1944- *Who 92*
**Agnew-Somerville,** Quentin 1929 *Who 92*
**Agnich,** Fred Joseph 1913- *WhoAmP 91*
**Agnich,** Richard John 1943- *WhoAmL 92, WhoAmP 91, WhoFI 92*
**Agnihotri,** Ram K 1933- *AmMWSc 92*
**Agnish,** Narsingh Dev 1940- *AmMWSc 92*
**Agno,** John G. 1940- *WhoMW 92*
**Agnoli,** Bruno 1911- *WhoAmP 91*
**Agnon,** S Y 1880-1970 *FacFETw*
**Agnon,** S. Y. 1888-1970 *LiExTwC*
**Agnon,** Shmuel Yosef 1888-1970 *WhoNob 90*
**Agnos,** Art 1938- *WhoAmP 91*
**Agnos,** Arthur Christ 1938- *WhoWest 92*
**Agnostak,** Harry Michael 1957- *WhoAmL 92*
**Ago,** Roberto 1907- *IntWW 91*
**Agogino,** George Allen 1920- *WhoWest 92*
**Agoglia,** Emmet John 1930- *WhoAmL 92*
**Agol,** Izrail' Iosifovich 1891-1937 *SovUnBD*
**Agonia,** Barbara Ann 1934- *WhoWest 92*
**Agonia,** Robert James 1938- *WhoHisp 92*
**Agonito,** Rosemary 1937- *WrDr 92*
**Agopian,** Ilie Z. 1942- *WhoEnt 92*
**Agosin,** Marjorie 1955- *WhoHisp 92*
**Agosin,** Moises 1922- *AmMWSc 92*
**Agosta,** Vito 1923- *AmMWSc 92*
**Agosta,** William Carleton 1933- *AmMWSc 92*
**Agostina** *EncAmaz 91*
**Agostinelli,** Robert Francesco 1953- *WhoFI 92*
**Agostini,** Gloria *WhoEnt 92*
**Agostini,** Romain Camille 1959- *AmMWSc 92*
**Agostini,** Wanda E 1927- *WhoAmP 91*
**Agosto,** Edwin 1956- *WhoHisp 92*
**Agoston,** Max Karl 1941- *AmMWSc 92*
**Agoston,** Thomas Charles 1957- *WhoAmL 92, WhoFI 92*
**Agoult,** Marie d' 1805-1876 *FrenWW*
**Agrait,** Fernando E. *WhoHisp 92*
**Agrama,** Frank *LesBEnT 92*
**Agramonte,** Ignacio 1841-1873 *HisDSpE*
**Agran,** Larry *WhoAmP 91*
**Agranat,** Simon 1906- *IntWW 91*
**Agranoff,** Bernard William 1926- *AmMWSc 92*
**Agranoff,** Gerald Neal 1946- *WhoAmL 92*
**Agras,** William Stewart 1929- *AmMWSc 92*
**Agrawal,** Andy 1962- *WhoAmL 92*
**Agrawal,** Arun Kumar 1945- *AmMWSc 92*
**Agrawal,** Atul 1958- *WhoFI 92*
**Agrawal,** Dharma Prakash 1945- *AmMWSc 92*
**Agrawal,** Govind P 1951- *AmMWSc 92*
**Agrawal,** Harish C 1939- *AmMWSc 92*
**Agrawal,** Krishna Chandra 1937- *AmMWSc 92*
**Agrawal,** Prabhu Lal 1926- *IntWW 91*
**Agrawal,** Pradeep Kumar 1946- *AmMWSc 92*
**Agrawal,** Subhash Chandra 1958- *WhoFI 92*
**Agrawal,** Suphal Prakash 1946- *AmMWSc 92*
**Agrawala,** Ashok Kumar 1943- *AmMWSc 92*
**Agrawala,** Surendra Kumar 1929- *IntWW 91*
**Agrawala,** Vasudeva Sharan 1904- *IntWW 91*
**Agraz-Guerena,** Jorge *WhoHisp 92*
**Agre,** Courtland LeVerne 1913- *AmMWSc 92*
**Agre,** Karl 1932- *AmMWSc 92*
**Agreda,** Victor Hugo 1953- *WhoHisp 92*
**Agres,** Stuart J. 1945- *WhoFI 92*
**Agress,** Clarence M 1912- *AmMWSc 92*
**Agresta,** Joseph 1929- *AmMWSc 92*
**Agresti,** David George 1938- *AmMWSc 92*
**Agresti,** William W 1946- *AmMWSc 92*
**Agricola,** Alexander 1446?-1506 *NewAmDM*
**Agrios,** George Nicholas 1936- *AmMWSc 92*
**Agrippina the Elder** d33 *EncAmaz 91*
**Agrippina the Younger** d60 *EncAmaz 91*
**Agris,** Paul F 1944- *AmMWSc 92*
**Agron,** Sam Lazrus 1920- *AmMWSc 92*
**Agrons,** Bernard Z 1922- *WhoAmP 91*
**Agronsky,** Martin *LesBEnT 92*
**Agruso,** Victor Michael 1959- *WhoMW 92*
**Agruss,** Neil Stuart 1939- *WhoMW 92*
**Agt,** Andries A. M. van 1931- *IntWW 91*
**Agthe,** Dale Robert 1953- *WhoWest 92*
**Agua,** Katherine Story 1929- *WhoWest 92*
**Aguado,** Pedro de 1538-1609? *HisDSpE*
**Agualongo,** Agustin 179-?- *HisDSpE*
**Aguayo,** Albert J *AmMWSc 92*
**Aguayo,** Jose 1941- *WhoHisp 92, WhoWest 92*
**Aguayo,** Patricia 1962- *WhoHisp 92*
**Aguayo-Rodriguez,** Luis A. 1950- *WhoHisp 92*
**Agudelio,** Rodrigo *WhoHisp 92*
**Agudelo Botero,** Orlando 1946- *WhoHisp 92*
**Aguero,** Bidal 1949- *WhoHisp 92*
**Aguero,** Joaquin 1816- *HisDSpE*
**Aguero,** Joseph Edward 1946- *WhoHisp 92*
**Aguero,** Kathleen *DrAPF 91*
**Aguero,** Ramon *WhoHisp 92*
**Aguero,** Yamile C. 1967- *WhoHisp 92*
**Agueros,** Jack 1934- *WhoHisp 92*
**Agueybana** *HisDSpE*
**Aguiar,** Adam Martin 1929- *AmMWSc 92*
**Aguiar,** Angel L. 1929- *WhoIns 92*
**Aguiar,** Anna *WhoHisp 92*
**Aguiar,** Antone Souza, Jr. 1930- *WhoAmL 92, WhoAmP 91*
**Aguiar,** Yvette M. 1959- *WhoHisp 92*
**Aguiar-Velez,** Deborah 1955- *WhoHisp 92*
**Aguila,** Gumersindo, Jr. 1959- *WhoEnt 92*
**Aguila,** Pancho *DrAPF 91*
**Aguilar,** Adolfo *WhoHisp 92*
**Aguilar,** Angel A. 1951- *WhoHisp 92*
**Aguilar,** Carlos A. 1943- *WhoHisp 92*

**Aguilar**, Charles, III 1944- *WhoFI 92*
**Aguilar**, Eduardo E., Sr. 1940- *WhoHisp 92*
**Aguilar**, Eleanor Garcia *WhoHisp 92*
**Aguilar**, Ernest Arthur 1942- *WhoHisp 92*
**Aguilar**, Ernest I. J. *WhoHisp 92*
**Aguilar**, Francis Joseph 1932- *WhoHisp 92*
**Aguilar**, George A. 1930- *WhoHisp 92*
**Aguilar**, Humberto Juan 1952- *WhoAmL 92*
**Aguilar**, Irma G. 1947- *WhoHisp 92*
**Aguilar**, Jeronimo de 1490?-1526 *HisDSpE*
**Aguilar**, John L. 1934- *WhoHisp 92*
**Aguilar**, Jose *BlkOlyM*
**Aguilar**, Karen 1952- *WhoHisp 92*
**Aguilar**, Larry 1949- *WhoHisp 92*
**Aguilar**, Lillian I. *WhoHisp 92*
**Aguilar**, Luis 1949- *WhoHisp 92*
**Aguilar**, Manuel 1750- *HisDSpE*
**Aguilar**, Manuel Jesus, Jr. 1952- *WhoHisp 92*
**Aguilar**, Margaret Hope 1951- *WhoWest 92*
**Aguilar**, Mario Roberto 1952- *WhoHisp 92*
**Aguilar**, Nicolas 1741-1818 *HisDSpE*
**Aguilar**, Octavio M. 1931- *WhoHisp 92*
**Aguilar**, Pat L. 1950- *WhoHisp 92*
**Aguilar**, Peter J. *WhoHisp 92*
**Aguilar**, Raul Abraham 1954- *WhoWest 92*
**Aguilar**, Ricardo *DrAPF 91*
**Aguilar**, Richard 1955- *WhoHisp 92*
**Aguilar**, Robert *WhoHisp 92*
**Aguilar**, Robert P. *WhoHisp 92*
**Aguilar**, Robert P. 1931- *WhoAmL 92*
**Aguilar**, Rodolfo J 1936- *AmMWSc 92*
**Aguilar**, Rodolfo Jesus 1936- *WhoHisp 92*
**Aguilar**, Steven, Jr. 1949- *WhoHisp 92*
**Aguilar Mawdsley**, Andres 1924- *IntWW 91*
**Aguilar-Melantzon**, Ricardo 1947- *WhoHisp 92*
**Aguilar y Seiyas**, Francisco d1698 *HisDSpE*
**Aguilera**, Elisa J. *WhoHisp 92*
**Aguilera**, Julio G. 1956- *WhoHisp 92*
**Aguilera**, Renato J. 1957- *WhoHisp 92*
**Aguilera**, Rick 1961- *WhoHisp 92*
**Aguilera**, Salvador, Jr. 1955- *WhoHisp 92*
**Aguillon**, Pablo R., Jr. 1945- *WhoHisp 92*
**Aguilo**, Adolfo 1928- *AmMWSc 92*
**Aguilo-Zambrana**, Juan M. 1933- *WhoHisp 92*
**Aguina**, Mary Elizabeth 1954- *WhoHisp 92*
**Aguinaldo**, Emilio 1869-1964 *HisDSpE*
**Aguinsky**, Richard Daniel 1958- *WhoFI 92*
**Aguirre**, Alejandro *WhoHisp 92*
**Aguirre**, Alicia Carmen 1955- *WhoHisp 92*
**Aguirre**, Benigno E. 1947- *WhoHisp 92*
**Aguirre**, Carlos Llerena 1952- *WhoHisp 92*
**Aguirre**, Doris Carolina 1959- *WhoHisp 92*
**Aguirre**, Edmundo Soto 1926- *WhoHisp 92*
**Aguirre**, Edward *WhoHisp 92*
**Aguirre**, Eugenio 1944- *IntAu&W 91*
**Aguirre**, Francisco *WhoHisp 92*
**Aguirre**, Francisco de 1500?-1580 *HisDSpE*
**Aguirre**, Gabriel Eloy 1935- *WhoHisp 92*
**Aguirre**, Guillermo de *HisDSpE*
**Aguirre**, Henry John 1931- *WhoHisp 92*
**Aguirre**, Horacio *WhoHisp 92*
**Aguirre**, Jesse 1944- *WhoHisp 92*
**Aguirre**, John *WhoWest 92*
**Aguirre**, John 1924- *WhoHisp 92*
**Aguirre**, Jose Luis 1961- *WhoHisp 92*
**Aguirre**, Juan Bautista 1725-1786 *HisDSpE*
**Aguirre**, Linda *WhoHisp 92*
**Aguirre**, Lope de 1511?-1561 *HisDSpE*
**Aguirre**, Marcelino O. *Who 92*
**Aguirre**, Maria Guadalupe d1991 *WhoHisp 92N*
**Aguirre**, Mark 1959- *WhoBlA 92, WhoHisp 92*
**Aguirre**, Marta Lucia 1963- *WhoHisp 92*
**Aguirre**, Martin 1948- *WhoHisp 92*
**Aguirre**, Michael Jules 1949- *WhoHisp 92*
**Aguirre**, Raul Ernesto 1955- *WhoHisp 92*
**Aguirre**, Robert 1964- *WhoEnt 92*
**Aguirre**, Robert D. 1961- *WhoHisp 92*
**Aguirre**, Roberta Pauline 1946- *WhoRel 92*
**Aguirre**, Vukoslav Eneas 1941- *WhoHisp 92*
**Aguirre Obarrio**, Eduardo Enrique 1923- *IntWW 91*
**Aguirre-Sacasa**, Rafael Eugenio 1951- *WhoFI 92*
**Aguirre Velazquez**, Ramon 1935- *IntWW 91*
**Agulian**, Samuel Kevork 1943- *AmMWSc 92*
**Aguolu**, Christian Chukwunedu 1940- *WrDr 92*
**Aguon**, John P 1944- *WhoAmP 91*
**Aguon**, Katherine Bordallo 1931- *WhoAmP 91*
**Agurs**, Donald Steele 1947- *WhoBlA 92*
**Agursky**, Mikhail d1991 *NewYTBS 91*
**Agus**, Zalman S 1941- *AmMWSc 92*
**Agusti**, Filiberto 1953- *WhoAmL 92, WhoFI 92*
**Agustini**, Delmira 1886-1914 *SpAmWW*
**Agustsson**, Helgi 1941- *Who 92*
**Agutter**, Jennifer Ann 1952- *ConAu 133, Who 92*
**Agutter**, Jenny *ConAu 133*
**Agutter**, Jenny 1952- *IntMPA 92, IntWW 91*
**Aguzzi-Barbagli**, Danilo Lorenzo 1924- *WhoWest 92*
**Agyeman**, Jaramogi Abebe 1911- *RelLAm 91*
**Agyilirah**, George Augustus 1947- *AmMWSc 92*
**Agypt**, Ronald G. 1956- *WhoIns 92*
**Agzigian**, Harry James 1943- *WhoAmL 92*
**Ah**, Hyong-Sun 1931- *AmMWSc 92*
**Ah-Chuen**, Moi Lin Jean 1911- *Who 92*
**Ahalt**, Arthur M. 1942- *WhoAmL 92*
**Ahalt**, Michael Chauncey 1946- *WhoMW 92*
**Aharoni**, Shaul Moshe 1933- *AmMWSc 92*
**Aharony**, David *AmMWSc 92*
**Ahart**, Thomas I. 1938- *WhoBlA 92*
**Ahde**, Matti Allan 1945- *IntWW 91*
**Ahearn**, Brian Smith 1933- *WhoAmL 92*
**Ahearn**, Donald G 1934- *AmMWSc 92*
**Ahearn**, Gregory Allen 1943- *AmMWSc 92*
**Ahearn**, James Joseph, Jr 1943- *AmMWSc 92*
**Ahearn**, John Douglas 1943- *WhoEnt 92*
**Ahearn**, John Stephen 1944- *AmMWSc 92*
**Ahearn**, Matthew Joseph 1936- *WhoFI 92*
**Ahearn**, Michael John 1936- *AmMWSc 92*
**Ahearn**, Patricia Jean 1936- *WhoAmL 92*
**Ahearne**, John Francis 1934- *AmMWSc 92, WhoAmP 91*
**Ahern**, Arleen Fleming 1922- *WhoWest 92*
**Ahern**, Bertie 1951- *IntWW 91*
**Ahern**, David George 1936- *AmMWSc 92*
**Ahern**, Francis Joseph 1944- *AmMWSc 92*
**Ahern**, Frank Gregory 1952- *WhoFI 92*
**Ahern**, George Irving, Jr. 1945- *WhoWest 92*
**Ahern**, Janet Mary 1961- *WhoAmL 92*
**Ahern**, John J. 1911- *Who 92*
**Ahern**, Joseph James, Jr. 1945- *WhoEnt 92, WhoMW 92*
**Ahern**, Judson Lewis 1951- *AmMWSc 92*
**Ahern**, Mary Eileen 1868-1938 *HanAmWH*
**Ahern**, Mary Margaret 1940- *WhoEnt 92*
**Ahern**, Michael John 1942- *IntWW 91, Who 92*
**Ahern**, Patrick V. 1919- *WhoRel 92*
**Ahern**, Richard Favor 1912- *WhoAmP 91*
**Ahern**, William F., Jr. 1931- *WhoAmL 92*
**Aherne**, Brian 1902-1986 *ConAu 135*
**Aherne**, Owen *IntAu&W 91X*
**Ahidjo**, Ahmadou 1924-1989 *FacFETw*
**Ahilyabai Holkar** d1795 *EncAmaz 91*
**Ahl**, Alwynelle S 1941- *AmMWSc 92*
**Ahl**, Edwin Eugene 1950- *WhoRel 92*
**Ahl**, Roger John 1963- *WhoEnt 92*
**Ahlberg**, Allan 1938- *IntAu&W 91, SmATA 68 [port], WrDr 92*
**Ahlberg**, Dan Leander 1926- *AmMWSc 92*
**Ahlberg**, Gus 1936- *WhoWest 92*
**Ahlberg**, Harold 1935- *WhoFI 92*
**Ahlberg**, Henry David 1939- *AmMWSc 92*
**Ahlberg**, James E. *WhoFI 92*
**Ahlberg**, James George 1951- *WhoAmL 92*
**Ahlberg**, Janet 1944- *SmATA 68*
**Ahlberg**, John Harold 1927- *AmMWSc 92*
**Ahlborn**, Boye 1933- *AmMWSc 92*
**Ahlborn**, Marvin James 1945- *WhoRel 92*
**Ahlborn**, Michael Wesley 1956- *WhoRel 92*
**Ahlbrandt**, Calvin Dale 1940- *AmMWSc 92*
**Ahlbrandt**, Thomas Stuart 1948- *AmMWSc 92*
**Ahlen**, Steven Paul 1949- *AmMWSc 92*
**Ahlenius**, William Matheson 1934- *WhoAmL 92*
**Ahler**, Kenneth James 1940- *WhoMW 92*
**Ahlers**, Bryan Eugene 1959- *WhoFI 92*
**Ahlers**, Dorothy M 1931- *WhoAmP 91*
**Ahlers**, Glen-Peter, Sr. 1955- *WhoAmL 92*
**Ahlers**, Guenter 1934- *AmMWSc 92*
**Ahlers**, John Peter 1951- *WhoAmL 92*
**Ahlers**, Pamela Kay 1952- *WhoFI 92*
**Ahlert**, Fred 1892-1953 *NewAmDM*
**Ahlert**, Robert Christian 1932- *AmMWSc 92*
**Ahlfeld**, Charles Edward 1940- *AmMWSc 92*
**Ahlfors**, Lars Valerian 1907- *AmMWSc 92, IntWW 91*
**Ahlgren**, Clifford Elmer 1922- *AmMWSc 92*
**Ahlgren**, George E 1931- *AmMWSc 92*
**Ahlgren**, Gibson-Taylor 1940- *WhoWest 92*
**Ahlgren**, Henry Lawrence 1908- *AmMWSc 92*
**Ahlgren**, Isabel Fulton 1924- *AmMWSc 92*
**Ahlgren**, Molly O 1957- *AmMWSc 92*
**Ahlgrimm**, John Calvin 1925- *WhoAmL 92*
**Ahlijanian**, Michael Kirk 1957- *WhoWest 92*
**Ahlmark**, Per 1939- *IntWW 91*
**Ahlquist**, John Bertil 1933- *WhoMW 92*
**Ahlrichs**, James Lloyd 1928- *AmMWSc 92*
**Ahlschwede**, Arthur Martin 1914- *WhoRel 92*
**Ahlschwede**, Margrethe P 1941- *WhoAmP 91*
**Ahlschwede**, William T 1942- *AmMWSc 92*
**Ahlsen**, Leopold 1927- *IntAu&W 91, IntWW 91*
**Ahlstrom**, Harlow G 1935- *AmMWSc 92*
**Ahlstrom**, John Keith 1942- *WhoWest 92*
**Ahlstrom**, Krister Harry 1940- *IntWW 91*
**Ahlstrom**, Michael Joseph 1953- *WhoAmL 92*
**Ahlstrom**, Patrick Carlton 1945- *WhoWest 92*
**Ahlstrom**, Tom *DcTwDes*
**Ahlswede**, Ann 1928- *TwCWW 91, WrDr 92*
**Ahluwalia**, Balwant Singh 1932- *AmMWSc 92*
**Ahluwalia**, Daljit Singh 1932- *AmMWSc 92*
**Ahluwalia**, Gurpreet S *AmMWSc 92*
**Ahluwalia**, Harjit Singh 1934- *AmMWSc 92, WhoWest 92*
**Ahlwardt**, Hermann 1846-1914 *EncTR 91*
**Ahmad**, Abdul Ajib bin 1947- *IntWW 91*
**Ahmad**, Anwar 1945- *WhoMW 92*
**Ahmad**, Awang Mohammed Yussof 1944- *IntWW 91*
**Ahmad**, Fazal *AmMWSc 92*
**Ahmad**, Imad-ad-Dean *WhoAmP 91*
**Ahmad**, Irshad 1939- *AmMWSc 92*
**Ahmad**, Jadwaa 1935- *WhoBlA 92*
**Ahmad**, Jameel 1941- *AmMWSc 92*
**Ahmad**, Khurshid 1934- *Who 92*
**Ahmad**, Mirza Ghulam Hazrat 1835-1908 *RelLAm 91*
**Ahmad**, Moid Uddin 1927- *AmMWSc 92*
**Ahmad**, Nazir 1936- *AmMWSc 92*
**Ahmad**, Othman Ibrahim al- 1942- *IntWW 91*
**Ahmad**, Shair 1934- *AmMWSc 92*
**Ahmad**, Shamim 1944- *AmMWSc 92*
**Ahmadjian**, Vernon 1930- *AmMWSc 92*
**Ahmadu-Suka**, Osman 1926- *IntWW 91*
**Ahmann**, Donald H 1920- *AmMWSc 92*
**Ahmann**, Mathew Hall *WhoBlA 92*
**Ahmed Ould Caid** *HisDSpE*
**Ahmed**, A Razzaque 1948- *AmMWSc 92*
**Ahmed**, Abdel-Rahim d1991 *NewYTBS 91*
**Ahmed**, Asad 1939- *AmMWSc 92*
**Ahmed**, Esam Mahmoud 1925- *AmMWSc 92*
**Ahmed**, Fakhruddin 1931- *IntWW 91*
**Ahmed**, Haroon 1936- *Who 92*
**Ahmed**, Ismail Yousef 1939- *AmMWSc 92*
**Ahmed**, Kazi Zafar 1940- *IntWW 91*
**Ahmed**, Khalil 1934- *AmMWSc 92*
**Ahmed**, Khandakar Moshtaque 1918- *IntWW 91*
**Ahmed**, Kyle *WhoEnt 92*
**Ahmed**, Mahmoud S 1942- *AmMWSc 92*
**Ahmed**, Moghisuddin 1950- *AmMWSc 92*
**Ahmed**, Mohamed el-Baghir 1927- *IntWW 91*
**Ahmed**, Moudud 1940- *IntWW 91*
**Ahmed**, Nasim 1927- *IntWW 91*
**Ahmed**, Nasir 1940- *AmMWSc 92*
**Ahmed**, Nasir Uddin 1934- *AmMWSc 92*
**Ahmed**, S Sultan 1937- *AmMWSc 92*
**Ahmed**, Saad Attia 1950- *AmMWSc 92, WhoMW 92*
**Ahmed**, Saiyed I 1941- *AmMWSc 92*
**Ahmed**, Shaffiq Uddin 1934- *AmMWSc 92*
**Ahmed**, Susan Wolofski 1946- *AmMWSc 92*
**Ahmed**, Syed Mahmood 1949- *AmMWSc 92*
**Ahmed**, Wase U 1931- *AmMWSc 92*
**Ahmed-Ansari**, Aftab 1944- *AmMWSc 92*
**Ahmed-Zaid**, Said 1956- *AmMWSc 92*
**Ahn**, Ho-Sam 1940- *AmMWSc 92*
**Ahn**, K Y 1930- *AmMWSc 92*
**Ahn**, Mark J. 1962- *WhoFI 92*
**Ahn**, Nolan S.B. 1948- *WhoFI 92*
**Ahn**, Peter Pyung-choo 1917- *WhoRel 92*
**Ahn**, Suhn Yung 1934- *WhoFI 92*
**Ahn**, Tae In 1947- *AmMWSc 92*
**Ahne**, Joseph Joo-Young 1943- *WhoRel 92*
**Aho**, Kalevi 1949- *ConCom 92*
**Aho**, Paul E 1934- *AmMWSc 92*
**'Aho**, Siaosi Taimani 1939- *Who 92*
**Ahokas**, Robert A *AmMWSc 92*
**Ahomadegbe**, Justin Tometin 1917- *IntWW 91*
**Ahotep** *EncAmaz 91*
**Ahr**, Deirdre O'Meara 1946- *WhoAmL 92*
**Ahr**, Wayne Merrill 1938- *AmMWSc 92*
**Ahren**, Uno 1897-1977 *DcTwDes, FacFETw*
**Ahrends**, Peter 1933- *IntWW 91, Who 92*
**Ahrenholz**, H William 1916- *AmMWSc 92*
**Ahrenkiel**, Richard K 1936- *AmMWSc 92*
**Ahrens**, Burton Joel 1937- *WhoAmL 92*
**Ahrens**, Carolyn 1959- *WhoAmL 92*
**Ahrens**, Edward Hamblin, Jr 1915- *AmMWSc 92*
**Ahrens**, Erick Karl Frederick 1949- *WhoWest 92*
**Ahrens**, Ernst H. 1929- *WhoWest 92*
**Ahrens**, Franklin Alfred 1936- *AmMWSc 92*
**Ahrens**, Frederick G 1915- *WhoAmP 91*
**Ahrens**, J. Benjamin 1960- *WhoAmL 92*
**Ahrens**, Jane A. 1948- *WhoEnt 92*
**Ahrens**, John Frederick 1929- *AmMWSc 92*
**Ahrens**, Joseph 1904- *IntWW 91*
**Ahrens**, Leigh P. *WhoFI 92*
**Ahrens**, M Conner 1922- *AmMWSc 92*
**Ahrens**, Richard August 1936- *AmMWSc 92*
**Ahrens**, Rolland William 1933- *AmMWSc 92*
**Ahrens**, Rudolf Martin 1928- *AmMWSc 92*
**Ahrens**, Thomas J 1936- *AmMWSc 92*
**Ahrensfeld**, Thomas Frederick 1923- *WhoAmL 92, WhoFI 92*
**Ahring**, Robert M 1928- *AmMWSc 92*
**Ahrland**, Karin Margareta 1931- *IntWW 91*
**Ahrold**, Robbin Liam 1943- *WhoEnt 92*
**Ahronovitch**, Yuri 1932- *IntWW 91*
**Ahrweiler**, Helene 1926- *IntWW 91*
**Ahsan**, Ahmad 1929- *WhoMW 92*
**Ahsanullah**, Mohammad *AmMWSc 92*
**Ahsen**, Akhter 1931- *WrDr 92*
**Ahshapanek**, Don Colesto 1932- *AmMWSc 92*
**Ahto**, Cheryl Lee 1957- *WhoMW 92*
**Ahuja**, Jagan N 1935- *AmMWSc 92*
**Ahuja**, Jagdish C *AmMWSc 92*
**Ahuja**, Jayant 1959- *WhoFI 92*
**Ahuja**, Narendra 1950- *AmMWSc 92, WhoMW 92*
**Ahuja**, Satinder 1933- *AmMWSc 92*
**Ahumada**, Albert Jil, Jr 1940- *AmMWSc 92*
**Ahvenlahti**, Olli 1949- *WhoEnt 92*
**Ai** *DrAPF 91*
**Ai** 1947- *ConLC 69 [port]*
**Ai Qing** 1910- *LiExTwC*
**Aibel**, Howard James 1929- *WhoAmL 92, WhoFI 92*
**Aichele**, Douglas B 1942- *AmMWSc 92*
**Aichele**, Murit Dean 1928- *AmMWSc 92*
**Aichinger**, Ilse 1921- *IntWW 91*
**Aickin**, Mikel G 1944- *AmMWSc 92*
**Aidinoff**, Merton Bernard 1929- *WhoAmL 92*
**Aidman**, Barton Terry 1947- *WhoFI 92*
**Aidman**, Charles *WhoEnt 92*
**Aidoo**, Ama Ata 1942- *IntAu&W 91, WrDr 92*
**Aiello**, Annette 1941- *AmMWSc 92*
**Aiello**, Barbara 1947- *WhoEnt 92*
**Aiello**, Danny 1933- *IntMPA 92, WhoEnt 92*
**Aiello**, Edward Lawrence 1928- *AmMWSc 92*
**Aiello**, Frank Mario 1943- *WhoAmL 92*
**Aiello**, Gennaro C. 1953- *WhoFI 92*
**Aiello**, Joseph Carmen 1940- *WhoEnt 92*
**Aiello**, Louis Peter 1932- *WhoWest 92*
**Aiello**, Neno Joseph 1928- *WhoWest 92*
**Aiello**, Rita *WhoEnt 92*
**Aife** *EncAmaz 91*
**Aig**, Dennis Ira 1950- *WhoEnt 92*
**Aigamaua**, Avegalio P *WhoAmP 91*
**Aiges**, Stanley L. 1931- *WhoAmL 92*
**Aigner**, Dennis John 1937- *WhoFI 92*
**Aigner**, Emily Burke 1920- *WhoRel 92*
**Aigner**, Herbert John 1929- *WhoAmP 91*
**Aigrain**, Pierre Raoul Roger 1924- *IntWW 91*
**Aikawa**, Jerry Kazuo 1921- *AmMWSc 92*
**Aikawa**, Masamichi 1931- *AmMWSc 92*
**Aiken**, Albert W. *BenetAL 91*
**Aiken**, Conrad 1889-1973 *BenetAL 91, FacFETw, ShSCr 9 [port]*
**Aiken**, Curtis Dale 1935- *WhoRel 92*
**Aiken**, David Vollmar 1943- *WhoEnt 92*
**Aiken**, George L. 1830-1876 *BenetAL 91*
**Aiken**, James G 1940- *AmMWSc 92*
**Aiken**, James Wavell 1943- *AmMWSc 92*

**Aiken**, Jefferson Kirksey, Jr. 1941- *WhoRel 92*
**Aiken**, Joan 1924- *ConAu 34NR, WrDr 92*
**Aiken**, Joan Delano 1924- *IntAu&W 91, Who 92*
**Aiken**, John 1921- *Who 92*
**Aiken**, John Macdonald 1880-1961 *TwCPaSc*
**Aiken**, Lewis R., Jr. 1931- *WrDr 92*
**Aiken**, Linda H 1943- *AmMWSc 92, IntWW 91, WrDr 92*
**Aiken**, Milam Worth 1958- *WhoWest 92*
**Aiken**, Patricia 1922- *WhoAmP 91*
**Aiken**, Phil Lund 1924- *WhoWest 92*
**Aiken**, Robert McCutchen 1930- *WhoFI 92*
**Aiken**, Robert McLean 1941- *AmMWSc 92*
**Aiken**, V Fred 1938- *WhoAmP 91*
**Aiken**, William 1934- *WhoBlA 92*
**Aiken**, William Minor 1932- *IntAu&W 91*
**Aikens**, Alexander E., III 1949- *WhoBlA 92*
**Aikens**, Chester Alfronza 1951- *WhoBlA 92*
**Aikens**, David Andrew 1932- *AmMWSc 92*
**Aikens**, Joan D 1928- *WhoAmP 91*
**Aikens**, Richard John Pearson 1948- *Who 92*
**Aikens**, Willie Mays 1954- *WhoBlA 92*
**Aikens-Young**, Linda Lee 1950- *WhoBlA 92*
**Aikin**, A M, III 1946- *WhoAmP 91*
**Aikin**, Arthur Coldren 1932- *AmMWSc 92*
**Aikin**, Jesse B. 1808-1900 *NewAmDM*
**Aikin**, Olga Lindholm 1934- *Who 92*
**Aikin**, William Edward Augustin 1807-1888 *BiInAmS*
**Aikins-Afful**, Nathaniel Akumanyi 1935- *WhoBlA 92*
**Aikman**, Albert Edward 1922- *WhoAmL 92, WhoFI 92*
**Aikman**, Ann *ConAu 34NR*
**Aikman**, Colin Campbell 1919- *Who 92*
**Aikman**, Elflora Anna 1929- *WhoMW 92*
**Aikman**, George Christopher Lawrence 1943- *AmMWSc 92*
**Aikman**, Peter Rentschler 1939- *WhoWest 92*
**Aikman**, Rosalie H *WhoAmP 91*
**Aiksnoras**, Peter J 1917- *WhoAmP 91*
**Ailes**, Aleita Joyce 1947- *WhoAmL 92*
**Ailes**, Roger *LesBEnT 92*
**Ailes**, Stephen 1912- *IntWW 91*
**Ailesbury**, Marquess of 1926- *Who 92*
**Ailey**, Alvin 1931-1989 *FacFETw [port], WhoBlA 92N*
**Ailion**, David Charles 1937- *AmMWSc 92*
**Ailsa**, Marquess of 1925- *Who 92*
**Ailshie**, Roger Allen 1962- *WhoWest 92*
**Aimee**, Anouk 1932- *IntWW 91*
**Aimee**, Anouk 1934?- *ConTFT 9, IntMPA 92*
**Aimee**, Joyce 1930- *WhoEnt 92*
**Ain**, Ross David 1946- *WhoAmL 92*
**Ain**, Sanford King 1947- *WhoAmL 92*
**Ainbinder**, Zarah 1937- *AmMWSc 92*
**Aines**, Philip Deane 1925- *AmMWSc 92*
**Aini**, Mohsen Ahmed al- 1932- *IntWW 91*
**Ainley**, Alfred John 1906- *Who 92*
**Ainley**, David Geoffrey 1924- *Who 92*
**Ainley**, David George 1946- *AmMWSc 92*
**Ainley**, John *Who 92*
**Aino**, Koichiro 1928- *IntWW 91*
**Ainsbury**, Ray *TwCSFW 91*
**Ainscow**, Robert Morrison 1936- *Who 92*
**Ainsley**, Sam 1950- *TwCPaSc*
**Ainsley**, Stuart Martin 1956- *WhoWest 92*
**Ainslie**, Harry Robert 1923- *AmMWSc 92*
**Ainslie**, Michael Lewis 1943- *WhoFI 92, WhoMW 92*
**Ainslie**, Peter, III 1867-1934 *AmPeW, RelLAm 91*
**Ainsman**, David Ira 1950- *WhoAmL 92*
**Ainsworth**, Cameron 1920- *AmMWSc 92*
**Ainsworth**, David *Who 92*
**Ainsworth**, David Vincent 1940- *WhoWest 92*
**Ainsworth**, Earl John 1933- *AmMWSc 92*
**Ainsworth**, Gordon Robert 1947- *WhoMW 92, WhoRel 92*
**Ainsworth**, Harriet *IntAu&W 91X*
**Ainsworth**, John 1947- *Who 92*
**Ainsworth**, John H *WhoAmP 91*
**Ainsworth**, Louis 1937- *AmMWSc 92*
**Ainsworth**, Mark 1954- *TwCPaSc*
**Ainsworth**, Mary D Salter 1913- *IntAu&W 91, WrDr 92*
**Ainsworth**, Michael Scott 1962- *WhoRel 92*
**Ainsworth**, Oscar Richard 1922- *AmMWSc 92*
**Ainsworth**, Patricia 1932- *IntAu&W 91, WrDr 92*
**Ainsworth**, Ruth 1908- *IntAu&W 91*
**Ainsworth**, Sterling K 1939- *AmMWSc 92*
**Ainsworth**, Thomas David 1926- *Who 92*
**Ainsworth**, William Harrison 1805-1882 *RfGEnL 91*
**Aiosa**, Frank John 1942- *WhoFI 92*
**Aipa**, Benson Nathaniel 1937- *IntWW 91*
**Airall**, Angela Maureen 1954- *WhoBlA 92*
**Airall**, Guillermo Evers 1919- *WhoBlA 92*
**Airall**, Zoila Erlinda 1951- *WhoBlA 92*
**Aird**, Alastair 1931- *Who 92*
**Aird**, Catherine *IntAu&W 91X*
**Aird**, Catherine 1930- *WrDr 92*
**Aird**, John 1940- *Who 92*
**Aird**, John Black 1923- *WhoFI 92*
**Aird**, Steven Douglas 1952- *AmMWSc 92*
**Airedale**, Baron 1915- *Who 92*
**Airee**, Shakti Kumar 1934- *AmMWSc 92*
**Airey**, Christian G. 1938- *WhoRel 92*
**Airey**, David Lawrence 1935- *Who 92*
**Airey**, Lawrence 1926- *IntWW 91, Who 92*
**Airey of Abingdon**, Baroness 1919- *Who 92*
**Airikyan**, Paruir Arshavirovich 1949- *SovUnBD*
**Airington**, Harold L. 1927- *WhoFI 92*
**Airkyan**, Paruir Arshavirovich 1949- *IntWW 91*
**Airlie**, Countess of 1933- *Who 92*
**Airlie**, Earl of 1926- *IntWW 91, Who 92*
**Airlie**, Catherine *IntAu&W 91X, WrDr 92*
**Airy**, Anna 1881-1964 *TwCPaSc*
**Airy**, Christopher 1934- *Who 92*
**Airy**, William W. 1954- *WhoWest 92*
**Aisen**, Jeffrey B. 1948- *WhoFI 92*
**Aisen**, Philip 1929- *AmMWSc 92*
**Aisenberg**, Alan Clifford 1926- *AmMWSc 92*
**Aisenberg**, Michele K 1924- *WhoAmP 91*
**Aisenberg**, Nadya 1928- *ConAu 135*
**Aisenberg**, Sol 1928- *AmMWSc 92*
**Aisenson**, David Judea 1924- *WhoAmL 92*
**Aisenstock**, Barry Alan 1947- *WhoAmL 92*
**Aisher**, Owen 1900- *Who 92*
**Aisin Ghiorroh Pujie** 1907- *IntWW 91*
**Aissen**, Michael Israel 1921- *AmMWSc 92*
**Aist**, James Robert 1945- *AmMWSc 92*
**Aistis**, Jonas 1904-1973 *LiExTwC*
**Aita**, Carolyn Rubin 1943- *AmMWSc 92*
**Aita**, John Andrew 1914- *AmMWSc 92*
**Aitay**, Victor *WhoEnt 92*
**Aitcheson**, Robert Day 1946- *WhoAmL 92*
**Aitchison**, Charles 1951- *Who 92*
**Aitchison**, Craigie 1926- *IntWW 91, TwCPaSc, Who 92*
**Aitchison**, Ian J. R. 1936- *WrDr 92*
**Aitchison**, June Rosemary *Who 92*
**Aitchison**, Robert Snyder 1913- *WhoMW 92*
**Aitken** *Who 92*
**Aitken**, Alfred H 1925- *AmMWSc 92*
**Aitken**, Bart Aaron 1959- *WhoFI 92*
**Aitken**, Donald Hector 1925- *IntWW 91*
**Aitken**, Donald W, Jr 1936- *AmMWSc 92*
**Aitken**, G J M 1936- *AmMWSc 92*
**Aitken**, Hugh 1922- *WrDr 92*
**Aitken**, Ian Levack 1927- *Who 92*
**Aitken**, James Henry 1927- *AmMWSc 92*
**Aitken**, Janet M 1916- *AmMWSc 92*
**Aitken**, John 1745-1831 *NewAmDM*
**Aitken**, John Eakin, Jr. 1941- *WhoWest 92*
**Aitken**, John Malcolm 1945- *AmMWSc 92*
**Aitken**, John Thomas 1913- *Who 92*
**Aitken**, Jonathan William Patrick 1942- *Who 92*
**Aitken**, Kristy Marie Moore 1955- *WhoEnt 92*
**Aitken**, Martin Jim 1922- *IntWW 91, Who 92*
**Aitken**, Max 1910-1985 *FacFETw*
**Aitken**, Michael Patrick 1963- *WhoWest 92*
**Aitken**, Philip Martin 1902- *WhoAmL 92*
**Aitken**, Robert *Who 92*
**Aitken**, Robert 1734-1802 *BenetAL 91*
**Aitken**, Robert 1939- *NewAmDM*
**Aitken**, Robert Grant 1864-1951 *FacFETw*
**Aitken**, Robert Stevenson 1901- *IntWW 91*
**Aitken**, Thomas Henry Gardiner 1912- *AmMWSc 92*
**Aitkin**, John Earnest 1881-1957 *TwCPaSc*
**Aitmatov**, Chingiz Torekulovich 1928- *IntWW 91*
**Aivaliotis**, Sharon 1951- *TwCPaSc*
**Aivazian**, Garabed Hagpop 1912- *AmMWSc 92*
**Aizawa**, Hideyuki *IntWW 91*
**Aizley**, Paul 1936- *AmMWSc 92*
**Ajalat**, Sol Peter 1932- *WhoAmL 92*
**Ajami**, Alfred Michel 1948- *AmMWSc 92*
**Ajanapon**, Pimon 1949- *WhoMW 92*
**Ajawara**, Augustus Chiedozie 1953- *WhoWest 92*
**Ajax**, Ernest Theodore 1926- *AmMWSc 92*
**Ajayi**, Jacob Festus Ade 1929- *IntWW 91, Who 92*
**Ajello**, Carl Richard 1932- *WhoAmP 91*
**Ajello**, Libero 1916- *AmMWSc 92*
**Ajemian**, Martin 1907- *AmMWSc 92*
**Ajersch**, Frank 1941- *AmMWSc 92*
**Ajibade**, Adeyemi Olanrewaju 1939- *IntAu&W 91*
**Ajifu**, Ralph K 1926- *WhoAmP 91*
**Ajl**, Samuel Jacob 1923- *AmMWSc 92*
**Ajmani**, Jagdish Chand 1930- *IntWW 91*
**Ajmone-Marsan**, Cosimo 1918- *AmMWSc 92*
**Ajzen**, Daniel 1950- *WhoHisp 92*
**Ajzenberg-Selove**, Fay 1926- *AmMWSc 92*
**Ajzenman**, Morris B. 1952- *WhoFI 92*
**Ak**, Dogan 1928- *WhoAmL 92*
**Akabusi**, Kriss 1958- *BlkOlyM*
**Akagi**, James Masuji 1927- *AmMWSc 92*
**Akaka**, Daniel K. 1924- *AlmAP 92 [port]*
**Akaka**, Daniel Kahikina 1924- *IntWW 91, WhoAmP 91, WhoWest 92*
**Akaka**, Ellen L. *WhoWest 92*
**Akalaitis**, JoAnne 1937- *WhoEnt 92*
**Akama**, Yoshihiro 1916- *IntWW 91*
**Akamine**, Ernest Kisei 1912- *AmMWSc 92*
**Akamine**, Ray S. 1946- *WhoWest 92*
**Akan**, Sally A. 1940- *WhoAmL 92*
**Akard**, Elizabeth 1950- *WhoMW 92*
**Akasaki**, Takeo 1936- *AmMWSc 92*
**Akasaki**, Toshiro 1925- *WhoFI 92*
**Akashi**, Toshio 1915- *IntWW 91*
**Akashi**, Yasushi 1931- *IntWW 91*
**Akasofu**, Syun-Ichi 1930- *AmMWSc 92, WhoWest 92*
**Akatani**, Genichi 1917- *IntWW 91*
**Akavia**, Miriam 1927- *IntAu&W 91*
**Akawie**, Richard Isidore 1923- *AmMWSc 92*
**Akay**, Adnan *AmMWSc 92*
**Akbar**, Huzoor *AmMWSc 92*
**Akbar**, Na'im 1944- *WhoBlA 92*
**Akbulut**, Yildirim 1935- *IntWW 91*
**Akcasu**, Ahmet Ziyaeddin 1924- *AmMWSc 92*
**Ake**, H. Worth 1923- *WhoIns 92*
**Ake**, Mary Katherine 1930- *WhoWest 92*
**Ake**, Simeon 1932- *IntWW 91*
**Ake**, Thomas Bellis, III 1949- *AmMWSc 92*
**Akehurst**, Daniel 1653?-1699? *DcNCBi 1*
**Akehurst**, John 1930- *Who 92*
**Akeley**, David Francis 1928- *AmMWSc 92*
**Akell**, Robert B 1921- *AmMWSc 92*
**Akella**, Jagannadham 1937- *AmMWSc 92, WhoWest 92*
**Akenhead**, Robert 1949- *Who 92*
**Akenside**, Mark 1721-1770 *DcLB 109 [port], RfGEnL 91*
**Akenson**, Donald Harman 1941- *IntWW 91*
**Aker**, Franklin David 1943- *AmMWSc 92*
**Akera**, Tai 1932- *AmMWSc 92*
**Akerbladh**, Alexander 1866- *TwCPaSc*
**Akerboom**, Jack 1928- *AmMWSc 92*
**Akerlof**, Carl W 1938- *AmMWSc 92*
**Akerlof**, George Arthur 1940- *Who 92*
**Akerlow**, Charles W 1940- *WhoAmP 91*
**Akerman**, Amos Tappan 1821-1880 *DcNCBi 1*
**Akerman**, Chantal *ReelWom*
**Akerman**, Chantal 1950- *IntDcF 2-2*
**Akerman**, Diane 1948- *ConPo 91*
**Akerman**, Johan 1925- *IntWW 91*
**Akerman**, Joseph Lax, Jr. 1950- *WhoEnt 92*
**Akerman**, Knut Lennart Alf 1923- *IntWW 91*
**Akers**, Alan Burt *IntAu&W 91X, WrDr 92*
**Akers**, Arthur 1927- *AmMWSc 92*
**Akers**, Bowden Clarence, Jr. 1934- *WhoRel 92*
**Akers**, CathayAnne Marie 1952- *WhoFI 92*
**Akers**, Charles Kenton 1942- *AmMWSc 92*
**Akers**, Deborah Rowley 1949- *WhoAmL 92*
**Akers**, Elizabeth 1832-1911 *BenetAL 91*
**Akers**, Ellery *DrAPF 91*
**Akers**, Floyd *ConAu 133*
**Akers**, Harley Eugene 1940- *WhoEnt 92*
**Akers**, John Fellows 1934- *IntWW 91, Who 92, WhoFI 92*
**Akers**, John Nance 1940- *WhoRel 92*
**Akers**, John Reynolds 1950- *WhoRel 92*
**Akers**, Lawrence Keith 1919- *AmMWSc 92*
**Akers**, Lex Alan 1950- *AmMWSc 92*
**Akers**, Lyman Leon 1954- *WhoEnt 92*
**Akers**, Michael James 1946- *AmMWSc 92*
**Akers**, Ottie Clay 1949- *WhoAmL 92*
**Akers**, Roger Lee 1950- *WhoRel 92*
**Akers**, Samuel Lee 1943- *WhoAmL 92*
**Akers**, Sheldon Buckingham, Jr 1926- *AmMWSc 92*
**Akers**, Steve Roy 1952- *WhoAmL 92*
**Akers**, Thomas Gilbert 1928- *AmMWSc 92*
**Akers**, Thomas Kenny 1931- *AmMWSc 92*
**Akers**, Wallace Allen 1888-1954 *FacFETw*
**Akers-Douglas** *Who 92*
**Akers-Jones**, David 1927- *IntWW 91, Who 92*
**Akert**, Konrad 1919- *IntWW 91*
**Akeson**, Richard Allan 1947- *AmMWSc 92*
**Akeson**, Walter Roy 1937- *AmMWSc 92*
**Akeson**, Wayne Henry 1928- *AmMWSc 92*
**Akesson**, Norman B 1914- *AmMWSc 92*
**Akgerman**, Aydin 1945- *AmMWSc 92*
**Akhanton**, Askia *DrAPF 91*
**Akhmadulina**, Bella 1937- *FacFETw*
**Akhmadulina**, Bella Akhatovna 1937- *IntWW 91, SovUnBD*
**Akhmatova**, Anna 1888-1966 *ConAu 35NR*
**Akhmatova**, Anna 1889-1966 *FacFETw*
**Akhmatova**, Anna Andreevna 1889-1966 *SovUnBD*
**Akhmedov**, Fikrat Gamidovich *IntWW 91*
**Akhromeev**, Sergey Fedorovich 1923- *SovUnBD*
**Akhromeyev**, Sergey Fyodorovich 1923- *IntWW 91*
**Akhtak**, Rashid Ahmed *AmMWSc 92*
**Akhtar**, Mohammad Humayoun 1943- *AmMWSc 92*
**Akhtar**, Muhammad 1933- *IntWW 91, Who 92*
**Akhund**, Iqbal Ahmad 1924- *IntWW 91*
**Aki**, James Hajime 1936- *WhoAmP 91*
**Aki**, Keiiti 1930- *AmMWSc 92, IntWW 91*
**Akihito** 1933- *FacFETw*
**Akihito**, Emperor of Japan 1933- *CurBio 91 [port], IntWW 91, Who 92*
**Akii-Bua**, John 1950- *BlkOlyM*
**Akil**, Huda 1945- *AmMWSc 92*
**Akilandam**, Perungalur Vaithialingam 1922- *IntWW 91*
**Akiman**, Nazmi 1929- *IntWW 91*
**Akimenko**, Fyodor 1876-1945 *NewAmDM*
**Akimov**, Nikolay Pavlovich 1901-1968 *SovUnBD*
**Akin**, Billy Larue 1933- *WhoIns 92*
**Akin**, Cavit 1931- *AmMWSc 92*
**Akin**, Ewen M., Jr. 1930- *WhoBlA 92*
**Akin**, Frank Jerrel 1941- *AmMWSc 92*
**Akin**, Gwynn Collins 1939- *AmMWSc 92*
**Akin**, Henry David 1900- *WhoAmL 92*
**Akin**, Jim Howard 1937- *AmMWSc 92*
**Akin**, John Stephen 1945- *WhoFI 92*
**Akin**, Lee Stanley 1927- *AmMWSc 92*
**Akin**, Lewis E. 1937- *WhoMW 92*
**Akin**, Ralph Hardie, Jr. 1938- *WhoFI 92*
**Akin**, W Todd 1947- *WhoAmP 91*
**Akin**, Wallace Elmus 1923- *AmMWSc 92, WhoMW 92*
**Akinaka**, Asa Masayoshi 1938- *WhoAmL 92*
**Akinkugbe**, Oladipo Olujimi 1933- *IntWW 91, Who 92*
**Akinmurele**, Akintunde 1949- *WhoFI 92*
**Akins**, Allen Clinton 1919- *WhoBlA 92*
**Akins**, Chip 1952- *WhoWest 92*
**Akins**, Claude 1926- *IntMPA 92*
**Akins**, Clinton Miles 1952- *WhoRel 92*
**Akins**, Ellen *ConAu 135*
**Akins**, George Charles 1917- *WhoFI 92, WhoWest 92*
**Akins**, Glenn Lee 1952- *WhoRel 92*
**Akins**, James E. 1926- *IntWW 91*
**Akins**, Richard Chisholm 1946- *WhoEnt 92*
**Akins**, Richard G 1934- *AmMWSc 92*
**Akins**, Vaughn Edward 1934- *WhoFI 92*
**Akins**, Virginia *AmMWSc 92*
**Akins**, Zoe 1886-1958 *BenetAL 91, FacFETw, ReelWom [port]*
**Akinwande Oluwole Soyinka** 1934- *WhoNob 90*
**Akira**, Yeiri 1928- *IntWW 91*
**Akiskal**, Hagop S 1944- *AmMWSc 92*
**Akita**, Richard Mitsuo 1939- *WhoWest 92*
**Akiwumi**, Viki *DrAPF 91*
**Akiya**, Einosuke 1930- *IntWW 91*
**Akiyama**, Carol Lynn 1946- *WhoEnt 92, WhoWest 92*
**Akiyama**, Junichi 1940- *WhoFI 92*
**Akiyama**, Kazuyoshi 1941- *NewAmDM*
**Akiyama**, Steven Ken *AmMWSc 92*
**Akiyoshi**, Toshiko 1929- *NewAmDM*
**Akkapeddi**, Murali Krishna 1942- *AmMWSc 92*
**Akkapeddi**, Prasad Rao 1943- *AmMWSc 92*
**Aklestad**, Gary C 1934- *WhoAmP 91*
**Aklilu**, Tesfaye 1944- *WhoBlA 92*
**Aklonis**, John Joseph 1940- *AmMWSc 92*
**Ako**, Harry Mu Kwong Ching 1945- *AmMWSc 92*
**Akoi**, Robert, Jr 1953- *WhoWest 92*
**Akonteh**, Benny Ambrose 1947- *AmMWSc 92*
**Akopov**, Pogos Semyonovich 1926- *IntWW 91*
**Akos**, Francis 1922- *WhoEnt 92*
**Akovali**, Yurdanur A *AmMWSc 92*
**Akporode Clark**, B. 1934- *IntWW 91*
**Akrabawi**, Salim S 1941- *AmMWSc 92*
**Akre**, Roger David 1937- *AmMWSc 92*
**Akridge**, Paul Bai 1952- *WhoBlA 92*
**Akrigg**, George Philip Vernon *WrDr 92*

**Akritidis**, Nicolaos 1935- *IntWW 91*
**Akruk**, Samir Rizk 1943- *AmMWSc 92*
**Aks**, Patricia 1926- *SmATA 68 [port]*
**Aksamit**, Robert Joseph 1947- *WhoMW 92*
**Aksamit**, Robert Rosooe *AmMWSc 92*
**Akselrad**, Aline 1935- *AmMWSc 92*
**Akselrad**, David Martin 1959- *WhoFI 92*
**Akselrad**, Harold Eaton 1953- *WhoEnt 92*
**Aksen**, Howard Stephen 1936- *WhoWest 92*
**Aksenov**, Aleksandr Nikiforovich 1924- *SovUnBD*
**Aksenov**, Nikolay Fedorovich 1928-1985 *SovUnBD*
**Aksenov**, Vasiliy Pavlovich 1932- *SovUnBD*
**Aksin**, Mustafa 1931- *IntWW 91*
**Akst**, Geoffrey R 1943- *AmMWSc 92*
**Aksu**, Abdulkadir 1944- *IntWW 91*
**Aksynov**, Vassily 1932- *FacFETw*
**Aksyonov**, Aleksandr Nikiforovich 1924- *IntWW 91*
**Aksyonov**, Vasiliy pavlovich 1932- *IntAu&W 91, IntWW 91*
**Aksyonov**, Vassily Pavlovich 1932- *LiExTwC*
**Akter**, Mahmood Ali Khan 1926- *IntMPA 92*
**Aktik**, Cetin 1953- *AmMWSc 92*
**Aktipis**, Stelios 1935- *AmMWSc 92*
**Akulov**, Ivan Aleksandrovich 1888-1939 *SovUnBD*
**Akurgal**, Ekrem 1911- *IntWW 91*
**Akutagawa**, Ryunosuke 1892-1927 *FacFETw*
**Akuzum**, Ilhan 1947- *IntWW 91*
**Akwaa'**, Mohamed Ali al- 1933- *IntWW 91*
**Akwei**, Richard Maximilian 1923- *IntWW 91*
**Akwue**, Francis Amaechi 1938- *WhoRel 92*
**Akyol**, Avni 1931- *IntWW 91*
**Akyuz**, Rint 1949- *WhoFI 92*
**Al Zhisheng** 1929- *IntWW 91*
**Al Zhongxin** 1931- *IntWW 91*
**Al-Aish**, Matti *AmMWSc 92*
**Al-Amin**, Jamil Abdullah 1943- *BlkLC [port], WhoBlA 92*
**Al-Askari**, Salah 1927- *AmMWSc 92*
**al-Assad**, Hafez 1930?- *News 92-1 [port]*
**Al-Awqati**, Qais 1939- *AmMWSc 92*
**Al-Azm**, Sadik J. *WrDr 92*
**Al-Azmeh**, Aziz 1947- *WhoRel 92*
**Al-Bazzaz**, Faiq J 1939- *AmMWSc 92*
**Al-Chalabi**, Margery Lee 1939- *WhoMW 92*
**Al-Doory**, Yousef 1924- *AmMWSc 92*
**Al-Fayed**, Mohamed 1933- *Who 92*
**al-Hafeez**, Huzema 1931- *WhoBlA 92*
**Al-Hajj Amin** 1895-1974 *BiDExR*
**Al-Husayni**, Muhammad Amin 1895-1974 *BiDExR*
**Al-Jurf**, Adel Saada *AmMWSc 92*
**Al-Kadhi**, Isam Nouri 1933- *WhoFI 92*
**Al-Khafaji**, Amir Wadi 1949- *WhoMW 92*
**Al-Khafaji**, Amir Wadi Nasif 1949- *AmMWSc 92*
**Al-Khalifa**, Abdul-Rahman Faris 1942- *Who 92*
**Al-lami**, Fadhil 1932- *AmMWSc 92*
**Al-Mansour**, Khalid Abdullah 1936- *WhoFI 92*
**Al-Marayati**, Abid A. 1931- *WrDr 92*
**Al-Mashat**, Mohamed Sadiq 1930- *Who 92*
**Al-Masih Haddad**, Abd *DcAmImH*
**Al-Mateen**, Cheryl Singleton 1959- *WhoBlA 92*
**Al-Mateen**, Kevin Bakeer 1958- *WhoBlA 92*
**Al-Nimr**, Nabih 1931- *Who 92*
**Al-Qaraguli**, Wahbi Abdul Razaq Fattah 1929- *Who 92*
**Al-Qazzaz**, Ayad 1941- *WhoWest 92*
**Al Saadi**, A Amir 1935- *AmMWSc 92*
**Al-Saadi**, Abdul A 1935- *AmMWSc 92*
**Al-Saadoon**, Faleh T 1943- *AmMWSc 92*
**Al-Sabah**, Saud Nasir 1944- *Who 92*
**Al Sabbagh**, Salman Abdul Wahab 1932- *Who 92*
**Al-Salihi**, Azmi Shafeeq 1934- *Who 92*
**Al-Sari**, Ahmad Mohammad 1947- *WhoFI 92*
**Al-Sarraf**, Muhyi 1938- *AmMWSc 92*
**Al-Shaieb**, Zuhair Fouad 1940- *AmMWSc 92*
**Al Shakar**, Karim Ebrahim 1945- *Who 92*
**Al-Shawi**, Hisham Ibrahim 1931- *Who 92*
**al-Shaykh**, Hanan 1945- *ConAu 135*
**Al-Suwaidi**, Salem Mohammed 1956- *WhoFI 92*
**Al-Tajir**, Mohamed Mahdi 1931- *Who 92*
**Al-Zamil**, Faisal Saleh 1955- *WhoFI 92*
**Al-Zubaidy**, Sarim Naji 1953- *AmMWSc 92*
**Alaan**, Mansour *WhoBlA 92*
**Alabaster**, William 1568-1640 *RfGEnL 91*
**Alabau**, Magali 1945- *WhoHisp 92*
**Alabyan**, Karo Semenovich 1897-1959 *SovUnBD*
**Aladjem**, Frederick 1921- *AmMWSc 92*
**Aladro**, Gerardo 1949- *WhoHisp 92*
**Alafouzo**, Antonia 1952- *WhoFI 92*
**Alagar**, Vangalur S 1940- *AmMWSc 92*
**Alaimo**, Anthony A. 1920- *WhoAmL 92*
**Alaimo**, Robert J 1940- *AmMWSc 92*
**Alaimo**, Stephen Charles 1939- *WhoEnt 92*
**Alain** 1868-1951 *GuFrLit 1, TwCLC 41 [port]*
**Alain**, Jehan 1911-1940 *NewAmDM*
**Alain**, Marie-Claire 1926- *IntWW 91, NewAmDM*
**Alain-Fournier** 1886-1914 *GuFrLit 1*
**Alaix**, Emperatriz 1949- *WhoHisp 92*
**Alam**, Abu Shafiul 1945- *AmMWSc 92*
**Alam**, Bassima Saleh 1935- *AmMWSc 92*
**Alam**, Jawed 1955- *AmMWSc 92*
**Alam**, Juan Shamsul 1946- *WhoHisp 92*
**Alam**, M Khairul *AmMWSc 92*
**Alam**, Maktoob 1942- *AmMWSc 92*
**Alam**, Mohammed Ashraful 1932- *AmMWSc 92*
**Alam**, Syed Qamar 1932- *AmMWSc 92*
**Alameda**, Lawrence G. *WhoHisp 92*
**Alameda**, Russell Raymond, Jr. 1945- *WhoWest 92*
**Alameda-Lozada**, Jose I. 1950- *WhoFI 92*
**Alami**, Ahmad 1939- *IntAu&W 91*
**Alami**, Sa'd Eddin 1911- *IntWW 91*
**Alami**, Shauna 1953- *WhoEnt 92*
**Alamia**, Richard Rene 1946- *WhoAmP 91*
**Alamilla**, Maclovio David 1942- *WhoHisp 92*
**Alamo**, Rafael 1952- *WhoHisp 92*
**Alamuddin**, Najib Salim 1909- *IntWW 91*
**Alan**, Christine Ann 1961- *WhoWest 92*
**Alan**, Mark 1939- *WhoEnt 92*
**Alan**, Roy 1955- *WhoEnt 92*
**Alanbrooke**, Viscount 1932- *Who 92*
**Alaniz**, Arnoldo Rene 1957- *WhoHisp 92*
**Alaniz**, Johnny Segura 1929- *WhoHisp 92*
**Alaniz**, Joseph J. 1956- *WhoHisp 92*
**Alaniz**, Miguel Jose Castaneda 1944- *WhoHisp 92*
**Alaniz**, Robert Manuel 1957- *WhoHisp 92*
**Alaniz**, Salvador, Sr. *WhoHisp 92*
**Alaniz**, Vicente A. 1945- *WhoHisp 92*
**Alarcon**, Alan F. 1948- *WhoHisp 92*
**Alarcon**, Arthur L *WhoAmP 91*
**Alarcon**, Arthur Lawrence 1925- *WhoAmL 92, WhoHisp 92*
**Alarcon**, Francisco X. 1954- *WhoHisp 92*
**Alarcon**, Francisco Xavier 1954- *WhoWest 92*
**Alarcon**, Graciela Solis 1942- *WhoHisp 92*
**Alarcon**, Guillermo Gerardo 1960- *WhoHisp 92*
**Alarcon**, Justo S. 1930- *WhoHisp 92*
**Alarcon**, Raul, Jr. *WhoHisp 92*
**Alarcon**, Renato D. 1942- *WhoHisp 92*
**Alarcon**, Richard Anthony 1953- *WhoHisp 92*
**Alarcon**, Terry Quentin 1948- *WhoAmL 92*
**Alarcon De Quesada**, Ricardo 1937- *IntWW 91*
**Alarcon Mantilla**, Luis Fernando 1951- *IntWW 91*
**Alarcon y Mendoza**, Juan Ruiz de *HisDSpE*
**Alari**, Steven K 1957- *WhoAmP 91*
**Alaric** 370?-410 *EncEarC*
**Alarid**, Albert Joseph 1948- *WhoWest 92*
**Alarid**, Albert Joseph, III 1948- *WhoHisp 92*
**Alarid**, Frank 1950- *WhoHisp 92*
**Alarid**, Jake Ignacio 1934- *WhoHisp 92*
**Alarid**, Michael *WhoAmP 91, WhoHisp 92*
**Alarie**, Yves 1939- *AmMWSc 92*
**Alario**, John A, Jr 1943- *WhoAmP 91*
**Alatalo**, Richard 1939- *WhoAmL 92*
**Alatas**, Ali 1932- *IntWW 91*
**Alatas**, Syed Hussein 1928- *IntWW 91*
**Alatorre**, Richard 1943- *WhoAmP 91, WhoHisp 92*
**Alatzas**, George 1940- *WhoFI 92*
**Alaupovic**, Petar 1923- *AmMWSc 92*
**Alavanja**, Michael Charles Robert 1948- *AmMWSc 92*
**Alavi**, Bozorg *LiExTwC*
**Alavi**, Misbahuddin Zafar 1946- *AmMWSc 92*
**Alavi**, Yousef 1929- *AmMWSc 92*
**Alaya**, Flavia 1935- *WrDr 92*
**Alazraki**, Jaime 1934- *WhoHisp 92, WrDr 92*
**Alba**, Duke of 1934- *IntWW 91*
**Alba**, Armando R. *WhoHisp 92*
**Alba**, Camilo Benjamin 1956- *WhoMW 92*
**Alba**, Ray *WhoHisp 92*
**Alba**, Victor 1916- *WrDr 92*
**Alba-Buffill**, Elio 1930- *WhoHisp 92*
**Albach**, Richard Allen 1931- *AmMWSc 92*
**Albach**, Roger Fred 1932- *AmMWSc 92*
**Albam**, Manny 1922- *WhoBlA 92*
**Alban** *EncEarC*
**Alban**, Roger Charles 1948- *WhoFI 92, WhoMW 92*
**Albanese**, Anthony August 1908- *AmMWSc 92*
**Albanese**, Donald Joseph 1937- *WhoAmP 91*
**Albanese**, Gerard, Jr. 1952- *WhoIns 92*
**Albanese**, Licia 1913- *NewAmDM*
**Albanese**, Lily Marie 1962- *WhoMW 92*
**Albanese**, Paul James 1949- *WhoMW 92*
**Albanese**, Rosemarie Ann 1942- *WhoAmP 91*
**Albanese**, Sal F 1949- *WhoAmP 91*
**Albanese**, Vincent Gandolfo 1949- *WhoFI 92*
**Albanese**, Vincent Michael 1926- *WhoAmP 91*
**Albanez**, Marguerite A. 1939- *WhoHisp 92*
**Albani**, Emma 1847-1930 *NewAmDM*
**Albani**, Suzanne Beardsley 1943- *WhoAmL 92*
**Albani**, Thomas J. 1942- *WhoFI 92*
**Albano**, Alfonso M 1939- *AmMWSc 92*
**Albano**, Andres, Jr. 1941- *WhoWest 92*
**Albano**, Marianita Madamba 1941- *AmMWSc 92*
**Albano**, Mark Joseph 1956- *WhoAmL 92*
**Albano**, Salvatore 1935- *WhoAmP 91*
**Albany**, George Martin 1945- *WhoIns 92*
**Albarella**, Joan *DrAPF 91*
**Albarn**, Keith 1939- *ConAu 135*
**Albats**, Paul 1941- *AmMWSc 92*
**Albaugh**, A Henry 1922- *AmMWSc 92*
**Albaugh**, Fred William 1917- *AmMWSc 92*
**Albeck**, Andy 1921- *IntMPA 92*
**Albeck**, Karen Kay 1948- *WhoAmP 91*
**Albee**, Arden Leroy 1928- *AmMWSc 92, WhoWest 92*
**Albee**, Don Dale 1935- *WhoFI 92*
**Albee**, Edward 1928- *BenetAL 91, FacFETw [port], IntAu&W 91, Who 92, WrDr 92*
**Albee**, Edward Franklin 1928- *IntWW 91, WhoEnt 92*
**Albee**, Howard F 1915- *AmMWSc 92*
**Albee**, Pauline Annette 1961- *WhoWest 92*
**Albemarle**, Countess of 1909- *Who 92*
**Albemarle**, Earl of 1965- *Who 92*
**Alben**, James O 1930- *AmMWSc 92*
**Alben**, Richard Samuel 1944- *AmMWSc 92*
**Albeniz**, Isaac 1860-1909 *FacFETw, NewAmDM*
**Alber**, Phillip George 1948- *WhoAmL 92*
**Alberch**, Pere 1954- *AmMWSc 92*
**Alberda**, Willis John 1936- *AmMWSc 92*
**Alberg**, Mildred Freed 1921- *WhoEnt 92*
**Alberg**, Tom Austin 1940- *WhoAmL 92*
**Alberger**, William Relph 1945- *WhoAmL 92, WhoAmP 91*
**Alberghetti**, Anna Maria 1936- *IntMPA 92, WhoEnt 92*
**Alberghini**, Christopher Robert 1965- *WhoEnt 92*
**Albergotti**, Jesse Clifton 1937- *AmMWSc 92*
**Albernaz**, Jose Geraldo 1923- *AmMWSc 92*
**Albero**, Richard Lewis 1945- *WhoEnt 92*
**Alberoni**, Julio 1664- *HisDSpE*
**Albers**, Anni 1899- *DcTwDes, FacFETw*
**Albers**, Charles Edgar 1940- *WhoFI 92*
**Albers**, Edwin Wolf 1930- *AmMWSc 92*
**Albers**, Francis C 1916- *AmMWSc 92*
**Albers**, Hans 1892-1960 *EncTR 91 [port]*
**Albers**, Hans 1925- *IntWW 91*
**Albers**, Henry 1925- *AmMWSc 92*
**Albers**, James Ray 1934- *AmMWSc 92*
**Albers**, James William 1937- *WhoMW 92, WhoRel 92*
**Albers**, John J 1941- *AmMWSc 92*
**Albers**, John Richard 1931- *WhoFI 92*
**Albers**, Josef 1888-1976 *DcTwDes, FacFETw*
**Albers**, Kenneth Lynn 1944- *WhoMW 92*
**Albers**, Peter Heinz 1943- *AmMWSc 92*
**Albers**, Robert Charles 1949- *AmMWSc 92*
**Albers**, Robert Edward 1931- *AmMWSc 92*
**Albers**, Robert Herbert 1940- *WhoRel 92*
**Albers**, Robert John 1941- *WhoFI 92*
**Albers**, Robert Wayne 1928- *AmMWSc 92*
**Albers**, Sheryl K 1954- *WhoAmP 91*
**Albers**, Thomas Leo 1940- *WhoRel 92*
**Albers**, Ursel K. 1930- *WhoFI 92*
**Albers**, Walter Anthony, Jr 1930- *AmMWSc 92, WhoMW 92*
**Albers**, William Edward 1943- *WhoFI 92*
**Albersheim**, Peter 1934- *AmMWSc 92*
**Albert I** 1875-1934 *FacFETw*
**Albert the Great** 1200?-1280 *DcLB 115 [port]*
**Albert**, Alan *DrAPF 91*
**Albert**, Alan S. 1950- *WhoEnt 92*
**Albert**, Alexis 1904- *Who 92*
**Albert**, Anthony Harold 1940- *AmMWSc 92*
**Albert**, Arthur 1946- *WhoEnt 92*
**Albert**, Arthur Edward 1935- *AmMWSc 92*
**Albert**, Calvin 1918- *IntWW 91*
**Albert**, Carl 1908- *Who 92*
**Albert**, Carl Bert 1908- *AmPolLe, IntWW 91, WhoAmP 91*
**Albert**, Charles Gregory 1955- *WhoBlA 92*
**Albert**, Donald Jack 1950- *WhoFI 92*
**Albert**, Donnie Ray 1950- *WhoBlA 92*
**Albert**, Eddie *LesBEnT 92*
**Albert**, Eddie 1908- *IntMPA 92, WhoEnt 92*
**Albert**, Edward 1951- *IntMPA 92, WhoEnt 92, WhoHisp 92*
**Albert**, Ernest Narinder 1937- *AmMWSc 92*
**Albert**, Eugene 1930- *AmMWSc 92*
**Albert**, Frank A 1938- *WhoAmP 91*
**Albert**, Frank Joseph 1954- *WhoEnt 92*
**Albert**, Harold Marcus 1919- *AmMWSc 92*
**Albert**, Harold William 1949- *WhoAmL 92*
**Albert**, Harrison Bernard 1936- *AmMWSc 92*
**Albert**, Harry Francis 1935- *WhoFI 92*
**Albert**, Janyce Louise 1932- *WhoFI 92, WhoMW 92*
**Albert**, Jeffrey B. 1946- *WhoAmL 92*
**Albert**, Jerry David 1937- *AmMWSc 92*
**Albert**, Kevin Karl 1952- *WhoFI 92*
**Albert**, Linda I 1939- *IntAu&W 91*
**Albert**, Luke Samuel 1927- *AmMWSc 92*
**Albert**, Marv *LesBEnT 92 [port]*
**Albert**, Marv 1943- *WhoEnt 92*
**Albert**, Marvin H *IntAu&W 91, TwCWW 91, WrDr 92*
**Albert**, Mary Roberts Forbes 1926- *AmMWSc 92*
**Albert**, Mimi *DrAPF 91*
**Albert**, Neale Malcolm 1937- *WhoAmL 92*
**Albert**, Octavia 1853-1899? *NotBlAW 92*
**Albert**, Otis William 1909- *WhoAmP 91*
**Albert**, Paul A 1926- *AmMWSc 92*
**Albert**, Paul Joseph 1946- *AmMWSc 92*
**Albert**, Philip Harold 1961- *WhoWest 92*
**Albert**, R E 1921- *AmMWSc 92*
**Albert**, Richard David 1922- *AmMWSc 92*
**Albert**, Richard K 1945- *AmMWSc 92*
**Albert**, Robert Hamilton 1931- *WhoAmL 92*
**Albert**, Robert Lawrence 1945- *WhoRel 92*
**Albert**, Robert Lee 1946- *AmMWSc 92*
**Albert**, Robin Jayne 1952- *WhoEnt 92*
**Albert**, Roger Charles 1944- *WhoFI 92*
**Albert**, Ross Alan 1958- *WhoAmL 92*
**Albert**, Roy Ernest 1924- *AmMWSc 92*
**Albert**, Samuel *DrAPF 91*
**Albert**, Stephen 1941- *NewAmDM*
**Albert**, Stephen Joel 1941- *WhoEnt 92*
**Albert**, Steven Wayne 1955- *WhoMW 92*
**Albert**, Sunny Elaine Judith *WhoEnt 92*
**Albert**, William Charles 1941- *WhoWest 92*
**Albert-Goldberg**, Nancy 1938- *WhoAmL 92*
**Alberte**, Randall Sheldon 1947- *AmMWSc 92*
**Alberti**, Domenico 1710?-1740 *NewAmDM*
**Alberti**, Joseph Alvin 1943- *WhoFI 92*
**Alberti**, Kurt George Matthew Mayer 1937- *Who 92*
**Alberti**, Peter W R M 1934- *AmMWSc 92*
**Alberti**, Rafael 1902- *DcLB 108 [port], FacFETw, LiExTwC*
**Albertine**, John Michael 1944- *WhoFI 92*
**Albertine**, Kurt H 1952- *AmMWSc 92*
**Albertini**, David Fred 1949- *AmMWSc 92*
**Albertini**, Richard Joseph 1935- *AmMWSc 92*
**Alberto**, John Peter 1951- *WhoFI 92*
**Alberts**, Al 1922- *WhoEnt 92*
**Alberts**, Alfred W 1931- *AmMWSc 92*
**Alberts**, Arnold A 1906- *AmMWSc 92*
**Alberts**, Bruce Michael 1938- *AmMWSc 92*
**Alberts**, Gene S 1937- *AmMWSc 92*
**Alberts**, Harold 1920- *WhoAmL 92*
**Alberts**, James Joseph 1943- *AmMWSc 92*
**Alberts**, John H., Jr. 1950- *WhoMW 92*
**Alberts**, Julien 1916-1986 *WorArt 1980 [port]*
**Alberts**, Robert Carman 1907- *IntAu&W 91, WrDr 92*
**Alberts**, Walter Watson 1929- *AmMWSc 92*
**Albertsen**, Kenneth Alan 1943- *WhoWest 92*
**Albertsen**, Ronald Lee 1953- *WhoMW 92*
**Albertson**, Bradley LeRoy 1955- *WhoMW 92*
**Albertson**, Charles Woodrow 1932- *WhoAmP 91*
**Albertson**, Christiern Gunnar 1931- *WhoEnt 92*
**Albertson**, Clarence E 1922- *AmMWSc 92*

**Albertson**, Harold D 1931- *AmMWSc 92*
**Albertson**, John Newman, Jr 1933- *AmMWSc 92*
**Albertson**, Mary A d1914 *BiInAmS*
**Albertson**, Michael Owen 1946- *AmMWSc 92*
**Albertson**, Noel Frederick 1915- *AmMWSc 92*
**Albertson**, Orris Earl 1933- *WhoWest 92*
**Albertson**, Robert Paul 1952- *WhoWest 92*
**Albertson**, Vernon D 1928- *AmMWSc 92*
**Albertson**, Wallace Thomson 1924- *WhoAmP 91*
**Albertsson**, Per-Ake 1930- *IntWW 91*
**Albertus Magnus** 1200?-1280 *DcLB 115 [port]*
**Alberty**, Robert Arnold 1921- *AmMWSc 92, IntWW 91*
**Albertyn**, Charles Henry 1928- *Who 92*
**Albertz**, Heinrich 1915- *IntWW 91*
**Albery**, Donald 1914-1988 *FacFETw*
**Albery**, Tim 1952- *Who 92*
**Albery**, Wyndham John 1936- *IntWW 91, Who 92*
**Albeverio Manzoni**, Solvejg 1939- *IntAu&W 91*
**Albicki**, Alexander 1941- *AmMWSc 92*
**Albiker**, Karl 1878-1961 *EncTR 91*
**Albin**, Leon 1925- *WhoAmP 91*
**Albin**, Randy Clark 1957- *WhoWest 92*
**Albin**, Robert Custer 1939- *AmMWSc 92*
**Albin**, Susan Lee 1950- *AmMWSc 92*
**Albinak**, Marvin Joseph 1928- *AmMWSc 92*
**Albinana Y Sanz**, Jose Maria 1883-1936 *BiDExR*
**Albinger**, William J., Jr. 1945- *WhoIns 92*
**Albini**, Franco 1905-1977 *DcTwDes*
**Albini**, Frank Addison 1936- *AmMWSc 92*
**Albinoni**, Tomaso Giovanni 1671-1750 *NewAmDM*
**Albinski**, Henry Stephen 1931- *WrDr 92*
**Albinson**, Don 1915- *DcTwDes*
**Albinus** 115?-170 *EncEarC*
**Albion**, Ken *TwCWW 91*
**Albisser**, Anthony Michael 1941- *AmMWSc 92*
**Albiston**, Marion H. 1930- *WhoEnt 92*
**Albo**, Dominic, Jr 1934- *AmMWSc 92*
**Albohn**, Arthur R *WhoAmP 91*
**Albohn**, Arthur R 1921- *AmMWSc 92*
**Albom**, Mitch 1958- *WrDr 92*
**Alboni**, Marietta 1826-1894 *NewAmDM*
**Albornoz**, Fernando 1950- *WhoHisp 92*
**Albosta**, Donald J 1925- *WhoAmP 91*
**Albosta**, Richard Francis 1936- *WhoFI 92*
**Albrecht**, Alberta Marie 1930- *AmMWSc 92*
**Albrecht**, Andreas Christopher 1927- *AmMWSc 92*
**Albrecht**, Ardon Du Wayne 1936- *WhoRel 92*
**Albrecht**, Arthur John 1931- *WhoFI 92*
**Albrecht**, Bohumil 1921- *AmMWSc 92*
**Albrecht**, Brian Michael 1944- *WhoRel 92*
**Albrecht**, Bruce Allen 1948- *AmMWSc 92*
**Albrecht**, Carolina 1962- *WhoEnt 92*
**Albrecht**, Charles 1759-1848 *NewAmDM*
**Albrecht**, Donald James 1951- *WhoEnt 92*
**Albrecht**, Duane Taylor 1927- *WhoWest 92*
**Albrecht**, Edward Daniel 1937- *AmMWSc 92, WhoMW 92*
**Albrecht**, Ernest Jacob 1937- *WhoEnt 92*
**Albrecht**, Ernst Carl Julius 1930- *IntWW 91*
**Albrecht**, Felix Robert 1926- *AmMWSc 92*
**Albrecht**, Frederick Xavier 1943- *AmMWSc 92*
**Albrecht**, G H 1932- *AmMWSc 92*
**Albrecht**, Herbert Richard 1909- *AmMWSc 92*
**Albrecht**, Howard 1926- *WhoEnt 92*
**Albrecht**, Irene Dorothy 1917- *WhoEnt 92*
**Albrecht**, Kenneth Adrian 1953- *AmMWSc 92*
**Albrecht**, Kenneth John 1933- *WhoAmP 91*
**Albrecht**, Leonard N. 1924- *WhoWest 92*
**Albrecht**, Mary Lewnes 1953- *AmMWSc 92, WhoMW 92*
**Albrecht**, Maureen Ann 1952- *WhoWest 92*
**Albrecht**, Paul 1925- *AmMWSc 92*
**Albrecht**, Richard Raymond 1932- *WhoFI 92*
**Albrecht**, Robert William 1935- *AmMWSc 92*
**Albrecht**, Ronald Frank 1937- *AmMWSc 92*
**Albrecht**, Ronald Lewis 1935- *WhoFI 92*
**Albrecht**, Ronald Norman 1952- *WhoMW 92*
**Albrecht**, Sally Kay 1954- *WhoEnt 92*
**Albrecht**, Stephan LaRowe 1943- *AmMWSc 92*
**Albrecht**, Suellen 1945- *WhoAmP 91*
**Albrecht**, Theodore 1945- *WhoEnt 92*
**Albrecht**, Theodore John 1945- *WhoMW 92*
**Albrecht**, Thomas Blair 1943- *AmMWSc 92*
**Albrecht**, Timothy Edward 1950- *WhoEnt 92*
**Albrecht**, William Lloyd 1933- *AmMWSc 92*
**Albrecht**, William Melvin 1926- *AmMWSc 92*
**Albrecht**, William Price, Jr. 1935- *WhoFI 92*
**Albrecht-Buehler**, Guenter Wilhelm 1942- *AmMWSc 92*
**Albrechtsberger**, Johann Georg 1736-1809 *NewAmDM*
**Albrechtsen**, Rulon S 1933- *AmMWSc 92*
**Albregts**, Earl Eugene 1929- *AmMWSc 92*
**Albrethsen**, A E 1929- *AmMWSc 92*
**Albridge**, Royal 1933- *AmMWSc 92*
**Albright**, Archie Earl, Jr. 1920- *WhoFI 92*
**Albright**, Bruce Calvin 1946- *AmMWSc 92*
**Albright**, Carl Howard 1933- *AmMWSc 92*
**Albright**, Charles Ellis 1943- *WhoMW 92*
**Albright**, Dale Lewis 1933- *WhoAmP 91*
**Albright**, Darryl Louis 1937- *AmMWSc 92*
**Albright**, David Foxwell 1932- *WhoAmL 92*
**Albright**, Edwin C 1915- *AmMWSc 92*
**Albright**, Fred Ronald 1944- *AmMWSc 92*
**Albright**, Gene McCrae 1937- *WhoEnt 92*
**Albright**, George 1956- *WhoAmP 91*
**Albright**, Harry Wesley, Jr. 1925- *WhoFI 92*
**Albright**, Ivan 1897-1983 *ModArCr 2 [port]*
**Albright**, Ivan de Lorraine 1897-1983 *FacFETw*
**Albright**, Jack Lawrence 1930- *AmMWSc 92*
**Albright**, James Alexander, III 1955- *WhoEnt 92*
**Albright**, James Andrew 1945- *AmMWSc 92*
**Albright**, James Curtice 1929- *AmMWSc 92*
**Albright**, Jay Donald 1933- *AmMWSc 92*
**Albright**, Jill Eileen 1965- *WhoMW 92*
**Albright**, Jimmy Lee 1942- *WhoRel 92*
**Albright**, John Grover 1934- *AmMWSc 92*
**Albright**, John Rupp 1937- *AmMWSc 92*
**Albright**, Joseph Finley 1927- *AmMWSc 92*
**Albright**, Joseph Paul 1938- *WhoAmP 91*
**Albright**, Julia W *AmMWSc 92*
**Albright**, Lawrence John 1941- *AmMWSc 92*
**Albright**, Lola 1924- *WhoEnt 92*
**Albright**, Lola 1925- *IntMPA 92*
**Albright**, Lovelia Fried 1934- *WhoFI 92*
**Albright**, Lyle F 1921- *AmMWSc 92*
**Albright**, Melvin A 1929- *AmMWSc 92*
**Albright**, Ray C 1934- *WhoAmP 91*
**Albright**, Robert, Jr. 1944- *WhoBlA 92*
**Albright**, Robert E *WhoAmP 91*
**Albright**, Robert James 1941- *WhoWest 92*
**Albright**, Robert Lee 1932- *AmMWSc 92*
**Albright**, Terrill D. 1938- *WhoAmL 92*
**Albright**, Thomas Hubert 1946- *WhoRel 92*
**Albright**, Warren Edward 1937- *WhoFI 92*
**Albright**, William 1944- *ConCom 92, NewAmDM*
**Albright**, William Dudley, Jr. 1949- *WhoBlA 92*
**Albright**, William Robert *WhoEnt 92*
**Albrigo**, Leo Gene 1940- *AmMWSc 92*
**Albrink**, Margaret Joralemon 1920- *AmMWSc 92*
**Albrink**, Wilhelm Stockman 1915- *AmMWSc 92*
**Albrittain**, James Sydney 1948- *WhoFI 92*
**Albritton**, Claude Carroll, Jr 1913- *AmMWSc 92*
**Albritton**, David Donald 1913- *BlkOlyM*
**Albritton**, Ken W 1936- *WhoAmP 91*
**Albritton**, Walter Matthew, Jr. 1932- *WhoRel 92*
**Albritton**, William Harold, III 1936- *WhoAmL 92, WhoAmP 91*
**Albritton**, William Leonard 1941- *AmMWSc 92*
**Albro**, Phillip William 1939- *AmMWSc 92*
**Albrow**, Desmond 1925- *IntAu&W 91, Who 92*
**Albu**, Austen Harry 1903- *Who 92*
**Albu**, Evelyn D 1938- *AmMWSc 92*
**Albu**, George 1944- *Who 92*
**Albu**, Marie *Who 92*
**Albuquerque**, Edson Xavier 1936- *AmMWSc 92*
**Alburger**, David Elmer 1920- *AmMWSc 92*
**Alburger**, James Reid 1950- *WhoEnt 92*
**Albus**, James S 1935- *AmMWSc 92*
**Alby**, James Francis Paul 1936- *WhoRel 92*
**Alby**, Pierre 1921- *IntWW 91*
**Alcaine**, Jose Luis 1938- *IntMPA 92*
**Alcala**, Dick 1950- *WhoHisp 92*
**Alcala**, Dora G. 1937- *WhoHisp 92*
**Alcala**, Jose Ramon 1940- *AmMWSc 92, WhoHisp 92, WhoMW 92*
**Alcala**, Luis A., Jr. 1943- *WhoHisp 92*
**Alcala Fonseca**, Josefina 1951- *WhoHisp 92*
**Alcamo**, I Edward 1941- *AmMWSc 92*
**Alcantar**, Joe 1947- *WhoHisp 92*
**Alcantara**, Emerita N 1943- *AmMWSc 92*
**Alcantara**, Miguel Baccay 1940- *WhoRel 92*
**Alcantara**, Theo 1941- *NewAmDM*
**Alcantara**, Victor Franco 1925- *AmMWSc 92, WhoFI 92*
**Alcaraz**, Ernest Charles 1935- *AmMWSc 92*
**Alcaraz**, Javier 1930- *WhoHisp 92*
**Alcaraz Figueroa**, Estanislao 1918- *WhoRel 92*
**Alcazar-Sabathie**, Jose A. 1959- *WhoHisp 92*
**Alcedo**, Antonio de 1734?-1812 *HisDSpE*
**Alcedo**, Richard 1951- *WhoHisp 92*
**Alcedo**, Thomas James 1949- *WhoHisp 92*
**Alcedo y Herrera**, Dionisio de 1690-1777 *HisDSpE*
**Alchouron**, Guillermo E. 1933- *IntWW 91*
**Alcina**, Francisco Ignacio de 1610-1674 *HisDSpE*
**Alcindor**, Lew 1947- *WhoBlA 92*
**Alcindor**, Lewis Ferdinand 1947- *WhoWest 92*
**Alcivar**, Bob *WhoEnt 92*
**Alcivar**, Michael Luis 1943- *WhoHisp 92*
**Alcocer**, Robert J. 1933- *WhoIns 92*
**Alcock and Brown** *FacFETw*
**Alcock**, Charles Benjamin 1923- *WhoMW 92*
**Alcock**, John William 1892-1919 *FacFETw*
**Alcock**, Leslie 1925- *Who 92*
**Alcock**, Robert James Michael 1936- *Who 92*
**Alcock**, Vivien 1924- *Au&Arts 8 [port], ChlLR 26 [port], IntAu&W 91*
**Alcock**, Vivien 1926- *WrDr 92*
**Alcon**, Emilio S 1926- *WhoAmP 91*
**Alcon**, Manuel Benjamin, Jr. 1926- *WhoHisp 92*
**Alconada Aramburu**, Carlos Roman Santiago 1920- *IntWW 91*
**Alcorn**, Daniel S 1955- *WhoAmP 91*
**Alcorn**, George Bennett 1910- *WhoWest 92*
**Alcorn**, Howard Ernest 1927- *WhoMW 92*
**Alcorn**, Hugh Meade, Jr 1907- *WhoAmP 91*
**Alcorn**, Randy Craig 1954- *WhoRel 92*
**Alcorn**, Stanley Marcus 1926- *AmMWSc 92*
**Alcorn**, Stephen Kenneth 1961- *WhoRel 92*
**Alcorn**, Troy Gene 1930- *WhoRel 92*
**Alcorn**, Wallace Arthur 1930- *WhoRel 92*
**Alcorn**, William R 1935- *AmMWSc 92, WhoMW 92*
**Alcosser**, Sandra *DrAPF 91*
**Alcott**, Abby 1800-1877 *HanAmWH*
**Alcott**, Bronson 1799-1888 *BenetAL 91*
**Alcott**, Kitty May 1923- *WhoAmP 91*
**Alcott**, Louisa May 1832-1888 *BenetAL 91, HanAmWH, RComAH*
**Alcott**, Mark Howard 1939- *WhoAmL 92*
**Alda**, Alan *LesBEnT 92 [port]*
**Alda**, Alan 1936- *IntMPA 92, IntWW 91, WhoEnt 92*
**Aldaco**, Roberto Flores 1938- *WhoHisp 92*
**Aldag**, Arthur William, Jr 1941- *AmMWSc 92*
**Aldag**, Jerome Marvin 1929- *WhoMW 92*
**Aldam**, Jeffery Heaton 1922- *Who 92*
**Aldama**, Andres *BlkOlyM*
**Aldama**, Benjamin, Jr. 1957- *WhoHisp 92*
**Aldama**, Ignacio de 1780-1811 *HisDSpE*
**Aldama**, Juan d1811 *HisDSpE*
**Aldama**, Miguel 1821-1888 *HisDSpE*
**Aldan**, Daisy *DrAPF 91*
**Aldana**, Antonio, Jr. *WhoHisp 92*
**Aldana**, Carl 1938- *WhoWest 92*
**Aldana**, Lorenzo de d1557 *HisDSpE*
**Aldanov**, Mark 1886-1957 *FacFETw, LiExTwC*
**Aldape**, Alina Alicia Catalina Elizabeth 1952- *WhoAmL 92*
**Aldave**, Barbara Bader 1938- *WhoAmL 92*
**Aldcroft**, Derek Howard 1936- *IntAu&W 91, WrDr 92*
**Aldea**, Patricia 1947- *WhoFI 92*
**Alden**, Carl L 1944- *AmMWSc 92*
**Alden**, Charles Henry 1836-1910 *BiInAmS*
**Alden**, David Wills 1948- *WhoAmL 92*
**Alden**, Eric M 1950- *WhoAmP 91*
**Alden**, Henry Mills 1836-1919 *BenetAL 91*
**Alden**, John 1599?-1687 *BenetAL 91*
**Alden**, John G. 1884-1962 *DcTwDes, FacFETw*
**Alden**, John R. 1908-1991 *ConAu 135*
**Alden**, John Richard 1908- *WrDr 92*
**Alden**, John Richard 1908-1991 *NewYTBS 91*
**Alden**, Linda N. 1952- *WhoFI 92*
**Alden**, Paulette Bates *DrAPF 91*
**Alden**, Raymond W, III 1949- *AmMWSc 92*
**Alden**, Robert Leslie 1937- *WhoRel 92*
**Alden**, Roland Herrick 1914- *AmMWSc 92*
**Alden**, Steven Michael 1945- *WhoAmL 92*
**Alden**, Sue *IntAu&W 91X, WrDr 92*
**Alden**, Thomas H 1933- *AmMWSc 92*
**Alden**, Timothy, Jr 1771-1839 *BiInAmS*
**Alden**, Vernon Roger 1923- *WhoFI 92*
**Alden**, William Lewis 1926- *WhoRel 92*
**Alden**, William Livingston 1837-1908 *ScFEYrs*
**Aldenham**, Baron 1948- *Who 92*
**Alder**, Althea Alice 1933- *WhoMW 92*
**Alder**, Berni Julian 1925- *AmMWSc 92, IntWW 91*
**Alder**, Edwin Francis 1927- *AmMWSc 92*
**Alder**, Gail Cecelia 1944- *WhoMW 92*
**Alder**, Henry Ludwig 1922- *AmMWSc 92*
**Alder**, Kurt 1902-1958 *FacFETw, WhoNob 90*
**Alder**, Lucette *Who 92*
**Alder**, Mark Edward 1961- *WhoFI 92*
**Alder**, Michael 1928- *Who 92*
**Alder**, Warner Stephen 1949- *WhoWest 92*
**Alder**, Zane Griffeth 1926- *WhoWest 92*
**Alderdice**, Marc Taylor 1948- *AmMWSc 92*
**Alderete**, Sam Albert 1941- *WhoHisp 92*
**Alderette**, Robert 1943- *WhoWest 92*
**Alderfer**, James Landes *AmMWSc 92*
**Alderfer**, Rodney Brent 1952- *WhoAmL 92*
**Alderfer**, Ronald Godshall 1943- *AmMWSc 92*
**Alderfer**, Russell Brunner 1913- *AmMWSc 92*
**Alderman**, Edwin Anderson 1861-1931 *DcNCBi 1*
**Alderman**, James E 1936- *WhoAmP 91*
**Alderman**, John Owen 1958- *WhoAmL 92*
**Alderman**, John Richard 1947- *WhoAmL 92*
**Alderman**, John Thomas 1853-1932 *DcNCBi 1*
**Alderman**, Michael 1946- *WhoEnt 92*
**Alderman**, Michael Harris 1936- *AmMWSc 92*
**Alderman**, Minnis Amelia 1928- *WhoFI 92, WhoRel 92, WhoWest 92*
**Alderman**, Richard Mark 1947- *WhoAmL 92*
**Alderman**, Robert K I 1942- *WhoAmP 91*
**Alderman**, Silvia Morell 1952- *WhoAmL 92*
**Alderman**, Thomas Ray 1948- *WhoAmP 91*
**Alderman**, Walter Arthur, Jr. 1945- *WhoFI 92*
**Alders**, C Dean 1924- *AmMWSc 92*
**Alders**, Hans 1942- *IntWW 91*
**Aldershof**, Kent LeRoy 1936- *WhoFI 92*
**Alderslade**, Richard 1947- *Who 92*
**Alderson**, Brian Wouldhave 1930- *IntAu&W 91, Who 92*
**Alderson**, Creed Flanary, Jr. 1933- *WhoFI 92*
**Alderson**, Daphne Elizabeth *Who 92*
**Alderson**, Harold B. d1991 *NewYTBS 91*
**Alderson**, John Cottingham 1922- *Who 92*
**Alderson**, Margaret Hanne 1959- *Who 92*
**Alderson**, Norris Eugene 1943- *AmMWSc 92*
**Alderson**, Richard Lynn 1947- *WhoWest 92*
**Alderson**, Sue Ann 1940- *WrDr 92*
**Alderson**, Thomas 1917- *AmMWSc 92*
**Alderton**, John 1940- *Who 92*
**Aldieri**, Dale Robert 1960- *WhoFI 92*
**Aldin**, Cecil 1870-1935 *TwCPaSc*
**Alding**, Peter *IntAu&W 91X, WrDr 92*
**Aldinger**, William F., III 1947- *WhoFI 92*
**Aldington**, Baron 1914- *IntWW 91, Who 92*
**Aldington**, Geoffrey 1907- *Who 92*
**Aldington**, Richard 1892-1962 *FacFETw, RfGEnL 91*
**Aldis**, Dorothy 1896?-1966 *ConAu 34NR*
**Aldiss**, Brian 1925- *ConNov 91, FacFETw, WrDr 92*
**Aldiss**, Brian W. 1925- *TwCSFW 91*
**Aldiss**, Brian Wilson 1925- *IntAu&W 91, IntWW 91, Who 92*
**Aldo-Benson**, Marlene Ann 1939- *AmMWSc 92*
**Aldock**, John Douglas 1942- *WhoAmL 92*
**Aldon**, Earl F 1930- *AmMWSc 92*
**Aldous**, Alan Harold 1923- *Who 92*
**Aldous**, Charles 1943- *Who 92*
**Aldous**, Duane Leo 1930- *AmMWSc 92*
**Aldous**, Lucette 1938- *Who 92*
**Aldous**, William 1936- *Who 92*

**Aldred,** Anthony T 1935- *AmMWSc 92*
**Aldred,** Cyril d1991 *Who 92N*
**Aldred,** Cyril 1914-1991 *ConAu 134*
**Aldredge,** James Earl 1939- *WhoBlA 92*
**Aldredge,** Theoni V 1932- *IntMPA 92*
**Aldredge,** Theoni Vachliotis 1932- *WhoEnt 92*
**Aldredge,** Thomas *ConTFT 9*
**Aldredge,** Tom 1928- *ConTFT 9*
**Aldrete,** Joaquin Salcedo 1936- *WhoHisp 92*
**Aldrete,** Jorge Antonio 1937- *AmMWSc 92*
**Aldrete,** Lori Johnson 1946- *WhoWest 92*
**Aldrich,** Ann 1927- *WhoAmL 92, WhoMW 92*
**Aldrich,** Bess Streeter 1881-1954 *BenetAL 91, TwCWW 91*
**Aldrich,** Bruce Elliott 1948- *WhoFI 92*
**Aldrich,** Charles 1828-1909 *BiInAmS*
**Aldrich,** Clarence Knight 1914- *AmMWSc 92*
**Aldrich,** David Lawrence 1948- *WhoWest 92*
**Aldrich,** David Virgil 1928- *AmMWSc 92*
**Aldrich,** Dell Stanley 1938- *WhoWest 92*
**Aldrich,** Duane Cannon 1943- *WhoAmL 92*
**Aldrich,** Frank Nathan 1923- *WhoFI 92*
**Aldrich,** Franklin Dalton 1929- *AmMWSc 92*
**Aldrich,** Frederic DeLong 1899- *WhoFI 92*
**Aldrich,** Frederick Allen 1927- *AmMWSc 92*
**Aldrich,** Frederick Cecil 1924- *WhoAmP 91*
**Aldrich,** Harl P, Jr 1923- *AmMWSc 92*
**Aldrich,** Haven Scott 1943- *AmMWSc 92*
**Aldrich,** Henry Carl 1941- *AmMWSc 92*
**Aldrich,** Hulbert Stratton 1907- *IntWW 91*
**Aldrich,** Jeffrey Richard 1949- *AmMWSc 92*
**Aldrich,** John Elliott, Jr. 1946- *WhoMW 92*
**Aldrich,** John Wesley, Jr. 1939- *WhoFI 92*
**Aldrich,** Jonathan *DrAPF 91*
**Aldrich,** Lovell Weld 1942- *WhoAmL 92*
**Aldrich,** Lyman Thomas 1917- *AmMWSc 92*
**Aldrich,** Mark Douglas 1950- *WhoMW 92*
**Aldrich,** Michael Ray 1942- *WhoWest 92*
**Aldrich,** Michele L 1942- *AmMWSc 92*
**Aldrich,** Nelson Wilmarth 1841-1915 *AmPolLe*
**Aldrich,** Paul E 1928- *AmMWSc 92*
**Aldrich,** Ralph Edward 1940- *AmMWSc 92*
**Aldrich,** Richard Dennis 1938- *WhoAmL 92*
**Aldrich,** Richard John 1925- *AmMWSc 92*
**Aldrich,** Robert 1918-1983 *IntDcF 2-2 [port]*
**Aldrich,** Robert A 1924- *AmMWSc 92*
**Aldrich,** Robert Anderson 1917- *AmMWSc 92*
**Aldrich,** Robert George 1940- *AmMWSc 92*
**Aldrich,** Samuel Roy 1917- *AmMWSc 92*
**Aldrich,** Spaulding Ross 1932- *WhoAmP 91*
**Aldrich,** Stephen Charles 1941- *WhoAmL 92*
**Aldrich,** Thomas Bailey 1836-1907 *BenetAL 91*
**Aldrich,** Thomas K 1950- *AmMWSc 92*
**Aldrich,** William C. 1932- *WhoIns 92*
**Aldrich,** William Rolland 1959- *WhoEnt 92*
**Aldridge,** A. Owen 1915- *WrDr 92*
**Aldridge,** Adele *DrAPF 91*
**Aldridge,** Arleen Rash 1949- *WhoHisp 92*
**Aldridge,** Charles Ray 1946- *WhoFI 92*
**Aldridge,** Claude Michael 1950- *WhoMW 92*
**Aldridge,** Danny Wayne 1947- *WhoFI 92*
**Aldridge,** David William 1952- *AmMWSc 92*
**Aldridge,** Delores Patricia *WhoBlA 92*
**Aldridge,** Donald Ray 1937- *WhoAmP 91*
**Aldridge,** Eileen 1916- *TwCPaSc*
**Aldridge,** Frederick Jesse 1915- *Who 92*
**Aldridge,** Gordon James 1916- *WrDr 92*
**Aldridge,** Holliday 1957- *WhoEnt 92*
**Aldridge,** Jack Paxton, III 1938- *AmMWSc 92*
**Aldridge,** James 1918- *ConNov 91, IntAu&W 91, IntWW 91, Who 92, WrDr 92*
**Aldridge,** James Richard 1949- *WhoEnt 92*
**Aldridge,** John 1905-1983 *TwCPaSc*
**Aldridge,** John Frederick Lewis 1926- *Who 92*
**Aldridge,** John W. 1922- *WrDr 92*
**Aldridge,** John Watson 1922- *IntAu&W 91*
**Aldridge,** Karen Beth 1952- *WhoBlA 92*
**Aldridge,** Marion Douglas 1947- *WhoRel 92*
**Aldridge,** Mary Hennen 1919- *AmMWSc 92*
**Aldridge,** Melvin D 1941- *AmMWSc 92*
**Aldridge,** Michael William Ffolliott 1920- *Who 92*
**Aldridge,** Noel Henry 1924- *WhoWest 92*
**Aldridge,** Richard *DrAPF 91*
**Aldridge,** Robert David 1944- *AmMWSc 92*
**Aldridge,** Roger Merle 1946- *WhoFI 92*
**Aldridge,** Ron *WhoAmP 91*
**Aldridge,** Susan Barham 1956- *WhoFI 92*
**Aldridge,** Trevor Martin 1933- *Who 92*
**Aldridge,** William Gordon 1934- *AmMWSc 92*
**Aldridge,** William Joseph 1955- *WhoAmL 92*
**Aldriedge,** Jean *DrAPF 91*
**Aldrin,** Buzz 1930- *Who 92*
**Aldrin,** Edwin E. *Who 92*
**Aldrin,** Edwin E, Jr 1930- *FacFETw*
**Aldrin,** Edwin Eugene, Jr. 1930- *IntWW 91*
**Alducin,** Don Jorge 1941- *WhoHisp 92*
**Aldworth,** Thomas Patrick 1947- *WhoRel 92*
**Aldyne,** Nathan *WrDr 92*
**Ale,** Suafanu'u T *WhoAmP 91*
**Ale,** Talavou S 1952- *WhoAmP 91*
**Alea,** Tomas Gutierrez *IntDcF 2-2*
**Aleandri,** Emelise Francesca *WhoEnt 92*
**Aleandro,** Norma *WhoHisp 92*
**Aleandro,** Norma 1941- *ConTFT 9, IntMPA 92*
**Alebua,** Ezekiel *IntWW 91*
**Aledort,** Paul Jeffrey 1954- *WhoFI 92*
**Aleem,** M I Hussain 1924- *AmMWSc 92*
**Alef,** Marvin James, Jr. 1944- *WhoFI 92, WhoMW 92*
**Alegre,** Francisco Javier 1729-1788 *HisDSpE*
**Alegria,** Ciro 1909-1967 *BenetAL 91, DcLB 113 [port]*
**Alegria,** Claribel 1924- *ConAu 15AS [port], LiExTwC, SpAmWW*
**Alegria,** Fernando 1918- *WhoHisp 92*
**Alegria,** Frank Anthony, Jr. 1957- *WhoHisp 92*
**Alegria,** Isabel L. 1951- *WhoHisp 92*
**Alegria,** Ricardo E. 1921- *WhoHisp 92*
**Alegria,** Richard Manuel 1944- *WhoAmP 91*
**Alegria-Ortega,** Idsa E. 1945- *WhoHisp 92*
**Aleichem,** Shalom 1859-1916 *BenetAL 91*
**Aleichem,** Sholom 1859-1916 *FacFETw*
**Aleinikoff,** John Nicholas 1950- *AmMWSc 92*
**Aleinikoff,** T. Alexander 1952- *WhoAmL 92*
**Aleixandre,** Vicente 1898-1984 *DcLB 108 [port], FacFETw*
**Aleixandre y Merlo,** Vicente Pio M 1898-1984 *WhoNob 90*
**Aleixo,** Theodore J, Jr 1942- *WhoAmP 91*
**Alejandro,** Esteban 1911- *WhoHisp 92*
**Alejandro,** Reynaldo Gamboa 1947- *WhoEnt 92*
**Alekhine,** Alexander Alexandrovich 1892-1946 *FacFETw*
**Alekman,** Stanley L 1938- *AmMWSc 92*
**Aleksander,** Igor 1937- *Who 92*
**Aleksandr,** Archbishop of Dmitrov 1941- *IntWW 91*
**Aleksandrov,** Aleksandr Danilovich 1912- *IntWW 91, SovUnBD*
**Aleksandrov,** Aleksandr Pavlovich 1943- *IntWW 91*
**Aleksandrov,** Anatoliy Petrovich 1903- *IntWW 91*
**Aleksandrov,** Georgij Nikolaevich 1930- *AmMWSc 92*
**Aleksandrov,** Grigory Vasil'evich 1903-1984 *SovUnBD*
**Aleksandrov,** Ivan Gavrilovich 1875-1936 *SovUnBD*
**Aleksandrovna,** Tamara *EncAmaz 91*
**Aleksankin,** Aleksandr Vasilevich 1929- *IntWW 91*
**Alekseev,** Mikhail Nikolaevich 1918- *SovUnBD*
**Alekseev,** Mikhail Pavlovich 1896-1981 *SovUnBD*
**Alekseev,** Sergey Sergeevich 1924- *SovUnBD*
**Alekseev,** Vasiliy 1942- *SovUnBD*
**Aleksey** 1929- *IntWW 91*
**Alekseyev,** Dmitri 1947- *IntWW 91*
**Alekseyev,** Michael Vasilyevich 1857-1918 *FacFETw*
**Aleksi,** Patriarch of Moscow 1877-1970 *SovUnBD*
**Aleksoff,** Carl Chris 1940- *AmMWSc 92*
**Aleman,** Dallas Ray 1951- *WhoFI 92*
**Aleman,** George 1944- *WhoHisp 92*
**Aleman,** Hector E. 1936- *WhoHisp 92*
**Aleman,** Joe, III 1963- *WhoHisp 92*
**Aleman,** Narciso L. 1946- *WhoHisp 92*
**Aleman,** Victor 1946- *WhoHisp 92*
**Alemann,** Roberto Teodoro 1922- *IntWW 91*
**Alemar,** Evelyn T. 1943- *WhoHisp 92*
**Alembert,** Jean Le Rond d' 1717-1783 *BlkwCEP*
**Alen,** Dick 1931- *WhoEnt 92*
**Alencar,** Jose Martiniano de 1829-1877 *BenetAL 91*
**Alenier,** Karren LaLonde *DrAPF 91*
**Alenier,** Karren LaLonde 1947- *IntAu&W 91*
**Alenikoff,** Frances 1920- *WhoEnt 92*
**Aleo,** Joseph John 1925- *AmMWSc 92*
**Alepoudelis** 1911- *WhoNob 90*
**Alepoudelis,** Odysseus *Who 92*
**Aleramo,** Sibilla 1876-1960 *DcLB 114 [port]*
**Alerding,** Kathy *DrAPF 91*
**Alers,** George A 1928- *AmMWSc 92*
**Alers,** Jose Oscar 1933- *WhoHisp 92*
**Alers,** Juan M. 1943- *WhoHisp 92*
**Alers,** Perry Baldwin 1926- *AmMWSc 92*
**Ales,** Michael Raymond 1958- *WhoMW 92*
**Aleschus,** Justine Lawrence 1925- *WhoFI 92*
**Aleshin,** Georgiy Vasil'evich 1931- *SovUnBD*
**Aleshire,** Joan *DrAPF 91*
**Aleshire,** Richard Joe 1947- *WhoMW 92*
**Aleshkovsky,** Yuz 1929- *LiExTwC*
**Alesia,** James Henry 1934- *WhoAmL 92, WhoMW 92*
**Alesia,** Patrick Lawrence 1948- *WhoFI 92*
**Alessi,** Joseph Gabriel, Jr. 1946- *WhoRel 92*
**Alessi,** Joseph N. 1959- *WhoEnt 92*
**Alessi,** Samuel Charles, Jr. 1932- *WhoAmL 92*
**Alessio,** George Paul, Jr. 1954- *WhoAmL 92*
**Alevizon,** William 1943- *AmMWSc 92*
**Alex,** Gregory K. 1948- *WhoBlA 92*
**Alex,** Jack Franklin 1928- *AmMWSc 92*
**Alex,** Leo James 1942- *AmMWSc 92*
**Alexa,** William E *WhoAmP 91*
**Alexander** *Who 92*
**Alexander** 1888-1934 *FacFETw*
**Alexander I** 1777-1825 *BlkwCEP*
**Alexander,** Baron 1905- *WrDr 92*
**Alexander of Alexandria** d328 *EncEarC*
**Alexander VI,** Pope 1431-1503 *HisDSpE*
**Alexander Severus** 208?-235 *EncEarC*
**Alexander,** Viscount 1990- *Who 92*
**Alexander,** A Allan 1928- *AmMWSc 92*
**Alexander,** A B d1916 *BiInAmS*
**Alexander,** A. Melvin 1943- *WhoBlA 92*
**Alexander,** Aaron D 1917- *AmMWSc 92*
**Alexander,** Albert Geoffrey 1932- *Who 92*
**Alexander,** Albert George, Jr 1929- *WhoAmP 91*
**Alexander,** Alex 1916- *IntWW 91*
**Alexander,** Alexander Sandor 1916- *Who 92*
**Alexander,** Alger Texas 1900-1954 *NewAmDM*
**Alexander,** Allen D. 1940- *WhoIns 92*
**Alexander,** Allen Leander 1910- *AmMWSc 92*
**Alexander,** Alma Duncan 1939- *WhoBlA 92*
**Alexander,** Alphonso, Jr. 1964- *WhoMW 92*
**Alexander,** Andrew Clive 1935- *Who 92*
**Alexander,** Andrew Lamar 1940- *IntWW 91*
**Alexander,** Andrew Lamar, Jr. *NewYTBS 91 [port]*
**Alexander,** Annie Lowrie 1864-1929 *DcNCBi 1*
**Alexander,** Anthony George Laurence 1938- *Who 92*
**Alexander,** Anthony Victor 1928- *Who 92*
**Alexander,** Archibald Ferguson 1928- *AmMWSc 92*
**Alexander,** Avery C 1910- *WhoAmP 91*
**Alexander,** Barbara Leah Shapiro 1943- *WhoMW 92*
**Alexander,** Barbara Lynne 1942- *WhoEnt 92*
**Alexander,** Barbara Toll 1948- *WhoFI 92*
**Alexander,** Barton 1951- *WhoWest 92*
**Alexander,** Ben B 1920- *WhoAmP 91*
**Alexander,** Benjamin H 1921- *AmMWSc 92*
**Alexander,** Benjamin Harold 1921- *WhoBlA 92*
**Alexander,** Bill 1948- *Who 92*
**Alexander,** Brett *WhoEnt 92*
**Alexander,** Brooke 1937- *IntWW 91*
**Alexander,** Bruce Donald 1943- *WhoFI 92*
**Alexander,** C. Philip 1929- *WhoMW 92*
**Alexander,** Cameron Madison 1932- *WhoRel 92*
**Alexander,** Catharine Coleman 1934- *WhoWest 92*
**Alexander,** Charles Edward, Jr 1930- *AmMWSc 92*
**Alexander,** Charles Fred, Jr. 1957- *WhoBlA 92*
**Alexander,** Charles G. 1923- *Who 92*
**Alexander,** Charles William 1931- *AmMWSc 92*
**Alexander,** Charlotte *DrAPF 91*
**Alexander,** Cherian *Who 92*
**Alexander,** Chester, Jr 1937- *AmMWSc 92*
**Alexander,** Christine Anne 1949- *IntAu&W 91*
**Alexander,** Christopher 1936- *DcTwDes, IntWW 91, WrDr 92*
**Alexander,** Claude Gordon 1924- *AmMWSc 92*
**Alexander,** Clifford L. 1933- *IntWW 91*
**Alexander,** Clifford L, Jr 1933- *WhoAmP 91, WhoBlA 92*
**Alexander,** Clifton Jack *WhoWest 92*
**Alexander,** Clyde 1946- *WhoAmP 91*
**Alexander,** Colleen Shirley 1926- *WhoAmP 91*
**Alexander,** Cornelia *WhoBlA 92*
**Alexander,** Cruzan 1918- *WhoAmL 92*
**Alexander,** Dana Jill 1964- *WhoEnt 92*
**Alexander,** Dave Almon 1915- *WhoAmL 92*
**Alexander,** David *LesBEnT 92, Who 92*
**Alexander,** David Andrew 1965- *WhoFI 92*
**Alexander,** David Cleon, III 1941- *WhoAmL 92, WhoWest 92*
**Alexander,** David Crichton 1926- *Who 92*
**Alexander,** David Michael 1941- *AmMWSc 92*
**Alexander,** Dawn Criket 1960- *WhoBlA 92*
**Alexander,** Dennis James 1941- *WhoEnt 92*
**Alexander,** Denton Eugene 1917- *AmMWSc 92*
**Alexander,** Diana Valdez 1963- *WhoHisp 92*
**Alexander,** Donald 1937- *WhoBlA 92*
**Alexander,** Donald Crichton 1921- *IntWW 91, WhoAmL 92*
**Alexander,** Donald Lee 1956- *WhoFI 92*
**Alexander,** Douglas 1936- *Who 92*
**Alexander,** Drew W 1948- *AmMWSc 92, WhoBlA 92*
**Alexander,** Duane Frederick 1940- *AmMWSc 92*
**Alexander,** E. Curtis 1941- *WhoBlA 92*
**Alexander,** Earl L, Jr 1920- *AmMWSc 92*
**Alexander,** Eben 1851-1910 *DcNCBi 1*
**Alexander,** Edward Cleve 1943- *AmMWSc 92, WhoBlA 92*
**Alexander,** Edwin 1870-1926 *TwCPaSc*
**Alexander,** Elizabeth 1962- *ConAu 135*
**Alexander,** Ellen Jo 1943- *WhoAmL 92*
**Alexander,** Emmit Calvin, Jr 1943- *AmMWSc 92*
**Alexander,** Errol D. 1940- *WhoFI 92*
**Alexander,** Errol D. 1941- *WhoBlA 92*
**Alexander,** Estella Conwill 1949- *WhoBlA 92*
**Alexander,** Ethel 1925- *WhoAmP 91*
**Alexander,** Evan Shelby 1767-1809 *DcNCBi 1*
**Alexander,** F. S. Jack 1930- *WhoBlA 92*
**Alexander,** Floyce *DrAPF 91*
**Alexander,** Floyce 1938- *WrDr 92*
**Alexander,** Forrest Doyle 1927- *AmMWSc 92*
**Alexander,** Frances 1888- *ConAu 35NR*
**Alexander,** Frances F *WhoAmP 91*
**Alexander,** Frank Creighton, Jr 1918- *AmMWSc 92*
**Alexander,** Frank Lyon 1939- *WhoFI 92*
**Alexander,** Frank Spruill 1952- *WhoAmL 92*
**Alexander,** Fred 1917- *AmMWSc 92*
**Alexander,** Fred Sharpe, III 1941- *WhoWest 92*
**Alexander,** Fritz W, II *WhoAmP 91*
**Alexander,** Fritz W., II 1926- *WhoAmL 92, WhoBlA 92*
**Alexander,** Gary 1941- *ConAu 135*
**Alexander,** Gary R 1942- *WhoAmP 91*
**Alexander,** George Jay 1925- *AmMWSc 92*
**Alexander,** George Jonathon 1931- *WhoWest 92*
**Alexander,** George Valentine 1936- *WhoRel 92*
**Alexander,** Gerald Corwin 1930- *AmMWSc 92*
**Alexander,** Gregory Stewart 1948- *WhoAmL 92*
**Alexander,** Guy B 1918- *AmMWSc 92*
**Alexander,** Haim 1915- *ConCom 92*
**Alexander,** Harold Campbell 1920- *WhoFI 92*
**Alexander,** Harold Edwin, Jr. 1949- *WhoWest 92*
**Alexander,** Harold Rupert Leofric George 1891-1969 *FacFETw*
**Alexander,** Harry 1905- *TwCPaSc*
**Alexander,** Harry 1953- *WhoEnt 92*
**Alexander,** Harry Toussaint 1924- *WhoBlA 92*
**Alexander,** Henry Alan 1953- *WhoRel 92, WhoWest 92*
**Alexander,** Henry R 1925- *AmMWSc 92*
**Alexander,** Herbert 1874-1946 *TwCPaSc*

Alexander, Herman Davis 1919- AmMWSc 92
Alexander, Hezekiah 1728-1801 DcNCBi 1
Alexander, Holmes 1906-1985 ConAu 36NR
Alexander, Hubbard Lindsay 1939- WhoBlA 92
Alexander, Hugh Quincy 1911- WhoAmP 91
Alexander, Ian Douglas Gavin 1941- Who 92
Alexander, Ira H 1920- AmMWSc 92
Alexander, Irene 1925- WhoRel 92
Alexander, J B 1926- WhoAmP 91
Alexander, Jack Edward 1963- WhoFI 92
Alexander, James 1691-1756 BiInAmS
Alexander, James, Jr. 1945- WhoBlA 92
Alexander, James B 1831- ScFEYrs
Alexander, James Brett 1948- WhoBlA 92
Alexander, James Craig 1926- AmMWSc 92
Alexander, James Crew 1942- AmMWSc 92
Alexander, James Kermott 1920- AmMWSc 92
Alexander, James King 1928- AmMWSc 92
Alexander, James Patrick 1944- WhoAmL 92
Alexander, James W. 1916- WhoBlA 92
Alexander, James Wesley 1934- AmMWSc 92
Alexander, Jane LesBEnT 92
Alexander, Jane 1939- IntMPA 92, WhoEnt 92
Alexander, Jane Marietta 1929- WhoAmP 91
Alexander, Jane Mayfield 1949- WhoEnt 92
Alexander, Jason 1959- IntMPA 92, WhoEnt 92
Alexander, Jeff 1953- WhoAmP 91
Alexander, Jessie Durrell 1919- WhoAmP 91
Alexander, Jim R 1946- WhoAmP 91
Alexander, Joan DrAPF 91
Alexander, John 1738?-1799 DcNCBi 1
Alexander, John 1923-1990 NewAmDM
Alexander, John 1962- WhoAmP 91
Alexander, John Brevard 1834-1911 DcNCBi 1
Alexander, John Charles 1915- WhoWest 92
Alexander, John Charles, Jr. 1946- WhoMW 92
Alexander, John David 1932- Who 92
Alexander, John David, Jr. 1932- WhoWest 92
Alexander, John Eric 1962- WhoEnt 92
Alexander, John Henry 1812-1867 BiInAmS
Alexander, John J 1940- AmMWSc 92
Alexander, John Lindsay 1920- IntWW 91, Who 92
Alexander, John M. 1954- WhoAmL 92
Alexander, John Macmillan, Jr 1931- AmMWSc 92
Alexander, John Malcolm 1921- Who 92
Alexander, John Noel 1941- WhoEnt 92
Alexander, John Stanley 1944- WhoBlA 92
Alexander, John Thorndike 1940- WrDr 92
Alexander, John Wesley, Jr. 1938- WhoBlA 92
Alexander, John William, Jr. 1933- WhoFI 92
Alexander, Johnnie Wilbert 1928- WhoBlA 92
Alexander, Jonathan James Graham 1935- IntWW 91, Who 92
Alexander, Joseph 1735?-1809 DcNCBi 1
Alexander, Joseph John Murphy 1933- WhoRel 92
Alexander, Joseph Kunkle 1940- AmMWSc 92
Alexander, Joseph Lee 1929- WhoBlA 92
Alexander, Joseph Walker 1947- AmMWSc 92
Alexander, Josephine WhoBlA 92
Alexander, Joyce London WhoBlA 92
Alexander, Judd Harris 1925- WhoFI 92
Alexander, Judith Dow Towsley 1937- WhoEnt 92
Alexander, Julia McGehee 1876-1957 DcNCBi 1
Alexander, Justin 1921- AmMWSc 92
Alexander, Karl DrAPF 91
Alexander, Karl 1944- ConAu 134
Alexander, Katharine Violet 1934- WhoAmL 92
Alexander, Kathleen Marie 1964- WhoWest 92
Alexander, Keith Milton 1951- WhoAmL 92
Alexander, Kelly Miller, Jr. 1948- WhoBlA 92
Alexander, Kenneth 1922- Who 92
Alexander, Kenneth Ross 1945- AmMWSc 92
Alexander, Kenneth Sidney 1958- WhoWest 92
Alexander, Kerry Duane 1935- WhoAmL 92
Alexander, Lamar 1940- CurBio 91 [port], News 91 [port], WhoAmP 91
Alexander, Lawrence R WhoAmP 91
Alexander, Lee 1927- WhoAmP 91
Alexander, Len 1947- WhoEnt 92
Alexander, Lenora Cole 1935- WhoBlA 92
Alexander, Leslie Luther 1917- AmMWSc 92
Alexander, Lindsay Who 92
Alexander, Lloyd 1924- WrDr 92
Alexander, Lloyd Ephraim 1902- AmMWSc 92
Alexander, Lorena 1954- WhoEnt 92
Alexander, Louis 1917- IntAu&W 91
Alexander, Louis 1954- WhoHisp 92
Alexander, Louis G. 1910- WhoBlA 92
Alexander, Louis George 1932- IntAu&W 91, WrDr 92
Alexander, Lucille Dillinger 1921- WhoEnt 92
Alexander, Lydia Lewis 1938- WhoBlA 92
Alexander, M. J. 1941- WrDr 92
Alexander, Marc 1929- ConAu 34NR
Alexander, Marcellus Winston, Jr. 1951- WhoBlA 92
Alexander, Margaret Walker 1915- WhoBlA 92
Alexander, Mark 1792-1883 DcNCBi 1
Alexander, Martin 1930- AmMWSc 92
Alexander, Martin Dale 1938- AmMWSc 92
Alexander, Mary Elsie 1947- WhoAmL 92
Alexander, Mary Louise 1926- AmMWSc 92
Alexander, Mason Gardner, Jr. 1959- WhoAmL 92
Alexander, Maurice Myron 1917- AmMWSc 92
Alexander, Max W. 1957- WhoEnt 92
Alexander, Meena DrAPF 91
Alexander, Meena 1951- ConPo 91, WrDr 92
Alexander, Mervin Franklin 1938- WhoBlA 92
Alexander, Mervyn Alban Newman Who 92
Alexander, Michael 1936- Who 92
Alexander, Michael Boyd 1951- WhoEnt 92
Alexander, Michael Charles 1920- IntAu&W 91, Who 92
Alexander, Michael Joseph 1941- IntAu&W 91
Alexander, Michael Lee 1959- WhoEnt 92
Alexander, Michael Norman 1941- AmMWSc 92
Alexander, Michael O'Donel Bjarne 1936- IntWW 91
Alexander, Miles Jordan 1931- WhoAmL 92
Alexander, Millard Henry 1943- AmMWSc 92
Alexander, Milton Otho 1923- WhoAmP 91
Alexander, Moses 1853-1924 DcAmImH
Alexander, Nancy J 1939- AmMWSc 92
Alexander, Nancy J 1947- AmMWSc 92
Alexander, Natalie 1926- AmMWSc 92
Alexander, Nathaniel 1756-1808 DcNCBi 1
Alexander, Nicholas Michael 1925- AmMWSc 92
Alexander, Norman Who 92
Alexander, Norman 1915- TwCPaSc
Alexander, Orin V 1924- WhoAmP 91
Alexander, Otis Douglas 1949- WhoBlA 92
Alexander, Padinjarethalakal Cherian 1921- IntWW 91
Alexander, Padınjarethalakkal Cherian 1921- Who 92
Alexander, Pamela DrAPF 91
Alexander, Pamela Gayle 1952- WhoBlA 92
Alexander, Patrick Byron 1950- WhoEnt 92
Alexander, Patrick Desmond William C. Who 92
Alexander, Patrick James 1926- WrDr 92
Alexander, Paul Crayton 1946- WhoBlA 92
Alexander, Paul Donald 1934- Who 92
Alexander, Paul Harrison 1933- WhoRel 92
Alexander, Paul Marion 1927- AmMWSc 92
Alexander, Peter Albert 1942- WhoFI 92
Alexander, Peter G. 1965- WhoEnt 92
Alexander, Preston Paul, Jr. 1952- WhoBlA 92
Alexander, Ralph IntMPA 92
Alexander, Ralph Holland 1936- WhoRel 92
Alexander, Ralph William 1911- AmMWSc 92
Alexander, Ralph William, Jr 1941- AmMWSc 92
Alexander, Randell Curtis 1950- WhoMW 92
Alexander, Randy 1958- WhoEnt 92
Alexander, Renee R 1932- AmMWSc 92
Alexander, Richard 1944- WhoAmL 92
Alexander, Richard Dale 1929- AmMWSc 92
Alexander, Richard Elmont 1924- WhoAmL 92, WhoMW 92
Alexander, Richard Goodman, Sr. 1950- WhoAmL 92
Alexander, Richard Raymond 1946- AmMWSc 92
Alexander, Richard Thain 1934- Who 92
Alexander, Robert 1875-1945 TwCPaSc
Alexander, Robert Allen 1932- AmMWSc 92
Alexander, Robert Benjamin 1917- AmMWSc 92
Alexander, Robert Darwood 1944- WhoAmP 91
Alexander, Robert Hugh 1933- WhoMW 92
Alexander, Robert I. 1913- WhoBlA 92
Alexander, Robert J. 1918- WrDr 92
Alexander, Robert John 1946- WhoWest 92
Alexander, Robert L 1923- AmMWSc 92
Alexander, Robert L. 1945- WhoBlA 92
Alexander, Robert Love 1913- Who 92
Alexander, Robert McN 1934- WrDr 92
Alexander, Robert McNeill 1934- IntWW 91, Who 92
Alexander, Robert Spence 1917- AmMWSc 92
Alexander, Robert William 1967- WhoRel 92
Alexander, Robin 1950- WhoBlA 92
Alexander, Rodger Norman 1947- WhoMW 92
Alexander, Rodney 1946- WhoAmP 91
Alexander, Roger Keith 1946- AmMWSc 92
Alexander, Roland E. 1935- WhoBlA 92
Alexander, Ronald Algernon 1950- WhoBlA 92
Alexander, Ronald Ralph 1947- WhoEnt 92
Alexander, Roosevelt Maurice 1941- WhoBlA 92
Alexander, Rosa M. 1928- WhoBlA 92
Alexander, Sadie 1898-1989 NotBlAW 92 [port]
Alexander, Sadie Tanner Mossell 1898-1989 WhoBlA 92N
Alexander, Samuel 1837?-1917 BiInAmS
Alexander, Samuel 1859-1938 FacFETw
Alexander, Samuel Allen, Jr. 1938- WhoFI 92
Alexander, Samuel Craighead, Jr 1930- AmMWSc 92
Alexander, Samuel P. WhoHisp 92
Alexander, Samuel Rudolph 1930- WhoEnt 92
Alexander, Shana 1925- WrDr 92
Alexander, Sidney H., Jr. 1919- WhoBlA 92
Alexander, Sigmund Bowman ScFEYrs
Alexander, Silas 1895- WhoBlA 92
Alexander, Stephen 1806-1883 BiInAmS
Alexander, Stephen 1948- AmMWSc 92
Alexander, Stephen Winthrop 1941- WhoMW 92
Alexander, Stuart David 1938- AmMWSc 92
Alexander, Sue 1933- IntAu&W 91, WrDr 92
Alexander, Susan Greig 1930- WhoAmP 91
Alexander, Sydenham Benoni 1840-1921 DcNCBi 1
Alexander, T. M., Sr. 1911- WhoIns 92
Alexander, Taylor Richard 1915- AmMWSc 92
Alexander, Tessa Elizabeth 1954- WhoWest 92
Alexander, Theodore Martin, Sr. 1909- WhoBlA 92
Alexander, Theodore Thomas, Jr. 1937- WhoBlA 92
Alexander, Thomas C 1956- WhoAmP 91
Alexander, Thomas Craig 1947- WhoRel 92
Alexander, Thomas Goodwin 1928- AmMWSc 92
Alexander, Thomas John 1940- Who 92
Alexander, Thomas Kennedy 1931- AmMWSc 92
Alexander, Timothy I. 1944- WhoRel 92
Alexander, Van 1915- WhoEnt 92
Alexander, Vera 1932- AmMWSc 92
Alexander, Vernell 1940- WhoRel 92
Alexander, Victor Nimrud 1943- WhoEnt 92
Alexander, Victor Theodore 1956- WhoFI 92
Alexander, W F ScFEYrs
Alexander, W J ScFEYrs
Alexander, Walter Gilbert, II 1922- WhoBlA 92
Alexander, Walter Ronald 1931- Who 92
Alexander, Wardine Towers 1955- WhoBlA 92
Alexander, Warren Dornell 1921- WhoBlA 92
Alexander, Willard A. 1931- WhoFI 92
Alexander, William 1726-1783 BiInAmS
Alexander, William B 1921- WhoAmP 91
Alexander, William Cameron, II 1938- WhoIns 92
Alexander, William Carter 1937- AmMWSc 92
Alexander, William D. d1991 NewYTBS 91
Alexander, William Davidson, III 1911- AmMWSc 92
Alexander, William DeWitt 1833-1913 BiInAmS
Alexander, William G 1951- WhoAmP 91
Alexander, William Gemmell 1918- Who 92
Alexander, William H 1930- WhoAmP 91, WhoBlA 92
Alexander, William Henry 1930- WhoAmL 92
Alexander, William Herbert 1941- WhoFI 92
Alexander, William Julius 1797-1857 DcNCBi 1
Alexander, William M., Jr. 1928- WhoBlA 92
Alexander, William Nebel 1929- AmMWSc 92
Alexander, William Nelson, II 1944- WhoAmL 92, WhoAmP 91
Alexander, William Polk, III 1947- WhoAmL 92
Alexander, William V., Jr. 1934- AlmAP 92 [port], WhoAmP 91
Alexander, Willie WhoBlA 92
Alexander-Grinalds, Julia C. 1947- WhoAmL 92
Alexander-Holland, Christina Ann IntAu&W 91
Alexander-Jackson, Eleanor Gertrude 1904- AmMWSc 92
Alexander of Ballochmyle, Claud Hagart- 1927- Who 92
Alexander of Potterhill, Baron 1905- Who 92
Alexander of Tunis, Earl 1935- Who 92
Alexander Of Weedon, Baron 1936- IntWW 91, Who 92
Alexander Ralston, Elreta 1919- NotBlAW 92
Alexander-Sinclair of Freswick, David B 1927- Who 92
Alexander-Whiting, Harriett 1947- WhoBlA 92
Alexanderson, Ernst 1878-1975 FacFETw
Alexanderson, Ernst F. W. d1975 LesBEnT 92
Alexanderson, Gerald Lee 1933- AmMWSc 92
Alexandra Fedorovna 1872-1918 FacFETw
Alexandra, Princess IntWW 91
Alexandra, Princess 1936 Who 92R
Alexandra, Queen of England 1844-1925 FacFETw
Alexandra, Danielle 1957- WhoEnt 92
Alexandratos, Spiro 1951- AmMWSc 92
Alexandre, Journel 1931- WhoBlA 92
Alexandre, Judith Lee 1944- WhoWest 92
Alexandridis, Alexander A 1949- AmMWSc 92
Alexandris, Efstathios IntWW 91
Alexandroff, Mirron 1923- WhoEnt 92, WhoMW 92
Alexandrov IntWW 91
Alexandru, Constantin 1953- IntWW 91
Alexandru, Lupu 1923- AmMWSc 92
Alexanian, Neshan 1921- WhoFI 92
Alexanian, Vazken Arsen 1943- AmMWSc 92
Alexeff, Igor 1931- AmMWSc 92
Alexeyev IntWW 91
Alexiadis, George 1911- IntWW 91
Alexiou, Arthur George 1930- AmMWSc 92
Alexiou, Margaret Beatrice 1939- WhoRel 92
Alexiou, Marina S. 1940- WhoFI 92
Alexis 1873-1970 FacFETw
Alexis, patriarch of Moscow & all Russia 1877-1970 DcEcMov
Alexis, Austin DrAPF 91
Alexis, Carlton Peter 1929- WhoBlA 92
Alexis, Doris Virginia 1921- WhoBlA 92
Alexis, Francis 1947- IntWW 91
Alexis, Geraldine M. 1948- WhoAmL 92
Alexis, Marcus 1932- WhoBlA 92
Alexis, Paul 1847-1901 ThHEIm [port]
Alexis, Paul Arthur 1946- WhoAmL 92

**Alexius**, Frederick Bernard 1941- *WhoAmL 92*
**Alexopoulos**, Helene *WhoEnt 92*
**Aley**, Charles R. 1956- *WhoAmL 92*
**Aley**, Thomas John 1938- *WhoMW 92*
**Alfano**, Blaise F. *WhoHisp 92*
**Alfano**, Franco 1875-1954 *NewAmDM*
**Alfano**, Michael Charles 1947- *AmMWSc 92*
**Alfano**, Robert R 1941- *AmMWSc 92*
**Alfaro**, Andreu 1929- *IntWW 91*
**Alfaro**, Armando Joffroy 1950- *WhoWest 92*
**Alfaro**, Armando Joffroy, Jr. 1950- *WhoHisp 92*
**Alfaro**, Felix Benjamin 1939- *WhoWest 92*
**Alfaro**, Ricardo 1961- *WhoHisp 92*
**Alfaro-Garcia**, Rafael 1941- *WhoHisp 92*
**Alfaro-Lopez**, Maria G. *WhoHisp 92*
**Alfarth**, Felix 1901-1923 *EncTR 91*
**Alfau**, Felipe 1902- *ConLC 66 [port], WhoHisp 92*
**Alfeld**, Peter 1950- *AmMWSc 92*
**Alfeld**, Philip Baker 1953- *WhoAmL 92*
**Alfert**, Max 1921- *AmMWSc 92*
**Alfhild** *EncAmaz 91*
**Alfidja**, Abderrahmane 1942- *IntWW 91*
**Alfieri**, Charles C 1922- *AmMWSc 92*
**Alfieri**, Dino 1886-1966 *BiDExR, EncTR 91*
**Alfieri**, Gaetano T 1926- *AmMWSc 92*
**Alfieri**, James Peter 1957- *WhoFI 92*
**Alfieri**, Lisa Gwyneth 1967- *WhoEnt 92*
**Alfieri**, Richard *WhoEnt 92*
**Alfieri**, Vittorio 1749-1803 *BlkwCEP*
**Alfiero**, Salvatore Harry 1937- *WhoFI 92*
**Alfin-Slater**, Roslyn Berniece 1916- *AmMWSc 92*
**Alfing**, Norman Lee 1933- *WhoWest 92*
**Alfinger**, Ambrosius d1533 *HisDSpE*
**Alfonsi**, William E. 1923- *WhoMW 92*
**Alfonsin**, Raul 1927- *FacFETw*
**Alfonsin**, Raul Ricardo 1927- *Who 92*
**Alfonsin Foulkes**, Raul 1926- *IntWW 91*
**Alfonso XIII** 1886-1941 *FacFETw*
**Alfonso**, Elisa J. 1955- *WhoHisp 92*
**Alfonso**, Kristian *WhoHisp 92*
**Alfonso**, Marco 1954- *WhoHisp 92*
**Alfonso**, Pedro 1948- *WhoBlA 92*
**Alfonso**, Ricardo Manuel 1959- *WhoMW 92*
**Alfonzo**, Carlos d1991 *NewYTBS 91*
**Alfonzo**, Carlos 1950-1991 *WhoHisp 92N*
**Alfonzo-Ravard**, Rafael *IntWW 91*
**Alford**, Alan Dean 1962- *WhoFI 92*
**Alford**, B. W. E. 1937- *WrDr 92*
**Alford**, Betty Bohon 1932- *AmMWSc 92*
**Alford**, Bobby R 1932- *AmMWSc 92*
**Alford**, Brenda 1947- *WhoBlA 92*
**Alford**, Cecil Orie 1933- *AmMWSc 92*
**Alford**, Charles Aaron, Jr 1928- *AmMWSc 92*
**Alford**, Cheryl Purdin 1953- *WhoAmP 91*
**Alford**, Dallas L, Jr *WhoAmP 91*
**Alford**, Dean 1953- *WhoAmP 91*
**Alford**, Donald Kay 1936- *AmMWSc 92*
**Alford**, Donald Sutton 1950- *WhoAmP 91*
**Alford**, Geary Simmons 1945- *AmMWSc 92*
**Alford**, Haile Lorraine 1949- *WhoBlA 92*
**Alford**, Harvey Edwin 1924- *AmMWSc 92*
**Alford**, Helen Johnson 1951- *WhoAmL 92*
**Alford**, J. Keith 1941- *WhoFI 92*
**Alford**, James Thomas 1948- *WhoWest 92*
**Alford**, Joan Franz 1940- *WhoFI 92*
**Alford**, John 1929-1960 *TwCPaSc*
**Alford**, John Richard 1919- *Who 92*
**Alford**, Kay Elizabeth *WhoMW 92*
**Alford**, Kenneth J 1930- *WhoAmP 91*
**Alford**, Kenneth Leon 1959- *WhoRel 92*
**Alford**, Marcus Richard 1953- *WhoEnt 92*
**Alford**, Mary Ann 1954- *WhoAmL 92*
**Alford**, Neill Herbert, Jr. 1919- *WhoAmL 92, WrDr 92*
**Alford**, Newell G., Jr. 1920- *WhoAmL 92, WhoFI 92*
**Alford**, Oteka Laverne 1948- *WhoAmL 92*
**Alford**, Paul Legare 1930- *WhoRel 92*
**Alford**, Richard Harding 1943- *Who 92*
**Alford**, Thomas Earl 1935- *WhoBlA 92*
**Alford**, Walter Helion 1938- *WhoAmL 92*
**Alford**, William Lumpkin 1924- *AmMWSc 92*
**Alford**, William P. 1948- *WhoAmL 92*
**Alford**, William Parker 1927- *AmMWSc 92*
**Alford**, Yvonne Marie 1936- *WhoAmP 91*
**Alfors**, John Theodore 1930- *AmMWSc 92*
**Alfred**, Dewitt C., Jr. 1937- *WhoBlA 92*
**Alfred**, James Jourdan 1933- *WhoAmP 91*
**Alfred**, Lindbergh Davis 1948- *WhoWest 92*
**Alfred**, Louis Charles Roland 1929- *AmMWSc 92*
**Alfred**, Montague 1925- *Who 92*
**Alfred**, Rayfield 1939- *WhoBlA 92*
**Alfred**, Stephen J 1934- *WhoAmP 91*
**Alfred**, Stephen Jay 1934- *WhoAmL 92*
**Alfred**, William 1922- *WrDr 92*
**Alfredeen**, Lennart Allan 1944- *WhoMW 92*
**Alfrey**, Clarence P, Jr 1930- *AmMWSc 92*
**Alfrey**, Thomas Neville 1944- *WhoAmL 92, WhoWest 92*
**Alfuth**, Terry J. 1945- *WhoIns 92*
**Alfven**, Hannes Olof Gosta 1908- *AmMWSc 92, FacFETw, IntWW 91, Who 92, WhoNob 90, WhoWest 92*
**Algabid**, Hamid *IntWW 91*
**Algar**, James 1912- *IntMPA 92*
**Algard**, Franklin Thomas 1922- *AmMWSc 92*
**Algard**, Ole 1921- *IntWW 91*
**Algarin**, Miguel 1941- *WhoHisp 92*
**Algarotti**, Francesco 1712-1764 *BlkwCEP*
**Algayer**, Jaromir 1935- *IntWW 91*
**Algaze**, Mario Arturo 1947- *WhoHisp 92*
**Algeo**, John 1930- *WrDr 92*
**Algeo**, Thomas Samuel 1956- *WhoAmL 92*
**Alger**, Daniel Richard 1950- *WhoFI 92*
**Alger**, David Townley 1945- *WhoRel 92*
**Alger**, Elizabeth A 1939- *AmMWSc 92*
**Alger**, Francis 1807-1863 *BiInAmS*
**Alger**, Horatio, Jr. *SmATA 67*
**Alger**, Horatio, Jr. 1832-1899 *BenetAL 91*
**Alger**, Matthew Dale 1959- *WhoAmL 92*
**Alger**, Nelda Elizabeth 1923- *AmMWSc 92*
**Algermissen**, Sylvester Theodore 1932- *AmMWSc 92*
**Algoma**, Bishop of 1928- *Who 92*
**Algood**, Alice Wright 1926- *WhoAmP 91*
**Algra**, Diana 1949- *WhoHisp 92*
**Algra**, Ronald James 1949- *WhoWest 92*
**Algren**, Nelson 1909-1981 *BenetAL 91, FacFETw*
**Alhadeff**, Jack Abraham 1943- *AmMWSc 92*
**Alhaji**, Alhaji Abubakar 1938- *IntWW 91*
**Alhegelan**, Faisal Abdul Aziz 1929- *Who 92*
**Alhegelan**, Faisal Abdul Aziz al- 1929- *IntWW 91*
**Alho**, Bonnie Kathleen 1942- *WhoRel 92*
**Alhossainy**, Effat M 1922- *AmMWSc 92*
**Ali**, Agha Shahid 1949- *ConPo 91, WrDr 92*
**Ali**, Ahmad Mohamed 1932- *IntWW 91*
**Ali**, Ahmed 1910- *ConAu 34NR, ConLC 69 [port], ConNov 91, IntAu&W 91, WrDr 92*
**Ali**, Fathi Mohamed *IntWW 91*
**Ali**, Fatima 1925- *WhoBlA 92*
**Ali**, Grace L. 1952- *WhoBlA 92*
**Ali**, H. A. Mukti 1923- *IntWW 91, WhoRel 92*
**Ali**, Hussien 1948- *WhoAmL 92*
**Ali**, Kamal Hassan 1921- *IntWW 91*
**Ali**, Kamal Hassan 1944- *WhoBlA 92*
**Ali**, Keramat *AmMWSc 92*
**Ali**, Mahamed Asgar 1934- *AmMWSc 92*
**Ali**, Marie Ida 1948- *WhoMW 92*
**Ali**, Michael N. *Who 92*
**Ali**, Mir Ahmed 1956- *WhoWest 92*
**Ali**, Mir Masoom 1929- *AmMWSc 92*
**Ali**, Mir Shawkat 1938- *IntWW 91, Who 92*
**Ali**, Mohamed Ather 1932- *AmMWSc 92*
**Ali**, Mohammed Yusuf 1937- *WhoMW 92*
**Ali**, Monica McCarthy 1941- *AmMWSc 92*
**Ali**, Moonis 1944- *AmMWSc 92*
**Ali**, Muhammad 1942- *BlkOlyM, ConBlB 2 [port], FacFETw [port], IntWW 91, RComAH, WhoBlA 92*
**Ali**, Naushad 1953- *AmMWSc 92*
**Ali**, Rasheedah Ziyadah 1950- *WhoBlA 92*
**Ali**, Rashied 1933- *WhoBlA 92*
**Ali**, Rashied 1935- *NewAmDM*
**Ali**, Rida A 1938- *AmMWSc 92*
**Ali**, Sadiq 1910- *IntWW 91*
**Ali**, Salah Omar Al- 1937- *IntWW 91*
**Ali**, Saleh Ahmad al- 1918- *IntWW 91*
**Ali**, Schavi Mali 1948- *WhoBlA 92*
**Ali**, Shahida Parvin 1942- *AmMWSc 92*
**Ali**, Shahrazad 1949- *WhoBlA 92*
**Ali**, Sultan Abu 1937- *IntWW 91*
**Ali**, Waleed Badie 1950- *WhoEnt 92*
**Ali**, Yusuf 1953- *AmMWSc 92*
**Ali**, Zine El Abidene ben 1936- *IntWW 91*
**Ali-Khan**, Ausat 1939- *AmMWSc 92*
**Ali Samater**, Mohammed 1931- *IntWW 91*
**Ali-Zadeh**, Franghiz 1947- *ConCom 92*
**Alia**, Ramiz 1925- *CurBio 91 [port], IntWW 91*
**Aliber**, Robert Z. 1930- *WhoMW 92, WrDr 92*
**Aliberti**, John A *WhoAmP 91*
**Alibrandi**, Joseph Francis 1928- *WhoFI 92, WhoWest 92*
**Alic**, John A 1941- *AmMWSc 92*
**Alice**, Princess 1901 *Who 92R*
**Alice**, Mary 1941- *WhoEnt 92*
**Alicea**, Benigno E. 1947- *WhoHisp 92*
**Alicea**, Victor Gabriel 1938- *WhoHisp 92*
**Alich**, Agnes Amelia 1932- *AmMWSc 92, WhoMW 92*
**Alich**, John A. 1942- *WhoFI 92*
**Alicino**, Nicholas J 1921- *AmMWSc 92*
**Alie**, Arthur H. 1939- *WhoIns 92*
**Alier**, Abel 1933- *IntWW 91*
**Aliesan**, Jody *DrAPF 91*
**Aliev**, Geydar Alievich 1923- *SovUnBD*
**Alieva**, Fazu 1932- *IntWW 91*
**Alig**, Frank Douglas Stalnaker 1921- *WhoFI 92, WhoMW 92*
**Alig**, Roger Casanova 1941- *AmMWSc 92*
**Aliger**, Margarita Iosifovna 1915- *IntWW 91, SovUnBD*
**Aliger**, Margarita Iosifovna 1915-1979 *FacFETw*
**Alikhan**, Muhammad Akhtar 1932- *AmMWSc 92*
**Aliki** *WrDr 92*
**Alimaras**, Gus 1958- *WhoAmL 92*
**Alimov**, Aleksandr Nikolayevich 1923- *IntWW 91*
**Alimov**, Timur Agzamovich 1936- *IntWW 91*
**Alin**, John Suemper 1940- *AmMWSc 92*
**Alin**, Morris *IntMPA 92*
**Alince**, Bohumil *AmMWSc 92*
**Alinder**, Mary Street 1946- *WhoWest 92*
**Alinova**, Durine Dieters 1947- *WhoEnt 92*
**Alinsky**, Saul 1909-1972 *ConAu 133*
**Aliosius**, David John 1965- *WhoMW 92*
**Alioto**, Angela Mia 1949- *WhoWest 92*
**Alioto**, Joseph Lawrence 1916- *IntWW 91*
**Aliprantis**, Charalambos Dionisios 1946- *AmMWSc 92*
**Alire**, Richard Marvin 1932- *AmMWSc 92*
**Alireza**, Ali A. *IntWW 91*
**Aliseda**, Jose Luis, Jr. 1956- *WhoHisp 92*
**Alishetti**, Bhoomaiah 1948- *WhoWest 92*
**Alisky**, Marvin 1923- *WrDr 92*
**Alison**, David 1882-1955 *TwCPaSc*
**Alison**, John Richardson 1956- *WhoAmL 92*
**Alison**, Michael James Hugh 1926- *Who 92*
**Alison**, Paul Nordell 1950- *WhoWest 92*
**Alison**, William Andrew Greig 1916- *Who 92*
**Alissandratos**, A D 1915- *WhoAmP 91*
**Alito**, Samuel Anthony, Jr. 1950- *WhoAmL 92, WhoAmP 91*
**Alivisatos**, A Paul 1959- *AmMWSc 92*
**Alivisatos**, Hamilkar Spiridonos 1887-1969 *DcEcMov*
**Alix**, Stephen J 1947- *IntAu&W 91*
**Alkadhi**, Karim A 1938- *AmMWSc 92*
**Alkalay-Gut**, Karen *DrAPF 91*
**Alkan**, Valentin 1813-1888 *NewAmDM*
**Alkema**, Robert A. *WhoIns 92*
**Alkezweeny**, Abdul Jabbar 1935- *AmMWSc 92*
**Alkhimov**, Vladimir Sergeyevich 1919- *IntWW 91*
**Alkire**, Betty Jo 1942- *WhoMW 92*
**Alkire**, David *WhoAmL 92*
**Alkire**, Richard Collin 1941- *AmMWSc 92, WhoMW 92*
**Alkjaersig**, Norma Kirstine 1921- *AmMWSc 92*
**Alkons**, James Joseph 1946- *WhoWest 92*
**Alks**, Vitauts 1938- *AmMWSc 92*
**Allaben**, Robert Dewitt 1930- *WhoMW 92*
**Allaben**, William Thomas 1939- *AmMWSc 92*
**Allaby**, John Michael 1933- *IntAu&W 91*
**Allaby**, Michael 1933- *WrDr 92*
**Allaby**, Stanley Reynolds 1931- *WhoRel 92*
**Alladaye**, Michel 1940- *IntWW 91*
**Allain**, Leon Gregory 1924- *WhoBlA 92, WhoRel 92*
**Allain**, William A 1928- *WhoAmP 91*
**Allaire**, Francis Raymond 1937- *AmMWSc 92*
**Allaire**, Mary E. 1955- *WhoEnt 92*
**Allaire**, Paul Arthur 1938- *Who 92, WhoFI 92*
**Allaire**, Paul Eugene 1941- *AmMWSc 92*
**Allais**, Maurice 1911- *IntWW 91, Who 92, WhoFI 92, WhoNob 90*
**Allam**, Peter John 1927- *Who 92*
**Allamandola**, Louis John 1946- *AmMWSc 92*
**Allan**, A J Gordon 1926- *AmMWSc 92*
**Allan**, Alexander Claud Stuart 1951- *Who 92*
**Allan**, Andrew Norman 1943- *Who 92*
**Allan**, Ann Gould 1940- *WhoMW 92*
**Allan**, Anthony James Allan H. *Who 92*
**Allan**, Barry David 1935- *AmMWSc 92*
**Allan**, Brian Shane 1967- *WhoRel 92*
**Allan**, Charles Lewis 1911- *Who 92*
**Allan**, Colin 1921- *Who 92*
**Allan**, Colin Faulds 1917- *Who 92*
**Allan**, Colin Hamilton 1921- *IntWW 91*
**Allan**, David Wayne 1936- *AmMWSc 92*
**Allan**, Diana Rosemary *Who 92*
**Allan**, Douglas *Who 92*
**Allan**, Elkan *IntAu&W 91, WrDr 92*
**Allan**, Frank Duane 1925- *AmMWSc 92*
**Allan**, George Alexander 1936- *Who 92*
**Allan**, George B 1935- *AmMWSc 92*
**Allan**, George Gordon 1934- *IntAu&W 91*
**Allan**, George Graham 1930- *AmMWSc 92*
**Allan**, Gordon Buchanan 1914- *Who 92*
**Allan**, Harper Keys 1946- *WhoWest 92*
**Allan**, Hugh James Pearson 1928- *Who 92, WhoRel 92*
**Allan**, Ian 1922- *Who 92*
**Allan**, J David 1945- *AmMWSc 92*
**Allan**, James Nicholas 1932- *IntWW 91, Who 92*
**Allan**, James Wilson 1945- *Who 92*
**Allan**, John 1950- *WrDr 92*
**Allan**, John Clifford 1920- *Who 92*
**Allan**, John Douglas 1941- *Who 92*
**Allan**, John Dykes 1925- *IntWW 91*
**Allan**, John Gray 1915- *Who 92*
**Allan**, John Mark 1960- *WhoAmP 91*
**Allan**, John R 1937- *AmMWSc 92*
**Allan**, John Ridgway 1947- *AmMWSc 92*
**Allan**, Julian Phelps 1892- *TwCPaSc*
**Allan**, Lewis *Who 92*
**Allan**, Luke d1962 *TwCWW 91*
**Allan**, Mabel Esther 1915- *IntAu&W 91, WrDr 92*
**Allan**, Ranald *IntAu&W 91*
**Allan**, Richard 1933- *TwCPaSc*
**Allan**, Richard Andrew 1948- *Who 92*
**Allan**, Richmond Frederick 1930- *WhoAmL 92*
**Allan**, Robert Emerson 1931- *AmMWSc 92*
**Allan**, Robert K 1940- *AmMWSc 92*
**Allan**, Robert Moffat, Jr. 1920- *WhoWest 92*
**Allan**, Robert Weir 1852-1942 *TwCPaSc*
**Allan**, Robin 1934- *WrDr 92*
**Allan**, Rosemary 1911- *TwCPaSc*
**Allan**, Ted *IntMPA 92*
**Allan**, Ted 1916- *IntAu&W 91, WrDr 92*
**Allan**, Walter Robert 1937- *WhoAmL 92*
**Allan**, William Roderick Buchanan 1945- *Who 92*
**Allan-Hodge**, Liz *WhoAmP 91*
**Allanbridge**, Lord 1925- *Who 92*
**Alland**, William 1916- *IntMPA 92*
**Allansmith**, Mathea R *AmMWSc 92*
**Allanson**, Garth Edward Christian 1969- *WhoEnt 92*
**Allanson-Winn** *Who 92*
**Allara**, David Lawrence 1937- *AmMWSc 92*
**Allard**, Edward Tiernan, III 1945- *WhoWest 92*
**Allard**, Geoffrey 1947- *TwCPaSc*
**Allard**, Gilles Olivier 1927- *AmMWSc 92*
**Allard**, Gordon 1909- *Who 92*
**Allard**, James Edward 1942- *WhoFI 92*
**Allard**, Jean 1924- *WhoAmL 92*
**Allard**, Jean Victor 1913- *Who 92*
**Allard**, Johane 1956- *AmMWSc 92*
**Allard**, Martine 1970- *WhoBlA 92*
**Allard**, Nanci A 1946- *WhoAmP 91*
**Allard**, Nona Mary 1928- *AmMWSc 92*
**Allard**, Robert Wayne 1919- *AmMWSc 92, WhoWest 92*
**Allard**, Stephen J *WhoAmP 91*
**Allard**, Thurman J. 1959- *WhoWest 92*
**Allard**, Wayne 1943- *AlmAP 92 [port], WhoAmP 91*
**Allard**, Wayne A. 1943- *WhoWest 92*
**Allard**, William Kenneth 1941- *AmMWSc 92*
**Allardice**, Bruce 1954- *WhoEnt 92*
**Allardice**, John McCarrell 1940- *WhoFI 92*
**Allardice**, William Arthur Llewellyn 1924- *Who 92*
**Allardt**, Erik Anders 1925- *IntWW 91*
**Allardt**, Linda *DrAPF 91*
**Allardyce**, Paula *WrDr 92*
**Allason**, James Harry 1912- *Who 92*
**Allason**, Rupert William Simon 1951- *Who 92*
**Allaudeen**, Hameedsulthan Sheik 1943- *AmMWSc 92*
**Allaun**, Frank 1913- *Who 92, WrDr 92*
**Allaway**, Ben Foster 1958- *WhoMW 92*
**Allaway**, Norman C 1922- *AmMWSc 92*
**Allaway**, Percy Albert 1915- *Who 92*
**Allbee**, Carlynne Marie 1947- *WhoWest 92*
**Allbee**, Charles Eugene 1937- *WhoWest 92*
**Allbee**, Robert George 1928- *WhoAmP 91*
**Allbee**, Sandra Moll 1947- *WhoWest 92*
**Allbery**, Debra *DrAPF 91*
**Allbeury**, Ted *ConAu 34NR*
**Allbeury**, Ted 1917- *IntAu&W 91*
**Allbeury**, Theodore Edward le Bouthillier 1917- *ConAu 34NR*
**Allbritton**, Cliff 1931- *WhoRel 92*
**Allbritton**, Joe Lewis 1924- *WhoEnt 92, WhoFI 92*
**Allbrooks**, Hubert Steven 1953- *WhoAmP 91*
**Allchin**, Arthur Macdonald 1930- *Who 92*
**Allchin**, Frank Raymond 1923- *IntWW 91, Who 92*
**Allcock**, Harry R 1932- *AmMWSc 92*
**Allcorn**, S. Robert 1947- *WhoAmL 92*
**Allcot**, Guy *IntAu&W 91X*

**Allcott,** Walter Herbert 1880-1951 *TwCPaSc*
**Allday,** Christopher J 1943- *AmMWSc 92*
**Allday,** Coningsby 1920- *Who 92*
**Allday,** Martin L *WhoAmP 91*
**Allday,** Martin Lewis 1926- *WhoAmL 92*
**Alldis,** Cecil Anderson 1918- *Who 92*
**Alldis,** John 1929- *NewAmDM, Who 92*
**Alldis,** Steve Allen 1953- *WhoWest 92*
**Alldredge,** Alice Louise 1949- *AmMWSc 92*
**Alldredge,** Gerald Palmer 1935- *AmMWSc 92*
**Alldredge,** Leroy Romney 1917- *AmMWSc 92*
**Alldredge,** Rendel Burdette 1920- *WhoWest 92*
**Alldredge,** Robert Louis 1922- *WhoFI 92, WhoWest 92*
**Alldridge,** Norman Alfred 1924- *AmMWSc 92*
**Alldrin,** Doris Reed 1930- *WhoWest 92*
**Alldritt,** Walter d1990 *Who 92N*
**Allee,** C. Ramon 1931- *WhoRel 92*
**Allee,** Henry Edward 1942- *WhoAmP 91*
**Allee,** Marshall Craig 1941- *AmMWSc 92*
**Allee,** Rita T 1947- *WhoAmP 91*
**Alleghanians,** The *NewAmDM*
**Allegra,** Peter Alexander 1953- *WhoFI 92*
**Allegrato,** Michael 1944- *WrDr 92*
**Allegre,** Charles Frederick 1911- *AmMWSc 92*
**Allegre,** Maurice Marie 1933- *IntWW 91*
**Allegret,** Yves 1907-1987 *FacFETw, IntDcF 2-2*
**Allegretti,** John E 1926- *AmMWSc 92*
**Allegrini,** Peter James 1952- *WhoFI 92*
**Allegro,** John 1923- *IntAu&W 91*
**Allegrucci,** Donald L 1936- *WhoAmP 91*
**Allegrucci,** Donald Lee 1936- *WhoAmL 92, WhoMW 92*
**Alleman,** Darrell Foster 1929- *WhoAmP 91*
**Alleman,** James H. 1941- *WhoMW 92*
**Alleman,** Raymond Henry 1934- *WhoFI 92*
**Allemand,** Charly D 1924- *AmMWSc 92*
**Allemann,** Sabina *WhoEnt 92*
**Allen** *Who 92*
**Allen,** Adela Artola *WhoHisp 92*
**Allen,** Alex B. *WrDr 92*
**Allen,** Alex James, Jr. 1934- *WhoBlA 92*
**Allen,** Alexander Charles 1933- *AmMWSc 92*
**Allen,** Alexander J. 1916- *WhoBlA 92*
**Allen,** Alfred Reginald 1876-1918 *BiInAmS*
**Allen,** Alistair 1947- *TwCPaSc*
**Allen,** Alma *EncAmaz 91*
**Allen,** Andrew A. 1921- *WhoBlA 92*
**Allen,** Anita Ford *WhoBlA 92*
**Allen,** Ann Tear 1963- *WhoMW 92*
**Allen,** Anna Marie 1955- *WhoMW 92*
**Allen,** Anneke S 1930- *AmMWSc 92*
**Allen,** Anthony John 1939- *Who 92*
**Allen,** Anthony Kenway 1917- *Who 92*
**Allen,** Anton Markert 1931- *AmMWSc 92*
**Allen,** Arch Turner 1875-1934 *DcNCBi 1*
**Allen,** Archie C 1929- *AmMWSc 92*
**Allen,** Aris Tee 1910-1991 *WhoBlA 92N*
**Allen,** Arnold Millman 1924- *Who 92*
**Allen,** Arnold Oral 1929- *AmMWSc 92*
**Allen,** Arthur 1928- *AmMWSc 92*
**Allen,** Arthur 1934- *AmMWSc 92*
**Allen,** Arthur Charles 1910- *AmMWSc 92*
**Allen,** Arthur Lee 1944- *AmMWSc 92*
**Allen,** Arthur T, Jr 1917- *AmMWSc 92*
**Allen,** Asa Alonzo 1911-1970 *RelLAm 91*
**Allen,** Augustine Oliver 1910- *AmMWSc 92*
**Allen,** B. D. 1935- *WhoFI 92*
**Allen,** Barbara *WhoAmP 91*
**Allen,** Barbara Ann 1956- *WhoEnt 92*
**Allen,** Barry Morgan 1939- *WhoFI 92*
**Allen,** Belle *WhoFI 92*
**Allen,** Ben Robert 1925- *WhoAmP 91*
**Allen,** Benjamin P., III 1942- *WhoBlA 92*
**Allen,** Bernestine 1944- *WhoBlA 92*
**Allen,** Bettie Jean 1926- *WhoBlA 92*
**Allen,** Betty *WhoBlA 92, WhoEnt 92*
**Allen,** Betty 1930- *NewAmDM*
**Allen,** Blair H 1933- *IntAu&W 91*
**Allen,** Blair Sidney 1952- *WhoBlA 92*
**Allen,** Bob L 1945- *WhoAmP 91*
**Allen,** Bonnie L 1924- *AmMWSc 92*
**Allen,** Bonnie Lynn 1957- *WhoWest 92*
**Allen,** Boyd Wilson, Jr. 1936- *WhoAmL 92*
**Allen,** Bradford Jon 1960- *WhoRel 92*
**Allen,** Brenda Foster 1947- *WhoBlA 92*
**Allen,** Browning E., Jr. 1925- *WhoBlA 92*
**Allen,** Bruce Michael 1949- *WhoMW 92*
**Allen,** Bruce S 1951- *WhoAmP 91*
**Allen,** Bruce Templeton 1938- *WhoFI 92, WhoMW 92*
**Allen,** Byron 1961- *WhoBlA 92, WhoEnt 92*
**Allen,** C Eugene 1939- *AmMWSc 92*
**Allen,** Cannon Fairfax 1961- *WhoAmL 92*
**Allen,** Carlton Barrington 1959- *WhoFI 92*
**Allen,** Carol M *WhoAmP 91*
**Allen,** Carolyn June 1935- *WhoFI 92*
**Allen,** Carrol V 1934- *WhoAmP 91*
**Allen,** Charles A 1933- *AmMWSc 92*
**Allen,** Charles C 1921- *AmMWSc 92*
**Allen,** Charles Claybourne 1935- *WhoBlA 92*
**Allen,** Charles E. 1931- *WhoBlA 92*
**Allen,** Charles E, Jr *WhoAmP 91*
**Allen,** Charles Edward 1947- *WhoBlA 92*
**Allen,** Charles Eugene 1939- *AmMWSc 92*
**Allen,** Charles Freeman 1928- *AmMWSc 92*
**Allen,** Charles H *WhoAmP 91*
**Allen,** Charles Lewis 1946- *WhoIns 92*
**Allen,** Charles Livingston 1913- *RelLAm 91*
**Allen,** Charles Marshall, Jr 1938- *AmMWSc 92*
**Allen,** Charles Marvin 1918- *AmMWSc 92*
**Allen,** Charles Michael 1942- *AmMWSc 92*
**Allen,** Charles Richard 1926- *WhoFI 92*
**Allen,** Charles W 1932- *AmMWSc 92*
**Allen,** Charles William 1932- *AmMWSc 92*
**Allen,** Charlotte Vale 1941- *WrDr 92*
**Allen,** Cheryl 1939- *AmMWSc 92*
**Allen,** Chester *TwCWW 91*
**Allen,** Christopher Edwards 1964- *WhoMW 92*
**Allen,** Christopher Whitney 1942- *AmMWSc 92*
**Allen,** Clarence Roderic 1925- *AmMWSc 92*
**Allen,** Clay *TwCWW 91*
**Allen,** Clifford Marsden 1927- *AmMWSc 92*
**Allen,** Clive Victor 1935- *WhoAmL 92, WhoFI 92*
**Allen,** Clyde Cecil 1943- *WhoBlA 92*
**Allen,** Clyde Thomas 1929- *WhoEnt 92*
**Allen,** Colin 1926- *TwCPaSc*
**Allen,** Colin Mervyn Gordon 1929- *Who 92*
**Allen,** Constance Olleen 1923- *WhoWest 92*
**Allen,** Corey 1934- *IntMPA 92*
**Allen,** Craig Adams 1941- *WhoAmP 91*
**Allen,** Crawford Leonard 1952- *WhoRel 92*
**Allen,** Daniel Ross 1949- *WhoRel 92*
**Allen,** David 1933- *Who 92*
**Allen,** David Charles 1944- *WhoWest 92*
**Allen,** David Christian 1949- *WhoMW 92*
**Allen,** David Christopher 1933- *WhoFI 92*
**Allen,** David Donald 1931- *WhoFI 92, WhoIns 92, WhoMW 92*
**Allen,** David Harlow 1930- *WhoWest 92*
**Allen,** David James 1935- *WhoAmL 92*
**Allen,** David Lynn 1954- *WhoFI 92*
**Allen,** David Mitchell 1938- *AmMWSc 92*
**Allen,** David Robert 1956- *WhoEnt 92*
**Allen,** David Searles 1934- *WhoRel 92*
**Allen,** David Thomas 1958- *AmMWSc 92*
**Allen,** David Watson 1956- *WhoRel 92*
**Allen,** David West *AmMWSc 92*
**Allen,** David Woodroffe 1944- *WhoFI 92*
**Allen,** Davis 1916- *DcTwDes*
**Allen,** Dayton 1919- *IntMPA 92*
**Allen,** Dean Ellis 1950- *WhoWest 92*
**Allen,** Debbie *WhoEnt 92*
**Allen,** Debbie 1950- *IntMPA 92, NotBlAW 92, WhoBlA 92*
**Allen,** Deborah *DrAPF 91*
**Allen,** Deborah Bourne 1953- *WhoAmL 92*
**Allen,** Deborah Leah 1953- *WhoRel 92*
**Allen,** Debra Janiece 1953- *WhoWest 92*
**Allen,** Dede *ReelWom*
**Allen,** Dede 1924?- *ConTFT 9, IntMPA 92*
**Allen,** Dell K 1931- *AmMWSc 92*
**Allen,** Delmas James 1937- *AmMWSc 92*
**Allen,** Deloran Matthew 1939- *AmMWSc 92*
**Allen,** DeMetrice Michealle 1958- *WhoBlA 92*
**Allen,** Dennis N. 1956- *WhoMW 92*
**Allen,** Dennis Patrick 1958- *WhoMW 92*
**Allen,** Derek William d1991 *Who 92N*
**Allen,** Deryck Norman de Garrs 1918- *Who 92*
**Allen,** Desi Wayne 1954- *WhoRel 92*
**Allen,** Devere 1891-1955 *AmPeW*
**Allen,** Dick *DrAPF 91*
**Allen,** Dick 1938- *WhoAmP 91*
**Allen,** Dick 1939- *WrDr 92*
**Allen,** Diogenes 1932- *IntAu&W 91, WhoRel 92, WrDr 92*
**Allen,** Don Lee 1934- *AmMWSc 92*
**Allen,** Donald Bruce 1941- *WhoWest 92*
**Allen,** Donald George 1930- *Who 92*
**Allen,** Donald M. 1912- *BenetAL 91*
**Allen,** Donald Orrie 1939- *AmMWSc 92*
**Allen,** Donald Stewart 1911- *AmMWSc 92*
**Allen,** Donald Vail 1928- *WhoFI 92, WhoWest 92*
**Allen,** Donald Wayne 1936- *WhoFI 92, WhoWest 92*
**Allen,** Doris 1936- *WhoAmP 91*
**Allen,** Douglas Albert Vivian *IntWW 91*
**Allen,** Douglas Charles 1940- *AmMWSc 92*
**Allen,** Dozier T, Jr 1931- *WhoAmP 91, WhoBlA 92*
**Allen,** Duane David 1943- *WhoEnt 92*
**Allen,** Dudley Dean 1943- *WhoAmL 92*
**Allen,** Dudley Peter 1852-1915 *BiInAmS*
**Allen,** Duff Shederic, Jr 1928- *AmMWSc 92*
**Allen,** Durward L. 1910- *WrDr 92*
**Allen,** Durward Leon 1910- *AmMWSc 92*
**Allen,** Eddie *TwCPaSc*
**Allen,** Eddie Dale *WhoFI 92*
**Allen,** Edgar 1892-1943 *FacFETw*
**Allen,** Edgar Burns 1929- *WhoWest 92*
**Allen,** Edgar Fredrick 1927- *WhoRel 92*
**Allen,** Edith Agnes 1939- *WhoFI 92*
**Allen,** Edna Rowery 1938- *WhoBlA 92*
**Allen,** Edward *DrAPF 91*
**Allen,** Edward David 1942- *AmMWSc 92*
**Allen,** Edward Franklin 1907- *AmMWSc 92*
**Allen,** Edward Lefebvre 1962- *WhoAmL 92*
**Allen,** Edward McDowell 1924- *WhoWest 92*
**Allen,** Edward Patrick 1943- *AmMWSc 92*
**Allen,** Edward Raymond 1913- *WhoWest 92*
**Allen,** Edwin Russell, Jr. 1949- *WhoRel 92*
**Allen,** Elbert E. 1921- *WhoBlA 92*
**Allen,** Eleazer 1692-1750 *DcNCBi 1*
**Allen,** Eliza 1826- *EncAmaz 91*
**Allen,** Elizabeth Morei *AmMWSc 92*
**Allen,** Emory Raworth 1935- *AmMWSc 92*
**Allen,** Eric 1916- *ConAu 133*
**Allen,** Eric Raymond 1932- *AmMWSc 92*
**Allen,** Ernest, Sr 1932- *WhoAmP 91*
**Allen,** Ernest E 1933- *AmMWSc 92*
**Allen,** Ernest Mason 1904- *AmMWSc 92*
**Allen,** Esther C 1905- *AmMWSc 92*
**Allen,** Esther Louisa 1912- *WhoBlA 92*
**Allen,** Ethan 1738-1789 *BenetAL 91, BlkwEAR*
**Allen,** Ethan Burdette, III 1954- *WhoAmL 92*
**Allen,** Eugene 1916- *AmMWSc 92*
**Allen,** F. C., Jr. 1933- *WhoAmL 92*
**Allen,** Fergus Hamilton 1921- *Who 92*
**Allen,** Frances Elizabeth 1932- *AmMWSc 92*
**Allen,** Frances Michael 1939- *WhoWest 92*
**Allen,** Francis A. 1919- *WrDr 92*
**Allen,** Francis Alfred 1919- *WhoAmL 92*
**Allen,** Francis Andrew 1933- *Who 92*
**Allen,** Frank B 1909- *AmMWSc 92*
**Allen,** Frank Graham 1920- *Who 92*
**Allen,** Frank Humphrey 1896- *TwCPaSc*
**Allen,** Frankie B. 1955- *WhoEnt 92*
**Allen,** Fred d1956 *LesBEnT 92*
**Allen,** Fred 1894-1956 *BenetAL 91, FacFETw*
**Allen,** Fred Ernest 1910- *AmMWSc 92*
**Allen,** Freddie Lewis 1947- *AmMWSc 92*
**Allen,** Frederic W. 1926- *WhoAmL 92, WhoAmP 91*
**Allen,** Frederick Graham 1923- *AmMWSc 92*
**Allen,** Frederick Lewis 1890-1954 *BenetAL 91*
**Allen,** Fulton 1907-1941 *DcNCBi 1*
**Allen,** G M *WhoAmP 91*
**Allen,** Garland Edward, III 1936- *AmMWSc 92*
**Allen,** Gary Curtiss 1939- *AmMWSc 92*
**Allen,** Gary James 1944- *IntWW 91, Who 92*
**Allen,** Gary Joe 1946- *WhoEnt 92*
**Allen,** Gary William 1944- *AmMWSc 92*
**Allen,** Gay Wilson 1903- *BenetAL 91, IntAu&W 91, WrDr 92*
**Allen,** Geoffrey 1928- *IntWW 91, Who 92*
**Allen,** George d1907 *DcLB 112*
**Allen,** George d1991 *NewYTBS 91 [port]*
**Allen,** George 1832-1907 *DcLB 106 [port]*
**Allen,** George 1922-1990 *AnObit 1990, CurBio 91N*
**Allen,** George 1955- *WhoBlA 92*
**Allen,** George, and Unwin Limited *DcLB 112*
**Allen,** George David, Jr. 1961- *WhoAmL 92*
**Allen,** George Felix 1952- *WhoAmP 91*
**Allen,** George Herbert 1923- *AmMWSc 92*
**Allen,** George Louis 1910- *WhoBlA 92*
**Allen,** George Mitchell 1932- *WhoBlA 92*
**Allen,** George Paul 1930- *WhoRel 92*
**Allen,** George Perry 1941- *AmMWSc 92*
**Allen,** George Rodger, Jr 1929- *AmMWSc 92*
**Allen,** George Venable 1903-1970 *DcNCBi 1*
**Allen,** George Warner 1916-1988 *TwCPaSc*
**Allen,** Georgia Mae 1944- *WhoMW 92*
**Allen,** Georgina 1954- *TwCPaSc*
**Allen,** Gerald Lee 1926- *WhoWest 92*
**Allen,** Gilbert *DrAPF 91*
**Allen,** Gladstone Wesley 1915- *WhoBlA 92*
**Allen,** Gloria Marie *WhoBlA 92*
**Allen,** Gordon Ainslie 1922- *AmMWSc 92*
**Allen,** Grace *WrDr 92*
**Allen,** Graham William 1953- *Who 92*
**Allen,** Grant 1848-1899 *ScFEYrs*
**Allen,** Gregory Bryce 1950- *WhoAmL 92*
**Allen,** Gregory D. 1949- *WhoEnt 92*
**Allen,** Gregory Scott 1955- *WhoWest 92*
**Allen,** Gregory Steven 1951- *WhoFI 92*
**Allen,** Hamish McEwan 1920- *Who 92*
**Allen,** Harold Don 1931- *AmMWSc 92*
**Allen,** Harold Norman 1912- *Who 92*
**Allen,** Harriette Louise 1943- *WhoBlA 92*
**Allen,** Harrison 1841-1897 *BiInAmS*
**Allen,** Harry Clay, Jr 1920- *AmMWSc 92*
**Allen,** Harry Cranbrook 1917- *Who 92, WrDr 92*
**Allen,** Harry E. 1894-1958 *TwCPaSc*
**Allen,** Harry Franklin 1956- *WhoFI 92*
**Allen,** Harry Prince 1938- *AmMWSc 92*
**Allen,** Heather Wild 1959- *WhoWest 92*
**Allen,** Henry 1908-1967 *NewAmDM*
**Allen,** Henry L 1945- *AmMWSc 92*
**Allen,** Henry Sermones, Jr. 1947- *WhoAmL 92*
**Allen,** Henry W. 1912- *BenetAL 91*
**Allen,** Henry Wilson 1912- *IntAu&W 91, TwCWW 91, WrDr 92*
**Allen,** Henry Wilson 1912-1991 *ConAu 135*
**Allen,** Herbert 1907- *AmMWSc 92*
**Allen,** Herbert 1908- *WhoFI 92*
**Allen,** Herbert Clifton, Jr 1917- *AmMWSc 92*
**Allen,** Herbert E 1939- *AmMWSc 92*
**Allen,** Herbert J. 1922- *WhoBlA 92*
**Allen,** Hervey 1889-1949 *BenetAL 91*
**Allen,** Hilary P 1911- *WhoAmP 91*
**Allen,** Horace N. *DcAmImH*
**Allen,** Howard Joseph 1941- *AmMWSc 92*
**Allen,** Howard Norman 1936- *WhoWest 92*
**Allen,** Howard Pfeiffer 1925- *WhoAmL 92, WhoFI 92, WhoWest 92*
**Allen,** Hugh *TwCWW 91*
**Allen,** Ingrid Victoria 1932- *Who 92*
**Allen,** Ira E 1913- *WhoAmP 91*
**Allen,** Irwin *IntMPA 92*
**Allen,** Irwin d1991 *NewYTBS 91 [port]*
**Allen,** Ivy Martell 1932- *WhoEnt 92*
**Allen,** J Frances 1916- *AmMWSc 92*
**Allen,** Jack Bradley 1925- *WhoRel 92*
**Allen,** Jack C, Jr 1935- *AmMWSc 92*
**Allen,** Jack Kenneth 1924- *WhoAmL 92*
**Allen,** Jacque *WhoAmP 91*
**Allen,** James *TwCPaSc*
**Allen,** James 1938- *WhoAmP 91*
**Allen,** James B. *DrAPF 91*
**Allen,** James Brown 1927- *WhoWest 92*
**Allen,** James Durwood 1935- *AmMWSc 92*
**Allen,** James Edward 1943- *WhoAmP 91*
**Allen,** James Frederick 1950- *AmMWSc 92*
**Allen,** James H. 1934- *WhoBlA 92*
**Allen,** James Harold 1935- *WhoRel 92*
**Allen,** James Lamar 1936- *AmMWSc 92*
**Allen,** James Lane 1849-1925 *BenetAL 91*
**Allen,** James Lucian 1928- *WhoAmL 92*
**Allen,** James O'Donnell 1949- *WhoMW 92*
**Allen,** James R, Jr 1927- *AmMWSc 92*
**Allen,** James Ralston 1938- *AmMWSc 92*
**Allen,** James Richard 1956- *WhoFI 92*
**Allen,** James Roy 1926- *AmMWSc 92*
**Allen,** James Sloan 1943- *WhoEnt 92*
**Allen,** James Stuart 1955- *WhoEnt 92*
**Allen,** James Trinton 1924- *WhoBlA 92*
**Allen,** James Ward 1941- *AmMWSc 92*
**Allen,** Jane 1928- *WhoEnt 92*
**Allen,** Jane Elizabeth 1945- *WhoBlA 92*
**Allen,** Janet Rosemary 1936- *Who 92*
**Allen,** Jantzen Courtney 1952- *WhoEnt 92*
**Allen,** Jasper Bryant, Jr. 1938- *WhoAmL 92*
**Allen,** Jay Presson *ReelWom*
**Allen,** Jay Presson 1922- *IntMPA 92, WhoEnt 92*
**Allen,** Jeanette Mary 1958- *WhoWest 92*
**Allen,** Jeffrey D. 1957- *WhoFI 92*
**Allen,** Jeffrey Michael 1948- *WhoAmL 92*
**Allen,** Jeffrey Rodgers 1953- *WhoAmL 92*
**Allen,** Jerry Clark 1939- *WhoFI 92*
**Allen,** Jesse Owen, III 1938- *WhoFI 92*
**Allen,** Jim *WhoAmP 91*
**Allen,** Joan 1956- *IntMPA 92*
**Allen,** Joe Bailey, III 1951- *WhoAmL 92*
**Allen,** Joe Frank 1934- *AmMWSc 92*
**Allen,** Joe Haskell 1939- *AmMWSc 92*
**Allen,** John *IntAu&W 91X*
**Allen,** John 1930- *News 92-1 [port]*
**Allen,** John Anthony *Who 92*
**Allen,** John Burton 1940- *AmMWSc 92*

**Allen,** John Carlton 1943- *WhoRel 92*
**Allen,** John Christopher 1935- *AmMWSc 92*
**Allen,** John E. 1921- *WrDr 92*
**Allen,** John Ed 1937- *AmMWSc 92*
**Allen,** John Edsall 1861-1944 *TwCPaSc*
**Allen,** John Edward 1932- *Who 92*
**Allen,** John Edward 1950- *WhoEnt 92*
**Allen,** John Edward, Jr 1945- *AmMWSc 92*
**Allen,** John Eliot 1908- *AmMWSc 92*
**Allen,** John Eugene 1939- *WhoRel 92*
**Allen,** John F. 1964- *WhoFI 92*
**Allen,** John Frank 1908- *IntWW 91, Who 92*
**Allen,** John Geoffrey Robyn 1923- *Who 92*
**Allen,** John Henry 1938- *WhoBlA 92*
**Allen,** John Hunter *Who 92*
**Allen,** John Jay 1932- *WrDr 92*
**Allen,** John Joseph, Jr 1899- *WhoAmP 91*
**Allen,** John Kay 1936- *AmMWSc 92*
**Allen,** John L 1931- *AmMWSc 92*
**Allen,** John Neville 1922- *WhoAmP 91*
**Allen,** John Piers 1912- *Who 92*
**Allen,** John Robert Lawrence 1932- *IntWW 91, Who 92*
**Allen,** John Robins 1869-1920 *BiInAmS*
**Allen,** John Rybolt 1926- *AmMWSc 92*
**Allen,** John Thomas, Jr. 1935- *WhoAmL 92, WhoFI 92*
**Allen,** John Walter 1928- *IntWW 91*
**Allen,** John William 1936- *WhoFI 92*
**Allen,** Jon Charles 1940- *AmMWSc 92*
**Allen,** Jonathan 1934- *AmMWSc 92*
**Allen,** Jonathan 1942- *AmMWSc 92*
**Allen,** Jonathan Adams 1787-1848 *BiInAmS*
**Allen,** Joseph, Jr 1914- *WhoAmP 91*
**Allen,** Joseph D., III 1945- *WhoIns 92*
**Allen,** Joseph Doorley, III 1945- *WhoAmL 92*
**Allen,** Joseph Dulles 1945- *WhoAmL 92*
**Allen,** Joseph Garrott 1912- *AmMWSc 92*
**Allen,** Joseph Hunter 1925- *AmMWSc 92*
**Allen,** Joseph Land 1928- *WhoRel 92*
**Allen,** Joseph Lee 1944- *WhoRel 92*
**Allen,** Joseph Stanley 1898- *Who 92*
**Allen,** Julia Natalia *AmMWSc 92*
**Allen,** Julian Myrick, Jr. 1956- *WhoFI 92*
**Allen,** Julius Cadden 1938- *AmMWSc 92*
**Allen,** Karen 1951- *IntMPA 92*
**Allen,** Karen Jane 1951- *WhoEnt 92*
**Allen,** Kathleen 1906- *TwCPaSc*
**Allen,** Keith W. 1953- *WhoEnt 92*
**Allen,** Kenneth *Who 92*
**Allen,** Kenneth Dale 1939- *WhoAmL 92*
**Allen,** Kenneth G D 1943- *AmMWSc 92*
**Allen,** Kenneth J. *WhoFI 92, WhoMW 92*
**Allen,** Kenneth William 1923- *Who 92*
**Allen,** Kenneth William 1930- *AmMWSc 92*
**Allen,** Kimberly A. 1959- *WhoAmL 92*
**Allen,** Lana Sue 1958- *WhoMW 92*
**Allen,** Larry Milton 1942- *AmMWSc 92*
**Allen,** Laura Jean *ConAu 133*
**Allen,** Lawrence David, Jr. 1952- *WhoFI 92*
**Allen,** Lawrence Harvey 1943- *AmMWSc 92*
**Allen,** Layman Edward 1927- *WhoAmL 92*
**Allen,** Leatrice Delorice 1948- *WhoMW 92*
**Allen,** Lee 1927- *WhoAmP 91*
**Allen,** Lee Harrison 1924- *WhoFI 92*
**Allen,** Leland Cullen 1926- *AmMWSc 92*
**Allen,** Leon Arthur, Jr. 1933- *WhoAmL 92*
**Allen,** Leonard Brown 1932- *WhoMW 92*
**Allen,** LeRoy Richard 1913- *AmMWSc 92*
**Allen,** Leslie 1958- *WhoAmL 92*
**Allen,** Leslie Christopher 1935- *WhoRel 92*
**Allen,** Lew, Jr 1925- *AmMWSc 92, IntWW 91, WhoWest 92*
**Allen,** Lewis 1905- *IntMPA 92*
**Allen,** Lewis Edwin 1937- *AmMWSc 92*
**Allen,** Lewis M 1922- *IntMPA 92*
**Allen,** Linda Kay 1944- *WhoWest 92*
**Allen,** Lindsay Helen 1946- *AmMWSc 92*
**Allen,** Linus Scott 1935- *AmMWSc 92*
**Allen,** Lisa Michelle 1963- *WhoRel 92*
**Allen,** Lois Arlene Height 1932- *WhoEnt 92, WhoMW 92*
**Allen,** Lois Brenda 1939- *AmMWSc 92*
**Allen,** Louis 1922- *WrDr 92*
**Allen,** Lowell Raymond 1933- *WhoWest 92*
**Allen,** Malaetasi *WhoAmP 91*
**Allen,** Malwina I *AmMWSc 92*
**Allen,** Marc 1956- *WhoAmP 91*
**Allen,** Marcia Katzman 1935- *AmMWSc 92*
**Allen,** Marcus 1924- *WhoBlA 92*
**Allen,** Marcus 1960- *WhoBlA 92, WhoWest 92*
**Allen,** Mark 1962- *WhoMW 92*
**Allen,** Mark Echalaz 1917- *Who 92*
**Allen,** Mark Hill 1956- *WhoAmL 92*
**Allen,** Marshall B, Jr 1927- *AmMWSc 92*
**Allen,** Martin 1918- *AmMWSc 92*
**Allen,** Martin Steven 1947- *WhoAmL 92*
**Allen,** Marvin Carrol 1939- *AmMWSc 92*
**Allen,** Mary A Mennes 1938- *AmMWSc 92*
**Allen,** Mary Elizabeth 1931- *WhoRel 92*
**Allen,** Mary Kathryn 1953- *WhoMW 92*
**Allen,** Maryon Pittman *WhoAmP 91*
**Allen,** Matthew Arnold 1930- *AmMWSc 92*
**Allen,** Max Scott 1911- *AmMWSc 92*
**Allen,** Maxine Bogues 1942- *WhoBlA 92*
**Allen,** Mel *LesBEnT 92*
**Allen,** Mel 1913- *IntMPA 92*
**Allen,** Merrill James 1918- *AmMWSc 92, WhoMW 92*
**Allen,** Michael A. 1951- *WhoWest 92*
**Allen,** Michael Thomas 1949- *AmMWSc 92*
**Allen,** Mildred Mesch *WhoHisp 92*
**Allen,** Milton B. 1917- *WhoBlA 92*
**Allen,** Minerva *DrAPF 91*
**Allen,** Minnie Louise 1956- *WhoBlA 92*
**Allen,** Nancy *WhoEnt 92*
**Allen,** Nancy 1950- *IntMPA 92*
**Allen,** Nathaniel 1755?-1805 *DcNCBi 1*
**Allen,** Neil Keith 1944- *AmMWSc 92*
**Allen,** Nelson Robert 1932- *WhoAmP 91*
**Allen,** Newton Perkins 1922- *WhoAmL 92*
**Allen,** Nina Stromgren 1935- *AmMWSc 92*
**Allen,** Noel Lee 1947- *WhoAmL 92*
**Allen,** Norman *Who 92*
**Allen,** Norman Lynn 1934- *WhoMW 92*
**Allen,** Norris Elliott 1939- *AmMWSc 92*
**Allen,** Oscar Dana 1836-1913 *BiInAmS*
**Allen,** Ottis Eugene, Jr. 1953- *WhoBlA 92*
**Allen,** Pamela 1934- *IntAu&W 91*
**Allen,** Patrick Joseph 1948- *WhoAmL 92*
**Allen,** Patrick Michael 1962- *WhoWest 92*
**Allen,** Paul *WhoWest 92*
**Allen,** Paul 1775-1826 *BenetAL 91*
**Allen,** Paul Alfred 1948- *WhoAmL 92*
**Allen,** Paul Howard 1954- *WhoFI 92*
**Allen,** Paul Steven 1956- *WhoFI 92*
**Allen,** Paula Gunn *DrAPF 91*
**Allen,** Paula Gunn 1939- *BenetAL 91, TwCWW 91, WrDr 92*
**Allen,** Percival 1917- *IntWW 91, Who 92*
**Allen,** Percy, II 1941- *WhoBlA 92*
**Allen,** Peter 1905- *Who 92, WrDr 92*
**Allen,** Peter 1929- *Who 92*
**Allen,** Peter 1944- *ConTFT 9*
**Allen,** Peter Christopher 1905- *IntWW 91*
**Allen,** Peter John 1956- *WhoRel 92*
**Allen,** Peter Martin 1947- *AmMWSc 92*
**Allen,** Peter William 1938- *Who 92*
**Allen,** Peter Zachary 1925- *AmMWSc 92*
**Allen,** Philip B 1942- *AmMWSc 92*
**Allen,** Philip C. 1936- *WhoBlA 92*
**Allen,** Philip G *AmMWSc 92*
**Allen,** Phillip E. 1931- *WhoAmL 92*
**Allen,** Phillip Stephen 1952- *WhoFI 92*
**Allen,** R. L. M. 1909- *WrDr 92*
**Allen,** Ralph Dean 1941- *WhoFI 92*
**Allen,** Ralph Gilmore 1934- *WhoEnt 92*
**Allen,** Ralph Orville, Jr 1943- *AmMWSc 92*
**Allen,** Randal Thomas 1964- *WhoWest 92*
**Allen,** Raymond A 1921- *AmMWSc 92*
**Allen,** Raymond Fulton 1938- *WhoRel 92*
**Allen,** Regina Ward 1959- *WhoEnt 92*
**Allen,** Reuben Arthur, Jr. 1941- *WhoFI 92*
**Allen,** Rex 1922- *IntMPA 92*
**Allen,** Richard *DcAmImH*
**Allen,** Richard 1760-1831 *RComAH*
**Allen,** Richard 1903- *Who 92*
**Allen,** Richard 1937- *WhoWest 92*
**Allen,** Richard 1949- *Who 92*
**Allen,** Richard, Sr. 1741-1832 *DcNCBi 1*
**Allen,** Richard Blose 1919- *WhoAmL 92*
**Allen,** Richard Charles 1942- *AmMWSc 92*
**Allen,** Richard Crenshaw, Jr 1933- *AmMWSc 92*
**Allen,** Richard Dean 1935- *AmMWSc 92, WhoWest 92*
**Allen,** Richard Glen 1952- *AmMWSc 92*
**Allen,** Richard Hinckley 1838-1908 *BiInAmS*
**Allen,** Richard Ian Gordon 1944- *Who 92*
**Allen,** Richard Marlow 1940- *WhoAmL 92*
**Allen,** Richard V. 1936- *IntWW 91*
**Allen,** Richie 1942- *WhoBlA 92*
**Allen,** Rick Martin 1962- *WhoEnt 92*
**Allen,** Robert *DrAPF 91*
**Allen,** Robert 1887- *ScFEYrs*
**Allen,** Robert B 1951- *AmMWSc 92*
**Allen,** Robert Carter 1930- *AmMWSc 92*
**Allen,** Robert Charles 1945- *AmMWSc 92*
**Allen,** Robert Dean 1959- *WhoFI 92*
**Allen,** Robert Dee 1928- *WhoAmL 92*
**Allen,** Robert English 1945- *WhoFI 92*
**Allen,** Robert Erwin 1941- *AmMWSc 92*
**Allen,** Robert Eugene 1935- *WhoFI 92*
**Allen,** Robert Eugene Barton 1940- *WhoAmL 92, WhoFI 92*
**Allen,** Robert F 1928- *WhoAmP 91*
**Allen,** Robert F. 1928-1987 *ConAu 36NR*
**Allen,** Robert H 1938- *AmMWSc 92*
**Allen,** Robert Harold 1928- *WhoFI 92*
**Allen,** Robert Harry 1956- *AmMWSc 92*
**Allen,** Robert Joseph 1954- *WhoMW 92*
**Allen,** Robert L. 1942- *WhoBlA 92*
**Allen,** Robert Loring 1921- *WhoFI 92*
**Allen,** Robert Max 1921- *AmMWSc 92*
**Allen,** Robert Nelson, Jr. 1956- *WhoAmL 92*
**Allen,** Robert Paul 1941- *AmMWSc 92*
**Allen,** Robert Ray 1920- *AmMWSc 92*
**Allen,** Robert S 1931- *WhoAmP 91*
**Allen,** Robert Thomas 1939- *AmMWSc 92*
**Allen,** Robert Wade 1950- *AmMWSc 92*
**Allen,** Robert Wayne 1963- *WhoWest 92*
**Allen,** Roberta *DrAPF 91*
**Allen,** Roberta Dodge 1948- *WhoMW 92*
**Allen,** Robin Leslie 1943- *AmMWSc 92*
**Allen,** Roger Baker 1929- *AmMWSc 92*
**Allen,** Roger W, Jr 1941- *AmMWSc 92*
**Allen,** Roland 1868-1947 *DcEcMov*
**Allen,** Roland E 1941- *AmMWSc 92*
**Allen,** Ronald *IntAu&W 91X*
**Allen,** Ronald Carl 1953- *WhoWest 92*
**Allen,** Ronald Jay 1948- *WhoAmL 92*
**Allen,** Ronald W. 1941- *WhoFI 92*
**Allen,** Rosanne Tibbals 1935- *WhoMW 92*
**Allen,** Rose Mary 1948- *WhoAmL 92*
**Allen,** Rowland Lancelot 1908- *Who 92*
**Allen,** Roy Leon 1950- *WhoAmP 91*
**Allen,** Roy Verl 1933- *WhoWest 92*
**Allen,** Russell H. 1963- *WhoMW 92*
**Allen,** Russell Plowman 1951- *WhoEnt 92*
**Allen,** S. Monique Nicole 1964- *WhoBlA 92*
**Allen,** Sally Lyman 1926- *AmMWSc 92*
**Allen,** Sally Rothfus 1941- *WhoFI 92, WhoWest 92*
**Allen,** Sam Raymond 1953- *WhoWest 92*
**Allen,** Samuel Joseph 1946- *WhoEnt 92*
**Allen,** Samuel Miller 1948- *AmMWSc 92*
**Allen,** Samuel W. *DrAPF 91*
**Allen,** Samuel Washington 1917- *WhoBlA 92*
**Allen,** Sandra Lee 1948- *AmMWSc 92*
**Allen,** Sanford 1939- *WhoBlA 92*
**Allen,** Seward Ellery 1920- *AmMWSc 92*
**Allen,** Sheila Rosalynd 1942- *ConAu 135*
**Allen,** Shirley Jeanne 1941- *WhoBlA 92*
**Allen,** Stanley M. 1941- *WhoBlA 92*
**Allen,** Stephen Dean 1943- *WhoMW 92*
**Allen,** Stephen Gregory 1952- *AmMWSc 92*
**Allen,** Stephen Ives 1914- *AmMWSc 92*
**Allen,** Stephen Valentine 1921- *IntAu&W 91*
**Allen,** Stephen Valentine Patrick William 1921- *WhoEnt 92*
**Allen,** Steve *LesBEnT 92*
**Allen,** Steve 1921- *BenetAL 91, FacFETw, IntMPA 92, NewAmDM, WrDr 92*
**Allen,** Steven 1927- *AmMWSc 92*
**Allen,** Steven Ernest 1959- *WhoEnt 92*
**Allen,** Steven Glen 1952- *WhoFI 92*
**Allen,** Steven Joe 1956- *WhoAmP 91*
**Allen,** Stuart *TwCSFW 91*
**Allen,** Stuart 1943- *WhoEnt 92, WhoFI 92*
**Allen,** Sture 1928- *IntWW 91*
**Allen,** Susan Au *WhoAmL 92*
**Allen,** Susan D 1944- *WhoAmP 91*
**Allen,** Susan Davis 1943- *AmMWSc 92*
**Allen,** Susan Macall 1944- *WhoWest 92*
**Allen,** Sydney Henry George 1929- *AmMWSc 92*
**Allen,** T.D. *TwCWW 91*
**Allen,** T. Diener *DrAPF 91*
**Allen,** Ted Tipton 1932- *AmMWSc 92*
**Allen,** Terrell Allison, III 1959- *WhoBlA 92*
**Allen,** Terry D 1908- *TwCWW 91*
**Allen,** Theresa O 1948- *AmMWSc 92*
**Allen,** Thomas 1944- *IntWW 91, Who 92*
**Allen,** Thomas Atherton 1949- *WhoAmL 92*
**Allen,** Thomas Charles 1948- *AmMWSc 92*
**Allen,** Thomas Cort, Jr 1931- *AmMWSc 92*
**Allen,** Thomas G. 1945- *WhoBlA 92*
**Allen,** Thomas Hunter 1914- *AmMWSc 92*
**Allen,** Thomas John 1931- *AmMWSc 92*
**Allen,** Thomas Lofton 1924- *AmMWSc 92*
**Allen,** Thomas Martin 1960- *WhoWest 92*
**Allen,** Thomas Oscar 1914- *AmMWSc 92*
**Allen,** Timothy Charles 1954- *WhoEnt 92*
**Allen,** Timothy Field 1837-1902 *BiInAmS*
**Allen,** Tom L *WhoAmP 91*
**Allen,** Toni K. 1940- *WhoAmL 92*
**Allen,** Trevor 1939- *TwCPaSc*
**Allen,** Ty W. 1961- *WhoBlA 92*
**Allen,** Van Sizar 1926- *WhoBlA 92*
**Allen,** Vernon R 1928- *AmMWSc 92*
**Allen,** Vivien Gore 1940- *AmMWSc 92*
**Allen,** W. George 1936- *WhoBlA 92*
**Allen,** W. Stannard 1913- *WrDr 92*
**Allen,** Walter 1911- *ConNov 91, WrDr 92*
**Allen,** Walter Brown 1946- *WhoMW 92*
**Allen,** Walter Ernest 1911- *IntAu&W 91, IntWW 91, Who 92*
**Allen,** Walter John Gardener 1916- *Who 92*
**Allen,** Walter Morrison 1867?-1909 *BiInAmS*
**Allen,** Walter R. 1930- *WhoBlA 92*
**Allen,** Warner Edward 1943- *WhoWest 92*
**Allen,** Warren William, Jr. 1924- *WhoFI 92*
**Allen,** Wayne Robert 1934- *AmMWSc 92*
**Allen,** Wendall E 1936- *AmMWSc 92*
**Allen,** Wendell 1947- *WhoBlA 92*
**Allen,** Wilbur Coleman 1925- *WhoAmL 92*
**Allen,** Wilford *ScFEYrs*
**Allen,** Willard C 1940- *WhoAmP 91*
**Allen,** Willard M 1904- *AmMWSc 92*
**Allen,** William *DcNCBi 1, DrAPF 91*
**Allen,** William 1784-1868 *AmPeW*
**Allen,** William 1803-1879 *DcNCBi 1*
**Allen,** William 1932- *Who 92*
**Allen,** William Alexander 1914- *Who 92*
**Allen,** William Alfred 1944- *WhoFI 92*
**Allen,** William Anthony 1949- *Who 92*
**Allen,** William Barclay 1944- *WhoAmP 91, WhoBlA 92*
**Allen,** William Bland, III 1947- *WhoAmP 91*
**Allen,** William C. 1957- *WhoEnt 92*
**Allen,** William Clifford 1937- *IntWW 91*
**Allen,** William Cola 1859-1952 *DcNCBi 1*
**Allen,** William Corwin 1934- *AmMWSc 92*
**Allen,** William Duncan 1906- *WhoBlA 92*
**Allen,** William F, Jr 1919- *AmMWSc 92*
**Allen,** William Frederick 1846-1915 *BiInAmS*
**Allen,** William Hayes 1926- *WhoAmL 92*
**Allen,** William Henry 1917- *WhoBlA 92*
**Allen,** William Kenneth 1907- *Who 92*
**Allen,** William Maurice 1931- *Who 92*
**Allen,** William Merle 1939- *AmMWSc 92*
**Allen,** William Oscar 1923- *WhoBlA 92*
**Allen,** William Peter 1927- *AmMWSc 92*
**Allen,** William Reynolds 1860-1921 *DcNCBi 1*
**Allen,** William Richard, Jr. 1940- *WhoFI 92*
**Allen,** William Riley 1953- *WhoAmL 92*
**Allen,** William Sheridan 1932- *WrDr 92*
**Allen,** William Sidney 1918- *IntWW 91, Who 92*
**Allen,** William Westhead 1921- *AmMWSc 92*
**Allen,** Willie B. 1921- *WhoBlA 92*
**Allen,** Winston Earle 1933- *WhoBlA 92*
**Allen,** Woody *NewYTBS 91 [port]*
**Allen,** Woody 1935- *BenetAL 91, FacFETw [port], IntAu&W 91, IntDcF 2-2 [port], IntMPA 92, IntWW 91, Who 92, WhoEnt 92, WrDr 92*
**Allen,** Zachariah 1795-1882 *BiInAmS*
**Allen-Jones,** John Ernest 1909- *Who 92*
**Allen-Noble,** Rosie Elizabeth 1938- *WhoBlA 92*
**Allen of Abbeydale,** Baron 1912- *Who 92*
**Allen-Rasheed,** Jamal Randy 1953- *WhoBlA 92*
**Allen-Woolfe,** Nicholas Richard 1944- *WhoEnt 92*
**Allenbach,** Charles Robert 1928- *AmMWSc 92*
**Allenbaugh,** G. Eric 1944- *WhoWest 92*
**Allenby** *Who 92*
**Allenby,** Viscount 1931- *Who 92*
**Allenby,** Edmund Henry Hynman 1861-1936 *FacFETw*
**Allenby,** Nicholas 1909- *Who 92*
**Allenby,** Richard John, Jr 1923- *AmMWSc 92*
**Allendale,** Viscount 1922- *Who 92*
**Allende,** Ignacio Jose de 1779-1821 *HisDSpE*
**Allende,** Isabel *IntAu&W 91*
**Allende,** Isabel 1942- *BenetAL 91, IntWW 91, LiExTwC, SpAmWW, WhoHisp 92*
**Allende Gossens,** Salvador 1908-1973 *FacFETw [port]*
**Allender,** David William 1947- *AmMWSc 92*
**Allender,** Eric Warren 1956- *AmMWSc 92*
**Allender,** John Roland 1950- *WhoAmL 92*
**Allender,** Patrick W. 1946- *WhoFI 92*
**Allender,** Peter John 1921- *WhoRel 92*
**Allendorf,** Frederick William 1947- *AmMWSc 92*
**Allendorf,** Peter F *WhoAmP 91*
**Allendorph,** Lewis Rogier 1927- *WhoMW 92*
**Allenson,** Douglas Rogers 1926- *AmMWSc 92*
**Allenspach,** Allan Leroy 1935- *AmMWSc 92*
**Allenstein,** Richard Van 1930- *AmMWSc 92*
**Allensworth,** Carl d1991 *NewYTBS 91*
**Allentoff,** Norman 1923- *AmMWSc 92*
**Allentuch,** Arnold 1930- *AmMWSc 92*
**Aller,** Harold Ernest 1934- *AmMWSc 92*
**Aller,** James Curwood 1921- *AmMWSc 92*

**Aller**, Lawrence Hugh 1913- AmMWSc 92, IntWW 91, WrDr 92
**Aller**, Margo Friedel 1938- AmMWSc 92, WhoMW 92
**Aller**, Robert Curwood 1950- AmMWSc 92
**Aller**, Robert Lundeen 1934- WhoFI 92
**Aller**, Ronald G. 1937- WhoIns 92
**Allerhand**, Adam 1937- AmMWSc 92
**Allerheiligen**, Robert Paul 1944- WhoFI 92, WhoWest 92
**Allers**, Franz 1905- WhoEnt 92
**Allers**, Marlene Elaine 1931- WhoFI 92, WhoMW 92
**Allerslev Jensen**, Erik 1911- IntWW 91
**Allerton**, Baron d1991 Who 92N
**Allerton**, Joseph 1919- AmMWSc 92
**Allerton**, Michael John 1935- WhoEnt 92
**Allerton**, Richard Christopher 1935- Who 92
**Allerton**, Samuel E 1933- AmMWSc 92
**Allessie**, Maurits 1945- AmMWSc 92
**Allest**, Frederic Jean Pierre d' 1940- IntWW 91
**Allestad**, Elaine Kinsey 1950- WhoAmP 91
**Alleva**, Frederic Remo 1933- AmMWSc 92
**Alleva**, John J 1928- AmMWSc 92
**Allewell**, Norma Mary AmMWSc 92
**Alley**, Alphonse 1930- IntWW 91
**Alley**, Anthea 1927- TwCPaSc
**Alley**, Barrett Le Quatte 1934- WhoEnt 92, WhoFI 92
**Alley**, Curtis J 1918- AmMWSc 92
**Alley**, Douglas Wayne 1951- WhoAmP 91
**Alley**, Earl Gifford 1935- AmMWSc 92
**Alley**, Felix Eugene 1873-1957 DcNCBi 1
**Alley**, Forrest C 1929- AmMWSc 92
**Alley**, Harold Pugmire 1924- AmMWSc 92
**Alley**, Henry Melton DrAPF 91
**Alley**, Henry Melton 1945- ConAu 35NR
**Alley**, John-Edward 1940- WhoAmL 92
**Alley**, Keith Edward 1943- AmMWSc 92
**Alley**, Kirstie WhoEnt 92
**Alley**, Kirstie 1955- IntMPA 92
**Alley**, Phillip Wayne 1932- AmMWSc 92
**Alley**, Reuben Edward, Jr 1918- AmMWSc 92
**Alley**, Rewi 1897-1987 ConAu 36NR
**Alley**, Richard Blaine 1957- AmMWSc 92
**Alley**, Richard Lee 1932- WhoMW 92
**Alley**, Robert S. 1932- WrDr 92
**Alley**, Ronald Edgar 1926- Who 92
**Alley**, Starling Kessler, Jr 1930- AmMWSc 92
**Alley**, Thomas 1946- WhoAmP 91
**Alley**, Wayne Edward 1932- WhoAmL 92
**Alley**, William J. 1929- IntWW 91
**Alley**, William Jack 1929- WhoFI 92, WhoIns 92
**Alley**, Willis David 1954- WhoMW 92
**Alleyne**, Edward D. 1928- WhoBlA 92
**Alleyne**, George 1932- Who 92
**Alleyne**, John WhoEnt 92
**Alleyne**, John 1928- Who 92
**Alleyne**, Mervyn C. 1933- WrDr 92
**Alleyne**, Reginald H., Jr. 1932- WhoAmL 92
**Alleyne**, Selwyn Eugene 1930- Who 92
**Alleyne**, Winston A. 1944- WhoBlA 92
**Allford**, David 1927- Who 92
**Allfrey**, Vincent George 1921- AmMWSc 92
**Allgaier**, Robert Stephen 1925- AmMWSc 92
**Allgeyer**, Edward J WhoAmP 91
**Allgeyer**, Glen Owen 1925- WhoMW 92
**Allgood**, Clarence W. 1902-1991 NewYTBS 91
**Allgood**, Clarence William 1902- WhoAmL 92
**Allgood**, Jimmy Eugene 1955- WhoMW 92
**Allgood**, Joseph Patrick 1927- AmMWSc 92
**Allgood**, Thomas Forrest 1928- WhoAmP 91
**Allgower**, Eugene L 1935- AmMWSc 92
**Allgyer**, Robert Earl 1944- WhoFI 92, WhoMW 92
**Allhusen**, Derek Swithin 1914- Who 92
**Alli**, Richard James, Jr. 1954- WhoAmL 92
**Alli**, Richard James, Sr. 1932- WhoFI 92, WhoMW 92
**Alliali**, Camille 1926- IntWW 91
**Alliance**, David 1932- Who 92
**Allibone**, Thomas Edward 1903- IntWW 91, Who 92
**Alliegro**, Richard Alan 1930- AmMWSc 92
**Alliet**, David F 1938- AmMWSc 92
**Alliger**, Jeremy David 1952- WhoEnt 92
**Alligood**, Douglass Lacy 1934- WhoBlA 92
**Allik**, Tiina Katrin 1951- WhoRel 92
**Alliluyeva**, Svetlana Iosifovna 1927- FacFETw
**Allimadi**, E. Otema 1929- IntWW 91
**Allin**, Arthur 1869-1903 BiInAmS
**Allin**, Craig Willard 1946- WhoMW 92
**Allin**, Edgar Francis 1939- AmMWSc 92
**Allin**, Elizabeth Josephine 1905- AmMWSc 92
**Allin**, George 1933- Who 92
**Allin**, John 1934- TwCPaSc
**Allin**, John Maury 1921- RelLAm 91, WhoRel 92
**Allin**, Lewis Frederick 1923- WhoRel 92
**Allin**, Robert Cameron 1938- WhoWest 92
**Alling**, David Wheelock 1918- AmMWSc 92
**Alling**, Norman Larrabee 1930- AmMWSc 92
**Allinger**, Norman Louis 1928- AmMWSc 92
**Allingham**, William 1824-1889 RfGEnL 91
**Allington**, Edward 1951- TwCPaSc
**Allington**, Robert W 1935- AmMWSc 92
**Allington**, Roger Walter 1933- WhoWest 92
**Allinson**, Adrian 1890-1959 TwCPaSc
**Allinson**, Leonard Who 92
**Allinson**, Michael 1920- WhoEnt 92
**Allinson**, Morris Jonathan Carl 1912- AmMWSc 92
**Allinson**, Sonya M. TwCPaSc
**Allinson**, Walter Leonard 1926- IntWW 91, Who 92
**Allio**, Rene 1924- IntDcF 2-2
**Allio**, Robert John 1931- WhoFI 92
**Alliott**, John 1932- Who 92
**Allis**, Andrew Parker B. 1938- WhoRel 92
**Allis**, John W 1939- AmMWSc 92
**Allis**, Willam Phelps 1901- AmMWSc 92
**Allish**, Richard Eugene, Jr. 1958- WhoFI 92
**Allison**, A. F. 1916- WrDr 92
**Allison**, Ann Estelle 1963- WhoAmL 92
**Allison**, Anthony Clifford AmMWSc 92
**Allison**, Benjamin 1717-1763 DcNCBi 1
**Allison**, Bonnie J WhoAmP 91
**Allison**, Brian George 1933- Who 92
**Allison**, Carol Wagner 1932- AmMWSc 92
**Allison**, Charles Ralph 1903- Who 92
**Allison**, Christopher FitzSimons 1927- WhoRel 92
**Allison**, Clay 1914-1978 TwCWW 91
**Allison**, Dale Clifford, Jr. 1955- WhoRel 92
**Allison**, David C 1924- WhoAmP 91
**Allison**, David C 1931- AmMWSc 92
**Allison**, David Coulter 1942- AmMWSc 92
**Allison**, David Lord 1942- WhoWest 92
**Allison**, Delburt E. 1924- WhoWest 92
**Allison**, Dennis 1932- Who 92
**Allison**, Dennis Ray 1953- WhoRel 92
**Allison**, Donald G. 1950- WhoFI 92
**Allison**, Dorothy DrAPF 91
**Allison**, E Lavonia Ingram WhoAmP 91
**Allison**, E. M. A. WrDr 92
**Allison**, Eric W. 1947- WrDr 92
**Allison**, Ferdinand V., Jr. 1923- WhoBlA 92
**Allison**, Fran d1989 FacFETw
**Allison**, Fred, Jr 1922- AmMWSc 92
**Allison**, Gaylene Delores 1948- IntAu&W 91
**Allison**, Grace 1946- WhoAmL 92, WhoFI 92
**Allison**, Graham T, Jr. 1940- ConAu 35NR
**Allison**, Harrison C 1917- ConAu 35NR
**Allison**, Henry E. 1937- ConAu 133
**Allison**, Ira Shimmin 1895- AmMWSc 92
**Allison**, James Abner, Jr. 1924- WhoRel 92
**Allison**, James Claybrooke, II 1942- WhoEnt 92
**Allison**, James Harold 1939- WhoWest 92
**Allison**, James M., Jr. 1926- WhoBlA 92
**Allison**, James Purney 1947- WhoAmP 91
**Allison**, Jean Batchelor 1931- AmMWSc 92
**Allison**, Jerry David 1948- AmMWSc 92
**Allison**, Joan Kelly 1935- WhoEnt 92
**Allison**, Joe Marion 1924- WhoEnt 92
**Allison**, John 1919- Who 92
**Allison**, John 1951- AmMWSc 92
**Allison**, John Everett 1917- AmMWSc 92
**Allison**, John P 1936- AmMWSc 92
**Allison**, John Robert 1945- WhoAmL 92
**Allison**, John Shakespeare 1943- Who 92
**Allison**, Kathleen Edler 1941- WhoMW 92
**Allison**, Kemper Clark 1960- WhoFI 92
**Allison**, Laird Burl 1917- WhoFI 92, WhoWest 92
**Allison**, Latham Lee 1933- WhoFI 92
**Allison**, Milton James 1931- AmMWSc 92
**Allison**, Mose 1927- NewAmDM
**Allison**, Munier Bernard 1927- IntAu&W 91
**Allison**, Nancy 1954- WhoEnt 92
**Allison**, R. Bruce 1949- WrDr 92
**Allison**, Richard C 1935- AmMWSc 92
**Allison**, Richard Clark 1924- IntWW 91, WhoAmL 92
**Allison**, Richard Gall 1943- AmMWSc 92
**Allison**, Ridgley Carleton 1950- WhoEnt 92
**Allison**, Robert Dean 1932- AmMWSc 92
**Allison**, Roderick Stuart 1936- Who 92
**Allison**, Ronald C 1945- AmMWSc 92
**Allison**, Ronald William Paul 1932- Who 92
**Allison**, Sam TwCWW 91
**Allison**, Samuel Dudleston 1911- WhoWest 92
**Allison**, Sandra Diane Arthur 1950- WhoAmP 91
**Allison**, Sherard Falkner 1907- IntWW 91, Who 92
**Allison**, Stephen Galender 1952- WhoEnt 92, WhoFI 92
**Allison**, Stephen William 1950- AmMWSc 92
**Allison**, Tomilea 1934- WhoAmP 91
**Allison**, Trenton B 1942- AmMWSc 92
**Allison**, W. Anthony 1926- WhoBlA 92
**Allison**, William Earl 1932- AmMWSc 92
**Allison**, William Hugh 1934- AmMWSc 92, WhoRel 92
**Allison**, William Robert 1941- WhoWest 92
**Allison**, William S 1935- AmMWSc 92
**Alliss**, Peter 1931- Who 92
**Alliston**, Charles Walter 1930- AmMWSc 92
**Allman Brothers**, The ConMus 6 [port]
**Allman Brothers Band** NewAmDM
**Allman**, Gregg 1947- WhoEnt 92
**Allman**, John DrAPF 91
**Allman**, John 1935- ConAu 15AS [port]
**Allman**, John Morgan 1943- AmMWSc 92
**Allman**, Linden Andrea 1958- WhoEnt 92
**Allman**, Marian Isabel 1946- WhoBlA 92
**Allman**, Peter Walter 1947- WhoEnt 92
**Allman**, Richard Lee 1937- WhoEnt 92
**Allman**, William Berthold 1927- WhoEnt 92
**Allmann**, David William 1935- AmMWSc 92
**Allmaras**, Raymond Richard 1926- AmMWSc 92
**Allmendinger**, E Eugene 1917- AmMWSc 92
**Allmendinger**, Paul Florin 1922- WhoFI 92
**Allmightey**, Jon 1963- WhoEnt 92
**Allmon**, Michael Bryan 1951- WhoFI 92
**Allmond**, Douglas Henry 1948- WhoEnt 92
**Allnatt**, Alan Richard 1933- AmMWSc 92
**Allner**, Walter Heinz 1909- WhoEnt 92
**Allnutt**, Alvin Howard 1932- WhoWest 92
**Allnutt**, Ian Peter 1917- Who 92
**Allnutt**, Robert Frederick 1935- WhoAmP 91
**Allocco**, Barbara 1946- WhoMW 92
**Allon**, Yigal 1918-1980 ConAu 36NR, FacFETw
**Allott**, Antony Nicolas 1924- Who 92
**Allott**, Miriam 1920- IntAu&W 91
**Allott**, Molly Greenwood 1918- Who 92
**Allott**, Robin Michael 1926- Who 92
**Allotta**, Robert 1961- WhoWest 92
**Allouache**, Merzak 1944- IntWW 91
**Alloway**, Anne Maureen Schubert 1954- WhoWest 92
**Alloway**, Debra Joan Elliott 1956- WhoMW 92
**Allport**, Charles William 1940- WhoMW 92
**Allport**, David Bruce 1954- WhoRel 92
**Allport**, Denis Ivor 1922- Who 92
**Allran**, Austin M 1951- WhoAmP 91
**Allread**, Ardith 1943- WhoRel 92
**Allred**, Albert Louis 1931- AmMWSc 92
**Allred**, Cary Dale 1947- WhoAmP 91
**Allred**, David Kris 1957- WhoWest 92
**Allred**, David R AmMWSc 92
**Allred**, Dorald Mervin 1923- AmMWSc 92
**Allred**, E R 1916 AmMWSc 92
**Allred**, Eugene Lyle 1949- WhoWest 92
**Allred**, Evan Leigh 1929- AmMWSc 92
**Allred**, Garland Howard 1922- WhoRel 92
**Allred**, Gloria Rachel 1941- WhoAmP 91
**Allred**, Jeffrey Allen 1965- WhoRel 92
**Allred**, John B 1934- AmMWSc 92
**Allred**, John C 1926- AmMWSc 92
**Allred**, John Thompson 1929- WhoAmL 92
**Allred**, Keith Reid 1925- AmMWSc 92
**Allred**, Kelly Wayne 1949- AmMWSc 92
**Allred**, Lawrence Ervin 1946- AmMWSc 92, WhoMW 92
**Allred**, Michael Sylvester 1945- WhoAmP 91
**Allred**, Rulon Clark 1906-1977 RelLAm 91
**Allred**, V Dean 1922- AmMWSc 92
**Allsbrook**, Ogden Olmstead, Jr. 1940- WhoFI 92
**Allsebrook**, Peter Winder d1991 Who 92N
**Allsep**, Larry Michael, Jr. 1958- WhoAmL 92
**Allshouse**, John 1951- WhoMW 92, WhoRel 92
**Allsop**, Peter Henry Bruce 1924- Who 92
**Allsopp** Who 92
**Allsopp**, Bruce Who 92
**Allsopp**, Bruce 1912- WrDr 92
**Allsopp**, Charles 1940- Who 92
**Allsopp**, Harold Bruce 1912- IntAu&W 91, Who 92
**Allsopp**, Mary Freiderica 1961- WhoMW 92
**Allsopp**, Michael Edmund 1942- WhoMW 92
**Allsopp**, William Wade 1951- WhoAmL 92
**Allston**, Joseph Blythe 1833-1904 BenetAL 91
**Allston**, Thomas Gray, III 1954- WhoBlA 92
**Allston**, Washington 1779-1843 BenetAL 91
**Allswang**, John Myers 1937- WhoWest 92
**Allum**, Frank Raymond 1936- AmMWSc 92
**Allum**, Geoffrey Michael 1957- WhoFI 92
**Allum**, Sarah Elizabeth Royle Who 92
**Allward**, Maurice 1923- WrDr 92
**Allwood**, Martin Samuel 1916- IntAu&W 91
**Ally**, Akbar F. 1943- WhoBlA 92
**Allyn**, Angela 1961- WhoEnt 92
**Allyson**, June 1917- IntMPA 92
**Allyson**, Kym WrDr 92
**Alm**, Alvin Arthur 1935- AmMWSc 92
**Alm**, James 1937- WhoFI 92
**Alm**, James Robert 1950- WhoFI 92
**Alm**, Robert M 1921- AmMWSc 92
**Almader**, Minnie 1957- WhoHisp 92
**Almagro**, Diego de 1475-1538 HisDSpE
**Almaguer**, Gilberto Francisco 1948- WhoEnt 92
**Almaguer**, Henry, Jr. 1947- WhoHisp 92
**Almaguer**, Imara Arredondo 1953- WhoHisp 92
**Almaguer**, Tomas 1948- WhoHisp 92
**Alman**, Emily Arnow 1922- WhoAmL 92
**Almand**, James Frederick 1948- WhoAmL 92, WhoAmP 91
**Almansi**, Guido 1931- WrDr 92
**Almanza-Lumpkin**, Carlota WhoHisp 92
**Almasi**, George Stanley 1938- AmMWSc 92
**Almasi**, Susan WhoEnt 92
**Almason**, Carmen Cristina 1954- AmMWSc 92
**Almassy**, Marcia Yamada 1944- WhoMW 92
**Almazan**, James A. 1935- WhoHisp 92
**Al'medingen**, Boris Alekseevich 1887-1960 SovUnBD
**Almeida**, Alfred 1931- WhoAmP 91
**Almeida**, Antonio WhoHisp 92
**Almeida**, Jacinto Rego de 1942- IntAu&W 91
**Almeida**, Laurindo 1917- NewAmDM, WhoEnt 92
**Almeida**, Silverio P 1933- AmMWSc 92
**Almeida**, Yolanda R. 1945- WhoHisp 92
**Almeida Braga**, Luis Carlos de Lima de 1890-1970 BiDExR
**Almeida Merino**, Adalberto 1916- WhoRel 92
**Almeling**, Guy Anthony 1949- WhoMW 92
**Almen**, Lowell Gordon 1941- WhoRel 92
**Almenara**, Juan Ramon 1933- WhoHisp 92
**Almenas**, Kazys Kestutis 1935- AmMWSc 92
**Almendarez**, Bob 1952- WhoHisp 92
**Almendro**, Jaime 1952- WhoHisp 92
**Almendros**, Nestor 1930- IntMPA 92, WhoEnt 92
**Almendros**, Nestor 1930-1992 WhoHisp 92N
**Alment**, Anthony 1922- Who 92
**Almeraz**, Ricardo 1940- WhoHisp 92
**Almerico**, Kendall Alan 1963- WhoAmL 92
**Almers**, Wolfhard 1943- AmMWSc 92
**Almeter**, Frank M 1929- AmMWSc 92
**Almeyda Medina**, Clodomiro 1923- IntWW 91
**Almgren**, Frederick Justin, Jr 1933- AmMWSc 92
**Almgren**, Peter Eric 1948- WhoWest 92
**Almirante**, Giorgio 1914-1988 BiDExR
**Almlie**, Curt WhoAmP 91
**Almodovar**, Pedro 1949?- ConAu 133
**Almodovar**, Pedro 1951?- IntDcF 2-2 [port], IntMPA 92, IntWW 91
**Almog**, Rami AmMWSc 92
**Almon**, Bert DrAPF 91
**Almon**, Reneau Pearson 1937- WhoAmL 92, WhoAmP 91
**Almon**, Richard Reiling 1946- AmMWSc 92
**Almond**, David R. WhoAmL 92

**Almond**, Edward M 1892-1979 *FacFETw*
**Almond**, Gabriel A. 1911- *WrDr 92*
**Almond**, Gabriel Abraham 1911- *IntWW 91*
**Almond**, Harold Russell, Jr 1934- *AmMWSc 92*
**Almond**, Hy 1914- *AmMWSc 92*
**Almond**, Joan 1934- *WhoFI 92*
**Almond**, Johnny Russell 1944- *WhoRel 92*
**Almond**, Lincoln C. 1936- *WhoAmL 92*
**Almond**, Paul 1931- *IntMPA 92, WhoEnt 92*
**Almond**, Peter R 1937- *AmMWSc 92*
**Almond**, Thomas Clive 1939- *Who 92*
**Almony**, Robert Allen, Jr. 1945- *WhoMW 92*
**Almquist**, Gregg Andrew 1948- *IntAu&W 91*
**Almquist**, Herman James 1903- *WhoWest 92*
**Alms**, Gregory Russell 1947- *AmMWSc 92*
**Almunia Amann**, Joaquin 1948- *IntWW 91*
**Almy**, Charles C, Jr 1935- *AmMWSc 92*
**Almy**, Lee Andrade, Jr. 1955- *WhoRel 92*
**Almy**, Linda L 1948- *WhoAmP 91*
**Almy**, R Christopher 1949- *WhoAmP 91*
**Almy**, Thomas Pattison 1915- *AmMWSc 92*
**Alo**, Richard Anthony *AmMWSc 92*
**Aloff**, Mindy *DrAPF 91*
**Aloff**, Mindy 1947- *ConAu 135, WhoEnt 92*
**Alofs**, John William, II 1955- *WhoWest 92*
**Aloia**, Richard Paul, Jr. 1967- *WhoEnt 92*
**Aloia**, Roland C 1943- *AmMWSc 92*
**Aloia**, Roland Craig 1943- *WhoWest 92*
**Alomar**, Roberto 1968- *WhoHisp 92*
**Alomar**, Sandy 1943- *WhoBlA 92, WhoHisp 92*
**Alomar**, Sandy, Jr. 1966- *WhoHisp 92*
**Alomar-Hamza**, Daisy 1940- *WhoHisp 92*
**Aloneftis**, Andreas P. 1945- *IntWW 91*
**Alonso**, Alicia 1921- *FacFETw, WhoEnt 92*
**Alonso**, Antonio Enrique 1924- *WhoAmL 92*
**Alonso**, Carmen 1946- *WhoAmL 92*
**Alonso**, Carol Travis 1941- *AmMWSc 92*
**Alonso**, Cecilia Holtz 1948- *WhoHisp 92*
**Alonso**, Damaso 1898-1990 *DcLB 108 [port], FacFETw*
**Alonso**, Danilo *WhoHisp 92*
**Alonso**, Francisco Manuel 1943- *WhoHisp 92*
**Alonso**, Joe 1964- *WhoEnt 92*
**Alonso**, Jose Ramon 1941- *AmMWSc 92*
**Alonso**, Kenneth B 1942- *AmMWSc 92*
**Alonso**, Manrique Domingo 1910- *WhoHisp 92*
**Alonso**, Marcelo 1921- *AmMWSc 92*
**Alonso**, Maria Conchita 1957- *IntMPA 92, WhoHisp 92*
**Alonso**, Miguel Angel 1930- *WhoHisp 92*
**Alonso**, Miriam *WhoHisp 92*
**Alonso**, Odon *WhoEnt 92A*
**Alonso**, Rafael *WhoHisp 92*
**Alonso**, Rafael Alonso *WhoAmP 91*
**Alonso**, Ricardo *DrAPF 91*
**Alonso**, Ricardo N 1954- *AmMWSc 92*
**Alonso**, Santos, Sr. *WhoHisp 92*
**Alonso**, Virgil *WhoHisp 92*
**Alonso-Alonso**, Rafael *WhoAmL 92*
**Alonso-Caplen**, Firelli V 1956- *AmMWSc 92*
**Alonso-Mendoza**, Emilio 1954- *WhoHisp 92*
**Alonso Schokel**, Luis 1920- *WhoRel 92*
**Alonso-Valls**, Fidel 1944- *WhoHisp 92*
**Alonzi**, Loreto Peter 1951- *WhoFI 92, WhoMW 92*
**Alonzo**, Angelo Anthony 1941- *WhoHisp 92*
**Alonzo**, John A. 1934- *IntMPA 92*
**Alonzo**, John A. 1936- *WhoHisp 92*
**Alonzo**, Mario *WhoEnt 92*
**Alonzo**, Martin Vincent 1931- *WhoFI 92*
**Alonzo**, R. Gregory 1954- *WhoWest 92*
**Alonzo**, Ralph Edward 1950- *WhoHisp 92*
**Alonzo**, Roberto R. 1956- *WhoHisp 92*
**Alonzo**, Ronald Thomas 1942- *WhoFI 92*
**Aloot**, Mariano Daniel 1947- *WhoWest 92*
**Alou**, Felipe Rojas 1935- *WhoHisp 92*
**Alou**, Jesus Maria Rojas 1942- *WhoHisp 92*
**Alou**, Matty 1938- *WhoHisp 92*
**Alou**, Moises 1966- *WhoHisp 92*
**Aloupis**, Angela Z 1943- *WhoAmP 91*
**Alousi**, Adawia A *AmMWSc 92*
**Alpaugh**, Walter G 1921- *WhoIns 92*
**Alpen**, Edward Lewis 1922- *AmMWSc 92*
**Alper**, Allen Myron 1932- *AmMWSc 92*
**Alper**, Carl 1920- *AmMWSc 92*
**Alper**, Cengiz 1939- *WhoFI 92*
**Alper**, Chester Allan 1931- *AmMWSc 92*
**Alper**, Howard 1941- *AmMWSc 92, IntWW 91*
**Alper**, Joseph Seth 1942- *AmMWSc 92*
**Alper**, Marshall Edward 1930- *AmMWSc 92*
**Alper**, Merlin Lionel 1932- *WhoFI 92*
**Alper**, Milton H 1930- *AmMWSc 92*
**Alper**, Richard H 1953- *AmMWSc 92*
**Alper**, Robert 1933- *AmMWSc 92*
**Alperen**, Martin Jay 1956- *WhoAmL 92*
**Alperin**, Harvey Albert 1929- *AmMWSc 92*
**Alperin**, Harvey Jacob 1950- *WhoEnt 92*
**Alperin**, Irwin Ephraim 1925- *WhoFI 92, WhoRel 92*
**Alperin**, Jack Bernard 1932- *AmMWSc 92*
**Alperin**, Jonathan L 1937- *AmMWSc 92*
**Alperin**, Morton 1918- *AmMWSc 92*
**Alperin**, Richard Junius 1941- *AmMWSc 92*
**Alpern**, Herbert P 1940- *AmMWSc 92*
**Alpern**, Mathew 1920- *AmMWSc 92*
**Alpern**, Michael Barry 1955- *WhoMW 92*
**Alpern**, Milton 1925- *AmMWSc 92*
**Alpern**, Robert Zellman 1928- *WhoRel 92*
**Alpers**, Antony 1919- *ConAu 35NR, IntAu&W 91, WrDr 92*
**Alpers**, Christian 1959- *WhoEnt 92*
**Alpers**, David Hershel 1935- *AmMWSc 92*
**Alpers**, John Hardesty, Jr. 1939- *WhoFI 92*
**Alpers**, Joseph Benjamin 1925- *AmMWSc 92*
**Alpers**, Robert Christopher 1949- *WhoWest 92*
**Alpers**, W. Frank 1924- *WhoEnt 92*
**Alpers**, William Charles 1851-1917 *BiInAmS*
**Alperstein**, Arthur Stuart 1940- *WhoAmP 91*
**Alperstein**, Pearl 1927- *WhoAmP 91*
**Alpert**, Ann Sharon 1938- *WhoFI 92*
**Alpert**, Barry Mark 1941- *WhoFI 92*
**Alpert**, Cathryn *DrAPF 91*
**Alpert**, Clark E. 1954- *WhoAmL 92*
**Alpert**, Daniel 1917- *AmMWSc 92*
**Alpert**, Daniel 1952- *WhoEnt 92*
**Alpert**, Dierdre *WhoAmP 91*
**Alpert**, Elliot 1936- *AmMWSc 92*
**Alpert**, Gordon Myles 1944- *WhoAmL 92*
**Alpert**, Herb 1935- *NewAmDM, WhoEnt 92*
**Alpert**, Herbert 1918- *WhoEnt 92*
**Alpert**, Hollis 1916- *WhoEnt 92, WrDr 92*
**Alpert**, Joel Jacobs 1930- *AmMWSc 92*
**Alpert**, Joseph M. 1938- *WhoFI 92*
**Alpert**, Joseph Stephen 1942- *IntWW 91*
**Alpert**, Leo 1915- *AmMWSc 92*
**Alpert**, Louis Katz 1907- *AmMWSc 92*
**Alpert**, Michael Edward 1942- *WhoAmL 92*
**Alpert**, Nelson Leigh 1925- *AmMWSc 92*
**Alpert**, Norman Roland 1922- *AmMWSc 92*
**Alpert**, Robert Lawrence 1955- *WhoRel 92*
**Alpert**, Ronald L 1941- *AmMWSc 92*
**Alpert**, Seymour 1918- *AmMWSc 92*
**Alpert**, Seymour Samuel 1930- *AmMWSc 92*
**Alpert**, Shirley Marcia 1936- *WhoWest 92*
**Alpert**, Wesley Simon 1926- *WhoFI 92*
**Alpha**, Andrew G 1912- *AmMWSc 92*
**Alpha**, Karen *DrAPF 91*
**Alphand**, Herve 1907- *IntWW 91, Who 92*
**Alpher**, David B. 1947- *WhoEnt 92*
**Alpher**, Ralph Asher 1921- *AmMWSc 92, FacFETw*
**Alphin**, Reevis Stancil 1929- *AmMWSc 92*
**Alphonso-Karkala**, John B 1923- *IntAu&W 91, WrDr 92*
**Alport** *Who 92*
**Alport**, Baron 1912- *IntWW 91, Who 92, WrDr 92*
**Alps**, Glen Earl 1914- *WhoWest 92*
**Alptemocin**, Ahmet Kurtcebe 1940- *IntWW 91*
**AlQahharIbnturiya**, Abdurrahman 1944- *WhoEnt 92*
**Alquen**, Gunter d' 1910- *EncTR 91*
**Alquire**, Mary Slanina 1943- *AmMWSc 92*
**Alquist**, Alfred E 1908- *WhoAmP 91*
**Alquist**, George Herman, Jr. 1952- *WhoRel 92*
**Alquist**, Lewis Russell 1946- *WhoWest 92*
**Alrich**, Alexis 1955- *WhoEnt 92*
**Alrude**, Countess of Bertinoro *EncAmaz 91*
**Alrutz**, Robert Willard 1921- *AmMWSc 92*
**Alsaker**, Robert John 1945- *WhoWest 92*
**Alsandor**, Jude 1938- *WhoBlA 92*
**Alsberg**, Henry 1921- *AmMWSc 92*
**Alsbro**, Donald Edgar 1940- *WhoMW 92*
**Alscher**, Ruth 1943- *AmMWSc 92*
**Alschuler**, Albert W. 1948- *WhoAmL 92*
**Alschuler**, George Arthur 1935- *WhoWest 92*
**Alsina**, Carlos Roque 1941- *ConCom 92*
**Alsmeyer**, Richard Harvey 1929- *AmMWSc 92*
**Alsmiller**, Rufard G, Jr 1927- *AmMWSc 92*
**Alsobrook**, Henry Herman 1917- *WhoAmP 91*
**Alson**, Eli 1929- *AmMWSc 92*
**Alsop**, David W 1939- *AmMWSc 92*
**Alsop**, Donald Douglas 1927- *WhoAmL 92, WhoMW 92*
**Alsop**, Frederick Joseph, III 1942- *AmMWSc 92*
**Alsop**, George 1638?- *BenetAL 91*
**Alsop**, Jack 1951- *WhoAmP 91*
**Alsop**, John Henry, III 1924- *AmMWSc 92*
**Alsop**, Joseph 1910- *BenetAL 91*
**Alsop**, Joseph Wright 1910- *WrDr 92*
**Alsop**, Leonard E 1930- *AmMWSc 92*
**Alsop**, Richard 1761-1815 *BenetAL 91*
**Alsop**, Roger Clark 1957- *WhoWest 92*
**Alsop**, Stewart 1914-1974 *BenetAL 91*
**Alspach**, Brian Roger 1938- *AmMWSc 92, WhoWest 92*
**Alspach**, Daniel Lee 1940- *AmMWSc 92*
**Alspach**, Donn E. 1931- *WhoMW 92*
**Alspach**, Philip Halliday 1923- *WhoFI 92, WhoWest 92*
**Alspaugh**, Dale W 1932- *AmMWSc 92*
**Alspaugh**, Dale William 1932- *WhoMW 92*
**Alspaugh**, John Wesley 1831-1912 *DcNCBi 1*
**Alstadt**, Don Martin 1921- *AmMWSc 92*
**Alstadt**, William Robert 1916- *WhoAmP 91*
**Alstead**, Stanley 1905- *Who 92*
**Alster**, Frank G. 1919- *WhoAmL 92*
**Alston**, Arthur Rex 1901- *Who 92*
**Alston**, Betty Bruner 1933- *WhoBlA 92*
**Alston**, Bettye Jo 1938- *WhoRel 92*
**Alston**, Casco, Jr. 1923- *WhoBlA 92*
**Alston**, Charles *IntAu&W 91X*
**Alston**, Denise Adele 1952- *WhoBlA 92*
**Alston**, Floyd William 1925- *WhoBlA 92*
**Alston**, Gerald 1951- *WhoBlA 92*
**Alston**, Gilbert C. 1931- *WhoBlA 92*
**Alston**, Harry L. 1914- *WhoBlA 92*
**Alston**, Harvey Hilbert 1947- *WhoMW 92*
**Alston**, J. Leo 1917- *Who 92*
**Alston**, James L. 1947- *WhoBlA 92*
**Alston**, Jimmy Albert 1942- *AmMWSc 92*
**Alston**, John 1673-1758 *DcNCBi 1*
**Alston**, Kathy Diane 1958- *WhoBlA 92*
**Alston**, Lela 1942- *WhoAmP 91, WhoWest 92*
**Alston**, Lemuel James 1760-1836 *DcNCBi 1*
**Alston**, Louis Watson 1884-1960 *DcNCBi 1*
**Alston**, Paul Douglas 1947- *WhoAmL 92*
**Alston**, Penny Kaye 1950- *WhoFI 92*
**Alston**, Peter Van 1946- *AmMWSc 92*
**Alston**, Philip 1745?-1791 *DcNCBi 1*
**Alston**, Quentin Lester Rohlfing 1918- *WhoWest 92*
**Alston**, Rex *Who 92*
**Alston**, Rex 1901- *WrDr 92*
**Alston**, Richard John William 1948- *Who 92, WhoEnt 92*
**Alston**, Robert John 1938- *IntWW 91, Who 92*
**Alston**, Robert Milton, Jr. 1949- *WhoBlA 92*
**Alston**, Robin Carfrae 1933- *Who 92*
**Alston**, Rowland Wright 1895-1958 *TwCPaSc*
**Alston**, Tracey Daniel 1961- *WhoBlA 92*
**Alston**, Willis 1769-1837 *DcNCBi 1*
**Alston-Garnjost**, Margaret 1929- *AmMWSc 92*
**Alston-Roberts-West**, George Arthur *Who 92*
**Alsum**, Donald James 1937- *AmMWSc 92*
**Alt**, Barbara Sue 1956- *WhoMW 92*
**Alt**, Betty Sowers 1931- *ConAu 133*
**Alt**, David D 1933- *AmMWSc 92*
**Alt**, Franz L 1910- *AmMWSc 92*
**Alt**, Gerhard Horst 1925- *AmMWSc 92*
**Alt**, James Edward 1946- *WhoFI 92*
**Alt**, Martha S. 1943- *WhoRel 92*
**Alta** *DrAPF 91*
**Altamirano**, Ben D *WhoAmP 91*
**Altamirano**, Ben D. 1930- *WhoHisp 92*
**Altamirano**, Fabricio Leon 1965- *WhoFI 92*
**Altamirano**, Ignacio Manuel 1834-1893 *BenetAL 91*
**Altamirano**, Salvador H. 1947- *WhoHisp 92*
**Altamont**, Earl of 1939- *Who 92*
**Altamura**, Carmela Elizabeth 1939- *WhoEnt 92, WhoWest 92*
**Altamura**, Michael Victor 1923- *WhoWest 92*
**Altamura**, Wendy Owen *WhoWest 92*
**Altamuro**, Stephen 1960- *WhoAmL 92*
**Altaner**, Berthold 1885-1964 *EncEarC*
**Altangerel**, Bat-Ochiryn 1934- *IntWW 91*
**Altares**, Timothy, Jr 1929- *AmMWSc 92*
**Altbach**, Philip 1941- *WhoFI 92*
**Altbach**, Philip G. 1941- *IntWW 91*
**Altemeier**, William Arthur, III 1936- *AmMWSc 92*
**Altemose**, Vincent O 1928- *AmMWSc 92*
**Alten**, Jerry 1931- *WhoEnt 92*
**Altenau**, Alan Giles 1938- *AmMWSc 92*
**Altenburg**, Lewis Conrad 1942- *AmMWSc 92*
**Altenkirch**, Robert Ames 1948- *AmMWSc 92*
**Altepeter**, Terry Vincent 1954- *WhoFI 92*
**Alter**, Amos Joseph 1916- *AmMWSc 92*
**Alter**, Brian Reid 1956- *WhoFI 92*
**Alter**, David 1807-1881 *BiInAmS*
**Alter**, David 1923- *WhoAmL 92*
**Alter**, Dean 1948- *WhoFI 92*
**Alter**, Edward T 1941- *WhoAmP 91, WhoWest 92*
**Alter**, Gerald L. 1910- *WhoFI 92, WhoWest 92*
**Alter**, Gerald M *AmMWSc 92*
**Alter**, Harvey 1932- *AmMWSc 92*
**Alter**, Harvey James 1935- *AmMWSc 92*
**Alter**, Henry Ward 1923- *AmMWSc 92*
**Alter**, Joanne Hammerman 1927- *WhoAmP 91*
**Alter**, John 1946- *WhoMW 92*
**Alter**, John Emanuel 1945- *AmMWSc 92*
**Alter**, Joseph Dinsmore 1923- *AmMWSc 92*
**Alter**, Judy 1938- *WrDr 92*
**Alter**, Milton 1929- *AmMWSc 92*
**Alter**, Ralph 1938- *AmMWSc 92*
**Alter**, Robert B 1935- *IntAu&W 91, WrDr 92*
**Alter**, Ronald 1939- *AmMWSc 92*
**Alter**, Steven Robert 1947- *WhoFI 92*
**Alter**, Susan D 1942- *WhoAmP 91*
**Alter**, Theodore Roberts 1946- *AmMWSc 92*
**Alter**, William 1944- *WhoAmP 91*
**Alter**, William A, III 1942- *AmMWSc 92*
**Altera**, Kenneth P 1936- *AmMWSc 92*
**Alterio**, Glenn 1958- *WhoAmL 92*
**Alterman**, Dean N. 1960- *WhoWest 92*
**Alterman**, Joseph George 1919- *IntMPA 92*
**Altermatt**, William Edward 1951- *WhoMW 92*
**Altes**, Frederik Korthals 1931- *IntWW 91*
**Altes**, Richard Alan 1941- *AmMWSc 92*
**Alteveer**, Robert Jan George 1935- *AmMWSc 92*
**Altevogt**, Raymond Fred 1940- *AmMWSc 92*
**Altfeld**, Richard Lewis 1918- *WhoMW 92*
**Altfeld**, Sheldon Isaac 1937- *WhoEnt 92, WhoFI 92*
**Altfest**, Lewis Jay 1940- *WhoFI 92*
**Altgeld**, John Peter 1847-1902 *DcAmImH*
**Altgeld**, John Peter 1847-1942 *BenetAL 91*
**Altgelt**, Klaus H 1927- *AmMWSc 92*
**Althaus**, David Steven 1945- *WhoFI 92*
**Althaus**, Keith *DrAPF 91*
**Althaus**, Nigel 1929- *Who 92*
**Althaus**, Ralph Elwood 1925- *AmMWSc 92*
**Althaus**, Rickert Ralph 1952- *WhoMW 92*
**Althaus**, William John 1948- *WhoAmP 91*
**Althaver**, Lambert Ewing 1931- *WhoFI 92, WhoMW 92*
**Altheimer**, Alan Milton 1940- *WhoMW 92*
**Alther**, Lisa 1944- *BenetAL 91, ConNov 91, IntAu&W 91, WrDr 92*
**Althoen**, Steven Clark 1946- *AmMWSc 92, WhoMW 92*
**Althoff**, Robert Roland 1952- *WhoFI 92*
**Altholz**, Josef L 1933- *ConAu 35NR*
**Althorp**, Viscount 1964- *Who 92*
**Althouse**, Paul 1889-1954 *NewAmDM*
**Althuis**, Thomas Henry 1941- *AmMWSc 92*
**Althusser**, Louis 1918-1990 *AnObit 1990, FacFETw*
**Altick**, Leslie L. *WhoFI 92*
**Altick**, Philip Lewis 1933- *AmMWSc 92*
**Altick**, Richard Daniel 1915- *IntAu&W 91, WrDr 92*
**Altier**, William John 1935- *WhoFI 92*
**Altieri**, A M 1907- *AmMWSc 92*
**Altieri**, Dario Carlo 1958- *AmMWSc 92*
**Altieri**, Maria Rita 1957- *WhoAmL 92*
**Altieri**, Peter Louis 1955- *WhoAmL 92*
**Altiero**, Nicholas James, Jr 1947- *AmMWSc 92*
**Altimari**, Frank X *WhoAmP 91*
**Altimari**, Frank X. 1928- *WhoAmL 92*
**Altinkaya**, Cengiz 1949- *IntWW 91*
**Altizer**, Barbara Walters 1948- *WhoFI 92*
**Altizer**, Nell *DrAPF 91*
**Altland**, Henry Wolf 1945- *AmMWSc 92*
**Altland**, Paul Daniel 1913- *AmMWSc 92*
**Altman**, Adele Rosenhain 1924- *WhoWest 92*
**Altman**, Albert 1932- *AmMWSc 92*
**Altman**, Allan 1929- *WhoAmL 92*
**Altman**, Allen Burchard 1942- *AmMWSc 92*
**Altman**, Barbara Jean Friedman 1947- *WhoAmL 92*
**Altman**, Barry Brent 1962- *WhoMW 92*
**Altman**, David 1920- *AmMWSc 92*
**Altman**, Dennis 1943- *ConAu 34NR, IntAu&W 91, WrDr 92*

**Altman,** Frances 1937- *IntAu&W 91, WrDr 92*
**Altman,** Herbert 1938- *WhoWest 92*
**Altman,** Jack 1923- *AmMWSc 92*
**Altman,** James Eston 1938- *WhoAmP 91*
**Altman,** Janice Mary 1938- *WhoRel 92*
**Altman,** Jeffrey Paul 1949- *WhoAmL 92*
**Altman,** Joseph 1925- *AmMWSc 92*
**Altman,** Joseph Henry 1921- *AmMWSc 92*
**Altman,** Kurt Ison 1919- *AmMWSc 92*
**Altman,** Landy B, Jr 1919- *AmMWSc 92*
**Altman,** Lawrence Jay 1941- *AmMWSc 92*
**Altman,** Lawrence Kimball 1937- *AmMWSc 92*
**Altman,** Leo Sidney 1911- *WhoAmL 92*
**Altman,** Leonard Charles 1944- *AmMWSc 92*
**Altman,** Lionel Phillips 1922- *Who 92*
**Altman,** Louis 1933- *WhoAmL 92*
**Altman,** Marcia 1938- *WhoEnt 92*
**Altman,** Michael J. 1944- *WhoEnt 92, WhoFI 92*
**Altman,** Mimi Angster 1935- *WhoMW 92*
**Al'tman,** Natan Isaevich 1889-1970 *SovUnBD*
**Altman,** Philip L 1924- *IntAu&W 91*
**Altman,** Philip Lawrence 1924- *AmMWSc 92*
**Altman,** Ray H 1943- *WhoAmP 91*
**Altman,** Robert 1925- *FacFETw, IntDcF 2-2 [port], IntMPA 92, IntWW 91, Who 92*
**Altman,** Robert Alan 1947- *WhoFI 92*
**Altman,** Robert B. 1925- *WhoEnt 92*
**Altman,** Robert Lee 1935- *WhoMW 92*
**Altman,** Robert Leon 1931- *AmMWSc 92*
**Altman,** Robert Linwood 1924- *WhoAmP 91*
**Altman,** Ruth B. 1933- *WhoEnt 92*
**Altman,** Samuel Pinover 1921- *AmMWSc 92*
**Altman,** Sheldon 1937- *WhoWest 92*
**Altman,** Sidney 1939- *AmMWSc 92, WhoNob 90*
**Altman,** Stuart Harold 1937- *IntWW 91*
**Altman,** William Kean 1944- *WhoAmL 92, WhoFI 92*
**Altmann,** Alan Fernand *WhoWest 92*
**Altmann,** Alexander 1906-1987 *ConAu 35NR*
**Altmann,** Klaus *EncTR 91*
**Altmann,** Stuart Allen 1930- *AmMWSc 92*
**Altmiller,** Dale Henry 1940- *AmMWSc 92*
**Altmiller,** Henry 1941- *AmMWSc 92*
**Altmiller,** John Connell 1936- *WhoAmL 92*
**Altner,** Peter Christian 1932- *AmMWSc 92*
**Altnikol,** Johann Christoph 1719-1759 *NewAmDM*
**Altnow,** Arthur R. 1916- *WhoFI 92*
**Altobello,** Henry D 1907- *WhoAmP 91*
**Altobello,** Mildred Frances 1953- *WhoFI 92*
**Altolaguirre,** Manuel 1905-1959 *DcLB 108 [port]*
**Altomare,** Edwin Paul 1954- *WhoFI 92*
**Altomari,** Mark Guido 1947- *WhoMW 92*
**Alton,** Alvin John 1913- *AmMWSc 92*
**Alton,** Ann Leslie 1945- *WhoAmL 92, WhoFI 92, WhoMW 92*
**Alton,** Ardyth *WhoEnt 92*
**Alton,** Colleen Edna 1959- *WhoWest 92*
**Alton,** David Patrick 1951- *Who 92*
**Alton,** Donald Alvin 1943- *AmMWSc 92*
**Alton,** Earl Robert 1933- *AmMWSc 92*
**Alton,** Elaine Vivian 1925- *AmMWSc 92*
**Alton,** Euan Beresford Seaton 1919- *Who 92*
**Alton,** Everett Donald 1915- *AmMWSc 92*
**Alton,** Gerald Dodd *AmMWSc 92*
**Alton,** Howard Robert, Jr. 1927- *WhoAmL 92*
**Alton,** John 1901- *IntMPA 92*
**Altose,** Murray D 1941- *AmMWSc 92*
**Altounian,** David Allen 1961- *WhoWest 92*
**Altpeter,** Lawrence L, Jr 1932- *AmMWSc 92*
**Altrichter,** Petr 1951- *WhoEnt 92*
**Altrincham,** Barony of 1934- *Who 92*
**Altrocchi,** Sally Archer 1960- *WhoEnt 92*
**Altrock,** Richard Charles 1940- *AmMWSc 92*
**Altschaeffl,** Adolph George 1930- *WhoMW 92*
**Altscher,** Siegfried 1922- *AmMWSc 92*
**Altschul,** Aaron Mayer 1914- *AmMWSc 92*
**Altschul,** Alfred Samuel 1939- *WhoFI 92*
**Altschul,** David Edwin 1947- *WhoAmL 92, WhoEnt 92*
**Altschul,** Joel Henry 1948- *WhoEnt 92*
**Altschul,** Rolf 1918- *AmMWSc 92*
**Altschul,** Stanford Marvin 1936- *WhoAmL 92*
**Altschule,** Mark David 1906- *AmMWSc 92*
**Altschuler,** David Edward 1952- *WhoFI 92*
**Altschuler,** Helmut Martin 1922- *AmMWSc 92*
**Altschuler,** Jonathan Bobrow 1936- *WhoFI 92*
**Altschuler,** Martin David 1940- *AmMWSc 92*
**Altshiller,** Arthur Leonard 1942- *WhoWest 92*
**Altshul,** Jeffrey Eliot 1956- *WhoAmL 92*
**Altshuler,** Bernard 1919- *AmMWSc 92*
**Altshuler,** Charles Haskell 1919- *AmMWSc 92*
**Altshuler,** Edward E 1931- *AmMWSc 92*
**Altshuler,** Harold Leon 1941- *AmMWSc 92*
**Altshuller,** Dmitry Alexander 1961- *WhoMW 92*
**Altstetter,** Carl J 1930- *AmMWSc 92*
**Altszuler,** Norman 1924- *AmMWSc 92*
**Altuch,** Peter Mark 1952- *WhoFI 92*
**Altunin,** Aleksandr Terent'evich 1921- *SovUnBD*
**Altura,** Bella T *AmMWSc 92*
**Altura,** Burton Myron 1936- *AmMWSc 92*
**Altwicker,** Elmar Robert 1930- *AmMWSc 92*
**Alu,** Al 1942- *WhoEnt 92*
**Aluise,** Timothy John 1956- *WhoAmL 92*
**Alukal,** Varghese George 1945- *WhoMW 92*
**Aluko,** T. M. 1918- *ConNov 91, WrDr 92*
**Aluko,** Timothy Mofolorunso 1918- *IntAu&W 91*
**Alukonis,** David J 1961- *WhoAmP 91*
**Alum,** Manuel Antonio 1943- *WhoHisp 92*
**Alum,** Roland Armando, Jr. *WhoHisp 92*
**Alumbaugh,** Debra Kay 1951- *WhoAmP 91*
**Alumnus** *AmPeW*
**Alun-Jones,** Derek 1933- *Who 92*
**Al'Uqdah,** William Mujahid 1953- *WhoMW 92*
**Aluri,** Rajarathnam Sudarshanam 1952- *WhoRel 92*
**Alurista** *DrAPF 91*
**Alurista** 1947- *WhoHisp 92*
**Alva** 1901-1973 *TwCPaSc*
**Alva,** Dinker 1933- *IntWW 91*
**Alva,** Luigi 1927- *NewAmDM*
**Alva Castro,** Luis *IntWW 91*
**Alva Ixtlilxochitl,** Fernando de 1577-1648 *HisDSpE*
**Alvager,** Torsten Karl Erik 1931- *AmMWSc 92*
**Alvarado,** Audrey Ramona 1952- *WhoHisp 92*
**Alvarado,** Blanca *WhoHisp 92*
**Alvarado,** Carlos R. 1960- *WhoFI 92*
**Alvarado,** Cipriano *WhoHisp 92*
**Alvarado,** Esteban P. 1962- *WhoHisp 92*
**Alvarado,** John Charles 1959- *WhoHisp 92*
**Alvarado,** Jose Antonio 1951- *WhoHisp 92*
**Alvarado,** Juan Manuel 1938- *WhoHisp 92*
**Alvarado,** Linda G. *WhoHisp 92*
**Alvarado,** Paul Henry 1939- *WhoHisp 92*
**Alvarado,** Raul, Jr. 1946- *WhoHisp 92*
**Alvarado,** Ricardo Raphael 1927- *WhoHisp 92*
**Alvarado,** Richard A. 1943- *WhoHisp 92*
**Alvarado,** Ronald Herbert 1933- *AmMWSc 92*
**Alvarado,** Ruben B. 1941- *WhoHisp 92*
**Alvarado,** Rudecindo 1792-1872 *HisDSpE*
**Alvarado,** Sam P. 1930- *WhoHisp 92*
**Alvarado,** Sully JF *WhoHisp 92*
**Alvarado,** Susan E. 1954- *WhoHisp 92*
**Alvarado,** Trini 1967- *IntMPA 92, WhoHisp 92*
**Alvarado,** Yolanda H. 1943- *WhoHisp 92*
**Alvarado de la Cueva,** Beatriz d1541 *HisDSpE*
**Alvarado Hidalgo,** Manuel 1775-1836 *HisDSpE*
**Alvarado-Tenorio,** Harold *DrAPF 91*
**Alvarado y Mesia,** Pedro de 1485?-1541 *HisDSpE*
**Alvares,** Alvito Peter 1935- *AmMWSc 92*
**Alvares,** Norman J 1933- *AmMWSc 92*
**Alvarez,** A. 1929- *ConNov 91, ConPo 91, FacFETw, WrDr 92*
**Alvarez,** Adolfo 1931- *WhoAmP 91*
**Alvarez,** Aida 1949- *WhoHisp 92*
**Alvarez,** Alfred 1929- *IntAu&W 91, Who 92*
**Alvarez,** Anne Maino 1941- *AmMWSc 92, WhoHisp 92*
**Alvarez,** Antonia V. 1951- *WhoHisp 92*
**Alvarez,** Avelino 1934- *WhoHisp 92*
**Alvarez,** Barry 1947- *WhoHisp 92*
**Alvarez,** Cesar L. *WhoHisp 92*
**Alvarez,** Daniel, Sr. 1924- *WhoHisp 92*
**Alvarez,** David 1931- *WhoHisp 92*
**Alvarez,** Eduardo 1951- *WhoHisp 92*
**Alvarez,** Eduardo J. 1935- *WhoHisp 92*
**Alvarez,** Eduardo Jorge *WhoRel 92*
**Alvarez,** Eduardo Jorge 1945- *WhoHisp 92*
**Alvarez,** Eduardo T. 1930- *WhoHisp 92*
**Alvarez,** Elvis *WhoHisp 92*
**Alvarez,** Everett, Jr. 1937- *WhoHisp 92*
**Alvarez,** F. Dennis 1945- *WhoHisp 92*
**Alvarez,** Felix Augusto 1954- *WhoHisp 92*
**Alvarez,** Ferdinand Chat, Jr. 1944- *WhoHisp 92*
**Alvarez,** Fernando 1935- *WhoHisp 92*
**Alvarez,** Francisco Alvarez 1957- *WhoHisp 92*
**Alvarez,** Frank D. *WhoHisp 92*
**Alvarez,** Fred T. 1937- *WhoHisp 92*
**Alvarez,** Fred W. 1949- *WhoHisp 92*
**Alvarez,** Hector Justo 1938- *WhoHisp 92*
**Alvarez,** Javier P. 1951- *WhoHisp 92*
**Alvarez,** Jeronimo *WhoHisp 92*
**Alvarez,** Jorge *DrAPF 91*
**Alvarez,** Jorge 1936- *WhoHisp 92*
**Alvarez,** Jose 1944- *WhoHisp 92*
**Alvarez,** Jose Armando 1949- *WhoFI 92*
**Alvarez,** Jose B. 1949- *WhoHisp 92*
**Alvarez,** Jose Jose 1951- *WhoHisp 92*
**Alvarez,** Jose M. *WhoHisp 92*
**Alvarez,** Jose Maria 1777-1820 *HisDSpE*
**Alvarez,** Jose O. 1947- *WhoHisp 92*
**Alvarez,** Juan Holquin 1944- *WhoHisp 92*
**Alvarez,** Juan Rafael 1956- *WhoHisp 92*
**Alvarez,** Julia *DrAPF 91, WhoHisp 92*
**Alvarez,** Julian Baltazar 1788-1843 *HisDSpE*
**Alvarez,** Julio E. *WhoHisp 92*
**Alvarez,** Laurence Richards 1937- *AmMWSc 92*
**Alvarez,** Lizette Ann 1964- *WhoHisp 92*
**Alvarez,** Louis Lefcourt 1955- *WhoEnt 92*
**Alvarez,** Luis 1911-1988 *FacFETw*
**Alvarez,** Luis Walter 1911-1988 *WhoNob 90*
**Alvarez,** Lynne *DrAPF 91*
**Alvarez,** Manuel Antonio, Sr. 1933- *WhoHisp 92*
**Alvarez,** Manuel G., Jr. *WhoHisp 92*
**Alvarez,** Maria Elena 1947- *WhoHisp 92*
**Alvarez,** Mario 1937- *WhoHisp 92*
**Alvarez,** Mario Roberto 1913- *IntWW 91*
**Alvarez,** Martin *WhoHisp 92*
**Alvarez,** Matt, Jr 1935- *WhoAmP 91*
**Alvarez,** Michael John 1949- *WhoHisp 92*
**Alvarez,** Mike, Jr. 1955- *WhoEnt 92*
**Alvarez,** Paul Hubert 1942- *WhoFI 92*
**Alvarez,** Pedro M. 1948- *WhoHisp 92*
**Alvarez,** Praxedes Eduardo 1958- *WhoHisp 92*
**Alvarez,** Ralph *WhoHisp 92*
**Alvarez,** Ramon A. 1937- *WhoHisp 92*
**Alvarez,** Ramon M. d1991 *WhoHisp 92N*
**Alvarez,** Raymond Angelo, Jr 1934- *AmMWSc 92*
**Alvarez,** Richard G. *WhoHisp 92*
**Alvarez,** Robert 1921- *AmMWSc 92*
**Alvarez,** Rodolfo 1936- *WhoAmP 91, WhoHisp 92*
**Alvarez,** Roman *WhoHisp 92*
**Alvarez,** Ronald Julian 1935- *AmMWSc 92, WhoHisp 92*
**Alvarez,** Santiago 1919- *IntDcF 2-2 [port]*
**Alvarez,** Sarah Lynn 1953- *WhoHisp 92*
**Alvarez,** Stephen Walter 1952- *WhoHisp 92*
**Alvarez,** Steven Grant 1955- *WhoHisp 92*
**Alvarez,** Thomas 1948- *WhoEnt 92, WhoMW 92*
**Alvarez,** Vernon Leon 1946- *AmMWSc 92*
**Alvarez,** Vincent Edward 1946- *AmMWSc 92*
**Alvarez,** Walter 1940- *AmMWSc 92*
**Alvarez,** Wilson 1970- *WhoHisp 92*
**Alvarez-Altman,** Grace de Jesus 1926- *WhoHisp 92*
**Alvarez Alvarez,** Jose Luis 1930- *IntWW 91*
**Alvarez Armellino,** Gregorio Conrado 1925- *IntWW 91*
**Alvarez Bischoff,** Ana Maria 1953- *WhoHisp 92*
**Alvarez-Breckenridge,** Carmen 1951- *WhoHisp 92*
**Alvarez-Buylla,** Ramon 1919- *AmMWSc 92*
**Alvarez de Arenales,** Jose Ildefonso 1793-1862 *HisDSpE*
**Alvarez de Arenales,** Juan Antonio 1770-1831 *HisDSpE*
**Alvarez de la Campa,** Alberto 1929- *WhoHisp 92*
**Alvarez del Castillo,** Ricardo Jon 1946- *WhoEnt 92*
**Alvarez de Toledo,** Juan Bautista 1655-1725 *HisDSpE*
**Alvarez de Toledo y Figueroa,** Francisco *HisDSpE*
**Alvarez-Glasman,** Arnold M. *WhoHisp 92*
**Alvarez-Gonzalez,** Jose Julian 1952- *WhoHisp 92*
**Alvarez-Gonzalez,** Rafael 1958- *AmMWSc 92*
**Alvarez-Lehman,** Amalia 1946- *WhoHisp 92*
**Alvarez-Mena,** Sergio O., III 1958- *WhoAmL 92*
**Alvarez-Moran,** Paul King 1965- *WhoEnt 92*
**Alvarez-Pont,** Victor 1949- *WhoHisp 92*
**Alvarez Ponte,** Antonio 1784-1820 *HisDSpE*
**Alvarez-Recio,** Emilio, Jr. 1938- *WhoHisp 92*
**Alvarez Rendueles,** Jose Ramon 1940- *IntWW 91, WhoFI 92*
**Alvarez-Renta,** Luis Rafael 1950- *WhoFI 92*
**Alvarez-Sharpe,** Maria Elena 1954- *WhoHisp 92*
**Alvarez Tena,** Victorino 1920- *WhoRel 92*
**Alvarino de Leira,** Angeles 1916- *AmMWSc 92*
**Alvaro,** Corredo 1896-1956 *LiExTwC*
**Alvary,** Lorenzo 1909- *WhoEnt 92*
**Alvear,** Carlos Antonio Jose de 1789-1852 *HisDSpE*
**Alvear,** Cecilia Estela *WhoHisp 92*
**Alvear y Ponce de Leon,** Diego de 1749-1830 *HisDSpE*
**Alveranga,** Glanvin L. 1928- *WhoBlA 92*
**Alverdes,** Paul 1897-1979 *EncTR 91*
**Alverio,** Daisy M. 1958- *WhoHisp 92*
**Alverio,** Diane *WhoHisp 92*
**Alvernaz,** Bil. 1947- *WhoWest 92*
**Alvernaz,** Rodrigo 1936- *WhoWest 92*
**Alverny,** Marie-Therese d' 1903- *IntWW 91*
**Alverson,** Dale C. 1945- *WhoWest 92*
**Alverson,** David Roy 1946- *AmMWSc 92*
**Alverson,** Dayton L 1924- *AmMWSc 92*
**Alverson,** Joy Ferguson 1954- *WhoWest 92*
**Alverson,** Marianne 1942- *IntAu&W 91*
**Alverson,** William March 1956- *WhoAmP 91*
**Alves,** Colin 1930- *Who 92*
**Alves,** Joseph Thomas 1921- *WhoRel 92*
**Alves,** Leo Manuel 1945- *AmMWSc 92*
**Alves,** Ronald V 1935- *AmMWSc 92*
**Alves,** Stephen D *WhoAmP 91*
**Alves,** William L, Jr 1935- *WhoAmP 91*
**Alvey,** Celine 1940- *WhoWest 92*
**Alvey,** David Dale 1932- *AmMWSc 92*
**Alvey,** John 1925- *IntWW 91, Who 92*
**Alvey,** Wilbur L 1912- *WhoAmP 91*
**Alvi,** Zahoor M 1932- *AmMWSc 92*
**Alvidrez,** Richard F. 1943- *WhoHisp 92*
**Alvidrez,** Richard Louis 1958- *WhoAmL 92*
**Alvin,** John 1917- *ConTFT 9, IntMPA 92*
**Alvine,** Robert 1938- *WhoFI 92*
**Alving,** Carl Richard 1939- *AmMWSc 92*
**Alvingham,** Baron 1926- *Who 92*
**Alvino,** Peter 1951- *WhoMW 92*
**Alvino,** William Michael 1939- *AmMWSc 92*
**Alvirez,** David 1936- *WhoHisp 92*
**Alvis,** Albert Lester, III 1959- *WhoAmL 92*
**Alvis,** Joel Lawrence, Jr. 1955- *WhoRel 92*
**Alviso,** Edward F. 1963- *WhoHisp 92*
**Alvord,** Benjamin 1813-1884 *BiInAmS*
**Alvord,** Burt *TwCWW 91*
**Alvord,** Donald C 1922- *AmMWSc 92*
**Alvord,** Edward Lorand 1950- *WhoAmL 92*
**Alvord,** Ellsworth Chapman, Jr 1923- *AmMWSc 92*
**Alvord,** Henry Elijah 1844-1904 *BiInAmS*
**Alvord,** Joel Barnes 1938- *WhoFI 92*
**Alwan,** Abdul Jabbar 1926- *WhoMW 92*
**Alwan,** Abdul-Mehsin 1927- *AmMWSc 92*
**Alwan,** Ameen *DrAPF 91*
**Alwan,** Georgia *DrAPF 91*
**Alwan,** Hamia 1930- *IntWW 91*
**Alward,** Ron E 1941- *AmMWSc 92*
**Alward,** Samuel A. *WhoFI 92*
**Alwardt,** Martha Alice 1947- *WhoMW 92*
**Alwilda** *EncAmaz 91*
**Alwin,** Jerry Lee 1942- *WhoAmP 91*
**Alwitt,** Robert 1933- *WhoMW 92*
**Alwitt,** Robert S 1933- *AmMWSc 92*
**Alworth,** William Lee 1939- *AmMWSc 92*
**Alwyn,** William 1905-1985 *FacFETw*
**Aly,** Abdel Fattah 1942- *AmMWSc 92*
**Aly,** Adel Ahmed 1944- *AmMWSc 92*
**Aly,** Hadi H 1930- *AmMWSc 92*
**Aly,** Hassan Youssef 1955- *WhoMW 92*
**Aly,** Raza 1935- *AmMWSc 92*
**Alydar** 1975-1990 *FacFETw*
**Alyea,** Ethan Davidson, Jr 1931- *AmMWSc 92*
**Alyea,** Fred Nelson 1938- *AmMWSc 92*
**Alyea,** Hubert Newcombe 1903- *AmMWSc 92*
**Alzaga,** Florinda 1930- *WhoHisp 92*
**Alzaga,** Martin de 1756- *HisDSpE*
**Alzamora,** Carlos 1926- *IntWW 91*
**Alzate y Ramirez,** Jose Antonio 1737-1799 *HisDSpE*
**Alzerreca,** Arnaldo 1943- *AmMWSc 92*
**Alzheimer,** William Edmund 1940- *WhoWest 92*
**Amabile,** George *DrAPF 91*
**Amabile,** George 1936- *WrDr 92*
**Amabile,** John Louis 1934- *WhoAmL 92*
**Amacher,** David E *AmMWSc 92*
**Amacher,** Maryanne 1943- *NewAmDM*
**Amacher,** Peter 1932- *AmMWSc 92*

**Amack**, Lewis Owen 1951- *WhoWest 92*
**Amad**, Hani Subhi al- 1938- *IntWW 91*
**Amadas**, Philip 1565?- *DcNCBi 1*
**Amadeo I** 1845-1890 *HisDSpE*
**Amadeo**, Mario 1911-1983 *BiDExR*
**Amadeus of the Heart of Jesus**, Mary 1846-1920 *RelLAm 91*
**Amadi**, Elechi 1934- *ConNov 91, IntAu&W 91, WrDr 92*
**Amado**, Jorge 1912- *BenetAL 91, ConAu 35NR, DcLB 113 [port], FacFETw, IntAu&W 91, IntWW 91, LiExTwC*
**Amado**, Patricia Ann 1960- *WhoWest 92*
**Amado**, Ralph 1932- *AmMWSc 92*
**Amado**, Richard Lewis 1964- *WhoWest 92*
**Amado**, Richard Steven 1948- *WhoMW 92*
**Amador**, Albert, III 1936- *WhoHisp 92*
**Amador**, Antonio Lucas 1948- *WhoHisp 92*
**Amador**, Dora 1948- *WhoHisp 92*
**Amador**, Elias 1932- *AmMWSc 92*
**Amador**, John Paul, Sr. 1945- *WhoHisp 92*
**Amador**, Michael George Sanchez 1936- *WhoHisp 92*
**Amador**, Richard S. *WhoHisp 92*
**Amador**, Rose Ann 1949- *WhoHisp 92*
**Amage** *EncAmaz 91*
**Amai**, Robert Lin Sung 1932- *AmMWSc 92*
**Amaker**, Norman Carey 1935- *WhoAmL 92, WhoBlA 92*
**Amaldi**, Edoardo 1908- *FacFETw*
**Amalrik**, Andrei Alekseyevich 1938-1980 *FacFETw*
**Amalrik**, Andrei Alekseyvich 1938-1980 *LiExTwC*
**Amal'rik**, Andrey Alekseevich 1938-1980 *SovUnBD*
**Aman**, Alfred Charles, Jr. 1945- *WhoAmL 92*
**Aman**, Gerald 1941- *WhoMW 92*
**Aman**, Joseph Patrick 1957- *WhoMW 92*
**Aman**, Karl E. 1928- *IntWW 91*
**Aman**, Mohammed M. 1940- *WhoBlA 92*
**Aman**, Reinhold Albert 1936- *WhoWest 92*
**Amandry**, Pierre 1912- *IntWW 91*
**Amann**, Charles A 1926- *AmMWSc 92*
**Amann**, Diane Marie 1957- *WhoAmL 92*
**Amann**, James A 1956- *WhoAmP 91*
**Amann**, James Francis 1945- *AmMWSc 92*
**Amann**, Max 1891-1957 *BiDExR, EncTR 91 [port]*
**Amann**, Rupert Preynoessl 1931- *AmMWSc 92*
**Amano**, Koei Hirofusa 1931- *WhoRel 92*
**Amano**, Kosei 1905- *IntWW 91*
**Amanshauser**, Gerhard 1928- *IntAu&W 91*
**Amantia**, Michael Anthony *WhoAmL 92*
**Amanuddin**, Syed *DrAPF 91*
**Amanullah Khan** 1892-1960 *FacFETw*
**Amar y Borbon**, Antonio d1819 *HisDSpE*
**Amara**, Lucine 1927- *NewAmDM, WhoEnt 92*
**Amara**, Roy C 1925- *AmMWSc 92*
**Amaral**, Annelle C 1948- *WhoAmP 91, WhoHisp 92*
**Amaral**, Pedro *WhoHisp 92*
**Amaranath**, L 1939- *AmMWSc 92*
**Amarasinghe**, N. 1935- *IntWW 91*
**Amarel**, John Anthony 1931- *WhoFI 92*
**Amarel**, S 1928- *AmMWSc 92*
**Amari**, John E 1948- *WhoAmP 91*
**Amarilio**, Joseph Daniel 1952- *WhoAmL 92*
**Amarilios**, John Alexander 1958- *WhoAmL 92, WhoFI 92*
**Amaro**, Hortensia *WhoHisp 92*
**Amaro**, Ruben 1936- *WhoBlA 92*
**Amarose**, Anthony Philip 1932- *AmMWSc 92*
**Amartey**, Prince *BlkOlyM*
**Amasino**, Richard M *AmMWSc 92*
**Amassian**, Vahe Eugene 1924- *AmMWSc 92*
**Amastris** *EncAmaz 91*
**Amat y Junient**, Manuel de *HisDSpE*
**Amata**, Charles David 1941- *AmMWSc 92*
**Amatangelo**, Nicholas S. 1935- *WhoFI 92, WhoMW 92*
**Amateau**, Rod *LesBEnT 92*
**Amateau**, Rod 1927- *IntMPA 92*
**Amati** *NewAmDM*
**Amati**, Andrea 1511?-1579? *NewAmDM*
**Amati**, Nicola 1596-1684 *NewAmDM*
**Amato**, Carol Joy 1944- *WhoWest 92*
**Amato**, Giuliano 1938- *IntWW 91*
**Amato**, John Dominick *WhoEnt 92*
**Amato**, Joseph Cono 1945- *AmMWSc 92*
**Amato**, R Stephen S 1936- *AmMWSc 92*
**Amato**, Rosemarie Helen 1950- *WhoMW 92*
**Amato**, Vincent Alfred 1915- *AmMWSc 92*
**Amato**, Vincent Anthony 1925- *WhoAmP 91*
**Amato**, Vincent Vito 1929- *WhoFI 92*
**Amatori**, Michael Louis 1951- *WhoEnt 92, WhoWest 92*
**Amatos**, Barbara Hansen 1944- *WhoMW 92*
**Amaudruz**, Gaston Armand 1920- *BiDExR*
**Amaya**, Abel *WhoHisp 92*
**Amaya**, Jorge 1954- *WhoHisp 92*
**Amaya**, Manuel Enrique 1953- *WhoHisp 92*
**Amaya**, Maria Alvarez 1955- *WhoHisp 92*
**Amaya**, Mario 1933-1986 *ConAu 36NR*
**Amazeen**, Paul Gerard 1939- *AmMWSc 92*
**Amazon of Letters**, The 1876-1972 *EncAmaz 91*
**Ambartsumian**, Sergey Aleksandrovich 1922- *IntWW 91*
**Ambartsumian**, Victor 1908- *Who 92*
**Ambartsumian**, Viktor Amazaspovich 1908- *FacFETw*
**Ambartsumov**, Yevgeniy Arshakovich 1929- *IntWW 91, SovUnBD*
**Ambartsumyan**, Victor Amazaspovich 1908- *IntWW 91*
**Ambasz**, Emilio 1943- *DcTwDes, WhoHisp 92*
**Ambeau**, Karen M. 1956- *WhoBlA 92*
**Ambegaokar**, Vinay 1934- *AmMWSc 92*
**Ambelang**, Joseph Carlyle 1914- *AmMWSc 92*
**Amber**, Douglas George 1956- *WhoAmL 92*
**Amber**, Lenny *NewAmDM*
**Amber**, Rich 1949- *WhoWest 92*
**Amberg**, Herman R 1920- *AmMWSc 92*
**Amberg**, Richard Hiller, Jr. 1942- *WhoFI 92*
**Amberley**, Viscount 1968- *Who 92*
**Amberley**, Richard *WrDr 92*
**Ambert**, Alba N. *DrAPF 91*
**Ambielli**, Robert John 1951- *WhoFI 92*
**Ambirajan**, Srinivasa 1936- *WrDr 92*
**Ambler**, David Samuel 1954- *WhoFI 92*
**Ambler**, Eric 1909- *ConNov 91, IntAu&W 91, IntWW 91, Who 92, WrDr 92*
**Ambler**, Ernest 1923- *AmMWSc 92*
**Ambler**, John Doss 1934- *Who 92, WhoFI 92*
**Ambler**, John Edward 1917- *AmMWSc 92*
**Ambler**, John Richard 1934- *WhoWest 92*
**Ambler**, Marjane 1948- *ConAu 135*
**Ambler**, Michael Ray 1947- *AmMWSc 92*
**Ambler**, Robert B 1927- *WhoAmP 91*
**Ambo**, George Somboba 1925- *Who 92*
**Amboian**, John Peter 1931- *WhoIns 92*
**Amborski**, Leonard Edward 1921- *AmMWSc 92*
**Ambraseys**, Nicholas 1929- *IntWW 91, Who 92*
**Ambre**, Emilie 1854-1898 *ThHEIm [port]*
**Ambre**, John Joseph 1937- *AmMWSc 92*
**Ambree**, Mary *EncAmaz 91*
**Ambriere**, Francis 1907- *IntAu&W 91, IntWW 91*
**Ambrister**, John Charles 1944- *WhoFI 92*
**Ambroggio**, Luis Alberto 1945- *WhoHisp 92*
**Ambrogio**, Anthony Pat 1937- *WhoFI 92*
**Ambromovage**, Anne Marie 1936- *AmMWSc 92*
**Ambron**, Richard Thomas 1943- *AmMWSc 92*
**Ambrose** 339?-397 *EncEarC*
**Ambrose**, Alice 1906- *WrDr 92*
**Ambrose**, Charles T 1929- *AmMWSc 92*
**Ambrose**, Donald Eric 1947- *WhoAmL 92*
**Ambrose**, Edmund Jack 1914- *Who 92*
**Ambrose**, Ernest R 1926- *AmMWSc 92*
**Ambrose**, Ethel L. 1930- *WhoBlA 92*
**Ambrose**, Harrison William, III 1938- *AmMWSc 92*
**Ambrose**, James R 1922- *WhoAmP 91*
**Ambrose**, James Walter Davy 1909- *Who 92*
**Ambrose**, John Augustine 1923- *AmMWSc 92*
**Ambrose**, John Charles 1954- *WhoFI 92*
**Ambrose**, John Daniel 1943- *AmMWSc 92*
**Ambrose**, John Russell 1940- *AmMWSc 92*
**Ambrose**, Leonard Gabriel, III 1947- *WhoAmL 92*
**Ambrose**, Myles Joseph 1926- *WhoAmP 91*
**Ambrose**, Paul Nicholas, Jr. 1953- *WhoAmL 92*
**Ambrose**, Raymond 1927- *TwCPaSc*
**Ambrose**, Richard Joseph 1942- *AmMWSc 92*
**Ambrose**, Robert T 1933- *AmMWSc 92*
**Ambrose**, Stephen 1936- *WrDr 92*
**Ambrose**, Thomas Cleary 1932- *WhoWest 92*
**Ambrose**, Thomas Neal 1962- *WhoFI 92*
**Ambrose**, Thomas William 1946- *WhoEnt 92, WhoMW 92*
**Ambrose**, Tommy W. 1926- *WhoFI 92*
**Ambrosiani**, Vincent F 1929- *AmMWSc 92*
**Ambrosiaster** *EncEarC*
**Ambrosino**, Carmen Felice 1948- *WhoFI 92*
**Ambrosio**, Gabriel M 1938- *WhoAmP 91*
**Ambrosio**, Michael Angelo 1945- *WhoAmL 92*
**Ambroson**, Gene Owen 1948- *WhoMW 92*
**Ambroziak**, Jacek 1941- *IntWW 91*
**Ambrozic**, Aloysius Matthew 1930- *WhoRel 92*
**Ambrus**, Clara Maria 1924- *AmMWSc 92*
**Ambrus**, Julian Lawrence 1924- *AmMWSc 92*
**Ambs**, Lawrence Lacy 1937- *AmMWSc 92*
**Ambs**, Marvin Nellis 1924- *WhoEnt 92*
**Ambs**, William Joseph 1929- *AmMWSc 92*
**Ambudkar**, Indu S 1954- *AmMWSc 92*
**Ambuel**, John Philip 1918- *AmMWSc 92*
**Amburgey**, Terry L 1940- *AmMWSc 92*
**Ambush**, Robert C. *WhoBlA 92*
**Amdahl**, Douglas Kenneth 1919- *WhoAmL 92*
**Amdahl**, Gene M 1922- *AmMWSc 92*
**Amdahl**, Gene Myron 1922- *WhoFI 92, WhoWest 92*
**Amdahl**, Myron 1948- *WhoAmP 91*
**Amdahl**, Timothy Henning 1955- *WhoAmP 91*
**Amdall**, William John 1953- *WhoFI 92*
**Amdur**, James Austin 1936- *WhoAmL 92*
**Amdur**, Martin Bennett 1942- *WhoAmL 92*
**Amdur**, Mary Ochsenhirt 1921- *AmMWSc 92*
**Amdur**, Millard Jason 1937- *AmMWSc 92*
**Ameche**, Don 1908- *IntMPA 92*
**Ameen**, Mark *DrAPF 91*
**Ameer**, George Albert 1931- *AmMWSc 92*
**Ameigh**, Michael Scott 1948- *WhoEnt 92*
**Amein**, Michael 1926- *AmMWSc 92*
**Ameliane de Glandeves** *EncAmaz 91*
**Ameliane du Puget** *EncAmaz 91*
**Amelin**, Charles Francis *AmMWSc 92*
**Ameling**, Elly 1938- *IntWW 91, NewAmDM*
**Amelio**, Gilbert Frank 1943- *AmMWSc 92, WhoFI 92, WhoWest 92*
**Amell**, Alexander Renton 1923- *AmMWSc 92*
**Amell**, Samuel 1948- *WhoHisp 92*
**Amelunxen**, Remi Edward 1928- *AmMWSc 92*
**Amemiya**, Frances Campbell 1915- *AmMWSc 92*
**Amemiya**, Kei *AmMWSc 92*
**Amemiya**, Kenjie *AmMWSc 92*
**Amemiya**, Koichi *WhoWest 92*
**Amemiya**, Minoru 1922- *AmMWSc 92*
**Amemiya**, Ronald Yoshihiko 1940- *WhoAmP 91*
**Amen**, Ralph DuWayne 1928- *AmMWSc 92*
**Amen**, Ronald Joseph 1943- *AmMWSc 92*
**Amend**, Bernhard Gottwald 1821?-1917 *BiInAmS*
**Amend**, Donald Ford 1939- *AmMWSc 92*
**Amend**, James Frederick 1943- *AmMWSc 92*
**Amend**, James Michael 1942- *WhoAmL 92*
**Amend**, John R. 1938- *WrDr 92*
**Amend**, John Robert 1938- *AmMWSc 92*
**Amende**, Lynn Meridith 1950- *AmMWSc 92*
**Amendola**, Giorgio 1907-1980 *FacFETw*
**Amendt**, John Hayward, Jr. 1955- *WhoMW 92*
**Amenomiya**, Yoshimitsu 1924- *AmMWSc 92*
**Ament**, Alison Stone 1948- *AmMWSc 92*
**Ament**, Don 1942- *WhoAmP 91*
**Ament**, Mark Steven 1951- *WhoAmL 92*
**Ament**, Marvin Earl 1938- *AmMWSc 92*
**Ament**, Richard Rand 1950- *WhoMW 92*
**Amenta**, Peter Sebastian 1927- *AmMWSc 92*
**Amer**, Kenneth Benjamin 1924- *WhoWest 92*
**Amer**, Mohamed Samir 1935- *AmMWSc 92*
**Amer**, Nabil Mahmoud 1942- *AmMWSc 92*
**Amer**, Patrick Joseph 1937- *WhoAmL 92*
**Amer**, Paul David 1953- *AmMWSc 92*
**Amerasinghe**, Chittharanjan Felix 1933- *IntWW 91*
**Amerine**, Anne Follette 1950- *WhoFI 92, WhoWest 92*
**Amerine**, Maynard Andrew 1911- *AmMWSc 92*
**Amerine**, Terry Lee 1964- *WhoMW 92*
**Ameringer**, Oscar 1870-1943 *AmPeW*
**Amerman**, Carroll R 1930- *AmMWSc 92*
**Amerman**, John Ellis 1944- *WhoAmL 92*
**Amerman**, John W. 1932- *WhoFI 92, WhoWest 92*
**Amerman**, Monique Gabrielle 1934- *WhoWest 92*
**Amero**, Bernard Alan 1948- *AmMWSc 92*
**Amero**, R C 1917- *AmMWSc 92*
**Amero**, Sally Ann 1952- *AmMWSc 92*
**Amerson**, Grady Malcolm 1939- *AmMWSc 92*
**Amerson**, Lucius Davenport 1933- *WhoAmP 91*
**Amery**, Carl *IntWW 91*
**Amery**, Carl 1922- *IntAu&W 91*
**Amery**, Colin Robert 1944- *Who 92*
**Amery**, H Julian 1919- *IntAu&W 91*
**Amery**, Julian 1919- *IntWW 91, Who 92, WrDr 92*
**Ames Brothers** *NewAmDM*
**Ames**, A. Gary 1944- *WhoFI 92, WhoWest 92*
**Ames**, Adelbert, III 1921- *AmMWSc 92*
**Ames**, Alison Winthrop 1945- *WhoEnt 92*
**Ames**, Bruce Nathan 1928- *AmMWSc 92, IntWW 91, WhoWest 92*
**Ames**, Clinton *TwCSFW 91*
**Ames**, Damaris 1944- *WhoFI 92*
**Ames**, Delano L. 1906- *WrDr 92*
**Ames**, Derrick Lee 1950- *WhoBlA 92*
**Ames**, Donald Paul 1922- *AmMWSc 92, WhoMW 92*
**Ames**, Edward R 1935- *AmMWSc 92*
**Ames**, Edward Scribner 1870-1958 *RelLAm 91*
**Ames**, Felicia *WrDr 92*
**Ames**, Fisher 1758-1808 *BenetAL 91*
**Ames**, Frank Anthony 1942- *WhoEnt 92*
**Ames**, G. Ronald 1939- *WhoIns 92*
**Ames**, Giovanna Ferro-Luzzi 1936- *AmMWSc 92*
**Ames**, Guy Chetwood, III 1951- *WhoRel 92*
**Ames**, Ira Harold 1937- *AmMWSc 92*
**Ames**, Irving 1929- *AmMWSc 92*
**Ames**, James Barr 1911- *WhoAmL 92*
**Ames**, Jane Irene 1950- *WhoMW 92*
**Ames**, Jesse Daniel 1883-1972 *HanAmWH*
**Ames**, John Cooper 1961- *WhoRel 92*
**Ames**, John Hersh 1943- *WhoFI 92*
**Ames**, John Wendell 1936- *AmMWSc 92*
**Ames**, Joseph Bushnell 1878-1928 *ScFEYrs*
**Ames**, Kenneth, Mrs. *Who 92*
**Ames**, Lawrence Coffin, Jr. 1925- *WhoWest 92*
**Ames**, Lawrence Lowell 1951- *AmMWSc 92*
**Ames**, Leon 1903- *IntMPA 92*
**Ames**, Leslie 1905-1990 *AnObit 1990*
**Ames**, Lloyd Leroy, Jr 1927- *AmMWSc 92*
**Ames**, Louis B. 1918- *IntMPA 92*
**Ames**, Lynford Lenhart 1938- *AmMWSc 92*
**Ames**, Marc L. 1943- *WhoAmL 92, WhoFI 92*
**Ames**, Mary Jane 1939- *WhoRel 92*
**Ames**, Mary L. Pulsifer 1845?-1902 *BiInAmS*
**Ames**, Matthew Martin 1947- *AmMWSc 92*
**Ames**, Michael McClean 1933- *IntWW 91, WhoWest 92*
**Ames**, Nathaniel 1708-1764 *BenetAL 91, BiInAmS*
**Ames**, Patricia Yvonne 1946- *WhoWest 92*
**Ames**, Peter L 1931- *AmMWSc 92*
**Ames**, Rachel *WrDr 92*
**Ames**, Raymond Gardner 1932- *WhoFI 92*
**Ames**, Robert San 1919- *WhoFI 92*
**Ames**, Roger Lyman 1933- *AmMWSc 92*
**Ames**, Sandra Patience 1947- *WhoFI 92, WhoMW 92*
**Ames**, Sarah Rachel 1922- *IntAu&W 91*
**Ames**, Stanley Richard 1918- *AmMWSc 92*
**Ames**, Stephen Charles 1938- *WhoFI 92*
**Ames**, Steven Reede 1951- *WhoFI 92*
**Ames**, William Clark 1950- *WhoWest 92*
**Ames**, William Eugene 1923- *WhoAmP 91*
**Ames**, Wilmer C. *WhoBlA 92*
**Amess**, David Anthony Andrew 1952- *Who 92*
**Amestoy**, Jeffrey L 1946- *WhoAmP 91*
**Amestoy**, Jeffrey Lee 1946- *WhoAmL 92*
**Amey**, Paul 1957- *TwCPaSc*
**Amey**, Rae 1947- *WhoEnt 92*
**Amey**, Ralph Leonard 1937- *AmMWSc 92*
**Amey**, William G 1918- *AmMWSc 92*
**Amezquita**, Jesusa Maria 1958- *WhoHisp 92*
**Amfiteatrov**, Aleksandr Valentinovich 1862-1938 *SovUnBD*
**Amfiteatrov**, Alexander Valentinovich 1862-1938 *FacFETw*
**Amft**, Robert Ernest 1916- *WhoMW 92*
**Amgott**, Madeline 1931- *WhoEnt 92*
**Amherst** *Who 92*
**Amherst**, Earl 1896- *Who 92*
**Amherst**, Jeffery 1717-1797 *BlkwEAR*
**Amherst**, Wes *TwCSFW 91*
**Amherst of Hackney**, Baron 1940- *Who 92*
**Amhowitz**, Harris J. 1934- *WhoAmL 92*
**Amichai**, Yehuda 1924- *FacFETw, LiExTwC*
**Amici**, Richard Victor 1953- *WhoAmL 92*

**Amick,** Carol Campbell *WhoAmP 91*
**Amick,** Charles James 1952- *AmMWSc 92*
**Amick,** James Albert 1928- *AmMWSc 92*
**Amick,** James L 1925- *AmMWSc 92*
**Amick,** Ollie C 1920- *WhoAmP 91*
**Amick,** Steven Hammond 1947- *WhoAmP 91*
**Amico,** Charles William 1942- *WhoFI 92, WhoWest 92*
**Amico,** David Michael 1951- *WhoWest 92*
**Amico,** Gina Maria 1936- *WhoRel 92*
**Amidei,** L. Neal 1933- *WhoWest 92*
**Amidon,** Eleanor H 1929- *WhoAmP 91*
**Amidon,** Richard Elkins 1927- *WhoAmP 91*
**Amidon,** Roger Welton 1914- *AmMWSc 92*
**Amidon,** Thomas Edward 1946- *AmMWSc 92*
**Amies,** Hardy 1909- *IntWW 91, Who 92*
**Amieva,** Marta Zenaida 1945- *WhoFI 92*
**Amiji,** Hatim M. 1939- *WhoBlA 92*
**Amiji,** Mohsin Mustafa 1960- *WhoFI 92*
**Amin,** Idi 1925?- *FacFETw [port]*
**Amin,** Karima 1947- *WhoBlA 92*
**Amin,** Mahmoud 1920- *IntWW 91*
**Amin,** Mirza Ruhul 1922- *IntWW 91*
**Amin,** Mostafa 1914- *IntAu&W 91, IntWW 91*
**Amin,** Omar M 1939- *AmMWSc 92*
**Amin,** Samir 1931- *ConAu 35NR, IntWW 91*
**Amin,** Sanjay Indubhai 1948- *AmMWSc 92*
**Amin Dada,** Idi 1925- *IntWW 91*
**Amina** *EncAmaz 91*
**Aminatu** *EncAmaz 91*
**Amini,** Ali 1905- *IntWW 91*
**Amini,** Bijan Khajehnouri 1943- *WhoFI 92*
**Aminoff,** David 1926- *AmMWSc 92*
**Amioka,** Wallace Shuzo 1914- *WhoFI 92, WhoWest 92*
**Amir Machmud** 1923- *IntWW 91*
**Amir-Moez,** Ali R 1919- *AmMWSc 92*
**Amiraian,** Kenneth 1926- *AmMWSc 92*
**Amirikia,** Hassan 1937- *WhoMW 92*
**Amirikian,** Arsham 1899- *AmMWSc 92*
**Amirkhanian,** Charles 1945- *NewAmDM*
**Amirkhanian,** John David 1927- *AmMWSc 92, WhoWest 92*
**Amirtharajah,** Appiah 1940- *AmMWSc 92*
**Amirvand,** Amir 1957- *WhoEnt 92*
**Amis,** Douglas Keith 1948- *WhoWest 92*
**Amis,** Eric J 1954- *AmMWSc 92*
**Amis,** Joan Skaggs 1934- *WhoRel 92*
**Amis,** Kingsley 1922- *CnDBLB 7 [port], ConNov 91, FacFETw, IntAu&W 91, IntWW 91, RfGEnL 91, TwCSFW 91, Who 92, WrDr 92*
**Amis,** Martin 1949- *ConNov 91, FacFETw, WrDr 92*
**Amis,** Martin Louis 1949- *IntAu&W 91, IntWW 91, Who 92*
**Amis,** Suzy 1962- *IntMPA 92*
**Amissah,** John Kodwo 1922-1991 *WhoRel 92*
**Amistad,** Glenn Repiedad 1955- *WhoWest 92*
**Amit,** Meir 1921- *IntWW 91*
**Amitay,** Noach 1930- *AmMWSc 92*
**Amith,** Avraham 1929- *AmMWSc 92*
**Amitin,** Mark Hall 1947- *WhoEnt 92*
**Amitsur,** Shimshon Avraham 1921- *IntWW 91*
**Amjad,** Zahid 1946- *AmMWSc 92*
**Amkraut,** Alfred A 1926- *AmMWSc 92*
**Amladi,** Prasad Ganesh 1941- *WhoFI 92, WhoMW 92*
**Amlaner,** Charles Joseph, Jr 1951- *AmMWSc 92*
**Amlen,** David 1961- *WhoEnt 92*
**Amling,** Frederick 1926- *ConAu 133*
**Amling,** Harry James 1931- *AmMWSc 92*
**Amlot,** Roy Douglas 1942- *Who 92*
**Amma,** Elmer Louis 1929- *AmMWSc 92*
**Amman,** Gene Doyle 1931- *AmMWSc 92*
**Ammann,** E O 1935- *AmMWSc 92*
**Ammann,** Harriet Maria 1939- *AmMWSc 92*
**Ammann,** Lillian Ann Nicholson 1946- *WhoFI 92*
**Ammann,** Othmar H 1875-1965 *DcTwDes, FacFETw*
**Ammar,** Mohamed Ali 1937- *IntWW 91*
**Ammar,** Raymond George 1932- *AmMWSc 92*
**Ammarell,** John Samuel 1920- *WhoFI 92*
**Amme,** Robert C. 1930- *WhoWest 92*
**Amme,** Robert Clyde 1930- *AmMWSc 92*
**Ammer,** Christine 1931- *WrDr 92*
**Ammer,** Mary Jane 1957- *WhoMW 92*
**Ammer,** William 1919- *WhoMW 92*
**Ammeraal,** Robert Neal 1936- *WhoMW 92*
**Ammerman,** Clarence Bailey 1929- *AmMWSc 92*
**Ammerman,** Dan Sheridan 1932- *WhoFI 92*
**Ammerman,** Gale Richard 1923- *AmMWSc 92*
**Ammerman,** James Harry, II 1951- *WhoAmL 92*
**Ammerman,** Joseph S 1924- *WhoAmP 91*
**Ammeson,** Charles F. 1953- *WhoAmL 92*
**Ammianus Marcellinus** 330?-400? *EncEarC*
**Ammirati,** Joseph Frank, Jr 1942- *AmMWSc 92*
**Ammirato,** Philip Vincent 1943- *AmMWSc 92*
**Ammlung,** Richard Lee 1952- *AmMWSc 92*
**Ammon,** Gunter Karl-Johannes 1918- *IntWW 91*
**Ammon,** Herman L 1936- *AmMWSc 92*
**Ammon,** Vernon Dale 1941- *AmMWSc 92*
**Ammonas** *EncEarC*
**Ammondson,** Clayton John 1923- *AmMWSc 92*
**Ammonius** *EncEarC*
**Ammonius of Alexandria** *EncEarC*
**Ammonius Saccas** 175?-244 *EncEarC*
**Ammons,** A.R. *DrAPF 91*
**Ammons,** A. R. 1926- *BenetAL 91, ConAu 36NR, ConPo 91, FacFETw, IntAu&W 91, WrDr 92*
**Ammons,** Albert 1907-1949 *NewAmDM*
**Ammons,** Bruce Carl 1961- *WhoRel 92*
**Ammons,** Edsel Albert 1924- *WhoBlA 92, WhoRel 92*
**Ammons,** Elias Milton 1860-1925 *DcNCBi 1*
**Ammons,** Gene 1925-1974 *NewAmDM*
**Ammons,** John 1831-1914 *DcNCBi 1*
**Ammons,** Tamara Nash 1957- *WhoBlA 92*
**Ammons,** Timothy Matthew 1958- *WhoAmL 92*
**Amo,** Tauraatua i *ConAu 133*
**Amols,** Howard Ira 1949- *AmMWSc 92*
**Amon,** Frank d1918 *BiInAmS*
**Amon,** Max 1939- *AmMWSc 92*
**Amon Parisi,** Cristina Hortensia 1956- *AmMWSc 92*
**Amondson,** Neil Arthur 1954- *WhoAmP 91*
**Amoore,** Frederick Andrew 1913- *Who 92*
**Amoore,** John Ernest 1930- *AmMWSc 92*
**Amore,** John *WhoIns 92*
**Amorello,** Matthew J *WhoAmP 91*
**Amortegui,** Antonio J. 1930- *WhoHisp 92*
**Amory** *Who 92*
**Amory,** Cleveland *IntAu&W 91*
**Amory,** Cleveland 1917- *BenetAL 91, WrDr 92*
**Amory,** Daniel 1946- *WhoAmL 92*
**Amory,** David William 1928- *AmMWSc 92*
**Amory,** Mark 1941- *ConAu 36NR*
**Amory,** Reginald L. 1936- *WhoBlA 92*
**Amory,** Robert 1842-1910 *BiInAmS*
**Amory,** Thomas Carhart 1933- *WhoWest 92*
**Amos,** Alan Thomas 1952- *Who 92*
**Amos,** Archie L, Jr 1947- *WhoAmP 91*
**Amos,** Barbara Mary D. *Who 92*
**Amos,** Charles Clinton 1940- *WhoFI 92*
**Amos,** Daniel Paul 1951- *WhoFI 92*
**Amos,** Dennis Bernard 1923- *AmMWSc 92*
**Amos,** Dewey Harold 1925- *AmMWSc 92, WhoMW 92*
**Amos,** Donald E 1929- *AmMWSc 92*
**Amos,** Eugene P *WhoAmP 91*
**Amos,** Francis John Clarke 1924- *Who 92*
**Amos,** George Henry, III 1959- *WhoWest 92*
**Amos,** Harold 1919- *AmMWSc 92*
**Amos,** Harton Douglas 1943- *WhoIns 92*
**Amos,** Henry Estill 1941- *AmMWSc 92*
**Amos,** James Larry 1938- *WhoRel 92*
**Amos,** John 1941- *IntMPA 92, WhoEnt 92*
**Amos,** John Beverly 1924- *WhoFI 92*
**Amos,** John Spencer, Jr. 1956- *WhoMW 92*
**Amos,** Joseph H. 1929- *WhoBlA 92*
**Amos,** Kent B. 1944- *WhoBlA 92*
**Amos,** Larry C. 1935- *WhoBlA 92*
**Amos,** Oris Elizabeth Carter *WhoBlA 92*
**Amos,** Paul Shelby 1926- *WhoFI 92*
**Amos,** Stanley Edd 1956- *WhoRel 92*
**Amos,** Valerie 1954- *Who 92*
**Amos,** Wally 1937- *WhoBlA 92*
**Amoss,** Max St Clair 1937- *AmMWSc 92*
**Amoss,** William H 1936- *WhoAmP 91*
**Amouzegar,** Jamshid 1923- *IntWW 91*
**Amowitz,** Georgette Weisz 1929- *WhoEnt 92*
**Amoyal,** Pierre Alain Wilfred 1949- *IntWW 91*
**Ampagoomian,** George Arakel 1943- *WhoFI 92*
**Ampagoomian,** Gregory Harold 1950- *WhoWest 92*
**Amper,** Leslie Ruth 1954- *WhoEnt 92*
**Amphilochius** 340?-394? *EncEarC*
**Amplatz,** Kurt 1924- *AmMWSc 92*
**Ampleforth,** Abbot of *Who 92*
**Ampthill,** Baron 1921- *Who 92*
**Ampulski,** Robert Stanley 1942- *AmMWSc 92*
**Ampy,** Franklin 1936- *AmMWSc 92*
**Ampy,** Franklin R. 1936- *WhoBlA 92*
**Amr,** Asad Tamer 1941- *WhoFI 92*
**Amr,** Sania *AmMWSc 92*
**Amram,** David 1930- *NewAmDM*
**Amram,** David Werner 1930- *WhoEnt 92*
**Amrein,** Yost Ursus Lucius 1918- *AmMWSc 92*
**Amri Sued,** Ismail 1942- *IntWW 91*
**Amrich,** Delores Elaine 1936- *WhoRel 92*
**Amrine,** Danny Andrew 1951- *WhoAmL 92*
**Amrine,** Harold Thomas 1916- *AmMWSc 92, WhoMW 92*
**Amritanand,** Joseph 1917- *IntWW 91, Who 92*
**Amritanandamayi,** Mataji 1953- *RelLAm 91*
**Amromin,** George David 1919- *AmMWSc 92*
**Amron,** Irving 1921- *AmMWSc 92*
**Amsbury,** David Leonard 1932- *AmMWSc 92*
**Amschler,** James Ralph 1943- *WhoAmL 92*
**Amsden,** Thomas William 1915- *AmMWSc 92*
**Amsel,** Abram 1922- *ConAu 35NR*
**Amsel,** Lewis Paul 1942- *AmMWSc 92*
**Amsel,** Robert Gary 1957- *WhoAmL 92*
**Amsler,** Laura Lynn 1963- *WhoRel 92*
**Amstadter,** Laurence 1922- *WhoMW 92*
**Amster,** Adolph Bernard 1924- *AmMWSc 92*
**Amster,** Caryn Meris 1941- *WhoMW 92*
**Amster,** Harvey Jerome 1928- *AmMWSc 92*
**Amsterdam,** Abraham 1939- *AmMWSc 92*
**Amsterdam,** Anthony Guy 1935- *WhoAmL 92*
**Amsterdam,** Daniel *AmMWSc 92*
**Amsterdam,** Mark Lemle 1944- *WhoAmL 92*
**Amsterdam,** Mark Russell 1957- *WhoEnt 92*
**Amsterdam,** Morey 1908- *ConTFT 9*
**Amsterdam,** Morey 1914- *IntMPA 92*
**Amstone,** Connie Sonja 1946- *WhoWest 92*
**Amstutz,** Gary Paul 1955- *WhoWest 92*
**Amstutz,** Harlan Cabot 1931- *AmMWSc 92*
**Amstutz,** Harold Emerson 1919- *AmMWSc 92*
**Amstutz,** James Louis 1960- *WhoRel 92*
**Amstutz,** Larry Ihrig 1941- *AmMWSc 92*
**Amstutz,** Ronald D *WhoAmP 91*
**Amte,** Baba *IntWW 91*
**Amudun Niyaz** 1932- *IntWW 91*
**Amuedo,** Jerry 1937- *WhoHisp 92*
**Amuedo,** Mark Gerard 1937- *WhoHisp 92*
**Amundrud,** Donald Lorne 1943- *AmMWSc 92*
**Amundsen,** Clifford C 1933- *AmMWSc 92*
**Amundsen,** Lawrence Hardin 1909- *AmMWSc 92*
**Amundsen,** Roald 1872-1928 *FacFETw [port]*
**Amundson,** Clyde Howard 1927- *AmMWSc 92*
**Amundson,** Eva Donalda 1911- *WhoWest 92*
**Amundson,** Karl Raymond 1961- *AmMWSc 92*
**Amundson,** Mark Douglas 1960- *WhoMW 92*
**Amundson,** Mary Jane 1936- *AmMWSc 92*
**Amundson,** Merle E 1936- *AmMWSc 92*
**Amundson,** Neal R 1916- *AmMWSc 92*
**Amundson,** Robert A. *WhoAmL 92, WhoMW 92*
**Amundson,** Robert Gale 1946- *AmMWSc 92*
**Amurri,** Franco 1958- *WhoEnt 92*
**Amuzegar,** Jahangir 1920- *WhoFI 92*
**Amwell,** Baron d1990 *Who 92N*
**Amwell,** Baron 1943- *Who 92*
**Amy,** Dennis Oldrieve 1932- *Who 92*
**Amy,** Gilbert 1936- *ConCom 92, NewAmDM*
**Amy,** Jonathan Weekes 1923- *AmMWSc 92*
**Amy,** Nancy Klein 1947- *AmMWSc 92*
**Amy,** Robert Lewis 1919- *AmMWSc 92*
**Amy-Moreno de Toro,** Angel Alberto 1945- *WhoHisp 92*
**Amyot,** Leopold Henri 1930- *Who 92*
**Amyot,** Rene 1926- *Who 92*
**Amzel,** L Mario 1942- *AmMWSc 92*
**An Gang** 1953- *IntWW 91*
**An Min** 1922- *IntWW 91*
**An Pingsheng** 1912- *IntWW 91*
**An Shiwei** 1919- *IntWW 91*
**An Tai-sung** 1931- *ConAu 133*
**An Zhendong** 1931- *IntWW 91*
**An Zhiwen** 1919- *IntWW 91*
**An Zhiyuan** d1987 *IntWW 91N*
**Ana-Alicia** *WhoEnt 92, WhoHisp 92*
**Anacker,** Heinrich 1901- *EncTR 91 [port]*
**Anacker,** R. David 1935- *WhoWest 92*
**Anacker,** Robert Leroy *AmMWSc 92*
**Anacletus** *EncEarC*
**Anaea** *EncAmaz 91*
**Anagnostakis,** Sandra Lee 1939- *AmMWSc 92*
**Anagnostis,** Nicholas Achilles 1942- *WhoEnt 92*
**Anagnostopoulos,** Constantine E 1922- *AmMWSc 92*
**Anagnostopoulos,** Constantine Emmanuel 1922- *WhoMW 92*
**Anagnostopoulos,** Constantine N 1944- *AmMWSc 92*
**Anagnostopoulos,** Madelaine Lynch 1941- *WhoFI 92*
**Anagnou,** Nicholas P 1947- *AmMWSc 92*
**Anahareo** *BenetAL 91*
**Anami,** Korechika 1887-1945 *FacFETw*
**Ananaba,** Agu Jackson, Jr. 1956- *WhoFI 92*
**Anand,** Amarjit Singh 1940- *AmMWSc 92*
**Anand,** Bal Krishan 1917- *IntWW 91*
**Anand,** Mulk Raj 1905- *ConNov 91, IntAu&W 91, IntWW 91, RfGEnL 91, WrDr 92*
**Anand,** Rajen S 1937- *AmMWSc 92*
**Anand,** Reema 1964- *IntAu&W 91*
**Anand,** Satish Chandra 1930- *AmMWSc 92*
**Anand,** Subhash Chandra 1933- *AmMWSc 92*
**Anand,** Suresh Chandra 1931- *WhoWest 92*
**Anand,** Yogindra Nath 1939- *WhoMW 92*
**Anand-Srivastava,** Madhu Bala *AmMWSc 92*
**Anandalingam,** G 1953- *AmMWSc 92*
**Anandamurti,** Shrii Shrii 1923- *RelLAm 91*
**Anandan,** Munisamy 1939- *AmMWSc 92*
**Ananev,** Anatoliy Andreyevich 1925- *IntWW 91*
**Anania,** Michael 1938- *IntAu&W 91*
**Anania,** Michael 1939- *WrDr 92*
**Anania,** Michael A. *DrAPF 91*
**Ananiashvili,** Nina 1963- *IntWW 91*
**Ananta Toer,** Pramoedya *IntWW 91*
**Anantha,** Narasipur Gundappa 1934- *AmMWSc 92*
**Anantha Narayanan,** Venkataraman 1936- *AmMWSc 92*
**Ananthanarayanan,** Vettaikkoru S 1938- *AmMWSc 92*
**Anantharaman,** Nagarajan 1952- *WhoFI 92*
**Ananthasouthone,** Thong Khoune 1923- *WhoRel 92*
**Anaporte-Easton,** Jean *DrAPF 91*
**Anas,** Demetra Economos 1960- *WhoAmL 92*
**Anast,** Constantine Spiro 1924- *AmMWSc 92*
**Anast,** David George 1955- *WhoWest 92*
**Anast,** Nick James 1947- *WhoFI 92*
**Anastanio,** Anthony J. *WhoIns 92*
**Anastaplo,** George 1925- *WhoMW 92*
**Anastas,** Peter *DrAPF 91*
**Anastas,** Terrence Joseph 1958- *WhoAmL 92*
**Anastasatu,** Constantin 1917- *IntWW 91*
**Anastasi,** Anne 1908- *WomPsyc*
**Anastasi,** Richard Joseph 1951- *WhoFI 92*
**Anastasia Nikolayevna** 1901-1918 *FacFETw*
**Anastasia,** Lawrence J *WhoAmP 91*
**Anastasio,** Betty Bodmer 1940- *WhoMW 92*
**Anastasio,** James 1930- *WhoFI 92, WhoIns 92*
**Anastasio,** Salvatore 1932- *AmMWSc 92*
**Anastasiou,** Clifford 1929 *WrDr 92*
**Anastasius I** *EncEarC*
**Anastasius II** *EncEarC*
**Anastasius Apocrisarius** d666 *EncEarC*
**Anastasius Monachus** d662 *EncEarC*
**Anastasius I of Antioch** *EncEarC*
**Anastasius II of Antioch** *EncEarC*
**Anastasius Sinaita** d700? *EncEarC*
**Anastassiou,** Dimitris 1952- *AmMWSc 92*
**Anastassy,** Metropolitan 1873-1965 *RelLAm 91*
**Anastor,** Peter 1941- *WhoAmL 92*
**Anathan,** Thomas Joseph 1944- *WhoFI 92*
**Anati,** Emmanuel 1930- *WrDr 92*
**Anatole** *IntAu&W 91X*
**Anawalt,** Howard Clarke 1938- *WhoAmL 92*
**Anawalt,** Patricia Rieff 1924- *WhoWest 92*
**Anawati,** Joseph Soliman 1941- *WhoWest 92*
**Anaya,** Gabriel 1937- *WhoAmP 91*
**Anaya,** George, Jr. 1964- *WhoHisp 92*
**Anaya,** M Steven 1956- *WhoAmP 91*
**Anaya,** Mary *WhoHisp 92*

**Anaya**, Richard Alfred, Jr. 1932- WhoFI 92
**Anaya**, Rudolfo A. DrAPF 91
**Anaya**, Rudolfo A. 1937- BenetAL 91, ConNov 91, TwCWW 91, WhoHisp 92, WrDr 92
**Anaya**, Rudolfo Alfonso 1937- WhoWest 92
**Anaya**, Toney 1941- WhoAmP 91, WhoHisp 92
**Anaya**, William Joseph 1952- WhoAmL 92
**Anayiotos**, George Constantinou 1959- WhoFI 92
**Anbar**, Michael 1927- AmMWSc 92
**Anbari**, Abdul-Amir al- 1934- IntWW 91
**Ancel**, Fredric D 1943- AmMWSc 92
**Ancell**, Robert M. 1942- WhoFI 92
**Ancerl**, Karel 1908-1973 NewAmDM
**Ancetti**, Carlo Guido 1933- WhoFI 92
**Anchel**, Marjorie Wolff 1910- AmMWSc 92
**Anchell**, Melvin 1919- WhoWest 92
**Anchishkin**, Aleksandr Ivanovich 1933- IntWW 91
**Anchondo**, Daniel 1946- WhoAmP 91
**Anchor**, Clifford James 1936- WhoEnt 92
**Anchorena**, Manuel de 1933- Who 92
**Ancier**, Garth LesBEnT 92
**Ancil**, Cynthia Ann 1945- WhoMW 92
**Ancira**, Ernesto, Jr. 1944- WhoHisp 92
**Ancira**, Oscar, Jr. WhoHisp 92
**Ancira**, Oscar, Sr. WhoHisp 92
**Ancker**, Clinton J, Jr 1919- AmMWSc 92
**Ancker-Johnson**, Betsy 1929- AmMWSc 92
**Ancona**, George 1929- WrDr 92
**Ancona**, George Efraim 1929- IntAu&W 91
**Ancona**, George Ephraim 1929- WhoWest 92
**Ancram**, Earl of 1945- Who 92
**Ancrile**, Joyce Irene 1942- WhoEnt 92
**Ancrom**, Nancy DrAPF 91
**Ancsin**, John 1933- AmMWSc 92
**Anctil**, Michel 1945- AmMWSc 92
**And**, Miekal DrAPF 91
**Anda**, Geza 1921-1976 NewAmDM
**Anda y Salazar**, Simon de 1719-1776 HisDSpE
**Andacht**, Herman William 1920- WhoMW 92
**Andagoya**, Pascual de 1495-1548 HisDSpE
**Andahazy**, Marius Joseph 1950- WhoEnt 92
**Andalafte**, Edward Ziegler 1935- AmMWSc 92
**Andary**, Thomas Joseph 1942- WhoWest 92
**Andeen**, Richard E 1927- AmMWSc 92
**Andelman**, Julian Barry 1931- AmMWSc 92
**Andelson**, Jonathan Gary 1949- AmMWSc 92
**Andelson**, Robert V. 1931- WrDr 92
**Andenaes**, Johannes 1912- IntWW 91
**Ander**, O. Fritiof 1903-1978 DcAmImH
**Ander**, Paul 1931- AmMWSc 92
**Andera**, Leonard E 1934- WhoAmP 91
**Anderberg**, Robert John 1967- WhoWest 92
**Anderberg**, Roy Anthony 1921- WhoWest 92
**Anderegg**, Doyle Edward 1930- AmMWSc 92
**Anderegg**, George Francis, Jr. 1937- WhoAmL 92
**Anderegg**, John William 1923- AmMWSc 92
**Anderegg**, Leisha Marie 1959- WhoWest 92
**Anderegg**, Robert James 1951- AmMWSc 92
**Anderle**, Richard 1926- AmMWSc 92
**Anderluh**, John Russell 1934- WhoMW 92
**Anderman**, Maureen WhoEnt 92
**Andermann**, George 1924- AmMWSc 92
**Andermann**, Greg WhoEnt 92
**Anders**, Barbara Lynne 1938- WhoEnt 92
**Anders**, Chris 1937- WhoEnt 92
**Anders**, Corrie Michael 1944- WhoBlA 92
**Anders**, Edward 1926- AmMWSc 92, IntWW 91, WhoMW 92
**Anders**, Edward B 1930- AmMWSc 92
**Anders**, Geoffrey Taylor 1950- WhoAmL 92, WhoFI 92
**Anders**, Jorge 1939- WhoEnt 92
**Anders**, Leslie 1922- WrDr 92
**Anders**, Louis Hart, Jr. 1938- WhoAmL 92
**Anders**, Mardellya Mary 1918- WhoAmP 91
**Anders**, Marion Walter 1936- AmMWSc 92
**Anders**, Mark Leslie 1955- WhoAmL 92
**Anders**, Milton Howard 1930- WhoAmL 92
**Anders**, Nedda Casson d1991 NewYTBS 91
**Anders**, Oswald Ulrich 1928- AmMWSc 92
**Anders**, Patricia Lee 1948- WhoWest 92
**Anders**, Rex TwCWW 91, WrDr 92
**Anders**, Richard H. 1925- WhoBlA 92
**Anders**, Robert Lee 1947- WhoWest 92
**Anders**, Shirley B DrAPF 91
**Anders**, Steven Lee 1951- WhoFI 92
**Anders**, William 1933- FacFETw
**Anders**, William A 1933- AmMWSc 92
**Anders**, William Alison 1933- IntWW 91, WhoFI 92, WhoMW 92
**Anders**, Wladyslaw 1892-1970 EncTR 91
**Anders-Richards**, Donald 1928- WrDr 92
**Andersdatter**, Karla M. DrAPF 91
**Andersen**, Alice Klopstad 1912- WhoAmP 91
**Andersen**, Anders 1912- IntWW 91
**Andersen**, Anton Chris 1960- WhoAmL 92
**Andersen**, Arnold E 1943- AmMWSc 92
**Andersen**, Axel Langvad 1914- AmMWSc 92
**Andersen**, Barrett Gene 1948- WhoFI 92
**Andersen**, Benny Allan 1929- IntAu&W 91
**Andersen**, Blaine Wright 1925- AmMWSc 92
**Andersen**, Burton 1932- AmMWSc 92
**Andersen**, Carl Marius 1936- AmMWSc 92
**Andersen**, Dale Gordon 1933- WhoWest 92
**Andersen**, Dale V WhoAmP 91
**Andersen**, Dana Suzanne 1964- WhoEnt 92
**Andersen**, Dean Martin 1931- AmMWSc 92
**Andersen**, Dewey Richard 1927- AmMWSc 92
**Andersen**, Donald Edward 1923- AmMWSc 92
**Andersen**, Doris 1909- IntAu&W 91
**Andersen**, Doris Evelyn 1923- WhoFI 92, WhoWest 92
**Andersen**, Elmer Lee 1909- WhoFI 92, WhoMW 92
**Andersen**, Emil Thorvald 1917- AmMWSc 92
**Andersen**, Ernest Christopher 1909- WhoWest 92
**Andersen**, Ferron Lee 1931- AmMWSc 92
**Andersen**, Frances Elizabeth Gold 1916- WhoRel 92
**Andersen**, Francis Ian 1925- WhoRel 92
**Andersen**, Frank Alan 1944- AmMWSc 92
**Andersen**, Frank Angelius 1953- WhoEnt 92
**Andersen**, G. Chris 1938- WhoFI 92
**Andersen**, Gunnar Aagaard 1919-1982 DcTwDes
**Andersen**, Hans Christian 1941- AmMWSc 92
**Andersen**, Hans George 1919- IntWW 91
**Andersen**, Hans Oliver 1935- WhoMW 92
**Andersen**, Harold Wayne 1923- WhoMW 92
**Andersen**, Harry Edward 1906- WhoFI 92, WhoMW 92
**Andersen**, Howard Arne 1916- AmMWSc 92
**Andersen**, Ib 1954- IntWW 91
**Andersen**, James A. 1924- WhoAmL 92, WhoAmP 91, WhoWest 92
**Andersen**, John Prinzing 1965- WhoRel 92
**Andersen**, John R 1928- AmMWSc 92
**Andersen**, Jon Alan 1938- AmMWSc 92
**Andersen**, Jonny 1935- AmMWSc 92
**Andersen**, Kenneth F 1945- AmMWSc 92
**Andersen**, Kenneth Frank 1945- WhoWest 92
**Andersen**, Kenneth J 1936- AmMWSc 92
**Andersen**, Kenneth K 1934- AmMWSc 92
**Andersen**, Kent Tucker 1942- WhoFI 92
**Andersen**, Kristin Marie 1952- WhoEnt 92
**Andersen**, L Bryce 1928- AmMWSc 92
**Andersen**, Leonard Christian 1911- WhoMW 92
**Andersen**, Loa Rae 1939- WhoEnt 92
**Andersen**, Lynne Cox WhoWest 92
**Andersen**, Michael Paul 1946- WhoWest 92
**Andersen**, Mogens 1916- IntWW 91
**Andersen**, Neil Richard 1935- AmMWSc 92
**Andersen**, Niels Hjorth 1943- AmMWSc 92
**Andersen**, Olaf Sparre 1945- AmMWSc 92
**Andersen**, R. Clifton 1933- WhoMW 92
**Andersen**, Richard 1931- WhoRel 92
**Andersen**, Richard Esten 1957- WhoAmL 92
**Andersen**, Richard Lee 1948- WhoMW 92
**Andersen**, Richard Nicolaj 1930- AmMWSc 92
**Andersen**, Robert Gary 1939- WhoMW 92
**Andersen**, Robert Michael 1950- WhoAmL 92
**Andersen**, Robert Neils 1928- AmMWSc 92
**Andersen**, Roger Allen 1930- AmMWSc 92
**Andersen**, Ronald 1939- AmMWSc 92
**Andersen**, Ronald Max 1939- IntWW 91
**Andersen**, Roy Stuart 1921- AmMWSc 92
**Andersen**, Ruth Emily 1951- WhoMW 92
**Andersen**, Sheree Hilton 1954- WhoWest 92
**Andersen**, Steven Mark 1945- WhoMW 92
**Andersen**, Svend 1915- IntWW 91
**Andersen**, Terrell Neils 1937- AmMWSc 92
**Andersen**, Thomas Gilbert 1951- WhoMW 92
**Andersen**, Thorkild Waino 1920- AmMWSc 92
**Andersen**, Torkild 1934- IntWW 91
**Andersen**, Valdemar Jens 1919- Who 92
**Andersen**, Victor Eugene 1956- WhoRel 92
**Andersen**, Wilford Hoyt 1924- AmMWSc 92
**Andersen**, Willem Hendrik Jan 1941- WhoWest 92
**Andersen**, William Alfred 1943- WhoFI 92
**Andersen**, William Ralph 1930- AmMWSc 92
**Andersen-Wyckoff**, R. G. 1940- WhoWest 92
**Andersland**, Mark Steven 1961- AmMWSc 92
**Andersland**, Orlando Baldwin 1929- AmMWSc 92, WhoMW 92
**Anderson** Who 92
**Anderson**, A Eugene 1916- AmMWSc 92
**Anderson**, A Keith 1924- AmMWSc 92
**Anderson**, A. Richard 1942- WhoFI 92
**Anderson**, Abbie H. 1928- WhoBlA 92
**Anderson**, Adelaide Mary 1863-1936 BiDBrF 2
**Anderson**, Al H., Jr. 1942- WhoBlA 92
**Anderson**, Alan, Jr. 1943- WrDr 92
**Anderson**, Alan B. 1934- ConAu 133
**Anderson**, Alan Brauer 1934- WhoRel 92
**Anderson**, Alan Marshall 1955- WhoAmL 92
**Anderson**, Alan Stewart 1948- WhoAmL 92
**Anderson**, Albert 1859-1932 DcNCBi 1
**Anderson**, Albert Douglas 1928- AmMWSc 92
**Anderson**, Albert Edward 1928- AmMWSc 92
**Anderson**, Albert Gordon 1945- AmMWSc 92
**Anderson**, Albert Sydney 1940- WhoAmL 92
**Anderson**, Aldon J. 1917- WhoAmL 92
**Anderson**, Alexander M. WhoFI 92
**Anderson**, Alfred Anthony 1961- WhoBlA 92
**Anderson**, Alfred Charles 1943- WhoAmP 91
**Anderson**, Alfred Titus, Jr 1937- AmMWSc 92
**Anderson**, Alice Marie 1931- WhoWest 92
**Anderson**, Alison Grey 1943- WhoAmL 92
**Anderson**, Alistair Andrew Gibson 1927- Who 92
**Anderson**, Allan George 1923- AmMWSc 92
**Anderson**, Alvin E. 1943- WhoIns 92
**Anderson**, Amel 1936- WhoBlA 92
**Anderson**, Amelia Veronica 1947- WhoBlA 92
**Anderson**, Amos Robert 1920- AmMWSc 92
**Anderson**, Ann 1952- WhoAmP 91
**Anderson**, Anna 1901-1984 FacFETw
**Anderson**, Anne Joyce 1946- AmMWSc 92
**Anderson**, Annelise Graebner 1938- WhoFI 92
**Anderson**, Ansel Cochran 1933- AmMWSc 92
**Anderson**, Anthony 1935- AmMWSc 92
**Anderson**, Anthony John 1938- Who 92
**Anderson**, Anthony LeClaire 1938- WhoAmL 92
**Anderson**, Archie A. 1960- WhoFI 92
**Anderson**, Arnett Artis 1931- WhoBlA 92
**Anderson**, Arnold C 1919- WhoAmP 91
**Anderson**, Arnold Lynn 1940- AmMWSc 92
**Anderson**, Arthur G, Jr 1918- AmMWSc 92
**Anderson**, Arthur George 1926- AmMWSc 92
**Anderson**, Arthur John Ritchie 1933- Who 92
**Anderson**, Arthur O 1945- AmMWSc 92
**Anderson**, Arthur R 1910- AmMWSc 92
**Anderson**, Arthur Roland 1910- WhoWest 92
**Anderson**, Arthur Stephen 1947- WhoAmL 92
**Anderson**, Arthur W 1914- AmMWSc 92
**Anderson**, Aubrey Lee 1940- AmMWSc 92
**Anderson**, Austin Gothard 1931- WhoAmL 92
**Anderson**, Avis Olivia 1949- WhoBlA 92
**Anderson**, Barbara 1926- ConNov 91
**Anderson**, Barbara Ann 1948- WhoFI 92
**Anderson**, Barbara Jenkins 1928- WhoBlA 92
**Anderson**, Barbara Louise WhoBlA 92
**Anderson**, Barbara Louise 1933- WhoWest 92
**Anderson**, Barbara McComas 1950- WhoAmL 92
**Anderson**, Barbara Smith 1932- WhoAmP 91
**Anderson**, Barry Stanley 1942- WhoWest 92
**Anderson**, Benjamin Stratman, Jr. 1936- WhoBlA 92
**Anderson**, Bernard A 1909- AmMWSc 92
**Anderson**, Bernard E. WhoBlA 92, WhoFI 92
**Anderson**, Bernard Jeffrey 1944- AmMWSc 92
**Anderson**, Bernard Joseph 1942- WhoAmP 91
**Anderson**, Bert Axel 1929- WhoRel 92
**Anderson**, Bertin W 1939- AmMWSc 92
**Anderson**, Beth DrAPF 91
**Anderson**, Beth 1950- ConCom 92, NewAmDM, WhoEnt 92
**Anderson**, Betty Keller 1951- WhoBlA 92
**Anderson**, Betty Radford 1954- WhoAmP 91
**Anderson**, Beverley Jean 1940- Who 92
**Anderson**, Beverly 1933- AmMWSc 92
**Anderson**, Bob 1932- WhoAmP 91, WhoMW 92
**Anderson**, Bradford William 1956- WhoWest 92
**Anderson**, Bradley Clark 1961- WhoWest 92
**Anderson**, Bradley Dale 1948- AmMWSc 92
**Anderson**, Brian David Outram 1941- Who 92
**Anderson**, Brian L. 1952- WhoIns 92
**Anderson**, Bruce Allan 1946- WhoBlA 92
**Anderson**, Bruce Carl 1949- WhoWest 92
**Anderson**, Bruce E WhoAmP 91
**Anderson**, Bruce Hamilton 1941- WhoAmL 92
**Anderson**, Bruce Holmes 1917- AmMWSc 92
**Anderson**, Bruce Martin 1942- AmMWSc 92
**Anderson**, Bruce Murray 1929- AmMWSc 92
**Anderson**, Bruce Nils 1939- WhoWest 92
**Anderson**, Bruce Ray 1937- WhoMW 92
**Anderson**, Bryan N. 1955- WhoBlA 92
**Anderson**, Bryon Don 1944- AmMWSc 92, WhoMW 92
**Anderson**, Burton Carl 1930- AmMWSc 92
**Anderson**, Byron 1941- AmMWSc 92
**Anderson**, Byron Edward 1954- WhoAmL 92
**Anderson**, Byron F 1953- WhoAmP 91
**Anderson**, C. Leonard 1946- WhoWest 92
**Anderson**, Calvin B 1948- WhoAmP 91
**Anderson**, Calvin James 1952- WhoAmP 91
**Anderson**, Campbell McCheyne 1941- IntWW 91, Who 92
**Anderson**, Carey Laine, Jr. 1950- WhoBlA 92
**Anderson**, Carl August 1929- WhoRel 92
**Anderson**, Carl D. 1905-1991 CurBio 91N, NewYTBS 91 [port]
**Anderson**, Carl D 1930- WhoAmP 91
**Anderson**, Carl D. 1931- WhoBlA 92
**Anderson**, Carl David d1991 IntWW 91N, Who 92N
**Anderson**, Carl David 1905- AmMWSc 92, FacFETw, WhoNob 90
**Anderson**, Carl Douglas 1958- WhoEnt 92
**Anderson**, Carl Edwin 1934- WhoBlA 92
**Anderson**, Carl Einar 1923- AmMWSc 92
**Anderson**, Carl F, III 1966- WhoAmP 91
**Anderson**, Carl Frederick AmMWSc 92
**Anderson**, Carl Henry 1938- WhoMW 92
**Anderson**, Carl Leonard 1901- AmMWSc 92
**Anderson**, Carl William 1944- AmMWSc 92
**Anderson**, Carl William 1950- AmMWSc 92
**Anderson**, Carlton Leon 1942- WhoBlA 92
**Anderson**, Carol Ann WhoAmL 92
**Anderson**, Carol Ann 1957- WhoAmP 91
**Anderson**, Carol Boyles 1953- WhoAmL 92
**Anderson**, Carol Byrd 1941- WhoBlA 92
**Anderson**, Carol Elaine 1948- WhoWest 92
**Anderson**, Carol Jean 1946- WhoFI 92
**Anderson**, Carol Lee 1943- WhoMW 92
**Anderson**, Carol Patricia 1946- AmMWSc 92
**Anderson**, Carol Ruth 1926- WhoWest 92
**Anderson**, Carole Lewis 1944- WhoFI 92
**Anderson**, Caroline Still 1848-1919 NotBlAW 92
**Anderson**, Carolyn Joyce 1947- WhoMW 92

**Anderson,** Carson Anthony 1951- *WhoWest 92*
**Anderson,** Cat 1916-1981 *NewAmDM*
**Anderson,** Charles *WhoAmP 91*
**Anderson,** Charles Alfred 1902- *AmMWSc 92*
**Anderson,** Charles Butler 1905- *WhoWest 92*
**Anderson,** Charles Courtney 1916- *Who 92*
**Anderson,** Charles Dean 1930- *AmMWSc 92*
**Anderson,** Charles E, Jr 1946- *AmMWSc 92*
**Anderson,** Charles Edward 1919- *AmMWSc 92*
**Anderson,** Charles Eugene 1934- *AmMWSc 92*
**Anderson,** Charles Hammond 1935- *AmMWSc 92*
**Anderson,** Charles Hill 1930- *WhoAmL 92*
**Anderson,** Charles Jordan 1932- *WhoWest 92*
**Anderson,** Charles Michael 1944- *WhoFI 92*
**Anderson,** Charles Palmerston 1864-1930 *RelLAm 91*
**Anderson,** Charles Ross 1937- *WhoFI 92, WhoWest 92*
**Anderson,** Charles Thomas 1921- *AmMWSc 92*
**Anderson,** Charles V 1933- *AmMWSc 92*
**Anderson,** Charles William 1934- *WhoMW 92*
**Anderson,** Chester 1932- *IntAu&W 91*
**Anderson,** Chester R. 1912- *WhoBlA 92*
**Anderson,** Christian Donald 1931- *AmMWSc 92*
**Anderson,** Christopher 1944- *IntWW 91*
**Anderson,** Christopher Marlowe 1941- *AmMWSc 92*
**Anderson,** Cindy Lynn 1958- *WhoAmL 92*
**Anderson,** Clarence Eugene 1938- *Who 92*
**Anderson,** Clifford Harold 1939- *AmMWSc 92*
**Anderson,** Clifton Einar 1923- *WhoRel 92, WhoWest 92*
**Anderson,** Clyde Lee 1926- *AmMWSc 92*
**Anderson,** Courtney *Who 92*
**Anderson,** Courtney 1906- *WrDr 92*
**Anderson,** Craig Alan 1955- *WhoAmL 92, WhoMW 92*
**Anderson,** Craig Barry 1942- *WhoRel 92*
**Anderson,** Craig Edgar 1947- *WhoAmL 92*
**Anderson,** Cromwell Adair 1926- *WhoAmL 92*
**Anderson,** Curt Lee 1952- *WhoFI 92*
**Anderson,** Curtis Benjamin 1932- *AmMWSc 92*
**Anderson,** Curtis Stovall 1949- *WhoAmP 91*
**Anderson,** Cynthia Lee 1956- *WhoEnt 92*
**Anderson,** D G *WhoAmP 91*
**Anderson,** Dale 1933- *WhoEnt 92, WhoFI 92*
**Anderson,** Dale Arden 1936- *AmMWSc 92*
**Anderson,** Dan Richard 1924- *WhoAmP 91*
**Anderson,** Dan Rogers 1951- *WhoFI 92*
**Anderson,** Dana Alan 1945- *WhoWest 92*
**Anderson,** Dana DeWitt 1948- *WhoWest 92*
**Anderson,** Daniel D 1948- *AmMWSc 92*
**Anderson,** Daniel Duane 1948- *WhoMW 92*
**Anderson,** Daniel L 1968- *WhoAmP 91*
**Anderson,** Daniel William 1939- *AmMWSc 92*
**Anderson,** Daniel William 1960- *WhoFI 92*
**Anderson,** Danita Ruth 1956- *WhoRel 92*
**Anderson,** Darel Burton 1927- *WhoFI 92*
**Anderson,** Darlene Yvonne 1953- *WhoWest 92*
**Anderson,** Darwin Wayne 1940- *AmMWSc 92*
**Anderson,** Daryl *WhoEnt 92*
**Anderson,** David *WhoAmP 91*
**Anderson,** David 1919- *Who 92*
**Anderson,** David 1937- *IntWW 91*
**Anderson,** David Arnold 1939- *WhoAmL 92*
**Anderson,** David Atlas 1930- *WhoBlA 92*
**Anderson,** David Bennett 1944- *AmMWSc 92*
**Anderson,** David Bowen 1948- *WhoAmL 92*
**Anderson,** David Boyd 1942- *WhoAmL 92*
**Anderson,** David Carl 1941- *WhoEnt 92*
**Anderson,** David Charles 1931- *WhoWest 92*
**Anderson,** David Charles 1944- *WhoEnt 92*
**Anderson,** David Colville 1916- *Who 92*
**Anderson,** David Cord 1948- *WhoFI 92*
**Anderson,** David Daniel 1924- *IntAu&W 91, WhoMW 92, WrDr 92*
**Anderson,** David Elliott 1964- *WhoWest 92*
**Anderson,** David Eugene 1926- *AmMWSc 92*
**Anderson,** David Everett 1939- *AmMWSc 92*
**Anderson,** David Franklin 1926- *WhoIns 92*
**Anderson,** David G 1928- *AmMWSc 92*
**Anderson,** David H 1939- *AmMWSc 92*
**Anderson,** David Heywood 1937- *Who 92*
**Anderson,** David J 1939- *AmMWSc 92*
**Anderson,** David John 1942- *AmMWSc 92*
**Anderson,** David Langley 1944- *WhoFI 92*
**Anderson,** David Laron 1955- *WhoFI 92*
**Anderson,** David Lawrence 1934- *WhoMW 92, WhoRel 92*
**Anderson,** David Lawrence 1948- *WhoAmL 92*
**Anderson,** David Leonard 1919- *AmMWSc 92*
**Anderson,** David Martin 1930- *AmMWSc 92*
**Anderson,** David Melvin 1944- *WhoWest 92*
**Anderson,** David Munro 1937- *Who 92*
**Anderson,** David O. 1947- *WhoMW 92*
**Anderson,** David Prewitt 1934- *AmMWSc 92*
**Anderson,** David R 1942- *AmMWSc 92*
**Anderson,** David Ralph 1946- *WhoAmL 92*
**Anderson,** David Richard 1943- *WhoRel 92*
**Anderson,** David Robert 1940- *AmMWSc 92*
**Anderson,** David Vincent 1941- *AmMWSc 92*
**Anderson,** David Walter 1937- *AmMWSc 92*
**Anderson,** David Wesley 1952- *AmMWSc 92*
**Anderson,** David William 1929- *Who 92*
**Anderson,** David William 1953- *WhoAmL 92*
**Anderson,** Davin Charles 1955- *WhoMW 92*
**Anderson,** Dean Herbert 1950- *WhoWest 92*
**Anderson,** Dean Mauritz 1947- *AmMWSc 92*
**Anderson,** Dean W 1927- *WhoAmP 91*
**Anderson,** Deann Joan 1962- *WhoWest 92*
**Anderson,** Deborah Jean 1949- *AmMWSc 92*
**Anderson,** Debra F *AmMWSc 92*
**Anderson,** Debra Jean 1957- *WhoAmL 92*
**Anderson,** Debra Rae 1949- *WhoAmP 91*
**Anderson,** Declan John 1920- *Who 92*
**Anderson,** Denise 1965- *WhoEnt 92*
**Anderson,** Dennis Albin 1937- *WhoRel 92*
**Anderson,** Dennis Elmo 1934- *AmMWSc 92*
**Anderson,** Dennis John 1957- *WhoMW 92*
**Anderson,** Dennis Keith 1956- *WhoMW 92*
**Anderson,** Diane Lynn 1968- *WhoWest 92*
**Anderson,** Don 1934- *WhoAmP 91*
**Anderson,** Don 1943- *WhoAmP 91*
**Anderson,** Don Eugene 1932- *WhoMW 92*
**Anderson,** Don L. 1933- *IntWW 91*
**Anderson,** Don Lynn 1933- *AmMWSc 92*
**Anderson,** Donald 1939- *Who 92*
**Anderson,** Donald Arthur 1918- *AmMWSc 92*
**Anderson,** Donald Bernard 1919- *WhoWest 92*
**Anderson,** Donald E 1931- *AmMWSc 92*
**Anderson,** Donald E. 1938- *WhoEnt 92*
**Anderson,** Donald Edward 1938- *WhoBlA 92*
**Anderson,** Donald Francis 1938- *WhoMW 92*
**Anderson,** Donald Gordon Marcus 1937- *AmMWSc 92*
**Anderson,** Donald Gregory 1945- *WhoEnt 92*
**Anderson,** Donald Hervin 1916- *AmMWSc 92*
**Anderson,** Donald K 1931- *AmMWSc 92*
**Anderson,** Donald K., Jr. 1922- *WrDr 92*
**Anderson,** Donald L. 1932- *WhoBlA 92*
**Anderson,** Donald Lindsay 1925- *AmMWSc 92*
**Anderson,** Donald Morgan 1930- *AmMWSc 92*
**Anderson,** Donald Norton, Jr. 1928- *WhoWest 92*
**Anderson,** Donald Oliver 1930- *AmMWSc 92*
**Anderson,** Donald T 1925- *AmMWSc 92*
**Anderson,** Donald Thomas 1931- *IntWW 91, Who 92*
**Anderson,** Donald Thomas, Jr. 1937- *WhoMW 92*
**Anderson,** Donald Werner 1938- *AmMWSc 92*
**Anderson,** Donald Whimbey 1931- *WhoRel 92*
**Anderson,** Donna 1925- *WhoEnt 92*
**Anderson,** Donna Kay 1935- *WhoEnt 92*
**Anderson,** Doreatha Madison 1943- *WhoBlA 92*
**Anderson,** Doris Ehlinger 1926- *WhoAmL 92*
**Anderson,** Doris J. 1933- *WhoBlA 92*
**Anderson,** Dorothy Fisher 1924- *WhoWest 92*
**Anderson,** Dorrine Ann Petersen 1923- *WhoMW 92*
**Anderson,** Douglas *DrAPF 91*
**Anderson,** Douglas Firth 1951- *WhoMW 92*
**Anderson,** Douglas I 1947- *AmMWSc 92*
**Anderson,** Douglas Jay 1957- *WhoMW 92*
**Anderson,** Douglas K *AmMWSc 92*
**Anderson,** Douglas Kenneth 1950- *WhoEnt 92*
**Anderson,** Douglas Leavon 1939- *WhoAmP 91*
**Anderson,** Douglas Poole 1939- *AmMWSc 92*
**Anderson,** Douglas Richard 1938- *AmMWSc 92*
**Anderson,** Douglas Scranton Hesley 1929- *WhoFI 92*
**Anderson,** Duwayne Marlo 1927- *AmMWSc 92*
**Anderson,** Dwight Daniel 1957- *WhoFI 92*
**Anderson,** Dwight Lyman 1935- *AmMWSc 92*
**Anderson,** E. Clive 1947- *WhoAmL 92*
**Anderson,** Earl L 1935- *WhoAmP 91*
**Anderson,** Edgar L. 1931- *WhoBlA 92*
**Anderson,** Edmund George 1928- *AmMWSc 92*
**Anderson,** Edmund Hughes 1924- *AmMWSc 92*
**Anderson,** Edward Everett 1919- *AmMWSc 92*
**Anderson,** Edward Everett 1941- *AmMWSc 92*
**Anderson,** Edward Frederick 1932- *AmMWSc 92*
**Anderson,** Edward P 1922- *AmMWSc 92*
**Anderson,** Edward Riley 1932- *WhoAmL 92*
**Anderson,** Edward V. 1953- *WhoAmL 92*
**Anderson,** Edwin Alexander 1860-1933 *DcNCBi 1*
**Anderson,** Edwin George 1942- *WhoFI 92*
**Anderson,** Edwin J 1939- *AmMWSc 92*
**Anderson,** Edwin Myron 1920- *AmMWSc 92*
**Anderson,** Eileen Ruth 1928- *WhoAmP 91*
**Anderson,** Einar Wulfsberg 1942- *WhoEnt 92*
**Anderson,** Eldon Thurlow 1935- *WhoRel 92*
**Anderson,** Eleanor M *WhoAmP 91*
**Anderson,** Elizabeth M. *WhoBlA 92*
**Anderson,** Ella *IntAu&W 91X, WrDr 92*
**Anderson,** Ella L. 1917- *WhoBlA 92*
**Anderson,** Elmer Ebert 1922- *AmMWSc 92*
**Anderson,** Eloise B. McMorris *WhoBlA 92*
**Anderson,** Emory Dean 1939- *AmMWSc 92*
**Anderson,** Ephraim Saul 1911- *Who 92*
**Anderson,** Eric *Who 92*
**Anderson,** Eric Anthony 1946- *WhoFI 92, WhoMW 92*
**Anderson,** Eric Keith 1957- *WhoAmL 92*
**Anderson,** Eric Severin 1943- *WhoAmL 92*
**Anderson,** Erik 1958- *WhoFI 92*
**Anderson,** Erland *DrAPF 91*
**Anderson,** Ernest R 1932- *AmMWSc 92*
**Anderson,** Ethel Avara *WhoFI 92*
**Anderson,** Ethel Irene 1924- *AmMWSc 92*
**Anderson,** Eugene *Who 92, WhoAmP 91*
**Anderson,** Eugene 1944- *WhoBlA 92*
**Anderson,** Evalyn Ruth 1931- *WhoAmL 92*
**Anderson,** Evans Leland 1914- *WhoWest 92*
**Anderson,** Felix Sylvester 1893- *WhoBlA 92*
**Anderson,** Ferguson *Who 92*
**Anderson,** Ferguson 1914- *WrDr 92*
**Anderson,** Flavia 1910- *WrDr 92*
**Anderson,** Fletcher N 1930- *AmMWSc 92*
**Anderson,** Fletcher Neal 1930- *WhoFI 92*
**Anderson,** Floyd Edmond 1915- *AmMWSc 92*
**Anderson,** Frances Jean 1937- *AmMWSc 92*
**Anderson,** Frances Margaret *Who 92*
**Anderson,** Francis David 1925- *AmMWSc 92*
**Anderson,** Francis Spilman 1920- *WhoEnt 92*
**Anderson,** Frank A 1914- *AmMWSc 92*
**Anderson,** Frank David 1927- *AmMWSc 92*
**Anderson,** Frank Wallace 1921- *AmMWSc 92*
**Anderson,** Frank Wylie 1928- *AmMWSc 92*
**Anderson,** Franz Elmer 1938- *AmMWSc 92, WhoWest 92*
**Anderson,** Frederick J 1912- *WhoAmP 91*
**Anderson,** Frederick Randolph, Jr. 1941- *WhoAmL 92*
**Anderson,** Frederick W 1866-1891 *BiInAmS*
**Anderson,** Frederick William 1953- *WhoFI 92*
**Anderson,** G Harvey 1941- *AmMWSc 92*
**Anderson,** G M 1921- *AmMWSc 92*
**Anderson,** Gary 1948- *AmMWSc 92*
**Anderson,** Gary 1961- *WhoBlA 92*
**Anderson,** Gary Bruce 1947- *AmMWSc 92*
**Anderson,** Gary David 1947- *WhoEnt 92*
**Anderson,** Gary Don 1943- *AmMWSc 92*
**Anderson,** Gary K *WhoAmP 91*
**Anderson,** Gary Lee *AmMWSc 92*
**Anderson,** Gene Ray 1934- *WhoRel 92*
**Anderson,** Geoffrey Allen 1947- *WhoAmL 92, WhoFI 92, WhoMW 92*
**Anderson,** George A. 1923- *WhoBlA 92*
**Anderson,** George Albert 1937- *AmMWSc 92*
**Anderson,** George Burgwyn 1831-1862 *DcNCBi 1*
**Anderson,** George Cameron 1926- *AmMWSc 92*
**Anderson,** George Edward 1938- *WhoFI 92, WhoWest 92*
**Anderson,** George Joseph 1960- *WhoAmL 92*
**Anderson,** George Lee 1934- *WhoMW 92*
**Anderson,** George Robert 1934- *AmMWSc 92*
**Anderson,** George Ross, Jr. 1929- *WhoAmL 92*
**Anderson,** George Walter 1932- *WhoEnt 92*
**Anderson,** George William 1924- *AmMWSc 92*
**Anderson,** George Wishart 1913- *IntWW 91, Who 92*
**Anderson,** Gerald 1939- *WhoAmP 91*
**Anderson,** Gerald Clifton 1920- *AmMWSc 92*
**Anderson,** Gerald Edwin 1931- *WhoFI 92*
**Anderson,** Gerald Harry 1930- *WhoRel 92*
**Anderson,** Gerald M 1935- *AmMWSc 92*
**Anderson,** Gerald S 1930- *AmMWSc 92*
**Anderson,** Gerald Verne 1931- *WhoWest 92*
**Anderson,** Geraldine Louise 1941- *WhoMW 92*
**Anderson,** Gerard Fenton 1951- *WhoFI 92*
**Anderson,** Gerry 1929- *IntMPA 92, IntWW 91*
**Anderson,** Gershon Freddie 1930- *WhoRel 92*
**Anderson,** Gillian Bunshaft 1943- *WhoEnt 92*
**Anderson,** Gladys Peppers *WhoBlA 92*
**Anderson,** Glen Clark 1944- *WhoAmL 92, WhoWest 92*
**Anderson,** Glen Douglas 1930- *AmMWSc 92*
**Anderson,** Glen H 1938- *WhoAmP 91*
**Anderson,** Glenn Allen 1948- *WhoRel 92*
**Anderson,** Glenn Arthur 1924- *AmMWSc 92*
**Anderson,** Glenn M. 1913- *AlmAP 92 [port], WhoAmP 91*
**Anderson,** Glenn Malcolm *WhoWest 92*
**Anderson,** Glenn Richard 1940- *WhoAmP 91*
**Anderson,** Gloria L. 1938- *WhoBlA 92*
**Anderson,** Gloria Long 1938- *AmMWSc 92*
**Anderson,** Gordon A 1924- *WhoAmP 91*
**Anderson,** Gordon Alexander 1931- *Who 92*
**Anderson,** Gordon Earl 1940- *WhoWest 92*
**Anderson,** Gordon Frederick 1934- *AmMWSc 92*
**Anderson,** Gordon Louis 1947- *WhoRel 92*
**Anderson,** Gordon MacKenzie 1932- *WhoFI 92, WhoWest 92*
**Anderson,** Gordon Sutherland 1934- *WhoWest 92*
**Anderson,** Gordon Wood 1936- *AmMWSc 92*
**Anderson,** Grady Lee 1931- *WhoBlA 92*
**Anderson,** Grant Allan 1963- *WhoWest 92*
**Anderson,** Granville Scott 1947- *WhoBlA 92*
**Anderson,** Gregg I. 1949- *WhoAmL 92*
**Anderson,** Gregg Winston 1953- *WhoRel 92*
**Anderson,** Gregor Munro 1932- *AmMWSc 92*
**Anderson,** Gregory 1946- *ConAu 135*
**Anderson,** Gregory Joseph 1944- *AmMWSc 92*
**Anderson,** Gregory Martin 1955- *WhoRel 92*
**Anderson,** Gregory Shane 1947- *WhoFI 92*
**Anderson,** Gregory Wayne 1964- *WhoBlA 92*
**Anderson,** Grieg Lowell 1943- *WhoFI 92*
**Anderson,** Gwen Adele 1930- *WhoAmP 91*
**Anderson,** H. John 1915- *Who 92*

**Anderson,** H. Michael 1957- *WhoRel 92*
**Anderson,** Hamilton Holland *AmMWSc 92*
**Anderson,** Harlan John 1926- *AmMWSc 92*
**Anderson,** Harlan U 1935- *AmMWSc 92*
**Anderson,** Harold 1939- *WhoBlA 92*
**Anderson,** Harold D 1940- *AmMWSc 92*
**Anderson,** Harold David 1923- *IntWW 91*
**Anderson,** Harold J. 1909- *WhoMW 92*
**Anderson,** Harold J 1928- *AmMWSc 92*
**Anderson,** Harold James 1934- *WhoRel 92*
**Anderson,** Harold Paul 1946- *WhoWest 92*
**Anderson,** Harrison Clarke 1932- *AmMWSc 92*
**Anderson,** Harry *WhoEnt 92*
**Anderson,** Harry 1952- *IntMPA 92*
**Anderson,** Harry Alan 1945- *WhoIns 92*
**Anderson,** Harvey L 1927- *AmMWSc 92*
**Anderson,** Helen Louise 1941- *WhoBlA 92*
**Anderson,** Henry J *WhoIns 92*
**Anderson,** Henry L. N. 1934- *WhoBlA 92*
**Anderson,** Henry Lee Norman 1934- *WhoWest 92*
**Anderson,** Henry Walter 1911- *AmMWSc 92*
**Anderson,** Herbert E. 1916- *WhoRel 92*
**Anderson,** Herbert Godwin, Jr 1931- *AmMWSc 92*
**Anderson,** Herbert Hale 1913- *AmMWSc 92*
**Anderson,** Herbert L 1914- *AmMWSc 92*
**Anderson,** Herbert Rudolph, Jr 1920- *AmMWSc 92*
**Anderson,** Herman Leroy *WhoRel 92*
**Anderson,** Herschel Vincent 1932- *WhoWest 92*
**Anderson,** Holly L. 1946- *WhoWest 92*
**Anderson,** Homer Lynn 1935- *WhoRel 92*
**Anderson,** Howard Alvin, Jr. 1920- *WhoEnt 92*
**Anderson,** Howard Benjamin 1914- *AmMWSc 92*
**Anderson,** Howard N. 1929- *WhoIns 92*
**Anderson,** Howard Palmer 1915- *WhoAmP 91*
**Anderson,** Howard W 1934- *AmMWSc 92*
**Anderson,** Hugh 1920- *Who 92*
**Anderson,** Hugh David 1951- *WhoRel 92*
**Anderson,** Hugh John 1926- *AmMWSc 92*
**Anderson,** Hugh Riddell 1932- *AmMWSc 92*
**Anderson,** Hugh Verity 1921- *AmMWSc 92*
**Anderson,** Iain *Who 92*
**Anderson,** Ingrid 1930- *AmMWSc 92*
**Anderson,** Iris Anita 1930- *WhoWest 92*
**Anderson,** Irvin Charles 1928- *AmMWSc 92*
**Anderson,** Irvin Neal 1923- *WhoAmP 91*
**Anderson,** Irvine Henry 1928- *WhoMW 92*
**Anderson,** Irving Edward, Jr. 1946- *WhoMW 92*
**Anderson,** J 1929- *AmMWSc 92*
**Anderson,** J Edward *AmMWSc 92*
**Anderson,** J. Mathew 1956- *WhoAmL 92*
**Anderson,** J. Morris 1936- *WhoBlA 92*
**Anderson,** J Robert 1934- *AmMWSc 92*
**Anderson,** J. Trent 1939- *WhoAmL 92*
**Anderson,** J. Wayne 1947- *IntMPA 92*
**Anderson,** Jack *DrAPF 91*
**Anderson,** Jack 1922- *FacFETw, WrDr 92*
**Anderson,** Jack Joe 1928- *WhoWest 92*
**Anderson,** Jack Leonard 1936- *WhoFI 92*
**Anderson,** Jacqueline Jones 1935- *WhoBlA 92*
**Anderson,** James *WrDr 92*
**Anderson,** James Alan 1948- *WhoBlA 92*
**Anderson,** James Albin 1936- *WhoRel 92*
**Anderson,** James B 1935- *AmMWSc 92*
**Anderson,** James Bell 1886-1938 *TwCPaSc*
**Anderson,** James Buell 1912- *WhoAmL 92*
**Anderson,** James Douglas 1948- *WhoFI 92*
**Anderson,** James E 1938- *AmMWSc 92*
**Anderson,** James Earl 1954- *WhoFI 92*
**Anderson,** James Edward 1926- *AmMWSc 92*
**Anderson,** James Frazer Gillan 1929- *Who 92*
**Anderson,** James Frederick 1927- *WhoRel 92*
**Anderson,** James G. 1936- *WrDr 92*
**Anderson,** James Gerard 1924- *AmMWSc 92, WhoMW 92*
**Anderson,** James Gerard 1944- *WhoMW 92*
**Anderson,** James Howard 1944- *AmMWSc 92*
**Anderson,** James Jay 1946- *AmMWSc 92*
**Anderson,** James L. 1931- *WhoFI 92*
**Anderson,** James L. 1943- *WhoIns 92*
**Anderson,** James Leroy 1926- *AmMWSc 92*
**Anderson,** James Leroy 1946- *AmMWSc 92*
**Anderson,** James Martin 1947- *WhoWest 92*
**Anderson,** James Michael 1943- *WhoWest 92*
**Anderson,** James Michael 1944- *WhoWest 92*
**Anderson,** James Milton 1941- *WhoFI 92*
**Anderson,** James Noel 1951- *WhoEnt 92*
**Anderson,** James Norman 1908- *IntAu&W 91, IntWW 91, Who 92*
**Anderson,** James R., Jr. 1922- *WhoBlA 92*
**Anderson,** James T 1921- *AmMWSc 92*
**Anderson,** James Wingo 1936- *AmMWSc 92*
**Anderson,** Jan Lee 1937- *WhoAmP 91*
**Anderson,** Janelle Marie 1954- *WhoFI 92*
**Anderson,** Janet Alm 1952- *WhoWest 92*
**Anderson,** Janice Linn 1943- *WhoFI 92*
**Anderson,** Janice Scott 1949- *WhoBlA 92*
**Anderson,** Jay Ennis 1937- *AmMWSc 92*
**Anderson,** Jay LaMar 1931- *AmMWSc 92*
**Anderson,** Jay Martin 1939- *AmMWSc 92*
**Anderson,** Jay Oscar 1921- *AmMWSc 92*
**Anderson,** Jay Rosamond 1953- *WhoBlA 92*
**Anderson,** Jean *DrAPF 91*
**Anderson,** Jean Blanche 1940- *WhoWest 92*
**Anderson,** Jeannie Ellen 1959- *WhoRel 92*
**Anderson,** Jeffery Stuart 1962- *WhoMW 92*
**Anderson,** Jeffery Wade 1963- *WhoFI 92*
**Anderson,** Jeffrey Chaddock 1950- *WhoMW 92*
**Anderson,** Jeffrey John 1953- *AmMWSc 92*
**Anderson,** Jeffrey L 1958- *WhoAmP 91*
**Anderson,** Jeffrey Lynn 1955- *WhoMW 92*
**Anderson,** Jeorgia 1954- *WhoEnt 92*
**Anderson,** Jerald Clayton 1934- *WhoAmP 91*
**Anderson,** Jerome Murphy 1957- *WhoRel 92*
**Anderson,** Jerry Allen 1947- *WhoFI 92*
**Anderson,** Jerry Lee 1941- *WhoEnt 92*
**Anderson,** Jerry William, Jr. 1926- *WhoFI 92, WhoMW 92*
**Anderson,** Jesse Lemond 1966- *WhoBlA 92*
**Anderson,** Jessica *IntAu&W 91, WrDr 92*
**Anderson,** Jessica 1916- *ConNov 91*
**Anderson,** Jim 1937- *ConAu 134*
**Anderson,** Joan *NewYTBS 91 [port]*
**Anderson,** Joe D. 1942- *WhoAmL 92*
**Anderson,** Joe Lewis, Sr. 1948- *WhoBlA 92*
**Anderson,** John 1909- *WrDr 92*
**Anderson,** John 1921- *Who 92*
**Anderson,** John 1922- *ConTFT 9, FacFETw*
**Anderson,** John 1936- *Who 92*
**Anderson,** John A. 1937- *WhoBlA 92*
**Anderson,** John Alfred, III 1946- *WhoAmL 92*
**Anderson,** John Allan Dalrymple 1926- *Who 92*
**Anderson,** John Ansel 1903- *AmMWSc 92*
**Anderson,** John Arthur 1932- *AmMWSc 92*
**Anderson,** John B 1922- *WhoAmP 91, WrDr 92*
**Anderson,** John B 1944- *AmMWSc 92*
**Anderson,** John Bayard 1922- *AmPolLe, IntWW 91*
**Anderson,** John C., Jr. 1917- *WhoBlA 92*
**Anderson,** John D 1930- *AmMWSc 92*
**Anderson,** John Denton 1912- *AmMWSc 92*
**Anderson,** John Donald 1935- *AmMWSc 92*
**Anderson,** John E. 1961- *WhoAmL 92*
**Anderson,** John Edward 1927- *AmMWSc 92*
**Anderson,** John Edward 1953- *WhoWest 92*
**Anderson,** John Evelyn 1916- *Who 92*
**Anderson,** John Filmore 1942- *WhoIns 92*
**Anderson,** John Firth 1928- *WhoRel 92*
**Anderson,** John Francis 1936- *AmMWSc 92*
**Anderson,** John Fredric 1936- *AmMWSc 92*
**Anderson,** John G 1922- *AmMWSc 92*
**Anderson,** John Graeme 1927- *Who 92*
**Anderson,** John Gregg 1948- *AmMWSc 92*
**Anderson,** John H, Jr 1916- *WhoAmP 91*
**Anderson,** John Henry 1936- *WhoAmP 91*
**Anderson,** John Henry 1950- *WhoFI 92*
**Anderson,** John Hope 1912- *WhoAmP 91*
**Anderson,** John Howard 1924- *AmMWSc 92*
**Anderson,** John Jerome 1930- *AmMWSc 92*
**Anderson,** John Joseph Baxter 1934- *AmMWSc 92*
**Anderson,** John Kerby 1951- *WhoRel 92*
**Anderson,** John Kinloch 1924- *Who 92*
**Anderson,** John L 1905- *ConAu 35NR*
**Anderson,** John Leonard 1945- *AmMWSc 92*
**Anderson,** John M 1924- *AmMWSc 92*
**Anderson,** John MacKenzie 1938- *WhoAmL 92*
**Anderson,** John Melvin 1946- *WhoAmP 91*
**Anderson,** John Muir 1914- *Who 92*
**Anderson,** John Murray 1926- *AmMWSc 92*
**Anderson,** John Neil 1922- *Who 92*
**Anderson,** John Nicholas 1946- *AmMWSc 92*
**Anderson,** John Norton 1937- *AmMWSc 92*
**Anderson,** John P 1939- *AmMWSc 92*
**Anderson,** John R. 1922- *WhoEnt 92*
**Anderson,** John R 1928- *AmMWSc 92*
**Anderson,** John Richard 1931- *AmMWSc 92*
**Anderson,** John Robert 1936- *WhoFI 92*
**Anderson,** John Roger *WhoRel 92*
**Anderson,** John Russell 1918- *Who 92*
**Anderson,** John Seymour 1936- *AmMWSc 92*
**Anderson,** John Stuart d1990 *Who 92N*
**Anderson,** John Stuart 1908- *IntWW 91*
**Anderson,** John Thomas 1930- *WhoAmL 92*
**Anderson,** John Thomas 1945- *AmMWSc 92*
**Anderson,** John Walberg 1927- *AmMWSc 92*
**Anderson,** John William 1934- *WhoAmP 91*
**Anderson,** John William 1953- *WhoEnt 92*
**Anderson,** JoLorene Miller Parker 1916- *WhoRel 92*
**Anderson,** Jon *DrAPF 91*
**Anderson,** Jon 1936- *ConAu 133*
**Anderson,** Jon 1940- *ConPo 91, WrDr 92*
**Anderson,** Jonathan Walfred 1957- *WhoAmL 92*
**Anderson,** Jonathan William 1955- *WhoRel 92*
**Anderson,** Jonpatrick Schuyler 1951- *WhoRel 92, WhoWest 92*
**Anderson,** Joseph F, Jr 1949- *WhoAmP 91*
**Anderson,** Joseph Fletcher, Jr. 1949- *WhoAmL 92*
**Anderson,** Joseph Manley 1943- *WhoFI 92*
**Anderson,** Josephine *Who 92*
**Anderson,** Josephine Margaret 1959- *WhoWest 92*
**Anderson,** Judith 1898- *IntMPA 92, IntWW 91, Who 92*
**Anderson,** Judith Wyckoff 1946- *WhoMW 92*
**Anderson,** Judson Truett 1933- *WhoWest 92*
**Anderson,** Julian Anthony 1938- *Who 92*
**Anderson,** Julianne E. 1949- *WhoMW 92*
**Anderson,** Julius Horne, Jr 1939- *AmMWSc 92*
**Anderson,** June 1952- *CurBio 91 [port]*
**Anderson,** Kari Kay 1940- *WhoMW 92*
**Anderson,** Karl E 1940- *AmMWSc 92*
**Anderson,** Karl Richard 1917- *WhoFI 92, WhoWest 92*
**Anderson,** Karl Stephen 1933- *WhoMW 92*
**Anderson,** Kathleen Gay 1950- *WhoAmL 92, WhoWest 92*
**Anderson,** Kathleen Wiley 1932- *WhoBlA 92*
**Anderson,** Kathryn Mae 1959- *WhoEnt 92*
**Anderson,** Keith Phillips 1919- *AmMWSc 92*
**Anderson,** Keith Russell 1955- *WhoAmP 91*
**Anderson,** Kelby John 1944- *AmMWSc 92*
**Anderson,** Kelly Elizabeth 1957- *WhoFI 92, WhoWest 92*
**Anderson,** Ken *DrAPF 91*
**Anderson,** Ken S. 1941- *WhoFI 92*
**Anderson,** Kenneth 1906- *Who 92*
**Anderson,** Kenneth Arthur 1942- *WhoRel 92*
**Anderson,** Kenneth Charles 1947- *WhoFI 92, WhoWest 92*
**Anderson,** Kenneth Ellsworth 1914- *AmMWSc 92*
**Anderson,** Kenneth Fritz 1928- *WhoEnt 92*
**Anderson,** Kenneth Jeffery 1954- *WhoWest 92*
**Anderson,** Kenneth Norman 1921- *IntAu&W 91, WrDr 92*
**Anderson,** Kenneth Richard 1936- *WhoBlA 92*
**Anderson,** Kenneth Verle 1938- *AmMWSc 92*
**Anderson,** Kenneth Wayne 1940- *WhoAmL 92*
**Anderson,** Kenning M 1933- *AmMWSc 92*
**Anderson,** Kenny *NewYTBS 91*
**Anderson,** Kent Taylor 1953- *WhoAmL 92, WhoFI 92*
**Anderson,** Kevin 1912- *Who 92*
**Anderson,** Kevin 1948- *WhoMW 92*
**Anderson,** Kevin 1960- *IntMPA 92*
**Anderson,** Kim Elizabeth 1960- *WhoMW 92*
**Anderson,** Kimball Richard 1952- *WhoAmL 92*
**Anderson,** Kimberly Muriel 1960- *WhoMW 92*
**Anderson,** Kinsey Amor 1926- *AmMWSc 92*
**Anderson,** Kristian Eric 1958- *WhoAmL 92*
**Anderson,** Kurt Michael 1953- *WhoAmL 92*
**Anderson,** L K 1935- *AmMWSc 92*
**Anderson,** LaCount Louis, III 1952- *WhoRel 92*
**Anderson,** Larrey 1953- *WhoAmP 91*
**Anderson,** Larry A 1945- *AmMWSc 92*
**Anderson,** Larry Bernard 1937- *AmMWSc 92*
**Anderson,** Larry Douglas 1947- *AmMWSc 92*
**Anderson,** Larry Ernest 1943- *AmMWSc 92, WhoWest 92*
**Anderson,** Larry Gene 1946- *AmMWSc 92*
**Anderson,** Larry John 1944- *WhoMW 92*
**Anderson,** Larry Robert 1960- *WhoEnt 92*
**Anderson,** Lars William James 1945- *AmMWSc 92*
**Anderson,** Laurence Ernest 1914- *WhoRel 92*
**Anderson,** Laurens 1920- *AmMWSc 92*
**Anderson,** Lauretta Mae 1936- *WhoMW 92*
**Anderson,** Lauri Arvid 1942- *WhoMW 92*
**Anderson,** Laurie 1947- *IntWW 91, NewAmDM, WorArt 1980 [port]*
**Anderson,** Lawrence Sven 1944- *AmMWSc 92*
**Anderson,** Lea E. 1954- *WhoAmL 92*
**Anderson,** Leif David 1963- *WhoRel 92*
**Anderson,** Leigh 1949- *AmMWSc 92*
**Anderson,** Leith Charles 1944- *WhoRel 92*
**Anderson,** Leon H. 1928- *WhoBlA 92*
**Anderson,** Leonard 1945- *WhoAmP 91*
**Anderson,** Leonard Mahlon 1944- *AmMWSc 92*
**Anderson,** Leone Castell 1923- *IntAu&W 91*
**Anderson,** Leroy 1908-1975 *NewAmDM*
**Anderson,** Lewis L 1935- *AmMWSc 92*
**Anderson,** Linda Carol 1955- *WhoAmL 92*
**Anderson,** Linda Cook 1943- *WhoAmP 91*
**Anderson,** Lindsay 1923- *FacFETw, IntDcF 2-2 [port], IntMPA 92, Who 92*
**Anderson,** Lindsay Gordon 1923- *IntWW 91, WhoEnt 92*
**Anderson,** Lloyd Crane 1947- *WhoAmL 92*
**Anderson,** Lloyd James 1917- *AmMWSc 92*
**Anderson,** Lloyd L 1933- *AmMWSc 92*
**Anderson,** Lloyd Vincent 1943- *WhoAmL 92*
**Anderson,** Loni 1945?- *ConTFT 9*
**Anderson,** Loni 1946- *IntMPA 92*
**Anderson,** Loni Kaye 1946- *WhoEnt 92*
**Anderson,** Lonzo *ConAu 35NR*
**Anderson,** Loran C 1936- *AmMWSc 92*
**Anderson,** Loren D *WhoAmP 91*
**Anderson,** Louie *WhoEnt 92*
**Anderson,** Louis Wilmer 1933- *AmMWSc 92*
**Anderson,** Louise Eleanor 1934- *AmMWSc 92*
**Anderson,** Louise Payne 1923- *WhoBlA 92*
**Anderson,** Louise Stout 1952- *WhoWest 92*
**Anderson,** Lowell Leonard 1930- *AmMWSc 92*
**Anderson,** Lowell Ray 1934- *AmMWSc 92*
**Anderson,** Lucia Lewis 1922- *AmMWSc 92*
**Anderson,** Lucy Macdonald 1942- *AmMWSc 92*
**Anderson,** Luke 1927- *WhoRel 92*
**Anderson,** Lyle Arthur 1931- *WhoFI 92*
**Anderson,** Lyman Frank 1926- *WhoAmP 91*
**Anderson,** Lynn *WhoEnt 92*
**Anderson,** Lynn 1947- *WhoEnt 92*
**Anderson,** Mabel M 1924- *WhoAmP 91*
**Anderson,** Madeline *ReelWom, WhoBlA 92*
**Anderson,** Maggie *DrAPF 91*
**Anderson,** Malachi *WhoAmP 91*
**Anderson,** Malcolm 1934- *WrDr 92*
**Anderson,** Malcolm Playfair 1879-1919 *BiInAmS*
**Anderson,** Marbury Earl 1923- *WhoRel 92*
**Anderson,** Marc Richard 1954- *WhoWest 92*
**Anderson,** Marcellus J., Sr. 1908- *WhoBlA 92*
**Anderson,** Margaret Caughman 1936- *WhoRel 92*
**Anderson,** Margret Elizabeth 1949- *WhoAmL 92*
**Anderson,** Marian 1900?- *NotBlAW 92 [port]*
**Anderson,** Marian 1902- *ConBlB 2 [port], FacFETw [port], IntWW 91, NewAmDM, RComAH, Who 92, WhoBlA 92*

Anderson, Marilyn Nelle 1942- *WhoWest 92*
Anderson, Marilyn P *AmMWSc 92*
Anderson, Marion C 1926- *AmMWSc 92*
Anderson, Marjo Elizabeth 1954- *WhoRel 92*
Anderson, Marjorie *WhoBlA 92*
Anderson, Marjorie Eleanor Amado 1939- *WhoBlA 92*
Anderson, Marjorie Elizabeth *AmMWSc 92*
Anderson, Mark *DrAPF 91*
Anderson, Mark Alan 1960- *WhoEnt 92*
Anderson, Mark Alexander 1953- *WhoAmL 92, WhoWest 92*
Anderson, Mark Allen 1962- *WhoRel 92*
Anderson, Mark Andrew 1952- *WhoWest 92*
Anderson, Mark Bo 1955- *WhoFI 92*
Anderson, Mark Eugene 1952- *WhoWest 92*
Anderson, Mark Magnus 1933- *WhoRel 92*
Anderson, Mark Robert 1951- *WhoWest 92*
Anderson, Mark T. 1953- *WhoFI 92*
Anderson, Marlin Dean 1934- *AmMWSc 92*
Anderson, Marshall W *AmMWSc 92*
Anderson, Martha 1953- *WhoMW 92*
Anderson, Martin Carl 1936- *WhoAmP 91*
Anderson, Marva Jean 1945- *WhoBlA 92*
Anderson, Marvin David 1938- *AmMWSc 92*
Anderson, Mary Ann 1946- *WhoWest 92*
Anderson, Mary Elizabeth *WhoBlA 92*
Anderson, Mary Elizabeth 1956- *AmMWSc 92*
Anderson, Mary Loucile 1940- *AmMWSc 92*
Anderson, Mary Mackenzie *Who 92*
Anderson, Mary Margaret 1932- *Who 92*
Anderson, Mary Margaret 1944- *WhoRel 92*
Anderson, Mary Pikul 1948- *AmMWSc 92*
Anderson, Mary Ruth 1939- *AmMWSc 92*
Anderson, Matthew Smith 1922- *IntAu&W 91, IntWW 91, WrDr 92*
Anderson, Mauritz Gunnar 1918- *AmMWSc 92*
Anderson, Max Elliot 1946- *WhoEnt 92, WhoMW 92*
Anderson, Max Leroy 1947- *WhoMW 92*
Anderson, Maxwell 1888-1959 *BenetAL 91, FacFETw*
Anderson, McKenny Willis 1943- *WhoAmP 91*
Anderson, Mel 1928- *WhoRel 92*
Anderson, Melissa Sue 1962- *IntMPA 92*
Anderson, Melody *WhoEnt 92*
Anderson, Melvern 1929- *WhoIns 92*
Anderson, Melvin Joseph 1927- *AmMWSc 92*
Anderson, Melvin Keith 1925- *WhoWest 92*
Anderson, Melvin Lee 1928- *AmMWSc 92, WhoMW 92*
Anderson, Melvin Robert 1925- *WhoRel 92*
Anderson, Melvin W 1937- *AmMWSc 92*
Anderson, Michael *DrAPF 91*
Anderson, Michael 1920- *IntMPA 92, IntWW 91*
Anderson, Michael 1942- *Who 92*
Anderson, Michael, Jr. 1943- *IntMPA 92*
Anderson, Michael George 1951- *WhoWest 92*
Anderson, Michael Granville Eric 1948- *WhoMW 92*
Anderson, Michael Joseph 1920- *WhoEnt 92*
Anderson, Michael L. 1958- *WhoFI 92*
Anderson, Michael Robert 1953- *WhoWest 92*
Anderson, Michael Wayne 1942- *WhoBlA 92*
Anderson, Mignon Holland *DrAPF 91*
Anderson, Milada Filko 1922- *WhoFI 92*
Anderson, Mildred White 1922- *WhoWest 92*
Anderson, Miles Edward 1926- *AmMWSc 92*
Anderson, Milo Vernette 1924- *AmMWSc 92*
Anderson, Milton Andrew 1927- *WhoMW 92*
Anderson, Milton Merrill 1943- *AmMWSc 92*
Anderson, Mitchell 1963- *WhoWest 92*
Anderson, Monroe 1947- *WhoBlA 92*
Anderson, Morris *WhoAmP 91*
Anderson, Morris Lynn 1951- *WhoRel 92*
Anderson, Moses B. *WhoBlA 92*
Anderson, Moses B. 1928- *WhoRel 92*
Anderson, Myron Kent 1950- *WhoAmL 92*
Anderson, N. Christian, III 1950- *WhoWest 92*
Anderson, Nathalie F. *DrAPF 91*
Anderson, Neal 1964- *WhoMW 92*
Anderson, Ned, Sr. 1943- *WhoWest 92*
Anderson, Neil *WhoEnt 92*
Anderson, Neil 1927- *Who 92*
Anderson, Neil Albert 1928- *AmMWSc 92*
Anderson, Neil Freeman 1954- *WhoRel 92*
Anderson, Neil Owen 1935- *AmMWSc 92*
Anderson, Neil Vincent 1933- *AmMWSc 92*
Anderson, Nels A, Jr 1939- *WhoAmP 91*
Anderson, Nels Carl, Jr 1936- *AmMWSc 92*
Anderson, Nicholas Charles 1953- *WhoBlA 92*
Anderson, Nick 1968- *WhoBlA 92*
Anderson, Norma V 1932- *WhoAmP 91*
Anderson, Norman *Who 92*
Anderson, Norman 1908- *WrDr 92*
Anderson, Norman 1932- *WhoAmP 91*
Anderson, Norman Foxen 1956- *WhoFI 92*
Anderson, Norman G. 1913- *ConAu 133*
Anderson, Norman Gulack 1919- *AmMWSc 92*
Anderson, Norman Herbert 1933- *AmMWSc 92*
Anderson, Norman Leigh 1949- *AmMWSc 92*
Anderson, Norman Robert 1941- *WhoWest 92*
Anderson, Norman Roderick 1921- *AmMWSc 92*
Anderson, O Roger 1937- *AmMWSc 92*
Anderson, Oddie 1937- *WhoBlA 92*
Anderson, Odin Waldemar 1914- *IntWW 91, WrDr 92*
Anderson, Olive Ruth 1926- *IntAu&W 91, IntWW 91, WrDr 92*
Anderson, Oliver Duncan 1940- *WhoFI 92*
Anderson, Oliver John 1928- *WhoFI 92*
Anderson, Olivo Margaret 1941- *AmMWSc 92*
Anderson, Olof W *ScFEYrs*
Anderson, Ora Sterling 1931- *WhoBlA 92*
Anderson, Oren P 1942- *AmMWSc 92*
Anderson, Orson Lamar 1924- *AmMWSc 92*
Anderson, Oscar Emmett 1916- *AmMWSc 92*
Anderson, Otis Lee, Jr. 1933- *WhoRel 92*
Anderson, Ottis Jerome 1957- *WhoBlA 92*
Anderson, Owen Conrad 1913- *WhoFI 92*
Anderson, Owen Thomas 1931- *AmMWSc 92*
Anderson, Pamela Jo 1951- *WhoAmL 92*
Anderson, Patricia Alice 1952- *WhoMW 92*
Anderson, Patricia Hebert 1945- *WhoBlA 92*
Anderson, Patricia Sue 1940- *WhoAmP 91*
Anderson, Patrick 1917-1979 *BenetAL 91*
Anderson, Patrick Michael 1953- *WhoWest 92*
Anderson, Patrick Mores 1954- *WhoAmL 92*
Anderson, Paul Dean 1940- *AmMWSc 92*
Anderson, Paul Dean 1946- *WhoMW 92*
Anderson, Paul Irving 1935- *WhoFI 92*
Anderson, Paul J 1925- *AmMWSc 92*
Anderson, Paul Knight 1927- *AmMWSc 92*
Anderson, Paul LeRoy 1935- *AmMWSc 92*
Anderson, Paul M 1938- *AmMWSc 92*
Anderson, Paul Maurice 1926- *AmMWSc 92*
Anderson, Paul Milton 1927- *AmMWSc 92*
Anderson, Paul Nathaniel 1937- *AmMWSc 92, WhoWest 92*
Anderson, Paul Simon 1943- *WhoMW 92*
Anderson, Pearl Corina 1898-1990 *WhoBlA 92N*
Anderson, Pearl G. 1950- *WhoBlA 92*
Anderson, Peer L. 1944- *WhoAmL 92*
Anderson, Peggy 1938- *WrDr 92*
Anderson, Peter Alexander Vallance 1951- *AmMWSc 92*
Anderson, Peter Avery 1942- *WhoAmL 92*
Anderson, Peter David 1940- *WhoAmP 91*
Anderson, Peter Glennie 1954- *AmMWSc 92*
Anderson, Peter Gordon 1940- *AmMWSc 92*
Anderson, Philip Carr 1930- *AmMWSc 92*
Anderson, Philip Pendleton, Jr. 1910- *WhoMW 92*
Anderson, Philip Sidney 1935- *WhoAmL 92*
Anderson, Philip W. 1923- *IntWW 91*
Anderson, Philip Warren 1923- *AmMWSc 92, FacFETw, Who 92, WhoFI 92, WhoNob 90*
Anderson, Phyllis Wynn *WhoEnt 92*
Anderson, Polly Gordon 1934- *WhoWest 92*
Anderson, Porter 1953- *WhoEnt 92*
Anderson, Poul *DrAPF 91*
Anderson, Poul 1926- *ConAu 34NR, TwCSFW 91, WrDr 92*
Anderson, Poul William 1926- *IntAu&W 91*
Anderson, Priscilla B 1935- *WhoAmP 91*
Anderson, Quentin 1912- *IntAu&W 91, WrDr 92*
Anderson, R F V 1943- *AmMWSc 92*
Anderson, R L 1927- *AmMWSc 92*
Anderson, R Lanier, III *WhoAmP 91*
Anderson, R M, Jr 1939- *AmMWSc 92*
Anderson, Rachel 1943- *IntAu&W 91, WrDr 92*
Anderson, Ralph *WhoAmP 91*
Anderson, Ralph Parker *ScFEYrs*
Anderson, Ralph Robert 1932- *AmMWSc 92*
Anderson, Randall Keith 1952- *WhoAmL 92*
Anderson, Randolph Thomas 1958- *WhoMW 92*
Anderson, Randy Robert 1963- *WhoWest 92*
Anderson, Rasmus B 1846-1936 *DcAmImH*
Anderson, Ray 1952- *ConMus 7 [port]*
Anderson, Ray Charles 1954- *WhoBlA 92*
Anderson, Ray Harold 1915- *AmMWSc 92*
Anderson, Raymond Charles 1958- *WhoWest 92*
Anderson, Raymond Ferdinand 1905- *WhoWest 92*
Anderson, Raymond Hartwell, Jr. 1932- *WhoWest 92*
Anderson, Raymond Kenneth 1928- *AmMWSc 92*
Anderson, Rebecca Jane 1949- *AmMWSc 92*
Anderson, Regina M. 1901- *NotBlAW 92*
Anderson, Reginald 1921- *Who 92*
Anderson, Reid Bryce 1949- *WhoEnt 92*
Anderson, Reuben V. 1942- *WhoAmL 92, WhoAmP 91*
Anderson, Reuben Vincent 1942- *WhoBlA 92*
Anderson, Rex Herbert, Jr. 1954- *WhoFI 92*
Anderson, Rhonda Jane 1961- *WhoMW 92*
Anderson, Richard 1926- *IntMPA 92*
Anderson, Richard Alan 1930- *AmMWSc 92*
Anderson, Richard Allen 1946- *AmMWSc 92*
Anderson, Richard Charles 1930- *AmMWSc 92*
Anderson, Richard Davis 1922- *AmMWSc 92*
Anderson, Richard Dean 1950- *IntMPA 92*
Anderson, Richard Ernest 1926- *WhoWest 92*
Anderson, Richard Ernest 1945- *AmMWSc 92, WhoWest 92*
Anderson, Richard Gilpin Wood 1940- *AmMWSc 92*
Anderson, Richard Gordon 1949- *WhoFI 92*
Anderson, Richard Gregory 1946- *AmMWSc 92*
Anderson, Richard H 1926- *WhoAmP 91*
Anderson, Richard John 1938- *AmMWSc 92*
Anderson, Richard L 1915- *AmMWSc 92*
Anderson, Richard Lee 1933- *AmMWSc 92*
Anderson, Richard Lee 1945- *AmMWSc 92*
Anderson, Richard Lloyd 1926- *WrDr 92*
Anderson, Richard Louis 1935- *AmMWSc 92*
Anderson, Richard M 1949- *WhoAmP 91*
Anderson, Richard Norman 1926- *WhoEnt 92, WhoWest 92*
Anderson, Richard Orr 1929- *AmMWSc 92*
Anderson, Richard Paul 1929- *WhoFI 92*
Anderson, Richard Paul 1946- *WhoAmP 91*
Anderson, Richard R 1944- *WhoAmP 91*
Anderson, Richard Sanford 1929- *WhoRel 92*
Anderson, Richmond K 1907- *AmMWSc 92*
Anderson, Robbin Colyer 1914- *AmMWSc 92*
Anderson, Robert 1917- *Who 92, WrDr 92*
Anderson, Robert 1920- *IntWW 91, WhoFI 92, WhoWest 92*
Anderson, Robert 1922- *WhoAmP 91*
Anderson, Robert Alan 1942- *AmMWSc 92*
Anderson, Robert Arthur 1945- *WhoWest 92*
Anderson, Robert Authur 1932- *AmMWSc 92*
Anderson, Robert Bernhard 1917- *WhoEnt 92*
Anderson, Robert Bruce 1956- *WhoAmL 92*
Anderson, Robert Bryce 1928- *WhoMW 92*
Anderson, Robert Burton 1833-1899 *DcNCBi 1*
Anderson, Robert C. 1945- *WhoIns 92*
Anderson, Robert Campbell, Jr. 1864-1955 *DcNCBi 1*
Anderson, Robert Christian 1918- *AmMWSc 92*
Anderson, Robert Clark 1926- *AmMWSc 92*
Anderson, Robert Clarke 1911- *AmMWSc 92*
Anderson, Robert Curtis 1941- *AmMWSc 92*
Anderson, Robert Dennis 1947- *WhoAmL 92*
Anderson, Robert E 1919- *AmMWSc 92*
Anderson, Robert E 1926- *AmMWSc 92*
Anderson, Robert E 1940- *AmMWSc 92*
Anderson, Robert Edwin 1931- *AmMWSc 92*
Anderson, Robert Emra 1924- *AmMWSc 92*
Anderson, Robert Ernest 1926- *WhoWest 92*
Anderson, Robert Floyd 1938- *WhoWest 92*
Anderson, Robert Geoffrey William 1944- *Who 92*
Anderson, Robert Glenn 1924- *AmMWSc 92*
Anderson, Robert Gordon 1926- *AmMWSc 92*
Anderson, Robert Gregg 1928- *WhoFI 92*
Anderson, Robert Henry 1942- *Who 92*
Anderson, Robert Hunt 1924- *AmMWSc 92*
Anderson, Robert Jeffries, Jr. 1954- *WhoRel 92*
Anderson, Robert Kieth 1955- *WhoMW 92*
Anderson, Robert L 1932- *AmMWSc 92*
Anderson, Robert L. 1940- *WhoBlA 92*
Anderson, Robert Lanier, III 1936- *WhoAmL 92*
Anderson, Robert LaZelle 1932- *WhoRel 92*
Anderson, Robert Leonard 1923- *WhoAmL 92*
Anderson, Robert Lester 1933- *AmMWSc 92*
Anderson, Robert Lewis *WhoAmP 91*
Anderson, Robert Lewis 1933- *AmMWSc 92*
Anderson, Robert Loyd 1945- *WhoWest 92*
Anderson, Robert Marshall 1933- *WhoRel 92*
Anderson, Robert Morris, Jr. 1939- *WhoFI 92*
Anderson, Robert Neil 1933- *AmMWSc 92*
Anderson, Robert Newman 1952- *WhoEnt 92*
Anderson, Robert Orville 1917- *IntWW 91, WhoAmP 91, WhoFI 92, WhoWest 92*
Anderson, Robert Philip 1950- *AmMWSc 92*
Anderson, Robert Simpers 1939- *AmMWSc 92*
Anderson, Robert Spencer 1922- *AmMWSc 92*
Anderson, Robert T 1945- *WhoAmP 91*
Anderson, Robert Theodore 1934- *WhoEnt 92*
Anderson, Robert Woodruff 1917- *BenetAL 91, IntAu&W 91, WhoEnt 92*
Anderson, Roberta Joan 1943- *WhoEnt 92*
Anderson, Roger Arthur 1935- *AmMWSc 92*
Anderson, Roger Clark 1941- *AmMWSc 92*
Anderson, Roger E. 1921- *IntWW 91*
Anderson, Roger E 1930- *AmMWSc 92*
Anderson, Roger Fabian 1914- *AmMWSc 92*
Anderson, Roger Gordon 1937- *WhoRel 92*
Anderson, Roger Harris 1930- *AmMWSc 92*
Anderson, Roger Lynn 1964- *WhoFI 92*
Anderson, Roger W 1924- *AmMWSc 92*
Anderson, Roger W 1943- *AmMWSc 92*
Anderson, Roger William 1951- *WhoAmL 92*
Anderson, Roger William, Jr. 1948- *WhoRel 92*
Anderson, Roger Yates 1927- *AmMWSc 92*
Anderson, Roland Carl 1934- *AmMWSc 92*
Anderson, Ron *WhoFI 92*
Anderson, Ronald A 1944- *WhoAmP 91*
Anderson, Ronald Anderson 1911- *WhoAmL 92*
Anderson, Ronald C. 1942- *WhoIns 92*
Anderson, Ronald E 1941- *AmMWSc 92*

**Anderson**, Ronald Edward 1948- *WhoBlA 92*
**Anderson**, Ronald Eugene 1920- *AmMWSc 92*
**Anderson**, Ronald G. 1930- *WhoMW 92*
**Anderson**, Ronald G 1949- *WhoAmP 91*
**Anderson**, Ronald Gene 1958- *WhoBlA 92*
**Anderson**, Ronald Gordon 1948- *WhoIns 92*
**Anderson**, Ronald Keith 1941- *AmMWSc 92*
**Anderson**, Ronald M 1935- *AmMWSc 92*
**Anderson**, Ronald Truman 1933- *WhoIns 92*
**Anderson**, Rosalind Coogan *AmMWSc 92*
**Anderson**, Roscoe Odell Dale 1913- *WhoWest 92*
**Anderson**, Ross Barrett 1951- *WhoFI 92*
**Anderson**, Ross Carl 1951- *WhoWest 92*
**Anderson**, Ross Jerrold 1955- *WhoRel 92*
**Anderson**, Roy Arnold 1920- *IntWW 91, Who 92*
**Anderson**, Roy Claude 1931- *IntAu&W 91*
**Anderson**, Roy Clayton 1926- *AmMWSc 92*
**Anderson**, Roy E 1918- *AmMWSc 92*
**Anderson**, Roy Malcolm 1947- *IntWW 91, Who 92*
**Anderson**, Royal J. 1914- *WhoFI 92, WhoWest 92*
**Anderson**, Russell D 1927- *AmMWSc 92*
**Anderson**, Russell K 1924- *AmMWSc 92*
**Anderson**, Russell Lloyd 1907- *WhoBlA 92*
**Anderson**, Ruth 1928- *WhoEnt 92*
**Anderson**, Ruth Bluford 1921- *WhoBlA 92*
**Anderson**, Ruth Mapes *AmMWSc 92*
**Anderson**, S. A. 1935- *WhoBlA 92*
**Anderson**, Sabra Sullivan 1939- *AmMWSc 92, WhoMW 92*
**Anderson**, Sally Ann 1943- *WhoAmL 92*
**Anderson**, Sally Jane 1942- *WhoWest 92*
**Anderson**, Sally Joan 1957- *WhoMW 92*
**Anderson**, Samuel 1934- *AmMWSc 92*
**Anderson**, Sandra Florence 1948- *WhoMW 92*
**Anderson**, Sandra Jo 1951- *WhoAmL 92*
**Anderson**, Sandy Fay *WhoMW 92*
**Anderson**, Sarah A. *WhoBlA 92*
**Anderson**, Sarah Jane 1943- *WhoAmL 92*
**Anderson**, Scot William 1958- *WhoAmL 92*
**Anderson**, Scott 1913- *AmMWSc 92*
**Anderson**, Scott Gale 1937- *WhoAmL 92*
**Anderson**, Sherwood 1876-1941 *BenetAL 91, FacFETw*
**Anderson**, Shirley Anne 1950- *WhoRel 92*
**Anderson**, Shirley Patricia 1933- *WhoEnt 92*
**Anderson**, Sigurd 1904-1990 *CurBio 91N*
**Anderson**, Sonia R 1939- *AmMWSc 92*
**Anderson**, Sparky 1934- *WhoMW 92*
**Anderson**, Stanley 1884-1966 *TwCPaSc*
**Anderson**, Stanley Daniel, Jr. 1937- *WhoMW 92*
**Anderson**, Stanley H 1939- *AmMWSc 92*
**Anderson**, Stanley Robert 1920- *AmMWSc 92*
**Anderson**, Stanley Willard 1923- *WhoFI 92*
**Anderson**, Stanley William 1921- *AmMWSc 92*
**Anderson**, Stefan Stolen 1934- *WhoFI 92*
**Anderson**, Stephen *WhoAmP 91*
**Anderson**, Stephen Francis 1950- *WhoMW 92*
**Anderson**, Stephen Hale 1932- *WhoAmL 92, WhoWest 92*
**Anderson**, Stephen J *WhoAmP 91*
**Anderson**, Stephen Joseph 1953- *WhoAmL 92*
**Anderson**, Stephen Mills 1946- *WhoFI 92*
**Anderson**, Stephen William 1956- *AmMWSc 92*
**Anderson**, Steven Clement 1936- *AmMWSc 92*
**Anderson**, Steven Keith 1948- *WhoEnt 92*
**Anderson**, Steven Robert 1955- *WhoAmL 92*
**Anderson**, Steven William 1956- *WhoMW 92*
**Anderson**, Sue Ann Debes 1947- *AmMWSc 92*
**Anderson**, Susan Blalock 1953- *WhoAmL 92*
**Anderson**, Susan Carol 1945- *WhoAmP 91*
**Anderson**, Susan Lynne 1964- *WhoWest 92*
**Anderson**, Sydney 1927- *AmMWSc 92*
**Anderson**, Sylvia *IntMPA 92*
**Anderson**, T. J. 1928- *NewAmDM*
**Anderson**, Tad Stephen 1955- *WhoMW 92*
**Anderson**, Talmadge 1932- *WhoBlA 92*
**Anderson**, Ted *WhoAmP 91*
**Anderson**, Ted L *AmMWSc 92*
**Anderson**, Tera Lougenia 1949- *AmMWSc 92*
**Anderson**, Teresa *DrAPF 91*
**Anderson**, Terrill Gordon 1952- *WhoAmP 91*
**Anderson**, Terry Lee 1947- *AmMWSc 92*
**Anderson**, Terry Ross 1944- *AmMWSc 92*
**Anderson**, Theodore Gustave 1902- *AmMWSc 92*
**Anderson**, Theodore Wellington 1941- *WhoFI 92*
**Anderson**, Theodore Wilbur 1918- *AmMWSc 92, IntWW 91*
**Anderson**, Thomas Alexander 1928- *AmMWSc 92*
**Anderson**, Thomas Caryl 1944- *WhoFI 92*
**Anderson**, Thomas Edward 1947- *AmMWSc 92*
**Anderson**, Thomas Ernest 1952- *AmMWSc 92*
**Anderson**, Thomas F *ScFEYrs*
**Anderson**, Thomas F. d1991 *NewYTBS 91*
**Anderson**, Thomas F & Umbstaetter, H D *ScFEYrs*
**Anderson**, Thomas Foxen 1911- *AmMWSc 92, IntWW 91*
**Anderson**, Thomas Frank 1939- *AmMWSc 92*
**Anderson**, Thomas Harold 1924- *WhoFI 92*
**Anderson**, Thomas Harrison 1942- *WhoWest 92*
**Anderson**, Thomas Jefferson 1919- *WhoAmP 91*
**Anderson**, Thomas Jefferson 1928- *WhoBlA 92*
**Anderson**, Thomas Jefferson, Jr. 1928- *WhoEnt 92*
**Anderson**, Thomas Jerome 1943- *WhoEnt 92*
**Anderson**, Thomas Kenneth 1949- *WhoWest 92*
**Anderson**, Thomas L 1936- *AmMWSc 92*
**Anderson**, Thomas Leif *WhoWest 92*
**Anderson**, Thomas Page 1918- *AmMWSc 92*
**Anderson**, Thomas Patrick 1934- *AmMWSc 92*
**Anderson**, Thomas R. 1944- *WhoFI 92*
**Anderson**, Thomas Ralph 1938- *WhoFI 92*
**Anderson**, Thomas Robert 1954- *WhoWest 92*
**Anderson**, Timothy Paul 1951- *WhoMW 92*
**Anderson**, Todd J. 1962- *WhoFI 92*
**Anderson**, Tom H 1946- *WhoAmP 91*
**Anderson**, Toni-Renee *WhoAmL 92*
**Anderson**, Tony 1947- *WhoBlA 92*
**Anderson**, Velma Lucille 1918- *WhoAmP 91*
**Anderson**, Verner J 1925- *WhoAmP 91*
**Anderson**, Vernon E 1908- *IntAu&W 91, WrDr 92*
**Anderson**, Vernon Russell 1931- *WhoFI 92*
**Anderson**, Victor Charles 1922- *AmMWSc 92*
**Anderson**, Victor Elving 1921- *AmMWSc 92*
**Anderson**, Victor H. 1917- *RelLAm 91*
**Anderson**, Vincent P. 1943- *WhoMW 92*
**Anderson**, Vinton Randolph *WhoRel 92*
**Anderson**, Vinton Randolph 1927- *WhoBlA 92*
**Anderson**, Virgil Lee 1922- *AmMWSc 92*
**Anderson**, Vivienne d1991 *NewYTBS 91*
**Anderson**, W E 1949- *WhoAmP 91*
**Anderson**, W. French *NewYTBS 91 [port]*
**Anderson**, W French 1936- *AmMWSc 92*
**Anderson**, W L 1922- *AmMWSc 92*
**Anderson**, W Robert *AmMWSc 92*
**Anderson**, W Townsend 1934- *WhoAmP 91*
**Anderson**, Wallace Ervin 1913- *AmMWSc 92*
**Anderson**, Wallace L 1922- *AmMWSc 92*
**Anderson**, Walter Charles 1910- *Who 92*
**Anderson**, Walter L 1922- *AmMWSc 92*
**Anderson**, Walter T 1923- *AmMWSc 92*
**Anderson**, Warren Boyd 1929- *AmMWSc 92*
**Anderson**, Warren M. 1921- *IntWW 91*
**Anderson**, Warren Mattice 1915- *WhoAmP 91*
**Anderson**, Warren R 1914- *AmMWSc 92*
**Anderson**, Wayne Arthur 1938- *AmMWSc 92*
**Anderson**, Wayne H 1936- *WhoAmP 91*
**Anderson**, Wayne I 1935- *AmMWSc 92*
**Anderson**, Wayne Keith 1941- *AmMWSc 92*
**Anderson**, Wayne Perry 1929- *WhoMW 92*
**Anderson**, Wayne Philpott 1942- *AmMWSc 92*
**Anderson**, Wendell R *WhoAmP 91*
**Anderson**, Wendell Richard 1933- *IntWW 91*
**Anderson**, Wendy *TwCPaSc*
**Anderson**, Wes d1991 *NewYTBS 91*
**Anderson**, Wesley Baxter 1932- *WhoRel 92*
**Anderson**, Weston Arthur 1928- *AmMWSc 92*
**Anderson**, Whitney T 1931- *WhoAmP 91*
**Anderson**, Wilbert Carl 1929- *WhoAmL 92*
**Anderson**, Wilaim Craig 1946- *WhoEnt 92*
**Anderson**, Willard Eugene 1933- *AmMWSc 92*
**Anderson**, Willard Woodbury 1939- *AmMWSc 92*
**Anderson**, William 1923- *WhoWest 92*
**Anderson**, William A. 1921- *WhoBlA 92*
**Anderson**, William A. 1937- *WhoBlA 92*
**Anderson**, William Alan 1941- *AmMWSc 92*
**Anderson**, William Augustus 1942- *WhoAmL 92*
**Anderson**, William B 1923- *AmMWSc 92*
**Anderson**, William Burke 1936- *WhoRel 92*
**Anderson**, William Burke 1962- *WhoWest 92*
**Anderson**, William C. *DrAPF 91*
**Anderson**, William C 1920- *IntAu&W 91*
**Anderson**, William Carl 1958- *WhoAmL 92*
**Anderson**, William Dewey, Jr 1933- *AmMWSc 92*
**Anderson**, William Eric 1936- *Who 92*
**Anderson**, William Ferguson 1914- *Who 92*
**Anderson**, William H. 1911- *IntMPA 92*
**Anderson**, William J 1922- *AmMWSc 92*
**Anderson**, William James 1949- *WhoMW 92*
**Anderson**, William John 1938- *AmMWSc 92*
**Anderson**, William L. 1941- *ConAu 135*
**Anderson**, William Leno 1935- *AmMWSc 92*
**Anderson**, William Loyd 1947- *AmMWSc 92*
**Anderson**, William McDowell 1951- *AmMWSc 92*
**Anderson**, William Miller 1940- *WhoEnt 92*
**Anderson**, William Niles, Jr 1939- *AmMWSc 92*
**Anderson**, William Phelps 1951- *WhoAmP 91*
**Anderson**, William Pike 1948- *WhoFI 92*
**Anderson**, William R. 1921- *IntWW 91*
**Anderson**, William Ray 1928- *WhoAmP 91*
**Anderson**, William Raymond 1911- *AmMWSc 92*
**Anderson**, William Russell 1942- *AmMWSc 92*
**Anderson**, William Scovil 1927- *WhoWest 92*
**Anderson**, William Summers 1919- *IntWW 91*
**Anderson**, William W 1933- *AmMWSc 92*
**Anderson**, Willie 1967- *BlkOlyM*
**Anderson**, Willie Lee, Jr. 1965- *WhoBlA 92*
**Anderson**, Willie Lloyd 1967- *WhoBlA 92*
**Anderson**, Wilmer Clayton 1909- *AmMWSc 92*
**Anderson**, Wyatt W 1939- *AmMWSc 92*
**Anderson**, Yvonne Ghislaine 1926- *TwCPaSc*
**Anderson-Coons**, Susan *DrAPF 91*
**Anderson-Imbert**, Enrique 1910- *IntWW 91*
**Anderson Janniere**, Iona Lucille 1919- *WhoBlA 92*
**Anderson-Mauser**, Linda Marie 1954- *AmMWSc 92*
**Anderson Olivo**, Margaret 1941- *AmMWSc 92*
**Anderson-Shaw**, Helen Lester 1936- *AmMWSc 92*
**Anderson-Shea**, Charlene 1957- *WhoFI 92*
**Anderson-Stout**, Zoe Estelle 1913- *AmMWSc 92*
**Anderson-Tanner**, Frederick T., Jr. 1937- *WhoBlA 92*
**Anderssen**, Anton 1960- *WhoHisp 92*
**Andersson**, Anne Respol 1943- *WhoRel 92*
**Andersson**, Bibi 1935- *IntMPA 92, IntWW 91*
**Andersson**, Borje 1930- *IntWW 91*
**Andersson**, Craig Remington 1937- *WhoFI 92*
**Andersson**, Georg 1936- *IntWW 91*
**Andersson**, Harriet 1932- *IntWW 91*
**Andersson**, Leif Christer Leander 1944- *IntWW 91*
**Andersson**, Leif Per Roland 1923- *WhoFI 92*
**Andersson**, Sten 1923- *IntWW 91*
**Andert**, David August 1946- *WhoRel 92*
**Andert**, Jeffrey Norman 1950- *WhoMW 92*
**Anderton**, Bob 1941- *WhoAmP 91*
**Anderton**, Cyril James 1932- *Who 92*
**Anderton**, James *Who 92*
**Anderton**, James 1904- *Who 92*
**Anderton**, James Franklin, IV 1943- *WhoFI 92*
**Anderton**, Laura Gaddes 1918- *AmMWSc 92*
**Anderton**, Roland Bush 1924- *WhoAmL 92*
**Andes**, Keith 1920- *IntMPA 92*
**Andes**, Larry Dale 1947- *WhoRel 92*
**Andes**, W Abe 1942- *AmMWSc 92*
**Andes**, William Francis, Jr. 1960- *WhoAmL 92*
**Andiievska**, Emma 1931- *LiExTwC*
**Anding**, Charles R 1928- *WhoAmP 91*
**Andlauer**, Lynn Anne 1959- *WhoEnt 92*
**Andonaegui**, Jose de 1685-1760 *HisDSpE*
**Andonian**, Arsavir Takfor 1950- *AmMWSc 92*
**Andora**, Anthony Dominick 1930- *WhoAmP 91*
**Andorka**, Frank Henry 1946- *WhoAmL 92*
**Andose**, Joseph D 1944- *AmMWSc 92*
**Andover**, Viscount 1974- *Who 92*
**Andow**, David A *AmMWSc 92*
**Andracke**, Gregory Edward 1943- *WhoEnt 92*
**Andrade**, Alfredo Rolando 1932- *WhoHisp 92*
**Andrade**, Augusto A. 1952- *WhoHisp 92*
**Andrade**, C. Roberto 1925- *WhoHisp 92*
**Andrade**, Carlos Drummond de 1902-1987 *BenetAL 91*
**Andrade**, Carolyn Marie *WhoAmP 91*
**Andrade**, Dino Santos 1963- *WhoEnt 92*
**Andrade**, Franklin Gabriel 1937- *WhoHisp 92*
**Andrade**, Jaime David 1933- *WhoWest 92*
**Andrade**, James Clyde 1953- *WhoHisp 92*
**Andrade**, Joe Russell 1947- *WhoWest 92*
**Andrade**, John Robert 1944- *AmMWSc 92, WhoFI 92*
**Andrade**, Jorge 1951- *WhoHisp 92*
**Andrade**, Joseph D 1941- *AmMWSc 92*
**Andrade**, Juan, Jr. 1947- *WhoHisp 92*
**Andrade**, Manuel 1939- *AmMWSc 92*
**Andrade**, Marcel Charles 1940- *WhoHisp 92*
**Andrade**, Mario de 1893- *BenetAL 91*
**Andrade**, Mario de 1893-1945 *TwCLC 43 [port]*
**Andrade**, Mary Juana 1943- *WhoHisp 92*
**Andrade**, Nancy Lee 1937- *WhoWest 92*
**Andrade**, Oswald de 1890-1954 *BenetAL 91*
**Andrade**, Rafael Gustavo 1964- *WhoHisp 92*
**Andrade**, Theresa Jane 1959- *WhoWest 92*
**Andrady**, Anthony Lakshman *AmMWSc 92*
**Andrako**, John 1924- *AmMWSc 92*
**Andras**, Sandor 1934- *LiExTwC*
**Andrasick**, James Stephen 1944- *WhoFI 92*
**Andrassy**, Timothy Francis 1948- *WhoMW 92*
**Andrasz**, Nicholas 1931- *WhoFI 92*
**Andre**, Brother 1845-1937 *RelLAm 91*
**Andre**, Albert 1888-1943 *ThHEIm*
**Andre**, Carl 1935- *IntWW 91*
**Andre**, Harvie 1940- *IntWW 91*
**Andre**, James H 1929- *WhoAmP 91*
**Andre**, Jerry P 1940- *WhoAmP 91*
**Andre**, John 1751-1780 *BenetAL 91*
**Andre**, Kenneth B., Jr. 1933- *WhoIns 92*
**Andre**, L. Aumund 1916- *WhoMW 92*
**Andre**, Maurice 1933- *IntWW 91, NewAmDM*
**Andre**, Michael *DrAPF 91*
**Andre**, Michael 1946- *WrDr 92*
**Andre**, Michael Paul 1951- *AmMWSc 92, WhoWest 92*
**Andre**, Paul Revere 1935- *WhoRel 92*
**Andre**, Peter P 1941- *AmMWSc 92*
**Andre**, Richard Henry 1953- *WhoAmL 92*
**Andre**, Yves Marie 1675-1764 *BlkwCEP*
**Andre-Schwartz**, Janine *AmMWSc 92*
**Andrea**, David Jeffrey 1961- *WhoFI 92*
**Andrea**, Elfreda C 1924- *WhoAmP 91*
**Andrea**, Frederick Wilhelm, III 1952- *WhoRel 92*
**Andrea**, Joseph F 1927- *WhoAmP 91*
**Andrea**, Marianne *DrAPF 91*
**Andrea**, Stephen Alfred 1938- *AmMWSc 92*
**Andreacchi**, Grace *DrAPF 91*
**Andreades**, Michael G. 1874-1959 *RelLAm 91*
**Andreadis**, Theodore George 1950- *AmMWSc 92*
**Andreadis**, Tim Dimitri 1951- *AmMWSc 92*
**Andreae**, Meinrat Otto *AmMWSc 92*
**Andreae-Jones**, William Pearce 1942- *Who 92*
**Andreano**, Ralph Louis 1929- *WhoMW 92*
**Andreas**, Barbara Kloha 1946- *AmMWSc 92*
**Andreas**, Dwayne Orville 1918- *WhoFI 92, WhoMW 92*
**Andreas**, John M 1912- *AmMWSc 92*
**Andreas**, Michael Dwayne 1948- *WhoFI 92*

**Andreasen,** Arman C. 1937- *WhoIns 92*
**Andreasen,** Arthur Albinus 1917- *AmMWSc 92*
**Andreasen,** James H 1931- *WhoAmP 91*
**Andreasen,** James Hallis 1931- *WhoAmL 92, WhoMW 92*
**Andreasen,** Nancy Coover *WhoMW 92*
**Andreasen,** Nancy Coover 1938- *AmMWSc 92*
**Andreasen,** Niels-Erik Albinns 1941- *WhoRel 92*
**Andreasen,** Phill E. 1949- *WhoRel 92*
**Andreasen,** Samuel Gene 1927- *WhoRel 92*
**Andreason,** Kurt Morris 1958- *WhoAmL 92*
**Andreatch,** Anthony J 1924- *AmMWSc 92*
**Andreatta,** Charles Edward 1955- *WhoFI 92*
**Andree,** Ellen 1857-1915? *ThHEIm [port]*
**Andree,** Michael Keith 1951- *WhoMW 92*
**Andree,** Richard Vernon 1919- *AmMWSc 92*
**Andreeff,** Margaret Ellen 1958- *WhoMW 92*
**Andreen,** Brian H 1934- *AmMWSc 92*
**Andreev,** Aleksandr Fyodorovich 1939- *IntWW 91*
**Andreev,** Leonid 1871-1919 *LiExTwC*
**Andregg,** Charles Harold 1917- *AmMWSc 92*
**Andrei,** Stefan 1931- *IntWW 91*
**Andreis,** Henry Jerome 1931- *AmMWSc 92*
**Andrekson,** Peter A 1960- *AmMWSc 92*
**Andren,** Carl-Gustaf 1922- *IntWW 91*
**Andreoff,** Christopher Andon 1947- *WhoAmL 92, WhoFI 92, WhoMW 92*
**Andreoli,** Anthony Joseph 1926- *AmMWSc 92*
**Andreoli,** Brian Eugene *WhoAmL 92*
**Andreoli,** Kathleen Gainor 1935- *AmMWSc 92, IntWW 91*
**Andreoli,** Peter Donald 1919- *WhoAmL 92*
**Andreoli,** Thomas E 1935- *AmMWSc 92*
**Andreopoulos,** Spyros George 1929- *WhoWest 92*
**Andreotti,** Giulio 1919- *IntWW 91, Who 92*
**Andreozzi,** Jack M. 1939- *WhoEnt 92*
**Andreozzi,** Louis Joseph 1959- *WhoAmL 92*
**Andres,** Alexander Francis 1942- *WhoFI 92*
**Andres,** Giuseppe A 1924- *AmMWSc 92*
**Andres,** John Milton 1927- *AmMWSc 92*
**Andres,** Klaus 1934- *AmMWSc 92*
**Andres,** Lloyd A 1928- *AmMWSc 92*
**Andres,** Marian Gail 1944- *WhoEnt 92*
**Andres,** Paul John 1959- *WhoAmL 92*
**Andres,** Prentice Lee 1939- *WhoIns 92*
**Andres,** Reubin 1923- *AmMWSc 92*
**Andres,** Ronald Paul 1938- *AmMWSc 92, WhoMW 92*
**Andres,** Scott Fitzgerald 1945- *AmMWSc 92*
**Andresen,** Brian Dean 1947- *AmMWSc 92, WhoWest 92*
**Andresen,** Malcolm 1917- *WhoAmL 92*
**Andresen,** Michael Christian 1949- *AmMWSc 92*
**Andresen,** Norman A 1943- *AmMWSc 92*
**Andreski,** Stanislav Leonard 1919- *IntAu&W 91, Who 92, WrDr 92*
**Andress,** Geneva Oak 1923- *WhoAmP 91*
**Andress,** Ursula 1936- *IntMPA 92*
**Andretta,** Robert Anthony 1942- *WhoAmL 92*
**Andretti,** Mario 1940- *FacFETw*
**Andretti,** Mario Gabriele 1940- *IntWW 91*
**Andreu-Garcia,** Jose Antonio 1937- *WhoHisp 92*
**Andreuzzi,** Denis 1931- *WhoFI 92*
**Andrevon,** Jean-Pierre 1937- *TwCSFW 91A*
**Andrew** *EncEarC*
**Andrew of Caesarea** *EncEarC*
**Andrew of Crete** 660?-740 *EncEarC*
**Andrew,** Agnelius 1908-1987 *FacFETw*
**Andrew,** Bryan Haydn 1939- *AmMWSc 92*
**Andrew,** Christopher M. 1941- *WrDr 92*
**Andrew,** Christopher Maurice 1941- *Who 92*
**Andrew,** Colin 1934- *Who 92*
**Andrew,** David Robert 1935- *AmMWSc 92*
**Andrew,** Edward Raymond 1921- *Who 92, WrDr 92*
**Andrew,** George McCoubrey 1929- *AmMWSc 92*
**Andrew,** Herbert Henry 1928- *Who 92*
**Andrew,** James F 1925- *AmMWSc 92*
**Andrew,** Jane Gana *DrAPF 91*
**Andrew,** Jane Hayes 1947- *WhoEnt 92*
**Andrew,** Jim *TwCPaSc*
**Andrew,** John Henry 1936- *WhoFI 92*
**Andrew,** Joseph Jerald 1960- *WhoMW 92*
**Andrew,** Kenneth L 1919- *AmMWSc 92*
**Andrew,** Lucilla *IntAu&W 91*
**Andrew,** Lucius Archibald David, III 1938- *WhoFI 92*
**Andrew,** Ludmilla *IntWW 91*
**Andrew,** Merle M 1920- *AmMWSc 92*
**Andrew,** Prudence 1924- *IntAu&W 91, WrDr 92*
**Andrew,** Ralph K 1943- *WhoAmP 91*
**Andrew,** Robert 1928- *Who 92*
**Andrew,** Robert Harry 1916- *AmMWSc 92*
**Andrew,** Seymour L. 1948- *WhoIns 92*
**Andrew,** Stephen J. 1958- *WhoFI 92*
**Andrew,** Sydney Percy Smith 1926- *IntWW 91, Who 92*
**Andrew,** William Treleaven 1921- *AmMWSc 92*
**Andrewartha,** Herbert George 1907- *WrDr 92*
**Andrewes,** Edward David Eden d1990 *Who 92N*
**Andrewes,** Lancelot 1555-1626 *RfGEnL 91*
**Andrews Sisters** *NewAmDM*
**Andrews,** A.A. *TwCWW 91*
**Andrews,** A. Noel 1946- *WhoWest 92*
**Andrews,** Adelia Smith 1914- *WhoBlA 92*
**Andrews,** Adolphus 1943- *WhoBlA 92*
**Andrews,** Albert O'Beirne, Jr. 1939- *WhoAmL 92*
**Andrews,** Alexander Boyd 1841-1915 *DcNCBi 1*
**Andrews,** Alexander Boyd, Jr. 1873-1946 *DcNCBi 1*
**Andrews,** Alice Elizabeth 1954- *WhoBlA 92*
**Andrews,** Allen 1913- *IntAu&W 91*
**Andrews,** Anthony 1948- *CurBio 91 [port], IntMPA 92, IntWW 91, WhoEnt 92*
**Andrews,** Anthony Darwin, Jr 1964- *WhoAmP 91*
**Andrews,** Arthur George 1939- *AmMWSc 92*
**Andrews,** Austin Michael, II 1943- *AmMWSc 92*
**Andrews,** Benny 1930- *WhoBlA 92*
**Andrews,** Bert J. 1929- *WhoBlA 92*
**Andrews,** Bethlehem Kottes 1936- *AmMWSc 92*
**Andrews,** Billy Franklin 1932- *AmMWSc 92*
**Andrews,** Bret William 1959- *WhoFI 92*
**Andrews,** Bruce *DrAPF 91*
**Andrews,** Bruce 1948- *ConPo 91, WrDr 92*
**Andrews,** Candace Lou 1957- *WhoWest 92*
**Andrews,** Carl R. 1926- *WhoBlA 92*
**Andrews,** Cecelia *WhoEnt 92*
**Andrews,** Cecil Hunter 1932- *AmMWSc 92*
**Andrews,** Charles Beresford Eaton B *Who 92*
**Andrews,** Charles Edward 1925- *AmMWSc 92*
**Andrews,** Charles Lawrence 1938- *AmMWSc 92*
**Andrews,** Chester W. 1936- *WhoRel 92*
**Andrews,** Christina 1944- *WhoAmL 92*
**Andrews,** Clara Padilla *WhoHisp 92*
**Andrews,** Clarence Adelbert 1912- *WrDr 92*
**Andrews,** Colin 1946- *ConAu 133*
**Andrews,** Colman Robert 1945- *WhoWest 92*
**Andrews,** Craig Eugene 1952- *WhoMW 92*
**Andrews,** Curtis D, Jr 1960- *WhoAmP 91*
**Andrews,** Cyril Blythe 1901- *WhoBlA 92*
**Andrews,** Dana 1909- *IntMPA 92*
**Andrews,** Daniel Keller 1924- *AmMWSc 92*
**Andrews,** David F 1943- *AmMWSc 92*
**Andrews,** David Ralph 1942- *WhoAmL 92*
**Andrews,** David Roger Griffith 1933- *IntWW 91, Who 92*
**Andrews,** Derek 1933- *Who 92*
**Andrews,** Dormer 1919- *Who 92*
**Andrews,** Douglas Guy 1917- *AmMWSc 92*
**Andrews,** E. Lee 1935- *WhoFI 92*
**Andrews,** Eamonn *LesBEnT 92*
**Andrews,** Ebenezer Baldwin 1821-1880 *BiInAmS*
**Andrews,** Edgar Harold 1932- *WrDr 92*
**Andrews,** Edmund 1824-1904 *BiInAmS*
**Andrews,** Edwin Joseph 1941- *AmMWSc 92*
**Andrews,** Emanuel Carl 1956- *WhoBlA 92*
**Andrews,** Eugene Raymond 1918- *AmMWSc 92*
**Andrews,** Evelyn F. 1958- *WhoAmL 92*
**Andrews,** Fannie Fern Phillips 1867-1950 *AmPeW*
**Andrews,** Frances Barbara 1936- *WhoFI 92*
**Andrews,** Frank Clinton 1932- *AmMWSc 92*
**Andrews,** Frank Lewis 1950- *WhoAmL 92*
**Andrews,** Frank Meredith 1935- *WhoMW 92*
**Andrews,** Frazier L. 1933- *WhoBlA 92*
**Andrews,** Fred Charles 1924- *AmMWSc 92*
**Andrews,** Fred Gordon 1933- *AmMWSc 92*
**Andrews,** Frederick B 1922- *WhoAmP 91*
**Andrews,** Frederick Newcomb 1914- *AmMWSc 92*
**Andrews,** Frederick T, Jr 1926- *AmMWSc 92*
**Andrews,** Garth E. 1943- *WhoWest 92*
**Andrews,** Gary Blaylock *WhoAmP 91*
**Andrews,** George Eyre 1938- *AmMWSc 92*
**Andrews,** George Harold 1932- *AmMWSc 92, WhoMW 92*
**Andrews,** George Lewis Williams 1910- *Who 92*
**Andrews,** George William 1929- *AmMWSc 92*
**Andrews,** Glendon Louis 1917- *WhoWest 92*
**Andrews,** Glenn Colton 1948- *AmMWSc 92*
**Andrews,** Gordon Louis 1945- *AmMWSc 92*
**Andrews,** Gregory Richard 1947- *AmMWSc 92*
**Andrews,** Harold Marcus E. *Who 92*
**Andrews,** Henry Nathaniel, Jr 1910- *AmMWSc 92, IntWW 91*
**Andrews,** Holdt 1946- *WhoFI 92*
**Andrews,** Howard Lucius 1906- *AmMWSc 92*
**Andrews,** Hugh Robert 1940- *AmMWSc 92*
**Andrews,** Hunter Booker 1921- *WhoAmP 91*
**Andrews,** Ike Franklin 1925- *WhoAmP 91*
**Andrews,** J. David 1933- *WhoAmL 92*
**Andrews,** J. S. 1934- *WrDr 92*
**Andrews,** James E. 1943- *WhoBlA 92*
**Andrews,** James Edgar 1928- *WhoRel 92*
**Andrews,** James Edward 1948- *WhoBlA 92*
**Andrews,** James Einar 1942- *AmMWSc 92*
**Andrews,** James F. 1918- *WhoBlA 92*
**Andrews,** James Roland Blake F. *Who 92*
**Andrews,** James Tucker 1921- *AmMWSc 92*
**Andrews,** James Whitmore, Jr. 1950- *WhoEnt 92, WhoWest 92*
**Andrews,** Jane 1833-1887? *BenetAL 91*
**Andrews,** Jay Donald 1916- *AmMWSc 92*
**Andrews,** Jenne R. *DrAPF 91*
**Andrews,** Jill C. 1943- *WhoWest 92*
**Andrews,** Jim *WrDr 92*
**Andrews,** John *WrDr 92*
**Andrews,** John Edwin 1922- *AmMWSc 92*
**Andrews,** John Frank 1930- *AmMWSc 92*
**Andrews,** John Hamilton 1933- *IntWW 91*
**Andrews,** John Hayward 1919- *Who 92*
**Andrews,** John Henry 1939- *WrDr 92*
**Andrews,** John Herrick 1946- *AmMWSc 92*
**Andrews,** John Kneeland 1920- *WhoWest 92*
**Andrews,** John Parray 1949- *AmMWSc 92*
**Andrews,** John Stevens, Jr 1927- *AmMWSc 92*
**Andrews,** John T. 1941- *WhoIns 92*
**Andrews,** John Thomas 1937- *AmMWSc 92*
**Andrews,** Joseph R. 1947- *WhoIns 92*
**Andrews,** Judis R. 1941- *WhoBlA 92*
**Andrews,** Julie 1935- *FacFETw, IntMPA 92, IntWW 91, NewAmDM, Who 92, WhoEnt 92, WrDr 92*
**Andrews,** Ken J 1947- *AmMWSc 92*
**Andrews,** Kenneth Raymond 1921- *IntWW 91, Who 92*
**Andrews,** Lawrence Donald 1960- *WhoFI 92*
**Andrews,** Lawrence James 1920- *AmMWSc 92*
**Andrews,** Leonard Gordon 1885-1960 *TwCPaSc*
**Andrews,** Lucilla 1919- *WrDr 92*
**Andrews,** Lucy Gordon 1941- *AmMWSc 92*
**Andrews,** Luther David 1923- *AmMWSc 92*
**Andrews,** Lyman 1938- *IntAu&W 91, WrDr 92*
**Andrews,** Lynn V. 1945- *RelLAm 91*
**Andrews,** M.S. *DrAPF 91*
**Andrews,** Malachi 1933- *WhoBlA 92*
**Andrews,** Mark 1926- *IntWW 91, WhoAmP 91*
**Andrews,** Mark Allen 1951- *AmMWSc 92*
**Andrews,** Mark Edward 1952- *WhoEnt 92*
**Andrews,** Mark J 1949- *WhoAmP 91*
**Andrews,** Martha Wilmoth 1960- *WhoRel 92*
**Andrews,** Mary Eloise Okeson 1923- *WhoAmP 91*
**Andrews,** Mary Raymond Shipman 1865?-1936 *BenetAL 91*
**Andrews,** Maxine Ramseur *WhoBlA 92*
**Andrews,** Merrill Leroy 1939- *AmMWSc 92*
**Andrews,** Michael 1928- *TwCPaSc*
**Andrews,** Michael A. 1944- *AlmAP 92 [port]*
**Andrews,** Michael Allen 1944- *WhoAmP 91*
**Andrews,** Myron Floyd 1924- *AmMWSc 92*
**Andrews,** Nancy *DrAPF 91*
**Andrews,** Neil Corbly 1916- *AmMWSc 92*
**Andrews,** Nelson Alexander Currie 1966- *WhoMW 92*
**Andrews,** Nelson Montgomery 1951- *WhoBlA 92*
**Andrews,** Oliver Augustus 1931- *AmMWSc 92*
**Andrews,** Patrick E. 1936- *TwCWW 91, WrDr 92*
**Andrews,** Peter Bruce 1937- *AmMWSc 92*
**Andrews,** Peter John 1946- *Who 92*
**Andrews,** Peter Walter 1950- *AmMWSc 92*
**Andrews,** Rawle 1926- *WhoBlA 92*
**Andrews,** Raymond *DrAPF 91*
**Andrews,** Raymond 1934- *LiExTwC, WhoBlA 92*
**Andrews,** Raymond Denzil Anthony 1925- *Who 92*
**Andrews,** Richard D 1933- *AmMWSc 92*
**Andrews,** Richard Nigel Lyon 1944- *AmMWSc 92*
**Andrews,** Richard Otis 1949- *WhoWest 92*
**Andrews,** Richard Vincent 1932- *AmMWSc 92*
**Andrews,** Robert *WhoAmP 91*
**Andrews,** Robert Derk 1937- *WhoAmL 92*
**Andrews,** Robert E. 1957- *AlmAP 92 [port]*
**Andrews,** Robert F. d1991 *NewYTBS 91*
**Andrews,** Robert Frederick 1927- *WhoRel 92*
**Andrews,** Robert Graham M. *Who 92*
**Andrews,** Robert Macon 1870-1947 *DcNCBi 1*
**Andrews,** Robert Sanborn 1935- *AmMWSc 92*
**Andrews,** Robert Taylor 1920- *WhoAmP 91*
**Andrews,** Robert V 1916- *AmMWSc 92*
**Andrews,** Robin M *AmMWSc 92*
**Andrews,** Rodney Denlinger, Jr 1922- *AmMWSc 92*
**Andrews,** Ronald Allen 1940- *AmMWSc 92*
**Andrews,** Roy Chapman 1884-1960 *BenetAL 91, FacFETw*
**Andrews,** Russell S, Jr 1942- *AmMWSc 92*
**Andrews,** Sally B. *WhoEnt 92*
**Andrews,** Samuel *DcNCBi 1*
**Andrews,** Stephen Brian 1944- *AmMWSc 92*
**Andrews,** Stephen Crandall 1941- *WhoFI 92*
**Andrews,** Stephen Pearl 1812-1886 *BenetAL 91*
**Andrews,** Stuart Morrison 1932- *Who 92*
**Andrews,** Susan Baldwin 1959- *WhoEnt 92*
**Andrews,** Susan Beth 1948- *WhoMW 92*
**Andrews,** Susan Michele 1955- *WhoMW 92*
**Andrews,** Sybil 1898- *TwCPaSc*
**Andrews,** Taylor Putney 1946- *WhoAmL 92*
**Andrews,** Theodore Francis 1917- *AmMWSc 92*
**Andrews,** Thomas H *WhoAmP 91*
**Andrews,** Thomas H. 1953- *AlmAP 92 [port]*
**Andrews,** Vincent Gerard 1954- *WhoEnt 92*
**Andrews,** W Thomas 1941- *WhoAmP 91*
**Andrews,** Wallace Henry 1943- *AmMWSc 92*
**Andrews,** William Allen 1922- *AmMWSc 92*
**Andrews,** William Denys Cathcart 1931- *Who 92*
**Andrews,** William Dorey 1931- *WhoAmL 92*
**Andrews,** William Frederick 1931- *WhoFI 92*
**Andrews,** William Henry 1919- *WhoBlA 92*
**Andrews,** William Henry 1929- *WhoRel 92*
**Andrews,** William Holmes d1905 *BiInAmS*
**Andrews,** William Joseph 1950- *WhoRel 92*
**Andrews,** William L., Sr. 1955- *WhoBlA 92*
**Andrews,** William Lester Self 1942- *AmMWSc 92*
**Andrews,** William Parker, Jr. 1949- *WhoAmL 92*
**Andrews,** William Phillip 1938- *WhoBlA 92*
**Andrews,** William S. 1949- *WhoAmL 92*
**Andreyev,** Andrei 1895-1971 *FacFETw*
**Andreyev,** Leonid 1871-1919 *FacFETw, LiExTwC*
**Andreyev,** Vadim 1903-1976 *LiExTwC*
**Andreyev,** Vladimir Alekseyevich 1930- *IntWW 91*

**Andreyeva**, Victoria *DrAPF 91*
**Andrezeski**, Anthony B 1947- *WhoAmP 91*
**Andria**, George D 1941- *AmMWSc 92*
**Andriacchi**, Dominic Francis 1943- *WhoAmL 92*
**Andriacchi**, Thomas Peter 1947- *AmMWSc 92*
**Andrianov**, Nikolay 1952- *SovUnBD*
**Andrianov**, Vasiliy Mikhaylovich 1902- *SovUnBD*
**Andriashev**, Anatoliy Petrovich 1910- *IntWW 91*
**Andric**, Ivo 1892-1975 *FacFETw, LiExTwC, WhoNob 90*
**Andrichuk**, John Michael 1926- *AmMWSc 92*
**Andriessen**, Franciscus H. J. J. 1929- *IntWW 91*
**Andriessen**, Frans 1929- *Who 92*
**Andriessen**, Jacobus Eije 1928- *IntWW 91*
**Andriessen**, Louis 1939- *ConCom 92*
**Andrieu**, Rene Gabriel 1920- *IntWW 91*
**Andrin**, Albert Antal 1928- *WhoAmL 92*
**Andringa**, Keimpe 1935- *AmMWSc 92*
**Andringa**, Robert Charles 1940- *WhoRel 92*
**Andriole**, Vincent T 1931- *AmMWSc 92*
**Andrisani**, Paul Joseph 1946- *WhoFI 92*
**Andrist**, Anson Harry 1943- *AmMWSc 92*
**Andritzky**, Frank William 1947- *WhoMW 92*
**Andrle**, Robert Francis 1927- *AmMWSc 92*
**Andro**, Michael John 1958- *WhoEnt 92*
**Androla**, Ron *DrAPF 91*
**Andron**, Alexander 1938- *WhoRel 92*
**Andropov**, Yuri 1914-1984 *FacFETw*
**Andropov**, Yuriy Vladimirovich 1914-1984 *SovUnBD*
**Andros**, Edmund 1637-1714 *BenetAL 91*
**Andros**, Stephen John 1955- *WhoWest 92*
**Androsch**, Hannes 1938- *IntWW 91*
**Androski**, Frank Nicholas, Jr. 1965- *WhoEnt 92*
**Andross**, Norman Ellsworth 1921- *WhoWest 92*
**Androus**, Melvin D 1925- *WhoAmP 91*
**Androutsopoulos**, Adamantios 1919- *IntWW 91*
**Andrulis**, Marilyn Ann 1940- *AmMWSc 92*
**Andrulis**, Peter Joseph, Jr 1940- *AmMWSc 92*
**Andrus**, Alan Richard 1943- *WhoWest 92*
**Andrus**, Cecil D. 1931- *AlmAP 92 [port], IntWW 91, WhoAmP 91*
**Andrus**, Cecil Dale 1931- *WhoWest 92*
**Andrus**, Francis Sedley 1915- *Who 92*
**Andrus**, Hyrum Leslie 1924- *WrDr 92*
**Andrus**, Jan Frederick 1932- *AmMWSc 92*
**Andrus**, Milton Henry, Jr 1938- *AmMWSc 92*
**Andrus**, Paul Grier 1925- *AmMWSc 92*
**Andrus**, Richard Edward 1941- *AmMWSc 92*
**Andrus**, Vance Robert 1947- *WhoAmP 91*
**Andrus**, William DeWitt, Jr 1928- *AmMWSc 92*
**Andrushkiw**, Roman Ihor 1937- *AmMWSc 92*
**Andrychuk**, Dmetro 1918- *AmMWSc 92*
**Andrykovitch**, George 1941- *AmMWSc 92*
**Andrys**, David Paul 1956- *WhoRel 92*
**Andrzjewski**, Jerzy 1909-1983 *FacFETw*
**Andujar**, Joaquin 1952- *WhoBlA 92, WhoHisp 92*
**Andujar**, Rafael 1946- *WhoFI 92*
**Andy**, Orlando Joseph 1920- *AmMWSc 92*
**Andzhaparidze**, Georgiy 1943- *IntWW 91*
**Anees**, Munawar Ahmad 1948- *WrDr 92*
**Aneja**, Viney P 1948- *AmMWSc 92*
**Anello**, Charles 1935- *AmMWSc 92*
**Anello**, John David, Jr. 1933- *WhoEnt 92*
**Anello**, Rick L. 1948- *WhoMW 92*
**Anema**, Durlynn Carol 1935- *WhoWest 92*
**Anerio**, Felice 1560?-1614 *NewAmDM*
**Anerio**, Giovanni Francesco 1567?-1630 *NewAmDM*
**Anestos**, Harry Peter 1917- *WhoAmL 92*
**Anet**, Frank Adrien Louis 1926- *AmMWSc 92*
**Anewalt**, Thomas C. 1953- *WhoAmL 92*
**Anex**, Basil Gideon 1931- *AmMWSc 92*
**Anfimov**, Oleg Georgiyevich 1937- *IntWW 91*
**Anfinsen**, Christian Boehmer 1916- *AmMWSc 92, FacFETw, IntWW 91, Who 92, WhoNob 90*
**Anfom**, Emmanuel E. *Who 92*
**Ang**, Alfredo H-S 1930- *AmMWSc 92*
**Ang**, Ien 1954- *ConAu 133*
**Ang**, James Alfred 1960- *WhoWest 92*
**Ang**, Ke Bing Cua 1950- *WhoFI 92*
**Ang**, Tjoan-Liem 1933- *AmMWSc 92*
**Angel**, Albalucia 1939- *SpAmWW*
**Angel**, Allen Robert 1942- *WhoFI 92*
**Angel**, Armando Carlos 1940- *WhoWest 92*
**Angel**, Aubie 1935- *AmMWSc 92*
**Angel**, Catherine Alice 1957- *WhoEnt 92*
**Angel**, Charles 1923- *AmMWSc 92*
**Angel**, Christopher Edward 1961- *WhoFI 92*
**Angel**, Dennis 1947- *WhoAmL 92*
**Angel**, Dennis Lee 1955- *WhoEnt 92*
**Angel**, Frank, Jr. 1914- *WhoHisp 92*
**Angel**, Frank Philip 1953- *WhoAmL 92*
**Angel**, Gerald Bernard Nathaniel Aylmer 1937- *Who 92*
**Angel**, Heather 1941- *IntAu&W 91, Who 92, WrDr 92*
**Angel**, Heather Hazel 1941- *IntWW 91*
**Angel**, Henry Seymour 1919- *AmMWSc 92*
**Angel**, James Joseph 1959- *WhoFI 92*
**Angel**, Joe 1949- *WhoHisp 92*
**Angel**, Joseph Francis 1940- *AmMWSc 92*
**Angel**, Marina 1944- *WhoAmL 92*
**Angel**, Ralph *DrAPF 91*
**Angel**, Robert 1950- *WhoAmL 92*
**Angel**, Steven Michael 1950- *WhoAmL 92*
**Angelakos**, Diogenes James 1919- *AmMWSc 92*
**Angelakos**, Evangelos Theodorou 1929- *AmMWSc 92*
**Angele** *ThHEIm*
**Angele**, Alfred Robert 1940- *WhoWest 92*
**Angeleri**, Lucy *DrAPF 91*
**Angeles**, Peter Adam 1931- *WhoWest 92*
**Angeles**, Victoria de los *NewAmDM, Who 92*
**Angeletti**, Ruth Hogue 1943- *AmMWSc 92*
**Angelici**, Robert Joe 1937- *AmMWSc 92*
**Angelides**, Kimon Jerry 1951- *AmMWSc 92*
**Angelini**, Arnaldo M 1909- *AmMWSc 92, IntWW 91*
**Angelini**, Corrado Italo 1941- *AmMWSc 92*
**Angelini**, Fiorenzo 1916- *WhoRel 92*
**Angelini**, Pio 1932- *AmMWSc 92*
**Angelino**, Charles F. 1935- *WhoIns 92*
**Angelino**, Norman J 1943- *AmMWSc 92*
**Angell**, Barbara Tanner *DrAPF 91*
**Angell**, C A 1933- *AmMWSc 92*
**Angell**, Charles Leslie 1926- *AmMWSc 92*
**Angell**, Charles Marshall 1946- *WhoIns 92*
**Angell**, Edgar O. *WhoBlA 92*
**Angell**, Frederick Franklyn 1937- *AmMWSc 92*
**Angell**, James Browne 1924- *AmMWSc 92*
**Angell**, Jean *WhoAmP 91*
**Angell**, John William 1920- *WhoRel 92*
**Angell**, Kenneth Anthony 1930- *WhoRel 92*
**Angell**, Norman 1873-1967 *FacFETw*
**Angell**, Norman 1874-1967 *WhoNob 90*
**Angell**, Robert 1929- *WhoWest 92*
**Angell**, Robert Walker 1929- *AmMWSc 92*
**Angell**, Roger *DrAPF 91*
**Angell**, Roger 1920- *WrDr 92*
**Angell**, Thomas Strong 1942- *AmMWSc 92*
**Angell**, Wayne D. *NewYTBS 91 [port]*
**Angell**, Wayne D. 1930- *IntWW 91, WhoAmP 91*
**Angell**, Wayne D. 1939- *WhoFI 92*
**Angell-James**, John 1901- *Who 92*
**Angello**, Stephen James 1918- *AmMWSc 92*
**Angelo**, Ernest, Jr 1934- *WhoAmP 91*
**Angelo**, Ian James 1938- *WhoFI 92*
**Angelo**, Margaret Ida 1960- *WhoFI 92*
**Angelo**, Ronald John 1952- *WhoFI 92*
**Angelo**, Rudolph J 1930- *AmMWSc 92*
**Angelo**, Steven V 1952- *WhoAmP 91*
**Angelone**, Alfred C. 1939- *WhoFI 92*
**Angelone**, Edgar Omar 1958- *WhoMW 92*
**Angelone**, James John 1947- *WhoFI 92*
**Angelone**, Luis 1919- *AmMWSc 92*
**Angeloni**, Francis M 1928- *AmMWSc 92*
**Angeloni**, Richard Anthony 1961- *WhoEnt 92*
**Angelopoulos**, Edith W 1936- *AmMWSc 92*
**Angelopoulos**, Theo 1936- *IntWW 91*
**Angelopoulos**, Theodorus 1935- *IntDcF 2-2*
**Angelos**, Peter Lewis 1952- *WhoWest 92*
**Angelou**, Maya *DrAPF 91, ReelWom*
**Angelou**, Maya 1928- *Au&Arts 7 [port], BenetAL 91, BlkLC [port], ConBlB 1 [port], ConPo 91, FacFETw [port], HanAmWH, IntAu&W 91, IntWW 91, ModAWWr, NotBlAW 92 [port], WhoBlA 92, WrDr 92*
**Angelow**, Angel George 1955- *WhoWest 92*
**Angeloz**, Eduardo Cesar 1931- *IntWW 91*
**Angenot**, Marc 1941- *IntWW 91*
**Anger**, Clifford D 1934- *AmMWSc 92*
**Anger**, David A W 1963- *WhoAmP 91*
**Anger**, Hal Oscar 1920- *AmMWSc 92*
**Anger**, Kenneth 1930- *IntDcF 2-2 [port]*
**Angerer**, J David 1942- *AmMWSc 92*
**Angerer**, Lynne Musgrave 1944- *AmMWSc 92*
**Angerer**, Paul 1927- *IntWW 91*
**Angerer**, Robert Clifford 1944- *AmMWSc 92*
**Angermann**, Christian 1950- *WhoEnt 92*
**Angermueller**, Hans H. 1924- *WhoFI 92*
**Angers**, Avril *IntMPA 92*
**Angers**, JoAnn Marie 1944- *WhoRel 92*
**Angers**, Roch 1934- *AmMWSc 92*
**Angevin**, Robert Perkins Brown 1963- *WhoFI 92, WhoWest 92*
**Angevine**, Jay Bernard, Jr 1928- *AmMWSc 92*
**Angevine**, Oliver Lawrence 1914- *AmMWSc 92*
**Anghaie**, Samim 1949- *AmMWSc 92*
**Anghelis**, Odysseus 1912-1987 *FacFETw*
**Angier**, Robert Bruce 1917- *AmMWSc 92*
**Angilletta**, Anthony 1963- *WhoFI 92*
**Angino**, Ernest Edward 1932- *AmMWSc 92*
**Angioli**, Renata Maria 1962- *WhoFI 92*
**Angione**, Howard Francis 1940- *WhoAmL 92*
**Anglace**, John Francis, Jr 1931- *WhoAmP 91*
**Angle**, Jim 1946- *ConAu 133*
**Angle**, John Charles 1923- *WhoFI 92, WhoMW 92*
**Angle**, John Edwin 1931- *WhoAmL 92*
**Angle**, Lisa Alison 1953- *WhoWest 92*
**Angle**, Margaret Susan 1948- *WhoAmL 92, WhoFI 92*
**Angle**, Roger R. *DrAPF 91, IntAu&W 91*
**Angle**, William Dodge 1926- *AmMWSc 92*
**Anglemier**, Allen Francis 1926- *AmMWSc 92*
**Anglemyer**, Roma Kathleen 1932- *WhoMW 92*
**Anglesey**, Marchioness of 1924- *Who 92*
**Anglesey**, Marquess of 1922- *Who 92, WrDr 92*
**Anglesey**, Henry 1922- *IntAu&W 91*
**Anglesey**, Zoe *DrAPF 91*
**Angleton**, George M 1927- *AmMWSc 92*
**Angleton**, James J 1917-1987 *FacFETw*
**Angley**, Ernest 1921- *RelLAm 91*
**Anglim**, Philip 1955- *WhoEnt 92*
**Anglim**, Timothy P. 1952- *WhoFI 92*
**Anglin**, Douglas 1923- *Who 92*
**Anglin**, Douglas G. 1923- *WrDr 92*
**Anglin**, Eric Jack 1923- *Who 92*
**Anglin**, J Hill, Jr 1922- *AmMWSc 92*
**Anglin**, John Edson 1946- *WhoEnt 92, WhoMW 92*
**Anglin**, Michael Williams 1946- *WhoAmL 92*
**Anglin**, Norman 1891- *ScFEYrs*
**Anglin**, Walter Michael 1958- *WhoRel 92*
**Angline**, Robert Alden 1915- *WhoRel 92*
**Anglund**, Joan Walsh 1926- *IntAu&W 91, WrDr 92*
**Angoff**, Charles 1902-1979 *BenetAL 91, DcAmImH*
**Angold**, Michael *WrDr 92*
**Angona**, Frank Anthony 1920- *AmMWSc 92*
**Angora**, Anne Louise 1947- *WhoWest 92*
**Angotti**, Don Robert 1932- *WhoAmP 91*
**Angotti**, Rodney 1937- *AmMWSc 92*
**Angremy**, Jean-Pierre 1937- *IntWW 91*
**Angrist**, Stanley W 1933- *AmMWSc 92*
**Angst**, Bim *DrAPF 91*
**Angst**, Carl L. 1921- *WhoFI 92*
**Angst**, Gerald L. 1950- *WhoAmL 92*
**Angstadt**, Carol Newborg 1935- *AmMWSc 92*
**Angstadt**, Eric Paul 1959- *WhoAmL 92*
**Angstadt**, Paul J 1939- *WhoAmP 91*
**Angstadt**, Robert B 1937- *AmMWSc 92*
**Angstrom**, Wayne Raymond 1939- *WhoFI 92*
**Angueira**, Alexander 1962- *WhoAmL 92*
**Anguera**, Joaquin 1943- *WhoHisp 92*
**Anguiano**, Lupe 1929- *WhoHisp 92*
**Anguiano**, Raul 1915- *IntWW 91*
**Angulo**, Albert W. 1936- *WhoHisp 92*
**Angulo**, Charles Bonin 1943- *WhoAmL 92, WhoFI 92*
**Angulo**, Eugenio Alberto 1952- *WhoHisp 92*
**Angulo**, Gerard Antonio 1956- *WhoFI 92*
**Angulo**, Gerardo Antonio 1956- *WhoHisp 92*
**Angulo**, Irma E. 1946- *WhoHisp 92*
**Angulo**, Lawrence George 1948- *WhoAmL 92*
**Angulo**, Manuel Rafael 1917- *WhoAmL 92*
**Angulo**, Mario L. 1945- *WhoHisp 92*
**Angulo**, Myriam B. 1955- *WhoHisp 92*
**Angulo**, Ramiro 1938- *WhoHisp 92*
**Angus and Robertson** *DcLB 112 [port]*
**Angus**, Ian *IntAu&W 91X, WrDr 92*
**Angus**, J. Colin 1907- *WrDr 92*
**Angus**, John Cotton 1934- *AmMWSc 92, WhoMW 92*
**Angus**, John Wakefield, III 1951- *WhoAmL 92*
**Angus**, Keith 1929- *Who 92*
**Angus**, Michael 1930- *Who 92*
**Angus**, Michael Richardson 1930- *IntWW 91*
**Angus**, Peggy 1905- *TwCPaSc*
**Angus**, Robert Carlyle, Jr. 1946- *WhoMW 92*
**Angus**, Ronald G. 1933- *WhoWest 92*
**Angus**, Russell Daniel 1945- *WhoMW 92*
**Angus**, Thomas Anderson 1915- *AmMWSc 92*
**Angus**, Thomas Roger 1937- *WhoMW 92*
**Angus-Butterworth**, Lionel 1900- *WrDr 92*
**Angus-Butterworth**, Lionel Milner 1900- *IntAu&W 91*
**Angyal**, Stephen John 1914- *IntWW 91*
**Anhalt**, Edward *IntMPA 92*
**Anhalt**, Grant James 1952- *AmMWSc 92*
**Anhalt**, Istvan 1919- *NewAmDM*
**Anheuser**, Eberhard 1880-1963 *FacFETw*
**Anianus** *EncEarC*
**Anianus** d453? *EncEarC*
**Anianus of Celeda** *EncEarC*
**Anicetus** *EncEarC*
**Anicich**, Gary Anthony 1949- *WhoWest 92*
**Aniebo**, I. N. C. 1939- *ConAu 134, ConNov 91, WrDr 92*
**Aniello**, Anthony Joseph 1941- *WhoMW 92*
**Anikouchine**, Nicolai William 1962- *WhoAmL 92*
**Anikst**, Aleksandr Abramovich 1910- *IntWW 91*
**Anikushin**, Mikhail Konstantinovich 1917- *SovUnBD*
**Anin**, Patrick Dankwa 1928- *IntWW 91*
**Anise**, Ladun Oladunjoye E. 1940- *WhoBlA 92*
**Anishchev**, Vladimir Petrovich 1935- *IntWW 91*
**Anisimov**, Anatoly Vasilevich 1919- *IntWW 91*
**Anisimov**, Pavel Petrovich 1928- *IntWW 91*
**Aniskovich**, Paul P. 1936- *WhoIns 92*
**Aniskovich**, William A *WhoAmP 91*
**Anissimov**, Alexandre 1947- *WhoEnt 92*
**Anjaneyulu**, P S R 1955- *AmMWSc 92*
**Anjard**, Ronald P. *WhoWest 92*
**Anjard**, Ronald P, Sr 1935- *AmMWSc 92*
**Anjard**, Ronald Paul, Sr. 1935- *WhoFI 92*
**Anka**, Paul 1941- *WhoEnt 92*
**Ankel**, Helmut K 1933- *AmMWSc 92*
**Ankel-Simons**, Friderun Annursel 1933- *AmMWSc 92*
**Ankenbrand**, Larry Joseph 1935- *WhoMW 92*
**Ankenbrandt**, Charles Martin 1939- *AmMWSc 92*
**Ankeney**, Jay Lloyd 1921- *AmMWSc 92*
**Ankeny**, Nesmith Cornett 1926- *AmMWSc 92*
**Anker**, Charlotte Miriam 1934- *WhoEnt 92*
**Anker**, Peter Louis 1935- *WhoFI 92*
**Anker**, Robert Alvin 1941- *WhoFI 92, WhoIns 92*
**Ankerberg**, William C. 1950- *WhoRel 92*
**Ankerman**, William Lewis 1947- *WhoAmL 92*
**Ankersmit**, Franklin Rudolf 1945- *IntWW 91*
**Anketell**, Judith 1952- *TwCPaSc*
**Ankner**, Terence Karl 1963- *WhoAmL 92*
**Ankrah**, Joseph Arthur 1915- *IntWW 91*
**Ankrom**, Robert Eugene 1939- *WhoEnt 92*
**Ankrom**, Robert Lynn 1959- *WhoRel 92*
**Ankrum**, Paul Denzel 1915- *AmMWSc 92*
**Ankum**, Hans 1930- *IntWW 91*
**Anlauf**, Kurt Guenther 1942- *AmMWSc 92*
**Anlyan**, William 1925- *IntWW 91*
**Anlyan**, William George 1925- *AmMWSc 92*
**Anmar**, Frank *IntAu&W 91X*
**Ann-Margret** 1941- *ConTFT 9, IntMPA 92, IntWW 91, WhoEnt 92*
**Annable**, James Edward 1943- *WhoFI 92, WhoMW 92*
**Annaheim**, Ellwood Joseph 1954- *WhoEnt 92*
**Annakin**, Kenneth *IntWW 91*
**Annakin**, Kenneth 1915- *IntMPA 92*
**Annakin**, Kenneth Cooper *WhoEnt 92*
**Annal**, Maria Theresia 1952- *WhoEnt 92*
**Annala**, Vilho 1888-1960 *BiDExR*
**Annals**, Michael 1938-1990 *AnObit 1990*
**Annaly**, Baron d1990 *Who 92N*
**Annaly**, Baron 1954- *Who 92*
**Annan** *Who 92*
**Annan**, Baron 1916- *IntWW 91, Who 92*
**Annan**, Dorothy 1907- *TwCPaSc*
**Annan**, Murvel Eugene 1920- *AmMWSc 92*
**Annan**, Noel Gilroy 1916- *WrDr 92*
**Annand**, James Earle 1929- *WhoRel 92*
**Annand**, James King 1908- *IntAu&W 91, WrDr 92*
**Annand**, John Angus 1926- *Who 92*
**Annand**, Richard Wallace 1914- *Who 92*

Annandale And Hartfell, Earl of 1941- Who 92
Annau, Zoltan 1936- AmMWSc 92
Annaud, Jean-Jacques 1943- IntMPA 92, IntWW 91, WhoEnt 92
Anne, Princess IntWW 91
Anne, Queen of England 1665-1714 EncAmaz 91
Anne, Sheila 1948- TwCPaSc
Annear, Paul Richard 1915- AmMWSc 92
Annee, Paul A. WhoMW 92
Annen, Edward James, Jr 1951- WhoAmP 91, WhoMW 92
Annenberg, Ted Max 1927- WhoAmL 92, WhoFI 92
Annenberg, Walter H. LesBEnT 92
Annenberg, Walter H. 1908- IntWW 91, Who 92
Annese, Joseph T., Jr. 1962- WhoEnt 92
Annesley Who 92
Annesley, Earl 1924- Who 92
Annesley, David 1936- TwCPaSc
Annesley, Hugh 1939- IntWW 91
Annesley, Hugh Norman 1939- Who 92
Annesley, Mabel 1881-1959 TwCPaSc
Annessi, Jean Ludeman 1958- WhoMW 92
Annestrand, Stig A 1933- AmMWSc 92
Annett, Bruce James, Jr. 1952- WhoMW 92
Annett, David Maurice 1917- Who 92
Annett, Robert Gordon 1941- AmMWSc 92
Annibale Padovano 1527?-1575 NewAmDM
Anning, Raymon Harry 1930- Who 92
Annino, Raymond 1927- AmMWSc 92
Annis, Brian Kitfield 1940- AmMWSc 92
Annis, David 1921- Who 92
Annis, Francesca IntWW 91
Annis, Francesca 1945- Who 92
Annis, Jason Carl 1930- AmMWSc 92
Annis, Philip Geoffrey Walter 1936- Who 92
Annis, Robert Lyndon 1949- WhoEnt 92
Anno, James Nelson 1934- AmMWSc 92
Annorkwei II, Nene 1900- IntWW 91
Annulis, John T 1945- AmMWSc 92
Annunzio, Frank 1915- AlmAP 92 [port], WhoAmP 91, WhoMW 92
Annunzio, Gabriele d' EncTR 91
Annur, Hanna Abdur DrAPF 91
Another Volunteer ScFEYrs
Anouchi, Abraham Y 1930- AmMWSc 92
Anouilh, Jean 1910- IntAu&W 91
Anouilh, Jean 1910-1987 FacFETw, GuFrLit 1
Anquin, Nimio de 1896- BiDExR
Anrep, Boris 1883-1969 TwCPaSc
Ansaldo Vejerano, Juan Antonio 1901-1958 BiDExR
Ansara, Michael 1922- IntMPA 92
Ansardi, Glenn B 1947- WhoAmP 91
Ansari, Ali 1934- AmMWSc 92
Ansari, Azam U 1940- AmMWSc 92
Ansari, Guhlam Ahmad Shakeel 1947- AmMWSc 92
Ansari, Megill Shakir 1957- WhoFI 92
Ansbacher, Rudi 1934- AmMWSc 92
Ansbacher, Stefan 1905- AmMWSc 92
Ansbro, David Anthony 1945- Who 92
Ansbro, James Michael WhoAmL 92, WhoEnt 92
Anscher, Bernard 1922- WhoFI 92
Anschutz, Phillip F. 1939- WhoFI 92, WhoWest 92
Anscombe, Francis John 1918- AmMWSc 92
Anscombe, Gertrude 1919- IntAu&W 91, WrDr 92
Anscombe, Gertrude Elizabeth Margaret 1919- Who 92
Anscombe, Isabelle Mary 1954- IntAu&W 91
Ansel, Howard Carl 1933- AmMWSc 92
Ansell, Barbara Mary 1923- IntWW 91, Who 92
Ansell, Daniel James 1953- WhoAmL 92
Ansell, Edward Orin 1926- WhoAmL 92
Ansell, Fred Asher 1945- WhoRel 92
Ansell, George S 1934- AmMWSc 92
Ansell, George Stephen 1934- WhoWest 92
Ansell, Graham Keith 1931- IntWW 91
Ansell, Julian Samuel 1922- AmMWSc 92
Ansell, Michael 1905- WrDr 92
Ansell, Michael Picton 1905- Who 92
Ansell, Nicholas George Picton 1937- Who 92
Anselm of Canterbury 1033-1109 DcLB 115 [port]
Anselme, Jean-Pierre L M 1936- AmMWSc 92
Anselmi, Donald Ray 1928- WhoAmP 91
Anselmi, Tina 1927- IntWW 91
Anselmini, Jean-Pierre 1940- WhoFI 92
Anselmo, Giovanni 1934- WorArt 1980
Anselmo, Vincent C 1930- AmMWSc 92
Anselone, Philip Marshall 1926- AmMWSc 92
Ansems, Tony Lambert 1940- WhoMW 92
Ansermet, Ernest 1883-1969 FacFETw, NewAmDM
Ansevin, Allen Thornburg 1928- AmMWSc 92
Anshel, Michael 1941- AmMWSc 92
Ansher, Sherry Singer 1957- AmMWSc 92
Anshus, Craig Lyman 1960- WhoMW 92
Ansi, Saud bin Salim al- 1949- IntWW 91
Ansimov, Georgiy Pavlovich 1922- IntWW 91
Ansley, Michael 1967- WhoBlA 92
Ansley, Shepard Bryan 1939- WhoAmL 92
Anson Who 92
Anson, Viscount 1978- Who 92
Anson, Charles Vernon 1944- Who 92
Anson, Christopher Martin 1954- WhoMW 92
Anson, Edward 1929- Who 92
Anson, Elizabeth Audrey 1931- Who 92
Anson, Fred 1933- AmMWSc 92
Anson, Fred Colvig 1933- WhoWest 92
Anson, Joan DrAPF 91
Anson, John 1930- IntWW 91, Who 92
Anson, Malcolm Allinson 1924- IntWW 91, Who 92
Anson, Peter 1924- Who 92
Anson, Peter Frederick 1889- TwCPaSc
Anson, Todd J. 1955- WhoAmL 92
Ansorge, Luella M. 1915- WhoMW 92
Ansorge, Richard James 1953- WhoWest 92
Anspach, Denny Sykes 1934- WhoWest 92
Anspach, Judith Ford 1940- WhoAmL 92
Anspach, Susan 1945- IntMPA 92
Anspacher, Louis 1878-1947 BenetAL 91
Anspaugh, Bruce Edward 1933- AmMWSc 92
Anspaugh, David 1946- IntMPA 92
Anspaugh, Lynn Richard 1937- AmMWSc 92
Anspon, Harry Davis 1917- AmMWSc 92
Anstee, Margaret Joan 1926- IntWW 91, Who 92
Anstey, Christopher 1724-1805 RfGEnL 91
Anstey, Edgar 1917- Who 92, WrDr 92
Anstey, John 1907- Who 92
Anstey, Robert L 1921- AmMWSc 92
Anstey, Sidney Herbert d1991 Who 92N
Anstey, Thomas Herbert 1917- AmMWSc 92
Anstine, Anne Baird 1924- WhoAmP 91
Anstruther-Gough-Calthorpe, Euan 1966- Who 92
Anstruther of that Ilk, Ralph 1921- Who 92
Ansul, Gerald R 1925- AmMWSc 92
Ant, Adam 1954- WhoEnt 92
Antakly, Tony 1951- AmMWSc 92
Antal, John Joseph 1926- AmMWSc 92
Antal, Michael Jerry, Jr 1947- AmMWSc 92
Antall, Jozsef 1932- IntWW 91
Antalpeter, Tibor 1930- Who 92
Antanaitis, Cynthia Emily 1954- WhoAmL 92
Antar, Ali A 1940- AmMWSc 92
Antar, Mohamed Abdelchany AmMWSc 92
Antaramian, Edward Richard 1959- WhoAmL 92
Antaramian, John Martin 1954- WhoAmP 91
Antcliffe, Kenneth Arthur Who 92
Ante, Antonio 1771-1836 HisDSpE
Antel, Jack Perry 1945- AmMWSc 92
Antelo, Armando A. 1953- WhoHisp 92
Antelo, Jose G. 1934- WhoHisp 92
Antenen, Ann Marie 1925- WhoAmP 91
Antequera y Castro, Jose de 1690- HisDSpE
Antes, Harry W 1930- AmMWSc 92
Antes, Horst 1936- IntWW 91, WorArt 1980
Antes, John 1740-1811 NewAmDM
Antes, Richard Louis 1936- WhoMW 92
Antheil, George 1900-1959 BenetAL 91, FacFETw, NewAmDM
Anthes, Clifford Charles 1907- WhoFI 92, WhoWest 92
Anthes, John Allen 1913- AmMWSc 92
Anthes, Richard A. 1944- WrDr 92
Anthes, Richard Allen 1944- AmMWSc 92
Anthis, Bill Clinton 1926- WhoMW 92
Antholine, William E 1943- AmMWSc 92
Anthonisen, Nicholas R 1933- AmMWSc 92
Anthony 251?-356 EncEarC
Anthony, Bishop 1935- WhoRel 92, WhoWest 92
Anthony, Metropolitan 1914- Who 92
Anthony Peter, Bishop 1907- WhoRel 92
Anthony, Adam 1923- AmMWSc 92
Anthony, Alexander Eddie, Jr. 1933- WhoWest 92
Anthony, Andrew John 1950- WhoAmL 92
Anthony, Bernard Winston 1945- WhoBlA 92
Anthony, Beryl F., Jr. 1938- AlmAP 92 [port]
Anthony, Beryl Franklin, Jr 1938- WhoAmP 91
Anthony, Betty Arlene 1926- WhoFI 92
Anthony, Bob WhoAmP 91
Anthony, C.L. ConAu 133, SmATA 65
Anthony, Clarence Edward 1959- WhoBlA 92
Anthony, Cushman D 1939- WhoAmP 91
Anthony, Dave 1949- WhoEnt 92
Anthony, David 1955- WhoAmP 91
Anthony, David Henry, III 1952- WhoBlA 92
Anthony, Deborah Pauletta 1955- WhoAmL 92
Anthony, Donald Barrett 1948- AmMWSc 92
Anthony, Donald Joseph 1922- AmMWSc 92
Anthony, Douglas Who 92
Anthony, Douglas 1929- IntWW 91
Anthony, Elaine Margaret 1932- WhoWest 92
Anthony, Elizabeth Youngblood 1953- AmMWSc 92
Anthony, Evelyn 1928- IntAu&W 91, Who 92, WrDr 92
Anthony, G. Doyle 1958- WhoAmL 92
Anthony, Graham George 1931- Who 92
Anthony, Graham Hudson 1892-1967 DcNCBi 1
Anthony, Harry D 1921- AmMWSc 92
Anthony, Homer Bruce 1934- WhoRel 92
Anthony, Jack Malcolm 1943- WhoAmL 92
Anthony, James R 1922- IntAu&W 91, WrDr 92
Anthony, Jeffrey Conrad 1949- WhoBlA 92
Anthony, Joan Caton 1939- WhoAmL 92
Anthony, John IntAu&W 91X, SmATA 65
Anthony, John Douglas 1929- Who 92
Anthony, John Gould 1804-1877 BiInAmS
Anthony, John Williams 1920- AmMWSc 92
Anthony, Kenneth C., Jr. 1954- WhoAmL 92
Anthony, Kenneth Christopher 1960- WhoRel 92
Anthony, Kenneth Leigh 1944- WhoEnt 92
Anthony, Leander Aldrich 1917- WhoBlA 92
Anthony, Lee Saunders 1932- AmMWSc 92
Anthony, Lillian Delores 1925- WhoBlA 92
Anthony, Linda J 1951- AmMWSc 92
Anthony, Margery Stuart 1924- AmMWSc 92
Anthony, Michael BlkOlyM
Anthony, Michael 1932- ConNov 91, WrDr 92
Anthony, Peter IntAu&W 91X
Anthony, Philip John 1952- AmMWSc 92
Anthony, Philip LeVern 1935- WhoAmP 91
Anthony, Piers 1934- IntAu&W 91, TwCSFW 91, WrDr 92
Anthony, R 1897-1942 ScFEYrs
Anthony, Rayford Gaines 1935- AmMWSc 92
Anthony, Rhonda Lea 1962- WhoRel 92
Anthony, Robert Armstrong 1931- WhoAmL 92
Anthony, Robert Holland 1948- WhoFI 92
Anthony, Ronald Desmond 1925- Who 92
Anthony, Ronald Lewis 1938- AmMWSc 92
Anthony, Ronald Ray 1944- WhoMW 92
Anthony, Sheila Foster 1940- WhoAmP 91
Anthony, Silas Reed, Jr. 1940- WhoFI 92
Anthony, Susan B. 1820-1906 BenetAL 91, HanAmWH, RComAH
Anthony, Susan B. 1916-1991 ConAu 134
Anthony, Thomas Richard 1941- AmMWSc 92
Anthony, Tony 1939- IntMPA 92
Anthony, Vivian Stanley 1938- Who 92
Anthony, W Brady 1916- AmMWSc 92
Anthony, W. Michael 1941- WhoWest 92
Anthony, William Arnold 1835-1908 BiInAmS
Anthony, Yancey Lamar 1922- WhoRel 92
Anthony-Twarog, Barbara Jean 1953- AmMWSc 92
Antia, Kersey H. 1936- WhoFI 92
Antianara EncAmaz 91
Antic, Michael 1963- WhoEnt 92
Antich, Rose Ann WhoAmP 91
Antico, Tristan 1923- IntWW 91, Who 92
Antigua Who 92
Antilla, Susan 1954- WhoFI 92
Antin, David DrAPF 91
Antin, David 1932- ConPo 91, WrDr 92
Antin, Eleanor DrAPF 91
Antin, Mary 1881-1949 BenetAL 91, DcAmImH
Antiochus of Ptolemais d408? EncEarC
Antiochus of Saba EncEarC
Antipa, Gregory Alexis 1941- AmMWSc 92, WhoWest 92
Antipolo, Virginia Cella 1959- WhoAmL 92
Antisdel, Louis Willard 1925- WhoAmP 91
Antisell, Thomas 1817-1893 BiInAmS
Antkiw, Stephen 1922- AmMWSc 92
Antkowiak, Wlodzimierz 1946- IntAu&W 91
Antle, Charles Edward 1930- AmMWSc 92
Antler DrAPF 91
Antler, Helayne Iris 1956- WhoEnt 92
Antler, Morton 1928- AmMWSc 92
Antley, Barry Thomas 1954- WhoRel 92
Antley, Eugene Brevard 1929- WhoRel 92
Antman, Stuart S 1939- AmMWSc 92
Antoch, Zdenek Vincent 1943- WhoWest 92
Antochewicz, Bernard 1931- IntAu&W 91
Antoci, Mario 1934- WhoWest 92
Antognoli, David L. 1953- WhoAmL 92
Antohin, Anatoly G. 1949- WhoEnt 92
Antoine, John Eugene 1937- AmMWSc 92
Antok, Jean Claude 1933- IntAu&W 91
Antokoletz, Elliott Maxim 1942- WhoEnt 92
Antokol'sky, Pavel Grigorievich 1896-1978 SovUnBD
Antolak, Arlyn Joe 1953- AmMWSc 92
Antoli Guarch, Miguel 1934- WhoRel 92
Antolovich, Stephen D 1939- AmMWSc 92
Antolski, Zdislaw Henryk 1953- IntAu&W 91
Anton, Aaron Harold 1921- AmMWSc 92, WhoMW 92
Anton, Alexander Elder 1922- Who 92
Anton, David 1958- WhoAmL 92
Anton, David L 1953- AmMWSc 92
Anton, Dene Hofheinz 1942- WhoEnt 92
Anton, Frank Leland 1930- WhoMW 92
Anton, Frederick W, III 1934- WhoIns 92
Anton, Harvey 1923- WhoFI 92
Anton, Howard 1939- AmMWSc 92
Anton, Ioan 1924- IntWW 91
Anton, James 1914- WhoAmP 91
Anton, John M. 1947- WhoAmL 92
Anton, Ludwig 1872- ScFEYrs
Anton, Mace Damon 1961- WhoFI 92
Anton, Nicholas Guy 1906- WhoFI 92
Anton, Ronald David 1933- WhoAmL 92
Anton, Susan WhoEnt 92
Anton, Susan 1951- IntMPA 92
Anton, Thomas 1931- WhoFI 92
Anton, Thomas Paul 1963- WhoFI 92
Anton, Victor 1909-1980 TwCPaSc
Anton, William WhoHisp 92
Antonacci, Anthony Eugene 1949- WhoFI 92, WhoMW 92
Antonaccio, Michael John 1943- AmMWSc 92
Antonakakis, Dimitris 1933- IntWW 91
Antonakakis, Suzana Maria 1935- IntWW 91
Antonanzas Perez-Egea, Juan Miguel 1932- IntWW 91
Antone, Nahil Peter 1952- WhoAmL 92
Antone, Steve 1921- WhoAmP 91
Antonecchia, Kelly Ann 1966- WhoWest 92
Antonelli, Ferdinando Giuseppe 1896- IntWW 91, WhoRel 92
Antonelli, Peter Louis 1941- AmMWSc 92
Antonescu, Ion 1882-1946 EncTR 91 [port], FacFETw
Antonetti, Richard P WhoAmP 91
Antoniades, Harry Nicholas 1923- AmMWSc 92
Antoniadi, Eugene Michael 1870-1944 FacFETw
Antoniak, Charles Edward 1940- AmMWSc 92
Antonic, James Paul 1943- WhoFI 92
Antonicello, Nicholas J, Jr 1960- WhoAmP 91
Antoniewicz, Peter R 1936- AmMWSc 92
Antonini, Joseph 1941- News 91
Antonini, Joseph E. 1941- WhoFI 92
Antonini, Louise EncAmaz 91
Antonini, Michael Joseph 1946- WhoWest 92
Antoninus, Brother BenetAL 91, WrDr 92
Antoninus Pius 86-161 EncEarC
Antonio Who 92
Antonio 1921- IntWW 91
Antonio, James Frederic 1939- WhoAmP 91
Antonio, Lou IntMPA 92
Antonio, Victor 1960- WhoRel 92
Antonioni, Michelangelo 1912- FacFETw, IntDcF 2-2 [port], IntWW 91, Who 92
Antonioni, Michelangelo 1913- IntMPA 92
Antonioni, Robert WhoAmP 91

**Antoniono**, James Richard 1945- *WhoAmP 91*
**Antoniou**, A 1938- *AmMWSc 92*
**Antoniou**, Antonios A 1923- *AmMWSc 92*
**Antoniou**, Theodore 1935- *NewAmDM*
**Antonoff**, Frederick Damian 1950- *WhoFI 92*
**Antonoff**, Marvin M 1930- *AmMWSc 92*
**Antonov**, Aleksey Innokent'evich 1896-1962 *SovUnBD*
**Antonov**, Aleksey Konstantinovich 1912- *SovUnBD*
**Antonov**, Sergei Fyodorovich 1911- *IntWW 91*
**Antonov**, Sergei Petrovich 1915- *IntAu&W 91, IntWW 91*
**Antonov-Ovseyenko**, Vladimir A 1884-1939? *FacFETw*
**Antonovich**, Michael Dennis *WhoAmP 91*
**Antonovich**, Michael Dennis 1939- *WhoWest 92*
**Antonowsky**, Marvin 1929- *IntMPA 92*
**Antonsen**, Conrad 1937- *WhoRel 92*
**Antonsen**, Donald Hans 1930- *AmMWSc 92*
**Antonson**, Joan Margaret 1951- *WhoWest 92*
**Antonson**, Newman Neil 1926- *WhoRel 92*
**Antonsson**, Erik Karl 1954- *AmMWSc 92*
**Antonucci**, Frank Ralph 1946- *AmMWSc 92*
**Antonucci**, John *WhoWest 92*
**Antosiewicz**, Henry Albert 1925- *AmMWSc 92*
**Antrim**, Earl of 1935- *Who 92*
**Antrim**, Minnie Faye 1916- *WhoFI 92*
**Antrobius**, David Shipley 1935- *WhoAmL 92*
**Antrobus**, John 1933- *IntAu&W 91, WrDr 92*
**Antrobus**, Philip Coutts 1908- *Who 92*
**Antunez**, Ellis Lewis 1950- *WhoHisp 92*
**Antupit**, Samuel Nathaniel 1932- *WhoEnt 92*
**Antzelevitch**, Charles 1951- *AmMWSc 92*
**Anum**, Isaac Boye 1943- *WhoMW 92*
**Anuras**, Sinn 1941- *AmMWSc 92*
**Anusavice**, Kenneth John 1940- *AmMWSc 92*
**Anuszkiewicz**, Richard Joseph 1930- *IntWW 91*
**Anuta**, Michael Joseph 1901- *WhoAmL 92, WhoMW 92*
**Anutta**, Lucile Jamison 1943- *WhoAmL 92*
**Anuzis**, Saul 1959- *WhoAmP 91*
**Anversa**, Piero 1938- *AmMWSc 92*
**Anvil**, Christopher *TwCSFW 91, WrDr 92*
**Anwar**, Imran 1962- *WhoEnt 92*
**Anwar**, Mohamed Samih 1924- *Who 92*
**Anwar**, Rashid Ahmad 1930- *AmMWSc 92*
**Anwar Sani**, Chaidir 1918- *IntWW 91*
**Anway**, Allen R 1941- *AmMWSc 92*
**Anwyl**, Shirley Anne *Who 92*
**Anwyl-Davies**, Marcus John 1923- *Who 92*
**Anyaoku**, Eleazar Chukwuemeka 1933- *IntWW 91, Who 92*
**Anyidoho**, Kofi 1947- *ConPo 91, WrDr 92*
**Anysas**, Jurgis Arvydas 1934- *AmMWSc 92*
**Anza**, Juan Bautista de 1735-1788 *BenetAL 91*
**Anzaldi**, James Anthony 1950- *WhoAmP 91*
**Anzaldua**, Gloria E. *DrAPF 91, WhoHisp 92*
**Anzalone**, Louis, Jr 1931- *AmMWSc 92*
**Anzalone**, William Francis 1951- *WhoAmL 92*
**Anzeveno**, Frank J, Jr 1958- *WhoAmP 91*
**Aoki**, John H. 1931- *WhoFI 92*
**Aoki**, Masanao 1931- *AmMWSc 92, WhoWest 92*
**Aotearoa**, Bishop of 1928- *Who 92*
**Aouita**, Said 1960- *BlkOlyM*
**Aoun**, Michel 1935- *IntWW 91*
**Apai**, Gustav Richard, II 1946- *AmMWSc 92*
**Apang**, Gegong 1945- *IntWW 91*
**Aparicio**, Frances R. 1955- *WhoHisp 92*
**Aparicio**, Luis 1934- *FacFETw*
**Aparicio**, Luis Ernesto Montiel 1934- *WhoHisp 92*
**Aparicio**, Sebastian de 1502-1600 *HisDSpE*
**Apatoff**, Michael John 1955- *WhoFI 92, WhoWest 92*
**Apatov**, Craig Allen 1958- *WhoEnt 92*
**Apea**, Joseph Bennet Kyeremateng 1932- *WhoBlA 92*
**Apel**, Carolyn Ruth 1943- *WhoEnt 92*
**Apel**, Charles Turner 1931- *AmMWSc 92*
**Apel**, Hans Eberhard 1932- *IntWW 91, Who 92*
**Apel**, John Ralph 1930- *AmMWSc 92*
**Apel**, Myrna L. 1942- *WhoMW 92*
**Apelfeld**, Aron 1931- *LiExTwC*
**Apelian**, Diran 1945- *AmMWSc 92*
**Apellaniz**, Joseph E P 1926- *AmMWSc 92*
**Apelles** *EncEarC*
**Apen**, Mark Brandon 1964- *WhoEnt 92*
**Apenbrink**, Edwin John 1946- *WhoAmL 92*
**Apes**, William 1798- *BenetAL 91*
**Apfel**, Edwin R. 1934- *IntMPA 92*
**Apfel**, Gary 1952- *WhoAmL 92*
**Apfel**, Necia H 1930- *IntAu&W 91*
**Apfel**, Robert Edmund 1943- *AmMWSc 92*
**Apfelbaum**, Marc Jeffrey 1955- *WhoAmL 92*
**Apfeldorf**, Morton 1949- *WhoAmL 92*
**Apgar**, Austin Craig 1838-1908 *BiInAmS*
**Apgar**, Barbara Jean 1936- *AmMWSc 92*
**Apgar**, Ellis A 1836-1905 *BiInAmS*
**Apgar**, Kenneth Edward 1946- *WhoAmL 92*
**Apgar**, Mahlon, IV 1941- *WhoFI 92*
**Apgar**, Robert Colin 1944- *WhoAmL 92*
**Aphraates** *EncEarC*
**Apirion**, David 1935- *AmMWSc 92*
**Apker**, Burton Marcellus, Jr. 1924- *WhoAmL 92, WhoWest 92*
**Apking**, Donald James 1950- *WhoWest 92*
**Apking**, William Tappan 1933- *WhoAmP 91*
**Aplan**, Frank F 1923- *AmMWSc 92*
**Apley**, Alan Graham 1914- *Who 92*
**Apley**, Martyn Linn 1938- *AmMWSc 92*
**Aplon**, Roger *DrAPF 91*
**Apo**, Peter K 1938- *WhoAmP 91*
**Apodaca**, Clara R. 1934- *WhoHisp 92*
**Apodaca**, Dennis Ray 1956- *WhoHisp 92*
**Apodaca**, Ed C. 1941- *WhoHisp 92*
**Apodaca**, Edward James 1948- *WhoHisp 92*
**Apodaca**, Esteban Corral 1952- *WhoHisp 92*
**Apodaca**, Francisco A. 1935- *WhoHisp 92*
**Apodaca**, Frank B. 1962- *WhoHisp 92*
**Apodaca**, James Max 1948- *WhoHisp 92*
**Apodaca**, Jerry 1934- *WhoAmP 91, WhoHisp 92*
**Apodaca**, Robert Anthony 1964- *WhoWest 92*
**Apodaca**, Rudy S. *DrAPF 91*
**Apodaca**, Rudy S. 1939- *WhoHisp 92*
**Apodaca**, Rudy Samuel 1939- *WhoWest 92*
**Apodaca**, Victor D., Jr. *WhoHisp 92*
**Apodaca**, Victor D., Jr. 1958- *WhoHisp 92*
**Apodaca-Thurmond**, Gidget 1954- *WhoHisp 92*
**Apolinsky**, Stephen Douglas 1961- *WhoAmL 92*
**Apollinaire**, Guillaume 1880-1918 *FacFETw, GuFrLit 1*
**Apollinaris of Hierapolis** *EncEarC*
**Apollinaris of Laodicea** 315?-392 *EncEarC*
**Aponius** *EncEarC*
**Aponte**, Angelo J. 1946- *WhoHisp 92*
**Aponte**, Antonio 1957- *WhoHisp 92*
**Aponte**, Carmen Iris 1951- *WhoHisp 92*
**Aponte**, Humberto 1924- *WhoAmP 91*
**Aponte**, Jesus S *WhoAmP 91*
**Aponte**, Jose *WhoAmP 91*
**Aponte**, Luis 1922- *WhoHisp 92*
**Aponte**, Mari Carmen 1946- *WhoHisp 92*
**Aponte**, Nestor S 1948- *WhoAmP 91, WhoHisp 92*
**Aponte**, Philip 1936- *WhoHisp 92*
**Aponte-Lebron**, Nilda I. 1944- *WhoHisp 92*
**Aponte Martinez**, Luis 1922- *IntWW 91, WhoRel 92*
**Aponte-Merced**, Luis Antonio 1946- *WhoHisp 92*
**Aponte Perez**, Francisco 1928- *WhoAmP 91*
**Aposhian**, Hurair Vasken 1926- *AmMWSc 92*
**Apostle to the Indians** *BenetAL 91*
**Apostol**, Ted James 1947- *WhoFI 92*
**Apostol**, Tom M 1923- *AmMWSc 92*
**Apostol**, William Peter 1950- *WhoEnt 92*
**Apostolakis**, James John 1942- *WhoFI 92*
**Apostolides**, Anthony Demetrios *WhoMW 92*
**Apostolos**, Margo Kay 1949- *WhoWest 92*
**App**, Alva A 1932- *AmMWSc 92*
**Appel**, Alfred, Jr. 1934- *ConAu 133, WrDr 92*
**Appel**, Allan *DrAPF 91*
**Appel**, Andre 1921- *IntWW 91*
**Appel**, Arthur Gary 1958- *AmMWSc 92*
**Appel**, Barry 1931- *WhoFI 92*
**Appel**, Brent Robert 1950- *WhoAmL 92*
**Appel**, David W 1924- *AmMWSc 92*
**Appel**, Dori *DrAPF 91*
**Appel**, Eric Michael 1960- *WhoAmL 92*
**Appel**, Irving Harold 1917- *WhoFI 92*
**Appel**, Jacob J. 1940- *WhoWest 92*
**Appel**, James B 1934- *AmMWSc 92*
**Appel**, Jeffrey Alan 1942- *AmMWSc 92*
**Appel**, Karel Christian 1921- *IntWW 91, Who 92*
**Appel**, Kenneth I 1932- *AmMWSc 92*
**Appel**, Martin Eliot 1948- *WhoEnt 92*
**Appel**, Max J 1929- *AmMWSc 92*
**Appel**, Michael Clayton 1947- *AmMWSc 92*
**Appel**, Nina S. 1936- *WhoAmL 92, WhoMW 92*
**Appel**, Robert Eugene 1958- *WhoAmL 92*
**Appel**, Russell Lewis 1961- *WhoFI 92*
**Appel**, Stanley Hersh 1933- *AmMWSc 92*
**Appel**, Toby *WhoEnt 92*
**Appel**, Warren Curtis 1944- *AmMWSc 92*
**Appelbaum**, Alan 1936- *WhoAmL 92*
**Appelbaum**, Bruce David 1957- *WhoWest 92*
**Appelbaum**, Emanuel 1894- *AmMWSc 92*
**Appelbaum**, Joel A 1941- *AmMWSc 92*
**Appelbaum**, Todd J. 1961- *WhoMW 92*
**Appelfeld**, Aharon 1931- *LiExTwC*
**Appelfeld**, Aharon 1932- *ConAu 133*
**Appelgren**, Walter Phon 1928- *AmMWSc 92*
**Appell**, Don *LesBEnT 92*
**Appell**, Keith Douglas 1941- *WhoRel 92*
**Appella**, Ettore 1933- *AmMWSc 92*
**Appelman**, Evan Hugh 1935- *AmMWSc 92, WhoMW 92*
**Appelman**, Mary Goold 1926- *WhoAmP 91*
**Appelquist**, Albin Ray 1918- *WhoRel 92*
**Appelquist**, Thomas 1941- *AmMWSc 92*
**Appelt**, Brian Gregory 1952- *WhoAmL 92*
**Appelt**, Glenn David 1935- *AmMWSc 92*
**Appelwick**, Marlin J *WhoAmP 91*
**Appenzeller**, Otto 1927- *AmMWSc 92, WhoWest 92*
**Apperley**, George Owen Wynne 1884-1960 *TwCPaSc*
**Apperson**, Bernard James 1956- *WhoAmL 92*
**Apperson**, Charles Hamilton 1925- *AmMWSc 92*
**Apperson**, Donna Lorraine 1956- *WhoEnt 92*
**Apperson**, Jeffrey A. 1954- *WhoAmL 92*
**Appert**, Hubert Ernest *AmMWSc 92*
**Appiah**, Joe d1990 *IntWW 91N*
**Appiah**, Joe 1918-1990 *AnObit 1990*
**Appiah**, Joseph Emmanuel 1918-1990 *FacFETw*
**Appiah**, Peggy 1921- *IntAu&W 91, WrDr 92*
**Appino**, James B 1931- *AmMWSc 92*
**Appl**, Franklin John 1937- *AmMWSc 92*
**Appl**, Fredric Carl 1932- *AmMWSc 92*
**Apple**, Andrew Thomas Geiger 1858-1918 *BiInAmS*
**Apple**, Daina Dravnieks 1944- *WhoFI 92*
**Apple**, Daniel Bryce 1951- *WhoWest 92*
**Apple**, David 1954- *WhoFI 92*
**Apple**, Douglas Merle 1963- *WhoRel 92*
**Apple**, Ed 1932- *WhoAmP 91*
**Apple**, Jacki *DrAPF 91, IntAu&W 91*
**Apple**, Jay Lawrence 1926- *AmMWSc 92*
**Apple**, Lowell D 1928- *WhoAmP 91*
**Apple**, Martin Allen 1939- *AmMWSc 92*
**Apple**, Max *DrAPF 91*
**Apple**, Max 1941- *WrDr 92*
**Apple**, Michael Whitman 1942- *WhoMW 92*
**Apple**, Robah Warren, Jr. 1955- *WhoEnt 92*
**Apple**, Spencer Butler, Jr 1912- *AmMWSc 92*
**Apple**, Steven Anthony 1954- *WhoWest 92*
**Applebaum**, Charles H 1942- *AmMWSc 92*
**Applebaum**, Charles Henry 1942- *WhoMW 92*
**Applebaum**, Elizabeth Liliane 1958- *WhoRel 92*
**Applebaum**, Emanuel 1922- *WhoRel 92*
**Applebaum**, Harvey Milton 1937- *WhoAmL 92*
**Applebaum**, Louis 1918- *NewAmDM, WhoEnt 92*
**Applebaum**, Michael Murray 1958- *WhoAmL 92*
**Applebaum**, Morton M. 1911- *WhoRel 92*
**Applebaum**, Stanley Seymour 1922- *WhoEnt 92*
**Applebee**, Leonard 1914- *TwCPaSc*
**Appleberry**, James Bruce 1938- *WhoMW 92*
**Appleberry**, Walter Thomas 1926- *WhoWest 92*
**Applebroog**, Ida 1929- *WorArt 1980*
**Applebury**, Meredithe L 1942- *AmMWSc 92*
**Appleby**, Alan 1937- *AmMWSc 92*
**Appleby**, Arnold Pierce 1935- *AmMWSc 92*
**Appleby**, Brian John 1930- *Who 92*
**Appleby**, Charlie L, Jr *WhoAmP 91*
**Appleby**, David Louis 1948- *WhoEnt 92*
**Appleby**, Douglas Edward Surtees 1929- *Who 92*
**Appleby**, Elizabeth 1942- *Who 92*
**Appleby**, James E 1904- *WhoAmP 91*
**Appleby**, James E 1936- *AmMWSc 92*
**Appleby**, Jerry Lee 1942- *WhoRel 92*
**Appleby**, John Frederick 1948- *AmMWSc 92*
**Appleby**, Malcolm Arthur 1946- *Who 92*
**Appleby**, Raphael 1931- *Who 92*
**Appleby**, Robert 1913- *Who 92*
**Appleby**, Robert H 1931- *AmMWSc 92*
**Appleby**, William Franklin, Sr. 1928- *WhoRel 92*
**Appleby-Young**, Sadye Pearl 1927- *WhoBlA 92*
**Applefeld**, Laurie Sue 1953- *WhoAmL 92*
**Appleford**, John Widman 1938- *WhoAmP 91*
**Applegarth**, Derek A 1937- *AmMWSc 92*
**Applegarth**, Virginia Bevington 1953- *WhoFI 92*
**Applegate**, Albert Augustus 1928- *WhoAmP 91*
**Applegate**, Douglas 1928- *AlmAP 92 [port], WhoAmP 91, WhoMW 92*
**Applegate**, Howard George 1922- *AmMWSc 92*
**Applegate**, James 1923- *WrDr 92*
**Applegate**, James Edward 1942- *AmMWSc 92*
**Applegate**, James Keith 1944- *AmMWSc 92*
**Applegate**, James L 1931- *WhoAmP 91*
**Applegate**, Karl Edwin 1923- *WhoAmL 92*
**Applegate**, Kenneth Ira 1958- *WhoRel 92*
**Applegate**, Lynn E 1941- *AmMWSc 92*
**Applegate**, Richard Lee 1936- *AmMWSc 92*
**Applegate**, William E, III 1942- *WhoAmP 91*
**Appleman**, Buford Marion 1925- *WhoFI 92*
**Appleman**, Daniel Everett 1931- *AmMWSc 92*
**Appleman**, Gabriel 1922- *AmMWSc 92*
**Appleman**, James R 1956- *AmMWSc 92*
**Appleman**, M Michael 1933- *AmMWSc 92*
**Appleman**, Marjorie *DrAPF 91*
**Appleman**, Morris 1922- *WhoRel 92*
**Appleman**, Philip *DrAPF 91*
**Appleman**, Philip 1926- *WrDr 92*
**Applequist**, Douglas Einar 1930- *AmMWSc 92*
**Applequist**, Jon Barr 1932- *AmMWSc 92, WhoMW 92*
**Appleseed**, Johnny 1774?-1847 *BenetAL 91*
**Appleson**, John Alan 1949- *WhoMW 92*
**Appleton**, B R 1937- *AmMWSc 92*
**Appleton**, Clevette Wilma *WhoBlA 92*
**Appleton**, Clyde Robert 1928- *WhoEnt 92*
**Appleton**, Edward Victor 1892-1965 *FacFETw, WhoNob 90*
**Appleton**, Everard Jack *ScFEYrs*
**Appleton**, George 1902- *IntWW 91, Who 92*
**Appleton**, John 1935- *WhoFI 92*
**Appleton**, John P 1934- *AmMWSc 92*
**Appleton**, Joseph Hayne 1927- *AmMWSc 92*
**Appleton**, Lawrence *ConAu 133*
**Appleton**, Martin David 1917- *AmMWSc 92*
**Appleton**, Peter Arthur 1941- *WhoEnt 92, WhoWest 92*
**Appleton**, Sarah *DrAPF 91*
**Appleton**, Sheldon Lee 1933- *WrDr 92*
**Appleton**, Victor *ScFEYrs, SmATA 67*
**Appleton**, Victor, II *SmATA 67*
**Applewhaite**, Leon B. 1927- *WhoBlA 92*
**Applewhite**, Francine Laura 1962- *WhoAmL 92*
**Applewhite**, James *DrAPF 91*
**Applewhite**, Thomas Hood 1924- *AmMWSc 92*
**Appleyard**, Edward Clair 1934- *AmMWSc 92*
**Appleyard**, Fred 1874-1963 *TwCPaSc*
**Appleyard**, Leonard Vincent 1938- *Who 92*
**Appleyard**, Raymond 1922- *Who 92*
**Appleyard**, Raymond K. 1922- *IntWW 91*
**Appleyard**, William James 1935- *Who 92*
**Appling**, Luke 1907-1991 *NewYTBS 91 [port]*
**Appling**, William David Love 1934- *AmMWSc 92*
**Appold**, Mark Leonard 1936- *WhoRel 92*
**Appratto**, Roberto 1951- *ConSpAP*
**Apps**, Michael John 1944- *AmMWSc 92*
**Aprahamian**, Ani 1958- *AmMWSc 92*
**Aprahamian**, Felix 1914- *IntWW 91*
**Ap Rees**, Thomas 1930- *Who 92*
**April**, Ernest W 1939- *AmMWSc 92*
**April**, Gary Charles 1940- *AmMWSc 92*
**April**, Rand Scott 1951- *WhoAmL 92*
**April**, Robert Wayne 1946- *AmMWSc 92*
**Aprill**, Arnold *DrAPF 91*
**Aprille**, Thomas Joseph, Jr 1943- *AmMWSc 92*
**Apringius of Beja** *EncEarC*
**Aprison**, Barry Steven 1953- *WhoMW 92*

**Aprison,** Morris Herman 1923- *AmMWSc 92*
**Ap Robert,** Hywel Wyn Jones 1923- *Who 92*
**Apruzese,** John Patrick 1948- *AmMWSc 92*
**Apruzzese,** Vincent John 1928- *WhoAmL 92*
**ApSimon,** John W 1935- *AmMWSc 92*
**Apsley,** Lord 1961- *Who 92*
**Apstein,** Theodore 1918- *WhoEnt 92*
**Apt,** Adam Jared 1955- *WhoFI 92*
**Apt,** Denise C 1929- *WhoAmP 91*
**Apt,** Kenneth Ellis 1945- *AmMWSc 92, WhoWest 92*
**Apt,** Walter James 1922- *AmMWSc 92*
**Apte,** Chidanand *AmMWSc 92*
**Apted,** Michael 1941- *IntMPA 92*
**Apted,** Michael D. 1941- *WhoEnt 92*
**Apter,** David Ernest 1924- *WrDr 92*
**Apter,** Julie Pasquariello 1958- *WhoAmL 92*
**Apter,** Michael John 1939- *WrDr 92*
**Apter,** Nathaniel Stanley 1913- *AmMWSc 92*
**Apter,** T. E. 1949- *ConAu 134*
**Aptheker,** Bettina 1944- *WrDr 92*
**Aptheker,** Bettina Fay 1944- *IntAu&W 91, WhoWest 92*
**Apthomas,** Ifan 1917- *WrDr 92*
**Apthorp,** John Dorrington 1935- *Who 92*
**Apuron,** Anthony Sablan 1945- *WhoRel 92, WhoWest 92*
**Apuzzio,** J J *AmMWSc 92*
**Apyan,** Roseanne Lucille 1949- *WhoWest 92*
**Aquarone,** Stanislas Raoul Adrien 1915- *IntWW 91*
**Aquila** *EncEarC*
**Aquila,** Evelyn J 1932- *WhoAmP 91*
**Aquila,** Francis Joseph 1957- *WhoAmP 91*
**Aquila,** Vincent Salvador 1963- *WhoRel 92*
**Aquilecchia,** Giovanni 1923- *Who 92*
**Aquilino,** Thomas Joseph, Jr. 1939- *WhoAmL 92*
**Aquinas,** Thomas 1224?-1274 *DcLB 115 [port]*
**Aquino,** Benigno *FacFETw*
**Aquino,** Carlos Alberto 1960- *WhoHisp 92*
**Aquino,** Corazon 1933- *FacFETw [port], IntWW 91*
**Aquino,** Dolores Catherine 1949- *AmMWSc 92*
**Aquino,** Francisco 1919- *IntWW 91*
**Aquino,** Humberto 1947- *WhoHisp 92*
**Aquino,** John Goddard 1960- *WhoFI 92*
**Aquino,** Luis 1965- *WhoHisp 92*
**Aquino,** Maria Corazon Cojuangco 1933- *Who 92*
**Aquino,** Michael A. 1946- *RelLAm 91*
**Arab-Ismaili,** Mohammad Sharif 1949- *AmMWSc 92*
**Arabe,** Michael Don 1947- *WhoWest 92*
**Arabia,** Paul 1938- *WhoAmL 92, WhoMW 92*
**Arabian,** Armand 1934- *WhoAmL 92, WhoWest 92*
**Arabian,** Armond A 1934- *WhoAmP 91*
**Arabyan,** Ara 1953- *AmMWSc 92*
**Arachidamia** *EncAmaz 91*
**Arad,** Yitshak 1926- *ConAu 134*
**Araeen,** Rasheed 1935- *TwCPaSc*
**Arafat,** Yasir 1929- *FacFETw [port]*
**Arafat,** Yasser 1929- *IntWW 91*
**Aragaki,** Minoru 1926- *AmMWSc 92*
**Aragon,** Arlene Bernice 1954- *WhoHisp 92*
**Aragon,** Bill John 1946- *WhoHisp 92*
**Aragon,** Carla Y. 1955- *WhoHisp 92*
**Aragon,** Ernest *WhoHisp 92*
**Aragon,** John A. 1930- *WhoHisp 92*
**Aragon,** Joseph M. *WhoHisp 92*
**Aragon,** Juan 1947- *WhoHisp 92*
**Aragon,** Louis 1897-1982 *FacFETw, GuFrLit 1*
**Aragon,** Manny *WhoHisp 92*
**Aragon,** Manny M *WhoAmP 91*
**Aragon,** Rafael De Jesus 1938- *WhoHisp 92*
**Aragon,** Sergio Ramiro 1949- *WhoHisp 92*
**Aragon Viamonte,** Andres 1946- *WhoWest 92*
**Arai,** Hisao Philip 1926- *AmMWSc 92*
**Arai,** Ken-Ichi 1942- *AmMWSc 92*
**Arai,** Kiyomaru 1918- *WhoFI 92*
**Arain,** Shafiq 1933- *IntWW 91, Who 92*
**Araiz,** Joseph Michael 1961- *WhoFI 92*
**Araiza,** Francisco 1950- *IntWW 91*
**Arajs,** Sigurds 1927- *AmMWSc 92*
**Arak,** Marcelle V. 1942- *WhoFI 92*
**Arakaki,** Dennis Akira 1947- *WhoAmP 91*
**Arakaki,** Wayne S. 1932- *WhoIns 92*
**Arakawa,** Edward Takashi 1929- *AmMWSc 92*
**Arakawa,** Kasumi 1926- *WhoMW 92*
**Arakelian,** Deborah *WhoEnt 92*
**Araki,** George Shoichi 1932- *AmMWSc 92*
**Araki,** James Tomomasa 1925- *WrDr 92*
**Araki,** Masasuke 1950- *AmMWSc 92*
**Araki,** Minoru S *AmMWSc 92*
**Araki,** Minoru S. 1931- *WhoWest 92*
**Araki,** Yoshiro 1921- *IntWW 91*
**Arakishvili,** Dmitriy Ignat'evich 1873-1953 *SovUnBD*
**Aral,** H. Cahit 1927- *IntWW 91*
**Arala-Chaves,** Mario Passalaqua 1939- *AmMWSc 92*
**Aramburo,** Sophie Watts 1931- *WhoBlA 92*
**Aramburu,** Albert 1934- *WhoHisp 92*
**Aramburu,** Juan Carlos 1912- *WhoRel 92*
**Aramini,** Jan Marie 1955- *AmMWSc 92*
**Arams,** F R 1925- *AmMWSc 92*
**Aran,** Alberto Joaquin 1954- *WhoHisp 92*
**Aran,** Fernando Santiago 1957- *WhoAmL 92*
**Arana,** Carlos Martin 1962- *WhoEnt 92*
**Arana,** Christina Alyce 1962- *WhoWest 92*
**Arana,** Helen *DrAPF 91*
**Arana,** Suelena M. 1958- *WhoHisp 92*
**Arana-Adams,** Therese A. 1945- *WhoIns 92*
**Arana-Adams,** Therese Anne 1945- *WhoFI 92*
**Arana Osorio,** Carlos Manuel 1918- *IntWW 91*
**Aranbarri,** Ricardo 1959- *WhoHisp 92*
**Aranda,** Conde de 1718-1799 *HisDSpE*
**Aranda,** Benjamin, III 1940- *WhoHisp 92*
**Aranda,** Jacob Velasco 1942- *AmMWSc 92*
**Aranda,** Jess Robert 1949- *WhoHisp 92*
**Aranda,** Thomas, Jr 1934- *WhoAmP 91*
**Araneo,** Barbara Ann *AmMWSc 92*
**Arangio-Ruiz,** Gaetano 1919- *IntWW 91*
**Arango,** Anthony Glenn 1945- *WhoFI 92*
**Arango,** Emilio 1927- *WhoAmL 92*
**Arango,** H. Humberto 1944- *WhoHisp 92*
**Arango,** J. A. *WhoHisp 92*
**Arango,** Jose O 1957- *WhoAmP 91*
**Arango y Parreno,** Francisco 1756-1837 *HisDSpE*
**Aranow,** Peter Jones 1946- *WhoFI 92*
**Aranow,** Ruth Lee Horwitz 1929- *AmMWSc 92*
**Arante,** Al *WhoHisp 92*
**Arany,** Janos 1817-1882 *NinCLC 34 [port]*
**Aranyi,** Jelly d' 1893-1966 *NewAmDM*
**Aranzadi Martinez,** Jose Claudio 1946- *IntWW 91*
**Arapasu,** Teoctist 1915- *WhoRel 92*
**Arapov,** Boris 1905- *ConCom 92*
**Arapov,** Boris Aleksandrovich 1905- *IntWW 91*
**Arashi,** Qadi Abdul Karim al- *IntWW 91*
**Araskog,** Rand V. 1931- *CurBio 91 [port]*
**Araskog,** Rand Vincent 1931- *IntWW 91, WhoFI 92*
**Arasmith,** Neil H 1930- *WhoAmP 91*
**Arata,** Dorothy 1928- *AmMWSc 92*
**Arata,** Sil Louis, Sr. 1930- *WhoWest 92*
**Arator** d550? *EncEarC*
**Araujo,** Denis 1917- *WhoRel 92*
**Araujo,** Jess J., Sr. 1947- *WhoHisp 92*
**Araujo,** Jose Emilio Goncalves 1922- *IntWW 91*
**Araujo,** Juan de 1646-1714 *HisDSpE*
**Araujo,** Julius C. 1926- *WhoHisp 92*
**Araujo,** Norman 1933- *WhoBlA 92*
**Araujo,** Oscar Eduardo 1927- *AmMWSc 92*
**Araujo,** Roger Jerome 1934- *AmMWSc 92*
**Araujo Sales,** Eugenio de 1920- *IntWW 91*
**Arauz,** Carlos Gaspar 1949- *WhoWest 92*
**Aravagiri,** Manickam 1952- *WhoWest 92*
**Arave,** Clive W 1931- *AmMWSc 92*
**Arb,** Tim Kent 1938- *WhoFI 92*
**Arbagi,** Martin George 1940- *WhoMW 92*
**Arbatov,** Georgiy Arkadevich 1923- *IntWW 91, SovUnBD*
**Arbeau,** Thoinot 1520-1595 *NewAmDM*
**Arbeeny,** Cynthia M *AmMWSc 92*
**Arbeid,** Ben *IntMPA 92*
**Arbeid,** Murray 1935- *IntWW 91*
**Arbeli-Almozlino,** Shoshana 1926- *IntWW 91*
**Arbenz,** Johann Kaspar 1918- *AmMWSc 92*
**Arbenz Guzman,** Jacobo 1913-1971 *FacFETw*
**Arber,** Carol H. 1942- *WhoAmL 92*
**Arber,** Werner *Who 92*
**Arber,** Werner 1929- *AmMWSc 92, FacFETw, IntWW 91, WhoNob 90*
**Arberry,** Morse, Jr 1953- *WhoAmP 91, WhoBlA 92*
**Arbhabhirama,** Anat 1938- *IntWW 91*
**Arbib,** John A. 1924- *WhoFI 92*
**Arbib,** Michael A 1940- *AmMWSc 92*
**Arbit,** Beryl Ellen 1949- *WhoAmL 92*
**Arbit,** Bruce 1954- *WhoFI 92*
**Arbit,** Terry Steven 1958- *WhoAmL 92*
**Arbiter,** Andrew Richard 1958- *WhoFI 92*
**Arbiter,** Nathaniel 1911- *AmMWSc 92*
**Arbogast,** David Lee 1945- *WhoMW 92*
**Arbogast,** Richard Terrance 1937- *AmMWSc 92*
**Arboleya,** Carlos Jose 1929- *WhoHisp 92*
**Arbor,** Jane *WrDr 92*
**Arbuckle,** Earl Francis, III 1950- *WhoEnt 92*
**Arbuckle,** Fatty 1887-1933 *FacFETw [port]*
**Arbuckle,** Kurt 1949- *WhoAmL 92*
**Arbuckle,** Matthew 1828-1883 *NewAmDM*
**Arbuckle,** Pamela Susan 1955- *WhoBlA 92*
**Arbuckle,** Philip Wayne 1954- *WhoMW 92*
**Arbuckle,** Ronald Lee, Sr. 1945- *WhoBlA 92*
**Arbulu,** Agustin 1928- *AmMWSc 92, WhoHisp 92*
**Arbulu,** Agustin Victor 1949- *WhoHisp 92*
**Arbulu,** Maria Azucena 1956- *WhoHisp 92*
**Arbulu Galliani,** Guillermo *IntWW 91*
**Arburtha,** Leodies U. 1923- *WhoBlA 92*
**Arbus,** Diane 1923-1971 *FacFETw*
**Arbus,** Diane Nemerov 1923-1971 *HanAmWH*
**Arbus,** Loreen Joy *WhoEnt 92*
**Arbuthnot,** Andrew Robert Coghill 1926- *Who 92*
**Arbuthnot,** James Norwich 1952- *Who 92*
**Arbuthnot,** John 1667-1735 *BlkwCEP*
**Arbuthnot,** John 1912- *Who 92*
**Arbuthnot,** Keith Robert Charles 1951- *Who 92*
**Arbuthnott** *Who 92*
**Arbuthnott,** Master of 1950- *Who 92*
**Arbuthnott,** Viscount of 1924- *Who 92*
**Arbuthnott,** Hugh James 1936- *Who 92*
**Arbuthnott,** John Peebles 1939- *Who 92*
**Arbuthnott,** Robert 1936- *Who 92*
**Arbuzov,** Aleksey Nikolaevich 1908-1986 *SovUnBD*
**Arbuzov,** Alexei Nikolayevich 1908- *FacFETw*
**Arbuzov,** Boris Aleksandrovich 1903- *IntWW 91*
**Arca,** Emil 1960- *WhoAmL 92*
**Arcadelt,** Jacob 1505?-1568 *NewAmDM*
**Arcadi,** John Albert 1924- *AmMWSc 92, WhoWest 92*
**Arcadipane,** Angelo Vincent 1941- *WhoAmL 92*
**Arcand,** Adrien 1899-1967 *BiDExR*
**Arcand,** Denys 1941- *ConAu 133, IntMPA 92, IntWW 91*
**Arcand,** George Myron 1924- *AmMWSc 92*
**Arcand,** Michel Roger 1949- *WhoEnt 92*
**Arcara,** James Paul 1934- *WhoEnt 92, WhoFI 92*
**Arcara,** Richard Joseph 1940- *WhoAmL 92*
**Arcari,** Anne Johnson 1939- *WhoAmP 91*
**Arcaro,** Eddie 1916- *FacFETw*
**Arcaro,** Harold Conrad, Jr. 1935- *WhoAmL 92*
**Arce,** A Anthony 1923- *AmMWSc 92, WhoHisp 92*
**Arce,** Carlos H. *WhoHisp 92*
**Arce,** Cecilia 1954- *WhoHisp 92*
**Arce,** Gina 1929- *AmMWSc 92*
**Arce,** Jose Antonio 1948- *WhoHisp 92*
**Arce,** Jose Edgar 1937- *AmMWSc 92*
**Arce,** Jose Martinez 1952- *WhoHisp 92*
**Arce,** Ligia A. *WhoHisp 92*
**Arce,** Manuel Jose 1787-1847 *HisDSpE*
**Arce,** Miguel Luis 1951- *WhoHisp 92*
**Arce,** Rafael 1944- *WhoHisp 92*
**Arce,** Rose Marie 1964- *WhoHisp 92*
**Arce Bello,** Jane *WhoHisp 92*
**Arce-Larreta,** Jorge J. 1939- *WhoHisp 92*
**Arce-Martinez,** Sergio Samuel 1924- *WhoRel 92*
**Arcenas,** Loy 1953?- *ConTFT 9*
**Arceneaux,** George, Jr. 1928- *WhoAmL 92*
**Arceneaux,** Joseph Lincoln 1941- *AmMWSc 92*
**Arceneaux,** Jules Menou, II 1953- *WhoRel 92*
**Arceo,** Andrew Michael 1961- *WhoFI 92*
**Arcese,** Paul Salvatore 1930- *AmMWSc 92*
**Arcesi,** Joseph A 1938- *AmMWSc 92*
**Arch,** Michael Alexis 1951- *WhoAmL 92*
**Arch,** Stephen William 1942- *AmMWSc 92*
**Archabal,** Nina Marchetti 1940- *WhoMW 92*
**Archambault,** John *ConAu 135, SmATA 67*
**Archambault,** John Kenehan 1938- *WhoFI 92, WhoMW 92*
**Archambeau,** John Orin 1925- *AmMWSc 92*
**Archangelsky,** Sergio 1931- *AmMWSc 92*
**Archard,** Howell Osborne 1929- *AmMWSc 92*
**Archbold,** Norbert L 1930- *AmMWSc 92*
**Archbold,** Phil Carlos 1936- *WhoRel 92*
**Archbold,** Thomas Frank 1933- *AmMWSc 92*
**Archdale,** Edward 1921- *Who 92*
**Archdale,** John 1642?-1710? *DcNCBi 1*
**Archdeacon,** John Robert 1919- *WhoWest 92*
**Archer,** Albert 1915- *Who 92*
**Archer,** Anne 1947- *IntMPA 92*
**Archer,** Arthur John 1924- *Who 92*
**Archer,** Bill 1928- *AlmAP 92 [port]*
**Archer,** Bruce *Who 92*
**Archer,** C. Russell 1918- *WhoRel 92*
**Archer,** Carl Marion 1920- *WhoAmP 91, WhoFI 92*
**Archer,** Cass L 1924- *AmMWSc 92*
**Archer,** Chalmers, Jr. 1938- *WhoBlA 92*
**Archer,** Chris James 1948- *WhoWest 92*
**Archer,** Clyde Vernon Harcourt 1904- *Who 92*
**Archer,** Colin 1832-1921 *DcTwDes*
**Archer,** David Horace 1928- *AmMWSc 92*
**Archer,** Dennis *TwCWW 91*
**Archer,** Dennis Wayne 1942- *WhoAmL 92, WhoAmP 91, WhoBlA 92, WhoMW 92*
**Archer,** Douglas Harley 1925- *AmMWSc 92*
**Archer,** Douglas R. 1948- *WhoWest 92*
**Archer,** Eva P. *WhoBlA 92*
**Archer,** Frank 1912- *TwCPaSc*
**Archer,** Frank Joseph 1912- *Who 92*
**Archer,** Fred 1915- *IntAu&W 91, WrDr 92*
**Archer,** George William 1939- *WhoWest 92*
**Archer,** Gleason Leonard 1916- *WrDr 92*
**Archer,** Glenn LeRoy, Jr. 1929- *WhoAmL 92, WhoAmP 91*
**Archer,** Graham Robertson 1939- *Who 92*
**Archer,** Ian W. 1960- *ConAu 135*
**Archer,** Jean Mary 1932- *Who 92*
**Archer,** Jeffrey 1940- *WrDr 92*
**Archer,** Jeffrey Howard 1940- *IntAu&W 91, IntWW 91, Who 92*
**Archer,** John *Who 92*
**Archer,** John 1915- *IntMPA 92*
**Archer,** John Dale 1923- *AmMWSc 92*
**Archer,** John Francis Ashweek 1925- *Who 92*
**Archer,** John Hall 1914- *WrDr 92*
**Archer,** John Norman 1921- *Who 92*
**Archer,** Juanita A. 1934- *WhoBlA 92*
**Archer,** Juanita Almetta 1934- *AmMWSc 92*
**Archer,** Jules 1915- *WrDr 92*
**Archer,** Keith 1955- *ConAu 135*
**Archer,** Kenneth Davidson 1940- *WhoAmL 92*
**Archer,** Lawrence H 1923- *AmMWSc 92*
**Archer,** Lee A., Jr. *WhoBlA 92*
**Archer,** Leonard Bruce 1922- *Who 92*
**Archer,** Mary Doreen 1944- *Who 92*
**Archer,** Mary Ellen 1943- *WhoFI 92*
**Archer,** Mildred 1911- *WrDr 92*
**Archer,** Mildred Agnes 1911- *Who 92*
**Archer,** Nuala *DrAPF 91*
**Archer,** Peter 1926- *Who 92*
**Archer,** Peter Kingsley 1926- *WrDr 92*
**Archer,** Richard A. 1927- *WhoIns 92*
**Archer,** Richard Earl 1945- *WhoFI 92*
**Archer,** Robert Allen 1936- *AmMWSc 92*
**Archer,** Robert James 1926- *AmMWSc 92*
**Archer,** Robert Raymond 1928- *AmMWSc 92*
**Archer,** Robert V *IntMPA 92*
**Archer,** Ron *TwCSFW 91, WrDr 92*
**Archer,** Ronald Dean 1932- *AmMWSc 92*
**Archer,** Ronald Walter 1929- *IntWW 91*
**Archer,** Sellers G. 1908-1980 *ConAu 134*
**Archer,** Stanley J 1944- *AmMWSc 92*
**Archer,** Stephen Murphy 1934- *WhoEnt 92*
**Archer,** Susie Coleman 1946- *WhoBlA 92*
**Archer,** Sydney 1917- *AmMWSc 92*
**Archer,** Val 1946- *TwCPaSc*
**Archer,** Van Henry, Jr 1940- *WhoAmP 91*
**Archer,** Vernon Shelby 1939- *AmMWSc 92*
**Archer,** Victor Eugene 1922- *AmMWSc 92*
**Archer,** Violet 1913- *ConCom 92, NewAmDM*
**Archer,** William Harley 1934- *WhoAmL 92*
**Archer,** William Reynolds, Jr 1928- *WhoAmP 91*
**Archerd,** Army *IntMPA 92*
**Archetto,** Paul H *WhoAmP 91*
**Archibald,** Barony of *Who 92*
**Archibald,** B. Milele 1945- *WhoBlA 92*
**Archibald,** Charles Arnold 1936- *WhoMW 92*
**Archibald,** Claudia Jane 1939- *WhoRel 92*
**Archibald,** Francis X 1931- *WhoAmP 91*
**Archibald,** Fred John 1922- *WhoFI 92*
**Archibald,** George Christopher 1926- *IntWW 91, Who 92*
**Archibald,** George William 1946- *WhoMW 92*
**Archibald,** Harry Munro 1915- *Who 92*
**Archibald,** James 1919- *AmMWSc 92*
**Archibald,** James Kenway 1949- *WhoAmL 92*
**Archibald,** Julius A, Jr 1931- *AmMWSc 92*
**Archibald,** Kenneth C 1927- *AmMWSc 92*
**Archibald,** Lane R. 1948- *WhoAmL 92*
**Archibald,** Liliana 1928- *Who 92*

**Archibald,** Munro *Who 92*
**Archibald,** Nate 1948- *WhoBlA 92*
**Archibald,** Nolan D. 1943- *WhoFI 92*
**Archibald,** Patricia Ann 1934- *AmMWSc 92*
**Archibald,** Rae William 1941- *WhoFI 92, WhoWest 92*
**Archibald,** Ralph George 1901- *AmMWSc 92*
**Archibald,** Reginald MacGregor 1910- *AmMWSc 92*
**Archibald,** Rupert Douglas 1919- *IntAu&W 91*
**Archibald,** William James 1912- *AmMWSc 92*
**Archie,** Charles Neill 1948- *AmMWSc 92*
**Archie,** Cornell B., Jr. 1948- *WhoBlA 92*
**Archie,** James Lee 1922- *WhoBlA 92*
**Archie,** Shirley Franklin 1944- *WhoBlA 92*
**Archie,** William C, Jr 1944- *AmMWSc 92*
**Archie-Hudson,** Marguerite *WhoAmP 91*
**Archimovich,** Alexander S 1892- *AmMWSc 92*
**Archipenko,** Alexander 1887-1965 *FacFETw*
**Archuleta,** Adelmo E. *WhoHisp 92*
**Archuleta,** Alfonso Luis 1931- *WhoHisp 92*
**Archuleta,** Celestino E. *WhoHisp 92*
**Archuleta,** Felipe Benito 1910-1991 *WhoHisp 92N*
**Archuleta,** Isaac Rivera 1933- *WhoHisp 92*
**Archuleta,** Katherine Lorraine 1947- *WhoHisp 92*
**Archuleta,** Ralph J. 1947- *WhoHisp 92*
**Archuleta,** Rudolph Alonzo 1950- *WhoHisp 92*
**Archuleta,** Steve A. 1951- *WhoHisp 92*
**Archuleta,** Teresa Ann 1957- *WhoHisp 92*
**Arciga,** Joseph 1930- *WhoHisp 92*
**Arciniaga,** Robert *WhoHisp 92*
**Arciniega,** Ricardo Jesus 1939- *WhoHisp 92*
**Arciniega,** Tomas A. 1937- *WhoHisp 92*
**Arciniega,** Tomas Abel 1937- *WhoWest 92*
**Arciniegas,** German 1900- *IntWW 91*
**Arciszewski,** Tomasz Tadeusz 1948- *WhoMW 92*
**Arconti,** Richard David 1952- *WhoAmL 92*
**Arcos,** Cresencio S *WhoAmP 91*
**Arcos,** Cresencio S., Jr. 1943- *WhoHisp 92*
**Arcos,** Joseph 1921- *AmMWSc 92*
**Arctic,** Bishop of The 1936- *Who 92*
**Arculus,** Ronald 1923- *IntWW 91, Who 92*
**Arcuni,** Anthony Oreste 1939- *WhoFI 92*
**Arcuri,** Edward Louis, III 1943- *WhoAmP 91*
**Arcuri,** Mary Anne 1947- *WhoAmP 91, WhoWest 92*
**Arcuri,** Shirley Copeland 1949- *WhoAmL 92*
**Ard,** Ben Neal, Jr. 1922- *WrDr 92*
**Ard,** William *TwCWW 91*
**Ard,** William Bryant, Jr 1927- *AmMWSc 92*
**Ardagh And Clonmacnoise,** Bishop of 1935- *Who 92*
**Ardant,** Fanny 1949- *IntMPA 92*
**Ardash,** Garin 1963- *WhoWest 92*
**Ardee,** Lord 1941- *Who 92*
**Ardell,** Alan Jay 1939- *AmMWSc 92*
**Ardell,** Jeffrey Laurence *AmMWSc 92*
**Ardelt,** Wojciech Joseph 1939- *AmMWSc 92*
**Ardema,** Mark D 1940- *AmMWSc 92*
**Arden,** Andrew Paul Russel 1948- *Who 92*
**Arden,** Daniel Douglas 1922- *AmMWSc 92*
**Arden,** Donald Seymour 1916- *Who 92*
**Arden,** Eve d1990 *LesBEnT 92*
**Arden,** Eve 1907?-1990 *CurBio 91N*
**Arden,** Eve 1908-1990 *AnObit 1990, FacFETw*
**Arden,** Eve 1912-1990 *News 91*
**Arden,** J E M *IntAu&W 91X*
**Arden,** John 1930- *IntAu&W 91, IntWW 91, RfGEnL 91, Who 92, WrDr 92*
**Arden,** Mary Howarth 1947- *Who 92*
**Arden,** Sheldon Bruce 1942- *AmMWSc 92*
**Arden,** William *IntAu&W 91X, WrDr 92*
**Arderne,** John d1710? *DcNCBi 1*
**Ardia,** Stephen Vincent 1941- *WhoFI 92*
**Ardiente,** Editha Mijares 1945- *WhoMW 92*
**Ardies,** Tom 1931- *IntAu&W 91, WrDr 92*
**Ardiles,** Miguel de 1515-1586 *HisDSpE*
**Ardis,** Colby V, Jr 1935- *AmMWSc 92*
**Arditti,** Joseph 1932- *AmMWSc 92*
**Arditti,** Mary Barrow 1946- *WhoFI 92*
**Ardizzone,** Charlotte 1943- *TwCPaSc*
**Ardizzone,** Edward 1900-1979 *TwCPaSc*
**Ardizzone,** Tony *DrAPF 91*
**Ardley,** Harry Mountcastle 1926- *WhoWest 92*
**Ardley,** Neil Richard 1937- *IntAu&W 91*
**Ardmore,** Jane Kesner 1915- *IntAu&W 91*
**Ardolino,** Emile *IntMPA 92*
**Ardoyno,** Dolores *WhoEnt 92*
**Ardrey,** Ross James 1943- *WhoWest 92*
**Ardrey,** Saundra Curry 1953- *WhoBlA 92*
**Ardrey,** Stephanie Dionne 1965- *WhoWest 92*
**Arduino,** Eugene 1961- *WhoEnt 92*
**Ardwick,** Baron 1910- *IntWW 91, Who 92*
**Areeda,** Phillip 1930- *WhoAmL 92, WrDr 92*
**Areen,** Judith Carol 1944- *WhoAmL 92*
**Aref,** Abdul Rahman Mohammed 1916- *IntWW 91*
**Aref,** Hassan 1950- *AmMWSc 92*
**Arehart,** Catherine Lee 1954- *WhoFI 92*
**Areias,** Rusty 1949- *WhoAmP 91*
**Areilza,** Jose Maria de 1909- *HisDSpE, IntWW 91*
**Arekapudi,** Kumar Vijaya Vasantha 1957- *WhoMW 92*
**Arekapudi,** Vijayalakshmi 1948- *WhoMW 92*
**Arel,** Bulent 1919- *NewAmDM*
**Arel,** Maurice Louis 1937- *WhoAmP 91*
**Arellanes,** Audrey Spencer 1920- *WhoWest 92*
**Arellano,** Albert E. *WhoHisp 92*
**Arellano,** Alfredo 1948- *WhoHisp 92*
**Arellano,** C. Rolando 1945- *WhoHisp 92*
**Arellano,** Eugene Walter 1927- *WhoFI 92*
**Arellano,** George R. 1933- *WhoHisp 92*
**Arellano,** Javier 1956- *WhoHisp 92*
**Arellano,** Jose M. 1944- *WhoHisp 92*
**Arellano,** Luis *WhoHisp 92*
**Arellano,** Silvia *WhoHisp 92*
**Arem,** Lawrence Jay 1950- *WhoAmL 92*
**Arena,** Alan Joseph 1950- *WhoWest 92*
**Arena,** Drew Charles 1947- *WhoAmL 92*
**Arena,** J. Sylvester 1961- *WhoWest 92*
**Arena,** Jay M 1909- *AmMWSc 92*
**Arena,** Joseph P 1954- *AmMWSc 92*
**Arena,** Mary Helen 1951- *WhoRel 92*
**Arena,** Paul Raymond 1958- *WhoFI 92*
**Arena,** Randall Ruggero Altavilla 1954- *WhoWest 92*
**Arena,** Salvatore F 1937- *WhoAmP 91*
**Arenal,** Julie *WhoEnt 92*
**Arenal,** Julie 1942- *WhoHisp 92*
**Arenales,** Juan Antonio Alvarez de *HisDSpE*
**Arenas,** Andrea-Teresa 1951- *WhoHisp 92*
**Arenas,** Braulio 1913-1988 *ConSpAP*
**Arenas,** Fernando George, Jr. 1937- *WhoHisp 92*
**Arenas,** George W. *WhoIns 92*
**Arenas,** Marion *DrAPF 91*
**Arenas,** Reinaldo 1943- *LiExTwC*
**Arenas,** Reinaldo 1943-1990 *BenetAL 91, ConAu 133, WhoHisp 92N*
**Arenas,** Rosa M. *DrAPF 91*
**Arenaz,** Pablo 1950- *AmMWSc 92*
**Arenberg,** David 1927- *AmMWSc 92*
**Arencibia,** Raul Antonio 1955- *WhoAmL 92*
**Arend,** Robert Lee 1944- *WhoWest 92*
**Arend,** William Phelps 1937- *AmMWSc 92*
**Arendale,** William Frank 1921- *AmMWSc 92*
**Arendes,** Joseph Michael 1939- *WhoFI 92*
**Arends,** Charles Bradford 1931- *AmMWSc 92*
**Arends,** John Godfrey 1740-1807 *DcNCBi 1*
**Arendsen,** David Lloyd 1942- *AmMWSc 92*
**Arendshorst,** William John 1944- *AmMWSc 92*
**Arendt,** Erich 1903-1984 *LiExTwC*
**Arendt,** Hannah 1906-1975 *BenetAL 91, ConLC 66 [port], FacFETw [port], HanAmWH, LiExTwC, WomSoc*
**Arendt,** Kenneth Albert 1925- *AmMWSc 92*
**Arendt,** Ronald H 1941- *AmMWSc 92*
**Arendt,** Volker Dietrich 1934- *AmMWSc 92*
**Arenella,** Peter Lee 1947- *WhoAmL 92*
**Arenivar,** John David 1957- *WhoMW 92*
**Arenowitz,** Albert Harold 1925- *WhoWest 92*
**Arens,** Egmont 1888-1966 *DcTwDes, FacFETw*
**Arens,** John Frederic 1939- *AmMWSc 92*
**Arens,** Max Quirin 1945- *AmMWSc 92*
**Arens,** Moshe 1925- *IntWW 91*
**Arens,** Richard Friederich 1919- *AmMWSc 92*
**Arens,** Yigal 1951- *AmMWSc 92, WhoWest 92*
**Arensky,** Anton 1861-1906 *NewAmDM*
**Arensman,** Kevin Keith 1959- *WhoRel 92*
**Arenson,** Barbara Levine 1947- *WhoWest 92*
**Arenson,** Donald L 1926- *AmMWSc 92*
**Arenstorf,** Richard F 1929- *AmMWSc 92*
**Arent,** Benno von 1898- *EncTR 91 [port]*
**Arent,** Patrice Marla 1956- *WhoAmL 92*
**Arents,** Albert 1840-1914 *BiInAmS*
**Arents,** John 1926- *AmMWSc 92*
**Arentz,** Andrew Albert 1928- *WhoFI 92*
**Arentz,** Dick 1935- *WhoWest 92*
**Arentzen,** Charles 1919- *WhoWest 92*
**Arenz,** Robert James 1924- *AmMWSc 92*
**Arenz,** Thomas Walter 1957- *WhoFI 92*
**Arese,** Francesco 1805-1881 *DcAmImH*
**Arespacochaga Y Felipe,** Juan de 1920- *IntWW 91*
**Aresty,** Jeffrey 1951- *WhoAmL 92*
**Aretz,** Tonya Marie 1959- *WhoAmL 92*
**Arevalo,** Alfred Daniel 1947- *WhoHisp 92*
**Arevalo,** Felizardo A. *WhoHisp 92*
**Arevalo,** Henrietta Martinez 1949- *WhoHisp 92*
**Arevalo,** Jorge Enrique 1940- *WhoHisp 92*
**Arevalo,** Juan Jose 1904-1990 *FacFETw*
**Arevalo,** Ricardo Vidal 1949- *WhoHisp 92*
**Arevalo,** Rodolfo 1946- *WhoHisp 92*
**Arezzo,** Guido d' *NewAmDM*
**Arfa,** Harvey Z. 1945- *WhoAmL 92*
**Arfin,** Stuart Michael 1936- *AmMWSc 92*
**Arfmann,** Dennis Leon 1951- *WhoAmP 91*
**Argabright,** Loren N 1933- *AmMWSc 92*
**Argabright,** Perry A 1929- *AmMWSc 92*
**Argall,** David G 1958- *WhoAmP 91*
**Argall,** Paul Richard 1951- *WhoFI 92*
**Argan,** Giulio Carlo 1909- *IntWW 91*
**Argana,** Luis Maria *IntWW 91*
**Arganbright,** A. Dean 1930- *WhoIns 92*
**Arganbright,** Donald G 1939- *AmMWSc 92*
**Arganbright,** Robert Philip 1923- *AmMWSc 92*
**Argauer,** Robert John 1937- *AmMWSc 92*
**Argenal-Arauz,** Roger 1937- *AmMWSc 92*
**Argenbright,** Barry Lyn 1953- *WhoEnt 92*
**Argenbright,** Ed *WhoAmP 91*
**Argenio,** Antonio 1961- *TwCPaSc*
**Argens,** Jean-Baptiste deBoyer, marquis d 1704-1771 *BlkwCEP*
**Argenson,** Rene-Louis deVoyer, marquis d' 1694-1757 *BlkwCEP*
**Argent,** Eric William 1923- *Who 92*
**Argent,** Malcolm 1935- *Who 92*
**Argentina,** Bishop of 1935- *Who 92*
**Argentine,** Peter Dominic 1948- *WhoFI 92*
**Argento,** Dominick 1927- *ConCom 92, NewAmDM*
**Argenziano,** Carmen Antimo 1943- *WhoEnt 92*
**Argenzio,** Robert Alan 1941- *AmMWSc 92*
**Argerich,** Martha 1941- *IntWW 91*
**Argeris,** George John 1931- *WhoAmL 92*
**Argersinger,** William John, Jr 1918- *AmMWSc 92*
**Argetsinger,** Cameron R. 1921- *WhoAmL 92*
**Argetsinger,** Gerald Scott 1946- *WhoEnt 92*
**Argetsinger,** J C *WhoAmP 91*
**Arghezi,** Tudor 1880-1967 *FacFETw*
**Argiris,** Spiros 1952- *WhoEnt 92*
**Argiz,** Antonio L. 1952- *WhoHisp 92*
**Argo,** Ellen *DrAPF 91*
**Argo,** Harold Virgil 1918- *AmMWSc 92*
**Argo,** Paul Emmett 1948- *AmMWSc 92*
**Argo,** Robert Eugene, Jr 1923- *WhoAmP 91*
**Argo,** Thomas Munro 1841-1909 *DcNCBi 1*
**Argo,** William Frank 1951- *WhoFI 92*
**Argon,** Ali Suphi 1930- *AmMWSc 92*
**Argos,** Patrick 1942- *AmMWSc 92*
**Argot,** Jeanne 1936- *AmMWSc 92*
**Argoudelis,** Chris J 1929- *AmMWSc 92*
**Argov,** Shlomo 1929- *IntWW 91, Who 92*
**Argow,** Keith Angevin 1936- *WhoFI 92*
**Argow,** Sylvia *DrAPF 91*
**Argraves,** W Scott 1956- *AmMWSc 92*
**Argrette,** Joseph 1931- *WhoBlA 92*
**Argudin,** Bernardo M. *WhoHisp 92*
**Argue,** Don Harvey 1939- *WhoRel 92*
**Argue,** Jim, Jr 1951- *WhoAmP 91*
**Argue,** John Clifford 1932- *WhoAmL 92*
**Arguedas,** Alcides 1879-1946 *BenetAL 91*
**Arguedas,** Jose Maria 1911-1969 *BenetAL 91, DcLB 113 [port]*
**Arguelles,** Fernando 1954- *WhoEnt 92*
**Arguelles,** Ivan *DrAPF 91*
**Arguelles,** John A *WhoAmP 91*
**Arguello,** Alexis 1952- *WhoHisp 92*
**Arguello,** Benjamin W. 1961- *WhoHisp 92*
**Arguello,** Javier Alberto 1961- *WhoFI 92*
**Arguello,** Roberto J. T., Sr. 1932- *WhoHisp 92*
**Arguello,** Roberto Jose 1955- *WhoHisp 92*
**Argueta,** Manlio *IntWW 91*
**Argueta,** Manlio 1935- *LiExTwC*
**Argueta Antillon,** Jose Luis 1932- *IntWW 91*
**Arguijo,** Conrad V. *WhoHisp 92*
**Argus,** George William 1929- *AmMWSc 92*
**Argus,** Mary Frances 1924- *AmMWSc 92*
**Argy,** Dimitri 1921- *AmMWSc 92*
**Argyle,** Michael 1925- *IntAu&W 91, WrDr 92*
**Argyle,** Michael Victor 1915- *Who 92*
**Argyll,** Duke of 1937- *Who 92*
**Argyll And The Isles,** Bishop of 1921- *Who 92*
**Argyll And The Isles,** Bishop of 1940- *Who 92*
**Argyll And The Isles,** Dean of *Who 92*
**Argyll And The Isles,** Provosts in *Who 92*
**Argyres,** Petros 1927- *AmMWSc 92*
**Argyris,** Bertie 1930- *AmMWSc 92*
**Argyris,** John 1913- *WrDr 92*
**Argyris,** John 1916- *IntWW 91, Who 92*
**Argyris,** Thomas Stephen 1923- *AmMWSc 92*
**Argyropoulos,** Stavros Andreas 1945- *AmMWSc 92*
**Argyros,** Ioannis Konstantinos 1956- *AmMWSc 92*
**Arhelger,** Roger Boyd 1932- *AmMWSc 92*
**Ari,** Bakuji 1922- *IntWW 91*
**Ariail,** Jacqueline *DrAPF 91*
**Arial,** Jean Claude 1958- *WhoEnt 92*
**Arian,** Charles Lawrence 1960- *WhoRel 92*
**Arian,** David *WhoWest 92*
**Ariano,** Marjorie Ann 1951- *AmMWSc 92*
**Ariarajah,** Wesley 1941- *IntWW 91*
**Ariarajah,** Wesley Seevaratnam 1941- *WhoRel 92*
**Arias,** Abelardo Antonio 1954- *WhoHisp 92*
**Arias,** Alejandro Antonio 1959- *WhoHisp 92*
**Arias,** Armando Antonio, Jr. 1953- *WhoHisp 92*
**Arias,** Arturo 1950- *LiExTwC*
**Arias,** David 1929- *WhoRel 92*
**Arias,** Ernesto G. 1943- *WhoHisp 92*
**Arias,** Illeana 1956- *WhoHisp 92*
**Arias,** Irwin Monroe 1926- *AmMWSc 92*
**Arias,** Jose Manuel 1954- *AmMWSc 92*
**Arias,** Margot Fonteyn De d1991 *Who 92N*
**Arias,** Margot Fonteyn de 1919-1991 *IntWW 91, -91N*
**Arias,** Mortimer 1924- *WhoRel 92*
**Arias,** Rafael 1937- *WhoHisp 92*
**Arias,** Ramon H. *WhoHisp 92*
**Arias,** Rita C. *WhoHisp 92*
**Arias,** Roberto Emilio 1918-1989 *FacFETw*
**Arias,** Ron *DrAPF 91*
**Arias,** Ronald F. 1941- *WhoHisp 92*
**Arias,** Steve 1944- *WhoHisp 92*
**Arias,** Victor, Jr. 1956- *WhoHisp 92*
**Arias,** Victor R., Jr. 1936- *WhoHisp 92*
**Arias,** William E. 1945- *WhoHisp 92*
**Arias de Avila,** Pedro *HisDSpE*
**Arias de Saavedra,** Hernando 1560-1634 *HisDSpE*
**Arias de Ugarte y Forero,** Hernando 1561-1638 *HisDSpE*
**Arias E.,** Ricardo M. 1912- *IntWW 91*
**Arias Madrid,** Arnulfo 1901-1988 *FacFETw*
**Arias-Misson,** Alain *DrAPF 91*
**Arias Navarro,** Carlos 1908- *HisDSpE*
**Arias Navarro,** Carlos 1908-1989 *FacFETw*
**Arias-Salgado Y Montalvo,** Fernando 1938- *IntWW 91, Who 92*
**Arias Sanches,** Oscar 1941- *WhoNob 90*
**Arias Sanchez,** Oscar 1941- *IntWW 91, Who 92*
**Arias Stella,** Javier 1924- *IntWW 91*
**Arico,** Anthony V, Jr 1936- *WhoAmP 91*
**Arida,** Naseeb *DcAmImH*
**Aridjis,** Homero 1940- *ConSpAP*
**Aridor,** Yoram 1933- *IntWW 91*
**Arie,** Thomas Harry David 1933- *IntWW 91, Who 92*
**Arieff,** Alex J 1908- *AmMWSc 92*
**Arieff,** Allen I *AmMWSc 92*
**Ariemma,** Sidney 1922- *AmMWSc 92*
**Aries,** Robert Sancier 1919- *WhoFI 92*
**Ariet,** Mario 1939- *AmMWSc 92*
**Arif,** Basil Mumtaz 1940- *AmMWSc 92*
**Arif,** Saleem 1949- *TwCPaSc*
**Arif,** Shoaib 1950- *AmMWSc 92*
**Arifin,** Bustanil 1925- *IntWW 91*
**Arifin,** Sjahabuddin 1928- *Who 92*
**Ariguzo,** Godwin 1958- *WhoFI 92*
**Arihood,** Herbert H. 1939- *WhoMW 92*
**Arik,** Leyla Hatice 1959- *WhoFI 92*
**Arik,** Tali 1956- *WhoWest 92*
**Arikan,** Vural 1929- *IntWW 91*
**Arikawa,** Hiroo 1926- *WhoFI 92*
**Arikpo,** Okoi 1916- *IntWW 91*
**Arimah,** Nina Calbazana 1957- *WhoEnt 92*
**Arimoto,** Suguru 1936- *AmMWSc 92*
**Arimura,** Akira 1923- *AmMWSc 92*
**Arin,** Kemal 1941- *AmMWSc 92*
**Aring,** Charles Dair 1904- *AmMWSc 92*
**Arinwine,** Kenneth Wayne 1934- *WhoBlA 92*
**Arinze,** Francis 1932- *WhoRel 92*
**Arinze,** Francis A. 1932- *IntWW 91*
**Arion,** Douglas 1957- *AmMWSc 92*
**Arion,** Douglas Norman 1957- *WhoWest 92*
**Arion,** William Joseph 1940- *AmMWSc 92*
**Aris,** John Bernard Benedict 1934- *Who 92*

Aris, Rutherford 1929- AmMWSc 92
Arisawa, Hiromi 1896- IntWW 91
Arison, Micky 1949- WhoFI 92
Ariss, David William 1939- WhoWest 92
Aristide, Jean Bertrand IntWW 91
Aristide, Jean-Bertrand 1953- CurBio 91 [port], News 91 [port], -91-3 [port]
Aristides EncEarC
Aristo of Pella EncEarC
Aristoclea of Larisa EncAmaz 91
Aristodomou, Chrystoforos 1927- WhoRel 92
Aristophanes 450?BC-385?BC DramC 2 [port]
Aristotle 384BC-324BC EncEarC
Aristov, Averkiy Borisovich 1903-1973 SovUnBD
Aristov, Boris Ivanovich 1925- IntWW 91
Arita, George Shiro 1940- WhoWest 92
Aritan, Atilla G. 1962- WhoFI 92
Ariturk, Haluk 1949- WhoIns 92
Arius 260?-336 EncEarC
Ariyan, Stephan 1941- AmMWSc 92
Ariyan, Zaven S 1933- AmMWSc 92
Ariyoshi, George Ryoichi 1926- IntWW 91, WhoAmP 91, WhoWest 92
Ariza, Ramon Enrique 1951- WhoHisp 92
Arizumi, Martha Helen Robbins 1952- WhoFI 92
Arizumi, Martha Robbins 1952- WhoWest 92
Arjona Perez, Marta Maria 1923- IntWW 91
Ark, Billie D 1924- WhoAmP 91
Arkansaw, Tim 1925- WhoBlA 92
Arkell, Alfred 1924- AmMWSc 92
Arkell, John Hardy 1939- Who 92
Arkell, John Heward 1909- Who 92
Arkfeld, Leo 1912- Who 92
Arkhipov, Vladimir Mikhailovich 1933- IntWW 91
Arkhipova, Irina Konstantinovna 1925- IntWW 91, SovUnBD
Arkhurst, Joyce Cooper 1921- WhoBlA 92
Arkilic, Galip Mehmet 1920- AmMWSc 92
Arkin, Alan 1934- IntMPA 92
Arkin, Alan Wolf 1934- IntWW 91, WhoEnt 92
Arkin, Arthur Malcolm 1921- AmMWSc 92
Arkin, Frieda DrAPF 91
Arkin, Gerald Franklin 1942- AmMWSc 92
Arkin, Jean Marie 1932- WhoRel 92
Arkin, Joseph 1923- AmMWSc 92
Arkin, L. Jules WhoAmL 92
Arkin, Marcus 1926- WrDr 92
Arkin, Michael Leonard 1950- WhoEnt 92
Arkin, Robert David 1954- WhoFI 92
Arking, Albert 1932- AmMWSc 92
Arking, Linda DrAPF 91
Arking, Lucille Musser 1936- WhoMW 92
Arking, Robert 1936- AmMWSc 92, WhoMW 92
Arkins, John A 1926- AmMWSc 92
Arkinstall, Leonard 1924- WhoWest 92
Arkle, Thomas, Jr 1918- AmMWSc 92
Arkles, Barry Charles 1949- AmMWSc 92
Arkley, Alfred Samuel 1937- WhoFI 92
Arkley, Arthur James 1919- WrDr 92
Arklin, Henry 1928- WhoAmP 91
Arko, Aloysius John 1940- AmMWSc 92
Arko, Suan Lynne 1958- WhoWest 92
Arkoff, Samuel Z. 1918- IntMPA 92, WhoEnt 92
Arkowitz, Martin Arthur 1935- AmMWSc 92
Arkus, Allen Sol 1946- WhoFI 92
Arkush, Allan 1948- IntMPA 92
Arkuss, Neil Philip 1945- WhoAmL 92
Arle, Edward J. 1944- WhoRel 92
Arledge, Patricia O'Brien 1934- WhoRel 92
Arledge, Roone LesBEnT 92 [port]
Arledge, Roone 1931- FacFETw, IntMPA 92, News 92-2 [port], WhoEnt 92, WhoFI 92
Arlein, Kenneth Alan 1946- WhoFI 92
Arlen, Gary Horatio Grant WhoEnt 92
Arlen, Harold 1905-1986 FacFETw, NewAmDM
Arlen, Jennifer Hall 1959- WhoAmL 92, WhoFI 92
Arlen, Michael 1895-1956 LiExTwC, RfGEnL 91
Arlen, Michael J. 1930- LiExTwC, WrDr 92
Arlen, Michael John 1930- IntAu&W 91
Arlene, Herbert WhoAmP 91
Arlene, Herbert 1917- WhoBlA 92
Arletty IntWW 91
Arlian, Larry George 1944- AmMWSc 92
Arline, Jean Evelyn 1947- WhoMW 92
Arling, Arthur E. 1906- IntMPA 92
Arlinghaus, Edward James 1925- WhoMW 92
Arlinghaus, Heinrich Franz 1958- AmMWSc 92
Arlinghaus, Ralph B 1935- AmMWSc 92
Arlinghaus, Sandra Judith Lach 1943- AmMWSc 92, WhoMW 92
Arlinghaus, William Charles 1944- WhoMW 92
Arlington Chemical Company ScFEYrs
Arlman, Paul 1946- IntWW 91
Arlook, Ira Arthur 1943- WhoMW 92
Arlook, Martin Maxwell 1932- WhoAmL 92
Arlook, Theodore David 1910- WhoMW 92
Arlott, John 1914- IntWW 91, Who 92, WrDr 92
Arlow, Arnold Jack 1933- WhoFI 92
Arlow, Jacob 1912- AmMWSc 92
Armacost, David Lee 1944- AmMWSc 92
Armacost, Michael H 1937- WhoAmP 91
Armacost, Michael Hayden 1937- IntWW 91
Armacost, Robert Leo 1942- WhoMW 92
Armacost, Samuel Henry 1939- IntWW 91, WhoFI 92
Armacost, William L 1941- AmMWSc 92
Armagh, Archbishop of 1917- Who 92
Armagh, Archbishop of 1937- Who 92
Armagh, Dean of Who 92
Armagost, Elsa Gafvert WhoFI 92
Armagost, Lesa Ann 1957- WhoRel 92
Armah, Ayi Kwei 1938- ConNov 91
Armah, Ayi Kwei 1939- BlkLC [port], LiExTwC, WrDr 92
Armaly, Bassem Farid 1937- AmMWSc 92
Armaly, Mansour F 1927- AmMWSc 92
Armamento, Eduardo T 1960- AmMWSc 92
Arman 1928- WorArt 1980 [port]
Arman, Ara 1930- AmMWSc 92
Armand, Inessa 1875-1920 SovUnBD
Armand, Patrick WhoEnt 92
Armani, Frank Henry 1927- WhoAmP 91
Armani, Giorgio 1934- IntWW 91, News 91 [port]
Armani, Giorgio 1935- DcTwDes, FacFETw
Armanini, Louis Anthony 1930- AmMWSc 92
Armant, D Randall 1951- AmMWSc 92
Armantrout, Guy Alan 1940- AmMWSc 92
Armantrout, Rae DrAPF 91
Armantrout, Rae 1947- IntAu&W 91
Armas, Jose DrAPF 91
Armas, Maureen V. WhoHisp 92
Armas, Tony 1953- WhoHisp 92
Armatis, Frank John, Jr. 1951- WhoMW 92
Armato, Ubaldo AmMWSc 92
Armatrading, Joan 1950- IntWW 91, WhoEnt 92
Armbrecht, Frank Maurice, Jr 1942- AmMWSc 92
Armbrecht, Harvey James 1947- AmMWSc 92
Armbrecht, William Henry, III 1929- WhoAmL 92
Armbrister, David Mason 1934- WhoRel 92
Armbrister, Kenneth 1941- WhoAmP 91
Armbrust, Mark William 1965- WhoWest 92
Armbruster, Charles William 1937- AmMWSc 92
Armbruster, David Charles 1939- AmMWSc 92
Armbruster, Frederick Carl 1931- AmMWSc 92, WhoMW 92
Armbruster, Gertrude D 1925- AmMWSc 92
Armbruster, Robert Paul 1952- WhoAmL 92
Armbrustmacher, Theodore J 1938- AmMWSc 92
Arme, Christopher 1939- Who 92
Armelagos, George John 1936- AmMWSc 92
Armellino, Michael Ralph 1940- WhoFI 92
Armen, Harry A, Jr 1940- AmMWSc 92
Armenakas, Anthony Emanuel 1924- AmMWSc 92
Armendarez, Peter X 1930- AmMWSc 92
Armendariz, David Esteban 1950- WhoHisp 92
Armendariz, Debra M. 1960- WhoHisp 92
Armendariz, Efraim Pacillas 1938- AmMWSc 92
Armendariz, Geraldine 1952- WhoAmL 92
Armendariz, Guadalupe M. 1943- WhoHisp 92
Armendariz, Lorenzo 1957- WhoHisp 92
Armendariz, Luis S. 1943- WhoHisp 92
Armendariz, Victor Manuel 1945- WhoHisp 92
Armendariz, Victor Parra 1953- WhoAmL 92
Armenia, John Williams 1938- WhoWest 92
Armeniades, Constantine D 1936- AmMWSc 92
Armenian, Raffi 1942- NewAmDM
Armenta, A. E. WhoHisp 92
Armentano, Louis Ernst 1954- AmMWSc 92
Armenti, Angelo, Jr 1940- AmMWSc 92
Armenti, Joseph Rocco 1950- WhoAmL 92
Armentor, Glenn John 1950- WhoAmL 92
Armentrout, Daryl Ralph 1942- AmMWSc 92
Armentrout, David Noel 1938- AmMWSc 92
Armentrout, Donald Smith 1939- WhoRel 92
Armentrout, Steve 1930- AmMWSc 92
Armentrout, Steven Alexander 1933- WhoWest 92
Armer, Alan Arthur 1922- WhoEnt 92
Armer, Sondra Audin DrAPF 91
Armer, Tony 1931- WhoFI 92
Armes, Jay J. WhoHisp 92
Armes, Roy 1937- IntAu&W 91, WrDr 92
Armesto, Eladio, III 1957- WhoHisp 92
Armey, Douglas Richard 1948- WhoRel 92, WhoWest 92
Armey, Richard K. 1940- AlmAP 92 [port]
Armey, Richard Keith 1940- WhoAmP 91
Armfield, Diana 1920- TwCPaSc
Armfield, Diana Maxwell 1920- Who 92
Armfield, Eugene Morehead 1904-1953 DcNCBi 1
Armfield, Joseph Franklin 1862-1910 DcNCBi 1
Armfield, Maxwell 1881-1972 TwCPaSc
Armfield, Robert Franklin 1829-1898 DcNCBi 1
Armfield, Wyatt Jackson 1843-1933 DcNCBi 1
Armidale, Bishop of 1934- Who 92
Armijo, Alan B. 1951- WhoHisp 92
Armijo, David C. 1916- WhoHisp 92
Armijo, Dennis 1940- WhoHisp 92
Armijo, Frances P 1947- WhoAmP 91
Armijo, Jacqulyn Doris 1938- WhoWest 92
Armijo, John Joe 1954- WhoHisp 92
Armijo, Joseph Sam 1938- AmMWSc 92
Arminana, Ruben 1947- WhoHisp 92
Armington, Alton 1927- AmMWSc 92
Armington, Ralph Elmer 1918- AmMWSc 92
Arminius, Jacobus 1560-1609 BenetAL 91
Armistead, Donna Lynne 1952- WhoEnt 92
Armistead, John Irving 1949- WhoFI 92
Armistead, Lewis Addison 1817-1863 DcNCBi 1
Armistead, Milton 1947- WhoBlA 92
Armistead, Thomas Boyd, III 1918- WhoEnt 92
Armistead, Willis William 1916- AmMWSc 92
Armitage, David Templeton WhoAmL 92
Armitage, Edward 1917- Who 92
Armitage, Frank ConAu 134
Armitage, Geoffrey Thomas Alexander 1917- Who 92
Armitage, Henry St John Basil 1924- Who 92
Armitage, Ian MacLeod 1947- AmMWSc 92
Armitage, John Brian 1927- AmMWSc 92
Armitage, John Vernon 1932- Who 92
Armitage, Kenneth 1916- IntWW 91, TwCPaSc, Who 92
Armitage, Kenneth Barclay 1925- AmMWSc 92
Armitage, Michael 1930- Who 92
Armitage, Peter 1924- Who 92
Armitage, Ronda 1943- IntAu&W 91, WrDr 92
Armitage, Simon 1963- ConAu 134
Armitage, William Kenneth Who 92
Armold, Judith Ann 1945- WhoFI 92
Armon, Norma 1937- WhoEnt 92, WhoHisp 92
Armor, John N 1944- AmMWSc 92, WhoFI 92
Armoudian, Garabed 1938- AmMWSc 92
Armour, Allan A. 1933- WhoEnt 92
Armour, Clifford Arnett, Jr. 1941- WhoRel 92
Armour, Eugene Arthur 1946- AmMWSc 92
Armour, Frances J ScFEYrs
Armour, George Denholm 1864-1949 TwCPaSc
Armour, George Porter 1921- WhoAmL 92
Armour, Gordon Charles 1929- WhoWest 92
Armour, Hazel 1894-1985 TwCPaSc
Armour, James Author 1943- WhoFI 92
Armour, James Lott 1938- WhoAmL 92
Armour, John TwCWW 91
Armour, John Andrew 1937- AmMWSc 92
Armour, John F ScFEYrs
Armour, Lawrence A. 1935- WhoFI 92
Armour, Mary 1902- TwCPaSc
Armour, Mary Nicol Neill 1902- Who 92
Armour, Peter James 1940- IntAu&W 91
Armour, Reginald 1895- IntMPA 92, WhoWest 92
Armour, Richard 1906- IntAu&W 91
Armour, Richard 1906-1989 BenetAL 91
Armour, William 1903- TwCPaSc
Armour-Lightner, Rosetta Amelia 1937- WhoBlA 92
Arms, Richard Woodworth, Jr. 1935- WhoWest 92
Arms, Suzanne 1944- WrDr 92
Armson, Frederick Simon 1948- Who 92
Armson, John Moss 1939- Who 92
Armson, Kenneth Avery 1927- AmMWSc 92
Armson, Simon Who 92
Armstead, Chapelle M. 1926- WhoBlA 92
Armstead, Ray 1960- BlkOlyM
Armstead, Robert Louis 1936- AmMWSc 92, WhoWest 92
Armstead, Ron E. 1947- WhoBlA 92
Armstead, Wilbert Edward, Jr. 1934- WhoBlA 92
Armstead, William M 1957- AmMWSc 92
Armster-Worrill, Cynthia Denise 1960- WhoBlA 92
Armstrong Who 92
Armstrong, A A, Jr 1921- AmMWSc 92
Armstrong, Alan Gordon 1937- Who 92
Armstrong, Alan Leigh 1945- WhoAmL 92
Armstrong, Albert Root 1951- WhoMW 92
Armstrong, Alexandra 1939- WhoFI 92
Armstrong, Alfred Ringgold 1911- AmMWSc 92
Armstrong, Alice Catt IntAu&W 91
Armstrong, Almetta WhoAmP 91
Armstrong, Andrew 1907- Who 92
Armstrong, Andrew Robert 1953- WhoWest 92
Armstrong, Andrew Thurman 1935- AmMWSc 92
Armstrong, Anna 1953- WhoFI 92
Armstrong, Anne Legendre 1927- IntWW 91, Who 92, WhoAmP 91
Armstrong, Annie Walker 1850-1938 RelLAm 91
Armstrong, Anthony TwCSFW 91
Armstrong, Arthur 1924- TwCPaSc
Armstrong, Arthur Hilary 1909- Who 92
Armstrong, B. J. 1967- WhoBlA 92
Armstrong, Baxter Hardin 1929- AmMWSc 92
Armstrong, Benita TwCPaSc
Armstrong, Benjamin Leighton 1923- WhoRel 92
Armstrong, Bess 1953- IntMPA 92
Armstrong, Bozena Wasilewski 1953- WhoEnt 92
Armstrong, Bruce O. 1948- WhoMW 92
Armstrong, C. Michael 1938- WhoFI 92
Armstrong, Campbell IntAu&W 91
Armstrong, Carol Hallow 1943- WhoAmP 91
Armstrong, Carter Michael 1950- AmMWSc 92
Armstrong, Charles P. 1951- WhoIns 92
Armstrong, Cheryl Burton 1956- WhoWest 92
Armstrong, Clay M 1934- AmMWSc 92
Armstrong, Connie Charles 1925- WhoAmP 91
Armstrong, Curtis Edward 1946- WhoEnt 92
Armstrong, Dale Dean 1927- AmMWSc 92
Armstrong, Daniel Wayne 1949- AmMWSc 92
Armstrong, David 1941- WhoAmP 91
Armstrong, David Anthony 1930- AmMWSc 92
Armstrong, David J. 1931- WhoAmL 92
Armstrong, David M 1944- AmMWSc 92
Armstrong, David Malet 1926- IntWW 91, WrDr 92
Armstrong, David Michael 1944- WhoWest 92
Armstrong, David Thomas 1929- AmMWSc 92
Armstrong, Deane 1934- WhoAmP 91
Armstrong, Diane Julie 1939- IntAu&W 91
Armstrong, Dickwin Dill 1934- WhoWest 92
Armstrong, Don L 1916- AmMWSc 92
Armstrong, Donald B 1937- AmMWSc 92
Armstrong, Donald James 1937- AmMWSc 92
Armstrong, Douglas Dean 1945- WhoEnt 92
Armstrong, Earlene 1947- AmMWSc 92
Armstrong, Edwin 1890-1954 FacFETw
Armstrong, Edwin Alan 1950- WhoAmL 92
Armstrong, Elmer Franklin 1931- WhoMW 92
Armstrong, Ernest 1915- Who 92
Armstrong, Ernest W., Sr. 1915- WhoBlA 92
Armstrong, Ernest Walter 1955- WhoRel 92

**Armstrong,** Evelyn Walker *WhoBlA 92*
**Armstrong,** F. Michael 1942- *WhoIns 92*
**Armstrong,** Frank 1920- *WhoAmP 91*
**Armstrong,** Frank Alton, Jr. 1902-1969 *DcNCBi 1*
**Armstrong,** Frank Bradley, Jr 1928- *AmMWSc 92*
**Armstrong,** Frank Clarkson Felix 1913- *AmMWSc 92*
**Armstrong,** Frank Wilbur 1940- *WhoRel 92*
**Armstrong,** Frank William 1931- *Who 92*
**Armstrong,** Fredric Michael 1942- *WhoFI 92*
**Armstrong,** Garner Ted 1930- *RelLAm 91*
**Armstrong,** Gary Murray 1943- *WhoRel 92*
**Armstrong,** Gene Lee 1922- *WhoFI 92, WhoWest 92*
**Armstrong,** Geoffrey *TwCSFW 91*
**Armstrong,** Geoffrey 1945- *TwCPaSc*
**Armstrong,** George Glaucus, Jr 1924- *AmMWSc 92*
**Armstrong,** George Michael 1938- *AmMWSc 92*
**Armstrong,** Gibson Edward 1943- *WhoAmP 91*
**Armstrong,** Gillian *ReelWom*
**Armstrong,** Gillian 1950- *IntDcF 2-2 [port], IntMPA 92*
**Armstrong,** Gordon 1937- *IntMPA 92*
**Armstrong,** Gregory Timon 1933- *WhoRel 92*
**Armstrong,** Hamilton Fish 1893-1973 *AmPeW*
**Armstrong,** Harriet Jane 1930- *WhoAmP 91*
**Armstrong,** Harry E. 1945- *WhoRel 92*
**Armstrong,** Hart Reid 1912- *WhoMW 92, WhoRel 92*
**Armstrong,** Helen Elizabeth 1943- *WhoEnt 92*
**Armstrong,** Henry 1912-1988 *FacFETw*
**Armstrong,** Herbert Stoker 1915- *AmMWSc 92*
**Armstrong,** Herbert W. 1892-1986 *RelLAm 91*
**Armstrong,** Hilary Jane 1945- *Who 92*
**Armstrong,** J.M. 1944- *WhoWest 92*
**Armstrong,** J. Niel 1907- *WhoBlA 92*
**Armstrong,** Jack *Who 92*
**Armstrong,** Jack Gilliland 1929- *WhoAmL 92*
**Armstrong,** James d1794 *DcNCBi 1*
**Armstrong,** James 1924- *WhoRel 92*
**Armstrong,** James Anthony 1943- *AmMWSc 92*
**Armstrong,** James Clyde 1933- *AmMWSc 92*
**Armstrong,** James Franklin *WhoRel 92*
**Armstrong,** James G 1924- *AmMWSc 92*
**Armstrong,** James Sinclair 1915- *WhoAmL 92*
**Armstrong,** Jan Robert 1953- *WhoAmL 92*
**Armstrong,** Jay John 1953- *WhoAmP 91*
**Armstrong,** Jim L *WhoAmP 91*
**Armstrong,** Joan Bernard *WhoBlA 92*
**Armstrong,** John 1709-1779 *RfGEnL 91*
**Armstrong,** John 1798-1844 *DcNCBi 1*
**Armstrong,** John 1893-1973 *TwCPaSc*
**Armstrong,** John 1905- *Who 92*
**Armstrong,** John A 1934- *AmMWSc 92*
**Armstrong,** John Alexander 1922- *IntAu&W 91, WrDr 92*
**Armstrong,** John Allan 1934- *WhoFI 92*
**Armstrong,** John Anderson d1990 *Who 92N*
**Armstrong,** John Archibald 1917- *IntWW 91, Who 92*
**Armstrong,** John Briggs *AmMWSc 92*
**Armstrong,** John Buchanan 1918- *AmMWSc 92*
**Armstrong,** John Edward 1912- *AmMWSc 92*
**Armstrong,** John Kremer 1934- *WhoAmL 92*
**Armstrong,** John Morrison 1936- *AmMWSc 92*
**Armstrong,** John William 1948- *AmMWSc 92*
**Armstrong,** Joseph E 1956- *WhoAmP 91*
**Armstrong,** Joseph Earl 1956- *WhoBlA 92*
**Armstrong,** Joseph Everett 1948- *AmMWSc 92*
**Armstrong,** Joseph M. 1943- *WhoBlA 92N*
**Armstrong,** Joseph N. 1939- *WhoBlA 92*
**Armstrong,** Joseph R d1919? *BiInAmS*
**Armstrong,** Judith 1935- *WrDr 92*
**Armstrong,** Karl R. 1958- *WhoEnt 92*
**Armstrong,** Kenneth William 1935- *AmMWSc 92*
**Armstrong,** Kenny Bryan 1953- *WhoRel 92*
**Armstrong,** Lee Ford 1955- *WhoAmL 92*
**Armstrong,** Leroy Robert, Jr. 1961- *WhoRel 92*
**Armstrong,** Lillian Hardin 1898-1971 *NotBlAW 92*
**Armstrong,** Lloyd, Jr 1940- *AmMWSc 92*
**Armstrong,** Loren Doyle 1947- *WhoRel 92*
**Armstrong,** Louis 1900-1970 *FacFETw [port]*
**Armstrong,** Louis 1900-1971 *ConBlB 2 [port], NewAmDM, RComAH*
**Armstrong,** Mark I *AmMWSc 92*
**Armstrong,** Mark Steven 1951- *WhoRel 92*
**Armstrong,** Martin 1739?-1808 *DcNCBi 1*
**Armstrong,** Martine Yvonne Katherine *AmMWSc 92*
**Armstrong,** Marvin Douglas 1918- *AmMWSc 92*
**Armstrong,** Mary Willems 1957- *ConAu 134*
**Armstrong,** Matthew Jordan, Jr. 1955- *WhoBlA 92*
**Armstrong,** Michael Allen 1956- *IntAu&W 91*
**Armstrong,** Michael David 1955- *WhoFI 92*
**Armstrong,** Michael Francis 1932- *WhoAmL 92*
**Armstrong,** Nancy 1924- *WrDr 92*
**Armstrong,** Nancy L. 1948- *WhoEnt 92*
**Armstrong,** Neal Earl 1941- *AmMWSc 92*
**Armstrong,** Neil A 1930- *AmMWSc 92, IntWW 91, Who 92*
**Armstrong,** Neil Alden 1930- *FacFETw*
**Armstrong,** Nelson 1950- *WhoBlA 92*
**Armstrong,** Orville 1929- *WhoAmL 92, WhoWest 92*
**Armstrong,** Owen Thomas 1923- *WhoAmL 92*
**Armstrong,** P Douglas 1941- *AmMWSc 92*
**Armstrong,** Patrick Hamilton 1941- *IntAu&W 91*
**Armstrong,** Peter Brownell 1939- *AmMWSc 92*
**Armstrong,** Philip E 1927- *AmMWSc 92*
**Armstrong,** Phillip Dale 1943- *WhoAmL 92, WhoFI 92, WhoMW 92*
**Armstrong,** R W 1934- *AmMWSc 92*
**Armstrong,** Reginald Donald, II 1958- *WhoBlA 92*
**Armstrong,** Richard 1943- *Who 92*
**Armstrong,** Richard B. 1956- *ConAu 134*
**Armstrong,** Richard Lee 1937- *AmMWSc 92*
**Armstrong,** Richard LeRoy 1953- *WhoAmL 92*
**Armstrong,** Richard Stoll 1924- *WhoRel 92*
**Armstrong,** Richard W 1936- *WhoAmP 91*
**Armstrong,** Richard William 1932- *WhoFI 92*
**Armstrong,** Robert A 1929- *AmMWSc 92*
**Armstrong,** Robert Beall 1940- *AmMWSc 92*
**Armstrong,** Robert Dean 1923- *WhoEnt 92, WhoWest 92*
**Armstrong,** Robert G 1928- *AmMWSc 92*
**Armstrong,** Robert George 1913- *Who 92*
**Armstrong,** Robert John 1939- *AmMWSc 92*
**Armstrong,** Robert Landis 1932- *WhoAmP 91*
**Armstrong,** Robert Laurence 1926- *WhoRel 92, WrDr 92*
**Armstrong,** Robert Lee 1939- *AmMWSc 92, WhoMW 92*
**Armstrong,** Robin Earl 1946- *IntAu&W 91*
**Armstrong,** Robin L 1935- *AmMWSc 92*
**Armstrong,** Robin Louis 1935- *IntWW 91*
**Armstrong,** Rodney E. 1935- *WhoFI 92*
**Armstrong,** Ronald 1948- *WhoFI 92*
**Armstrong,** Ronnie Clyde 1953- *WhoMW 92*
**Armstrong,** Rosa Mae 1937- *AmMWSc 92*
**Armstrong,** Sean Frederick 1962- *WhoWest 92*
**Armstrong,** Seth 1941- *WhoAmP 91*
**Armstrong,** Shearer 1894- *TwCPaSc*
**Armstrong,** Sheila Ann 1942- *IntWW 91, Who 92*
**Armstrong,** Terence Edward 1920- *Who 92*
**Armstrong,** Theodore Morelock 1939- *WhoFI 92*
**Armstrong,** Thomas Errol 1959- *WhoAmP 91*
**Armstrong,** Thomas Henry Wait 1898- *IntWW 91, Who 92*
**Armstrong,** Thomas Herschel 1937- *WhoAmP 91*
**Armstrong,** Thomas Peyton 1941- *AmMWSc 92*
**Armstrong,** Tommy *WhoAmP 91*
**Armstrong,** Tommy Gene 1941- *WhoAmP 91*
**Armstrong,** Vickie *WhoAmP 91*
**Armstrong,** Victor Munro 1946- *WhoEnt 92*
**Armstrong,** Wallace Dowan, Jr. 1926- *WhoWest 92*
**Armstrong,** Walter 1948- *WhoBlA 92*
**Armstrong,** Walter Preston, Jr. 1916- *WhoAmL 92*
**Armstrong,** Ward Lynn 1956- *WhoAmP 91*
**Armstrong,** Warren Bruce 1933- *WhoMW 92*
**Armstrong,** Wiley T. 1909- *WhoBlA 92*
**Armstrong,** William David 1944- *AmMWSc 92*
**Armstrong,** William Edward 1938- *WhoAmL 92*
**Armstrong,** William H. 1914- *WrDr 92*
**Armstrong,** William Henry 1943- *WhoAmL 92*
**Armstrong,** William L 1937- *WhoAmP 91, WhoWest 92*
**Armstrong,** William Lawrence 1939- *AmMWSc 92*
**Armstrong,** Willis Coburn 1912- *WhoFI 92*
**Armstrong-Jones** *Who 92*
**Armstrong Of Ilminster,** Baron 1927- *IntWW 91, Who 92*
**Armstrong-Seward,** Catherine A. 1915- *WhoWest 92*
**Armytage,** David George 1929- *Who 92*
**Armytage,** Martin 1933- *Who 92*
**Armytage,** Walter Harry Green 1915- *Who 92*
**Arn,** Kenneth Dale 1921- *WhoMW 92*
**Arnaboldi,** Leo Peter, III 1959- *WhoAmL 92*
**Arnade,** Charles W. 1927- *WrDr 92*
**Arnal,** Robert Emile 1922- *AmMWSc 92*
**Arnall,** Ellis Gibbs 1907- *IntMPA 92, IntWW 91, WhoAmP 91*
**Arnall,** Joseph Henry 1947- *WhoAmP 91*
**Arnaout,** M Amin 1949- *AmMWSc 92*
**Arnas,** Ozer Ali 1936- *AmMWSc 92*
**Arnason,** Barry Gilbert Wyatt 1933- *AmMWSc 92*
**Arnason,** Tomas 1923- *IntWW 91*
**Arnatt,** Ray 1934- *TwCPaSc*
**Arnaud,** Claude 1919- *IntWW 91*
**Arnaud,** Claude Donald, Jr 1929- *AmMWSc 92*
**Arnaud,** Jean-Loup 1942- *IntWW 91*
**Arnaud,** Jules Arsene *ThHEIm [port]*
**Arnaud,** Paul Henri, Jr 1924- *AmMWSc 92*
**Arnaud,** Philippe 1935- *AmMWSc 92*
**Arnauld,** Antoine 1612-1694 *BlkwCEP*
**Arnauskas,** Leonas Semenovich 1921- *IntWW 91*
**Arnaz,** Desi d1986 *LesBEnT 92*
**Arnaz,** Desi 1917-1986 *FacFETw*
**Arnaz,** Desi, Jr. 1953- *IntMPA 92, WhoHisp 92*
**Arnaz,** Lucie 1951- *IntMPA 92, WhoHisp 92*
**Arnaz,** Lucie Desiree 1951- *WhoEnt 92*
**Arnberg,** Robert Lewis 1945- *AmMWSc 92, WhoFI 92*
**Arndt,** Elizabeth Moore 1920- *WhoAmP 91*
**Arndt,** Heinz Wolfgang 1915- *IntAu&W 91, IntWW 91, WrDr 92*
**Arndt,** Henry Clifford 1945- *AmMWSc 92*
**Arndt,** Karl 1903- *WrDr 92*
**Arndt,** Karl John Richard 1903- *IntAu&W 91*
**Arndt,** Kenneth Eugene 1933- *WhoFI 92*
**Arndt,** Marcia Ann Menn 1958- *WhoMW 92*
**Arndt,** Mary Jo 1933- *WhoAmP 91*
**Arndt,** Michael Paul 1930- *WhoWest 92*
**Arndt,** Otto 1920- *IntWW 91*
**Arndt,** Richard Allen 1933- *AmMWSc 92*
**Arndt,** Roger Edward Anthony 1935- *AmMWSc 92*
**Arndt,** Sven William 1936- *WhoFI 92*
**Arndt,** Ulrich W. 1924- *IntWW 91*
**Arndt,** Ulrich Wolfgang 1924- *Who 92*
**Arndt,** Walter 1891-1944 *EncTR 91*
**Arndts,** John Christian 1962- *WhoAmL 92*
**Arne,** Michael 1741-1786 *NewAmDM*
**Arne,** Thomas Augustine 1710-1778 *NewAmDM*
**Arnedo Orbananos,** Miguel Angel 1944- *IntWW 91*
**Arnell,** John Carstairs 1918- *AmMWSc 92*
**Arnell,** Peter *IntMPA 92*
**Arnell,** Richard Anthony 1938- *WhoMW 92*
**Arnell,** Richard Anthony Sayer 1917- *IntWW 91, Who 92*
**Arnell,** Walter James 1924- *AmMWSc 92*
**Arnell,** Walter James William 1924- *WhoWest 92*
**Arnelle,** Hugh Jesse 1933- *WhoBlA 92*
**Arneman,** Harold Frederick 1915- *AmMWSc 92*
**Arner,** Dale H 1920- *AmMWSc 92*
**Arnesen,** Deborah Arnie 1953- *WhoAmP 91*
**Arneson,** Dora Williams 1947- *AmMWSc 92, WhoMW 92*
**Arneson,** George Stephen 1925- *WhoMW 92*
**Arneson,** James Herman 1952- *WhoAmL 92*
**Arneson,** Marc W. 1927- *WhoFI 92*
**Arneson,** Phil Alan 1940- *AmMWSc 92*
**Arneson,** Richard Michael 1938- *AmMWSc 92*
**Arneson,** Robert 1930- *WorArt 1980 [port]*
**Arness,** James *LesBEnT 92*
**Arness,** James 1923- *FacFETw, IntMPA 92*
**Arnet,** William Francis 1948- *WhoAmL 92*
**Arnett,** Alex Mathews 1888-1945 *DcNCBi 1*
**Arnett,** Benjamin William, Jr. 1838-1906 *RelLAm 91*
**Arnett,** Carroll *DrAPF 91*
**Arnett,** Carroll D. 1946- *WhoWest 92*
**Arnett,** Edward McCollin 1922- *AmMWSc 92, IntWW 91*
**Arnett,** Foster Deaver 1920- *WhoAmL 92*
**Arnett,** Gerald Alan 1962- *WhoEnt 92*
**Arnett,** Gregory Scott 1965- *WhoRel 92*
**Arnett,** James Edward 1912- *WhoFI 92, WhoMW 92*
**Arnett,** James Edward, II 1955- *WhoFI 92*
**Arnett,** Jerry Butler 1938- *AmMWSc 92*
**Arnett,** Michael Kent 1941- *WhoIns 92*
**Arnett,** Patricia Marie 1945- *WhoAmL 92*
**Arnett,** Peter *IntWW 91, LesBEnT 92*
**Arnett,** Peter 1934- *CurBio 91 [port]*
**Arnett,** Ross Harold, Jr 1919- *AmMWSc 92*
**Arnett,** Silas W. *DcNCBi 1*
**Arnett,** William David 1940- *AmMWSc 92*
**Arnett,** William Harold 1928- *AmMWSc 92*
**Arnette,** Dorothy Deanna 1942- *WhoBlA 92*
**Arnette,** Mack L. 1954- *WhoFI 92*
**Arnette,** Robert *ConAu 36NR, TwCSFW 91*
**Arnette,** Walter Gregory, Jr 1947- *WhoAmP 91*
**Arney,** Randall *WhoEnt 92*
**Arney,** Rex Odell 1940- *WhoAmP 91*
**Arney,** William Ray 1950- *WhoWest 92*
**Arnez,** Nancy L. 1928- *WhoBlA 92*
**Arnfield,** Anthony John 1945- *AmMWSc 92*
**Arnheim,** Norman 1938- *AmMWSc 92*
**Arnheim,** Rudolf 1904- *DcTwDes, FacFETw, IntAu&W 91, WrDr 92*
**Arnheiter,** Heinz 1951- *AmMWSc 92*
**Arnholt,** Philip John 1940- *AmMWSc 92*
**Arnick,** John Stephen 1933- *WhoAmP 91*
**Arning,** John Fredrick 1925- *WhoAmL 92*
**Arnison,** Paul Grenville 1949- *AmMWSc 92*
**Arno,** Madame *EncAmaz 91*
**Arno,** Andrew Ralph 1942- *WhoWest 92*
**Arno,** Daniel James 1950- *WhoAmL 92*
**Arno,** Peter 1904-1968 *FacFETw*
**Arno,** Stephen Francis 1943- *AmMWSc 92*
**Arnobius** d327? *EncEarC*
**Arnobius The Younger** d451? *EncEarC*
**Arnoff,** E Leonard 1922- *AmMWSc 92*
**Arnoff,** Judith Unger 1946- *WhoFI 92*
**Arnold,** Adrian K 1932- *WhoAmP 91*
**Arnold,** Allan *ScFEYrs*
**Arnold,** Allen Parker 1923- *AmMWSc 92*
**Arnold,** Alton A., Jr. 1932- *WhoBlA 92*
**Arnold,** Alva Lee C 1919- *WhoAmP 91*
**Arnold,** Ann 1936- *TwCPaSc*
**Arnold,** Anthony 1928- *WhoWest 92*
**Arnold,** Armin 1931- *IntWW 91*
**Arnold,** Arnold F. 1929- *WrDr 92*
**Arnold,** Arthur Palmer 1946- *AmMWSc 92*
**Arnold,** Barbara Eileen 1924- *WhoAmP 91*
**Arnold,** Benedict 1741-1801 *BenetAL 91, BlkwEAR, RComAH*
**Arnold,** Benjamin McLean 1953- *WhoAmL 92*
**Arnold,** Billy L 1926- *WhoAmP 91*
**Arnold,** Bob *DrAPF 91*
**Arnold,** Bob 1943- *WhoAmP 91*
**Arnold,** Bradford Henry 1916- *AmMWSc 92*
**Arnold,** C W 1923- *AmMWSc 92*
**Arnold,** Charles, Jr 1930- *AmMWSc 92*
**Arnold,** Charles Geoffrey 1915- *TwCPaSc*
**Arnold,** Charles Harvey 1920- *WhoRel 92*
**Arnold,** Charles Ryan, Jr. 1960- *WhoRel 92*
**Arnold,** Cheryl Christine 1951- *WhoEnt 92*
**Arnold,** Clarence Edward, Jr. 1944- *WhoBlA 92*
**Arnold,** Clifford Delos 1920- *WhoAmP 91*
**Arnold,** Craig C. 1945- *WhoFI 92*
**Arnold,** Craig Glen 1949- *IntAu&W 91*
**Arnold,** Cynthia Jean 1942- *WhoMW 92*
**Arnold,** D S 1920- *AmMWSc 92*
**Arnold,** Dale Eugene 1953- *WhoWest 92*
**Arnold,** Daniel Michael 1937- *WhoFI 92*
**Arnold,** Daniel W. 1954- *WhoIns 92*
**Arnold,** Danny *LesBEnT 92*
**Arnold,** Danny 1925- *IntMPA 92*
**Arnold,** Daryl 1924- *IntWW 91, WhoAmP 91*
**Arnold,** David 1946- *WhoBlA 92, WrDr 92*
**Arnold,** David M 1939- *AmMWSc 92*
**Arnold,** David Paul 1942- *WhoMW 92*
**Arnold,** David Walker 1936- *AmMWSc 92*

**Arnold**, David Wayne 1958- *WhoEnt 92*
**Arnold**, Dean Edward 1939- *AmMWSc 92*
**Arnold**, Deborah Kaye 1955- *WhoFI 92*
**Arnold**, Delos d1909 *BiInAmS*
**Arnold**, Denis Midgley 1926- *IntAu&W 91*
**Arnold**, Don *WhoAmP 91*
**Arnold**, Donald Robert 1935- *AmMWSc 92*
**Arnold**, Doris Foltz 1926- *WhoRel 92*
**Arnold**, Duane Wade-Hampton 1953- *WhoMW 92, WhoRel 92*
**Arnold**, Eberhard 1883-1935 *RelLAm 91*
**Arnold**, Ed 1943- *WhoAmP 91*
**Arnold**, Eddy 1918- *IntMPA 92, NewAmDM, WhoEnt 92*
**Arnold**, Eddy William 1951- *WhoEnt 92*
**Arnold**, Edmund Clarence 1913- *WrDr 92*
**Arnold**, Edward 1857-1942 *DcLB 112*
**Arnold**, Edwin L 1857-1935 *TwCSFW 91*
**Arnold**, Edwin Lester 1857-1935 *ScFEYrs*
**Arnold**, Edwin Roy 1962- *WhoMW 92*
**Arnold**, Edwin T. 1947- *ConAu 134*
**Arnold**, Elliott 1912-1980 *TwCWW 91*
**Arnold**, Elliott, Mrs. *Who 92*
**Arnold**, Emil 1932- *AmMWSc 92*
**Arnold**, Emily *DrAPF 91*
**Arnold**, Ernest Woodrow 1914- *WhoRel 92*
**Arnold**, Ethel N. 1924- *WhoBlA 92*
**Arnold**, Ferris Lucien 1946- *WhoAmL 92*
**Arnold**, Frank R 1910- *AmMWSc 92*
**Arnold**, Frank Steele, Jr. 1939- *WhoFI 92*
**Arnold**, Fred English 1938- *WhoAmL 92*
**Arnold**, Frederic G 1923- *AmMWSc 92*
**Arnold**, G. Dewey, Jr. 1925- *WhoFI 92*
**Arnold**, Gary Howard 1942- *WhoEnt 92*
**Arnold**, George 1834-1865 *BenetAL 91*
**Arnold**, George Feversham 1914- *Who 92*
**Arnold**, George W 1923- *AmMWSc 92*
**Arnold**, Gordon Thomas 1960- *WhoAmL 92*
**Arnold**, Gottfried 1666-1714 *EncEarC*
**Arnold**, Graham 1932- *TwCPaSc*
**Arnold**, Guy 1932- *IntAu&W 91, WrDr 92*
**Arnold**, H F *ScFEYrs*
**Arnold**, H. J. P. 1932- *WrDr 92*
**Arnold**, Hans Redlef 1923- *IntWW 91*
**Arnold**, Harriet Amelia Chapman 1937- *WhoBlA 92*
**Arnold**, Harry L, Jr 1912- *AmMWSc 92*
**Arnold**, Harry Loren, Jr. 1912- *WhoWest 92*
**Arnold**, Harvey James 1933- *AmMWSc 92*
**Arnold**, Haskell N., Jr. 1945- *WhoBlA 92*
**Arnold**, Heinz Ludwig 1940- *IntAu&W 91*
**Arnold**, Helen E. 1924- *WhoBlA 92*
**Arnold**, Helen T 1927- *WhoAmP 91*
**Arnold**, Henry Albert 1914- *AmMWSc 92*
**Arnold**, Henry Harley 1886-1950 *FacFETw*
**Arnold**, Hubert Andrew 1912- *AmMWSc 92*
**Arnold**, Ion *ScFEYrs*
**Arnold**, J Barto, III 1950- *AmMWSc 92*
**Arnold**, Jack 1912- *IntMPA 92*
**Arnold**, Jacques Arnold 1947- *Who 92*
**Arnold**, James A. 1936- *WhoBlA 92*
**Arnold**, James Darrell 1937- *AmMWSc 92*
**Arnold**, James Edward 1956- *WhoAmL 92*
**Arnold**, James Keith 1959- *WhoAmP 91*
**Arnold**, James Norman 1949- *AmMWSc 92*
**Arnold**, James R. 1923- *IntWW 91*
**Arnold**, James Richard 1923- *AmMWSc 92, WhoWest 92*
**Arnold**, James S 1911- *AmMWSc 92*
**Arnold**, James Schoonover 1923- *AmMWSc 92*
**Arnold**, James Tracy 1920- *AmMWSc 92*
**Arnold**, Janet 1932- *IntAu&W 91, WrDr 92*
**Arnold**, Janet Drew 1951- *WhoRel 92*
**Arnold**, Jeffrey Stephen 1964- *WhoAmL 92*
**Arnold**, Jerome Gilbert *WhoAmL 92*
**Arnold**, Jesse Charles 1937- *AmMWSc 92*
**Arnold**, Jimmy Thomas 1941- *AmMWSc 92*
**Arnold**, Joe R 1942- *WhoAmP 91*
**Arnold**, John 1946- *WhoAmP 91*
**Arnold**, John Burleigh 1931- *WhoAmP 91*
**Arnold**, John David 1951- *WhoEnt 92*
**Arnold**, John Dirk 1950- *WhoEnt 92*
**Arnold**, John Edward 1936- *WhoMW 92*
**Arnold**, John Emery 1940- *WhoWest 92*
**Arnold**, John Fox 1937- *WhoAmP 91*
**Arnold**, John Henry 1927- *WhoAmP 91*
**Arnold**, John Hudson 1931- *WhoFI 92*
**Arnold**, John Lewis 1915- *Who 92*
**Arnold**, John Miller 1936- *AmMWSc 92*
**Arnold**, John P. 1946- *WhoAmL 92*
**Arnold**, John Richard 1956- *AmMWSc 92*
**Arnold**, John Robert 1923- *WhoAmP 91*
**Arnold**, John Robert 1933- *Who 92*
**Arnold**, John Ronald 1910- *AmMWSc 92*
**Arnold**, Jonathan 1953- *AmMWSc 92*
**Arnold**, Joseph H. *WrDr 92*
**Arnold**, Joshua David 1951- *WhoFI 92*
**Arnold**, June 1926-1982 *ConAu 133*
**Arnold**, Kathy Spelts 1941- *WhoAmP 91*
**Arnold**, Keith Alan 1937- *AmMWSc 92*
**Arnold**, Keith Appleby 1926- *Who 92*
**Arnold**, Kenneth James 1914- *AmMWSc 92*
**Arnold**, Kenneth James 1927- *WhoAmL 92*
**Arnold**, Kenneth L. *DrAPF 91*
**Arnold**, Landis Stevens 1960- *WhoWest 92*
**Arnold**, Larkin 1942- *WhoBlA 92*
**Arnold**, Larry Robert 1958- *WhoRel 92*
**Arnold**, Leonard J. 1947- *WhoWest 92*
**Arnold**, Leslie K 1938- *AmMWSc 92*
**Arnold**, Linda Gayle 1947- *WhoMW 92*
**Arnold**, Lionel A. 1921- *WhoBlA 92*
**Arnold**, Louis Walker 1914- *WhoRel 92*
**Arnold**, Luther Bishop, Jr 1907- *AmMWSc 92*
**Arnold**, Magda Blondiay 1903- *IntAu&W 91*
**Arnold**, Malcolm 1921- *ConCom 92, IntWW 91, NewAmDM, Who 92*
**Arnold**, Maria 1915- *WhoRel 92*
**Arnold**, Mary B 1924- *AmMWSc 92*
**Arnold**, Matthew 1822-1888 *BenetAL 91, CnDBLB 4 [port], RfGEnL 91*
**Arnold**, Michael James 1946- *WhoWest 92*
**Arnold**, Michael Neal 1947- *WhoWest 92*
**Arnold**, Morris Fairchild 1915- *WhoRel 92*
**Arnold**, Morris Sheppard 1941- *WhoAmL 92*
**Arnold**, Peter *TwCPaSc*
**Arnold**, Peter 1943- *WrDr 92*
**Arnold**, Ralph Gunther 1928- *AmMWSc 92*
**Arnold**, Ralph Leo, III 1949- *WhoFI 92*
**Arnold**, Ralph M. 1928- *WhoBlA 92*
**Arnold**, Richard Bentham 1932- *Who 92*
**Arnold**, Richard S 1936- *WhoAmP 91*
**Arnold**, Richard Sheppard 1936- *WhoAmL 92*
**Arnold**, Richard Thomas 1913- *AmMWSc 92*
**Arnold**, Richard Walker 1947- *WhoFI 92*
**Arnold**, Robert Edwin 1948- *WhoRel 92*
**Arnold**, Robert Fairbanks 1940- *AmMWSc 92*
**Arnold**, Robert Lloyd 1952- *WhoFI 92*
**Arnold**, Rollo Davis 1926- *WrDr 92*
**Arnold**, Ronald Henri 1937- *WhoWest 92*
**Arnold**, Roseanne *NewYTBS 91 [port]*
**Arnold**, Roseanne 1953- *WhoEnt 92*
**Arnold**, Roy Gary 1941- *AmMWSc 92*
**Arnold**, Rudolph P. 1948- *WhoBlA 92*
**Arnold**, Scott Gregory 1961- *WhoMW 92*
**Arnold**, Sheila 1929- *WhoAmP 91, WhoWest 92*
**Arnold**, Shirlee 1926- *WhoAmP 91*
**Arnold**, Simon Rory 1933- *Who 92*
**Arnold**, Stephen George 1961- *WhoAmP 91*
**Arnold**, Steven Lloyd 1949- *AmMWSc 92*
**Arnold**, Susan R. 1960- *WhoEnt 92*
**Arnold**, Terrence Eugene 1955- *WhoWest 92*
**Arnold**, Thomas 1742-1816 *BlkwCEP*
**Arnold**, Thomas 1947- *Who 92*
**Arnold**, Thomas Brent 1950- *WhoAmL 92*
**Arnold**, Thurman Wesley 1891-1969 *AmPolLe*
**Arnold**, Val John 1949- *WhoMW 92*
**Arnold**, Vere Arbuthnot 1902- *Who 92*
**Arnold**, Vince G. 1962- *WhoMW 92*
**Arnold**, Vladimir Igorevich 1937- *IntWW 91*
**Arnold**, Wallace C. 1938- *WhoBlA 92*
**Arnold**, Walter Frank 1920- *AmMWSc 92*
**Arnold**, Watson Caufield 1945- *AmMWSc 92*
**Arnold**, Wilfred Niels 1936- *AmMWSc 92*
**Arnold**, William 1953- *Who 92*
**Arnold**, William Archibald 1904- *AmMWSc 92*
**Arnold**, William Edwin 1938- *WhoFI 92*
**Arnold**, William Howard, Jr 1931- *AmMWSc 92*
**Arnold**, William Vance 1936- *WhoEnt 92*
**Arnold-Baker**, Charles 1918- *Who 92*
**Arnoldi**, Robert Alfred 1921- *AmMWSc 92*
**Arnoldi**, Walter Edwin 1917- *AmMWSc 92*
**Arnolds**, John William Schmidt 1846-1888 *BiInAmS*
**Arnoldson**, Klas 1844-1916 *FacFETw*
**Arnoldson**, Klas Pontus 1844-1916 *WhoNob 90*
**Arnoldy**, Roger L 1934- *AmMWSc 92*
**Arnon**, Daniel I 1910- *AmMWSc 92, IntWW 91*
**Arnon**, Michael 1925- *WhoFI 92*
**Arnone**, Arthur Richard 1942- *AmMWSc 92*
**Arnone**, Michael J 1932- *WhoAmP 91*
**Arnott**, Alexander John Maxwell 1975- *Who 92*
**Arnott**, Howard Joseph 1928- *AmMWSc 92*
**Arnott**, Jacob Willard 1918- *WhoRel 92*
**Arnott**, Margaret Anne 1916- *IntAu&W 91*
**Arnott**, Marilyn Sue 1943- *AmMWSc 92*
**Arnott**, Melville *Who 92*
**Arnott**, Robert A 1941- *AmMWSc 92*
**Arnott**, Robert Douglas 1954- *WhoFI 92*
**Arnott**, Struther 1934- *AmMWSc 92, IntWW 91, Who 92*
**Arnott**, William, III 1942- *WhoAmP 91*
**Arnott**, William Melville 1909- *Who 92*
**Arnoul**, Francoise 1931- *IntWW 91*
**Arnould**, Richard Julius 1941- *WhoMW 92*
**Arnould**, Robert C 1953- *WhoAmP 91*
**Arnouts**, Robert Aloysius 1943- *WhoFI 92*
**Arnovick**, George 1925- *AmMWSc 92*
**Arnow**, Arthur Emanuel 1932- *WhoAmL 92*
**Arnow**, Diana Irene 1958- *WhoEnt 92*
**Arnow**, Harriette Simpson 1908-1986 *BenetAL 91*
**Arnow**, Ted J. *IntMPA 92*
**Arnow**, Theodore 1921- *AmMWSc 92*
**Arnow**, Winston Eugene 1911- *WhoAmL 92*
**Arnowich**, Beatrice 1930- *AmMWSc 92*
**Arnowitt**, Richard Lewis 1928- *AmMWSc 92*
**Arnrich**, Lotte 1911- *AmMWSc 92*
**Arns**, Paulo Evarist 1921- *WhoRel 92*
**Arns**, Paulo Evaristo 1921- *IntWW 91*
**Arns**, Robert George 1933- *AmMWSc 92*
**Arnsdorf**, Dennis Abraham 1953- *WhoFI 92*
**Arnsdorf**, Morton Frank 1940- *WhoMW 92*
**Arnshtam**, Leo Oskarovich 1905- *SovUnBD*
**Arnst**, Albert 1909- *WhoWest 92*
**Arnsteen**, Katy Keck 1934- *SmATA 68 [port]*
**Arnstein**, Flora J. *DrAPF 91*
**Arnstein**, Sherry Phyllis *WhoFI 92*
**Arnston**, Guy C. 1952- *WhoEnt 92*
**Arntzen**, Charles Joel 1941- *AmMWSc 92*
**Arntzen**, Clyde Edward 1915- *AmMWSc 92*
**Arnush**, Donald 1936- *AmMWSc 92*
**Arnwine**, William Carrol 1929- *AmMWSc 92*
**Arny**, Deane Cedric 1917- *AmMWSc 92*
**Arny**, Margaret Jane 1948- *AmMWSc 92*
**Arny**, Thomas Travis 1940- *AmMWSc 92*
**Aro**, Glenn Scott 1948- *WhoWest 92*
**Arocho**, Juan R. 1947- *WhoHisp 92*
**Aroesty**, Julian Max 1931- *AmMWSc 92*
**Aroesty**, Sidney A. 1946- *WhoFI 92*
**Aroesty**, Steven Mitchell 1961- *WhoAmL 92*
**Aroian**, Leo Avedis 1907- *AmMWSc 92*
**Aron**, Gert 1927- *AmMWSc 92*
**Aron**, Jean-Paul 1925-1988 *FacFETw*
**Aron**, Mark G. 1943- *WhoAmL 92, WhoFI 92*
**Aron**, Martin Warren 1957- *WhoAmL 92*
**Aron**, Paul Harvey 1921-1991 *NewYTBS 91 [port]*
**Aron**, Raymond 1905-1983 *FacFETw*
**Aron**, Roberto 1915- *WhoAmL 92*
**Aron**, Susan Marlene 1956- *WhoEnt 92*
**Aron**, Walter Arthur 1921- *AmMWSc 92*
**Aron**, William Irwin 1930- *AmMWSc 92*
**Aronberg**, Charles 1930- *WhoAmP 91*
**Aronfeld**, Mandel L. 1914- *WhoAmL 92*
**Aroni**, Samuel 1927- *AmMWSc 92, WhoWest 92*
**Aronin**, Lewis Richard 1919- *AmMWSc 92*
**Aronoff**, George R 1950- *AmMWSc 92*
**Aronoff**, Samuel 1915- *AmMWSc 92*
**Aronoff**, Stanley J 1932- *WhoAmP 91*
**Aronoff**, Stanley Jerome 1932- *WhoMW 92*
**Aronofsky**, Julius S 1921- *AmMWSc 92*
**Aronov**, Victor Abraham 1937- *WhoMW 92*
**Aronovic**, Sanford Maxwell 1926- *AmMWSc 92*
**Aronovich**, Victor Efimovich 1940- *WhoEnt 92*
**Aronovitch**, Roberta Gail 1949- *WhoRel 92*
**Aronovsky**, Ronald George 1955- *WhoAmL 92*
**Aronow**, Geoffrey Francis 1955- *WhoAmL 92*
**Aronow**, Lewis 1927- *AmMWSc 92*
**Aronow**, Richard Avery 1953- *WhoAmL 92*
**Aronow**, Saul 1917- *AmMWSc 92*
**Aronow**, Saul 1923- *AmMWSc 92*
**Aronow**, Wilbert Solomon 1931- *AmMWSc 92*
**Aronowitz**, Frederick 1935- *AmMWSc 92*
**Arons**, Arnold Boris 1916- *AmMWSc 92*
**Arons**, John Clark 1952- *WhoRel 92*
**Arons**, Jonathan 1943- *AmMWSc 92*
**Arons**, Leonard Frank 1952- *WhoAmP 91*
**Arons**, Mark David 1958- *WhoAmL 92*
**Arons**, Michael Eugene 1939- *AmMWSc 92*
**Aronsohn**, Lotte Therese *Who 92*
**Aronson**, A L 1933- *AmMWSc 92*
**Aronson**, Adam 1916- *WhoMW 92*
**Aronson**, Arnold H. 1935- *WhoFI 92*
**Aronson**, Arthur H 1935- *AmMWSc 92*
**Aronson**, Arthur Ian 1930- *AmMWSc 92*
**Aronson**, Bernard William 1946- *IntWW 91*
**Aronson**, Carl Edward 1936- *AmMWSc 92*
**Aronson**, Casper Jacob 1916- *AmMWSc 92*
**Aronson**, Clifford Hank 1955- *WhoAmL 92*
**Aronson**, David Emmert 1953- *WhoMW 92*
**Aronson**, Donald Gary 1929- *AmMWSc 92*
**Aronson**, Eva Beer *WhoFI 92*
**Aronson**, Frederick Rupp 1953- *WhoWest 92*
**Aronson**, Geoffrey Fraser 1914- *Who 92*
**Aronson**, Hazel Josephine 1946- *Who 92*
**Aronson**, Herbert 1923- *AmMWSc 92*
**Aronson**, J Richard 1937- *ConAu 34NR*
**Aronson**, James Ries 1932- *AmMWSc 92*
**Aronson**, Jason 1928- *WhoFI 92*
**Aronson**, Jay E 1953- *AmMWSc 92*
**Aronson**, Jerome Melville 1930- *AmMWSc 92*
**Aronson**, John Ferguson *AmMWSc 92*
**Aronson**, John Noel 1934- *AmMWSc 92*
**Aronson**, Jonathan David 1949- *WhoWest 92*
**Aronson**, Josh 1951- *WhoEnt 92*
**Aronson**, Leon 1935- *WhoAmL 92*
**Aronson**, Louis Vincent, II 1923- *WhoFI 92*
**Aronson**, M 1919- *AmMWSc 92*
**Aronson**, Mark Berne 1941- *WhoFI 92*
**Aronson**, Martin Stanley 1939- *WhoEnt 92*
**Aronson**, Michael M. 1945- *WhoMW 92*
**Aronson**, Nathan Ned, Jr 1940- *AmMWSc 92*
**Aronson**, Peter S 1947- *AmMWSc 92*
**Aronson**, Raphael 1928- *AmMWSc 92*
**Aronson**, Robert Bernard 1930- *AmMWSc 92*
**Aronson**, Ronald 1938- *ConAu 133*
**Aronson**, Ronald Stephen 1944- *AmMWSc 92*
**Aronson**, Samuel Harry 1942- *AmMWSc 92*
**Aronson**, Seymour 1929- *AmMWSc 92*
**Aronson**, Sherlee Holmes 1931- *WhoEnt 92*
**Aronson**, Stanley Maynard 1922- *AmMWSc 92*
**Aronson**, Theo 1930- *IntAu&W 91, WrDr 92*
**Arora**, Harbans Lall 1921- *AmMWSc 92*
**Arora**, Jasbir Singh 1943- *AmMWSc 92*
**Arora**, Kartar Singh 1954- *WhoMW 92*
**Arora**, Narinder *AmMWSc 92*
**Arora**, Prince Kumar *AmMWSc 92*
**Arora**, Sardari Lal 1929- *WhoMW 92*
**Arora**, Swarnjit Singh 1940- *WhoFI 92, WhoMW 92*
**Arora**, Vijay Kumar 1945- *AmMWSc 92*
**Aros**, Jesse Richard *WhoWest 92*
**Aros**, Olga M. 1950- *WhoHisp 92*
**Arosa**, Gustave 1835?-1900? *ThHEIm*
**Arosemena Monroy**, Carlos Julio 1920- *IntWW 91*
**Arots**, Joseph B 1923- *AmMWSc 92*
**Arouna**, Mounkella 1938- *IntWW 91*
**Arova**, Sonia 1928- *WhoEnt 92*
**Aroyan**, H J 1921- *AmMWSc 92*
**Arp**, Alissa Jan 1954- *AmMWSc 92*
**Arp**, Bill *BenetAL 91*
**Arp**, Daniel James 1954- *AmMWSc 92*
**Arp**, Fred Allen 1944- *WhoWest 92*
**Arp**, Gerald Kench 1947- *AmMWSc 92*
**Arp**, Gregory Gene 1945- *WhoMW 92*
**Arp**, Halton Christian 1927- *AmMWSc 92*
**Arp**, Jean 1887-1966 *DcTwDes, FacFETw*
**Arp**, Leon Joseph 1930- *AmMWSc 92*
**Arp**, Robert Kelley 1962- *WhoRel 92*
**Arp**, Vincent D 1930- *AmMWSc 92*
**Arpaia**, Pasquale J 1932- *AmMWSc 92*
**Arpaillange**, Pierre Raymond 1924- *IntWW 91*
**Arpinati**, Leandro 1892-1945 *BiDExR*
**Arpino**, Gerald 1928- *FacFETw*
**Arpino**, Gerald Peter 1928- *WhoEnt 92*
**Arpke**, Charles Kenneth 1921- *AmMWSc 92*
**Arquette**, Gordon James 1925- *AmMWSc 92*
**Arquette**, Lewis 1935- *WhoEnt 92*
**Arquette**, Rosanna *IntWW 91*
**Arquette**, Rosanna 1959- *IntMPA 92, WhoEnt 92*
**Arquilla**, Edward R 1922- *AmMWSc 92*
**Arrabal**, Fernando 1932- *IntAu&W 91, IntWW 91, LiExTwC*
**Arraj**, Alfred Albert 1906- *WhoAmL 92, WhoWest 92*
**Arran**, Earl of 1938- *Who 92*
**Arranaga**, Christopher Lee 1960- *WhoHisp 92*
**Arranaga**, Robert C., Sr. *WhoHisp 92*

**Arrathoon**, Leigh Adelaide 1942- *WhoMW 92*
**Arrau**, Claudio d1991 *Who 92N*
**Arrau**, Claudio 1903- *IntWW 91*
**Arrau**, Claudio 1903-1991 *CurBio 91N, NewAmDM, NewYTBS 91 [port], News 92-1, WhoHisp 92N*
**Arreaga**, Michael Joseph 1952- *WhoHisp 92*
**Arreaza Arreaza**, Julio Cesar 1923- *IntWW 91*
**Arredondo**, Jo Marie 1940- *WhoHisp 92*
**Arredondo**, Lorenzo 1941- *WhoHisp 92*
**Arredondo**, P. Ben *WhoHisp 92*
**Arredondo**, Patricia Maria 1945- *WhoHisp 92*
**Arredondo**, Richard Cortez 1949- *WhoHisp 92*
**Arredondo**, Rudy, Sr. 1942- *WhoHisp 92*
**Arreguin**, Alfredo Mendoza 1935- *WhoHisp 92*
**Arreguin**, Arturo B. 1937- *WhoHisp 92*
**Arreguin**, Esteban Jose 1958- *WhoWest 92*
**Arreola**, Daniel David 1950- *WhoHisp 92*
**Arreola**, Juan Jose 1918- *DcLB 113 [port]*
**Arreola**, Philip 1940- *WhoHisp 92*
**Arreola**, Rafael A. *WhoHisp 92*
**Arrese Y Magra**, Jose Luis de 1905-1986 *BiDExR*
**Arrhenius**, Gustaf Olof Svante 1922- *AmMWSc 92*
**Arrhenius**, Svante August 1859-1927 *WhoNob 90*
**Arrhenius**, Svante August 1859-1929 *FacFETw*
**Arriaga**, Kaulza de 1915- *IntWW 91*
**Arriaga**, Maria Alexandra 1963- *WhoHisp 92*
**Arriaga**, Pablo Jose de 1564-1622 *HisDSpE*
**Arriaga y Rivera**, Julian de 1696-1776 *HisDSpE*
**Arrick**, Douglas Lee 1949- *WhoFI 92*
**Arrick**, Ronald M. 1946- *WhoAmL 92*
**Arrieta**, Roman 1924- *WhoRel 92*
**Arrieta**, Ruben O. 1935- *WhoHisp 92*
**Arrieta-Walden**, Frances Damaris 1958- *WhoHisp 92*
**Arrieu**, Claude 1903- *NewAmDM*
**Arrighi**, Frances Ellen 1924- *AmMWSc 92*
**Arrighi**, Mel 1933- *IntAu&W 91*
**Arrighi De Casanova**, Emile 1920- *IntWW 91*
**Arrighie**, Raymond Joseph 1938- *WhoAmP 91*
**Arrigoni**, Louis 1916- *WhoWest 92*
**Arrillaga**, Josu 1934- *IntWW 91*
**Arrillaga**, Maria 1940- *WhoHisp 92*
**Arrindell**, Clement Athelston 1931- *Who 92*
**Arrindell**, Clement Athelston 1932- *IntWW 91*
**Arrington**, Alfred W. 1810-1867 *BenetAL 91*
**Arrington**, Archibald Hunter 1809-1872 *DcNCBi 1*
**Arrington**, Charles Hammond, Jr 1920- *AmMWSc 92*
**Arrington**, Grady P 1923- *WhoAmP 91*
**Arrington**, Harold Mitchell 1947- *WhoBlA 92*
**Arrington**, Harriet Ann 1924- *WhoWest 92*
**Arrington**, Henry 1932- *WhoBlA 92*
**Arrington**, Irby N 1917- *WhoAmP 91*
**Arrington**, Jack Phillip 1942- *AmMWSc 92*
**Arrington**, John B 1919- *WhoAmP 91*
**Arrington**, John Leslie, Jr. 1931- *WhoAmL 92*
**Arrington**, John N. 1939- *WhoWest 92*
**Arrington**, Katherine Clark Pendleton 1876-1955 *DcNCBi 1*
**Arrington**, Keith 1914- *WhoMW 92*
**Arrington**, Lloyd M., Jr. 1947- *WhoBlA 92*
**Arrington**, Louis Carroll 1936- *AmMWSc 92*
**Arrington**, Marvin *WhoBlA 92*
**Arrington**, Michael *WhoAmP 91*
**Arrington**, Michael Browne 1943- *WhoFI 92, WhoMW 92*
**Arrington**, Pamela Gray 1953- *WhoBlA 92*
**Arrington**, Richard, Jr 1934- *AmMWSc 92, WhoAmP 91, WhoBlA 92*
**Arrington**, Robert Erskin 1920- *WhoAmP 91*
**Arrington**, Robyn James, Jr. 1944- *WhoBlA 92*
**Arrington**, Ronald K. 1955- *WhoAmL 92*
**Arrington**, Saul 1930- *WhoBlA 92*
**Arrington**, Teresa Ross 1949- *WhoRel 92*
**Arrington**, Wendell S 1936- *AmMWSc 92*
**Arriola**, Carlos L. 1946- *WhoHisp 92*
**Arriola**, Elizabeth P 1928- *WhoAmP 91*
**Arriola**, Gustavo Montano 1917- *WhoHisp 92*
**Arriola**, Helen Dolores 1943- *WhoHisp 92*
**Arriola**, John 1956- *WhoAmP 91*
**Arriola**, Jose Ricardo, Jr. 1947- *WhoHisp 92*
**Arriola**, Pedro Cogure 1954- *WhoAmP 91*
**Arriola**, Pedro Sablan *WhoAmP 91*
**Arrivi**, Francesco 1915- *BenetAL 91*
**Arrivi**, Francisco 1915- *WhoHisp 92*
**Arrizurieta**, Luis *WhoHisp 92*
**Arrobus**, Sydney 1901- *TwCPaSc*
**Arroe**, Hack 1920- *AmMWSc 92*
**Arrol**, John 1923- *WhoFI 92*
**Arron**, Henck Alphonsus Eugene 1936- *IntWW 91*
**Arron**, Judith Hagerty 1942- *WhoEnt 92, WhoFI 92*
**Arronge**, Steven William 1947- *WhoAmL 92*
**Arronte**, Albert Ray 1944- *WhoHisp 92*
**Arrott**, Anthony 1928- *AmMWSc 92*
**Arrow**, Kenneth 1921- *WrDr 92*
**Arrow**, Kenneth J 1921- *AmMWSc 92, IntWW 91*
**Arrow**, Kenneth Joseph 1921- *Who 92, WhoFI 92, WhoNob 90, WhoWest 92*
**Arrow**, William *TwCSFW 91, WrDr 92*
**Arrowood**, Catharine Biggs 1951- *WhoAmL 92*
**Arrowood**, Lisa Gayle 1956- *WhoAmL 92*
**Arrowood**, Roy Mitchell, Jr *AmMWSc 92*
**Arrowsmith**, Edwin 1909- *Who 92*
**Arrowsmith**, Isaac d1871 *DcLB 106*
**Arrowsmith**, J.W. d1913 *DcLB 106*
**Arrowsmith**, John 1798-1873 *ThHEIm*
**Arrowsmith**, Pat 1930- *Who 92*
**Arrowsmith**, Sue 1950- *TwCPaSc*
**Arrowsmith**, William 1924- *WrDr 92*
**Arrowsmith**, William Rankin 1910- *AmMWSc 92*
**Arroyave**, Carlos Mariano *AmMWSc 92*
**Arroyave**, Guillermo *AmMWSc 92*
**Arroyo**, Andrea 1962- *WhoHisp 92*
**Arroyo**, Antonio Perez 1950- *WhoHisp 92*
**Arroyo**, Carlos 1954- *WhoHisp 92*
**Arroyo**, Carmen 1943- *WhoHisp 92*
**Arroyo**, Eduardo 1937- *WorArt 1980*
**Arroyo**, Eva G. 1954- *WhoHisp 92*
**Arroyo**, Felix D. 1948- *WhoHisp 92*
**Arroyo**, Frank V., Sr. 1926- *WhoHisp 92*
**Arroyo**, Gilberto 1935- *WhoHisp 92*
**Arroyo**, Jose Antonio 1931- *WhoHisp 92*
**Arroyo**, Judith Angelica 1954- *WhoHisp 92*
**Arroyo**, Lourdes Maria 1953- *WhoHisp 92*
**Arroyo**, Martina *WhoBlA 92, WhoHisp 92*
**Arroyo**, Martina 1936- *NewAmDM*
**Arroyo**, Melissa Juanita 1949- *WhoHisp 92*
**Arroyo**, Nelson 1959- *WhoRel 92*
**Arroyo**, Nicolas Rene 1917- *WhoHisp 92*
**Arroyo**, Robert F. 1938- *WhoHisp 92*
**Arroyos**, Alexander Garcia, Sr. 1936- *WhoHisp 92*
**Arrupe**, Pedro 1907-1991 *CurBio 91N, IntWW 91, -91N, NewYTBS 91 [port]*
**Arruza**, Andrew Luis 1940- *WhoHisp 92*
**Arscott**, David Gifford 1944- *WhoFI 92*
**Arscott**, George Henry 1923- *AmMWSc 92*
**Arsenault**, Anzia Kubicek 1926- *WhoEnt 92*
**Arsenault**, Guy Pierre 1930- *AmMWSc 92*
**Arsenault**, Henri H 1937- *AmMWSc 92*
**Arseneau**, Donald Francis 1928- *AmMWSc 92*
**Arsenis**, Gerasimos 1931- *IntWW 91*
**Arseny**, Bishop 1866-1945 *RelLAm 91*
**Arsham**, Gary Martin 1941- *WhoWest 92*
**Arsiennieva**, Natalia 1903- *LiExTwC*
**Arsinoe** *EncAmaz 91*
**Arsinoe III Cleopatra** *EncAmaz 91*
**Arsinoe II Philadelphus** d269?BC *EncAmaz 91*
**Arslancan**, Ahmet N *AmMWSc 92*
**Arsove**, Maynard Goodwin 1922- *AmMWSc 92*
**Arstrom**, Folke 1907- *DcTwDes*
**Arsura**, Edward Louis 1950- *WhoWest 92*
**Art**, Henry Warren 1944- *AmMWSc 92*
**Artakama** *EncAmaz 91*
**Artaud**, Antonin 1896-1948 *FacFETw, GuFrLit 1, LiExTwC*
**Arteaga**, Alfred *DrAPF 91*
**Arteaga**, Gilda *WhoHisp 92*
**Arteaga**, Leonardo E. 1943- *WhoHisp 92*
**Arteaga**, Lucio 1924- *AmMWSc 92*
**Arteh Ghalib**, Omar 1930- *IntWW 91*
**Artem'ev**, Pavel Artem'evich 1897-1979 *SovUnBD*
**Artemiadis**, Nicholas 1917- *AmMWSc 92*
**Artemisia** *EncAmaz 91*
**Artemisia II** *EncAmaz 91*
**Arterberry**, Trent 1951- *WhoEnt 92*
**Arterbery**, Vivian J. *WhoBlA 92*
**Arterburn**, David Roe 1939- *AmMWSc 92*
**Arterburn**, Stephen Forrest 1953- *WhoRel 92*
**Artes**, Richard H 1926- *AmMWSc 92*
**Artes-Gomez**, Mariano 1947- *IntWW 91*
**Arth**, Joseph George, Jr 1945- *AmMWSc 92*
**Arth**, Lawrence J. 1943- *WhoIns 92*
**Arth**, Lawrence Joseph 1943- *WhoFI 92*
**Arthaud**, Raymond Louis 1921- *AmMWSc 92*
**Arthen**, Andras Corban 1949- *RelLAm 91*
**Arthen**, Deirdre Pulgram 1956- *RelLAm 91*
**Arthington-Davy**, Humphrey Augustine 1920- *Who 92*
**Arthur** *Who 92*
**Arthur**, Alan Thorne 1942- *AmMWSc 92*
**Arthur**, Allen James Vincent 1915- *Who 92*
**Arthur**, Beatrice *LesBEnT 92*
**Arthur**, Beatrice 1926- *IntMPA 92, WhoEnt 92*
**Arthur**, Burt 1899?-1975 *TwCWW 91*
**Arthur**, Charles Gemmell, IV 1965- *WhoMW 92*
**Arthur**, Chester A 1829-1886 *RComAH*
**Arthur**, Chester A. 1830-1886 *BenetAL 91*
**Arthur**, Chester Alan 1830-1886 *AmPolLe [port]*
**Arthur**, David Allen 1938- *WhoAmP 91*
**Arthur**, David Tallmadge 1936- *WhoMW 92*
**Arthur**, Elizabeth *DrAPF 91*
**Arthur**, Elizabeth Ann 1953- *IntAu&W 91*
**Arthur**, Gary David 1950- *WhoMW 92*
**Arthur**, Geoffrey Herbert 1916- *Who 92*
**Arthur**, George Kenneth 1933- *WhoBlA 92*
**Arthur**, George Kenneth 1934- *WhoAmP 91*
**Arthur**, Glenn N 1932- *WhoAmP 91*
**Arthur**, Herbert *TwCWW 91*
**Arthur**, James Alan 1936- *AmMWSc 92*
**Arthur**, James Greig 1944- *AmMWSc 92, IntWW 91*
**Arthur**, James M 1917- *WhoAmP 91*
**Arthur**, James Stanley 1923- *Who 92*
**Arthur**, Jean 1900?-1991 *CurBio 91N, NewYTBS 91 [port]*
**Arthur**, Jean 1901?-1991 *News 92-1*
**Arthur**, Jett Clinton, Jr 1918- *AmMWSc 92*
**Arthur**, John Morrison 1922- *WhoFI 92*
**Arthur**, John Norman 1931- *Who 92*
**Arthur**, John Preston 1851-1916 *DcNCBi 1*
**Arthur**, John Read, Jr 1931- *AmMWSc 92*
**Arthur**, John Rhys 1923- *Who 92*
**Arthur**, John W 1937- *AmMWSc 92*
**Arthur**, Karen *ReelWom*
**Arthur**, Karen 1941- *IntMPA 92*
**Arthur**, Katherine Elizabeth 1914- *WhoEnt 92*
**Arthur**, Lawrence 1943- *TwCPaSc*
**Arthur**, Margaret 1930- *TwCPaSc*
**Arthur**, Marion Abrahams 1911- *AmMWSc 92*
**Arthur**, Michael Allan 1948- *AmMWSc 92*
**Arthur**, Michael Anthony 1950- *Who 92*
**Arthur**, Norman *Who 92*
**Arthur**, Paul D 1925- *AmMWSc 92*
**Arthur**, Paul Keith 1931- *WhoWest 92*
**Arthur**, Peter *TwCSFW 91*
**Arthur**, Peter Bernard 1923- *Who 92*
**Arthur**, Randy Lee 1955- *WhoAmL 92, WhoWest 92*
**Arthur**, Rasjid Arthur James 1928- *IntAu&W 91*
**Arthur**, Richard J 1924- *AmMWSc 92*
**Arthur**, Robert David 1942- *AmMWSc 92*
**Arthur**, Robert Gordon 1909- *Who 92*
**Arthur**, Robert M 1924- *AmMWSc 92*
**Arthur**, Robert Siple 1916- *AmMWSc 92*
**Arthur**, Stephen 1953- *Who 92*
**Arthur**, Stephen E. 1955- *WhoAmL 92*
**Arthur**, Susan Peterson 1949- *AmMWSc 92*
**Arthur**, Thomas Hahn 1937- *WhoEnt 92*
**Arthur**, Timothy Shay 1809-1885 *BenetAL 91*
**Arthur**, Wallace 1932- *AmMWSc 92*
**Arthur**, Warren DuPree, IV 1948- *WhoAmP 91*
**Arthur**, William Brian 1946- *AmMWSc 92, WhoFI 92*
**Arthur**, William Lynn 1954- *WhoWest 92*
**Arthure**, Humphrey George Edgar *Who 92*
**Arthurhultz**, Phillip James 1947- *WhoAmP 91*
**Arthurs**, Harry William 1935- *IntWW 91, Who 92*
**Arties**, Lucy Elvira Yvonne *WhoBlA 92*
**Arties**, Walter Eugene, III 1941- *WhoBlA 92*
**Artigas**, Jose Gervasio 1764-1850 *HisDSpE*
**Artigue**, Ray Joseph 1954- *WhoWest 92*
**Artiles-Leon**, Noel 1957- *WhoHisp 92*
**Artime**, Luis Mariano 1950- *WhoAmL 92*
**Artin**, Michael 1934- *AmMWSc 92*
**Artingstall**, Thomas 1920- *WhoWest 92*
**Artis**, Andre Keith 1954- *WhoBlA 92*
**Artis**, Anthony Joel 1951- *WhoBlA 92*
**Artis**, Michael John 1938- *Who 92*
**Artis**, Myrle Everett 1924- *WhoBlA 92*
**Artison**, Richard E. 1933- *WhoBlA 92*
**Artisst**, Robert Irving 1932- *WhoBlA 92*
**Artist**, Everette Ward 1954- *WhoWest 92*
**Artist**, J William 1945- *WhoAmP 91*
**Artist**, Russell 1911- *AmMWSc 92*
**Artman**, Joseph Oscar 1926- *AmMWSc 92*
**Artman**, Paul Compton, Jr. 1951- *WhoEnt 92*
**Artmann**, William Charlie 1957- *WhoFI 92*
**Artna-Cohen**, Agda 1930- *AmMWSc 92*
**Artom**, Camillo 1893-1970 *DcNCBi 1*
**Arton**, A. T. B. *Who 92*
**Artope**, William 1943- *WhoBlA 92*
**Artrip**, William J 1924- *WhoAmP 91*
**Artro Morris**, John Evan 1925- *Who 92*
**Artru**, Alan Arthur 1949- *AmMWSc 92*
**Artschwager**, Richard 1923- *WorArt 1980 [port]*
**Artschwager**, Richard Ernst 1923- *IntWW 91*
**Artsybashev**, Mikhail Petrovich 1878-1927 *FacFETw*
**Artura**, Richard Frank 1958- *WhoAmL 92*
**Artus**, Ronald Edward 1931- *Who 92*
**Artusio**, Joseph F, Jr 1917- *AmMWSc 92*
**Artwick**, Frederic 1944- *WhoAmL 92*
**Arty**, Mary Ann 1926- *WhoAmP 91*
**Artyomov**, Vyacheslav 1940- *ConCom 92*
**Artyukhina**, Aleksandra Vasil'evna 1889-1969 *SovUnBD*
**Artz**, Bob 1946- *IntMPA 92*
**Artz**, Daniel James 1954- *WhoAmL 92*
**Artz**, Frederick James 1949- *WhoFI 92*
**Artzt**, Alice Josephine 1943- *IntWW 91, WhoEnt 92*
**Artzt**, Edwin Lewis 1930- *IntWW 91, WhoFI 92, WhoMW 92*
**Artzt**, Karen 1942- *AmMWSc 92*
**Aruca**, Francisco G. 1940- *WhoHisp 92*
**Aruego**, Jose 1932- *SmATA 68 [port]*
**Arumi**, Francisco Noe 1940- *AmMWSc 92*
**Arunasalam**, Vickramasingam 1935- *AmMWSc 92*
**Arundel**, Ian Bresson 1914- *WhoFI 92, WhoWest 92*
**Arundel And Brighton**, Bishop of 1932- *Who 92*
**Arundel And Surrey**, Earl of 1956- *Who 92*
**Arundell** *Who 92*
**Arup**, Ove 1895- *DcTwDes, FacFETw*
**Arutiunian**, Suren Gurgenovich 1938- *IntWW 91*
**Arutyunyan**, Suren Gurgenovich 1939- *SovUnBD*
**Arvan**, Dean Andrew 1933- *AmMWSc 92*
**Arvan**, Peter *AmMWSc 92*
**Arvani**, Christopher Carl 1937- *WhoFI 92*
**Arvatov**, Boris Ignatievich 1896-1940 *SovUnBD*
**Arvay**, Nancy Joan 1952- *WhoFI 92*
**Arvedson**, Peter Fredrick 1937- *WhoRel 92*
**Arvelo**, Alan 1962- *WhoFI 92*
**Arveschoug**, Steve 1958- *WhoAmP 91*
**Arvesen**, James Norman 1942- *AmMWSc 92*
**Arveson**, William Barnes 1934- *AmMWSc 92*
**Arvidson**, Fred B. 1949- *WhoAmL 92*
**Arvidson**, Raymond Ernst 1948- *AmMWSc 92*
**Arvidson**, Robert Benjamin, Jr. 1920- *WhoMW 92*
**Arvill**, Robert *Who 92*
**Arvin**, Charles Stanford 1931- *WhoMW 92*
**Arvizu**, John Henry 1945- *WhoHisp 92*
**Arvizu**, Ray *WhoHisp 92*
**Arvizu**, Robert E. 1943- *WhoHisp 92*
**ARW** *DrAPF 91*
**Ary**, Dennis 1950- *AmMWSc 92*
**Ary**, Donald Eugene 1930- *WhoMW 92*
**Ary**, T S 1925- *WhoFI 92*
**Ary**, Thomas Edward 1950- *AmMWSc 92*
**Arya**, Atam Parkash 1934- *AmMWSc 92*
**Arya**, Satya Pal Singh 1939- *AmMWSc 92*
**Aryal**, Krishna Raj 1928- *IntWW 91*
**Aryutyunyan**, Aleksandr Grigorevich 1920- *IntWW 91, SovUnBD*
**Arza**, Maria Cecilia 1956- *WhoMW 92*
**Arzac**, Adriana Maria 1947- *WhoHisp 92*
**Arzaga**, Ronald Dean 1963- *WhoWest 92*
**Arzbaecher**, Robert 1931- *AmMWSc 92*
**Arzberger**, Gus 1921- *WhoAmP 91*
**Arzner**, Dorothy 1900-1979 *HanAmWH, IntDcF 2-2 [port], ReelWom [port]*
**Arzoumanidis**, Gregory G 1936- *AmMWSc 92*
**Arzruni**, Sahan 1943- *WhoEnt 92*
**Arzt**, Sholom 1929- *AmMWSc 92*
**Arzube**, Juan Alfredo 1918- *WhoRel 92, WhoWest 92*
**Asa**, Sylvia L 1953- *AmMWSc 92*
**Asaad**, Fikry Naguib M. *Who 92*
**Asaad**, Magdi Mikhaeil 1940- *AmMWSc 92*
**Asada**, Shizuo 1911- *IntWW 91*
**Asadi**, Asad 1946- *WhoMW 92*
**Asadov**, Eduard Arkadevich 1923- *IntWW 91*
**Asadulla**, Syed 1933- *AmMWSc 92*

**Asaf'ev,** Boris Vladimirovich 1884-1949 *SovUnBD*
**Asahara,** Stella L. T. *WhoWest 92*
**Asahina,** Robert James 1950- *WhoFI 92*
**Asai,** David J 1953- *AmMWSc 92*
**Asakawa,** Takako 1939- *WhoEnt 92*
**Asakura,** Toshio 1935- *AmMWSc 92*
**Asal,** Nabih Rafia 1938- *AmMWSc 92*
**Asalde-Infante,** Yrene 1952- *WhoHisp 92*
**Asangono,** Evuna Owono 1944- *IntWW 91*
**Asano,** Akira 1923- *AmMWSc 92*
**Asano,** Teiji 1906- *IntWW 91*
**Asano,** Tomoaki 1929- *AmMWSc 92*
**Asante,** Kariamu Welsh 1949- *WhoBlA 92*
**Asante,** Kwaku Baprui 1924- *Who 92*
**Asante,** Molefi K. *WrDr 92*
**Asante,** Molefi Kete 1942- *WhoBlA 92*
**Asante,** Samuel Kwadwo Boaten 1933- *IntWW 91, WhoAmL 92*
**Asanuma,** Hiroshi 1926- *AmMWSc 92*
**Asare,** Meshack 1945- *WrDr 92*
**Asare,** Seth Ohene 1946- *WhoRel 92*
**Asarnow,** Herman Lewis 1950- *WhoEnt 92*
**Asaro,** Andi 1961- *WhoEnt 92*
**Asaro,** Robert John 1945- *AmMWSc 92*
**Asati,** Charles 1945- *BlkOlyM*
**Asato,** Goro 1931- *AmMWSc 92*
**Asato,** Yukio 1934- *AmMWSc 92*
**Asay,** Carlos Egan 1926- *WhoRel 92*
**Asay,** E Verl 1922- *WhoAmP 91*
**Asay,** Kay Harris 1933- *AmMWSc 92*
**Asay,** Tom 1926- *WhoAmP 91*
**Asbell,** Bernard 1923- *WrDr 92*
**Asbell,** Fred Thomas 1948- *WhoAmP 91*
**Asbell-Swanger,** Lea 1960- *WhoEnt 92*
**Asbill,** Mac, Jr. 1922- *WhoAmL 92*
**Asbridge,** John Robert 1928- *AmMWSc 92*
**Asbrink,** Erik 1947- *IntWW 91*
**Asbury,** Charles Theodore, Jr 1938- *WhoAmP 91*
**Asbury,** Chris Merlin 1952- *WhoWest 92*
**Asbury,** Daniel 1762-1825 *DcNCBi 1*
**Asbury,** Francis 1745-1816 *BenetAL 91, BlkwEAR, DcNCBi 1*
**Asbury,** Herbert 1891-1963 *BenetAL 91, ScFEYrs*
**Asbury,** Joseph G 1938- *AmMWSc 92*
**Asbury,** Joseph George 1938- *WhoMW 92*
**Asbury,** Mary Ruth 1954- *WhoRel 92*
**Asbury,** William W. 1943- *WhoBlA 92*
**Ascah,** Ralph Gordon 1918- *AmMWSc 92*
**Ascanio,** Montiano *WhoHisp 92*
**Ascarelli,** Gianni 1931- *AmMWSc 92*
**Ascenio,** Diego C. *WhoHisp 92*
**Ascensao,** Joao L 1948- *AmMWSc 92*
**Ascenzi,** Joseph Michael 1949- *AmMWSc 92*
**Ascenzo,** Brian William 1957- *WhoEnt 92*
**Asch,** Beth Jessica 1958- *WhoFI 92*
**Asch,** Bonnie Bradshaw *AmMWSc 92*
**Asch,** Frank 1946- *IntAu&W 91, SmATA 66 [port], WrDr 92*
**Asch,** Harold Lawrence 1943- *AmMWSc 92*
**Asch,** Moses 1905-1986 *FacFETw*
**Asch,** Nathan 1902-1964 *BenetAL 91*
**Asch,** Nolan E. 1949- *WhoIns 92*
**Asch,** Peter 1937-1990 *ConAu 133*
**Asch,** Sholem 1880-1957 *BenetAL 91, DcAmImH, LiExTwC*
**Asch,** Sunny Charla *WhoEnt 92*
**Aschaffenburg,** Walter Eugene 1927- *WhoEnt 92*
**Ascham,** Roger 1515?-1568 *RfGEnL 91*
**Aschauer,** Charles Joseph, Jr. 1928- *WhoFI 92, WhoMW 92*
**Aschbacher,** Michael 1944- *AmMWSc 92*
**Aschbacher,** Peter William 1928- *AmMWSc 92*
**Aschenbrener,** Thomas David 1944- *WhoWest 92*
**Aschenbrenner,** Frank Aloysious 1924- *WhoFI 92, WhoWest 92*
**Aschenbrenner,** John E. 1949- *WhoIns 92*
**Ascher,** Carol *DrAPF 91*
**Ascher,** Eduard 1915- *AmMWSc 92*
**Ascher,** Everett S. 1936- *WhoWest 92*
**Ascher,** James John 1928- *WhoFI 92, WhoMW 92*
**Ascher,** Marcia 1935- *AmMWSc 92*
**Ascher,** Michael S 1942- *AmMWSc 92*
**Ascher,** Robert 1931- *AmMWSc 92*
**Ascher,** Sheila *DrAPF 91*
**Ascher,** Steven Peter 1955- *WhoEnt 92*
**Ascherl,** Jack 1937- *WhoAmP 91*
**Ascherman,** Herbert, Jr 1947- *WhoEnt 92*
**Ascherson,** Neal 1932- *Who 92, WrDr 92*
**Ascherson,** Pamela 1923- *TwCPaSc*
**Aschleman,** James Allan 1944- *WhoAmL 92*
**Aschmann,** Mary Francis 1921- *WhoRel 92*
**Aschner,** Joseph Felix 1922- *AmMWSc 92*
**Aschner,** Michael 1955- *AmMWSc 92*
**Aschoff,** Jurgen Walter Ludwig 1913- *IntWW 91*
**Aschoff,** Karl Albert Ludwig 1866-1942 *FacFETw*
**Ascoli,** Giulio 1922- *AmMWSc 92*
**Ascoli,** Mario 1951- *AmMWSc 92*
**Ascot,** James Dennis 1949- *WhoMW 92*
**Ascott,** Roy 1934- *TwCPaSc*
**Asculai,** Samuel Simon 1942- *AmMWSc 92*
**Aseer,** Ghulam Nabi 1940- *WhoFI 92*
**Aseev,** Nikolay Nikolaevich 1889-1963 *SovUnBD*
**Asefa,** Sisay 1950- *WhoFI 92*
**Aseff,** George V 1921- *AmMWSc 92*
**Asekoff,** Stanley Louis 1944- *WhoRel 92*
**Asen,** Shel F. 1937- *WhoFI 92*
**Asendorf,** Robert Harry 1927- *AmMWSc 92*
**Asenio-Wunderlich,** Julio 1911- *IntWW 91*
**Asenjo,** Florencio Gonzalez 1926- *AmMWSc 92, WhoHisp 92*
**Aserinsky,** Eugene 1921- *AmMWSc 92*
**Aseyev,** Nikolai Nikolayevich 1889-1963 *FacFETw*
**Asfa Wossen Haile Sellassie,** Merd A 1916- *Who 92*
**Asfahl,** C Ray 1938- *AmMWSc 92*
**Asfeld,** Ludwig Nicholas 1931- *WhoMW 92*
**Asgar,** Kamal 1922- *AmMWSc 92*
**Asgeirsson,** Asgeir 1894-1972 *FacFETw*
**Asghar,** Khursheed 1940- *AmMWSc 92*
**Asgrimsson,** Halldor 1947- *IntWW 91*
**Ash,** Arlene Sandra 1946- *AmMWSc 92*
**Ash,** Bernadette 1934- *TwCPaSc*
**Ash,** Brian 1936- *IntAu&W 91*
**Ash,** Brian Maxwell 1941- *Who 92*
**Ash,** Eric 1928- *Who 92*
**Ash,** Eric Albert 1928- *IntWW 91*
**Ash,** Eric Duane 1959- *WhoRel 92*
**Ash,** Fayola Foltz 1926- *WhoEnt 92*
**Ash,** Fenton *TwCSFW 91*
**Ash,** Fenton 1840-1927 *ScFEYrs*
**Ash,** Hiram Newton 1934- *WhoEnt 92*
**Ash,** J Marshall 1940- *AmMWSc 92, WhoMW 92*
**Ash,** James Lee, Jr. 1945- *WhoRel 92*
**Ash,** James Mathew 1958- *WhoWest 92*
**Ash,** John 1948- *ConPo 91, IntAu&W 91, WrDr 92*
**Ash,** Kenneth Owen 1936- *AmMWSc 92*
**Ash,** Lawrence Robert 1933- *AmMWSc 92*
**Ash,** Major McKinley, Jr 1921- *AmMWSc 92*
**Ash,** Mary Kay Wagner *WhoFI 92*
**Ash,** Maurice Anthony 1917- *Who 92*
**Ash,** Michael 1939- *WhoAmL 92*
**Ash,** Michael 1955- *WhoEnt 92*
**Ash,** Michael Edward 1937- *AmMWSc 92*
**Ash,** Peter 1947- *WhoFI 92*
**Ash,** Raymond 1928- *Who 92*
**Ash,** Raymond H 1939- *AmMWSc 92*
**Ash,** Rene 1939- *IntMPA 92*
**Ash,** Rene Lee 1939- *WhoEnt 92*
**Ash,** Richard Larry 1959- *WhoBlA 92*
**Ash,** Robert B 1935- *AmMWSc 92*
**Ash,** Robert Lafayette 1941- *AmMWSc 92*
**Ash,** Roy L 1918- *WhoAmP 91*
**Ash,** Roy Lawrence 1918- *IntWW 91*
**Ash,** Roy Phillip 1943- *AmMWSc 92*
**Ash,** Russell 1946- *WrDr 92*
**Ash,** Sidney Roy 1928- *AmMWSc 92*
**Ash,** Virginia Maria 1918- *WhoEnt 92*
**Ash,** Walter Brinker 1932- *WhoAmL 92, WhoWest 92*
**Ash,** Walter William Hector 1906- *Who 92*
**Ash,** William 1917- *IntAu&W 91*
**Ash,** William Franklin 1917- *WrDr 92*
**Ash,** William James 1931- *AmMWSc 92*
**Ash,** William Noel 1921- *Who 92*
**Ash,** William Wesley 1941- *AmMWSc 92*
**Ashabranner,** Brent 1921- *SmATA 67 [port], SmATA 14AS [port]*
**Ashabranner,** Melissa 1950- *ConAu 134*
**Ashadawi,** Ahmed Ali 1939- *WhoFI 92*
**Ashanti,** Baron James *DrAPF 91*
**Ashanti,** Baron James 1950- *IntAu&W 91*
**Ashbach,** David Laurence 1942- *WhoMW 92*
**Ashbach,** Robert O 1916- *WhoAmP 91*
**Ashbacher,** Charles David 1954- *WhoMW 92*
**Ashbaugh,** Ann Marie 1945- *WhoWest 92*
**Ashbaugh,** Donald Le Roy 1954- *WhoMW 92*
**Ashbeck,** David Kilian 1942- *WhoRel 92*
**Ashbee,** Charles Robert 1863-1942 *DcTwDes*
**Ashbee,** Paul 1918- *Who 92*
**Ashbery,** John *DrAPF 91*
**Ashbery,** John 1927- *BenetAL 91, ConPo 91, FacFETw, WrDr 92*
**Ashbery,** John Lawrence 1927- *IntWW 91*
**Ashbolt,** Allan 1921- *WrDr 92*
**Ashbourne,** Baron 1933- *Who 92*
**Ashbridge,** Elizabeth 1713-1755 *BenetAL 91*
**Ashbridge,** Elizabeth Sampson 1713-1755 *HanAmWH*
**Ashbrock,** David Paul 1956- *WhoEnt 92*
**Ashbrook,** Viscount 1905- *Who 92*
**Ashbrook,** Allan William 1929- *AmMWSc 92*
**Ashbrook,** James Barbour 1925- *WhoRel 92, WrDr 92*
**Ashbrook,** Kate Jessie 1955- *Who 92*
**Ashbrook,** William Sinclair, Jr. 1922- *WhoEnt 92*
**Ashburn,** Allen David 1933- *AmMWSc 92*
**Ashburn,** Edward V 1910- *AmMWSc 92*
**Ashburn,** Marian 1954- *TwCPaSc*
**Ashburn,** William Lee 1933- *AmMWSc 92*
**Ashburner,** Charles Albert 1854-1889 *BiInAmS*
**Ashburner,** Michael 1942- *Who 92*
**Ashburnham,** Denny Reginald 1916- *Who 92*
**Ashburton,** Baron d1991 *Who 92N*
**Ashburton,** Baron 1928- *Who 92*
**Ashby** *Who 92*
**Ashby,** Baron 1904- *IntWW 91, Who 92, WrDr 92*
**Ashby,** B B 1930- *AmMWSc 92*
**Ashby,** Bernadette Evalle 1963- *WhoRel 92*
**Ashby,** Bruce Allan 1922- *AmMWSc 92*
**Ashby,** Carl Toliver 1905- *AmMWSc 92*
**Ashby,** Carter *TwCWW 91*
**Ashby,** Cliff 1919- *IntAu&W 91, WrDr 92*
**Ashby,** Clifford Charles 1925- *WhoEnt 92*
**Ashby,** Dale Cottrell 1952- *WhoFI 92*
**Ashby,** David Glynn 1940- *Who 92*
**Ashby,** Derek 1926- *TwCPaSc*
**Ashby,** Dorothy J. 1932- *WhoBlA 92*
**Ashby,** Eric *WrDr 92*
**Ashby,** Ernestine Arnold 1928- *WhoBlA 92*
**Ashby,** Eugene Christopher 1930- *AmMWSc 92*
**Ashby,** Francis Dalton 1920- *Who 92*
**Ashby,** Godfrey William Ernest Candler 1930- *Who 92*
**Ashby,** Gwynneth Margaret 1922- *IntAu&W 91, WrDr 92*
**Ashby,** Hal 1932-1988 *IntDcF 2-2 [port]*
**Ashby,** Harold Kenneth 1925- *WhoEnt 92*
**Ashby,** John Edmund, Jr. 1936- *WhoFI 92*
**Ashby,** John Forsythe 1929- *WhoRel 92*
**Ashby,** Jon Kenneth 1941- *AmMWSc 92*
**Ashby,** Laura Lee 1954- *WhoWest 92*
**Ashby,** Lucius Antoine 1944- *WhoBlA 92*
**Ashby,** Lucius Antone 1944- *WhoFI 92, WhoWest 92*
**Ashby,** Michael Farries 1935- *IntWW 91, Who 92*
**Ashby,** Neil 1934- *AmMWSc 92*
**Ashby,** Norma Rae Beatty 1935- *WhoEnt 92*
**Ashby,** Paul David 1959- *WhoEnt 92*
**Ashby,** Philip H. 1916- *WrDr 92*
**Ashby,** Reginald W. *WhoBlA 92*
**Ashby,** Roger Arthur 1940- *WhoFI 92*
**Ashby,** T.H.W. 1927- *TwCPaSc*
**Ashby,** Val Jean 1923- *AmMWSc 92*
**Ashby,** William Clark 1922- *AmMWSc 92, WhoMW 92*
**Ashby,** William M. 1889-1991 *NewYTBS 91 [port]*
**Ashcom,** John M. 1945- *WhoFI 92*
**Ashcombe,** Baron 1924- *Who 92*
**Ashcraft,** Aaron Edward 1940- *WhoWest 92*
**Ashcraft,** Arnold Clifton, Jr 1938- *AmMWSc 92*
**Ashcraft,** Bernard 1941- *WhoBlA 92*
**Ashcraft,** David Lee 1946- *WhoFI 92*
**Ashcraft,** Percy C, II 1957- *WhoAmP 91*
**Ashcraft,** Thomas J. *WhoAmL 92*
**Ashcroft,** Dale Leroy 1926- *AmMWSc 92*
**Ashcroft,** David 1920- *Who 92*
**Ashcroft,** Frederick H 1953- *AmMWSc 92*
**Ashcroft,** James Geoffrey 1928- *Who 92*
**Ashcroft,** John *IntWW 91*
**Ashcroft,** John 1942- *AlmAP 92 [port]*
**Ashcroft,** John David 1942- *WhoAmP 91, WhoMW 92*
**Ashcroft,** John Kevin 1948- *Who 92*
**Ashcroft,** Lawrence 1901- *Who 92*
**Ashcroft,** Neil William 1938- *AmMWSc 92*
**Ashcroft,** Peggy d1991 *Who 92N*
**Ashcroft,** Peggy 1907- *IntWW 91*
**Ashcroft,** Peggy 1907-1991 *CurBio 91N, FacFETw, NewYTBS 91 [port], News 92-1*
**Ashcroft,** Philip Giles 1926- *Who 92*
**Ashcroft,** Richard Carter 1942- *WhoMW 92*
**Ashcroft,** Richard Thomas 1934- *WhoWest 92*
**Ashdjian,** Vilma 1954- *WhoWest 92*
**Ashdown,** Dulcie Margaret 1946- *IntAu&W 91*
**Ashdown,** Franklin Donald 1942- *WhoWest 92*
**Ashdown,** Jeremy John Durham 1941- *IntWW 91, Who 92*
**Ashdown,** Marie Matranga *WhoEnt 92*
**Ashdown,** Philomena Saldanha 1958- *WhoAmL 92*
**Ashe,** Arthur 1943- *ConAu 35NR, ConBlB 1 [port], SmATA 65 [port], WrDr 92*
**Ashe,** Arthur James, III 1940- *AmMWSc 92*
**Ashe,** Arthur R., Jr. 1943- *WhoBlA 92*
**Ashe,** Arthur Robert 1943- *FacFETw, IntWW 91*
**Ashe,** Bernard Flemming 1936- *WhoAmL 92*
**Ashe,** Claire Clyde 1934- *WhoWest 92*
**Ashe,** Derick 1919- *Who 92*
**Ashe,** Derick Rosslyn 1919- *IntWW 91*
**Ashe,** Geoffrey Thomas 1923- *IntAu&W 91, WrDr 92*
**Ashe,** James S 1947- *AmMWSc 92*
**Ashe,** John 1725-1781 *DcNCBi 1*
**Ashe,** John Baptist 1748-1802 *DcNCBi 1*
**Ashe,** John Baptista d1734 *DcNCBi 1*
**Ashe,** John Herman 1944- *AmMWSc 92, WhoWest 92*
**Ashe,** Oliver Richard 1933- *WhoFI 92*
**Ashe,** Robert Lawrence, Jr. 1940- *WhoAmL 92*
**Ashe,** Samuel 1725-1813 *DcNCBi 1*
**Ashe,** Samuel A'Court 1840-1938 *DcNCBi 1*
**Ashe,** Thomas 1770- *BenetAL 91*
**Ashe,** Thomas Samuel 1812-1887 *DcNCBi 1*
**Ashe,** Victor Henderson 1945- *WhoAmP 91*
**Ashe,** Warren 1929- *AmMWSc 92*
**Ashe,** William Shepperd 1814-1862 *DcNCBi 1*
**Ashe,** William Willard 1872-1932 *DcNCBi 1*
**Ashe Lincoln,** Fredman *Who 92*
**Ashear,** Linda *DrAPF 91*
**Asheghian,** Parviz 1943- *WhoFI 92*
**Asheim,** David Clair 1955- *WhoFI 92*
**Ashen,** Philip 1915- *AmMWSc 92*
**Ashendel,** Curtis Lloyd 1955- *AmMWSc 92*
**Ashendon,** Edward James 1896- *TwCPaSc*
**Ashendorf,** Linda *WhoAmP 91*
**Ashenhurst,** Francis Ernest 1933- *Who 92*
**Ashenhurst,** Robert Lovett 1929- *AmMWSc 92*
**Asher,** Alvin Bernard 1920- *WhoWest 92*
**Asher,** Betty Turner 1944- *WhoMW 92*
**Asher,** David 1946- *WhoIns 92*
**Asher,** David Michael 1937- *AmMWSc 92*
**Asher,** Garland Parker 1944- *WhoFI 92*
**Asher,** Howard Ralph 1947- *WhoWest 92*
**Asher,** J. William 1927- *WhoMW 92*
**Asher,** James Edward 1931- *WhoWest 92*
**Asher,** James Leonard 1947- *WhoFI 92*
**Asher,** James Michael 1949- *WhoAmL 92*
**Asher,** Jane 1946- *ConAu 133, IntAu&W 91, IntMPA 92, IntWW 91, Who 92*
**Asher,** Jefferson William, Jr. 1924- *WhoWest 92*
**Asher,** John Alexander 1921- *WrDr 92*
**Asher,** Kamlesh 1953- *WhoFI 92*
**Asher,** Kathleen May 1932- *WhoAmP 91*
**Asher,** Maxine Klein 1935- *WhoWest 92*
**Asher,** Miriam *ConAu 34NR*
**Asher,** Peter 1944- *WhoEnt 92*
**Asher,** Robert B 1937- *WhoAmP 91*
**Asher,** Sandy 1942- *SmATA 13AS [port]*
**Asher,** Steven Alan 1947- *WhoAmL 92*
**Asher,** William *LesBEnT 92*
**Asher,** William 1919- *ConTFT 9*
**Asherin,** Duane Arthur 1940- *AmMWSc 92*
**Ashford,** Albert Reginald 1914- *Who 92*
**Ashford,** Brad 1949- *WhoAmP 91*
**Ashford,** Clinton Rutledge 1925- *WhoAmL 92*
**Ashford,** Evelyn 1957- *BlkOlyM [port], WhoBlA 92*
**Ashford,** George Francis 1911- *Who 92*
**Ashford,** James Knox 1937- *WhoFI 92*
**Ashford,** Jeffrey *IntAu&W 91X, WrDr 92*
**Ashford,** L. Jerome 1937- *WhoBlA 92*
**Ashford,** Laplois 1935- *WhoBlA 92*
**Ashford,** Nicholas 1943- *WhoBlA 92*
**Ashford,** Percival Leonard 1927- *Who 92*
**Ashford,** Reginald *Who 92*
**Ashford,** Ronald Gordon 1931- *Who 92*
**Ashford,** Ross 1926- *AmMWSc 92*
**Ashford,** Victor Aaron 1942- *AmMWSc 92*
**Ashford,** William Stanton 1924- *IntWW 91, Who 92*
**Ashforth,** Alden 1933- *WhoEnt 92*
**Ashihara,** Yoshinobu 1918- *IntWW 91*
**Ashimov,** Baiken Ashimovich 1917- *IntWW 91*
**Ashiotis,** Costas 1908- *Who 92*
**Ashjian,** Mesrob 1941- *WhoRel 92*
**Ashken,** Kenneth Richard 1945- *Who 92*
**Ashkenasi,** Shmuel 1941- *IntWW 91*
**Ashkenaz,** David Elliot 1950- *WhoMW 92*
**Ashkenazy,** Vladimir 1937- *FacFETw [port], IntWW 91, NewAmDM, SovUnBD, Who 92*

**Ashkenazy**, Vladimir Davidovich 1937- WhoEnt 92
**Ashkin**, Arthur 1922- AmMWSc 92
**Ashkin**, Rajasperi Maliapen 1956- WhoMW 92
**Ashkin**, Ronald Evan 1957- WhoFI 92, WhoMW 92
**Ashkinaze**, Alan Steven 1960- WhoAmL 92
**Ashland**, Calvin Kolle 1933- WhoAmL 92, WhoWest 92
**Ashler**, Philip Frederic 1914- WhoAmP 91
**Ashley**, Lord 1977- Who 92
**Ashley**, Alvin 1934- NewYTBS 91 [port]
**Ashley**, Bernard 1926- Who 92
**Ashley**, Bernard 1935- IntAu&W 91, WrDr 92
**Ashley**, Bob 1953- WhoAmP 91
**Ashley**, Cedric 1936- Who 92
**Ashley**, Charles Allen 1923- AmMWSc 92
**Ashley**, Corlanders 1951- WhoBlA 92
**Ashley**, Don William 1948- WhoFI 92
**Ashley**, Douglas Daniels WhoEnt 92
**Ashley**, Doyle Allen 1932- AmMWSc 92
**Ashley**, Elizabeth 1939- IntMPA 92
**Ashley**, Elizabeth 1941- WhoEnt 92
**Ashley**, Franklin DrAPF 91
**Ashley**, Franklin Bascom 1942- WhoEnt 92
**Ashley**, Fred TwCSFW 91
**Ashley**, George d1991 NewYTBS 91
**Ashley**, George Edward 1919- WhoAmL 92
**Ashley**, Harrison Everett 1876-1911 BiInAmS
**Ashley**, Holt 1923- AmMWSc 92, WhoFI 92
**Ashley**, J Robert 1927- AmMWSc 92
**Ashley**, Jack 1922- IntAu&W 91, Who 92, WrDr 92
**Ashley**, James Wheeler 1923- WhoAmL 92
**Ashley**, John 1934- IntMPA 92
**Ashley**, John M, Jr WhoAmP 91
**Ashley**, Kenneth R 1941- AmMWSc 92
**Ashley**, Laura 1926-1985 DcTwDes, FacFETw
**Ashley**, Leonard R N 1928- IntAu&W 91, WrDr 92
**Ashley**, Lillard Governor 1909- WhoBlA 92
**Ashley**, Lynn 1920- WhoMW 92
**Ashley**, Marshall Douglas 1942- AmMWSc 92
**Ashley**, Martha E 1955- WhoAmP 91
**Ashley**, Maurice 1907- IntAu&W 91, WrDr 92
**Ashley**, Maurice Percy 1907- Who 92
**Ashley**, Merrill WhoEnt 92
**Ashley**, Ona Christine 1954- WhoMW 92
**Ashley**, Paula Claire 1939- WhoWest 92
**Ashley**, Renee A. DrAPF 91
**Ashley**, Richard Allan 1941- AmMWSc 92
**Ashley**, Robert 1930- ConCom 92, NewAmDM
**Ashley**, Roger Parkmand 1940- AmMWSc 92
**Ashley**, Rosalind Minor 1923- WhoWest 92
**Ashley**, Samuel Stanford 1819-1887 DcNCBi 1
**Ashley**, Sharon Anita 1948- WhoWest 92
**Ashley**, Ted LesBEnT 92
**Ashley**, Ted 1922- IntMPA 92
**Ashley**, Terry Fay 1942- AmMWSc 92
**Ashley**, Thomas Ludlow 1923- WhoAmP 91
**Ashley**, Thomas William Ludlow 1923- NewYTBS 91 [port]
**Ashley**, Warren Cotton 1904- AmMWSc 92
**Ashley**, Willard Walden C., Sr. 1953- WhoRel 92
**Ashley-Cooper** Who 92
**Ashley-Farrand**, Margalo 1944- WhoAmL 92
**Ashley Harris**, Dolores B. WhoBlA 92
**Ashley-Miller**, Michael 1930- Who 92
**Ashley-Smith**, Jonathan 1946- Who 92
**Ashliman**, Joseph Lyle, Jr. 1927- WhoFI 92
**Ashlock**, Bruce E. 1948- WhoRel 92
**Ashlock**, James Allen 1955- WhoRel 92
**Ashlock**, Ken WhoRel 92
**Ashlock**, Peter Dunning 1929- AmMWSc 92
**Ashman**, Bruce Lorn 1951- WhoMW 92
**Ashman**, Charles Henry 1924- WhoRel 92
**Ashman**, Glen Edward 1956- WhoAmL 92
**Ashman**, Howard d1991 NewYTBS 91 [port]
**Ashman**, Howard 1950-1991 ConAu 133, ConTFT 9
**Ashman**, Joyce Elaine 1939- WhoRel 92
**Ashman**, Michael Nathan 1940- AmMWSc 92
**Ashman**, Robert F 1938- AmMWSc 92
**Ashman**, William Alfred, Jr. 1954- WhoWest 92
**Ashmann**, Jon 1950- WhoMW 92
**Ashmead**, Allez Morrill 1916- WhoWest 92
**Ashmead**, Graham Gaylord 1951- WhoMW 92
**Ashmead**, William Harris 1855-1908 BiInAmS
**Ashmole**, David 1949- Who 92
**Ashmore**, Alick 1920- Who 92
**Ashmore**, Andrea Lynn 1954- WhoBlA 92
**Ashmore**, Charles Robert 1934- AmMWSc 92
**Ashmore**, Edward 1919- IntWW 91, Who 92
**Ashmore**, Owen 1920- IntAu&W 91
**Ashmore**, Peter 1921- Who 92
**Ashmore**, Philip George 1916- Who 92
**Ashmore**, William Thomas, Jr. 1912- WhoFI 92
**Ashnault**, Paul O WhoAmP 91
**Ashok**, S 1947- AmMWSc 92
**Ashpole**, William Emory 1929- WhoRel 92
**Ashrawi**, Hanan NewYTBS 91 [port]
**Ashtal**, Abdalla Saleh al- 1940- IntWW 91
**Ashtekar**, Abhay Vasant 1949- AmMWSc 92
**Ashton** Who 92
**Ashton**, Alan C. WhoFI 92
**Ashton**, Ann WrDr 92
**Ashton**, Anthony Southcliffe 1916- Who 92
**Ashton**, Bruce Leland 1945- WhoAmL 92
**Ashton**, David Hugh 1939- AmMWSc 92
**Ashton**, Dore WrDr 92
**Ashton**, Elizabeth WrDr 92
**Ashton**, Floyd Milton 1922- AmMWSc 92
**Ashton**, Francis T AmMWSc 92
**Ashton**, Frederick 1906-1988 FacFETw
**Ashton**, Geoffrey C 1925- AmMWSc 92
**Ashton**, George Arthur 1921- Who 92
**Ashton**, Graham 1948- TwCPaSc
**Ashton**, John IntMPA 92
**Ashton**, John Howard 1938- WhoEnt 92
**Ashton**, John Peter 1945- WhoAmL 92
**Ashton**, John Russell 1925- Who 92
**Ashton**, John William 1881-1963 TwCPaSc
**Ashton**, Joseph Benjamin 1930- AmMWSc 92
**Ashton**, Joseph William 1933- Who 92
**Ashton**, Juliet H AmMWSc 92
**Ashton**, Katherine 1960- WhoAmL 92
**Ashton**, Kenneth Bruce 1925- Who 92
**Ashton**, Leonard 1915- Who 92
**Ashton**, Margaret 1856-1937 BiDBrF 2
**Ashton**, Mark Randolph 1955- WhoAmP 91
**Ashton**, Norman 1913- Who 92
**Ashton**, Norman Henry 1913- IntWW 91
**Ashton**, Patrick Thomas 1916- Who 92
**Ashton**, Peter Shaw 1934- AmMWSc 92
**Ashton**, Price Richard 1917- WhoAmL 92
**Ashton**, Rick James 1945- WhoWest 92
**Ashton**, Robert 1924- IntAu&W 91, Who 92, WrDr 92
**Ashton**, Robert W. 1937- WhoAmL 92
**Ashton**, Roy 1928- Who 92
**Ashton**, Ruth Mary 1939- Who 92
**Ashton**, Stewart Leslie 1920- WhoFI 92
**Ashton**, Tony 1948- TwCPaSc
**Ashton**, Vivian Christina R. 1910- WhoBlA 92
**Ashton Hill**, Norman 1918- Who 92
**Ashton of Hyde**, Baron 1926- Who 92
**Ashton-Warner**, Sylvia 1908-1984 FacFETw
**Ashtown**, Baron d1990 Who 92N
**Ashtown**, Baron 1916- Who 92
**Ashutosh**, Kumar 1940- AmMWSc 92
**Ashwell**, G Gilbert 1916- AmMWSc 92
**Ashwin**, James Guy 1926- AmMWSc 92
**Ashwood**, Andrew Mark 1957- WhoEnt 92
**Ashworth**, Brent Ferrin 1949- WhoAmL 92, WhoFI 92
**Ashworth**, Edwin Robert 1927- AmMWSc 92
**Ashworth**, Elinor Gene 1942- WhoFI 92
**Ashworth**, Geoffrey Hugh 1950- WhoIns 92
**Ashworth**, Graham William 1935- Who 92
**Ashworth**, Harry Arthur 1943- AmMWSc 92
**Ashworth**, Herbert 1910- Who 92
**Ashworth**, Ian Edward 1930- Who 92
**Ashworth**, James Louis 1906- Who 92
**Ashworth**, John Blackwood 1910- Who 92
**Ashworth**, John Michael 1938- IntWW 91, Who 92
**Ashworth**, John R. 1942- TwCPaSc
**Ashworth**, Lawrence Nelson 1942- WhoFI 92
**Ashworth**, Lee Jackson, Jr 1926- AmMWSc 92
**Ashworth**, Peter Anthony Frank 1935- Who 92
**Ashworth**, Piers 1931- Who 92
**Ashworth**, Robert Archibald 1871-1959 RelLAm 91
**Ashworth**, Robert David 1940- AmMWSc 92
**Ashworth**, T 1940- AmMWSc 92
**Ashworth**, William d1991 Who 92N
**Ashworth**, William 1920-1991 ConAu 134
**Ashworth**, William 1942- ConAu 133
**Ashworth**, William Bruce, Jr 1943- AmMWSc 92
**Ashy**, Peter Jawad 1940- AmMWSc 92
**Asia**, Daniel Isaac 1953- WhoWest 92
**Asik**, Joseph R 1937- AmMWSc 92
**Asilis**, Carlos Manuel 1962- WhoFI 92
**Asimakis**, Gregory K 1947- AmMWSc 92
**Asimakopulos**, Athanasios 1930- IntWW 91
**Asimov**, Isaac DrAPF 91
**Asimov**, Isaac 1920- AmMWSc 92, BenetAL 91, ConAu 36NR, ConNov 91, FacFETw [port], IntAu&W 91, IntWW 91, ScFEYrs, TwCSFW 91, Who 92, WhoEnt 92, WrDr 92
**Asimov**, Isaac, Waugh, C C & Greenberg ScFEYrs
**Asimov**, Isaac & Cote, Jean Marc ScFEYrs A
**Asimov**, Janet 1926- ConAu 36NR
**Asimov**, Janet Jeppson 1926- WrDr 92
**Asimov**, Janet O. Jeppson 1926- IntAu&W 91
**Asimov**, Mukhamed Saifitdinovich 1920- IntWW 91
**Asimow**, Michael R. 1939- WhoAmL 92
**Asinof**, Eliot 1919- WrDr 92
**Asinor**, Freddie Andrew 1955- WhoBlA 92
**Asip**, Patricia Victoria WhoHisp 92
**Asiroglu**, Vahap 1916- Who 92
**Askanazi**, Jeffrey 1951- AmMWSc 92
**Askari**, Amir 1930- AmMWSc 92
**Aske**, Conan 1912- Who 92
**Askeland**, Donald Raymond 1942- AmMWSc 92
**Askenase**, Philip William AmMWSc 92
**Askenov**, Vassily Pavlovich 1932- LiExTwC
**Askew**, Barry Reginald William 1936- Who 92
**Askew**, Bonny Lamar 1955- WhoBlA 92
**Askew**, Bryan 1930- Who 92
**Askew**, Eldon Wayne 1942- AmMWSc 92
**Askew**, Homer L 1913- WhoAmP 91
**Askew**, James R. 1925-1979 WhoBlA 92N
**Askew**, John Marjoribanks Eskdale 1908- Who 92
**Askew**, Jonathan Stephen 1950- WhoEnt 92
**Askew**, Michael Eugene, Sr. 1957- WhoRel 92
**Askew**, Raymond Fike 1935- AmMWSc 92
**Askew**, Reginald James Albert 1928- Who 92
**Askew**, Reubin O'D 1928- WhoAmP 91
**Askew**, Reubin O'Donovan 1928- IntWW 91
**Askew**, Rilla DrAPF 91
**Askew**, Roger L. 1931- WhoBlA 92
**Askew**, Victor 1909- TwCPaSc
**Askew**, William Crews 1940- AmMWSc 92
**Askey**, Richard Allen 1933- AmMWSc 92
**Askill**, John 1939- AmMWSc 92, WhoMW 92
**Askin**, A. Bradley 1943- WhoFI 92
**Askin**, Elisa Mullinex 1953- WhoIns 92
**Askin**, Leon 1907- WhoEnt 92
**Askin**, Richard Henry, Jr. 1947- WhoEnt 92, WhoWest 92
**Askin**, Ronald Gene 1953- AmMWSc 92
**Askins**, Arthur James 1944- WhoFI 92
**Askins**, Gregory Patrick 1965- WhoWest 92
**Askins**, Harold Williams, Jr 1939- AmMWSc 92
**Askins**, Keith WhoBlA 92
**Askins**, Wallace Boyd 1930- WhoFI 92
**Askoldov**, Sergey 1871-1945 SovUnBD
**Askonas**, Brigitte Alice 1923- IntWW 91, Who 92
**Askwith**, Betty Ellen 1909- Who 92
**Aslam**, Khalid Saleem 1949- WhoWest 92
**Aslan**, Ana 1897-1988 FacFETw
**Aslan**, Sam Sarkis 1952- WhoWest 92
**Asleson**, Gary Lee 1948- AmMWSc 92
**Asleson**, Johan Arnold 1918- AmMWSc 92
**Aslet**, Clive William 1955- Who 92
**Asling**, Clarence Willet 1913- AmMWSc 92
**Asling**, Nils Gunnar 1927- IntWW 91
**Asma**, Lawrence Francis 1947- WhoRel 92
**Asma**, Thomas M. WhoBlA 92
**Asmar**, Laila Michelle 1957- WhoAmL 92
**Asmar**, Mark A. 1945- WhoAmL 92
**Asmodi**, Herbert 1923- IntWW 91
**Asmonas**, Vladas 1910- WhoWest 92
**Asmundson**, Robert Mark 1950- WhoWest 92
**Asmus**, John Fredrich 1937- AmMWSc 92
**Asmus**, Marvin Louis, Jr. 1925- WhoMW 92
**Asmussen**, Hans Christian 1898-1968 EncTR 91
**Asmussen**, William Wallace 1948- WhoEnt 92
**Asner**, Bernarad A, Jr 1933- AmMWSc 92
**Asner**, Edward LesBEnT 92
**Asner**, Edward 1929- IntMPA 92, WhoEnt 92
**Asner**, Marie A. DrAPF 91
**Asnes**, Andrew WhoEnt 92
**Asnes**, Clara F 1946- AmMWSc 92
**Aso** EncAmaz 91
**Asofsky**, Richard Marcy 1933- AmMWSc 92
**Asom**, Moses T. 1958- WhoBlA 92
**Asonsky**, George WhoRel 92, WhoWest 92
**Asp**, Carl W 1931- AmMWSc 92
**Asp**, Eero Rafael 1922- IntWW 91
**Aspatore**, George Alfred 1949- WhoAmL 92
**Aspbury**, Herbert F. 1944- WhoFI 92
**Aspden**, Robert George 1927- AmMWSc 92
**Aspel**, Michael IntMPA 92
**Aspel**, Michael Terence 1933- Who 92
**Aspelin**, Gary B 1939- AmMWSc 92
**Aspell**, Gerald Laycock 1915- Who 92
**Aspell**, James Fitzgerald 1961- WhoAmL 92
**Aspen**, Alfred William 1927- WhoFI 92
**Aspen**, Janet Elizabeth 1958- WhoAmL 92
**Aspen**, Marvin Edward 1934- WhoAmL 92, WhoMW 92
**Aspenberg**, Gary Alan DrAPF 91
**Asper**, Israel Harold 1932- IntWW 91, WhoEnt 92, WhoFI 92
**Asper**, Samuel Phillips 1916- AmMWSc 92
**Asperger**, Donald Paul 1955- WhoAmL 92, WhoWest 92
**Asperger**, Paul 1928- WhoAmL 92
**Asperger**, Robert George, Sr 1937- AmMWSc 92
**Aspero**, Benedict Vincent 1940- WhoAmL 92
**Aspey**, Frederick M. 1947- WhoAmL 92
**Aspin**, Les 1938- AlmAP 92 [port], WhoAmP 91, WhoMW 92
**Aspin**, Norman 1922- Who 92
**Aspinall**, Gerald Oliver 1924- AmMWSc 92
**Aspinall**, John Victor 1926- Who 92
**Aspinall**, Norman 1929- TwCPaSc
**Aspinall**, Owen Stewart 1927- WhoAmP 91
**Aspinall**, Wilfred 1942- Who 92
**Aspinwall**, Jack Heywood 1933- Who 92
**Aspiotou**, Koula 1946- WhoFI 92
**Aspland**, John Richard 1936- AmMWSc 92
**Aspland**, Joseph R. 1928- WhoIns 92
**Aspler**, Tony 1939- IntAu&W 91
**Asplin**, Syd 1902-1971 TwCPaSc
**Asplund**, Bronwyn Lorraine 1947- WhoAmP 91
**Asplund**, Erik Gunnar 1885-1940 FacFETw
**Asplund**, Gunnar 1885-1940 DcTwDes
**Asplund**, John Malcolm AmMWSc 92
**Asplund**, Russell Owen 1928- AmMWSc 92
**Aspnes**, David E 1939- AmMWSc 92
**Aspnes**, Lynne Adair 1952- WhoMW 92
**Aspray**, Rodney George 1934- Who 92
**Asprey**, Algernon d1991 Who 92N
**Asprey**, Larned Brown 1919- AmMWSc 92
**Asprey**, Robert Brown 1923- WrDr 92
**Asprey**, Winifred Alice 1917- AmMWSc 92
**Asprin**, Robert 1946- IntAu&W 91, TwCSFW 91, WrDr 92
**Aspuru**, Carlos M. 1936- WhoHisp 92
**Aspuru**, Eugenio WhoHisp 92
**Asque**, Michael Webb 1945- WhoMW 92
**Asquith** Who 92
**Asquith**, Viscount 1952- Who 92
**Asquith**, Anthony 1902-1968 IntDcF 2-2 [port]
**Asquith**, Cynthia 1887-1960 ScFEYrs
**Asquith**, George Benjamin 1936- AmMWSc 92
**Asquith**, Herbert Henry 1852-1928 FacFETw
**Asquith**, Ward 1929- WhoEnt 92
**Asrar**, Jawed 1949- AmMWSc 92
**Asri Bin Haji Muda**, Mohamed 1923- IntWW 91
**Assad**, Hafez al- 1930- FacFETw [port]
**Assad**, Hafiz al- 1928- IntWW 91
**Assad**, Nassir El-Din El- 1923- IntWW 91
**Assadi**, Barbara Seeley 1951- WhoWest 92
**Assadourian**, Fred 1915- AmMWSc 92
**Assael**, Henry 1935- WhoFI 92
**Assael**, Michael 1949- WhoAmL 92, WhoFI 92

**Assaf**, Ali Youssef 1947- WhoFI 92
**Assali**, Nicholas S 1916- AmMWSc 92
**Assalone**, John Richard 1942- WhoAmP 91
**Assanis**, Dennis N 1959- AmMWSc 92
**Assante**, Armand 1949- IntMPA 92, WhoEnt 92
**Assante**, Carole Anne 1937- WhoIns 92
**Assante**, Katharine DrAPF 91
**Assault** 1943-1971 FacFETw
**Assaykeen**, Tatiana Anna 1939- AmMWSc 92
**Asscher**, William 1931- Who 92
**Asselin**, John Thomas 1951- WhoAmL 92
**Asselineau**, Roger Maurice 1915- IntAu&W 91
**Assenmacher**, Ivan 1927- IntWW 91
**Assennato**, Vincent Thomas 1950- WhoIns 92
**Assenzo**, Joseph Robert 1932- AmMWSc 92
**Asser**, Tobias 1838-1913 FacFETw
**Asser**, Tobias Michael Carel 1838-1913 WhoNob 90
**Asseyev**, Tamara IntMPA 92
**Assheton** Who 92
**Assheton**, Caroline 1961- TwCPaSc
**Assink**, Anne Hoekstra 1948- WhoAmL 92
**Assink**, Roger Alyn 1945- AmMWSc 92
**Assisi**, Rita Fernandez 1943- WhoWest 92
**Assmus**, Alexi Josephine 1962- AmMWSc 92
**Assmus**, Edward F, Jr 1931- AmMWSc 92
**Assoian**, Richard Kenneth 1954- AmMWSc 92
**Assony**, Steven James 1920- AmMWSc 92
**Assousa**, George Elias 1936- AmMWSc 92
**Assue**, Clare Melba 1922- WhoBlA 92
**Ast**, David Bernard 1902- AmMWSc 92
**Ast**, Joseph Daniel 1966- WhoMW 92
**Asta**, Richard A. 1956- WhoFI 92
**Astacio**, Julio Ernesto 1932- IntWW 91
**Astaf'ev**, Viktor Petrovich 1924- SovUnBD
**Astafiev**, Viktor Petrovich 1924- IntWW 91
**Astaire**, Fred d1984 LesBEnT 92
**Astaire**, Fred 1899-1987 FacFETw [port], NewAmDM, RComAH
**Astaire**, Jarvis Joseph 1923- Who 92
**Astakhova**, Anna Mikhaylovna 1886-1971 SovUnBD
**Astaurov**, Boris L'vovich 1904-1974 SovUnBD
**Astbury**, William Thomas 1889-1961 FacFETw
**Astell**, Caroline R AmMWSc 92
**Astell**, Mary 1668-1731 BlkwCEP
**Aster**, Jeannette Ursula 1948- WhoEnt 92
**Aster**, Robert Wesley 1953- AmMWSc 92
**Asteriadis**, George Thomas, Jr 1944- AmMWSc 92
**Asterita**, Mary Frances AmMWSc 92
**Asterius** d341? EncEarC
**Astheimer**, Robert W 1922- AmMWSc 92
**Astill**, Bernard Douglas 1925- AmMWSc 92
**Astill**, Kenneth Norman 1923- AmMWSc 92
**Astill**, Michael John 1938- Who 92
**Astin**, Alan Edgar 1930- IntWW 91
**Astin**, John 1930- IntMPA 92
**Astin**, John Allen 1930- WhoEnt 92
**Astin**, Sean 1971- IntMPA 92
**Astle**, Doris J. 1948- WhoAmL 92
**Astle**, John C 1943- WhoAmP 91
**Astley** Who 92
**Astley**, Eugene Roy 1926- AmMWSc 92, WhoWest 92
**Astley**, Francis Jacob Dugdale 1908- Who 92
**Astley**, Philip Sinton 1943- Who 92
**Astley**, Thea 1925- ConNov 91, IntAu&W 91, WrDr 92
**Astley**, William RfGEnL 91
**Astling**, Alistair Vivian 1943- Who 92
**Astling**, Elford George 1937- AmMWSc 92
**Aston**, Archdeacon of Who 92
**Aston**, Anthony BenetAL 91
**Aston**, Athina Leka 1934- IntAu&W 91
**Aston**, Duane Ralph 1932- AmMWSc 92
**Aston**, Francis William 1877-1945 FacFETw, WhoNob 90
**Aston**, Harold 1923- Who 92
**Aston**, James William 1911- IntWW 91
**Aston**, Peter George 1938- Who 92
**Aston**, Raymond Boyd 1948- WhoMW 92
**Aston**, Richard 1936- AmMWSc 92
**Aston**, Roy 1929- AmMWSc 92
**Aston**, Steven Wesley 1953- WhoEnt 92
**Aston**, William 1916- Who 92
**Aston-Jones**, Gary Stephen 1951- AmMWSc 92
**Astor** Who 92
**Astor**, Viscount 1951- Who 92
**Astor**, Brooke NewYTBS 91 [port]
**Astor**, David Langhorne 1912- IntWW 91
**Astor**, David Waldorf 1943- Who 92
**Astor**, Francis David 1912- Who 92
**Astor**, Frank Charles 1927- WhoHisp 92
**Astor**, Gerald IntAu&W 91, WrDr 92
**Astor**, Hugh Waldorf 1920- Who 92
**Astor**, John 1918- Who 92
**Astor**, John Jacob 1763-1848 BenetAL 91, RComAH
**Astor**, John Jacob 1864-1912 ScFEYrs
**Astor**, Nancy Witcher 1879-1964 BiDBrF 2
**Astor**, Susan DrAPF 91
**Astor de Carbonell**, Annie 1958- WhoHisp 92
**Astor of Hever**, Baron 1946- Who 92
**Astorga**, Alicia Albacete 1947- WhoHisp 92
**Astorga**, Tony Manuel 1945- WhoFI 92
**Astrachan**, Boris Morton 1931- AmMWSc 92
**Astrachan**, George Jules 1939- WhoRel 92
**Astrachan**, Lazarus 1925- AmMWSc 92
**Astrachan**, Max 1909- AmMWSc 92
**Astrachan**, Samuel DrAPF 91
**Astrahan**, Melvin Alan 1952- AmMWSc 92
**Astrahan**, Morton M 1924- AmMWSc 92
**Astrin**, Marvin H. 1925- WhoEnt 92
**Astrologes**, Gary William 1949- AmMWSc 92
**Astromoff**, Andrew 1932- AmMWSc 92
**Astroth**, Frank Sisto 1936- WhoAmL 92
**Astroth**, John 1955- WhoFI 92
**Astruc**, Alexandre 1923- IntDcF 2-2
**Astruc**, Jean 1684-1766 BlkwCEP
**Astruc**, Juan 1933- AmMWSc 92
**Astruc**, Zacharie 1833-1907 ThHEIm
**Astrue**, Robert William 1928- AmMWSc 92
**Astudillo**, Hector A. 1942- WhoHisp 92
**Astumian**, Raymond Dean 1956- AmMWSc 92
**Asturias**, Miguel Angel 1899-1974 BenetAL 91, DcLB 113 [port], FacFETw, LiExTwC, WhoNob 90
**Astwood**, James 1923- Who 92
**Astwood**, Jeffrey 1907- Who 92
**Asuega**, Fitifiti 1938- WhoAmP 91
**Asukata**, Ichio 1915- IntWW 91
**Aswad**, A Adnan 1933- AmMWSc 92
**Aswad**, Richard Nejm 1936- WhoAmL 92
**Asylmuratova**, Altynai 1962- IntWW 91
**Aszalos**, Adorjan 1929- AmMWSc 92
**Atack**, Douglas 1923- AmMWSc 92
**Atahuallpa** d1533 HisDSpE
**Atai**, Grant A. WhoBlA 92
**Ataie**, Ata Jennati 1934- WhoWest 92
**Atal**, Bishnu S 1933- AmMWSc 92
**Atala Nazzal**, Cesar 1917- IntWW 91
**Atalay**, Bulent Ismail 1940- AmMWSc 92
**Atall**, Peter BenetAL 91
**Atalla**, Rajai Hanna 1935- AmMWSc 92
**Atalla**, Robert E 1929- AmMWSc 92
**Atallah**, Laila Kathleen 1957- WhoAmL 92
**Atallah**, Mikhail Jibrayil 1953- AmMWSc 92
**Atallo**, Robert Alan 1958- WhoFI 92
**Atam-Alibeckoff**, Galib-Bey 1923- AmMWSc 92, WhoFI 92
**Atamian**, Alan Elliott 1961- WhoEnt 92
**Atanasoff**, John Vincent 1903- AmMWSc 92
**Atanasov**, Georgi Ivanov 1933- IntWW 91
**Atasi**, Khalil Ziad 1951- WhoMW 92
**Atasoy**, Veysel 1947- IntWW 91
**Atassi**, Nureddin 1929- IntWW 91
**Atassi**, Zouhair 1934- AmMWSc 92
**Ataturk**, Mustapha Kemal 1880-1938 FacFETw [port]
**Atcher**, Randy 1918- WhoEnt 92
**Atcher**, Robert Whitehill 1951- WhoMW 92
**Atcherley**, Harold Winter 1918- Who 92
**Atcheson**, J D 1917- AmMWSc 92
**Atcheson**, Sue Hart WhoWest 92
**Atchison**, Arthur Mark 1944- WhoMW 92
**Atchison**, Calvin O. 1920- WhoBlA 92
**Atchison**, Charles Marvin 1933- WhoWest 92
**Atchison**, David Rice 1807-1886 AmPolLe
**Atchison**, F Stanley 1918- AmMWSc 92
**Atchison**, Jeannine Cowell 1929- WhoAmP 91
**Atchison**, Leon H. 1928- WhoBlA 92
**Atchison**, Lillian Elizabeth 1919- WhoBlA 92
**Atchison**, Michael David 1938- WhoFI 92
**Atchison**, Oliver Cromwell 1918- WhoWest 92
**Atchison**, Robert Wayne 1930- AmMWSc 92
**Atchison**, Thomas Andrew 1937- AmMWSc 92
**Atchison**, Thomas Calvin, Jr 1922- AmMWSc 92
**Atchison**, William Franklin 1918- AmMWSc 92
**Atchity**, Kenneth John DrAPF 91
**Atchley**, Anthony A 1957- AmMWSc 92
**Atchley**, Ben 1930- WhoAmP 91
**Atchley**, Bill Lee AmMWSc 92
**Atchley**, Dana W. DrAPF 91
**Atchley**, Daniel Gene 1942- WhoFI 92
**Atchley**, William Reid 1942- AmMWSc 92
**Atcitty**, Thomas E 1935- WhoAmP 91
**Ateiga**, Abdalla Ali 1958- WhoWest 92
**Atema**, Jelle 1940- AmMWSc 92
**Aten**, Carl Faust, Jr 1932- AmMWSc 92
**Aten**, Gary Jon 1938- WhoRel 92
**Aten**, Kenneth Lamont 1933- WhoMW 92
**Atencio**, Alonzo C 1929- AmMWSc 92
**Atencio**, Alonzo Cristobal 1929- WhoHisp 92
**Atencio**, Denise L. 1953- WhoHisp 92
**Atencio**, Dolores WhoHisp 92
**Atencio**, Paulette M. 1947- WhoHisp 92
**Atencio**, Robert James 1962- WhoMW 92
**Ater**, Al 1953- WhoAmP 91
**Aterman**, Kurt 1913- AmMWSc 92
**Ates**, J. Robert 1945- WhoAmL 92
**Atget**, Eugene 1856-1927 FacFETw
**Atha**, Bernard Peter 1928- Who 92
**Athabasca**, Bishop of 1942- Who 92
**Athaliah** d878BC EncAmaz 91
**Athanas**, Verne 1917-1962 TwCWW 91
**Athanasius** 300?-373 EncEarC
**Athanason**, Arthur Nicholas 1937- WhoEnt 92
**Athanassiades**, Ted WhoFI 92
**Athanassiades**, Thomas J AmMWSc 92
**Athanassoulas**, Sotirios 1936- WhoRel 92
**Athans**, Mary Christine 1932- WhoRel 92
**Athans**, Michael 1937- AmMWSc 92
**Athappilly**, Kuriakose Kunjuvarkey 1937- WhoMW 92
**Athar**, Mohammed Aqueel 1939- AmMWSc 92
**Athas**, Daphne DrAPF 91
**Athas**, Daphne 1923- WrDr 92
**Athas**, Gus James 1936- WhoAmL 92
**Athas**, Robert Thomas 1946- WhoRel 92
**Athearn**, Hope DrAPF 91
**Atheling**, William, Jr. SmATA 66
**Athelstan**, Gary Thomas 1936- AmMWSc 92, WhoMW 92
**Athen**, Joan Iversen 1944- WhoAmP 91
**Athenagoras** EncEarC
**Athenagoras I** 1886-1972 DcEcMov [port]
**Athenagoras**, Patriarch 1886-1972 RelLAm 91
**Athens**, Andrew A. WhoRel 92
**Athens**, John William 1923- AmMWSc 92
**Atherly**, Alan G 1936- AmMWSc 92
**Atherton**, Alan Royle 1931- Who 92
**Atherton**, Alexander Simpson 1913- WhoWest 92
**Atherton**, Alfred Leroy, Jr. 1921- IntWW 91
**Atherton**, David 1944- IntWW 91, Who 92, WhoEnt 92
**Atherton**, Gertrude 1857-1948 BenetAL 91, ScFEYrs, TwCWW 91
**Atherton**, Gertrude Franklin Horn 1857-1948 HanAmWH
**Atherton**, James Bernard 1927- Who 92
**Atherton**, Kevin 1950- TwCPaSc
**Atherton**, Lucius ConAu 133
**Atherton**, Michael James 1949- WhoFI 92
**Atherton**, Robert W 1946- AmMWSc 92
**Atherton**, Shirley Joelle 1938- WhoAmP 91
**Atherton**, William 1947- IntMPA 92, WhoEnt 92
**Athey**, Henry and Bowers, A Herbert ScFEYrs
**Athey**, Robert Douglas, Jr 1936- AmMWSc 92
**Athey**, Robert Jackson 1925- AmMWSc 92
**Athey**, Sharon Elizabeth 1961- WhoFI 92
**Athey**, Tyras S 1927- WhoAmP 91
**Athfield**, Ian Charles 1940- IntWW 91
**Athineos**, Emil 1933- WhoMW 92
**Athlone Press** DcLB 112
**Atholl**, Duke of 1931- Who 92
**Atholl**, Desmond 1956- ConAu 134
**Athon**, Troy A WhoAmP 91
**Athos**, Anthony G. 1934- WrDr 92
**Athos**, Anthony George 1934- WhoFI 92
**Athow**, Kirk Leland 1920- AmMWSc 92
**Athreya**, Krishna Balasundaram 1939- AmMWSc 92
**Atia**, Ali Ezz Eldin 1941- AmMWSc 92
**Atieh**, Michael Gerard 1953- WhoFI 92
**Atigbi**, Kofitunde Jolomi 1961- WhoFI 92
**Atinmo**, Tola 1945- AmMWSc 92
**Atiqi**, Abdel-Rahman Salim al- 1928- IntWW 91
**Atiya**, Aziz Suryal 1898- IntWW 91
**Atiyah**, Michael 1929- Who 92
**Atiyah**, Michael Francis 1929- IntWW 91
**Atiyah**, P. S. 1931- WrDr 92
**Atiyah**, Patrick Selim 1931- Who 92
**Atiyeh**, Victor G. 1923- IntWW 91, WhoAmP 91
**Atkeson**, Timothy Granger 1957- WhoWest 92
**Atkey**, Bertram 1880-1952 ScFEYrs
**Atkin**, Alec Field 1925- Who 92
**Atkin**, Arlo Kay 1956- WhoWest 92
**Atkin**, Eugene L. 1936- WhoMW 92
**Atkin**, Flora B. 1919- WrDr 92
**Atkin**, Flora Blumethal 1919- IntAu&W 91
**Atkin**, Gerald Clifford 1936- WhoFI 92
**Atkin**, Hillary C. 1956- WhoEnt 92
**Atkin**, J Myron 1927- AmMWSc 92
**Atkin**, James Blakesley 1930- WhoAmL 92
**Atkin**, John 1959- TwCPaSc
**Atkin**, John W WhoAmP 91
**Atkin**, Rupert Lloyd 1918- AmMWSc 92
**Atkin**, Ruth 1958- WhoWest 92
**Atkins** Who 92
**Atkins**, Aaron Ardene 1960- WhoAmL 92
**Atkins**, Arthur Harold 1910- IntAu&W 91
**Atkins**, Brenda J. 1954- WhoBlA 92
**Atkins**, Carl Clyde 1914- WhoAmL 92
**Atkins**, Carl J. WhoEnt 92
**Atkins**, Carl J. 1945- WhoBlA 92
**Atkins**, Carolyn Vaughn 1930- WhoBlA 92
**Atkins**, Charles Gilmore 1939- AmMWSc 92
**Atkins**, Chester G. 1948- AlmAP 92 [port], WhoAmP 91
**Atkins**, Chet 1924- NewAmDM
**Atkins**, Cholly 1913- WhoEnt 92
**Atkins**, Chris Alan 1954- WhoRel 92
**Atkins**, Christopher 1961- IntMPA 92
**Atkins**, David 1937- TwCPaSc
**Atkins**, David Lynn 1935- AmMWSc 92
**Atkins**, Don Carlos, Jr 1921- AmMWSc 92
**Atkins**, Edmund E. 1944- WhoBlA 92
**Atkins**, Edna R. 1945- WhoBlA 92
**Atkins**, Eileen 1934- Who 92
**Atkins**, Elisha 1920- AmMWSc 92
**Atkins**, Ferrel 1924- AmMWSc 92
**Atkins**, Fredd Glossie 1952- WhoBlA 92
**Atkins**, Fredd Lewis Stanley 1952- WhoAmP 91
**Atkins**, George Douglas 1943- WhoMW 92
**Atkins**, George Roy 1930- WhoAmP 91
**Atkins**, George T 1906- AmMWSc 92
**Atkins**, H A 1821-1885 BiInAmS
**Atkins**, H. Kent WhoFI 92
**Atkins**, Hannah Diggs 1923- WhoAmP 91, WhoBlA 92
**Atkins**, Harold Lewis 1926- AmMWSc 92
**Atkins**, Harry Samuel, Jr. 1944- WhoAmL 92
**Atkins**, Henry Pearce 1915- AmMWSc 92
**Atkins**, Henry St J. 1896- Who 92
**Atkins**, Howard Ian 1951- WhoFI 92
**Atkins**, Humphrey Edward IntWW 91
**Atkins**, Irvin Stanley 1917- WhoWest 92
**Atkins**, James, Jr. 1850-1923 DcNCBi 1
**Atkins**, James Lawrence 1947- AmMWSc 92
**Atkins**, Jane Hudson 1937- WhoAmP 91
**Atkins**, Jaspard Harvey 1926- AmMWSc 92
**Atkins**, Jeannine DrAPF 91
**Atkins**, Jerilyn Horne 1954- WhoMW 92
**Atkins**, John 1938- WhoEnt 92
**Atkins**, John Alfred 1916- IntAu&W 91, WrDr 92
**Atkins**, John Marshall 1941- AmMWSc 92
**Atkins**, Joseph Blackshear 1961- WhoAmL 92
**Atkins**, Kenneth R. 1920- WrDr 92
**Atkins**, Leonard B. W. Who 92
**Atkins**, Marvin C 1931- AmMWSc 92
**Atkins**, Meg Elizabeth IntAu&W 91
**Atkins**, Michael B. 1914- WhoAmL 92
**Atkins**, Michael Barton 1941- WhoMW 92
**Atkins**, Nelson Lawrence 1939- WhoBlA 92
**Atkins**, Orin Ellsworth 1924- IntWW 91
**Atkins**, Patrick Riley 1942- AmMWSc 92
**Atkins**, Paul C 1942- AmMWSc 92
**Atkins**, Pervis 1935- WhoBlA 92
**Atkins**, Peter Allan 1943- WhoAmL 92, WhoFI 92
**Atkins**, Peter Geoffrey 1936- Who 92
**Atkins**, Ray 1937- TwCPaSc
**Atkins**, Rev E C ScFEYrs
**Atkins**, Richard Bart 1951- WhoEnt 92
**Atkins**, Richard Elton 1919- AmMWSc 92
**Atkins**, Richard G. WhoFI 92
**Atkins**, Robert 1695?-1731 DcNCBi 1
**Atkins**, Robert Alan, Jr. 1949- WhoRel 92
**Atkins**, Robert Charles 1944- AmMWSc 92
**Atkins**, Robert James 1946- Who 92
**Atkins**, Robert M. 1948- WhoMW 92
**Atkins**, Robert S. 1931- WhoAmL 92
**Atkins**, Robert W 1917- AmMWSc 92
**Atkins**, Ron 1938- TwCPaSc
**Atkins**, Ronald Henry 1916- Who 92
**Atkins**, Ronald Leroy 1939- AmMWSc 92
**Atkins**, Ronald Raymond 1933- WhoAmL 92
**Atkins**, Russell DrAPF 91
**Atkins**, Russell 1926- WhoBlA 92, WrDr 92
**Atkins**, S Lee 1943- WhoAmP 91
**Atkins**, Sam Oillie 1934- WhoBlA 92
**Atkins**, Samuel James, III 1944- WhoFI 92

**Atkins**, Simon Green 1863-1934 *DcNCBi 1*
**Atkins**, Spencer Bert 1951- *WhoAmL 92*
**Atkins**, Spencer Wyatt 1923- *WhoAmP 91*
**Atkins**, Stuart 1914- *WrDr 92*
**Atkins**, Thomas *DrAPF 91*
**Atkins**, Thomas Herman 1939- *WhoAmL 92*
**Atkins**, Thomas Irving 1939- *WhoBlA 92*
**Atkins**, Thomas Jay 1943- *WhoAmL 92, WhoFI 92*
**Atkins**, Thomas Kent 1947- *WhoRel 92*
**Atkins**, Todd Findley 1960- *WhoMW 92*
**Atkins**, Tom 1938- *WhoEnt 92*
**Atkins**, William Austin 1933- *WhoAmP 91*
**Atkins**, William M *AmMWSc 92*
**Atkinson**, Alan *DrAPF 91*
**Atkinson**, Alec *Who 92*
**Atkinson**, Anthony 1929- *TwCPaSc*
**Atkinson**, Anthony Barnes 1944- *IntAu&W 91, IntWW 91, Who 92, WrDr 92*
**Atkinson**, Arlis 1945- *WhoFI 92*
**Atkinson**, Arthur John, Jr 1938- *AmMWSc 92*
**Atkinson**, Arthur Kingsley Hall 1926- *Who 92*
**Atkinson**, Barbara *AmMWSc 92*
**Atkinson**, Bernard 1936- *Who 92*
**Atkinson**, Brooks 1894-1984 *BenetAL 91, FacFETw*
**Atkinson**, Burr Gervais 1937- *AmMWSc 92*
**Atkinson**, Charles 1913- *WhoEnt 92*
**Atkinson**, Charles N. 1931- *WhoBlA 92*
**Atkinson**, Charles O. *DrAPF 91*
**Atkinson**, Clinton Ashley *WhoAmP 91*
**Atkinson**, Clinton Jones, Jr. 1927- *WhoEnt 92*
**Atkinson**, Colin Ronald Michael d1991 *Who 92N*
**Atkinson**, Conrad 1940- *IntWW 91, TwCPaSc*
**Atkinson**, Curtis L. 1934- *WhoBlA 92*
**Atkinson**, Dale 1962- *TwCPaSc*
**Atkinson**, Daniel Edward 1921- *AmMWSc 92*
**Atkinson**, David 1924- *Who 92*
**Atkinson**, David Anthony 1940- *Who 92*
**Atkinson**, David Rowland 1930- *Who 92*
**Atkinson**, Don Joseph 1940- *WhoEnt 92*
**Atkinson**, Dorothy Gillis 1929- *WhoWest 92*
**Atkinson**, Edward Neely 1953- *AmMWSc 92*
**Atkinson**, Edward Redmond 1912- *AmMWSc 92*
**Atkinson**, Eric 1928- *TwCPaSc*
**Atkinson**, Eugene D. 1944- *WhoFI 92*
**Atkinson**, Eugene Vincent 1927- *WhoAmP 91*
**Atkinson**, Eugenia C. 1943- *WhoBlA 92*
**Atkinson**, Frank d1991 *Who 92N*
**Atkinson**, Frank 1924- *Who 92*
**Atkinson**, Frank 1925- *IntAu&W 91*
**Atkinson**, Frank 1927- *WrDr 92*
**Atkinson**, Frederick John 1919- *IntWW 91, Who 92*
**Atkinson**, Gean Brook 1944- *WhoAmP 91*
**Atkinson**, Geoffrey Arthur 1931- *Who 92*
**Atkinson**, George Francis 1854-1918 *BiInAmS*
**Atkinson**, George Francis 1932- *AmMWSc 92*
**Atkinson**, Gladys Whitted 1932- *WhoBlA 92*
**Atkinson**, Gordon 1930- *AmMWSc 92*
**Atkinson**, Harold Russell 1937- *AmMWSc 92*
**Atkinson**, Harold Witherspoon 1914- *WhoFI 92*
**Atkinson**, Harry Hindmarsh 1929- *IntWW 91, Who 92*
**Atkinson**, Henry 1782-1842 *DcNCBi 1*
**Atkinson**, Henry Avery 1877-1960 *AmPeW*
**Atkinson**, J. Edward 1914- *WhoBlA 92*
**Atkinson**, James 1914- *IntAu&W 91, Who 92, WrDr 92*
**Atkinson**, James Byron *AmMWSc 92*
**Atkinson**, James Oscar 1867-1940 *DcNCBi 1*
**Atkinson**, James T N 1923- *AmMWSc 92*
**Atkinson**, James William 1942- *AmMWSc 92*
**Atkinson**, Jeff John Frederick 1948- *WhoAmL 92*
**Atkinson**, Jeffrey Scott 1962- *WhoMW 92*
**Atkinson**, John Alexander 1919- *Who 92*
**Atkinson**, John Brian 1942- *AmMWSc 92*
**Atkinson**, John Christopher 1948- *WhoWest 92*
**Atkinson**, John Patterson 1943- *AmMWSc 92*
**Atkinson**, Joseph George 1935- *AmMWSc 92*
**Atkinson**, Joseph Mayo 1820-1891 *DcNCBi 1*
**Atkinson**, Kathleen Lois 1955- *WhoRel 92*
**Atkinson**, Kelly C 1951- *WhoAmP 91*
**Atkinson**, Kendall E 1940- *AmMWSc 92*
**Atkinson**, Kenneth Neil 1931- *Who 92*
**Atkinson**, Larry P 1941- *AmMWSc 92*
**Atkinson**, Lawrence 1873-1931 *TwCPaSc*
**Atkinson**, Lenette Rogers 1899- *AmMWSc 92*
**Atkinson**, Leonard Allan 1906- *Who 92*
**Atkinson**, Leonard Henry d1990 *IntWW 91N*
**Atkinson**, Leslie 1913- *Who 92*
**Atkinson**, Lewis K. 1924- *WhoBlA 92*
**Atkinson**, Linda 1941- *ConAu 135*
**Atkinson**, Lloyd Charles 1942- *WhoFI 92*
**Atkinson**, Marilyn Gore 1946- *TwCPaSc*
**Atkinson**, Mark Arthur Leonard 1952- *AmMWSc 92*
**Atkinson**, Mary *Who 92*
**Atkinson**, Michael William 1932- *Who 92*
**Atkinson**, Myron H, Jr 1927- *WhoAmP 91*
**Atkinson**, Nolan N., Jr. *WhoBlA 92*
**Atkinson**, Norman 1923- *Who 92*
**Atkinson**, Paul H 1943- *AmMWSc 92*
**Atkinson**, Peggy Lee 1948- *WhoEnt 92*
**Atkinson**, Percy *ScFEYrs*
**Atkinson**, Peter Gordon 1952- *Who 92*
**Atkinson**, R. S. 1927- *WrDr 92*
**Atkinson**, Reay *Who 92*
**Atkinson**, Regina Elizabeth 1952- *WhoBlA 92*
**Atkinson**, Richard C 1929- *AmMWSc 92*
**Atkinson**, Richard Chatham 1929- *WhoAmP 91, WhoWest 92*
**Atkinson**, Richard Frederick 1926- *WhoAmP 91*
**Atkinson**, Richard John Copland 1920- *Who 92*
**Atkinson**, Richard L, Jr 1942- *AmMWSc 92*
**Atkinson**, Rick 1952- *ConAu 133*
**Atkinson**, Robert 1916- *IntWW 91, Who 92*
**Atkinson**, Robert Poland 1927- *WhoRel 92*
**Atkinson**, Roger 1945- *AmMWSc 92*
**Atkinson**, Ron *DrAPF 91*
**Atkinson**, Ronald Field 1928- *WrDr 92*
**Atkinson**, Rowan Sebastian 1955- *Who 92*
**Atkinson**, Russell H 1922- *AmMWSc 92*
**Atkinson**, Shannon K C 1956- *AmMWSc 92*
**Atkinson**, Sheridan Earle 1945- *WhoAmL 92, WhoFI 92, WhoWest 92*
**Atkinson**, Susan D. 1944- *WhoEnt 92*
**Atkinson**, Terry 1939- *TwCPaSc*
**Atkinson**, Thomas 1807-1881 *DcNCBi 1*
**Atkinson**, Thomas 1924- *Who 92*
**Atkinson**, Thomas Grisedale 1929- *AmMWSc 92*
**Atkinson**, Tomasine 1939- *WhoWest 92*
**Atkinson**, Whittier C. 1893- *WhoBlA 92*
**Atkinson**, William Christopher 1902- *Who 92*
**Atkinson**, William Edward 1939- *WhoAmL 92*
**Atkinson**, William Reay 1926- *Who 92*
**Atkinson**, William Walker 1862-1932 *RelLAm 91*
**Atkinson-Templeman**, Kristine Hofgren 1947- *AmMWSc 92*
**Atkinston**, Ronald A 1944- *AmMWSc 92*
**Atlan**, Liliane 1932- *IntAu&W 91*
**Atlantov**, Vladimir Andreevich 1933- *IntWW 91*
**Atlantov**, Vladimir Andreevich 1939- *SovUnBD*
**Atlas**, Allan Jay 1952- *WhoAmL 92*
**Atlas**, Craig Mitchell 1959- *WhoAmL 92*
**Atlas**, Dalia *WhoEnt 92*
**Atlas**, David 1924- *AmMWSc 92*
**Atlas**, James *DrAPF 91*
**Atlas**, Jay David 1945- *WhoWest 92*
**Atlas**, John D 1943- *WhoAmP 91*
**Atlas**, John Wesley 1941- *WhoBlA 92*
**Atlas**, Liane Wiener *WhoFI 92*
**Atlas**, Morris 1926- *WhoAmP 91*
**Atlas**, Ronald M 1946- *AmMWSc 92*
**Atlas**, Scott Jerome 1950- *WhoAmL 92*
**Atlas**, Seth Jackson 1958- *WhoAmL 92*
**Atlas**, Steven Alan 1946- *AmMWSc 92*
**Atlass**, H. Leslie d1960 *LesBEnT 92*
**Atlee**, Philip *WrDr 92*
**Atlee**, Philip d1991 *NewYTBS 91*
**Atluri**, Satya N 1945- *AmMWSc 92*
**Atneosen**, Richard Allen 1934- *AmMWSc 92*
**Atnip**, Jerry Ronald 1955- *WhoEnt 92*
**Atnip**, Robert Lee 1928- *AmMWSc 92*
**Atnipp**, Douglas Clay 1959- *WhoAmL 92*
**Atoji**, Masao 1925- *AmMWSc 92*
**Aton**, Thomas John 1948- *AmMWSc 92*
**Ator**, Lloyd George, Jr. 1944- *WhoAmL 92*
**Atrakchi**, Aisar Hasan 1955- *AmMWSc 92*
**Atrash**, Muhammad al- 1934- *IntWW 91*
**Atreya**, Arvind 1954- *AmMWSc 92*
**Atreya**, Sushil Kumar 1946- *AmMWSc 92*
**Attaingnant**, Pierre 1494?-1552 *NewAmDM*
**Attakullakulla** 1705-1779 *DcNCBi 1*
**Attali**, Bernard 1943- *IntWW 91*
**Attali**, Jacques 1943- *IntWW 91, NewYTBS 91 [port]*
**Attalla**, Albert 1931- *AmMWSc 92*
**Attallah**, A M 1944- *AmMWSc 92*
**Attallah**, Naim Ibrahim 1931- *IntWW 91, Who 92*
**Attanasio**, A A 1951- *TwCSFW 91*
**Attanasio**, John Baptist 1954- *WhoAmL 92, WhoMW 92*
**Attao**, Jesus Torres *WhoAmP 91*
**Attao**, Maximo *WhoAmP 91*
**Attao**, Vicente Torres 1947- *WhoAmP 91*
**Attardi**, Giuseppe M 1923- *AmMWSc 92*
**Attardo**, Lewis Charles 1950- *WhoFI 92*
**Attas**, Ely Michael 1952- *AmMWSc 92*
**Attas**, Haydar Abu Bakr al- *IntWW 91*
**Attassi**, Louai 1926- *IntWW 91*
**Attaway**, Cecil Reid 1940- *AmMWSc 92*
**Attaway**, David Henry 1938- *AmMWSc 92*
**Attaway**, John Allen 1930- *AmMWSc 92*
**Attaway**, John David 1929- *WhoBlA 92*
**Attaway**, Robert J. 1940- *WhoAmL 92*
**Attaway**, William 1911- *BenetAL 91*
**Attaway**, William 1911?-1986 *BlkLC [port]*
**Atteberry**, William Duane 1920- *WhoFI 92*
**Attebery**, Billy Joe 1927- *AmMWSc 92*
**Attebery**, Louie Wayne 1927- *WhoWest 92*
**Attebury**, Janice Marie 1954- *WhoFI 92*
**Attebury**, William Hugh 1929- *WhoFI 92*
**Attenborough**, David 1926- *IntMPA 92, Who 92, WrDr 92*
**Attenborough**, David Frederick 1926- *IntAu&W 91, IntWW 91*
**Attenborough**, John Philip 1901- *Who 92*
**Attenborough**, Peter John 1938- *Who 92*
**Attenborough**, Philip John 1936- *IntWW 91, Who 92*
**Attenborough**, Richard 1923- *IntMPA 92, IntWW 91, Who 92, WhoEnt 92*
**Atter**, Gordon Francis 1905- *WhoRel 92*
**Atterbury**, Francis 1663-1732 *BlkwCEP*
**Atterbury**, Malcolm 1907- *IntMPA 92*
**Atterbury**, Robert Rennie, III 1937- *WhoAmL 92*
**Atterbury**, Thomas J. 1931- *WhoMW 92*
**Atterley**, Joseph 1775-1861 *ScFEYrs*
**Attermeier**, Fredric Joseph 1946- *WhoAmL 92*
**Attersee** 1942- *IntWW 91*
**Atterton**, David Valentine 1927- *Who 92*
**Attewell**, Brian 1937- *Who 92*
**Atteya**, Ahmad Mamdouh 1923- *IntWW 91*
**Atthill**, Robin 1912- *WrDr 92*
**Atticus** *ConAu 135*
**Attie**, Alan D 1955- *AmMWSc 92*
**Attig**, Thomas George 1946- *AmMWSc 92*
**Attila** d453 *EncEarC*
**Attinger**, Ernst Otto 1922- *AmMWSc 92*
**Attipoe**, Lebene Kofi 1957- *IntAu&W 91*
**Attix**, Frank Herbert 1925- *AmMWSc 92*
**Attlee** *Who 92*
**Attlee**, Earl d1991 *NewYTBS 91, Who 92N*
**Attlee**, Earl 1956- *Who 92*
**Attlee**, Clement 1883-1967 *EncTR 91 [port], FacFETw [port]*
**Attlee**, Donald Laurence 1922- *Who 92*
**Attles**, Alvin *WhoBlA 92*
**Attrep**, Moses, Jr 1939- *AmMWSc 92*
**Attride**, Roy Ronald Buxton 1942- *WhoFI 92*
**Attridge**, Elizabeth Ann Johnston 1934- *Who 92*
**Attridge**, Richard Byron 1933- *WhoAmL 92*
**Attwell**, Arthur Henry d1991 *Who 92N*
**Attwell**, Kirby 1935- *WhoFI 92*
**Attwood**, David Thomas, Jr 1941- *AmMWSc 92*
**Attwood**, George Kenneth 1922- *WhoMW 92*
**Attwood**, Thomas 1765-1838 *NewAmDM*
**Attwood**, Thomas Jaymril 1931- *Who 92*
**Attygalle**, Don Sepala 1921- *Who 92*
**Atwater**, Caleb 1778-1867 *BiInAmS*
**Atwater**, Edward Congdon 1926- *AmMWSc 92*
**Atwater**, Evelyn Louise Lowe 1921- *WhoEnt 92*
**Atwater**, Florence 1896-1979 *ConAu 135, SmATA 66*
**Atwater**, Franklin Simpson 1916- *WhoFI 92*
**Atwater**, Harry Albert 1921- *AmMWSc 92*
**Atwater**, Horace Brewster, Jr. 1931- *WhoFI 92, WhoMW 92*
**Atwater**, John Wilbur 1840-1910 *DcNCBi 1*
**Atwater**, Lee 1951-1991 *CurBio 91N, NewYTBS 91 [port], News 91*
**Atwater**, N. William 1934- *WhoFI 92*
**Atwater**, Norman Willis 1926- *AmMWSc 92*
**Atwater**, P.M.H. 1937- *ConAu 133*
**Atwater**, Richard 1892-1948 *ConAu 135, SmATA 66*
**Atwater**, Richard Merlin 1946- *WhoMW 92*
**Atwater**, Stephen Dennis 1966- *WhoBlA 92*
**Atwater**, Tanya Maria 1942- *AmMWSc 92*
**Atwater**, Wilbur Olin 1844-1907 *BiInAmS*
**Atwell**, Charles McHugh 1939- *WhoFI 92*
**Atwell**, Constance Woodruff 1942- *AmMWSc 92*
**Atwell**, Eleanor C 1936- *WhoAmP 91*
**Atwell**, John 1911- *Who 92*
**Atwell**, Laura Eckman 1953- *WhoWest 92*
**Atwell**, William Alan 1951- *AmMWSc 92*
**Atwell**, William Henry 1936- *AmMWSc 92*
**Atwill**, John 1926- *Who 92*
**Atwood**, Ann 1913- *IntAu&W 91*
**Atwood**, Barry Thomas 1940- *Who 92*
**Atwood**, Charles LeRoy 1951- *AmMWSc 92*
**Atwood**, Clare 1866-1962 *TwCPaSc*
**Atwood**, Clark Dennis 1953- *WhoFI 92*
**Atwood**, Donald J 1924- *AmMWSc 92*
**Atwood**, Donald Keith 1933- *AmMWSc 92*
**Atwood**, Genevieve 1946- *WhoAmP 91*
**Atwood**, Gilbert Richard 1928- *AmMWSc 92*
**Atwood**, Glenn A 1935- *AmMWSc 92*
**Atwood**, Harold Leslie 1937- *AmMWSc 92*
**Atwood**, James R. 1944- *WhoAmL 92*
**Atwood**, Jerry Lee 1942- *AmMWSc 92*
**Atwood**, Jim D 1950- *AmMWSc 92*
**Atwood**, John Leland 1904- *AmMWSc 92, IntWW 91*
**Atwood**, John Rawson 1946- *WhoAmP 91*
**Atwood**, John William 1941- *AmMWSc 92*
**Atwood**, Kelly Palmer 1946- *WhoWest 92*
**Atwood**, Kenneth W 1922- *AmMWSc 92*
**Atwood**, Linda 1946- *AmMWSc 92*
**Atwood**, Luther 1826-1868 *BiInAmS*
**Atwood**, Margaret *DrAPF 91*
**Atwood**, Margaret 1939- *BenetAL 91, ConNov 91, ConPo 91, FacFETw, IntAu&W 91, IntWW 91, RfGEnL 91, Who 92, WrDr 92*
**Atwood**, Mark William 1952- *WhoAmL 92*
**Atwood**, Mark Wyllie 1942- *AmMWSc 92*
**Atwood**, Mary Sanford 1935- *WhoWest 92*
**Atwood**, Nathaniel Ellis 1807-1886 *BiInAmS*
**Atwood**, Richard Kenneth 1964- *WhoAmL 92*
**Atwood**, Robert Bruce 1907- *WhoWest 92*
**Atwood**, Sherrell Jean Townsend 1944- *WhoWest 92*
**Atwood**, William 1830-1884 *BiInAmS*
**Atyeo**, Warren Thomas 1927- *AmMWSc 92*
**Atzmon**, Moshe 1931- *IntWW 91, WhoEnt 92*
**Au**, Alice Miu-Hing 1958- *WhoFI 92*
**Au**, Chi-Kwan 1946- *AmMWSc 92*
**Au**, Lawrence 1938- *WhoRel 92*
**Au**, Mary Wai-Yin *WhoWest 92*
**Au**, Matthew Kam-Yuen 1964- *WhoFI 92*
**Au**, Tung 1923- *AmMWSc 92*
**Au**, William August, III 1949- *WhoRel 92*
**Aub**, Max 1903-1972 *LiExTwC*
**Aubee**, Caleb Babatunde 1942- *Who 92*
**Aubel**, Joseph Lee 1936- *AmMWSc 92*
**Auber**, Daniel-Francois-Esprit 1782-1871 *NewAmDM*
**Auberger**, Bernard 1937- *IntWW 91*
**Auberjonois**, Rene 1940- *IntMPA 92*
**Auberjonois**, Rene Murat 1940- *WhoEnt 92*
**Aubert**, Alvin *DrAPF 91*
**Aubert**, Alvin 1930- *ConPo 91, WrDr 92*
**Aubert**, Alvin Bernard 1930- *WhoBlA 92*
**Aubert**, Maurice 1924- *IntWW 91*
**Aubert**, Pierre 1927- *IntWW 91*
**Aubert de Gaspe**, Phillippe 1786-1871 *BenetAL 91*
**Aubertin**, Gerald Martin 1931- *AmMWSc 92*
**Aubespin**, Francis Borgia 1935- *WhoBlA 92*
**Aubespin**, Mervin R. 1937- *WhoBlA 92*
**Aubin**, Jane E 1950- *AmMWSc 92*
**Aubin**, Penelope 1679?-1731 *BlkwCEP*
**Aubin**, William Mark 1929- *WhoFI 92*
**Aubock**, Carl 1924- *DcTwDes, FacFETw*
**Auborn**, James John 1940- *AmMWSc 92*
**Aubouin**, Jean Armand 1928- *IntWW 91*
**Aubrecht**, Gordon James, II 1943- *AmMWSc 92, WhoMW 92*
**Aubrey**, David Glenn 1950- *AmMWSc 92*
**Aubrey**, Debra Elizabeth 1960- *WhoWest 92*
**Aubrey**, Frank *TwCSFW 91*
**Aubrey**, Frank 1840-1927 *ScFEYrs*
**Aubrey**, James T. *LesBEnT 92*
**Aubrey**, James T., Jr. 1918- *IntMPA 92*
**Aubrey**, John 1626-1697 *RfGEnL 91*
**Aubrey**, John Melbourn 1921- *Who 92*
**Aubrey**, Lisabeth Louise *WhoEnt 92*

Aubrey, Oliver Warren 1921- WhoEnt 92
Aubrey-Fletcher Who 92
Aubrey-Fletcher, John 1912- Who 92
Aubry, James Guy 1947- WhoFI 92
Aubuchon, Joseph Ramey 1944- WhoAmL 92
Auburn, Sandy Korman 1945- WhoMW 92
Auchampaugh, George Fredrick 1939- AmMWSc 92
Auchincloss, Adele Lawrence d1991 NewYTBS 91
Auchincloss, Gordon 1917- WhoEnt 92
Auchincloss, Hugh, Jr 1949- AmMWSc 92
Auchincloss, Joseph Howland, Jr 1921- AmMWSc 92
Auchincloss, Louis DrAPF 91
Auchincloss, Louis 1917- BenetAL 91, ConNov 91, WrDr 92
Auchincloss, Louis Stanton 1917- IntWW 91, Who 92
Auchinleck, Claude John Eyre 1884-1981 FacFETw
Auchinloss, Louis Stanton 1917- IntAu&W 91
Auchmuty, Giles 1945- AmMWSc 92
Auchmuty, James Francis Giles 1945- AmMWSc 92
Auchter, Harry A 1920- AmMWSc 92
Auchter, John R 1922- WhoAmP 91
Auckerman, Raymond A. 1944- WhoIns 92
Auckland, Archdeacon of Who 92
Auckland, Assistant Bishop of Who 92
Auckland, Baron 1926- Who 92
Auckland, Bishop of 1937- Who 92
Auckland, Bishop of 1938- Who 92
Auclair, Alphonse Felix 1924- WhoAmP 91
Auclair, Jacques Lucien 1923- AmMWSc 92
Auclair, Joan 1960- SmATA 68
Auclair, Walter 1933- AmMWSc 92
AuCoin, Les 1942- AlmAP 92 [port], WhoAmP 91, WhoWest 92
Aucoin, Paschal Joseph, Jr 1932- AmMWSc 92
Aucott, George W. 1934- WhoFI 92
Aucott, George William 1934- IntWW 91
Aucutt, Ronald David 1945- WhoAmL 92
Audain, Linz 1959- WhoAmL 92
Audata EncAmaz 91
Audemars, Pierre 1909- IntAu&W 91
Auden, W. H. 1907-1973 BenetAL 91, CnDBLB 6 [port], FacFETw [port], LiExTwC, RfGEnL 91
Auderska, Halina 1904- IntAu&W 91, IntWW 91
Audesirk, Gerald Joseph 1948- AmMWSc 92
Audesirk, Teresa Eck 1950- AmMWSc 92
Audet, Leonard 1932- WhoRel 92
Audet, Rene 1920- WhoRel 92
Audett, Theophilus Bernard 1905- WhoWest 92
Audi, Pierre Raymond 1957- WhoEnt 92
Audino, David Lawrence 1953- WhoMW 92
Audino, Joseph Vincent 1949- WhoWest 92
Audland, Christopher 1926- Who 92
Audley, Baron 1914- Who 92
Audley, Bernard 1924- Who 92
Audley, Nancy Karin Mallette 1950- WhoEnt 92
Audley, Robert John 1928- Who 92
Audley, Thomas Joseph 1939- WhoMW 92
Audley-Charles, Michael Geoffrey 1935- Who 92
Audlin, James David 1954- WhoRel 92
Audrain, Paul Andre Marie 1945- IntWW 91
Audran, Stephane IntWW 91
Audran, Stephane 1938- IntMPA 92
Audry, Colette d1990 IntWW 91N
Audsley, Mary 1919- TwCPaSc
Audu, Ishaya Shu'aibu 1927- Who 92
Audubon, John James 1785-1851 BenetAL 91, BiInAmS, RComAH
Audus, Leslie John 1911- Who 92, WrDr 92
Aue, Craig S. 1954- WhoRel 92
Aue, Donald Henry 1942- AmMWSc 92
Aue, Walter Alois 1935- AmMWSc 92
Auel, Jean M. DrAPF 91
Auel, Jean M. 1936- Au&Arts 7 [port], CurBio 91 [port], WrDr 92
Auelua, Pone M 1919- WhoAmP 91
Auen, Michael H. 1946- WhoAmL 92
Auer, Alfons 1915- WhoRel 92
Auer, Delmar L 1929- WhoAmP 91
Auer, Henry Ernest 1938- AmMWSc 92
Auer, J P 1953- WhoAmP 91
Auer, James M. 1928- ConAu 133
Auer, Jan Willem 1942- AmMWSc 92
Auer, Lawrence H 1941- AmMWSc 92
Auer, Leopold 1845-1930 NewAmDM
Auer, Marilyn Mills 1936- WhoFI 92
Auer, Peter Louis 1928- AmMWSc 92
Auer, Ron 1950- WhoAmP 91
Auerbach, Alan Bennett WhoFI 92
Auerbach, Andrew Bernard 1948- AmMWSc 92
Auerbach, Arleen D 1937- AmMWSc 92
Auerbach, Arnold 1898-1978 TwCPaSc
Auerbach, Arnold Jacob 1917- FacFETw
Auerbach, Arthur Henry 1928- AmMWSc 92
Auerbach, Bob Shipley 1919- WhoAmP 91
Auerbach, Bradford Carlton 1957- WhoAmL 92, WhoWest 92
Auerbach, Carl Abraham 1915- WhoAmL 92, WhoMW 92
Auerbach, Charlotte Who 92
Auerbach, Charlotte 1899- IntWW 91
Auerbach, Clemens 1923- AmMWSc 92
Auerbach, Daniel J 1942- AmMWSc 92
Auerbach, David Hillel 1938- WhoRel 92
Auerbach, Earl AmMWSc 92
Auerbach, Elliot H 1932- AmMWSc 92
Auerbach, Erich 1892-1957 LiExTwC, TwCLC 43
Auerbach, Erna 1897-1975 TwCPaSc
Auerbach, Ernest Sigmund 1936- WhoAmL 92, WhoFI 92
Auerbach, Frank 1931- IntWW 91, TwCPaSc, WorArt 1980
Auerbach, Frank Helmuth 1931- Who 92
Auerbach, Irving 1919- AmMWSc 92
Auerbach, Isaac L 1921- AmMWSc 92, WhoFI 92
Auerbach, Jeffrey Ira 1953- WhoAmL 92
Auerbach, Jerome Martin 1944- AmMWSc 92
Auerbach, Jonathan Louis 1942- WhoFI 92
Auerbach, Joseph 1916- WhoAmL 92, WhoFI 92
Auerbach, Lee David 1952- WhoAmL 92
Auerbach, Leonard B 1929- AmMWSc 92
Auerbach, Marshall Jay 1932- WhoAmL 92, WhoFI 92, WhoMW 92
Auerbach, Michael Howard 1943- AmMWSc 92
Auerbach, Nina 1943- ConAu 34NR
Auerbach, Norbert T. 1923- IntMPA 92
Auerbach, Oscar 1905- AmMWSc 92
Auerbach, Philip Bernstein 1953- WhoFI 92
Auerbach, Philip Gary 1932- WhoAmL 92
Auerbach, Robert 1929- AmMWSc 92
Auerbach, Ronald Jay 1965- WhoFI 92
Auerbach, Stanley Irving 1921- AmMWSc 92, IntWW 91
Auerbach, Stephen Michael 1942- AmMWSc 92
Auerbach, Victor 1917- AmMWSc 92
Auerbach, Victor Hugo 1928- AmMWSc 92
Auerback, Alfred 1915- AmMWSc 92
Auerback, Sandra Jean 1946- WhoWest 92
Auernheimer, Brent 1958- WhoFI 92
Auernheimer, Leonardo 1936- WhoHisp 92
Auersperg, Nelly 1928- AmMWSc 92
Aufdemberge, Theodore Paul 1934- AmMWSc 92, WhoMW 92
Aufderheide, Karl John 1948- AmMWSc 92
Aufderheide, May 1888-1972 NewAmDM
Aufdermarsh, Carl Albert, Jr 1932- AmMWSc 92
Aufenkamp, Darrel Don 1927- AmMWSc 92
Auffant, James Robert 1949- WhoHisp 92
Auffenberg, Walter 1928- AmMWSc 92
Aufhauser, Siegfried 1884-1969 EncTR 91
Aufrecht, Michael D. 1940- WhoAmL 92
Aug, Ellen W. DrAPF 91
Aug, Stephen M. 1936- WhoFI 92
Augarde, Anthony John 1936- IntAu&W 91
Augelli, John Pat 1921- WhoMW 92
Augenlicht, Leonard Harold 1946- AmMWSc 92
Augensen, Harry John 1951- AmMWSc 92
Augenstein, Bruno 1923- AmMWSc 92
Augenstein, Karen Lynn 1968- WhoMW 92
Augenstein, Moshe 1947- AmMWSc 92
Auger, Arleen 1939- IntWW 91, WhoEnt 92
Auger, David J. WhoWest 92
Auger, Pierre Victor 1899- FacFETw, IntWW 91, Who 92
Auger, Simone WhoEnt 92
Aughenbaugh, Nolan B 1928- AmMWSc 92
Aughey, Samuel 1831-1912 BiInAmS
Augier, Emile 1820-1889 GuFrLit 1, NinCLC 31 [port]
Augier, Marc 1908- BiDExR
Augl, Joseph Michael 1932- AmMWSc 92
Augmon, Stacey 1968- BlkOlyM
Augood, Derek Raymond 1928- AmMWSc 92
Augsburger, Aaron Donald 1925- WhoRel 92
Augsburger, John Bird 1934- WhoAmP 91
Augsburger, Larry Louis 1940- AmMWSc 92
Augspurger, Carol Kathleen AmMWSc 92
Augspurger, Terry Lee 1954- WhoMW 92
Augstein, Rudolf 1923- IntWW 91
Augstkalns, Valdis Ansis 1939- AmMWSc 92
Augur, Marilyn Hussman 1938- WhoFI 92
August Wilhelm 1887-1949 EncTR 91 [port]
August, Bille 1948- IntMPA 92, IntWW 91
August, Busby Harris 1941- WhoFI 92
August, Joseph Thomas 1927- AmMWSc 92
August, Lawrence I. 1959- WhoEnt 92
August, Leon Stanley 1926- AmMWSc 92
August, Melissa Blaire 1965- WhoEnt 92
August, Paul Rudolph 1966- WhoAmP 91
August, Richard Bruce 1952- WhoWest 92
August, Robert William 1944- WhoMW 92
Auguste, Yves L. IntWW 91
Augusteijn, Marijke Francina 1946- AmMWSc 92
Augustin, Jorg A L 1930- AmMWSc 92
Augustina, the Maid of Saragossa 1788-1857 EncAmaz 91
Augustine 354-430 DcLB 115 [port], EncEarC
Augustine of Canterbury d610? EncEarC
Augustine, Bradford Gordon 1959- WhoWest 92
Augustine, Fennis Lincoln 1932- Who 92
Augustine, James Robert 1946- AmMWSc 92
Augustine, Jane DrAPF 91
Augustine, Jim Henry 1942- WhoMW 92
Augustine, Matthew 1944- WhoBlA 92
Augustine, Mildred ConAu 134, SmATA 65
Augustine, Nicholas E. 1950- WhoFI 92
Augustine, Norman R 1935- AmMWSc 92
Augustine, Norman Ralph 1935- WhoFI 92
Augustine, Patricia C 1937- AmMWSc 92
Augustine, Robert Leo 1932- AmMWSc 92
Augustine, Robert Mark 1953- WhoMW 92
Augustine, Robertson J 1933- AmMWSc 92
Augustine, Sheryle Joan 1952- WhoFI 92
Augustine, Tawnita Lynn 1959- WhoMW 92
Augustine, William E. 1949- WhoWest 92
Augustinus, Aurelius 354-430 DcLB 115 [port]
Augusto, Antonio C. 1937- WhoHisp 92
Augustus 63BC-14AD EncEarC
Augustus II 1670-1733 BlkwCEP
Augustus III 1696-1763 BlkwCEP
Augustus, Franklin J. P. 1950- WhoBlA 92
Augustyn, Joan Mary AmMWSc 92
Augustyn, Noel James 1946- WhoAmL 92
Aujaleu, Eugene Jean Yves d1990 IntWW 91N
Aukerman, James Vance 1948- WhoAmP 91
Aukerman, Lee William 1923- AmMWSc 92
Aukin, David 1942- IntWW 91, Who 92
Aukland, Duncan Dayton 1954- WhoAmL 92
Aukland, Jerry C 1931- AmMWSc 92
Aukrust, Egil 1933- AmMWSc 92
Auksmann, Boris 1927- AmMWSc 92
Aulbekov, Erkin Nurzhanovich 1930- IntWW 91
Auld, Alasdair Alpin 1930- Who 92
Auld, Albert Michael 1943- WhoBlA 92
Auld, David Stuart 1937- AmMWSc 92
Auld, Edward George 1936- AmMWSc 92
Auld, Georgie 1919- NewAmDM
Auld, John H 1940- WhoAmP 91
Auld, Lorna Bergeson 1944- WhoAmP 91
Auld, Margaret Gibson 1932- Who 92
Auld, Nancy Slomer WhoMW 92
Auld, Peter A McF 1928- AmMWSc 92
Auld, Robin Ernest 1937- Who 92
Auld, Rose A. 1946- WhoBlA 92
Aulenbach, Donald Bruce 1928- AmMWSc 92
Aulenti, Gae 1927- DcTwDes
Aulerich, Richard J 1936- AmMWSc 92
Auletta, Carol Spence 1942- AmMWSc 92
Auletta, Joan Miglorisi 1940- WhoFI 92
Auletta, Louis John, Sr. 1938- WhoFI 92
Auletta, Nancy Ellen 1954- WhoFI 92
Aulick, Louis H AmMWSc 92
Aull, Charles Edward 1927- AmMWSc 92
Aull, Elizabeth Berryman 1951- WhoMW 92
Aull, Felice 1938- AmMWSc 92
Aull, James Stroud 1931- WhoRel 92
Aull, John Louis 1939- AmMWSc 92
Aull, Luther Bachman, III 1929- AmMWSc 92
Aulsebrook, Lucille Hagan 1925- AmMWSc 92
Aulson, Patrick J. 1951- WhoIns 92
Ault, Addison 1933- AmMWSc 92
Ault, Charles Rollin 1923- WhoAmL 92
Ault, George Mervin 1921- AmMWSc 92
Ault, James Mase 1918- WhoRel 92
Ault, Jeffrey Michael 1947- WhoRel 92
Ault, Lynn Baxley 1934- WhoAmL 92
Ault, N N 1922- AmMWSc 92
Ault, Robert Harris 1954- WhoMW 92
Ault, Thomas Jefferson, III 1911- WhoFI 92, WhoMW 92
Ault, Wayne Urban 1923- AmMWSc 92
Ault, Wendy L WhoAmP 91
Aumale, Christian d' 1918- IntWW 91
Auman, Jason Reid 1937- AmMWSc 92
Auman, William David 1961- WhoAmL 92
Aumand, Ernest James, III WhoWest 92
Aumann, Glenn D 1930- AmMWSc 92
Aumann, Hartmut Hans-Georg 1940- AmMWSc 92
Aumann, R. Karl 1960- WhoAmL 92
Aumann, Robert John 1930- AmMWSc 92
Aumbry, Alan IntAu&W 91X
Aumoeualogo, Salanoa WhoAmP 91
Aumonier, Eric TwCPaSc
Aumonier, William TwCPaSc
Aumons, Jean-Pierre IntWW 91
Aumont, Jean Pierre 1909- IntMPA 92
Aumont, Jean-Pierre 1911- WhoEnt 92
Aumueller, Ronald Fred 1942- WhoFI 92
Aune, David Edward 1939- WhoRel 92
Aune, Gregory John 1953- WhoEnt 92
Aune, Janet AmMWSc 92
Aune, Kirk Carl 1942- AmMWSc 92
Aune, Leif Jorgen 1925- IntWW 91
Aung San Suu Kyi IntWW 91
Aung, Taing 1944- AmMWSc 92
Aung San Suu Kyi, Daw 1945- NewYTBS 91
Aungst, Bruce J 1952- AmMWSc 92
Aunon, Jorge Ignacio 1942- AmMWSc 92, WhoHisp 92
Aunspach, Dale Ervin 1927- WhoMW 92
Aura, Matti Ilmari 1943- IntWW 91
Aura, Teuvo Ensio 1912- IntWW 91
Aurand, Charles Henry, Jr. 1932- WhoEnt 92
Aurand, Douglas R 1941- WhoAmP 91
Aurand, Henry Spiese, Jr 1924- AmMWSc 92
Aurand, Leonard William 1920- AmMWSc 92
Aurbach, Gerald D. d1991 NewYTBS 91
Aurbach, Gerald Donald 1927- AmMWSc 92
Aurelian 212?-275 EncEarC
Aurelian, Laure 1939- AmMWSc 92
Aurelius, George M. 1911- IntMPA 92
Auric, Georges 1899-1963 FacFETw
Auric, Georges 1899-1983 NewAmDM
Auriemmo, Frank J., Jr. 1942- WhoIns 92
Aurilia, Christine Marie 1962- WhoEnt 92
Auringer, Tim James 1949- WhoEnt 92
Auriol, Vincent 1884-1966 FacFETw
Aurner, Robert Ray, II 1937- WhoFI 92
Aurnhammer, Thomas Walter 1958- WhoWest 92
Aurobindo, Sri 1872-1950 RelLAm 91
Auroux, Jean 1942- IntWW 91
Aurrecoechea, Rafael 1962- WhoHisp 92
Aurthur, Robert Alan d1978 LesBEnT 92
Aurthur, Robert Alan 1922-1978 ConAu 34NR
Aus, Roger David 1940- WhoRel 92
Ausberry, Marshal Lee 1957- WhoFI 92
Ausbrooks, Beth Nelson 1930- WhoBlA 92
Ausburn, Grayce Pomeroy 1930- WhoEnt 92
Ausby, Ellsworth Augustus 1942- WhoBlA 92
Ausenda, Marco 1955- Who 92
Ausere, Joe Morris 1929- WhoFI 92
Ausich, Rodney L 1953- AmMWSc 92
Ausich, William Irl 1952- AmMWSc 92, WhoMW 92
Ausiello, Dennis Arthur 1945- AmMWSc 92
Auskaps, Aina Marija 1921- AmMWSc 92
Auslander, Bernice Liberman 1930- AmMWSc 92
Auslander, David Scott 1961- WhoAmL 92
Auslander, Edith S. WhoHisp 92
Auslander, Jay Stuart DrAPF 91
Auslander, Jay Stuart 1964- WhoAmL 92
Auslander, Joseph 1897-1965 BenetAL 91
Auslander, Joseph 1930- AmMWSc 92
Auslander, Louis 1928- AmMWSc 92
Auslander, Maurice 1926- AmMWSc 92
Ausman, Jon Michael 1953- WhoAmP 91
Ausman, Robert K 1933- AmMWSc 92
Ausnehmer, John Edward 1954- WhoAmL 92
Ausonius 310?-395? EncEarC
Auspitz, Josiah Lee 1941- WhoAmP 91

**Auspos,** Lawrence Arthur 1917- *AmMWSc 92*
**Aussem,** James Scott 1949- *WhoAmL 92*
**Aust,** Anthony Ivall 1942- *Who 92*
**Aust,** Catherine Cowan 1946- *AmMWSc 92*
**Aust,** Gerald Aldric 1950- *WhoFI 92*
**Aust,** J Bradley 1926- *AmMWSc 92*
**Aust,** Karl T 1925- *AmMWSc 92*
**Aust,** Richard Bert 1938- *AmMWSc 92*
**Aust,** Steven Douglas 1938- *AmMWSc 92*
**Austad,** Randall John 1956- *WhoAmP 91*
**Austad,** Tore 1935- *IntWW 91*
**Austen,** Alice 1866-1952 *HanAmWH*
**Austen,** Hallie Iglehart 1947- *WhoWest 92*
**Austen,** Jane 1775-1817 *CnDBLB 3 [port], NinCLC 33 [port], RfGEnL 91*
**Austen,** John Joseph 1948- *WhoEnt 92*
**Austen,** K Frank 1928- *AmMWSc 92, IntWW 91*
**Austen,** Karl 1964- *WhoEnt 92*
**Austen,** Peter Townsend 1852-1907 *BiInAmS*
**Austen,** W Gerald 1930- *AmMWSc 92*
**Austen-Smith,** Roy 1924- *Who 92*
**Austenson,** Herman Milton 1924- *AmMWSc 92*
**Auster,** Albert 1940- *WhoEnt 92*
**Auster,** Lawrence Scott 1947- *WhoIns 92*
**Auster,** Paul 1947- *ConNov 91, WrDr 92*
**Austerberry,** Sidney Denham 1908- *Who 92*
**Austern,** Barry M 1942- *AmMWSc 92*
**Austern,** Norman 1926- *AmMWSc 92*
**Austero,** Wayne Joseph 1945- *WhoAmL 92*
**Austgen,** Robert Joseph 1932- *WrDr 92*
**Austic,** Richard Edward 1941- *AmMWSc 92*
**Austick,** David 1920- *Who 92*
**Austin,** Abraham Lincoln 1906- *WhoMW 92*
**Austin,** Alfred 1835-1913 *RfGEnL 91*
**Austin,** Alfred Ells 1920- *AmMWSc 92*
**Austin,** Arthur Converse 1911- *WhoRel 92*
**Austin,** Arthur Leroy 1929- *AmMWSc 92*
**Austin,** Bert Peter 1946- *AmMWSc 92*
**Austin,** Billy Ray 1940- *AmMWSc 92*
**Austin,** Bobby William 1944- *WhoBlA 92*
**Austin,** Brett *IntAu&W 91X, TwCWW 91*
**Austin,** Brian Patrick 1938- *Who 92*
**Austin,** Carl Fulton 1932- *AmMWSc 92*
**Austin,** Carl Fulton, Sr. 1932- *WhoWest 92*
**Austin,** Catherine Kerwin 1946- *WhoFI 92*
**Austin,** Cathy Kiselyak 1954- *WhoAmL 92*
**Austin,** Cedric Ronald Jonah 1912- *WrDr 92*
**Austin,** Charles Marshall 1941- *WhoRel 92*
**Austin,** Charles Ward 1932- *AmMWSc 92*
**Austin,** Coe Finch 1831-1880 *BiInAmS*
**Austin,** Colin Francois Lloyd 1941- *IntWW 91, Who 92*
**Austin,** Colin Russell 1914- *Who 92*
**Austin,** Danforth Whitley 1946- *WhoFI 92*
**Austin,** Daniel Frank 1943- *AmMWSc 92*
**Austin,** Daniel Lynn 1952- *WhoWest 92*
**Austin,** Daniel William 1949- *WhoAmL 92*
**Austin,** Darrell Glen 1936- *WhoWest 92*
**Austin,** David Fletcher 1927- *WhoWest 92*
**Austin,** David Leonard, II 1928- *WhoRel 92, WhoWest 92*
**Austin,** Donald Franklin 1937- *AmMWSc 92*
**Austin,** Donald Guy 1926- *AmMWSc 92*
**Austin,** Donald Murray 1938- *AmMWSc 92*
**Austin,** Doris Jean *DrAPF 91*
**Austin,** Dorothy Mayover 1931- *WhoFI 92*
**Austin,** Ed *WhoAmP 91*
**Austin,** Edith 1907- *WhoAmP 91*
**Austin,** Edward Marvin 1933- *WhoFI 92*
**Austin,** Ellen Jane *WhoAmP 91*
**Austin,** Ernest Augustus 1932- *WhoBlA 92*
**Austin,** Faye Carol 1944- *AmMWSc 92*
**Austin,** Florence Edith *ScFEYrs*
**Austin,** Frank *TwCWW 91*
**Austin,** Frank 1933- *WhoBlA 92*
**Austin,** Fred 1936- *AmMWSc 92*
**Austin,** Fred C. *WhoFI 92*
**Austin,** Frederick Britten 1885-1941 *ScFEYrs*
**Austin,** Frederick George 1902- *TwCPaSc*
**Austin,** George Bernard 1931- *Who 92*
**Austin,** George M 1916- *AmMWSc 92*
**Austin,** George Stephen 1936- *AmMWSc 92*
**Austin,** George T 1914- *AmMWSc 92*
**Austin,** Glenn Thomas, Jr. 1948- *WhoFI 92*
**Austin,** Harry *ConAu 34NR*
**Austin,** Harry Gregory 1936- *WhoAmL 92*
**Austin,** Henry Wilfred 1906- *WrDr 92*
**Austin,** Homer Wellington 1944- *AmMWSc 92*
**Austin,** Howard *ScFEYrs*
**Austin,** Jack Kenneth 1923- *WhoMW 92*
**Austin,** Jack Spencer 1936- *WhoRel 92*
**Austin,** Jacob 1932- *Who 92*
**Austin,** James Albert 1931- *WhoWest 92*
**Austin,** James Bliss 1904- *AmMWSc 92*
**Austin,** James Henry 1925- *AmMWSc 92*
**Austin,** James Murdoch 1915- *AmMWSc 92*
**Austin,** James P. 1900- *WhoBlA 92*
**Austin,** James Ray 1952- *WhoRel 92*
**Austin,** Jane Goodwin 1831-1894 *BenetAL 91*
**Austin,** Janice Gayle 1948- *WhoFI 92*
**Austin,** Janyth Yvonne 1958- *WhoBlA 92*
**Austin,** Jeanie Reed 1933- *WhoAmP 91*
**Austin,** Jesse Hinnant, III 1954- *WhoAmL 92*
**Austin,** John 1923- *IntMPA 92*
**Austin,** John DeLong 1935- *WhoAmL 92*
**Austin,** John H 1929- *AmMWSc 92*
**Austin,** John Langshaw 1911-1960 *FacFETw*
**Austin,** Joseph Riley 1939- *WhoAmL 92*
**Austin,** Joseph Wells 1930- *AmMWSc 92*
**Austin,** Kent Arlon 1940- *WhoRel 92*
**Austin,** L. Kathleen 1949- *WhoWest 92*
**Austin,** Larry 1930- *ConCom 92, NewAmDM*
**Austin,** Larry Don 1930- *WhoEnt 92*
**Austin,** Lemuel, Jr *WhoAmP 91*
**Austin,** Leonard G 1929- *AmMWSc 92*
**Austin,** Lloyd James 1915- *Who 92*
**Austin,** M. M. 1943- *WrDr 92*
**Austin,** Margot 1909?-1990 *SmATA 66*
**Austin,** Marshall Edward 1957- *WhoFI 92*
**Austin,** Mary 1868-1934 *BenetAL 91, TwCWW 91*
**Austin,** Mary Jane 1935- *WhoBlA 92*
**Austin,** Max E 1933- *AmMWSc 92*
**Austin,** Michael 1927- *Who 92*
**Austin,** Mike Gerard 1954- *WhoAmP 91*
**Austin,** Moses *HisDSpE*
**Austin,** Nancy Elizabeth 1953- *IntAu&W 91*
**Austin,** Oliver Luther, Jr 1903- *AmMWSc 92*
**Austin,** Patricia Mae 1953- *WhoRel 92*
**Austin,** Paul Rolland 1906- *AmMWSc 92*
**Austin,** Pauline Morrow 1916- *AmMWSc 92*
**Austin,** Peter 1921- *Who 92*
**Austin,** Phil Lee 1960- *WhoMW 92*
**Austin,** Philip Robert 1955- *WhoMW 92*
**Austin,** Ray 1932- *IntMPA 92*
**Austin,** Raymond Darrel 1953- *WhoAmL 92*
**Austin,** Regina 1956- *WhoEnt 92*
**Austin,** Richard 1926- *WrDr 92*
**Austin,** Richard H 1913- *WhoAmP 91, WhoBlA 92*
**Austin,** Richard Henry 1913- *WhoMW 92*
**Austin,** Robert 1895-1973 *TwCPaSc*
**Austin,** Robert Alan 1954- *WhoEnt 92*
**Austin,** Robert Andrae 1938- *AmMWSc 92*
**Austin,** Robert Clarke 1931- *WhoWest 92*
**Austin,** Robert Eugene, Jr. 1937- *WhoAmL 92, WhoFI 92*
**Austin,** Robert Farias 1948- *WhoEnt 92*
**Austin,** Robert Lee 1918- *WhoAmL 92*
**Austin,** Roger Mark 1940- *Who 92*
**Austin,** Roswell W 1920- *AmMWSc 92*
**Austin,** Russell Anderson, Jr. 1930- *WhoAmL 92, WhoAmP 91*
**Austin,** Sam M 1933- *AmMWSc 92*
**Austin,** Sarah Short 1933- *WhoBlA 92*
**Austin,** Spencer Peter 1909- *WhoRel 92*
**Austin,** Stephen F 1793-1836 *RComAH*
**Austin,** Stephen Fuller 1793-1836 *BenetAL 91*
**Austin,** Steven Arthur 1948- *AmMWSc 92*
**Austin,** T Louis, Jr *AmMWSc 92*
**Austin,** T. Louis, Jr. 1919- *WhoFI 92*
**Austin,** Thomas Howard 1937- *AmMWSc 92*
**Austin,** Tom Al 1943- *AmMWSc 92*
**Austin,** Walter J 1920- *AmMWSc 92*
**Austin,** William 1778-1841 *BenetAL 91*
**Austin,** William Bouldin 1949- *WhoRel 92*
**Austin,** William W 1915- *AmMWSc 92*
**Austin,** William W 1920- *IntAu&W 91, WrDr 92*
**Austin,** William Winter 1945- *WhoAmL 92*
**Austin-Lucas,** Barbara Etta 1951- *WhoRel 92*
**Austin-Smith,** Michael Gerard 1944- *Who 92*
**Auston,** David H 1940- *AmMWSc 92*
**Australia,** North-West, Bishop of 1927- *Who 92*
**Austregesilo De Athayde,** Belarmino Maria 1898- *IntWW 91*
**Austreim,** Douglas John 1948- *WhoMW 92*
**Austrian,** Marjorie Beryl 1934- *WhoEnt 92*
**Austrian,** Mark Louis 1945- *WhoAmL 92*
**Austrian,** Robert 1916- *AmMWSc 92, IntWW 91*
**Austrin,** Harvey Robert 1924- *WhoMW 92*
**Austwick,** Kenneth 1927- *Who 92*
**Ausubel,** Frederick Michael 1945- *AmMWSc 92*
**Ausubel,** Jesse Huntley 1951- *AmMWSc 92*
**Ausubel,** Marvin Victor 1927- *WhoAmL 92*
**Autant-Lara,** Claude *IntMPA 92*
**Autant-Lara,** Claude 1901- *IntWW 91*
**Autant-Lara,** Claude 1903- *IntDcF 2-2*
**Autele,** Faofamo *WhoAmP 91*
**Auten,** Dean Garland 1937- *WhoAmP 91*
**Auten,** Gerald Earle 1945- *WhoFI 92*
**Autenrieth,** John Stork 1916- *AmMWSc 92*
**Auterinen,** Olli 1921- *WhoRel 92*
**Auteuil,** Daniel 1950- *IntMPA 92*
**Auth,** David C 1940- *AmMWSc 92*
**Auth,** Robert Ralph 1926- *WhoWest 92*
**Authement,** Ray Paul 1929- *AmMWSc 92*
**Autian,** John 1924- *AmMWSc 92*
**Autin,** A. Anthony, Jr. 1938- *WhoFI 92*
**Autin,** Jean Georges 1921-1991 *IntWW 91, -91N*
**Autobee,** George 1949- *WhoHisp 92*
**Autolitano,** Astrid 1938- *WhoHisp 92*
**Auton,** David Lee 1939- *AmMWSc 92*
**Autor,** Anne Pomeroy 1935- *AmMWSc 92*
**Autor,** Erik Orm 1957- *WhoAmL 92*
**Autrey,** Henry Edward 1952- *WhoAmL 92*
**Autrey,** Joseph Latrell 1940- *WhoFI 92*
**Autrey,** Robert Luis 1932- *AmMWSc 92*
**Autrum,** Hansjochem 1907- *IntWW 91*
**Autry,** Gene *LesBEnT 92*
**Autry,** Gene 1907- *FacFETw, IntMPA 92, NewAmDM, WhoEnt 92, WhoFI 92, WhoWest 92*
**Autry,** James A. 1933- *ConAu 135*
**Autry,** Micajah 1794?-1836 *DcNCBi 1*
**Autry,** Sharon Louise 1963- *WhoAmL 92*
**Autton,** Norman 1920- *IntAu&W 91, WrDr 92*
**Auty,** Giles 1934- *TwCPaSc*
**Auty,** Richard Mossop 1920- *Who 92*
**Auvil,** Paul R, Jr 1937- *AmMWSc 92*
**Auvil,** Paul Reeves 1937- *WhoMW 92*
**Auvinen,** Thomas Roger 1939- *WhoIns 92*
**Auwarter,** Franklin Paul 1934- *WhoAmL 92*
**Auwi** *EncTR 91*
**Auxenfans,** Bernard Paul 1944- *WhoMW 92*
**Auxentios,** Bishop 1953- *WhoRel 92*
**Auxentius** *EncEarC*
**Auxentius** d374 *EncEarC*
**Auxier,** Allen Glen 1948- *WhoEnt 92*
**Auxier,** John A 1925- *AmMWSc 92*
**Au-Yeung,** Hang Stephen 1953- *WhoWest 92*
**Auyeung,** Kenneth 1941- *WhoRel 92*
**Auyong,** Theodore Koon-Hook 1925- *AmMWSc 92*
**Auza,** Enrique Alfredo 1942- *WhoWest 92*
**Avadhani,** Narayan G 1941- *AmMWSc 92*
**Avakian,** Peter 1933- *AmMWSc 92*
**Avakoff,** Joseph Carnegie 1936- *WhoWest 92*
**Avallone,** Anthony John, Jr. 1960- *WhoFI 92*
**Avallone,** Anthony Vincent 1947- *WhoAmP 91*
**Avallone,** Michael 1924- *WrDr 92*
**Avallone,** Michael Angelo, Jr 1924- *IntAu&W 91*
**Avalon,** Frankie 1940- *IntMPA 92, WhoEnt 92*
**Avalone,** Ronnie 1922- *WhoRel 92*
**Avalos,** Andy Anthony 1956- *WhoHisp 92*
**Avalos,** Luis 1946- *WhoEnt 92*
**Avalos,** Martin Eduardo 1959- *WhoHisp 92*
**Avans,** Joy Marie 1961- *WhoEnt 92*
**Avant,** David Louis 1943- *WhoAmP 91*
**Avant,** Grady, Jr. 1932- *WhoAmL 92*
**Avants,** Aubrey Lee 1943- *WhoFI 92*
**Avants,** Beecher *WhoAmP 91*
**Avara,** R Charles 1932- *WhoAmP 91*
**Avarese,** John Vincent 1957- *WhoEnt 92*
**Avault,** James W, Jr 1935- *AmMWSc 92*
**Avcin,** Matthew John, Jr 1943- *AmMWSc 92*
**Avdul,** Donald D. 1943- *WhoMW 92*
**Ave,** Gregory Richardson 1964- *WhoWest 92*
**Ave Lallemant,** Hans Gerhard 1938- *AmMWSc 92*
**Avebury,** Baron 1928- *Who 92*
**Avebury,** Lady 1934- *Who 92*
**Avedis,** Howard Aghanigian *WhoEnt 92*
**Avedon,** Bruce 1928- *WhoMW 92*
**Avedon,** Doe *IntMPA 92*
**Avedon,** Richard 1923- *DcTwDes, FacFETw, IntWW 91, WrDr 92*
**Avegeropoulos,** G 1934- *AmMWSc 92*
**Avelar,** Carlos *WhoHisp 92*
**Aveline,** Claude 1901- *IntWW 91*
**Aveling,** Alan John 1928- *Who 92*
**Aveling,** J. C. H. 1917- *WrDr 92*
**Avellaneda,** Gertrudis Gomez de *HisDSpE*
**Avellino,** Bernard Joseph 1937- *WhoAmP 91*
**Avellon,** Guy Thomas 1945- *WhoMW 92*
**Avelsgaard,** Roger A 1932- *AmMWSc 92*
**Avemanay,** Lorenza *EncAmaz 91*
**Aven,** Manuel 1924- *AmMWSc 92*
**Aven,** Russell E 1923- *AmMWSc 92*
**Avendano,** Fausto 1941- *WhoHisp 92*
**Aveni,** Anthony 1938- *AmMWSc 92*
**Aveni,** Anthony Joseph 1938- *WhoAmL 92, WhoMW 92*
**Aveni,** Virginia Lee 1933- *WhoAmP 91*
**Avenna,** Paul Robert 1943- *WhoHisp 92*
**Avens,** John Stewart 1940- *AmMWSc 92*
**Avenson,** Donald Dean 1944- *WhoAmP 91*
**Avent,** Jacques Myron 1940- *WhoBlA 92*
**Avent,** Jon C 1934- *AmMWSc 92*
**Avent,** Robert M 1942- *AmMWSc 92*
**Avera,** Alan James 1955- *WhoRel 92*
**Avera,** Fitzhugh Lee 1906- *AmMWSc 92*
**Averbach,** B L 1919- *AmMWSc 92*
**Averbach,** Benjamin L 1919- *WhoAmP 91*
**Averback,** Hy 1925- *IntMPA 92*
**Averbakh,** Leopold Leonovich 1903-1939 *SovUnBD*
**Averett,** John E 1943- *AmMWSc 92*
**Averill,** Bruce Alan 1948- *AmMWSc 92*
**Averill,** Esther 1902- *WrDr 92*
**Averill,** Frank Wallace *AmMWSc 92*
**Averill,** H.C. *TwCWW 91*
**Averill,** Lawrence Herman, Jr. 1940- *WhoAmL 92*
**Averill,** Lloyd James, Jr. 1923- *WhoRel 92*
**Averill,** Marilyn 1946- *WhoAmL 92*
**Averill,** Seward Junior 1921- *AmMWSc 92*
**Averill,** Thomas Fox *DrAPF 91*
**Averill,** William Allen 1948- *AmMWSc 92*
**Averitt,** Paul 1908- *AmMWSc 92*
**Averitt,** Richard Garland, III 1945- *WhoFI 92*
**Averoff-Tositsas,** Evangelos 1910-1990 *FacFETw*
**Averoff-Tossitsas,** Evangelos 1910-1990 *AnObit 1990*
**Averoff-Tossizza,** Evangelos 1910- *IntAu&W 91*
**Averona,** William E. 1947- *WhoAmL 92*
**Averre,** Charles Wilson, III 1932- *AmMWSc 92*
**Averroes** 1126-1198 *CIMLC 7 [port], DcLB 115 [port]*
**Avers,** Charlotte J 1926- *AmMWSc 92*
**Avery,** Alphonso Calhoun 1835-1913 *DcNCBi 1*
**Avery,** Bruce Edward 1949- *WhoAmL 92*
**Avery,** Bryce David 1965- *WhoWest 92*
**Avery,** Cameron Scott 1938- *WhoAmL 92*
**Avery,** Carl Gershom 1935- *WhoMW 92, WhoRel 92*
**Avery,** Charles Carrington 1933- *AmMWSc 92*
**Avery,** Charles Ellery 1848?-1916 *BiInAmS*
**Avery,** Clark Moulton 1819-1864 *DcNCBi 1*
**Avery,** Dennis T 1946- *WhoAmP 91*
**Avery,** Donald Hills 1937- *AmMWSc 92*
**Avery,** Emerson Roy, Jr. 1954- *WhoAmL 92*
**Avery,** Fred 1907-1980 *FacFETw*
**Avery,** Gerald Kenneth 1953- *WhoMW 92*
**Avery,** Gillian 1926- *IntAu&W 91, WrDr 92*
**Avery,** Gillian Elise 1926- *Who 92*
**Avery,** Gordon B 1931- *AmMWSc 92*
**Avery,** Graham John Lloyd 1943- *Who 92*
**Avery,** Herbert B. 1933- *WhoBlA 92*
**Avery,** Howard S 1906- *AmMWSc 92*
**Avery,** Isaac Erwin 1828-1863 *DcNCBi 1*
**Avery,** Isaac Erwin 1871-1904 *DcNCBi 1*
**Avery,** Isaac Thomas 1785-1864 *DcNCBi 1*
**Avery,** James Knuckey 1921- *AmMWSc 92*
**Avery,** James Royle 1925- *Who 92*
**Avery,** James S. 1923- *WhoBlA 92*
**Avery,** James Thomas, III 1945- *WhoAmL 92*
**Avery,** Jeromye Lee 1949- *WhoBlA 92*
**Avery,** John Ernest 1940- *Who 92*
**Avery,** Julia May 1917- *WhoWest 92*
**Avery,** Lee Ann 1957- *WhoFI 92*
**Avery,** Luther James 1923- *WhoAmL 92*
**Avery,** Mark Douglas 1957- *WhoRel 92*
**Avery,** Mark Hermanson 1964- *WhoAmL 92*
**Avery,** Martha Gallison Moore 1851-1929 *RelLAm 91*
**Avery,** Mary Ellen 1927- *AmMWSc 92, IntWW 91*
**Avery,** Milton 1893-1965 *FacFETw*
**Avery,** Oswald Theodore 1877-1955 *FacFETw*
**Avery,** Paul Eric 1959- *WhoAmL 92*
**Avery,** Percy Leonard 1915- *Who 92*
**Avery,** Richard *TwCSFW 91*
**Avery,** Richard Eugene 1935- *WhoWest 92*
**Avery,** Robert 1921- *AmMWSc 92*
**Avery,** Robert David 1953- *WhoAmL 92*

**Avery**, Roy *Who 92*
**Avery**, Stephen Goodrich 1938- *WhoAmP 91*
**Avery**, Steven Miller 1942- *WhoAmL 92*
**Avery**, Susan Kathryn 1950- *AmMWSc 92*
**Avery**, Waddell 1928- *WhoBlA 92*
**Avery**, Waightstill 1741-1821 *DcNCBi 1*
**Avery**, William Cushman 1832?-1894 *BiInAmS*
**Avery**, William Henry 1911- *WhoAmP 91*
**Avery**, William Hinckley 1912- *AmMWSc 92, IntWW 91*
**Avery**, William Waightstill 1816-1864 *DcNCBi 1*
**Avery**, Willoughby Francis 1843-1876 *DcNCBi 1*
**Avery Jones**, Francis 1910- *Who 92*
**Avery Jones**, John Francis 1940- *Who 92*
**Avery-Peck**, Alan Jeffery 1953- *WhoRel 92*
**Averyt**, Gayle Owen 1933- *WhoIns 92*
**Avetisyan**, Minas Karapetovich 1928-1975 *SovUnBD*
**Avey**, Ruby Doreen 1927- *IntAu&W 91*
**Avgerakis**, George Harris 1949- *WhoEnt 92*
**Avgerakis**, Maria Rosa 1953- *WhoEnt 92*
**Avgerinos**, Cecily T Grazio 1945- *IntAu&W 91*
**Avgerinos**, Paul Costas 1957- *WhoEnt 92*
**Avgeris**, George Nicholas 1939- *WhoAmL 92*
**Avgeropoulos**, George N 1934- *AmMWSc 92*
**Avi** 1937- *ChlLR 24 [port], WrDr 92*
**Aviado**, Domingo Mariano 1924- *AmMWSc 92*
**Avian**, Bob 1937- *WhoEnt 92*
**Avice**, Edwige 1945- *IntWW 91*
**Avicenna** 980-1037 *DcLB 115 [port]*
**Avidano**, Raymond Anthony 1938- *WhoRel 92*
**Avidom**, Menahem 1908- *IntWW 91*
**Aviel**, Jo Ann B. Fagot 1942- *WhoWest 92*
**Avigad**, Gad 1930- *AmMWSc 92*
**Avigan**, Joel 1920- *AmMWSc 92*
**Avigdor**, Isaac Chaim 1920- *WhoRel 92*
**Avignone**, Frank Titus, III 1932- *AmMWSc 92*
**Avil**, Richard D., Jr. 1948- *WhoAmL 92*
**Avila**, Arthur Julian 1917- *WhoMW 92*
**Avila**, Carlos Francisco 1925- *WhoHisp 92*
**Avila**, Charles Francis 1906- *AmMWSc 92*
**Avila**, David A. 1953- *WhoHisp 92*
**Avila**, Eduardo E. 1948- *WhoHisp 92*
**Avila**, Eli Narciso 1959- *WhoHisp 92*
**Avila**, Elza S. 1931- *WhoHisp 92*
**Avila**, Fernando Bastos de 1918- *IntWW 91*
**Avila**, Francisco de 1573-1647 *HisDSpE*
**Avila**, Humberto Nuno 1954- *WhoHisp 92*
**Avila**, Jesus 1945- *AmMWSc 92*
**Avila**, Joaquin G. 1948- *WhoHisp 92*
**Avila**, Joe Martinez 1937- *WhoHisp 92*
**Avila**, John *WhoHisp 92*
**Avila**, Juan Marcos 1959- *WhoHisp 92*
**Avila**, Pablo 1949- *WhoHisp 92*
**Avila**, Pedro Arias de 1442-1531 *HisDSpE*
**Avila**, Rafael Urbano 1930- *WhoHisp 92*
**Avila**, Ralph 1957- *WhoHisp 92*
**Avila**, Raul 1959- *WhoHisp 92*
**Avila**, Vernon L. 1941- *WhoHisp 92*
**Avila**, Vernon Lee 1941- *AmMWSc 92*
**Avila**, William Thaddeus 1954- *WhoAmL 92*
**Avildsen**, John G. *IntMPA 92*
**Avildsen**, John Guilbert 1935- *WhoEnt 92*
**Aviles**, Brian Andrew 1959- *WhoHisp 92*
**Aviles**, Carmelo Anibal, Sr. 1932- *WhoHisp 92*
**Aviles**, Christopher B. 1957- *WhoHisp 92*
**Aviles**, Joseph B 1927- *AmMWSc 92*
**Aviles**, Juan 1905- *WhoHisp 92*
**Aviles**, Juan Carlos 1957- *WhoHisp 92*
**Aviles**, Rafael G 1952- *AmMWSc 92*
**Aviles**, Rosemarie 1957- *WhoHisp 92*
**Aviles Cordero**, Leonor 1941- *WhoHisp 92*
**Avina**, Philip Indalecio 1940- *WhoWest 92*
**Avina-Rhodes**, Nina Alvarado 1944- *WhoFI 92*
**Avineri**, Shlomo 1933- *IntWW 91*
**Avino Pepls**, Joaquin *WhoHisp 92*
**Avins**, Jack 1911- *AmMWSc 92*
**Avioli**, Louis 1931- *AmMWSc 92*
**Aviram**, Ari 1937- *AmMWSc 92*
**Avirappattu**, George Antony 1962- *WhoMW 92*
**Avirett**, James Battle 1835-1912 *DcNCBi 1*
**Avirom**, Cheryl Ruth 1951- *WhoEnt 92*
**Avis**, Kenneth Edward 1918- *AmMWSc 92*
**Avis**, Paul David Loup 1947- *WhoRel 92*
**Avis**, Robert Grier 1931- *WhoFI 92*
**Avise**, John C 1948- *AmMWSc 92*
**Avison**, Margaret 1918- *BenetAL 91, ConPo 91, RfGEnL 91*
**Avitabile**, George P *WhoAmP 91*
**Avitus** 450-518 *EncEarC*
**Avitzur**, Betzalel 1925- *AmMWSc 92*
**Avizienis**, Algirdas 1932- *AmMWSc 92*
**Avizonis**, Petras V 1935- *AmMWSc 92*
**Avner**, Barry P 1944- *AmMWSc 92*
**Avner**, Brett Kim 1949- *WhoMW 92*
**Avner**, Ellis David 1948- *AmMWSc 92*
**Avner**, Sanford Eldon 1940- *WhoWest 92*
**Avner**, Yehuda 1928- *IntWW 91, Who 92*
**Avnet**, Jon 1949- *IntMPA 92*
**Avnet**, Jonathan Michael 1949- *WhoEnt 92*
**Avni**, Abraham 1921- *WrDr 92*
**Avni**, Haim 1930- *ConAu 133*
**Avni**, Ran 1941- *WhoEnt 92*
**Avolio**, Wendy Freedman 1953- *WhoWest 92*
**Avonda**, Frank Peter 1924- *AmMWSc 92*
**Avonside**, Lady 1917- *Who 92*
**Avonside**, Lord 1914- *Who 92*
**Avouris**, Phaedon 1945- *AmMWSc 92*
**Avramides**, Anita 1952- *ConAu 133*
**Avramis**, Vassilios Ioannis 1950- *WhoWest 92*
**Avramovic**, Dragoslav 1919- *WrDr 92*
**Avrett**, Eugene Hinton 1933- *AmMWSc 92*
**Avriel**, Ehud 1917-1980 *ConAu 133*
**Avril**, Pierre 1930- *IntWW 91*
**Avril**, Prosper *IntWW 91*
**Avrin**, William F 1953- *AmMWSc 92*
**Avruch**, Joseph 1941- *AmMWSc 92*
**Avshalomov**, Aaron 1894-1965 *NewAmDM*
**Avshalomov**, Jacob 1919- *NewAmDM*
**Avtsyn**, Aleksandr Pavlovich 1908- *IntWW 91*
**Avveduto**, Saverio 1924- *IntWW 91*
**Awad**, Albert T 1928- *AmMWSc 92*
**Awad**, Atif B *AmMWSc 92*
**Awad**, Elias M 1934- *AmMWSc 92*
**Awad**, Essam A 1932- *AmMWSc 92*
**Awad**, Muhammad Hadi 1934- *IntWW 91, Who 92*
**Awad**, William Michel, Jr 1927- *AmMWSc 92*
**Awadalla**, Farouk Tawfik 1951- *AmMWSc 92*
**Awadalla**, Nabil G 1945- *AmMWSc 92*
**Awadallah**, Babikir 1917- *IntWW 91*
**Awak**, Shehu 1932- *Who 92*
**Awakessien**, Herbert Simon 1957- *WhoFI 92*
**Awapara**, Jorge 1918- *AmMWSc 92*
**Awashonks** *EncAmaz 91*
**Awasthi**, Yogesh C 1939- *AmMWSc 92*
**Awbrey**, Frank Thomas 1932- *AmMWSc 92*
**Awdry**, Christopher Vere 1940- *SmATA 67*
**Awdry**, Daniel 1924- *Who 92*
**Awdry**, W V 1911- *IntAu&W 91, WrDr 92*
**Awdry**, Wilbert Vere 1911- *SmATA 67 [port], Who 92*
**Awkard**, Julita Castro 1929- *WhoBlA 92*
**Awoonor**, Kofi *DrAPF 91*
**Awoonor**, Kofi 1935- *ConPo 91, IntAu&W 91, LiExTwC, WrDr 92*
**Awoonor**, Kofi Nyidevu 1935- *IntWW 91*
**Awramik**, Stanley Michael 1946- *AmMWSc 92, WhoWest 92*
**Awschalom**, Miguel 1927- *AmMWSc 92*
**Awume** *WhoRel 92*
**Awwad**, Hanan Ahmad 1951- *IntAu&W 91*
**Ax**, Emanuel 1949- *IntWW 91, NewAmDM*
**Ax**, Toni Sue 1940- *WhoAmL 92*
**Axam**, John Arthur 1930- *WhoBlA 92*
**Axdahl**, Evelyn Irene 1929- *WhoAmP 91*
**Axe**, John Donald 1933- *AmMWSc 92*
**Axe**, William Nelson 1909- *AmMWSc 92*
**Axel**, Bernard 1946- *WhoFI 92*
**Axel**, Gabriel 1920?- *IntMPA 92*
**Axel**, John Werner 1941- *WhoFI 92*
**Axel**, Leon 1947- *AmMWSc 92*
**Axel**, Richard 1946- *AmMWSc 92*
**Axel-Lute**, Paul 1945- *WhoAmL 92*
**Axelman**, Arthur 1944- *WhoEnt 92*
**Axelrad**, Arthur Aaron 1923- *AmMWSc 92*
**Axelrad**, D R 1910- *AmMWSc 92*
**Axelrad**, George 1929- *AmMWSc 92*
**Axelrad**, Jeffrey 1942- *WhoAmL 92*
**Axelrod**, Abraham Edward 1912- *AmMWSc 92*
**Axelrod**, Arnold Raymond 1921- *AmMWSc 92*
**Axelrod**, Bernadette Bonner 1963- *WhoEnt 92*
**Axelrod**, Bernard 1914- *AmMWSc 92*
**Axelrod**, Bradley Neal 1961- *WhoMW 92*
**Axelrod**, Charles Paul 1941- *WhoAmL 92*
**Axelrod**, Daniel 1948- *AmMWSc 92*
**Axelrod**, Daniel Isaac 1910- *AmMWSc 92*
**Axelrod**, David *AmMWSc 92*
**Axelrod**, David B. *DrAPF 91*
**Axelrod**, David E 1940- *AmMWSc 92*
**Axelrod**, George 1922- *BenetAL 91, IntMPA 92, WhoEnt 92, WrDr 92*
**Axelrod**, Jack 1930- *WhoEnt 92*
**Axelrod**, Joel Nathan 1932- *WhoFI 92*
**Axelrod**, John Neal 1966- *WhoEnt 92*
**Axelrod**, Jonathan 1950- *IntMPA 92*
**Axelrod**, Joseph H. d1991 *NewYTBS 91*
**Axelrod**, Julius 1912- *AmMWSc 92, FacFETw, IntWW 91, Who 92, WhoNob 90*
**Axelrod**, Leonard 1950- *WhoMW 92*
**Axelrod**, Lloyd 1942- *AmMWSc 92*
**Axelrod**, M.R. *DrAPF 91*
**Axelrod**, Norman Nathan 1934- *AmMWSc 92, WhoFI 92*
**Axelrod**, Stephen Lee 1951- *WhoWest 92*
**Axelrod**, Steven Gould 1944- *WhoWest 92*
**Axelrod**, Susan Rita *DrAPF 91*
**Axelroth**, Lynn Robin 1954- *WhoAmL 92*
**Axelson**, Eric 1913- *WrDr 92*
**Axelson**, Joseph Allen 1927- *WhoWest 92*
**Axelson**, Marta Lynne 1953- *AmMWSc 92*
**Axen**, David 1938- *AmMWSc 92*
**Axen**, Kenneth 1943- *AmMWSc 92*
**Axen**, Udo Friedrich 1935- *AmMWSc 92*
**Axenrod**, Theodore 1935- *AmMWSc 92*
**Axer**, Erwin 1917- *IntWW 91*
**Axford**, David Norman 1934- *IntWW 91, Who 92*
**Axford**, Elizabeth Carole 1958- *WhoEnt 92*
**Axford**, Roy Arthur 1928- *AmMWSc 92, WhoFI 92, WhoMW 92*
**Axford**, Warren Scott 1956- *WhoRel 92*
**Axford**, William Ian 1933- *IntWW 91, Who 92*
**Axilrod**, Stephen Harvey 1926- *WhoFI 92*
**Axinn**, Donald Everett *DrAPF 91*
**Axis Sally** 1900-1988 *FacFETw*
**Axisa**, John Francis 1906- *Who 92*
**Axler**, David Allan 1942- *AmMWSc 92*
**Axler**, Sheldon 1949- *WhoMW 92*
**Axley**, Frederick William 1941- *WhoAmL 92*
**Axley**, Hartman 1931- *WhoFI 92*
**Axley**, John Harold 1915- *AmMWSc 92*
**Axmann**, Arthur 1913- *EncTR 91 [port]*
**Axmann**, Artur 1913- *BiDExR*
**Axselle**, Ralph Lewis, Jr 1943- *WhoAmP 91*
**Ax:son Johnson**, Antonia Margaret 1943- *WhoFI 92*
**Axt**, Veronica Renee 1960- *WhoBlA 92*
**Axtell**, Darrell Dean 1944- *AmMWSc 92*
**Axtell**, John David 1934- *AmMWSc 92*
**Axtell**, Ralph William 1928- *AmMWSc 92*
**Axtell**, Richard Charles 1932- *AmMWSc 92*
**Axthelm**, Deon D 1920- *AmMWSc 92*
**Axthelm**, Pete d1991 *NewYTBS 91 [port]*
**Axthelm**, Pete 1943?-1991 *News 91, -91-3*
**Axtman**, Ben *WhoAmP 91*
**Axtman**, Benjamin J. 1933- *WhoMW 92*
**Axtman**, Carol E. 1937- *WhoMW 92*
**Axtmann**, Robert Clark 1925- *AmMWSc 92*
**Axtmayer Prado**, Robert W. 1950- *WhoHisp 92*
**Axton**, David *ConAu 36NR, WrDr 92*
**Axton**, Henry Stuart 1923- *Who 92*
**Axton**, Hoyt Wayne 1938- *WhoEnt 92*
**Axworthy**, Geoffrey 1923- *Who 92*
**Aya**, Edgar H. 1943- *WhoHisp 92*
**Aya**, Roderick Honeyman 1916- *WhoFI 92, WhoWest 92*
**Ayad**, Boulos Ayad 1928- *WhoWest 92*
**Ayadi**, Naida Anita 1932- *WhoMW 92*
**Ayala**, Anthony Eugene 1957- *WhoHisp 92*
**Ayala**, Arthur Angel 1934- *WhoHisp 92*
**Ayala**, Bernardo Lozano 1938- *WhoHisp 92*
**Ayala**, Cesar J. 1960- *WhoHisp 92*
**Ayala**, Felix C. 1960- *WhoHisp 92*
**Ayala**, Francisco 1906- *LiExTwC*
**Ayala**, Francisco Jose 1934- *AmMWSc 92, IntWW 91, WhoHisp 92, WrDr 92*
**Ayala**, Gonzalo F. 1949- *WhoHisp 92*
**Ayala**, Helen *WhoHisp 92*
**Ayala**, Jaime Z. de *Who 92*
**Ayala**, John 1943- *WhoWest 92*
**Ayala**, John Louis 1943- *WhoHisp 92*
**Ayala**, Manuel 1959- *WhoHisp 92*
**Ayala**, Marta Stiefel 1937- *WhoHisp 92*
**Ayala**, Raymond Gerard 1961- *WhoAmL 92*
**Ayala**, Reginald P. 1931- *WhoBlA 92, WhoHisp 92*
**Ayala**, Reynaldo 1934- *WhoHisp 92, WhoWest 92*
**Ayala**, Ruben, Sr. 1934- *WhoHisp 92*
**Ayala**, Ruben S 1922- *WhoAmP 91, WhoHisp 92*
**Ayala**, Ruben Samuel 1922- *WhoWest 92*
**Ayala**, Xenaro Gonzalez 1943- *WhoHisp 92*
**Ayalon**, David 1914- *IntWW 91*
**Ayandho**, Bernard Christian 1930- *IntWW 91*
**Ayari**, Chedli 1933- *IntWW 91*
**Ayars**, Albert Lee 1917- *IntAu&W 91, WrDr 92*
**Ayars**, James Earl 1943- *AmMWSc 92*
**Aycinena**, Jose de *HisDSpE*
**Aycinena**, Juan Fermin *HisDSpE*
**Ayckbourn**, Alan 1939- *FacFETw, IntAu&W 91, IntWW 91, RfGEnL 91, Who 92, WrDr 92*
**Aycock**, Alice 1946- *WorArt 1980 [port]*
**Aycock**, Benjamin Franklin 1922- *AmMWSc 92*
**Aycock**, Charles Brantley 1859-1912 *DcNCBi 1*
**Aycock**, Charles Broughton, III 1946- *WhoAmL 92*
**Aycock**, Charles Ronald 1940- *WhoAmL 92*
**Aycock**, Marvin Kenneth, Jr 1935- *AmMWSc 92*
**Aycock**, Pamela Gayle 1961- *WhoFI 92*
**Aycock**, Robert 1919- *AmMWSc 92*
**Aycock**, Shirley *DrAPF 91*
**Aydalot**, Maurice 1905- *IntWW 91*
**Aydelott**, Alfred Lewis, III 1943- *WhoFI 92*
**Aydelott**, Madison P., III 1954- *WhoAmL 92*
**Aydelott**, Martin Vaden 1944- *WhoAmL 92*
**Aydelotte**, Margaret Beesley 1934- *AmMWSc 92*
**Aydelotte**, Myrtle K 1917- *AmMWSc 92*
**Aydin**, Mehmet 1928- *IntWW 91*
**Aydlett**, Louise Clate 1941- *AmMWSc 92*
**Aydlette**, D L 1938- *WhoAmP 91*
**Aydy**, Catherine *IntAu&W 91X, WrDr 92*
**Aye**, Maung Tin 1941- *AmMWSc 92*
**Ayen**, Richard J 1938- *AmMWSc 92*
**Ayenew**, Mesfin 1949- *WhoWest 92*
**Ayengar**, Padmasini 1924- *AmMWSc 92*
**Ayeni**, Babatunde J 1954- *AmMWSc 92*
**Ayensu**, Edward Solomon 1935- *WhoBlA 92*
**Ayer**, A J 1910- *FacFETw*
**Ayer**, A J 1910-1989 *ConAu 34NR*
**Ayer**, Alfred Jules 1910- *IntAu&W 91*
**Ayer**, Anne 1917- *IntAu&W 91*
**Ayer**, B Frederick 1913- *WhoAmP 91*
**Ayer**, Darrell 1908- *AmMWSc 92*
**Ayer**, Donald Belton 1949- *WhoAmL 92*
**Ayer**, G. W. *WhoRel 92*
**Ayer**, Gertrude Elise 1884-1971 *NotBlAW 92 [port]*
**Ayer**, Hilary *DrAPF 91*
**Ayer**, Howard Earle 1924- *AmMWSc 92*
**Ayer**, John Butler 1948- *WhoMW 92*
**Ayer**, John Demeritt 1936- *WhoAmL 92, WhoFI 92*
**Ayer**, Ramani *WhoIns 92*
**Ayer**, William Alfred 1932- *AmMWSc 92*
**Ayers**, Alvin Dearing 1909- *AmMWSc 92*
**Ayers**, Arthur Raymond 1947- *AmMWSc 92*
**Ayers**, Carlos R 1932- *AmMWSc 92*
**Ayers**, Caroline LeRoy 1941- *AmMWSc 92*
**Ayers**, Cheryl S. 1957- *WhoRel 92*
**Ayers**, Deanne Campbell 1964- *WhoAmL 92*
**Ayers**, Donald Clayton 1950- *WhoMW 92*
**Ayers**, Everette Lee 1940- *WhoWest 92*
**Ayers**, Gaylord Lew 1935- *WhoEnt 92*
**Ayers**, George E. 1938- *WhoBlA 92*
**Ayers**, George Waldon, Jr. 1931- *WhoBlA 92*
**Ayers**, Jack Duane 1941- *AmMWSc 92*
**Ayers**, James Cordon 1934- *WhoMW 92*
**Ayers**, James Edson 1932- *WhoFI 92*
**Ayers**, James Lee 1919- *WhoWest 92*
**Ayers**, Jeffrey David 1960- *WhoAmL 92*
**Ayers**, Jerry Bart 1939- *AmMWSc 92*
**Ayers**, John E 1941- *AmMWSc 92*
**Ayers**, John Gilbert 1922- *Who 92*
**Ayers**, Joseph Leonard, Jr 1947- *AmMWSc 92*
**Ayers**, Jule 1911- *WhoRel 92*
**Ayers**, Mary Alice *DrAPF 91*
**Ayers**, Orval Edwin 1932- *AmMWSc 92*
**Ayers**, Oscar L. 1927- *WhoIns 92*
**Ayers**, Paul Wayne 1936- *AmMWSc 92*
**Ayers**, Randy *WhoBlA 92*
**Ayers**, Raymond Dean 1940- *AmMWSc 92*
**Ayers**, Richard Wayne 1945- *WhoMW 92*
**Ayers**, Robert G. 1897- *WhoBlA 92*
**Ayers**, Roderick Glen, Jr. 1947- *WhoAmL 92*
**Ayers**, Sharon Kay 1961- *WhoAmL 92*
**Ayers**, Thomas G. 1915- *IntWW 91*
**Ayers**, Timothy F. 1958- *WhoBlA 92*
**Ayers**, Will 1927- *WhoAmP 91*
**Ayers**, William Arthur 1924- *AmMWSc 92*
**Ayers**, William Scott 1950- *WhoAmL 92*
**Ayers-Elliott**, Cindy 1956- *WhoBlA 92*
**Ayerst**, David 1904- *IntAu&W 91*
**Ayerst**, Edward Richard *Who 92*
**Ayesha** 614?-678? *EncAmaz 91*
**Aygi**, Gennadi Nikolaevich 1934- *IntWW 91*
**Ayguesparse**, Albert 1900- *IntAu&W 91*
**Ayick**, Paul 1947- *WhoEnt 92*
**Aykal**, Gurer 1942- *WhoEnt 92*
**Aykan**, Kamran 1930- *AmMWSc 92*
**Aykroyd**, Cecil William 1905- *Who 92*

**Aykroyd**, Dan *LesBEnT 92*
**Aykroyd**, Dan 1952- *IntMPA 92*
**Aykroyd**, Daniel Edward 1952- *IntWW 91, WhoEnt 92*
**Aykroyd**, William Miles 1923- *Who 92*
**Aykut**, Imren 1941- *IntWW 91*
**Aylard**, Richard John 1952- *Who 92*
**Aylen**, Ian Gerald 1910- *Who 92*
**Aylen**, Leo *IntAu&W 91, WrDr 92*
**Aylen**, Walter Stafford 1937- *Who 92*
**Ayler**, Albert 1936-1970 *NewAmDM*
**Ayler**, Maynard Franklin 1922- *AmMWSc 92, WhoWest 92*
**Ayles**, George Burton 1945- *AmMWSc 92*
**Aylesford**, Earl of 1918- *Who 92*
**Aylestone**, Baron 1905- *IntWW 91, Who 92*
**Aylesworth**, John Bansley 1928- *WhoEnt 92*
**Aylesworth**, Julie Ann 1953- *WhoEnt 92*
**Aylesworth**, Merlin Hall d1952 *LesBEnT 92*
**Aylesworth**, Thomas Gibbons 1927- *AmMWSc 92*
**Ayliffe**, Gerald Ray 1947- *WhoEnt 92*
**Ayling**, June E *AmMWSc 92*
**Ayling**, Peter William 1925- *Who 92*
**Ayling**, Richard Cecil 1916- *Who 92*
**Ayling**, Stanley 1909- *WrDr 92*
**Ayling**, Stanley Edward 1909- *IntAu&W 91*
**Ayllon**, Lucas Vasquez de 1480?-1526 *DcNCBi 1*
**Aylmer** *Who 92*
**Aylmer**, Baron 1923- *Who 92*
**Aylmer**, G E 1926- *IntAu&W 91, WrDr 92*
**Aylmer**, Gerald Edward 1926- *IntWW 91, Who 92*
**Aylmer**, John Francis 1934- *WhoAmP 91*
**Aylmer**, Richard John 1937- *Who 92*
**Aylor**, Donald Earl 1940- *AmMWSc 92*
**Aylor**, Gary Leon 1947- *WhoRel 92*
**Aylor**, James Hiram 1946- *AmMWSc 92*
**Ayloush**, Cynthia Marie 1950- *WhoFI 92*
**Aylward**, Christopher Paul 1967- *WhoRel 92*
**Aylward**, J. Patrick 1951- *WhoWest 92*
**Aylward**, Jayne Anne 1956- *WhoAmP 91*
**Aylward**, Marcus *ConAu 34NR*
**Aylward**, Margaret Fayerweather 1918- *WhoAmP 91*
**Aylward**, Paul Leon 1908- *WhoAmL 92*
**Aylward**, Ronald Lee 1930- *WhoFI 92, WhoMW 92*
**Aylward**, Susan Marie 1964- *WhoAmL 92*
**Aylward**, Thomas James, Jr. 1923- *WhoEnt 92*
**Aylwin**, Patricio 1919- *IntWW 91*
**Ayme**, Marcel 1902-1967 *ChlLR 25 [port], GuFrLit 1*
**Aymond**, Gregory M. *WhoRel 92*
**Aymond**, Gregory Ray 1956- *WhoAmL 92*
**Aynardi**, Martha Whitman *AmMWSc 92*
**Aynes**, Richard Lee 1949- *WhoAmL 92*
**Ayo**, Donald Joseph 1934- *AmMWSc 92*
**Ayoola**, Emmanuel Olayinka 1933- *IntWW 91*
**Ayotte**, Gaston Arthur 1933- *WhoAmP 91*
**Ayoub**, Christine Williams 1922- *AmMWSc 92*
**Ayoub**, Elia Moussa 1928- *AmMWSc 92*
**Ayoub**, George Wafik Youseef 1953- *WhoEnt 92*
**Ayoub**, John Edward Moussa 1908- *Who 92*
**Ayoub**, Mahmoud A 1942- *AmMWSc 92*
**Ayoub**, Mohamed Mohamed 1931- *AmMWSc 92*
**Ayoub**, Raymond G Dimitri 1923- *AmMWSc 92*
**Ayoung**, Judith Mary 1965- *WhoFI 92*
**Ayr**, Michael 1953- *ConTFT 9*
**Ayral-Kaloustian**, Semiramis *AmMWSc 92*
**Ayre**, J. Randolph *WhoAmL 92*
**Ayre**, John Randolph 1938- *WhoAmP 91*
**Ayre**, Thornton *TwCSFW 91*
**Ayres**, Anne 1816-1896 *RelLAm 91*
**Ayres**, Arthur James John 1902- *TwCPaSc*
**Ayres**, Brown 1856-1919 *BilnAmS*
**Ayres**, David Edson 1947- *WhoFI 92*
**Ayres**, David H. 1945- *WhoFI 92*
**Ayres**, David Smith 1939- *AmMWSc 92*
**Ayres**, Elizabeth *DrAPF 91*
**Ayres**, Gerald *IntMPA 92*
**Ayres**, Gilbert Haven 1904- *AmMWSc 92*
**Ayres**, Gillian 1930- *IntWW 91, TwCPaSc, Who 92*
**Ayres**, Ian 1959- *WhoAmL 92*
**Ayres**, James Walter 1942- *AmMWSc 92*
**Ayres**, Janice Ruth 1930- *WhoWest 92*
**Ayres**, John Clifton 1913- *AmMWSc 92*
**Ayres**, Kathleen N *AmMWSc 92*
**Ayres**, Keith Allen 1954- *WhoEnt 92*
**Ayres**, Leonard Porter 1879-1946 *DcAmImH*
**Ayres**, Lew 1908- *FacFETw, IntMPA 92*
**Ayres**, Philip 1944- *ConAu 134*
**Ayres**, Ralph D 1948- *WhoAmP 91*
**Ayres**, Robert Allen 1946- *AmMWSc 92*
**Ayres**, Robert U 1932- *AmMWSc 92*
**Ayres**, Ronald Keith 1946- *WhoMW 92*
**Ayres**, Stephen McClintock 1929- *AmMWSc 92*
**Ayres**, Ted Dean 1947- *WhoAmL 92, WhoMW 92*
**Ayres**, Wesley P 1924- *AmMWSc 92*
**Ayres**, William Orville 1817-1887 *BilnAmS*
**Ayroud**, Abdul-Mejid 1926- *AmMWSc 92*
**Ayrton**, Elisabeth 1910- *WrDr 92*
**Ayrton**, Elizabeth 1910- *IntAu&W 91*
**Ayrton**, Michael 1921-1975 *TwCPaSc*
**Ayrton**, Norman Walter 1924- *Who 92*
**Ayscue**, Brian Thomas 1948- *WhoEnt 92*
**Aytch**, Donald M, Sr 1930- *WhoAmP 91*
**Aytch**, Donald Melvin 1930- *WhoBlA 92*
**Aytmatov**, Chingiz Torekulovich 1928- *SovUnBD*
**Ayton**, Robert 1569?-1638 *RfGEnL 91*
**Ayub Khan**, Mohammed 1908-1974 *FacFETw*
**Ayuso**, Katharine 1918- *AmMWSc 92*
**Ayvazian**, L Fred 1919- *AmMWSc 92*
**Ayyagari**, L Rao 1940- *AmMWSc 92*
**Ayyangar**, Komanduri M 1940- *AmMWSc 92*
**Ayyappan**, Duraiswamy Periaswamy 1950- *WhoEnt 92*
**Ayyaswamy**, Portonovo S 1942- *AmMWSc 92*
**Ayyildiz**, Judy Light *DrAPF 91*
**Ayyoubi**, Mahmoud Ben Saleh al- 1932- *IntWW 91*
**Az-Zawi**, Taher Ahmad *WhoRel 92*
**Azaceta**, Luis Cruz 1942- *WhoHisp 92, WorArt 1980 [port]*
**Azad**, Abdu F 1942- *AmMWSc 92*
**Azad**, Abdur Rehman 1930- *IntAu&W 91*
**Azad**, Hardam Singh 1938- *AmMWSc 92*
**Azaid** *SmATA 66*
**Azam**, Farooq *AmMWSc 92*
**Azana**, Manuel 1880-1940 *FacFETw*
**Azar**, Anthony C *WhoAmP 91*
**Azar**, Edward E. d1991 *NewYTBS 91*
**Azar**, Edward E. 1938-1991 *ConAu 134*
**Azar**, Henry A 1927- *AmMWSc 92*
**Azar**, Jamal J 1937- *AmMWSc 92*
**Azar**, Miguel M 1936- *AmMWSc 92, WhoMW 92*
**Azar**, Oren Bentley 1964- *WhoAmL 92*
**Azar**, Richard Thomas 1954- *WhoFI 92*
**Azar**, Suzanne S *WhoAmP 91*
**Azara**, Felix de 1752-1821 *HisDSpE*
**Azari**, Parviz 1930- *AmMWSc 92*
**Azariah**, Vedanayagam Samuel 1874-1945 *DcEcMov*
**Azarloza**, Armando E. 1965- *WhoHisp 92*
**Azarmi**, Fariborz Ted *WhoMW 92*
**Azarnoff**, Daniel L. 1926- *IntWW 91*
**Azarnoff**, Daniel Lester 1926- *AmMWSc 92, WhoFI 92, WhoWest 92*
**Azaroff**, Leonid Vladimirovich 1926- *AmMWSc 92*
**Azaroff**, Marcella Marie 1938- *WhoFI 92*
**Azbel**, Mark 1932- *AmMWSc 92*
**Azbell**, William 1906- *AmMWSc 92, WhoMW 92*
**Azcarraga**, Emilio *WhoHisp 92*
**Azcarraga**, Emilio, Sr. d1973 *LesBEnT 92*
**Azcona Del Hoyo**, Jose 1927- *IntWW 91*
**Azcue**, Pedro Arturo 1955- *WhoWest 92*
**Azcuenaga**, Mary L 1945- *WhoAmP 91, WhoHisp 92*
**Azcuenaga**, Mary Laurie 1945- *WhoAmL 92, WhoFI 92*
**Azcuna**, Adolfo 1939- *IntWW 91*
**Azen**, Edwin Allan 1931- *AmMWSc 92*
**Azeredo Da Silveira**, Antonio Francisco 1917- *IntWW 91*
**Azevedo**, Aluizio de 1857-1913 *BenetAL 91*
**Azevedo**, Arthur Victor 1942- *WhoAmL 92*
**Azevedo**, Carlos de 1918- *IntWW 91*
**Azhar**, Salman *AmMWSc 92*
**Azikiwe**, Benjamin 1904- *FacFETw*
**Azikiwe**, Nnamdi 1904- *IntWW 91, Who 92*
**Azimov**, Sarvar Alimdjanovich 1923- *IntWW 91*
**Azios**, A. D. *WhoHisp 92*
**Aziz**, Datin Paduka Rafidah 1943- *IntWW 91*
**Aziz**, Kareem A. 1951- *WhoBlA 92*
**Aziz**, Khalid 1936- *AmMWSc 92*
**Aziz**, Martha Dianne 1945- *WhoMW 92*
**Aziz**, Philip Michael 1924- *AmMWSc 92*
**Aziz**, Ronald A 1928- *AmMWSc 92*
**Aziz**, Samimah 1960- *WhoBlA 92*
**Aziz**, Suhail Ibne 1937- *Who 92*
**Aziz**, Tariq 1936- *CurBio 91 [port], IntWW 91*
**Aziz**, Ungku Abdul 1922- *IntWW 91*
**Azizi**, Sayed Ausim 1954- *AmMWSc 92*
**Azkoul**, Karim 1915- *IntWW 91*
**Azmanarashvili**, V. *WhoEnt 92*
**Aznam**, Ahmad 1928- *Who 92*
**Aznar Gerner**, Agustin 1911-1984 *BiDExR*
**Aznavour**, Charles 1924- *IntMPA 92*
**Aznavourian**, Varenagh 1924- *IntWW 91*
**Azneer**, J. Leonard 1921- *WrDr 92*
**Azocar**, Oscar 1965- *WhoHisp 92*
**Azoff**, Edward Arthur 1945- *AmMWSc 92*
**Azon**, Glenn 1956- *WhoHisp 92*
**Azorsky**, Tami Lyn 1959- *WhoAmL 92*
**Azpeitia**, Alfonso Gil 1922- *AmMWSc 92*
**Azpilcueta**, Martin de 1491-1586 *HisDSpE*
**Azpurua**, Antonio Jose 1956- *WhoFI 92*
**Azrael**, Judith Anne *DrAPF 91*
**Azrak**, Janice A. 1951- *WhoEnt 92*
**Azua**, Ernest R. 1941- *WhoHisp 92*
**Azua**, Miguel Angel 1965- *WhoHisp 92*
**Azuela**, Arturo 1938- *IntWW 91*
**Azuela**, Mariano 1873-1952 *BenetAL 91*
**Azuma**, Hiroshi 1926- *IntWW 91*
**Azumano**, George Ichiro 1918- *WhoWest 92*
**Azumaya**, Goro 1920- *AmMWSc 92*
**Azurduy**, Juana *EncAmaz 91*
**Azurduy de Padilla**, Juana 1781-1862 *HisDSpE*
**Azus**, Louis 1936- *WhoIns 92*
**Azzam**, Rasheed M A 1945- *AmMWSc 92*
**Azzarello**, Russell J 1942- *WhoAmP 91*
**Azzaro**, Albert J *AmMWSc 92*
**Azzato**, Louis E. 1930- *IntWW 91*
**Azzato**, Louis Enrico 1930- *WhoFI 92*
**Azziz**, Ricardo 1958- *WhoHisp 92*
**Azzolina**, Joseph 1926- *WhoAmP 91*
**Azzouni**, Jody *DrAPF 91*

# B

**B B** *IntAu&W 91X*
**B.L.T.** *BenetAL 91*
**Ba Jin** 1904- *IntAu&W 91, IntWW 91*
**Ba,** Babacar 1930- *IntWW 91*
**Ba,** Elhadjdia 1958- *BlkOlyM*
**Baab,** David John 1956- *WhoFI 92*
**Baack,** Dennis 1946- *WhoAmP 91*
**Baad,** Michael Francis 1941- *AmMWSc 92*
**Baade,** Paul T 1940- *WhoAmP 91*
**Baade,** Wilhelm Heinrich Walter 1893-1960 *FacFETw*
**Baader,** Andreas *FacFETw*
**Baader-Meinhof Group** *FacFETw*
**Baadsgaard,** Halfdan 1929- *AmMWSc 92*
**Baak,** David P. *WhoRel 92*
**Baalman,** Robert J 1939- *AmMWSc 92*
**Baaqee,** Susanne Inez 1952- *WhoBlA 92*
**Baar,** James A. 1929- *WhoFI 92*
**Baar,** John Greenfield, II 1952- *WhoMW 92*
**Baar,** Kenneth Donald 1926- *WhoRel 92*
**Baarda,** David Gene 1937- *AmMWSc 92*
**Baarda,** Tjitze 1932- *WhoRel 92*
**Baars,** Bruce Terry 1952- *WhoMW 92*
**Baars,** Donald Lee 1928- *AmMWSc 92, WhoMW 92*
**Baars,** Jan 1903- *BiDExR*
**Baarsma,** William Henry 1942- *WhoAmP 91*
**Baas,** Jacquelynn 1948- *WhoWest 92*
**Baasel,** William David 1932- *AmMWSc 92*
**Baaske,** David Michael 1947- *AmMWSc 92*
**Baastad,** Babbis Friis *ConAu 134*
**Baba Ould Hassena** *HisDSpE*
**Baba,** Anthony John 1936- *AmMWSc 92*
**Baba,** Corneliu 1906- *IntWW 91*
**Baba,** Encik Abdul Ghafar Bin 1925- *IntWW 91*
**Baba,** Isamu 1923- *WhoFI 92*
**Baba,** Jason Nobuo 1957- *WhoAmL 92*
**Baba,** Marietta Lynn 1949- *WhoMW 92*
**Baba,** Paul David 1932- *AmMWSc 92*
**Baba,** Thomas Frank 1957- *WhoFI 92*
**Babad,** Harry 1936- *AmMWSc 92*
**Babadzhan,** Ramz 1921- *IntWW 91*
**Babadzhanyan,** Arno Harutyuni 1921-1983 *SovUnBD*
**Babakhanov,** Ziyautdin 1908-1982 *SovUnBD*
**Babangida,** Ibrahim 1941- *IntWW 91*
**Babaoglu,** Rehim 1946- *WhoAmL 92*
**Babar,** Raza Ali 1947- *WhoFI 92*
**Babauta,** Gabriel Boki *WhoAmP 91*
**Babauta,** Juan N 1953- *WhoAmP 91*
**Babauta,** Juan Nekai 1953- *WhoWest 92*
**Babayan,** Vigen Khachig 1913- *AmMWSc 92*
**Babayans,** Emil 1951- *WhoFI 92, WhoWest 92*
**Babayev,** Agadzhan Geldevich 1929- *IntWW 91*
**Babayevsky,** Semyon Petrovich 1909- *IntAu&W 91, IntWW 91*
**Babb,** Albert L 1925- *AmMWSc 92*
**Babb,** Albert Leslie 1925- *IntWW 91*
**Babb,** Billie Margaret 1918- *WhoAmP 91*
**Babb,** Daniel Paul 1939- *AmMWSc 92*
**Babb,** David Daniel 1928- *AmMWSc 92*
**Babb,** Frank Edward 1932- *WhoAmL 92*
**Babb,** Robert Massey 1938- *AmMWSc 92*
**Babb,** Sanora 1907- *IntAu&W 91, WrDr 92*
**Babb,** Stanley Nicholson 1874-1957 *TwCPaSc*
**Babb,** Valerie M. 1955- *WhoBlA 92*
**Babb,** Wylie Sherrill 1940- *WhoRel 92*
**Babbage,** Robert *WhoAmP 91*
**Babbage,** Stuart Barton 1916- *WrDr 92*
**Babbel,** David Frederick 1949- *WhoFI 92*
**Babbes,** Thom A. 1958- *WhoEnt 92*
**Babbie,** Leon F 1926- *WhoAmP 91*
**Babbin,** Jacqueline *LesBEnT 92*
**Babbin,** Jed Lloyd 1950- *WhoAmL 92*
**Babbis,** Eleanor *ConAu 134*
**Babbitt,** Bruce E 1938- *WhoAmP 91*
**Babbitt,** Bruce Edward 1938- *WhoWest 92*
**Babbitt,** Donald George 1936- *AmMWSc 92*
**Babbitt,** Irving 1865-1933 *BenetAL 91, FacFETw*
**Babbitt,** Milton 1916- *ConCom 92, FacFETw, NewAmDM*
**Babbitt,** Milton Byron 1916- *IntWW 91, WhoEnt 92*
**Babbitt,** Natalie *WrDr 92*
**Babbitt,** Natalie 1932- *SmATA 68 [port]*
**Babbitt,** Thomas Michael 1952- *WhoEnt 92*
**Babbo,** Thomas John 1971- *WhoEnt 92*
**Babbott,** Frank Lusk, Jr 1919- *AmMWSc 92*
**Babbs,** Charles Frederick 1946- *AmMWSc 92*
**Babbs,** Junious C., Sr. 1924- *WhoBlA 92*
**Babbush,** Howard Edward 1941- *WhoAmP 91*
**Babcock,** Alpheus 1785-1842 *NewAmDM*
**Babcock,** Anita Kathleen 1948- *AmMWSc 92*
**Babcock,** Barbara Allen 1938- *WhoAmL 92*
**Babcock,** Byron D 1931- *AmMWSc 92*
**Babcock,** Carmel A 1929- *WhoAmP 91*
**Babcock,** Caroline Lexow 1882-1980 *HanAmWH*
**Babcock,** Charles Henry 1899-1967 *DcNCBi 1*
**Babcock,** Charles Lynde, IV 1949- *WhoAmL 92*
**Babcock,** Charles Witten 1941- *WhoAmL 92*
**Babcock,** Clarence Lloyd 1904- *AmMWSc 92*
**Babcock,** Dale F 1906- *AmMWSc 92*
**Babcock,** Daniel Lawrence 1930- *AmMWSc 92, WhoMW 92*
**Babcock,** Donald Eric 1907- *AmMWSc 92*
**Babcock,** Dwight V. 1909- *IntMPA 92*
**Babcock,** Elkanah Andrew 1941- *AmMWSc 92*
**Babcock,** George *ScFEYrs*
**Babcock,** George, Jr 1916- *AmMWSc 92*
**Babcock,** Gerald Thomas 1946- *AmMWSc 92*
**Babcock,** Harold Delos 1882-1968 *FacFETw*
**Babcock,** Henry Homes 1832-1881 *BiInAmS*
**Babcock,** Horace W 1912- *AmMWSc 92, IntWW 91*
**Babcock,** Horace Welcome 1912- *FacFETw, Who 92*
**Babcock,** James Francis 1844-1897 *BiInAmS*
**Babcock,** Janice Beatrice 1942- *WhoFI 92, WhoMW 92*
**Babcock,** Jeff Charles 1960- *WhoFI 92*
**Babcock,** John Bodine 1925- *WhoEnt 92*
**Babcock,** John Montran 1949- *WhoRel 92*
**Babcock,** Judith Ann 1956- *WhoEnt 92*
**Babcock,** Keith Moss 1951- *WhoAmL 92*
**Babcock,** Lewis Thornton 1943- *WhoAmL 92*
**Babcock,** Lyndon Ross 1934- *AmMWSc 92*
**Babcock,** Lyndon Ross, Jr. 1934- *WhoMW 92*
**Babcock,** Malin Marie 1939- *AmMWSc 92*
**Babcock,** Mary Reynolds 1908-1953 *DcNCBi 1*
**Babcock,** Michael Joseph 1941- *WhoFI 92*
**Babcock,** Michael Ward 1944- *WhoMW 92*
**Babcock,** Peter H. 1949- *WhoWest 92*
**Babcock,** Philip Arnold 1932- *AmMWSc 92*
**Babcock,** Robert E 1937- *AmMWSc 92*
**Babcock,** Robert Frederick 1930- *AmMWSc 92*
**Babcock,** Stephen Lee 1939- *WhoAmL 92*
**Babcock,** Stephen Moulton 1843-1931 *FacFETw*
**Babcock,** Warner King 1951- *WhoFI 92*
**Babcock,** Wendell Keith 1925- *WhoMW 92, WhoRel 92*
**Babcock,** William Edward 1922- *AmMWSc 92*
**Babcock,** William James Verner 1912- *AmMWSc 92*
**Babcock,** William Richards 1929- *WhoEnt 92*
**Babe,** Thomas 1941- *IntAu&W 91, WhoEnt 92, WrDr 92*
**Babel,** Frederick John 1911- *AmMWSc 92*
**Babel,** Gary Richard 1947- *WhoMW 92*
**Babel,** Henry Wolfgang 1933- *WhoWest 92*
**Babel,** Isaac Emmanuelovich 1894-1941 *FacFETw*
**Babel',** Isaak Emmanuilovich 1894-1941? *SovUnBD*
**Babenco,** Hector 1946- *IntDcF 2-2 [port], IntMPA 92*
**Babenko,** Alexander Alexandrovich 1935- *IntWW 91*
**Babenko,** Hector 1946- *IntWW 91*
**Baber,** Asa *DrAPF 91*
**Baber,** Burl B, Jr 1928- *AmMWSc 92*
**Baber,** Ceola Ross 1950- *WhoBlA 92*
**Baber,** Ernest George 1924- *Who 92*
**Baber,** Lucky Larry 1949- *WhoBlA 92*
**Baber,** Wilbur H., Jr. 1926- *WhoAmL 92, WhoFI 92*
**Babero,** Andras F. 1955- *WhoHisp 92*
**Babero,** Bert Bell 1918- *AmMWSc 92, WhoBlA 92*
**Babers,** Alonzo 1961- *BlkOlyM*
**Babeuf,** Francois-Noel 1760-1797 *BlkwCEP*
**Babiarz,** Francis Stanley 1948- *WhoAmL 92*
**Babiarz,** John Edward 1915- *WhoAmP 91*
**Babiarz,** Joseph Francis, Jr. 1951- *WhoAmL 92*
**Babic,** Michael Walter 1951- *WhoAmL 92*
**Babich,** Adam 1955- *WhoAmL 92*
**Babich,** Harvey 1947- *AmMWSc 92*
**Babich,** Michael Wayne 1945- *AmMWSc 92*
**Babicky,** Charlotte L. *DrAPF 91*
**Babics,** Antal 1902- *IntWW 91*
**Babicz,** Laurence Walter 1961- *WhoEnt 92*
**Babikian,** George H. *WhoWest 92*
**Babikian,** Khatchik Diran 1924- *IntWW 91*
**Babilla,** Terrence Michael 1962- *WhoAmL 92*
**Babilonia,** Ana J. *WhoHisp 92*
**Babin,** Joyce Bradley 1954- *WhoAmL 92*
**Babin,** Maria Teresa 1910-1988 *WhoHisp 92N*
**Babin,** Victor 1908-1972 *NewAmDM*
**Babin,** William Albert, Jr 1929- *WhoAmP 91*
**Babineau,** G Raymond 1937- *AmMWSc 92*
**Babinec,** Gehl P. *WhoAmL 92*
**Babinec,** George Frederick 1957- *WhoWest 92*
**Babington,** Anthony Patrick 1920- *Who 92, WrDr 92*
**Babington,** Charles Martin, III 1944- *WhoAmL 92*
**Babington,** Rennie Frederic 1938- *WhoWest 92*
**Babington,** Robert John 1920- *Who 92*
**Babington,** William 1916- *Who 92*
**Babington-Browne,** Gillian Brenda 1949- *Who 92*
**Babington Smith,** Constance 1912- *IntAu&W 91*
**Babiniec,** Dennis Henry 1956- *WhoAmL 92*
**Babior,** Bernard M 1935- *AmMWSc 92*
**Babish,** John George 1946- *AmMWSc 92*
**Babish,** Richard Constantine 1918- *WhoFI 92*
**Babish,** Timothy James 1951- *WhoWest 92*
**Babitch,** Joseph Aaron 1942- *AmMWSc 92*
**Babiuc,** Vicor *IntWW 91*
**Babiuch,** Edward 1927- *IntWW 91*
**Babiuk,** Lorne A 1946- *AmMWSc 92*
**Bablanian,** Rostom 1929- *AmMWSc 92*
**Babler,** James Harold 1944- *AmMWSc 92*
**Babler,** Wayne E. 1915- *WhoAmL 92*
**Babler,** Wayne E., Jr. 1942- *WhoAmL 92*
**Bablitch,** William A. 1941- *WhoAmL 92, WhoAmP 91, WhoMW 92*
**Babochkin,** Boris Andreevich 1904-1975 *SovUnBD*
**Baboian,** Robert 1934- *AmMWSc 92*
**Baboukis,** John Nicholaou 1955- *WhoMW 92*
**Babrauskas,** Vytenis 1946- *AmMWSc 92*
**Babrov,** Harold J 1926- *AmMWSc 92*
**Babson,** Arthur Lawrence 1927- *AmMWSc 92*
**Babson,** Irving K. 1936- *WhoFI 92*
**Babson,** Marian *IntAu&W 91, WrDr 92*
**Babst,** Dean Voris 1921- *WhoWest 92*
**Babu,** Suresh Chandra 1961- *WhoFI 92*
**Babu,** Suresh Pandurangam 1941- *AmMWSc 92*
**Babu,** Uma Mahesh 1947- *AmMWSc 92*
**Babula,** William 1943- *WhoWest 92*
**Babur** 1483-1530 *LitC 18*
**Babuska,** Ivo Milan 1926- *AmMWSc 92*
**Babyak,** Michael, Jr. 1937- *WhoFI 92*

**Babyface** *WhoEnt 92*
**Baca,** Augustine Christobal 1944- *WhoHisp 92*
**Baca,** Bernal C. 1952- *WhoHisp 92*
**Baca,** Dorothy M. *WhoHisp 92*
**Baca,** Edward Dionicio 1938- *WhoWest 92*
**Baca,** Elmo L. 1953- *WhoHisp 92*
**Baca,** Fernie 1939- *WhoHisp 92*
**Baca,** Geraldine Tomasita 1962- *WhoHisp 92*
**Baca,** Glenn 1943- *AmMWSc 92*
**Baca,** Gloria Yvonne 1957- *WhoHisp 92*
**Baca,** Guy A. 1936- *WhoHisp 92*
**Baca,** Jim R. 1945- *WhoHisp 92*
**Baca,** Jimmy Santiago 1952- *WhoBlA 92, WhoHisp 92*
**Baca,** Joe 1947- *WhoHisp 92*
**Baca,** Jose J. *WhoHisp 92*
**Baca,** Joseph F 1936- *WhoAmP 91*
**Baca,** Joseph Francis 1936- *WhoAmL 92, WhoHisp 92, WhoWest 92*
**Baca,** Joseph P. *WhoHisp 92*
**Baca,** Judith *WhoHisp 92*
**Baca,** Lee F., Jr. 1944- *WhoHisp 92*
**Baca,** Maria A. *WhoHisp 92*
**Baca,** Mary Lou *WhoHisp 92*
**Baca,** Milton L. *WhoHisp 92*
**Baca,** Oswald G. 1942- *WhoHisp 92*
**Baca,** Oswald Gilbert 1942- *AmMWSc 92*
**Baca,** Patricia V *WhoAmP 91*
**Baca,** Polly B. 1941- *WhoHisp 92*
**Baca,** Richard 1942- *WhoHisp 92*
**Baca,** Robert T. *WhoHisp 92*
**Baca,** Rowena Joyce *WhoHisp 92*
**Baca,** Ruben Albert 1936- *WhoHisp 92*
**Baca,** Sacramento Henry, Jr. 1939- *WhoHisp 92*
**Baca,** Samuel Valdez 1949- *WhoHisp 92*
**Baca,** Ted Paul 1941- *WhoHisp 92*
**Baca,** Theresa Marie 1950- *WhoHisp 92*
**Baca,** Virginia G. 1933- *WhoHisp 92*
**Baca,** Wilfred Ruben 1940- *WhoHisp 92*
**Baca-Barragan,** Polly 1941- *WhoAmP 91*
**Baca Zinn,** Maxine 1942- *WhoHisp 92*
**Bacal,** Glenn Spencer 1953- *WhoAmL 92*
**Bacalis,** Nicholas George 1942- *WhoRel 92*
**Bacall,** Lauren 1924- *FacFETw, IntMPA 92, IntWW 91, WhoEnt 92, WrDr 92*
**Bacaner,** Marvin Bernard 1923- *AmMWSc 92*
**Bacani,** Nicanor-Guglielmo Vila 1947- *WhoFI 92*
**Bacardi Moreau,** Emilio 1844-1922 *HisDSpE*
**Bacarella,** Mary Martha 1958- *WhoEnt 92*
**Bacas,** William Augustus 1932- *WhoAmL 92*
**Bacastow,** Robert Bruce 1930- *AmMWSc 92*
**Baccala,** John Patrick 1960- *WhoEnt 92*
**Baccanari,** David Patrick 1947- *AmMWSc 92*
**Baccei,** Louis Joseph 1941- *AmMWSc 92*
**Bacchetti,** Fausto 1917- *IntWW 91*
**Bacchetti,** Silvia 1939- *AmMWSc 92*
**Bacchilega,** Cristina 1955- *IntAu&W 91*
**Bacchus,** Brian Michel 1957- *WhoEnt 92*
**Bacchus,** Habeeb 1928- *AmMWSc 92*
**Bacchus,** James L. 1949- *AlmAP 92 [port]*
**Bacchus,** Jim 1949- *WhoAmP 91*
**Bacci,** Donald Robert 1952- *WhoWest 92*
**Baccigaluppi,** Roger John 1934- *WhoFI 92, WhoWest 92*
**Baccini,** Laurance Ellis 1945- *WhoAmL 92*
**Baccouche,** Hedi 1930- *IntWW 91*
**Bacevicius,** John Anthony 1953- *WhoMW 92*
**Bacewicz,** Grazyna 1909-1969 *NewAmDM*
**Bach,** Aleksey Nikolaevich 1857-1946 *SovUnBD*
**Bach,** Anna Magdelena 1701-1760 *NewAmDM*
**Bach,** Carl Philipp Emanuel 1714-1788 *BlkwCEP, NewAmDM*
**Bach,** Catherine 1954- *IntMPA 92*
**Bach,** Claudia Stewart 1956- *WhoEnt 92*
**Bach,** Darwyn Paul 1964- *WhoFI 92*
**Bach,** David Rudolph 1924- *AmMWSc 92*
**Bach,** Elizabeth Marie 1952- *WhoMW 92*
**Bach,** Eric 1952- *AmMWSc 92*
**Bach,** Frederick L 1921- *AmMWSc 92*
**Bach,** Hartwig C 1930- *AmMWSc 92*
**Bach,** Jan Morris 1937- *WhoEnt 92, WhoMW 92*
**Bach,** Johann Christian 1735-1782 *BlkwCEP, NewAmDM*
**Bach,** Johann Christoph 1642-1703 *NewAmDM*
**Bach,** Johann Christoph Friedrich 1732-1795 *NewAmDM*
**Bach,** Johann Sebastian 1685-1750 *NewAmDM*
**Bach,** John Alfred 1935- *AmMWSc 92*
**Bach,** John Crittenden 1951- *WhoAmL 92*
**Bach,** Marilyn Lee 1937- *AmMWSc 92*
**Bach,** Martin Wayne 1940- *WhoWest 92*
**Bach,** Michael Klaus 1931- *AmMWSc 92*
**Bach,** P.D.Q. *NewAmDM*
**Bach,** Ricardo O 1917- *AmMWSc 92*
**Bach,** Richard 1936- *WrDr 92*
**Bach,** Russ *WhoEnt 92*
**Bach,** Shirley 1931- *AmMWSc 92*
**Bach,** Vincent 1890-1976 *NewAmDM*
**Bach,** Walther Debele, Jr 1939- *AmMWSc 92*
**Bach,** Wilhelm Friedemann 1710-1784 *NewAmDM*
**Bach-Y-Rita,** Paul 1934- *AmMWSc 92*
**Bach-Zelewski,** Erich von dem 1899-1972 *EncTR 91 [port]*
**Bach-Zelewsky,** Erich von dem 1899-1972 *FacFETw*
**Bacha,** Edmar Lisboa 1942- *IntWW 91*
**Bacha,** Habib *WhoRel 92*
**Bacha,** John D 1941- *AmMWSc 92*
**Bacha,** William Joseph, Jr 1930- *AmMWSc 92*
**Bacharach,** Burt 1928- *IntMPA 92, NewAmDM*
**Bacharach,** Burt 1929- *WhoEnt 92*
**Bacharach,** Martin Max 1925- *AmMWSc 92*
**Bachauer,** Gina 1913-1976 *FacFETw, NewAmDM*
**Bachaumont,** Louis Petit de 1690-1771 *BlkwCEP*
**Bache,** Alexander Dallas 1806-1867 *BiInAmS*
**Bache,** Andrew Philip Foley 1939- *Who 92*
**Bache,** David 1926- *DcTwDes, FacFETw*
**Bache,** Doug Albert 1951- *WhoAmP 91*
**Bache,** Ellyn *DrAPF 91*
**Bache,** Ellyn 1942- *WrDr 92*
**Bache,** Franklin 1792-1864 *BiInAmS*
**Bache,** Gerald Michael 1927- *WhoFI 92*
**Bache,** Robert James 1938- *AmMWSc 92*
**Bache,** Sarah Franklin 1743-1808 *BlkwEAR*
**Bache,** Theodore Stephen 1936- *WhoEnt 92*
**Bache,** Thomas H 1826?-1912 *BiInAmS*
**Bachel,** Larry F. 1949- *WhoIns 92*
**Bachelard,** Gaston 1884-1962 *GuFrLit 1*
**Bachelder,** Oscar Louis 1852-1935 *DcNCBi 1*
**Bachelder,** Robert Stephen 1951- *WhoRel 92*
**Bachelis,** Gregory Frank 1941- *AmMWSc 92*
**Bacheller,** Irving 1859-1950 *BenetAL 91*
**Bachelor,** Frank William 1928- *AmMWSc 92*
**Bachenheimer,** Cara Conway 1961- *WhoAmL 92*
**Bachenheimer,** Steven Larry 1945- *AmMWSc 92*
**Bacher,** Andrew Dow 1938- *AmMWSc 92*
**Bacher,** Frederick Addison 1915- *AmMWSc 92*
**Bacher,** Judith St. George 1946- *WhoFI 92*
**Bacher,** Lutz 1941- *WhoEnt 92*
**Bacher,** Robert Fox 1905- *AmMWSc 92, IntWW 91*
**Bacher,** Rosalie Wride 1925- *WhoWest 92*
**Bachert,** Alan Harold 1942- *WhoRel 92*
**Bachert,** Sharon Kay 1969- *WhoRel 92*
**Bachi,** Roberto 1909- *IntWW 91*
**Bachiarius** *EncEarC*
**Bachicha,** Joseph A. *WhoHisp 92*
**Bachicha,** Joseph Alfred *WhoMW 92*
**Bachicha,** Willie A. 1952- *WhoHisp 92*
**Bachik,** Mark 1955- *WhoFI 92*
**Bachini,** Robert F 1933- *WhoAmP 91*
**Bachir Mustapha Sayed** 1950?- *HisDSpE*
**Bachir,** Ahmed Ould Brahim Ould El 1918- *HisDSpE*
**Bachkatov,** Nina 1946- *ConAu 134*
**Bachko,** Nicholas d1991 *NewYTBS 91*
**Bachko,** Nicholas 1919- *WhoFI 92*
**Bachle,** Anne Elizabeth 1956- *WhoRel 92*
**Bachman,** A. A. *WhoRel 92*
**Bachman,** Bonnie Jean Wilson 1950- *AmMWSc 92*
**Bachman,** Brian Richard 1945- *WhoWest 92*
**Bachman,** Carol Christine 1959- *WhoFI 92*
**Bachman,** Gary Edward 1952- *WhoMW 92*
**Bachman,** Gary Eugene 1951- *WhoFI 92*
**Bachman,** George 1929- *AmMWSc 92*
**Bachman,** George O 1920- *AmMWSc 92*
**Bachman,** George S 1915- *AmMWSc 92*
**Bachman,** Gerald Lee 1932- *AmMWSc 92*
**Bachman,** Henry L 1930- *AmMWSc 92*
**Bachman,** Ilse 1924- *WhoAmP 91*
**Bachman,** James Vernon 1946- *WhoRel 92*
**Bachman,** Joan Marie 1938- *WhoMW 92*
**Bachman,** John 1790-1874 *BiInAmS*
**Bachman,** John W. 1916- *WrDr 92*
**Bachman,** Katharine Elizabeth 1953- *WhoAmL 92*
**Bachman,** Kenneth Charles 1922- *AmMWSc 92*
**Bachman,** Kenneth Leroy, Jr. 1943- *WhoAmL 92*
**Bachman,** Marvin Charles 1921- *AmMWSc 92*
**Bachman,** Neal Kenyon 1950- *WhoMW 92*
**Bachman,** Paul Lauren 1939- *AmMWSc 92*
**Bachman,** Richard *WrDr 92*
**Bachman,** Richard Thomas 1943- *AmMWSc 92*
**Bachman,** Robert Jay 1945- *WhoAmL 92*
**Bachman,** Walter Crawford 1911- *AmMWSc 92*
**Bachmann,** Barbara Joyce 1924- *AmMWSc 92*
**Bachmann,** Fedor W 1927- *AmMWSc 92*
**Bachmann,** Ingebord 1926-1973 *LiExTwC*
**Bachmann,** Ingeborg 1926-1973 *ConLC 69 [port], FacFETw*
**Bachmann,** John Henry, Jr 1944- *AmMWSc 92*
**Bachmann,** John William 1938- *WhoFI 92*
**Bachmann,** Kenneth Allen 1946- *AmMWSc 92*
**Bachmann,** Richard Arthur 1944- *WhoFI 92*
**Bachmann,** Roger Werner 1934- *AmMWSc 92*
**Bachmeier,** Adam Bernard 1938- *WhoRel 92*
**Bachner,** Annette *WhoEnt 92*
**Bachner,** Donald Joseph 1930- *WhoFI 92*
**Bachner,** Frank Joseph 1940- *AmMWSc 92*
**Bachner,** John Philip 1944- *WhoFI 92*
**Bachop,** William Earl 1926- *AmMWSc 92*
**Bachrach,** Alice R. d1991 *NewYTBS 91*
**Bachrach,** Anne Jameson 1919- *WhoAmP 91*
**Bachrach,** Arthur Julian 1923- *AmMWSc 92*
**Bachrach,** David Arthur 1952- *WhoEnt 92*
**Bachrach,** George *WhoAmP 91*
**Bachrach,** Howard L 1920- *AmMWSc 92, IntWW 91*
**Bachrach,** Ira Nathaniel 1938- *WhoFI 92*
**Bachrach,** Jonathan David 1946- *WhoAmL 92*
**Bachrach,** Joseph 1918- *AmMWSc 92*
**Bachrach,** Peter 1918- *WrDr 92*
**Bachrach,** Robert Zelman 1942- *AmMWSc 92*
**Bachstein,** Harry Samuel 1943- *WhoAmL 92*
**Bachtel,** Ann Elizabeth 1928- *WhoWest 92*
**Bachtel,** John Wayne 1938- *WhoWest 92*
**Bachtold,** Thomas Eugene 1935- *WhoMW 92*
**Bachur,** Nicholas R, Sr 1933- *AmMWSc 92*
**Bachus,** Benson Floyd 1917- *WhoFI 92, WhoWest 92*
**Bachus,** Marie Darsey 1940- *WhoBlA 92*
**Bachus,** Spencer *WhoAmP 91*
**Bachus,** William Earl 1940- *WhoAmP 91*
**Bachvaroff,** Radoslav J 1935- *AmMWSc 92*
**Bachvarova,** Rosemary Faulkner 1938- *AmMWSc 92*
**Bachynski,** Morrel Paul 1930- *AmMWSc 92, IntWW 91*
**Bacigalupa,** Andrea 1923- *WhoWest 92*
**Bacigalupo,** Charles Anthony 1934- *WhoFI 92*
**Bacin,** William Fredric 1923- *WhoEnt 92*
**Bacino,** Kathy E 1940- *WhoAmP 91*
**Back,** Birger Bo 1946- *AmMWSc 92*
**Back,** George *LesBEnT 92*
**Back,** George Leonard 1939- *WhoEnt 92*
**Back,** J. H., Mrs. *Who 92*
**Back,** James Arthur 1951- *WhoMW 92*
**Back,** Jerry Lee 1933- *WhoRel 92*
**Back,** Kenneth Charles 1925- *AmMWSc 92*
**Back,** Kenneth John Campbell 1925- *Who 92*
**Back,** Leon B. 1912- *IntMPA 92*
**Back,** Margaret Helen 1929- *AmMWSc 92*
**Back,** Nathan 1925- *AmMWSc 92*
**Back,** Patrick 1917- *Who 92*
**Back,** Robert Arthur 1929- *AmMWSc 92*
**Back,** Robert Wyatt 1936- *WhoFI 92*
**Back,** Sven-Erik 1919- *ConCom 92*
**Back,** William 1925- *AmMWSc 92*
**Backalenick,** Irene Margolis 1921- *WhoEnt 92*
**Backberg,** Bruce Allen 1948- *WhoFI 92*
**Backe,** Herbert 1896-1947 *BiDExR, EncTR 91 [port]*
**Backe,** John D. *LesBEnT 92*
**Backe,** John David 1932- *IntMPA 92, IntWW 91*
**Backe,** Pamela Renee 1955- *WhoWest 92*
**Backenstoss,** Henry Brightbill 1912- *WhoFI 92*
**Backer,** Bruce Everett 1955- *WhoWest 92*
**Backer,** Donald Charles 1943- *AmMWSc 92*
**Backer,** Gracia Yancy 1950- *WhoAmP 91*
**Backer,** Lisa Henriksen 1961- *WhoFI 92*
**Backer,** Paul Allen 1957- *WhoEnt 92*
**Backer,** Ronald Charles 1943- *AmMWSc 92*
**Backer,** William Montague 1926- *WhoFI 92*
**Backes,** Richard J 1925- *WhoAmP 91*
**Backett,** Edward Maurice 1916- *Who 92*
**Backhaus,** Ralph Andrew 1951- *WhoWest 92*
**Backhaus,** Wilhelm 1884-1969 *FacFETw, NewAmDM*
**Backhouse,** David Miles 1939- *Who 92*
**Backhouse,** John d1784? *DcNCBi 1*
**Backhouse,** Jonathan 1907- *Who 92*
**Backhouse,** Jonathan Roger 1939- *Who 92*
**Backhouse,** Roger Bainbridge 1938- *Who 92*
**Backhuus,** Troy Alan 1966- *WhoRel 92*
**Backlund,** Daniel Steven 1956- *WhoEnt 92*
**Backlund,** Gordon 1940- *WhoAmP 91*
**Backlund,** Larry Robert 1945- *WhoEnt 92*
**Backman,** Cecilia Ann 1950- *WhoMW 92*
**Backman,** Gerald Stephen 1938- *WhoAmL 92*
**Backman,** Jack H 1922- *WhoAmP 91*
**Backman,** Keith Cameron 1947- *AmMWSc 92*
**Backman,** Paul Anthony 1944- *AmMWSc 92*
**Backman,** Stephen John 1949- *WhoMW 92*
**Backofen,** Donald Wayne 1918- *WhoMW 92*
**Backofen,** Walter A 1925- *AmMWSc 92*
**Backstrom,** Charles Herbert 1926- *WhoAmL 92*
**Backstrom,** Don 1941- *WhoBlA 92*
**Backus,** Bertha Gilman 1946- *WhoAmP 91*
**Backus,** Bradley 1950- *WhoBlA 92*
**Backus,** Charles E 1937- *AmMWSc 92*
**Backus,** George Edward 1930- *AmMWSc 92, IntWW 91, WrDr 92*
**Backus,** Isaac 1724-1806 *BenetAL 91, BlkwEAR*
**Backus,** Jan 1947- *WhoAmP 91*
**Backus,** Jim 1913-1989 *FacFETw*
**Backus,** John 1911- *AmMWSc 92*
**Backus,** John 1924- *AmMWSc 92, IntWW 91*
**Backus,** John King 1925- *AmMWSc 92*
**Backus,** Kevin Michael 1956- *WhoRel 92*
**Backus,** Leland Eugene 1947- *WhoAmL 92*
**Backus,** Milo M 1932- *AmMWSc 92*
**Backus,** Richard Haven 1922- *AmMWSc 92*
**Backus,** W Elwyn *ScFEYrs*
**Backus,** William 1926- *ConAu 135*
**Baclawski,** Leona Marie 1945- *AmMWSc 92*
**Bacmeister,** Rhoda W. 1893-1991 *ConAu 133*
**Bacoate,** Matthew, Jr. 1931- *WhoBlA 92*
**Bacoats,** Inez B. 1899- *WhoBlA 92*
**Bacon** *Who 92*
**Bacon,** Baroness *Who 92*
**Bacon,** Albert S. 1942- *WhoBlA 92*
**Bacon,** Arthur Dennis 1948- *WhoMW 92, WhoRel 92*
**Bacon,** Arthur Lorenza 1937- *AmMWSc 92*
**Bacon,** Barbara Crumpler 1943- *WhoBlA 92*
**Bacon,** Brett Kermit 1947- *WhoAmL 92*
**Bacon,** Charles A 1860?-1901 *BiInAmS*
**Bacon,** Charles Wilson *AmMWSc 92*
**Bacon,** Charlotte Meade *WhoBlA 92*
**Bacon,** Darwin Dee 1947- *WhoRel 92*
**Bacon,** David W 1935- *AmMWSc 92*
**Bacon,** Deanna Maria 1943- *WhoMW 92*
**Bacon,** Delia 1811-1859 *BenetAL 91*
**Bacon,** Denise 1920- *WhoEnt 92*
**Bacon,** Donald C. 1935- *ConAu 133*
**Bacon,** Edgar Mayhew *ScFEYrs*
**Bacon,** Edmond James 1944- *AmMWSc 92*
**Bacon,** Edmund N. 1910- *WrDr 92*
**Bacon,** Edmund Norwood 1910- *IntWW 91*
**Bacon,** Egbert King 1900- *AmMWSc 92*
**Bacon,** Ernst 1898- *NewAmDM*
**Bacon,** Francis 1561-1626 *BlkwCEP, CnDBLB 1 [port], LitC 18, RfGEnL 91, ScFEYrs*
**Bacon,** Francis 1909- *FacFETw, IntWW 91, TwCPaSc, Who 92*
**Bacon,** Francis Thomas 1904- *IntWW 91, Who 92*
**Bacon,** Frank 1864-1922 *BenetAL 91*
**Bacon,** Frank Rider 1914- *AmMWSc 92, WhoMW 92*
**Bacon,** Frederick J. 1871-1948 *NewAmDM*
**Bacon,** George Adam, Jr. 1929- *WhoFI 92*
**Bacon,** George Edgar 1932- *AmMWSc 92*
**Bacon,** George Edward 1917- *Who 92, WrDr 92*
**Bacon,** George Hughes 1935- *WhoFI 92*
**Bacon,** Gloria Jackson 1937- *WhoBlA 92*

**Bacon**, Henry, Jr. 1866-1924 *DcNCBi 1*
**Bacon**, J M *ScFEYrs*
**Bacon**, James Richard 1914- *WhoEnt 92*
**Bacon**, Jennifer Helen 1945- *Who 92*
**Bacon**, John, Jr 1817-1881 *BiInAmS*
**Bacon**, Josephine Dodge 1876-1961 *BenetAL 91*
**Bacon**, Kevin 1958- *IntMPA 92, WhoEnt 92*
**Bacon**, Larry Dean 1938- *AmMWSc 92*
**Bacon**, Lawrence E. 1938- *WhoIns 92*
**Bacon**, Lawrence Edward 1938- *WhoFI 92*
**Bacon**, Leonard 1887-1954 *BenetAL 91*
**Bacon**, Leonard Anthony 1931- *WhoFI 92, WhoHisp 92, WhoWest 92*
**Bacon**, Lloyd 1890-1955 *IntDcF 2-2 [port]*
**Bacon**, Lyle C, Jr 1931- *AmMWSc 92*
**Bacon**, Margaret *WrDr 92*
**Bacon**, Marion 1914- *AmMWSc 92*
**Bacon**, Marjorie May 1902- *TwCPaSc*
**Bacon**, Merle D 1931- *AmMWSc 92*
**Bacon**, Nathaniel 1647-1676 *BenetAL 91*
**Bacon**, Nicholas 1953- *Who 92*
**Bacon**, Oscar Gray 1919- *AmMWSc 92*
**Bacon**, Patricia S. 1942- *WhoRel 92*
**Bacon**, Paul 1907- *IntWW 91*
**Bacon**, Paul Caldwell, Sr. 1945- *WhoWest 92*
**Bacon**, Paul Erwin 1942- *WhoRel 92*
**Bacon**, Peggy 1895-1987 *BenetAL 91*
**Bacon**, R. L. 1924- *WrDr 92*
**Bacon**, Ralph Gordon 1923- *WhoRel 92*
**Bacon**, Randall C. 1937- *WhoBlA 92*
**Bacon**, Reba Broyles 1908- *WhoAmP 91*
**Bacon**, Reginald W. 1949- *WhoEnt 92*
**Bacon**, Robert *DrAPF 91*
**Bacon**, Robert 1860-1919 *AmPolLe*
**Bacon**, Robert Charles 1952- *WhoFI 92*
**Bacon**, Robert Elwin 1934- *AmMWSc 92*
**Bacon**, Robert John, Jr. 1948- *WhoBlA 92*
**Bacon**, Roger 1214?-1292 *DcLB 115 [port]*
**Bacon**, Roger 1926- *AmMWSc 92, WhoMW 92*
**Bacon**, Sidney 1919- *Who 92*
**Bacon**, Susan M. *WhoMW 92*
**Bacon**, Sylvia 1931- *WhoAmL 92*
**Bacon**, Vicky Lee 1950- *WhoFI 92, WhoWest 92*
**Bacon**, Vinton Walker 1916- *AmMWSc 92*
**Bacon**, Wallace Alger 1914- *WhoWest 92*
**Bacon**, Warren H. d1991 *NewYTBS 91*
**Bacon**, Warren H. 1923- *WhoBlA 92*
**Bacon**, Wesley D. 1940- *WhoIns 92*
**Bacon**, William Edward 1917- *AmMWSc 92*
**Bacon**, William Francis 1956- *WhoAmL 92*
**Bacon**, William Louis 1936- *WhoBlA 92*
**Bacon Richards**, Bille J. *WhoBlA 92*
**Bacopoulos**, Nicholas G 1949- *AmMWSc 92*
**Bacot**, John Carter 1933- *WhoFI 92*
**Bacot**, Marie 1942- *WhoFI 92*
**Bacque**, Odon Lessley, Jr 1944- *WhoAmP 91*
**Bacquier**, Gabriel 1924- *IntWW 91*
**Bacs**, Ludovic 1930- *IntWW 91*
**Bacskai**, Robert 1930- *AmMWSc 92*
**Bacus**, James Nevill 1948- *AmMWSc 92*
**Bacus**, James William 1941- *AmMWSc 92*
**Bacus**, Terrence Lee 1944- *WhoMW 92*
**Baczek**, Stanley Karl 1946- *AmMWSc 92*
**Bada**, Jeffrey L 1942- *AmMWSc 92*
**Badal**, Robert Samuel 1945- *WhoMW 92*
**Badalamenti**, Anthony 1940- *WhoFI 92, WhoMW 92*
**Badalamenti**, Anthony Francis 1943- *AmMWSc 92*
**Badalewski**, Barbara Ann 1953- *WhoRel 92*
**Badami**, Rose Mary Rita 1929- *WhoRel 92*
**Badamo**, Thomas John 1965- *WhoRel 92*
**Badani**, Abdulla 1955- *WhoIns 92*
**Badash**, Lawrence 1934- *AmMWSc 92*
**Badavas**, Robert Peter *WhoFI 92*
**Badawi**, Abdel Halim 1930- *IntWW 91*
**Badawi**, Abdullah Bin Haj 1939- *IntWW 91*
**Badawi**, Mohamed Mustafa 1925- *IntAu&W 91, WrDr 92*
**Badcock**, Christopher Robert 1946- *IntAu&W 91, WrDr 92*
**Badcock**, John Michael Watson 1922- *Who 92*
**Baddeley**, Alan David 1934- *Who 92*
**Baddeley**, Hermione 1906?-1986 *ConAu 133*
**Baddeley**, John 1938- *Who 92*
**Baddeley**, William Pye 1914- *Who 92*
**Badder**, Elliott Michael 1943- *AmMWSc 92*
**Baddiley**, James 1918- *AmMWSc 92, IntWW 91, Who 92*
**Badding**, Victor George 1935- *AmMWSc 92*
**Baddour**, Raymond F 1925- *AmMWSc 92*
**Bade**, Maria Leipelt 1925- *AmMWSc 92*
**Bade**, William George 1924- *AmMWSc 92*
**Badea**, Christian *WhoEnt 92, WhoMW 92*
**Badeau**, Roger R 1936- *WhoAmP 91*
**Badeer**, Henry Sarkis 1915- *AmMWSc 92*
**Baden**, Ernest 1924- *AmMWSc 92*
**Baden**, Harry Christian 1923- *AmMWSc 92*
**Baden**, Howard Philip 1931- *AmMWSc 92*
**Baden**, John 1928- *Who 92*
**Baden-Powell** *Who 92*
**Baden-Powell**, Baron 1936- *Who 92*
**Baden-Powell**, Lady 1936- *Who 92*
**Baden-Powell**, Robert 1857-1941 *FacFETw*
**Badenhop**, Arthur Fredrick 1941- *AmMWSc 92*
**Badenhuizen**, Nicolaas Pieter 1910- *AmMWSc 92*
**Badeni**, June 1925- *WrDr 92*
**Badenoch**, Alec William d1991 *Who 92N*
**Badenoch**, James 1945- *Who 92*
**Badenoch**, John 1920- *Who 92*
**Bader**, Albert Xavier, Jr. 1932- *WhoAmL 92*
**Bader**, Charles W 1940- *WhoAmP 91*
**Bader**, Edward E. 1955- *WhoEnt 92*
**Bader**, Eliot Mark 1961- *WhoAmL 92*
**Bader**, Gerald Louis, Jr. 1934- *WhoAmL 92*
**Bader**, Gregory Vincent 1948- *WhoAmL 92*
**Bader**, Henry 1920- *AmMWSc 92*
**Bader**, Hermann 1927- *AmMWSc 92*
**Bader**, Izaak Walton 1922- *WhoAmL 92*
**Bader**, Kenneth L 1934- *AmMWSc 92*
**Bader**, Michael Haley 1929- *WhoEnt 92*
**Bader**, Richard Eugene *WhoEnt 92*
**Bader**, Richard Frederick W 1931- *AmMWSc 92*
**Bader**, Richard Frederick William 1931- *IntWW 91*
**Bader**, Robert Smith 1925- *AmMWSc 92*
**Bader**, Samuel David 1947- *AmMWSc 92*
**Bader**, Stephen Leigh 1942- *WhoFI 92*
**Bader**, W. Reece 1941- *WhoAmL 92*
**Bader-Molnar**, Katarina Elisabeth *IntAu&W 91*
**Baderman**, Alfred Carl 1927- *WhoRel 92*
**Badertscher**, Robert F 1922- *AmMWSc 92*
**Badge**, Peter Gilmour Noto 1931- *Who 92*
**Badger**, Alison Mary 1935- *AmMWSc 92*
**Badger**, Bryant D. 1938- *WhoRel 92*
**Badger**, David Harry 1931- *WhoAmL 92*
**Badger**, Geoffrey Malcolm 1916- *IntWW 91, Who 92*
**Badger**, George Edmund 1795-1866 *DcNCBi 1*
**Badger**, George Franklin 1907- *AmMWSc 92*
**Badger**, Joseph 1848-1909 *ScFEYrs*
**Badger**, Lloyd, Jr. 1950- *WhoBlA 92*
**Badger**, Michael Jay 1946- *WhoWest 92*
**Badger**, Rodney Allan 1943- *AmMWSc 92*
**Badger**, Rodney Seymour 1952- *WhoWest 92*
**Badgerow**, John Nicholas 1951- *WhoAmL 92*
**Badgett**, Allen A 1943- *AmMWSc 92*
**Badgett**, Edward 1935- *WhoBlA 92*
**Badgley**, Delores Romelia 1963- *WhoHisp 92*
**Badgley**, Edmund Kirk, Jr. 1923- *WhoWest 92*
**Badgley**, Franklin Ilsley 1914- *AmMWSc 92*
**Badgley**, John Herbert 1930- *WrDr 92*
**Badgley**, John Roy 1922- *WhoWest 92*
**Badgley**, Judeth Birdwell 1954- *WhoWest 92*
**Badgley**, Patrick Ryan 1942- *WhoMW 92*
**Badham**, Douglas George 1914- *Who 92*
**Badham**, Edward Leslie 1873-1944 *TwCPaSc*
**Badham**, John 1939- *IntMPA 92*
**Badham**, John 1943- *IntDcF 2-2*
**Badham**, John MacDonald 1939- *WhoEnt 92*
**Badham**, Leonard 1923- *IntWW 91, Who 92*
**Badham**, Robert E. 1929- *WhoWest 92*
**Badham**, Robert Edward 1929- *WhoAmP 91*
**Badham**, Walker Percy, III 1957- *WhoAmL 92*
**Badhwar**, Gautam D 1940- *AmMWSc 92*
**Badia-Batalla**, Francesc 1923- *WhoRel 92*
**Badian**, Ernst 1925- *IntWW 91, Who 92, WrDr 92*
**Badias**, Maria Elena 1959- *WhoHisp 92*
**Badie**, Ronald Peter 1942- *WhoFI 92*
**Badillo**, Herman 1929- *WhoAmP 91, WhoHisp 92*
**Badillo-Martinez**, Diana 1946- *WhoHisp 92*
**Badin**, Elmer John 1917- *AmMWSc 92*
**Badings**, Henk 1907- *IntWW 91*
**Badings**, Henk 1907-1987 *NewAmDM*
**Badini**, Aldo Anthony 1958- *WhoAmL 92*
**Badinter**, Robert 1928- *IntWW 91*
**Badish**, Kenneth Michael 1951- *WhoWest 92*
**Badler**, Norman Ira 1948- *AmMWSc 92*
**Badman**, John, III 1944- *WhoFI 92*
**Badmin**, S.R. 1906-1989 *TwCPaSc*
**Badner**, Barry 1937- *WhoFI 92*
**Bado**, Kenneth Steve 1941- *WhoMW 92*
**Bado-Santana**, Eduardo 1950- *WhoHisp 92*
**Badoglio**, Pietro 1871-1956 *EncTR 91 [port], FacFETw*
**Badolato**, Dominic J *WhoAmP 91*
**Badonnel**, Marie-Claude H M 1939- *AmMWSc 92*
**Badovinich**, Roberta Lynn 1952- *WhoMW 92*
**Badovinus**, Wayne L. 1943- *WhoWest 92*
**Badoyannis**, Helen Litman 1959- *AmMWSc 92*
**Badr**, Mostafa 1950- *AmMWSc 92*
**Badra**, Robert George 1933- *WhoMW 92*
**Badran**, Mudar 1934- *IntWW 91*
**Badre**, Albert Nasib 1945- *AmMWSc 92*
**Badua**, Raymond Martin 1960- *WhoWest 92*
**Badura-Skoda**, Paul 1927- *IntWW 91, NewAmDM*
**Bae**, Jae Ho 1939- *AmMWSc 92*
**Baebler**, Drew Charles 1960- *WhoAmL 92*
**Baechle**, James Joseph 1932- *WhoAmL 92, WhoFI 92*
**Baechler**, Bruce Andrew 1955- *WhoAmP 91*
**Baechler**, Charles Albert 1934- *AmMWSc 92*
**Baechler**, Raymond Dallas 1945- *AmMWSc 92*
**Baeck**, Leo 1873-1956 *EncTR 91 [port]*
**Baeck**, Martin Gerald 1953- *WhoEnt 92*
**Baeckelandt**, David Warren 1962- *WhoFI 92*
**Baedecker**, Mary Jo 1941- *AmMWSc 92*
**Baedecker**, Philip A 1939- *AmMWSc 92*
**Baeder**, Donald L 1925- *AmMWSc 92*
**Baeder**, Donald Lee 1925- *WhoFI 92*
**Baehr**, Anne-Ruth Ediger *DrAPF 91*
**Baehr**, Geoffrey George 1955- *WhoWest 92*
**Baehr**, Patricia 1952- *ConAu 35NR, SmATA 65*
**Baehr**, Theodore 1946- *WhoRel 92*
**Baekeland**, Frederick 1928- *AmMWSc 92*
**Baelz**, Peter Richard 1923- *Who 92*
**Baena**, Robert B. 1930- *WhoHisp 92*
**Baena**, Scott Louis 1949- *WhoAmL 92*
**Baender**, Margaret Woodruff 1921- *WhoWest 92*
**Baenziger**, Norman Charles 1922- *AmMWSc 92*
**Baer**, Adela 1931- *AmMWSc 92*
**Baer**, Adrian Donald 1942- *AmMWSc 92*
**Baer**, Agnes Marie 1921- *WhoRel 92*
**Baer**, Barbara 1936- *WhoRel 92*
**Baer**, Byron M 1929- *WhoAmP 91*
**Baer**, David, Jr. 1905- *WhoAmL 92*
**Baer**, Donald Ray 1947- *AmMWSc 92*
**Baer**, Donald Robert 1928- *AmMWSc 92*
**Baer**, Eric 1932- *AmMWSc 92*
**Baer**, Ferdinand 1929- *AmMWSc 92*
**Baer**, George M 1936- *AmMWSc 92*
**Baer**, Gordon *WhoMW 92*
**Baer**, Hans Helmut 1926- *AmMWSc 92*
**Baer**, Harold 1918- *AmMWSc 92*
**Baer**, Helmut W 1939- *AmMWSc 92*
**Baer**, Henry Philip 1935- *WhoAmL 92*
**Baer**, Herman 1933- *AmMWSc 92*
**Baer**, Howard A 1957- *AmMWSc 92*
**Baer**, Jack Mervyn Frank 1924- *Who 92*
**Baer**, James L 1935- *AmMWSc 92*
**Baer**, Jerome I 1936- *WhoIns 92*
**Baer**, Jerry W. 1936- *WhoMW 92*
**Baer**, Jo Webb 1936- *WhoAmP 91*
**Baer**, John Elson 1917- *AmMWSc 92*
**Baer**, John G. 1934- *IntMPA 92*
**Baer**, John Richard Frederick 1941- *WhoAmL 92, WhoMW 92*
**Baer**, Joseph d1991 *NewYTBS 91*
**Baer**, Ledolph 1929- *AmMWSc 92*
**Baer**, Lewis Byron 1946- *WhoAmL 92*
**Baer**, Luke 1950- *WhoAmL 92*
**Baer**, Max Adelbert, Jr. 1937- *WhoEnt 92*
**Baer**, Max Frank 1912- *WhoRel 92*
**Baer**, Michael Lee 1954- *WhoRel 92*
**Baer**, Norbert Sebastian 1938- *AmMWSc 92*
**Baer**, Olaf 1957- *IntWW 91*
**Baer**, Paul Nathan 1921- *AmMWSc 92*
**Baer**, Ralph Norman 1948- *AmMWSc 92*
**Baer**, Richard 1953- *AmMWSc 92*
**Baer**, Richard Myron 1928- *WhoFI 92*
**Baer**, Robert J. 1937- *WhoFI 92*
**Baer**, Robert Lloyd 1931- *AmMWSc 92*
**Baer**, Robert W 1948- *AmMWSc 92*
**Baer**, Rudolf L 1910- *AmMWSc 92*
**Baer**, Thomas James 1927- *WhoAmL 92*
**Baer**, Thomas Strickland 1942- *AmMWSc 92*
**Baer**, Timothy Robert 1951- *WhoAmP 91*
**Baer**, Tomas 1939- *AmMWSc 92*
**Baer**, Walter S 1937- *AmMWSc 92*
**Baer**, Wayne Graf 1957- *WhoMW 92*
**Baer**, William Bruce 1938- *WhoWest 92*
**Baer**, William Edward 1948- *WhoMW 92*
**Baer**, William Harold 1947- *WhoFI 92*
**Baerg**, David Carl 1938- *AmMWSc 92*
**Baerg**, Harry John 1909- *IntAu&W 91, WrDr 92*
**Baerg**, Marlene Annette 1966- *WhoWest 92*
**Baerg**, William 1938- *AmMWSc 92*
**Baerga**, Carlos 1968- *WhoHisp 92*
**Baerlein**, Richard Edgar 1915- *Who 92*
**Baermann**, Donna Lee Roth 1939- *WhoMW 92*
**Baernstein**, Albert, II 1941- *AmMWSc 92, WhoMW 92*
**Baertsch**, Richard D 1936- *AmMWSc 92*
**Baerwald**, Hans H 1927- *IntAu&W 91, WrDr 92*
**Baerwald**, John E 1925- *AmMWSc 92*
**Baerwald**, John Edward 1925- *WhoWest 92*
**Baerwald**, Susan *LesBEnT 92*
**Baerwald**, Susan Grad 1944- *WhoEnt 92*
**Baes**, Charles Frederick, Jr 1924- *AmMWSc 92*
**Baesler**, Scotty 1941- *WhoAmP 91*
**Baeta**, Christian Goncalves Kwami 1908- *DcEcMov*
**Baetke**, Edward A 1937- *AmMWSc 92*
**Baety**, Edward L. 1944- *WhoBlA 92*
**Baetz**, Albert L 1938- *AmMWSc 92*
**Baetz**, W. Timothy 1944- *WhoAmL 92, WhoFI 92*
**Baetz-Matthews**, Katrina Sue 1955- *WhoEnt 92*
**Baetzold**, Roger C 1942- *AmMWSc 92*
**Baeumler**, Alfred 1887-1968 *EncTR 91*
**Baeumler**, Howard William 1921- *AmMWSc 92*
**Baev**, Aleksandr Aleksandrovich 1904- *SovUnBD*
**Baez**, Albert Vinicio 1912- *AmMWSc 92, WhoHisp 92*
**Baez**, Joan 1941- *FacFETw, IntWW 91, NewAmDM*
**Baez**, Joan C. 1941- *HanAmWH*
**Baez**, Joan Chandos 1941- *WhoEnt 92, WhoHisp 92*
**Baez**, Julio A. 1954- *WhoHisp 92*
**Baez**, Luis 1948- *WhoHisp 92*
**Baez**, Mary Belinda 1955- *WhoHisp 92*
**Baez**, Silvio 1915- *AmMWSc 92*
**Baeza**, Abelardo 1944- *WhoHisp 92*
**Baeza**, Mario Leon 1951- *WhoAmL 92*
**Baezconde-Garbanati**, Lourdes A. 1955- *WhoHisp 92*
**Baffi**, Paolo 1911-1989 *FacFETw*
**Bafia**, Jerzy 1926- *IntWW 91*
**Bafile**, Corrado 1903- *IntWW 91, WhoRel 92*
**Bafunno**, Valerie Lynn 1955- *WhoMW 92*
**Bag**, Jnanankur 1947- *AmMWSc 92*
**Bagarazzi**, James Michael 1951- *WhoAmL 92*
**Bagarry**, Alexander Anthony, III 1949- *WhoWest 92*
**Bagasra**, Omar 1948- *AmMWSc 92*
**Bagaza**, Jean-Baptiste 1946- *IntWW 91*
**Bagbeni Adeito Nzengeya** 1941- *IntWW 91*
**Bagby**, Daniel Gordon 1941- *WhoRel 92*
**Bagby**, Frederick L 1920- *AmMWSc 92*
**Bagby**, George William 1828-1883 *BenetAL 91*
**Bagby**, Glen Stovall 1944- *WhoAmL 92, WhoFI 92*
**Bagby**, Gregory John *AmMWSc 92*
**Bagby**, Grover Carlton 1942- *AmMWSc 92*
**Bagby**, John R, Jr 1919- *AmMWSc 92*
**Bagby**, Marvin Orville 1932- *AmMWSc 92, WhoMW 92*
**Bagby**, Myron Rex 1944- *WhoFI 92*
**Bagby**, Rachel L 1956- *WhoBlA 92*
**Bagby**, Roland Mohler *AmMWSc 92*
**Bagby**, William Rardin 1910- *WhoAmL 92*
**Bagchi**, Amitabha 1945- *AmMWSc 92*
**Bagchi**, Mihir 1938- *AmMWSc 92*
**Bagchi**, Pranab 1946- *AmMWSc 92*
**Bagchi**, Sakti Prasad 1931- *AmMWSc 92*
**Bagdasarian**, Andranik 1935- *AmMWSc 92, WhoWest 92*
**Bagdasarian**, Ross 1949- *WhoEnt 92*
**Bagdikian**, Ben Haig 1920- *WhoWest 92, WrDr 92*
**Bagdon**, Robert Edward 1927- *AmMWSc 92*
**Bagdon**, Walter Joseph 1938- *AmMWSc 92*
**Bagdonas**, Kathy Joann 1953- *WhoAmL 92*
**Bage**, Robert 1728-1801 *RfGEnL 91*
**Bagert**, Bernard J, Jr 1944- *WhoAmP 91*
**Bagg**, Robert *DrAPF 91*
**Bagg**, Thomas Campbell 1917- *AmMWSc 92*
**Bagga**, Jaswant Singh 1948- *WhoMW 92*
**Bagga**, Kunwarjit Singh 1952- *WhoMW 92*

**Bagge**, Jeremy 1945- Who 92
**Bagge**, Michael Charles 1950- WhoAmL 92
**Bagge**, Traugott 1729-1800 DcNCBi 1
**Baggenstoss**, Archie Herbert 1908- AmMWSc 92
**Bagger**, Ralph William 1923- WhoRel 92
**Bagger**, Richard Hartvig 1960- WhoAmL 92
**Baggerly**, Leo L 1928- AmMWSc 92
**Baggerly**, Leo Lon 1928- WhoWest 92
**Baggett**, Agnes Beahn 1905- WhoAmP 91
**Baggett**, Billy 1928- AmMWSc 92
**Baggett**, George Edward 1928- WhoEnt 92
**Baggett**, James Alex 1932- WhoAmP 91
**Baggett**, James Ronald 1928- AmMWSc 92
**Baggett**, Kelsea Kindrick 1937- WhoWest 92
**Baggett**, Lawrence W 1939- AmMWSc 92
**Baggett**, Lee, Jr. 1927- IntWW 91
**Baggett**, Lester Marchant 1920- AmMWSc 92
**Baggett**, Louis Burney 1949- WhoRel 92
**Baggett**, Millicent 1939- AmMWSc 92
**Baggett**, Neil Vance 1938- AmMWSc 92
**Baggett**, Rebecca DrAPF 91
**Baggett**, Terrance L. WhoIns 92
**Baggett Boozer**, Linda Dianne 1956- WhoAmL 92
**Baggi**, Denis Louis 1945- AmMWSc 92
**Baggio**, Sebastiano 1913- IntWW 91, WhoRel 92
**Baggish**, Joy 1950- WhoEnt 92
**Baggley**, Charles David Aubrey 1923- Who 92
**Baggot**, J Desmond 1939- AmMWSc 92
**Baggott**, James Patrick 1941- AmMWSc 92
**Baggott**, John Wayne 1918- WhoFI 92
**Baghzouz**, Yahia 1956- WhoWest 92
**Bagier**, Gordon Alexander Thomas 1924- Who 92
**Bagilhole**, Robin 1942- TwCPaSc
**Baginski**, F C 1923- AmMWSc 92
**Baginski**, Joseph Anthony 1957- WhoEnt 92
**Bagirov**, Kyamran Mamed Ogly 1933- IntWW 91
**Bagirov**, Mir Dzhafar Abassovich 1896-1956 SovUnBD
**Bagley**, Brian G 1934- AmMWSc 92
**Bagley**, Cherie Albertha 1954- WhoMW 92
**Bagley**, Clyde Pattison 1951- AmMWSc 92
**Bagley**, Colleen 1954- WhoFI 92
**Bagley**, Constance Elizabeth 1952- WhoAmL 92
**Bagley**, Donald Neff 1927- WhoEnt 92
**Bagley**, Dudley Warren 1889-1964 DcNCBi 1
**Bagley**, Edythe Scott 1924- WhoEnt 92
**Bagley**, Floyd Caldwell 1922- WhoAmP 91
**Bagley**, Gary J. 1946- WhoRel 92
**Bagley**, George Everett 1933- AmMWSc 92
**Bagley**, Gregory P. 1930- WhoBlA 92
**Bagley**, Jay M 1925- AmMWSc 92
**Bagley**, John 1960- WhoBlA 92
**Bagley**, John D 1935- AmMWSc 92
**Bagley**, John Joseph 1908- IntAu&W 91, WrDr 92
**Bagley**, Lawrence Miles 1928- WhoWest 92
**Bagley**, Margaret Ann 1944- WhoAmP 91
**Bagley**, Peter B. E. 1935- WhoBlA 92
**Bagley**, Philip Joseph, III 1941- WhoAmL 92
**Bagley**, Richard Marshall 1927- WhoAmP 91
**Bagley**, Robert Waller 1921- AmMWSc 92
**Bagley**, Ronald Michael 1950- WhoRel 92
**Bagley**, Sarah G. HanAmWH
**Bagley**, Stanley B. 1935- WhoBlA 92
**Bagley**, Thomas Steven 1952- WhoMW 92
**Bagley**, Worth 1874-1898 DcNCBi 1
**Bagli**, Ibrahim Taher al- 1942- IntWW 91
**Bagli**, Jenanbux Framroz 1928- AmMWSc 92
**Baglin**, Raymond Eugene, Jr 1944- AmMWSc 92
**Baglin**, Richard John 1942- Who 92
**Baglini**, Norman A. 1942- WhoIns 92
**Baglio**, Joseph Anthony 1939- AmMWSc 92
**Baglio**, Vincent Paul 1960- WhoFI 92
**Baglioni**, Corrado 1933- AmMWSc 92
**Bagliore**, Virginia DrAPF 91
**Baglivo**, Jenny Antoinette 1948- AmMWSc 92
**Bagnal**, Charles W., Jr. 1957- WhoFI 92
**Bagnal**, Harry Stroman 1928- WhoAmP 91
**Bagnall**, Graham Edward 1948- WhoFI 92
**Bagnall**, Kenneth Reginald 1927- Who 92
**Bagnall**, Larry Owen 1935- AmMWSc 92
**Bagnall**, Nigel 1927- IntWW 91, Who 92
**Bagnall**, Richard Herbert 1923- AmMWSc 92
**Bagnall**, Richard Maurice 1917- IntWW 91, Who 92
**Bagnara**, Joseph Thomas 1929- AmMWSc 92
**Bagnariol**, John A 1932- WhoAmP 91
**Bagnell**, Carol A 1952- AmMWSc 92
**Bagneris**, Dennis R, Sr 1948- WhoAmP 91
**Bagneris**, Vernel 1949- ConTFT 9
**Bagnold**, Enid 1889-1981 RfGEnL 91
**Bagnold**, Ralph Alger d1990 IntWW 91N
**Bagot** Who 92
**Bagot**, Baron 1914- Who 92
**Bagot**, Walter Morrison 1935- WhoMW 92
**Bagri**, Durgadas S. 1942- WhoWest 92
**Bagritsky**, Eduard Georgievich 1895-1934 SovUnBD
**Bagshaw**, Joseph Charles 1943- AmMWSc 92
**Bagshaw**, Malcolm A 1925- AmMWSc 92
**Bagshawe**, Kenneth Dawson 1925- IntWW 91, Who 92
**Bague**, Jeffrey Steven 1957- WhoWest 92
**Bagus**, Paul Saul 1937- AmMWSc 92
**Bagwell**, Ervin Eugene 1936- AmMWSc 92
**Bagwell**, Gerald Ezra 1936- WhoRel 92
**Bagwell**, Kathleen Kay 1951- WhoMW 92
**Bagwell**, Sara Ruth 1919- WhoRel 92
**Bagwill**, John Williams, Jr. 1930- WhoFI 92
**Baha**, Daniel Scott 1955- WhoWest 92
**Bahadur**, Birendra 1949- AmMWSc 92
**Bahadur**, Chance 1942- WhoFI 92
**Bahadur**, K. C. Kaisher 1907- IntWW 91
**Bahadur**, Raghu Raj 1924- AmMWSc 92
**Bahadur**, Raj 1912- IntWW 91
**Bahal**, Neeta 1965- AmMWSc 92
**Bahal**, Surendra Mohan 1935- AmMWSc 92
**Baham**, Arnold 1943- AmMWSc 92
**Bahar**, Abdul Aziz Ahmed al- 1929- IntWW 91
**Bahar**, Ezekiel 1933- AmMWSc 92
**Bahar**, Leon Y 1928- AmMWSc 92
**Baharna**, Husain Mohammad al- 1932- IntWW 91
**Bahary**, William S 1936- AmMWSc 92
**Baha'u'llah** 1817-1892 RelLAm 91
**Bahcall**, John Norris 1934- AmMWSc 92, IntWW 91
**Bahcall**, Neta Assaf 1942- AmMWSc 92
**Bahe**, Lowell W 1927- AmMWSc 92
**Baher**, Constance Whitman 1942- WhoWest 92
**Bahill**, A Terry 1946- AmMWSc 92
**Bahl**, Franklin TwCSFW 91
**Bahl**, Inder Jit 1944- AmMWSc 92
**Bahl**, Lalit R 1943- AmMWSc 92
**Bahl**, Om Parkash 1927- AmMWSc 92
**Bahler**, Beth DrAPF 91
**Bahler**, Brent Norman 1953- WhoAmP 91
**Bahler**, Mabel Madelyn 1933- WhoMW 92
**Bahler**, Thomas Lee 1920- AmMWSc 92
**Bahler**, Thomas Lee 1943- WhoEnt 92
**Bahlman**, William Thorne, Jr. 1920- WhoAmL 92
**Bahlo**, Peter 1959- WhoWest 92
**Bahls**, Gene Charles 1929- WhoFI 92
**Bahm**, Archie J. 1907- WrDr 92
**Bahmani-Oskooee**, Mohsen 1951- WhoFI 92
**Bahmann**, Manfred Kurt 1930- WhoRel 92
**Bahn**, Arthur Nathaniel 1926- AmMWSc 92
**Bahn**, Charles Frederick, Jr. 1954- WhoAmL 92
**Bahn**, David Louis 1951- WhoRel 92
**Bahn**, Emil Lawrence, Jr 1924- AmMWSc 92
**Bahn**, Gilbert S 1922- AmMWSc 92
**Bahn**, Gilbert Schuyler 1922- WhoWest 92
**Bahn**, Robert Carlton 1925- AmMWSc 92
**Bahner**, Carl Tabb 1908- AmMWSc 92
**Bahner**, George Washington 1937- WhoRel 92
**Bahner**, Sue WhoEnt 92
**Bahner**, Thomas Maxfield 1933- WhoAmL 92
**Bahnfleth**, Donald R 1927- AmMWSc 92
**Bahnfleth**, Donald Robert 1927- WhoFI 92
**Bahnfleth**, William Parry 1957- WhoMW 92
**Bahng**, John Deuck Ryong 1927- AmMWSc 92
**Bahnini**, M'Hammed 1914- IntWW 91
**Bahniuk**, Eugene 1926- AmMWSc 92, WhoMW 92
**Bahns**, Mary AmMWSc 92
**Bahnsen**, Uwe 1930- DcTwDes
**Bahnson**, Agnew Hunter 1886-1966 DcNCBi 1
**Bahnson**, Frederic Fries 1876-1944 DcNCBi 1
**Bahnson**, Henry Theodore 1845-1917 DcNCBi 1
**Bahr**, Charles Chester 1958- AmMWSc 92
**Bahr**, Donald Walter 1927- AmMWSc 92
**Bahr**, Edward Richard 1941- WhoEnt 92
**Bahr**, Egon 1922- IntWW 91
**Bahr**, Ehrhard 1932- IntAu&W 91, WhoWest 92, WrDr 92
**Bahr**, Gustave Karl 1929- AmMWSc 92
**Bahr**, James Theodore 1942- AmMWSc 92
**Bahr**, Janice M AmMWSc 92
**Bahr**, Jerome 1909- WrDr 92
**Bahr**, Jolynn Perry 1966- WhoMW 92
**Bahr**, Karl Edward 1933- AmMWSc 92
**Bahr**, Kevin Michael 1955- WhoMW 92
**Bahr**, Leonard M, Jr 1940- AmMWSc 92
**Bahr**, Mel James 1945- WhoMW 92
**Bahr**, Richard Allen 1964- WhoMW 92
**Bahr**, Robert 1940- WrDr 92
**Bahr**, Sheila Kay 1956- WhoMW 92
**Bahr**, Thomas Gordon 1940- AmMWSc 92
**Bahr**, William Am End 1928- WhoFI 92
**Bahre**, Tom 1943- WhoAmP 91
**Bahti**, Mark Tomas 1950- WhoWest 92
**Bahus**, Karen Lizabeth 1953- WhoMW 92
**Bai Dongcai** 1949- IntWW 91
**Bai Hua** 1930- IntWW 91
**Bai Jiefu** 1921- IntWW 91
**Bai Jinian** 1926- IntWW 91
**Bai Lichen** 1941- IntWW 91
**Bai Rubing** 1912- IntWW 91
**Bai Shangwu** 1928- IntWW 91
**Bai Shouyi** 1909- IntWW 91
**Bai Xueshi** 1915- IntWW 91
**Bai Yang** 1920- IntWW 91
**Bai**, Hua 1930- IntAu&W 91
**Bai**, Zhi Dong 1943- AmMWSc 92
**Baiamonte**, Frank C. WhoIns 92
**Baiamonte**, Vernon D 1934- AmMWSc 92
**Baiardi**, John Charles 1918- AmMWSc 92
**Baich**, Annette 1930- AmMWSc 92, WhoMW 92
**Baide**, Maria EncAmaz 91
**Baiden**, Tim 1937- WhoMW 92
**Baidins**, Andrejs 1930- AmMWSc 92
**Baie**, Lyle Fredrick 1942- AmMWSc 92
**Baier**, George Patrick 1945- WhoAmL 92
**Baier**, John Christopher 1959- WhoWest 92
**Baier**, Joseph George 1908- AmMWSc 92
**Baier**, Robert Edward 1939- AmMWSc 92
**Baier**, William H 1922- AmMWSc 92
**Baier**, Wolfgang 1923- AmMWSc 92
**Baierbach**, William WhoEnt 92
**Baierlein**, Ralph Frederick 1936- AmMWSc 92
**Baig**, Mirza Mansoor 1942- AmMWSc 92
**Baigell**, Matthew 1933- IntAu&W 91, WrDr 92
**Baigent**, Beryl 1937- IntAu&W 91
**Baigi**, Marla Jean 1959- WhoMW 92
**Baik**, Hyo Whi 1942- WhoWest 92
**Bail**, Caroline 1953- WhoRel 92
**Bail**, Murray 1941- ConNov 91, WrDr 92
**Bail**, Richard Paul 1955- WhoFI 92
**Bailar**, Barbara Ann 1935- AmMWSc 92
**Bailar**, Benjamin Franklin 1934- IntWW 91
**Bailar**, John Christian, III 1932- AmMWSc 92
**Bailar**, John Christian, Jr 1904- AmMWSc 92
**Baildon**, John David 1943- AmMWSc 92
**Baile**, Clifton Augustus, III 1940- AmMWSc 92
**Bailer**, Bonnie Lynn 1946- WhoBlA 92
**Bailer**, Kermit Gamaliel 1921- WhoBlA 92
**Bailes Brothers** NewAmDM
**Bailes**, Alyson Judith Kirtley 1949- Who 92
**Bailes**, Dale Alan DrAPF 91
**Bailes**, George L, Jr WhoAmP 91
**Bailes**, Gordon Lee 1946- AmMWSc 92
**Bailes**, Margaret Johnson 1951- BlkOlyM
**Bailey** Who 92
**Bailey**, A. Peter 1938- WhoBlA 92
**Bailey**, A. V. 1921- WhoRel 92
**Bailey**, Adrienne Yvonne 1944- WhoBlA 92
**Bailey**, Agnes Jackson 1931- WhoBlA 92
**Bailey**, Alan 1931- Who 92
**Bailey**, Alan J. WhoEnt 92
**Bailey**, Alan Marshall 1931- IntWW 91
**Bailey**, Alex Stuart 1952- WhoWest 92
**Bailey**, Alfred Goldsworthy 1905- IntAu&W 91
**Bailey**, Alice LaTrobe Bateman 1880-1949 RelLAm 91
**Bailey**, Allen Jackson 1931- Who 92
**Bailey**, Amos Purnell 1918- WhoRel 92
**Bailey**, Angela 1962- BlkOlyM
**Bailey**, Ann 1936- WhoAmP 91
**Bailey**, Anne Penny Lee 1894-1975 RelLAm 91
**Bailey**, Annette Lee 1958- WhoFI 92
**Bailey**, Annie L 1918- WhoAmP 91
**Bailey**, Anthony 1933- WrDr 92
**Bailey**, Anthony Cowper 1933- IntAu&W 91
**Bailey**, Antoinette M. 1949- WhoBlA 92
**Bailey**, Arthur WhoBlA 92
**Bailey**, Arthur W 1938- AmMWSc 92
**Bailey**, Barbara J. 1942- WhoAmL 92
**Bailey**, Barry Dee 1954- WhoFI 92
**Bailey**, Benny Ray 1944- WhoAmP 91
**Bailey**, Bert Heald 1875-1917 BiInAmS
**Bailey**, Betty Jane 1931- WhoRel 92
**Bailey**, Bob Carl 1935- WhoBlA 92
**Bailey**, Brad Duane 1958- WhoAmL 92
**Bailey**, Brad Sterling 1959- WhoFI 92
**Bailey**, Brian 1923- Who 92
**Bailey**, Brian Dennis 1952- WhoWest 92
**Bailey**, Brian Lloyd 1958- WhoMW 92
**Bailey**, Bruce C. 1948- WhoAmL 92
**Bailey**, Bruce M 1928- AmMWSc 92
**Bailey**, Burck 1934- WhoAmL 92
**Bailey**, Buster 1902-1967 NewAmDM
**Bailey**, Byron James 1934- AmMWSc 92
**Bailey**, Calvin 1909- WhoBlA 92
**Bailey**, Calvin Dean 1955- WhoEnt 92
**Bailey**, Carl Franklin 1930- WhoFI 92
**Bailey**, Carl Leonard 1918- AmMWSc 92
**Bailey**, Carl Williams, III 1941- AmMWSc 92
**Bailey**, Carroll Edward 1940- AmMWSc 92
**Bailey**, Catherine Hayes 1921- AmMWSc 92
**Bailey**, Cecil 1907- TwCPaSc
**Bailey**, Cecil Dewitt 1921- AmMWSc 92
**Bailey**, Charles Basil Mansfield 1930- AmMWSc 92
**Bailey**, Charles Edward 1932- AmMWSc 92
**Bailey**, Charles Lavon 1942- AmMWSc 92
**Bailey**, Charles R 1929- WhoAmP 91
**Bailey**, Charles Stanley 1949- WhoFI 92
**Bailey**, Charles Waldo 1929- WrDr 92
**Bailey**, Charles Waldo, II 1929- IntAu&W 91
**Bailey**, Charles William 1932- WhoMW 92
**Bailey**, Chauncey Wendell, Jr. 1949- WhoBlA 92
**Bailey**, Chip 1944- WhoAmP 91
**Bailey**, Christopher Thomas 1835-1895 DcNCBi 1
**Bailey**, Clarence Walter 1933- WhoBlA 92
**Bailey**, Claudia F AmMWSc 92
**Bailey**, Clayton George 1939- WhoWest 92
**Bailey**, Cleta Sue 1945- AmMWSc 92
**Bailey**, Cliff WhoAmP 91
**Bailey**, Clover Thomasson 1952- WhoRel 92
**Bailey**, Curtis Darnell 1954- WhoBlA 92
**Bailey**, Curtiss Merkel 1927- AmMWSc 92
**Bailey**, D. R. Shackleton 1917- Who 92, WrDr 92
**Bailey**, Dana Kavanagh 1916- AmMWSc 92
**Bailey**, D'Army 1941- WhoBlA 92
**Bailey**, Daryl Wayne 1957- WhoAmL 92
**Bailey**, David 1938- IntWW 91, Who 92
**Bailey**, David Emmett 1942- WhoAmP 91
**Bailey**, David George 1940- AmMWSc 92
**Bailey**, David Nelson 1945- AmMWSc 92
**Bailey**, David Newton 1941- AmMWSc 92
**Bailey**, David R Shackleton 1917- IntAu&W 91, IntWW 91
**Bailey**, David Scott 1965- WhoMW 92
**Bailey**, David Tiffany 1942- AmMWSc 92
**Bailey**, DeFord 1899-1982 NewAmDM
**Bailey**, Denis Mahlon 1935- AmMWSc 92
**Bailey**, Dennis 1931- Who 92
**Bailey**, Derrick Thomas Louis 1918- Who 92
**Bailey**, Desmond Patrick 1907- Who 92
**Bailey**, Didi Giselle 1948- WhoBlA 92, WhoWest 92
**Bailey**, Don 1945- WhoAmP 91
**Bailey**, Donald Coleman 1901-1985 FacFETw
**Bailey**, Donald Etheridge 1931- AmMWSc 92
**Bailey**, Donald Forest 1939- AmMWSc 92
**Bailey**, Donald Leroy 1922- AmMWSc 92
**Bailey**, Donald Leroy 1939- AmMWSc 92
**Bailey**, Donald Wayne 1926- AmMWSc 92
**Bailey**, Donald Wycoff 1933- AmMWSc 92
**Bailey**, Donn Fritz 1932- WhoBlA 92
**Bailey**, Donna 1938- SmATA 68 [port]
**Bailey**, Donna Jean 1960- WhoMW 92
**Bailey**, Doris Adeline 1924- WhoRel 92
**Bailey**, Doug 1951- WhoAmP 91
**Bailey**, Douglas Kent 1949- WhoWest 92
**Bailey**, Duane W 1936- AmMWSc 92
**Bailey**, Dudley Graham 1924- Who 92
**Bailey**, Duwain 1957- WhoBlA 92
**Bailey**, Earl Eugene 1927- WhoRel 92
**Bailey**, Edward D 1931- AmMWSc 92
**Bailey**, Edward Hopkins 1939- WhoWest 92
**Bailey**, Elden C. WhoEnt 92
**Bailey**, Elizabeth Ellery 1938- WhoFI 92
**Bailey**, Emilie Kathryn 1946- WhoFI 92
**Bailey**, Emmanuel Franklin 1954- WhoRel 92
**Bailey**, Emmanuel McDonald 1920- BlkOlyM
**Bailey**, Eric 1913- Who 92
**Bailey**, Eugene Ridgeway 1938- WhoBlA 92

**Bailey,** Everett Murl, Jr 1940- *AmMWSc 92*
**Bailey,** Exine Margaret Anderson 1922- *WhoEnt 92*
**Bailey,** F Lee 1933- *FacFETw, WrDr 92*
**Bailey,** F Wallace 1929- *AmMWSc 92*
**Bailey,** Francis 1735?-1815 *BenetAL 91*
**Bailey,** Francis Lee 1933- *WhoAmL 92*
**Bailey,** Frank I, Jr *WhoAmP 91*
**Bailey,** Frank Kelton d1909 *BiInAmS*
**Bailey,** Fred Coolidge 1925- *AmMWSc 92*
**Bailey,** Frederick 1946- *ConAu 133*
**Bailey,** Frederick Eugene, Jr 1927- *AmMWSc 92, WhoFI 92*
**Bailey,** Frederick George 1924- *WrDr 92*
**Bailey,** Fredric L 1935- *WhoAmP 91*
**Bailey,** Fredric Nelson 1932- *AmMWSc 92*
**Bailey,** Garland Howard 1890- *AmMWSc 92*
**Bailey,** Gary Lewis 1944- *WhoMW 92*
**Bailey,** George Hampton 1937- *WhoAmP 91*
**Bailey,** George Rufus 1925- *WhoAmP 91*
**Bailey,** George Screven 1951- *WhoAmL 92*
**Bailey,** George William 1930- *AmMWSc 92*
**Bailey,** George William 1933- *AmMWSc 92*
**Bailey,** Gilbert E 1933- *WhoAmP 91*
**Bailey,** Glenn Charles 1930- *AmMWSc 92*
**Bailey,** Glenn E. 1954- *WhoRel 92*
**Bailey,** Glenn Ross 1929- *WhoRel 92*
**Bailey,** Glenn Waldemar 1925- *WhoFI 92*
**Bailey,** Gordon 1936- *IntAu&W 91, WrDr 92*
**Bailey,** Gordon Burgess 1934- *AmMWSc 92*
**Bailey,** Gracie Massenberg 1936- *WhoBlA 92*
**Bailey,** Guy Burdette, Jr. 1939- *WhoAmL 92*
**Bailey,** H. Barry 1926- *WhoRel 92*
**Bailey,** Hannah Clark Johnston 1839-1923 *AmPeW*
**Bailey,** Harley Evan 1915- *WhoAmP 91*
**Bailey,** Harold 1899- *Who 92*
**Bailey,** Harold 1914- *Who 92*
**Bailey,** Harold 1946- *WhoBlA 92*
**Bailey,** Harold Edwards 1906- *AmMWSc 92*
**Bailey,** Harold Stevens 1922- *AmMWSc 92*
**Bailey,** Harold Walter 1899- *IntWW 91*
**Bailey,** Harry *WhoAmP 91*
**Bailey,** Harry A., Jr. 1932- *WhoBlA 92*
**Bailey,** Harry Hudson 1921- *AmMWSc 92*
**Bailey,** Harvey Alan 1937- *WhoWest 92*
**Bailey,** Heather 1956- *WhoFI 92*
**Bailey,** Herbert R 1925- *AmMWSc 92*
**Bailey,** Howard Robert 1932- *WhoRel 92*
**Bailey,** Howland Haskell 1912- *WhoWest 92*
**Bailey,** Ian James 1957- *WhoWest 92*
**Bailey,** Ian L 1940- *AmMWSc 92*
**Bailey,** Irving Widmer, II 1941- *WhoFI 92*
**Bailey,** J Chalmers Da Costa 1931- *WhoAmP 91*
**Bailey,** J Earl 1933- *AmMWSc 92*
**Bailey,** J. Hugh 1936- *WhoIns 92*
**Bailey,** J. Lee 1942- *WhoMW 92*
**Bailey,** Jack d1979 *LesBEnT 92*
**Bailey,** Jack Arthur 1930- *Who 92*
**Bailey,** Jack Clinton 1936- *AmMWSc 92*
**Bailey,** Jack Moore, Jr. 1951- *WhoAmL 92*
**Bailey,** Jackson Holbrook 1925- *WhoMW 92*
**Bailey,** Jacob Whitman 1811-1857 *BiInAmS*
**Bailey,** Jacqueline 1961- *WhoBlA 92*
**Bailey,** James 1922- *TwCPaSc*
**Bailey,** James Allen 1934- *AmMWSc 92*
**Bailey,** James E 1944- *AmMWSc 92*
**Bailey,** James Edward 1942- *AmMWSc 92*
**Bailey,** James J 1944- *WhoAmP 91*
**Bailey,** James L 1930- *AmMWSc 92*
**Bailey,** James L. 1957- *WhoBlA 92*
**Bailey,** James M. 1841-1894 *BenetAL 91*
**Bailey,** James Martin 1929- *WhoRel 92*
**Bailey,** James Richard 1938- *WhoMW 92*
**Bailey,** James Russell 1935- *WhoIns 92*
**Bailey,** James Spencer 1830-1883 *BiInAmS*
**Bailey,** James Stephen 1942- *AmMWSc 92*
**Bailey,** James Stuart 1921- *AmMWSc 92*
**Bailey,** James W. 1922- *WhoBlA 92*
**Bailey,** Jane *DrAPF 91*
**Bailey,** Jerry Dean 1950- *WhoBlA 92*
**Bailey,** Jerry Wayne 1948- *WhoWest 92*
**Bailey,** Jewell R 1920- *WhoAmP 91*
**Bailey,** John *Who 92*
**Bailey,** John 1942- *IntMPA 92, WhoEnt 92*
**Bailey,** John Albert 1937- *AmMWSc 92*
**Bailey,** John Bilsland 1928- *Who 92*
**Bailey,** John Bryon 1959- *WhoFI 92*
**Bailey,** John Clark 1942- *AmMWSc 92*
**Bailey,** John Everett Creighton 1905- *Who 92*
**Bailey,** John M, III 1942- *WhoIns 92*
**Bailey,** John Martyn 1929- *AmMWSc 92*
**Bailey,** John Preston 1951- *WhoAmP 91*
**Bailey,** John Robert 1958- *WhoEnt 92*
**Bailey,** John Taylor 1958- *WhoWest 92*
**Bailey,** Jon Nelson 1954- *WhoRel 92*
**Bailey,** Jonathan Sansbury 1940- *Who 92*
**Bailey,** Joseph Alexander, II 1935- *WhoBlA 92*
**Bailey,** Joseph Randle 1913- *AmMWSc 92*
**Bailey,** Joseph T 1937- *AmMWSc 92*
**Bailey,** Josiah William 1873-1946 *DcNCBi 1*
**Bailey,** K. Ronald 1947- *WhoAmL 92*
**Bailey,** Keels Dale 1936- *WhoRel 92*
**Bailey,** Kenneth Elvin 1946- *WhoAmP 91*
**Bailey,** Kent Joseph 1956- *WhoWest 92*
**Bailey,** Kerry Douglas 1950- *WhoWest 92*
**Bailey,** Kevin E 1951- *WhoAmP 91*
**Bailey,** Kincheon Hubert, Jr 1921- *AmMWSc 92*
**Bailey,** Kristen 1952- *WhoMW 92*
**Bailey,** Larrie 1934- *WhoAmP 91*
**Bailey,** Lawrence R., Sr. 1918- *WhoBlA 92*
**Bailey,** Lawrence Randolph, Jr. 1949- *WhoAmL 92*
**Bailey,** Lawrence Randolph, Sr. 1918- *WhoFI 92*
**Bailey,** Lee 1926- *WrDr 92*
**Bailey,** Leo L 1922- *AmMWSc 92*
**Bailey,** Leonard Charles 1936- *AmMWSc 92*
**Bailey,** Leonard Lee 1942- *AmMWSc 92, WhoWest 92*
**Bailey,** Leslie Edgar 1931- *AmMWSc 92*
**Bailey,** Linda F. 1951- *WhoBlA 92*
**Bailey,** Loraine Dolar 1936- *AmMWSc 92*
**Bailey,** Louie Lee 1946- *WhoEnt 92*
**Bailey,** Lynn Bonnette 1948- *AmMWSc 92*
**Bailey,** Marcia Barnes 1961- *WhoRel 92*
**Bailey,** Marion Crawford 1937- *AmMWSc 92*
**Bailey,** Mark Leroy 1950- *WhoRel 92*
**Bailey,** Marolyn Leslie 1953- *WhoBlA 92*
**Bailey,** Marshall Lee 1927- *WhoAmP 91*
**Bailey,** Martha Clark *WhoFI 92*
**Bailey,** Martin 1947- *ConAu 134, IntAu&W 91*
**Bailey,** Martin Jean 1927- *WhoFI 92*
**Bailey,** Maurice Eugene 1916- *AmMWSc 92*
**Bailey,** Michael John 1953- *AmMWSc 92, WhoWest 92*
**Bailey,** Michael Keith 1956- *WhoAmL 92*
**Bailey,** Mildred 1907-1951 *NewAmDM*
**Bailey,** Mildred T. 1920- *WhoBlA 92*
**Bailey,** Milton 1917- *AmMWSc 92*
**Bailey,** Milton 1924- *AmMWSc 92*
**Bailey,** Mona Humphries 1932- *WhoBlA 92*
**Bailey,** Moreen Deloris 1957- *WhoEnt 92, WhoMW 92*
**Bailey,** Nan Parker 1955- *WhoFI 92*
**Bailey,** Nathan d1742 *BlkwCEP*
**Bailey,** Norman 1931- *WrDr 92*
**Bailey,** Norman Sprague 1912- *AmMWSc 92*
**Bailey,** Norman Stanley 1933- *IntWW 91, Who 92*
**Bailey,** Odessa 1941- *WhoEnt 92*
**Bailey,** Orville Taylor 1909- *AmMWSc 92*
**Bailey,** P. Diane 1966- *WhoWest 92*
**Bailey,** Patricia L 1936- *WhoAmP 91*
**Bailey,** Patricia Lawson 1944- *WhoFI 92*
**Bailey,** Patricia Price 1937- *WhoAmL 92*
**Bailey,** Patrick Edward Robert 1925- *Who 92*
**Bailey,** Paul 1937- *ConNov 91, IntAu&W 91, IntWW 91, Who 92, WrDr 92*
**Bailey,** Paul Townsend 1939- *AmMWSc 92*
**Bailey,** Pearl 1918-1990 *AnObit 1990, ConTFT 9, NewAmDM, News 91, NotBlAW 92 [port], WhoBlA 92N*
**Bailey,** Pearl Mae 1918-1990 *FacFETw [port]*
**Bailey,** Peter 1944- *TwCPaSc*
**Bailey,** Philip James 1816-1902 *RfGEnL 91*
**Bailey,** Philip Sigmon 1916- *AmMWSc 92*
**Bailey,** Phyllis Ann 1957- *WhoBlA 92*
**Bailey,** R L 1916- *AmMWSc 92*
**Bailey,** R. Richard 1953- *WhoRel 92*
**Bailey,** R V 1932- *AmMWSc 92*
**Bailey,** R Wendell 1940- *WhoAmP 91*
**Bailey,** Ralph E. 1924- *IntWW 91*
**Bailey,** Randall Charles 1947- *WhoBlA 92*
**Bailey,** Raymond H. *WhoRel 92*
**Bailey,** Raymond Victor 1923- *AmMWSc 92*
**Bailey,** Reginald Bertram 1916- *Who 92*
**Bailey,** Richard 1923- *Who 92*
**Bailey,** Richard Declan 1957- *WhoFI 92*
**Bailey,** Richard E. d1991 *NewYTBS 91*
**Bailey,** Richard Elmore 1929- *AmMWSc 92*
**Bailey,** Richard Hendricks 1946- *AmMWSc 92*
**Bailey,** Richard Williams 1933- *WhoAmL 92*
**Bailey,** Ricky E. 1959- *WhoAmL 92*
**Bailey,** Robert 1937- *WhoEnt 92*
**Bailey,** Robert, Jr. 1945- *WhoFI 92, WhoMW 92*
**Bailey,** Robert B., III 1929- *WhoBlA 92*
**Bailey,** Robert Brian 1950- *AmMWSc 92*
**Bailey,** Robert C. 1936- *WhoWest 92*
**Bailey,** Robert Clifton 1941- *AmMWSc 92*
**Bailey,** Robert David 1939- *WhoFI 92*
**Bailey,** Robert David 1951- *WhoRel 92*
**Bailey,** Robert Donald 1953- *WhoMW 92*
**Bailey,** Robert E 1931- *AmMWSc 92*
**Bailey,** Robert Elliott 1932- *WhoFI 92*
**Bailey,** Robert G. 1943- *WhoIns 92*
**Bailey,** Robert Greg 1954- *WhoAmL 92*
**Bailey,** Robert Laurence 1938- *WhoFI 92*
**Bailey,** Robert Leroy 1940- *AmMWSc 92*
**Bailey,** Robert Leslie 1945- *WhoRel 92*
**Bailey,** Robert Marshall 1954- *WhoAmL 92*
**Bailey,** Robert Ray 1938- *WhoEnt 92, WhoWest 92*
**Bailey,** Robert Short 1931- *WhoMW 92*
**Bailey,** Robert W. 1944- *WhoIns 92*
**Bailey,** Robin 1919- *IntMPA 92*
**Bailey,** Rodney Lawrence 1937- *WhoWest 92*
**Bailey,** Ronald Albert 1933- *AmMWSc 92*
**Bailey,** Ronald Bruce 1934- *WhoWest 92*
**Bailey,** Ronald C *WhoAmP 91*
**Bailey,** Ronald W. 1938- *WhoBlA 92*
**Bailey,** Ronald William 1917- *Who 92*
**Bailey,** Roy Alden 1929- *AmMWSc 92*
**Bailey,** Roy Horton, Jr 1921- *AmMWSc 92*
**Bailey,** Ruth Hill 1916- *WhoRel 92*
**Bailey,** Ryburn H. 1929- *WhoIns 92*
**Bailey,** Samuel David 1915- *AmMWSc 92*
**Bailey,** Scott Field 1916- *WhoRel 92*
**Bailey,** Shelby Jean 1947- *WhoRel 92*
**Bailey,** Stacey Dwayne 1960- *WhoBlA 92*
**Bailey,** Stanley 1926- *Who 92*
**Bailey,** Steven Scott 1948- *WhoWest 92*
**Bailey,** Sturges Williams 1919- *AmMWSc 92*
**Bailey,** Susan Goodman 1940- *AmMWSc 92*
**Bailey,** T Wayne 1935- *WhoAmP 91*
**Bailey,** Ted Edward 1950- *WhoMW 92*
**Bailey,** Temple 187-?-1953 *BenetAL 91*
**Bailey,** Thomas *WhoAmP 91*
**Bailey,** Thomas Aubrey 1912- *Who 92*
**Bailey,** Thomas Daniel 1945- *AmMWSc 92*
**Bailey,** Thomas Everett 1936- *WhoWest 92*
**Bailey,** Thomas L, III 1923- *AmMWSc 92*
**Bailey,** Thomas Morgan, Jr. 1927- *WhoIns 92*
**Bailey,** Thurl 1961- *WhoBlA 92*
**Bailey,** Velma Neal 1938- *WhoAmL 92*
**Bailey,** Vernon Leslie, Jr 1941- *AmMWSc 92*
**Bailey,** Virginia Hurt 1937- *WhoWest 92*
**Bailey,** Wayne L 1942- *AmMWSc 92*
**Bailey,** Weltman D., Sr. 1927- *WhoBlA 92*
**Bailey,** Wendell 1940- *WhoMW 92*
**Bailey,** Wilford Sherrill 1921- *AmMWSc 92*
**Bailey,** Wilfrid 1910- *Who 92*
**Bailey,** William 1948- *WhoAmP 91*
**Bailey,** William Alvin 1934- *WhoMW 92*
**Bailey,** William C 1939- *AmMWSc 92*
**Bailey,** William Charles 1939- *AmMWSc 92*
**Bailey,** William Francis 1946- *AmMWSc 92*
**Bailey,** William Gene 1939- *WhoMW 92*
**Bailey,** William H. 1927- *WhoBlA 92*
**Bailey,** William Henry 1831-1925 *DcNCBi 1*
**Bailey,** William John 1921- *AmMWSc 92*
**Bailey,** William John 1940- *Who 92*
**Bailey,** William O. 1926- *WhoFI 92*
**Bailey,** William R. 1935- *WhoBlA 92*
**Bailey,** William T 1936- *AmMWSc 92*
**Bailey,** William Whitman 1848-1914 *BiInAmS*
**Bailey,** William Wilder 1953- *WhoEnt 92*
**Bailey,** Zeno Earl 1921- *AmMWSc 92*
**Bailey-Bok,** Sharon Lee 1949- *WhoMW 92*
**Bailey-Brock,** Julie Helen *AmMWSc 92*
**Bailey-Serres,** Julia 1958- *AmMWSc 92*
**Bailhache,** Philip Martin 1946- *Who 92*
**Bailhe,** Jacques Pierre 1952- *WhoWest 92*
**Bailie,** Michael David 1936- *AmMWSc 92*
**Bailie,** Richard Colsten 1928- *AmMWSc 92*
**Bailie,** Robin John 1937- *Who 92*
**Bailie,** Wayne E 1932- *AmMWSc 92*
**Bailin,** Gary 1936- *AmMWSc 92*
**Bailin,** George *DrAPF 91*
**Bailin,** Lionel J 1928- *AmMWSc 92*
**Bailit,** Howard L 1937- *AmMWSc 92*
**Baillargeon,** Victor Paul 1958- *AmMWSc 92*
**Baille,** Baptiste 1841-1918 *ThHEIm*
**Baillie** *Who 92*
**Baillie,** Alastair Turner 1932- *IntWW 91, Who 92*
**Baillie,** Allan Stuart 1943- *IntAu&W 91*
**Baillie,** Andrew Dollar 1912- *AmMWSc 92*
**Baillie,** Bruce 1931- *IntDcF 2-2*
**Baillie,** Donald Chesley 1915- *AmMWSc 92*
**Baillie,** Gawaine George Hope 1934- *Who 92*
**Baillie,** Ian Fowler 1921- *Who 92*
**Baillie,** James Leonard 1942- *WhoAmL 92*
**Baillie,** Joanna 1762-1851 *RfGEnL 91*
**Baillie,** John 1944- *Who 92*
**Baillie,** Patricia Ann 1952- *WhoWest 92*
**Baillie,** Priscilla Woods 1935- *AmMWSc 92*
**Baillie,** Thomas Allan 1948- *AmMWSc 92*
**Baillie,** William 1923- *TwCPaSc*
**Baillie,** William James Laidlaw 1923- *Who 92*
**Baillie-Hamilton** *Who 92*
**Baillie-Scott,** Mackay Hugh 1865-1945 *DcTwDes, FacFETw*
**Baillieu** *Who 92*
**Baillieu,** Baron 1950- *Who 92*
**Baillieu,** Colin Clive 1930- *Who 92*
**Baillod,** Charles Robert 1941- *AmMWSc 92*
**Bailly,** Jean Paul Marie Henri 1921- *IntWW 91*
**Bailly,** Paul Alain 1926- *WhoWest 92*
**Bailly,** Richard Craig 1944- *WhoMW 92*
**Bailon,** Gilbert Herculano 1959- *WhoHisp 92*
**Bailon,** Roberto 1938- *WhoHisp 92*
**Baily,** Douglas B 1937- *WhoAmP 91*
**Baily,** Douglas Boyd 1937- *WhoAmL 92, WhoWest 92*
**Baily,** Dykeman Waldron 1871-1953 *DcNCBi 1*
**Baily,** Everett M 1938- *AmMWSc 92*
**Baily,** Everett Minnich 1938- *WhoWest 92*
**Baily,** John T. 1944- *WhoIns 92*
**Baily,** Nathan A. 1920- *WrDr 92*
**Baily,** Norman Arthur 1915- *AmMWSc 92*
**Baily,** Walter Lewis, Jr 1930- *AmMWSc 92*
**Bailyn,** Bernard 1922- *IntAu&W 91, IntWW 91, WrDr 92*
**Bailyn,** Martin H 1928- *AmMWSc 92*
**Bain,** Andrew David 1936- *Who 92*
**Bain,** Barbara *WhoEnt 92*
**Bain,** Barbara 1932- *AmMWSc 92*
**Bain,** Brian Andrew 1968- *WhoEnt 92*
**Bain,** Bruce Alan 1957- *WhoFI 92*
**Bain,** C. Randall 1934- *WhoAmL 92*
**Bain,** Charles Robert 1926- *WhoAmP 91*
**Bain,** Clinton Dwight 1960- *WhoRel 92*
**Bain,** Conrad Stafford 1923- *WhoEnt 92*
**Bain,** Donald 1904-1979 *TwCPaSc*
**Bain,** Donald Knight 1935- *WhoAmL 92*
**Bain,** Donald William 1841-1892 *DcNCBi 1*
**Bain,** Douglas Cogburn, Jr. 1940- *WhoRel 92*
**Bain,** Douglas John 1924- *Who 92*
**Bain,** Erlin 1950- *WhoBlA 92*
**Bain,** George Sayers 1939- *Who 92*
**Bain,** Gordon Orville 1926- *AmMWSc 92*
**Bain,** Iain Andrew 1949- *Who 92*
**Bain,** James Arthur 1918- *AmMWSc 92*
**Bain,** Jeff *WrDr 92*
**Bain,** John Taylor 1912- *Who 92*
**Bain,** Josie Gray *WhoBlA 92*
**Bain,** Kenneth 1923- *WrDr 92*
**Bain,** Lawrence David 1950- *WhoMW 92*
**Bain,** Lee J 1939- *AmMWSc 92*
**Bain,** Linda Valerie 1947- *WhoBlA 92, WhoFI 92*
**Bain,** Margaret Anne *Who 92*
**Bain,** Mary Anderson 1911- *WhoAmP 91*
**Bain,** Neville Clifford 1940- *Who 92*
**Bain,** Patricia Money 1942- *WhoRel 92*
**Bain,** Ralph Ben, Jr. 1968- *WhoWest 92*
**Bain,** Raymone Kaye 1954- *WhoBlA 92*
**Bain,** Roger J 1940- *AmMWSc 92*
**Bain,** Samuel McCutchen 1869-1914 *BiInAmS*
**Bain,** Ted *TwCSFW 91*
**Bain,** Travis Whitsett, II 1934- *WhoFI 92*
**Bain,** Walt 1932- *WhoAmP 91*
**Bain,** William Murray 1928- *AmMWSc 92*
**Bainborough,** Arthur Raymond 1918- *AmMWSc 92*
**Bainbridge,** Beryl 1934- *ConNov 91, IntAu&W 91, IntWW 91, Who 92, WrDr 92*
**Bainbridge,** Cyril 1928- *Who 92*
**Bainbridge,** Dennis Ray 1945- *WhoIns 92*
**Bainbridge,** Eric 1955- *TwCPaSc*
**Bainbridge,** Henry 1903- *Who 92*
**Bainbridge,** John 1913- *WrDr 92*
**Bainbridge,** John 1918-1978 *TwCPaSc*
**Bainbridge,** John Seaman 1915- *WhoAmL 92*
**Bainbridge,** Kenneth Tompkins 1904- *AmMWSc 92, IntWW 91*

**Bainbridge,** Russell Benjamin, Jr. 1945- *WhoFI 92*
**Bainbridge,** Simon 1952- *ConCom 92*
**Bainbridge,** Stephen Mark 1958- *WhoAmL 92*
**Bainbridge,** William L. 1945- *WhoMW 92*
**Baine,** Herman 1940- *WhoBlA 92*
**Baine,** James Everitt 1941- *WhoAmL 92, WhoFI 92*
**Baine,** John Stephen 1947- *WhoFI 92*
**Baine,** William Brennan 1945- *AmMWSc 92*
**Bainer,** Roy 1902- *AmMWSc 92*
**Baines,** A D 1934- *AmMWSc 92*
**Baines,** Anthony Cuthbert 1912- *Who 92*
**Baines,** Clare *TwCPaSc*
**Baines,** Elaine M. 1959- *WhoEnt 92*
**Baines,** George G. *Who 92*
**Baines,** Harold Douglas 1959- *WhoBlA 92*
**Baines,** John Robert 1946- *Who 92*
**Baines,** Kim Marie 1960- *AmMWSc 92*
**Baines,** Ruth Etta *AmMWSc 92*
**Baines,** Tyrone Randolph 1943- *WhoBlA 92*
**Baines,** William Douglas 1926- *AmMWSc 92*
**Bains,** Harrison MacKellar, Jr. 1943- *WhoFI 92*
**Bains,** Lawrence Arthur 1920- *Who 92*
**Bains,** Leslie Elizabeth 1943- *WhoFI 92*
**Bains,** Malcolm Arnold 1921- *Who 92*
**Bains,** Malkiat Singh 1932- *AmMWSc 92*
**Bainter,** M Juanita 1919- *WhoAmP 91*
**Bainter,** Stan 1931- *WhoAmP 91*
**Bainter,** Thomas Nolan 1957- *WhoMW 92*
**Bainton,** Cedric R *AmMWSc 92*
**Bainton,** Denise Marlene 1949- *WhoAmL 92*
**Bainton,** Donald J. 1931- *WhoFI 92*
**Bainton,** Dorothy Ford 1933- *AmMWSc 92, WhoWest 92*
**Bainton,** John Joseph 1947- *WhoAmL 92*
**Bainum,** Duke *WhoAmP 91*
**Bainum,** Peter Montgomery 1938- *AmMWSc 92*
**Bainum,** Stewart 1919- *WhoFI 92*
**Bainum,** Stewart, Jr 1946- *WhoAmP 91*
**Bainville,** Jacques 1879-1936 *BiDExR*
**Baio,** Scott 1961- *IntMPA 92, WhoEnt 92*
**Bair,** Anna Withers 1916- *WhoEnt 92*
**Bair,** Bruce B. 1928- *WhoAmL 92*
**Bair,** Dale Leroy 1926- *WhoRel 92*
**Bair,** Deirdre 1935- *WrDr 92*
**Bair,** Edward Jay 1922- *AmMWSc 92*
**Bair,** Harvey Edward 1936- *AmMWSc 92*
**Bair,** Joe Keagy 1918- *AmMWSc 92*
**Bair,** Kenneth Walter 1948- *AmMWSc 92*
**Bair,** Myrna Lynn 1940- *WhoAmP 91*
**Bair,** Sheldon Eugene 1954- *WhoEnt 92*
**Bair,** Thomas De Pinna 1922- *AmMWSc 92*
**Bair,** Thomas Irvin 1938- *AmMWSc 92*
**Bair,** William J 1924- *AmMWSc 92*
**Baird,** Alan C. 1951- *WhoEnt 92, WhoWest 92*
**Baird,** Albert Washington, III 1940- *WhoRel 92*
**Baird,** Alfred Michael 1948- *AmMWSc 92*
**Baird,** Ansie *DrAPF 91*
**Baird,** Anthony *Who 92*
**Baird,** Barbara A 1951- *AmMWSc 92*
**Baird,** Bill 1904-1987 *FacFETw*
**Baird,** Brian David 1963- *WhoAmL 92*
**Baird,** Charles Bruce 1935- *WhoAmL 92*
**Baird,** Charles Fitz 1922- *Who 92, WhoFI 92*
**Baird,** Charles Henry 1938- *WhoMW 92*
**Baird,** Charles Robert 1935- *AmMWSc 92*
**Baird,** Clay P *WhoAmP 91*
**Baird,** Craig Riska 1939- *AmMWSc 92*
**Baird,** D C 1928- *AmMWSc 92*
**Baird,** David Charles 1912- *Who 92*
**Baird,** David George 1963- *WhoWest 92*
**Baird,** David Leach, Jr. 1945- *WhoFI 92*
**Baird,** David Tennent 1935- *Who 92*
**Baird,** Delpha A 1930- *WhoAmP 91*
**Baird,** Donald 1926- *AmMWSc 92*
**Baird,** Donald George 1946- *WhoRel 92*
**Baird,** Donald Heston 1921- *AmMWSc 92*
**Baird,** Douglas Gordon 1953- *WhoAmL 92*
**Baird,** Douglas James 1962- *WhoFI 92*
**Baird,** Dugald Euan 1937- *IntWW 91, WhoFI 92*
**Baird,** Edward 1904-1949 *TwCPaSc*
**Baird,** Eric Anthony 1920- *Who 92*
**Baird,** Gordon Cardwell 1946- *AmMWSc 92*
**Baird,** Harry Russell 1918- *WhoRel 92*
**Baird,** Henry W, III 1922- *AmMWSc 92*
**Baird,** Henry Welles 1952- *WhoFI 92*
**Baird,** Herbert Wallace 1936- *AmMWSc 92*
**Baird,** Jack R 1931- *AmMWSc 92*
**Baird,** Jack Vernon 1928- *AmMWSc 92*
**Baird,** James 1915- *Who 92*
**Baird,** James Clyde 1931- *AmMWSc 92*
**Baird,** James Hewson 1944- *Who 92*
**Baird,** James Kenneth 1951- *WhoEnt 92*
**Baird,** James Kern 1941- *AmMWSc 92*
**Baird,** James Leroy, Jr 1934- *AmMWSc 92*
**Baird,** James Richard Gardiner 1913- *Who 92*
**Baird,** John Charlton 1938- *IntAu&W 91*
**Baird,** John Jeffers 1921- *AmMWSc 92*
**Baird,** John Logie d1946 *LesBEnT 92*
**Baird,** John Logie 1888-1946 *FacFETw*
**Baird,** John Wallace 1873-1919 *BiInAmS*
**Baird,** Joseph Arthur 1922- *WhoRel 92*
**Baird,** Joyce Elizabeth Leslie 1929- *Who 92*
**Baird,** Julian William 1859-1911 *BiInAmS*
**Baird,** Keith E. 1923- *WhoBlA 92*
**Baird,** Kenneth MacClure 1923- *AmMWSc 92*
**Baird,** Kenneth William 1950- *Who 92*
**Baird,** Larry Don 1949- *WhoRel 92*
**Baird,** Lourdes G. *WhoAmL 92*
**Baird,** Lourdes G. 1935- *WhoHisp 92*
**Baird,** Malcolm Barry 1943- *AmMWSc 92*
**Baird,** Malcolm Henry Inglis 1935- *AmMWSc 92*
**Baird,** Mark Stephen 1962- *WhoEnt 92*
**Baird,** Merton Denison 1940- *AmMWSc 92*
**Baird,** Michael 1929- *TwCPaSc*
**Baird,** Michael 1945- *WhoEnt 92*
**Baird,** Michael Jefferson 1939- *AmMWSc 92*
**Baird,** Norman Colin 1942- *AmMWSc 92*
**Baird,** Patricia A *AmMWSc 92*
**Baird,** Paul Theodore 1944- *WhoAmP 91*
**Baird,** Quincey Lamar 1932- *AmMWSc 92*
**Baird,** Ramon Condie 1929- *AmMWSc 92*
**Baird,** Randy Michael 1955- *WhoRel 92*
**Baird,** Richard Leroy 1931- *AmMWSc 92*
**Baird,** Robert Dahlen 1933- *WhoMW 92, WhoRel 92*
**Baird,** Robert Dean 1933- *WhoRel 92*
**Baird,** Robert R. 1929- *WhoIns 92*
**Baird,** Ronald 1930- *Who 92*
**Baird,** Ronald C 1936- *AmMWSc 92*
**Baird,** Ronald James 1930- *AmMWSc 92*
**Baird,** Russell Miller 1916- *WhoAmL 92*
**Baird,** Russell N. 1922- *WrDr 92*
**Baird,** Russell Norman 1922- *IntAu&W 91*
**Baird,** Spencer Fullerton 1823-1887 *BiInAmS*
**Baird,** Stacy Avery 1958- *WhoEnt 92*
**Baird,** Susan 1940- *Who 92*
**Baird,** Tadeusz 1928-1981 *NewAmDM*
**Baird,** Thomas 1924- *Who 92*
**Baird,** Thomas Bryan, Jr. 1931- *WhoAmL 92*
**Baird,** Thomas Joseph 1958- *WhoFI 92*
**Baird,** Thomas Terence 1916- *Who 92*
**Baird,** Troy Alan 1954- *AmMWSc 92*
**Baird,** W. Blake 1960- *WhoFI 92*
**Baird,** William 1927- *Who 92*
**Baird,** William C, Jr 1933- *AmMWSc 92*
**Baird,** William McKenzie 1944- *AmMWSc 92, WhoMW 92*
**Baird,** William Robb 1924- *WhoRel 92*
**Baird,** Zoe 1952- *WhoAmL 92, WhoFI 92*
**Bairsto,** Peter 1926- *Who 92*
**Bairstow,** John 1930- *Who 92*
**Bairstow,** Lynne Rae 1959- *WhoFI 92*
**Bairstow,** Richard Raymond 1917- *WhoAmL 92*
**Baisch,** Steven Dale 1955- *WhoMW 92*
**Baisden,** Charles Robert 1939- *AmMWSc 92*
**Baisden,** Eleanor Marguerite 1935- *WhoFI 92, WhoMW 92*
**Baisden,** Patricia Ann 1949- *AmMWSc 92*
**Baish,** James William 1957- *AmMWSc 92*
**Baisley,** Charles William 1930- *WhoAmL 92*
**Baisley,** James Mahoney 1932- *WhoAmL 92*
**Baisley,** Robert William 1923- *WhoEnt 92*
**Baisted,** Derek John 1934- *AmMWSc 92*
**Baitinger,** William F, Jr 1935- *AmMWSc 92*
**Baity,** Alton Philip 1950- *WhoAmL 92*
**Baity,** Gail Owens 1952- *WhoBlA 92*
**Baity,** Herman Glenn 1895-1975 *DcNCBi 1*
**Baity,** Isaiah, Jr. 1955- *WhoEnt 92*
**Baity,** John Cooley 1933- *WhoAmL 92*
**Baitz,** Jon Robin 1961- *ConAu 134*
**Baizan,** Gabriel *WhoHisp 92*
**Baize,** Timothy Brent 1944- *WhoEnt 92*
**Baizer,** Eric *DrAPF 91*
**Baizer,** Joan Susan 1946- *AmMWSc 92*
**Baj,** Enrico 1924- *FacFETw*
**Bajaj,** Jagmohan 1954- *AmMWSc 92*
**Bajaj,** Prem Nath 1932- *AmMWSc 92*
**Bajaj,** Rahul 1938- *IntWW 91*
**Bajaj,** Ram 1946- *AmMWSc 92*
**Bajaj,** Ramkrishna 1923- *IntWW 91*
**Bajaj,** S Paul 1946- *AmMWSc 92*
**Bajars,** Laimonis 1908- *AmMWSc 92*
**Bajcsy,** Ruzena K 1933- *AmMWSc 92*
**Bajema,** Carl J 1937- *AmMWSc 92*
**Bajer,** Andrew 1928- *AmMWSc 92*
**Bajer,** Frederik 1837-1922 *FacFETw*
**Bajer,** Fredrik 1837-1922 *WhoNob 90*
**Bajikar,** Sateesh S 1965- *AmMWSc 92*
**Bajoie,** Diana E 1948- *WhoAmP 91*
**Bajor,** James Henry 1953- *WhoEnt 92, WhoMW 92*
**Bajorek,** Christopher Henry 1943- *AmMWSc 92*
**Bajos,** Orlando L. *WhoHisp 92*
**Bajpai,** Praphulla K 1936- *AmMWSc 92*
**Bajpai,** Rajendra Kumari 1925- *IntWW 91*
**Bajpai,** Rakesh Kumar 1950- *AmMWSc 92*
**Bajt,** Aleksander 1921- *IntWW 91*
**Bajwa,** Wajeeh 1952- *WhoMW 92*
**Bajzak,** Denes 1933- *AmMWSc 92*
**Bajzer,** William Xavier 1940- *AmMWSc 92*
**Bak,** Chan Soo 1936- *AmMWSc 92*
**Bak,** David Arthur 1939- *AmMWSc 92*
**Bak,** Mary Magnuson 1953- *WhoAmL 92*
**Bak,** Michael Joe 1962- *WhoRel 92*
**Bak,** Per 1947- *AmMWSc 92*
**Baka,** Wladyslaw 1936- *IntWW 91*
**Bakac,** Andreja *AmMWSc 92*
**Bakal,** Abraham I 1936- *AmMWSc 92*
**Bakaletz,** Lauren Opremcak 1957- *WhoMW 92*
**Bakaly,** Charles G, Jr 1927- *WhoAmP 91*
**Bakaly,** Charles George, Jr. 1927- *WhoAmL 92*
**Bakane,** John Louis 1951- *WhoFI 92*
**Bakanowski,** Stephen Michael 1945- *AmMWSc 92*
**Bakatin,** Vadim Viktorovich 1937- *IntWW 91, SovUnBD*
**Bakay,** Louis 1917- *AmMWSc 92*
**Bakelman,** Ilya J 1928- *AmMWSc 92*
**Bakels,** Kees *WhoEnt 92*
**Bakely,** Donald Carlisle 1928- *WhoRel 92*
**Bakeman,** Carol Ann 1934- *WhoWest 92*
**Bakemeier,** Robert Farnum 1957- *WhoAmL 92*
**Baker,** A Leroy 1939- *AmMWSc 92*
**Baker,** Adelaide N. 1894-1974 *ConAu 134*
**Baker,** Adolph 1917- *AmMWSc 92*
**Baker,** Al 1956- *WhoBlA 92*
**Baker,** Alan 1939- *IntWW 91, Who 92, WrDr 92*
**Baker,** Alan Gardner 1947- *AmMWSc 92*
**Baker,** Alan Paul 1938- *AmMWSc 92*
**Baker,** Alex Anthony 1922- *Who 92*
**Baker,** Alexander Shelley 1915- *Who 92*
**Baker,** Allan Ivor 1908- *Who 92*
**Baker,** Allen Jerome 1936- *AmMWSc 92*
**Baker,** Almina Rogers 1923- *WhoAmP 91*
**Baker,** Alton Fletcher, Jr. 1919- *WhoWest 92*
**Baker,** Andrew Eliot 1949- *WhoRel 92*
**Baker,** Andrew Hartill 1948- *WhoFI 92*
**Baker,** Andrew Newton, Jr 1928- *AmMWSc 92*
**Baker,** Andrew Zachariah 1919- *WhoAmP 91*
**Baker,** Anita 1958- *WhoBlA 92*
**Baker,** Anita Diane 1955- *WhoAmL 92, WhoFI 92*
**Baker,** Ann Maureen *Who 92*
**Baker,** Anthony Baxter 1923- *Who 92*
**Baker,** Anthony Castelli 1921- *Who 92*
**Baker,** Archibald 1812-1878 *DcNCBi 1*
**Baker,** Arnold Barry 1946- *WhoFI 92*
**Baker,** Arthur A 1897- *AmMWSc 92*
**Baker,** Arthur John 1928- *Who 92*
**Baker,** Arthur John 1942- *WhoMW 92*
**Baker,** Augusta 1911- *NotBlAW 92 [port]*
**Baker,** Avery Dean 1935- *WhoIns 92*
**Baker,** Barry *WhoEnt 92*
**Baker,** Bart 1915- *WhoAmP 91*
**Baker,** Barton 1901- *WhoAmL 92*
**Baker,** Barton Scofield 1941- *AmMWSc 92*
**Baker,** Benjamin Franklin 1811-1889 *NewAmDM*
**Baker,** Benjamin Joseph 1954- *WhoAmL 92*
**Baker,** Bernard Ray 1932- *AmMWSc 92*
**Baker,** Bernard S 1936- *AmMWSc 92*
**Baker,** Betty 1928- *IntAu&W 91*
**Baker,** Beverly Poole 1944- *WhoBlA 92*
**Baker,** Billy Ross 1937- *WhoRel 92*
**Baker,** Blake 1730?-1769 *DcNCBi 1*
**Baker,** Blake, Jr. 1755?-1818 *DcNCBi 1*
**Baker,** Blanche 1956- *IntMPA 92*
**Baker,** Bonnie Ann 1946- *WhoFI 92*
**Baker,** Boyd Odell 1961- *WhoAmP 91*
**Baker,** Brenda Sue 1948- *AmMWSc 92*
**Baker,** Brian Courtney 1944- *WhoFI 92*
**Baker,** Brian Reed 1949- *WhoWest 92*
**Baker,** Bridget Downey 1955- *WhoWest 92*
**Baker,** Bruce Allen 1938- *WhoFI 92*
**Baker,** Bruce Frederick 1930- *WhoFI 92*
**Baker,** Bruce J. 1954- *WhoAmL 92*
**Baker,** Bruce Jay 1954- *WhoAmL 92, WhoMW 92*
**Baker,** Bruce Lee 1958- *WhoRel 92*
**Baker,** Bryan, Jr 1923- *AmMWSc 92*
**Baker,** C. Edwin 1947- *WhoAmL 92*
**Baker,** C.J. *ConAu 135*
**Baker,** C Ray *WhoAmP 91*
**Baker,** Calvin Daniel, Jr. 1949- *WhoAmL 92*
**Baker,** Cameron 1937- *WhoAmL 92, WhoFI 92*
**Baker,** Carl Gwin 1920- *AmMWSc 92*
**Baker,** Carl Leroy 1943- *WhoFI 92*
**Baker,** Carl TenEyck 1951- *WhoAmL 92*
**Baker,** Carleton Harold 1930- *AmMWSc 92*
**Baker,** Carol *DrAPF 91*
**Baker,** Carroll 1931- *IntAu&W 91, IntMPA 92, IntWW 91, WhoEnt 92*
**Baker,** Cary Scott 1955- *WhoEnt 92*
**Baker,** Cecil John 1915- *Who 92*
**Baker,** Charles A. *Who 92*
**Baker,** Charles Adams d1991 *NewYTBS 91*
**Baker,** Charles DeWitt 1932- *WhoWest 92*
**Baker,** Charles Duane *WhoAmP 91*
**Baker,** Charles Edward 1931- *AmMWSc 92*
**Baker,** Charles Ernest 1946- *WhoFI 92*
**Baker,** Charles Gordan 1944- *WhoMW 92*
**Baker,** Charles Henry Collins 1880-1959 *TwCPaSc*
**Baker,** Charles Lynn 1934- *WhoFI 92*
**Baker,** Charles Michael 1948- *WhoFI 92*
**Baker,** Charles Michael 1961- *WhoMW 92*
**Baker,** Charles P 1910- *AmMWSc 92*
**Baker,** Charles Ray 1932- *AmMWSc 92*
**Baker,** Charles Taft 1939- *AmMWSc 92*
**Baker,** Charles Wayne 1940- *WhoAmL 92, WhoAmP 91*
**Baker,** Charles Wesley 1945- *AmMWSc 92*
**Baker,** Charlotte 1954- *TwCPaSc*
**Baker,** Chester Bird 1918- *WhoFI 92*
**Baker,** Chet 1929-1988 *FacFETw, NewAmDM*
**Baker,** Chris 1944- *TwCPaSc*
**Baker,** Christopher John 1948- *ConAu 135, WrDr 92*
**Baker,** Christopher Paul 1938- *Who 92*
**Baker,** Christopher Perry 1952- *WhoFI 92*
**Baker,** Claire Anne 1943- *WhoMW 92*
**Baker,** Clarence Albert, Sr. 1919- *WhoFI 92, WhoMW 92*
**Baker,** Claude Douglas 1944- *WhoMW 92*
**Baker,** Clifford Howard 1932- *WhoFI 92*
**Baker,** Cosette Marlyn 1933- *WhoRel 92*
**Baker,** D B 1920- *AmMWSc 92*
**Baker,** D James 1937- *AmMWSc 92*
**Baker,** Dale E 1930- *AmMWSc 92*
**Baker,** Danial Edwin 1955- *WhoWest 92*
**Baker,** Daniel Alex 1957- *WhoMW 92*
**Baker,** Daniel Neal 1948- *AmMWSc 92*
**Baker,** Daniel Richard 1932- *WhoFI 92*
**Baker,** Darrell F. 1926- *WhoWest 92*
**Baker,** Darrius Gene 1946- *WhoIns 92*
**Baker,** Darryl Brent 1955- *WhoBlA 92*
**Baker,** Dave E. 1943- *WhoBlA 92*
**Baker,** David *DrAPF 91*
**Baker,** David 1931- *NewAmDM*
**Baker,** David A 1954- *IntAu&W 91*
**Baker,** David Bruce 1936- *AmMWSc 92*
**Baker,** David Duane 1958- *WhoMW 92*
**Baker,** David E. 1934- *WhoRel 92*
**Baker,** David H 1925- *AmMWSc 92*
**Baker,** David H 1939- *AmMWSc 92*
**Baker,** David Harris 1955- *WhoAmL 92*
**Baker,** David Kenneth 1923- *AmMWSc 92*
**Baker,** David Nathaniel, Jr. 1931- *WhoBlA 92*
**Baker,** David Remember 1932- *WhoAmL 92, WhoFI 92*
**Baker,** David Scott 1946- *WhoWest 92*
**Baker,** David Thomas 1925- *AmMWSc 92*
**Baker,** David Warren 1939- *AmMWSc 92*
**Baker,** Deborah Ann 1956- *WhoWest 92*
**Baker,** Delbert Wayne 1953- *WhoBlA 92*
**Baker,** Dennis John 1940- *AmMWSc 92*
**Baker,** Dennis Newton 1944- *WhoRel 92*
**Baker,** Denys Marie 1948- *WhoWest 92*
**Baker,** Derek *Who 92*
**Baker,** Dexter Farrington 1927- *WhoFI 92*
**Baker,** Diane *WhoEnt 92*
**Baker,** Diane 1938- *IntMPA 92*
**Baker,** Don 1931- *IntMPA 92*
**Baker,** Don G. 1934- *WhoMW 92*
**Baker,** Don H, Jr 1924- *AmMWSc 92*
**Baker,** Don M. 1932- *WhoIns 92*
**Baker,** Don R. 1948- *WhoEnt 92*
**Baker,** Don Robert 1933- *AmMWSc 92, WhoWest 92*
**Baker,** Donald 1929- *WhoAmL 92*
**Baker,** Donald Brien 1939- *WhoFI 92*
**Baker,** Donald Edward 1944- *WhoFI 92*
**Baker,** Donald Gardner 1923- *AmMWSc 92*
**Baker,** Donald Granville 1924- *AmMWSc 92*
**Baker,** Donald Matthew 1925- *WhoAmP 91*
**Baker,** Donald Roy 1927- *AmMWSc 92*
**Baker,** Donald W. *DrAPF 91*
**Baker,** Donna Anne 1939- *IntAu&W 91*
**Baker,** Doris 1921- *AmMWSc 92*
**Baker,** Douglas J 1938- *WhoAmP 91*

**Baker**, Douglas Robert Pelham 1929- *Who 92*
**Baker**, Douglas Wayne 1948- *WhoRel 92*
**Baker**, Dudley Duggan, III 1936- *AmMWSc 92*
**Baker**, Durwood L 1919- *AmMWSc 92*
**Baker**, Dusty 1949- *WhoBlA 92*
**Baker**, E LaMar 1915- *WhoAmP 91*
**Baker**, Earl M 1940- *WhoAmP 91*
**Baker**, Earl Wayne 1928- *AmMWSc 92*
**Baker**, Ed *DrAPF 91*
**Baker**, Edgar Eugene, Jr 1913- *AmMWSc 92*
**Baker**, Edgar Gates Stanley 1909- *AmMWSc 92*
**Baker**, Edward Thomas 1945- *AmMWSc 92*
**Baker**, Edward William 1914- *AmMWSc 92*
**Baker**, Edwin Clarence 1925- *WhoIns 92*
**Baker**, Edwin Herbert 1934- *WhoAmL 92*
**Baker**, Edwin Moody 1923- *WhoWest 92*
**Baker**, Edwin Stuart 1944- *WhoWest 92*
**Baker**, Elizabeth 1941- *WhoAmP 91*
**Baker**, Elizabeth McIntosh 1945- *AmMWSc 92*
**Baker**, Elizabeth N 1933- *WhoAmP 91*
**Baker**, Ella 1903-1986 *FacFETw, NotBlAW 92 [port], PorAmW [port], RComAH*
**Baker**, Elliott 1922- *ConNov 91, WrDr 92*
**Baker**, Elmer Earl 1927- *WhoMW 92*
**Baker**, Eric Nolan 1951- *WhoEnt 92*
**Baker**, Ernest Waldo, Jr. 1926- *WhoMW 92*
**Baker**, Ethelyn Johnson 1928- *WhoMW 92*
**Baker**, Eugene 1938- *WhoBlA 92*
**Baker**, Eugene Manigault 1951- *WhoWest 92*
**Baker**, Falcon 1916- *ConAu 135*
**Baker**, Floyd Edward 1920- *WhoBlA 92*
**Baker**, Francis Edward, Jr 1944- *AmMWSc 92*
**Baker**, Francis Edward N. *Who 92*
**Baker**, Francis Ellsworth 1929- *WhoFI 92*
**Baker**, Francis Eustace 1933- *Who 92*
**Baker**, Francis Todd 1942- *AmMWSc 92*
**Baker**, Frank 1841-1918 *BiInAmS*
**Baker**, Frank 1910- *IntAu&W 91, WrDr 92*
**Baker**, Frank 1936- *AmMWSc 92*
**Baker**, Frank Bernard 1947- *WhoFI 92*
**Baker**, Frank Hamon 1923- *AmMWSc 92*
**Baker**, Frank Sloan, Jr 1921- *AmMWSc 92*
**Baker**, Frank Weir 1938- *AmMWSc 92*
**Baker**, Frank William 1935- *AmMWSc 92*
**Baker**, Fred Greentree 1950- *WhoWest 92*
**Baker**, Frederick Charles 1948- *AmMWSc 92*
**Baker**, Frederick Lloyd, III 1941- *WhoFI 92*
**Baker**, Frederick Milton, Jr. 1949- *WhoAmL 92*
**Baker**, Frederick Waller 1949- *WhoIns 92*
**Baker**, Gail Dyer 1954- *WhoAmL 92*
**Baker**, Garrison Buford 1955- *WhoAmP 91*
**Baker**, Gary Dwain 1951- *WhoRel 92*
**Baker**, Gary Hugh 1947- *WhoAmL 92*
**Baker**, Gene Stewart 1937- *WhoAmP 91*
**Baker**, Geoffrey 1925- *Who 92*
**Baker**, Geoffrey Alan 1881- *TwCPaSc*
**Baker**, Geoffrey Hunter 1916- *Who 92*
**Baker**, George 1931- *IntMPA 92*
**Baker**, George Allen 1903- *AmMWSc 92*
**Baker**, George Allen, Jr 1932- *AmMWSc 92*
**Baker**, George H 1919- *WhoAmP 91*
**Baker**, George Lorimer d1909 *BiInAmS*
**Baker**, George Pierce 1866-1935 *BenetAL 91, FacFETw*
**Baker**, George Pierce 1903- *IntWW 91*
**Baker**, George Severt 1927- *AmMWSc 92*
**Baker**, George Thomas, III 1940- *AmMWSc 92*
**Baker**, George William 1917- *Who 92*
**Baker**, Georgette Latoofa 1954- *WhoEnt 92*
**Baker**, Gerald Allen 1939- *WhoWest 92*
**Baker**, Gilbert Jens 1946- *WhoMW 92*
**Baker**, Gladys Corvera 1950- *WhoHisp 92*
**Baker**, Gladys Elizabeth 1908- *AmMWSc 92, WhoWest 92*
**Baker**, Glen Bryan 1947- *AmMWSc 92*
**Baker**, Gloria Beth 1942- *WhoFI 92*
**Baker**, Gordon Meldrum 1941- *Who 92*
**Baker**, Graeme Levo 1925- *AmMWSc 92*
**Baker**, Gregory Lynn 1954- *WhoAmL 92*
**Baker**, Griffin Jonathan 1917- *AmMWSc 92*
**Baker**, Guy Eugene 1945- *WhoFI 92*
**Baker**, Gwendolyn Calvert 1931- *WhoBlA 92*
**Baker**, Harlan Robert 1947- *WhoAmP 91*
**Baker**, Harold A *WhoAmP 91*
**Baker**, Harold Albert 1929- *WhoAmL 92*
**Baker**, Harold Cecil 1954- *WhoFI 92*
**Baker**, Harold Lawrence 1918- *AmMWSc 92*
**Baker**, Harold Nordean 1943- *AmMWSc 92*
**Baker**, Harold Weldon 1931- *AmMWSc 92*
**Baker**, Henry 1952- *WhoEnt 92*
**Baker**, Henry W., Sr. 1937- *WhoBlA 92*
**Baker**, Herbert George 1920- *AmMWSc 92*
**Baker**, Herman 1926- *AmMWSc 92*
**Baker**, Herman Dupree 1928- *WhoAmL 92*
**Baker**, Herschel C 1914-1990 *DcLB 111 [port]*
**Baker**, Houston A., Jr. 1943- *WhoBlA 92*
**Baker**, Houston Alfred, Jr 1943- *IntAu&W 91, WrDr 92*
**Baker**, Houston Richard 1940- *AmMWSc 92*
**Baker**, Howard 1905- *ConPo 91*
**Baker**, Howard Crittenden 1943- *WhoMW 92*
**Baker**, Howard Crittendon 1943- *AmMWSc 92*
**Baker**, Howard H, Jr 1925- *WhoAmP 91*
**Baker**, Howard Henry, Jr. 1925- *IntWW 91, Who 92*
**Baker**, Hugh D. R. 1937- *WrDr 92*
**Baker**, Ian Helstrip 1927- *Who 92*
**Baker**, Ian Michael 1947- *Who 92*
**Baker**, Israel 1921- *NewAmDM*
**Baker**, Ivor *Who 92*
**Baker**, J. A. 1944- *WhoFI 92*
**Baker**, J. Edwin 1914- *IntMPA 92*
**Baker**, Jackson Arnold 1938- *WhoFI 92*
**Baker**, James A., III 1930- *News 91 [port], WhoAmP 91*
**Baker**, James Addison 1922- *AmMWSc 92*
**Baker**, James Addison, III 1930- *AmPolLe [port], IntWW 91, Who 92, WhoFI 92*
**Baker**, James Bert 1939- *AmMWSc 92*
**Baker**, James Chamberlain 1879-1969 *RelLAm 91*
**Baker**, James Donald 1930- *WhoRel 92*
**Baker**, James E 1931- *AmMWSc 92*
**Baker**, James E. 1935- *WhoBlA 92*
**Baker**, James Edward Sproul 1912- *WhoAmL 92, WhoMW 92*
**Baker**, James Estes 1935- *WhoAmP 91*
**Baker**, James Gilbert 1914- *AmMWSc 92*
**Baker**, James Haskell 1940- *AmMWSc 92*
**Baker**, James Kendrick 1931- *WhoFI 92*
**Baker**, James LeRoy 1944- *AmMWSc 92*
**Baker**, James McNair 1821-1892 *DcNCBi 1*
**Baker**, James Robert 1941- *AmMWSc 92*
**Baker**, James Rupert 1925- *WrDr 92*
**Baker**, James W. 1926- *ConAu 133, SmATA 65 [port]*
**Baker**, Jane Elaine 1923- *WhoAmP 91, WhoWest 92*
**Baker**, Janet 1933- *FacFETw, IntWW 91, NewAmDM, Who 92*
**Baker**, Janet Abbott 1933- *WhoEnt 92*
**Baker**, Jeanette Sledge 1947- *WhoWest 92*
**Baker**, Jeannie 1950- *WrDr 92*
**Baker**, Jeffrey J. 1953- *WhoAmL 92*
**Baker**, Jeffrey John Wheeler 1931- *AmMWSc 92*
**Baker**, Jeffrey Stephen 1947- *WhoEnt 92*
**Baker**, Joe Benny 1948- *WhoRel 92*
**Baker**, Joe Don 1936- *IntMPA 92, WhoEnt 92*
**Baker**, Joe M, Jr 1927- *WhoAmP 91*
**Baker**, Joel L. 1934- *WhoBlA 92*
**Baker**, Joffre B 1947- *AmMWSc 92*
**Baker**, Joffre Bernard 1947- *AmMWSc 92*
**Baker**, John A. 1939- *WhoIns 92*
**Baker**, John Alexander 1939- *AmMWSc 92*
**Baker**, John Arnold 1925- *Who 92*
**Baker**, John Austin *Who 92*
**Baker**, John Austin 1928- *IntWW 91*
**Baker**, John B. *Who 92*
**Baker**, John Bee 1927- *AmMWSc 92*
**Baker**, John Burkett 1931- *Who 92*
**Baker**, John Charles 1954- *WhoFI 92*
**Baker**, John Christopher 1952- *AmMWSc 92*
**Baker**, John David 1949- *AmMWSc 92*
**Baker**, John E. 1954- *WhoMW 92*
**Baker**, John Edward 1917- *WhoAmP 91*
**Baker**, John Gatch 1946- *WhoAmL 92*
**Baker**, John Hamilton 1944- *IntWW 91, Who 92*
**Baker**, John Keith 1942- *AmMWSc 92*
**Baker**, John Martin 1944- *WhoAmP 91*
**Baker**, John P 1923- *AmMWSc 92*
**Baker**, John Richard 1938- *WhoFI 92*
**Baker**, John Rowland 1934- *AmMWSc 92*
**Baker**, John Russell 1926- *WhoFI 92*
**Baker**, John Stevenson 1931- *WhoMW 92*
**Baker**, John Warren 1936- *AmMWSc 92*
**Baker**, John William 1937- *IntWW 91, Who 92*
**Baker**, Joni Elizabeth 1959- *WhoAmP 91*
**Baker**, Joseph Edmond 1940- *WhoAmP 91*
**Baker**, Joseph Henry 1831-1902 *DcNCBi 1*
**Baker**, Joseph Roderick, III 1947- *WhoWest 92*
**Baker**, Joseph Willard 1924- *AmMWSc 92*
**Baker**, Josephine 1906-1975 *FacFETw [port], HanAmWH, NotBlAW 92 [port], RComAH*
**Baker**, Josephine 1906-1979 *NewAmDM*
**Baker**, Josephine L. Redenius 1920- *WhoRel 92*
**Baker**, Joyce Irene 1929- *WhoAmP 91*
**Baker**, Julian Meredith 1857-1935 *DcNCBi 1*
**Baker**, Julius 1915- *NewAmDM, WhoEnt 92*
**Baker**, June Frankland *DrAPF 91*
**Baker**, June Marshall 1922- *AmMWSc 92*
**Baker**, Kandra 1959- *WhoEnt 92*
**Baker**, Kathy 1950- *IntMPA 92*
**Baker**, Kay Dayne 1934- *AmMWSc 92*
**Baker**, Keith Leon 1950- *WhoAmL 92*
**Baker**, Keith Michael 1938- *WhoWest 92*
**Baker**, Kelly Shane 1962- *WhoWest 92*
**Baker**, Ken *WhoAmP 91*
**Baker**, Kenneth 1934- *IntWW 91, Who 92*
**Baker**, Kenneth Frank 1908- *AmMWSc 92*
**Baker**, Kenneth L 1919- *AmMWSc 92*
**Baker**, Kenneth Melvin 1947- *AmMWSc 92*
**Baker**, Kenny 1926- *NewAmDM*
**Baker**, Kenrick Martin, Jr. 1923- *WhoRel 92*
**Baker**, Kent Alfred 1948- *WhoEnt 92, WhoWest 92*
**Baker**, Kent Steven 1945- *WhoAmP 91*
**Baker**, Kerry Allen 1949- *WhoFI 92*
**Baker**, Kimberley Renee 1965- *WhoBlA 92*
**Baker**, Kirby Alan 1940- *AmMWSc 92*
**Baker**, Larry 1942- *WhoAmP 91*
**Baker**, Larry Curtis 1945- *WhoRel 92, WhoWest 92*
**Baker**, Larry Lane 1960- *WhoEnt 92*
**Baker**, Larry Neal 1950- *WhoRel 92*
**Baker**, Laura *DrAPF 91*
**Baker**, Lauren Charles 1939- *WhoRel 92*
**Baker**, Laurence 1745-1805 *DcNCBi 1*
**Baker**, Laurence Simmons 1830-1907 *DcNCBi 1*
**Baker**, LaVolia Ealy 1925- *WhoBlA 92*
**Baker**, Lawrence Colby, Jr. 1935- *WhoIns 92*
**Baker**, Lee Edward 1924- *AmMWSc 92*
**Baker**, Lenox Dial 1902- *AmMWSc 92*
**Baker**, Leon *DrAPF 91*
**Baker**, Leonard Graham Derek 1931- *Who 92*
**Baker**, Leonard Morton 1934- *AmMWSc 92*
**Baker**, Leslie Marie 1959- *WhoAmL 92*
**Baker**, Lewis Norman 1955- *WhoWest 92*
**Baker**, Lillian L. 1921- *WhoWest 92*
**Baker**, Lloyd Harvey 1927- *WhoAmL 92*
**Baker**, Lloyd J 1931- *WhoAmP 91*
**Baker**, Lonny 1942- *WhoWest 92*
**Baker**, Loretta Ann 1949- *WhoAmL 92*
**Baker**, Louis, Jr 1927- *AmMWSc 92*
**Baker**, Louis Coombs Weller 1921- *AmMWSc 92*
**Baker**, Lucinda 1916- *WrDr 92*
**Baker**, Malchus Brooks, Jr 1941- *AmMWSc 92*
**Baker**, Marcus 1849-1903 *BiInAmS*
**Baker**, Margaret J 1918- *IntAu&W 91, WrDr 92*
**Baker**, Margery Claire 1948- *WhoEnt 92*
**Baker**, Marian Gray *WhoMW 92*
**Baker**, Marian Irene Arbaugh 1935- *WhoWest 92*
**Baker**, Marilyn Verna 1935- *WhoAmP 91*
**Baker**, Mark Alexander Wyndham 1940- *Who 92*
**Baker**, Mark R. 1954- *WhoAmL 92*
**Baker**, Martyn Murray 1944- *Who 92*
**Baker**, Mary Ann 1940- *AmMWSc 92*
**Baker**, Mary Anne *WhoMW 92*
**Baker**, Mary Elizabeth 1961- *WhoEnt 92*
**Baker**, Mary Evelyn 1912- *WhoRel 92*
**Baker**, Maurice S. 1911- *Who 92*
**Baker**, Max Leslie 1943- *AmMWSc 92*
**Baker**, Merl 1924- *AmMWSc 92*
**Baker**, Michael 1926- *WhoEnt 92*
**Baker**, Michael A. *NewYTBS 91 [port]*
**Baker**, Michael Allen 1943- *AmMWSc 92*
**Baker**, Michael Findlay 1943- *Who 92*
**Baker**, Michael Harris 1945- *WhoAmL 92*
**Baker**, Michael Harry 1916- *AmMWSc 92*
**Baker**, Michael John 1935- *Who 92*
**Baker**, Michael John 1950- *WhoMW 92*
**Baker**, Michael John David 1934- *Who 92*
**Baker**, Michael Lyndon 1949- *WhoRel 92*
**Baker**, Milton Baretz 1908- *WhoFI 92*
**Baker**, Moorean Ann *WhoBlA 92*
**Baker**, Nardin Long 1958- *WhoFI 92*
**Baker**, Nathan Larry 1937- *WhoRel 92*
**Baker**, Neal Kenton 1945- *AmMWSc 92*
**Baker**, Neil 1958- *WhoEnt 92*
**Baker**, Newton Diehl 1871-1937 *AmPeW, AmPolLe, FacFETw*
**Baker**, Nicholas Brian 1938- *Who 92*
**Baker**, Nicholson 1957- *ConAu 135*
**Baker**, Nigel Robert James 1942- *Who 92*
**Baker**, Nikito John 1954- *WhoFI 92*
**Baker**, Nome 1927- *AmMWSc 92*
**Baker**, Norman Hodgson 1931- *AmMWSc 92*
**Baker**, Oscar Wilson 1911- *WhoBlA 92*
**Baker**, Pamela J 1947- *SmATA 66*
**Baker**, Patricia Ann 1929- *WhoAmP 91*
**Baker**, Patricia J *AmMWSc 92*
**Baker**, Paul 1911- *WhoEnt 92*
**Baker**, Paul, Jr 1921- *AmMWSc 92*
**Baker**, Paul R 1927- *IntAu&W 91, WrDr 92*
**Baker**, Paul T. 1927- *IntWW 91*
**Baker**, Paul Thornell 1927- *AmMWSc 92*
**Baker**, Paul Vivian 1923- *Who 92*
**Baker**, Peter 1926- *IntAu&W 91, WrDr 92*
**Baker**, Peter C 1933- *AmMWSc 92*
**Baker**, Peter Maxwell 1930- *Who 92*
**Baker**, Peter Thomas 1932- *Who 92*
**Baker**, Philip S d1901 *BiInAmS*
**Baker**, Philip Schaffner 1916- *AmMWSc 92*
**Baker**, Phillip 1938- *WhoRel 92*
**Baker**, Phillip John 1935- *AmMWSc 92*
**Baker**, R Ralph 1924- *AmMWSc 92*
**Baker**, Ralph D 1924- *WhoAmP 91*
**Baker**, Ralph Robinson 1928- *AmMWSc 92*
**Baker**, Ralph Stanley 1927- *AmMWSc 92*
**Baker**, Ralph Thomas 1953- *AmMWSc 92*
**Baker**, Ray Stannard 1870-1946 *AmPeW, BenetAL 91*
**Baker**, Raymond Milton 1940- *AmMWSc 92*
**Baker**, Rebecca Louise 1951- *WhoEnt 92*
**Baker**, Rees Terence Keith 1938- *AmMWSc 92*
**Baker**, Reginald Ralph 1924- *WhoWest 92*
**Baker**, Richard A 1934- *AmMWSc 92*
**Baker**, Richard Dean 1913- *AmMWSc 92*
**Baker**, Richard Douglas James 1925- *Who 92*
**Baker**, Richard Earl 1928- *WhoWest 92*
**Baker**, Richard Eugene 1939- *WhoEnt 92*
**Baker**, Richard Freligh 1910- *AmMWSc 92*
**Baker**, Richard Graves 1938- *AmMWSc 92*
**Baker**, Richard H 1921- *AmMWSc 92*
**Baker**, Richard H 1936- *AmMWSc 92*
**Baker**, Richard H. 1948- *AlmAP 92 [port]*
**Baker**, Richard Hugh 1935- *Who 92*
**Baker**, Richard Hugh 1948- *WhoAmP 91*
**Baker**, Richard J. 1931- *WhoIns 92*
**Baker**, Richard Joint 1931- *WhoAmL 92*
**Baker**, Richard M., Jr. 1924-1978 *ConAu 135*
**Baker**, Richard Southworth 1929- *WhoAmL 92*
**Baker**, Richard W. 1945- *WhoWest 92*
**Baker**, Richard W.S. 1933- *WhoIns 92*
**Baker**, Richard William 1941- *AmMWSc 92*
**Baker**, Robert Andrew 1925- *AmMWSc 92*
**Baker**, Robert Carl 1921- *AmMWSc 92*
**Baker**, Robert Charles 1930- *AmMWSc 92*
**Baker**, Robert David 1929- *AmMWSc 92*
**Baker**, Robert Donald 1927- *AmMWSc 92*
**Baker**, Robert Edward 1930- *WhoFI 92*
**Baker**, Robert Eric 1959- *WhoFI 92*
**Baker**, Robert Flowers 1935- *WhoAmL 92*
**Baker**, Robert Frank 1936- *AmMWSc 92*
**Baker**, Robert G 1918- *AmMWSc 92*
**Baker**, Robert George 1940- *AmMWSc 92*
**Baker**, Robert George Humphrey S. *Who 92*
**Baker**, Robert H. 1943- *IntMPA 92*
**Baker**, Robert Hart 1954- *WhoEnt 92*
**Baker**, Robert Henry 1908- *AmMWSc 92*
**Baker**, Robert Henry, Jr 1934- *AmMWSc 92*
**Baker**, Robert J, Jr 1938- *AmMWSc 92*
**Baker**, Robert John 1938- *AmMWSc 92*
**Baker**, Robert K. 1946- *WhoFI 92*
**Baker**, Robert Lisle 1942- *WhoAmL 92*
**Baker**, Robert Norton 1923- *AmMWSc 92*
**Baker**, Robert S. 1916- *IntMPA 92*
**Baker**, Robert Stevens 1916- *WhoEnt 92*
**Baker**, Robert William 1946- *WhoWest 92*
**Baker**, Robert Woodward 1944- *WhoFI 92*
**Baker**, Rod 1945- *WhoEnt 92*
**Baker**, Rodney Lee 1950- *WhoWest 92*
**Baker**, Roger Lorin 1934- *WhoAmP 91*
**Baker**, Roland C. 1938- *WhoIns 92*
**Baker**, Roland Charles 1938- *WhoBlA 92*
**Baker**, Roland Jerald 1938- *WhoWest 92*
**Baker**, Rollin Harold 1916- *AmMWSc 92*
**Baker**, Ronald G 1939- *AmMWSc 92*
**Baker**, Ronald Lee 1927- *WhoAmL 92*
**Baker**, Ronald Phillip 1942- *WhoMW 92*
**Baker**, Ronald Ray 1943- *WhoFI 92*
**Baker**, Ronnie 1967- *WhoRel 92*
**Baker**, Rosalyn 1946- *WhoAmP 91*
**Baker**, Roy *IntMPA 92*

**Baker,** Roy E. 1927- *WhoFI 92*
**Baker,** Russell 1925- *IntAu&W 91, WrDr 92*
**Baker,** Russell Wayne 1925- *IntWW 91*
**Baker,** S Josephine 1873-1945 *DcAmImH*
**Baker,** Sally 1932- *WhoEnt 92, WhoWest 92*
**Baker,** Samuel I 1934- *AmMWSc 92*
**Baker,** Saul Phillip 1924- *AmMWSc 92, WhoMW 92*
**Baker,** Scott *Who 92*
**Baker,** Sharon *DrAPF 91*
**Baker,** Sharon 1938- *IntAu&W 91, TwCSFW 91*
**Baker,** Sharon L. 1958- *WhoBlA 92*
**Baker,** Sharon Smith 1949- *WhoBlA 92*
**Baker,** Sheldon S. 1936- *WhoAmL 92*
**Baker,** Sheridan 1918- *WrDr 92*
**Baker,** Shorty 1913-1966 *NewAmDM*
**Baker,** Simmons Jones 1775-1853 *DcNCBi 1*
**Baker,** Stephen 1921- *IntAu&W 91, WrDr 92*
**Baker,** Stephen 1926- *Who 92*
**Baker,** Stephen Denio 1936- *AmMWSc 92*
**Baker,** Stephen Phillip 1948- *AmMWSc 92*
**Baker,** Steven Wright 1947- *WhoAmL 92*
**Baker,** Susan Elizabeth 1954- *WhoWest 92*
**Baker,** Susan Leigh 1962- *WhoFI 92*
**Baker,** Susan Pardee 1930- *AmMWSc 92*
**Baker,** Theodore Paul 1949- *AmMWSc 92*
**Baker,** Theodore Robert 1956- *WhoEnt 92*
**Baker,** Thomas Brent 1960- *WhoRel 92*
**Baker,** Thomas Earl 1958- *WhoAmL 92*
**Baker,** Thomas Edgar 1931- *WhoFI 92*
**Baker,** Thomas Edward 1923- *WhoAmL 92*
**Baker,** Thomas G 1949- *WhoAmP 91*
**Baker,** Thomas G, Jr 1956- *WhoAmP 91*
**Baker,** Thomas George Adames 1920- *Who 92*
**Baker,** Thomas Harrison 1933- *WrDr 92*
**Baker,** Thomas Irving 1931- *AmMWSc 92*
**Baker,** Thomas Scott 1937- *Who 92*
**Baker,** Thompson Simkins 1905- *WhoFI 92*
**Baker,** Thurbert E *WhoAmP 91*
**Baker,** Timothy Alan 1954- *WhoWest 92*
**Baker,** Timothy D 1925- *AmMWSc 92*
**Baker,** Timothy Lee 1957- *WhoEnt 92*
**Baker,** Tom *WhoAmP 91*
**Baker,** V. Lilith 1935- *WhoWest 92*
**Baker,** Venetta Denise 1955- *WhoRel 92*
**Baker,** Vera Lee 1925- *IntAu&W 91*
**Baker,** Victor Richard 1945- *AmMWSc 92*
**Baker,** Vincent S. *WhoBlA 92*
**Baker,** Virginia Marie 1935- *WhoAmP 91*
**Baker,** Wallis James 1931- *Who 92*
**Baker,** Walter A 1937- *WhoAmP 91*
**Baker,** Walter E. 1936- *WhoFI 92*
**Baker,** Walter L 1924- *AmMWSc 92*
**Baker,** Walter M 1927- *WhoAmP 91*
**Baker,** Walter Robert 1951- *WhoWest 92*
**Baker,** Walter Wolf 1924- *AmMWSc 92*
**Baker,** Warren J 1938- *AmMWSc 92*
**Baker,** Warren Joseph 1938- *WhoWest 92*
**Baker,** Wayne D. 1932- *WhoFI 92, WhoIns 92*
**Baker,** Wilber Winston 1934- *AmMWSc 92*
**Baker,** Wilbur Francis 1931- *WhoMW 92*
**Baker,** Wilfred E 1924- *AmMWSc 92*
**Baker,** Willfred Harold Kerton 1920- *Who 92*
**Baker,** William Buck 1954- *WhoMW 92*
**Baker,** William Costello, Jr. 1959- *WhoAmL 92*
**Baker,** William D 1932- *WhoAmP 91*
**Baker,** William F. *LesBEnT 92*
**Baker,** William F. 1944- *IntMPA 92*
**Baker,** William Franklin 1942- *WhoEnt 92, WhoFI 92*
**Baker,** William George 1935- *WhoFI 92*
**Baker,** William Harris 1945- *WhoAmL 92*
**Baker,** William Kaufman 1919- *AmMWSc 92*
**Baker,** William L. 1945- *WhoIns 92*
**Baker,** William Oliver 1915- *AmMWSc 92, IntWW 91, WhoFI 92*
**Baker,** William P 1940- *WhoAmP 91*
**Baker,** William Parr 1946- *WhoAmL 92*
**Baker,** William Scott d1990 *Who 92N*
**Baker,** Willie Arthur, Jr 1933- *AmMWSc 92*
**Baker,** Willie J. 1938- *WhoBlA 92*
**Baker,** Willie L., Jr. 1941- *WhoBlA 92*
**Baker,** Wilson 1900- *IntWW 91, Who 92*
**Baker,** Winslow Furber *AmMWSc 92*
**Baker,** Winthrop Patterson, Jr. 1931- *WhoEnt 92*
**Baker-Bates,** Merrick Stuart 1939- *Who 92*
**Baker-Carr,** John 1906- *Who 92*
**Baker-Cohen,** Katherine France 1928- *AmMWSc 92*
**Baker-Lievanos,** Nina Gillson 1950- *WhoWest 92*
**Baker Wilbraham,** Richard 1934- *Who 92*
**Bakerman,** Jane Adelle 1931- *WhoMW 92*
**Bakerman,** Seymour 1924- *AmMWSc 92*
**Bakes,** Robert Eldon 1932- *WhoAmL 92, WhoAmP 91, WhoWest 92*
**Bakewell,** Joan Dawson 1933- *Who 92*
**Bakewell,** Kenneth 1931- *WrDr 92*
**Bakewell,** Kenneth Graham Bartlett 1931- *IntAu&W 91*
**Bakfark,** Balint 1507-1576 *NewAmDM*
**Bakh,** Aleksey Nikolaevich 1857-1946 *SovUnBD*
**Bakhiet,** Atef 1941- *AmMWSc 92*
**Bakhiet,** Nouna 1956- *WhoWest 92*
**Bakhru,** Hassaram 1937- *AmMWSc 92*
**Bakhshi,** Narendra Nath 1928- *AmMWSc 92*
**Bakhshi,** Vidya Sagar 1939- *AmMWSc 92*
**Bakht,** Sikander 1918- *IntWW 91*
**Bakhtiar,** Shahpur 1916-1991 *NewYTBS 91 [port]*
**Bakhtiar,** Shapour 1916- *IntWW 91*
**Bakhtin,** Mikhail 1895-1975 *FacFETw*
**Bakhtin,** Mikhail Mikhaylovich 1895-1975 *SovUnBD*
**Baki** 1947- *WhoBlA 92*
**Baki,** Boulaem 1922- *IntWW 91*
**Bakinowski,** Daniel Vincent 1950- *WhoAmL 92*
**Bakis,** Raimo 1933- *AmMWSc 92*
**Bakish,** Robert 1926- *AmMWSc 92*
**Bakka,** Richard S. 1940- *WhoIns 92*
**Bakke,** Allan *FacFETw*
**Bakke,** Hallvard 1943- *IntWW 91*
**Bakke,** Jerome E 1931- *AmMWSc 92*
**Bakke,** Karl Edward 1930- *WhoAmP 91*
**Bakke,** M. Russell 1945- *WhoFI 92*
**Bakken,** Aimee Hayes 1941- *AmMWSc 92*
**Bakken,** Anne-Lise 1952- *IntWW 91*
**Bakken,** Arnold 1921- *AmMWSc 92*
**Bakken,** Dick *DrAPF 91*
**Bakken,** Earl E 1924- *AmMWSc 92*
**Bakken,** George Stewart 1943- *AmMWSc 92, WhoMW 92*
**Bakken,** Gordon Morris 1943- *WhoAmL 92*
**Bakken,** John Edgar 1930- *WhoWest 92*
**Bakkenkist,** Siebrand Cornelis 1914- *IntWW 91*
**Bakker,** Cornelis Bernardus 1929- *AmMWSc 92*
**Bakker,** Gerald Robert 1933- *AmMWSc 92*
**Bakker,** Jaap Jelle 1929- *AmMWSc 92*
**Bakker,** Jim 1941- *RelLAm 91*
**Bakker,** Paul Michel 1956- *WhoFI 92*
**Bakker,** Robert T. *News 91, -91-3*
**Bakker,** Sandra Kay 1957- *WhoMW 92*
**Bakker,** Tammy Faye 1942- *RelLAm 91*
**Bakker-Arkema,** Frederik Wilte 1932- *AmMWSc 92*
**Bakkum,** Barclay W 1957- *AmMWSc 92*
**Baklanov,** Grigoriy Yakovlevich 1923- *IntWW 91, SovUnBD*
**Baklanov,** Oleg Dmitrievich 1932- *IntWW 91, SovUnBD*
**Bakle,** John Lewis 1937- *WhoMW 92, WhoRel 92*
**Bako,** David John 1952- *WhoAmP 91*
**Bakos,** Gustav Alfons 1918- *AmMWSc 92*
**Bakos,** Jack David, Jr 1940- *AmMWSc 92*
**Bakos,** Roger Paul 1939- *WhoEnt 92*
**Bakr,** Ahmed Hassan 1914-1982 *FacFETw*
**Bakr,** Rashid El Tahir 1930- *IntWW 91*
**Baksay,** Laszlo Andras 1945- *AmMWSc 92*
**Baksheev,** Vasiliy Nikolaevich 1862-1958 *SovUnBD*
**Bakshi,** Manmohan K. *WhoAmL 92*
**Bakshi,** Moneesh Krishan 1964- *WhoAmL 92*
**Bakshi,** Pradip M 1936- *AmMWSc 92*
**Bakshi,** Ralph *WhoEnt 92*
**Bakshi,** Ralph 1938- *IntMPA 92*
**Bakshi,** Trilochan Singh 1925- *AmMWSc 92*
**Bakshian,** Aram, Jr 1944- *WhoAmP 91*
**Baksi,** Samarendra Nath 1940- *AmMWSc 92*
**Bakst,** David Allan 1939- *WhoAmL 92*
**Bakst,** Edward 1950- *WhoEnt 92*
**Bakst,** Leon Samoylovich 1866-1924 *FacFETw*
**Baktscharow,** Marie *EncAmaz 91*
**Bakula,** Scott *WhoEnt 92*
**Bakule,** Ronald David 1936- *AmMWSc 92*
**Bakun,** Andrew 1939- *AmMWSc 92*
**Bakun,** William Henry 1941- *AmMWSc 92*
**Bakus,** Gerald Joseph 1934- *AmMWSc 92*
**Bakuzis,** Egolfs Voldemars 1912- *AmMWSc 92*
**Baky,** Laszlo 1898-1946 *BiDExR*
**Bal,** Arya Kumar 1934- *AmMWSc 92*
**Bala,** Gary Ganesh 1958- *WhoAmL 92*
**Bala,** John *IntMPA 92*
**Bala,** Shukal 1951- *AmMWSc 92*
**Balaam** *IntAu&W 91X, WrDr 92*
**Balaba,** Willy Mukama 1953- *AmMWSc 92*
**Balaban,** Bob 1945- *IntMPA 92*
**Balaban,** Elmer *IntMPA 92*
**Balaban,** John *DrAPF 91*
**Balaban,** John 1943- *IntAu&W 91*
**Balaban,** Martin 1930- *AmMWSc 92*
**Balaban,** Robert S 1953- *AmMWSc 92*
**Balabanian,** Norman 1922- *AmMWSc 92*
**Balachandran,** Kashi Ramamurthi 1941- *AmMWSc 92*
**Balachandran,** Swaminathan 1946- *WhoMW 92*
**Balada,** Leonardo 1933- *WhoEnt 92*
**Baladi,** Andre 1934- *WhoFI 92*
**Balado,** Manuel *WhoHisp 92*
**Balafrej,** Ahmed 1908- *IntWW 91*
**Balagna,** John Paul 1920- *AmMWSc 92*
**Balagot,** Reuben Castillo 1920- *AmMWSc 92*
**Balaguer,** Joaquin 1907- *FacFETw*
**Balaguer,** Joaquin 1950- *WhoHisp 92*
**Balaguer Ricardo,** Joaquin 1907- *IntWW 91*
**Balagura,** Saul 1943- *AmMWSc 92*
**Balaguru,** Perumalsamy N 1947- *AmMWSc 92*
**Balaguy,** Daniel Jason 1964- *WhoWest 92*
**Balahtsis,** Dede Z. 1964- *WhoMW 92*
**Balaita,** George 1935- *IntWW 91*
**Balajee,** Shankverm R 1939- *AmMWSc 92*
**Balak,** William Martin 1937- *WhoFI 92*
**Balakian,** Nona d1991 *NewYTBS 91 [port]*
**Balakian,** Nona 1919-1991 *ConAu 134*
**Balakian,** Peter *DrAPF 91*
**Balakirev,** Mily Alexeyevich 1837-1910 *NewAmDM*
**Balakrishnan,** A V 1922- *AmMWSc 92*
**Balakrishnan,** Narayana Swamy *AmMWSc 92*
**Balakrishnan,** Narayanaswany 1956- *AmMWSc 92*
**Balakrishnan,** P. V. 1959- *WhoMW 92*
**Balakrishnan,** V K *AmMWSc 92*
**Balakshin,** Pyotr P. 1898- *SovUnBD*
**Balam,** Baxish Singh 1930- *AmMWSc 92*
**Balames,** Thomas Stephen 1958- *WhoFI 92*
**Balamuth,** David P 1942- *AmMWSc 92*
**Balanchine,** George 1904-1983 *FacFETw [port], RComAH, SovUnBD*
**Balanchivadze,** Andrey Melitonovich 1906- *SovUnBD*
**Balanchivadze,** George 1904-1983 *SovUnBD*
**Balandin,** Anatoliy Nikiforovich 1927- *IntWW 91*
**Balandin,** Yuriy Nikolayevich 1925- *IntWW 91*
**Balandrin,** Manuel F 1952- *AmMWSc 92*
**Balanis,** Constantine A 1938- *AmMWSc 92*
**Balanis,** George Nick 1944- *WhoFI 92*
**Balanoff,** Clement *WhoAmP 91*
**Balanoff,** Miriam *WhoAmP 91*
**Balanza,** Virgilio Domine 1930- *WhoRel 92*
**Balart,** Luis A. 1948- *WhoHisp 92*
**Balas,** Egon *AmMWSc 92*
**Balas,** John Paul, III 1940- *WhoRel 92*
**Balash,** Jeffrey Linke 1948- *WhoFI 92, WhoWest 92*
**Balash,** Muriel Hope *WhoEnt 92*
**Balasinski,** Artur 1957- *AmMWSc 92*
**Balasko,** John Allan 1941- *AmMWSc 92*
**Balassa,** Bela 1928- *IntAu&W 91, IntWW 91, WrDr 92*
**Balassa,** Bela 1928-1991 *ConAu 134*
**Balassa,** Bela A. d1991 *NewYTBS 91*
**Balassa,** Ivan 1917- *IntWW 91*
**Balassa,** Leslie Ladislaus 1903- *AmMWSc 92*
**Balassa,** Sandor 1935- *ConCom 92, IntWW 91*
**Balasubrahmanyan,** Vriddhachalam K 1926- *AmMWSc 92*
**Balasubramanian,** Krishnan 1956- *AmMWSc 92*
**Balasuriya,** Stanislaus Tissa 1924- *IntWW 91*
**Balatka,** Hans 1826-1899 *NewAmDM*
**Balayan,** Roman Gurgenovich 1941- *IntWW 91*
**Balaye,** Simone 1925- *IntWW 91*
**Balazovich,** Kenneth J 1954- *AmMWSc 92*
**Balazs,** Artur Krzysztof 1952- *IntWW 91*
**Balazs,** Endre Alexander 1920- *AmMWSc 92*
**Balazs,** Eva H. 1915- *IntWW 91*
**Balazs,** Frederic E. *WhoEnt 92*
**Balazs,** Louis A P 1937- *AmMWSc 92*
**Balazs,** Mary *DrAPF 91*
**Balazs,** Nandor Laszlo 1926- *AmMWSc 92*
**Balazs,** Tibor 1922- *AmMWSc 92*
**Balbach,** Edward, Jr 1839-1910 *BiInAmS*
**Balbach,** Stanley Byron 1919- *WhoAmL 92*
**Balbes,** Raymond 1940- *AmMWSc 92*
**Balbin,** Julius *DrAPF 91*
**Balbinder,** Elias 1926- *AmMWSc 92*
**Balbo,** Italo 1896-1940 *BiDExR, EncTR 91*
**Balboa,** Marcelo *WhoHisp 92*
**Balboa,** Richard Mario 1936- *WhoHisp 92*
**Balboa,** Vasco Nunez de 1475-1517 *HisDSpE*
**Balboni,** Edward Raymond 1930- *AmMWSc 92*
**Balboni,** Michael A L 1959- *WhoAmP 91*
**Balbuena,** Bernardo de d1637 *HisDSpE*
**Balcarce** *HisDSpE*
**Balcazar-Monzon,** Gustavo 1927- *Who 92*
**Balcer,** Lukasz 1935- *IntWW 91*
**Balcer,** Rene Chenevert 1954- *WhoEnt 92*
**Balcer-Brownstein,** Josefine P 1948- *AmMWSc 92*
**Balcerowicz,** Leszek 1947- *IntWW 91*
**Balcerzak,** Marion John 1933- *AmMWSc 92*
**Balcerzak,** Stanley Paul 1930- *AmMWSc 92*
**Balcerzak-Dyer,** Judith Geneva 1949- *WhoWest 92*
**Balch,** Alan Lee 1940- *AmMWSc 92*
**Balch,** Alfred Hudson 1928- *AmMWSc 92*
**Balch,** Charles Mitchell 1942- *AmMWSc 92*
**Balch,** Donald James 1922- *AmMWSc 92*
**Balch,** Emily Greene 1867-1961 *AmPeW, FacFETw, HanAmWH, WhoNob 90, WomSoc*
**Balch,** Frank *ScFEYrs*
**Balch,** Glenn McClain, Jr. 1937- *WhoRel 92, WhoWest 92*
**Balch,** Hezekiah James 1745-1776 *DcNCBi 1*
**Balch,** Pamela Mae 1950- *WhoWest 92*
**Balch,** Thomas Willing 1866-1927 *AmPeW*
**Balch,** William E 1949- *AmMWSc 92*
**Balchin,** John Alfred 1914- *Who 92*
**Balchin,** Robert George Alexander 1942- *Who 92*
**Balchin,** William George Victor 1916- *Who 92, WrDr 92*
**Balchum,** Oscar Joseph 1917- *AmMWSc 92*
**Balchunas,** Gerard Andrew 1955- *WhoEnt 92*
**Balciar,** Gerald George 1942- *WhoWest 92*
**Balcom,** Gloria Darleen 1939- *WhoFI 92, WhoWest 92*
**Balcom,** Orville 1937- *WhoWest 92*
**Balcomb,** M. Michelle 1927- *WhoWest 92*
**Balcomb,** Raymond Everett 1923- *WhoRel 92*
**Balcombe,** Alfred John 1925- *Who 92*
**Balcombe,** Frederick James 1911- *Who 92*
**Balcombe,** John *Who 92*
**Balcon,** Raphael 1936- *Who 92*
**Balcziak,** Louis William 1918- *AmMWSc 92*
**Bald,** Kenneth Charles 1930- *AmMWSc 92*
**Balda,** Juan Carlos 1956- *WhoHisp 92*
**Balda,** Russell Paul 1939- *AmMWSc 92*
**Baldacci,** John E *WhoAmP 91*
**Baldassarre,** Joseph Anthony 1950- *WhoEnt 92*
**Baldauf,** Gunther H 1923- *AmMWSc 92*
**Baldauf,** Kent Edward 1943- *WhoAmL 92*
**Balder,** James Ellsworth *WhoMW 92*
**Balder,** Jay Royal 1941- *AmMWSc 92*
**Baldermann,** Ingo Herbert 1929- *WhoRel 92*
**Balderrama,** Fred *WhoHisp 92*
**Balderrama,** Sylvia Ramirez 1952- *WhoHisp 92*
**Balderson,** Margaret *IntAu&W 91*
**Balderson,** Margaret 1935- *WrDr 92*
**Balderston,** Frederick E. 1923- *ConAu 133*
**Balderston,** Jean *DrAPF 91*
**Balderston,** Thomas William 1941- *WhoFI 92*
**Balderstone,** James 1921- *Who 92*
**Balderstone,** James Schofield 1921- *IntWW 91*
**Baldeschwieler,** John Dickson 1933- *AmMWSc 92, IntWW 91*
**Baldessari,** John 1931- *CurBio 91 [port], News 91 [port], WorArt 1980 [port]*
**Baldessarini,** Ross John 1937- *AmMWSc 92*
**Baldi,** Robert Otjen 1949- *WhoAmL 92*
**Baldin,** Aleksandr Mikhailovich 1926- *IntWW 91*
**Baldini,** James Thomas 1927- *AmMWSc 92*
**Baldino,** Frank, Jr 1953- *AmMWSc 92*
**Baldizar,** Barbara J 1947- *WhoAmP 91*
**Baldocchi,** Dennis D 1955- *AmMWSc 92*
**Baldock,** Bobby R *WhoAmP 91*
**Baldock,** Bobby Ray 1936- *WhoAmL 92, WhoWest 92*
**Baldock,** Brian Ford 1934- *Who 92*
**Baldock,** John Markham 1915- *Who 92*
**Baldock,** Lionel Trevor 1936- *Who 92*
**Baldon,** Cleo 1927- *WhoWest 92*
**Baldonado,** Arthur *WhoHisp 92*
**Baldonado,** Michael *WhoHisp 92*
**Baldonado,** Orlino Castro 1942- *WhoFI 92*

**Baldoni**, Andrew Ateleo 1916- *AmMWSc 92*
**Baldoni**, John Peter 1962- *WhoMW 92*
**Baldoni**, Lauren Patricia 1958- *WhoWest 92*
**Baldorioty de Castro**, Ramon 1822-1889 *HisDSpE*
**Baldrey**, Keith 1958- *ConAu 133*
**Baldridge**, Charlene *DrAPF 91*
**Baldridge**, Elizabeth McIntosh 1949- *WhoFI 92*
**Baldridge**, Robert Crary 1921- *AmMWSc 92*
**Baldridge**, Warren Scott 1945- *AmMWSc 92*
**Baldry**, Antony Brian 1950- *Who 92*
**Baldry**, Harold Caparne 1907- *Who 92, WrDr 92*
**Baldry**, Jack Thomas 1911- *Who 92*
**Baldry**, Tony *Who 92*
**Balducci**, Carolyn *DrAPF 91*
**Balducci**, Lodovico 1944- *AmMWSc 92*
**Balducci**, Richard J 1942- *WhoAmP 91*
**Baldus**, Alvin J 1926- *WhoAmP 91*
**Baldus**, Tom James 1954- *WhoMW 92*
**Baldus**, William Phillip 1932- *AmMWSc 92*
**Balduzzi**, Piero 1928- *AmMWSc 92*
**Baldwin** *Who 92*
**Baldwin**, A Quillian, Jr *WhoAmP 91*
**Baldwin**, Adam 1962- *IntMPA 92*
**Baldwin**, Alan Charles 1948- *Who 92*
**Baldwin**, Alan Dale 1961- *WhoEnt 92*
**Baldwin**, Alec 1958- *IntMPA 92*
**Baldwin**, Alexander Rae, III 1958- *WhoEnt 92*
**Baldwin**, Alice Mary 1879-1960 *DcNCBi 1*
**Baldwin**, Anne Norris 1938- *IntAu&W 91, WrDr 92*
**Baldwin**, Anthony Blair 1928- *WhoFI 92*
**Baldwin**, Arthur Dwight, Jr 1938- *AmMWSc 92*
**Baldwin**, Arthur Richard 1918- *AmMWSc 92*
**Baldwin**, Barbara Gearldine 1935- *WhoRel 92*
**Baldwin**, Barrett S, Jr 1921- *AmMWSc 92*
**Baldwin**, Benjamin 1913- *DcTwDes*
**Baldwin**, Bernard Arthur 1940- *AmMWSc 92*
**Baldwin**, Bernell Elwyn 1924- *AmMWSc 92*
**Baldwin**, Bertha Marjorie *IntAu&W 91*
**Baldwin**, Betty Jo 1925- *WhoWest 92*
**Baldwin**, Brent Winfield 1952- *WhoAmL 92*
**Baldwin**, Brewster 1919- *AmMWSc 92*
**Baldwin**, Brooks *WhoEnt 92*
**Baldwin**, Carrie Marie 1965- *WhoWest 92*
**Baldwin**, Chandler Milnes 1951- *AmMWSc 92*
**Baldwin**, Charlene Marie 1946- *WhoWest 92*
**Baldwin**, Charles Carroll 1956- *WhoIns 92*
**Baldwin**, Charles Franklin, Jr. 1916- *WhoMW 92*
**Baldwin**, Charles Henry 1942- *WhoFI 92*
**Baldwin**, Cynthia A. 1945- *WhoBlA 92*
**Baldwin**, Cynthia Ackron 1945- *WhoAmL 92*
**Baldwin**, Dalton 1931- *NewAmDM*
**Baldwin**, Dana Clark 1959- *WhoRel 92*
**Baldwin**, David Allen 1938- *WhoMW 92*
**Baldwin**, David Arthur 1936- *Who 92*
**Baldwin**, David Dwight 1831-1912 *BiInAmS*
**Baldwin**, David Ellis 1936- *AmMWSc 92*
**Baldwin**, David Hale 1936- *AmMWSc 92*
**Baldwin**, David Robert 1948- *WhoEnt 92*
**Baldwin**, Douglas Parks 1936- *WhoAmP 91*
**Baldwin**, Edwin Steedman 1932- *WhoAmL 92*
**Baldwin**, Elaine Marshall 1947- *WhoAmP 91*
**Baldwin**, Eldon Dean 1939- *AmMWSc 92*
**Baldwin**, Ewart Merlin 1915- *AmMWSc 92*
**Baldwin**, Faith 1893-1978 *BenetAL 91, FacFETw*
**Baldwin**, Frederick Stephen 1946- *WhoRel 92*
**Baldwin**, Garry Wayne 1954- *WhoRel 92*
**Baldwin**, George C 1917- *AmMWSc 92*
**Baldwin**, George Clifton 1921- *Who 92*
**Baldwin**, George Koehler 1919- *WhoFI 92, WhoMW 92*
**Baldwin**, George R. 1934- *WhoBlA 92*
**Baldwin**, Gerald Erwin 1950- *WhoWest 92*
**Baldwin**, Gilbert Louis 1949- *WhoMW 92*
**Baldwin**, Gladys Jane 1924- *WhoWest 92*
**Baldwin**, Gordo *IntAu&W 91X, TwCWW 91*
**Baldwin**, Gordon Brewster 1929- *WhoAmL 92*
**Baldwin**, Gordon C 1908- *IntAu&W 91, TwCWW 91, WrDr 92*
**Baldwin**, Grant Kermit 1953- *WhoWest 92*
**Baldwin**, Gregory Alan 1946- *WhoAmL 92*
**Baldwin**, Hanson W. 1903-1991 *NewYTBS 91 [port]*
**Baldwin**, Henry Furlong 1932- *WhoFI 92*
**Baldwin**, Henry Ives 1896- *AmMWSc 92*
**Baldwin**, Howard Wesley 1928- *AmMWSc 92*
**Baldwin**, Huntley *WhoFI 92*
**Baldwin**, Jack Edward 1938- *IntWW 91, Who 92*
**Baldwin**, Jack Okey 1949- *WhoRel 92*
**Baldwin**, Jack Timothy 1945- *AmMWSc 92*
**Baldwin**, James 1924-1987 *AfrAmW, BenetAL 91, BlkLC [port], ConBlB 1 [port], ConLC 67 [port], DramC 1 [port], LiExTwC, RComAH*
**Baldwin**, James 1924-1989 *FacFETw [port]*
**Baldwin**, James Allen 1944- *WhoMW 92*
**Baldwin**, James Gordon 1945- *AmMWSc 92, WhoFI 92*
**Baldwin**, James Mark 1949- *WhoRel 92*
**Baldwin**, James Patric 1954- *WhoMW 92*
**Baldwin**, James W, Jr 1929- *AmMWSc 92*
**Baldwin**, Jeffrey Kenton 1954- *WhoAmL 92, WhoAmP 91*
**Baldwin**, Jerome Charles 1941- *WhoAmP 91*
**Baldwin**, John 1923- *Who 92*
**Baldwin**, John 1937- *TwCPaSc*
**Baldwin**, John 1949- *BlkOlyM*
**Baldwin**, John Chandler 1945- *WhoAmL 92*
**Baldwin**, John Charles 1948- *AmMWSc 92*
**Baldwin**, John E 1937- *AmMWSc 92*
**Baldwin**, John Evan 1931- *Who 92*
**Baldwin**, John H. 1913- *WhoBlA 92*
**Baldwin**, John Theodore 1944- *AmMWSc 92*
**Baldwin**, Joseph Glover 1815-1864 *BenetAL 91*
**Baldwin**, Kate M 1940- *AmMWSc 92*
**Baldwin**, Keith Malcolm 1928- *AmMWSc 92*
**Baldwin**, Kenneth M 1942- *AmMWSc 92*
**Baldwin**, Larell Hardison 1940- *WhoFI 92*
**Baldwin**, Laurie 1942- *TwCPaSc*
**Baldwin**, Leroy Franklin 1934- *WhoRel 92*
**Baldwin**, Lewis V. 1949- *ConAu 135*
**Baldwin**, Lionel V 1932- *AmMWSc 92*
**Baldwin**, Loammi 1740-1807 *BiInAmS*
**Baldwin**, Loammi, Jr 1780-1838 *BiInAmS*
**Baldwin**, Louis J. *WhoBlA 92*
**Baldwin**, Margaret *ConAu 34NR*
**Baldwin**, Maria Louise 1856-1922 *HanAmWH, NotBlAW 92 [port]*
**Baldwin**, Mark Phillip 1958- *AmMWSc 92*
**Baldwin**, Mark Steven 1960- *WhoAmL 92*
**Baldwin**, Merri Anne 1962- *WhoAmL 92*
**Baldwin**, Mervyn 1934- *TwCPaSc*
**Baldwin**, Mitchell Cardell 1958- *WhoBlA 92*
**Baldwin**, Neil *DrAPF 91*
**Baldwin**, Olivia McNair 1943- *WhoBlA 92*
**Baldwin**, Peter 1922- *Who 92*
**Baldwin**, Peter Alan Charles 1927- *Who 92*
**Baldwin**, Ransom Leland 1935- *AmMWSc 92*
**Baldwin**, Richard Eugene 1940- *WhoWest 92*
**Baldwin**, Richard H 1927- *AmMWSc 92*
**Baldwin**, Robert Charles 1942- *AmMWSc 92*
**Baldwin**, Robert Lesh 1927- *AmMWSc 92*
**Baldwin**, Robert Roy 1920- *IntWW 91*
**Baldwin**, Robert Russel 1916- *AmMWSc 92*
**Baldwin**, Robert William 1927- *AmMWSc 92*
**Baldwin**, Roger 1884-1981 *FacFETw*
**Baldwin**, Roger Allan 1931- *AmMWSc 92*
**Baldwin**, Roger Nash 1884-1981 *AmPeW*
**Baldwin**, Ronald 1934- *WhoEnt 92*
**Baldwin**, Ronald Martin 1947- *AmMWSc 92*
**Baldwin**, Ruth Ann *ReelWom*
**Baldwin**, Scott 1928- *WhoAmL 92*
**Baldwin**, Stanley 1867-1947 *FacFETw*
**Baldwin**, Susan Olin 1954- *WhoAmL 92, WhoMW 92*
**Baldwin**, Thomas James 1955- *WhoFI 92*
**Baldwin**, Thomas O 1938- *AmMWSc 92*
**Baldwin**, Thomas Oakley 1947- *AmMWSc 92*
**Baldwin**, Vincent Curtis 1902- *WhoAmL 92*
**Baldwin**, Virgil Clark, Jr 1940- *AmMWSc 92*
**Baldwin**, W George 1938- *AmMWSc 92*
**Baldwin**, Wilhelmina F. 1923- *WhoBlA 92*
**Baldwin**, William 1779-1819 *BiInAmS*
**Baldwin**, William 1903-1984 *DcTwDes*
**Baldwin**, William A. 1949- *WhoHisp 92*
**Baldwin**, William David 1939- *WhoIns 92*
**Baldwin**, William E 1948- *WhoAmP 91*
**Baldwin**, William Lee 1928- *WhoFI 92*
**Baldwin**, William Ray 1956- *WhoRel 92*
**Baldwin**, William Russell 1926- *AmMWSc 92*
**Baldwin**, William Walter 1940- *AmMWSc 92*
**Baldwin of Bewdley**, Earl 1938- *Who 92*
**Baldy**, Anderson Lacy, III 1960- *WhoAmL 92*
**Baldy**, Marian Wendorf 1944- *AmMWSc 92*
**Baldy**, Richard Wallace 1942- *AmMWSc 92*
**Bale**, Christian 1974- *IntMPA 92*
**Bale**, Don 1937- *WrDr 92*
**Bale**, Harold David 1927- *AmMWSc 92*
**Bale**, John 1495-1563 *RfGEnL 91*
**Bale**, Joy *DrAPF 91*
**Balenciaga**, Cristobal 1895-1972 *DcTwDes, FacFETw*
**Balentine**, J Douglas 1937- *AmMWSc 92*
**Bales**, Barney Leroy 1939- *AmMWSc 92*
**Bales**, Bradley R. 1959- *WhoRel 92*
**Bales**, Connie Watkins 1954- *AmMWSc 92*
**Bales**, Dorothy Johnson 1927- *WhoEnt 92*
**Bales**, Edward Wagner 1939- *WhoMW 92*
**Bales**, Howard E 1912- *AmMWSc 92*
**Bales**, Jerry F *WhoAmP 91*
**Bales**, John Foster, III 1940- *WhoAmL 92*
**Bales**, Kenneth Frederick 1931- *Who 92*
**Bales**, Norman Lane 1935- *WhoRel 92*
**Bales**, Richard Henry Horner 1915- *WhoEnt 92*
**Balestier**, Wolcott 1861-1891 *BenetAL 91*
**Balestre**, Jean-Marie 1921- *IntWW 91*
**Balestri**, John 1947- *WhoAmP 91*
**Balestrini**, Silvio J 1922- *AmMWSc 92*
**Balestrino**, Charles Joseph 1941- *WhoFI 92*
**Balevski**, Angel Tonchev 1910- *IntWW 91*
**Balewa**, Alhaji 1912-1966 *FacFETw*
**Baley**, James M., Jr. 1912- *WhoAmL 92*
**Balfe**, Michael William 1808-1870 *NewAmDM*
**Balfe**, Richard Andrew 1944- *Who 92*
**Balfour** *Who 92*
**Balfour**, Earl of 1925- *Who 92*
**Balfour**, Andrew 1737-1782 *DcNCBi 1*
**Balfour**, Arthur 1848-1930 *EncTR 91 [port]*
**Balfour**, Arthur James 1848-1930 *FacFETw*
**Balfour**, Dale Elliman 1941- *WhoAmP 91*
**Balfour**, David Mathers 1910- *Who 92*
**Balfour**, Douglas James 1952- *WhoAmL 92*
**Balfour**, Elizabeth Jean 1927- *Who 92*
**Balfour**, Eve 1898-1990 *AnObit 1990*
**Balfour**, George Ian Mackintosh 1912- *Who 92*
**Balfour**, Henry H, Jr 1940- *AmMWSc 92*
**Balfour**, Hugh Maxwell 1933- *Who 92*
**Balfour**, Jean *Who 92*
**Balfour**, John Charles 1919- *Who 92*
**Balfour**, Mark Robin 1927- *Who 92*
**Balfour**, Michael 1908- *IntAu&W 91, WrDr 92*
**Balfour**, Michael John 1925- *Who 92*
**Balfour**, Nancy 1911- *Who 92*
**Balfour**, Neil Roxburgh 1944- *Who 92*
**Balfour**, Peter Edward Gerald 1921- *Who 92*
**Balfour**, Raymond Lewis 1923- *Who 92*
**Balfour**, Richard Creighton 1916- *Who 92*
**Balfour**, Robert George Victor FitzGeorge *Who 92*
**Balfour**, Walter Joseph 1941- *AmMWSc 92*
**Balfour**, William Mayo 1914- *AmMWSc 92*
**Balfour of Burleigh**, Lord 1927- *Who 92*
**Balfour of Inchrye**, Baron 1924- *Who 92*
**Balfour-Paul**, Glencairn 1917- *Who 92*
**Balgeman**, Richard Vernon 1929- *WhoMW 92*
**Balgonie**, Lord 1954- *Who 92*
**Balgooyen**, Thomas Gerrit 1943- *AmMWSc 92*
**Balguy**, John 1686-1748 *BlkwCEP*
**Balhajav**, Tserenpiliin 1928- *IntWW 91*
**Balhorn**, Rod Lowell 1947- *WhoWest 92*
**Balhuizen**, John Ross 1959- *WhoAmL 92*
**Balian**, Lorna 1929- *IntAu&W 91, WrDr 92*
**Balich**, Nicholas Samuel 1936- *WhoFI 92, WhoWest 92*
**Balick**, Helen Shaffer *WhoAmL 92*
**Balicki**, Zdzislaw 1930- *IntWW 91*
**Baliga**, B Surendra 1935- *AmMWSc 92*
**Baliga**, Jayant 1948- *AmMWSc 92*
**Balikov**, Henry R. 1946- *WhoFI 92*
**Baliles**, Gerald L. 1940- *IntWW 91, WhoAmP 91*
**Balin**, Arthur Kirsner 1948- *AmMWSc 92*
**Balin**, Ina 1937-1990 *ConTFT 9*
**Balin**, Marty 1942- *WhoEnt 92*
**Baline**, Israel *NewAmDM*
**Balinski**, Michel Louis 1933- *AmMWSc 92*
**Balinsky**, Doris 1934- *AmMWSc 92*
**Balint**, Daniel Lynn 1961- *WhoRel 92*
**Balint**, Enid *WrDr 92*
**Balint**, Francis Joseph 1932- *AmMWSc 92*
**Balint**, John Alexander 1925- *AmMWSc 92*
**Balint**, Joseph Philip 1948- *WhoWest 92*
**Balintfy**, Joseph L 1924- *AmMWSc 92*
**Baliozian**, Kevin Mardick 1962- *WhoFI 92*
**Balis**, John Ulysses 1932- *AmMWSc 92*
**Balis**, Moses Earl 1921- *AmMWSc 92*
**Balish**, Edward 1935- *AmMWSc 92*
**Baljon**, Johannes Marinus Simon 1919- *WhoRel 92*
**Balk**, Christianne *DrAPF 91*
**Balk**, Kenneth 1934- *WhoMW 92*
**Balk**, Pieter 1924- *AmMWSc 92*
**Balka**, Don Stephen 1946- *AmMWSc 92*
**Balka**, Sigmund Ronell 1935- *WhoAmL 92*
**Balkan**, Kenneth J. 1948- *WhoAmL 92*
**Balkany**, Thomas Jay *AmMWSc 92*
**Balkcom**, Ralph J *WhoAmP 91*
**Balke**, Bruno 1907- *AmMWSc 92*
**Balke**, Nelson Edward 1949- *AmMWSc 92*
**Balke**, Victor H. 1931- *WhoRel 92*
**Balkin**, Alan G. 1946- *WhoAmL 92*
**Balkin**, Jack M. 1956- *WhoAmL 92*
**Balkin**, Ruth Goldring 1951- *WhoAmL 92*
**Balkin**, Steven M. 1946- *WhoFI 92*
**Balkissoon**, Basdeo 1922- *AmMWSc 92*
**Balko**, George Anthony, III 1955- *WhoAmL 92*
**Balko**, Gregg Brian 1951- *WhoWest 92*
**Balkwill**, Bryan Havell 1922- *Who 92*
**Balkwill**, David Lee 1949- *AmMWSc 92*
**Ball**, Alfred 1921- *Who 92*
**Ball**, Alwyn Martin 1937- *WhoWest 92*
**Ball**, Angela *DrAPF 91*
**Ball**, Angela 1952- *ConAu 135*
**Ball**, Anthony George 1934- *Who 92*
**Ball**, Arthur Beresford 1923- *Who 92*
**Ball**, Ben C., Jr. 1928- *WhoFI 92*
**Ball**, Bill 1923- *WhoWest 92*
**Ball**, Billie Joe 1929- *AmMWSc 92*
**Ball**, Billy Joe 1925- *AmMWSc 92*
**Ball**, Blair Evan 1954- *WhoFI 92*
**Ball**, Brian N 1932- *IntAu&W 91*
**Ball**, Carroll Raybourne 1925- *AmMWSc 92*
**Ball**, Charles 1924- *Who 92*
**Ball**, Christopher 1935- *Who 92*
**Ball**, Christopher John Elinger 1935- *IntWW 91*
**Ball**, Christopher John Watkins 1939- *IntWW 91, Who 92*
**Ball**, Claire Melvin, Jr 1941- *WhoAmP 91*
**Ball**, Clarence M., Jr. 1949- *WhoBlA 92*
**Ball**, Clelland J *ScFEYrs*
**Ball**, Darrell Wayne 1960- *WhoMW 92*
**Ball**, David G. 1941- *WhoEnt 92*
**Ball**, David Lynn 1945- *WhoWest 92*
**Ball**, David Ralph 1940- *AmMWSc 92*
**Ball**, Davis Frederick 1938- *WhoEnt 92*
**Ball**, Denis William 1928- *Who 92*
**Ball**, Derek Harry 1931- *AmMWSc 92*
**Ball**, Donald Edmon 1942- *WhoWest 92*
**Ball**, Donald Lee 1931- *AmMWSc 92*
**Ball**, Douglas 1920- *AmMWSc 92*
**Ball**, Drexel Bernard 1948- *WhoBlA 92*
**Ball**, Earl Ellsworth 1930- *WhoRel 92*
**Ball**, Edward D 1950- *AmMWSc 92*
**Ball**, Edward James 1948- *AmMWSc 92*
**Ball**, Elizabeth Pierce 1959- *WhoEnt 92*
**Ball**, Eric Clinton 1966- *WhoBlA 92*
**Ball**, Eric Greaham 1955- *WhoRel 92*
**Ball**, Ernest R. 1878-1927 *NewAmDM*
**Ball**, Frances Louise 1924- *AmMWSc 92*
**Ball**, Frank Jervery 1919- *AmMWSc 92*
**Ball**, Frank P *ScFEYrs*
**Ball**, Fred 1924- *WhoFI 92*
**Ball**, Fred Shelton 1932- *WhoWest 92*
**Ball**, Gene V 1931- *AmMWSc 92*
**Ball**, George 1909- *WrDr 92*
**Ball**, George Eugene 1926- *AmMWSc 92*
**Ball**, George Wildman 1909- *IntWW 91, WhoAmP 91*
**Ball**, George William 1941- *AmMWSc 92*
**Ball**, Gordon Charles 1942- *AmMWSc 92*
**Ball**, Gregory Francis 1955- *AmMWSc 92*
**Ball**, Guy David 1953- *WhoWest 92*
**Ball**, Harold James 1919- *AmMWSc 92, WhoMW 92*
**Ball**, Harold William 1926- *Who 92*
**Ball**, Haywood Moreland 1939- *WhoAmL 92*
**Ball**, Irvin Joseph 1944- *AmMWSc 92*
**Ball**, James *IntWW 91, Who 92*
**Ball**, James Bryan 1932- *AmMWSc 92*
**Ball**, James Herington 1942- *WhoAmL 92, WhoFI 92*
**Ball**, James Stutsman 1934- *AmMWSc 92*
**Ball**, James William 1942- *WhoFI 92*
**Ball**, Jane Lee 1930- *WhoBlA 92*
**Ball**, Jerry Lee 1964- *WhoBlA 92*
**Ball**, Jo-Anne Moreland 1930- *WhoWest 92*
**Ball**, John 1911- *IntAu&W 91*
**Ball**, John Allen 1935- *AmMWSc 92*
**Ball**, John Bradley 1932- *IntAu&W 91*
**Ball**, John Calvin, Sr. 1924- *WhoBlA 92*
**Ball**, John Charles 1949- *WhoWest 92*

**Ball,** John Geoffrey 1916- *Who 92*
**Ball,** John Macleod 1948- *Who 92*
**Ball,** John Nelson 1938- *WhoRel 92*
**Ball,** John Sigler 1914- *AmMWSc 92*
**Ball,** Joseph Anthony 1947- *AmMWSc 92*
**Ball,** Joseph Edward 1904- *WhoWest 92*
**Ball,** Karen Susan 1947- *WhoAmP 91*
**Ball,** Kathleen Curry 1953- *WhoAmL 92*
**Ball,** Kenneth Leon 1932- *WhoFI 92, WhoMW 92*
**Ball,** Kenneth Steven 1960- *AmMWSc 92*
**Ball,** Laurence Andrew 1944- *AmMWSc 92*
**Ball,** Lawrence Ernest 1935- *AmMWSc 92, WhoMW 92*
**Ball,** Leslie David 1944- *WhoFI 92*
**Ball,** Louis Alvin 1921- *WhoMW 92*
**Ball,** Lucille d1989 *LesBEnT 92 [port]*
**Ball,** Lucille 1911-1989 *FacFETw [port]*
**Ball,** M Isabel 1929- *AmMWSc 92*
**Ball,** Mahlon M 1931- *AmMWSc 92*
**Ball,** Markham 1934- *WhoAmL 92*
**Ball,** Martin 1948- *TwCPaSc*
**Ball,** Mary Uhrich 1944- *AmMWSc 92*
**Ball,** Michael Owen 1950- *AmMWSc 92*
**Ball,** Michael Thomas *Who 92*
**Ball,** Nelson 1942- *ConAu 134*
**Ball,** Owen Keith, Jr. 1950- *WhoAmL 92*
**Ball,** Peter Eugene *TwCPaSc*
**Ball,** Peter John *Who 92*
**Ball,** Peter William 1930- *Who 92*
**Ball,** R.C. 1910- *TwCPaSc*
**Ball,** Raiford Mill 1941- *AmMWSc 92*
**Ball,** Ralph Adrian 1926- *WhoEnt 92*
**Ball,** Ralph Wayne 1925- *AmMWSc 92*
**Ball,** Rex Harrison 1943- *WhoAmP 91*
**Ball,** Richard E. 1918- *WhoBlA 92*
**Ball,** Richard William 1923- *AmMWSc 92*
**Ball,** Robert 1918- *TwCPaSc*
**Ball,** Robert Bates, Sr *WhoAmP 91*
**Ball,** Robert Edwin 1935- *WhoWest 92*
**Ball,** Robert Hamilton 1902- *IntAu&W 91*
**Ball,** Robert James 1933- *IntWW 91, Who 92*
**Ball,** Robert James 1949- *WhoRel 92*
**Ball,** Robert Kenneth, II 1937- *WhoAmL 92*
**Ball,** Robert Spencer 1941- *WhoAmL 92*
**Ball,** Robin Ann 1963- *WhoMW 92*
**Ball,** Roger Alford 1944- *WhoAmP 91*
**Ball,** Rosemary Louise 1957- *WhoMW 92*
**Ball,** Roy Orville 1945- *WhoFI 92*
**Ball,** Russell Martin 1927- *AmMWSc 92*
**Ball,** Stanton Mock 1933- *AmMWSc 92*
**Ball,** Thomas Eric 1956- *WhoRel 92*
**Ball,** Troy Eugene 1946- *WhoWest 92*
**Ball,** Wilbur Perry 1923- *AmMWSc 92*
**Ball,** Wilfred R. 1932- *WhoBlA 92*
**Ball,** William d1991 *NewYTBS 91 [port]*
**Ball,** William 1923- *WhoAmP 91*
**Ball,** William 1931- *IntWW 91*
**Ball,** William 1931-1991 *CurBio 91N*
**Ball,** William Batten 1928- *WhoBlA 92*
**Ball,** William David 1937- *AmMWSc 92*
**Ball,** William E 1930- *AmMWSc 92*
**Ball,** William Henry Warren 1921- *AmMWSc 92*
**Ball,** William James 1910- *WhoMW 92*
**Ball,** William James, Jr 1942- *AmMWSc 92*
**Ball,** William L 1948- *WhoAmP 91*
**Ball,** William Paul 1913- *AmMWSc 92, WhoWest 92*
**Ball,** William Raymond 1952- *WhoEnt 92*
**Ball-Kilbourne,** Debra Gayle 1951- *WhoRel 92*
**Ball-Kilbourne,** Gary Lee 1953- *WhoRel 92*
**Ball-Sundine,** Sandra Jean 1963- *WhoWest 92*
**Balla,** Bulcsu 1934- *WhoFI 92, WhoMW 92*
**Balla,** Giacomo 1871-1958 *FacFETw*
**Balladur,** Edouard 1929- *IntWW 91*
**Ballal,** S K 1938- *AmMWSc 92, WhoAmP 91*
**Ballam,** Joseph 1917- *AmMWSc 92*
**Ballam,** Michael L. 1951- *WhoWest 92*
**Ballam,** Samuel Humes, Jr. 1919- *WhoFI 92*
**Ballance,** Frank Winston, Jr 1942- *WhoAmP 91, WhoBlA 92*
**Ballance,** Robert Michael 1957- *WhoFI 92*
**Ballanfant,** Kathleen Gamber 1945- *WhoFI 92*
**Ballantine,** Beverly Neblett 1941- *WhoAmL 92*
**Ballantine,** C S 1929- *AmMWSc 92*
**Ballantine,** David Stephen 1922- *AmMWSc 92*
**Ballantine,** Duncan Smith 1912- *IntWW 91*
**Ballantine,** Grant 1941- *Who 92*
**Ballantine,** Ian 1916- *IntWW 91*
**Ballantine,** John Tilden 1931- *WhoAmL 92*
**Ballantine,** Larry Gene 1944- *AmMWSc 92*
**Ballantine,** Mary Keith 1926- *WhoAmP 91*
**Ballantine,** Morley Cowles 1925- *WhoFI 92, WhoWest 92*
**Ballantine,** Thomas Austin, Jr. 1926- *WhoAmL 92*
**Ballantyne,** Bryan 1934- *AmMWSc 92*
**Ballantyne,** Colin Sandergrove d1988 *Who 92N*
**Ballantyne,** David John 1931- *AmMWSc 92*
**Ballantyne,** Donald Lindsay 1922- *AmMWSc 92*
**Ballantyne,** Garth H 1951- *AmMWSc 92*
**Ballantyne,** Jerome Brooks 1947- *WhoMW 92*
**Ballantyne,** John 1917- *WrDr 92*
**Ballantyne,** Joseph M 1934- *AmMWSc 92*
**Ballantyne,** R. M. 1825-1894 *RfGEnL 91*
**Ballantyne,** Sheila *DrAPF 91*
**Ballarat,** Bishop of 1924- *Who 92*
**Ballarat,** Bishop of 1930- *Who 92*
**Ballard,** Alden G *WhoAmP 91*
**Ballard,** Alexandrous L.W. 1965- *WhoEnt 92*
**Ballard,** Alice Walker 1948- *WhoAmL 92*
**Ballard,** Allen Butler, Jr. 1930- *WhoBlA 92*
**Ballard,** Billy Ray 1940- *WhoBlA 92*
**Ballard,** Billy Ward 1925- *WhoAmP 91*
**Ballard,** Bruce Laine 1939- *WhoBlA 92*
**Ballard,** Carroll 1937- *IntMPA 92*
**Ballard,** Charles Joseph 1943- *WhoRel 92*
**Ballard,** Christine G. 1947- *WhoEnt 92*
**Ballard,** Clark Tilton, Jr. 1941- *WhoWest 92*
**Ballard,** Clifford Frederick 1910- *Who 92*
**Ballard,** Clyde 1936- *WhoAmP 91*
**Ballard,** Eddie 1929- *WhoAmP 91*
**Ballard,** Edna Anne Wheeler 1886-1971 *RelLAm 91*
**Ballard,** Edward Hunter 1900- *WhoBlA 92*
**Ballard,** Edward Parke 1916- *WhoAmP 91*
**Ballard,** Emmett Jessee, II 1950- *WhoAmL 92*
**Ballard,** Frederic Lyman, Jr. 1941- *WhoAmL 92*
**Ballard,** Gerald Porter 1936- *WhoMW 92, WhoRel 92*
**Ballard,** Greg 1955- *WhoBlA 92*
**Ballard,** Guy Warren 1878-1939 *RelLAm 91*
**Ballard,** Harold 1903-1990 *AnObit 1990, FacFETw*
**Ballard,** Harold Noble 1919- *AmMWSc 92*
**Ballard,** Harold Stanley 1927- *WhoBlA 92*
**Ballard,** J.G. *DrAPF 91*
**Ballard,** J. G. 1930- *ConNov 91, FacFETw, RfGEnL 91, TwCSFW 91, WrDr 92*
**Ballard,** Jack Stokes 1928- *WhoWest 92*
**Ballard,** Jackie Wayne 1954- *WhoMW 92*
**Ballard,** James Alan 1929- *AmMWSc 92*
**Ballard,** James Graham 1930- *IntAu&W 91, IntWW 91, Who 92*
**Ballard,** James M., Jr. 1938- *WhoBlA 92*
**Ballard,** Janet Jones 1930- *WhoBlA 92*
**Ballard,** John David 1936- *WhoIns 92*
**Ballard,** John Frederick 1943- *Who 92*
**Ballard,** John Houston, III 1944- *WhoIns 92*
**Ballard,** John Stuart 1922- *WhoAmP 91*
**Ballard,** Joseph Grant 1928- *WhoMW 92*
**Ballard,** Juliet Lyle Brooke 1913- *IntAu&W 91*
**Ballard,** Kathryn W. 1930- *WhoBlA 92*
**Ballard,** Kathryn Wise 1930- *AmMWSc 92*
**Ballard,** Kaye *WhoEnt 92*
**Ballard,** Kaye 1926- *IntMPA 92*
**Ballard,** Kenneth J 1930- *AmMWSc 92*
**Ballard,** Larry Coleman 1935- *WhoFI 92, WhoIns 92, WhoMW 92*
**Ballard,** Lewis Franklin 1934- *AmMWSc 92*
**Ballard,** Louis W. 1931- *NewAmDM*
**Ballard,** Louis Wayne 1931- *WhoEnt 92*
**Ballard,** Lowell Douglas 1933- *WhoFI 92*
**Ballard,** Marguerite Candler 1920- *AmMWSc 92*
**Ballard,** Marshall 1942- *WhoFI 92*
**Ballard,** Melvin Russell, Jr. 1928- *WhoRel 92*
**Ballard,** Michael d1991 *NewYTBS 91*
**Ballard,** Michael Alan 1960- *WhoRel 92*
**Ballard,** Michael Eugene 1953- *WhoAmL 92*
**Ballard,** Myrtle Ethel 1930- *WhoBlA 92*
**Ballard,** Neil Brian 1938- *AmMWSc 92*
**Ballard,** Orville 1935- *WhoEnt 92*
**Ballard,** Ralph Campbell 1926- *AmMWSc 92*
**Ballard,** Robert D 1942- *AmMWSc 92*
**Ballard,** Roger K. 1935- *WhoFI 92*
**Ballard,** Ronald Alfred 1925- *Who 92*
**Ballard,** Ronald Lee 1947- *WhoAmL 92*
**Ballard,** Ronald Michael 1958- *WhoAmL 92*
**Ballard,** Stanley Sumner 1908- *AmMWSc 92*
**Ballard,** Wade Hampton, II 1904- *WhoAmP 91*
**Ballard,** Walter W. 1928- *WhoBlA 92*
**Ballard,** William Donaldson 1927- *WhoAmP 91*
**Ballard,** William Ralph 1926- *WhoWest 92*
**Ballard,** Willis Todhunter 1903-1980 *TwCWW 91*
**Ballarini,** Roberto 1958- *WhoMW 92*
**Ballas,** Zuhari K *AmMWSc 92*
**Ballas-Traynor,** Lucia Veronica 1964- *WhoHisp 92*
**Ballato,** Arthur 1936- *AmMWSc 92*
**Balle,** Francis 1939- *IntWW 91*
**Balleisen,** Donald Herbert 1924- *WhoAmL 92*
**Ballen,** Robert Gerald 1956- *WhoAmL 92*
**Ballengee,** James Richard 1935- *WhoFI 92*
**Ballenger,** Cass 1926- *AlmAP 92 [port]*
**Ballenger,** Hurley Rene 1946- *WhoFI 92, WhoMW 92*
**Ballenger,** James Caudell 1944- *AmMWSc 92*
**Ballenger,** Thomas Cass 1926- *WhoAmP 91*
**Ballentine,** Alva Ray 1931- *AmMWSc 92*
**Ballentine,** J. Gregory 1948- *WhoFI 92*
**Ballentine,** Krim Menelik 1936- *WhoAmP 91, WhoBlA 92*
**Ballentine,** Lee Kenney 1954- *WhoWest 92*
**Ballentine,** Leslie Edward 1940- *AmMWSc 92*
**Ballentine,** Michael C. d1991 *NewYTBS 91*
**Ballentine,** Robert 1914- *AmMWSc 92*
**Ballentine,** Rudolph Miller 1941- *AmMWSc 92, WhoFI 92*
**Ballentyne,** Donald Francis 1929- *Who 92*
**Baller,** Robert Stuart 1936- *WhoMW 92*
**Ballerini,** Rocco 1958- *AmMWSc 92*
**Balleroy,** Albert de 1828-1873 *ThHEIm [port]*
**Balles,** John Joseph 1921- *WhoFI 92*
**Ballestero,** Manuel 1937- *WhoHisp 92*
**Ballestero,** Thomas P 1953- *AmMWSc 92*
**Ballesteros,** David 1933- *WhoHisp 92*
**Ballesteros,** Frank Trujillo 1948- *WhoHisp 92*
**Ballesteros,** Hugo 1923- *WhoHisp 92*
**Ballesteros,** Juventino Ray, Jr. 1953- *WhoRel 92*
**Ballesteros,** Mario Alberto 1952- *WhoHisp 92*
**Ballesteros,** Severiano 1957- *Who 92*
**Ballesteros Sota,** Severiano 1957- *IntWW 91*
**Ballestrero,** Anastasio Alberto 1913- *IntWW 91, WhoRel 92*
**Ballew,** Charles *TwCWW 91*
**Ballew,** David Wayne 1940- *AmMWSc 92*
**Ballew,** Frederick Keith 1938- *WhoAmP 91*
**Ballew,** Glenn L. 1948- *WhoIns 92*
**Ballew,** Leighton Milton 1916- *WhoEnt 92*
**Ballew,** Royce Avery 1935- *WhoRel 92*
**Ballhaus,** Michael 1935- *IntMPA 92, WhoEnt 92*
**Ballhaus,** William F 1918- *AmMWSc 92*
**Ballhaus,** William Francis 1918- *WhoFI 92*
**Ballhaus,** William Francis, Jr 1945- *AmMWSc 92, WhoWest 92*
**Balliett,** John William 1947- *WhoFI 92*
**Balliett,** Whitney 1926- *WhoEnt 92, WrDr 92*
**Ballif,** Claude 1924- *ConCom 92*
**Ballif,** Jae R 1931- *AmMWSc 92*
**Ballin,** Ernst Hirsch *IntWW 91*
**Ballina,** Rudolph August 1934- *AmMWSc 92*
**Balling,** Jan Walter 1934- *AmMWSc 92*
**Ballinger,** Carter M 1922- *AmMWSc 92*
**Ballinger,** Charles A. 1942- *WhoEnt 92*
**Ballinger,** Charles Edwin 1935- *WhoWest 92*
**Ballinger,** Charles Kenneth 1950- *WhoWest 92*
**Ballinger,** Glenn Thomas 1943- *WhoIns 92*
**Ballinger,** James N 1914- *WhoAmP 91*
**Ballinger,** Laura 1957- *WhoRel 92*
**Ballinger,** Peter Richard 1932- *AmMWSc 92*
**Ballinger,** Philip Albert 1957- *WhoWest 92*
**Ballinger,** Richard Achilles 1858-1922 *AmPolLe*
**Ballinger,** Royce Eugene 1942- *AmMWSc 92*
**Ballinger,** Ruth Ann 1960- *WhoWest 92*
**Ballinger,** Walter Elmer 1926- *AmMWSc 92*
**Ballinger,** Walter F, II 1925- *AmMWSc 92*
**Ballintulo,** Gillian Nataniel *WhoEnt 92*
**Balliro,** Joseph James 1928- *WhoAmL 92*
**Ballman,** B. George 1931- *WhoAmL 92*
**Ballman,** Donna Marie 1959- *WhoAmL 92*
**Ballmann,** Donald Lawrence 1927- *AmMWSc 92*
**Ballmer,** Ray Wayne 1926- *IntWW 91, WhoFI 92*
**Ballot,** Michael Harvey 1940- *WhoFI 92*
**Ballotti,** Geoffrey A. 1961- *WhoFI 92*
**Ballou,** Adin 1803-1890 *AmPeW, BenetAL 91*
**Ballou,** Arthur W. 1915-1981 *ConAu 134*
**Ballou,** Clinton Edward 1923- *AmMWSc 92, IntWW 91*
**Ballou,** David Penfield 1942- *AmMWSc 92, WhoMW 92*
**Ballou,** Donald Henry 1908- *AmMWSc 92*
**Ballou,** Donald Pollard 1940- *AmMWSc 92*
**Ballou,** Esther 1915-1973 *NewAmDM*
**Ballou,** John Edgerton 1925- *AmMWSc 92*
**Ballou,** Nathan Elmer 1919- *AmMWSc 92*
**Ballou,** Richard A 1945- *WhoAmP 91*
**Ballou,** Ronald Herman 1937- *WhoMW 92*
**Ballou,** Timothy Joseph 1964- *WhoEnt 92*
**Ballow,** Yvonne *TwCPaSc*
**Ballowe,** James *DrAPF 91*
**Balls,** Alastair Gordon 1944- *Who 92*
**Balluffi,** R W 1924- *AmMWSc 92*
**Ballweg,** Larry Veneard 1944- *WhoAmP 91*
**Ballweg,** Mary Lou 1948- *WhoMW 92*
**Ballweg,** Mitchell Joseph 1958- *WhoAmL 92*
**Bally,** Albert Walter 1925- *AmMWSc 92*
**Balm-Demmel,** Darline Dawn Miller 1933- *WhoRel 92*
**Balmain,** Keith George 1933- *AmMWSc 92*
**Balmain,** Pierre 1904-1982 *DcTwDes*
**Balmaseda,** Elizabeth R. 1959- *WhoHisp 92*
**Balmer,** Barbara 1929- *TwCPaSc*
**Balmer,** Clifford Earl 1921- *AmMWSc 92*
**Balmer,** David Gregory 1962- *WhoAmP 91*
**Balmer,** Derek 1934- *TwCPaSc*
**Balmer,** Edwin 1883-1959 *ScFEYrs*
**Balmer,** Horace Dalton, Sr. 1939- *WhoBlA 92*
**Balmer,** Joseph 1899- *Who 92*
**Balmer,** Robert Theodore 1938- *AmMWSc 92*
**Balmer,** Thomas Ancil 1952- *WhoAmL 92*
**Balmforth,** Anthony James 1926- *Who 92*
**Balmforth,** Dennis 1930- *AmMWSc 92*
**Balmont,** Boris Vladimirovich 1927- *IntWW 91*
**Balmont,** Konstantin Dmitrievich 1864-1943 *LiExTwC*
**Balnicky,** Robert Gabriel 1922- *WhoRel 92*
**Balniel,** Lord 1958- *Who 92*
**Balodis,** Janis 1950- *ConAu 134, WrDr 92*
**Balog,** B.E. *DrAPF 91*
**Balog,** George 1928- *AmMWSc 92*
**Balog,** James 1928- *WhoFI 92*
**Balog,** Richard Thomas 1951- *WhoFI 92*
**Balog,** Rita Jean 1930- *WhoMW 92*
**Balogh,** Charles B 1929- *AmMWSc 92*
**Balogh,** Connie Lee 1949- *WhoWest 92*
**Balogh,** Karoly 1930- *AmMWSc 92*
**Balogh,** Lajos 1931- *WhoEnt 92*
**Balogh,** Linda Jean 1950- *WhoFI 92*
**Balogun,** Kolawole 1926- *IntWW 91*
**Baloian,** James C. *DrAPF 91*
**Balon,** Eugene Kornel 1930- *AmMWSc 92*
**Balonon,** Peter M. 1945- *WhoHisp 92*
**Balota,** D.A. 1954- *ConAu 135*
**Baloun,** Calvin H 1928- *AmMWSc 92*
**Balousek,** John B. *WhoFI 92*
**Balow,** James E 1942- *AmMWSc 92*
**Baloyra,** Enrique Antonio 1942- *WhoHisp 92*
**Balph,** David Finley 1931- *AmMWSc 92*
**Balph,** Martha Hatch 1943- *AmMWSc 92*
**Bals,** Jerry John 1941- *WhoMW 92, WhoRel 92*
**Balsai,** Istvan 1947- *IntWW 91*
**Balsam,** Artur 1906- *NewAmDM*
**Balsam,** Martin 1919- *IntMPA 92*
**Balsam,** Martin Henry 1919- *IntWW 91, WhoEnt 92*
**Balsano,** Joseph Silvio 1937- *AmMWSc 92*
**Balsbaugh,** Edward Ulmont, Jr 1933- *AmMWSc 92*
**Balsbaugh,** Jesse Dale 1951- *WhoMW 92*
**Balseiro,** Jose Agustin 1900- *WhoHisp 92*
**Balsemao,** Francisco Pinto *IntWW 91*
**Balser,** Elnora Marie 1952- *WhoWest 92*
**Balser,** Walter Thomas 1925- *WhoAmP 91*
**Balsiger,** David Wayne 1945- *WhoRel 92, WhoWest 92*
**Balsley,** Ben Burton 1932- *AmMWSc 92, WhoWest 92*
**Balsley,** Philip Elwood 1939- *WhoEnt 92*
**Balstad,** Jan 1937- *IntWW 91*
**Balster,** Clifford Arthur 1922- *AmMWSc 92*
**Balster,** Robert L 1944- *AmMWSc 92*
**Balsters,** Harold Walter 1930- *WhoMW 92*
**Balston,** Antony Francis 1939- *Who 92*
**Baltake,** Joe 1945- *WhoEnt 92*
**Baltakis,** Paul Antanas 1925- *WhoRel 92*
**Baltakis,** Paulius *DcAmImH*

**Baltay**, Charles 1937- AmMWSc 92
**Baltazar**, Eulalio WrDr 92
**Baltazzi**, Evan S 1919- AmMWSc 92
**Baltensperger**, Arden Albert 1922- AmMWSc 92
**Baltensperger**, David Dwight 1953- AmMWSc 92
**Balter**, Alan WhoEnt 92
**Balthaser**, James Harvey 1954- WhoAmL 92
**Balthaser**, Lawrence Harold 1937- AmMWSc 92
**Balthazar**, Brandon 1955- WhoFI 92
**Balthazar**, Earl Edward 1918- WhoMW 92
**Balthazard**, Mark Joseph 1957- WhoAmL 92
**Balthazor**, Terrell Mack 1949- AmMWSc 92
**Balthis**, Bill W WhoAmP 91
**Balthrop**, David Scott 1959- WhoEnt 92
**Balthrope**, Jacqueline Morehead WhoBlA 92
**Balthus** IntWW 91
**Baltierra**, Ronald J. WhoHisp 92
**Baltimore**, David 1938- AmMWSc 92, FacFETw, IntWW 91, Who 92, WhoNob 90
**Baltimore**, Richard Lewis, III 1947- WhoBlA 92
**Baltimore**, Roslyn Lois 1942- WhoBlA 92
**Baltl**, Hermann Josef 1918- IntWW 91
**Baltodano**, Guiselle 1944- WhoHisp 92
**Balton**, Kirkwood R. 1935- WhoBlA 92
**Balton**, Nancy Crain 1935- WhoAmP 91
**Baltrusaitis**, Rose Mary 1950- AmMWSc 92
**Baltrusitis**, Arleane 1951- WhoHisp 92
**Baltsa**, Agnes IntWW 91
**Baltuch**, Marc 1945- WhoFI 92
**Baltus**, Rita Kleiber 1925- WhoMW 92
**Baltz**, Anthony John 1942- AmMWSc 92
**Baltz**, Howard Burl 1930- AmMWSc 92
**Baltz**, Michael Thomas 1948- WhoMW 92
**Baltz**, Walter F 1938- WhoAmP 91
**Baltzer**, Cynthia Louise 1955- WhoEnt 92
**Baltzer**, Kimberly Lenore 1964- WhoMW 92
**Baltzer**, Otto John 1916- AmMWSc 92
**Baltzer**, Philip Keene 1924- AmMWSc 92
**Baluda**, Marcel A 1930- AmMWSc 92
**Baluni**, Alice 1945- WhoWest 92
**Balut**, George Samuel 1955- WhoMW 92
**Balvanz**, Brenda Marie 1966- WhoMW 92
**Balverde-Sanchez**, Laura WhoHisp 92
**Balwanz**, William Walter 1913- AmMWSc 92
**Balwierczak**, Joseph Leonard 1954- AmMWSc 92
**Baly**, Elaine Vivienne 1922- IntAu&W 91
**Baly**, Hilda 1966- WhoHisp 92
**Balyo**, John Gabriel 1920- WhoRel 92, WhoWest 92
**Balz**, Frank Joseph 1950- WhoFI 92
**Balzac**, Honore de 1799-1850 GuFrLit 1, ScFEYrs
**Balzer**, Giorgio 1940- WhoIns 92
**Balzer**, Howard Marc 1951- WhoMW 92
**Balzer**, Joel 1956- WhoRel 92
**Balzhiser**, Richard E 1932- AmMWSc 92
**Bam**, Brigalia Hlophe 1933- DcEcMov
**Bamba**, George 1951- WhoAmP 91
**Bamba**, Joseph George 1951- WhoWest 92
**Bambace**, Angela 1898-1975 DcAmImH
**Bambace**, Robert Shelly 1930- WhoAmL 92
**Bambacus**, John N 1945- WhoAmP 91
**Bambara**, Robert Anthony 1949- AmMWSc 92
**Bambara**, Toni Cade DrAPF 91
**Bambara**, Toni Cade 1939- BenetAL 91, BlkLC [port], WhoBlA 92
**Bambenek**, Mark A 1934- AmMWSc 92
**Bamber**, Anthony 1941- TwCPaSc
**Bamber**, Frederick Boyd 1943- WhoFI 92
**Bamber**, George DrAPF 91
**Bamberg**, Harold Rolf 1923- Who 92
**Bamberger**, Carlos Enrique Leopoldo 1933- AmMWSc 92
**Bamberger**, Charles 1944- WhoHisp 92
**Bamberger**, Curt 1900- AmMWSc 92
**Bamberger**, Henry 1935- WhoRel 92
**Bamberger**, Judy 1952- AmMWSc 92
**Bamberger**, Michael 1960- ConAu 134
**Bamberger**, Michael Albert 1936- WhoAmL 92
**Bamberger**, Phylis Skloot 1939- WhoAmL 92
**Bamberry**, Carol Ross WhoFI 92
**Bamborough**, John Bernard 1921- Who 92
**Bambrey**, Thomas Edward 1946- WhoWest 92
**Bambrick**, James Alan 1946- WhoIns 92
**Bambrick**, James Joseph 1917- WhoMW 92
**Bambuck**, Roger 1945- BlkOlyM
**Bamburg**, James Robert 1943- AmMWSc 92
**Bame**, Samuel Jarvis, Jr 1924- AmMWSc 92
**Bamfield**, Clifford 1922- Who 92
**Bamford**, Alan George 1930- Who 92
**Bamford**, Anthony 1945- Who 92
**Bamford**, Brian Reginald 1932- WrDr 92
**Bamford**, Clement Henry 1912- IntWW 91, Who 92
**Bamford**, Ian 1948-1975 TwCPaSc
**Bamford**, Joseph Cyril 1916- Who 92
**Bamford**, Louis Neville Jules 1932- Who 92
**Bamford**, Robert Wendell 1937- AmMWSc 92
**Bamforth**, Betty Jane 1923- AmMWSc 92
**Bamforth**, Stuart Shoosmith 1926- AmMWSc 92
**Bammer**, Richard Earl 1950- WhoEnt 92
**Bammes**, Donald Ray 1938- WhoMW 92
**Bampfylde** Who 92
**Bampton**, Rose 1909- NewAmDM
**Bampton**, Rose Elizabeth 1907- WhoEnt 92
**Bamrick**, Eileen Marie 1964- WhoFI 92
**Bamrick**, John Francis 1926- AmMWSc 92, WhoMW 92
**Ban**, John Robert 1931- WhoMW 92
**Ban**, Stephen Dennis 1940- AmMWSc 92
**Ban**, Stephen Peter 1962- WhoMW 92
**Ban**, Thomas Arthur 1929- AmMWSc 92, WrDr 92
**Ban**, Vladimir Sinisa 1941- AmMWSc 92
**Banach**, Art John 1931- WhoFI 92, WhoMW 92
**Banahan**, Christopher 1958- TwCPaSc
**Banai**, Moshe 1948- WhoFI 92
**Banaitis**, Daiva Audenas 1940- WhoWest 92
**Banakar**, Umesh Virupaksh 1956- AmMWSc 92
**Banales**, Frank 1945- WhoHisp 92
**Banales**, Irma 1956- WhoHisp 92
**Banales**, J. Manuel WhoHisp 92
**Banana**, Canaan Sodindo 1936- IntWW 91, Who 92
**Bananal**, Eduardo Florendo 1911- WhoWest 92
**Banas**, Emil Mike 1921- WhoWest 92
**Banas**, Richard Frederick 1948- WhoFI 92
**Banasiak**, Dennis Stephen 1950- AmMWSc 92
**Banasik**, Orville James 1919- AmMWSc 92
**Banasik**, Robert Casmer 1942- WhoFI 92, WhoMW 92
**Banaszak**, John Dennis 1945- WhoMW 92
**Banaszak**, Leonard Jerome 1933- AmMWSc 92
**Banaugh**, Robert Peter 1922- AmMWSc 92
**Banavar**, Jayanth Ramarao 1953- AmMWSc 92
**Banay-Schwartz**, Miriam 1929- AmMWSc 92
**Banbury** Who 92
**Banbury**, Frederick Harold Frith 1912- Who 92
**Banbury**, Frith Who 92
**Banbury**, Frith 1912- IntWW 91
**Banbury**, Jeffrey Edward 1951- WhoEnt 92
**Banbury**, Philip 1914- WrDr 92
**Banbury**, William 1871- TwCPaSc
**Banbury of Southam**, Baron 1953- Who 92
**Banchero**, J T 1914- AmMWSc 92
**Banchero**, Joseph Jerry 1937- WhoWest 92
**Banchero**, Natalio 1935- AmMWSc 92
**Banchieri**, Adriano 1568-1634 NewAmDM
**Banchs**, Jaime 1946- WhoHisp 92
**Bancquart**, Alain 1934- ConCom 92
**Bancroft** Who 92
**Bancroft**, Baron 1922- IntWW 91, Who 92
**Bancroft**, Alexander Clerihew 1938- WhoAmL 92
**Bancroft**, Anne 1923- IntAu&W 91, WrDr 92
**Bancroft**, Anne 1931- IntMPA 92, IntWW 91, WhoEnt 92
**Bancroft**, Bruce Richard 1940- WhoAmL 92, WhoMW 92
**Bancroft**, Charles E. 1925- WhoIns 92
**Bancroft**, Dennison 1911- AmMWSc 92
**Bancroft**, Edward 1744-1821 BlInAmS
**Bancroft**, Elizabeth Abercrombie 1947- WhoFI 92
**Bancroft**, George 1800-1891 BenetAL 91, RComAH
**Bancroft**, George Michael 1942- AmMWSc 92
**Bancroft**, Harold Ramsey 1932- AmMWSc 92
**Bancroft**, Hubert Howe 1832-1918 BenetAL 91
**Bancroft**, Iris 1922- IntAu&W 91
**Bancroft**, John Basil 1929- AmMWSc 92
**Bancroft**, Laura ConAu 133
**Bancroft**, Lewis Clinton 1929- AmMWSc 92
**Bancroft**, Margaret Armstrong 1938- WhoAmL 92
**Bancroft**, Paul, III 1930- WhoFI 92
**Bancroft**, Paul Marshall 1954- WhoFI 92, WhoIns 92
**Bancroft**, Richard Anderson 1918- WhoBlA 92
**Bancroft**, Richard Wolcott 1916- AmMWSc 92
**Bancroft**, Ronald Mann 1943- WhoFI 92
**Band**, The FacFETw, NewAmDM
**Band**, Albert 1924- IntMPA 92
**Band**, Charles 1951- IntMPA 92
**Band**, David 1942- Who 92, WhoFI 92
**Band**, David 1959- TwCPaSc
**Band**, Hans Eduard 1924- AmMWSc 92
**Band**, Jonathan 1959- WhoAmL 92
**Band**, Jordan Clifford 1923- WhoAmL 92
**Band**, Pierre Robert 1935- AmMWSc 92
**Band**, Robert Murray Niven 1919- Who 92
**Band**, Rudolph Neal 1929- AmMWSc 92
**Band**, Thomas Mollison 1934- Who 92
**Band**, William 1906- AmMWSc 92
**Band**, Yehuda Benzion 1946- AmMWSc 92
**Banda**, Aleke Kadonaphani 1939- IntWW 91
**Banda**, Hastings Kamuzu 1905- Who 92
**Banda**, Hastings Kamuzu 1906- FacFETw, IntWW 91
**Banda**, Rupiah Bwezani 1937- IntWW 91
**Banda**, Siva S 1951- AmMWSc 92
**Bandar Ibn Sultan Ibn Abdulaziz Al-Saud** 1949- IntWW 91
**Bandaranaike**, Sirimavo 1916- FacFETw, Who 92
**Bandaranaike**, Sirimavo Ratwatte Dias 1916- IntWW 91
**Bandaranaike**, Solomon West Ridgeway Dias 1899-1959 FacFETw
**Bande**, Andres 1944- WhoHisp 92
**Bande**, Andres B. WhoMW 92
**Bandeen**, Robert Angus 1930- IntWW 91
**Bandeen**, William Reid 1926- AmMWSc 92
**Bandeira**, Manuel 1886-1968 BenetAL 91
**Bandeira De Mello**, Lydio Machado 1901- IntWW 91
**Bandel**, Ehud 1956- WhoRel 92
**Bandel**, Hannskarl 1925- AmMWSc 92
**Bandel**, Herman William 1916- AmMWSc 92
**Bandel**, Vernon Allan 1937- AmMWSc 92
**Bandelier**, Adolph DcAmImH
**Bandelier**, Adolph Francis Alphonse 1840-1914 BenetAL 91, BlInAmS
**Bander**, Edward Julius 1923- WhoAmL 92
**Bander**, Myron 1937- AmMWSc 92
**Bander**, Norman Robert WhoFI 92
**Bander**, Thomas Samuel 1924- WhoMW 92
**Banderas**, Antonio WhoHisp 92
**Banderas**, Quintin 1834-1906 HisDSpE
**Bandes**, Dean 1944- AmMWSc 92
**Bandes**, Herbert 1914- AmMWSc 92
**Bandi**, William R 1924- AmMWSc 92
**Bandick**, Neal Raymond 1938- AmMWSc 92
**Bandier**, Martin WhoEnt 92
**Bandish**, Dennis Michael 1948- WhoFI 92
**Bandler**, John William 1941- AmMWSc 92, IntWW 91
**Bandman**, Everett 1947- AmMWSc 92
**Bando**, Thelma Preyer 1919- WhoBlA 92
**Bandong**, Paul Anthony 1956- WhoFI 92, WhoWest 92
**Bandoni**, Robert Joseph 1926- AmMWSc 92
**Bandopadhyaya**, Amitava 1957- WhoMW 92
**Bandow**, Douglas Leighton 1957- WhoAmP 91
**Bandstra**, Richard WhoAmP 91
**Bandur**, Stanley Raymond 1953- WhoMW 92
**Bandura**, Albert 1925- WrDr 92
**Bandurski**, Robert Stanley 1924- AmMWSc 92
**Bandy**, Alan Ray 1940- AmMWSc 92
**Bandy**, Albert WhoEnt 92
**Bandy**, Mary Lea 1943- IntMPA 92
**Bandy**, Moe 1944- NewAmDM
**Bandy**, Percy John 1927- AmMWSc 92
**Bandy**, Riley Thomas, Sr. 1920- WhoBlA 92
**Bane**, Frank B 1893-1983 FacFETw
**Bane**, Gilbert Winfield 1931- AmMWSc 92
**Bane**, John McGuire, Jr 1946- AmMWSc 92
**Bane**, Margo Ewing 1949- WhoAmP 91
**Bane**, Marilyn Annette 1943- WhoFI 92
**Bane**, Tom 1913- WhoAmP 91
**Banegas**, Estevan Brown 1941- WhoFI 92
**Banerjee**, Amit 1958- WhoMW 92
**Banerjee**, Amiya Kumar 1936- AmMWSc 92
**Banerjee**, Chandra Madhab 1932- AmMWSc 92
**Banerjee**, Debendranath 1935- AmMWSc 92
**Banerjee**, Dipak Kumar 1947- AmMWSc 92
**Banerjee**, Kali Shankar 1914- AmMWSc 92
**Banerjee**, Mihir R 1927- AmMWSc 92
**Banerjee**, Mukul Ranjan 1937- AmMWSc 92
**Banerjee**, Prasanta Kumar 1941- AmMWSc 92
**Banerjee**, Prashant 1962- WhoMW 92
**Banerjee**, Prithviraj 1960- AmMWSc 92
**Banerjee**, R L 1933- AmMWSc 92
**Banerjee**, Ranjit 1948- AmMWSc 92
**Banerjee**, Samarendranath 1932- WhoMW 92
**Banerjee**, Sanjay Kumar 1958- AmMWSc 92
**Banerjee**, Sipra 1939- AmMWSc 92
**Banerjee**, Subir Kumar 1938- AmMWSc 92
**Banerjee**, Surath Kumar 1938- AmMWSc 92, WhoMW 92
**Banerjee**, Sushanta Kumar 1927- AmMWSc 92
**Banerjee**, Umesh Chandra 1937- AmMWSc 92
**Banerjee**, Utpal 1942- AmMWSc 92
**Banerjee**, Victor 1946- ConTFT 9
**Banerji**, Asoka Nath 1917- IntWW 91
**Banerji**, Ranan Bihari 1928- AmMWSc 92
**Banerji**, Sara Ann 1932- IntAu&W 91
**Banerji**, Shankha K 1936- AmMWSc 92
**Banerji**, Tapan Kumar 1940- AmMWSc 92
**Banes**, Albert Joseph 1947- AmMWSc 92
**Banes**, Jackie Kyle 1964- WhoRel 92
**Baness**, Bridget 1939- TwCPaSc
**Baness**, Jerome Alex 1936- WhoAmP 91
**Banet**, D Beatrice WhoAmP 91
**Baney**, Ronald Howard 1932- AmMWSc 92, WhoMW 92
**Banez**, Domingo 1528-1607 HisDSpE
**Banfer**, Franklin Arthur, II 1959- WhoFI 92
**Banfield**, A. W. Frank 1918- WrDr 92
**Banfield**, Alexander William Francis 1918- AmMWSc 92
**Banfield**, Anne L. 1925- WhoBlA 92
**Banfield**, David John 1933- Who 92
**Banfield**, Edison H. 1924- WhoBlA 92
**Banfield**, William Gethin 1920- AmMWSc 92
**Bang**, Nils Ulrik 1929- AmMWSc 92
**Bang**, Otto T, Jr 1931- WhoAmP 91
**Bangaru**, Babu Rajendra Prasad 1947- WhoWest 92
**Bangdiwala**, Ishver Surchand 1922- AmMWSc 92
**Bange**, David W 1945- AmMWSc 92
**Bangel**, Herbert K. 1928- WhoAmL 92
**Bangemann**, Martin 1934- IntWW 91, Who 92
**Bangert**, John T 1919- AmMWSc 92
**Bangerter**, Hans Ernst 1924- IntWW 91
**Bangerter**, Jack M 1925- WhoAmP 91
**Bangerter**, Norman H. 1933- AlmAP 92 [port], WhoAmP 91
**Bangerter**, Norman Howard 1933- IntWW 91, WhoWest 92
**Bangerter**, Roger Odell 1939- AmMWSc 92
**Bangerter**, William Grant 1918- WhoRel 92, WhoWest 92
**Bangham**, Alec Douglas 1921- Who 92
**Bangham**, Robert Arthur 1942- WhoWest 92
**Banghart**, Frank W 1923- AmMWSc 92
**Banghart**, William 1948- WhoAmP 91
**Bangiola**, Paul 1923- WhoAmL 92
**Bangle**, Richard Morris 1941- WhoWest 92
**Bangor**, Bishop of 1922- Who 92
**Bangor**, Dean of Who 92
**Bangor**, Viscount 1905- Who 92
**Bangs**, Carl Oliver 1922- WhoRel 92
**Bangs**, Carol Jane DrAPF 91
**Bangs**, Cate 1951- WhoWest 92
**Bangs**, J K 1862-1922 ScFEYrs
**Bangs**, James William, III 1959- WhoWest 92
**Bangs**, John Kendrick 1862-1922 BenetAL 91
**Bangs**, John Kendrick 1920- WhoAmL 92
**Bangs**, John Wesley, III 1941- WhoWest 92
**Bangs**, Leigh Buchanan 1936- AmMWSc 92
**Bangs**, Nelson A. WhoAmL 92
**Bangs**, Richard Johnston 1950- WhoWest 92
**Bangsund**, Edward Lee 1935- WhoWest 92
**Bangura**, T. S. WhoRel 92
**Banham**, Belinda Joan Who 92
**Banham**, John Michael Middlecott 1940- IntWW 91, Who 92
**Banham**, Reyner 1920-1988 DcTwDes
**Banham**, Reyner 1922-1988 ConAu 35NR
**Banharn Silpaarcha**, Nai 1932- IntWW 91
**Banholzer**, William Frank AmMWSc 92

**Bani-Sadr**, Abolhasan 1933- *IntWW 91*
**Baniak**, Sheila Mary 1953- *WhoMW 92*
**Banick**, William Michael, Jr 1932- *AmMWSc 92*
**Banigan**, Thomas Franklin, Jr 1920- *AmMWSc 92*
**Banik**, Douglas Heil 1947- *WhoMW 92*
**Banik**, Narendra Lal 1938- *AmMWSc 92*
**Banim**, John 1798-1842 *RfGEnL 91, ScFEYrs*
**Banis**, Richard P. 1943- *WhoFI 92*
**Banis**, Robert Joseph 1943- *WhoFI 92*
**Banister**, Barbara *TwCPaSc*
**Banister**, Eric Wilton 1932- *AmMWSc 92*
**Banister**, George R 1950- *WhoAmP 91*
**Banister**, John 1650-1692 *BiInAmS*
**Banister**, Kenneth Dell 1946- *WhoWest 92*
**Banister**, Stephen Michael Alvin 1918- *Who 92*
**Baniszewski**, David Edmund 1954- *WhoRel 92*
**Banitt**, Elden Harris 1937- *AmMWSc 92*
**Banjanin**, Tom 1942- *WhoAmP 91*
**Banjerjee**, Victor *IntMPA 92*
**Banjo**, Casper 1937- *WhoBlA 92*
**Banjoko**, Alimi Ajimon 1954- *WhoFI 92*
**Bank**, Arthur 1935- *AmMWSc 92*
**Bank**, Charles Nicky 1943- *WhoFI 92*
**Bank**, Harvey L 1943- *AmMWSc 92*
**Bank**, Norman 1925- *AmMWSc 92*
**Bank**, Shelton 1932- *AmMWSc 92*
**Bank**, Steven Barry 1939- *AmMWSc 92*
**Bank**, Susan Johnston 1953- *WhoAmL 92*
**Bank**, William Julius 1913- *WhoFI 92*
**Bank-Anthony**, Mobolaji d1991 *Who 92N*
**Bank-Anthony**, Mobolaji 1907- *IntWW 91*
**Bank-Schlegel**, Susan Pamela *AmMWSc 92*
**Banker**, Barron E. 1948- *WhoEnt 92*
**Banker**, Dave Vinodkumar 1943- *WhoFI 92*
**Banker**, Gary A 1946- *AmMWSc 92*
**Banker**, Gilbert Stephen 1931- *AmMWSc 92*
**Banker**, Nancy Sirmay 1944- *WhoWest 92*
**Bankert**, Ralph Allen 1918- *AmMWSc 92*
**Bankert**, Richard Burton 1940- *AmMWSc 92*
**Bankes**, Lyn 1941- *WhoAmP 91*
**Bankett**, William Daniel 1930- *WhoBlA 92*
**Bankhead**, Patricia Ann 1947- *WhoBlA 92*
**Bankhead**, Porter Lee 1941- *WhoBlA 92*
**Bankhead**, Tallulah 1903-1968 *FacFETw*
**Bankhead**, William Brockman 1874-1940 *AmPolLe*
**Bankhead**, William G 1941- *WhoAmP 91*
**Bankhurst**, Arthur Dale 1937- *WhoWest 92*
**Bankoff**, S George 1921- *AmMWSc 92*
**Bankowski**, Raymond Adam 1914- *AmMWSc 92*
**Banks** *Who 92*
**Banks**, Baron 1918- *Who 92*
**Banks**, Alan George 1911- *Who 92*
**Banks**, Allen *WhoFI 92*
**Banks**, Alvin Samuel 1944- *WhoWest 92*
**Banks**, Anna Delceina 1952- *WhoFI 92*
**Banks**, Arthur C., Jr. 1915- *WhoBlA 92*
**Banks**, Barbara *DrAPF 91*
**Banks**, Beatrice 1936- *WhoBlA 92*
**Banks**, Bradley Carter 1952- *WhoAmP 91*
**Banks**, Brenda L. 1953- *WhoBlA 92*
**Banks**, Brian 1939- *TwCPaSc*
**Banks**, Carl 1962- *WhoBlA 92*
**Banks**, Carl A. 1903- *WhoBlA 92*
**Banks**, Carl L. 1932- *WhoWest 92*
**Banks**, Carlton Luther 1958- *WhoBlA 92*
**Banks**, Caroline Long 1940- *WhoBlA 92*
**Banks**, Carolyn *DrAPF 91*
**Banks**, Carolyn Long 1940- *WhoAmP 91*
**Banks**, Cecil J. 1947- *WhoBlA 92*
**Banks**, Charles A. *WhoAmL 92*
**Banks**, Charlie 1931- *WhoBlA 92*
**Banks**, Chip 1959- *WhoBlA 92*
**Banks**, Colin 1932- *Who 92*
**Banks**, Cullen W. 1946- *WhoBlA 92*
**Banks**, Dallas O 1928- *AmMWSc 92*
**Banks**, Deirdre Margaret 1934- *WhoRel 92*
**Banks**, Diane Lewis *WhoBlA 92*
**Banks**, Donald Jack 1930- *AmMWSc 92*
**Banks**, Dwayne Martin 1961- *WhoBlA 92*
**Banks**, Ellen *WhoBlA 92*
**Banks**, Ephraim 1918- *AmMWSc 92*
**Banks**, Eric Kendall 1955- *WhoAmL 92*
**Banks**, Ernest 1931- *FacFETw*
**Banks**, Ernie 1931- *WhoBlA 92*
**Banks**, Frank David 1933- *Who 92*
**Banks**, Fred L., Jr. 1942- *WhoBlA 92*
**Banks**, Fred Lee, Jr 1942- *WhoAmP 91*
**Banks**, Garnie 1932- *WhoBlA 92*
**Banks**, Gene 1959- *WhoBlA 92*
**Banks**, Gillian Theresa 1933- *Who 92*
**Banks**, Gordon 1958- *WhoBlA 92*
**Banks**, Grace Ann 1942- *AmMWSc 92*
**Banks**, Harlan Parker 1913- *AmMWSc 92*
**Banks**, Harold Chamberlain 1909-1985 *FacFETw*
**Banks**, Harold Douglas 1943- *AmMWSc 92*
**Banks**, Harvey Oren 1910- *AmMWSc 92*
**Banks**, Henry H 1921- *AmMWSc 92*
**Banks**, Henry Stephen 1920- *WhoFI 92*
**Banks**, Iain 1954- *IntAu&W 91*
**Banks**, Iain M 1954- *TwCSFW 91*
**Banks**, Iola Kelley 1935- *WhoAmP 91*
**Banks**, J B 1926- *WhoAmP 91*
**Banks**, J. B. 1934- *WhoBlA 92*
**Banks**, James Albert 1941- *IntAu&W 91, WhoBlA 92, WrDr 92*
**Banks**, James Houston 1925- *WhoFI 92*
**Banks**, James R., II 1955- *WhoRel 92*
**Banks**, James S. 1938- *WhoBlA 92*
**Banks**, Jeffrey Laurence 1953- *WhoBlA 92*
**Banks**, Jerry 1939- *AmMWSc 92*
**Banks**, Jerry L. 1943- *WhoBlA 92*
**Banks**, Jessie 1921- *WhoAmP 91*
**Banks**, John 1653?-1706 *RfGEnL 91*
**Banks**, John 1920- *Who 92*
**Banks**, Joyce P. 1930- *WhoBlA 92*
**Banks**, Karl Marvin 1949- *WhoAmP 91*
**Banks**, Keith L *AmMWSc 92*
**Banks**, Kenneth E. 1943- *WhoBlA 92*
**Banks**, Laura N. 1921- *WhoBlA 92*
**Banks**, Loubertha May *WhoBlA 92*
**Banks**, Lynne Reid 1929- *ConNov 91, IntAu&W 91, Who 92*
**Banks**, Manley E. 1913- *WhoBlA 92*
**Banks**, Margaret Downie 1950- *WhoEnt 92, WhoMW 92*
**Banks**, Marguerita C. 1946- *WhoBlA 92*
**Banks**, Marshall D. 1940- *WhoBlA 92*
**Banks**, Maurice Alfred Lister d1991 *Who 92N*
**Banks**, Nathaniel Prentiss 1816-1894 *AmPolLe [port]*
**Banks**, Norman Guy 1940- *AmMWSc 92*
**Banks**, Patricia 1949- *WhoBlA 92*
**Banks**, Paul Edward 1938- *WhoFI 92*
**Banks**, Perry L. 1955- *WhoBlA 92*
**Banks**, Peter 1938- *TwCPaSc*
**Banks**, Peter Louis 1938- *WhoAmP 91*
**Banks**, Peter Morgan 1937- *AmMWSc 92*
**Banks**, Philip Alan 1952- *AmMWSc 92, WhoWest 92*
**Banks**, Philip Oren 1937- *AmMWSc 92*
**Banks**, Price Terrance 1943- *WhoAmL 92*
**Banks**, Priscilla Sneed 1941- *WhoBlA 92*
**Banks**, Reginald, Sr. 1951- *WhoBlA 92*
**Banks**, Richard Alford 1902- *Who 92*
**Banks**, Richard C 1940- *AmMWSc 92*
**Banks**, Richard Charles 1931- *AmMWSc 92*
**Banks**, Richard Edward 1960- *WhoBlA 92*
**Banks**, Richard L. 1930- *WhoBlA 92*
**Banks**, Robert 1911- *TwCPaSc*
**Banks**, Robert B 1922- *AmMWSc 92*
**Banks**, Robert George 1937- *Who 92*
**Banks**, Robert J. 1928- *WhoRel 92*
**Banks**, Robert John 1939- *WhoRel 92*
**Banks**, Robert L 1921- *AmMWSc 92*
**Banks**, Robert Louis 1946- *WhoMW 92*
**Banks**, Robert O *AmMWSc 92*
**Banks**, Robert R 1925- *AmMWSc 92*
**Banks**, Robert Thomas 1931- *WhoRel 92*
**Banks**, Ronald 1951- *WhoBlA 92*
**Banks**, Ronald Trenton 1947- *WhoBlA 92*
**Banks**, Russell *DrAPF 91*
**Banks**, Russell 1919- *WhoFI 92*
**Banks**, Russell 1940- *ConAu 15AS [port], ConNov 91, IntAu&W 91, WrDr 92*
**Banks**, Ruth R. 1943- *WhoBlA 92*
**Banks**, Saundra Elizabeth 1948- *WhoBlA 92*
**Banks**, Sharon P. 1942- *WhoBlA 92*
**Banks**, Stanley E. *DrAPF 91*
**Banks**, Tazewell 1932- *WhoBlA 92*
**Banks**, Terry Michael 1947- *WhoBlA 92*
**Banks**, Thomas 1949- *AmMWSc 92*
**Banks**, Tony *Who 92*
**Banks**, Trevor Albert 1934- *WhoRel 92*
**Banks**, Waldo R., Sr. 1928- *WhoBlA 92*
**Banks**, William Hartley 1909- *Who 92*
**Banks**, William Henry, Jr. *DrAPF 91*
**Banks**, William J P 1949- *WhoAmP 91*
**Banks**, William Jasper, Jr. 1944- *WhoBlA 92*
**Banks**, William Joseph, Jr 1938- *AmMWSc 92*
**Banks**, William Louis, Jr 1936- *AmMWSc 92*
**Banks**, William Maron, III 1943- *WhoBlA 92*
**Banks**, William Michael 1914- *AmMWSc 92*
**Banks-Williams**, Lula 1947- *WhoBlA 92*
**Bankson**, Daniel Duke 1956- *AmMWSc 92*
**Bankson**, Douglas Henneck 1920- *WhoEnt 92, WhoWest 92*
**Bankston**, Archie M. 1937- *WhoBlA 92*
**Bankston**, Archie Moore, Jr. 1937- *WhoAmL 92*
**Bankston**, Charles A, Jr 1935- *AmMWSc 92*
**Bankston**, David Russell 1961- *WhoAmL 92*
**Bankston**, Donald Carl 1938- *AmMWSc 92*
**Bankston**, Jesse H 1907- *WhoAmP 91*
**Bankston**, Larry S 1951- *WhoAmP 91*
**Bann**, Robert 1921- *AmMWSc 92*
**Banna**, Salim M 1947- *AmMWSc 92*
**Bannai**, Eichi 1946- *AmMWSc 92*
**Bannan**, Elmer Alexander 1928- *AmMWSc 92*
**Bannard**, Robert Alexander Brock 1922- *AmMWSc 92*
**Bannatyne**, Jack *WrDr 92*
**Bannatyne**, Lesley Pratt 1953- *WhoEnt 92*
**Banneker**, Benjamin 1731-1806 *BiInAmS, BlkwEAR [port], RComAH*
**Bannen**, Carol 1951- *WhoAmL 92*
**Bannen**, Ian 1928- *IntMPA 92, IntWW 91*
**Bannen**, Ian 1931- *WhoEnt 92*
**Bannen**, John T. 1951- *WhoAmL 92*
**Bannenberg**, Jon 1929- *Who 92*
**Banner**, Abraham L. 1929- *WhoAmL 92*
**Banner**, Angela 1923- *ChlLR 24, IntAu&W 91, WrDr 92*
**Banner**, Bob *LesBEnT 92*
**Banner**, Bob 1921- *IntMPA 92, WhoEnt 92*
**Banner**, David Lee 1942- *AmMWSc 92*
**Banner**, Delmar, Mrs. *Who 92*
**Banner**, Earl J 1937- *WhoWest 92*
**Banner**, James J 1921- *WhoAmP 91*
**Banner**, Melvin Edward 1914- *WhoBlA 92*
**Banner**, Stephen Edward 1938- *WhoAmL 92*
**Banner**, William Augustus 1915- *WhoBlA 92*
**Bannerman**, Afrakuma 1950- *TwCPaSc*
**Bannerman**, David 1935- *Who 92*
**Bannerman**, Douglas George 1917- *AmMWSc 92*
**Bannerman**, James Knox 1946- *AmMWSc 92*
**Bannerman-Richter**, Gabriel 1931- *WhoBlA 92*
**Bannes**, Lorenz Theodore 1935- *WhoFI 92*
**Bannes**, Stephen William 1958- *WhoMW 92*
**Bannett**, Gary E. 1965- *WhoFI 92*
**Banning**, Cyrus Wayne 1932- *WhoMW 92*
**Banning**, Jon Willroth 1947- *AmMWSc 92*
**Banning**, Lloyd H 1909- *AmMWSc 92*
**Banning**, Margaret Culkin 1891-1982 *BenetAL 91*
**Bannister**, Alan *WhoBlA 92*
**Bannister**, Brian 1926- *AmMWSc 92*
**Bannister**, Bryant 1926- *AmMWSc 92*
**Bannister**, Charles E *WhoAmP 91*
**Bannister**, Daniel Richard 1930- *WhoFI 92*
**Bannister**, George Benjamin 1957- *WhoRel 92*
**Bannister**, Henry Martyn 1844-1920 *BiInAmS*
**Bannister**, Kenneth 1960- *WhoBlA 92*
**Bannister**, Lee Kenneth 1939- *WhoFI 92, WhoWest 92*
**Bannister**, Peter Robert 1938- *AmMWSc 92*
**Bannister**, Robert Grimshaw 1925- *AmMWSc 92*
**Bannister**, Roger 1929- *FacFETw [port], Who 92, WrDr 92*
**Bannister**, Roger G. 1929- *IntWW 91*
**Bannister**, Thomas Turpin 1930- *AmMWSc 92*
**Bannister**, Wes 1936- *WhoAmP 91*
**Bannister**, William Warren 1929- *AmMWSc 92*
**Bannock**, Graham 1932- *WrDr 92*
**Bannon**, George 1925- *WhoFI 92*
**Bannon**, James Andrew 1953- *AmMWSc 92*
**Bannon**, John Charles *IntWW 91*
**Bannon**, John Kernan 1916- *Who 92*
**Bannon**, Joseph Kevin 1949- *WhoFI 92*
**Bannon**, Peter *IntAu&W 91X, WrDr 92*
**Bannon**, Robert Edward 1910- *AmMWSc 92*
**Bannon**, Robert Patrick 1927- *AmMWSc 92*
**Banoff**, Sheldon Irwin 1949- *WhoAmL 92*
**Banos**, Jose Luis 1918- *WhoAmL 92*
**Banos-Milton**, Margarita 1952- *WhoHisp 92*
**Banovic**, Zlatko Josip 1951- *WhoFI 92*
**Banowetz**, Joseph Murray 1934- *WhoEnt 92*
**Banquer**, Myra *WhoRel 92*
**Bansak**, Stephen A., Jr. 1939- *WhoFI 92*
**Banschbach**, Martin Wayne 1946- *AmMWSc 92*
**Banse**, Ewald 1883-1953 *EncTR 91*
**Banse**, Karl 1929- *AmMWSc 92*
**Banse**, Perry Ray 1958- *WhoRel 92*
**Banse**, Robert Lee 1927- *WhoAmL 92, WhoFI 92*
**Bansemer**, Richard Frederick 1940- *WhoRel 92*
**Bansil**, Arun 1948- *AmMWSc 92*
**Bansil**, Rama 1947- *AmMWSc 92*
**Banta**, Don Arthur 1926- *WhoAmL 92*
**Banta**, James E 1927- *AmMWSc 92*
**Banta**, Marion Calvin 1934- *AmMWSc 92*
**Banta**, William Claude 1941- *AmMWSc 92*
**Bantadtan**, Banyat 1942- *IntWW 91*
**Banter**, John C 1931- *AmMWSc 92*
**Bantham**, Russel A. *WhoAmL 92*
**Banther**, Barry *WhoRel 92*
**Banther**, Michael Robert 1957- *WhoWest 92*
**Banting**, Frederick Grant 1891-1941 *FacFETw, WhoNob 90*
**Banting**, John 1902-1972 *TwCPaSc*
**Bantjes**, John Henry 1955- *WhoMW 92*
**Bantle**, John Albert 1946- *AmMWSc 92*
**Bantle**, Louis Francis 1928- *WhoFI 92*
**Bantock**, Gavin 1939- *ConPo 91, IntAu&W 91*
**Bantock**, Geoffrey Herman 1914- *IntAu&W 91, Who 92, WrDr 92*
**Bantock**, John Leonard 1927- *Who 92*
**Bantom**, Michael Allen 1951- *BlkOlyM*
**Banton**, Coy *IntAu&W 91X, TwCWW 91*
**Banton**, John T., Jr. *WhoIns 92*
**Banton**, Michael Parker 1926- *Who 92*
**Banton**, Stephen Chandler 1947- *WhoAmP 91*
**Banton**, William C., II 1922- *WhoBlA 92*
**Bantry**, Bryan 1956- *WhoFI 92*
**Banttari**, Ernest E 1932- *AmMWSc 92*
**Bantuveris**, Mike 1935- *WhoFI 92*
**Bantz**, Charles Richard 1949- *WhoWest 92*
**Banucci**, Eugene George 1943- *AmMWSc 92*
**Banuelas**, Arturo 1949- *WhoHisp 92*
**Banuelos**, Rodrigo 1954- *WhoHisp 92*
**Banuelos**, Romana Acosta 1925- *WhoHisp 92*
**Banus**, Mario Douglas 1921- *AmMWSc 92*
**Banville**, Bertrand 1931- *AmMWSc 92*
**Banville**, Guy Rene 1934- *WhoMW 92*
**Banville**, John *IntWW 91*
**Banville**, John 1945- *ConNov 91, IntAu&W 91, WrDr 92*
**Banville**, Marcel 1933- *AmMWSc 92*
**Banville**, Theodore de 1823-1891 *ThHEIm*
**Banville**, Theodore Faullain de 1823-1891 *GuFrLit 1*
**Banwart**, George J 1926- *AmMWSc 92*
**Banwart**, Keith Gary, Jr. 1965- *WhoRel 92*
**Banwart**, Wayne Lee 1948- *AmMWSc 92*
**Banwell**, Derick Frank 1919- *Who 92*
**Banwell**, John G 1930- *AmMWSc 92*
**Banyard**, Alfred Lothian 1908- *WhoRel 92*
**Banyard**, Rosemary Elizabeth 1958- *WhoFI 92*
**Banyas**, James J. 1936- *WhoIns 92*
**Banyasz**, Rezso 1931- *Who 92*
**Banz**, Clint James 1958- *WhoRel 92*
**Banzer**, Cindy 1947- *WhoAmP 91*
**Banzer Suarez**, Hugo 1926- *IntWW 91*
**Banzett**, Robert B 1947- *AmMWSc 92*
**Banzhaf** *LesBEnT 92*
**Banzhaf**, John F., III 1940- *WhoAmL 92*
**Bao Cong** *IntWW 91*
**Bao Dai** 1913- *FacFETw*
**Bao Tong** *IntWW 91*
**Bao Tongzhi** 1931- *IntWW 91*
**Bao Wenkui** 1916- *IntWW 91*
**Bao**, Joseph Yue-Se 1937- *WhoWest 92*
**Bao**, Qingcheng 1948- *AmMWSc 92*
**Bapatla**, Krishna M 1936- *AmMWSc 92*
**Bappoo**, Sheilabai 1947- *IntWW 91*
**Baptist**, Errol Christopher 1945- *WhoMW 92*
**Baptist**, James 1930- *AmMWSc 92*
**Baptist**, Victor Harry 1923- *AmMWSc 92*
**Baptista**, Howard 1930- *WhoBlA 92*
**Baptista**, Jose Antonio 1939- *AmMWSc 92*
**Baptista**, Luis Felipe 1941- *WhoWest 92*
**Baptista**, Robert Charles, Jr. 1948- *WhoAmL 92*
**Baptista**, Ronald 1932- *WhoWest 92*
**Baptiste**, Clarence Boysie 1941- *WhoRel 92*
**Baptiste**, Hansom P., Jr. 1939- *WhoBlA 92*
**Baptiste**, Kirk 1963- *BlkOlyM*
**Baquet**, Charles *WhoAmP 91*
**Baquet**, Claudia *AmMWSc 92*
**Bar**, Christopher Velten 1955- *WhoMW 92*
**Bar**, Jacques Jean Louis 1921- *IntMPA 92*
**Bar-Cohen**, Yoseph 1947- *AmMWSc 92*
**Bar-Illan**, David 1930- *NewAmDM*
**Bar-Illan**, David Jacob 1930- *WhoEnt 92*
**Bar-Lev**, Haim 1924- *IntWW 91*
**Bar-Shavit**, Rachel 1953- *AmMWSc 92*
**Bar-Shavit**, Zvi *AmMWSc 92*
**Bar-Yam**, Zvi H 1928- *AmMWSc 92*
**Bar-Yishay**, Ephraim 1948- *AmMWSc 92*
**Bar-Zohar**, Michael 1938- *ConAu 35NR*
**Bara**, John V 1926- *WhoAmP 91*
**Bara**, Leonard Joard 1941- *WhoFI 92*
**Bara**, Theda 1890-1955 *FacFETw*
**Barab**, Marvin 1927- *WhoWest 92*
**Barabanov**, Yevgeniy Viktorovich 1943- *IntWW 91*

**Barabas**, Gabor 1948- *ConAu 134*
**Barabas**, SuzAnne 1949- *ConAu 134*
**Barabino**, William Albert 1932- *WhoFI 92*
**Barac-Nieto**, Mario 1940- *AmMWSc 92*
**Barach**, John Paul 1935- *AmMWSc 92*
**Barack**, Joseph Anthony 1949- *WhoFI 92*
**Baracks**, Barbara *DrAPF 91*
**Baracos**, Andrew 1925- *AmMWSc 92*
**Barad**, Jill Elikann 1951- *WhoFI 92*
**Baradat**, Raymond Alphonse 1942- *WhoEnt 92*
**Baraff**, Gary Wayne 1957- *WhoWest 92*
**Baraff**, Gene Allen 1930- *AmMWSc 92*
**Baragar**, William Robert Arthur 1926- *AmMWSc 92*
**Baraheni**, Reza *LiExTwC*
**Barajas**, Charles 1944- *WhoHisp 92*
**Barajas**, Felipe Lara 1938- *WhoRel 92*
**Barajas**, Gil Cuevas 1952- *WhoHisp 92*
**Barajas**, Luciano 1933- *AmMWSc 92*
**Barajas**, Richard 1953- *WhoHisp 92*
**Barak**, Anthony Joseph 1922- *AmMWSc 92*
**Barak**, Eve Ida 1948- *AmMWSc 92*
**Barak**, Gregg 1948- *ConAu 35NR*
**Barak**, Michael *ConAu 35NR*
**Baraka**, Amiri *DrAPF 91*
**Baraka**, Amiri 1934- *AfrAmW, BenetAL 91, BlkLC [port], ConBlB 1 [port], ConPo 91, FacFETw, IntAu&W 91, PoeCrit 4 [port]*
**Baraka**, Imamu Amiri *WrDr 92*
**Baraka**, Imamu Amiri 1934- *WhoBlA 92*
**Barakat**, Gamal Eddin 1921- *IntWW 91*
**Barakat**, Hisham A 1943- *AmMWSc 92*
**Barakat**, Russell G 1940- *WhoAmP 91*
**Baraket**, Edmund S., Jr. 1947- *WhoFI 92*
**Barald**, Kate Francesca 1945- *AmMWSc 92*
**Baran**, George Roman 1950- *AmMWSc 92*
**Baran**, John Stanislaus 1929- *AmMWSc 92*
**Baranano**, Carlos, Sr. *WhoHisp 92*
**Baranano**, Ildefonso Gerardo *WhoWest 92*
**Baranco**, Beverly Victor, Jr. *WhoBlA 92*
**Baranco**, Gordon S. 1948- *WhoBlA 92*
**Baranco**, Gregory T. *WhoBlA 92*
**Baranco**, Raphael Alvin 1932- *WhoBlA 92*
**Baranczak**, Stanislaw *DrAPF 91*
**Baranczak**, Stanislaw 1946- *LiExTwC*
**Baranczuk**, Richard John 1943- *AmMWSc 92*
**Baranek**, Paul Peter 1914- *WhoWest 92*
**Baranger**, Elizabeth Urey 1927- *AmMWSc 92*
**Baranger**, Michel 1927- *AmMWSc 92*
**Barankiewicz**, Jerzy Andrzej 1942- *AmMWSc 92, WhoWest 92*
**Baranow**, Joan *DrAPF 91*
**Baranowski**, Carl 1957- *WhoAmL 92*
**Baranowski**, Edwin Michael 1947- *WhoEnt 92, WhoMW 92*
**Baranowski**, Richard Matthew 1928- *AmMWSc 92*
**Baranowski**, Robert Louis *AmMWSc 92*
**Baranowski**, Tom 1946- *AmMWSc 92*
**Baranski**, Christine 1952- *WhoEnt 92*
**Baranski**, Dennis Anthony 1950- *WhoMW 92*
**Baranski**, Michael Joseph 1946- *AmMWSc 92*
**Baranwal**, Krishna Chandra 1936- *AmMWSc 92*
**Barany**, Francis 1957- *AmMWSc 92*
**Barany**, George 1955- *AmMWSc 92*
**Barany**, James W 1930- *AmMWSc 92*
**Barany**, James Walter 1930- *WhoMW 92*
**Barany**, Kate *AmMWSc 92*
**Barany**, Michael 1921- *AmMWSc 92*
**Barany**, Robert 1876-1936 *FacFETw, WhoNob 90*
**Barany**, Ronald 1928- *AmMWSc 92*
**Barasch**, Clarence Sylvan 1912- *WhoAmL 92*
**Barasch**, Frances K. 1928- *WrDr 92*
**Barasch**, Guy Errol 1937- *AmMWSc 92*
**Barasch**, Mal Livingston 1929- *WhoAmL 92*
**Barasch**, Werner 1919- *AmMWSc 92*
**Barash**, Alan Jeffrey 1942- *WhoAmL 92*
**Barash**, Anthony Harlan 1943- *WhoAmL 92*
**Barash**, Moshe M 1922- *AmMWSc 92*
**Barash**, Paul G 1942- *AmMWSc 92*
**Barash**, Samuel T. 1921- *WrDr 92*
**Barati**, George 1913- *WhoEnt 92*
**Baratka**, Thomas Edward 1946- *WhoFI 92*
**Baratoff**, Alexis 1937- *AmMWSc 92*
**Baratta**, Anthony J 1945- *AmMWSc 92*
**Baratta**, Anthony Joseph, Jr. 1943- *WhoFI 92*
**Baratta**, Edmond John 1928- *AmMWSc 92*
**Baratta**, Pamela Amelia 1960- *WhoEnt 92*
**Baratta-Lorton**, Robert 1939- *WhoWest 92*
**Baratz**, Robert Sears 1946- *AmMWSc 92*
**Baraya**, Antonio 1770-1816 *HisDSpE*
**Barayon**, Ramon Sender *DrAPF 91*
**Baraz**, Robert H. d1991 *NewYTBS 91*
**Barazoto**, David Joseph 1964- *WhoFI 92*
**Barb**, C Richard 1948- *AmMWSc 92*
**Barb**, Earl C. 1920- *WhoMW 92*
**Barba**, Carlos 1935- *WhoHisp 92*
**Barba**, Harry *DrAPF 91*
**Barba**, Harry 1922- *WrDr 92*
**Barba**, John 1950- *WhoHisp 92*
**Barba**, Julius William 1923- *WhoAmP 91*
**Barba**, Ralph N. *WhoHisp 92*
**Barba**, Raymond Felix 1923- *WhoHisp 92*
**Barba**, Sharon *DrAPF 91*
**Barba**, William P, II 1922- *AmMWSc 92*
**Barbacci**, Mario R 1945- *AmMWSc 92*
**Barbachano**, Fernando G. R. 1926- *WhoFI 92*
**Barback**, Joseph 1937- *AmMWSc 92*
**Barback**, Ronald Henry 1919- *Who 92*
**Barbagallo**, Ralph A. 1942- *WhoAmL 92*
**Barbalet**, Margaret Evelyn Hardy 1949- *IntAu&W 91*
**Barban**, Stanley 1921- *AmMWSc 92*
**Barbanel**, Jack Allen 1950- *WhoAmL 92*
**Barbanell**, Robert Louis 1930- *WhoFI 92*
**Barbano**, Frances Elizabeth Dufresne 1944- *IntAu&W 91*
**Barbara of Erecourt** 1609- *EncAmaz 91*
**Barbara**, Saint *EncAmaz 91*
**Barbara**, Agatha 1923- *IntWW 91, Who 92*
**Barbaree**, James Martin 1940- *AmMWSc 92*
**Barbarese**, J.T. *DrAPF 91*
**Barbarese**, J.T. 1948- *ConAu 135*
**Barbarich**, Stanley Joseph 1945- *WhoWest 92*
**Barbaris**, Lisa 1963- *WhoEnt 92*
**Barbarito**, Luigi 1922- *Who 92*
**Barbaro**, Frank J 1927- *WhoAmP 91*
**Barbaro**, Frank Pasquale 1943- *WhoAmP 91*
**Barbaro**, John Calogero 1956- *WhoFI 92*
**Barbaro**, Leo Michael 1959- *WhoFI 92*
**Barbaro**, Ronald D 1933- *AmMWSc 92*
**Barbarosh**, Milton Harvey 1955- *WhoFI 92*
**Barbarowicz**, Robert Paul 1946- *WhoAmL 92*
**Barbas**, John Theophani *AmMWSc 92*
**Barbas**, Rex Martin 1951- *WhoAmL 92*
**Barbash**, Lillian 1927- *WhoEnt 92, WhoFI 92*
**Barbat**, William Franklin 1905- *AmMWSc 92*
**Barbato**, Silvio *WhoEnt 92*
**Barbauld**, Anna 1743-1825 *RfGEnL 91*
**Barbauld**, Anna Laetitia 1743-1825 *BlkwCEP, DcLB 107 [port], -109 [port]*
**Barbe**, Betty Catherine 1930- *WhoMW 92*
**Barbe**, David Franklin 1939- *AmMWSc 92*
**Barbe**, Henri 1902-1966 *BiDExR*
**Barbeau**, Adrienne *IntMPA 92, WhoEnt 92*
**Barbeau**, Edward Joseph, Jr 1938- *AmMWSc 92*
**Barbee**, Allen Cromwell 1910- *WhoAmP 91*
**Barbee**, Bobby H, Sr 1927- *WhoAmP 91*
**Barbee**, Donna L. 1948- *WhoFI 92*
**Barbee**, Elizabeth Joann 1940- *WhoWest 92*
**Barbee**, Joe Ed 1934- *WhoAmL 92, WhoWest 92*
**Barbee**, Lloyd Augustus 1925- *WhoAmP 91, WhoBlA 92, WhoMW 92*
**Barbee**, Phyllis May 1930- *WhoAmP 91*
**Barbee**, R Wayne 1956- *AmMWSc 92*
**Barbee**, Victor 1954- *WhoEnt 92*
**Barbehenn**, Elizabeth Kern 1933- *AmMWSc 92*
**Barbehenn**, Kyle Ray 1928- *AmMWSc 92*
**Barbeito**, Nelson 1946- *WhoHisp 92*
**Barbella**, Victor Gerard 1960- *WhoEnt 92*
**Barbenel**, Joseph Cyril 1937- *IntWW 91*
**Barber** *Who 92*
**Barber**, Baron 1920- *IntWW 91, Who 92*
**Barber**, Albert Alcide 1929- *AmMWSc 92*
**Barber**, Albert W 1930- *WhoAmP 91*
**Barber**, Arnold *IntMPA 92*
**Barber**, Barry 1945- *WhoFI 92*
**Barber**, Benjamin R. *DrAPF 91*
**Barber**, Benjamin R. 1939- *WrDr 92*
**Barber**, Brian Harold *AmMWSc 92*
**Barber**, Charles Edward 1939- *WhoFI 92*
**Barber**, Charles Finch 1917- *WhoFI 92*
**Barber**, Charles Laurence 1915- *IntAu&W 91, WrDr 92*
**Barber**, Charles Turner 1941- *WhoMW 92*
**Barber**, Chris *Who 92*
**Barber**, Clarence Lyle 1917- *IntWW 91*
**Barber**, Claudia Adeline 1959- *WhoEnt 92*
**Barber**, David Gilmer 1953- *WhoRel 92*
**Barber**, Derek *Who 92*
**Barber**, Donald Chris 1930- *Who 92*
**Barber**, Donald E 1931- *AmMWSc 92*
**Barber**, Earl Eugene 1939- *WhoMW 92*
**Barber**, Edward Bruce 1937- *WhoMW 92*
**Barber**, Edwin AtLee 1851-1916 *BiInAmS*
**Barber**, Edwin B. 1927- *WhoIns 92*
**Barber**, Elton Dude 1926- *WhoWest 92*
**Barber**, Esler 1905- *Who 92*
**Barber**, Eugene Douglas 1943- *AmMWSc 92*
**Barber**, Eugene John 1918- *AmMWSc 92*
**Barber**, Frances 1957- *ConTFT 9, IntMPA 92*
**Barber**, Frank 1923- *Who 92*
**Barber**, Franklin Weston 1912- *AmMWSc 92*
**Barber**, Gary *WhoEnt 92*
**Barber**, Gary Frank 1953- *WhoRel 92*
**Barber**, George 1878-1939 *FacFETw*
**Barber**, George Alfred 1925- *AmMWSc 92*
**Barber**, George Arthur 1929- *AmMWSc 92*
**Barber**, Giles Gaudard 1930- *Who 92*
**Barber**, Hargrow Dexter 1956- *WhoBlA 92*
**Barber**, Herbert Bradford 1943- *WhoWest 92*
**Barber**, J C 1916- *AmMWSc 92*
**Barber**, James David 1921- *WhoAmP 91*
**Barber**, James David 1930- *IntAu&W 91, WrDr 92*
**Barber**, James Michael 1939- *WhoAmL 92*
**Barber**, James Peden 1931- *Who 92*
**Barber**, James Richard 1942- *AmMWSc 92*
**Barber**, James W. 1936- *WhoBlA 92*
**Barber**, Janet Katheryne 1949- *WhoRel 92*
**Barber**, Janice Denise 1952- *WhoBlA 92*
**Barber**, Jeffrey Ryan 1963- *WhoAmL 92*
**Barber**, Jesse B., Jr. 1924- *WhoBlA 92*
**Barber**, Jim Robert 1952- *WhoFI 92*
**Barber**, John 1944- *WrDr 92*
**Barber**, John L. *Who 92*
**Barber**, John Linder 1946- *WhoAmL 92*
**Barber**, John Norman Romney *Who 92*
**Barber**, John Norman Romney 1919- *IntWW 91*
**Barber**, John Paul 1961- *WhoAmL 92*
**Barber**, John Threlfall 1937- *AmMWSc 92*
**Barber**, Kathleen Ann Starks 1950- *WhoWest 92*
**Barber**, Kathleen Lucas 1924- *WhoAmP 91*
**Barber**, Larry Lee 1939- *WhoFI 92*
**Barber**, Lloyd Ingram 1932- *IntWW 91*
**Barber**, Lynn 1944- *IntAu&W 91*
**Barber**, M R 1931- *AmMWSc 92*
**Barber**, Melanie Margaret Cecilia 1958- *WhoAmL 92*
**Barber**, Michael d1991 *Who 92N*
**Barber**, Michael James 1950- *AmMWSc 92*
**Barber**, Morgan Allison, Jr. 1933- *WhoEnt 92*
**Barber**, Nathan Lewis 1945- *WhoRel 92*
**Barber**, Nicholas Charles Faithorn 1940- *Who 92*
**Barber**, Noel John Lysberg 1909- *IntAu&W 91*
**Barber**, Norman Frederick 1909- *IntWW 91*
**Barber**, Patrick George 1942- *AmMWSc 92*
**Barber**, Paul 1941- *ConAu 134*
**Barber**, Paul D *WhoAmP 91*
**Barber**, Paul Everard *Who 92*
**Barber**, Perry Oscar, Jr. 1938- *WhoAmL 92, WhoFI 92*
**Barber**, Phillip Mark 1944- *WhoAmL 92*
**Barber**, Phillip Robert, III 1959- *WhoEnt 92*
**Barber**, Putnam 1940- *WhoWest 92*
**Barber**, Rahe Darlynn 1944- *WhoAmP 91*
**Barber**, Red *LesBEnT 92*
**Barber**, Richard 1941- *WrDr 92*
**Barber**, Richard A. 1911- *WhoAmL 92*
**Barber**, Richard William 1941- *IntAu&W 91*
**Barber**, Robert A, Jr 1949- *WhoAmP 91*
**Barber**, Robert Charles 1936- *AmMWSc 92*
**Barber**, Robert Edwin 1932- *AmMWSc 92*
**Barber**, Russell Brooks Butler 1934- *WhoEnt 92*
**Barber**, Samuel 1910-1981 *FacFETw, NewAmDM*
**Barber**, Saul Benjamin 1920- *AmMWSc 92*
**Barber**, Sherburne Frederick 1907- *AmMWSc 92*
**Barber**, Stanley Arthur 1921- *AmMWSc 92*
**Barber**, Theodore Francis 1931- *WhoWest 92*
**Barber**, Thomas King 1923- *AmMWSc 92*
**Barber**, Thomas Lynwood 1934- *AmMWSc 92*
**Barber**, Tina Sandra 1949- *WhoFI 92*
**Barber**, Walter Carlisle 1919- *AmMWSc 92*
**Barber**, William 1905- *Who 92*
**Barber**, William, Jr. 1942- *WhoBlA 92*
**Barber**, William Austin 1924- *AmMWSc 92*
**Barber**, William J *AmMWSc 92*
**Barber**, William Joseph 1925- *Who 92*
**Barber**, Yvonne Jeanne *WhoEnt 92*
**Barbera**, Frank Anthony 1935- *WhoFI 92*
**Barbera**, Joseph *WhoEnt 92*
**Barbera**, Joseph R. 1911- *IntMPA 92*
**Barbera**, Michael Anthony 1952- *WhoFI 92*
**Barbera**, Vincent Joseph 1956- *WhoAmP 91*
**Barberena**, Eduardo J. 1957- *WhoHisp 92*
**Barberi**, Robert Obed 1945- *WhoAmL 92*
**Barberia**, Richard A 1944- *WhoAmP 91*
**Barberis**, Grace H 1932- *WhoAmP 91*
**Barberis**, Pierre Georges 1942- *IntWW 91*
**Barbero**, Giulio J 1923- *AmMWSc 92*
**Barbery**, Gilles A 1943- *AmMWSc 92*
**Barbet**, Pierre 1925- *IntAu&W 91*
**Barbey d'Aurevilly**, Jules-Amedee 1808-1889 *GuFrLit 1*
**Barbeyrac**, Jean 1674-1744 *BlkwCEP*
**Barbezat**, Eugene LaVar 1936- *WhoWest 92*
**Barbi**, Josef Walter 1949- *WhoMW 92*
**Barbie**, Klaus *FacFETw*
**Barbie**, Klaus 1913- *EncTR 91*
**Barbie**, Klaus 1913-1991 *NewYTBS 91 [port], News 92-2*
**Barbie**, Niklaus 1913- *BiDExR*
**Barbieri**, Arthur Robert 1926- *WhoFI 92*
**Barbieri**, Enrique 1959- *WhoHisp 92*
**Barbieri**, Fedora 1919- *IntWW 91*
**Barbieri**, Marco Renato 1969- *WhoEnt 92*
**Barbieri**, Margaret Elizabeth 1947- *Who 92*
**Barbiero**, Michael F. 1949- *WhoEnt 92*
**Barbin**, Allen R 1934- *AmMWSc 92*
**Barbirolli**, Evelyn *NewAmDM*
**Barbirolli**, John 1899-1970 *FacFETw, NewAmDM*
**Barbo**, Dorothy M 1932- *AmMWSc 92*
**Barbor**, John Howard 1952- *WhoAmL 92*
**Barborak**, James Carl 1941- *AmMWSc 92*
**Barboriak**, Joseph Jan 1923- *AmMWSc 92*
**Barbosa**, Jose 1857-1921 *HisDSpE*
**Barbosa**, Miguel 1925- *IntAu&W 91*
**Barbosa-Canovas**, Gustavo Victor 1949- *WhoHisp 92*
**Barbot**, Ivan 1937- *IntWW 91*
**Barbour**, Alan G. 1933- *IntMPA 92*
**Barbour**, Clyde D 1935- *AmMWSc 92*
**Barbour**, Douglas 1940- *ConPo 91, IntAu&W 91, WrDr 92*
**Barbour**, Haley Reeves 1947- *WhoAmP 91*
**Barbour**, Hugh 1921- *WrDr 92*
**Barbour**, Hugh Revell 1929- *WhoRel 92*
**Barbour**, Ian Graeme 1923- *WhoRel 92*
**Barbour**, James Keith 1948- *WhoFI 92*
**Barbour**, John 1316-1395 *RfGEnL 91*
**Barbour**, John Dickinson 1951- *WhoRel 92*
**Barbour**, Joseph Pius, Jr. 1923- *WhoBlA 92*
**Barbour**, Julian B. 1937- *ConAu 133*
**Barbour**, Kenneth O. *WhoRel 92*
**Barbour**, Malcolm 1934- *IntMPA 92*
**Barbour**, Michael G 1942- *AmMWSc 92*
**Barbour**, Michael Thomas 1947- *AmMWSc 92*
**Barbour**, Patricia Jeanne *WhoAmP 91*
**Barbour**, Philip Pendleton 1783-1841 *AmPolLe*
**Barbour**, Ralph Henry 1870-1944 *BenetAL 91*
**Barbour**, Robert Alexander Stewart 1921- *IntWW 91, Who 92*
**Barbour**, Robert Gordon 1947- *WhoWest 92*
**Barbour**, Roger William 1919- *AmMWSc 92*
**Barbour**, Ross Edwin 1928- *WhoEnt 92*
**Barbour**, Stephen D 1942- *AmMWSc 92*
**Barbour**, Sue Jennifer 1950- *WhoEnt 92*
**Barbour**, Thomas 1884-1946 *BenetAL 91*
**Barbour**, Volney G d1901 *BiInAmS*
**Barbour**, Walworth 1908- *Who 92*
**Barbour**, William E, Jr 1909- *AmMWSc 92*
**Barbour**, Williams H., Jr. 1941- *WhoAmL 92*
**Barbour**, Worth L. 1929- *WhoBlA 92*
**Barboza**, Mario G. *Who 92*
**Barbre**, John H. 1934- *WhoIns 92*
**Barbul**, Adrian 1950- *AmMWSc 92*
**Barbusse**, Henri 1873-1935 *FacFETw*
**Barbut**, Erol 1940- *WhoWest 92*
**Barca**, George Gino 1937- *WhoFI 92, WhoWest 92*
**Barca**, Kathleen 1946- *WhoFI 92, WhoWest 92*
**Barca**, Peter William 1958- *WhoAmP 91*
**Barcella**, Mary Lashley 1949- *WhoFI 92*
**Barcellona**, Wayne J 1940- *AmMWSc 92*
**Barcelo**, Alvaro 1952- *WhoHisp 92*
**Barcelo**, John James, III 1940- *WhoAmL 92*
**Barcelo**, Miguel 1957- *WorArt 1980 [port]*
**Barcelo**, Randy 1946- *WhoEnt 92*
**Barcelo**, Raymond 1931- *AmMWSc 92*
**Barcelona**, Michael Joseph 1949- *AmMWSc 92*
**Barcenas**, Jude Ramon Legaspi 1956- *WhoFI 92*
**Barcey**, Harold Edward Dean 1949- *WhoMW 92*

**Barchas**, Jack D 1935- *AmMWSc 92*
**Barchet**, William Richard 1943- *AmMWSc 92*
**Barchfeld**, Francis John 1935- *AmMWSc 92*
**Barcia**, James A 1952- *WhoAmP 91*
**Barcikowski**, Kazimierz 1927- *IntWW 91*
**Barcilon**, Albert I 1937- *AmMWSc 92*
**Barcilon**, Victor 1939- *AmMWSc 92*
**Barckett**, Joseph Anthony 1955- *AmMWSc 92*
**Barclay**, Alexander 1475?-1552 *RfGEnL 91*
**Barclay**, Alexander Primrose Hutcheson 1913- *AmMWSc 92*
**Barclay**, Andrew Michael 1941- *WhoMW 92*
**Barclay**, Arthur S 1932- *AmMWSc 92*
**Barclay**, Bill *TwCSFW 91*
**Barclay**, Carl Archie 1922- *WhoBlA 92*
**Barclay**, Christopher Francis Robert 1919- *Who 92*
**Barclay**, Colville Herbert Sanford 1913- *Who 92*
**Barclay**, David Cave 1950- *WhoAmL 92*
**Barclay**, David Keating 1952- *WhoFI 92*
**Barclay**, David Ronald 1932- *WhoBlA 92*
**Barclay**, Francis Walter 1931- *AmMWSc 92*
**Barclay**, George M. 1936- *WhoFI 92*
**Barclay**, Hugh Maben 1927- *Who 92*
**Barclay**, Jack Kenneth 1938- *AmMWSc 92*
**Barclay**, James A 1918- *AmMWSc 92*
**Barclay**, James Christopher 1945- *Who 92*
**Barclay**, James Edward 1941- *WhoFI 92*
**Barclay**, John Allen 1951- *WhoAmL 92*
**Barclay**, John Arthur 1942- *AmMWSc 92*
**Barclay**, John Bruce 1909- *IntAu&W 91*
**Barclay**, L P d1908 *BiInAmS*
**Barclay**, Lawrence Ross Coates 1928- *AmMWSc 92*
**Barclay**, Lawrence V. *WhoBlA 92*
**Barclay**, Patrick George 1959- *WhoMW 92*
**Barclay**, Peter Maurice 1926- *Who 92*
**Barclay**, Richard L 1937- *WhoAmP 91*
**Barclay**, Robert, Jr 1928- *AmMWSc 92*
**Barclay**, Robin Marie 1956- *WhoBlA 92*
**Barclay**, Roderick 1909- *Who 92*
**Barclay**, Roderick Edward 1909- *IntWW 91*
**Barclay**, Ronald David 1934- *WhoFI 92*
**Barclay**, Stephen 1961- *TwCPaSc*
**Barclay**, Terry Anne 1957- *WhoMW 92*
**Barclay**, W J 1912- *AmMWSc 92*
**Barclay**, William R 1919- *AmMWSc 92*
**Barclay**, Yvonne Fay *Who 92*
**Barclift**, William C., III 1949- *WhoAmL 92*
**Barco**, Virgilio 1921- *IntWW 91*
**Barcos**, Maurice P 1935- *AmMWSc 92*
**Barcroft**, Douglas Morgan 1958- *WhoRel 92*
**Barcroft**, Henry 1904- *IntWW 91, Who 92*
**Barcroft**, John Hill *WhoMW 92*
**Barcroft**, Joseph 1872-1947 *FacFETw*
**Barcun**, Seymour 1932- *WhoFI 92*
**Barcus**, Benjamin Franklin 1960- *WhoWest 92*
**Barcus**, David Lynn 1949- *WhoMW 92*
**Barcus**, Gilbert Martin 1937- *WhoFI 92*
**Barcus**, Mary Evelyn 1938- *WhoMW 92*
**Barcus**, Robert Gene 1937- *WhoMW 92*
**Barcus**, William Dickson, Jr 1929- *AmMWSc 92*
**Barczak**, Virgil J 1931- *AmMWSc 92*
**Bard**, Allen J. 1933- *IntWW 91*
**Bard**, Allen Joseph 1933- *AmMWSc 92*
**Bard**, Basil Joseph Asher 1914- *Who 92*
**Bard**, Charleton Cordery 1924- *AmMWSc 92*
**Bard**, David S 1935- *AmMWSc 92*
**Bard**, Enzo 1938- *AmMWSc 92*
**Bard**, Eugene Dwight 1928- *AmMWSc 92*
**Bard**, Gily Epstein 1924- *AmMWSc 92*
**Bard**, Imre 1928- *WhoWest 92*
**Bard**, James Richard *AmMWSc 92*
**Bard**, John 1716-1799 *BiInAmS*
**Bard**, John C 1925- *AmMWSc 92*
**Bard**, Martin 1942- *AmMWSc 92*
**Bard**, Raymond Camillo 1918- *AmMWSc 92*
**Bard**, Richard James 1923- *AmMWSc 92*
**Bard**, Samuel 1742-1821 *BiInAmS*
**Bard**, Sandra Ann 1936- *WhoFI 92*
**Bard**, Terry Ross 1944- *WhoRel 92*
**Bardach**, John E 1915- *AmMWSc 92*
**Bardach**, Sheldon Gilbert 1937- *WhoAmL 92*
**Bardack**, David 1932- *AmMWSc 92*
**Bardacke**, Paul G 1944- *WhoAmP 91*
**Bardaglio**, Wrexie Lainson 1946- *WhoAmP 91*
**Bardana**, Emil John, Jr 1935- *AmMWSc 92*
**Bardanouve**, Francis 1917- *WhoAmP 91*
**Bardasis**, Angelo 1936- *AmMWSc 92*
**Bardasz**, Ewa Alice *AmMWSc 92*
**Bardawil**, Wadi Antonio 1921- *AmMWSc 92*
**Barde**, Lloyd Stuart 1950- *WhoEnt 92*
**Bardeche**, Maurice 1907- *IntWW 91*
**Bardeche**, Maurice 1909- *BiDExR*
**Bardeen**, James Maxwell 1939- *AmMWSc 92*
**Bardeen**, John d1991 *IntWW 91N, Who 92N*
**Bardeen**, John 1908- *AmMWSc 92, WhoNob 90*
**Bardeen**, John 1908-1991 *CurBio 91N, FacFETw*
**Bardeen**, William A 1941- *AmMWSc 92*
**Bardell**, David *AmMWSc 92*
**Bardell**, Eunice Bonow 1915- *AmMWSc 92*
**Bardell**, Eunice Ruth 1915- *WhoMW 92*
**Bardem**, Juan Antonio 1922- *IntDcF 2-2 [port]*
**Barden**, Don H. 1943- *WhoBlA 92*
**Barden**, Graham Arthur 1896-1967 *DcNCBi 1*
**Barden**, John Allan 1936- *AmMWSc 92*
**Barden**, Karl Alvin 1940- *WhoRel 92*
**Barden**, Kenneth Eugene 1955- *WhoAmL 92, WhoMW 92*
**Barden**, Laing 1931- *Who 92*
**Barden**, Lawrence Samuel 1942- *AmMWSc 92*
**Barden**, Nicholas 1946- *AmMWSc 92*
**Barden**, Robert Christopher 1954- *WhoMW 92*
**Barden**, Roland Eugene 1942- *AmMWSc 92, WhoMW 92*
**Bardenwerper**, Walter William 1951- *WhoAmL 92*
**Barder**, Brian Leon 1934- *IntWW 91, Who 92*
**Bardesanes** 154?-222 *EncEarC*
**Bardi**, Giovanni de' 1534-1612 *NewAmDM*
**Bardin**, Clyde Wayne 1934- *AmMWSc 92*
**Bardin**, Ivan Pavlovich 1883-1960 *SovUnBD*
**Bardin**, Rodney Norman, II 1957- *WhoEnt 92*
**Bardin**, Russell Keith 1932- *AmMWSc 92*
**Bardin**, Tsing Tchao 1938- *AmMWSc 92*
**Bardini**, Adolfo 1915- *IntWW 91*
**Bardini**, Aleksander 1913- *IntWW 91*
**Bardis**, Panos D. 1924- *IntWW 91, WrDr 92*
**Bardis**, Panos Demetrios 1924- *IntAu&W 91*
**Bardo**, Richard Dale *AmMWSc 92*
**Bardoliwalla**, Dinshaw Framroze 1945- *AmMWSc 92*
**Bardon**, Diane Marie 1949- *WhoWest 92*
**Bardon**, Marcel 1927- *AmMWSc 92*
**Bardoner**, James Leo 1918- *WhoFI 92*
**Bardonnet**, Daniel 1931- *IntWW 91*
**Bardos**, Denes I 1938- *AmMWSc 92*
**Bardos**, Karoly 1942- *WhoEnt 92*
**Bardos**, Thomas Joseph 1915- *AmMWSc 92*
**Bardot**, Brigitte 1934- *FacFETw [port], IntMPA 92, IntWW 91*
**Bardsley**, Andrew Tromlow 1927- *Who 92*
**Bardsley**, Charles Edward 1921- *AmMWSc 92*
**Bardsley**, Cuthbert K. N. 1907-1991 *ConAu 133*
**Bardsley**, Cuthbert Killick Norman d1991 *Who 92N*
**Bardsley**, Elizabeth S 1931- *WhoAmP 91*
**Bardsley**, James Norman 1941- *AmMWSc 92*
**Barduhn**, Allen J 1918- *AmMWSc 92*
**Bardwell**, Denver *TwCWW 91*
**Bardwell**, Elizabeth M 1832?-1899 *BiInAmS*
**Bardwell**, George 1924- *AmMWSc 92*
**Bardwell**, Jennifer Ann 1957- *AmMWSc 92*
**Bardwell**, John Alexander Eddie 1921- *AmMWSc 92*
**Bardwell**, Rufus B., III 1937- *WhoBlA 92*
**Bardwell**, Steven Jack 1949- *AmMWSc 92*
**Bardwick**, John, III 1931- *AmMWSc 92*
**Bardwick**, Judith M. 1933- *WrDr 92*
**Bardwick**, Judith Marcia 1933- *WhoFI 92*
**Bardwil**, Joseph Anthony 1928- *WhoFI 92*
**Bardyguine**, Patricia Wilde 1928- *WhoEnt 92*
**Bare**, B. Bruce 1942- *WhoWest 92*
**Bare**, Barry Bruce 1942- *AmMWSc 92*
**Bare**, Charles L 1932- *AmMWSc 92*
**Bare**, Donald Richard 1931- *WhoAmP 91*
**Bare**, Joseph Edward, Jr. 1923- *WhoAmL 92*
**Bare**, Richard L. *IntMPA 92*
**Bare**, Richard W., Jr. 1963- *WhoMW 92*
**Bare**, Robert Joseph 1935- *WhoEnt 92*
**Bare**, Thomas M 1942- *AmMWSc 92*
**Bared**, Jose *WhoHisp 92*
**Barefield**, Eddie d1991 *NewYTBS 91*
**Barefield**, Edward Emanuel 1909-1991 *WhoBlA 92N*
**Barefield**, Edward Kent 1943- *AmMWSc 92*
**Barefield**, Morris 1939- *WhoBlA 92*
**Barefield**, Ollie Delores 1930- *WhoBlA 92*
**Barefield**, Thomas A. *WhoIns 92*
**Barefoot**, Aldos Cortez, Jr 1927- *AmMWSc 92*
**Barefoot**, Brian Miller 1943- *WhoFI 92*
**Bareham**, Terence 1937- *IntAu&W 91, WrDr 92*
**Bareis**, David W 1922- *AmMWSc 92*
**Bareis**, Donna Lynn 1954- *AmMWSc 92*
**Bareiss**, Erwin Hans 1922- *AmMWSc 92*
**Barel**, Monique 1952- *AmMWSc 92*
**Barela**, Esmerlindo Jaramillo 1948- *WhoWest 92*
**Barela**, George Larry 1948- *WhoHisp 92*
**Barela**, Henry T. *WhoHisp 92*
**Barela**, Linel G. 1947- *WhoHisp 92*
**Baren**, David Morris 1923- *WhoFI 92*
**Baren**, Harvey M. 1931- *IntMPA 92*
**Barenberg**, Ernest J 1929- *AmMWSc 92*
**Barenberg**, Sumner 1945- *AmMWSc 92, WhoMW 92*
**Barenboim**, Daniel 1942- *FacFETw, IntWW 91, NewAmDM, Who 92, WhoEnt 92, WhoMW 92*
**Barendregt**, Rene William 1950- *AmMWSc 92*
**Barengo**, Robert R 1941- *WhoAmP 91*
**Barenholtz**, Ben 1935- *IntMPA 92*
**Barenis**, Pat Peaster 1951- *WhoWest 92*
**Barents**, Brian Edward 1944- *WhoFI 92*
**Barer**, Michael Gary 1952- *WhoAmL 92*
**Barer**, Ralph David 1922- *AmMWSc 92*
**Barer**, Seymour 1923- *WhoFI 92*
**Bares**, Allen R 1936- *WhoAmP 91*
**Bares**, William Anthony 1935- *AmMWSc 92*
**Baresi**, Larry *AmMWSc 92*
**Baretti**, Giuseppe 1719-1789 *BlkwCEP*
**Barfett**, Thomas 1916- *Who 92*
**Barfield**, Billy Joe 1938- *AmMWSc 92*
**Barfield**, Bourdon Rea 1926- *WhoFI 92*
**Barfield**, Clementine 1950- *WhoBlA 92*
**Barfield**, Deborah Denise 1963- *WhoBlA 92*
**Barfield**, Jesse Lee 1959- *WhoBlA 92*
**Barfield**, John E. *WhoBlA 92*
**Barfield**, Leila Millford 1923- *WhoBlA 92*
**Barfield**, Liston 1945- *WhoAmP 91*
**Barfield**, Michael 1934- *AmMWSc 92*
**Barfield**, Owen 1898- *IntAu&W 91, WrDr 92*
**Barfield**, Quay F. 1912- *WhoBlA 92*
**Barfield**, Robert F 1933- *AmMWSc 92*
**Barfield**, Rufus L. 1929- *WhoBlA 92*
**Barfield**, Walter David 1928- *AmMWSc 92*
**Barfoot**, Fisher *WhoAmP 91*
**Barford**, Lee Alton 1961- *WhoWest 92*
**Barford**, Leonard 1908- *Who 92*
**Barford**, Robert A 1936- *AmMWSc 92*
**Barfuss**, Delon Willis 1942- *AmMWSc 92*
**Barg**, James Michael 1956- *WhoEnt 92*
**Bargabos**, Sheree Lynn 1955- *WhoWest 92*
**Bargas**, Joe G., Sr. 1927- *WhoHisp 92*
**Barge**, Jean Marie 1927- *WhoRel 92*
**Barge**, Jeffrey Thomas 1957- *WhoWest 92*
**Bargellini**, P L 1914- *AmMWSc 92*
**Bargen**, Walter *DrAPF 91*
**Barger**, A Clifford 1917- *AmMWSc 92*
**Barger**, Catherine Harden 1954- *WhoAmP 91*
**Barger**, James Daniel 1917- *AmMWSc 92*
**Barger**, James Edwin 1934- *AmMWSc 92*
**Barger**, Kathleen Carson 1948- *WhoAmL 92*
**Barger**, Louise Baldwin 1938- *WhoRel 92*
**Barger**, Maurice W., Jr. 1931- *WhoIns 92*
**Barger**, Ralph 1923- *WhoAmP 91*
**Barger**, Richards D. 1928- *WhoIns 92*
**Barger**, Samuel Floyd 1936- *AmMWSc 92*
**Barger**, Stephen Richard 1950- *WhoWest 92*
**Barger**, Vernon Duane 1938- *AmMWSc 92, WhoMW 92*
**Barger**, William James 1944- *WhoFI 92*
**Bargeron**, Cecil Brent 1943- *AmMWSc 92*
**Bargeron**, Emory E 1927- *WhoAmP 91*
**Bargeron**, Lionel Malcolm, Jr 1923- *AmMWSc 92*
**Bargfrede**, James Allen 1928- *WhoFI 92*
**Barghini**, Sandra Jean 1951- *WhoWest 92*
**Barghoorn**, Frederick C. d1991 *NewYTBS 91*
**Barghoorn**, Frederick C. 1911- *WrDr 92*
**Barghusen**, Herbert Richard 1933- *AmMWSc 92*
**Bargmann**, Rolf Erwin 1921- *AmMWSc 92*
**Bargmann**, Valentine 1908- *AmMWSc 92*
**Bargon**, Joachim 1939- *AmMWSc 92*
**Bargreen**, Melinda Lueth 1947- *WhoEnt 92*
**Barham**, Bruce 1949- *WhoEnt 92*
**Barham**, Charles C *WhoAmP 91*
**Barham**, Charles Dewey, Jr. 1930- *WhoAmL 92, WhoFI 92*
**Barham**, Jean 1924- *TwCPaSc*
**Barham**, Richard Harris 1788-1845 *RfGEnL 91*
**Barham**, Robert Edward 1942- *WhoWest 92*
**Barham**, Warren Sandusky 1919- *AmMWSc 92*
**Barham**, Wilbur Stectson 1955- *WhoBlA 92*
**Barham Hill**, Brenda Marie 1948- *WhoWest 92*
**Barhydt**, Hamilton 1928- *AmMWSc 92*
**Bari**, Robert Allan 1943- *AmMWSc 92*
**Bari**, Susan Phillips 1945- *WhoAmP 91*
**Bari**, Wagih A *AmMWSc 92*
**Baria**, Dorab Naoroze 1942- *AmMWSc 92*
**Barial**, Ellen V. *WhoAmL 92*
**Bariani**, Didier 1943- *IntWW 91*
**Baric**, Lee Wilmer 1932- *AmMWSc 92*
**Barica**, Jan M 1933- *AmMWSc 92*
**Barich**, Bill 1943- *WrDr 92*
**Barie**, Philip S 1953- *AmMWSc 92*
**Barie**, Walter Peter, Jr 1926- *AmMWSc 92*
**Barieau**, Robert 1915- *AmMWSc 92*
**Bariff**, Martin Louis 1944- *WhoMW 92*
**Baril**, Albert, Jr 1926- *AmMWSc 92*
**Baril**, Earl Francis 1930- *AmMWSc 92*
**Barile**, Andrew J. 1942- *WhoIns 92*
**Barile**, Diane Dunmire 1940- *AmMWSc 92*
**Barile**, George Conrad 1948- *AmMWSc 92*
**Barile**, Michael Frederick 1924- *AmMWSc 92*
**Barile**, Raymond Conrad 1936- *AmMWSc 92*
**Barilich**, Thomas Anthony 1955- *WhoFI 92, WhoMW 92*
**Barilla**, Anita White 1952- *WhoRel 92*
**Baring** *Who 92*
**Baring**, Arnulf Martin 1932- *IntWW 91*
**Baring**, George Rowland Stanley 1918-1991 *NewYTBS 91 [port]*
**Baring**, John 1947- *Who 92*
**Baring**, John Francis Harcourt 1928- *IntWW 91*
**Baring**, Maurice 1874-1945 *RfGEnL 91, ScFEYrs*
**Baring**, Nicholas Hugo 1934- *Who 92*
**Baring**, Peter 1935- *Who 92*
**Baring**, Robin 1931- *TwCPaSc*
**Baring**, Rose 1909- *Who 92*
**Baring-Gould**, Sabine 1834-1924 *RfGEnL 91*
**Baringer**, J Richard 1935- *AmMWSc 92*
**Bariola**, Louis Anthony 1932- *AmMWSc 92*
**Baris**, David H. 1944- *WhoAmL 92*
**Barisas**, Bernard George, Jr 1945- *AmMWSc 92, WhoWest 92*
**Barish**, Barry C 1936- *AmMWSc 92*
**Barish**, George 1938- *WhoAmL 92*
**Barish**, Jonas A. 1922- *WrDr 92*
**Barish**, Jonas Alexander 1922- *IntAu&W 91, WhoWest 92*
**Barish**, Keith *IntMPA 92*
**Barish**, Leo 1930- *AmMWSc 92*
**Barish**, Robert John 1946- *AmMWSc 92*
**Barist**, Jeffrey A. 1941- *WhoAmL 92*
**Barjacoba**, Pedro 1934- *WhoHisp 92*
**Barjavel**, Rene 1911- *TwCSFW 91A*
**Bark**, Evelyn 1900- *Who 92*
**Bark**, Laurence Dean 1926- *AmMWSc 92*
**Barka**, Tibor 1926- *AmMWSc 92*
**Barka**, Wasyl 1908- *LiExTwC*
**Barkai**, Amiram I 1936- *AmMWSc 92*
**Barkalow**, Derek Talbot 1951- *AmMWSc 92*
**Barkalow**, Fern J 1960- *AmMWSc 92*
**Barkan**, Alexander Elias 1909-1990 *FacFETw*
**Barkan**, P 1925- *AmMWSc 92*
**Barkan**, Shaul 1949- *WhoWest 92*
**Barkan**, Stanley H. *DrAPF 91*
**Barkate**, John Albert 1936- *AmMWSc 92*
**Barkauskas**, Antanas Stasevich 1917- *IntWW 91*
**Barkauskas**, Anthony Edward 1946- *AmMWSc 92*
**Barke**, Harvey Ellis 1917- *AmMWSc 92*
**Barkelew**, Chandler H 1919- *AmMWSc 92*
**Barkeley**, James Norman 1954- *WhoAmL 92*
**Barkeley**, Norman A. *IntWW 91*
**Barken**, Bernard Allen 1924- *WhoAmL 92, WhoMW 92*
**Barker** *Who 92*
**Barker**, A. L. 1918- *ConNov 91, IntAu&W 91, WrDr 92*
**Barker**, Albert Penick 1954- *WhoAmL 92*
**Barker**, Alfred Stanley, Jr 1933- *AmMWSc 92*
**Barker**, Allen 1937- *TwCPaSc*
**Barker**, Allen Vaughan 1937- *AmMWSc 92, WhoAmP 91*
**Barker**, Alwyn 1900- *Who 92*
**Barker**, Anne Judith *Who 92*
**Barker**, Anthony 1944- *Who 92*
**Barker**, Arthur *DcLB 112*
**Barker**, Arthur Vincent 1911- *Who 92*
**Barker**, Arthur W *ScFEYrs*
**Barker**, Audrey Lilian 1918- *Who 92*
**Barker**, Barbara Bache 1937- *WhoAmL 92*

**Barker,** Barbara Elizabeth *AmMWSc 92*
**Barker,** Barry 1929- *Who 92*
**Barker,** Ben D 1931- *AmMWSc 92*
**Barker,** Bob *LesBEnT 92*
**Barker,** Brian John 1945- *Who 92*
**Barker,** C L R 1930- *AmMWSc 92*
**Barker,** Charles *WhoEnt 92*
**Barker,** Clayton Robert, III 1957- *WhoAmL 92, WhoFI 92*
**Barker,** Clifford Conder 1926- *Who 92*
**Barker,** Clive 1940- *TwCPaSc*
**Barker,** Clive 1952- *IntAu&W 91, WrDr 92*
**Barker,** Clyde Frederick 1932- *AmMWSc 92*
**Barker,** Colin 1926- *Who 92*
**Barker,** Colin G 1939- *AmMWSc 92*
**Barker,** Dana Marie 1961- *WhoMW 92*
**Barker,** Daniel Stephen 1934- *AmMWSc 92*
**Barker,** David 1922- *Who 92*
**Barker,** David 1932- *Who 92*
**Barker,** David 1940- *TwCPaSc*
**Barker,** David Alan 1957- *WhoRel 92*
**Barker,** David J. P. 1938- *WrDr 92*
**Barker,** David Lowell 1941- *AmMWSc 92*
**Barker,** David Walker 1949- *TwCPaSc*
**Barker,** Dee H 1921- *AmMWSc 92*
**Barker,** Dennis 1929- *IntAu&W 91, WrDr 92*
**Barker,** Donald Young 1925- *AmMWSc 92*
**Barker,** Dorothy Jean 1929- *WhoAmP 91*
**Barker,** Earl Stephens 1920- *AmMWSc 92*
**Barker,** Ed *WhoAmP 91*
**Barker,** Edmund William 1920- *IntWW 91*
**Barker,** Edward 1909- *Who 92*
**Barker,** Edward 1942- *WhoAmL 92*
**Barker,** Edwin Bogue 1954- *WhoEnt 92*
**Barker,** Edwin Stephen 1940- *AmMWSc 92*
**Barker,** Eileen 1938- *WrDr 92*
**Barker,** Eric 1912-1990 *AnObit 1990*
**Barker,** Frank Granville 1923- *IntAu&W 91*
**Barker,** Franklin Brett 1923- *AmMWSc 92*
**Barker,** Franklin Luther 1871-1920 *BiInAmS*
**Barker,** Fred 1928- *AmMWSc 92*
**Barker,** Frederick Henry, Jr. 1953- *WhoFI 92*
**Barker,** Garry *DrAPF 91*
**Barker,** Garry 1943- *WrDr 92*
**Barker,** George *DrAPF 91*
**Barker,** George 1913- *ConPo 91, LiExTwC, RfGEnL 91, WrDr 92*
**Barker,** George Edward 1928- *AmMWSc 92*
**Barker,** George Ernest 1907- *AmMWSc 92*
**Barker,** George Frederick 1835-1910 *BiInAmS*
**Barker,** George Granville 1913- *IntAu&W 91, IntWW 91, Who 92*
**Barker,** George Granville 1913-1991 *ConAu 135*
**Barker,** Graeme William Walter 1946- *Who 92*
**Barker,** Hal B 1925- *AmMWSc 92*
**Barker,** Harley Granville- 1877-1946 *RfGEnL 91*
**Barker,** Harold 1919- *Who 92*
**Barker,** Harold Clinton 1922- *AmMWSc 92*
**Barker,** Harold Grant 1917- *AmMWSc 92*
**Barker,** Harry Heaton 1898- *Who 92*
**Barker,** Horace Albert 1907- *AmMWSc 92, IntWW 91*
**Barker,** Howard 1946- *IntAu&W 91, Who 92, WrDr 92*
**Barker,** James Cathey 1945- *AmMWSc 92*
**Barker,** James Edward, Jr. 1936- *WhoWest 92*
**Barker,** James Hadley 1946- *WhoFI 92*
**Barker,** James J 1922- *AmMWSc 92*
**Barker,** James Joseph 1922- *WhoWest 92*
**Barker,** James McClure 1934- *WhoAmP 91*
**Barker,** James Nelson 1784-1858 *BenetAL 91*
**Barker,** James Peter 1935- *WhoAmP 91*
**Barker,** James Robert 1958- *WhoFI 92*
**Barker,** Jane Ellen 1935- *AmMWSc 92*
**Barker,** Jeffery Lange 1943- *AmMWSc 92*
**Barker,** Jeffrey Dillon 1959- *WhoWest 92*
**Barker,** Jim L 1935- *WhoAmP 91*
**Barker,** Jo Ann 1948- *WhoRel 92*
**Barker,** John Francis Holroyd 1925- *Who 92*
**Barker,** John L, Jr 1937- *AmMWSc 92*
**Barker,** John Lindsay 1910- *Who 92*
**Barker,** John M 1916- *WhoAmP 91*
**Barker,** John Michael Adrian 1932- *Who 92*
**Barker,** John Perronet 1930- *Who 92*
**Barker,** John Roger 1943- *AmMWSc 92*
**Barker,** Judy 1941- *WhoFI 92*
**Barker,** June Northrop 1928- *AmMWSc 92*
**Barker,** Keith 1947- *ConAu 135*
**Barker,** Keith Rene 1928- *WhoFI 92, WhoMW 92*
**Barker,** Kenneth 1934- *Who 92*
**Barker,** Kenneth Leroy 1939- *AmMWSc 92*
**Barker,** Kenneth Neil 1937- *AmMWSc 92*
**Barker,** Kenneth Reece 1932- *AmMWSc 92*
**Barker,** Kit 1916-1988 *TwCPaSc*
**Barker,** Laren Dee Stacy 1942- *AmMWSc 92*
**Barker,** Lawrence Edward 1938- *WhoRel 92*
**Barker,** Lee Charles 1952- *WhoRel 92*
**Barker,** LeRoy N 1928- *AmMWSc 92*
**Barker,** Lewellys Franklin 1933- *AmMWSc 92*
**Barker,** Louis Allen 1941- *AmMWSc 92*
**Barker,** Lynn Marshall 1928- *AmMWSc 92*
**Barker,** Margaret 1907- *TwCPaSc*
**Barker,** Mary Elizabeth 1930- *AmMWSc 92*
**Barker,** Mary Katherine 1921- *WhoMW 92*
**Barker,** Mason Clement, Jr. 1944- *WhoRel 92*
**Barker,** Michael 1951- *WhoEnt 92*
**Barker,** Michael W. 1954- *IntMPA 92*
**Barker,** Mildred *DrAPF 91*
**Barker,** Mildred 1897- *NewAmDM*
**Barker,** Morris Wayne 1945- *AmMWSc 92*
**Barker,** Nancie Lynne 1942- *WhoWest 92*
**Barker,** Nancy Lepard 1936- *WhoMW 92*
**Barker,** Nicolas John 1932- *Who 92*
**Barker,** Norman Bruce 1956- *WhoEnt 92*
**Barker,** Norval Glen 1925- *AmMWSc 92*
**Barker,** Pat 1943- *WrDr 92*
**Barker,** Patricia Margaret 1943- *IntAu&W 91*
**Barker,** Paul 1935- *IntAu&W 91, Who 92*
**Barker,** Paul Kenneth 1949- *AmMWSc 92*
**Barker,** Pauline J. 1930- *WhoBlA 92*
**Barker,** Penelope 1728-1796 *DcNCBi 1*
**Barker,** Peter Eugene *AmMWSc 92*
**Barker,** Peter William 1928- *Who 92*
**Barker,** Philip 1929- *WrDr 92*
**Barker,** Philip Shaw 1933- *AmMWSc 92*
**Barker,** Raymond Henry, Jr. 1946- *WhoWest 92*
**Barker,** Revel 1944- *IntAu&W 91*
**Barker,** Richard Alexander 1947- *WhoWest 92*
**Barker,** Richard Canfield 1935- *WhoFI 92*
**Barker,** Richard Clark 1926- *AmMWSc 92*
**Barker,** Richard Gordon 1937- *AmMWSc 92*
**Barker,** Richard Philip 1939- *Who 92*
**Barker,** Rick Albert 1952- *WhoEnt 92*
**Barker,** Robert 1928- *AmMWSc 92*
**Barker,** Robert Edward, Jr 1930- *AmMWSc 92*
**Barker,** Robert Henry 1937- *AmMWSc 92*
**Barker,** Robert Jeffery 1946- *WhoWest 92*
**Barker,** Robert Leigh 1933- *WhoFI 92*
**Barker,** Robert William *IntMPA 92, WhoEnt 92*
**Barker,** Ronald Hugh 1915- *Who 92*
**Barker,** Ronnie 1929- *Who 92*
**Barker,** Roy Edwin 1925- *WhoAmP 91*
**Barker,** Roy Jean 1924- *AmMWSc 92*
**Barker,** S Omar 1894-1985 *TwCWW 91*
**Barker,** Samuel Booth 1912- *AmMWSc 92*
**Barker,** Samuel Lamar 1942- *AmMWSc 92*
**Barker,** Sandra Mills 1958- *WhoFI 92*
**Barker,** Sarah Evans 1943- *WhoAmL 92, WhoMW 92*
**Barker,** Stephen Richards 1955- *WhoFI 92*
**Barker,** Susan Vera *Who 92*
**Barker,** Theodore Cardwell 1923- *Who 92, WrDr 92*
**Barker,** Thomas 1713-1789 *DcNCBi 1*
**Barker,** Thomas Christopher 1928- *Who 92*
**Barker,** Timothy Gwynne 1940- *Who 92*
**Barker,** Timothy T. 1948- *WhoBlA 92*
**Barker,** Tom 1943- *WhoAmP 91*
**Barker,** Trevor 1935- *Who 92*
**Barker,** Verlyn Lloyd 1931- *WhoMW 92, WhoRel 92*
**Barker,** Wayne Melvin 1928- *WhoMW 92*
**Barker,** Wendy *DrAPF 91*
**Barker,** Wiley Franklin 1919- *AmMWSc 92*
**Barker,** William 1909- *Who 92*
**Barker,** William Alfred 1919- *AmMWSc 92*
**Barker,** William Barney 1950- *WhoAmL 92*
**Barker,** William George 1922- *AmMWSc 92*
**Barker,** William Griffith, Jr. 1933- *WhoEnt 92*
**Barker,** William H *WhoAmP 91*
**Barker,** William Hamblin, II 1948- *AmMWSc 92*
**Barker,** William Onico 1934- *WhoAmP 91*
**Barker,** William Shirmer, II 1934- *WhoRel 92*
**Barker,** William T 1941- *AmMWSc 92*
**Barker,** William Thomas 1947- *WhoMW 92*
**Barker,** Winona Clinton 1938- *AmMWSc 92*
**Barkett,** Diane DeMichele *DrAPF 91*
**Barkett,** Rosemary 1939- *WhoAmP 91*
**Barkett,** Steve 1950- *IntMPA 92*
**Barkey,** Kenneth Thomas 1916- *AmMWSc 92*
**Barkey,** Lisa Marie 1965- *WhoMW 92*
**Barkhausen,** David N 1950- *WhoAmP 91*
**Barkhausen,** Heinrich Georg 1881-1956 *FacFETw*
**Barkhin,** Grigoriy Borisovich 1880-1969 *SovUnBD*
**Barkhordar,** Parviz *WhoWest 92*
**Barkhorn,** Gerhard 1919-1983 *EncTR 91 [port]*
**Barkhoudarian,** Sarkis 1938- *WhoWest 92*
**Barkhouse,** Joyce Carman 1913- *IntAu&W 91*
**Barkin,** Carol 1944- *ConAu 135, WrDr 92*
**Barkin,** Ellen 1954- *IntMPA 92*
**Barkin,** Ellen 1955- *WhoEnt 92*
**Barkin,** Jill *WrDr 92*
**Barkin,** Marvin E. 1933- *WhoAmL 92*
**Barkin,** Michael Adam 1963- *WhoAmL 92*
**Barkin,** Richard Bruce 1952- *WhoAmL 92*
**Barkin,** Solomon 1907- *WhoFI 92*
**Barkin,** Stanley M 1926- *AmMWSc 92*
**Barking,** Bishop of 1936- *Who 92*
**Barkis,** Marvin William 1943- *WhoAmP 91*
**Barkla,** Charles Glover 1877-1944 *FacFETw, WhoNob 90*
**Barkley,** Alan 1944- *TwCPaSc*
**Barkley,** Alben 1877-1956 *FacFETw*
**Barkley,** Alben William 1877-1956 *AmPolLe*
**Barkley,** Alben William, II 1944- *WhoAmP 91*
**Barkley,** Bronson Lee 1949- *WhoRel 92*
**Barkley,** Charles *NewYTBS 91 [port], WhoBlA 92*
**Barkley,** Charles 1963- *CurBio 91 [port]*
**Barkley,** Drew S. *WhoIns 92*
**Barkley,** Dwight G 1932- *AmMWSc 92*
**Barkley,** John Montieth 1910- *Who 92*
**Barkley,** John R 1938- *AmMWSc 92*
**Barkley,** Joseph Richard 1942- *WhoFI 92*
**Barkley,** Lloyd Blair 1925- *AmMWSc 92*
**Barkley,** Mark E. 1932- *WhoBlA 92*
**Barkley,** Richard C. 1932- *IntWW 91, WhoAmP 91*
**Barkley,** Rufus, Jr. 1949- *WhoBlA 92*
**Barkley,** Theodore Mitchell 1934- *AmMWSc 92, WhoMW 92*
**Barkley,** Thierry Vincent 1955- *WhoAmL 92, WhoWest 92*
**Barkley,** William Donald 1941- *WhoWest 92*
**Barkman,** Alma 1939- *ConAu 35NR*
**Barkman,** Annette Shaulis 1948- *WhoFI 92*
**Barkman,** Jon Albert 1947- *WhoAmL 92*
**Barkman,** Robert Cloyce 1942- *AmMWSc 92*
**Barko,** John William 1947- *AmMWSc 92*
**Barkoff,** Rupert Mitchell 1948- *WhoAmL 92*
**Barkoff,** Sarah Elizabeth *WhoEnt 92*
**Barkow,** Al 1932- *IntAu&W 91, WrDr 92*
**Barks,** Coleman *DrAPF 91*
**Barks,** Coleman 1937- *ConPo 91*
**Barks,** Coleman Bryan 1937- *IntAu&W 91, WrDr 92*
**Barks,** Paul Allan 1936- *AmMWSc 92, WhoMW 92*
**Barks,** Ronald Edward 1938- *WhoWest 92*
**Barksdale,** Charles Madsen 1947- *AmMWSc 92*
**Barksdale,** Clarence Caulfield 1932- *WhoFI 92*
**Barksdale,** Donald Argee 1923- *BlkOlyM*
**Barksdale,** Hudson L. 1907- *WhoBlA 92*
**Barksdale,** James Bryan, Jr 1940- *AmMWSc 92*
**Barksdale,** James Love 1943- *WhoFI 92*
**Barksdale,** Lane W 1914- *AmMWSc 92*
**Barksdale,** Mary Frances 1934- *WhoBlA 92*
**Barksdale,** Rhesa H *WhoAmP 91*
**Barksdale,** Rhesa H. 1944- *WhoAmL 92*
**Barksdale,** Richard Dillon 1938- *AmMWSc 92*
**Barksdale,** Richard Kenneth 1915- *WhoBlA 92*
**Barksdale,** Rita Phillips 1920- *WhoWest 92*
**Barksdale,** Thomas Henry 1932- *AmMWSc 92*
**Barksdale Hall,** Roland C. 1960- *WhoBlA 92*
**Barkshire,** John *Who 92*
**Barkshire,** Robert Hugh 1909- *Who 92*
**Barkshire,** Robert Renny St. John 1935- *Who 92*
**Barkstall,** Vernon L. 1929- *WhoBlA 92*
**Barkum,** Jerome Phillip 1950- *WhoBlA 92*
**Barkun,** Michael 1938- *ConAu 135*
**Barkworth,** Mary Elizabeth 1941- *AmMWSc 92*
**Barkworth,** Peter Wynn 1929- *Who 92*
**Barlach,** Ernst 1870-1938 *EncTR 91, FacFETw*
**Barland,** Thomas Howard 1930- *WhoAmL 92*
**Barlar,** Rebecca Nance 1950- *WhoEnt 92*
**Barlas,** Julie S 1944- *AmMWSc 92*
**Barlay,** Stephen 1930- *IntAu&W 91, WrDr 92*
**Barlett,** James Edward 1944- *WhoFI 92*
**Barletta,** Michael Anthony 1942- *AmMWSc 92*
**Barletta,** Naomi Lockwood *DrAPF 91*
**Barletta,** Nicolas Ardito 1938- *IntWW 91*
**Barley,** Barron Philip 1961- *WhoRel 92*
**Barley,** John Alvin 1940- *WhoAmL 92*
**Barley,** John E 1945- *WhoAmP 91*
**Barley,** M. W. *ConAu 134*
**Barley,** Maurice Willmore d1991 *Who 92N*
**Barley,** Maurice Willmore 1909-1991 *ConAu 134*
**Barley,** Michael Steven 1961- *WhoRel 92*
**Barley,** Vernon 1934- *WhoAmP 91*
**Barlich,** Jack F 1922- *WhoAmP 91*
**Barling,** Gerald Edward 1949- *Who 92*
**Barlis,** Thomas George 1960- *WhoAmL 92*
**Barloco,** Gerard H. 1944- *WhoIns 92*
**Barlog,** Agnieszka 1909- *IntAu&W 91*
**Barlog,** Boleslaw 1906- *IntWW 91*
**Barlok,** S. M. Electa 1931- *WhoRel 92*
**Barlow,** Anthony 1938- *AmMWSc 92*
**Barlow,** August Ralph, Jr. 1934- *WhoRel 92*
**Barlow,** Becky Ann 1949- *WhoRel 92*
**Barlow,** Bohuslav 1947- *TwCPaSc*
**Barlow,** Charles F 1923- *AmMWSc 92*
**Barlow,** Christopher Hilaro 1929- *Who 92*
**Barlow,** Clyde Howard *AmMWSc 92*
**Barlow,** David Hearnshaw 1949- *Who 92*
**Barlow,** David John 1937- *Who 92*
**Barlow,** David Michael Rigby 1936- *Who 92*
**Barlow,** Donald Spiers Monteagle 1905- *Who 92*
**Barlow,** Edward Dawson 1938- *WhoAmP 91*
**Barlow,** Edward J 1920- *AmMWSc 92*
**Barlow,** Frank 1911- *IntAu&W 91, Who 92, WrDr 92*
**Barlow,** Frank John 1914- *WhoFI 92*
**Barlow,** Franklin Sackett 1912- *WhoMW 92*
**Barlow,** George *DrAPF 91*
**Barlow,** George 1926- *AmMWSc 92*
**Barlow,** George Francis 1939- *Who 92*
**Barlow,** George Webber 1929- *AmMWSc 92*
**Barlow,** George William 1924- *Who 92*
**Barlow,** Gillian 1944- *TwCPaSc*
**Barlow,** Grover S. 1934- *WhoBlA 92*
**Barlow,** Haven J 1922- *WhoAmP 91*
**Barlow,** Herman Zulch, Jr. 1949- *WhoWest 92*
**Barlow,** Horace B. 1921- *IntWW 91*
**Barlow,** Horace Basil 1921- *Who 92*
**Barlow,** Howard 1892-1972 *NewAmDM*
**Barlow,** Howard William 1927- *WhoAmL 92*
**Barlow,** James A, Jr 1923- *AmMWSc 92*
**Barlow,** James Edwin 1928- *WhoAmL 92*
**Barlow,** Janet Rosalyn Herman 1953- *WhoEnt 92*
**Barlow,** Joel 1754-1812 *BenetAL 91, BlkwEAR*
**Barlow,** Joel William 1942- *AmMWSc 92*
**Barlow,** John 1924- *WrDr 92*
**Barlow,** John 1934- *Who 92*
**Barlow,** John Aden 1942- *WhoAmL 92*
**Barlow,** John Noble 1861-1917 *TwCPaSc*
**Barlow,** John Sutton 1925- *AmMWSc 92*
**Barlow,** Jon Charles 1935- *AmMWSc 92*
**Barlow,** Joyce Krutick 1946- *WhoAmL 92*
**Barlow,** Linda Ann 1944- *WhoFI 92*
**Barlow,** Lolete Falck 1932- *IntAu&W 91*
**Barlow,** Loren Call 1926- *WhoWest 92*
**Barlow,** Mark Owens 1946- *AmMWSc 92*
**Barlow,** Maude 1947- *ConAu 135*
**Barlow,** Nicholas 1940- *TwCPaSc*
**Barlow,** Patrick 1947- *Who 92*
**Barlow,** Phil *IntMPA 92*
**Barlow,** Phyllida 1944- *TwCPaSc*
**Barlow,** Richard Eugene 1931- *AmMWSc 92*
**Barlow,** Robert Brown, Jr 1939- *AmMWSc 92*
**Barlow,** Ronald Rand 1941- *WhoEnt 92*
**Barlow,** Roy Oxspring 1927- *Who 92*
**Barlow,** Samuel L. 1892-1982 *NewAmDM*
**Barlow,** Thomas 1914- *Who 92*
**Barlow,** Thomas James 1922- *IntWW 91*

**Barlow,** Thomas Martin 1935- *WhoWest 92*
**Barlow,** Wayne Brewster 1912- *NewAmDM*
**Barlow,** Wilfred 1915- *WrDr 92*
**Barlow,** William *Who 92*
**Barlow,** William 1924- *IntWW 91*
**Barlow,** William Pusey, Jr. 1934- *WhoFI 92, WhoWest 92*
**Barlowe,** Arthur *DcNCBi 1*
**Barlowe,** Raleigh 1914- *WrDr 92*
**Barlowe,** Wayne Douglas 1958- *ConAu 134*
**Barlowe,** William Terry 1953- *WhoRel 92*
**Barlozzari,** Teresa 1954- *AmMWSc 92*
**Barltrop,** Robert 1922- *WrDr 92*
**Barltrop,** Robert Arthur Horace 1922- *IntAu&W 91*
**Barltrop,** Roger Arnold Rowlandson 1930- *IntWW 91, Who 92*
**Barlund,** Kaj-Ole Johannes 1945- *IntWW 91*
**Barmack,** Neal Herbert 1942- *AmMWSc 92*
**Barman,** Susan Marie 1949- *AmMWSc 92*
**Barmann,** Bernard Charles, Sr. 1932- *WhoAmL 92*
**Barmann,** Lawrence 1932- *IntAu&W 91, WrDr 92*
**Barmat** *EncTR 91*
**Barmatz,** Martin Bruce 1938- *AmMWSc 92*
**Barmby,** David Stanley 1928- *AmMWSc 92*
**Barmby,** John G 1922- *AmMWSc 92*
**Barmen,** Stewart B. 1940- *WhoAmL 92*
**Barmeyer,** John R. 1946- *WhoIns 92*
**Barmine,** Alexander G 1899-1987 *FacFETw*
**Barmore,** Frank E 1938- *AmMWSc 92*
**Barmore,** Frank Edward 1938- *WhoMW 92*
**Barna,** Ed *DrAPF 91*
**Barna,** Gabriel George 1946- *AmMWSc 92*
**Barna,** Lillian Carattini 1929- *WhoWest 92*
**Barna,** Tibor 1919- *Who 92*
**Barnaal,** Dennis E 1936- *AmMWSc 92*
**Barnabas,** John Henry *ScFEYrs*
**Barnabeo,** Austin Emidio 1933- *AmMWSc 92*
**Barnabeo,** Susan Patricia 1960- *WhoAmL 92*
**Barnaby,** Bruce E 1929- *AmMWSc 92*
**Barnaby,** Charles Frank 1927- *IntAu&W 91, IntWW 91, WrDr 92*
**Barnack,** Oscar 1879-1936 *DcTwDes, FacFETw*
**Barnala,** Surjit Singh 1925- *IntWW 91*
**Barnard,** Baron 1923- *Who 92*
**Barnard,** Adam Johannes 1929- *AmMWSc 92*
**Barnard,** Ann Watson 1930- *WhoMW 92*
**Barnard,** Anthony C L 1932- *AmMWSc 92*
**Barnard,** Arthur Thomas 1893- *Who 92*
**Barnard,** Aurora Caro 1908- *WhoAmP 91*
**Barnard,** Charlotte D. 1936- *WhoWest 92*
**Barnard,** Christaan 1922- *IntAu&W 91, WrDr 92*
**Barnard,** Christiaan Neethling 1922- *FacFETw [port], IntWW 91, Who 92*
**Barnard,** Clare Amundson 1927- *WhoAmP 91*
**Barnard,** Donald Roy 1946- *AmMWSc 92*
**Barnard,** Dorothy Gaskill 1925- *WhoRel 92*
**Barnard,** Doug, Jr. 1922- *AlmAP 92 [port]*
**Barnard,** Douglas Craig 1958- *WhoAmL 92*
**Barnard,** Druie Douglas, Jr 1922- *WhoAmP 91*
**Barnard,** Edith Ethel 1880-1914 *BiInAmS*
**Barnard,** Elaine Patricia 1930- *WhoEnt 92*
**Barnard,** Eric Albert 1927- *IntWW 91, Who 92*
**Barnard,** Ernest Edward Peter 1927- *Who 92*
**Barnard,** Frederick Augustus Porter 1809-1889 *BiInAmS*
**Barnard,** Frederick Mechner 1921- *WrDr 92*
**Barnard,** Garland Ray 1932- *AmMWSc 92*
**Barnard,** George Alfred 1915- *Who 92*
**Barnard,** George Edward 1907- *Who 92*
**Barnard,** George Smith *WhoAmL 92*
**Barnard,** Gwen 1912- *TwCPaSc*
**Barnard,** H B *WhoAmP 91*
**Barnard,** Jerald Scott 1965- *WhoEnt 92*
**Barnard,** Jerry Laurens 1928- *AmMWSc 92*
**Barnard,** John 1681-1770 *BiInAmS*
**Barnard,** John Gross 1815-1882 *BiInAmS*
**Barnard,** John Michael 1936- *Who 92*
**Barnard,** John Wesley 1946- *AmMWSc 92*
**Barnard,** Joseph 1928- *Who 92*
**Barnard,** Joseph Edwin 1870-1949 *FacFETw*
**Barnard,** Kate 1875-1930 *HanAmWH*
**Barnard,** Kate 1941- *TwCPaSc*
**Barnard,** Kathleen Rainwater 1927- *WhoMW 92*
**Barnard,** Kathryn E 1938- *AmMWSc 92*
**Barnard,** Lance Herbert 1919- *IntWW 91, Who 92*
**Barnard,** Lukas Daniel 1949- *IntWW 91*
**Barnard,** Marjorie Faith *TwCSFW 91*
**Barnard,** Mary *DrAPF 91*
**Barnard,** Michael Dana 1946- *WhoWest 92*
**Barnard,** Michael Richard 1951- *WhoEnt 92, WhoWest 92*
**Barnard,** Michael Walker 1946- *WhoEnt 92*
**Barnard,** R James *AmMWSc 92*
**Barnard,** Robert 1936- *IntAu&W 91, WrDr 92*
**Barnard,** Robert C. 1913- *WhoAmL 92*
**Barnard,** Robert D, Jr 1929- *AmMWSc 92*
**Barnard,** Robert N. 1947- *WhoAmL 92*
**Barnard,** Robert William 1946- *WhoFI 92*
**Barnard,** Roger W 1942- *AmMWSc 92*
**Barnard,** Rollin Dwight 1922- *WhoFI 92, WhoWest 92*
**Barnard,** Scott Henry 1943- *WhoEnt 92*
**Barnard,** Seph 1956- *WhoEnt 92*
**Barnard,** Sheri *WhoWest 92*
**Barnard,** Sheri S 1937- *WhoAmP 91*
**Barnard,** Thomas *Who 92*
**Barnard,** Thomas H. 1939- *WhoAmL 92*
**Barnard,** Thomas Henslow 1898- *TwCPaSc*
**Barnard,** Walther M 1937- *AmMWSc 92*
**Barnard,** William C. 1935- *WhoAmL 92*
**Barnard,** William Marion 1949- *WhoWest 92*
**Barnard,** William Sprague 1925- *AmMWSc 92*
**Barnard,** William Stebbins 1849-1887 *BiInAmS*
**Barnartt,** Sidney 1919- *AmMWSc 92*
**Barnathan,** Julius *LesBEnT 92*
**Barnathan,** Julius 1927- *WhoEnt 92, WhoFI 92*
**Barnawell,** Earl B 1922- *AmMWSc 92*
**Barncastle,** Delia Garcia 1925- *WhoAmP 91*
**Barnden,** Hugh 1948- *TwCPaSc*
**Barndorff-Nielsen,** Ole Eiler 1935- *IntWW 91*
**Barndt,** Richard V. 1931- *WhoAmL 92*
**Barne,** Nicholas Michael Lancelot 1943- *Who 92*
**Barnea,** Uri N. 1943- *WhoEnt 92, WhoWest 92*
**Barnebey,** Malcolm 1927- *WhoAmP 91*
**Barneby,** Henry Habington 1909- *Who 92*
**Barnekow,** Russell George, Jr 1932- *AmMWSc 92*
**Barner,** Brett Lee 1963- *WhoFI 92*
**Barner,** Bruce Monroe 1951- *WhoMW 92*
**Barner,** Hendrick Boyer 1933- *AmMWSc 92*
**Barnerjee,** Shailesh Prasad 1940- *AmMWSc 92*
**Barnes** *Who 92*
**Barnes,** A James 1942- *WhoAmP 91*
**Barnes,** Aaron 1939- *AmMWSc 92*
**Barnes,** Adrian Francis Patrick 1943- *Who 92*
**Barnes,** Alan Robert 1927- *Who 92*
**Barnes,** Alfred 1872-1951 *ThHElm*
**Barnes,** Alice Josephine 1912- *IntWW 91, Who 92*
**Barnes,** Allan Marion 1924- *AmMWSc 92*
**Barnes,** Allan Randall 1946- *WhoWest 92*
**Barnes,** Allen Lawrence 1932- *AmMWSc 92*
**Barnes,** Andre LaMont 1957- *WhoEnt 92*
**Barnes,** Anne Craig 1932- *WhoAmP 91*
**Barnes,** Anne T. 1940- *WhoBlA 92*
**Barnes,** Anthony Hugh 1931- *Who 92*
**Barnes,** Archibald George 1887- *TwCPaSc*
**Barnes,** Arnold Appleton, Jr 1930- *AmMWSc 92*
**Barnes,** Arthur K 1911-1969 *TwCSFW 91*
**Barnes,** Asa, Jr 1933- *AmMWSc 92*
**Barnes,** Audra Guyton 1921- *WhoWest 92*
**Barnes,** Barnabe 1569?-1609 *RfGEnL 91*
**Barnes,** Benjamin Warren Grant 1948- *WhoAmL 92*
**Barnes,** Benny 1951- *WhoBlA 92*
**Barnes,** Bill Lloyd 1926- *WhoMW 92, WhoRel 92*
**Barnes,** Bobby T. 1938- *WhoEnt 92*
**Barnes,** Boisey O. 1943- *WhoBlA 92*
**Barnes,** Bruce Herbert 1931- *AmMWSc 92*
**Barnes,** Burton Verne 1930- *AmMWSc 92*
**Barnes,** Byron Ashwood 1927- *AmMWSc 92*
**Barnes,** C. V. *WrDr 92*
**Barnes,** C W, Jr 1927- *AmMWSc 92*
**Barnes,** Calvin K. 1929- *WhoFI 92*
**Barnes,** Carl Eldon 1936- *AmMWSc 92*
**Barnes,** Carnella 1911- *NotBlAW 92*
**Barnes,** Carolyn S. Machalec 1957- *WhoAmL 92*
**Barnes,** Charles Ahrens 1938- *WhoAmP 91*
**Barnes,** Charles Andrew 1921- *AmMWSc 92*
**Barnes,** Charles Dee 1935- *AmMWSc 92*
**Barnes,** Charles M 1922- *AmMWSc 92*
**Barnes,** Charles Patrick 1958- *WhoMW 92*
**Barnes,** Charles Reid 1858-1910 *BiInAmS*
**Barnes,** Charles Winfred 1934- *AmMWSc 92*
**Barnes,** Charlie James 1930- *AmMWSc 92*
**Barnes,** Charlotte Mary Sanford 1818-1863 *BenetAL 91*
**Barnes,** Christopher John Andrew 1944- *Who 92*
**Barnes,** Christopher Richard 1940- *AmMWSc 92, IntWW 91*
**Barnes,** Clifford Adrian 1905- *AmMWSc 92*
**Barnes,** Clive 1927- *WrDr 92*
**Barnes,** Clive Alexander 1927- *IntAu&W 91, IntWW 91, Who 92, WhoEnt 92*
**Barnes,** Craig Eliot 1955- *AmMWSc 92*
**Barnes,** Craig Martin 1949- *WhoFI 92*
**Barnes,** Cyril Arthur 1926- *Who 92*
**Barnes,** Daniel Henry 1785-1828 *BiInAmS*
**Barnes,** Daniel Sennett 1924- *Who 92*
**Barnes,** Dave *TwCSFW 91*
**Barnes,** David *Who 92, WhoAmP 91*
**Barnes,** David Alexander 1819-1892 *DcNCBi 1*
**Barnes,** David Fitz 1921- *AmMWSc 92*
**Barnes,** David Kennedy 1923- *AmMWSc 92*
**Barnes,** David Michael 1943- *Who 92*
**Barnes,** David Robert, Jr. 1952- *WhoWest 92*
**Barnes,** Delorise Creecy 1947- *WhoBlA 92*
**Barnes,** Denis 1914- *Who 92*
**Barnes,** Dennis Norman 1940- *WhoAmL 92*
**Barnes,** Derek A 1933- *AmMWSc 92*
**Barnes,** Diane 1961- *WhoBlA 92*
**Barnes,** Djuna 1892-1982 *BenetAL 91, FacFETw, LiExTwC*
**Barnes,** Don B 1924- *WhoAmP 91*
**Barnes,** Donald Frederic 1914- *WhoIns 92*
**Barnes,** Donald Kay 1935- *AmMWSc 92*
**Barnes,** Donald L. 1943- *WhoIns 92*
**Barnes,** Donald McLeod 1921- *AmMWSc 92*
**Barnes,** Donald Michael 1943- *WhoAmL 92*
**Barnes,** Donald Wesley 1944- *AmMWSc 92*
**Barnes,** Douglas 1927- *IntAu&W 91, WrDr 92*
**Barnes,** Earl Russell 1942- *AmMWSc 92*
**Barnes,** Edward Campbell 1928- *Who 92*
**Barnes,** Edward Larrabee 1915- *IntWW 91*
**Barnes,** Edwin Ellsworth 1929- *AmMWSc 92*
**Barnes,** Edwin Ronald 1935- *Who 92*
**Barnes,** Eileen Stout 1945- *WhoAmP 91*
**Barnes,** Eric Charles 1924- *Who 92*
**Barnes,** Ernest Eugene, Jr. 1938- *WhoBlA 92*
**Barnes,** Ernest John 1917- *Who 92*
**Barnes,** Ernest Leon 1946- *WhoRel 92*
**Barnes,** Eugene M. 1931- *WhoBlA 92*
**Barnes,** Eugene Miller, Jr 1943- *AmMWSc 92*
**Barnes,** Fannie Burrell *WhoBlA 92*
**Barnes,** Francis M, III 1918- *WhoAmP 91*
**Barnes,** Francis Walter Ibbetson 1914- *Who 92*
**Barnes,** Frank Stephenson 1932- *AmMWSc 92*
**Barnes,** Frederic Wood, Jr. 1943- *WhoEnt 92*
**Barnes,** Frederick Walter, Jr 1909- *AmMWSc 92*
**Barnes,** G Richard 1922- *AmMWSc 92*
**Barnes,** Garrett Henry, Jr 1926- *AmMWSc 92*
**Barnes,** Gene 1926- *WhoEnt 92*
**Barnes,** Gene A 1935- *AmMWSc 92*
**Barnes,** Geoffrey Thomas 1932- *Who 92*
**Barnes,** George 1909- *TwCPaSc*
**Barnes,** George 1921- *AmMWSc 92*
**Barnes,** George Edgar 1943- *AmMWSc 92*
**Barnes,** George Emerson 1944- *WhoFI 92*
**Barnes,** George Lewis 1920- *AmMWSc 92*
**Barnes,** Gerald Joseph 1936- *AmMWSc 92*
**Barnes,** Gilbert J. 1954- *WhoFI 92, WhoWest 92*
**Barnes,** Glover William 1923- *AmMWSc 92*
**Barnes,** H Verdain 1935- *AmMWSc 92*
**Barnes,** Harold 1936- *Who 92*
**Barnes,** Harper Henderson 1937- *WhoEnt 92*
**Barnes,** Harry Elmer 1889-1968 *AmPeW*
**Barnes,** Harry George, Jr. 1926- *IntWW 91, WhoAmP 91*
**Barnes,** Henson Perrymoore 1934- *WhoAmP 91*
**Barnes,** Herbert M 1918- *AmMWSc 92*
**Barnes,** Herman Verdain 1935- *WhoMW 92*
**Barnes,** Howard Clarence 1912- *AmMWSc 92*
**Barnes,** Howard G. 1913- *WhoEnt 92*
**Barnes,** Hoyt Michael 1943- *AmMWSc 92*
**Barnes,** Hubert Lloyd 1928- *AmMWSc 92*
**Barnes,** Ingrid Victoria *Who 92*
**Barnes,** Ira Lynus 1928- *AmMWSc 92*
**Barnes,** Iraline G. *WhoBlA 92*
**Barnes,** Isabel Janet 1936- *WhoMW 92*
**Barnes,** Ivan 1931- *AmMWSc 92*
**Barnes,** J Bradford 1957- *WhoFI 92*
**Barnes,** Jack Leonard 1935- *WhoRel 92*
**Barnes,** James 1855-1936 *ScFEYrs*
**Barnes,** James A 1951- *WhoAmP 91*
**Barnes,** James Alford 1944- *AmMWSc 92*
**Barnes,** James Allen 1933- *AmMWSc 92*
**Barnes,** James Byron 1942- *WhoMW 92*
**Barnes,** James David 1936- *Who 92*
**Barnes,** James Edwin 1917- *Who 92*
**Barnes,** James Frederick 1932- *Who 92*
**Barnes,** James Garland, Jr. 1940- *WhoAmL 92*
**Barnes,** James George 1908- *Who 92*
**Barnes,** James J. 1931- *WrDr 92*
**Barnes,** James Mark 1956- *WhoRel 92*
**Barnes,** James Milton 1923- *AmMWSc 92*
**Barnes,** James Neil 1944- *WhoFI 92*
**Barnes,** James Ray 1940- *AmMWSc 92*
**Barnes,** James Woodrow 1918- *WhoEnt 92*
**Barnes,** Jane *DrAPF 91*
**Barnes,** Jane Ellen 1943- *IntAu&W 91*
**Barnes,** Jane M 1926- *WhoAmP 91*
**Barnes,** Jeffery Dwayne 1966- *WhoMW 92*
**Barnes,** Jeffrey Lee *AmMWSc 92*
**Barnes,** Jerry 1931- *WhoAmP 91*
**Barnes,** Jim *DrAPF 91*
**Barnes,** Jim 1941- *BlkOlyM*
**Barnes,** Jodie Kay 1959- *WhoMW 92*
**Barnes,** John *Who 92*
**Barnes,** John 1917- *IntWW 91*
**Barnes,** John Alfred 1930- *Who 92*
**Barnes,** John Arundel 1918- *IntWW 91, Who 92, WrDr 92*
**Barnes,** John B., Sr. 1922- *WhoBlA 92*
**Barnes,** John David 1939- *AmMWSc 92*
**Barnes,** John E. 1933- *WhoBlA 92*
**Barnes,** John Earl 1956- *WhoAmL 92*
**Barnes,** John Fayette 1930- *AmMWSc 92, WhoWest 92*
**Barnes,** John J. 1924- *WhoIns 92*
**Barnes,** John Maurice 1931- *AmMWSc 92*
**Barnes,** John Stanley, Jr 1931- *WhoAmP 91*
**Barnes,** John Wadsworth 1920- *WhoEnt 92*
**Barnes,** Jonathan 1942- *Who 92, WrDr 92*
**Barnes,** Joseph Curtis 1913- *WhoFI 92, WhoWest 92*
**Barnes,** Joseph Harry George 1930- *Who 92*
**Barnes,** Joseph Nathan 1950- *WhoBlA 92*
**Barnes,** Josephine *Who 92*
**Barnes,** Josephine 1912- *WrDr 92*
**Barnes,** Joshua 1813-1890 *DcNCBi 1*
**Barnes,** Joy Chappell 1950- *WhoAmL 92*
**Barnes,** Julian 1946- *ConNov 91, IntAu&W 91, IntWW 91, WrDr 92*
**Barnes,** Julian Patrick 1946- *Who 92*
**Barnes,** Juliana *EncAmaz 91*
**Barnes,** Karen Louise 1942- *AmMWSc 92*
**Barnes,** Kate *DrAPF 91*
**Barnes,** Kathleen Joyce 1962- *WhoFI 92*
**Barnes,** Kenneth 1922- *Who 92*
**Barnes,** Kenneth James 1930- *Who 92*
**Barnes,** Lahna Harris 1947- *WhoMW 92*
**Barnes,** Larry D *AmMWSc 92*
**Barnes,** Lawrence Gayle 1945- *AmMWSc 92*
**Barnes,** Lee 1933- *WhoAmP 91*
**Barnes,** Leonard C. 1922- *WhoBlA 92*
**Barnes,** Linda 1949- *WrDr 92*
**Barnes,** Louie Burton, III 1948- *WhoAmL 92, WhoFI 92*
**Barnes,** Loutricia *ConAu 135*
**Barnes,** Luther Matthew, III 1936- *WhoFI 92*
**Barnes,** Marc Willis 1959- *WhoMW 92*
**Barnes,** Margaret Ayer 1886-1967 *BenetAL 91*
**Barnes,** Mark 1960- *WhoAmL 92*
**Barnes,** Marshall Hayes, II 1937- *WhoMW 92*
**Barnes,** Martin G. 1948- *WhoBlA 92*
**Barnes,** Martin McRae 1920- *AmMWSc 92*
**Barnes,** Mary Westergaard 1927- *AmMWSc 92*
**Barnes,** Matthew Molena, Jr. 1933- *WhoBlA 92*
**Barnes,** Melvyn Peter Keith 1942- *Who 92*
**Barnes,** Michael *Who 92*
**Barnes,** Michael Carl 1958- *WhoFI 92*
**Barnes,** Michael Cecil John 1932- *Who 92*
**Barnes,** Michael Darr 1943- *WhoAmP 91*
**Barnes,** Michael Earl 1963- *WhoMW 92*
**Barnes,** Michael Horace 1937- *WhoRel 92*
**Barnes,** Michael Patrick 1940- *Who 92*
**Barnes,** Molly Mock 1936- *WhoWest 92*
**Barnes,** N. Kurt 1947- *WhoBlA 92*

**Barnes**, Nancy DrAPF 91
**Barnes**, Paul Douglas 1946- WhoBlA 92
**Barnes**, Paul McClung 1914- WhoAmL 92
**Barnes**, Paul Richard 1936- AmMWSc 92
**Barnes**, Peter 1931- ConAu 34NR, IntAu&W 91, Who 92, WrDr 92
**Barnes**, Peter David 1937- AmMWSc 92
**Barnes**, Peter Robert 1921- Who 92
**Barnes**, Peter William 1939- WhoWest 92
**Barnes**, Philip W. WhoIns 92
**Barnes**, Priscilla 1955- ConTFT 9
**Barnes**, Ralph Craig 1914- AmMWSc 92
**Barnes**, Ralph W 1936- AmMWSc 92
**Barnes**, Ramon M 1940- AmMWSc 92
**Barnes**, Ramona L 1938- WhoAmP 91
**Barnes**, Richard DrAPF 91
**Barnes**, Richard Lewis, Jr. 1953- WhoWest 92
**Barnes**, Richard N 1928- AmMWSc 92
**Barnes**, Richard O 1921- WhoAmP 91
**Barnes**, Richard Walter 1943- WhoAmP 91
**Barnes**, Robert Drane 1927- AmMWSc 92
**Barnes**, Robert F 1933- AmMWSc 92, WhoMW 92
**Barnes**, Robert Henry 1921- IntWW 91, WhoWest 92
**Barnes**, Robert Keith 1925- AmMWSc 92
**Barnes**, Robert Lee 1935- AmMWSc 92
**Barnes**, Robert Sandford 1924- Who 92
**Barnes**, Roderick Arthur 1920- AmMWSc 92
**Barnes**, Roland 1907- Who 92
**Barnes**, Ronald B. WhoRel 92
**Barnes**, Ronnie C 1941- AmMWSc 92
**Barnes**, Rosemary Lois 1946- WhoMW 92, WhoRel 92
**Barnes**, Rosemary Susan 1946- Who 92
**Barnes**, Ross Owen 1946- AmMWSc 92
**Barnes**, Roy E 1948- WhoAmP 91
**Barnes**, Rudolph Counts 1917- WhoAmL 92
**Barnes**, Russell Hanlon 1959- WhoWest 92
**Barnes**, Samuel Henry 1931- WrDr 92
**Barnes**, Sandra Henley 1943- WhoFI 92, WhoMW 92
**Barnes**, Scott Young 1946- WhoAmL 92
**Barnes**, Simon 1951- WrDr 92
**Barnes**, Stan Oscar 1961- WhoAmP 91
**Barnes**, Stephanie DrAPF 91
**Barnes**, Stephen Darryl 1953- WhoBlA 92
**Barnes**, Stephen Paul 1957- WhoFI 92
**Barnes**, Steven 1952- TwCSFW 91, WrDr 92
**Barnes**, Steven Lee 1950- WhoMW 92
**Barnes**, Symiria Peters WhoEnt 92
**Barnes**, Thomas 1936- WhoBlA 92
**Barnes**, Thomas Aaron, Sr 1928- WhoAmP 91, WhoWest 92
**Barnes**, Thomas G. 1930- WhoAmL 92
**Barnes**, Thomas Grogard 1911- AmMWSc 92
**Barnes**, Thomas John 1943- WhoAmL 92
**Barnes**, Thomas V 1936- WhoAmP 91
**Barnes**, Thomas Vernon 1936- WhoMW 92
**Barnes**, Tim DrAPF 91
**Barnes**, Timothy Paul 1944- Who 92
**Barnes**, Virgil Everett 1903- AmMWSc 92
**Barnes**, Virgil Everett, II 1935- AmMWSc 92
**Barnes**, Vivian Leigh 1946- WhoBlA 92
**Barnes**, W.D. DrAPF 91
**Barnes**, Wade 1917- WhoEnt 92
**Barnes**, Wallace Edward 1920- AmMWSc 92
**Barnes**, Wayne Morris 1947- AmMWSc 92
**Barnes**, Wilfred E 1924- AmMWSc 92
**Barnes**, William 1801-1886 RfGEnL 91
**Barnes**, William Anderson 1944- WhoFI 92, WhoWest 92
**Barnes**, William Charles 1934- AmMWSc 92
**Barnes**, William G. 1927- WhoMW 92
**Barnes**, William Gartin 1927- AmMWSc 92
**Barnes**, William L. 1936- WhoBlA 92
**Barnes**, William Mattison, Jr. 1954- WhoRel 92
**Barnes**, William Shafer 1951- WhoRel 92
**Barnes**, William Shelley 1947- AmMWSc 92
**Barnes**, William Wayne 1927- AmMWSc 92
**Barnes**, Willie R. 1931- WhoAmL 92, WhoBlA 92
**Barnes**, Wilson Edward 1938- WhoBlA 92
**Barnes**, Winston Herbert Frederick d1990 Who 92N
**Barnes**, Zane Edison 1921- WhoFI 92
**Barnes-Svarney**, Patricia L. 1953- ConAu 135, SmATA 67 [port]
**Barness**, Lewis Abraham 1921- AmMWSc 92
**Barnet**, Ann B AmMWSc 92
**Barnet**, Boris 1902-1965 IntDcF 2-2
**Barnet**, Boris Vasil'evich 1902-1965 SovUnBD
**Barnet**, Charlie 1913- NewAmDM
**Barnet**, Charlie 1913-1991 NewYTBS 91 [port]
**Barnet**, Harry Nathan 1923- AmMWSc 92
**Barnet**, Peter M. WhoFI 92
**Barnet**, Robert Joseph 1929- WhoWest 92
**Barnet**, Vern 1942- WhoRel 92
**Barnett** Who 92
**Barnett**, Baron 1923- IntWW 91, Who 92
**Barnett**, Alfreda W. Duster 1904- WhoBlA 92
**Barnett**, Alice Ray 1886-1975 NewAmDM
**Barnett**, Allen d1991 NewYTBS 91
**Barnett**, Allen 1937- AmMWSc 92
**Barnett**, Allen M 1940- AmMWSc 92
**Barnett**, Alva P. 1947- WhoBlA 92
**Barnett**, Arthur Doak 1921- IntAu&W 91, WrDr 92
**Barnett**, Audrey 1933- AmMWSc 92
**Barnett**, Bill B 1946- AmMWSc 92
**Barnett**, Bill H WhoAmP 91
**Barnett**, Bobby Dale 1927- AmMWSc 92
**Barnett**, Bradley Gault 1953- WhoMW 92
**Barnett**, Charles Jackson 1942- AmMWSc 92, WhoFI 92
**Barnett**, Charles Radcliffe 1934- WhoEnt 92
**Barnett**, Christopher Andrew 1953- Who 92
**Barnett**, Christopher John Anthony 1936- Who 92
**Barnett**, Clarence Franklin 1924- AmMWSc 92
**Barnett**, Claude C 1928- AmMWSc 92
**Barnett**, Colin Michael 1929- Who 92
**Barnett**, Correlli 1927- IntAu&W 91, Who 92, WrDr 92
**Barnett**, Correlli Douglas 1927- IntWW 91
**Barnett**, Darrell d1991 NewYTBS 91
**Barnett**, David 1940- AmMWSc 92
**Barnett**, David Austin 1945- WhoAmL 92
**Barnett**, David M 1939- AmMWSc 92
**Barnett**, Deanna Louise 1964- WhoMW 92
**Barnett**, Denis Hensley Fulton 1906- Who 92
**Barnett**, Don Marvin 1940- WhoAmL 92
**Barnett**, Don R 1935- AmMWSc 92
**Barnett**, Douglas Eldon 1944- AmMWSc 92, WhoFI 92
**Barnett**, Douglas Eugene 1961- WhoRel 92
**Barnett**, Edith 1942- WhoAmL 92
**Barnett**, Edward 1960- WhoRel 92
**Barnett**, Edward McLain 1947- WhoMW 92
**Barnett**, Edward William 1933- WhoAmL 92
**Barnett**, Elizabeth Hale 1940- WhoFI 92
**Barnett**, Ethel S 1929- WhoAmP 91, WhoBlA 92
**Barnett**, Etta Moten 1901- WhoBlA 92
**Barnett**, Etta Moten 1902- NotBlAW 92 [port]
**Barnett**, Eugene Victor 1932- AmMWSc 92
**Barnett**, Evelyn Brooks 1945- WhoBlA 92
**Barnett**, Ewin Harvey, III 1952- WhoMW 92
**Barnett**, Geoffrey Grant Fulton 1943- Who 92
**Barnett**, George Leonard 1915- WrDr 92
**Barnett**, Gordon Dean 1924- AmMWSc 92
**Barnett**, Guy Octo 1930- AmMWSc 92
**Barnett**, H J M 1922- AmMWSc 92
**Barnett**, Henry Lewis 1914- AmMWSc 92
**Barnett**, Henry William 1927- WhoAmP 91
**Barnett**, Herald Alva 1923- AmMWSc 92
**Barnett**, James Allen 1908- WhoFI 92
**Barnett**, James Monroe 1925- WhoRel 92
**Barnett**, James P 1935- AmMWSc 92
**Barnett**, Jeffrey Charles 1946- AmMWSc 92
**Barnett**, Jenifer W. Who 92
**Barnett**, Jeremy John 1941- Who 92
**Barnett**, John Brian 1945- AmMWSc 92
**Barnett**, John Dean 1930- AmMWSc 92
**Barnett**, John William 1941- AmMWSc 92
**Barnett**, Joseph Anthony 1931- Who 92
**Barnett**, Joseph W 1929- WhoAmP 91
**Barnett**, Judith Anne 1938- WhoAmP 91
**Barnett**, Kenneth Thomas 1921- Who 92
**Barnett**, Kenneth Wayne 1940- AmMWSc 92
**Barnett**, Lauren Ileene 1956- WhoEnt 92
**Barnett**, Leland Bruce 1935- AmMWSc 92
**Barnett**, Lena Sue 1959- WhoAmL 92
**Barnett**, Leonard 1919- WrDr 92
**Barnett**, Lewis Brinkley 1934- AmMWSc 92
**Barnett**, Lloyd Eldon 1941- WhoMW 92
**Barnett**, Lloyd M. H. 1930- IntWW 91
**Barnett**, Margaret Edwina 1949- WhoMW 92
**Barnett**, Marguerite Ross 1942- NotBlAW 92, WhoBlA 92
**Barnett**, Marie WhoFI 92
**Barnett**, Mark 1957- AmMWSc 92
**Barnett**, Mark W 1954- WhoAmP 91
**Barnett**, Mark William 1954- WhoAmL 92, WhoMW 92
**Barnett**, Martha Walters 1947- WhoAmL 92
**Barnett**, Mary Louise 1941- WhoWest 92
**Barnett**, Michael Peter 1929- AmMWSc 92
**Barnett**, Mickey Dee 1951- WhoAmP 91
**Barnett**, Mikky Dean 1947- WhoWest 92
**Barnett**, Murphy Eugene 1935- WhoRel 92
**Barnett**, Murray Alan 1946- WhoFI 92
**Barnett**, Neal Mason 1937- AmMWSc 92
**Barnett**, O M WhoAmP 91
**Barnett**, Oliver 1907- Who 92
**Barnett**, Ortus Webb, Jr 1939- AmMWSc 92
**Barnett**, Paul Edward 1936- AmMWSc 92
**Barnett**, Paul le Page 1949- IntAu&W 91
**Barnett**, Paul William 1935- Who 92
**Barnett**, Peter Leonard 1930- IntAu&W 91, IntWW 91
**Barnett**, Peter Ralph 1951- WhoFI 92
**Barnett**, Phillip Charles 1963- WhoRel 92
**Barnett**, R Michael 1944- AmMWSc 92
**Barnett**, Richard Mark 1950- WhoAmL 92
**Barnett**, Robert 1938- WhoBlA 92
**Barnett**, Robert Alan 1959- WhoEnt 92
**Barnett**, Robert Bruce 1946- WhoAmL 92, WhoEnt 92
**Barnett**, Robert Eugene 1957- WhoMW 92
**Barnett**, Robert Glenn 1933- WhoAmL 92
**Barnett**, Robert Steven 1950- WhoFI 92
**Barnett**, Ronald David 1943- AmMWSc 92
**Barnett**, Ronald E 1942- AmMWSc 92
**Barnett**, Ross 1898-1987 FacFETw
**Barnett**, S. Anthony 1915- WrDr 92
**Barnett**, Samuel B. 1931- WhoBlA 92
**Barnett**, Samuel C 1922- AmMWSc 92
**Barnett**, Scott A AmMWSc 92
**Barnett**, Scott Brian 1960- WhoEnt 92
**Barnett**, Stanley Kendall 1953- WhoAmP 91
**Barnett**, Stanley M 1936- AmMWSc 92
**Barnett**, Stephen R. 1935- WhoAmL 92
**Barnett**, Steven McLellan 1955- WhoEnt 92
**Barnett**, Stockton Gordon, III 1939- AmMWSc 92
**Barnett**, Susanne La Mar 1946- WhoMW 92
**Barnett**, Teddy 1948- WhoBlA 92
**Barnett**, Theresa Ann 1952- WhoAmL 92
**Barnett**, Thomas Buchanan 1919- AmMWSc 92
**Barnett**, Tommy Joe 1937- WhoRel 92
**Barnett**, Vera Smith 1927- WhoAmP 91
**Barnett**, William 1917- WhoBlA 92
**Barnett**, William Arnold 1941- AmMWSc 92, WhoMW 92
**Barnett**, William Edgar 1934- AmMWSc 92
**Barnett**, William Evans 1937- Who 92
**Barnett**, William Oscar 1922- AmMWSc 92
**Barnette**, Curtis Handley 1935- WhoAmL 92, WhoFI 92
**Barnette**, Dennis Arthur 1941- WhoFI 92
**Barnette**, Marge C. 1944- WhoFI 92
**Barnevik**, Percy 1941- Who 92
**Barnevik**, Percy Nils 1941- IntWW 91, WhoFI 92
**Barneville**, Marie-Catherine Le Jumel de 1650?-1705 FrenWW
**Barnewall** Who 92
**Barnewall**, Reginald Robert 1924- Who 92
**Barney**, Arthur Livingston 1918- AmMWSc 92
**Barney**, Bob 1942- WhoAmP 91
**Barney**, Charles Wesley 1915- AmMWSc 92
**Barney**, Christopher Carroll 1951- AmMWSc 92
**Barney**, Clarence Lyle 1934- WhoBlA 92
**Barney**, Duane Lowell 1928- AmMWSc 92
**Barney**, Duane R. 1956- WhoMW 92
**Barney**, Gary Scott 1942- AmMWSc 92
**Barney**, Gerald O. 1937- WhoFI 92
**Barney**, James Earl, II 1926- AmMWSc 92
**Barney**, John A. 1929- WhoRel 92
**Barney**, John Stewart 1868-1925 ScFEYrs
**Barney**, Mary Margaret 1917- WhoAmP 91
**Barney**, Natalie 1876-1972 LiExTwC
**Barney**, Nora Stanton Blatch 1883-1971 AmPeW
**Barney**, Patrick Earl 1954- WhoAmL 92
**Barney**, William Joshua, Jr. d1991 NewYTBS 91 [port]
**Barney**, Willie J. 1927- WhoBlA 92
**Barnfield**, Richard 1574?-1627 RfGEnL 91
**Barngrover**, Debra Anne AmMWSc 92
**Barnham**, Denis 1920- TwCPaSc
**Barnham**, Nicholas 1939- TwCPaSc
**Barnhard**, Howard Jerome 1925- AmMWSc 92
**Barnhard**, Sherwood Arthur 1921- WhoFI 92
**Barnhardt**, Robert Alexander 1937- AmMWSc 92
**Barnhardt**, Terry Wayne 1948- WhoEnt 92
**Barnhardt**, Zeb Elonzo, Jr. 1941- WhoAmL 92
**Barnhart**, Barry B 1936- AmMWSc 92
**Barnhart**, Benjamin J 1935- AmMWSc 92
**Barnhart**, Beverly Homyak 1929- WhoAmP 91
**Barnhart**, Charles Elmer 1923- AmMWSc 92
**Barnhart**, Cynthia 1959- AmMWSc 92
**Barnhart**, David M 1933- AmMWSc 92
**Barnhart**, Forrest Gregory 1951- WhoAmL 92
**Barnhart**, James Lee AmMWSc 92
**Barnhart**, James William 1935- AmMWSc 92
**Barnhart**, Marion Isabel 1921- AmMWSc 92
**Barnhart**, Ray Anderson 1928- WhoFI 92
**Barnhart**, Stephen Paul 1947- WhoRel 92
**Barnhart**, Steven Robert 1956- WhoFI 92, WhoWest 92
**Barnhart**, Timothy Coleman 1956- WhoAmP 91, WhoMW 92
**Barnhart**, Timothy V 1947- WhoAmP 91
**Barnhill**, Charles William 1943- WhoFI 92
**Barnhill**, David Stan 1949- WhoAmL 92
**Barnhill**, Donald Clayton 1932- WhoRel 92
**Barnhill**, Helen Iphigenia 1937- WhoBlA 92
**Barnhill**, Howard Clinton WhoAmP 91
**Barnhill**, Kenneth Smaltz, Jr. 1928- WhoRel 92
**Barnhill**, Maurice Victor 1887-1963 DcNCBi 1
**Barnhill**, Maurice Victor, III 1940- AmMWSc 92
**Barnhill**, Robert E 1939- AmMWSc 92
**Barnhisel**, Richard I 1938- AmMWSc 92
**Barnhizer**, David R. 1944- WhoAmL 92
**Barnholdt**, Terry Joseph 1954- WhoAmL 92
**Barnholtz**, Barry 1945- IntMPA 92
**Barnhouse**, Donald Grey 1895-1960 RelLAm 91
**Barnhouse**, Ruth Tiffany WhoRel 92
**Barnidge**, Mary Shen DrAPF 91
**Barnie**, John 1941- WrDr 92
**Barnoff**, Robert Mark 1926- AmMWSc 92
**Barnoski**, Michael K 1940- AmMWSc 92
**Barnoski**, Richard Lee 1936- WhoWest 92
**Barnothy**, Jeno Michael 1904- AmMWSc 92
**Barnouw**, Erik LesBEnT 92
**Barnouw**, Erik 1908- WhoEnt 92, WrDr 92
**Barns**, Justine 1925- WhoAmP 91
**Barns**, Robert L 1927- AmMWSc 92
**Barns-Graham**, Wilhelmina 1912- TwCPaSc
**Barnsley Brothers** DcTwDes
**Barnsley**, Eric Arthur 1934- AmMWSc 92
**Barnsley**, Ernest 1863-1926 DcTwDes
**Barnsley**, Sidney 1865-1926 DcTwDes
**Barnsley**, Thomas Edward 1919- Who 92
**Barnstaple**, Archdeacon of Who 92
**Barnstein**, Charles Hansen 1925- AmMWSc 92
**Barnston**, Betsy Hahn 1935- WhoFI 92
**Barnstone**, Aliki DrAPF 91
**Barnstone**, Willis DrAPF 91
**Barnstone**, Willis 1927- ConAu 15AS [port]
**Barnthouse**, Lawrence Warner 1946- AmMWSc 92
**Barnum**, Dennis W 1931- AmMWSc 92
**Barnum**, Donald Alfred 1918- AmMWSc 92
**Barnum**, Emmett Raymond 1913- AmMWSc 92
**Barnum**, James Alymer 1950- WhoAmL 92
**Barnum**, James Robert 1944- AmMWSc 92
**Barnum**, John Charles 1947- WhoEnt 92
**Barnum**, John Wallace 1928- WhoAmL 92, WhoAmP 91
**Barnum**, Mel Bloyce 1949- WhoFI 92
**Barnum**, Nan Martin 1951- WhoFI 92
**Barnum**, P. T. 1810-1891 BenetAL 91, NewAmDM
**Barnum**, Phineas T 1810-1891 RComAH
**Barnum**, Richard SmATA 67
**Barnum**, William Douglas 1946- WhoFI 92
**Barnum**, William Laird 1916- WhoWest 92
**Barnwell**, Adrienne Knox 1938- WhoMW 92
**Barnwell**, Charles Brison, Jr. 1942- WhoAmL 92
**Barnwell**, David Ray 1953- WhoFI 92
**Barnwell**, Franklin Hershel 1937- AmMWSc 92
**Barnwell**, Henry Lee 1934- WhoBlA 92
**Barnwell**, J.O. TwCWW 91
**Barnwell**, Ray Ervin, Sr. 1945- WhoRel 92
**Barnwell**, Thomas Osborn, Jr 1947- AmMWSc 92

**Barnwell,** William 1943- *IntAu&W 91, TwCSFW 91, WrDr 92*
**Baro,** Robert Aristides 1948- *WhoHisp 92*
**Barocas,** Ralph David 1949- *WhoHisp 92*
**Barocci,** Robert Louis 1942- *WhoFI 92*
**Baroczy,** Charles J 1924- *AmMWSc 92*
**Baroff,** Lynn Elliott 1949- *WhoWest 92*
**Barolini,** Helen *DrAPF 91*
**Baron de Hirsch** *DcAmImH*
**Baron di Novara** 1940- *WhoFI 92*
**Baron,** The *ScFEYrs*
**Baron,** Alec *IntAu&W 91*
**Baron,** Alexander *Who 92*
**Baron,** Arthur L *AmMWSc 92*
**Baron,** Carol Kitzes *WhoEnt 92*
**Baron,** Carolyn 1940- *WhoFI 92*
**Baron,** Charles Hillel 1936- *WhoAmL 92*
**Baron,** David Alan 1951- *AmMWSc 92*
**Baron,** Denis Neville 1924- *WrDr 92*
**Baron,** Elaine Hilton 1936- *WhoAmP 91*
**Baron,** Frank A 1933- *AmMWSc 92*
**Baron,** Franklin Andrew 1923- *IntWW 91*
**Baron,** Franklin Andrew Merrifield 1923- *Who 92*
**Baron,** Hazen Jay 1934- *AmMWSc 92*
**Baron,** Helena *WhoEnt 92*
**Baron,** Jean-Jacques 1909- *IntWW 91*
**Baron,** Jeffrey 1942- *AmMWSc 92, WhoMW 92*
**Baron,** Jeffrey Isaac 1947- *WhoAmL 92*
**Baron,** John Herschel 1936- *WhoEnt 92*
**Baron,** Joseph Alexander 1917- *Who 92*
**Baron,** Judson R 1924- *AmMWSc 92*
**Baron,** Judy Kaplan 1952- *WhoFI 92*
**Baron,** Linda Michelle *DrAPF 91*
**Baron,** Louis Sol 1924- *AmMWSc 92*
**Baron,** Mark *IntMPA 92*
**Baron,** Mary *DrAPF 91*
**Baron,** Melvin L 1927- *AmMWSc 92*
**Baron,** Mitchell Neal 1947- *WhoAmL 92*
**Baron,** Myrna 1934- *WhoWest 92*
**Baron,** Neville A. 1933- *WhoBlA 92*
**Baron,** Robert 1932- *AmMWSc 92*
**Baron,** Robert Howard *WhoAmL 92*
**Baron,** Robert Walter 1947- *AmMWSc 92*
**Baron,** Ronald Harvey 1950- *WhoFI 92*
**Baron,** Salo Wittmayer 1895-1989 *FacFETw*
**Baron,** Samuel 1925- *NewAmDM*
**Baron,** Samuel 1928- *AmMWSc 92*
**Baron,** Sandy David 1952- *WhoAmL 92*
**Baron,** Seymour 1923- *AmMWSc 92*
**Baron,** Suze *DrAPF 91*
**Baron,** Wendy 1937- *Who 92, WrDr 92*
**Baron,** William F. *WhoAmL 92*
**Baron,** William Robert 1947- *AmMWSc 92*
**Baron Crespo,** Enrique 1944- *IntWW 91*
**Baron Crespo,** Enrique Carlos 1944- *Who 92*
**Barona,** Andres, Jr. 1945- *WhoHisp 92*
**Barona,** Narses 1932- *AmMWSc 92*
**Barondes,** Samuel Herbert 1933- *AmMWSc 92, WhoWest 92*
**Barondess,** Jeremiah A 1924- *AmMWSc 92*
**Barone,** Dennis *DrAPF 91*
**Barone,** Frank Carmen 1949- *AmMWSc 92*
**Barone,** James Patrick 1956- *WhoAmP 91*
**Barone,** John A 1924- *AmMWSc 92*
**Barone,** John B *AmMWSc 92*
**Barone,** Leesa M 1958- *AmMWSc 92*
**Barone,** Louis J 1929- *AmMWSc 92*
**Barone,** Milo C 1941- *AmMWSc 92*
**Barone,** Patricia *DrAPF 91*
**Barone,** Sandra M 1946- *WhoAmP 91*
**Baronet,** Clifford Nelson 1934- *AmMWSc 92*
**Baroni,** Geno C. 1930-1984 *DcAmImH*
**Baronian,** Maureen Murphy 1934- *WhoAmP 91*
**Barons of Rhythm** *NewAmDM*
**Barons,** Christopher Macon 1953- *WhoEnt 92*
**Barooah,** Dev Kanta 1914- *IntWW 91*
**Baroody,** Benjamin C 1946- *WhoAmP 91*
**Baroody,** Georgio 1956- *WhoEnt 92*
**Baroody,** Michael Elias 1946- *WhoAmP 91*
**Baroody,** William J, Jr 1937- *WhoAmP 91*
**Barosky,** Bertha Elizabeth 1929- *WhoAmP 91*
**Baross,** John Allen 1941- *AmMWSc 92*
**Barot,** Madeleine 1909- *DcEcMov [port]*
**Baroudy,** Bahige M 1950- *AmMWSc 92*
**Baroudy,** Bahige Mourad 1950- *WhoFI 92, WhoMW 92*
**Barouki,** Robert 1957- *AmMWSc 92*
**Barpal,** Isaac Ruben 1940- *AmMWSc 92*
**Barquet,** Jesus Jose 1953- *WhoHisp 92*
**Barquin,** Ramon Carlos 1942- *WhoHisp 92*
**Barr,** A. W. Cleeve 1910- *Who 92*
**Barr,** Alfred Hamilton, Jr 1902-1981 *FacFETw*
**Barr,** Alfred L 1933- *AmMWSc 92*
**Barr,** Allan Ralph 1926- *AmMWSc 92*
**Barr,** Alwyn 1938- *WrDr 92*
**Barr,** Amelia E. 1831-1919 *BenetAL 91*
**Barr,** Amelia Edith Huddleston 1831-1919 *RelLAm 91*
**Barr,** Anthony 1921- *IntMPA 92, WhoEnt 92, WhoFI 92*
**Barr,** B Griffith 1923- *AmMWSc 92*
**Barr,** Bill Ray 1960- *WhoMW 92*
**Barr,** Bruce Reid 1935- *WhoAmP 91*
**Barr,** Burton S *WhoAmP 91*
**Barr,** Charles 1922- *AmMWSc 92*
**Barr,** Charles E 1929- *AmMWSc 92*
**Barr,** Charles Harvey 1936- *WhoAmL 92*
**Barr,** Charles Richard 1932- *AmMWSc 92*
**Barr,** Cynthia 1957- *WhoEnt 92*
**Barr,** David 1925- *Who 92*
**Barr,** David Charles 1950- *WhoFI 92*
**Barr,** David John 1939- *AmMWSc 92*
**Barr,** David Lawrence 1942- *WhoRel 92*
**Barr,** David Ross 1932- *AmMWSc 92*
**Barr,** David Wallace 1943- *AmMWSc 92*
**Barr,** Dennis Brannon 1943- *AmMWSc 92*
**Barr,** Densil *IntAu&W 91, WrDr 92*
**Barr,** Donald Eugene 1934- *AmMWSc 92*
**Barr,** Donald John Stoddart 1937- *AmMWSc 92*
**Barr,** Donald R 1938- *AmMWSc 92*
**Barr,** Donald Roy 1938- *WhoWest 92*
**Barr,** Donald Westwood 1932- *AmMWSc 92*
**Barr,** Douglas *WhoEnt 92*
**Barr,** Frank T 1910- *AmMWSc 92*
**Barr,** Fred S 1926- *AmMWSc 92*
**Barr,** George E 1937- *AmMWSc 92*
**Barr,** Ginger 1947- *WhoAmP 91*
**Barr,** Harry 1904- *AmMWSc 92*
**Barr,** Harry L 1922- *AmMWSc 92*
**Barr,** Ian 1927- *Who 92*
**Barr,** Ian 1946- *TwCPaSc*
**Barr,** James 1862-1923 *ScFEYrs*
**Barr,** James 1924- *IntWW 91, Who 92, WhoRel 92, WrDr 92*
**Barr,** James Houston, III 1941- *WhoAmL 92*
**Barr,** John Alexander James Pooler 1939- *Who 92*
**Barr,** John Baldwin 1932- *AmMWSc 92*
**Barr,** John Douglas, II 1963- *WhoAmP 91*
**Barr,** John H. 1955- *WhoAmL 92*
**Barr,** John Michael 1957- *WhoFI 92*
**Barr,** John Robert 1936- *WhoAmL 92, WhoAmP 91*
**Barr,** John Tilman, IV 1948- *WhoWest 92*
**Barr,** John W. 1943- *WhoFI 92*
**Barr,** Joseph Walker 1918- *IntWW 91*
**Barr,** Kenneth Glen 1941- *Who 92*
**Barr,** Kenneth John 1926- *WhoFI 92, WhoWest 92*
**Barr,** Kevin Patrick 1944- *AmMWSc 92*
**Barr,** Lawrence Dale 1930- *AmMWSc 92*
**Barr,** LeRoy 1936- *WhoBlA 92*
**Barr,** Lloyd 1929- *AmMWSc 92*
**Barr,** Marlene Joy 1935- *WhoMW 92*
**Barr,** Martin 1925- *AmMWSc 92*
**Barr,** Marylin Lytle *DrAPF 91*
**Barr,** Mason, Jr 1935- *AmMWSc 92*
**Barr,** Michael 1937- *AmMWSc 92*
**Barr,** Michael Blanton 1948- *WhoAmL 92*
**Barr,** Michael Charles 1947- *WhoFI 92*
**Barr,** Morris Alfred 1922- *IntWW 91*
**Barr,** Murray Llewellyn 1908- *AmMWSc 92, IntWW 91, Who 92*
**Barr,** Nathaniel Frank 1927- *AmMWSc 92*
**Barr,** Patricia 1934- *WrDr 92*
**Barr,** Patricia Miriam 1934- *IntAu&W 91*
**Barr,** Reginald Alfred 1920- *Who 92*
**Barr,** Richard 1947- *TwCPaSc*
**Barr,** Richard Arthur 1925- *AmMWSc 92*
**Barr,** Richard Louis 1949- *WhoEnt 92*
**Barr,** Rita 1929- *AmMWSc 92, WhoMW 92*
**Barr,** Robert *WhoRel 92, WhoWest 92*
**Barr,** Robert 1850-1912 *ScFEYrs*
**Barr,** Robert Edward 1956- *WhoFI 92*
**Barr,** Robert Ortha, Jr 1940- *AmMWSc 92*
**Barr,** Roger Coke 1942- *AmMWSc 92*
**Barr,** Ronald Duncan 1943- *AmMWSc 92*
**Barr,** Ronald Edward 1936- *AmMWSc 92*
**Barr,** Rosanne 1953- *IntMPA 92*
**Barr,** Roseanne 1953- *WhoEnt 92*
**Barr,** Sanford Lee 1952- *WhoMW 92*
**Barr,** Scott 1916- *WhoAmP 91*
**Barr,** Shirley Ann 1946- *WhoMW 92*
**Barr,** Stringfellow 1897-1982 *BenetAL 91*
**Barr,** Sue 1942- *WhoAmP 91*
**Barr,** Sumner 1938- *AmMWSc 92*
**Barr,** Susan Hartline 1942- *AmMWSc 92, WhoMW 92*
**Barr,** Terence David 1945- *WhoRel 92*
**Barr,** Tery Lynn 1939- *AmMWSc 92*
**Barr,** Thomas Albert, Jr 1924- *AmMWSc 92*
**Barr,** Thomas Delbert 1931- *WhoAmL 92*
**Barr,** Tina *DrAPF 91*
**Barr,** William A 1921- *AmMWSc 92*
**Barr,** William Frederick 1920- *AmMWSc 92*
**Barr,** William Greig 1917- *Who 92*
**Barr,** William Hoffman *WhoEnt 92*
**Barr,** William J 1919- *AmMWSc 92*
**Barr,** William Lee 1925- *AmMWSc 92*
**Barr,** William Pelham *NewYTBS 91*
**Barr,** William Pelham 1950- *WhoAmL 92*
**Barr,** William Richard 1934- *WhoRel 92*
**Barr Young,** Gavin Neil 1939- *Who 92*
**Barra,** Francesca Luisa 1952- *WhoEnt 92*
**Barrack,** Carroll Marlin 1927- *AmMWSc 92*
**Barrack,** Evelyn Ruth *AmMWSc 92*
**Barrack,** Martin Jonathan 1961- *WhoAmL 92*
**Barrack,** William Peter 1959- *WhoFI 92*
**Barrack,** William Sample, Jr. 1929- *Who 92, WhoFI 92*
**Barraclough,** Charles Arthur 1926- *AmMWSc 92*
**Barraclough,** John 1918- *Who 92*
**Barraclough,** Kenneth 1907- *Who 92*
**Barraclough,** Steve 1953- *TwCPaSc*
**Barraco,** Robin Anthony 1945- *AmMWSc 92*
**Barrad,** Catherine Marie 1953- *WhoAmL 92*
**Barradas,** Remigio Germano 1928- *AmMWSc 92*
**Barraford,** Nora Mary 1913- *WhoEnt 92*
**Barraga,** Thomas Francis 1943- *WhoAmP 91*
**Barragan,** Charles J., III 1958- *WhoWest 92*
**Barragan,** Linda Diane 1950- *WhoRel 92*
**Barragan,** Luis 1902-1988 *DcTwDes, FacFETw*
**Barragan,** Miguel F. *WhoHisp 92*
**Barraine,** Elsa 1910- *ConCom 92*
**Barrall,** Edward Martin, II 1934- *AmMWSc 92*
**Barrall,** Raymond Charles 1930- *AmMWSc 92*
**Barran,** David Haven 1912- *IntWW 91, Who 92*
**Barran,** John 1934- *Who 92*
**Barran,** Leslie Rohit 1939- *AmMWSc 92*
**Barranco,** Sam Christopher, III 1938- *AmMWSc 92*
**Barrand,** Paul 1959- *TwCPaSc*
**Barranger,** John Arthur 1945- *AmMWSc 92*
**Barranger,** John P 1930- *AmMWSc 92*
**Barranger,** M. S. 1937- *WrDr 92*
**Barranger,** Milly S. 1937- *WhoEnt 92*
**Barrante,** James Richard 1938- *AmMWSc 92*
**Barraque,** Jean 1928-1973 *NewAmDM*
**Barrar,** Richard Blaine 1923- *AmMWSc 92*
**Barras,** Charles M. 1826-1873 *BenetAL 91*
**Barras,** Donald J 1932- *AmMWSc 92*
**Barras,** Jonetta Rose *DrAPF 91*
**Barras,** Stanley J 1936- *AmMWSc 92*
**Barrass,** Gordon Stephen 1940- *Who 92*
**Barrat,** Joseph George 1922- *AmMWSc 92*
**Barratt,** Eric George 1938- *WhoFI 92*
**Barratt,** Francis Russell 1924- *Who 92*
**Barratt,** Gilbert Alexander 1930- *Who 92*
**Barratt,** Herbert George Harold 1905- *Who 92*
**Barratt,** J. Scott 1946- *WhoAmL 92*
**Barratt,** Krome 1924- *TwCPaSc*
**Barratt,** Lawrence 1927- *Who 92*
**Barratt,** Michael Fieldhouse 1928- *Who 92*
**Barratt,** Michael George 1927- *AmMWSc 92, Who 92*
**Barratt,** Raymond William 1920- *AmMWSc 92*
**Barratt,** Richard 1928- *Who 92*
**Barratt,** Robin Alexander 1945- *Who 92*
**Barratt,** Thomas Keating 1927- *WhoWest 92*
**Barratt-Boyes,** Brian 1924- *Who 92*
**Barratt-Boyes,** Brian Gerald 1924- *IntWW 91*
**Barratt Brown,** Michael 1918- *WrDr 92*
**Barrau,** Liberte *EncAmaz 91*
**Barraud,** Henry 1900- *IntWW 91*
**Barrault,** Jean-Louis 1910- *FacFETw, IntWW 91, Who 92*
**Barrault,** Marie-Christine 1944- *IntMPA 92*
**Barrax,** Gerald *DrAPF 91*
**Barraza,** Rosaleo N. 1947- *WhoHisp 92*
**Barraza,** Santa C. 1951- *WhoHisp 92*
**Barraza,** Viola Y. 1951- *WhoHisp 92*
**Barre,** Gabriel 1957- *WhoEnt 92*
**Barre,** Isaac 1726-1802 *BlkwEAR*
**Barre,** Laura Kohlman 1931- *WhoAmP 91*
**Barre,** Raymond 1924- *IntWW 91, Who 92*
**Barreas Arrechea,** Ricardo Alfredo 1934- *IntWW 91*
**Barreda,** Antonio 1942- *WhoHisp 92*
**Barredo,** Maniya *WhoEnt 92*
**Barreiro,** Mauricio Enrique 1961- *WhoAmL 92*
**Barrekette,** Euval S 1931- *AmMWSc 92*
**Barrell,** Anthony Charles 1933- *Who 92*
**Barrell,** Charles Alden 1909- *WhoAmP 91*
**Barrell,** Joseph 1869-1919 *BiInAmS*
**Barrell,** Sarah Sayward *BenetAL 91*
**Barren,** Bruce Willard 1942- *WhoFI 92*
**Barren,** Jean VanAken 1917- *WhoAmP 91*
**Barren,** Michael James 1958- *WhoAmL 92*
**Barrentine,** Jimmy Lloyd 1946- *WhoRel 92*
**Barrer,** Daniel Edward 1949- *AmMWSc 92*
**Barrer,** Richard Maling 1910- *IntWW 91, Who 92*
**Barrera,** Cecilio Richard 1942- *AmMWSc 92*
**Barrera,** Ernest C. 1950- *WhoHisp 92*
**Barrera,** Felix N. 1936- *WhoHisp 92*
**Barrera,** Frank 1917- *AmMWSc 92*
**Barrera,** Joseph S 1941- *AmMWSc 92*
**Barrera,** Laz 1924-1991 *NewYTBS 91 [port]*
**Barrera,** Manuel, Jr. 1943- *WhoHisp 92*
**Barrera,** Mario 1939- *WhoHisp 92*
**Barrera,** Oscar d1991 *NewYTBS 91*
**Barrera,** Ralph A. 1959- *WhoHisp 92*
**Barrera,** Rodolfo Luis 1938- *WhoAmP 91*
**Barrera,** Ruben Rivera 1939- *WhoFI 92*
**Barrera,** Victor T. *WhoHisp 92*
**Barrera Lombana,** Jose Pablo 1956- *WhoHisp 92*
**Barreras,** Amelita Manoto 1954- *WhoFI 92*
**Barreras,** Raymond Domingo 1949- *WhoHisp 92*
**Barreras,** Raymond Joseph 1940- *AmMWSc 92*
**Barreras del Rio,** Petra *WhoHisp 92*
**Barrere,** Clem A, Jr 1939- *AmMWSc 92*
**Barrere,** Georges 1876-1944 *NewAmDM*
**Barres,** Auguste Maurice 1862-1923 *BiDExR*
**Barres,** Maurice 1862-1923 *GuFrLit 1*
**Barresi,** Dorothy *DrAPF 91*
**Barreto,** Ernesto 1934- *AmMWSc 92*
**Barreto,** Hector *WhoHisp 92*
**Barreto,** Kathleen Anne 1954- *WhoWest 92*
**Barreto,** Martin O. 1957- *WhoHisp 92*
**Barrett,** Alan H d1991 *NewYTBS 91*
**Barrett,** Alan H 1927- *AmMWSc 92*
**Barrett,** Andrea *DrAPF 91*
**Barrett,** Andrew *WhoFI 92*
**Barrett,** Andrew 1953- *WhoEnt 92*
**Barrett,** Anthony A. 1941- *ConAu 134*
**Barrett,** Anthony Gerard Martin 1952- *AmMWSc 92*
**Barrett,** Arthur Michael 1932- *Who 92*
**Barrett,** Barbara McConnell 1950- *WhoAmL 92, WhoWest 92*
**Barrett,** Benjamin F. 1940- *WhoAmL 92*
**Barrett,** Brenda Lee 1964- *WhoMW 92*
**Barrett,** Brian Lee 1959- *WhoRel 92*
**Barrett,** Bruce Richard 1939- *AmMWSc 92, WhoWest 92*
**Barrett,** C Brent 1955- *AmMWSc 92*
**Barrett,** Carol *DrAPF 91*
**Barrett,** Carrie Geroux 1964- *WhoAmL 92*
**Barrett,** Charles D. 1933- *WhoRel 92*
**Barrett,** Charles Kingsley 1917- *IntAu&W 91, IntWW 91, Who 92, WrDr 92*
**Barrett,** Charles S. 1902- *IntWW 91*
**Barrett,** Charles Sanborn 1902- *AmMWSc 92*
**Barrett,** Christopher 1954- *TwCPaSc*
**Barrett,** Connor 1908-1987 *TwCPaSc*
**Barrett,** David 1930- *IntWW 91, Who 92*
**Barrett,** David Eugene 1955- *WhoAmL 92*
**Barrett,** David J. *WhoEnt 92*
**Barrett,** David William S. *Who 92*
**Barrett,** Deborah Joan 1951- *WhoAmL 92*
**Barrett,** Denis Everett 1911- *Who 92*
**Barrett,** Dennis 1936- *AmMWSc 92*
**Barrett,** Dennis Charles T. *Who 92*
**Barrett,** Dennis John 1945- *WhoAmL 92*
**Barrett,** Don 1946- *WhoEnt 92*
**Barrett,** Donald John 1927- *WhoWest 92*
**Barrett,** Edmond Fox 1928- *Who 92*
**Barrett,** Edward Joseph 1931- *AmMWSc 92*
**Barrett,** Ellen Faye 1944- *AmMWSc 92*
**Barrett,** Ernest 1917- *Who 92*
**Barrett,** Ethel *ConAu 134*
**Barrett,** Evan Donald 1945- *WhoAmP 91*
**Barrett,** Frank 1848-1926 *ScFEYrs*
**Barrett,** Frederick Charles 1949- *WhoFI 92*
**Barrett,** Gary Wayne 1940- *AmMWSc 92*
**Barrett,** Geoffrey John 1928- *TwCWW 91, WrDr 92*
**Barrett,** George West 1908- *WhoWest 92*
**Barrett,** Gerald Van 1936- *WhoAmL 92, WhoMW 92*
**Barrett,** Harrison D. 1863-1911 *RelLAm 91*
**Barrett,** Harrison Hooker 1939- *AmMWSc 92*
**Barrett,** Herbert 1910- *WhoEnt 92*
**Barrett,** Ian Timothy 1965- *WhoEnt 92*
**Barrett,** Izadore 1926- *AmMWSc 92, WhoWest 92*
**Barrett,** J Carl 1946- *AmMWSc 92*
**Barrett,** Jack Wheeler 1912- *Who 92*
**Barrett,** James A. 1932- *WhoBlA 92*

**Barrett**, James E. 1922- WhoAmL 92, WhoWest 92
**Barrett**, James E 1942- AmMWSc 92
**Barrett**, James Martin 1920- AmMWSc 92
**Barrett**, James P. 1936- WhoAmL 92
**Barrett**, James Passmore 1931- AmMWSc 92
**Barrett**, James Peter 1924- WhoWest 92
**Barrett**, James Thomas 1927- AmMWSc 92
**Barrett**, Jane Hayes 1947- WhoAmL 92
**Barrett**, Janie Porter 1865-1948 NotBlAW 92 [port]
**Barrett**, Jeffrey Scott 1949- WhoMW 92
**Barrett**, Jerry Wayne 1936- AmMWSc 92
**Barrett**, John 1866-1938 AmPeW
**Barrett**, John, III 1947- WhoAmP 91
**Barrett**, John Adams 1937- WhoAmL 92
**Barrett**, John Charles Allanson 1943- Who 92, WhoRel 92
**Barrett**, John Edward 1931- Who 92
**Barrett**, John F. 1949- WhoIns 92
**Barrett**, John G. 1921- WrDr 92
**Barrett**, John Harold 1926- AmMWSc 92
**Barrett**, John Henry 1913- WrDr 92
**Barrett**, John James, Jr. 1948- WhoAmL 92
**Barrett**, John Neil 1943- AmMWSc 92
**Barrett**, John Richard 1926- WhoAmL 92
**Barrett**, John Victor 1952- WhoRel 92
**Barrett**, Joseph Anthony, Jr. 1963- WhoMW 92
**Barrett**, Joseph John 1936- AmMWSc 92
**Barrett**, Judi 1941- IntAu&W 91, WrDr 92
**Barrett**, Julie Ann 1957- WhoEnt 92
**Barrett**, Kate Harwood Waller 1857-1925 RelLAm 91
**Barrett**, Kate Waller 1858-1925 DcAmImH
**Barrett**, Kim Elaine 1958- WhoWest 92
**Barrett**, Lida Kittrell 1927- AmMWSc 92
**Barrett**, Linton Lomas 1904-1972 ConAu 134
**Barrett**, Lois Yvonne 1947- WhoRel 92
**Barrett**, Louis Carl 1924- AmMWSc 92
**Barrett**, Lynne DrAPF 91
**Barrett**, Marshall 1943- WhoFI 92
**Barrett**, Marvin DrAPF 91
**Barrett**, Mary Lou 1941- WhoAmP 91
**Barrett**, Matthew Anderson 1947- WhoBlA 92
**Barrett**, Matthew W. 1944- IntWW 91, WhoFI 92
**Barrett**, Max 1937- TwCPaSc
**Barrett**, Michael Who 92
**Barrett**, Michael Dennis 1947- WhoWest 92
**Barrett**, Michael Henry 1932- WhoFI 92, WhoWest 92
**Barrett**, Michael J 1948- WhoAmP 91
**Barrett**, Nancy Smith 1942- WhoFI 92, WrDr 92
**Barrett**, Neal, Jr TwCSFW 91, WrDr 92
**Barrett**, O'Neill, Jr 1929- AmMWSc 92
**Barrett**, Paul Henry 1922- AmMWSc 92
**Barrett**, Peter 1935- TwCPaSc
**Barrett**, Peter Fowler 1939- AmMWSc 92
**Barrett**, Peter Van Doren 1934- AmMWSc 92
**Barrett**, Reginald Haughton 1942- WhoWest 92
**Barrett**, Richard 1959- ConCom 92
**Barrett**, Richard Daniel 1944- WhoFI 92
**Barrett**, Richard H 1930- WhoAmP 91
**Barrett**, Richard Hewins 1949- WhoWest 92
**Barrett**, Richard John 1945- AmMWSc 92
**Barrett**, Richard John 1949- AmMWSc 92
**Barrett**, Richard O. 1923- WhoBlA 92
**Barrett**, Robert 1914- AmMWSc 92
**Barrett**, Robert Dulaney 1935- WhoRel 92
**Barrett**, Robert James, III 1944- WhoFI 92
**Barrett**, Robert Matthew 1948- WhoAmL 92
**Barrett**, Robert S, IV WhoAmP 91
**Barrett**, Roderic 1920- TwCPaSc
**Barrett**, Roger Watson 1915- WhoAmL 92
**Barrett**, Rolin F 1937- AmMWSc 92
**Barrett**, Rona IntMPA 92, LesBEnT 92, WhoEnt 92
**Barrett**, Ronald Keith 1948- WhoBlA 92
**Barrett**, Sherman L. 1945- WhoBlA 92
**Barrett**, Spencer Charles Hilton 1948- AmMWSc 92
**Barrett**, Stephen Jeremy 1931- Who 92
**Barrett**, Stephen W. 1956- WhoIns 92
**Barrett**, Steven Keith 1962- WhoMW 92
**Barrett**, Susan Patricia 1948- WhoAmP 91
**Barrett**, Thomas Joseph 1934- WhoFI 92
**Barrett**, Thomas Leon Francis 1938- WhoFI 92
**Barrett**, Thomas M 1953- WhoAmP 91
**Barrett**, Tom Hans 1930- IntWW 91, WhoFI 92, WhoMW 92
**Barrett**, Walter Carlin, Jr. 1947- WhoBlA 92
**Barrett**, Walter Edward 1921- AmMWSc 92
**Barrett**, William 1929- AlmAP 92 [port]
**Barrett**, William Avon 1930- AmMWSc 92
**Barrett**, William E ScFEYrs
**Barrett**, William E 1929- WhoAmP 91, WhoMW 92
**Barrett**, William Edmund 1900-1986 BenetAL 91
**Barrett**, William Joel 1939- WhoFI 92
**Barrett**, William Jordan 1916- AmMWSc 92
**Barrett**, William L. D. 1938- WhoAmL 92
**Barrett**, William Louis 1933- AmMWSc 92
**Barrett**, William Spencer 1914- Who 92
**Barrett**, William Waldo 1945- WhoAmL 92
**Barrett-Connor**, Elizabeth L 1935- AmMWSc 92
**Barrett-Lennard**, Hugh 1917- Who 92
**Barrette**, Daniel Claude 1943- AmMWSc 92
**Barrette**, Jean 1946- AmMWSc 92
**Barrette**, Sarah Catharine 1936- WhoMW 92
**Barrick**, Donald Edward 1938- AmMWSc 92
**Barrick**, Elliott Roy 1915- AmMWSc 92
**Barrick**, P L 1914- AmMWSc 92
**Barrick**, William Henry 1916- WhoAmL 92
**Barrie and Jenkins** DcLB 112
**Barrie and Rockliff** DcLB 112
**Barrie**, Alexander 1923- WrDr 92
**Barrie**, Barbara 1931- IntMPA 92
**Barrie**, David Scott 1952- WhoFI 92
**Barrie**, Dennis Ray 1947- WhoMW 92
**Barrie**, George 1918- IntMPA 92
**Barrie**, George Napier 1940- IntWW 91
**Barrie**, Herbert 1927- Who 92
**Barrie**, J.M. 1860-1937 RfGEnL 91
**Barrie**, James DcLB 112
**Barrie**, James M. 1860-1937 CnDBLB 5 [port]
**Barrie**, James Matthew 1860-1937 FacFETw
**Barrie**, Leonard Arthur AmMWSc 92
**Barrie**, Mardi 1946- TwCPaSc
**Barrie**, Robert 1927- AmMWSc 92
**Barrie**, Susan WrDr 92
**Barrie-Wilson**, Wendy WhoEnt 92
**Barrientos**, Ben 1946- WhoAmP 91
**Barrientos**, Celso Saquitan 1936- AmMWSc 92
**Barrientos**, Gonzalo 1941- WhoAmP 91, WhoHisp 92
**Barrientos**, Julian Adolph WhoHisp 92
**Barrientos**, Pedro Nolasco 1734-1810 HisDSpE
**Barrientos**, Raul Ernesto 1942- WhoHisp 92
**Barrientos**, Robert John 1953- WhoFI 92
**Barriera**, Iris D. 1944- WhoHisp 92
**Barriera**, Victor M 1925- WhoAmP 91
**Barriga**, Omar Oscar 1938- AmMWSc 92
**Barriger**, John Walker, IV 1927- WhoFI 92, WhoMW 92
**Barringer**, Daniel Laurens 1788-1852 DcNCBi 1
**Barringer**, Daniel Moreau 1806-1873 DcNCBi 1
**Barringer**, Daniel Moreau 1860-1929 FacFETw
**Barringer**, Daniel Moreau, Jr. 1860-1929 DcNCBi 1
**Barringer**, Donald F, Jr 1932- AmMWSc 92
**Barringer**, Paul 1778-1844 DcNCBi 1
**Barringer**, Paul Brandon 1857-1941 DcNCBi 1
**Barringer**, Rufus Clay 1821-1895 DcNCBi 1
**Barringer**, Russell Newton 1903- WhoAmP 91
**Barringer**, Thomas Lawson 1940- WhoAmP 91
**Barringer**, Victor Clay 1827-1896 DcNCBi 1
**Barringer**, William Charles 1934- AmMWSc 92
**Barrington**, A E 1921- AmMWSc 92
**Barrington**, Alexander 1909- Who 92
**Barrington**, Bruce David 1942- WhoFI 92
**Barrington**, David Stanley 1948- AmMWSc 92
**Barrington**, Deborah Douglas 1947- WhoAmL 92
**Barrington**, Gordon P 1923- AmMWSc 92
**Barrington**, Judith DrAPF 91
**Barrington**, Judith Mary 1944- IntAu&W 91
**Barrington**, Mary Diane 1952- WhoMW 92
**Barrington**, Nevitt H J 1908- AmMWSc 92
**Barrington**, Nicholas John 1934- IntWW 91, Who 92
**Barrington**, Rodney Craig 1953- WhoMW 92
**Barrington**, Ronald Eric 1931- AmMWSc 92
**Barrington**, Thomas Joseph 1916- WrDr 92
**Barrington-Carlson**, Sharyn Marie 1946- WhoMW 92
**Barrington-Ward**, Simon Who 92
**Barrington-Ward**, Simon 1930- IntWW 91
**Barrio**, Guilmo 1939- WhoHisp 92
**Barrio**, Raymond DrAPF 91
**Barrio**, Raymond 1921- ConAu 15AS [port], WhoHisp 92, WrDr 92
**Barrio**, Tony 1933- WhoHisp 92
**Barrionuevo Pena**, Jose 1942- IntWW 91
**Barrios**, Alfred Angel 1933- WhoHisp 92, WhoWest 92
**Barrios**, Earl P 1917- AmMWSc 92
**Barrios**, Eduardo 1884-1963 BenetAL 91
**Barrios**, Enrique 1955- WhoEnt 92
**Barrios**, Mary Elizabeth Heck 1960- WhoAmL 92
**Barrios**, Zulma X. 1943- WhoHisp 92
**Barrios de Chamorro**, Violeta 1939?- IntWW 91
**Barris**, Chuck IntAu&W 91, LesBEnT 92, WrDr 92
**Barris**, Willis Hervey 1821?-1901 BiInAmS
**Barrison**, Steven Mark 1956- WhoAmL 92
**Barritt**, Gordon Emerson 1920- Who 92
**Barrnett**, Russell Joffree 1920- AmMWSc 92
**Barro**, John 1643?-1718 DcNCBi 1
**Barro**, Mary Helen 1938- WhoEnt 92, WhoHisp 92
**Barrois**, Bertrand C 1952- AmMWSc 92
**Barroll**, John Leeds WhoAmL 92
**Barroll**, Katherine Brandt 1957- WhoAmL 92
**Barron**, Alfred 1829-1893 AmPeW
**Barron**, Almen Leo 1926- AmMWSc 92
**Barron**, Anthony Ramirez 1954- WhoEnt 92
**Barron**, Arthur LesBEnT 92
**Barron**, Arthur Ray 1934- IntMPA 92
**Barron**, Barbara Jane 1959- WhoAmL 92
**Barron**, Bernie Garcia 1956- WhoHisp 92
**Barron**, Bob 1945- TwCPaSc
**Barron**, Brian Munro 1940- Who 92
**Barron**, Bruce Albrecht 1934- AmMWSc 92
**Barron**, Caroline Joan 1958- WhoWest 92
**Barron**, Charles Irwin 1916- AmMWSc 92
**Barron**, Clarence 1855-1928 FacFETw
**Barron**, Clemente 1943- WhoHisp 92
**Barron**, David Anthony 1959- WhoAmL 92
**Barron**, David Henry 1953- WhoAmP 91
**Barron**, Dempsey James 1922- WhoAmP 91
**Barron**, Derek Donald 1929- Who 92
**Barron**, Donald 1921- Who 92
**Barron**, Donald James 1921- IntWW 91
**Barron**, Dora Jones 1960- WhoFI 92
**Barron**, Douglas Shield 1904- Who 92
**Barron**, Edward Carroll 1939- WhoRel 92
**Barron**, Edward J 1927- AmMWSc 92
**Barron**, Emmanuel Nicholas 1949- AmMWSc 92
**Barron**, Eric James 1951- AmMWSc 92
**Barron**, Ernesto Alvarez 1946- WhoHisp 92
**Barron**, Eugene Clyde 1952- WhoRel 92
**Barron**, Eugene D. 1958- WhoFI 92
**Barron**, Eugene Roy 1941- AmMWSc 92
**Barron**, Francis Patrick 1951- WhoAmL 92
**Barron**, Glenn Eugene 1944- WhoMW 92
**Barron**, Grover Cleveland, III 1948- WhoRel 92
**Barron**, Harold Sheldon 1936- WhoAmL 92
**Barron**, Iann Marchant 1936- Who 92
**Barron**, Inge Falk 1927- WhoFI 92
**Barron**, Jerome Aure 1933- WhoAmL 92
**Barron**, John Arthur 1947- AmMWSc 92
**Barron**, John Penrose 1934- IntWW 91, Who 92
**Barron**, John Robert 1932- AmMWSc 92
**Barron**, Kevin D 1929- AmMWSc 92
**Barron**, Kevin John 1946- Who 92
**Barron**, Lowell Ray 1942- WhoAmP 91
**Barron**, Margaret Louise 1933- WhoMW 92
**Barron**, Martin George 1963- WhoWest 92
**Barron**, Milton L 1918- IntAu&W 91
**Barron**, Myra Hymovich 1938- WhoAmL 92
**Barron**, Patrick Harold Falkiner 1911- Who 92
**Barron**, Pepe 1937- WhoHisp 92
**Barron**, Randall DeWayne 1929- WhoMW 92
**Barron**, Randall F 1936- AmMWSc 92
**Barron**, Reginald WhoBlA 92
**Barron**, Richard Edward 1940- Who 92
**Barron**, Robert 1918- Who 92
**Barron**, Robert Anthony 1933- WhoAmL 92
**Barron**, Robert V. 1932- WhoEnt 92
**Barron**, Roberta 1940- WhoMW 92
**Barron**, Ronald Michael 1948- AmMWSc 92
**Barron**, Russell J. 1946- WhoAmL 92
**Barron**, Saul 1917- AmMWSc 92
**Barron**, Stephanie 1950- WhoWest 92
**Barron**, Wendell WhoBlA 92
**Barron**, William M. 1945- WhoAmL 92
**Barrone**, Gerald Doran 1931- WhoFI 92, WhoWest 92
**Barrons**, John Lawson 1932- Who 92
**Barronton**, D. Neal 1937- WhoEnt 92
**Barros**, Anthony Eugene 1950- WhoRel 92
**Barros**, Dana Bruce 1967- WhoBlA 92
**Barros**, Henry 1960- WhoHisp 92
**Barros de San Milan**, Manuel d1599 HisDSpE
**Barroso**, Gustavo Dodt 1888-1959 BiDExR
**Barrow**, Bernard Elliott 1927- WhoEnt 92
**Barrow**, Bernard Gibbs 1937- WhoAmP 91
**Barrow**, Charles Wallace 1921- WhoAmL 92
**Barrow**, Chelmer Lee Roy, Jr. 1961- WhoMW 92
**Barrow**, Claude Norton 1934- WhoMW 92
**Barrow**, Clyde FacFETw
**Barrow**, Denise 1943- WhoBlA 92
**Barrow**, Emily Mildred Stacy 1927- AmMWSc 92
**Barrow**, Errol W 1920-1987 FacFETw
**Barrow**, G. W. S. 1924- WrDr 92
**Barrow**, Geoffrey Wallis Steuart 1924- Who 92
**Barrow**, Gordon M 1923- AmMWSc 92
**Barrow**, Iris Lena 1933- IntAu&W 91
**Barrow**, James Howell, Jr 1920- AmMWSc 92
**Barrow**, Jocelyn 1929- Who 92
**Barrow**, John 1643?-1718 DcNCBi 1
**Barrow**, John 1903- TwCPaSc
**Barrow**, John D. 1952- WrDr 92
**Barrow**, John Frederick 1918- Who 92
**Barrow**, John Jenkins 1955- WhoAmP 91
**Barrow**, Julian 1939- TwCPaSc
**Barrow**, Lance Ward 1955- WhoEnt 92
**Barrow**, Lionel Ceon, Jr. 1926- WhoBlA 92
**Barrow**, Mark Steven 1958- WhoAmL 92
**Barrow**, Michael Ernest 1932- Who 92
**Barrow**, Nita Who 92
**Barrow**, Nita 1916- DcEcMov
**Barrow**, Pamela WrDr 92
**Barrow**, Richard John Uniacke 1933- Who 92
**Barrow**, Robert Ruffin 1798-1875 DcNCBi 1
**Barrow**, Robin 1944- IntAu&W 91, WrDr 92
**Barrow**, Ruth Nita IntWW 91, WhoRel 92
**Barrow**, Ruth Nita 1916- Who 92
**Barrow**, Thomas D 1924- AmMWSc 92
**Barrow**, Thomas Davies 1924- WhoFI 92
**Barrow**, Thomas Joe 1949- WhoBlA 92
**Barrow**, Ursula Helen 1955- IntWW 91
**Barrow**, William 1765-1823 DcNCBi 1
**Barrow**, Willie B. 1924- NotBlAW 92, WhoBlA 92
**Barrowclough**, Anthony 1924- Who 92
**Barrowclough**, Anthony Richard 1924- IntWW 91
**Barrowman**, James Adams 1936- AmMWSc 92
**Barrows**, Anita DrAPF 91
**Barrows**, Austin Willard 1937- AmMWSc 92
**Barrows**, Blair 1932- WhoAmP 91
**Barrows**, Charles Clifford 1857-1916 BiInAmS
**Barrows**, Edward Myron 1946- AmMWSc 92
**Barrows**, Frank David WhoAmP 91
**Barrows**, G M ScFEYrs
**Barrows**, Harold Lindsey 1926- WhoMW 92
**Barrows**, John Frederick 1928- AmMWSc 92
**Barrows**, Joseph Howard 1950- WhoAmP 91
**Barrows**, Michael John 1949- WhoMW 92
**Barrows**, Robert G. 1946- WhoMW 92
**Barrows**, Robert Guy 1926- WhoEnt 92, WhoWest 92
**Barrows**, Ronald Thomas 1954- WhoAmL 92
**Barrows**, Samuel June 1845-1909 AmPeW
**Barrows**, Sidney 1918- WhoAmL 92
**Barrows**, Sydney 1952- IntAu&W 91
**Barrozo**, Tobin G. WhoMW 92
**Barrs**, Norman 1917- WhoEnt 92
**Barrueto**, Richard Benigno 1928- AmMWSc 92
**Barrull**, Agustin 1933- WhoHisp 92
**Barrundia**, Jose Francisco 1784-1854 HisDSpE
**Barrus**, Edward Murray 1923- WhoWest 92
**Barry** IntAu&W 91X
**Barry**, Allan Ronald 1945- WhoFI 92
**Barry**, Arthur John 1909- AmMWSc 92

**Barry,** Arthur Leland 1932- *AmMWSc 92*
**Barry,** B Austin 1917- *AmMWSc 92*
**Barry,** B. H. 1940- *WhoEnt 92*
**Barry,** Brian Michael 1936- *IntWW 91, Who 92*
**Barry,** Carole Joyce 1933- *WhoWest 92*
**Barry,** Christopher John 1947- *WhoAmL 92*
**Barry,** Colman James 1921- *WhoRel 92*
**Barry,** Cornelius 1934- *AmMWSc 92*
**Barry,** Daniel 1928- *Who 92*
**Barry,** Dave 1947- *ConAu 134, News 91 [port], WrDr 92*
**Barry,** David Earl 1945- *WhoAmL 92*
**Barry,** David N., III *WhoAmL 92*
**Barry,** Desmond Thomas, Jr. 1945- *WhoAmL 92*
**Barry,** Don Cary 1941- *AmMWSc 92*
**Barry,** Donald Lee 1953- *WhoFI 92*
**Barry,** Donald Martin 1944- *WhoFI 92*
**Barry,** Douglas Albert 1961- *WhoFI 92*
**Barry,** Edward *Who 92*
**Barry,** Edward Gail 1933- *AmMWSc 92*
**Barry,** Edward Louis 1951- *WhoAmL 92*
**Barry,** Edward Norman 1920- *Who 92*
**Barry,** Gene 1919- *WhoEnt 92*
**Barry,** Gene 1921- *IntMPA 92*
**Barry,** Gerald 1952- *ConCom 92*
**Barry,** Gerald, Mother 1881-1961 *HanAmWH*
**Barry,** Gordon Richard 1948- *WhoAmL 92*
**Barry,** Gregory Steven 1959- *WhoFI 92*
**Barry,** Guerin Spencer 1942- *WhoEnt 92*
**Barry,** Henry F 1923- *AmMWSc 92*
**Barry,** Henry Ford 1923- *WhoWest 92*
**Barry,** Herbert, III 1930- *AmMWSc 92*
**Barry,** Hilary D *WhoAmP 91*
**Barry,** Hugh Collis 1912- *WrDr 92*
**Barry,** Jack *DrAPF 91*
**Barry,** Jack d1984 *LesBEnT 92*
**Barry,** James Dale 1942- *AmMWSc 92*
**Barry,** James Edward 1938- *Who 92*
**Barry,** James Michael 1956- *WhoWest 92*
**Barry,** James P 1918- *IntAu&W 91, WrDr 92*
**Barry,** James Paul 1953- *WhoWest 92*
**Barry,** James Potvin 1918- *WhoMW 92*
**Barry,** James Russell 1960- *WhoAmL 92*
**Barry,** Jan *DrAPF 91*
**Barry,** Jane 1925- *TwCWW 91, WrDr 92*
**Barry,** Janet Gail 1938- *WhoAmP 91*
**Barry,** Joan 1953- *AmMWSc 92*
**Barry,** Joan LeBlanc 1937- *WhoWest 92*
**Barry,** Jocelyn *IntAu&W 91X*
**Barry,** John 1933- *IntMPA 92*
**Barry,** John Decatur 1839-1867 *DcNCBi 1*
**Barry,** John Eduard 1959- *WhoAmL 92*
**Barry,** John J. *WhoFI 92*
**Barry,** John Kevin 1925- *WhoAmL 92*
**Barry,** John Willard 1934- *WhoWest 92*
**Barry,** Jonathan B 1945- *WhoAmP 91*
**Barry,** Kevin Arnold 1954- *WhoAmL 92*
**Barry,** Kevin Gerard 1923- *AmMWSc 92*
**Barry,** Kevin Jerome 1942- *WhoAmL 92*
**Barry,** Lawrence Edward 1939- *Who 92*
**Barry,** Leah Carol 1964- *WhoAmL 92*
**Barry,** Leonora Kearney 1849-1930 *DcAmImH*
**Barry,** Lynda *WhoEnt 92*
**Barry,** Lynda 1956?- *News 92-1 [port], WrDr 92*
**Barry,** Margaret Stuart 1927- *IntAu&W 91, WrDr 92*
**Barry,** Marion 1936- *News 91 [port]*
**Barry,** Marion S, Jr 1936- *WhoAmP 91*
**Barry,** Marion Shepilov, Jr. 1936- *IntWW 91, WhoBlA 92*
**Barry,** Maryanne Trump 1937- *WhoAmL 92*
**Barry,** Michael Anhalt 1953- *AmMWSc 92*
**Barry,** Michael Lee 1935- *AmMWSc 92*
**Barry,** Michael Thomas 1945- *WhoAmP 91*
**Barry,** Mike *WrDr 92*
**Barry,** Miranda Robbins 1951- *WhoEnt 92*
**Barry,** Norman P. 1944- *ConAu 134*
**Barry,** Patrick 1917- *Who 92*
**Barry,** Peter 1928- *IntWW 91, Who 92*
**Barry,** Philip 1896-1949 *BenetAL 91, FacFETw*
**Barry,** Philip, Jr. *LesBEnT 92*
**Barry,** Philip M 1938- *WhoAmP 91*
**Barry,** Philip Semple 1923- *WhoEnt 92*
**Barry,** Philip Stuart M. *Who 92*
**Barry,** Ray *ConTFT 9*
**Barry,** Raymond *ConTFT 9*
**Barry,** Raymond J. 1939- *ConTFT 9*
**Barry,** Richard Francis, III 1943- *WhoFI 92*
**Barry,** Richard Hugh 1908- *Who 92*
**Barry,** Robert David 1954- *WhoWest 92*
**Barry,** Robert Everett 1931- *WrDr 92*
**Barry,** Robert L 1934- *WhoAmP 91*
**Barry,** Roger Donald 1935- *AmMWSc 92, WhoMW 92*
**Barry,** Roger Graham 1935- *AmMWSc 92*
**Barry,** Ronald A 1950- *AmMWSc 92*
**Barry,** Ronald Everett, Jr 1947- *AmMWSc 92*
**Barry,** Sebastian 1955- *IntAu&W 91*
**Barry,** Sheila Anne *ConAu 135*
**Barry,** Simon 1962- *TwCPaSc*
**Barry,** Sue-Ning C 1932- *AmMWSc 92*
**Barry,** Thomas James 1957- *WhoFI 92*
**Barry,** Thomas Joseph 1955- *WhoAmL 92*
**Barry,** Tobias Gerald 1924- *WhoAmL 92*
**Barry,** Tom 1898-1980 *FacFETw*
**Barry,** Vivian 1938- *WhoAmP 91*
**Barry,** William Burdette 1961- *WhoFI 92*
**Barry,** William Eugene 1928- *AmMWSc 92*
**Barry,** William James 1948- *AmMWSc 92*
**Barry,** William Logan 1926- *WhoAmP 91*
**Barry,** William M 1959- *WhoAmP 91*
**Barry,** William W. *WhoFI 92*
**Barrymore** *FacFETw [port]*
**Barrymore,** Drew 1975- *IntMPA 92*
**Barrymore,** Ethel 1879-1959 *BenetAL 91, FacFETw [port]*
**Barrymore,** Georgiana Drew 1856-1893 *BenetAL 91*
**Barrymore,** John 1882-1942 *BenetAL 91*
**Barrymore,** John 1882-1944 *FacFETw [port]*
**Barrymore,** John Drew 1932- *IntMPA 92*
**Barrymore,** Lionel 1878-1954 *BenetAL 91, FacFETw [port]*
**Barrymore,** Maurice 1847-1905 *BenetAL 91*
**Barrymores,** The *BenetAL 91*
**Bars,** Itzhak 1943- *AmMWSc 92, WhoWest 92*
**Bars,** Ivars John 1954- *WhoAmL 92*
**Barsalona,** Frank Samuel 1938- *WhoEnt 92, WhoFI 92*
**Barsalou,** Yves 1932- *IntWW 91*
**Barsamian,** John Albert 1934- *WhoAmL 92*
**Barsamian,** Khajag Sarkis 1951- *WhoRel 92*
**Barsan,** Richard Emil 1945- *WhoWest 92*
**Barsan,** Robert Blake 1948- *WhoMW 92*
**Barsauma** 415?-495? *EncEarC*
**Barsch,** Gerhard Richard 1927- *AmMWSc 92*
**Barschall,** Henry Herman 1915- *AmMWSc 92, IntWW 91*
**Barsdate,** Mary Kathryn 1933- *WhoWest 92*
**Barsdate,** Robert John 1934- *AmMWSc 92*
**Barselou,** Paul Edgar 1922- *WhoEnt 92*
**Barsh,** Gregory Scott 1961- *WhoAmL 92*
**Barsh,** Harry Edward, Jr. 1930- *WhoAmL 92*
**Barshai,** Rudolf 1924- *NewAmDM*
**Barshai,** Rudolf Borisovich 1924- *IntWW 91, WhoEnt 92*
**Barshay,** Jacob 1940- *AmMWSc 92*
**Barshay,** Rudol'f Borisovich 1924- *SovUnBD*
**Barsis,** Edwin Howard 1940- *AmMWSc 92, WhoWest 92*
**Barske,** Philip 1917- *AmMWSc 92*
**Barsky,** Bernard *WhoRel 92*
**Barsky,** Brian Andrew 1954- *AmMWSc 92*
**Barsky,** Constance Kay 1944- *AmMWSc 92*
**Barsky,** David 1929- *WhoMW 92*
**Barsky,** James 1925- *AmMWSc 92*
**Barsky,** Joseph Mitchell, III 1949- *WhoMW 92*
**Barsky,** Martin 1927- *WhoWest 92*
**Barsom,** John M *AmMWSc 92*
**Barsova,** Valeriya Vladimirovna 1892-1967 *SovUnBD*
**Barss,** Walter Malcomson 1917- *AmMWSc 92*
**Barst,** Fran *DrAPF 91*
**Barston,** Eugene Myron 1935- *AmMWSc 92*
**Barstow,** David Robbins 1947- *AmMWSc 92*
**Barstow,** Josephine Clare 1940- *IntWW 91, Who 92*
**Barstow,** Leon E 1940- *AmMWSc 92*
**Barstow,** Leon ElRoy 1940- *WhoWest 92*
**Barstow,** Stan 1928- *ConNov 91, IntAu&W 91, Who 92, WrDr 92*
**Bart,** A. S. *Who 92*
**Bart,** Edward 1917- *WhoIns 92*
**Bart,** George Raymond *AmMWSc 92*
**Bart,** Jill *DrAPF 91*
**Bart,** Lionel 1930- *IntAu&W 91, IntWW 91, NewAmDM, Who 92, WrDr 92*
**Bart,** Peter *IntMPA 92*
**Bart,** Peter 1932- *IntAu&W 91, WrDr 92*
**Barta,** James Joseph 1940- *WhoAmL 92*
**Barta,** James Omer 1931- *WhoMW 92, WhoRel 92*
**Barta,** Karen Ann 1939- *WhoRel 92*
**Barta,** Marie Laura 1917- *WhoEnt 92*
**Barta,** Ota 1931- *AmMWSc 92*
**Barta,** Paula Gene 1952- *WhoFI 92*
**Barta,** Peter Claude 1965- *WhoEnt 92*
**Barta,** Richard Francis 1926- *WhoMW 92*
**Bartak,** Gary J. 1953- *WhoFI 92*
**Bartal,** Arie H 1947- *AmMWSc 92*
**Barteau,** Betty Anne 1935- *WhoAmL 92*
**Barteau,** John Frank 1928- *WhoFI 92*
**Barteau,** Mark Alan 1956- *AmMWSc 92*
**Barteau,** Mary Alice 1963- *WhoMW 92*
**Bartee,** Darrell H. *DrAPF 91*
**Bartee,** Russell Floyd 1954- *WhoRel 92*
**Bartek,** Edward J 1921- *IntAu&W 91, WrDr 92*
**Bartek,** Gordon Luke 1925- *WhoMW 92*
**Bartel,** Allen Hawley 1923- *AmMWSc 92*
**Bartel,** Arthur Gabriel 1934- *WhoWest 92*
**Bartel,** David Scott 1954- *WhoAmL 92*
**Bartel,** Donald L 1939- *AmMWSc 92*
**Bartel,** Fred F 1917- *AmMWSc 92*
**Bartel,** Herbert H, Jr 1924- *AmMWSc 92*
**Bartel,** Lavon L 1951- *AmMWSc 92*
**Bartel,** Lewis Clark 1934- *AmMWSc 92*
**Bartel,** Monroe H 1936- *AmMWSc 92*
**Bartel,** Paul 1938- *IntMPA 92, WhoEnt 92*
**Bartel,** Richard Joseph 1950- *WhoFI 92*
**Bartel,** Robert Joseph 1955- *WhoAmL 92*
**Bartel,** Sheryl June 1949- *WhoWest 92*
**Bartelink,** Dirk Jan 1933- *AmMWSc 92*
**Bartell,** Anne *Who 92*
**Bartell,** Clelmer Kay 1934- *AmMWSc 92*
**Bartell,** Daniel P 1944- *AmMWSc 92*
**Bartell,** Kenneth George William 1914- *Who 92*
**Bartell,** Lawrence Sims 1923- *AmMWSc 92, WhoMW 92*
**Bartell,** Lee 1910- *WhoRel 92*
**Bartell,** Marvin H 1938- *AmMWSc 92*
**Bartell,** Steven Michael 1948- *AmMWSc 92*
**Bartelle,** Talmadge Louis *WhoBlA 92*
**Bartelme,** Joe d1991 *LesBEnT 92, NewYTBS 91*
**Bartelme,** Lois Ann 1941- *WhoMW 92*
**Bartels,** Adolf 1862-1945 *BiDExR, EncTR 91*
**Bartels,** Brenda L. 1959- *WhoAmL 92*
**Bartels,** Brian Desmond 1957- *WhoFI 92*
**Bartels,** George William, Jr 1928- *AmMWSc 92*
**Bartels,** Joachim Conrad 1938- *WhoFI 92*
**Bartels,** John Ries 1897- *WhoAmL 92*
**Bartels,** Paul George 1934- *AmMWSc 92*
**Bartels,** Peter H 1929- *AmMWSc 92*
**Bartels,** Richard Alfred 1938- *AmMWSc 92*
**Bartels,** Richard Harold 1939- *AmMWSc 92*
**Bartels,** Robert Christian Frank 1911- *AmMWSc 92*
**Bartelski,** Leslaw 1920- *IntAu&W 91, IntWW 91*
**Bartelstone,** Ted Henry 1950- *WhoAmL 92*
**Bartelt,** John Eric 1955- *AmMWSc 92*
**Bartelt,** Martin William 1941- *AmMWSc 92*
**Bartelt,** Paul Douglas 1960- *WhoEnt 92, WhoWest 92*
**Bartelt,** Paul Eugene 1952- *WhoMW 92*
**Barten,** John Michael 1951- *WhoMW 92*
**Bartenfelder,** A Joseph 1957- *WhoAmP 91*
**Bartenstein,** Louis 1946- *WhoIns 92*
**Barter,** James T 1930- *AmMWSc 92*
**Barter,** John William, III 1946- *WhoFI 92*
**Barter,** Paul 1935- *TwCPaSc*
**Barter,** Ruby Sunshine *WhoFI 92*
**Bartfeld,** Harry 1913- *AmMWSc 92*
**Bartfield,** William 1932- *WhoWest 92*
**Barth,** Alvin Ludwig, Jr 1936- *WhoAmP 91*
**Barth,** Andrew Francis 1961- *WhoFI 92*
**Barth,** Charles Adolph 1930- *AmMWSc 92*
**Barth,** David Victor 1942- *WhoWest 92*
**Barth,** Else M. 1928- *IntWW 91*
**Barth,** Eugene Howard 1913- *WhoRel 92*
**Barth,** Howard Gordon 1946- *AmMWSc 92*
**Barth,** Ilene Joan 1944- *ConAu 134*
**Barth,** J Robert 1931- *IntAu&W 91, WrDr 92*
**Barth,** Jeffrey Lynn 1951- *WhoAmL 92*
**Barth,** John *DrAPF 91*
**Barth,** John 1930- *BenetAL 91, ConNov 91, IntAu&W 91, IntWW 91, WrDr 92*
**Barth,** John 1930-1990 *FacFETw*
**Barth,** Karl 1886-1968 *ConAu 134, DcEcMov, EncTR 91 [port], FacFETw*
**Barth,** Karl Frederick 1938- *AmMWSc 92*
**Barth,** Karl Luther 1924- *WhoRel 92*
**Barth,** Karl M 1927- *AmMWSc 92*
**Barth,** Kevin Mitchell 1957- *WhoAmL 92*
**Barth,** Mark Harold 1951- *WhoAmL 92*
**Barth,** Markus 1915- *WrDr 92*
**Barth,** Markus Karl 1915- *WhoRel 92*
**Barth,** Michael Carl 1941- *WhoFI 92*
**Barth,** Richard 1931- *WhoFI 92*
**Barth,** Richard 1943- *WrDr 92*
**Barth,** Robert Hood, Jr 1934- *AmMWSc 92*
**Barth,** Rolf Frederick 1937- *AmMWSc 92, WhoMW 92*
**Barth,** Thomas Frederik 1928- *IntWW 91*
**Bartha,** Denes 1908- *IntWW 91*
**Bartha,** Richard 1934- *AmMWSc 92*
**Bartha,** Tibor 1912- *IntWW 91*
**Barthe,** Richmond 1901-1989 *WhoBlA 92N*
**Barthel,** David William 1959- *WhoFI 92*
**Barthel,** Harold O 1925- *AmMWSc 92*
**Barthel,** Ludwig Friedrich 1898-1962 *EncTR 91*
**Barthel,** Max 1893-1975 *EncTR 91*
**Barthel,** Romard 1924- *AmMWSc 92*
**Barthel,** Willard Otto 1922- *WhoAmP 91*
**Barthel,** William Frederick 1915- *AmMWSc 92*
**Barthelemy,** Sidney John 1942- *WhoAmP 91, WhoBlA 92*
**Barthelemy,** Victor 1906- *BiDExR*
**Barthell,** Ronald Lewis 1935- *WhoRel 92*
**Barthelmas,** Ned Kelton 1927- *WhoFI 92, WhoMW 92*
**Barthelme,** Donald 1931-1989 *BenetAL 91*
**Barthelme,** Donald 1931-1990 *FacFETw*
**Barthelme,** Frederick 1943- *BenetAL 91, ConNov 91, IntAu&W 91, WrDr 92*
**Barthelmeh,** Hans Adolf 1923- *IntWW 91*
**Barthes,** Roland 1915-1980 *FacFETw, GuFrLit 1*
**Barthold,** Clementine B. 1921- *WhoMW 92*
**Barthold,** Lauren Swayne 1965- *WhoRel 92*
**Barthold,** Lionel O 1926- *AmMWSc 92*
**Barthold,** Stephen William 1945- *AmMWSc 92*
**Bartholdi,** Auguste Frederick 1834-1904 *DcAmImH*
**Bartholdi,** Marty Frank 1952- *AmMWSc 92*
**Bartholdson,** John Robert 1944- *WhoFI 92*
**Bartholdt,** Richard 1855-1932 *AmPeW*
**Bartholet,** Elizabeth 1940- *WhoAmL 92*
**Bartholmey,** Sandra Jean 1942- *AmMWSc 92*
**Bartholomay,** William C. 1928- *WhoFI 92, WhoIns 92*
**Bartholome,** Paul Albert 1848-1928 *ThHEIm*
**Bartholomew,** Arthur Peck, Jr. 1918- *WhoFI 92*
**Bartholomew,** Barbara 1941- *ConAu 135*
**Bartholomew,** Barbara Gillett 1950- *WhoWest 92*
**Bartholomew,** Calvin Henry 1943- *AmMWSc 92*
**Bartholomew,** Carroll Eugene 1935- *WhoRel 92*
**Bartholomew,** Darrell Thomas 1947- *AmMWSc 92*
**Bartholomew,** Dave 1960- *WhoEnt 92*
**Bartholomew,** David Cleaver 1960- *WhoRel 92*
**Bartholomew,** David John 1931- *Who 92*
**Bartholomew,** Donald Dekle 1929- *WhoFI 92, WhoMW 92*
**Bartholomew,** Duane P 1934- *AmMWSc 92*
**Bartholomew,** Freddie 1924- *IntMPA 92*
**Bartholomew,** Gary Alan 1956- *WhoEnt 92*
**Bartholomew,** George Adelbert 1919- *AmMWSc 92*
**Bartholomew,** Gilbert Alfred 1922- *AmMWSc 92*
**Bartholomew,** James 1950- *IntAu&W 91*
**Bartholomew,** James Collins 1942- *AmMWSc 92*
**Bartholomew,** James Ira 1938- *WhoAmL 92*
**Bartholomew,** Jean *ConAu 134, IntAu&W 91X, SmATA 68, WrDr 92*
**Bartholomew,** Lee Houck 1950- *WhoWest 92*
**Bartholomew,** Lindsay 1944- *TwCPaSc*
**Bartholomew,** Lloyd Gibson 1921- *AmMWSc 92*
**Bartholomew,** Marshall 1885-1978 *NewAmDM*
**Bartholomew,** Mervin Jerome 1942- *AmMWSc 92*
**Bartholomew,** Reginald 1936- *WhoAmP 91*
**Bartholomew,** Roger Frank 1937- *AmMWSc 92*
**Bartholomew,** Tracy, II 1952- *WhoFI 92*
**Bartholomew,** William Lee 1950- *WhoMW 92, WhoRel 92*
**Bartholow,** George William 1930- *AmMWSc 92*
**Bartholow,** Lester C 1936- *AmMWSc 92*
**Barthwell,** Jack Clinton, III 1950- *WhoBlA 92*
**Bartilucci,** Andrew J 1922- *AmMWSc 92*
**Bartimes,** George F 1935- *AmMWSc 92*
**Bartis,** James Thomas 1945- *AmMWSc 92*
**Bartish,** Charles Michael Christopher 1947- *AmMWSc 92*
**Bartizal,** John Frank, Jr. 1933- *WhoMW 92*

**Bartke**, Andrzej 1939- *AmMWSc 92, WhoMW 92*
**Bartkevich**, Leonard Leopoldovich 1932- *IntWW 91*
**Bartko**, John 1931- *AmMWSc 92*
**Bartko**, John Jaroslav 1937- *AmMWSc 92*
**Bartkoski**, Michael John, Jr 1945- *AmMWSc 92, WhoMW 92*
**Bartkowech**, R. *DrAPF 91*
**Bartkowiak**, Andrzej 1950- *IntMPA 92*
**Bartkowiak**, Daniel James 1950- *WhoRel 92*
**Bartkowiak**, Tadeusz Ludwik 1942- *IntAu&W 91*
**Bartkowski**, Eugene H. 1934- *WhoIns 92*
**Bartkowski**, William Patrick 1951- *WhoFI 92*
**Bartkus**, Edward Peter 1920- *AmMWSc 92*
**Bartkus**, Robert Edward 1946- *WhoAmL 92*
**Bartl**, Paul 1928- *AmMWSc 92*
**Bartle**, Emery Warness 1943- *WhoAmL 92*
**Bartle**, Robert Gardner 1927- *AmMWSc 92, WhoMW 92*
**Bartle**, Ronald David 1929- *Who 92*
**Bartleet**, David Henry *Who 92*
**Bartles**, James Richard *AmMWSc 92*
**Bartles-Smith**, Douglas Leslie 1937- *Who 92*
**Bartleson**, John David 1917- *AmMWSc 92*
**Bartlett**, Alan C 1934- *AmMWSc 92*
**Bartlett**, Albert Allen 1923- *AmMWSc 92*
**Bartlett**, Allen Lyman, Jr. 1929- *WhoRel 92*
**Bartlett**, Arthur Eugene 1933- *WhoFI 92*
**Bartlett**, Boyd C. 1925- *IntWW 91*
**Bartlett**, Bruce R. 1951- *WrDr 92*
**Bartlett**, Bruce Reeves 1951- *WhoFI 92*
**Bartlett**, Bud 1940- *WhoEnt 92, WhoMW 92*
**Bartlett**, Charles *Who 92*
**Bartlett**, Charles 1921- *TwCPaSc*
**Bartlett**, Charles Samuel, Jr 1929- *AmMWSc 92*
**Bartlett**, Christopher Bartholomew 1964- *WhoEnt 92*
**Bartlett**, Christopher John 1931- *IntAu&W 91, WrDr 92*
**Bartlett**, D. Brook 1937- *WhoAmL 92*
**Bartlett**, David Carson 1944- *WhoAmP 91*
**Bartlett**, David Farnham 1938- *AmMWSc 92*
**Bartlett**, David Vangelder 1959- *WhoEnt 92*
**Bartlett**, David W. 1946- *WhoWest 92*
**Bartlett**, Dede Thompson 1943- *WhoFI 92*
**Bartlett**, Desmond William 1931- *WhoFI 92*
**Bartlett**, Donald, Jr 1937- *AmMWSc 92*
**Bartlett**, Doreen Zeh 1955- *WhoAmL 92*
**Bartlett**, Douglas Hoyt 1957- *WhoFI 92*
**Bartlett**, Duane Edward 1947- *WhoWest 92*
**Bartlett**, Edwin S 1928- *AmMWSc 92*
**Bartlett**, Elizabeth *DrAPF 91*
**Bartlett**, Elizabeth 1924- *ConPo 91, WrDr 92*
**Bartlett**, Elizabeth Susan 1927- *WhoEnt 92*
**Bartlett**, Eric George 1920- *IntAu&W 91, WrDr 92*
**Bartlett**, Frank David 1928- *AmMWSc 92*
**Bartlett**, Frederick Charles 1886-1969 *FacFETw*
**Bartlett**, George Robert 1944- *Who 92*
**Bartlett**, Gerald Lloyd 1939- *AmMWSc 92*
**Bartlett**, Gordon E 1926- *WhoAmP 91*
**Bartlett**, Grant Rogers 1912- *AmMWSc 92*
**Bartlett**, Hall 1925- *IntMPA 92*
**Bartlett**, Hall 1929- *WhoEnt 92, WhoFI 92, WhoWest 92*
**Bartlett**, Harold Charles 1921- *Who 92*
**Bartlett**, Henry Francis 1916- *Who 92*
**Bartlett**, J Frederick 1936- *AmMWSc 92*
**Bartlett**, James Holly 1904- *AmMWSc 92*
**Bartlett**, James Kenneth 1925- *AmMWSc 92*
**Bartlett**, James Williams, Jr 1926- *AmMWSc 92*
**Bartlett**, James Wilson, III 1946- *WhoAmL 92*
**Bartlett**, Janeth Marie 1946- *AmMWSc 92*
**Bartlett**, Jeffrey Leon 1939- *WhoBIA 92*
**Bartlett**, Jennifer 1941- *IntWW 91, WorArt 1980 [port]*
**Bartlett**, Joe 1926- *WhoAmP 91*
**Bartlett**, John 1820-1905 *BenetAL 91*
**Bartlett**, John 1938- *Who 92*
**Bartlett**, John Bruen 1941- *WhoFI 92*
**Bartlett**, John Laurence 1942- *WhoAmL 92*
**Bartlett**, John Leonard 1926- *Who 92*
**Bartlett**, John Russell 1843-1904 *BiInAmS*
**Bartlett**, John Vernon 1927- *IntWW 91, Who 92*
**Bartlett**, John W 1935- *AmMWSc 92*
**Bartlett**, Joseph Warren 1933- *WhoAmL 92*
**Bartlett**, Katharine Tiffany 1947- *WhoAmL 92*
**Bartlett**, Landell *ScFEYrs*
**Bartlett**, Lee *DrAPF 91*
**Bartlett**, Leonard 1893-1971 *TwCPaSc*
**Bartlett**, Linda Gail 1943- *WhoAmL 92*
**Bartlett**, Mary 1940- *WhoAmP 91*
**Bartlett**, Maurice Stevenson 1910- *Who 92*
**Bartlett**, Neil 1932- *AmMWSc 92, FacFETw, IntWW 91, Who 92*
**Bartlett**, Oliver Richard 1945- *WhoAmP 91*
**Bartlett**, Paul A 1948- *AmMWSc 92*
**Bartlett**, Paul Alexander *DrAPF 91*
**Bartlett**, Paul Arthur 1954- *WhoMW 92*
**Bartlett**, Paul Dana, Jr. 1919- *WhoFI 92, WhoMW 92*
**Bartlett**, Paul Doughty 1907- *AmMWSc 92, FacFETw, IntWW 91*
**Bartlett**, Paul Eugene 1926- *AmMWSc 92*
**Bartlett**, Peter Greenough 1930- *WhoFI 92, WhoMW 92*
**Bartlett**, R W 1933- *AmMWSc 92*
**Bartlett**, Richard Wrelton 1939- *WhoWest 92*
**Bartlett**, Richmond J 1927- *AmMWSc 92*
**Bartlett**, Robert Perry, Jr. 1938- *WhoAmL 92*
**Bartlett**, Robert Watkins 1933- *WhoWest 92*
**Bartlett**, Robert William 1941- *WhoAmL 92*
**Bartlett**, Rodney Joseph 1944- *AmMWSc 92*
**Bartlett**, Roger Danforth 1949- *WhoMW 92*
**Bartlett**, Roger James 1942- *AmMWSc 92*
**Bartlett**, Shirley Anne 1933- *WhoMW 92*
**Bartlett**, Stephen 1942- *TwCPaSc*
**Bartlett**, Steve 1947- *WhoAmP 91*
**Bartlett**, Steven Thade 1962- *WhoWest 92*
**Bartlett**, Thomas Alva 1930- *WhoWest 92*
**Bartlett**, Thomas Henry 1931- *WhoWest 92*
**Bartlett**, Vanessa Ann 1961- *WhoAmL 92*
**Bartlett**, Victoria 1940- *TwCPaSc*
**Bartlett**, Walter E. 1928- *WhoFI 92*
**Bartlett**, William Clair 1950- *WhoRel 92*
**Bartlett**, William Donald, Jr. 1950- *WhoRel 92*
**Bartlett**, William Holms Chambers 1804-1893 *BiInAmS*
**Bartlett**, William Pitt Greenwood 1837-1865 *BiInAmS*
**Bartlett**, William Rosebrough 1943- *AmMWSc 92*
**Bartlett**, William S, Jr 1930- *WhoAmP 91*
**Bartlett Diaz**, Manuel 1936- *IntWW 91*
**Bartlette**, Donald Lloyd 1939- *WhoMW 92*
**Bartley**, David Michael 1935- *WhoAmP 91*
**Bartley**, Diana Esther Pelaez Rivera 1940- *WhoMW 92*
**Bartley**, Edward Francis 1916- *AmMWSc 92*
**Bartley**, Eugene *WhoFI 92*
**Bartley**, John C *WhoAmP 91*
**Bartley**, John C 1932- *AmMWSc 92*
**Bartley**, Kurt Douglas 1958- *WhoRel 92*
**Bartley**, Mary Margaret *WhoEnt 92*
**Bartley**, Murray Hill 1933- *WhoWest 92*
**Bartley**, Murray Hill, Jr 1933- *AmMWSc 92*
**Bartley**, Opelene 1924- *WhoWest 92*
**Bartley**, Robert LeRoy 1937- *WhoFI 92*
**Bartley**, Robert T. d1988 *LesBEnT 92*
**Bartley**, Talmadge O. 1920- *WhoBIA 92*
**Bartley**, William Call 1932- *AmMWSc 92*
**Bartley**, William J 1935- *AmMWSc 92*
**Bartley**, William Raymond 1944- *WhoBIA 92*
**Bartley**, William Warren, III 1934- *IntAu&W 91*
**Bartling**, Charles Edwin 1938- *WhoMW 92*
**Bartling**, Judd Quentin 1936- *AmMWSc 92*
**Bartling**, Wayne Earl *WhoAmP 91*
**Bartlit**, John R 1934- *AmMWSc 92*
**Bartlo**, Sam D. 1919- *WhoAmL 92*
**Bartlow**, Thomas L 1942- *AmMWSc 92*
**Bartman**, Joeffrey *DrAPF 91*
**Bartmess**, Geary, III 1948- *WhoAmL 92*
**Bartnick**, Merle *WhoAmP 91*
**Bartnicki**, Stanley Thomas 1933- *WhoAmL 92*
**Bartnicki-Garcia**, Salomon 1935- *AmMWSc 92*
**Bartnik**, Jerry C 1943- *WhoAmP 91*
**Bartnikas**, Ray 1936- *AmMWSc 92*
**Bartnoff**, Judith 1949- *WhoAmL 92*
**Bartnoff**, Shepard 1919- *AmMWSc 92*
**Bartocha**, Bodo 1928- *AmMWSc 92*
**Bartok**, Bela 1881-1945 *FacFETw [port], NewAmDM*
**Bartok**, Michael Frederick 1959- *WhoEnt 92*
**Bartok**, William 1930- *AmMWSc 92*
**Bartol**, Ernest Thomas 1946- *WhoAmL 92*
**Bartol**, Walter W. 1931- *WhoWest 92*
**Bartoletti**, Bruno 1926- *NewAmDM, WhoEnt 92*
**Bartoletti**, Marietta Louise 1949- *WhoFI 92*
**Bartoli**, Diane S. 1938- *WhoFI 92*
**Bartolini**, Anthony Louis 1931- *WhoAmL 92*
**Bartolini**, Bruce Anthony 1950- *WhoFI 92*
**Bartolini**, Daniel John 1935- *WhoAmL 92*
**Bartolini**, Davio *DcTwDes*
**Bartolini**, Kathleen Barry 1947- *WhoAmP 91*
**Bartolini**, Lucia *DcTwDes*
**Bartolini**, Robert Alfred 1942- *AmMWSc 92*
**Bartolo**, Donna M. 1941- *WhoFI 92*
**Bartolucci**, Luis A. 1946- *WhoHisp 92*
**Barton**, Alan Joel 1938- *WhoAmL 92*
**Barton**, Alexander James 1924- *AmMWSc 92*
**Barton**, Ann Elizabeth 1923- *WhoWest 92*
**Barton**, Anne *Who 92*
**Barton**, Anne 1933- *IntWW 91*
**Barton**, Anthony Blackshaw 1947- *WhoAmL 92*
**Barton**, Babette B. 1930- *WhoAmL 92*
**Barton**, Barbara Ann 1954- *AmMWSc 92*
**Barton**, Barbara Anne 1933- *Who 92*
**Barton**, Benjamin Smith 1766-1815 *BenetAL 91, BiInAmS*
**Barton**, Bernard Alan, Jr. 1948- *WhoAmL 92*
**Barton**, Beverly E 1954- *AmMWSc 92*
**Barton**, Bruce 1886-1967 *RelLAm 91*
**Barton**, C. Robert 1926- *WhoIns 92*
**Barton**, Carrie Maxey 1954- *WhoWest 92*
**Barton**, Charles Andrews, Jr. 1916- *WhoRel 92*
**Barton**, Charles David 1954- *WhoRel 92*
**Barton**, Charles John Greenwood 1936- *Who 92*
**Barton**, Charles Julian, Sr 1912- *AmMWSc 92*
**Barton**, Clara 1821-1912 *BenetAL 91, HanAmWH, RComAH*
**Barton**, Cliff S 1919- *AmMWSc 92*
**Barton**, David Joseph 1956- *WhoAmL 92*
**Barton**, David Knox 1927- *AmMWSc 92*
**Barton**, Derek Harold Richard 1918- *AmMWSc 92, FacFETw, IntWW 91, Who 92, WhoNob 90*
**Barton**, Donald Wilber 1921- *AmMWSc 92*
**Barton**, Eric Walter 1928- *Who 92*
**Barton**, Erle *TwCSFW 91, WrDr 92*
**Barton**, Ernesto F. 1930- *WhoHisp 92*
**Barton**, Erwin W 1931- *WhoAmP 91*
**Barton**, Evan Mansfield 1903- *AmMWSc 92*
**Barton**, Francis Christopher 1916- *Who 92*
**Barton**, Franklin Ellwood, II 1942- *AmMWSc 92*
**Barton**, Frederick 1949- *WhoAmP 91*
**Barton**, Fredrick *DrAPF 91*
**Barton**, Furman W 1932- *AmMWSc 92*
**Barton**, Gerald Blackett 1917- *AmMWSc 92*
**Barton**, Glenys 1944- *TwCPaSc*
**Barton**, Graham George 1928- *WhoMW 92*
**Barton**, Gregory Edward 1961- *WhoAmL 92*
**Barton**, Harvey Eugene 1936- *AmMWSc 92*
**Barton**, Henry Ruwe, Jr 1944- *AmMWSc 92*
**Barton**, Hildor Arnold 1929- *WhoMW 92*
**Barton**, J. S. *WhoRel 92*
**Barton**, Jack *TwCWW 91*
**Barton**, Jacqueline K 1952- *AmMWSc 92*
**Barton**, James *WrDr 92*
**Barton**, James Brockman 1944- *AmMWSc 92*
**Barton**, James Cary 1940- *WhoAmL 92*
**Barton**, James Charles 1944- *WhoMW 92*
**Barton**, James Don, Jr 1929- *AmMWSc 92*
**Barton**, James T. 1940- *WhoFI 92*
**Barton**, Janice Sweeny 1939- *AmMWSc 92*
**Barton**, Jery Edward 1947- *WhoMW 92*
**Barton**, Joe Linus 1949- *AlmAP 92 [port], WhoAmP 91*
**Barton**, John 1946- *WhoIns 92*
**Barton**, John 1948- *Who 92*
**Barton**, John Bernard Adie 1928- *IntWW 91, Who 92*
**Barton**, John Greenwood *Who 92*
**Barton**, John Hays 1936- *WhoAmL 92*
**Barton**, John R *AmMWSc 92*
**Barton**, Jon *WrDr 92*
**Barton**, Judith Marie 1953- *WhoAmL 92*
**Barton**, Kenneth Ray 1936- *AmMWSc 92*
**Barton**, Larry Lumir 1940- *AmMWSc 92*
**Barton**, Lawrence 1938- *AmMWSc 92*
**Barton**, Lee *IntAu&W 91X, TwCSFW 91, WrDr 92*
**Barton**, Lewis 1940- *WhoFI 92*
**Barton**, Margaret 1897- *Who 92*
**Barton**, Marie Tidwell 1937- *WhoAmL 92*
**Barton**, Mark Q 1928- *AmMWSc 92*
**Barton**, Mary *WhoEnt 92*
**Barton**, May Hollis *SmATA 67*
**Barton**, Nelda Ann Lambert 1929- *WhoAmP 91*
**Barton**, Paul 1936- *AmMWSc 92*
**Barton**, Paul Booth, Jr 1930- *AmMWSc 92*
**Barton**, Paul Douglas 1960- *WhoWest 92*
**Barton**, Paule 1916-1974 *LiExTwC*
**Barton**, Pauline 1923- *WhoMW 92*
**Barton**, Peter *ConTFT 9*
**Barton**, Randolph, Jr 1941- *AmMWSc 92*
**Barton**, Rhonda L. 1966- *WhoBIA 92*
**Barton**, Richard Donald 1936- *AmMWSc 92*
**Barton**, Richard J 1928- *AmMWSc 92*
**Barton**, Robert L., Jr. 1943- *WhoAmL 92*
**Barton**, Roger 1945- *Who 92*
**Barton**, Samuel *ScFEYrs*
**Barton**, Stanley 1927- *WhoFI 92*
**Barton**, Stephen, Jr. 1806-1865 *DcNCBi 1*
**Barton**, Stuart Samuel 1922- *AmMWSc 92*
**Barton**, Thomas Donald 1949- *WhoAmL 92*
**Barton**, Thomas J 1940- *AmMWSc 92*
**Barton**, Walter E 1906- *AmMWSc 92*
**Barton**, Wayne 1944- *TwCWW 91, WrDr 92*
**Barton**, William Arnold 1948- *WhoAmL 92*
**Barton**, William E. 1861-1930 *BenetAL 91*
**Barton**, William Henry, II 1921- *WhoWest 92*
**Barton**, William Hickson 1917- *IntWW 91*
**Barton**, William L 1939- *WhoAmP 91*
**Barton**, William Paul Crillon 1786-1856 *BiInAmS*
**Barton**, William Thomas 1933- *WhoAmP 91*
**Barton-Chapple**, Dorothy *Who 92*
**Bartoo**, James Breese 1921- *AmMWSc 92*
**Bartos**, Dagmar 1929- *AmMWSc 92*
**Bartos**, Frantisek 1926- *AmMWSc 92*
**Bartosek**, Karel 1930- *IntWW 91*
**Bartoshevich**, Gennadiy Georgievich 1934- *IntWW 91*
**Bartoshuk**, Linda May *AmMWSc 92*
**Bartosic**, Florian 1926- *WhoAmL 92*
**Bartosiewicz**, Thomas 1948- *WhoAmP 91*
**Bartosik**, Alexander Michael 1924- *AmMWSc 92*
**Bartosik**, Delphine 1937- *AmMWSc 92*
**Bartosik**, Josef C. 1917- *Who 92*
**Bartoszcze**, Roman Boleslaw 1946- *IntWW 91*
**Bartoszewski**, Wladyslaw 1922- *IntAu&W 91*
**Bartov**, Omer 1954- *ConAu 135*
**Bartovics**, Albert 1916- *AmMWSc 92*
**Bartow**, Charles Louis 1937- *WhoRel 92*
**Bartow**, David Winfield 1939- *WhoRel 92*
**Bartow**, Jerome E. *WhoIns 92*
**Bartow**, Jerome Edward *WhoBIA 92*
**Bartram**, James F 1926- *AmMWSc 92*
**Bartram**, John 1699-1777 *BenetAL 91, BiInAmS*
**Bartram**, Judith Ames 1956- *WhoAmL 92*
**Bartram**, Maynard Cleveland, Jr. 1926- *WhoFI 92*
**Bartram**, Ralph Herbert 1929- *AmMWSc 92*
**Bartram**, William 1739-1823 *BiInAmS, DcNCBi 1*
**Bartram**, William 1739-1833 *BenetAL 91*
**Bartruff**, Bryce Duane 1950- *WhoRel 92*
**Bartruff**, Robert David 1927- *WhoAmP 91*
**Bartsch**, Glenn Emil 1928- *AmMWSc 92*
**Bartsch**, Richard Alan 1950- *WhoWest 92*
**Bartsch**, Richard Allen 1940- *AmMWSc 92*
**Bartschmid**, Betty Rains 1949- *AmMWSc 92*
**Bartson**, Ronald John 1941- *WhoMW 92*
**Barttelot**, Brian Walter de Stopham 1941- *Who 92*
**Bartter**, Brit Jeffrey 1949- *WhoMW 92*
**Bartucca**, Frank Richard 1943- *WhoFI 92*
**Bartunek**, Robert Richard, Jr. 1946- *WhoAmL 92*
**Barturen Duenas** 1936- *IntWW 91*
**Bartus**, Raymond T 1947- *AmMWSc 92*
**Bartus**, Raymond Thomas 1947- *WhoWest 92*
**Bartusis**, Constance *DrAPF 91*
**Bartuska**, Doris G *AmMWSc 92*
**Bartz**, Albert 1933- *WrDr 92*
**Bartz**, David John 1955- *WhoAmL 92*
**Bartz**, Jerry A 1942- *AmMWSc 92*
**Bartz**, Merlin E 1961- *WhoAmP 91*
**Bartz**, Paul Alan 1948- *WhoMW 92*
**Bartz**, Richard Earl 1936- *WhoRel 92*
**Bartz**, Warren F 1913- *AmMWSc 92*
**Bartz**, William Walter 1959- *WhoEnt 92*
**Bartzatt**, Ronald Lee 1953- *WhoMW 92*
**Baruch**, Andre *IntMPA 92*
**Baruch**, Andre d1991 *NewYTBS 91*
**Baruch**, Bernard 1870-1965 *BenetAL 91*
**Baruch**, Bernard M. 1870-1965 *FacFETw [port], RComAH*

**Baruch,** Bernard Mannes 1870-1965 *AmPolLe*
**Baruch,** Izak Zacharias 1917- *WhoRel 92*
**Baruch,** Jordan J 1923- *AmMWSc 92*
**Baruch,** Marjory Jean 1951- *AmMWSc 92*
**Baruch,** Michael Amnon 1965- *WhoWest 92*
**Baruch,** Ralph M. *LesBEnT 92*
**Baruch,** Ralph M. 1923- *IntMPA 92*
**Baruch,** Ruth-Marion Evelyn 1922- *WhoWest 92*
**Baruch,** Sulamita B 1936- *AmMWSc 92*
**Barudin,** Theodore William 1951- *WhoAmL 92*
**Barus,** Carl 1919- *AmMWSc 92*
**Barusch,** Lawrence Roos 1949- *WhoAmL 92*
**Barusch,** Maurice R 1919- *AmMWSc 92*
**Barusch,** Ronald Charles 1953- *WhoAmL 92*
**Barut,** Asim Orhan 1926- *AmMWSc 92*
**Baruzdin,** Sergey Alekseevich 1926- *IntWW 91, SovUnBD*
**Barve,** Kumar P 1958- *WhoAmP 91*
**Barville,** Rebecca Penelope 1936- *WhoWest 92*
**Barwell,** Cindy Ann 1957- *WhoAmL 92*
**Barwell,** David John Frank 1938- *Who 92*
**Barwick,** David Robert 1927- *Who 92*
**Barwick,** Garfield 1903- *Who 92*
**Barwick,** Garfield Edward John 1903- *IntWW 91*
**Barwick,** Plato Collins, Jr 1937- *WhoAmP 91*
**Barwick,** Steven William 1959- *AmMWSc 92*
**Barwig,** Regis Norbert James 1932- *WhoRel 92*
**Barwood,** Hal *IntMPA 92*
**Barwood,** Lee *DrAPF 91*
**Barykin,** Victor *WhoEnt 92*
**Baryshnikov,** Mikhail 1948- *ConAu 133, FacFETw [port], IntMPA 92, IntWW 91, SovUnBD, Who 92, WhoEnt 92*
**Barz,** Diane 1943- *WhoWest 92*
**Barz,** Diane G *WhoAmP 91*
**Barz,** Diane Gay 1943- *WhoAmL 92*
**Barz,** Richard Alfred 1939- *WhoEnt 92*
**Barzani,** Mustafa 1904-1979 *FacFETw*
**Barzdukas,** Robert Charles 1944- *WhoWest 92*
**Barzel,** Rainer 1924- *IntWW 91*
**Barzel,** Rainer C. 1924- *Who 92*
**Barzel,** Uriel S 1929- *AmMWSc 92*
**Barzelay,** Walter Moshe 1914- *WrDr 92*
**Barzey,** Raymond Clifford, II *WhoBlA 92*
**Barzin,** Leon 1900- *NewAmDM*
**Barzini,** Luigi 1908-1984 *FacFETw*
**Barzun,** Jacques 1907- *BenetAL 91, IntWW 91, Who 92, WrDr 92*
**Barzun,** Jacques Martin 1907- *FacFETw*
**Barzune,** Dolores 1939- *WhoHisp 92*
**Barzyk,** James E. 1954- *WhoFI 92*
**Basaldella,** Afro 1912- *IntWW 91*
**Basang** 1937- *IntWW 91*
**Basarah,** Saleh 1928- *Who 92*
**Basart,** John Philip 1938- *AmMWSc 92, WhoMW 92*
**Basavaiah,** Suryadevara 1938- *AmMWSc 92*
**Basbaum,** Carol Beth *AmMWSc 92*
**Basch,** Buddy 1922- *IntMPA 92*
**Basch,** David *WhoFI 92*
**Basch,** Harry 1926- *WhoEnt 92*
**Basch,** Jay Justin 1932- *AmMWSc 92*
**Basch,** Paul Frederick 1933- *AmMWSc 92*
**Basch,** Ross S 1937- *AmMWSc 92*
**Basci,** Joseph Ronald 1948- *WhoAmP 91*
**Basco,** N 1929- *AmMWSc 92*
**Basco y Vargas,** Jose de *HisDSpE*
**Bascom,** Donna L. *WhoEnt 92*
**Bascom,** Earl Wesley 1906- *WhoWest 92*
**Bascom,** Harold A. 1951- *ConAu 135*
**Bascom,** John G. 1943- *WhoFI 92*
**Bascom,** Willard 1916- *AmMWSc 92*
**Bascom,** Willard D 1931- *AmMWSc 92*
**Bascom,** William Russel 1912- *IntAu&W 91*
**Bascombe,** Ronald D. *DrAPF 91*
**Basconcillo,** Lindy 1943- *WhoWest 92*
**Bascunana,** Jose Luis 1927- *AmMWSc 92, WhoFI 92*
**Basdekas,** Nicholas Leonidas 1924- *AmMWSc 92*
**Basdekis,** Costas H 1921- *AmMWSc 92*
**Basden,** Barbara Holz 1940- *WhoWest 92*
**Basden,** Cameron *WhoEnt 92*
**Base,** Graeme 1958- *ConAu 134, SmATA 67 [port]*
**Basefsky,** Stuart Mark 1949- *WhoAmL 92*
**Baseley,** Godfrey 1904- *IntAu&W 91*
**Baseman,** Alan Howard 1953- *WhoAmL 92*
**Baseman,** Joel Barry 1942- *AmMWSc 92*
**Baseman,** Robert Lynn 1932- *WhoMW 92*
**Basendwah,** Mohamed Salem 1935- *IntWW 91*
**Baserga,** Renato 1925- *AmMWSc 92*
**Baserva,** Guillermo *WhoHisp 92*
**Basevi,** Giorgio 1938- *IntWW 91*
**Basey,** Glen Robert 1942- *WhoRel 92*
**Basey,** Ovetta T. 1920- *WhoBlA 92*
**Basford,** James Orlando 1931- *WhoFI 92, WhoMW 92*
**Basford,** Robert Eugene 1923- *AmMWSc 92*
**Basford,** Ronald 1932- *IntWW 91*
**Basgall,** Bernard A., Jr. 1940- *WhoIns 92*
**Bash,** Charles Dayton 1949- *WhoAmL 92*
**Bash,** Elton 1950- *TwCPaSc*
**Bash,** Frank N. 1937- *WrDr 92*
**Bash,** Frank Ness 1937- *AmMWSc 92*
**Bash,** Paul Anthony 1952- *AmMWSc 92*
**Basha,** Leigh-Alexandra 1960- *WhoAmL 92*
**Basham,** Brian Arthur 1943- *Who 92*
**Basham,** Charles W 1934- *AmMWSc 92*
**Basham,** Donald Wilson 1926-1989 *RelLAm 91*
**Basham,** Jack T 1926- *AmMWSc 92*
**Basham,** Jerald F 1942- *AmMWSc 92*
**Basham,** Ray S 1921- *AmMWSc 92*
**Basham,** Samuel Jerome, Jr 1927- *AmMWSc 92*
**Basham,** Teresa 1947- *AmMWSc 92*
**Basham,** Terry 1953- *WhoAmP 91*
**Bashara,** N M 1917- *AmMWSc 92*
**Bashaw,** Elexis Cook 1923- *AmMWSc 92*
**Bashe,** Philip 1954- *ConAu 134*
**Bashe,** Winslow Jerome, Jr 1920- *AmMWSc 92*
**Bashevis,** Isaac *ConAu 134, IntAu&W 91X, SmATA 68*
**Bashevkin,** Albert 1907- *WhoFI 92*
**Bashey,** Reza Ismail 1932- *AmMWSc 92*
**Bashford,** Humphrey John Charles 1920- *Who 92*
**Bashford,** William L. 1925- *WhoWest 92*
**Bashful,** Emmett W. 1917- *WhoBlA 92*
**Bashilov,** Sergei Vasilievich 1923- *IntWW 91*
**Bashinski,** Leonard C. 1943- *WhoIns 92*
**Bashir,** Anthony 1898-1966 *RelLAm 91*
**Bashir,** Omar Hassan Ahmad al- *IntWW 91*
**Bashirelahi,** Nasir 1935- *AmMWSc 92*
**Bashkin,** Lloyd Scott 1951- *WhoFI 92*
**Bashkin,** Stanley 1923- *AmMWSc 92*
**Bashkirov,** Dmitriy Aleksandrovich 1931- *SovUnBD*
**Bashkow,** Theodore R 1921- *AmMWSc 92*
**Bashline,** Terry Lee Morgan 1953- *WhoAmL 92*
**Basho,** Matsuo 1644?-1694 *PoeCrit 3 [port]*
**Bashore,** George Willis 1934- *WhoRel 92*
**Bashour,** Fouad A 1924- *AmMWSc 92*
**Bashwiner,** Steven Lacelle 1941- *WhoAmL 92*
**Basich,** Bob *WhoAmP 91*
**Basichis,** Gordon Allen 1947- *WhoEnt 92, WhoWest 92*
**Basichis,** Marcia Hammond *WhoEnt 92*
**Basie,** Count *ConAu 134*
**Basie,** Count 1904-1984 *NewAmDM*
**Basie,** William 1904-1984 *FacFETw [port]*
**Basie,** William James 1904?-1984 *ConAu 134*
**Basil of Ancyra** d363? *EncEarC*
**Basil of Caesarea** 330-379 *EncEarC*
**Basil of Seleucia** d468? *EncEarC*
**Basila,** Michael Robert 1930- *AmMWSc 92*
**Basile,** Dominick V 1931- *AmMWSc 92*
**Basile,** Francis X. *WhoFI 92*
**Basile,** Frank Michel 1939- *WhoMW 92*
**Basile,** Louis Joseph 1924- *AmMWSc 92, WhoMW 92*
**Basile,** Michael 1948- *WhoAmL 92*
**Basile,** Paul Louis, Jr. 1945- *WhoAmL 92, WhoFI 92, WhoWest 92*
**Basile,** Robert Manlius 1916- *AmMWSc 92*
**Basilevsky,** Alexander 1943- *AmMWSc 92*
**Basili,** Victor Robert 1940- *AmMWSc 92*
**Basilico,** Claudio 1936- *AmMWSc 92*
**Basilides** *EncEarC*
**Basilio,** Eleanor Vasco 1961- *WhoWest 92*
**Basilius Celix** *EncEarC*
**Basilone,** Peter J 1920- *WhoAmP 91*
**Basin,** M A 1929- *AmMWSc 92*
**Basing,** Baron 1939- *Who 92*
**Basinger,** Earl *WhoRel 92*
**Basinger,** Jeanine 1936- *IntAu&W 91, WrDr 92*
**Basinger,** Kim 1953- *IntMPA 92, IntWW 91, WhoEnt 92A*
**Basinger,** Richard Craig 1938- *AmMWSc 92*
**Basinger,** Richard Lee 1941- *WhoAmL 92, WhoWest 92*
**Basingstoke,** Archdeacon of *Who 92*
**Basingstoke,** Bishop Suffragan of 1927- *Who 92*
**Basinski,** Anthony Joseph 1947- *WhoAmL 92*
**Basinski,** Michael *DrAPF 91*
**Basinski,** Zbigniew Stanislaw 1928- *IntWW 91, Who 92*
**Basir,** Ismail 1927- *IntWW 91*
**Baska,** James Louis 1927- *WhoFI 92*
**Baskakov,** Vladimir Yvtikhianovich 1921- *IntWW 91*
**Baske,** C. Alan 1927- *WhoMW 92*
**Basker,** Robin Michael 1936- *Who 92*
**Baskervill,** Charles Thornton 1953- *WhoAmL 92*
**Baskerville,** Charles 1870-1922 *DcNCBi 1*
**Baskerville,** Charles Alexander 1928- *AmMWSc 92, WhoBlA 92*
**Baskerville,** Gordon Lawson 1933- *AmMWSc 92*
**Baskerville,** John 1706-1775 *BlkwCEP*
**Baskerville,** Pearl 1929- *WhoBlA 92*
**Baskerville,** Penelope Anne 1946- *WhoBlA 92*
**Baskerville,** Randolph 1949- *WhoBlA 92*
**Baskerville,** Samuel J., Jr. 1933- *WhoBlA 92*
**Baskerville,** Tim 1949- *WhoEnt 92*
**Baskes,** Michael I 1943- *AmMWSc 92*
**Baskett,** Charles Henry 1872-1953 *TwCPaSc*
**Baskett,** Kenneth Gerald 1942- *WhoBlA 92*
**Baskett,** Thomas Sebree 1916- *AmMWSc 92, WhoMW 92*
**Baskette,** Ernest E., Jr. 1944- *WhoBlA 92*
**Baskette,** F Kenneth, Jr 1940- *WhoAmP 91*
**Baskin,** Andrew Lewis 1951- *WhoBlA 92*
**Baskin,** Charles Richard 1926- *WhoFI 92*
**Baskin,** Clarence L. 1927- *WhoBlA 92*
**Baskin,** Denis George 1941- *AmMWSc 92*
**Baskin,** E. F. 1939- *WhoMW 92*
**Baskin,** Elya 1950- *WhoEnt 92*
**Baskin,** Jerry Mack 1940- *AmMWSc 92*
**Baskin,** Leonard 1922- *FacFETw*
**Baskin,** Ronald J 1935- *AmMWSc 92*
**Baskin,** Shale Donald 1927- *WhoMW 92*
**Baskin,** Steven Ivan 1942- *AmMWSc 92*
**Baskin,** William Maxwell, Sr. 1921- *WhoAmL 92*
**Baskin,** Yvonne E. 1951- *WhoBlA 92*
**Baskins,** Lewis C. 1932- *WhoBlA 92*
**Baskir,** Emanuel 1929- *AmMWSc 92*
**Baskow,** Jacqueline 1951- *WhoEnt 92*
**Basler,** Eddie, Jr 1924- *AmMWSc 92*
**Basler,** John Michell 1926- *WhoWest 92*
**Basler,** Richard Alan 1939- *WhoWest 92*
**Basler,** Roy Prentice 1935- *AmMWSc 92*
**Basler,** Sabra *DrAPF 91*
**Basler,** Wayne Gordon 1930- *WhoFI 92*
**Basmadjian,** Diran 1929- *AmMWSc 92*
**Basmajian,** John Aram 1929- *AmMWSc 92*
**Basmajian,** John V 1921- *AmMWSc 92*
**Basmajian,** Walter 1922- *WhoAmP 91*
**Basmeson,** Gustavo Adolfo 1952- *WhoHisp 92*
**Basnett,** Patricia Moreland 1953- *WhoAmL 92*
**Basnight,** Marc 1947- *WhoAmP 91*
**Basolo,** Fred 1920- *AmMWSc 92, IntWW 91*
**Basore,** B L 1922- *AmMWSc 92*
**Basov,** Nikolai Gennadievich 1922- *Who 92, WhoNob 90*
**Basov,** Nikolai Gennadiievich 1922- *IntWW 91*
**Basov,** Vladimir Pavlovich d1987 *IntWW 91N*
**Basque,** David 1927- *WhoAmP 91*
**Basquiat,** Jean Michel 1960-1988 *WorArt 1980 [port]*
**Basri,** Gibor Broitman 1951- *WhoBlA 92*
**Basri,** Hasan *WhoRel 92*
**Basri,** Saul Abraham 1926- *AmMWSc 92*
**Bass** *Who 92*
**Bass Family** *NewYTBS 91 [port]*
**Bass,** Alice Cabaniss *DrAPF 91*
**Bass,** Allan Delmage 1910- *AmMWSc 92*
**Bass,** Anthony Duane 1960- *WhoBlA 92*
**Bass,** Arnold Marvin 1922- *AmMWSc 92*
**Bass,** Arthur 1941- *AmMWSc 92*
**Bass,** Barbara DeJong 1946- *WhoEnt 92*
**Bass,** Bernard M. 1925- *WrDr 92*
**Bass,** Brian John 1933- *IntAu&W 91*
**Bass,** Bryan Geoffrey 1934- *Who 92*
**Bass,** Charles Daniel 1934- *WhoRel 92*
**Bass,** Charles Foster 1952- *WhoAmP 91*
**Bass,** Charles Morris 1949- *WhoFI 92*
**Bass,** Charlotta Spears 1880-1969 *NotBlAW 92*
**Bass,** David A 1941- *AmMWSc 92*
**Bass,** David Eli *AmMWSc 92*
**Bass,** David Jason 1954- *WhoWest 92*
**Bass,** Dorothy Ussery *DrAPF 91*
**Bass,** Edgar Wales 1843-1918 *BiInAmS*
**Bass,** Ellen *DrAPF 91*
**Bass,** Eugene L 1942- *AmMWSc 92*
**Bass,** Floyd L. 1921- *WhoBlA 92*
**Bass,** Frank *TwCWW 91*
**Bass,** George F 1932- *AmMWSc 92*
**Bass,** George Harold 1936- *WhoRel 92*
**Bass,** George Houston 1938-1990 *WhoBlA 92N*
**Bass,** Harry Godfrey Mitchell 1914- *Who 92*
**Bass,** Henry Ellis 1943- *AmMWSc 92*
**Bass,** Herbert H. 1929- *WhoBlA 92*
**Bass,** Howard 1923- *IntAu&W 91, WrDr 92*
**Bass,** Hyman 1932- *AmMWSc 92*
**Bass,** Jack 1934- *IntAu&W 91, WrDr 92*
**Bass,** Jack 1938- *AmMWSc 92*
**Bass,** James Edwin 1953- *WhoRel 92*
**Bass,** James Gifford 1936- *WhoFI 92*
**Bass,** James L. 1899- *WhoBlA 92*
**Bass,** James Orin 1910- *WhoAmL 92, WhoFI 92*
**Bass,** James W 1930- *AmMWSc 92*
**Bass,** Jeffrey Stephen 1952- *WhoFI 92*
**Bass,** John F 1926- *WhoAmP 91*
**Bass,** John Franklin 1946- *WhoFI 92*
**Bass,** Jon Dolf 1933- *AmMWSc 92*
**Bass,** Jonathan Langer 1938- *AmMWSc 92*
**Bass,** Joseph Frank 1938- *WhoBlA 92*
**Bass,** Joseph Oscar 1933- *WhoRel 92*
**Bass,** Josie A. 1947- *WhoBlA 92*
**Bass,** Kenneth Carrington, III 1944- *WhoAmL 92, WhoAmP 91*
**Bass,** Kevin Charles 1959- *WhoBlA 92*
**Bass,** Leonard Channing 1941- *WhoBlA 92*
**Bass,** Leonard Joel 1943- *AmMWSc 92*
**Bass,** Manuel N 1927- *AmMWSc 92*
**Bass,** Marshall Brent *WhoBlA 92*
**Bass,** Mary Anna 1930- *AmMWSc 92*
**Bass,** Max H 1934- *AmMWSc 92*
**Bass,** Michael 1939- *AmMWSc 92*
**Bass,** Michael Lawrence 1945- *AmMWSc 92*
**Bass,** Milton *DrAPF 91*
**Bass,** Norman Herbert 1936- *AmMWSc 92*
**Bass,** Paul 1928- *AmMWSc 92*
**Bass,** Paul Eric 1925- *Who 92*
**Bass,** Perkins 1912- *WhoAmP 91*
**Bass,** Perry Richardson 1914- *WhoFI 92*
**Bass,** Richard O., Sr. *WhoRel 92*
**Bass,** Richard Samuel 1938- *WhoWest 92*
**Bass,** Rick 1958- *IntAu&W 91*
**Bass,** Robert Gerald 1933- *AmMWSc 92*
**Bass,** Robert Muse 1948- *WhoFI 92*
**Bass,** Robert P, Jr 1923- *WhoAmP 91*
**Bass,** Robert Thrane 1949- *WhoAmP 91*
**Bass,** Ronald *WhoEnt 92*
**Bass,** Ross 1918- *WhoAmP 91*
**Bass,** Saul 1920- *IntMPA 92, WhoEnt 92*
**Bass,** Saul 1921- *DcTwDes*
**Bass,** Steven Craig 1943- *AmMWSc 92*
**Bass,** Steven Murray 1957- *WhoEnt 92, WhoFI 92*
**Bass,** T J 1932- *TwCSFW 91, WrDr 92*
**Bass,** Thomas A. 1951- *WrDr 92*
**Bass,** Tim Lee 1953- *WhoEnt 92*
**Bass,** Tonya Raye 1963- *WhoEnt 92*
**Bass,** Treva Bell 1955- *WhoEnt 92*
**Bass,** William Marvin, III 1928- *AmMWSc 92*
**Bass,** William Thomas 1942- *AmMWSc 92*
**Bassani,** Giorgio 1916- *IntWW 91*
**Bassani,** Giuseppe Franco 1929- *IntWW 91*
**Bassano,** Louis 1942- *WhoAmP 91*
**Bassard,** Yvonne Brooks 1937- *WhoBlA 92*
**Basseches,** Harold 1923- *AmMWSc 92*
**Basseches,** Robert Treinis 1934- *WhoAmL 92*
**Bassel,** Robert Harold 1928- *AmMWSc 92*
**Bassermann,** Lujo *ConAu 36NR*
**Basset,** Bryan Ronald 1932- *Who 92*
**Basset,** Elizabeth 1908- *Who 92*
**Basset,** Michail Edward Rainton 1938- *IntWW 91*
**Bassett** *TwCPaSc*
**Bassett,** Alice Cook 1925- *WhoAmP 91*
**Bassett,** Alton Herman 1930- *AmMWSc 92*
**Bassett,** Arthur L 1935- *AmMWSc 92*
**Bassett,** Arthur Ray 1935- *WhoWest 92*
**Bassett,** Charles Andrew Loockerman 1924- *AmMWSc 92*
**Bassett,** David R 1939- *AmMWSc 92*
**Bassett,** Donald Edwin 1928- *WhoFI 92*
**Bassett,** Douglas Anthony 1927- *Who 92*
**Bassett,** Elizabeth Ewing 1937- *IntAu&W 91*
**Bassett,** Emmett W 1921- *AmMWSc 92*
**Bassett,** Henry Gordon 1924- *AmMWSc 92, WhoWest 92*
**Bassett,** Hurley *WhoRel 92*
**Bassett,** Jack *TwCWW 91*
**Bassett,** James Wilbur 1923- *AmMWSc 92*
**Bassett,** John Spencer 1867-1928 *BenetAL 91, DcNCBi 1*
**Bassett,** John Walden, Jr. 1938- *WhoAmL 92*
**Bassett,** John White Hughes 1915- *WhoEnt 92*
**Bassett,** Joseph M. 1948- *WhoFI 92*

**Bassett**, Joseph Yarnall, Jr 1927- *AmMWSc 92*
**Bassett**, Lawrence C 1931- *WhoFI 92*
**Bassett**, Leslie 1923- *ConCom 92, NewAmDM*
**Bassett**, Leslie Raymond 1923- *WhoEnt 92*
**Bassett**, Linda *IntMPA 92*
**Bassett**, Mark Julian 1940- *AmMWSc 92*
**Bassett**, Michelle Segall 1955- *WhoFI 92*
**Bassett**, Nigel F. *Who 92*
**Bassett**, Paul Merritt 1935- *WhoRel 92*
**Bassett**, Paul Robert 1945- *WhoWest 92*
**Bassett**, Ralph Edward 1944- *WhoEnt 92*
**Bassett**, Ronald Leslie 1924- *IntAu&W 91*
**Bassett**, Scott Gregory 1956- *WhoAmL 92*
**Bassett**, Tina *WhoFI 92*
**Bassett**, William Akers 1931- *AmMWSc 92*
**Bassett**, William Henry 1935- *WhoEnt 92*
**Bassett**, William W. 1932- *ConAu 34NR*
**Bassey**, Jennifer E. 1944- *WhoEnt 92*
**Bassey**, Linus A. *WhoBlA 92*
**Bassford**, Daniel Joseph 1949- *WhoMW 92*
**Bassham**, Genevieve Prieto 1939- *WhoHisp 92*
**Bassham**, James Alan 1922- *AmMWSc 92*
**Bassi**, Robert Amos 1942- *WhoMW 92*
**Bassi**, Sukh D *AmMWSc 92*
**Bassichis**, William 1937- *AmMWSc 92*
**Bassim**, Mohamad Nabil 1944- *AmMWSc 92*
**Bassin**, Robert Harris 1938- *AmMWSc 92*
**Bassingthwaighte**, James B 1929- *AmMWSc 92*
**Bassingthwaighte**, Keith 1943- *Who 92*
**Bassiouni**, M. Cherif 1937- *ConAu 34NR*
**Bassiouny**, Mohamed Abdel-Aziz 1937- *IntWW 91*
**Bassiouny**, Mohamed Ali 1941- *AmMWSc 92*
**Bassiri**, Mohammed Sidi Ibrahim 1942?- *HisDSpE*
**Bassner**, Sherri Lynn 1962- *AmMWSc 92*
**Basso**, Hamilton 1904-1964 *BenetAL 91*
**Basso**, Robert 1948- *WhoFI 92*
**Bassoff**, Joel Michael 1956- *WhoAmL 92*
**Bassole**, Bazomboue Leandre 1946- *IntWW 91*
**Bassuk**, Craig Allan 1956- *WhoEnt 92*
**Bast**, Robert Clinton, Jr *AmMWSc 92*
**Bast**, William *LesBEnT 92*
**Bast**, William Edwin 1931- *WhoEnt 92*
**Bastarache**, Julie Rico 1957- *WhoHisp 92*
**Bastardi**, Marilyn Patricia 1945- *WhoFI 92*
**Bastedo**, Wayne Webster 1948- *WhoAmL 92, WhoFI 92*
**Basten**, Henry *Who 92*
**Basti**, Fuli 1957- *IntWW 91*
**Bastiaans**, Glenn John 1947- *AmMWSc 92*
**Bastiaans**, Robert Henry 1948- *WhoFI 92*
**Bastiaanse**, Gerard C. 1935- *WhoAmL 92*
**Bastian**, Donald Noel 1925- *WhoRel 92*
**Bastian**, Dwight Ralph 1942- *WhoRel 92*
**Bastian**, Gert 1923- *IntWW 91*
**Bastian**, James W 1926- *AmMWSc 92*
**Bastian**, John F 1951- *AmMWSc 92*
**Bastian**, Joseph 1944- *AmMWSc 92*
**Bastian**, Walter 1922- *WhoMW 92*
**Bastianini**, Giuseppe 1899-1961 *BiDExR*
**Bastid**, Suzanne 1906- *IntWW 91*
**Bastida**, Elena Beck 1950- *WhoHisp 92*
**Bastidas**, Micaela *EncAmaz 91*
**Bastidas**, Rodrigo de 1460-1526 *HisDSpE*
**Bastidas**, Rodrigo de 1498-1570 *HisDSpE*
**Bastide**, Francois-Regis 1926- *IntWW 91*
**Bastidos**, Hugo A. *WhoHisp 92*
**Bastien**, Christopher Paul 1958- *WhoAmL 92*
**Bastin**, Edson Sewell 1843-1897 *BiInAmS*
**Bastin**, Gary 1950- *WhoAmP 91*
**Bastin**, John Andrew 1929- *Who 92*
**Bastin**, Jules 1889-1944 *FacFETw*
**Bastine**, Lillian Beatrice d1989 *WhoBlA 92N*
**Basto**, La Donna Joan 1933- *WhoMW 92*
**Bastoky**, Bruce Michael 1953- *WhoFI 92, WhoMW 92*
**Baston**, Elvira 1944- *WhoHisp 92*
**Baston**, Janet Evelyn 1941- *AmMWSc 92*
**Bastress**, E Karl 1929- *AmMWSc 92*
**Basu**, Asit Prakas 1937- *AmMWSc 92*
**Basu**, Debabrata 1924- *AmMWSc 92*
**Basu**, Jyoti 1914- *IntWW 91*
**Basu**, Manju 1942- *AmMWSc 92*
**Basu**, Mitali 1951- *AmMWSc 92*
**Basu**, Prasanta Kumar 1922- *AmMWSc 92*
**Basu**, Subhash Chandra 1938- *AmMWSc 92*
**Basu**, Tapan Kumar *AmMWSc 92*
**Basu-Mullick**, Sabyasachi 1958- *WhoFI 92*
**Basulto**, Maria 1949- *WhoHisp 92*
**Basurto**, Luis G 1921- *IntAu&W 91*
**Basye**, Paul Edmond 1901- *WhoWest 92*
**Bat-Uul**, Erdeniin 1957- *IntWW 91*
**Bata**, Rudolph Andrew, Jr. 1947- *WhoAmL 92*
**Bata**, Thomas John 1914- *IntWW 91*
**Bataille**, Henri 1872-1922 *GuFrLit 1*
**Bataille**, Jacques Albert 1926- *WhoBlA 92*
**Bataillon**, Joseph Francis 1949- *WhoAmP 91*
**Batalden**, Paul B 1941- *AmMWSc 92*
**Batalin**, Yuriy Petrovich 1927- *IntWW 91, SovUnBD*
**Batalov**, Aleksey Vladimirovich 1928- *IntWW 91, SovUnBD*
**Batalov**, Nikolay Petrovich 1899-1937 *SovUnBD*
**Batanides**, Arthur 1923- *WhoEnt 92*
**Batarse**, Anthony Abraham, Jr. 1933- *WhoHisp 92, WhoWest 92*
**Batarse**, Elizabeth Carina 1935- *WhoHisp 92*
**Batarseh**, Issa Eid 1961- *WhoMW 92*
**Batastini**, Armando Emilio, Jr 1930- *WhoAmP 91*
**Batay-Csorba**, Peter Andrew 1945- *AmMWSc 92*
**Batayneh**, Ghassan Jason Rizek 1960- *WhoFI 92*
**Batbayar**, Bat-Erdeniin 1955- *IntWW 91*
**Batbedat**, Jean 1926- *IntWW 91*
**Batchelder**, Alice M. 1944- *WhoAmL 92*
**Batchelder**, Anne Stuart 1920- *WhoMW 92*
**Batchelder**, Arthur Roland 1932- *AmMWSc 92*
**Batchelder**, Bruce Anderson 1942- *WhoRel 92*
**Batchelder**, David G 1920- *AmMWSc 92*
**Batchelder**, Gerald M 1925- *AmMWSc 92*
**Batchelder**, John Montgomery 1811-1892 *BiInAmS*
**Batchelder**, John Thomas Hutchins 1956- *WhoAmL 92*
**Batchelder**, Kenneth Atherton 1927- *WhoRel 92*
**Batchelder**, Kenneth Thomas 1932- *WhoIns 92*
**Batchelder**, Loren Harrison 1846- *BiInAmS*
**Batchelder**, William F *WhoAmP 91*
**Batchelder**, William F. 1926- *WhoAmL 92*
**Batchelder**, William George 1942- *WhoAmP 91*
**Batchelder**, William George, III 1942- *WhoMW 92*
**Batcheller**, Joseph Ann 1932- *WhoFI 92*
**Batchelor**, Asbury Collins 1929- *WhoBlA 92*
**Batchelor**, B D 1928- *AmMWSc 92*
**Batchelor**, Bernard Phillip 1924- *TwCPaSc*
**Batchelor**, David 1943- *WrDr 92*
**Batchelor**, David Brook Lockhart 1943- *IntAu&W 91*
**Batchelor**, Fines Frank, Jr. 1927- *WhoAmL 92*
**Batchelor**, George Keith 1920- *IntWW 91, Who 92, WrDr 92*
**Batchelor**, Ivor 1916- *Who 92*
**Batchelor**, James Kent 1934- *WhoWest 92*
**Batchelor**, John 1942- *WrDr 92*
**Batchelor**, John Barham 1942- *IntAu&W 91*
**Batchelor**, John Calvin 1948- *IntAu&W 91, TwCSFW 91, WrDr 92*
**Batchelor**, John W 1914- *AmMWSc 92*
**Batchelor**, Reg *TwCWW 91*
**Batchelor**, Richard 1931- *Who 92*
**Batchelor**, Suzanne Marie 1961- *WhoAmL 92*
**Batcher**, Kenneth Edward 1935- *AmMWSc 92*
**Batchman**, John Clifford 1944- *WhoEnt 92, WhoMW 92*
**Batchman**, Theodore E 1940- *AmMWSc 92*
**Batcho**, Andrew David 1934- *AmMWSc 92*
**Batdorf**, Robert Ludwig 1926- *AmMWSc 92*
**Batdorf**, Samuel Burbridge 1914- *AmMWSc 92*
**Bate**, David 1916- *Who 92*
**Bate**, Edwin 1901- *Who 92*
**Bate**, Francis 1853-1950 *TwCPaSc*
**Bate**, Geoffrey 1929- *AmMWSc 92*
**Bate**, George Lee 1924- *AmMWSc 92*
**Bate**, Jennifer Lucy 1944- *IntWW 91*
**Bate**, Jonathan 1958- *ConAu 134*
**Bate**, Marilyn Anne 1939- *WhoMW 92*
**Bate**, Robert Thomas 1931- *AmMWSc 92*
**Bate**, W Jackson 1918- *IntAu&W 91*
**Bate**, Walter Jackson 1918- *Who 92, WrDr 92*
**Bate**, William 1920- *Who 92*
**Bate**, William Joseph, Jr 1934- *WhoAmP 91*
**Bateham**, Josephine Abiah Penfield C. 1829-1901 *RelLAm 91*
**Bately**, Janet Margaret 1932- *Who 92*
**Bateman**, Andrew 1959- *AmMWSc 92*
**Bateman**, Ann Creighton 1943- *WhoRel 92, WhoWest 92*
**Bateman**, Barry Lynn 1943- *AmMWSc 92*
**Bateman**, Bradley William 1956- *WhoMW 92*
**Bateman**, Cecil 1910- *Who 92*
**Bateman**, David Alfred 1946- *WhoAmL 92*
**Bateman**, Dottye Jane Spencer *WhoFI 92*
**Bateman**, Durward F 1934- *AmMWSc 92*
**Bateman**, Felice Davidson 1922- *AmMWSc 92*
**Bateman**, Geoffrey 1906- *Who 92*
**Bateman**, Giles Hirst Litton 1944- *WhoFI 92*
**Bateman**, H.M. 1887-1970 *TwCPaSc*
**Bateman**, Harold Harding 1923- *WhoMW 92*
**Bateman**, Herbert H. 1928- *AlmAP 92 [port]*
**Bateman**, Herbert Harvell 1928- *WhoAmP 91*
**Bateman**, James 1893-1959 *TwCPaSc*
**Bateman**, Jason 1969- *IntMPA 92*
**Bateman**, John Henry 1934- *WhoFI 92*
**Bateman**, John Hugh 1941- *AmMWSc 92*
**Bateman**, John Laurens 1926- *AmMWSc 92*
**Bateman**, Joseph R 1922- *AmMWSc 92*
**Bateman**, Justine 1966- *IntMPA 92, WhoEnt 92*
**Bateman**, Leslie Clifford 1915- *IntWW 91, Who 92*
**Bateman**, Mary-Rose Christine 1935- *Who 92*
**Bateman**, Michael Allen 1952- *WhoBlA 92*
**Bateman**, Mildred Mitchell 1922- *AmMWSc 92*
**Bateman**, Paul Terence 1946- *Who 92*
**Bateman**, Paul Trevier 1919- *AmMWSc 92*
**Bateman**, Ralph 1910- *IntWW 91, Who 92*
**Bateman**, Raymond Henry 1927- *WhoAmP 91*
**Bateman**, Richard George Saumarez La T. *Who 92*
**Bateman**, Robert McLellan 1930- *IntWW 91*
**Bateman**, Rocklin *WhoAmP 91*
**Bateman**, Samuel T, Jr 1936- *WhoAmP 91*
**Bateman**, Sidney Frances 1823-1881 *BenetAL 91*
**Batemarco**, Robert John 1952- *WhoFI 92*
**Batenburg**, Andries 1922- *IntWW 91*
**Bates**, Alan 1934- *IntMPA 92, IntWW 91, Who 92, WhoEnt 92*
**Bates**, Alfred 1944- *Who 92*
**Bates**, Allan Frederick 1911- *Who 92*
**Bates**, Alonzo W. 1939- *WhoBlA 92*
**Bates**, Amy 1961- *WhoMW 92*
**Bates**, Arlo 1850-1918 *BenetAL 91*
**Bates**, Arthur Verdi 1916- *WhoBlA 92*
**Bates**, Bart S 1963- *WhoAmP 91*
**Bates**, Betty F 1931- *WhoAmP 91*
**Bates**, Billie Rae 1968- *WhoMW 92*
**Bates**, Bonnie-Jo Grieve 1949- *WhoMW 92*
**Bates**, Bradford 1937- *WhoMW 92*
**Bates**, Brian Edward 1957- *WhoAmL 92*
**Bates**, Carl H 1939- *AmMWSc 92*
**Bates**, Charles Carpenter 1918- *AmMWSc 92*
**Bates**, Charles Emerson 1946- *WhoWest 92*
**Bates**, Charles Johnson 1930- *AmMWSc 92, WhoMW 92*
**Bates**, Charles Walter 1953- *WhoFI 92, WhoWest 92*
**Bates**, Clayton Wilson, Jr 1932- *AmMWSc 92, WhoBlA 92*
**Bates**, Craig Dana 1952- *WhoWest 92*
**Bates**, Daisy *WhoBlA 92*
**Bates**, Daisy 1920- *NotBlAW 92 [port]*
**Bates**, David 1916- *Who 92*
**Bates**, David 1952- *WorArt 1980 [port]*
**Bates**, David Frank 1928- *Who 92*
**Bates**, David James 1928- *AmMWSc 92*
**Bates**, David Martin 1934- *AmMWSc 92*
**Bates**, David Robert 1916- *IntWW 91*
**Bates**, David Vincent 1922- *AmMWSc 92, IntWW 91*
**Bates**, David Vliet 1938- *WhoRel 92*
**Bates**, Dawson *Who 92*
**Bates**, Donald F *WhoAmP 91*
**Bates**, Donald George 1933- *AmMWSc 92*
**Bates**, Donald W 1918- *AmMWSc 92*
**Bates**, Douglas Martin 1949- *AmMWSc 92*
**Bates**, Dwight Lee 1943- *WhoWest 92*
**Bates**, Edward John 1911- *Who 92*
**Bates**, Edward Lawrence 1948- *WhoWest 92*
**Bates**, Edward Payson 1844?-1919 *BiInAmS*
**Bates**, Elisha 1781-1861 *AmPeW*
**Bates**, Eric 1908- *Who 92*
**Bates**, Ernest Alphonso 1936- *WhoBlA 92*
**Bates**, Ernest Sutherland 1879-1939 *BenetAL 91*
**Bates**, G William 1940- *AmMWSc 92*
**Bates**, Geoffrey Voltelin 1921- *Who 92*
**Bates**, George Edmonds 1933- *WhoRel 92, WhoWest 92*
**Bates**, George Winston *AmMWSc 92*
**Bates**, Gerald Earl 1933- *WhoRel 92*
**Bates**, Gladys Noel 1920- *WhoBlA 92*
**Bates**, Gordon *Who 92*
**Bates**, Grace Elizabeth 1914- *AmMWSc 92*
**Bates**, Grace Kamp 1917- *WhoWest 92*
**Bates**, Guy Allen 1958- *WhoWest 92*
**Bates**, H E 1905-1974 *ConAu 34NR, FacFETw, RfGEnL 91*
**Bates**, Harold Brennan, Jr 1935- *AmMWSc 92*
**Bates**, Harry 1900- *TwCSFW 91*
**Bates**, Henry Melvin 1918- *WhoBlA 92*
**Bates**, Herbert T 1913- *AmMWSc 92*
**Bates**, Howard Francis 1927- *AmMWSc 92*
**Bates**, J Lambert 1928- *AmMWSc 92*
**Bates**, James 1926- *WrDr 92*
**Bates**, James P. M. *Who 92*
**Bates**, Janice 1955- *WhoFI 92*
**Bates**, Jefferson D 1920- *ConAu 34NR*
**Bates**, Jim 1941- *WhoAmP 91, WhoWest 92*
**Bates**, John *Who 92*
**Bates**, John 1904- *Who 92*
**Bates**, John Bertram 1914- *AmMWSc 92*
**Bates**, John Bryant 1942- *AmMWSc 92*
**Bates**, John Burnham 1918- *WhoAmL 92*
**Bates**, John Cecil, Jr. 1936- *WhoAmL 92*
**Bates**, John Dawson 1921- *Who 92*
**Bates**, John Dodd 1934- *WhoWest 92*
**Bates**, John Gerald Higgs 1936- *Who 92*
**Bates**, John Milton 1914- *WhoBlA 92*
**Bates**, John Norman 1954- *WhoRel 92*
**Bates**, John Robert 1947- *WhoMW 92*
**Bates**, Joseph H 1933- *AmMWSc 92*
**Bates**, Katharine Lee 1850-1929 *BenetAL 91*
**Bates**, Kathy *NewYTBS 91 [port]*
**Bates**, Kathy 1948- *CurBio 91 [port], IntMPA 92, WhoEnt 92*
**Bates**, Kathy 1949?- *News 91 [port]*
**Bates**, Kenneth Norris 1949- *WhoWest 92*
**Bates**, Kermit Francis, Jr *WhoAmP 91*
**Bates**, Laurence William 1958- *WhoAmL 92*
**Bates**, Leslie Fleetwood 1897-1978 *FacFETw*
**Bates**, Lionel Ray, Sr. 1955- *WhoBlA 92*
**Bates**, Lloyd M 1924- *AmMWSc 92*
**Bates**, Louise Rebecca 1932- *WhoBlA 92*
**Bates**, Lura Wheeler 1932- *WhoFI 92*
**Bates**, Lynn Shannon 1940- *AmMWSc 92*
**Bates**, Malcolm Rowland 1934- *WhoFI 92*
**Bates**, Marel Kenneth 1943- *WhoWest 92*
**Bates**, Margaret Westbrook 1926- *AmMWSc 92*
**Bates**, Mark Alan 1963- *WhoMW 92*
**Bates**, Mark Roger 1956- *WhoAmL 92*
**Bates**, Martin 1939- *TwCPaSc*
**Bates**, Mary Lynn Dovith 1947- *WhoAmL 92*
**Bates**, Merrick Stuart B. *Who 92*
**Bates**, Milton J 1945- *IntAu&W 91*
**Bates**, Nathaniel Rubin 1931- *WhoAmP 91, WhoBlA 92*
**Bates**, Oric 1883-1918 *BiInAmS*
**Bates**, Paul Spencer 1940- *Who 92*
**Bates**, Percy 1932- *WhoBlA 92*
**Bates**, Peter Edward Gascoigne 1924- *Who 92*
**Bates**, Peter Miller 1955- *WhoMW 92*
**Bates**, Peter William 1947- *AmMWSc 92*
**Bates**, Ralph 1899- *Who 92*
**Bates**, Ralph 1940- *ConTFT 9*
**Bates**, Rex James 1923- *WhoFI 92, WhoMW 92*
**Bates**, Richard Doane, Jr 1944- *AmMWSc 92*
**Bates**, Richard Heaton Tunstall d1990 *IntWW 91N*
**Bates**, Richard Pierce 1926- *AmMWSc 92*
**Bates**, Robert Brown 1933- *AmMWSc 92*
**Bates**, Robert Clair 1944- *AmMWSc 92*
**Bates**, Robert E., Jr. 1934- *WhoBlA 92*
**Bates**, Robert Latimer 1912- *AmMWSc 92*
**Bates**, Robert P 1932- *AmMWSc 92*
**Bates**, Robert Wesley 1904- *AmMWSc 92*
**Bates**, Robert William 1961- *WhoAmL 92*
**Bates**, Rodney Lin 1946- *WhoMW 92*
**Bates**, Roger 1947- *TwCPaSc*
**Bates**, Roger Gordon 1912- *AmMWSc 92*
**Bates**, Scott *DrAPF 91*
**Bates**, Stephen 1958- *IntAu&W 91*
**Bates**, Stephen Roger 1944- *AmMWSc 92*
**Bates**, Steven Latimer 1940- *WhoMW 92*
**Bates**, Stewart Taverner 1926- *Who 92*
**Bates**, Sturgis Goodwin, III 1937- *WhoAmP 91*
**Bates**, Thomas Edward 1926- *AmMWSc 92*
**Bates**, Thomas Fulcher 1917- *AmMWSc 92*
**Bates**, Timothy 1950- *WhoAmP 91*
**Bates**, Timothy Dexter 1948- *WhoAmL 92, WhoAmP 91*
**Bates**, Timothy Mark 1960- *WhoAmL 92*

**Bates,** Tom 1938- *WhoAmP 91*
**Bates,** Trevor 1921- *TwCPaSc*
**Bates,** Walter Alan 1925- *WhoAmL 92*
**Bates,** William, III 1949- *WhoAmL 92*
**Bates,** William J. 1952- *WhoBlA 92*
**Bates,** William K 1936- *AmMWSc 92*
**Bates,** William Stanley 1920- *Who 92*
**Bates,** Willie Earl 1940- *WhoBlA 92*
**Bates-George,** Mary Beth 1955- *WhoEnt 92*
**Bates-Parker,** Linda 1944- *WhoBlA 92*
**Bateson** *Who 92*
**Bateson,** Andrew James 1925- *Who 92*
**Bateson,** John Swinburne 1942- *Who 92*
**Bateson,** Marion 1935- *WhoWest 92*
**Bateson,** Patrick 1938- *Who 92*
**Bateson,** Paul Patrick Gordon 1938- *IntWW 91*
**Bateson,** Robert Neil 1931- *AmMWSc 92*
**Bateson,** William 1861-1926 *FacFETw*
**Batey,** Harry Hallsted, Jr 1923- *AmMWSc 92*
**Batey,** Robert William 1918- *AmMWSc 92*
**Batey,** Tom *WrDr 92*
**Bath,** Archdeacon of *Who 92*
**Bath,** Marquess of 1905- *Who 92*
**Bath,** Alan Alfred 1924- *Who 92*
**Bath,** David E *WhoAmP 91*
**Bath,** Donald Alan 1947- *AmMWSc 92*
**Bath,** Donna Swarts 1944- *WhoEnt 92*
**Bath,** James Edmond 1938- *AmMWSc 92*
**Bath,** Patricia E. 1942- *WhoBlA 92*
**Bath,** Peter Donald Henry 1952- *WhoFI 92, WhoMW 92*
**Bath And Wells,** Bishop of 1936- *Who 92*
**Batha,** Howard Dean 1925- *AmMWSc 92*
**Bathala,** Mohinder S 1940- *AmMWSc 92*
**Bathen,** Karl Hans 1934- *AmMWSc 92*
**Bather,** Paul Charles 1947- *WhoAmP 91, WhoBlA 92*
**Bathiat,** Leonie 1898- *IntWW 91*
**Bathke,** Warren E. *WhoRel 92*
**Batho,** Edward Hubert 1925- *AmMWSc 92*
**Batho,** Peter 1939- *Who 92*
**Batho,** Walter James Scott 1925- *Who 92*
**Bathon,** Thomas Neil 1961- *WhoFI 92*
**Bathum,** Richard Willis 1951- *WhoAmL 92*
**Bathurst** *Who 92*
**Bathurst,** Bishop of 1942- *Who 92*
**Bathurst,** Earl 1927- *Who 92*
**Bathurst,** Benjamin 1936- *Who 92*
**Bathurst,** Bill *DrAPF 91*
**Bathurst,** Frederick Peter Methuen Hervey 1903- *Who 92*
**Bathurst,** Joan Caroline *Who 92*
**Bathurst,** Maurice 1913- *Who 92*
**Bathurst Norman,** George Alfred 1939- *Who 92*
**Batich,** Christopher David 1943- *AmMWSc 92*
**Batiffol,** Henri 1905- *IntWW 91*
**Batine,** Rafael 1947- *WhoBlA 92*
**Batista,** Alberto Victor 1963- *WhoAmL 92, WhoHisp 92*
**Batista,** Duane R. 1934- *WhoAmL 92*
**Batista,** George *WhoHisp 92*
**Batista,** Juan E. 1936- *WhoHisp 92*
**Batista,** Julio G. *WhoHisp 92*
**Batista,** Leon Felix 1964- *WhoHisp 92*
**Batista,** Santiago 1931- *WhoHisp 92*
**Batista Gaston,** Melchor Ignacio 1944- *WhoHisp 92*
**Batista-Wales,** Maria del Carmen 1960- *WhoHisp 92*
**Batista y Zaldivar,** Fulgencio 1901-1973 *FacFETw*
**Batiste,** Edna E. 1931- *WhoBlA 92*
**Batiste,** Mary Virginia 1925- *WhoBlA 92*
**Batiste,** Robert Joseph 1950- *WhoFI 92*
**Batiste,** Spencer Lee 1945- *Who 92*
**Batitsky,** Pavel Fedorovich 1910- *SovUnBD*
**Batiz Campbell,** Enrique 1942- *IntWW 91*
**Batiza,** Rodey 1947- *WhoWest 92*
**Batjer,** Cameron McVicar 1919- *WhoAmP 91*
**Batki,** John *DrAPF 91*
**Batkin,** Stanley 1912- *AmMWSc 92*
**Batla,** Raymond John, Jr. 1947- *WhoAmL 92, WhoFI 92*
**Batley,** Frank 1920- *AmMWSc 92*
**Batley,** John Geoffrey 1930- *Who 92*
**Batley,** Walter 1850-1936 *TwCPaSc*
**Batliner,** Gerard 1928- *IntWW 91*
**Batlivala,** Robert Bomi D. 1940- *WhoFI 92, WhoMW 92*
**Batlogg,** Bertram *AmMWSc 92*
**Batmunh,** Jambyn 1926- *IntWW 91*
**Batoni,** Pompeo Girolamo 1708-1787 *BlkwCEP*
**Bator,** Francis Michel 1925- *WhoFI 92*
**Bator,** Robert J. 1939- *WhoMW 92*
**Batorewicz,** Wadim 1934- *AmMWSc 92*
**Batory,** Ronald Louis 1950- *WhoFI 92, WhoMW 92*
**Batozech,** Jeffrey 1960- *WhoIns 92*
**Batra,** Gopal Krishan 1943- *AmMWSc 92*
**Batra,** Inder Paul 1942- *AmMWSc 92*
**Batra,** Karam Vir 1932- *AmMWSc 92*
**Batra,** Lekh Raj 1929- *AmMWSc 92*
**Batra,** Narendra K 1943- *AmMWSc 92*
**Batra,** Peter Rakesh 1965- *WhoMW 92*
**Batra,** Prem Parkash 1936- *AmMWSc 92*
**Batra,** Romesh Chander 1947- *AmMWSc 92, WhoMW 92*
**Batra,** Subhash Kumar 1935- *AmMWSc 92*
**Batra,** Suzanne Wellington Tubby 1937- *AmMWSc 92*
**Batra,** Tilak Raj 1936- *AmMWSc 92*
**Batres,** Eduardo *WhoEnt 92*
**Batrin,** George Leslie 1957- *AmMWSc 92*
**Batsakis,** John G 1929- *AmMWSc 92*
**Batsanov,** Boris Terentevich 1927- *IntWW 91*
**Batsanyi,** Janos 1763-1845 *BlkwCEP*
**Batscha,** Robert Michael 1945- *WhoEnt 92, WhoFI 92*
**Batsford,** B.T. d1904 *DcLB 106 [port]*
**Batsford,** Brian Caldwell Cook d1991 *Who 92N*
**Batshaw,** Mark Levitt 1945- *AmMWSc 92*
**Batson,** Alan Percy 1932- *AmMWSc 92*
**Batson,** Blair Everett 1920- *AmMWSc 92*
**Batson,** Charles Alvin 1916- *WhoEnt 92*
**Batson,** David Banks 1944- *AmMWSc 92*
**Batson,** David Warren 1956- *WhoAmL 92*
**Batson,** Flora 1864-1906 *NewAmDM, NotBlAW 92*
**Batson,** Gordon B 1932- *AmMWSc 92*
**Batson,** Margaret Bailly 1914- *AmMWSc 92*
**Batson,** Oscar Randolph 1916- *AmMWSc 92*
**Batson,** Raymond Milner 1931- *WhoWest 92*
**Batson,** Richard Neal 1941- *WhoAmL 92*
**Batson,** Ruth Marion *WhoBlA 92*
**Batson,** William Cleveland, III 1951- *WhoRel 92*
**Batson,** William Edward, Jr 1942- *AmMWSc 92*
**Batsukh,** Damdinsurengiin 1952- *IntWW 91*
**Batt,** David L 1934- *WhoAmP 91*
**Batt,** Ellen Rae 1934- *AmMWSc 92*
**Batt,** Neil Leonard Charles 1937- *IntWW 91*
**Batt,** Nick 1952- *WhoAmL 92, WhoFI 92, WhoMW 92*
**Batt,** Philip E *WhoAmP 91*
**Batt,** Raymond Warren 1933- *WhoAmL 92*
**Batt,** Reginald Joseph Alexander d1991 *Who 92N*
**Batt,** Robert E 1933- *WhoAmP 91*
**Batt,** Russell Howard 1938- *AmMWSc 92*
**Batt,** William 1931- *AmMWSc 92*
**Battaglia,** Adolfo 1930- *IntWW 91*
**Battaglia,** Basil Richard 1935- *WhoAmP 91*
**Battaglia,** David P 1931- *WhoAmP 91*
**Battaglia,** Frederick Camillo 1932- *AmMWSc 92*
**Battaglia,** Joseph Paul 1950- *WhoEnt 92*
**Battaglia,** Michael Salvatore 1944- *WhoFI 92*
**Battaglia,** Raymond A. 1957- *WhoEnt 92*
**Battaglia,** Raymond William 1958- *WhoAmL 92*
**Battaglia,** Richard Alfred 1943- *WhoMW 92*
**Battaglia,** Richard Anthony 1955- *WhoWest 92*
**Battaglia,** Robert Kenneth 1939- *WhoWest 92*
**Battaile,** Julian 1925- *AmMWSc 92*
**Battan,** Louis Joseph 1923- *AmMWSc 92*
**Battarbee,** Harold Douglas 1940- *AmMWSc 92*
**Batte,** Edward G 1921- *AmMWSc 92*
**Batte,** William Granville 1927- *AmMWSc 92*
**Batteast,** Margaret W. 1904- *WhoBlA 92*
**Batteast,** Robert V. 1931- *WhoBlA 92*
**Batten,** Alan Gary 1943- *WhoEnt 92*
**Batten,** Alan Henry 1933- *AmMWSc 92, IntWW 91*
**Batten,** Anne K 1932- *WhoAmP 91*
**Batten,** Bruce Edgar *AmMWSc 92*
**Batten,** Charles Francis 1942- *AmMWSc 92*
**Batten,** Frank 1927- *WhoFI 92*
**Batten,** George L, Jr 1952- *AmMWSc 92*
**Batten,** George Washington, Jr 1937- *AmMWSc 92*
**Batten,** Grace Ruth 1943- *WhoBlA 92*
**Batten,** James Knox 1936- *WhoFI 92*
**Batten,** James William 1919- *WrDr 92*
**Batten,** John 1924- *Who 92*
**Batten,** John Charles 1924- *IntWW 91*
**Batten,** Mark Wilfred 1905- *TwCPaSc*
**Batten,** Mark Wilfrid *Who 92*
**Batten,** Michael Ellsworth 1940- *WhoFI 92, WhoMW 92*
**Batten,** Patti Sue 1961- *WhoRel 92*
**Batten,** Roger Lyman 1923- *AmMWSc 92*
**Batten,** Stephen Duval 1945- *Who 92*
**Batten,** T. R. 1904- *WrDr 92*
**Batten,** Tony 1935- *WhoBlA 92*
**Batten,** William Milfred 1909- *IntWW 91*
**Battenberg,** Thomas V. 1941- *WhoEnt 92*
**Battenburg,** Joseph R 1934- *AmMWSc 92*
**Battenhouse,** Roy W. 1912- *WrDr 92*
**Batter,** John F, Jr 1931- *AmMWSc 92*
**Batter,** John Frederic, III 1957- *WhoAmL 92*
**Batterbury,** Paul Tracy Shepherd 1934- *Who 92*
**Batterman,** Boris William 1930- *AmMWSc 92*
**Batterman,** Robert Coleman 1911- *AmMWSc 92, WhoWest 92*
**Batterman,** Steven C 1937- *AmMWSc 92*
**Battern,** Timothy Hill 1950- *WhoAmL 92*
**Battersby,** Alan Rushton 1925- *IntWW 91, Who 92*
**Battersby,** Matthew Richard 1953- *WhoAmL 92*
**Battersby,** Patricia Josephine 1951- *WhoAmL 92*
**Battersby,** Robert Christopher 1924- *Who 92*
**Battershell,** Robert Dean 1931- *AmMWSc 92*
**Batterson,** J. Robert 1937- *WhoIns 92*
**Batterson,** James Robert, Sr. 1937- *WhoAmL 92*
**Batterson,** Steven L 1950- *AmMWSc 92*
**Batterson,** William Mark, III 1954- *WhoEnt 92*
**Battestin,** Martin Carey 1930- *IntAu&W 91, WrDr 92*
**Batteux,** Charles 1713-1780 *BlkwCEP*
**Battey,** James F 1952- *AmMWSc 92*
**Battey,** Richard Howard 1929- *WhoAmL 92*
**Battey,** Robert 1828-1895 *BiInAmS*
**Battiato,** David Alan 1952- *WhoAmL 92*
**Battie,** David 1942- *ConAu 135*
**Battie,** William 1704-1776 *BlkwCEP*
**Batties,** Paul Terry 1941- *WhoBlA 92*
**Battifora,** Hector A 1930- *AmMWSc 92*
**Battigelli,** Mario C 1927- *AmMWSc 92*
**Battin,** B W 1941- *IntAu&W 91*
**Battin,** Cynthia Ann Price 1957- *WhoWest 92*
**Battin,** James Franklin 1925- *WhoAmL 92, WhoWest 92*
**Battin,** M. Pabst *DrAPF 91*
**Battin,** Richard H 1925- *AmMWSc 92*
**Battin,** Wendy *DrAPF 91*
**Battin,** William James 1920- *AmMWSc 92*
**Battin,** William T 1927- *AmMWSc 92*
**Battino,** Rubin 1931- *AmMWSc 92, WhoMW 92*
**Battiscombe,** Christopher Charles Richard 1940- *Who 92*
**Battiscombe,** Georgina 1905- *Who 92, WrDr 92*
**Battiscombe,** Georgina 1911- *IntAu&W 91*
**Battishill,** Anthony 1937- *Who 92*
**Battison,** John Henry 1915- *WhoEnt 92*
**Battista,** Arthur Francis 1920- *AmMWSc 92*
**Battista,** Nicholas Rudolph 1951- *WhoFI 92*
**Battista,** Orlando Aloysius 1917- *AmMWSc 92, IntWW 91*
**Battista,** Sam P 1924- *AmMWSc 92*
**Battistati,** Louisa *EncAmaz 91*
**Battiste,** David Ray 1946- *AmMWSc 92*
**Battiste,** Merle Andrew 1933- *AmMWSc 92*
**Battisti,** Angelo James 1945- *AmMWSc 92*
**Battisti,** Frank Joseph 1922- *WhoAmL 92*
**Battisti,** Frank L. 1931- *WhoEnt 92*
**Battisto,** Jack Richard 1922- *AmMWSc 92*
**Battisto,** Joseph W 1931- *WhoAmP 91*
**Battistoli,** Geraldine 1945- *WhoAmL 92*
**Battiston,** Donald Lino 1941- *WhoRel 92*
**Battjes,** Carl Robert 1929- *WhoWest 92*
**Battle,** Bernard J., Sr. 1927- *WhoBlA 92*
**Battle,** Charles E. 1953- *WhoBlA 92*
**Battle,** Cullen Andrews 1829-1905 *DcNCBi 1*
**Battle,** Dennis Frank Orlando 1942- *Who 92*
**Battle,** Edward Gene 1931- *WhoFI 92, WhoWest 92*
**Battle,** Elisha 1723-1799 *DcNCBi 1*
**Battle,** Ephraim d1798 *DcNCBi 1*
**Battle,** Felix *IntAu&W 91X*
**Battle,** George Edward, Jr. 1947- *WhoRel 92*
**Battle,** George Gordon 1868-1949 *DcNCBi 1*
**Battle,** Gloria Jean 1950- *WhoBlA 92*
**Battle,** Helen Irene 1903- *AmMWSc 92*
**Battle,** Herbert Bemerton 1862-1929 *DcNCBi 1*
**Battle,** Jacob 1852-1916 *DcNCBi 1*
**Battle,** Jacqueline 1962- *WhoBlA 92*
**Battle,** James Smith 1786-1854 *DcNCBi 1*
**Battle,** Joe David 1958- *WhoMW 92*
**Battle,** Joe Turner 1941- *WhoBlA 92*
**Battle,** Joel 1779-1829 *DcNCBi 1*
**Battle,** John Dominic 1951- *Who 92*
**Battle,** John Sidney 1962- *WhoBlA 92*
**Battle,** John Thomas Johnson 1859-1940 *DcNCBi 1*
**Battle,** Joseph F 1937- *WhoAmP 91*
**Battle,** Kathleen *IntWW 91, WhoBlA 92*
**Battle,** Kathleen 1948- *ConMus 6 [port], NewAmDM*
**Battle,** Kathleen Deanna *WhoEnt 92*
**Battle,** Kemp Davis 1888-1973 *DcNCBi 1*
**Battle,** Kemp Plummer 1831-1919 *DcNCBi 1*
**Battle,** Kemp Plummer, Jr. 1859-1922 *DcNCBi 1*
**Battle,** Kenny 1964- *WhoBlA 92*
**Battle,** Leonard Carroll 1929- *WhoAmL 92*
**Battle,** Lucius D 1918- *WhoAmP 91*
**Battle,** Lucius Durham 1918- *IntWW 91*
**Battle,** Mark G. 1924- *WhoBlA 92*
**Battle,** Maurice Tazwell 1926- *WhoBlA 92*
**Battle,** Richard Henry 1835-1912 *DcNCBi 1*
**Battle,** Samuel Westray 1854-1927 *DcNCBi 1*
**Battle,** Thomas Cornell 1946- *WhoBlA 92*
**Battle,** Thomas Hall 1860-1936 *DcNCBi 1*
**Battle,** Thomas Peyton 1942- *WhoAmL 92*
**Battle,** Turner Charles, III 1926- *WhoBlA 92*
**Battle,** Turner Westray 1899-1944 *DcNCBi 1*
**Battle,** Vann DuWayne 1957- *WhoRel 92*
**Battle,** Walter Leroy 1921- *WhoBlA 92*
**Battle,** Willa Lee Grant 1924- *WhoRel 92*
**Battle,** William Cullen 1920- *WhoFI 92*
**Battle,** William Elzie 1899- *WhoBlA 92*
**Battle,** William Horn 1802-1879 *DcNCBi 1*
**Battle,** William R. 1924- *WhoIns 92*
**Battle,** William Smith 1823-1915 *DcNCBi 1*
**Battles,** Brett Eric 1962- *WhoWest 92*
**Battles,** Gary Dennis 1950- *WhoWest 92*
**Battles,** James E 1930- *AmMWSc 92*
**Battles,** Robert Winfield, Jr. 1938- *WhoRel 92*
**Battles,** Ronald Lee 1948- *WhoAmL 92*
**Battles,** Roxy Edith Baker 1921- *IntAu&W 91*
**Battles,** Willis Ralph 1914- *AmMWSc 92*
**Battley,** Edwin Hall 1925- *AmMWSc 92*
**Battocletti,** Joseph H 1925- *AmMWSc 92*
**Batton,** Calvert Vorwerk 1926- *WhoFI 92*
**Batton,** Monica Kim 1956- *WhoFI 92*
**Batton,** Roy Eugene 1949- *WhoFI 92*
**Battoni,** Pompeo Girolamo 1708-1787 *BlkwCEP*
**Battram,** Richard L. 1934- *WhoFI 92, WhoMW 92*
**Batts,** Billy Stuart 1934- *AmMWSc 92*
**Batts,** Carlton Sherrod 1961- *WhoEnt 92*
**Batts,** Henry Lewis, Jr 1922- *AmMWSc 92*
**Batts,** Michael Stanley 1929- *WhoWest 92*
**Batts,** Nathaniell 1620?-1679? *DcNCBi 1*
**Batts,** Terry Milburn 1914- *WhoBlA 92*
**Batts,** Warren Leighton 1932- *IntWW 91, WhoFI 92, WhoMW 92*
**Battson,** Bradford Lee 1957- *WhoAmL 92*
**Batty,** Byron A 1941- *WhoAmP 91*
**Batty,** Hugh Kenworthy *WhoWest 92*
**Batty,** Joseph Clair 1939- *AmMWSc 92*
**Batty,** Joseph H d1906 *BiInAmS*
**Batty,** Peter 1931- *IntMPA 92*
**Batty,** Peter Wright 1931- *Who 92*
**Batty,** Ronald, Mrs. *Who 92*
**Batty,** William 1913- *IntWW 91, Who 92*
**Batu Bagen** 1924- *IntWW 91*
**Baty,** Reginald Clement 1937- *WhoBlA 92*
**Baty,** Richard Samuel 1937- *AmMWSc 92*
**Batye,** Clifford Wayne 1947- *WhoRel 92*
**Batz,** William George 1947- *WhoFI 92*
**Batzar,** Kenneth 1938- *AmMWSc 92*
**Batzel,** Roger Elwood 1921- *AmMWSc 92, WhoWest 92*
**Batzer,** Harold Otto 1928- *AmMWSc 92*
**Batzing,** Barry Lewis 1945- *AmMWSc 92*
**Batzli,** George Oliver 1936- *AmMWSc 92*
**Bau,** Annette Marion 1963- *WhoFI 92*
**Bau,** Haim Heinrich 1947- *AmMWSc 92*
**Bau,** Robert 1944- *AmMWSc 92*
**Bauch,** Thomas Jay 1943- *WhoAmL 92, WhoWest 92*
**Bauchens,** Anne 1882-1967 *ReelWom*
**Bauchens,** Robert Norman 1942- *WhoEnt 92*
**Bauchwitz,** Peter S 1920- *AmMWSc 92*
**Bauck,** Jerald Lee 1955- *WhoMW 92*
**Baucom,** Ben *WhoIns 92*
**Baucom,** Sidney George 1930- *WhoAmL 92*
**Baucus,** Max 1941- *AlmAP 92 [port], IntWW 91, WhoAmP 91*
**Baucus,** Max S. 1941- *WhoWest 92*
**Baude,** Frederic John 1938- *AmMWSc 92*
**Baudelaire,** Charles 1821-1867 *GuFrLit 1*
**Baudelaire,** Charles Pierre 1821-1867 *ThHEIm*

**Baudendistel**, Daniel *WhoEnt 92*
**Bauder**, James Warren 1947- *AmMWSc 92*
**Bauder**, Kenneth F. 1946- *WhoMW 92*
**Bauder**, Kevin Thomas 1955- *WhoRel 92*
**Baudet**, Henri 1919- *ConAu 134*
**Baudler**, Bryan John 1940- *WhoAmL 92*
**Baudo**, Serge 1927- *IntWW 91*
**Baudot**, Jeanne 1877-1957 *ThHEIm*
**Baudouin I** 1930- *IntWW 91*
**Baudouin**, Jean-Louis 1938- *IntWW 91*
**Baudrier**, Jacqueline 1922- *IntAu&W 91*
**Baudrier**, Jaqueline 1922- *IntWW 91*
**Baudrier**, Yves 1906- *NewAmDM*
**Bauduit**, Harold S. 1930- *WhoBlA 92*
**Bauer** *Who 92*
**Bauer**, Baron 1915- *IntWW 91, Who 92*
**Bauer**, Adolphus Gustavus 1858-1898 *DcNCBi 1*
**Bauer**, Albert N, Jr 1928- *WhoAmP 91*
**Bauer**, Armand 1924- *AmMWSc 92*
**Bauer**, Armand W 1900- *WhoAmP 91*
**Bauer**, Arthur James 1947- *WhoMW 92*
**Bauer**, August Robert, Jr. 1928- *WhoWest 92*
**Bauer**, Bernard Oswald 1957- *WhoWest 92*
**Bauer**, Betty Lee 1945- *WhoRel 92*
**Bauer**, Beverly Ann 1949- *AmMWSc 92*
**Bauer**, Bruce F. 1912- *WhoWest 92*
**Bauer**, Burnett Calix 1916- *WhoAmP 91*
**Bauer**, Burnett Patrick 1944- *WhoAmP 91*
**Bauer**, C L 1933- *AmMWSc 92*
**Bauer**, C. William *WhoMW 92*
**Bauer**, Carl August 1916- *AmMWSc 92*
**Bauer**, Caroline Feller *WhoWest 92*
**Bauer**, Caroline Feller 1935- *IntAu&W 91, WrDr 92*
**Bauer**, Catherine Marie 1954- *WhoRel 92*
**Bauer**, Charles Edward *AmMWSc 92*
**Bauer**, Christian Schmid, Jr 1944- *AmMWSc 92*
**Bauer**, Daniel A 1952- *AmMWSc 92*
**Bauer**, Daniel George 1960- *WhoFI 92*
**Bauer**, Daniel Yehuda 1963- *WhoEnt 92*
**Bauer**, David August 1960- *WhoMW 92*
**Bauer**, David Francis 1940- *AmMWSc 92*
**Bauer**, David Robert 1949- *AmMWSc 92*
**Bauer**, Dennis Paul 1948- *AmMWSc 92*
**Bauer**, Dietrich Charles 1931- *AmMWSc 92*
**Bauer**, Douglas *DrAPF 91*
**Bauer**, Douglas Clifford 1938- *AmMWSc 92*
**Bauer**, Douglas F. 1942- *WhoAmL 92*
**Bauer**, Earl William 1934- *WhoWest 92*
**Bauer**, Elaine Louise 1949- *WhoEnt 92*
**Bauer**, Ernest 1927- *AmMWSc 92*
**Bauer**, Ernst Georg 1928- *AmMWSc 92*
**Bauer**, Eugene Andrew 1942- *AmMWSc 92*
**Bauer**, Evgeni 1865-1917 *IntDcF 2-2*
**Bauer**, Frances Brand 1923- *AmMWSc 92*
**Bauer**, Frederick William 1922- *AmMWSc 92*
**Bauer**, Gary Haywood 1950- *WhoEnt 92*
**Bauer**, Grace *DrAPF 91*
**Bauer**, Gustav 1870-1944 *EncTR 91 [port]*
**Bauer**, Gustav Eric 1935- *AmMWSc 92*
**Bauer**, Harald P. 1928- *IntMPA 92*
**Bauer**, Harold 1873-1951 *NewAmDM*
**Bauer**, Heinz 1914- *AmMWSc 92*
**Bauer**, Henry 1914- *AmMWSc 92*
**Bauer**, Henry Hermann 1931- *AmMWSc 92*
**Bauer**, Henry Leland 1928- *WhoAmL 92, WhoWest 92*
**Bauer**, Henry Raymond, III 1943- *AmMWSc 92*
**Bauer**, James H 1922- *AmMWSc 92*
**Bauer**, James L. 1947- *WhoFI 92*
**Bauer**, Jere Marklee 1915- *AmMWSc 92*
**Bauer**, Jerome Leo, Jr. 1938- *WhoWest 92*
**Bauer**, John Goodwin 1954- *WhoAmL 92*
**Bauer**, John Harry 1943- *AmMWSc 92*
**Bauer**, Josef Martin 1901-1970 *EncTR 91*
**Bauer**, Joseph Bruce 1961- *WhoEnt 92*
**Bauer**, Joseph Peter 1945- *WhoAmL 92*
**Bauer**, Judy Marie 1947- *WhoRel 92*
**Bauer**, Karl Gerard 1964- *WhoEnt 92*
**Bauer**, Karl Jack 1926- *IntAu&W 91*
**Bauer**, Kurt W 1929- *AmMWSc 92, WhoMW 92*
**Bauer**, Logan Probst 1940- *WhoWest 92*
**Bauer**, Lois Darlene 1938- *WhoAmP 91*
**Bauer**, Ludwig 1908- *IntWW 91*
**Bauer**, Ludwig 1926- *AmMWSc 92*
**Bauer**, Marion 1887-1955 *NewAmDM*
**Bauer**, Marvin E 1943- *AmMWSc 92*
**Bauer**, Max William 1957- *WhoWest 92*
**Bauer**, Michael Anthony 1948- *AmMWSc 92*
**Bauer**, Nyles Jason 1961- *WhoWest 92*
**Bauer**, Otto 1881-1938 *EncTR 91*
**Bauer**, Paul David 1943- *WhoFI 92*
**Bauer**, Penelope Jane Hanchey 1942- *AmMWSc 92*
**Bauer**, Peter 1932- *AmMWSc 92*
**Bauer**, Peter Thomas 1915- *IntAu&W 91, WrDr 92*
**Bauer**, Philip Lane 1941- *WhoWest 92*
**Bauer**, Randy Mark 1946- *WhoWest 92*
**Bauer**, Raymond 1958- *WhoMW 92*
**Bauer**, Raymond Gale 1934- *WhoFI 92*
**Bauer**, Riccardo 1896-1982 *FacFETw*
**Bauer**, Richard G 1935- *AmMWSc 92*
**Bauer**, Richard H. 1913- *WhoRel 92*
**Bauer**, Richard Lee 1943- *WhoFI 92*
**Bauer**, Richard M 1928- *AmMWSc 92*
**Bauer**, Robert 1926- *AmMWSc 92*
**Bauer**, Robert Alan 1952- *WhoMW 92*
**Bauer**, Robert Forest 1918- *AmMWSc 92*
**Bauer**, Robert Oliver 1918- *AmMWSc 92*
**Bauer**, Robert Steven 1944- *AmMWSc 92*
**Bauer**, Roger Duane 1932- *AmMWSc 92*
**Bauer**, Ronald Sherman 1932- *AmMWSc 92*
**Bauer**, Rudolf Wilhelm 1928- *AmMWSc 92*
**Bauer**, Sharon Ann 1947- *WhoAmL 92*
**Bauer**, Simon Harvey 1911- *AmMWSc 92*
**Bauer**, Stephen Michael 1952- *WhoMW 92*
**Bauer**, Stephen Walter 1960- *WhoAmL 92*
**Bauer**, Steven *DrAPF 91*
**Bauer**, Steven 1956- *IntMPA 92, WhoHisp 92*
**Bauer**, Steven Albert 1948- *IntAu&W 91*
**Bauer**, Steven Michael 1949- *WhoFI 92, WhoWest 92*
**Bauer**, Steven Michael 1957- *WhoAmL 92*
**Bauer**, Stewart Thomas 1909- *AmMWSc 92*
**Bauer**, Teresa Mary 1960- *WhoEnt 92*
**Bauer**, Tricia *DrAPF 91*
**Bauer**, Walter 1935- *AmMWSc 92*
**Bauer**, Wendy Hagen 1950- *AmMWSc 92*
**Bauer**, William, Jr 1936- *AmMWSc 92*
**Bauer**, William Eugene 1933- *AmMWSc 92*
**Bauer**, William Henry 1915- *WhoEnt 92*
**Bauer**, William J 1926- *WhoAmP 91*
**Bauer**, William Joseph 1926- *WhoAmL 92, WhoMW 92*
**Bauer**, William R 1939- *AmMWSc 92*
**Bauer**, Yehuda 1926- *IntAu&W 91, WrDr 92*
**Bauerle**, Ronald H 1937- *AmMWSc 92*
**Bauerly**, Jerry J 1943- *WhoAmP 91*
**Bauerly**, Ronald John 1953- *WhoMW 92*
**Bauermeister**, Herman Otto 1914- *AmMWSc 92*
**Bauernfeind**, Jacob C 1914- *AmMWSc 92*
**Bauers**, John Allen 1950- *WhoWest 92*
**Bauersfeld**, Carl Frederick 1916- *WhoAmL 92*
**Bauge**, Cynthia Wise 1943- *WhoFI 92*
**Baugh**, Ann Lawrence 1938- *AmMWSc 92*
**Baugh**, C. Don *WhoRel 92*
**Baugh**, Charles M 1931- *AmMWSc 92*
**Baugh**, Florence Ellen 1935- *WhoBlA 92*
**Baugh**, James Edward 1941- *WhoBlA 92*
**Baugh**, Jerry Phelps 1933- *WhoAmL 92*
**Baugh**, John Frank 1916- *WhoFI 92*
**Baugh**, John Trevor 1932- *Who 92*
**Baugh**, Joyce Ann 1959- *WhoBlA 92*
**Baugh**, Kenneth Lee O'Neil 1941- *IntWW 91*
**Baugh**, L. Darrell 1930- *WhoWest 92*
**Baugh**, Lynnette 1949- *WhoBlA 92*
**Baugh**, Mark Anthony 1958- *WhoRel 92*
**Baugh**, Robert Franklin 1942- *WhoWest 92*
**Baughan**, Blanche 1870-1958 *RfGEnL 91*
**Baughan**, Julian James 1944- *Who 92*
**Baughan**, Peter Edward 1934- *IntAu&W 91, WrDr 92*
**Baughcum**, Steven Lee 1950- *AmMWSc 92, WhoWest 92*
**Baughen**, Michael Alfred *Who 92*
**Baugher**, Forrest *WhoAmP 91*
**Baugher**, Gary Lee 1942- *WhoAmP 91*
**Baugher**, Shirley L. 1948- *WhoMW 92*
**Baughman**, Donald LeRoy, Jr. 1958- *WhoWest 92*
**Baughman**, George Larkins 1938- *AmMWSc 92*
**Baughman**, Glenn Laverne 1931- *AmMWSc 92*
**Baughman**, J Ross 1953- *IntAu&W 91*
**Baughman**, Leonora Knoblock 1956- *WhoAmL 92*
**Baughman**, Ray Henry 1943- *AmMWSc 92*
**Baughman**, Robert J 1937- *WhoAmP 91*
**Baughman**, Robert Neil 1952- *WhoFI 92*
**Baughman**, Robert Patrick 1938- *WhoMW 92*
**Baughman**, Russell George *AmMWSc 92*
**Baughman**, Ruth Elizabeth 1920- *WhoWest 92*
**Baughn**, Alfred Fairhurst 1912- *WhoAmL 92, WhoWest 92*
**Baughn**, Charles, Jr 1921- *AmMWSc 92*
**Baughn**, Robert Elroy 1940- *AmMWSc 92*
**Baughn**, William Hubert 1918- *WhoWest 92*
**Bauguess**, Carl Thomas, Jr 1928- *AmMWSc 92*
**Bauguess**, Milt *WhoIns 92*
**Bauhs**, Marian Sayles 1928- *WhoAmP 91*
**Bauknecht**, Sharon Mary 1947- *WhoAmP 91*
**Bauknight**, Charles William, Jr 1959- *AmMWSc 92*
**Bauknight**, Clarence Brock 1936- *WhoFI 92*
**Bauknight**, Tillman 1933- *WhoBlA 92*
**Baukus**, Erwin John 1936- *WhoMW 92*
**Bauld**, Alison 1944- *ConCom 92*
**Bauld**, Nathan Louis 1934- *AmMWSc 92*
**Bauld**, Nelson Robert, Jr 1931- *AmMWSc 92*
**Bauldock**, Gerald 1957- *WhoBlA 92*
**Bauldrick**, Walter Ryland, Sr. 1946- *WhoFI 92, WhoMW 92*
**Baule**, Gerhard M 1934- *AmMWSc 92*
**Bauleke**, Howard Paul 1959- *WhoAmL 92*
**Baulieu**, Etienne-Emile 1926- *IntWW 91*
**Baum**, Alan Stuart 1955- *WhoAmL 92*
**Baum**, Allyn Zelton 1924- *WhoFI 92*
**Baum**, Alvin John, Jr. 1918- *WhoEnt 92*
**Baum**, Bernard 1924- *AmMWSc 92*
**Baum**, Bernard H. 1926- *WrDr 92*
**Baum**, Bernard R 1937- *AmMWSc 92*
**Baum**, Bernard Rene 1937- *IntWW 91*
**Baum**, Bruce J 1945- *AmMWSc 92*
**Baum**, Burton Murry 1934- *AmMWSc 92*
**Baum**, Carl E 1940- *AmMWSc 92*
**Baum**, Carl Edward 1940- *WhoWest 92*
**Baum**, David 1927- *AmMWSc 92*
**Baum**, David 1940- *Who 92*
**Baum**, Dennis Willard 1940- *AmMWSc 92*
**Baum**, Derek Michael 1935- *WhoWest 92*
**Baum**, Eleanor Kushel *AmMWSc 92*
**Baum**, Gary Allen 1939- *AmMWSc 92*
**Baum**, George 1933- *AmMWSc 92*
**Baum**, Gerald A 1929- *AmMWSc 92*
**Baum**, Gerald L 1924- *AmMWSc 92*
**Baum**, Gerald Robert 1947- *WhoWest 92*
**Baum**, Harry 1915- *AmMWSc 92*
**Baum**, Herbert Merrill 1936- *WhoFI 92*
**Baum**, Howard Richard 1936- *AmMWSc 92*
**Baum**, J Clayton 1946- *AmMWSc 92*
**Baum**, Joan 1937- *ConAu 134*
**Baum**, John 1927- *AmMWSc 92*
**Baum**, John Daniel 1918- *AmMWSc 92*
**Baum**, John W 1931- *AmMWSc 92*
**Baum**, John William 1940- *AmMWSc 92*
**Baum**, Jonathan Klee 1957- *WhoAmL 92*
**Baum**, Joseph Herman 1927- *AmMWSc 92*
**Baum**, Jules Leonard 1931- *AmMWSc 92*
**Baum**, Kerry Robert 1939- *WhoWest 92*
**Baum**, L. Frank *ConAu 134, SmATA 66*
**Baum**, L. Frank 1856-1919 *BenetAL 91, ConAu 133, FacFETw, ScFEYrs*
**Baum**, Lawrence Stephen 1938- *AmMWSc 92*
**Baum**, Lester Jerome 1928- *WhoAmP 91*
**Baum**, Linda Louise 1945- *AmMWSc 92*
**Baum**, Louis 1948- *WrDr 92*
**Baum**, Louis F. *ConAu 133*
**Baum**, Martin 1924- *IntMPA 92*
**Baum**, Martin David 1941- *AmMWSc 92*
**Baum**, Michael 1937- *Who 92*
**Baum**, Michael Scott 1952- *WhoAmL 92*
**Baum**, O Eugene 1916- *AmMWSc 92*
**Baum**, Parker Bryant 1923- *AmMWSc 92*
**Baum**, Paul Frank 1936- *AmMWSc 92*
**Baum**, Paul M 1935- *AmMWSc 92*
**Baum**, Peter Alan 1947- *WhoAmL 92*
**Baum**, Peter Joseph 1943- *AmMWSc 92*
**Baum**, Phyllis Gardner 1930- *WhoWest 92*
**Baum**, Ray 1955- *WhoAmP 91*
**Baum**, Raymond Nathan 1944- *WhoAmL 92*
**Baum**, Rebecca Marie 1947- *WhoFI 92*
**Baum**, Richard D. 1932- *WhoIns 92*
**Baum**, Richard T 1919- *AmMWSc 92*
**Baum**, Richard Theodore 1919- *WhoFI 92*
**Baum**, Robert Harold 1936- *AmMWSc 92*
**Baum**, Sandra Roslyn 1951- *WhoFI 92*
**Baum**, Sanford 1924- *AmMWSc 92*
**Baum**, Sherry Liss *WhoAmP 91*
**Baum**, Siegmund Jacob 1920- *AmMWSc 92*
**Baum**, Simeon Harold 1954- *WhoAmL 92*
**Baum**, Stanley 1929- *AmMWSc 92*
**Baum**, Stanley M. 1944- *WhoAmL 92*
**Baum**, Stephen Graham 1937- *AmMWSc 92*
**Baum**, Stuart J 1939- *AmMWSc 92*
**Baum**, Vicki 1888-1960 *EncTR 91, LiExTwC*
**Baum**, Warren C. 1922- *IntWW 91*
**Baum**, Werner A 1923- *AmMWSc 92*
**Baum**, William Alvin 1924- *AmMWSc 92*
**Baum**, William Wakefield 1926- *IntWW 91, RelLAm 91, WhoRel 92*
**Baumal**, Reuben 1939- *AmMWSc 92*
**Bauman**, Bernard D 1946- *AmMWSc 92*
**Bauman**, Dale E 1942- *AmMWSc 92*
**Bauman**, David Benjamin 1919- *WhoRel 92*
**Bauman**, Earl William 1916- *WhoFI 92, WhoWest 92*
**Bauman**, Eric Robert 1946- *WhoEnt 92*
**Bauman**, Frederick Carl 1952- *WhoAmL 92*
**Bauman**, George Fredrick 1920- *WhoAmP 91*
**Bauman**, Gus Bloch 1949- *WhoAmL 92*
**Bauman**, Howard Eugene 1925- *AmMWSc 92*
**Bauman**, Janina 1926- *ConAu 134*
**Bauman**, Jeffrey Allen 1955- *WhoWest 92*
**Bauman**, Jeffrey Thomas 1957- *WhoFI 92*
**Bauman**, John Andrew 1921- *WhoAmL 92*
**Bauman**, John E, Jr 1933- *AmMWSc 92*
**Bauman**, John Gregory 1957- *WhoWest 92*
**Bauman**, John W, Jr 1918- *AmMWSc 92*
**Bauman**, Judith C *WhoAmP 91*
**Bauman**, Karl Yanovich 1892-1937 *SovUnBD*
**Bauman**, Louis Sylvester 1875-1950 *RelLAm 91*
**Bauman**, Loyal Frederick 1920- *AmMWSc 92*
**Bauman**, M. Garrett *DrAPF 91*
**Bauman**, Michael Edward 1950- *WhoMW 92, WhoRel 92*
**Bauman**, Neale Lorman 1949- *WhoMW 92*
**Bauman**, Norman 1932- *AmMWSc 92*
**Bauman**, Raquel 1948- *WhoHisp 92*
**Bauman**, Richard Gilbert 1924- *AmMWSc 92*
**Bauman**, Robert Andrew 1923- *AmMWSc 92*
**Bauman**, Robert D. 1940- *WhoIns 92*
**Bauman**, Robert Patten 1931- *IntWW 91, Who 92, WhoFI 92*
**Bauman**, Robert Poe 1928- *AmMWSc 92*
**Bauman**, Thomas Trost 1939- *AmMWSc 92, WhoMW 92*
**Bauman**, William Winter 1961- *WhoWest 92*
**Bauman**, Zygmunt 1925- *IntWW 91, WrDr 92*
**Baumann**, Arthur Nicholas 1922- *AmMWSc 92*
**Baumann**, Carl August 1906- *AmMWSc 92*
**Baumann**, Carol Edler 1932- *IntAu&W 91, WrDr 92*
**Baumann**, Daniel E. 1937- *WhoMW 92*
**Baumann**, David Jonathan 1953- *WhoWest 92*
**Baumann**, Dwight Maylon Billy 1933- *AmMWSc 92*
**Baumann**, E Robert 1921- *AmMWSc 92*
**Baumann**, Elizabeth Wilson *AmMWSc 92*
**Baumann**, Erwin Wesley 1953- *WhoMW 92*
**Baumann**, Frederick 1930- *AmMWSc 92, WhoWest 92*
**Baumann**, Gary Joseph 1949- *WhoMW 92*
**Baumann**, Gary N. 1941- *WhoIns 92*
**Baumann**, George P 1919- *AmMWSc 92*
**Baumann**, Gerhard 1941- *AmMWSc 92*
**Baumann**, Gerhard Paul 1941- *WhoMW 92*
**Baumann**, Gregory William 1947- *WhoMW 92*
**Baumann**, Hans 1914- *EncTR 91*
**Baumann**, Hans D *AmMWSc 92*
**Baumann**, Herbert Karl Wilhelm 1925- *IntWW 91*
**Baumann**, Jacob Bruce 1932- *AmMWSc 92*
**Baumann**, James L 1931- *WhoAmP 91*
**Baumann**, Julian Henry, Jr. 1943- *WhoAmL 92*
**Baumann**, Marion Muns 1928- *WhoAmP 91*
**Baumann**, Norman Paul 1927- *AmMWSc 92*
**Baumann**, Paul C 1946- *AmMWSc 92*
**Baumann**, Peter 1953- *WhoEnt 92*
**Baumann**, Richard Charles 1935- *WhoWest 92*
**Baumann**, Richard Gordon 1938- *WhoAmL 92*
**Baumann**, Richard William 1940- *AmMWSc 92*
**Baumann**, Robert Jay 1940- *AmMWSc 92*
**Baumann**, Ronald Edwin 1933- *WhoFI 92*
**Baumann**, Thiema Wolf 1921- *AmMWSc 92*
**Baumann**, Wolfgang J 1936- *AmMWSc 92*
**Baumbach**, Jonathan *DrAPF 91*
**Baumbach**, Jonathan 1933- *ConNov 91, IntAu&W 91, WrDr 92*
**Baumbach**, Werner 1916-1953 *EncTR 91 [port]*
**Baumber**, John Scott 1937- *AmMWSc 92*
**Baumber**, Michael 1935- *ConAu 133*
**Baumberger**, Benjamin L. 1962- *WhoMW 92*
**Baumberger**, Charles Henry 1941- *WhoAmL 92*
**Baumberger**, David Lee 1955- *WhoAmL 92*
**Baume**, William James 1947- *WhoMW 92*
**Baumeister**, Carl Frederick 1907- *AmMWSc 92*

**Baumeister,** Philip Werner 1929- *AmMWSc 92*
**Baumeister,** Richard Thomas, Jr. 1961- *WhoFI 92*
**Baumeister,** Willi 1889-1955 *FacFETw*
**Baumel,** Herbert 1919- *WhoEnt 92*
**Baumel,** Jacques 1918- *IntWW 91*
**Baumel,** Judith *DrAPF 91*
**Baumel,** Julian Joseph 1922- *AmMWSc 92*
**Baumel,** Philip 1932- *AmMWSc 92*
**Baumer,** Martha Ann 1938- *WhoRel 92*
**Baumes,** Louise Houssaye de *EncAmaz 91*
**Baumeyer,** Joel Bernard 1936- *AmMWSc 92*
**Baumgaertel,** Marc Warren *WhoWest 92*
**Baumgardner,** Brian J. 1959- *WhoMW 92*
**Baumgardner,** F Wesley *AmMWSc 92*
**Baumgardner,** John Ellwood, Jr. 1951- *WhoAmL 92*
**Baumgardner,** Kandy Diane 1946- *AmMWSc 92*
**Baumgardner,** Marion F 1926- *AmMWSc 92*
**Baumgardner,** Ray K 1933- *AmMWSc 92*
**Baumgardt,** Arden Charles 1941- *WhoIns 92*
**Baumgardt,** Billy Ray 1933- *AmMWSc 92, WhoMW 92*
**Baumgart,** James R *WhoAmP 91*
**Baumgart,** Richard 1947- *AmMWSc 92*
**Baumgarten,** Alexander 1935- *AmMWSc 92*
**Baumgarten,** Alexander Gottlieb 1717-1762 *BlkwCEP*
**Baumgarten,** Alice Marie 1939- *WhoMW 92*
**Baumgarten,** Craig 1949- *IntMPA 92*
**Baumgarten,** Gustav 1837-1910 *BiInAmS*
**Baumgarten,** Henry Ernest 1921- *AmMWSc 92*
**Baumgarten,** Herbert Joseph 1935- *WhoAmL 92*
**Baumgarten,** Joseph Russell 1928- *AmMWSc 92*
**Baumgarten,** Paul Anthony 1934- *WhoAmL 92*
**Baumgarten,** Reuben Lawrence 1934- *AmMWSc 92*
**Baumgarten,** Ronald J 1935- *AmMWSc 92*
**Baumgarten,** Sidney 1933- *WhoAmL 92*
**Baumgarten,** Werner 1914- *AmMWSc 92*
**Baumgartner,** Anton Edward 1948- *WhoWest 92*
**Baumgartner,** Cary 1948- *WhoFI 92*
**Baumgartner,** Elaine Ann 1950- *WhoMW 92*
**Baumgartner,** Ferdinand 1931- *IntWW 91*
**Baumgartner,** George Julius 1924- *AmMWSc 92*
**Baumgartner,** Harold Floyd 1936- *WhoWest 92*
**Baumgartner,** Ingeborg 1936- *WhoMW 92*
**Baumgartner,** John F 1947- *WhoAmP 91*
**Baumgartner,** Leona d1991 *NewYTBS 91 [port]*
**Baumgartner,** Leona 1902- *AmMWSc 92*
**Baumgartner,** Leona 1902-1991 *CurBio 91N*
**Baumgartner,** Nancy Helen 1956- *WhoAmL 92*
**Baumgartner,** Rena V 1934- *WhoAmP 91*
**Baumgartner,** Reuben Albert 1912- *WhoMW 92*
**Baumgartner,** Robert Van 1956- *WhoMW 92*
**Baumgartner,** Ronald Julian 1930- *WhoFI 92*
**Baumgartner,** Werner Andreas 1935- *AmMWSc 92*
**Baumgartner,** William Hans, Jr. 1955- *WhoAmL 92*
**Baumhefner,** David Paul 1941- *AmMWSc 92*
**Baumhoff,** Walter Henry 1937- *WhoWest 92*
**Baumiller,** Robert Cahill 1931- *AmMWSc 92*
**Baummer,** J Charles, Jr 1945- *AmMWSc 92*
**Baumol,** William J. 1922- *WrDr 92*
**Baumol,** William Jack 1922- *IntWW 91, WhoFI 92*
**Baumrucker,** Craig Richard 1944- *AmMWSc 92*
**Baumslag,** Gilbert 1933- *AmMWSc 92*
**Baumstark,** John Spann 1927- *AmMWSc 92*
**Baumunk,** Jon Adam 1960- *WhoFI 92*
**Baun,** Terrence Michal 1947- *WhoMW 92*
**Baunach,** Phyllis Jo 1947- *WhoAmL 92*
**Baur,** Christopher Frank 1942- *Who 92*
**Baur,** Clara 1835-1912 *NewAmDM*
**Baur,** Ferdinand Christian 1792-1860 *EncEarC*
**Baur,** Fredric John, Jr 1918- *AmMWSc 92*
**Baur,** Georg Hermann Carl Ludwig 1859-1898 *BiInAmS*
**Baur,** James Francis 1938- *AmMWSc 92*
**Baur,** James Gerard 1940- *WhoFI 92*
**Baur,** Jean *DrAPF 91*
**Baur,** John Edward 1922- *WrDr 92*
**Baur,** John M 1939- *AmMWSc 92*
**Baur,** Mario Elliott 1934- *AmMWSc 92*
**Baur,** Robert F 1945- *WhoAmP 91*
**Baur,** Thomas George 1944- *AmMWSc 92*
**Baur,** Werner Heinz 1931- *AmMWSc 92*
**Baurer,** Theodore 1924- *AmMWSc 92*
**Baus,** Bernard V 1925- *AmMWSc 92*
**Baus,** Herbert Michael 1914- *WrDr 92*
**Baus,** John Villars, Jr. 1956- *WhoAmL 92*
**Baus,** M. Walker 1959- *WhoAmL 92*
**Baus,** Ruth Brumme 1917- *WhoFI 92*
**Bausch,** Donna Kay 1957- *WhoAmL 92*
**Bausch,** Henry 1859?-1909 *BiInAmS*
**Bausch,** Richard *DrAPF 91*
**Bausch,** Richard 1945- *ConAu 14AS [port], WrDr 92*
**Bausch,** Robert 1945- *ConAu 14AS [port]*
**Bauschard,** Richard Bach 1944- *WhoMW 92*
**Bausher,** Larry Paul 1939- *AmMWSc 92*
**Bausher,** Michael George 1945- *AmMWSc 92*
**Bausher,** Mildred Jordan 1901-1982 *ConAu 133*
**Bausher,** Verne Charles *WhoFI 92*
**Baussus von Luetzow,** Hans Gerhard 1921- *AmMWSc 92*
**Baust,** John G 1942- *AmMWSc 92*
**Baustian,** Robert Frederick 1921- *WhoEnt 92*
**Bausum,** Howard Thomas 1933- *AmMWSc 92*
**Bautch,** Dorette Marie 1952- *WhoMW 92*
**Bauter,** Robert Theodore 1929- *WhoFI 92*
**Bautier,** Robert-Henri 1922- *IntWW 91*
**Bautista,** Daniel 1952- *BlkOlyM*
**Bautista,** Liberato de la Cruz 1959- *WhoRel 92*
**Bautista,** Manny Hector, Jr. 1958- *WhoHisp 92*
**Bautista,** Pilar 1958- *WhoHisp 92*
**Bautz,** Gordon T *AmMWSc 92*
**Bautz,** Laura Patricia 1940- *AmMWSc 92*
**Bauza,** Mario 1911- *WhoEnt 92*
**Bavadra,** Adi Kuini Teimumu Vuikaba 1949- *IntWW 91*
**Bavarel,** Michel 1940- *ConAu 35NR*
**Bavaria,** Duke of 1905- *IntWW 91*
**Bavaud,** Maurice 1916-1941 *EncTR 91*
**Bavel,** Zamir 1929- *WhoMW 92*
**Baverstock,** Donald Leighton 1924- *Who 92*
**Bavin,** Alfred Robert Walter 1917- *Who 92*
**Bavin,** Timothy John *Who 92*
**Bavin,** Timothy John 1935- *IntWW 91*
**Bavis,** Karen Ann 1962- *WhoFI 92*
**Bavisotto,** Vincent 1925- *AmMWSc 92*
**Bavister,** Barry Douglas 1943- *AmMWSc 92*
**Bavley,** Abraham 1915- *AmMWSc 92*
**Bavlinka,** Barbara Jean Clark 1930- *WhoRel 92*
**Baw,** Philemon S H 1939- *AmMWSc 92*
**Bawa,** Kamaljit S 1939- *AmMWSc 92*
**Bawa,** Mohendra S 1931- *AmMWSc 92*
**Bawden,** Charles Roskelly 1924- *Who 92*
**Bawden,** Edward 1903-1989 *TwCPaSc*
**Bawden,** Frederick Charles 1908- *FacFETw*
**Bawden,** Harry Reginald 1921- *IntAu&W 91*
**Bawden,** James Wyatt 1930- *AmMWSc 92*
**Bawden,** Monte Paul 1943- *AmMWSc 92*
**Bawden,** Nina 1925- *ConNov 91, WrDr 92*
**Bawden,** Nina Mary 1925- *IntAu&W 91, IntWW 91, Who 92*
**Bawden,** Richard 1936- *TwCPaSc*
**Bawdon,** Roger Everett 1939- *AmMWSc 92*
**Bawn,** Cecil Edwin Henry 1908- *IntWW 91, Who 92*
**Baworowsky,** John Michael 1959- *WhoMW 92*
**Bawtree,** David Kenneth 1937- *Who 92*
**Bax,** Ad 1956- *AmMWSc 92*
**Bax,** Arnold 1883-1953 *FacFETw, NewAmDM*
**Bax,** Clifford 1886-1962 *RfGEnL 91*
**Bax,** Martin 1933- *WrDr 92*
**Bax,** Nicholas John *AmMWSc 92*
**Bax,** Roger *WrDr 92*
**Baxandall,** David Kighley 1905- *Who 92*
**Baxandall,** Michael David Kighley 1933- *IntWW 91, Who 92*
**Baxendale,** James Edward 1940- *WhoIns 92*
**Baxendell,** Peter 1925- *Who 92*
**Baxendell,** Peter Brian 1925- *IntWW 91*
**Baxley,** John Michael 1956- *WhoAmP 91*
**Baxley,** Phillip Kent 1957- *WhoAmL 92*
**Baxley,** William Allison 1933- *AmMWSc 92*
**Baxley,** William Duane 1952- *WhoRel 92*
**Baxley,** William J 1941- *WhoAmP 91*
**Baxman,** Horace Roy 1921- *AmMWSc 92*
**Baxt,** George 1923- *IntAu&W 91, WrDr 92*
**Baxter,** Albert James, II 1935- *WhoBlA 92*
**Baxter,** Andrew 1686-1750 *BlkwCEP*
**Baxter,** Ann Webster 1917- *AmMWSc 92*
**Baxter,** Annie 1864-1944 *HanAmWH*
**Baxter,** Augustus, Sr. 1928- *WhoBlA 92*
**Baxter,** Belgium Nathan 1921- *WhoBlA 92*
**Baxter,** Billy 1926- *IntMPA 92*
**Baxter,** Brian *WrDr 92*
**Baxter,** Carol Cairns 1940- *WhoWest 92*
**Baxter,** Charles *DrAPF 91*
**Baxter,** Charles D. 1926- *WhoIns 92*
**Baxter,** Charles F., Jr. 1959- *WhoBlA 92*
**Baxter,** Charles Rufus 1929- *AmMWSc 92*
**Baxter,** Charles T. 1959- *WhoEnt 92*
**Baxter,** Claude Frederick 1923- *AmMWSc 92*
**Baxter,** Craig 1929- *IntAu&W 91, WrDr 92*
**Baxter,** Curtis Michael 1952- *WhoFI 92*
**Baxter,** Denver O 1925- *AmMWSc 92*
**Baxter,** Donald Henry 1916- *AmMWSc 92*
**Baxter,** Donald William 1926- *AmMWSc 92*
**Baxter,** Douglas Gordon 1920- *TwCPaSc*
**Baxter,** Duby Yvonne 1953- *WhoWest 92*
**Baxter,** E.R. *DrAPF 91*
**Baxter,** Elaine 1933- *WhoMW 92*
**Baxter,** Elaine Bland 1933- *WhoAmP 91*
**Baxter,** Elisha 1827-1899 *DcNCBi 1*
**Baxter,** Frank Edward 1936- *WhoFI 92*
**Baxter,** Fred Edwin, Jr. 1943- *WhoFI 92*
**Baxter,** Gene Francis 1922- *AmMWSc 92*
**Baxter,** George Arthur, Jr 1940- *WhoAmP 91*
**Baxter,** George Owen *TwCWW 91*
**Baxter,** George T 1919- *AmMWSc 92*
**Baxter,** Glen 1944- *IntWW 91, TwCPaSc*
**Baxter,** Gregory Stephen 1948- *WhoAmL 92*
**Baxter,** Harry Stevens 1915- *WhoAmL 92*
**Baxter,** Harry Youngs 1930- *WhoAmP 91*
**Baxter,** Ian Stuart 1937- *Who 92*
**Baxter,** J. R. 1887-1960 *NewAmDM*
**Baxter,** James Hubert 1913- *AmMWSc 92*
**Baxter,** James K. 1926-1972 *RfGEnL 91*
**Baxter,** James Thomas, III 1947- *WhoAmL 92*
**Baxter,** James Watson 1927- *AmMWSc 92*
**Baxter,** Jeremy Richard d1991 *Who 92N*
**Baxter,** John *IntAu&W 91X*
**Baxter,** John 1819-1886 *DcNCBi 1*
**Baxter,** John 1896-1975 *IntDcF 2-2*
**Baxter,** John 1939- *IntAu&W 91, TwCSFW 91, WrDr 92*
**Baxter,** John Darling 1940- *AmMWSc 92*
**Baxter,** John Edwards 1937- *AmMWSc 92*
**Baxter,** John Lawson 1939- *Who 92*
**Baxter,** John Lewis 1925- *AmMWSc 92*
**Baxter,** John Walter 1917- *Who 92*
**Baxter,** Joseph Diedrich 1937- *WhoMW 92*
**Baxter,** Keith 1933- *IntMPA 92*
**Baxter,** Keith 1935- *ConAu 135*
**Baxter,** Lawrence Gerald 1952- *WhoAmL 92*
**Baxter,** Lincoln, II 1924- *AmMWSc 92*
**Baxter,** Luther Willis, Jr 1924- *AmMWSc 92*
**Baxter,** Marvin 1940- *WhoAmP 91*
**Baxter,** Marvin R. 1940- *WhoAmL 92, WhoWest 92*
**Baxter,** Meredith *LesBEnT 92*
**Baxter,** Meredith 1947- *ConTFT 9, IntMPA 92*
**Baxter,** Michael St. Patrick 1955- *WhoAmL 92*
**Baxter,** Murdoch Scott 1944- *Who 92*
**Baxter,** Neal Edward 1908- *AmMWSc 92*
**Baxter,** Pat Ann 1929- *WhoWest 92*
**Baxter,** Phyllis *ConAu 35NR*
**Baxter,** Ralph Felix 1925- *WhoFI 92*
**Baxter,** Randolph 1946- *WhoAmL 92*
**Baxter,** Ray 1952- *WhoAmP 91*
**Baxter,** Raymond Frederic 1922- *IntAu&W 91, Who 92*
**Baxter,** Richard Reeve 1921-1980 *AmPeW*
**Baxter,** Robert Dale 1953- *WhoEnt 92*
**Baxter,** Robert Henry 1940- *WhoFI 92*
**Baxter,** Robert MacCallum 1926- *AmMWSc 92*
**Baxter,** Robert Scott 1952- *WhoEnt 92*
**Baxter,** Robert Wilson 1914- *AmMWSc 92*
**Baxter,** Rodney James 1940- *IntWW 91, Who 92*
**Baxter,** Roger George 1940- *Who 92*
**Baxter,** Ronald Dale 1934- *AmMWSc 92*
**Baxter,** Ross M 1918- *AmMWSc 92*
**Baxter,** Samuel G *AmMWSc 92*
**Baxter,** Sarah Elizabeth 1931- *WhoAmP 91*
**Baxter,** Shane V *IntAu&W 91X, TwCWW 91*
**Baxter,** Stanley 1928- *IntMPA 92*
**Baxter,** Thomas Gregory 1946- *WhoEnt 92*
**Baxter,** Turner Butler 1922- *WhoFI 92*
**Baxter,** Walter 1915- *Who 92*
**Baxter,** Wendy Marie 1952- *WhoBlA 92*
**Baxter,** Willard Ellis 1929- *AmMWSc 92*
**Baxter,** William 1929- *WhoAmP 91*
**Baxter,** William D 1936- *AmMWSc 92*
**Baxter,** William Francis 1929- *WhoAmL 92, WhoFI 92*
**Baxter,** William John 1935- *AmMWSc 92*
**Baxter,** William John Ernest 1914- *RelLAm 91*
**Baxter,** William Leroy 1929- *AmMWSc 92*
**Baxter,** William MacNeil 1923- *WhoRel 92*
**Baxter,** William T. 1906- *Who 92, WrDr 92*
**Baxter,** Zenobia 1910- *WhoBlA 92*
**Baxter-Birney,** Meredith *ConTFT 9*
**Baxter-Birney,** Meredith 1947- *WhoEnt 92*
**Baxter-Wright,** Keith 1935- *ConAu 135*
**Baxtresser,** Jeanne *WhoEnt 92*
**Bay,** Ben *WhoAmP 91*
**Bay,** Darrell Edward 1942- *AmMWSc 92*
**Bay,** Donald Eugene 1934- *WhoMW 92*
**Bay,** Ernest C 1929- *AmMWSc 92*
**Bay,** Marvin Lee 1938- *WhoWest 92*
**Bay,** Melburn Earl 1913- *WhoEnt 92, WhoMW 92*
**Bay,** Peter 1957- *WhoEnt 92, WhoMW 92*
**Bay,** Richard Anthony 1948- *WhoWest 92*
**Bay,** Roger Rudolph 1931- *AmMWSc 92*
**Bay,** Susan Louise 1946- *WhoMW 92*
**Bay,** Theodosios 1931- *AmMWSc 92*
**Bay,** Zoltan Lajos 1900- *AmMWSc 92*
**Bayar,** Celal 1882-1986 *FacFETw*
**Bayard,** Elizabeth Cornell 1761?-1854 *DcNCBi 1*
**Bayard,** Franck 1917- *WhoBlA 92*
**Bayard,** Hippolyte 1801-1887 *ThHEIm*
**Bayard,** Kenneth Howard 1959- *WhoMW 92*
**Bayard,** Thomas Francis 1828-1898 *AmPolLe*
**Baybars,** Taner 1936- *ConPo 91, IntAu&W 91, WrDr 92*
**Baybayan,** Ronald Alan 1946- *WhoAmL 92, WhoFI 92*
**Baybutt,** Arlene Evans 1921- *WhoAmP 91*
**Bayda,** Edward Dmytro 1931- *Who 92, WhoWest 92*
**Baye,** Lawrence James J. 1933- *WhoBlA 92*
**Baye,** Michael Roy 1958- *WhoFI 92*
**Baye,** Nathalie 1948- *IntWW 91*
**Bayer,** Arthur Craig 1946- *AmMWSc 92*
**Bayer,** Barbara Moore 1948- *AmMWSc 92*
**Bayer,** Charlene Warres 1950- *AmMWSc 92*
**Bayer,** David E 1926- *AmMWSc 92*
**Bayer,** Frederick Merkle 1921- *AmMWSc 92*
**Bayer,** George Herbert 1924- *AmMWSc 92*
**Bayer,** Herbert 1900- *DcTwDes*
**Bayer,** Herbert 1900-1985 *FacFETw*
**Bayer,** Horst Otto 1934- *AmMWSc 92*
**Bayer,** Josh Samuel 1952- *WhoEnt 92*
**Bayer,** Karel 1931- *WhoRel 92*
**Bayer,** Manfred Erich 1928- *AmMWSc 92*
**Bayer,** Margret Helene Janssen 1931- *AmMWSc 92*
**Bayer,** Oswald 1939- *IntWW 91*
**Bayer,** Raymond George 1935- *AmMWSc 92*
**Bayer,** Richard Eugene 1932- *AmMWSc 92*
**Bayer,** Robert Clark 1944- *AmMWSc 92*
**Bayer,** Shirley Ann 1940- *AmMWSc 92*
**Bayer,** Thomas Norton 1934- *AmMWSc 92*
**Bayer,** Thomas Paul 1958- *WhoAmL 92*
**Bayer,** William 1939- *IntAu&W 91, WhoEnt 92, WrDr 92*
**Bayero,** Alhaji Ado 1930- *IntWW 91*
**Bayes,** Gilbert 1872-1953 *TwCPaSc*
**Bayes,** Kyle D 1935- *AmMWSc 92*
**Bayes,** Ronald H. *DrAPF 91*
**Bayes,** Walter 1869-1956 *TwCPaSc*
**Bayev,** Aleksandr Aleksandrovich 1904- *IntWW 91*
**Bayev,** Alexander A 1904- *AmMWSc 92*
**Bayfield,** Anthony Michael 1946- *Who 92*
**Bayh,** Birch 1928- *WhoAmP 91*
**Bayh,** Birch Evans, Jr. 1928- *IntWW 91*
**Bayh,** Evan 1955- *AlmAP 92 [port], IntWW 91, WhoAmP 91, WhoMW 92*
**Bayhurst,** Barbara P 1926- *AmMWSc 92*
**Bayi,** Filbert 1953- *BlkOlyM, IntWW 91*
**Baykam,** Bedri 1957- *IntWW 91*
**Baykara,** Zeyyad 1918- *IntWW 91*
**Bayko,** Emil Thomas 1947- *WhoAmL 92*
**Bayle,** Francois 1932- *ConCom 92*
**Bayle,** Generes Dufour 1933- *WhoFI 92*
**Bayle,** Henry Robert Auguste 1915- *IntWW 91*
**Bayle,** Pierre 1647-1706 *BlkwCEP*
**Baylen,** Joseph O 1920- *IntAu&W 91, WrDr 92*
**Bayler,** Lavon 1933- *WhoRel 92*
**Bayles,** Donald Hamilton, Jr. 1949- *WhoAmL 92*
**Bayles,** Martha 1948- *ConAu 134*
**Bayless,** Charles Edward 1942- *WhoAmL 92*

**Bayless**, David Lee 1938- *AmMWSc 92*
**Bayless**, James Leavell, Jr 1952- *WhoAmP 91*
**Bayless**, Kathryn Reed 1950- *WhoAmL 92*
**Bayless**, Laurence Emery 1938- *AmMWSc 92*
**Bayless**, Mary Lou 1948- *WhoWest 92*
**Bayless**, Paul Clifton 1935- *WhoBlA 92*
**Bayless**, Philip Leighton 1928- *AmMWSc 92*
**Bayless**, Romaine Belle 1945- *WhoMW 92*
**Bayless**, Samuel Holliman 1947- *WhoAmL 92*
**Baylet**, Jean-Michel 1946- *IntWW 91*
**Bayley**, Barrington John 1937- *IntAu&W 91, TwCSFW 91, WrDr 92*
**Bayley**, Donovan *ScFEYrs*
**Bayley**, Gordon Vernon 1920- *Who 92*
**Bayley**, Henry Shaw 1938- *AmMWSc 92*
**Bayley**, Iris *Who 92*
**Bayley**, John *WhoAmP 91*
**Bayley**, John 1925- *WrDr 92*
**Bayley**, John Oliver 1925- *IntWW 91, Who 92*
**Bayley**, Nancy 1899- *WomPsyc*
**Bayley**, Nicola Mary 1949- *Who 92*
**Bayley**, Oscar Stewart Morris 1926- *Who 92*
**Bayley**, Peter 1921- *IntAu&W 91, WrDr 92*
**Bayley**, Peter Charles 1921- *Who 92*
**Bayley**, Peter James 1944- *Who 92*
**Bayley**, Ray Waldo Gustavus 1919- *WhoRel 92*
**Bayley**, Stanley Thomas 1926- *AmMWSc 92*
**Bayley**, Stephen 1951- *IntWW 91, WrDr 92*
**Bayley**, Stephen 1952- *DcTwDes*
**Bayley**, Stephen Paul 1951- *Who 92*
**Bayley**, T Donovan 1881- *ScFEYrs*
**Bayliff**, Brad 1959- *WhoAmP 91*
**Bayliff**, Edgar W. 1927- *WhoAmL 92*
**Bayliff**, William Henry 1928- *AmMWSc 92*
**Baylin**, George Jay 1911- *AmMWSc 92*
**Baylin**, Lee 1943- *WhoAmL 92*
**Baylink**, David J 1931- *AmMWSc 92*
**Baylis**, Clifford Henry 1915- *Who 92*
**Baylis**, Jeffrey Rowe 1945- *AmMWSc 92*
**Baylis**, John 1946- *WrDr 92*
**Baylis**, John Robert, Jr 1927- *AmMWSc 92*
**Baylis**, Robert Goodwin 1925- *Who 92*
**Baylis**, Robert Montague 1938- *WhoFI 92*
**Baylis**, William Eric 1939- *AmMWSc 92*
**Bayliss**, A E 1892-1961 *ScFEYrs*
**Bayliss**, Colin Edward 1936- *AmMWSc 92*
**Bayliss**, Frederic Joseph 1926- *Who 92*
**Bayliss**, Gene 1927- *WhoEnt 92*
**Bayliss**, J C 1919- *ScFEYrs*
**Bayliss**, John 1934- *Who 92*
**Bayliss**, John Temple 1939- *AmMWSc 92*
**Bayliss**, Larry Dale 1940- *WhoFI 92*
**Bayliss**, Noel 1906- *Who 92*
**Bayliss**, Noel Stanley 1906- *IntWW 91*
**Bayliss**, Peter *AmMWSc 92*
**Bayliss**, Richard 1917- *Who 92*
**Bayliss**, Richard Ian Samuel 1917- *IntWW 91*
**Bayliss**, Timothy *IntAu&W 91X, WrDr 92*
**Bayliss**, Valerie June 1944- *Who 92*
**Bayliss**, William Maddock 1860-1924 *FacFETw*
**Baylon**, David Anthony 1945- *WhoWest 92*
**Baylor**, Charles, Jr 1940- *AmMWSc 92*
**Baylor**, Denis Aristide 1940- *AmMWSc 92*
**Baylor**, Don Edward 1949- *WhoBlA 92*
**Baylor**, Elgin 1934- *WhoBlA 92*
**Baylor**, Elgin Gay 1934- *FacFETw, WhoWest 92*
**Baylor**, Emmett R., Jr. 1933- *WhoBlA 92*
**Baylor**, Hugh Murray 1913- *WhoEnt 92*
**Baylor**, John E 1922- *AmMWSc 92*
**Baylor**, Solomon 1922- *WhoBlA 92*
**Baylouny**, Raymond Anthony 1932- *AmMWSc 92*
**Baylson**, Michael Morris 1939- *WhoAmL 92*
**Bayly**, Christopher Alan 1945- *Who 92*
**Bayly**, George W *ScFEYrs*
**Bayly**, Joseph 1920- *IntAu&W 91*
**Bayly**, M Brian 1929- *AmMWSc 92*
**Bayly**, Patrick 1914- *Who 92*
**Baym**, Gordon A 1935- *AmMWSc 92*
**Baym**, Gordon Alan 1935- *IntWW 91*
**Bayma**, Joseph 1816-1892 *BiInAmS*
**Bayman**, Benjamin 1930- *AmMWSc 92*
**Bayman**, Dawn Wiley 1959- *WhoEnt 92*
**Baymiller**, Lynda Doern 1943- *WhoMW 92*
**Bayne**, Adele Wehman *WhoEnt 92*
**Bayne**, Brian Leicester 1938- *Who 92*
**Bayne**, Charles Kenneth 1944- *AmMWSc 92*
**Bayne**, Christopher Jeffrey 1941- *AmMWSc 92*
**Bayne**, David Roberge 1941- *AmMWSc 92*
**Bayne**, Donald Storm 1949- *WhoAmL 92*
**Bayne**, Ellen Kahn 1949- *AmMWSc 92*
**Bayne**, Gilbert M 1921- *AmMWSc 92*
**Bayne**, Henry G. 1925- *WhoBlA 92*
**Bayne**, Henry Godwin 1925- *AmMWSc 92*
**Bayne**, James Elwood 1940- *WhoFI 92*
**Bayne**, James Thomas, Jr. 1934- *WhoRel 92*
**Bayne**, John *Who 92*
**Bayne**, Nicholas Peter 1937- *IntWW 91, Who 92*
**Bayne**, Robert Donald, Jr. 1953- *WhoRel 92*
**Bayne**, Steven Eric 1959- *WhoWest 92*
**Bayne**, William 1929- *WhoWest 92*
**Bayne-Powell**, Robert Lane 1910- *Who 92*
**Baynes**, John 1928- *Who 92, WrDr 92*
**Baynes**, John William 1940- *AmMWSc 92*
**Baynes**, Keith 1887-1977 *TwCPaSc*
**Baynes**, Pauline Diana 1922- *Who 92*
**Baynes**, Robert Gene 1939- *WhoAmL 92*
**Baynham**, Alexander Christopher 1935- *Who 92*
**Baynham**, Henry Wellesley Forster 1933- *WrDr 92*
**Baynham**, James Donald 1946- *WhoFI 92*
**Baynton**, Harold Wilbert 1920- *AmMWSc 92*
**Bayo**, Eduardo 1954- *WhoWest 92*
**Bayoumi**, Tamim Andrew 1959- *WhoFI 92*
**Bayramoglu**, Fuat 1912- *IntWW 91*
**Bayrd**, Edwin Dorrance 1917- *AmMWSc 92*
**Bayrer**, Ralph L. *WhoFI 92*
**Bays**, Carrson W., Jr. 1943- *WhoFI 92*
**Bays**, Donna Jean 1958- *WhoAmL 92*
**Bays**, Eric *Who 92*
**Bays**, Eric 1932- *WhoRel 92, WhoWest 92*
**Bays**, James Philip 1941- *AmMWSc 92*
**Bays**, Karl D 1933- *AmMWSc 92*
**Bays**, Robert Earl 1921- *WhoEnt 92*
**Bayster**, R. Jeffrey 1953- *WhoFI 92*
**Bayton**, John 1930- *Who 92*
**Bayulken**, Umit Haluk 1921- *IntWW 91, Who 92*
**Bayusik**, Robert Edward 1927- *WhoRel 92*
**Bayuzick**, Robert J 1937- *AmMWSc 92*
**Baz**, Amr Mahmoud Sabry 1945- *AmMWSc 92*
**Bazaine**, Jean 1904- *IntWW 91*
**Bazalgette**, Derek Willoughby 1924- *Who 92*
**Bazan**, Alfonso M. *WhoHisp 92*
**Bazan**, Elias, Jr. 1943- *WhoHisp 92*
**Bazan**, Jose Luis 1946- *WhoHisp 92*
**Bazan**, Nicolas Guillermo 1942- *AmMWSc 92*
**Bazan**, Patricia 1957- *WhoHisp 92*
**Bazant**, Zdenek P 1937- *AmMWSc 92*
**Bazao-Turunku** *EncAmaz 91*
**Bazargan**, Mehdi 1907- *IntWW 91*
**Bazarov**, Vladimir Aleksandrovich 1874-1939 *SovUnBD*
**Baze**, Ted F. 1934- *WhoEnt 92*
**Bazela**, Jean Ann 1947- *WhoMW 92*
**Bazelon**, David 1909- *FacFETw*
**Bazelon**, David L. *LesBEnT 92*
**Bazelon**, Irwin 1922- *ConCom 92*
**Bazelon**, Irwin Allen 1922- *WhoEnt 92*
**Bazemore**, Dennis Neal 1955- *WhoRel 92*
**Bazer**, Fuller Warren 1938- *AmMWSc 92*
**Bazer**, Jack 1924- *AmMWSc 92*
**Bazett-Jones**, David Paul 1953- *AmMWSc 92*
**Bazhbeuk-Melikyan**, Aleksandr A. 1891-1966 *SovUnBD*
**Baziga**, David *WhoRel 92*
**Bazil**, Anne Marie 1956- *WhoAmL 92*
**Bazil**, Ronald 1937- *WhoBlA 92*
**Bazile**, Leo *WhoBlA 92*
**Bazille**, Frederic 1841-1870 *ThHEIm [port]*
**Bazin**, Herve *IntWW 91*
**Bazin**, John Robert 1953- *WhoFI 92, WhoMW 92*
**Bazin**, Marc Louis 1932- *IntWW 91*
**Bazinet**, George Frederick 1937- *AmMWSc 92*
**Bazinet**, James Richard *WhoAmP 91*
**Bazinet**, Maurice L 1918- *AmMWSc 92*
**Baziotes**, William 1912-1963 *FacFETw*
**Bazire**, Reginald Victor d1990 *Who 92N*
**Bazis**, Albert J. *WhoFI 92*
**Bazler**, Frank Ellis 1930- *WhoAmL 92*
**Bazley**, Colin Frederick *Who 92*
**Bazley**, Thomas Stafford 1907- *Who 92*
**Bazluke**, Francine Tilewick 1954- *WhoAmL 92*
**Bazovsky**, Vladimir Nikolayevich 1917- *IntWW 91*
**Bazzarre**, John Thomas 1930- *WhoFI 92*
**Bazzaz**, Fakhri Al 1933- *AmMWSc 92*
**Bazzaz**, Maarib Bakri 1940- *AmMWSc 92*
**BB** *SmATA 66*
**Be Ment**, Spencer L 1937- *AmMWSc 92*
**Bea**, Augustin 1881-1968 *DcEcMov*
**Bea**, Robert G *AmMWSc 92*
**Beabout**, Douglas Howard 1950- *WhoMW 92*
**Beach** *Who 92*
**Beach Boys**, The *FacFETw, NewAmDM*
**Beach**, Alfred Ely 1826-1896 *BiInAmS*
**Beach**, Amy Marcy Cheney 1867-1944 *FacFETw, HanAmWH*
**Beach**, Arthur O'Neal 1945- *WhoFI 92, WhoWest 92*
**Beach**, Barbara Purse 1947- *WhoAmL 92*
**Beach**, Betty Laura *AmMWSc 92*
**Beach**, Charles Maynard 1876-1959 *DcNCBi 1*
**Beach**, Daniel Magee, IV 1962- *WhoEnt 92*
**Beach**, Daniel Raymond 1946- *WhoRel 92*
**Beach**, David H 1939- *AmMWSc 92*
**Beach**, Douglas Ryder 1948- *WhoAmL 92*
**Beach**, Edward L. *DrAPF 91*
**Beach**, Edward L. 1918- *WrDr 92*
**Beach**, Eliot Frederick 1911- *AmMWSc 92*
**Beach**, Eugene Huff 1918- *AmMWSc 92*
**Beach**, Frank Ambrose 1911- *AmMWSc 92*
**Beach**, George Kimmich 1935- *WhoRel 92*
**Beach**, George Winchester 1913- *AmMWSc 92*
**Beach**, H.H.A., Mrs. 1867-1944 *NewAmDM*
**Beach**, Harry Lee, Jr 1944- *AmMWSc 92*
**Beach**, Henry Harris Aubrey 1843-1910 *BiInAmS*
**Beach**, Hugh 1923- *Who 92*
**Beach**, Louis Andrew 1925- *AmMWSc 92*
**Beach**, Mary *DrAPF 91*
**Beach**, Mildred A 1924- *WhoAmP 91*
**Beach**, Morrison H. 1917- *IntWW 91*
**Beach**, Neil William 1928- *AmMWSc 92*
**Beach**, R K 1918- *AmMWSc 92*
**Beach**, Rex 1877-1949 *BenetAL 91, TwCWW 91*
**Beach**, Robert C 1935- *WhoAmP 91*
**Beach**, Robert L 1938- *AmMWSc 92*
**Beach**, Robert Preston 1916- *WhoFI 92*
**Beach**, Roger C. 1936- *WhoWest 92*
**Beach**, Sharon Sickel 1946- *AmMWSc 92*
**Beach**, Stephen Holbrook 1915- *WhoAmL 92*
**Beach**, Sylvia 1887-1962 *BenetAL 91, FacFETw*
**Beach**, Walter G., II *WhoBlA 92*
**Beach**, William Vincent 1903- *Who 92*
**Beacham**, Andrea Jeanette 1957- *WhoAmL 92*
**Beacham**, Arthur 1913- *Who 92*
**Beacham**, Billy, Jr. 1954- *WhoRel 92*
**Beachcroft**, Ellinor Nina 1931- *IntAu&W 91*
**Beachcroft**, Nina 1931- *WrDr 92*
**Beachem**, Cedric D 1932- *AmMWSc 92*
**Beachem**, Constance 1921- *WhoBlA 92*
**Beachem**, William Perry 1932- *WhoBlA 92*
**Beachey**, Edwin Henry *AmMWSc 92*
**Beachler**, Charles S 1870-1894 *BiInAmS*
**Beachler**, Kenneth Clarke 1935- *WhoMW 92*
**Beachley**, Norman Henry 1933- *AmMWSc 92*
**Beachley**, Orville Theodore, Jr 1937- *AmMWSc 92*
**Beachum**, Christopher Mark 1966- *WhoEnt 92, WhoRel 92*
**Beachy**, Roger Neil 1944- *AmMWSc 92*
**Beachy**, William 1948- *WhoAmP 91*
**Beacom**, Stanley Ernest 1927- *AmMWSc 92*
**Beadel**, Stephen Jay 1949- *WhoMW 92*
**Beadell**, Len 1923- *WrDr 92*
**Beadell**, Leonard 1923- *IntAu&W 91*
**Beadle**, Buell Wesley 1911- *AmMWSc 92*
**Beadle**, Charles *ScFEYrs*
**Beadle**, Charles Wilson 1930- *AmMWSc 92*
**Beadle**, Erastus F. 1821-1894 *BenetAL 91*
**Beadle**, George Wells 1903- *AmMWSc 92, FacFETw*
**Beadle**, George Wells 1903-1989 *WhoNob 90*
**Beadle**, John Grant 1932- *WhoFI 92*
**Beadle**, Peter Campbell 1945- *WhoMW 92*
**Beadle**, Ralph Eugene 1943- *AmMWSc 92*
**Beadle**, Sue M 1944- *WhoAmP 91*
**Beadles**, John Kenneth 1931- *AmMWSc 92*
**Beadleston**, Alfred N 1912- *WhoAmP 91*
**Beadling**, Leslie Craig 1946- *AmMWSc 92*
**Beagle**, Gail Joyce 1935- *WhoAmP 91*
**Beagle**, John Gordon 1943- *WhoWest 92*
**Beagle**, Peter S. *DrAPF 91*
**Beagle**, Peter S. 1939- *WrDr 92*
**Beagle**, William Gerhardt 1946- *WhoRel 92*
**Beagley**, Thomas Lorne 1919- *Who 92*
**Beagrie**, George Simpson 1925- *AmMWSc 92*
**Beahm**, Edward Charles 1939- *AmMWSc 92*
**Beahn**, Raymond Anglum, II 1932- *WhoFI 92*
**Beaird**, Betty *WhoEnt 92*
**Beaird**, Daniel R 1944- *WhoAmP 91*
**Beaird**, Eric Thomas 1954- *WhoEnt 92*
**Beaird**, Pat C. 1960- *WhoFI 92*
**Beak**, Peter 1936- *AmMWSc 92*
**Beake**, John *WhoWest 92*
**Beakley**, George Carroll, Jr 1922- *AmMWSc 92*
**Beal**, Anthony Ridley 1925- *Who 92*
**Beal**, Bernard B. *NewYTBS 91 [port]*
**Beal**, Bob 1949- *WrDr 92*
**Beal**, David R. 1963- *WhoEnt 92*
**Beal**, Diane Lynn 1950- *WhoFI 92*
**Beal**, Foster Ellenborough Lascelles 1840-1916 *BiInAmS*
**Beal**, Fred Erwin 1896-1954 *DcNCBi 1*
**Beal**, Graham William John 1947- *WhoMW 92*
**Beal**, Gregory John 1942- *WhoAmP 91*
**Beal**, Helen Marjorie 1887-1965 *DcNCBi 1*
**Beal**, Jack Lewis 1923- *AmMWSc 92*
**Beal**, Jacqueline Jean 1960- *WhoBlA 92*
**Beal**, James Burton, Jr 1932- *AmMWSc 92*
**Beal**, Jim C 1933- *AmMWSc 92*
**Beal**, John 1909- *IntMPA 92, WhoEnt 92*
**Beal**, John Anthony 1945- *AmMWSc 92*
**Beal**, Kathleen Grabaskas 1951- *AmMWSc 92*
**Beal**, M.F. *DrAPF 91*
**Beal**, Mary Christine 1957- *WhoEnt 92*
**Beal**, Myron Clarence 1920- *AmMWSc 92, WhoMW 92*
**Beal**, Philip Franklin, III 1922- *AmMWSc 92*
**Beal**, Richard Sidney, Jr 1916- *AmMWSc 92*
**Beal**, Robert Carl 1940- *AmMWSc 92*
**Beal**, Robert George *Who 92*
**Beal**, Robert Lawrence 1941- *WhoFI 92*
**Beal**, Stuart Kirkham 1932- *AmMWSc 92*
**Beal**, Thomas Ellis 1930- *WhoFI 92, WhoMW 92*
**Beal**, Thomas R 1929- *AmMWSc 92*
**Beal**, Virginia Asta 1918- *AmMWSc 92*
**Beal**, Wesley Arnold, Jr 1946- *WhoAmP 91*
**Beal**, Winona Roark 1924- *WhoRel 92*
**Beale**, Anthony John 1932- *Who 92*
**Beale**, Charles Willing 1845-1932 *ScFEYrs*
**Beale**, Edward *Who 92*
**Beale**, Geoffrey Herbert 1913- *IntWW 91, Who 92*
**Beale**, Georgia Robison 1905- *WhoFI 92*
**Beale**, Guy Otis 1944- *AmMWSc 92*
**Beale**, Josiah Edward Michael 1928- *Who 92*
**Beale**, Larry D. 1949- *WhoBlA 92*
**Beale**, Lawrence L. 1932- *WhoRel 92*
**Beale**, Luther A 1923- *AmMWSc 92*
**Beale**, Nancy Lee 1956- *WhoRel 92*
**Beale**, Paul Drew 1955- *AmMWSc 92*
**Beale**, Peter John 1934- *Who 92*
**Beale**, Philippa 1946- *TwCPaSc*
**Beale**, Samuel I 1942- *AmMWSc 92*
**Beale**, Sara Sun 1949- *WhoAmL 92*
**Beale**, Stephen Bruce 1958- *WhoWest 92*
**Beale**, Thomas Edward 1904- *Who 92*
**Beale**, Walter Michael 1955- *WhoFI 92*
**Beale**, William 1908- *Who 92*
**Bealer**, Steven Lee 1949- *AmMWSc 92*
**Beales**, D. E. D. 1931- *IntAu&W 91, WrDr 92*
**Beales**, Derek Edward Dawson 1931- *Who 92*
**Beales**, Francis William 1919- *AmMWSc 92*
**Beales**, John Howard, III 1950- *WhoFI 92*
**Beales**, Peter Leslie 1936- *Who 92*
**Bealey**, Frank 1922- *IntAu&W 91, WrDr 92*
**Bealey**, Frank William 1922- *Who 92*
**Beall**, Arthur Charles, Jr 1929- *AmMWSc 92*
**Beall**, Charles M 1920- *WhoAmP 91*
**Beall**, DeWitt Talmadge 1940- *WhoWest 92*
**Beall**, Donald Ray 1938- *IntWW 91, WhoFI 92, WhoWest 92*
**Beall**, Frank Carroll 1933- *AmMWSc 92, WhoWest 92*
**Beall**, Gary Wayne 1950- *AmMWSc 92*
**Beall**, George Halsey 1935- *AmMWSc 92*
**Beall**, Gildon Noel 1928- *AmMWSc 92*
**Beall**, Herbert 1939- *AmMWSc 92*
**Beall**, J Glenn, Jr 1927- *WhoAmP 91*
**Beall**, James Howard 1945- *AmMWSc 92*
**Beall**, James Robert 1940- *AmMWSc 92*
**Beall**, John 1942- *WhoEnt 92*
**Beall**, John Robert 1962- *WhoFI 92*
**Beall**, Karen Friedmann *WhoMW 92*
**Beall**, Lester 1903-1969 *DcTwDes*
**Beall**, Paula Thornton 1946- *AmMWSc 92*
**Beall**, Pauline 1937- *WhoEnt 92*
**Beall**, Robert Allan 1920- *AmMWSc 92*
**Beall**, Robert Joseph 1943- *AmMWSc 92*
**Beall**, Robert Milton 1944- *WhoFI 92*
**Beall**, Russell G 1922- *WhoAmP 91*
**Beall**, S E, Jr 1919- *AmMWSc 92*
**Beall**, Ware Thompson, Jr. 1940- *WhoMW 92*

**Beall**, William Charles 1955- *WhoAmL 92*
**Bealmear**, Michael William 1947- *WhoFI 92*
**Bealmear**, Patricia Maria 1929- *AmMWSc 92*
**Bealor**, Mark Dabney 1921- *AmMWSc 92*
**Beals**, Duane J. *WhoRel 92*
**Beals**, Edward Wesley 1933- *AmMWSc 92*
**Beals**, Harold Oliver 1931- *AmMWSc 92*
**Beals**, Jennifer 1963- *IntMPA 92, WhoEnt 92*
**Beals**, Jessie Tarbox 1870-1942 *HanAmWH*
**Beals**, Kenneth Albert 1946- *WhoRel 92*
**Beals**, Kim A. 1955- *WhoAmL 92*
**Beals**, Paul Archer 1924- *WhoRel 92*
**Beals**, R Michael 1954- *AmMWSc 92*
**Beals**, Richard William 1938- *AmMWSc 92*
**Beals**, Robert J 1923- *AmMWSc 92*
**Beals**, Rodney K 1931- *AmMWSc 92*
**Beals**, Terrence Roger 1941- *WhoWest 92*
**Beals**, Vaughn LeRoy, Jr. 1928- *WhoFI 92*
**Beam**, Alex 1954- *ConAu 135*
**Beam**, Beebe *EncAmaz 91*
**Beam**, C Arlen 1930- *WhoAmP 91*
**Beam**, Carl Adams 1920- *AmMWSc 92*
**Beam**, Charles Fitzhugh, Jr 1940- *AmMWSc 92*
**Beam**, Clarence Arlen 1930- *WhoAmL 92, WhoMW 92*
**Beam**, Francis H., Jr. 1935- *WhoFI 92*
**Beam**, Frank Letts 1942- *WhoFI 92*
**Beam**, Jacob D. 1908- *Who 92*
**Beam**, James Harold 1934- *WhoAmP 91*
**Beam**, Jeffery *DrAPF 91*
**Beam**, John E 1931- *AmMWSc 92*
**Beam**, John Scott 1944- *WhoAmP 91*
**Beam**, Karen Grace Kloos 1942- *WhoFI 92, WhoMW 92*
**Beam**, Kurt George, Jr 1945- *AmMWSc 92*
**Beam**, Lillian Kennedy 1924- *WhoBlA 92*
**Beam**, Margaret Anne Ridgeway 1948- *WhoAmL 92*
**Beam**, Steven Gerald 1956- *WhoRel 92*
**Beam**, Thomas Roger 1946- *AmMWSc 92*
**Beam**, Walter R 1928- *AmMWSc 92*
**Beam**, William Washington, III 1960- *WhoFI 92*
**Beaman**, Blaine Lee 1942- *AmMWSc 92*
**Beaman**, Donald Robert 1933- *AmMWSc 92*
**Beaman**, Jack 1924- *WhoAmP 91*
**Beaman**, John Homer 1929- *AmMWSc 92*
**Beaman**, Joyce Proctor 1931- *WrDr 92*
**Beaman**, Larry Gene 1946- *WhoAmL 92*
**Beame**, Abraham David 1906- *IntWW 91, WhoAmP 91*
**Beament**, George Edwin 1908- *IntWW 91*
**Beament**, James 1921- *IntWW 91, Who 92*
**Beamer**, Charles Christian 1950- *WhoRel 92*
**Beamer**, Gregory Alan 1963- *WhoEnt 92*
**Beamer**, Paul Donald 1914- *AmMWSc 92*
**Beamer**, Robert Lewis 1933- *AmMWSc 92*
**Beamer**, Robert William 1937- *WhoWest 92*
**Beamer-Patton**, June Elizabeth 1944- *WhoWest 92*
**Beames**, Calvin G, Jr 1930- *AmMWSc 92*
**Beames**, R M 1931- *AmMWSc 92*
**Beamish**, Adrian John 1939- *Who 92*
**Beamish**, Arthur Russell 1929- *WhoMW 92*
**Beamish**, Cecil Howard 1915- *Who 92*
**Beamish**, Frederick William Henry 1935- *AmMWSc 92*
**Beamish**, Robert Earl 1916- *AmMWSc 92*
**Beamish**, Thomas Bryce 1958- *WhoMW 92*
**Beamon**, Bob 1946- *FacFETw*
**Beamon**, Reginald Glenn 1951- *WhoAmP 91*
**Beamon**, Robert 1946- *BlkOlyM [port]*
**Beamon**, Teresa Kristine Nkenge Zola 1954- *WhoBlA 92*
**Beamont**, Roland Prosper 1920- *Who 92*
**Beams**, Harold William 1903- *AmMWSc 92*
**Bean**, Alan 1932- *FacFETw*
**Bean**, Alan LaVern 1932- *WhoEnt 92*
**Bean**, Albert C., III 1946- *WhoWest 92*
**Bean**, Amelia *TwCWW 91*
**Bean**, Barbara Louise 1948- *AmMWSc 92*
**Bean**, Barry 1942- *AmMWSc 92*
**Bean**, Basil 1931- *Who 92*
**Bean**, Brent Leroy 1941- *AmMWSc 92*
**Bean**, Bruce Winfield 1941- *WhoAmL 92, WhoFI 92*
**Bean**, C Thomas, Jr 1920- *AmMWSc 92*
**Bean**, Charles Palmer 1923- *AmMWSc 92*
**Bean**, Daniel Joseph 1934- *AmMWSc 92*
**Bean**, David Ira Mitchell 1954- *WhoRel 92*
**Bean**, Donna Rae 1950- *WhoWest 92*
**Bean**, Edwin Lee, Jr. 1950- *WhoAmL 92*
**Bean**, Elizabeth Harriman 1923- *WhoAmP 91*
**Bean**, Erik Paul 1962- *WhoFI 92*
**Bean**, George A 1933- *AmMWSc 92*
**Bean**, George E. 1903-1977 *ConAu 133*
**Bean**, Gerritt Post 1929- *AmMWSc 92*
**Bean**, Glen Atherton 1962- *WhoMW 92*
**Bean**, Hugh 1929- *Who 92*
**Bean**, James J 1903- *AmMWSc 92*
**Bean**, James L, Jr 1932- *WhoAmP 91*
**Bean**, James Woolson, Jr. 1947- *WhoFI 92*
**Bean**, John Condon 1950- *AmMWSc 92*
**Bean**, John David 1947- *WhoIns 92*
**Bean**, John Victor 1925- *Who 92*
**Bean**, Karen Edmundson 1955- *WhoEnt 92*
**Bean**, Leonard 1914- *Who 92*
**Bean**, Marion Talpey 1926- *WhoRel 92*
**Bean**, Marisa *Who 92*
**Bean**, Mark William 1955- *WhoAmL 92*
**Bean**, Marvin Day 1921- *WhoRel 92*
**Bean**, Maurice Darrow 1928- *WhoBlA 92*
**Bean**, Michael Arthur 1940- *AmMWSc 92*
**Bean**, Orson 1928- *IntMPA 92, WhoEnt 92*
**Bean**, Oscar Belmont 1923- *WhoAmP 91*
**Bean**, Pamela B 1942- *WhoAmP 91*
**Bean**, Ralph J 1933- *AmMWSc 92*
**Bean**, Robert Jay 1924- *AmMWSc 92*
**Bean**, Robert Taylor 1913- *AmMWSc 92*
**Bean**, Ross Coleman 1924- *AmMWSc 92*
**Bean**, Sean *IntMPA 92*
**Bean**, Stephen Michael 1953- *WhoAmP 91*
**Bean**, Tarleton Hoffman 1846-1916 *BiInAmS*
**Bean**, Vern Ellis 1937- *AmMWSc 92*
**Bean**, Walter Dempsey 1912- *WhoBlA 92*
**Bean**, Wendell Clebern 1934- *AmMWSc 92*
**Bean**, William Bennett *IntWW 91N*
**Bean**, William Bennett 1909- *AmMWSc 92*
**Bean**, William Clifton 1938- *AmMWSc 92*
**Bean**, William J, Jr 1945- *AmMWSc 92*
**Beane**, C. Ernest 1940- *WhoAmL 92, WhoMW 92*
**Beane**, Donald Gene 1929- *AmMWSc 92*
**Beane**, J D 1963- *WhoAmP 91*
**Beane**, Mark Christopher 1956- *WhoRel 92*
**Beane**, Patricia Jean 1944- *WhoBlA 92*
**Beane**, Robert Hubert 1947- *WhoBlA 92*
**Beane**, Wendell Charles 1935- *WhoRel 92*
**Beaney**, Jan *ConAu 35NR*
**Beans**, Elroy William 1931- *AmMWSc 92, WhoMW 92*
**Bear**, David George 1950- *AmMWSc 92*
**Bear**, Frederick Thomas 1937- *WhoFI 92*
**Bear**, Greg 1951- *ConAu 35NR, IntAu&W 91, SmATA 65, TwCSFW 91, WrDr 92*
**Bear**, Herbert S, Jr 1929- *AmMWSc 92*
**Bear**, Herbert Stanley, Jr. 1929- *WhoWest 92*
**Bear**, Jeffrey Warren 1945- *WhoWest 92*
**Bear**, John L 1934- *AmMWSc 92*
**Bear**, Larry Alan 1928- *WhoFI 92*
**Bear**, Leslie William 1911- *Who 92*
**Bear**, Phyllis Dorothy 1931- *AmMWSc 92*
**Bear**, Richard Scott 1908- *AmMWSc 92*
**Bear**, Sharon Louise 1946- *WhoEnt 92*
**Bear**, William Edward 1931- *WhoWest 92*
**Bearak**, Corey Becker 1955- *WhoAmL 92*
**Bearce**, Denny N 1934- *AmMWSc 92*
**Bearce**, Winfield Hutchinson 1937- *AmMWSc 92*
**Beard**, Allan Geoffrey 1919- *Who 92*
**Beard**, Benjamin H 1918- *AmMWSc 92*
**Beard**, Bill Lawrence 1932- *WhoEnt 92*
**Beard**, Charles A. 1874-1948 *BenetAL 91, RComAH*
**Beard**, Charles Austin 1874-1948 *AmPeW, FacFETw*
**Beard**, Charles Irvin 1916- *AmMWSc 92*
**Beard**, Charles Julian 1943- *WhoBlA 92*
**Beard**, Charles Noble 1906- *AmMWSc 92*
**Beard**, Charles Richard 1929- *WhoAmL 92, WhoMW 92*
**Beard**, Charles Walter 1932- *AmMWSc 92*
**Beard**, Christopher Nigel 1936- *Who 92*
**Beard**, Cindy York 1961- *WhoAmL 92*
**Beard**, Constance Rachelle 1949- *WhoWest 92*
**Beard**, Daniel C. 1850-1941 *BenetAL 91*
**Beard**, Daniel Perry 1943- *WhoAmP 91*
**Beard**, David Breed 1922- *AmMWSc 92*
**Beard**, Derek 1930- *Who 92*
**Beard**, Elizabeth L 1932- *AmMWSc 92*
**Beard**, Elmer 1937- *WhoAmP 91*
**Beard**, Geoffrey 1929- *WrDr 92*
**Beard**, George B 1924- *AmMWSc 92*
**Beard**, George Plummer, Jr 1921- *WhoAmP 91*
**Beard**, Hazel *WhoAmP 91*
**Beard**, Israel 1932- *WhoBlA 92*
**Beard**, James 1903-1985 *FacFETw*
**Beard**, James B 1935- *AmMWSc 92*
**Beard**, James David 1937- *AmMWSc 92*
**Beard**, James Taylor 1939- *AmMWSc 92*
**Beard**, James William, Jr. 1941- *WhoBlA 92*
**Beard**, Jean 1934- *AmMWSc 92*
**Beard**, John, Jr. 1797-1876 *DcNCBi 1*
**Beard**, Joseph James 1933- *WhoAmL 92*
**Beard**, Kenneth Van Kirke 1937- *AmMWSc 92*
**Beard**, Laronce D. 1949- *WhoBlA 92*
**Beard**, Leo Roy 1917- *AmMWSc 92*
**Beard**, Lewis 1754-1820 *DcNCBi 1*
**Beard**, Lillian McLean *WhoBlA 92*
**Beard**, Luther Stanford 1929- *AmMWSc 92*
**Beard**, Malcolm E 1919- *WhoAmP 91*
**Beard**, Margaret Elzada 1941- *AmMWSc 92*
**Beard**, Martin Luther 1926- *WhoBlA 92*
**Beard**, Mary 1876-1958 *HanAmWH*
**Beard**, Mary R. 1876-1958 *BenetAL 91, RComAH*
**Beard**, Melvin Charles 1935- *WhoBlA 92*
**Beard**, Michael Carl 1956- *WhoMW 92, WhoRel 92*
**Beard**, Montgomery, Jr. 1932- *WhoBlA 92*
**Beard**, Nigel *Who 92*
**Beard**, Owen Wayne 1916- *AmMWSc 92*
**Beard**, Patrick 1947- *WhoAmP 91*
**Beard**, R D 1923- *WhoAmP 91*
**Beard**, Randall Everet 1957- *WhoRel 92*
**Beard**, Richard B 1922- *AmMWSc 92*
**Beard**, Richard William 1931- *Who 92*
**Beard**, Rodney Allen 1961- *WhoAmL 92*
**Beard**, Rodney Rau 1911- *AmMWSc 92*
**Beard**, Ronald Stratton 1939- *WhoAmL 92*
**Beard**, Sherilyn F. 1952- *WhoEnt 92*
**Beard**, Stephen Ross 1950- *WhoAmL 92*
**Beard**, Virginia H. 1941- *WhoBlA 92*
**Beard**, William Clarence 1934- *AmMWSc 92*
**Beard**, William Quinby, Jr 1932- *AmMWSc 92*
**Beard**, Wolcott LeClear 1867-1937 *ScFEYrs*
**Beardall**, John Smith 1939- *AmMWSc 92*
**Bearde**, Chris *LesBEnT 92*
**Bearden**, Alan Joyce 1931- *AmMWSc 92*
**Bearden**, Alfred Douglas 1954- *WhoRel 92*
**Bearden**, Bessye 1888-1943 *NotBlAW 92*
**Bearden**, Henry Joe 1926- *AmMWSc 92*
**Bearden**, Mike R 1948- *WhoAmP 91*
**Bearden**, Romare 1912-1988 *ConBlB 2 [port]*
**Bearden**, William Harlie 1949- *AmMWSc 92*
**Beardmore**, Alexander Francis 1931- *Who 92*
**Beardmore**, John Alec 1930- *Who 92*
**Beardmore**, Peter 1935- *AmMWSc 92*
**Beardmore**, William Boone 1925- *AmMWSc 92*
**Beards**, Paul Francis Richmond 1916- *Who 92*
**Beardslee**, Ann Nesmith 1929- *WhoRel 92*
**Beardslee**, Bethany 1927- *NewAmDM*
**Beardslee**, Ronald Allen 1946- *AmMWSc 92*
**Beardslee**, William Armitage 1916- *WhoRel 92*
**Beardsley**, Arthur 1843-1920 *BiInAmS*
**Beardsley**, Bruce Robert 1953- *WhoFI 92*
**Beardsley**, Charles Mitchell 1921- *WhoFI 92, WhoIns 92*
**Beardsley**, George Peter 1940- *AmMWSc 92*
**Beardsley**, Irene Adelaide 1935- *AmMWSc 92*
**Beardsley**, Jacob Edward 1928- *WhoFI 92*
**Beardsley**, James H, II 1945- *WhoAmP 91, WhoMW 92*
**Beardsley**, John Douglas 1941- *IntAu&W 91*
**Beardsley**, John Wyman, Jr 1926- *AmMWSc 92*
**Beardsley**, Robert Alan 1961- *WhoMW 92*
**Beardsley**, Robert Cruce 1942- *AmMWSc 92*
**Beardsley**, Robert Eugene 1923- *AmMWSc 92*
**Beardsley**, Theodore S., Jr. 1930- *WrDr 92*
**Beardsworth**, Simon John 1929- *Who 92*
**Beare**, Robin Lyell Blin 1922- *Who 92*
**Beare**, Steven Douglas 1944- *AmMWSc 92*
**Beare**, Stuart Newton 1936- *Who 92*
**Beare-Rogers**, Joyce Louise 1927- *AmMWSc 92*
**Bearer**, Elaine L *AmMWSc 92*
**Bearg**, Martin Lee 1952- *WhoAmL 92*
**Bearley**, William Leon 1938- *WhoWest 92*
**Bearman**, Richard John 1929- *AmMWSc 92*
**Bearmon**, Lee *WhoAmL 92*
**Bearn**, Alexander Gordon 1923- *AmMWSc 92, IntWW 91, Who 92*
**Bearn**, Margaret Slocum 1924- *WhoAmL 92*
**Bearne**, Guy 1908- *Who 92*
**Bearrows**, Thomas Robert 1957- *WhoAmL 92*
**Bearse**, Gordon Everett 1907- *AmMWSc 92*
**Bearse**, Robert Carleton 1938- *AmMWSc 92*
**Bearss**, Joyce C 1930- *WhoAmP 91*
**Bearsted**, Viscount 1911- *Who 92*
**Bearwald**, Jean Haynes 1924- *WhoWest 92*
**Beary**, Dexter F 1924- *AmMWSc 92*
**Beary**, Shirley Lorraine 1928- *WhoRel 92*
**Beasley**, Alice Margaret 1945- *WhoBlA 92*
**Beasley**, Andrew Bowie 1931- *AmMWSc 92*
**Beasley**, Anne Vickers 1917- *WhoBlA 92*
**Beasley**, Annie Ruth 1928- *WhoBlA 92*
**Beasley**, Anthony L. 1960- *WhoMW 92*
**Beasley**, Arlene Audrey 1943- *WhoBlA 92*
**Beasley**, Barbara Starin 1955- *WhoFI 92*
**Beasley**, Bruce Miller 1939- *WhoWest 92*
**Beasley**, Clark Wayne 1942- *AmMWSc 92*
**Beasley**, Cloyd O, Jr 1933- *AmMWSc 92*
**Beasley**, Daniel L. 1910- *WhoBlA 92*
**Beasley**, David Muldrow 1957- *WhoAmP 91*
**Beasley**, Debbie Sue *AmMWSc 92*
**Beasley**, Delilah Leontium 1867-1934 *NotBlAW 92*
**Beasley**, Dorothy Toth *WhoAmL 92*
**Beasley**, Douglas Kent 1954- *WhoRel 92*
**Beasley**, Edward 1958- *WhoWest 92*
**Beasley**, Edward, III *WhoBlA 92*
**Beasley**, Edward Evans 1924- *AmMWSc 92*
**Beasley**, Eula Daniel 1958- *WhoBlA 92*
**Beasley**, Frederic 1777-1845 *DcNCBi 1*
**Beasley**, George Garland 1932- *WhoEnt 92*
**Beasley**, J Lamar 1936- *WhoAmP 91*
**Beasley**, James Edwin 1926- *WhoAmL 92*
**Beasley**, James Gordon 1928- *AmMWSc 92*
**Beasley**, Jesse C. 1929- *WhoBlA 92*
**Beasley**, John P *WhoAmP 91*
**Beasley**, John T. *Who 92*
**Beasley**, Johnny Mark 1952- *WhoEnt 92*
**Beasley**, Joseph Noble 1924- *AmMWSc 92*
**Beasley**, Kim Allen 1952- *WhoFI 92*
**Beasley**, Lois Rene 1960- *WhoAmL 92*
**Beasley**, Malcolm Roy 1940- *AmMWSc 92*
**Beasley**, Michael Charles 1924- *Who 92*
**Beasley**, Oscar Homer 1925- *WhoAmL 92*
**Beasley**, Paul Lee 1950- *WhoBlA 92*
**Beasley**, Philip Gene 1927- *AmMWSc 92*
**Beasley**, Phoebe 1943- *NotBlAW 92*
**Beasley**, Robert Scott 1949- *WhoFI 92*
**Beasley**, Rule Curtis 1931- *WhoEnt 92*
**Beasley**, Ruth 1942- *ConAu 135*
**Beasley**, Ulysses Christian, Jr. 1928- *WhoBlA 92*
**Beasley**, Victor Mario 1956- *WhoBlA 92*
**Beasley**, Wayne M 1922- *AmMWSc 92*
**Beasley**, William Gerald 1919- *IntAu&W 91, Who 92, WrDr 92*
**Beasley**, William Harold 1944- *AmMWSc 92*
**Beasley**, William Rex 1934- *WhoAmL 92*
**Beasley-Murray**, George Raymond 1916- *IntAu&W 91, Who 92, WrDr 92*
**Beasley-Murray**, Paul 1944- *Who 92*
**Beason**, James Douglas 1953- *WhoWest 92*
**Beason**, Margaret Eva 1933- *WhoAmP 91*
**Beason**, Robert Curtis 1946- *AmMWSc 92*
**Beastall**, John Sale 1941- *Who 92*
**Beat**, Janet 1937- *ConCom 92*
**Beath**, Betty 1932- *ConCom 92*
**Beath**, Cynthia Mathis 1944- *WhoWest 92*
**Beath**, Paul R. *BenetAL 91*
**Beathard**, Bobby 1937- *WhoWest 92*
**Beatie**, Rita *WhoEnt 92*
**Beatie**, Russel Harrison, Jr. 1938- *WhoAmL 92*
**Beatles**, The *FacFETw [port], NewAmDM*
**Beatley**, Janice Carson 1919- *AmMWSc 92*
**Beato**, Maritza 1949- *WhoHisp 92*
**Beaton**, Albert E 1931- *AmMWSc 92*
**Beaton**, Arthur Charles d1990 *Who 92N*
**Beaton**, Cecil 1904-1980 *FacFETw*
**Beaton**, Daniel H 1910- *AmMWSc 92*
**Beaton**, Dennis Wayne 1949- *WhoWest 92*
**Beaton**, George *IntAu&W 91X*
**Beaton**, George Hector 1929- *AmMWSc 92*
**Beaton**, James Donald 1940- *WhoWest 92*
**Beaton**, James Duncan 1930- *AmMWSc 92*
**Beaton**, James Wallace 1943- *Who 92*
**Beaton**, John McCall 1944- *AmMWSc 92*
**Beaton**, John Rogerson 1925- *AmMWSc 92*
**Beaton**, Lyle Glen 1935- *WhoMW 92*
**Beaton**, Nancy C 1955- *WhoAmP 91*
**Beaton**, Roy Howard 1916- *AmMWSc 92*
**Beaton**, William Henry 1921- *IntWW 91*
**Beatrix**, Queen of the Netherlands 1938- *IntWW 91*
**Beatson**, Jack 1948- *Who 92*
**Beattie**, Alan Gilbert 1934- *AmMWSc 92*
**Beattie**, Alexander 1912- *Who 92*
**Beattie**, Ann *DrAPF 91*
**Beattie**, Ann 1947- *BenetAL 91, ConNov 91, FacFETw, WrDr 92*
**Beattie**, Anne Heather *Who 92*
**Beattie**, Arthur James 1914- *Who 92*
**Beattie**, Basil 1935- *TwCPaSc*

**Beattie,** Charles Kenneth 1923- *WhoAmP 91*
**Beattie,** Charles Noel 1912- *Who 92*
**Beattie,** Craig W 1943- *AmMWSc 92*
**Beattie,** David 1924- *Who 92*
**Beattie,** David 1938- *Who 92*
**Beattie,** David Stuart 1924- *IntWW 91*
**Beattie,** Diana Scott 1934- *AmMWSc 92*
**Beattie,** Donald A 1929- *AmMWSc 92*
**Beattie,** Edward J 1918- *AmMWSc 92*
**Beattie,** George Chapin 1919- *WhoWest 92*
**Beattie,** Gregory Paul 1954- *WhoMW 92*
**Beattie,** Horace S 1909- *AmMWSc 92*
**Beattie,** James 1735-1803 *DcLB 109 [port], RfGEnL 91*
**Beattie,** James Monroe 1921- *AmMWSc 92*
**Beattie,** Jessie Louise 1896- *IntAu&W 91*
**Beattie,** John 1915-1990 *AnObit 1990*
**Beattie,** Lane 1951- *WhoAmP 91*
**Beattie,** Randall Chester 1945- *AmMWSc 92*
**Beattie,** Thomas Brunton 1924- *Who 92*
**Beattie,** Thomas Robert 1940- *AmMWSc 92*
**Beattie,** Willard Horatio 1927- *AmMWSc 92*
**Beattie,** William John Hunt Montgomery *Who 92*
**Beatts,** Anne Patricia 1947- *WhoEnt 92*
**Beatty,** Earl 1946- *Who 92*
**Beatty,** Charles Eugene, Sr. 1909- *WhoBlA 92*
**Beatty,** Charles Lee 1939- *AmMWSc 92*
**Beatty,** Clarissa Hager 1919- *AmMWSc 92*
**Beatty,** Conny Davinroy 1959- *WhoAmL 92*
**Beatty,** David Delmar 1935- *AmMWSc 92*
**Beatty,** David Lawrence 1952- *WhoAmP 91*
**Beatty,** David Ross 1942- *WhoFI 92*
**Beatty,** Donald W 1952- *WhoAmP 91*
**Beatty,** Garry Hamilton 1935- *WhoFI 92*
**Beatty,** Hugh Tyrrell 1939- *WhoWest 92*
**Beatty,** James D *WhoAmP 91*
**Beatty,** James Joseph 1952- *WhoEnt 92*
**Beatty,** James Wayne, Jr 1934- *AmMWSc 92*
**Beatty,** Jerry Alfred 1947- *WhoEnt 92*
**Beatty,** John C 1947- *AmMWSc 92*
**Beatty,** John Townsend, Jr. 1936- *WhoFI 92*
**Beatty,** Joseph John 1947- *AmMWSc 92*
**Beatty,** K O, Jr 1913- *AmMWSc 92*
**Beatty,** Kenneth Wilson 1929- *AmMWSc 92*
**Beatty,** Linda L 1942- *WhoAmP 91*
**Beatty,** Martha Nell 1933- *WhoWest 92*
**Beatty,** Martin Clarke *WhoBlA 92*
**Beatty,** Marvin Theodore 1928- *AmMWSc 92*
**Beatty,** Michael Alexander *WhoAmP 91*
**Beatty,** Michael L. 1947- *WhoAmL 92, WhoFI 92*
**Beatty,** Millard Fillmore, Jr 1930- *AmMWSc 92*
**Beatty,** Ned 1937- *IntMPA 92, WhoEnt 92*
**Beatty,** Oren Alexander 1901- *AmMWSc 92*
**Beatty,** Otto, Jr *WhoAmP 91*
**Beatty,** Otto, Jr. 1940- *WhoBlA 92*
**Beatty,** Ozell Kakaskus 1921- *WhoBlA 92*
**Beatty,** Patricia 1922- *IntAu&W 91, WrDr 92*
**Beatty,** Patricia Robbins d1991 *NewYTBS 91*
**Beatty,** Patricia Robbins 1922-1991 *ConAu 134, SmATA 68*
**Beatty,** Paul Francis 1934- *WhoAmL 92*
**Beatty,** Pearl 1935- *WhoBlA 92*
**Beatty,** Perrin 1950- *IntWW 91, Who 92*
**Beatty,** Robert 1909- *IntMPA 92*
**Beatty,** Robert 1937- *WhoFI 92*
**Beatty,** Robert L. 1939- *WhoBlA 92*
**Beatty,** Samuel Alston 1923- *WhoAmP 91*
**Beatty,** Tina Marie 1955- *WhoFI 92*
**Beatty,** Vander L. 1941-1990 *WhoBlA 92N*
**Beatty,** Warren *NewYTBS 91 [port]*
**Beatty,** Warren 1937- *IntMPA 92, IntWW 91, WhoEnt 92*
**Beatty,** William Clemens 1925- *WhoAmL 92*
**Beatty,** William Louis 1925- *WhoAmL 92, WhoMW 92*
**Beatty-Brown,** Florence R. 1912- *WhoBlA 92*
**Beaty,** Arthur David 1919- *IntAu&W 91*
**Beaty,** Betty *IntAu&W 91, WrDr 92*
**Beaty,** David 1919- *WrDr 92*
**Beaty,** David Wayne 1953- *AmMWSc 92*
**Beaty,** Earl Claude 1930- *AmMWSc 92*
**Beaty,** Earl Richard 1934- *WhoMW 92*
**Beaty,** Frederick Lee 1926- *WhoMW 92*
**Beaty,** James Ralph 1929- *WhoRel 92*
**Beaty,** John Thurston, Jr. 1944- *WhoFI 92*
**Beaty,** Orren, III 1945- *AmMWSc 92*
**Beaty,** Paul Richard 1946- *WhoWest 92*
**Beaty,** Richard Eugene 1931- *WhoMW 92*
**Beaty,** Robert Leon 1936- *WhoFI 92*
**Beaty,** Rufus F. 1958- *WhoFI 92*
**Beaty,** Warren 1937- *IntAu&W 91*
**Beaubien,** George H. 1937- *WhoBlA 92*
**Beaubien,** Stewart James 1919- *AmMWSc 92*
**Beaubouef,** Judith Schnabel 1946- *WhoAmL 92*
**Beaucaire,** Daniel Edward 1948- *WhoMW 92*
**Beauchamp,** Arthur Paul 1914- *WhoAmP 91*
**Beauchamp,** Charles 1949- *TwCPaSc*
**Beauchamp,** Christopher Radstock Proctor- 1935- *Who 92*
**Beauchamp,** Edward William 1942- *WhoRel 92*
**Beauchamp,** Edwin Knight 1930- *AmMWSc 92*
**Beauchamp,** Eric G 1936- *AmMWSc 92*
**Beauchamp,** Finis Pierre 1956- *WhoRel 92*
**Beauchamp,** Gary Keith 1943- *AmMWSc 92*
**Beauchamp,** Jack *WhoAmP 91*
**Beauchamp,** Jerry J *WhoAmP 91*
**Beauchamp,** Jesse Lee 1942- *AmMWSc 92*
**Beauchamp,** John J 1937- *AmMWSc 92*
**Beauchamp,** Kathleen Mansfield 1888-1923 *ConAu 134*
**Beauchamp,** Kenneth 1939- *WrDr 92*
**Beauchamp,** Lilia Marie *AmMWSc 92*
**Beauchamp,** Mark Thomas 1951- *WhoEnt 92*
**Beauchamp,** Patrick L. *WhoBlA 92*
**Beauchamp,** Paul 1948- *TwCPaSc*
**Beauchamp,** Rollin Odell 1950- *WhoRel 92*
**Beauchane,** Judith Ann Orrben 1941- *WhoRel 92*
**Beauchene,** Roy E 1925- *AmMWSc 92*
**Beauchesne,** Wilfred P 1923- *WhoAmP 91*
**Beauclerk** *Who 92*
**Beauclerk,** Charles Frederic Aubrey de V 1915-1988 *FacFETw*
**Beaudet,** Arthur L 1942- *AmMWSc 92*
**Beaudet,** Jean-Marie 1908-1971 *NewAmDM*
**Beaudet,** Robert A 1935- *AmMWSc 92*
**Beaudette,** Robert Lee 1943- *WhoMW 92*
**Beaudin,** John Anthony 1946- *WhoMW 92*
**Beaudine,** Frank Richard 1923- *WhoFI 92*
**Beaudoin,** Adrien Robert 1940- *AmMWSc 92*
**Beaudoin,** Allan Roger 1927- *AmMWSc 92*
**Beaudoin,** Gerald-A. 1929- *IntWW 91*
**Beaudoin,** Kenneth L. *DrAPF 91*
**Beaudoin,** Laurent 1938- *WhoFI 92*
**Beaudoin,** Monica 1937- *WhoAmP 91*
**Beaudoin,** Robert Lawrence 1933- *WhoFI 92, WhoMW 92*
**Beaudouin,** David *DrAPF 91*
**Beaudreau,** George Stanley 1925- *AmMWSc 92*
**Beaudreau,** Louise F 1928- *WhoAmP 91*
**Beaudrot,** Charles Rufus, Jr. 1951- *WhoAmL 92*
**Beaudry,** Bernard Joseph 1932- *AmMWSc 92*
**Beaudry,** G. Ward 1941- *WhoAmL 92*
**Beaudry,** Janis Stonier 1956- *WhoWest 92*
**Beauduin,** Lambert 1873-1960 *DcEcMov*
**Beaufait,** Frederick W 1936- *AmMWSc 92*
**Beaufait,** Frederick William 1936- *WhoFI 92, WhoMW 92*
**Beauford,** Fred 1940- *WhoBlA 92*
**Beauford,** Willie, Jr. 1944- *WhoWest 92*
**Beaufort,** Duke of 1928- *Who 92*
**Beaufort,** John David 1912- *WhoEnt 92*
**Beauglie,** Madame de *EncAmaz 91*
**Beaugureau,** David Lee 1949- *WhoAmL 92*
**Beaujeu-Garnier,** Jacqueline 1917- *IntWW 91*
**Beauland,** Frank 1936- *TwCPaSc*
**Beaulieu,** Alan Louis 1948- *WhoWest 92*
**Beaulieu,** Edith S 1937- *WhoAmP 91*
**Beaulieu,** Hyacinthe 1916- *WhoAmP 91*
**Beaulieu,** J A 1929- *AmMWSc 92*
**Beaulieu,** John David 1944- *AmMWSc 92*
**Beaulne,** Joseph-Charles-Leonard Yvon 1919- *IntWW 91*
**Beauman,** Katharine Bentley *WrDr 92*
**Beauman,** Katharine Burgoyne Bentley 1903- *IntAu&W 91*
**Beauman,** Sally 1944?- *ConAu 134*
**Beaumarchais,** Pierre-Augustin Caron de 1732-1799 *BlkwCEP, BlkwEAR*
**Beaumariage,** D C 1925- *AmMWSc 92*
**Beaumariage,** Terrence Gilbert 1961- *AmMWSc 92*
**Beaumont** *Who 92*
**Beaumont,** Bill *Who 92*
**Beaumont,** Charles 1929-1967 *TwCSFW 91*
**Beaumont,** Christopher *Who 92*
**Beaumont,** Christopher Hubert 1926- *Who 92*
**Beaumont,** David Colin Baskcomb 1942- *Who 92*
**Beaumont,** Diana Jean 1948- *WhoEnt 92*
**Beaumont,** Dina G *WhoAmP 91*
**Beaumont,** Edward Nicholas 1929- *Who 92*
**Beaumont,** Enid Franklin 1930- *WhoFI 92*
**Beaumont,** Francis 1584?-1616 *CnDBLB 1 [port], RfGEnL 91*
**Beaumont,** Francis, and John Fletcher *CnDBLB 1 [port]*
**Beaumont,** George Howland Francis 1924- *Who 92*
**Beaumont,** Herbert Christopher 1912- *Who 92*
**Beaumont,** James Rawlings 1956- *WhoEnt 92*
**Beaumont,** John 1582-1627 *RfGEnL 91*
**Beaumont,** Joseph 1616-1699 *RfGEnL 91*
**Beaumont,** Leonard 1891-1986 *TwCPaSc*
**Beaumont,** Michael 1927- *Who 92*
**Beaumont,** Mona *WhoWest 92*
**Beaumont,** Nicholas *Who 92*
**Beaumont,** Peter John Luther 1944- *Who 92*
**Beaumont,** Ralph Harrison, Jr 1923- *AmMWSc 92*
**Beaumont,** Randolph Campbell 1941- *AmMWSc 92, WhoWest 92*
**Beaumont,** Richard Ashton 1912- *IntWW 91, Who 92*
**Beaumont,** Richard Austin 1925- *WhoFI 92*
**Beaumont,** Ross Allen 1914- *AmMWSc 92*
**Beaumont,** William 1785-1853 *BiInAmS*
**Beaumont,** William Anderson 1924- *Who 92*
**Beaumont,** William Blackledge 1952- *Who 92*
**Beaumont-Dark,** Anthony Michael 1932- *Who 92*
**Beaumont of Whitley,** Baron 1928- *Who 92*
**Beaupeurt,** Joseph Eugene 1912- *WhoWest 92*
**Beaupre,** Elaine Marcia Kenow 1942- *WhoMW 92*
**Beaupre,** Jon Norman 1953- *WhoEnt 92*
**Beaupre,** Odette *WhoEnt 92*
**Beaupre,** Roland O 1931- *WhoAmP 91*
**Beauregard,** Raymond A 1943- *AmMWSc 92*
**Beaurepaire,** Beryl 1923- *Who 92*
**Beaurepaire,** Ian Francis 1922- *Who 92*
**Beaurline,** Andrew Anderson 1952- *WhoFI 92*
**Beausang,** Michael Francis, Jr. 1936- *WhoAmL 92*
**Beausay,** Florence E 1911- *IntAu&W 91*
**Beausoleil,** Beau *DrAPF 91*
**Beauvais,** Edward R. 1936- *WhoWest 92*
**Beauvoir,** Simone de *FacFETw*
**Beauvoir,** Simone de 1908-1986 *FrenWW, GuFrLit 1, WomSoc*
**Beaux,** Cecilia 1855-1942 *HanAmWH*
**Beauzee,** Nicolas 1717-1789 *BlkwCEP*
**Beavan** *Who 92*
**Beaven,** John Lewis 1930- *Who 92*
**Beaven,** Mark W. 1961- *WhoEnt 92*
**Beaven,** Michael Anthony 1936- *AmMWSc 92*
**Beaven,** Peter Jamieson 1925- *IntWW 91*
**Beaven,** Vida Helms 1939- *AmMWSc 92*
**Beaver,** Bonnie Veryle *AmMWSc 92*
**Beaver,** Bruce 1928- *ConPo 91, IntAu&W 91, WrDr 92*
**Beaver,** Donald Loyd 1943- *AmMWSc 92*
**Beaver,** Earl Richard 1945- *AmMWSc 92*
**Beaver,** Frank Eugene 1938- *WhoEnt 92*
**Beaver,** H H 1925- *AmMWSc 92*
**Beaver,** Harold 1929- *LiExTwC*
**Beaver,** James Norman, Jr. 1950- *WhoEnt 92*
**Beaver,** Joseph T., Jr. 1922- *WhoBlA 92*
**Beaver,** Patrick 1923- *IntAu&W 91, WrDr 92*
**Beaver,** Paul 1953- *WrDr 92*
**Beaver,** Paul Chester 1905- *AmMWSc 92*
**Beaver,** Paul Eli 1953- *IntAu&W 91*
**Beaver,** Randy Lynn 1954- *WhoMW 92*
**Beaver,** Robert John 1937- *AmMWSc 92*
**Beaver,** W Don 1924- *AmMWSc 92*
**Beaver,** W L 1920- *AmMWSc 92*
**Beaver,** William Lee, Jr. 1917- *WhoMW 92*
**Beaver,** William Thomas 1933- *AmMWSc 92*
**Beaverbrook,** Baron 1951- *Who 92*
**Beaverbrook,** William Maxwell Aitken 1879-1964 *FacFETw [port]*
**Beavers,** Dorothy Johnson 1927- *AmMWSc 92*
**Beavers,** Ellington McHenry *AmMWSc 92*
**Beavers,** George A. 1891- *WhoBlA 92N*
**Beavers,** Gordon Stanley 1936- *AmMWSc 92*
**Beavers,** Graten Don Hogan 1949- *WhoAmL 92*
**Beavers,** John Parrish 1947- *WhoAmL 92*
**Beavers,** Leo Earice 1920- *AmMWSc 92*
**Beavers,** Louise 1902-1962 *NotBlAW 92*
**Beavers,** Nathan Howard, Jr. 1928- *WhoBlA 92*
**Beavers,** Peggy Jones 1946- *WhoBlA 92*
**Beavers,** Robert M., Jr. 1944- *WhoBlA 92*
**Beavers,** Willet I 1933- *AmMWSc 92*
**Beavers,** William *WhoAmP 91*
**Beavis,** Michael 1929- *Who 92*
**Beavo,** Joseph A *AmMWSc 92*
**Beavon,** Joseph Charles 1943- *WhoRel 92*
**Beazer,** Brian Cyril 1935- *Who 92*
**Beazley,** Christopher John Pridham 1952- *Who 92*
**Beazley,** Hamilton Scott 1943- *WhoFI 92*
**Beazley,** Kim Christian 1948- *IntWW 91, Who 92*
**Beazley,** Peter George 1922- *Who 92*
**Bebb,** Herbert Barrington 1935- *AmMWSc 92*
**Bebb,** Michael Schuck 1833-1895 *BiInAmS*
**Bebbington,** D. W. 1949- *ConAu 133*
**Bebbington,** W P 1915- *AmMWSc 92*
**Bebchuk,** Lucian Arye 1955- *WhoAmL 92*
**Bebear,** Claude *NewYTBS 91 [port]*
**Beber,** Robert H. 1933- *WhoAmL 92*
**Bebernes,** Jerrold William 1935- *AmMWSc 92*
**Bebey,** Francis 1929- *LiExTwC*
**Bebout,** David James 1951- *WhoAmL 92*
**Bebout,** Don Gray 1931- *AmMWSc 92*
**Bebout,** Eli D 1946- *WhoAmP 91*
**Becan,** Daniel Joseph 1932- *WhoAmP 91*
**Beccaria,** Cesare Bonesana di 1738-1794 *BlkwCEP*
**Becchetti,** Frederick Daniel 1943- *AmMWSc 92*
**Becella,** Tadeusz 1907- *IntAu&W 91*
**Becerra,** Abel 1936- *WhoHisp 92*
**Becerra,** Felipe Edgardo 1958- *WhoHisp 92*
**Becerra,** Francisco 1932- *WhoHisp 92*
**Becerra,** Francisco J., Jr. 1961- *WhoHisp 92*
**Becerra,** Guillermo *WhoEnt 92*
**Becerra,** Jose Carlos 1936-1970 *ConSpAP*
**Becerra,** Rosina M. 1939- *WhoHisp 92*
**Becerra,** Xavier 1958- *WhoAmP 91, WhoHisp 92*
**Becerra Barney,** Manuel Francisco 1951- *IntWW 91*
**Becerra Tanco,** Luis 1602-1672 *HisDSpE*
**Bechac,** A Denis 1939- *WhoAmP 91*
**Bechara,** Ibrahim 1943- *AmMWSc 92*
**Bechara,** Jose A., Jr. 1944- *WhoHisp 92*
**Bechard,** Paul Francis 1926- *WhoFI 92*
**Bechdolt,** Frederick R. 1874-1950 *TwCWW 91*
**Bechdolt,** Jack 1884-1954 *ScFEYrs*
**Becher,** Andrew Clifford 1946- *WhoAmL 92*
**Becher,** Edmund Theodore 1904- *WhoWest 92*
**Becher,** Johannes R. 1891-1958 *EncTR 91, LiExTwC*
**Becher,** Kurt 1909- *EncTR 91*
**Becher,** Paul 1918- *AmMWSc 92*
**Becher,** Ulrich 1910- *IntAu&W 91, IntWW 91*
**Becher,** William D 1929- *AmMWSc 92*
**Becher,** William Don 1929- *WhoMW 92*
**Becher,** William Fane Wrixon- 1915- *Who 92*
**Becherer,** Hans Walter 1935- *IntWW 91, WhoFI 92, WhoMW 92*
**Becherer,** John 1949- *WhoMW 92*
**Bechert,** Heinz 1932- *IntWW 91*
**Bechervaise,** John M 1910- *IntAu&W 91*
**Bechervaise,** John Mayston 1910- *WrDr 92*
**Bechet,** Sidney 1897?-1959 *NewAmDM*
**Bechhofer,** Robert E 1919- *AmMWSc 92*
**Bechily,** Maria Concepcion 1949- *WhoHisp 92*
**Bechis,** Dennis John 1951- *AmMWSc 92*
**Bechis,** Kenneth Paul 1949- *AmMWSc 92*
**Bechko,** P A 1950- *IntAu&W 91, TwCWW 91, WrDr 92*
**Bechler,** Lawrence Edgar 1950- *WhoAmL 92*
**Bechman,** Charles Edward 1922- *WhoAmP 91*
**Bechmann,** Mary 1957- *WhoFI 92*
**Becht,** Charles, IV 1954- *AmMWSc 92*
**Becht,** Paul Frederick 1937- *WhoAmP 91*
**Bechtel,** Donald Bruce 1949- *AmMWSc 92*
**Bechtel,** James Harvey 1945- *AmMWSc 92*
**Bechtel,** Leslie Ann *WhoAmL 92*
**Bechtel,** Peter John 1943- *AmMWSc 92*
**Bechtel,** Richard Neil 1932- *WhoMW 92*
**Bechtel,** Riley *WhoFI 92, WhoWest 92*
**Bechtel,** Robert D 1931- *AmMWSc 92*
**Bechtel,** Roy 1948- *WhoMW 92*
**Bechtel,** Stephen D, Jr 1925- *AmMWSc 92*
**Bechtel,** Stephen Davison 1900-1989 *FacFETw*
**Bechtel,** Stephen Davison, Jr. *IntWW 91N*
**Bechtel,** Stephen Davison, Jr. 1925- *WhoFI 92, WhoWest 92*
**Bechtelheimer,** Robert Russell 1932- *WhoWest 92*

**Bechtle,** Daniel Wayne 1949- *AmMWSc 92*
**Bechtle,** Gerald Francis 1921- *AmMWSc 92*
**Bechtle,** Louis Charles 1927- *WhoAmL 92*
**Bechtle,** Perry Stevens 1926- *WhoAmL 92*
**Bechtler,** Christopher 1782-1842? *DcNCBi 1*
**Bechtol,** John Beatty 1947- *WhoAmL 92*
**Bechtol,** Kathleen B 1945- *AmMWSc 92*
**Bechtol,** William M 1931- *ConAu 34NR*
**Bechtold,** Linda Helen 1963- *WhoEnt 92*
**Bechtold,** Max Frederick 1915- *AmMWSc 92*
**Bechtold,** Susan Hatfield 1948- *WhoAmL 92*
**Bechtold,** William Eric 1952- *AmMWSc 92*
**Bechtoldt,** Richard Blaine 1947- *WhoMW 92*
**Beck,** Aaron Temkin 1921- *AmMWSc 92*
**Beck,** Alan Edward *AmMWSc 92*
**Beck,** Albert 1928- *WhoFI 92*
**Beck,** Albert J 1935- *AmMWSc 92*
**Beck,** Alexander J. 1926- *IntMPA 92*
**Beck,** Allen Earl 1937- *WhoEnt 92*
**Beck,** Anatole 1930- *AmMWSc 92*
**Beck,** Andrew James 1948- *WhoAmL 92, WhoFI 92*
**Beck,** Ariadne Plumis 1933- *WhoMW 92*
**Beck,** Arnold Hugh William *Who 92*
**Beck,** Art *DrAPF 91*
**Beck,** Arthello, Jr. 1941- *WhoBlA 92*
**Beck,** Barbara North *AmMWSc 92*
**Beck,** Beatrix Marie 1914- *IntWW 91*
**Beck,** Benny Lee 1932- *AmMWSc 92*
**Beck,** Betty Anne 1922- *AmMWSc 92*
**Beck,** Brenda Faye 1952- *WhoFI 92*
**Beck,** Brian Edgar 1933- *IntWW 91, Who 92*
**Beck,** Carl 1856-1911 *BiInAmS*
**Beck,** Charles Beverley 1927- *AmMWSc 92*
**Beck,** Charlotte Hudgens 1937- *WhoEnt 92*
**Beck,** Christopher Alan 1953- *WhoAmL 92*
**Beck,** Clark E. 1929- *WhoBlA 92*
**Beck,** Clifford Wallace 1908- *WhoAmP 91*
**Beck,** Clive 1937- *Who 92*
**Beck,** Conrad 1901- *IntWW 91*
**Beck,** Curt B 1924- *AmMWSc 92*
**Beck,** Curt Werner 1927- *AmMWSc 92*
**Beck,** David Paul 1944- *AmMWSc 92*
**Beck,** Donald Edward 1934- *AmMWSc 92*
**Beck,** Donald Richardson 1940- *AmMWSc 92*
**Beck,** Doris Jean *AmMWSc 92*
**Beck,** Earl Ray 1916- *IntAu&W 91, WrDr 92*
**Beck,** Edgar 1911- *IntWW 91, Who 92*
**Beck,** Edgar Philip 1934- *Who 92*
**Beck,** Edward C 1918- *AmMWSc 92*
**Beck,** Edward Henry, III 1950- *WhoAmL 92*
**Beck,** Edward Nelson 1949- *WhoRel 92*
**Beck,** Edward William 1944- *WhoAmL 92*
**Beck,** Eugene Jerome 1929- *WhoMW 92*
**Beck,** Frances Patricia *WhoEnt 92*
**Beck,** Franklin H 1920- *AmMWSc 92*
**Beck,** Gail Edwin 1923- *AmMWSc 92*
**Beck,** Gary 1939- *WhoAmP 91*
**Beck,** Greg Dudley 1948- *WhoRel 92*
**Beck,** Harold Lawrence 1938- *AmMWSc 92*
**Beck,** Harry *TwCWW 91*
**Beck,** Henry M., Jr. 1951- *WhoAmL 92*
**Beck,** Henry Nelson 1927- *AmMWSc 92*
**Beck,** Henry Sanford, III 1945- *WhoRel 92*
**Beck,** Henry V 1920- *AmMWSc 92*
**Beck,** Hershell P. 1940- *WhoBlA 92*
**Beck,** Ivan Thomas 1924- *AmMWSc 92*
**Beck,** Jackson *IntMPA 92*
**Beck,** James 1930- *WrDr 92*
**Beck,** James Donald 1940- *AmMWSc 92*
**Beck,** James Hayes 1935- *WhoAmL 92*
**Beck,** James Henry John 1920- *Who 92*
**Beck,** James M 1917- *WhoAmP 91*
**Beck,** James Richard 1931- *AmMWSc 92, WhoMW 92*
**Beck,** James S 1931- *AmMWSc 92*
**Beck,** James Toomey, II 1956- *WhoMW 92*
**Beck,** James V 1930- *AmMWSc 92*
**Beck,** Jan Scott 1955- *WhoAmL 92*
**Beck,** Jay Vern 1912- *AmMWSc 92*
**Beck,** Jeanne Crawford 1943- *AmMWSc 92*
**Beck,** Jeff 1944- *WhoEnt 92*
**Beck,** Jeffrey Haines 1949- *WhoAmL 92*
**Beck,** Joan Wagner 1923- *WhoMW 92*
**Beck,** John *WhoAmP 91*
**Beck,** John 1943?- *ConTFT 9, IntMPA 92*
**Beck,** John Albert 1925- *WhoAmL 92*
**Beck,** John C. 1924- *IntWW 91*
**Beck,** John Christen 1959- *WhoWest 92*
**Beck,** John Christian 1924- *AmMWSc 92, WhoWest 92*
**Beck,** John Dixon 1950- *WhoWest 92*
**Beck,** John G. 1925- *WhoIns 92*
**Beck,** John Louis 1931- *AmMWSc 92*
**Beck,** John R 1929- *AmMWSc 92*
**Beck,** John Robert 1953- *AmMWSc 92*
**Beck,** John Robert, Jr. 1952- *WhoEnt 92, WhoFI 92, WhoMW 92*
**Beck,** John Roland 1929- *WhoFI 92, WhoWest 92*
**Beck,** John Swanson 1928- *Who 92*
**Beck,** Jozef 1894-1944 *EncTR 91 [port]*
**Beck,** Julian 1925-1985 *FacFETw*
**Beck,** Karl Maurice 1922- *AmMWSc 92*
**Beck,** Keith Lindell 1946- *WhoWest 92*
**Beck,** Keith Russell 1944- *AmMWSc 92*
**Beck,** Kenneth Charles *AmMWSc 92*
**Beck,** Kimberly 1956- *ConTFT 9*
**Beck,** Lewis Alfred 1919- *WhoWest 92*
**Beck,** Lewis Caleb 1798-1853 *BiInAmS*
**Beck,** Lewis White 1913- *WrDr 92*
**Beck,** Lloyd Willard 1919- *AmMWSc 92*
**Beck,** Lowell R. 1934- *WhoIns 92*
**Beck,** Lucille Bluso 1949- *AmMWSc 92*
**Beck,** Ludwig 1880-1944 *EncTR 91 [port]*
**Beck,** Mae Lucille 1930- *AmMWSc 92*
**Beck,** Marilyn Mohr 1928- *WhoEnt 92*
**Beck,** Mary Constance 1946- *WhoFI 92*
**Beck,** Mary Jean 1934- *WhoAmP 91*
**Beck,** Mat *WhoEnt 92*
**Beck,** Maxine Louise 1917- *WhoWest 92*
**Beck,** Meryl Hershey 1946- *WhoMW 92*
**Beck,** Michael 1949- *IntMPA 92*
**Beck,** Myrl Emil, Jr 1933- *AmMWSc 92*
**Beck,** Norman Arthur 1933- *WhoRel 92*
**Beck,** Paul Adams 1908- *AmMWSc 92*
**Beck,** Paul Augustine 1936- *WhoAmL 92*
**Beck,** Paul Edward 1937- *AmMWSc 92*
**Beck,** Paul W 1916- *AmMWSc 92*
**Beck,** Philip *Who 92*
**Beck,** Raymond Edward 1939- *WhoAmP 91*
**Beck,** Raymond Warren 1925- *AmMWSc 92*
**Beck,** Richard A 1933- *WhoAmP 91*
**Beck,** Richard P. 1943- *WhoAmL 92*
**Beck,** Richard R. 1930- *WhoIns 92*
**Beck,** Richard Theodore 1905- *Who 92*
**Beck,** Robert A. 1925- *IntWW 91, WhoIns 92*
**Beck,** Robert Arthur 1925- *WhoFI 92*
**Beck,** Robert Cory 1954- *WhoWest 92*
**Beck,** Robert Edward 1941- *AmMWSc 92*
**Beck,** Robert Frederick 1943- *AmMWSc 92*
**Beck,** Robert Lee 1921- *WhoMW 92*
**Beck,** Robert N. *WhoFI 92*
**Beck,** Robert Nason 1928- *AmMWSc 92*
**Beck,** Robert Randall 1940- *WhoFI 92*
**Beck,** Robert Raymond 1940- *WhoRel 92*
**Beck,** Robin Lynn 1968- *WhoMW 92*
**Beck,** Rod *WhoAmP 91*
**Beck,** Roger Jay 1941- *WhoMW 92*
**Beck,** Roland Arthur 1913- *AmMWSc 92*
**Beck,** Rolf d1991 *Who 92N*
**Beck,** Ronald Richard 1934- *AmMWSc 92*
**Beck,** Roswell Nathaniel *WhoBlA 92*
**Beck,** Saul L. 1928- *WhoBlA 92*
**Beck,** Sheryl Gene 1951- *WhoMW 92*
**Beck,** Sidney L 1935- *AmMWSc 92*
**Beck,** Sidney Louis *WhoMW 92*
**Beck,** Sidney M 1919- *AmMWSc 92*
**Beck,** Simone 1904-1991 *NewYTBS 91 [port]*
**Beck,** Stanley Dwight 1919- *AmMWSc 92*
**Beck,** Stanton Phillip 1961- *WhoAmL 92*
**Beck,** Stephen D 1930- *AmMWSc 92*
**Beck,** Steven R 1947- *AmMWSc 92*
**Beck,** Swanson *Who 92*
**Beck,** T. Mihaly 1929- *IntWW 91*
**Beck,** Tamas 1929- *IntWW 91*
**Beck,** Theodore R 1926- *AmMWSc 92*
**Beck,** Theodric Romeyn 1791-1855 *BiInAmS*
**Beck,** Thomas Arthur, III 1929- *WhoBlA 92*
**Beck,** Thomas Edwin 1946- *WhoWest 92*
**Beck,** Thomas W 1948- *AmMWSc 92*
**Beck,** Timothy Daniel 1953- *WhoWest 92*
**Beck,** Tom 1939- *WhoAmP 91*
**Beck,** Vilhelm *DcAmImH*
**Beck,** Warren *DrAPF 91*
**Beck,** Warren Albert 1918- *IntAu&W 91, WrDr 92*
**Beck,** Warren Albert 1918-1991 *ConAu 135*
**Beck,** Warren R 1918- *AmMWSc 92*
**Beck,** William Carl 1907- *AmMWSc 92*
**Beck,** William F 1938- *AmMWSc 92*
**Beck,** William Harold, Jr. 1928- *WhoAmL 92, WhoFI 92*
**Beck,** William J 1921- *AmMWSc 92*
**Beck,** William Samson 1923- *AmMWSc 92*
**Beck-von-Peccoz,** Stephen George Wolfgang 1933- *WhoWest 92*
**Becke,** Shirley Cameron 1917- *Who 92*
**Becke,** William Hugh Adamson 1916- *Who 92*
**Beckel,** Charles Leroy 1928- *AmMWSc 92, WhoWest 92*
**Beckel,** Graham *ConTFT 9*
**Beckelhymer,** Hunter 1919- *WrDr 92*
**Beckemeier,** Edward A. 1925- *WhoIns 92*
**Becken,** Bradford Albert 1924- *AmMWSc 92*
**Becken,** Eugene D 1911- *AmMWSc 92*
**Becken,** Garold Wallace 1953- *WhoWest 92*
**Beckenbauer,** Franz 1945- *FacFETw, IntWW 91*
**Beckendorf,** Steven K 1944- *AmMWSc 92*
**Beckendorf,** Steven Kent 1944- *WhoWest 92*
**Beckenstein,** Edward 1940- *AmMWSc 92*
**Becker,** Aaron Jay 1940- *AmMWSc 92*
**Becker,** Adolph Eric 1925- *WhoBlA 92*
**Becker,** Aharon 1906- *IntWW 91*
**Becker,** Alan I. 1946- *WhoAmL 92*
**Becker,** Alex 1935- *AmMWSc 92*
**Becker,** Anthony David 1958- *WhoMW 92*
**Becker,** Anthony J, Jr 1948- *AmMWSc 92*
**Becker,** Anthony Joseph 1922- *WhoRel 92*
**Becker,** Arlene 1948- *WhoAmP 91*
**Becker,** Arnold *LesBEnT 92*
**Becker,** Barbara 1932- *AmMWSc 92*
**Becker,** Becky Lynne 1955- *WhoRel 92*
**Becker,** Benjamin 1916- *AmMWSc 92*
**Becker,** Boris 1967- *FacFETw, IntWW 91*
**Becker,** Brian Elden 1949- *WhoFI 92*
**Becker,** Bruce Carl, II 1948- *WhoMW 92*
**Becker,** Bruce Clare 1929- *AmMWSc 92*
**Becker,** Carl 1873-1945 *BenetAL 91*
**Becker,** Carl Frederick 1948- *WhoAmL 92*
**Becker,** Carl George 1936- *AmMWSc 92*
**Becker,** Carl Johan 1915- *IntWW 91*
**Becker,** Carl Kline 1926- *WhoRel 92*
**Becker,** Carol *DrAPF 91*
**Becker,** Carter Miles 1940- *AmMWSc 92*
**Becker,** Charles J *WhoAmP 91*
**Becker,** Charles McVey 1937- *WhoFI 92*
**Becker,** Clarence Dale 1930- *AmMWSc 92*
**Becker,** Clarence F 1920- *AmMWSc 92*
**Becker,** David Leigh 1960- *WhoAmL 92*
**Becker,** David Mandel 1935- *WhoAmL 92*
**Becker,** David Michael 1955- *WhoRel 92*
**Becker,** David Stewart 1945- *AmMWSc 92*
**Becker,** David Victor 1923- *AmMWSc 92*
**Becker,** Debra Denise 1960- *WhoEnt 92*
**Becker,** Dennis Carl 1951- *WhoAmL 92*
**Becker,** Dismas Paul 1936- *WhoAmP 91*
**Becker,** Donald A 1938- *AmMWSc 92*
**Becker,** Donald Arthur 1938- *AmMWSc 92*
**Becker,** Donald Eugene 1923- *AmMWSc 92*
**Becker,** Douglas Jay 1955- *WhoAmL 92*
**Becker,** Edward A. 1938- *WhoFI 92*
**Becker,** Edward Brooks 1931- *AmMWSc 92*
**Becker,** Edward R *WhoAmP 91*
**Becker,** Edward Roy 1933- *WhoAmL 92*
**Becker,** Edward Samuel 1929- *AmMWSc 92*
**Becker,** Edwin Demuth 1930- *AmMWSc 92*
**Becker,** Edwin Norbert 1922- *AmMWSc 92*
**Becker,** Eileen *WhoRel 92*
**Becker,** Elizabeth Ann 1950- *AmMWSc 92*
**Becker,** Elmer Lewis 1918- *AmMWSc 92*
**Becker,** Ernest I 1918- *AmMWSc 92*
**Becker,** Eugene *WhoEnt 92*
**Becker,** Eugene Bruno 1942- *WhoFI 92*
**Becker,** Eugene E. *WhoIns 92*
**Becker,** F K 1924- *AmMWSc 92*
**Becker,** Fred Paul 1926- *WhoWest 92*
**Becker,** Frederick F 1931- *AmMWSc 92*
**Becker,** Gary S. 1930- *WrDr 92*
**Becker,** Gary Stanley 1930- *IntWW 91, WhoFI 92, WhoMW 92*
**Becker,** Gary Wayne 1952- *WhoAmL 92*
**Becker,** Gaylynn Leigh 1950- *WhoMW 92*
**Becker,** Gene *WhoFI 92*
**Becker,** George Charles 1935- *AmMWSc 92*
**Becker,** George Ferdinand 1847-1919 *BiInAmS*
**Becker,** Gerald Anthony 1924- *AmMWSc 92*
**Becker,** Gerald Arthur 1941- *WhoMW 92*
**Becker,** Gerald Leonard 1940- *AmMWSc 92*
**Becker,** Gert 1933- *IntWW 91*
**Becker,** Gordon Alan 1953- *WhoWest 92*
**Becker,** Gordon Edward 1920- *AmMWSc 92*
**Becker,** Gordon Maurice 1924- *WhoMW 92*
**Becker,** Gregory R *WhoAmP 91*
**Becker,** Haidee 1950- *TwCPaSc*
**Becker,** Harold *IntMPA 92*
**Becker,** Harry 1865-1928 *TwCPaSc*
**Becker,** Harry Carroll 1913- *AmMWSc 92*
**Becker,** Henry A 1929- *AmMWSc 92*
**Becker,** Horst Carl E. 1924- *IntWW 91*
**Becker,** Howard S. 1928- *ConAu 134*
**Becker,** Isidore A. 1926- *IntWW 91*
**Becker,** Jacques 1906-1960 *IntDcF 2-2 [port]*
**Becker,** Jeffrey Marvin 1943- *AmMWSc 92*
**Becker,** Jeffrey Scott 1960- *WhoFI 92*
**Becker,** Jerry Page 1937- *AmMWSc 92*
**Becker,** Jillian 1932- *IntAu&W 91*
**Becker,** John Alphonsis 1942- *WhoMW 92*
**Becker,** John Angus 1936- *AmMWSc 92*
**Becker,** John Henry 1948- *AmMWSc 92*
**Becker,** John J. 1886-1961 *NewAmDM*
**Becker,** Jon Scott 1953- *WhoAmL 92*
**Becker,** Joseph F 1927- *AmMWSc 92*
**Becker,** Joseph Whitney 1943- *AmMWSc 92*
**Becker,** Joshua A 1932- *AmMWSc 92*
**Becker,** Jurek 1937- *IntWW 91, LiExTwC*
**Becker,** Jurgen 1932- *IntWW 91*
**Becker,** Karl Martin 1943- *WhoAmL 92*
**Becker,** Kenneth Louis 1931- *AmMWSc 92*
**Becker,** Kevin Dale 1958- *WhoRel 92*
**Becker,** Kevin Paul 1958- *WhoWest 92*
**Becker,** Kurt H 1953- *AmMWSc 92*
**Becker,** Kurt Heinrich 1953- *AmMWSc 92*
**Becker,** Lanson 1941- *WhoMW 92*
**Becker,** Larry Keith 1948- *WhoIns 92*
**Becker,** Larry Wayne 1946- *WhoWest 92*
**Becker,** Lawrence Charles 1934- *AmMWSc 92*
**Becker,** Leslee *DrAPF 91*
**Becker,** Lewis Charles *AmMWSc 92*
**Becker,** Lillie Elaine 1950- *WhoWest 92*
**Becker,** Lisa Jane 1961- *WhoAmL 92*
**Becker,** Lucille Frackman 1929- *IntAu&W 91, WrDr 92*
**Becker,** Marie G. 1955- *WhoHisp 92*
**Becker,** Marsha Faye 1955- *WhoEnt 92*
**Becker,** Marshall Hilford 1940- *AmMWSc 92*
**Becker,** Martha Jane 1916- *WhoEnt 92*
**Becker,** Martin 1940- *AmMWSc 92*
**Becker,** Martin Joseph *AmMWSc 92*
**Becker,** Marvin Burton 1922- *WhoMW 92*
**Becker,** Mary E. 1945- *WhoAmL 92*
**Becker,** Michael Allen 1940- *AmMWSc 92*
**Becker,** Michael Craig 1955- *WhoFI 92*
**Becker,** Michael F. 1946- *WhoFI 92*
**Becker,** Michael Franklin 1947- *AmMWSc 92*
**Becker,** Michael Richard 1945- *WhoFI 92, WhoMW 92*
**Becker,** Millard William Herman, Jr. 1934- *WhoAmL 92*
**Becker,** Milton 1920- *AmMWSc 92*
**Becker,** Murray Leonard 1933- *WhoFI 92*
**Becker,** Nancy Lyn 1959- *WhoEnt 92*
**Becker,** Norwin Howard 1930- *AmMWSc 92*
**Becker,** Patricia W. *WhoAmL 92*
**Becker,** Paul Albert 1939- *WhoFI 92*
**Becker,** Paul Lewis 1953- *WhoFI 92*
**Becker,** Ralph Edward 1931- *WhoEnt 92*
**Becker,** Ralph Elihu 1907- *WhoAmL 92*
**Becker,** Ralph Leonard 1927- *WhoMW 92*
**Becker,** Ralph M. 1937- *WhoFI 92*
**Becker,** Ralph Sherman 1925- *AmMWSc 92*
**Becker,** Randolph Armin 1924- *AmMWSc 92*
**Becker,** Randolph William 1946- *WhoRel 92*
**Becker,** Richard Alan 1949- *AmMWSc 92*
**Becker,** Richard Logan 1929- *AmMWSc 92*
**Becker,** Richard Thomas 1935- *WhoAmL 92*
**Becker,** Robert Adolph 1913- *AmMWSc 92*
**Becker,** Robert Allen 1942- *WhoMW 92*
**Becker,** Robert Charles, Jr. 1950- *WhoFI 92*
**Becker,** Robert Clarence 1927- *WhoRel 92*
**Becker,** Robert Hugh 1934- *AmMWSc 92*
**Becker,** Robert Jerome 1922- *WhoMW 92*
**Becker,** Robert Joseph 1946- *WhoMW 92*
**Becker,** Robert O 1923- *AmMWSc 92*
**Becker,** Robert Paul 1942- *AmMWSc 92*
**Becker,** Robert Richard 1923- *AmMWSc 92*
**Becker,** Robin *DrAPF 91*
**Becker,** Roger Jackson 1944- *AmMWSc 92*
**Becker,** Roger Vern 1947- *WhoAmL 92, WhoWest 92*
**Becker,** Roland Frederick 1912- *AmMWSc 92*
**Becker,** Rolf-Walter 1935- *WhoRel 92*
**Becker,** Rudolph Frederick, III 1934- *WhoAmL 92*
**Becker,** Samuel L. d1991 *NewYTBS 91*
**Becker,** Sheldon Theodore 1938- *AmMWSc 92*
**Becker,** Stanley J 1921- *AmMWSc 92*
**Becker,** Stanley Leonard 1929- *AmMWSc 92*
**Becker,** Stanley R. *WhoFI 92*
**Becker,** Stephen *DrAPF 91*
**Becker,** Stephen 1927- *ConNov 91, WrDr 92*
**Becker,** Stephen David 1927- *WhoEnt 92*

**Becker,** Stephen Fraley 1942- *AmMWSc 92*
**Becker,** Stephen William 1955- *WhoMW 92*
**Becker,** Steven Allan 1938- *AmMWSc 92*
**Becker,** Susan Kaplan 1948- *WhoFI 92*
**Becker,** Suzette Toledano 1955- *WhoAmL 92*
**Becker,** Therese *DrAPF 91*
**Becker,** Thomas Bruce 1964- *WhoMW 92*
**Becker,** Tim August 1949- *WhoFI 92*
**Becker,** Tony *WhoEnt 92*
**Becker,** Ulrich J 1938- *AmMWSc 92*
**Becker,** Vanetta G 1949- *WhoAmP 91*
**Becker,** W. John 1945- *WhoIns 92*
**Becker,** Walter *WhoEnt 92*
**Becker,** Walter Alvin 1920- *AmMWSc 92*
**Becker,** Walter Francis, Jr. 1956- *WhoAmL 92*
**Becker,** Wayne Marvin 1940- *AmMWSc 92*
**Becker,** Wilhelm 1942- *AmMWSc 92*
**Becker,** William Adolph 1933- *WhoFI 92*
**Becker,** William Gerard 1958- *WhoFI 92*
**Becker,** William Hartshorne 1935- *WhoRel 92*
**Becker,** William Henry 1909- *WhoAmL 92*
**Becker-Slaton,** Nellie Frances 1921- *WhoBlA 92*
**Becker-Theye,** Betty 1935- *WhoMW 92*
**Beckerle,** John C 1923- *AmMWSc 92*
**Beckerman,** Barry Lee 1941- *AmMWSc 92*
**Beckerman,** Joel Leonard 1963- *WhoEnt 92*
**Beckerman,** Wilfred 1925- *IntAu&W 91, Who 92, WrDr 92*
**Beckermann,** Christoph 1960- *AmMWSc 92*
**Beckers,** Jacques Maurice 1934- *AmMWSc 92*
**Beckert,** William Henry 1920- *AmMWSc 92*
**Beckett** *Who 92*
**Beckett,** Arnold Heyworth 1920- *Who 92*
**Beckett,** Bradley Arthur 1953- *WhoAmP 91*
**Beckett,** Bruce Probart 1924- *Who 92*
**Beckett,** Charles Campbell 1912- *WhoBlA 92*
**Beckett,** Denis Arthur 1917- *Who 92*
**Beckett,** Edwin Horace Alexander 1937- *Who 92*
**Beckett,** Evette Olga 1956- *WhoBlA 92*
**Beckett,** Grace 1912- *WhoFI 92, WhoMW 92*
**Beckett,** Jack Brown 1925- *AmMWSc 92*
**Beckett,** James Anthony 1951- *WhoRel 92*
**Beckett,** James Camlin 1912- *Who 92*
**Beckett,** James Reid 1946- *AmMWSc 92*
**Beckett,** John Michael 1929- *IntWW 91, Who 92*
**Beckett,** Justin Francis 1963- *WhoFI 92*
**Beckett,** Kenneth Albert 1929- *IntAu&W 91*
**Beckett,** Margaret M. 1943- *Who 92*
**Beckett,** Margaret-Mary 1943- *IntWW 91*
**Beckett,** Martyn 1918- *TwCPaSc*
**Beckett,** Martyn Gervase 1918- *Who 92*
**Beckett,** Noel George Stanley d1990 *Who 92N*
**Beckett,** Ralph Lawrence 1923- *AmMWSc 92*
**Beckett,** Ray Herbert, Jr. 1928- *WhoWest 92*
**Beckett,** Richard Gervase 1944- *Who 92*
**Beckett,** Royce E 1923- *AmMWSc 92*
**Beckett,** Samuel 1905-1989 *FacFETw [port]*
**Beckett,** Samuel 1906- *IntAu&W 91*
**Beckett,** Samuel 1906-1989 *CnDBLB 7 [port], ConTFT 9, GuFrLit 1, LiExTwC, RfGEnL 91*
**Beckett,** Samuel Barclay 1906- *WhoNob 90*
**Beckett,** Sanford Ray 1946- *WhoMW 92, WhoRel 92*
**Beckett,** Sarah 1946- *TwCPaSc*
**Beckett,** Sidney D 1932- *AmMWSc 92*
**Beckett,** Sydney A. 1943- *WhoBlA 92*
**Beckett,** Terence 1923- *IntWW 91, Who 92*
**Beckett,** Theodore Charles 1929- *WhoAmL 92*
**Beckett,** Theodore Cornwall 1952- *WhoAmL 92, WhoFI 92, WhoMW 92*
**Beckett,** Thomas Allen 1949- *WhoWest 92*
**Beckett,** William Cartwright 1929- *Who 92*
**Beckett-Rinker,** Peggy *WhoAmP 91*
**Beckey,** Sylvia Louise 1946- *WhoAmL 92, WhoFI 92*
**Beckfield,** William John 1920- *AmMWSc 92*
**Beckford,** Ernest Raul 1958- *WhoAmL 92*
**Beckford,** William 1760-1844 *BlkwCEP, RfGEnL 91*
**Beckh,** Harald J. von 1917- *IntWW 91*
**Beckham,** Barry 1944- *BlkLC [port], ConNov 91, WrDr 92*
**Beckham,** Barry Earl 1944- *WhoBlA 92*
**Beckham,** Charles Wickliffe 1856-1888 *BiInAmS*
**Beckham,** Edgar Frederick 1933- *WhoBlA 92*
**Beckham,** Janice Louise 1950- *WhoRel 92*
**Beckham,** Robert R 1915- *AmMWSc 92*
**Beckham,** Robert Warren 1966- *WhoEnt 92*
**Beckham,** Stephen Andrew 1959- *WhoFI 92*
**Beckham,** Stephen Dow 1941- *WhoWest 92*
**Beckham,** Stephen Robert 1952- *WhoAmL 92*
**Beckham,** Walter Hull, III 1948- *WhoAmL 92*
**Beckham,** Walter Hull, Jr. 1920- *WhoAmL 92*
**Beckham,** William Arthur 1927- *WhoRel 92*
**Beckham,** William J., Jr. 1940- *WhoBlA 92*
**Beckhoff,** Gerhard Franz 1929- *AmMWSc 92*
**Beckhorn,** Edward John *AmMWSc 92*
**Becking,** Rudolf 1922- *AmMWSc 92*
**Beckingham,** Charles Fraser 1914- *IntWW 91, Who 92, WrDr 92*
**Beckingham,** Kathleen Mary 1946- *AmMWSc 92*
**Beckinsale,** Robert Percy 1908- *IntAu&W 91, WrDr 92*
**Becklake,** Ernest John Stephen 1943- *Who 92*
**Becklake,** Margaret Rigsby 1922- *AmMWSc 92*
**Beckler,** Richard William 1940- *WhoAmL 92*
**Beckles,** Benita Harris 1950- *WhoBlA 92*
**Beckles Willson,** Robina Elizabeth 1930- *IntAu&W 91*
**Beckley,** David Lenard 1946- *WhoBlA 92*
**Beckley,** Robert Howard 1920- *WhoRel 92*
**Beckley,** Ronald Scott 1944- *AmMWSc 92*
**Beckman,** Alexander Lynn 1941- *AmMWSc 92*
**Beckman,** Arnold Orville 1900- *AmMWSc 92, WhoWest 92*
**Beckman,** Barbara Stuckey *AmMWSc 92*
**Beckman,** Carl Harry 1923- *AmMWSc 92*
**Beckman,** David Allen 1950- *AmMWSc 92*
**Beckman,** David Lee 1939- *AmMWSc 92*
**Beckman,** Ernestine Elizabeth 1930- *WhoAmP 91*
**Beckman,** Frank Samuel 1921- *AmMWSc 92*
**Beckman,** Gail M. 1938- *WrDr 92*
**Beckman,** Gail McKnight 1938- *WhoAmL 92*
**Beckman,** Gunnel 1910- *ChILR 25 [port]*
**Beckman,** James Wallace Bim 1936- *WhoFI 92, WhoWest 92*
**Beckman,** Jean Catherine 1951- *AmMWSc 92*
**Beckman,** John Coyle 1919- *WhoWest 92*
**Beckman,** Joseph Alfred 1937- *AmMWSc 92*
**Beckman,** Judy Kay 1959- *WhoFI 92*
**Beckman,** Kenneth Oren 1948- *WhoEnt 92*
**Beckman,** Michael David 1932- *Who 92*
**Beckman,** Patricia *WhoRel 92*
**Beckman,** Richard C. 1937- *WhoWest 92*
**Beckman,** Tad Alan 1936- *WhoWest 92*
**Beckman,** Tracy L 1945- *WhoAmP 91*
**Beckman,** William A 1935- *AmMWSc 92*
**Beckmann,** Dennis Drake 1954- *WhoMW 92*
**Beckmann,** Donald McElligott 1944- *WhoRel 92*
**Beckmann,** Jon Michael 1936- *WhoFI 92*
**Beckmann,** Max 1884-1950 *EncTR 91 [port], FacFETw, WorArt 1980*
**Beckmann,** Petr 1924- *AmMWSc 92*
**Beckmann,** Robert B 1918- *AmMWSc 92*
**Beckmann,** William Carl 1934- *WhoRel 92*
**Beckmeyer,** Henry Ernest 1939- *WhoMW 92*
**Becknell,** Charles E. 1941- *WhoBlA 92*
**Becknell,** Patricia Ann 1950- *WhoFI 92*
**Becknell,** William 1790?-1832? *BenetAL 91*
**Beckner,** Donald Lee 1939- *WhoAmL 92*
**Beckner,** Everet Hess 1935- *AmMWSc 92*
**Beckner,** Suzanne K 1950- *AmMWSc 92*
**Beckstead,** Jay H 1948- *AmMWSc 92*
**Beckstead,** Leo William 1949- *AmMWSc 92*
**Beckstead,** Lucy 1920- *WhoAmP 91*
**Beckstedt,** John Edgar 1947- *WhoFI 92*
**Beckstrom,** James Clifford 1937- *WhoAmL 92*
**Beckstrom,** John H. 1932- *WhoAmL 92*
**Beckwith,** Athelstan Laurence Johnson 1930- *IntWW 91, Who 92*
**Beckwith,** Barbara Jean 1948- *WhoMW 92*
**Beckwith,** Burnham Putnam 1904- *IntAu&W 91, WrDr 92*
**Beckwith,** Edward Jay 1949- *WhoAmL 92*
**Beckwith,** Geoffrey Clifton 1958- *WhoAmP 91*
**Beckwith,** George Cone 1801-1870 *AmPeW*
**Beckwith,** John 1785-1870 *DcNCBi 1*
**Beckwith,** John 1927- *NewAmDM, WhoEnt 92*
**Beckwith,** John Bruce 1933- *AmMWSc 92*
**Beckwith,** John Charles 1941- *WhoFI 92*
**Beckwith,** John Gordon d1991 *Who 92N*
**Beckwith,** John Gordon 1918- *WrDr 92*
**Beckwith,** John Lionel 1947- *Who 92*
**Beckwith,** John Watrus 1831-1890 *DcNCBi 1*
**Beckwith,** Jonathan Roger 1935- *AmMWSc 92*
**Beckwith,** Lillian 1916- *IntAu&W 91, WrDr 92*
**Beckwith,** Merle Ray *DrAPF 91*
**Beckwith,** Peter Michael 1945- *Who 92*
**Beckwith,** Richard Edward 1927- *AmMWSc 92*
**Beckwith,** Rodney Fisk 1935- *WhoFI 92*
**Beckwith,** Sandra Shank 1943- *WhoAmL 92*
**Beckwith,** Sterling 1905- *AmMWSc 92*
**Beckwith,** Steven Van Walter 1951- *AmMWSc 92*
**Beckwith,** William Boynton 1911- *WhoFI 92*
**Beckwith,** William Frederick 1934- *AmMWSc 92*
**Beckwith,** William Hunter 1896- *WhoRel 92*
**Beckwitt,** Richard David 1949- *AmMWSc 92*
**Beckworth,** John Barney 1958- *WhoAmL 92*
**Beckwourth,** James P. 1798-1867? *BenetAL 91*
**Becofsky,** Arthur Luke 1950- *WhoEnt 92*
**Becote,** Fohliette W. 1958- *WhoBlA 92*
**Becque,** Henry 1837-1899 *GuFrLit 1*
**Becquerel,** Antoine Henri 1852-1908 *FacFETw, WhoNob 90*
**Becraft,** Lloyd G 1936- *AmMWSc 92*
**Bective,** Earl of 1959- *Who 92*
**Becton,** Eddie Lee, Jr. 1963- *WhoMW 92*
**Becton,** Henry P., Jr. *LesBEnT 92*
**Becton,** Henry Prentiss, Jr. 1943- *WhoEnt 92*
**Becton,** Julius Wesley, Jr 1926- *WhoAmP 91, WhoBlA 92*
**Becton,** Rudolph 1930- *WhoBlA 92*
**Becton,** Sharvell *WhoBlA 92*
**Becvar,** James Edgar *AmMWSc 92*
**Becwar,** Gregory Eugene 1943- *WhoMW 92*
**Bedard,** Donna Lee 1947- *AmMWSc 92*
**Bedau,** Hugo Adam 1926- *IntAu&W 91, WrDr 92*
**Bedbrook,** George 1921- *Who 92*
**Bedbrook,** George Montario 1921- *IntWW 91*
**Bedbrook,** Jack Harry 1924- *Who 92*
**Beddall,** Hugh Richard Muir 1922- *Who 92*
**Beddard,** Nicholas Elliot 1934- *Who 92*
**Beddingfield,** Eugene Crocker 1862-1926 *DcNCBi 1*
**Beddington,** Charles Richard 1911- *Who 92*
**Beddington,** Roy 1910- *IntAu&W 91*
**Beddoe,** Jack Eglinton d1990 *Who 92N*
**Beddoes,** John Geoffrey Genior 1925- *Who 92*
**Beddoes,** M P 1924- *AmMWSc 92*
**Beddoes,** Thomas Lovell 1803-1849 *RfGEnL 91*
**Beddome,** John MacDonald 1930- *IntWW 91, WhoFI 92, WhoWest 92*
**Beddor,** Sandy M. 1953- *WhoWest 92*
**Beddow,** Jean T *WhoAmP 91*
**Beddow,** Richard Harold 1932- *WhoAmL 92*
**Bede** 673?-735 *EncEarC*
**Bedelia,** Bonnie 1946- *IntMPA 92*
**Bedelia,** Bonnie 1948- *WhoEnt 92*
**Bedell,** Berkley Warren 1921- *WhoAmP 91*
**Bedell,** Eileen Hanna 1952- *WhoFI 92*
**Bedell,** Frederick Delano 1934- *WhoBlA 92*
**Bedell,** Gaynell Pack *WhoRel 92*
**Bedell,** George Noble 1922- *AmMWSc 92*
**Bedell,** Kenneth Berkley 1947- *WhoRel 92*
**Bedell,** Louis Robert 1939- *AmMWSc 92*
**Bedell,** Ralph Clairon 1904- *IntWW 91*
**Bedell,** Richard Munro 1958- *WhoFI 92*
**Bedell,** Thomas Erwin 1931- *AmMWSc 92*
**Bedenbaugh,** Angela Lea Owen 1939- *AmMWSc 92*
**Bedenbaugh,** John Holcombe 1931- *AmMWSc 92*
**Bedenbaugh,** Mary Evelyn 1935- *WhoRel 92*
**Bederson,** Benjamin 1921- *AmMWSc 92*
**Bedford,** Archdeacon of *Who 92*
**Bedford,** Bishop Suffragan of 1929- *Who 92*
**Bedford,** Duke of 1917- *Who 92*
**Bedford,** Alfred William 1920- *Who 92*
**Bedford,** Anthony 1938- *AmMWSc 92*
**Bedford,** Barbara Lynn 1946- *AmMWSc 92*
**Bedford,** Brian 1935- *WhoEnt 92*
**Bedford,** Celia 1904-1959 *TwCPaSc*
**Bedford,** Clay P. d1991 *NewYTBS 91*
**Bedford,** Daniel Ross 1945- *WhoFI 92*
**Bedford,** David 1937- *ConCom 92, IntWW 91, NewAmDM, Who 92*
**Bedford,** Eric *Who 92*
**Bedford,** Henry Frederick 1931- *WrDr 92*
**Bedford,** James William 1942- *AmMWSc 92*
**Bedford,** Joel S 1938- *AmMWSc 92*
**Bedford,** John Michael 1932- *AmMWSc 92*
**Bedford,** Judith *WhoEnt 92*
**Bedford,** Kenneth *TwCWW 91*
**Bedford,** Pat 1948- *WhoEnt 92*
**Bedford,** Richard 1883-1967 *TwCPaSc*
**Bedford,** Roger, Jr 1956- *WhoAmP 91*
**Bedford,** Ronald Ernest 1930- *AmMWSc 92*
**Bedford,** Steuart John Rudolf 1939- *IntWW 91, Who 92*
**Bedford,** Sybille 1911- *ConNov 91, IntAu&W 91, Who 92, WrDr 92*
**Bedford,** William 1963- *WhoBlA 92*
**Bedford,** William Brian 1947- *AmMWSc 92*
**Bedgood,** Dale Ray 1932- *AmMWSc 92*
**Bedi,** Bishan Singh 1946- *IntWW 91*
**Bedi,** Rahul 1941- *WhoFI 92*
**Bedie,** Henri Konan 1934- *IntWW 91*
**Bedient,** Jack DeWitt 1926- *AmMWSc 92*
**Bedient,** Phillip E 1922- *AmMWSc 92*
**Bedikian,** Mary Aslanian 1950- *WhoAmL 92*
**Bedikian,** Rhonda Colette 1950- *WhoFI 92*
**Bedinger,** Charles Arthur, Jr 1942- *AmMWSc 92*
**Bedinger,** Frank Cleveland, Jr. 1916- *WhoAmL 92*
**Bedingfeld** *Who 92*
**Bedingfield,** Charles H 1916- *AmMWSc 92*
**Bedingfield,** Christopher Ohl Macredie 1935- *Who 92*
**Bedini,** Silvio A. 1917- *WrDr 92*
**Bedjaoui,** Mohammed 1929- *IntWW 91*
**Bednar,** Carolyn Diane 1953- *WhoMW 92*
**Bednar,** Jonnie Bee 1941- *AmMWSc 92*
**Bednar,** Michael Charles 1958- *WhoAmL 92*
**Bednar,** Rodney Allan 1955- *AmMWSc 92*
**Bednar,** Rudy Gerard 1951- *WhoEnt 92*
**Bednarcyk,** Norman Earle 1938- *AmMWSc 92*
**Bednarek,** Alexander R 1933- *AmMWSc 92*
**Bednarek,** Jana Marie *AmMWSc 92*
**Bednarek,** Stanley Michael 1904- *WhoAmP 91*
**Bednarowski,** Mary Farrell 1942- *WhoRel 92*
**Bednarski,** Henryk 1934- *IntWW 91*
**Bednarz,** Paul Robert 1950- *WhoIns 92*
**Bednarz,** Susan Clare 1955- *WhoMW 92*
**Bednekoff,** Alexander G 1932- *AmMWSc 92*
**Bedner,** Mark Allen 1948- *WhoFI 92*
**Bednorz,** George 1950- *IntWW 91*
**Bednorz,** J. George 1950- *Who 92*
**Bednorz,** Johannes Georg 1950- *AmMWSc 92, WhoNob 90*
**Bednowitz,** Allan Lloyd 1939- *AmMWSc 92*
**Bedny,** Demyan 1883-1945 *FacFETw*
**Bedo,** Donald Elro 1929- *AmMWSc 92*
**Bedoit,** William Clarence, Jr 1922- *AmMWSc 92*
**Bedon,** Pedro 1555-1621 *HisDSpE*
**Bedore,** Michael Paul 1956- *WhoWest 92*
**Bedoya,** Consuelo *WhoHisp 92*
**Bedoya,** Jaime J. 1948- *WhoFI 92*
**Bedoya,** Luis 1939- *WhoHisp 92*
**Bedoya,** Roberto Eligio 1951- *WhoHisp 92*
**Bedoya Velez,** Luis 1920- *IntWW 91*
**Bedrick,** Jeffrey Keith 1960- *WhoWest 92*
**Bedrick,** Melvin Leonard 1932- *WhoAmL 92*
**Bedrosian,** E 1922- *AmMWSc 92*
**Bedrosian,** Edward Robert 1932- *WhoFI 92*
**Bedrosian,** Karakian 1933- *AmMWSc 92*
**Bedrosian,** Samuel D 1921- *AmMWSc 92*
**Bedrossian,** Robert Haig 1924- *WhoAmP 91*
**Bedser,** Alec Victor 1918- *IntWW 91, Who 92*
**Bedsole,** Ann Smith 1930- *WhoAmP 91*
**Bedsworth,** James Howard 1936- *WhoFI 92*
**Bedwell,** Thomas Howard 1915- *AmMWSc 92*
**Bedworth,** David D 1932- *AmMWSc 92*

**Bee,** Adeline Mary 1954- *WhoAmP 91*
**Bee,** Charles Michael 1950- *WhoAmL 92*
**Bee,** Jay *SmATA 65*
**Bee,** Keith 1965- *WhoAmP 91*
**Beebe,** B. F. 1920- *WrDr 92*
**Beebe,** Charles William 1887-1962 *FacFETw*
**Beebe,** David Lewis 1931- *WhoRel 92*
**Beebe,** George Warren 1936- *AmMWSc 92*
**Beebe,** Gilbert Wheeler 1912- *AmMWSc 92*
**Beebe,** Joseph A. 1832-1903 *RelLAm 91*
**Beebe,** Leo Clair 1917- *WhoFI 92*
**Beebe,** Lucy Cresap Ord 1939- *IntAu&W 91*
**Beebe,** Mike 1946- *WhoAmP 91*
**Beebe,** Ralph K. 1932- *WrDr 92*
**Beebe,** Raymond Mark 1942- *WhoAmL 92*
**Beebe,** Richard Townsend 1902- *AmMWSc 92*
**Beebe,** Robert R. 1928- *WhoWest 92*
**Beebe,** Robert Ray 1928- *AmMWSc 92*
**Beebe,** William 1851-1917 *BiInAmS*
**Beebe,** William 1877-1962 *BenetAL 91*
**Beebee,** John Christopher 1941- *AmMWSc 92*
**Beeber,** Allan Howard 1951- *WhoRel 92*
**Beeby,** Clarence Edward 1902- *IntWW 91, Who 92, WrDr 92*
**Beeby,** George Harry 1902- *Who 92*
**Beeby,** Kenneth Jack 1936- *WhoAmL 92*
**Beech,** E. Martin 1950- *WhoEnt 92*
**Beech,** H. R. 1925- *WrDr 92*
**Beech,** Harvey Elliott 1924- *WhoBlA 92*
**Beech,** Joseph, III 1945- *WhoAmL 92*
**Beech,** Patrick Mervyn 1912- *Who 92*
**Beecham,** Alice *TwCSFW 91*
**Beecham,** Curtis Michael 1947- *AmMWSc 92*
**Beecham,** Jeremy Hugh 1944- *Who 92*
**Beecham,** John Charles *ScFEYrs*
**Beecham,** John Stratford Roland 1942- *Who 92*
**Beecham,** Thomas 1879-1961 *FacFETw [port], NewAmDM*
**Beecher,** Catharine 1800-1878 *HanAmWH, PorAmW [port], RComAH*
**Beecher,** Catherine E. 1800-1878 *BenetAL 91*
**Beecher,** Charles Emerson 1856-1904 *BiInAmS*
**Beecher,** Christopher W W 1948- *AmMWSc 92*
**Beecher,** Donald A. 1942- *ConAu 135*
**Beecher,** Earl Stephens 1928- *WhoWest 92*
**Beecher,** Earl William 1942- *WhoFI 92*
**Beecher,** Edward 1803-1895 *BenetAL 91*
**Beecher,** Gary Richard 1939- *AmMWSc 92*
**Beecher,** Graciela F. 1927- *WhoHisp 92*
**Beecher,** Henry Ward 1813-1887 *BenetAL 91, RelLAm 91*
**Beecher,** James Francis 1940- *WhoMW 92*
**Beecher,** Lyman 1775-1863 *BenetAL 91*
**Beecher,** Robert William 1931- *WhoFI 92*
**Beecher,** Thomas Wylie 1958- *WhoAmL 92*
**Beecher,** William John 1914- *AmMWSc 92*
**Beechey,** Robert Harry 1963- *WhoFI 92*
**Beeching,** Charles Train, Jr. 1930- *WhoAmL 92*
**Beeching,** Jack 1922- *IntAu&W 91*
**Beeching,** Richard 1913-1985 *FacFETw*
**Beeching-Prieto,** Marian Train 1912- *IntAu&W 91*
**Beechler,** Barbara Jean 1928- *AmMWSc 92*
**Beechner,** Richard Ash 1934- *WhoMW 92*
**Beeckmans,** Jan Maria 1930- *AmMWSc 92*
**Beecroft,** Norma 1934- *NewAmDM*
**Beed,** David James 1945- *WhoFI 92*
**Beede,** Charles Herbert 1934- *AmMWSc 92*
**Beedham,** Brian James 1928- *Who 92*
**Beedle,** Lynn Simpson 1917- *AmMWSc 92*
**Beeghley,** Jesse Wirt, Jr. 1923- *WhoAmL 92*
**Beegle,** Eugene S. *WhoRel 92*
**Beehler,** Jerry R 1943- *AmMWSc 92*
**Beehler,** Roger Earl 1934- *AmMWSc 92*
**Beehner,** Mark Edward 1952- *WhoMW 92*
**Beek,** John 1906- *AmMWSc 92*
**Beeke,** Joel Robert 1952- *WhoRel 92*
**Beeker,** Marvin Ray 1941- *WhoWest 92*
**Beekman,** Allan 1913- *WrDr 92*
**Beekman,** Bruce Edward 1930- *AmMWSc 92*
**Beekman,** John 1918-1980 *ConAu 135*
**Beekman,** John Alfred 1931- *AmMWSc 92*
**Beekman,** Philip E. 1931- *WhoFI 92, WhoMW 92*
**Beekman,** William Bedloe 1949- *WhoAmL 92*
**Beekman,** William David 1946- *WhoMW 92*
**Beel,** John Addis 1921- *AmMWSc 92*
**Beel,** Louis J M 1902-1977 *FacFETw*
**Beeler,** Barbara Louise 1963- *WhoWest 92*
**Beeler,** Bruce A. 1941- *WhoMW 92*
**Beeler,** Charlotte Jean 1928- *WhoMW 92*
**Beeler,** David Lee 1945- *WhoFI 92*
**Beeler,** Donald A 1931- *AmMWSc 92*
**Beeler,** Donald Daryl 1935- *WhoFI 92, WhoMW 92*
**Beeler,** George W, Jr 1938- *AmMWSc 92*
**Beeler,** James Mario 1954- *WhoRel 92*
**Beeler,** Joe R, Jr 1924- *AmMWSc 92*
**Beeler,** John Charles 1942- *WhoEnt 92*
**Beeler,** Myrton Freeman 1922- *AmMWSc 92*
**Beeler,** Thomas Joseph 1933- *WhoAmL 92, WhoFI 92*
**Beeler,** Troy James *AmMWSc 92*
**Beeler,** Virgil L. 1931- *WhoAmL 92*
**Beeley,** Harold 1909- *IntWW 91, Who 92*
**Beelik,** Andrew 1924- *AmMWSc 92*
**Beelman,** Robert B 1944- *AmMWSc 92*
**Beem,** Jack Darrel 1931- *WhoAmL 92*
**Beem,** John Kelly 1942- *AmMWSc 92, WhoMW 92*
**Beem,** Marc O 1923- *AmMWSc 92*
**Beeman,** Bette Jane 1927- *WhoWest 92*
**Beeman,** Bob Joe 1952- *WhoRel 92*
**Beeman,** Carol Ann *DrAPF 91*
**Beeman,** Curt Pletcher 1944- *AmMWSc 92*
**Beeman,** David Edmund, Jr 1938- *AmMWSc 92*
**Beeman,** Joseph Henry 1833-1909 *DcNCBi 1*
**Beeman,** Richard E. 1945- *WhoFI 92*
**Beeman,** Robert D 1932- *AmMWSc 92*
**Beeman,** S W 1879- *ScFEYrs*
**Beeman,** William Waldron 1911- *AmMWSc 92*
**Beemer,** Elvin Homer 1919- *WhoAmP 91*
**Beemon,** Karen Louise 1947- *AmMWSc 92*
**Beemster,** Joseph Robert 1941- *WhoFI 92, WhoMW 92*
**Been,** Hans Henrik 1949- *WhoWest 92*
**Been,** Kent Douglas 1958- *WhoMW 92*
**Beene,** Geoffrey 1927- *DcTwDes, FacFETw, IntWW 91*
**Beene,** James Robert 1947- *AmMWSc 92*
**Beene,** Sophia Darlynn Benavidas 1949- *WhoMW 92*
**Beenstock,** Michael 1946- *Who 92*
**Beer,** Alan E 1937- *AmMWSc 92*
**Beer,** Albert Carl 1920- *AmMWSc 92*
**Beer,** Anthony Stafford 1926- *Who 92*
**Beer,** Bernard *AmMWSc 92*
**Beer,** Charles 1923- *AmMWSc 92*
**Beer,** Charles Thomas 1954- *WhoMW 92*
**Beer,** Clem *TwCPaSc*
**Beer,** Colin Gordon 1933- *AmMWSc 92*
**Beer,** Craig 1927- *AmMWSc 92*
**Beer,** Ferdinand P 1915- *AmMWSc 92*
**Beer,** George Atherley 1935- *AmMWSc 92*
**Beer,** George Louis 1872-1920 *AmPeW*
**Beer,** Gillian 1935- *WrDr 92*
**Beer,** Gillian Patricia Kempster 1935- *Who 92*
**Beer,** Hans L. 1927- *WhoEnt 92*
**Beer,** Ian David Stafford 1931- *Who 92*
**Beer,** James Edmund 1931- *Who 92*
**Beer,** Janos Miklos 1923- *Who 92*
**Beer,** John Bernard 1926- *Who 92*
**Beer,** John Joseph 1927- *AmMWSc 92*
**Beer,** Joseph Ernest 1959- *WhoWest 92*
**Beer,** Lawrence Brad 1954- *WhoMW 92*
**Beer,** Michael 1926- *AmMWSc 92*
**Beer,** Otto F. 1910- *IntWW 91*
**Beer,** Patricia 1924- *ConPo 91, IntAu&W 91, Who 92, WrDr 92*
**Beer,** Peter George 1941- *Who 92*
**Beer,** Peter Hill 1928- *WhoAmL 92*
**Beer,** Ralph 1947- *TwCWW 91, WrDr 92*
**Beer,** Reinhard 1935- *AmMWSc 92*
**Beer,** Richard 1928- *TwCPaSc*
**Beer,** Robert Edward 1918- *AmMWSc 92*
**Beer,** Samuel 1911- *WrDr 92*
**Beer,** Samuel Hutchison 1911- *IntWW 91*
**Beer,** Stafford *Who 92*
**Beer,** Stafford 1926- *WrDr 92*
**Beer,** Steven Vincent 1941- *AmMWSc 92*
**Beer,** Sylvan Zavi 1929- *AmMWSc 92*
**Beer,** Thomas 1889-1940 *BenetAL 91*
**Beer,** Walter R, Jr 1926- *WhoAmP 91*
**Beer-Bottle Gustav** *EncTR 91*
**Beer-Hoffmann,** Richard 1866-1945 *LiExTwC*
**Beer-Hofmann,** Richard 1866-1945 *EncTR 91*
**Beerbohm,** Max 1872-1956 *FacFETw, RfGEnL 91, TwCPaSc*
**Beerbower,** Cynthia Gibson 1949- *WhoAmL 92*
**Beerbower,** James Richard 1927- *AmMWSc 92*
**Beering,** John George 1936- *WhoFI 92*
**Beering,** Steven Claus 1932- *AmMWSc 92, IntWW 91, WhoMW 92*
**Beerling,** John William 1937- *Who 92*
**Beerman,** Albert Lowell 1934- *WhoFI 92*
**Beerman,** Bernard Marvin 1936- *WhoAmL 92*
**Beerman,** Burton 1943- *WhoEnt 92*
**Beerman,** Herman 1901- *AmMWSc 92*
**Beermann,** Allen J. 1940- *WhoMW 92*
**Beermann,** Allen Jay 1940- *WhoAmP 91*
**Beermann,** Donald Harold 1949- *AmMWSc 92*
**Beermann Kappaladonna,** Judith Countesa A 1945- *WhoFI 92*
**Beernaert,** Auguste Marie Francois 1829-1912 *WhoNob 90*
**Beernink,** Darrell W. 1937- *WhoIns 92*
**Beers,** Burton Floyd 1927- *IntAu&W 91, WrDr 92*
**Beers,** Charlotte L. 1935- *WhoFI 92*
**Beers,** Clifford 1876-1943 *BenetAL 91*
**Beers,** Darrell 1927- *WhoAmP 91*
**Beers,** Deborah Merkamp 1949- *WhoAmL 92*
**Beers,** Donald Osborne 1949- *WhoAmL 92*
**Beers,** Ethel Lynn 1827-1879 *BenetAL 91*
**Beers,** Greg *WhoAmP 91*
**Beers,** John R 1933- *AmMWSc 92*
**Beers,** Kenneth Norman, Sr. 1930- *WhoMW 92*
**Beers,** Orvas E 1918- *WhoAmP 91, WhoMW 92*
**Beers,** Robert Wilson 1947- *WhoAmP 91*
**Beers,** Robin 1943- *TwCPaSc*
**Beers,** Roland Frank, Jr 1923- *AmMWSc 92*
**Beers,** Thomas Wesley 1930- *AmMWSc 92*
**Beers,** V. Gilbert 1928- *ConAu 36NR, IntAu&W 91*
**Beers,** Victor Gilbert 1928- *WhoRel 92*
**Beers,** William Howard 1943- *AmMWSc 92*
**Beers,** William O. 1914- *IntWW 91*
**Beers,** Yardley 1913- *AmMWSc 92*
**Beerstecher,** Ernest, Jr 1919- *AmMWSc 92*
**Beery,** Dwight Beecher 1937- *AmMWSc 92*
**Beery,** John Wray 1939- *WhoMW 92*
**Beery,** Mary *WrDr 92*
**Beery,** Neil L. 1926- *WhoRel 92*
**Beery,** Noah 1916- *WhoEnt 92*
**Beery,** Noah, Jr. 1916- *IntMPA 92*
**Beesack,** Paul Richard 1924- *AmMWSc 92*
**Beese,** J. Carter, Jr. 1956- *WhoFI 92*
**Beese,** Ronald Elroy 1929- *AmMWSc 92*
**Beesley,** David 1938- *WhoWest 92*
**Beesley,** David 1947- *WhoAmP 91*
**Beesley,** Edward Maurice 1915- *AmMWSc 92*
**Beesley,** Ian Blake 1942- *Who 92*
**Beesley,** Michael Edwin 1924- *Who 92*
**Beesley,** Mike 1944- *TwCPaSc*
**Beesley,** R. A. *WhoRel 92*
**Beesley,** Richard Clarence 1922- *WhoAmL 92*
**Beesley,** Robert Charles *AmMWSc 92*
**Beesley,** Walter Wade, Jr 1948- *WhoAmP 91*
**Beesley,** William Harry 1926- *WhoEnt 92*
**Beeson,** Brant Robert 1951- *WhoAmL 92*
**Beeson,** Diane *DrAPF 91*
**Beeson,** Edward Lee, Jr 1928- *AmMWSc 92*
**Beeson,** Jack 1921- *NewAmDM*
**Beeson,** Jack Hamilton 1921- *WhoEnt 92*
**Beeson,** Jane 1930- *TwCPaSc*
**Beeson,** Justin Leo 1930- *AmMWSc 92*
**Beeson,** Paul Bruce 1908- *AmMWSc 92, Who 92*
**Beeson,** Rachel 1932- *WhoRel 92*
**Beeson,** Trevor Randall 1926- *Who 92, WrDr 92*
**Beeson,** W Malcolm *AmMWSc 92*
**Beestman,** George Bernard 1939- *AmMWSc 92*
**Beeston,** Alfred Felix Landon 1911- *Who 92*
**Beeston,** L J *ScFEYrs*
**Beetch,** Ellsworth Benjamin *AmMWSc 92*
**Beetham,** Bruce Craig 1936- *IntWW 91*
**Beetham,** Michael 1923- *IntWW 91, Who 92*
**Beetham,** Roger Campbell 1937- *Who 92*
**Beetham,** Stanley Williams 1933- *WhoFI 92, WhoWest 92*
**Beetham,** Thomas Mark 1951- *WhoAmL 92*
**Beethoven,** Ludwig van 1770-1827 *NewAmDM*
**Beeton,** Emerson, Doughty, & Murray *ScFEYrs*
**Beeton,** Alan 1880-1942 *TwCPaSc*
**Beeton,** Alfred Merle 1927- *AmMWSc 92*
**Beeton,** David Christopher 1939- *Who 92*
**Beeton,** S.O. d1877 *DcLB 106 [port]*
**Beeton,** Samuel Orchart 1831-1877 *ScFEYrs*
**Beets,** F. Lee 1922- *WhoMW 92*
**Beetz,** Jean 1927- *IntWW 91*
**Beevers,** Harry 1924- *AmMWSc 92, IntWW 91*
**Beevers,** Leonard 1934- *AmMWSc 92*
**Beevis,** David 1940- *AmMWSc 92*
**Beevor,** Antony Romer 1940- *Who 92*
**Beevor,** Miles 1900- *Who 92*
**Beevor,** Thomas Agnew 1929- *Who 92*
**Beezer,** Robert Arnold 1958- *WhoWest 92*
**Beezer,** Robert R *WhoAmP 91*
**Beezer,** Robert Renaut 1928- *WhoAmL 92*
**Beezley,** Frederick Ernest 1921- *Who 92*
**Beezley,** Linda *WhoAmP 91*
**Beezley,** William M 1917- *WhoAmP 91*
**Befeler,** Benjamin 1939- *AmMWSc 92*
**Befera,** Frank Christopher 1966- *WhoEnt 92*
**Beffa,** Jean-Louis Guy Henri 1941- *IntWW 91, Who 92*
**Befort,** Alois George, Jr 1927- *WhoAmP 91*
**Befoure,** Jeannine Marie 1923- *WhoFI 92*
**Befu,** Ben 1927- *WhoWest 92*
**Befus,** A Dean 1948- *AmMWSc 92*
**Beg,** Mirza Abdul Baqi 1934- *AmMWSc 92*
**Beg,** Mirza Aslam 1931- *IntWW 91*
**Bega,** Robert V 1928- *AmMWSc 92*
**Begala,** Arthur James 1940- *AmMWSc 92*
**Begam,** Robert G 1928- *WhoAmP 91*
**Begam,** Robert George 1928- *WhoAmL 92*
**Begay,** Frederick 1932- *AmMWSc 92*
**Begaye,** Helen Christine 1943- *WhoRel 92*
**Begbie,** David 1956- *TwCPaSc*
**Begell,** William 1928- *AmMWSc 92*
**Begg,** Alexander Charles 1912- *WrDr 92*
**Begg,** David A 1943- *AmMWSc 92*
**Begg,** Neil 1915- *Who 92, WrDr 92*
**Begg,** Peter Robert 1951- *WhoFI 92*
**Begg,** Robert William 1922- *Who 92*
**Begg,** Varyl 1908- *IntWW 91, Who 92*
**Beggiani,** Seely 1935- *WhoRel 92*
**Beggs,** Bill 1950- *WhoMW 92*
**Beggs,** David 1909- *WrDr 92*
**Beggs,** Guy 1947- *TwCPaSc*
**Beggs,** Harry Mark 1941- *WhoAmL 92, WhoWest 92*
**Beggs,** James Montgomery 1926- *IntWW 91, WhoAmP 91*
**Beggs,** Joe Edward 1946- *WhoAmP 91*
**Beggs,** Richard 1942- *WhoEnt 92*
**Beggs,** Robert Cameron 1940- *WhoEnt 92*
**Beggs,** Roy 1936- *Who 92*
**Beggs,** William H 1935- *AmMWSc 92*
**Beggs,** William John 1942- *AmMWSc 92*
**Beghe,** Renato 1933- *WhoAmL 92*
**Beghini,** Victor Gene 1934- *WhoFI 92*
**Begich,** Joseph R 1930- *WhoAmP 91*
**Begiebing,** Robert John 1946- *IntAu&W 91*
**Begin,** Gerard Henry 1949- *WhoRel 92*
**Begin,** Louis Nazaire 1840-1925 *RelLAm 91*
**Begin,** Menachem 1913- *FacFETw, IntWW 91, Who 92*
**Begin,** Menachim Wolfovitch 1913- *WhoNob 90*
**Begin,** Robert T. *WhoRel 92*
**Begin,** Roger Normand 1952- *WhoAmP 91*
**Begin-Heick,** Nicole 1937- *AmMWSc 92*
**Beglarian,** Grant 1927- *WhoEnt 92*
**Beglau,** David Alan 1958- *AmMWSc 92*
**Begleiter,** Henri 1935- *AmMWSc 92*
**Begleiter,** Martin David 1945- *WhoAmL 92*
**Begleiter,** Ralph J. 1949- *WhoEnt 92*
**Begley,** David Donald 1957- *WhoAmL 92*
**Begley,** Ed, Jr. 1949- *IntMPA 92, WhoEnt 92*
**Begley,** Jack 1934- *WhoAmP 91*
**Begley,** James Andrew 1942- *AmMWSc 92*
**Begley,** Jeanne F 1930- *WhoAmP 91*
**Begley,** Louis 1933- *WhoAmL 92*
**Begnaud,** Wayne Jacque 1955- *WhoWest 92*
**Begougne De Juniac,** Gontran 1908- *IntWW 91*
**Begovac,** Paul C 1956- *AmMWSc 92*
**Begovich,** Michael 1959- *WhoAmL 92*
**Begovich,** Nicholas A 1921- *AmMWSc 92*
**Begue,** William John 1931- *AmMWSc 92*
**Beguesse,** Barry Osmund, Jr. 1950- *WhoBlA 92*
**Beguin,** Bernard 1923- *IntAu&W 91, IntWW 91*
**Beguin,** Fred P 1909- *AmMWSc 92*
**Begun,** George Murray 1921- *AmMWSc 92*
**Behal,** Francis Joseph 1931- *AmMWSc 92*
**Behan,** Brendan 1923-1964 *CnDBLB 7 [port], FacFETw, RfGEnL 91*
**Behan,** John d1991 *NewYTBS 91*
**Behan,** John 1944- *WhoAmP 91*
**Behan,** Mark Joseph 1931- *AmMWSc 92*
**Behan,** Peter 1939- *TwCPaSc*
**Behan,** Walter A. 1911- *WhoIns 92*
**Behan-Pelletier,** Valerie Mary 1948- *AmMWSc 92*
**Behannon,** Kenneth Wayne 1934- *AmMWSc 92*
**Behar,** Leon Isidore 1956- *WhoAmL 92*
**Behar,** Marjam Gojchlerner 1925- *AmMWSc 92*

**Behar**, Robert *WhoHisp 92*
**Behara**, Minaketan 1937- *AmMWSc 92*
**Behbehani**, Abbas M 1925- *AmMWSc 92*
**Behdad**, Sohrab 1943- *WhoFI 92, WhoMW 92*
**Beheim-Schwarzbach**, Martin 1900-1985 *EncTR 91*
**Beheler**, Laura *DrAPF 91*
**Beher**, William Tyers 1922- *AmMWSc 92*
**Behera**, Prasanta Kumar 1965- *WhoWest 92*
**Behforooz**, Ali 1942- *AmMWSc 92*
**Behki**, Ram M 1932- *AmMWSc 92*
**Behl**, Richard Allen 1941- *WhoRel 92*
**Behl**, Wishvender K 1935- *AmMWSc 92*
**Behle**, William Harroun 1909- *AmMWSc 92, WrDr 92*
**Behlen**, Charles *DrAPF 91*
**Behling**, Dorothy Unseth 1939- *WhoMW 92*
**Behling**, Robert Edward 1941- *AmMWSc 92*
**Behlman**, William Richard 1952- *WhoFI 92*
**Behlmer**, Curt Randolph 1960- *WhoEnt 92, WhoFI 92, WhoWest 92*
**Behlmer**, Rudy H., Jr. 1926- *WhoEnt 92, WhoWest 92*
**Behlow**, Herbert Wallace 1930- *WhoMW 92*
**Behlow**, Robert Frank 1926- *AmMWSc 92*
**Behm**, David Harold 1949- *WhoMW 92*
**Behm**, Forrest Edwin 1919- *WhoFI 92*
**Behm**, Roy 1930- *AmMWSc 92*
**Behme**, Ronald John 1938- *AmMWSc 92*
**Behmer**, David J 1941- *AmMWSc 92*
**Behn**, Aphra 1640?-1689 *RfGEnL 91*
**Behn**, Noel 1928- *IntAu&W 91, WrDr 92*
**Behn**, Robert Dietrich 1941- *WhoAmP 91*
**Behn**, Robin *DrAPF 91*
**Behne**, Edmond Rowlands 1906- *Who 92*
**Behne**, Noel David 1936- *WhoWest 92*
**Behner**, Elton Dale 1952- *WhoMW 92*
**Behney**, Charles Augustus, Jr. 1929- *WhoWest 92*
**Behning**, Laurel Jean 1948- *WhoMW 92*
**Behnke**, Carl Gilbert 1945- *WhoWest 92*
**Behnke**, Charles Norman 1943- *WhoMW 92*
**Behnke**, James Ralph 1943- *AmMWSc 92*
**Behnke**, Roy Herbert 1921- *AmMWSc 92*
**Behnke**, Wallace B, Jr 1926- *AmMWSc 92*
**Behnke**, Wallace Blanchard, Jr. 1926- *WhoFI 92*
**Behnke**, William David 1941- *AmMWSc 92*
**Behof**, Anthony F, Jr 1937- *AmMWSc 92*
**Behr**, Barbara Ellen 1934- *WhoAmL 92*
**Behr**, Carl Triplett 1952- *WhoMW 92*
**Behr**, Edward 1926- *IntAu&W 91, WrDr 92*
**Behr**, Eldon August 1918- *AmMWSc 92*
**Behr**, Hans Hermann 1818-1904 *BiInAmS*
**Behr**, Inga 1923- *AmMWSc 92*
**Behr**, Ira Steven 1953- *WhoEnt 92*
**Behr**, Lawrence Van der Poel 1940- *WhoAmP 91*
**Behr**, Lyell Christian 1916- *AmMWSc 92*
**Behr**, Norman Isaac 1922- *Who 92*
**Behr**, Peter Howell 1915- *WhoWest 92*
**Behr**, Randall *WhoEnt 92*
**Behr**, Stephen Richard 1952- *AmMWSc 92*
**Behr**, Ted Arthur 1934- *WhoRel 92*
**Behravesh**, Mohamad Martin 1945- *AmMWSc 92*
**Behrenbruch**, William David 1946- *WhoWest 92*
**Behrend**, Donald Fraser 1931- *AmMWSc 92, WhoWest 92*
**Behrend**, Frank Ludwig 1938- *WhoMW 92*
**Behrend**, George 1922- *WrDr 92*
**Behrend**, George Henry Sandham 1922- *IntAu&W 91*
**Behrend**, Hilde 1917- *IntWW 91*
**Behrend**, Jack 1929- *WhoEnt 92*
**Behrend**, Siegfried 1933- *IntWW 91*
**Behrend-Updike**, Susan Lynn 1954- *WhoAmL 92*
**Behrends**, Ralph Eugene 1926- *AmMWSc 92*
**Behrendt**, John Charles 1932- *AmMWSc 92*
**Behrendt**, Richard L. *WhoMW 92*
**Behrendt**, Timothy Hume 1937- *WhoRel 92*
**Behrens**, Donald Warren 1949- *WhoWest 92*
**Behrens**, Earl William 1935- *AmMWSc 92*
**Behrens**, Ernst Wilhelm 1931- *AmMWSc 92*
**Behrens**, H Wilhelm 1935- *AmMWSc 92*
**Behrens**, Herbert Charles 1904- *AmMWSc 92*
**Behrens**, Herbert Ernest 1915- *AmMWSc 92*
**Behrens**, Hildegard *IntWW 91*
**Behrens**, John C. 1933- *WrDr 92*
**Behrens**, June Adelle 1925- *WhoWest 92*
**Behrens**, Laura Suzanne 1956- *WhoEnt 92*
**Behrens**, Mary 1942- *WhoAmP 91*
**Behrens**, Mildred Esther 1922- *AmMWSc 92*
**Behrens**, Otto Karl 1911- *AmMWSc 92*
**Behrens**, Peter 1868-1940 *DcTwDes, FacFETw*
**Behrens**, Richard 1921- *AmMWSc 92*
**Behrens**, Richard John 1946- *WhoFI 92*
**Behrens**, Robert George 1943- *AmMWSc 92*
**Behrens**, Roy Richard 1946- *WhoMW 92*
**Behrens**, Thomas A 1957- *WhoAmP 91*
**Behrens**, Tim 1937- *TwCPaSc*
**Behrens**, William Blade 1956- *WhoEnt 92*
**Behrens**, Willy A 1938- *AmMWSc 92*
**Behrents**, Rolf Gordon 1947- *AmMWSc 92*
**Behring**, Daniel William 1940- *WhoMW 92*
**Behring**, Emil Adolf von 1854-1917 *FacFETw*
**Behring**, Kenneth E. 1928- *WhoWest 92*
**Behringer**, Robert Ernest 1931- *AmMWSc 92*
**Behrisch**, Hans Werner 1941- *AmMWSc 92*
**Behrle**, Franklin C 1922- *AmMWSc 92*
**Behrman**, A Sidney 1892- *AmMWSc 92*
**Behrman**, Edward Joseph 1930- *AmMWSc 92, WhoMW 92*
**Behrman**, Harold R 1939- *AmMWSc 92*
**Behrman**, Jack Newton 1922- *WrDr 92*
**Behrman**, Richard Elliot 1931- *AmMWSc 92, IntWW 91*
**Behrman**, Richard H 1944- *AmMWSc 92*
**Behrman**, S. N. 1893-1973 *BenetAL 91*
**Behrman**, Samuel J 1920- *AmMWSc 92*
**Behrmann**, Eleanor Mitts 1917- *AmMWSc 92*
**Behrmann**, Serge T. 1937- *WhoBlA 92*
**Behroozi**, Feredoon 1941- *AmMWSc 92*
**Behrstock**, Roger W. 1937- *WhoWest 92*
**Behymer**, Christopher Glenn 1954- *WhoFI 92*
**Behymer**, Richard Eugene 1947- *WhoWest 92*
**Bei Dao** 1949- *IntAu&W 91, IntWW 91, LiExTwC*
**Bei Ling** *LiExTwC*
**Bei Shizhang** 1903- *IntWW 91*
**Beichl**, George John 1918- *AmMWSc 92*
**Beichle**, Kent Danny 1958- *WhoFI 92*
**Beichman**, Arnold 1913- *WhoWest 92*
**Beickel**, Sharon Lynne 1943- *WhoWest 92*
**Beickler**, Ferdinand 1922- *IntWW 91*
**Beideman**, Ronald Paul 1926- *WhoMW 92*
**Beider**, Andrew Michael 1951- *WhoMW 92*
**Beiderbecke**, Bix 1903-1931 *FacFETw, NewAmDM*
**Beidleman**, James C 1936- *AmMWSc 92*
**Beidleman**, Richard Gooch 1923- *AmMWSc 92*
**Beidler**, Lloyd M 1922- *AmMWSc 92*
**Beier**, Eugene William 1940- *AmMWSc 92*
**Beier**, Friedrich-Karl 1926- *IntWW 91*
**Beier**, Ross Carlton 1946- *AmMWSc 92*
**Beier**, Sandra Jean 1943- *WhoMW 92*
**Beier**, Ulli 1922- *IntAu&W 91*
**Beierwaites**, William Henry 1916- *AmMWSc 92*
**Beierwaltes**, Andrew Joseph 1959- *WhoFI 92*
**Beigel**, Allan 1940- *AmMWSc 92*
**Beigelman**, Paul Maurice 1924- *AmMWSc 92*
**Beighey**, Lawrence Jerome 1938- *WhoFI 92*
**Beighle**, Douglas Paul 1932- *WhoAmL 92, WhoFI 92*
**Beighley**, Clair M 1924- *AmMWSc 92*
**Beight**, Janice Marie 1947- *WhoMW 92*
**Beightler**, Charles Sprague 1924- *AmMWSc 92*
**Beighton**, Leonard John Hobhouse 1934- *Who 92*
**Beigl**, William 1950- *WhoMW 92*
**Beiko**, Alexandra *EncAmaz 91*
**Beil**, Gary Milton 1938- *AmMWSc 92*
**Beil**, Richard Oliver 1955- *WhoFI 92*
**Beil**, Robert J 1924- *AmMWSc 92*
**Beilby**, Alvin Lester 1932- *AmMWSc 92, WhoWest 92*
**Beilby**, George Thomas 1850-1924 *FacFETw*
**Beilenson**, Anthony C. 1932- *AlmAP 92 [port], WhoAmP 91*
**Beilenson**, Anthony Charles 1932- *WhoWest 92*
**Beilenson**, Norton Y. 1937- *WhoAmL 92*
**Beiler**, Theodore Wiseman 1924- *AmMWSc 92*
**Beilhart**, Jacob 1867-1908 *RelLAm 91*
**Beilharz**, Amy Rosemarie 1957- *WhoFI 92*
**Beill**, Alfred 1931- *Who 92*
**Beilman**, Michael Edward 1948- *WhoMW 92*
**Beilstein**, Henry Richard 1920- *AmMWSc 92*
**Beim**, Norman *IntAu&W 91, WhoEnt 92*
**Beimers**, George Jacob 1930- *WhoFI 92*
**Beimfohr**, Douglas Alan 1960- *WhoAmL 92*
**Beimler**, Hans 1895-1936 *EncTR 91*
**Bein**, Donald 1934- *AmMWSc 92*
**Beindorff**, Arthur Baker 1925- *AmMWSc 92*
**Beinecke**, William Sperry 1914- *IntWW 91*
**Beineix**, Jean-Jacques 1946- *IntDcF 2-2, IntWW 91*
**Beineke**, Lowell Wayne 1939- *AmMWSc 92, WhoMW 92*
**Beineke**, Walter Frank 1938- *AmMWSc 92*
**Beinert**, Helmut 1913- *AmMWSc 92*
**Beinfest**, Sidney 1917- *AmMWSc 92*
**Beinfield**, Malcolm Sydney 1921- *WhoFI 92*
**Beinfield**, William Harvey 1918- *AmMWSc 92*
**Beinhocker**, Gilbert David 1932- *WhoFI 92*
**Beining**, Guy R. *DrAPF 91*
**Beining**, Paul R 1923- *AmMWSc 92*
**Beinum**, Eduard van *NewAmDM*
**Beique**, Rene Alexandre 1925- *AmMWSc 92*
**Beirn**, Terence U. d1991 *NewYTBS 91*
**Beirne**, Alice 1960- *WhoAmL 92*
**Beirne**, Bryan Patrick 1918- *AmMWSc 92*
**Beirne**, John Peter 1952- *WhoAmL 92*
**Beirne**, Kilian 1896-1976 *ConAu 134*
**Beirne**, Martin Douglas 1944- *WhoAmL 92*
**Beisecker**, Thomas David 1941- *WhoMW 92*
**Beisel**, James Richard, Jr. 1955- *WhoAmL 92*
**Beisel**, William R 1923- *AmMWSc 92*
**Beiser**, Carl A 1929- *AmMWSc 92*
**Beiser**, Helen R 1914- *AmMWSc 92*
**Beiser**, Morton 1936- *AmMWSc 92*
**Beishline**, Robert Raymond 1930- *AmMWSc 92*
**Beishon**, John 1930- *Who 92*
**Beisler**, John Albert 1937- *AmMWSc 92*
**Beisner**, John Herbert 1953- *WhoAmL 92*
**Beisner**, Ralph Andrew 1942- *WhoAmL 92*
**Beisner**, Robert L. 1936- *WrDr 92*
**Beispiel**, Myron 1931- *AmMWSc 92*
**Beissel**, Conrad 1690-1768 *NewAmDM*
**Beissel**, Henry 1929- *IntAu&W 91, WrDr 92*
**Beissel**, Heribert 1933- *WhoEnt 92*
**Beisser**, Arnold Ray 1925- *AmMWSc 92*
**Beisser**, Fredrick George 1942- *WhoFI 92*
**Beissner**, Robert Edward 1933- *AmMWSc 92*
**Beistel**, Donald W 1936- *AmMWSc 92*
**Beiswanger**, Gary Lee 1938- *WhoAmL 92*
**Beit**, Alfred Lane 1903- *Who 92*
**Beit-Arie**, Malachi 1937- *IntWW 91*
**Beitch**, Irwin 1937- *AmMWSc 92*
**Beitcher**, Robert *IntMPA 92*
**Beitchman**, Burton David 1926- *AmMWSc 92*
**Beitelspacher**, Ronald J 1945- *WhoAmP 91*
**Beiter**, Phyllis Elizabeth 1937- *WhoRel 92*
**Beith**, Alan James 1943- *Who 92*
**Beith**, Carsten 1959- *WhoFI 92*
**Beith**, John 1914- *Who 92*
**Beith**, John Greville Stanley 1914- *IntWW 91*
**Beith**, John William 1909- *Who 92*
**Beitinger**, Thomas Lee 1945- *AmMWSc 92*
**Beitins**, Inese Zinta *AmMWSc 92*
**Beitlich**, Paul Donald 1957- *WhoAmL 92*
**Beitman**, Lawrence 1954- *WhoFI 92*
**Beitner**, Geoffrey Sherwood 1948- *WhoFI 92*
**Beitner**, Norman Harry 1954- *WhoAmL 92*
**Beitz**, Alvin James 1949- *AmMWSc 92*
**Beitz**, Berthold 1913- *IntWW 91*
**Beitz**, Donald Clarence 1940- *AmMWSc 92, WhoMW 92*
**Beitz**, Helen Joy 1958- *WhoMW 92*
**Beitz**, Michael B 1942- *WhoAmP 91*
**Beizer**, Boris 1934- *AmMWSc 92*
**Beizer**, Lance Kurt 1938- *WhoAmL 92*
**Beizer**, Lawrence H 1909- *AmMWSc 92*
**Beizer**, Matthew Robert 1958- *WhoFI 92*
**Beja**, Morris 1935- *IntAu&W 91, WrDr 92*
**Bejarano**, Carmen 1944- *WhoHisp 92*
**Bejarano**, Richard Xavier, Sr. 1950- *WhoHisp 92*
**Bejart**, Maurice 1927- *IntWW 91, Who 92*
**Bejart**, Maurice 1928- *FacFETw*
**Bejart**, Maurice Jean 1927- *WhoEnt 92*
**Bejerot**, Nils 1921-1988 *FacFETw*
**Bejnar**, Thaddeus Putnam 1948- *WhoAmL 92*
**Bejnar**, Waldemere 1920- *AmMWSc 92*
**Bek**, Aleksandr Alfredovich 1902-1972 *SovUnBD*
**Bek**, Wieslaw Marian 1929- *IntAu&W 91, IntWW 91*
**Bek-Nazarov**, Amo Ivanovich 1892-1965 *SovUnBD*
**Bekavac**, Nancy Yavor 1947- *WhoWest 92*
**Bekederemo**, J. P. Clark *ConPo 91, RfGEnL 91*
**Bekefi**, George 1925- *AmMWSc 92*
**Bekemeyer**, Dennis Lee 1943- *WhoAmL 92*
**Bekenstein**, Jacob David 1947- *AmMWSc 92*
**Beker**, George 1945- *WhoEnt 92*
**Beker**, Henry Joseph 1951- *Who 92*
**Bekersky**, Ihor 1940- *AmMWSc 92*
**Bekesi**, Laszlo 1942- *IntWW 91*
**Bekey**, George A 1928- *AmMWSc 92*
**Bekey**, George Albert 1928- *WhoWest 92*
**Bekhor**, Isaac *AmMWSc 92*
**Bekhteev**, Vladimir Georgievich 1878-1971 *SovUnBD*
**Bekhterev**, Vladimir Mikhaylovich 1857-1927 *SovUnBD*
**Bekhtereva**, Natalya Petrovna 1924- *IntWW 91*
**Bekir**, Nagwa Esmat 1944- *WhoWest 92*
**Bekkedahl**, Brad Douglas 1957- *WhoMW 92*
**Bekoe**, Daniel Adzei 1928- *Who 92*
**Bekoff**, Anne C 1947- *AmMWSc 92*
**Bekoff**, Marc 1945- *AmMWSc 92*
**Bel**, Matyas 1684-1749 *BlkwCEP*
**Bel Bruno**, Joseph James 1952- *AmMWSc 92*
**Bel Geddes**, Barbara 1922- *IntMPA 92, WhoEnt 92*
**Bel Geddes**, Joan 1916- *IntAu&W 91*
**Bel Geddes**, Norman 1893-1958 *DcTwDes, FacFETw*
**Belady**, Laszlo Antal 1928- *AmMWSc 92*
**Belafonte**, Harry *DcAmImH*
**Belafonte**, Harry 1927- *FacFETw, IntMPA 92, IntWW 91, WhoBlA 92, WhoEnt 92*
**Belafonte**, Shari 1954- *IntMPA 92*
**Belaga**, Julie D *WhoAmP 91*
**Belaid**, Moncef 1942- *IntWW 91*
**Belalcazar**, Sebastian de *HisDSpE*
**Belam**, Noel Stephen d1991 *Who 92N*
**Belan**, Albert V 1930- *WhoAmP 91*
**Belan**, William Wells 1950- *WhoEnt 92*
**Belancourt**, Dunet Francois 1928- *WhoBlA 92*
**Beland**, Gary LaVern 1942- *AmMWSc 92*
**Beland**, Pierre 1947- *AmMWSc 92*
**Belanger**, A. Kenneth 1942- *WhoRel 92*
**Belanger**, Alain 1947- *AmMWSc 92*
**Belanger**, Brian Charles 1941- *AmMWSc 92*
**Belanger**, David Gerald 1944- *AmMWSc 92*
**Belanger**, Francois-Joseph 1744-1818 *BlkwCEP*
**Belanger**, Gerard 1940- *IntWW 91*
**Belanger**, Guy *WhoEnt 92*
**Belanger**, Jacqueline M R 1954- *AmMWSc 92*
**Belanger**, James Henry 1943- *WhoAmL 92*
**Belanger**, JoAnn Lynn 1944- *WhoMW 92*
**Belanger**, Luc 1948- *AmMWSc 92*
**Belanger**, Michel 1929- *IntWW 91*
**Belanger**, Patrice Charles 1940- *AmMWSc 92*
**Belanger**, Pierre Andre 1941- *AmMWSc 92*
**Belanger**, Pierre Rolland 1937- *AmMWSc 92*
**Belanger**, Ronald Joseph 1939- *WhoAmP 91*
**Belanger**, Thomas V 1948- *AmMWSc 92*
**Belanger**, William V, Jr 1928- *WhoAmP 91*
**Belany**, Archibald Stansfeld *BenetAL 91*
**Belardi**, Fred 1942- *WhoAmP 91*
**Belardinelli**, Luiz *AmMWSc 92*
**Belardo de O'Neal**, Lilliana 1944- *WhoAmP 91, WhoBlA 92*
**Belasco**, David 1853-1931 *FacFETw*
**Belasco**, David 1859-1931 *BenetAL 91*
**Belashova**, Yekaterina Fedorovna 1906-1971 *SovUnBD*
**Belatti**, Richard G *WhoAmP 91*
**Belau**, Jane Carol Gullickson 1934- *WhoFI 92*
**Belaunde Terry**, Fernando 1913- *IntWW 91*
**Belbeck**, L W 1943- *AmMWSc 92*
**Belbruno**, Diana Rousseau 1952- *WhoAmL 92*
**Belcastro**, Patrick Frank 1920- *AmMWSc 92*
**Belch**, Alexander Ross 1920- *Who 92*
**Belch**, Charles Henry 1938- *WhoAmP 91*
**Belch**, Kenneth James 1944- *WhoRel 92*
**Belchak**, Frank Robert 1943- *WhoMW 92*
**Belcher**, Bascom Anthony 1902- *AmMWSc 92*

**Belcher,** Dennis Irl 1951- *WhoAmL 92*
**Belcher,** Edward Loring 1926- *WhoFI 92*
**Belcher,** George 1875-1948 *TwCPaSc*
**Belcher,** George 1941- *WhoWest 92*
**Belcher,** Jennifer M 1944- *WhoAmP 91*
**Belcher,** John Davis 1955- *WhoMW 92*
**Belcher,** John Rashleigh 1917- *Who 92*
**Belcher,** Larry Ray 1946- *WhoFI 92*
**Belcher,** Leon H. 1930- *WhoBlA 92*
**Belcher,** Lewis, Jr. 1931- *WhoBlA 92*
**Belcher,** Louis D 1939- *WhoAmP 91*
**Belcher,** Margaret L. 1922- *WhoBlA 92*
**Belcher,** Melvin B 1925- *AmMWSc 92*
**Belcher,** Nathaniel L. 1929- *WhoBlA 92*
**Belcher,** Paul E. 1933- *WhoBlA 92*
**Belcher,** Richard Neil 1954- *WhoAmL 92*
**Belcher,** Robert Orange 1918- *AmMWSc 92*
**Belcher,** Ronald Harry 1916- *Who 92*
**Belcher,** Supply 1751-1836 *NewAmDM*
**Belcher,** Taylor Garrison 1920- *WhoAmP 91*
**Belcher,** William Walter, Jr. 1943- *WhoWest 92*
**Belchev,** Belcho Antonov 1932- *IntWW 91*
**Belchior,** Murillo 1913- *IntWW 91*
**Belcourt,** Mignonne L. 1945- *WhoFI 92*
**Beldam,** Roy 1925- *Who 92*
**Belden,** David Leigh 1935- *WhoFI 92*
**Belden,** Don Alexander, Jr 1926- *AmMWSc 92*
**Belden,** Everett Lee 1938- *AmMWSc 92*
**Belden,** Glen William 1937- *WhoFI 92, WhoMW 92*
**Belden,** H. Reginald 1907- *WhoAmL 92*
**Belden,** Jerry Lee 1935- *WhoRel 92*
**Belden,** Richard O 1934- *WhoAmP 91*
**Belden,** Stephen Frederic 1954- *WhoAmL 92*
**Belden,** Ursula 1947- *WhoEnt 92*
**Belding,** Lyman 1829-1917 *BiInAmS*
**Belding,** Ralph Cedric 1915- *AmMWSc 92*
**Beldock,** Myron 1929- *WhoAmL 92*
**Belefant,** Martin S. 1925- *WhoAmL 92*
**Belefant,** Sterling Bernard 1962- *WhoEnt 92*
**Belenski,** Richard Paul 1955- *WhoFI 92*
**Beleson,** Robert Brian 1950- *WhoFI 92*
**Beless,** Rosemary June 1947- *WhoAmL 92*
**Belew,** Adrian *WhoEnt 92*
**Belew,** David Lee 1931- *WhoMW 92*
**Belew,** David Owen, Jr. 1920- *WhoAmL 92*
**Belew,** Joe Duncan 1949- *WhoAmP 91*
**Belew,** John Seymour 1920- *AmMWSc 92*
**Belew-Noah,** Patricia W 1940- *AmMWSc 92*
**Belfanti,** Robert Edward, Jr 1948- *WhoAmP 91*
**Belfast,** Dean of *Who 92*
**Belfast,** Earl of 1952- *Who 92*
**Belfer,** Hal B. *IntMPA 92*
**Belfield,** Judy *DrAPF 91*
**Belfiore,** Dennis 1954- *WhoFI 92*
**Belfiore,** Evelina *WhoRel 92*
**Belford,** Barbara 1935- *WrDr 92*
**Belford,** Geneva Grosz 1932- *AmMWSc 92*
**Belford,** Julius 1920- *AmMWSc 92*
**Belford,** R Linn 1931- *AmMWSc 92*
**Belford,** Virginia Helen Wisdom 1948- *WhoMW 92, WhoRel 92*
**Belfort,** Georges 1940- *AmMWSc 92*
**Belfort,** Marlene 1945- *AmMWSc 92*
**Belfrage,** Cedric 1904-1990 *AnObit 1990*
**Belfrage,** Leif Axel Lorentz d1990 *Who 92N*
**Belfrage,** Leif Axel Lorentz 1910- *IntWW 91*
**Belfrage,** Sally 1936- *SmATA 65 [port]*
**Belgium,** King BaudouinI of *IntWW 91*
**Belgrano,** Manuel 1770-1820 *BlkwCEP, HisDSpE*
**Belham,** David Ernest 1914- *Who 92*
**Belhaven,** Master of 1953- *Who 92*
**Belhaven and Stenton,** Lord 1927- *Who 92*
**Belhorn,** Paul Christy 1941- *WhoRel 92*
**Beliaev,** Aleksandr Romanovich 1884-1942 *ScFEYrs*
**Belian,** Richard Duane 1938- *AmMWSc 92*
**Beliard,** Edouard 1835-1902 *ThHEIm*
**Beliard,** Jean 1919- *IntWW 91*
**Belica,** Marina Elena 1959- *WhoEnt 92*
**Belich,** James 1927- *Who 92*
**Belichick,** Bill *WhoMW 92*
**Beligan,** Radu 1918- *IntWW 91*
**Belikov,** Valeriy Aleksandrovich *IntWW 91*
**Beliles,** Robert Pryor 1932- *AmMWSc 92*
**Belille,** Ronald 1947- *WhoWest 92*
**Belin,** Carl A, Jr 1934- *WhoAmP 91*
**Belin,** David William 1928- *WhoAmL 92, WhoFI 92*
**Belin,** Jacob Chapman 1914- *WhoFI 92*
**Belin,** Roger 1916- *IntWW 91*
**Belina,** Peter 1963- *WhoFI 92*
**Belinfante,** Alexander Erik Ernst 1944- *WhoFI 92*
**Belinfante,** Frederik J 1913- *AmMWSc 92*
**Belinfante,** Geoffrey Warren 1947- *WhoEnt 92*
**Belinfante,** Johan G F 1940- *AmMWSc 92*
**Belinske,** Barbara *WhoRel 92*
**Belinsky,** Steven Alan 1956- *AmMWSc 92*
**Belisle,** Barbara Wolfanger 1951- *AmMWSc 92*
**Belisle,** Denton 1948- *Who 92*
**Belisle,** Gilles 1923- *WhoRel 92*
**Belisle,** John Adrien 1942- *WhoFI 92*
**Belisle,** Samuel Darrel 1954- *WhoRel 92*
**Belitskus,** David 1938- *AmMWSc 92*
**Belitsos,** Michael *WhoFI 92*
**Belitt,** Ben *DrAPF 91*
**Belitt,** Ben 1911- *ConPo 91, IntAu&W 91, WrDr 92*
**Belitz,** Paul Edward 1951- *WhoAmL 92*
**Beliveau,** Jean Arthur 1931- *FacFETw*
**Beliveau,** Jules 1942- *WhoRel 92*
**Beliveau,** Severin Matthew 1938- *WhoAmP 91*
**Beljan,** John Richard 1930- *AmMWSc 92*
**Belk,** Gene Denton 1938- *AmMWSc 92*
**Belk,** Henry 1898-1972 *DcNCBi 1*
**Belk,** Irwin 1922- *WhoFI 92*
**Belk,** John Blanton 1925- *WhoWest 92*
**Belk,** John M. 1920- *WhoFI 92*
**Belk,** Samuel Ellison, III 1920- *WhoRel 92*
**Belk,** Thomas Milburn 1925- *WhoFI 92*
**Belk,** William Henry 1862-1952 *DcNCBi 1*
**Belkaid,** Aboubakr 1934- *IntWW 91*
**Belker,** Loren Richard 1935- *WhoWest 92*
**Belkhodja,** Mohamed Moncef 1932- *IntWW 91*
**Belkhodja,** Muhammad Habir *WhoRel 92*
**Belkin,** Alan 1947- *WhoAmL 92*
**Belkin,** Barry 1940- *AmMWSc 92*
**Belkin,** Harriet Tauba 1931- *WhoEnt 92*
**Belkin,** Herbert Allen 1939- *WhoEnt 92, WhoFI 92*
**Belkin,** Janet Ehrenreich 1938- *WhoAmL 92*
**Belkin,** Norman 1924- *WhoEnt 92*
**Belknap,** Allen Roger 1941- *WhoEnt 92*
**Belknap,** Daniel 1771-1815 *NewAmDM*
**Belknap,** George Eugene 1832-1903 *BiInAmS*
**Belknap,** Jeremy 1744-1798 *BenetAL 91*
**Belknap,** John Corbould 1946- *WhoFI 92*
**Belknap,** John Kenneth 1943- *AmMWSc 92*
**Belknap,** Michael H. P. 1940- *WhoFI 92*
**Belknap,** Norton 1925- *WhoEnt 92*
**Belknap,** Robert Ernest, III 1938- *WhoFI 92*
**Belknap,** Robert L. 1929- *WrDr 92*
**Belknap,** Robert Wayne 1924- *AmMWSc 92*
**Belknap,** William Bernhard 1927- *WhoFI 92*
**Belknap,** William Worth 1829-1890 *AmPolLe*
**Bell and Daldy** *DcLB 106*
**Bell and Hyman Ltd.** *DcLB 106*
**Bell,** A Earl 1918- *AmMWSc 92*
**Bell,** A Jean 1926- *WhoAmP 91*
**Bell,** Agrippa Nelson 1820-1911 *BiInAmS*
**Bell,** Alan Edward 1948- *AmMWSc 92*
**Bell,** Albert Jerome 1960- *WhoAmL 92*
**Bell,** Albert Leo 1930- *WhoAmL 92*
**Bell,** Alexander F. 1904-1986 *WhoBlA 92N*
**Bell,** Alexander Gilmour 1933- *Who 92*
**Bell,** Alexander Graham 1847-1922 *BenetAL 91, DcTwDes, FacFETw, RComAH*
**Bell,** Alexander Melville 1819-1905 *BenetAL 91*
**Bell,** Alexander Scott 1941- *Who 92*
**Bell,** Alexis T 1942- *AmMWSc 92*
**Bell,** Alfred Lee Loomis, Jr 1923- *AmMWSc 92*
**Bell,** Alistair Watson 1930- *Who 92*
**Bell,** Allen L 1937- *AmMWSc 92*
**Bell,** Alois Adrian 1934- *AmMWSc 92*
**Bell,** Alphonzo 1914- *WhoAmP 91*
**Bell,** Andrew Montgomery 1940- *Who 92*
**Bell,** Anthony Dewitt 1964- *WhoBlA 92*
**Bell,** Anthony E 1937- *AmMWSc 92*
**Bell,** Archibald Angus 1923- *Who 92*
**Bell,** Arthur *Who 92*
**Bell,** Barbara 1922- *AmMWSc 92*
**Bell,** Barbara H 1920- *IntAu&W 91*
**Bell,** Benjamin Clayton, Jr. 1959- *WhoFI 92*
**Bell,** Bernard Raymond 1912- *WhoFI 92*
**Bell,** Beverly June 1950- *WhoEnt 92*
**Bell,** Blake Allen 1958- *WhoAmL 92*
**Bell,** Brian James Kennard 1932- *WhoWest 92*
**Bell,** Brian Mayes 1940- *WhoAmL 92*
**Bell,** Brian Reed 1964- *WhoEnt 92*
**Bell,** Bruce Arnold 1944- *AmMWSc 92*
**Bell,** Bryan 1918- *WhoFI 92*
**Bell,** C Gordon 1934- *AmMWSc 92*
**Bell,** Camille Marie 1956- *WhoMW 92*
**Bell,** Carl Compton 1947- *WhoBlA 92*
**Bell,** Carl F 1933- *AmMWSc 92*
**Bell,** Carlos G, Jr 1922- *AmMWSc 92*
**Bell,** Carol Jean 1964- *WhoMW 92*
**Bell,** Carolyn Shaw 1920- *WhoFI 92*
**Bell,** Catherine *WrDr 92*
**Bell,** Charles Bernard, Jr 1928- *AmMWSc 92*
**Bell,** Charles E, Jr 1931- *AmMWSc 92*
**Bell,** Charles Eugene, Jr 1932- *AmMWSc 92, WhoFI 92, WhoMW 92*
**Bell,** Charles G. 1916- *WrDr 92*
**Bell,** Charles Greenleaf *DrAPF 91*
**Bell,** Charles Greenleaf 1916- *IntAu&W 91*
**Bell,** Charles H. 1927- *WhoFI 92*
**Bell,** Charles J 1854-1903 *BiInAmS*
**Bell,** Charles Smith 1934- *WhoBlA 92*
**Bell,** Charles Trevor 1927- *Who 92*
**Bell,** Charles Vester 1934- *AmMWSc 92*
**Bell,** Charles W 1931- *AmMWSc 92*
**Bell,** Charlotte Renee 1949- *WhoWest 92*
**Bell,** Christopher Ross 1956- *WhoFI 92*
**Bell,** Clara Ellen 1934- *WhoBlA 92*
**Bell,** Clara G 1937- *AmMWSc 92*
**Bell,** Clarence Deshong 1914- *WhoAmP 91*
**Bell,** Clarence E 1912- *WhoAmP 91*
**Bell,** Clive 1881-1962 *FacFETw*
**Bell,** Clyde Ritchie 1921- *AmMWSc 92*
**Bell,** Cool Papa 1903-1991 *WhoBlA 92N*
**Bell,** Craig Marshall 1952- *WhoAmL 92*
**Bell,** Curtis Calvin *AmMWSc 92*
**Bell,** Curtis Porter 1934- *AmMWSc 92*
**Bell,** Cyril Felix 1942- *WhoAmP 91*
**Bell,** Dan G. 1953- *WhoFI 92*
**Bell,** Daniel 1919- *WrDr 92*
**Bell,** Daniel Carroll 1940- *WhoWest 92*
**Bell,** Daniel Long, Jr. 1929- *WhoAmL 92, WhoFI 92*
**Bell,** Darryl *WhoEnt 92*
**Bell,** David Arthur 1943- *WhoFI 92*
**Bell,** David Elliott 1919- *IntWW 91*
**Bell,** David S. 1964- *WhoRel 92*
**Bell,** Deborah Dolores 1961- *WhoMW 92*
**Bell,** Dennis Arthur 1934- *WhoAmL 92*
**Bell,** Dennis Lawrence 1941- *WhoEnt 92*
**Bell,** Dennis Philip 1948- *WhoBlA 92*
**Bell,** Derrick Albert 1930- *WhoAmL 92*
**Bell,** Derrick Albert, Jr. 1930- *WhoBlA 92*
**Bell,** Diana Lynne 1952- *WhoBlA 92*
**Bell,** Don Wayne 1945- *WhoFI 92, WhoWest 92*
**Bell,** Donald Atkinson 1941- *Who 92*
**Bell,** Donald L. *Who 92*
**Bell,** Donald Munro 1934- *Who 92*
**Bell,** Donald Robert 1928- *WhoWest 92*
**Bell,** Donald William 1936- *WhoWest 92*
**Bell,** Douglas Maurice 1914- *Who 92*
**Bell,** Drucilla Emma 1951- *WhoAmL 92*
**Bell,** Duncan Hadley 1952- *AmMWSc 92*
**Bell,** Earnest Franklin 1913- *WhoBlA 92*
**Bell,** Edith Alice 1919- *Who 92*
**Bell,** Edward Percy d1987 *Who 92N*
**Bell,** Edward Percy 1902- *Who 92*
**Bell,** Edwin Graham 1939- *WhoAmP 91*
**Bell,** Edwin Lewis, II 1926- *AmMWSc 92*
**Bell,** Eileen 1907- *TwCPaSc*
**Bell,** Eldrin A. *WhoBlA 92*
**Bell,** Elmer A. 1941- *WhoBlA 92*
**Bell,** Emerson 1861-1930 *ScFEYrs*
**Bell,** Ernest Arthur 1926- *IntWW 91, Who 92*
**Bell,** Eudorus N. 1866-1923 *RelLAm 91*
**Bell,** Eugene 1918- *AmMWSc 92*
**Bell,** Evalyn Lurene Krueger *WhoWest 92*
**Bell,** Everett Thomas 1909- *WhoBlA 92*
**Bell,** Ewart *Who 92*
**Bell,** Felix C. 1936- *WhoBlA 92*
**Bell,** Forest Stirling *DrAPF 91*
**Bell,** Frank *ConAu 134, SmATA 65*
**Bell,** Frank 1904- *Who 92*
**Bell,** Frank F 1915- *AmMWSc 92*
**Bell,** Frank Ouray, Jr. 1940- *WhoAmL 92*
**Bell,** Franklin R 1943- *WhoAmP 91*
**Bell,** Fred E 1925- *AmMWSc 92*
**Bell,** G. Wilbur 1912- *WhoMW 92*
**Bell,** Gail Marie 1951- *WhoFI 92*
**Bell,** Gawain 1909- *Who 92*
**Bell,** Geoffrey Lakin 1939- *IntWW 91, Who 92*
**Bell,** George *WhoBlA 92*
**Bell,** George 1814-1890 *DcLB 106 [port]*
**Bell,** George 1959- *WhoHisp 92*
**Bell,** George, and Sons *DcLB 106*
**Bell,** George Allen Kennedy 1883-1958 *DcEcMov [port]*
**Bell,** George Antonio 1959- *WhoBlA 92*
**Bell,** George de Benneville 1924- *WhoFI 92*
**Bell,** George Douglas Hutton 1905- *IntWW 91, Who 92*
**Bell,** George Edwin 1923- *WhoFI 92*
**Bell,** George Irving 1926- *AmMWSc 92*
**Bell,** George Raymond 1916- *IntWW 91, Who 92*
**Bell,** George W *ScFEYrs*
**Bell,** Gordon M 1920- *AmMWSc 92*
**Bell,** Graham 1910-1943 *TwCPaSc*
**Bell,** Graham Arthur Charlton 1949- *AmMWSc 92*
**Bell,** Graydon Dee 1923- *AmMWSc 92*
**Bell,** Gregory C 1930- *BlkOlyM*
**Bell,** Gregory Joseph 1948- *WhoAmP 91*
**Bell,** Gregory Leon 1962- *WhoBlA 92*
**Bell,** Gregory S. 1948- *WhoAmL 92*
**Bell,** Griffin B. 1918- *Who 92, WhoAmL 92, WhoAmP 91*
**Bell,** Griffin Boyette 1918- *IntWW 91*
**Bell,** Guy Davies 1933- *Who 92*
**Bell,** H. B. 1938- *WhoBlA 92*
**Bell,** H R 1920- *AmMWSc 92*
**Bell,** Harold 1932- *AmMWSc 92*
**Bell,** Harold E 1926- *AmMWSc 92*
**Bell,** Harold Morton 1940- *AmMWSc 92*
**Bell,** Harry Edward 1947- *WhoMW 92*
**Bell,** Henry Haywood 1808-1868 *DcNCBi 1*
**Bell,** Herbert Sidney 1929- *WhoMW 92*
**Bell,** Howard E 1937- *AmMWSc 92*
**Bell,** Howard Eugene 1920- *WhoBlA 92*
**Bell,** Howard Holman 1913- *WhoBlA 92*
**Bell,** Howard Wesley, Jr. 1948- *WhoMW 92*
**Bell,** Hubert Thomas, Jr. 1942- *WhoBlA 92*
**Bell,** Ian 1932- *AmMWSc 92*
**Bell,** Ian Wright 1913- *Who 92*
**Bell,** J. A. Gordon 1929- *WhoFI 92*
**Bell,** J M 1935- *AmMWSc 92*
**Bell,** Jack Perkins 1940- *AmMWSc 92*
**Bell,** James 1903-1991 *FacFETw, NewYTBS 91 [port]*
**Bell,** James A. *WhoBlA 92*
**Bell,** James Bacon 1952- *WhoMW 92*
**Bell,** James David 1932- *WhoRel 92*
**Bell,** James Edward 1926- *WhoBlA 92*
**Bell,** James Edward 1941- *WrDr 92*
**Bell,** James F 1914- *AmMWSc 92*
**Bell,** James Frederick 1922- *WhoAmL 92*
**Bell,** James H. 1916- *WhoBlA 92*
**Bell,** James Henry 1917- *AmMWSc 92*
**Bell,** James Kenton 1937- *WrDr 92*
**Bell,** James L., Jr. 1921- *WhoBlA 92*
**Bell,** James M., Sr. 1928- *WhoRel 92*
**Bell,** James Madison 1826-1902 *BlkLC, TwCLC 43 [port]*
**Bell,** James Milton 1921- *AmMWSc 92, WhoBlA 92*
**Bell,** James Paul 1934- *AmMWSc 92*
**Bell,** James Scott *DrAPF 91*
**Bell,** James Steven 1914- *Who 92*
**Bell,** Janet Sharon 1947- *WhoBlA 92*
**Bell,** Janis Callen 1950- *WhoMW 92*
**Bell,** Jeannette Lois 1941- *WhoAmP 91*
**Bell,** Jeffrey 1952- *AmMWSc 92*
**Bell,** Jeffrey Donald 1956- *WhoFI 92*
**Bell,** Jerry *WhoMW 92*
**Bell,** Jerry Alan 1936- *AmMWSc 92*
**Bell,** Jesse Spencer 1906-1967 *DcNCBi 1*
**Bell,** Jimmy 1944- *WhoBlA 92*
**Bell,** Jimmy Holt 1935- *AmMWSc 92*
**Bell,** Jimmy Todd 1938- *AmMWSc 92*
**Bell,** Jocelyn *Who 92*
**Bell,** Joe W *WhoAmP 91*
**Bell,** John 1797-1869 *AmPolLe [port]*
**Bell,** John Alexander Gordon 1929- *IntWW 91*
**Bell,** John Alton 1958- *WhoAmL 92*
**Bell,** John Anthony 1924- *Who 92*
**Bell,** John David 1947- *WhoFI 92*
**Bell,** John Frederick 1924- *AmMWSc 92*
**Bell,** John G 1812-1889 *BiInAmS*
**Bell,** John Hutson 1933- *WhoMW 92*
**Bell,** John Lewis 1942- *WhoFI 92*
**Bell,** John Lowthian 1960- *Who 92*
**Bell,** John Milton 1922- *AmMWSc 92, IntWW 91*
**Bell,** John Perry 1948- *WhoRel 92*
**Bell,** John Raymond 1954- *WhoMW 92*
**Bell,** John Stewart d1990 *IntWW 91N, Who 92N*
**Bell,** John Urwin 1948- *AmMWSc 92*
**Bell,** John Wright 1925- *WhoAmL 92*
**Bell,** Jonathan George *AmMWSc 92*
**Bell,** Jonathan Robert 1947- *WhoAmL 92*
**Bell,** Joseph Curtis 1933- *WhoBlA 92*
**Bell,** Joseph Denis Milburn 1920- *Who 92*
**Bell,** Joseph Ernest, II 1941- *WhoAmP 91*
**Bell,** Joseph James *WhoAmP 91*
**Bell,** Joseph N. 1948- *WhoBlA 92*
**Bell,** Joshua 1967- *IntWW 91*
**Bell,** Juanita 1923- *WhoAmP 91*
**Bell,** Judith Endicott 1932- *WhoEnt 92*
**Bell,** Julian 1952- *TwCPaSc*
**Bell,** Juliette B 1955- *AmMWSc 92*
**Bell,** Kasandra Lynn Nordine 1945- *WhoEnt 92*
**Bell,** Kathleen *TwCPaSc*
**Bell,** Kathleen Myra 1920- *Who 92*
**Bell,** Katie Roberson 1936- *WhoBlA 92*
**Bell,** Kenneth J 1930- *AmMWSc 92*
**Bell,** Kenneth M. 1941- *WhoBlA 92*
**Bell,** Kinith John 1951- *WhoRel 92*
**Bell,** L. M. *WhoRel 92*
**Bell,** Lanette 1961- *WhoEnt 92*
**Bell,** Larry Stuart 1939- *WhoWest 92*
**Bell,** Laura Jeane 1922- *WhoMW 92*
**Bell,** Laurie 1952- *WhoEnt 92*
**Bell,** Lawrence F. 1958- *WhoBlA 92*
**Bell,** Lawrence R. 1941- *WhoIns 92*

**Bell**, Lee Phillip *WhoEnt 92*
**Bell**, Leland 1922-1991 *NewYTBS 91*
**Bell**, Lemuel Nelson 1894-1973 *DcNCBi 1*
**Bell**, Leo S. 1913- *WhoWest 92*
**Bell**, Leon 1930- *WhoBlA 92*
**Bell**, Leslie 1906-1962 *NewAmDM*
**Bell**, Leslie B. 1947- *WhoMW 92*
**Bell**, Leslie Gladstone 1919- *Who 92*
**Bell**, M W Jack 1927- *AmMWSc 92*
**Bell**, Madison Smartt *DrAPF 91*
**Bell**, Madison Smartt 1957- *ConNov 91, WrDr 92*
**Bell**, Malcolm Rice 1928- *AmMWSc 92*
**Bell**, Marcus Arthur Money 1935- *AmMWSc 92*
**Bell**, Marian Whieldon *WhoAmP 91*
**Bell**, Marie 1946- *WhoAmP 91*
**Bell**, Marilyn Lenora 1943- *WhoBlA 92*
**Bell**, Martha Jane 1943- *WhoAmP 91*
**Bell**, Martha Lue 1945- *WhoBlA 92*
**Bell**, Martha McFarlane McGee 1735-1820 *DcNCBi 1*
**Bell**, Martin 1938- *Who 92*
**Bell**, Martin George Henry 1935- *Who 92*
**Bell**, Marvin *DrAPF 91*
**Bell**, Marvin 1937- *ConAu 14AS [port], ConPo 91, WrDr 92*
**Bell**, Marvin Carl 1921- *AmMWSc 92*
**Bell**, Marvin Drake 1929- *AmMWSc 92*
**Bell**, Marvin Hartley 1937- *IntAu&W 91*
**Bell**, Mary 1937- *AmMWSc 92*
**Bell**, Mary Allison 1936- *AmMWSc 92*
**Bell**, Mary E. Beniteau 1937- *WhoFI 92*
**Bell**, Mary L. *WhoBlA 92*
**Bell**, Maurice Evan 1910- *AmMWSc 92*
**Bell**, Max Ewart 1927- *AmMWSc 92*
**Bell**, Maxine T 1931- *WhoAmP 91*
**Bell**, Melvyn Clarence 1944- *WhoBlA 92*
**Bell**, Michael Allen 1947- *AmMWSc 92*
**Bell**, Michael Bruce 1943- *WhoFI 92*
**Bell**, Michael John Vincent 1941- *Who 92*
**Bell**, Michael S. *DrAPF 91*
**Bell**, Mildred Bailey 1928- *WhoAmL 92, WhoFI 92*
**Bell**, Millicent *ConAu 36NR*
**Bell**, Millicent 1919- *DcLB 111 [port]*
**Bell**, Milo C 1905- *AmMWSc 92*
**Bell**, Mitchel Alan 1962- *WhoFI 92*
**Bell**, Napoleon A. 1927- *WhoBlA 92*
**Bell**, Nathan James 1946- *WhoAmP 91*
**Bell**, Nikki 1959- *TwCPaSc*
**Bell**, Nikki, and Langlands, Ben *TwCPaSc*
**Bell**, Norman Francis 1948- *WhoWest 92*
**Bell**, Norman H 1931- *AmMWSc 92*
**Bell**, Norman Martin 1907-1970 *TwCPaSc*
**Bell**, Norman R 1918- *AmMWSc 92*
**Bell**, Normand W. 1930- *WhoIns 92*
**Bell**, Olin Nile 1939- *WhoAmL 92*
**Bell**, Orion Hancock, III 1936- *WhoRel 92*
**Bell**, Paul, Jr. 1921- *WhoBlA 92*
**Bell**, Paul Burton, Jr 1946- *AmMWSc 92*
**Bell**, Paul Hadley 1914- *AmMWSc 92*
**Bell**, Persa Raymond 1913- *AmMWSc 92*
**Bell**, Peter M 1934- *AmMWSc 92*
**Bell**, Peter Robert 1920- *Who 92*
**Bell**, Peter Robert Frank 1938- *Who 92*
**Bell**, Quentin 1910- *IntAu&W 91, TwCPaSc, Who 92, WrDr 92*
**Bell**, Raleigh Berton 1915- *WhoBlA 92*
**Bell**, Randall 1943- *WhoRel 92*
**Bell**, Randall Keith 1962- *WhoRel 92*
**Bell**, Raymond *IntWW 91, Who 92*
**Bell**, Raymond M. 1907- *WrDr 92*
**Bell**, Raymond Martin 1907- *AmMWSc 92*
**Bell**, Reaver Garland *WhoMW 92*
**Bell**, Reva Pearl 1925- *WhoBlA 92*
**Bell**, Richard 1920- *WhoAmL 92, WhoAmP 91*
**Bell**, Richard Dennis 1937- *AmMWSc 92*
**Bell**, Richard Eugene 1934- *WhoFI 92*
**Bell**, Richard Eugene 1947- *WhoRel 92*
**Bell**, Richard G. 1947- *WhoFI 92*
**Bell**, Richard Oman 1933- *AmMWSc 92*
**Bell**, Richard Russell 1926- *WhoMW 92*
**Bell**, Richard Thomas 1937- *AmMWSc 92*
**Bell**, Ricky Lynn 1955-1984 *WhoBlA 92N*
**Bell**, Robbie Hancock 1955- *WhoAmL 92*
**Bell**, Robert Alan 1934- *AmMWSc 92*
**Bell**, Robert Anning 1863-1933 *TwCPaSc*
**Bell**, Robert Arnold 1950- *WhoFI 92*
**Bell**, Robert Cecil 1951- *WhoWest 92*
**Bell**, Robert Charles 1917- *WrDr 92*
**Bell**, Robert Collins 1912- *WhoAmL 92, WhoFI 92*
**Bell**, Robert Donald Murray 1916- *Who 92*
**Bell**, Robert Edward 1918- *AmMWSc 92, IntWW 91, Who 92*
**Bell**, Robert Eugene 1914- *AmMWSc 92, WrDr 92*
**Bell**, Robert Holmes 1944- *WhoAmL 92*
**Bell**, Robert Hudson 1929- *WhoAmP 91*
**Bell**, Robert John 1934- *AmMWSc 92*
**Bell**, Robert L. 1934- *WhoBlA 92*
**Bell**, Robert Lloyd 1923- *AmMWSc 92*
**Bell**, Robert Mack 1943- *WhoBlA 92*
**Bell**, Robert Maurice 1944- *AmMWSc 92*
**Bell**, Robert Morrall 1936- *WhoAmL 92*
**Bell**, Robert Vaughn *TwCWW 91, WrDr 92*
**Bell**, Robert Wesley 1918- *WhoBlA 92*
**Bell**, Robin 1945- *WrDr 92*
**Bell**, Robin Graham 1942- *AmMWSc 92*
**Bell**, Rodger 1939- *Who 92*
**Bell**, Roger 1947- *WrDr 92*
**Bell**, Roger Alistair 1935- *AmMWSc 92*
**Bell**, Roma Raines 1944- *AmMWSc 92*
**Bell**, Ronald Leslie 1929- *Who 92*
**Bell**, Ronald Percy 1907- *IntWW 91, Who 92*
**Bell**, Rondal E 1933- *AmMWSc 92*
**Bell**, Roseann P. 1945- *WhoBlA 92*
**Bell**, Ross Taylor 1929- *AmMWSc 92*
**Bell**, Rouzeberry 1934- *WhoBlA 92*
**Bell**, Russell A 1935- *AmMWSc 92*
**Bell**, S. Aaron 1924- *WhoBlA 92*
**Bell**, Samuel Frank 1962- *WhoFI 92*
**Bell**, Samuel H. 1925- *WhoAmL 92, WhoMW 92*
**Bell**, Samuel P, III 1939- *WhoAmP 91*
**Bell**, Sandra Lucille 1935- *AmMWSc 92*
**Bell**, Scott *Who 92*
**Bell**, Scott Lee 1954- *WhoRel 92*
**Bell**, Sharon Kaye 1943- *WhoFI 92*
**Bell**, Sheila Trice 1949- *WhoBlA 92*
**Bell**, Stanley C 1931- *AmMWSc 92*
**Bell**, Stanley Joseph 1921- *WhoAmL 92*
**Bell**, Stephen Robert 1942- *WhoAmL 92*
**Bell**, Steve 1951- *WhoAmP 91*
**Bell**, Steven 1943- *WhoFI 92*
**Bell**, Stewart Edward 1919- *Who 92*
**Bell**, Stewart Lynn 1945- *WhoAmL 92*
**Bell**, Stoughton 1923- *AmMWSc 92*
**Bell**, Stuart 1938- *Who 92*
**Bell**, Susan *WhoEnt 92*
**Bell**, Susan J 1948- *WhoAmP 91*
**Bell**, T *ScFEYrs*
**Bell**, Tenolian Rodney, Sr. 1949- *WhoRel 92*
**Bell**, Terrel H 1921- *WhoAmP 91*
**Bell**, Terrel Howard 1921- *IntWW 91*
**Bell**, Terry Allen 1952- *WhoAmL 92*
**Bell**, Thaddeus Gibson 1923- *AmMWSc 92*
**Bell**, Theodore Augustus 1946- *WhoFI 92*
**Bell**, Theodore Joshua, II 1961- *WhoBlA 92*
**Bell**, Theron J. 1931- *WhoBlA 92*
**Bell**, Thom R. 1943- *WhoBlA 92*
**Bell**, Thomas 1903-1961 *BenetAL 91*
**Bell**, Thomas Devereaux, Jr. 1949- *WhoFI 92*
**Bell**, Thomas James, Jr. 1946- *WhoIns 92*
**Bell**, Thomas Johnston 1914- *IntWW 91*
**Bell**, Thomas Norman 1932- *AmMWSc 92*
**Bell**, Thomas Porter 1943- *WhoAmL 92*
**Bell**, Thomas Wayne 1951- *AmMWSc 92*
**Bell**, Thornton *TwCSFW 91, WrDr 92*
**Bell**, Timothy Alexander 1942- *WhoAmP 91*
**Bell**, Timothy John Leigh 1941- *IntWW 91, Who 92*
**Bell**, Todd Anthony 1958- *WhoBlA 92*
**Bell**, Tom 1932?- *ConTFT 9, IntMPA 92*
**Bell**, Tommy Lee, III 1948- *WhoBlA 92*
**Bell**, Travers J., Sr. *WhoBlA 92*
**Bell**, Trenton Grandville 1924- *WhoBlA 92*
**Bell**, Trevor *Who 92*
**Bell**, Trevor 1930- *TwCPaSc*
**Bell**, Vanessa 1879-1961 *FacFETw, TwCPaSc*
**Bell**, Vernon Lee, Jr 1927- *AmMWSc 92*
**Bell**, Victory 1934- *WhoAmP 91, WhoBlA 92*
**Bell**, Vincent Patrick *WhoMW 92*
**Bell**, Wallace Edward 1950- *WhoRel 92*
**Bell**, Wallace William 1953- *WhoRel 92*
**Bell**, Walter 1909- *Who 92*
**Bell**, Warren, Jr. 1951- *WhoBlA 92*
**Bell**, Warren Napier 1921- *AmMWSc 92*
**Bell**, Wayne Steven 1954- *WhoAmL 92, WhoWest 92*
**Bell**, Wendolyn Yvonne 1928-1988 *WhoBlA 92N*
**Bell**, Wilfred Joseph 1927- *WhoAmP 91*
**Bell**, Wilhemenia 1954- *WhoBlA 92*
**Bell**, William 1783-1867 *DcNCBi 1*
**Bell**, William A. *WhoBlA 92*
**Bell**, William Archibald Ottley Juxon 1919- *Who 92*
**Bell**, William Augustus, II 1917- *WhoBlA 92*
**Bell**, William Averill 1934- *AmMWSc 92*
**Bell**, William Bradshaw 1935- *Who 92*
**Bell**, William Charles 1945- *WhoBlA 92*
**Bell**, William E 1929- *AmMWSc 92*
**Bell**, William Edwin 1926- *IntWW 91, Who 92*
**Bell**, William Ewart 1924- *Who 92*
**Bell**, William Fletcher 1929- *WhoAmP 91*
**Bell**, William H. D. M. *Who 92*
**Bell**, William Hall 1951- *WhoAmL 92*
**Bell**, William Harrison 1927- *AmMWSc 92*
**Bell**, William Jerry 1934- *WhoBlA 92*
**Bell**, William Joseph 1939- *WhoEnt 92*
**Bell**, William Lewis 1919- *Who 92*
**Bell**, William McKinley 1926- *WhoBlA 92*
**Bell**, William Robert, Jr *AmMWSc 92*
**Bell**, William Rupert Graham 1920- *Who 92*
**Bell**, William Vaughn 1941- *WhoBlA 92*
**Bell**, William W. 1956- *WhoAmL 92*
**Bell**, William Woodward 1938- *WhoAmL 92*
**Bell**, Winston Alonzo 1930- *WhoBlA 92*
**Bell**, Yolanda Maria 1949- *WhoBlA 92*
**Bell**, Yvonne Lola 1953- *WhoBlA 92*
**Bell**, Zane W 1952- *AmMWSc 92*
**Bell Burnell**, Jocelyn 1943- *Who 92*
**Bell Davies**, Lancelot 1926- *Who 92*
**Bell-Patten**, Karen 1944- *WhoWest 92*
**Bell-Scott**, Patricia 1950- *WhoBlA 92*
**Bella**, Imre E *AmMWSc 92*
**Bella**, Vincent J 1927- *WhoAmP 91*
**Bellabarba**, Diego 1935- *AmMWSc 92*
**Bellace**, Janice Rose 1949- *WhoAmL 92*
**Bellack**, Jack H 1926- *AmMWSc 92*
**Bellacosa**, Joseph W. 1937- *WhoAmL 92, WhoAmP 91*
**Bellah**, James Warner 1899-1976 *BenetAL 91, TwCWW 91*
**Bellah**, Michael Dean 1949- *WhoRel 92*
**Bellah**, Robert Glenn 1927- *AmMWSc 92*
**Bellah**, Robert N. 1927- *WrDr 92*
**Bellah**, Robert Neelly 1927- *WhoRel 92*
**Bellair**, Berg *ScFEYrs*
**Bellaire**, Rosemary 1947- *WhoFI 92*
**Bellairs**, Angus d'Albini d1990 *Who 92N*
**Bellairs**, Angus D'Albini 1918- *WrDr 92*
**Bellairs**, John 1938- *IntAu&W 91, WrDr 92*
**Bellairs**, John 1938-1991 *ConAu 133, SmATA 66, -68 [port]*
**Bellairs**, John A. d1991 *NewYTBS 91*
**Bellairs**, Malcolm Keith, IV 1943- *WhoAmL 92*
**Bellak**, John George 1930- *Who 92*
**Bellak**, Leopold 1916- *AmMWSc 92*
**Bellamah**, Joseph Louis 1914- *WhoEnt 92*
**Bellamann**, Henry 1882-1945 *BenetAL 91*
**Bellamy**, Albert John 1915- *Who 92*
**Bellamy**, Alexander 1909- *Who 92*
**Bellamy**, Angela Robinson 1952- *WhoBlA 92*
**Bellamy**, Audrey Virginia 1931- *WhoAmP 91*
**Bellamy**, Bill C 1949- *WhoAmP 91*
**Bellamy**, Carol 1942- *WhoAmP 91*
**Bellamy**, Christopher William 1946- *Who 92*
**Bellamy**, David 1926- *AmMWSc 92*
**Bellamy**, David James 1933- *IntAu&W 91, IntWW 91, Who 92, WrDr 92*
**Bellamy**, David P 1944- *AmMWSc 92*
**Bellamy**, Earl 1917- *IntMPA 92*
**Bellamy**, Earl De Laine 1930- *WhoFI 92*
**Bellamy**, Edmund Henry 1923- *Who 92*
**Bellamy**, Edward 1850-1898 *BenetAL 91, ScFEYrs, TwCSFW 91*
**Bellamy**, Elizabeth 1837-1900 *ScFEYrs*
**Bellamy**, Everett 1949- *WhoAmL 92*
**Bellamy**, Guy 1935- *ConAu 34NR*
**Bellamy**, Herbert L 1931- *WhoAmP 91, WhoBlA 92*
**Bellamy**, Ivory Gandy 1952- *WhoBlA 92*
**Bellamy**, James Leslie, Jr. 1947- *WhoEnt 92*
**Bellamy**, Joe David *DrAPF 91*
**Bellamy**, Joe David 1941- *ConAu 34NR*
**Bellamy**, John C 1915- *AmMWSc 92*
**Bellamy**, John Cary 1915- *WhoWest 92*
**Bellamy**, John Dillard 1853-1942 *DcNCBi 1*
**Bellamy**, Joseph 1719-1790 *BenetAL 91*
**Bellamy**, Kenneth Rex 1928- *Who 92*
**Bellamy**, Peter d1991 *NewYTBS 91*
**Bellamy**, Ralph 1904- *IntMPA 92*
**Bellamy**, Ralph 1904-1991 *NewYTBS 91 [port]*
**Bellamy**, Ralph Rexford 1904- *WhoEnt 92*
**Bellamy**, Ronald Frank *AmMWSc 92*
**Bellamy**, Verdelle B. 1928- *WhoBlA 92*
**Bellamy**, Walter 1939- *BlkOlyM, WhoAmP 91, WhoBlA 92*
**Bellamy**, William 1770-1846 *DcNCBi 1*
**Bellamy**, Winthrop Dexter 1915- *AmMWSc 92*
**Bellan**, Paul Murray 1948- *AmMWSc 92*
**Bellan**, Ruben Carl 1918- *WrDr 92*
**Belland**, Rene Jean 1954- *AmMWSc 92*
**Bellandi**, Wilma 1914- *WhoWest 92*
**Bellando**, John W. 1956- *WhoFI 92*
**Bellanger**, Maurice G 1941- *AmMWSc 92*
**Bellanger**, Serge Rene 1933- *WhoFI 92*
**Bellante**, Donald J. 1945- *WhoFI 92*
**Bellanti**, Joseph A 1934- *AmMWSc 92*
**Bellantoni**, Barbara 1962- *WhoFI 92*
**Bellantoni**, Maureen Blanchfield 1949- *WhoFI 92*
**Bellany**, Ian 1941- *Who 92*
**Bellany**, John 1942- *IntWW 91, TwCPaSc, Who 92*
**Bellas**, Albert Constantine 1942- *WhoFI 92*
**Bellavance**, David Walter 1943- *AmMWSc 92*
**Bellavance**, Joseph Arthur, III 1939- *WhoFI 92*
**Belle**, Charles E. 1940- *WhoBlA 92*
**Belle**, Euris E. 1955- *WhoBlA 92*
**Belle**, John Otis 1922- *WhoBlA 92*
**Belle**, Pamela 1952- *WrDr 92*
**Belle**, Regina 1963- *ConBlB 1 [port], ConMus 6 [port]*
**Belle**, Regina 1964- *WhoBlA 92*
**Belleau**, Bernard Roland 1925- *AmMWSc 92*
**Bellegarde-Smith**, Patrick 1947- *WhoBlA 92*
**Bellego**, Herve Melaine 1947- *WhoFI 92*
**Bellelli Family** *ThHEIm [port]*
**Bellen**, Heinz 1927- *IntWW 91*
**Bellenger**, Dominic Aidan 1950- *WhoRel 92*
**Bellenger**, Dominic Terence Joseph 1950- *Who 92*
**Bellenot**, Steven F 1948- *AmMWSc 92*
**Beller**, Barry M 1935- *AmMWSc 92*
**Beller**, Fritz K 1924- *AmMWSc 92*
**Beller**, Gary A. 1938- *WhoAmL 92*
**Beller**, George Allan 1940- *AmMWSc 92*
**Beller**, Gerald Stephen 1935- *WhoFI 92, WhoWest 92*
**Beller**, Martin Leonard 1924- *AmMWSc 92*
**Beller**, Michael E. 1957- *WhoAmL 92*
**Beller**, Miles 1951- *ConAu 134*
**Beller**, Sam Edward 1934- *WhoFI 92*
**Beller**, Steven 1958- *ConAu 133*
**Bellermann**, Peter Robert Wilhelm 1939- *WhoFI 92*
**Bellerose**, Edgar G *WhoAmP 91*
**Belles**, Anita Louise 1948- *WhoFI 92*
**Belles**, Christine Fugiel 1945- *WhoMW 92*
**Belles**, Frank Edward 1923- *AmMWSc 92*
**Bellet**, Eugene Marshall 1940- *AmMWSc 92*
**Bellet**, Pierre Remy 1911- *IntWW 91*
**Bellet**, Richard Joseph 1927- *AmMWSc 92*
**Belletire**, John Lewis 1943- *AmMWSc 92*
**Belletz**, Louise *EncAmaz 91*
**Belleville**, Philip Frederick 1934- *WhoAmL 92*
**Bellew** *Who 92*
**Bellew**, Baron 1920- *Who 92*
**Bellew**, George 1899- *Who 92*
**Bellew**, Joseph Michael 1958- *WhoAmL 92*
**Bellflower**, Nellie 1946- *WhoEnt 92*
**Bellfort**, Joseph *IntMPA 92*
**Bellhorn**, Margaret Burns 1939- *AmMWSc 92*
**Belli**, Carlos German 1927- *BenetAL 91, ConSpAP*
**Belli**, Melvin 1907- *FacFETw*
**Belli**, Melvin M 1907- *ConAu 34NR*
**Belli**, Pedro 1939- *WhoFI 92*
**Belliard**, Rafael Leonidas 1961- *WhoHisp 92*
**Bellido**, Ramon 1951- *WhoEnt 92*
**Bellido**, Ricardo L. 1953- *WhoHisp 92*
**Bellin**, David 1951- *WhoFI 92*
**Bellin**, Gerald H. 1946- *WhoMW 92*
**Bellin**, Harvey Forrest 1944- *WhoEnt 92*
**Bellina**, Joseph Henry 1942- *AmMWSc 92*
**Bellina**, Joseph James, Jr 1940- *AmMWSc 92*
**Bellina**, Russell Frank 1942- *AmMWSc 92*
**Bellinger**, Cindy *DrAPF 91*
**Bellinger**, Clyde Wesley 1950- *WhoMW 92*
**Bellinger**, Edgar Thomson 1929- *WhoAmL 92*
**Bellinger**, Elizabeth Smith 1948- *WhoRel 92*
**Bellinger**, George M. 1932- *WhoBlA 92*
**Bellinger**, Harold 1951- *WhoBlA 92*
**Bellinger**, Larry Lee 1947- *AmMWSc 92*
**Bellinger**, Luther Garic 1933- *WhoBlA 92*
**Bellinger**, Mary Anne 1939- *WhoBlA 92*
**Bellinger**, Peter F 1921- *AmMWSc 92*
**Bellinger**, Reb *WhoAmP 91*
**Bellinger**, Robert 1910- *Who 92*
**Bellinger**, William Hagood, Jr. 1949- *WhoRel 92*
**Bellingham**, Brenda 1931- *IntAu&W 91*
**Bellingham**, Henry Campbell 1955- *Who 92*
**Bellingham**, Noel 1943- *Who 92*
**Bellini**, Mario 1935- *DcTwDes*
**Bellini**, Vincenzo 1801-1835 *NewAmDM*
**Bellink**, Alan A. 1948- *WhoEnt 92*
**Bellino**, Francis Leonard 1938- *AmMWSc 92*
**Belliny**, Daniel S. 1915- *WhoBlA 92*
**Bellio**, Georges de 1835-1894 *ThHEIm*
**Bellion**, Edward 1944- *AmMWSc 92*
**Bellis**, Arthur Albert 1928- *WhoFI 92*
**Bellis**, Bertram Thomas 1927- *Who 92*
**Bellis**, Carroll Joseph *WhoWest 92*
**Bellis**, Edward David 1927- *AmMWSc 92*
**Bellis**, Harold E 1930- *AmMWSc 92*
**Bellis**, John Herbert 1930- *Who 92*
**Bellis**, Vincent J, Jr 1938- *AmMWSc 92*

**Bellisario,** Donald *LesBEnT 92*
**Bellissimo,** Dominic G. d1991 *NewYTBS 91*
**Belliston,** Edward Glen 1958- *WhoFI 92*
**Bellitto,** Robert B. 1941- *WhoAmL 92*
**Bellius,** Matthias 1684-1749 *BlkwCEP*
**Belliveau,** Louis J 1926- *AmMWSc 92*
**Bellizzi,** John J. 1919- *WhoAmL 92*
**Bellman,** Samuel I. 1926- *WrDr 92*
**Bellman,** Willard Franklin 1920- *WhoEnt 92*
**Bellmer,** Elizabeth Henry 1927- *AmMWSc 92*
**Bellmon,** Henry L 1921- *WhoAmP 91*
**Bellmore,** Lawrence Robert, Jr. 1947- *WhoFI 92*
**Bellmore,** Mandell 1935- *AmMWSc 92*
**Bellmyre,** Carole *WhoWest 92*
**Bello,** Andres 1781-1865 *BenetAL 91*
**Bello,** Andres V. 1952- *WhoHisp 92*
**Bello,** Doris M. 1948- *WhoHisp 92*
**Bello,** George E. 1935- *WhoFI 92*
**Bello,** Heinz 1920-1944 *EncTR 91*
**Bello,** Jake 1928- *AmMWSc 92*
**Bello,** Judith Hippler *WhoAmL 92*
**Bello,** Mohammed 1930- *Who 92*
**Bello,** P 1929- *AmMWSc 92*
**Bello,** Raul N. 1948- *WhoHisp 92*
**Bello,** Roberto 1933- *WhoHisp 92*
**Bello,** Victor Manuel 1945- *WhoMW 92*
**Bello Lopez,** Andres 1781-1865 *HisDSpE*
**Bello Ruiz,** Rafael 1926- *WhoRel 92*
**Belloc,** Hilaire 1870-1953 *FacFETw, RfGEnL 91, ScFEYrs*
**Bellocchio,** Marco 1939- *IntDcF 2-2, IntMPA 92*
**Belloff,** Lord 1913- *IntAu&W 91*
**Belloli,** Robert Charles 1942- *AmMWSc 92*
**Bellomo,** Gaspare Michael 1930- *WhoFI 92*
**Bellon,** Ricardo Sinesio 1955- *WhoHisp 92*
**Belloncik,** Serge 1944- *AmMWSc 92*
**Bellone,** Clifford John 1941- *AmMWSc 92*
**Bellone,** Paul 1938- *WhoIns 92*
**Bellotte,** Gregory Alan 1963- *WhoEnt 92*
**Bellotti,** David Frank 1943- *Who 92*
**Bellotti,** Francis Xavier 1923- *WhoAmP 91*
**Bellow** *Who 92*
**Bellow,** Alexandra 1935- *AmMWSc 92*
**Bellow,** Donald Grant 1931- *AmMWSc 92*
**Bellow,** Gary 1935- *WhoAmL 92*
**Bellow,** Saul *DcAmImH, DrAPF 91*
**Bellow,** Saul 1915- *BenetAL 91, ConNov 91, FacFETw [port], IntAu&W 91, IntWW 91, RComAH, Who 92, WhoMW 92, WhoNob 90, WrDr 92*
**Bellows,** George 1882-1925 *FacFETw*
**Bellows,** James Gilbert 1922- *Who 92*
**Bellows,** Laurel Gordon 1948- *WhoAmL 92*
**Bellport,** Bernard Philip 1907- *AmMWSc 92*
**Bellrose,** Robert Bruce 1947- *WhoFI 92*
**Bellson,** Louis 1924- *NewAmDM*
**Bellson,** Louis Paul 1924- *WhoEnt 92*
**Bellucci,** Patricia Marie 1954- *WhoEnt 92*
**Belluce,** Lawrence P 1932- *AmMWSc 92*
**Bellugi,** Piero 1924- *IntWW 91*
**Bellum,** John Curtis 1945- *AmMWSc 92*
**Belluomini,** Frank Stephen 1934- *WhoFI 92, WhoWest 92*
**Bellus,** Ronald Joseph 1951- *WhoWest 92*
**Belluschi,** Anthony C. 1941- *WhoMW 92*
**Belluschi,** Pietro 1899- *IntWW 91*
**Bellve,** Anthony Rex 1940- *AmMWSc 92*
**Bellville,** Ralph Earl 1925- *WhoFI 92, WhoWest 92*
**Bellward,** Gail Dianne 1939- *AmMWSc 92*
**Bellwin,** Baron 1923- *Who 92*
**Belly,** Robert T 1945- *AmMWSc 92*
**Belmaker,** Robert Henry 1947- *AmMWSc 92*
**Belman,** Murray Joel 1935- *WhoAmL 92*
**Belman,** Sidney 1926- *AmMWSc 92*
**Belmar,** Warren 1942- *WhoAmL 92*
**Belmear,** Horace Edward 1916- *WhoBIA 92*
**Belmondo,** Jean-Paul 1933- *FacFETw, IntMPA 92, IntWW 91*
**Belmont,** Daniel Thomas 1957- *AmMWSc 92*
**Belmont,** Herman S 1920- *AmMWSc 92*
**Belmont,** Larry Miller 1936- *WhoWest 92*
**Belmont,** Roy John 1946- *WhoEnt 92*
**Belmonte,** Albert Anthony 1944- *AmMWSc 92*
**Belmonte,** Anamaria 1944- *WhoHisp 92*
**Belmonte,** Edgar C. 1940- *WhoHisp 92*
**Belmonte,** Rocco George 1915- *AmMWSc 92*
**Belmore,** Earl of 1951- *Who 92*
**Belmore,** F. Martin 1944- *WhoAmL 92*
**Belnap,** Jayne *AmMWSc 92*
**Belnap,** Jeffry Paul 1957- *WhoEnt 92*
**Belnap,** Norma Lee Madsen 1927- *WhoEnt 92*
**Belnick,** Mark Alan 1946- *WhoAmL 92*
**Belo,** Alfred Horatio 1839-1901 *DcNCBi 1*
**Belo,** Frederick Edward 1811-1883 *DcNCBi 1*
**Beloff** *Who 92*
**Beloff,** Baron 1913- *IntWW 91, Who 92*
**Beloff,** Lord 1913- *WrDr 92*
**Beloff,** Leland M 1942- *WhoAmP 91*
**Beloff,** Michael Jacob 1942- *Who 92*
**Beloff,** Nora 1919- *IntAu&W 91, Who 92, WrDr 92*
**Belohlavek,** Jiri 1946- *IntWW 91, WhoEnt 92*
**Belohoubek,** Erwin F 1929- *AmMWSc 92*
**Belon,** Albert Edward 1930- *AmMWSc 92*
**Belongia,** Kenneth John 1955- *WhoAmL 92*
**Belonogov,** Aleksandr M. 1931- *IntWW 91*
**Beloof,** Robert Lawrence 1923- *WrDr 92*
**Belousov,** Igor' Sergeevich 1928- *SovUnBD*
**Belousov,** Igor Sergeyevich 1928- *IntWW 91*
**Belousova,** Ludmila Yevgen'evna 1935- *SovUnBD*
**Belov,** Andrei Ivanovich 1917- *IntWW 91*
**Belov,** Vasiliy Ivanovich 1932- *IntWW 91, SovUnBD*
**Belova,** Yelena 1947- *SovUnBD*
**Belove,** Charles 1925- *AmMWSc 92*
**Belove,** Edward Jay 1950- *WhoFI 92*
**Beloz,** George *WhoHisp 92*
**Belozersky,** Andrey Nikolaevich 1905-1972 *SovUnBD*
**Belper,** Baron 1912- *Who 92*
**Belsare,** Jayant Vishnu 1938- *WhoMW 92*
**Belser,** James Burkey 1947- *WhoEnt 92*
**Belser,** William Luther, Jr 1925- *AmMWSc 92*
**Belserene,** Emilia Pisani 1922- *AmMWSc 92*
**Belshaw,** Cyril Shirley 1921- *IntWW 91*
**Belshaw,** George Phelps Mellick 1928- *WhoRel 92*
**Belshe,** John Francis 1935- *AmMWSc 92*
**Belsheim,** Robert Oscar 1924- *AmMWSc 92*
**Belskis,** David 1954- *WhoEnt 92*
**Belsky,** Franta 1921- *Who 92*
**Belsky,** Igor' Dmitrievich 1925- *SovUnBD*
**Belsky,** Igor Dmitriyevich 1925- *IntWW 91*
**Belsky,** Martin Henry 1944- *WhoAmL 92*
**Belsky,** Melvin Myron 1926- *AmMWSc 92*
**Belsky,** Theodore 1930- *AmMWSc 92*
**Belsley,** David Alan 1939- *WhoFI 92*
**Belsly,** John Robert 1930- *WhoFI 92*
**Belson,** James A 1931- *WhoAmP 91*
**Belson,** James Anthony 1931- *WhoAmL 92*
**Belson,** Jerry *IntMPA 92, LesBEnT 92*
**Belstead,** Baron 1932- *IntWW 91, Who 92*
**Belt,** Audrey Evon 1948- *WhoWest 92*
**Belt,** Bradley Deck 1958- *WhoAmL 92, WhoFI 92*
**Belt,** Charles Banks, Jr 1931- *AmMWSc 92*
**Belt,** Edward Scudder 1933- *AmMWSc 92*
**Belt,** Roger Francis 1929- *AmMWSc 92*
**Belt,** Warner Duane 1925- *AmMWSc 92*
**Belt-Mendoza,** Mercedes M. 1958- *WhoHisp 92*
**Belter,** Martin G. 1952- *WhoEnt 92*
**Belter,** Wesley R 1913- *WhoAmP 91*
**Belter,** Wesley R 1945- *WhoAmP 91*
**Belth,** Joseph M. 1929- *WhoIns 92*
**Belth,** Joseph Morton 1929- *WhoMW 92*
**Belthoff,** Richard Charles, Jr. 1958- *WhoAmL 92*
**Belton,** C. Ronald 1948- *WhoBIA 92*
**Belton,** David Freeman 1958- *WhoFI 92*
**Belton,** Edward DeVaughn 1935- *WhoBIA 92*
**Belton,** Geoffrey Richard 1934- *AmMWSc 92*
**Belton,** Howard G. 1934- *WhoBIA 92*
**Belton,** John Thomas 1947- *WhoAmL 92*
**Belton,** Michael J S 1934- *AmMWSc 92*
**Belton,** Peter 1930- *AmMWSc 92*
**Belton,** Robert 1935- *WhoBIA 92*
**Beltram,** Geoffrey 1921- *Who 92*
**Beltrami,** Edward J 1934- *AmMWSc 92*
**Beltrami,** Giacomo Constantino 1779-1855 *DcAmImH*
**Beltramo,** Michael Norman 1942- *WhoFI 92*
**Beltran,** Anthony Natalicio 1938- *WhoWest 92*
**Beltran,** Armando 1949- *WhoHisp 92*
**Beltran,** Celestino Martinez 1945- *WhoHisp 92*
**Beltran,** Eusebius Joseph 1934- *WhoRel 92*
**Beltran,** German T. 1932- *WhoHisp 92*
**Beltran,** Lourdes Luz 1961- *WhoHisp 92*
**Beltran,** Manuela *EncAmaz 91*
**Beltran,** Mario Alberto 1952- *WhoHisp 92*
**Beltran,** Robert Adame 1953- *WhoEnt 92*
**Beltran,** Washington 1914- *IntWW 91*
**Beltran Espantoso,** Pedro Gerardo 1897-1979 *FacFETw*
**Beltrao,** Alexandre Fontana 1924- *IntWW 91*
**Beltrao,** Helio Marcos Penna 1916- *IntWW 91*
**Beltz,** Charles R 1913- *AmMWSc 92*
**Beltz,** Richard Edward 1929- *AmMWSc 92*
**Beltz,** Robert Roy 1952- *WhoAmL 92*
**Belushi,** James 1954- *IntMPA 92, WhoEnt 92*
**Belushi,** Judith Jacklin 1951- *WhoEnt 92*
**Belveal,** Jon Michael 1950- *WhoEnt 92*
**Bely,** Andrei 1880-1934 *FacFETw*
**Bely,** Andrey 1880-1934 *SovUnBD*
**Belyaev,** Aleksandr 1884-1942 *TwCSFW 91A*
**Belyaev,** Dmitriy Konstantinovich 1917-1985 *SovUnBD*
**Belyaev,** Nikolay Il'ich 1903-1966 *SovUnBD*
**Belyaev,** Nikolay Konstantinovich 1899-1937 *SovUnBD*
**Belyak,** Konstantin Nikitovich 1916- *IntWW 91*
**Belyakov,** Oleg Sergeevich 1933- *SovUnBD*
**Belyakov,** Oleg Sergeyevich 1933- *IntWW 91*
**Belyakov,** Rostislav Appolonovich 1919- *IntWW 91*
**Belyamani,** Seddik 1942- *WhoFI 92*
**Belyayev,** Albert Andreyevich 1928- *IntWW 91*
**Belyayev,** Pavel 1925-1970 *FacFETw*
**Belyayev,** Spartak Timofeyevich 1923- *IntWW 91*
**Belyea,** Glenn Young 1943- *AmMWSc 92*
**Belyew,** Paul Lawrence 1913- *WhoAmP 91*
**Belz,** Joel 1941- *WhoRel 92*
**Belzberg,** Brent Stanley 1951- *WhoFI 92*
**Belzberg,** Samuel 1928- *WhoFI 92, WhoWest 92*
**Belzberg,** William 1932- *WhoWest 92*
**Belzer,** Alan 1932- *WhoFI 92*
**Belzer,** Folkert O 1930- *AmMWSc 92*
**Belzer,** Richard 1944- *WhoEnt 92*
**Belzile,** Rene 1930- *AmMWSc 92*
**Bem,** Sandra Lipsitz 1944- *WomPsyc*
**Bemberg,** Maria Luisa 1925- *IntDcF 2-2*
**Bemberis,** Ivars 1941- *WhoFI 92*
**Bemelmans,** Ludwig 1898-1962 *BenetAL 91*
**Bement,** A L, Jr 1932- *AmMWSc 92*
**Bement,** Robert Earl 1918- *AmMWSc 92*
**BeMiller,** James Noble 1933- *AmMWSc 92*
**BeMiller,** Paraskevi Mavridis *AmMWSc 92*
**Bemis,** Curtis Elliot, Jr 1940- *AmMWSc 92*
**Bemis,** Hal Lawall 1912- *WhoFI 92*
**Bemis,** Samuel Flagg 1891-1973 *BenetAL 91*
**Bemis,** William Putnam 1922- *AmMWSc 92*
**Bempong,** Maxwell A. 1938- *WhoBIA 92*
**Bempong,** Maxwell Alexander 1938- *AmMWSc 92*
**Bemrick,** William Joseph 1927- *AmMWSc 92*
**Bemrose and Sons** *DcLB 106*
**Bemrose,** William d1880 *DcLB 106 [port]*
**Ben & Jerry** *News 91 [port], -91-3 [port]*
**Ben,** Manuel 1916- *AmMWSc 92*
**Ben,** Max 1926- *AmMWSc 92*
**Ben Abbes,** Youssef 1921- *IntWW 91*
**Ben Abdallah,** Moncef 1946- *IntWW 91*
**Ben-Akiva,** Moshe E 1944- *AmMWSc 92*
**Ben-Ari,** Neal 1952- *ConTFT 9*
**Ben-Asher,** M. David 1931- *WhoWest 92*
**Ben Bella,** Mohammed 1916- *IntWW 91*
**Ben Bella,** Mohammed Ahmed 1916- *FacFETw*
**Ben-David,** Zadok 1949- *IntWW 91, TwCPaSc*
**Ben Elissar,** Eliaju 1932- *IntWW 91*
**Ben Gurion,** David 1886-1973 *FacFETw [port]*
**Ben Haim,** Paul 1897-1984 *FacFETw, NewAmDM*
**Ben-Israel,** Adi 1933- *AmMWSc 92*
**Ben Jelloun,** Tahar 1944- *ConAu 135*
**Ben-Jonathan,** Nira 1940- *AmMWSc 92*
**Ben-Natan,** Asher 1921- *IntWW 91*
**Ben-Porat,** Tamar 1929- *AmMWSc 92*
**Ben Shimon Halevi,** Zev *WrDr 92*
**Ben-Sorek,** Esor Winer 1933- *WhoRel 92*
**Ben-Tovim,** Atarah 1940- *Who 92*
**Ben-Yaacov,** Miriam *DrAPF 91*
**Ben-Yoseph,** Yoav 1941- *AmMWSc 92*
**Ben-Ze'ev,** Avri 1947- *AmMWSc 92*
**Ben-Zvi,** Phillip Norman 1942- *WhoFI 92, WhoIns 92*
**Benabdeljalil,** Mohamed-Mehdi 1930- *Who 92*
**Benacerraf,** Baruj 1920- *AmMWSc 92, IntWW 91, Who 92, WhoNob 90*
**Benach,** Jorge L 1945- *AmMWSc 92*
**Benach,** Sharon Ann 1944- *WhoWest 92*
**Benachenhou,** Mouroud 1938- *IntWW 91*
**Benagh,** Christine P. 1947- *WhoAmL 92*
**Benak,** James Donald 1954- *WhoAmL 92*
**Benalcazar,** Sebastian de 1490-1551 *HisDSpE*
**Benally,** Raymond A. 1953- *WhoWest 92*
**Benamati,** Dennis Charles 1948- *WhoAmL 92*
**Benanzer,** Elizabeth Jean 1947- *WhoMW 92*
**Benard,** Andre Pierre Jacques 1922- *IntWW 91, Who 92*
**Benard,** Bernard 1933- *AmMWSc 92*
**Benard,** Jean Pierre 1908- *IntWW 91*
**Benard,** Mark 1944- *AmMWSc 92*
**Benarde,** Melvin Albert 1923- *AmMWSc 92*
**Benarde,** Melvin Albert 1924- *WrDr 92*
**Benaroya,** Haym 1954- *AmMWSc 92*
**Benarroch,** Heather Mary *Who 92*
**Benassi,** August Louis 1942- *WhoFI 92*
**Benassi,** James P. 1947- *WhoAmL 92*
**Benasutti,** Marion 1908- *WrDr 92*
**Benatar,** Pat 1953- *WhoEnt 92*
**Benatar,** Solomon Robert 1942- *AmMWSc 92*
**Benaud,** Richard 1930- *IntWW 91, Who 92*
**Benaud,** Richie 1930- *WrDr 92*
**Benavente,** Diego Tenorio 1959- *WhoAmP 91*
**Benavente,** Luis Arriola 1939- *WhoAmP 91*
**Benavente,** Luis Cepeda 1948- *WhoAmP 91*
**Benavente,** Toribio de 1482?-1569 *HisDSpE*
**Benavente y Martinez,** Jacinto 1866-1954 *FacFETw, WhoNob 90*
**Benavides,** Alonso de 1580-1636 *HisDSpE*
**Benavides,** Fortunato P. *WhoHisp 92*
**Benavides,** George Henry 1944- *WhoHisp 92*
**Benavides,** Jesse *WhoHisp 92*
**Benavides,** Luis Jordan 1949- *WhoFI 92*
**Benavides,** Miguel de 1552-1607 *HisDSpE*
**Benavides,** Norma *WhoHisp 92*
**Benavides,** Raul Falcon 1950- *WhoHisp 92*
**Benavides,** Steven Mel 1963- *WhoHisp 92*
**Benavides,** Tomas R 1939- *WhoAmP 91*
**Benavides,** Vicente 1777-1822 *HisDSpE*
**Benavides Escobar,** Cesar Raul 1920- *IntWW 91*
**Benavidez,** Celina G. *WhoHisp 92*
**Benavidez,** Frank Gregory 1927- *WhoHisp 92*
**Benavidez,** Jose Modesto 1941- *WhoHisp 92*
**Benavidez,** Michael D. 1959- *WhoHisp 92*
**Benavidez,** Roy Perez 1935- *WhoHisp 92*
**Benavidez,** Thomas R. *WhoHisp 92*
**Benawa,** Abdul Raouf 1913- *IntWW 91*
**Benberry,** Cuesta Ray 1923- *WhoMW 92*
**Benbow,** De Witt Clinton 1832-1902 *DcNCBi 1*
**Benbow,** Donald Wallace 1936- *WhoMW 92*
**Benbow,** Richard Addison 1949- *WhoWest 92*
**Benbow,** Robert Michael 1943- *AmMWSc 92*
**Benbow,** Terence Howard 1929- *WhoAmL 92*
**Benbrook,** Charles M 1949- *AmMWSc 92*
**Benbury,** Thomas 1736-1793 *DcNCBi 1*
**Bencala,** Kenneth Edward 1951- *AmMWSc 92*
**Bence,** Alfred Edward 1940- *AmMWSc 92*
**Bence,** Clarence Luther 1944- *WhoRel 92*
**Bence,** Cyril Raymond 1902- *Who 92*
**Bence-Jones,** Mark 1930- *IntAu&W 91, WrDr 92*
**Bench,** Dan A. 1934- *WhoIns 92*
**Bench,** Johnny 1947- *ConAu 133, FacFETw*
**Bench,** Russell W. 1950- *WhoAmL 92*
**Bench,** Stuart Thomas 1951- *WhoAmL 92*
**Benchimol,** Alberto 1932- *WhoWest 92*
**Benchley,** Nathaniel 1915-1981 *BenetAL 91*
**Benchley,** Peter 1940- *BenetAL 91, ConAu 35NR, IntAu&W 91, WrDr 92*
**Benchley,** Peter Bradford 1940- *WhoEnt 92*
**Benchley,** Robert 1889-1945 *BenetAL 91*
**Benchley,** Robert Charles 1889-1945 *FacFETw*
**Bencini,** Sara Haltiwanger 1926- *WhoEnt 92*
**Bencivenga,** Ernest V. 1918- *WhoFI 92*
**Bencke,** Ronald Lee 1940- *WhoFI 92*
**Benckenstein,** John Henry 1903- *WhoAmL 92*
**Bencomo,** Jose A 1946- *AmMWSc 92*
**Bencomo,** Yolanda Elinora 1937- *WhoHisp 92*
**Bencosme,** Sergio Arturo 1920- *AmMWSc 92*
**Bencsath,** Katalin A 1945- *AmMWSc 92*

**Benczik**, Terry Ann 1957- *WhoEnt 92*
**Bend**, John Richard 1942- *AmMWSc 92*
**Benda**, Ernst 1925- *IntWW 91*
**Benda**, Gerd Thomas Alfred 1927- *AmMWSc 92*
**Benda**, Harry J. 1919-1971 *ConAu 134*
**Benda**, Julien 1867-1956 *FacFETw, GuFrLit 1*
**Benda**, Miroslav 1944- *AmMWSc 92*
**Benda**, Vaclav 1946- *IntWW 91*
**Bendall**, David Vere 1920- *Who 92*
**Bendall**, Eve Rosemarie Duffield 1927- *Who 92*
**Bendall**, Victor Ivor 1935- *AmMWSc 92*
**Bendall**, Vivian Walter Hough 1938- *Who 92*
**Bendapudi**, Kasi Visweswararao 1946- *AmMWSc 92*
**Bendat**, Julius Samuel 1923- *AmMWSc 92*
**Bendayan**, Moise 1949- *AmMWSc 92*
**Bendel**, Warren Lee 1925- *AmMWSc 92*
**Bendelac**, Roger Emile 1956- *WhoFI 92*
**Bendell**, Don *DrAPF 91*
**Bender**, Arlene Louise 1953- *WhoAmL 92*
**Bender**, Arnold 1918- *WrDr 92*
**Bender**, Arnold Eric 1918- *IntWW 91, Who 92*
**Bender**, Barbara A. 1939- *WhoBlA 92*
**Bender**, Bert Arthur 1938- *WhoWest 92*
**Bender**, Bill 1919- *WhoWest 92*
**Bender**, Brian Geoffrey 1949- *Who 92*
**Bender**, Carl Martin 1943- *AmMWSc 92*
**Bender**, Charles Christian 1936- *WhoFI 92*
**Bender**, Coleman 1921- *IntAu&W 91*
**Bender**, Coleman C. 1921- *WhoWest 92*
**Bender**, Daniel Frank 1936- *AmMWSc 92*
**Bender**, Daniel Henry 1866-1945 *RelLAm 91*
**Bender**, David 1939- *WhoAmL 92*
**Bender**, David Bowman 1942- *AmMWSc 92*
**Bender**, David Christian 1952- *WhoMW 92*
**Bender**, Donald Lee 1931- *AmMWSc 92*
**Bender**, Douglas Ray 1953- *WhoBlA 92*
**Bender**, Edward Anton 1942- *AmMWSc 92*
**Bender**, Edward Trotter 1916- *WhoAmP 91*
**Bender**, Graham I. 1939- *WhoFI 92*
**Bender**, Harold 1910- *WhoFI 92*
**Bender**, Harold S. 1897-1962 *RelLAm 91*
**Bender**, Harold Stauffer 1897-1962 *AmPeW*
**Bender**, Harvey A. 1933- *WhoMW 92*
**Bender**, Harvey Alan 1933- *AmMWSc 92*
**Bender**, Howard L 1893- *AmMWSc 92*
**Bender**, Howard Sanford 1935- *AmMWSc 92*
**Bender**, Ivette Merrilee 1946- *WhoMW 92*
**Bender**, Jack Sinclair, III 1944- *WhoAmL 92*
**Bender**, Joel Charles 1939- *WhoAmL 92*
**Bender**, John Charles 1940- *WhoAmL 92, WhoFI 92*
**Bender**, Kathleen Laura 1961- *WhoWest 92*
**Bender**, Lauretta 1897-1987 *FacFETw*
**Bender**, Leonard Franklin 1925- *AmMWSc 92*
**Bender**, Leslie 1952- *WhoAmL 92*
**Bender**, Margaret McLean 1916- *AmMWSc 92*
**Bender**, Max 1914- *AmMWSc 92*
**Bender**, Michael A 1929- *AmMWSc 92*
**Bender**, Michael E 1939- *AmMWSc 92*
**Bender**, Michael Lee 1942- *WhoAmL 92*
**Bender**, Myron L. *IntWW 91N*
**Bender**, Patrick Kevin 1953- *AmMWSc 92*
**Bender**, Pattie Sue 1950- *WhoAmP 91*
**Bender**, Paul A 1931- *AmMWSc 92*
**Bender**, Paul Edward 1951- *WhoAmL 92*
**Bender**, Paul Elliot 1942- *AmMWSc 92*
**Bender**, Paul J 1917- *AmMWSc 92*
**Bender**, Peter Leopold 1930- *AmMWSc 92*
**Bender**, Phillip R 1927- *AmMWSc 92*
**Bender**, Rick S 1949- *WhoAmP 91*
**Bender**, Robert 1936- *WhoAmP 91*
**Bender**, Robert Algerd 1946- *AmMWSc 92*
**Bender**, Robert Frank, Jr. 1951- *WhoRel 92*
**Bender**, Ross Thomas 1929- *WhoRel 92*
**Bender**, Thomas 1944- *ConAu 35NR, WrDr 92*
**Bender**, Todd K 1936- *IntAu&W 91, WrDr 92*
**Bender**, Virginia Best 1945- *WhoMW 92*
**Bender**, Welcome W 1915- *AmMWSc 92*
**Bendersky**, Martin 1945- *AmMWSc 92*
**Bendersky**, Pamela May H. *Who 92*
**Benderson**, Bruce *DrAPF 91*
**Bendetsen**, Karl R. *DcAmImH*
**Bendheim**, Sam, III 1935- *IntMPA 92*
**Bendich**, Adrianne *AmMWSc 92*
**Bendich**, Arnold Jay 1942- *AmMWSc 92*
**Bendick**, Jeanne 1919- *SmATA 68 [port]*
**Bendick**, Robert *LesBEnT 92*
**Bendick**, Robert 1917- *IntMPA 92*
**Bendick**, Robert Louis 1917- *WhoEnt 92*
**Bendiner**, Robert 1909- *IntAu&W 91, WrDr 92*
**Bendinger**, Bruce H. 1944- *WhoMW 92*
**Bendire**, Charles Emil 1836-1897 *BiInAmS*
**Bendisz**, Kazimierz 1914- *AmMWSc 92*
**Benditt**, Earl Philip 1916- *AmMWSc 92, IntWW 91*
**Bendix**, Frances *DrAPF 91*
**Bendix**, Helen Irene 1952- *WhoAmL 92*
**Bendix**, Reinhard d1991 *NewYTBS 91*
**Bendix**, Reinhard 1916- *IntAu&W 91, WrDr 92*
**Bendix**, Reinhard 1916-1991 *ConAu 133*
**Bendix**, Richard Charles 1948- *WhoWest 92*
**Bendix**, Selina 1930- *AmMWSc 92*
**Bendix**, William d1964 *LesBEnT 92*
**Bendix**, William Emanuel 1935- *WhoFI 92*
**Bendixen**, Arturo 1950- *WhoHisp 92*
**Bendixen**, Henrik H 1923- *AmMWSc 92*
**Bendixen**, Leo E 1923- *AmMWSc 92*
**Bendixen**, Sergio 1948- *WhoAmP 91*
**Bendixson**, Terence 1934- *WrDr 92*
**Bendjedid**, Chadli *IntWW 91*
**Bendler**, John Thomas 1944- *AmMWSc 92*
**Bendrihem**, Jack David 1959- *WhoFI 92*
**Bendt**, Philip Joseph 1919- *AmMWSc 92*
**Bendure**, Leona Jensen 1912- *WhoEnt 92*
**Bendure**, Raymond Lee 1943- *AmMWSc 92*
**Bendure**, Robert J 1920- *AmMWSc 92*
**Benecke**, Tex 1914- *NewAmDM*
**Benedek**, Andrew 1943- *AmMWSc 92*
**Benedek**, Elissa Leah 1936- *WhoMW 92*
**Benedek**, George Bernard 1928- *AmMWSc 92*
**Benedek**, Laslo 1907- *IntMPA 92*
**Benedek**, Roy 1945- *AmMWSc 92*
**Benedek**, William Clark 1957- *WhoRel 92*
**Benedetti**, David *DrAPF 91*
**Benedetti**, Jacqueline Kay 1948- *AmMWSc 92*
**Benedetti**, Joseph Benedict 1929- *WhoAmP 91*
**Benedetti**, Joseph Carmelo 1942- *WhoAmL 92*
**Benedetti**, Mario 1920- *ConSpAP, DcLB 113 [port], IntWW 91, LiExTwC*
**Benedetti**, Robert Lawrence 1939- *WhoEnt 92*
**Benedetto**, John 1939- *AmMWSc 92*
**Benedetto**, Robert Joseph 1950- *WhoRel 92*
**Benedict XIV** 1675-1758 *BlkwCEP*
**Benedict XV** 1854-1922 *FacFETw*
**Benedict**, Monseigneur Friar 1917- *WhoRel 92*
**Benedict of Nursia** 480?-540 *EncEarC*
**Benedict**, Al 1929- *WhoAmP 91*
**Benedict**, Albert Alfred 1921- *AmMWSc 92*
**Benedict**, Amy Elizabeth 1964- *WhoEnt 92*
**Benedict**, Anthony John 1944- *WhoAmL 92*
**Benedict**, Barry Arden 1942- *AmMWSc 92*
**Benedict**, Bruce Kevin 1955- *WhoWest 92*
**Benedict**, Bruce Whitlock, Sr. 1937- *WhoFI 92*
**Benedict**, Burton 1923- *WhoWest 92*
**Benedict**, C R 1930- *AmMWSc 92*
**Benedict**, Chauncey 1930- *AmMWSc 92*
**Benedict**, Cleve 1935- *WhoAmP 91*
**Benedict**, Dale Mark 1958- *WhoFI 92*
**Benedict**, Dirk 1945- *IntMPA 92, WhoEnt 92*
**Benedict**, Elinor *DrAPF 91*
**Benedict**, Ellen Maring 1931- *AmMWSc 92*
**Benedict**, Gary Francis 1954- *WhoWest 92*
**Benedict**, George Frederick 1945- *AmMWSc 92*
**Benedict**, Helen *DrAPF 91*
**Benedict**, James Harold 1922- *AmMWSc 92*
**Benedict**, James Nelson 1949- *WhoAmL 92*
**Benedict**, John Comerford 1955- *WhoFI 92*
**Benedict**, John Howard, Jr 1944- *AmMWSc 92*
**Benedict**, Joseph T 1920- *AmMWSc 92*
**Benedict**, Julius 1804-1885 *NewAmDM*
**Benedict**, Leopold *BenetAL 91*
**Benedict**, Linda J. 1942- *WhoIns 92*
**Benedict**, Manson 1907- *AmMWSc 92*
**Benedict**, Paul 1938- *IntMPA 92, WhoEnt 92*
**Benedict**, Philip 1949- *WrDr 92*
**Benedict**, Rex 1920- *IntAu&W 91, WrDr 92*
**Benedict**, Robert C. 1951- *WhoIns 92*
**Benedict**, Robert Curtis 1932- *AmMWSc 92*
**Benedict**, Robert Edward 1923- *WhoFI 92*
**Benedict**, Robert Glenn 1911- *AmMWSc 92*
**Benedict**, Ruth 1887-1948 *FacFETw*
**Benedict**, Ruth F. 1887-1948 *BenetAL 91*
**Benedict**, Ruth Fulton 1887-1948 *HanAmWH*
**Benedict**, Samuel S. 1930- *WhoMW 92*
**Benedict**, Shelton L. 1956- *WhoAmL 92*
**Benedict**, Steve *WhoAmP 91*
**Benedict**, Winfred Gerald 1919- *AmMWSc 92*
**Benedicto**, Roberto S. 1917- *IntWW 91*
**Benedictus**, David 1938- *ConNov 91, IntAu&W 91, WrDr 92*
**Benedictus**, David Henry 1938- *Who 92*
**Benedicty**, Mario 1922- *AmMWSc 92*
**Benedikt**, Bozidar D. 1938- *WhoEnt 92*
**Benedikt**, Michael *DrAPF 91*
**Benedikt**, Michael 1935- *ConPo 91, IntAu&W 91, WrDr 92*
**Benediktsson**, Einar 1931- *IntWW 91, Who 92*
**Benediktsson**, Jakob 1907- *IntWW 91*
**Benedix**, Gary Ray 1957- *WhoMW 92*
**Benedosso**, Anthony Nechols 1949- *WhoAmL 92*
**Benedyktowicz**, Witold 1921- *IntWW 91*
**Benefield**, Barry 1877-1956 *BenetAL 91*
**Benefield**, Jimmy W *WhoAmP 91*
**Benegal**, Shyam 1934- *IntDcF 2-2*
**Beneke**, Everett Smith 1918- *AmMWSc 92*
**Beneke**, Sarah Emblen 1924- *WhoAmP 91*
**Benekohal**, Rahim Farahnak 1953- *WhoMW 92*
**Benemann**, John Rudiger 1943- *AmMWSc 92*
**Benenati**, R F 1921- *AmMWSc 92*
**Benenson**, Abram Salmon 1914- *AmMWSc 92, WhoWest 92*
**Benenson**, Claire Berger *WhoFI 92*
**Benenson**, David Maurice 1927- *AmMWSc 92*
**Benenson**, Donald Lloyd 1956- *WhoFI 92*
**Benenson**, Raymond Elliott 1925- *AmMWSc 92*
**Benenson**, Walter 1936- *AmMWSc 92*
**Benepal**, Parshotam S 1933- *AmMWSc 92*
**Benerito**, Ruth Rogan 1916- *AmMWSc 92*
**Benes**, Eduard 1884-1948 *FacFETw*
**Benes**, Edvard 1884-1948 *EncTR 91 [port]*
**Benes**, Elinor Simson 1924- *AmMWSc 92*
**Benes**, Norman Stanley 1921- *AmMWSc 92, WhoWest 92*
**Benes**, Philip Charles 1955- *WhoMW 92*
**Benes**, Vaclav Edvard 1930- *AmMWSc 92*
**Benesch**, Katherine 1946- *WhoAmL 92*
**Benesch**, Ruth Erica 1925- *AmMWSc 92*
**Benesch**, Samuel Eli 1924- *AmMWSc 92*
**Benesch**, William Milton 1922- *AmMWSc 92*
**Benet**, Laura 1884-1979 *BenetAL 91*
**Benet**, Leslie Z 1937- *AmMWSc 92*
**Benet**, Stephen Vincent 1898-1943 *BenetAL 91, FacFETw [port]*
**Benet**, William Rose 1886-1950 *BenetAL 91, FacFETw*
**Benetton**, Giuliana 1938- *FacFETw*
**Benevenga**, Norlin Jay 1934- *AmMWSc 92*
**Benevento**, Louis Anthony 1940- *AmMWSc 92*
**Benevides**, Alfredo *WhoHisp 92*
**Benezet**, Anthony 1713-1784 *AmPeW, BenetAL 91*
**Benfer**, David William 1946- *WhoMW 92*
**Benfer**, James Elmer, III 1954- *WhoAmL 92*
**Benfey**, Bruno Georg 1917- *AmMWSc 92*
**Benfey**, Otto Theodor 1925- *AmMWSc 92*
**Benfield**, Charles W 1921- *AmMWSc 92*
**Benfield**, Derek 1926- *IntAu&W 91*
**Benfield**, Ernest Frederick 1942- *AmMWSc 92*
**Benfield**, John R 1931- *AmMWSc 92*
**Benfield**, Warren Abraham 1913- *WhoEnt 92*
**Benfield**, William Floyd, Sr. 1940- *WhoRel 92*
**Benflis**, Ali 1944- *IntWW 91*
**Benforado**, Joseph Mark 1921- *AmMWSc 92*
**Benford**, Arthur E 1931- *AmMWSc 92*
**Benford**, Clare E. 1939- *WhoBlA 92*
**Benford**, Gregory 1941- *TwCSFW 91, WrDr 92*
**Benford**, Gregory A 1941- *AmMWSc 92*
**Benford**, Gregory Albert 1941- *IntAu&W 91*
**Benford**, Harry 1917- *AmMWSc 92*
**Benfreha**, Ahmed 1940- *IntWW 91*
**Bengele**, Howard Henry 1937- *AmMWSc 92*
**Bengelloun**, Ahmed Majid 1927- *IntWW 91*
**Bengelsdorf**, Irving Swem 1922- *AmMWSc 92*
**Bengelsdorf**, Seth Dan 1957- *WhoEnt 92*
**Benghiat**, Russell Alan 1948- *WhoMW 92*
**Bengis**, Ingrid *DrAPF 91*
**Bengisu**, Murat 1963- *WhoWest 92*
**Benglis**, Lynda 1941- *WorArt 1980 [port]*
**Bengoechea**, Aurora 1948- *TwCPaSc*
**Bengough**, Piers 1929- *Who 92*
**Bengsch**, Alfred 1921-1979 *FacFETw*
**Bengson**, Pam 1945- *WhoAmP 91*
**Bengson**, Stuart A. 1943- *WhoWest 92*
**Bengston**, Billy Al 1934- *IntWW 91*
**Bengston-Brue**, Debra 1956- *WhoRel 92*
**Bengtson**, Bo Nils 1944- *IntAu&W 91*
**Bengtson**, David *DrAPF 91*
**Bengtson**, Esther G 1927- *WhoAmP 91*
**Bengtson**, Felix Jan 1927- *WhoRel 92*
**Bengtson**, George Wesley 1930- *AmMWSc 92*
**Bengtson**, Harlan Holger 1941- *AmMWSc 92*
**Bengtson**, Hermann d1989 *IntWW 91N*
**Bengtson**, Kermit 1922- *AmMWSc 92*
**Bengtson**, Larry Edwin 1939- *WhoAmP 91*
**Bengtson**, Roger D 1941- *AmMWSc 92*
**Bengtson**, Torsten Stanley 1914- *IntWW 91*
**Bengtson**, Vern L. 1941- *WrDr 92*
**Bengtsson**, Ingemund 1919- *IntWW 91*
**Bengzon**, Cesar 1896- *IntWW 91*
**Benham**, Craig John 1946- *AmMWSc 92*
**Benham**, Ida Whipple 1849- *AmPeW*
**Benham**, Isabel Hamilton 1909- *WhoFI 92*
**Benham**, John Richard 1948- *WhoWest 92*
**Benham**, Judith Laureen *AmMWSc 92*
**Benham**, Lee Kenneth 1940- *WhoFI 92, WhoMW 92*
**Benham**, Paul Burrus, Jr 1921- *WhoAmP 91*
**Benham**, Robert *WhoAmL 92*
**Benham**, Robert 1946- *WhoAmP 91, WhoBlA 92*
**Benham**, Ross Stephen 1911- *AmMWSc 92*
**Benhamouda**, Boualem 1933- *IntWW 91*
**Benhart**, Gary Len 1949- *WhoAmL 92*
**Benhima**, Mohamed 1924- *IntWW 91*
**Beni**, Gerardo 1946- *AmMWSc 92*
**Benicewicz**, Brian Chester 1954- *AmMWSc 92*
**Benich**, Roy Krsto 1938- *WhoFI 92*
**Benichou**, Jacques 1922- *IntWW 91*
**Benichou**, Pascal *WhoEnt 92*
**Benigno**, Thomas Daniel 1954- *WhoAmL 92, WhoFI 92*
**Benin**, David B 1941- *AmMWSc 92*
**Beninati**, Francis Anthony 1947- *WhoAmL 92*
**Benincasa**, Caterina *EncAmaz 91*
**Bening**, Annette 1958- *ConTFT 9, IntMPA 92, News 92-1 [port]*
**Beninger**, Richard J 1950- *AmMWSc 92*
**Benington**, Frederick *AmMWSc 92*
**Benington**, John 1921-1969 *ConAu 134*
**Benioff**, Paul 1930- *AmMWSc 92, WhoMW 92*
**Benirschke**, Kurt 1924- *AmMWSc 92, WhoWest 92*
**Benisek**, William Frank 1938- *AmMWSc 92*
**Benison**, Betty Bryant 1939- *AmMWSc 92*
**Benison**, Peter 1950- *WhoEnt 92*
**Benitez**, Carlos Humberto 1967- *WhoHisp 92*
**Benitez**, Celeste *WhoAmP 91, WhoHisp 92*
**Benitez**, Daniel 1940- *WhoHisp 92*
**Benitez**, Felipe Santiago 1926- *WhoRel 92*
**Benitez**, Francisco Manuel 1950- *AmMWSc 92*
**Benitez**, Horacio A., Jr. 1943- *WhoHisp 92*
**Benitez**, Jose Rafael 1949- *WhoHisp 92*
**Benitez**, Margarita *WhoHisp 92*
**Benitez**, Maurice Manuel 1928- *WhoRel 92*
**Benitez**, Robert J. *WhoHisp 92*
**Benitez**, Ruben A. 1928- *WhoHisp 92*
**Benitez-Hodge**, Grissel Minerva 1950- *WhoHisp 92*
**Benizelos**, Philothey *EncAmaz 91*
**Benjamin**, Anglia Sue 1957- *WhoAmL 92*
**Benjamin**, Anthony 1931- *TwCPaSc*
**Benjamin**, Arthur 1893-1960 *NewAmDM*
**Benjamin**, Arthur, Jr. 1938- *WhoBlA 92*
**Benjamin**, Ben d1991 *NewYTBS 91*
**Benjamin**, Ben Monte 1923- *AmMWSc 92*
**Benjamin**, Benoit 1964- *WhoBlA 92*
**Benjamin**, Bernard 1910- *Who 92*
**Benjamin**, Brooke *Who 92*
**Benjamin**, Burton d1988 *LesBEnT 92*
**Benjamin**, Cecil R. 1945- *WhoBlA 92*
**Benjamin**, Chester Ray 1923- *AmMWSc 92*
**Benjamin**, Christopher Edwin 1950- *WhoEnt 92*
**Benjamin**, David Charles 1936- *AmMWSc 92*
**Benjamin**, David Marshall 1946- *AmMWSc 92*
**Benjamin**, Don C., Jr. 1942- *WhoRel 92*
**Benjamin**, Donald F. 1925- *WhoBlA 92*
**Benjamin**, Donald S. 1938- *WhoBlA 92*
**Benjamin**, Edward Bernard 1897-1980 *ConAu 133*
**Benjamin**, Edward Bernard, Jr. 1923- *WhoAmL 92*
**Benjamin**, Esther P. 1910- *WhoBlA 92*

**Benjamin**, Fred Berthold 1912- *AmMWSc 92*
**Benjamin**, Gary Adams 1951- *WhoAmL 92*
**Benjamin**, Gary Duane 1941- *WhoRel 92*
**Benjamin**, George 1960- *ConCom 92*
**Benjamin**, George William John 1960- *IntWW 91, Who 92*
**Benjamin**, Harvey E. 1941- *WhoAmL 92*
**Benjamin**, Hiram Bernard 1901- *AmMWSc 92*
**Benjamin**, Irb 1946- *WhoAmP 91*
**Benjamin**, James William 1926- *WhoAmL 92*
**Benjamin**, Janice Yukon 1951- *WhoMW 92*
**Benjamin**, Jeffrey 1945- *WhoAmL 92*
**Benjamin**, Jeffrey Royce 1954- *WhoFI 92, WhoWest 92*
**Benjamin**, Jerry Dean 1937- *WhoRel 92*
**Benjamin**, John Joseph 1965- *WhoFI 92*
**Benjamin**, Judah Philip 1811-1884 *AmPolLe*
**Benjamin**, Karen Jean 1951- *WhoWest 92*
**Benjamin**, Karl Stanley 1925- *WhoWest 92*
**Benjamin**, Louis 1922- *Who 92*
**Benjamin**, Marc Andrew 1964- *WhoEnt 92*
**Benjamin**, Monica G. 1947- *WhoBlA 92*
**Benjamin**, Park 1809-1864 *BenetAL 91*
**Benjamin**, Pauline *Who 92*
**Benjamin**, Philip Palamoottil 1932- *AmMWSc 92*
**Benjamin**, Ralph 1922- *Who 92*
**Benjamin**, Richard 1938- *WhoEnt 92*
**Benjamin**, Richard 1939- *IntMPA 92*
**Benjamin**, Richard Keith 1922- *AmMWSc 92*
**Benjamin**, Richard Walter 1935- *AmMWSc 92*
**Benjamin**, Robba Lee 1947- *WhoFI 92, WhoWest 92*
**Benjamin**, Robert Fredric 1945- *AmMWSc 92*
**Benjamin**, Robert Myles 1927- *AmMWSc 92*
**Benjamin**, Robert S. d1979 *LesBEnT 92*
**Benjamin**, Robert Stephen 1943- *AmMWSc 92*
**Benjamin**, Roland John 1928- *AmMWSc 92*
**Benjamin**, Ronald 1941- *WhoBlA 92*
**Benjamin**, Rose Mary 1933- *WhoBlA 92*
**Benjamin**, Ruth *DrAPF 91*
**Benjamin**, Stephen Alfred 1939- *AmMWSc 92*
**Benjamin**, Steven James 1953- *WhoWest 92*
**Benjamin**, Thomas Brooke 1929- *IntWW 91, Who 92*
**Benjamin**, Tritobia Hayes 1944- *WhoBlA 92*
**Benjamin**, Vernon Henry 1949- *WhoAmP 91*
**Benjamin**, Walter 1892-1940 *LiExTwC*
**Benjamin**, Wayne Ronald 1953- *WhoAmL 92*
**Benjamin**, William B 1934- *AmMWSc 92*
**Benjamin**, William Chase 1947- *WhoAmL 92*
**Benjamine**, Elbert 1882-1951 *RelLAm 91*
**Benjamini**, Eli 1929- *WhoWest 92*
**Benjamini**, Eliezer 1929- *AmMWSc 92*
**Benjaminov**, Benjamin S 1923- *AmMWSc 92*
**Benjamins**, Joyce Ann 1941- *AmMWSc 92*
**Benjaminson**, Morris Aaron 1930- *AmMWSc 92*
**Benjelloun**, Tahar 1944- *IntWW 91*
**Benjenk**, Munir P. 1924- *IntWW 91*
**Benke**, Robin Paul 1953- *WhoFI 92*
**Benkendorf**, Carol Ann 1940- *AmMWSc 92*
**Benkert**, Joseph Philip, Jr. 1958- *WhoAmL 92*
**Benkeser**, Robert Anthony 1920- *AmMWSc 92*
**Benkovic**, Stephen J 1938- *AmMWSc 92*
**Benkovitz**, Miriam J 1911- *IntAu&W 91*
**Benlon**, Lisa L 1953- *WhoAmP 91*
**Benlowes**, Edward 1603?-1676 *RfGEnL 91*
**Benmaati**, Nadir 1944- *IntWW 91*
**Benmaman**, Joseph David 1924- *AmMWSc 92*
**Benn**, Anthony 1912- *Who 92*
**Benn**, Douglas Frank 1936- *WhoFI 92*
**Benn**, Edward 1922- *Who 92*
**Benn**, Edward Glanvill 1905- *Who 92*
**Benn**, Gottfried 1886-1956 *BiDExR, EncTR 91 [port], FacFETw*
**Benn**, Ishmael 1919-1978 *WhoBlA 92N*
**Benn**, J.W. d1922 *DcLB 106*
**Benn**, J W, and Brothers *DcLB 106*
**Benn**, James Jonathan 1933- *Who 92*
**Benn**, John Meriton 1908- *Who 92*
**Benn**, Jonathan *Who 92*
**Benn**, Matthew *ConAu 135*
**Benn**, Patrick 1922- *Who 92*
**Benn**, Timothy John 1936- *Who 92*
**Benn**, Tony 1925- *FacFETw, IntAu&W 91, IntWW 91, Who 92, WrDr 92*
**Benn**, Tony 1956- *TwCPaSc*
**Bennack**, Frank Anthony, Jr. 1933- *WhoEnt 92, WhoFI 92*
**Bennafield**, Donald E.J. 1931- *WhoEnt 92*
**Bennane**, Michael J 1945- *WhoAmP 91*
**Bennani**, Ben *DrAPF 91*
**Bennardo**, Brian Joseph 1967- *WhoEnt 92*
**Benne**, Kenneth Dean 1908- *WrDr 92*
**Bennehan**, Richard 1743-1825 *DcNCBi 1*
**Benner**, Blair Richard 1947- *AmMWSc 92*
**Benner**, Dorothy Spurlock 1938- *WhoWest 92*
**Benner**, Gereld Stokes 1933- *AmMWSc 92*
**Benner**, Henry d1901 *BiInAmS*
**Benner**, Patrick 1923- *Who 92*
**Benner**, Robert E *AmMWSc 92*
**Benner**, Russell Edward 1925- *AmMWSc 92*
**Benner**, Wilbur Wayne 1929- *WhoRel 92*
**Bennert**, Arthur James 1926- *WhoFI 92, WhoIns 92*
**Bennet** *Who 92*
**Bennet**, Archie Wayne 1937- *AmMWSc 92*
**Bennet**, Douglas J., Jr. 1938- *IntWW 91*
**Bennet**, Douglas Joseph, Jr 1938- *WhoAmP 91, WhoEnt 92, WhoFI 92*
**Bennet**, George Kemble, Jr 1940- *AmMWSc 92*
**Bennet**, Glin 1927- *WrDr 92*
**Bennet**, R A 1870-1954 *ScFEYrs*
**Bennet**, William Samuel, II 1952- *WhoWest 92*
**Bennett**, A D 1909- *AmMWSc 92*
**Bennett**, Al *WhoAmP 91, WhoBlA 92*
**Bennett**, Alan 1934- *ConAu 35NR, FacFETw, IntAu&W 91, IntMPA 92, IntWW 91, Who 92, WrDr 92*
**Bennett**, Alan Jerome 1941- *AmMWSc 92, WhoFI 92*
**Bennett**, Albert Edward 1931- *Who 92*
**Bennett**, Albert Farrell 1944- *AmMWSc 92*
**Bennett**, Albert George, Jr 1937- *AmMWSc 92*
**Bennett**, Albert Joseph 1913- *Who 92*
**Bennett**, Alexander *Who 92*
**Bennett**, Alexander Elliot 1940- *WhoAmL 92*
**Bennett**, Alexander Robert 1929- *WhoEnt 92*
**Bennett**, Andrea *WhoAmP 91*
**Bennett**, Andrew Francis 1939- *Who 92*
**Bennett**, Andrew John 1942- *Who 92*
**Bennett**, Anna Dell 1935- *WhoRel 92*
**Bennett**, Anna Katherine 1954- *WhoAmL 92*
**Bennett**, Anthony Jude 1948- *WhoMW 92*
**Bennett**, Archie Wayne 1937- *AmMWSc 92*
**Bennett**, Arnold 1867-1931 *CnDBLB 5 [port], FacFETw, RfGEnL 91*
**Bennett**, Arthur T. 1933- *WhoBlA 92*
**Bennett**, Barbara 1949- *WhoEnt 92*
**Bennett**, Barbara 1952- *WhoAmL 92*
**Bennett**, Barbara Esther 1953- *WhoFI 92*
**Bennett**, Basil Taylor 1944- *AmMWSc 92*
**Bennett**, Belle Harris 1852-1922 *RelLAm 91*
**Bennett**, Bessye Warren 1938- *WhoBlA 92*
**Bennett**, Billy Joe 1953- *WhoRel 92*
**Bennett**, Bobby 1944- *WhoBlA 92*
**Bennett**, Bradford Carl 1953- *WhoWest 92*
**Bennett**, Brian Erland 1942- *WhoAmL 92*
**Bennett**, Brian O'Leary 1955- *WhoWest 92*
**Bennett**, Bruce *DrAPF 91*
**Bennett**, Bruce 1909- *IntMPA 92*
**Bennett**, Bruce David 1948- *WhoWest 92*
**Bennett**, Bruce W., Jr. 1930- *WhoFI 92*
**Bennett**, Bruce Webb 1948- *WhoWest 92*
**Bennett**, Byron J 1920- *AmMWSc 92*
**Bennett**, C Frank 1956- *AmMWSc 92*
**Bennett**, C Leonard 1939- *AmMWSc 92*
**Bennett**, Carl Allen 1921- *AmMWSc 92*
**Bennett**, Carl Leroy 1935- *AmMWSc 92*
**Bennett**, Carl McGhie 1933- *WhoWest 92*
**Bennett**, Carlen Brett 1955- *WhoMW 92*
**Bennett**, Carol Elise 1938- *WhoEnt 92*
**Bennett**, Carroll G 1933- *AmMWSc 92*
**Bennett**, Carroll O 1921- *AmMWSc 92*
**Bennett**, Cecil Jackson 1927- *AmMWSc 92*
**Bennett**, Chad Daniel 1967- *WhoRel 92*
**Bennett**, Charles 1899- *IntMPA 92*
**Bennett**, Charles Alfred 1899- *WhoEnt 92*
**Bennett**, Charles Dodson 1940- *WhoAmL 92*
**Bennett**, Charles E. 1910- *AlmAP 92 [port], WhoAmP 91*
**Bennett**, Charles Franklin 1926- *AmMWSc 92*
**Bennett**, Charles H 1828-1867 *ScFEYrs*
**Bennett**, Charles James, Jr. 1956- *WhoBlA 92*
**Bennett**, Charles John Michael 1906- *Who 92*
**Bennett**, Charles L 1956- *AmMWSc 92*
**Bennett**, Charles Leon 1951- *WhoWest 92*
**Bennett**, Charles Lougheed 1949- *AmMWSc 92*
**Bennett**, Charles Moihi 1913- *Who 92*
**Bennett**, Charles Moihi To Arawaka 1913- *IntWW 91*
**Bennett**, Charles O'Brien 1927- *WhoRel 92*
**Bennett**, Charles Turner 1932- *WhoWest 92*
**Bennett**, Charles William 1962- *WhoWest 92*
**Bennett**, Clarence Edwin 1902- *AmMWSc 92*
**Bennett**, Cleaves M 1934- *AmMWSc 92*
**Bennett**, Clifton Francis 1925- *AmMWSc 92*
**Bennett**, Colin 1946- *AmMWSc 92*
**Bennett**, Collin B. 1931- *WhoBlA 92*
**Bennett**, Courtney Ajaye 1959- *WhoBlA 92*
**Bennett**, D C T 1910-1986 *FacFETw*
**Bennett**, Dale T. 1930- *WhoIns 92*
**Bennett**, Dave 1930- *WhoAmL 92*
**Bennett**, David Arthur 1942- *AmMWSc 92*
**Bennett**, David Brian 1960- *WhoAmL 92*
**Bennett**, David M. 1963- *WhoFI 92*
**Bennett**, David William 1948- *WhoRel 92*
**Bennett**, Debra A *AmMWSc 92*
**Bennett**, Debra Quinette 1958- *WhoBlA 92*
**Bennett**, Delores *WhoBlA 92*
**Bennett**, Dennis Ray 1944- *WhoBlA 92*
**Bennett**, DeRobigne Mortimer 1818-1882 *RelLAm 91*
**Bennett**, Donald Raymond 1926- *AmMWSc 92, WhoMW 92*
**Bennett**, Dorothea 1929- *AmMWSc 92*
**Bennett**, Douglas 1955- *WhoWest 92*
**Bennett**, Douglas Carleton 1946- *WhoWest 92*
**Bennett**, Douglas Marshall 1947- *WhoFI 92*
**Bennett**, Dwight *IntAu&W 91X, TwCWW 91, WrDr 92*
**Bennett**, Dwight G, Jr 1935- *AmMWSc 92*
**Bennett**, Dyke D. 1949- *WhoAmL 92*
**Bennett**, Edgar F 1929- *AmMWSc 92*
**Bennett**, Edith Lillian 1931- *WhoRel 92*
**Bennett**, Edward *Who 92*
**Bennett**, Edward A. *WhoEnt 92*
**Bennett**, Edward Henry 1917- *WhoFI 92*
**Bennett**, Edward J 1925- *WhoAmP 91*
**Bennett**, Edward J 1937- *WhoAmP 91*
**Bennett**, Edward James 1941- *WhoAmL 92, WhoFI 92*
**Bennett**, Edward Leigh 1921- *AmMWSc 92*
**Bennett**, Edward M. 1927- *WrDr 92*
**Bennett**, Edward N. 1936- *WhoIns 92*
**Bennett**, Edward Nevill 1936- *WhoFI 92*
**Bennett**, Edward Owen 1926- *AmMWSc 92*
**Bennett**, Elbert White 1929- *AmMWSc 92*
**Bennett**, Emerson 1822-1905 *BenetAL 91*
**Bennett**, Emmett Leslie 1918- *IntWW 91*
**Bennett**, Erik Peter 1928- *Who 92*
**Bennett**, Ernest Walter 1921- *WrDr 92*
**Bennett**, Eugene F. 1923- *WhoIns 92*
**Bennett**, F Lawrence 1939- *AmMWSc 92*
**Bennett**, Floyd 1890-1928 *FacFETw*
**Bennett**, Foster Clyde 1914- *AmMWSc 92*
**Bennett**, Fred Lawrence 1939- *WhoWest 92*
**Bennett**, Frederic 1918- *Who 92*
**Bennett**, Frederick Dewey 1917- *AmMWSc 92*
**Bennett**, Frederick Leander, Jr. 1948- *WhoAmL 92*
**Bennett**, Frederick Onslow Alexander 1913- *Who 92*
**Bennett**, Frederick Onslow Alexander G. 1913- *IntWW 91*
**Bennett**, G F 1935- *AmMWSc 92*
**Bennett**, Garner Ray 1955- *WhoFI 92*
**Bennett**, Gary Colin 1939- *AmMWSc 92*
**Bennett**, Gary L. *DrAPF 91*
**Bennett**, Gary Lee 1951- *AmMWSc 92*
**Bennett**, Gary Oliver 1953- *WhoEnt 92*
**Bennett**, George 1920-1969 *ConAu 134*
**Bennett**, George Kemble 1940- *AmMWSc 92*
**Bennett**, George Nelson *AmMWSc 92*
**Bennett**, George P. 1927- *WhoBlA 92*
**Bennett**, George Thomas 1952- *WhoEnt 92*
**Bennett**, George Willis 1919- *WhoRel 92*
**Bennett**, Gerald William 1933- *AmMWSc 92*
**Bennett**, Gertrude Ryder *IntAu&W 91*
**Bennett**, Glenn Allen 1938- *AmMWSc 92*
**Bennett**, Glenn Taylor 1956- *AmMWSc 92*
**Bennett**, Gordon C. *DrAPF 91*
**Bennett**, Gordon Daniel 1931- *AmMWSc 92*
**Bennett**, Gordon Fraser 1930- *AmMWSc 92*
**Bennett**, Gudrun Staub 1940- *AmMWSc 92*
**Bennett**, Gwendolyn 1902-1981 *NotBlAW 92 [port]*
**Bennett**, H. O. *WrDr 92*
**Bennett**, Hal *DrAPF 91*
**Bennett**, Hal 1936- *WrDr 92*
**Bennett**, Hal Zina 1936- *IntAu&W 91*
**Bennett**, Harold Clark 1924- *WhoRel 92*
**Bennett**, Harold Earl 1929- *AmMWSc 92*
**Bennett**, Harry 1895- *AmMWSc 92*
**Bennett**, Harry Daniel 1955- *WhoWest 92*
**Bennett**, Harry Graham 1921- *Who 92*
**Bennett**, Harry Jackson 1904- *AmMWSc 92*
**Bennett**, Harve *LesBEnT 92*
**Bennett**, Harve 1930- *IntMPA 92, WhoEnt 92*
**Bennett**, Henry Stanley 1910- *AmMWSc 92*
**Bennett**, Holly Vander Laan 1957- *AmMWSc 92*
**Bennett**, Hubert 1909- *Who 92*
**Bennett**, Hugh Deevereaux 1918- *AmMWSc 92*
**Bennett**, Hugh Hammond 1881-1960 *DcNCBi 1*
**Bennett**, Hugh Peter Derwyn 1943- *Who 92*
**Bennett**, Hywel *IntMPA 92*
**Bennett**, Hywel 1944- *ConTFT 9, IntWW 91*
**Bennett**, Hywel Thomas 1944- *Who 92*
**Bennett**, Ian Cecil 1931- *AmMWSc 92*
**Bennett**, Ivan Frank 1919- *AmMWSc 92*
**Bennett**, Ivan Loveridge, Jr. d1990 *IntWW 91N*
**Bennett**, Ivan Loveridge, Jr 1922- *AmMWSc 92*
**Bennett**, Ivy Hooker 1951- *WhoBlA 92*
**Bennett**, J. William 1935- *WhoAmL 92*
**Bennett**, Jack D. 1937- *WhoEnt 92*
**Bennett**, Jack Franklin 1924- *IntWW 91*
**Bennett**, Jackson 1927- *WhoMW 92*
**Bennett**, Jacqueline Beekman 1946- *WhoWest 92*
**Bennett**, James Anthony 1948- *AmMWSc 92*
**Bennett**, James Austin 1915- *AmMWSc 92*
**Bennett**, James Clark *ScFEYrs*
**Bennett**, James Davison 1938- *WhoAmL 92*
**Bennett**, James Gordon 1795-1872 *BenetAL 91*
**Bennett**, James Gordon, Jr 1841-1918 *RComAH*
**Bennett**, James Gordon, Sr 1795-1872 *RComAH*
**Bennett**, James Gordy, Jr 1932- *AmMWSc 92*
**Bennett**, James Peter 1944- *AmMWSc 92*
**Bennett**, James Richard 1932- *WrDr 92*
**Bennett**, James Ronald 1940- *WhoAmP 91*
**Bennett**, James Stark 1947- *WhoEnt 92*
**Bennett**, James T. 1942- *WhoFI 92*
**Bennett**, Jean McPherson 1930- *AmMWSc 92*
**Bennett**, Jesse Harland 1936- *AmMWSc 92*
**Bennett**, Jill d1990 *IntWW 91N, Who 92N*
**Bennett**, Jill 1931-1990 *AnObit 1990, FacFETw*
**Bennett**, Joan d1990 *Who 92N*
**Bennett**, Joan 1910-1990 *AnObit 1990, ConTFT 9, FacFETw, News 91*
**Bennett**, Joan Carol 1949- *WhoAmL 92*
**Bennett**, Joan Wennstrom 1942- *AmMWSc 92*
**Bennett**, Joe *WhoRel 92*
**Bennett**, Joe Claude 1933- *AmMWSc 92*
**Bennett**, John *DrAPF 91*
**Bennett**, John 1865-1956 *BenetAL 91*
**Bennett**, John 1912- *Who 92, WhoAmP 91*
**Bennett**, John 1920- *WrDr 92*
**Bennett**, John A. 1937- *WhoWest 92*
**Bennett**, John Campbell White 1948- *WhoAmL 92*
**Bennett**, John Coleman 1902- *RelLAm 91*
**Bennett**, John E 1933- *AmMWSc 92*
**Bennett**, John Francis 1925- *AmMWSc 92*
**Bennett**, John M. *DrAPF 91*
**Bennett**, John M 1933- *AmMWSc 92*
**Bennett**, John M. 1942- *WrDr 92*
**Bennett**, John O 1948- *WhoAmP 91*
**Bennett**, John Richard 1952- *WhoFI 92*
**Bennett**, Jonathan David 1954- *WhoAmL 92*
**Bennett**, Joseph L. 1942- *WhoMW 92*
**Bennett**, Julia Hubert 1925- *WhoBlA 92*
**Bennett**, June Newton 1926- *WhoWest 92*
**Bennett**, Keith 1956- *WhoBlA 92*
**Bennett**, Kenneth A 1935- *AmMWSc 92*
**Bennett**, Larry E 1940- *AmMWSc 92*
**Bennett**, Laurie Edward 1919- *WhoAmP 91*
**Bennett**, Lawrence Allen 1923- *WhoWest 92*
**Bennett**, Lawrence E 1923- *WhoAmP 91*
**Bennett**, Lawrence Herman 1930- *AmMWSc 92*
**Bennett**, Lee Cotton, Jr 1933- *AmMWSc 92*
**Bennett**, Leon 1927- *AmMWSc 92*

**Bennett,** Leonard Lee, Jr 1920- *AmMWSc 92*
**Bennett,** Lerone, Jr. 1928- *WhoBlA 92*
**Bennett,** Leslie R 1918- *AmMWSc 92*
**Bennett,** Leslie Robert 1918- *WhoWest 92*
**Bennett,** Lewis Tilton, Jr. 1940- *WhoEnt 92, WhoWest 92*
**Bennett,** Lloyd M 1928- *AmMWSc 92*
**Bennett,** Lonnie Truman 1933- *AmMWSc 92*
**Bennett,** Louis Lowell d1991 *NewYTBS 91*
**Bennett,** Louise 1919- *BlkLC [port], ConPo 91, RfGEnL 91, WrDr 92*
**Bennett,** Louise Lynette 1947- *WhoEnt 92*
**Bennett,** M. J. *ConAu 35NR*
**Bennett,** Maisha B. H. 1948- *WhoBlA 92*
**Bennett,** Manu Augustus 1916- *Who 92*
**Bennett,** Marcia J 1945- *ConAu 35NR*
**Bennett,** Marion D. 1936- *WhoBlA 92*
**Bennett,** Marion T 1914- *WhoAmP 91*
**Bennett,** Marion Tinsley 1914- *WhoAmL 92*
**Bennett,** Mark Jay 1954- *WhoAmL 92*
**Bennett,** Marlin John 1939- *WhoWest 92*
**Bennett,** Marshall Goodloe 1943- *WhoAmP 91*
**Bennett,** Mary Katherine 1940- *AmMWSc 92*
**Bennett,** Mary Katherine Jones 1864-1950 *RelLAm 91*
**Bennett,** Mary Letitia Somerville 1913- *Who 92*
**Bennett,** Maxwell Richard 1939- *IntWW 91*
**Bennett,** Maybelle Taylor 1949- *WhoBlA 92*
**Bennett,** Michael 1936- *AmMWSc 92*
**Bennett,** Michael 1943-1987 *FacFETw*
**Bennett,** Michael Vander Laan 1931- *AmMWSc 92, IntWW 91*
**Bennett,** Miriam Frances 1928- *AmMWSc 92*
**Bennett,** Nancy 1958- *WhoEnt 92*
**Bennett,** Neville 1937- *WrDr 92*
**Bennett,** Neville Hough 1934- *WhoWest 92*
**Bennett,** Nicholas Jerome 1949- *Who 92*
**Bennett,** Ovell Francis 1929- *AmMWSc 92*
**Bennett,** Pamela McHardy 1947- *WhoEnt 92*
**Bennett,** Patricia A. *WhoBlA 92*
**Bennett,** Patrick 1924- *Who 92*
**Bennett,** Paul *DrAPF 91*
**Bennett,** Paul Edward 1947- *WhoAmL 92*
**Bennett,** Paul Lester 1946- *WhoWest 92*
**Bennett,** Peter 1917-1990? *ConTFT 9*
**Bennett,** Peter Bellew 1945- *WhoAmL 92*
**Bennett,** Peter Brian 1931- *AmMWSc 92*
**Bennett,** Peter Howard 1937- *AmMWSc 92*
**Bennett,** Peter Ward *Who 92*
**Bennett,** Philip Hugh Penberthy 1919- *Who 92*
**Bennett,** Philip Oliver 1913- *WhoEnt 92*
**Bennett,** Phillip 1928- *Who 92*
**Bennett,** Polly Cathryn 1938- *WhoWest 92*
**Bennett,** Ralph Featherstone 1923- *Who 92*
**Bennett,** Raymond Clayton Watson 1939- *Who 92*
**Bennett,** Raymond Dudley 1931- *AmMWSc 92*
**Bennett,** Reginald 1911- *Who 92*
**Bennett,** Richard Alan 1963- *WhoAmP 91*
**Bennett,** Richard Bedford 1870-1947 *FacFETw*
**Bennett,** Richard Bond 1932- *AmMWSc 92*
**Bennett,** Richard Carl 1933- *WhoMW 92*
**Bennett,** Richard Harold 1939- *AmMWSc 92*
**Bennett,** Richard Henry 1944- *AmMWSc 92*
**Bennett,** Richard L. 1952- *WhoEnt 92*
**Bennett,** Richard Rodney 1936- *ConCom 92, IntWW 91, NewAmDM, Who 92*
**Bennett,** Rick *WhoAmP 91*
**Bennett,** Risden Tyler 1840-1913 *DcNCBi 1*
**Bennett,** Robert *LesBEnT 92 [port]*
**Bennett,** Robert A. 1933- *WhoBlA 92*
**Bennett,** Robert Bowen 1927- *AmMWSc 92*
**Bennett,** Robert D 1928- *WhoAmP 91*
**Bennett,** Robert Frederick 1927- *IntWW 91, WhoAmP 91, WhoMW 92*
**Bennett,** Robert John 1948- *Who 92*
**Bennett,** Robert Louis 1925- *WhoWest 92*
**Bennett,** Robert M 1940- *AmMWSc 92*
**Bennett,** Robert Putnam 1932- *AmMWSc 92*
**Bennett,** Robert Russell 1894-1981 *NewAmDM*
**Bennett,** Robert Thomas 1939- *WhoAmP 91*
**Bennett,** Robert William 1941- *WhoAmL 92*
**Bennett,** Robin 1934- *Who 92*
**Bennett,** Roger Spurgeon 1954- *WhoRel 92*
**Bennett,** Ronald 1930- *Who 92*
**Bennett,** Ronald Alistair 1922- *Who 92*
**Bennett,** Roy Frederick 1928- *IntWW 91*
**Bennett,** Roy Grissell 1917- *Who 92*
**Bennett,** Sara Neville 1931- *AmMWSc 92*
**Bennett,** Saul 1936- *WhoFI 92*
**Bennett,** Scott Lawrence 1949- *WhoAmL 92*
**Bennett,** Shirley M 1936- *WhoAmP 91*
**Bennett,** Stanley T 1947- *WhoAmP 91*
**Bennett,** Stephen Lawrence 1938- *AmMWSc 92, WhoMW 92*
**Bennett,** Stewart 1933- *AmMWSc 92*
**Bennett,** T. James *WhoRel 92*
**Bennett,** Thomas Edward 1950- *AmMWSc 92*
**Bennett,** Thomas Mitchell 1945- *WhoMW 92*
**Bennett,** Thomas P 1937- *AmMWSc 92*
**Bennett,** Thomas Wesley 1936- *WhoAmL 92*
**Bennett,** Timothy Bernard 1951- *WhoWest 92*
**Bennett,** Tony 1926- *WhoEnt 92*
**Bennett,** Tony L 1940- *WhoAmP 91*
**Bennett,** Tracy d1991 *NewYTBS 91*
**Bennett,** W A C 1911-1979 *FacFETw*
**Bennett,** W Donald 1924- *AmMWSc 92*
**Bennett,** W Scott 1929- *AmMWSc 92*
**Bennett,** W W, Jr 1940- *WhoAmP 91*
**Bennett,** Wallace F *WhoAmP 91*
**Bennett,** Ward 1917- *DcTwDes, FacFETw*
**Bennett,** Wayne 1927- *WhoAmP 91*
**Bennett,** Will *DrAPF 91*
**Bennett,** William *WhoEnt 92*
**Bennett,** William 1932- *FacFETw*
**Bennett,** William Andrew 1963- *WhoWest 92*
**Bennett,** William Donald 1939- *WhoBlA 92*
**Bennett,** William E. *WhoFI 92*
**Bennett,** William Earl 1923- *AmMWSc 92*
**Bennett,** William Ernest 1928- *AmMWSc 92*
**Bennett,** William Franklin *AmMWSc 92*
**Bennett,** William Frederick 1927- *AmMWSc 92*
**Bennett,** William Gordon 1924- *WhoFI 92, WhoWest 92*
**Bennett,** William J 1943- *WhoAmP 91*
**Bennett,** William John 1911- *Who 92*
**Bennett,** William John 1943- *AmPolLe, IntWW 91*
**Bennett,** William Leffis 1924- *WhoRel 92*
**Bennett,** William M 1938- *AmMWSc 92*
**Bennett,** William Ralph 1904- *AmMWSc 92*
**Bennett,** William Ralph 1933- *WhoAmP 91*
**Bennett,** William Ralph, Jr 1930- *AmMWSc 92*
**Bennett,** William Richards 1932- *IntWW 91, Who 92*
**Bennett,** William Ronald 1935- *WhoBlA 92*
**Bennett,** William Tapley, Jr. 1917- *IntWW 91, WhoAmP 91*
**Bennett,** Winston George, III 1965- *WhoBlA 92*
**Bennett,** Word Brown, Jr 1915- *AmMWSc 92*
**Bennett-England,** Rodney 1936- *WrDr 92*
**Bennett-England,** Rodney Charles 1936- *IntAu&W 91*
**Bennett Spector Greenfield,** Veronica 1943- *WhoEnt 92*
**Bennette,** Connie E. 1951- *WhoBlA 92*
**Bennette,** Jerry Mac 1952- *AmMWSc 92*
**Bennetton,** Giuliana 1938- *DcTwDes*
**Benney,** Adrian Gerald Sallis 1930- *IntWW 91*
**Benney,** Douglas Mabley 1922- *WhoFI 92*
**Benney,** Gerald 1930- *Who 92*
**Bennick,** Anders *AmMWSc 92*
**Bennighof,** R H 1928- *AmMWSc 92*
**Bennin,** Bruce 1943- *WhoMW 92*
**Benning,** Carl J, Jr 1930- *AmMWSc 92*
**Benning,** Emma Bowman 1928- *WhoBlA 92*
**Benninger,** Fred 1917- *WhoWest 92*
**Benninghoff,** William Shiffer 1918- *AmMWSc 92*
**Bennington,** James Lynne 1935- *AmMWSc 92*
**Bennington,** Kenneth Oliver 1916- *AmMWSc 92*
**Bennington,** Leslie Orville, Jr. 1946- *WhoWest 92*
**Bennington,** Ronald Kent 1936- *WhoAmL 92*
**Bennington,** William Lewis 1946- *WhoWest 92*
**Bennink,** Maurice Ray 1944- *AmMWSc 92*
**Bennion,** Douglas Noel 1935- *AmMWSc 92*
**Bennion,** Douglas Wilford 1931- *AmMWSc 92*
**Bennion,** Francis Alan Roscoe 1923- *Who 92*
**Bennion,** John W. *WhoWest 92*
**Bennis,** Warren 1925- *IntAu&W 91, WrDr 92*
**Bennis,** Warren Gameliel 1925- *WhoFI 92, WhoWest 92*
**Bennison,** Allan P 1918- *AmMWSc 92*
**Bennison,** Bertrand Earl 1915- *AmMWSc 92*
**Bennison,** Charles E. 1917- *WhoWest 92*
**Bennison,** Charles Ellsworth, Jr. 1943- *WhoRel 92*
**Bennitt,** Michael Paul 1955- *WhoFI 92*
**Bennitt,** Mortimer Wilmot 1910- *Who 92*
**Bennun,** Alfred 1934- *AmMWSc 92*
**Benny,** Jack d1974 *LesBEnT 92*
**Benny,** Jack 1894-1974 *FacFETw*
**Beno,** Carolyn Elizabeth 1953- *WhoWest 92*
**Beno,** John Richardson 1931- *WhoAmP 91*
**Beno-Clark,** Candice Lynn 1951- *WhoFI 92*
**Benois,** Alexandre 1870-1960 *FacFETw*
**Benoist,** Alain Marie de 1943- *BiDExR*
**Benoist,** Jean-Marie Jules 1942- *IntAu&W 91*
**Benoist-Mechin,** Jacques Michel Gabriel P 1901-1983 *BiDExR*
**Benoit,** Edith B. 1918- *WhoBlA 92*
**Benoit,** Gary 1953- *WhoAmP 91*
**Benoit,** Guy J C 1926- *AmMWSc 92*
**Benoit,** Harry L 1940- *WhoAmP 91*
**Benoit,** Henri 1921- *IntWW 91*
**Benoit,** Karen Virginia 1945- *WhoAmP 91*
**Benoit,** Kenneth Roger 1952- *WhoEnt 92*
**Benoit,** Nancy L 1944- *WhoAmP 91*
**Benoit,** Normand George 1949- *WhoAmL 92*
**Benoit,** Peter Wells 1939- *AmMWSc 92*
**Benoit,** Pierre 1886-1962 *ScFEYrs*
**Benoit,** Richard J 1922- *AmMWSc 92*
**Benoit,** Sharon B 1944- *WhoAmP 91*
**Benoit,** William Lyon 1953- *WhoMW 92*
**Benoit-Christian,** Paulette Therese 1947- *WhoWest 92*
**Benoit De Coignac,** Henri Elie Marie 1935- *IntWW 91*
**Benoiton,** Normand Leo 1932- *AmMWSc 92*
**Benokraitis,** Vitalius 1941- *AmMWSc 92*
**Benolken,** Robert Marshall 1932- *AmMWSc 92*
**Benos,** Dale John 1950- *AmMWSc 92*
**Benowitz,** Roy 1924- *WhoEnt 92*
**Benrud,** Charles Harris 1921- *AmMWSc 92*
**Bens,** Frederick Peter 1913- *AmMWSc 92*
**Bens Argandona,** Francisco 1867-1949 *HisDSpE*
**Bensadoun,** Andre 1931- *AmMWSc 92*
**Bensch,** Klaus George 1928- *AmMWSc 92*
**Benscheidt,** Steven Eugene 1954- *WhoWest 92*
**Benschip,** Gary John 1947- *WhoFI 92*
**Benschoter,** Reba Ann 1930- *AmMWSc 92*
**Bensel,** Bill 1956- *WhoAmP 91*
**Bensel,** John Phillip 1945- *AmMWSc 92*
**Bensel,** Mary *WhoEnt 92*
**Benseler,** Rolf Wilhelm 1932- *AmMWSc 92, WhoWest 92*
**Bensen,** Alice R. 1911- *WrDr 92*
**Bensen,** Annette Wolf 1938- *WhoFI 92*
**Bensen,** Clark Hamilton 1952- *WhoAmP 91*
**Bensen,** Craig Lee 1948- *WhoRel 92*
**Bensen,** David Warren 1928- *AmMWSc 92*
**Bensen,** Jack F 1923- *AmMWSc 92*
**Bensen,** Robert *DrAPF 91*
**Benser,** Frank LeRoy 1945- *WhoAmP 91*
**Bensheimer,** Virginia *DrAPF 91*
**Benshoof,** Terrence James 1946- *WhoAmL 92*
**Bensinger,** David August 1926- *AmMWSc 92*
**Bensinger,** James Robert 1941- *AmMWSc 92*
**Bensinger,** Peter Benjamin 1936- *WhoAmP 91*
**Bensinger,** Steven J. 1955- *WhoIns 92*
**Bension,** Marc *WhoEnt 92*
**Bension,** Shmuel 1945- *WhoEnt 92*
**Benski,** Raymond 1931- *WhoAmP 91*
**Benskina,** Princess Orelia *WhoEnt 92*
**Bensko,** John *DrAPF 91*
**Bensley,** Connie 1929- *ConAu 135*
**Benslimane,** Abdelkader 1932- *IntWW 91*
**Bensmiller,** Jean Pullin 1933- *WhoAmP 91*
**Benson** *Who 92*
**Benson,** Baron 1909- *IntWW 91, Who 92*
**Benson,** A.C. 1862-1925 *FacFETw*
**Benson,** Adam *IntAu&W 91X*
**Benson,** Alfred M. 1941- *WhoWest 92*
**Benson,** Andrew Alm 1917- *AmMWSc 92, IntWW 91*
**Benson,** Andrew Jay 1954- *WhoWest 92*
**Benson,** Ann Marie *AmMWSc 92*
**Benson,** Annette R. 1946- *WhoEnt 92*
**Benson,** Arthur A., II 1944- *WhoAmL 92, WhoAmP 91*
**Benson,** Barrett Wendell 1939- *AmMWSc 92*
**Benson,** Betty G 1943- *WhoAmP 91*
**Benson,** Bradley Duane 1959- *WhoWest 92*
**Benson,** Brent W 1941- *AmMWSc 92*
**Benson,** Bruce Buzzell 1922- *AmMWSc 92*
**Benson,** Bruce D 1938- *WhoAmP 91*
**Benson,** Bruce Lowell 1949- *WhoFI 92*
**Benson,** Byron Obie 1944- *WhoMW 92*
**Benson,** Carl Sidney 1927- *AmMWSc 92*
**Benson,** Carleton J *WhoAmP 91*
**Benson,** Carolyn Roberts 1931- *WhoAmL 92*
**Benson,** Charles Edward 1912- *WhoFI 92*
**Benson,** Charles Everett 1937- *AmMWSc 92*
**Benson,** Christopher 1933- *Who 92*
**Benson,** Christopher John 1933- *IntWW 91*
**Benson,** Craig Burgess 1945- *WhoEnt 92*
**Benson,** Dale B 1930- *AmMWSc 92*
**Benson,** Daniel *IntAu&W 91X, WrDr 92*
**Benson,** David Alan 1953- *WhoFI 92*
**Benson,** David Ernest 1944- *WhoMW 92, WhoRel 92*
**Benson,** David Holford 1938- *Who 92*
**Benson,** David Michael 1945- *AmMWSc 92*
**Benson,** Dean Clifton 1918- *AmMWSc 92*
**Benson,** Debra Ann 1953- *WhoEnt 92*
**Benson,** Dee Vance 1948- *WhoAmL 92*
**Benson,** Dennis Alan 1944- *AmMWSc 92*
**Benson,** Dennis Keith 1946- *WhoMW 92*
**Benson,** Donald Charles 1927- *AmMWSc 92*
**Benson,** Donald Erick 1930- *WhoFI 92*
**Benson,** Donald Warren 1921- *AmMWSc 92*
**Benson,** Duane D 1945- *WhoAmP 91*
**Benson,** E F 1867-1940 *FacFETw, RfGEnL 91*
**Benson,** E F 1867-1942 *ScFEYrs*
**Benson,** E. Stephen 1947- *WhoFI 92*
**Benson,** Edgar John 1923- *IntWW 91*
**Benson,** Edmund Walter 1938- *AmMWSc 92*
**Benson,** Elizabeth P 1924- *ConAu 35NR, SmATA 65*
**Benson,** Ellis Starbranch 1919- *AmMWSc 92*
**Benson,** Ernest Phillip, Jr 1936- *AmMWSc 92*
**Benson,** Ezra Taft 1899- *AmPolLe, IntWW 91, RelLAm 91, WhoRel 92, WhoWest 92*
**Benson,** Francis M. 1958- *WhoWest 92*
**Benson,** Frank Atkinson 1921- *Who 92, WrDr 92*
**Benson,** Fred J 1914- *AmMWSc 92*
**Benson,** Frederic Rupert 1915- *AmMWSc 92*
**Benson,** George 1943- *WhoBlA 92, WhoEnt 92*
**Benson,** George Campbell 1919- *AmMWSc 92*
**Benson,** George Michael 1960- *WhoRel 92*
**Benson,** Gilbert 1930- *WhoBlA 92*
**Benson,** Gilbert Thomas 1929- *AmMWSc 92*
**Benson,** Harriet 1941- *AmMWSc 92*
**Benson,** Harry Peter 1917- *Who 92*
**Benson,** Hayward J., Jr. 1936- *WhoBlA 92*
**Benson,** Herbert 1935- *AmMWSc 92*
**Benson,** Herbert Linne, Jr 1934- *AmMWSc 92*
**Benson,** Horace Burford 1904- *Who 92*
**Benson,** Hugh *IntMPA 92*
**Benson,** J. Jeffrey 1957- *WhoAmL 92*
**Benson,** Jackson J. 1930- *DcLB 111 [port], WrDr 92*
**Benson,** Jackson Jerald 1930 *IntAu&W 91, WhoWest 92*
**Benson,** James 1925- *Who 92*
**Benson,** James Bernard, Jr. 1930- *WhoWest 92*
**Benson,** James DeWitt 1922- *WhoAmL 92*
**Benson,** James R 1942- *AmMWSc 92*
**Benson,** James Russell 1933- *WhoBlA 92*
**Benson,** Jeffrey *Who 92*
**Benson,** Jeffrey Scott 1963- *WhoFI 92*
**Benson,** Jeremy Henry 1925- *Who 92*
**Benson,** Joan *WhoEnt 92*
**Benson,** Joanne 1943- *WhoAmP 91*
**Benson,** Joanne C *WhoAmP 91*
**Benson,** John Alexander, Jr 1921- *AmMWSc 92, WhoWest 92*
**Benson,** John Schuler McKinney, Sr. 1927- *WhoFI 92*
**Benson,** Joseph Kenneth 1943- *WhoFI 92*
**Benson,** Joyce Lorentzson *DrAPF 91*
**Benson,** Katherine Alice 1938- *AmMWSc 92*
**Benson,** Keith Rodney 1948- *AmMWSc 92*
**Benson,** Kenneth Peter 1927- *WhoFI 92, WhoWest 92*

**Benson,** Kenneth Samuel 1937- WhoFI 92
**Benson,** Lenni Beth 1958- WhoAmL 92
**Benson,** Leon IntMPA 92
**Benson,** Libby 1953- WhoEnt 92
**Benson,** Lloyd Kenneth 1954- WhoFI 92
**Benson,** Loren Allen 1932- AmMWSc 92
**Benson,** Loyd L 1940- WhoAmP 91
**Benson,** Lucy Wilson 1927- WhoAmP 91
**Benson,** Lyman 1909- IntAu&W 91
**Benson,** Marvin Wayne 1946- WhoRel 92
**Benson,** Mary 1919- IntAu&W 91
**Benson,** Melvoid J WhoAmP 91
**Benson,** Mildred 1905- ConAu 134, SmATA 65 [port]
**Benson,** Mildred Wirt ConAu 134, SmATA 65
**Benson,** Moses, Jr. 1943- WhoMW 92
**Benson,** Norman G 1923- AmMWSc 92
**Benson,** Paul 1918- WhoAmL 92
**Benson,** Paul George 1946- WhoMW 92
**Benson,** Peter Who 92
**Benson,** Peter H. 1935- WhoMW 92
**Benson,** Peter Herbert 1923- Who 92
**Benson,** Phillip Stanley 1943- WhoWest 92
**Benson,** R.H. 1871-1914 FacFETw, ScFEYrs
**Benson,** Ralph C, Jr 1942- AmMWSc 92
**Benson,** Randolph 1923- WrDr 92
**Benson,** Richard C 1944- AmMWSc 92
**Benson,** Richard Carter 1951- AmMWSc 92
**Benson,** Richard Edward 1920- AmMWSc 92
**Benson,** Richard Hall 1929- AmMWSc 92
**Benson,** Richard Norman 1935- AmMWSc 92
**Benson,** Robby 1956- IntMPA 92
**Benson,** Robert C., II 1914- WhoRel 92
**Benson,** Robert Clinton, Jr. 1946- WhoFI 92
**Benson,** Robert Franklin 1941- AmMWSc 92
**Benson,** Robert Frederick 1935- AmMWSc 92
**Benson,** Robert Haynes 1924- AmMWSc 92
**Benson,** Robert Leland 1941- AmMWSc 92
**Benson,** Robert Wilmer 1924- AmMWSc 92
**Benson,** Robert Winston 1948- WhoWest 92
**Benson,** Rodney E. 1954- WhoAmL 92
**Benson,** Roxanne M. 1951- WhoHisp 92
**Benson,** Royal H 1925- AmMWSc 92
**Benson,** Rubin Author 1946- WhoBlA 92
**Benson,** Sally 1900-1972 BenetAL 91
**Benson,** Sharon Marie 1959- WhoBlA 92
**Benson,** Sidney William 1918- AmMWSc 92, IntWW 91
**Benson,** Stan Alan 1953- WhoFI 92
**Benson,** Stella 1892-1933 RfGEnL 91
**Benson,** Stephen Harold 1943- WhoMW 92
**Benson,** Steve DrAPF 91
**Benson,** Steven Clark 1954- WhoFI 92
**Benson,** Steven Verner 1952- WhoWest 92
**Benson,** Suzanne Mireille WhoEnt 92
**Benson,** Thomas W and Wolfe, Charles S ScFEYrs
**Benson,** Walter Roderick 1929- AmMWSc 92
**Benson,** Walter Russell 1920- AmMWSc 92
**Benson,** Warren 1924- NewAmDM
**Benson,** Warren Frank 1924- WhoEnt 92
**Benson,** Warren Sten 1929- WhoRel 92
**Benson,** William Edward Barnes 1919- AmMWSc 92
**Benson,** William Hazlehurst 1954- AmMWSc 92
**Benson,** William Jeffrey 1922- IntWW 91, Who 92
**Bensoussan,** Abraham 1948- WhoRel 92
**Benstock,** Bernard 1930- IntAu&W 91, WrDr 92
**Benstock,** Shari 1944- WrDr 92
**Benston,** George James 1932- WhoFI 92
**Benston,** Margaret Lowe 1937- AmMWSc 92
**Bensuaski,** Fernando 1949- WhoWest 92
**Bent,** Brian E 1960- AmMWSc 92
**Bent,** Daniel A. 1947- WhoAmL 92
**Bent,** Donald Frederick 1925- AmMWSc 92
**Bent,** Henry Albert 1926- AmMWSc 92
**Bent,** Ian David 1938- WhoEnt 92
**Bent,** Michael William 1951- WhoFI 92, WhoWest 92
**Bent,** Richard Lincoln 1917- AmMWSc 92
**Bent,** Robert Demo 1928- AmMWSc 92
**Bent,** Robert Oliver, II 1941- WhoFI 92
**Bent,** Samuel W 1955- AmMWSc 92
**Bent,** Silas 1820-1887 BiInAmS
**Bent,** Ted DrAPF 91
**Bentall,** Hugh Henry 1920- Who 92
**Bentall,** Leonard Edward 1939- Who 92
**Bentall,** Ray 1917- AmMWSc 92
**Bentall,** Rowan 1911- Who 92
**Bentall,** Shirley Franklyn 1926- WhoRel 92
**Bentch,** Sue Todd 1945- WhoAmL 92
**Bentcover,** Bruce Jay 1954- WhoFI 92
**Benteen,** John TwCWW 91
**Bentele,** Raymond F. 1936- IntWW 91
**Benter,** George H., Jr. 1942- WhoFI 92
**Benthall,** Arthur Paul 1902- Who 92
**Benthall,** Jonathan Charles Mackenzie 1941- Who 92
**Benthall,** Paul Who 92
**Bentham,** Edward 1707-1776 BlkwCEP
**Bentham,** Ethel 1861-1931 BiDBrF 2
**Bentham,** Jeremy 1748-1832 BlkwCEP, DcLB 107 [port]
**Bentham,** Richard Walker 1930- IntWW 91, Who 92
**Benthic,** Arch E. ConAu 35NR
**Bentinck** Who 92
**Bentkowski,** Aleksander 1941- IntWW 91
**Bentley,** Albert 1960- WhoBlA 92
**Bentley,** Alfred Young, Jr. 1943- WhoFI 92
**Bentley,** Anthony Philip 1948- Who 92
**Bentley,** Antoinette C. 1937- WhoIns 92
**Bentley,** Barbara Lee 1942- AmMWSc 92
**Bentley,** Beth DrAPF 91
**Bentley,** Carol Jane 1945- WhoAmP 91
**Bentley,** Charles Raymond 1929- AmMWSc 92, WhoMW 92
**Bentley,** Danny L. 1958- WhoIns 92
**Bentley,** David Edward Who 92
**Bentley,** David Jeffrey 1935- Who 92
**Bentley,** David R 1940- AmMWSc 92
**Bentley,** David Ronald 1942- Who 92
**Bentley,** Donald Lyon 1935- AmMWSc 92
**Bentley,** Earl Wilson, Jr. 1920- WhoFI 92
**Bentley,** Eric 1916- BenetAL 91, IntAu&W 91, WrDr 92
**Bentley,** Frank William Henry 1934- Who 92
**Bentley,** Fred 1914- IntWW 91
**Bentley,** Fred Douglas, Sr. 1926- WhoAmL 92, WhoFI 92
**Bentley,** Geoffrey Bryan 1909- Who 92
**Bentley,** George 1936- Who 92
**Bentley,** Gerald Eades 1901- IntAu&W 91, WrDr 92
**Bentley,** Gerald Eades, Jr. 1930- IntWW 91
**Bentley,** Glenn E 1946- AmMWSc 92
**Bentley,** Gregory Smith 1949- WhoAmL 92
**Bentley,** Harry Thomas, III 1942- AmMWSc 92
**Bentley,** Helen Delich IntWW 91, WhoFI 92
**Bentley,** Helen Delich 1923- AlmAP 92 [port], WhoAmP 91
**Bentley,** Herbert Dean 1940- WhoBlA 92
**Bentley,** Herschel Lamar 1939- AmMWSc 92
**Bentley,** J Peter 1931- AmMWSc 92
**Bentley,** James Robert 1942- WhoFI 92
**Bentley,** Joe Richard 1957- WhoMW 92
**Bentley,** John Joseph 1946- AmMWSc 92
**Bentley,** John Ransome 1940- Who 92
**Bentley,** Kenneth Chessar 1935- AmMWSc 92
**Bentley,** Kenneth Pershing 1940- WhoRel 92
**Bentley,** Kenton Earl 1927- AmMWSc 92
**Bentley,** Leonard Douglas 1953- WhoMW 92
**Bentley,** Michael David 1939- AmMWSc 92
**Bentley,** Ormond L. 1935- WhoIns 92
**Bentley,** Orville G 1918- WhoAmP 91
**Bentley,** Orville George 1918- AmMWSc 92
**Bentley,** Peter John 1930- AmMWSc 92
**Bentley,** Philip Who 92
**Bentley,** Philip Jay 1945- WhoRel 92
**Bentley,** Richard d1871 DcLB 106 [port]
**Bentley,** Richard 1662-1742 BlkwCEP
**Bentley,** Richard, and Son DcLB 106 [port]
**Bentley,** Robert 1913- WhoAmP 91
**Bentley,** Ronald 1922- AmMWSc 92
**Bentley,** Russell 1946- WhoAmP 91
**Bentley,** Steven Wayne Tolton 1956- WhoWest 92
**Bentley,** Timothy 1949- WhoFI 92
**Bentley,** Timothy Edward 1953- WhoAmP 91
**Bentley,** William 1927- IntWW 91, Who 92
**Bently,** Donald Emery 1924- WhoFI 92, WhoWest 92
**Benton,** Allen Haydon 1921- AmMWSc 92
**Benton,** Allen William 1931- AmMWSc 92
**Benton,** Angelo Ames 1837-1912 DcNCBi 1
**Benton,** Anthony Stuart 1949- WhoAmL 92
**Benton,** Arthur Lester 1909- AmMWSc 92, WhoMW 92
**Benton,** Auburn Edgar 1926- WhoAmL 92
**Benton,** Barbi 1950- ConTFT 9
**Benton,** Ben 1947- WhoAmP 91
**Benton,** Brook 1931-1988 ConMus 7 [port]
**Benton,** Byrl E 1912- AmMWSc 92
**Benton,** Calvin B. 1931- WhoBlA 92
**Benton,** Charles Herbert 1925- AmMWSc 92
**Benton,** Daniel K. 1952- WhoEnt 92
**Benton,** Deborah Sally 1958- WhoAmL 92
**Benton,** Donald Stewart 1924- WhoAmL 92
**Benton,** Duane Allen 1931- AmMWSc 92
**Benton,** Duane Marshall 1933- AmMWSc 92
**Benton,** Edward Henry 1950- WhoAmL 92
**Benton,** Edward Rowell 1934- AmMWSc 92
**Benton,** Eugene Vladimir 1937- AmMWSc 92
**Benton,** Francis Lee 1912- AmMWSc 92
**Benton,** Frank 1852-1919 BiInAmS
**Benton,** Gary Lee 1959- WhoAmL 92
**Benton,** George A. 1933- WhoBlA 92
**Benton,** George Stock 1917- AmMWSc 92
**Benton,** Gladys Gay 1906- WhoWest 92
**Benton,** Gordon Nance 1952- WhoRel 92
**Benton,** Homer Grabill 1926- WhoFI 92, WhoWest 92
**Benton,** Hugh Arthur 1929- WhoMW 92
**Benton,** Ishmael Claud 1920- WhoAmP 91
**Benton,** Jack Mitchell 1941- WhoFI 92
**Benton,** James Wilbert, Jr. 1944- WhoBlA 92
**Benton,** Jean Elizabeth 1943- WhoMW 92
**Benton,** John William, Jr 1930- AmMWSc 92
**Benton,** Joseph Edward 1933- Who 92
**Benton,** Juanita 1959- WhoBlA 92
**Benton,** Kenneth 1909- WrDr 92
**Benton,** Kenneth Carter 1909- IntAu&W 91, Who 92
**Benton,** Kenneth Curtis 1941- AmMWSc 92
**Benton,** Lemuel 1754-1818 DcNCBi 1
**Benton,** Leonard D. 1939- WhoBlA 92
**Benton,** Louise White 1920- WhoEnt 92
**Benton,** Luther 1947- WhoBlA 92
**Benton,** Marjorie Craig 1933- WhoAmP 91
**Benton,** Michael Kenneth 1950- WhoMW 92
**Benton,** Nelkane O. 1935- WhoBlA 92
**Benton,** Nelson d1988 LesBEnT 92
**Benton,** Nicholas 1926- WhoEnt 92
**Benton,** Patricia 1907- IntAu&W 91
**Benton,** Peggie 1906- IntAu&W 91
**Benton,** Peter Faulkner 1934- IntWW 91, Who 92
**Benton,** Philip Eglin, Jr. 1928- WhoFI 92, WhoMW 92
**Benton,** Quinnie Etta 1898-1985 WhoBlA 92N
**Benton,** Richardson D 1914- WhoAmP 91
**Benton,** Robert 1932- IntDcF 2-2, IntMPA 92, WhoEnt 92
**Benton,** Robert Wilmer 1931- WhoRel 92, WhoWest 92
**Benton,** Samuel d1770 DcNCBi 1
**Benton,** Stephen Anthony 1941- AmMWSc 92
**Benton,** Thomas Hart 1782-1858 AmPolLe [port], BenetAL 91, DcNCBi 1
**Benton,** Thomas Hart 1889-1975 BenetAL 91, FacFETw
**Benton,** Thomas Iden 1946- WhoAmP 91
**Benton,** Will TwCWW 91
**Benton,** William J 1933- AmMWSc 92
**Benton,** William Pettigrew 1923- WhoFI 92
**Benton-Borghi,** Beatrice Hope 1946- WhoMW 92
**Benton Jones,** Simon W. F. Who 92
**Bentov,** Mordechai 1900- IntAu&W 91
**Bentrude,** Wesley George 1935- AmMWSc 92
**Bentsen,** Harry R. 1932- WhoIns 92
**Bentsen,** Lloyd 1921- AlmAP 92 [port], FacFETw
**Bentsen,** Lloyd Millard 1921- WhoAmP 91
**Bentsen,** Lloyd Millard, Jr. 1921- IntWW 91, Who 92
**Bentyne,** Cheryl WhoEnt 92
**Bentz,** Alan P 1927- AmMWSc 92
**Bentz,** Gregory Dean 1945- AmMWSc 92
**Bentz,** Ralph Wagner 1919- AmMWSc 92
**Bentz,** Warren Worthington 1926- WhoAmL 92
**Bentzel,** Carl Johan 1934- AmMWSc 92
**Bentzin,** Charles Gilbert 1932- WhoIns 92
**Bentzon,** Niels Viggo 1919- ConCom 92, IntWW 91
**Benuck,** Myron 1934- AmMWSc 92
**Benumof,** Reuben 1912- AmMWSc 92
**Benveniste,** Asa 1925- IntAu&W 91, WrDr 92
**Benveniste,** Jacob 1921- AmMWSc 92
**Benveniste,** Rachelle DrAPF 91
**Benvenisti,** Meron 1934- ConAu 35NR
**Benvenuto,** Emil Vincent 1931- WhoAmP 91
**Benvenuto,** Sergio, Sr. 1930- WhoHisp 92
**Benvenuto-Nichele,** Virginia Alison 1959- WhoHisp 92
**Beny,** Roloff 1924-1984 FacFETw
**Benya,** Anton 1912- IntWW 91
**Benyajati,** Siribhinya AmMWSc 92
**Benyard,** William B., Jr. 1948- WhoBlA 92
**Benyon,** John TwCSFW 91
**Benyon,** Thomas Yates 1942- Who 92
**Benyon,** William Richard 1930- Who 92
**Benyshek,** Larry L 1947- AmMWSc 92
**Benz,** Allen 1945- WhoWest 92
**Benz,** Dorothee Elisabeth 1965- WhoFI 92
**Benz,** Edmund Woodward 1911- AmMWSc 92
**Benz,** Edward John 1923- AmMWSc 92
**Benz,** Frederick W 1944- AmMWSc 92
**Benz,** George William 1922- AmMWSc 92
**Benz,** Karl 1844-1929 DcTwDes
**Benz,** M G 1935- AmMWSc 92
**Benz,** Rachel Berman 1963- WhoEnt 92
**Benz,** Richard 1884-1966 EncTR 91
**Benz,** Steven Frank 1960- WhoAmL 92
**Benz,** William Robert 1931- WhoAmP 91
**Benz,** Wolfgang 1932- AmMWSc 92
**Benzak,** Louis Richard 1939- WhoFI 92
**Benzaquen,** Moises 1952- WhoRel 92
**Benzecry,** Mario WhoEnt 92
**Benzeevi,** Benny Simon 1962- WhoWest 92
**Benzel,** William Marc 1953- WhoWest 92
**Benzell,** Mimi 1922-1970 NewAmDM
**Benzer,** Seymour 1921- AmMWSc 92, IntWW 91, WhoWest 92
**Benzi,** Roberto 1937- IntWW 91, WhoEnt 92
**Benzie,** William 1930- WrDr 92
**Benzien,** Christian Ludwig 1753-1811 DcNCBi 1
**Benziger,** Peter Hamilton 1926- WhoFI 92
**Benziger,** Theodore Michell 1922- AmMWSc 92
**Benzil,** Philip Stanley 1933- WhoAmP 91
**Benzing,** Cynthia Dell 1951- WhoFI 92
**Benzing,** David H 1937- AmMWSc 92
**Benzing,** David Warren 1953- WhoWest 92
**Benzing,** George, III 1926- AmMWSc 92
**Benzinger,** Harold Edward, Jr 1940- AmMWSc 92
**Benzinger,** James Robert 1922- AmMWSc 92
**Benzinger,** Rolf Hans 1935- AmMWSc 92
**Benzinger,** William Donald 1940- AmMWSc 92
**Benzle,** Curtis Munhall 1949- WhoMW 92
**Benzo,** Camillo Anthony 1942- AmMWSc 92
**Benzoni,** Girolamo 1519-1572 HisDSpE
**Benzor-Cox,** Betty WhoHisp 92
**Beougher,** Elton Earl 1940- AmMWSc 92, WhoMW 92
**Beozzo,** Sylvester Anthony 1952- WhoAmL 92
**Bepko,** Gerald Lewis 1940- WhoMW 92
**Bequette,** B Wayne 1957- AmMWSc 92
**Ber,** Andre Marie-Antoine 1920- IntAu&W 91
**Beral,** Harold 1939- WhoFI 92
**Berall,** Erik Dustin 1959- WhoRel 92
**Beran,** Andrew Nast 1958- WhoWest 92
**Beran,** Donald Wilmer 1935- AmMWSc 92
**Beran,** George Wesley 1928- AmMWSc 92, WhoMW 92
**Beran,** Jo Allan 1942- AmMWSc 92
**Beran,** Mark Jay 1930- AmMWSc 92
**Beran,** Robert Lynn 1943- AmMWSc 92
**Beran,** Rudolf Jaroslav Vaclav 1943- WhoWest 92
**Beranbaum,** Samuel Louis 1915- AmMWSc 92
**Beranek,** David T 1944- AmMWSc 92
**Beranek,** Leo Leroy 1914- AmMWSc 92
**Beranek,** William, Jr 1946- AmMWSc 92
**Beranger,** Clara 1886-1956 ReelWom
**Beranger,** Pierre Jean de 1780-1857 NinCLC 34 [port]
**Berard,** Andre 1940- WhoFI 92
**Berard,** Anthony D, Jr 1942- AmMWSc 92
**Berard,** Costan William 1932- AmMWSc 92
**Berard,** Michael F 1938- AmMWSc 92
**Berard,** Paul 1823-1905 ThHEIm
**Berardesco,** Michael Richard 1951- WhoFI 92
**Berardinelli,** Frank Michael 1920- AmMWSc 92
**Berardo,** Peter Antonio 1939- AmMWSc 92
**Beras Rojas,** Octavio Antonio 1906-1990 IntWW 91, -91N
**Berbano,** Marrino 1936- WhoWest 92
**Berbari,** Edward J 1949- AmMWSc 92
**Berbee,** John Gerard 1925- AmMWSc 92
**Berberet,** Grace Margaret 1915- WhoAmP 91
**Berberian,** Cathy 1925-1983 NewAmDM
**Berberian,** Paul Anthony 1945- AmMWSc 92

**Berberian**, Sterling Khazag 1926- *AmMWSc 92*
**Berberick**, James Andrew 1940- *WhoFI 92*
**Berberova**, Nina 1901- *LiExTwC*
**Berbit**, Warren Eric 1943- *WhoAmL 92*
**Berbrich**, Joan D. 1925- *WrDr 92*
**Bercaw**, Donald C 1930- *WhoAmP 91*
**Bercaw**, James Robert 1923- *AmMWSc 92*
**Bercaw**, John Edward 1944- *AmMWSc 92, WhoWest 92*
**Berch**, Julian 1916- *AmMWSc 92*
**Berch**, Rebecca White 1955- *WhoAmL 92*
**Berch**, William O. *ConAu 134*
**Berchem**, Douglas Martin 1951- *WhoFI 92*
**Berchem**, Robert Lee, Sr. 1941- *WhoAmL 92*
**Berchman**, Robert Michael 1951- *WhoRel 92*
**Berchowitz**, David Montague 1952- *WhoMW 92*
**Berchtold**, Glenn Allen 1932- *AmMWSc 92*
**Berck**, Cindy Jo 1963- *WhoFI 92*
**Berck**, Harry 1921- *WhoIns 92*
**Berckmans**, Prosper J A 1829?-1910 *BiInAmS*
**Bercot**, Pierre 1903- *IntWW 91*
**Bercov**, Ronald David 1937- *AmMWSc 92*
**Bercovici**, Eric *LesBEnT 92*
**Bercovici**, Konrad 1882-1961 *BenetAL 91*
**Bercovici**, Martin William 1942- *WhoAmL 92*
**Bercovitz**, Arden Bryan 1945- *AmMWSc 92*
**Bercq**, Alexis Claude 1960- *WhoWest 92*
**Berczi**, Istvan 1938- *AmMWSc 92*
**Berdahl**, Donald Richard 1954- *AmMWSc 92*
**Berdahl**, Paul Hilland 1945- *AmMWSc 92*
**Berdan**, Craig Randal 1964- *WhoFI 92*
**Berdan**, Jean Milton 1916- *AmMWSc 92*
**Berdanier**, Carolyn Dawson 1936- *AmMWSc 92*
**Berdell**, James Russell 1944- *WhoWest 92*
**Berdelle**, Richard Lee, Jr. 1953- *WhoAmL 92*
**Berdes**, Jane Louise Baldauf 1931- *WhoEnt 92*
**Berdick**, Leonard Stanley 1938- *WhoFI 92*
**Berdick**, Murray 1920- *AmMWSc 92*
**Berdrow**, Stanton K. 1928- *WhoFI 92, WhoWest 92*
**Berdyaev**, Nicolas 1874-1948 *DcEcMov*
**Berdyaev**, Nikolai Aleksandrovich 1874-1948 *FacFETw*
**Berdyaev**, Nikolai Alexandrovich 1874-1948 *LiExTwC*
**Bere**, James Frederick 1922- *WhoFI 92, WhoMW 92*
**Bere**, Rennie 1907- *IntAu&W 91*
**Bere**, Rennie Montague d1991 *Who 92N*
**Bere**, Rennie Montague 1907- *WrDr 92*
**Bere**, Richard L. *WhoFI 92*
**Berebitsky**, Michael Jay 1948- *WhoAmL 92*
**Berecek**, Kathleen Helen *AmMWSc 92*
**Beregovoy**, Georgiy Timofeyevich 1921- *IntWW 91*
**Beregovoy**, Georgy 1921- *FacFETw*
**Beregovoy**, Pierre 1925- *Who 92*
**Beregovoy**, Pierre Eugene 1925- *IntWW 91*
**Berek**, Jonathan S 1948- *AmMWSc 92*
**Berella**, Henry *WhoHisp 92*
**Bereman**, Robert Deane 1943- *AmMWSc 92*
**Beren**, Joel Stuart 1957- *WhoFI 92, WhoMW 92*
**Beren**, Sheldon *WhoRel 92*
**Beren**, Sheldon Kuciel 1922- *AmMWSc 92*
**Berenato**, Mark Anthony 1958- *WhoAmL 92*
**Berenbaum**, May Roberta 1953- *AmMWSc 92*
**Berenbaum**, Morris Benjamin 1924- *AmMWSc 92*
**Berenberg**, Danny Bob 1944- *WhoMW 92*
**Berenberg**, William 1915- *AmMWSc 92*
**Berenblum**, Isaac 1903- *IntWW 91*
**Berenbom**, Max 1919- *AmMWSc 92*
**Berend**, Alice 1878-1938 *EncTR 91*
**Berend**, Robert William 1931- *WhoAmL 92*
**Berend**, T. Ivan 1930- *IntWW 91*
**Berendes**, Heinz Werner 1925- *AmMWSc 92*
**Berendonck**, Gerd 1924- *IntWW 91*
**Berendsen**, Peter Barney 1937- *AmMWSc 92*
**Berendsohn**, Walter A 1884-1984? *ConAu 34NR*
**Berendzen**, Richard 1938- *AmMWSc 92*
**Berendzen**, Richard Earl 1938- *WhoEnt 92*
**Berengaria of Navarre** 1172?-1230? *EncAmaz 91*
**Berenger**, Paul Raymond 1945- *IntWW 91*
**Berenger**, Tom 1950- *ConTFT 9, IntMPA 92*
**Berenguer**, Amanda 1922- *ConSpAP*
**Berenguer**, Ana Helena *WhoEnt 92*
**Berenguer**, Elba F. 1940- *WhoHisp 92*
**Berenguer**, Juan Bautista 1954- *WhoHisp 92*
**Berenguer y Fueste**, Damaso 1873-1953 *HisDSpE*
**Berenholtz**, Jim 1957- *WhoEnt 92*
**Berenice I** *EncAmaz 91*
**Berenice II of Cyrene** 273BC-245?BC *EncAmaz 91*
**Berens**, Alan Paul 1934- *AmMWSc 92*
**Berens**, Alan Robert 1925- *AmMWSc 92*
**Berens**, Mark H. 1928- *WhoIns 92*
**Berens**, Mark Harry 1928- *WhoAmL 92*
**Berens**, Randolph Lee 1943- *AmMWSc 92*
**Berens**, William Joseph 1952- *WhoAmL 92*
**Berens-Totenohl**, Josefa 1891-1969 *EncTR 91*
**Berensohn**, Roger 1933- *WhoHisp 92*
**Berenson**, Bernard 1865-1959 *BenetAL 91, FacFETw*
**Berenson**, Gerald Sanders 1922- *AmMWSc 92*
**Berenson**, Malcolm Mark *AmMWSc 92*
**Berenson**, Marisa 1947- *IntMPA 92*
**Berenson**, Paul Stewart 1944- *WhoEnt 92*
**Berenson**, Robert Leonard 1939- *WhoFI 92*
**Berenson**, William Keith 1954- *WhoAmL 92*
**Berenstain**, Jan 1923- *ConAu 36NR*
**Berenstain**, Michael 1951- *ConAu 36NR*
**Berenstain**, Stan 1923- *ConAu 36NR*
**Berenstein**, Marvin Stuart 1936- *WhoAmL 92*
**Berent**, Stanley 1941- *AmMWSc 92*
**Berentsen**, Kurtis George 1953- *WhoEnt 92, WhoWest 92*
**Berenzweig**, Jack Charles 1942- *WhoAmL 92*
**Berenzy**, Alix 1957- *ConAu 133, SmATA 65 [port]*
**Bereola**, Enitan Olu 1947- *WhoBlA 92*
**Bereolos**, Demetrius Theodore 1954- *WhoAmL 92*
**Berera**, Geetha Poonacha *AmMWSc 92*
**Beres**, John Joseph 1947- *AmMWSc 92*
**Beres**, Kenneth David 1931- *WhoRel 92*
**Beres**, Larry A. 1946- *WhoFI 92*
**Beres**, Mary Elizabeth 1942- *WhoFI 92*
**Beres**, Michael John 1950- *WhoMW 92*
**Beres**, William Philip 1936- *AmMWSc 92, WhoMW 92*
**Beresford** *Who 92*
**Beresford**, Alexander Paul 1946- *Who 92*
**Beresford**, Anne 1929- *ConPo 91, WrDr 92*
**Beresford**, Anne Ellen Hamburger 1928- *IntAu&W 91*
**Beresford**, Bruce 1940- *IntDcF 2-2, IntMPA 92, IntWW 91, WhoEnt 92*
**Beresford**, Douglas Lincoln 1956- *WhoAmL 92*
**Beresford**, Elisabeth *IntAu&W 91, WrDr 92*
**Beresford**, Frank Ernest 1881-1967 *TwCPaSc*
**Beresford**, J D 1873-1947 *ScFEYrs, TwCSFW 91*
**Beresford**, Leslie *ScFEYrs*
**Beresford**, Maurice 1920- *WrDr 92*
**Beresford**, Maurice Warwick 1920- *Who 92*
**Beresford**, Meg 1937- *IntWW 91, Who 92*
**Beresford**, Richard 1930- *WhoAmL 92*
**Beresford**, William Anthony 1936- *AmMWSc 92*
**Beresford-Howe**, Constance 1922- *WrDr 92*
**Beresford-Howe**, Constance Elizabeth 1922- *IntAu&W 91*
**Beresford-Peirse**, Henry Grant de la Poer 1933- *Who 92*
**Beresford-West**, Michael Charles 1928- *Who 92*
**Beresheim**, James T. 1948- *WhoMW 92*
**Beresniewicz**, Aleksander 1927- *AmMWSc 92*
**Beresovsky**, Boris 1969- *IntWW 91*
**Berestecki**, Philip P. 1944- *WhoAmL 92*
**Bereston**, Eugene Sydney 1914- *AmMWSc 92*
**Berestynski**, Adam S. 1927- *WhoWest 92*
**Berets**, Donald Joseph 1926- *AmMWSc 92*
**Beretta**, Giordano Bruno 1951- *WhoWest 92*
**Beretz**, Paul Basil 1938- *WhoFI 92, WhoWest 92*
**Bereuter**, Doug 1939- *AlmAP 92 [port]*
**Bereuter**, Douglas K 1939- *WhoAmP 91*
**Bereuter**, Douglas Kent 1939- *WhoMW 92*
**Berezin**, Alec 1947- *WhoAmL 92*
**Berezin**, Alexander A 1944- *AmMWSc 92*
**Berezin**, Harold Stephen 1955- *WhoAmL 92*
**Berezin**, Tanya Harriet 1941- *WhoEnt 92*
**Berezney**, Ronald 1943- *AmMWSc 92*
**Bereznoff**, Gregory Michael 1951- *WhoAmL 92*
**Berfield**, Morton Lang 1933- *WhoAmL 92*
**Berg**, A Scott 1949- *IntAu&W 91, WrDr 92*
**Berg**, Adrian 1929- *IntWW 91, TwCPaSc*
**Berg**, Aksel Ivanovich 1893-1979 *FacFETw*
**Berg**, Alban 1885-1935 *FacFETw, NewAmDM*
**Berg**, Andrew N. 1952- *WhoAmL 92*
**Berg**, Arthur R 1937- *AmMWSc 92*
**Berg**, Benjamin Nathan 1897- *AmMWSc 92*
**Berg**, Bernard 1931- *IntWW 91*
**Berg**, Carl John, Jr 1944- *AmMWSc 92*
**Berg**, Carolyn Nourse 1938- *WhoWest 92*
**Berg**, Charles A 1927- *WhoAmP 91*
**Berg**, Charles Ramirez 1947- *WhoHisp 92*
**Berg**, Christian 1944- *IntWW 91*
**Berg**, Claire M 1937- *AmMWSc 92*
**Berg**, Clyde C 1936- *AmMWSc 92*
**Berg**, Clyde H O 1915- *AmMWSc 92*
**Berg**, Dana B 1921- *AmMWSc 92*
**Berg**, Daniel 1929- *AmMWSc 92*
**Berg**, Dave 1920- *WrDr 92*
**Berg**, Dave 1948- *WhoWest 92*
**Berg**, David 1920- *IntAu&W 91*
**Berg**, David Howard 1942- *WhoAmL 92*
**Berg**, Dick *IntMPA 92*
**Berg**, Eduard 1928- *AmMWSc 92*
**Berg**, Eivinn 1931- *IntWW 91*
**Berg**, Eric Lennart 1956- *WhoAmL 92*
**Berg**, Eric Wilhelm 1921- *WhoAmP 91*
**Berg**, Eugene Walter 1926- *AmMWSc 92*
**Berg**, Evelynne Marie *WhoMW 92*
**Berg**, Frederick John 1956- *WhoMW 92*
**Berg**, George G 1919- *AmMWSc 92*
**Berg**, Gerald 1928- *AmMWSc 92*
**Berg**, Gertrude d1966 *LesBEnT 92*
**Berg**, Gordon 1927- *WhoAmP 91*
**Berg**, Gordon Hercher 1937- *WhoFI 92*
**Berg**, Gunnar Johannes 1930- *AmMWSc 92*
**Berg**, Hans Fredrik 1936- *WhoAmL 92*
**Berg**, Harry K 1943- *WhoAmP 91*
**Berg**, Helen MacDuffee 1932- *WhoWest 92*
**Berg**, Henry Clay 1929- *AmMWSc 92*
**Berg**, Howard Curtis 1934- *AmMWSc 92*
**Berg**, Howard Martin 1942- *AmMWSc 92*
**Berg**, Ian 1932- *IntAu&W 91*
**Berg**, Ira David 1931- *AmMWSc 92*
**Berg**, J Robert 1915- *AmMWSc 92*
**Berg**, James Irving 1940- *AmMWSc 92*
**Berg**, Jean Horton 1913- *IntAu&W 91*
**Berg**, Jean Stewart 1934- *WhoMW 92, WhoRel 92*
**Berg**, Jeff 1947- *IntMPA 92*
**Berg**, Jeffrey Howard 1943- *AmMWSc 92*
**Berg**, Jeffrey Spencer 1947- *WhoEnt 92*
**Berg**, John Calvin 1937- *AmMWSc 92*
**Berg**, John J. *Who 92*
**Berg**, John Richard 1932- *AmMWSc 92*
**Berg**, John Thomas 1961- *WhoWest 92*
**Berg**, Jonathan Albert 1943- *WhoFI 92*
**Berg**, Jonathan H 1947- *AmMWSc 92*
**Berg**, Jonathan Henry 1947- *WhoMW 92*
**Berg**, Joseph Wilbur, Jr 1920- *AmMWSc 92*
**Berg**, Kimberly *DrAPF 91*
**Berg**, Knut 1925- *IntWW 91*
**Berg**, Lawrence Andrew 1937- *WhoMW 92*
**Berg**, Lee Michael 1948- *WhoFI 92*
**Berg**, Leila 1917- *WrDr 92*
**Berg**, Leila Rita 1917- *IntAu&W 91*
**Berg**, Lev Semenovich 1876-1950 *SovUnBD*
**Berg**, Linda Lee 1955- *WhoRel 92*
**Berg**, Lloyd 1914- *AmMWSc 92*
**Berg**, Lloyd Olin 1953- *WhoEnt 92*
**Berg**, Lonette Lamb 1958- *WhoAmL 92*
**Berg**, M 1921- *AmMWSc 92*
**Berg**, Marie Hirsch 1909- *AmMWSc 92*
**Berg**, Marie Majella 1916- *WhoRel 92*
**Berg**, Marjorie Ann 1935- *WhoWest 92*
**Berg**, Mark Alan 1958- *AmMWSc 92*
**Berg**, Michael Clemens 1935- *WhoMW 92*
**Berg**, Myles Renver 1932- *AmMWSc 92*
**Berg**, Norman J *AmMWSc 92*
**Berg**, Patty 1918- *FacFETw*
**Berg**, Paul 1926- *AmMWSc 92, IntWW 91, Who 92, WhoNob 90, WhoWest 92*
**Berg**, Paul Edward 1941- *WhoFI 92*
**Berg**, Paul Walter 1925- *AmMWSc 92*
**Berg**, Randall Challen, Jr. 1949- *WhoAmL 92*
**Berg**, Regena May 1923- *WhoAmP 91*
**Berg**, Richard A 1945- *AmMWSc 92*
**Berg**, Richard Allen 1942- *AmMWSc 92*
**Berg**, Richard Blake 1937- *AmMWSc 92*
**Berg**, Richard Harold 1937- *AmMWSc 92*
**Berg**, Richard Roland 1947- *WhoRel 92*
**Berg**, Rick A 1959- *WhoAmP 91*
**Berg**, Robert Jeffrey 1957- *WhoAmL 92*
**Berg**, Robert R 1924- *AmMWSc 92*
**Berg**, Robert W 1917- *AmMWSc 92*
**Berg**, Robert Warren, Jr. 1954- *WhoRel 92*
**Berg**, Robert William 1963- *WhoFI 92*
**Berg**, Roger Langton 1935- *WhoMW 92*
**Berg**, Roy Torgny 1927- *AmMWSc 92*
**Berg**, Sandra 1947- *WhoAmP 91*
**Berg**, Sandra Irene 1953- *WhoEnt 92*
**Berg**, Stanton Oneal 1928- *WhoFI 92, WhoMW 92*
**Berg**, Stephen *DrAPF 91*
**Berg**, Stephen 1934- *ConPo 91, WrDr 92*
**Berg**, Stephen Warren 1948- *WhoFI 92*
**Berg**, Steven Paul 1948- *AmMWSc 92*
**Berg**, Tab Aaron 1964- *WhoWest 92*
**Berg**, Teodor Sodergren 1939- *WhoWest 92*
**Berg**, Tom 1943- *WhoWest 92*
**Berg**, Virginia Marie 1932- *WhoAmP 91*
**Berg**, Virginia Seymour 1948- *AmMWSc 92*
**Berg**, Walter Gilman 1858-1908 *BiInAmS*
**Berg**, William Albert 1930- *AmMWSc 92*
**Berg**, William Eugene 1918- *AmMWSc 92*
**Berg**, William James 1942- *WhoMW 92*
**Berg**, William Keith 1943- *AmMWSc 92*
**Berg-Johnson**, Karen Ann 1959- *WhoMW 92*
**Bergalis**, Kimberly d1991 *NewYTBS 91 [port]*
**Bergamo**, Ron *WhoEnt 92*
**Bergan**, Edmund Paul, Jr. 1950- *WhoFI 92*
**Bergan**, William Luke 1939- *WhoAmL 92*
**Bergano y Villegas**, Simon 1781-1828 *HisDSpE*
**Bergansky**, Suzanne M *WhoAmP 91*
**Berganza**, Teresa *Who 92*
**Berganza**, Teresa 1935- *IntWW 91, NewAmDM, WhoEnt 92*
**Bergasse**, Nicolas 1750-1832 *BlkwCEP*
**Bergau**, Frank Conrad 1926- *WhoFI 92*
**Bergbreiter**, David Edward 1948- *AmMWSc 92*
**Bergdall**, Obera Jean 1929- *WhoAmP 91*
**Bergdoll**, Merlin Scott 1916- *AmMWSc 92*
**Bergdolt**, Vollmar Edgar 1918- *AmMWSc 92*
**Berge**, Carol *DrAPF 91*
**Berge**, Carol 1928- *ConPo 91, WrDr 92*
**Berge**, Douglas G 1938- *AmMWSc 92*
**Berge**, Gunnar 1940- *IntWW 91*
**Berge**, Hans Cornelis ten 1938- *IntAu&W 91*
**Berge**, John Williston 1930- *AmMWSc 92*
**Berge**, Jon Peter 1935- *AmMWSc 92*
**Berge**, Kenneth G 1926- *AmMWSc 92*
**Berge**, Pierre 1930- *WhoFI 92*
**Berge**, Pierre Vital Georges 1930- *IntWW 91*
**Berge**, Robert Allen 1952- *WhoMW 92*
**Berge**, Trygve O *AmMWSc 92*
**Bergee**, Harold Ellet 1931- *WhoMW 92*
**Bergel**, Hans 1925- *IntAu&W 91*
**Bergeland**, Martin E 1935- *AmMWSc 92*
**Bergeland**, Nathan Daniel 1958- *WhoFI 92*
**Bergelin**, Olaf P 1911- *AmMWSc 92*
**Bergeman**, Thomas H 1933- *AmMWSc 92*
**Bergen**, Bruce Harry 1955- *WhoAmL 92*
**Bergen**, Candice 1946- *IntMPA 92, WhoEnt 92, WrDr 92*
**Bergen**, Candice Patricia 1946- *IntWW 91*
**Bergen**, Catharine Mary 1912- *AmMWSc 92*
**Bergen**, Charles S. 1955- *WhoAmL 92*
**Bergen**, Christopher Brooke 1949- *WhoWest 92*
**Bergen**, D. Thomas 1930- *WhoFI 92*
**Bergen**, Donna Catherine 1945- *AmMWSc 92*
**Bergen**, Edgar d1978 *LesBEnT 92*
**Bergen**, Edgar 1903-1978 *FacFETw*
**Bergen**, Eric Lincoln 1960- *WhoFI 92*
**Bergen**, G. S. Peter 1936- *WhoAmL 92*
**Bergen**, Gerald Roy 1933- *WhoMW 92*
**Bergen**, James David 1932- *AmMWSc 92*
**Bergen**, Jeffrey Marc 1955- *WhoMW 92*
**Bergen**, John Thomas 1953- *WhoMW 92*
**Bergen**, Joseph Young 1851-1917 *BiInAmS*
**Bergen**, Lawrence *AmMWSc 92*
**Bergen**, Margarita 1946- *WhoHisp 92*
**Bergen**, Polly *WhoEnt 92*
**Bergen**, Polly 1930- *IntMPA 92*
**Bergen**, Robert Dale 1954- *WhoRel 92*
**Bergen**, Robert Ludlum, Jr 1929- *AmMWSc 92*
**Bergen**, Stanley S, Jr 1929- *AmMWSc 92*
**Bergen**, Werner Gerhard 1943- *AmMWSc 92, WhoMW 92*
**Bergen**, William Benjamin 1915- *IntWW 91*
**Bergenback**, Richard Edward 1926- *AmMWSc 92*
**Bergendahl**, Maximilian Hilmar 1921- *AmMWSc 92*
**Bergendoff**, Conrad John Immanuel 1895- *WhoRel 92*
**Bergenfeld**, Nathan *DrAPF 91*
**Bergengruen**, Werner 1892-1962 *LiExTwC*
**Bergengruen**, Werner 1892-1964 *EncTR 91 [port]*
**Bergenstrom**, Stig Gullmar 1909- *IntWW 91*

**Berger**, A. Fred 1934- *WhoAmL 92*
**Berger**, Alan Eric 1946- *AmMWSc 92*
**Berger**, Alan I. 1933- *WhoAmL 92*
**Berger**, Alan Lewis 1939- *WhoRel 92*
**Berger**, Albert Jeffrey 1943- *AmMWSc 92*
**Berger**, Andrew John 1915- *AmMWSc 92*
**Berger**, Andrew L. 1946- *WhoFI 92*
**Berger**, Andrew Robert 1955- *WhoAmL 92*
**Berger**, Ann Elizabeth *AmMWSc 92*
**Berger**, Arion 1965- *WhoEnt 92*
**Berger**, Arthur 1912- *NewAmDM*
**Berger**, Arthur A 1933- *IntAu&W 91, WrDr 92*
**Berger**, Arthur Asa 1933- *WhoEnt 92*
**Berger**, Arthur Victor 1912- *WhoEnt 92*
**Berger**, Bernard Ben 1912- *AmMWSc 92*
**Berger**, Beverly Jane 1939- *AmMWSc 92*
**Berger**, Beverly Kobre 1946- *AmMWSc 92*
**Berger**, Bruce *DrAPF 91*
**Berger**, Bruce 1938- *WrDr 92*
**Berger**, Bruce Jeffrey 1950- *WhoAmL 92*
**Berger**, Bruce Keith 1946- *WhoMW 92*
**Berger**, Bruce S 1932- *AmMWSc 92*
**Berger**, Byron Roland 1944- *AmMWSc 92*
**Berger**, Charles Lee 1947- *WhoAmL 92*
**Berger**, Charles W 1936- *WhoAmP 91*
**Berger**, Curtis Jay 1926- *WhoAmL 92*
**Berger**, Daniel Lawrence 1954- *WhoAmL 92*
**Berger**, Daniel Richard 1933- *AmMWSc 92*
**Berger**, Daniel S 1923- *AmMWSc 92*
**Berger**, David 1912- *WhoAmL 92*
**Berger**, David G. *WhoRel 92*
**Berger**, David Joseph 1954- *WhoAmP 91*
**Berger**, Diane DeWoskin 1963- *WhoMW 92*
**Berger**, Diane Klein 1946- *WhoWest 92*
**Berger**, Edmond Louis 1939- *AmMWSc 92*
**Berger**, Edward Alan 1948- *AmMWSc 92*
**Berger**, Edward B. 1929- *WhoAmL 92*
**Berger**, Edward Michael 1944- *AmMWSc 92*
**Berger**, Erna 1900-1990 *FacFETw*
**Berger**, Eugenia Hepworth 1925- *WhoWest 92*
**Berger**, Francine Ellis 1949- *WhoEnt 92*
**Berger**, Frank Milan 1913- *AmMWSc 92*
**Berger**, Frank Stanley 1936- *WhoFI 92*
**Berger**, Franklin Gordon 1947- *AmMWSc 92*
**Berger**, Fredericka Nolde 1932- *WhoRel 92*
**Berger**, Geoffrey Leslie 1958- *WhoFI 92*
**Berger**, George 1936- *WhoAmL 92*
**Berger**, George John 1944- *WhoAmL 92*
**Berger**, Gilda 1935- *ConAu 134*
**Berger**, Gottfried O. 1924- *WhoIns 92*
**Berger**, Gottlob 1896-1975 *BiDExR, EncTR 91 [port]*
**Berger**, Harold 1925- *WhoAmL 92, WhoFI 92*
**Berger**, Harold 1926- *AmMWSc 92*
**Berger**, Harold 1927- *AmMWSc 92*
**Berger**, Harold D 1921- *WhoAmP 91*
**Berger**, Harold Phillip 1947- *WhoAmL 92*
**Berger**, Harvey J 1950- *AmMWSc 92*
**Berger**, Helmut 1942- *IntMPA 92, IntWW 91*
**Berger**, Howard Martin 1927- *WhoWest 92*
**Berger**, Jacques 1934- *AmMWSc 92*
**Berger**, James Charles 1941- *WhoFI 92*
**Berger**, James Dennis 1942- *AmMWSc 92*
**Berger**, James Edward 1935- *AmMWSc 92*
**Berger**, Jan Paul 1955- *WhoFI 92*
**Berger**, Jay Manton 1927- *AmMWSc 92*
**Berger**, Jay Vari 1944- *WhoWest 92*
**Berger**, Jean 1909- *NewAmDM*
**Berger**, Jerry Eugene 1933- *AmMWSc 92*
**Berger**, Joel Gilbert 1937- *AmMWSc 92*
**Berger**, John 1926- *ConNov 91, IntAu&W 91, IntWW 91, RfGEnL 91, Who 92, WrDr 92*
**Berger**, John Peter 1926- *FacFETw*
**Berger**, John Torrey, Jr. 1938- *WhoAmL 92*
**Berger**, Josef 1940- *AmMWSc 92*
**Berger**, Judith Ann 1947- *WhoMW 92*
**Berger**, Kenneth Walter 1924- *AmMWSc 92*
**Berger**, L E *WhoAmP 91*
**Berger**, Lance Allen 1943- *WhoFI 92*
**Berger**, Lawrence 1926- *AmMWSc 92*
**Berger**, Lawrence Howard 1947- *WhoAmL 92*
**Berger**, Leland Roger 1956- *WhoAmL 92*
**Berger**, Leo *WhoAmP 91*
**Berger**, Leslie Ralph 1928- *AmMWSc 92*
**Berger**, Luc 1933- *AmMWSc 92*
**Berger**, Marilyn *LesBEnT 92*
**Berger**, Martin 1926- *AmMWSc 92*
**Berger**, Martin Jacob 1922- *AmMWSc 92*
**Berger**, Maurice 1927- *WhoEnt 92*
**Berger**, Maxon Alexander 1946- *WhoEnt 92*
**Berger**, Melvin 1950- *AmMWSc 92*
**Berger**, Melvin Gerald 1943- *WhoAmL 92*
**Berger**, Melvyn Stuart 1939- *AmMWSc 92*
**Berger**, Meyer 1912- *WhoAmP 91*
**Berger**, Michael Harvey 1950- *WhoAmL 92*
**Berger**, Miles Lee 1930- *WhoMW 92*
**Berger**, Miriam Roskin 1934- *WhoEnt 92*
**Berger**, Mitchell Harvey 1949- *AmMWSc 92*
**Berger**, Neal Jeffrey 1952- *WhoAmP 91*
**Berger**, Neil Everett 1942- *AmMWSc 92*
**Berger**, Newell James, Jr. 1926- *WhoWest 92*
**Berger**, Pat Patricia Eve 1929- *WhoWest 92*
**Berger**, Paul Raymond 1963- *AmMWSc 92*
**Berger**, Peter 1925- *Who 92*
**Berger**, Peter Ludwig 1929- *WhoRel 92*
**Berger**, Phil *WhoEnt 92*
**Berger**, Philip Jeffrey 1943- *AmMWSc 92*
**Berger**, Philmore 1927- *WhoRel 92*
**Berger**, Ralph Francis 1951- *WhoMW 92*
**Berger**, Ralph Jacob 1937- *AmMWSc 92*
**Berger**, Richard Donald 1934- *AmMWSc 92*
**Berger**, Richard L. 1939- *IntMPA 92*
**Berger**, Richard Lee 1935- *AmMWSc 92*
**Berger**, Richard Leo 1944- *AmMWSc 92*
**Berger**, Richard S 1929- *AmMWSc 92*
**Berger**, Rick 1958- *WhoEnt 92*
**Berger**, Robert *LesBEnT 92*
**Berger**, Robert 1938- *AmMWSc 92*
**Berger**, Robert Bertram 1924- *WhoAmL 92*
**Berger**, Robert Elliott 1947- *AmMWSc 92*
**Berger**, Robert Glenn 1954- *WhoFI 92*
**Berger**, Robert Lewis 1925- *AmMWSc 92*
**Berger**, Robert Michael 1942- *WhoAmL 92*
**Berger**, Robert S 1933- *AmMWSc 92*
**Berger**, S Edmund 1922- *AmMWSc 92*
**Berger**, Selman A 1942- *AmMWSc 92*
**Berger**, Shelby Louise 1941- *AmMWSc 92*
**Berger**, Sheldon 1928- *AmMWSc 92*
**Berger**, Stanley A 1934- *AmMWSc 92*
**Berger**, Stephen 1939- *WhoFI 92*
**Berger**, Steven Barry 1946- *AmMWSc 92*
**Berger**, Steven R. 1945- *WhoAmL 92*
**Berger**, Stuart David 1943- *WhoMW 92*
**Berger**, Susan May Collins 1952- *WhoAmL 92*
**Berger**, Suzanne E. *DrAPF 91*
**Berger**, Terry 1933- *IntAu&W 91*
**Berger**, Thomas 1924- *BenetAL 91, ConNov 91, TwCWW 91, WrDr 92*
**Berger**, Thomas Robert 1941- *WhoMW 92*
**Berger**, Toby 1940- *AmMWSc 92*
**Berger**, Victor Louis 1860-1929 *AmPolLe*
**Berger**, Vivian Olivia 1944- *WhoAmL 92*
**Berger**, Wilhelm Georg 1929- *IntWW 91*
**Berger**, William Ernest 1918- *WhoFI 92*
**Berger**, William J 1921- *AmMWSc 92*
**Berger**, Wolfgang H. 1937- *WhoWest 92*
**Berger**, Wolfgang Helmut 1937- *AmMWSc 92*
**Bergerac**, Jacques 1927- *IntMPA 92*
**Bergeret**, Albert Hamilton 1948- *WhoEnt 92*
**Bergeron**, Andre Louis 1922- *IntWW 91*
**Bergeron**, Belvin Francis 1924- *WhoAmP 91*
**Bergeron**, Clifton George 1925- *AmMWSc 92, WhoMW 92*
**Bergeron**, Clyde J, Jr 1932- *AmMWSc 92*
**Bergeron**, Earleen Fournet 1938- *WhoEnt 92*
**Bergeron**, Georges Albert 1916- *AmMWSc 92*
**Bergeron**, Jeffrey David 1953- *WhoMW 92*
**Bergeron**, John Albert 1929- *AmMWSc 92*
**Bergeron**, John Joseph Marcel 1946- *AmMWSc 92*
**Bergeron**, Kenneth Donald 1946- *AmMWSc 92*
**Bergeron**, Louis E. 1934- *WhoIns 92*
**Bergeron**, Michel *AmMWSc 92*
**Bergeron**, Robert F, Jr 1942- *AmMWSc 92*
**Bergersen**, Fraser John 1929- *IntWW 91, Who 92*
**Bergerson**, David Raymond 1939- *WhoAmL 92, WhoFI 92*
**Bergerud**, Vivian Grotte 1923- *WhoAmP 91*
**Bergery**, Gaston Frank 1892-1974 *BiDExR*
**Berges**, David Alan 1941- *AmMWSc 92*
**Berges**, Ronald Ray 1959- *WhoMW 92*
**Bergeson**, Debra JoAnn 1951- *WhoRel 92*
**Bergeson**, Haven Eldred 1933- *AmMWSc 92*
**Bergeson**, John Henning 1919- *WhoRel 92, WhoWest 92*
**Bergeson**, Marian 1927- *WhoAmP 91*
**Bergevin**, Louis W 1922- *WhoAmP 91*
**Bergey**, Gregory Kent 1949- *AmMWSc 92*
**Bergey**, James L 1945- *AmMWSc 92*
**Bergford**, James W. *WhoFI 92*
**Berggol'ts**, Ol'ga Fedorovna 1910-1975 *SovUnBD*
**Berggren**, Bo Erik Gunnar 1936- *IntWW 91*
**Berggren**, Gerard Thomas, Jr 1946- *AmMWSc 92*
**Berggren**, Michael J 1939- *AmMWSc 92*
**Berggren**, Paul Walter 1922- *WhoRel 92*
**Berggren**, Ronald B 1931- *AmMWSc 92*
**Berggren**, Ronald Bernard 1931- *WhoMW 92*
**Berggren**, Thommy 1937- *IntWW 91*
**Berggren**, William Alfred 1931- *AmMWSc 92*
**Bergh**, Arpad A 1930- *AmMWSc 92*
**Bergh**, Berthold Orphie 1925- *AmMWSc 92*
**Bergh**, Birger 1925- *IntWW 91*
**Bergh**, David Morgan 1947- *WhoWest 92*
**Bergh**, Donald Charles 1945- *WhoWest 92*
**Berghahn**, Volker R. 1938- *WrDr 92*
**Berghash**, Rachel *DrAPF 91*
**Berghaus**, Ruth 1927- *IntWW 91*
**Berghoefer**, Fred G 1921- *AmMWSc 92*
**Berghoefer**, Fred George 1921- *WhoAmP 91*
**Berghof**, Herbert 1909-1990 *AnObit 1990, FacFETw*
**Berghold**, Joseph Philip 1938- *WhoFI 92*
**Bergholz**, George Frederick 1963- *WhoMW 92*
**Bergholz**, Julie Lynn 1958- *WhoEnt 92*
**Berghuis**, Peter Lange 1951- *WhoWest 92*
**Berghuser**, Hugo 1935- *Who 92*
**Bergin**, Edward Daniel 1943- *WhoAmP 91*
**Bergin**, John Francis 1924- *WhoFI 92*
**Bergin**, Marion Joseph 1927- *AmMWSc 92*
**Bergin**, Thomas F. 1924- *WhoAmL 92*
**Bergius**, Friedrich Karl Rudolph 1884-1949 *WhoNob 90*
**Bergjans**, Lucy Ellen 1927- *WhoMW 92*
**Bergland**, Robert Selmer 1928- *IntWW 91*
**Berglas**, Frank E. 1940- *WhoIns 92*
**Bergle**, Kenneth Charles 1956- *WhoEnt 92*
**Bergleitner**, George Charles, Jr. 1935- *WhoFI 92*
**Bergles**, Arthur E 1935- *AmMWSc 92*
**Berglin**, Linda L 1944- *WhoAmP 91*
**Berglund**, Brian Winston 1956- *WhoAmL 92*
**Berglund**, Carl Neil 1938- *AmMWSc 92*
**Berglund**, Larry Glenn 1938- *AmMWSc 92*
**Berglund**, Paavo Allan Engelbert 1929- *IntWW 91, WhoEnt 92*
**Berglund**, Sharon Marie 1956- *WhoMW 92*
**Bergman**, Abraham 1932- *AmMWSc 92*
**Bergman**, Alan *IntMPA 92, WhoEnt 92*
**Bergman**, Andrew 1945- *IntMPA 92, WhoEnt 92*
**Bergman**, Barry 1944- *WhoEnt 92*
**Bergman**, Bradley Anthony 1953- *WhoMW 92*
**Bergman**, Bruce Jeffrey 1944- *WhoFI 92*
**Bergman**, Charles Carroll 1932- *WhoWest 92*
**Bergman**, Charles Emmett 1924- *WhoFI 92*
**Bergman**, David *DrAPF 91*
**Bergman**, David Clinton 1957- *WhoMW 92*
**Bergman**, Denise *DrAPF 91*
**Bergman**, Edward, III 1954- *WhoAmL 92*
**Bergman**, Elliot 1930- *AmMWSc 92*
**Bergman**, Emmett Norlin 1929- *AmMWSc 92*
**Bergman**, Erik 1911- *ConCom 92*
**Bergman**, Ernest L 1922- *AmMWSc 92*
**Bergman**, Ernst Ingmar 1918- *Who 92*
**Bergman**, Eugene 1930- *ConAu 135*
**Bergman**, Fred Wayne 1953- *WhoMW 92*
**Bergman**, Hannah E. 1925-1981 *ConAu 135*
**Bergman**, Harlan W. 1932- *WhoIns 92*
**Bergman**, Harold Lee 1941- *AmMWSc 92*
**Bergman**, Heidi Suzanne 1958- *WhoEnt 92*
**Bergman**, Hyman Chaim 1905- *AmMWSc 92*
**Bergman**, Ingmar *Who 92*
**Bergman**, Ingmar 1918- *FacFETw [port], IntDcF 2-2 [port], IntMPA 92, IntWW 91, WhoEnt 92*
**Bergman**, Ingrid 1915-1982 *FacFETw*
**Bergman**, Janet Louise 1920- *WhoEnt 92*
**Bergman**, Jerry Rae 1946- *WhoMW 92*
**Bergman**, John *WhoRel 92*
**Bergman**, Judson Taft 1957- *WhoFI 92*
**Bergman**, Jules d1988 *LesBEnT 92*
**Bergman**, Kenneth David 1949- *AmMWSc 92*
**Bergman**, Kenneth Harris 1935- *AmMWSc 92*
**Bergman**, Klaus 1931- *WhoFI 92*
**Bergman**, Marilyn *IntMPA 92*
**Bergman**, Marilyn Keith *WhoEnt 92*
**Bergman**, Mark Steven 1956- *WhoAmL 92*
**Bergman**, Moe 1916- *AmMWSc 92*
**Bergman**, Norman 1926- *AmMWSc 92*
**Bergman**, Paul Bruce 1943- *WhoAmL 92*
**Bergman**, Peter Jay 1944- *WhoEnt 92*
**Bergman**, Ray E 1928- *AmMWSc 92*
**Bergman**, Richard N 1944- *AmMWSc 92*
**Bergman**, Robert 1931- *AmMWSc 92*
**Bergman**, Robert Aaron 1928- *WhoWest 92*
**Bergman**, Robert Clayton 1935- *WhoEnt 92*
**Bergman**, Robert George 1942- *AmMWSc 92*
**Bergman**, Robert Ira 1954- *WhoAmL 92*
**Bergman**, Robert K 1934- *AmMWSc 92*
**Bergman**, Ronald Arly 1927- *AmMWSc 92*
**Bergman**, Stephanie 1946- *TwCPaSc*
**Bergman**, Stephenie Jane 1946- *IntWW 91*
**Bergman**, Theodore L 1956- *AmMWSc 92*
**Bergman**, Torbern Olof 1735-1784 *BlkwCEP*
**Bergman**, Walter Chester 1949- *WhoEnt 92*
**Bergmanis**, Ilmars 1930- *WhoMW 92*
**Bergmann**, Alan Spencer *WhoEnt 92*
**Bergmann**, Allan Dale 1928- *WhoMW 92*
**Bergmann**, Barbara Rose 1927- *WhoFI 92*
**Bergmann**, Carl Kenzig 1929- *WhoFI 92*
**Bergmann**, Charles Arnold 1938- *WhoWest 92*
**Bergmann**, Dietrich R 1938- *AmMWSc 92*
**Bergmann**, Ernest Eisenhardt 1942- *AmMWSc 92*
**Bergmann**, Felix 1908- *IntWW 91*
**Bergmann**, Fred Heinz 1928- *AmMWSc 92*
**Bergmann**, Otto 1925- *AmMWSc 92*
**Bergmann**, Peter Gabriel 1915- *AmMWSc 92*
**Bergmann**, Steven R 1951- *AmMWSc 92*
**Bergmann**, Ted *LesBEnT 92*
**Bergmark**, William R 1940- *AmMWSc 92*
**Bergna**, Horacio Enrique 1924- *AmMWSc 92*
**Bergner**, Jane Cohen 1943- *WhoAmL 92*
**Bergo**, Conrad Hunter 1943- *AmMWSc 92*
**Bergo**, Edward Arthur 1938- *WhoWest 92*
**Bergoffen**, Debra Beth 1941- *WhoRel 92*
**Bergofsky**, Edward Harold 1927- *AmMWSc 92*
**Bergold**, Harry E, Jr 1931- *WhoAmP 91*
**Bergomi**, Angelo 1933- *AmMWSc 92*
**Bergonzi**, Bernard 1929- *IntAu&W 91, ScFEYrs, Who 92, WrDr 92*
**Bergonzi**, Carlo 1924- *FacFETw, IntWW 91, NewAmDM*
**Bergougnou**, Maurice A 1928- *AmMWSc 92*
**Bergquist**, Barry Darril 1945- *WhoAmP 91*
**Bergquist**, David Erik 1963- *WhoAmL 92*
**Bergquist**, Harlan Richard 1908- *AmMWSc 92*
**Bergquist**, James William 1928- *AmMWSc 92*
**Bergquist**, Patricia Rose 1933- *IntWW 91*
**Bergreen**, Laurence 1950- *WrDr 92*
**Bergs**, Mary A. 1954- *WhoMW 92*
**Bergs**, Victor Visvaldis 1923- *AmMWSc 92*
**Bergs**, William F. 1947- *WhoIns 92*
**Bergsagel**, Daniel Egil 1925- *AmMWSc 92*
**Bergsagel**, Ernest 1955- *WhoAmP 91*
**Bergsagel**, John Dagfinn 1928- *IntWW 91*
**Bergseth**, Robert Reid 1945- *WhoMW 92*
**Bergsma**, Derke Peter 1927- *WhoRel 92*
**Bergsma**, William 1921- *NewAmDM*
**Bergsma**, William Laurence 1921- *WhoEnt 92*
**Bergsmann**, Bobby 1956- *WhoEnt 92*
**Bergson**, Abram 1914- *IntWW 91, WhoFI 92, WrDr 92*
**Bergson**, Henri 1859-1941 *FacFETw, GuFrLit 1*
**Bergson**, Henri Louis 1859-1941 *WhoNob 90*
**Bergson**, Maria *WhoEnt 92*
**Bergstedt**, Alan W. 1936- *WhoRel 92*
**Bergstein**, Daniel Gerard 1943- *WhoAmL 92*
**Bergstein**, Eleanor *DrAPF 91*
**Bergstein**, Jerry Michael *AmMWSc 92*
**Bergstein**, Scott Dryfuss 1952- *WhoEnt 92*
**Bergsten**, Anita Ingegerd 1936- *WhoFI 92*
**Bergsten**, C Fred 1941- *WhoAmP 91, WhoFI 92*
**Bergsten**, Jane Williams 1927- *AmMWSc 92*
**Bergstraesser**, Edward William 1935- *WhoMW 92, WhoRel 92*
**Bergstralh**, Jay Thor 1943- *AmMWSc 92*
**Bergstrand**, Wilton Everet 1909- *WhoRel 92*
**Bergstresser**, Kenneth A 1912- *AmMWSc 92*
**Bergstresser**, Paul Richard 1941- *AmMWSc 92*
**Bergstrom**, Clarence George 1925- *AmMWSc 92*
**Bergstrom**, Donald Eugene 1943- *AmMWSc 92*
**Bergstrom**, Elaine 1946- *WhoAmP 91*
**Bergstrom**, Gary Carlton 1953- *AmMWSc 92*

**Bergstrom,** George Frederick 1950- WhoMW 92
**Bergstrom,** Janice 1947- WhoMW 92
**Bergstrom,** John Andrew 1867-1910 BiInAmS
**Bergstrom,** K Sune D 1916- AmMWSc 92
**Bergstrom,** Robert Charles 1922- AmMWSc 92
**Bergstrom,** Robert Edward 1923- AmMWSc 92
**Bergstrom,** Rolf Olof Bernhard 1934- WhoFI 92
**Bergstrom,** Scott E. 1952- WhoEnt 92
**Bergstrom,** Stig Magnus 1935- AmMWSc 92
**Bergstrom,** Sune 1916- Who 92, WhoNob 90
**Bergstrom,** William H 1921- AmMWSc 92
**Bergsund,** Richard T. 1927- WhoIns 92
**Bergtraum,** Howard Michael 1946- WhoAmL 92
**Bergtrom,** Gerald 1945- AmMWSc 92
**Bergus,** Donald Clayton 1920- WhoAmP 91
**Bergvig,** Chyrl Rae 1949- WhoMW 92
**Bergwall,** Karin Laverne 1944- WhoFI 92
**Berhe,** Annette Toney WhoBlA 92
**Beri,** Avinash Chandra 1949- AmMWSc 92
**Beria,** Lavrenti 1899-1953 FacFETw
**Beria,** Lavrentiy Pavlovich 1899-1953 SovUnBD
**Beric,** Berislav 1927- IntWW 91
**Berigan,** Bunny 1908-1942 NewAmDM
**Berigan,** Patrick Tierney 1956- WhoAmL 92
**Bering,** Charles Lawrence 1947- AmMWSc 92
**Bering,** Edgar Andrew, III 1946- AmMWSc 92
**Bering,** Edgar Andrew, Jr 1917- AmMWSc 92
**Beringer,** Robert 1917- AmMWSc 92
**Beringer,** Roberta Jeanne 1964- WhoAmL 92
**Beringer,** Theodore Michael 1944- AmMWSc 92
**Beringer,** William Ernst 1928- WhoFI 92
**Berington,** Simon 1680-1755 ScFEYrs
**Berinsky,** Burton d1991 NewYTBS 91
**Berio,** Luciano 1925- ConCom 92, IntWW 91, NewAmDM, Who 92, WhoEnt 92
**Beriosova,** Svetlana 1932- IntWW 91
**Beriozova,** Svetlana 1932- Who 92
**Berisavljevic,** Zivan 1935- Who 92
**Berk,** Alan S. 1934- WhoFI 92
**Berk,** Ann E. WhoEnt 92
**Berk,** Aristid D 1925- AmMWSc 92
**Berk,** Arnold J 1949- AmMWSc 92
**Berk,** Bernard 1915- AmMWSc 92
**Berk,** Charles Michael 1951- WhoAmL 92
**Berk,** Harlan Joseph 1942- WhoMW 92
**Berk,** Jack Edward 1911- AmMWSc 92
**Berk,** James Edward 1945- WhoFI 92
**Berk,** James Lawrence, II 1960- WhoEnt 92, WhoFI 92
**Berk,** Jeremiah E. 1941- WhoAmL 92
**Berk,** Joseph 1952- WhoMW 92
**Berk,** Karen M. 1943- WhoWest 92
**Berk,** Kenneth N 1938- AmMWSc 92
**Berk,** Peggy Faith 1951- WhoFI 92
**Berk,** Richard Samuel 1928- AmMWSc 92
**Berk,** Robert Norton 1930- AmMWSc 92
**Berk,** Toby Steven 1944- AmMWSc 92
**Berk,** William Stewart 1957- WhoAmL 92
**Berka,** Ladislav Henry 1936- AmMWSc 92
**Berke,** Alice Karen 1963- WhoAmL 92
**Berke,** Amy Turner 1942- WhoMW 92
**Berke,** Judith DrAPF 91
**Berke,** Michael 1939- WhoFI 92
**Berke,** Nancy DrAPF 91
**Berke,** Thomas Sertac 1956- WhoFI 92
**Berkebile,** Charles Alan 1938- AmMWSc 92
**Berkedal,** Thomas Robert 1953- WhoFI 92
**Berkeley,** Baroness 1905- Who 92
**Berkeley,** Arthur Eliot 1943- WhoAmL 92
**Berkeley,** Busby 1895-1976 FacFETw, IntDcF 2-2 [port]
**Berkeley,** Edmund 1912- ConAu 133
**Berkeley,** Frederic George 1919- Who 92
**Berkeley,** George 1685-1753 BlkwCEP
**Berkeley,** George 1685-1783 BenetAL 91
**Berkeley,** Humphry John 1926- IntAu&W 91, Who 92
**Berkeley,** Jill Brenda 1950- WhoAmL 92
**Berkeley,** Lennox 1903-1989 FacFETw, NewAmDM
**Berkeley,** Lennox 1903-1990 ConCom 92
**Berkeley,** Maurice d1991 Who 92N
**Berkeley,** Michael 1948- ConCom 92
**Berkeley,** Michael Fitzhardinge 1948- IntWW 91, Who 92
**Berkeley,** William 1606-1677 BenetAL 91
**Berkeley Milne,** Alexander Who 92
**Berkelhamer,** Louis H 1912- AmMWSc 92
**Berkelhammer,** Gerald 1931- AmMWSc 92
**Berkelhammer,** Jane AmMWSc 92
**Berkelman,** Karl 1933- AmMWSc 92
**Berkelman,** Thomas Roger 1949- WhoAmP 91
**Berkenpas,** Darlis Ann 1949- WhoRel 92
**Berker,** Ahmet Nihat 1949- AmMWSc 92
**Berkery,** Peter Michael, Jr. 1961- WhoAmL 92
**Berkes,** John Stephan 1940- AmMWSc 92
**Berkes,** Leslie John 1946- WhoWest 92
**Berkes,** Milton 1924- WhoAmP 91
**Berkett,** Marian Mayer 1913- WhoAmL 92
**Berkey,** Dennis Dale 1947- AmMWSc 92
**Berkey,** Donald C AmMWSc 92
**Berkey,** Gordon Bruce 1942- AmMWSc 92
**Berkheimer,** Henry Edward 1929- AmMWSc 92
**Berkheiser,** Samuel William 1922- AmMWSc 92
**Berkhof,** Hendrikus 1914- DcEcMov
**Berkhof,** Louis 1873-1957 RelLAm 91
**Berkhout,** Aart W J 1939- AmMWSc 92
**Berkhouwer,** Cornelis 1919- Who 92
**Berking,** Max 1917- WhoAmP 91
**Berkland,** James Omer 1930- AmMWSc 92
**Berkland,** Terrill Raymond 1941- AmMWSc 92
**Berklav,** Eduard Karlovich 1914- SovUnBD
**Berklavs,** Eduards 1914- IntWW 91, SovUnBD
**Berkley,** Constance E. DrAPF 91
**Berkley,** Constance Elaine 1931- WhoBlA 92
**Berkley,** David A 1940- AmMWSc 92
**Berkley,** John Lee 1948- AmMWSc 92
**Berkley,** Peter Lee 1939- WhoAmL 92
**Berkley,** Richard 1931- WhoAmP 91
**Berkley,** Robert John 1933- WhoWest 92
**Berkley,** Thomas Lucius 1915- WhoBlA 92
**Berkley,** William R. 1945- WhoIns 92
**Berkman,** Aaron d1991 NewYTBS 91
**Berkman,** Alexander DcAmImH
**Berkman,** Craig Lamont 1941- WhoAmP 91
**Berkman,** Isidoro 1940- WhoAmL 92
**Berkman,** James Israel 1913- AmMWSc 92
**Berkman,** Marsha Lee DrAPF 91
**Berkman,** Michael G 1917- AmMWSc 92
**Berkman,** Samuel 1935- AmMWSc 92
**Berkman,** Stanley Peter 1960- WhoFI 92
**Berkman,** Susan C. Josephs 1953- WhoWest 92
**Berkman,** Sylvia DrAPF 91
**Berkman,** William Roger 1928- WhoAmL 92
**Berkner,** Klaus Hans 1938- AmMWSc 92
**Berko,** Stephan 1924- AmMWSc 92
**Berkof,** Richard Stanley 1941- AmMWSc 92
**Berkoff,** Charles Edward 1932- AmMWSc 92, WhoFI 92
**Berkoff,** Steven 1937- IntAu&W 91, IntMPA 92, Who 92
**Berkoff,** Steven 1939- WrDr 92
**Berkoff,** Stevn 1937- IntWW 91
**Berkos,** Christy S 1926- WhoAmP 91
**Berkove,** Lawrence Ivan 1930- ConAu 36NR, WhoMW 92
**Berkovitch,** Boris S. 1921- WhoFI 92
**Berkovits,** Shimshon 1936- AmMWSc 92
**Berkovitz,** Jay R. 1951- ConAu 134
**Berkovitz,** Leonard David 1924- AmMWSc 92, WhoMW 92
**Berkow,** Albert Joseph 1923- WhoFI 92
**Berkower,** Ira 1948- AmMWSc 92
**Berkowitz,** Adena Karen 1959- WhoAmL 92
**Berkowitz,** Alan Robert 1942- WhoAmL 92
**Berkowitz,** Barry Alan 1942- AmMWSc 92
**Berkowitz,** David Andrew 1952- AmMWSc 92
**Berkowitz,** David J 1941- WhoAmP 91
**Berkowitz,** Harry Leo 1937- AmMWSc 92
**Berkowitz,** Herbert Mattis 1947- WhoAmL 92
**Berkowitz,** Howard Perry 1940- WhoFI 92
**Berkowitz,** Irving 1951- WhoMW 92
**Berkowitz,** Jerome 1928- AmMWSc 92
**Berkowitz,** Jesse M 1928- AmMWSc 92
**Berkowitz,** Joan B 1931- AmMWSc 92
**Berkowitz,** Jonathan Mark DrAPF 91
**Berkowitz,** Joseph 1930- AmMWSc 92
**Berkowitz,** Lewis Maurice 1931- AmMWSc 92
**Berkowitz,** Philip 1938- WhoRel 92
**Berkowitz,** Raymond S 1923- AmMWSc 92
**Berkowitz,** Robert Carl 1940- WhoWest 92
**Berkowitz,** Robert S. 1951- WhoEnt 92
**Berkowitz,** Sidney 1921- AmMWSc 92
**Berkowitz,** Steve WhoFI 92
**Berkshire,** Archdeacon of Who 92
**Berkshire,** Gerald Lynn 1951- WhoFI 92
**Berkshire,** Steven David 1947- WhoWest 92
**Berkson,** Bill DrAPF 91
**Berkson,** Bill 1939- ConPo 91, IntAu&W 91, WrDr 92
**Berkson,** David M 1928- AmMWSc 92
**Berkson,** David Mayer 1934- Who 92
**Berkson,** Earl Robert 1934- AmMWSc 92
**Berkson,** Harold 1929- AmMWSc 92
**Berkson,** Jacob Benjamin 1925- WhoAmL 92
**Berkson,** Jonathan Milton 1941- AmMWSc 92
**Berkson,** Robert Gary 1939- WhoFI 92
**Berkson,** William Craig 1939- WhoWest 92
**Berkstresser,** Jerry William 1934- WhoAmL 92
**Berkus,** David William 1941- WhoWest 92
**Berkut,** Michael Kalen 1915- AmMWSc 92
**Berky,** John James 1924- AmMWSc 92
**Berl,** Soll 1918- AmMWSc 92
**Berl,** Walter G 1917- AmMWSc 92
**Berlad,** Abraham Leon 1921- AmMWSc 92, WhoWest 92
**Berlage,** Hendrikus Petrus 1856-1934 DcTwDes
**Berland,** Howard DrAPF 91
**Berlandi,** Francis Joseph 1941- AmMWSc 92
**Berlanga,** David, Jr. 1943- WhoHisp 92
**Berlanga,** Hugo 1948- WhoAmP 91, WhoHisp 92
**Berlanga,** Luis Garcia IntDcF 2-2
**Berle,** Adolf Augustus, Jr 1895-1971 FacFETw
**Berle,** Milton LesBEnT 92 [port]
**Berle,** Milton 1908- FacFETw, IntMPA 92, WhoEnt 92
**Berlekamp,** Elwyn R 1940- AmMWSc 92
**Berler,** Joan Irma 1961- WhoEnt 92
**Berlew,** Frank Kingston 1930- WhoAmL 92
**Berley,** David 1930- AmMWSc 92
**Berley,** David Richard 1942- WhoAmL 92
**Berliet,** Paul 1918- IntWW 91
**Berlin,** Alan Daniel 1939- WhoAmL 92, WhoFI 92
**Berlin,** Andrew WhoWest 92
**Berlin,** Barry Neil 1954- WhoFI 92
**Berlin,** Byron Sanford 1921- AmMWSc 92
**Berlin,** Charles I 1933- AmMWSc 92
**Berlin,** Cheston Milton 1936- AmMWSc 92
**Berlin,** Donald Nelson 1944- WhoMW 92
**Berlin,** Donald Robert 1936- WhoRel 92
**Berlin,** Ellin Mackay 1903-1988 BenetAL 91
**Berlin,** Elliott 1934- AmMWSc 92
**Berlin,** Fred S 1941- AmMWSc 92
**Berlin,** Graydon Lennis 1943- AmMWSc 92
**Berlin,** Irving 1888-1989 BenetAL 91, FacFETw [port], NewAmDM, RComAH
**Berlin,** Irving Norman 1917- AmMWSc 92
**Berlin,** Isaiah 1909- IntWW 91, Who 92, WrDr 92
**Berlin,** Jerome Clifford 1942- WhoFI 92
**Berlin,** Jerry D 1934- AmMWSc 92
**Berlin,** Kathryn E. 1937- WhoMW 92
**Berlin,** Kenneth 1947- WhoAmL 92
**Berlin,** Kenneth Darrell 1933- AmMWSc 92
**Berlin,** Mark A. 1944- WhoAmL 92
**Berlin,** Michael Alan 1953- WhoEnt 92, WhoFI 92
**Berlin,** Nathaniel Isaac 1920- AmMWSc 92
**Berlin,** Steve WhoHisp 92
**Berlin,** Steven Benjamin 1949- WhoAmL 92
**Berlin,** Steven Ritt 1944- WhoFI 92
**Berlin,** Sven 1911- TwCPaSc
**Berlincourt,** Ted Gibbs 1925- AmMWSc 92
**Berlind,** Allan 1942- AmMWSc 92
**Berlind,** Bruce DrAPF 91
**Berlind,** Roger Stuart 1930- WhoEnt 92
**Berliner,** Alan Frederick 1951- WhoAmL 92
**Berliner,** Charles Alan 1946- WhoEnt 92
**Berliner,** Ernst 1915- AmMWSc 92
**Berliner,** Frances 1921- AmMWSc 92
**Berliner,** Hans Jack 1929- AmMWSc 92
**Berliner,** Henry A, Jr 1934- WhoAmP 91
**Berliner,** Judith A 1939- AmMWSc 92
**Berliner,** Lawrence J 1941- AmMWSc 92
**Berliner,** Lori Monica 1960- WhoAmL 92
**Berliner,** Martha D 1928- AmMWSc 92
**Berliner,** Robert W. 1915- IntWW 91
**Berliner,** Robert William 1915- AmMWSc 92
**Berliner,** William Michael 1923- WhoFI 92
**Berling,** Judith Ann 1945- WhoRel 92
**Berlinger,** Robert William 1958- WhoEnt 92
**Berlinger,** Warren 1937- IntMPA 92, WhoEnt 92
**Berlinghieri,** Joel Carl 1942- AmMWSc 92
**Berlinguer,** Enrico 1922-1984 FacFETw
**Berlinrood,** Martin 1943- AmMWSc 92
**Berlins,** Marcel Joseph 1941- Who 92
**Berlioz,** Georges Louis 1943- WhoFI 92
**Berlioz,** Hector 1803-1869 NewAmDM
**Berlman,** Isadore B 1922- AmMWSc 92
**Berlo,** Robert Christopher 1941- WhoWest 92
**Berlow,** Robert Alan 1947- WhoAmL 92, WhoFI 92
**Berlow,** Stanley 1921- AmMWSc 92
**Berlowitz,** Allan J. 1940- WhoAmL 92
**Berlowitz Tarrant,** Laurence 1934- AmMWSc 92
**Berlusconi,** Silvio LesBEnT 92 [port]
**Berlusconi,** Silvio 1936- IntWW 91
**Berlyn,** Graeme Pierce 1933- AmMWSc 92
**Berlyn,** Mary Berry 1938- AmMWSc 92
**Berlyn,** Robin Wilfrid 1934- AmMWSc 92
**Berlyne,** Geoffrey Merton 1931- AmMWSc 92
**Berman,** Abraham S 1921- AmMWSc 92
**Berman,** Alan 1925- AmMWSc 92
**Berman,** Alex 1914- AmMWSc 92
**Berman,** Alvin Leonard 1924- AmMWSc 92
**Berman,** Andrew Jay 1959- WhoAmL 92
**Berman,** Arthur Leonard 1935- WhoAmP 91, WhoMW 92
**Berman,** Barbara P 1938- WhoAmP 91
**Berman,** Barry L 1936- AmMWSc 92
**Berman,** Baruch 1925- WhoWest 92
**Berman,** Bernard Mayer 1940- WhoAmL 92
**Berman,** Boris 1948- WhoEnt 92
**Berman,** Brad Laurence 1957- WhoAmL 92, WhoFI 92
**Berman,** Bruce WhoEnt 92
**Berman,** Carol 1923- WhoAmP 91
**Berman,** Cassia DrAPF 91
**Berman,** Claire 1936- IntAu&W 91, WrDr 92
**Berman,** Daniel Katzel 1954- WhoFI 92
**Berman,** Daniel Micah 1957- WhoAmL 92
**Berman,** Daniel S. 1921- WhoAmL 92
**Berman,** David 1934- WhoAmL 92
**Berman,** David 1942- ConAu 135
**Berman,** David Albert 1917- AmMWSc 92, WhoWest 92
**Berman,** David Alvin 1924- AmMWSc 92
**Berman,** David Michael 1946- AmMWSc 92
**Berman,** David S 1940- AmMWSc 92
**Berman,** David Samuel 1946- WhoEnt 92
**Berman,** David Theodore 1920- AmMWSc 92
**Berman,** Edward David 1941- Who 92
**Berman,** Eleanor 1921- AmMWSc 92
**Berman,** Eleanore 1928- WhoWest 92
**Berman,** Ellen Myra 1957- AmMWSc 92
**Berman,** Elliot 1930- AmMWSc 92
**Berman,** Eric M. 1948- WhoAmL 92, WhoEnt 92
**Berman,** Florence R. 1957- WhoFI 92
**Berman,** Franklin Delow 1939- Who 92
**Berman,** Frederic Sanford 1927- WhoAmL 92
**Berman,** Gerald 1924- AmMWSc 92
**Berman,** Gerald Adrian 1934- AmMWSc 92
**Berman,** Harold Jesse 1948- WhoRel 92
**Berman,** Harvey Paul 1939- WhoAmL 92
**Berman,** Helen Miriam 1943- AmMWSc 92
**Berman,** Henry Louis 1952- WhoEnt 92
**Berman,** Herbert E 1933- WhoAmP 91
**Berman,** Herbert Joshua 1924- AmMWSc 92
**Berman,** Horace Aaron 1915- AmMWSc 92
**Berman,** Howard 1952- WhoEnt 92
**Berman,** Howard Allen 1949- WhoMW 92, WhoRel 92
**Berman,** Howard C. 1951- WhoAmL 92
**Berman,** Howard L. 1941- AlmAP 92 [port], WhoAmP 91
**Berman,** Howard Lawrence 1941- WhoWest 92
**Berman,** Howard Mitchell 1936- AmMWSc 92
**Berman,** Irwin 1924- AmMWSc 92
**Berman,** Irwin 1925- AmMWSc 92
**Berman,** Jack 1957- WhoAmL 92
**Berman,** Jacob 1948- WhoFI 92
**Berman,** Jakub 1901-1984 FacFETw
**Berman,** Jay Harris 1958- WhoAmL 92
**Berman,** Jay Michael 1952- WhoMW 92
**Berman,** Jeffrey 1945- ConAu 134
**Berman,** Jerome Richard 1920- AmMWSc 92
**Berman,** Joanna WhoEnt 92
**Berman,** Joel David 1943- AmMWSc 92
**Berman,** John Arthur 1932- WhoAmP 91
**Berman,** Joshua Mordecai 1938- WhoAmL 92
**Berman,** Julian 1924- AmMWSc 92

**Berman**, Julius 1935- *WhoAmL 92*
**Berman**, Keith 1942- *WhoAmL 92*
**Berman**, Lawrence Sam 1928- *Who 92*
**Berman**, Lawrence Uretz 1919- *AmMWSc 92, WhoMW 92*
**Berman**, Layne Alan 1956- *WhoFI 92*
**Berman**, Lazar 1930- *WhoEnt 92*
**Berman**, Lazar Naumovich 1930- *SovUnBD*
**Berman**, Leo 1917- *WhoMW 92*
**Berman**, Leo 1935- *WhoAmP 91*
**Berman**, Louis 1903- *AmMWSc 92*
**Berman**, M Lawrence 1929- *AmMWSc 92*
**Berman**, Mark Laurence 1940- *WhoWest 92*
**Berman**, Marlene Oscar 1939- *AmMWSc 92*
**Berman**, Martin 1938- *AmMWSc 92*
**Berman**, Maxine 1946- *WhoAmP 91*
**Berman**, Michael Barry 1942- *WhoAmL 92*
**Berman**, Michael Roy 1947- *AmMWSc 92*
**Berman**, Mona S. 1925- *WhoEnt 92*
**Berman**, Monty M. 1912- *IntMPA 92*
**Berman**, Nancy Elizabeth Johnson 1946- *AmMWSc 92*
**Berman**, Neil Sheldon 1933- *AmMWSc 92*
**Berman**, Pandro S. 1905- *IntMPA 92*
**Berman**, Pandro Samuel 1905- *WhoEnt 92*
**Berman**, Patricia Dondanville 1956- *WhoRel 92*
**Berman**, Paul 1949- *SmATA 66*
**Berman**, Paul J. 1951- *WhoAmL 92*
**Berman**, Paul Ronald 1945- *AmMWSc 92*
**Berman**, Philip I. 1915- *WhoFI 92*
**Berman**, Reuben 1908- *AmMWSc 92*
**Berman**, Rhoda Gelfond *DrAPF 91*
**Berman**, Richard Bruce 1951- *WhoAmL 92*
**Berman**, Richard Iles 1940- *WhoMW 92*
**Berman**, Richard Miles 1943- *WhoAmL 92, WhoFI 92*
**Berman**, Robert Hiram 1948- *AmMWSc 92*
**Berman**, Ronald Charles 1949- *WhoAmL 92, WhoMW 92*
**Berman**, Rosalind *WhoAmP 91*
**Berman**, Sam Morris 1933- *AmMWSc 92*
**Berman**, Sanford 1927- *AmMWSc 92*
**Berman**, Sanford 1933- *WrDr 92*
**Berman**, Saul J. 1946- *WhoWest 92*
**Berman**, Shier 1929- *AmMWSc 92*
**Berman**, Simeon Moses 1935- *AmMWSc 92*
**Berman**, Sonia *WhoEnt 92*
**Berman**, Steve 1967- *WhoMW 92*
**Berman**, Steve William 1954- *WhoWest 92*
**Berman**, Steven H. 1952- *IntMPA 92, WhoEnt 92*
**Berman**, Tony 1933- *WhoAmL 92*
**Berman**, Yitzhak 1913- *IntWW 91*
**Berman-Hammer**, Susan 1950- *WhoMW 92*
**Bermann**, George Alan 1945- *WhoAmL 92*
**Bermant**, Chaim 1929- *ConNov 91, WrDr 92*
**Bermant**, Chaim Icyk 1929- *IntAu&W 91, Who 92*
**Bermant**, George Wilson 1926- *WhoAmL 92*
**Bermas**, Stephen 1925- *WhoFI 92*
**Bermello**, Willy *WhoHisp 92*
**Bermes**, Boris John 1926- *AmMWSc 92*
**Bermes**, Edward William, Jr 1932- *AmMWSc 92*
**Bermingham**, Gerald Edward 1940- *Who 92*
**Bermingham**, John Scott 1951- *WhoMW 92*
**Bermingham**, Joseph Daniel 1938- *WhoAmL 92*
**Bermingham**, Richard P. 1939- *WhoWest 92*
**Bermon**, Stuart 1936- *AmMWSc 92*
**Bermont**, Peter Leslie 1945- *WhoFI 92*
**Bermoy**, Emiliano Simacio 1946- *WhoRel 92*
**Bermuda**, Bishop of 1934- *Who 92*
**Bermudes**, Mariano Reyes *WhoAmP 91*
**Bermudez**, Diana *WhoHisp 92*
**Bermudez**, Eduardo *WhoHisp 92*
**Bermudez**, Enrique d1991 *IntWW 91N*
**Bermudez**, Gloria 1930- *WhoHisp 92*
**Bermudez**, Jose Francisco 1782-1831 *HisDSpE*
**Bermudez**, Juan 1941- *WhoHisp 92*
**Bermudez**, Manuel Enrique 1957- *WhoHisp 92*
**Bermudez**, Victor Manuel 1947- *AmMWSc 92*
**Bermudez Colom**, Helcias Daniel 1947- *WhoHisp 92*
**Bern**, Howard Alan 1920- *AmMWSc 92, IntWW 91*
**Bern**, Lars A. V. 1942- *IntWW 91*
**Bern**, Marc Jay 1950- *WhoAmL 92*
**Bern**, Ronald Lawrence 1936- *WhoFI 92*
**Bernabe**, Teresa 1970- *WhoHisp 92*
**Bernabei**, Amy Bosio 1961- *WhoFI 92*
**Bernabei**, Austin M 1928- *AmMWSc 92*
**Bernabei**, Ettore 1921- *IntWW 91*
**Bernabei**, Stefano 1944- *AmMWSc 92*
**Bernabie**, Carmen Ralph 1942- *WhoMW 92*
**Bernabo-Brea**, Luigi 1910- *IntWW 91*
**Bernabucci**, John R, Jr 1930- *WhoAmP 91*
**Bernac**, Pierre 1899-1979 *NewAmDM*
**Bernacchi**, Richard Lloyd 1938- *WhoAmL 92*
**Bernacki**, Ralph J 1946- *AmMWSc 92*
**Bernadicou**, Paul Joseph 1933- *WhoRel 92*
**Bernadotte**, Folke 1895-1948 *EncTR 91 [port], FacFETw*
**Bernadotte**, Lennart 1909- *IntWW 91*
**Bernadotte**, Sigvard 1907- *DcTwDes, FacFETw*
**Bernadotte**, Sigvard Oscar Fredrik 1907- *IntWW 91*
**Bernadou**, John Baptiste 1858-1908 *BiInAmS*
**Bernady**, Karel Francis 1941- *AmMWSc 92*
**Bernal**, Albert Louis 1947- *WhoAmL 92*
**Bernal**, Armando, Jr. *WhoHisp 92*
**Bernal**, Arthur W. d1991 *NewYTBS 91*
**Bernal**, Harriet Jean 1931- *WhoWest 92*
**Bernal**, Henrietta *WhoHisp 92*
**Bernal**, Ivan 1931- *AmMWSc 92, WhoHisp 92*
**Bernal**, Jesus Rodriguez 1953- *WhoHisp 92*
**Bernal**, Joe J 1927- *WhoAmP 91*
**Bernal**, Lynda Evelyn 1959- *WhoWest 92*
**Bernal**, Margarita Solano 1954- *WhoHisp 92*
**Bernal**, Marie-Louise 1939- *WhoAmL 92*
**Bernal**, Martha E. 1931- *WhoHisp 92*
**Bernal**, Mike *WhoHisp 92*
**Bernal**, Philip Vincent 1944- *WhoHisp 92*
**Bernal G**, Enrique 1938- *AmMWSc 92*
**Bernal Jimenez**, Miguel 1910-1956 *NewAmDM*
**Bernal-Pereira**, Waldo 1934- *Who 92*
**Bernal Vargas**, Jorge 1929- *WhoRel 92*
**Bernal y del Rio**, Victor 1917- *WhoHisp 92*
**Bernal Y Garcia Pimentel**, Ignacio 1910- *IntWW 91*
**Bernanos**, Georges 1888-1948 *GuFrLit 1, LiExTwC*
**Bernar Castellanos**, Ignacio 1929- *IntWW 91*
**Bernard of Chartres** 1060?-1124? *DcLB 115*
**Bernard**, Alexander 1952- *WhoWest 92*
**Bernard**, Andre M. R. *WhoFI 92*
**Bernard**, Bernie Boyd 1952- *AmMWSc 92*
**Bernard**, Canute Clive 1924- *WhoBlA 92*
**Bernard**, Christopher *DrAPF 91*
**Bernard**, Dale Anthony 1959- *WhoAmL 92*
**Bernard**, Dallas 1926- *Who 92*
**Bernard**, Dane Thomas 1948- *AmMWSc 92*
**Bernard**, David A. 1945- *WhoFI 92*
**Bernard**, Davy Lee 1936- *AmMWSc 92*
**Bernard**, Donald Ray 1932- *WhoAmL 92*
**Bernard**, Donald Ray 1936- *WhoAmP 91*
**Bernard**, Douglas Alan 1953- *AmMWSc 92*
**Bernard**, Eddie Nolan 1946- *AmMWSc 92*
**Bernard**, Edwin Young 1936- *WhoRel 92*
**Bernard**, Elyssa Lynn 1964- *WhoWest 92*
**Bernard**, Emile 1868-1941 *ThHEIm*
**Bernard**, Eric 1943-1991 *NewYTBS 91*
**Bernard**, Ernest Charles 1950- *AmMWSc 92*
**Bernard**, Francis 1712?-1779 *BlkwEAR*
**Bernard**, Frank Charles 1908- *WhoMW 92*
**Bernard**, Gary Dale 1938- *AmMWSc 92*
**Bernard**, George W 1925- *AmMWSc 92*
**Bernard**, Harold O. 1938- *WhoBlA 92*
**Bernard**, Henry 1912- *IntWW 91*
**Bernard**, Jacques Niels 1938- *WhoFI 92*
**Bernard**, James William 1937- *WhoWest 92*
**Bernard**, Jami 1956- *WhoEnt 92*
**Bernard**, Jeffrey Joseph 1932- *Who 92*
**Bernard**, Jerry Wayne 1937- *WhoRel 92*
**Bernard**, Jessie 1903- *WomSoc*
**Bernard**, Joan Constance 1918- *Who 92*
**Bernard**, Joan Kovalic 1948- *WhoAmL 92*
**Bernard**, John 1756-1828 *BenetAL 91*
**Bernard**, John Milford 1933- *AmMWSc 92*
**Bernard**, John Wilfrid 1928- *AmMWSc 92*
**Bernard**, Judd *WhoEnt 92*
**Bernard**, Kenneth *DrAPF 91*
**Bernard**, Kenneth 1930- *WhoEnt 92, WrDr 92*
**Bernard**, Kent Bede 1942- *BlkOlyM*
**Bernard**, Lewis W. *WhoFI 92*
**Bernard**, Louis Joseph 1925- *WhoBlA 92*
**Bernard**, Lucien 1913- *IntWW 91*
**Bernard**, Marvin A. 1934- *IntMPA 92*
**Bernard**, Mary E 1908- *WhoAmP 91*
**Bernard**, Michael Mark 1926- *WhoAmL 92*
**Bernard**, Michelle Denise 1963- *WhoAmL 92, WhoBlA 92*
**Bernard**, Nesta Hyacinth *WhoBlA 92*
**Bernard**, Oliver 1925- *IntAu&W 91, WrDr 92*
**Bernard**, Pamela Jenks 1955- *WhoAmL 92*
**Bernard**, Paul T 1951- *WhoAmP 91*
**Bernard**, Peter Simon 1950- *AmMWSc 92*
**Bernard**, Pierre 1946- *ConCom 92*
**Bernard**, Pierre Arnold 1875-1955 *RelLAm 91*
**Bernard**, Randolph John, Sr. 1962- *WhoAmL 92*
**Bernard**, Richard Fernand 1934- *AmMWSc 92*
**Bernard**, Richard Lawson 1926- *AmMWSc 92*
**Bernard**, Richard Ryerson 1917- *AmMWSc 92*
**Bernard**, Robert *IntAu&W 91X, WrDr 92*
**Bernard**, Robert Scales 1946- *AmMWSc 92*
**Bernard**, Ronald Charles 1943- *WhoEnt 92*
**Bernard**, Rudy Andrew 1930- *AmMWSc 92*
**Bernard**, Selden Robert 1925- *AmMWSc 92*
**Bernard**, Sharon Elaine 1943- *WhoBlA 92*
**Bernard**, Thelma Rene *WhoWest 92*
**Bernard**, Walter Joseph 1923- *AmMWSc 92*
**Bernard**, William 1927- *AmMWSc 92*
**Bernard**, William Bayle 1807-1875 *BenetAL 91*
**Bernard**, William Henry 1837-1918 *DcNCBi 1*
**Bernard**, William Hickman 1932- *AmMWSc 92*
**Bernard**, William Stanly 1867-1938 *DcNCBi 1*
**Bernard-Castillo**, Debra Lee 1958- *WhoWest 92*
**Bernard-Stevens**, David F 1951- *WhoAmP 91*
**Bernardez**, Teresa 1931- *AmMWSc 92, WhoHisp 92*
**Bernardi**, James Edward 1946- *WhoMW 92*
**Bernardi**, Mario 1930- *NewAmDM, WhoEnt 92, WhoWest 92*
**Bernardin**, James Irwin 1929- *WhoFI 92*
**Bernardin**, John Emile 1937- *AmMWSc 92*
**Bernardin**, Joseph L. 1928- *IntWW 91*
**Bernardin**, Joseph Louis 1928- *RelLAm 91, WhoMW 92, WhoRel 92*
**Bernardin**, Leo J 1930- *AmMWSc 92*
**Bernardin de Saint-Pierre**, Jacques-Henri 1737-1814 *BlkwCEP*
**Bernardis**, Lee L 1926- *AmMWSc 92*
**Bernardo**, Everett *WhoHisp 92*
**Bernardo**, Jose Raul 1938- *WhoHisp 92*
**Bernardo**, Manuel Anthony 1945- *WhoAmL 92*
**Bernards**, Solomon Schnair 1914- *WhoRel 92*
**Bernardy**, Amy A 1879-1959 *DcAmImH*
**Bernasconi**, Bruno Lawrence 1944- *WhoWest 92*
**Bernasconi**, Claude Francois 1939- *AmMWSc 92*
**Bernasek**, Steven Lynn 1949- *AmMWSc 92*
**Bernat**, John Paul 1952- *WhoAmL 92*
**Bernat-Ciechan**, Anna Marianna 1946- *IntAu&W 91*
**Bernath**, L 1921- *AmMWSc 92*
**Bernath**, Peter Francis 1953- *AmMWSc 92*
**Bernath**, Tibor 1934- *AmMWSc 92*
**Bernatowicz**, Felix Jan Brzozowski 1920- *WhoFI 92*
**Bernatowicz**, Frank Allen 1954- *WhoMW 92*
**Bernau**, Bill 1964- *WhoAmP 91*
**Bernau**, Simon J 1937- *AmMWSc 92*
**Bernauer**, Edmund Michael 1926- *AmMWSc 92*
**Bernays**, Anne *DrAPF 91*
**Bernays**, Edward L. 1891- *WrDr 92*
**Bernays**, Elizabeth Anna 1940- *AmMWSc 92*
**Bernays**, Peter Michael 1918- *AmMWSc 92*
**Bernbach**, John Lincoln 1944- *WhoFI 92*
**Berndt**, Alan Fredric 1932- *AmMWSc 92*
**Berndt**, Bruce Carl 1939- *AmMWSc 92*
**Berndt**, Donald Carl 1935- *AmMWSc 92*
**Berndt**, Ernst Rudolf 1946- *WhoFI 92*
**Berndt**, Joan Gassaway 1936- *WhoEnt 92*
**Berndt**, Jule F *WhoAmP 91*
**Berndt**, Robert J 1918- *WhoAmP 91*
**Berndt**, Ronald Murray 1916- *IntAu&W 91, WrDr 92*
**Berndt**, Thomas Joseph 1949- *WhoMW 92*
**Berndt**, Thomas Theodore, Jr. 1947- *WhoEnt 92*
**Berndt**, William F 1956- *WhoAmP 91*
**Berndt**, William O 1933- *AmMWSc 92, WhoMW 92*
**Berndtson**, William Everett 1944- *AmMWSc 92*
**Berne**, Bernard H 1938- *AmMWSc 92*
**Berne**, Bruce J 1940- *AmMWSc 92*
**Berne**, Robert Matthew 1918- *AmMWSc 92, IntWW 91*
**Berne**, Stanley *DrAPF 91*
**Bernea**, Horia Mihai 1938- *IntWW 91*
**Bernecker**, Richard Rudolph 1936- *AmMWSc 92*
**Bernee**, Andrea Lorel 1960- *WhoWest 92*
**Berneis**, Kenneth Stanley 1951- *WhoMW 92*
**Berner**, Arthur Samuel 1943- *WhoAmL 92, WhoFI 92*
**Berner**, Frederic George, Jr. 1943- *WhoAmL 92*
**Berner**, Gary *WhoAmP 91*
**Berner**, Jeff *DrAPF 91*
**Berner**, Leo Dewitte, Jr 1922- *AmMWSc 92*
**Berner**, Lewis 1915- *AmMWSc 92*
**Berner**, Peter 1924- *IntWW 91*
**Berner**, Robert A 1935- *AmMWSc 92*
**Berner**, Robert Lee, Jr. 1931- *WhoAmL 92*
**Berner**, Robert Leslie 1928- *WhoMW 92*
**Berner**, Urs 1944- *IntAu&W 91*
**Berners**, Baroness 1901- *Who 92*
**Berners**, Edgar Davis 1927- *AmMWSc 92*
**Bernett**, Theodore Byron 1924- *WhoFI 92*
**Bernetti**, Raffaele 1932- *AmMWSc 92*
**Berney**, Charles V 1931- *AmMWSc 92*
**Berney**, James E. *WhoRel 92*
**Berney**, Joseph Henry 1932- *WhoFI 92*
**Berney**, Julian 1952- *Who 92*
**Berney**, Rex Leroy 1950- *AmMWSc 92*
**Berney**, Robert Edward 1932- *WhoFI 92, WhoWest 92*
**Berney**, Steven 1935- *AmMWSc 92*
**Berney**, Stuart Alan 1945- *AmMWSc 92*
**Bernfeld**, Peter 1912- *AmMWSc 92*
**Bernfeld**, William Steven 1950- *WhoFI 92*
**Bernfield**, Merton Ronald 1938- *AmMWSc 92*
**Bernhagen**, John Joseph 1934- *WhoAmP 91*
**Bernhagen**, Ralph John 1910- *AmMWSc 92*
**Bernhard Leopold Frederik Everhard J.** *IntWW 91*
**Bernhard**, Alexander Alfred 1936- *WhoAmL 92*
**Bernhard**, Berl 1929- *WhoAmL 92*
**Bernhard**, Georg 1875-1944 *EncTR 91*
**Bernhard**, George Kenneth 1944- *WhoAmL 92*
**Bernhard**, Harry Barnett 1933- *WhoFI 92*
**Bernhard**, Harvey 1924- *IntMPA 92, WhoEnt 92*
**Bernhard**, Jason Ruggles 1965- *WhoFI 92*
**Bernhard**, Jeffrey David 1951- *AmMWSc 92*
**Bernhard**, Johnnie Alicia 1962- *WhoMW 92*
**Bernhard**, Jon Casper 1961- *WhoWest 92*
**Bernhard**, Lucian 1883-1972 *DcTwDes*
**Bernhard**, Richard Allan 1923- *AmMWSc 92*
**Bernhard**, Richard Harold 1933- *AmMWSc 92*
**Bernhard**, Sandra 1955- *IntMPA 92*
**Bernhard**, Thomas 1931-1989 *FacFETw*
**Bernhard**, Victor Montwid 1927- *AmMWSc 92*
**Bernhard**, William Allen 1942- *AmMWSc 92*
**Bernhardt**, Anthony F 1945- *AmMWSc 92*
**Bernhardt**, Arthur Dieter 1937- *WhoFI 92*
**Bernhardt**, Ernest C 1923- *AmMWSc 92*
**Bernhardt**, Herbert Nelson *WhoAmL 92*
**Bernhardt**, Melvin *WhoEnt 92*
**Bernhardt**, Michael Howard 1937- *WhoAmP 91*
**Bernhardt**, Randal Jay 1956- *AmMWSc 92*
**Bernhardt**, Robert L, III 1939- *AmMWSc 92*
**Bernhardt**, Roger 1934- *WhoWest 92*
**Bernhardt**, Sarah 1844-1923 *FacFETw [port]*
**Bernhart**, Scott Russell 1959- *WhoEnt 92*
**Bernheim**, Frederick 1905- *AmMWSc 92*
**Bernheim**, Gotthardt Dellman 1827-1916 *DcNCBi 1*
**Bernheim**, Guy Felix 1951- *WhoFI 92*
**Bernheim**, Joyce Mary 1952- *WhoAmL 92*
**Bernheim**, Robert A 1933- *AmMWSc 92*
**Bernheimer**, Alan *DrAPF 91*
**Bernheimer**, Alan Weyl 1913- *AmMWSc 92*
**Bernheimer**, Charles 1942- *ConAu 134*
**Bernheimer**, Harriet P 1919- *AmMWSc 92*
**Bernheimer**, Martin 1936- *WhoWest 92*
**Bernholc**, Jerzy 1952- *AmMWSc 92*
**Bernholz**, William Francis 1924- *AmMWSc 92*
**Berni**, Betty Catherine 1942- *WhoWest 92*
**Berni**, Ralph John 1931- *AmMWSc 92*
**Bernick**, David M. 1954- *WhoAmL 92*
**Bernick**, Sol 1915- *AmMWSc 92*
**Bernier**, Charles L 1907- *AmMWSc 92*
**Bernier**, Claude 1931- *AmMWSc 92*
**Bernier**, John Gerard 1958- *WhoEnt 92*

Bernier, Joseph Leroy 1909- AmMWSc 92
Bernier, Paul Emile 1911- AmMWSc 92, WhoWest 92
Bernikow, Louise DrAPF 91
Berning, Paul Wilson 1948- WhoAmL 92
Berning, Randall Karl 1950- WhoAmL 92
Berning, Robert Hull, Jr. 1947- WhoEnt 92
Berning, Warren Walt 1920- AmMWSc 92
Berninger, Virginia Wise 1946- WhoWest 92
Bernini, Carlo IntWW 91
Bernius, Mark Thomas 1957- AmMWSc 92
Bernius, Robert Charles 1946- WhoAmL 92
Bernknopf, Al d1991 NewYTBS 91
Bernkopf, Michael 1927- AmMWSc 92
Bernlohr, Robert William 1933- AmMWSc 92
Bernoco, Domenico 1935- AmMWSc 92, WhoWest 92
Bernofsky, Carl 1933- AmMWSc 92
Bernor, Raymond Louis 1949- AmMWSc 92
Bernoudy, James Logan 1919- WhoBlA 92
Bernoulli, Daniel 1700-1782 BlkwCEP
Bernoulli, Jakob 1655-1705 BlkwCEP
Bernoulli, Johann 1667-1748 BlkwCEP
Berns, Donald Sheldon 1934- AmMWSc 92
Berns, Kenneth 1938- AmMWSc 92
Berns, Michael W 1942- AmMWSc 92
Berns, Norman C. 1942- WhoEnt 92
Berns, Sheldon 1932- WhoAmL 92
Berns, Wally Kay 1929- WhoEnt 92
Bernsen, Corbin 1954- IntMPA 92, WhoEnt 92
Bernsen, Sidney A 1928- AmMWSc 92
Bernstein Who 92
Bernstein, Baron 1899- IntWW 91, Who 92
Bernstein, Aaron 1904- WhoFI 92
Bernstein, Abram Bernard 1935- AmMWSc 92
Bernstein, Alan 1926- AmMWSc 92
Bernstein, Alan D 1938- AmMWSc 92
Bernstein, Alexander 1936- Who 92
Bernstein, Allen Richard 1941- AmMWSc 92, WhoFI 92
Bernstein, Alvin Stanley 1929- AmMWSc 92
Bernstein, Armyan IntMPA 92
Bernstein, Aron 1931- AmMWSc 92
Bernstein, Arthur Harold 1925- WhoFI 92
Bernstein, Barbara Elaine 1948- AmMWSc 92
Bernstein, Barry 1930- AmMWSc 92
Bernstein, Barry Selwyn 1946- WhoAmL 92
Bernstein, Barton Jannen 1936- WrDr 92
Bernstein, Basil 1924- WrDr 92
Bernstein, Basil Bernard 1924- Who 92
Bernstein, Bernard 1929- WhoFI 92
Bernstein, Bob IntMPA 92
Bernstein, Bradley Alan 1951- AmMWSc 92
Bernstein, Bruce 1959- WhoFI 92
Bernstein, Burton DrAPF 91
Bernstein, Burton 1920- AmMWSc 92
Bernstein, Burton 1932- WrDr 92
Bernstein, Carl FacFETw
Bernstein, Carl 1944- WrDr 92
Bernstein, Carol 1941- AmMWSc 92
Bernstein, Caryl Salomon 1933- WhoAmL 92, WhoFI 92
Bernstein, Charles DrAPF 91
Bernstein, Charles 1950- ConPo 91, WrDr 92
Bernstein, Charles Harry 1943- WhoEnt 92
Bernstein, Charles Marc 1952- WhoWest 92
Bernstein, David 1910- AmMWSc 92
Bernstein, David Howard 1956- WhoAmL 92
Bernstein, David Maier 1947- AmMWSc 92
Bernstein, Donald Chester 1942- WhoAmL 92
Bernstein, Donald Scott 1953- WhoAmL 92
Bernstein, Dorothy Lewis 1914- AmMWSc 92
Bernstein, Douglas Lon 1958- WhoEnt 92
Bernstein, Edwin S. 1930- WhoAmL 92
Bernstein, Elaine Katz 1922- AmMWSc 92
Bernstein, Elliot R 1941- AmMWSc 92
Bernstein, Elmer 1922- IntMPA 92, NewAmDM, WhoWest 92
Bernstein, Emil Oscar 1929- AmMWSc 92
Bernstein, Eric Martin 1957- WhoAmL 92
Bernstein, Eugene F 1930- AmMWSc 92
Bernstein, Eugene H AmMWSc 92
Bernstein, Eugene Merle 1931- AmMWSc 92
Bernstein, Gerald Sanford 1928- AmMWSc 92
Bernstein, Gerald William 1947- WhoWest 92
Bernstein, H. Bruce 1943- WhoAmL 92
Bernstein, Harris 1934- AmMWSc 92, WhoWest 92
Bernstein, Herbert J 1943- AmMWSc 92
Bernstein, Herbert Jacob 1944- AmMWSc 92
Bernstein, Herbert L. 1930- WhoAmL 92
Bernstein, Honey 1952- WhoAmL 92
Bernstein, I Leonard 1924- AmMWSc 92
Bernstein, I Melvin 1938- AmMWSc 92
Bernstein, Ingeborg 1931- Who 92
Bernstein, Ira Borah 1924- AmMWSc 92
Bernstein, Irwin Frederick 1933- WhoFI 92
Bernstein, Irwin S 1934- AmMWSc 92
Bernstein, Irwin Samuel 1933- AmMWSc 92
Bernstein, Isadore A 1919- AmMWSc 92
Bernstein, Jack B. 1937- IntMPA 92
Bernstein, Jack Barry 1937- WhoEnt 92
Bernstein, Jane DrAPF 91
Bernstein, Jane 1949- WhoEnt 92
Bernstein, Jason Asher 1958- WhoAmL 92
Bernstein, Jay 1927- AmMWSc 92, WhoMW 92
Bernstein, Jay 1937- IntMPA 92
Bernstein, Jay S 1942- WhoAmP 91
Bernstein, Jerald Jack 1934- AmMWSc 92
Bernstein, Jeremy 1929- AmMWSc 92
Bernstein, Jeremy Marshall 1952- WhoAmL 92
Bernstein, Jerry Daniel 1949- WhoAmL 92
Bernstein, Jesse Aaron 1948- WhoMW 92
Bernstein, Joel Edward 1943- AmMWSc 92
Bernstein, Jonathan 1951- WhoWest 92
Bernstein, Joseph 1930- WhoAmL 92, WhoFI 92
Bernstein, Joseph N 1945- AmMWSc 92
Bernstein, Kenneth Alan 1956- WhoAmL 92
Bernstein, Lawrence 1940- AmMWSc 92
Bernstein, Leonard d1990 IntWW 91N, LesBEnT 92, Who 92N
Bernstein, Leonard 1918-1990 AnObit 1990, BenetAL 91, ConCom 92, FacFETw [port], NewAmDM, News 91, RComAH
Bernstein, LeRoy G WhoAmP 91
Bernstein, Leslie 1924- AmMWSc 92
Bernstein, Leslie 1939- AmMWSc 92
Bernstein, Lionel M 1923- AmMWSc 92
Bernstein, Lisa DrAPF 91
Bernstein, Louis 1927- WhoRel 92
Bernstein, Margaret Esther 1959- WhoBlA 92
Bernstein, Marvin Harry 1943- AmMWSc 92
Bernstein, Maurice Harry 1923- AmMWSc 92
Bernstein, Maurice Jeremy 1939- WhoEnt 92
Bernstein, Merton Clay 1923- WhoAmL 92
Bernstein, Michael Irwin 1938- WhoAmL 92
Bernstein, Mitchell Harris 1949- WhoAmL 92
Bernstein, Norman Xavier 1930- WhoRel 92
Bernstein, Ralph 1933- AmMWSc 92
Bernstein, Richard 1923-1990 AnObit 1990
Bernstein, Richard A. 1946- WhoFI 92
Bernstein, Richard Barry d1990 IntWW 91N
Bernstein, Richard Barry 1923- AmMWSc 92
Bernstein, Robert Alan 1958- WhoAmL 92
Bernstein, Robert Jay 1948- WhoAmL 92, WhoEnt 92
Bernstein, Robert Lee 1944- AmMWSc 92
Bernstein, Robert Louis 1923- IntWW 91
Bernstein, Robert Steven 1943- AmMWSc 92
Bernstein, Robert Steven 1954- WhoAmL 92
Bernstein, Ronald Harold 1918- Who 92
Bernstein, Sanford Irwin 1953- AmMWSc 92
Bernstein, Seldon Edwin 1926- AmMWSc 92
Bernstein, Sheldon 1927- AmMWSc 92
Bernstein, Sidney 1899- IntMPA 92
Bernstein, Sidney 1938- WhoFI 92
Bernstein, Sidney Ralph 1907- WhoMW 92
Bernstein, Sol 1927- AmMWSc 92, WhoWest 92
Bernstein, Stanley Carl 1937- AmMWSc 92
Bernstein, Stanley H 1924- AmMWSc 92
Bernstein, Stephen 1933- AmMWSc 92
Bernstein, Stephen Michael 1941- WhoAmL 92
Bernstein, Stuart 1919- WhoAmL 92
Bernstein, Susan Lisa 1965- WhoWest 92
Bernstein, Theodore 1926- AmMWSc 92
Bernstein, Walter 1919- IntMPA 92
Bernstein, William 1933- IntMPA 92, WhoEnt 92, WhoFI 92
Bernstein, Zalman C. WhoFI 92
Bernstein-Medlyn, Jeanne Ann 1947- WhoMW 92
Bernstine, Daniel O. 1947- WhoBlA 92
Bernstine, Daniel O'Neal 1947- WhoAmL 92
Bernstine, Rod Earl 1965- WhoBlA 92
Bernstorf, Betty James 1925- WhoAmP 91
Bernstorf, Earl Cranston 1921- AmMWSc 92
Bernt, Benno Anthony 1931- WhoFI 92
Bernthal, Frederick M 1943- WhoAmP 91
Bernthal, Frederick Michael 1943- AmMWSc 92
Bernthal, John E 1940- AmMWSc 92
Berntsen, Robert Andyv 1917- AmMWSc 92
Bero, James Louis 1942- WhoFI 92
Berolzheimer, Karl 1932- WhoAmL 92
Beron, Alberto 1940- WhoWest 92
Beron, Gail Laskey 1943- WhoMW 92
Beron, Kurt James 1956- WhoFI 92
Beron, Patrick 1952- AmMWSc 92
Beros, Svetlana 1961- WhoMW 92
Beroza, Morton 1917- AmMWSc 92
Berquist, James Richard 1928- WhoIns 92
Berquist, Jon Laurence 1963- WhoRel 92
Berquist, Robert James 1960- WhoMW 92
Berra, Paul M 1925- WhoAmP 91
Berra, Tim Martin 1943- AmMWSc 92
Berra, Yogi 1925- FacFETw
Berragan, Gerald Brian 1933- Who 92
Berrend, Robert E 1925- AmMWSc 92
Berresford, Geoffrey Case 1944- AmMWSc 92
Berresford, John Wickham 1950- WhoAmL 92
Berreth, Julius R 1929- AmMWSc 92
Berrett, Delwyn Green 1935- AmMWSc 92
Berrett, Lamar Cecil 1926- WhoRel 92
Berrett, Paul O 1928- AmMWSc 92
Berrettini, Wade Hayhurst 1951- AmMWSc 92
Berrey, Robert Forrest 1939- WhoAmL 92, WhoFI 92
Berrey, Robert Wilson, III 1929- WhoMW 92
Berri 1934- IntWW 91
Berri, Claude 1934- IntMPA 92
Berri, Nabih 1939- IntWW 91
Berridge, Donald Roy 1922- Who 92
Berridge, Elizabeth 1919- IntAu&W 91
Berridge, Michael John 1938- Who 92
Berridge, Paul Thomas 1937- WhoRel 92
Berridge, Thomas E. 1946- WhoIns 92
Berrie, David William 1937- AmMWSc 92
Berrie, John Archibald Alexander 1887-1962 TwCPaSc
Berriedale, Lord 1981- Who 92
Berrier, David Jewell 1934- WhoWest 92
Berrier, Harry Hilbourn 1917- AmMWSc 92
Berrigan brothers FacFETw, RelLAm 91
Berrigan, Daniel DrAPF 91
Berrigan, Daniel 1921- AmPeW, BenetAL 91, ConPo 91, FacFETw
Berrigan, Daniel J 1921- IntAu&W 91, RelLAm 91, WrDr 92
Berrigan, Elizabeth McAlister AmPeW
Berrigan, Philip 1923- AmPeW, FacFETw, RelLAm 91
Berrigan, Philip Francis 1923- BenetAL 91
Berrill, Kenneth 1920- IntWW 91, Who 92
Berrill, Michael 1944- AmMWSc 92
Berrill, Norman John 1903- IntAu&W 91, IntWW 91, Who 92, WrDr 92
Berriman, David 1928- Who 92
Berriman, Lester P 1925- AmMWSc 92
Berring, Robert Charles, Jr. 1949- WhoAmL 92
Berrington, Craig Anthony 1943- WhoAmL 92
Berrington, Hugh Bayard 1928- WrDr 92
Berrington, John IntAu&W 91X
Berrios, Angel O 1940- WhoAmP 91
Berrios, Joseph 1952- WhoAmP 91, WhoHisp 92
Berrios, Suzette Nanovic 1962- WhoAmL 92
Berrios Cuadrado, Jose Diego 1934- WhoHisp 92
Berrios de Santos, Elsa I. WhoHisp 92
Berriozabal, Manuel Phillip 1931- WhoHisp 92
Berriozabal, Maria Antonietta 1941- WhoAmP 91, WhoHisp 92
Berrisford, Peter 1932- TwCPaSc
Berritt, Harold Edward 1936- WhoAmL 92, WhoFI 92
Berro, Michael Bruce 1955- WhoEnt 92
Berroa, Billy WhoHisp 92
Berry Who 92
Berry, Adrian M 1937- IntAu&W 91, WrDr 92
Berry, Albert G. 1933- WhoBlA 92
Berry, Anthony Arthur 1915- Who 92
Berry, Anthony Scyld 1954- Who 92
Berry, Archie Paul 1935- WhoBlA 92
Berry, Arthur 1925- TwCPaSc
Berry, B S 1929- AmMWSc 92
Berry, Barbara 1937- WrDr 92
Berry, Benjamin Donaldson 1939- WhoBlA 92
Berry, Bernard David 1948- WhoMW 92
Berry, Beverly A. 1939- WhoMW 92
Berry, Bob Ray 1938- WhoFI 92
Berry, Bradford William 1941- AmMWSc 92
Berry, Brian J 1958- WhoAmP 91
Berry, Brian Joe Lobley 1934- IntAu&W 91, IntWW 91, WhoFI 92, WrDr 92
Berry, Charles d1765 DcNCBi 1
Berry, Charles Arthur 1929- AmMWSc 92
Berry, Charles Dennis 1940- AmMWSc 92
Berry, Charles Eugene 1950- WhoAmP 91
Berry, Charles Gordon 1950- WhoAmL 92
Berry, Charles Richard 1927- AmMWSc 92
Berry, Charles Richard 1948- WhoAmL 92
Berry, Charles Richard, Jr 1945- AmMWSc 92
Berry, Christine Albachten 1946- AmMWSc 92
Berry, Christine Anne 1949- WhoWest 92
Berry, Chu 1908-1941 NewAmDM
Berry, Chuck 1926- FacFETw [port], IntWW 91, NewAmDM, RComAH, WhoBlA 92
Berry, Cicely 1926- WrDr 92
Berry, Cicely Frances 1926- Who 92
Berry, Clark Green 1908- AmMWSc 92
Berry, Clyde Marvin 1913- AmMWSc 92
Berry, Colin Leonard 1937- Who 92
Berry, D.C. DrAPF 91
Berry, Daisilee H AmMWSc 92
Berry, Dan C WhoAmP 91
Berry, David Michael 1951- WhoMW 92
Berry, Dean Lester 1935- WhoAmL 92
Berry, Deborah 1961- WhoEnt 92, WhoWest 92
Berry, DeMaris Anne 1943- WhoMW 92
Berry, Don 1932- TwCWW 91, WrDr 92
Berry, Donald Kent 1953- WhoRel 92
Berry, Donald Lee 1940- WhoFI 92
Berry, Donald S 1911- AmMWSc 92
Berry, Douglas R. 1952- WhoFI 92
Berry, E Janet 1917- AmMWSc 92
Berry, Edward Alan 1952- AmMWSc 92
Berry, Edward DeJarnette 1949- WhoAmP 91
Berry, Edwin X 1935- AmMWSc 92, WhoWest 92
Berry, Eve Marie 1950- WhoFI 92
Berry, Faith 1939- ConAu 133
Berry, Frances Miriam BenetAL 91
Berry, Francis 1915- ConPo 91, IntAu&W 91, Who 92, WrDr 92
Berry, Fraser Who 92
Berry, Frederick E 1949- WhoAmP 91
Berry, Frederick Joseph 1940- WhoBlA 92
Berry, Gail W 1939- AmMWSc 92
Berry, Garrett Richard 1951- WhoEnt 92
Berry, George Willard 1915- AmMWSc 92
Berry, George William 1907- AmMWSc 92
Berry, Glenn 1929- WhoWest 92
Berry, Gordon Dana 1959- WhoEnt 92
Berry, Gordon L. WhoBlA 92
Berry, Gregory Franklin 1943- AmMWSc 92
Berry, Guy C 1935- AmMWSc 92
Berry, Harriet Morehead 1877-1940 DcNCBi 1
Berry, Henry Gordon 1940- AmMWSc 92
Berry, Herbert Weaver 1913- AmMWSc 92
Berry, Ila F 1922- IntAu&W 91
Berry, Ivan Leroy 1937- AmMWSc 92
Berry, James 1925- ConAu 135, ConPo 91, SmATA 67 [port], WrDr 92
Berry, James D., III 1938- WhoFI 92
Berry, James Frederick 1927- AmMWSc 92
Berry, James Frederick 1947- AmMWSc 92
Berry, James G 1925- AmMWSc 92
Berry, James Heird 1910- WhoWest 92
Berry, James Lee 1961- WhoRel 92
Berry, James Terrance 1946- WhoMW 92
Berry, James Wesley 1926- AmMWSc 92
Berry, James William 1931- Who 92
Berry, James William 1935- AmMWSc 92
Berry, Janice Rae 1937- WhoWest 92
Berry, Janis Marie 1949- WhoAmL 92
Berry, Jeffrey Alan 1958- WhoEnt 92
Berry, Jerome 1950- WhoBlA 92
Berry, Jewel Edward 1926- AmMWSc 92
Berry, Jo 1933- IntAu&W 91
Berry, Joe Gene 1944- AmMWSc 92
Berry, John DrAPF 91
Berry, John 1798-1870 DcNCBi 1
Berry, John 1907- Who 92
Berry, John 1917- IntMPA 92
Berry, John Charles 1938- WhoWest 92

**Berry,** John Douglas 1944- *WhoFI 92*
**Berry,** John Fredrick 1955- *WhoAmL 92*
**Berry,** Joy *ConAu 134*
**Berry,** Joy Wilt 1944- *ConAu 134*
**Berry,** June *TwCPaSc*
**Berry,** Keith O 1938- *AmMWSc 92*
**Berry,** Keith Oran 1938- *WhoWest 92*
**Berry,** Keith Thomas 1936- *WhoRel 92*
**Berry,** Ken 1933- *IntMPA 92*
**Berry,** Ken A. 1958- *WhoEnt 92*
**Berry,** L. Michael 1937- *IntWW 91*
**Berry,** Latin 1967- *WhoBlA 92*
**Berry,** Lee Allen 1945- *AmMWSc 92*
**Berry,** Lee Roy, Jr. 1943- *WhoBlA 92*
**Berry,** Lemuel, Jr. 1946- *WhoBlA 92, WhoEnt 92*
**Berry,** Leonard 1930- *AmMWSc 92*
**Berry,** Leonidas H. 1902- *WhoBlA 92*
**Berry,** Leonidas Harris 1902- *AmMWSc 92*
**Berry,** LeRoy 1920- *WhoBlA 92*
**Berry,** Linda Tomlinson 1946- *WhoFI 92*
**Berry,** Lisbon C., Jr. 1922- *WhoBlA 92*
**Berry,** Lloyd E. 1935-1977 *ConAu 133*
**Berry,** Lorraine L 1949- *WhoAmP 91*
**Berry,** Louise Spaulding 1927- *WhoAmP 91*
**Berry,** Margaret Loree 1927- *WhoAmP 91*
**Berry,** Mary Alice 1951- *WhoRel 92*
**Berry,** Mary Frances 1938- *NotBlAW 92 [port], WhoBlA 92*
**Berry,** Max Nathan 1935- *WhoAmL 92, WhoAmP 91*
**Berry,** Maxwell 1910- *AmMWSc 92*
**Berry,** Michael G. 1957- *WhoEnt 92*
**Berry,** Michael James 1947- *AmMWSc 92*
**Berry,** Michael John 1940- *AmMWSc 92*
**Berry,** Michael Victor 1941- *Who 92*
**Berry,** Michelle 1932- *WhoRel 92*
**Berry,** Myron Garland 1919- *AmMWSc 92*
**Berry,** Ondra Lamon 1958- *WhoBlA 92*
**Berry,** Paul 1919- *IntAu&W 91, WrDr 92*
**Berry,** Paul 1946- *TwCPaSc*
**Berry,** Paul Lawrence 1944- *WhoBlA 92*
**Berry,** Peter Austin 1935- *Who 92*
**Berry,** Peter Fremantle 1944- *Who 92*
**Berry,** Philip Alfonso 1950- *WhoBlA 92*
**Berry,** Phillip Reid 1950- *WhoMW 92*
**Berry,** Phillip Samuel 1937- *WhoAmL 92*
**Berry,** Ralph Eugene 1940- *AmMWSc 92*
**Berry,** Richard C 1928- *AmMWSc 92*
**Berry,** Richard Emerson 1933- *AmMWSc 92*
**Berry,** Richard G 1916- *AmMWSc 92*
**Berry,** Richard Lee 1942- *AmMWSc 92*
**Berry,** Richard Morgan 1945- *WhoAmL 92*
**Berry,** Richard Stephen 1931- *AmMWSc 92, IntWW 91*
**Berry,** Richard Warren 1933- *AmMWSc 92*
**Berry,** Robert Bass 1948- *WhoFI 92*
**Berry,** Robert Courtland 1931- *WhoRel 92*
**Berry,** Robert Craven 1936- *WhoAmL 92, WhoEnt 92*
**Berry,** Robert Eddy 1930- *AmMWSc 92*
**Berry,** Robert Edward Fraser 1926- *Who 92, WhoRel 92*
**Berry,** Robert James 1934- *Who 92*
**Berry,** Robert John 1929- *AmMWSc 92*
**Berry,** Robert Langley Page 1918- *Who 92*
**Berry,** Robert Taylor 1949- *WhoMW 92*
**Berry,** Robert Vaughan 1933- *WhoFI 92*
**Berry,** Robert Wade 1930- *AmMWSc 92*
**Berry,** Robert Walter 1928- *AmMWSc 92*
**Berry,** Robert Wayne 1944- *AmMWSc 92*
**Berry,** Robert William 1944- *WhoRel 92*
**Berry,** Robert Worth 1926- *WhoAmL 92, WhoFI 92, WhoWest 92*
**Berry,** Rodney T 1948- *WhoAmP 91*
**Berry,** Roger Julian 1935- *Who 92*
**Berry,** Roger Simon 1948- *Who 92*
**Berry,** Ron 1920- *IntAu&W 91, WrDr 92*
**Berry,** Ronald 1917- *Who 92*
**Berry,** Roscoe Darewood, Jr. 1921- *WhoBlA 92*
**Berry,** Roy Alfred, Jr 1933- *AmMWSc 92*
**Berry,** Scyld *Who 92*
**Berry,** Simon *Who 92*
**Berry,** Spencer Julian 1933- *AmMWSc 92*
**Berry,** Stanley Z 1930- *AmMWSc 92*
**Berry,** Stephen Pressley 1951- *WhoRel 92*
**Berry,** Theodore M. 1905- *WhoBlA 92*
**Berry,** Thomas 1914- *WrDr 92*
**Berry,** Thomas A. 1939- *WhoAmL 92*
**Berry,** Thomas Clayton 1948- *WhoWest 92*
**Berry,** Thomas Eugene 1923- *WhoAmL 92*
**Berry,** Todd Andrew 1951- *WhoMW 92*
**Berry,** Turney Powers 1961- *WhoAmL 92*
**Berry,** Vern Vincent 1941- *AmMWSc 92*
**Berry,** Vinod K 1936- *AmMWSc 92*
**Berry,** Virgil Jennings, Jr. 1928- *WhoFI 92*
**Berry,** Wallace Taft 1928- *WrDr 92*
**Berry,** Walter 1929- *IntWW 91, WhoEnt 92*
**Berry,** Weldon H. *WhoBlA 92*
**Berry,** Wendell 1934- *BenetAL 91, ConPo 91, FacFETw, IntWW 91, WrDr 92*
**Berry,** Wendell E. *DrAPF 91*
**Berry,** William B 1931- *AmMWSc 92*
**Berry,** William Benjamin Newell 1931- *AmMWSc 92*
**Berry,** William Fouts 1943- *WhoMW 92*
**Berry,** William Lee 1927- *AmMWSc 92*
**Berry,** William Martin 1920- *WhoFI 92, WhoMW 92*
**Berry-Caban,** Cristobal S. *WhoHisp 92*
**Berryessa,** Richard Greaves 1947- *WhoWest 92*
**Berryhill,** David Lee 1944- *AmMWSc 92*
**Berryhill,** Michael *DrAPF 91*
**Berryhill,** Stuart Randall 1951- *WhoWest 92*
**Berryman,** Alan Andrew 1937- *AmMWSc 92*
**Berryman,** George Hugh 1914- *AmMWSc 92*
**Berryman,** Jack Holmes 1921- *AmMWSc 92*
**Berryman,** James Cleo 1935- *WhoRel 92*
**Berryman,** James Garland 1947- *AmMWSc 92*
**Berryman,** John 1914-1972 *BenetAL 91, ConAu 35NR, FacFETw*
**Berryman,** Macon M. 1908- *WhoBlA 92*
**Berryman,** Matilene S. *WhoBlA 92*
**Berryman,** Richard Byron 1932- *WhoAmL 92*
**Bers,** Abraham 1930- *AmMWSc 92*
**Bers,** Edith D. *WhoEnt 92*
**Bers,** Lipman 1914- *AmMWSc 92, IntWW 91*
**Bersch,** Charles Frank 1927- *AmMWSc 92*
**Bersch,** Lynn A. 1962- *WhoAmL 92*
**Berscheidt,** Joanne Marie 1944- *WhoAmL 92*
**Bershad,** Andrew David 1955- *WhoAmL 92*
**Bershad,** Jack R. 1930- *WhoFI 92*
**Bershad,** Neil Jeremy 1937- *AmMWSc 92*
**Bershader,** Daniel 1923- *AmMWSc 92*
**Bersohn,** Malcolm 1925- *AmMWSc 92*
**Bersohn,** Richard 1925- *AmMWSc 92*
**Berson,** Alan *AmMWSc 92*
**Berson,** David William 1954- *WhoFI 92*
**Berson,** Jerome Abraham 1924- *AmMWSc 92, IntWW 91*
**Berson,** Norman S 1926- *WhoAmP 91*
**Berssenbrugge,** Mei-Mei *DrAPF 91*
**Bersted,** Bruce Howard 1940- *AmMWSc 92*
**Berstein,** Irving Aaron 1926- *WhoFI 92*
**Berstein,** Israel 1926- *AmMWSc 92*
**Bersticker,** Albert Charles 1934- *WhoMW 92*
**Bersu,** Edward Thorwald 1946- *AmMWSc 92*
**Bert,** Charles Wesley 1929- *AmMWSc 92*
**Bert,** Eddie 1922- *WhoEnt 92*
**Bert,** Jack Michael 1947- *WhoMW 92*
**Bert,** Mark Henry 1916- *AmMWSc 92*
**Bert,** Norman Allen 1942- *WhoWest 92*
**Berta,** Joseph Michel 1940- *WhoEnt 92*
**Bertagnolli,** Leslie *DrAPF 91*
**Bertain,** George Joseph, Jr. 1929- *WhoAmL 92, WhoWest 92*
**Bertalanffy,** Felix D 1926- *AmMWSc 92*
**Bertani,** Dante G 1931- *WhoAmP 91*
**Bertani,** Giuseppe 1923- *AmMWSc 92*
**Bertani,** Lillian Elizabeth 1931- *AmMWSc 92*
**Bertaut,** Edgard Francis 1931- *AmMWSc 92*
**Bertea,** Hyla Holmes 1940- *WhoWest 92*
**Berteau,** Peter Edmund 1929- *AmMWSc 92*
**Bertell,** Rosalie 1929- *AmMWSc 92*
**Bertelo,** Christopher Anthony 1947- *AmMWSc 92*
**Bertelsen,** Bruce I 1926- *AmMWSc 92*
**Bertelsen,** Michael William 1951- *WhoAmL 92*
**Bertelsen,** Ole *WhoRel 92*
**Bertelsman,** William Odis 1936- *WhoAmL 92*
**Bertelson,** Robert Calvin 1931- *AmMWSc 92, WhoMW 92*
**Bertenshaw,** Bobbi Cherrelle 1961- *WhoEnt 92*
**Bertenshaw,** William Howard, III 1930- *WhoEnt 92*
**Bertera,** James H 1948- *AmMWSc 92*
**Bertero,** Vitelmo V. *WhoWest 92*
**Berthelot,** Yves M. 1937- *IntWW 91*
**Berthelsdorf,** Siegfried 1911- *WhoWest 92*
**Berthelsen,** Asger 1928- *IntWW 91*
**Berthelsen,** John Robert 1954- *WhoFI 92, WhoMW 92*
**Berthelsen,** Marilyn A 1929- *WhoAmP 91*
**Berthiaume,** John Lloyd 1956- *WhoMW 92*
**Berthiaume,** Marc Andre 1956- *WhoEnt 92*
**Berthoin,** Georges Paul 1925- *IntWW 91, Who 92*
**Berthold,** Fred, Jr. 1922- *WhoRel 92*
**Berthold,** George Charles 1935- *WhoRel 92*
**Berthold,** John William, III 1945- *AmMWSc 92*
**Berthold,** Joseph Ernest 1947- *AmMWSc 92*
**Berthold,** Robert, Jr 1941- *AmMWSc 92*
**Berthold,** Robert R. 1945- *WhoMW 92*
**Bertholf,** Dennis E 1941- *AmMWSc 92*
**Berthollet,** Claude-Louis 1748-1822 *BlkwCEP*
**Berthon,** Stephen 1922- *Who 92*
**Berthoud,** Ferdinand 1727-1807 *BlkwCEP*
**Berthoud,** Jacques Alexandre 1935- *Who 92*
**Berthoud,** Kenneth H., Jr. 1928- *WhoBlA 92*
**Berthoud,** Martin 1931- *IntWW 91, Who 92*
**Berthouex,** Paul Mac 1940- *AmMWSc 92*
**Berthrong,** Morgan 1918- *AmMWSc 92*
**Berti,** Luciano 1922- *IntWW 91*
**Bertie** *Who 92*
**Bertie,** John E 1936- *AmMWSc 92*
**Bertin,** John Joseph 1938- *AmMWSc 92*
**Bertin,** Michael C 1942- *AmMWSc 92*
**Bertin,** Michael Stephen 1951- *WhoWest 92*
**Bertin,** Robert Ian 1952- *AmMWSc 92*
**Bertinelli,** Valerie 1960- *IntMPA 92, WhoEnt 92*
**Bertini,** Gary 1927- *WhoEnt 92*
**Bertini,** Hugo W 1926- *AmMWSc 92*
**Bertino,** Frank Christen 1938- *WhoWest 92*
**Bertino,** Joseph R 1930- *AmMWSc 92*
**Bertinuson,** Teresalee *WhoAmP 91*
**Bertke,** Eldridge Melvin *AmMWSc 92*
**Bertland,** Alexander U 1931- *AmMWSc 92*
**Bertler,** Mark John 1950- *WhoMW 92*
**Bertles,** John F 1925- *AmMWSc 92*
**Bertness,** Janette Ann 1957- *WhoAmL 92*
**Bertnolli,** Edward Clarence 1935- *AmMWSc 92*
**Bertocci,** Ugo 1926- *AmMWSc 92*
**Bertog,** Eugene Tracy 1930- *WhoMW 92*
**Bertoia,** Harry 1915-1978 *DcTwDes, FacFETw*
**Bertola,** Giuseppe M. 1910- *IntWW 91*
**Bertolacini,** Ralph James 1925- *AmMWSc 92*
**Bertolami,** Charles Nicholas 1949- *AmMWSc 92, WhoWest 92*
**Bertolatus,** Roy Edward 1952- *WhoAmL 92*
**Bertoldi,** Gilbert LeRoy 1938- *AmMWSc 92*
**Bertoldo,** Joseph Ramon 1950- *WhoAmL 92*
**Bertolette,** W deB 1914- *AmMWSc 92*
**Bertoletti,** Marisa Capriolo 1930- *WhoAmP 91*
**Bertoli,** Paolo 1908- *IntWW 91, WhoRel 92*
**Bertolini,** Donald R 1949- *AmMWSc 92*
**Bertolino,** James *DrAPF 91*
**Bertolino,** James 1942- *ConPo 91, IntAu&W 91, WrDr 92*
**Bertolucci,** Bernardo 1940- *FacFETw, IntDcF 2-2 [port], IntMPA 92, IntWW 91*
**Bertolucci,** Bernardo 1941- *WhoEnt 92*
**Berton,** John Andrew 1930- *AmMWSc 92*
**Berton,** Pierre 1920- *CurBio 91 [port], WrDr 92*
**Berton,** Pierre Francis Demarigny 1920- *IntAu&W 91*
**Berton,** Stuart Irwin 1940- *WhoEnt 92*
**Berton,** William Morris 1924- *AmMWSc 92*
**Bertonazzi,** Louis Peter 1933- *WhoAmP 91*
**Bertoncini,** Peter Joseph 1939- *AmMWSc 92*
**Bertone,** Flaminio 1903- *DcTwDes, FacFETw*
**Bertone,** Nuccio 1914- *DcTwDes, FacFETw*
**Bertoni,** Henry Louis 1938- *AmMWSc 92*
**Bertoniere,** Noelie Rita 1936- *AmMWSc 92*
**Bertossa,** Robert C 1916- *AmMWSc 92*
**Bertouille,** Andre 1932- *IntWW 91*
**Bertozzi,** Eugene R 1915- *AmMWSc 92*
**Bertozzi,** William 1931- *AmMWSc 92*
**Bertram,** Adolf 1859-1945 *EncTR 91 [port]*
**Bertram,** Brian Colin Ricardo 1944- *Who 92*
**Bertram,** Christoph 1937- *Who 92*
**Bertram,** Debbie Kay 1958- *WhoMW 92*
**Bertram,** Edward Arthur 1939- *WhoWest 92*
**Bertram,** Ernst 1884-1957 *EncTR 91*
**Bertram,** J E 1927- *AmMWSc 92*
**Bertram,** Jack Renard 1943- *WhoWest 92*
**Bertram,** James 1910- *IntAu&W 91, WrDr 92*
**Bertram,** Jeff *WhoAmP 91*
**Bertram,** Joe Leo, Sr 1954- *WhoAmP 91*
**Bertram,** Kate 1912- *Who 92*
**Bertram,** Leon Leroy 1917- *AmMWSc 92*
**Bertram,** Manya M. *WhoAmL 92*
**Bertram,** Phyllis Ann 1954- *WhoAmL 92*
**Bertram,** Robert David Darney 1941- *Who 92*
**Bertram,** Robert William 1942- *AmMWSc 92*
**Bertram,** Sidney 1913- *AmMWSc 92*
**Bertram,** Timothy Allyn 1955- *AmMWSc 92*
**Bertramson,** Bertram Rodney 1914- *AmMWSc 92*
**Bertran,** Ross Frederick 1952- *WhoEnt 92*
**Bertrand,** Aloysius 1807-1841 *NinCLC 31 [port]*
**Bertrand,** Charlotte Marie 1969- *WhoEnt 92*
**Bertrand,** Donald Ernest 1946- *WhoAmL 92*
**Bertrand,** Forest 1918- *AmMWSc 92*
**Bertrand,** Fred Edmond 1938- *AmMWSc 92*
**Bertrand,** Frederic Howard 1936- *WhoFI 92*
**Bertrand,** Gary Lane 1935- *AmMWSc 92*
**Bertrand,** Helen Anne 1939- *AmMWSc 92*
**Bertrand,** Helmut 1937- *AmMWSc 92*
**Bertrand,** Joseph Aaron 1933- *AmMWSc 92*
**Bertrand,** Joseph E 1924- *AmMWSc 92*
**Bertrand,** Joseph G., Sr. 1931-1990 *WhoBlA 92N*
**Bertrand,** Marsha 1950- *WhoMW 92*
**Bertrand,** Rene Robert 1936- *AmMWSc 92*
**Bertrand,** Ronald Ralph 1942- *WhoWest 92*
**Bertrand,** Terry Dale 1951- *WhoRel 92*
**Bertranou,** Armando Victorio 1942- *IntWW 91*
**Bertrew,** Berton *ScFEYrs*
**Bertsch,** Audrey *WhoRel 92*
**Bertsch,** Charles Rudolph 1931- *AmMWSc 92*
**Bertsch,** Frank Henry 1925- *WhoMW 92*
**Bertsch,** George Frederick 1942- *AmMWSc 92*
**Bertsch,** Hans 1944- *AmMWSc 92*
**Bertsch,** James L. 1944- *WhoFI 92*
**Bertsch,** Marguerite d1967 *ReelWom [port]*
**Bertsch,** Mark Alan 1959- *WhoAmL 92*
**Bertsch,** Robert Joseph 1948- *AmMWSc 92*
**Bertsch,** Wolfgang 1940- *AmMWSc 92*
**Bertucelli,** Robert Edward 1948- *WhoFI 92*
**Berty,** Jozsef M 1922- *AmMWSc 92*
**Bertz,** Steven Howard 1950- *AmMWSc 92*
**Beru,** Nega 1951- *AmMWSc 92*
**Berube,** Georgette B *WhoAmP 91*
**Berube,** Robert 1935- *AmMWSc 92*
**Berutowicz,** Wlodzimierz 1914- *IntWW 91*
**Berv,** Harry *WhoEnt 92*
**Berven,** Norman Lee 1945- *WhoMW 92*
**Bervid,** Joseph Leo 1953- *WhoAmL 92*
**Bervin-Mitchell,** Gabrielle 1955- *WhoBlA 92*
**Berwald,** Franz 1796-1868 *NewAmDM*
**Berwick,** Edward *ScFEYrs*
**Bery,** Mahendera K *AmMWSc 92*
**Bery,** Rajendra Nath 1930- *WhoFI 92*
**Berz,** Martin 1960- *WhoMW 92*
**Berzins,** Erna Marija 1914- *WhoMW 92*
**Berzins,** Valdis Andris 1951- *WhoWest 92*
**Berzinski,** Vivian Lee Hobbs *WhoAmL 92*
**Berzofsky,** Jay Arthur 1946- *AmMWSc 92*
**Berzow,** Harold Steven 1946- *WhoAmL 92*
**Besabe,** Renato C. 1945- *WhoFI 92*
**Besancon,** Robert Martin 1910- *AmMWSc 92*
**Besant,** Annie Wood 1847-1933 *RelLAm 91*
**Besant,** Walter 1836-1901 *RfGEnL 91, ScFEYrs*
**Besch,** Anthony John Elwyn 1924- *Who 92*
**Besch,** Bernice Kathleen 1924- *WhoMW 92*
**Besch,** Emerson Louis 1928- *AmMWSc 92*
**Besch,** Gordon Otto Carl 1922- *AmMWSc 92*
**Besch,** Henry Roland, Jr 1942- *AmMWSc 92*
**Besch,** Paige Keith 1931- *AmMWSc 92*
**Besch,** Werner Walter 1928- *IntWW 91*
**Bescherer,** Edwin A., Jr. 1933- *WhoFI 92*
**Beschloss,** Michael Richard 1955- *NewYTBS 91 [port]*
**Beschorner,** W E 1947- *AmMWSc 92*
**Besel,** Karl William 1968- *WhoRel 92*
**Besel,** Robert Curtis 1960- *WhoWest 92*
**Besen,** Aaron Jay 1958- *WhoAmL 92*
**Besen,** Stanley Martin 1937- *WhoFI 92*
**Beserra,** Frank J 1947- *WhoAmP 91*

Beshar, Christine 1929- WhoAmL 92
Beshar, Robert Peter 1928- WhoAmL 92
Besharov, Douglas John 1945- WhoAmL 92
Besharse, Joseph Culp 1944- AmMWSc 92
Beshear, Betty Jean 1941- WhoAmP 91
Beshear, Steven L. 1944- WhoAmL 92, WhoAmP 91
Beshears, Kelsy 1898- WhoBlA 92
Beshears, William Joseph 1930- WhoRel 92
Beshers, Daniel N 1928- AmMWSc 92
Besinaiz, Carlos WhoHisp 92
Besio, Suzanne Knapp 1959- WhoMW 92
Besjakov, Dan Viktor 1961- WhoFI 92
Beskid, George 1929- AmMWSc 92
Beskow, Elsa 1874-1953 ConAu 135
Besley, Christopher 1916- Who 92
Besman, Michael IntMPA 92
Besmann, Theodore Martin 1949- AmMWSc 92
Besnard, Paul Albert 1849-1934 ThHEIm
Besner, Michel 1947- AmMWSc 92
Besnette, Francis Frank Henry 1939- WhoWest 92
Besnoff, Larry 1951- WhoAmL 92
Besosa, Frank Louis 1963- WhoFI 92
Besoyan, Rick 1924-1970 NewAmDM
Besozzi, Alfio Joseph 1921- AmMWSc 92
Besozzi, Paul Charles 1947- WhoAmL 92
Bespalec, Dale Anthony 1951- WhoMW 92
Bespalov, Yuri Aleksandrovich 1939- IntWW 91
Bess, Henry David 1939- WhoFI 92, WhoWest 92
Bess, James Earnest 1950- WhoEnt 92
Bess, John Clifford 1937- AmMWSc 92
Bess, Robert Carl 1944- AmMWSc 92
Bess, William Louis, Jr. 1941- WhoEnt 92
Bessala, Jean Joseph 1941- BlkOlyM
Bessalel, Menajem Moises 1932- WhoFI 92, WhoHisp 92
Bessant, Shanna Elizabeth 1966- WhoWest 92
Bessborough, Earl of 1913- Who 92
Besse, John C 1933- AmMWSc 92
Besse, Robert Gale 1923- WhoWest 92
Bessell, Frank D. 1944- WhoEnt 92
Bessell, Iris Karen 1948- WhoEnt 92
Bessell, Peter 1921-1985 FacFETw
Bessell, Ted 1942- ConTFT 9
Bessels, Emil 1847-1888 BiInAmS
Bessent, Hattie 1926- WhoBlA 92
Bessenyei, Gyorgy 1747-1811 BlkwCEP
Besser, John Edward 1942- WhoAmL 92, WhoFI 92
Besser, John Edwin 1947- AmMWSc 92
Bessette, France Marie 1944- AmMWSc 92
Bessette, Russell Romulus 1940- AmMWSc 92
Bessette, Steven Mark 1961- WhoAmL 92
Bessette, Thomas Alan 1952- WhoAmL 92
Bessey, Charles Edwin 1845-1915 BiInAmS
Bessey, Edward A d1910 BiInAmS
Bessey, Edward Cushing 1934- WhoFI 92
Bessey, Gordon Scott 1910- Who 92
Bessey, Paul Mack 1925- AmMWSc 92
Bessey, Robert John 1916- AmMWSc 92
Bessey, William Higgins 1913- AmMWSc 92
Bessiah, Boulaem 1930- IntWW 91
Bessie, Alvah DrAPF 91
Bessie, Dan 1932- WhoEnt 92
Bessie, Simon Michael 1916- IntWW 91
Bessis, Marcel Claude 1917- IntWW 91
Bessler, Stephen Craig 1951- WhoEnt 92
Bessman, Alice Neuman 1922- AmMWSc 92
Bessman, Joel David AmMWSc 92
Bessman, Maurice Jules 1928- AmMWSc 92
Bessman, Samuel Paul 1921- AmMWSc 92
Bessmertnova, Natalya Igorevna 1941- IntWW 91, SovUnBD
Bessmertnykh, Aleksandr IntWW 91
Bessmertnykh, Aleksandr A. 1933- CurBio 91 [port]
Bessmertnykh, Aleksandr Aleksandrovich 1933- NewYTBS 91 [port], SovUnBD
Besso, Michael M 1930- AmMWSc 92
Besson, Luc 1959- IntWW 91
Besson, Paul Smith 1953- WhoBlA 92
Best Who 92
Best, Alfred Charles 1904- Who 92
Best, Barbara 1921- IntMPA 92, WhoWest 92
Best, Carlton Eugene 1929- WhoRel 92
Best, Cecil H 1928- AmMWSc 92
Best, Charles Edmund 1926- WhoAmP 91
Best, Dale Edwin 1947- WhoMW 92
Best, David M 1945- AmMWSc 92
Best, Edgar Allan 1925- AmMWSc 92
Best, Edward Wallace 1917- Who 92
Best, Eleanor d1958 TwCPaSc
Best, Elizabeth Allaire 1956- WhoAmL 92
Best, Ernest 1917- ConAu 35NR, Who 92
Best, Eugene Crawford, Jr. 1939- WhoEnt 92
Best, Franklin Luther, Jr. 1945- WhoAmL 92
Best, Gary Keith 1938- AmMWSc 92
Best, Gary Thorman 1944- WhoWest 92
Best, Geoffrey Francis Andrew 1928- Who 92
Best, Geoffry D. C. 1943- WhoAmL 92
Best, George E 1912- AmMWSc 92
Best, George Harold 1920- AmMWSc 92
Best, Giles Bernard 1925- Who 92
Best, James 1926- IntMPA 92
Best, Jay Boyd AmMWSc 92
Best, Jennings H. 1925- WhoBlA 92
Best, John T. 1936- WhoBlA 92
Best, Judah 1932- WhoAmL 92
Best, Karl Rudolf Werner 1903- BiDExR
Best, Keith 1949- Who 92
Best, LaVar 1931- AmMWSc 92
Best, Louis Brown 1944- AmMWSc 92
Best, Philip Ernest 1938- AmMWSc 92
Best, Prince Albert, Jr. 1938- WhoBlA 92
Best, Richard 1933- Who 92
Best, Richard Allen, Jr. 1957- WhoFI 92, WhoWest 92
Best, Richard Stuart 1945- Who 92
Best, Robert Wayne 1946- WhoFI 92
Best, Roberta Louise 1941- WhoWest 92
Best, Roger Donald 1934- WhoRel 92
Best, Roger Norman 1949- WhoWest 92
Best, Sheila Diane 1956- WhoBlA 92
Best, Stanley Gordon 1918- AmMWSc 92
Best, Troy Lee 1945- AmMWSc 92
Best, Werner 1903- EncTR 91 [port]
Best, William Andrew 1949- WhoBlA 92
Best, William Callahan, Jr. 1954- WhoAmL 92
Best, William Robert 1922- AmMWSc 92
Best, Willie Armster 1954- WhoBlA 92
Best, Winfield Judson 1919- WhoEnt 92
Best-Shaw, John 1924- Who 92
Bestard, Jose M. 1943- WhoHisp 92
Beste, Charles Edward 1939- AmMWSc 92
Bestehorn, Ute Wiltrud 1930- WhoMW 92
Besteiro, Ollie 1936- WhoHisp 92
Besteni, Barbara Amnerys 1958- WhoEnt 92
Bester, Alfred 1913- IntAu&W 91
Bester, Alfred 1913-1987 ConAu 36NR, TwCSFW 91
Bester-Toadvin, Josephine Vesella 1926- WhoMW 92
Besterman, Edwin Melville Mack 1924- Who 92
Bestervelt, Peggy Lee 1961- WhoFI 92
Bestgen, William Henry, Jr. 1947- WhoFI 92
Bestler, Gerald Milton 1929- WhoMW 92
Beston, Henry 1888-1968 BenetAL 91
Bestor, Arthur 1908- Who 92
Bestor, Arthur E. 1908- WrDr 92
Bestor, Arthur Eugene 1908- IntWW 91
Bestor, Charles Lemon 1924- WhoEnt 92
Bestul, Alden Beecher 1921- AmMWSc 92
Besunder, Lewis 1944- WhoIns 92
Beswick, Bobbie 1933- TwCPaSc
Beswick, John Reginald 1919- Who 92
Beszterczey, Lesley Margaret 1945- WhoFI 92
Betances, Ramon Emerito 1827-1898 HisDSpE
Betances, Samuel WhoHisp 92
Betancourt, Adolfo Garza 1922- WhoHisp 92
Betancourt, Antonio L. 1944- WhoHisp 92
Betancourt, Hector Mainhard 1949- WhoWest 92
Betancourt, Ingrid WhoHisp 92
Betancourt, Ismael, Jr. 1938- WhoFI 92
Betancourt, John 1950- WhoHisp 92
Betancourt, Jose Luis 1956- WhoHisp 92
Betancourt, Pedro de 1626-1667 HisDSpE
Betancourt, Romulo 1908-1981 FacFETw
Betancourt y Davalos, Pedro 1858-1933 HisDSpE
Betancur Cuartas, Belisario 1923- IntWW 91
Betanzos, Amalia WhoHisp 92
Betanzos, Louis 1936- WhoHisp 92
Betanzos, Ramon James 1933- WhoHisp 92
Betanzos-Palacios, Odon 1926- WhoHisp 92
Beteille, Andre 1934- WrDr 92
Betenson, Lula Parker 1884-1980 ConAu 133
Beth, Eric Walter 1912- AmMWSc 92
Bethancourt, Tomas Ernesto 1932- WhoEnt 92
Bethany, John A. 1929- WhoIns 92
Bethe, Hans A 1906- FacFETw
Bethe, Hans Albrecht 1906- AmMWSc 92, IntWW 91, Who 92, WhoNob 90
Bethea, Charles 1933- WhoFI 92
Bethea, Cynthia Louise 1952- AmMWSc 92
Bethea, Edwin Ayers 1931- WhoBlA 92
Bethea, Gregory Austin 1952- WhoBlA 92
Bethea, John Dow 1947- WhoFI 92
Bethea, Joseph Benjamin 1932- WhoRel 92
Bethea, Mollie Ann 1949- WhoBlA 92
Bethea, Neil Graham 1872-1957 DcNCBi 1
Bethea, Robert Morrison 1935- AmMWSc 92
Bethea, Tristram Walker, III 1938- AmMWSc 92
Betheil, Joseph Jay 1924- AmMWSc 92
Bethel, David Percival 1923- Who 92
Bethel, Dell 1929- WrDr 92
Bethel, Doreen Izetta 1956- WhoMW 92
Bethel, Edward Lee 1926- AmMWSc 92
Bethel, Gar DrAPF 91
Bethel, James Samuel 1915- AmMWSc 92
Bethel, Jesse Moncell, Sr. 1922- WhoBlA 92
Bethel, Kathleen Evonne 1953- WhoBlA 92
Bethel, Lander Louis, Jr. 1957- WhoRel 92
Bethel, Leonard Leslie 1939- WhoBlA 92
Bethel, Mark Davis 1951- WhoMW 92
Bethel, Martin 1943- Who 92
Bethel, Robert George 1931- WhoMW 92
Bethell Who 92
Bethell, Baron 1938- Who 92
Bethell, Leslie Michael 1937- Who 92
Bethell, Mary Ursula 1874-1945 RfGEnL 91
Bethell, Nicholas 1938- IntAu&W 91, WrDr 92
Bethell, Richard Anthony 1922- Who 92
Bethell, William 1744-1804 DcNCBi 1
Bethge, Friedrich 1891-1963 EncTR 91 [port]
Bethke, Philip Martin 1930- AmMWSc 92
Bethke, Terry Joseph 1948- WhoWest 92
Bethlahmy, Nedavia 1918- AmMWSc 92
Bethlen, T. D. ConAu 36NR
Bethmann, Erich 1904- IntAu&W 91
Bethmann-Hollweg, Theobald von 1856-1921 FacFETw
Bethune, Alexander Maitland Sharp 1909- Who 92
Bethune, Angus 1908- Who 92
Bethune, Donald Stimson 1948- AmMWSc 92
Bethune, Ed 1935- WhoAmP 91
Bethune, John 1751-1815 DcNCBi 1
Bethune, John Edmund 1927- AmMWSc 92
Bethune, John Johnson 1956- WhoFI 92
Bethune, John Lemuel 1925- AmMWSc 92
Bethune, Lauchlin 1785-1874 DcNCBi 1
Bethune, Lebert DrAPF 91
Bethune, Lonnie Jay 1951- WhoMW 92
Bethune, Mary McLeod 1875-1955 FacFETw, HanAmWH, NotBlAW 92 [port], RComAH, RelLAm 91
Bethune, Robert William 1954- WhoEnt 92
Bethune, Thomas 1849-1908 NewAmDM
Bethune, Zina 1944- IntMPA 92
Bethune, Zina 1950?- ConTFT 9, WhoEnt 92, WhoWest 92
Beti, Mongo 1932- BlkLC [port], LiExTwC
Betjeman, John 1906-1984 CnDBLB 7 [port], FacFETw, RfGEnL 91
Betkoski, John W, III 1952- WhoAmP 91
Beto, George John 1916- WhoRel 92
Beton, John Allen 1950- WhoFI 92
Betros, Anthony Francis 1963- WhoEnt 92
Betrozoff, John W WhoAmP 91
Betsalel, Harvey 1947- WhoFI 92
Betsch, Madeline WhoFI 92
Betschart, Antoinette 1939- AmMWSc 92
Betso, Stephen Richard 1945- AmMWSc 92
Betsworth, Roger G. 1933- WhoRel 92
Bett, Michael 1935- Who 92
Bettac, Robert Edward 1949- WhoAmL 92
Bettag, Tom LesBEnT 92
Bettan, Anita Esther 1928- WhoMW 92
Bettan, Philip Warren 1942- WhoEnt 92
Bettany, Peter 1945- TwCPaSc
Bettelheim, Bruno 1903- IntAu&W 91
Bettelheim, Bruno 1903-1990 AnObit 1990, BenetAL 91, FacFETw
Bettelheim, Charles 1913- IntWW 91
Bettelheim, Frederick A 1923- AmMWSc 92
Bettelini, Lauro 1938- IntAu&W 91
Betten, J Robert 1932- AmMWSc 92
Bettencourt, Joseph S, Jr 1940- AmMWSc 92
Bettencourt, Lawrence J WhoAmP 91
Bettencourt Santos, Humberto 1940- IntWW 91
Bettendorf, James Bernard 1933- WhoMW 92, WhoRel 92
Bettenhausen, Elizabeth Ann 1942- WhoRel 92
Better, William Joel 1951- WhoWest 92
Betteridge, Anne IntAu&W 91X, WrDr 92
Bettermann, Hilda 1942- WhoAmP 91
Bettersworth, Alexander Pitts ScFEYrs
Betterton, Jesse O, Jr 1920- AmMWSc 92
Bettes, Richard S., III 1951- WhoFI 92
Bettger, Lyle 1915- IntMPA 92
Bettger, William Joseph 1953- AmMWSc 92
Betti, John A 1931- AmMWSc 92, WhoFI 92
Bettice, John Allen 1942- AmMWSc 92
Bettilyon, Mark M. 1958- WhoAmL 92
Bettinger, Abraham Leon 1934- WhoFI 92
Bettinger, Donald John 1927- AmMWSc 92
Bettinger, Judith Pedersen WhoEnt 92
Bettinger, Richard Thomas 1931- AmMWSc 92
Bettiol, Marie E. 1943- WhoWest 92
Bettis, Anne Katherine 1949- WhoBlA 92
Bettis, Artilla Elizabeth 1906- WhoRel 92
Bettis, Barry Phillip 1954- WhoAmL 92
Bettis, John Gregory 1946- WhoEnt 92, WhoWest 92
Bettis, Joseph Dabney 1936- WhoRel 92
Bettis, Robert Allen 1955- WhoRel 92
Bettisworth, Robert H WhoAmP 91
Bettley, F. Ray 1909- Who 92
Bettman, Gary Bruce 1952- WhoAmL 92, WhoEnt 92, WhoFI 92
Bettman, Jerome Wolf 1909- AmMWSc 92
Bettman, Maur DrAPF 91
Bettman, Max 1925- AmMWSc 92
Betton, Joe Stewart 1952- WhoRel 92
Bettonville, Paul John 1918- AmMWSc 92
Bettridge, Ben 1952- WhoAmP 91
Bettridge, John Bryan 1932- Who 92
Betts, Alan Osborn 1927- Who 92
Betts, Alexander Davis 1832-1918 DcNCBi 1
Betts, Ann Brantly 1947- WhoFI 92
Betts, Attie L 1916- AmMWSc 92
Betts, Austin Wortham 1912- AmMWSc 92
Betts, Barbara Lang 1926- WhoAmL 92, WhoWest 92
Betts, Burr Joseph 1945- AmMWSc 92
Betts, Charles Stephen 1919- Who 92
Betts, Clive James Charles 1950- Who 92
Betts, Donald Drysdale 1929- AmMWSc 92, IntWW 91
Betts, Doris DrAPF 91
Betts, Floyd O 1915- WhoAmP 91
Betts, Henry Brognard 1928- AmMWSc 92
Betts, James Anthony 1896-1980 TwCPaSc
Betts, James William, Jr. 1923- WhoFI 92, WhoWest 92
Betts, Leah Warrington 1932- WhoAmP 91
Betts, Lillian W d1938 DcAmImH
Betts, Lily Edna Minerva Who 92
Betts, Raymond Frederick 1925- IntAu&W 91, WrDr 92
Betts, Sheri Elaine 1958- WhoBlA 92
Betts, Simon 1957- TwCPaSc
Betts, Stanley Woodley 1912- Who 92
Betts, Stephen Who 92
Betts, William Wilson, Jr. 1926- WrDr 92
Betty, Lewis Stafford 1942- WhoRel 92, WhoWest 92
Betty, Warren Randall 1931- WhoBlA 92
Betuel, Jonathan IntMPA 92
Betunada, Rosco Julio 1949- WhoWest 92
Betz, A Lorris 1947- AmMWSc 92
Betz, Carl d1978 LesBEnT 92
Betz, Don 1946- WhoAmP 91
Betz, Ebon Elbert 1914- AmMWSc 92
Betz, Edward Bergan 1934- WhoFI 92
Betz, Frank Herbert 1933- WhoFI 92
Betz, Frank Herbert, III 1933- WhoAmP 91
Betz, George 1934- AmMWSc 92
Betz, Hans Dieter 1931- WhoRel 92
Betz, John Vianney 1937- AmMWSc 92
Betz, Mathew J 1932- AmMWSc 92
Betz, Norman Leo 1938- AmMWSc 92
Betz, Otto Wilhelm 1917- WhoRel 92
Betz, Robert F 1923- AmMWSc 92
Betz, Ronald Philip 1933- WhoMW 92
Betz, Valerie P 1933- WhoAmP 91
Betz, William J 1943- AmMWSc 92
Betzer, Peter Robin 1942- AmMWSc 92
Beu, Marjorie Janet 1921- WhoEnt 92
Beuc, Rudolph, Jr. 1931- WhoFI 92, WhoMW 92
Beuchat, Carol Ann 1955- AmMWSc 92
Beuchat, Larry Ray 1943- AmMWSc 92
Beuerman, Roger Wilmer 1943- AmMWSc 92
Beug, Michael William 1944- AmMWSc 92
Beugel, Ernst Hans van der 1918- IntWW 91
Beuhler, Robert James, Jr 1942- AmMWSc 92
Beukema, John Frederick 1947- WhoAmL 92
Beukens, Roelf Pieter 1943- AmMWSc 92
Beukes, Wiets Daniel 1927- IntWW 91
Beum, Robert DrAPF 91

**Beumel,** Wilford J. 1935- *WhoWest 92*
**Beumelburg,** Werner 1899-1963 *EncTR 91 [port]*
**Beumer,** Richard Eugene 1938- *WhoFI 92, WhoMW 92*
**Beumler,** Henry Weber 1913- *WhoAmL 92*
**Beuret,** Jules William 1914- *WhoWest 92*
**Beuret,** Kevin Paul 1945- *WhoMW 92*
**Beuret,** Stephen George 1955- *WhoEnt 92*
**Beus,** Stanley S 1930- *AmMWSc 92*
**Beus,** Stanley Spencer 1930- *WhoWest 92*
**Beusch,** John U 1938- *AmMWSc 92*
**Beussink,** Donald Raymond 1955- *WhoMW 92*
**Beute,** Marvin Kenneth 1935- *AmMWSc 92*
**Beutel,** Eugene William 1927- *WhoRel 92*
**Beutel,** Paul Wayne 1950- *WhoEnt 92*
**Beuter,** John H 1935- *AmMWSc 92*
**Beuter,** Richard William 1942- *WhoMW 92*
**Beuther,** Harold 1917- *AmMWSc 92*
**Beutler,** Albert Jacob 1929- *WhoMW 92*
**Beutler,** Arthur Julius 1924- *WhoMW 92*
**Beutler,** Christopher John 1944- *WhoAmP 91*
**Beutler,** Ernest 1928- *AmMWSc 92, IntWW 91, WhoWest 92*
**Beutler,** Frederick J 1926- *AmMWSc 92*
**Beutler,** Martin K. 1956- *WhoMW 92*
**Beutler,** Stephen Albert 1952- *WhoRel 92*
**Beutner,** Edward C 1939- *AmMWSc 92*
**Beutner,** Ernst Herman 1923- *AmMWSc 92*
**Beuttenmuller,** Rudolf William 1953- *WhoAmL 92*
**Beutter,** Robert Charles 1935- *WhoAmP 91*
**Beuve-Mery,** Hubert 1902- *IntAu&W 91*
**Beuve-Mery,** Hubert 1902-1989 *FacFETw*
**Beuys,** Joseph 1921-1986 *FacFETw*
**Bevacqua,** Ronald Anthony 1945- *WhoFI 92*
**Bevak,** Joseph Perry 1929- *AmMWSc 92*
**Bevan,** Andrew David Gilroy 1928- *Who 92*
**Bevan,** Aneurin 1897-1960 *FacFETw*
**Bevan,** Beth Ann 1962- *WhoFI 92*
**Bevan,** Charles Albert, Jr. 1944- *WhoRel 92*
**Bevan,** Christopher Martin 1923- *Who 92*
**Bevan,** David Gilroy *Who 92*
**Bevan,** Donald Edward 1921- *AmMWSc 92*
**Bevan,** Edward Julian 1940- *Who 92*
**Bevan,** Gloria *ConAu 134, IntAu&W 91, WrDr 92*
**Bevan,** Hugh Keith 1922- *Who 92*
**Bevan,** James 1930- *WrDr 92*
**Bevan,** John Acton 1930- *AmMWSc 92*
**Bevan,** John Penry Vaughan 1947- *Who 92*
**Bevan,** John Stuart 1935- *Who 92*
**Bevan,** Julian *Who 92*
**Bevan,** Kenneth Graham 1898- *Who 92*
**Bevan,** Martyn Evan E. *Who 92*
**Bevan,** Michael Guy Molesworth 1926- *Who 92*
**Bevan,** Nicolas 1942- *Who 92*
**Bevan,** Oliver 1941- *TwCPaSc*
**Bevan,** Peter Gilroy 1922- *Who 92*
**Bevan,** Richard Justin William 1922- *Who 92*
**Bevan,** Richard Thomas 1914- *Who 92*
**Bevan,** Robert 1865-1925 *TwCPaSc*
**Bevan,** Robert Lewis 1928- *WhoAmL 92, WhoFI 92*
**Bevan,** Rosemary D *AmMWSc 92*
**Bevan,** Thomas Roy 1936- *WhoRel 92*
**Bevan,** Timothy 1927- *Who 92*
**Bevan,** Timothy Hugh 1927- *IntWW 91*
**Bevan,** Timothy Michael 1931- *Who 92*
**Bevan,** Tony 1951- *TwCPaSc*
**Bevan,** Walter Harold 1916- *Who 92*
**Bevan,** William 1922- *AmMWSc 92, IntWW 91*
**Bevans,** Rowland S 1919- *AmMWSc 92*
**Bevc,** Vladislav 1932- *AmMWSc 92*
**Bevel,** James Luther 1936- *WhoBlA 92*
**Bevelacqua,** Joseph John 1949- *AmMWSc 92*
**Bevelander,** Gerrit 1905- *AmMWSc 92*
**Bevens,** Floyd d1991 *NewYTBS 91*
**Bever,** Christopher Theodore 1919- *AmMWSc 92*
**Bever,** James Edward 1920- *AmMWSc 92*
**Bever,** John William 1959- *WhoFI 92*
**Bever,** Michael B 1911- *AmMWSc 92*
**Bever,** Robert Lynn 1953- *WhoAmL 92, WhoAmP 91*
**Bever,** Timothy Michael 1953- *WhoMW 92*
**Beverett,** Andrew Jackson 1917- *WhoFI 92, WhoWest 92*
**Beveridge,** Albert J 1862-1927 *FacFETw*
**Beveridge,** Albert Jeremiah 1862-1927 *AmPolLe*
**Beveridge,** Albert Jeremiah, III 1935- *WhoAmL 92*
**Beveridge,** Crawford William 1945- *Who 92*
**Beveridge,** David L 1938- *AmMWSc 92*
**Beveridge,** Gordon Smith Grieve 1933- *IntWW 91, Who 92*
**Beveridge,** James MacDonald Richardson 1912- *AmMWSc 92*
**Beveridge,** John Caldwell 1937- *Who 92*
**Beveridge,** Lowell P. 1905-1991 *NewYTBS 91*
**Beveridge,** Norwood Pierson, Jr. 1936- *WhoAmL 92*
**Beveridge,** William 1908- *WrDr 92*
**Beveridge,** William Henry 1879-1963 *FacFETw*
**Beveridge,** William Ian Beardmore 1908- *IntAu&W 91, Who 92*
**Beverley,** Henry 1935- *Who 92*
**Beverley,** Jane Taylor 1918- *WhoMW 92*
**Beverley,** Robert 1673?-1722 *BenetAL 91*
**Beverley-Burton,** Mary 1930- *AmMWSc 92*
**Beverloo,** Cornelis Van 1922- *IntWW 91*
**Beverly,** Benjamin Franklin 1938- *WhoBlA 92*
**Beverly,** Creigs C. 1942- *WhoBlA 92*
**Beverly,** Frankie *WhoBlA 92*
**Beverly,** Robert Edward, III 1948- *AmMWSc 92*
**Beverly,** Robert Graham 1925- *WhoAmP 91*
**Beverly,** Rose Jackson 1938- *WhoBlA 92*
**Beverly,** Theria M. 1931- *WhoWest 92*
**Beverly,** Thomas More 1958- *WhoAmL 92*
**Beverly,** Urias Harrison 1941- *WhoRel 92*
**Beverly,** William C., Jr. 1943- *WhoBlA 92*
**Bevers,** Robert Joe 1937- *WhoMW 92*
**Bevers,** William Leon 1945- *WhoAmP 91*
**Beverton,** Raymond John Heaphy 1922- *IntWW 91, Who 92*
**Beverung,** Warren Neil, Jr 1941- *AmMWSc 92*
**Bevier,** Lillian Riemer 1939- *WhoAmL 92*
**Bevier,** Mary Lou 1953- *AmMWSc 92*
**Bevilacqua,** Anthony J. 1923- *RelLAm 91*
**Bevilacqua,** Anthony Joseph 1923- *WhoRel 92*
**Bevilacqua,** Don *WhoHisp 92*
**Bevilacqua,** Francis J 1923- *WhoAmP 91*
**Bevilacqua,** John J *WhoAmP 91*
**Bevill,** Burnie L *ScFEYrs*
**Bevill,** Evangeline 1928- *IntAu&W 91*
**Bevill,** Richard F, Jr 1934- *AmMWSc 92*
**Bevill,** Tom 1921- *AlmAP 92 [port], WhoAmP 91*
**Bevill,** Vincent 1928- *AmMWSc 92*
**Beville,** Hugh M., Jr. 1908- *IntMPA 92*
**Beville,** Norborne P, Jr 1941- *WhoAmP 91*
**Beville,** R. Harwood 1940- *WhoFI 92*
**Bevin,** A Griswold 1935- *AmMWSc 92*
**Bevin,** Ernest 1879-1951 *FacFETw*
**Bevin,** Ernest 1881-1951 *EncTR 91*
**Bevington,** Edmund Milton 1928- *WhoFI 92*
**Bevington,** Eric Raymond 1914- *Who 92*
**Bevins,** John Reginald 1908- *Who 92*
**Bevins,** Kenneth Milton 1918- *Who 92*
**Bevins,** Robert Jackson 1928- *WhoFI 92*
**Bevis,** Herbert A 1929- *AmMWSc 92*
**Bevis,** Jean Harwell 1939- *AmMWSc 92*
**Bevk,** Joze 1943- *AmMWSc 92*
**Bevolo,** Albert Joseph 1940- *AmMWSc 92*
**Bewes,** Richard 1934- *WrDr 92*
**Bewes,** Richard Thomas 1934- *IntAu&W 91, Who 92*
**Bewick,** Herbert 1911- *Who 92*
**Bewicke-Copley** *Who 92*
**Bewkes,** Jeff *LesBEnT 92, WhoEnt 92*
**Bewley,** Edward de Beauvoir 1931- *Who 92*
**Bewley,** Glenn Carl 1942- *AmMWSc 92*
**Bewley,** Harrison James 1957- *WhoWest 92*
**Bewley,** Joe L *WhoAmP 91*
**Bewley,** John Derek 1943- *AmMWSc 92*
**Bewley,** Judy Baker 1942- *WhoAmP 91*
**Bewley,** Loyal V 1898- *AmMWSc 92*
**Bewley,** Thomas Henry 1926- *IntWW 91, Who 92*
**Bewtra,** Jatinder Kumar 1935- *AmMWSc 92*
**Bex,** Craig Alan 1953- *WhoRel 92*
**Bex,** Frederick James 1947- *AmMWSc 92*
**Bexar,** Phil *TwCWW 91*
**Bexon,** Roger 1926- *IntWW 91, Who 92*
**Bey,** Turhan 1920- *IntMPA 92*
**Beyad,** Mohammed Hossain 1950- *AmMWSc 92*
**Beyard,** Thomas Blaine 1955- *WhoAmP 91*
**Beye,** Holly *DrAPF 91*
**Beyea,** Jan Edgar 1939- *AmMWSc 92*
**Beyen,** Werner J 1929- *AmMWSc 92*
**Beyenbach,** Klaus Werner 1943- *AmMWSc 92*
**Beyer,** Aaron Jay 1946- *WhoAmL 92*
**Beyer,** Ann L 1951- *AmMWSc 92*
**Beyer,** Arthur Frederick *AmMWSc 92*
**Beyer,** Baldwin Martin 1926- *WhoRel 92*
**Beyer,** Barbara Lynn 1947- *WhoFI 92*
**Beyer,** Brenda Maxine 1952- *WhoWest 92*
**Beyer,** Carl Fredrick 1947- *AmMWSc 92*
**Beyer,** Charlotte Bishop 1947- *WhoFI 92*
**Beyer,** Craig Franklin 1958- *WhoMW 92*
**Beyer,** Daniel G. 1954- *WhoAmL 92*
**Beyer,** Donald S, Jr *WhoAmP 91*
**Beyer,** Edgar Herman 1931- *AmMWSc 92*
**Beyer,** Elmo Monroe, Jr 1941- *AmMWSc 92*
**Beyer,** Emil E, Jr 1929- *WhoAmP 91, WhoMW 92*
**Beyer,** Erik 1936- *WhoAmP 91*
**Beyer,** Frank Michael 1928- *IntWW 91*
**Beyer,** Gene *WhoAmP 91*
**Beyer,** George Leidy 1919- *AmMWSc 92*
**Beyer,** Gerhard H 1923- *AmMWSc 92*
**Beyer,** Gerry Wayne 1956- *WhoAmL 92*
**Beyer,** Henry Gustav 1850-1918 *BiInAmS*
**Beyer,** Herbert Albert 1923- *WhoMW 92*
**Beyer,** James B 1931- *AmMWSc 92*
**Beyer,** Jennifer Elmer 1963- *WhoAmL 92*
**Beyer,** Karl Henry, Jr 1914- *AmMWSc 92*
**Beyer,** Lee Louis 1948- *WhoWest 92*
**Beyer,** Lisa Catherine 1959- *WhoMW 92*
**Beyer,** Louis Martin 1939- *AmMWSc 92*
**Beyer,** Richard G. *DrAPF 91*
**Beyer,** Robert Edward 1928- *AmMWSc 92*
**Beyer,** Robert Harold 1933- *WhoFI 92*
**Beyer,** Robert Thomas 1920- *AmMWSc 92*
**Beyer,** Terry 1939- *AmMWSc 92*
**Beyer,** W Nelson 1950- *AmMWSc 92*
**Beyer,** Wayne Cartwright 1946- *WhoAmL 92*
**Beyer,** Wayne Herman 1956- *WhoMW 92*
**Beyer,** Werner W. 1911- *WrDr 92*
**Beyer,** Werner William 1911- *IntAu&W 91*
**Beyer,** William A 1924- *AmMWSc 92*
**Beyer,** William Hyman 1930- *AmMWSc 92*
**Beyerlein,** Douglas Craig 1950- *WhoWest 92*
**Beyerlein,** Floyd Hilbert 1942- *AmMWSc 92*
**Beyers,** Charlotte Kempner 1931- *WhoWest 92*
**Beyers,** James Daley 1939- *WhoMW 92*
**Beyers,** Robert John 1933- *AmMWSc 92*
**Beyersdorf,** Marguerite Mulloy 1922- *WhoWest 92*
**Beyfus,** Drusilla *IntAu&W 91, WrDr 92*
**Beyfus,** Drusilla Norman *Who 92*
**Beyler,** Roger Eldon 1922- *AmMWSc 92*
**Beylerian,** Nurel 1937- *AmMWSc 92*
**Beymer,** Richard *WhoEnt 92*
**Beymer,** Richard 1939- *ConTFT 9, IntMPA 92*
**Beyner,** Ronald Eugene 1947- *WhoWest 92*
**Beynon,** Ernest Geoffrey 1926- *Who 92*
**Beynon,** Granville *Who 92*
**Beynon,** Huw 1942- *IntAu&W 91, WrDr 92*
**Beynon,** James Royston 1907- *Who 92*
**Beynon,** John David Emrys 1939- *IntWW 91, Who 92*
**Beynon,** John Herbert 1923- *IntWW 91, Who 92*
**Beynon,** Timothy George 1939- *Who 92*
**Beynon,** William John Granville 1914- *IntWW 91, Who 92*
**Beyster,** J Robert *AmMWSc 92*
**Beyster,** John Robert 1924- *WhoWest 92*
**Beytagh,** Francis Xavier, Jr. 1935- *WhoAmL 92*
**Beytagh-Maldonado,** Guillermo Jose 1957- *WhoHisp 92*
**Bezahler,** Donald Jay 1932- *WhoAmL 92*
**Bezanski,** Ilia Metodiev 1941- *WhoFI 92*
**Bezanson,** Randall Peter 1946- *WhoAmL 92*
**Bezanson,** Ronald Scott, Jr. 1936- *WhoRel 92*
**Bezar,** Leonard Raymond 1933- *WhoFI 92*
**Bezdek,** James Christian 1939- *AmMWSc 92*
**Bezdicek,** David Fred 1938- *AmMWSc 92*
**Bezella,** Winfred August 1935- *AmMWSc 92*
**Bezer,** David Leon 1943- *WhoWest 92*
**Bezigian,** Thomas 1955- *WhoMW 92*
**Bezkorovainy,** Anatoly 1935- *AmMWSc 92*
**Bezman,** Richard David 1946- *AmMWSc 92*
**Bezobrazov,** Alexander Mikhailovich 1866-1933 *FacFETw*
**Bezold,** Richard Michael 1956- *WhoAmL 92*
**Bezombes,** Roger 1913- *IntWW 91*
**Bezos,** Beatriz M. 1958- *WhoHisp 92*
**Bezou,** Henry Charles 1913- *WhoRel 92*
**Bezrodny,** Igor *WhoEnt 92*
**Bezuszka,** Stanley John 1914- *AmMWSc 92*
**Bezwada,** Rao Srinivasa 1945- *AmMWSc 92*
**Bezymensky,** Aleksandr Il'ich 1898-1973 *SovUnBD*
**Bhabha,** J. J. 1914- *IntWW 91*
**Bhada,** Rohinton K 1935- *AmMWSc 92*
**Bhada,** Rohinton Khurshed 1935- *WhoWest 92*
**Bhaduri,** Saumya 1942- *AmMWSc 92*
**Bhagat,** Bali Ram 1922- *IntWW 91*
**Bhagat,** Dhanraj 1917- *IntWW 91*
**Bhagat,** Goberdhan 1928- *WrDr 92*
**Bhagat,** H. K. L. *IntWW 91*
**Bhagat,** Hitesh Rameshchandra *AmMWSc 92*
**Bhagat,** Phiroz Maneck 1948- *AmMWSc 92*
**Bhagat,** Pramode Kumar 1944- *AmMWSc 92*
**Bhagat,** Satindar M 1933- *AmMWSc 92*
**Bhagat,** Surinder Kumar 1935- *AmMWSc 92*
**Bhagavan,** Hemmige 1934- *AmMWSc 92*
**Bhagavan,** Nadhipuram V 1931- *AmMWSc 92*
**Bhagavantam,** Suri 1909- *IntWW 91*
**Bhagavatula,** VijayaKumar 1953- *AmMWSc 92*
**Bhagia,** Gobind Shewakram 1935- *AmMWSc 92*
**Bhagwan,** Sudhir 1942- *WhoFI 92, WhoWest 92*
**Bhagwat,** Subhash Bhaskar 1941- *WhoFI 92*
**Bhagwati,** Prafulla Chandra 1921- *IntWW 91*
**Bhajan Lal,** Chaudhri 1930- *IntWW 91*
**Bhakar,** Balram Singh 1937- *AmMWSc 92*
**Bhala,** Rakesh Kumar 1962- *WhoAmL 92*
**Bhalla,** Amar S *AmMWSc 92*
**Bhalla,** Chander P 1932- *AmMWSc 92*
**Bhalla,** Deepak Kumar 1946- *WhoWest 92*
**Bhalla,** Ramesh C 1935- *AmMWSc 92*
**Bhalla,** Ranbir J R Singh 1943- *AmMWSc 92*
**Bhalla,** Sushil K 1939- *AmMWSc 92*
**Bhalla,** Vinod Kumar 1940- *AmMWSc 92*
**Bhamidipaty,** Kameswara Rao 1955- *WhoWest 92*
**Bhandari,** Anil Kumar 1953- *WhoWest 92*
**Bhandari,** Sunder Singh 1921- *IntWW 91*
**Bhandarkar,** Dileep Pandurang 1949- *AmMWSc 92*
**Bhandarkar,** Mangalore Dilip 1946- *AmMWSc 92*
**Bhandarkar,** Suhas D 1964- *AmMWSc 92*
**Bhansali,** Praful V 1949- *AmMWSc 92*
**Bhanu,** Bir 1951- *AmMWSc 92*
**Bhapkar,** Vasant Prabhakar 1931- *AmMWSc 92*
**Bhappu,** Roshan B 1926- *AmMWSc 92*
**Bharadvaj,** Bala Krishnan 1952- *AmMWSc 92*
**Bharadwaj,** Prem Datta 1931- *AmMWSc 92*
**Bharath,** Ramachandran 1935- *WhoMW 92*
**Bharati,** Agehananda 1923- *WrDr 92*
**Bharati,** Agehananda 1923-1991 *ConAu 134, NewYTBS 91*
**Bharati,** Saroja *AmMWSc 92*
**Bhardwj,** Neelam Bala 1950- *WhoFI 92*
**Bhargava,** Ashok 1943- *WhoFI 92*
**Bhargava,** Hemendra Nath 1942- *AmMWSc 92*
**Bhargava,** Hridaya Nath 1935- *AmMWSc 92*
**Bhargava,** Madhu Mittra *AmMWSc 92*
**Bhargava,** Rameshwar Nath 1939- *AmMWSc 92*
**Bhargava,** Triloki Nath 1933- *AmMWSc 92*
**Bharj,** Sarjit Singh 1950- *AmMWSc 92*
**Bhartendu,** Srivastava 1935- *AmMWSc 92*
**Bhartia,** Prakash 1944- *AmMWSc 92*
**Bharucha,** Keki Rustomji 1928- *AmMWSc 92*
**Bharucha,** Nana R 1926- *AmMWSc 92*
**Bhasin,** Madan M 1938- *AmMWSc 92*
**Bhaskar,** Krishan Nath 1945- *Who 92*
**Bhaskar,** Rahul 1963- *WhoMW 92*
**Bhaskar,** Surindar Nath 1923- *AmMWSc 92*
**Bhaskaran,** Govindan 1935- *AmMWSc 92*
**Bhat,** Gopal Krishna 1925- *AmMWSc 92*
**Bhat,** Mulki Radhakrishna 1930- *AmMWSc 92*
**Bhat,** Rama B 1943- *AmMWSc 92*
**Bhat,** Uggappakodi Narayan 1933- *AmMWSc 92*
**Bhat,** Venkatramana Kakekochi 1933- *AmMWSc 92*
**Bhatarai,** Krishna Prasad *IntWW 91*
**Bhathena,** Sam Jehangirji 1936- *AmMWSc 92*
**Bhatia,** Anand K 1934- *AmMWSc 92*
**Bhatia,** Darshan Singh 1923- *AmMWSc 92*
**Bhatia,** Hans Raj 1904-1979 *ConAu 133*
**Bhatia,** Jamunadevi 1919- *WrDr 92*
**Bhatia,** Jamundavi 1919- *IntAu&W 91*
**Bhatia,** June *IntAu&W 91X, WrDr 92*

**Bhatia**, Kishan 1936- *AmMWSc 92*
**Bhatia**, Mahesh Vishnu 1944- *WhoFI 92*
**Bhatia**, Nam Parshad 1932- *AmMWSc 92*
**Bhatia**, Navin Chandra 1942- *WhoFI 92*
**Bhatia**, Prem Narain 1911- *IntWW 91*
**Bhatia**, Shyam Sunder 1924- *AmMWSc 92*
**Bhatia**, Suraj Prakash 1954- *WhoFI 92*
**Bhatla**, Manmohan N *AmMWSc 92*
**Bhatnagar**, Ajay Sahai 1942- *AmMWSc 92*
**Bhatnagar**, Dinech C 1934- *AmMWSc 92*
**Bhatnagar**, Gopal Mohan 1937- *AmMWSc 92*
**Bhatnagar**, Kunwar Prasad 1934- *AmMWSc 92*
**Bhatnagar**, Mary Elizabeth 1943- *WhoAmL 92*
**Bhatnagar**, Rajendra Sahai 1936- *AmMWSc 92*
**Bhatnagar**, Ranbir Krishna *AmMWSc 92*
**Bhatnagar**, Yogendra Mohan 1945- *AmMWSc 92*
**Bhatnager**, Deepak 1949- *AmMWSc 92*
**Bhatt**, Girish M 1946- *AmMWSc 92*
**Bhatt**, Harry Vishnuprasad 1945- *WhoFI 92*
**Bhatt**, Jagdish J 1939- *AmMWSc 92, WrDr 92*
**Bhatt**, Mukesh Balvantray 1958- *WhoWest 92*
**Bhatt**, Padmamabh P 1957- *AmMWSc 92*
**Bhatt**, Pravin Nanabhai *AmMWSc 92*
**Bhatt**, Ravindra Nautam 1952- *AmMWSc 92*
**Bhatt**, Sujata 1956- *IntAu&W 91*
**Bhatt**, Uddhav Deo 1932- *IntWW 91*
**Bhattacharjee**, Himangshu Ranjan 1942- *AmMWSc 92*
**Bhattacharjee**, Jnanendra K 1936- *AmMWSc 92*
**Bhattacharji**, Somdev 1932- *AmMWSc 92*
**Bhattacharya**, Amar Nath 1934- *AmMWSc 92*
**Bhattacharya**, Amit 1961- *WhoEnt 92*
**Bhattacharya**, Anindya Kumar 1946- *WhoFI 92*
**Bhattacharya**, Ashok Kumar 1935- *AmMWSc 92*
**Bhattacharya**, Basu 1936- *IntWW 91*
**Bhattacharya**, Bhabani 1906- *IntAu&W 91*
**Bhattacharya**, Debanshu 1947- *AmMWSc 92*
**Bhattacharya**, Jahar 1946- *AmMWSc 92*
**Bhattacharya**, Malaya 1946- *AmMWSc 92*
**Bhattacharya**, Pallab Kumar 1949- *AmMWSc 92*
**Bhattacharya**, Prabir 1948- *AmMWSc 92*
**Bhattacharya**, Pradeep Kumar 1940- *AmMWSc 92, WhoMW 92*
**Bhattacharya**, Rabi Sankar 1948- *AmMWSc 92, WhoMW 92*
**Bhattacharya**, Rabindra Nath 1937- *AmMWSc 92, WhoMW 92*
**Bhattacharya**, Syamal Kanti 1949- *AmMWSc 92*
**Bhattacharya-Chatterjee**, Malaya 1946- *AmMWSc 92*
**Bhattacharyya**, Ashim Kumar 1936- *AmMWSc 92*
**Bhattacharyya**, Bibhuti Bhusan 1938- *AmMWSc 92*
**Bhattacharyya**, Bibhuti Bhushan 1935- *AmMWSc 92*
**Bhattacharyya**, Birendra Kumar 1924- *IntAu&W 91, IntWW 91*
**Bhattacharyya**, Gouri Kanta 1940- *AmMWSc 92*
**Bhattacharyya**, Maryka Horsting 1943- *AmMWSc 92*
**Bhattacharyya**, Mohit Lal 1944- *AmMWSc 92*
**Bhattacharyya**, Pranab K 1938- *AmMWSc 92*
**Bhattacharyya**, Ramendra Kumar 1931- *AmMWSc 92*
**Bhattacharyya**, Samit Kumar 1947- *AmMWSc 92*
**Bhattacharyya**, Santosh Kumar 1927- *WhoFI 92*
**Bhattacharyya**, Shankar P 1946- *AmMWSc 92*
**Bhattacharyya**, Sugato 1957- *WhoFI 92*
**Bhattacharyya**, Sushantha Kumar 1940- *Who 92*
**Bhatti**, Masood Akram 1962- *WhoFI 92*
**Bhatti**, Rashid 1939- *AmMWSc 92*
**Bhatti**, Waqar Hamid 1931- *AmMWSc 92*
**Bhaumik**, Mani Lal 1932- *AmMWSc 92*
**Bhavanandan**, Veer P 1936- *AmMWSc 92*
**Bhavnani**, Bhagu R 1936- *AmMWSc 92*
**Bhayani**, Kiran Lilachand 1944- *WhoWest 92*
**Bhichai Rattakul**, Nai 1926- *IntWW 91*
**Bhogilal**, Pratap 1916- *IntWW 91*
**Bhorjee**, Jaswant S 1935- *AmMWSc 92*
**Bhown**, Ajit Singh *AmMWSc 92*
**Bhugra**, Satnam Singh 1933- *WhoMW 92*
**Bhuiyan**, Rabia 1944- *IntWW 91*
**Bhumibol Adulyadej** 1927- *IntWW 91*
**Bhushan**, Bharat 1949- *AmMWSc 92, WhoWest 92*
**Bhushan**, Shanti 1925- *IntWW 91*
**Bhuta**, Ramesh 1946- *WhoWest 92*
**Bhutto**, Benazir 1953- *FacFETw [port], IntWW 91, Who 92*
**Bhutto**, Nusrat 1934- *IntWW 91*
**Bhutto**, Zulfikar Ali 1928-1977 *FacFETw [port]*
**Bhuva**, Rohit L 1954- *AmMWSc 92*
**Bhuvaneswaran**, Chidambaram 1934- *AmMWSc 92*
**Bhuyan**, Bijoy Kumar 1930- *AmMWSc 92*
**Bhyrappa**, Santeshivara Lingannaiah 1934- *IntAu&W 91*
**Bi Dexian** 1908- *IntWW 91*
**Biaett**, Doddridge Hewitt, III 1942- *WhoAmL 92*
**Biafore**, Gabriel J *WhoAmP 91*
**Biagas**, Edward D. 1948- *WhoBlA 92*
**Biagetti**, Richard Victor 1940- *AmMWSc 92*
**Biaggi**, Mario 1917- *IntWW 91*
**Biaggioni**, Italo 1954- *AmMWSc 92*
**Biagi**, L D *ScFEYrs*
**Biagini**, Raymond E 1949- *AmMWSc 92*
**Biaglow**, John E 1937- *AmMWSc 92*
**Bial**, Morrison David 1917- *WhoRel 92*
**Bialas**, Wayne Francis 1949- *AmMWSc 92*
**Biale**, Rachel Korati 1952- *WhoWest 92*
**Bialecke**, Edward P 1934- *AmMWSc 92*
**Bialek**, Richard Walter 1957- *WhoFI 92*
**Bialer**, Irving 1925- *WhoFI 92*
**Bialick**, David W. 1942- *WhoFI 92*
**Bialik**, Ghayim Nachman 1873-1934 *LiExTwC*
**Bialk**, Elisa *SmATA 65*
**Bialkin**, Kenneth Jules 1929- *WhoAmL 92, WhoFI 92*
**Bialkowski**, Diana *WhoRel 92*
**Bialla**, Rowley 1914- *WhoAmL 92*
**Biallas**, Leonard John 1939- *WhoMW 92, WhoRel 92*
**Bialo**, Kenneth Marc 1946- *WhoAmL 92*
**Bialosky**, Marshall Howard 1923- *WhoEnt 92*
**Bialy**, Harvey *DrAPF 91*
**Bianca**, Andrew Michael 1956- *WhoFI 92*
**Biancani**, Piero 1944- *AmMWSc 92*
**Biancheri**, Boris 1930- *IntWW 91, Who 92*
**Bianchi**, Al *NewYTBS 91 [port]*
**Bianchi**, Carmine Paul 1927- *AmMWSc 92*
**Bianchi**, Charles Paul 1945- *WhoFI 92*
**Bianchi**, Don 1938- *WhoAmP 91*
**Bianchi**, Donald Ernest 1933- *AmMWSc 92*
**Bianchi**, Ettore Carlo 1959- *WhoFI 92*
**Bianchi**, Eugene Carl 1930- *IntAu&W 91, WrDr 92*
**Bianchi**, Icilio W, Jr *WhoAmP 91*
**Bianchi**, Marco Berkeley 1939- *WhoFI 92*
**Bianchi**, Michele 1883-1930 *BiDExR, EncTR 91*
**Bianchi**, Richard A. 1940- *WhoIns 92*
**Bianchi**, Robert George 1925- *AmMWSc 92*
**Bianchi**, Ronald Bruce 1938- *WhoAmL 92*
**Bianchi**, Ted J, Jr. 1940- *WhoIns 92*
**Bianchine**, Joseph Raymond 1929- *AmMWSc 92*
**Bianchini**, Robert Joseph 1956- *WhoFI 92*
**Bianchini**, Robert V 1940- *WhoAmP 91*
**Bianchini**, Victor Eugene *WhoAmL 92*
**Bianchino**, Bernard Anthony 1948- *WhoAmL 92*
**Biancini**, Angelo 1911- *IntWW 91*
**Bianco**, Anthony 1953- *ConAu 134*
**Bianco**, Benjamin Joseph 1933- *WhoWest 92*
**Bianco**, Don Christopher 1947- *WhoMW 92*
**Bianco**, Gerardo 1931- *IntWW 91*
**Bianco**, Jean-Louis 1943- *IntWW 91*
**Bianco**, Michael Fabius Patrick 1940- *WhoWest 92*
**Bianco**, Nicole Ann 1949- *WhoWest 92*
**Bianco**, Peter 1963- *WhoEnt 92*
**Bianco**, Phillip, Jr 1939- *WhoAmP 91*
**Bianco**, Ralph D. 1948- *WhoWest 92*
**Bianco**, Sal C 1944- *WhoAmP 91*
**Bianconi**, Lorenzo 1946- *ConAu 134*
**Biard**, James R 1931- *AmMWSc 92*
**Bias**, Dana G. 1959- *WhoAmL 92*
**Bias**, Steven Eugene 1953- *WhoRel 92*
**Bias**, Wilma B 1928- *AmMWSc 92*
**Biasell**, Laverne R 1915- *AmMWSc 92*
**Biasin**, Gian-Paolo 1933- *WhoWest 92*
**Biasin**, Gian-Polo 1933- *WrDr 92*
**Biassey**, Earle Lambert 1920- *WhoBlA 92*
**Biava**, Luis *WhoEnt 92*
**Bibalo**, Antonio 1922- *ConCom 92*
**Bibart**, Richard Lee 1942- *WhoFI 92*
**Bibas**, Frank Percy 1917- *IntMPA 92*
**Bibb**, Daniel Roland 1951- *WhoFI 92*
**Bibb**, Harold David 1940- *AmMWSc 92*
**Bibb**, James Richard 1952- *WhoMW 92*
**Bibb**, Robert Cushman 1922- *WhoAmL 92*
**Bibb**, T. Clifford 1938- *WhoBlA 92*
**Bibb**, William Robert 1932- *AmMWSc 92*
**Bibber**, John Walter 1947- *WhoMW 92*
**Bibbo**, James V, Jr 1919- *WhoAmP 91*
**Bibbo**, Marluce 1939- *AmMWSc 92*
**Bibbs**, Janice Denise 1958- *WhoBlA 92*
**Bibbs**, Lona Carol 1948- *WhoMW 92*
**Bibby**, Benjamin *Who 92*
**Bibby**, Deirdre L. 1951- *WhoBlA 92*
**Bibby**, Derek 1922- *Who 92*
**Bibby**, Douglas M. 1946- *WhoFI 92*
**Bibby**, John Benjamin 1929- *Who 92*
**Bibby**, John E 1920- *WhoAmP 91*
**Bibby**, John F 1934- *ConAu 35NR*
**Bibby**, John Franklin 1934- *WhoAmP 91*
**Bibby**, Judy 1947- *TwCPaSc*
**Bibby**, Malcolm 1939- *AmMWSc 92*
**Bibby**, Peter Leonard 1940- *IntAu&W 91*
**Bibeau**, Armand A 1924- *AmMWSc 92*
**Bibeau**, Thomas Clifford 1949- *AmMWSc 92*
**Bibel**, Debra Jan 1945- *AmMWSc 92*
**Biber**, Heinrich Johann Franz von 1644-1704 *NewAmDM*
**Biber**, Margaret Clare Boadle 1943- *AmMWSc 92*
**Biber**, Thomas U L *AmMWSc 92*
**Biberger**, Erich Ludwig 1927- *IntAu&W 91*
**Biberman**, Lucien Morton 1919- *AmMWSc 92*
**Biberstein**, Ernst Ludwig 1922- *AmMWSc 92*
**Bibin**, Leonid Alekseyevich 1930- *IntWW 91*
**Bible**, Frances 1927- *NewAmDM*
**Bible**, Francis Lillian *WhoEnt 92*
**Bible**, Geoffrey Cyril 1937- *WhoFI 92*
**Bible**, Keith Christopher 1958- *WhoMW 92*
**Bible**, Paul Alfred 1940- *WhoAmL 92*
**Bibler**, Ned Eugene 1937- *AmMWSc 92*
**Biblis**, Evangelos J 1929- *AmMWSc 92*
**Biblo**, Mary 1927- *WhoBlA 92*
**Bibolet**, R H *IntAu&W 91X, WrDr 92*
**Bibring**, Thomas *AmMWSc 92*
**Bic**, Lubomir 1951- *AmMWSc 92*
**Bicat**, Andre 1909- *TwCPaSc*
**Bice**, David Earl 1938- *AmMWSc 92*
**Bice**, Debra Louise 1953- *WhoAmL 92*
**Bice**, Scott Haas 1943- *WhoAmL 92*
**Bicester**, Baron 1932- *Who 92*
**Bich**, Marcel 1914- *IntWW 91*
**Bichachi**, Olga Victoria 1952- *WhoHisp 92*
**Bichat**, Marie-Francois-Xavier 1771-1802 *BlkwCEP*
**Bichlmeier**, Germanus Joseph 1939- *WhoFI 92*
**Bichotte**, Rodrigue Ben *WhoRel 92*
**Bichsel**, Hans 1924- *AmMWSc 92*
**Bichteler**, Klaus Richard 1938- *AmMWSc 92*
**Bick**, David Greer 1953- *WhoFI 92, WhoMW 92*
**Bick**, George Herman 1914- *AmMWSc 92*
**Bick**, Jerry 1927- *IntMPA 92*
**Bick**, Katherine Livingstone 1932- *AmMWSc 92*
**Bick**, Kenneth F 1932- *AmMWSc 92*
**Bick**, Kenneth Roland 1955- *WhoAmL 92*
**Bick**, Martin James M. *Who 92*
**Bick**, Peter Hamilton 1948- *AmMWSc 92*
**Bick**, Robert Steven 1961- *WhoAmL 92*
**Bick**, Rodger Lee 1942- *AmMWSc 92, WhoWest 92*
**Bick**, Theodore A 1930- *AmMWSc 92*
**Bickar**, Betty Arlene 1931- *WhoWest 92*
**Bickart**, Theodore Albert 1935- *AmMWSc 92, WhoMW 92*
**Bickel**, Bertram Watkins 1925- *WhoFI 92*
**Bickel**, David Robert 1944- *WhoAmL 92*
**Bickel**, Edwin David 1941- *AmMWSc 92*
**Bickel**, Floyd Gilbert, III 1944- *WhoFI 92*
**Bickel**, John Henry 1950- *AmMWSc 92*
**Bickel**, Kenneth Robert 1952- *WhoRel 92*
**Bickel**, Lennard 1923- *WrDr 92*
**Bickel**, Nancy Kramer 1941- *WhoEnt 92, WhoWest 92*
**Bickel**, Peter J 1940- *AmMWSc 92*
**Bickel**, Robert John 1916- *AmMWSc 92*
**Bickel**, Stephen Douglas 1939- *WhoFI 92, WhoIns 92*
**Bickel**, Thomas Fulcher 1937- *AmMWSc 92*
**Bickel**, William Samuel 1937- *AmMWSc 92*
**Bickelhaupt**, Pamela Dianne 1945- *WhoMW 92*
**Bickelhaupt**, R E 1928- *AmMWSc 92*
**Bickerdike**, John 1893- *TwCPaSc*
**Bickerman**, Hylan A 1913- *AmMWSc 92*
**Bickerman**, Peter Bruce 1952- *WhoAmL 92*
**Bickerstaff**, Bernard Tyrone, Sr. 1943- *WhoBlA 92*
**Bickerstaff**, Bernie Lavelle 1944- *WhoWest 92*
**Bickerstaff**, Edwin Robert 1920- *WrDr 92*
**Bickerstaff**, Isaac *BenetAL 91*
**Bickerstaff**, Isaac 1733-1808? *RfGEnL 91*
**Bickerstaff**, Patsy Anne *DrAPF 91*
**Bickersteth**, John Monier 1921- *Who 92*
**Bickert**, William George 1937- *AmMWSc 92*
**Bickerton**, Frank Donald 1917- *Who 92*
**Bickerton**, John Thorburn 1930- *WhoFI 92*
**Bickerton**, Robert Keith 1934- *AmMWSc 92*
**Bickerton**, Thomas James 1958- *WhoRel 92*
**Bickes**, Paul Frank 1926- *WhoRel 92*
**Bicket**, Zenas Johan 1932- *WhoRel 92*
**Bickett**, Dianne Leslie 1965- *WhoRel 92*
**Bickett**, Thomas Walter 1869-1921 *DcNCBi 1*
**Bickford**, Charlene Nora 1944- *WhoAmP 91*
**Bickford**, David 1953- *ConAu 133, WhoEnt 92*
**Bickford**, Drucilla 1925- *WhoAmP 91*
**Bickford**, Gary *WhoAmP 91*
**Bickford**, George Percival 1901- *WhoFI 92*
**Bickford**, James David Prydeaux 1940- *Who 92*
**Bickford**, Jewelle Wooten 1941- *WhoFI 92*
**Bickford**, Lawrence Richardson 1921- *AmMWSc 92*
**Bickford**, Marion Eugene 1932- *AmMWSc 92*
**Bickford**, Reginald G 1913- *AmMWSc 92*
**Bickford Smith**, John Roger 1915- *Who 92*
**Bickford-Wimer**, Paula Cole 1956- *WhoWest 92*
**Bickham**, Jack M 1930- *IntAu&W 91, TwCWW 91, WrDr 92*
**Bickham**, John W 1949- *AmMWSc 92*
**Bickham**, L. B. 1923- *WhoBlA 92*
**Bickham**, Noel 1919- *WhoAmP 91*
**Bickley**, Dawn 1947- *TwCPaSc*
**Bickley**, Martin 1947- *TwCPaSc*
**Bickley**, Susan Louise 1959- *WhoAmL 92*
**Bickley**, William Elbert 1914- *AmMWSc 92*
**Bickling**, Charles Robert 1924- *AmMWSc 92*
**Bickmann**, Joan Mary 1951- *WhoFI 92*
**Bickmore**, Albert Smith 1839-1914 *BiInAmS*
**Bickmore**, John Tarry 1928- *AmMWSc 92*
**Bicknell**, Arthur Dwayne 1933- *WhoWest 92*
**Bicknell**, Brian Keith 1957- *WhoMW 92*
**Bicknell**, Christine Betty 1919- *Who 92*
**Bicknell**, Claud 1910- *Who 92*
**Bicknell**, Edward J 1928- *AmMWSc 92*
**Bicknell**, Gioconda *Who 92*
**Bicknell**, John 1958- *TwCPaSc*
**Bicknell**, Nadyne C. 1935- *WhoWest 92*
**Bicknell**, Nadyne Cooke 1935- *WhoAmP 91*
**Bicknell**, Robert C 1929- *WhoAmP 91*
**Bicknell**, William Edmund 1935- *AmMWSc 92*
**Bicknell-Brown**, Ellen 1944- *AmMWSc 92*
**Bickner**, Bruce Pierce 1943- *WhoMW 92*
**Bickner**, Deborah Kimmel 1959- *WhoMW 92*
**Bicks**, David Peter 1933- *WhoAmL 92*
**Bicks**, Mark Steven 1948- *WhoAmL 92*
**Bickwit**, Andrew Roy 1959- *WhoAmL 92*
**Bidart**, Frank 1939- *BenetAL 91, ConPo 91, WrDr 92*
**Bidart de Satulsky**, Gay-Darlene *WhoHisp 92*
**Bidault**, Georges 1899-1983 *FacFETw*
**Bidawid**, Raphael I. *WhoRel 92*
**Biddelman**, Mark Jay 1943- *WhoRel 92*
**Biddinger**, Brian Edward 1957- *WhoFI 92*
**Biddington**, William Robert 1925- *AmMWSc 92*
**Biddiss**, Michael Denis 1942- *IntAu&W 91, IntWW 91, WrDr 92*
**Biddle**, Adrian *WhoEnt 92*
**Biddle**, Allen Alexander 1939- *WhoRel 92*
**Biddle**, Anthony Joseph Drexel, III 1948- *WhoFI 92*
**Biddle**, Bruce Jesse 1928- *WrDr 92*
**Biddle**, Donald Ray 1936- *WhoFI 92, WhoWest 92*
**Biddle**, Jack, III *WhoAmP 91*
**Biddle**, Jane Lammert 1926- *WhoAmP 91*
**Biddle**, Martin 1937- *IntWW 91, Who 92*
**Biddle**, Mary Duke 1887-1960 *DcNCBi 1*
**Biddle**, Nicholas 1786-1844 *AmPolLe*
**Biddle**, Owen 1737-1799 *BiInAmS*
**Biddle**, Richard Albert 1930- *AmMWSc 92*
**Biddle**, Stanton F. 1943- *WhoBlA 92*
**Biddle**, Wayne *DrAPF 91*
**Biddlecom**, William Gerard 1942- *AmMWSc 92*
**Biddlecome**, Robert *WhoEnt 92*
**Biddulph** *Who 92*
**Biddulph**, Baron 1959- *Who 92*
**Biddulph**, Constance *Who 92*
**Biddulph**, Ian D'Olier 1940- *Who 92*
**Biddy**, Ernest C, Jr. 1945- *WhoIns 92*
**Biddy**, Fred Douglas 1932- *WhoAmP 91*
**Bide**, Austin 1915- *IntWW 91, Who 92*
**Bide**, Martin John 1951- *AmMWSc 92*

**Bide**, Richard W 1939- *AmMWSc 92*
**Bideau**, Edwin H, III *WhoAmP 91*
**Bidelman**, William Pendry 1918- *AmMWSc 92*
**Biden**, Joseph R., Jr. 1942- *AlmAP 92 [port]*
**Biden**, Joseph Robinette, Jr. 1942- *IntWW 91, WhoAmP 91*
**Bider**, John Roger 1932- *AmMWSc 92*
**Biderman**, Sumiko 1924- *WhoAmP 91*
**Bidgood**, Bryant Frederick 1937- *AmMWSc 92*
**Bidgood**, John Claude 1914- *Who 92*
**Bidinosti**, Dino Ronald 1933- *AmMWSc 92*
**Bidlack**, Donald Eugene 1932- *AmMWSc 92*
**Bidlack**, Jerald Dean 1935- *WhoFI 92*
**Bidlack**, Verne Claude, Jr 1923- *AmMWSc 92*
**Bidlack**, Wayne Ross 1944- *AmMWSc 92, WhoWest 92*
**Bidlake**, Mark Forrest 1954- *WhoMW 92*
**Bidleman**, Terry Frank 1942- *AmMWSc 92*
**Bidlingmayer**, William Lester 1920- *AmMWSc 92*
**Bidlingmeyer**, Brian Arthur 1944- *AmMWSc 92*
**Bidstrup**, Lesley 1916- *Who 92*
**Bidwell**, Arline M 1914- *WhoAmP 91*
**Bidwell**, Bennett E. 1927- *WhoFI 92*
**Bidwell**, Bennette E. 1927- *IntWW 91*
**Bidwell**, Benson 1835- *ScFEYrs*
**Bidwell**, Charles Edward 1932- *IntWW 91*
**Bidwell**, Hugh 1934- *Who 92*
**Bidwell**, James Truman, Jr. 1934- *WhoAmL 92*
**Bidwell**, Lawrence Romaine 1931- *AmMWSc 92*
**Bidwell**, Leonard Nathan 1934- *AmMWSc 92*
**Bidwell**, Lorena Louise 1961- *WhoMW 92*
**Bidwell**, Orville Willard 1918- *AmMWSc 92*
**Bidwell**, Robert Edward 1932- *WhoMW 92*
**Bidwell**, Roger Grafton Shelford 1927- *AmMWSc 92, IntWW 91*
**Bidwell**, Sydney James 1917- *Who 92*
**Bidwill**, William V. *WhoWest 92*
**Bie**, Helen *WhoAmP 91*
**Bie**, James Edward 1927- *WhoWest 92*
**Bie**, Oskar 1864-1938 *EncTR 91*
**Biebel**, Curt Fred, Jr. 1947- *WhoMW 92*
**Biebel**, Frederick K 1926- *WhoAmP 91*
**Biebel**, Mary J. 1952- *WhoAmL 92*
**Biebel**, Paul Joseph 1928- *AmMWSc 92*
**Bieber**, Allan Leroy 1934- *AmMWSc 92*
**Bieber**, Harold H 1927- *AmMWSc 92*
**Bieber**, Herman 1930- *AmMWSc 92*
**Bieber**, Irving d1991 *NewYTBS 91*
**Bieber**, Irving 1908- *AmMWSc 92*
**Bieber**, Loran Lamoine 1933- *AmMWSc 92*
**Bieber**, Mark Allan 1946- *AmMWSc 92*
**Bieber**, Owen F. 1929- *IntWW 91, WhoFI 92*
**Bieber**, Raymond W *AmMWSc 92*
**Bieber**, Samuel 1926- *AmMWSc 92*
**Bieber**, Theodore Immanuel 1925- *AmMWSc 92*
**Bieber-Meek**, Susan Kay 1951- *WhoAmL 92*
**Bieberman**, Robert Arthur 1923- *AmMWSc 92*
**Bieberstein**, Heinz Gunther 1930- *WhoMW 92*
**Biebuyck**, Daniel P. 1925- *WrDr 92*
**Biebuyck**, Julien Francois 1935- *AmMWSc 92*
**Bieck**, Robert Barton, Jr. 1952- *WhoAmL 92*
**Biedebach**, Mark Conrad 1932- *AmMWSc 92*
**Biedenbender**, Michael David 1961- *AmMWSc 92*
**Biedenharn**, Lawrence Christian, Jr 1922- *AmMWSc 92*
**Biedenkopf**, Kurt Hans 1930- *IntWW 91*
**Biederman**, Brian Maurice 1954- *AmMWSc 92*
**Biederman**, Donald Ellis 1934- *WhoAmL 92, WhoEnt 92, WhoWest 92*
**Biederman**, Edwin Williams, Jr 1930- *AmMWSc 92*
**Biederman**, Marcia *DrAPF 91*
**Biederman**, Ronald R 1938- *AmMWSc 92*
**Biederman-Thorson**, Marguerite Ann 1936- *AmMWSc 92*
**Biedermann**, Brooke 1950- *WhoFI 92*
**Biederwolf**, Robert Isadore 1928- *WhoEnt 92, WhoMW 92*
**Biederwolf**, William Edward 1867-1939 *RelLAm 91*
**Biedler**, June Lee 1925- *AmMWSc 92*
**Biefeld**, Paul Franklin 1925- *AmMWSc 92*
**Biege**, Philip E. 1919- *WhoIns 92*
**Biegel**, David Eli 1946- *WhoMW 92*
**Biegel**, John E 1925- *AmMWSc 92*
**Biegel**, Paul Johannes 1925- *IntAu&W 91*
**Biegelsen**, David K 1943- *AmMWSc 92*
**Biegelsen**, Elaine Lander 1939- *WhoFI 92*
**Biegen**, Arnold Irwin 1933- *WhoAmL 92*
**Bieger**, Detlef 1939- *AmMWSc 92*
**Bieger**, R. Cyril 1934- *WhoWest 92*
**Bieging**, David Arthur 1949- *WhoAmP 91*
**Biegler**, Lorenz Theodor 1956- *AmMWSc 92*
**Biegler**, Louis W. 1914- *WhoIns 92*
**Biehl**, Dallis Derrick 1938- *WhoEnt 92*
**Biehl**, Edward Robert 1932- *AmMWSc 92*
**Biehl**, Francis Walter 1928- *WhoFI 92*
**Biehl**, Joseph Park 1922- *AmMWSc 92*
**Biehl**, Michael M. 1951- *WhoAmL 92*
**Biehler**, Gregory Lee 1957- *WhoAmL 92*
**Biehler**, Rod William 1947- *WhoEnt 92*
**Biehler**, Shawn 1937- *AmMWSc 92*
**Biehn**, Michael 1957- *IntMPA 92*
**Biel**, Jacquelyn 1945- *WhoEnt 92*
**Biel**, Michael Jay 1946- *WhoEnt 92*
**Bielajew**, Alexander Frederick 1953- *AmMWSc 92*
**Bielak**, Jacobo *AmMWSc 92*
**Bielak**, Robert Stanley 1946- *WhoEnt 92*
**Bielat**, Kenneth L 1945- *AmMWSc 92*
**Bielaus**, Edward Henry 1955- *WhoEnt 92*
**Bielawa**, Dan 1950- *WhoMW 92*
**Bielawski**, Anthony *WhoAmP 91*
**Bielby**, Lorence Jon 1956- *WhoAmL 92*
**Biele**, Hugh Irving 1942- *WhoAmL 92*
**Bielecki**, Edwin J 1924- *AmMWSc 92*
**Bielecki**, Jan Krzysztof 1951- *IntWW 91*
**Bielecki**, John D. 1958- *WhoMW 92*
**Bielecki**, Paul Michael 1947- *WhoFI 92*
**Bielecki**, Richard Anthony 1956- *WhoFI 92*
**Bielen**, Casimir S. 1960- *WhoEnt 92*
**Bielenberg**, Leonard Herman 1927- *WhoAmL 92*
**Bieler**, Barrie Hill 1929- *AmMWSc 92*
**Bieler**, Leslie Foulds 1951- *WhoMW 92*
**Bieler**, Manfred 1934- *IntWW 91*
**Bieler**, Rudiger 1955- *AmMWSc 92*
**Bieley**, Peggy M. 1934- *WhoFI 92*
**Bielfeldt**, Donald Wayne 1930- *WhoMW 92*
**Bielinska**, Jzabela 1925- *IntAu&W 91*
**Bielinski**, Daniel Walter 1961- *WhoFI 92*
**Bielka**, Robert Bruce 1950- *WhoFI 92*
**Bielke**, Patricia Anne 1949- *WhoMW 92*
**Biellier**, Harold Victor 1921- *AmMWSc 92*
**Bielory**, Abraham Melvin 1946- *WhoAmL 92*
**Bielory**, Leonard 1954- *WhoFI 92*
**Bielski**, Alison 1925- *WrDr 92*
**Bielski**, Alison Joy Prosser 1925- *IntAu&W 91*
**Bielski**, Benon H J 1927- *AmMWSc 92*
**Bieluch**, William Charles 1918- *WhoAmL 92*
**Biemann**, Klaus 1926- *AmMWSc 92*
**Biempica**, Luis 1925- *AmMWSc 92*
**Bien**, Clark David 1953- *WhoMW 92*
**Bien**, Darl Dean 1940- *WhoFI 92*
**Bien**, Julius 1826-1909 *BiInAmS*
**Bien**, Michael W. 1955- *WhoAmL 92*
**Bien**, Peter A. 1930- *WrDr 92*
**Bien**, Richard N. 1957- *WhoAmL 92*
**Bienemann**, Charles Edward, Jr. 1941- *WhoAmL 92*
**Bienen**, Leigh Buchanan *DrAPF 91*
**Bienenstock**, Arthur Irwin 1935- *AmMWSc 92*
**Bienfang**, Paul Kenneth 1948- *AmMWSc 92*
**Bieniawski**, Zdzislaw Tadeusz 1936- *AmMWSc 92*
**Bieniek**, Maciej P 1927- *AmMWSc 92*
**Bieniek**, Ronald James 1948- *AmMWSc 92*
**Bieniewski**, Thomas M 1936- *AmMWSc 92*
**Bienkowski**, John Richard 1947- *WhoFI 92*
**Bienstock**, D 1917- *AmMWSc 92*
**Bienstock**, Daniel 1960- *AmMWSc 92*
**Bienstock**, Freddy 1928- *WhoEnt 92*
**Bienstock**, Terry Scott 1954- *WhoEnt 92*
**Bienvenu**, Robert Charles 1922- *WhoWest 92*
**Bienvenue**, Gordon Raymond 1946- *AmMWSc 92*
**Bienz**, Darrel Rudolph 1926- *AmMWSc 92*
**Bier**, Dennis Martin 1941- *AmMWSc 92*
**Bier**, Jesse 1925- *WhoWest 92*
**Bier**, John Leo 1936- *WhoIns 92*
**Bier**, Milan 1920- *AmMWSc 92*
**Bierbauer**, Charles J. *LesBEnT 92*
**Bierbaum**, Christopher John 1966- *WhoMW 92*
**Bierbaum**, Paul Martin, Jr. 1946- *WhoWest 92*
**Bierbaum**, Veronica Marie 1948- *AmMWSc 92*
**Bierce**, Ambrose 1842-1914 *BenetAL 91, FacFETw, ScFEYrs, ShSCr 9 [port], TwCLC 44 [port]*
**Bierce**, James Malcolm 1931- *WhoAmL 92*
**Bierds**, Linda *DrAPF 91*
**Bierdz**, Thom *WhoEnt 92*
**Bierenbaum**, Marvin L 1926- *AmMWSc 92*
**Bierhorst**, John 1936- *WrDr 92*
**Bieri**, Jacqueline Elizabeth 1962- *WhoFI 92*
**Bieri**, John Genther 1920- *AmMWSc 92*
**Bieri**, Robert 1926- *AmMWSc 92*
**Bierich**, Marcus 1926- *IntWW 91, Who 92*
**Bierig**, Jack R. 1947- *WhoAmL 92*
**Bierkamper**, George G *AmMWSc 92*
**Bierlein**, James A 1921- *AmMWSc 92*
**Bierlein**, James Allison 1921- *WhoMW 92*
**Bierlein**, John Carl 1936- *AmMWSc 92, WhoMW 92*
**Bierlein**, John David 1940- *AmMWSc 92*
**Bierlein**, Theo Karl 1924- *AmMWSc 92*
**Bierley**, John Charles 1936- *WhoAmL 92*
**Bierley**, Paul Edmund 1926- *WhoEnt 92*
**Bierly**, Eugene Wendell 1931- *AmMWSc 92*
**Bierly**, James N, Jr 1922- *AmMWSc 92*
**Bierly**, Mahlon Zwingli, Jr 1922- *AmMWSc 92*
**Bierly**, Richard A. 1946- *WhoAmL 92*
**Bierman**, Arthur 1925- *AmMWSc 92*
**Bierman**, Charles John 1938- *WhoRel 92*
**Bierman**, Edwin Lawrence 1930- *AmMWSc 92, WhoWest 92*
**Bierman**, Everett E 1924- *WhoAmP 91*
**Bierman**, Howard Richard 1915- *AmMWSc 92*
**Bierman**, James Norman 1945- *WhoAmL 92*
**Bierman**, Laurence William 1933- *WhoWest 92*
**Bierman**, Mary Jo *WhoAmP 91*
**Bierman**, Sidney Roy 1928- *AmMWSc 92*
**Bierman**, Steven M. 1952- *WhoAmL 92*
**Biermann**, Alan Wales 1939- *AmMWSc 92*
**Biermann**, Bruce Robert 1965- *WhoEnt 92*
**Biermann**, Christopher James 1958- *AmMWSc 92*
**Biermann**, Janet Sybil 1961- *AmMWSc 92*
**Biermann**, Theodore Frank 1943- *WhoMW 92*
**Biermann**, Todd Allen 1964- *WhoRel 92*
**Biermann**, Wolf 1936- *LiExTwC*
**Biernacki-Poray**, Wlad Otton 1924- *WhoFI 92*
**Biernaski**, Eugene Edward 1930- *WhoFI 92*
**Biernbaum**, Charles Knox 1946- *AmMWSc 92*
**Bieron**, Joseph F 1937- *AmMWSc 92*
**Bierring**, Ole 1926- *IntWW 91*
**Bierschenk**, William Henry 1926- *AmMWSc 92*
**Bierschwale**, Bryan Walter 1950- *WhoAmP 91*
**Biersdorf**, John Edgar 1930- *WhoMW 92*
**Biersdorf**, William Richard 1925- *AmMWSc 92*
**Biersmith**, Edward L, III 1942- *AmMWSc 92*
**Biersner**, Robert John 1941- *AmMWSc 92*
**Bierstedt**, Peter Richard 1943- *WhoAmL 92, WhoFI 92*
**Bierut**, Boleslaw 1892-1956 *EncTR 91*
**Bierwag**, Gerald O. 1936- *WhoFI 92*
**Bierwagen**, Gordon Paul 1943- *AmMWSc 92*
**Bierwirth**, John Cocks 1924- *IntWW 91*
**Biery**, Evelyn Hudson 1946- *WhoAmL 92*
**Biery**, Richard Martin 1942- *WhoMW 92*
**Bierzychudek**, Paulette F 1951- *AmMWSc 92*
**Bies**, David Alan 1925- *AmMWSc 92*
**Biesele**, John Julius 1918- *AmMWSc 92*
**Biesemeyer**, Marilyn Jean 1931- *WhoMW 92*
**Biesenberger**, Joseph A 1935- *AmMWSc 92*
**Biesheuvel**, Barend Willem 1920- *IntWW 91*
**Bieshu**, Mariya Lukyanovna 1934- *IntWW 91*
**Biesinger**, John William, III 1949- *WhoAmL 92*
**Biesiot**, Patricia Marie 1950- *AmMWSc 92*
**Biestek**, John Paul 1935- *WhoMW 92*
**Biester**, John Louis 1918- *AmMWSc 92*
**Biesterfeld**, Craig Stewart 1953- *WhoMW 92*
**Bietry**, Pierre 1872-1918 *BiDExR*
**Bietz**, Elmer A *WhoAmP 91*
**Bietz**, Jerold Allen 1942- *AmMWSc 92*
**Biever**, Keith James 1936- *WhoWest 92*
**Biever**, Kenneth Duane 1940- *AmMWSc 92*
**Biever**, Robert Henry 1931- *WhoFI 92*
**Biever**, Violet S 1911- *WhoAmP 91*
**Biezup**, John Thomas 1929- *WhoAmL 92*
**Biffen**, John 1930- *IntAu&W 91, IntWW 91, Who 92*
**Biffi**, Giacomo 1928- *IntWW 91, WhoRel 92*
**Biffle**, Jerome Cousins 1928- *BlkOlyM*
**Biffle**, Richard Lee, III 1949- *WhoWest 92*
**Biffot**, Laurent Marie 1925- *IntWW 91*
**Big Eagle**, Duane *DrAPF 91*
**Big-Foot Wallace** 1817-1899 *BenetAL 91*
**Bigard**, Barney 1906-1980 *ConAu 134, NewAmDM*
**Bigart**, Homer 1907-1991 *CurBio 91N, NewYTBS 91 [port]*
**Bigas**, Johnny 1929- *WhoHisp 92*
**Bigbee**, John Franklin, Jr 1934- *WhoAmP 91*
**Bigbie**, Charles Roy, III 1959- *WhoFI 92*
**Bigbie**, Scott Woodson 1946- *WhoWest 92*
**Bigby-Young**, Betty 1930- *WhoBlA 92*
**Bigeleisen**, Jacob 1919- *AmMWSc 92, IntWW 91*
**Bigelow**, Artemas 1818-1901 *BiInAmS*
**Bigelow**, Charles C 1928- *AmMWSc 92*
**Bigelow**, Charles Russell 1947- *WhoMW 92*
**Bigelow**, Daniel James 1935- *WhoMW 92*
**Bigelow**, David Skinner, III 1931- *WhoFI 92*
**Bigelow**, E. Thayer *LesBEnT 92*
**Bigelow**, Howard Elson 1923- *AmMWSc 92*
**Bigelow**, Jacob 1786-1879 *BiInAmS*
**Bigelow**, Jane 1933- *WhoRel 92*
**Bigelow**, John 1817-1911 *BenetAL 91*
**Bigelow**, John E 1929- *AmMWSc 92*
**Bigelow**, John Edward 1922- *AmMWSc 92*
**Bigelow**, Margaret Elizabeth Barr 1923- *AmMWSc 92*
**Bigelow**, Martha Mitchell 1921- *WhoMW 92*
**Bigelow**, Michael *WhoEnt 92*
**Bigelow**, Michael Allan 1959- *WhoRel 92*
**Bigelow**, Newton J.T. d1991 *NewYTBS 91*
**Bigelow**, Sanford Walker 1956- *AmMWSc 92*
**Bigelow**, Thayer *WhoEnt 92*
**Bigelow**, W. T. 1929- *WhoBlA 92*
**Bigelow**, Wilbur Charles 1923- *AmMWSc 92, WhoMW 92*
**Bigelow-Lourie**, Anne Edwige 1946- *WhoEnt 92*
**Bigg**, Donald Michael 1945- *WhoMW 92*
**Bigg**, Dort Sharon 1930- *WhoAmP 91*
**Biggam**, Robin Adair 1938- *IntWW 91, Who 92*
**Biggar**, Andrew 1915- *Who 92*
**Biggar**, Barry P. 1952- *WhoAmL 92*
**Biggar**, James McCrea 1928- *WhoMW 92*
**Biggart**, Norman 1930- *Who 92*
**Biggart**, Waddell Alexander 1935- *WhoAmL 92*
**Bigge**, Morris L 1908- *IntAu&W 91, WrDr 92*
**Bigger**, B. Frank 1942- *WhoFI 92*
**Bigger**, Cynthia Anita Hopwood 1942- *AmMWSc 92*
**Bigger**, J Thomas, Jr 1935- *AmMWSc 92*
**Biggers**, Charles James 1935- *AmMWSc 92*
**Biggers**, Earl Derr 1884-1933 *BenetAL 91*
**Biggers**, Howard David 1950- *WhoRel 92*
**Biggers**, James Virgil 1928- *AmMWSc 92*
**Biggers**, Janis R. 1951- *WhoFI 92*
**Biggers**, John Dennis 1923- *AmMWSc 92*
**Biggers**, Neal Brooks, Jr. 1935- *WhoAmL 92*
**Biggers**, Ralph Lee 1941- *WhoFI 92*
**Biggers**, Samuel Loring, Jr. 1935- *WhoBlA 92*
**Biggerstaff**, John A 1931- *AmMWSc 92*
**Biggerstaff**, Randy Lee 1951- *WhoMW 92*
**Biggerstaff**, Robert Huggins 1927- *AmMWSc 92*
**Biggerstaff**, Warren Richard 1918- *AmMWSc 92*
**Biggini**, Carlo Alberto 1902-1945 *BiDExR*
**Biggins**, John 1936- *AmMWSc 92*
**Biggle**, Lloyd, Jr. 1923- *ConAu 35NR, IntAu&W 91, SmATA 65 [port], TwCSFW 91, WrDr 92*
**Biggs** *Who 92*
**Biggs**, Alan Richard 1953- *AmMWSc 92*
**Biggs**, Albert Wayne 1926- *AmMWSc 92*
**Biggs**, Arlene *DrAPF 91*
**Biggs**, Asa 1811-1878 *DcNCBi 1*
**Biggs**, Cynthia DeMari 1953- *WhoBlA 92*
**Biggs**, David Frederick 1939- *AmMWSc 92*
**Biggs**, Donald Lee 1920- *AmMWSc 92*
**Biggs**, Dorothy Elnora 1941- *WhoWest 92*
**Biggs**, Douglas Craig 1950- *AmMWSc 92*
**Biggs**, E. Power 1906-1977 *NewAmDM*
**Biggs**, Ervie Glenn 1930- *WhoRel 92*
**Biggs**, Frank 1927- *AmMWSc 92*
**Biggs**, Homer Gates 1930- *AmMWSc 92*
**Biggs**, J. O. 1925- *WhoAmL 92*
**Biggs**, James Crawford 1872-1960 *DcNCBi 1*
**Biggs**, Joel Gilson, Jr. 1947- *WhoWest 92*
**Biggs**, John 1933- *Who 92*
**Biggs**, John Burville 1934- *WrDr 92*

**Biggs**, John H. 1936- *WhoIns 92*
**Biggs**, John Herron 1936- *WhoFI 92*
**Biggs**, Luther C. 1958- *WhoRel 92*
**Biggs**, Margaret Annette 1933- *IntAu&W 91*
**Biggs**, Margaret Key *DrAPF 91*
**Biggs**, Mark McCampbell 1954- *WhoEnt 92*
**Biggs**, Mary *DrAPF 91*
**Biggs**, Maurice Earl 1921- *AmMWSc 92*
**Biggs**, Michael Worthington 1911- *Who 92*
**Biggs**, Norman 1907- *Who 92*
**Biggs**, Norman Parris 1907- *IntWW 91*
**Biggs**, Paul 1913- *AmMWSc 92*
**Biggs**, Peter Martin 1926- *IntWW 91, Who 92*
**Biggs**, R B 1937- *AmMWSc 92*
**Biggs**, R Dale 1928- *AmMWSc 92*
**Biggs**, R. Tipton 1939- *WhoEnt 92*
**Biggs**, Richard Lee 1949- *WhoBlA 92*
**Biggs**, Robert Hilton 1931- *AmMWSc 92*
**Biggs**, Ronald C 1938- *AmMWSc 92*
**Biggs**, Shirley Ann 1938- *WhoBlA 92*
**Biggs**, Thomas Wylie 1950- *WhoWest 92*
**Biggs**, Timothy d1684? *DcNCBi 1*
**Biggs**, Tyrell 1960- *BlkOlyM*
**Biggs**, Walter Clark, Jr 1931- *AmMWSc 92*
**Bigham** *Who 92*
**Bigham**, Clifford Bruce 1928- *AmMWSc 92*
**Bigham**, Darrel Eugene 1942- *WhoMW 92*
**Bigham**, Eric Cleveland 1947- *AmMWSc 92*
**Bigham**, James John 1937- *WhoFI 92*
**Bigham**, Reta Lacy 1949- *WhoBlA 92*
**Bigham**, Robert Eric 1940- *AmMWSc 92*
**Bighley**, Mark Steven 1954- *WhoEnt 92*
**Bigler**, Carole Lindemann 1940- *WhoEnt 92*
**Bigler**, Rodney Errol 1941- *AmMWSc 92*
**Bigler**, Stuart Grazier 1927- *AmMWSc 92*
**Bigler**, William Norman 1937- *AmMWSc 92*
**Bigley**, Harry Andrew, Jr 1913- *AmMWSc 92*
**Bigley**, Nancy Jane 1932- *AmMWSc 92*
**Bigley**, Robert Harry 1929- *AmMWSc 92*
**Bigley**, William Joseph, Jr. 1924- *WhoFI 92*
**Bigliani**, Gabriele 1952- *WhoWest 92*
**Bigliano**, Robert P 1929- *AmMWSc 92*
**Bigliardi**, Matthew Paul 1920- *WhoRel 92*
**Bigliardi**, Patricia Ann 1943- *WhoRel 92*
**Biglieri**, Edward George 1925- *AmMWSc 92*
**Bigly**, Cantell A 1817-1859 *ScFEYrs*
**Bigman**, Anton W. 1929- *WhoAmL 92*
**Bignall**, John Reginald 1913- *Who 92*
**Bignall**, Robert 1730?-1787 *DcNCBi 1*
**Bignell**, Richard Carl 1943- *AmMWSc 92*
**Bignone**, Reynaldo Benito 1928- *IntWW 91*
**Bigongiari**, Mary Julia 1945- *WhoMW 92*
**Bigras**, Francine Jeanne 1948- *AmMWSc 92*
**Bigsby**, C. W. E. 1941- *WrDr 92*
**Bigsby**, Christopher William Edgar 1941- *IntAu&W 91*
**Biguenet**, John *DrAPF 91*
**Bigus**, Lawrence Weaver 1955- *WhoAmL 92*
**Bihalji-Merin**, Oto 1904- *ConAu 34NR, IntWW 91*
**Bihari**, Barna Laszlo 1965- *WhoWest 92*
**Bihler**, Ivan 1924- *AmMWSc 92*
**Bihler**, Penny Harter *DrAPF 91*
**Bihovsky**, Ron 1948- *AmMWSc 92*
**Bijou**, Rachelle *DrAPF 91*
**Bijou**, Sidney William 1908- *AmMWSc 92*
**Bijur**, Peter I. *WhoFI 92*
**Bijur**, Peter Isaac 1942- *Who 92*
**Bikales**, Norbert M 1929- *AmMWSc 92*
**Bikales**, Norman Allen 1935- *WhoAmL 92*
**Bikel**, Theodore 1924- *NewAmDM, WhoEnt 92*
**Bikerman**, Michael 1934- *AmMWSc 92*
**Bikila**, Abebe 1932-1973 *BlkOlyM [port]*
**Bikin**, Henry 1918- *AmMWSc 92*
**Bikkal**, Cecilia G. 1954- *WhoHisp 92*
**Bikkenin**, Nail Barievich 1931- *IntWW 91, SovUnBD*
**Bikle**, Daniel David 1944- *AmMWSc 92*
**Bikle**, Paul F. d1991 *NewYTBS 91*
**Biko**, Steve 1947-1977 *FacFETw [port]*
**Bikulege**, Vivian Irene 1958- *WhoFI 92*
**Bilal**, Melvin Asim 1942- *WhoBlA 92*
**Bilali**, Irahim *BlkOlyM*
**Bilan**, M Victor 1922- *AmMWSc 92*
**Bilandic**, M 1923- *WhoAmP 91*
**Bilandic**, Michael A. 1923- *WhoMW 92*
**Bilaniuk**, Larissa Tetiana 1941- *AmMWSc 92*
**Bilaniuk**, Oleksa-Myron 1926- *AmMWSc 92*
**Bilbao**, Francisco Ernesto 1933- *WhoHisp 92*
**Bilbao**, Marcia Kepler 1931- *AmMWSc 92*
**Bilbao**, Maria Antonieta 1950- *WhoHisp 92*
**Bilbo**, Claude V, Jr 1941- *WhoAmP 91*
**Bilbo**, Hal Andrew 1955- *WhoRel 92*
**Bilbo**, Theodore 1877-1947 *RelLAm 91*
**Bilbray**, James 1938- *AlmAP 92 [port]*
**Bilbray**, James Hubert 1938- *WhoAmP 91, WhoWest 92*
**Bilbrey**, Bruce Martin 1943- *WhoWest 92*
**Bilby**, Bruce Alexander 1922- *IntWW 91, Who 92*
**Bilby**, Kenneth W. *LesBEnT 92*
**Bilby**, Kenneth W. 1918- *IntMPA 92*
**Bilby**, Richard Mansfield 1931- *WhoAmL 92, WhoWest 92*
**Bild**, Frank 1911- *WhoAmP 91, WhoMW 92*
**Bild**, Richard Wayne 1946- *AmMWSc 92*
**Bilder**, James Gerard *WhoMW 92*
**Bilderback**, David Earl 1943- *AmMWSc 92*
**Bilderback**, Diane Elizabeth 1951- *WhoWest 92*
**Bilderback**, Donald Heywood 1947- *AmMWSc 92*
**Bilderdijk**, Willem 1756-1831 *ScFEYrs A*
**Bildersee**, Robert Alan 1942- *WhoAmL 92*
**Bildstein**, Keith Louis 1950- *AmMWSc 92*
**Bildt**, Carl 1949- *IntWW 91*
**Bile**, Abdi *NewYTBS 91 [port]*
**Bilecki**, Mary Lydia 1929- *WhoRel 92*
**Bilecki**, Ronald Allan 1942- *WhoFI 92*
**Bilello**, John Charles 1938- *AmMWSc 92, WhoMW 92*
**Bilello**, Michael Anthony 1924- *AmMWSc 92*
**Biles**, Charles Morgan 1939- *AmMWSc 92*
**Biles**, John Alexander 1923- *AmMWSc 92*
**Biles**, Kevin F. 1947- *WhoEnt 92*
**Biles**, Robert Wayne 1947- *AmMWSc 92*
**Biles**, W R 1923- *AmMWSc 92*
**Biletch**, Harry 1922- *AmMWSc 92*
**Bilezikjian**, Edward Andrew 1950- *WhoWest 92*
**Bilezikjian**, John Haig 1948- *WhoEnt 92*
**Bilge**, Ali Suat 1921- *IntWW 91*
**Bilger**, David Victor 1945- *WhoEnt 92*
**Bilger**, Hans Rudolf 1935- *AmMWSc 92*
**Bilgrav-Nielsen**, Jens 1936- *IntWW 91*
**Bilgutay**, Nihat Mustafa 1952- *AmMWSc 92*
**Bilheimer**, Charlene Frances 1956- *WhoAmL 92*
**Bilheimer**, Robert S. 1917- *DcEcMov*
**Bilheimer**, Robert Sperry 1917- *IntWW 91*
**Bilhorn**, John Merlyn 1926- *AmMWSc 92*
**Bilimoria**, Minoo Hormasji 1930- *AmMWSc 92*
**Bilimoria**, N. M. 1922- *IntMPA 92*
**Bilinski**, Stanley Michael 1953- *WhoRel 92*
**Bilirakis**, Michael 1930- *AlmAP 92 [port], WhoAmP 91*
**Bilistiche of Magnesia** *EncAmaz 91*
**Bill**, Geoffrey 1924- *Who 92*
**Bill**, Gregory Stuart 1946- *WhoWest 92*
**Bill**, James A. 1929- *WrDr 92*
**Bill**, Karen S. 1951- *WhoEnt 92*
**Bill**, Lester Henry 1910- *WhoRel 92*
**Bill**, Max 1908- *DcTwDes, FacFETw, IntWW 91*
**Bill**, Tony 1940- *IntMPA 92, WhoEnt 92*
**Bill'-Belotserkovsky**, Vladimir Naumovich 1884-1970 *SovUnBD*
**Billak**, James Robert 1950- *WhoMW 92*
**Billard**, William Thomas 1946- *WhoMW 92*
**Billaud**, Bernard 1942- *IntWW 91*
**Billauer**, Barbara Pfeffer 1951- *WhoAmL 92*
**Billen**, Daniel 1924- *AmMWSc 92*
**Billenstien**, Dorothy Corinne 1921- *AmMWSc 92*
**Biller**, Alan David 1944- *WhoFI 92*
**Biller**, Henry B 1940- *ConAu 35NR*
**Biller**, James Francis 1941- *WhoMW 92*
**Biller**, Joel Wilson 1929- *WhoFI 92*
**Biller**, Jose 1948- *AmMWSc 92*
**Biller**, Leslie Stuart 1948- *WhoFI 92*
**Billera**, Louis Joseph 1943- *AmMWSc 92*
**Billerbeck**, Jeffrey George 1954- *WhoRel 92*
**Billesbach**, David P 1956- *AmMWSc 92*
**Billeskov-Jansen**, Frederik Julius 1907- *IntWW 91*
**Billet**, Bret Lee 1962- *WhoFI 92*
**Billet**, Georges 1920- *IntWW 91*
**Billetdoux**, Francois-Paul 1927- *IntWW 91*
**Billett**, Paul Rodney 1921- *Who 92*
**Billette**, Jacques 1940- *AmMWSc 92*
**Billey**, Steven Ray 1956- *WhoMW 92*
**Billheimer**, Foster E 1936- *AmMWSc 92*
**Billheimer**, Jeffrey Thomas 1946- *AmMWSc 92*
**Billias**, George Athan 1919- *WrDr 92*
**Billica**, Harry Robert 1919- *AmMWSc 92*
**Billick**, David Joseph 1947- *WhoMW 92*
**Billick**, L. Larkin 1948- *WhoFI 92*
**Billig**, Erwin H. 1927- *WhoMW 92*
**Billig**, Etel Jewel 1932- *WhoMW 92*
**Billig**, Franklin A 1923- *AmMWSc 92*
**Billig**, Frederick S 1933- *AmMWSc 92*
**Billig**, Otto 1910- *AmMWSc 92*
**Billig**, Thomas Clifford 1930- *WhoMW 92*
**Billigheimer**, Claude Elias 1930- *AmMWSc 92*
**Billimoria**, F. Bill 1943- *WhoFI 92*
**Billing**, Graham 1936- *ConNov 91, WrDr 92*
**Billing**, Graham John 1936- *IntAu&W 91*
**Billing**, Melvin George 1906- *Who 92*
**Billing**, Oliver Donald, Jr. 1949- *WhoMW 92*
**Billingham**, Carol Jean 1926- *WhoFI 92*
**Billingham**, Edward J, Jr 1934- *AmMWSc 92*
**Billingham**, John 1930- *AmMWSc 92*
**Billingham**, Rupert Everett 1921- *AmMWSc 92, IntWW 91, Who 92*
**Billinghurst**, Alfred John 1880-1963 *TwCPaSc*
**Billings**, Brian Lee 1957- *WhoAmP 91*
**Billings**, Bruce Hadley 1915- *AmMWSc 92, WhoWest 92*
**Billings**, Charles Edgar 1925- *AmMWSc 92*
**Billings**, Charles Edgar 1929- *WhoWest 92*
**Billings**, Charles Edgar, Jr 1929- *AmMWSc 92*
**Billings**, Chester, Jr. 1924- *WhoAmL 92*
**Billings**, Clarence David 1943- *WhoFI 92*
**Billings**, Cora Marie 1939- *WhoBlA 92*
**Billings**, Frank Seaver 1845-1912 *BiInAmS*
**Billings**, Franklin S, Jr 1922- *WhoAmP 91*
**Billings**, Franklin Swift, Jr. 1922- *WhoAmL 92*
**Billings**, George Washington, III 1944- *WhoAmL 92*
**Billings**, John Shaw 1838-1913 *BiInAmS*
**Billings**, Josh 1818-1885 *BenetAL 91*
**Billings**, Judith 1939- *WhoAmP 91*
**Billings**, Leon *WhoAmP 91*
**Billings**, Marland Pratt 1902- *AmMWSc 92*
**Billings**, Patricia Anne 1943- *WhoFI 92*
**Billings**, Peggy Marie 1928- *WhoRel 92*
**Billings**, Peter, Jr *WhoAmP 91*
**Billings**, R Gail 1934- *AmMWSc 92*
**Billings**, Robert Northrop 1947- *WhoIns 92*
**Billings**, Thomas Neal 1931- *WhoFI 92, WhoWest 92*
**Billings**, Thomas Trevor 1951- *WhoAmL 92*
**Billings**, William 1746-1800 *NewAmDM*
**Billings**, William Dwight 1910- *AmMWSc 92*
**Billings**, William H 1921- *WhoAmP 91*
**Billingslea**, Edgar D. 1910- *WhoBlA 92*
**Billingslea**, Monroe L. 1933- *WhoBlA 92*
**Billingsley**, Andrew 1926- *WhoBlA 92*
**Billingsley**, Lance W. 1940- *WhoAmL 92*
**Billingsley**, Lance William 1940- *WhoAmP 91*
**Billingsley**, Mary Lee 1952- *WhoMW 92*
**Billingsley**, Orzell, Jr. 1924- *WhoBlA 92*
**Billingsley**, Patrick Paul 1925- *AmMWSc 92*
**Billingsley**, Ray C. 1957- *WhoBlA 92*
**Billingsley**, Robert Thaine 1954- *WhoAmL 92*
**Billington**, Barry E. 1940- *WhoAmL 92*
**Billington**, Clyde, Jr. 1934- *WhoBlA 92*
**Billington**, David P. 1927- *ConAu 134*
**Billington**, David Perkins 1927- *AmMWSc 92*
**Billington**, Douglas S 1912- *AmMWSc 92*
**Billington**, James Hadley 1929- *IntWW 91, Who 92*
**Billington**, Ken 1946- *WhoEnt 92*
**Billington**, Kevin 1934- *IntWW 91, Who 92*
**Billington**, Michael 1939- *IntAu&W 91, Who 92, WrDr 92*
**Billington**, Peter James 1948- *WhoWest 92*
**Billington**, Rachel 1942- *ConNov 91, Who 92, WrDr 92*
**Billington**, Rachel Mary 1942- *IntAu&W 91*
**Billington**, Ray 1930- *WrDr 92*
**Billington**, Scott Thomas 1951- *WhoEnt 92*
**Billington**, Steven Miles 1952- *WhoEnt 92*
**Billinson**, George David 1954- *WhoAmL 92*
**Billinton**, Roy 1935- *AmMWSc 92, WhoWest 92*
**Billiot**, John Alvas 1933- *WhoAmP 91*
**Billitteri**, Salvatore 1921- *IntMPA 92*
**Billman**, Brookes D., Jr. 1949- *WhoAmL 92*
**Billman**, Frank Henry 1952- *WhoRel 92*
**Billman**, Fred Richard 1943- *AmMWSc 92*
**Billman**, George Edward 1954- *AmMWSc 92, WhoMW 92*
**Billman**, John Henry 1912- *AmMWSc 92*
**Billman**, Kenneth William 1933- *AmMWSc 92*
**Billman**, Larry Edward 1938- *WhoEnt 92*
**Billmeyer**, Fred W., Jr. 1919- *WrDr 92*
**Billmeyer**, Fred Wallace, Jr 1919- *AmMWSc 92*
**Billo**, Edward Joseph 1938- *AmMWSc 92*
**Billops**, Camille 1933- *NotBlAW 92*
**Billops**, Camille J. 1933- *WhoBlA 92*
**Billot**, Barbara Kathleen 1920- *Who 92*
**Billotte**, Pierre 1906- *IntWW 91*
**Billow**, Andrew, Jr *WhoAmP 91*
**Bills**, Charles Wayne 1924- *AmMWSc 92*
**Bills**, Daniel Granville 1924- *AmMWSc 92*
**Bills**, Donald Duane 1932- *AmMWSc 92*
**Bills**, Fred Dean 1943- *WhoFI 92*
**Bills**, James LaVar 1935- *AmMWSc 92*
**Bills**, John Lawrence 1920- *AmMWSc 92*
**Bills**, Johnny Bernard 1949- *WhoBlA 92*
**Billups**, Clinton Ford, Jr. 1947- *WhoEnt 92*
**Billups**, Florence W. 1921- *WhoBlA 92*
**Billups**, Janet Noelle 1952- *WhoAmL 92*
**Billups**, Mattie Lou 1935- *WhoBlA 92*
**Billups**, Myles E., Sr. 1926- *WhoBlA 92*
**Billups**, Norman Frederick 1934- *AmMWSc 92*
**Billups**, W Edward 1939- *AmMWSc 92*
**Billy the Kid** 1859-1881 *BenetAL 91*
**Billy**, Dennis Joseph 1953- *WhoRel 92*
**Bilock**, John M. 1916- *WhoRel 92*
**Bilodeau**, Brent Laurence 1962- *WhoMW 92*
**Bilodeau**, Gerald Gustave 1929- *AmMWSc 92*
**Bilodeau**, Robert David 1947- *WhoFI 92*
**Biloen**, Paul 1939- *AmMWSc 92*
**Bilotta**, Diane Briley 1953- *WhoMW 92*
**Bilous**, Edward W. 1957- *WhoEnt 92*
**Bilow**, Norman 1928- *AmMWSc 92*
**Bilow**, Steven Craig 1960- *WhoWest 92*
**Bilpuch**, Edward George 1927- *AmMWSc 92*
**Bils**, Robert F 1931- *AmMWSc 92*
**Bilski**, Peter 1918- *WhoEnt 92*
**Bilson**, Bruce 1928- *IntMPA 92, WhoEnt 92*
**Bilson**, Malcolm 1935- *NewAmDM*
**Biltonen**, Rodney Lincoln 1937- *AmMWSc 92*
**Biltz**, Thomas William 1960- *WhoMW 92*
**Bily**, Mikhail Ulyanovich 1922- *IntWW 91*
**Bilyeu**, Byron Lee 1936- *WhoAmP 91*
**Bilyeu**, Charles Edward 1917- *WhoAmP 91*
**Bilyeu**, Russell Gene 1930- *AmMWSc 92*
**Bilz**, Reed Kenworthey 1935- *WhoAmL 92*
**Bimber**, Russell Morrow 1929- *AmMWSc 92*
**Bimler**, Richard William 1940- *WhoRel 92*
**Bin Xin** 1900- *LiExTwC*
**bin Yeop**, Abdul Aziz 1916- *Who 92*
**Bina**, Melvin Joseph 1931- *WhoWest 92*
**Bina**, Minou 1945- *AmMWSc 92*
**Binaisa**, Godfrey Lukwongwa 1920- *IntWW 91*
**Bincer**, Adam Marian 1930- *AmMWSc 92*
**Binchois**, Gilles 1400?-1460? *NewAmDM*
**Binchy**, Maeve *IntAu&W 91*
**Binchy**, Maeve 1940- *ConAu 134, ConNov 91, WrDr 92*
**Binder**, Amy Finn 1955- *WhoFI 92*
**Binder**, Bernd R 1945- *AmMWSc 92*
**Binder**, Bernhard 1936- *AmMWSc 92*
**Binder**, Carl Vincent 1949- *WhoFI 92*
**Binder**, Daniel 1927- *AmMWSc 92*
**Binder**, David A. 1934- *WhoAmL 92*
**Binder**, David Franklin 1935- *WhoAmL 92, WhoFI 92*
**Binder**, Eando 1911-1974 *TwCSFW 91*
**Binder**, Erwin 1934- *WhoWest 92*
**Binder**, Franklin Lewis 1945- *AmMWSc 92*
**Binder**, Gary 1944- *WhoFI 92*
**Binder**, Henry J 1936- *AmMWSc 92*
**Binder**, Irwin 1949- *AmMWSc 92*
**Binder**, James Kauffman 1920- *WhoWest 92*
**Binder**, Janet O'Harra 1927- *WhoMW 92*
**Binder**, John 1930- *WhoRel 92*
**Binder**, John Joseph 1956- *WhoFI 92*
**Binder**, Madeline Dotti 1942- *WhoMW 92*
**Binder**, Marc David 1949- *AmMWSc 92*
**Binder**, Matthew J 1917- *WhoAmP 91*
**Binder**, Maurice d1991 *NewYTBS 91*
**Binder**, Michael 1951- *AmMWSc 92*
**Binder**, Otto *TwCSFW 91*
**Binder**, Paul Julius 1928- *WhoRel 92*
**Binder**, Robert Lawrence 1951- *WhoAmL 92*
**Binder**, Steve *IntMPA 92, LesBEnT 92, WhoEnt 92*
**Binder**, Theodor 1919- *IntWW 91*
**Binder**, William Harry 1922- *WhoFI 92*
**Bindesboll**, Thorwald 1846-1908 *DcTwDes*
**Binding**, Gunther 1936- *IntWW 91*
**Binding**, Rudolf Georg 1867-1938 *EncTR 91 [port]*
**Bindley**, William Edward 1940- *WhoFI 92*

**Bindloss**, Harold 1866-1945 *TwCWW 91*
**Bindloss**, William 1937- *AmMWSc 92*
**Bindra**, Jasjit Singh 1942- *AmMWSc 92*
**Bindseil**, Lee Anton, III 1938- *WhoFI 92*
**Binegar**, Gwendolyn Ann 1924- *WhoWest 92*
**Bines**, Harvey Ernest 1941- *WhoAmL 92*
**Binet**, Alfred 1857-1911 *DcAmImH, FacFETw*
**Binet**, Rene Valentin 1914-1957 *BiDExR*
**Binford**, Gregory Glenn 1948- *WhoAmL 92*
**Binford**, Helen Bills Titsworth 1885-1952 *DcNCBi 1*
**Binford**, Henry C. 1944- *WhoBlA 92*
**Binford**, Jesse Stone, Jr 1928- *AmMWSc 92*
**Binford**, Laurence C. 1935- *WrDr 92*
**Binford**, Laurence Charles 1935- *AmMWSc 92*
**Binford**, Michael W 1951- *AmMWSc 92*
**Binford**, Raymond 1876-1951 *DcNCBi 1*
**Bing**, Arthur 1916- *AmMWSc 92*
**Bing**, Dave 1943- *WhoBlA 92*
**Bing**, David H 1938- *AmMWSc 92*
**Bing**, George Franklin 1924- *AmMWSc 92*
**Bing**, Inigo Geoffrey 1944- *Who 92*
**Bing**, Kurt 1914- *AmMWSc 92*
**Bing**, Oscar H L 1935- *AmMWSc 92*
**Bing**, Ralph Sol 1917- *WhoWest 92*
**Bing**, Richard F 1941- *AmMWSc 92*
**Bing**, Richard John 1909- *AmMWSc 92*
**Bing**, Richard McPhail 1950- *WhoAmL 92*
**Bing**, Rubell M. 1938- *WhoBlA 92*
**Bing**, Rudolf 1902- *IntWW 91, Who 92*
**Bing**, Rudolf 1902-1988 *NewAmDM*
**Bing**, Rudolph 1902- *FacFETw*
**Bing**, Samuel 1838-1919 *DcTwDes*
**Bingaman**, Anne Kovacovich 1943- *WhoAmL 92*
**Bingaman**, Jeff 1943- *AlmAP 92 [port], IntWW 91, WhoAmP 91, WhoWest 92*
**Bingel**, Audrey Susanna *AmMWSc 92*
**Bingeman**, Michael Robert 1958- *WhoFI 92*
**Binger**, Glenn H 1931- *WhoAmP 91*
**Binger**, Wilson Valentine 1917- *AmMWSc 92*
**Binggeli**, Richard Lee 1937- *AmMWSc 92*
**Bingham** *Who 92*
**Bingham**, Lord 1967- *Who 92*
**Bingham**, Arthur E. 1906- *WhoBlA 92*
**Bingham**, Billy Elias 1931- *AmMWSc 92*
**Bingham**, Caleb 1757-1817 *BenetAL 91*
**Bingham**, Carleton Dille 1929- *AmMWSc 92*
**Bingham**, Caroline 1938- *WrDr 92*
**Bingham**, Caroline Margery Conyers 1938- *IntAu&W 91, Who 92*
**Bingham**, Carrol R 1938- *AmMWSc 92*
**Bingham**, Charlotte 1942- *WrDr 92*
**Bingham**, Charlotte Marie-Therese 1942- *IntAu&W 91*
**Bingham**, Charlotte Mary Therese 1942- *Who 92*
**Bingham**, Christopher 1937- *AmMWSc 92*
**Bingham**, Donna Guydon 1961- *WhoBlA 92*
**Bingham**, Eardley Max 1927- *Who 92*
**Bingham**, Edwin Theodore 1936- *AmMWSc 92*
**Bingham**, Eula 1929- *AmMWSc 92*
**Bingham**, Felton Wells 1935- *AmMWSc 92*
**Bingham**, Gene Austin *AmMWSc 92*
**Bingham**, George Caleb 1811-1879 *BenetAL 91*
**Bingham**, Glenn George 1955- *WhoWest 92*
**Bingham**, Harry H, Jr 1931- *AmMWSc 92*
**Bingham**, Hiram 1789-1869 *BenetAL 91*
**Bingham**, Hiram 1831-1908 *BenetAL 91*
**Bingham**, Hiram 1875-1956 *BenetAL 91, FacFETw*
**Bingham**, James d1990 *Who 92N*
**Bingham**, Jinsie Scott 1935- *WhoEnt 92*
**Bingham**, John 1908- *IntAu&W 91*
**Bingham**, John 1930- *IntWW 91, Who 92*
**Bingham**, June 1919- *IntAu&W 91*
**Bingham**, June Rossbach 1919- *WrDr 92*
**Bingham**, Lemuel 1795-1885 *DcNCBi 1*
**Bingham**, Mary Lily Kenan Flagler 1867-1917 *DcNCBi 1*
**Bingham**, Max *Who 92*
**Bingham**, Michael Lee 1957- *WhoRel 92*
**Bingham**, Nelson Preston 1925- *WhoAmP 91*
**Bingham**, Rebecca Josephine 1928- *WhoBlA 92*
**Bingham**, Richard Charles 1944- *AmMWSc 92*
**Bingham**, Richard Donnelly 1937- *WhoFI 92, WhoMW 92*
**Bingham**, Richard Martin 1915- *Who 92*
**Bingham**, Richard S, Jr 1924- *AmMWSc 92*
**Bingham**, Robert 1838-1927 *DcNCBi 1*
**Bingham**, Robert Dorsey 1948- *WhoFI 92*
**Bingham**, Robert Evan 1918- *WhoAmL 92*
**Bingham**, Robert J 1932- *AmMWSc 92*
**Bingham**, Robert Lodewijk 1930- *AmMWSc 92*
**Bingham**, Robert Worth 1871-1937 *DcNCBi 1*
**Bingham**, Sallie *DrAPF 91*
**Bingham**, Sallie 1937- *WhoEnt 92, WrDr 92*
**Bingham**, Samuel Wayne 1929- *AmMWSc 92*
**Bingham**, Seth 1882-1972 *NewAmDM*
**Bingham**, Thomas 1933- *Who 92*
**Bingham**, Walter D. 1921- *WhoRel 92*
**Bingham**, William 1754-1826 *DcNCBi 1*
**Bingham**, William 1835-1873 *DcNCBi 1*
**Bingham**, William Allen 1962- *WhoRel 92*
**Bingham**, William James 1802-1866 *DcNCBi 1*
**Bingle**, Donald J. 1954- *WhoAmL 92*
**Bingler**, Edward Charles 1935- *AmMWSc 92*
**Bingley**, Clive 1936- *WrDr 92*
**Bingley**, David Ernest 1920-1985 *TwCWW 91*
**Bingley**, Edward J. 1934- *WhoIns 92*
**Bingley**, Juliet Martin 1925- *Who 92*
**Bingo-Duggins**, Karen Leiko 1942- *WhoFI 92*
**Binhammer**, Robert T 1929- *AmMWSc 92*
**Bini**, Dante Natale 1932- *WhoWest 92*
**Binienda**, John Joseph, Sr 1947- *WhoAmP 91*
**Binion**, Rudolph 1927- *IntAu&W 91, WrDr 92*
**Binkerd**, Gordon 1916- *NewAmDM*
**Binkley**, Barbara Jeanne 1944- *WhoEnt 92*
**Binkley**, Charlotte Kay 1942- *WhoMW 92, WhoRel 92*
**Binkley**, Johne 1953- *WhoAmP 91*
**Binkley**, Jonathan Andrew 1940- *WhoMW 92*
**Binkley**, Luther John 1925- *WrDr 92*
**Binkley**, Marguerite Hall 1926- *WhoAmP 91*
**Binkley**, Olin Trivette 1908- *WhoRel 92*
**Binkley**, Roger Wendell 1941- *AmMWSc 92*
**Binkley**, Sue Ann 1944- *AmMWSc 92*
**Binkley**, Thomas 1931- *ConAu 135, NewAmDM*
**Binkley**, Thomas Eden *WhoEnt 92*
**Binkowski**, Edward Stephan 1948- *WhoAmL 92*
**Binkowski**, Francis Stanley 1937- *AmMWSc 92*
**Binkowski**, Johannes Aloysius Joseph 1908- *IntAu&W 91, IntWW 91*
**Binn**, Leonard Norman 1927- *AmMWSc 92*
**Binner**, Kathy M. 1956- *WhoMW 92*
**Binney**, Amos 1803-1847 *BiInAmS*
**Binney**, Caroline Thorn *WhoEnt 92*
**Binney**, H. A. Roy 1907- *Who 92*
**Binney**, Marcus Hugh Crofton *IntAu&W 91, Who 92*
**Binney**, Wiliam Greene 1833-1909 *BiInAmS*
**Binnicker**, Pamela Caroline 1938- *AmMWSc 92*
**Binnie**, David Stark 1922- *Who 92*
**Binnie**, Nancy Catherine 1937- *WhoWest 92*
**Binnie**, William Hugh 1939- *AmMWSc 92*
**Binnig**, Gerd 1947- *AmMWSc 92, IntWW 91*
**Binnig**, Gerd Karl 1947- *Who 92, WhoNob 90*
**Binning**, Lord 1985- *Who 92*
**Binning**, Byron Dee 1935- *WhoWest 92*
**Binning**, J. Boyd 1944- *WhoAmL 92*
**Binning**, John Harlan 1923- *WhoIns 92*
**Binning**, Kenneth George Henry 1928- *Who 92*
**Binning**, Larry Keith 1942- *AmMWSc 92*
**Binning**, Robert Christie 1921- *AmMWSc 92*
**Binning**, William Charles 1944- *WhoAmP 91, WhoMW 92*
**Binninger**, David Michael *AmMWSc 92*
**Binnion**, John Edward 1918- *WhoAmP 91*
**Binns**, Archie 1899-1971 *BenetAL 91, ConAu 133*
**Binns**, David John 1929- *Who 92*
**Binns**, Geoffrey John 1930- *Who 92*
**Binns**, Jack Robert 1933- *WhoAmP 91*
**Binns**, Malcolm 1936- *IntWW 91, Who 92*
**Binns**, Michael Ferrers Elliott 1923- *WrDr 92*
**Binns**, Silas Odell 1920- *WhoBlA 92*
**Binns**, St John 1914- *Who 92*
**Binns**, Walter Gordon, Jr. 1929- *WhoFI 92*
**Binns**, Walter Robert 1940- *AmMWSc 92*
**Binns**, Walter Scot 1941- *WhoWest 92*
**Binns**, William Arthur 1925- *WhoMW 92*
**Binny**, John Anthony Francis 1911- *Who 92*
**Bins**, Milton 1934- *WhoBlA 92*
**Binsfeld**, Connie 1924- *WhoAmP 91*
**Binsfeld**, Connie Berube 1924- *WhoMW 92*
**Binsinger**, Richard 1940- *WhoFI 92*
**Binstock**, Michael 1948- *WhoEnt 92*
**Bint-Anat** *EncAmaz 91*
**Bintinger**, David L *AmMWSc 92*
**Bintley**, David Julian 1957- *Who 92*
**Bintliff**, Barbara Ann 1953- *WhoAmL 92*
**Bintz**, Gary Luther 1941- *AmMWSc 92*
**Binyon**, Helen 1904-1979 *TwCPaSc*
**Binyon**, Laurence 1869-1943 *RfGEnL 91*
**Binz**, Carl Michael 1947- *AmMWSc 92*
**Biobaku**, Saburi Oladeni 1918- *IntWW 91, Who 92*
**Bioke Malabo**, Cristino Seriche *IntWW 91*
**Biolchini**, Robert Fredrick 1939- *WhoAmL 92, WhoFI 92*
**Bioleau**, Luc J R *AmMWSc 92*
**Biolsi**, Louis, Jr 1940- *AmMWSc 92*
**Biondi**, Christine A 1952- *WhoAmP 91*
**Biondi**, Frank *LesBEnT 92*
**Biondi**, Frank J., Jr 1945- *IntMPA 92, WhoEnt 92, WhoFI 92*
**Biondi**, Lawrence 1938- *WhoMW 92, WhoRel 92*
**Biondi**, Manfred Anthony 1924- *AmMWSc 92*
**Biondo**, Dino Dominick 1958- *WhoMW 92*
**Biondo**, Frank X 1927- *AmMWSc 92*
**Biorn**, David Olaf 1942- *WhoMW 92*
**Bioy Casares**, Adolfo 1914- *DcLB 113 [port], IntWW 91*
**Bippes**, Bernece 1918- *WhoAmP 91*
**Bippus**, David Paul 1949- *WhoFI 92, WhoMW 92*
**Biran**, Yoav 1939- *Who 92*
**Birbara**, Linda Hope 1963- *WhoFI 92*
**Birch**, A.G. *ScFEYrs*
**Birch**, Albert Francis 1903- *AmMWSc 92*
**Birch**, Alexander Hope 1913- *Who 92*
**Birch**, Anthony Harold 1924- *IntAu&W 91, Who 92, WrDr 92*
**Birch**, Arthur John 1915- *IntWW 91, Who 92*
**Birch**, Bryan John 1931- *IntWW 91, Who 92*
**Birch**, Clifford Wadsworth, Jr 1920- *WhoAmP 91*
**Birch**, Dean W. 1960- *WhoAmL 92*
**Birch**, Dennis Arthur 1925- *Who 92*
**Birch**, Frank Stanley Heath 1939- *Who 92*
**Birch**, Jean Gordon 1921- *WhoAmP 91*
**Birch**, John A 1943- *WhoAmP 91*
**Birch**, John Allan 1935- *Who 92*
**Birch**, John Anthony 1929- *Who 92*
**Birch**, L. Charles 1918- *IntWW 91*
**Birch**, Martin Christopher 1944- *AmMWSc 92*
**Birch**, Michael Ray 1962- *WhoEnt 92*
**Birch**, Michael Scott 1949- *WhoAmL 92*
**Birch**, Peter Gibbs 1937- *Who 92*
**Birch**, Philip Thomas 1927- *Who 92*
**Birch**, Raymond E 1905- *AmMWSc 92*
**Birch**, Reginald 1914- *Who 92*
**Birch**, Robert Edward Thomas 1917- *Who 92*
**Birch**, Robert William 1935- *WhoMW 92*
**Birch**, Robin Arthur 1939- *Who 92*
**Birch**, Roger 1930- *Who 92*
**Birch**, Ruth Ellen 1952- *AmMWSc 92*
**Birch**, S.J. Lamorna 1869-1955 *TwCPaSc*
**Birch**, Sheryl Joyce 1958- *WhoAmL 92*
**Birch**, Stanley F, Jr *WhoAmP 91*
**Birch**, Stanley F., Jr. 1945- *WhoAmL 92*
**Birch**, Teresa Christine 1961- *WhoEnt 92*
**Birch**, Thomas 1705-1766 *BlkwCEP*
**Birch**, William 1925- *Who 92*
**Birch**, William Henry David 1895-1968 *TwCPaSc*
**Birchak**, James Robert 1939- *AmMWSc 92*
**Birchall**, Derek 1930- *Who 92*
**Birchall**, James Derek 1930- *IntWW 91*
**Bircham**, Deric Neale 1934- *IntAu&W 91*
**Birchby**, Kenneth Lee 1915- *WhoFI 92*
**Birchem**, Regina *AmMWSc 92*
**Birchenall**, Charles Ernest 1922- *AmMWSc 92*
**Birchenough**, Michael 1923- *Who 92*
**Bircher**, Edgar Allen 1934- *WhoAmL 92, WhoFI 92*
**Birchette**, William Ashby, III 1942- *WhoBlA 92*
**Birchette-Pierce**, Cheryl L. 1945- *WhoBlA 92*
**Birchfield**, Gene Edward 1928- *AmMWSc 92*
**Birchfield**, John Kermit, Jr. 1940- *WhoAmL 92*
**Birchfield**, Wray 1920- *AmMWSc 92*
**Birchler**, James Arthur 1950- *AmMWSc 92*
**Birckbichler**, Paul Joseph 1942- *AmMWSc 92*
**Bird** *NewAmDM*
**Bird**, Adrian Peter 1947- *Who 92*
**Bird**, Agnes Thornton 1921- *WhoAmL 92, WhoAmP 91*
**Bird**, Andrew Reid, Jr. 1909- *WhoRel 92*
**Bird**, Anthony 1917-1974 *ConAu 135*
**Bird**, Anthony Peter 1931- *Who 92*
**Bird**, Arthur *ScFEYrs*
**Bird**, C 1843?-1910 *BiInAmS*
**Bird**, Caroline 1915- *WrDr 92*
**Bird**, Charles Albert 1947- *WhoWest 92*
**Bird**, Charles Coleman 1945- *WhoAmL 92*
**Bird**, Charles Durham 1932- *AmMWSc 92*
**Bird**, Charles Edward 1931- *AmMWSc 92*
**Bird**, Charles Mark 1955- *WhoRel 92*
**Bird**, Charles Norman 1929- *AmMWSc 92*
**Bird**, Colin Richard 1933- *Who 92*
**Bird**, Daniel Woodrow, Jr 1938- *WhoAmP 91*
**Bird**, David 1945- *WhoAmP 91*
**Bird**, David Darrell 1946- *WhoAmL 92*
**Bird**, David Jacobs 1954- *WhoAmL 92*
**Bird**, Dennis Leslie 1930- *WrDr 92*
**Bird**, Elias Neal 1940- *WhoEnt 92*
**Bird**, Elizabeth Anne 1950- *WhoAmL 92*
**Bird**, Francis Marion 1902- *WhoAmL 92*
**Bird**, Francis Marion, Jr. 1938- *WhoAmL 92*
**Bird**, George Richmond 1925- *AmMWSc 92*
**Bird**, George W 1939- *AmMWSc 92*
**Bird**, Glenn V 1949- *WhoAmP 91*
**Bird**, Gordon Winslow 1943- *AmMWSc 92*
**Bird**, Harold L, Jr 1921- *AmMWSc 92*
**Bird**, Harvey Harold 1934- *AmMWSc 92*
**Bird**, Hector Ramon 1939- *WhoHisp 92*
**Bird**, Henry Richard 1909- *TwCPaSc*
**Bird**, Herbert Roderick 1912- *AmMWSc 92*
**Bird**, Jack Richard, Jr. 1957- *WhoAmL 92*
**Bird**, James Gurth 1909- *Who 92*
**Bird**, James Harold 1923- *WrDr 92*
**Bird**, John Alfred William *Who 92*
**Bird**, John Eric 1958- *WhoWest 92*
**Bird**, John Malcolm 1931- *AmMWSc 92*
**Bird**, John Rossey, II 1947- *WhoEnt 92*
**Bird**, John T *WhoAmP 91*
**Bird**, John Tullis 1948- *WhoMW 92*
**Bird**, John William Clyde 1932- *AmMWSc 92*
**Bird**, Joseph Francis 1930- *AmMWSc 92*
**Bird**, Joseph G 1915- *AmMWSc 92*
**Bird**, Judith Tieman 1946- *WhoMW 92*
**Bird**, Kenneth D. d1991 *NewYTBS 91*
**Bird**, Kenneth Woodward 1946- *WhoMW 92*
**Bird**, L. Raymond 1914- *WhoFI 92*
**Bird**, Lesley Ann 1963- *WhoWest 92*
**Bird**, Leslie V 1929- *AmMWSc 92*
**Bird**, Luther Smith 1921- *AmMWSc 92*
**Bird**, Matthew Alexius 1957- *WhoMW 92*
**Bird**, Michael Anthony 1955- *WhoMW 92*
**Bird**, Michael C 1939- *WhoAmP 91*
**Bird**, Michael Gwynne 1921- *Who 92*
**Bird**, Michael James 1935- *Who 92*
**Bird**, Michael Larry 1949- *WhoAmP 91*
**Bird**, Michael Wesley 1942- *AmMWSc 92*
**Bird**, Peter 1951- *AmMWSc 92*
**Bird**, Phillip Craig 1947- *WhoMW 92*
**Bird**, R Byron 1924- *AmMWSc 92*
**Bird**, Ralph Gordon 1933- *WhoFI 92*
**Bird**, Randall Charles 1949- *WhoWest 92*
**Bird**, Richard *Who 92*
**Bird**, Richard 1938- *WrDr 92*
**Bird**, Richard 1950- *Who 92*
**Bird**, Richard Dawnay M. *Who 92*
**Bird**, Richard Geoffrey Chapman 1935- *Who 92*
**Bird**, Richard Herries 1932- *Who 92*
**Bird**, Richard Putnam 1938- *AmMWSc 92*
**Bird**, Robert Earl 1943- *AmMWSc 92*
**Bird**, Robert Montgomery 1806-1854 *BenetAL 91*
**Bird**, Ronald Charles 1936- *WhoAmP 91*
**Bird**, Rose Elizabeth 1936- *IntWW 91, WhoAmP 91, WhoWest 92*
**Bird**, Samuel Oscar, II 1934- *AmMWSc 92*
**Bird**, Stephanie J 1948- *AmMWSc 92*
**Bird**, Stephen C 1939- *WhoAmP 91*
**Bird**, Thomas Joseph 1927- *AmMWSc 92*
**Bird**, Valentine d1679? *DcNCBi 1*
**Bird**, Vere Cornwall 1910- *Who 92*
**Bird**, Vere Cornwall, Sr. 1909- *IntWW 91*
**Bird**, Wendell Raleigh 1954- *WhoAmL 92*
**Bird**, Whitworth F. 1932- *WhoIns 92*
**Bird**, William Ernest 1890-1975 *DcNCBi 1*
**Bird-Wilson**, Harold Arthur Cooper 1919- *Who 92*
**Birdlebough**, Harold 1928- *WhoWest 92*
**Birdsall**, Arthur Anthony 1947- *WhoMW 92*
**Birdsall**, Charles Kennedy 1925- *AmMWSc 92*
**Birdsall**, David Lee 1954- *WhoWest 92*
**Birdsall**, David Robert 1960- *WhoMW 92*
**Birdsall**, Derek Walter 1934- *Who 92*
**Birdsall**, Doris 1915- *Who 92*
**Birdsall**, Kevin Jay 1962- *WhoEnt 92*
**Birdsall**, Marion Ivens 1940- *AmMWSc 92*
**Birdsall**, Theodore G 1927- *AmMWSc 92*

**Birdsall,** William John 1944- *AmMWSc 92*
**Birdsell,** Dale Carl 1940- *AmMWSc 92*
**Birdseye,** Clarence 1886-1956 *FacFETw*
**Birdseye,** Tom 1951- *ConAu 133, SmATA 66*
**Birdsong,** James Cook 1843-1918 *DcNCBi 1*
**Birdsong,** Jimmy 1925- *WhoAmP 91*
**Birdsong,** Kenneth Wilson 1927- *WhoAmP 91*
**Birdsong,** Michael Howard 1945- *WhoEnt 92*
**Birdsong,** Otis 1955- *WhoBlA 92*
**Birdsong,** Ray Stuart 1935- *AmMWSc 92*
**Birdwell,** Carolyn Campbell 1947- *WhoEnt 92*
**Birdwell,** Edward R. 1936- *WhoEnt 92, WhoWest 92*
**Birdwell,** William A. 1946- *WhoAmL 92*
**Birdwhistell,** Ralph Kenton 1924- *AmMWSc 92*
**Birdwood** *Who 92*
**Birdwood,** Baron 1938- *Who 92*
**Birdzell,** Floyd Douglas 1930- *WhoAmL 92*
**Birecka,** Helena M 1921- *AmMWSc 92*
**Birecki,** Henryk 1948- *AmMWSc 92*
**Bireley,** Marlene Kay 1936- *WhoRel 92*
**Birely,** John H 1939- *AmMWSc 92*
**Birenbaum,** Barbara 1941- *SmATA 65 [port]*
**Birenbaum,** David Elias 1937- *WhoAmL 92*
**Birenbaum,** William M. 1923- *WrDr 92*
**Birendra Bir Bikram Shah Dev** 1945- *FacFETw, IntWW 91*
**Birendra Singh,** Rao 1921- *IntWW 91*
**Bires,** Dennis Eugene 1954- *WhoAmL 92*
**Birge,** Ann Chamberlain 1925- *AmMWSc 92*
**Birge,** Robert Richards 1946- *AmMWSc 92*
**Birge,** Robert Walsh 1924- *AmMWSc 92*
**Birge,** Wesley Joe 1929- *AmMWSc 92*
**Birgeneau,** Robert Joseph 1942- *AmMWSc 92*
**Birido,** Omer Yousif 1939- *IntWW 91*
**Birincioglu,** Ahmet Ihsan 1923- *IntWW 91*
**Biringer,** Paul P 1924- *AmMWSc 92*
**Biritz,** Helmut 1940- *AmMWSc 92*
**Biriuk,** George 1928- *AmMWSc 92*
**Birk** *Who 92*
**Birk,** Baroness *Who 92*
**Birk,** James Peter 1941- *AmMWSc 92*
**Birk,** Kathy *NewYTBS 91 [port]*
**Birk,** Robert Louis 1940- *WhoMW 92*
**Birk,** Roger Emil 1930- *IntWW 91, WhoFI 92*
**Birkbeck,** Morris *DcAmImH*
**Birkbeck,** Morris 1764-1825 *BenetAL 91*
**Birkby,** Walter H 1931- *AmMWSc 92*
**Birkby,** Walter Hudson 1931- *WhoWest 92*
**Birke,** Adolf Matthias 1939- *IntWW 91*
**Birke,** Ronald Lewis 1939- *AmMWSc 92*
**Birkebak,** Richard C 1934- *AmMWSc 92*
**Birkedal Hansen,** Henning *AmMWSc 92*
**Birkeland,** Arthur C 1904- *WhoAmP 91*
**Birkeland,** Charles John 1916- *AmMWSc 92*
**Birkeland,** Peter Wessel 1934- *AmMWSc 92*
**Birkelund,** John Peter 1930- *WhoFI 92*
**Birkelund,** Palle 1912- *IntWW 91*
**Birkemeier,** William P 1927- *AmMWSc 92*
**Birken,** Steven 1945- *AmMWSc 92*
**Birkenfeld,** Rose Maria 1931- *WhoRel 92*
**Birkenhauer,** Robert Joseph 1916- *AmMWSc 92*
**Birkenhead,** Bishop Suffragan of 1926- *Who 92*
**Birkenhead,** Thomas Bruce 1931- *WhoEnt 92*
**Birkenholz,** Dale Eugene *AmMWSc 92*
**Birkenstock,** Arthur O. 1928- *WhoIns 92*
**Birkerts,** Sven 1951- *ConAu 133*
**Birkes,** David Spencer 1942- *AmMWSc 92*
**Birkett** *Who 92*
**Birkett,** Baron 1929- *Who 92*
**Birkett,** James Davis 1936- *AmMWSc 92*
**Birkett,** Michael 1929- *WhoEnt 92*
**Birkett,** Peter Vidler 1948- *Who 92*
**Birkhahn,** Jonathan 1953- *WhoEnt 92*
**Birkhahn,** Ronald H *AmMWSc 92*
**Birkhead,** Paul Kenneth 1928- *AmMWSc 92*
**Birkhead,** Thomas Larry 1941- *WhoRel 92*
**Birkhoff,** Garrett 1911- *AmMWSc 92, IntWW 91, WrDr 92*
**Birkhoff,** Neil Vincent 1955- *WhoAmL 92*
**Birkhoff,** Robert D 1925- *AmMWSc 92*
**Birkholm,** Michael Peter 1952- *WhoWest 92*
**Birkholz,** Gabriella Sonja 1938- *WhoFI 92, WhoMW 92*
**Birkholz,** Janice Kay 1949- *WhoFI 92*
**Birkimer,** Donald Leo 1941- *AmMWSc 92*
**Birkin,** Derek *Who 92*
**Birkin,** Derek 1929- *IntWW 91*
**Birkin,** John 1953- *Who 92*
**Birkin,** John Derek 1929- *Who 92*
**Birkinbine,** John 1844-1915 *BiInAmS*
**Birkinbine,** John, II 1930- *WhoWest 92*
**Birkinbine,** John L, Jr 1946- *WhoAmP 91*
**Birkinshaw,** John Howard 1894- *Who 92*
**Birkitt,** James Nelson, Jr. 1956- *WhoRel 92*
**Birkle,** A John 1930- *AmMWSc 92*
**Birkmaier,** Robert David 1955- *WhoAmL 92*
**Birkmyre,** Henry 1898- *Who 92*
**Birkner,** Hans-Joachim 1931- *WhoRel 92*
**Birks,** George Drummond 1919- *WhoFI 92*
**Birks,** Jack 1920- *IntWW 91, Who 92*
**Birks,** John William 1946- *AmMWSc 92*
**Birks,** Michael 1920- *Who 92*
**Birks,** Michael Lynn 1958- *WhoRel 92*
**Birks,** Neil 1935- *AmMWSc 92*
**Birks,** Peter Brian Herrenden 1941- *Who 92*
**Birky,** Carl William, Jr 1937- *AmMWSc 92*
**Birky,** John Edward 1934- *WhoFI 92*
**Birla,** Basant Kumar 1921- *IntWW 91*
**Birla,** Ganga Prasad 1922- *IntWW 91*
**Birle,** James Robb 1936- *WhoFI 92, WhoWest 92*
**Birle,** John David 1939- *AmMWSc 92*
**Birleffi,** Lynn *WhoAmP 91*
**Birley,** Anthony Addison 1920- *Who 92*
**Birley,** Derek 1926- *Who 92*
**Birley,** Eric 1906- *Who 92*
**Birley,** James Leatham Tennant 1928- *Who 92*
**Birley,** Michael Pellew 1920- *Who 92*
**Birley,** Oswald 1880-1952 *TwCPaSc*
**Birley,** Susan Joyce *Who 92*
**Birman,** Joan Sylvia 1927- *AmMWSc 92*
**Birman,** Joseph Harold 1924- *AmMWSc 92*
**Birman,** Joseph Leon 1927- *AmMWSc 92*
**Birman,** S.P. d1937 *SovUnBD*
**Birman,** Serafima Germanovna 1890-1976 *SovUnBD*
**Birmele,** Raymond Elsworth 1948- *WhoMW 92*
**Birmelin,** Jerry *WhoAmP 91*
**Birmingham,** Archbishop of 1929- *Who 92*
**Birmingham,** Archdeacon of *Who 92*
**Birmingham,** Auxiliary Bishop of *Who 92*
**Birmingham,** Bishop of 1936- *Who 92*
**Birmingham,** Provost of *Who 92*
**Birmingham,** Brendan Charles 1945- *AmMWSc 92*
**Birmingham,** John J. 1939- *WhoIns 92*
**Birmingham,** Linda Lee 1962- *WhoMW 92*
**Birmingham,** Maisie *WrDr 92*
**Birmingham,** Maisie Poynter 1914- *IntAu&W 91*
**Birmingham,** Marion Krantz 1917- *AmMWSc 92*
**Birmingham,** Mary Irene 1926- *WhoAmP 91*
**Birmingham,** Paul A. 1937- *IntMPA 92*
**Birmingham,** Richard Francis 1949- *WhoAmL 92*
**Birmingham,** Richard Joseph 1953- *WhoAmL 92*
**Birmingham,** Stephen 1931- *WrDr 92*
**Birmingham,** Thomas Edward 1951- *WhoWest 92*
**Birmingham,** Thomas F *WhoAmP 91*
**Birmingham,** Thomas Joseph 1938- *AmMWSc 92*
**Birmingham,** Walter 1913- *WrDr 92*
**Birmingham,** Walter Barr 1913- *IntAu&W 91*
**Birmingham,** William Joseph 1923- *WhoAmL 92, WhoMW 92*
**Birn,** Raymond Francis 1935- *IntAu&W 91, WrDr 92*
**Birnbach,** Martin 1929- *WrDr 92*
**Birnbach,** Martin David 1937- *WhoEnt 92*
**Birnbaum,** David 1940- *AmMWSc 92*
**Birnbaum,** Denise Barbara 1951- *WhoWest 92*
**Birnbaum,** Donald Howard 1946- *WhoAmL 92*
**Birnbaum,** Edward R. 1943- *WhoWest 92*
**Birnbaum,** Edward Robert 1943- *AmMWSc 92*
**Birnbaum,** Ernest Rodman 1933- *AmMWSc 92*
**Birnbaum,** George 1919- *AmMWSc 92*
**Birnbaum,** George I 1931- *AmMWSc 92*
**Birnbaum,** H K 1932- *AmMWSc 92*
**Birnbaum,** Hermann 1905- *AmMWSc 92*
**Birnbaum,** Irwin Morton 1935- *WhoAmL 92*
**Birnbaum,** Joan Welker 1923- *WhoRel 92*
**Birnbaum,** Joel S *AmMWSc 92*
**Birnbaum,** Leon S 1916- *AmMWSc 92*
**Birnbaum,** Linda Silber 1946- *AmMWSc 92*
**Birnbaum,** Lucia Chiavola 1924- *WhoRel 92*
**Birnbaum,** Milton 1920- *AmMWSc 92*
**Birnbaum,** Nathan 1956- *WhoEnt 92*
**Birnbaum,** Robert J. 1927- *IntWW 91*
**Birnbaum,** Robert Jack 1927- *WhoAmL 92, WhoFI 92*
**Birnbaum,** S. Elizabeth 1958- *WhoAmL 92*
**Birnbaum,** Sidney 1928- *AmMWSc 92*
**Birnbaum,** Solomon 1891-1989 *FacFETw*
**Birnbaum,** Stephen d1991 *NewYTBS 91 [port]*
**Birnbaum,** Stevan Allen 1943- *WhoWest 92*
**Birnbaumer,** Lutz 1939- *AmMWSc 92*
**Birnboim,** Hyman Chaim 1936- *AmMWSc 92*
**Birnbrook,** Leroy Allan 1940- *WhoRel 92*
**Birndorf,** Theodore 1932- *WhoAmL 92*
**Birne,** Kenneth Andrew 1956- *WhoAmL 92*
**Birne,** Robert Eric 1959- *WhoAmL 92*
**Birney,** Alice Lotvin 1938- *IntAu&W 91, WrDr 92*
**Birney,** David 1940- *IntMPA 92*
**Birney,** David Bell, IV *WhoFI 92*
**Birney,** David Edwin *WhoEnt 92*
**Birney,** David Martin 1956- *AmMWSc 92*
**Birney,** Dion Scott, Jr 1926- *AmMWSc 92*
**Birney,** Earle *DrAPF 91*
**Birney,** Earle 1904- *BenetAL 91, ConPo 91, IntAu&W 91, IntWW 91, RfGEnL 91, WrDr 92*
**Birney,** Elmer Clea 1940- *AmMWSc 92*
**Birney,** Hoffman 1891-1958 *TwCWW 91*
**Birney,** James Gillespie 1792-1857 *AmPolLe*
**Birney,** Lawrence Preston 1917- *WhoFI 92*
**Birney,** Leroy 1942- *WhoRel 92*
**Birnhak,** Sandra Jean 1945- *WhoEnt 92*
**Birnholz,** Jason Cordell 1942- *AmMWSc 92*
**Birnholz,** Richard Joseph 1945- *WhoRel 92*
**Birnie,** Richard Williams 1944- *AmMWSc 92*
**Birnir,** Bjorn 1953- *AmMWSc 92*
**Birnkrant,** Henry Joseph 1955- *WhoAmL 92*
**Birnkrant,** Jeanne Ann *WhoEnt 92*
**Birnkrant,** Sherwin Maurice 1927- *WhoAmL 92*
**Birns,** Ira Michael 1962- *WhoFI 92*
**Birnstiel,** Charles 1929- *AmMWSc 92*
**Birnstiel,** Max Luciano 1933- *IntWW 91*
**Biro,** B. *SmATA 67 [port]*
**Biro,** B S 1921- *SmATA 67 [port]*
**Biro,** George P 1938- *AmMWSc 92*
**Biro,** Ladislao Jose 1899-1985 *FacFETw*
**Biro,** Val *IntAu&W 91X, SmATA 67 [port]*
**Biro,** Val 1921- *IntAu&W 91, SmATA 13AS [port], WrDr 92*
**Biroc,** Joseph F. 1900- *IntMPA 92*
**Biron,** Christine A 1951- *AmMWSc 92*
**Birosik,** Patti 1956- *WhoEnt 92*
**Birrell,** James Drake 1933- *Who 92*
**Birrell,** James Peter 1928- *WrDr 92*
**Birren,** James E *AmMWSc 92*
**Birren,** Jeffrey Emmett 1951- *WhoAmL 92*
**Birrenkott,** Glen Peter, Jr 1951- *AmMWSc 92*
**Birri,** Fernando 1925- *IntDcF 2-2*
**Birss,** Fraser William 1932- *AmMWSc 92*
**Birss,** Viola Ingrid *AmMWSc 92*
**Birstein,** Ann *DrAPF 91*
**Birstein,** Ann 1927- *IntAu&W 91, WrDr 92*
**Birstein,** Seymour J 1927- *AmMWSc 92*
**Birt,** Arthur Robert 1906- *AmMWSc 92*
**Birt,** David 1936- *ConAu 35NR*
**Birt,** Diane Feickert 1949- *AmMWSc 92*
**Birt,** John *LesBEnT 92*
**Birt,** John 1944- *IntWW 91, Who 92*
**Birt,** Kay B 1924- *WhoAmP 91*
**Birt,** Lindsay Michael 1932- *IntWW 91*
**Birt,** Michael 1932- *Who 92*
**Birt,** Walter Arthur 1915- *WhoAmP 91*
**Birt,** William Raymond 1911- *Who 92*
**Birtalan,** Stefan 1948- *IntWW 91*
**Birtch,** Alan Grant 1932- *AmMWSc 92*
**Birtcher,** Normand Harold 1955- *WhoWest 92*
**Birtel,** Frank T 1932- *AmMWSc 92*
**Birtha,** Becky *DrAPF 91*
**Birtha,** Jessie M. 1920- *WhoBlA 92*
**Birts,** Peter William 1946- *Who 92*
**Birtwell,** Francis J d1901 *BiInAmS*
**Birtwistle,** Archibald Cull 1927- *Who 92*
**Birtwistle,** Harrison 1934- *ConCom 92, IntWW 91, NewAmDM, Who 92*
**Birx,** Deborah L 1956- *AmMWSc 92*
**Biryukova,** Aleksandra Pavlovna 1929- *IntWW 91, SovUnBD*
**Biryuzov,** Sergey Semenovich 1904-1964 *SovUnBD*
**Bis,** Richard F 1935- *AmMWSc 92*
**Bisaillon,** Andre 1943- *AmMWSc 92*
**Bisalputra,** Thana 1932- *AmMWSc 92*
**Bisar,** Muhammad Abdul Rahman 1910?- *IntWW 91*
**Bisbee,** David George 1947- *WhoAmL 92*
**Bisbee,** Eugene Shade *ScFEYrs*
**Bisbee,** Gerald Elftman, Jr. 1942- *WhoFI 92*
**Bisby,** Mark A 1946- *AmMWSc 92*
**Biscardi,** Chester 1948- *WhoEnt 92*
**Biscaye,** Pierre Eginton 1935- *AmMWSc 92*
**Bischof,** Harrington 1935- *WhoFI 92*
**Bischof,** John Edward George 1936- *WhoAmL 92*
**Bischof,** Merriem Lanova *WhoEnt 92*
**Bischof,** Steven Donald 1954- *WhoMW 92*
**Bischoff,** Arthur John 1943- *WhoMW 92*
**Bischoff,** Bernhard 1906- *IntWW 91*
**Bischoff,** David F 1951- *IntAu&W 91, TwCSFW 91, WrDr 92*
**Bischoff,** Elmer 1916-1991 *NewYTBS 91*
**Bischoff,** Eric Richard 1938- *AmMWSc 92*
**Bischoff,** Harry William 1922- *AmMWSc 92*
**Bischoff,** James Louden 1940- *AmMWSc 92*
**Bischoff,** Joyce Arlene 1938- *WhoFI 92*
**Bischoff,** Kenneth Bruce 1936- *AmMWSc 92*
**Bischoff,** Robert Francis 1943- *AmMWSc 92*
**Bischoff,** Robert John 1941- *WhoAmP 91*
**Bischoff,** Winfried Franz Wilhelm 1941- *IntWW 91, Who 92*
**Biscoe,** Alec Julian T. *Who 92*
**Biscoe,** Timothy John 1932- *Who 92*
**Biscotti,** Joseph Charles 1959- *WhoEnt 92*
**Bise,** Christopher John 1950- *AmMWSc 92*
**Bisel,** Harry Ferree 1918- *AmMWSc 92*
**Bisenius,** Stephen William 1947- *WhoAmP 91*
**Bisers,** Ilmars 1930- *SovUnBD*
**Bisgaard,** Edward Lawrence, Jr. 1946- *WhoWest 92*
**Bisgaard,** Soren 1951- *AmMWSc 92*
**Bisgard,** Gerald Edwin 1937- *AmMWSc 92, WhoMW 92*
**Bish,** Anthony Steven 1960- *WhoEnt 92*
**Bish,** David Lee 1952- *AmMWSc 92*
**Bish,** Milan D 1929- *WhoAmP 91*
**Bish,** Milan David 1929- *WhoMW 92*
**Bish,** William Howard 1957- *WhoWest 92*
**Bishar,** John Joseph, Jr. 1950- *WhoAmL 92*
**Bishara,** Abdulla Yacoub 1936- *IntWW 91*
**Bishara,** Michael Nageeb 1933- *AmMWSc 92*
**Bishara,** Rafik Hanna 1941- *AmMWSc 92*
**Bishara,** Samir Edward 1935- *AmMWSc 92*
**Bisher,** Ilmar Olgertovich 1930- *IntWW 91, SovUnBD*
**Bisher,** James Furman 1918- *IntAu&W 91*
**Bishir,** John William 1933- *AmMWSc 92*
**Bishoff,** W. Ray, Jr. 1944- *WhoFI 92*
**Bishop** *Who 92*
**Bishop,** A A 1913- *AmMWSc 92*
**Bishop,** Al 1925- *WhoAmP 91*
**Bishop,** Alan Henry 1929- *Who 92*
**Bishop,** Albert B 1929- *AmMWSc 92*
**Bishop,** Albert Bentley 1929- *WhoMW 92*
**Bishop,** Alfred A. 1923- *WhoBlA 92*
**Bishop,** Alfred Chilton, Jr. 1942- *WhoAmL 92*
**Bishop,** Allen David, Jr 1938- *AmMWSc 92*
**Bishop,** Andre 1948- *ConTFT 9*
**Bishop,** Angela Marie 1964- *WhoEnt 92*
**Bishop,** Arthur Clive 1930- *Who 92*
**Bishop,** Asa Orin, Jr 1938- *AmMWSc 92*
**Bishop,** Barney Tipton, III 1951- *WhoFI 92*
**Bishop,** Betty Josephine 1947- *WhoFI 92, WhoWest 92*
**Bishop,** Beverly Petterson 1922- *AmMWSc 92*
**Bishop,** Bruce William 1948- *WhoRel 92*
**Bishop,** C. Diane 1943- *WhoWest 92*
**Bishop,** Cecil *WhoRel 92*
**Bishop,** Cecil 1930- *WhoBlA 92*
**Bishop,** Charles 1920- *AmMWSc 92*
**Bishop,** Charles Anthony 1934- *AmMWSc 92*
**Bishop,** Charles Dean 1937- *WhoAmP 91*
**Bishop,** Charles E. 1930- *WhoIns 92*
**Bishop,** Charles Franklin 1918- *AmMWSc 92*
**Bishop,** Charles Johnson 1920- *AmMWSc 92, IntWW 91*
**Bishop,** Charles Joseph 1941- *AmMWSc 92, WhoMW 92*
**Bishop,** Christine Fath 1958- *WhoAmP 91*
**Bishop,** Claire Huchet *ConAu 36NR, WrDr 92*
**Bishop,** Clarence 1959- *WhoBlA 92*
**Bishop,** Claude Titus 1925- *AmMWSc 92*
**Bishop,** Clay Massey, Jr. 1953- *WhoAmL 92*
**Bishop,** Clifford Leofric Purdy 1908- *Who 92*
**Bishop,** Corinth, II 1963- *WhoAmL 92*

**Bishop,** David 1954- *WhoEnt 92*
**Bishop,** David Hugh Langler 1937- *AmMWSc 92, Who 92*
**Bishop,** David Michael 1936- *AmMWSc 92*
**Bishop,** David Nolan 1940- *WhoFI 92*
**Bishop,** David Rudolph 1924- *WhoBlA 92*
**Bishop,** David Stewart 1933- *WhoRel 92, WhoWest 92*
**Bishop,** David T 1929- *WhoAmP 91*
**Bishop,** David Wakefield 1912- *AmMWSc 92*
**Bishop,** Diane 1943- *WhoAmP 91*
**Bishop,** Donald Curtis 1939- *WhoFI 92*
**Bishop,** Donald Harold 1920- *WhoRel 92*
**Bishop,** Dori Suzanne 1957- *WhoFI 92*
**Bishop,** Edna Noe 1912- *WhoAmP 91*
**Bishop,** Edward 1902- *TwCPaSc*
**Bishop,** Edwin Burnett 1921- *WhoWest 92*
**Bishop,** Edwin Lyman 1930- *WhoRel 92*
**Bishop,** Edwin Vandewater 1935- *AmMWSc 92, WhoMW 92*
**Bishop,** Eliza Honey 1920- *WhoEnt 92*
**Bishop,** Elizabeth 1911-1979 *BenetAL 91, FacFETw, LiExTwC, ModAWWr, PoeCrit 3 [port]*
**Bishop,** Elizabeth Shreve 1951- *WhoMW 92*
**Bishop,** Elizabeth Susan Lisa 1954- *WhoEnt 92*
**Bishop,** Ernest Merrill 1927- *WhoWest 92*
**Bishop,** Errett A 1928- *AmMWSc 92*
**Bishop,** Eugene H 1933- *AmMWSc 92*
**Bishop,** Finley Charles 1949- *AmMWSc 92*
**Bishop,** Frederick 1915- *Who 92*
**Bishop,** Gale Arden 1942- *AmMWSc 92*
**Bishop,** Gavin John 1946- *IntAu&W 91*
**Bishop,** Gene Herbert 1930- *WhoFI 92*
**Bishop,** George 1913- *Who 92*
**Bishop,** George Robert 1927- *Who 92*
**Bishop,** George Sidney 1913- *IntWW 91*
**Bishop,** George Victor 1924- *WhoEnt 92*
**Bishop,** Geraldine Evelyn 1941- *WhoAmL 92*
**Bishop,** Gordon Bruce 1938- *WhoFI 92*
**Bishop,** Grant William 1961- *WhoWest 92*
**Bishop,** Guy William 1926- *AmMWSc 92*
**Bishop,** H G *ScFEYrs A*
**Bishop,** Harold 1909- *AmMWSc 92*
**Bishop,** Hayward S. 1945- *WhoEnt 92*
**Bishop,** Henry 1868-1939 *TwCPaSc*
**Bishop,** Ian Benjamin 1927- *IntAu&W 91*
**Bishop,** Irving Prescott 1849-1912 *BiInAmS*
**Bishop,** Ivan D. 1940- *WhoIns 92*
**Bishop,** J Hampton *ScFEYrs*
**Bishop,** Jack Belmont 1943- *AmMWSc 92*
**Bishop,** Jack Garland 1919- *AmMWSc 92*
**Bishop,** Jack King 1935- *WhoFI 92*
**Bishop,** Jack Lawson, Jr. 1939- *WhoMW 92*
**Bishop,** Jack Lynn 1929- *AmMWSc 92*
**Bishop,** James, Jr. 1930- *WhoBlA 92*
**Bishop,** James Allen 1950- *WhoWest 92*
**Bishop,** James Drew 1929- *IntAu&W 91, IntWW 91, Who 92, WrDr 92*
**Bishop,** James F. 1940- *WhoMW 92*
**Bishop,** James Francis 1937- *WhoFI 92*
**Bishop,** James K *WhoAmP 91*
**Bishop,** James Keough 1938- *IntWW 91*
**Bishop,** James Martin 1936- *AmMWSc 92*
**Bishop,** Jay Lyman 1932- *AmMWSc 92, WhoWest 92*
**Bishop,** Jim *DrAPF 91*
**Bishop,** John Edward 1935- *Who 92*
**Bishop,** John J. 1950- *WhoFI 92*
**Bishop,** John J, Jr 1927- *WhoAmP 91*
**Bishop,** John Joseph 1948- *WhoAmP 91*
**Bishop,** John Melville 1946- *WhoEnt 92*
**Bishop,** John Michael 1936- *AmMWSc 92, Who 92, WhoNob 90, WhoWest 92*
**Bishop,** John Peal 1892-1944 *LiExTwC*
**Bishop,** John Peale 1892-1944 *BenetAL 91*
**Bishop,** John Russell 1920- *AmMWSc 92*
**Bishop,** John Watson 1938- *AmMWSc 92*
**Bishop,** John William 1916- *AmMWSc 92*
**Bishop,** Jonathan S 1925- *AmMWSc 92*
**Bishop,** Joseph Michael 1943- *AmMWSc 92*
**Bishop,** Joyce 1896- *Who 92*
**Bishop,** Kathryn Diane 1955- *WhoEnt 92*
**Bishop,** Kathryn Elizabeth 1945- *WhoEnt 92*
**Bishop,** Keith C, III 1947- *AmMWSc 92*
**Bishop,** Lawrence Ray 1934- *WhoAmL 92*
**Bishop,** Leo Kenneth 1911- *WhoRel 92*
**Bishop,** Louise 1933- *WhoAmP 91*
**Bishop,** Margaret S 1906- *AmMWSc 92*
**Bishop,** Marilyn Frances 1950- *AmMWSc 92*
**Bishop,** Martin *TwCWW 91*
**Bishop,** Marvin 1945- *AmMWSc 92*
**Bishop,** Mary Kathryn 1935- *WhoAmP 91*
**Bishop,** Mary Lucille 1918- *WhoEnt 92*
**Bishop,** Michael *Who 92*
**Bishop,** Michael 1945- *TwCSFW 91, WrDr 92*
**Bishop,** Michael David 1942- *Who 92*
**Bishop,** Michael Joseph 1951- *WhoEnt 92*
**Bishop,** Michael Lawson 1945- *IntAu&W 91*
**Bishop,** Michael William 1941- *Who 92*
**Bishop,** Morris 1893-1973 *BenetAL 91*
**Bishop,** Muriel Boyd 1928- *AmMWSc 92*
**Bishop,** Nancy Horschel 1936- *AmMWSc 92*
**Bishop,** Norman Ivan 1928- *AmMWSc 92*
**Bishop,** Oliver Richard 1928- *WhoMW 92*
**Bishop,** Paul Edward 1940- *AmMWSc 92*
**Bishop,** Paul Leslie 1945- *AmMWSc 92*
**Bishop,** Peter Orlebar 1917- *IntWW 91, Who 92*
**Bishop,** Ralph Clayton, Jr. 1959- *WhoAmL 92*
**Bishop,** Rand *DrAPF 91*
**Bishop,** Randall Warren 1958- *WhoFI 92*
**Bishop,** Richard 1950- *WhoBlA 92*
**Bishop,** Richard Arthur 1918- *WhoAmL 92*
**Bishop,** Richard Lawrence 1931- *AmMWSc 92*
**Bishop,** Richard Ray 1938- *AmMWSc 92*
**Bishop,** Richard Stearns 1945- *AmMWSc 92*
**Bishop,** Robert d1991 *NewYTBS 91 [port]*
**Bishop,** Robert 1938- *ConAu 35NR, IntAu&W 91, WrDr 92*
**Bishop,** Robert 1938-1991 *ConAu 135*
**Bishop,** Robert Charles 1929- *WhoWest 92*
**Bishop,** Robert H *AmMWSc 92*
**Bishop,** Robert Vance 1949- *WhoFI 92*
**Bishop,** Robert Welch 1955- *WhoAmL 92*
**Bishop,** Robert Whitsitt 1949- *WhoAmL 92*
**Bishop,** Robert William 1951- *WhoAmP 91*
**Bishop,** Robert Willis 1943- *WhoAmL 92*
**Bishop,** Ronald Clare 1921- *WhoMW 92*
**Bishop,** Ronald E. *WhoFI 92*
**Bishop,** Ronald Eric 1903-1989 *FacFETw*
**Bishop,** Ronald T. 1934- *WhoEnt 92*
**Bishop,** Roy Lovitt 1939- *AmMWSc 92*
**Bishop,** Ruth Ann 1942- *WhoEnt 92, WhoMW 92*
**Bishop,** Samuel P. *TwCWW 91, WrDr 92*
**Bishop,** Sanford Dixon, Jr 1947- *WhoAmP 91*
**Bishop,** Sanford Parsons 1936- *AmMWSc 92*
**Bishop,** Sereno Edwards 1827-1909 *BiInAmS*
**Bishop,** Sid Glenwood 1923- *WhoFI 92*
**Bishop,** Sidney Willard 1926- *WhoIns 92*
**Bishop,** Stanley Victor 1916- *Who 92*
**Bishop,** Stephen *Who 92*
**Bishop,** Stephen 1952- *WhoEnt 92*
**Bishop,** Stephen Gray 1939- *AmMWSc 92*
**Bishop,** Stephen Hurst 1936- *AmMWSc 92*
**Bishop,** Terence Alan Martyn 1907- *Who 92*
**Bishop,** Thomas A 1955- *WhoAmP 91*
**Bishop,** Thomas Brigham 1835-1905 *BenetAL 91*
**Bishop,** Thomas Burke, Jr. 1951- *WhoEnt 92*
**Bishop,** Thomas Parker 1936- *AmMWSc 92*
**Bishop,** Tilman M 1933- *WhoAmP 91*
**Bishop,** Tilman Malcolm 1933- *WhoWest 92*
**Bishop,** Vannoy Gray 1946- *WhoAmL 92*
**Bishop,** Verissa Rene 1954- *WhoBlA 92*
**Bishop,** Vernon S *AmMWSc 92*
**Bishop,** W H 1847-1928 *ScFEYrs*
**Bishop,** Walton B 1917- *AmMWSc 92*
**Bishop,** Warner Bader 1918- *WhoFI 92*
**Bishop,** Wendy *DrAPF 91*
**Bishop,** William Alfred d1991 *Who 92N*
**Bishop,** William Avery 1894-1956 *FacFETw*
**Bishop,** William F. 1936- *WhoRel 92*
**Bishop,** William P 1940- *AmMWSc 92*
**Bishop,** William T. 1940- *WhoFI 92*
**Bishop,** William Wade 1939- *WhoFI 92*
**Bishop,** Yvonne M M 1925- *AmMWSc 92*
**Bishop-Gaines,** Lynn McKenzie 1947- *WhoEnt 92*
**Bishop-Kovacevich,** Stephen 1940- *IntWW 91, Who 92*
**Bisignani,** Giovanni 1946- *IntWW 91*
**Bisignani,** J D 1947- *ConAu 35NR*
**Bisignano,** Tony 1952- *WhoAmP 91*
**Bisio,** Atillio L 1930- *AmMWSc 92*
**Biskeborn,** Merle Chester 1907- *AmMWSc 92*
**Bisland,** Elizabeth 1861-1929 *ScFEYrs*
**Bismanis,** Jekabs Edwards 1911- *AmMWSc 92*
**Bismarck,** Klaus von 1912- *IntWW 91*
**Bisno,** Alan Lester 1936- *AmMWSc 92*
**Bispham,** David 1857-1921 *NewAmDM*
**Bispham,** Frank L. 1924- *WhoBlA 92*
**Bisque,** Ramon Edward 1931- *AmMWSc 92*
**Biss,** Ellen Graf *DrAPF 91*
**Bissat,** Bahaeddine 1923- *IntWW 91*
**Bissell,** A Keith 1941- *WhoAmP 91*
**Bissell,** Brent John 1950- *WhoMW 92*
**Bissell,** Charles Lynn 1939- *AmMWSc 92*
**Bissell,** Claude T. 1916- *IntWW 91*
**Bissell,** Claude Thomas 1916- *Who 92*
**Bissell,** Dwight Montgomery 1940- *AmMWSc 92*
**Bissell,** Eugene Richard 1928- *AmMWSc 92*
**Bissell,** Frances Mary 1946- *Who 92*
**Bissell,** Glenn Daniel 1935- *AmMWSc 92*
**Bissell,** Grosvenor Willse 1915- *AmMWSc 92*
**Bissell,** Harold Joseph 1913- *AmMWSc 92*
**Bissell,** Howard William 1952- *WhoEnt 92*
**Bissell,** James Dougal, III 1951- *WhoEnt 92*
**Bissell,** John Howard 1935- *WhoFI 92*
**Bissell,** John W. 1940- *WhoAmL 92*
**Bissell,** LeClair 1928- *ConAu 133*
**Bissell,** Michael G 1947- *AmMWSc 92*
**Bissell,** Michael Gilbert 1947- *WhoWest 92*
**Bissell,** Mina Jahan 1940- *AmMWSc 92*
**Bissell,** Richard 1913-1977 *BenetAL 91*
**Bissell,** Richard Etter 1946- *WhoAmP 91*
**Bissell,** William Grosvenor 1870-1919 *BiInAmS*
**Bissert,** Ellen Marie *DrAPF 91*
**Bisset,** Davies W, Jr. 1930- *WhoIns 92*
**Bisset,** Donald 1910- *IntAu&W 91, WrDr 92*
**Bisset,** Jacqueline 1944- *IntMPA 92, IntWW 91*
**Bisset,** Jacqueline 1946- *WhoEnt 92*
**Bisset,** Suzanne 1949- *WhoRel 92*
**Bissett,** Barbara Anne 1950- *WhoMW 92*
**Bissett,** Bill 1939- *ConPo 91, IntAu&W 91, WrDr 92*
**Bissett,** J R 1910- *AmMWSc 92*
**Bissett,** John J 1836?-1915 *BiInAmS*
**Bissett,** Marjorie Louise 1925- *AmMWSc 92*
**Bissett,** Phil *WhoAmP 91*
**Bissette,** Winston Louis, Jr 1943- *WhoAmP 91*
**Bissey,** Luther Trauger 1912- *AmMWSc 92*
**Bisshopp,** Frederic Edward 1934- *AmMWSc 92*
**Bissil,** George 1896-1973 *TwCPaSc*
**Bissing,** Donald Eugene 1934- *AmMWSc 92*
**Bissing,** Donald Ray 1943- *AmMWSc 92*
**Bissinger,** Barnard Hinkle 1918- *AmMWSc 92*
**Bissinger,** Frederick Lewis 1911- *IntWW 91*
**Bissinger,** H. G. 1954- *WrDr 92*
**Bissman,** Peter 1939- *WhoEnt 92*
**Bisson,** Andre 1929- *WhoFI 92*
**Bisson,** Edmond E 1916- *AmMWSc 92*
**Bisson,** Gordon 1918- *Who 92*
**Bisson,** Linda Gale 1946- *WhoFI 92*
**Bisson,** Mary A 1948- *AmMWSc 92*
**Bisson,** Peter Andre 1945- *AmMWSc 92*
**Bisson,** Todd Dunham 1966- *WhoEnt 92*
**Bisson,** Wheelock Alexander 1898-1985 *WhoBlA 92N*
**Bissonette,** John Alfred 1941- *AmMWSc 92*
**Bissonnette,** Gary Kent 1947- *AmMWSc 92*
**Bissonnette,** Howard Louis 1927- *AmMWSc 92*
**Bissonnette,** John Maurice 1939- *AmMWSc 92*
**Bissonnette,** Marcel Ivan 1957- *WhoEnt 92*
**Bissoondath,** Neil 1955- *LiExTwC*
**Bissoondoyal,** Basdeo 1906- *IntAu&W 91, WrDr 92*
**Bissot,** Thomas Charles 1930- *AmMWSc 92*
**Bista,** Kirti Nidhi 1927- *IntWW 91*
**Bistany,** Diane V. 1939- *WhoIns 92*
**Bisti,** Dmitriy Spiridonovich 1925- *SovUnBD*
**Bistline,** F. Walter, Jr. 1950- *WhoAmL 92*
**Bistline,** Stephen *WhoAmP 91*
**Bistline,** Stephen 1921- *WhoAmL 92, WhoWest 92*
**Bistrian,** Bruce Ryan 1939- *AmMWSc 92*
**Biswal,** Nilambar 1934- *AmMWSc 92*
**Biswas,** Asit Kumar 1939- *AmMWSc 92*
**Biswas,** Chitra 1936- *AmMWSc 92*
**Biswas,** Dipak R 1949- *AmMWSc 92*
**Biswas,** Nripendra Nath 1930- *AmMWSc 92*
**Biswas,** Prosanto K 1934- *AmMWSc 92, WhoBlA 92*
**Biswas,** Robin Michael 1942- *AmMWSc 92*
**Biswas,** Shib D 1940- *AmMWSc 92*
**Bisztyga,** Jan 1933- *IntWW 91, Who 92*
**Bita,** Lili *ConAu 36NR, DrAPF 91*
**Bita,** Lili 1935- *WhoEnt 92*
**Bitat,** Rabah 1925- *IntWW 91*
**Bitcover,** Ezra Harold 1920- *AmMWSc 92*
**Biteler,** Cornelius Royal 1931- *WhoMW 92*
**Bitensky,** Mark Wolfe 1934- *AmMWSc 92*
**Bitensky,** Susan Helen 1948- *WhoAmL 92*
**Bitetti,** Ernesto G. 1943- *WhoEnt 92*
**Bitgood,** J James 1940- *AmMWSc 92*
**Bitha,** Panayota *AmMWSc 92*
**Bither,** Stephen Donald 1948- *WhoEnt 92*
**Bitler,** William Reynolds 1927- *AmMWSc 92*
**Bitman,** Joel 1926- *AmMWSc 92*
**Bitner,** Denver William 1947- *WhoRel 92*
**Bitner,** Harry 1916- *WhoAmL 92*
**Bitner,** John William 1948- *WhoFI 92*
**Bito,** Laszlo Z 1934- *AmMWSc 92*
**Bitondo,** Domenic 1925- *AmMWSc 92*
**Bitonte,** David Alan 1954- *WhoMW 92*
**Bitov,** Andrei Georgevich 1937- *IntWW 91*
**Bitov,** Andrey Georgievich 1937- *SovUnBD*
**Bitsch,** Hans-Ullrich 1946- *IntWW 91*
**Bitsianes,** Gust 1919- *AmMWSc 92*
**Bittar,** Evelyn Edward 1928- *AmMWSc 92*
**Bittenbender,** Brad James 1948- *WhoWest 92*
**Bitter Bierce** *BenetAL 91*
**Bitter,** Gary G 1940- *AmMWSc 92*
**Bitterman,** Gregory Val 1960- *WhoAmL 92*
**Bitterman,** Mary G F 1944- *WhoAmP 91*
**Bitterman,** Melvin Lee 1938- *WhoWest 92*
**Bitterman,** Morton Edward 1921- *AmMWSc 92*
**Bitters,** Conrad Lee 1946- *WhoWest 92*
**Bitters,** Willard Paul 1915- *AmMWSc 92*
**Bitterwolf,** Thomas Edwin 1947- *WhoWest 92*
**Bitting,** Robin David 1957- *WhoMW 92*
**Bittinger,** David Lowell 1952- *WhoRel 92*
**Bittinger,** Marvin Lowell 1941- *AmMWSc 92*
**Bittings,** Rosemary Brooks 1951- *WhoBlA 92*
**Bittke,** Brian Edmund 1937- *WhoMW 92*
**Bittker,** Boris Irving 1916- *WhoAmL 92*
**Bittker,** David *WhoRel 92*
**Bittker,** David Arthur 1927- *AmMWSc 92*
**Bittle,** D. Denise 1957- *WhoFI 92*
**Bittle,** Edgar H. 1942- *WhoAmL 92*
**Bittle,** Harley Earnest 1937- *WhoAmP 91*
**Bittle,** James Long 1927- *AmMWSc 92*
**Bittle,** Russell Harry 1938- *WhoAmP 91*
**Bittman,** James Michael 1936- *WhoMW 92*
**Bittman,** Robert 1942- *AmMWSc 92*
**Bittman,** William Omar 1931- *WhoAmL 92*
**Bittner,** Burt James 1921- *AmMWSc 92*
**Bittner,** Harlan Fletcher 1951- *AmMWSc 92*
**Bittner,** James Anthony 1911- *WhoEnt 92*
**Bittner,** John William 1926- *AmMWSc 92*
**Bittner,** Mary Ellen 1947- *WhoAmL 92*
**Bitton,** Gabriel 1940- *AmMWSc 92*
**Bitton,** Isaac 1926- *WhoMW 92*
**Bittrich,** Gustav 1937- *WhoEnt 92*
**Bitts,** Todd Michael 1946- *WhoEnt 92*
**Bitzegaio,** Harold James 1921- *WhoAmL 92*
**Bitzer,** Donald L 1934- *AmMWSc 92*
**Bitzer,** Jeffrey T. 1952- *WhoAmL 92*
**Bitzer,** John Frederick, Jr. 1936- *WhoFI 92*
**Bitzer,** Morris Jay 1936- *AmMWSc 92*
**Bitzer,** Richard Allen 1939- *AmMWSc 92*
**Bitzer,** Warren W. *WhoRel 92*
**Bivens,** Richard Lowell 1939- *AmMWSc 92*
**Bivens,** Shelia Reneea 1954- *WhoBlA 92*
**Bivens,** Stephen Dale 1946- *WhoAmP 91*
**Biver,** Carl John, Jr 1932- *AmMWSc 92*
**Bivins,** Brack Allen 1943- *AmMWSc 92*
**Bivins,** C. Benny 1956- *WhoEnt 92*
**Bivins,** Edward Byron 1929- *WhoBlA 92*
**Bivins,** Ollie B., Jr. 1923- *WhoBlA 92*
**Bivins,** Susan Steinbach 1941- *WhoWest 92*
**Bivins,** Teel 1947- *WhoAmP 91*
**Bivona,** Thomas Charles 1949- *WhoAmL 92*
**Biwott,** Amos 1947- *BlkOlyM*
**Bixby,** Allan Barton 1936- *WhoFI 92*
**Bixby,** Bill *LesBEnT 92*
**Bixby,** Bill 1934- *ConTFT 9, IntMPA 92*
**Bixby,** Brian Dale 1952- *WhoAmL 92*
**Bixby,** Frank Lyman 1928- *WhoAmL 92*
**Bixby,** Joseph Reynolds 1925- *WhoIns 92*
**Bixby,** R. Burdell d1991 *NewYTBS 91*
**Bixby,** Robert *DrAPF 91*
**Bixby,** Robert Hardwick 1952- *WhoAmL 92*
**Bixby,** Tom 1947- *WhoEnt 92*
**Bixby,** W Herbert 1906- *AmMWSc 92*
**Bixby,** Walter E. 1932- *WhoIns 92*
**Bixel,** Janet Kennedy 1936- *WhoMW 92*
**Bixler,** David 1929- *AmMWSc 92, WhoMW 92*
**Bixler,** Dean A 1919- *AmMWSc 92*
**Bixler,** John Wilson 1937- *AmMWSc 92*
**Bixler,** Joseph H. 1945- *WhoIns 92*
**Bixler,** Martha Harrison 1927- *WhoEnt 92*
**Bixler,** Otto C 1916- *AmMWSc 92*

**Bixler**, Roy Russell 1927- *WhoEnt 92*
**Bixler**, William Elwell 1947- *WhoFI 92*
**Bixler-Marquez**, Dennis J. 1945- *WhoHisp 92*
**Biya**, Paul 1933- *IntWW 91*
**Bizar**, Irving 1932- *WhoAmL 92*
**Bizet**, Georges 1838-1875 *NewAmDM*
**Bizios**, Rena 1943- *AmMWSc 92*
**Bizub**, Johanna Catherine 1957- *WhoAmL 92*
**Bizzaro**, Patrick *DrAPF 91*
**Bizzell**, Kinchen Carey 1954- *WhoAmL 92*
**Bizzi**, Emilio 1933- *AmMWSc 92*
**Bizzoco**, Richard Lawrence Weiss 1940- *AmMWSc 92*
**Bjarnason**, Gudmundur 1944- *IntWW 91*
**Bjarnason**, Matthias 1921- *IntWW 91*
**Bjarnason**, Sigurdur 1915- *Who 92*
**Bjarngard**, Bengt E 1934- *AmMWSc 92*
**Bjartveit**, Eleonore 1924- *IntWW 91*
**Bjelke-Petersen**, Johannes 1911- *IntWW 91, Who 92*
**Bjelkhagen**, Teresa Grace 1951- *IntAu&W 91*
**Bjella**, Brian Raymond 1952- *WhoMW 92*
**Bjelland**, Harley LeRoy 1926- *WhoWest 92*
**Bjelland**, Timothy Dean 1959- *WhoMW 92*
**Bjercke**, Alf Richard 1921- *WhoFI 92*
**Bjerkaas**, Allan Wayne 1944- *AmMWSc 92*
**Bjerknes**, Michael Leif 1956- *WhoEnt 92*
**Bjerregaard**, Richard S 1943- *AmMWSc 92*
**Bjerring**, Nicolas 1831- *RelLAm 91*
**Bjerrum**, Jannik 1909- *IntWW 91*
**Bjerve**, Petter Jakob 1913- *IntWW 91*
**Bjoerk**, Christina 1938- *ConAu 135, SmATA 67*
**Bjontegard**, Arthur Martin, Jr. 1938- *WhoFI 92*
**Bjorhovde**, Reidar 1941- *AmMWSc 92*
**Bjork**, Anita 1923- *IntWW 91*
**Bjork**, Carl Kenneth, Sr 1926- *AmMWSc 92*
**Bjork**, Christina *ConAu 135*
**Bjork**, Janeen 1956- *WhoEnt 92*
**Bjork**, John Gary 1940- *WhoFI 92*
**Bjork**, Philip R 1940- *AmMWSc 92*
**Bjork**, Robert David, Jr. 1946- *WhoAmL 92*
**Bjorken**, James D 1934- *AmMWSc 92*
**Bjorkholm**, John Ernst 1939- *AmMWSc 92*
**Bjorkholm**, Paul J 1942- *AmMWSc 92*
**Bjorkland**, John A 1923- *AmMWSc 92*
**Bjorklund**, Gary Carl 1946- *AmMWSc 92*
**Bjorklund**, Ilkka-Christian 1947- *IntWW 91*
**Bjorklund**, Janet Vinsen 1947- *WhoWest 92*
**Bjorklund**, Katharine Browne 1952- *WhoWest 92*
**Bjorklund**, Leland Lee Robert 1940- *WhoMW 92*
**Bjorklund**, Mary Jean 1941- *WhoAmL 92*
**Bjorklund**, Richard Carl 1930- *WhoMW 92*
**Bjorklund**, Richard Guy 1928- *AmMWSc 92*
**Bjorkman**, Edwin August 1866-1951 *DcNCBi 1*
**Bjorkman**, Olle Erik 1933- *AmMWSc 92, IntWW 91, WhoWest 92*
**Bjorkman**, Pamela J 1956- *AmMWSc 92*
**Bjorkquist**, David Carl 1932- *WhoMW 92*
**Bjorksten**, Johan Augustus 1907- *AmMWSc 92*
**Bjorkstrand**, Hilding Gustav Mattias 1941- *IntWW 91*
**Bjorling**, Joel Victor 1952- *WhoRel 92*
**Bjorling**, Jussi 1911-1960 *FacFETw, NewAmDM*
**Bjorn**, Acton 1910- *DcTwDes*
**Bjorn**, H. Lars Olof 1936- *IntWW 91*
**Bjornbak**, Mark Philip 1958- *WhoFI 92*
**Bjorncrantz**, Carl Eduard 1944- *WhoFI 92*
**Bjorndahl**, Jay Mark 1955- *AmMWSc 92*
**Bjorndal**, Arne Magne 1916- *AmMWSc 92*
**Bjornerud**, Egil Kristoffer 1925- *AmMWSc 92*
**Bjornholm**, Sven 1927- *IntWW 91*
**Bjornson**, August Sven 1922- *AmMWSc 92*
**Bjornson**, Bjornstjerne Martinius 1832-1910 *WhoNob 90*
**Bjornson**, Carroll Norman 1929- *WhoFI 92*
**Bjornson**, Maria *WhoEnt 92*
**Bjornstad**, James 1940- *WhoRel 92*
**Bjornvig**, Thorkild Strange 1918- *IntWW 91*
**Bjotvedt**, George 1929- *AmMWSc 92*
**Bjugstad**, Ardell Jerome 1933- *AmMWSc 92*
**Bjurstrom**, Per Gunnar 1928- *IntWW 91*
**Blaauw**, Russell Wayne 1944- *WhoMW 92*
**Blaber**, Leo B. 1930- *WhoFI 92*
**Blabey**, Eugene Hulbert, II 1939- *WhoEnt 92*
**Blache**, Alice *IntDcF 2-2*
**Blache**, Alice Guy 1875-1968 *HanAmWH, ReelWom [port]*
**Blacher**, Alan J. 1947- *WhoEnt 92*
**Blacher**, Boris 1903-1975 *NewAmDM*
**Blacher**, Joan Helen 1928- *WhoWest 92*
**Blachere**, Jean R 1937- *AmMWSc 92*
**Blachford**, Cameron W 1931- *AmMWSc 92*
**Blachly**, Jack Lee 1942- *WhoAmL 92, WhoFI 92*
**Blachman**, Arthur Gilbert 1926- *AmMWSc 92*
**Blachman**, Michael Joel 1944- *WhoAmL 92, WhoAmP 91*
**Blachman**, Nelson Merle 1923- *AmMWSc 92*
**Blachut**, T J 1915- *AmMWSc 92*
**Black Agnes** 1300?-1369? *EncAmaz 91*
**Black Crowes**, The *ConMus 7 [port]*
**Black Elk** 1863-1950 *BenetAL 91, RelLAm 91*
**Black Hawk** 1767-1838 *BenetAL 91, RComAH*
**Black Virgin**, The *EncAmaz 91*
**Black**, Alastair Kenneth Lamond 1929- *Who 92*
**Black**, Alex 1906- *AmMWSc 92*
**Black**, Alexander 1859-1940 *BenetAL 91*
**Black**, Alexander 1914- *WhoAmL 92, WhoFI 92*
**Black**, Alexander Chisholm 1954- *WhoAmL 92*
**Black**, Alexander F. 1918- *IntMPA 92*
**Black**, Alyssa Jo 1963- *WhoEnt 92*
**Black**, Anthony Edward Norman 1938- *Who 92*
**Black**, Archibald Niel 1912- *Who 92*
**Black**, Arthur Herman 1919- *AmMWSc 92*
**Black**, Arthur Leo 1922- *AmMWSc 92*
**Black**, Asa C, Jr 1943- *AmMWSc 92*
**Black**, Barbara Aronstein 1933- *WhoAmL 92*
**Black**, Barbara Robinson 1936- *WhoBlA 92*
**Black**, Barrington 1932- *Who 92*
**Black**, Barry Maitland 1945- *WhoEnt 92*
**Black**, Ben E 1940- *WhoAmP 91*
**Black**, Bert 1956- *WhoAmP 91*
**Black**, Betty Lynne 1946- *AmMWSc 92*
**Black**, Billy C, II 1937- *AmMWSc 92*
**Black**, Billy Charleston 1937- *WhoBlA 92*
**Black**, Blane Alan 1956- *WhoAmL 92*
**Black**, Bobby C. 1933- *WhoRel 92*
**Black**, Bonnie-Leigh Anne 1952- *WhoEnt 92*
**Black**, Boyd Carson 1926- *WhoFI 92*
**Black**, Calvin Douglas 1933- *WhoMW 92*
**Black**, Campbell *IntAu&W 91X*
**Black**, Candace *DrAPF 91*
**Black**, Carl Clifton, II 1955- *WhoRel 92*
**Black**, Carl Dean 1929- *WhoMW 92*
**Black**, Charles Allen 1916- *AmMWSc 92*
**Black**, Charles E. 1943- *WhoBlA 92*
**Black**, Charles Lund, Jr. 1915- *WrDr 92*
**Black**, Charles Robert 1935- *WhoFI 92*
**Black**, Charles W M d1902 *BiInAmS*
**Black**, Charlie J. 1934- *WhoBlA 92*
**Black**, Christina Ellen 1959- *WhoFI 92*
**Black**, Clanton Candler, Jr 1931- *AmMWSc 92*
**Black**, Clementina 1854-1922 *BiDBrF 2*
**Black**, Clint *WhoEnt 92*
**Black**, Clinton V. 1918- *WrDr 92*
**Black**, Cobey 1922- *WhoWest 92*
**Black**, Colin Hyndmarsh 1930- *Who 92*
**Black**, Conrad M. 1944- *IntWW 91*
**Black**, Conrad Moffat 1944- *Who 92, WhoFI 92*
**Black**, Craig C 1932- *AmMWSc 92*
**Black**, Craig Call 1932- *WhoWest 92*
**Black**, Craig Patrick 1946- *AmMWSc 92*
**Black**, Curtis Doersam 1951- *AmMWSc 92*
**Black**, Cyril 1902- *Who 92*
**Black**, Daniel L., Jr. 1945- *WhoBlA 92*
**Black**, David *DrAPF 91, Who 92*
**Black**, David 1941- *ConPo 91, IntAu&W 91, WrDr 92*
**Black**, David 1945- *WhoEnt 92, WhoWest 92*
**Black**, David Alan 1952- *WhoRel 92*
**Black**, David Charles 1943- *AmMWSc 92*
**Black**, David Ian 1946- *WhoEnt 92*
**Black**, David Luther 1934- *WhoFI 92*
**Black**, David Scott 1961- *WhoFI 92*
**Black**, David Wayne 1962- *WhoAmL 92*
**Black**, Davidson 1884-1934 *FacFETw*
**Black**, Dean 1942- *AmMWSc 92*
**Black**, Dennis H 1939- *WhoAmP 91*
**Black**, DeWitt Carlisle, Jr. 1930- *WhoAmL 92*
**Black**, Don Gene 1945- *WhoBlA 92, WhoMW 92*
**Black**, Donald I. *WhoRel 92*
**Black**, Donald K 1936- *AmMWSc 92*
**Black**, Donald Leighton 1928- *AmMWSc 92*
**Black**, Douglas 1913- *Who 92, WrDr 92*
**Black**, Douglas Andrew Kilgour 1913- *IntWW 91*
**Black**, Douglas D. 1961- *WhoMW 92*
**Black**, Duncan d1991 *Who 92N*
**Black**, Eileen Mary 1944- *WhoWest 92*
**Black**, Eric 1958- *WhoEnt 92*
**Black**, Erroll Vic 1945- *WhoFI 92*
**Black**, Eugene R. 1898- *Who 92*
**Black**, Francis Lee 1926- *AmMWSc 92*
**Black**, Frank S. 1941- *WhoBlA 92*
**Black**, Franklin Owen 1937- *AmMWSc 92*
**Black**, Fraser 1960- *WhoWest 92*
**Black**, Frederick Evan 1944- *WhoAmL 92*
**Black**, Frederick Harrison 1921- *WhoBlA 92*
**Black**, Gail 1950- *WhoBlA 92*
**Black**, Gary Eugene 1953- *WhoRel 92*
**Black**, Gavin *WrDr 92*
**Black**, Geoffrey 1954- *WhoEnt 92*
**Black**, George Philip 1932- *Who 92*
**Black**, Gerald Joseph 1946- *WhoAmL 92*
**Black**, Greene Vardiman 1836-1915 *BiInAmS*
**Black**, H S 1898- *AmMWSc 92*
**Black**, Harold *DrAPF 91*
**Black**, Henry W *WhoAmP 91*
**Black**, Homer Selton 1935- *AmMWSc 92*
**Black**, Howard 1947- *WhoAmL 92*
**Black**, Howard Charles 1912- *AmMWSc 92*
**Black**, Hugh Elias 1938- *AmMWSc 92*
**Black**, Hugh Lawrance 1942- *WhoAmL 92, WhoWest 92*
**Black**, Hugo 1886-1971 *RComAH*
**Black**, Hugo L 1886-1971 *FacFETw*
**Black**, Hugo LaFayette 1886-1971 *AmPolLe [port]*
**Black**, Iain James *Who 92*
**Black**, Ira B *AmMWSc 92*
**Black**, Isaac J. *DrAPF 91*
**Black**, Jacinth Baubblitz 1944- *WhoMW 92*
**Black**, Jacob Leslie 1921- *WhoRel 92*
**Black**, James *AmMWSc 92*
**Black**, James 1924- *IntWW 91*
**Black**, James B 1935- *WhoAmP 91*
**Black**, James Francis 1919- *AmMWSc 92*
**Black**, James H 1921- *AmMWSc 92*
**Black**, James Isaac, III 1951- *WhoAmL 92*
**Black**, James Michael 1951- *WhoAmL 92*
**Black**, James Robert 1948- *WhoMW 92*
**Black**, James Tillman 1934- *WhoBlA 92*
**Black**, James W. 1924- *WhoNob 90*
**Black**, James Walter 1941- *Who 92*
**Black**, James Whyte 1924- *Who 92*
**Black**, Jane Rogers 1922- *WhoAmP 91*
**Black**, Jeffrey Howard 1943- *AmMWSc 92*
**Black**, Jeremiah Sullivan 1810-1883 *AmPolLe*
**Black**, Jeremy 1932- *Who 92*
**Black**, Jerry Bernard 1940- *WhoAmL 92*
**Black**, Jessie Kate *AmMWSc 92*
**Black**, Joe Bernard 1933- *AmMWSc 92*
**Black**, Joe David 1939- *WhoAmP 91*
**Black**, John Alexander 1940- *AmMWSc 92*
**Black**, John B 1939- *AmMWSc 92*
**Black**, John David 1908- *AmMWSc 92*
**Black**, John Harry 1949- *AmMWSc 92*
**Black**, John Newman 1925- *Who 92*
**Black**, John Nicholson 1922- *Who 92*
**Black**, John Wilson 1906- *AmMWSc 92*
**Black**, John Woodland 1925- *WhoAmP 91*
**Black**, Joseph 1728-1799 *BlkwCEP*
**Black**, Joseph 1921- *Who 92*
**Black**, Joseph 1924- *WhoBlA 92*
**Black**, Joseph Wayne 1953- *WhoWest 92*
**Black**, Joseph Willard 1923- *WhoMW 92*
**Black**, Karen 1942- *IntMPA 92, WhoEnt 92*
**Black**, Kaylene Slay 1945- *WhoFI 92*
**Black**, Kenneth, Jr. 1925- *WhoIns 92*
**Black**, Kenneth Eldon 1922 *AmMWSc 92*
**Black**, Kenneth Wallace 1912- *WhoAmP 91*
**Black**, Kirby Samuel 1954- *AmMWSc 92*
**Black**, Kristine Mary 1953- *WhoWest 92*
**Black**, L. Alexander *WhoRel 92*
**Black**, Larry 1951- *BlkOlyM*
**Black**, Larry David 1949- *WhoMW 92*
**Black**, Laura *IntAu&W 91X, WrDr 92*
**Black**, Layton 1940- *WhoAmP 91*
**Black**, Lee Roy 1937- *WhoBlA 92*
**Black**, Leona R. 1924- *WhoBlA 92*
**Black**, Lindsay MacLeod 1907- *AmMWSc 92*
**Black**, Lord James Joseph 1949- *WhoAmL 92*
**Black**, Louis Engleman 1943- *WhoAmL 92*
**Black**, Louise Roseanne 1952- *WhoAmP 91*
**Black**, Lowell Lynn 1938- *AmMWSc 92*
**Black**, Lucius, Sr *WhoAmP 91, WhoBlA 92*
**Black**, Lydia T. 1925- *WhoWest 92*
**Black**, Malcolm Charles Lamont 1928- *WhoEnt 92*
**Black**, Malcolm Mazique 1937- *WhoBlA 92*
**Black**, Mansell *WrDr 92*
**Black**, Marcel *WhoAmP 91*
**Black**, Margaret McLeod 1912- *Who 92*
**Black**, Mark Morris *AmMWSc 92*
**Black**, Martin *AmMWSc 92*
**Black**, Matthew 1908- *IntWW 91, Who 92*
**Black**, Max 1909- *WrDr 92*
**Black**, Michael R. 1960- *WhoEnt 92*
**Black**, Mike 1937- *WhoBlA 92*
**Black**, Misha 1910-1977 *ConAu 133, DcTwDes, FacFETw*
**Black**, Neil Cathcart 1932- *Who 92*
**Black**, Noel 1940- *IntMPA 92*
**Black**, Noel Anthony 1937- *WhoEnt 92, WhoWest 92*
**Black**, Norman William 1931- *WhoAmL 92*
**Black**, Patricia Eileen 1955- *WhoWest 92*
**Black**, Patricia Reed 1957- *WhoAmL 92*
**Black**, Paul Emmerson 1962- *WhoMW 92*
**Black**, Paul H 1930- *AmMWSc 92*
**Black**, Paul Joseph 1930- *Who 92*
**Black**, Percy 1922- *IntAu&W 91, WrDr 92*
**Black**, Perry 1930- *AmMWSc 92*
**Black**, Pete 1946- *WhoAmP 91*
**Black**, Peter Blair 1917- *Who 92*
**Black**, Peter Elliott 1934- *AmMWSc 92*
**Black**, Randall William 1960- *WhoAmL 92*
**Black**, Richard H 1925- *AmMWSc 92*
**Black**, Richard James 1944- *WhoWest 92*
**Black**, Robert 1906- *Who 92*
**Black**, Robert 1947- *Who 92*
**Black**, Robert 1950- *NewAmDM*
**Black**, Robert Allen 1954- *WhoAmL 92*
**Black**, Robert Andrew 1951- *WhoFI 92*
**Black**, Robert Corl 1941- *AmMWSc 92*
**Black**, Robert David 1929- *Who 92*
**Black**, Robert Denis Collison 1922- *IntWW 91, Who 92*
**Black**, Robert Durward 1952- *WhoRel 92*
**Black**, Robert Earl Lee 1928- *AmMWSc 92*
**Black**, Robert James 1955- *WhoWest 92*
**Black**, Robert L 1930- *AmMWSc 92*
**Black**, Robert L., Jr. 1917- *WhoAmL 92, WhoRel 92*
**Black**, Robert Lincoln 1930- *IntWW 91*
**Black**, Robert Perry 1927- *WhoFI 92, WrDr 92*
**Black**, Robin *Who 92*
**Black**, Ronald E 1935- *WhoAmP 91*
**Black**, Ronald L 1943- *WhoAmP 91*
**Black**, Ronnie Delane 1947- *WhoRel 92*
**Black**, Rosa Walston *WhoBlA 92*
**Black**, Roy E. *NewYTBS 91 [port]*
**Black**, Roy Eric 1945- *WhoAmL 92*
**Black**, Samuel Harold 1930- *AmMWSc 92*
**Black**, Samuel P W 1916- *AmMWSc 92*
**Black**, Shaun Dennis 1954- *WhoMW 92*
**Black**, Sheila 1920- *Who 92*
**Black**, Shirley Temple 1928- *IntWW 91, WhoAmP 91, WhoEnt 92*
**Black**, Simon 1917- *AmMWSc 92*
**Black**, Spencer 1950- *WhoAmP 91*
**Black**, Stanley *IntMPA 92*
**Black**, Stanley 1913- *IntWW 91*
**Black**, Stanley Warren, III 1939- *WhoFI 92*
**Black**, Susan Harrell 1943- *WhoAmL 92*
**Black**, Sydney D 1915- *AmMWSc 92*
**Black**, Terance Timothy 1954- *WhoEnt 92*
**Black**, Terry Paul 1960- *WhoFI 92*
**Black**, Theodore Halsey 1928- *WhoFI 92*
**Black**, Theodore R. 1906- *IntMPA 92*
**Black**, Thomas Donald 1920- *WhoRel 92*
**Black**, Thomas John 1943- *WhoFI 92*
**Black**, Truman D 1937- *AmMWSc 92*
**Black**, V Anne 1922- *WhoAmP 91*
**Black**, Veronica *IntAu&W 91X, WrDr 92*
**Black**, Veronica Correll 1946- *WhoBlA 92*
**Black**, Virginia H 1941- *AmMWSc 92*
**Black**, Wallace Gordon 1922- *AmMWSc 92*
**Black**, Walter Evan, Jr. 1926- *WhoAmL 92*
**Black**, Walter Kerrigan 1915- *WhoBlA 92*
**Black**, Walter Weldon, Jr. *WhoBlA 92*
**Black**, Wayne Edward 1935- *AmMWSc 92*
**Black**, Wendell C. 1935- *WhoBlA 92*
**Black**, Wilford Rex, Jr 1920- *WhoAmP 91, WhoWest 92*
**Black**, Willa 1915- *WhoBlA 92*
**Black**, William Alan 1953- *WhoFI 92*
**Black**, William B 1941- *WhoAmP 91*
**Black**, William Bruce 1923- *AmMWSc 92*
**Black**, William Gordon 1927- *WhoFI 92*
**Black**, William Grant 1920- *WhoRel 92*
**Black**, William H 1931- *WhoAmP 91*
**Black**, William Hubert 1927- *WhoIns 92*
**Black**, William Z 1940- *AmMWSc 92*
**Black-Keefer**, Sharon Kay 1949- *WhoFI 92*
**Black-Rhodes**, Diana Karen 1953- *WhoEnt 92*

**Blackadar,** Alfred Kimball 1920- *AmMWSc 92*
**Blackadar,** Bruce Evan 1948- *AmMWSc 92*
**Blackadar,** Robert Gordon 1928- *AmMWSc 92*
**Blackadder,** Elizabeth 1931- *TwCPaSc*
**Blackall,** Willard Thomas 1934- *WhoAmP 91*
**Blackard,** William Griffith 1933- *AmMWSc 92*
**Blackbeard** d1718 *BenetAL 91*
**Blackbeard the Pirate** 1680?-1718 *DcNCBi 1*
**Blackbird,** George Michael 1942- *WhoAmP 91*
**Blackbourn,** David Gordon 1949- *IntWW 91*
**Blackburn,** Archdeacon of *Who 92*
**Blackburn,** Bishop of 1937- *Who 92*
**Blackburn,** Provost of *Who 92*
**Blackburn,** Alberta 1924- *WhoBlA 92*
**Blackburn,** Anthony 1945- *Who 92*
**Blackburn,** Archie Barnard 1938- *AmMWSc 92*
**Blackburn,** Benjamin Allan, II 1940- *WhoBlA 92*
**Blackburn,** Catherine Elaine 1953- *WhoAmL 92*
**Blackburn,** Chancey 1947- *WhoEnt 92*
**Blackburn,** Charles Edward 1939- *WhoWest 92*
**Blackburn,** Charles M. 1937- *WhoBlA 92*
**Blackburn,** Dale Warren 1926- *AmMWSc 92*
**Blackburn,** Daniel Glenn 1952- *AmMWSc 92*
**Blackburn,** David Craig 1947- *WhoMW 92*
**Blackburn,** Edmond Spencer 1868-1912 *DcNCBi 1*
**Blackburn,** Edward Victor 1944- *AmMWSc 92*
**Blackburn,** Elizabeth Helen 1948- *AmMWSc 92*
**Blackburn,** Gary Ray 1946- *AmMWSc 92*
**Blackburn,** George L 1936- *AmMWSc 92*
**Blackburn,** Grover Kelly, Jr. 1956- *WhoRel 92*
**Blackburn,** Guy 1911- *Who 92*
**Blackburn,** Henry Webster, Jr 1925- *AmMWSc 92*
**Blackburn,** Isaac W 1851?-1911 *BiInAmS*
**Blackburn,** Jack Bailey 1922- *AmMWSc 92*
**Blackburn,** Jacob Floyd 1918- *AmMWSc 92*
**Blackburn,** Jeffrey Michael 1941- *Who 92*
**Blackburn,** John 1923- *WrDr 92*
**Blackburn,** John 1945- *Who 92*
**Blackburn,** John Fenwick Anderson 1923- *IntAu&W 91*
**Blackburn,** John Gill 1935- *AmMWSc 92*
**Blackburn,** John Gilmer 1927- *WhoAmL 92*
**Blackburn,** John Graham 1933- *Who 92*
**Blackburn,** John Lewis 1913- *AmMWSc 92, WhoWest 92*
**Blackburn,** John Robert 1945- *AmMWSc 92*
**Blackburn,** Julie Prlina 1954- *WhoAmL 92*
**Blackburn,** Lou Jean 1928- *WhoWest 92*
**Blackburn,** Marsh Hanly 1929- *WhoFI 92*
**Blackburn,** Martha Grace 1944- *WhoMW 92*
**Blackburn,** McKinley Lee 1930- *WhoAmP 91*
**Blackburn,** Michael *Who 92*
**Blackburn,** Michael Dale 1951- *WhoAmL 92*
**Blackburn,** Michael John 1930- *Who 92*
**Blackburn,** Michael N 1944- *AmMWSc 92*
**Blackburn,** Michael Scott 1936- *Who 92*
**Blackburn,** Mitchell Derek 1961- *WhoAmL 92*
**Blackburn,** Paul 1926-1971 *BenetAL 91, ConAu 34NR*
**Blackburn,** Paul Edward 1924- *AmMWSc 92*
**Blackburn,** Peter Hugh 1940- *Who 92*
**Blackburn,** Richard Wallace 1942- *WhoAmL 92, WhoFI 92*
**Blackburn,** Robert McGrady 1919- *WhoRel 92*
**Blackburn,** Roger Lloyd 1946- *WhoAmL 92*
**Blackburn,** Ronald Henry Albert 1924- *Who 92*
**Blackburn,** Sharon Lovelace 1950- *WhoAmL 92*
**Blackburn,** Steven Peter 1952- *WhoRel 92*
**Blackburn,** Terry Michael 1951- *WhoMW 92*
**Blackburn,** Thomas Henry 1923- *AmMWSc 92*
**Blackburn,** Thomas Roy 1936- *AmMWSc 92*
**Blackburn,** Wilbert Howard 1941- *AmMWSc 92*
**Blackburn,** Will R 1936- *AmMWSc 92*
**Blackburn,** William Howard 1941- *AmMWSc 92*
**Blackburn,** William Keaton 1947- *WhoAmP 91*
**Blackburn,** William Maxwell 1899-1972 *DcNCBi 1*
**Blackburn,** Wyatt Douglas 1954- *WhoFI 92*
**Blackburn Rodriguez,** Thomas Richard 1946- *WhoHisp 92*
**Blackburne,** Hugh Charles 1912- *Who 92*
**Blackburne,** Neville 1913- *WrDr 92*
**Blackburne,** Neville Alfred Edmund 1913- *IntAu&W 91*
**Blacken,** John D 1930- *WhoAmP 91*
**Blacker,** Anthony Stephen Jeremy 1939- *Who 92*
**Blacker,** Carmen Elizabeth 1924- *Who 92*
**Blacker,** Cecil 1916- *Who 92*
**Blacker,** Derek Charles 1929- *Who 92*
**Blacker,** Ian T. 1954- *WhoRel 92*
**Blacker,** Kate 1955- *TwCPaSc*
**Blacker,** Nordin Francis 1937- *WhoAmL 92*
**Blacker,** Norman 1938- *Who 92*
**Blacker,** Richard Alan 1937- *WhoAmL 92*
**Blacker,** Robert George 1947- *WhoEnt 92*
**Blacker,** Thetis *TwCPaSc*
**Blackerby,** Bruce Alfred 1936- *AmMWSc 92*
**Blackerby,** James William 1950- *WhoFI 92*
**Blacketor,** Paul G 1927- *WhoAmP 91*
**Blacketor,** Paul Garber 1927- *WhoRel 92*
**Blackett,** Donald Watson 1926- *AmMWSc 92*
**Blackett,** George 1906- *Who 92*
**Blackett,** Patrick Maynard Stuart 1897-1974 *WhoNob 90*
**Blackett,** Shirley Allart 1928- *AmMWSc 92*
**Blackett,** Vivien 1955- *TwCPaSc*
**Blackett-Ord,** Andrew James 1921- *Who 92*
**Blackfield,** Cecilia Malik 1915- *WhoWest 92*
**Blackford,** Eugene Gilbert 1839-1904 *BiInAmS*
**Blackford,** Jason Collier 1938- *WhoAmL 92*
**Blackford,** Leo Price 1951- *WhoFI 92*
**Blackford,** Robert Newton 1937- *WhoFI 92*
**Blackford,** Thomas Earl 1961- *WhoRel 92*
**Blackham,** Angus Udell 1926- *AmMWSc 92*
**Blackham,** Ann Rosemary 1927- *WhoAmP 91, WhoFI 92*
**Blackham,** Joseph Leslie 1912- *Who 92*
**Blackhurst,** Eric Paul 1961- *WhoAmL 92*
**Blackie,** James Randall 1958- *WhoWest 92*
**Blacking,** John 1928-1990 *AnObit 1990*
**Blackiston,** Henry Curtis, III 1943- *WhoAmL 92*
**Blackketter,** Dennis O 1932- *AmMWSc 92*
**Blackledge,** Sheri Dione 1968- *WhoWest 92*
**Blackledge,** William d1828 *DcNCBi 1*
**Blackledge,** William Salter 1793-1857 *DcNCBi 1*
**Blackler,** Antonie W C 1931- *AmMWSc 92*
**Blackley,** Allan Baillie 1937- *Who 92*
**Blacklidge,** Raymond Mark 1960- *WhoAmL 92*
**Blacklin,** Malcolm *IntAu&W 91X*
**Blacklow,** Neil Richard 1938- *AmMWSc 92*
**Blackman,** Carl F 1941- *AmMWSc 92*
**Blackman,** David Ira 1951- *WhoWest 92*
**Blackman,** Diane Dailey 1946- *WhoFI 92*
**Blackman,** Donald George 1935- *IntWW 91*
**Blackman,** Edwin Jackson 1947- *WhoMW 92*
**Blackman,** Frank 1926- *Who 92*
**Blackman,** George Raymond 1960- *WhoAmL 92*
**Blackman,** Gilbert Albert Waller 1925- *Who 92*
**Blackman,** Harold Alphonso 1940- *IntWW 91*
**Blackman,** Honor *IntMPA 92, IntWW 91*
**Blackman,** Ian Richard 1959- *WhoEnt 92*
**Blackman,** J S 1907- *AmMWSc 92*
**Blackman,** James Timothy 1951- *WhoFI 92*
**Blackman,** Jeffrey William 1948- *WhoAmL 92, WhoWest 92*
**Blackman,** Jerome 1928- *AmMWSc 92*
**Blackman,** Kenneth Robert 1941- *WhoAmL 92*
**Blackman,** Lionel Cyril Francis 1930- *Who 92*
**Blackman,** Marc Roy 1946- *AmMWSc 92*
**Blackman,** Murray 1920- *WhoRel 92*
**Blackman,** Murray Ivan 1945- *WhoAmL 92*
**Blackman,** Paul Charles 1941- *WhoFI 92*
**Blackman,** Randell Dean 1940- *WhoRel 92*
**Blackman,** Raymond Victor Bernard 1910- *IntAu&W 91*
**Blackman,** Rolando 1959- *WhoBlA 92*
**Blackman,** Samuel William 1913- *AmMWSc 92*
**Blackman,** Scott Harris 1960- *WhoAmL 92*
**Blackmar,** Charles A. 1944- *WhoAmL 92*
**Blackmar,** Charles B 1922- *WhoAmP 91*
**Blackmar,** Charles Blakey 1922- *WhoAmL 92, WhoMW 92*
**Blackmer,** Donald L. M. 1929- *WrDr 92*
**Blackmer,** Sidney Alderman 1895-1973 *DcNCBi 1*
**Blackmon,** Anthony Wayne 1957- *WhoBlA 92*
**Blackmon,** Bobby Glenn 1940- *AmMWSc 92*
**Blackmon,** Clinton Ralph 1919- *AmMWSc 92*
**Blackmon,** Daniel M 1947- *WhoAmP 91*
**Blackmon,** Edward, Jr 1947- *WhoAmP 91, WhoBlA 92*
**Blackmon,** Evelyn Kinnison 1924- *WhoAmP 91*
**Blackmon,** James B 1938- *AmMWSc 92*
**Blackmon,** John G 1928- *WhoAmP 91*
**Blackmon,** John R 1930- *AmMWSc 92*
**Blackmon,** Joyce McAnulty 1937- *WhoBlA 92*
**Blackmon,** Larry Terry 1946- *WhoRel 92*
**Blackmon,** Maurice Lee 1940- *AmMWSc 92*
**Blackmon,** Michael Dale 1958- *WhoMW 92, WhoRel 92*
**Blackmon,** Mosetta Whitaker 1950- *WhoBlA 92*
**Blackmon,** Terrell David 1933- *WhoRel 92*
**Blackmon,** W. E. B. 1951- *WhoAmL 92*
**Blackmore,** Denis Louis 1943- *AmMWSc 92*
**Blackmore,** Howard Loftus 1917- *IntAu&W 91*
**Blackmore,** June *WrDr 92*
**Blackmore,** Michael Howell 1928- *Who 92*
**Blackmore,** Peter Fredrick *AmMWSc 92*
**Blackmore,** Richard 1654-1729 *RfGEnL 91*
**Blackmore,** Richard D. 1825-1900 *RfGEnL 91*
**Blackmore,** Stephen 1952- *Who 92*
**Blackmun,** Harry A 1908- *FacFETw [port], IntWW 91, Who 92*
**Blackmun,** Harry Andrew 1908- *WhoAmL 92, WhoAmP 91*
**Blackmur,** Richard 1904-1965 *BenetAL 91*
**Blacknall,** John 1690?-1749 *DcNCBi 1*
**Blacknall,** Oscar William 1852-1918 *DcNCBi 1*
**Blackney,** Kathleen Ann 1956- *WhoMW 92*
**Blackorby,** Lila Rose *WhoAmP 91*
**Blackshaw,** Alan 1933- *Who 92*
**Blackshaw,** George Lansing 1936- *AmMWSc 92*
**Blackshaw,** William Simon 1930- *Who 92*
**Blackshear,** A. T., Jr. 1942- *WhoAmL 92*
**Blackshear,** Julian W., Jr. 1941- *WhoBlA 92*
**Blackshear,** L. T., Sr. *WhoRel 92*
**Blackshear,** Perry L, Jr 1921- *AmMWSc 92*
**Blackshear,** William 1935- *WhoBlA 92*
**Blacksnake,** George *TwCWW 91*
**Blackstad,** Theodor Wilhelm 1925- *IntWW 91*
**Blackstead,** Howard Allan 1940- *AmMWSc 92*
**Blackstock,** Charity *IntAu&W 91, WrDr 92*
**Blackstock,** David Theobald 1930- *AmMWSc 92*
**Blackstock,** James Fielding 1947- *WhoWest 92*
**Blackstock,** Larry Lee 1954- *WhoEnt 92*
**Blackstock,** Lee *WrDr 92*
**Blackstock,** LeRoy 1914- *WhoAmL 92*
**Blackstock,** Narvel Wayne 1956- *WhoEnt 92*
**Blackstock,** Rebecca 1943- *AmMWSc 92*
**Blackstock,** Robert William 1927- *WhoAmL 92*
**Blackstone,** Baroness 1942- *IntWW 91, Who 92, WrDr 92*
**Blackstone,** Harry Bouton, Jr. 1934- *WhoEnt 92*
**Blackstone,** Tessa Ann Vosper 1942- *IntAu&W 91*
**Blackstone,** William 1723-1780 *BlkwCEP, BlkwEAR*
**Blackton,** J. Stuart 1875-1941 *IntDcF 2-2 [port]*
**Blackton,** Jay Schwartzdorf 1909- *WhoEnt 92*
**Blackwelder,** Blake Winfield 1945- *AmMWSc 92*
**Blackwelder,** Boyce W. 1913-1976 *ConAu 135*
**Blackwelder,** Ron F 1941- *AmMWSc 92*
**Blackwell,** Alan Trevor 1942- *AmMWSc 92*
**Blackwell,** Albert T, Jr *WhoAmP 91*
**Blackwell,** Alice Stone 1857-1950 *HanAmWH*
**Blackwell,** Anna Derby 1932- *WhoWest 92*
**Blackwell,** Annie Walker 1862-1922 *RelLAm 91*
**Blackwell,** Antoinette 1825-1921 *HanAmWH*
**Blackwell,** Antoinette Brown 1825-1921 *RelLAm 91*
**Blackwell,** Arthur Brendhal, III 1953- *WhoBlA 92*
**Blackwell,** B.H. d1885 *DcLB 106*
**Blackwell,** B H d1924 *DcLB 106*
**Blackwell,** Barry M 1934- *AmMWSc 92*
**Blackwell,** Basil 1889-1984 *DcLB 106 [port]*
**Blackwell,** Basil 1922- *Who 92*
**Blackwell,** Basil, and Mott, Limited *DcLB 106*
**Blackwell,** Bennie Francis 1941- *AmMWSc 92*
**Blackwell,** Charles C, Jr 1933- *AmMWSc 92*
**Blackwell,** Charles Wilfred 1930- *WhoMW 92*
**Blackwell,** Crist Scott 1945- *AmMWSc 92*
**Blackwell,** Dan Page 1952- *WhoWest 92*
**Blackwell,** David 1919- *AmMWSc 92*
**Blackwell,** David Harold 1919- *WhoBlA 92*
**Blackwell,** Dill 1929- *WhoAmP 91*
**Blackwell,** Donald Eustace 1921- *Who 92*
**Blackwell,** Douglas A. 1950- *WhoEnt 92*
**Blackwell,** Douglas Charles 1938- *Who 92*
**Blackwell,** Elizabeth 1821-1910 *BiInAmS, HanAmWH, RComAH*
**Blackwell,** Faiger Megrea 1955- *WhoBlA 92*
**Blackwell,** Faye Brown 1942- *WhoBlA 92*
**Blackwell,** Floyd Oris 1925- *AmMWSc 92*
**Blackwell,** Frederick Wayne 1937- *WhoWest 92*
**Blackwell,** G. L. *WhoRel 92*
**Blackwell,** Gus Ray 1955- *WhoRel 92*
**Blackwell,** Harold Richard 1921- *AmMWSc 92*
**Blackwell,** Harvel E. 1937- *WhoBlA 92*
**Blackwell,** Helen Reddy 1941- *WhoAmP 91*
**Blackwell,** Henry Barlow, II 1928- *WhoMW 92*
**Blackwell,** J Kenneth 1948- *WhoAmP 91, WhoBlA 92*
**Blackwell,** James E. 1926- *ConAu 133, WhoBlA 92*
**Blackwell,** John 1942- *AmMWSc 92, WhoMW 92*
**Blackwell,** John 1945- *WhoAmL 92*
**Blackwell,** John Charles 1935- *Who 92*
**Blackwell,** John Henry 1921- *AmMWSc 92*
**Blackwell,** Julian 1929- *Who 92*
**Blackwell,** Julian Toby 1929- *IntWW 91*
**Blackwell,** Lawrence A 1931- *AmMWSc 92*
**Blackwell,** Leo Herman 1934- *AmMWSc 92*
**Blackwell,** Leonard Adam, II 1942- *WhoAmL 92*
**Blackwell,** Lucien E *WhoAmP 91*
**Blackwell,** Lucien E. 1931- *WhoBlA 92*
**Blackwell,** Lyle Marvin 1932- *AmMWSc 92*
**Blackwell,** Marlin Earl, Jr. 1941- *WhoIns 92*
**Blackwell,** Menefee Davis 1916- *WhoMW 92*
**Blackwell,** Meredith 1940- *AmMWSc 92*
**Blackwell,** Milford 1921- *WhoBlA 92*
**Blackwell,** Morton Clyde 1939- *WhoAmP 91*
**Blackwell,** Nathan, Jr. 1951- *WhoRel 92*
**Blackwell,** Noble Virgil 1934- *WhoBlA 92*
**Blackwell,** Patricia A. 1943- *WhoBlA 92*
**Blackwell,** Paul K, II 1931- *AmMWSc 92*
**Blackwell,** Randolph Talmadge 1927- *WhoBlA 92*
**Blackwell,** Rebecca Maxine 1954- *WhoFI 92*
**Blackwell,** Richard J. 1929- *WrDr 92*
**Blackwell,** Richard Manning 1940- *WhoFI 92*
**Blackwell,** Richard Quentin 1918- *AmMWSc 92*
**Blackwell,** Robert B. 1924- *WhoBlA 92*
**Blackwell,** Robert Brendall 1924- *WhoAmP 91*
**Blackwell,** Robert Jerry 1925- *AmMWSc 92*
**Blackwell,** Robert Leighton 1924- *AmMWSc 92*
**Blackwell,** Robert Lester 1895-1918 *DcNCBi 1*

**Blackwell**, Samuel Eugene 1930- *WhoAmP 91*
**Blackwell**, Scott Wesley 1953- *WhoFI 92*
**Blackwell**, Terry Lynn 1947- *WhoWest 92*
**Blackwell**, Thomas 1701-1757 *BlkwCEP*
**Blackwell**, Thomas F. 1961- *WhoAmL 92*
**Blackwell**, Thomas Francis 1942- *WhoAmL 92*
**Blackwell**, Unita *WhoAmP 91*
**Blackwell**, Waller Taylor, Jr. 1958- *WhoFI 92*
**Blackwell**, William A 1920- *AmMWSc 92*
**Blackwell**, William Thomas 1839-1903 *DcNCBi 1*
**Blackwell**, Willie 1954- *WhoBlA 92*
**Blackwood** *Who 92*
**Blackwood**, Algernon 1869-1951 *ScFEYrs*
**Blackwood**, Andrew W 1942- *AmMWSc 92*
**Blackwood**, Bill 1936- *WhoAmP 91*
**Blackwood**, Caroline 1931- *ConNov 91, IntAu&W 91, WrDr 92*
**Blackwood**, Easley 1933- *NewAmDM*
**Blackwood**, George Douglas 1909- *Who 92*
**Blackwood**, Robert Lee 1952- *WhoFI 92*
**Blackwood**, Ronald A 1926- *WhoAmP 91, WhoBlA 92*
**Blackwood**, Roy, Jr. 1925- *WhoRel 92*
**Blackwood**, William d1990 *Who 92N*
**Blacque**, Taurean *WhoBlA 92, WhoEnt 92*
**Blad**, Blaine L 1939- *AmMWSc 92*
**Blade**, Alexander *ConAu 36NR, TwCSFW 91*
**Blade**, Gary Alvin 1934- *WhoMW 92*
**Blade**, Mary Ellen 1953- *WhoAmL 92*
**Blade**, Robert Eric 1923- *WhoRel 92*
**Blade**, Thomas 1943- *WhoAmL 92*
**Blades**, Ann 1947- *WrDr 92*
**Blades**, Arthur Taylor 1926- *AmMWSc 92*
**Blades**, Bennie 1966- *WhoBlA 92*
**Blades**, Brian Keith 1965- *WhoBlA 92*
**Blades**, Herbert William 1908- *WhoFI 92*
**Blades**, James 1901- *WrDr 92*
**Blades**, James Bishop 1856-1918 *DcNCBi 1*
**Blades**, John Dieterle 1924- *AmMWSc 92*
**Blades**, Leslie Burton *ScFEYrs*
**Blades**, Lucille 1922- *WhoAmP 91*
**Blades**, Ruben 1948- *IntMPA 92, WhoHisp 92*
**Blades**, Steven Paul 1951- *WhoWest 92*
**Blades**, William Howard 1947- *WhoWest 92*
**Bladh**, Katherine Laing 1947- *AmMWSc 92*
**Bladh**, Kenneth W 1947- *AmMWSc 92*
**Bladon**, Richard Anthony 1943- *WhoWest 92*
**Blaedel**, Walter John 1916- *AmMWSc 92, WhoMW 92*
**Blaese**, R Michael 1939- *AmMWSc 92*
**Blaess**, Darrell L. 1937- *WhoIns 92*
**Blaettler**, Richard Bruce 1938- *WhoWest 92*
**Blaffer**, Sarah C. *ConAu 35NR*
**Blager**, Florence Berman 1928- *AmMWSc 92*
**Blagonravov**, Anatoli Arkad'evich 1894-1975 *FacFETw*
**Blagowidow**, George *DrAPF 91*
**Blaha**, Eli William 1927- *AmMWSc 92*
**Blaha**, Gordon C 1934- *AmMWSc 92*
**Blaha**, John E. *NewYTBS 91 [port]*
**Blaha**, Joseph Wade 1938- *WhoFI 92*
**Blahd**, William Henry 1921- *AmMWSc 92*
**Blaher**, Neal Jonathan 1960- *WhoAmL 92*
**Blahetka**, Russell Ernest 1952- *WhoWest 92*
**Blahnik**, Bernard E. 1928- *WhoIns 92*
**Blahnik**, Manolo 1943- *IntWW 91*
**Blahnik**, Miloslav 1927- *IntWW 91*
**Blahut**, Eric Ronald 1943- *WhoRel 92*
**Blahut**, Richard E 1937- *AmMWSc 92*
**Blahuta**, Renee Maria 1932- *WhoAmP 91*
**Blaich**, Larry Mason 1949- *WhoFI 92*
**Blaidsell**, Machrina L. *WhoRel 92*
**Blaige**, Thomas Edward 1962- *WhoFI 92*
**Blaikley**, Robert Marcel 1916- *Who 92*
**Blaiklock**, Robert George 1940- *AmMWSc 92*
**Blaim**, Leland C., II 1955- *WhoMW 92*
**Blain**, Alexander, III 1918- *WhoMW 92*
**Blain**, Francis Rene 1943- *IntWW 91*
**Blain**, Gerard 1930- *IntMPA 92*
**Blain**, Peter Charles 1949- *WhoAmL 92*
**Blaine**, Allan 1930- *WhoRel 92*
**Blaine**, Charles Gillespie 1925- *WhoAmL 92*
**Blaine**, Dorothea Constance Ragette 1930- *WhoAmL 92, WhoWest 92*
**Blaine**, Edward Homer 1940- *AmMWSc 92*
**Blaine**, James G. 1830-1893 *BenetAL 91, RComAH*
**Blaine**, James Gillespie 1830-1893 *AmPolLe [port]*
**Blaine**, Jeff *TwCWW 91*
**Blaine**, John *SmATA 65*
**Blaine**, Joseph Kirby 1955- *WhoFI 92*
**Blaine**, Vivian 1921- *IntMPA 92*
**Blainey**, Geoffrey Norman 1930- *IntAu&W 91, IntWW 91, WrDr 92*
**Blair**, Alan Huntley 1933- *AmMWSc 92*
**Blair**, Alastair Campbell 1908- *Who 92*
**Blair**, Alfred Francis 1927- *WhoMW 92*
**Blair**, Anthony Charles Lynton 1953- *IntWW 91, Who 92*
**Blair**, Barbara Ann 1926- *AmMWSc 92*
**Blair**, Betsy 1923- *IntMPA 92, WhoEnt 92*
**Blair**, Bruce Graeme Donald 1946- *Who 92*
**Blair**, Bruce Reynolds 1940- *WhoFI 92*
**Blair**, Carol Dean 1942- *AmMWSc 92, WhoWest 92*
**Blair**, Chandos 1919- *Who 92*
**Blair**, Charles E. 1920- *WhoRel 92*
**Blair**, Charles Eugene 1949- *AmMWSc 92*
**Blair**, Charles Melvin, Jr 1910- *AmMWSc 92*
**Blair**, Charles Michael 1947- *WhoBlA 92*
**Blair**, Chester Laughton Ellison 1928- *WhoBlA 92*
**Blair**, Claude 1922- *IntAu&W 91, Who 92, WrDr 92*
**Blair**, Clay Drewry 1925- *WrDr 92*
**Blair**, Damian J. W. 1957- *WhoEnt 92*
**Blair**, David Reston 1953- *WhoMW 92*
**Blair**, David W 1929- *AmMWSc 92*
**Blair**, Dennis Alan 1960- *WhoMW 92*
**Blair**, Dennis Earl 1947- *WhoFI 92*
**Blair**, Dennis Lance *WhoEnt 92*
**Blair**, Diane Divers 1938- *WhoAmP 91*
**Blair**, Donald George Ralph 1932- *AmMWSc 92*
**Blair**, Edward McCormick, Jr. 1942- *WhoFI 92*
**Blair**, Edward Payson 1910- *WhoRel 92*
**Blair**, Edward Thomas H. *Who 92*
**Blair**, Emil 1923- *AmMWSc 92*
**Blair**, Emily Newell 1877-1952 *HanAmWH*
**Blair**, Eric Arthur *RfGEnL 91*
**Blair**, Ernest *WhoHisp 92*
**Blair**, Etcyl Howell 1922- *AmMWSc 92*
**Blair**, Francis Preston 1791-1876 *AmPolLe*
**Blair**, Frank *LesBEnT 92*
**Blair**, Fred 1940- *WhoAmP 91*
**Blair**, Fred Edward 1933- *WhoMW 92*
**Blair**, Frederick David 1946- *WhoWest 92*
**Blair**, Gary Charles 1938- *WhoWest 92*
**Blair**, George Ellis, Jr. 1932- *WhoBlA 92*
**Blair**, George Richard 1920- *AmMWSc 92*
**Blair**, George S. 1924- *WrDr 92*
**Blair**, George W *WhoAmP 91*
**Blair**, Glenn Myers 1908- *IntAu&W 91, WrDr 92*
**Blair**, Gordon Purves 1937- *IntWW 91, Who 92*
**Blair**, Graham Kerin 1951- *WhoAmL 92*
**Blair**, Grant Clark 1965- *AmMWSc 92*
**Blair**, H. David 1940- *WhoAmL 92*
**Blair**, H W d1884 *BiInAmS*
**Blair**, Hannah Millikan 1756-1852 *DcNCBi 1*
**Blair**, Homer Orrin 1925- *WhoAmL 92*
**Blair**, Hugh 1718-1800 *BlkwCEP*
**Blair**, James 1655-1743 *BenetAL 91*
**Blair**, James B 1935- *WhoAmP 91*
**Blair**, James Bryan 1944- *AmMWSc 92*
**Blair**, James Burton 1935- *WhoFI 92*
**Blair**, James Douglas d1991 *Who 92N*
**Blair**, James Edward 1935- *AmMWSc 92*
**Blair**, James H. 1926- *WhoBlA 92*
**Blair**, Janet 1921- *IntMPA 92*
**Blair**, Jayne 1952- *WhoEnt 92*
**Blair**, Jean Marie 1947- *WhoEnt 92*
**Blair**, John 1929- *AmMWSc 92*
**Blair**, John Martin 1957- *WhoAmL 92*
**Blair**, John Milton 1938- *WhoWest 92*
**Blair**, John Morris 1919- *AmMWSc 92*
**Blair**, John Orlando, Jr. 1941- *WhoFI 92*
**Blair**, John Sanborn 1923- *AmMWSc 92*
**Blair**, Jonnie Carlisle 1940- *WhoFI 92*
**Blair**, Joseph E, Jr. 1931- *WhoIns 92*
**Blair**, Judith Ann 1952- *WhoWest 92*
**Blair**, Karen Elaine 1948- *WhoWest 92*
**Blair**, Kathryn *WrDr 92*
**Blair**, Kenneth B. 1929- *WhoFI 92*
**Blair**, Kerrie Jane 1956- *WhoWest 92*
**Blair**, Lacy Gordon 1937- *WhoBlA 92*
**Blair**, Laurel Gotshall 1909- *WhoMW 92*
**Blair**, Linda 1959- *IntMPA 92*
**Blair**, Linda Denise 1959- *WhoEnt 92*
**Blair**, Louis Curtis 1954- *AmMWSc 92*
**Blair**, Louise 1958- *TwCPaSc*
**Blair**, Margaret Mendenhall 1950- *WhoFI 92*
**Blair**, Martha Longwell 1948- *AmMWSc 92*
**Blair**, Michael Campbell 1941- *Who 92*
**Blair**, Michael W. 1955- *WhoAmL 92*
**Blair**, Murray Reid, Jr 1928- *AmMWSc 92*
**Blair**, Norma *DrAPF 91*
**Blair**, Paul V 1929- *AmMWSc 92*
**Blair**, Philip M. 1928-1979 *ConAu 133*
**Blair**, Phyllis Beebe 1931- *AmMWSc 92*
**Blair**, R.A. d1902 *BiInAmS*
**Blair**, R. Cary 1939- *WhoIns 92*
**Blair**, Ralph, Jr 1942- *WhoAmP 91*
**Blair**, Randall Howell 1946- *WhoEnt 92*
**Blair**, Rebecca Gay 1956- *WhoMW 92*
**Blair**, Rhonda Louise 1951- *WhoEnt 92*
**Blair**, Richard Bryson 1945- *WhoAmL 92*
**Blair**, Richard Eugene 1923- *WhoAmL 92*
**Blair**, Robert 1699-1746 *RfGEnL 91*
**Blair**, Robert 1933- *AmMWSc 92*
**Blair**, Robert Allen 1946- *WhoAmL 92*
**Blair**, Robert G 1936- *AmMWSc 92*
**Blair**, Robert Louie 1927- *AmMWSc 92*
**Blair**, Robert Park 1950- *WhoWest 92*
**Blair**, Robert William *AmMWSc 92*
**Blair**, Robert William 1917- *AmMWSc 92*
**Blair**, Russell 1949- *WhoAmP 91*
**Blair**, Ruth Van Ness 1912- *WrDr 92*
**Blair**, Samuel Davidson 1927- *WhoFI 92*
**Blair**, Sidney Robert 1929- *WhoFI 92, WhoWest 92*
**Blair**, Sloan Blackmon 1929- *WhoAmL 92*
**Blair**, Stephen Alexander 1947- *WhoWest 92*
**Blair**, Steven Douglas 1960- *WhoMW 92*
**Blair**, Stewart D. 1950- *IntMPA 92, WhoWest 92*
**Blair**, Thomas 1926- *WrDr 92*
**Blair**, Thomas Alexander 1916- *Who 92*
**Blair**, Tony *Who 92*
**Blair**, Virginia Ann 1925- *WhoMW 92*
**Blair**, W Richardson 1908- *WhoAmP 91*
**Blair**, Walter 1900- *BenetAL 91, IntAu&W 91*
**Blair**, Warren Emerson 1916- *WhoAmL 92*
**Blair**, Watson Bayard 1954- *WhoAmL 92*
**Blair**, William Allen 1859-1948 *DcNCBi 1*
**Blair**, William David 1943- *AmMWSc 92, WhoMW 92*
**Blair**, William Emanuel 1934- *AmMWSc 92*
**Blair**, William LeRoy 1928- *WhoFI 92*
**Blair**, William Travis 1925- *WhoMW 92*
**Blair-Hastings**, Fredrika 1918-1990 *WhoEnt 92*
**Blair-Kerr**, William Alexander 1911- *Who 92*
**Blair-Oliphant**, David Nigel Kington 1911- *Who 92*
**Blairman**, Jacqueline *WrDr 92*
**Blais**, Benoit U 1918- *WhoAmP 91*
**Blais**, Burton W 1963- *AmMWSc 92*
**Blais**, J A Rodrigue 1941- *AmMWSc 92*
**Blais**, Jean Jacques 1940- *Who 92*
**Blais**, Leo D 1929- *WhoAmP 91*
**Blais**, Marie-Claire 1939- *BenetAL 91, IntWW 91*
**Blais**, Norman Joseph 1929- *WhoFI 92*
**Blais**, Normand C 1926- *AmMWSc 92*
**Blais**, Pierre 1948- *WhoFI 92*
**Blais**, Richard Leo 1927- *WhoEnt 92*
**Blais**, Roger A 1926- *AmMWSc 92*
**Blais**, Roger Nathaniel 1944- *AmMWSc 92*
**Blais**, Thomas Lionel 1965- *WhoEnt 92*
**Blais-Grenier**, Suzanne *IntWW 91*
**Blaisdell**, Anne *IntAu&W 91X*
**Blaisdell**, Clesson J 1926- *WhoAmP 91*
**Blaisdell**, Ernest Atwell, Jr 1940- *AmMWSc 92*
**Blaisdell**, Fred W 1911- *AmMWSc 92*
**Blaisdell**, James Pershing 1918- *AmMWSc 92*
**Blaisdell**, John Lewis 1935- *AmMWSc 92*
**Blaisdell**, Richard Kekuni 1925- *AmMWSc 92*
**Blaisdell**, Robert Keith 1934- *WhoEnt 92*
**Blaisdell**, Robert R *WhoAmP 91*
**Blaisdell**, Russell Carter 1936- *WhoRel 92*
**Blaise**, Clark *DrAPF 91*
**Blaise**, Clark 1940- *BenetAL 91, ConNov 91, WrDr 92*
**Blaising**, Craig Alan 1949- *WhoRel 92*
**Blaize**, Herbert Augustus 1918-1989 *FacFETw*
**Blaize**, Mavis 1927- *WhoBlA 92*
**Blake** *Who 92*
**Blake**, Baron 1916- *IntWW 91, Who 92*
**Blake**, Lord *WrDr 92*
**Blake**, Alan Craig 1952- *WhoFI 92*
**Blake**, Albert Jefferson, Jr 1926- *WhoAmP 91*
**Blake**, Alexander 1920- *AmMWSc 92*
**Blake**, Alfred *WrDr 92*
**Blake**, Alfred 1915- *Who 92*
**Blake**, Alphonso R. 1935- *WhoBlA 92*
**Blake**, Andrew *WrDr 92*
**Blake**, Anthony *TwCSFW 91*
**Blake**, Barbara Sandra 1939- *WhoFI 92*
**Blake**, Blind 1895?-1935 *NewAmDM*
**Blake**, Bobby *ConTFT 9*
**Blake**, Brian 1918- *WrDr 92*
**Blake**, Bruce *WhoRel 92*
**Blake**, Carl 1925- *AmMWSc 92*
**Blake**, Carl LeRoy 1951- *WhoBlA 92*
**Blake**, Carl Thomas 1926- *AmMWSc 92*
**Blake**, Carlton Hugh 1934- *WhoBlA 92*
**Blake**, Carolyn Louise 1944- *WhoEnt 92*
**Blake**, Charles 1940- *WhoRel 92*
**Blake**, Charles Edward 1940- *RelLAm 91*
**Blake**, Charles Henry 1912- *Who 92*
**Blake**, Christopher 1926- *Who 92*
**Blake**, Clarence John 1843-1919 *BiInAmS*
**Blake**, Craig Thomas 1946- *WhoWest 92*
**Blake**, Daniel Bryan 1939- *AmMWSc 92, WhoMW 92*
**Blake**, Daniel Melvin 1943- *AmMWSc 92*
**Blake**, Darcie Kay 1958- *WhoEnt 92*
**Blake**, Darlene Evelyn 1947- *WhoMW 92*
**Blake**, David 1936- *ConCom 92*
**Blake**, David Andrew 1941- *AmMWSc 92*
**Blake**, David Charles 1936- *Who 92*
**Blake**, David Gordon 1946- *WhoAmL 92*
**Blake**, David Leonard 1936- *Who 92*
**Blake**, David M. 1948- *IntMPA 92*
**Blake**, Eli Whitney 1795-1886 *BiInAmS*
**Blake**, Eli Whitney, Jr 1836-1895 *BiInAmS*
**Blake**, Elias, Jr. 1929- *WhoBlA 92*
**Blake**, Emily Calvin 1882- *ScFEYrs*
**Blake**, Emmet Reid 1908- *AmMWSc 92*
**Blake**, Eubie 1883-1983 *FacFETw, NewAmDM*
**Blake**, Eugene Carson 1906-1985 *DcEcMov, RelLAm 91*
**Blake**, Forrester *TwCWW 91*
**Blake**, Francis 1850-1913 *BiInAmS*
**Blake**, Francis Michael 1943- *Who 92*
**Blake**, Frank Burgay 1924- *WhoMW 92*
**Blake**, Gary 1944- *WhoFI 92*
**Blake**, Geoffrey Lewis 1962- *WhoEnt 92*
**Blake**, George E. 1775?-1871 *NewAmDM*
**Blake**, George Henry, Jr 1922- *AmMWSc 92*
**Blake**, George Marston 1932- *AmMWSc 92*
**Blake**, George Rowland 1918- *AmMWSc 92*
**Blake**, Gilbert Easton 1953- *WhoFI 92*
**Blake**, Hayward Robert 1925- *WhoEnt 92*
**Blake**, Henry Vincent 1912- *Who 92*
**Blake**, Howard 1938- *ConCom 92*
**Blake**, Ian Fraser 1941- *AmMWSc 92*
**Blake**, J Bernard 1935- *AmMWSc 92*
**Blake**, J. Herman 1934- *WhoBlA 92*
**Blake**, J. Paul 1950- *WhoBlA 92*
**Blake**, James 1815-1893 *BiInAmS*
**Blake**, James Elwood 1938- *AmMWSc 92*
**Blake**, James G. 1944- *WhoBlA 92*
**Blake**, James J 1937- *AmMWSc 92*
**Blake**, James Neal 1933- *AmMWSc 92*
**Blake**, Jane Salley 1937- *WhoFI 92*
**Blake**, Jeff Herbert 1944- *WhoMW 92*
**Blake**, Jeffrey Vincent 1952- *WhoEnt 92*
**Blake**, Jennifer *IntAu&W 91X, WrDr 92*
**Blake**, Joan Johnston Wallman 1930- *WhoEnt 92*
**Blake**, John Archibald *AmMWSc 92*
**Blake**, John Ballard 1922- *WrDr 92*
**Blake**, John Clemens 1945- *IntWW 91*
**Blake**, John Clifford 1901- *Who 92*
**Blake**, John Freeman 1950- *WhoFI 92*
**Blake**, John H 1808-1899 *BiInAmS*
**Blake**, John L. 1921- *WhoBlA 92*
**Blake**, John Marcus 1831?-1920 *BiInAmS*
**Blake**, John Michael 1948- *Who 92*
**Blake**, John Philip 1956- *WhoAmL 92*
**Blake**, Jon 1954- *ConAu 135*
**Blake**, Joseph Thomas 1919- *AmMWSc 92*
**Blake**, Jules 1924- *AmMWSc 92*
**Blake**, Justin *IntAu&W 91X, WrDr 92*
**Blake**, Katherine Devereux 1858-1950 *AmPeW*
**Blake**, Ken *IntAu&W 91X, WrDr 92*
**Blake**, Lamont Vincent 1913- *AmMWSc 92*
**Blake**, LeRoy Carl 1935- *WhoFI 92*
**Blake**, Les 1913- *IntAu&W 91*
**Blake**, Lillie Devereux 1835-1913 *DcNCBi 1*
**Blake**, Lillie Devereux 1835-1915 *ScFEYrs*
**Blake**, Louis Harvey 1943- *AmMWSc 92*
**Blake**, Lucien Ira 1854-1916 *BiInAmS*
**Blake**, Marianne Teresa *Who 92*
**Blake**, Martin Irving 1923- *AmMWSc 92*
**Blake**, Mary Netterville 1922- *Who 92*
**Blake**, Melville Edgar, III 1954- *WhoFI 92*
**Blake**, Michael Herbert 1944- *WhoWest 92*
**Blake**, Michael James 1943- *WhoFI 92*
**Blake**, Michael James 1956- *WhoMW 92*
**Blake**, Milton Clark, Jr 1932- *AmMWSc 92*
**Blake**, Milton James 1934- *WhoBlA 92*
**Blake**, Naomi 1924- *TwCPaSc*
**Blake**, Nicholas *ConAu 34NR, FacFETw*
**Blake**, Nick *WrDr 92*
**Blake**, Norman Francis 1934- *IntAu&W 91, WrDr 92*
**Blake**, Norman Perkins, Jr. 1941- *WhoFI 92*
**Blake**, Pat *WhoAmP 91*
**Blake**, Patrick *IntAu&W 91X, WrDr 92*
**Blake**, Paul M, Jr 1946- *WhoAmP 91*
**Blake**, Peter 1920- *WrDr 92*
**Blake**, Peter 1932- *TwCPaSc*
**Blake**, Peter 1948- *IntWW 91*
**Blake**, Peter Thomas 1932- *IntWW 91*

**Blake,** Philip Edward 1944- *WhoWest 92*
**Blake,** Quentin 1932- *WrDr 92*
**Blake,** Quentin Saxby 1932- *IntWW 91, Who 92*
**Blake,** Richard *Who 92*
**Blake,** Richard Charles 1938- *WhoAmL 92*
**Blake,** Richard D 1932- *AmMWSc 92*
**Blake,** Richard Frederick William 1948- *Who 92*
**Blake,** Richard L 1937- *AmMWSc 92*
**Blake,** Richard Louis 1949- *WhoRel 92*
**Blake,** Richard Ronald 1930- *WhoRel 92, WhoWest 92*
**Blake,** Robby *ConTFT 9*
**Blake,** Robert 1916- *IntAu&W 91, WrDr 92*
**Blake,** Robert 1933?- *ConTFT 9, IntMPA 92*
**Blake,** Robert 1949- *WhoRel 92*
**Blake,** Robert George 1906- *AmMWSc 92*
**Blake,** Robert L 1933- *AmMWSc 92*
**Blake,** Robert Wesley 1945- *AmMWSc 92*
**Blake,** Roland Charles 1920- *AmMWSc 92*
**Blake,** Rolland Laws 1924- *AmMWSc 92*
**Blake,** Roy M 1928- *WhoAmP 91*
**Blake,** Sally *WrDr 92*
**Blake,** Stacey *ScFEYrs*
**Blake,** Stephanie *WrDr 92*
**Blake,** Thomas Gaynor 1917- *WhoMW 92*
**Blake,** Thomas Lewis 1946- *AmMWSc 92*
**Blake,** Thomas Mathews 1920- *AmMWSc 92*
**Blake,** Thomas R 1938- *AmMWSc 92*
**Blake,** Thomas Richard 1942- *Who 92*
**Blake,** Tom *AmMWSc 92*
**Blake,** Vernon 1885-1930 *TwCPaSc*
**Blake,** Victor Harold 1935- *WhoIns 92*
**Blake,** Vincent *Who 92*
**Blake,** Wendell Owen 1940- *WhoBlA 92*
**Blake,** Weston, Jr 1930- *AmMWSc 92*
**Blake,** William 1757-1827 *BlkwCEP, CnDBLB 3 [port], RfGEnL 91*
**Blake,** William George 1949- *WhoAmL 92*
**Blake,** William Henry 1913- *WhoMW 92*
**Blake,** William King 1942- *AmMWSc 92*
**Blake,** William Phipps 1825-1910 *BiInAmS*
**Blake,** Wilson 1934- *AmMWSc 92*
**Blakeley,** Denis 1931- *IntAu&W 91*
**Blakeley,** Johnston 1781-1814 *DcNCBi 1*
**Blakeley,** Ulysses Buckley, Sr. 1911- *WhoBlA 92*
**Blakely,** Allison *WhoBlA 92*
**Blakely,** Charles 1951- *WhoBlA 92*
**Blakely,** Colin 1930-1987 *FacFETw*
**Blakely,** Edward James 1938- *WhoBlA 92*
**Blakely,** Eleanor Alice 1947- *AmMWSc 92*
**Blakely,** Everett Jordan 1941- *WhoMW 92*
**Blakely,** J M 1936- *AmMWSc 92*
**Blakely,** Lawrence Eldon 1941- *WhoEnt 92*
**Blakely,** Lawrence Mace 1934- *AmMWSc 92*
**Blakely,** Maurilia Ortiz 1928- *WhoHisp 92*
**Blakely,** Robert Fraser 1921- *AmMWSc 92*
**Blakely,** Susan 1950- *IntMPA 92*
**Blakely,** William H., Jr. 1927- *WhoBlA 92*
**Blakely,** Zelma 1922-1978 *TwCPaSc*
**Blakeman,** Beth R. *DrAPF 91*
**Blakeman,** Marlene Magdalen *WhoMW 92*
**Blakeman,** Royal Edwin 1923- *WhoAmL 92, WhoEnt 92*
**Blakemore,** Colin 1944- *IntAu&W 91, WrDr 92*
**Blakemore,** Colin Brian 1944- *IntWW 91, Who 92*
**Blakemore,** John Sydney 1927- *AmMWSc 92*
**Blakemore,** Michael Howell 1928- *IntWW 91*
**Blakemore,** Paul Henry, Jr. 1925- *WhoWest 92*
**Blakemore,** Richard Peter 1942- *AmMWSc 92*
**Blakemore,** Sally Gay 1947- *WhoEnt 92*
**Blakemore,** William Stephen 1920- *AmMWSc 92*
**Blakeney,** Allan Emrys 1925- *IntWW 91, Who 92*
**Blakeney,** Harrell *WhoAmP 91*
**Blakenham,** Viscount 1938- *IntWW 91, Who 92*
**Blakenship,** Cheryl L. 1950- *WhoBlA 92*
**Blaker,** George Blaker 1912- *Who 92*
**Blaker,** J Warren 1934- *AmMWSc 92*
**Blaker,** John 1935- *Who 92*
**Blaker,** Margaret *DrAPF 91*
**Blaker,** Peter 1922- *Who 92*
**Blaker,** Robert Hockman 1920- *AmMWSc 92*
**Blakeslee,** A Eugene 1928- *AmMWSc 92*
**Blakeslee,** Dennis L 1938- *AmMWSc 92*
**Blakeslee,** Diane Pusey 1933- *WhoFI 92*
**Blakeslee,** Edward Eaton 1921- *WhoAmL 92*
**Blakeslee,** George Hubbard 1871-1954 *AmPeW*
**Blakeslee,** George M 1946- *AmMWSc 92*
**Blakeslee,** James Rankin, Jr. 1933- *WhoMW 92*
**Blakesley,** Christopher Lee 1945- *WhoAmL 92*
**Blakesley,** Wayne Lavere, Jr. 1926- *WhoMW 92*
**Blakey,** Art d1990 *IntWW 91N*
**Blakey,** Art 1919-1990 *AnObit 1990, CurBio 91N, FacFETw, NewAmDM, News 91, WhoBlA 92N*
**Blakey,** Douglas Bert 1960- *WhoMW 92*
**Blakey,** Lewis Horrigan 1933- *AmMWSc 92*
**Blakey,** Scott Chaloner 1936- *WhoWest 92*
**Blakey,** William A. 1943- *WhoBlA 92*
**Blakey,** William Arthur 1943- *WhoAmL 92*
**Blakiston,** Ferguson Arthur James 1963- *Who 92*
**Blakley,** Barry Raymond 1949- *AmMWSc 92*
**Blakley,** Benjamin Spencer, III 1952- *WhoAmL 92*
**Blakley,** Donna De Lano 1956- *WhoMW 92*
**Blakley,** George Robert 1932- *AmMWSc 92*
**Blakley,** Raymond L 1926- *AmMWSc 92*
**Blakney,** William G G 1926- *AmMWSc 92*
**Blakstad,** Michael Bjorn 1940- *Who 92*
**Blalock,** Alfred 1899-1964 *FacFETw*
**Blalock,** Hubert M., Jr. 1926-1991 *ConAu 133*
**Blalock,** Hubert Morse, Jr. 1926- *IntWW 91*
**Blalock,** J Edwin 1949- *AmMWSc 92*
**Blalock,** James Edwin 1949- *AmMWSc 92*
**Blalock,** Jeffrey W. 1961- *WhoEnt 92*
**Blalock,** Joyce 1929- *WhoAmL 92*
**Blalock,** Marion Gale 1948- *WhoFI 92*
**Blalock,** Marion W. 1947- *WhoBlA 92*
**Blalock,** Michael David 1951- *WhoAmL 92*
**Blalock,** Nelson Gales 1836-1913 *DcNCBi 1*
**Blalock,** Sarah M P and William McKesson *DcNCBi 1*
**Blalock,** Sarah Malinda Pritchard 1840?-1901 *DcNCBi 1*
**Blalock,** Sherrill 1945- *WhoFI 92*
**Blalock,** Theron Vaughn 1934- *AmMWSc 92*
**Blalock,** Wallace Davis 1931- *WhoFI 92*
**Blama,** Robert James 1937- *WhoFI 92, WhoWest 92*
**Blamey,** Norman 1914- *TwCPaSc*
**Blamey,** Norman Charles 1914- *IntWW 91, Who 92*
**Blamire,** Roger Victor 1923- *Who 92*
**Blamire-Brown,** John 1915- *Who 92*
**Blamires,** Harry 1916- *IntAu&W 91, WrDr 92*
**Blamont,** Jacques Emile 1926- *IntWW 91*
**Blamont,** Philippe Lucien 1927- *IntWW 91*
**Blampied,** Edmund 1886-1966 *TwCPaSc*
**Blan,** Kennith William, Jr. 1946- *WhoAmL 92, WhoMW 92*
**Blanc,** Charles 1813-1882 *ThHEIm*
**Blanc,** David Abraham 1957- *WhoMW 92*
**Blanc,** Esther Silverstein 1913- *SmATA 66 [port]*
**Blanc,** Francis Louis 1916- *AmMWSc 92*
**Blanc,** Frederic C 1939- *AmMWSc 92*
**Blanc,** Georges 1943- *IntWW 91*
**Blanc,** Joseph 1930- *AmMWSc 92*
**Blanc,** Marcel 1925- *IntWW 91*
**Blanc,** Mel d1989 *LesBEnT 92*
**Blanc,** Mel 1908-1989 *FacFETw*
**Blanc,** Michel H. A. 1929- *ConAu 133*
**Blanc,** Pierre-Louis 1926- *IntWW 91*
**Blanc,** Raymond Rene 1949- *Who 92*
**Blanc,** Raymond Rene Alfred 1949- *IntWW 91*
**Blanc,** Robert Peter 1946- *AmMWSc 92*
**Blanc,** Roger David 1945- *WhoAmL 92*
**Blanc,** William Andre 1922- *AmMWSc 92*
**Blanc-Lapierre,** Andre Joseph Lucien 1915- *IntWW 91*
**Blancard,** Jean Raymond Edouard 1914- *IntWW 91*
**Blancart Kubber,** Teresa *WhoHisp 92*
**Blancas Bustamante,** Carlos 1946- *IntWW 91*
**Blancato,** Robert B 1951- *WhoAmP 91*
**Blancato,** William Alfred 1957- *WhoAmL 92*
**Blancett-Maddock,** V. Diane 1956- *WhoAmL 92*
**Blanch** *Who 92*
**Blanch,** Baron 1918- *IntWW 91, Who 92*
**Blanch,** E. W., Jr. 1936- *WhoIns 92*
**Blanch,** Harvey Warren 1947- *AmMWSc 92*
**Blanch,** Lesley 1907- *IntAu&W 91, Who 92, WrDr 92*
**Blanch,** Roy Lavern 1946- *WhoFI 92*
**Blanch,** Stuart Yarworth 1918- *IntAu&W 91, WhoRel 92, WrDr 92*
**Blanchaer,** Marcel Corneille 1921- *AmMWSc 92*
**Blanchar,** Robert W 1937- *AmMWSc 92*
**Blanchard,** Andrew 1728-1787 *DcNCBi 1*
**Blanchard,** Bruce 1932- *AmMWSc 92*
**Blanchard,** Charles Albert 1848-1925 *RelLAm 91*
**Blanchard,** Chuck *WhoAmP 91*
**Blanchard,** Converse Herrick 1923- *AmMWSc 92*
**Blanchard,** Daniel Gordon 1959- *WhoFI 92*
**Blanchard,** Diane Marie 1951- *WhoMW 92*
**Blanchard,** Donald Edward 1930- *WhoRel 92*
**Blanchard,** Dorothy Minnie 1921- *WhoMW 92*
**Blanchard,** Duncan Cromwell 1924- *AmMWSc 92*
**Blanchard,** E L 1820-1889 *ScFEYrs*
**Blanchard,** Fletcher A, Jr 1924- *AmMWSc 92*
**Blanchard,** Francis 1916- *IntWW 91, Who 92*
**Blanchard,** Frank Nelson 1931- *AmMWSc 92*
**Blanchard,** Fred Ayres 1923- *AmMWSc 92, WhoMW 92*
**Blanchard,** Frederick 1843- *BiInAmS*
**Blanchard,** Gerald Lee 1953- *WhoAmL 92*
**Blanchard,** Gordon Carlton 1932- *AmMWSc 92*
**Blanchard,** H Percy 1862- *ScFEYrs*
**Blanchard,** James 1940- *AmMWSc 92*
**Blanchard,** James J. 1942- *IntWW 91*
**Blanchard,** James Johnston 1942- *WhoAmP 91*
**Blanchard,** Jonathan 1811-1892 *RelLAm 91*
**Blanchard,** Jonathan Ewart 1921- *AmMWSc 92*
**Blanchard,** Joseph Procter 1945- *WhoFI 92*
**Blanchard,** Joshua Pollard 1782-1868 *AmPeW*
**Blanchard,** MaryAnn 1942- *WhoAmP 91*
**Blanchard,** Richard Beirn 1951- *WhoAmL 92*
**Blanchard,** Richard Frederick 1933- *WhoFI 92*
**Blanchard,** Richard Lee 1933- *AmMWSc 92*
**Blanchard,** Robert Osborn 1939- *AmMWSc 92*
**Blanchard,** Tim *WhoRel 92*
**Blanchard,** Townsend Eugene 1931- *WhoFI 92*
**Blanchard,** William 1922- *WrDr 92*
**Blanchard,** William Clifford 1933- *WhoFI 92*
**Blanchard,** William Graham 1944- *WhoEnt 92*
**Blanchard,** William Henry 1922- *WhoWest 92*
**Blanchard,** William Paul 1955- *WhoRel 92*
**Blanchard Wildman,** Suzanne 1940- *WhoEnt 92*
**Blanche of Rossi** *EncAmaz 91*
**Blanche,** Arundel 1583-1649 *EncAmaz 91*
**Blanche,** Ella *DrAPF 91*
**Blanche,** Ernest Evred 1912- *AmMWSc 92*
**Blanche,** Jacques-Emile 1861-1942 *ThHEIm*
**Blanche,** Joe Advincula 1954- *WhoWest 92*
**Blanchet,** Bertrand 1932- *WhoRel 92*
**Blanchet,** Waldo W E 1910- *AmMWSc 92*
**Blanchet,** Waldo Willie E. 1910- *WhoBlA 92*
**Blanchet-Sadri,** Francine 1953- *AmMWSc 92*
**Blanchette,** David Paul 1960- *WhoMW 92*
**Blanchette,** James Edward 1924- *WhoWest 92*
**Blanchette,** Kevin Phillip 1954- *WhoAmP 91*
**Blanchette,** Patti 1952- *WhoAmP 91*
**Blanchette,** Robert, Jr 1959- *WhoAmP 91*
**Blanchette,** Robert Anthony 1951- *AmMWSc 92, WhoMW 92*
**Blanchette,** Robert Wilfred 1932- *WhoAmL 92*
**Blanchette,** Stephen, Jr. 1964- *WhoWest 92*
**Blanchflower,** David Graham 1952- *WhoFI 92*
**Blanck,** Andrew R 1925- *AmMWSc 92*
**Blanck,** Harvey F, Jr 1932- *AmMWSc 92*
**Blanco,** Alberto 1951- *ConSpAP*
**Blanco,** Betty M 1927- *AmMWSc 92*
**Blanco,** Bruce M. 1949- *WhoHisp 92*
**Blanco,** Jorge S. 1948- *WhoHisp 92*
**Blanco,** Julio A. 1939- *WhoHisp 92*
**Blanco,** Julio C. 1931- *WhoHisp 92*
**Blanco,** Julio R. 1951- *WhoHisp 92*
**Blanco,** Kathleen Babineaux 1942- *WhoAmP 91*
**Blanco,** Laura 1956- *WhoEnt 92*
**Blanco,** Michael *WhoHisp 92*
**Blanco,** Ray 1955- *WhoAmP 91*
**Blanco,** Ray Stephen 1955- *WhoEnt 92, WhoHisp 92*
**Blanco,** Raymond D, Jr. 1932- *WhoIns 92*
**Blanco,** Richard M. *IntMPA 92*
**Blanco,** Salvador Jorge 1926- *IntWW 91*
**Blanco,** Serge 1958- *IntWW 91*
**Blanco,** Victor 1936- *WhoAmP 91*
**Blanco,** Victor Manuel 1918- *AmMWSc 92*
**Blanco,** Yolanda Maria 1954- *WhoHisp 92*
**Blanco-Cervantes,** Raul 1903- *IntWW 91*
**Blanco Estrade,** Juan Carlos 1934- *IntWW 91*
**Blanco Fombona,** Rufino 1874-1944 *BenetAL 91*
**Blanco-Gonzalez,** Manuel 1932- *WhoHisp 92*
**Blanco Pi,** Wilfredo G. *WhoHisp 92*
**Blanco White,** Thomas Anthony 1915- *Who 92*
**Blanco-Zavala,** David 1946- *IntWW 91*
**Blancpain,** Marc 1909- *IntAu&W 91, IntWW 91*
**Bland,** Arthur H. 1923- *WhoBlA 92*
**Bland,** Beatrice 1869-1951 *TwCPaSc*
**Bland,** Brian Herbert 1943- *AmMWSc 92*
**Bland,** Carl Nathaniel 1961- *WhoBlA 92*
**Bland,** Celia *DrAPF 91*
**Bland,** Charles E 1943- *AmMWSc 92*
**Bland,** Christopher 1938- *Who 92*
**Bland,** Clifford J 1936- *AmMWSc 92*
**Bland,** E 1858-1924 *ScFEYrs*
**Bland,** Edward *WhoBlA 92*
**Bland,** Edward d1653 *DcNCBi 1*
**Bland,** Henry 1909- *Who 92*
**Bland,** Hester Beth 1906- *AmMWSc 92*
**Bland,** Heyward 1918- *WhoBlA 92*
**Bland,** James A. 1854-1911 *BenetAL 91, NewAmDM*
**Bland,** James H B 1832?-1911 *BiInAmS*
**Bland,** James Kevin 1963- *WhoFI 92*
**Bland,** James Theodore, Jr. 1950- *WhoAmL 92*
**Bland,** Jane Cooper d1991 *NewYTBS 91*
**Bland,** Janeese Myra 1960- *WhoWest 92*
**Bland,** Jeffrey S 1946- *AmMWSc 92*
**Bland,** Jennifer *IntAu&W 91X*
**Bland,** John 1917- *AmMWSc 92*
**Bland,** Kirby Isaac 1942- *AmMWSc 92*
**Bland,** Laurel Le Mieux 1926- *WhoWest 92*
**Bland,** Louise Sarah *Who 92*
**Bland,** Mary Groves 1936- *WhoAmP 91*
**Bland,** Peter 1934- *ConPo 91, WrDr 92*
**Bland,** Richard 1710-1776 *BlkwEAR*
**Bland,** Richard David 1940- *AmMWSc 92*
**Bland,** Richard P 1928- *AmMWSc 92*
**Bland,** Richard Parks 1835-1899 *AmPolLe*
**Bland,** Robert Arthur 1938- *WhoBlA 92*
**Bland,** Robert Gary 1948- *AmMWSc 92*
**Bland,** Roger Gladwin 1939- *AmMWSc 92*
**Bland,** Simon 1923- *Who 92*
**Bland,** Thomas 1809-1885 *BiInAmS*
**Bland,** William M, Jr 1922- *AmMWSc 92*
**Blanden,** Lee Ernest 1942- *WhoBlA 92*
**Blander,** Milton 1927- *AmMWSc 92, WhoMW 92*
**Blandford,** Marquess of 1955- *Who 92*
**Blandford,** Donald Joseph 1938- *WhoAmP 91*
**Blandford,** Eric George 1916- *Who 92*
**Blandford,** Heinz Hermann 1908- *Who 92*
**Blandford,** Percy 1912- *WrDr 92*
**Blandford,** Robert Roy 1937- *AmMWSc 92*
**Blandford,** Roger David 1949- *AmMWSc 92, Who 92, WhoWest 92*
**Blandina** d177 *EncEarC*
**Blanding,** Larry 1953- *WhoAmP 91, WhoBlA 92*
**Blanding,** Mary Rhonella 1950- *WhoBlA 92*
**Blandy,** John Frederic 1936- *WhoWest 92*
**Blandy,** John Peter 1927- *IntWW 91, Who 92*
**Blane,** Edith Littefield 1929- *WhoAmP 91*
**Blane,** Howard Thomas 1926- *AmMWSc 92*
**Blane,** John 1929- *WhoAmP 91*
**Blane,** Ralph 1914- *IntMPA 92*
**Blaney,** Dennis Joseph 1932- *WhoRel 92*
**Blaney,** Donald John 1926- *AmMWSc 92*
**Blaney,** James Bernard 1961- *WhoAmL 92*
**Blaney,** James Thomas 1952- *WhoEnt 92*
**Blaney,** Robert William 1931- *WhoRel 92*
**Blanford,** Colvin 1938- *WhoBlA 92*
**Blanford,** George Emmanuel, Jr 1940- *AmMWSc 92*
**Blanford,** Virginia L. *DrAPF 91*
**Blangiardo,** Thomas Michael 1948- *WhoMW 92*
**Blank,** Albert Abraham 1924- *AmMWSc 92*
**Blank,** Allan 1925- *WhoEnt 92*
**Blank,** Andrew Russell 1945- *WhoAmL 92*
**Blank,** Benjamin 1931- *AmMWSc 92*
**Blank,** Benjamin Henry 1954- *WhoEnt 92*
**Blank,** Carl Herbert 1927- *AmMWSc 92*

**Blank,** Carla Maria 1941- *WhoEnt 92*
**Blank,** Charles Anthony 1922- *AmMWSc 92*
**Blank,** David 1923- *WhoFI 92*
**Blank,** Edward Leo 1943- *WhoEnt 92*
**Blank,** Gregory Scott 1954- *AmMWSc 92*
**Blank,** Harvey 1918- *AmMWSc 92*
**Blank,** Irvin H 1902- *AmMWSc 92*
**Blank,** J.N. 1957- *TwCPaSc*
**Blank,** John Edward 1942- *AmMWSc 92*
**Blank,** Kenneth Charles 1946- *WhoRel 92*
**Blank,** Lawrence Francis 1932- *WhoFI 92, WhoWest 92*
**Blank,** Leland T 1944- *AmMWSc 92*
**Blank,** Martin 1933- *AmMWSc 92*
**Blank,** Maurice Victor 1942- *Who 92*
**Blank,** Myron 1911- *IntMPA 92*
**Blank,** Myron Nathan 1911- *WhoEnt 92*
**Blank,** Peter Harris 1942- *WhoEnt 92*
**Blank,** Peter Joseph 1933- *WhoFI 92*
**Blank,** Rebecca Margaret 1955- *WhoMW 92*
**Blank,** Richard Earl 1947- *WhoFI 92*
**Blank,** Robert H 1926- *AmMWSc 92*
**Blank,** Robert H. 1943- *WrDr 92*
**Blank,** Stuart Lawrence 1942- *AmMWSc 92*
**Blank,** Thomas Craig 1956- *WhoAmL 92*
**Blank,** Thomas Rannels 1952- *WhoFI 92*
**Blank,** Timothy Charles 1958- *WhoAmL 92*
**Blank,** Uel 1921- *WhoFI 92, WhoMW 92*
**Blank,** Zvi *AmMWSc 92*
**Blanke,** Jordan Matthew 1954- *AmMWSc 92*
**Blanke,** Richard B. 1954- *WhoAmL 92*
**Blanke,** Robert Vernon 1924- *AmMWSc 92*
**Blankenbaker,** Ronald Gail 1941- *WhoMW 92*
**Blankenbaker,** Virginia Murphy 1933- *WhoAmP 91*
**Blankenbecler,** Richard 1933- *AmMWSc 92*
**Blankenhorn,** David Henry 1924- *AmMWSc 92*
**Blankenhorn,** Herbert d1991 *Who 92N*
**Blankenhorn,** Paul Richard 1944- *AmMWSc 92*
**Blankenship,** A. B. 1914- *WrDr 92*
**Blankenship,** Asa Lee 1926- *WhoFI 92*
**Blankenship,** Barbara Stewart 1949- *WhoFI 92*
**Blankenship,** C A 1903- *WhoAmP 91*
**Blankenship,** Chrisanne 1959- *WhoMW 92*
**Blankenship,** Dale Clifford 1957- *WhoWest 92*
**Blankenship,** Daniel W. 1957- *WhoFI 92*
**Blankenship,** Dwight David 1944- *WhoFI 92*
**Blankenship,** Eddie L. 1925- *WhoBlA 92*
**Blankenship,** Edward G. 1943- *WhoWest 92*
**Blankenship,** Floyd Allen 1930- *AmMWSc 92*
**Blankenship,** Geoffrey King 1961- *WhoMW 92*
**Blankenship,** Glenn Rayford 1948- *WhoBlA 92*
**Blankenship,** J. Frantiska 1947- *WhoWest 92*
**Blankenship,** James Emery 1941- *AmMWSc 92*
**Blankenship,** James Lynn 1931- *AmMWSc 92*
**Blankenship,** James W 1928- *AmMWSc 92*
**Blankenship,** James William 1943- *AmMWSc 92, WhoWest 92*
**Blankenship,** Keith Scott 1965- *WhoEnt 92*
**Blankenship,** Lytle Houston 1927- *AmMWSc 92*
**Blankenship,** Mark Earl 1964- *WhoEnt 92*
**Blankenship,** Randall Auston 1960- *WhoFI 92*
**Blankenship,** Robert Eugene 1948- *AmMWSc 92*
**Blankenship,** Robert Taylor 1953- *WhoFI 92*
**Blankenship,** Terry Lee 1945- *WhoFI 92*
**Blankenship,** Victor D 1934- *AmMWSc 92*
**Blanker,** Charles H. 1951- *WhoFI 92*
**Blankespoor,** Harvey Dale 1939- *AmMWSc 92*
**Blankespoor,** Ronald Lee 1946- *AmMWSc 92*
**Blankfield,** Alan 1932- *AmMWSc 92*
**Blankfort,** Lowell Arnold 1926- *WhoFI 92, WhoWest 92*
**Blankinship,** G. L., Jr. 1955- *WhoBlA 92*
**Blankinship,** Henry Massie 1942- *WhoFI 92*
**Blankley,** Bruce Travis 1950- *WhoMW 92*
**Blankley,** Clifton John 1942- *AmMWSc 92, WhoMW 92*
**Blankley,** Walter Elwood 1935- *WhoFI 92*
**Blankner,** Frederika *DrAPF 91*
**Blanks,** Delilah B. 1936- *WhoBlA 92*
**Blanks,** Herbert Beverly 1915- *WhoWest 92*
**Blanks,** Howard John 1932- *Who 92*
**Blanks,** Janet Marie 1944- *AmMWSc 92*
**Blanks,** Lance 1966- *WhoBlA 92*
**Blanks,** Robert F 1936- *AmMWSc 92, WhoMW 92*
**Blanks,** Wilhelmina E. 1905- *WhoBlA 92*
**Blankschtein,** Daniel 1951- *AmMWSc 92*
**Blankstein,** Mary Freeman 1931- *WhoEnt 92*
**Blann,** H Marshall 1935- *AmMWSc 92*
**Blanning,** Timothy Charles William 1942- *IntWW 91, Who 92*
**Blanpain,** Jan E 1930- *AmMWSc 92*
**Blanpied,** Gary Stephen 1949- *AmMWSc 92*
**Blanpied,** George David 1930- *AmMWSc 92*
**Blanpied,** Pamela Wharton *DrAPF 91*
**Blanpied,** William Antoine 1933- *AmMWSc 92*
**Blanquet,** Richard Steven 1940- *AmMWSc 92*
**Blanshan,** Eugene H 1948- *WhoAmP 91*
**Blanshard,** Brand 1892- *IntAu&W 91*
**Blanshard,** Paul 1892-1980 *ConAu 135*
**Blanshard,** Paul Beecher 1892-1980 *RelLAm 91*
**Blanton,** Barbara 1937- *WhoAmP 91*
**Blanton,** Ben Wayne 1956- *WhoAmL 92*
**Blanton,** Betty J. 1937- *WhoRel 92*
**Blanton,** Charles DeWitt, Jr 1937- *AmMWSc 92*
**Blanton,** Hoover Clarence 1925- *WhoAmL 92*
**Blanton,** Jackson Orin 1939- *AmMWSc 92*
**Blanton,** James B., III 1949- *WhoBlA 92*
**Blanton,** James Cleveland 1930- *WhoIns 92*
**Blanton,** Jeremy 1939- *WhoEnt 92*
**Blanton,** Jimmy 1918-1942 *NewAmDM*
**Blanton,** John Arthur 1928- *WhoFI 92, WhoWest 92*
**Blanton,** John David 1927- *AmMWSc 92*
**Blanton,** L Ray 1930- *WhoAmP 91*
**Blanton,** Leonard Ray 1930- *IntWW 91*
**Blanton,** Linda Gayle 1940- *WhoMW 92*
**Blanton,** Patricia Louise 1941- *AmMWSc 92*
**Blanton,** Ricky *WhoBlA 92*
**Blanton,** Ronald Edward 1952- *AmMWSc 92*
**Blanton,** W. C. 1946- *WhoAmL 92*
**Blanton,** William George 1930- *AmMWSc 92*
**Blanton,** William W *WhoAmP 91*
**Blantyre,** Archbishop of 1924- *Who 92*
**Blantz,** Roland C *AmMWSc 92*
**Blas,** Franklin F 1941- *WhoAmP 91*
**Blasbalg,** Herman 1925- *AmMWSc 92*
**Blasch,** Howard F. 1928- *WhoIns 92*
**Blasch,** Robert Edward 1931- *WhoEnt 92*
**Blasch,** Tracy Marie 1959- *WhoMW 92*
**Blaschek,** Hans P 1952- *AmMWSc 92*
**Blaschke,** Janet Winter 1959- *WhoWest 92*
**Blaschke,** Lawrence Raymond 1950- *WhoMW 92*
**Blaschko,** Hermann 1900- *IntWW 91*
**Blaschko,** Hermann Karl Felix 1900- *Who 92*
**Blasco Ibanez,** Vicente 1867-1928 *LiExTwC*
**Blasdell,** Robert Ferris 1929- *AmMWSc 92*
**Blase,** Charles David 1940- *WhoRel 92*
**Blase,** Edwin W 1923- *AmMWSc 92*
**Blaser,** Dwight A 1943- *AmMWSc 92*
**Blaser,** Klauspeter 1939- *WhoRel 92*
**Blaser,** Martin Jack 1948- *AmMWSc 92*
**Blaser,** Robert U 1916- *AmMWSc 92*
**Blaser,** Robin 1925- *ConPo 91, WrDr 92*
**Blaser,** Robin Francis 1925- *IntAu&W 91*
**Blaser,** Stephen Jeffery *WhoAmL 92*
**Blasetti,** Alessandro 1900-1987 *IntDcF 2-2 [port]*
**Blashford-Snell,** John Nicholas 1936- *IntAu&W 91, IntWW 91, Who 92, WrDr 92*
**Blasi,** Anthony T 1924- *WhoAmP 91*
**Blasi,** Edward Joseph 1935- *WhoFI 92*
**Blasi,** Vincent A. 1943- *WhoAmL 92*
**Blasie,** J Kent 1943- *AmMWSc 92*
**Blasing,** Herman Thomas 1955- *WhoEnt 92*
**Blasing,** Mutlu Konuk 1944- *ConAu 35NR*
**Blasing,** Randy *DrAPF 91*
**Blasing,** Randy 1943- *ConAu 35NR*
**Blasing,** Terence Jack 1943- *AmMWSc 92*
**Blasingame,** Benjamin P 1918- *AmMWSc 92*
**Blasingame,** James Carter 1866-1941 *DcNCBi 1*
**Blasingham,** Mary Cynthia 1948- *AmMWSc 92*
**Blasinski,** Clare Marie 1950- *WhoMW 92*
**Blasius,** Donald Charles 1929- *WhoFI 92*
**Blasius,** William 1818-1899 *BiInAmS*
**Blaskovic,** Dionyz 1913- *IntWW 91*
**Blaskowitz,** Johannes 1883-1948 *EncTR 91 [port]*
**Blasky,** Harold Frederic 1912- *WhoAmL 92*
**Blasor-Bernhardt,** Donna Jo 1944- *WhoWest 92*
**Blass,** Andreas Raphael 1947- *WhoMW 92*
**Blass,** Bill 1922- *DcTwDes, FacFETw*
**Blass,** Bill Ralph 1922- *IntWW 91*
**Blass,** Elliott Martin 1940- *AmMWSc 92*
**Blass,** Ernst 1890-1939 *EncTR 91*
**Blass,** Gerhard Alois 1916- *AmMWSc 92, WhoFI 92*
**Blass,** Joel W. 1917- *WhoAmL 92*
**Blass,** John P 1937- *AmMWSc 92*
**Blass,** Joseph J 1940- *AmMWSc 92*
**Blass,** W Joel *WhoAmP 91*
**Blass,** Walter Paul 1930- *WhoFI 92*
**Blass,** William Errol 1937- *AmMWSc 92*
**Blass,** William John 1933- *WhoFI 92*
**Blasse,** George 1934- *IntWW 91*
**Blassie,** Freddy 1918- *WhoEnt 92*
**Blassingame,** Gary Joe 1955- *WhoAmL 92*
**Blassingame,** John W. 1940- *WhoBlA 92*
**Blaszczyk,** Miroslaw Jacek 1959- *WhoEnt 92*
**Blaszkowski,** Thomas P 1934- *AmMWSc 92*
**Blaszyk,** Christopher Paul 1957-1990 *WhoRel 92*
**Blatch** *Who 92*
**Blatch,** Baroness 1937- *Who 92*
**Blatch,** Harriet Stanton 1856-1940 *HanAmWH*
**Blatchford,** John Kerslake 1925- *AmMWSc 92*
**Blatchford,** Joseph H 1934- *WhoAmP 91*
**Blatchley,** Geraldine *Who 92*
**Blatchly,** John Marcus 1932- *Who 92*
**Blatherwick,** David Elliott Spiby 1941- *Who 92*
**Blatherwick,** Gerald D. 1936- *WhoFI 92*
**Blatner,** Barbara A. *DrAPF 91*
**Blatnick,** John A d1991 *NewYTBS 91*
**Blatnik,** John A. d1991 *NewYTBS 91*
**Blatnik,** Lawrence Edward 1952- *WhoAmL 92*
**Blatnik,** Thais Frances 1919- *WhoAmP 91*
**Blatov,** Anatoliy Ivanovich d1988 *IntWW 91N*
**Blatstein,** Ira M 1944- *AmMWSc 92*
**Blatt,** Beverly Faye 1944- *WhoWest 92*
**Blatt,** Carl Roger 1938- *AmMWSc 92*
**Blatt,** Daniel *IntMPA 92*
**Blatt,** David Howard 1956- *WhoWest 92*
**Blatt,** Edward A. 1903-1991 *NewYTBS 91*
**Blatt,** Elizabeth Kempske 1936- *AmMWSc 92*
**Blatt,** Frank Joachim 1924- *AmMWSc 92*
**Blatt,** Genevieve 1913- *WhoAmL 92*
**Blatt,** Harvey 1931- *AmMWSc 92*
**Blatt,** James Joseph 1932- *WhoMW 92*
**Blatt,** Jeremiah Lion 1920- *AmMWSc 92*
**Blatt,** Joel Herman 1938- *AmMWSc 92*
**Blatt,** Joel Martin 1942- *AmMWSc 92, WhoMW 92*
**Blatt,** Leslie Alan 1944- *WhoEnt 92*
**Blatt,** Melanie Judith 1946- *WhoWest 92*
**Blatt,** Morton Bernard 1923- *WhoWest 92*
**Blatt,** Richard Lee 1940- *WhoAmL 92*
**Blatt,** S Leslie 1935- *AmMWSc 92*
**Blatt,** Sidney Israel 1921- *WhoMW 92*
**Blatt,** Solomon, Jr. 1921- *WhoAmL 92*
**Blatt,** Sylvia 1918- *AmMWSc 92*
**Blatteis,** Clark Martin 1932- *AmMWSc 92*
**Blattenberg,** Robert C. 1919- *WhoIns 92*
**Blatter,** Alfred 1937- *WhoEnt 92*
**Blattmachr,** Jonathan George 1945- *WhoAmL 92*
**Blattman,** Rubin Joseph 1948- *WhoFI 92*
**Blattner,** Frederick Russell 1940- *AmMWSc 92*
**Blattner,** H.W. *DrAPF 91*
**Blattner,** Meera McCuaig 1930- *AmMWSc 92, WhoFI 92, WhoWest 92*
**Blattner,** Robert 1952- *IntMPA 92, WhoWest 92*
**Blattner,** Robert J 1931- *AmMWSc 92*
**Blattner,** William Albert 1943- *AmMWSc 92*
**Blatty,** William 1928- *WrDr 92*
**Blatty,** William Peter *IntMPA 92*
**Blatty,** William Peter 1928- *IntWW 91, WhoEnt 92*
**Blatz,** Kathleen 1954- *WhoAmP 91*
**Blatz,** Paul E 1923- *AmMWSc 92*
**Blau,** Alan Lee 1958- *WhoEnt 92*
**Blau,** Francine D. 1946- *WrDr 92*
**Blau,** Francine Dee 1946- *WhoMW 92*
**Blau,** George Gafford, III 1936- *WhoAmL 92*
**Blau,** Harvey Isaac 1942- *AmMWSc 92*
**Blau,** Harvey Ronald 1935- *WhoFI 92*
**Blau,** Helen Margaret 1948- *AmMWSc 92*
**Blau,** Henry Hess, Jr 1930- *AmMWSc 92*
**Blau,** Herbert 1926- *ConAu 36NR, WhoEnt 92*
**Blau,** Jeffrey Alan 1951- *WhoAmL 92*
**Blau,** Julian Herman 1917- *AmMWSc 92*
**Blau,** Lawrence Martin 1938- *AmMWSc 92*
**Blau,** Leslie Alan 1945- *WhoAmL 92*
**Blau,** Martin 1924- *IntMPA 92*
**Blau,** Monte 1926- *AmMWSc 92*
**Blau,** Peter M. 1918- *WrDr 92*
**Blau,** Peter Michael 1918- *IntWW 91*
**Blaudin De The,** Guy *IntWW 91*
**Blauer,** Aaron Clyde 1939- *AmMWSc 92*
**Blauer,** Joanne 1950- *WhoAmL 92*
**Blauer,** Roland Eugene 1947- *WhoWest 92*
**Blaufox,** Morton D 1934- *AmMWSc 92*
**Blaug,** Mark 1927- *Who 92*
**Blaugher,** Kurt Edwin 1952- *WhoEnt 92*
**Blaugrund,** David Scott 1953- *WhoAmL 92, WhoMW 92*
**Blaukopf,** Henry 1949- *WhoEnt 92*
**Blaum,** Kevin 1952- *WhoAmP 91*
**Blauner,** Bob 1929- *WrDr 92*
**Blauner,** Laurie *DrAPF 91*
**Blaunstein,** Robert P 1939- *AmMWSc 92*
**Blauschild,** Robert Alan 1948- *AmMWSc 92*
**Blaustein,** Albert P. 1921- *WrDr 92*
**Blaustein,** Albert Paul 1921- *IntWW 91, WhoFI 92*
**Blaustein,** Andrew Richard 1949- *AmMWSc 92*
**Blaustein,** Bernard Daniel 1929- *AmMWSc 92*
**Blaustein,** Ernest Herman 1921- *AmMWSc 92*
**Blaustein,** Julian 1913- *IntMPA 92*
**Blaustein,** Mordecai P 1935- *AmMWSc 92*
**Blauth,** Eugene Karl 1945- *WhoWest 92*
**Blauvelt,** Arthur Abram 1951- *WhoAmL 92*
**Blauvelt,** Howard W. 1917- *IntWW 91*
**Blavatsky,** Helena Petrovna 1831-1891 *BenetAL 91, RelLAm 91*
**Blavatsky,** Helena Petrovna Hahn *ScFEYrs B*
**Blaw,** Michael Ervin 1927- *AmMWSc 92*
**Blawie,** James Louis 1928- *WhoAmL 92, WhoWest 92*
**Blaxall,** Martha Ossoff 1942- *WhoFI 92*
**Blaxter,** Kenneth d1991 *IntWW 91N*
**Blaxter,** Kenneth 1919- *IntWW 91*
**Blaxter,** Kenneth Lyon d1991 *Who 92N*
**Blay,** Andre *IntMPA 92*
**Blay,** Eddie *BlkOlyM*
**Blay,** George Albert 1932- *AmMWSc 92*
**Blaya,** Joaquin F. *WhoHisp 92*
**Blayden,** Lee Chandler 1941- *AmMWSc 92*
**Blaydes,** David Fairchild 1934- *AmMWSc 92*
**Blaylock,** Chet 1924- *WhoAmP 91*
**Blaylock,** Enid V. 1925- *WhoBlA 92*
**Blaylock,** James Carl 1938- *WhoRel 92*
**Blaylock,** James P 1950- *TwCSFW 91*
**Blaylock,** Layton Moore 1954- *WhoEnt 92*
**Blaylock,** Lester Samuel 1936- *WhoEnt 92*
**Blaylock,** Mookie 1967- *WhoBlA 92*
**Blaylock,** W Kenneth 1931- *AmMWSc 92*
**Blayney,** Elizabeth Carmel 1925- *Who 92*
**Blayre,** Christopher 1861-1943 *ScFEYrs, TwCSFW 91*
**Blayton-Taylor,** Betty 1937- *WhoBlA 92*
**Blaz,** Anthony Crisostomo 1958- *WhoAmP 91*
**Blaz,** Ben 1928- *AlmAP 92 [port], WhoWest 92*
**Blaz,** Ben Garnido 1928- *WhoAmP 91*
**Blazar,** Beverly A 1934- *AmMWSc 92*
**Blaze** *WrDr 92*
**Blaze-Gosden,** Anthony Alfred 1931- *IntAu&W 91*
**Blazek,** Doris Defibaugh 1943- *WhoAmL 92*
**Blazek,** Douglas *DrAPF 91*
**Blazek,** Jizi 1923- *WhoEnt 92*
**Blazek,** John Howard 1953- *WhoMW 92*
**Blazek,** Vladimir 1929- *IntWW 91*
**Blazel,** Robert Patrick 1942- *WhoMW 92*
**Blazer,** Dan German 1944- *AmMWSc 92*
**Blazer,** Sondra Kay 1937- *WhoAmP 91*
**Blazevic,** Donna Jean 1931- *AmMWSc 92, WhoAmL 92*
**Blazevic,** Jakov 1912- *IntWW 91*
**Blazey,** Leland Way 1913- *AmMWSc 92*
**Blazey,** Richard N 1941- *AmMWSc 92*
**Blazier,** John Edward 1950- *WhoFI 92, WhoIns 92*
**Blazier,** Kenneth Dean 1933- *WhoRel 92*
**Blazkovec,** Andrew A 1936- *AmMWSc 92*
**Blazquez Y Servin,** Carlos Humberto 1926- *AmMWSc 92*
**Blazyk,** Jack 1947- *AmMWSc 92*
**Blea,** Daniel Anthoney 1949- *WhoHisp 92*
**Blea,** Irene Isabel 1946- *WhoHisp 92*
**Bleackley,** David 1919- *Who 92*
**Bleackley,** Horace 1868-1931 *ScFEYrs*
**Bleackley,** Robert Christopher 1952- *AmMWSc 92*
**Bleakley,** David Wylie 1925- *IntAu&W 91, Who 92, WrDr 92*

**Bleakley**, Frederick Walter 1960- *WhoAmL 92*
**Bleakley**, Peter Kimberley 1936- *WhoAmL 92*
**Bleakney**, John Sherman 1928- *AmMWSc 92*
**Bleakney**, Walker 1901- *AmMWSc 92*
**Bleaney**, Brebis 1915- *IntWW 91, Who 92*
**Bleasdale**, Alan 1946- *IntAu&W 91, Who 92, WrDr 92*
**Bleasdale**, Cyril 1934- *Who 92*
**Blease** *Who 92*
**Blease**, Baron 1914- *Who 92*
**Blech**, Harry 1910- *IntWW 91, Who 92*
**Blecha**, David R. 1948- *WhoMW 92*
**Blecha**, Karl 1933- *IntWW 91*
**Blecher**, F H 1929- *AmMWSc 92*
**Blecher**, George M. *DrAPF 91*
**Blecher**, Marvin 1940- *AmMWSc 92*
**Blecher**, Melvin 1922- *AmMWSc 92*
**Blechman**, Burt 1927- *ConNov 91, IntAu&W 91*
**Blechman**, Corey Edward 1949- *WhoEnt 92*
**Blechman**, Harry 1918- *AmMWSc 92*
**Blechman**, R. O. 1930- *WhoEnt 92*
**Blechner**, Jack Norman 1933- *AmMWSc 92*
**Bleck**, Rainer 1939- *AmMWSc 92*
**Bleck**, Thomas Frank 1929- *WhoMW 92*
**Bleck**, Virginia Eleanore 1929- *WhoMW 92*
**Blecker**, Harry Herman 1927- *AmMWSc 92*
**Blecker**, Marvin 1946- *WhoWest 92*
**Blecker**, Naomi Perle 1956- *WhoFI 92*
**Bleckinger**, Robert Thomas 1952- *WhoIns 92*
**Bleckmann**, Charles Allen 1944- *AmMWSc 92*
**Bleckner**, Jeff 1943- *IntMPA 92*
**Bleckner**, Ross 1949- *WorArt 1980 [port]*
**Bleckstein**, Ted Craig 1953- *WhoMW 92*
**Bledisloe**, Viscount 1934- *Who 92*
**Bledsoe**, Carl Beverly 1923- *WhoAmP 91, WhoWest 92*
**Bledsoe**, Caroline Hazel 1949- *WhoFI 92*
**Bledsoe**, Carolyn E. Lewis 1946- *WhoBlA 92*
**Bledsoe**, Donald Scott 1956- *WhoMW 92*
**Bledsoe**, Frank S. 1891- *WhoBlA 92*
**Bledsoe**, Horace Willie Lee 1944- *AmMWSc 92*
**Bledsoe**, James L. 1947- *WhoBlA 92*
**Bledsoe**, James O, Jr 1938- *AmMWSc 92*
**Bledsoe**, Janeva Leigh 1949- *WhoMW 92*
**Bledsoe**, Jules 1898-1943 *NewAmDM*
**Bledsoe**, Lewis Jackson 1942- *AmMWSc 92*
**Bledsoe**, Lucy Jane *DrAPF 91*
**Bledsoe**, Michael Stewart 1944- *WhoFI 92*
**Bledsoe**, Milton Hargis, Jr. 1941- *WhoBlA 92*
**Bledsoe**, Moses Andrew 1822-1905 *DcNCBi 1*
**Bledsoe**, Tempestt *WhoBlA 92*
**Bledsoe**, Tommy Dalton 1942- *WhoRel 92*
**Bledsoe**, Woodrow Wilson 1921- *AmMWSc 92*
**Bleech**, Peter 1918- *WhoAmP 91*
**Bleeck**, Oliver *WrDr 92*
**Bleecker**, Ann Eliza 1752-1783 *BenetAL 91*
**Bleecker**, Eugene R 1943- *AmMWSc 92*
**Bleecker**, Margit 1943- *AmMWSc 92*
**Bleehen**, Norman Montague 1930- *IntWW 91, Who 92*
**Bleeke**, John Richard 1954- *AmMWSc 92*
**Blees**, Robert *IntMPA 92*
**Blefko**, Robert L 1932- *AmMWSc 92*
**Blegen**, Judith *IntWW 91*
**Blegen**, Judith 1941- *NewAmDM*
**Blegen**, Theodore C. 1891-1969 *DcAmImH*
**Blegvad**, Erik 1923- *SmATA 66 [port]*
**Blegvad**, Lenore 1926- *SmATA 66*
**Blegvad**, Mogens 1917- *IntWW 91*
**Blehert**, Dean *DrAPF 91*
**Blei**, Franz 1871-1942 *EncTR 91*
**Blei**, Ira 1931- *AmMWSc 92*
**Blei**, K. *WhoRel 92*
**Blei**, Norbert *DrAPF 91*
**Blei**, Ron Charles 1945- *AmMWSc 92*
**Bleiberg**, Leon William 1932- *WhoWest 92*
**Bleiberg**, Marvin Jay 1928- *AmMWSc 92*
**Bleiberg**, Robert Marvin 1924- *WhoFI 92*
**Bleiberg**, Steven David 1959- *WhoFI 92*
**Bleibtreu**, Adam David 1958- *WhoEnt 92*
**Bleibtreu**, Hermann Karl 1933- *AmMWSc 92*
**Bleich**, David Lloyd 1943- *WhoAmL 92*
**Bleicher**, Beatrice Koretsky 1942- *WhoAmL 92*
**Bleicher**, Michael N 1935- *WhoAmP 91*
**Bleicher**, Michael Nathaniel 1935- *AmMWSc 92, WhoMW 92*
**Bleicher**, Sheldon Joseph 1931- *AmMWSc 92*
**Bleick**, Willard Evan 1907- *AmMWSc 92*
**Bleicken**, Jochen 1926- *IntWW 91*
**Bleidner**, William Egidius 1921- *AmMWSc 92*
**Bleier**, Alan 1948- *AmMWSc 92*
**Bleier**, Barbara Schlachet *WhoEnt 92*
**Bleier**, Edward *LesBEnT 92*
**Bleier**, Edward 1929- *IntMPA 92*
**Bleier**, Frank P 1913- *AmMWSc 92*
**Bleier**, William Joseph 1947- *AmMWSc 92*
**Bleifuss**, Rodney L 1928- *AmMWSc 92*
**Bleil**, Carl Edward 1923- *AmMWSc 92*
**Bleil**, David F 1908- *AmMWSc 92*
**Bleistein**, Norman 1939- *AmMWSc 92*
**Bleiweis**, Arnold Sheldon 1937- *AmMWSc 92*
**Bleiweis**, Phyllis Rosenblum 1937- *WhoAmP 91*
**Bleiweiss**, Max Phillip 1944- *AmMWSc 92, WhoWest 92*
**Blejer**, Hector P 1933- *AmMWSc 92*
**Blejwas**, Thomas Edward 1946- *AmMWSc 92*
**Blelloch**, John Niall Henderson 1930- *Who 92*
**Blem**, Charles R 1943- *AmMWSc 92*
**Blemker**, Margaret Ruth 1915- *WhoRel 92, WhoWest 92*
**Blencowe**, Paul Sherwood 1953- *WhoAmL 92*
**Blend**, Charles D. 1918-1971 *ConAu 134*
**Blenden**, Donald C 1929- *AmMWSc 92*
**Blender**, Leon Philip 1920- *IntMPA 92*
**Blenderman**, Ronald John, Jr. 1927- *WhoFI 92*
**Blendon**, Robert J. 1942- *IntWW 91*
**Blendon**, Robert Jay 1942- *AmMWSc 92*
**Blenkarn**, Kenneth Ardley 1929- *AmMWSc 92*
**Blenkinsop**, Dorothy 1931- *Who 92*
**Blenkinsopp**, Joseph 1927- *WrDr 92*
**Blenko**, Walter John, Jr. 1926- *WhoAmL 92, WhoFI 92*
**Blennerhassett**, Adrian 1940- *Who 92*
**Blennerhassett**, Francis Alfred 1916- *Who 92*
**Blennerhassett**, Harman 1765-1831 *BenetAL 91*
**Bleriot**, Louis 1872-1936 *DcTwDes, FacFETw*
**Bles**, Geoffrey 1886-1957 *DcLB 112*
**Blesch**, Carl Lee 1952- *WhoMW 92*
**Blesch**, Robert William 1959- *WhoAmL 92*
**Bless**, Robert Charles 1927- *AmMWSc 92*
**Blesser**, Barry Allen 1943- *AmMWSc 92*
**Blesser**, William B 1924- *AmMWSc 92*
**Blessey**, Gerald Henry 1942- *WhoAmP 91*
**Blessing**, Buck 1963- *WhoWest 92*
**Blessing**, Donald Carl 1955- *WhoAmL 92*
**Blessing**, Gerald Vincent 1942- *AmMWSc 92*
**Blessing**, John A 1946- *AmMWSc 92*
**Blessing**, Linda Jane 1951- *WhoWest 92*
**Blessing**, Louis W, Jr 1948- *WhoAmP 91*
**Blessing**, Robert Harry 1941- *AmMWSc 92*
**Blessing**, Ronald John 1951- *WhoWest 92*
**Blessing**, Vicki L. 1954- *WhoWest 92*
**Blessinger**, Michael Anthony 1956- *AmMWSc 92*
**Blessington**, F.C. *DrAPF 91*
**Blessington**, Francis C. 1942- *WrDr 92*
**Blessley**, Kenneth Harry 1914- *Who 92*
**Blest Gana**, Alberto 1830-1920 *BenetAL 91*
**Blethen**, Frank A. 1945- *WhoWest 92*
**Bletner**, James Karl 1912- *AmMWSc 92*
**Blettner**, James Donald 1924- *WhoMW 92*
**Bleuer**, Ned Kermit 1943- *AmMWSc 92*
**Bleunard**, A 1852- *ScFEYrs*
**Bleustein-Blanchet**, Marcel 1906- *IntWW 91*
**Blevin**, William Roderick 1929- *IntWW 91*
**Blevins**, Charles Edward 1924- *AmMWSc 92*
**Blevins**, Charles Russell 1942- *WhoFI 92*
**Blevins**, Dale Glenn 1943- *AmMWSc 92*
**Blevins**, Donn Irving *DrAPF 91*
**Blevins**, Gary Lynn 1941- *WhoFI 92*
**Blevins**, Gilbert Sanders 1927- *AmMWSc 92*
**Blevins**, Jeffrey Alexander 1955- *WhoAmL 92*
**Blevins**, Leon Wilford 1937- *WhoRel 92*
**Blevins**, Maurice Everett 1928- *AmMWSc 92*
**Blevins**, Michael Wayne 1947- *WhoAmL 92*
**Blevins**, Patricia M *WhoAmP 91*
**Blevins**, R W 1923- *AmMWSc 92*
**Blevins**, Raymond Dean 1939- *AmMWSc 92*
**Blevins**, Robert L 1931- *AmMWSc 92*
**Blevins**, Walter, Jr 1950- *WhoAmP 91*
**Blevins**, William Edward 1927- *WhoFI 92, WhoMW 92*
**Blevis**, Bertram Charles 1932- *AmMWSc 92*
**Bleviss**, Zegmund O 1922- *AmMWSc 92*
**Blewett**, Charles William 1943- *AmMWSc 92*
**Blewett**, John P 1910- *AmMWSc 92*
**Blewett**, Myrtle Hildred 1911- *AmMWSc 92*
**Blewett**, Neal 1933- *IntWW 91*
**Blewett**, Patrick Alan 1956- *WhoRel 92*
**Blewitt**, Shane 1935- *Who 92*
**Bley**, Carla 1938- *NewAmDM*
**Bley**, Carla Borg 1938- *IntWW 91, WhoEnt 92*
**Bley**, Margalo Anne 1936- *WhoMW 92*
**Bley**, Paul 1932- *NewAmDM*
**Bleyer**, Ann Katzenstein 1918- *WhoEnt 92*
**Bleyl**, Katherine Lorraine 1949- *WhoWest 92*
**Bleyl**, Robert Lingren 1936- *AmMWSc 92, WhoWest 92*
**Bleyle**, John A. 1944- *WhoIns 92*
**Bleyle**, John Allen 1944- *WhoFI 92*
**Bleyman**, Lea Kanner 1936- *AmMWSc 92*
**Blezzard**, Judith 1944- *ConAu 134*
**Blicher**, Adolph *AmMWSc 92*
**Blick**, Ambler Montquire 1947- *WhoFI 92*
**Blick**, Benny George 1943- *WhoAmP 91*
**Blick**, Edward F 1932- *AmMWSc 92*
**Blickensderfer**, Peter W 1932- *AmMWSc 92*
**Blickensderfer**, Tom 1957- *WhoAmP 91*
**Blickenstaff**, Robert Theron 1921- *AmMWSc 92*
**Blickman**, Bernard I. d1991 *NewYTBS 91*
**Blickstein**, Stuart I 1939- *AmMWSc 92*
**Blickwede**, D J 1920- *AmMWSc 92*
**Blide**, Todd David Foster 1959- *WhoEnt 92*
**Bliek**, Beatrice 1925- *WhoRel 92*
**Blier**, Bernard Benedict 1917- *WhoFI 92*
**Blier**, Bertrand 1939- *IntDcF 2-2 [port], IntMPA 92, IntWW 91*
**Bliese**, John C W 1913- *AmMWSc 92*
**Bliesener**, Mark Edward 1949- *WhoEnt 92*
**Blievernicht**, Gary Wayne 1951- *WhoEnt 92*
**Bligh** *Who 92*
**Bligh**, Aurora *DrAPF 91*
**Bligh**, John 1922- *AmMWSc 92*
**Bligh**, Thomas Percival 1941- *AmMWSc 92*
**Blight**, John 1913- *ConPo 91, IntAu&W 91, WrDr 92*
**Bliley**, Thomas J., Jr. 1932- *AlmAP 92 [port], WhoAmP 91*
**Blim**, Richard Don *AmMWSc 92*
**Blim**, Richard Don 1927- *IntWW 91*
**Blin-Stoyle**, Roger John 1924- *IntWW 91, Who 92*
**Blincoe**, Clifton 1926- *AmMWSc 92*
**Blind**, William Charles 1911- *WhoAmL 92*
**Blinder**, Alan S. 1945- *WrDr 92*
**Blinder**, Alan Stuart 1945- *WhoFI 92*
**Blinder**, Albert Allan 1925- *WhoAmL 92*
**Blinder**, Martin S. 1946- *WhoFI 92, WhoWest 92*
**Blinder**, Seymour Michael 1932- *AmMWSc 92*
**Blinderman**, Charles 1930- *ConAu 135*
**Blindt**, David A. 1953- *WhoEnt 92*
**Blink**, James Allen 1948- *AmMWSc 92*
**Blinken**, Robert James 1929- *WhoFI 92*
**Blinks**, John Rogers 1931- *AmMWSc 92*
**Blinks**, Lawrence Rogers 1900- *AmMWSc 92*
**Blinn**, Dean Ward 1941- *AmMWSc 92*
**Blinn**, Elliott L 1940- *AmMWSc 92*
**Blinn**, James Frederick 1949- *AmMWSc 92*
**Blinn**, John Randolph 1943- *WhoAmL 92*
**Blinn**, Lorena Virginia 1939- *AmMWSc 92, WhoMW 92*
**Blinn**, Walter Craig 1930- *AmMWSc 92*
**Blinn**, William *LesBEnT 92*
**Blinn**, William Ferguson 1947- *WhoEnt 92*
**Blinn**, William Frederick 1937- *WhoEnt 92*
**Blinoff**, Mark 1939- *WhoEnt 92*
**Blint**, Richard Joseph 1945- *AmMWSc 92*
**Blischke**, Wallace Robert 1934- *AmMWSc 92, WhoWest 92*
**Blish**, Eugene Sylvester 1912- *WhoWest 92*
**Blish**, James 1921-1975 *BenetAL 91, SmATA 66, TwCSFW 91*
**Blish**, John Harwood 1937- *WhoAmL 92*
**Blish**, Nelson Adrian 1945- *WhoAmL 92*
**Blishen**, Anthony Owen 1932- *Who 92*
**Blishen**, Edward 1920- *IntAu&W 91, SmATA 66 [port], Who 92, WrDr 92*
**Bliss**, A. J. *ConAu 134*
**Bliss**, Alan 1921-1985 *ConAu 134*
**Bliss**, Anthony A. 1913-1991 *CurBio 91N, NewYTBS 91 [port]*
**Bliss**, Anthony Addison 1913- *IntWW 91*
**Bliss**, Arthur 1891-1975 *NewAmDM*
**Bliss**, Arthur Dean 1927- *AmMWSc 92*
**Bliss**, Brenda D. 1955- *WhoMW 92*
**Bliss**, Bruce James 1935- *WhoAmP 91*
**Bliss**, Christopher John Emile 1940- *Who 92*
**Bliss**, Corinne Demas *DrAPF 91*
**Bliss**, Daniel Howard 1961- *WhoAmL 92*
**Bliss**, David Francis 1946- *AmMWSc 92*
**Bliss**, Donald Allan 1932- *WhoWest 92*
**Bliss**, Dorothy Crandall 1916- *AmMWSc 92*
**Bliss**, Douglas Percy 1900-1984 *TwCPaSc*
**Bliss**, Edwin Crosby 1923- *WhoWest 92*
**Bliss**, Erlan S 1941- *AmMWSc 92*
**Bliss**, Eugene Lawrence 1918- *AmMWSc 92*
**Bliss**, Fredrick Allen 1938- *AmMWSc 92*
**Bliss**, James C 1933- *AmMWSc 92*
**Bliss**, James Ireland 1944- *WhoFI 92*
**Bliss**, John Cordeux 1914- *Who 92*
**Bliss**, John Everett 1948- *WhoRel 92*
**Bliss**, John William Michael 1941- *IntWW 91*
**Bliss**, Julia Christine 1953- *WhoAmL 92*
**Bliss**, Kathleen 1908-1989 *DcEcMov*
**Bliss**, Laura 1916- *AmMWSc 92*
**Bliss**, Lawrence Carroll 1929- *AmMWSc 92*
**Bliss**, Lowell Scott 1912- *WhoAmP 91*
**Bliss**, Matthew Todd 1964- *WhoRel 92*
**Bliss**, Philip Paul 1838-1876 *RelLAm 91*
**Bliss**, Robert Landers 1907- *WhoAmP 91*
**Bliss**, Rodney David, III 1942- *WhoIns 92*
**Bliss**, Rosalind 1937- *TwCPaSc*
**Bliss**, S.W. *DrAPF 91*
**Bliss**, Stanley Michael 1939- *WhoFI 92*
**Bliss**, Tasker Howard 1853-1930 *AmPeW*
**Bliss**, William Dwight Porter 1856-1926 *RelLAm 91*
**Blissett**, Alfreda Rose *Who 92*
**Blissett**, William 1921- *IntWW 91*
**Blitch**, Peg *WhoAmP 91*
**Blitman**, Bruce Alan 1956- *WhoAmL 92*
**Blitstein**, John 1938- *AmMWSc 92*
**Blitz**, Bert Allan 1935- *WhoAmL 92*
**Blitz**, Daniel 1920- *WhoFI 92*
**Blitz**, Mark 1946- *WhoAmP 91*
**Blitz**, Peggy Sanderfur 1940- *WhoMW 92*
**Blitz**, Robert Harmon 1956- *WhoAmL 92*
**Blitz**, Stephen M. 1941- *WhoAmL 92*
**Blitz-Weisz**, Sally 1954- *WhoWest 92*
**Blitzer**, David Mayers 1948- *WhoFI 92*
**Blitzer**, Leon 1915- *AmMWSc 92*
**Blitzer**, Sidney Milton, Jr. 1944- *WhoAmL 92*
**Blitzstein**, Marc 1905-1964 *BenetAL 91, FacFETw, NewAmDM*
**Blitzstein**, William 1920- *AmMWSc 92*
**Blivaiss**, Ben Burton 1917- *AmMWSc 92*
**Bliven**, Bruce 1916- *IntAu&W 91*
**Bliven**, Floyd E, Jr 1921- *AmMWSc 92*
**Blivess**, Michael P. 1947- *WhoIns 92*
**Bliwas**, James Charles 1946- *WhoFI 92*
**Bliwas**, Philip R. 1920- *WhoFI 92*
**Bliwise**, Lester Martin 1945- *WhoAmL 92*
**Blix**, Hans 1928- *Who 92*
**Blix**, Hans Martin 1928- *IntWW 91*
**Blix**, Susanne 1949- *AmMWSc 92*
**Blixt**, Roy Elof 1915- *WhoAmL 92, WhoMW 92*
**Bliznakov**, Emile George 1926- *AmMWSc 92*
**Blizzard**, Robert M 1924- *AmMWSc 92*
**Blobaum**, Gary Duane 1952- *WhoRel 92*
**Blobel**, Gunter 1936- *AmMWSc 92*
**Blobel**, Paul 1894-1951 *EncTR 91*
**Bloch**, Aaron N 1942- *AmMWSc 92*
**Bloch**, Aaron Nixon 1942- *AmMWSc 92*
**Bloch**, Alan 1915- *AmMWSc 92*
**Bloch**, Alan Neil 1932- *WhoAmL 92*
**Bloch**, Alexander 1923- *AmMWSc 92*
**Bloch**, Alice *DrAPF 91*
**Bloch**, Andrew L. 1951- *WhoEnt 92*
**Bloch**, Anthony Michael 1955- *WhoMW 92*
**Bloch**, Chana *DrAPF 91*
**Bloch**, Clifford Alan 1953- *WhoWest 92*
**Bloch**, Daniel R 1940- *AmMWSc 92*
**Bloch**, Donald Martin 1939- *WhoAmL 92*
**Bloch**, Edward Henry 1914- *AmMWSc 92*
**Bloch**, Eric 1928- *AmMWSc 92*
**Bloch**, Erich 1925- *AmMWSc 92*
**Bloch**, Ernest 1880-1959 *FacFETw, NewAmDM*
**Bloch**, Ernest 1921- *WhoFI 92*
**Bloch**, Ernst 1885-1977 *ConAu 34NR*
**Bloch**, Felix 1905-1983 *WhoNob 90*
**Bloch**, Frank Samuel 1945- *WhoAmL 92*
**Bloch**, Henry *WhoEnt 92*
**Bloch**, Henry Wollman 1922- *WhoMW 92*
**Bloch**, Herbert A. 1904-1965 *ConAu 134*
**Bloch**, Herman Samuel 1912- *AmMWSc 92*
**Bloch**, Ingram 1920- *AmMWSc 92*
**Bloch**, Jane Ellen 1960- *WhoEnt 92*
**Bloch**, Jonathan Michael 1952- *WhoFI 92*
**Bloch**, Joseph Meyer 1917- *WhoEnt 92*
**Bloch**, Konrad 1912- *IntWW 91*
**Bloch**, Konrad E. 1912- *Who 92, WhoNob 90*
**Bloch**, Konrad Emil 1912- *AmMWSc 92*
**Bloch**, Kurt Julius 1929- *AmMWSc 92*

**Bloch,** Lester Bernard 1930- *WhoFI 92*
**Bloch,** Louis Mayer, Jr. 1918- *WhoMW 92*
**Bloch,** Lucienne S *DrAPF 91*
**Bloch,** Marie Halun 1910- *IntAu&W 91, WrDr 92*
**Bloch,** Martin 1883-1954 *TwCPaSc*
**Bloch,** Maurice Emile Felix 1939- *Who 92*
**Bloch,** Merle Florence *Who 92*
**Bloch,** Philip Alan 1953- *WhoWest 92*
**Bloch,** Raymond 1914- *IntWW 91*
**Bloch,** Robert *DrAPF 91*
**Bloch,** Robert 1917- *IntAu&W 91, IntMPA 92, TwCSFW 91, WrDr 92*
**Bloch,** Robert Albert 1917- *WhoEnt 92*
**Bloch,** Robert Joseph 1946- *AmMWSc 92*
**Bloch,** Salman 1945- *AmMWSc 92*
**Bloch,** Stuart Fulton 1933- *WhoAmP 91*
**Bloch,** Stuart Marshall 1942- *WhoAmL 92*
**Bloch,** Sylvan C 1931- *AmMWSc 92*
**Bloch,** Thomas Morton 1954- *WhoMW 92*
**Bloch,** William A, Jr. 1942- *WhoIns 92*
**Bloch-Laine,** Francois 1912- *IntWW 91*
**Blocher,** John Milton, Jr 1919- *AmMWSc 92*
**Block,** A Jay 1938- *AmMWSc 92*
**Block,** Adam Johnstone Cheyne 1908- *Who 92*
**Block,** Alan Peter 1964- *WhoAmL 92*
**Block,** Alex Benjamin 1946- *WhoEnt 92*
**Block,** Allan *DrAPF 91*
**Block,** Allan Martin 1942- *WhoMW 92*
**Block,** Bartley C 1933- *AmMWSc 92*
**Block,** Carolyn B. 1942- *WhoBlA 92*
**Block,** Daniel Isaac 1943- *WhoRel 92*
**Block,** David Arthur Kennedy William 1908- *Who 92*
**Block,** David Greenberg 1936- *Who 92*
**Block,** David L 1939- *AmMWSc 92*
**Block,** Dennis Jeffery 1942- *WhoAmL 92*
**Block,** Douglas Alfred 1921- *AmMWSc 92*
**Block,** Duane Llewellyn 1926- *AmMWSc 92*
**Block,** Edward R 1944- *AmMWSc 92*
**Block,** Eric 1942- *AmMWSc 92*
**Block,** Ethel Lasher 1919- *WhoAmP 91*
**Block,** Franklin L 1936- *WhoAmP 91*
**Block,** Gene David 1948- *AmMWSc 92*
**Block,** George E 1926- *AmMWSc 92*
**Block,** Gregory Scott 1964- *WhoMW 92*
**Block,** Henry William 1941- *AmMWSc 92*
**Block,** Herbert Lawrence 1909- *IntWW 91*
**Block,** I Edward 1924- *AmMWSc 92*
**Block,** Ira 1941- *AmMWSc 92*
**Block,** Irving H 1916- *AmMWSc 92*
**Block,** Jacob 1936- *AmMWSc 92*
**Block,** James A 1944- *AmMWSc 92*
**Block,** James Harold 1945- *WhoWest 92*
**Block,** Jeanne Humphrey 1923-1981 *WomPsyc*
**Block,** Jerome Bernard 1931- *AmMWSc 92*
**Block,** Jerome D. 1948- *WhoHisp 92*
**Block,** Joel Christopher 1945- *WhoEnt 92*
**Block,** John Harvey 1938- *AmMWSc 92*
**Block,** John R *WhoAmP 91*
**Block,** John Rusling 1935- *IntWW 91*
**Block,** Julia Chang 1942- *WhoAmP 91*
**Block,** Lawrence *DrAPF 91*
**Block,** Lawrence 1938- *WrDr 92*
**Block,** Lawrence Howard 1941- *AmMWSc 92*
**Block,** Leonard Nathan 1911- *WhoFI 92*
**Block,** Lester Edmund 1935- *WhoEnt 92*
**Block,** M Sabel 1917- *AmMWSc 92*
**Block,** Martin M 1925- *AmMWSc 92*
**Block,** Michael David 1958- *WhoRel 92*
**Block,** Michael I 1956- *WhoIns 92*
**Block,** Michael Joseph 1942- *AmMWSc 92*
**Block,** Neal Jay 1942- *WhoAmL 92*
**Block,** Pamela Jo 1947- *WhoFI 92*
**Block,** Philip Dee, III 1937- *WhoMW 92*
**Block,** Philip M. 1940- *WhoAmL 92*
**Block,** Richard B 1934- *AmMWSc 92*
**Block,** Richard Blanchard 1934- *WhoWest 92*
**Block,** Richard C. *LesBEnT 92*
**Block,** Richard Earl 1931- *AmMWSc 92*
**Block,** Richard Raphael 1938- *WhoAmL 92*
**Block,** Robert Charles 1929- *AmMWSc 92*
**Block,** Robert Jay 1935- *AmMWSc 92*
**Block,** Ronald Edward 1941- *AmMWSc 92*
**Block,** S. Lester 1917- *WhoAmL 92, WhoFI 92*
**Block,** Seymour Stanton 1918- *AmMWSc 92*
**Block,** Stanley 1926- *AmMWSc 92*
**Block,** Stanley L 1923- *AmMWSc 92*
**Block,** Stanley M 1922- *AmMWSc 92*
**Block,** Stephan Michael 1951- *WhoFI 92*
**Block,** Steven Robert 1955- *WhoAmL 92*
**Block,** Thomas H 1945- *IntAu&W 91, WrDr 92*
**Block,** Thomas Ray 1953- *WhoEnt 92*
**Block,** Toby Fran 1949- *AmMWSc 92*
**Block,** Walter *WhoWest 92*
**Block,** Walter David 1911- *AmMWSc 92*
**Block,** Willard 1930- *IntMPA 92*
**Block,** William 1915- *WhoMW 92*
**Block,** William Karl, Jr. 1944- *WhoMW 92*
**Block,** William Kenneth 1950- *WhoAmL 92, WhoFI 92*
**Blocker,** Dirk 1957- *WhoEnt 92*
**Blocker,** Helen Powell 1923- *WhoBlA 92*
**Blocker,** Henry Derrick 1932- *AmMWSc 92*
**Blocker,** Michael Owen 1951- *WhoIns 92*
**Blocker,** Robert Lewis 1946- *WhoEnt 92*
**Blocksom,** Rita Verlene Haynes 1952- *WhoMW 92*
**Blockson,** Charles L. 1933- *WhoBlA 92*
**Blockstein,** David Edward 1956- *AmMWSc 92*
**Blockstein,** William Leonard 1925- *AmMWSc 92*
**Blodget,** Lorin 1823-1901 *BiInAmS*
**Blodget,** Michael 1963- *TwCPaSc*
**Blodget,** Robert Newton 1927- *WhoRel 92*
**Blodgett,** Elsie Grace 1921- *WhoFI 92, WhoWest 92*
**Blodgett,** Forrest Clinton 1927- *WhoFI 92, WhoWest 92*
**Blodgett,** Frank Caleb 1927- *WhoFI 92, WhoMW 92*
**Blodgett,** Frederic Maurice 1920- *AmMWSc 92*
**Blodgett,** Omer William 1917- *WhoMW 92*
**Blodgett,** Robert Bell 1916- *AmMWSc 92*
**Blodgett,** Stephen Sargent 1944- *WhoAmP 91*
**Blodgett,** William Arthur 1937- *WhoFI 92*
**Blodi,** Frederick Christopher 1917- *AmMWSc 92*
**Bloede,** Louis William 1928- *WhoRel 92*
**Bloede,** Victor Carl 1917- *WhoAmL 92, WhoWest 92*
**Bloedel,** James R 1940- *AmMWSc 92*
**Bloedel,** Philip John 1931- *WhoAmL 92*
**Bloem,** Walter 1868-1951 *EncTR 91*
**Bloem,** William Dirk 1956- *WhoMW 92*
**Bloembergen,** Nicolaas 1920- *AmMWSc 92, IntWW 91, Who 92, WhoNob 90, WrDr 92*
**Bloemer,** Rosemary Celeste 1930- *WhoMW 92*
**Bloemer,** William Louis 1947- *AmMWSc 92*
**Bloemfontein,** Bishop of 1932- *Who 92*
**Bloemsma,** Marco Paul 1924- *WhoFI 92*
**Bloesch,** Donald George 1928- *WrDr 92*
**Bloesser,** Rex William 1952- *WhoWest 92*
**Blofeld,** John Christopher Calthorpe 1932- *Who 92*
**Blogoslawski,** Walter 1943- *AmMWSc 92*
**Blohm,** Gary Lee 1942- *WhoEnt 92*
**Blohm,** Thomas Robert 1920- *AmMWSc 92*
**Blois,** Charles 1939- *Who 92*
**Blois,** Flavia 1914- *TwCPaSc*
**Blois,** Marsden Scott, Jr 1919- *AmMWSc 92*
**Blok,** Aleksandr Aleksandrovich 1880-1921 *SovUnBD*
**Blok,** Alexander 1880-1921 *FacFETw*
**Blok,** Bobbi Helene 1953- *WhoAmP 91*
**Blokh,** Alexandre 1923- *Who 92*
**Blokhin,** Nikolay Nikolayevich 1912- *IntWW 91*
**Blokhin,** Oleg 1953- *IntWW 91, SovUnBD*
**Blokzijl,** Marius Hugh Louis Wilhelm 1884-1946 *BiDExR*
**Blom,** August 1869-1947 *IntDcF 2-2*
**Blom,** C. James 1928- *WhoFI 92*
**Blom,** Christian James 1928- *AmMWSc 92*
**Blom,** Daniel Charles 1919- *WhoAmL 92, WhoIns 92*
**Blom,** Gaston Eugene 1920- *AmMWSc 92*
**Blom,** Kark Arne 1946- *IntAu&W 91*
**Blom,** Richard Frederick 1932- *WhoFI 92*
**Blom-Cooper,** Louis Jacques 1926- *IntWW 91, Who 92*
**Blomain,** Karen *DrAPF 91*
**Blomberg,** Bonnie B 1948- *AmMWSc 92*
**Blomberg,** Werner von 1878-1946 *EncTR 91 [port]*
**Blomefield,** Charles 1948- *Who 92*
**Blomen,** Constance 1929- *WhoAmP 91*
**Blomer,** Philip Joseph 1948- *WhoAmL 92*
**Blomfield,** Adelaide *DrAPF 91*
**Blomfield,** John Reginald 1916- *Who 92*
**Blomgren,** David Kenneth 1940- *WhoRel 92*
**Blomgren,** George Earl 1931- *AmMWSc 92*
**Blomgren,** Harry LeRoy 1938- *WhoMW 92*
**Blommers,** Elizabeth Ann 1923- *AmMWSc 92*
**Blomquist,** Alan Charles 1953- *WhoEnt 92*
**Blomquist,** Carl Arthur 1947- *WhoFI 92*
**Blomquist,** Charles Howard 1933- *AmMWSc 92*
**Blomquist,** Dian 1940- *WhoAmP 91*
**Blomquist,** Ernest R., III 1946- *WhoAmL 92*
**Blomquist,** Gary James 1947- *AmMWSc 92*
**Blomquist,** Richard Frederick 1912- *AmMWSc 92*
**Blomquist,** Thomas Melville 1957- *WhoWest 92*
**Blomqvist,** Carl Gunnar 1931- *AmMWSc 92*
**Blomstedt,** Henrik Lennart 1921- *IntWW 91*
**Blomstedt,** Herbert 1927- *NewAmDM*
**Blomstedt,** Herbert Thorson 1927- *IntWW 91, WhoWest 92*
**Blomster,** Galen Grant 1942- *WhoFI 92*
**Blomster,** Ralph N 1931- *AmMWSc 92*
**Blomstrom,** Dale Clifton 1927- *AmMWSc 92*
**Blomstrom,** John Paul, Sr. 1949- *WhoEnt 92*
**Blond,** Anthony 1928- *IntAu&W 91*
**Blond,** Barton Saffran 1938- *WhoAmL 92*
**Blond,** Maxwell 1943- *TwCPaSc*
**Blondeau,** Jacques Patrick Adrien 1944- *WhoIns 92*
**Blondel,** Jacques-Francois 1705-1774 *BlkwCEP*
**Blondel,** Jean 1929- *WrDr 92*
**Blondel,** Jean Fernand Pierre 1929- *IntAu&W 91, Who 92*
**Blondel,** John deCarteret 1956- *WhoFI 92*
**Blondi** d1945 *EncTR 91 [port]*
**Blondin,** Antoine 1922- *IntAu&W 91, IntWW 91*
**Blondin,** John Michael 1960- *AmMWSc 92*
**Blood,** Sweat and Tears *ConMus 7 [port], NewAmDM*
**Blood,** Benjamin Donald 1914- *AmMWSc 92*
**Blood,** Benjamin Paul 1832-1919 *BenetAL 91*
**Blood,** Bindon 1920- *Who 92*
**Blood,** Charles Allen, Jr 1923- *AmMWSc 92*
**Blood,** Dwight Melvin 1932- *WhoFI 92*
**Blood,** Edward Linford 1945- *WhoFI 92*
**Blood,** Elizabeth Reid 1951- *AmMWSc 92*
**Blood,** Eric 1931- *TwCPaSc*
**Blood,** Marje *WrDr 92*
**Bloodgood,** Patricia Annette 1947- *WhoWest 92*
**Bloodgood,** Robert Alan 1948- *AmMWSc 92*
**Bloodstein,** Oliver 1920- *AmMWSc 92*
**Bloodworth,** A W Franklin 1935- *WhoAmL 92*
**Bloodworth,** James Morgan Bartow, Jr 1925- *AmMWSc 92*
**Bloodworth,** M E 1920- *AmMWSc 92*
**Bloodworth,** Timothy 1736-1814 *DcNCBi 1*
**Bloom,** Alan 1945- *WhoAmL 92, WhoFI 92*
**Bloom,** Alan S 1947- *AmMWSc 92*
**Bloom,** Allan 1930- *FacFETw, IntWW 91, WrDr 92*
**Bloom,** Allen 1943- *AmMWSc 92, WhoAmL 92, WhoFI 92*
**Bloom,** Andre Borisovich *Who 92*
**Bloom,** Arnold Lapin 1923- *AmMWSc 92*
**Bloom,** Arnold Sanford 1942- *WhoAmL 92, WhoFI 92*
**Bloom,** Arthur David 1934- *AmMWSc 92*
**Bloom,** Arthur Leroy 1928- *AmMWSc 92*
**Bloom,** Barry Malcolm 1928- *AmMWSc 92*
**Bloom,** Barry R 1937- *AmMWSc 92*
**Bloom,** Bruce H. 1949- *WhoMW 92*
**Bloom,** Charles 1940- *Who 92*
**Bloom,** Charles Joseph 1946- *WhoAmL 92*
**Bloom,** Claire 1931- *IntMPA 92, IntWW 91, Who 92, WhoEnt 92*
**Bloom,** Daniel 1949- *WhoWest 92*
**Bloom,** David Ronald 1943- *WhoFI 92*
**Bloom,** Donald Eugene 1928- *WhoIns 92*
**Bloom,** Eda Terri 1945- *AmMWSc 92*
**Bloom,** Edward A. 1914- *WrDr 92*
**Bloom,** Elaine 1937- *WhoAmP 91*
**Bloom,** Elliott D 1940- *AmMWSc 92*
**Bloom,** Everett E *AmMWSc 92*
**Bloom,** Floyd Elliott 1936- *AmMWSc 92*
**Bloom,** Frank *AmMWSc 92*
**Bloom,** G. Cromarty 1910- *Who 92*
**Bloom,** Gary J. 1942- *WhoMW 92*
**Bloom,** Harold 1930- *BenetAL 91, IntWW 91, WhoRel 92, WrDr 92*
**Bloom,** Harold Edward 1946- *WhoFI 92*
**Bloom,** James Armin 1952- *WhoAmP 91*
**Bloom,** James Edward 1941- *WhoFI 92, WhoMW 92*
**Bloom,** James Martin 1932- *WhoRel 92*
**Bloom,** James R 1924- *AmMWSc 92*
**Bloom,** Janet *DrAPF 91*
**Bloom,** Janet Carol 1958- *WhoMW 92*
**Bloom,** Jeffrey Brian 1953- *WhoAmP 91*
**Bloom,** Jeffrey Phillip 1956- *WhoAmL 92*
**Bloom,** Jerome H 1924- *AmMWSc 92*
**Bloom,** Jessie L 1933- *WhoAmP 91*
**Bloom,** John 1953- *WhoEnt 92*
**Bloom,** John Andrew 1949- *WhoRel 92*
**Bloom,** John Scott 1946- *WhoAmP 91*
**Bloom,** Joseph Morris 1937- *AmMWSc 92*
**Bloom,** Kerry Steven 1953- *AmMWSc 92*
**Bloom,** L R 1914- *AmMWSc 92*
**Bloom,** Lawrence S 1943- *WhoAmP 91*
**Bloom,** Lynn 1934- *WrDr 92*
**Bloom,** Lynn Marie Zimmerman 1934- *IntAu&W 91*
**Bloom,** Max Robert 1916- *WhoFI 92*
**Bloom,** Michael 1950- *WhoEnt 92*
**Bloom,** Michael Anthony 1947- *WhoAmL 92*
**Bloom,** Michael Eugene 1947- *WhoFI 92, WhoWest 92*
**Bloom,** Michael Jay 1958- *WhoAmL 92*
**Bloom,** Michael Joel 1950- *WhoAmL 92*
**Bloom,** Miriam 1934- *AmMWSc 92*
**Bloom,** Murray Teigh 1916- *WrDr 92*
**Bloom,** Myer 1928- *AmMWSc 92, IntWW 91*
**Bloom,** Peter Herbert 1949- *WhoEnt 92*
**Bloom,** Rodney Merlin 1933- *WhoFI 92*
**Bloom,** Roger Fredric 1934- *WhoAmL 92*
**Bloom,** Ronald 1926- *Who 92*
**Bloom,** Rube 1902-1976 *NewAmDM*
**Bloom,** Samuel W. 1921- *WrDr 92*
**Bloom,** Samuel W. 1924- *NewYTBS 91 [port]*
**Bloom,** Sanford Gilbert 1937- *AmMWSc 92*
**Bloom,** Sherman 1934- *AmMWSc 92*
**Bloom,** Stanley 1924- *AmMWSc 92*
**Bloom,** Stephen Allen 1947- *AmMWSc 92*
**Bloom,** Stephen Earl 1941- *AmMWSc 92*
**Bloom,** Steven Paul 1944- *WhoAmP 91*
**Bloom,** Stewart Dave 1923- *AmMWSc 92*
**Bloom,** Verna 1939- *IntMPA 92*
**Bloom,** Victor 1931- *AmMWSc 92, WhoMW 92*
**Blooman,** Michael 1942- *TwCPaSc*
**Bloomberg,** Arthur H 1913- *WhoAmP 91*
**Bloomberg,** Robert Joseph 1947- *WhoWest 92*
**Bloomberg,** Ronald William 1954- *WhoAmL 92*
**Bloomberg,** Wilfred 1905- *AmMWSc 92*
**Bloomdahl,** Jeffrey Kent 1954- *WhoMW 92*
**Bloomer,** Amelia 1818-1894 *BenetAL 91*
**Bloomer,** Amelia Jenks 1818-1894 *HanAmWH*
**Bloomer,** Harold Franklin, Jr. 1933- *WhoAmL 92*
**Bloomer,** James L 1939- *AmMWSc 92*
**Bloomer,** John H 1930- *WhoAmP 91*
**Bloomer,** Oscar T 1923- *AmMWSc 92*
**Bloomer,** Robert A 1921- *WhoAmP 91*
**Bloomer,** Stephen J 1947- *IntMPA 92*
**Bloomer,** William Arthur 1933- *WhoWest 92*
**Bloomfield,** Anthony John Westgate 1922- *IntAu&W 91*
**Bloomfield,** Arthur Irving 1914- *WhoFI 92*
**Bloomfield,** Arthur John 1931- *WhoEnt 92*
**Bloomfield,** Barry 1931- *WrDr 92*
**Bloomfield,** Barry Cambray 1931- *IntAu&W 91, Who 92*
**Bloomfield,** Coleman *WhoIns 92*
**Bloomfield,** Daniel Kermit 1926- *AmMWSc 92*
**Bloomfield,** David Peter 1938- *AmMWSc 92*
**Bloomfield,** Dennis Alexander 1933- *AmMWSc 92*
**Bloomfield,** Edward Jackson 1947- *WhoMW 92*
**Bloomfield,** Harold H 1944- *AmMWSc 92*
**Bloomfield,** John Stoughton d1989 *Who 92N*
**Bloomfield,** Jordan Jay 1930- *AmMWSc 92, WhoWest 92*
**Bloomfield,** Keith Martin 1951- *WhoFI 92*
**Bloomfield,** Kenneth Percy 1931- *IntWW 91, Who 92*
**Bloomfield,** Lawrence B. 1938- *WhoEnt 92*
**Bloomfield,** Lincoln P. 1920- *WrDr 92*
**Bloomfield,** Louis Aub 1956- *AmMWSc 92*
**Bloomfield,** Louis J. 1936- *WhoIns 92*
**Bloomfield,** Mary Sue 1940- *WhoAmL 92*
**Bloomfield,** Maureen *DrAPF 91*
**Bloomfield,** Philip Earl 1934- *AmMWSc 92*
**Bloomfield,** Randall D. 1923- *WhoBlA 92*
**Bloomfield,** Robert 1766-1823 *RfGEnL 91*
**Bloomfield,** Robert Russell, Jr. 1955- *WhoEnt 92*
**Bloomfield,** Saul 1925- *AmMWSc 92*
**Bloomfield,** Theodore 1923- *NewAmDM*
**Bloomfield,** Victor Alfred 1938- *AmMWSc 92*
**Bloomgarden,** Alina 1944- *WhoEnt 92*
**Bloomgarden,** Kathleen Finn 1949- *WhoFI 92*
**Bloomingdale,** Arthur Lee, Jr. 1930- *WhoIns 92*
**Bloomquist,** Dennis Howard 1942- *WhoAmL 92*
**Bloomquist,** Edward Robert 1924- *WhoWest 92*
**Bloomquist,** Eunice 1940- *AmMWSc 92*

**Bloomquist,** George Elmer 1939- *WhoRel 92*
**Bloomquist,** Kenneth Gene 1931- *WhoEnt 92*
**Bloomquist,** Marvin Robert 1930- *WhoRel 92*
**Bloomsburg,** George L 1931- *AmMWSc 92*
**Bloor,** Colin Mercer 1933- *AmMWSc 92*
**Bloor,** David 1937- *Who 92*
**Bloor,** John E 1929- *AmMWSc 92*
**Bloor,** W Spencer 1918- *AmMWSc 92*
**Blos,** Joan 1928- *WrDr 92*
**Bloser,** Dieter 1944- *WhoMW 92*
**Bloskas,** John D. 1928- *WhoFI 92*
**Bloss,** Fred Donald 1920- *AmMWSc 92*
**Bloss,** Homer Earl 1933- *AmMWSc 92*
**Bloss,** Julie L. 1959- *WhoAmL 92*
**Bloss,** Richard 1934- *WhoFI 92*
**Blosse,** Richard Hely L. *Who 92*
**Blosser,** Henry Gabriel 1928- *AmMWSc 92*
**Blosser,** James Carlisle 1945- *AmMWSc 92*
**Blosser,** James Lee 1953- *WhoFI 92*
**Blosser,** Patricia Ellen 1931- *WhoMW 92*
**Blosser,** Timothy Hobert 1920- *AmMWSc 92*
**Blossey,** Erich Carl 1935- *AmMWSc 92*
**Blossom,** Beverly 1926- *WhoEnt 92*
**Blossom,** Charles N. 1935- *WhoIns 92*
**Blossom,** Laurel *DrAPF 91*
**Blossom,** Tifanie Theylon 1947- *WhoRel 92*
**Blostein,** Maier Lionel 1932- *AmMWSc 92*
**Blostein,** Rhoda 1936- *AmMWSc 92*
**Blot,** Jean *Who 92*
**Blot,** Thomas *ScFEYrs*
**Blot,** William James 1943- *AmMWSc 92*
**Blotcky,** Alan Jay 1930- *AmMWSc 92, WhoMW 92*
**Blotkamp,** Robert 1956- *WhoAmP 91*
**Blotner,** Joseph 1923- *ConAu 35NR, DcLB 111 [port], IntAu&W 91, WrDr 92*
**Blotnick,** Srully 1941- *WrDr 92*
**Blotzer,** Timothy Robert 1952- *WhoWest 92*
**Blouch,** Timothy Craig 1954- *WhoFI 92*
**Blouet,** Brian Walter 1936- *AmMWSc 92*
**Blough,** Herbert Allen 1929- *AmMWSc 92*
**Blough,** William LeRoy 1946- *WhoEnt 92*
**Blouin,** Andre 1945- *AmMWSc 92*
**Blouin,** Florine Alice 1931- *AmMWSc 92*
**Blouin,** Francis Xavier, Jr. 1946- *WhoMW 92*
**Blouin,** Georges Henri 1921- *IntWW 91*
**Blouin,** Glenn M 1919- *AmMWSc 92*
**Blouin,** Leonard Thomas 1930- *AmMWSc 92*
**Blouin,** Rose Louise 1948- *WhoBlA 92*
**Blount,** Bertie Kennedy 1907- *Who 92*
**Blount,** Charles E 1931- *AmMWSc 92*
**Blount,** Charlotte Renee 1952- *WhoBlA 92*
**Blount,** Clarence W 1921- *WhoAmP 91, WhoBlA 92*
**Blount,** David Laurence 1954- *WhoAmL 92*
**Blount,** Don Houston 1929- *AmMWSc 92*
**Blount,** Eugene Irving 1927- *AmMWSc 92*
**Blount,** Evelyn 1942- *WhoRel 92*
**Blount,** Floyd Eugene 1922- *AmMWSc 92*
**Blount,** Frederick 1778-1823 *DcNCBi 1*
**Blount,** Harry Neil 1944- *WhoWest 92*
**Blount,** Helon Jacqueline 1929- *WhoEnt 92*
**Blount,** Henry Clayton, Jr. 1925- *WhoRel 92*
**Blount,** Jacob 1726-1789 *DcNCBi 1*
**Blount,** James d1686 *DcNCBi 1*
**Blount,** John 1671-1726 *DcNCBi 1*
**Blount,** John Gray 1752-1833 *DcNCBi 1*
**Blount,** Joseph Lamar 1946- *WhoAmP 91*
**Blount,** Julius A 1926- *WhoAmP 91*
**Blount,** Larry Elisha 1950- *WhoBlA 92*
**Blount,** Lisa *IntMPA 92*
**Blount,** Mary Sumner 1777-1822 *DcNCBi 1*
**Blount,** Melvin Cornell 1948- *WhoBlA 92*
**Blount,** Michael 1963- *WhoFI 92*
**Blount,** Michael Eugene 1949- *WhoMW 92*
**Blount,** Nancy Munjiovi *WhoAmL 92*
**Blount,** Nathaniel 1748?-1816 *DcNCBi 1*
**Blount,** Reading 1757-1807 *DcNCBi 1*
**Blount,** Robert Arthur 1949- *WhoAmL 92*
**Blount,** Robert Grier 1938- *WhoFI 92*
**Blount,** Roy, Jr. 1941- *WrDr 92*
**Blount,** Roy Alton, Jr 1941- *WhoEnt 92*
**Blount,** Thomas d1706? *DcNCBi 1*
**Blount,** Thomas 1759-1812 *DcNCBi 1*
**Blount,** Tom *DcNCBi 1*
**Blount,** Walter 1917- *Who 92*
**Blount,** Wilbur Clanton 1929- *WhoBlA 92, WhoMW 92*
**Blount,** William *WhoAmP 91*
**Blount,** William 1749-1800 *DcNCBi 1*
**Blount,** William Allan 1954- *WhoAmP 91*
**Blount,** William Augustus 1792-1867 *DcNCBi 1*
**Blount,** William Grainger 1784-1827 *DcNCBi 1*
**Blount,** Willie 1768-1835 *DcNCBi 1*
**Blount,** Winton Malcolm 1921- *IntWW 91*
**Blount,** Winton Malcolm, III 1943- *WhoFI 92*
**Blouse,** Louis E, Jr 1931- *AmMWSc 92*
**Bloustein,** Laurence Charles 1949- *WhoWest 92*
**Blout,** Elkan R. 1919- *IntWW 91*
**Blout,** Elkan Rogers 1919- *AmMWSc 92*
**Blovits,** Larry John 1936- *WhoMW 92*
**Blow,** David Mervyn 1931- *IntWW 91, Who 92*
**Blow,** George 1928- *WhoAmL 92*
**Blow,** John 1649-1708 *NewAmDM*
**Blow,** John Needham 1905- *WhoWest 92*
**Blow,** Joyce 1929- *Who 92*
**Blow,** Sandra 1925- *IntWW 91, TwCPaSc, Who 92*
**Blow,** Sarah Parsons 1921- *WhoBlA 92*
**Blow,** Susan Elizabeth 1843-1916 *HanAmWH*
**Blowers,** Anthony John 1926- *Who 92*
**Blowers,** Bobbie 1944- *WhoMW 92*
**Blowers,** LaVerne Palmer 1940- *WhoMW 92, WhoRel 92*
**Bloxham,** Don Dee *AmMWSc 92*
**Bloxham,** Joseph A. 1933- *WhoWest 92*
**Bloxham,** Laurence Hastings 1945- *AmMWSc 92*
**Bloxom,** Donna Raye 1957- *WhoAmP 91*
**Bloxom,** Robert Spurgeon 1937- *WhoAmP 91*
**Bloy,** Francis Eric Irving 1904- *Who 92*
**Bloy,** Leon 1846-1917 *GuFrLit 1*
**Blozis,** George G 1929- *AmMWSc 92*
**Bluck,** Duncan Robert Yorke 1927- *IntWW 91, Who 92*
**Bludlworth,** David H. *NewYTBS 91 [port]*
**Bludman,** Sidney Arnold 1927- *AmMWSc 92*
**Bludson-Francis,** Vernett Michelle 1951- *WhoBlA 92*
**Blue Devils** *NewAmDM*
**Blue Jay Singers** *NewAmDM*
**Blue Sky Boys** *NewAmDM*
**Blue,** Betty Venus 1950- *WhoMW 92*
**Blue,** Bob 1943- *WhoEnt 92*
**Blue,** Charles Leroy 1915- *WhoFI 92*
**Blue,** Daniel T, Jr 1949- *WhoAmP 91*
**Blue,** Daniel Terry, Jr. 1949- *WhoBlA 92*
**Blue,** Daniel W., Jr. 1939- *WhoBlA 92*
**Blue,** E M 1912- *AmMWSc 92*
**Blue,** Harold Darrell 1937- *WhoEnt 92*
**Blue,** James Guthrie 1920- *WhoWest 92*
**Blue,** James Lawrence 1940- *AmMWSc 92*
**Blue,** James Monroe 1941- *WhoAmL 92*
**Blue,** James R, Sr 1939- *WhoAmP 91*
**Blue,** John Ronald 1935- *WhoRel 92*
**Blue,** Joseph Edward 1936- *AmMWSc 92*
**Blue,** Lionel 1930- *Who 92*
**Blue,** Marie Muffy 1961- *WhoFI 92*
**Blue,** Marts Donald 1932- *AmMWSc 92*
**Blue,** Michael Henry 1929- *AmMWSc 92*
**Blue,** Richard Arthur 1936- *AmMWSc 92*
**Blue,** Robert Linson 1912- *WhoFI 92*
**Blue,** Sherwood 1905- *WhoAmL 92*
**Blue,** Tyson 1952- *WhoEnt 92*
**Blue,** Victor 1865-1928 *DcNCBi 1*
**Blue,** Vida, Jr. 1949- *WhoBlA 92*
**Blue,** William Guard 1923- *AmMWSc 92*
**Blue Cloud,** Peter *DrAPF 91*
**Bluechel,** Alan Joseph 1924- *WhoAmP 91*
**Bluefarb,** Samuel M 1912- *AmMWSc 92*
**Bluemel,** Van 1934- *AmMWSc 92*
**Bluemle,** Lewis W, Jr 1921- *AmMWSc 92*
**Bluemle,** Paul Edward 1926- *WhoWest 92*
**Bluemle,** Robert Louis 1933- *WhoAmL 92*
**Bluestein,** Allen Channing 1926- *AmMWSc 92*
**Bluestein,** Ben Alfred 1918- *AmMWSc 92*
**Bluestein,** Bernard Richard 1925- *AmMWSc 92*
**Bluestein,** Burt 1939- *WhoEnt 92*
**Bluestein,** Claire 1926- *AmMWSc 92*
**Bluestein,** Edwin A., Jr. 1930- *WhoAmL 92*
**Bluestein,** Harold 1950- *WhoAmL 92*
**Bluestein,** Harry Gilbert 1939- *AmMWSc 92*
**Bluestein,** Howard Bruce 1948- *AmMWSc 92*
**Bluestein,** Judith Ann 1948- *WhoRel 92*
**Bluestein,** Maurice 1941- *WhoMW 92*
**Bluestein,** Paul Harold 1923- *WhoFI 92, WhoMW 92*
**Bluestein,** Steve Franklin 1947- *WhoEnt 92*
**Bluestein,** Theodore 1934- *AmMWSc 92*
**Bluestein,** Venus Weller 1933- *WhoMW 92*
**Bluestone,** Ellen Jane 1937- *WhoRel 92*
**Bluestone,** Henry 1914- *AmMWSc 92*
**Bluestone,** Irving 1917- *WhoAmP 91*
**Bluestone,** Jeffrey A 1953- *AmMWSc 92*
**Bluestone,** Stanton J. 1944- *WhoMW 92*
**Bluett,** Thomas Byron, Sr. 1931- *WhoMW 92*
**Bluford,** Grady L. 1930- *WhoBlA 92*
**Bluford,** Guion 1942- *FacFETw*
**Bluford,** Guion Stewart, Jr 1942- *AmMWSc 92, WhoBlA 92*
**Bluford,** Guy 1942- *ConBlB 2 [port]*
**Bluglass,** Robert Saul 1930- *Who 92*
**Bluh,** Bonnie *DrAPF 91*
**Bluher,** Hans 1888-1955 *EncTR 91*
**Bluhm,** Aaron Leo 1924- *AmMWSc 92*
**Bluhm,** Donna Fay 1932- *WhoAmP 91*
**Bluhm,** Harold Frederick 1927- *AmMWSc 92*
**Bluhm,** Heinz 1907- *WrDr 92*
**Bluhm,** Leslie 1940- *AmMWSc 92*
**Bluhm,** Myron Dean 1934- *WhoMW 92*
**Bluhm,** Neil G. 1938- *WhoFI 92*
**Bluhm,** Terry Lee 1947- *AmMWSc 92*
**Bluitt,** Benjamin 1924- *WhoBlA 92*
**Blum,** Albert A. 1924- *WrDr 92*
**Blum,** Alexandra Lynne 1956- *WhoFI 92*
**Blum,** Alvin Seymour 1926- *AmMWSc 92*
**Blum,** Andre 1931- *WhoMW 92*
**Blum,** Barbara Bennett 1930- *WhoAmP 91*
**Blum,** Barry 1940- *WhoWest 92*
**Blum,** Barton Morrill 1932- *AmMWSc 92*
**Blum,** Bruce I *AmMWSc 92*
**Blum,** David Arthur 1962- *WhoWest 92*
**Blum,** Edward H 1940- *AmMWSc 92*
**Blum,** Edward Howard 1940- *WhoFI 92*
**Blum,** Eleanor Goodfriend 1940- *WhoAmP 91*
**Blum,** Eric M. 1955- *WhoEnt 92*
**Blum,** Etta *DrAPF 91*
**Blum,** Eva Tansky 1949- *WhoAmL 92*
**Blum,** Fred A 1939- *AmMWSc 92*
**Blum,** Fred Andrew 1939- *WhoWest 92*
**Blum,** Harold A 1921- *AmMWSc 92*
**Blum,** Harry 1924- *AmMWSc 92*
**Blum,** Harry N. 1932- *IntMPA 92*
**Blum,** Ivan Jack 1947- *WhoWest 92*
**Blum,** Jacob Joseph 1926- *AmMWSc 92*
**Blum,** James Arnold 1942- *WhoIns 92*
**Blum,** Jeffrey Stuart 1947- *WhoAmL 92*
**Blum,** Jerome 1913- *WrDr 92*
**Blum,** John Alan 1933- *WhoWest 92*
**Blum,** John Bennett 1952- *AmMWSc 92*
**Blum,** John Christian 1784-1854 *DcNCBi 1*
**Blum,** John Leo 1917- *AmMWSc 92*
**Blum,** Jon H. 1944- *WhoMW 92*
**Blum,** Joseph 1919- *AmMWSc 92*
**Blum,** Kenneth 1939- *AmMWSc 92*
**Blum,** Kevin John 1956- *WhoMW 92*
**Blum,** Lee M 1956- *AmMWSc 92*
**Blum,** Lenore Carol 1942- *AmMWSc 92*
**Blum,** Leon 1872-1950 *EncTR 91, FacFETw*
**Blum,** Leon Leib 1908- *AmMWSc 92*
**Blum,** Lesser 1934- *AmMWSc 92*
**Blum,** Manuel 1938- *AmMWSc 92*
**Blum,** Marc Paul 1942- *WhoAmL 92*
**Blum,** Mark 1950- *IntMPA 92*
**Blum,** Mark Emanuel 1937- *IntAu&W 91*
**Blum,** Marvin 1928- *AmMWSc 92*
**Blum,** Michael Stephen 1939- *WhoFI 92, WhoMW 92*
**Blum,** Murray Sheldon 1929- *AmMWSc 92*
**Blum,** Norbert 1935- *IntWW 91*
**Blum,** Norman Allen 1932- *AmMWSc 92*
**Blum,** Patricia Rae 1948- *AmMWSc 92*
**Blum,** Peter 1950- *WhoFI 92*
**Blum,** Richard 1913- *AmMWSc 92*
**Blum,** Richard A 1943- *IntAu&W 91*
**Blum,** Richard Arthur 1943- *WhoEnt 92*
**Blum,** Richard L., Jr. d1991 *NewYTBS 91*
**Blum,** Robert Allan 1938- *AmMWSc 92*
**Blum,** Samuel Emil 1920- *AmMWSc 92*
**Blum,** Seymour L 1925- *AmMWSc 92*
**Blum,** Sheri Ellen 1957- *WhoRel 92*
**Blum,** Stanley Walter 1933- *AmMWSc 92*
**Blum,** Susan Waite 1940- *IntAu&W 91*
**Blum,** Udo 1939- *AmMWSc 92*
**Blum,** Walter J. 1918- *WhoAmL 92, WhoMW 92*
**Blum,** William Henry 1933- *WhoWest 92*
**Blum,** William L 1952- *WhoAmP 91*
**Blum,** Yehuda Z. 1931- *IntWW 91*
**Blumberg,** Alan Fred 1948- *AmMWSc 92*
**Blumberg,** Arnold 1925- *IntAu&W 91, WrDr 92*
**Blumberg,** Avrom Aaron 1928- *AmMWSc 92*
**Blumberg,** Baruch Samuel 1925- *AmMWSc 92, FacFETw, IntWW 91, Who 92, WhoNob 90*
**Blumberg,** Daniel Edward 1959- *WhoAmL 92*
**Blumberg,** David Russell 1956- *WhoAmP 91*
**Blumberg,** Edward Robert 1951- *WhoAmL 92*
**Blumberg,** Grace Ganz 1940- *WhoAmL 92*
**Blumberg,** Harold 1909- *AmMWSc 92*
**Blumberg,** Jeffrey Bernard 1945- *AmMWSc 92*
**Blumberg,** John Philip 1949- *WhoAmL 92*
**Blumberg,** Laurence James 1961- *WhoFI 92*
**Blumberg,** Leroy Norman 1929- *AmMWSc 92*
**Blumberg,** Mark Stuart 1924- *AmMWSc 92*
**Blumberg,** Patricia Helene 1956- *WhoAmL 92*
**Blumberg,** Peter Mitchell 1949- *AmMWSc 92*
**Blumberg,** Phillip I 1919- *ConAu 35NR*
**Blumberg,** Phillip Irvin 1919- *WhoAmL 92, WrDr 92*
**Blumberg,** Rhoda 1917- *WrDr 92*
**Blumberg,** Richard Winston 1914- *AmMWSc 92*
**Blumberg,** Robert Lee 1942- *WhoFI 92, WhoWest 92*
**Blumberg,** Robert S. 1943- *WhoFI 92*
**Blumberg,** Stuart Lester 1947- *WhoEnt 92*
**Blumberg,** William Emil 1930- *AmMWSc 92*
**Blume,** Arthur Joel 1941- *AmMWSc 92*
**Blume,** August Gerard 1927- *WhoEnt 92*
**Blume,** Frederick Duane 1933- *AmMWSc 92*
**Blume,** Hans-Juergen Christian 1926- *AmMWSc 92*
**Blume,** James Donald 1950- *WhoAmL 92*
**Blume,** John A 1909- *AmMWSc 92*
**Blume,** Judy 1938- *BenetAL 91, IntAu&W 91, WrDr 92*
**Blume,** Judy Sussman 1938- *WhoEnt 92*
**Blume,** Lawrence Dayton 1948- *WhoAmL 92*
**Blume,** Marshall Edward 1941- *WhoFI 92*
**Blume,** Martin 1932- *AmMWSc 92*
**Blume,** Norbert L 1922- *WhoAmP 91*
**Blume,** Paul Chiappe 1929- *WhoAmL 92, WhoMW 92*
**Blume,** Peter 1906- *IntWW 91*
**Blume,** Sheila Bierman 1934- *AmMWSc 92*
**Blume,** Willis Leon 1944- *WhoEnt 92*
**Blumen,** William 1931- *AmMWSc 92*
**Blumenbach,** Johann Friedrich 1752-1840 *BlkwCEP*
**Blumenfeld,** Charles Raban 1944- *WhoAmL 92*
**Blumenfeld,** Eli 1933- *WhoAmL 92*
**Blumenfeld,** Gerald Martin 1939- *WhoAmL 92*
**Blumenfeld,** Harold 1905?-1991 *ConAu 133*
**Blumenfeld,** Henry A 1925- *AmMWSc 92*
**Blumenfeld,** Jack Barry 1952- *WhoAmL 92*
**Blumenfeld,** John Allen, Jr. 1954- *WhoAmL 92*
**Blumenfeld,** Martin 1941- *AmMWSc 92*
**Blumenfeld,** Michael Hugh 1957- *WhoMW 92*
**Blumenfeld,** Olga O 1923- *AmMWSc 92*
**Blumenfeld,** Sue Deborah 1952- *WhoAmL 92*
**Blumenfield,** David 1928- *AmMWSc 92*
**Blumenkrantz,** Jeff 1965- *WhoEnt 92*
**Blumenkrantz,** Steven Jay 1946- *WhoFI 92*
**Blumenreich,** Julia *DrAPF 91*
**Blumenshine,** Mahlon 1928- *WhoMW 92*
**Blumenson,** Leslie Eli 1934- *AmMWSc 92*
**Blumenson,** Martin 1918- *WrDr 92*
**Blumenstein,** Michael 1947- *AmMWSc 92*
**Blumenstock,** David A 1927- *AmMWSc 92*
**Blumenstock,** Michael Allen 1959- *WhoFI 92*
**Blumenstock,** Sid *IntMPA 92*
**Blumenthal,** Bob 1940- *WhoEnt 92*
**Blumenthal,** Charles S 1924- *WhoAmP 91*
**Blumenthal,** Gary Howard 1954- *WhoAmP 91*
**Blumenthal,** George Ray 1945- *AmMWSc 92*
**Blumenthal,** Gerda Renee 1923- *WrDr 92*
**Blumenthal,** Harold Jay 1926- *AmMWSc 92, WhoMW 92*
**Blumenthal,** Herbert 1925- *AmMWSc 92*
**Blumenthal,** Herman T 1913- *AmMWSc 92*
**Blumenthal,** Howard J. 1952- *WhoEnt 92*
**Blumenthal,** Irwin S 1925- *AmMWSc 92*
**Blumenthal,** John Frederick 1949- *WhoEnt 92*
**Blumenthal,** Kenneth Michael 1945- *AmMWSc 92*
**Blumenthal,** Marcia *DrAPF 91*
**Blumenthal,** Michael 1949- *BenetAL 91*
**Blumenthal,** Michael C. *DrAPF 91*
**Blumenthal,** Ralph Herbert 1925- *AmMWSc 92*
**Blumenthal,** Richard *WhoAmL 92, WhoAmP 91*
**Blumenthal,** Richard Cary 1951- *WhoWest 92*
**Blumenthal,** Robert Allan 1951- *AmMWSc 92*
**Blumenthal,** Robert Martin 1951- *AmMWSc 92*
**Blumenthal,** Robert McCallum 1931- *AmMWSc 92*
**Blumenthal,** Robert N 1934- *AmMWSc 92*

**Blumenthal**, Robert Paul 1938- *AmMWSc 92*
**Blumenthal**, Ronnie 1944- *WhoAmL 92*
**Blumenthal**, Rosa Lee *WhoAmP 91*
**Blumenthal**, Rosalyn D 1959- *AmMWSc 92*
**Blumenthal**, Saul 1935- *AmMWSc 92*
**Blumenthal**, Sidney 1948- *IntAu&W 91, WrDr 92*
**Blumenthal**, Thomas *AmMWSc 92*
**Blumenthal**, W. Michael 1926- *IntWW 91, Who 92, WhoAmP 91*
**Blumenthal**, Werner Michael 1926- *WhoFI 92, WhoMW 92*
**Blumenthal**, William 1955- *WhoAmL 92*
**Blumer**, Abraham *DcAmImH*
**Blumer**, Jeffrey L 1951- *AmMWSc 92*
**Blumer**, Rodney Milnes 1936- *Who 92*
**Blumfield**, Clifford William 1922- *Who 92*
**Blumgart**, Leslie Harold 1931- *IntWW 91, Who 92*
**Blumhagen**, Vern Allen 1929- *AmMWSc 92*
**Blumhardt**, Jon Howard 1951- *WhoWest 92*
**Bluming**, Sidney David 1944- *WhoAmL 92*
**Blumkin**, Linda Ruth 1944- *WhoAmL 92*
**Blumm**, Michael Charles 1950- *WhoWest 92*
**Blummer**, Kathleen Ann 1945- *WhoWest 92*
**Blumofe**, Robert F. *IntMPA 92*
**Blumofe**, Robert Fulton *WhoEnt 92*
**Blumrosen**, Alfred William 1928- *WhoAmL 92*
**Blumrosen**, Ruth Gerber 1927- *WhoAmL 92*
**Blumstein**, Alexandre 1930- *AmMWSc 92*
**Blumstein**, Alfred 1930- *AmMWSc 92*
**Blumstein**, Andree Kahn 1945- *WhoAmL 92*
**Blumstein**, Carl Joseph 1942- *AmMWSc 92*
**Blumstein**, Edward 1933- *WhoAmL 92*
**Blumstein**, James Franklin 1945- *WhoAmL 92*
**Blumstein**, Rita Blattberg 1937- *AmMWSc 92*
**Blumstein**, William A. 1948- *WhoFI 92*
**Blunck**, Hans Friedrich 1888-1961 *EncTR 91 [port]*
**Blunck**, Hanz Freidrich 1888-1961 *BiDExR*
**Blunck**, Lawrence Paul 1956- *WhoAmL 92*
**Blundell**, Daphne Mary 1916- *Who 92*
**Blundell**, Derek 1929- *ConAu 135*
**Blundell**, Derek John 1933- *Who 92*
**Blundell**, George Phelan *AmMWSc 92*
**Blundell**, James *WhoRel 92*
**Blundell**, James Kenneth 1949- *AmMWSc 92*
**Blundell**, Michael 1907- *IntWW 91, Who 92*
**Blundell**, Thomas Leon 1942- *IntWW 91, Who 92*
**Blundell**, William Richard Charles 1927- *IntWW 91, WhoFI 92*
**Blunden**, Edmund 1896-1974 *RfGEnL 91*
**Blunden**, George 1922- *IntWW 91, Who 92*
**Blunden**, Philip 1922- *Who 92*
**Blunden**, Vide Rebecca 1912- *WhoEnt 92*
**Blundon**, Joseph Andrew 1926- *WhoAmL 92*
**Blundstone**, Ferdinand Victor 1882-1951 *TwCPaSc*
**Blunk**, Christian Raymond 1958- *WhoAmL 92*
**Blunkett**, David 1947- *Who 92*
**Blunson**, Samuel James 1931- *WhoFI 92*
**Blunt**, Anthony 1907-1983 *FacFETw*
**Blunt**, Charles William 1951- *IntWW 91, Who 92*
**Blunt**, David John 1944- *Who 92*
**Blunt**, David Richard Reginald Harvey 1938- *Who 92*
**Blunt**, Don *IntAu&W 91X, TwCWW 91, WrDr 92*
**Blunt**, Edmund 1799-1866 *BiInAmS*
**Blunt**, Edmund March 1770-1862 *BiInAmS*
**Blunt**, George William 1802-1878 *BiInAmS*
**Blunt**, Leroy 1921- *WhoAmP 91*
**Blunt**, Madelyne Bowen *WhoBlA 92*
**Blunt**, Peter 1923- *Who 92*
**Blunt**, Peter Howe 1945- *WhoWest 92*
**Blunt**, Raymond Stewart 1943- *WhoAmP 91*
**Blunt**, Robert Matteson 1916- *WhoWest 92*
**Blunt**, Roger Reckling 1930- *WhoBlA 92*
**Blunt**, Roy D 1950- *WhoAmP 91, WhoMW 92*
**Blunt**, Tom 1675?-1739? *DcNCBi 1*
**Blunt**, Wilfrid Scawen 1840-1922 *RfGEnL 91*
**Blurton**, Keith F 1940- *AmMWSc 92*
**Blute**, Joseph Galvin 1957- *WhoAmL 92*
**Blute**, Peter I 1956- *WhoAmP 91*
**Bluth**, Don *IntMPA 92*
**Bluthardt**, Edward Earl 1916- *WhoAmP 91*
**Bluthner**, Julius *NewAmDM*
**Blutstein**, Harvey M. 1927- *WhoIns 92*
**Blutza**, Steven Jay 1945- *WhoMW 92*
**Bluyssen**, Johannes Wilhelmus Maria 1926- *IntWW 91*
**Bluzer**, Nathan 1947- *AmMWSc 92*
**Bly**, Belden G, Jr *WhoAmP 91*
**Bly**, Belden Gerald, Jr. 1914- *WhoAmL 92*
**Bly**, Carol *DrAPF 91*
**Bly**, Chauncey Goodrich 1920- *AmMWSc 92*
**Bly**, David Alan 1953- *WhoWest 92*
**Bly**, Donald David 1936- *AmMWSc 92*
**Bly**, Nellie *BenetAL 91*
**Bly**, Nellie 1865-1922 *HanAmWH*
**Bly**, Robert *DrAPF 91*
**Bly**, Robert 1926- *BenetAL 91, ConPo 91, FacFETw, IntAu&W 91, IntWW 91, WrDr 92*
**Bly**, Robert Stewart 1929- *AmMWSc 92*
**Bly**, Sara A 1946- *AmMWSc 92*
**Bly**, William J. *DrAPF 91*
**Blye**, Allan, and Bearde, Chris *LesBEnT 92*
**Blye**, Cecil A., Sr. 1927- *WhoBlA 92*
**Blye**, Douglas William Alfred 1924- *Who 92*
**Blye**, Margaret Jane *WhoEnt 92*
**Blye**, Richard Perry 1932- *AmMWSc 92*
**Blyholder**, George Donald 1931- *AmMWSc 92*
**Blyler**, Lee Landis, Jr 1938- *AmMWSc 92*
**Blyler**, William Edward 1936- *WhoAmL 92*
**Blymyer**, William Hervey 1865-1939 *AmPeW*
**Blystone**, Robert Vernon 1943- *AmMWSc 92*
**Blytas**, George Constantin 1930- *AmMWSc 92*
**Blyth** *Who 92*
**Blyth**, Baron 1931- *Who 92*
**Blyth**, Alan Geoffrey 1929- *WrDr 92*
**Blyth**, Ann 1928- *IntMPA 92*
**Blyth**, Ann Marie 1949- *WhoMW 92*
**Blyth**, Charles 1940- *Who 92*
**Blyth**, Chay 1940- *IntAu&W 91, WrDr 92*
**Blyth**, Colin Ross 1922- *AmMWSc 92*
**Blyth**, James 1940- *IntWW 91, Who 92*
**Blyth**, John *WrDr 92*
**Blyth**, John Douglas Morrison 1924- *Who 92*
**Blyth**, John E. 1931- *WhoAmL 92*
**Blyth**, John Stevenson 1931- *WhoFI 92*
**Blyth**, Michael Leslie 1950- *WhoFI 92*
**Blyth**, Myrna 1939- *IntAu&W 91*
**Blythe**, David K 1917- *AmMWSc 92*
**Blythe**, Jack Gordon 1922- *AmMWSc 92*
**Blythe**, James David, II 1940- *WhoAmL 92*
**Blythe**, James Forbes 1917- *Who 92*
**Blythe**, Mark Andrew 1943- *Who 92*
**Blythe**, Mary Algeron 1932- *WhoRel 92*
**Blythe**, Philip Anthony 1937- *AmMWSc 92*
**Blythe**, Rex Arnold 1928- *Who 92*
**Blythe**, Robert Richard 1949- *WhoRel 92*
**Blythe**, Ronald 1922- *WrDr 92*
**Blythe**, Ronald George 1922- *IntAu&W 91*
**Blythe**, William Brevard 1928- *AmMWSc 92*
**Blythe**, William Jackson, Jr 1935- *WhoAmP 91*
**Blythe**, William Richard 1931- *AmMWSc 92*
**Blyukher**, Vasiliy Konstantinovich 1890-1938 *SovUnBD*
**Blyumenental'-Tamarina**, Maria M. 1859-1938 *SovUnBD*
**Bo Yibo** 1908- *IntWW 91*
**Bo**, Jorgen 1919- *IntWW 91*
**Bo**, Ning 1960- *WhoWest 92*
**Bo**, Walter John 1923- *AmMWSc 92*
**Bo-Boliko Lokonga Monse Mihomo** 1934- *IntWW 91*
**Boa**, Kenneth Dale 1945- *WhoRel 92*
**Boackle**, Robert J *AmMWSc 92*
**Boade**, Rodney Russett 1935- *AmMWSc 92*
**Boadicea** *EncAmaz 91*
**Boado**, Ruben Jose 1955- *WhoWest 92*
**Boadt**, Lawrence Edward 1942- *WhoRel 92*
**Boadway**, John Douglas 1922- *AmMWSc 92*
**Boag**, David Archibald 1934- *AmMWSc 92*
**Boag**, John Wilson 1911- *Who 92*
**Boag**, Thomas Johnson 1922- *AmMWSc 92*
**Boags**, Charles D. 1929- *WhoBlA 92*
**Boak**, Bruce Gordon 1947- *WhoRel 92*
**Boal**, Brett Alan 1960- *WhoFI 92*
**Boal**, David Harold 1948- *AmMWSc 92*
**Boal**, Dean 1931- *WhoEnt 92*
**Boal**, Graham 1943- *Who 92*
**Boal**, Jan List 1930- *AmMWSc 92*
**Boal**, Marcia Anne Riley 1944- *WhoMW 92*
**Boal**, Peter Cadbury 1965- *WhoEnt 92*
**Boalch**, Donald Howard 1914- *WrDr 92*
**Boam**, Jeffrey David 1949- *WhoEnt 92*
**Boam**, Thomas Anthony 1932- *Who 92*
**Boan**, William D 1949- *WhoAmP 91*
**Boand**, Charles Wilbur 1908- *WhoAmL 92, WhoFI 92, WhoMW 92*
**Board**, Dwaine 1956- *WhoBlA 92*
**Board**, James Ellery 1948- *AmMWSc 92*
**Board**, John Arnold 1931- *AmMWSc 92*
**Board**, Joseph Breckinridge 1931- *WhoAmP 91*
**Boardley**, Curtestine May 1943- *WhoBlA 92*
**Boardman** *Who 92*
**Boardman**, Baron 1919- *IntWW 91, Who 92*
**Boardman**, Donald Peter 1939- *WhoRel 92*
**Boardman**, Eleanor d1991 *NewYTBS 91*
**Boardman**, Eunice 1926- *WhoEnt 92*
**Boardman**, Fon W, Jr 1911- *IntAu&W 91, WrDr 92*
**Boardman**, Gregory Dale 1950- *AmMWSc 92*
**Boardman**, Harold 1907- *Who 92*
**Boardman**, Harold Frederick, Jr. 1939- *WhoAmL 92, WhoFI 92*
**Boardman**, John 1927- *IntAu&W 91, Who 92, WrDr 92*
**Boardman**, John 1932- *AmMWSc 92*
**Boardman**, John Michael 1938- *AmMWSc 92*
**Boardman**, Katherine Anne 1961- *WhoRel 92*
**Boardman**, Kay Irene 1939- *WhoWest 92*
**Boardman**, Kenneth 1914- *Who 92*
**Boardman**, Lowell Jay 1948- *WhoWest 92*
**Boardman**, Mark R 1950- *AmMWSc 92*
**Boardman**, Mark Robert 1950- *WhoMW 92*
**Boardman**, Mark Seymour 1958- *WhoAmL 92*
**Boardman**, Michael Neil 1942- *WhoAmL 92*
**Boardman**, Norman D. 1932- *WhoIns 92*
**Boardman**, Norman Keith 1926- *IntWW 91, Who 92*
**Boardman**, Richard John 1940- *WhoAmL 92*
**Boardman**, Robert Emmett 1932- *WhoAmP 91*
**Boardman**, Rosanne Virginia 1946- *WhoWest 92*
**Boardman**, Shelby Jett 1944- *AmMWSc 92*
**Boardman**, True Eames 1909- *WhoEnt 92*
**Boardman**, William Jarvis 1939- *AmMWSc 92*
**Boardman**, William Penniman 1941- *WhoMW 92*
**Boardman**, William Todd 1949- *WhoAmL 92*
**Boardman**, William Walter, Jr 1916- *AmMWSc 92*
**Boaretto**, Claire 1947- *ConAu 134*
**Boarini**, Edward James 1949- *WhoFI 92, WhoWest 92*
**Boarman**, Gerald Jude 1940- *WhoFI 92*
**Boarman**, Patrick Madigan 1922- *WhoWest 92*
**Boas**, Frank 1930- *WhoAmL 92*
**Boas**, Franz 1858-1942 *FacFETw*
**Boas**, Mary Layne 1917- *AmMWSc 92*
**Boas**, Norman Francis 1922- *AmMWSc 92*
**Boas**, Ralph Philip, Jr 1912- *AmMWSc 92*
**Boase**, Martin 1932- *IntWW 91, Who 92*
**Boast**, Charles Warren 1943- *AmMWSc 92*
**Boast**, Philip 1952- *ConAu 135*
**Boast**, W B 1909- *AmMWSc 92*
**Boat**, Ronald Allen 1947- *WhoWest 92*
**Boaten**, Frank Edmund 1923- *IntWW 91*
**Boateng**, Ernest Amano 1920- *IntWW 91, Who 92*
**Boateng**, Paul Yaw 1951- *Who 92*
**Boatman**, Edwin S 1921- *AmMWSc 92*
**Boatman**, Joe Francis 1949- *AmMWSc 92*
**Boatman**, Kara Teevan 1962- *WhoFI 92*
**Boatman**, Ralph Henry, Jr 1921- *AmMWSc 92*
**Boatman**, Sandra 1939- *AmMWSc 92*
**Boatner**, Lynn Allen 1938- *AmMWSc 92*
**Boatner**, Roy Alton 1941- *WhoAmP 91*
**Boatright**, Joanna Morson 1958- *WhoFI 92*
**Boatwright**, Charlotte Jeanne 1937- *WhoFI 92*
**Boatwright**, Christopher Monroe 1954- *WhoEnt 92*
**Boatwright**, Daniel E 1930- *WhoAmP 91*
**Boatwright**, Helen 1916- *NewAmDM*
**Boatwright**, Howard 1918- *NewAmDM*
**Boatwright**, John Baker, III 1952- *WhoAmL 92*
**Boatwright**, Joseph Weldon 1949- *WhoBlA 92*
**Boatwright**, M Tracy 1942- *WhoAmP 91*
**Boatwright**, Mary H 1920- *WhoAmP 91*
**Boatwright**, McHenry 1928- *NewAmDM*
**Boatwright**, McHenry Rutherford 1928- *WhoBlA 92*
**Boatwright**, P J, Jr. d1991 *NewYTBS 91*
**Boaz**, David Paul 1944- *AmMWSc 92*
**Boaz**, James D. *WhoEnt 92*
**Boaz**, John Knox 1938- *WhoMW 92*
**Boaz**, Patricia Anne 1922- *AmMWSc 92*
**Boaz**, Stephen Scott 1948- *WhoAmL 92*
**Bob and Ray** *FacFETw*
**Bobadilla**, Francisco de d1502 *HisDSpE*
**Bobadilla**, Jose Roberto 1959- *WhoFI 92*
**Bobadilla**, Tomasito Nilson 1961- *WhoEnt 92*
**Bobalek**, Edward G 1915- *AmMWSc 92*
**Bobb**, Dusan 1949- *WhoEnt 92*
**Bobb**, Harold Daniel 1952- *WhoMW 92*
**Bobb**, L. Edward 1951- *WhoIns 92*
**Bobb**, Marvin Lester 1911- *AmMWSc 92*
**Bobbin**, Richard Peter 1942- *AmMWSc 92*
**Bobbio**, Norberto 1909- *IntWW 91*
**Bobbitt**, Donald Robert 1956- *AmMWSc 92*
**Bobbitt**, Jesse LeRoy 1933- *AmMWSc 92*
**Bobbitt**, Leroy 1943- *WhoBlA 92*
**Bobbitt**, Oliver Bierne 1917- *AmMWSc 92*
**Bobbitt**, Philip Chase 1948- *WhoAmL 92*
**Bobco**, William David, Jr. 1946- *WhoMW 92*
**Bobcock**, Floyd C. *WhoRel 92*
**Bobear**, Jean B 1922- *AmMWSc 92*
**Bobechko**, Walter Peter 1932- *AmMWSc 92*
**Bobeck**, Andrew H 1926- *AmMWSc 92*
**Bobel**, Ronald Emmett 1939- *WhoAmP 91*
**Bober**, Anne Marie 1948- *WhoFI 92*
**Bober**, Harold Lewis 1936- *WhoWest 92*
**Bober**, Lawrence Harold 1924- *WhoFI 92*
**Bober**, William 1930- *AmMWSc 92*
**Boberski**, William George 1947- *WhoMW 92*
**Bobette** *ConAu 35NR*
**Bobier**, Bill *WhoAmP 91*
**Bobillo**, Raymond Manuel 1929- *WhoFI 92, WhoMW 92*
**Bobino**, Rita Florencia 1934- *WhoBlA 92*
**Bobinski**, George S. 1929- *WrDr 92*
**Bobinski**, George Sylvan 1929- *IntAu&W 91*
**Bobinski**, Mary Anne 1962- *WhoAmL 92*
**Bobisud**, Larry Eugene 1940- *AmMWSc 92*
**Bobka**, Rudolph J 1928- *AmMWSc 92*
**Bobko**, Edward 1925- *AmMWSc 92*
**Bobko**, John B. 1956- *WhoFI 92*
**Bobkov**, Filipp Denisovich 1925- *IntWW 91*
**Boblitt**, Robert LeRoy 1925- *AmMWSc 92*
**Bobo**, Edwin Ray 1938- *AmMWSc 92*
**Bobo**, Jack E. 1924- *WhoIns 92*
**Bobo**, Jack Edward 1924- *WhoFI 92*
**Bobo**, Leslie Joyner 1958- *WhoAmL 92*
**Bobo**, Melvin 1924- *AmMWSc 92*
**Bobo**, Richard Lee 1940- *WhoEnt 92*
**Bobo**, Roscoe Lemual 1912- *WhoBlA 92*
**Boboc**, Nicolae 1920- *WhoEnt 92*
**Bobonich**, Harry Michael 1924- *AmMWSc 92*
**Bobonis**, Augusto 1907- *AmMWSc 92*
**Bobovikov**, Ratmir Stepanovich 1927- *IntWW 91*
**Bobowick**, Morton 1942- *WhoAmL 92*
**Bobrick**, William David 1955- *WhoAmP 91*
**Bobrinskoy**, Charles Kellogg 1959- *WhoFI 92*
**Bobroff**, Harold 1920- *WhoAmP 91*
**Bobrofsky**, Albert C 1933- *WhoAmP 91*
**Bobrow**, Alvan Lee 1949- *WhoEnt 92, WhoFI 92*
**Bobrow**, Andrew C. 1949- *WhoEnt 92*
**Bobrow**, Daniel G 1935- *AmMWSc 92*
**Bobrow**, Leonard S 1940- *AmMWSc 92*
**Bobrow**, Martin 1938- *Who 92*
**Bobrowski**, Czeslaw 1904- *IntWW 91*
**Bobrowski**, Joseph Anthony, Jr. 1962- *WhoFI 92*
**Bobst**, Albert M 1939- *AmMWSc 92*
**Bobykin**, Leonid Fedorovich 1930- *IntWW 91*
**Bobyshev**, Dmitri Vasilevich 1936- *IntWW 91*
**Bobyshev**, Dmitriy Vasil'evich 1936- *SovUnBD*
**Bocaccio** *DrAPF 91*
**Bocage**, Ronald J. 1946- *WhoBlA 92*
**Bocanegra**, Gertrudis d1817 *EncAmaz 91*
**Bocarsly**, Andrew B 1954- *AmMWSc 92*
**Bocca**, Julio *WhoEnt 92, WhoHisp 92*
**Boccabella**, Anthony Vincent *AmMWSc 92*
**Boccara**, Bruno 1958- *WhoFI 92*
**Boccella**, Claire M. 1955- *WhoAmL 92*
**Boccherini**, Luigi 1743-1805 *NewAmDM*
**Bocchini**, Arturo 1880-1940 *BiDExR*
**Bocchini**, Joseph L, Jr 1944- *WhoAmP 91*
**Bocchino**, Linda Elizabeth 1948- *WhoFI 92*
**Bocchino**, Robert Louis 1936- *WhoEnt 92*

**Boccia,** Allison Briner 1957- *WhoEnt 92*
**Boccia,** Maria Liboria 1953- *WhoWest 92*
**Boccio,** Karen Corinne *DrAPF 91*
**Boccioni,** Umberto *DcTwDes*
**Boccitto,** Bonnie L. 1949- *WhoIns 92*
**Boccitto,** Elio *WhoFI 92*
**Boch,** Henry Lawrence 1946- *WhoFI 92*
**Bochco,** Steve 1943- *WhoEnt 92*
**Bochco,** Steven *LesBEnT 92*
**Bochco,** Steven 1943- *CurBio 91 [port], IntMPA 92*
**Bochenek,** Wieslaw Janusz 1938- *AmMWSc 92*
**Bochenski,** Joseph 1902- *IntWW 91*
**Bocher,** Maxime 1867-1918 *BiInAmS*
**Bochet,** Bernard Adrien Jacques 1926- *IntWW 91*
**Bochinski,** Pamela D. 1941- *WhoAmL 92*
**Bochner,** Barry Ronald *AmMWSc 92*
**Bochner,** Hart 1956- *IntMPA 92, WhoEnt 92*
**Bochner,** Lloyd 1924- *IntMPA 92, WhoEnt 92*
**Bock,** Arthur E 1916- *AmMWSc 92*
**Bock,** Bennie W, II 1942- *WhoAmP 91*
**Bock,** Carl E 1942- *AmMWSc 92*
**Bock,** Charles Walter 1945- *AmMWSc 92*
**Bock,** Claus Victor 1926- *Who 92*
**Bock,** Darilyn Winifred 1946- *WhoAmL 92, WhoFI 92*
**Bock,** Darrell Lane 1953- *WhoRel 92*
**Bock,** Edward John 1916- *IntWW 91*
**Bock,** Ernst 1929- *AmMWSc 92*
**Bock,** Fedor von 1880-1945 *EncTR 91 [port]*
**Bock,** Frank F 1912- *WhoAmP 91*
**Bock,** Fred 1939- *WhoWest 92*
**Bock,** Fred G 1923- *AmMWSc 92*
**Bock,** Frederick *DrAPF 91*
**Bock,** Fritz 1911- *IntWW 91*
**Bock,** Gregory William 1951- *WhoMW 92*
**Bock,** Hans 1928- *IntWW 91*
**Bock,** J. John 1931- *WhoMW 92*
**Bock,** Jane Haskett 1936- *AmMWSc 92*
**Bock,** Jeffrey William 1950- *WhoWest 92*
**Bock,** Jerry 1928- *IntWW 91, NewAmDM, WhoEnt 92*
**Bock,** Joseph Gerard 1957- *WhoAmP 91*
**Bock,** Keith Charles 1954- *WhoFI 92*
**Bock,** Lothar *LesBEnT 92*
**Bock,** Mark Gary 1946- *AmMWSc 92*
**Bock,** Mitchell 1951- *WhoEnt 92*
**Bock,** Paul 1926- *AmMWSc 92*
**Bock,** Paul John 1922- *WhoRel 92*
**Bock,** Peter Ernest 1948- *WhoAmP 91*
**Bock,** Philip Karl 1934- *WrDr 92*
**Bock,** Robert M. d1991 *NewYTBS 91*
**Bock,** Robert Manley 1923- *AmMWSc 92*
**Bock,** S Allan 1946- *AmMWSc 92*
**Bock,** Walter Joseph 1933- *AmMWSc 92*
**Bock,** Wayne Dean 1932- *AmMWSc 92*
**Bock/Pallant,** Layeh *DrAPF 91*
**Bockel,** Otto 1859-1923 *BiDExR, EncTR 91*
**Bockelman,** Charles Kincaid 1922- *AmMWSc 92*
**Bockelman,** John Richard 1925- *WhoAmL 92, WhoFI 92, WhoMW 92*
**Bockelmann,** John B 1915- *AmMWSc 92*
**Bockemuehl,** R R 1927- *AmMWSc 92*
**Bockemuehl,** Richard George 1939- *WhoAmP 91*
**Bocker,** Gerard Joseph 1958- *WhoEnt 92*
**Bockerstette,** Joseph A. 1957- *WhoFI 92*
**Bockhoff,** Frank James 1928- *AmMWSc 92*
**Bockholt,** Anton John 1930- *AmMWSc 92*
**Bockian,** James Bernard 1936- *WhoFI 92*
**Bockle,** Franz 1921- *IntWW 91*
**Bockman,** Dale Edward 1935- *AmMWSc 92*
**Bockman,** Miriam Levine 1931- *WhoAmP 91*
**Bockman,** Richard Steven 1941- *AmMWSc 92*
**Bockmon,** Harthia W 1932- *WhoAmP 91*
**Bocko,** Mark Frederick 1956- *AmMWSc 92*
**Bockosh,** George R 1951- *AmMWSc 92*
**Bockover,** James D. 1945- *WhoFI 92*
**Bockrath,** Bradley Charles 1942- *AmMWSc 92*
**Bockrath,** Richard Charles, Jr 1938- *AmMWSc 92*
**Bockris,** John O'Mara 1923- *AmMWSc 92*
**Bockris,** Victor *DrAPF 91*
**Bocksch,** Robert Donald 1931- *AmMWSc 92*
**Bockstahler,** Larry Earl 1934- *AmMWSc 92*
**Bockstahler,** Theodore Edwin 1920- *AmMWSc 92*
**Bockstein,** Herbert 1943- *WhoAmL 92*
**Bockus,** C. Barry 1934- *WhoFI 92*
**Bocock,** Maclin *DrAPF 91*
**Bocock,** Robert James 1940- *WrDr 92*
**Bocock,** Robert James 1942- *IntAu&W 91*
**Bocquet,** Philip E 1918- *AmMWSc 92*
**Boctor,** Magdy 1930- *AmMWSc 92*
**Bocuse,** Paul 1926- *IntWW 91*
**Boczar,** Barbara Ann 1951- *AmMWSc 92*
**Boczkowski,** Ronald James 1943- *AmMWSc 92*
**Bod,** Peter Akos 1951- *IntWW 91*
**Boda,** James Marvin 1924- *AmMWSc 92*
**Bod'a,** Koloman 1927- *IntWW 91*
**Boda,** Rexford A. *WhoRel 92*
**Boda,** Veronica Constance 1952- *WhoAmL 92*
**Bodack,** Leonard J 1932- *WhoAmP 91*
**Bodager,** Ben F. 1932- *WhoMW 92*
**Bodahl,** Larry D 1947- *WhoAmP 91*
**Bodaly,** Richard Andrew 1949- *AmMWSc 92*
**Bodamer,** George Willoughby 1916- *AmMWSc 92*
**Bodammer,** Joel Edward 1942- *AmMWSc 92*
**Bodansky,** David 1924- *AmMWSc 92*
**Bodansky,** Robert Lee *WhoAmL 92*
**Bodanszky,** Miklos 1915- *AmMWSc 92*
**Bodard,** Lucien Albert 1914- *IntWW 91*
**Bodde,** William, Jr 1931- *WhoAmP 91*
**Bodden,** James Manoah, II 1951- *WhoFI 92*
**Bodden,** John Meredith 1930- *WhoFI 92*
**Bodden,** Wendell N. 1930- *WhoBlA 92*
**Boddie,** Algernon Owens 1933- *WhoBlA 92*
**Boddie,** Arthur Walker 1910- *WhoBlA 92*
**Boddie,** Daniel W. 1922- *WhoBlA 92*
**Boddie,** Don O'Mar 1944- *WhoEnt 92*
**Boddie,** Gwendolyn M. 1957- *WhoBlA 92*
**Boddie,** Lewis F., Sr. 1913- *WhoBlA 92*
**Boddie,** Lewis Franklin, Sr. 1913- *WhoWest 92*
**Boddie,** Louise 1935- *WhoBlA 92*
**Boddie,** Reginald Alonzo 1959- *WhoAmL 92*
**Boddie,** William Willis 1945- *WhoMW 92*
**Boddington,** Craig Thornton 1952- *IntAu&W 91*
**Boddington,** Ewart Agnew 1927- *Who 92*
**Boddington,** Lewis 1907- *Who 92*
**Boddy,** David Edwin 1936- *AmMWSc 92*
**Boddy,** Dennis Warren 1922- *AmMWSc 92*
**Boddy,** Jack Richard 1922- *Who 92*
**Boddy,** Janice 1951- *ConAu 134*
**Boddy,** Philip J 1933- *AmMWSc 92*
**Bode,** Arthur Palfrey 1953- *AmMWSc 92*
**Bode,** Carl *DrAPF 91*
**Bode,** Carl 1911- *WrDr 92*
**Bode,** Donald Edward 1922- *AmMWSc 92*
**Bode,** Hugh J. 1952- *WhoAmL 92*
**Bode,** James Adolph 1938- *WhoAmP 91*
**Bode,** James Daniel 1923- *AmMWSc 92*
**Bode,** John William 1955- *WhoAmP 91*
**Bode,** Joyce Scruggs 1953- *WhoAmL 92*
**Bode,** Nancy M. 1951- *WhoMW 92*
**Bode,** Ralf *IntMPA 92*
**Bode,** Timothy Alan 1961- *WhoRel 92*
**Bode,** Vernon Cecil 1933- *AmMWSc 92*
**Bode,** William Morris 1943- *AmMWSc 92*
**Bodecker,** N M 1922- *IntAu&W 91*
**Bodek,** Arie 1947- *AmMWSc 92*
**Bodell,** Robert Edwayne 1948- *WhoRel 92*
**Bodell,** William J *AmMWSc 92*
**Bodelschwingh,** Friedrich von 1877-1946 *EncTR 91 [port]*
**Bodelun,** Rogelio 1936- *IntWW 91*
**Bodem,** Beverly 1940- *WhoAmP 91*
**Boden,** Edward Arthur 1911- *Who 92*
**Boden,** Guenther 1935- *AmMWSc 92*
**Boden,** Herbert 1932- *AmMWSc 92*
**Boden,** Leonard 1911- *Who 92*
**Boden,** Margaret A. 1936- *WrDr 92*
**Boden,** Margaret Ann 1936- *IntWW 91, Who 92*
**Boden,** Thomas Bennion 1915- *Who 92*
**Bodenheim,** Maxwell 1892-1954 *TwCLC 44 [port]*
**Bodenheim,** Maxwell 1893-1954 *BenetAL 91*
**Bodenheimer,** Peter Herman 1937- *AmMWSc 92*
**Bodenhorn,** Howard Nelson 1959- *WhoFI 92*
**Bodenlos,** Alfred John 1918- *AmMWSc 92*
**Bodensieck,** Ernest Justus 1923- *WhoWest 92*
**Bodenstein,** Ira 1954- *WhoAmL 92*
**Bodenstein,** Kenneth Alan 1937- *WhoFI 92*
**Bodenstein,** Max Ernst August 1871-1942 *FacFETw*
**Bodenstein,** Robert Quentin 1936- *WhoIns 92*
**Bodenstein,** Walter 1914- *WhoRel 92*
**Bodensteiner,** Richard *WhoAmP 91*
**Boderman,** Mary Lou 1953- *WhoWest 92*
**Bodett,** Thomas Edward 1955- *WhoWest 92*
**Bodett,** Tom 1955- *WrDr 92*
**Bodewitz,** Hendrik Wilhelm 1939- *IntWW 91*
**Bodey,** David Roderick Lessiter 1947- *Who 92*
**Bodey,** Gerald Paul, Sr 1934- *AmMWSc 92*
**Bodey,** Richard Allen 1930- *WhoRel 92*
**Bodfish,** Ralph E 1922- *AmMWSc 92*
**Bodger** *Who 92*
**Bodi,** Lewis Joseph 1924- *AmMWSc 92*
**Bodian,** David 1910- *AmMWSc 92, IntWW 91*
**Bodie,** Elizabeth Idella Fallaw 1925- *IntAu&W 91*
**Bodiford,** Vincent Walter 1962- *WhoWest 92*
**Bodiford,** William Marvin 1955- *WhoRel 92*
**Bodig,** Jozsef *WhoWest 92*
**Bodig,** Jozsef 1934- *AmMWSc 92*
**Bodiker,** Richard W 1936- *WhoAmP 91*
**Bodilly,** Jocelyn 1913- *Who 92*
**Bodily,** David Martin 1933- *AmMWSc 92*
**Bodily,** Stephen M 1936- *WhoAmP 91*
**Bodin,** Jerome Irwin 1930- *AmMWSc 92*
**Bodine,** Arthur William 1943- *WhoFI 92*
**Bodine,** Bernadette 1935- *WhoRel 92*
**Bodine,** Carlton Wright, Jr. 1948- *WhoRel 92*
**Bodine,** Donaldson 1866-1916? *BiInAmS*
**Bodine,** J.D. *TwCWW 91*
**Bodine,** Janice M 1937- *WhoAmP 91*
**Bodine,** Jerry *WhoAmP 91*
**Bodine,** John Jermain 1941- *WhoRel 92*
**Bodine,** Laurence 1950- *WhoAmL 92*
**Bodine,** Peter Van Nest 1958- *AmMWSc 92*
**Bodine,** Richard Shearon 1946- *AmMWSc 92*
**Bodine,** Robert Y 1933- *AmMWSc 92*
**Bodine,** Willis Ramsey, Jr. 1935- *WhoEnt 92*
**Bodinson,** Holt 1941- *WhoWest 92*
**Bodisco,** Michael Andrew 1941- *WhoWest 92*
**Bodkin,** Francis Fisher, Jr. 1944- *WhoFI 92*
**Bodkin,** Henry Grattan, Jr. 1921- *WhoAmL 92*
**Bodkin,** Lawrence Edward 1927- *WhoFI 92*
**Bodkin,** Norlyn L 1937- *AmMWSc 92*
**Bodkins,** Douglas Wayne 1950- *WhoMW 92*
**Bodley Head** *DcLB 112*
**Bodley,** Harley Ryan, Jr 1936- *IntAu&W 91*
**Bodley,** Herbert Daniel, II 1939- *AmMWSc 92*
**Bodley,** James William 1937- *AmMWSc 92*
**Bodley,** Joshua 1705-1775 *DcNCBi 1*
**Bodley,** Rachel Littler 1831-1888 *BiInAmS*
**Bodman,** Geoffrey Baldwin 1894- *AmMWSc 92*
**Bodman,** Richard Stockwell 1938- *WhoFI 92*
**Bodman,** Roger Alan 1952- *WhoAmP 91*
**Bodman,** Samuel Wright, III 1938- *AmMWSc 92, IntWW 91, WhoFI 92*
**Bodman,** Whitney Shepard 1950- *WhoRel 92*
**Bodman-Bustamante,** Denise Ann 1951- *WhoWest 92*
**Bodmer,** Arnold R 1929- *AmMWSc 92*
**Bodmer,** Jacques *WhoEnt 92*
**Bodmer,** Johann Jakob 1698-1783 *BlkwCEP*
**Bodmer,** Walter 1936- *Who 92, WrDr 92*
**Bodmer,** Walter Fred 1936- *AmMWSc 92, IntWW 91*
**Bodmin,** Archdeacon of *Who 92*
**Bodnar,** Donald George 1941- *AmMWSc 92*
**Bodnar,** John, III 1958- *WhoFI 92*
**Bodnar,** Louis Eugene 1929- *AmMWSc 92*
**Bodnar,** Robert John 1949- *AmMWSc 92*
**Bodnar,** Stephen J 1925- *AmMWSc 92*
**Bodnar,** Stephen Joseph 1955- *WhoFI 92, WhoWest 92*
**Bodnaruk,** Bohdan J. *WhoMW 92*
**Bodnaryk,** Robert Peter 1940- *AmMWSc 92*
**Bodner,** Emanuel 1947- *WhoFI 92*
**Bodner,** George Michael 1946- *AmMWSc 92*
**Bodner,** John, Jr. 1927- *WhoAmL 92*
**Bodner,** Mark Steven 1960- *WhoAmL 92*
**Bodner,** Paul Martin 1937- *WhoAmL 92*
**Bodner,** Randall Wayne 1959- *WhoAmL 92*
**Bodner,** Sol R 1929- *AmMWSc 92*
**Bodner,** Stephen E 1939- *AmMWSc 92*
**Bodney,** David Jeremy 1954- *WhoAmL 92*
**Bodney,** John Andrew 1948- *WhoAmL 92*
**Bodo,** John Rainer 1920- *WhoRel 92*
**Bodoni,** Giambattista 1740-1813 *BlkwCEP*
**Bodonyi,** Richard James 1943- *AmMWSc 92*
**Bodor,** Bruce Timothy 1959- *WhoEnt 92*
**Bodre,** Robert Joseph 1921- *AmMWSc 92*
**Bodrick,** Leonard Eugene 1953- *WhoBlA 92*
**Bodson,** Victor Hubert Joseph 1902- *IntWW 91*
**Bodstrom,** Lennart 1928- *IntWW 91*
**Bodsworth,** Fred 1918- *BenetAL 91, ConNov 91, WrDr 92*
**Bodtke,** Richard *DrAPF 91*
**Bodvarsson,** Gunnar 1916- *AmMWSc 92*
**Bodwell,** Clarence Eugene 1935- *AmMWSc 92*
**Body,** Geoffrey 1929- *WrDr 92*
**Body,** Richard 1927- *Who 92*
**Body,** Ronald Gilmour 1959- *WhoRel 92*
**Bodzy,** Glen Alan 1952- *WhoAmL 92*
**Boe,** Arthur Amos 1933- *AmMWSc 92*
**Boe,** David Stephen 1936- *WhoEnt 92*
**Boe,** Deborah *DrAPF 91*
**Boe,** Eric Neil 1965- *WhoWest 92*
**Boe,** Marianne Guerrini 1954- *WhoAmL 92*
**Boe,** Myron Timothy 1948- *WhoAmL 92, WhoFI 92*
**Boe,** Nils A 1913- *WhoAmP 91*
**Boe,** Nils Andreas 1913- *WhoAmL 92*
**Boe,** Norman Wallace 1943- *Who 92*
**Boe,** Randall J. 1962- *WhoAmL 92*
**Boe,** William Donald, Jr. 1949- *WhoAmL 92*
**Boecher,** Otto Hermann Konrad 1935- *WhoRel 92*
**Boeck,** Larry James 1947- *WhoWest 92*
**Boeck,** William Louis 1939- *AmMWSc 92*
**Boeckel,** Florence Brewer 1885- *AmPeW*
**Boecker,** Bruce Bernard 1932- *AmMWSc 92*
**Boeckman,** Charles 1920- *IntAu&W 91*
**Boeckman,** Robert K, Jr 1944- *AmMWSc 92*
**Boeckman,** Steven Emil 1952- *WhoAmP 91*
**Boeckx,** Roger L. O. 1946- *WhoMW 92*
**Boeddeker,** Timothy Mark 1948- *WhoMW 92*
**Boedeker,** Richard Roy 1933- *AmMWSc 92*
**Boeder,** Bruce Arthur 1950- *WhoAmL 92*
**Boeder,** Floyd Victor 1932- *WhoMW 92*
**Boeder,** Thomas L. 1944- *WhoAmL 92, WhoWest 92*
**Boedtker,** Olaf A 1924- *AmMWSc 92*
**Boedtker Doty,** Helga 1924- *AmMWSc 92*
**Boegner,** Jean-Marc 1913- *Who 92*
**Boegner,** Marc 1881-1970 *DcEcMov*
**Boehle,** John, Jr 1932- *AmMWSc 92*
**Boehler,** Conrad Joseph 1930- *WhoAmP 91*
**Boehler,** Gabriel D 1926- *AmMWSc 92*
**Boehler,** Robert A 1924- *AmMWSc 92*
**Boehlert,** George Walter 1950- *AmMWSc 92*
**Boehlert,** Sherwood 1936- *AlmAP 92 [port]*
**Boehlert,** Sherwood Louis 1936- *WhoAmP 91*
**Boehlje,** Michael Dean 1943- *AmMWSc 92*
**Boehlke,** Craig Alan 1947- *WhoRel 92*
**Boehlke,** Robert Richard 1925- *WhoRel 92*
**Boehlke,** William Fredrick 1946- *WhoWest 92*
**Boehm,** Barry William 1935- *AmMWSc 92*
**Boehm,** David Oscar 1922- *WhoAmL 92*
**Boehm,** Felix H 1924- *AmMWSc 92*
**Boehm,** Gottfried Karl 1942- *IntWW 91*
**Boehm,** James *WhoAmP 91*
**Boehm,** John Joseph 1929- *AmMWSc 92*
**Boehm,** Paul David 1948- *AmMWSc 92*
**Boehm,** Richard W 1926- *WhoAmP 91*
**Boehm,** Robert Foty 1940- *AmMWSc 92*
**Boehm,** Robert Louis 1925- *AmMWSc 92*
**Boehm,** Theobald 1793-1881 *NewAmDM*
**Boehm,** Thomas Wayne, II 1962- *WhoEnt 92*
**Boehme,** Hollis 1933- *AmMWSc 92*
**Boehme,** Ronald Edward 1937- *WhoMW 92*
**Boehme,** Werner Richard 1920- *AmMWSc 92*
**Boehmer,** Clifford Bernard 1927- *WhoWest 92*
**Boehmer,** Gerhard Walter 1935- *IntWW 91*
**Boehmer,** Raquel Davenport 1938- *WhoEnt 92*
**Boehmer,** Ronald Glenn 1947- *WhoWest 92*
**Boehmler,** E. William 1940- *WhoFI 92*
**Boehms,** Charles Nelson 1931- *AmMWSc 92*
**Boehne,** Edward George 1940- *WhoFI 92*
**Boehne,** John William 1921- *AmMWSc 92*
**Boehnen,** David Leo 1946- *WhoAmL 92*
**Boehner,** Edward Haub *WhoAmL 92*
**Boehner,** John A. 1949- *AlmAP 92 [port], WhoMW 92*
**Boehner,** John Andrew 1949- *WhoAmP 91*
**Boehner,** Leonard Bruce 1930- *WhoAmL 92*
**Boehnke,** David Neal 1939- *AmMWSc 92*

**Boehnke**, John Henry 1932- *WhoRel 92*
**Boehr**, Gary 1945- *WhoFI 92*
**Boeing**, William Edward 1881-1956 *FacFETw*
**Boeke**, Chet Lee 1945- *WhoAmP 91*
**Boeke**, Norbert Henry 1940- *WhoFI 92, WhoMW 92*
**Boekelheide**, Virgil Carl 1919- *AmMWSc 92, IntWW 91*
**Boekenheide**, Russell William 1930- *WhoFI 92*
**Boeker**, Elizabeth Anne 1941- *AmMWSc 92*
**Boeker**, Paul Harold 1938- *IntWW 91, WhoAmP 91*
**Boele**, Michael Edward 1950- *WhoWest 92*
**Boelhower**, Gary John 1950- *WhoRel 92*
**Boell**, Edgar John 1906- *AmMWSc 92*
**Boell**, Robert Paul 1962- *WhoMW 92*
**Boellstorff**, John David 1940- *AmMWSc 92*
**Boelter**, Don Howard 1933- *AmMWSc 92*
**Boelter**, Edwin D, Jr 1928- *AmMWSc 92*
**Boelz**, Thomas Leonard 1935- *WhoMW 92*
**Boen**, Bradley Nelson 1936- *WhoMW 92*
**Boen**, Dan L. 1950- *WhoMW 92*
**Boen**, James Robert 1932- *AmMWSc 92*
**Boendermaker**, Johannes Pieter 1925- *WhoRel 92*
**Boeniger**, Henry R 1947- *WhoAmP 91*
**Boenigk**, John William 1918- *AmMWSc 92*
**Boening**, John W. 1942- *WhoMW 92*
**Boening**, Paul Henrik 1953- *AmMWSc 92*
**Boenisch**, Peter H. 1927- *IntWW 91*
**Boensch**, Arthur Cranwell 1933- *WhoAmL 92*
**Boer**, Charles 1939- *IntAu&W 91, WrDr 92*
**Boer**, Jeffrey Kent 1951- *WhoRel 92*
**Boer**, Karl Wolfgang 1926- *AmMWSc 92*
**Boerboom**, Jim *WhoAmP 91*
**Boerboom**, Lawrence E *AmMWSc 92*
**Boercker**, David Bryan 1949- *AmMWSc 92*
**Boere**, Rene Theodoor 1957- *AmMWSc 92*
**Boerema**, Bert Edward 1938- *WhoMW 92*
**Boergers**, Mary H 1946- *WhoAmP 91*
**Boerhaave**, Hermann 1668-1738 *BlkwCEP*
**Boeri**, Cini 1924- *DcTwDes*
**Boerlage**, Frans Theodoor 1930- *WhoEnt 92*
**Boerma**, Addeke Hendrik 1912- *IntWW 91, Who 92*
**Boerner**, Ralph E J 1948- *AmMWSc 92*
**Boernke**, William E 1944- *AmMWSc 92*
**Boers**, Jack E 1935- *AmMWSc 92*
**Boersig**, David Scott 1964- *WhoMW 92*
**Boersma**, Arden Dale 1956- *WhoMW 92*
**Boersma**, Diana Lurie 1956- *WhoAmL 92*
**Boersma**, Lawrence Allan 1932- *WhoWest 92*
**Boersma**, P Dee 1946- *AmMWSc 92*
**Boerste**, Dean William 1952- *WhoAmP 91*
**Boertje**, Stanley 1930- *AmMWSc 92*
**Boes**, Ardel J 1937- *AmMWSc 92*
**Boes**, Lawrence William 1935- *WhoAmL 92*
**Boesak**, Allan 1946- *IntWW 91*
**Boesak**, Allan Aubrey 1946- *WhoRel 92*
**Boesch**, Francis Theodore *AmMWSc 92*
**Boesch**, Lawrence Michael 1951- *WhoAmL 92*
**Boesch**, William J 1923- *AmMWSc 92*
**Boeschenstein**, William Wade 1925- *IntWW 91, WhoFI 92, WhoMW 92*
**Boese**, Eleanor Jane 1940- *WhoAmP 91*
**Boese**, Gilbert Karyle 1937- *AmMWSc 92*
**Boese**, Jody Alan 1951- *WhoEnt 92*
**Boese**, Mark Alan 1960- *WhoMW 92*
**Boesel**, Milton Charles, Jr. 1928- *WhoAmL 92, WhoFI 92, WhoMW 92*
**Boesgaard**, Ann Merchant 1939- *AmMWSc 92*
**Boeshaar**, Patricia Chikotas 1947- *AmMWSc 92*
**Boetcker**, Ruth Elizabeth *WhoFI 92*
**Boethius** 480?-524? *DcLB 115 [port], EncEarC*
**Boethius** 1240?- *DcLB 115*
**Boethius of Dacia** 1240?- *DcLB 115*
**Boetius of Sweden** 1240?- *DcLB 115*
**Boetsch**, Frederick Paul 1940- *WhoWest 92*
**Boettcher**, Armin Schlick 1941- *WhoFI 92*
**Boettcher**, Arthur Lee 1935- *AmMWSc 92*
**Boettcher**, F Peter 1932- *AmMWSc 92*
**Boettcher**, Frederick Hans Rudolf 1935- *WhoAmP 91*
**Boettcher**, Harold P 1923- *AmMWSc 92*
**Boettcher**, Steven Michael 1962- *WhoWest 92*
**Boettcher**, Wilfried 1929- *IntWW 91, WhoEnt 92*
**Boettger**, George Albert 1947- *WhoWest 92*
**Boettger**, Susan D 1952- *AmMWSc 92*
**Boettger**, William F. 1945- *WhoWest 92*
**Boetticher**, Budd 1916- *IntDcF 2-2, IntMPA 92*
**Boettinger**, William James 1946- *AmMWSc 92*
**Boettner**, Dorothy Ellen 1917- *WhoAmP 91*
**Boettner**, Edward Alvin 1915- *AmMWSc 92*
**Boettner**, Fred Easterday 1918- *AmMWSc 92*
**Boevey**, Thomas C. *Who 92*
**Boeynants**, Paul Van Den 1919- *IntWW 91*
**Boff**, Leonardo Genezio Darci 1938- *IntWW 91*
**Boffa**, Lidia C 1945- *AmMWSc 92*
**Boffa**, Robert Charles 1935- *WhoAmL 92*
**Boffetti**, Raymond John 1924- *WhoAmP 91*
**Boffman**, James 1929- *WhoBlA 92*
**Boffo**, Dion Louis 1947- *WhoRel 92*
**Bofill**, Angela 1954- *WhoBlA 92*
**Bofill**, Ricardo 1939- *IntWW 91*
**Bofinger**, Diane P 1951- *AmMWSc 92*
**Bofinger**, Karl Kurt 1938- *WhoMW 92*
**Bogaard**, William Joseph 1938- *WhoAmL 92, WhoFI 92*
**Bogaers**, Petrus Clemens Wilhelmus Maria 1924- *IntWW 91*
**Bogaev**, Paul Harry 1953- *WhoEnt 92*
**Bogan**, Denis John 1941- *AmMWSc 92*
**Bogan**, James J. *DrAPF 91*
**Bogan**, Louise 1897-1970 *BenetAL 91, FacFETw, ModAWWr*
**Bogan**, Mary Flair 1948- *WhoFI 92*
**Bogan**, Neil Earnest 1945- *WhoFI 92*
**Bogan**, Richard Herbert 1926- *AmMWSc 92*
**Bogan**, Robert L 1926- *AmMWSc 92*
**Bogan**, Roy Turner 1931- *WhoIns 92*
**Bogar**, John A. 1918- *WhoIns 92*
**Bogar**, Louis Charles 1932- *AmMWSc 92*
**Bogar**, Thomas John 1947- *AmMWSc 92*
**Bogard**, Andrew Dale 1915- *AmMWSc 92*
**Bogard**, Carole Christine *WhoEnt 92*
**Bogard**, David Kenneth 1953- *WhoWest 92*
**Bogard**, Donald Dale 1940- *AmMWSc 92*
**Bogard**, Hazel Zinamon 1925- *WhoBlA 92*
**Bogard**, Lawrence Joseph *WhoAmL 92*
**Bogard**, Terry L 1936- *AmMWSc 92*
**Bogard**, Travis 1918- *WrDr 92*
**Bogard-Reynolds**, Christine Elizabeth 1954- *WhoWest 92*
**Bogarde**, Dirk *Who 92*
**Bogarde**, Dirk 1921?- *ConTFT 9, IntAu&W 91, IntMPA 92, IntWW 91, WrDr 92*
**Bogardus**, Carl Robert, Jr 1933- *AmMWSc 92*
**Bogardus**, Egbert Hal 1931- *AmMWSc 92*
**Bogardus**, John A, Jr. 1927- *WhoIns 92*
**Bogarin**, Russell Samuel 1931- *WhoMW 92*
**Bogart**, Alvin Seymour 1921- *WhoFI 92*
**Bogart**, Bruce Ian 1939- *AmMWSc 92*
**Bogart**, Homer Gordon 1922- *WhoFI 92*
**Bogart**, Humphrey 1899-1957 *FacFETw [port]*
**Bogart**, John Thomas 1937- *WhoMW 92*
**Bogart**, Keith Charles 1936- *WhoMW 92*
**Bogart**, Kenneth Paul 1943- *AmMWSc 92*
**Bogart**, Larry 1914-1991 *NewYTBS 91 [port]*
**Bogart**, Marcel J P 1913- *AmMWSc 92*
**Bogart**, Paul *LesBEnT 92*
**Bogart**, Paul 1919- *IntMPA 92, WhoEnt 92*
**Bogart**, Wanda Lee 1939- *WhoWest 92*
**Bogart**, William Harry 1931- *WhoAmL 92*
**Bogash**, R 1922- *AmMWSc 92*
**Bogasky**, Michael 1958- *WhoEnt 92*
**Bogaty**, Herman 1918- *AmMWSc 92*
**Bogatyrev**, Pyotr Grigor'evich 1893-1971 *SovUnBD*
**Bogdan**, Livius Silviu 1932- *WhoFI 92, WhoWest 92*
**Bogdan**, Victor Michael 1933- *AmMWSc 92*
**Bogdanoff**, John Lee 1916- *AmMWSc 92*
**Bogdanoff**, Leonard 1930- *WhoEnt 92*
**Bogdanor**, Vernon 1943- *ConAu 35NR, IntAu&W 91, WrDr 92*
**Bogdanov**, Aleksandr Aleksandrovich 1873-1928 *SovUnBD*
**Bogdanov**, Michael 1938- *IntWW 91, Who 92*
**Bogdanov**, Petr Alekseevich 1882-1939 *SovUnBD*
**Bogdanove**, Emanuel Mendel 1925- *AmMWSc 92*
**Bogdanovich**, Peter 1939- *IntAu&W 91, IntDcF 2-2 [port], IntMPA 92, IntWW 91, Who 92, WhoEnt 92, WrDr 92*
**Bogdanowicz-Bindert**, Christine Anne 1951- *WhoFI 92*
**Bogdanski**, Donald Frank 1928- *AmMWSc 92*
**Bogden**, Arthur Eugene 1921- *AmMWSc 92*
**Bogden**, John Dennis 1945- *AmMWSc 92*
**Bogdon**, Glendon Joseph 1935- *WhoMW 92*
**Bogdonoff**, Maurice Lambert 1926- *WhoMW 92*
**Bogdonoff**, Morton David 1925- *AmMWSc 92*
**Bogdonoff**, Philip David, Jr 1927- *AmMWSc 92*
**Bogdonoff**, Seymour 1921- *AmMWSc 92*
**Boge**, Ronald Stephen, Sr. 1934- *WhoFI 92*
**Bogen**, Andrew E. 1941- *WhoAmL 92*
**Bogen**, Don *DrAPF 91*
**Bogen**, Edward J., Jr. 1944- *WhoAmL 92*
**Bogen**, Karen Iris *DrAPF 91*
**Bogen**, Laurel Ann *DrAPF 91*
**Bogen**, Laurel Ann 1950- *ConAu 35NR*
**Bogen**, Nancy *DrAPF 91*
**Bogenschneider**, Neil E 1948- *WhoAmP 91*
**Bogenschutz**, J. David 1944- *WhoAmL 92*
**Bogenschutz**, Robert Parks 1933- *AmMWSc 92*
**Boger**, Carolyn S. 1967- *WhoEnt 92*
**Boger**, Dale L 1953- *AmMWSc 92*
**Boger**, Dan Calvin 1946- *WhoFI 92*
**Boger**, Edwin August, Sr 1923- *AmMWSc 92*
**Boger**, Friedrich Wilhelm 1906-1977 *EncTR 91 [port]*
**Boger**, George 1782-1865 *DcNCBi 1*
**Boger**, Gilbert Lee 1927- *WhoAmP 91*
**Boger**, Phillip David 1943- *AmMWSc 92*
**Boger**, Richard Edwin, Jr. 1952- *WhoRel 92*
**Boger**, Robert Shelton 1947- *AmMWSc 92*
**Boger**, William Pierce 1913- *AmMWSc 92*
**Bogert**, Bruce Plympton 1923- *AmMWSc 92*
**Bogert**, Charles Norman 1940- *WhoMW 92*
**Bogert**, Frank M *WhoAmP 91*
**Bogert**, George Taylor 1920- *WhoAmL 92*
**Boggan**, Daniel, Jr. 1945- *WhoBlA 92, WhoWest 92*
**Boggan**, Patrick 1725?-1817 *DcNCBi 1*
**Boggess**, Albert 1929- *AmMWSc 92*
**Boggess**, Gary Thomas 1952- *WhoEnt 92*
**Boggess**, Gary Wade 1936- *AmMWSc 92*
**Boggess**, Nancy Weber 1929- *AmMWSc 92*
**Boggess**, Thomas Phillip, III 1921- *WhoMW 92*
**Boggess**, William Randolph 1913- *AmMWSc 92*
**Boggio**, Dennis Ray 1953- *WhoWest 92*
**Boggio**, Joseph E 1936- *AmMWSc 92*
**Boggio**, Miriam A. 1952- *WhoIns 92*
**Boggis-Rolfe**, Hume 1911- *Who 92*
**Boggs**, Corinne Morrison Claiborne 1916- *WhoAmP 91*
**Boggs**, Dane Ruffner 1931- *AmMWSc 92*
**Boggs**, Danny J *WhoAmP 91*
**Boggs**, Danny Julian 1944- *WhoAmL 92, WhoMW 92*
**Boggs**, David Robert 1941- *WhoRel 92*
**Boggs**, Diane Kay 1952- *WhoEnt 92*
**Boggs**, Dock 1898-1971 *NewAmDM*
**Boggs**, Donald Gordon 1953- *WhoEnt 92*
**Boggs**, Eddie Arnold 1945- *WhoEnt 92*
**Boggs**, Edward Louis, III 1951- *WhoMW 92*
**Boggs**, George Edward, Jr. 1946- *WhoWest 92*
**Boggs**, George Johnson 1949- *AmMWSc 92*
**Boggs**, George Trenholm 1947- *WhoAmL 92*
**Boggs**, J Caleb 1909- *WhoAmP 91*
**Boggs**, James 1919- *WhoBlA 92*
**Boggs**, James Ashley 1934- *WhoMW 92*
**Boggs**, James Ernest 1921- *AmMWSc 92*
**Boggs**, James H 1921- *AmMWSc 92*
**Boggs**, Jean Sutherland 1922- *IntAu&W 91*
**Boggs**, Jesse Ernest 1954- *WhoRel 92*
**Boggs**, John Steven 1960- *WhoMW 92*
**Boggs**, John William 1951- *WhoMW 92*
**Boggs**, Joseph D 1921- *AmMWSc 92*
**Boggs**, Judith Roslyn 1939- *WhoAmP 91*
**Boggs**, Judith Susan 1946- *WhoAmL 92*
**Boggs**, Lawrence Allen 1910- *AmMWSc 92*
**Boggs**, Linda Farnsworth 1956- *WhoMW 92*
**Boggs**, Nathaniel 1926- *WhoBlA 92*
**Boggs**, Paul Thomas 1944- *AmMWSc 92*
**Boggs**, Robert J *WhoAmP 91*
**Boggs**, Robert Wayne 1941- *AmMWSc 92*
**Boggs**, Ross, Jr *WhoAmP 91*
**Boggs**, Sallie Patton Slaughter 1937- *AmMWSc 92*
**Boggs**, Sam, Jr 1928- *AmMWSc 92*
**Boggs**, Steven A 1946- *AmMWSc 92*
**Boggs**, Thomas Hale, Jr. 1940- *WhoAmL 92*
**Boggs**, William Brady 1943- *WhoFI 92*
**Boggs**, William Emmerson 1924- *AmMWSc 92*
**Boggs**, William O. *DrAPF 91*
**Boggus**, Francis Oliver 1947- *WhoBlA 92*
**Boghaert**, Arnold *WhoRel 92*
**Bogholtz**, William E. 1959- *WhoRel 92*
**Boghossian**, Skunder 1937- *WhoBlA 92*
**Bogianckino**, Massimo 1922- *IntWW 91*
**Bogie**, David Wilson 1946- *Who 92*
**Bogier**, Lawrence, Jr. 1941- *WhoRel 92*
**Bogin**, Abba 1925- *WhoEnt 92*
**Bogin**, Magda *DrAPF 91*
**Bogin**, Nina *DrAPF 91*
**Bogina**, August, Jr 1927- *WhoAmP 91*
**Bogitsh**, Burton Jerome 1929- *AmMWSc 92*
**Bogle**, David Blyth 1903- *Who 92*
**Bogle**, Ellen Gray 1941- *IntWW 91, Who 92*
**Bogle**, James 1817-1873 *DcNCBi 1*
**Bogle**, JoeAnn Rose 1934- *WhoMW 92*
**Bogle**, John Clifton 1929- *WhoFI 92*
**Bogle**, Margaret L *AmMWSc 92*
**Bogle**, Robert 1817-1860? *DcNCBi 1*
**Bogle**, Robert Worthington 1918- *AmMWSc 92*
**Bogle**, Tommy Earl 1940- *AmMWSc 92*
**Bognar**, Charles Ralph 1926- *WhoWest 92*
**Bognar**, Jozsef 1917- *IntWW 91*
**Bogner**, Fred K 1939- *AmMWSc 92*
**Bogner**, Jonathan Scott *WhoEnt 92*
**Bogner**, Phyllis Holt 1930- *AmMWSc 92*
**Bogner**, Willy 1942- *IntWW 91*
**Bognon**, Pierre Desire 1940- *WhoFI 92*
**Bogoch**, Samuel 1928- *AmMWSc 92*
**Bogoliubov**, Nikolai Nikolaevich 1909- *FacFETw*
**Bogolyubov**, Klavdiy Mikhailovich 1909- *IntWW 91*
**Bogolyubov**, Mikhail Nikolayevich 1918- *IntWW 91*
**Bogolyubov**, Nikolay Ivanovich 1899-1980 *SovUnBD*
**Bogolyubov**, Nikolay Nikolayevich 1909- *IntWW 91*
**Bogomolets**, Aleksandr Aleksandrovich 1881-1946 *SovUnBD*
**Bogomolov**, Aleksey Fedorovich 1913- *IntWW 91*
**Bogomolov**, Oleg 1927- *IntWW 91*
**Bogomolov**, Oleg Timofeevich 1927- *SovUnBD*
**Bogomolov**, Sergey Aleksandrovich 1926- *IntWW 91*
**Bogorad**, Lawrence 1921- *AmMWSc 92, IntWW 91*
**Bogoroch**, Rita *AmMWSc 92*
**Bogorodsky**, Fedor Semenovich 1895-1959 *SovUnBD*
**Bogosian**, Eric 1953- *IntMPA 92, WhoEnt 92*
**Bogosian**, Gregg *AmMWSc 92*
**Bogosian**, Philip Stephen 1943- *WhoRel 92*
**Bogosian**, Richard W 1937- *WhoAmP 91*
**Bograd**, Sandra Lynn 1958- *WhoAmL 92*
**Bograkos**, William Louis 1954- *WhoMW 92*
**Bogsch**, Arpad 1919- *Who 92*
**Bogucki**, Raymond Francis 1928- *AmMWSc 92*
**Bogue**, Andrew Wendell 1919- *WhoMW 92*
**Bogue**, David d1856 *DcLB 106*
**Bogue**, Donald Chapman 1932- *AmMWSc 92*
**Bogue**, Ernest Everett 1864-1907 *BiInAmS*
**Bogue**, Lucile *DrAPF 91*
**Bogue**, Lucile Maxfield 1911- *IntAu&W 91, WrDr 92*
**Bogue**, Nancy Lynn 1953- *WhoMW 92*
**Bogue**, Virgil Gay 1846-1916 *BiInAmS*
**Bogue**, William Shields 1938- *WhoMW 92*
**Bogues**, Leon Franklin 1926- *WhoBlA 92*
**Bogues**, Tyrone 1965- *WhoBlA 92*
**Bogus**, Carl Thomas 1948- *WhoAmL 92*
**Bogus**, Houston, Jr. 1951- *WhoBlA 92*
**Bogus**, SDiane *DrAPF 91*
**Bogus**, SDiane Adams 1946- *WhoBlA 92*
**Bogusky**, Alf 1947- *WhoMW 92*
**Boguslaski**, Robert Charles 1941- *AmMWSc 92*
**Boguslavsky**, Mark Moiseevich 1924- *SovUnBD*
**Boguslavsky**, Mark Moiseyevich *IntWW 91*
**Bogut**, John Carl, Jr. 1961- *WhoAmL 92*
**Bogutz**, Jerome Edwin 1935- *WhoAmL 92*
**Bogyo**, Thomas P 1918- *AmMWSc 92*
**Bohacek**, Peter Karl 1936- *AmMWSc 92*
**Bohachevsky**, Ihor O 1928- *AmMWSc 92*
**Bohacs**, Kevin Michael 1954- *AmMWSc 92*
**Bohacz**, Michael Anthony 1958- *WhoEnt 92*
**Bohan**, Marc 1926- *IntWW 91*
**Bohan**, William Joseph 1929- *Who 92*
**Bohanan**, David John 1946- *WhoFI 92*
**Bohandy**, Joseph 1938- *AmMWSc 92*

**Bohannan,** Jules Kirby 1917- WhoFI 92
**Bohannan,** Paul 1920- WrDr 92
**Bohannon,** Bill Carl 1939- WhoEnt 92
**Bohannon,** Derek Shawn 1963- WhoRel 92
**Bohannon,** James Everett 1944- WhoEnt 92
**Bohannon,** Judith WhoEnt 92
**Bohannon,** Marshall Topping, Jr. 1930- WhoAmL 92
**Bohannon,** Raymond Lawrence 1954- WhoMW 92
**Bohannon,** Richard Wallace 1953- AmMWSc 92
**Bohannon,** Robert Arthur 1922- AmMWSc 92
**Bohannon,** Robert Gary 1949- AmMWSc 92
**Bohannon-Kaplan,** Margaret Anne 1937- WhoFI 92
**Bohanon,** Joseph Terril 1939- WhoMW 92
**Bohanon,** Richard Lee 1935- WhoAmL 92
**Bohanske,** Robert Thomas 1953- WhoWest 92
**Boharski,** William E 1961- WhoAmP 91
**Bohart,** Richard Mitchell 1913- AmMWSc 92
**Bohata,** Emil Anton 1918- WhoMW 92
**Bohen,** Frederick M 1937- WhoAmP 91
**Bohen,** Joseph Michael 1946- AmMWSc 92
**Bohi,** Lynn 1947- WhoAmP 91
**Bohigas Guardiola,** Oriol 1925- IntWW 91
**Bohigian,** Robert J WhoAmP 91
**Bohigian,** Valerie IntAu&W 91
**Bohinski,** Robert Clement 1940- AmMWSc 92
**Bohl,** Robert W 1925- AmMWSc 92
**Bohle,** Ernst Wilhelm 1903-1960 EncTR 91 [port]
**Bohlen,** Harold Glenn 1946- AmMWSc 92
**Bohlen,** Richard William 1935- WhoFI 92, WhoWest 92
**Bohlen,** Steven Ralph 1952- AmMWSc 92
**Bohlen,** Walter Franklin 1938- AmMWSc 92
**Bohlender,** Hugh Darrow 1951- WhoAmL 92
**Bohler,** Jennifer Denise 1955- WhoEnt 92
**Bohler,** William J. 1957- WhoAmL 92
**Bohlin,** John David 1939- AmMWSc 92
**Bohlin,** Ralph Charles 1943- AmMWSc 92
**Bohlken,** Deborah Kay 1952- WhoFI 92
**Bohlken,** Donald Walter 1952- WhoAmL 92
**Bohlmann,** Daniel Robert 1948- WhoAmL 92, WhoWest 92
**Bohlmann,** Edward Gustav 1917- AmMWSc 92
**Bohlmann,** Melvin A. 1927- WhoMW 92
**Bohlmann,** Ralph Arthur 1932- WhoMW 92, WhoRel 92
**Bohls,** Cleo Evelyn 1924- WhoAmP 91
**Bohls,** Sally Ruth 1956- WhoEnt 92
**Bohm,** Arno 1936- AmMWSc 92
**Bohm,** Bruce Arthur 1935- AmMWSc 92
**Bohm,** David 1917- Who 92
**Bohm,** Doker Gest 1945- WhoEnt 92
**Bohm,** Georg G A 1935- AmMWSc 92
**Bohm,** Henry Victor 1929- AmMWSc 92
**Bohm,** Howard A 1943- AmMWSc 92
**Bohm,** Jack Nelson 1924- WhoAmL 92
**Bohm,** James Glenn 1962- WhoAmL 92
**Bohm,** Joel Lawrence 1942- WhoFI 92
**Bohm,** Karl 1894-1981 FacFETw, NewAmDM
**Bohm,** Michael Neil 1952- WhoRel 92
**Bohm,** Robert Dean 1945- WhoAmL 92
**Bohman,** Gosta 1911- IntWW 91
**Bohman,** Verle Rudolph 1924- AmMWSc 92, WhoWest 92
**Bohme,** Diethard Kurt 1941- AmMWSc 92
**Bohme,** Hans-Joachim 1931- IntWW 91
**Bohme,** Helmut 1936- IntWW 91
**Bohme,** Herbert 1907-1971 EncTR 91
**Bohmer,** Heinrich Everhard 1931- AmMWSc 92
**Bohmont,** Dale W 1922- AmMWSc 92
**Bohmrich,** Marion Letcher d1991 NewYTBS 91
**Bohn,** Charlotte Galitz 1930- WhoFI 92, WhoMW 92
**Bohn,** Cheryl Metcalfe 1955- WhoWest 92
**Bohn,** Dennis Allen 1942- WhoEnt 92, WhoWest 92
**Bohn,** H. G. d1884 DcLB 106 [port]
**Bohn,** Hinrich Lorenz 1934- AmMWSc 92
**Bohn,** Melvin Michael 1942- WhoMW 92
**Bohn,** Ralph Carl 1930- WhoWest 92
**Bohn,** Randy G 1941- AmMWSc 92
**Bohn,** Robert John 1946- WhoWest 92
**Bohn,** Robert K 1939- AmMWSc 92
**Bohn,** Sherman Elwood 1927- AmMWSc 92
**Bohn,** Walter Moro 1939- WhoEnt 92
**Bohnen,** Michael J. 1947- WhoAmL 92
**Bohnenberger,** Dale Vincent 1952- WhoWest 92
**Bohnenblust,** Kenneth E 1923- AmMWSc 92
**Bohnengel,** Andrew Charles 1949- WhoMW 92
**Bohner,** Robert Windsor 1952- WhoAmL 92
**Bohnert,** Janice Lee AmMWSc 92
**Bohning,** Daryl Eugene 1941- AmMWSc 92
**Bohning,** James Joel 1934- AmMWSc 92
**Bohnsack,** Kurt K 1920- AmMWSc 92
**Bohon,** Robert Lynn 1925- AmMWSc 92
**Bohor,** Bruce Forbes 1932- AmMWSc 92
**Bohorquez,** Pedro 1602?-1667 HisDSpE
**Bohoskey,** Bernice Fleming 1918- WhoFI 92, WhoWest 92
**Bohr,** Aage 1922- AmMWSc 92
**Bohr,** Aage Niels 1922- FacFETw, IntWW 91, Who 92, WhoNob 90
**Bohr,** David Francis 1915- AmMWSc 92
**Bohr,** Niels Hendrik David 1885-1962 FacFETw [port]
**Bohr,** Niels Henrik David 1885-1962 WhoNob 90
**Bohren,** Bernard Benjamin 1914- AmMWSc 92
**Bohren,** Craig Frederick 1940- AmMWSc 92
**Bohren,** Michael Oscar 1947- WhoAmP 91
**Bohrer,** James Calvin 1923- AmMWSc 92
**Bohrer,** Richard William 1926- WhoRel 92
**Bohrer,** Robert Arnold 1949- WhoWest 92
**Bohrer,** Robert Edward 1939- AmMWSc 92
**Bohrer,** Thomas Carl 1939- AmMWSc 92
**Bohrer,** Vorsila Laurene 1931- AmMWSc 92
**Bohrman,** David Ellis 1954- WhoEnt 92
**Bohrman,** Jeffrey Stephen 1944- AmMWSc 92
**Bohusz-Szyszko,** Cicely Who 92
**Boiarski,** Phil DrAPF 91
**Boice,** Craig Kendall 1952- WhoFI 92
**Boice,** James Montgomery 1938- IntAu&W 91, WrDr 92
**Boice,** John D, Jr 1945- AmMWSc 92
**Boieldieu,** Adrien 1775-1834 NewAmDM
**Boies,** Wilber H. 1944- WhoAmL 92
**Boikess,** Robert S 1937- AmMWSc 92
**Boiko,** Viktor Grigorevich 1931- IntWW 91
**Boileau,** Guy 1935- Who 92
**Boileau,** Oliver C 1927- AmMWSc 92
**Boileau,** Oliver Clark, Jr. 1927- IntWW 91
**Boiman,** Donna Rae 1946- WhoMW 92
**Boime,** Irving 1941- AmMWSc 92
**Boire,** Richard Larry 1952- WhoAmL 92
**Boireau,** Gerard WhoEnt 92
**Bois,** Melville Roma 1946- WhoMW 92
**Boisclair,** David Richard 1955- WhoRel 92
**Boisdeffre,** Pierre Jules Marie Raoul 1926- IntWW 91
**Boisdefre,** Pierre Jules Marie Raoul 1926- IntAu&W 91
**Boise,** Glen Richard 1951- WhoMW 92
**Boise,** Ola Irene 1946- WhoMW 92
**Boisen,** Anton Theophilus 1876-1965 RelLAm 91
**Boisfontaine,** Curtis Rich 1929- WhoAmL 92
**Boisgilbert,** Edmund, MD 1831-1901 ScFEYrs
**Boisi,** James O. 1919- IntWW 91
**Boismortier,** Joseph Bodin de 1689-1755 NewAmDM
**Boisse,** Norman Robert 1947- AmMWSc 92
**Boisseau,** Jerry Philip 1939- WhoFI 92
**Boisseau,** Michelle DrAPF 91
**Boisseau,** Richard Robert 1944- WhoAmL 92
**Boisselle,** Arthur Henry 1933- WhoWest 92
**Boisset,** Caroline 1955- ConAu 134
**Boisset,** Yves 1939- IntWW 91
**Boissevain,** Inez Milholland 1886-1916 AmPeW
**Boissevain,** Jean Tennyson d1991 NewYTBS 91
**Boissevain,** Jeremy 1928- IntAu&W 91
**Boissier,** Roger Humphrey 1930- Who 92
**Boissieu Dean De Luigne,** Alain Henri de 1914- IntWW 91
**Boissy,** Raymond E 1954- AmMWSc 92
**Boisvenue,** Rudolph Joseph 1926- AmMWSc 92
**Boisvert,** Beryl Mildred 1942- WhoFI 92
**Boisvert,** Robert Charles, Jr. 1960- WhoAmL 92
**Boisvert,** Ronald Fernand 1951- AmMWSc 92
**Boisvert,** William E. 1942- WhoFI 92
**Boit,** Michael 1949- BlkOlyM
**Boito,** Arrigo 1842-1918 NewAmDM
**Boitsov,** Vasiliy Vasiliyevich 1908- IntWW 91
**Boivin,** Alberic 1919- AmMWSc 92
**Boivin,** Claude 1934- WhoFI 92
**Boivin,** Daniel J. 1956- WhoAmL 92
**Boivin,** Louis-Philippe 1944- AmMWSc 92
**Boizot,** Peter James 1929- Who 92
**Bojalil,** Luis Felipe 1925- AmMWSc 92
**Bojangles** NewAmDM
**Bojanic,** Ranko 1924- AmMWSc 92
**Bojar,** Samuel 1915- AmMWSc 92
**Bojarski,** Ronald Henry 1934- WhoRel 92
**Bojart Ortega,** Rafael 1920- IntWW 91
**Bojaxhiu,** Agnes Gonxha Who 92
**Bojaxhiu,** Agnes Gonxha 1910- WhoNob 90, WhoRel 92
**Bojer,** Johan BenetAL 91
**Bojesen,** Kai 1886-1938 DcTwDes
**Bok,** Bart Jan 1906- FacFETw
**Bok,** Derek 1930- IntWW 91, Who 92, WrDr 92
**Bok,** Edward DcAmImH
**Bok,** Edward 1863-1930 RComAH
**Bok,** Edward W. 1863-1930 BenetAL 91
**Bok,** Joan Toland 1929- WhoFI 92
**Bok,** Kooshti IntAu&W 91X
**Bok,** Mary Louise Curtis 1876-1970 NewAmDM
**Bok,** P Dean 1939- AmMWSc 92
**Bok,** Sissela 1934- WrDr 92
**Bokassa,** Jean-Bedel 1921- FacFETw, IntWW 91
**Boke,** Norman Hill 1913- AmMWSc 92
**Bokelman,** Delwin Lee 1934- AmMWSc 92
**Bokelmann,** Stanley Otto 1923- WhoWest 92
**Boker,** George Henry 1823-1890 BenetAL 91
**Boklan,** Abbey Lenore 1939- WhoAmL 92
**Bokoch,** Gary M 1954- AmMWSc 92
**Bokov,** Nikolai Konstantinovich 1945- IntWW 91
**Bokros,** J C 1931- AmMWSc 92
**Boksay,** Istvan Janos Endre 1940- AmMWSc 92
**Boksenberg,** Alexander 1936- IntWW 91, Who 92
**Bokser,** Zelman Lewis 1951- WhoEnt 92
**Bokuniewicz,** Henry Joseph 1949- AmMWSc 92
**Bol,** Douglas John 1935- WhoRel 92
**Bol,** Kees 1925- AmMWSc 92
**Bol,** Manute WhoBlA 92
**Bol,** Manute 1963- ConBlB 1 [port]
**Bolaffi,** Janice Lerner AmMWSc 92
**Bolaji,** Rotimi Michael 1952- WhoFI 92
**Bolak,** Halil Dogan 1961- WhoFI 92
**Bolam,** James 1938- Who 92
**Bolan,** Barbara A. 1952- WhoEnt 92
**Bolan,** James IntMPA 92
**Bolan,** Robert S. 1941- WhoMW 92
**Bolan,** Thomas Anthony 1924- WhoAmL 92
**Bolan,** William F. WhoRel 92
**Boland,** Ann Shaughnessy 1958- WhoFI 92
**Boland,** Ardney James, Sr 1920- WhoAmP 91
**Boland,** Eavan 1944- ConLC 67 [port]
**Boland,** Edward P 1911- WhoAmP 91
**Boland,** Gerald Lee 1946- WhoFI 92
**Boland,** James P 1931- AmMWSc 92
**Boland,** John Anthony 1931- Who 92
**Boland,** John Louis, II 1954- WhoFI 92
**Boland,** Joseph Patrick 1952- WhoFI 92
**Boland,** Joseph S, III 1939- AmMWSc 92
**Boland,** Michael Joseph 1942- WhoAmP 91
**Boland,** Paula L 1940- WhoAmP 91
**Boland,** Raymond James 1932- WhoRel 92
**Boland,** Thomas Edwin 1934- WhoFI 92
**Boland,** W Robert 1937- AmMWSc 92
**Boland-Robillard,** Virginia Anne 1958- WhoWest 92
**Bolande,** Robert Paul 1926- AmMWSc 92
**Bolander,** Glen S., Jr. 1946- WhoFI 92
**Bolander,** Henry Nicholas 1831?-1897 BiInAmS
**Bolander,** Richard 1940- AmMWSc 92
**Bolander,** Robert C WhoAmP 91
**Bolanos,** Alberto Antonio 1962- WhoHisp 92
**Bolanos,** Alvaro Felix 1955- WhoHisp 92
**Bolanos,** Benjamin AmMWSc 92
**Bolanos,** Jack 1930- WhoHisp 92
**Bolanos,** Luis de 1550-1629 HisDSpE
**Bolar,** Marlin L 1927- AmMWSc 92
**Bolas,** Gerald Douglas 1949- WhoWest 92
**Bolasni,** Saul WhoEnt 92
**Bolch,** Ben Wilsman 1938- WhoFI 92
**Bolch,** William Emmett, Jr 1935- AmMWSc 92
**Bolcom,** William 1938- ConCom 92, NewAmDM
**Bolcom,** William Elden 1938- WhoEnt 92, WhoMW 92
**Bold,** Alan 1943- ConPo 91, IntAu&W 91, WrDr 92
**Bo'ld,** Paul 1880-1951 ScFEYrs
**Boldan,** Kelton John 1956- WhoMW 92
**Bolden,** Betty A. 1944- WhoBlA 92
**Bolden,** Buddy 1868?-1931 NewAmDM
**Bolden,** Charles E. 1941- WhoBlA 92
**Bolden,** Charles Frank, Jr. 1946- WhoBlA 92
**Bolden,** Dorothy Lee 1920- WhoBlA 92
**Bolden,** Frank Augustus 1942- WhoBlA 92
**Bolden,** J. Taber, III 1926- WhoBlA 92
**Bolden,** James Lee 1936- WhoBlA 92
**Bolden,** Jeanette 1960- BlkOlyM
**Bolden,** John Henry 1922- WhoBlA 92
**Bolden,** Melvin Wilberforce, Jr. 1941- WhoAmL 92
**Bolden,** Michael Geronia 1953- WhoWest 92
**Bolden,** Raymond A. 1933- WhoBlA 92
**Bolden,** Theodore E. 1920- WhoBlA 92
**Bolden,** Theodore Edward 1920- AmMWSc 92
**Bolden,** Wiley Speights 1918- WhoBlA 92
**Boldi,** Lana Lorraine 1941- WhoAmP 91
**Boldi,** Nick Richard 1934- WhoEnt 92
**Boldin,** Valeriy Ivanovich 1935- IntWW 91, SovUnBD
**Bolding,** Amy 1910- WrDr 92
**Boldon,** Billy Gragg 1962- WhoMW 92
**Boldrewood,** Rolf 1826-1915 RfGEnL 91
**Boldridge,** David William 1954- AmMWSc 92
**Boldridge,** William Franklin 1917- AmMWSc 92
**Boldt,** Charles Eugene 1928- AmMWSc 92
**Boldt,** David H AmMWSc 92
**Boldt,** Deborah Elizabeth 1947- WhoEnt 92
**Boldt,** Elihu 1931- AmMWSc 92
**Boldt,** Frederick Frank 1946- WhoRel 92
**Boldt,** Michael Herbert 1950- WhoAmL 92
**Boldt,** Richard Charles 1958- WhoAmL 92
**Boldt,** Roger Earl 1928- AmMWSc 92
**Bolduc,** Dennis R 1959- WhoAmP 91
**Bolduc,** Donald Raymond 1946- WhoFI 92
**Bolduc,** Reginald J 1939- AmMWSc 92
**Boldyrev,** Ivan Sergeyevich 1937- IntWW 91
**Boldyrev,** Vil Konstantinovich 1924- IntWW 91
**Bole,** Filipe Nagera 1936- IntWW 91
**Bole,** Giles G 1928- AmMWSc 92
**Boleat,** Mark John 1949- Who 92
**Bolef,** Dan Isadore 1921- AmMWSc 92
**Bolejack,** J. Rodney 1953- WhoRel 92
**Bolema,** Thomas William 1951- WhoEnt 92
**Bolemon,** Jay S 1941- AmMWSc 92
**Bolen,** Bob 1926- WhoAmP 91
**Bolen,** David B. 1927- WhoBlA 92
**Bolen,** David Benjamin 1923- WhoAmP 91
**Bolen,** David Wayne 1942- AmMWSc 92
**Bolen,** Eric George 1937- AmMWSc 92
**Bolen,** James Alta 1927- WhoEnt 92
**Bolen,** Kenneth James 1947- WhoIns 92
**Bolen,** Lee Napier, Jr 1937- AmMWSc 92
**Bolen,** Lin LesBEnT 92
**Bolen,** Lynne N. 1954- WhoWest 92
**Bolen,** Max Carlton 1919- AmMWSc 92
**Bolender,** Carroll H 1919- AmMWSc 92
**Bolender,** Charles L 1932- AmMWSc 92
**Bolender,** David Leslie 1947- AmMWSc 92
**Bolender,** James Henry 1937- WhoFI 92
**Bolender,** Robert P 1938- AmMWSc 92
**Bolender,** Todd 1919- WhoEnt 92, WhoMW 92
**Boles,** David LaVelle 1937- WhoAmL 92
**Boles,** Donald Michael 1951- WhoAmL 92
**Boles,** Hal WrDr 92
**Boles,** Harold Wilson 1915- WrDr 92
**Boles,** James Richard 1944- AmMWSc 92
**Boles,** Jeremy John Fortescue 1932- Who 92
**Boles,** John Culson 1953- WhoEnt 92
**Boles,** John Dennis 1925- Who 92
**Boles,** Robert Joe 1916- AmMWSc 92
**Boles,** Stamey Llewellyn 1931- WhoWest 92
**Bolet,** Jorge 1914- IntWW 91, NewAmDM
**Bolet,** Jorge 1914-1990 AnObit 1990, FacFETw, WhoHisp 92N
**Boley,** Bruno Adrian 1924- AmMWSc 92
**Boley,** Charles Daniel 1943- AmMWSc 92
**Boley,** Dennis Lynn 1951- WhoFI 92
**Boley,** Donna Jean 1935- WhoAmP 91
**Boley,** Forrest Irving 1925- AmMWSc 92
**Boley,** Robert B 1928- AmMWSc 92
**Boley,** Scott Jason AmMWSc 92
**Bolger,** Edward M 1938- AmMWSc 92
**Bolger,** James B. 1935- Who 92
**Bolger,** James Brendan 1935- IntWW 91
**Bolger,** Jeanne Marie 1928- WhoAmP 91
**Bolger,** P Michael 1949- AmMWSc 92
**Bolger,** Ray 1906-1987 FacFETw
**Bolger,** Robert Joseph 1922- WhoFI 92
**Bolger,** Timothy Joseph 1955- WhoFI 92
**Bolgiano,** Louis Paul, Jr 1922- AmMWSc 92
**Bolgiano,** Nicholas Charles 1923- AmMWSc 92
**Bolgiano,** Ralph, Jr 1922- AmMWSc 92

**Bolhofer**, William Alfred 1920- *AmMWSc 92*
**Bolhuis**, Reinder L H 1945- *AmMWSc 92*
**Bolich**, Gregory Gordon 1953- *WhoRel 92*
**Bolick**, Margaret Ruth 1950- *AmMWSc 92*
**Bolick**, Stephanie Corinne 1952- *WhoAmP 91*
**Bolie**, Victor Wayne 1924- *AmMWSc 92*
**Boliek**, Irene 1907- *AmMWSc 92*
**Bolin**, Bertil 1923- *IntWW 91*
**Bolin**, Bruce Martin 1950- *WhoAmP 91*
**Bolin**, Daniel Stuart 1952- *WhoRel 92*
**Bolin**, Elizabeth Anne 1947- *WhoAmP 91*
**Bolin**, Harold R 1930- *AmMWSc 92*
**Bolin**, James Edwin, Jr. 1941- *WhoAmL 92*
**Bolin**, Jane M. 1908- *NotBlAW 92*
**Bolin**, John Seelye 1943- *WhoEnt 92*
**Bolin**, Lionel E. 1927- *WhoBlA 92*
**Bolin**, Michael Patrick 1957- *WhoFI 92*
**Bolin**, Richard Luddington 1923- *WhoWest 92*
**Bolin**, Vernon Spencer 1913- *WhoWest 92*
**Bolin**, Vladimir Dustin 1965- *WhoWest 92*
**Bolind**, Lawrence, Jr. 1954- *WhoAmL 92*
**Bolinder**, William H. *WhoIns 92*
**Bolinder**, William Howard 1943- *WhoMW 92*
**Boling**, Edward J. 1922- *IntWW 91*
**Boling**, James A *AmMWSc 92*
**Boling**, Karen O'Reilly 1961- *WhoWest 92*
**Boling**, Mark Edward 1954- *WhoEnt 92*
**Boling**, Robert Gordon 1930- *WhoRel 92*
**Bolingbroke**, Viscount 1927- *Who 92*
**Bolingbroke**, Henry Saint John 1678-1751 *BlkwCEP*
**Bolingbroke**, Robert A. 1938- *WhoFI 92, WhoWest 92*
**Bolinger**, Corbin Eugene 1929- *WhoFI 92*
**Bolinger**, Dwight LeMerton 1907- *WrDr 92*
**Bolinger**, Robert E 1919- *AmMWSc 92*
**Bolino**, August C. 1922- *WrDr 92*
**Bolino**, Gloria Jean 1954- *WhoAmL 92*
**Bolitho**, Simon Edward d1991 *Who 92N*
**Bolivar**, Simon 1783-1830 *HisDSpE*
**Bolker**, Ethan D 1938- *AmMWSc 92*
**Bolker**, Henry Irving 1926- *AmMWSc 92*
**Bolkiah Mu'izzuddin Waddaulah**, Muda H. 1946- *IntWW 91*
**Bolkow**, Ludwig 1912- *IntWW 91*
**Bolks**, Ervin Jay 1941- *WhoFI 92, WhoMW 92*
**Boll**, H J 1930- *AmMWSc 92*
**Boll**, Heinrich 1917-1985 *FacFETw, WhoNob 90*
**Boll**, Jacob 1828-1880 *BiInAmS*
**Boll**, William George 1921- *AmMWSc 92*
**Bolla**, Robert Irving 1943- *AmMWSc 92*
**Bollag**, Jean-Marc 1935- *AmMWSc 92*
**Bolland**, David Michael 1947- *Who 92*
**Bolland**, Edwin 1922- *Who 92*
**Bolland**, Guy Alfred 1909- *Who 92*
**Bolland**, John 1920- *Who 92*
**Bolland**, Michael *Who 92*
**Bollandus**, John 1596-1665 *EncEarC*
**Bollard**, Edward George 1920- *IntWW 91*
**Bollard**, R John H 1927- *AmMWSc 92*
**Bollback**, Anthony George 1922- *WhoRel 92*
**Bolle**, Dale J 1923- *WhoAmP 91*
**Bolle**, Donald Martin 1933- *AmMWSc 92*
**Bolle**, James Dougan 1931- *WhoEnt 92*
**Bollenbacher**, Herbert Kenneth 1933- *WhoMW 92*
**Boller**, Francois 1938- *AmMWSc 92*
**Boller**, John Hall, Jr. 1949- *WhoRel 92*
**Boller**, Kirk Alan 1961- *WhoFI 92*
**Boller**, Paul F., Jr. 1916- *WrDr 92*
**Boller**, Ronald Cecil 1939- *WhoFI 92*
**Bollers**, Harold 1915- *Who 92*
**Bolles**, A. Lynn 1949- *WhoBlA 92*
**Bolles**, Donald Scott 1936- *WhoAmL 92*
**Bolles**, Edmund Blair 1942- *WrDr 92*
**Bolles**, Frank 1856-1894 *BiInAmS*
**Bolles**, Richard Nelson 1927- *WrDr 92*
**Bolles**, Ronald Kent 1948- *WhoWest 92*
**Bolles**, Theodore Frederick 1940- *AmMWSc 92*
**Bolles**, William Palmer d1916 *BiInAmS*
**Bollet**, Alfred Jay 1926- *AmMWSc 92*
**Bolleter**, William Theodore 1927- *AmMWSc 92*
**Bollier**, John Albert 1927- *WhoRel 92*
**Bolling**, Bruce C. *WhoBlA 92*
**Bolling**, Bryant Bernard 1954- *WhoEnt 92*
**Bolling**, Claude 1930- *IntWW 91*
**Bolling**, Deborah A. 1957- *WhoBlA 92*
**Bolling**, G. Fredric 1931- *WhoMW 92*
**Bolling**, George Richard, Sr 1937- *WhoAmP 91*
**Bolling**, Gustaf Fredric 1931- *AmMWSc 92*
**Bolling**, Richard 1916-1991 *ConAu 134, CurBio 91N*
**Bolling**, Richard W. d1991 *NewYTBS 91*
**Bolling**, Royal, Jr. 1944- *WhoBlA 92*
**Bolling**, Royal L, Sr *WhoAmP 91*
**Bolling**, Tiffany 1951- *WhoEnt 92*
**Bollinger**, Bob James 1953- *WhoFI 92*
**Bollinger**, Debra Marie 1956- *WhoAmL 92*
**Bollinger**, Donald G 1915- *WhoAmP 91*
**Bollinger**, Donald T 1949- *WhoAmP 91*
**Bollinger**, Edward H 1926- *AmMWSc 92*
**Bollinger**, Frederick W 1918- *AmMWSc 92*
**Bollinger**, Gilbert A 1931- *AmMWSc 92*
**Bollinger**, John G 1935- *AmMWSc 92*
**Bollinger**, John Gustave 1935- *WhoMW 92*
**Bollinger**, Lee 1941- *WhoEnt 92*
**Bollinger**, Lee Carroll 1946- *WhoAmL 92*
**Bollinger**, Lowell Moyer 1923- *AmMWSc 92*
**Bollinger**, Ralph R 1944- *AmMWSc 92*
**Bollinger**, Richard Amsey 1928- *WhoRel 92*
**Bollinger**, Richard Coleman 1932- *AmMWSc 92*
**Bollinger**, Robert Otto 1939- *AmMWSc 92*
**Bollinger**, William Hugh 1947- *AmMWSc 92*
**Bollman**, Charles Harvey 1868-1889 *BiInAmS*
**Bollnow**, Otto Friedrich 1903- *IntWW 91*
**Bollock**, Margot *DrAPF 91*
**Bolls**, Imogene L. *DrAPF 91*
**Bolls**, Nathan J, Jr 1931- *AmMWSc 92*
**Bollum**, Frederick James 1927- *AmMWSc 92*
**Bollyky**, L Joseph 1932- *AmMWSc 92*
**Bolman**, William Merton 1929- *AmMWSc 92*
**Bolmarcich**, Joseph John 1942- *AmMWSc 92*
**Bolme**, Donald W 1928- *AmMWSc 92*
**Bolme**, Mark W 1952- *AmMWSc 92*
**Bolmer**, Perce W 1928- *AmMWSc 92*
**Bolmey**, Carlos Alberto 1950- *WhoMW 92*
**Bolnick**, Howard J 1945- *WhoIns 92*
**Bolnick**, Howard Jeffrey 1945- *WhoFI 92*
**Bolocofsky**, David N. 1947- *WhoAmL 92, WhoWest 92*
**Bologna**, Calogero Antonio 1957- *WhoFI 92*
**Bologna**, Joseph 1938- *ConTFT 9, IntMPA 92, WhoEnt 92*
**Bologna-Garagozlo**, Patricia Ellen 1961- *WhoAmL 92*
**Bolognesi**, Dani Paul 1941- *AmMWSc 92*
**Bolois**, Robert Wayne 1946- *WhoRel 92*
**Bolon**, Albert Eugene 1939- *AmMWSc 92*
**Bolon**, Donald A 1934- *AmMWSc 92*
**Bolon**, Roger B 1939- *AmMWSc 92*
**Bolotin**, Herbert Howard 1930- *AmMWSc 92*
**Bolotin**, Moshe 1922- *AmMWSc 92*
**Bolotowsky**, Andrew Ilyitch 1949- *WhoEnt 92*
**Bolotowsky**, Gideon *WhoRel 92*
**Bolotowsky**, Ilya 1907-1981 *FacFETw*
**Bols**, Niels Christian 1948- *AmMWSc 92*
**Bolsaitis**, Pedro 1937- *AmMWSc 92*
**Bolsinger**, Don Clark 1931- *WhoAmL 92*
**Bolson**, David Edward 1961- *WhoEnt 92*
**Bolstad**, James Joseph 1951- *WhoMW 92*
**Bolstad**, Luther 1918- *AmMWSc 92*
**Bolstein**, Arnold Richard 1940- *AmMWSc 92*
**Bolster**, Christopher Pearce 1964- *WhoFI 92*
**Bolster**, Paul D 1944- *WhoAmP 91*
**Bolster**, Sally M *WhoAmP 91*
**Bolster**, William Lawrence 1943- *WhoMW 92*
**Bolsterli**, Mark 1930- *AmMWSc 92*
**Bolt**, Arthur Seymour 1907- *Who 92*
**Bolt**, Bruce 1930- *WrDr 92*
**Bolt**, Bruce A 1930- *AmMWSc 92*
**Bolt**, David Ernest 1921- *Who 92*
**Bolt**, Douglas John 1939- *AmMWSc 92*
**Bolt**, Fred Felton 1952- *WhoRel 92*
**Bolt**, Jay A 1911- *AmMWSc 92*
**Bolt**, John Ryan 1940- *AmMWSc 92*
**Bolt**, Richard 1923- *Who 92*
**Bolt**, Richard Henry 1911- *AmMWSc 92*
**Bolt**, Robert 1924- *ConAu 35NR, FacFETw, IntAu&W 91, IntMPA 92, WrDr 92*
**Bolt**, Robert James 1920- *AmMWSc 92*
**Bolt**, Robert O'Connor 1917- *AmMWSc 92*
**Bolt**, Robert Oxton 1924- *IntWW 91, Who 92*
**Bolt**, Robert William 1961- *WhoMW 92*
**Bolt**, Thomas *DrAPF 91*
**Bolt**, Thomas 1959- *WrDr 92*
**Bolt**, Thomas Alvin Waldrep 1956- *WhoAmP 91*
**Boltanski**, Christian 1944- *IntWW 91*
**Boltax**, Alvin 1930- *AmMWSc 92*
**Bolte**, Edouard 1931- *AmMWSc 92*
**Bolte**, Frank Richard 1913- *WhoAmL 92*
**Bolte**, John R 1929- *AmMWSc 92*
**Bolte**, Keith Alan 1944- *WhoWest 92*
**Bolter**, Andrew 1820-1900 *BiInAmS*
**Bolter**, Ernst A 1935- *AmMWSc 92*
**Bolter**, Norman *WhoEnt 92*
**Boltho**, Andrea 1939- *WrDr 92*
**Bolthouse**, Warren Jay 1927- *WhoRel 92*
**Boltin**, Lee 1917-1991 *NewYTBS 91*
**Boltinghouse**, Joseph C 1919- *AmMWSc 92*
**Bolton**, Archdeacon of *Who 92*
**Bolton**, Baron 1929- *Who 92*
**Bolton**, Bishop Suffragan of 1934- *Who 92*
**Bolton**, Ann D 1930- *WhoAmP 91*
**Bolton**, Arthur Key 1922- *WhoAmP 91*
**Bolton**, Benjamin A 1928- *AmMWSc 92*
**Bolton**, Benjamin Arthur 1928- *WhoMW 92*
**Bolton**, Charles Thomas 1943- *AmMWSc 92*
**Bolton**, David 1932- *Who 92*
**Bolton**, David C 1952- *AmMWSc 92*
**Bolton**, Dennis Rudolph 1953- *WhoRel 92*
**Bolton**, Earl Clinton 1919- *WhoWest 92*
**Bolton**, Ellis Truesdale 1922- *AmMWSc 92*
**Bolton**, Eric James 1935- *Who 92*
**Bolton**, Evelyn *WrDr 92*
**Bolton**, F H *ScFEYrs*
**Bolton**, Frederic 1921- *Who 92*
**Bolton**, Geoffrey Curgenven 1931- *Who 92*
**Bolton**, Guy Reginald 1894-1979 *FacFETw*
**Bolton**, Henry Carrington 1843-1903 *BiInAmS*
**Bolton**, James R 1937- *AmMWSc 92*
**Bolton**, James Ross 1921- *WhoIns 92*
**Bolton**, John Eveleigh 1920- *Who 92*
**Bolton**, John Robert 1948- *WhoAmL 92, WhoAmP 91*
**Bolton**, Joseph Aloysius 1939- *AmMWSc 92*
**Bolton**, Julian Taylor 1949- *WhoBlA 92*
**Bolton**, Kenneth Albert 1941- *WhoFI 92*
**Bolton**, Laura Lee 1944- *AmMWSc 92*
**Bolton**, Martha O. 1951- *WhoEnt 92, WhoWest 92*
**Bolton**, Michael *WhoEnt 92*
**Bolton**, Richard Andrew Ernest 1939- *AmMWSc 92*
**Bolton**, Robert Floyd 1942- *WhoWest 92*
**Bolton**, Roger Edwin 1938- *WhoFI 92*
**Bolton**, Ruth A. 1952- *WhoMW 92*
**Bolton**, Steven Alfred 1953- *WhoAmL 92*
**Bolton**, Sylbert 1959- *TwCPaSc*
**Bolton**, W Kline *AmMWSc 92*
**Bolton**, Wanda E. 1914- *WhoBlA 92*
**Bolton**, Wesson Dudley 1922- *AmMWSc 92*
**Bolton-Smith**, Carlile, Jr. 1937- *WhoAmL 92, WhoFI 92*
**Boltralik**, John Joseph 1926- *AmMWSc 92*
**Boltuck**, Richard Dale 1955- *WhoFI 92*
**Boltwood**, Bertram Borden 1870-1927 *FacFETw*
**Boltwood**, Russell Lewis 1963- *WhoFI 92*
**Boltz**, Daryl Lynn 1959- *WhoFI 92*
**Boltz**, David Thomas 1961- *WhoEnt 92*
**Boltz**, Gerald Edmund 1931- *WhoAmL 92*
**Boltz**, Mary Ann 1923- *WhoFI 92*
**Boltz**, Richard Alan 1932- *WhoAmL 92*
**Boltz**, Robert Charles, Jr 1945- *AmMWSc 92*
**Bolus**, Michael 1934- *TwCPaSc*
**Boly**, Craig Spencer 1944- *WhoWest 92*
**Boly**, Jeffrey Elwyn 1942- *WhoAmL 92*
**Bolyard**, Robert Delano 1936- *WhoMW 92*
**Bolz**, Eugen 1881-1945 *EncTR 91*
**Bolz**, Farrell Paul 1945- *WhoAmL 92*
**Bolz**, Harold A 1911- *AmMWSc 92*
**Bolz**, Harriett *WhoEnt 92*
**Bolz**, Jody *DrAPF 91*
**Bolz**, R E 1918- *AmMWSc 92*
**Boman**, Gregory Mark 1960- *WhoMW 92*
**Boman**, Primavera Roxan 1946- *WhoEnt 92*
**Boman**, Samuel R. *WhoRel 92*
**Boman**, Sten Arvid Stigsson 1953- *WhoRel 92*
**Bomani**, Paul Lazaro 1925- *IntWW 91*
**Bomar**, Lucien Clay 1947- *AmMWSc 92*
**Bomba**, Steven James 1937- *AmMWSc 92*
**Bombacci**, Nicolo 1879-1945 *BiDExR*
**Bombal**, Maria Luisa 1910-1980 *BenetAL 91, SpAmWW*
**Bombardier**, Paul Alfred 1953- *WhoRel 92*
**Bombassei Frascani De Vettor**, Giorgio 1910- *IntWW 91*
**Bombay**, Archbishop of 1920- *Who 92*
**Bombeck**, Charles Thomas, III 1937- *AmMWSc 92*
**Bombeck**, Erma 1927- *BenetAL 91, WrDr 92*
**Bombeck**, Erma Louise 1927- *IntAu&W 91, WhoEnt 92*
**Bombela**, Rose Mary 1950- *WhoHisp 92*
**Bomberg**, David 1890-1957 *TwCPaSc*
**Bomberger**, H B, Jr 1922- *AmMWSc 92*
**Bomberger**, Russell Branson 1934- *WhoAmL 92*
**Bomer**, Elton 1935- *WhoAmP 91*
**Bomers**, Henricus J. A. 1936- *IntWW 91*
**Bomes**, Stephen D. 1948- *WhoAmL 92, WhoWest 92*
**Bomford**, Nicholas Raymond 1939- *Who 92*
**Bomgarden**, Stanley Ralph 1946- *WhoRel 92*
**Bomke**, Hans Alexander 1910- *AmMWSc 92*
**Bommer**, Minnie L. 1940- *WhoBlA 92*
**Bompart**, Billy Earl 1933- *AmMWSc 92*
**Bompas**, Donald George 1920- *Who 92*
**Bompas**, William Carpenter 1834-1906 *RelLAm 91*
**Bompey**, Stuart Howard 1940- *WhoAmL 92*
**Bomse**, Frederick 1939- *AmMWSc 92*
**Bomsey**, Edward Norman 1944- *WhoAmL 92*
**Bon**, Christoph Rudolf 1921- *Who 92*
**Bon**, Naftali 1945- *BlkOlyM*
**Bon**, William Andrew, Jr. 1954- *WhoAmL 92*
**Bon Jovi**, Jon 1962- *WhoEnt 92*
**Bona**, Jerry Lloyd 1945- *AmMWSc 92*
**Bona**, Thomas Mark 1955- *WhoAmL 92*
**Bonacci**, John C 1935- *AmMWSc 92*
**Bonacci**, Richard John 1946- *WhoWest 92*
**Bonaccorso**, Anthony 1929- *WhoRel 92*
**Bonachea**, Rolando *WhoHisp 92*
**Bonacic**, John J 1942- *WhoAmP 91*
**Bonacorsi**, Mary Catherine 1949- *WhoAmL 92*
**Bonahoom**, Otto M. 1930- *WhoMW 92*
**Bonakdarpour**, Akbar *AmMWSc 92*
**Bonallack**, Michael Francis 1934- *Who 92*
**Bonallack**, Richard 1904- *Who 92*
**Bonan**, Eugene J 1923- *AmMWSc 92*
**Bonanno**, Frederick Ramon 1927- *WhoRel 92*
**Bonanno**, Giacomo Francesco 1954- *WhoFI 92*
**Bonanno**, Louie 1961- *IntMPA 92*
**Bonapart**, Alan David 1930- *WhoAmL 92*
**Bonaparte**, Charles Lucien 1803-1857 *BiInAmS*
**Bonaparte**, Lois Ann 1941- *WhoBlA 92*
**Bonaparte**, Lucien *BiInAmS*
**Bonaparte**, Napoleon *BlkwCEP*
**Bonaparte**, Napoleon 1769-1821 *HisDSpE*
**Bonaparte**, Norton Nathaniel, Jr. 1953- *WhoBlA 92*
**Bonaparte**, Tony Hillary 1939- *WhoBlA 92*
**Bonaparte**, Wallace Tyrone 1942- *WhoMW 92*
**Bonar**, Clayton Lloyd 1934- *WhoRel 92*
**Bonar**, Daniel Donald 1938- *AmMWSc 92*
**Bonar**, Herbert 1907- *Who 92*
**Bonar**, Lucian George 1934- *WhoFI 92*
**Bonar**, Robert Addison 1925- *AmMWSc 92*
**Bonar**, Veronica *SmATA 68*
**Bonasso**, Miguel *LiExTwC*
**Bonat**, Michelle Marie 1962- *WhoMW 92*
**Bonati**, Gina Angeline *DrAPF 91*
**Bonaventura**, Celia Jean 1941- *AmMWSc 92*
**Bonaventura**, Joseph 1942- *AmMWSc 92*
**Bonaventura**, Leo Mark 1945- *WhoMW 92*
**Bonaventure** 1217?-1274 *DcLB 115 [port]*
**Bonavida**, Benjamin 1940- *AmMWSc 92*
**Bonavita**, Nino Louis 1931- *AmMWSc 92*
**Bonazzi**, Elaine Claire *WhoEnt 92*
**Bonbright**, Harry Ward, Jr. 1932- *WhoMW 92*
**Boncek**, Barbara *DrAPF 91*
**Bonch-Bruevich**, Vladimir Dmitrievich 1873-1955 *SovUnBD*
**Boncy**, Roger Richard 1944- *WhoAmL 92*
**Bond**, Adrienne *DrAPF 91*
**Bond**, Alan *LesBEnT 92, WhoFI 92*
**Bond**, Alan 1938- *IntWW 91, Who 92*
**Bond**, Alan D. 1945- *WhoBlA 92*
**Bond**, Albert F 1930- *AmMWSc 92*
**Bond**, Albert Haskell, Jr 1940- *AmMWSc 92*
**Bond**, Aleck C 1922- *AmMWSc 92*
**Bond**, Andrew 1927- *AmMWSc 92*
**Bond**, Anson 1914- *IntMPA 92*
**Bond**, Armand Paul 1933- *AmMWSc 92*
**Bond**, Arthur Chalmer 1917- *AmMWSc 92*
**Bond**, C. 1945- *WrDr 92*
**Bond**, Carl Eldon 1920- *AmMWSc 92*
**Bond**, Carrie 1861-1946 *NewAmDM*
**Bond**, Carrie Jacobs 1862-1946 *BenetAL 91*
**Bond**, Cecil Walton, Jr. 1937- *WhoBlA 92*
**Bond**, Charles Dailey 1932- *WhoAmP 91*
**Bond**, Charles Earl 1958- *WhoWest 92*
**Bond**, Charles Eugene 1930- *AmMWSc 92*
**Bond**, Christopher S. 1939- *AlmAP 92 [port]*
**Bond**, Christopher Samuel 1939- *IntWW 91, WhoAmP 91, WhoMW 92*
**Bond**, Clifford Walter 1937- *AmMWSc 92*
**Bond**, Derek *Who 92*
**Bond**, Derek 1920- *IntMPA 92*
**Bond**, Edward 1934- *FacFETw, IntAu&W 91, IntWW 91, RfGEnL 91, Who 92, WrDr 92*
**Bond**, Edwin Joshua 1927- *AmMWSc 92*
**Bond**, Edwina Elaine 1954- *WhoRel 92*

**Bond,** Elizabeth Dux 1923- *AmMWSc 92*
**Bond,** Ennie Angel 1950- *WhoWest 92*
**Bond,** Frederick E 1920- *AmMWSc 92*
**Bond,** Frederick Thomas 1936- *AmMWSc 92*
**Bond,** Gary Carl 1942- *AmMWSc 92*
**Bond,** Geoffrey 1924-1978 *ConAu 134*
**Bond,** George Clement 1936- *WhoBlA 92*
**Bond,** George F 1915-1983 *FacFETw*
**Bond,** George Phillips 1825-1865 *BiInAmS*
**Bond,** George Walter 1944- *AmMWSc 92*
**Bond,** Gerard C 1940- *AmMWSc 92*
**Bond,** Gillian *IntAu&W 91X*
**Bond,** Gladys B. 1914- *WhoBlA 92*
**Bond,** Godfrey William 1925- *Who 92*
**Bond,** Guy Hugh 1934- *AmMWSc 92*
**Bond,** Harold *DrAPF 91*
**Bond,** Harold 1939- *WrDr 92*
**Bond,** Harry David 1952- *WhoFI 92, WhoMW 92*
**Bond,** Henry Mark Garneys 1922- *Who 92*
**Bond,** Howard Edward 1930- *AmMWSc 92*
**Bond,** Howard Emerson 1942- *AmMWSc 92*
**Bond,** Howard H. 1938- *WhoBlA 92*
**Bond,** J. Max, Sr. d1991 *NewYTBS 91*
**Bond,** James Anthony 1952- *AmMWSc 92*
**Bond,** James Arthur 1917- *WhoBlA 92*
**Bond,** James Arthur, II 1917- *AmMWSc 92*
**Bond,** James G. 1924- *WhoBlA 92*
**Bond,** James G. 1944- *WhoBlA 92*
**Bond,** James Max, Jr. 1935- *WhoBlA 92*
**Bond,** Jenny Taylor 1939- *AmMWSc 92*
**Bond,** John Adikes 1955- *WhoAmL 92*
**Bond,** John Percy, III 1937- *WhoBlA 92*
**Bond,** John Reed, Jr. 1952- *WhoWest 92*
**Bond,** Jon Patterson 1946- *WhoAmL 92*
**Bond,** Judith 1940- *AmMWSc 92*
**Bond,** Julian 1940- *ConBlB 2 [port], FacFETw, IntWW 91, WhoAmP 91, WhoBlA 92*
**Bond,** June Marilyn 1950- *WhoRel 92*
**Bond,** Kenneth 1920- *IntWW 91, Who 92*
**Bond,** Kerry Layne 1957- *WhoRel 92*
**Bond,** Lawrence Wade 1946- *WhoMW 92*
**Bond,** Leslie Fee 1928- *WhoBlA 92*
**Bond,** Lewis *TwCWW 91*
**Bond,** Lilian d1991 *NewYTBS 91*
**Bond,** Lloyd 1941- *WhoBlA 92*
**Bond,** Lora 1917- *AmMWSc 92*
**Bond,** Louis Grant 1947- *WhoBlA 92*
**Bond,** M G 1932- *WhoAmP 91*
**Bond,** Margaret Sigogne 1920- *WhoFI 92*
**Bond,** Martha W 1946- *AmMWSc 92*
**Bond,** Marvin Thomas 1930- *AmMWSc 92*
**Bond,** Michael *IntAu&W 91, WrDr 92*
**Bond,** Michael 1926- *Who 92*
**Bond,** Michael Richard 1936- *Who 92*
**Bond,** Myron Humphrey 1938- *WhoFI 92*
**Bond,** Nancy 1945- *ConAu 36NR, SmATA 13AS [port], WrDr 92*
**Bond,** Nancy Barbara 1945- *IntAu&W 91*
**Bond,** Nelson Leighton, Jr. 1935- *WhoFI 92*
**Bond,** Nelson S. 1908- *TwCSFW 91, WrDr 92*
**Bond,** Norman T 1920- *AmMWSc 92*
**Bond,** Octavia Zollikoffer 1846- *ScFEYrs*
**Bond,** Ollie P. 1925- *WhoBlA 92*
**Bond,** Peter Danford 1940- *AmMWSc 92*
**Bond,** Richard Ewing 1953- *WhoAmL 92*
**Bond,** Richard L. 1935- *WhoMW 92*
**Bond,** Richard Lee 1935- *WhoAmP 91*
**Bond,** Richard Milton 1924- *WhoAmP 91*
**Bond,** Richard N 1950- *WhoAmP 91*
**Bond,** Richard Randolph 1927- *AmMWSc 92, WhoAmP 91*
**Bond,** Robert Augustine 1928- *WhoEnt 92*
**Bond,** Robert Franklin 1937- *AmMWSc 92*
**Bond,** Robert Harold 1936- *AmMWSc 92*
**Bond,** Robert Levi 1940- *AmMWSc 92*
**Bond,** Robert Sumner 1925- *AmMWSc 92*
**Bond,** Roger 1937- *WhoFI 92*
**Bond,** Ruskin 1934- *IntAu&W 91, WrDr 92*
**Bond,** Russell, Jr. 1937- *WhoMW 92*
**Bond,** Stephon Thomas 1934- *AmMWSc 92*
**Bond,** Thomas Alden 1938- *WhoWest 92*
**Bond,** Thomas Lester 1954- *WhoMW 92*
**Bond,** Thomas Moore, Jr. 1930- *WhoWest 92*
**Bond,** Thomas Ross 1926- *WhoEnt 92*
**Bond,** Timothy 1942- *WhoEnt 92*
**Bond,** Victor Potter 1919- *AmMWSc 92*
**Bond,** Victoria 1950- *NewAmDM*
**Bond,** Victoria Ellen 1945- *WhoEnt 92*
**Bond,** Vincent Earl 1947- *WhoWest 92*
**Bond,** Walter D 1932- *AmMWSc 92*
**Bond,** Wilbert, Sr. 1925- *WhoBlA 92*
**Bond,** William Bennett 1815-1906 *RelLAm 91*
**Bond,** William Bradford 1929- *AmMWSc 92, WhoMW 92*
**Bond,** William Chramer, Jr. 1954- *WhoRel 92*
**Bond,** William Cranch 1789-1859 *BiInAmS*
**Bond,** William H 1916- *AmMWSc 92*
**Bond,** William Payton 1941- *AmMWSc 92*
**Bond,** William Robert 1839-1922 *DcNCBi 1*
**Bond-Upson,** Deborah Gwendolyn 1949- *WhoWest 92*
**Bond-Williams,** Noel Ignace 1914- *Who 92*
**Bonda,** Alva Ted 1917- *WhoMW 92*
**Bondar,** Richard Jay Laurent 1940- *AmMWSc 92*
**Bondarchuk,** Sergei 1920- *FacFETw*
**Bondarchuk,** Sergey Fedorovich 1920- *IntWW 91*
**Bondareff,** William 1930- *AmMWSc 92*
**Bondarenko,** Aleksandr Pavlovich 1922- *IntWW 91*
**Bondarev,** Yuriy Vasil'evich 1924- *SovUnBD*
**Bondarev,** Yuriy Vasiliyevich 1924- *IntWW 91*
**Bonde,** Brian James 1958- *WhoMW 92*
**Bonde,** Erik Kauffmann 1922- *AmMWSc 92*
**Bonde,** Morris Reiner 1945- *AmMWSc 92*
**Bonde,** Peder 1923- *IntWW 91*
**Bondelevitch,** David Joseph 1963- *WhoEnt 92*
**Bondelid,** James E. 1954- *WhoMW 92*
**Bondelid,** Rollon Oscar 1923- *AmMWSc 92*
**Bonder,** Seth 1932- *AmMWSc 92*
**Bonderman,** Dean P 1936- *AmMWSc 92*
**Bondeson,** Stephen Ray 1952- *AmMWSc 92*
**Bondevik,** Kjell Magne 1947- *IntWW 91*
**Bondi,** Amedeo 1912- *AmMWSc 92*
**Bondi,** Bert Roger 1945- *WhoWest 92*
**Bondi,** Gene L 1913- *WhoAmP 91*
**Bondi,** Hermann 1919- *FacFETw, IntWW 91, Who 92*
**Bondi,** Richard John 1951- *WhoRel 92*
**Bondi-Stoddard,** Annamarie 1958- *WhoAmL 92*
**Bondinell,** William Edward 1942- *AmMWSc 92*
**Bondoc,** Rommel 1938- *WhoAmL 92*
**Bonds,** Barry Lamar 1964- *WhoBlA 92*
**Bonds,** Bill *LesBEnT 92*
**Bonds,** Bobby Lee 1946- *WhoBlA 92*
**Bonds,** Christopher Noonan 1942- *WhoEnt 92*
**Bonds,** Josephene Tabb 1952- *WhoEnt 92*
**Bonds,** Margaret 1913-1972 *NewAmDM, NotBlAW 92*
**Bondurant,** Byron L 1925- *AmMWSc 92*
**Bondurant,** Charles W, Jr 1918- *AmMWSc 92*
**Bondurant,** David William 1948- *WhoWest 92*
**Bondurant,** James A 1926- *AmMWSc 92*
**Bondurant,** Kathleen Alice 1958- *WhoEnt 92*
**Bondurant,** Mary Williams 1961- *WhoAmL 92*
**Bondurant,** Stuart 1929- *AmMWSc 92, IntWW 91*
**Bondy,** Donald Clarence 1932- *AmMWSc 92*
**Bondy,** Michael F 1923- *AmMWSc 92*
**Bondy,** Philip K 1917- *AmMWSc 92*
**Bondy,** Stephen Claude 1938- *AmMWSc 92*
**Bondy,** Susan 1948- *WhoMW 92*
**Bondybey,** Vladimir E 1940- *AmMWSc 92*
**Bone,** Alan Clarke 1938- *WhoRel 92*
**Bone,** Bruce Charles 1928- *WhoFI 92*
**Bone,** Charles 1926- *Who 92*
**Bone,** Charles Hugh 1937- *WhoMW 92*
**Bone,** Glenn Daniel, III 1963- *WhoFI 92*
**Bone,** Hugh A. 1909- *WrDr 92*
**Bone,** J F 1916- *IntAu&W 91, TwCSFW 91, WrDr 92*
**Bone,** Jack Norman 1919- *AmMWSc 92*
**Bone,** Jesse Franklin 1916- *AmMWSc 92*
**Bone,** John Frank Ewan *Who 92*
**Bone,** Larry Irvin 1935- *AmMWSc 92*
**Bone,** Leon Wilson 1945- *AmMWSc 92*
**Bone,** Marie Alexander 1956- *WhoFI 92*
**Bone,** Maurice Edgar 1924- *WhoAmL 92*
**Bone,** Muirhead 1876-1953 *TwCPaSc*
**Bone,** Quentin 1931- *IntWW 91, Who 92*
**Bone,** Ralph George 1959- *WhoIns 92*
**Bone,** Robert Earl 1957- *WhoMW 92*
**Bone,** Robert William 1932- *WhoWest 92*
**Bone,** Roger Bridgland 1944- *Who 92*
**Bone,** Roger C 1941- *AmMWSc 92*
**Bone,** Stephen 1904-1958 *TwCPaSc*
**Bone,** Stephen, Mrs. *Who 92*
**Bone,** Thomas Renfrew 1935- *Who 92*
**Bone,** Winston S. 1932- *WhoBlA 92*
**Bonebrake,** Alan Ray 1954- *WhoMW 92*
**Bonee,** John Leon, III 1947- *WhoAmL 92*
**Boneham,** Roger Frederick 1935- *AmMWSc 92*
**Bonehill,** Ralph *SmATA 67*
**Bonell,** Carlos Antonio 1949- *IntWW 91*
**Bonelli,** Joseph Edward 1946- *WhoWest 92*
**Bonelli,** Norma Lee 1945- *WhoEnt 92*
**Bonelli Hernando,** Emilio 1854-1910 *HisDSpE*
**Bonem,** Rena Mae 1948- *AmMWSc 92*
**Boner,** Donald Leslie 1944- *WhoMW 92*
**Boner,** John Henry 1845-1903 *DcNCBi 1*
**Boner,** William Hill 1945- *WhoAmP 91*
**Bonerz,** Peter 1938- *WhoEnt 92*
**Bones,** Ricky 1969- *WhoHisp 92*
**Bones,** Walter I 1927- *WhoAmP 91*
**Bonesio,** Woodrow Michael 1943- *WhoAmL 92*
**Boness,** Michael John 1940- *AmMWSc 92*
**Bonessa,** Dennis R. 1948- *WhoAmL 92*
**Bonessio di Terzet,** Ettore *IntAu&W 91*
**Bonestell,** Chesley 1888-1986 *FacFETw*
**Bonet,** Antonio 1913- *DcTwDes*
**Bonet,** Guillermo A. 1942- *WhoHisp 92*
**Bonet,** Lisa *WhoEnt 92*
**Bonet,** Lisa 1967- *IntMPA 92, WhoBlA 92*
**Bonet,** Nai *IntMPA 92*
**Bonett,** Emery *WrDr 92*
**Bonett,** John *IntAu&W 91X, WrDr 92*
**Bonetti,** Mattia 1952- *IntWW 91*
**Bonewits,** Philip Emmons Isaac 1949- *RelLAm 91*
**Bonewitz,** Robert Allen 1943- *AmMWSc 92*
**Boney,** Guy Thomas Knowles 1944- *Who 92*
**Boney,** J. Don 1928- *WhoBlA 92*
**Boney,** William Andrew 1933- *WhoFI 92*
**Boney,** William Arthur, Jr 1916- *AmMWSc 92*
**Bonfield,** Andrew Joseph 1924- *WhoWest 92*
**Bonfield,** Arthur Earl 1936- *WhoAmL 92*
**Bonfield,** Gordon Bradley, Jr. 1926- *WhoFI 92*
**Bonfield,** Peter Leahy 1944- *IntWW 91, Who 92*
**Bonfiglio,** Gregory Alan 1952- *WhoAmL 92*
**Bonfiglio,** Joel David 1958- *WhoAmL 92*
**Bonfiglio,** Michael 1917- *AmMWSc 92*
**Bonfiglio,** Robert 1956- *WhoEnt 92*
**Bonga,** Jan Max 1929- *AmMWSc 92*
**Bongarten,** Bruce C 1951- *AmMWSc 92*
**Bongartz,** Ferdinand A 1923- *WhoAmP 91*
**Bongartz,** Seth 1954- *WhoAmP 91*
**Bongers,** Paul Nicholas 1943- *Who 92*
**Bongiorni,** Domenic Frank 1908- *AmMWSc 92*
**Bongiorno,** Anthony Michael 1959- *WhoAmL 92*
**Bongiorno,** John Jacques 1938- *WhoFI 92*
**Bongiorno,** Salvatore F 1939- *AmMWSc 92*
**Bongiovanni,** Alfred Marius 1921- *AmMWSc 92*
**Bongmba,** Elias Kifon 1953- *WhoRel 92*
**Bongo,** Albert-Bernard 1935- *IntWW 91*
**Bongo,** Martin 1940- *IntWW 91*
**Bongo,** Omar 1935- *ConBlB 1 [port]*
**Bonhag,** Thomas Edward 1952- *WhoFI 92*
**Bonham,** Antony Lionel Thomas 1916- *Who 92*
**Bonham,** Barbara 1926- *IntAu&W 91, WrDr 92*
**Bonham,** Charles D 1937- *AmMWSc 92*
**Bonham,** Charlie Leonard 1939- *WhoWest 92*
**Bonham,** Clifford Vernon 1921- *WhoWest 92*
**Bonham,** Frank 1914- *IntAu&W 91*
**Bonham,** Frank 1914-1988 *TwCWW 91*
**Bonham,** Frank 1914-1989 *ConAu 36NR*
**Bonham,** Harold F, Jr 1928- *AmMWSc 92*
**Bonham,** Harold Florian 1928- *WhoWest 92*
**Bonham,** James Paul 1940- *WhoFI 92*
**Bonham,** John Stephen Henry 1936- *WhoRel 92*
**Bonham,** Kelshaw 1909- *AmMWSc 92*
**Bonham,** Lawrence Cook 1920- *AmMWSc 92*
**Bonham,** Nicholas 1948- *Who 92*
**Bonham,** Robert Logan 1927- *WhoFI 92*
**Bonham,** Russell Aubrey 1931- *AmMWSc 92*
**Bonham,** Terrence James 1938- *WhoWest 92*
**Bonham,** Vence L., Jr. *WhoBlA 92*
**Bonham,** Vence Lee, Jr. 1956- *WhoAmL 92*
**Bonham Carter** *Who 92*
**Bonham-Carter,** Baron 1922- *Who 92*
**Bonham-Carter,** Helena 1966- *IntMPA 92, IntWW 91, WhoEnt 92*
**Bonham-Carter,** John Arkwright 1915- *Who 92*
**Bonham Carter,** Raymond Henry 1929- *Who 92*
**Bonham Carter,** Richard Erskine 1910- *Who 92*
**Bonham-Carter,** Victor 1913- *IntAu&W 91, Who 92, WrDr 92*
**Bonham-Yeaman,** Doria 1932- *WhoAmL 92*
**Bonhoeffer,** Dietrich 1906-1945 *DcEcMov, EncTR 91 [port], FacFETw*
**Bonhoeffer,** Klaus 1901-1945 *EncTR 91 [port]*
**Bonhorst,** Carl W 1917- *AmMWSc 92*
**Bonhote,** Elizabeth 1744-1818 *BlkwCEP*
**Boni,** John Anthony 1937- *WhoEnt 92*
**Boni,** Michal 1954- *IntWW 91*
**Boni,** Robert Eugene 1928- *AmMWSc 92, WhoFI 92*
**Bonica,** John Joseph 1917- *AmMWSc 92, WrDr 92*
**Bonicelli,** Derito 1918- *WhoAmP 91*
**Bonicelli,** Joanne 1951- *WhoWest 92*
**Boniface I** *EncEarC*
**Boniface II** *EncEarC*
**Boniface,** John, Jr. 1944- *WhoMW 92*
**Bonifacio,** Andres 1863-1897 *HisDSpE*
**Bonifas,** Barbara J. 1947- *WhoFI 92*
**Bonifaz Nuno,** Ruben 1923- *ConSpAP*
**Bonifazi,** Stephen 1924- *AmMWSc 92*
**Bonifield,** Dale Robert 1960- *WhoWest 92*
**Bonifield,** Eugene 1933- *WhoIns 92*
**Bonilla,** Amalia *EncAmaz 91*
**Bonilla,** Anthony Cruz 1950- *WhoHisp 92*
**Bonilla,** Bobby 1963- *News 92-2 [port], WhoBlA 92, WhoHisp 92*
**Bonilla,** Eduardo *WhoHisp 92*
**Bonilla,** Frank *WhoHisp 92*
**Bonilla,** Gladys *WhoHisp 92*
**Bonilla,** Hector *WhoHisp 92*
**Bonilla,** Henry 1954- *WhoHisp 92*
**Bonilla,** Julio 1957- *WhoHisp 92*
**Bonilla,** Manuel George 1920- *AmMWSc 92*
**Bonilla,** Maria O. 1952- *WhoHisp 92*
**Bonilla,** Ruben, Jr. *WhoHisp 92*
**Bonilla,** Tony 1936- *WhoHisp 92*
**Bonilla,** Tony Correa 1940- *WhoHisp 92*
**Bonilla-Santiago,** Gloria 1954- *WhoHisp 92*
**Bonime,** Florence *DrAPF 91*
**Bonime-Blanc,** Andrea 1957- *WhoAmL 92*
**Bonin,** Bernard 1936- *IntWW 91*
**Bonin,** John H 1919- *AmMWSc 92*
**Bonin,** Keith Donald 1956- *AmMWSc 92*
**Bonington,** Chris 1934- *ConAu 34NR, WrDr 92*
**Bonington,** Christian John Storey 1934- *IntAu&W 91, IntWW 91, Who 92*
**Bonini,** William E 1926- *AmMWSc 92*
**Boniol,** Eddie Eugene 1931- *WhoFI 92*
**Bonior,** David E. 1945- *AlmAP 92 [port], WhoAmP 91*
**Bonior,** David Edward 1945- *WhoMW 92*
**Bonis,** Laszlo Joseph 1931- *WhoFI 92*
**Bonito,** Joseph Gerard 1958- *WhoFI 92*
**Bonitsis,** Theologos Homer 1953- *WhoFI 92*
**Bonitz,** August Heinrich Christian Julius 1841-1891 *DcNCBi 1*
**Bonk,** David Thomas 1956- *WhoAmL 92*
**Bonk,** James *DrAPF 91*
**Bonk,** James F 1931- *AmMWSc 92*
**Bonk,** James Raymond 1953- *WhoMW 92*
**Bonk,** Leslie Lynn 1962- *WhoMW 92*
**Bonker,** Don L 1937- *WhoAmP 91*
**Bonkovsky,** Herbert Lloyd *AmMWSc 92*
**Bonkowski,** Ronald L 1938- *WhoAmP 91*
**Bonkowski,** Ronald Lawrence 1938- *WhoMW 92*
**Bonmartini,** Francesco 1926- *WhoFI 92*
**Bonn,** Ethel May 1925- *AmMWSc 92*
**Bonn,** Eva Louise 1927- *WhoEnt 92*
**Bonn,** Ferdinand J 1943- *AmMWSc 92*
**Bonn,** Johann Jacob 1733-1781 *DcNCBi 1*
**Bonn,** Stanley Eils 1924- *WhoEnt 92*
**Bonn,** T H 1923- *AmMWSc 92*
**Bonn,** William Gordon 1946- *AmMWSc 92*
**Bonnard,** Abel Jean Desire 1883-1968 *BiDExR*
**Bonnard,** Pierre 1867-1947 *FacFETw*
**Bonne,** Ulrich 1937- *AmMWSc 92, WhoMW 92*
**Bonnefous,** Edouard 1907- *IntWW 91*
**Bonnefous,** Marc 1924- *IntWW 91*
**Bonnefoy,** Yves 1923- *FacFETw, GuFrLit 1*
**Bonnefoy,** Yves Jean 1923- *IntAu&W 91, IntWW 91*
**Bonnell,** David William 1943- *AmMWSc 92*
**Bonnell,** James Monroe 1922- *AmMWSc 92*
**Bonnell,** Paula *DrAPF 91*
**Bonnell,** William Everal 1941- *WhoWest 92*
**Bonnell,** William Richard 1942- *WhoMW 92*
**Bonner,** Alan L. 1947- *WhoEnt 92*
**Bonner,** Alice A. 1941- *WhoBlA 92*
**Bonner,** Alice Carol 1948- *WhoBlA 92*
**Bonner,** Anthony 1968- *WhoBlA 92*
**Bonner,** Arthur 1922- *ConAu 135, WrDr 92*
**Bonner,** Bester Davis *WhoBlA 92*

**Bonner,** Billy Edward 1939- *AmMWSc 92*
**Bonner,** Brian 1917- *WrDr 92*
**Bonner,** Bruce Albert 1929- *AmMWSc 92*
**Bonner,** Charles Douglass 1917-1990 *WhoBlA 92N*
**Bonner,** Daniel Patrick 1945- *AmMWSc 92*
**Bonner,** David Calhoun 1946- *AmMWSc 92, WhoMW 92*
**Bonner,** Della M. 1929- *WhoBlA 92*
**Bonner,** Edwin Knight 1914- *WhoFI 92*
**Bonner,** Elena Georgievna 1923- *IntWW 91*
**Bonner,** Eugene Aloysius 1951- *WhoAmL 92*
**Bonner,** Francis Joseph 1934- *AmMWSc 92*
**Bonner,** Francis Truesdale 1921- *AmMWSc 92*
**Bonner,** Frederick Ernest 1923- *Who 92*
**Bonner,** Herbert Covington 1891-1965 *DcNCBi 1*
**Bonner,** Hugh Warren 1944- *AmMWSc 92*
**Bonner,** Jack *TwCWW 91*
**Bonner,** James 1910- *AmMWSc 92, IntWW 91*
**Bonner,** James Frederick 1910- *FacFETw*
**Bonner,** James Jose 1950- *AmMWSc 92, WhoMW 92*
**Bonner,** Jill Christine 1937- *AmMWSc 92*
**Bonner,** John 1643?-1725? *BiInAmS*
**Bonner,** John Arthur 1929- *WhoEnt 92*
**Bonner,** John Franklin, Jr 1917- *AmMWSc 92*
**Bonner,** John Tyler 1920- *AmMWSc 92, IntWW 91, WrDr 92*
**Bonner,** Lorraine *WhoAmP 91*
**Bonner,** Lyman Gaylord 1912- *AmMWSc 92*
**Bonner,** Mary Winstead 1924- *WhoBlA 92*
**Bonner,** Michael 1924- *TwCWW 91, WrDr 92*
**Bonner,** Norman Andrew 1920- *AmMWSc 92*
**Bonner,** Oscar Davis 1917- *AmMWSc 92*
**Bonner,** Parker *TwCWW 91*
**Bonner,** Patricia J. 1939- *WhoWest 92*
**Bonner,** Paul Max 1934- *IntWW 91, Who 92*
**Bonner,** Philip Hallinder *AmMWSc 92*
**Bonner,** R Alan 1939- *AmMWSc 92*
**Bonner,** Raymond Thomas 1942- *IntAu&W 91*
**Bonner,** Robert 1942- *WhoAmP 91*
**Bonner,** Robert Cleve 1942- *WhoAmL 92*
**Bonner,** Robert Dubois 1926- *AmMWSc 92*
**Bonner,** Robert F, Jr. d1991 *NewYTBS 91*
**Bonner,** Robert William 1920- *IntWW 91*
**Bonner,** Sherwood *BenetAL 91*
**Bonner,** Stephen Jacob, III 1946- *WhoMW 92*
**Bonner,** Theophulis W. 1917- *WhoBlA 92*
**Bonner,** Tom Ivan 1942- *AmMWSc 92*
**Bonner,** Walter Daniel, Jr 1919- *AmMWSc 92*
**Bonner,** Walter Joseph 1925- *WhoAmL 92*
**Bonner,** Willard Hallam, Jr 1928- *AmMWSc 92*
**Bonner,** William Andrew 1919- *AmMWSc 92*
**Bonner,** William Haven 1921- *WhoRel 92*
**Bonner,** William Joel, Jr. 1956- *WhoAmL 92*
**Bonner,** William L. *WhoRel 92*
**Bonner,** William Neely, Jr. 1923- *WhoAmL 92*
**Bonner,** William Paul 1931- *AmMWSc 92*
**Bonner,** Yelena Georgievna 1923- *SovUnBD*
**Bonnes,** Charles Andrew 1941- *WhoAmL 92, WhoFI 92*
**Bonnesar,** David 1946- *WhoWest 92*
**Bonnet,** C. M. *Who 92*
**Bonnet,** Charles 1720-1793 *BlkwCEP*
**Bonnet,** Christian 1921- *IntWW 91*
**Bonnet,** Felix A. 1955- *WhoHisp 92*
**Bonnet,** Juan A, Jr 1939- *AmMWSc 92*
**Bonnet,** Peter Robert Frank 1936- *Who 92*
**Bonnet,** Stede d1718 *DcNCBi 1*
**Bonnett,** Aubrey Wendell 1942- *WhoWest 92*
**Bonnett,** Daniel Lee 1953- *WhoAmL 92*
**Bonnett,** Raymond 1931- *Who 92*
**Bonnett,** Richard Brian 1939- *AmMWSc 92*
**Bonnette,** Della T 1936- *AmMWSc 92*
**Bonneville,** Benjamin Louis Eulalie de 1769-1878 *BenetAL 91*
**Bonneville,** Mary Agnes 1931- *AmMWSc 92*
**Bonney,** Allan L 1917- *WhoAmP 91*
**Bonney,** Anne 1700-1722? *EncAmaz 91*
**Bonney,** Bill *TwCWW 91*
**Bonney,** Donald Ernest 1952- *WhoWest 92*
**Bonney,** George Louis William 1920- *Who 92*
**Bonney,** Hal James, Jr. 1929- *WhoAmL 92*
**Bonney,** J. Dennis 1930- *IntWW 91*
**Bonney,** John Dennis 1930- *WhoFI 92*
**Bonney,** Mary Lucinda 1816-1900 *RelLAm 91*
**Bonney,** Robert John 1942- *AmMWSc 92*
**Bonney,** Weston Leonard 1925- *WhoFI 92*
**Bonney,** William H. *BenetAL 91*
**Bonney,** William Wallace *AmMWSc 92*
**Bonnichsen,** Bill 1937- *AmMWSc 92*
**Bonnichsen,** Martha Miller 1941- *AmMWSc 92*
**Bonnici,** Carmelo M. *Who 92*
**Bonnici,** Emanuel 1928- *IntWW 91*
**Bonnici,** Karmenu Mifsud *IntWW 91*
**Bonnici,** Ugo Mifsud *IntWW 91*
**Bonnicksen,** Andrea Lynn 1947- *WhoMW 92*
**Bonnicksen-Jones,** Holly Christine *WhoMW 92*
**Bonnie and Clyde** *FacFETw [port]*
**Bonnie,** Richard Jeffrey 1945- *WhoAmL 92*
**Bonnielizabethoag** *DrAPF 91*
**Bonnin,** Gertrude 1876-1938 *RComAH*
**Bonnin,** Gertrude Simmons 1876-1938 *HanAmWH*
**Bonnin Julia,** Sebastian, III 1951- *WhoHisp 92*
**Bonnington,** Vicki Van Velson 1950- *WhoFI 92*
**Bonnor,** William Bowen 1920- *IntAu&W 91, WrDr 92*
**Bonnoront,** Hugh Edward 1938- *WhoMW 92*
**Bonny,** Anne *ScFEYrs*
**Bonny,** Michael Sinclair 1926- *WhoMW 92*
**Bonnycastle,** Charles 1792-1840 *BiInAmS*
**Bono Vox** 1960- *IntWW 91*
**Bono,** Alexander Dominic 1952- *WhoAmL 92*
**Bono,** Anthony Salvatore Emanuel, II 1946- *WhoFI 92*
**Bono,** Emilio de 1866-1944 *EncTR 91 [port]*
**Bono,** Sonny *WhoAmP 91*
**Bono,** Sonny 1935- *IntMPA 92, News 92-2 [port]*
**Bono,** Sonny Salvatore 1935- *WhoEnt 92, WhoWest 92*
**Bono,** Vincent Horace, Jr 1933- *AmMWSc 92*
**Bonomi,** John Gurnee 1923- *WhoAmL 92*
**Bonomo,** Jacqueline *DrAPF 91*
**Bononcini,** Giovanni 1670-1747 *NewAmDM*
**Bonora,** Anthony Charles 1943- *AmMWSc 92*
**Bonow,** Raysa Rose 1930- *WhoEnt 92*
**Bonowski,** Stephen John 1949- *WhoWest 92*
**Bonpane,** Theresa Killeen 1935- *WhoWest 92*
**Bonsack,** James Paul 1932- *AmMWSc 92*
**Bonsack,** Rose Mary Hatem *WhoAmP 91*
**Bonsack,** Walter Karl 1932- *AmMWSc 92*
**Bonsal,** Richard Irving 1920- *WhoFI 92*
**Bonsall,** Arthur 1917- *Who 92*
**Bonsall,** Crosby 1921- *IntAu&W 91, WrDr 92*
**Bonsall,** Frank Featherstone 1920- *Who 92*
**Bonsall,** Joseph Sloan, Jr. 1948- *WhoEnt 92*
**Bonser,** David *Who 92*
**Bonser,** Pamela Elizabeth 1960- *WhoEnt 92*
**Bonser,** Quentin 1920- *WhoWest 92*
**Bonser,** Sidney Henry 1924- *WhoMW 92*
**Bonser,** Stanley Haslam 1916- *Who 92*
**Bonsey,** Mary *Who 92*
**Bonsi,** Conrad K 1950- *AmMWSc 92*
**Bonsib,** Richard Eugene 1931- *WhoFI 92, WhoMW 92*
**Bonsib,** Stephen M *AmMWSc 92*
**Bonsiepe,** Gui 1934- *DcTwDes*
**Bonsignore,** Michael Robert 1941- *WhoMW 92*
**Bonsignore,** Patrick Vincent 1929- *AmMWSc 92*
**Bonsignore,** Robert James 1958- *WhoAmL 92*
**Bonsky,** Jack Alan 1938- *WhoFI 92*
**Bonsor,** Nicholas 1942- *Who 92*
**Bonstead,** Douglas Lyal 1947- *WhoMW 92*
**Bonta,** Diana Maria 1950- *WhoHisp 92*
**Bontadelli,** James Albert 1929- *AmMWSc 92*
**Bonte,** Frederick James 1922- *AmMWSc 92*
**Bontempo,** John A 1930- *AmMWSc 92*
**Bontempo,** Paul N 1951- *WhoAmP 91*
**Bontemps,** Arna 1902-1973 *BenetAL 91, BlkLC [port], ConAu 35NR*
**Bontemps,** Jacqueline Marie Fonvielle *WhoBlA 92*
**Bonting,** Sjoerd Lieuwe 1924- *AmMWSc 92*
**Bontly,** Thomas *DrAPF 91*
**Bonuccelli,** Charles Louis 1955- *WhoFI 92*
**Bonuomo,** Nancy Hope 1955- *WhoAmL 92*
**Bonura,** Thomas 1947- *AmMWSc 92*
**Bonus,** Harold William 1941- *WhoMW 92*
**Bonutti,** Alexander Carl 1951- *WhoWest 92*
**Bonventre,** Peter Frank 1928- *AmMWSc 92*
**Bonventre,** Joseph A. 1957- *WhoAmL 92*
**Bonvicino,** Guido Eros 1921- *AmMWSc 92*
**Bonvillian,** John Doughty 1948- *AmMWSc 92*
**Bonvin,** Francois 1817-1887 *ThHEIm*
**Bonwick,** Roy Edwin 1929- *WhoFI 92*
**Bony,** Jean V. 1908- *Who 92*
**Bonynge,** Jeanne Redfield 1925- *WhoAmL 92*
**Bonynge,** Joan *Who 92*
**Bonynge,** Richard 1930- *IntWW 91, NewAmDM, Who 92, WhoEnt 92*
**Boo,** Ben 1925- *WhoAmP 91*
**Boo,** Daniel 1959- *IntAu&W 91*
**Boochever,** Robert 1917- *WhoAmL 92, WhoAmP 91, WhoWest 92*
**Boocock,** Stephen William 1948- *WhoAmL 92*
**Boodman,** David Morris 1923- *AmMWSc 92*
**Boodman,** Norman S 1927- *AmMWSc 92*
**Boody,** Bertha M. 1877-1951 *DcAmImH*
**Boody,** Irving Rickerson, Jr. 1917- *WhoFI 92*
**Boody,** Janet 1946- *WhoAmP 91*
**Booe,** J M 1906- *AmMWSc 92*
**Booe,** James Marvin 1906- *WhoFI 92, WhoMW 92*
**Boohar,** Richard Kenneth 1935- *AmMWSc 92*
**Booher,** Alice Ann 1941- *WhoAmL 92*
**Booher,** Charles Forest 1944- *WhoMW 92*
**Booher,** Dianna Daniels 1948- *IntAu&W 91, WhoFI 92*
**Booher,** Edward E. d1990 *IntWW 91N*
**Booher,** Harold Hasting 1929- *WhoRel 92*
**Booher,** John Arthur 1942- *WhoRel 92*
**Book,** David Lincoln 1939- *AmMWSc 92*
**Book,** Jeffrey S 1959- *WhoAmP 91*
**Book,** John Kenneth 1950- *WhoFI 92*
**Book,** Linda Sue 1946- *AmMWSc 92*
**Book,** Raymond Thomas 1925- *WhoAmP 91*
**Book,** Ronald Lee 1952- *WhoAmP 91*
**Book,** Stephen Alan 1941- *AmMWSc 92*
**Book,** Steven Arnold 1945- *AmMWSc 92*
**Book,** William Joseph 1942- *WhoMW 92*
**Bookbinder,** Ronald Eric 1949- *WhoAmP 91*
**Bookchin,** Murray 1921- *WrDr 92*
**Bookchin,** Robert M 1935- *AmMWSc 92*
**Booke,** Henry Edward 1932- *AmMWSc 92*
**Booke,** Sorrell 1930- *IntMPA 92*
**Booker,** Alex 1956- *TwCPaSc*
**Booker,** Anne M. 1951- *WhoBlA 92*
**Booker,** Betty *DrAPF 91*
**Booker,** Bruce E. *WhoIns 92*
**Booker,** Carl Granger, Sr. 1928- *WhoBlA 92*
**Booker,** Christopher John Penrice 1937- *IntAu&W 91, Who 92*
**Booker,** Clifford R. 1926- *WhoBlA 92*
**Booker,** Cyrus L. 1956- *WhoAmL 92*
**Booker,** Daniel I. 1947- *WhoAmL 92*
**Booker,** Garvall H. 1925- *WhoBlA 92*
**Booker,** Gary P. 1959- *WhoBlA 92*
**Booker,** Henry George *IntWW 91N*
**Booker,** Henry George 1910- *AmMWSc 92*
**Booker,** Irvin B. *WhoBlA 92*
**Booker,** J F 1934- *AmMWSc 92*
**Booker,** James Avery, Jr. 1936- *WhoBlA 92*
**Booker,** James Douglas 1933- *WhoAmL 92*
**Booker,** James E. 1926- *WhoBlA 92*
**Booker,** Janice Leah 1929- *WhoEnt 92*
**Booker,** John, III 1947- *WhoBlA 92*
**Booker,** John Ratcliffe 1942- *AmMWSc 92*
**Booker,** Larry Frank 1950- *WhoFI 92*
**Booker,** Lewis Thomas 1929- *WhoAmL 92*
**Booker,** Matilda 1887-1957 *NotBlAW 92*
**Booker,** Merrel Daniel, Sr. *WhoBlA 92*
**Booker,** Michael Eugene 1951- *WhoAmP 91*
**Booker,** Patricia Kathleen 1965- *WhoMW 92*
**Booker,** Robert Joseph 1935- *WhoBlA 92*
**Booker,** Simeon S. 1918- *WhoBlA 92*
**Booker,** Teresa Hillary Clarke 1963- *WhoBlA 92*
**Booker,** Thurman D. 1937- *WhoBlA 92*
**Booker,** Venerable Francis 1920- *WhoBlA 92*
**Booker,** Walter M. 1907-1988 *WhoBlA 92N*
**Booker-Milburn,** Donald 1940- *Who 92*
**Bookert,** Charles C. 1918- *WhoBlA 92*
**Bookhammer,** Eugene Donald 1918- *WhoAmP 91*
**Bookholder,** Ronald Michael 1943- *WhoAmL 92*
**Bookhout,** Cazlyn Green 1907- *AmMWSc 92*
**Bookhout,** Theodore Arnold 1931- *AmMWSc 92*
**Bookman,** Mark 1952- *WhoAmL 92*
**Bookman,** Robert *IntMPA 92*
**Bookman,** Robert 1947- *WhoEnt 92*
**Bookman,** Terry Allen 1950- *WhoRel 92*
**Bookmyer,** Beverly Brandon *AmMWSc 92*
**Bookout,** Jerry 1933- *WhoAmP 91*
**Bookout,** John Frank, Jr. 1922- *IntWW 91*
**Bookout,** Ruth Lorraine 1940- *WhoAmP 91*
**Bookspan,** Martin 1926- *WhoEnt 92*
**Bookspan,** Michael Lloyd 1929- *WhoEnt 92*
**Bookstein,** Abraham 1940- *AmMWSc 92, WhoMW 92*
**Bookstein,** Fred Leon 1947- *AmMWSc 92*
**Bookstein,** Joseph Jacob 1929- *AmMWSc 92*
**Bookwalter,** George Norman 1924- *AmMWSc 92*
**Boolchand,** Punit *AmMWSc 92*
**Boole,** John Allen, Jr 1921- *AmMWSc 92*
**Boolell,** Satcam 1920- *IntWW 91, Who 92*
**Boolootian,** Richard Andrew 1927- *AmMWSc 92, WhoWest 92*
**Boom,** Roger Wright 1923- *AmMWSc 92*
**Booman,** Keith Albert 1928- *AmMWSc 92*
**Boomershine,** Donald Eugene 1931- *WhoFI 92*
**Booms,** Hans 1924- *IntWW 91*
**Booms,** Robert Edward 1945- *AmMWSc 92*
**Boomsliter,** Paul Colgan 1915- *AmMWSc 92*
**Boomstra,** Sjoerd 1913- *IntWW 91*
**Boon,** George Counsell 1927- *Who 92*
**Boon,** Henrik Nicolaas 1911- *IntWW 91*
**Boon,** Ina M. 1927- *WhoBlA 92*
**Boon,** John Daniel, Jr 1914- *AmMWSc 92*
**Boon,** John Trevor 1916- *IntWW 91, Who 92*
**Boon,** Peter Coleman 1916- *Who 92*
**Boon,** Ratliff 1781-1844 *DcNCBi 1*
**Boon,** William Robert 1911- *IntWW 91, Who 92*
**Boone,** Ashley A., Jr. 1938- *IntMPA 92*
**Boone,** Blind 1864-1927 *NewAmDM*
**Boone,** Bradley Gilbert 1950- *AmMWSc 92*
**Boone,** Carol Marie 1945- *WhoBlA 92*
**Boone,** Celia Trimble 1953- *WhoAmL 92*
**Boone,** Charles 1930- *WhoBlA 92*
**Boone,** Charles 1939- *NewAmDM*
**Boone,** Charles Walter 1925- *AmMWSc 92*
**Boone,** Cheryl Annette 1961- *WhoFI 92*
**Boone,** Clarence Donald 1939- *WhoBlA 92*
**Boone,** Clarence Wayne 1931- *WhoBlA 92*
**Boone,** Clifford Scott 1948- *WhoWest 92*
**Boone,** Clinton Caldwell 1922- *WhoBlA 92*
**Boone,** Daniel 1734-1820 *BenetAL 91, DcNCBi 1, RComAH*
**Boone,** Daniel R. 1927- *WrDr 92*
**Boone,** Daniel Richard 1927- *IntAu&W 91*
**Boone,** Deborah Ann 1956- *WhoEnt 92*
**Boone,** Don Maxwell 1949- *WhoRel 92*
**Boone,** Donald Joe 1943- *AmMWSc 92*
**Boone,** Donald Milford 1918- *AmMWSc 92*
**Boone,** Elwood Bernard, Jr. 1943- *WhoBlA 92*
**Boone,** Eugene Lawrence 1937- *WhoAmP 91*
**Boone,** Frederick Oliver 1941- *WhoBlA 92*
**Boone,** Gary M 1929- *AmMWSc 92*
**Boone,** Ike *TwCWW 91*
**Boone,** J. Fred 1919- *WhoAmL 92*
**Boone,** J. William 1952- *WhoAmL 92*
**Boone,** James Edward 1927- *AmMWSc 92*
**Boone,** James Lightholder 1932- *AmMWSc 92*
**Boone,** James Robert 1939- *AmMWSc 92*
**Boone,** James Ronald 1946- *AmMWSc 92*
**Boone,** James Virgil 1933- *WhoWest 92*
**Boone,** Jesse 1935- *WhoEnt 92*
**Boone,** John Clay 1947- *WhoRel 92*
**Boone,** John Lewis 1927- *WhoRel 92*
**Boone,** Joy Bale *DrAPF 91*
**Boone,** Kimberlie Ann 1960- *WhoEnt 92*
**Boone,** Larry Murphy 1937- *WhoWest 92*
**Boone,** Lawrence Rudolph, III 1948- *AmMWSc 92*
**Boone,** Louis Eugene 1941- *WhoFI 92*
**Boone,** Mark Philip 1951- *WhoWest 92*
**Boone,** Marvin Lester, Sr. 1931- *WhoEnt 92*
**Boone,** Michelle Terresa 1961- *WhoEnt 92*
**Boone,** Pat 1934- *IntMPA 92, WhoEnt 92, WrDr 92*
**Boone,** Raymond Harold 1938- *WhoBlA 92*
**Boone,** Richard Winston 1941- *WhoAmL 92*
**Boone,** Robert Franklin 1949- *WhoBlA 92*
**Boone,** Robert Lawrence 1947- *WhoAmP 91*
**Boone,** Ronald Bruce 1946- *WhoBlA 92*
**Boone,** Squire 1696-1765 *DcNCBi 1*
**Boone,** Thomas Caleb 1957- *WhoAmL 92*

**Boone,** Thomas John 1957- *WhoMW 92*
**Boone,** Willie Belle 1934- *WhoAmP 91*
**Boone,** Zola Ernest 1937- *WhoBlA 92*
**Boonieh,** Obi Anthony 1957- *WhoBlA 92*
**Boonstra,** Bram B 1912- *AmMWSc 92*
**Boonstra,** John C. *WhoRel 92*
**Boonyachai,** Sonthi 1917- *IntWW 91*
**Boonzaier,** Hugh Murray 1933- *IntWW 91*
**Boop,** Warren Clark, Jr 1933- *AmMWSc 92*
**Boor,** Myron Vernon 1942- *WhoMW 92*
**Booraem,** Robert Elmer 1856-1918 *BiInAmS*
**Booras,** Tommy George 1957- *WhoEnt 92*
**Boord,** Nicolas 1936- *Who 92*
**Boord,** Robert Lennis 1926- *AmMWSc 92*
**Booren,** Steve Michael 1956- *WhoFI 92*
**Boorman,** Derek 1930- *Who 92*
**Boorman,** Edwin Roy Pratt 1935- *Who 92*
**Boorman,** Gary Alexis 1942- *AmMWSc 92*
**Boorman,** Henry Roy Pratt 1900- *Who 92*
**Boorman,** John 1933- *IntDcF 2-2 [port], IntMPA 92, IntWW 91*
**Boorman,** Philip Michael 1939- *AmMWSc 92*
**Boorman,** Stanley Harold 1939- *WhoEnt 92*
**Boorn,** Andrew William 1954- *AmMWSc 92*
**Boorne,** Ronald Albert 1926- *AmMWSc 92*
**Booros,** James L. 1929- *WhoIns 92*
**Boorse,** Henry Abraham 1904- *AmMWSc 92*
**Boorstein,** Beverly Weinger 1941- *WhoAmL 92*
**Boorstein,** Lucille Paula 1927- *WhoAmL 92*
**Boorstin,** Daniel J. 1914- *IntWW 91, Who 92, WrDr 92*
**Boorstin,** Daniel Joseph 1914- *IntAu&W 91, WhoAmP 91*
**Boorstin,** Jon *ConAu 134*
**Boorstin,** Ruth F. *ConAu 134*
**Boorstin,** Ruth Frankel 1917- *ConAu 134*
**Boorstyn,** Robert Roy 1937- *AmMWSc 92*
**Boos,** Dennis Dale 1948- *AmMWSc 92*
**Boos,** H. Gordon 1958- *WhoEnt 92*
**Boosalis,** Michael Gus 1917- *AmMWSc 92*
**Boose,** Jerry Dale 1942- *WhoAmP 91*
**Boose,** Maryetta Kelsick *DrAPF 91*
**Booser,** E R 1922- *AmMWSc 92*
**Boosey,** John Arthur 1929- *WhoFI 92*
**Boosman,** Jaap Wim 1935- *AmMWSc 92*
**Booss,** John 1938- *AmMWSc 92*
**Booster,** Dean Emerson 1926- *AmMWSc 92*
**Boot,** John C. G. 1936- *WrDr 92*
**Boot,** William *IntAu&W 91X*
**Boote,** Charles Geoffrey Michael 1909- *Who 92*
**Boote,** Kenneth Jay 1945- *AmMWSc 92*
**Boote,** Robert Edward 1920- *Who 92*
**Booth** *Who 92*
**Booth,** Alan Edward 1951- *WhoEnt 92*
**Booth,** Alan Shore 1922- *Who 92*
**Booth,** Albert Edward 1928- *IntWW 91, Who 92*
**Booth,** Alex 1924- *WhoRel 92*
**Booth,** Amanda Jane 1962- *AmMWSc 92*
**Booth,** Andrew Donald 1918- *AmMWSc 92*
**Booth,** Anna-Marie 1946- *WhoAmL 92*
**Booth,** Anna Maxine 1917- *WhoAmP 91*
**Booth,** Anthony John 1939- *Who 92*
**Booth,** Ballington 1857-1940 *RelLAm 91*
**Booth,** Beatrice Crosby 1938- *AmMWSc 92*
**Booth,** Bert 1925- *WhoAmP 91*
**Booth,** Bradford Allen 1878-1919 *BiInAmS*
**Booth,** Brian George 1942- *Who 92*
**Booth,** Bruce L 1938- *AmMWSc 92*
**Booth,** Charles E. 1947- *WhoBlA 92*
**Booth,** Charles E 1952- *AmMWSc 92*
**Booth,** Charles Edward 1947- *WhoMW 92, WhoRel 92*
**Booth,** Charles Leonard 1925- *IntWW 91, Who 92*
**Booth,** Charles Loomis, Jr. 1933- *WhoFI 92*
**Booth,** Christopher 1924- *Who 92*
**Booth,** Clive 1943- *Who 92*
**Booth,** David Eugene 1949- *WhoMW 92*
**Booth,** David Herbert 1907- *Who 92*
**Booth,** David Layton 1939- *AmMWSc 92*
**Booth,** Donald Campbell 1950- *AmMWSc 92*
**Booth,** Douglas Allen 1949- *Who 92*
**Booth,** Edward d1917 *BiInAmS*
**Booth,** Edwin *IntAu&W 91, TwCWW 91, WrDr 92*
**Booth,** Edwin 1833-1893 *BenetAL 91*
**Booth,** Edwina d1991 *NewYTBS 91*
**Booth,** Eric Stuart 1914- *IntWW 91, Who 92*
**Booth,** Evangeline Cory 1865-1950 *RelLAm 91*
**Booth,** Frank 1943- *AmMWSc 92*
**Booth,** Gary Edwin 1940- *AmMWSc 92*
**Booth,** Gary Lynn 1952- *WhoFI 92*
**Booth,** Gary Melvon 1940- *AmMWSc 92*
**Booth,** Geoffrey *WrDr 92*
**Booth,** Gordon 1921- *Who 92*
**Booth,** Gordon Dean, Jr. 1939- *WhoAmL 92*
**Booth,** Gordon J 1931- *WhoAmP 91*
**Booth,** Harold W. 1934- *WhoIns 92*
**Booth,** Harold Waverly 1934- *WhoAmL 92*
**Booth,** Howard John 1938- *WhoMW 92, WhoRel 92*
**Booth,** I. MacAllister 1931- *IntWW 91*
**Booth,** Ian Jeremy 1960- *AmMWSc 92*
**Booth,** Irwin *TwCSFW 91*
**Booth,** Israel MacAllister 1931- *WhoFI 92*
**Booth,** James 1914- *Who 92*
**Booth,** James Curtis 1810-1888 *BiInAmS*
**Booth,** James Samuel 1927- *AmMWSc 92*
**Booth,** Jim 1946- *WhoAmP 91*
**Booth,** John Antony W. *Who 92*
**Booth,** John Austin 1929- *AmMWSc 92*
**Booth,** John Barton 1937- *Who 92*
**Booth,** John Dick L *Who 92*
**Booth,** John Evans 1956- *WhoRel 92*
**Booth,** John Lord 1907- *WhoEnt 92*
**Booth,** John Louis 1933- *WhoFI 92, WhoWest 92*
**Booth,** John Nicholls 1912- *WhoRel 92*
**Booth,** John Wells 1903- *Who 92*
**Booth,** John Wilkes 1838-1865 *BenetAL 91*
**Booth,** Junius Brutus 1769-1852 *BenetAL 91*
**Booth,** Ken 1943- *WrDr 92*
**Booth,** Lavaughn Venchael 1919- *WhoBlA 92*
**Booth,** Lawrence A 1934- *AmMWSc 92*
**Booth,** Le-Quita 1946- *WhoBlA 92*
**Booth,** Margaret 1898- *IntMPA 92, ReelWom [port]*
**Booth,** Margaret 1933- *Who 92*
**Booth,** Margaret Ann 1946- *WhoFI 92*
**Booth,** Martin 1944- *IntAu&W 91, WrDr 92*
**Booth,** Maud Ballington 1865-1948 *RelLAm 91*
**Booth,** Michael Addison John W. *Who 92*
**Booth,** Newell Ormond 1940- *AmMWSc 92*
**Booth,** Nicholas Henry 1923- *AmMWSc 92*
**Booth,** Norman E 1930- *AmMWSc 92*
**Booth,** Pat 1942- *WrDr 92*
**Booth,** Pat 1945- *IntAu&W 91*
**Booth,** Paul Wayne 1929- *WhoRel 92*
**Booth,** Peter John Richard 1949- *Who 92*
**Booth,** Philip *DrAPF 91*
**Booth,** Philip 1925- *BenetAL 91, ConPo 91, IntAu&W 91, WrDr 92*
**Booth,** Powers 1949- *IntMPA 92*
**Booth,** Ray S 1938- *AmMWSc 92*
**Booth,** Raymond 1929- *TwCPaSc*
**Booth,** Raymond George 1960- *AmMWSc 92*
**Booth,** Richard Alan 1950- *WhoAmL 92*
**Booth,** Richard George William Pitt 1938- *Who 92*
**Booth,** Richard H. *WhoIns 92*
**Booth,** Richard W 1924- *AmMWSc 92*
**Booth,** Robert 1916- *Who 92*
**Booth,** Robert Edwin 1921- *AmMWSc 92*
**Booth,** Robert John 1943- *WhoEnt 92*
**Booth,** Samuel Colton 1812-1895 *BiInAmS*
**Booth,** Sheldon James 1945- *AmMWSc 92*
**Booth,** Shirley 1899- *IntMPA 92*
**Booth,** Steven Craig 1959- *WhoRel 92*
**Booth,** Taylor Lockwood 1933- *AmMWSc 92*
**Booth,** Thomas Edward 1952- *AmMWSc 92*
**Booth,** Tony Hood, Jr. 1948- *WhoEnt 92*
**Booth,** Wayne C. 1921- *BenetAL 91*
**Booth,** Wayne Clayson 1921- *IntAu&W 91, WhoRel 92, WrDr 92*
**Booth,** William 1829-1912 *RelLAm 91*
**Booth,** William H. 1922- *WhoBlA 92*
**Booth,** William James 1939- *Who 92*
**Booth-Clibborn,** Stanley Eric Francis *Who 92*
**Booth-Clibborn,** Stanley Eric Francis 1924- *IntWW 91*
**Boothby,** Lord 1900-1986 *FacFETw*
**Boothby,** Brooke 1949- *Who 92*
**Boothby,** Guy 1867-1905 *ScFEYrs*
**Boothby,** James M 1959- *WhoAmP 91*
**Boothby,** William Munger 1918- *AmMWSc 92, WhoMW 92*
**Boothe,** Clare *BenetAL 91*
**Boothe,** Garland Cecil, Jr. 1932- *WhoAmL 92*
**Boothe,** James Howard 1916- *AmMWSc 92*
**Boothe,** Jeffrey Ferris 1955- *WhoAmL 92, WhoAmP 91*
**Boothe,** Raymond Lynn 1953- *WhoMW 92*
**Boothe,** Ronald G 1947- *AmMWSc 92*
**Boothman,** Campbell Lester 1942- *Who 92*
**Boothman,** Derek Arnold 1932- *Who 92*
**Boothman,** Sherre L. 1953- *WhoRel 92*
**Boothroyd,** Basil 1910- *IntAu&W 91*
**Boothroyd,** Betty 1929- *Who 92*
**Boothroyd,** Carl William 1915- *AmMWSc 92*
**Boothroyd,** Geoffrey 1932- *AmMWSc 92*
**Bootle,** William Augustus 1902- *WhoAmL 92*
**Bootle-Wilbraham** *Who 92*
**Booton,** Ray L. 1937- *WhoRel 92*
**Booton,** Richard C, Jr 1926- *AmMWSc 92*
**Boots,** Marvin Robert 1937- *AmMWSc 92*
**Boots,** Sharon G 1939- *AmMWSc 92*
**Boott,** Francis 1792-1863 *BiInAmS*
**Boott,** William 1805-1887 *BiInAmS*
**Booty,** John Everitt 1925- *WhoRel 92*
**Bootz,** Heidi Alice 1956- *WhoFI 92*
**Booysen,** Peter de Villiers 1930- *IntWW 91*
**Booz,** Gretchen Arlene 1933- *WhoMW 92*
**Booze,** Thomas Franklin 1955- *WhoWest 92*
**Boozer,** Allen Hayne 1944- *AmMWSc 92*
**Boozer,** Charles 1927- *AmMWSc 92*
**Boozer,** Emerson, Jr. 1943- *WhoBlA 92*
**Boozer,** F Vernon 1936- *WhoAmP 91*
**Boozer,** Reuben Bryan 1925- *AmMWSc 92*
**Boozer,** Robert 1937- *BlkOlyM*
**Boozman,** Catherine Armistead 1951- *WhoAmL 92*
**Bope,** Frank Willis 1918- *AmMWSc 92*
**Bopp,** Bernard William 1947- *AmMWSc 92*
**Bopp,** C Dan 1923- *AmMWSc 92*
**Bopp,** Edward Sidney 1930- *WhoAmP 91*
**Bopp,** Frederick, III *AmMWSc 92*
**Bopp,** Gordon R 1934- *AmMWSc 92*
**Bopp,** James, Jr. 1948- *WhoMW 92*
**Bopp,** Lawrence Howard 1949- *AmMWSc 92*
**Bopp,** Lynn A. *WhoRel 92*
**Bopp,** Thomas Theodore 1941- *AmMWSc 92*
**Bopp,** William Clarence 1943- *WhoFI 92*
**Boquet,** Donald James 1945- *AmMWSc 92*
**Bor,** Jonathan 1953- *ConAu 133*
**Bor,** Walter George 1916- *Who 92*
**Bora,** Alexander 1916- *WhoWest 92*
**Bora,** Irfan Ahmed 1960- *WhoFI 92*
**Bora,** Sunder S 1938- *AmMWSc 92*
**Borah,** Kripanath 1931- *AmMWSc 92*
**Borah,** Lyn R 1939- *WhoAmP 91*
**Borah,** William E 1865-1940 *RComAH*
**Borah,** William Edgar 1865-1940 *AmPolLe, FacFETw*
**Boraker,** David Kenneth 1939- *AmMWSc 92*
**Boram,** Clifford Wayne, Jr. 1933- *WhoMW 92*
**Boratyn,** George Michael, Jr. 1947- *WhoMW 92*
**Borax,** Eugene 1919- *AmMWSc 92*
**Boraz,** Robert Alan 1951- *WhoMW 92*
**Borch,** Otto Rose 1921- *IntWW 91*
**Borch,** Richard Frederic 1941- *AmMWSc 92*
**Borchard,** Edwin Montefiore 1884-1951 *AmPeW*
**Borchard,** Ronald Eugene 1939- *AmMWSc 92*
**Borchard,** William Marshall 1938- *WhoEnt 92*
**Borchardt,** Frank L 1938- *IntAu&W 91, WrDr 92*
**Borchardt,** Georg Hermann *EncTR 91*
**Borchardt,** Glenn 1942- *AmMWSc 92*
**Borchardt,** Hans J 1930- *AmMWSc 92*
**Borchardt,** Jack A 1916- *AmMWSc 92*
**Borchardt,** John Keith 1946- *AmMWSc 92*
**Borchardt,** Kenneth 1928- *AmMWSc 92*
**Borchardt,** Ronald T 1944- *AmMWSc 92*
**Borchardt,** Rudolf 1877-1945 *EncTR 91, LiExTwC*
**Borcherding,** Duthiel Harry 1920- *WhoMW 92*
**Borchers,** Edward Alan 1925- *AmMWSc 92*
**Borchers,** Elisabeth 1926- *IntWW 91*
**Borchers,** Harold Allison 1935- *AmMWSc 92*
**Borchers,** Patrick Joseph 1961- *WhoAmL 92*
**Borchers,** Raymond 1916- *AmMWSc 92*
**Borchers,** Robert Reece 1936- *WhoWest 92*
**Borchers,** Webber 1906- *WhoAmP 91*
**Borchert,** Gerald L. 1932- *ConAu 36NR*
**Borchert,** Gerald Leo 1932- *WhoRel 92*
**Borchert,** Harold R 1940- *AmMWSc 92*
**Borchert,** Peter Jochen 1923- *AmMWSc 92*
**Borchert,** Rolf 1933- *AmMWSc 92*
**Borchert,** Wilhelm *IntWW 91N*
**Borcherts,** Robert H 1936- *AmMWSc 92*
**Borchman,** Norman John 1923- *WhoFI 92*
**Bord,** Andre 1922- *IntWW 91*
**Borda,** Deborah 1949- *WhoEnt 92*
**Borda,** Richard Joseph 1931- *WhoFI 92, WhoWest 92*
**Bordaberry Arocena,** Juan Maria 1928- *IntWW 91*
**Bordallo,** Madeleine Mary 1933- *WhoAmP 91, WhoWest 92*
**Bordan,** Jack 1926- *AmMWSc 92*
**Bordao,** Rafael *DrAPF 91*
**Bordas,** Juana *WhoHisp 92*
**Bordass,** Dorothy 1905- *TwCPaSc*
**Bordaz,** Robert 1908- *IntWW 91*
**Borde,** Mark 1948- *WhoEnt 92*
**Bordeau,** Renee 1770-1828 *EncAmaz 91*
**Bordeaux Pilgrim** *EncEarC*
**Bordeaux,** Thomas Eugene 1950- *WhoRel 92*
**Bordeaux,** Tom *WhoAmP 91*
**Bordeleau,** Jo Ann 1938- *WhoMW 92*
**Bordeleau,** Lucien Mario 1940- *AmMWSc 92*
**Bordelon,** Scott Edward 1955- *WhoFI 92*
**Borden,** Christopher, III 1925- *WhoAmP 91*
**Borden,** Craig W 1915- *AmMWSc 92*
**Borden,** David 1938- *NewAmDM*
**Borden,** David M *WhoAmP 91*
**Borden,** Edward B 1949- *AmMWSc 92*
**Borden,** Ernest Carleton 1939- *AmMWSc 92*
**Borden,** Gail 1801-1874 *BiInAmS*
**Borden,** Gavin Gail d1991 *NewYTBS 91*
**Borden,** George Wayne 1937- *AmMWSc 92*
**Borden,** Harold F., Jr. 1942- *WhoBlA 92*
**Borden,** James B 1927- *AmMWSc 92*
**Borden,** John Harvey 1938- *AmMWSc 92*
**Borden,** Kenneth Duane 1940- *AmMWSc 92*
**Borden,** Lee 1953- *WhoFI 92*
**Borden,** Lizzie 1860-1927 *BenetAL 91*
**Borden,** Louise 1949- *SmATA 68 [port]*
**Borden,** Margaret Susan 1938- *WhoMW 92*
**Borden,** Maurice Anthony 1957- *WhoAmL 92*
**Borden,** Morton 1925- *WhoWest 92*
**Borden,** Nancy Higgen 1938- *WhoAmP 91*
**Borden,** Richard Stanley 1962- *WhoWest 92*
**Borden,** Robert Laird 1854-1937 *FacFETw*
**Borden,** Roger R 1930- *AmMWSc 92*
**Borden,** Simeon 1798-1856 *BiInAmS*
**Borden,** Stanley Perry 1917- *WhoRel 92*
**Borden,** Steelman Jonathan 1950- *WhoRel 92*
**Borden,** Thomas Allen 1937- *WhoWest 92*
**Borden,** Weston Thatcher 1943- *AmMWSc 92*
**Borden,** William *DrAPF 91*
**Borden,** William Vickers 1938- *WhoEnt 92*
**Borden,** Winston Wendell 1943- *WhoAmP 91*
**Bordenca,** Carl 1916- *AmMWSc 92*
**Border,** James Robert 1956- *WhoAmL 92*
**Border,** Larry 1951- *WhoAmP 91*
**Border,** Wayne Allen 1943- *AmMWSc 92*
**Bordereau,** Joanne *EncAmaz 91*
**Borders,** Alvin Marshall 1914- *AmMWSc 92*
**Borders,** Charles LaMonte, Jr 1942- *AmMWSc 92*
**Borders,** Charlie 1948- *WhoAmP 91*
**Borders,** Donald B 1932- *AmMWSc 92*
**Borders,** Florence Edwards 1924- *WhoBlA 92*
**Borders,** Frances Roma B. 1933- *WhoRel 92*
**Borders,** James Alan 1941- *AmMWSc 92*
**Borders,** Joe H 1861?- *ScFEYrs*
**Borders,** Margaret James 1939- *WhoRel 92*
**Borders,** Michael G. 1946- *WhoBlA 92*
**Borders,** William Alexander 1939- *ConAu 134*
**Borders,** William Donald 1913- *WhoRel 92*
**Bordes,** Peter Anthony 1927- *WhoEnt 92*
**Bordet,** Jules Jean Baptiste Vincent 1870-1961 *FacFETw, WhoNob 90*
**Bordett,** Robert Daniel 1948- *WhoFI 92*
**Bordeu,** Theophile de 1722-1776 *BlkwCEP*
**Bordier,** Primrose 1929- *IntWW 91*
**Bordier,** Roger 1923- *IntWW 91*
**Bordin,** Gerald M 1940- *AmMWSc 92*
**Bordine,** Burton W 1934- *AmMWSc 92*
**Bordley,** James, III 1900-1979 *ConAu 133*
**Bordley,** John Beal 1727-1804 *BiInAmS*
**Bordner,** Charles Albert, Jr 1937- *AmMWSc 92*
**Bordner,** Gregory Wilson 1959- *WhoWest 92*
**Bordner,** Jon D B 1940- *AmMWSc 92*
**Bordogna,** Joseph 1933- *AmMWSc 92*
**Bordoloi,** Kiron 1934- *AmMWSc 92*
**Bordoni,** Faustina 1693-1783 *NewAmDM*
**Bordow,** Robert Alexander 1954- *WhoWest 92*
**Bordson,** Nancy Carlson 1961- *WhoEnt 92*
**Bordwell,** Frederick George 1916- *AmMWSc 92*
**Bordy,** Bill 1930- *WhoEnt 92*

**Borecki,** Kenneth Michael 1955- *WhoFI 92*
**Borecky,** Isidore 1911- *WhoRel 92*
**Boreel,** Francis 1926- *Who 92*
**Boreel,** Wendela 1895-1985 *TwCPaSc*
**Boreen,** John Mark 1945- *WhoAmL 92*
**Boreham,** Arthur John 1925- *IntWW 91*
**Boreham,** John 1925- *Who 92*
**Boreham,** Leslie Kenneth Edward *Who 92*
**Borei,** Hans Georg 1914- *AmMWSc 92*
**Boreiko,** Craig John 1951- *AmMWSc 92*
**Borek,** Carmia Ganz 1937- *AmMWSc 92*
**Borek,** Felix 1926- *AmMWSc 92*
**Borek,** Thomas William 1936- *WhoEnt 92*
**Borel,** Armand 1923- *AmMWSc 92*
**Borel,** Jacques 1925- *IntWW 91*
**Borel,** Jacques Paul 1927- *IntWW 91*
**Borel,** James David 1951- *WhoWest 92*
**Borel,** Petrus 1809-1859 *GuFrLit 1*
**Borel,** Richard Wilson 1943- *WhoFI 92*
**Borel,** Yves *AmMWSc 92*
**Borella,** Luis Enrique 1930- *AmMWSc 92*
**Borelli,** Giovanni Alfonso 1608-1679 *BlkwCEP*
**Borelli,** Richard 1964- *WhoFI 92*
**Boreman,** John George, Jr 1948- *AmMWSc 92*
**Boren,** David L. 1941- *IntWW 91*
**Boren,** David Lyle 1941- *AlmAP 92 [port], WhoAmP 91*
**Boren,** Edward Daniel 1936- *WhoRel 92*
**Boren,** James Edgar 1949- *WhoAmL 92*
**Boren,** James Lewis, Jr. 1928- *WhoAmL 92*
**Boren,** Kenneth Ray 1945- *WhoWest 92*
**Boren,** William Meredith 1924- *WhoFI 92*
**Borenfreund,** Ellen 1922- *AmMWSc 92*
**Borenstein,** Audrey *DrAPF 91*
**Borenstein,** Benjamin 1928- *AmMWSc 92*
**Borenstein,** Emily *DrAPF 91*
**Borenstein,** Emily 1923- *WrDr 92*
**Borenstein,** Eugene Reed 1944- *WhoAmL 92*
**Borenstein,** Eve Rose 1955- *WhoAmL 92*
**Borenstein,** Henry I. 1949- *WhoWest 92*
**Borenstein,** Max 1920- *WhoFI 92*
**Borenstein,** Milton Conrad 1914- *WhoAmL 92, WhoFI 92*
**Borenstine,** Alvin Jerome 1933- *WhoFI 92, WhoMW 92*
**Borensztein,** Eduardo Roberto 1954- *WhoFI 92*
**Borer,** Anton Joseph 1916- *WhoRel 92*
**Borer,** Edward Turner 1938- *WhoFI 92*
**Borer,** Jeffrey Stephen 1945- *AmMWSc 92*
**Borer,** Katarina Tomljenovic 1940- *AmMWSc 92*
**Borer,** Mary Cathcart 1906- *WrDr 92*
**Borer,** Mary Irene Cathcart 1906- *IntAu&W 91*
**Borer,** Philip N 1945- *AmMWSc 92*
**Boresi,** Arthur Peter *AmMWSc 92*
**Boretz,** Benjamin 1934- *NewAmDM*
**Borg,** Alan Charles Nelson 1942- *IntWW 91, Who 92*
**Borg,** Bjoern 1956- *ConAu 134*
**Borg,** Bjorn *ConAu 134*
**Borg,** Bjorn 1956- *FacFETw*
**Borg,** Bjorn Rune 1956- *IntWW 91, Who 92*
**Borg,** Donald Cecil 1926- *AmMWSc 92*
**Borg,** Iris Y P 1928- *AmMWSc 92*
**Borg,** Jack *TwCWW 91*
**Borg,** Kim 1919- *IntWW 91*
**Borg,** Lars Goran 1913- *IntWW 91*
**Borg,** Malcolm Austin 1938- *WhoFI 92*
**Borg,** Marcus Joel 1942- *WhoRel 92*
**Borg,** Parker W 1939- *WhoAmP 91*
**Borg,** Richard John 1925- *AmMWSc 92*
**Borg,** Robert Munson 1910- *AmMWSc 92*
**Borg,** Sidney Fred 1916- *AmMWSc 92*
**Borg,** Thomas K 1943- *AmMWSc 92*
**Borg Costanzi,** Edwin J. 1925- *Who 92*
**Borgaonkar,** Digamber Shankarrao 1932- *AmMWSc 92*
**Borgatta,** Marie Lentini 1925- *WhoWest 92*
**Borgatti,** Alfred Lawrence 1928- *AmMWSc 92*
**Borge,** Donald Robert 1934- *WhoMW 92*
**Borge,** Tracy Ann 1958- *WhoAmL 92*
**Borge,** Victor 1909- *IntMPA 92, IntWW 91, NewAmDM, WhoEnt 92*
**Borge Martinez,** Tomas 1930- *IntWW 91*
**Borgeat,** Pierre 1947- *AmMWSc 92*
**Borgeaud,** Pierre 1934- *IntWW 91*
**Borgen,** Kjell 1939- *IntWW 91*
**Borgen,** Ole Edvard 1925- *WhoRel 92*
**Borgenicht,** Miriam 1915- *WrDr 92*
**Borgens,** Richard Ben 1946- *AmMWSc 92*
**Borger,** David Paul 1950- *WhoRel 92*
**Borger,** Edward M., Jr. 1947- *WhoWest 92*
**Borger,** Gary Alan 1944- *WhoEnt 92*
**Borger,** Gary L. 1947- *WhoAmL 92*
**Borger,** Michael Hinton Ivers 1951- *WhoMW 92*
**Borger,** Mitchell F. 1957- *WhoAmL 92*
**Borger,** Riekele 1929- *IntWW 91*
**Borgerding,** Shirley Ruth 1929- *WhoAmP 91*
**Borges,** Carlos Rego 1939- *AmMWSc 92, WhoWest 92*
**Borges,** Dain Edward 1954- *WhoHisp 92*
**Borges,** Evelyn 1951- *WhoHisp 92*
**Borges,** Francisco L 1951- *WhoAmP 91, WhoBlA 92*
**Borges,** Jacobo 1931- *IntWW 91*
**Borges,** Jorge Luis 1899- *IntAu&W 91*
**Borges,** Jorge Luis 1899-1986 *BenetAL 91, DcLB 113 [port], FacFETw, TwCSFW 91A*
**Borges,** Jose Joaquim Almeida 1910- *IntWW 91*
**Borges,** Juan Roberto 1950- *WhoHisp 92*
**Borges,** Lynne MacFarlane 1952- *WhoBlA 92*
**Borges,** Max E., Jr. 1942- *WhoHisp 92*
**Borges,** Ramon F. 1939- *WhoHisp 92*
**Borges,** Thomas William Alfred 1923- *Who 92*
**Borges,** Wayne Howard 1919- *AmMWSc 92*
**Borges,** William, III 1948- *WhoWest 92*
**Borges Rodriguez,** Nicasio 1912-1991 *WhoHisp 92N*
**Borgese,** Giuseppe 1882-1952 *LiExTwC*
**Borgese,** John A. 1951- *WhoAmL 92*
**Borgese,** Thomas A 1929- *AmMWSc 92*
**Borgeson,** David P 1935- *AmMWSc 92*
**Borgeson,** Earl Charles 1922- *WhoAmL 92*
**Borgeson,** Jon Timothy 1957- *WhoEnt 92*
**Borgeson,** Ralph Irwin, Jr 1932- *WhoAmP 91*
**Borgeson,** Vernon R 1920- *WhoAmP 91*
**Borgford,** Norma Jeanne 1933- *WhoRel 92*
**Borghesani,** James Michael 1958- *WhoEnt 92*
**Borghese,** Junio Valerio 1906-1974 *BiDExR*
**Borgia,** Gerald 1949- *AmMWSc 92*
**Borgia,** John F. 1940- *WhoHisp 92*
**Borgia,** Julian Frank 1943- *AmMWSc 92*
**Borgia,** Mary Regina Seber 1955- *WhoEnt 92*
**Borgic,** Rosemary Aurora 1927- *WhoMW 92*
**Borgie,** Jerald Richard 1936- *WhoRel 92*
**Borginis,** Sarah d1866? *EncAmaz 91*
**Borgiotti,** Giorgio V 1932- *AmMWSc 92*
**Borgkvist,** Joseph, Jr. 1944- *WhoRel 92*
**Borglum,** Gerald Baltzer 1933- *AmMWSc 92*
**Borglum,** Gutzon 1870-1941 *BenetAL 91*
**Borglum,** John Gutzon de la Mothe 1867-1941 *FacFETw*
**Borglum,** Keith Carsten 1951- *WhoWest 92*
**Borgman,** James Mark 1954- *ConAu 133*
**Borgman,** Jan 1929- *IntWW 91*
**Borgman,** Jim *ConAu 133*
**Borgman,** Leon Emry 1928- *AmMWSc 92*
**Borgman,** Robert F 1926- *AmMWSc 92*
**Borgman,** Robert John 1942- *AmMWSc 92*
**Borgman,** Robert P 1930- *AmMWSc 92*
**Borgnaes,** Dan 1935- *AmMWSc 92*
**Borgnine,** Ernest 1917- *IntWW 91, WhoEnt 92*
**Borgnine,** Ernest 1918- *IntMPA 92*
**Borgomeo,** Pasquale 1933- *IntWW 91*
**Borgstadt,** Marcia Ann 1958- *WhoMW 92*
**Borgstedt,** Harold Heinrich 1929- *AmMWSc 92*
**Borgstrom,** Georg Arne 1912- *AmMWSc 92*
**Borgwardt,** Robert G. 1922- *WhoRel 92*
**Borhi,** Carol 1949- *WhoFI 92*
**Bori,** Lucrezia 1887-1960 *FacFETw*
**Borich,** Michael *DrAPF 91*
**Borie,** Bernard Simon 1924- *AmMWSc 92*
**Boring,** Charles Marion 1943- *WhoWest 92*
**Boring,** John Rutledge, III 1930- *AmMWSc 92*
**Boring,** John Wayne 1929- *AmMWSc 92*
**Boring,** Phyllis Zatlin *ConAu 36NR*
**Boringdon,** Viscount 1956- *Who 92*
**Borinstein,** Dennis Ivan 1949- *WhoWest 92*
**Boris III** 1894-1943 *EncTR 91, FacFETw*
**Boris III,** King of Bulgaria 1894-1943 *CurBio 91N*
**Boris,** Kathleen Vaughan 1947- *WhoAmP 91*
**Boris,** Martin *DrAPF 91*
**Boris,** Robert 1945- *IntMPA 92*
**Boris,** Ruthanna 1918- *WhoEnt 92*
**Boris,** William O. 1939- *WhoFI 92, WhoMW 92*
**Borisenok,** Walter A 1923- *AmMWSc 92*
**Borisevich,** Nikolai Aleksandrovich 1923- *IntWW 91*
**Borish,** Irvin Max 1913- *AmMWSc 92*
**Borison,** Herbert Leon 1922- *AmMWSc 92*
**Borisy,** Gary Guy 1942- *AmMWSc 92*
**Borisyak,** Aleksey Alekseevich 1872-1944 *SovUnBD*
**Boritzer,** Rafael B. 1943- *WhoEnt 92*
**Borja,** Dale Raymond Paras 1959- *WhoWest 92*
**Borja,** Francisco Manglona *WhoAmP 91*
**Borja,** Juan de 1564-1628 *HisDSpE*
**Borja Cevallos,** Rodrigo 1937- *IntWW 91*
**Borjas,** George Jesus 1950- *WhoFI 92*
**Borjon,** Robert Patrick 1935- *WhoHisp 92*
**Bork,** Alfred Morton 1926- *AmMWSc 92*
**Bork,** Kennard Baker 1940- *AmMWSc 92, WhoMW 92*
**Bork,** Ned Lawrence, III 1955- *WhoAmL 92*
**Bork,** Robert H 1927- *FacFETw*
**Bork,** Robert Heron 1927- *IntWW 91, WhoAmL 92, WhoAmP 91*
**Borkan,** Gene 1947- *WhoEnt 92*
**Borkan,** Harold 1927- *AmMWSc 92*
**Borkan,** Leonard Michael 1957- *WhoFI 92*
**Borkan,** William Noah 1956- *WhoFI 92*
**Borke,** Louise Ilene 1955- *WhoFI 92*
**Borke,** Mitchell Louis 1919- *AmMWSc 92*
**Borker,** Wallace Jacob 1919- *WhoAmL 92*
**Borkh,** Inge 1921- *IntWW 91*
**Borkman,** Raymond Francis 1940- *AmMWSc 92*
**Borko,** Harold 1922- *WrDr 92*
**Borkon,** Eli Leroy 1908- *AmMWSc 92*
**Borkovec,** Alexej B 1925- *AmMWSc 92*
**Borkovitz,** Henry S 1935- *AmMWSc 92*
**Borkowski,** Mark Stephen 1958- *WhoWest 92*
**Borkowski,** Raymond P 1934- *AmMWSc 92*
**Borkowsky,** William 1947- *AmMWSc 92*
**Borland,** Barbara Dodge 1904?-1991 *ConAu 133*
**Borland,** David Morton 1911- *Who 92*
**Borland,** Hal 1900- *TwCWW 91*
**Borland,** Hal 1900-1978 *BenetAL 91*
**Borland,** John Nelson 1828-1890 *BiInAmS*
**Borland,** Kathryn 1916- *WrDr 92*
**Borland,** Lorelei Joy 1941- *WhoAmL 92*
**Borland,** Solon 1811-1864 *DcNCBi 1*
**Borland,** William K. 1942- *WhoIns 92*
**Borlase,** Deidre 1925- *TwCPaSc*
**Borlaug,** Allen 1941- *WhoAmP 91*
**Borlaug,** David P. 1956- *WhoMW 92*
**Borlaug,** Norman Ernest 1914- *AmMWSc 92, FacFETw, IntWW 91, Who 92, WhoNob 90*
**Borle,** Andre Bernard 1930- *AmMWSc 92*
**Borlenghi,** Matthew Andrew 1967- *WhoEnt 92*
**Borley,** Lester 1931- *Who 92*
**Borm,** Alfred Ervin 1937- *AmMWSc 92*
**Borman,** Aleck 1919- *AmMWSc 92*
**Borman,** Amy Joanne 1954- *WhoAmL 92*
**Borman,** Frank 1928- *FacFETw, IntWW 91*
**Borman,** Gary Lee 1932- *AmMWSc 92*
**Bormann,** Barbara-Jean Anne 1958- *AmMWSc 92*
**Bormann,** Frederick Herbert 1922- *AmMWSc 92*
**Bormann,** Martin 1900-1945 *BiDExR, EncTR 91 [port], FacFETw*
**Born,** Alfred Ernest 1945- *WhoMW 92*
**Born,** Allen 1933- *WhoFI 92*
**Born,** Brooksley Elizabeth 1940- *WhoAmL 92*
**Born,** George Henry 1939- *AmMWSc 92*
**Born,** Gordon Stuart 1933- *AmMWSc 92*
**Born,** Gustav Victor Rudolf 1921- *IntWW 91, Who 92*
**Born,** Harold Joseph 1922- *AmMWSc 92*
**Born,** Helena 1860-1901 *BiDBrF 2*
**Born,** Ignaz Edler von 1742-1791 *BlkwCEP*
**Born,** James E. 1934- *WhoMW 92*
**Born,** John 1937- *WhoAmP 91*
**Born,** Leonard Loth 1906- *WhoFI 92*
**Born,** Max 1882-1970 *FacFETw, WhoNob 90*
**Born,** Samuel Roydon, II 1945- *WhoAmL 92*
**Born,** Steven Murray 1947- *WhoWest 92*
**Borne,** Allen Helwick, Jr. 1959- *WhoAmL 92*
**Borne,** Bonita H. 1953- *WhoEnt 92*
**Borne,** Leon L 1938- *WhoAmP 91*
**Borne,** Ronald Francis 1938- *AmMWSc 92*
**Borneman,** Donald William 1949- *WhoFI 92*
**Borneman,** George Howard 1915- *WhoMW 92, WhoRel 92*
**Borneman,** John Paul 1958- *WhoWest 92*
**Bornemann,** Alfred 1906- *AmMWSc 92*
**Bornemann,** Alfred H. d1991 *NewYTBS 91*
**Bornemann,** Alfred H. 1908-1991 *ConAu 134*
**Bornemeier,** Dwight D 1934- *AmMWSc 92*
**Borner,** Silvio 1941- *IntWW 91*
**Borner,** William J. 1959- *WhoAmL 92*
**Bornewasser,** Hans 1924- *IntWW 91*
**Bornfriend,** Jacob 1904-1976 *TwCPaSc*
**Bornheimer,** Allen Millard 1942- *WhoAmL 92*
**Bornholdt,** Robert Mark 1961- *WhoWest 92*
**Bornhuetter,** Ronald L. 1932- *WhoIns 92*
**Bornmann,** Carl Malcolm 1936- *WhoAmL 92*
**Bornmann,** John Arthur 1930- *AmMWSc 92*
**Bornmann,** Lewis Joseph 1936- *WhoWest 92*
**Bornmann,** Patricia L 1958- *AmMWSc 92*
**Bornmann,** Robert Clare 1931- *AmMWSc 92*
**Borns,** David James 1950- *WhoWest 92*
**Borns,** Harold William, Jr 1927- *AmMWSc 92*
**Borns,** Robert Aaron 1935- *WhoFI 92, WhoMW 92*
**Bornside,** George Harry 1925- *AmMWSc 92*
**Bornslaeger,** Elayne A 1960- *AmMWSc 92*
**Bornstein,** Alan Arnold 1950- *AmMWSc 92*
**Bornstein,** Deborah H. 1953- *WhoAmL 92*
**Bornstein,** George 1941- *IntAu&W 91, WrDr 92*
**Bornstein,** Joseph 1921- *AmMWSc 92*
**Bornstein,** Joseph 1925- *AmMWSc 92*
**Bornstein,** Lawrence A 1923- *AmMWSc 92*
**Bornstein,** Michael 1940- *AmMWSc 92*
**Bornstein,** Morris 1927- *WhoFI 92, WhoMW 92*
**Bornstein,** Paul 1934- *AmMWSc 92*
**Bornstein,** Robert D 1942- *AmMWSc 92*
**Borny,** Walter Michael 1948- *WhoWest 92*
**Borock,** Herb *WhoAmP 91*
**Borod,** Donald Lee 1947- *WhoAmL 92, WhoFI 92*
**Borod,** Ronald Sam 1941- *WhoAmL 92*
**Borodale,** Viscount 1973- *Who 92*
**Borodin,** Alexander Porphyrevich 1833-1887 *NewAmDM*
**Borodin,** George *Who 92*
**Borodinsky,** Samuel 1941- *IntMPA 92*
**Borofsky,** Jonathan 1942- *WorArt 1980 [port]*
**Borom,** Lawrence H. 1937- *WhoBlA 92*
**Borom,** Marcus P 1934- *AmMWSc 92*
**Boron,** Frank Thomas 1941- *WhoFI 92*
**Boron,** Jeffrey Robert 1960- *WhoFI 92*
**Boron,** Walter Frank 1949- *AmMWSc 92*
**Boros,** Dov Lewis 1932- *AmMWSc 92*
**Borosh,** Itshak 1938- *AmMWSc 92*
**Boroskin,** Alan 1942- *WhoWest 92*
**Boross,** Peter 1928- *IntWW 91*
**Borotra,** Jean 1898- *IntWW 91*
**Boroughs,** Thaddeus Calhoun, III 1950- *WhoRel 92*
**Borovik-Romanov,** Viktor-Andrey S. 1920- *IntWW 91*
**Borovkov,** Aleksandr Alekseyevich 1931- *IntWW 91*
**Borovoy,** Marc Allen 1960- *WhoMW 92*
**Borovoy,** Vitali 1916- *DcEcMov*
**Borovsky,** Dov 1943- *AmMWSc 92*
**Borow,** Aaron 1933- *WhoRel 92*
**Borow,** Richard Henry 1935- *WhoAmL 92*
**Borowczyk,** Walerian 1923- *IntDcF 2-2*
**Borowiecki,** Barbara Zakrzewska 1924- *AmMWSc 92*
**Borowitz,** Albert Ira 1930- *WhoAmL 92*
**Borowitz,** Grace Burchman 1934- *AmMWSc 92*
**Borowitz,** Irving Julius 1930- *AmMWSc 92*
**Borowitz,** Joseph Leo 1932- *AmMWSc 92*
**Borowitz,** Michael J 1950- *AmMWSc 92*
**Borowitz,** Sidney 1918- *AmMWSc 92*
**Borowski,** Jennifer Lucile 1934- *WhoFI 92*
**Borowski,** John Michael 1948- *WhoAmL 92*
**Borowski,** Tadeusz 1922-1951 *EncTR 91*
**Borowsky,** Betty Marian 1943- *AmMWSc 92*
**Borowsky,** Harry Herbert 1914- *AmMWSc 92*
**Borowsky,** Richard Lewis 1943- *AmMWSc 92*
**Borowy,** Frank Rhine 1948- *WhoAmL 92*
**Borr,** Mitchell 1924- *AmMWSc 92*
**Borra,** Ermanno Franco 1943- *AmMWSc 92*
**Borradaile,** Earl Edward 1930- *WhoAmL 92*
**Borradaile,** Hugh Alastair 1907- *Who 92*
**Borras,** Caridad 1942- *AmMWSc 92*
**Borreca,** John Peter 1953- *WhoFI 92*
**Borrego,** Jose M 1931- *AmMWSc 92*
**Borrego,** Joseph Thomas 1939- *AmMWSc 92*
**Borrell,** Jerry 1952- *WhoEnt 92, WhoFI 92*
**Borrell,** Richard Thomas 1951- *WhoFI 92*
**Borrelli,** Damon Joseph 1962- *WhoAmL 92*
**Borrelli,** Mario 1922- *IntWW 91*
**Borrelli,** Nicholas Francis 1936- *AmMWSc 92*
**Borrelli,** Robert L 1932- *AmMWSc 92*
**Borrello,** Michael Lucas 1964- *WhoEnt 92*
**Borrero,** I. Michael *WhoHisp 92*

**Borrero-de Jesus**, Nydia 1963- *WhoHisp 92*
**Borreson**, Glenn Leland 1944- *WhoRel 92*
**Borrett**, Charles Walter 1916- *Who 92*
**Borrett**, Louis Albert Frank 1924- *Who 92*
**Borrie**, Gordon 1931- *IntWW 91, Who 92*
**Borrie**, John 1915- *WrDr 92*
**Borrie**, Wilfred David 1913- *IntWW 91*
**Borror**, Alan L 1934- *AmMWSc 92*
**Borror**, Arthur Charles 1935- *AmMWSc 92*
**Borror**, Caywood Joseph 1930- *WhoAmL 92*
**Borrow**, George 1803-1881 *RfGEnL 91*
**Borrowman**, S Ralph 1918- *AmMWSc 92*
**Borsa**, Joseph 1938- *AmMWSc 92*
**Borsari**, Bruno 1961- *AmMWSc 92*
**Borsch**, Frederick Houk 1935- *WhoRel 92, WhoWest 92*
**Borschke**, Daniel Christopher 1952- *WhoMW 92*
**Borsden**, John F. 1953- *WhoEnt 92*
**Borse**, Garold Joseph 1940- *AmMWSc 92*
**Borselle**, Marianne Patricia 1962- *WhoEnt 92*
**Borseth**, Donald George 1950- *WhoMW 92*
**Borsick**, Marlin Lester 1953- *WhoFI 92, WhoMW 92*
**Borski**, Chester L. *WhoRel 92*
**Borski**, Robert A. 1948- *AlmAP 92 [port], WhoAmP 91*
**Borski**, Thomas Anthony 1941- *WhoFI 92*
**Borso**, Charles S 1946- *AmMWSc 92*
**Borson**, Daniel Benjamin 1946- *WhoWest 92*
**Borson**, Robert Oliver 1938- *WhoWest 92*
**Borson**, Roo 1952- *ConPo 91*
**Borsos**, Miklos d1990 *IntWW 91N*
**Borsos**, Tibor 1927- *AmMWSc 92*
**Borst**, Daryll C 1940- *AmMWSc 92*
**Borst**, David W *AmMWSc 92*
**Borst**, John, Jr. 1927- *WhoAmL 92*
**Borst**, Lawrence Marion 1927- *WhoAmP 91*
**Borst**, Lyle Benjamin 1912- *AmMWSc 92*
**Borst**, Philip Craig 1950- *WhoAmP 91, WhoMW 92*
**Borst**, Philip Wayne 1941- *WhoAmL 92*
**Borst**, Roger Lee 1930- *AmMWSc 92*
**Borst**, Terry *DrAPF 91*
**Borst**, Walter Ludwig 1938- *AmMWSc 92*
**Borst-Eilers**, Else *AmMWSc 92*
**Borsting**, Jack Raymond 1929- *AmMWSc 92, WhoFI 92, WhoWest 92*
**Borsuk**, Gerald M 1944- *AmMWSc 92*
**Borsum**, James Carl 1958- *WhoFI 92*
**Borta**, James Robert 1947- *WhoMW 92*
**Bortel**, Calvin Stanley 1925- *WhoFI 92*
**Bortel**, Maureen A. Mason 1942- *WhoFI 92*
**Bortell**, Glen *WhoAmP 91*
**Borten**, Per 1913- *IntWW 91*
**Borthwick** *Who 92*
**Borthwick**, Lord 1905- *Who 92*
**Borthwick**, Master of 1940- *Who 92*
**Borthwick**, J. S. *WrDr 92*
**Borthwick**, Jason *Who 92*
**Borthwick**, John Thomas 1917- *Who 92*
**Borthwick**, Kenneth W. 1915- *Who 92*
**Borthwick**, Paul Monroe 1954- *WhoRel 92*
**Borthwick**, William Jason 1910- *Who 92*
**Bortin**, Mortimer M *AmMWSc 92*
**Bortko**, Edward Joseph 1929- *WhoMW 92*
**Bortner**, Ernest Edward 1930- *WhoRel 92*
**Bortner**, Michael E 1949- *WhoAmP 91*
**Bortnick**, Newman Mayer 1921- *AmMWSc 92*
**Bortoff**, Alexander 1932- *AmMWSc 92*
**Bortolan**, Peter Roger 1937- *WhoAmL 92*
**Bortolozzi**, Jehud 1940- *AmMWSc 92*
**Bortolussi**, Michael Richard 1956- *WhoWest 92*
**Bortoluzzi**, Paolo 1938- *IntWW 91*
**Borton**, Anthony 1933- *AmMWSc 92*
**Borton**, Douglas Child 1926- *WhoFI 92*
**Borton**, George Robert 1922- *WhoWest 92*
**Borton**, Robert Ernest 1942- *WhoAmL 92*
**Borton**, Thomas Ernest 1942- *AmMWSc 92*
**Borton**, William Monroe 1914- *WhoWest 92*
**Bortone**, Stephen Anthony 1946- *AmMWSc 92*
**Borts**, Robert Edward 1962- *WhoEnt 92*
**Bortz**, Alfred Benjamin 1944- *AmMWSc 92*
**Bortz**, Garry Lynden 1953- *WhoRel 92*
**Bortz**, Mark Vaughn 1958- *WhoEnt 92*
**Bortz**, Paul Isaac 1937- *WhoEnt 92*
**Boruch**, Marianne *DrAPF 91*
**Boruchowitz**, Stephen Alan 1952- *WhoWest 92*
**Borucki**, William Joseph 1939- *AmMWSc 92*
**Boruff**, John David 1930- *WhoMW 92*
**Borum**, Isabel *WhoAmP 91*
**Borum**, Olin H 1917- *AmMWSc 92*
**Borum**, Peggy R 1946- *AmMWSc 92*
**Borum**, Regina A. 1938- *WhoBlA 92*
**Borum**, Rodney Lee 1929- *WhoFI 92*
**Borunda**, Daniel Manuel 1959- *WhoHisp 92*
**Borunda**, Ernest *WhoHisp 92*
**Borunda**, Kathy *WhoHisp 92*
**Borunda**, Luis G. 1935- *WhoHisp 92*
**Borunda**, Mario Rene 1952- *WhoHisp 92*
**Borunda**, Patrick 1947- *WhoWest 92*
**Boruszak**, James Martin 1930- *WhoMW 92*
**Borwein**, David 1924- *AmMWSc 92*
**Borwick** *Who 92*
**Borwick**, Baron 1917- *Who 92*
**Bory**, Chak 1939- *WhoWest 92*
**Borysenko**, Myrin 1942- *AmMWSc 92*
**Borysewicz**, Mary Louise *WhoMW 92*
**Borysko**, Emil 1918- *AmMWSc 92*
**Borzaga**, Marita 1936- *WhoAmP 91*
**Borzage**, Frank 1893-1962 *IntDcF 2-2*
**Borzelleca**, Joseph Francis 1930- *AmMWSc 92*
**Borzov**, Valeriy 1949- *IntWW 91, SovUnBD*
**Borzutzky**, Silvia 1946- *WhoHisp 92*
**Bos**, A. David *WhoRel 92*
**Bos**, Carole Dianne 1949- *WhoMW 92*
**Bos**, John Arthur 1933- *WhoWest 92*
**Bosakov**, Joseph Blagoev 1942- *WhoRel 92*
**Bosanquet**, Louis Percival 1931- *AmMWSc 92*
**Bosart**, Lance Frank 1942- *AmMWSc 92*
**Boscarine**, Leonard G. 1944- *WhoWest 92*
**Boscawen** *Who 92*
**Boscawen**, Robert Thomas 1923- *Who 92*
**Bosch**, Arthur James 1928- *AmMWSc 92*
**Bosch**, Brian A. 1959- *WhoAmL 92*
**Bosch**, Carl 1874-1940 *FacFETw, WhoNob 90*
**Bosch**, Guillermo L. 1949- *WhoHisp 92*
**Bosch**, Henry G. 1914- *ConAu 135*
**Bosch**, Juan 1909- *FacFETw, IntWW 91*
**Bosch**, Samuel Henry 1934- *WhoFI 92*
**Boschan**, Robert Herschel 1925- *AmMWSc 92*
**Boschert**, Douglas Francis 1921- *WhoAmP 91*
**Boschmann**, Erwin 1939- *AmMWSc 92, WhoMW 92*
**Boschulte**, Joseph Clement 1931- *WhoBlA 92*
**Boschung**, Herbert Theodore 1925- *AmMWSc 92*
**Boschwitz**, Rudy 1930- *IntWW 91, WhoAmP 91*
**Bosco**, Anthony Gerard 1927- *WhoRel 92*
**Bosco**, Douglas H 1946- *WhoAmP 91*
**Bosco**, Giacinto 1905- *IntWW 91*
**Bosco**, Jay William 1951- *WhoMW 92*
**Bosco**, Joseph A 1938- *WhoAmP 91*
**Bosco**, Philip 1930- *IntMPA 92*
**Bosco**, Philip Michael 1930- *WhoEnt 92*
**Boscolo**, Benjamin Tederick 1961- *WhoAmL 92*
**Bose**, Ajay Kumar 1925- *AmMWSc 92*
**Bose**, Amar G 1929- *AmMWSc 92*
**Bose**, Anil Kumar 1929- *AmMWSc 92*
**Bose**, Animesh 1953- *WhoFI 92*
**Bose**, Anjan 1946- *AmMWSc 92*
**Bose**, Bimal K 1932- *AmMWSc 92*
**Bose**, Deepak 1941- *AmMWSc 92*
**Bose**, Henry Robert, Jr 1940- *AmMWSc 92*
**Bose**, Jagadis Chandra 1858-1937 *FacFETw*
**Bose**, Mihir 1947- *Who 92*
**Bose**, Nirmal K 1940- *AmMWSc 92*
**Bose**, Romen 1970- *WhoWest 92*
**Bose**, Samir K 1934- *AmMWSc 92*
**Bose**, Satyendra Nath 1894-1974 *FacFETw*
**Bose**, Shyamalendu M 1939- *AmMWSc 92*
**Bose**, Subir Kumar 1931- *AmMWSc 92, WhoMW 92*
**Bose**, Subir Kumar 1939- *AmMWSc 92*
**Bose**, Tapan Kumar 1938- *AmMWSc 92*
**Bosee**, Roland Andrew 1910- *AmMWSc 92*
**Boseker**, Barbara Jean 1944- *WhoMW 92*
**Boserup**, Ester Talke 1910- *IntWW 91*
**Bosetti**, Guy C. *WhoAmL 92*
**Boshart**, Charles Ralph 1932- *AmMWSc 92*
**Boshart**, Gregory Lew 1933- *AmMWSc 92*
**Boshell**, Buris Raye 1926- *AmMWSc 92*
**Bosher**, John Francis 1929- *IntWW 91*
**Boshes**, Benjamin 1907- *AmMWSc 92*
**Boshes**, Louis D 1908- *AmMWSc 92*
**Boshier**, Derek 1937- *TwCPaSc*
**Boshkov**, Stefan 1918- *AmMWSc 92*
**Boshoff**, Carel Willem Hendrik 1927- *IntWW 91*
**Bosin**, Talmage R 1941- *AmMWSc 92*
**Boskey**, Adele Ludin 1943- *AmMWSc 92*
**Boskey**, Bennett 1916- *WhoAmL 92*
**Boskin**, Joseph 1929- *WrDr 92*
**Boskin**, Michael Jay 1945- *IntWW 91, WhoAmP 91, WhoFI 92*
**Boskoff**, Alvin 1924- *WrDr 92*
**Boskovski**, Jozo T 1933- *IntAu&W 91*
**Boskovsky**, Willi 1909-1991 *IntWW 91, -91N, NewAmDM*
**Bosland**, Chelcie Clayton 1901- *WrDr 92*
**Boslaugh**, Leslie 1917- *WhoAmL 92, WhoAmP 91*
**Bosley**, Daniel Edward 1953- *WhoAmP 91*
**Bosley**, David Emerson 1927- *AmMWSc 92*
**Bosley**, Elizabeth Caswell 1912- *AmMWSc 92*
**Bosley**, Freeman Robertson, Jr. 1954- *WhoBlA 92*
**Bosley**, Gary Oscar 1944- *WhoWest 92*
**Bosley**, Harold Augustus 1907-1975 *DcNCBi 1*
**Bosley**, Keith 1937- *ConPo 91, WrDr 92*
**Bosley**, Keith Anthony 1937- *IntAu&W 91*
**Bosley**, Thad 1956- *WhoBlA 92*
**Bosley**, Tom *LesBEnT 92*
**Bosley**, Tom 1927- *IntMPA 92, WhoEnt 92*
**Boslow**, Harold Meyer 1915- *AmMWSc 92*
**Bosma**, Brian Charles 1957- *WhoAmP 91*
**Bosma**, Charles Edward 1922- *WhoAmP 91*
**Bosma**, James F 1916- *AmMWSc 92*
**Bosmajian**, George 1921- *AmMWSc 92*
**Bosmajian**, Haig 1928- *WrDr 92*
**Bosmajian**, Haig Aram 1928- *IntAu&W 91*
**Bosman**, Evelyn 1939- *WhoMW 92*
**Bosman**, Paul Wray 1929- *WhoWest 92*
**Bosmann**, Harold Bruce 1942- *AmMWSc 92*
**Bosniack**, David S 1932- *AmMWSc 92*
**Bosniak**, Morton A 1929- *AmMWSc 92*
**Bosnjak**, Zeljko J *AmMWSc 92*
**Bosnyak**, Paul Steven 1939- *WhoIns 92*
**Bosomworth**, Peter Palliser 1930- *AmMWSc 92*
**Bosone**, Reva Beck 1895-1978 *HanAmWH*
**Bosonnet**, Paul Graham 1932- *Who 92*
**Bosque**, George d1991 *NewYTBS 91*
**Bosquet**, Alain 1919- *IntAu&W 91, IntWW 91*
**Bosquez**, Jess 1935- *WhoHisp 92*
**Bosquez**, Juan Manuel 1941- *WhoHisp 92*
**Bosquez**, Melinda Jane Dondlinger 1956- *WhoAmL 92*
**Bosron**, William F 1944- *AmMWSc 92*
**Boss**, Alan Paul 1951- *AmMWSc 92*
**Boss**, Benjamin *FacFETw*
**Boss**, Charles Ben 1945- *AmMWSc 92*
**Boss**, Charles Frederick 1888-1965 *AmPeW*
**Boss**, Kenneth Jay 1935- *AmMWSc 92*
**Boss**, Laura *DrAPF 91*
**Boss**, Lenard Barrett 1960- *WhoAmL 92*
**Boss**, Lewis 1846-1912 *BiInAmS, FacFETw*
**Boss**, Manley Leon 1924- *AmMWSc 92*
**Bossano**, Joe 1938- *IntWW 91*
**Bossano**, Joseph 1939- *Who 92*
**Bossard**, Andre 1926- *IntWW 91*
**Bossard**, David Charles 1940- *AmMWSc 92*
**Bossard**, Gerard Scott 1960- *WhoEnt 92*
**Bossard**, Mary Jeanette 1954- *AmMWSc 92*
**Bossbach**, Shirley Cagle 1941- *WhoAmP 91*
**Bosse**, David Ross 1943- *WhoAmL 92*
**Bosse**, Fred Charles 1949- *WhoIns 92*
**Bosse**, Fred M 1947- *WhoAmP 91*
**Bosse**, Leigh Dennis 1947- *WhoAmP 91*
**Bosse**, Malcolm J. *DrAPF 91*
**Bosse**, Virginia Mae 1927- *WhoAmP 91*
**Bossen**, David August 1927- *WhoWest 92*
**Bossen**, Douglas C 1941- *AmMWSc 92*
**Bossen**, Wendell John 1933- *WhoFI 92*
**Bossenbroek**, Albertus George 1910- *WhoRel 92*
**Bosses**, Stevan J. 1937- *WhoAmL 92*
**Bosshard**, John, III 1946- *WhoAmL 92*
**Bosshardt**, David Kirn 1916- *AmMWSc 92*
**Bosshart**, Karen Anne *WhoAmL 92*
**Bosshart**, Robert Perry 1942- *AmMWSc 92*
**Bossi**, William J, Jr. 1956- *WhoIns 92*
**Bossidy**, Lawrence Arthur 1935- *IntWW 91, WhoFI 92*
**Bossie**, Robert F 1942- *WhoAmP 91*
**Bossler**, John David 1936- *AmMWSc 92*
**Bossman**, David Manuel 1938- *WhoRel 92*
**Bossmeyer**, Glenn David *WhoAmL 92*
**Bosso**, Joseph Frank 1931- *AmMWSc 92*
**Bossom**, Clive 1918- *Who 92*
**Bosson**, Bernard 1948- *IntWW 91*
**Bossone**, Dennis J. 1898- *WhoEnt 92*
**Bossone**, Richard M. 1924- *WrDr 92*
**Bossy**, Michael Joseph Frederick 1929- *Who 92*
**Bost**, Annie Kizer 1883-1961 *DcNCBi 1*
**Bost**, Fred M. 1938- *WhoBlA 92*
**Bost**, Howard William 1924- *AmMWSc 92*
**Bost**, Patricia James 1943- *WhoFI 92*
**Bost**, Robert Orion 1943- *AmMWSc 92*
**Bost**, Stephen M 1956- *WhoAmP 91*
**Bost**, Thomas Glen 1942- *WhoAmL 92, WhoWest 92*
**Bost**, William Thomas 1878-1951 *DcNCBi 1*
**Bostedt**, Marina Debellagente *DrAPF 91*
**Boster**, Andrew Reynolds 1951- *WhoMW 92*
**Boster**, Davis Eugene 1920- *WhoAmP 91*
**Boster**, Thomas Arthur 1936- *AmMWSc 92*
**Bosterud**, Helen 1940- *IntWW 91*
**Bostian**, Carey Hoyt 1907- *AmMWSc 92*
**Bostian**, Charles William 1940- *AmMWSc 92*
**Bostian**, Harry 1933- *AmMWSc 92*
**Bostian**, Harry Edward 1933- *WhoMW 92*
**Bostic**, Dorothy *WhoBlA 92*
**Bostic**, James Edward, Jr. 1947- *WhoBlA 92*
**Bostic**, Lee H. 1935- *WhoBlA 92*
**Bosticco**, Mary *WrDr 92*
**Bostick**, Edgar E 1926- *AmMWSc 92*
**Bostick**, Henry *WhoAmP 91*
**Bostick**, Laurence Herbert 1913-1990 *WhoBlA 92N*
**Bostick**, Robert L. 1909- *IntMPA 92*
**Bostick**, Virginia Halton Lord 1912- *WhoEnt 92*
**Bostick**, Warren Lithgow 1914- *AmMWSc 92*
**Bostick**, Winston H. d1991 *NewYTBS 91*
**Bostick**, Winston Harper 1916- *AmMWSc 92*
**Bostleman**, Richard Lee 1944- *WhoMW 92*
**Bostock**, David 1936- *WrDr 92*
**Bostock**, David John 1948- *Who 92*
**Bostock**, Donald Ivan 1924- *WrDr 92*
**Bostock**, Douglas 1955- *WhoEnt 92*
**Bostock**, James Edward 1917- *Who 92*
**Bostock**, Judith Louise *AmMWSc 92*
**Bostock**, Peter Geoffrey 1911- *Who 92*
**Boston** *Who 92*
**Boston**, Baron 1939- *Who 92*
**Boston**, Andrew Chester 1941- *AmMWSc 92*
**Boston**, Archie, Jr. 1943- *WhoBlA 92*
**Boston**, Ben 1961- *WhoAmL 92*
**Boston**, Betty Lee 1935- *WhoFI 92*
**Boston**, Betty Roach 1926- *WhoWest 92*
**Boston**, Billie 1939- *WhoEnt 92*
**Boston**, Bruce Ormand 1940- *WhoRel 92*
**Boston**, Charles Ray 1928- *AmMWSc 92*
**Boston**, David Merrick 1931- *Who 92*
**Boston**, Eugene Alfred 1928- *WhoAmP 91*
**Boston**, Frank D, Jr 1938- *WhoAmP 91*
**Boston**, Garry 1936- *WhoAmP 91*
**Boston**, George David 1923- *WhoBlA 92*
**Boston**, Horace Oscar 1934- *WhoBlA 92*
**Boston**, James Robert, Jr. 1958- *WhoAmL 92*
**Boston**, James Terrell 1947- *WhoRel 92*
**Boston**, John Robert 1942- *AmMWSc 92*
**Boston**, Leona 1914- *WhoRel 92*
**Boston**, Lucy 1892-1990 *AnObit 1990*
**Boston**, Paul B. 1958- *WhoFI 92*
**Boston**, Ralph 1939- *WhoBlA 92*
**Boston**, Ralph Harold 1939- *BlkOlyM*
**Boston**, Richard 1938- *Who 92*
**Boston**, Robert Wesley 1932- *AmMWSc 92*
**Boston**, Wallace Ellsworth, Jr. 1954- *WhoFI 92*
**Boston**, William Clayton 1934- *WhoAmL 92*
**Boston of Faversham**, Baron 1930- *Who 92*
**Bostrack**, Jack M 1931- *AmMWSc 92*
**Bostrom**, Carl Otto 1932- *AmMWSc 92*
**Bostrom**, Curt 1926- *IntWW 91*
**Bostrom**, Robert Christian 1920- *AmMWSc 92*
**Bostrom**, Rolf Gustav 1936- *IntWW 91*
**Bostwick**, Barry 1945- *IntMPA 92, WhoEnt 92*
**Bostwick**, Richard Raymond 1918- *WhoAmL 92, WhoWest 92*
**Bosustow**, Nick 1940- *IntMPA 92*
**Bosustow**, Nick Onslow 1940- *WhoEnt 92, WhoWest 92*
**Bosustow**, Ted 1938- *IntMPA 92*
**Bosveld**, Jennifer Groce Welch *DrAPF 91*
**Bosville Macdonald of Sleat**, Ian Godfrey 1947- *Who 92*
**Boswall**, Alford H. *Who 92*
**Boswall**, Jeffery 1931- *IntMPA 92*
**Boswell**, Alexander 1928- *Who 92*
**Boswell**, Arnita J. *WhoBlA 92*
**Boswell**, Arthur W. 1909- *WhoBlA 92*
**Boswell**, Bennie, Jr. 1948- *WhoBlA 92*
**Boswell**, Bernell N. *WhoWest 92*
**Boswell**, Bernell Nephi 1925- *WhoWest 92*
**Boswell**, Cathy 1962- *BlkOlyM*
**Boswell**, Dan Alan 1947- *WhoFI 92*
**Boswell**, David E 1949- *WhoAmP 91*
**Boswell**, Donald Eugene 1934- *AmMWSc 92*
**Boswell**, Dorothye Harris 1924- *WhoBlA 92*

**Boswell,** Frank William Charles 1924- *AmMWSc 92*
**Boswell,** Fred Carlen 1930- *AmMWSc 92*
**Boswell,** Gary Taggart 1937- *WhoFI 92*
**Boswell,** George A 1932- *AmMWSc 92*
**Boswell,** George Marion, Jr. 1920- *WhoFI 92*
**Boswell,** Hamilton Theodore 1914- *WhoRel 92*
**Boswell,** James *IntAu&W 91X*
**Boswell,** James 1740-1795 *BlkwCEP, CnDBLB 2 [port], RfGEnL 91*
**Boswell,** James 1906-1971 *TwCPaSc*
**Boswell,** John 1947- *WrDr 92*
**Boswell,** John Howard 1932- *WhoAmL 92*
**Boswell,** Larry Ray 1940- *WhoMW 92*
**Boswell,** Leonard L 1934- *WhoAmP 91*
**Boswell,** Nathalie Spence 1924- *WhoMW 92*
**Boswell,** Paul P. 1905- *WhoBlA 92*
**Boswell,** Philip John 1949- *WhoEnt 92*
**Boswell,** Tamara 1945- *WhoFI 92*
**Boswell,** Timothy Eric 1942- *Who 92*
**Boswell,** William Douglas 1918- *WhoAmL 92*
**Boswell,** William Paret 1946- *WhoAmL 92*
**Boswick,** John A 1926- *AmMWSc 92*
**Boswood,** Anthony Richard 1947- *Who 92*
**Bosworth,** Allan R. 1901-1986 *TwCWW 91*
**Bosworth,** Bruce Leighton 1942- *WhoWest 92*
**Bosworth,** David *DrAPF 91*
**Bosworth,** David 1936- *IntAu&W 91*
**Bosworth,** Frank *TwCWW 91*
**Bosworth,** Jeffrey Willson 1948- *WhoMW 92*
**Bosworth,** Michael 1921- *Who 92*
**Bosworth,** Michael Francis 1950- *WhoMW 92*
**Bosworth,** Neville 1918- *Who 92*
**Bosworth,** R. J. B. 1943- *WrDr 92*
**Bosworth,** Richard James Boon 1943- *IntAu&W 91*
**Bosworth,** Stephen Warren 1939- *WhoAmP 91*
**Bosworth,** Thomas Lawrence 1930- *WhoWest 92*
**Boszormeny,** Zoltan 1893- *BiDExR*
**Botana,** William Amadeo 1920- *WhoHisp 92*
**Botchkareva,** Maria *EncAmaz 91*
**Botein,** Michael 1945- *WhoEnt 92*
**Botelho,** Bruce M 1948- *WhoAmP 91*
**Botelho,** Bruce Manuel 1948- *WhoWest 92*
**Botelho,** Eugene G.E. *DrAPF 91*
**Botelho,** Joao 1949- *IntWW 91*
**Botelho,** Lynne H Parker *AmMWSc 92*
**Botelho,** Stella Yates 1919- *AmMWSc 92*
**Botelho,** Stephen M. *WhoHisp 92*
**Botella,** Rita Ann 1951- *WhoHisp 92*
**Botello,** John Lynn, Sr. 1953- *WhoHisp 92*
**Botello,** Jorge Alberto 1969- *WhoHisp 92*
**Botello,** Michael Steven 1950- *WhoHisp 92*
**Botello,** Troy James 1953- *WhoWest 92*
**Botero** 1932- *IntWW 91*
**Botero,** Bernardo Merino *WhoRel 92*
**Botero,** Fernando 1932- *FacFETw*
**Botero,** J M 1929- *AmMWSc 92*
**Botero Restrepo,** Oscar 1933- *IntWW 91*
**Botez,** Dan 1948- *AmMWSc 92*
**Both,** Robert Allen 1952- *WhoEnt 92*
**Botha,** Jan Christoffel Greyling 1929- *IntWW 91*
**Botha,** Louis 1862-1919 *FacFETw*
**Botha,** Matthys 1913- *Who 92*
**Botha,** Matthys Izak 1913- *IntWW 91*
**Botha,** P W 1916- *FacFETw*
**Botha,** Pieter Willem 1916- *IntWW 91, Who 92*
**Botha,** Roelof Frederik 1932- *IntWW 91, Who 92*
**Botham,** Ian Terence 1955- *IntWW 91*
**Bothast,** Rodney Jacob 1945- *AmMWSc 92*
**Bothe,** Arthur George 1931- *WhoEnt 92*
**Bothe,** Danny Walter 1949- *WhoFI 92, WhoMW 92*
**Bothe,** Walther Wilhelm Georg 1891-1957 *WhoNob 90*
**Bothe,** Walther Wilhelm Georg Franz 1891-1957 *FacFETw*
**Bothmann,** Hans 1911-1946 *EncTR 91*
**Bothner,** Richard Charles 1929- *AmMWSc 92*
**Bothner,** Wallace Arthur 1941- *AmMWSc 92*
**Bothner-By,** Aksel Arnold 1921- *AmMWSc 92*
**Bothuel,** Ethel C. S. 1941- *WhoBlA 92*
**Bothwell,** Alfred Lester Meador 1949- *AmMWSc 92*
**Bothwell,** Frank Edgar 1918- *AmMWSc 92*
**Bothwell,** John Charles 1926- *Who 92, WhoRel 92*
**Bothwell,** Max Lewis 1946- *AmMWSc 92*
**Bothwell,** Robert Otto 1937- *WhoFI 92*
**Bothwell,** Thomas Hamilton 1926- *IntWW 91*
**Bothwell-Murphy,** Linda Ann 1954- *WhoMW 92*
**Botic,** Donald A. 1943- *WhoRel 92*
**Botifoll,** Luis J. *WhoHisp 92*
**Botimer,** Allen Ray 1930- *WhoWest 92*
**Botinelly,** Donna 1950- *WhoMW 92*
**Botkin,** B. A. 1901-1975 *BenetAL 91*
**Botkin,** Daniel Benjamin 1937- *AmMWSc 92*
**Botkin,** Merwin P 1922- *AmMWSc 92*
**Botkin,** Monty Lane 1951- *WhoFI 92*
**Botman,** Selma 1950- *ConAu 135*
**Botros,** Raouf 1932- *AmMWSc 92*
**Botsaris,** Gregory D 1930- *AmMWSc 92*
**Botsch,** Sharyn 1950- *WhoMW 92*
**Botsco,** Ronald Joseph 1937- *WhoWest 92*
**Botsford,** James L 1942- *AmMWSc 92*
**Botsford,** Ronald Arthur 1933- *WhoRel 92*
**Botsford,** Ward 1927- *SmATA 66*
**Botssi,** Despo *EncAmaz 91*
**Botstein,** David 1942- *AmMWSc 92, IntWW 91*
**Bott,** Amy Jo 1963- *WhoMW 92*
**Bott,** Frederick Reynolds 1933- *WhoAmL 92*
**Bott,** George 1920- *IntAu&W 91*
**Bott,** George Fredrick 1926- *WhoRel 92*
**Bott,** Harold Sheldon 1933- *WhoMW 92*
**Bott,** Ian Bernard 1932- *Who 92*
**Bott,** Jerry Frederick 1936- *AmMWSc 92*
**Bott,** John Charles 1960- *WhoAmP 91*
**Bott,** Kenneth F 1936- *AmMWSc 92*
**Bott,** Martin Harold Phillips 1926- *IntWW 91, Who 92*
**Bott,** Raoul 1923- *IntWW 91*
**Bott,** Raoul H 1923- *AmMWSc 92*
**Bott,** Thomas Lee 1940- *AmMWSc 92*
**Botta,** Mario 1943- *DcTwDes*
**Bottai,** Bruno 1930- *IntWW 91, Who 92*
**Bottai,** Giuseppe 1895-1959 *BiDExR, EncTR 91*
**Bottar,** Anthony Samuel 1950- *WhoAmL 92*
**Bottaro,** Timothy Shanahan 1958- *WhoAmP 91*
**Bottcher,** Ron d1991 *NewYTBS 91*
**Bottei,** Rudolph Santo 1929- *AmMWSc 92*
**Bottel,** Helen 1914- *WrDr 92*
**Botteri,** Richard M. 1945- *WhoAmL 92*
**Botteri,** Richard Merlo 1945- *WhoAmP 91*
**Bottesini,** Giovanni 1821-1889 *NewAmDM*
**Bottger,** Gary Lee 1938- *AmMWSc 92*
**Bottger,** Lorna Conley 1910- *WhoAmP 91*
**Bottger,** Tracy Ann 1956- *WhoMW 92*
**Bottger,** William Carl, Jr. 1941- *WhoAmL 92*
**Botti,** Richard Charles 1939- *WhoWest 92*
**Botticelli,** Charles Robert 1928- *AmMWSc 92*
**Bottiger,** Lars Erik 1924- *IntWW 91*
**Bottiger,** R Ted 1932- *WhoAmP 91*
**Bottin,** Rob 1959?- *ConTFT 9*
**Bottinelli,** Terry Paul 1951- *WhoAmL 92*
**Botting,** David Francis Edmund 1937- *Who 92*
**Botting,** Douglas 1934- *WrDr 92*
**Botting,** Douglas Scott 1934- *IntAu&W 91*
**Botting,** Louise 1939- *Who 92*
**Bottini,** Albert Thomas 1932- *AmMWSc 92*
**Bottini,** Reginald Norman 1916- *Who 92*
**Bottino,** Carroll Ann 1938- *WhoEnt 92*
**Bottino,** Nestor Rodolfo 1925- *AmMWSc 92*
**Bottino,** Paul James 1941- *AmMWSc 92*
**Bottje,** Will Gay 1925- *WhoEnt 92*
**Bottjer,** David John 1951- *AmMWSc 92*
**Bottjer,** William George 1931- *AmMWSc 92*
**Bottka,** Nicholas 1939- *AmMWSc 92*
**Botto,** Antony Alan 1938- *WhoEnt 92*
**Botto,** Robert Irving 1949- *AmMWSc 92*
**Botto De Barros,** Adwaldo Cardoso 1925- *IntWW 91, Who 92*
**Bottom,** Virgil Eldon 1911- *AmMWSc 92*
**Bottome,** Margaret McDonald 1827-1906 *RelLAm 91*
**Bottomley,** Baron 1907- *Who 92*
**Bottomley,** Lady 1906- *Who 92*
**Bottomley,** Frank 1941- *AmMWSc 92*
**Bottomley,** Gordon 1874-1948 *RfGEnL 91*
**Bottomley,** James 1920- *Who 92*
**Bottomley,** James Reginald Alfred 1920- *IntWW 91*
**Bottomley,** Lawrence Andrew 1950- *AmMWSc 92*
**Bottomley,** Paul Arthur 1953- *AmMWSc 92*
**Bottomley,** Peter James 1944- *Who 92*
**Bottomley,** Richard H 1933- *AmMWSc 92*
**Bottomley,** Sylvia Stakle 1934- *AmMWSc 92*
**Bottomley,** Virginia Hilda Brunette M 1948- *Who 92*
**Bottomore,** Thomas 1920- *WrDr 92*
**Bottomore,** Thomas Burton 1920- *IntAu&W 91*
**Bottoms,** Albert Maitland 1925- *AmMWSc 92*
**Bottoms,** Anthony Edward 1939- *Who 92*
**Bottoms,** David *DrAPF 91*
**Bottoms,** Gerald Doyle 1930- *AmMWSc 92*
**Bottoms,** Joseph 1954- *IntMPA 92*
**Bottoms,** Robert Garvin 1944- *WhoMW 92*
**Bottoms,** Sam 1955- *IntMPA 92, WhoEnt 92*
**Bottoms,** Timothy 1951- *IntMPA 92, WhoEnt 92*
**Bottoms,** William Clay, Jr. 1946- *WhoWest 92*
**Bottone,** Edward Joseph 1934- *AmMWSc 92*
**Bottorff,** Dennis C. 1944- *WhoFI 92*
**Bottorff,** Edmond Milton 1916- *AmMWSc 92*
**Bottorff,** James L 1944- *WhoAmP 91*
**Bottrall,** Margaret 1909- *WrDr 92*
**Bottrall,** Margaret F S 1909- *IntAu&W 91*
**Bottrell,** Kriston Lynn 1957- *WhoMW 92*
**Botts,** Ronald Wesley 1944- *WhoMW 92*
**Botts,** Truman Arthur 1917- *AmMWSc 92*
**Bottum,** Thomas George 1950- *WhoIns 92*
**Botvin,** Aleksandr Platonovich 1918- *IntWW 91*
**Botvinnik,** Mikhail Moiseevich 1911- *SovUnBD*
**Botvinnik,** Mikhail Moiseyevich 1911- *FacFETw, IntWW 91*
**Botvinnik,** Mikhail Moisseyevich 1911- *Who 92*
**Botwood,** Richard Price 1932- *Who 92*
**Botz,** Wayne Ray 1957- *WhoFI 92*
**Botzler,** Richard George 1942- *AmMWSc 92*
**Bouabid,** Maati 1927- *IntWW 91*
**Boubai,** Wilfred Brass 1947- *WhoFI 92, WhoMW 92*
**Boubalina,** Lascarina 1783-1825 *EncAmaz 91*
**Boubel,** Richard W 1927- *AmMWSc 92*
**Boublik,** Miloslav 1927- *AmMWSc 92*
**Bouboulis,** Constantine Joseph 1928- *AmMWSc 92*
**Boucek,** George Washington 1912- *WhoAmL 92*
**Boucetta,** M'Hamed 1925- *IntWW 91*
**Bouchard,** Andre G. 1961- *WhoAmL 92*
**Bouchard,** Benoit 1940- *IntWW 91*
**Bouchard,** Giorgio 1929- *WhoRel 92*
**Bouchard,** James Paul 1961- *WhoMW 92*
**Bouchard,** Michael J 1956- *WhoAmP 91*
**Bouchard,** Michel Andre 1948- *AmMWSc 92*
**Bouchard,** Paul Eugene 1946- *WhoWest 92*
**Bouchard,** Peter T 1947- *WhoAmP 91*
**Bouchard,** Philippe Ovide 1932- *WhoMW 92*
**Bouchard,** Raymond William 1944- *AmMWSc 92*
**Bouchard,** Rene Joseph, Jr 1931- *WhoAmP 91*
**Bouchard,** Richard Emile 1926- *AmMWSc 92*
**Bouchard,** Stephen Alfred 1958- *WhoAmL 92*
**Bouchard,** Velma Mae 1931- *WhoAmP 91*
**Bouchardeau,** Huguette 1935- *IntWW 91*
**Bouchaud,** Jean Max d1990 *IntWW 91N*
**Boucher,** Anthony 1911-1968 *TwCSFW 91*
**Boucher,** Bill Antonio 1934- *WhoWest 92*
**Boucher,** Charles Victor 1955- *WhoRel 92*
**Boucher,** David 1951- *ConAu 135*
**Boucher,** Francois 1703-1770 *BlkwCEP*
**Boucher,** Gene 1933- *WhoEnt 92*
**Boucher,** H A *WhoAmP 91*
**Boucher,** Henry Joseph 1947- *WhoFI 92*
**Boucher,** Henry Mason 1907- *WhoAmP 91*
**Boucher,** John H 1930- *AmMWSc 92*
**Boucher,** Jonathan 1738-1804 *BenetAL 91*
**Boucher,** Joseph William 1951- *WhoAmL 92, WhoFI 92*
**Boucher,** Laurence James 1938- *AmMWSc 92*
**Boucher,** Laurent J 1915- *WhoAmP 91*
**Boucher,** Lionel R 1931- *WhoAmP 91*
**Boucher,** Louis Jack 1922- *AmMWSc 92*
**Boucher,** Mayo Terry 1918- *WhoWest 92*
**Boucher,** Merle *WhoAmP 91*
**Boucher,** Michael Charles 1968- *WhoRel 92*
**Boucher,** Raymond 1906- *AmMWSc 92*
**Boucher,** Rick 1946- *AlmAP 92 [port], WhoAmP 91*
**Boucher,** Thomas Owen 1942- *AmMWSc 92*
**Boucher,** William Paul 1930- *WhoAmP 91*
**Bouchey,** Myrna *DrAPF 91*
**Bouchier,** Chili 1909- *IntMPA 92*
**Bouchier,** Ian Arthur Dennis 1932- *IntWW 91, Who 92*
**Bouchillon,** Charles W 1931- *AmMWSc 92*
**Boucicault,** Dion 1820-1890 *BenetAL 91, RfGEnL 91*
**Bouck,** G Benjamin 1933- *AmMWSc 92*
**Bouck,** Gerald R 1934- *AmMWSc 92*
**Bouck,** John F 1941- *WhoAmP 91*
**Bouck,** Noel 1936- *AmMWSc 92*
**Boucot,** Arthur James 1924- *AmMWSc 92*
**Boucot,** Barbara Pierce 1926- *WhoAmP 91*
**Boudakian,** Max Minas 1925- *AmMWSc 92*
**Boudart,** Michel 1924- *AmMWSc 92, IntWW 91, WhoWest 92*
**Boudette,** Eugene L 1926- *AmMWSc 92*
**Boudicca** d62? *EncAmaz 91*
**Boudin,** Eugene 1824-1898 *ThHEIm*
**Boudin,** Jean *DrAPF 91*
**Boudin,** Michael 1939- *WhoAmL 92*
**Boudinot,** Elias 1740-1821 *BenetAL 91*
**Boudinot,** Elias 1803?-1839 *BenetAL 91*
**Boudinot,** Frank Douglas 1956- *AmMWSc 92*
**Boudjouk,** Philip Raymond 1942- *AmMWSc 92*
**Boudouris,** Georges 1919- *IntWW 91*
**Boudreau,** Cathe Anne 1964- *WhoEnt 92*
**Boudreau,** Edward Joseph, Jr. 1944- *WhoFI 92*
**Boudreau,** James Charles 1936- *AmMWSc 92*
**Boudreau,** James Lawton 1935- *WhoFI 92*
**Boudreau,** Jay Edmond 1946- *AmMWSc 92*
**Boudreau,** Jean Claude *DrAPF 91*
**Boudreau,** Kathryn Lynda Sattler 1947- *WhoWest 92*
**Boudreau,** Keith Ernest 1953- *WhoMW 92*
**Boudreau,** Louis 1917- *FacFETw, WhoEnt 92*
**Boudreau,** Nancy Anna 1947- *WhoFI 92*
**Boudreau,** Paul J. 1938- *WhoIns 92*
**Boudreau,** Robert Austin 1927- *WhoEnt 92*
**Boudreau,** Robert Donald 1931- *AmMWSc 92*
**Boudreau,** Robert James 1950- *WhoMW 92*
**Boudreau,** William F 1914- *AmMWSc 92*
**Boudreaux,** Edward A 1933- *AmMWSc 92*
**Boudreaux,** Henry Bruce 1914- *AmMWSc 92*
**Boudreaux,** Jack Lawrence 1960- *WhoAmP 91*
**Boudreaux,** Kenneth Justin 1943- *WhoFI 92*
**Boudreaux,** Olan J. 1953- *WhoAmL 92*
**Boudreaux,** Warren Louis 1918- *WhoRel 92*
**Boue,** Michel 1936-1971 *DcTwDes, FacFETw*
**Boueil,** Sylvain R. 1952- *WhoIns 92*
**Bouer,** Judith 1942- *WhoFI 92*
**Bouey,** Gerald Keith 1920- *IntWW 91*
**Bougainville,** Louis Antoine de 1729-1811 *BlkwCEP*
**Bougas,** James Andrew 1924- *AmMWSc 92*
**Bougas,** Nick Arthur 1955- *WhoEnt 92*
**Bough,** Francis Joseph 1933- *Who 92*
**Bough,** Wayne Arnold 1943- *AmMWSc 92*
**Boughey,** John 1959- *Who 92*
**Boughey,** Joseph Fenton C. *Who 92*
**Boughn,** Stephen Paul 1946- *AmMWSc 92*
**Boughner,** Leslie C. *WhoIns 92*
**Boughton,** Donald William 1935- *WhoAmP 91*
**Boughton,** James Murray 1944- *WhoFI 92*
**Boughton,** John Harland 1932- *AmMWSc 92*
**Boughton,** Robert Ivan, Jr 1942- *AmMWSc 92*
**Boughton,** William Hart 1937- *WhoWest 92*
**Bougie,** Jacques 1947- *WhoFI 92*
**Bouhet,** Jacques Emile 1942- *WhoFI 92*
**Bouhler,** Philipp 1899-1945 *BiDExR, EncTR 91 [port]*
**Bouhoutsos,** Jacqueline Cotcher *WhoWest 92*
**Bouie,** Merceline 1929- *WhoBlA 92*
**Bouie,** Preston L. 1926- *WhoBlA 92*
**Bouie,** Simon Pinckney 1939- *WhoBlA 92*
**Bouillant,** Alain Marcel 1928- *AmMWSc 92*
**Bouilliant-Linet,** Francis Jacques 1932- *WhoFI 92*
**Bouis,** Paul Andre 1945- *AmMWSc 92*
**Boukidis,** Constantine Michael 1959- *WhoWest 92*
**Bouknight,** Reynard Ronald 1946- *WhoBlA 92*
**Boulainviller,** Henri de 1658-1722 *BlkwCEP*
**Boulanger,** Jean Baptiste 1922- *AmMWSc 92*
**Boulanger,** Lili 1893-1918 *NewAmDM*
**Boulanger,** Nadia 1887-1979 *FacFETw [port], NewAmDM*
**Boulanger,** Nicolas-Antoine 1722-1759 *BlkwCEP*

**Boulanger**, Paul 1905- IntWW 91
**Boulanger**, Philomena M WhoAmP 91
**Boulanger**, Pierre 1886-1950 DcTwDes, FacFETw
**Boulant**, Jack A AmMWSc 92
**Boulay**, Marc Norman 1958- WhoFI 92
**Bouldes**, Charlene 1945- WhoBlA 92
**Bouldin**, Danny Lee 1953- WhoWest 92
**Bouldin**, David Ritchey 1926- AmMWSc 92
**Bouldin**, Richard H 1942- AmMWSc 92
**Boulding**, Elise Bjorn-Hansen 1920- AmPeW
**Boulding**, Kenneth Ewart 1910- AmPeW, IntAu&W 91, IntWW 91, WhoFI 92, WrDr 92
**Bouldry**, John M 1917- AmMWSc 92
**Boulet**, Gilles 1926- IntWW 91, Who 92
**Boulet**, J Lionel 1919- AmMWSc 92
**Boulet**, Jean-Claude 1941- IntWW 91
**Boulet**, Marcel 1919- AmMWSc 92
**Boulet**, Roger Henri 1944- WhoWest 92
**Boulet**, Tami Lee 1958- WhoWest 92
**Bouley**, Richard L 1938- WhoAmP 91
**Boulez**, Pierre 1925- ConCom 92, FacFETw [port], IntWW 91, NewAmDM, Who 92, WhoEnt 92
**Boulger**, Francis W 1913- AmMWSc 92
**Boulger**, William Charles 1924- WhoAmL 92
**Boulind**, Joan 1912- Who 92
**Boulle**, Pierre 1912- TwCSFW 91A
**Boullee**, Etienne-Louis 1728-1799 BlkwCEP
**Boullier**, David Renaud 1699-1759 BlkwCEP
**Boullin**, David John 1931- AmMWSc 92
**Boullion**, Lois Ann 1948- WhoAmL 92
**Boullion**, Thomas L 1940- AmMWSc 92
**Boulos**, Badi Mansour 1930- AmMWSc 92
**Boulos**, Edward Nashed 1941- WhoMW 92
**Bouloucon**, Peter 1935- AmMWSc 92
**Bouloukos**, Don P. WhoEnt 92
**Boulpaep**, Emile L 1938- AmMWSc 92
**Boulse**, Gerald Lee 1950- WhoWest 92
**Boult**, Adrian 1889-1983 FacFETw, NewAmDM
**Boulter**, Beau 1942- WhoAmP 91
**Boulter**, Donald 1926- Who 92
**Boulter**, Patrick Stewart 1927- Who 92
**Boulting Brothers** FacFETw
**Boulting**, John 1913- FacFETw
**Boulting**, John 1913-1985 IntDcF 2-2 [port]
**Boulting**, Roy 1913- IntDcF 2-2 [port], IntMPA 92, IntWW 91, Who 92
**Boulting**, Roy 1913-1985 FacFETw
**Boulting**, S. A. Who 92
**Boulton**, Alan Arthur 1936- AmMWSc 92
**Boulton**, Christian Who 92
**Boulton**, Clifford 1930- Who 92
**Boulton**, David 1935- IntAu&W 91, IntWW 91, WrDr 92
**Boulton**, Edwin Charles 1928- WhoMW 92, WhoRel 92
**Boulton**, Geoffrey Stewart 1940- Who 92
**Boulton**, Grace 1926- WhoAmP 91
**Boulton**, Harold Hugh Christian 1918- Who 92
**Boulton**, James T. 1924- WrDr 92
**Boulton**, James Thompson 1924- IntAu&W 91, Who 92
**Boulton**, Peter Henry 1925- Who 92
**Boulton**, Peter Irwin Paul 1934- AmMWSc 92
**Boulton**, Roger Brett 1949- AmMWSc 92
**Boulton**, William 1912- Who 92
**Boulton**, William Richard 1942- WhoFI 92
**Boulware**, David G 1937- AmMWSc 92
**Boulware**, Fay D. WhoBlA 92
**Boulware**, James L. 1921- WhoRel 92
**Boulware**, Patricia A. 1949- WhoBlA 92
**Boulware**, Ralph Frederick 1917- AmMWSc 92
**Boulware**, Richard Stark 1935- WhoWest 92
**Boulware**, William H. 1949- WhoBlA 92
**Bouma**, Arnold Heiko 1932- AmMWSc 92
**Bouma**, Hessel, III 1950- AmMWSc 92
**Bouma**, J. L. WrDr 92
**Bouma**, J.L. d1978? TwCWW 91
**Bouma**, Johannes 1940- IntWW 91
**Bouma**, Robert Edwin 1938- WhoAmL 92
**Bouman**, Thomas David 1940- AmMWSc 92
**Bouman**, Walter Richard 1929- WhoMW 92, WhoRel 92
**Boumann**, Robert Lyle 1946- WhoAmL 92, WhoWest 92
**Boumedienne**, Houari 1925-1978 FacFETw
**Boumgarden**, David Lewis 1951- WhoRel 92
**Boundas**, Louise Gooch WhoEnt 92
**Bounds**, Harold C 1940- AmMWSc 92
**Bounds**, Laurence Harold 1922- WhoFI 92
**Bounds**, Nancy 1928- WhoMW 92
**Bounds**, Peter 1943- Who 92
**Bounds**, Shelton E 1929- WhoAmP 91
**Bounds**, Sydney J. 1920- WrDr 92
**Boundy**, Donna J 1949- IntAu&W 91
**Boundy**, Ray Harold 1903- AmMWSc 92
**Bouquet**, Henri DcAmImH
**Bouquot**, Jerry Elmer 1945- AmMWSc 92
**Bour**, Jean-Antoine 1934- WhoWest 92
**Bouras**, James Charles 1941- WhoEnt 92
**Bourassa**, Alphonse J 1941- WhoAmP 91
**Bourassa**, Robert 1933- IntWW 91, Who 92
**Bourbaki**, Nicolas FacFETw
**Bourbakis**, Niklaos G 1950- AmMWSc 92
**Bourbon Busset**, Jacques Louis R. M. de 1912- IntWW 91
**Bourbour**, Valerie Marianne 1959- WhoRel 92
**Bourchier**, Robert James 1927- AmMWSc 92
**Bourdais de Charbonniere**, Eric 1939- WhoFI 92
**Bourdeau**, Bernard N. 1948- WhoIns 92
**Bourdeau**, James Edward 1948- AmMWSc 92
**Bourdeau**, Paul Layman 1955- WhoAmL 92
**Bourdeau**, Paul T. WhoIns 92
**Bourdeau de Fontenay**, Alain Jean-Marie D 1940- WhoFI 92
**Bourdeaux**, Michael Alan 1934- Who 92, WhoRel 92, WrDr 92
**Bourdet**, Claude 1909- IntWW 91
**Bourdieu**, Pierre 1930- IntWW 91
**Bourdillon**, Antony John 1944- AmMWSc 92
**Bourdillon**, Henry Townsend d1991 Who 92N
**Bourdillon**, Mervyn Leigh 1924- Who 92
**Bourdo**, Eric A, Jr 1917- AmMWSc 92
**Bourdon**, David 1934- WrDr 92
**Bourdon**, Derek Conway 1932- Who 92
**Boureau**, Edouard 1913- IntWW 91
**Bourekis**, James George 1930- WhoWest 92
**Bourell**, David Lee 1953- AmMWSc 92
**Bourgault**, Priscilla C 1928- AmMWSc 92
**Bourgaux**, Pierre 1934- AmMWSc 92
**Bourgeois**, Adam 1929- WhoBlA 92
**Bourgeois**, Glenn Michael 1940- WhoAmL 92
**Bourgeois**, John Edward 1949- WhoMW 92
**Bourgeois**, Leon-Victor Auguste 1851-1925 WhoNob 90
**Bourgeois**, Louis 1510?-1561? NewAmDM
**Bourges**, Herve 1933- IntWW 91
**Bourges**, Yvon 1921- IntWW 91
**Bourges-Maunoury**, Maurice 1914- IntWW 91
**Bourget**, Edwin 1946- AmMWSc 92
**Bourget**, Paul 1852-1935 GuFrLit 1
**Bourget**, Ronald William 1959- WhoAmL 92
**Bourget**, Sylvio-J 1930- AmMWSc 92
**Bourgholtzer**, Frank LesBEnT 92
**Bourgin**, David Gordon 1900- AmMWSc 92
**Bourgoignie**, Jacques J AmMWSc 92
**Bourgoine**, Ella Florence 1935- WhoAmP 91
**Bourgon**, Marcel 1926- AmMWSc 92
**Bourgoyne**, Adam T, Jr 1944- AmMWSc 92
**Bourguiba**, Habib 1903- FacFETw
**Bourguiba**, Habib, Jr. 1927- IntWW 91
**Bourguiba**, Habib Ben Ali 1903- IntWW 91
**Bourguignon**, Lilly Y W 1946- AmMWSc 92
**Bourguignon**, Philippe Etienne 1948- WhoFI 92
**Bouricius**, Terry 1954- WhoAmP 91
**Bouris**, Michael Lee 1942- WhoIns 92
**Bourjaily**, Vance DrAPF 91
**Bourjaily**, Vance 1922- BenetAL 91, ConNov 91, IntWW 91, WrDr 92
**Bourke** Who 92
**Bourke**, Charles Francis ScFEYrs
**Bourke**, Christopher John 1926- Who 92
**Bourke**, Gerard Joseph 1926- WhoRel 92
**Bourke**, John Butts 1934- AmMWSc 92
**Bourke**, John Gregory 1846-1896 BiInAmS
**Bourke**, Lyle James 1963- WhoWest 92
**Bourke**, Michael 1941- Who 92
**Bourke**, Robert Hathaway 1938- AmMWSc 92
**Bourke**, Roger 1945- TwCPaSc
**Bourke**, Vernon J 1907- IntAu&W 91, WrDr 92
**Bourke**, William Oliver 1927- IntWW 91, WhoFI 92
**Bourke-White**, Margaret 1904-1971 RComAH
**Bourke-White**, Margaret 1906-1971 BenetAL 91, FacFETw, HanAmWH
**Bourkoff**, Etan 1949- AmMWSc 92
**Bourland**, Charles Thomas 1937- AmMWSc 92
**Bourland**, Freddie Marshall 1948- AmMWSc 92
**Bourland**, John Daniel 1956- WhoMW 92
**Bourliere**, Francois 1913- IntWW 91
**Bourman**, Nadia WhoEnt 92
**Bourn**, Harry Joseph 1940- WhoFI 92, WhoMW 92
**Bourn**, James 1917- Who 92
**Bourn**, John Bryant 1934- Who 92
**Bourn**, William M AmMWSc 92
**Bourne**, Beal Vernon, II 1950- WhoBlA 92
**Bourne**, Bob 1939- TwCPaSc
**Bourne**, Carol Elizabeth Mulligan 1948- AmMWSc 92
**Bourne**, Charles Beresford 1921- IntWW 91
**Bourne**, Charles Percy 1931- AmMWSc 92
**Bourne**, Daniel DrAPF 91
**Bourne**, Earl Whitfield 1938- AmMWSc 92
**Bourne**, Frederick John 1937- Who 92
**Bourne**, Gordon Lionel 1921- Who 92
**Bourne**, Henry C, Jr 1921- AmMWSc 92
**Bourne**, Henry Clark 1893-1972 DcNCBi 1
**Bourne**, Henry Clay 1840-1911 DcNCBi 1
**Bourne**, Henry R 1940- AmMWSc 92
**Bourne**, James Gerald 1906- Who 92
**Bourne**, John David 1937- WhoFI 92
**Bourne**, John Ross 1944- AmMWSc 92
**Bourne**, John Wilfrid 1922- Who 92
**Bourne**, Judith Louise 1945- WhoBlA 92
**Bourne**, Kenneth 1930- IntAu&W 91, IntWW 91, Who 92, WrDr 92
**Bourne**, Larry Stuart 1939- IntWW 91, WrDr 92
**Bourne**, Malcolm Cornelius 1926- AmMWSc 92
**Bourne**, Margaret Janet 1931- Who 92
**Bourne**, Peter 1939- AmMWSc 92
**Bourne**, Philip Eric 1953- AmMWSc 92
**Bourne**, Ralph W, Jr. 1936- WhoIns 92
**Bourne**, Randolph 1886-1918 BenetAL 91
**Bourne**, Randolph S 1886-1918 DcAmImH
**Bourne**, Randolph Silliman 1886-1918 AmPeW
**Bourne**, Richard IntAu&W 91, Who 92
**Bourne**, Russell 1928- ConAu 133
**Bourne**, Samuel G 1916- AmMWSc 92
**Bourne**, Wilfrid Who 92
**Bourne-Arton**, Anthony Temple 1913- Who 92
**Bourne-Jones**, Derek 1928- IntAu&W 91
**Bournia**, Anthony 1925- AmMWSc 92
**Bournias-Vardiabasis**, Nicole 1954- AmMWSc 92
**Bournique**, Raymond August 1913- AmMWSc 92
**Bourns**, Arthur Newcombe 1919- Who 92
**Bourns**, Thomas Kenneth Richard 1924- AmMWSc 92
**Bourquardez**, Earl Constant 1948- WhoFI 92
**Bourque**, Ann J 1941- WhoAmP 91
**Bourque**, Daniel J. 1955- WhoAmL 92
**Bourque**, Don Philippe 1942- AmMWSc 92
**Bourque**, George J 1913- WhoAmP 91
**Bourque**, Jude David 1961- WhoAmL 92
**Bourque**, Linda Anne Brookover 1941- WhoWest 92
**Bourque**, Paul N 1927- AmMWSc 92
**Bourquin**, Al Willis J 1943- AmMWSc 92
**Bourquin**, Paul Henry James 1916- WrDr 92
**Bours**, William A, III 1918- AmMWSc 92
**Bourseiller**, Antoine 1930- IntWW 91
**Bourton**, Cyril Leonard 1916- Who 92
**Bousbib**, Gabriel 1965- WhoFI 92
**Bouscaren**, Timothy Lincoln 1943- WhoAmL 92
**Bouse**, Walter Harold 1932- WhoMW 92
**Bouseman**, John Keith 1936- AmMWSc 92
**Bousfield**, Aldridge Knight 1941- AmMWSc 92
**Bousfield**, Edward Lloyd 1926- AmMWSc 92, IntWW 91
**Boush**, George Mallory 1926- AmMWSc 92
**Bousley**, Gloria Diane Parrish 1932- WhoMW 92
**Bousono**, Carlos 1923- DcLB 108 [port]
**Bousquet**, William F 1933- AmMWSc 92
**Bousquette**, William C. 1936- WhoFI 92
**Boussac**, Marcel 1889-1980 FacFETw
**Boussena**, Sadek 1948- IntWW 91
**Boussenard**, Louis 1847-1910 ScFEYrs
**Boussod and Valadon** ThHEIm
**Boustany**, Kamel 1941- AmMWSc 92
**Boutaib**, Moulay Brahim 1967- BlkOlyM
**Boutaleb**, Abdelhadi 1923- IntWW 91
**Bouteflika**, Abdul Aziz 1937- IntWW 91
**Boutelle**, Sara Holmes WhoWest 92
**Boutet**, Benoit 1960- WhoEnt 92
**Bouthillette**, Ronald Joseph 1950- WhoRel 92
**Boutilier**, Bradford WhoAmP 91
**Boutilier**, Robert Francis 1937- AmMWSc 92
**Boutillier**, Robert John 1924- WhoFI 92
**Boutin**, Bernard Louis 1923- IntWW 91
**Bouton**, James 1939- FacFETw
**Bouton**, Thomas Chester 1939- AmMWSc 92
**Boutos**, Ioannis 1925- IntWW 91
**Boutris**, Demetrios Aristides 1961- WhoAmL 92
**Boutros**, Fouad 1920- IntWW 91
**Boutros**, Naji Emile 1964- WhoFI 92
**Boutros**, Osiris Wahba 1928- AmMWSc 92
**Boutros**, Susan Noblit 1942- AmMWSc 92
**Boutros Ghali**, Boutros 1922- IntWW 91
**Boutte**, Alvin J. 1929- WhoBlA 92
**Boutte**, David Gray 1944- WhoAmL 92, WhoFI 92
**Boutte**, Ernest John 1943- WhoBlA 92
**Boutte**, Jean-Luc IntWW 91
**Boutton**, Thomas William 1951- AmMWSc 92
**Bouture**, Didier WhoEnt 92
**Boutwell**, Charles Edward 1938- WhoMW 92
**Boutwell**, Joseph Haskell AmMWSc 92
**Boutwell**, Ralph S 1926- WhoAmP 91
**Boutwell**, Roswell Knight 1917- AmMWSc 92
**Boutwell**, Wayne Allison 1944- WhoFI 92
**Bouvard**, Marguerite 1937- IntAu&W 91
**Bouvard**, Marguerite Guzman DrAPF 91
**Bouve**, Edward T ScFEYrs
**Bouve**, Thomas Tracy 1815-1896 BiInAmS
**Bouverie** Who 92
**Bouvier**, Christian Rene 1940- WhoFI 92
**Bouvier**, Marshall Andre 1923- WhoAmL 92, WhoWest 92
**Bouw**, Gerardus Dingeman 1945- WhoMW 92
**Bouw**, Lois Marie Schlaegel 1929- WhoRel 92
**Bouwkamp**, John C 1942- AmMWSc 92
**Bouwsma**, Ward D 1935- AmMWSc 92
**Bouygues**, Francis LesBEnT 92
**Bouygues**, Francis Georges 1922- IntWW 91
**Bouyoucos**, John Vinton 1926- AmMWSc 92
**Bouzeghoub**, Mohamed Tahar 1947- IntWW 91
**Bova**, Ben 1932- IntAu&W 91, SmATA 68 [port], TwCSFW 91, WrDr 92
**Bova**, Jeffrey Stephen 1953- WhoEnt 92
**Bova**, Vincent Arthur, Jr. 1946- WhoAmL 92
**Bovaird**, Brendan Peter 1948- WhoAmL 92, WhoEnt 92
**Bovan**, Patricia Marie 1955- WhoAmL 92
**Bovard**, Freeman Carroll 1921- AmMWSc 92
**Bovard**, John Morrow 1944- WhoFI 92
**Bovard**, Kenly Paul 1928- AmMWSc 92
**Bovasso**, Julie d1991 NewYTBS 91 [port]
**Bovasso**, Julie 1930- WrDr 92
**Bovay**, Harry Elmo, Jr 1914- AmMWSc 92
**Bovbjerg**, Dana H AmMWSc 92
**Bovbjerg**, Richard Viggo 1919- AmMWSc 92
**Bove**, Alfred Anthony AmMWSc 92
**Bove**, John L 1928- AmMWSc 92
**Bove**, Joseph Richard 1926- AmMWSc 92
**Bove**, Kevin E AmMWSc 92
**Bove**, Marilyn June 1932- WhoWest 92
**Bove**, Marylou Goodman 1958- WhoMW 92
**Bove**, Nicholas Joseph, Jr. 1952- WhoAmL 92
**Bove**, Patricia Ann 1953- WhoAmL 92
**Bovee**, Kenneth C 1936- AmMWSc 92
**Bovee**, Spence 1962- WhoEnt 92
**Bovell**, Carlton Rowland 1924- AmMWSc 92
**Bovell**, Stewart 1906- Who 92
**Bovenizer**, Bruce 1945- WhoIns 92
**Bovenizer**, Vernon Gordon Fitzell 1908- Who 92
**Bovenzi**, John Francis 1952- WhoFI 92
**Boverini**, Walter John 1925- WhoAmP 91
**Boverman**, Harold 1927- WhoWest 92
**Boves**, Joaquin Lorenzo 1949- WhoFI 92
**Boves**, Jose Tomas 1770?- HisDSpE
**Bovet**, Daniel 1907- FacFETw, IntWW 91, Who 92, WhoNob 90
**Bovet**, Eric David 1900- WhoFI 92
**Bovey**, Frank Alden 1918- AmMWSc 92
**Bovey**, John DrAPF 91
**Bovey**, Leonard 1924- Who 92
**Bovey**, Philip Henry 1948- Who 92
**Bovey**, Rodney William 1934- AmMWSc 92
**Bovey**, Terry Robinson 1948- WhoFI 92, WhoWest 92
**Boville**, Byron Walter 1920- AmMWSc 92
**Bovin**, Aleksandr Yevgenevich 1930- SovUnBD
**Bovin**, Aleksandr Yevgeniyevich 1930- IntWW 91
**Boving**, Bent Giede 1920- AmMWSc 92
**Bovingdon**, George Geil 1934- WhoAmL 92

**Bovitz**, J. Scott 1955- *WhoAmL 92*
**Bovon**, Francois 1938- *WhoRel 92*
**Bovopoulos**, Andreas D 1958- *AmMWSc 92*
**Bovy**, Philippe R 1951- *AmMWSc 92*
**Bow**, Clara 1905-1965 *FacFETw*
**Bow**, Kenneth Earl 1939- *WhoMW 92*
**Bow**, Sing Tze 1924- *WhoMW 92*
**Bowater**, Euan David Vansittart 1935- *Who 92*
**Bowater**, J. Vansittart 1918- *Who 92*
**Bowcott**, Diane Lorene Phelps 1966- *WhoEnt 92*
**Bowd**, Douglas Gordon 1918- *WrDr 92*
**Bowdan**, Elizabeth Segal *AmMWSc 92*
**Bowdash** *EncAmaz 91*
**Bowden** *Who 92*
**Bowden**, Andrew 1930- *Who 92*
**Bowden**, Charles Malcolm 1933- *AmMWSc 92*
**Bowden**, Charles Ronald 1949- *AmMWSc 92*
**Bowden**, David Clark 1940- *AmMWSc 92*
**Bowden**, David Merle 1929- *AmMWSc 92*
**Bowden**, Douglas Mchose 1937- *AmMWSc 92*
**Bowden**, Drummond Hyde 1924- *AmMWSc 92*
**Bowden**, Elbert Victor 1924- *WhoFI 92*
**Bowden**, Frank Houston 1909- *Who 92*
**Bowden**, George Timothy 1945- *AmMWSc 92*
**Bowden**, Gerald Francis 1935- *Who 92*
**Bowden**, Howard Kent 1955- *WhoFI 92*
**Bowden**, Howard W 1935- *WhoAmP 91*
**Bowden**, Hugh Kent 1933- *WhoFI 92*
**Bowden**, Hugh Winslow *WhoAmP 91*
**Bowden**, James Alvin 1948- *WhoFI 92*
**Bowden**, James H. *DrAPF 91*
**Bowden**, Jean 1928- *IntAu&W 91*
**Bowden**, Jim *WrDr 92*
**Bowden**, Jim 1923- *TwCWW 91*
**Bowden**, Joe Allen 1940- *AmMWSc 92*
**Bowden**, Leonard 1933-1979 *ConAu 134*
**Bowden**, Logan S. *Who 92*
**Bowden**, Mary W 1941- *IntAu&W 91, WrDr 92*
**Bowden**, Maxine 1943- *WhoRel 92*
**Bowden**, Murrae John Stanley 1943- *AmMWSc 92*
**Bowden**, Otis Hearne, II 1928- *WhoFI 92*
**Bowden**, Rick 1947- *WhoAmP 91*
**Bowden**, Robert D *WhoAmP 91*
**Bowden**, Robert Lee, Jr 1933- *AmMWSc 92*
**Bowden**, Roland Heywood 1916- *IntAu&W 91, WrDr 92*
**Bowden**, Ruth Elizabeth Mary 1915- *Who 92*
**Bowden**, Sally Ann 1943- *WhoEnt 92*
**Bowden**, Warren W 1925- *AmMWSc 92*
**Bowdish**, Frank W 1917- *AmMWSc 92*
**Bowditch**, Henry Pickering 1840-1911 *BiInAmS*
**Bowditch**, Jonathan Ingersoll 1806-1889 *BiInAmS*
**Bowditch**, Nathaniel 1773-1838 *BenetAL 91, BiInAmS*
**Bowdle**, Donald Nelson 1935- *WhoRel 92*
**Bowdler**, Anthony John 1928- *AmMWSc 92*
**Bowdoin**, James 1726-1790 *BiInAmS, BlkwEAR*
**Bowdoin**, Robert E. 1929- *WhoBlA 92*
**Bowdon**, Edward K, Sr 1935- *AmMWSc 92*
**Bowdon**, Thomas Michael 1944- *WhoRel 92*
**Bowdring**, Paul 1946- *ConAu 135*
**Bowe**, Barbara Ellen 1945- *WhoRel 92*
**Bowe**, David Robert 1953- *Who 92*
**Bowe**, Howard Howie Andrew 1924- *WhoEnt 92*
**Bowe**, Joseph Charles 1921- *AmMWSc 92*
**Bowe**, Peter Armistead 1956- *WhoFI 92*
**Bowe**, Riddick 1967- *BlkOlyM*
**Bowe**, Robert Looby 1925- *AmMWSc 92*
**Bowe**, Roger Lee 1954- *WhoWest 92*
**Bowe**, William John 1942- *WhoAmL 92*
**Bowen**, Adam Bruce 1964- *WhoWest 92*
**Bowen**, Anabel Smith 1950- *WhoAmP 91*
**Bowen**, 'Asta 1955- *WhoWest 92*
**Bowen**, Barbara C 1937- *IntAu&W 91, WrDr 92*
**Bowen**, Benjamin Arthur 1959- *WhoMW 92*
**Bowen**, Billy M. 1935- *WhoIns 92*
**Bowen**, Blannie Evans 1953- *WhoBlA 92*
**Bowen**, Bradley William 1961- *WhoAmL 92*
**Bowen**, Brenda Lee Matistic 1960- *WhoAmL 92*
**Bowen**, Bruce Montague 1951- *WhoFI 92*
**Bowen**, Bryan Morris 1932- *Who 92*
**Bowen**, Catherine Drinker 1897-1973 *BenetAL 91*
**Bowen**, Charles E 1936- *AmMWSc 92*
**Bowen**, Clotilde Dent 1923- *WhoBlA 92, WhoWest 92*
**Bowen**, Daniel Edward 1944- *AmMWSc 92*
**Bowen**, David Allen 1963- *WhoWest 92*
**Bowen**, David Aubrey Llewellyn 1924- *Who 92*
**Bowen**, David Hywel Michael 1939- *AmMWSc 92*
**Bowen**, David Reece 1932- *WhoAmP 91*
**Bowen**, Denis 1921- *TwCPaSc*
**Bowen**, Donald Edgar 1939- *AmMWSc 92*
**Bowen**, Donnell *AmMWSc 92*
**Bowen**, Duane Glenn 1935- *WhoAmP 91*
**Bowen**, Dudley Hollingsworth, Jr. 1941- *WhoAmL 92*
**Bowen**, Edmund John 1898- *FacFETw*
**Bowen**, Edward C 1923- *WhoAmP 91*
**Bowen**, Edward Farquharson 1945- *Who 92*
**Bowen**, Edward George d1991 *Who 92N*
**Bowen**, Elizabeth 1899-1973 *CnDBLB 7 [port], ConAu 35NR, FacFETw, RfGEnL 91*
**Bowen**, Emma L. 1916- *WhoBlA 92*
**Bowen**, Erva J. 1919- *WhoBlA 92*
**Bowen**, Esmond John 1922- *Who 92*
**Bowen**, Evan Roderic 1913- *Who 92*
**Bowen**, Francis Lee 1932- *WhoWest 92*
**Bowen**, Frank 1930- *Who 92*
**Bowen**, Geoffrey Fraser *Who 92*
**Bowen**, George Hamilton, Jr 1925- *AmMWSc 92*
**Bowen**, George Thomas 1803-1828 *BiInAmS*
**Bowen**, Gilbert Willard 1931- *WhoMW 92, WhoRel 92*
**Bowen**, Gordon d1991 *Who 92N*
**Bowen**, Gwen Lorrayne *WhoEnt 92*
**Bowen**, H Kent 1941- *AmMWSc 92*
**Bowen**, Henry Dittimus 1921- *AmMWSc 92*
**Bowen**, Howard Rothmann *IntWW 91N*
**Bowen**, Ira Sprague 1898-1973 *FacFETw*
**Bowen**, J. Donald 1944- *WhoAmL 92*
**Bowen**, J Hartley, Jr 1914- *AmMWSc 92*
**Bowen**, J Ray 1934- *AmMWSc 92*
**Bowen**, James *WhoEnt 92*
**Bowen**, James David 1962- *WhoWest 92*
**Bowen**, James Milton 1935- *AmMWSc 92*
**Bowen**, James Ross 1935- *WhoWest 92*
**Bowen**, James Thomas 1948- *WhoMW 92*
**Bowen**, John 1924- *ConNov 91, WrDr 92*
**Bowen**, John Griffith 1924- *IntAu&W 91, Who 92*
**Bowen**, John Metcalf 1933- *AmMWSc 92*
**Bowen**, John Pearson 1953- *WhoEnt 92*
**Bowen**, John Richard 1934- *WhoFI 92*
**Bowen**, John Wesley Edward, IV 1954- *WhoAmL 92*
**Bowen**, Joshua Shelton, Jr 1919- *AmMWSc 92*
**Bowen**, Kenneth Alan 1942- *AmMWSc 92*
**Bowen**, Kit Hansel 1948- *AmMWSc 92*
**Bowen**, Lawrence 1914- *Who 92*
**Bowen**, Lawrence Hoffman 1934- *AmMWSc 92*
**Bowen**, Lela Irene 1949- *WhoAmL 92*
**Bowen**, Lionel Frost 1922- *IntWW 91, Who 92*
**Bowen**, Mark Edward Mortimer 1958- *Who 92*
**Bowen**, Michael 1951- *ConAu 134*
**Bowen**, Michael Anthony 1951- *WhoAmL 92*
**Bowen**, Michael George *Who 92*
**Bowen**, Michael George 1930- *IntWW 91*
**Bowen**, Michael Martin 1953- *WhoMW 92*
**Bowen**, Michael Ray 1954- *WhoRel 92*
**Bowen**, Nancy Lynn 1955- *WhoWest 92*
**Bowen**, Nigel 1911- *Who 92*
**Bowen**, Nigel Hubert 1911- *IntWW 91*
**Bowen**, Otis R 1918- *WhoAmP 91*
**Bowen**, Otis Ray 1918- *IntWW 91*
**Bowen**, Patrick Harvey 1939- *WhoAmL 92, WhoFI 92*
**Bowen**, Paul Ross 1902- *AmMWSc 92*
**Bowen**, Paul Tyner *AmMWSc 92*
**Bowen**, Peggy Lear 1949- *WhoAmP 91*
**Bowen**, Peter 1932- *AmMWSc 92*
**Bowen**, Peter Geoffrey 1939- *WhoWest 92*
**Bowen**, Rafael Lee 1925- *AmMWSc 92*
**Bowen**, Ray M 1936- *AmMWSc 92*
**Bowen**, Raymond C. 1934- *WhoBlA 92*
**Bowen**, Richard, Jr. 1942- *WhoBlA 92*
**Bowen**, Richard Eli 1932- *AmMWSc 92*
**Bowen**, Richard Lee 1929- *AmMWSc 92*
**Bowen**, Richard Lee 1933- *WhoWest 92*
**Bowen**, Robert Allen 1946- *WhoIns 92*
**Bowen**, Robert Allen 1958- *WhoFI 92*
**Bowen**, Robert Alphonzo, Jr. 1953- *WhoMW 92*
**Bowen**, Robert Callender 1925- *WhoFI 92*
**Bowen**, Robert O. 1920- *WrDr 92*
**Bowen**, Robert Otis 1952- *WhoAmL 92*
**Bowen**, Robert William 1960- *WhoFI 92*
**Bowen**, Robin Diane 1955- *WhoWest 92*
**Bowen**, Roderic *Who 92*
**Bowen**, Rooney L 1933- *WhoAmP 91*
**Bowen**, Ruth J. 1930- *WhoBlA 92*
**Bowen**, Ruth Justice 1942- *AmMWSc 92*
**Bowen**, Samuel Philip 1939- *AmMWSc 92*
**Bowen**, Sandra Dixon 1941- *WhoAmP 91*
**Bowen**, Sarane Thompson 1927- *AmMWSc 92*
**Bowen**, Scott Michael 1956- *AmMWSc 92*
**Bowen**, Shayne M. 1954- *WhoFI 92*
**Bowen**, Stanley 1910- *Who 92*
**Bowen**, Stephen Hartman 1949- *AmMWSc 92*
**Bowen**, Stephen Stewart 1946- *WhoAmL 92*
**Bowen**, Steven Holmes 1946- *WhoAmL 92*
**Bowen**, Theodore 1928- *AmMWSc 92*
**Bowen**, Thomas Earle, Jr 1938- *AmMWSc 92*
**Bowen**, Thomas Edward Ifor L. *Who 92*
**Bowen**, Tim *WhoEnt 92*
**Bowen**, Vaughan Tabor 1915- *AmMWSc 92*
**Bowen**, William 1933- *WrDr 92*
**Bowen**, William 1942- *TwCPaSc*
**Bowen**, William Donald 1948- *AmMWSc 92*
**Bowen**, William F 1929- *WhoAmP 91, WhoBlA 92*
**Bowen**, William G. 1933- *Who 92*
**Bowen**, William Gordon 1933- *IntWW 91*
**Bowen**, William H 1933- *AmMWSc 92*
**Bowen**, William Joseph 1934- *WhoFI 92*
**Bowen**, William R 1936- *AmMWSc 92*
**Bowen**, Zack 1934- *WrDr 92*
**Bowen**, Zeddie Paul 1937- *AmMWSc 92*
**Bowen-Judd**, Sara *WrDr 92*
**Bowens**, Johnny Wesley 1946- *WhoBlA 92*
**Bowens**, Joseph T. *WhoRel 92*
**Bower**, Allan Maxwell 1936- *WhoAmL 92*
**Bower**, Amy Sue 1959- *AmMWSc 92*
**Bower**, Annette 1933- *AmMWSc 92*
**Bower**, B. M. 1871-1940 *BenetAL 91, TwCWW 91*
**Bower**, B M 1874-1940 *ScFEYrs*
**Bower**, Barbara Louise 1959- *WhoAmL 92*
**Bower**, Barbara Rose 1946- *WhoAmP 91*
**Bower**, Beverly Lynne 1951- *WhoBlA 92*
**Bower**, Bruce Edward 1950- *WhoFI 92, WhoMW 92*
**Bower**, Charles Arthur 1916- *AmMWSc 92*
**Bower**, Christopher James 1957- *WhoWest 92*
**Bower**, Dallas 1907- *IntMPA 92*
**Bower**, David Roy Eugene 1934- *AmMWSc 92*
**Bower**, Donald Edward 1920- *WhoWest 92*
**Bower**, Douglas William 1948- *WhoRel 92*
**Bower**, Fay Louise 1929- *WhoWest 92*
**Bower**, Frank H 1921- *AmMWSc 92*
**Bower**, G Kevin 1951- *WhoAmP 91*
**Bower**, George Myron 1925- *AmMWSc 92*
**Bower**, Glen Landis 1949- *WhoAmP 91*
**Bower**, Glenn Laurence 1953- *WhoAmL 92*
**Bower**, Gordon 1932- *IntWW 91*
**Bower**, Henry 1833-1896 *BiInAmS*
**Bower**, Holly *WhoEnt 92*
**Bower**, J R, Jr 1915- *AmMWSc 92*
**Bower**, Jean Helen 1933- *WhoWest 92*
**Bower**, Kenneth F. 1942- *WhoMW 92*
**Bower**, Larry Kenneth 1940- *WhoEnt 92, WhoMW 92*
**Bower**, Leslie William Clement d1991 *Who 92N*
**Bower**, Marvin D. 1924- *WhoFI 92, WhoIns 92, WhoMW 92*
**Bower**, Michael Douglas 1942- *Who 92*
**Bower**, Monty Lee 1954- *WhoRel 92*
**Bower**, Nathan Wayne 1951- *AmMWSc 92*
**Bower**, Norma L. 1939- *WhoRel 92*
**Bower**, Norman d1990 *Who 92N*
**Bower**, Oliver Kenneth 1902- *AmMWSc 92*
**Bower**, Paul George 1933- *WhoAmL 92*
**Bower**, Raymond Kenneth 1927- *AmMWSc 92*
**Bower**, Richard James 1939- *WhoRel 92*
**Bower**, Richard William 1947- *WhoRel 92*
**Bower**, Robert Hewitt 1949- *WhoMW 92*
**Bower**, Roger *DrAPF 91*
**Bower**, Ronald Edward 1944- *WhoMW 92*
**Bower**, Roy Donald 1939- *WhoRel 92*
**Bower**, Sandra Irwin 1946- *WhoMW 92*
**Bower**, Stephen Ernest D. *Who 92*
**Bower**, Susan Mae 1951- *AmMWSc 92*
**Bower**, William David 1964- *WhoWest 92*
**Bower**, William Horton 1850-1910 *DcNCBi 1*
**Bower**, William Walter 1945- *AmMWSc 92, WhoMW 92*
**Bowerfind**, Edgar Sihler, Jr 1924- *AmMWSc 92*
**Bowering**, Christine 1936- *Who 92*
**Bowering**, George 1935- *BenetAL 91*
**Bowering**, George 1936- *ConPo 91, IntAu&W 91*
**Bowering**, George 1938- *WrDr 92*
**Bowering**, George Harry 1936- *WhoWest 92*
**Bowering**, Gerhard 1939- *WhoRel 92*
**Bowering**, Jean 1939- *AmMWSc 92*
**Bowering**, Marilyn 1949- *ConPo 91, IntAu&W 91, WrDr 92*
**Bowering**, Michael Ernest 1935- *Who 92*
**Bowerman**, David Alexander 1903- *Who 92*
**Bowerman**, Earl Harry 1942- *AmMWSc 92*
**Bowerman**, Ernest William 1905- *AmMWSc 92*
**Bowers**, Arthur Robert 1919- *WhoAmP 91*
**Bowers**, Beth Baker *DrAPF 91*
**Bowers**, C Edward 1919- *AmMWSc 92*
**Bowers**, Claude 1878-1958 *BenetAL 91, FacFETw*
**Bowers**, Darl Eugene 1921- *AmMWSc 92*
**Bowers**, David A 1952- *WhoAmP 91*
**Bowers**, Dorothy C *WhoAmP 91*
**Bowers**, Douglas Edward 1947- *WhoFI 92*
**Bowers**, Edgar 1924- *ConPo 91, IntAu&W 91, WrDr 92*
**Bowers**, Edgar R 1937- *WhoAmP 91*
**Bowers**, Frank Dana 1936- *AmMWSc 92*
**Bowers**, Fredson d1991 *NewYTBS 91*
**Bowers**, Fredson 1905- *IntAu&W 91*
**Bowers**, Fredson 1905-1991 *ConAu 134*
**Bowers**, Fredson Thayer d1991 *Who 92N*
**Bowers**, Fredson Thayer 1905-1991 *DcLB Y91N [port]*
**Bowers**, George Henry, III 1923- *AmMWSc 92*
**Bowers**, George Robert 1935- *WhoMW 92*
**Bowers**, Gideon Mark 1940- *WhoAmL 92*
**Bowers**, Grayson Hunter 1897- *WhoFI 92*
**Bowers**, Greg *DrAPF 91*
**Bowers**, Jack 1947- *WhoWest 92*
**Bowers**, James Charles, Jr. 1943- *WhoMW 92*
**Bowers**, James Clark 1934- *AmMWSc 92*
**Bowers**, Jane Ann 1940- *AmMWSc 92, WhoMW 92*
**Bowers**, Jeffrey Lynn 1952- *WhoWest 92*
**Bowers**, John *DrAPF 91*
**Bowers**, John 1928- *WrDr 92*
**Bowers**, John C. 1939- *WhoWest 92*
**Bowers**, John Carl 1943- *WhoRel 92*
**Bowers**, John Dalton 1915- *AmMWSc 92*
**Bowers**, John E 1954- *AmMWSc 92*
**Bowers**, Joseph Thomas 1918- *RelLAm 91*
**Bowers**, Kathryn Inez 1943- *WhoAmP 91*
**Bowers**, Kevin Lynn 1956- *WhoRel 92*
**Bowers**, Klaus Dieter 1929- *AmMWSc 92*
**Bowers**, Larry Donald 1950- *AmMWSc 92*
**Bowers**, Marianne 1919- *WhoRel 92*
**Bowers**, Marion Deane 1952- *AmMWSc 92*
**Bowers**, Mary Blair 1930- *AmMWSc 92*
**Bowers**, Maynard C 1930- *AmMWSc 92*
**Bowers**, Michael John 1933- *Who 92*
**Bowers**, Michael Joseph 1941- *WhoAmL 92, WhoAmP 91*
**Bowers**, Michael Raymond 1956- *WhoWest 92*
**Bowers**, Michael Thomas 1939- *AmMWSc 92*
**Bowers**, Mirion Perry 1935- *WhoBlA 92*
**Bowers**, Patricia Eleanor Fritz 1928- *WhoFI 92*
**Bowers**, Paul Alan 1947- *WhoEnt 92*
**Bowers**, Paul Applegate 1911- *AmMWSc 92*
**Bowers**, Peter George 1937- *AmMWSc 92*
**Bowers**, Phillip Frederick 1947- *AmMWSc 92*
**Bowers**, Richard Stewart, Jr. 1946- *WhoAmL 92, WhoFI 92*
**Bowers**, Robert Charles 1937- *AmMWSc 92*
**Bowers**, Robert Clarence 1922- *AmMWSc 92*
**Bowers**, Rodney V *WhoAmP 91*
**Bowers**, Roger George 1942- *Who 92*
**Bowers**, Roger Raymond 1944- *AmMWSc 92*
**Bowers**, Roy Anderson 1913- *AmMWSc 92*
**Bowers**, Russel Todd 1956- *WhoFI 92*
**Bowers**, Terrell L. 1945- *TwCWW 91, WrDr 92*
**Bowers**, Thomas J. 1836-1885 *NewAmDM*
**Bowers**, Wayne Alexander 1919- *AmMWSc 92*
**Bowers**, William E 1938- *AmMWSc 92*
**Bowers**, William Sigmond 1935- *AmMWSc 92*
**Bowers-Broadbent**, Christopher Joseph 1945- *IntWW 91*
**Bowersock**, Terry Lynn 1953- *WhoMW 92*
**Bowersock**, Von K 1943- *WhoIns 92*
**Bowersox**, Glen 1920- *WhoRel 92, WhoWest 92*
**Bowersox**, Thomas H. 1941- *WhoFI 92*
**Bowersox**, Thomas Omar 1947- *WhoFI 92*
**Bowersox**, Todd Wilson 1941- *AmMWSc 92*
**Bowery**, Norman George 1944- *Who 92*
**Bowes**, A. Wendell 1945- *WhoRel 92*
**Bowes**, Alan Theodore 1936- *WhoAmL 92*
**Bowes**, Florence 1925- *WhoWest 92*
**Bowes**, Frederick, III 1941- *WhoFI 92*
**Bowes**, George Ernest 1942- *AmMWSc 92*

**Bowes,** Richard Noel 1928- *Who 92*
**Bowes,** Roger Norman 1943- *Who 92*
**Bowes Lyon** *Who 92*
**Bowes Lyon,** Simon Alexander 1932- *Who 92*
**Bowett,** Derek W. 1927- *WrDr 92*
**Bowett,** Derek William 1927- *Who 92*
**Bowett,** Druie 1924- *TwCPaSc*
**Bowey,** Angela Marilyn 1940- *Who 92*
**Bowey,** Olwyn 1936- *TwCPaSc, Who 92*
**Bowhers,** Vincent Carroll 1928- *WhoFI 92*
**Bowhill,** Sidney Allan 1927- *AmMWSc 92*
**Bowick,** David Marshall 1923- *Who 92*
**Bowick,** Mark John 1957- *AmMWSc 92*
**Bowie,** Alexander Glen 1928- *Who 92*
**Bowie,** Andrew 1952- *ConAu 134*
**Bowie,** Andrew Gwynn, Jr. 1945- *WhoAmL 92*
**Bowie,** Andrew J 1923- *AmMWSc 92*
**Bowie,** David 1947- *FacFETw, IntMPA 92, IntWW 91, NewAmDM, Who 92, WhoEnt 92*
**Bowie,** David Bernard 1954- *WhoRel 92*
**Bowie,** Edward John Walter 1925- *AmMWSc 92*
**Bowie,** Glen *Who 92*
**Bowie,** Graham Maitland 1931- *Who 92*
**Bowie,** Hallie Myers 1964- *WhoMW 92*
**Bowie,** James Dwight 1941- *AmMWSc 92*
**Bowie,** James Smith 1939- *WhoAmP 91*
**Bowie,** Jim *IntAu&W 91X, TwCWW 91*
**Bowie,** Joanne Walker 1937- *WhoAmP 91*
**Bowie,** Joel Frank 1942- *WhoAmL 92*
**Bowie,** Jonathan Munford 1951- *WhoAmL 92*
**Bowie,** Karen Lorraine 1961- *WhoFI 92*
**Bowie,** Lemuel James 1944- *AmMWSc 92*
**Bowie,** Norman E. 1942- *WrDr 92*
**Bowie,** Oliver Wendell 1947- *WhoBlA 92*
**Bowie,** Oscar L 1921- *AmMWSc 92*
**Bowie,** Sam *TwCWW 91*
**Bowie,** Sam 1961- *WhoBlA 92*
**Bowie,** Stanley Hay Umphray 1917- *IntWW 91, Who 92*
**Bowie,** Thomas Contee 1876-1947 *DcNCBi 1*
**Bowie,** Timothy Jon 1963- *WhoMW 92*
**Bowie,** Walter C 1925- *AmMWSc 92, WhoBlA 92*
**Bowie,** Walter Russell 1882-1969 *RelLAm 91*
**Bowin,** Carl Otto 1934- *AmMWSc 92*
**Bowin,** William Ferdinand 1937- *WhoMW 92*
**Bowis,** John Crocket 1945- *Who 92*
**Bowker,** Albert Hosmer 1919- *AmMWSc 92*
**Bowker,** Alfred Johnstone 1922- *Who 92*
**Bowker,** David Edwin 1928- *AmMWSc 92*
**Bowker,** John Westerdale 1935- *IntAu&W 91, Who 92, WrDr 92*
**Bowker,** Judi Ann *WhoEnt 92*
**Bowker,** Laura Lee 1957- *WhoAmL 92*
**Bowker,** Richard George 1946- *AmMWSc 92*
**Bowker,** Robin Marsland *WrDr 92*
**Bowker,** Robin Marsland 1920- *IntAu&W 91*
**Bowkett,** Gerald Edson 1926- *WhoWest 92*
**Bowkett,** Stephen 1953- *ConAu 134, SmATA 67 [port]*
**Bowkley,** Herbert Louis 1921- *AmMWSc 92*
**Bowland,** Creig Dean 1957- *WhoMW 92*
**Bowland,** John Patterson 1924- *AmMWSc 92*
**Bowland,** Virginia Long 1914- *WhoAmP 91*
**Bowlby,** Anthony Hugh Mostyn 1906- *Who 92*
**Bowlby,** John 1907-1990 *AnObit 1990, ConAu 34NR*
**Bowlby,** Richard Eric 1939- *WhoFI 92, WhoMW 92*
**Bowlby,** Ronald Oliver 1926- *Who 92*
**Bowlden,** Henry James 1925- *AmMWSc 92*
**Bowlen,** Patrick Dennis 1944- *WhoWest 92*
**Bowler,** Barbara B 1932- *WhoAmP 91*
**Bowler,** Brian *WhoWest 92*
**Bowler,** David Livingstone 1926- *AmMWSc 92*
**Bowler,** Edward Joseph, Jr. 1956- *WhoFI 92*
**Bowler,** Geoffrey 1924- *Who 92*
**Bowler,** Ian John 1920- *Who 92*
**Bowler,** John Patrick 1959- *WhoEnt 92*
**Bowler,** Orson Lloyd 1931- *WhoAmP 91*
**Bowles,** Barbara Landers 1947- *WhoBlA 92, WhoFI 92*
**Bowles,** Bruce W. 1930- *WhoFI 92*
**Bowles,** Chester 1901-1986 *FacFETw*
**Bowles,** Chester Bliss 1901-1986 *AmPolLe*
**Bowles,** Cyril William Johnston 1916- *Who 92*
**Bowles,** Edna Mathilda 1928- *WhoFI 92*
**Bowles,** Edward Houghton, Jr. 1935- *WhoMW 92*
**Bowles,** Eva del Vakia 1875-1943 *NotBlAW 92 [port], RelLAm 91*
**Bowles,** Gilbert 1869-1960 *AmPeW*
**Bowles,** Godfrey Edward 1935- *Who 92*
**Bowles,** Howard Roosevelt 1932- *WhoBlA 92*
**Bowles,** James Harold, Sr. 1921- *WhoBlA 92*
**Bowles,** Jane 1917-1973 *BenetAL 91, ConLC 68 [port], FacFETw*
**Bowles,** Jane Auer 1917-1973 *LiExTwC*
**Bowles,** Jean Alyce 1929- *AmMWSc 92*
**Bowles,** Jessee Groover 1921- *WhoAmP 91*
**Bowles,** John 1830-1900 *ScFEYrs*
**Bowles,** John Bedell 1933- *AmMWSc 92*
**Bowles,** Joseph Edward 1929- *AmMWSc 92*
**Bowles,** Kenneth Ludlam 1929- *AmMWSc 92*
**Bowles,** Lawrence Thompson 1931- *AmMWSc 92*
**Bowles,** Marcia Ann 1940- *WhoAmL 92*
**Bowles,** Margo La Joy 1949- *WhoAmL 92*
**Bowles,** Paul *DrAPF 91*
**Bowles,** Paul 1910- *BenetAL 91, ConNov 91, FacFETw, IntAu&W 91, IntWW 91, LiExTwC, WrDr 92*
**Bowles,** Paul Frederick 1910- *WhoEnt 92*
**Bowles,** Paul Richard 1953- *WhoAmL 92*
**Bowles,** Peter 1936- *Who 92*
**Bowles,** Richard Joseph 1944- *WhoRel 92*
**Bowles,** Samuel 1797-1851 *BenetAL 91*
**Bowles,** Samuel 1826-1878 *BenetAL 91*
**Bowles,** Walter Donald 1923- *WhoFI 92*
**Bowles,** William Allen 1939- *AmMWSc 92*
**Bowles,** William E 1934- *WhoAmP 91*
**Bowles,** William Howard 1936- *AmMWSc 92*
**Bowles,** William Lisle 1762-1850 *RfGEnL 91*
**Bowley,** Curtis S 1954- *WhoAmP 91*
**Bowley,** Donovan Robin 1945- *AmMWSc 92*
**Bowley,** George Andrew 1937- *WhoEnt 92*
**Bowley,** Martin Richard 1936- *Who 92*
**Bowley,** Rex Lyon 1925- *WrDr 92*
**Bowley,** Wallace William 1932- *AmMWSc 92*
**Bowlin,** Kenneth Green 1944- *WhoMW 92*
**Bowlin,** Lyndon Ross 1954- *WhoMW 92*
**Bowlin,** Robert Henderson 1946- *WhoRel 92*
**Bowlin,** Selden Clay 1959- *WhoMW 92, WhoRel 92*
**Bowling,** Ann L 1943- *AmMWSc 92*
**Bowling,** Arthur Lee, Jr 1947- *AmMWSc 92*
**Bowling,** Clarence C 1926- *AmMWSc 92*
**Bowling,** David Ivan 1940- *AmMWSc 92*
**Bowling,** Floyd E 1911- *AmMWSc 92*
**Bowling,** Frank 1936- *TwCPaSc, WhoBlA 92*
**Bowling,** Franklin Lee 1909- *AmMWSc 92*
**Bowling,** Harry 1931- *IntAu&W 91*
**Bowling,** James Chandler 1928- *WhoFI 92*
**Bowling,** Lance Christopher 1948- *WhoEnt 92*
**Bowling,** Lloyd Spencer, Sr 1930- *AmMWSc 92*
**Bowling,** Michael Dean 1956- *WhoAmP 91*
**Bowling,** Nina Richardson 1956- *WhoWest 92*
**Bowling,** Robert Edward 1926- *AmMWSc 92*
**Bowling,** Sue Ann 1941- *AmMWSc 92*
**Bowling,** Thomas B 1932- *WhoIns 92*
**Bowling,** W C 1927- *WhoAmP 91*
**Bowlt,** John Ellis 1943- *WhoWest 92, WrDr 92*
**Bowman** *Who 92*
**Bowman,** Allen Lee 1931- *AmMWSc 92*
**Bowman,** Ann L. *DrAPF 91*
**Bowman,** Arthur Tolliver, III 1947- *WhoMW 92*
**Bowman,** Arthur Wagner 1938- *WhoWest 92*
**Bowman,** Barbara Hyde 1930- *AmMWSc 92*
**Bowman,** Barbara Sheryl 1953- *WhoFI 92*
**Bowman,** Barry J 1946- *AmMWSc 92*
**Bowman,** Bernard Ulysses, Jr 1926- *AmMWSc 92*
**Bowman,** Bill *WhoAmP 91*
**Bowman,** Bruce 1938- *WhoWest 92*
**Bowman,** Bruce T 1942- *AmMWSc 92*
**Bowman,** C W 1930- *AmMWSc 92*
**Bowman,** Carlos Morales 1935- *AmMWSc 92*
**Bowman,** Catherine McKenzie 1962- *WhoAmL 92*
**Bowman,** Charles D 1935- *AmMWSc 92*
**Bowman,** Christopher David 1962- *WhoRel 92*
**Bowman,** Craig T 1939- *AmMWSc 92*
**Bowman,** David F 1920- *AmMWSc 92*
**Bowman,** David Wesley 1940- *WhoAmL 92, WhoFI 92*
**Bowman,** Derek 1931- *IntAu&W 91*
**Bowman,** Donald Edwin 1908- *AmMWSc 92*
**Bowman,** Donald Houts 1911- *AmMWSc 92*
**Bowman,** Donald W. 1928- *WhoIns 92*
**Bowman,** Douglas Clyde 1925- *AmMWSc 92*
**Bowman,** Earl W., Jr. 1927- *WhoBlA 92*
**Bowman,** Ed Howard, Jr. 1946- *WhoFI 92*
**Bowman,** Edward Randolph 1927- *AmMWSc 92*
**Bowman,** Edwin Geoffrey 1946- *Who 92*
**Bowman,** Eric Joseph 1929- *Who 92*
**Bowman,** Eugene W 1910- *AmMWSc 92*
**Bowman,** Fletcher C, Jr 1936- *WhoAmP 91*
**Bowman,** Gary Martin 1943- *WhoWest 92*
**Bowman,** Geoffrey *Who 92*
**Bowman,** George 1923- *Who 92*
**Bowman,** George Arthur, Jr. 1917- *WhoMW 92*
**Bowman,** George McKinley 1925- *WhoAmP 91*
**Bowman,** H Frederick 1941- *AmMWSc 92*
**Bowman,** Harlan Gilbert 1921- *WhoMW 92*
**Bowman,** Harry Joseph 1944- *WhoMW 92*
**Bowman,** Isaiah 1878-1950 *AmPeW*
**Bowman,** Jacob Weaver 1831-1905 *DcNCBi 1*
**Bowman,** Jacquelynne Jeanette 1955- *WhoBlA 92*
**Bowman,** James David 1939- *AmMWSc 92*
**Bowman,** James E 1923- *AmMWSc 92*
**Bowman,** James E., Jr. 1923- *WhoBlA 92*
**Bowman,** James Floyd, II 1932- *AmMWSc 92*
**Bowman,** James Fred 1927- *WhoAmP 91*
**Bowman,** James Sheppard 1928- *AmMWSc 92*
**Bowman,** James Talton 1937- *AmMWSc 92*
**Bowman,** James Thomas 1941- *Who 92*
**Bowman,** Janet Wilson *WhoBlA 92*
**Bowman,** Jean Louise 1938- *WhoWest 92*
**Bowman,** Jeffery 1935- *Who 92*
**Bowman,** Joel Mark 1948- *AmMWSc 92*
**Bowman,** John 1916- *IntWW 91*
**Bowman,** John B. 1961- *WhoAmL 92*
**Bowman,** John Christopher 1933- *Who 92*
**Bowman,** John Francis 1927- *Who 92*
**Bowman,** John Paget 1904- *Who 92*
**Bowman,** Joseph E., Jr. 1950- *WhoBlA 92*
**Bowman,** Joseph Kie 1956- *WhoRel 92*
**Bowman,** Kenneth Aaron 1948- *AmMWSc 92*
**Bowman,** Kimiko Osada 1927- *AmMWSc 92*
**Bowman,** Larry Alan 1948- *WhoFI 92*
**Bowman,** Lawrence Sieman 1934- *AmMWSc 92*
**Bowman,** Leo Henry 1934- *AmMWSc 92*
**Bowman,** Leonard Joseph 1941- *WhoRel 92*
**Bowman,** Leslie Greene 1956- *WhoWest 92*
**Bowman,** Lewis Wilmer 1928- *AmMWSc 92*
**Bowman,** Locke E., Jr. 1927- *WhoRel 92*
**Bowman,** Louis Charles 1945- *WhoAmL 92*
**Bowman,** Malcolm James 1942- *AmMWSc 92*
**Bowman,** Marven Owen, II 1929- *WhoFI 92*
**Bowman,** Monroe Bengt 1901- *WhoFI 92, WhoMW 92*
**Bowman,** Ned David 1948- *WhoFI 92*
**Bowman,** Newell Stedman 1924- *AmMWSc 92*
**Bowman,** Pasco M 1933- *WhoAmP 91*
**Bowman,** Pasco Middleton, II 1933- *WhoAmL 92, WhoMW 92*
**Bowman,** Peyton Graham, III 1929- *WhoAmL 92*
**Bowman,** Phil Bryan 1939- *AmMWSc 92*
**Bowman,** Phillip Jess 1948- *WhoBlA 92*
**Bowman,** Ray Douglas 1942- *AmMWSc 92*
**Bowman,** Richard John 1951- *WhoAmP 91*
**Bowman,** Robert A *WhoAmP 91*
**Bowman,** Robert Clark, Jr 1945- *AmMWSc 92*
**Bowman,** Robert Mathews 1940- *AmMWSc 92*
**Bowman,** Robert Samuel 1917- *AmMWSc 92*
**Bowman,** Robert William 1947- *WhoRel 92*
**Bowman,** Rodney Martin 1957- *WhoRel 92*
**Bowman,** Roger Holmes 1924- *AmMWSc 92*
**Bowman,** Roger M. 1950- *WhoIns 92*
**Bowman,** Ronald Lee 1954- *WhoWest 92*
**Bowman,** Ronald Paul 1956- *WhoAmL 92*
**Bowman,** Rose *WhoAmP 91*
**Bowman,** Rufus David 1899-1952 *AmPeW*
**Bowman,** Sheridan Gail Esther 1950- *Who 92*
**Bowman,** Steven Ellis 1944- *WhoAmP 91*
**Bowman,** Thea 1939-1990 *WhoBlA 92N*
**Bowman,** Thelma Shanks *WhoAmP 91*
**Bowman,** Theodore Allen 1953- *WhoAmL 92*
**Bowman,** Thomas Edwin 1926- *WhoWest 92*
**Bowman,** Thomas Elliot 1918- *AmMWSc 92*
**Bowman,** Thomas Eugene 1938- *AmMWSc 92*
**Bowman,** Vivian Lee 1942- *WhoAmP 91*
**Bowman,** Walker H 1924- *AmMWSc 92*
**Bowman,** Walker Hill, III 1924- *WhoMW 92*
**Bowman,** Wilfred William 1941- *AmMWSc 92*
**Bowman,** William Henry 1938- *AmMWSc 92*
**Bowman,** William McKinley *WhoRel 92*
**Bowman,** William McKinley, Sr. 1914- *WhoBlA 92*
**Bowman,** William Powell 1932- *Who 92*
**Bowman,** Woods 1941- *WhoAmP 91*
**Bowman-Dalton,** Burdene Kathryn 1937- *WhoMW 92*
**Bowman-Shaw,** Neville 1930- *Who 92*
**Bowman-Webb,** Loetta 1956- *WhoBlA 92*
**Bowmar,** Erskine 1913- *Who 92*
**Bowmer,** Richard Glenn 1931- *AmMWSc 92, WhoWest 92*
**Bowmont And Cessford,** Marquis of 1981- *Who 92*
**Bown,** Jane Hope 1925- *IntWW 91, Who 92*
**Bown,** Lalage Jean 1927- *Who 92*
**Bown,** Patti 1931- *WhoEnt 92*
**Bown,** Thomas Michael 1946- *AmMWSc 92*
**Bownds,** John Marvin 1941- *AmMWSc 92*
**Bownds,** M Deric 1942- *AmMWSc 92*
**Bowne,** Borden Parker 1847-1910 *RelLAm 91*
**Bowne,** Samuel Winter, Jr 1925- *AmMWSc 92*
**Bowne,** Shirlee Pearson 1936- *WhoAmP 91*
**Bownes,** Hugh Henry 1920- *WhoAmL 92*
**Bowness,** Alan 1928- *IntWW 91, Who 92, WrDr 92*
**Bowness,** Colin 1929- *AmMWSc 92*
**Bowness,** Peter 1943- *Who 92*
**Bowns,** Beverly Henry *AmMWSc 92*
**Bowring,** Edgar Rennie Harvey 1915- *IntWW 91, Who 92*
**Bowring,** John Humphrey Stephen 1913- *Who 92*
**Bowring,** John Ivan Roy 1923- *Who 92*
**Bowring,** Peter 1923- *IntWW 91, Who 92*
**Bowring,** Richard John 1947- *Who 92*
**Bowron,** John Lewis 1924- *Who 92*
**Bowron,** Les 1957- *WhoAmP 91*
**Bowron,** Robert Henry, Jr. 1927- *WhoAmL 92*
**Bows,** Robert Alan 1949- *WhoEnt 92*
**Bowser,** Anita Olga 1920- *WhoAmP 91*
**Bowser,** Benjamin Paul 1946- *WhoBlA 92*
**Bowser,** Carl 1937- *AmMWSc 92*
**Bowser,** Charles Emanuel 1959- *WhoBlA 92*
**Bowser,** David Stewart 1926- *Who 92*
**Bowser,** Edward Albert 1837-1910 *BiInAmS*
**Bowser,** Eileen 1928- *IntMPA 92, WhoEnt 92*
**Bowser,** Hamilton Victor, Sr. 1928- *WhoBlA 92*
**Bowser,** Harry E 1931- *WhoAmP 91*
**Bowser,** James A. 1913- *WhoBlA 92*
**Bowser,** James Ralph 1949- *AmMWSc 92*
**Bowser,** Mary Elizabeth 1839- *NotBlAW 92*
**Bowser,** McEva R. 1922- *WhoBlA 92*
**Bowser,** Robert Louis 1935- *WhoBlA 92*
**Bowser,** Vivian Roy 1926- *WhoBlA 92*
**Bowsher,** Arthur LeRoy 1917- *AmMWSc 92*
**Bowsher,** Charles Arthur 1931- *WhoFI 92*
**Bowsher,** Harry Fred 1931- *AmMWSc 92*
**Bowsher,** Peter Charles 1935- *Who 92*
**Bowsher,** Robert Reynard 1946- *WhoFI 92*
**Bowtell,** Ann Elizabeth 1938- *Who 92*
**Bowyer** *Who 92*
**Bowyer,** C Stuart 1934- *AmMWSc 92*
**Bowyer,** Charles Lester 1939- *WhoRel 92*
**Bowyer,** Charles Stuart 1934- *WhoWest 92*
**Bowyer,** Edna L 1917- *WhoAmP 91*
**Bowyer,** Gary Neal 1947- *WhoFI 92*
**Bowyer,** Gordon Arthur 1923- *Who 92*
**Bowyer,** J M, Jr 1920- *AmMWSc 92*
**Bowyer,** Jane Baker 1934- *WhoWest 92*
**Bowyer,** Kern M 1928- *AmMWSc 92*
**Bowyer,** Mathew Justice 1926- *WrDr 92*
**Bowyer,** William 1926- *IntWW 91, TwCPaSc, Who 92*
**Bowyer-Smyth,** T. W. *Who 92*
**Box,** Barry Glenn 1958- *WhoFI 92*

**Box**, Betty 1920- *IntMPA 92*
**Box**, Betty Evelyn *Who 92*
**Box**, Betty Evelyn 1949- *IntWW 91*
**Box**, Charles 1951- *WhoBlA 92*
**Box**, Charles Dewey 1943- *WhoEnt 92*
**Box**, Charles E *WhoAmP 91*
**Box**, Donald Stewart 1917- *Who 92*
**Box**, E. 1919-1988 *TwCPaSc*
**Box**, Edgar *IntAu&W 91X, WrDr 92*
**Box**, Edith Darrow 1922- *AmMWSc 92*
**Box**, George Edward Pelham 1919- *AmMWSc 92, Who 92*
**Box**, Glenn *WhoAmP 91*
**Box**, Harold C 1925- *AmMWSc 92*
**Box**, James Ellis, Jr 1931- *AmMWSc 92*
**Box**, Larry 1939- *AmMWSc 92*
**Box**, Michael Allister 1947- *AmMWSc 92*
**Box**, Michael Edward 1954- *WhoAmP 91*
**Box**, Muriel Violette 1905- *IntAu&W 91*
**Box**, Richard 1943- *TwCPaSc*
**Box**, Roland 1945- *TwCPaSc*
**Box**, Thadis Wayne 1929- *AmMWSc 92*
**Box**, Vernon G S 1946- *AmMWSc 92*
**Boxall**, Bernard 1906- *Who 92*
**Boxall**, Lewis, Mrs. *Who 92*
**Boxcar Willie** 1931- *WhoEnt 92*
**Boxenbaum**, Harold George 1942- *AmMWSc 92*
**Boxer**, Alan 1916- *Who 92*
**Boxer**, Alan Lee 1935- *WhoWest 92*
**Boxer**, Arabella *WrDr 92*
**Boxer**, Barbara 1940- *AlmAP 92 [port], WhoAmP 91, WhoWest 92*
**Boxer**, Charles Ian 1926- *Who 92*
**Boxer**, Charles Ralph 1904- *Who 92*
**Boxer**, Harry 1946- *WhoWest 92*
**Boxer**, Henry Everard Crichton 1914- *Who 92*
**Boxer**, Jerome Harvey 1930- *WhoWest 92*
**Boxer**, Laurence A 1940- *AmMWSc 92*
**Boxer**, Laurence Alan 1940- *WhoMW 92*
**Boxer**, Leonard 1939- *WhoAmL 92*
**Boxer**, Lester 1935- *WhoAmL 92*
**Boxer**, Mark 1931-1988 *FacFETw*
**Boxer**, Richard James 1947- *WhoMW 92*
**Boxer**, Robert Jacob 1935- *AmMWSc 92*
**Boxer**, Sandor Theodore 1939- *WhoAmL 92*
**Boxer**, Steven George 1947- *AmMWSc 92*
**Boxer**, Tim 1934- *WhoEnt 92*
**Boxeur**, Dennis Serge 1951- *WhoAmL 92*
**Boxill**, Edith Hillman 1926- *WhoEnt 92*
**Boxill**, Gale Clark 1919- *AmMWSc 92*
**Boxleitner**, Bruce 1950- *IntMPA 92, WhoEnt 92*
**Boxman**, Raymond Leon 1946- *AmMWSc 92*
**Boy**, Michael David 1965- *WhoRel 92*
**Boyajian**, Aram *DrAPF 91*
**Boyajian**, Carole L. 1948- *WhoEnt 92*
**Boyan**, William Lawrence 1927- *WhoAmL 92*
**Boyar**, Jeffrey Wayne 1956- *WhoFI 92*
**Boyar**, Robert Anselm 1923- *WhoEnt 92*
**Boyar**, Sully 1923- *WhoEnt 92*
**Boyars**, Albert *IntMPA 92*
**Boyarsky**, Abraham Joseph 1946- *AmMWSc 92*
**Boyarsky**, Israel 1923- *WhoEnt 92*
**Boyarsky**, Lila Harriet 1921- *AmMWSc 92*
**Boyarsky**, Louis Lester 1919- *AmMWSc 92*
**Boyarsky**, Saul 1923- *AmMWSc 92, WhoAmL 92, WhoMW 92*
**Boyatt**, Thomas D 1933- *WhoAmP 91*
**Boyazis**, James *WhoAmL 92*
**Boyce**, Charles N. 1935- *WhoBlA 92*
**Boyce**, Charles Riddle 1959- *WhoFI 92*
**Boyce**, Daniel Hobbs 1953- *WhoFI 92*
**Boyce**, David 1922- *WhoRel 92*
**Boyce**, David H. 1946- *WhoFI 92*
**Boyce**, Deborah Susan *WhoMW 92*
**Boyce**, Donald Joe 1931- *AmMWSc 92*
**Boyce**, Donald Nelson 1938- *WhoFI 92*
**Boyce**, Doreen Elizabeth 1934- *WhoFI 92*
**Boyce**, Douglas F. 1949- *WhoMW 92*
**Boyce**, Frederick Fitzherbert 1903- *AmMWSc 92*
**Boyce**, George L 1942- *WhoAmP 91*
**Boyce**, Gerard Robert 1954- *WhoAmL 92*
**Boyce**, Graham Hugh 1945- *Who 92*
**Boyce**, Henry Emerson *WhoFI 92*
**Boyce**, Henry Worth, Jr 1930- *AmMWSc 92*
**Boyce**, James H 1922- *WhoAmP 91*
**Boyce**, James John 1938- *WhoFI 92*
**Boyce**, John Charles 1941- *WhoFI 92*
**Boyce**, John G. 1935- *WhoBlA 92*
**Boyce**, Joseph Frederick 1926- *Who 92*
**Boyce**, Joseph Nelson 1937- *WhoBlA 92*
**Boyce**, Kerry Marcus 1957- *WhoWest 92*
**Boyce**, Laura E. 1962- *WhoBlA 92*
**Boyce**, Lester Fred, Jr. 1924- *WhoFI 92*
**Boyce**, Mark Donald 1958- *WhoFI 92*
**Boyce**, Mark S 1950- *AmMWSc 92*
**Boyce**, Mark Stephen 1950- *WhoWest 92*
**Boyce**, Mary Cecelia 1930- *WhoRel 92*
**Boyce**, Michael Cecil 1943- *Who 92*
**Boyce**, Michael David 1937- *Who 92*
**Boyce**, Paul Graham 1954- *WhoFI 92*
**Boyce**, Peter Bradford 1936- *AmMWSc 92*
**Boyce**, Peter John 1935- *Who 92*
**Boyce**, Richard Joseph 1939- *AmMWSc 92*
**Boyce**, Richard P 1928- *AmMWSc 92*
**Boyce**, Robert Abbott 1942- *WhoWest 92*
**Boyce**, Robert Leslie 1962- *Who 92*
**Boyce**, Roland G. 1943- *WhoRel 92*
**Boyce**, Ronald Reed 1931- *WhoWest 92*
**Boyce**, Sheldon William, Jr. 1953- *WhoAmL 92*
**Boyce**, Sonia 1962- *TwCPaSc*
**Boyce**, Stephen Gaddy 1924- *AmMWSc 92*
**Boyce**, Stephen Scott 1942- *AmMWSc 92*
**Boyce**, Steven Edward 1954- *WhoAmL 92*
**Boyce**, Timothy John 1954- *WhoFI 92*
**Boyce**, Walter Edwin 1918- *Who 92*
**Boyce**, William 1711-1779 *NewAmDM*
**Boyce**, William Edward 1930- *AmMWSc 92*
**Boyce**, William Henry 1918- *AmMWSc 92*
**Boyce**, William M. 1928- *WhoBlA 92*
**Boychuck**, Stanley Victor 1951- *WhoAmL 92*
**Boychuk**, Bohdan 1927- *LiExTwC*
**Boycott**, Brian Blundell 1924- *IntWW 91, Who 92*
**Boycott**, Geoff 1940- *WrDr 92*
**Boycott**, Geoffrey 1940- *FacFETw, IntAu&W 91, IntWW 91, Who 92*
**Boycott-Brown**, Michael 1910- *TwCPaSc*
**Boyd** *Who 92*
**Boyd and Evans** *TwCPaSc*
**Boyd**, Adam 1738-1803 *DcNCBi 1*
**Boyd**, Alamo *TwCWW 91*
**Boyd**, Alan Conduitt 1926- *WhoMW 92*
**Boyd**, Alan Stephenson 1922- *IntWW 91*
**Boyd**, Alexander Walter 1934- *Who 92*
**Boyd**, Alfred Colton, Jr 1929- *AmMWSc 92*
**Boyd**, Allen 1945- *WhoAmP 91*
**Boyd**, Alvah L 1948- *WhoAmP 91*
**Boyd**, Aquilino Edgardo 1921- *IntWW 91*
**Boyd**, Arthur 1920- *TwCPaSc*
**Boyd**, Arthur Merric Bloomfield 1920- *IntWW 91, Who 92*
**Boyd**, Atarah *Who 92*
**Boyd**, Bernard Henry 1910-1975 *DcNCBi 1*
**Boyd**, Betty 1924- *WhoAmP 91*
**Boyd**, Beverley Randolph 1947- *WhoAmL 92*
**Boyd**, Blanche McCrary *DrAPF 91*
**Boyd**, Bruce L 1938- *WhoIns 92*
**Boyd**, C. Dewayne 1956- *WhoEnt 92*
**Boyd**, Candy Dawson 1946- *WhoBlA 92*
**Boyd**, Carl M 1933- *AmMWSc 92*
**Boyd**, Charles Curtis 1943- *AmMWSc 92*
**Boyd**, Charles Flynn 1938- *WhoBlA 92*
**Boyd**, Charles Hixson 1934- *WhoFI 92*
**Boyd**, Christopher *Who 92*
**Boyd**, Christopher Thomas 1962- *WhoEnt 92*
**Boyd**, Claude Elson 1939- *AmMWSc 92*
**Boyd**, Curtis 1940- *WhoEnt 92*
**Boyd**, Danny Douglass 1933- *WhoFI 92*
**Boyd**, David Charles 1942- *AmMWSc 92*
**Boyd**, David Eugene 1955- *WhoMW 92*
**Boyd**, David John 1935- *Who 92*
**Boyd**, David Malcolm 1951- *WhoMW 92*
**Boyd**, David Parker 1957- *WhoAmL 92*
**Boyd**, David Preston 1943- *WhoFI 92*
**Boyd**, David Raymond 1941- *WhoMW 92*
**Boyd**, David William 1941- *AmMWSc 92*
**Boyd**, Dean Weldon 1941- *AmMWSc 92, WhoFI 92*
**Boyd**, Deborah Jean 1949- *WhoAmP 91*
**Boyd**, Delores Rosetta 1950- *WhoBlA 92*
**Boyd**, Delsie 1956- *WhoMW 92*
**Boyd**, Dennis Galt 1931- *Who 92*
**Boyd**, Derek Ashley 1941- *AmMWSc 92*
**Boyd**, Diana Lynn 1959- *WhoWest 92*
**Boyd**, Donald Bradford 1941- *AmMWSc 92, WhoMW 92*
**Boyd**, Donald Edward 1933- *AmMWSc 92*
**Boyd**, Donald Wilkin 1927- *AmMWSc 92*
**Boyd**, Doris Regina 1952- *WhoBlA 92*
**Boyd**, Earl Neal 1922- *AmMWSc 92*
**Boyd**, Eddie L. 1939- *WhoBlA 92*
**Boyd**, Edward Hascal 1934- *WhoWest 92*
**Boyd**, Eleanor H 1935- *AmMWSc 92*
**Boyd**, Elizabeth French 1905- *WrDr 92*
**Boyd**, Ernest 1887-1946 *BenetAL 91*
**Boyd**, Evelyn Shipps *WhoBlA 92*
**Boyd**, Felix *TwCSFW 91*
**Boyd**, Fionnuala 1944- *TwCPaSc*
**Boyd**, Francis *Who 92*
**Boyd**, Francis R 1926- *AmMWSc 92*
**Boyd**, Frank McCalla 1929- *AmMWSc 92*
**Boyd**, Frederick Mervin 1939- *AmMWSc 92*
**Boyd**, Frederick Tilghman 1913- *AmMWSc 92*
**Boyd**, Frolly 1950- *WhoIns 92*
**Boyd**, Gary Delane 1932- *AmMWSc 92*
**Boyd**, Gavin 1928- *Who 92*
**Boyd**, George Addison 1907- *AmMWSc 92*
**Boyd**, George Arthur 1928- *WhoBlA 92*
**Boyd**, George Dillard 1797-1886 *DcNCBi 1*
**Boyd**, George Edward 1911- *AmMWSc 92*
**Boyd**, Greg *DrAPF 91*
**Boyd**, Gregory 1951- *WhoEnt 92*
**Boyd**, Gregory Bruce 1959- *WhoRel 92*
**Boyd**, Gregory Kenneth 1950- *WhoEnt 92*
**Boyd**, Harry Dalton 1923- *WhoAmL 92*
**Boyd**, Henry Allen 1876-1959 *RelLAm 91*
**Boyd**, Howard Taney 1909- *IntWW 91*
**Boyd**, Ian Robertson 1922- *Who 92*
**Boyd**, Jack 1932- *ConAu 34NR*
**Boyd**, James 1888-1944 *BenetAL 91, DcNCBi 1*
**Boyd**, James Brown 1937- *AmMWSc 92*
**Boyd**, James Duncan 1958- *WhoRel 92*
**Boyd**, James Edmund 1845-1935 *DcNCBi 1*
**Boyd**, James Edward 1928- *Who 92*
**Boyd**, James Emory 1906- *AmMWSc 92*
**Boyd**, James Felton 1930- *BlkOlyM*
**Boyd**, James Fleming 1920- *Who 92*
**Boyd**, James Harold Allen 1951- *WhoAmP 91*
**Boyd**, James Preston, Jr 1929- *WhoAmP 91*
**Boyd**, James S *ScFEYrs*
**Boyd**, Jamie 1948- *TwCPaSc*
**Boyd**, Jeffery Hawthorne 1956- *WhoAmL 92*
**Boyd**, Jeffrey Allen 1958- *AmMWSc 92*
**Boyd**, Joe Dan 1934- *WhoFI 92*
**Boyd**, John 1919- *TwCSFW 91, WrDr 92*
**Boyd**, John 1957- *TwCPaSc*
**Boyd**, John A. 1928- *WhoIns 92*
**Boyd**, John Addison, Jr. 1930- *WhoFI 92*
**Boyd**, John Dixon Ikle 1936- *Who 92*
**Boyd**, John E. *WhoRel 92*
**Boyd**, John Edward 1932- *AmMWSc 92*
**Boyd**, John Francis 1910- *Who 92*
**Boyd**, John Garth 1942- *WhoWest 92*
**Boyd**, John Kent 1910- *WhoFI 92*
**Boyd**, John Marvin 1943- *WhoRel 92*
**Boyd**, John Morton 1925- *Who 92*
**Boyd**, John Philip 1951- *AmMWSc 92*
**Boyd**, John Wells 1950- *WhoAmL 92*
**Boyd**, John William 1931- *AmMWSc 92*
**Boyd**, Joseph A *ScFEYrs*
**Boyd**, Joseph Arthur, Jr 1916- *WhoAmP 91*
**Boyd**, Joseph Aubrey 1921- *IntWW 91*
**Boyd**, Joseph Ian 1935- *WhoRel 92*
**Boyd**, Joseph L. 1947- *WhoBlA 92*
**Boyd**, Josephine Watson 1927- *AmMWSc 92*
**Boyd**, Juanell N 1942- *AmMWSc 92*
**Boyd**, Julia Margaret 1921- *WhoRel 92*
**Boyd**, Kenneth James 1935- *WhoRel 92*
**Boyd**, Kenneth Ray 1959- *WhoEnt 92*
**Boyd**, Kevin Bruce 1969- *WhoEnt 92*
**Boyd**, Kevin Robert 1955- *WhoRel 92*
**Boyd**, L L 1923- *AmMWSc 92*
**Boyd**, Leona Potter 1907- *WhoWest 92*
**Boyd**, Leroy Houston 1935- *AmMWSc 92*
**Boyd**, Leslie Balfour 1914- *Who 92*
**Boyd**, Liona 1950?- *ConMus 7 [port], NewAmDM*
**Boyd**, Liona Maria *WhoEnt 92*
**Boyd**, Louis Jefferson 1928- *AmMWSc 92*
**Boyd**, Louise A. 1877-1972 *HanAmWH*
**Boyd**, Louise Yvonne 1959- *WhoBlA 92*
**Boyd**, Lucille I. 1906- *WhoBlA 92*
**Boyd**, Luke Howard, Jr. 1933- *WhoAmL 92*
**Boyd**, Lynn 1800-1859 *AmPolLe*
**Boyd**, Malcolm 1923- *RelLAm 91, WhoRel 92, WrDr 92*
**Boyd**, Malcolm 1932- *IntAu&W 91*
**Boyd**, Malcolm R 1924- *AmMWSc 92*
**Boyd**, Martin 1893-1972 *RfGEnL 91*
**Boyd**, Mary H. 1929- *WhoWest 92*
**Boyd**, Mary K 1960- *AmMWSc 92*
**Boyd**, Mary Olert 1930- *WhoAmP 91*
**Boyd**, Megan *DrAPF 91*
**Boyd**, Michael Alan 1937- *WhoAmL 92, WhoFI 92*
**Boyd**, Michael Delen 1956- *WhoFI 92*
**Boyd**, Michael Joel 1938- *WhoIns 92*
**Boyd**, Michael R *AmMWSc 92*
**Boyd**, Miles Farris 1953- *WhoRel 92*
**Boyd**, Miller W., Jr. 1934- *WhoBlA 92*
**Boyd**, Milton John 1941- *AmMWSc 92*
**Boyd**, Milton Matthew 1937- *WhoEnt 92*
**Boyd**, Morgan Alistair 1934- *Who 92*
**Boyd**, Muriel Isabel Belton 1910- *WhoBlA 92*
**Boyd**, Murray Middleton 1934- *WhoRel 92*
**Boyd**, Nancy *BenetAL 91*
**Boyd**, Obie Dale 1925- *WhoAmP 91*
**Boyd**, Oil Can 1959- *WhoBlA 92*
**Boyd**, Peter James 1919- *WhoAmL 92*
**Boyd**, Randall M. 1946- *WhoIns 92*
**Boyd**, Richard Hays 1929- *AmMWSc 92*
**Boyd**, Richard Henry 1843-1922 *RelLAm 91*
**Boyd**, Richard Nelson 1940- *AmMWSc 92*
**Boyd**, Robert 1922- *Who 92*
**Boyd**, Robert B *AmMWSc 92*
**Boyd**, Robert Edward, Sr 1927- *AmMWSc 92*
**Boyd**, Robert Friend 1927- *WhoAmL 92*
**Boyd**, Robert Friend, Jr. 1954- *WhoRel 92*
**Boyd**, Robert Henry 1932- *AmMWSc 92*
**Boyd**, Robert Hugh Steele 1924- *IntWW 91*
**Boyd**, Robert Lewis Fullarton 1922- *IntWW 91*
**Boyd**, Robert Nathaniel, III 1928- *WhoBlA 92*
**Boyd**, Robert Sprott 1941- *WhoAmL 92*
**Boyd**, Robert Stanley 1927- *Who 92*
**Boyd**, Robert Thompson 1914- *WhoRel 92*
**Boyd**, Robert William 1948- *AmMWSc 92*
**Boyd**, Robin 1919-1971 *ConAu 133*
**Boyd**, Rodney Carney 1943- *WhoEnt 92, WhoMW 92*
**Boyd**, Roger Lee 1947- *AmMWSc 92, WhoMW 92*
**Boyd**, Ronald 1946- *TwCPaSc*
**Boyd**, Rozelle 1934- *WhoAmP 91, WhoBlA 92*
**Boyd**, Russell Jaye 1945- *AmMWSc 92*
**Boyd**, Ruth R. 1936- *WhoBlA 92*
**Boyd**, Sandra Hughes 1938- *WhoRel 92*
**Boyd**, Sara Dixon 1957- *WhoFI 92*
**Boyd**, Sharon 1945- *WhoAmL 92*
**Boyd**, Shyla *DrAPF 91*
**Boyd**, Stephen Blake 1954- *WhoRel 92*
**Boyd**, Stephen Curtis 1949- *WhoWest 92*
**Boyd**, Stephen Kent 1945- *WhoMW 92*
**Boyd**, Steven Don 1957- *WhoAmL 92*
**Boyd**, Stewart Craufurd 1943- *Who 92*
**Boyd**, Sue Abbott *DrAPF 91*
**Boyd**, Theophilus B., III 1947- *WhoBlA 92*
**Boyd**, Thomas d1715? *DcNCBi 1*
**Boyd**, Thomas 1942- *WhoBlA 92*
**Boyd**, Thomas Alexander 1898-1935 *BenetAL 91*
**Boyd**, Thomas Andrew 1952- *WhoMW 92*
**Boyd**, Thomas Christopher 1916- *Who 92*
**Boyd**, Thomas Marshall 1946- *WhoAmL 92*
**Boyd**, Tom 1928- *WhoAmP 91*
**Boyd**, Virginia Ann Lewis 1944- *AmMWSc 92*
**Boyd**, Vivienne 1926- *Who 92*
**Boyd**, W. Harland 1912- *WrDr 92*
**Boyd**, Waldo T. 1918- *WrDr 92*
**Boyd**, Wayne Edwin 1939- *WhoAmP 91*
**Boyd**, Wilda Mae 1936- *WhoAmP 91*
**Boyd**, Wilford Perry, Jr. 1946- *WhoEnt 92*
**Boyd**, Willard Lee 1927- *WhoAmL 92, WhoMW 92*
**Boyd**, William 1885-1979 *ConAu 135*
**Boyd**, William 1941- *WhoAmP 91*
**Boyd**, William 1952- *ConNov 91, IntAu&W 91, WrDr 92*
**Boyd**, William Allen 1957- *WhoRel 92*
**Boyd**, William Andrew Murray 1952- *IntWW 91, Who 92*
**Boyd**, William Arthur, II 1953- *WhoWest 92*
**Boyd**, William B. *IntWW 91*
**Boyd**, William Clouser 1903- *FacFETw*
**Boyd**, William Elkins 1947- *WhoWest 92*
**Boyd**, William Harland 1912- *WhoWest 92*
**Boyd**, William Kenneth 1879-1938 *DcNCBi 1*
**Boyd**, William Lee 1926- *AmMWSc 92*
**Boyd**, William Stewart 1952- *WhoBlA 92*
**Boyd-Carpenter** *Who 92*
**Boyd-Carpenter**, Baron 1908- *IntWW 91, Who 92*
**Boyd-Carpenter**, Thomas Patrick John 1938- *Who 92*
**Boyd-Clinkscales**, Mary Elizabeth 1918- *WhoBlA 92*
**Boyd-Foy**, Mary Louise 1936- *WhoBlA 92*
**Boyd Of Merton**, Viscount 1939- *IntWW 91, Who 92*
**Boyd Orr**, John 1880-1971 *FacFETw*
**Boyde**, Patrick 1934- *Who 92*
**Boydell**, Brian 1917- *ConCom 92*
**Boydell**, Peter Thomas Sherrington 1920- *Who 92*
**Boyden**, Bruce Robert 1949- *WhoAmL 92*
**Boyden**, Christopher Wayne 1952- *WhoAmL 92*
**Boyden**, Donald Philip 1957- *WhoMW 92*
**Boyden**, James 1910- *Who 92*
**Boyden**, Nathaniel 1796-1873 *DcNCBi 1*
**Boyden**, Seth 1788-1870 *BiInAmS*
**Boyden**, Thomas Newhall 1940- *WhoFI 92*
**Boyden**, Uriah Atherton 1804-1879 *BiInAmS*
**Boyden**, Walter Lincoln 1932- *WhoAmL 92*
**Boydston**, James Christopher 1947- *WhoWest 92*
**Boydstun**, Jimmy Earl 1946- *WhoWest 92*
**Boye**, Charles Andrew, Jr 1928- *AmMWSc 92*
**Boye**, Frederick C 1923- *AmMWSc 92*
**Boye**, Ibrahima 1924- *IntWW 91*
**Boye**, Karin 1900-1941 *TwCSFW 91A*
**Boye**, Martin Hans 1812-1909 *BiInAmS*

**Boye,** Mohamed Mahjoub Ould 1947- IntWW 91
**Boye,** Robert James 1934- AmMWSc 92
**Boye,** Thore Albert 1912- IntWW 91
**Boyer,** Andrew Ben 1958- WhoAmL 92
**Boyer,** Barbara Conta 1942- AmMWSc 92
**Boyer,** Carl, III 1937- WhoWest 92
**Boyer,** Charles 1897-1978 FacFETw [port]
**Boyer,** Cinda Marie 1954- AmMWSc 92
**Boyer,** Delmar Lee 1926- AmMWSc 92
**Boyer,** Don Eric 1959- WhoEnt 92
**Boyer,** Don Lamar 1938- AmMWSc 92
**Boyer,** Don Raymond 1929- AmMWSc 92
**Boyer,** Don W. 1930- WhoMW 92
**Boyer,** Donald Wayne 1929- AmMWSc 92
**Boyer,** Elroy G 1920- WhoAmP 91
**Boyer,** Ernest LeRoy 1928- WhoAmP 91
**Boyer,** Ernest Wendell 1937- AmMWSc 92
**Boyer,** Ford Sylvester 1934- WhoWest 92
**Boyer,** Geoffrey Frederick 1945- WhoFI 92
**Boyer,** George Edward, Jr. 1955- WhoFI 92
**Boyer,** Harold Edwin 1925- AmMWSc 92
**Boyer,** Harry Starr 1950- WhoRel 92
**Boyer,** Herbert Wayne 1936- AmMWSc 92, FacFETw
**Boyer,** Horace Clarence 1935- WhoBlA 92
**Boyer,** James B. 1934- WhoBlA 92
**Boyer,** James Gambrell 1928- WhoAmP 91
**Boyer,** James Lorenzen 1936- AmMWSc 92
**Boyer,** Jay DrAPF 91
**Boyer,** Jay Marcus 1947- WhoWest 92
**Boyer,** Jere Michael 1946- AmMWSc 92
**Boyer,** Joe L. WhoBlA 92
**Boyer,** John Frederick 1941- AmMWSc 92
**Boyer,** John Leslie 1926- Who 92
**Boyer,** John Strickland 1937- AmMWSc 92
**Boyer,** Joseph Henry 1922- AmMWSc 92
**Boyer,** Laura Mercedes 1934- WhoWest 92
**Boyer,** LeRoy T 1937- AmMWSc 92
**Boyer,** Lester Leroy 1937- AmMWSc 92
**Boyer,** Marcus Aurelius 1945- WhoBlA 92
**Boyer,** Mark WhoAmP 91
**Boyer,** Markley Holmes 1932- AmMWSc 92
**Boyer,** Max Kevin 1953- WhoAmL 92
**Boyer,** Michael George 1925- AmMWSc 92
**Boyer,** Paul Delos 1918- AmMWSc 92, IntWW 91
**Boyer,** Phil 1940- IntMPA 92
**Boyer,** Raymond Foster 1910- AmMWSc 92
**Boyer,** Richard Donald 1957- WhoRel 92
**Boyer,** Richard Edward 1944- WhoAmP 91
**Boyer,** Rick 1943- WrDr 92
**Boyer,** Robert Allan 1934- WhoFI 92
**Boyer,** Robert Allen 1916- AmMWSc 92
**Boyer,** Robert Elston 1939- AmMWSc 92
**Boyer,** Robert Ernst 1929- AmMWSc 92
**Boyer,** Robert Jay 1951- WhoWest 92
**Boyer,** Rodney Frederick 1942- AmMWSc 92
**Boyer,** Rodney Raymond 1939- AmMWSc 92
**Boyer,** Samuel H, IV 1924- AmMWSc 92
**Boyer,** Spencer H. 1938- WhoBlA 92
**Boyer,** Stanley Clark 1927- WhoAmP 91
**Boyer,** Timothy Howard 1941- AmMWSc 92
**Boyer,** Vincent Lee 1956- WhoFI 92
**Boyer,** Vincent S 1918- AmMWSc 92
**Boyer,** Wayne Allen 1937- WhoEnt 92
**Boyer,** Wayne Wendell 1941- WhoRel 92
**Boyer,** Wilbur Bookman, Jr. 1945- WhoFI 92
**Boyer,** William Davis 1924- AmMWSc 92
**Boyer,** William F. DcTwDes
**Boyer Salvador,** Miguel 1939- IntWW 91
**Boyers,** Albert Sage 1940- AmMWSc 92
**Boyers,** Carol Ann 1948- WhoRel 92
**Boyers,** Howard 1915- Who 92
**Boyers,** Janeth Mauree 1931- WhoMW 92
**Boyers,** Matthew Erin 1959- WhoRel 92
**Boyers,** Robert 1942- WrDr 92
**Boyes,** Brian Gerald B. Who 92
**Boyes,** Glenn Mervin 1955- WhoRel 92
**Boyes,** James Ashley 1924- Who 92
**Boyes,** Karl W 1936- WhoAmP 91
**Boyes,** Kate Emily Tyrrell 1918- Who 92
**Boyes,** Megan 1923- WrDr 92
**Boyes,** Roland Who 92
**Boyesen,** Hjalmar Hjorth 1848-1895 BenetAL 91
**Boyett,** Robert Lee IntMPA 92, WhoEnt 92
**Boyette,** Joseph Greene 1929- AmMWSc 92
**Boyette,** Richard Alexander 1934- WhoFI 92
**Boyington,** Gregory 1912-1988 FacFETw
**Boykan,** Martin 1931- WhoEnt 92
**Boykin,** A. Wade, Jr. 1947- WhoBlA 92
**Boykin,** David Withers, Jr 1939- AmMWSc 92
**Boykin,** Glenda Darnell 1944- WhoRel 92
**Boykin,** Hamilton Haight 1939- WhoAmL 92
**Boykin,** James Lester 1928- WhoWest 92
**Boykin,** Joel S. 1926- WhoBlA 92
**Boykin,** Lorraine Stith 1931- AmMWSc 92
**Boykin,** Marybeth Trescher 1926- WhoAmP 91
**Boykin,** Nancy Merritt WhoAmP 91, WhoMW 92
**Boykin,** Randson C. 1949- WhoBlA 92
**Boykin,** Raymond Francis 1953- WhoWest 92
**Boykin,** Robert Heath 1926- WhoFI 92
**Boykin,** William H, Jr 1938- AmMWSc 92
**Boykin,** Willie 1916- WhoBlA 92
**Boykin-Chase,** Susan Michelle 1958- WhoWest 92
**Boykins,** Billie Anthony 1946- WhoAmP 91
**Boykins,** Ernest A. 1931- WhoBlA 92
**Boykins,** Ernest Aloysius, Jr 1931- AmMWSc 92
**Boyko,** Christopher Allan 1954- WhoAmL 92, WhoMW 92
**Boyko,** Edward Raymond 1930- AmMWSc 92
**Boylan,** Brian Richard 1936- WhoRel 92
**Boylan,** Clare 1948- ConNov 91, WrDr 92
**Boylan,** Clare 1950- IntAu&W 91
**Boylan,** D R 1922- AmMWSc 92
**Boylan,** Edward S 1938- AmMWSc 92
**Boylan,** Elizabeth S 1946- AmMWSc 92
**Boylan,** Gary Francis 1944- WhoMW 92
**Boylan,** Gary Lynn 1952- WhoEnt 92
**Boylan,** Gerard William WhoFI 92
**Boylan,** James George 1937- WhoAmL 92
**Boylan,** John Patrick 1941- WhoEnt 92
**Boylan,** John Patrick 1959- WhoWest 92
**Boylan,** John W 1914- AmMWSc 92
**Boylan,** Patrick John 1939- Who 92
**Boylan,** Paul Charles 1939- WhoEnt 92
**Boylan,** Paul F 1919- WhoAmP 91
**Boylan,** Paul Gerard 1950- WhoAmL 92
**Boylan,** Richard John 1939- WhoWest 92
**Boylan,** William 1777-1861 DcNCBi 1
**Boylan,** William Alvin 1924- WhoAmL 92, WhoFI 92
**Boylan,** William J 1929- AmMWSc 92
**Boylan,** William John 1929- WhoMW 92
**Boyland,** Dorian Scott 1955- WhoBlA 92
**Boyland,** Eric 1905- IntWW 91, Who 92
**Boyland,** Mark Charles 1963- WhoAmL 92
**Boyland,** William Frank WhoAmP 91
**Boyle** Who 92
**Boyle,** Viscount 1960- Who 92
**Boyle,** A R 1920- AmMWSc 92
**Boyle,** Alan Gordon 1949- Who 92
**Boyle,** Alicia 1908- TwCPaSc
**Boyle,** Andrew 1919-1991 ConAu 134, NewYTBS 91 [port]
**Boyle,** Andrew Philip More d1991 Who 92N
**Boyle,** Andrew Philip More 1919- IntAu&W 91
**Boyle,** Antonia Barnes 1939- WhoEnt 92
**Boyle,** Archibald Cabbourn 1918- Who 92
**Boyle,** Barbara D. 1935- IntMPA 92
**Boyle,** Barbara Dorman 1935- WhoEnt 92
**Boyle,** Brian J WhoAmP 91
**Boyle,** Bryan Douglas 1956- WhoFI 92
**Boyle,** Carolyn Anne 1940- WhoIns 92
**Boyle,** Carolyn Moore 1937- WhoWest 92
**Boyle,** Christopher 1956- WhoAmP 91
**Boyle,** David 1958- ConAu 133
**Boyle,** Dermot 1904- Who 92
**Boyle,** Dermot Alexander 1904- IntWW 91
**Boyle,** Eugene P WhoAmP 91
**Boyle,** Eugene Philip 1946- WhoMW 92
**Boyle,** Francis Joseph 1927- WhoAmL 92
**Boyle,** Francis Joseph 1945- WhoFI 92
**Boyle,** Francis William 1951- WhoWest 92
**Boyle,** Frank James 1945- WhoAmP 91
**Boyle,** Frederick 1814-1883? ScFEYrs
**Boyle,** Gary William 1956- WhoAmL 92
**Boyle,** James B. 1955- WhoEnt 92
**Boyle,** James Martin 1942- AmMWSc 92
**Boyle,** James Michael 1953- WhoFI 92
**Boyle,** James P 1904- WhoAmP 91
**Boyle,** Jim WhoBlA 92
**Boyle,** Jimmy 1945- TwCPaSc
**Boyle,** John Aloysius, Jr 1950- AmMWSc 92
**Boyle,** John Joseph 1930- AmMWSc 92
**Boyle,** John Leo 1934- WhoFI 92
**Boyle,** John Phillips 1931- WhoRel 92
**Boyle,** John Sebastian d1991 Who 92N
**Boyle,** John T. 1921- WhoIns 92
**Boyle,** John William 1929- WhoFI 92
**Boyle,** Joseph, III 1934- AmMWSc 92
**Boyle,** Kathryn Moyne Ward Dittemore AmMWSc 92
**Boyle,** Kay DrAPF 91
**Boyle,** Kay 1902- ConNov 91, ConPo 91, IntAu&W 91, LiExTwC, Who 92, WrDr 92
**Boyle,** Kay 1903- BenetAL 91
**Boyle,** Lara Flynn 1971- IntMPA 92
**Boyle,** Larry Monroe 1943- WhoAmL 92, WhoAmP 91, WhoWest 92
**Boyle,** Lawrence Dennis 1942- WhoWest 92
**Boyle,** Leonard Butler 1913- Who 92
**Boyle,** Mark 1934- TwCPaSc
**Boyle,** Mary O 1941- WhoAmP 91
**Boyle,** Michael 1944- WhoAmP 91
**Boyle,** Michael Dermot 1949- AmMWSc 92
**Boyle,** Patricia J 1937- WhoAmP 91
**Boyle,** Patricia Jean WhoAmL 92, WhoMW 92
**Boyle,** Peter 1933?- ConTFT 9, IntMPA 92, WhoEnt 92
**Boyle,** Richard James 1927- AmMWSc 92
**Boyle,** Richard James 1943- WhoFI 92
**Boyle,** Robert 1627-1691 BlkwCEP
**Boyle,** Robert Daniel 1965- WhoFI 92
**Boyle,** Robert H. 1928- SmATA 65
**Boyle,** Roger 1621-1679 RfGEnL 91
**Boyle,** Stephen Gurney 1962- Who 92
**Boyle,** T. Coraghessan DrAPF 91
**Boyle,** T. Coraghessan 1948- BenetAL 91, CurBio 91 [port]
**Boyle,** Terence 1952- WhoAmL 92
**Boyle,** Terrence W. 1945- WhoAmL 92
**Boyle,** Walter Gordon, Jr 1928- AmMWSc 92
**Boyle,** Willard Sterling 1924- AmMWSc 92
**Boyle,** William Anthony 1904-1985 FacFETw
**Boyle,** William C 1936- AmMWSc 92
**Boyle,** William Johnston, Jr 1944- AmMWSc 92
**Boyle,** William Robert 1932- AmMWSc 92
**Boylen,** Charles William 1942- AmMWSc 92
**Boylen,** Joyce Beatrice 1926- AmMWSc 92
**Boyles,** Ann 1954- WhoRel 92
**Boyles,** Clarence Scott, Jr. TwCWW 91
**Boyles,** Edgar William 1921- Who 92
**Boyles,** Harlan E 1929- WhoAmP 91
**Boyles,** James Glenn 1937- AmMWSc 92
**Boyles,** James McGregor 1926- AmMWSc 92
**Boyles,** Janet AmMWSc 92
**Boyles,** Robert Joseph 1955- WhoWest 92
**Boyles,** William Archer 1951- WhoAmL 92
**Boyless,** James Andrus 1945- WhoHisp 92
**Boyll,** David Lloyd 1940- WhoEnt 92
**Boylston,** Benjamin Calvin 1932- WhoFI 92
**Boylston,** Zabdiel 1680-1766 BiInAmS
**Boyne,** Viscount 1931- Who 92
**Boyne,** Donald Arthur Colin Aydon 1921- Who 92
**Boyne,** Henry Brian 1910- Who 92
**Boyne,** John 1932- Who 92
**Boyne,** Philip John 1924- AmMWSc 92
**Boyne,** Walter J. 1929- WrDr 92
**Boyne,** William Joseph 1926- AmMWSc 92
**Boynton,** Asa Terrell, Sr. 1945- WhoBlA 92
**Boynton,** Buck William 1920- WhoWest 92
**Boynton,** Charles Lawrence 1864-1943 DcNCBi 1
**Boynton,** Donald Arthur 1940- WhoWest 92
**Boynton,** Ernest B., Jr. 1936-1984 WhoBlA 92N
**Boynton,** Henry W. 1869-1947 BenetAL 91
**Boynton,** Irvin Parker 1937- WhoMW 92
**Boynton,** John 1918- Who 92
**Boynton,** John E 1938- AmMWSc 92
**Boynton,** John E 1950- AmMWSc 92
**Boynton,** Marjorie Chase 1925- WhoAmP 91
**Boynton,** Percy H. 1875-1946 BenetAL 91
**Boynton,** Robert Granville 1951- WhoWest 92
**Boynton,** Robert Lyman 1916- WhoAmL 92
**Boynton,** Robert M 1924- AmMWSc 92
**Boynton,** Robert Merrill 1924- IntWW 91
**Boynton,** Sandra 1953- IntAu&W 91
**Boynton,** W W 1904- AmMWSc 92
**Boynton,** Walter Raymond 1947- AmMWSc 92
**Boynton,** William Lewis 1928- WhoFI 92, WhoWest 92
**Boynton,** William Vandegrift 1944- AmMWSc 92
**Boyriven,** Mariette Hartley 1940- WhoEnt 92
**Boys,** Penelope Ann 1947- Who 92
**Boys-Smith,** Humphry Gilbert 1904- Who 92
**Boys Smith,** John Sandwith 1901- Who 92
**Boys Smith,** Stephen Wynn 1946- Who 92
**Boyse,** Edward A 1923- AmMWSc 92
**Boyse,** Edward Arthur 1923- IntWW 91, Who 92
**Boysen,** Connie Jean 1958- WhoAmL 92
**Boysen,** Lars 1948- WhoFI 92
**Boysen,** Melicent Pearl 1943- WhoFI 92, WhoMW 92
**Boyson,** Rhodes 1925- Who 92
**Boyson,** Sally J. 1952- WhoWest 92
**Boyte,** George Griffin 1925- WhoAmL 92
**Boyte,** Robert Howard 1930- WhoRel 92
**Boytim,** Joan Frey 1933- WhoEnt 92
**Boza,** Juan 1941-1991 WhoHisp 92N
**Bozak,** Richard Edward 1934- AmMWSc 92
**Bozanga,** Simon-Narcisse 1942- IntWW 91
**Bozarth,** Gene Allen 1941- AmMWSc 92
**Bozarth,** Robert F 1930- AmMWSc 92
**Bozdech,** Marek Jiri 1946- AmMWSc 92
**Boze,** Fred Adwell 1946- WhoFI 92
**Bozeman,** Adda 1908- WrDr 92
**Bozeman,** Adda Bruemmer 1908- IntAu&W 91
**Bozeman,** Beverley Jean 1927- WhoEnt 92
**Bozeman,** Bruce L. 1944- WhoBlA 92
**Bozeman,** Bruce Lee 1944- WhoAmL 92
**Bozeman,** Carlton Michael 1957- WhoAmL 92
**Bozeman,** Cary E 1940- WhoAmP 91
**Bozeman,** Catherine E. 1904- WhoBlA 92
**Bozeman,** F Marilyn 1927- AmMWSc 92
**Bozeman,** John Russell 1935- AmMWSc 92
**Bozeman,** Maggie Simmons 1929- WhoBlA 92
**Bozeman,** Samuel Richmond 1915- AmMWSc 92
**Bozeman,** Theodore Dwight WhoRel 92
**Bozer,** Ali Husrev 1925- IntWW 91
**Bozian,** Richard C 1919- AmMWSc 92
**Bozian,** Richard Charles 1919- WhoMW 92
**Bozick,** Peter A WhoAmP 91
**Bozler,** Carl O 1941- AmMWSc 92
**Bozler,** Emil 1901- AmMWSc 92
**Bozman,** Bennett WhoAmP 91
**Bozniak,** Eugene George 1942- AmMWSc 92
**Bozo,** Dominique 1935- IntWW 91
**Bozoki,** George Edward 1930- AmMWSc 92
**Bozoki-Gombosi,** Eva S AmMWSc 92
**Bozorth,** Squire Newland 1935- WhoAmL 92
**Bozza,** Eugene 1905- NewAmDM
**Bozzelli,** Joseph William 1942- AmMWSc 92
**Bozzo,** Ana Cristina d1991 NewYTBS 91
**Bozzoli,** Guerino Renzo 1911- Who 92
**Bozzuti,** John Anthony 1965- WhoFI 92
**Bozzuto,** Carl Richard 1947- AmMWSc 92
**Bozzuto,** Richard Carl 1930- WhoFI 92
**Bozzuto,** Victor J 1921- WhoAmP 91
**Braams,** Cornelis Marius 1925- IntWW 91
**Braasch,** Norman L 1928- AmMWSc 92
**Braasch,** William Michael 1947- WhoWest 92
**Braaten,** David A 1955- AmMWSc 92
**Braaten,** Mark Hendricks 1955- WhoRel 92
**Braaten,** Melvin Ole 1934- AmMWSc 92
**Braatz,** James Anthony 1943- AmMWSc 92
**Braatz,** Thomas Myron 1933- WhoMW 92
**Brabander,** Herbert Joseph 1932- AmMWSc 92
**Brabazon** Who 92
**Brabazon,** James 1923- IntAu&W 91, WrDr 92
**Brabazon of Tara,** Baron 1946- Who 92
**Brabb,** Earl Edward 1929- AmMWSc 92, WhoWest 92
**Brabham,** Jack 1926- IntWW 91
**Brabham,** John Arthur 1926- Who 92
**Brabourne,** Baron 1924- IntWW 91, Who 92
**Brabourne,** John 1924- IntMPA 92
**Brabson,** Bennet Bristol 1938- AmMWSc 92
**Brabson,** George Dana, Jr 1935- AmMWSc 92
**Brabson,** Howard V. 1925- WhoBlA 92
**Brabson,** Howard Victor 1925- WhoMW 92
**Braby,** Dorothea 1909-1987 TwCPaSc
**Braby,** Gudvor Wikane 1899- WhoAmP 91
**Braby,** Leslie Alan 1941- AmMWSc 92
**Bracali,** Giampaolo 1941- WhoEnt 92
**Bracamonte,** Oscar WhoHisp 92
**Bracco,** Donato John 1921- AmMWSc 92
**Bracco,** Lorraine 1955- IntMPA 92
**Brace,** C Loring 1930- AmMWSc 92
**Brace,** Charles Loring 1826-1890 DcAmImH
**Brace,** DeWitt Bristol 1859-1905 BiInAmS
**Brace,** Edward Roy 1936- WhoEnt 92
**Brace,** Gerald Warner 1901-1978 BenetAL 91
**Brace,** John Michael 1942- WhoMW 92
**Brace,** John Pierce 1793-1872 BiInAmS
**Brace,** John Wells 1926- AmMWSc 92
**Brace,** Larry Harold 1929- AmMWSc 92
**Brace,** Neal Orin 1922- AmMWSc 92
**Brace,** Nebraska Odell 1929- WhoAmP 91
**Brace,** Robert Allen 1948- AmMWSc 92

**Brace**, William Francis 1926- *AmMWSc 92, IntWW 91*
**Bracegirdle**, Brian 1933- *IntAu&W 91, Who 92, WrDr 92*
**Bracete**, Juan Manuel 1951- *WhoAmL 92*
**Braceti**, Mariana *EncAmaz 91*
**Bracewell**, Joyanne 1934- *Who 92*
**Bracewell**, Michael 1958- *ConAu 135*
**Bracewell**, Robert Edward Lee 1930- *WhoFI 92*
**Bracewell**, Ronald Newbold 1921- *AmMWSc 92*
**Bracewell-Milnes**, Barry 1931- *WrDr 92*
**Bracewell-Milnes**, John Barry 1931- *IntAu&W 91*
**Bracewell-Smith**, Charles 1955- *Who 92*
**Bracey**, Cookie Frances Lee 1945- *WhoRel 92*
**Bracey**, Henry J. 1949- *WhoBlA 92*
**Bracey**, John Henry, Jr. 1941- *WhoBlA 92*
**Bracey**, William Rubin 1920- *WhoBlA 92*
**Bracey**, Willie Earl 1950- *WhoBlA 92*
**Brach**, Eugene Jeno 1928- *AmMWSc 92*
**Brach**, Raymond M 1934- *AmMWSc 92*
**Bracher**, George 1909- *WhoWest 92*
**Bracher**, Karl Dietrich 1922- *IntWW 91*
**Bracher**, Katherine 1938- *AmMWSc 92*
**Bracher**, Peter Scholl 1932- *WhoMW 92*
**Braches**, Ernst 1930- *IntWW 91*
**Brachet**, Jean Louis Auguste 1909- *FacFETw*
**Brachfeld**, Norman 1927- *AmMWSc 92*
**Brachlow**, Stephen John 1947- *WhoRel 92*
**Brachman**, Malcolm K 1926- *AmMWSc 92*
**Brachman**, Philip Sigmund 1927- *AmMWSc 92*
**Brachman**, Richard John, II 1951- *WhoMW 92*
**Bracho**, Coral 1951- *ConSpAP*
**Bracht**, Franz 1877-1933 *EncTR 91*
**Brachtenbach**, Robert F *WhoAmP 91*
**Brachtenbach**, Robert F. 1931- *WhoAmL 92, WhoWest 92*
**Braciale**, Thomas Joseph, Jr 1946- *AmMWSc 92*
**Braciale**, Vivian Lam 1948- *AmMWSc 92*
**Brack**, Karl 1923- *AmMWSc 92*
**Brack**, Reginald Kufeld, Jr. 1937- *WhoFI 92*
**Brack**, Rita MacDonaid 1918- *WhoAmP 91*
**Brack**, Ron Kevin 1960- *WhoRel 92*
**Brack**, Steve 1949- *WhoFI 92*
**Brack**, Viktor 1904-1948 *EncTR 91 [port]*
**Brack-Hanes**, Sheila Delfeld 1939- *AmMWSc 92*
**Brackbill**, Jeremiah U 1941- *AmMWSc 92*
**Brackelsberg**, Paul O 1939- *AmMWSc 92*
**Bracken**, Barton William 1955- *WhoIns 92*
**Bracken**, Brendan 1901-1958 *FacFETw*
**Bracken**, Eddie 1920- *IntMPA 92, WhoEnt 92*
**Bracken**, James Donald 1934- *WhoRel 92*
**Bracken**, John P. 1938- *WhoAmL 92*
**Bracken**, Joseph Andrew 1930- *WhoRel 92*
**Bracken**, Linda K. 1963- *WhoMW 92*
**Bracken**, Louis Everett 1947- *WhoFI 92*
**Brackenbury**, Alison 1953- *ConPo 91, WrDr 92*
**Brackenbury**, Michael Palmer 1930- *Who 92*
**Brackenbury**, Robert William 1948- *AmMWSc 92*
**Brackenrich**, James D 1936- *WhoAmP 91*
**Brackenridge**, David Ross 1938- *AmMWSc 92*
**Brackenridge**, Henry Marie 1786-1871 *BenetAL 91*
**Brackenridge**, Hugh Henry 1748-1816 *BenetAL 91*
**Brackenridge**, John Bruce 1927- *AmMWSc 92*
**Brackenridge**, Robert L 1941- *WhoAmP 91*
**Brackenridge**, William Dunlop 1810-1893 *BiInAmS*
**Bracker**, Charles E 1938- *AmMWSc 92*
**Bracker**, Jonathan *DrAPF 91*
**Brackett**, Benjamin Gaylord 1938- *AmMWSc 92*
**Brackett**, Charles 1892-1969 *BenetAL 91*
**Brackett**, Cyrus Fogg 1833-1915 *BiInAmS*
**Brackett**, David Lynn 1961- *WhoRel 92*
**Brackett**, Edward Boone, III 1936- *WhoMW 92*
**Brackett**, Foster H 1863?-1900 *BiInAmS*
**Brackett**, Leigh 1915-1978 *ReelWom, TwCSFW 91*
**Brackett**, Martin Luther, Jr. 1947- *WhoAmL 92*
**Brackett**, Noy E 1913- *WhoAmP 91*
**Brackett**, Randall Carr 1955- *WhoWest 92*
**Brackett**, Robert E 1953- *AmMWSc 92*
**Brackett**, Robert Giles 1930- *AmMWSc 92*
**Brackett**, Ronald E. 1942- *WhoFI 92*
**Brackin**, Eddy Joe 1945- *AmMWSc 92*
**Brackin**, John LeRoy 1949- *WhoRel 92*
**Brackman**, David Herman 1960- *WhoMW 92*
**Brackmann**, Richard Theodore 1930- *AmMWSc 92*
**Bracquemond**, Felix 1833-1914 *ThHEIm*
**Bracquemond**, Marie 1841-1916 *ThHEIm*
**Bracy**, Arnold Lee 1938- *WhoRel 92*
**Bracy**, Ursula J. 1908- *WhoBlA 92*
**Bracy**, Warren D 1942- *WhoAmP 91*
**Bradac**, Jaroslav 1945- *TwCPaSc*
**Bradbeer**, Clive 1933- *AmMWSc 92*
**Bradbeer**, Derek 1931- *Who 92*
**Bradberry**, Brent Alan 1939- *WhoWest 92*
**Bradberry**, Bruce Martin 1948- *WhoWest 92*
**Bradberry**, Richard Paul 1951- *WhoBlA 92*
**Bradbrook**, Muriel Clara 1909- *IntAu&W 91, IntWW 91, Who 92, WrDr 92*
**Bradburd**, Ervin M 1920- *AmMWSc 92*
**Bradburn**, Gregory Russell 1955- *AmMWSc 92, WhoMW 92*
**Bradburn**, John 1915- *Who 92*
**Bradbury** *Who 92*
**Bradbury**, Agnew and Company *DcLB 106*
**Bradbury and Evans** *DcLB 106 [port]*
**Bradbury**, Baron 1914- *Who 92*
**Bradbury**, Anita Jean *Who 92*
**Bradbury**, Donald 1917- *AmMWSc 92*
**Bradbury**, E Morton 1933- *AmMWSc 92*
**Bradbury**, Edgar 1927- *Who 92*
**Bradbury**, Edward P *TwCSFW 91*
**Bradbury**, Edwin Morton 1933- *WhoWest 92*
**Bradbury**, Ellen Adele 1940- *WhoWest 92*
**Bradbury**, Elmer J 1917- *AmMWSc 92*
**Bradbury**, Eric 1911- *Who 92*
**Bradbury**, Jack W 1941- *AmMWSc 92*
**Bradbury**, James Clifford 1918- *AmMWSc 92*
**Bradbury**, James Norris 1935- *AmMWSc 92*
**Bradbury**, James Thomas 1906- *AmMWSc 92*
**Bradbury**, John Daniels 1941- *WhoFI 92*
**Bradbury**, John Wymond 1960- *WhoWest 92*
**Bradbury**, Malcolm 1932- *ConNov 91, WrDr 92*
**Bradbury**, Malcolm Stanley 1932- *IntAu&W 91, IntWW 91, Who 92*
**Bradbury**, Margaret G 1927- *AmMWSc 92*
**Bradbury**, Matthew D. 1961- *WhoFI 92*
**Bradbury**, Michael Don 1942- *WhoAmL 92*
**Bradbury**, Michael Wayne 1953- *AmMWSc 92*
**Bradbury**, Norris Edwin 1909- *AmMWSc 92*
**Bradbury**, Patricia Nofer 1954- *WhoEnt 92*
**Bradbury**, Phyllis Clarke *AmMWSc 92*
**Bradbury**, Ray *DrAPF 91*
**Bradbury**, Ray 1920- *BenetAL 91, ConNov 91, FacFETw [port], IntAu&W 91, IntWW 91, TwCSFW 91, WrDr 92*
**Bradbury**, Ray Douglas 1920- *Who 92*
**Bradbury**, Thomas Henry 1922- *Who 92*
**Bradbury**, William Chapman 1949- *WhoAmP 91*
**Bradby**, David Henry 1942- *Who 92*
**Bradby**, Edward Lawrence 1907- *Who 92*
**Braddock**, Carol T. 1942- *WhoBlA 92*
**Braddock**, Dennis *WhoAmP 91*
**Braddock**, Donald Layton 1941- *WhoAmL 92*
**Braddock**, James J 1905-1974 *FacFETw*
**Braddock**, Joseph V 1929- *AmMWSc 92*
**Braddock**, Marilyn Eugenia 1955- *WhoBlA 92*
**Braddock**, Nonnie Clarke *WhoRel 92*
**Braddock**, Richard S. 1941- *WhoFI 92*
**Braddock**, Robert L. 1937- *WhoBlA 92*
**Braddock**, Walter David, III 1936- *WhoFI 92, WhoMW 92*
**Braddock**, William A 1929- *AmMWSc 92*
**Braddon**, M E 1835-1915 *ScFEYrs*
**Braddon**, Mary Elizabeth 1835-1915 *RfGEnL 91*
**Braddon**, Russell 1921- *WrDr 92*
**Braddon**, Russell Reading 1921- *IntAu&W 91, Who 92*
**Brademas**, John 1927- *WhoAmP 91*
**Braden**, Bernard 1916- *Who 92*
**Braden**, Betty L. 1944- *WhoFI 92, WhoMW 92*
**Braden**, Charles Hosea 1926- *AmMWSc 92*
**Braden**, Charles McMurray 1918- *AmMWSc 92*
**Braden**, Dennis *DrAPF 91*
**Braden**, Everette Arnold 1932- *WhoBlA 92*
**Braden**, Henry E, IV 1944- *WhoAmP 91, WhoBlA 92*
**Braden**, Hugh Reginald 1923- *Who 92*
**Braden**, James Dale 1934- *WhoAmP 91, WhoMW 92*
**Braden**, John Black 1950- *WhoMW 92*
**Braden**, Stanton Connell 1960- *WhoAmL 92, WhoBlA 92*
**Braden**, Verlon Patrick 1934- *WhoWest 92*
**Braden**, Waldo W. 1911- *WrDr 92*
**Braden**, William 1939- *IntMPA 92*
**Braden**, William Edward 1919- *WhoFI 92*
**Braden**, William Lou 1944- *WhoMW 92*
**Bradenburg**, Hubertus *WhoRel 92*
**Brader**, Walter Howe, Jr 1927- *AmMWSc 92*
**Bradesca**, Donna Marie 1938- *WhoRel 92*
**Bradfield**, Clarence McKinley 1942- *WhoBlA 92*
**Bradfield**, Horace Ferguson 1913- *WhoBlA 92*
**Bradfield**, James E 1944- *AmMWSc 92*
**Bradfield**, John Richard Grenfell 1925- *Who 92*
**Bradfield**, Nancy 1913- *WrDr 92*
**Bradfield**, Nellie Evangeline 1925- *WhoAmP 91*
**Bradfield**, Robert B 1928- *AmMWSc 92*
**Bradfield**, Scott William 1959- *WhoEnt 92*
**Bradfield**, Stephanie Alison 1950- *WhoWest 92*
**Bradfisch**, Otto 1903- *EncTR 91*
**Bradford**, Archdeacon of *Who 92*
**Bradford**, Bishop of *Who 92*
**Bradford**, Earl of 1947- *Who 92*
**Bradford**, Provost of *Who 92*
**Bradford**, Archie J. 1931- *WhoBlA 92*
**Bradford**, Arvine M. 1915- *WhoBlA 92*
**Bradford**, Barbara Reed 1948- *WhoFI 92*
**Bradford**, Barbara Taylor *IntAu&W 91*
**Bradford**, Barbara Taylor 1933- *CurBio 91 [port], IntWW 91, SmATA 66 [port], WrDr 92*
**Bradford**, Charles Edward 1925- *WhoBlA 92, WhoRel 92*
**Bradford**, Charles Lobdell 1936- *WhoFI 92*
**Bradford**, Christina 1942- *WhoMW 92*
**Bradford**, Columbus 1901-1938 *ScFEYrs*
**Bradford**, Dallas Hansen 1941- *WhoFI 92*
**Bradford**, David Jeffrey 1952- *WhoAmL 92*
**Bradford**, David Paul 1955- *WhoWest 92*
**Bradford**, David S 1936- *AmMWSc 92*
**Bradford**, David Thomas 1961- *WhoAmL 92*
**Bradford**, Dennis Doyle 1945- *WhoFI 92*
**Bradford**, Donald Wray 1944- *WhoIns 92*
**Bradford**, Dorothy 1918- *TwCPaSc*
**Bradford**, Douglas Munroe 1957- *WhoWest 92*
**Bradford**, Edward Alexander Slade 1952- *Who 92*
**Bradford**, Elwood Walter 1909- *WhoAmP 91*
**Bradford**, Equilla Forrest 1931- *WhoBlA 92*
**Bradford**, Eric Watts 1919- *Who 92*
**Bradford**, G Eric 1929- *AmMWSc 92*
**Bradford**, Gamaliel 1863-1932 *BenetAL 91*
**Bradford**, Garrett Eugene 1970- *WhoWest 92*
**Bradford**, Gary C. 1956- *WhoBlA 92*
**Bradford**, Georgia Walton 1935- *WhoAmP 91*
**Bradford**, Harold R 1909- *AmMWSc 92*
**Bradford**, Henry Bartlett 1761-1833 *DcNCBi 1*
**Bradford**, Henry Bernard, Jr 1942- *AmMWSc 92*
**Bradford**, Howard 1919- *WhoWest 92*
**Bradford**, James C 1930- *AmMWSc 92*
**Bradford**, James Carrow 1930- *AmMWSc 92*
**Bradford**, James Edward 1928- *BlkOlyM*
**Bradford**, James Edward 1943- *WhoBlA 92*
**Bradford**, Jay 1940- *WhoAmP 91*
**Bradford**, John 1749-1830 *BenetAL 91*
**Bradford**, John C 1940- *WhoAmP 91*
**Bradford**, John Carroll 1924- *WhoEnt 92*
**Bradford**, John Norman 1931- *AmMWSc 92*
**Bradford**, John R 1922- *AmMWSc 92*
**Bradford**, Joshua Taylor 1818-1871 *BiInAmS*
**Bradford**, Karleen 1936- *IntAu&W 91*
**Bradford**, Laura Sample 1945- *AmMWSc 92*
**Bradford**, Lawrence Glenn 1939- *AmMWSc 92*
**Bradford**, M. E. 1934- *WrDr 92*
**Bradford**, M. Ray, Jr. 1946- *WhoAmL 92*
**Bradford**, Marion McKinley 1946- *AmMWSc 92*
**Bradford**, Martina Lewis 1952- *WhoBlA 92*
**Bradford**, Michael Lee 1942- *WhoRel 92*
**Bradford**, Milton Douglas 1930- *WhoFI 92*
**Bradford**, Orcelia Sylvia 1953- *WhoMW 92*
**Bradford**, Peter Amory 1942- *WrDr 92*
**Bradford**, Phillips Verner 1940- *AmMWSc 92*
**Bradford**, Ray 1954- *WhoHisp 92*
**Bradford**, Reagan Howard 1932- *AmMWSc 92*
**Bradford**, Richard 1932- *TwCWW 91, WrDr 92*
**Bradford**, Richard J 1932- *WhoAmP 91*
**Bradford**, Richard Roark 1932- *WhoEnt 92*
**Bradford**, Roark 1896-1948 *BenetAL 91*
**Bradford**, Robert Edward 1931- *WhoFI 92, WhoWest 92*
**Bradford**, Robert Ernest *WhoEnt 92, WhoFI 92*
**Bradford**, Robert Wm. 1931- *WhoWest 92*
**Bradford**, Roy Hamilton 1921- *Who 92*
**Bradford**, Royal Bird 1844-1914 *BiInAmS*
**Bradford**, Samuel Arthur 1928- *AmMWSc 92*
**Bradford**, Walter L. *DrAPF 91*
**Bradford**, Will *TwCWW 91*
**Bradford**, William 1590-1657 *AmPolLe, BenetAL 91, RComAH*
**Bradford**, William 1663-1752 *BenetAL 91*
**Bradford**, William 1722-1791 *BenetAL 91*
**Bradford**, William Dalton 1931- *AmMWSc 92*
**Bradford**, William E. 1933- *IntWW 91*
**Bradford**, William Hollis, Jr. 1937- *WhoAmL 92, WhoAmP 91*
**Bradford**, Willis Warren 1922- *AmMWSc 92*
**Bradford-Eaton**, Zee 1953- *WhoBlA 92*
**Bradfute**, Oscar E *AmMWSc 92*
**Bradham**, Caleb Davis 1867-1934 *DcNCBi 1*
**Bradham**, Gilbert Bowman 1931- *AmMWSc 92*
**Bradham**, Laurence Stobo 1929- *AmMWSc 92*
**Bradhering**, Walter Jon 1957- *WhoEnt 92*
**Bradie**, Peter Richard 1937- *WhoAmL 92*
**Brading**, Charles *WhoAmP 91*
**Brading**, Keith 1917- *Who 92*
**Bradish**, John Patrick 1923- *AmMWSc 92*
**Bradlaw**, June A 1936- *AmMWSc 92*
**Bradlaw**, Robert 1905- *Who 92*
**Bradlee**, Ben 1921- *WrDr 92*
**Bradlee**, Benjamin 1921- *FacFETw*
**Bradlee**, Benjamin C. 1921- *NewYTBS 91 [port]*
**Bradley**, A Freeman 1932- *AmMWSc 92*
**Bradley**, Alan Dean 1951- *WhoMW 92*
**Bradley**, Alfred 1925-1991 *ConAu 134*
**Bradley**, Allen 1951- *WhoAmP 91*
**Bradley**, Andrew Mortimer 1951- *WhoEnt 92*
**Bradley**, Andrew Thomas, Sr. 1948- *WhoBlA 92*
**Bradley**, Anthony Wilfred 1934- *Who 92*
**Bradley**, Ardyth *DrAPF 91*
**Bradley**, Arthur 1926- *AmMWSc 92*
**Bradley**, Beth Ann 1963- *WhoFI 92*
**Bradley**, Bill 1921- *IntMPA 92*
**Bradley**, Bill 1943- *AlmAP 92 [port], IntWW 91, WhoAmP 91*
**Bradley**, Bob J. 1957- *WhoEnt 92*
**Bradley**, Bobbie Jean 1936- *WhoMW 92*
**Bradley**, Bonnie 1951- *WhoEnt 92*
**Bradley**, Burton Gyrth B. *Who 92*
**Bradley**, Charles Clive 1937- *Who 92*
**Bradley**, Charles Ernest 1962- *WhoEnt 92*
**Bradley**, Charles H 1922- *WhoAmP 91*
**Bradley**, Charles Harvey, Jr. 1923- *WhoAmL 92*
**Bradley**, Charles Lowrance 1938- *WhoRel 92*
**Bradley**, Charles Stuart 1936- *Who 92*
**Bradley**, Charles William 1923- *WhoWest 92*
**Bradley**, Clive 1934- *IntWW 91, Who 92*
**Bradley**, Concho *TwCWW 91*
**Bradley**, Craig Allen 1963- *WhoEnt 92*
**Bradley**, Craig MacDowell 1945- *WhoAmL 92*
**Bradley**, Daniel Joseph 1928- *IntWW 91, Who 92*
**Bradley**, Daniel Joseph 1949- *AmMWSc 92*
**Bradley**, David *DrAPF 91*
**Bradley**, David 1950- *BenetAL 91, BlkLC [port], ConNov 91, WrDr 92*
**Bradley**, David Gilbert 1916- *WhoRel 92*
**Bradley**, David Hammond 1936- *WhoAmP 91*
**Bradley**, David Henry, Jr. 1950- *WhoBlA 92*
**Bradley**, David John 1937- *Who 92*
**Bradley**, David Lee 1950- *WhoAmP 91*
**Bradley**, David R. 1950- *WhoIns 92*
**Bradley**, David Rice 1938- *Who 92*
**Bradley**, David Richard 1960- *WhoEnt 92*
**Bradley**, Donald Charlton 1924- *IntWW 91, Who 92*
**Bradley**, Donald Edward 1943- *WhoAmL 92*
**Bradley**, Doris P 1932- *AmMWSc 92*
**Bradley**, Dorothy 1947- *WhoAmP 91*
**Bradley**, Duane Michael 1954- *WhoEnt 92*
**Bradley**, E. Michael 1939- *WhoAmL 92, WhoFI 92*

**Bradley,** Ed *LesBEnT 92 [port]*
**Bradley,** Ed 1941- *ConBlB 2 [port], IntMPA 92*
**Bradley,** Edgar Leonard 1917- *Who 92*
**Bradley,** Edward R. *WhoBlA 92*
**Bradley,** Edwin Luther, Jr 1943- *AmMWSc 92*
**Bradley,** Elihu F 1917- *AmMWSc 92*
**Bradley,** Ernest Cerel 1915- *WhoMW 92*
**Bradley,** Eugene Bradford 1932- *AmMWSc 92*
**Bradley,** Francis *BiInAmS*
**Bradley,** Francis H 1846-1924 *FacFETw*
**Bradley,** Francis J 1926- *AmMWSc 92*
**Bradley,** Francis MacLeod 1921- *WhoRel 92*
**Bradley,** Frank Howe 1838-1879 *BiInAmS*
**Bradley,** Frank Michael 1948- *WhoEnt 92*
**Bradley,** Fred 1931- *WhoAmP 91*
**Bradley,** Gary Morrison, Jr. 1958- *WhoRel 92*
**Bradley,** George *DrAPF 91*
**Bradley,** George 1953- *ConAu 134*
**Bradley,** George Alexander 1926- *AmMWSc 92*
**Bradley,** George Havis 1937- *WhoAmL 92*
**Bradley,** Gerald Allen 1927- *WhoAmP 91*
**Bradley,** Gordon Roy 1921- *WhoAmP 91*
**Bradley,** Guy M 1870-1905 *BiInAmS*
**Bradley,** H B 1920- *AmMWSc 92*
**Bradley,** Harris Walton 1915- *AmMWSc 92*
**Bradley,** Helen 1900-1979 *TwCPaSc*
**Bradley,** Hilbert L. 1920- *WhoBlA 92*
**Bradley,** Hugh Edward *AmMWSc 92*
**Bradley,** J. Robert 1920- *WhoBlA 92*
**Bradley,** Jack Carter 1919- *WhoBlA 92*
**Bradley,** James 1693-1762 *BlkwCEP*
**Bradley,** James 1919- *TwCPaSc*
**Bradley,** James George 1940- *WhoBlA 92*
**Bradley,** James Henry Stobart 1933- *AmMWSc 92*
**Bradley,** James Howard, Jr. 1936- *WhoBlA 92*
**Bradley,** James Monroe, Jr. 1934- *WhoBlA 92*
**Bradley,** James T *AmMWSc 92*
**Bradley,** James Vandiver 1924- *WrDr 92*
**Bradley,** Jane *DrAPF 91*
**Bradley,** Jeb E 1952- *WhoAmP 91*
**Bradley,** Jeffrey 1963- *WhoBlA 92*
**Bradley,** Jenny 1886-1983 *FacFETw*
**Bradley,** Jesse J., Jr. 1929- *WhoBlA 92*
**Bradley,** Jessie Mary *WhoBlA 92*
**Bradley,** John *DrAPF 91*
**Bradley,** John Albertson 1908- *WhoAmP 91*
**Bradley,** John Andrew 1930- *WhoFI 92*
**Bradley,** John Daniel, III 1946- *WhoAmP 91*
**Bradley,** John Douglas 1945- *WhoFI 92*
**Bradley,** John Floyd 1914- *WhoAmP 91*
**Bradley,** John Lewis 1917- *IntAu&W 91, WrDr 92*
**Bradley,** John Samuel 1923- *AmMWSc 92*
**Bradley,** John Spurgeon 1934- *AmMWSc 92*
**Bradley,** Julius Roscoe, Jr 1940- *AmMWSc 92*
**Bradley,** Kathy Annette 1956- *WhoAmL 92*
**Bradley,** Keith John Charles 1950- *Who 92*
**Bradley,** Kenneth Daniel 1949- *WhoWest 92*
**Bradley,** Kim Alexandra 1955- *WhoFI 92*
**Bradley,** Kirk Jackson 1962- *WhoFI 92*
**Bradley,** Laurence A 1949- *AmMWSc 92*
**Bradley,** Lawrence D., Jr. 1920- *WhoAmL 92*
**Bradley,** Lee Carrington, III 1926- *AmMWSc 92*
**Bradley,** Leon Charles 1938- *WhoEnt 92*
**Bradley,** Lola 1921- *WhoAmP 91*
**Bradley,** London M., Jr. 1943- *WhoBlA 92*
**Bradley,** M. Louise 1920- *WhoBlA 92*
**Bradley,** Margaret Ann 1950- *WhoEnt 92*
**Bradley,** Marion Zimmer 1930- *TwCSFW 91, WrDr 92*
**Bradley,** Marshall Rice 1951- *AmMWSc 92*
**Bradley,** Martin 1931- *TwCPaSc*
**Bradley,** Matthews Ogden 1942- *AmMWSc 92, WhoFI 92*
**Bradley,** Melvin 1938- *WhoAmP 91*
**Bradley,** Melvin LeRoy 1938- *WhoBlA 92*
**Bradley,** Michael Douglas 1938- *AmMWSc 92*
**Bradley,** Michael H. *WhoAmL 92*
**Bradley,** Michael John 1933- *Who 92*
**Bradley,** Michael Lynn 1955- *WhoRel 92*
**Bradley,** Omar 1893-1981 *RComAH*
**Bradley,** Omar Nelson 1893-1981 *FacFETw*
**Bradley,** Patricia 1951- *WhoAmP 91*
**Bradley,** Paul Joseph 1945- *WhoRel 92*
**Bradley,** Paul William 1961- *WhoWest 92*
**Bradley,** Peter Edward Moore 1914- *Who 92*
**Bradley,** Phil Poole 1959- *WhoBlA 92*
**Bradley,** Philip Tibbs 1938- *WhoAmP 91*
**Bradley,** Preston 1888-1983 *RelLAm 91*
**Bradley,** R. C. 1929- *WrDr 92*
**Bradley,** Ralph Allan 1923- *AmMWSc 92*
**Bradley,** Raymond Stuart 1948- *AmMWSc 92*
**Bradley,** Rebecca Maye Arend 1957- *WhoWest 92*
**Bradley,** Richard Alan 1925- *Who 92*
**Bradley,** Richard Crane 1922- *AmMWSc 92*
**Bradley,** Richard Crane, Jr 1950- *AmMWSc 92*
**Bradley,** Richard E 1926- *AmMWSc 92*
**Bradley,** Richard E 1927- *AmMWSc 92*
**Bradley,** Richard John 1946- *Who 92*
**Bradley,** Richard Paul 1959- *WhoMW 92*
**Bradley,** Robert Foster 1940- *AmMWSc 92*
**Bradley,** Robert Lester, Jr 1933- *AmMWSc 92*
**Bradley,** Robert Martin 1939- *AmMWSc 92*
**Bradley,** Roberta Palm 1947- *WhoBlA 92*
**Bradley,** Roger Thubron 1936- *Who 92*
**Bradley,** Roger William 1944- *WhoAmL 92*
**Bradley,** Ronald W 1936- *AmMWSc 92*
**Bradley,** Ronald William 1936- *WhoMW 92*
**Bradley,** Sandra Wentworth 1946- *WhoEnt 92*
**Bradley,** Stanley Edward 1913- *AmMWSc 92*
**Bradley,** Stanley Walter 1927- *Who 92*
**Bradley,** Sterling Gaylen 1932- *AmMWSc 92*
**Bradley,** Steven Arthur 1949- *AmMWSc 92*
**Bradley,** Stuart *Who 92*
**Bradley,** Stuart B. 1907-1990 *WhoAmL 92*
**Bradley,** Ted Ray 1940- *AmMWSc 92*
**Bradley,** Terrye Singletary 1950- *WhoBlA 92*
**Bradley,** Thomas 1917- *ConBlB 2 [port], IntWW 91, WhoAmP 91, WhoBlA 92, WhoWest 92*
**Bradley,** Thomas Andrew 1957- *WhoIns 92*
**Bradley,** Thomas Bernard, Jr 1928- *AmMWSc 92*
**Bradley,** Thomas George 1926- *Who 92*
**Bradley,** Thomas J. d1991 *NewYTBS 91*
**Bradley,** Thomas Reid, Sr. 1923- *WhoFI 92*
**Bradley,** Vincent Gerard 1939- *WhoAmL 92*
**Bradley,** W E 1913- *AmMWSc 92*
**Bradley,** Wade Harlow *WhoWest 92*
**Bradley,** Walter D. 1946- *WhoFI 92, WhoWest 92*
**Bradley,** Walter Dwight 1946- *WhoAmP 91*
**Bradley,** Walter Thomas, Jr. 1925- *WhoBlA 92*
**Bradley,** Wayne W. 1948- *WhoBlA 92*
**Bradley,** Will H. 1868-1962 *DcTwDes*
**Bradley,** William Arthur 1921- *AmMWSc 92*
**Bradley,** William B. 1926- *WhoBlA 92*
**Bradley,** William Bryan 1929- *WhoEnt 92*
**Bradley,** William Crane 1925- *AmMWSc 92*
**Bradley,** William Ewart 1910- *Who 92*
**Bradley,** William Robinson 1908- *AmMWSc 92*
**Bradley,** William Sutton 1935- *WhoFI 92*
**Bradley,** William W 1922- *AmMWSc 92*
**Bradley Goodman,** Michael *Who 92*
**Bradlow,** Frank Rosslyn 1913- *WrDr 92*
**Bradlow,** Herbert Leon 1924- *AmMWSc 92*
**Bradman,** Donald 1908- *FacFETw, Who 92, WrDr 92*
**Bradman,** Donald George 1908- *IntWW 91*
**Bradman,** Godfrey Michael 1936- *Who 92*
**Bradna,** Joanne Justice 1952- *WhoMW 92*
**Bradner,** Hugh 1915- *AmMWSc 92*
**Bradner,** James Holland, Jr. 1941- *WhoAmL 92*
**Bradner,** Mead 1914- *AmMWSc 92*
**Bradner,** William Murray, Jr. 1926- *WhoAmL 92*
**Bradner,** William Turnbull 1924- *AmMWSc 92*
**Bradney,** John Robert 1931- *Who 92*
**Brado,** Michael Wayne 1958- *WhoWest 92*
**Bradpiece,** Sarah 1954- *TwCPaSc*
**Bradrick,** Roy Burton, Jr. 1953- *WhoAmL 92*
**Bradrick,** William G. 1939- *WhoMW 92*
**Bradsell,** Kenneth Raymond 1948- *WhoRel 92*
**Bradshaw,** Afton B *WhoAmP 91*
**Bradshaw,** Anthony David 1926- *IntWW 91, Who 92*
**Bradshaw,** Aubrey Swift 1910- *AmMWSc 92*
**Bradshaw,** Billy Dean 1940- *WhoMW 92*
**Bradshaw,** Brian 1923- *TwCPaSc*
**Bradshaw,** Buck *TwCWW 91*
**Bradshaw,** Carl John 1930- *WhoAmL 92*
**Bradshaw,** Dale E. 1925- *WhoAmL 92*
**Bradshaw,** Doris Marion 1928- *WhoBlA 92*
**Bradshaw,** Gerald Haywood 1934- *WhoBlA 92*
**Bradshaw,** Gillian 1956- *WrDr 92*
**Bradshaw,** Gordon 1931- *TwCPaSc*
**Bradshaw,** Gordon Van Rensselaer 1931- *AmMWSc 92*
**Bradshaw,** Howard Holt 1937- *WhoFI 92*
**Bradshaw,** Ira Webb 1929- *WhoFI 92*
**Bradshaw,** James Daniel 1950- *WhoRel 92*
**Bradshaw,** James R. 1938- *WhoWest 92*
**Bradshaw,** Jean Paul, II 1956- *WhoAmL 92*
**Bradshaw,** Jerald Sherwin 1932- *AmMWSc 92*
**Bradshaw,** Joel C 1946- *WhoAmP 91*
**Bradshaw,** John 1933- *News 92-1 [port]*
**Bradshaw,** John Alden 1919- *AmMWSc 92*
**Bradshaw,** John Stratlii 1927- *AmMWSc 92*
**Bradshaw,** Kenneth 1922- *Who 92*
**Bradshaw,** Larry Leo 1943- *WhoMW 92*
**Bradshaw,** Lawrence A. 1932- *WhoBlA 92*
**Bradshaw,** Lawrence Jack 1924- *AmMWSc 92*
**Bradshaw,** Mae Concemi 1945- *WhoAmL 92*
**Bradshaw,** Mark Davis 1954- *WhoAmL 92*
**Bradshaw,** Martin Clark 1935- *Who 92*
**Bradshaw,** Martin Daniel 1936- *AmMWSc 92*
**Bradshaw,** Maurice Bernard 1903- *Who 92*
**Bradshaw,** Murray Charles 1930- *WhoEnt 92, WhoWest 92*
**Bradshaw,** Nanci Marie 1940- *WhoFI 92*
**Bradshaw,** Peter 1935- *IntWW 91, Who 92*
**Bradshaw,** Ralph Alden 1941- *AmMWSc 92*
**Bradshaw,** Rebecca Christina 1963- *WhoEnt 92*
**Bradshaw,** Richard 1920- *Who 92*
**Bradshaw,** Robert 1917-1978 *FacFETw*
**Bradshaw,** Robert V. 1938- *WhoWest 92*
**Bradshaw,** Robert Wallace, Jr 1933- *WhoAmP 91*
**Bradshaw,** Timothy Ashley 1962- *WhoAmL 92*
**Bradshaw,** Walter H., Jr. 1938- *WhoBlA 92*
**Bradshaw,** Wayne *WhoBlA 92*
**Bradshaw,** Willard Henry 1925- *AmMWSc 92*
**Bradshaw,** William David 1928- *WhoMW 92*
**Bradshaw,** William Emmons 1942- *AmMWSc 92*
**Bradshaw,** William Newman 1928- *AmMWSc 92*
**Bradshaw,** William Peter 1936- *Who 92*
**Bradshaw,** William R 1851-1927 *ScFEYrs*
**Bradshaw,** William S 1937- *AmMWSc 92*
**Bradsher,** Charles Kilgo 1912- *AmMWSc 92*
**Bradsher,** Henry S. 1931- *ConAu 133*
**Bradstreet,** Anne 1612?-1672 *BenetAL 91, HanAmWH*
**Bradstreet,** Raymond Bradford 1901- *AmMWSc 92*
**Bradstreet,** Simon 1603- *BenetAL 91*
**Bradt,** Hale Van Dorn 1930- *AmMWSc 92*
**Bradt,** Patricia Thornton 1930- *AmMWSc 92*
**Bradt,** Richard Carl 1938- *AmMWSc 92*
**Bradwardina,** Thomas de 1295?-1349 *DcLB 115*
**Bradwardine,** Thomas 1295?-1349 *DcLB 115*
**Bradway,** Becky *DrAPF 91*
**Bradway,** Keith E 1926- *AmMWSc 92*
**Bradwell,** Area Bishop of 1927- *Who 92*
**Bradwell,** Carl Richard 1950- *WhoMW 92*
**Bradwell,** James *IntAu&W 91X, WrDr 92*
**Bradwhaw,** Samuel Lockwood, Jr 1937- *AmMWSc 92*
**Brady,** Alexander *WhoEnt 92*
**Brady,** Allan Jordan 1927- *AmMWSc 92*
**Brady,** Allen H 1934- *AmMWSc 92*
**Brady,** Allen Roy 1933- *AmMWSc 92*
**Brady,** Anne M 1926- *IntAu&W 91*
**Brady,** Barry Hugh Garnet 1942- *AmMWSc 92*
**Brady,** Bill *WhoAmP 91*
**Brady,** Brian T 1938- *AmMWSc 92*
**Brady,** Bruce Dale 1961- *WhoEnt 92*
**Brady,** Carolyn L 1941- *WhoAmP 91*
**Brady,** Charles A. 1945- *WhoBlA 92*
**Brady,** Charles John 1952- *WhoMW 92*
**Brady,** Colleen Anne 1951- *WhoWest 92*
**Brady,** Conor 1949- *IntWW 91*
**Brady,** Cyrus Townsend 1861-1920 *BenetAL 91*
**Brady,** David D 1937- *WhoAmP 91*
**Brady,** Dennis Patrick 1949- *AmMWSc 92*
**Brady,** Donald R 1939- *AmMWSc 92*
**Brady,** Donna Elizabeth 1955- *WhoEnt 92*
**Brady,** Donnie Gayle 1940- *AmMWSc 92*
**Brady,** Douglas MacPherson 1943- *AmMWSc 92*
**Brady,** Ernest William 1917- *Who 92*
**Brady,** Eugene F 1927- *AmMWSc 92*
**Brady,** Francis *WhoEnt 92*
**Brady,** Francis R, Jr 1931- *WhoAmP 91*
**Brady,** Frank 1924-1986 *DcLB 111 [port]*
**Brady,** Frank 1934- *IntAu&W 91*
**Brady,** Frank Owen 1944- *AmMWSc 92, WhoMW 92*
**Brady,** Franklin Paul 1931- *AmMWSc 92*
**Brady,** George Moore 1959- *WhoAmL 92*
**Brady,** George W 1921- *AmMWSc 92*
**Brady,** Gordon Leonard, Jr. 1945- *WhoFI 92*
**Brady,** Harvey Joe 1944- *WhoAmP 91*
**Brady,** Holland, Jr. 1925- *WhoFI 92*
**Brady,** James Edward 1938- *AmMWSc 92*
**Brady,** James Joseph 1904- *AmMWSc 92*
**Brady,** James Joseph 1944- *WhoAmL 92, WhoAmP 91*
**Brady,** James Patrick 1945- *WhoWest 92*
**Brady,** James S. 1940- *CurBio 91 [port], News 91 [port]*
**Brady,** James S. 1944- *IntWW 91*
**Brady,** James Winston 1928- *IntAu&W 91*
**Brady,** Jane Mariette 1955- *WhoWest 92*
**Brady,** John Albert 1923- *WhoFI 92*
**Brady,** John David 1956- *WhoAmP 91*
**Brady,** John Everett 1860-1941 *DcNCBi 1*
**Brady,** John F 1928- *AmMWSc 92*
**Brady,** John Patrick, Jr. 1929- *WhoWest 92*
**Brady,** John Paul 1928- *AmMWSc 92*
**Brady,** Joseph Vincent 1922- *AmMWSc 92*
**Brady,** Joyce Lynn 1963- *WhoEnt 92*
**Brady,** Julio A. 1942- *WhoBlA 92*
**Brady,** Kathleen *DrAPF 91*
**Brady,** Keith Bryan Craig 1954- *AmMWSc 92*
**Brady,** Kevin 1955- *WhoAmP 91*
**Brady,** Lawrence Lee 1936- *AmMWSc 92*
**Brady,** Lawrence Peter 1940- *WhoAmL 92*
**Brady,** Leonard Everett 1928- *AmMWSc 92*
**Brady,** Luther Weldon, Jr 1925- *AmMWSc 92*
**Brady,** Lynn R 1933- *AmMWSc 92*
**Brady,** Lynne Ellen 1946- *WhoAmL 92*
**Brady,** Martin R, Jr. 1938- *WhoIns 92*
**Brady,** Mathew 1823?-1896 *RComAH*
**Brady,** Mathew B. 1823?-1896 *BenetAL 91*
**Brady,** Maureen *DrAPF 91*
**Brady,** Maureen Elizabeth 1945- *WhoMW 92*
**Brady,** Michael 1945- *Who 92*
**Brady,** Michael Cameron 1957- *WhoFI 92*
**Brady,** Michael Jeff 1941- *WhoAmP 91*
**Brady,** Nelvia M. 1948- *WhoBlA 92, WhoMW 92*
**Brady,** Nicholas F. 1930- *IntWW 91*
**Brady,** Nicholas Frederick 1930- *Who 92, WhoAmP 91, WhoFI 92*
**Brady,** Nyle C 1920- *AmMWSc 92*
**Brady,** Phillip Donley 1951- *WhoAmL 92*
**Brady,** Richard Alan 1934- *WhoAmL 92*
**Brady,** Robert Frederick, Jr 1942- *AmMWSc 92*
**Brady,** Robert James 1927- *AmMWSc 92*
**Brady,** Robert Lindsay 1946- *WhoFI 92*
**Brady,** Rodney Howard 1933- *WhoEnt 92*
**Brady,** Roscoe Owen 1923- *AmMWSc 92, IntWW 91*
**Brady,** Ruth Mary 1924- *AmMWSc 92*
**Brady,** Ryder *DrAPF 91*
**Brady,** Sarah 1942- *News 91 [port]*
**Brady,** Scott T 1950- *AmMWSc 92*
**Brady,** Shaun Michael 1957- *WhoFI 92*
**Brady,** Stephen Francis 1941- *AmMWSc 92*
**Brady,** Stephen W 1941- *AmMWSc 92*
**Brady,** Terence Joseph 1939- *IntAu&W 91, Who 92*
**Brady,** Terrence Joseph 1940- *WhoAmL 92*
**Brady,** Thomas 1938- *WhoAmP 91*
**Brady,** Thomas Carl 1947- *WhoAmL 92*
**Brady,** Thomas Denis 1955- *WhoFI 92, WhoWest 92*
**Brady,** Thomas E 1941- *AmMWSc 92*
**Brady,** Thomas Edward 1947- *WhoWest 92*
**Brady,** Thomas P. 1949- *WhoAmL 92*
**Brady,** Ullman Eugene, Jr 1933- *AmMWSc 92*
**Brady,** Wallace Anthony 1921- *WhoAmL 92*
**Brady,** William Gordon 1923- *AmMWSc 92*
**Brady,** William Robert 1956- *WhoAmP 91*
**Brady,** William S *TwCWW 91, WrDr 92*
**Brady,** William Thomas 1933- *AmMWSc 92*
**Brady,** Wray Grayson 1918- *AmMWSc 92*
**Brady,** Yolanda J 1956- *AmMWSc 92*
**Braeden,** Eric *IntMPA 92*

**Braekevelt**, Charlie Roger 1942- *AmMWSc 92*
**Braemer**, Allen C 1930- *AmMWSc 92*
**Braendel**, Gregory George 1944- *WhoWest 92*
**Braendle**, Donald Harold 1927- *AmMWSc 92*
**Braestrup**, Peter 1929- *IntAu&W 91*
**Braeutigam**, Ronald Ray 1947- *WhoFI 92, WhoMW 92*
**Brafford**, William Charles 1932- *WhoAmL 92, WhoFI 92*
**Braga**, Daniel 1946- *WhoFI 92*
**Braga**, Sonia 1951- *IntMPA 92*
**Bragalone**, Jeffrey Ray 1962- *WhoAmL 92*
**Bragdon**, Claude Fayette 1866-1946 *BenetAL 91*
**Bragdon**, Paul Errol 1927- *WhoWest 92*
**Bragdon**, Robert Wright 1922- *AmMWSc 92*
**Brager**, Walter S. 1925- *WhoFI 92*
**Bragg**, Billy 1957- *ConMus 7 [port]*
**Bragg**, Braxton 1817-1876 *DcNCBi 1*
**Bragg**, Darrell Brent 1933- *WhoWest 92*
**Bragg**, David Gordon 1933- *AmMWSc 92*
**Bragg**, Denver Dayton 1915- *AmMWSc 92*
**Bragg**, Elizabeth Jean 1945- *WhoRel 92*
**Bragg**, Ellis Meredith, Jr. 1947- *WhoAmL 92*
**Bragg**, George Freeman, Jr. 1863-1940 *RelLAm 91*
**Bragg**, Gordon McAlpine 1939- *AmMWSc 92*
**Bragg**, Harland W *WhoAmP 91*
**Bragg**, James Randolph 1946- *WhoFI 92*
**Bragg**, Jay Miller 1950- *WhoAmP 91*
**Bragg**, Jeffrey S. 1949- *WhoIns 92*
**Bragg**, Jeffrey Steven 1949- *WhoAmP 91*
**Bragg**, JoAnn M. 1955- *WhoFI 92*
**Bragg**, John 1806-1878 *DcNCBi 1*
**Bragg**, John Kendal 1919- *AmMWSc 92*
**Bragg**, John Thomas 1918- *WhoAmP 91*
**Bragg**, Joseph L. 1937- *WhoBlA 92*
**Bragg**, Kenneth Lawrence, Jr. 1959- *WhoMW 92*
**Bragg**, Leslie B 1902- *AmMWSc 92*
**Bragg**, Lincoln Ellsworth 1936- *AmMWSc 92*
**Bragg**, Louis Hairston 1928- *AmMWSc 92*
**Bragg**, Louis Richard 1931- *AmMWSc 92*
**Bragg**, Melvin 1939- *IntAu&W 91*
**Bragg**, Melvyn 1939- *ConNov 91, IntWW 91, Who 92, WrDr 92*
**Bragg**, Michael Ellis 1947- *WhoAmL 92, WhoFI 92, WhoMW 92*
**Bragg**, Philip Dell 1932- *AmMWSc 92*
**Bragg**, Robert G. 1955- *WhoEnt 92*
**Bragg**, Robert H 1919- *AmMWSc 92*
**Bragg**, Robert Henry 1919- *WhoBlA 92*
**Bragg**, Robert Lloyd 1916- *WhoBlA 92*
**Bragg**, Stephen Lawrence 1923- *Who 92*
**Bragg**, Susan Lynn 1953- *AmMWSc 92*
**Bragg**, Thomas 1810-1872 *DcNCBi 1*
**Bragg**, Thomas Braxton 1938- *AmMWSc 92*
**Bragg**, W.F. 1892-1967 *TwCWW 91*
**Bragg**, William David 1962- *WhoEnt 92*
**Bragg**, William Henry 1862-1942 *FacFETw [port], WhoNob 90*
**Bragg**, William J. 1946- *WhoEnt 92*
**Bragg**, William Lawrence 1890-1971 *FacFETw, WhoNob 90*
**Braggins**, Derek Henry 1931- *Who 92*
**Bragin**, Joseph 1939- *AmMWSc 92*
**Braginski**, Aleksander Ignace 1929- *AmMWSc 92*
**Braginton-Smith**, Brian S. 1953- *WhoFI 92*
**Bragman**, David Geoffrey 1953- *WhoEnt 92*
**Bragman**, Michael J 1940- *WhoAmP 91*
**Bragole**, Robert Anthony 1936- *AmMWSc 92*
**Bragonier**, John Robert 1937- *AmMWSc 92*
**Bragonier**, Wendell Hughell 1910- *AmMWSc 92*
**Braha**, Thomas I. 1947- *WhoFI 92*
**Braham**, Allan 1937- *WrDr 92*
**Braham**, Allan John Witney 1937- *IntWW 91, Who 92*
**Braham**, Delphine Doris 1946- *WhoMW 92*
**Braham**, Harold 1907- *Who 92*
**Braham**, Howard Wallace 1942- *AmMWSc 92*
**Braham**, Jeanne *DrAPF 91*
**Braham**, Phil 1959- *TwCPaSc*
**Braham**, Roscoe Riley, Jr 1921- *AmMWSc 92*
**Brahana**, Thomas Roy 1926- *AmMWSc 92*
**Brahen**, Leonard Samuel 1921- *AmMWSc 92*
**Brahimi**, Abdelhamid 1936- *IntWW 91*
**Brahimi**, Lakhdar 1934- *IntWW 91, Who 92*
**Brahma**, Chandra Sekhar 1941- *AmMWSc 92*
**Brahmananda**, Palahally Ramaiya 1926- *IntWW 91, WrDr 92*
**Brahmi**, Zacharie *AmMWSc 92*
**Brahms**, Johannes 1833-1897 *NewAmDM*
**Brahs**, Stuart J. 1940- *WhoIns 92*
**Braibant**, Guy 1927- *IntWW 91*
**Braica**, Viorel Liviu *WhoEnt 92*
**Braid**, Andrew 1846-1919 *BiInAmS*
**Braid**, Thomas Hamilton 1925- *AmMWSc 92*
**Braide**, Robert David 1953- *WhoEnt 92*
**Braiden**, Rose Margaret 1922- *WhoWest 92*
**Braids**, Olin Capron 1938- *AmMWSc 92*
**Braidwood**, Clinton Alexander 1914- *AmMWSc 92*
**Braidwood**, Robert John 1907- *IntWW 91*
**Brailey**, Troy *WhoAmP 91*
**Brailey**, Troy 1916- *WhoBlA 92*
**Brailovsky**, Carlos Alberto 1939- *AmMWSc 92*
**Brailow**, David Gregory 1950- *WhoMW 92*
**Brailsford**, Alan David 1930- *AmMWSc 92*
**Brain** *Who 92*
**Brain**, Baron 1926- *Who 92*
**Brain**, Albert Edward Arnold 1917- *Who 92*
**Brain**, Carlos W *AmMWSc 92*
**Brain**, Dennis 1921-1957 *FacFETw, NewAmDM*
**Brain**, Devin King 1926- *AmMWSc 92*
**Brain**, Donald Chester 1917- *WhoIns 92*
**Brain**, Donald Chester, Jr. 1954- *WhoFI 92*
**Brain**, Joseph David 1940- *AmMWSc 92*
**Brain**, Norman 1907- *Who 92*
**Brainard**, Alan J 1936- *AmMWSc 92*
**Brainard**, Cecilia Manguerra *DrAPF 91*
**Brainard**, James C. 1954- *WhoMW 92*
**Brainard**, James R *AmMWSc 92*
**Brainard**, Joe *DrAPF 91*
**Brainard**, John Gardiner Calkins 1796-1828 *BenetAL 91*
**Brainard**, Norton Hammond, III 1953- *WhoAmL 92*
**Braine**, Bernard 1914- *Who 92*
**Braine**, John 1922-1985 *FacFETw*
**Braine**, John 1922-1986 *CnDBLB 7 [port], RfGEnL 91*
**Braine**, John Gerard 1922- *IntAu&W 91*
**Braine**, Richard Allix 1900- *Who 92*
**Braine**, Robert 1832- *ScFEYrs*
**Brainerd**, Barron 1928- *AmMWSc 92*
**Brainerd**, David 1718-1747 *BenetAL 91*
**Brainerd**, Jerome J 1932- *AmMWSc 92*
**Brainerd**, John Grist 1904-1988 *FacFETw*
**Brainerd**, John W 1918- *SmATA 65*
**Brainerd**, Walter Scott 1936- *AmMWSc 92*
**Brainerd**, Winthrop John 1939- *WhoRel 92*
**Brainin**, Constance Spears 1932- *WhoMW 92*
**Brainin**, Norbert 1923- *IntWW 91, Who 92*
**Brainin-Rodriguez**, Laura 1951- *WhoHisp 92*
**Braisher**, Mark H. 1963- *WhoRel 92*
**Braiterman**, Thea G 1927- *WhoAmP 91*
**Braithwaite**, Bernard Richard 1917- *Who 92*
**Braithwaite**, Charles Henry 1920- *WhoWest 92*
**Braithwaite**, Charles Henry, Jr 1920- *AmMWSc 92*
**Braithwaite**, E. R. 1922- *WrDr 92*
**Braithwaite**, Eustace Adolphe 1922- *IntAu&W 91, IntWW 91*
**Braithwaite**, Eustace Edward Adolph R 1922- *Who 92*
**Braithwaite**, Franklin 1917- *Who 92*
**Braithwaite**, Gordon L. *WhoBlA 92*
**Braithwaite**, J. William 1928- *WhoAmL 92*
**Braithwaite**, James Roland 1927- *WhoBlA 92, WhoEnt 92*
**Braithwaite**, John Geden North 1920- *AmMWSc 92*
**Braithwaite**, Mark Winston 1954- *WhoBlA 92*
**Braithwaite**, Nicholas Paul Dallon 1939- *WhoEnt 92*
**Braithwaite**, Raymond George 1943- *WhoFI 92*
**Braithwaite**, Rodric 1932- *Who 92*
**Braithwaite**, Rodric Quentin 1932- *IntWW 91*
**Braithwaite**, Walt Waldiman 1945- *WhoWest 92*
**Braithwaite**, William Stanley 1878-1962 *BenetAL 91, BlkLC [port]*
**Braithwaithe**, Edward 1930- *LiExTwC*
**Braitman**, Mary Beth 1950- *WhoAmL 92*
**Brake**, Dan Lee 1947- *WhoMW 92*
**Brake**, Timothy L. 1948- *WhoAmL 92*
**Brakefield**, James Charles 1944- *AmMWSc 92*
**Brakeley**, George Archibald, III 1939- *WhoFI 92*
**Brakeman**, Fred Ellis 1950- *WhoWest 92*
**Brakemeier**, Gottfried 1937- *WhoRel 92*
**Brakensiek**, Donald Lloyd 1928- *AmMWSc 92*
**Brakensiek**, Jay Clemence 1954- *WhoWest 92*
**Braker**, William Paul 1926- *WhoMW 92*
**Brakey**, Robert G. 1938- *WhoIns 92*
**Brakhage**, James Stanley 1933- *WhoEnt 92*
**Brakhage**, Stan 1933- *IntDcF 2-2 [port], WrDr 92*
**Brakke**, Myron Kendall 1921- *AmMWSc 92, IntWW 91*
**Brakov**, Yergeniy Alekseyevich 1937- *IntWW 91*
**Braks**, Gerrit J. M. 1933- *IntWW 91*
**Braley**, Edna Christine 1937- *WhoMW 92, WhoRel 92*
**Bralla**, James George 1926- *WhoFI 92*
**Bralley**, James Alexander 1916- *AmMWSc 92*
**Bralow**, S Philip 1921- *AmMWSc 92*
**Bralver**, Peter Jeffrey 1943- *WhoWest 92*
**Braly**, Bobby Key 1938- *WhoRel 92*
**Braly**, George Webster 1948- *WhoAmL 92*
**Braly**, Terrell Alfred 1953- *WhoFI 92*
**Bram**, Christopher 1952- *IntAu&W 91*
**Bram**, Isabelle Mary Rickey McDonough *WhoMW 92*
**Bram**, Joseph 1926- *AmMWSc 92*
**Bram**, Ralph A 1932- *AmMWSc 92*
**Bramah**, Ernest 1868-1942 *ScFEYrs*
**Bramall** *Who 92*
**Bramall**, Baron 1923- *Who 92*
**Bramall**, Life Peer 1923- *IntWW 91*
**Bramall**, Ashley 1916- *Who 92*
**Bramall**, Margaret Elaine 1916- *Who 92*
**Braman**, Heather Ruth 1934- *WhoMW 92*
**Braman**, Robert Steven 1930- *AmMWSc 92*
**Braman**, Sandra *DrAPF 91*
**Bramante**, A Donald 1930- *WhoAmP 91*
**Bramante**, Pietro Ottavio 1920- *AmMWSc 92*
**Brambell**, Francis William Rogers 1901-1970 *FacFETw*
**Brambila**, Art Peralta 1941- *WhoHisp 92*
**Brambila**, Robert Luis 1949- *WhoWest 92*
**Brambl**, Robert Morgan 1942- *AmMWSc 92*
**Bramble**, Barry B. 1953- *WhoAmL 92*
**Bramble**, James H 1930- *AmMWSc 92*
**Bramble**, John Myles 1946- *WhoWest 92*
**Bramble**, Ronald Lee 1937- *WhoAmL 92, WhoFI 92*
**Bramble**, William Clark 1907- *AmMWSc 92*
**Bramblett**, Claud Allen 1939- *AmMWSc 92*
**Bramblett**, Garold Eugene 1926- *WhoAmL 92*
**Bramblett**, Richard Lee 1935- *AmMWSc 92*
**Bramblett**, Stephen Walter 1958- *WhoRel 92*
**Brame**, Arden Howell, II 1934- *WhoWest 92*
**Brame**, Edward Grant, Jr 1927- *AmMWSc 92*
**Brame**, Marillyn A. 1928- *WhoWest 92*
**Brame**, Walter Melvyn 1946- *WhoBlA 92*
**Bramesco**, Norton J. d1991 *NewYTBS 91*
**Bramfitt**, Bruce Livingston 1938- *AmMWSc 92*
**Bramhall**, Eugene Hulbert *WhoAmL 92*
**Bramhall**, John Shepherd 1950- *AmMWSc 92*
**Bramhall**, Robert Richard 1927- *WhoFI 92*
**Bramlage**, William Joseph 1937- *AmMWSc 92*
**Bramlet**, Roland C 1921- *AmMWSc 92*
**Bramlett**, Lonnie L., Jr 1943- *WhoMW 92*
**Bramlett**, Paul Kent 1944- *WhoAmL 92*
**Bramlett**, William 1942- *AmMWSc 92*
**Bramlette**, William 1911- *AmMWSc 92*
**Bramley**, Paul 1923- *Who 92*
**Bramley**, Russell 1945- *WhoAmP 91*
**Bramma**, Harry Wakefield 1936- *Who 92*
**Brammer**, Anthony John 1942- *AmMWSc 92*
**Brammer**, Forest E 1913- *AmMWSc 92*
**Brammer**, Kenneth Leo 1924- *WhoMW 92*
**Brammer**, Lee 1963- *AmMWSc 92*
**Brammer**, Leonard Griffith 1906- *TwCPaSc, Who 92*
**Brammer**, Phil 1932- *WhoAmP 91*
**Brammer**, William Evert 1952- *WhoMW 92*
**Bramnik**, Robert Paul 1949- *WhoAmL 92*
**Brampton**, Sally Jane 1955- *Who 92*
**Brams**, Stewart L 1914- *AmMWSc 92*
**Bramson**, Berenice Louise 1929- *WhoEnt 92*
**Bramson**, Leon 1930- *WrDr 92*
**Bramwell**, Charlotte *WrDr 92*
**Bramwell**, Fitzgerald Burton 1945- *AmMWSc 92, WhoBlA 92*
**Bramwell**, George Youngs 1937- *WhoAmL 92*
**Bramwell**, Henry 1919- *WhoAmL 92, WhoBlA 92*
**Bramwell**, Marvel Lynnette 1947- *WhoWest 92*
**Bramwell**, Patricia Ann 1941- *WhoBlA 92*
**Bramwell**, Richard Mervyn 1944- *Who 92*
**Bran**, Edgar Antonio 1934- *WhoHisp 92*
**Brana-Lopez**, Angel Rafael 1950- *WhoHisp 92*
**Branagh**, Kenneth 1960- *ConTFT 9, IntMPA 92, IntWW 91, News 92-2 [port], WhoEnt 92*
**Branagh**, Kenneth Charles 1960- *Who 92*
**Branahl**, Erwin Fred 1922- *AmMWSc 92*
**Branan**, Carolyn Benner 1953- *WhoAmL 92*
**Branand**, Robert Edwin 1948- *WhoAmL 92*
**Branca**, Andrew A 1950- *AmMWSc 92*
**Branca**, Glenn 1948- *ConCom 92*
**Branca**, John Gregory 1950- *WhoEnt 92*
**Branca**, John R 1924- *WhoAmP 91*
**Branca**, Robert G., Jr. 1962- *WhoAmL 92*
**Branca**, Vittore 1913- *IntWW 91*
**Brancaglione**, John William 1945- *WhoMW 92*
**Brancato**, Carolyn Kay 1945- *WhoFI 92*
**Brancato**, Emanuel L 1914- *AmMWSc 92*
**Brancato**, Kathleen Madlyn 1957- *WhoEnt 92*
**Brancato**, Leo J 1922- *AmMWSc 92*
**Brancel**, Ben 1950- *WhoAmP 91*
**Branch**, Addison A., Sr. 1903- *WhoBlA 92*
**Branch**, Alan E. 1933- *WrDr 92*
**Branch**, Alan Edward 1933- *IntAu&W 91*
**Branch**, Alan Henry 1942- *WhoWest 92*
**Branch**, Andre Jose 1959- *WhoBlA 92*
**Branch**, Anna Hempstead 1875-1937 *BenetAL 91*
**Branch**, B. Lawrence 1937- *WhoBlA 92*
**Branch**, Barrington Heath 1940- *WhoFI 92*
**Branch**, Ben Shirley 1943- *WhoFI 92*
**Branch**, Bill J 1932- *WhoAmP 91*
**Branch**, Charles Edwin, Sr. 1940- *WhoRel 92*
**Branch**, Clarence Joseph 1940- *AmMWSc 92*
**Branch**, Clifford 1948- *WhoBlA 92*
**Branch**, Daniel Hugh 1958- *WhoAmL 92*
**Branch**, David Reed 1942- *AmMWSc 92*
**Branch**, Dorothy L. 1912- *WhoBlA 92*
**Branch**, Douglas McKinley 1908-1963 *DcNCBi 1*
**Branch**, Edgar Marquess 1913- *IntAu&W 91, WrDr 92*
**Branch**, Eldridge Stanley 1906- *WhoBlA 92*
**Branch**, G. Murray 1914- *WhoBlA 92*
**Branch**, Garland Marion, Jr 1922- *AmMWSc 92*
**Branch**, George 1928- *WhoBlA 92*
**Branch**, Geraldine Burton 1908- *WhoBlA 92*
**Branch**, Harllee, Jr. 1906- *IntWW 91*
**Branch**, Harrison 1947- *WhoBlA 92*
**Branch**, John 1782-1863 *DcNCBi 1*
**Branch**, John Curtis 1934- *AmMWSc 92*
**Branch**, Lawrence O'Bryan 1820-1862 *DcNCBi 1*
**Branch**, Lyn Clarke 1953- *AmMWSc 92*
**Branch**, Mary E. 1881-1944 *NotBlAW 92 [port]*
**Branch**, Michael Arthur 1940- *Who 92*
**Branch**, Otis Linwood 1943- *WhoBlA 92*
**Branch**, Paul Sheldon, Jr 1925- *WhoAmP 91*
**Branch**, Rob Hardin 1939- *WhoWest 92*
**Branch**, Robert Anthony 1942- *AmMWSc 92*
**Branch**, Rocky Lee 1959- *WhoRel 92*
**Branch**, Stanley Keith 1950- *WhoFI 92*
**Branch**, Taylor 1947- *IntAu&W 91*
**Branch**, Thomas Broughton, III 1936- *WhoAmL 92*
**Branch**, Thomas Harry 1928- *WhoAmP 91*
**Branch**, Tobie 1927- *WhoAmP 91*
**Branch**, Tricia Alison 1958- *WhoEnt 92*
**Branch**, Turner Williamson 1938- *WhoAmL 92*
**Branch**, William Allan Patrick 1915- *Who 92*
**Branch**, William Augustus Blount 1847-1910 *DcNCBi 1*
**Branch**, William Blackwell 1927- *WhoBlA 92, WhoEnt 92*
**Branch**, William Dean 1950- *AmMWSc 92*
**Branch**, William McKinley 1918- *WhoBlA 92*
**Branch-Simpson**, Germaine Gail 1950- *WhoBlA 92*
**Branchaw**, Bernadine Patricia 1933- *WhoMW 92*
**Branche**, Gilbert M. 1932- *WhoBlA 92*
**Branche**, William C., Jr. 1934- *WhoBlA 92*
**Branchflower**, Lyle 1940- *WhoFI 92*

**Branchini,** Bruce Robert 1950- *AmMWSc 92*
**Branciforte,** James Thomas 1961- *WhoFI 92*
**Brancker,** Theodore 1909- *Who 92*
**Branco,** James 1951- *WhoIns 92*
**Branco,** Joaquim Rafael 1953- *IntWW 91*
**Brancusi,** Constantin 1876-1957 *DcTwDes, FacFETw*
**Brand** *Who 92*
**Brand,** Lord 1923- *Who 92*
**Brand,** Alexander George 1918- *Who 92*
**Brand,** Alice G. *DrAPF 91*
**Brand,** Bryan P. 1944- *WhoMW 92*
**Brand,** Carl F. 1892-1981 *ConAu 133*
**Brand,** Charles Peter 1923- *Who 92*
**Brand,** Clay *IntAu&W 91X, TwCWW 91*
**Brand,** David William Robert *Who 92*
**Brand,** Dollar 1934- *WhoBlA 92*
**Brand,** Donald A *AmMWSc 92*
**Brand,** Donald A. 1940- *WhoWest 92*
**Brand,** Edward Cabell 1923- *WhoAmP 91*
**Brand,** Eugene Dew 1924- *AmMWSc 92*
**Brand,** Frank Amery 1924- *WhoFI 92*
**Brand,** Geoffrey Arthur 1930- *Who 92*
**Brand,** Grover Junior 1930- *WhoMW 92*
**Brand,** Jay Lloyd 1959- *WhoWest 92*
**Brand,** Jerry Jay 1941- *AmMWSc 92*
**Brand,** Joel 1906-1964 *EncTR 91 [port]*
**Brand,** John S 1938- *AmMWSc 92*
**Brand,** John William 1932- *WhoAmL 92*
**Brand,** John William 1947- *WhoFI 92*
**Brand,** Joseph Lyon 1936- *WhoAmL 92, WhoFI 92*
**Brand,** Joshua, and Falsey, John *LesBEnT 92*
**Brand,** Karl Gerhard 1922- *AmMWSc 92*
**Brand,** Leonard 1923- *AmMWSc 92*
**Brand,** Leonard Roy 1941- *AmMWSc 92, WhoWest 92*
**Brand,** Ludwig 1932- *AmMWSc 92*
**Brand,** Malcolm Leigh 1935- *WhoAmL 92*
**Brand,** Mary Lou 1934- *WhoWest 92*
**Brand,** Max *BenetAL 91*
**Brand,** Max 1891-1944 *ScFEYrs*
**Brand,** Max 1892-1944 *TwCWW 91*
**Brand,** Max 1896-1980 *NewAmDM*
**Brand,** Milton Irving 1925- *WhoMW 92*
**Brand,** Mona 1915- *WrDr 92*
**Brand,** Myles 1942- *WhoWest 92*
**Brand,** Neville 1921- *IntMPA 92*
**Brand,** Oscar 1920- *IntAu&W 91, WhoEnt 92, WrDr 92*
**Brand,** Othal Eugene 1919- *WhoAmP 91*
**Brand,** Paul Hyman 1940- *AmMWSc 92*
**Brand,** Philip Preston 1961- *WhoMW 92*
**Brand,** Ray Manning 1922- *WhoAmL 92*
**Brand,** Raymond Howard 1928- *AmMWSc 92*
**Brand,** Richard Clyde, Jr. 1943- *WhoRel 92*
**Brand,** Ronald Alvah 1952- *WhoAmL 92*
**Brand,** Ronald S 1919- *AmMWSc 92*
**Brand,** Samson 1943- *AmMWSc 92*
**Brand,** Stefanie Alice 1960- *WhoAmL 92*
**Brand,** Steve Aaron 1948- *WhoAmL 92, WhoMW 92*
**Brand,** Victor *IntAu&W 91X*
**Brand,** Wayne Leslie 1942- *WhoAmP 91*
**Brand,** William J 1958- *WhoAmP 91*
**Brand,** William Wayne 1944- *AmMWSc 92*
**Brandaleone,** Harold 1907- *AmMWSc 92*
**Brandau,** Betty Lee *AmMWSc 92*
**Brandau,** Eugene Clinton 1934- *WhoWest 92*
**Brandauer,** Carl M 1924- *AmMWSc 92*
**Brandauer,** Klaus Maria 1944- *IntMPA 92, IntWW 91, WhoEnt 92*
**Brandeau,** Margaret Louise 1955- *AmMWSc 92*
**Brandeberry,** James E 1939- *AmMWSc 92*
**Brandegee,** Mary Katharine Layne Curran 1844-1920 *BiInAmS*
**Brandeis,** Linda Miyake 1949- *WhoWest 92*
**Brandeis,** Louis D. 1856-1941 *BenetAL 91, FacFETw, RComAH*
**Brandeis,** Louis Dembitz 1856-1941 *AmPolLe [port]*
**Brandelik,** Donna M. 1944- *WhoMW 92*
**Brandell,** Bruce Reeves 1926- *AmMWSc 92*
**Brandemuehl,** David A 1931- *WhoAmP 91*
**Brandemuehl,** Jenny Angela 1963- *WhoWest 92*
**Branden,** Nathaniel 1930- *WrDr 92*
**Brandenberg,** Aliki *IntAu&W 91*
**Brandenberg,** Franz 1932- *IntAu&W 91, WrDr 92*
**Brandenberger,** Arthur J 1916- *AmMWSc 92*
**Brandenberger,** John Russell 1939- *AmMWSc 92, WhoMW 92*
**Brandenberger,** Robert H 1954- *AmMWSc 92*
**Brandenberger,** Stanley George 1930- *AmMWSc 92*
**Brandenburg,** Aliki 1929- *WrDr 92*
**Brandenburg,** Carlos Enrique 1948- *WhoHisp 92*
**Brandenburg,** Elizabeth Diane 1965- *WhoMW 92*
**Brandenburg,** Glen Ray 1950- *WhoWest 92*
**Brandenburg,** James David 1958- *WhoMW 92*
**Brandenburg,** James H 1930- *AmMWSc 92*
**Brandenburg,** Robert Fairchild, Jr. 1938- *WhoAmL 92*
**Brandenburg,** Robert O 1918- *AmMWSc 92*
**Brandenburg,** Ronald William 1954- *WhoAmL 92*
**Brandenburg,** Rosemary 1956- *WhoEnt 92*
**Brandenburgh,** Donald Carter 1931- *WhoWest 92*
**Brandenstein,** Robert Lewis 1923- *WhoRel 92*
**Brander,** John *DrAPF 91*
**Brander,** Reynolds A., Jr. 1937- *WhoAmL 92*
**Brandes,** George *WhoHisp 92*
**Brandes,** Joel R. 1943- *WhoAmL 92*
**Brandes,** Joseph 1928- *WrDr 92*
**Brandes,** Lawrence Henry 1924- *Who 92*
**Brandes,** Raymond S. 1924- *WhoHisp 92*
**Brandewie,** Ray 1940- *WhoAmP 91*
**Brandewie,** Richard A 1936- *AmMWSc 92*
**Brandewyne,** Rebecca 1955- *IntAu&W 91, WrDr 92*
**Brandfonbrener,** Martin 1927- *AmMWSc 92*
**Brandford,** Napoleon, III 1952- *WhoBlA 92*
**Brandhorst,** Henry William, Jr 1936- *AmMWSc 92*
**Brandi,** Jay Thomas 1947- *WhoFI 92*
**Brandi,** John *DrAPF 91*
**Brandi,** John 1943- *ConPo 91, WrDr 92*
**Brandies,** Warren 1939- *WhoFI 92*
**Brandin,** Ake H. 1924- *WhoIns 92*
**Brandin,** Alf Elvin 1912- *WhoWest 92*
**Brandin,** Donald Nelson 1921- *WhoMW 92*
**Brandin,** Robert Eric 1926- *WhoWest 92*
**Brandinger,** Jay J 1927- *AmMWSc 92*
**Brandis,** Alan D. 1956- *WhoWest 92*
**Brandis,** Bernardine *WhoEnt 92*
**Brandish,** Stephen *ScFEYrs*
**Brandl,** John Edward 1937- *WhoAmP 91, WhoFI 92, WhoMW 92*
**Brandler,** Philip 1943- *AmMWSc 92*
**Brandli,** Henry William 1937- *AmMWSc 92*
**Brandmaier,** Harold Edmund 1926- *AmMWSc 92*
**Brandman,** Harold A 1941- *AmMWSc 92*
**Brandman,** Rusti 1945- *WhoEnt 92*
**Brandmeier,** John Francis 1956- *WhoEnt 92*
**Brandmuller,** Walter 1929- *WhoRel 92*
**Brandner,** John David 1910- *AmMWSc 92*
**Brandner,** Margaret Anne Shaw 1937- *WhoWest 92*
**Brando,** Jocelyn 1919- *IntMPA 92*
**Brando,** Marlon 1924- *FacFETw, IntMPA 92, IntWW 91, Who 92*
**Brando,** Marlon, Jr. 1924- *WhoEnt 92*
**Brandofino,** Ralph J. 1954- *WhoEnt 92*
**Brandolino,** Joseph Anthony 1961- *WhoAmL 92*
**Brandom,** William Franklin 1926- *AmMWSc 92*
**Brandon** *Who 92*
**Brandon,** Allen DeWain 1957- *WhoWest 92*
**Brandon,** Brumsic, Jr. 1927- *WhoBlA 92*
**Brandon,** Burt 1937- *WhoEnt 92*
**Brandon,** Carl Ray 1953- *WhoBlA 92*
**Brandon,** Carter Jeffrey 1954- *WhoFI 92*
**Brandon,** Clement Edwin 1915- *AmMWSc 92*
**Brandon,** David Lawrence 1946- *AmMWSc 92*
**Brandon,** Doug 1932- *WhoAmP 91*
**Brandon,** Edward Bermetz 1931- *WhoFI 92, WhoMW 92*
**Brandon,** Elvis Denby, III 1954- *WhoFI 92*
**Brandon,** Frank *TwCSFW 91*
**Brandon,** Frank Bayard 1927- *AmMWSc 92*
**Brandon,** Henry 1916- *IntAu&W 91, IntWW 91, Who 92, WrDr 92*
**Brandon,** James Hamilton 1956- *WhoFI 92*
**Brandon,** James Kenneth 1940- *AmMWSc 92*
**Brandon,** James L *WhoAmP 91*
**Brandon,** Jay Robert 1953- *WhoAmL 92*
**Brandon,** Joan Mack 1930- *WhoMW 92*
**Brandon,** Joe *IntAu&W 91X*
**Brandon,** Kathryn Elizabeth Beck 1916- *WhoWest 92*
**Brandon,** Lawrence G. 1936- *WhoIns 92*
**Brandon,** Liane *WhoEnt 92*
**Brandon,** Michael *IntMPA 92*
**Brandon,** Percy Samuel 1916- *Who 92*
**Brandon,** Phyllis Dillaha 1935- *WhoAmP 91*
**Brandon,** Raymond Wilson 1959- *WhoFI 92*
**Brandon,** Richard Leonard 1951- *WhoFI 92*
**Brandon,** Ronald Arthur 1933- *AmMWSc 92*
**Brandon,** Sheila *IntAu&W 91X, WrDr 92*
**Brandon,** Walter Wiley, Jr 1929- *AmMWSc 92*
**Brandon-Bravo,** Martin Maurice 1932- *Who 92*
**Brandon Of Oakbrook,** Baron 1920- *IntWW 91, Who 92*
**Brandow,** Baird H 1935- *AmMWSc 92*
**Brandow,** Floyd E. 1925- *WhoAmL 92*
**Brandow,** Wayne Robert 1952- *WhoRel 92*
**Brandreth,** Dale Alden 1931- *AmMWSc 92*
**Brandreth,** Gyles 1948- *IntAu&W 91, WrDr 92*
**Brandreth,** Gyles Daubeney 1948- *Who 92*
**Brandrick,** David Guy 1932- *Who 92*
**Brandriss,** Marjorie C 1949- *AmMWSc 92*
**Brandriss,** Michael W 1931- *AmMWSc 92*
**Brandrup,** Douglas Warren 1940- *WhoAmL 92*
**Brands,** Allen J 1914- *AmMWSc 92*
**Brands,** Alvira Bernice 1922- *AmMWSc 92*
**Brands,** James Edwin 1937- *WhoFI 92*
**Brands,** Robert Christopher 1958- *WhoWest 92*
**Brandstetter,** Albin 1932- *AmMWSc 92*
**Brandstetter,** Bruce George 1956- *WhoFI 92*
**Brandstrader,** Fred Lucas 1938- *WhoRel 92*
**Brandstrom,** Charlotte 1959- *WhoEnt 92*
**Brandt,** Bill 1905-1983 *FacFETw*
**Brandt,** Bruce Losure 1941- *AmMWSc 92*
**Brandt,** Carl David 1928- *AmMWSc 92*
**Brandt,** Carl Raymond 1923- *WhoFI 92*
**Brandt,** Carlos Villeneuva 1957- *TwCPaSc*
**Brandt,** Catherine Ann 1962- *WhoAmL 92*
**Brandt,** Charles Lawrence 1925- *AmMWSc 92*
**Brandt,** Cornelis J. 1913- *IntWW 91*
**Brandt,** David Dean 1947- *WhoFI 92, WhoMW 92*
**Brandt,** Donald Edward 1962- *WhoFI 92*
**Brandt,** E J *AmMWSc 92*
**Brandt,** Eddie August 1922- *WhoEnt 92*
**Brandt,** Edward Newman, Jr 1933- *AmMWSc 92*
**Brandt,** Elizabeth Anne 1945- *WhoWest 92*
**Brandt,** G Donald 1925- *AmMWSc 92*
**Brandt,** Gene Stuart 1950- *WhoMW 92*
**Brandt,** Gerald Bennett 1938- *AmMWSc 92*
**Brandt,** Gerald H 1933- *AmMWSc 92*
**Brandt,** H 1925- *AmMWSc 92*
**Brandt,** Howard Allen 1946- *AmMWSc 92*
**Brandt,** I. Marvin 1942- *WhoFI 92*
**Brandt,** Ira Kive 1923- *AmMWSc 92*
**Brandt,** J Leonard 1919- *AmMWSc 92*
**Brandt,** James Bradford 1951- *WhoEnt 92*
**Brandt,** James David 1956- *WhoWest 92*
**Brandt,** James Zahn 1949- *WhoFI 92*
**Brandt,** Jerrold Thurston, Jr. 1946- *WhoEnt 92*
**Brandt,** Jo *WhoAmP 91*
**Brandt,** John Ashworth 1950- *WhoMW 92*
**Brandt,** John Edward 1946- *WhoMW 92*
**Brandt,** John T 1948- *AmMWSc 92*
**Brandt,** Jon A. 1947- *WhoMW 92*
**Brandt,** Jon Alan 1947- *AmMWSc 92*
**Brandt,** Joseph Michael *WhoMW 92*
**Brandt,** Karl 1904-1948 *EncTR 91 [port]*
**Brandt,** Karl Garet 1938- *AmMWSc 92*
**Brandt,** Kenneth 1938- *WhoAmP 91*
**Brandt,** Kenneth Edward 1959- *WhoRel 92*
**Brandt,** Konrad *WhoRel 92*
**Brandt,** Leslie F. 1919- *WrDr 92*
**Brandt,** Lillian B. 1919- *WhoBlA 92*
**Brandt,** Luther Warren 1920- *AmMWSc 92*
**Brandt,** Manuel 1915- *AmMWSc 92*
**Brandt,** Marianne 1893- *DcTwDes*
**Brandt,** Michael Earl 1950- *WhoAmL 92*
**Brandt,** Nancy Claire 1950- *WhoMW 92*
**Brandt,** Nat 1929- *WrDr 92*
**Brandt,** Paul Nicholas 1937- *Who 92*
**Brandt,** Peter Augustus 1931- *Who 92*
**Brandt,** Philip Williams 1930- *AmMWSc 92*
**Brandt,** Richard Bernard 1934- *AmMWSc 92*
**Brandt,** Richard Charles 1940- *AmMWSc 92*
**Brandt,** Richard Gustave 1936- *AmMWSc 92*
**Brandt,** Richard M. 1922- *WrDr 92*
**Brandt,** Richard Paul 1927- *IntMPA 92, WhoFI 92*
**Brandt,** Robert Barry 1948- *WhoRel 92*
**Brandt,** Ronald Lee 1947- *WhoAmL 92*
**Brandt,** Sharon K. 1957- *WhoMW 92*
**Brandt,** Stephen Bernard 1950- *AmMWSc 92*
**Brandt,** Susan Lorae 1950- *WhoWest 92*
**Brandt,** Tom *IntAu&W 91X*
**Brandt,** Victor Leonard 1920- *WhoRel 92*
**Brandt,** Walter 1912-1937 *EncTR 91*
**Brandt,** Walter Edmund 1935- *AmMWSc 92*
**Brandt,** Werner W 1938- *WhoAmP 91*
**Brandt,** Werner Wilfried 1927- *AmMWSc 92*
**Brandt,** William Arthur, Jr. 1949- *WhoFI 92, WhoMW 92*
**Brandt,** William Henry 1927- *AmMWSc 92*
**Brandt,** Willy 1913- *FacFETw [port], IntWW 91, Who 92, WhoNob 90*
**Brandts,** John Frederick 1934- *AmMWSc 92*
**Brandvik,** Paul Allen 1937- *WhoMW 92*
**Brandvold,** Donald Keith 1936- *AmMWSc 92*
**Brandvold,** Lynn Airheart 1940- *WhoWest 92*
**Brandvold,** Steven C. 1943- *WhoMW 92*
**Brandwajn,** Alexandre 1948- *WhoWest 92*
**Brandwein,** Bernard Jay 1927- *AmMWSc 92*
**Brandys,** Kazimierz 1916- *LiExTwC*
**Branen,** Alfred Larry 1945- *AmMWSc 92, WhoWest 92*
**Branfield,** John 1931- *WrDr 92*
**Branfield,** John Charles 1931- *IntAu&W 91*
**Brangan,** Pamela J 1944- *AmMWSc 92*
**Branges,** Louis de 1932- *AmMWSc 92*
**Brangwyn,** Frank 1867-1956 *TwCPaSc*
**Branham,** Andrew Criddle 1953- *WhoAmL 92*
**Branham,** Dawn Louise 1960- *WhoWest 92*
**Branham,** George, III 1962- *WhoBlA 92*
**Branham,** Hudson 1921- *WhoAmL 92*
**Branham,** Joseph Morhart 1932- *AmMWSc 92*
**Branham,** Luther George 1930- *WhoFI 92*
**Branham,** Mack Carison, Jr. 1931- *WhoRel 92*
**Branham,** William Marrion 1909-1965 *RelLAm 91*
**Braniff,** William *WhoAmL 92*
**Branigan,** Donald William 1933- *WhoWest 92*
**Branigan,** Keith 1940- *IntAu&W 91, WrDr 92*
**Branigan,** Patrick 1906- *Who 92*
**Branigin,** Roger D., Jr. 1931- *WhoAmL 92*
**Branin,** Joan Julia 1944- *WhoFI 92*
**Branitzki,** Heinz 1929- *IntWW 91*
**Branker,** Julian Michael *WhoBlA 92*
**Brankovic,** Slobodan Svetomir 1923- *WhoFI 92*
**Brankovich,** Mark J. 1922- *WhoWest 92*
**Branley,** Franklyn M 1915- *AmMWSc 92, SmATA 68 [port]*
**Branman,** Martin Jeffrey 1955- *WhoFI 92*
**Brann,** Alton Joseph 1941- *WhoFI 92*
**Brann,** Darrell Wayne 1958- *AmMWSc 92*
**Brann,** Donald Treasurer 1929- *WhoMW 92*
**Brann,** Edward Rommel 1920- *WhoFI 92, WhoMW 92*
**Brann,** Herman Ivelaw 1942- *WhoBlA 92*
**Brann,** Lester William, Jr. 1925- *WhoMW 92*
**Brann,** Richard R. 1943- *WhoAmL 92*
**Brann,** William Cowper 1855-1898 *BenetAL 91*
**Brann,** William Norman 1915- *Who 92*
**Brannan,** Charles Franklin 1903- *Who 92*
**Brannan,** Curtis Ward 1931- *WhoRel 92*
**Brannan,** George W 1932- *WhoAmP 91*
**Brannan,** James Bernard, Jr. 1951- *WhoAmL 92*
**Brannan,** Pat White 1930- *WhoAmP 91*
**Brannan,** William Breece 1958- *WhoAmL 92*
**Brannan,** William C. 1949- *WhoFI 92*
**Brannen,** Eric 1921- *AmMWSc 92*
**Brannen,** James H., III 1940- *WhoBlA 92*
**Brannen,** John Howard 1949- *WhoAmL 92*
**Brannen,** Jonathan *DrAPF 91*
**Brannen,** Malcolm Erskine 1946- *WhoEnt 92*
**Brannen,** Perry, Jr. 1940- *WhoAmL 92*
**Brannen,** William Thomas, Jr 1936- *AmMWSc 92*
**Brannian,** Ross E 1925- *WhoAmP 91*
**Brannigan,** David 1941- *AmMWSc 92*
**Brannigan,** Joseph C *WhoAmP 91*
**Brannigan,** Russ *TwCWW 91*
**Branning,** Peter Sterry 1947- *WhoAmL 92*
**Brannon,** Brian Ray 1944- *WhoWest 92*
**Brannon,** Clifton Woodrow 1912- *WhoRel 92*

**Brannon,** Donald Ray 1939- *AmMWSc 92*
**Brannon,** Donn *DrAPF 91*
**Brannon,** Dottie 1935- *WhoMW 92*
**Brannon,** H Raymond, Jr 1926- *AmMWSc 92*
**Brannon,** James R. 1943- *WhoBlA 92*
**Brannon,** Lester Travis, Jr. 1926- *WhoAmL 92*
**Brannon,** Max R *WhoAmP 91*
**Brannon,** Nancy Ruth 1947- *WhoAmP 91*
**Brannon,** Patsy M *AmMWSc 92*
**Brannon,** Paul J 1935- *AmMWSc 92*
**Brannon,** Richard Scott 1926- *WhoRel 92*
**Brannon,** Ronald Roy 1928- *WhoRel 92*
**Brannon,** William Earl 1936- *WhoAmL 92*
**Brans,** Carl Henry 1935- *AmMWSc 92, FacFETw*
**Branscom,** James Jefferson 1939- *WhoWest 92*
**Branscomb,** Anne Wells 1928- *WhoAmL 92*
**Branscomb,** Elbert Warren 1935- *AmMWSc 92*
**Branscomb,** Lewis McAdory 1926- *AmMWSc 92, IntWW 91, WhoFI 92*
**Branscomb,** Ralph Stafford 1944- *WhoAmL 92*
**Branscum,** Alfred Dean 1952- *WhoRel 92*
**Branscum,** David Lawdon 1958- *WhoAmP 91*
**Branscum,** Herby, Jr 1941- *WhoAmP 91*
**Bransford,** Mallory Watkins 1912- *WhoRel 92*
**Bransford,** Paris 1930- *WhoBlA 92*
**Bransford,** Stephen 1949- *ConAu 134*
**Bransford,** William L. 1924- *WhoBlA 92*
**Bransome,** Edwin D, Jr 1933- *AmMWSc 92*
**Branson,** Albert Harold 1935- *WhoAmL 92*
**Branson,** Allegra 1934- *WhoEnt 92*
**Branson,** Branley Allan 1929- *AmMWSc 92*
**Branson,** Bruce William 1927- *AmMWSc 92*
**Branson,** Cecil Robert Peter Charles 1924- *Who 92*
**Branson,** Dan E 1928- *AmMWSc 92*
**Branson,** Dean Russell 1941- *AmMWSc 92*
**Branson,** Dorothy Swingle 1921- *AmMWSc 92*
**Branson,** Edward James 1918- *Who 92*
**Branson,** Eli d1818? *DcNCBi 1*
**Branson,** Eugene Cunningham 1861-1933 *DcNCBi 1*
**Branson,** Farrel Allen 1919- *AmMWSc 92*
**Branson,** Fredine McBryde 1931- *WhoAmP 91*
**Branson,** Harley Kenneth 1942- *WhoFI 92*
**Branson,** Herman Russell 1914- *AmMWSc 92, WhoBlA 92*
**Branson,** Jay Wallace 1956- *WhoFI 92*
**Branson,** Jessie M *WhoAmP 91*
**Branson,** Levi 1832-1903 *DcNCBi 1*
**Branson,** Margaret Aber 1927- *WhoAmP 91*
**Branson,** Philip B. 1941- *WhoRel 92*
**Branson,** Richard 1950- *IntWW 91*
**Branson,** Richard Charles Nicholas 1950- *Who 92*
**Branson,** Robert Bailey 1960- *WhoAmL 92*
**Branson,** Terry Fred 1935- *AmMWSc 92*
**Branson,** William Rainforth 1905- *Who 92*
**Branstad,** Clifford 1924- *WhoAmP 91*
**Branstad,** Terry E. 1946- *AlmAP 92 [port]*
**Branstad,** Terry Edward 1946- *IntWW 91, WhoAmP 91, WhoMW 92*
**Branstetter,** Cecil Dewey, Sr. 1920- *WhoAmL 92*
**Branstetter,** Daniel G 1950- *AmMWSc 92*
**Branstetter,** Olin 1929- *WhoAmP 91*
**Branstetter,** Russell Wayne 1946- *WhoRel 92*
**Branstner,** Karl Christian 1931- *WhoMW 92*
**Branstool,** Charles Eugene 1936- *WhoAmP 91, WhoMW 92*
**Brant,** Albert Wade 1919- *AmMWSc 92*
**Brant,** Beth *DrAPF 91*
**Brant,** Colin Trevor 1929- *Who 92*
**Brant,** Daniel 1921- *AmMWSc 92*
**Brant,** Gerald Allen 1953- *WhoAmP 91*
**Brant,** Henry 1913- *ConCom 92, NewAmDM*
**Brant,** John Ira 1872- *ScFEYrs*
**Brant,** John Sidney 1939- *WhoFI 92*
**Brant,** Jonathan Jay 1952- *WhoMW 92*
**Brant,** Joseph 1742-1807 *BenetAL 91, BlkwEAR [port]*
**Brant,** Larry James 1946- *AmMWSc 92*
**Brant,** Lewis *TwCWW 91*
**Brant,** Mary 1736?-1796 *BlkwEAR*
**Brant,** Russell Alan 1919- *AmMWSc 92*
**Branthaver,** Jan Franklin 1936- *AmMWSc 92, WhoWest 92*
**Branting,** Karl Hjalmar 1860-1925 *WhoNob 90*
**Brantingham,** Charles Ross 1917- *AmMWSc 92, WhoWest 92*
**Brantingham,** Patricia Louise 1943- *WhoWest 92*
**Brantingham,** Paul Jeffrey 1943- *WhoWest 92*
**Brantley,** Bobby Lynn 1948- *WhoAmP 91*
**Brantley,** Booker Terry, Jr. 1935- *WhoBlA 92*
**Brantley,** Daniel 1944- *WhoBlA 92*
**Brantley,** Edward J. 1923- *WhoBlA 92*
**Brantley,** Ellen B. 1948- *WhoAmL 92*
**Brantley,** Etta Renae 1953- *WhoMW 92*
**Brantley,** Haskew Hawthorne, Jr 1922- *WhoAmP 91*
**Brantley,** John Randolph 1951- *WhoAmL 92*
**Brantley,** Lee Reed 1906- *AmMWSc 92*
**Brantley,** Montague Delano 1919- *WhoBlA 92*
**Brantley,** Sandra Benson 1960- *WhoAmL 92*
**Brantley,** Susan Louise 1958- *AmMWSc 92*
**Brantley,** William Arthur 1941- *AmMWSc 92*
**Brantley,** William Cain, Jr 1949- *AmMWSc 92*
**Brantley,** William Henry 1938- *AmMWSc 92*
**Brantley,** William Stanley 1956- *WhoRel 92*
**Brantly,** William Tomlinson 1787-1845 *DcNCBi 1*
**Branton,** Daniel 1932- *AmMWSc 92*
**Branton,** Leo, Jr. 1922- *WhoBlA 92*
**Branton,** Philip Edward 1943- *AmMWSc 92*
**Branton,** Raymond 1924- *WhoAmP 91*
**Branton,** Wiley Austin 1923-1988 *FacFETw*
**Branton,** William Strobel 1939- *WhoAmP 91*
**Branzer,** John Paul 1942- *WhoEnt 92*
**Branzi,** Andrea 1928- *DcTwDes*
**Braque,** Georges 1882-1963 *FacFETw*
**Braquet,** Pierre G 1947- *AmMWSc 92*
**Bras,** Luisa A. *WhoHisp 92*
**Bras,** Rafael Luis 1950- *AmMWSc 92*
**Brasch,** Frederick Martin, Jr 1943- *AmMWSc 92*
**Brasch,** John Michael 1955- *WhoWest 92*
**Brasch,** Klaus Rainer 1940- *AmMWSc 92, WhoWest 92*
**Brasch,** Rudolph 1912- *IntAu&W 91, WhoRel 92, WrDr 92*
**Braschler,** Todd Clifton 1962- *WhoRel 92*
**Brascho,** Donn Joseph 1933- *AmMWSc 92*
**Brasda,** Bernard William 1938- *WhoWest 92*
**Brase,** David Arthur 1945- *AmMWSc 92*
**Brase,** Paul *DrAPF 91*
**Brasel,** Jo Anne 1934- *AmMWSc 92*
**Braselton,** James Todd 1952- *WhoWest 92*
**Braselton,** Webb Emmett, Jr 1941- *AmMWSc 92*
**Brasen,** Steven John 1966- *WhoEnt 92*
**Brasey,** Henry L. 1937- *WhoBlA 92*
**Brasfield,** David Williamson 1956- *WhoFI 92*
**Brasfield,** Evans Booker 1932- *WhoAmL 92, WhoFI 92*
**Brasfield,** James *DrAPF 91*
**Brash,** Alan Anderson 1913- *DcEcMov, Who 92*
**Brash,** Donald Thomas 1940- *IntWW 91*
**Brash,** Edward *DrAPF 91*
**Brash,** John Law 1937- *AmMWSc 92*
**Brash,** Robert 1924- *Who 92*
**Brash,** Sally Miller 1911- *WhoEnt 92*
**Brashear,** Berlaind Leander 1934- *WhoBlA 92*
**Brashear,** John Alfred 1840-1920 *BiInAmS*
**Brashear,** Kermit, II 1944- *WhoAmP 91*
**Brashear,** Kermit Allen, II 1944- *WhoAmL 92*
**Brashear,** Robert Laird 1949- *WhoRel 92*
**Brashear,** Russ 1954- *WhoRel 92*
**Brasher,** Christopher 1928- *WrDr 92*
**Brasher,** Christopher William 1928- *IntAu&W 91, Who 92*
**Brasher,** Gary Vaughn 1950- *WhoEnt 92*
**Brasher,** Norman Henry 1922- *WrDr 92*
**Brasher,** Richard Curtis 1931- *WhoFI 92*
**Brasher,** Richard Madison, Sr. 1954- *WhoAmL 92*
**Brashier,** Clyde Kenneth 1933- *AmMWSc 92*
**Brashier,** Joseph Clarence 1956- *WhoRel 92*
**Brashler,** William 1947- *WrDr 92*
**Brasic,** Gregory Lee 1961- *WhoMW 92*
**Brasie,** Jeffrey Dean 1947- *WhoMW 92*
**Brasillach,** Robert 1909-1945 *BiDExR, GuFrLit 1*
**Brasitus,** Thomas *AmMWSc 92*
**Brasitus,** Thomas Albert 1945- *WhoMW 92*
**Braslau,** Norman 1931- *AmMWSc 92*
**Brasley,** John Anthony 1960- *WhoAmL 92*
**Brasloff,** Stanley H. 1930- *IntMPA 92*
**Brasmer,** Randall Dane 1952- *WhoWest 92*
**Brasnett,** John 1929- *Who 92*
**Brass,** John 1908- *Who 92*
**Brass,** William 1921- *Who 92*
**Brassai** 1899-1984 *FacFETw*
**Brassard,** Andre 1933- *AmMWSc 92*
**Brassell,** Gilbert W. *WhoHisp 92*
**Brassell,** Roselyn Strauss 1930- *WhoAmL 92, WhoWest 92*
**Brasselle,** Keefe d1981 *LesBEnT 92*
**Brasseur,** Claude 1936- *IntWW 91*
**Brassey** *Who 92*
**Brassey,** Peter 1907- *Who 92*
**Brassey of Apethorpe,** Baron 1932- *Who 92*
**Brassfield,** Eugene Everett 1933- *WhoMW 92*
**Brasted,** Robert Crocker 1915- *AmMWSc 92*
**Brastins,** Auseklis 1925- *AmMWSc 92*
**Brasunas,** Anton Des 1919- *AmMWSc 92*
**Brasunas,** John Charles 1952- *AmMWSc 92*
**Braswell,** Carlton Samuel 1959- *WhoRel 92*
**Braswell,** Edwin Maurice, Jr. 1952- *WhoAmL 92*
**Braswell,** Emory Harold 1932- *AmMWSc 92*
**Braswell,** Erin Christine 1954- *WhoEnt 92*
**Braswell,** James Craig 1868-1951 *DcNCBi 1*
**Braswell,** Louis Erskine 1937- *WhoAmL 92*
**Braswell,** Palmira 1928- *WhoBlA 92*
**Braswell,** Pearl Eva 1914- *WhoMW 92*
**Braswell,** Robert Neil 1932- *AmMWSc 92*
**Braswell,** Thomas Edward, Jr 1921- *WhoAmP 91*
**Brata,** Sasthi 1939- *ConNov 91, WrDr 92*
**Brataas,** Nancy 1928- *WhoMW 92*
**Brataas,** Nancy Osborn 1928- *WhoAmP 91*
**Bratby,** Jean Esme Oregon *Who 92*
**Bratby,** John 1928- *IntWW 91, TwCPaSc*
**Bratby,** John Randall 1928- *Who 92, WrDr 92*
**Bratchenko,** Boris Fedorovich 1912- *IntWW 91*
**Bratcher,** Dennis Ray 1947- *WhoRel 92*
**Bratcher,** Thomas Lester 1942- *AmMWSc 92*
**Bratenahl,** Alexander 1918- *AmMWSc 92*
**Brater,** D Craig *AmMWSc 92*
**Braterman,** Paul S 1938- *AmMWSc 92*
**Brathovde,** James Robert 1926- *AmMWSc 92*
**Brathwaite,** Edward 1930- *BenetAL 91*
**Brathwaite,** Edward Kamau *DrAPF 91*
**Brathwaite,** Edward Kamau 1930- *ConPo 91, RfGEnL 91, WrDr 92*
**Brathwaite,** Errol 1924- *ConNov 91*
**Brathwaite,** Errol 1929- *WrDr 92*
**Brathwaite,** Errol Freeman 1924- *IntAu&W 91*
**Brathwaite,** Kamau 1930- *IntAu&W 91*
**Bratina,** Woymir John 1916- *AmMWSc 92*
**Bratkowski,** Charles J 1949- *WhoAmP 91*
**Bratnober,** Patricia Ray 1925- *WhoMW 92*
**Bratschun,** William R 1931- *AmMWSc 92*
**Bratt,** Albertus Dirk 1933- *AmMWSc 92*
**Bratt,** Bengt Erik 1922- *AmMWSc 92*
**Bratt,** C. Griffith 1914- *WhoEnt 92*
**Bratt,** Carolyn Schmoll 1943- *WhoAmL 92*
**Bratt,** Guy Maurice 1920- *Who 92*
**Bratt,** Herbert Sidney 1931- *WhoAmL 92*
**Bratt,** John Albert 1938- *WhoMW 92*
**Bratt,** Nicholas 1948- *WhoFI 92*
**Bratt,** Peter Raymond 1929- *AmMWSc 92*
**Brattain,** Arlene Jane Clark 1938- *WhoMW 92*
**Brattain,** Bruce Douglas 1950- *WhoAmL 92*
**Brattain,** Frank Konrad 1959- *WhoMW 92*
**Brattain,** Michael Gene 1947- *AmMWSc 92*
**Brattain,** Walter Houser 1902-1987 *FacFETw, WhoNob 90*
**Brattain,** William Edwin 1938- *WhoEnt 92*
**Brattgard,** Helge Axel Kristian 1920- *WhoRel 92*
**Brattle,** Thomas 1658-1713 *BenetAL 91, BiInAmS*
**Bratton,** Conrad Christopher 1941- *WhoRel 92*
**Bratton,** Daniel Lindsay 1932- *WhoEnt 92*
**Bratton,** George Stanford 1941- *WhoRel 92*
**Bratton,** Gerald Roy 1942- *AmMWSc 92*
**Bratton,** J. S. 1945- *WrDr 92*
**Bratton,** Priscilla Hoffman 1951- *WhoEnt 92*
**Bratton,** Richard Waldo 1933- *WhoAmP 91*
**Bratton,** Susan Power 1948- *AmMWSc 92*
**Bratton,** William Edward 1919- *WhoFI 92*
**Brattsten,** Lena B *AmMWSc 92*
**Brattstrom,** Bayard Holmes 1929- *AmMWSc 92*
**Bratus',** Sergey Nikitich 1904- *SovUnBD*
**Bratz,** Robert Davis 1920- *AmMWSc 92*
**Bratza,** Nicolas Dusan 1945- *Who 92*
**Brau,** Charles Allen 1938- *AmMWSc 92*
**Brau,** James Edward 1946- *AmMWSc 92*
**Brauch,** Manfred T. *WhoRel 92*
**Braucher,** Jane Alberta Elliott *WhoAmL 92*
**Brauchi,** John Tony 1927- *AmMWSc 92*
**Brauchitsch,** Walther von 1881-1948 *EncTR 91 [port]*
**Brauchli,** Bernard *WhoEnt 92*
**Braucht,** Carol Jean 1939- *WhoMW 92*
**Braucht,** La Vere T, Jr. 1929- *WhoIns 92*
**Braucht,** Stephanie Ann Sirotnak 1948- *WhoMW 92*
**Braud,** Harry J 1935- *AmMWSc 92*
**Braude,** Abraham Isaac 1917- *AmMWSc 92*
**Braude,** George Leon 1918- *AmMWSc 92*
**Braude,** Michael 1936- *WhoFI 92, WhoMW 92*
**Braude,** Monique Colsenet 1925- *AmMWSc 92*
**Braude,** Samuel 1918- *WhoFI 92*
**Braudel,** Fernand 1902-1985 *FacFETw*
**Braudy,** Leo 1941- *WrDr 92*
**Braudy,** Leo Beal 1941- *IntAu&W 91*
**Brauer,** Arik 1929- *IntWW 91*
**Brauer,** Fred 1932- *AmMWSc 92*
**Brauer,** Fred Gunther 1932- *WhoMW 92*
**Brauer,** George Ulrich 1927- *AmMWSc 92, WhoMW 92*
**Brauer,** Gerhard Max 1919- *AmMWSc 92*
**Brauer,** Harrol Andrew, Jr. 1920- *WhoEnt 92, WhoFI 92*
**Brauer,** Jerald C. 1921- *WrDr 92*
**Brauer,** Jerald Carl 1921- *IntWW 91*
**Brauer,** John Robert 1943- *AmMWSc 92*
**Brauer,** Joseph B 1930- *AmMWSc 92*
**Brauer,** Mark Alan 1952- *WhoWest 92*
**Brauer,** Max 1887-1973 *EncTR 91*
**Brauer,** Michael 1949- *WhoFI 92, WhoWest 92*
**Brauer,** Philip Roger 1955- *WhoMW 92*
**Brauer,** Ralph Werner 1921- *AmMWSc 92*
**Brauer,** Roger L *AmMWSc 92*
**Brauer,** Stephen Franklin 1945- *WhoFI 92*
**Braughler,** John Mark 1950- *AmMWSc 92, WhoMW 92*
**Braughton,** Michael Lynn 1947- *WhoMW 92*
**Brault,** Adelard Lionel 1909- *WhoAmP 91*
**Brault,** Gayle Lorain 1944- *WhoWest 92*
**Brault,** James William 1932- *AmMWSc 92*
**Brault,** Margaret A *AmMWSc 92*
**Brault,** Michel 1928- *WhoEnt 92*
**Brault,** Robert George 1918- *AmMWSc 92*
**Brauman,** John I 1937- *AmMWSc 92, IntWW 91*
**Brauman,** Sharon K 1939- *AmMWSc 92*
**Braumiller,** Allen Spooner 1934- *WhoFI 92*
**Braun,** Alan James 1942- *WhoRel 92*
**Braun,** Alvin Joseph 1915- *AmMWSc 92*
**Braun,** Andrey Georgevich 1937- *IntWW 91*
**Braun,** Andrey Georgievich 1937- *SovUnBD*
**Braun,** Arlo David 1938- *WhoWest 92*
**Braun,** Artur 1925- *DcTwDes*
**Braun,** Berton Gilman 1932- *WhoAmL 92*
**Braun,** Carl P *WhoAmP 91*
**Braun,** Carol Moseley E 1947- *WhoAmP 91*
**Braun,** Charles Louis 1937- *AmMWSc 92*
**Braun,** Clait E 1939- *AmMWSc 92*
**Braun,** Craig Allen 1939- *WhoEnt 92*
**Braun,** Dennis Duane 1943- *WhoMW 92*
**Braun,** Donald E 1930- *AmMWSc 92*
**Braun,** Donald Peter 1950- *AmMWSc 92*
**Braun,** Edward 1936- *ConAu 134*
**Braun,** Eldon John 1937- *AmMWSc 92*
**Braun,** Eric Douglas 1921- *IntAu&W 91*
**Braun,** Eunice Hockspeier *WhoRel 92*
**Braun,** Eva 1912-1945 *EncTR 91 [port]*
**Braun,** Fernand 1925- *IntWW 91*
**Braun,** George Wesley 1908- *WhoFI 92*
**Braun,** Gerry Cole 1948- *WhoWest 92*
**Braun,** Helen Marie *WhoFI 92*
**Braun,** Henry *DrAPF 91*
**Braun,** James John 1962- *WhoEnt 92*
**Braun,** Jeffrey Louis 1946- *WhoAmL 92*
**Braun,** Jerome Irwin 1929- *WhoAmL 92*
**Braun,** Joseph C. *WhoMW 92*
**Braun,** Juergen Hans 1927- *AmMWSc 92*
**Braun,** Karl Ferdinand 1850-1918 *FacFETw, WhoNob 90*
**Braun,** Kazimierz Pawel 1936- *WhoEnt 92*
**Braun,** Keith Brian 1959- *WhoAmL 92*
**Braun,** Larry C. 1959- *WhoMW 92*
**Braun,** Lewis Timothy 1923- *AmMWSc 92*
**Braun,** Lilian Jackson *WrDr 92*
**Braun,** Loren L 1929- *AmMWSc 92*
**Braun,** Ludwig 1926- *AmMWSc 92*

**Braun,** Martin 1941- *AmMWSc 92*
**Braun,** Matt 1932- *TwCWW 91, WrDr 92*
**Braun,** Max d1951 *DcTwDes*
**Braun,** Michael 1722?-1807 *DcNCBi 1*
**Braun,** Michael Alan 1949- *WhoFI 92*
**Braun,** Michael Thomas 1956- *WhoEnt 92*
**Braun,** Nancy Lynn 1952- *WhoAmL 92*
**Braun,** Otto 1872-1955 *EncTR 91*
**Braun,** Peter Eric 1939- *AmMWSc 92*
**Braun,** Phyllis C 1953- *AmMWSc 92*
**Braun,** Pinkas 1923- *IntWW 91*
**Braun,** Randy Kenneth 1953- *WhoMW 92*
**Braun,** Raymond William 1957- *WhoAmL 92*
**Braun,** Richard Emil *DrAPF 91*
**Braun,** Richard Emil 1934- *ConPo 91, WrDr 92*
**Braun,** Richard Lane 1917- *WhoAmL 92*
**Braun,** Richard Lane, II 1948- *WhoAmL 92*
**Braun,** Robert Alexander 1910- *WhoMW 92*
**Braun,** Robert Clare 1928- *WhoFI 92, WhoMW 92*
**Braun,** Robert Denton 1943- *AmMWSc 92*
**Braun,** Robert Leore 1936- *AmMWSc 92*
**Braun,** Robert William 1938- *WhoAmL 92*
**Braun,** Sigismund von 1911- *IntWW 91*
**Braun,** Stephen Baker 1942- *WhoFI 92*
**Braun,** Stephen Hughes 1942- *WhoWest 92*
**Braun,** Stephen J *WhoAmP 91*
**Braun,** Virginia Mary 1917- *WhoAmP 91*
**Braun,** Walter G 1917- *AmMWSc 92*
**Braun,** Warren Lloyd 1922- *WhoEnt 92*
**Braun,** Werner Heinz 1945- *AmMWSc 92*
**Braun,** Werner von 1912-1977 *FacFETw*
**Braun,** Wernher von 1912-1977 *EncTR 91 [port]*
**Braun,** Willi Karl 1931- *AmMWSc 92*
**Braun,** William J. 1925- *WhoIns 92*
**Braun,** Zev *LesBEnT 92, WhoEnt 92*
**Braun-Munzinger,** Peter 1946- *AmMWSc 92*
**Braunbehrens,** Volkmar 1941- *ConAu 134*
**Braund,** Allin 1915- *TwCPaSc*
**Braundmeier,** Arthur John, Jr 1943- *AmMWSc 92*
**Braune,** Maximillian O 1932- *AmMWSc 92*
**Brauner,** Joseph Eli 1961- *WhoEnt 92*
**Brauner,** Kenneth Martin 1927- *AmMWSc 92*
**Brauner,** Phyllis Ambler 1916- *AmMWSc 92*
**Brauner,** Ronald Allan 1939- *WhoRel 92*
**Braunfeld,** Peter George 1930- *AmMWSc 92*
**Braunfels,** Michael 1917- *IntWW 91*
**Braunlich,** Peter Fritz 1937- *AmMWSc 92*
**Brauns,** Heinrich 1868-1939 *EncTR 91*
**Braunschweiger,** Christian Carl 1926- *AmMWSc 92*
**Braunschweiger,** Paul G 1947- *AmMWSc 92*
**Braunsdorf,** James Allen 1938- *WhoMW 92*
**Braunsdorf,** Paul Raymond 1943- *WhoAmL 92*
**Braunstein,** David Michael 1942- *AmMWSc 92*
**Braunstein,** George Gregory 1947- *IntMPA 92, WhoEnt 92*
**Braunstein,** Glenn David 1944- *AmMWSc 92*
**Braunstein,** Helen Mentcher 1925- *AmMWSc 92*
**Braunstein,** Herbert 1926- *AmMWSc 92, WhoWest 92*
**Braunstein,** Jerry 1922- *AmMWSc 92*
**Braunstein,** Joseph David 1943- *AmMWSc 92*
**Braunstein,** Jules 1913- *AmMWSc 92*
**Braunstein,** Rubin 1922- *AmMWSc 92*
**Braunthal,** Gerard 1923- *WrDr 92*
**Braunwald,** Eugene 1929- *AmMWSc 92*
**Braus,** Stephen Vincent 1952- *WhoRel 92*
**Brause,** Allan R 1942- *AmMWSc 92*
**Brause,** Dorsey Wayland 1927- *WhoRel 92*
**Brauth,** Steven Earle 1947- *AmMWSc 92*
**Brautigam,** Hans Otto 1931- *IntWW 91*
**Brautigan,** David L 1950- *AmMWSc 92*
**Brautigan,** Lynn Margaret 1966- *WhoFI 92*
**Brautigan,** Richard 1935-1984 *BenetAL 91, ConAu 34NR, FacFETw*
**Brauweiler,** Daniel Charles 1961- *WhoAmL 92*
**Brauwerman,** Jeffrey Norman 1945- *WhoAmL 92*
**Brauwerman,** Suzan Carol 1948- *WhoAmL 92*
**Brauza,** Ellen Lederer 1950- *WhoRel 92*
**Brave,** Georgine Frances 1940- *WhoAmL 92*
**Bravenec,** Edward V 1930- *AmMWSc 92*
**Bravener,** Lee Carin 1950- *WhoWest 92*
**Braver,** Barbara Leix 1938- *WhoRel 92*
**Braverman,** Burt Alan 1946- *WhoAmL 92*
**Braverman,** Charles 1944- *IntMPA 92*
**Braverman,** Charles Dell 1944- *WhoEnt 92*
**Braverman,** David J 1934- *AmMWSc 92*
**Braverman,** Donna Caryn 1947- *WhoWest 92*
**Braverman,** Douglas Mark 1952- *WhoEnt 92*
**Braverman,** Ernest 1933- *WhoFI 92*
**Braverman,** Irwin Merton 1929- *AmMWSc 92*
**Braverman,** Kate 1950- *ConLC 67 [port]*
**Braverman,** Louise Marcia 1948- *WhoFI 92*
**Braverman,** Philip 1933- *WhoFI 92*
**Bravo,** Carlos E. 1959- *WhoHisp 92*
**Bravo,** Carlos Eduardo 1959- *WhoFI 92*
**Bravo,** Facundo D. 1941- *WhoHisp 92*
**Bravo,** Jaime A. 1958- *WhoEnt 92*
**Bravo,** Justo Baladjay 1917- *AmMWSc 92*
**Bravo,** Leonardo 1764-1812 *HisDSpE*
**Bravo,** Martin Maurice B. *Who 92*
**Bravo,** Raul H. 1931- *WhoWest 92*
**Bravo,** Rose Marie 1951- *WhoFI 92*
**Bravo,** Ruben 1913- *WhoHisp 92*
**Brawer,** James Robin 1944- *AmMWSc 92*
**Brawer,** Marc Harris 1946- *WhoAmL 92*
**Brawer,** Steven Arnold 1941- *AmMWSc 92*
**Brawerman,** George 1927- *AmMWSc 92*
**Brawley,** Barry Wade 1965- *WhoEnt 92*
**Brawley,** Benjamin 1882-1939 *BenetAL 91*
**Brawley,** C Robert 1944- *WhoAmP 91*
**Brawley,** Edward M. 1851-1923 *RelLAm 91*
**Brawley,** Ernest *DrAPF 91*
**Brawley,** Ernest 1937- *WrDr 92*
**Brawley,** Joel Vincent, Jr 1938- *AmMWSc 92*
**Brawley,** Susan Howard 1951- *AmMWSc 92*
**Brawn,** Linda Curtis 1947- *WhoAmP 91*
**Brawn,** Mary Karen 1955- *AmMWSc 92*
**Brawne,** Michael 1925- *IntAu&W 91, WrDr 92*
**Brawner,** Thomas A 1945- *AmMWSc 92*
**Braxton,** Anthony 1945- *ConCom 92, NewAmDM*
**Braxton,** Edward Kenneth 1944- *WhoBlA 92*
**Braxton,** Harriet E. 1926- *WhoBlA 92*
**Braxton,** Jodi *DrAPF 91*
**Braxton,** John Ledger 1945- *WhoBlA 92*
**Braxton,** Malva 1905- *WhoAmP 91*
**Bray,** A Philip 1933- *AmMWSc 92*
**Bray,** Absalom Francis, Jr. 1918- *WhoAmL 92*
**Bray,** Allen Anthony 1949- *WhoWest 92*
**Bray,** Austin Coleman, Jr. 1941- *WhoAmL 92*
**Bray,** Bonnie Anderson 1929- *AmMWSc 92*
**Bray,** Bruce G 1930- *AmMWSc 92*
**Bray,** Claude A, Jr 1931- *WhoAmP 91*
**Bray,** Dale Frank 1922- *AmMWSc 92*
**Bray,** David Maurice 1941- *WhoFI 92*
**Bray,** Denis Campbell 1926- *Who 92*
**Bray,** Donald James 1923- *AmMWSc 92*
**Bray,** Donald Lawrence 1942- *WhoRel 92*
**Bray,** Frank T J 1948- *WhoAmP 91*
**Bray,** Gail Etheridge 1948- *WhoAmP 91*
**Bray,** George A 1931- *AmMWSc 92*
**Bray,** James Houston 1926- *WhoAmP 91*
**Bray,** James Wallace, II 1952- *WhoRel 92*
**Bray,** James William 1948- *AmMWSc 92*
**Bray,** Jeremy 1930- *WrDr 92*
**Bray,** Jeremy William 1930- *Who 92*
**Bray,** Joan Lynne 1935- *AmMWSc 92*
**Bray,** John Arthur 1950- *WhoRel 92*
**Bray,** John Donald 1938- *WhoWest 92*
**Bray,** John Jefferson 1912- *IntAu&W 91, IntWW 91, Who 92, WrDr 92*
**Bray,** John R 1929-1978 *FacFETw*
**Bray,** John Roger 1929- *AmMWSc 92*
**Bray,** John Thomas 1944- *AmMWSc 92*
**Bray,** Kenneth Noel Corbett 1929- *Who 92*
**Bray,** Lane *WhoAmP 91*
**Bray,** Larry Evan 1955- *WhoEnt 92*
**Bray,** Laurack Doyle 1949- *WhoAmL 92*
**Bray,** Maureen Elizabeth 1946- *WhoRel 92*
**Bray,** Nicholas 1948- *ConAu 135*
**Bray,** Norman Francis 1938- *AmMWSc 92*
**Bray,** Paul Sheldon 1936- *Who 92*
**Bray,** Philip James 1925- *AmMWSc 92*
**Bray,** Phyllis 1911- *TwCPaSc*
**Bray,** Ralph 1921- *AmMWSc 92, WhoMW 92*
**Bray,** Richard D *WhoAmP 91*
**Bray,** Richard Newton 1945- *AmMWSc 92*
**Bray,** Robert 1942- *DcTwDes*
**Bray,** Robert Bruce 1924- *WhoEnt 92*
**Bray,** Robert Harris 1946- *WhoMW 92*
**Bray,** Robert S 1927- *AmMWSc 92*
**Bray,** Theodor 1905- *Who 92*
**Bray,** William Albert 1924- *WhoFI 92*
**Bray,** William Davenport 1913- *WhoRel 92*
**Bray,** William Howard 1952- *WhoRel 92*
**Bray,** William John 1911- *Who 92*
**Bray,** Winston 1910- *Who 92*
**Braybrook,** Edward John 1911- *Who 92*
**Braybrooke,** Baron 1932- *Who 92*
**Braybrooke,** David 1924- *IntWW 91*
**Braybrooke,** Marcus Christopher Rossi 1938- *Who 92*
**Braybrooke,** Neville 1928- *WrDr 92*
**Braybrooke,** Neville Patrick Bellairs 1925- *Who 92*
**Braye,** Baroness 1941- *Who 92*
**Brayer,** Donald J. 1942- *WhoIns 92*
**Brayer,** Kenneth 1941- *AmMWSc 92*
**Brayer,** Yves d1990 *IntWW 91N*
**Brayfield,** Celia 1945- *WrDr 92*
**Brayfield,** Celia Frances 1945- *IntAu&W 91*
**Brayman,** Harold Halliday 1935- *WhoAmP 91*
**Braymen,** Phyllis A. 1953- *WhoMW 92*
**Braymer,** Hugh Douglas 1933- *AmMWSc 92*
**Brayne,** Richard Bolding 1924- *Who 92*
**Brayne-Baker,** John 1905- *Who 92*
**Brayne-Nicholls,** Brian 1914- *Who 92*
**Braynen,** Alvin 1904- *Who 92*
**Braynon,** Edward J., Jr. 1928- *WhoBlA 92*
**Brayshaw,** Joseph 1912- *Who 92*
**Brayshaw,** Thomas Carlton 1946- *WhoWest 92*
**Brayson,** Albert Aloysius, II 1953- *WhoFI 92*
**Braz,** Darline Kristina 1940- *WhoAmL 92*
**Braz,** Evandro Freitas 1943- *WhoFI 92*
**Brazauskas,** Algirdas-Mikolas Kazevich 1932- *IntWW 91, SovUnBD*
**Brazauskas,** Beverly Mae 1944- *WhoRel 92*
**Brazdil,** James Frank 1953- *WhoMW 92*
**Brazdys,** Antanas 1939- *TwCPaSc*
**Brazdzionis,** Bernardas 1907- *LiExTwC*
**Brazeau,** Gayle A 1957- *AmMWSc 92*
**Brazeau,** Willoughby F. d1991 *NewYTBS 91*
**Brazee,** James Louis, Jr. 1943- *WhoAmL 92*
**Brazee,** Ross D 1930- *AmMWSc 92, WhoMW 92*
**Brazeir,** Thomas J 1930- *WhoAmP 91*
**Brazel,** Anthony James *AmMWSc 92*
**Brazell,** John L. 1939- *WhoIns 92*
**Brazelton,** David Todd 1954- *WhoRel 92*
**Brazelton,** Edgar, Jr. 1913- *WhoBlA 92*
**Brazelton,** William T 1921- *AmMWSc 92*
**Brazer,** Harvey E. 1922-1991 *ConAu 134*
**Brazier,** John Richard 1940- *WhoWest 92*
**Brazier,** Julian William Hendy 1953- *Who 92*
**Brazier,** Martin George 1943- *WhoBlA 92*
**Brazier,** Mary A B *AmMWSc 92*
**Brazier,** Robert G. *WhoWest 92*
**Brazier,** Robert H. B. d1837 *DcNCBi 1*
**Brazier,** Wesley R. 1917- *WhoBlA 92*
**Brazier,** William H. 1922- *WhoBlA 92*
**Brazier-Creagh,** Rupert 1909- *Who 92*
**Brazil,** Ernest L. 1943- *WhoBlA 92*
**Brazil,** Gino T. 1956- *WhoHisp 92*
**Brazil,** Robert D. 1939- *WhoBlA 92*
**Brazile,** Robert Lorenzo, Jr. 1953- *WhoBlA 92*
**Brazina,** Rhonda Freedman 1951- *WhoMW 92*
**Brazington,** Andrew Paul 1918- *WhoBlA 92*
**Brazinsky,** Irving 1936- *AmMWSc 92*
**Brazis,** A Richard 1926- *AmMWSc 92*
**Brazle,** Kenneth Dale 1957- *WhoAmL 92*
**Brazy,** Peter C 1946- *AmMWSc 92*
**Brazzeal,** Marie *WhoAmP 91*
**Brazzel,** Stephen Ray 1964- *WhoRel 92*
**Brazzi,** Rossano 1916- *IntMPA 92*
**Brdas,** Mary Alexine 1929- *WhoRel 92*
**Brea,** Luis C. 1932- *WhoHisp 92*
**Breach,** Gerald Ernest John 1932- *Who 92*
**Breadalbane And Holland,** Earl of 1919- *Who 92*
**Breaden,** Robert William 1937- *Who 92*
**Breakefield,** Xandra Owens 1942- *AmMWSc 92*
**Breaker,** Charles 1906- *TwCPaSc*
**Breaker,** Melanie Kay 1966- *WhoWest 92*
**Breaker,** Richard Carroll 1926- *WhoWest 92*
**Breakey,** Donald Ray 1927- *AmMWSc 92*
**Breakstone,** Alan M 1950- *AmMWSc 92*
**Breakstone,** Donald S. 1945- *WhoAmL 92*
**Breakstone,** Kay Louise 1936- *WhoFI 92*
**Breakwell,** Glynis M. 1952- *WrDr 92*
**Breakwell,** Ian 1943- *TwCPaSc*
**Breakwell,** John 1917- *AmMWSc 92*
**Brealey,** Richard Arthur 1936- *Who 92*
**Bream,** Antony 1943- *TwCPaSc*
**Bream,** Charles Anthony 1915- *AmMWSc 92*
**Bream,** Julian 1933- *IntWW 91, NewAmDM, Who 92, WhoEnt 92*
**Breare,** William Robert Ackrill 1916- *Who 92*
**Brearley,** Christopher John Scott 1943- *Who 92*
**Brearley,** Harrington C, Jr 1926- *AmMWSc 92*
**Brearley,** John Michael 1942- *IntWW 91*
**Brearley,** Michael 1942- *Who 92*
**Brearley,** Mike 1942- *WrDr 92*
**Brears,** Peter C. D. 1944- *WrDr 92*
**Brears,** Peter Charles David 1944- *IntAu&W 91, Who 92*
**Breasher,** Philip M. 1941- *WhoWest 92*
**Breasure,** Rebecca Ann *WhoAmP 91*
**Breathitt,** Edward Thompson, Jr 1924- *WhoAmP 91, WhoFI 92*
**Breathnach,** Aodan S. 1922- *WrDr 92*
**Breault,** George Omer 1942- *AmMWSc 92*
**Breault,** Joseph Lawrence 1949- *WhoMW 92*
**Breault,** Theodore Edward 1938- *WhoAmL 92*
**Breaux,** Billie J *WhoAmP 91*
**Breaux,** Clifton Lynn 1954- *WhoRel 92*
**Breaux,** Helen Isabel 1934- *WhoRel 92*
**Breaux,** John B. 1944- *AlmAP 92 [port], IntWW 91, WhoAmP 91*
**Breaux,** Michael Joseph 1949- *WhoAmL 92*
**Breaux,** Paul Joseph 1942- *WhoAmL 92*
**Breazeale,** Almut Frerichs 1938- *AmMWSc 92*
**Breazeale,** Mack Alfred 1930- *AmMWSc 92*
**Breazeale,** Michael John 1964- *WhoEnt 92*
**Breazeale,** Robert David 1935- *AmMWSc 92*
**Breazeale,** Vicki Diane 1949- *WhoWest 92*
**Breazeale,** William Horace, Jr 1938- *AmMWSc 92*
**Breazile,** James E 1934- *AmMWSc 92*
**Brebner,** Jean Ann 1923- *WhoEnt 92*
**Brebrick,** Robert Frank, Jr 1925- *AmMWSc 92*
**Brechbill,** Susan Reynolds 1943- *WhoWest 92*
**Brecher,** Armin G. 1942- *WhoAmL 92*
**Brecher,** Arthur Seymour 1928- *AmMWSc 92*
**Brecher,** Aviva 1945- *AmMWSc 92*
**Brecher,** Charles 1932- *AmMWSc 92*
**Brecher,** George 1913- *AmMWSc 92*
**Brecher,** Irving *WhoEnt 92*
**Brecher,** Irving 1914- *IntMPA 92*
**Brecher,** Kenneth 1943- *AmMWSc 92*
**Brecher,** Michael 1925- *IntAu&W 91, IntWW 91, WrDr 92*
**Brecher,** Peter I 1940- *AmMWSc 92*
**Brechin,** Bishop of 1932- *Who 92*
**Brechin,** Dean of *Who 92*
**Brechner,** Beverly Lorraine 1936- *AmMWSc 92*
**Brechner,** Larry Allen 1955- *WhoEnt 92*
**Brecht,** Bertolt 1891-1956 *FacFETw [port]*
**Brecht,** Bertolt 1898-1956 *ConAu 133, EncTR 91 [port], LiExTwC*
**Brecht,** Patrick Ernest 1946- *AmMWSc 92*
**Brecht,** Paul Nicholas, Jr. 1935- *WhoMW 92*
**Brecht,** Sally Ann 1951- *WhoFI 92*
**Breck,** Allen du Pont 1914- *WhoWest 92*
**Brecke,** Barry John 1947- *AmMWSc 92*
**Breckenridge,** Adam 1916- *WrDr 92*
**Breckenridge,** Alasdair Muir 1937- *IntWW 91, Who 92*
**Breckenridge,** Alexander Douglas 1966- *WhoMW 92*
**Breckenridge,** Bruce 1926- *AmMWSc 92*
**Breckenridge,** Carl 1942- *AmMWSc 92*
**Breckenridge,** Franklin E. *WhoBlA 92*
**Breckenridge,** Gerald 1899-1964 *ScFEYrs*
**Breckenridge,** Jackie B. 1941- *WhoBlA 92*
**Breckenridge,** James 1935- *WhoRel 92*
**Breckenridge,** Jill *DrAPF 91*
**Breckenridge,** John L. 1913- *WhoBlA 92*
**Breckenridge,** John Robert 1920- *AmMWSc 92*
**Breckenridge,** Ray E. 1932- *WhoAmL 92*
**Breckenridge,** Robert A 1924- *AmMWSc 92*
**Breckenridge,** Robert Paul 1955- *WhoWest 92*
**Breckenridge,** William Callow 1951- *WhoRel 92*
**Breckenridge,** William H 1941- *AmMWSc 92*
**Brecker,** Jeffrey Ross 1953- *WhoAmL 92*
**Brecker,** Randal Edward 1945- *WhoEnt 92*
**Breckinridge,** James Bernard 1939- *AmMWSc 92*
**Breckinridge,** John Cabell 1821-1875 *AmPolLe*
**Breckinridge,** Sophonisba 1886-1948 *WomSoc*
**Breckner,** Anthony Jacob 1953- *WhoFI 92*
**Breckner,** Jane McMillin 1915- *WhoMW 92*
**Brecknock,** Earl of 1965- *Who 92*
**Breda,** Malcolm J. 1934- *WhoBlA 92*
**Bredahl,** Edward Arlan 1937- *AmMWSc 92*
**Breddan,** Joe 1950- *WhoWest 92*
**Bredeck,** Henry E 1927- *AmMWSc 92*
**Bredehoeft,** John Dallas 1933- *AmMWSc 92*

**Bredehoft**, Elaine Charlson 1958- *WhoAmL 92*
**Bredehoft**, John Michael 1958- *WhoAmL 92*
**Bredel**, Willi 1907-1964 *EncTR 91*
**Bredenberg**, Carl Eric 1940- *AmMWSc 92*
**Breder**, Charles Vincent 1940- *AmMWSc 92*
**Bredes**, Don *DrAPF 91*
**Bredesen**, Philip Norman 1943- *WhoFI 92*
**Bredeson**, Dean Kardell 1921- *WhoFI 92*
**Bredeson**, James Clemens 1956- *WhoRel 92*
**Bredeweg**, Robert Allen 1941- *AmMWSc 92*
**Bredfeldt**, John Creighton 1947- *WhoMW 92*
**Brediceanu**, Mihai 1920- *WhoEnt 92*
**Bredin**, Humphrey Edgar Nicholson 1916- *Who 92*
**Bredin**, James John 1924- *Who 92*
**Bredon**, Glen E 1932- *AmMWSc 92*
**Bredsdorff**, Elias 1912- *IntWW 91*
**Bredsdorff**, Elias Lunn 1912- *WrDr 92*
**Bredt**, Jack B. 1926- *WhoFI 92*
**Bree**, Alan V 1932- *AmMWSc 92*
**Bree**, Germaine 1907- *ConAu 15AS [port], IntWW 91, WrDr 92*
**Breece**, Harry T, III 1939- *AmMWSc 92*
**Breece**, Viola 1911- *WhoMW 92*
**Breecher**, Sheila Rae 1953- *WhoAmL 92*
**Breed**, Carol Sameth 1933- *AmMWSc 92*
**Breed**, Daniel 1825?- *BiInAmS*
**Breed**, Eileen Judith 1945- *WhoMW 92*
**Breed**, Ernest Spencer 1913- *AmMWSc 92*
**Breed**, Helen Illick 1925- *AmMWSc 92*
**Breed**, Henry Eltinge 1915- *AmMWSc 92*
**Breed**, James Lincoln 1944- *WhoRel 92*
**Breed**, Laurence Woods 1924- *AmMWSc 92*
**Breed**, Michael Dallam 1951- *AmMWSc 92*
**Breed**, William Joseph 1928- *AmMWSc 92*
**Breeden**, David *DrAPF 91, WhoEnt 92*
**Breeden**, Douglas Tower 1950- *WhoFI 92*
**Breeden**, James Pleasant 1934- *WhoBlA 92*
**Breeden**, John Elbert 1931- *AmMWSc 92*
**Breeden**, Kenneth Ray 1938- *WhoFI 92, WhoWest 92*
**Breeden**, Rex Earl 1920- *WhoMW 92*
**Breeden**, Richard C *WhoAmP 91, WhoFI 92*
**Breeden**, Richard C. 1949- *NewYTBS 91 [port], WhoAmL 92*
**Breeding**, Carl L. 1932- *WhoBlA 92*
**Breeding**, Carl Wayne 1954- *WhoAmL 92*
**Breeding**, J Ernest, Jr 1938- *AmMWSc 92*
**Breedlove**, Charles B 1916- *AmMWSc 92*
**Breedlove**, Joseph Penn 1874-1955 *DcNCBi 1*
**Breedlove**, Keith R *WhoAmP 91*
**Breedlove**, Michael M 1940- *WhoAmP 91*
**Breedlove**, S. Marc 1954- *WhoWest 92*
**Breen**, Barton James 1962- *WhoRel 92*
**Breen**, Dale H 1925- *AmMWSc 92*
**Breen**, Daniel Anthony 1928- *WhoFI 92*
**Breen**, David Hart 1960- *WhoAmL 92*
**Breen**, Faith Fei-Mei Lee 1951- *WhoFI 92*
**Breen**, Gail Anne Marie *AmMWSc 92*
**Breen**, Geoffrey Brian 1944- *Who 92*
**Breen**, George Edward 1911- *IntAu&W 91*
**Breen**, James Langhorne 1926- *AmMWSc 92*
**Breen**, John E 1932- *AmMWSc 92*
**Breen**, John Richard 1934- *WhoFI 92*
**Breen**, Jon L. 1943- *WrDr 92*
**Breen**, Joseph John 1942- *AmMWSc 92*
**Breen**, Marie 1902- *Who 92*
**Breen**, Marilyn 1944- *AmMWSc 92*
**Breen**, Moira 1923- *AmMWSc 92*
**Breen**, Nelson Edward 1945- *WhoEnt 92*
**Breen**, Paula Virginia 1943- *WhoRel 92*
**Breen**, Riobart Eadbard 1967- *WhoRel 92*
**Breen**, Thomas John 1948- *WhoFI 92*
**Breen**, Walter Henry 1928- *WhoWest 92*
**Breene**, William Michael 1930- *AmMWSc 92*
**Breer**, Carl 1883-1970 *DcTwDes*
**Breese**, Claude Rader 1930- *WhoAmL 92*
**Breese**, George Richard 1936- *AmMWSc 92*
**Breese**, Gerald 1912- *WrDr 92*
**Breese**, John Allen 1951- *WhoFI 92, WhoMW 92*
**Breese**, Mary 1721-1799 *EncAmaz 91*
**Breese**, Sydney Salisbury, Jr 1922- *AmMWSc 92*
**Breeze**, Alastair Jon 1934- *Who 92*
**Breeze**, David John 1944- *IntAu&W 91*
**Breeze**, William Hancock 1923- *WhoFI 92, WhoIns 92*
**Breg**, Leslie Dove 1942- *WhoMW 92*
**Breg**, William Roy 1923- *AmMWSc 92*
**Bregar**, William S 1941- *AmMWSc 92*
**Breger**, Brian *DrAPF 91*
**Breger**, Marshall Jordan 1946- *WhoAmP 91*
**Breggin**, Janis Ann 1955- *WhoAmL 92*
**Breggin**, Peter R 1936- *ConAu 34NR*
**Breglia**, Rudolph John 1947- *AmMWSc 92*
**Bregman**, Allyn A 1941- *AmMWSc 92*
**Bregman**, Arthur Randolph 1946- *WhoAmL 92*
**Bregman**, David 1940- *AmMWSc 92*
**Bregman**, Jacob I 1923- *WhoAmP 91*
**Bregman**, Jacob Israel 1923- *AmMWSc 92*
**Bregman**, Jenn Swenson 1960- *WhoAmL 92*
**Bregman**, Martin *WhoEnt 92*
**Bregman**, Martin 1931- *IntMPA 92*
**Bregou**, Christian Robert 1941- *IntWW 91*
**Bregvadze**, Nani Georgevna 1938- *IntWW 91*
**Brehm**, Bertram George, Jr 1926- *AmMWSc 92*
**Brehm**, Bruno 1892-1974 *EncTR 91 [port]*
**Brehm**, Frederick Carl 1930- *WhoFI 92*
**Brehm**, John Joseph 1934- *AmMWSc 92*
**Brehm**, Lawrence Paul 1948- *AmMWSc 92*
**Brehm**, Warren John 1925- *AmMWSc 92*
**Brehm**, William Allen, Jr. 1945- *WhoMW 92*
**Brehm**, William Frederick 1940- *AmMWSc 92*
**Brehme**, Robert W 1930- *AmMWSc 92*
**Brehmer**, Morris Leroy 1925- *AmMWSc 92*
**Brehob**, W M 1936- *AmMWSc 92*
**Brehon**, James Gloster 1740?-1819 *DcNCBi 1*
**Brehony**, John Albert Noel 1936- *Who 92*
**Breidenbach**, Cherie Elizabeth 1952- *WhoAmL 92*
**Breidenbach**, Rowland William 1935- *AmMWSc 92*
**Breidenthal**, Robert Edward 1951- *WhoWest 92*
**Breig**, Edward Louis 1932- *AmMWSc 92*
**Breig**, Marvin L 1934- *AmMWSc 92*
**Breil**, David A 1938- *AmMWSc 92*
**Breil**, Sandra J 1937- *AmMWSc 92*
**Breiland**, John Gustavson 1905- *AmMWSc 92*
**Breillatt**, Julian Paul, Jr 1938- *AmMWSc 92*
**Breimer**, Stephen Fabian 1951- *WhoEnt 92*
**Breimyer**, Harold F. 1914- *WrDr 92*
**Breinburg**, Petronella 1927- *IntAu&W 91*
**Breiner**, Richard Harry 1935- *WhoAmL 92, WhoWest 92*
**Breiner**, Rosemary 1937- *WhoHisp 92*
**Breiner**, Sheldon 1936- *AmMWSc 92*
**Breines**, Paul 1941- *WrDr 92*
**Breipohl**, Arthur M 1931- *AmMWSc 92*
**Breipohl**, Walter Eugene 1953- *WhoMW 92*
**Breisch**, Eric Alan 1950- *AmMWSc 92*
**Breit**, Gregory 1899- *FacFETw*
**Breit**, Jeffrey Arnold 1955- *WhoAmL 92*
**Breit**, John Louis 1947- *WhoAmL 92*
**Breit**, Luke *DrAPF 91*
**Breitbart**, Barbara Renee 1935- *WhoWest 92*
**Breitbarth**, Richard Jay 1948- *WhoFI 92*
**Breitbarth**, S. Robert 1925- *WhoFI 92*
**Breitbarth**, Steven Eldor 1949- *WhoRel 92*
**Breitbeil**, Fred W, III 1931- *AmMWSc 92*
**Breitel**, Charles D. d1991 *NewYTBS 91 [port]*
**Breitenbach**, Douglas Lee 1944- *WhoAmL 92*
**Breitenbach**, E A 1936- *AmMWSc 92*
**Breitenbach**, Eugene Allen 1936- *WhoWest 92*
**Breitenbach**, Robert Peter 1923- *AmMWSc 92*
**Breitenbeck**, Joseph M. 1914- *WhoRel 92*
**Breitenberger**, Ernst 1924- *AmMWSc 92*
**Breitenfeld**, Frederick, Jr. 1931- *WhoEnt 92*
**Breitenstein**, Bill Douglas 1943- *WhoFI 92*
**Breithaupt**, Lea Joseph, Jr 1929- *AmMWSc 92*
**Breitkreutz**, Anne Marie 1965- *WhoAmL 92*
**Breitman**, Theodore Ronald 1931- *AmMWSc 92*
**Breitmann**, Hans *BenetAL 91*
**Breitmayer**, Theodore 1922- *AmMWSc 92*
**Breitnauer**, Paul J. 1939- *WhoIns 92*
**Breitner**, Gerard T. 1947- *WhoFI 92*
**Breitscheid**, Rudolf 1874-1944 *EncTR 91 [port]*
**Breitschwerdt**, Edward B 1948- *AmMWSc 92*
**Breitschwerdt**, Werner 1927- *IntWW 91*
**Breittholz**, Brian Eric 1963- *WhoMW 92*
**Breitweiser**, James Russell 1936- *WhoFI 92*
**Breitwieser**, Charles J 1910- *AmMWSc 92*
**Breitwieser**, R. *WhoRel 92*
**Breitzer**, Gerard Martin 1948- *WhoMW 92*
**Breker**, Arlo 1900- *EncTR 91 [port]*
**Breker-Cooper**, Steven Mark 1947- *WhoAmL 92*
**Brekhov**, Konstantin Ivanovich 1907- *IntWW 91*
**Brekhovskikh**, Leonid Maksimovich 1917- *IntWW 91*
**Brekke**, Clark Joseph 1944- *AmMWSc 92*
**Brekke**, Elizabeth Marie 1942- *WhoMW 92*
**Brekke**, Joanne J *WhoAmP 91*
**Brekke**, Kris 1954- *WhoAmP 91*
**Brekke**, Lola M 1931- *WhoAmP 91*
**Brekke**, Paul Norman 1956- *WhoFI 92*
**Brel**, Jacques 1929-1978 *FacFETw*
**Breland**, Allen McInnis 1958- *WhoFI 92*
**Breland**, Annis Pepper 1938- *WhoAmL 92*
**Breland**, H Terrell *WhoAmP 91*
**Breland**, Mark 1963- *BlkOlyM*
**Breland**, Rupert Earl 1935- *WhoAmP 91*
**Brelis**, Matthew 1957- *IntAu&W 91*
**Breman**, Jan 1936- *IntWW 91*
**Breman**, Joseph Eliot 1945- *WhoAmL 92*
**Bremberg**, Ginger *WhoAmP 91*
**Bremberg**, Virginia *WhoWest 92*
**Bremby**, Roderick LeMar 1960- *WhoBlA 92*
**Bremel**, Robert Duane 1945- *AmMWSc 92*
**Bremen**, Ronald David 1950- *WhoAmL 92*
**Brement**, Marshall 1932- *WhoAmP 91*
**Bremer**, Charles E. 1941- *WhoBlA 92*
**Bremer**, Christine Agnes 1953- *WhoAmL 92*
**Bremer**, Christine Dodge 1952- *WhoMW 92*
**Bremer**, Donald Duane 1934- *WhoWest 92*
**Bremer**, Frederika 1801-1865 *BenetAL 91*
**Bremer**, Hans 1927- *AmMWSc 92*
**Bremer**, John Paul 1926- *WhoFI 92*
**Bremer**, John Paul 1941- *WhoFI 92*
**Bremer**, Jon 1928- *IntWW 91*
**Bremer**, Keith George 1927- *AmMWSc 92*
**Bremer**, Kevin Louis 1958- *WhoMW 92*
**Bremer**, L Paul 1941- *WhoAmP 91*
**Bremer**, Sidney Hillyer 1944- *WhoMW 92*
**Bremermann**, Hans J 1926- *AmMWSc 92*
**Bremmer**, Bart J 1930- *AmMWSc 92*
**Bremner**, D Roger 1937- *WhoAmP 91*
**Bremner**, John McColl 1922- *AmMWSc 92*
**Bremner**, Raymond Wilson 1904- *AmMWSc 92*
**Bremner**, Steven Scott 1950- *WhoWest 92*
**Bremner**, William John 1943- *AmMWSc 92*
**Bremridge**, John 1925- *Who 92*
**Bremridge**, John Henry 1925- *IntWW 91*
**Brems**, David Paul 1950- *WhoWest 92*
**Brems**, Hans J 1915- *IntAu&W 91, WrDr 92*
**Brems**, Hans Julius 1915- *WhoFI 92, WhoMW 92*
**Bremser**, George, Jr. 1928- *WhoWest 92*
**Bremser**, Ray *DrAPF 91*
**Bremser**, Ray 1934- *ConPo 91, WrDr 92*
**Brenan**, Gerald *IntAu&W 91X*
**Brenan**, Gerald 1894- *IntAu&W 91*
**Brenchley**, Gayle Anne 1951- *AmMWSc 92*
**Brenchley**, Jean Elnora 1944- *AmMWSc 92*
**Brenchley**, Thomas Frank 1918- *IntWW 91, Who 92*
**Brendel**, Alfred 1931- *IntWW 91, NewAmDM, Who 92*
**Brendel**, Klaus 1933- *AmMWSc 92*
**Brenden**, John C, II 1941- *WhoAmP 91*
**Brender**, Ronald Franklin 1943- *AmMWSc 92*
**Brendle**, Kenneth Lee *WhoIns 92*
**Brendley**, William H, Jr 1938- *AmMWSc 92*
**Brendlinger**, Darwin 1934- *AmMWSc 92*
**Brendlinger**, Jack Allen 1933- *WhoEnt 92*
**Brendon**, Piers 1940- *WrDr 92*
**Brendon**, Piers George Rundle 1940- *IntAu&W 91*
**Brendon**, Rupert Timothy Rundle 1943- *WhoFI 92*
**Brendsel**, Leland C. *WhoFI 92*
**Breneman**, David Clinton, II 1959- *WhoEnt 92*
**Breneman**, Edwin Jay 1927- *AmMWSc 92*
**Breneman**, William C 1941- *AmMWSc 92*
**Breneman**, William Dudley 1943- *WhoAmL 92*
**Brener**, Rochelle Diane 1945- *IntAu&W 91*
**Brener**, Roland 1942- *TwCPaSc*
**Brenerman**, David H 1951- *WhoAmP 91*
**Brengel**, Fred Lenhardt 1923- *WhoFI 92, WhoMW 92*
**Brengelman**, Fred 1928- *ConAu 134*
**Brengelmann**, George Leslie *AmMWSc 92*
**Brengle**, Samuel Logan 1860-1939 *RelLAm 91*
**Brengle**, Thomas Alan 1952- *WhoWest 92*
**Brengle**, Timothy James 1954- *WhoWest 92*
**Brenholdt**, Irving R *AmMWSc 92*
**Brenikov**, Paul 1921- *Who 92*
**Brenkert**, Dennis Richard 1945- *WhoWest 92*
**Brenkert**, Karl, Jr 1921- *AmMWSc 92*
**Brennan**, Anthony John Edward 1927- *Who 92*
**Brennan**, Archibald Orr *Who 92*
**Brennan**, Barbara Jane 1936- *WhoWest 92*
**Brennan**, Bernard Francis 1938- *WhoFI 92, WhoMW 92*
**Brennan**, Brian John 1918- *Who 92*
**Brennan**, C.J. 1870-1932 *RfGEnL 91*
**Brennan**, Charles Martin, III 1942- *WhoFI 92*
**Brennan**, Christopher Patrick 1953- *WhoRel 92*
**Brennan**, Ciaran Brendan 1944- *WhoFI 92, WhoWest 92*
**Brennan**, Daniel Christopher 1954- *WhoAmL 92*
**Brennan**, Daniel Edward, Jr. 1942- *WhoAmL 92*
**Brennan**, Daniel Joseph 1929- *AmMWSc 92*
**Brennan**, Daniel Joseph 1942- *Who 92*
**Brennan**, Daniel Macauley 1930- *WhoEnt 92*
**Brennan**, David Leo 1931- *WhoFI 92, WhoMW 92*
**Brennan**, David Michael 1929- *AmMWSc 92*
**Brennan**, Dennis Joseph 1937- *WhoAmL 92*
**Brennan**, Doris Alene 1920- *WhoAmP 91*
**Brennan**, Edward 1915- *WhoAmP 91*
**Brennan**, Edward A. 1934- *IntWW 91, Who 92, WhoFI 92, WhoMW 92*
**Brennan**, Eileen 1935- *IntMPA 92*
**Brennan**, Eileen Regina 1935- *WhoEnt 92*
**Brennan**, Francis 1895-1968 *RelLAm 91*
**Brennan**, Francis W. 1919- *WhoAmL 92*
**Brennan**, Gerard 1928- *Who 92*
**Brennan**, James 1952- *WhoAmP 91*
**Brennan**, James A 1920- *AmMWSc 92*
**Brennan**, James Gerard 1927- *AmMWSc 92*
**Brennan**, James Joseph 1936- *WhoAmL 92*
**Brennan**, James Joseph 1950- *WhoAmL 92*
**Brennan**, James Patrick, Sr. 1947- *WhoAmL 92*
**Brennan**, James Robert 1930- *AmMWSc 92*
**Brennan**, James Robert 1935- *WhoMW 92*
**Brennan**, James Thomas 1916- *AmMWSc 92*
**Brennan**, Jerry Michael 1944- *WhoWest 92*
**Brennan**, John 1949- *TwCPaSc*
**Brennan**, John A, Jr 1945- *WhoAmP 91*
**Brennan**, John Christopher 1949- *IntAu&W 91*
**Brennan**, John Edward 1928- *WhoFI 92*
**Brennan**, John Francis, Jr. 1935- *WhoAmL 92*
**Brennan**, John Joseph 1938- *AmMWSc 92*
**Brennan**, John Joseph 1951- *WhoRel 92*
**Brennan**, John Joseph 1958- *WhoAmL 92*
**Brennan**, John Merritt 1935- *WhoFI 92*
**Brennan**, John V. 1934- *WhoIns 92*
**Brennan**, Joseph Edward 1934- *IntWW 91, WhoAmP 91*
**Brennan**, Joseph Francis Xavier 1939- *WhoIns 92*
**Brennan**, Joseph Patrick, Jr. 1944- *WhoAmL 92*
**Brennan**, Joseph Payne 1918- *IntAu&W 91*
**Brennan**, Lawrence Edward 1927- *AmMWSc 92*
**Brennan**, Louise Smith 1922- *WhoAmP 91*
**Brennan**, Maeve *DrAPF 91*
**Brennan**, Martin A 1946- *WhoIns 92*
**Brennan**, Mary 1954- *WhoAmP 91*
**Brennan**, Mary Alice 1937- *WhoMW 92*
**Brennan**, Mary Murphy 1919- *WhoAmL 92*
**Brennan**, Matthew *DrAPF 91*
**Brennan**, Matthew John 1961- *WhoMW 92*
**Brennan**, Michael Edward 1941- *AmMWSc 92*
**Brennan**, Michael James 1921- *AmMWSc 92*
**Brennan**, Michael Patrick 1944- *WhoEnt 92*
**Brennan**, Murray F 1940- *AmMWSc 92*
**Brennan**, Neil F. 1923- *WrDr 92*
**Brennan**, Patricia Conlon 1932- *AmMWSc 92*
**Brennan**, Patrick Francis 1931- *WhoFI 92, WhoMW 92*
**Brennan**, Patrick Joseph 1938- *AmMWSc 92*
**Brennan**, Paul Joseph 1920- *AmMWSc 92*
**Brennan**, Richard Grey 1956- *WhoEnt 92*
**Brennan**, Richard Robert, Jr. 1954- *WhoWest 92*

Brennan, Richard Snyder 1938- WhoAmL 92
Brennan, Robert Emmet 1957- WhoWest 92
Brennan, Robert Francis 1959- WhoAmL 92
Brennan, Robert Walter 1934- WhoMW 92
Brennan, Seamus 1948- IntWW 91
Brennan, Stephen Michael 1964- WhoMW 92
Brennan, T. Casey 1948- WhoMW 92
Brennan, Thomas Emmett 1929- WhoAmL 92
Brennan, Thomas Michael 1941- AmMWSc 92
Brennan, Tim SmATA 65
Brennan, Timothy Louis 1957- WhoAmP 91
Brennan, Walt TwCWW 91
Brennan, Will TwCWW 91
Brennan, William Collins, Jr. 1951- WhoAmL 92
Brennan, William J, Jr 1906- FacFETw [port], WhoAmP 91
Brennan, William Joseph, Jr. 1906- IntWW 91, Who 92, WhoAmL 92
Brennan, William Thomas 1925- WhoFI 92
Brennecke, Allen Eugene 1937- WhoAmL 92
Brennecke, Henry Martin 1924- AmMWSc 92
Brennecke, Llewellyn F 1923- AmMWSc 92
Brenneis, Donald Lawrence 1946- WhoWest 92
Brenneman, Frederica S. 1926- WhoAmL 92
Brenneman, Helen Good 1925- WrDr 92
Brenneman, Hugh Warren, Jr. 1945- WhoAmL 92, WhoMW 92
Brenneman, James Alden 1943- AmMWSc 92, WhoMW 92
Brenneman, John 1945- WhoFI 92
Brenneman, John David 1942- WhoAmP 91, WhoWest 92
Brenneman, John M. 1816-1895 AmPeW
Brenneman, Mary Louise 1923- WhoWest 92
Brennemann, Andrew E, Jr 1925- AmMWSc 92
Brennen, William Elbert 1930- WhoFI 92
Brennenstuhl, Henry Brent WhoAmL 92
Brenner, Abner 1908- AmMWSc 92
Brenner, Alan 1946- AmMWSc 92
Brenner, Albert 1926- WhoEnt 92
Brenner, Alfred Ephraim 1931- AmMWSc 92
Brenner, Barbara 1925- SmATA 14AS [port]
Brenner, Barry Morton 1937- AmMWSc 92
Brenner, Daeg Scott 1939- AmMWSc 92
Brenner, Daniel L. 1951- WhoAmL 92
Brenner, David 1945- ConAu 133, WhoEnt 92
Brenner, Donald Charles 1955- WhoEnt 92
Brenner, Donald Leonard 1939- WhoMW 92
Brenner, Donald Robert 1936- WhoFI 92
Brenner, Dori ConTFT 9
Brenner, Douglas 1938- AmMWSc 92
Brenner, Edgar H. 1930- WhoAmL 92
Brenner, Edward John 1923- WhoAmL 92
Brenner, Egon 1925- AmMWSc 92
Brenner, Fivel Cecil 1918- AmMWSc 92
Brenner, Frederic J 1936- AmMWSc 92
Brenner, George Marvin 1943- AmMWSc 92
Brenner, Gerald Donald 1963- WhoRel 92
Brenner, Gerald Stanley 1934- AmMWSc 92
Brenner, Gilbert J 1933- AmMWSc 92
Brenner, Henry Clifton 1946- AmMWSc 92
Brenner, Howard 1929- AmMWSc 92
Brenner, Janet Maybin Walker WhoAmL 92
Brenner, John Francis 1941- AmMWSc 92
Brenner, Jonathan Andrew 1960- WhoAmL 92
Brenner, Joseph 1918- IntMPA 92
Brenner, Lorry Jack 1923- AmMWSc 92
Brenner, Mark 1942- AmMWSc 92
Brenner, Mark Lee 1942- WhoMW 92
Brenner, Marshall Leib 1933- WhoAmL 92, WhoFI 92
Brenner, Michael James 1949- WhoMW 92
Brenner, Mortimer W 1912- AmMWSc 92
Brenner, Raymond Anthony 1943- WhoRel 92
Brenner, Reeve Robert 1936- WhoRel 92
Brenner, Rena Claudy WhoFI 92
Brenner, Richard Joseph 1953- AmMWSc 92
Brenner, Robert Murray 1929- AmMWSc 92
Brenner, Saul Daniel 1962- WhoAmL 92
Brenner, Sidney S 1927- AmMWSc 92
Brenner, Stephen Louis 1948- AmMWSc 92
Brenner, Summer DrAPF 91
Brenner, Susan Woolf 1947- WhoAmL 92
Brenner, Sydney 1927- FacFETw, IntWW 91, Who 92
Brenner, Yehojachin Simon 1926- WrDr 92
Brennert, Alan Michael 1954- WhoEnt 92
Brennessel, Barbara A 1948- AmMWSc 92
Brenniman, Gary Russell 1942- AmMWSc 92
Brenon, Herbert 1880-1958 IntDcF 2-2 [port]
Brenon, John Gene 1948- WhoAmL 92
Brenowitz, A Harry 1918- AmMWSc 92
Brenson, Verdel Lee 1925- WhoBlA 92
Brent, Andrew Jackson 1918- WhoAmL 92
Brent, Anne Marie 1926- WhoAmP 91
Brent, Benny Earl 1937- AmMWSc 92
Brent, Charles Henry 1862-1929 DcEcMov
Brent, Charles Ray 1931- AmMWSc 92
Brent, Daniel Franklin 1945- WhoAmL 92
Brent, David L. 1929- WhoBlA 92
Brent, Ira Martin 1944- WhoWest 92
Brent, J Allen 1921- AmMWSc 92
Brent, Jason G. 1936- WhoAmL 92
Brent, John Clinton, Jr. 1937- WhoBlA 92
Brent, Leslie 1925- Who 92
Brent, Loring 1892-1967 ScFEYrs
Brent, Madeleine WrDr 92
Brent, Michael Leon 1936- Who 92
Brent, Morgan McKenzie 1923- AmMWSc 92
Brent, Paul Leslie 1916- WhoWest 92
Brent, Paul M. 1960- WhoAmL 92
Brent, Richard Peirce 1946- IntWW 91
Brent, Richard Samuel 1949- WhoWest 92
Brent, Robert Leonard 1927- AmMWSc 92
Brent, Ruth Stumpe 1951- WhoMW 92
Brent, Thomas Peter 1937- AmMWSc 92
Brent, William B 1924- AmMWSc 92
Brentano, Lowell 1895-1950 BenetAL 91
Brentford, Viscount 1933- Who 92
Brenti, Francesco WhoMW 92
Brentjens, Jan R 1936- AmMWSc 92
Brentlinger, Paul Smith 1927- WhoFI 92
Brenton, Howard 1942- IntAu&W 91, IntWW 91, Who 92, WrDr 92
Brenton, June Grimm 1918- AmMWSc 92
Brenton, Marianne WhoAmP 91
Brents, Barbara Gayle 1957- WhoWest 92
Brentwood, Bishop of 1936- Who 92
Brereton, Donald 1945- Who 92
Brereton, F S 1872-1957 ScFEYrs
Brereton, John BenetAL 91
Bres, Philip Wayne 1950- WhoWest 92
Bresani, Federico Fernando 1945- WhoFI 92
Brescia, Vincent Thomas 1930- AmMWSc 92
Bresciani, Italo 1890-1964 BiDExR
Bresee, Phineas 1838-1915 RelLAm 91
Bresee, Wilmer Edgar 1910- WhoFI 92
Bresette, Linna Eleanor d1960 HanAmWH
Breshears, Jon Chandler 1945- WhoRel 92
Breshears, Wilbert Dale 1939- AmMWSc 92
Breshkovskaya, Ekaterina EncAmaz 91
Bresis, Vilnis-Edvin Gedertovich 1938- SovUnBD
Bresis, Vilnis-Edvins 1938- IntWW 91
Breske, Roger M WhoAmP 91
Bresky, Jan Barton 1951-1991 WhoRel 92
Breslau, Barry Richard 1942- AmMWSc 92
Breslau, Leigh Stanton 1956- WhoMW 92
Breslauer, Samuel Daniel 1942- WhoRel 92
Breslawsky, Marc C. 1942- WhoFI 92
Bresler, Aaron D 1924- AmMWSc 92
Bresler, B 1918- AmMWSc 92
Bresler, Boris 1918- WhoRel 92
Bresler, Jack Barry 1923- AmMWSc 92
Bresler, Martin I. 1931- WhoAmL 92
Breslerman, Lee Howard 1950- WhoAmL 92
Breslin, Hugh Joseph, III 1955- WhoEnt 92
Breslin, Jimmy 1930- WrDr 92
Breslin, John Bernard 1943- WhoRel 92
Breslin, John P 1919- AmMWSc 92
Breslin, Mark James 1959- WhoWest 92
Breslin, Mary 1936- WhoRel 92
Breslin, Michael Edward 1937- WhoAmL 92
Breslin, Michael Francis 1944- WhoEnt 92
Breslin, Patricia 1959- WhoAmL 92
Breslin, Peg McDonnell 1946- WhoAmP 91
Breslin, Thomas Raymond 1944- WhoFI 92
Breslow, David Samuel 1916- AmMWSc 92
Breslow, Esther M G 1931- AmMWSc 92
Breslow, Jan Leslie 1943- AmMWSc 92
Breslow, John WhoAmP 91
Breslow, Lester 1915- AmMWSc 92, IntWW 91
Breslow, Maurice 1935- ConAu 133
Breslow, Michael DrAPF 91
Breslow, Norman Edward 1941- AmMWSc 92
Breslow, Ronald 1931- AmMWSc 92
Breslow, Ronald Charles 1931- IntWW 91
Bresnahan, Arthur Stephen 1944- WhoAmL 92
Bresnahan, David Parsons 1930- WhoIns 92
Bresnahan, James Patrick 1954- WhoWest 92
Bresnan, William J. LesBEnT 92
Bresnick, Edward 1930- AmMWSc 92
Bresnick, Martin 1944- ConCom 92
Bresnick, Martin 1946- WhoEnt 92
Bresnick, William Orrin 1949- WhoAmL 92
Bress, Michael E. 1933- WhoAmL 92
Bress, Sol 1948- WhoEnt 92
Bressan, Paul Louis 1947- WhoAmL 92
Bressani, Ricardo 1926- IntWW 91
Bressel, Bernd 1966- WhoEnt 92
Bressi, Betty DrAPF 91
Bressler, Arnold Nacht 1949- WhoAmL 92
Bressler, Barry Evan 1947- WhoAmL 92
Bressler, Bernard 1917- AmMWSc 92
Bressler, Bernard Harvey 1944- AmMWSc 92
Bressler, Carl 1955- WhoEnt 92
Bressler, David Wilson 1923- AmMWSc 92
Bressler, Gary David 1956- WhoAmL 92
Bressler, Jerome George, Jr. 1948- WhoFI 92
Bressler, Philip Jack 1954- WhoFI 92
Bressler, Richard Main 1930- WhoFI 92, WhoWest 92
Bressler, Rubin AmMWSc 92
Bressler, Steven L 1951- AmMWSc 92
Bresson, Clarence Richard 1925- AmMWSc 92
Bresson, Robert 1901- IntWW 91, Who 92
Bresson, Robert 1907- FacFETw, IntDcF 2-2 [port], IntMPA 92
Bressoud, David Marius 1950- AmMWSc 92
Brest, Albert N 1928- AmMWSc 92
Brest, Alexander 1894- WhoEnt 92
Brest, Martin 1951- IntMPA 92, WhoEnt 92
Brest, Paul 1940- WhoAmL 92
Brestel, William Jack 1950- WhoMW 92
Brester, Ronald Bernard 1950- WhoMW 92
Breston, Joseph N 1912- AmMWSc 92
Bret, David 1952- ConAu 134
Bret-Harte, Margaret Sparks 1935- WhoWest 92
Brethauer, Tom Lee 1943- WhoWest 92
Bretherick, Ronald David 1950- WhoRel 92
Bretherton, Francis P 1935- AmMWSc 92
Bretherton, Russell Frederick d1991 Who 92N
Brethour, John Raymond 1934- AmMWSc 92, WhoMW 92
Bretnor, Reginald 1911- IntAu&W 91, TwCSFW 91, WrDr 92
Bretoi, Remus Nicolae 1925- WhoWest 92
Breton, Albert 1929- WrDr 92
Breton, Andre 1896-1966 FacFETw, GuFrLit 1, LiExTwC
Breton, J Raymond 1931- AmMWSc 92
Breton, Nicholas 1545?-1626? RfGEnL 91
Bretones, Reynaldo 1936- WhoHisp 92
Bretos, Miguel A. 1943- WhoHisp 92
Bretsch, Darwin O. WhoMW 92
Bretscher, Anthony P 1950- AmMWSc 92
Bretscher, Barbara Mary Frances Who 92
Bretscher, Manuel Martin 1928- AmMWSc 92
Bretscher, Mark Steven 1940- IntWW 91, Who 92
Bretschneider, Barry Eastburn 1947- WhoAmL 92
Bretschneider, Charles Leroy 1920- AmMWSc 92
Bretsky, Peter William 1938- AmMWSc 92
Brett Who 92
Brett, Arthur Cushman, Jr. 1928- WhoFI 92
Brett, Barrie Sheila WhoEnt 92
Brett, Betty Lou Hilton 1952- AmMWSc 92
Brett, Carlton Elliot 1951- AmMWSc 92
Brett, Charles 1928- Who 92
Brett, Christian TwCPaSc
Brett, Cliff WhoEnt 92
Brett, Donna W. 1947- ConAu 134
Brett, Dorothy 1883-1987 TwCPaSc
Brett, Edward T. 1944- ConAu 134
Brett, George Howard 1953- WhoMW 92
Brett, James T WhoAmP 91
Brett, Jan Churchill 1949- IntAu&W 91
Brett, Jay Elliot 1931- WhoAmP 91
Brett, Jeremy 1933- IntMPA 92
Brett, Jeremy 1935- Who 92
Brett, John Alfred 1915- Who 92
Brett, John Michael IntAu&W 91X
Brett, John Roland 1918- AmMWSc 92
Brett, Larry Richard 1944- WhoEnt 92
Brett, Leo TwCSFW 91, WrDr 92
Brett, Lionel Who 92
Brett, Michael IntAu&W 91X, WrDr 92
Brett, Michael 1928- WrDr 92
Brett, Michael John Lee 1939- Who 92
Brett, Molly IntAu&W 91
Brett, Peter DrAPF 91
Brett, Philip 1937- WhoEnt 92
Brett, Raymond Laurence 1917- IntAu&W 91, Who 92, WrDr 92
Brett, Richard John 1921- WhoMW 92
Brett, Robin 1935- AmMWSc 92
Brett, Rosalind WrDr 92
Brett, Simon 1945- WrDr 92
Brett, Simon Anthony Lee 1945- IntAu&W 91
Brett, Stephen M. WhoAmL 92
Brett, Stephen Noel 1946- WhoIns 92
Brett, Thomas Marshall 1916- WhoAmL 92
Brett, Thomas Rutherford 1931- WhoAmL 92
Brett, Timothy Andrew 1953- WhoAmP 91
Brett, Vane IntAu&W 91X
Brett, William Henry 1942- Who 92
Brett, William John 1923- AmMWSc 92
Brett-Major, Lin 1943- WhoAmL 92
Brettell, Herbert R 1921- AmMWSc 92
Brettell, Richard R. 1949- WrDr 92
Bretten, George Rex 1942- Who 92
Bretthauer, Roger K 1935- AmMWSc 92
Bretton, R H 1918- AmMWSc 92
Bretton-Granatoor, Gary Martin 1956- WhoRel 92
Bretz, Michael 1938- AmMWSc 92
Bretz, Philip Eric 1953- AmMWSc 92
Bretz, Ronald James 1951- WhoMW 92
Bretz, Thurman Wilbur 1934- WhoAmL 92
Bretz, William Franklin 1937- WhoMW 92
Bretzmann, Gary L 1939- WhoAmP 91
Breu, George 1954- WhoMW 92
Breuer, Charles B 1931- AmMWSc 92
Breuer, Delmar W 1925- AmMWSc 92
Breuer, George Michael 1944- AmMWSc 92
Breuer, Lee 1937- WrDr 92
Breuer, Marcel 1902-1981 DcTwDes, FacFETw
Breuer, Max Everett 1938- AmMWSc 92
Breuer, Melvin A 1938- AmMWSc 92
Breuer, Melvin Allen 1938- WhoWest 92
Breuer, Rolf E. IntWW 91
Breuer, Ronald Karl, Sr. 1945- WhoFI 92
Breuer, Stephen Ernest 1936- WhoRel 92, WhoWest 92
Breuhaus, W O 1918- AmMWSc 92
Breum, Arlene Adair 1936- WhoAmP 91
Breunig, Robert Henry 1926- WhoWest 92
Breuning, Siegfried M 1924- AmMWSc 92
Breuninger, Tyrone 1939- WhoEnt 92
Brevard, Alexander 1755-1829 DcNCBi 1
Brevard, John, II 1716-1790 DcNCBi 1
Brevard, Joseph 1766-1821 DcNCBi 1
Brevig, Eric WhoEnt 92
Brevig, Per WhoEnt 92
Brew, David Alan 1930- AmMWSc 92
Brew, Kwesi 1928- ConPo 91
Brew, O. H. Kwesi 1928- WrDr 92
Brew, Richard Maddock 1930- Who 92
Brew, William Barnard 1913- AmMWSc 92
Breward, Ian 1934- WrDr 92
Brewbaker, James Lynn 1926- AmMWSc 92, WhoWest 92
Brewbaker, William Styne, III 1959- WhoAmL 92
Brewen, J Grant 1939- AmMWSc 92
Brewer, Albert Preston 1928- WhoAmP 91
Brewer, Allen A 1911- AmMWSc 92
Brewer, Alvin L. 1946- WhoBlA 92
Brewer, Arnold, Jr WhoAmP 91
Brewer, Arthur David 1941- AmMWSc 92
Brewer, Barry Dominic 1946- WhoMW 92
Brewer, Carl Robert 1912- AmMWSc 92
Brewer, Cecil 1894-1972 DcTwDes
Brewer, Charles Edward 1866-1941 DcNCBi 1
Brewer, Charles H., Jr. WhoRel 92
Brewer, Charles Moulton 1931- WhoAmL 92
Brewer, Curtis d1991 NewYTBS 91 [port]
Brewer, Curtis 1925- WhoBlA 92
Brewer, Curtis Fred 1944- AmMWSc 92
Brewer, Dana Alice 1950- AmMWSc 92

**Brewer,** Daniel Hanley 1951- *WhoAmL 92*
**Brewer,** David J. 1837-1910 *FacFETw*
**Brewer,** David Madison 1953- *WhoAmL 92, WhoFI 92*
**Brewer,** Derek Stanley 1923- *IntWW 91, Who 92*
**Brewer,** Douglas G 1935- *AmMWSc 92*
**Brewer,** Franklin Douglas 1938- *AmMWSc 92*
**Brewer,** Garry D. 1941- *WrDr 92*
**Brewer,** George E F 1909- *AmMWSc 92*
**Brewer,** George Maxted Kenneth 1930- *Who 92*
**Brewer,** George R 1922- *AmMWSc 92*
**Brewer,** George Warner, Jr. 1925- *WhoWest 92*
**Brewer,** Glenn A, Jr 1927- *AmMWSc 92*
**Brewer,** Glynn Douglas, Jr. 1961- *WhoEnt 92*
**Brewer,** Gregory J *AmMWSc 92*
**Brewer,** H Bryan, Jr 1938- *AmMWSc 92*
**Brewer,** H. Michael 1954- *WhoRel 92*
**Brewer,** Harper, Jr 1937- *WhoAmP 91*
**Brewer,** Howard Eugene 1910- *AmMWSc 92*
**Brewer,** James A., Sr. 1931- *WhoBlA 92*
**Brewer,** James Turner 1951- *BlkOlyM*
**Brewer,** James W 1942- *AmMWSc 92*
**Brewer,** Jameson 1916- *WhoEnt 92*
**Brewer,** Janice Kay 1944- *WhoAmP 91*
**Brewer,** Janice Los 1963- *WhoMW 92*
**Brewer,** Jerome 1919- *AmMWSc 92*
**Brewer,** Jesse Wayne 1940- *AmMWSc 92*
**Brewer,** John *Who 92*
**Brewer,** John Bruce 1846-1929 *DcNCBi 1*
**Brewer,** John Gilbert 1937- *AmMWSc 92*
**Brewer,** John Michael 1938- *AmMWSc 92*
**Brewer,** Joyce M. 1948- *WhoWest 92*
**Brewer,** Katherine Kristin C. 1955- *WhoAmL 92*
**Brewer,** Kenneth Alvin 1938- *AmMWSc 92, WhoMW 92*
**Brewer,** Kenneth W. *DrAPF 91*
**Brewer,** Kevin Duane 1960- *WhoWest 92*
**Brewer,** Leo 1919- *AmMWSc 92, IntWW 91*
**Brewer,** LeRoy Earl, Jr 1936- *AmMWSc 92*
**Brewer,** Lewis Gordon 1946- *WhoAmL 92*
**Brewer,** Mark 1955- *WhoFI 92*
**Brewer,** Mark Courtland 1955- *WhoAmL 92*
**Brewer,** Mary Morland 1947- *WhoMW 92*
**Brewer,** Max C 1924- *AmMWSc 92*
**Brewer,** Moses 1947- *WhoBlA 92*
**Brewer,** Nathan Ronald 1904- *AmMWSc 92*
**Brewer,** Oliver Gordon, Jr. 1936- *WhoFI 92*
**Brewer,** Paul 1946- *TwCPaSc*
**Brewer,** Paul Huie 1934- *WhoFI 92*
**Brewer,** Ralph Wright, Jr. 1928- *WhoAmL 92*
**Brewer,** Richard 1933- *AmMWSc 92*
**Brewer,** Richard George 1928- *AmMWSc 92, IntWW 91*
**Brewer,** Richard W. 1947- *WhoFI 92*
**Brewer,** Robert Franklin 1927- *AmMWSc 92, WhoWest 92*
**Brewer,** Robert Hyde 1931- *AmMWSc 92*
**Brewer,** Robert Nelson 1934- *AmMWSc 92*
**Brewer,** Ronald James 1950- *WhoAmP 91*
**Brewer,** Ronald Ray 1951- *WhoRel 92*
**Brewer,** Rose Marie 1947- *WhoBlA 92*
**Brewer,** Roy Edward 1949- *WhoWest 92*
**Brewer,** Roy M. 1909- *IntMPA 92*
**Brewer,** Soila Padilla 1942- *WhoHisp 92*
**Brewer,** Stanley R. 1937- *WhoFI 92*
**Brewer,** Stephen Michael 1948- *WhoAmP 91*
**Brewer,** Stephen Wiley, Jr 1941- *AmMWSc 92*
**Brewer,** Thomas Bowman 1932- *WhoWest 92*
**Brewer,** Thomas Daniel 1960- *WhoMW 92*
**Brewer,** Thomas Mayo 1814-1880 *BiInAmS*
**Brewer,** Tim Dee 1959- *WhoWest 92*
**Brewer,** Timothy R. 1956- *WhoEnt 92*
**Brewer,** Tina Rene 1955- *WhoRel 92*
**Brewer,** Webster L. 1935- *WhoBlA 92*
**Brewer,** William Augustus 1930- *AmMWSc 92*
**Brewer,** William Dane 1961- *WhoAmL 92*
**Brewer,** William Dodd 1922- *WhoAmP 91*
**Brewer,** William Henry 1828-1910 *BiInAmS*
**Brewer,** Willis 1844-1912 *ScFEYrs*
**Brewer,** Willis Ralph 1919- *WhoWest 92*
**Brewer-Mangum,** Ernestine Tywanna 1936- *WhoBlA 92*
**Brewington,** Percy, Jr 1930- *AmMWSc 92*
**Brewington,** Rudolph W. 1946- *WhoBlA 92*
**Brewington,** Thomas E., Jr. 1943- *WhoBlA 92*
**Brews,** Lee 1944- *TwCPaSc*
**Brewster,** Benjamin *IntAu&W 91X, WrDr 92*
**Brewster,** Bill 1941- *AlmAP 92 [port]*
**Brewster,** Bill K 1941- *WhoAmP 91*
**Brewster,** Clark Otto 1956- *WhoAmL 92*
**Brewster,** Daniel Fergerson 1916- *WhoRel 92*
**Brewster,** David *DrAPF 91*
**Brewster,** Donald William 1930- *WhoAmP 91*
**Brewster,** Elizabeth 1922- *BenetAL 91, ConAu 15AS [port], ConPo 91, WrDr 92*
**Brewster,** Elizabeth Susan 1943- *WhoWest 92*
**Brewster,** Franklin *IntAu&W 91X*
**Brewster,** Gary Scott 1965- *WhoRel 92*
**Brewster,** George d1991 *Who 92N*
**Brewster,** Gerry Leiper *WhoAmP 91*
**Brewster,** Gerry Leiper 1957- *WhoAmL 92*
**Brewster,** James Henry 1922- *AmMWSc 92*
**Brewster,** Jonathan 1593-1659 *BiInAmS*
**Brewster,** Luther George 1942- *WhoBlA 92*
**Brewster,** Marcus Quinn 1955- *AmMWSc 92*
**Brewster,** Marjorie Ann 1940- *AmMWSc 92*
**Brewster,** Mark Price 1962- *WhoAmL 92*
**Brewster,** Martyn 1952- *TwCPaSc*
**Brewster,** Nadine Pinnell 1916- *WhoAmP 91*
**Brewster,** Robert Charles 1921- *WhoAmP 91*
**Brewster,** Robert Gene 1938- *WhoEnt 92*
**Brewster,** Rudi Milton 1932- *WhoAmL 92, WhoWest 92*
**Brewster,** Seward B. 1927- *WhoAmL 92*
**Brewster,** Stephen Thomas 1942- *WhoMW 92*
**Brewster,** Townsend Tyler 1924- *IntAu&W 91*
**Brewster,** William 1851-1919 *BiInAmS*
**Brewster,** William Howard 1962- *WhoAmL 92*
**Brewton,** Butler E. 1935- *WhoBlA 92*
**Brewton,** Marjorie Gwynn *WhoWest 92*
**Brey,** R N 1920- *AmMWSc 92*
**Brey,** Wallace Siegfried, Jr 1922- *AmMWSc 92*
**Breyer,** Arthur Charles 1925- *AmMWSc 92*
**Breyer,** James William 1961- *WhoFI 92*
**Breyer,** Norman Nathan 1921- *AmMWSc 92*
**Breyer,** Stephen G *WhoAmP 91*
**Breyer,** Stephen Gerald 1938- *WhoAmL 92*
**Breyere,** Edward Joseph 1927- *AmMWSc 92*
**Breytenbach,** Breyten 1939- *FacFETw, LiExTwC*
**Brezenoff,** Henry Evans 1940- *AmMWSc 92*
**Brezhnev,** Leonid Il'ich 1906-1982 *SovUnBD*
**Brezhnev,** Leonid Ilyich 1906-1982 *FacFETw [port]*
**Brezhnev,** Vladimir Arkadevich 1931- *IntWW 91*
**Brezhnev,** Yuriy Leonidovich 1933- *IntWW 91*
**Brezinski,** Darlene Rita 1941- *AmMWSc 92*
**Brezis,** Haim 1944- *IntWW 91*
**Breznak,** John Allen 1944- *AmMWSc 92*
**Brezner,** Jerome 1931- *AmMWSc 92*
**Brezonik,** Patrick Lee 1941- *AmMWSc 92*
**Brhel,** Martin Charles, Jr. 1947- *WhoAmL 92*
**Bria,** Francis Leonard 1930- *WhoWest 92*
**Brialy,** Jean-Claude 1933- *IntMPA 92*
**Brian,** Alexis Morgan, Jr. 1928- *WhoAmL 92*
**Brian,** David 1914- *IntMPA 92*
**Brian,** P L Thibaut 1930- *AmMWSc 92*
**Brian,** Tom 1948- *WhoAmP 91*
**Briand,** Aristide 1862-1932 *EncTR 91 [port], FacFETw [port], WhoNob 90*
**Briand,** Frederic Jean-Paul 1949- *AmMWSc 92*
**Briant,** Bernard Christian 1917- *Who 92*
**Briant,** Clyde Leonard 1948- *AmMWSc 92*
**Briante,** Nicholas Michael 1937- *WhoIns 92*
**Briarton,** Grendel *TwCSFW 91, WrDr 92*
**Briault,** Eric William Henry 1911- *Who 92*
**Bricall,** Josep M. 1936- *IntWW 91*
**Briccetti,** Joan Therese 1948- *WhoEnt 92*
**Brice,** Ann Nuala 1937- *Who 92*
**Brice,** Carol 1918-1985 *NewAmDM, NotBlAW 92*
**Brice,** David Kenneth 1933- *AmMWSc 92*
**Brice,** Donat B 1920- *AmMWSc 92*
**Brice,** Eric John 1917- *Who 92*
**Brice,** Eugene Clay 1929- *WhoBlA 92*
**Brice,** Fanny 1891-1951 *FacFETw, NewAmDM*
**Brice,** Geoffrey James Barrington Groves 1938- *Who 92*
**Brice,** Gregory Richard 1954- *WhoFI 92*
**Brice,** James Coble 1920- *AmMWSc 92*
**Brice,** Janette Rae 1939- *WhoWest 92*
**Brice,** Luther Kennedy 1928- *AmMWSc 92*
**Brice,** Nuala *Who 92*
**Brice,** Percy A., Jr. 1923- *WhoBlA 92*
**Brice,** Roger Thomas 1948- *WhoAmL 92*
**Brice,** William Charles 1947- *WhoMW 92*
**Brichta,** Paul 1931- *WhoFI 92*
**Brick,** Ann Veta 1947- *WhoAmL 92*
**Brick,** Barrett Lee 1954- *WhoAmL 92*
**Brick,** Cary R 1945- *WhoAmP 91*
**Brick,** David Joseph 1947- *WhoIns 92*
**Brick,** Irving B 1914- *AmMWSc 92*
**Brick,** Robert Wayne 1939- *AmMWSc 92*
**Brickbauer,** Elwood Arthur *AmMWSc 92*
**Brickdale,** Eleanor Fortescue 1871-1945 *TwCPaSc*
**Brickel,** Bernard Michael 1940- *WhoEnt 92*
**Brickell,** Beth *WhoEnt 92*
**Brickell,** Christopher David 1932- *Who 92*
**Brickell,** John *DcNCBi 1*
**Bricker,** Clark Eugene 1918- *AmMWSc 92*
**Bricker,** Dale Eugene, Sr 1925- *WhoAmP 91*
**Bricker,** Donald Clark 1949- *WhoAmL 92*
**Bricker,** Gerald Wayne 1947- *WhoMW 92*
**Bricker,** Jerome Gough 1928- *AmMWSc 92*
**Bricker,** Neal S 1927- *AmMWSc 92, IntWW 91*
**Bricker,** Owen P, III 1936- *AmMWSc 92*
**Bricker,** Richard James 1943- *WhoWest 92*
**Bricker,** Ruth 1930- *WhoWest 92*
**Bricker,** Seymour Murray 1924- *WhoAmL 92, WhoEnt 92*
**Brickey,** James Nelson 1942- *WhoAmL 92*
**Brickey,** Paris Manaford 1931- *AmMWSc 92*
**Brickhill,** Paul d1991 *NewYTBS 91*
**Brickhill,** Paul Chester Jerome d1991 *Who 92N*
**Brickhill,** Paul Chester Jerome 1916- *IntAu&W 91*
**Brickhill,** Paul Chester Jerome 1916-1991 *ConAu 134*
**Bricklebank,** Peter *DrAPF 91*
**Brickler,** John Weise 1944- *WhoAmL 92*
**Brickley,** David Guy 1944- *WhoAmP 91*
**Brickley,** James H. 1928- *WhoAmL 92, WhoAmP 91, WhoMW 92*
**Brickman,** Bruce Kenneth 1944- *WhoAmL 92*
**Brickman,** Howard Joseph 1946- *WhoFI 92*
**Brickman,** John Michael 1944- *WhoAmL 92*
**Brickman,** Marshall *WhoEnt 92*
**Brickman,** Marshall 1941- *IntMPA 92*
**Brickman,** Paul *IntMPA 92, WhoEnt 92*
**Brickner,** Gerald Bernard 1938- *WhoMW 92*
**Brickner,** Paul 1940- *WhoMW 92*
**Brickner,** Ralph Gregg 1951- *WhoWest 92*
**Brickner,** Richard P. *DrAPF 91*
**Brickner,** Sally Ann 1942- *WhoRel 92*
**Brickner,** Samuel Max 1867-1916 *BiInAmS*
**Bricks,** Bernard Gerard 1941- *AmMWSc 92*
**Brickson,** Richard Alan 1948- *WhoAmL 92*
**Bricktop** 1894-1984 *FacFETw*
**Brickus,** John W. 1919- *WhoBlA 92*
**Brickwedde,** Richard James 1944- *WhoAmL 92*
**Brickwood,** Basil 1923- *Who 92*
**Brickwood,** Susan Callaghan 1946- *WhoAmL 92*
**Brico,** Antonia 1902-1989 *FacFETw [port], NewAmDM*
**Bricusse,** Leslie 1931- *ConTFT 9*
**Briddell,** Robert Albert 1963- *WhoMW 92*
**Bride,** John William 1937- *WhoEnt 92*
**Bride,** Robert Fairbanks 1953- *WhoFI 92*
**Bride,** Thomas Robert 1940- *WhoRel 92*
**Briden,** James Christopher 1938- *Who 92*
**Bridenbaugh,** Peter R 1940- *AmMWSc 92*
**Bridendall,** John Philip 1950- *WhoFI 92*
**Bridenstine,** Eugene *WhoAmP 91*
**Bridge** *Who 92*
**Bridge,** Alan G 1936- *AmMWSc 92*
**Bridge,** Andrew *WhoEnt 92*
**Bridge,** Antony Cyprian 1914- *Who 92*
**Bridge,** Frank 1879-1941 *FacFETw, NewAmDM*
**Bridge,** Herbert Sage 1919- *AmMWSc 92*
**Bridge,** Horatio 1806-1893 *BenetAL 91*
**Bridge,** John 1915- *Who 92*
**Bridge,** John F 1933- *AmMWSc 92*
**Bridge,** Keith James 1929- *Who 92*
**Bridge,** Ronald George Blacker 1932- *Who 92*
**Bridge,** Thomas E 1925- *AmMWSc 92*
**Bridge of Harwich,** Baron 1917- *Who 92*
**Bridgeford,** Douglas Joseph 1926- *AmMWSc 92*
**Bridgeford,** Gary James 1947- *WhoFI 92*
**Bridgeforth,** Arthur Mac, Jr. 1965- *WhoBlA 92*
**Bridgeforth,** Barbara 1943- *WhoBlA 92*
**Bridgeman** *Who 92*
**Bridgeman,** Viscount 1930- *Who 92*
**Bridgeman,** Donald Earl 1939- *WhoBlA 92*
**Bridgeman,** Garry Wayne 1953- *WhoFI 92*
**Bridgeman,** Harriet 1942- *IntAu&W 91*
**Bridgeman,** John Michael 1931- *Who 92*
**Bridgeman,** John Wilfred 1895- *Who 92*
**Bridgeman,** June 1932- *Who 92*
**Bridgeman,** Junior 1953- *WhoBlA 92*
**Bridgeman,** Michael *Who 92*
**Bridgeo,** William Alphonsus 1927- *AmMWSc 92*
**Bridger,** Adam *IntAu&W 91X, TwCWW 91*
**Bridger,** Gordon Frederick 1932- *Who 92*
**Bridger,** James 1804-1881 *BenetAL 91*
**Bridger,** Pearl 1912- *Who 92*
**Bridger,** Wagner H 1928- *AmMWSc 92*
**Bridger,** William Aitken 1941- *AmMWSc 92*
**Bridgers,** Ann Preston 1891-1967 *DcNCBi 1*
**Bridgers,** Henry Clark 1876-1951 *DcNCBi 1*
**Bridgers,** John Luther 1821-1884 *DcNCBi 1*
**Bridgers,** John Luther, Jr. 1850-1932 *DcNCBi 1*
**Bridgers,** Robert Rufus 1819-1888 *DcNCBi 1*
**Bridgers,** Sue Ellen *DrAPF 91*
**Bridgers,** Sue Ellen 1942- *Au&Arts 8 [port], ConAu 36NR, WrDr 92*
**Bridgers,** William Frank 1932- *AmMWSc 92*
**Bridges** *Who 92*
**Bridges,** Baron 1927- *IntWW 91, Who 92*
**Bridges,** Alan 1927- *IntMPA 92, IntWW 91*
**Bridges,** Alfred Renton Bryant 1901-1990 *FacFETw*
**Bridges,** Alvin Leroy 1925- *WhoBlA 92*
**Bridges,** Beau 1941- *IntMPA 92, WhoEnt 92*
**Bridges,** Ben *TwCWW 91, WrDr 92*
**Bridges,** Bill 1939- *WhoBlA 92*
**Bridges,** Bobby Lawrence 1949- *WhoRel 92*
**Bridges,** Brian 1937- *Who 92*
**Bridges,** C David 1933- *AmMWSc 92*
**Bridges,** Charles Hubert 1921- *AmMWSc 92*
**Bridges,** Charlie Glenn 1960- *WhoRel 92*
**Bridges,** David Manning 1936- *WhoAmL 92*
**Bridges,** Dewi Morris *Who 92*
**Bridges,** Donald Norris 1936- *AmMWSc 92*
**Bridges,** E 1931- *AmMWSc 92*
**Bridges,** Frank G *AmMWSc 92*
**Bridges,** Gailen Wayne 1933- *WhoAmL 92*
**Bridges,** Gerald Dean 1929- *WhoRel 92*
**Bridges,** Harry 1901-1990 *AnObit 1990*
**Bridges,** James 1936- *IntMPA 92, WhoEnt 92*
**Bridges,** James Wilfrid 1938- *Who 92*
**Bridges,** James Wilson 1935- *WhoBlA 92*
**Bridges,** Jeff 1949- *IntMPA 92, IntWW 91*
**Bridges,** Jeff 1950- *CurBio 91 [port]*
**Bridges,** Jeff 1951- *WhoEnt 92*
**Bridges,** John Robert 1944- *AmMWSc 92*
**Bridges,** Joseph Henry 1943- *WhoFI 92*
**Bridges,** Joseph Lewis 1940- *WhoEnt 92*
**Bridges,** Kent Wentworth 1941- *AmMWSc 92*
**Bridges,** Lee *DrAPF 91*
**Bridges,** Leon 1932- *WhoBlA 92*
**Bridges,** Les *DrAPF 91*
**Bridges,** Lloyd *WhoEnt 92*
**Bridges,** Lloyd 1913- *IntMPA 92*
**Bridges,** Lucille W. 1923- *WhoBlA 92*
**Bridges,** Mary 1930- *Who 92*
**Bridges,** Peter Scott 1932- *WhoAmP 91*
**Bridges,** Peter Sydney Godfrey 1925- *Who 92*
**Bridges,** Phillip 1922- *Who 92*
**Bridges,** Phillip Rodney 1922- *IntWW 91*
**Bridges,** Robert 1806-1882 *BiInAmS*
**Bridges,** Robert 1844-1930 *CnDBLB 5 [port], FacFETw, RfGEnL 91*
**Bridges,** Robert McSteen 1914- *WhoWest 92*
**Bridges,** Robert Stafford 1947- *AmMWSc 92*
**Bridges,** Roger Dean 1937- *WhoMW 92*
**Bridges,** Thomas James 1923- *AmMWSc 92*

**Bridges,** Timothy Arthur 1957- *WhoMW 92*
**Bridges,** Webster E, Jr 1933- *WhoAmP 91*
**Bridges,** William B 1934- *AmMWSc 92*
**Bridges,** William Bruce 1934- *WhoWest 92*
**Bridges,** William G 1942- *AmMWSc 92*
**Bridges-Adams,** John Nicholas William 1930- *Who 92*
**Bridgetower,** George 1780-1860 *NewAmDM*
**Bridgett-Chisolm,** Karen 1956- *WhoBlA 92*
**Bridgewater,** Albert Louis 1941- *WhoBlA 92*
**Bridgewater,** Albert Louis, Jr 1941- *AmMWSc 92*
**Bridgewater,** Allan 1936- *Who 92*
**Bridgewater,** Bentley Powell Conyers 1911- *Who 92*
**Bridgewater,** Herbert Jeremiah, Jr. 1942- *WhoBlA 92, WhoEnt 92*
**Bridgewater,** Nancy 1940- *WhoAmP 91*
**Bridgewater,** Paul *WhoBlA 92*
**Bridgforth,** Robert Moore, Jr 1918- *AmMWSc 92, WhoFI 92, WhoWest 92*
**Bridgland,** Milton Deane 1922- *Who 92*
**Bridgman,** Charles James 1930- *AmMWSc 92, WhoMW 92*
**Bridgman,** George Henry 1940- *AmMWSc 92*
**Bridgman,** George Ross 1947- *WhoAmL 92*
**Bridgman,** Howard Allen 1944- *AmMWSc 92*
**Bridgman,** James Campbell 1950- *WhoAmL 92, WhoWest 92*
**Bridgman,** John Francis 1925- *AmMWSc 92*
**Bridgman,** Percy Williams 1882-1961 *FacFETw, WhoNob 90*
**Bridgman,** Raymond Landon 1848-1925 *AmPeW*
**Bridgman,** Thomas Francis 1933- *WhoAmL 92*
**Bridgman,** Wilbur Benjamin 1913- *AmMWSc 92*
**Bridgwater,** Alan 1903- *TwCPaSc*
**Bridgwater,** John 1938- *Who 92*
**Bridie,** James 1888-1951 *RfGEnL 91*
**Bridle,** Alan Henry 1942- *AmMWSc 92*
**Bridle,** Gordon Walter 1923- *Who 92*
**Bridle,** Ronald Jarman 1930- *Who 92*
**Bridport,** Viscount 1948- *Who 92*
**Bridston,** Keith Richard 1924- *WhoRel 92*
**Bridston,** Paul Joseph 1928- *WhoFI 92*
**Bridwell,** Charmaine Claudette 1953- *WhoFI 92, WhoWest 92*
**Bridwell,** Herbert H. 1928- *WhoBlA 92*
**Bridwell,** Norman 1928- *SmATA 68 [port]*
**Bridwell,** Norman Ray 1928- *IntAu&W 91, WrDr 92*
**Bridwell,** Wilburn Fowler 1933- *WhoWest 92*
**Bridwell-Jones,** Margaret *DrAPF 91*
**Brieaddy,** Lawrence Edward 1944- *AmMWSc 92*
**Brieant,** Charles La Monte, Jr. 1923- *WhoAmL 92*
**Bried,** Henry William 1933- *WhoFI 92*
**Brief,** Henry 1924- *WhoEnt 92*
**Brief,** Neil 1934- *WhoRel 92*
**Brieff,** Frank 1912- *WhoEnt 92*
**Briegel,** Geoffrey Michael Olver 1923- *Who 92*
**Briegel,** William Eugene 1949- *WhoFI 92*
**Brieger,** Gert Henry 1932- *AmMWSc 92*
**Brieger,** Gottfried 1935- *AmMWSc 92*
**Brieger,** Stephen Gustave 1935- *WhoWest 92*
**Briegleb,** Philip Anthes 1906- *AmMWSc 92*
**Briehl,** Robin Walt 1928- *AmMWSc 92*
**Brien,** Alan 1925- *IntAu&W 91, Who 92*
**Brien,** Albert George 1940- *WhoAmP 91*
**Brien,** Francis Staples 1908- *AmMWSc 92*
**Brien,** James Frederick 1945- *AmMWSc 92*
**Brien,** Lois Ann 1928- *WhoWest 92*
**Brien,** Marilyn Biggs 1938- *WhoAmP 91*
**Brien,** Robert L. 1937- *WhoFI 92*
**Brient,** Charles E 1934- *AmMWSc 92*
**Brient,** Samuel John, Jr 1930- *AmMWSc 92*
**Brienza,** Michael Joseph 1939- *AmMWSc 92*
**Brier,** Charles James 1937- *WhoWest 92*
**Brier,** Harriet 1922- *WhoEnt 92*
**Brier,** Jack H 1946- *WhoAmP 91*
**Brier,** Kenneth Paul 1952- *WhoAmL 92*
**Briere,** Normand 1937- *AmMWSc 92*
**Brierley,** Christopher Wadsworth 1929- *Who 92*
**Brierley,** Corale Louise 1945- *AmMWSc 92*
**Brierley,** David 1936- *IntAu&W 91*
**Brierley,** Gerald Philip 1931- *AmMWSc 92*
**Brierley,** James Alan 1938- *AmMWSc 92*
**Brierley,** John David 1918- *Who 92*
**Brierley,** Richard Greer 1915- *WhoWest 92*
**Brierley,** Ronald 1937- *Who 92*
**Brierley,** Ronald Alfred 1937- *IntWW 91*
**Brierley,** Zachry 1920- *Who 92*
**Brierly,** Keppel 1909- *WhoWest 92*
**Briers,** Richard 1934- *ConTFT 9*
**Briers,** Richard David 1934- *IntWW 91, Who 92*
**Brierton,** John 1572?-1619? *BenetAL 91*
**Brierton,** Maureen 1956- *WhoEnt 92*
**Brierton,** Robert Sylvester 1948- *WhoAmL 92*
**Briese,** Leonard Arden 1933- *WhoWest 92*
**Brieske,** Thomas John 1939- *AmMWSc 92*
**Brieve-Martin,** Ila Corrinna 1939- *WhoBlA 92*
**Briganti,** Debra Ann 1953- *WhoAmL 92*
**Brigantti-Hughes,** Mary Ann *WhoHisp 92*
**Brigden,** Richard T. 1944- *WhoFI 92*
**Brigden,** Wallace 1916- *Who 92*
**Briggaman,** Robert Alan 1934- *AmMWSc 92*
**Briggerman,** Steven Leslie 1943- *WhoAmL 92*
**Briggins,** Charles E. 1930- *WhoBlA 92*
**Briggle,** Leland Wilson 1920- *AmMWSc 92*
**Briggle,** Stockton Frederick 1942- *WhoEnt 92*
**Briggs** *Who 92*
**Briggs,** Baron 1921- *IntWW 91, Who 92*
**Briggs,** Alan Leonard 1942- *WhoAmL 92*
**Briggs,** Arthur Harold 1930- *AmMWSc 92*
**Briggs,** Asa 1921- *IntAu&W 91, ScFEYrs, WrDr 92*
**Briggs,** Charles Augustus 1841-1913 *RelLAm 91*
**Briggs,** Charles Frederick 1804-1877 *BenetAL 91*
**Briggs,** Cyril 1888-1955 *AmPeW*
**Briggs,** Dale Edward 1930- *AmMWSc 92*
**Briggs,** Darinka Zigic 1932- *AmMWSc 92*
**Briggs,** David Griffith 1932- *AmMWSc 92*
**Briggs,** David R 1899- *AmMWSc 92*
**Briggs,** David Sheldon 1956- *WhoEnt 92*
**Briggs,** Dean Winfield 1953- *WhoWest 92*
**Briggs,** Dinus Marshall 1940- *WhoWest 92*
**Briggs,** Donald K 1924- *AmMWSc 92*
**Briggs,** Douglas Lloyd 1956- *WhoWest 92*
**Briggs,** Eddie 1949- *WhoAmP 91*
**Briggs,** Edward Burton, Jr. 1939- *WhoRel 92*
**Briggs,** Edward M *AmMWSc 92*
**Briggs,** Everett Ellis 1934- *WhoAmP 91*
**Briggs,** Faye Alaye 1947- *AmMWSc 92*
**Briggs,** Fred Norman 1924- *AmMWSc 92*
**Briggs,** Garrett 1934- *AmMWSc 92*
**Briggs,** Gary Philip 1952- *WhoFI 92*
**Briggs,** Geoffrey 1914- *Who 92*
**Briggs,** George Cardell 1910- *Who 92*
**Briggs,** George Madison 1927- *WhoFI 92*
**Briggs,** George McSpadden 1919- *AmMWSc 92*
**Briggs,** George Roland 1924- *AmMWSc 92*
**Briggs,** Hilton Marshall 1913- *AmMWSc 92*
**Briggs,** Isabel Diana *Who 92*
**Briggs,** Janet Marie Louise 1951- *WhoMW 92*
**Briggs,** Jeffrey L *AmMWSc 92*
**Briggs,** Joe Bob 1953- *WhoEnt 92*
**Briggs,** John *Who 92*
**Briggs,** John C. 1945- *WhoAmL 92*
**Briggs,** John Carmon 1920- *AmMWSc 92*
**Briggs,** John Dorian 1926- *AmMWSc 92*
**Briggs,** John Mancel, III 1942- *WhoAmL 92*
**Briggs,** John Porter 1953- *WhoFI 92*
**Briggs,** Josephine P 1944- *AmMWSc 92*
**Briggs,** Kenneth 1934- *WrDr 92*
**Briggs,** Kenneth Ray 1934- *IntAu&W 91*
**Briggs,** Leslie Ray 1944- *WhoMW 92*
**Briggs,** Lloyd Clark 1942- *WhoIns 92*
**Briggs,** Marjorie Crowder 1946- *WhoAmL 92*
**Briggs,** Michael 1951- *ConAu 135*
**Briggs,** Michael Peter 1944- *Who 92*
**Briggs,** Mikel S. 1957- *WhoMW 92*
**Briggs,** Patrick David 1940- *Who 92*
**Briggs,** Paul Wellington 1922- *WhoFI 92*
**Briggs,** Peter *Who 92*
**Briggs,** Peter John 1928- *Who 92*
**Briggs,** Philip 1928- *WhoFI 92, WhoIns 92*
**Briggs,** Phillip D 1937- *AmMWSc 92*
**Briggs,** Raymond 1934- *SmATA 66 [port], WrDr 92*
**Briggs,** Raymond Redvers 1934- *IntAu&W 91, IntWW 91, Who 92*
**Briggs,** Reginald Peter 1929- *AmMWSc 92*
**Briggs,** Richard Julian 1937- *AmMWSc 92*
**Briggs,** Robert 1822-1882 *BiInAmS*
**Briggs,** Robert Chester 1944- *AmMWSc 92*
**Briggs,** Robert Eugene 1927- *AmMWSc 92*
**Briggs,** Robert Henry 1937- *WhoMW 92*
**Briggs,** Robert Nathan 1946- *WhoWest 92*
**Briggs,** Robert Stephen 1949- *WhoIns 92*
**Briggs,** Robert Wilbur 1934- *AmMWSc 92*
**Briggs,** Stephen Alan 1951- *WhoWest 92*
**Briggs,** Steve Clement 1947- *WhoAmL 92*
**Briggs,** Taylor Rastrick 1933- *WhoAmL 92*
**Briggs,** Thomas 1933- *AmMWSc 92*
**Briggs,** Thomas Henry 1847-1928 *DcNCBi 1*
**Briggs,** Thomas N *AmMWSc 92*
**Briggs,** Thomas Vallack 1906- *Who 92*
**Briggs,** Wallace Neal 1915- *WhoEnt 92*
**Briggs,** Ward W. 1945- *ConAu 135*
**Briggs,** William 1836-1922 *RelLAm 91*
**Briggs,** William Cyrus 1861-1918 *DcNCBi 1*
**Briggs,** William Egbert 1925- *AmMWSc 92*
**Briggs,** William Morse 1931- *WhoWest 92*
**Briggs,** William Scott 1941- *AmMWSc 92*
**Briggs,** Willis Grandy 1875-1954 *DcNCBi 1*
**Briggs,** Winslow Russell 1928- *AmMWSc 92, IntWW 91, WhoWest 92*
**Briggs-Graves,** Anasa *WhoBlA 92*
**Brigham,** Besmilr *DrAPF 91*
**Brigham,** Eugene Foster 1930- *WhoFI 92*
**Brigham,** Jerry Powell 1947- *WhoAmP 91*
**Brigham,** John Allen, Jr. 1942- *WhoWest 92*
**Brigham,** Kenneth Larry 1939- *AmMWSc 92*
**Brigham,** Nelson Allen 1915- *AmMWSc 92*
**Brigham,** Raymond Dale 1926- *AmMWSc 92*
**Brigham,** Samuel Townsend Jack, III 1939- *WhoAmL 92*
**Brigham,** Warren Ulrich 1942- *AmMWSc 92*
**Brigham,** William Everett 1929- *AmMWSc 92*
**Brighouse,** Harold 1882-1958 *RfGEnL 91*
**Brighouse,** Timothy Robert Peter 1940- *Who 92*
**Bright,** Alfred Lee 1940- *WhoBlA 92, WhoMW 92*
**Bright,** Arthur Aaron 1946- *AmMWSc 92*
**Bright,** Colin Charles 1948- *Who 92*
**Bright,** Craig Bartley 1931- *WhoAmL 92*
**Bright,** Donald Bolton 1930- *WhoWest 92*
**Bright,** Donald Edward 1934- *AmMWSc 92*
**Bright,** E Shippen 1956- *WhoAmP 91*
**Bright,** George Walter 1945- *AmMWSc 92*
**Bright,** Gordon Stanley 1915- *AmMWSc 92*
**Bright,** Graham Frank James 1942- *Who 92*
**Bright,** Harold Frederick 1913- *AmMWSc 92*
**Bright,** Harvey R. 1920- *WhoFI 92*
**Bright,** Herbert L., Sr. 1941- *WhoBlA 92*
**Bright,** Jean Marie 1915- *WhoBlA 92*
**Bright,** John Calvin 1915- *WhoRel 92*
**Bright,** Joseph Converse 1940- *WhoAmL 92*
**Bright,** Kate 1964- *TwCPaSc*
**Bright,** Keith 1931- *IntWW 91, Who 92*
**Bright,** Louvenia Dorsey 1941- *WhoAmP 91*
**Bright,** Marilyn Agnes 1946- *WhoFI 92*
**Bright,** Myron H. 1919- *ConAu 134, WhoAmL 92, WhoMW 92*
**Bright,** Pamela Mary 1937- *WhoRel 92*
**Bright,** Peter Bowman 1937- *AmMWSc 92*
**Bright,** Richard *IntMPA 92, WhoEnt 92*
**Bright,** Richard S. 1936- *IntMPA 92*
**Bright,** Robert C 1928- *AmMWSc 92*
**Bright,** Ronnell Lovelace 1930- *WhoEnt 92*
**Bright,** Simon 1702?-1777? *DcNCBi 1*
**Bright,** Simon 1757?-1802 *DcNCBi 1*
**Bright,** Simon, Jr. 1734?-1776 *DcNCBi 1*
**Bright,** Stanley J. 1940- *WhoMW 92*
**Bright,** Stephen Brooks 1948- *WhoAmL 92*
**Bright,** Thomas J 1937- *AmMWSc 92*
**Bright,** Thomas Lynn 1948- *WhoAmL 92*
**Bright,** Willard Mead 1914- *AmMWSc 92*
**Bright,** William Rohl 1921- *RelLAm 91*
**Bright,** Willie S. 1934- *WhoBlA 92*
**Brightbill,** David John 1942- *WhoAmP 91*
**Brightbill,** Lorenzo Otis, III 1936- *WhoFI 92*
**Brightfield,** Richard 1927- *ConAu 35NR, SmATA 65*
**Brightfield,** Rick *ConAu 35NR, SmATA 65*
**Brightling,** Peter Henry Miller 1921- *Who 92*
**Brightman** *Who 92*
**Brightman,** Baron 1911- *IntWW 91, Who 92*
**Brightman,** Edgar Sheffield 1884-1953 *FacFETw, RelLAm 91*
**Brightman,** I Jay 1909- *AmMWSc 92*
**Brightman,** Milton Wilfred 1923- *AmMWSc 92*
**Brightman,** Peggy 1938- *WhoEnt 92*
**Brightman,** Sarah *WhoEnt 92*
**Brightman,** Vernon 1930- *AmMWSc 92*
**Brighton,** Carl T 1931- *AmMWSc 92*
**Brighton,** Catherine 1943- *SmATA 65*
**Brighton,** Gerald David 1920- *WhoFI 92*
**Brighton,** John Austin 1934- *AmMWSc 92*
**Brighton,** Peter 1933- *Who 92*
**Brighton,** Ruth Louise 1931- *WhoRel 92*
**Brightup,** Robert Leroy 1936- *WhoMW 92, WhoRel 92*
**Brightwell,** Dennis Richard 1946- *AmMWSc 92*
**Brighty,** Anthony David 1939- *Who 92*
**Briginshaw** *Who 92*
**Briginshaw,** Baron *Who 92*
**Brigitha,** Enith Salle 1955- *BlkOlyM*
**Brigneau,** Francois 1919- *BiDExR*
**Brignoli Gable,** Carol 1945- *AmMWSc 92*
**Brignolo,** Joseph Bartholemew 1920- *WhoFI 92*
**Brigstocke** *Who 92*
**Brigstocke,** Baroness 1929- *Who 92*
**Brigstocke,** John Richard 1945- *Who 92*
**Briles,** Connally Oran 1919- *AmMWSc 92*
**Briles,** David Elwood 1945- *AmMWSc 92*
**Briles,** George Herbert 1937- *AmMWSc 92*
**Briles,** James E 1926- *WhoAmP 91*
**Briles,** Margaret Stevenson 1925- *WhoAmL 92*
**Briles,** Worthie Elwood 1918- *AmMWSc 92*
**Briley,** Bruce Edwin 1936- *AmMWSc 92*
**Briley,** John 1925- *IntAu&W 91*
**Briley,** John Richard 1925- *WhoEnt 92*
**Briley,** Martha Clark 1949- *WhoFI 92*
**Brilhart,** Arnold Ross 1904- *WhoEnt 92*
**Brill,** A. A. 1874-1948 *BenetAL 91*
**Brill,** A Bertrand 1928- *AmMWSc 92*
**Brill,** Alan Richard 1942- *WhoEnt 92, WhoFI 92, WhoMW 92*
**Brill,** Arthur Sylvan 1927- *AmMWSc 92*
**Brill,** Billy Allen 1950- *WhoEnt 92*
**Brill,** Dieter Rudolf 1933- *AmMWSc 92*
**Brill,** Ernie *DrAPF 91*
**Brill,** Frederick 1920-1984 *TwCPaSc*
**Brill,** James Lathrop 1951- *WhoFI 92, WhoWest 92*
**Brill,** Joel Victor 1956- *WhoWest 92*
**Brill,** Joseph Warren 1950- *AmMWSc 92*
**Brill,** Kenneth Gray, Jr 1910- *AmMWSc 92*
**Brill,** Moredecai Louis 1910- *WhoRel 92*
**Brill,** Newton Clyde 1936- *WhoAmL 92*
**Brill,** Newton Clyde, Jr 1936- *WhoAmP 91*
**Brill,** Raymond Julian 1954- *WhoMW 92*
**Brill,** Reginald 1902-1974 *TwCPaSc*
**Brill,** Robert H 1929- *AmMWSc 92*
**Brill,** Steven 1950- *WhoFI 92*
**Brill,** Steven Charles 1953- *WhoAmL 92*
**Brill,** Steven I. 1954- *WhoAmL 92*
**Brill,** Steven M. 1958- *WhoEnt 92*
**Brill,** Thomas Barton 1944- *AmMWSc 92*
**Brill,** Wilfred G 1930- *AmMWSc 92*
**Brill,** William Franklin 1923- *AmMWSc 92*
**Brill,** Winston J 1939- *AmMWSc 92*
**Brill,** Winston Jonas 1939- *WhoFI 92*
**Brill,** Yvonne Claeys 1924- *AmMWSc 92*
**Briller,** Stanley A 1922- *AmMWSc 92*
**Brillhart,** Donald D 1918- *AmMWSc 92*
**Brilliana,** Harley 1598?-1643 *EncAmaz 91*
**Brilliande,** Robert 1909- *WhoFI 92*
**Brilliant,** Alan 1936- *WrDr 92*
**Brilliant,** Barbara 1935- *WhoEnt 92*
**Brilliant,** Fredda *Who 92*
**Brilliant,** Howard Michael 1945- *AmMWSc 92*
**Brilliant,** Lawrence Brent 1944- *AmMWSc 92*
**Brilliant,** Martin Barry 1931- *AmMWSc 92*
**Brilliant,** Richard 1929- *WrDr 92*
**Brillinger,** David Ross 1937- *AmMWSc 92, IntWW 91*
**Brillson,** Leonard Jack 1945- *AmMWSc 92*
**Brillstein,** Bernie 1931- *IntMPA 92*
**Brim,** Charles A 1924- *AmMWSc 92*
**Brim,** Orville G, Jr 1923- *AmMWSc 92, IntWW 91*
**Brimacombe,** John Stuart 1935- *Who 92*
**Brimacombe,** Robert Kenneth 1957- *AmMWSc 92*
**Brimelow** *Who 92*
**Brimelow,** Baron 1915- *IntWW 91, Who 92*
**Brimelow,** Peter 1947- *ConAu 133*
**Brimer,** Kenneth Kimberlin, Jr 1945- *WhoAmP 91*
**Brimer,** Philip G 1950- *WhoIns 92*
**Brimhall,** George H 1947- *AmMWSc 92*
**Brimhall,** J L 1937- *AmMWSc 92*
**Brimhall,** James Elmore 1936- *AmMWSc 92*
**Brimhall,** John Clark 1928- *WhoEnt 92*
**Brimhall,** Owen DeMar 1958- *WhoWest 92*
**Brimijoin,** William Stephen 1942- *AmMWSc 92*

**Brimley,** Clement Samuel 1863-1946 *DcNCBi 1*
**Brimley,** Herbert Hutchinson 1861-1946 *DcNCBi 1*
**Brimley,** Wilford 1934- *IntMPA 92, WhoEnt 92*
**Brimm,** Charles Edwin 1924- *WhoBlA 92*
**Brimm,** David Ross 1952- *WhoMW 92*
**Brimm,** Eugene Oskar 1915- *AmMWSc 92*
**Brimmekamp,** Carl Gerd 1928- *WhoFI 92*
**Brimmer,** Andrew F. 1926- *ConBlB 2 [port], WhoBlA 92*
**Brimmer,** Andrew Felton 1926- *IntWW 91*
**Brimmer,** Clarence Addison 1922- *WhoAmL 92*
**Brimmer,** Steven Richard 1949- *WhoEnt 92*
**Brin,** David 1950- *IntAu&W 91, SmATA 65 [port], TwCSFW 91, WrDr 92*
**Brin,** Myron 1923- *AmMWSc 92*
**Brin,** Royal Henry, Jr. 1919- *WhoAmL 92*
**Brinch-Hansen,** Per 1938- *AmMWSc 92*
**Brinck-Johnsen,** Truls 1926- *AmMWSc 92*
**Brinckerhoff,** Walter Remsen 1874-1911 *BiInAmS*
**Brinckman,** Donald Wesley 1931- *WhoFI 92, WhoMW 92*
**Brinckman,** Frederick Edward, Jr 1928- *AmMWSc 92*
**Brinckman,** Theodore 1932- *Who 92*
**Brincko,** Andrew John 1951- *WhoMW 92*
**Brind,** Henry 1927- *Who 92*
**Brind,** Peter Holmes Walter 1912- *Who 92*
**Brinda,** Wayne 1950- *WhoEnt 92*
**Brindel,** June Rachuy *DrAPF 91*
**Brindle,** Barbara Ann 1923- *WhoRel 92*
**Brindle,** David Lowell 1948- *WhoRel 92*
**Brindle,** James d1991 *NewYTBS 91 [port]*
**Brindle,** Reginald Smith 1917- *ConCom 92*
**Brindle,** Van Roger 1939- *WhoRel 92*
**Brindley,** Giles Skey 1926- *IntWW 91, Who 92*
**Brindley,** Joseph Warren, II 1945- *WhoAmP 91*
**Brindus,** Nicolae 1935- *IntWW 91*
**Brine,** Charles James 1950- *AmMWSc 92*
**Brine,** Jane 1940- *TwCPaSc*
**Brine,** John 1920- *TwCPaSc*
**Brinegar,** Claude Stout 1926- *WhoFI 92, WhoWest 92*
**Brinegar,** Don Eugene 1929- *WhoWest 92*
**Brinegar,** Todd Williams 1959- *WhoEnt 92*
**Brinen,** Jacob Solomon 1934- *AmMWSc 92*
**Briner,** Pamela Joan 1950- *WhoWest 92*
**Briner,** William Watson 1928- *AmMWSc 92*
**Briney,** Robert Edward 1933- *AmMWSc 92*
**Bring,** Dale Vincent 1949- *WhoAmL 92*
**Bring,** Harry Victor 1943- *WhoEnt 92*
**Bring,** Karl Elmer 1959- *WhoWest 92*
**Bring,** Murray 1935- *WhoAmL 92, WhoFI 92*
**Bringelson,** Mark Alan 1957- *WhoEnt 92*
**Bringer,** Robert Paul 1930- *AmMWSc 92*
**Bringewatt,** Ronald Mark 1963- *WhoFI 92*
**Bringham,** William Talbert 1924- *WhoMW 92*
**Bringhurst,** Robert *DrAPF 91*
**Bringhurst,** Robert 1946- *ConPo 91, IntAu&W 91, WhoWest 92, WrDr 92*
**Bringhurst,** Royce S 1918- *AmMWSc 92*
**Brings,** Allen Stephen 1934- *WhoEnt 92*
**Brings,** Virginia Natalie 1932- *WhoAmP 91*
**Bringuier,** Jean-Claude 1925- *ConAu 133*
**Brinig,** Myron 1896-1991 *NewYTBS 91 [port]*
**Brinig,** Myron 1900- *TwCWW 91*
**Brinig,** Myron 1901-1991 *BenetAL 91*
**Brinigar,** William Seymour, Jr 1930- *AmMWSc 92*
**Brinitzer,** Michael Werner 1932- *WhoAmL 92*
**Brink,** Andre 1935- *ConNov 91, WrDr 92*
**Brink,** Andre Philippus 1935- *IntAu&W 91, IntWW 91, Who 92*
**Brink,** Andries Jacob 1923- *IntWW 91*
**Brink,** Carol 1895-1981 *BenetAL 91*
**Brink,** Carol Ryrie 1895-1981 *TwCWW 91*
**Brink,** Charles Oscar 1907- *Who 92*
**Brink,** Charles Patrick 1955- *WhoAmL 92*
**Brink,** David Liddell 1917- *AmMWSc 92*
**Brink,** David Maurice 1930- *IntWW 91, Who 92*
**Brink,** David Ryrie 1919- *WhoAmL 92*
**Brink,** Derek Eron 1960- *WhoFI 92*
**Brink,** Edwin Wallace 1934- *WhoWest 92*
**Brink,** Frank, Jr 1910- *AmMWSc 92, IntWW 91*
**Brink,** Frederick Wright 1940- *WhoEnt 92*
**Brink,** Gary Jerome 1963- *WhoRel 92, WhoWest 92*
**Brink,** Gilbert Oscar 1929- *AmMWSc 92*
**Brink,** Jean Renee 1942- *WhoWest 92*
**Brink,** John Arthur 1954- *WhoFI 92*
**Brink,** John Jerome 1934- *AmMWSc 92*
**Brink,** John William 1945- *WhoFI 92*
**Brink,** Judith Kay 1947- *WhoMW 92*
**Brink,** Kenneth Harold 1949- *AmMWSc 92*
**Brink,** Kenneth Maurice 1932- *AmMWSc 92*
**Brink,** Linda Holk 1944- *AmMWSc 92*
**Brink,** Marion Francis 1932- *AmMWSc 92*
**Brink,** Norman George 1920- *AmMWSc 92*
**Brink,** Randall Wilson 1955- *WhoAmP 91, WhoWest 92*
**Brink,** Robert *WhoEnt 92*
**Brink,** T L 1949- *ConAu 34NR*
**Brink,** William P. 1916- *WhoRel 92*
**Brinker,** Barry Joe 1953- *WhoFI 92*
**Brinker,** Connie Juge 1928- *WhoWest 92*
**Brinker,** Kenneth Chris 1953- *WhoAmL 92*
**Brinker,** Nancy 1946- *ConAu 134*
**Brinker,** Russell Charles 1908- *AmMWSc 92*
**Brinker,** Thomas Michael 1933- *WhoFI 92*
**Brinkerhoff,** Allan T. 1947- *WhoAmL 92*
**Brinkerhoff,** Martin Louis 1951- *WhoEnt 92*
**Brinkerhoff,** Richard Noel 1930- *WhoAmP 91*
**Brinkerhoff,** Tom J. 1939- *WhoMW 92*
**Brinkhaus,** Armand Joseph 1935- *WhoAmP 91*
**Brinkhous,** Kenneth Merle 1908- *AmMWSc 92, IntWW 91*
**Brinkhues,** Josef 1913- *IntWW 91*
**Brinkhuis,** Boudewijn H 1946- *AmMWSc 92*
**Brinkhurst,** Ralph O 1933- *AmMWSc 92*
**Brinkley,** Alan 1949- *IntAu&W 91, WrDr 92*
**Brinkley,** Amy Woods 1956- *WhoFI 92*
**Brinkley,** Charles H., Sr. 1942- *WhoBlA 92*
**Brinkley,** Christie Lee 1954- *IntAu&W 91*
**Brinkley,** David *LesBEnT 92 [port]*
**Brinkley,** David 1920- *FacFETw, IntMPA 92, IntWW 91*
**Brinkley,** Eston Clyde, Jr. 1943- *WhoEnt 92*
**Brinkley,** Jack Thomas 1930- *WhoAmP 91, WhoEnt 92*
**Brinkley,** John Michael 1944- *AmMWSc 92*
**Brinkley,** John Romulus 1885-1942 *DcNCBi 1*
**Brinkley,** Linda Lee 1943- *AmMWSc 92*
**Brinkley,** Norman, Jr. 1931- *WhoBlA 92*
**Brinkley,** Stanley Alan 1950- *WhoAmP 91*
**Brinkley,** William John 1925- *WhoMW 92*
**Brinkmam-Mendoza,** Nancy L 1949- *WhoAmP 91*
**Brinkman,** Allan 1948- *WhoIns 92*
**Brinkman,** Bernard J *WhoAmP 91*
**Brinkman,** Charles R 1937- *AmMWSc 92*
**Brinkman,** Clarence Arthur 1929- *WhoMW 92*
**Brinkman,** Dale Thomas 1952- *WhoAmL 92*
**Brinkman,** Daniel John 1950- *WhoMW 92*
**Brinkman,** Edwin Lee 1934- *WhoMW 92*
**Brinkman,** Gabriel 1924- *WhoRel 92*
**Brinkman,** Herbert Charles 1926- *WhoAmL 92*
**Brinkman,** John Anthony 1934- *WhoMW 92*
**Brinkman,** Joyce Elaine 1944- *WhoAmP 91*
**Brinkman,** Kathleen M. 1943- *WhoAmL 92*
**Brinkman,** Leonard Cornelis 1948- *IntWW 91*
**Brinkman,** Michael Phil 1944- *WhoEnt 92*
**Brinkman,** William F 1938- *AmMWSc 92*
**Brinkmann,** Robert Joseph 1950- *WhoAmL 92*
**Brinkmann,** Robert S. 1961- *WhoEnt 92*
**Brinkmeyer,** Raymond Samuel 1948- *AmMWSc 92*
**Brinks,** Donald Anthony 1928- *WhoMW 92*
**Brinks,** James S 1934- *AmMWSc 92*
**Brinley,** Charles A 1847-1919 *BiInAmS*
**Brinley,** Floyd John, Jr 1930- *AmMWSc 92*
**Brinley Jones,** Robert *Who 92*
**Brinn,** Chauncey J. 1932- *WhoBlA 92*
**Brinn,** Jack Elliott, Jr 1942- *AmMWSc 92*
**Brinnin,** John Malcolm *DrAPF 91*
**Brinnin,** John Malcolm 1916- *BenetAL 91, ConPo 91, IntAu&W 91, IntWW 91, WrDr 92*
**Brinon,** Fernand de 1885-1947 *BiDExR*
**Brinsfield,** Shirley D. 1922- *WhoFI 92*
**Brinsley,** John Harrington 1933- *WhoAmL 92*
**Brinsmade,** Herman Hine *ScFEYrs*
**Brinsmade,** Lyon Louis 1924- *WhoAmL 92*
**Brinsmead,** H F *IntAu&W 91X*
**Brinsmead,** H. F. 1922- *WrDr 92*
**Brinsmead Hungerford,** Hesba Fay 1922- *IntAu&W 91*
**Brinson,** Gay Creswell, Jr. 1925- *WhoAmL 92*
**Brinson,** Mark McClellan 1943- *AmMWSc 92*
**Brinson,** Melville Gibbons, III 1961- *WhoAmL 92*
**Brinson,** Samuel Mitchell 1870-1922 *DcNCBi 1*
**Brinster,** Kenneth Joseph 1953- *WhoWest 92*
**Brinster,** Ralph L 1932- *AmMWSc 92*
**Brint,** Armand *DrAPF 91*
**Brinton,** Bradford Hickman 1935- *WhoAmL 92*
**Brinton,** Charles Chester, Jr 1926- *AmMWSc 92*
**Brinton,** Crane 1898-1968 *BenetAL 91*
**Brinton,** Daniel Garrison 1837-1899 *BenetAL 91, BiInAmS*
**Brinton,** Dilworth Carlos 1917- *WhoWest 92*
**Brinton,** Donald Eugene 1927- *WhoAmP 91*
**Brinton,** Edward 1924- *AmMWSc 92*
**Brinton,** Ellen Starr 1886-1954 *AmPeW*
**Brinton,** Howard Haines 1884-1973 *RelLAm 91*
**Brinton,** Richard Kirk 1946- *WhoWest 92*
**Brinton,** Timothy Denis 1929- *Who 92*
**Brinzo,** John S. 1942- *WhoFI 92*
**Brion,** Christopher Edward 1937- *AmMWSc 92*
**Briones,** Robert A. *WhoHisp 92*
**Brisbane,** Archbishop of 1916- *Who 92*
**Brisbane,** Archbishop of 1935- *Who 92*
**Brisbane,** Assistant Bishops of *Who 92*
**Brisbane,** Albert 1809-1890 *BenetAL 91*
**Brisbane,** Samuel Chester 1914- *WhoBlA 92*
**Brisbin,** Doreen A 1926- *AmMWSc 92*
**Brisbin,** I Lehr, Jr 1940- *AmMWSc 92*
**Brisbin,** Robert Edward 1946- *WhoWest 92*
**Brisby,** Stewart *DrAPF 91*
**Brischetto,** Stephen Louis 1952- *WhoAmL 92*
**Brisco,** Donald Gilfrid 1920- *Who 92*
**Brisco,** P A *IntAu&W 91X, WrDr 92*
**Brisco,** Patty *IntAu&W 91X, WrDr 92*
**Brisco-Hooks,** Valerie 1960- *BlkOlyM [port], WhoBlA 92*
**Briscoe,** Alex Shell *ScFEYrs*
**Briscoe,** Anne M 1918- *AmMWSc 92*
**Briscoe,** Arthur 1873-1943 *TwCPaSc*
**Briscoe,** Barrie 1936- *TwCPaSc*
**Briscoe,** Brian Anthony 1945- *Who 92*
**Briscoe,** Charles Victor 1930- *AmMWSc 92*
**Briscoe,** Edward Gans 1937- *WhoBlA 92*
**Briscoe,** Glenn *WhoAmP 91*
**Briscoe,** Hattie Ruth Elam 1916- *WhoBlA 92*
**Briscoe,** Jack Clayton 1920- *WhoAmL 92*
**Briscoe,** James E 1942- *WhoAmP 91*
**Briscoe,** John 1911- *Who 92*
**Briscoe,** John 1948- *AmMWSc 92, WhoAmL 92, WhoWest 92*
**Briscoe,** John Frederick, Jr. 1952- *WhoWest 92*
**Briscoe,** John Hanson 1934- *WhoAmP 91*
**Briscoe,** John William 1917- *AmMWSc 92*
**Briscoe,** June T. 1961- *WhoBlA 92*
**Briscoe,** Leonard E. 1940- *WhoBlA 92*
**Briscoe,** Marianne Grier 1945- *WhoWest 92*
**Briscoe,** Melbourne George 1941- *AmMWSc 92*
**Briscoe,** Sidney Edward, Jr. 1929- *WhoBlA 92*
**Briscoe,** Thomas F. 1910- *WhoBlA 92*
**Briscoe,** William Travis *AmMWSc 92*
**Brise** *Who 92*
**Brisebois,** Marcel 1933- *WhoMW 92*
**Briseno,** Alex 1950- *WhoHisp 92*
**Briseno,** Fernando Antonio 1967- *WhoHisp 92*
**Briseno,** Francisco P. *WhoHisp 92*
**Briske,** Bonnie Belle 1943- *WhoAmP 91*
**Briske,** David D 1951- *AmMWSc 92*
**Brisker,** Lawrence 1934- *WhoBlA 92*
**Briskin,** Bernard 1924- *WhoFI 92*
**Briskin,** Jacqueline 1927- *IntAu&W 91, WrDr 92*
**Briskin,** Jonathan Kalonymus 1960- *WhoEnt 92*
**Briskin,** Mae *DrAPF 91*
**Briskin,** Mae 1924- *ConAu 134*
**Briskin,** Mort 1919- *IntMPA 92*
**Brisley,** Chester L 1914- *AmMWSc 92*
**Brisley,** Stuart 1933- *TwCPaSc*
**Brislin,** Ralph Francis 1955- *WhoMW 92*
**Brison,** Kenneth E 1939- *WhoAmP 91*
**Brison,** William Stanley 1929- *Who 92, WhoRel 92*
**Brissenden,** Alan 1932- *WrDr 92*
**Brissenden,** Alan Theo 1932- *IntAu&W 91*
**Brissenden,** Robert Francis 1928- *IntWW 91*
**Brissette,** Martha Blevins 1959- *WhoAmL 92*
**Brisson,** Elsa Ramirez 1954- *WhoHisp 92*
**Brisson,** Germain J 1920- *AmMWSc 92*
**Brisson,** Pat 1951- *ConAu 134, SmATA 67 [port]*
**Brissot,** Jacques Pierre 1754-1793 *BlkwCEP*
**Brissot de Warville,** Jacques Pierre 1754-1793 *BlkwCEP*
**Brister,** Arthur Mack, Sr. 1937- *WhoRel 92*
**Brister,** C. W. 1926- *WhoRel 92*
**Brister,** Mark Allen 1951- *WhoRel 92*
**Brister,** Richard 1915- *IntAu&W 91, WrDr 92*
**Brister,** Thomas Stanley 1940- *WhoFI 92*
**Brister,** William Arthur Francis 1925- *Who 92*
**Bristley,** Calvin Wesley, Jr. 1926- *WhoAmL 92, WhoAmP 91*
**Bristol,** Archdeacon of *Who 92*
**Bristol,** Bishop of *IntWW 91*
**Bristol,** Bishop of 1936- *Who 92*
**Bristol,** Dean of *Who 92*
**Bristol,** Marquess of 1954- *Who 92*
**Bristol,** Benton Keith 1920- *AmMWSc 92*
**Bristol,** David *DrAPF 91*
**Bristol,** Douglas Walter 1940- *AmMWSc 92*
**Bristol,** Fred A., III 1952- *WhoEnt 92*
**Bristol,** John Richard 1938- *AmMWSc 92*
**Bristol,** Melvin Lee 1936- *AmMWSc 92*
**Bristol,** Ralph Buffum, Jr. 1931- *WhoFI 92*
**Bristow,** Alan Edgar 1923- *Who 92*
**Bristow,** Benjamin Helm 1832-1896 *AmPolLe*
**Bristow,** Charles William 1953- *WhoWest 92*
**Bristow,** Clinton, Jr. 1949- *WhoBlA 92*
**Bristow,** George Frederick 1825-1898 *NewAmDM*
**Bristow,** Gwen 1903-1980 *BenetAL 91, TwCWW 91*
**Bristow,** John David 1928- *AmMWSc 92*
**Bristow,** Lonnie Robert 1930- *AmMWSc 92*
**Bristow,** Lucille May 1937- *WhoAmP 91*
**Bristow,** Peter 1913- *Who 92*
**Bristow,** Peter Richard 1946- *AmMWSc 92*
**Bristow,** Robert James 1935- *WhoAmP 91*
**Bristow,** Robert O'Neil 1926- *IntAu&W 91, WrDr 92*
**Bristow,** Tom *WhoAmP 91*
**Bristow,** Walter James, Jr. 1924- *WhoAmL 92*
**Bristow,** Wayne Douglass 1949- *WhoRel 92*
**Bristowe,** William Warren 1940- *AmMWSc 92*
**Britain,** Dan *IntAu&W 91X, WrDr 92*
**Britain,** James Edward 1950- *WhoAmL 92*
**Britain,** Lucille Helen 1933- *WhoAmP 91*
**Britain,** Radie 1908- *WhoEnt 92*
**Britell,** Peter Stuart 1940- *WhoAmL 92*
**British Royal Family** *NewYTBS 91*
**British Columbia,** Bishop of 1926- *Who 92*
**British Columbia,** Metropolitan of *Who 92*
**Britnell,** Charlie *WhoAmP 91*
**Brito,** Aristeo 1942- *WhoHisp 92*
**Brito,** Christi L 1955- *WhoAmP 91*
**Brito,** Dagobert Llanos 1941- *WhoFI 92, WhoHisp 92*
**Brito,** John Solomon 1945- *WhoHisp 92*
**Brito,** Jose Manuel 1948- *WhoHisp 92*
**Brito,** Maria Teresa 1952- *WhoAmL 92*
**Brito,** Phil 1915- *WhoEnt 92*
**Brito,** Silvia E. 1933- *WhoHisp 92*
**Britschgi,** Brenton Carl 1935- *WhoAmP 91*
**Britt,** Alan *DrAPF 91*
**Britt,** Brian Michael 1964- *WhoRel 92*
**Britt,** Charles Robin 1942- *WhoAmP 91*
**Britt,** Clifford Calvin 1948- *WhoAmP 91*
**Britt,** Danny Gilbert 1946- *AmMWSc 92*
**Britt,** David Van Buren 1937- *WhoFI 92*
**Britt,** Dewey Duane, Jr. 1959- *WhoAmL 92*
**Britt,** Douglas Lee 1946- *AmMWSc 92*
**Britt,** Edward Joseph 1941- *AmMWSc 92*
**Britt,** Eugene Leslie 1941- *WhoWest 92*
**Britt,** Eugene Maurice 1924- *AmMWSc 92*
**Britt,** George Gittion, Jr. 1949- *WhoFI 92*
**Britt,** Glenn Alan 1949- *WhoFI 92*
**Britt,** Harold Curran 1934- *AmMWSc 92*
**Britt,** Henry Middleton 1919- *WhoAmL 92, WhoAmP 91*
**Britt,** James Jefferson 1861-1939 *DcNCBi 1*
**Britt,** John Francis 1927- *WhoMW 92*
**Britt,** Katrina *WrDr 92*
**Britt,** Maisha Dorrah *WhoAmL 92, WhoFI 92*
**Britt,** N Wilson 1913- *AmMWSc 92*
**Britt,** Patricia Marie 1931- *AmMWSc 92*
**Britt,** Paul D., Jr. 1951- *WhoBlA 92*
**Britt,** Ronald Leroy 1935- *WhoMW 92*

**Britt**, Susan Fagen 1947- WhoAmL 92
**Britt**, Teresa Marie 1961- WhoFI 92
**Britt**, W. Earl 1932- WhoAmL 92
**Brittain**, Alfred, III 1922- IntWW 91
**Brittain**, Bill DrAPF 91, WrDr 92
**Brittain**, Bradley Bernard, Jr. 1948- WhoBlA 92
**Brittain**, David B 1925- AmMWSc 92
**Brittain**, Donald 1928-1989 FacFETw
**Brittain**, Gary Ray 1957- WhoRel 92
**Brittain**, Jack Oliver 1928- WhoAmL 92, WhoAmP 91
**Brittain**, Jeffrey Charles 1949- WhoWest 92
**Brittain**, John O 1920- AmMWSc 92
**Brittain**, Paul Alfred Robert 1949- WhoRel 92
**Brittain**, Ross 1951- WhoEnt 92
**Brittain**, Thomas M 1934- AmMWSc 92
**Brittain**, Vera RfGEnL 91
**Brittain**, Vera 1894-1970 FacFETw
**Brittain**, Vera Mary 1893-1970 BiDBrF 2
**Brittain**, William 1930- WrDr 92
**Brittain**, William Joseph 1955- AmMWSc 92
**Brittan**, Leon 1939- IntWW 91, Who 92
**Brittan**, Martin Ralph 1922- AmMWSc 92
**Brittan**, Samuel 1933- IntAu&W 91, IntWW 91, Who 92, WrDr 92
**Brittany**, Morgan 1951- IntMPA 92
**Brittelli**, David Ross 1944- AmMWSc 92
**Britten**, Alan Edward Marsh 1938- Who 92
**Britten**, Benjamin 1913-1976 FacFETw [port], NewAmDM
**Britten**, Bill WhoEnt 92
**Britten**, Bryan Terrence 1933- AmMWSc 92
**Britten**, Edward James 1915- AmMWSc 92
**Britten**, Emma Hardinge 1823-1899 RelLAm 91
**Britten**, George Vallette 1909- Who 92
**Britten**, Gerald 1930- WhoAmP 91
**Britten**, Michel 1960- AmMWSc 92
**Britten**, Rae Gordon 1920- Who 92
**Britten**, Robert Wallace Tudor 1922- Who 92
**Britten**, Roy John 1919- AmMWSc 92, IntWW 91
**Britten**, William Harry 1921- WhoMW 92
**Brittenden**, Arthur 1924- Who 92
**Brittin**, Dorothy Helen Clark 1938- AmMWSc 92
**Brittin**, Norman Aylsworth 1906- WrDr 92
**Brittin**, Wesley E 1917- AmMWSc 92
**Britting**, Robert Joseph 1948- WhoFI 92
**Britto**, Ronald 1937- WhoFI 92
**Britton**, Albert B., Jr. 1922- WhoBlA 92
**Britton**, Allen Perdue 1914- WhoEnt 92
**Britton**, Andrew James Christie 1940- Who 92
**Britton**, Benjamin Jay 1958- WhoEnt 92
**Britton**, Carlton M 1944- AmMWSc 92
**Britton**, Charles Cooper 1922- AmMWSc 92
**Britton**, Charles Harvey 1941- WhoRel 92
**Britton**, Charles William 1918-1985 RelLAm 91
**Britton**, Clarence Keith 1930- WhoRel 92
**Britton**, Clarold Lawrence 1932- WhoAmL 92
**Britton**, Denis 1920- WrDr 92
**Britton**, Denis King 1920- Who 92
**Britton**, Donald MacPhail 1923- AmMWSc 92
**Britton**, Doyle 1930- AmMWSc 92
**Britton**, Edward 1909- Who 92
**Britton**, Edward Charles 1955- WhoAmL 92
**Britton**, Elizabeth 1930- WhoBlA 92
**Britton**, Erwin Adelbert 1915- WhoRel 92
**Britton**, Gwendolyn Faye 1937- WhoMW 92
**Britton**, John H., Jr. 1937- WhoBlA 92
**Britton**, John William 1936- Who 92
**Britton**, Joseph Scott 1957- WhoAmL 92
**Britton**, Lionel 1887- ScFEYrs
**Britton**, Marvin Gale 1922- AmMWSc 92
**Britton**, Mary Kay 1939- WhoWest 92
**Britton**, Maxwell Edwin 1912- AmMWSc 92
**Britton**, Otha Leon 1945- AmMWSc 92
**Britton**, Scott Richard 1960- WhoAmL 92
**Britton**, Steven Loyal 1948- AmMWSc 92
**Britton**, Theodore R., Jr. 1925- WhoBlA 92
**Britton**, Theodore Roosevelt, Jr 1925- WhoAmP 91
**Britton**, Thomas Warren, Jr. 1944- WhoWest 92
**Britton**, Tony 1924- IntMPA 92
**Britton**, Walter Martin 1939- AmMWSc 92
**Britton**, William Giering 1921- AmMWSc 92
**Britz**, Diane Edward 1952- WhoFI 92
**Britz**, Galen C 1939- AmMWSc 92
**Britz**, Jack 1930- Who 92
**Britz**, Lewis 1933- Who 92
**Britz**, Steven J 1949- AmMWSc 92
**Britzman**, Darwin Gene 1931- AmMWSc 92
**Brixey**, John Clark 1904- AmMWSc 92
**Brixner**, Lothar Heinrich 1928- AmMWSc 92
**Brixton**, Denby ScFEYrs
**Brixworth**, Bishop Suffragan of 1935- Who 92
**Brizgys**, Bernardas Justinas 1915- WhoMW 92
**Brizgys**, Vincas DcAmImH
**Brizgys**, Vincentas 1903- WhoRel 92
**Brizio-Molteni**, Loredana 1927- AmMWSc 92
**Brizzee**, Kenneth Raymond 1916- AmMWSc 92
**Brizzi**, Nancy Lee 1965- WhoEnt 92
**Brizzolara**, Paul Thomas 1957- WhoAmL 92
**Broach**, Robert William 1949- AmMWSc 92
**Broach**, S. Elizabeth WhoBlA 92
**Broach**, Wilson J 1915- AmMWSc 92
**Broach-Sowels**, Ethylean Holly 1952- WhoMW 92
**Broackes**, Nigel 1934- IntWW 91, Who 92
**Broad**, Alfred Carter 1922- AmMWSc 92
**Broad**, Charlie Dunbar 1887-1971 FacFETw
**Broad**, Eli 1933- WhoWest 92
**Broad**, Michael 1951- WhoAmL 92
**Broadaway**, Gerald WhoRel 92
**Broadbear**, Michael Webster 1941- WhoAmL 92
**Broadbent**, Amalia Sayo Castillo 1956- WhoEnt 92, WhoFI 92
**Broadbent**, Donald 1926- IntAu&W 91, WrDr 92
**Broadbent**, Donald Eric 1926- IntWW 91, Who 92
**Broadbent**, Edward Granville 1923- IntWW 91, Who 92
**Broadbent**, Ewen 1924- Who 92
**Broadbent**, Francis Everett 1922- AmMWSc 92
**Broadbent**, George 1935- Who 92
**Broadbent**, Hyrum Smith 1920- AmMWSc 92
**Broadbent**, John Edward 1936- IntWW 91
**Broadbent**, Michael 1927- Who 92
**Broadbent**, Noel Daniel 1946- AmMWSc 92
**Broadbent**, Simon Hope 1942- Who 92
**Broadbooks**, Harold Eugene 1915- AmMWSc 92
**Broadbridge** Who 92
**Broadbridge**, Baron 1938- Who 92
**Broaddus**, Charles D 1930- AmMWSc 92
**Broaddus**, Charles David 1930- WhoFI 92
**Broaddus**, John Alfred, Jr. 1939- WhoFI 92
**Broaddus**, William WhoAmP 91
**Broadfield**, Aubrey Alfred 1910- WrDr 92
**Broadfoot**, Albert Lyle 1930- AmMWSc 92
**Broadhead**, Garland Carr 1827-1912 BiInAmS
**Broadhead**, James Lowell 1935- WhoFI 92
**Broadhead**, Paul WhoEnt 92
**Broadhead**, Ronald Frigon 1955- AmMWSc 92, WhoWest 92
**Broadhurst**, Austin 1917- WhoAmL 92
**Broadhurst**, Austin, Jr. 1947- WhoFI 92
**Broadhurst**, Edwin Borden 1915-1965 DcNCBi 1
**Broadhurst**, George H. 1866-1952 BenetAL 91
**Broadhurst**, Harry 1905- Who 92
**Broadhurst**, Martin Gilbert 1932- AmMWSc 92
**Broadhurst**, Norman Neil 1946- WhoFI 92, WhoWest 92
**Broadley**, Denise 1913- TwCPaSc
**Broadley**, John Kenneth Elliott 1936- Who 92
**Broadman**, Richard James 1946- WhoEnt 92
**Broadnax**, David IntMPA 92, WhoEnt 92
**Broadnax**, Madison 1914- WhoBlA 92
**Broadnax**, Melvin F. 1929- WhoBlA 92
**Broadright**, Larry Raymond 1956- WhoRel 92
**Broadus**, Clyde R. WhoBlA 92
**Broadus**, James Matthew 1947- AmMWSc 92
**Broadus**, John Albert 1827-1895 RelLAm 91
**Broadus**, Joseph Edward 1946- WhoAmL 92
**Broadwater**, Douglas Dwight 1944- WhoAmL 92
**Broadwater**, Tommie, Jr 1942- WhoAmP 91, WhoBlA 92
**Broadway**, Judith Lee 1935- WhoAmP 91
**Broadway**, Roxanne Meyer 1951- AmMWSc 92
**Broadwell**, Clyde ScFEYrs
**Broadwell**, James E 1921- AmMWSc 92
**Broadwell**, Richard Dow 1945- AmMWSc 92
**Broadwin**, Joseph Louis 1930- WhoAmL 92
**Broadwood**, John 1732-1812 NewAmDM
**Broady**, Earl Clifford 1904- WhoBlA 92
**Broback**, Art WhoAmP 91
**Brobeck**, John R. 1914- IntWW 91
**Brobeck**, John Raymond 1914- AmMWSc 92
**Broberg**, Joel Wilbur 1910- AmMWSc 92
**Brobst**, Donald Albert 1925- AmMWSc 92
**Brobst**, Duane Franklin 1923- AmMWSc 92
**Brobst**, Kenneth Martin 1915- AmMWSc 92
**Brobst**, Robert Arthur 1922- WhoMW 92
**Broca**, Philippe de 1933- IntDcF 2-2
**Brocard**, Dominique Nicolas AmMWSc 92
**Brocas**, Viscount 1950- Who 92
**Brocato**, Vincent Joseph, Jr. 1954- WhoFI 92
**Broccoli**, Albert 1909- IntMPA 92
**Broccoli**, Albert Romolo 1909- IntWW 91, WhoEnt 92
**Broccoli**, Anthony Joseph 1956- AmMWSc 92
**Broch**, Harald Beyer 1944- ConAu 135
**Broch**, Hermann 1886-1951 EncTR 91, FacFETw, LiExTwC
**Brochand**, Christian Pierre 1935- IntWW 91
**Broches**, Aron 1914- IntWW 91
**Brochmann-Hanssen**, Einar 1917- AmMWSc 92
**Brochner-Mortensen**, Knud 1906- IntWW 91
**Brock** Who 92
**Brock**, Bernard Lee 1932- WhoMW 92
**Brock**, Betty 1923- WrDr 92
**Brock**, Carolyn Pratt 1946- AmMWSc 92
**Brock**, Charles Marquis 1941- WhoAmL 92, WhoFI 92, WhoMW 92
**Brock**, David A WhoAmP 91
**Brock**, David Allen 1936- WhoAmL 92
**Brock**, Delia SmATA 65
**Brock**, Donald R AmMWSc 92
**Brock**, Edwin 1927- ConPo 91, IntAu&W 91, WrDr 92
**Brock**, Ernest George 1926- AmMWSc 92
**Brock**, Foster C., Jr. 1945- WhoRel 92
**Brock**, Fred Vincent 1932- AmMWSc 92
**Brock**, Gary Lynn 1942- WhoRel 92
**Brock**, Geoffrey E 1930- AmMWSc 92
**Brock**, George William 1920- AmMWSc 92
**Brock**, Gerald 1932- WhoBlA 92
**Brock**, Harry Blackwell, Jr. 1926- WhoFI 92
**Brock**, Ignatius Wadsworth 1866-1950 DcNCBi 1
**Brock**, James Harvey 1957- AmMWSc 92
**Brock**, James Hassel 1941- WhoFI 92
**Brock**, James Leslie 1944- WhoWest 92
**Brock**, James Rush 1937- AmMWSc 92
**Brock**, James Sidney 1913- WhoAmL 92
**Brock**, John 1932- WhoAmP 91
**Brock**, John E 1918- AmMWSc 92
**Brock**, John H 1937- WhoAmP 91
**Brock**, John Morgan, Jr. 1956- WhoEnt 92
**Brock**, Karena Diane 1942- WhoEnt 92
**Brock**, Katherine Middleton 1938- AmMWSc 92
**Brock**, Kenneth Jack 1937- AmMWSc 92
**Brock**, Larry Raymond 1946- WhoWest 92
**Brock**, Laura Lindley 1960- WhoEnt 92
**Brock**, Lila Mae 1915- WhoBlA 92
**Brock**, Lonnie Rex 1950- WhoWest 92
**Brock**, Louis Clark 1939- FacFETw, WhoBlA 92
**Brock**, Louis Milton 1943- AmMWSc 92
**Brock**, Margaret Martin WhoAmP 91
**Brock**, Mary Anne 1932- AmMWSc 92
**Brock**, Michael 1920- WrDr 92
**Brock**, Michael George 1920- Who 92
**Brock**, Patrick Laurence 1918- WhoRel 92
**Brock**, Patrick Willet Grote 1932- AmMWSc 92
**Brock**, Paul Warrington 1928- WhoAmL 92
**Brock**, Peter de Beauvoir 1920- WrDr 92
**Brock**, Ralph Eldon 1926- WhoRel 92
**Brock**, Randall DrAPF 91
**Brock**, Ray Leonard, Jr 1922- WhoAmP 91
**Brock**, Richard Eugene 1943- AmMWSc 92
**Brock**, Richard Linton 1945- WhoAmL 92
**Brock**, Richard R 1938- AmMWSc 92
**Brock**, Robert H, Jr 1933- AmMWSc 92
**Brock**, Robert Lee 1924- WhoAmP 91
**Brock**, Rose WrDr 92
**Brock**, Sebastian Paul 1938- Who 92
**Brock**, Stephen Francis 1959- WhoAmL 92
**Brock**, Stuart TwCWW 91
**Brock**, Susan Ann 1947- WhoMW 92
**Brock**, Thomas 1847-1922 TwCPaSc
**Brock**, Thomas Dale 1926- AmMWSc 92
**Brock**, Thomas Leon 1946- WhoRel 92
**Brock**, Tommy A AmMWSc 92
**Brock**, Van K. DrAPF 91
**Brock**, Walter Edgar, Jr. 1952- WhoAmL 92
**Brock**, William Allen, III 1941- WhoFI 92, WhoMW 92
**Brock**, William Emerson 1872-1950 DcNCBi 1
**Brock**, William Emerson 1930- IntWW 91
**Brock**, William Emerson, III 1930- WhoAmP 91
**Brock**, William Hodson 1936- WrDr 92
**Brock**, William Ranulf 1916- IntAu&W 91, IntWW 91, Who 92, WrDr 92
**Brock-Broido**, Lucie DrAPF 91
**Brocka**, Bruce 1959- WhoMW 92
**Brocka**, Lino d1991 NewYTBS 91
**Brocka**, Lino 1940- IntDcF 2-2
**Brockbank**, Albert Ernest 1862-1958 TwCPaSc
**Brockbank**, Gary H WhoAmP 91
**Brockbank**, James Tyrrell 1920- Who 92
**Brockbank**, John Myles 1921- Who 92
**Brockbank**, Tyrrell Who 92
**Brocke**, Rainer H 1933- AmMWSc 92
**Brockelman**, Michael D 1939- WhoAmP 91
**Brockemeyer**, Eugene William 1929- AmMWSc 92
**Brockenborough**, Joseph Antonio 1921-1990 WhoBlA 92N
**Brockenbrough**, Edwin C 1930- AmMWSc 92
**Brockerhoff**, Hans 1928- AmMWSc 92
**Brocket**, Baron 1952- Who 92
**Brockett**, Charles A. 1937- WhoBlA 92
**Brockett**, John Henry, Jr. 1915- WhoBlA 92
**Brockett**, Oscar Gross 1923- IntAu&W 91, WrDr 92
**Brockett**, Patrick Lee 1948- AmMWSc 92
**Brockett**, Roger Ware 1938- AmMWSc 92
**Brockett**, Ronald WhoBlA 92
**Brockfeld**, Russell G 1926- WhoAmP 91
**Brockhaus**, Robert Herold, Sr. 1940- WhoFI 92, WhoMW 92
**Brockhoff**, Jack 1908- Who 92
**Brockholes**, Michael John F. Who 92
**Brockhouse**, Bertram Neville 1918- AmMWSc 92, Who 92
**Brockhouse**, James Edward 1943- WhoFI 92
**Brockhurst**, Gerald 1890-1978 TwCPaSc
**Brockie**, Edward Simmons, Jr. 1925- WhoIns 92
**Brockington**, Benjamin 1933- WhoBlA 92
**Brockington**, Colin Fraser 1903- Who 92
**Brockington**, Donella P. 1952- WhoBlA 92
**Brockington**, Eugene Alfonzo 1931- WhoBlA 92
**Brockington**, Howard Burnell 1922- WhoEnt 92
**Brockington**, Ian Fraser 1935- IntWW 91
**Brockington**, James Wallace 1943- AmMWSc 92
**Brockington**, Joseph Lawrence 1951- WhoMW 92
**Brockish**, Robert Francis 1931- WhoWest 92
**Brocklebank**, Aubrey 1952- Who 92
**Brocklebank-Fowler**, Christopher 1934- Who 92
**Brocklehurst**, Arthur Evers 1905- Who 92
**Brocklehurst**, John Charles 1924- Who 92
**Brocklehurst**, Robert James 1899- Who 92
**Brocklesby**, David William 1929- Who 92
**Brocklesby**, John 1811-1889 BiInAmS
**Brockman**, Charles Thurston 1927- WhoMW 92
**Brockman**, David Dean 1922- AmMWSc 92
**Brockman**, Ellis R 1934- AmMWSc 92
**Brockman**, Estes David 1937- WhoAmL 92
**Brockman**, Harold W 1922- AmMWSc 92
**Brockman**, Harold William 1922- WhoMW 92
**Brockman**, Herman E 1934- AmMWSc 92
**Brockman**, Howard Lyle, Jr 1944- AmMWSc 92
**Brockman**, John A, Jr 1920- AmMWSc 92
**Brockman**, John J. 1946- IntMPA 92
**Brockman**, John Paul 1950- WhoMW 92
**Brockman**, John St Leger 1928- Who 92
**Brockman**, Michael 1938- IntMPA 92
**Brockman**, Peter 1938- WhoAmP 91
**Brockman**, Philip AmMWSc 92
**Brockman**, Robert W 1924- AmMWSc 92
**Brockman**, Ronald 1909- Who 92
**Brockman**, Terry James 1955- WhoFI 92
**Brockman**, Thomas Charles D. Who 92
**Brockman**, William Henry 1950- WhoFI 92
**Brockman**, William Warner 1942- AmMWSc 92
**Brockmann**, Helen Jane 1947- AmMWSc 92
**Brockmeier**, Norman Frederick 1937- AmMWSc 92

**Brockmeier,** Richard Taber 1937- *AmMWSc 92*
**Brocks-Shedd,** Virgia Lee 1943- *WhoBlA 92*
**Brocksbank,** Robert Wayne 1924- *WhoFI 92*
**Brocksome,** Brent 1946- *WhoAmP 91*
**Brockway,** Alan Priest 1936- *AmMWSc 92*
**Brockway,** David Hunt 1943- *WhoAmL 92*
**Brockway,** Fenner 1888- *IntAu&W 91*
**Brockway,** Fenner 1888-1988 *FacFETw*
**Brockway,** Fred John 1860-1901 *BiInAmS*
**Brockway,** George Pond 1915- *WhoFI 92*
**Brockway,** Merrill LaMonte 1923- *WhoEnt 92*
**Brockway,** Michael 1919- *TwCPaSc*
**Brockwell,** Peter John 1937- *AmMWSc 92*
**Brockwell,** Sherwood Battle 1885-1953 *DcNCBi 1*
**Brocoum,** Stephan John 1941- *AmMWSc 92*
**Brod,** Donald Frederick 1932- *WhoMW 92*
**Brod,** Max 1884-1960 *EncTR 91 [port]*
**Brod,** Max 1884-1968 *FacFETw, LiExTwC*
**Brod,** Stanford 1932- *WhoEnt 92*
**Broda,** Betty Lorraine 1932- *WhoAmP 91*
**Brodasky,** Thomas Francis 1930- *AmMWSc 92*
**Brodd,** Ralph James 1928- *AmMWSc 92*
**Brode,** David B. 1946- *WhoMW 92*
**Brode,** Marvin Jay 1931- *WhoAmL 92, WhoAmP 91*
**Brode,** William Edward 1929- *AmMWSc 92*
**Brodecki,** Joseph Michael 1946- *WhoFI 92*
**Broder,** Bill *DrAPF 91*
**Broder,** Douglas Fisher 1948- *WhoAmL 92*
**Broder,** Ernst-Gunther 1927- *IntWW 91, Who 92*
**Broder,** Irvin 1930- *AmMWSc 92*
**Broder,** Joe Arnold 1939- *WhoAmP 91*
**Broder,** Joseph Arnold 1939- *WhoAmL 92*
**Broder,** Martin Ivan 1936- *AmMWSc 92*
**Broder,** Samuel 1945- *AmMWSc 92*
**Broderick,** Anthony James 1943- *WhoFI 92*
**Broderick,** Beth Alison 1959- *WhoEnt 92*
**Broderick,** Damien 1944- *TwCSFW 91, WrDr 92*
**Broderick,** Damien Francis 1944- *IntAu&W 91*
**Broderick,** David Francis 1958- *WhoAmL 92*
**Broderick,** Dennis J. *WhoAmL 92*
**Broderick,** Edward M, III 1947- *WhoIns 92*
**Broderick,** Edward Michael, III 1947- *WhoAmL 92, WhoFI 92, WhoWest 92*
**Broderick,** Glen Allen 1945- *AmMWSc 92*
**Broderick,** Glen Reid 1943- *WhoWest 92*
**Broderick,** Harold Christian 1925- *WhoWest 92*
**Broderick,** James Anthony 1943- *WhoAmL 92*
**Broderick,** John 1940- *AmMWSc 92*
**Broderick,** Kilian J. *WhoRel 92*
**Broderick,** Laurence 1935- *TwCPaSc*
**Broderick,** Matthew 1962- *IntMPA 92, IntWW 91, WhoEnt 92*
**Broderick,** Richard James 1921- *WhoFI 92*
**Broderick,** Terry 1945- *WhoIns 92*
**Broderick,** Vincent Lyons 1920- *WhoAmL 92*
**Broderius,** Steven James 1943- *AmMWSc 92*
**Brodersen,** Arthur James 1939- *AmMWSc 92*
**Brodersen,** Robert W *AmMWSc 92*
**Broderson,** Stevan Hardy 1938- *AmMWSc 92*
**Brodeur,** Alfred L 1948- *WhoAmP 91*
**Brodeur,** Armand Edward 1922- *AmMWSc 92*
**Brodeur,** Paul 1931- *IntAu&W 91, WrDr 92*
**Brodeur,** Richard Dennis 1953- *WhoFI 92*
**Brodey,** Jim *DrAPF 91*
**Brodhag,** Alex Edgar, Jr 1924- *AmMWSc 92*
**Brodhead,** Charles Nelson, III 1963- *WhoRel 92*
**Brodhead,** David Crawmer 1934- *WhoAmL 92, WhoFI 92*
**Brodhead,** James Easton 1932- *WhoEnt 92*
**Brodhead,** William McNulty 1941- *WhoAmP 91*
**Brodhurst,** Albert Edward 1934- *WhoAmL 92*
**Brodian,** Laura 1947- *WhoEnt 92*
**Brodie,** Alan David 1960- *WhoWest 92*
**Brodie,** Ann Elizabeth 1943- *AmMWSc 92*
**Brodie,** Benjamin David Ross 1925- *Who 92*
**Brodie,** Bernard Beryl 1907- *AmMWSc 92*
**Brodie,** Bernard Beryl 1909-1989 *FacFETw*
**Brodie,** Bruce Orr 1924- *AmMWSc 92, WhoMW 92*
**Brodie,** Colin Alexander 1929- *Who 92*
**Brodie,** David Alan 1929- *AmMWSc 92*
**Brodie,** Don E 1929- *AmMWSc 92*
**Brodie,** Donald Crum 1908- *AmMWSc 92*
**Brodie,** Donald Gibbs 1938- *WhoFI 92*
**Brodie,** Edmund Darrell, Jr 1941- *AmMWSc 92*
**Brodie,** Elizabeth *Who 92*
**Brodie,** Harlow Keith Hammond 1939- *AmMWSc 92, IntWW 91, WhoAmL 92*
**Brodie,** Harry Joseph 1928- *AmMWSc 92*
**Brodie,** Howard 1915- *WhoWest 92*
**Brodie,** Ivor 1928- *AmMWSc 92*
**Brodie,** James Kennedy 1947- *WhoAmP 91*
**Brodie,** James William 1920- *IntWW 91*
**Brodie,** Jan Lois 1947- *WhoAmL 92*
**Brodie,** Janis 1938- *WhoAmL 92*
**Brodie,** Jean Pamela 1953- *AmMWSc 92*
**Brodie,** Jonathan D 1938- *AmMWSc 92*
**Brodie,** Laird Charles 1922- *AmMWSc 92*
**Brodie,** M. J. 1936- *WhoFI 92*
**Brodie,** Malcolm 1926- *IntAu&W 91*
**Brodie,** Mark S *AmMWSc 92*
**Brodie,** Norman 1920- *WhoIns 92*
**Brodie,** Peter Philip d1990 *Who 92N*
**Brodie,** Philip Hope 1950- *Who 92*
**Brodie,** Robert 1938- *Who 92*
**Brodie,** Stanley Eric 1930- *Who 92*
**Brodie,** Thomas 1903- *Who 92*
**Brodie-Hall,** Laurence Charles 1910- *Who 92*
**Brodie of Brodie,** Ninian 1912- *Who 92*
**Brodigan,** George Dimond 1928- *WhoAmL 92*
**Brodis,** Nellie Fannie 1916- *WhoBlA 92*
**Brodish,** Alvin 1925- *AmMWSc 92*
**Brodkey,** Andrew Alan 1956- *WhoAmL 92*
**Brodkey,** Donald 1910- *WhoAmP 91*
**Brodkey,** Harold *DrAPF 91*
**Brodkey,** Harold 1930- *BenetAL 91, ConNov 91, IntAu&W 91, WrDr 92*
**Brodkey,** Jerald Steven 1934- *AmMWSc 92*
**Brodkey,** R S 1928- *AmMWSc 92*
**Brodkey,** Robert Stanley 1928- *WhoMW 92*
**Brodkin,** Herbert d1991 *LesBEnT 92*
**Brodkin,** Herbert 1912-1990 *FacFETw*
**Brodkorb,** Pierce 1908- *AmMWSc 92*
**Brodmann,** John Milton 1933- *AmMWSc 92*
**Brodnax,** Edward Travis 1796-1874 *DcNCBi 1*
**Brodnax,** John Grammar 1829-1907 *DcNCBi 1*
**Brodney,** Oscar 1905- *IntMPA 92*
**Brodnik,** Carl Joseph, Jr. 1949- *WhoFI 92*
**Brodoff,** Bernard Noah 1923- *AmMWSc 92*
**Brodovitch,** Alexey 1898-1971 *DcTwDes, FacFETw*
**Brodoway,** Nicolas 1922- *AmMWSc 92*
**Brodribb,** Gerald 1915- *WrDr 92*
**Brodrick** *Who 92*
**Brodrick,** Alex 1944- *WhoRel 92*
**Brodrick,** Dorothy Lynn 1961- *WhoAmL 92*
**Brodrick,** Michael John Lee 1941- *Who 92*
**Brodrick,** Norman John Lee 1912- *Who 92*
**Brodsky,** Allen 1928- *AmMWSc 92*
**Brodsky,** Barry 1948- *WhoEnt 92*
**Brodsky,** Carroll M 1922- *AmMWSc 92*
**Brodsky,** David M. 1943- *WhoAmL 92*
**Brodsky,** Frances M *AmMWSc 92*
**Brodsky,** Frederick 1940- *WhoFI 92*
**Brodsky,** Iosif Aleksandrovich 1940- *IntAu&W 91, SovUnBD*
**Brodsky,** Isaak Izraelevich 1884-1939 *SovUnBD*
**Brodsky,** Jack 1932- *IntMPA 92*
**Brodsky,** Jeffrey Allan 1956- *WhoRel 92*
**Brodsky,** Joseph 1940- *BenetAL 91, FacFETw [port], LiExTwC, WrDr 92*
**Brodsky,** Joseph Aleksandrovich 1940- *IntWW 91*
**Brodsky,** Joseph Alexandrovich 1940- *NewYTBS 91 [port], Who 92, WhoNob 90*
**Brodsky,** Marc Herbert 1938- *AmMWSc 92*
**Brodsky,** Marshall David 1935- *WhoAmL 92*
**Brodsky,** Merwyn Berkley 1930- *AmMWSc 92*
**Brodsky,** Noel 1961- *WhoMW 92*
**Brodsky,** Philip Hyman 1942- *AmMWSc 92*
**Brodsky,** Richard Louis 1946- *WhoAmP 91*
**Brodsky,** Robert Jay 1939- *WhoFI 92*
**Brodsky,** Stanley Jerome 1940- *AmMWSc 92*
**Brodsky,** William Aaron 1918- *AmMWSc 92*
**Brodsky,** William J. 1944- *WhoFI 92*
**Brodsky,** William Martin 1941- *WhoAmL 92*
**Brodwick,** Malcolm Stephen 1944- *AmMWSc 92*
**Brodwin,** Morris E 1924- *AmMWSc 92*
**Brody,** Aaron Leo 1930- *AmMWSc 92*
**Brody,** Alan 1937- *WhoEnt 92*
**Brody,** Alan Jeffrey 1952- *WhoFI 92*
**Brody,** Alexander 1933- *WhoFI 92*
**Brody,** Alfred Walter 1920- *AmMWSc 92*
**Brody,** Arnold R 1943- *AmMWSc 92*
**Brody,** Bernard B 1922- *AmMWSc 92*
**Brody,** Burton Alan 1942- *AmMWSc 92*
**Brody,** Clark Louis 1914- *WhoEnt 92*
**Brody,** David 1930- *WhoWest 92*
**Brody,** David Allan 1916- *WhoAmL 92*
**Brody,** Edward Norman 1939- *AmMWSc 92*
**Brody,** Elly Rosemary 1941- *WhoWest 92*
**Brody,** Eugene B 1921- *AmMWSc 92*
**Brody,** Garry Sidney 1932- *AmMWSc 92*
**Brody,** Harold 1923- *AmMWSc 92*
**Brody,** Harold D 1939- *AmMWSc 92*
**Brody,** Harry *DrAPF 91*
**Brody,** Howard 1932- *AmMWSc 92*
**Brody,** Jacob A 1931- *AmMWSc 92*
**Brody,** Jane E. 1941- *WrDr 92*
**Brody,** Jane Ellen 1941- *IntWW 91*
**Brody,** Jean *DrAPF 91*
**Brody,** Jeffrey David *WhoEnt 92*
**Brody,** Jerome Ira 1928- *AmMWSc 92*
**Brody,** Jerome Saul 1934- *AmMWSc 92*
**Brody,** Leslie *DrAPF 91*
**Brody,** Marcia 1929- *AmMWSc 92*
**Brody,** Michael J 1934- *AmMWSc 92*
**Brody,** Morton *WhoAmP 91*
**Brody,** Nancy Louise 1954- *WhoAmL 92, WhoFI 92*
**Brody,** Paula 1936- *WhoEnt 92*
**Brody,** Randy 1951- *WhoEnt 92*
**Brody,** Richard David 1952- *WhoEnt 92*
**Brody,** Richard Eric 1947- *WhoAmL 92*
**Brody,** Richard Simon 1950- *AmMWSc 92*
**Brody,** Robert 1948- *WhoMW 92*
**Brody,** Seymour Steven 1927- *AmMWSc 92*
**Brody,** Sigmund A. 1941- *WhoIns 92*
**Brody,** Steven I. 1959- *WhoAmL 92*
**Brody,** Stuart 1937- *AmMWSc 92*
**Brody,** Stuart Martin 1936- *AmMWSc 92*
**Brody,** Theodore Meyer 1920- *AmMWSc 92*
**Brody-Watts,** Stella 1939- *WhoWest 92*
**Brodzinski,** Ronald Lee 1941- *AmMWSc 92*
**Brodzky,** Horace 1885-1969 *TwCPaSc*
**Broecker,** Eugene W 1931- *WhoIns 92*
**Broecker,** Eugene William 1931- *WhoFI 92*
**Broecker,** Howard William 1940- *WhoAmL 92*
**Broecker,** Wallace 1931- *AmMWSc 92*
**Broeder,** Robert Frederick 1958- *WhoMW 92*
**Broeg,** Charles Burton 1916- *AmMWSc 92*
**Broekema,** Dirk, Jr. 1936- *WhoFI 92*
**Broeker,** Barbara Ann 1946- *WhoMW 92*
**Broeker,** Galen 1920-1978 *ConAu 133*
**Broeker,** John Milton 1940- *WhoAmL 92*
**Broekhuysen,** Martin *DrAPF 91*
**Broemeling,** Lyle David 1939- *AmMWSc 92*
**Broene,** Gilbert Richard 1948- *WhoRel 92*
**Broene,** Herman Henry 1919- *AmMWSc 92*
**Broer,** Lawrence R. 1938- *WrDr 92*
**Broer,** Matthijs Meno 1956- *AmMWSc 92*
**Broer,** Roger L. 1945- *WhoWest 92*
**Broerman,** F S 1938- *AmMWSc 92*
**Broers,** Alec N 1938- *AmMWSc 92*
**Broers,** Alec Nigel 1938- *IntWW 91, Who 92*
**Broersma,** Delmar B 1934- *AmMWSc 92*
**Broersma,** Sybrand 1919- *AmMWSc 92*
**Brof,** Janet *DrAPF 91*
**Brofazi,** Frederick R 1933- *AmMWSc 92*
**Brofman,** Lance Mark 1949- *WhoFI 92*
**Brog,** Terrence Kenyon 1957- *WhoWest 92*
**Brogan,** Amy Genthner 1956- *WhoAmL 92*
**Brogan,** Elise *WrDr 92*
**Brogan,** George Edward 1944- *AmMWSc 92*
**Brogan,** James *WrDr 92*
**Brogan,** John Aloysius 1931- *WhoFI 92*
**Brogan,** Jonathan William 1959- *WhoAmL 92*
**Brogan,** Joyce Alice 1940- *WhoMW 92*
**Brogan,** Kevin Herbert 1953- *WhoAmL 92*
**Brogan,** Mervyn 1915- *Who 92*
**Brogan,** Ronald Edward 1946- *WhoMW 92*
**Brogan,** Thomas Patrick 1955- *WhoFI 92*
**Brogan,** William L 1935- *AmMWSc 92*
**Brogden,** Curtis Hooks 1816-1901 *DcNCBi 1*
**Brogdon,** Byron Gilliam 1929- *AmMWSc 92*
**Broge,** Robert Walter 1920- *AmMWSc 92*
**Broger,** Karl 1886-1944 *EncTR 91*
**Broggi,** Michael Joseph 1942- *WhoFI 92*
**Brogin,** Ira Michael 1947- *WhoFI 92*
**Brogle,** Richard Charles 1927- *AmMWSc 92*
**Brogliatti,** Barbara Spencer 1946- *WhoFI 92, WhoWest 92*
**Broglie,** Louis-Victor Pierre Raymond de 1892-1987 *WhoNob 90*
**Brogno,** August, Jr. 1935- *WhoFI 92*
**Brogoitti,** Robert A 1920- *WhoAmP 91*
**Broida,** Helen 1916- *IntAu&W 91*
**Broida,** Theodore Ray 1928- *AmMWSc 92*
**Broido,** Abraham 1924- *AmMWSc 92*
**Broido,** Arnold Peace 1920- *WhoEnt 92, WhoFI 92*
**Broido,** Debra Ann 1954- *WhoWest 92*
**Broido,** Jeffrey Hale 1934- *AmMWSc 92*
**Broido,** Thomas Alan 1953- *WhoEnt 92*
**Broiles,** Melvyn *WhoEnt 92*
**Broiles,** Rowland David 1938- *WhoAmL 92*
**Broin,** Thayne Leo 1922- *AmMWSc 92*
**Broinowski,** John Herbert 1911- *Who 92*
**Broitman,** Selwyn Arthur 1931- *AmMWSc 92*
**Brojanac,** Rosaline Rose 1924- *WhoAmP 91*
**Brokamp,** Joyce Marie 1954- *WhoMW 92*
**Brokaw,** Beth Fletcher 1955- *WhoWest 92*
**Brokaw,** Bryan Edward 1949- *AmMWSc 92*
**Brokaw,** Carol Ann 1946- *WhoBlA 92*
**Brokaw,** Cary Scott 1951- *WhoEnt 92*
**Brokaw,** Charles Jacob 1934- *AmMWSc 92*
**Brokaw,** George Young 1921- *AmMWSc 92*
**Brokaw,** Jim *WhoAmP 91*
**Brokaw,** Kurt John 1938- *WhoRel 92*
**Brokaw,** Norman R. 1927- *IntMPA 92*
**Brokaw,** Norman Robert 1927- *WhoEnt 92, WhoFI 92*
**Brokaw,** Richard Spohn 1923- *AmMWSc 92*
**Brokaw,** Thomas John 1940- *IntWW 91*
**Brokaw,** Tom *LesBEnT 92 [port]*
**Brokaw,** Tom 1940- *IntMPA 92*
**Broke** *Who 92*
**Broke,** George Robin Straton 1946- *Who 92*
**Broke,** Robert Straton 1913- *Who 92*
**Brokensha,** John Joseph 1926- *WhoEnt 92*
**Broker,** Jeffrey John 1949- *WhoFI 92*
**Broker,** Thomas Richard 1944- *AmMWSc 92*
**Brokering,** T. Mark 1952- *WhoRel 92*
**Brokhoff,** John Rudolph 1913- *WhoRel 92*
**Brokke,** Catherine Juliet 1926- *WhoMW 92, WhoRel 92*
**Brolin,** James *WhoEnt 92*
**Brolin,** James 1940- *IntMPA 92*
**Brolin,** Robert Edward 1948- *AmMWSc 92*
**Brolley,** John Edward, Jr 1919- *AmMWSc 92*
**Brolmann,** John Bernardus 1920- *AmMWSc 92*
**Brom,** Joseph March, Jr 1942- *AmMWSc 92*
**Brom,** Rafael 1952- *WhoEnt 92*
**Brom,** Robert H. 1938- *WhoRel 92, WhoWest 92*
**Bromberg,** Alan Robert 1928- *WhoAmL 92*
**Bromberg,** Barbara Schwartz 1941- *WhoAmL 92*
**Bromberg,** Eleazer 1913- *AmMWSc 92*
**Bromberg,** Frank Wallace, Jr 1955- *WhoAmP 91*
**Bromberg,** J Philip 1936- *AmMWSc 92*
**Bromberg,** John E. 1946- *WhoAmL 92*
**Bromberg,** Lee Carl 1943- *WhoAmL 92*
**Bromberg,** Milton Jay 1923- *AmMWSc 92*
**Bromberg,** R 1921- *AmMWSc 92*
**Bromberg,** Rachelle 1960- *WhoAmL 92*
**Bromberger,** Samuel H 1941- *AmMWSc 92*
**Bromberger-Barnea,** Baruch 1918- *AmMWSc 92*
**Brombert,** Victor 1923- *WrDr 92*
**Brome,** Richard 1590?-1652 *RfGEnL 91*
**Brome,** Thomas Reed 1942- *WhoAmL 92*
**Brome,** Vincent *IntAu&W 91, Who 92, WrDr 92*
**Bromeland,** Andrew Allan 1948- *WhoAmP 91*
**Bromell,** Henry *DrAPF 91*
**Bromell,** Henry 1947- *WrDr 92*
**Bromenschenkel,** Gib H. 1930- *WhoMW 92, WhoRel 92*
**Bromer,** William Wallis 1927- *AmMWSc 92*
**Bromery,** Keith Marcel 1948- *WhoBlA 92*
**Bromery,** Randolph Wilson 1926- *AmMWSc 92, WhoBlA 92*
**Bromet,** Evelyn J 1944- *AmMWSc 92*
**Bromet,** Jean *Who 92*
**Bromfield,** Calvin Stanton 1923- *AmMWSc 92*

**Bromfield,** John Farron 1922- *WhoEnt 92*
**Bromfield,** Kenneth Raymond 1922- *AmMWSc 92*
**Bromfield,** Louis 1896-1956 *BenetAL 91*
**Bromfield,** Louis Brucker 1896-1956 *LiExTwC*
**Bromhead,** David M. 1960- *IntMPA 92*
**Bromhead,** John Desmond Gonville *Who 92*
**Bromhead,** Peter Alexander 1919- *WrDr 92*
**Bromige,** David *DrAPF 91*
**Bromige,** David 1933- *WrDr 92*
**Bromige,** David Mansfield 1933- *IntAu&W 91*
**Bromige,** Iris 1910- *WrDr 92*
**Bromiley,** Geoffrey William 1915- *WrDr 92*
**Bromke,** Adam 1928- *WrDr 92*
**Bromley,** Archdeacon of *Who 92*
**Bromley,** Daniel Wood 1940- *WhoFI 92*
**Bromley,** David Allan 1926- *AmMWSc 92, IntWW 91*
**Bromley,** Ernest W. *WhoHisp 92*
**Bromley,** John Robert 1940- *WhoMW 92*
**Bromley,** Lance Lee 1920- *Who 92*
**Bromley,** Le Roy Alton 1919- *AmMWSc 92*
**Bromley,** Leonard John 1929- *Who 92*
**Bromley,** Peter Mann 1922- *Who 92*
**Bromley,** Robert LeVan 1931- *WhoRel 92*
**Bromley,** Rupert Charles 1936- *Who 92*
**Bromley,** Stephen C 1938- *AmMWSc 92*
**Bromley,** Yulian Vladimirovich d1990 *IntWW 91N*
**Bromley,** Yulian Vladimirovich 1921-1990 *SovUnBD*
**Bromley-Davenport,** William Arthur 1935- *Who 92*
**Bromm,** Frederick Whittemore 1953- *WhoAmL 92*
**Bromm,** Robert Dale, Sr. 1950- *WhoWest 92*
**Brommer,** Gerald Frederick 1927- *WhoWest 92*
**Broms,** Charles Howard 1942- *WhoFI 92*
**Bromund,** Richard Hayden 1940- *AmMWSc 92*
**Bromund,** Werner Hermann 1909- *AmMWSc 92*
**Bromwell,** Thomas L 1949- *WhoAmP 91*
**Bromwich,** Michael 1941- *Who 92*
**Bromwich,** Michael Ray 1953- *WhoAmL 92*
**Bron,** Anthony John 1936- *Who 92*
**Bron,** Eleanor *Who 92*
**Bron,** Eleanor 1934- *IntMPA 92*
**Bron,** Guillermo 1951- *WhoHisp 92*
**Bron,** Robert Philip 1942- *WhoEnt 92*
**Bron,** Walter Ernest 1930- *AmMWSc 92*
**Bronaugh,** Bert Allen 1918- *WhoRel 92*
**Bronaugh,** Edwin Lee 1932- *AmMWSc 92*
**Bronaugh,** Robert Lewis 1942- *AmMWSc 92*
**Bronck,** Jonas *DcAmImH*
**Bronco,** Charles John 1928- *AmMWSc 92*
**Brondfield,** Jerome 1913- *IntMPA 92*
**Brondo,** Robert Stanley 1951- *WhoFI 92*
**Brondsted,** Morgens 1918- *IntWW 91*
**Brondyke,** Kenneth J 1922- *AmMWSc 92*
**Brondz,** Boris Davidovich 1934- *AmMWSc 92*
**Broner,** E.M. *DrAPF 91*
**Broner,** E. M. 1930- *ConNov 91, WrDr 92*
**Bronfeld,** Stewart 1929- *WhoEnt 92*
**Bronfenbrenner,** Martin 1914- *IntWW 91*
**Bronfenbrenner,** Urie 1917- *IntWW 91*
**Bronfin,** Fred 1918- *WhoAmL 92*
**Bronfman,** Charles Rosner 1931- *IntWW 91, WhoFI 92*
**Bronfman,** Edgar M. *WhoRel 92*
**Bronfman,** Edgar M. 1929- *IntWW 91*
**Bronfman,** Edgar Miles 1929- *Who 92, WhoFI 92*
**Bronfman,** Yefim 1958- *ConMus 6 [port]*
**Brong,** Gerald Russell 1939- *WhoWest 92*
**Bronger,** Jerry 1935- *WhoAmP 91*
**Broniarek,** Zygmunt 1925- *IntWW 91*
**Bronikowski,** Thomas Andrew 1932- *AmMWSc 92*
**Bronis,** Stephen J. 1947- *WhoAmL 92*
**Bronislawski,** Jerzy-Stanislaw Kudas 1930- *IntAu&W 91*
**Bronk,** Burt V 1935- *AmMWSc 92*
**Bronk,** Detlev Wulf 1897-1975 *FacFETw*
**Bronk,** John Ramsey 1929- *AmMWSc 92*
**Bronk,** William *DrAPF 91*
**Bronk,** William 1918- *ConPo 91, IntAu&W 91, WrDr 92*
**Bronkar,** Carolyn *WhoRel 92*
**Bronkema,** Frederick Hollander 1934- *WhoRel 92*
**Bronkesh,** Annette Cylia 1956- *WhoFI 92*
**Bronn,** Leslie Joan Boyle 1948- *WhoMW 92*
**Bronnen,** Arnolt 1895-1959 *EncTR 91 [port]*
**Bronner,** Arne 1895-1959 *EncTR 91 [port]*
**Bronner,** Edwin Blaine 1920- *WrDr 92*
**Bronner,** Felix 1921- *AmMWSc 92*
**Bronner,** James Russell 1943- *WhoAmL 92*
**Bronner,** Nathaniel, Sr. *WhoBlA 92*
**Bronner,** Stephen Eric 1949- *WhoFI 92*
**Bronnes,** Robert L 1924- *AmMWSc 92*
**Bronocco,** Terri Lynn 1953- *WhoFI 92*
**Bronowski,** Jacob 1908-1974 *FacFETw*
**Brons,** Cornelius Hendrick 1955- *AmMWSc 92*
**Brons,** Kenneth Allyn 1929- *AmMWSc 92*
**Bronsky,** Albert J 1928- *AmMWSc 92*
**Bronson,** Charles *WhoEnt 92*
**Bronson,** Charles 1920- *IntMPA 92*
**Bronson,** Charles 1922- *IntWW 91*
**Bronson,** Franklin Herbert *AmMWSc 92*
**Bronson,** Fred James 1935- *WhoBlA 92*
**Bronson,** Gwendolyn T 1937- *WhoAmP 91*
**Bronson,** Irlo Overstreet, Jr 1936- *WhoAmP 91*
**Bronson,** Jeff Donaldson 1938- *AmMWSc 92*
**Bronson,** Kenneth 1934- *WhoAmL 92*
**Bronson,** Kenneth Caldean 1933- *WhoMW 92*
**Bronson,** L T *TwCSFW 91*
**Bronson,** Lee *TwCWW 91*
**Bronson,** Oswald P. 1927- *WhoBlA 92*
**Bronson,** Oswald Perry 1927- *WhoRel 92*
**Bronson,** Roy DeBolt 1920- *AmMWSc 92*
**Bronson,** Terrence Philip 1949- *WhoAmL 92*
**Bronsted,** Johannes Nicolaus 1879-1947 *FacFETw*
**Bronsted,** Roger Lewis 1925- *WhoRel 92*
**Bronsteen,** Peter 1954- *WhoFI 92*
**Bronstein,** Arthur J. 1914- *WhoWest 92, WrDr 92*
**Bronstein,** Daniel A. 1942- *WhoAmL 92*
**Bronstein,** Glen Max 1960- *WhoAmL 92*
**Bronstein,** Herbert 1930- *WhoRel 92*
**Bronstein,** Irena Y *AmMWSc 92*
**Bronstein,** Lynne *DrAPF 91*
**Bronstein,** Robert 1919- *WhoAmL 92*
**Bronstein,** Steve 1954- *WhoEnt 92*
**Bronston,** Benjamin William 1964- *WhoAmL 92*
**Bronston,** Edythe Lee 1936- *WhoAmL 92*
**Bronston,** Samuel 1908- *IntMPA 92, IntWW 91*
**Bronte,** Anne 1820-1849 *RfGEnL 91*
**Bronte,** Charlotte 1816-1855 *CnDBLB 4 [port], NinCLC 33 [port], RfGEnL 91*
**Bronte,** Emily 1818-1848 *CnDBLB 4 [port], RfGEnL 91*
**Bronte,** Louisa *WrDr 92*
**Bronte,** Patricia Ann 1957- *WhoAmL 92*
**Bronz,** Lois Gougis Taplin 1927- *WhoBlA 92*
**Bronzan,** Bruce 1947- *WhoAmP 91*
**Bronzan,** John Brayton 1937- *AmMWSc 92*
**Bronzini,** Michael Stephen 1944- *AmMWSc 92*
**Bronzino,** Joseph Daniel 1937- *AmMWSc 92*
**Bronzo,** Mark Peter 1960- *WhoIns 92*
**Broo,** Kenneth Robert 1952- *WhoEnt 92*
**Broodo,** Archie 1925- *AmMWSc 92*
**Broodthaers,** Marcel 1924-1976 *WorArt 1980*
**Brook,** Adrian G. 1924- *IntWW 91*
**Brook,** Adrian Gibbs 1924- *AmMWSc 92*
**Brook,** Anthony Donald 1936- *Who 92*
**Brook,** David 1932- *WrDr 92*
**Brook,** David Conway Grant 1935- *Who 92*
**Brook,** Donna *DrAPF 91*
**Brook,** Gary Fred 1961- *WhoFI 92*
**Brook,** Gerald Robert 1928- *Who 92*
**Brook,** Helen 1907- *Who 92*
**Brook,** Itzhak 1941- *AmMWSc 92*
**Brook,** Leopold 1912- *Who 92*
**Brook,** Marx 1920- *AmMWSc 92*
**Brook,** Peter 1925- *FacFETw, IntMPA 92*
**Brook,** Peter 1927- *TwCPaSc*
**Brook,** Peter Stephen Paul 1925- *IntWW 91, Who 92*
**Brook,** Ralph Ellis *Who 92*
**Brook,** Richard John 1938- *Who 92*
**Brook,** Robert *Who 92*
**Brook,** Robert H 1943- *AmMWSc 92, IntWW 91*
**Brook,** Robin 1908- *IntWW 91, Who 92*
**Brook,** Susan G. 1949- *WhoMW 92*
**Brook,** Ted Stephens 1926- *AmMWSc 92*
**Brook,** Victor John, Jr. 1946- *WhoAmL 92*
**Brook,** William Edward 1922- *Who 92*
**Brook,** Winston Rollins 1931- *WhoEnt 92, WhoWest 92*
**Brook-Partridge,** Bernard 1927- *Who 92*
**Brookbank,** John Warren 1927- *AmMWSc 92, WhoWest 92*
**Brooke** *Who 92*
**Brooke,** Lord 1957- *Who 92*
**Brooke,** Alistair Weston 1947- *Who 92*
**Brooke,** Arthur Caffin 1919- *Who 92*
**Brooke,** Bryan Nicholas 1915- *IntAu&W 91, Who 92, WrDr 92*
**Brooke,** Charles Patrick 1914- *WhoWest 92*
**Brooke,** Christopher N. L. 1927- *WrDr 92*
**Brooke,** Christopher Nugent Lawrence 1927- *IntWW 91, Who 92*
**Brooke,** Christopher Roger 1931- *Who 92*
**Brooke,** Clive 1942- *Who 92*
**Brooke,** Edna Mae 1923- *WhoFI 92, WhoWest 92*
**Brooke,** Edward W 1919- *FacFETw*
**Brooke,** Edward William 1919- *AmPolLe, IntWW 91, WhoAmP 91, WhoBlA 92*
**Brooke,** Frances 1724-1789 *BenetAL 91*
**Brooke,** Francis 1963- *Who 92*
**Brooke,** Henry 1703?-1783 *RfGEnL 91*
**Brooke,** Henry 1936- *Who 92*
**Brooke,** James B. 1955- *ConAu 135*
**Brooke,** Jeffrey Franklin 1963- *WhoAmL 92*
**Brooke,** John Mercer 1826-1906 *BiInAmS*
**Brooke,** John Percival 1933- *AmMWSc 92*
**Brooke,** M 1913- *AmMWSc 92*
**Brooke,** Marion Murphy 1913- *AmMWSc 92*
**Brooke,** Michael Zachary 1921- *IntAu&W 91*
**Brooke,** Patricia Cynthia 1953- *WhoAmL 92*
**Brooke,** Penny Simpson 1945- *WhoAmL 92*
**Brooke,** Peter 1934- *IntWW 91*
**Brooke,** Peter Leonard 1934- *Who 92*
**Brooke,** Ralph Ian *AmMWSc 92*
**Brooke,** Richard 1915- *Who 92*
**Brooke,** Richard, Jr 1926- *WhoIns 92*
**Brooke,** Robert Larry 1949- *WhoAmL 92*
**Brooke,** Rodney George 1939- *Who 92*
**Brooke,** Roger *Who 92*
**Brooke,** Rupert 1887-1915 *CnDBLB 6 [port], FacFETw, RfGEnL 91*
**Brooke,** Susan Rogers 1951- *WhoAmL 92*
**Brooke,** Vivian M 1943- *WhoAmP 91*
**Brooke,** Wallace Sands *WhoWest 92*
**Brooke,** William J. 1946- *ConAu 134*
**Brooke-Little,** John 1927- *WrDr 92*
**Brooke-Little,** John Philip 1927- *IntAu&W 91*
**Brooke-Little,** John Philip Brooke 1927- *Who 92*
**Brooke of Ystradfellte,** Baroness 1908- *Who 92*
**Brooke-Rose,** Christine *ConNov 91, Who 92, WrDr 92*
**Brooke-Rose,** Christine 1923- *TwCSFW 91*
**Brooke Turner,** Alan 1926- *Who 92*
**Brookeborough,** Viscount 1952- *Who 92*
**Brooker,** Alan Bernard 1931- *Who 92*
**Brooker,** Clark *IntAu&W 91X, TwCWW 91*
**Brooker,** Donald Brown 1916- *AmMWSc 92*
**Brooker,** Gary 1942- *AmMWSc 92*
**Brooker,** Hampton Ralph 1934- *AmMWSc 92*
**Brooker,** Jewel Spears 1940- *ConAu 135*
**Brooker,** Moe Albert 1940- *WhoBlA 92*
**Brooker,** Neil 1962- *WhoWest 92*
**Brooker,** Norton William, Jr. 1944- *WhoAmL 92*
**Brooker,** Robert Elton 1905- *IntWW 91*
**Brooker,** Robert Elton, Jr. 1937- *WhoFI 92*
**Brooker,** Robert Munro 1918- *AmMWSc 92*
**Brooker,** Rosalind Poll 1928- *WhoAmP 91*
**Brooker,** Thomas Kimball 1939- *WhoFI 92, WhoMW 92*
**Brooker,** William 1918- *TwCPaSc*
**Brookes** *Who 92*
**Brookes,** Baron 1909- *IntWW 91, Who 92*
**Brookes,** Beata 1931- *Who 92*
**Brookes,** Bernard L. 1950- *WhoBlA 92*
**Brookes,** Iveson Lewis 1793-1865 *DcNCBi 1*
**Brookes,** James Robert 1941- *Who 92*
**Brookes,** John 1933- *Who 92*
**Brookes,** Neville 1939- *AmMWSc 92*
**Brookes,** Pamela 1922- *WrDr 92*
**Brookes,** Peter C. *Who 92*
**Brookes,** Valentine 1913- *WhoWest 92*
**Brookes,** Victor Jack 1926- *AmMWSc 92*
**Brookes,** Warren T. d1991 *NewYTBS 91*
**Brookes,** Wilfred 1906- *Who 92*
**Brookhart,** John Mills 1913- *AmMWSc 92*
**Brookhart,** Maurice S 1942- *AmMWSc 92*
**Brookhouse,** Christopher *DrAPF 91*
**Brooking,** Patrick Guy 1937- *Who 92*
**Brooking,** Trevor David 1948- *Who 92*
**Brookins,** Dolores 1948- *WhoBlA 92*
**Brookins,** Douglas Gridley 1936- *AmMWSc 92*
**Brookins,** H. Hartford 1925- *WhoBlA 92*
**Brookins,** Howard B 1932- *WhoAmP 91*
**Brookins,** Howard B., Sr. 1932- *WhoBlA 92*
**Brookman,** Anthony Raymond 1922- *WhoAmL 92, WhoFI 92, WhoWest 92*
**Brookman,** David Joseph 1943- *AmMWSc 92*
**Brookman,** Eileen B 1921- *WhoAmP 91*
**Brookmeyer,** Bobby 1929- *NewAmDM*
**Brookner,** Anita *Who 92*
**Brookner,** Anita 1925- *IntAu&W 91*
**Brookner,** Anita 1928- *ConNov 91, FacFETw, WrDr 92*
**Brookner,** Anita 1938- *IntWW 91*
**Brookner,** Eli 1931- *AmMWSc 92*
**Brookover,** George David 1947- *WhoMW 92*
**Brookover,** Thomas Wilbur 1944- *WhoAmL 92*
**Brookover,** Wilbur 1911- *WrDr 92*
**Brooks** *Who 92*
**Brooks,** A. Raymond d1991 *NewYTBS 91 [port]*
**Brooks,** A. Russell 1906- *WhoBlA 92, WrDr 92*
**Brooks,** Alan 1935- *Who 92*
**Brooks,** Albert *NewYTBS 91 [port]*
**Brooks,** Albert 1947- *IntMPA 92, WhoEnt 92*
**Brooks,** Albert 1948?- *News 91 [port]*
**Brooks,** Alexander Dobbin 1940- *WhoMW 92, WhoRel 92*
**Brooks,** Alfred Austin, Jr 1921- *AmMWSc 92*
**Brooks,** Alvin Lee 1932- *WhoBlA 92*
**Brooks,** Andree Aelion 1937- *ConAu 133*
**Brooks,** Annmarie Manzi 1953- *WhoFI 92*
**Brooks,** Antone L 1938- *AmMWSc 92*
**Brooks,** Arkles Clarence, Jr. 1943- *WhoBlA 92*
**Brooks,** Arthur S 1943- *AmMWSc 92*
**Brooks,** Aubrey Lee 1871-1958 *DcNCBi 1*
**Brooks,** Austin Edward 1938- *AmMWSc 92*
**Brooks,** Avery 1949- *ConTFT 9, WhoBlA 92*
**Brooks,** Barbara Alice 1934- *AmMWSc 92*
**Brooks,** Ben *DrAPF 91*
**Brooks,** Benjamin Rix 1942- *WhoMW 92*
**Brooks,** Bernard E. 1935- *WhoBlA 92*
**Brooks,** Bernard W. 1939- *WhoBlA 92*
**Brooks,** Bradford O 1951- *AmMWSc 92*
**Brooks,** Bradford Oldham 1951- *WhoWest 92*
**Brooks,** Brent Thomas 1953- *WhoRel 92*
**Brooks,** Bruce 1950- *Au&Arts 8 [port], ChlLR 25 [port]*
**Brooks,** Byron A 1845-1911 *ScFEYrs*
**Brooks,** Carl 1949- *WhoBlA 92*
**Brooks,** Carol Lorraine 1955- *WhoBlA 92*
**Brooks,** Carolyn Branch 1946- *WhoBlA 92*
**Brooks,** Chandler McCuskey 1905- *AmMWSc 92*
**Brooks,** Charles Alvin 1871-1931 *DcAmImH*
**Brooks,** Charles Joseph 1952- *WhoEnt 92*
**Brooks,** Charlie R 1931- *AmMWSc 92*
**Brooks,** Charlotte Kendrick 1918- *WhoBlA 92*
**Brooks,** Chet Edward 1935- *WhoAmP 91*
**Brooks,** Christine D. *WhoBlA 92*
**Brooks,** Cleanth 1906- *BenetAL 91, ConAu 35NR, FacFETw, IntWW 91, Who 92, WrDr 92*
**Brooks,** Clifton Rowland 1925- *WhoHisp 92*
**Brooks,** Clyde Henry 1941- *WhoBlA 92*
**Brooks,** Clyde S 1917- *AmMWSc 92*
**Brooks,** Clyde Scott 1948- *WhoEnt 92*
**Brooks,** Daisy *WhoEnt 92*
**Brooks,** Daisy M. Anderson *WhoBlA 92*
**Brooks,** Dana DeMarco 1951- *WhoBlA 92*
**Brooks,** Daniel Rusk 1951- *AmMWSc 92*
**Brooks,** Daniel Townley 1941- *WhoAmL 92*
**Brooks,** David Arthur 1943- *AmMWSc 92*
**Brooks,** David C 1936- *AmMWSc 92*
**Brooks,** David Patrick 1952- *AmMWSc 92*
**Brooks,** David-Vincent 1960- *WhoEnt 92*
**Brooks,** Dawne Lea *WhoRel 92*
**Brooks,** Debra Lee 1952- *WhoMW 92*
**Brooks,** Dee W 1952- *AmMWSc 92*
**Brooks,** Delores Jean 1944- *WhoBlA 92*
**Brooks,** Derl 1930- *AmMWSc 92*
**Brooks,** Dick *IntMPA 92*
**Brooks,** Dolores Ann 1931- *WhoAmP 91*
**Brooks,** Don Locellus 1953- *WhoBlA 92*
**Brooks,** Doris F *WhoAmP 91*
**Brooks,** Dorothy Lynn 1935- *AmMWSc 92*
**Brooks,** Douglas 1928- *Who 92*
**Brooks,** Douglas L 1916- *ConAu 35NR*
**Brooks,** Douglas Lee 1916- *AmMWSc 92*
**Brooks,** Dwight 1931- *WhoEnt 92*
**Brooks,** Edward Howard 1921- *WhoWest 92*
**Brooks,** Edward Morgan 1916- *AmMWSc 92*
**Brooks,** Edward Pennell d1991 *NewYTBS 91*
**Brooks,** Edwin 1929- *Who 92, WrDr 92*
**Brooks,** Elbridge S. 1846-1902 *BenetAL 91*
**Brooks,** Elwood Ralph 1934- *AmMWSc 92*
**Brooks,** Emmit Horace 1935- *WhoEnt 92*

**Brooks,** Eric Arthur Swatton 1907- *Who 92*
**Brooks,** Eugene Clyde 1871-1947 *DcNCBi 1*
**Brooks,** Forest Clyde 1947- *WhoWest 92*
**Brooks,** Forrest W., Sr. *WhoRel 92*
**Brooks,** Francis Gerard *Who 92*
**Brooks,** Francis K 1943- *WhoAmP 91*
**Brooks,** Frank Pickering 1920- *AmMWSc 92*
**Brooks,** Frederick P, Jr 1931- *AmMWSc 92*
**Brooks,** Garnett Ryland, Jr 1936- *AmMWSc 92*
**Brooks,** Garth *WhoEnt 92*
**Brooks,** Garth 1962- *News 92-1 [port]*
**Brooks,** Gary 1934- *WhoFI 92*
**Brooks,** Gary Allen 1946- *WhoAmP 91*
**Brooks,** Gary Leon 1950- *WhoAmL 92*
**Brooks,** Gene Edward 1931- *WhoAmL 92*
**Brooks,** George *ConAu 133, WhoAmP 91*
**Brooks,** George Andrew 1900- *WhoAmL 92, WhoFI 92*
**Brooks,** George E, Jr 1933- *IntAu&W 91, WrDr 92*
**Brooks,** George H 1919- *AmMWSc 92*
**Brooks,** George Savage, II 1950- *WhoAmL 92*
**Brooks,** George Washington 1821-1882 *DcNCBi 1*
**Brooks,** George Wilson 1920- *AmMWSc 92*
**Brooks,** Gilbert 1934- *WhoBlA 92*
**Brooks,** Glenn Allen 1960- *WhoWest 92*
**Brooks,** Grover Lee 1938- *WhoMW 92*
**Brooks,** Gwendolyn *DrAPF 91*
**Brooks,** Gwendolyn 1917- *AfrAmW, BenetAL 91, BlkLC [port], ConBlB 1 [port], ConPo 91, FacFETw [port], HanAmWH, IntAu&W 91, IntWW 91, ModAWWr, NotBlAW 92 [port], WhoMW 92, WrDr 92*
**Brooks,** Gwendolyn Elizabeth 1917- *WhoBlA 92*
**Brooks,** H. Allen 1925- *WrDr 92*
**Brooks,** Harold 1907-1990 *AnObit 1990*
**Brooks,** Harold Kelly 1924- *AmMWSc 92*
**Brooks,** Harold W. 1948- *WhoBlA 92*
**Brooks,** Harry W., Jr. 1928- *WhoBlA 92*
**Brooks,** Harvey 1915- *AmMWSc 92, IntWW 91*
**Brooks,** Henry Marcellus 1942- *WhoBlA 92*
**Brooks,** Hindi *WhoEnt 92*
**Brooks,** Hubie 1956- *WhoBlA 92*
**Brooks,** Hunter O. 1929- *WhoBlA 92*
**Brooks,** Jack 1922- *AlmAP 92 [port], WhoAmP 91*
**Brooks,** Jack Carlton 1941- *AmMWSc 92*
**Brooks,** James *DrAPF 91*
**Brooks,** James 1906- *IntWW 91*
**Brooks,** James Elwood 1925- *AmMWSc 92*
**Brooks,** James Keith 1938- *AmMWSc 92*
**Brooks,** James L. *LesBEnT 92*
**Brooks,** James L. 1940- *IntMPA 92, WhoEnt 92*
**Brooks,** James Lee 1937- *AmMWSc 92*
**Brooks,** James Mark 1947- *AmMWSc 92*
**Brooks,** James O 1930- *AmMWSc 92*
**Brooks,** James O'Neil 1922- *WhoBlA 92*
**Brooks,** James Reed 1955- *AmMWSc 92*
**Brooks,** James Robert 1958- *WhoBlA 92*
**Brooks,** James Wright 1942- *WhoRel 92*
**Brooks,** Janice Willena 1946- *WhoBlA 92*
**Brooks,** Jeanne *ConAu 135*
**Brooks,** Jeremy 1926- *IntAu&W 91, WrDr 92*
**Brooks,** Jerome 1931- *WhoMW 92*
**Brooks,** Jerry Claude 1936- *WhoFI 92*
**Brooks,** Jerry R 1930- *AmMWSc 92*
**Brooks,** Jo 1949- *WhoAmL 92*
**Brooks,** John 1920- *WrDr 92*
**Brooks,** John A 1916- *AmMWSc 92*
**Brooks,** John Ashton 1928- *Who 92*
**Brooks,** John Bill 1929- *AmMWSc 92*
**Brooks,** John C *WhoAmP 91*
**Brooks,** John J 1948- *AmMWSc 92*
**Brooks,** John Langdon 1920- *AmMWSc 92*
**Brooks,** John Robinson 1918- *AmMWSc 92*
**Brooks,** John S J 1948- *AmMWSc 92*
**Brooks,** John White 1936- *WhoAmL 92*
**Brooks,** Joseph *IntMPA 92, WhoEnt 92*
**Brooks,** Josephine 1934- *WhoAmP 91*
**Brooks,** Julie Anne 1945- *WhoAmL 92*
**Brooks,** Karl B 1956- *WhoAmP 91*
**Brooks,** Kenneth Conrad 1947- *AmMWSc 92*
**Brooks,** Kevin P 1944- *WhoIns 92*
**Brooks,** Larry 1950- *WhoBlA 92*
**Brooks,** Leo Austin 1932- *WhoBlA 92*
**Brooks,** Leslie James 1916- *Who 92*
**Brooks,** Lewis William, Jr 1944- *WhoAmP 91*
**Brooks,** Linda Thomas 1963- *WhoMW 92*
**Brooks,** Louise 1906-1985 *ConAu 134, FacFETw*
**Brooks,** Marcellus 1941- *WhoBlA 92*
**Brooks,** Marguerite *WhoEnt 92*
**Brooks,** Maria 1794?-1845 *BenetAL 91*
**Brooks,** Marion Jackson 1920- *WhoBlA 92*
**Brooks,** Mark Hunter 1960- *WhoFI 92*
**Brooks,** Marsha Storper 1951- *WhoAmL 92, WhoEnt 92*
**Brooks,** Martha *SmATA 68 [port]*
**Brooks,** Martin 1950- *WhoEnt 92*
**Brooks,** Marvin Alan 1945- *AmMWSc 92*
**Brooks,** Mary Campbell 1964- *WhoEnt 92*
**Brooks,** Mary Elizabeth *WhoAmP 91*
**Brooks,** Mel *LesBEnT 92*
**Brooks,** Mel 1926- *FacFETw, IntAu&W 91, IntDcF 2-2 [port], IntMPA 92, IntWW 91, Who 92, WhoEnt 92*
**Brooks,** Mel, Mrs. 1931- *WhoEnt 92*
**Brooks,** Merle Eugene 1916- *AmMWSc 92*
**Brooks,** Morris Jackson, Jr 1954- *WhoAmP 91*
**Brooks,** Nathan Eugene 1933- *BlkOlyM*
**Brooks,** Nicholas Peter 1941- *Who 92*
**Brooks,** Noah 1830-1903 *BenetAL 91*
**Brooks,** Nona Lovell 1861-1945 *RelLAm 91*
**Brooks,** Norman H 1928- *AmMWSc 92*
**Brooks,** Norman Leon 1932- *WhoBlA 92*
**Brooks,** Norward J. 1934- *WhoBlA 92*
**Brooks,** Oscar Stephenson 1928- *WhoRel 92*
**Brooks,** P. A., II *WhoRel 92*
**Brooks,** Patrick William 1943- *WhoAmL 92*
**Brooks,** Paul 1909- *IntAu&W 91, WrDr 92*
**Brooks,** Perry 1954- *WhoBlA 92*
**Brooks,** Peter 1952- *WhoAmL 92*
**Brooks,** Peter Stuyvesant 1942- *WhoFI 92*
**Brooks,** Peter T *WhoAmP 91*
**Brooks,** Peter Wright 1920- *IntAu&W 91, WrDr 92*
**Brooks,** Philip Barron 1914- *WhoFI 92*
**Brooks,** Philip Russell 1938- *AmMWSc 92*
**Brooks,** Phillip Daniel 1946- *WhoBlA 92*
**Brooks,** Phillips 1835-1893 *BenetAL 91, RelLAm 91*
**Brooks,** Porter Harrison 1926- *WhoRel 92*
**Brooks,** Preston Smith 1819-1857 *AmPolLe*
**Brooks,** R Daniel 1946- *WhoIns 92*
**Brooks,** Rachelle Marie 1960- *WhoEnt 92*
**Brooks,** Ray O. 1923- *WhoRel 92*
**Brooks,** Richard 1912- *IntAu&W 91, IntDcF 2-2 [port], IntMPA 92, IntWW 91, WhoEnt 92, WrDr 92*
**Brooks,** Richard Dickinson 1944- *WhoAmL 92*
**Brooks,** Richard Leonard 1934- *WhoBlA 92*
**Brooks,** Richard Mallon 1928- *WhoFI 92*
**Brooks,** Richard Thomas 1955- *WhoAmL 92*
**Brooks,** Robert 1957- *WhoWest 92*
**Brooks,** Robert Alan 1924- *AmMWSc 92*
**Brooks,** Robert Alexander 1944- *WhoFI 92*
**Brooks,** Robert E 1921- *AmMWSc 92*
**Brooks,** Robert Earl, Jr 1956- *WhoAmP 91*
**Brooks,** Robert Franklin 1928- *AmMWSc 92*
**Brooks,** Robert Franklin 1939- *WhoAmL 92*
**Brooks,** Robert M 1938- *AmMWSc 92*
**Brooks,** Robert Nathaniel 1888-1953 *DcNCBi 1*
**Brooks,** Robert R 1944- *AmMWSc 92*
**Brooks,** Robert Terrance, Jr. 1963- *WhoRel 92*
**Brooks,** Rodney Alan, Sr. 1953- *WhoBlA 92*
**Brooks,** Rodney Norman 1954- *WhoBlA 92*
**Brooks,** Roger Alan 1944- *WhoMW 92*
**Brooks,** Roger K 1937- *WhoIns 92*
**Brooks,** Roger Kay 1937- *WhoFI 92*
**Brooks,** Romaine 1874-1970 *HanAmWH*
**Brooks,** Ron Esta *WhoRel 92*
**Brooks,** Ronald James 1941- *AmMWSc 92*
**Brooks,** Roy Howard, Jr. 1923- *WhoAmL 92*
**Brooks,** Roy LaVerne Wilson 1955- *WhoAmP 91*
**Brooks,** Roy Lavon *WhoAmL 92*
**Brooks,** Roy Lavon 1950- *WhoBlA 92*
**Brooks,** Sam Raymond 1940- *AmMWSc 92*
**Brooks,** Samuel Carroll 1928- *AmMWSc 92*
**Brooks,** Sharon Lee Kopsky 1942- *WhoEnt 92*
**Brooks,** Sharon Lynn 1944- *AmMWSc 92*
**Brooks,** Sheila Dean 1956- *WhoBlA 92*
**Brooks,** Sheila Jeanne 1944- *WhoWest 92*
**Brooks,** Sheilagh Thompson 1923- *AmMWSc 92*
**Brooks,** Shelton 1886-1975 *NewAmDM*
**Brooks,** Sidney Joseph 1935- *WhoBlA 92*
**Brooks,** Steven Doyle 1958- *WhoMW 92*
**Brooks,** Stuart Merrill 1936- *AmMWSc 92*
**Brooks,** Sumner 1928- *WhoAmP 91*
**Brooks,** Suzanne R. 1941- *WhoBlA 92*
**Brooks,** Terry *DrAPF 91*
**Brooks,** Theodore Roosevelt, Jr. 1930- *WhoBlA 92*
**Brooks,** Thomas Benton 1836-1900 *BiInAmS*
**Brooks,** Thomas E. 1907-1982 *WhoBlA 92N*
**Brooks,** Thomas Furman 1943- *AmMWSc 92*
**Brooks,** Thomas Joseph, Jr 1916- *AmMWSc 92*
**Brooks,** Thomas L *WhoAmP 91*
**Brooks,** Thomas R 1925- *ConAu 34NR*
**Brooks,** Tilford Uthratese 1925- *WhoBlA 92*
**Brooks,** Timothy Don 1956- *WhoMW 92*
**Brooks,** Timothy Gerald Martin 1929- *Who 92*
**Brooks,** Todd Frederick 1954- *WhoBlA 92*
**Brooks,** Tommy N *WhoAmP 91*
**Brooks,** Tyrone *WhoEnt 92*
**Brooks,** Tyrone L 1945- *WhoAmP 91*
**Brooks,** Van Wyck 1886-1963 *BenetAL 91, FacFETw*
**Brooks,** Vernon Bernard 1923- *AmMWSc 92*
**Brooks,** W. Webster *WhoBlA 92*
**Brooks,** Wadell, Sr. 1933- *WhoBlA 92*
**Brooks,** Walter Lyda 1923- *AmMWSc 92*
**Brooks,** Walter S 1932- *WhoAmP 91*
**Brooks,** Wayne Maurice 1939- *AmMWSc 92*
**Brooks,** Wendell V F 1925- *AmMWSc 92*
**Brooks,** William C. *WhoBlA 92*
**Brooks,** William Donald Wykeham 1905- *Who 92*
**Brooks,** William H *WhoIns 92*
**Brooks,** William Hamilton 1932- *AmMWSc 92*
**Brooks,** William Joseph 1961- *WhoAmL 92*
**Brooks,** William Keith 1848-1908 *BiInAmS*
**Brooks,** William P. 1934- *WhoBlA 92*
**Brooks-Gunn,** Jeanne 1946- *ConAu 135*
**Brooks of Tremorfa,** Baron 1927- *Who 92*
**Brooks-Schmitz,** Nancy 1942- *WhoEnt 92*
**Brooks Springs,** Suzanne Beth 1935- *AmMWSc 92*
**Brooksbank,** Edward Nicholas 1944- *Who 92*
**Brooksbank,** Nicholas *Who 92*
**Brooksbank,** Randolph Wood 1947- *WhoEnt 92*
**Brooksby,** John Burns 1914- *Who 92*
**Brookshaw,** Valjean Bispham, Jr. 1931- *WhoFI 92*
**Brookshear,** James Glenn 1944- *AmMWSc 92*
**Brooksher,** K. Dane *WhoMW 92*
**Brookshier,** Tom *LesBEnT 92*
**Brookshire,** James Earl 1951- *WhoAmL 92*
**Broom,** Arthur Davis 1937- *AmMWSc 92, WhoWest 92*
**Broom,** Donald Maurice 1942- *Who 92*
**Broom,** Ivor 1920- *Who 92*
**Broom,** Linda Christine 1962- *WhoWest 92*
**Broom,** Richard Stuart 1948- *WhoAmL 92*
**Broom,** Robert 1866-1951 *FacFETw*
**Broomall,** Lowell d1991 *NewYTBS 91*
**Broomall,** Robert W. 1946- *TwCWW 91, WrDr 92*
**Brooman,** Eric William 1940- *AmMWSc 92*
**Broome,** Barry Dean 1942- *WhoFI 92*
**Broome,** Carmen Rose 1939- *AmMWSc 92*
**Broome,** Claire V 1949- *AmMWSc 92*
**Broome,** David 1940- *IntWW 91, Who 92*
**Broome,** Dean Carl 1918- *WhoAmP 91*
**Broome,** Henry George, Jr. 1941- *WhoAmL 92*
**Broome,** Hugh Wilson, III 1936- *WhoAmP 91*
**Broome,** John Lawson 1943- *Who 92*
**Broome,** Paul W 1932- *AmMWSc 92*
**Broome,** Pershing 1921- *WhoBlA 92*
**Broome,** Randall 1954- *WhoRel 92*
**Broomes,** Lloyd Rudy 1936- *WhoBlA 92*
**Broomfield,** Clarence A 1930- *AmMWSc 92*
**Broomfield,** Mary Elizabeth 1935- *WhoBlA 92*
**Broomfield,** Nigel Hugh Robert Allen 1937- *Who 92*
**Broomfield,** Oree, Sr. *WhoRel 92*
**Broomfield,** Robert Cameron 1933- *WhoAmL 92*
**Broomfield,** William S. 1922- *AlmAP 92 [port], WhoAmP 91, WhoMW 92*
**Broomhall,** William Maurice 1897- *Who 92*
**Broonzy,** Big Bill 1893-1958 *NewAmDM*
**Brooten,** Bernadette Joan 1951- *WhoRel 92*
**Brooten,** Dorothy 1942- *AmMWSc 92*
**Brooten,** Kenneth Edward, Jr. 1942- *WhoAmL 92*
**Brophy,** Brigid 1929- *ConNov 91, FacFETw, IntAu&W 91, IntWW 91, Who 92, WrDr 92*
**Brophy,** Gerald Patrick 1926- *AmMWSc 92*
**Brophy,** Gilbert Thomas 1926- *WhoAmL 92*
**Brophy,** James John d1991 *NewYTBS 91*
**Brophy,** James John 1926- *AmMWSc 92*
**Brophy,** Jere H 1934- *AmMWSc 92*
**Brophy,** Jere Hall 1934- *WhoMW 92*
**Brophy,** John Allen 1924- *AmMWSc 92*
**Brophy,** Joseph T *WhoIns 92*
**Brophy,** Joseph Thomas 1933- *WhoFI 92*
**Brophy,** Mary O'Reilly 1948- *AmMWSc 92*
**Brophy,** Michael John Mary 1937- *Who 92*
**Brophy,** Theodore F. 1923- *IntWW 91, WhoFI 92*
**Brophy,** Todd Randall 1954- *WhoWest 92*
**Broquist,** Harry Pearson 1919- *AmMWSc 92*
**Brorby,** Wade *WhoAmP 91*
**Brorby,** Wade 1934- *WhoAmL 92*
**Brosa,** Carol Joanne 1933- *WhoMW 92*
**Brosan,** George Stephen 1921- *Who 92*
**Brosbe,** Edwin Allan 1918- *AmMWSc 92*
**Broschat,** Kay O *AmMWSc 92*
**Brose,** David Stephen 1939- *AmMWSc 92*
**Brose,** Gregory Lee 1964- *WhoRel 92*
**Broseghini,** Albert L 1932- *AmMWSc 92*
**Broselow,** Stanley David 1925- *WhoWest 92*
**Brosemer,** Ronald Webster 1934- *AmMWSc 92*
**Brosens,** Frank Peter 1957- *WhoFI 92*
**Brosens,** Pierre Joseph 1933- *AmMWSc 92*
**Broshar,** Wayne Cecil 1933- *AmMWSc 92*
**Brosig,** Michael Francis, Sr. 1950- *WhoFI 92*
**Brosilow,** Coleman B 1934- *AmMWSc 92*
**Brosin,** Henry Walter 1904- *AmMWSc 92*
**Brosious,** Paul Romain 1938- *AmMWSc 92*
**Brosius,** Gene N. 1950- *WhoRel 92*
**Brosky,** John G. 1920- *WhoAmL 92*
**Brosman,** Catharine Savage *DrAPF 91*
**Brosnahan,** James Jerome 1934- *WhoAmL 92*
**Brosnahan,** Kenneth William 1963- *WhoAmL 92*
**Brosnahan,** L. F. 1922- *WrDr 92*
**Brosnahan,** Leonard Francis 1922- *IntAu&W 91*
**Brosnan,** John 1947- *TwCSFW 91*
**Brosnan,** John Thomas 1943- *AmMWSc 92*
**Brosnan,** Margaret Eileen 1942- *AmMWSc 92*
**Brosnan,** Pierce 1953- *IntMPA 92, WhoEnt 92*
**Brosnan,** Shaun *TwCPaSc*
**Brosnan,** Thomas Francis 1921- *WhoAmL 92*
**Brosnihan,** K Bridget 1941- *AmMWSc 92*
**Bross,** Irwin D J 1921- *IntAu&W 91, WrDr 92*
**Bross,** Irwin Dudley Jackson 1921- *AmMWSc 92*
**Bross,** James Lee 1944- *WhoAmL 92*
**Bross,** John Joseph 1939- *WhoFI 92*
**Bross,** Steward Richard, Jr. 1922- *WhoAmL 92*
**Brossard,** Chandler *DrAPF 91*
**Brossard,** Chandler 1922- *BenetAL 91, IntAu&W 91, WrDr 92*
**Brossard,** Nicole 1943- *BenetAL 91*
**Brosseau,** George Emile, Jr 1930- *AmMWSc 92*
**Brosseau,** James Dean 1944- *WhoMW 92*
**Brosseau,** Jon Hubert 1945- *WhoAmL 92*
**Brosses,** Charles de 1709-1777 *BlkwCEP*
**Brossette,** Alvin, Jr. 1942- *WhoBlA 92*
**Brost,** Erich Eduard 1903- *IntWW 91*
**Brostoff,** Steven Warren 1942- *AmMWSc 92*
**Brostow,** Witold Konrad 1934- *AmMWSc 92*
**Brostowin,** P.R. *DrAPF 91*
**Brostrom,** Charles Otto 1942- *AmMWSc 92*
**Brostrom,** Margaret Ann 1941- *AmMWSc 92*
**Brostron,** Judith Curran 1950- *WhoAmL 92*
**Brosz,** Don Gayle, Jr. 1954- *WhoMW 92*
**Brot,** Frederick Elliot 1941- *AmMWSc 92*
**Brot,** Nathan 1931- *AmMWSc 92*
**Brotak,** Edward Allen 1948- *AmMWSc 92*
**Brotbeck,** George Nathan 1946- *WhoFI 92*
**Brotcke,** Paul Norman 1944- *WhoFI 92*
**Broten,** Norman W 1921- *AmMWSc 92*
**Brother Antoninus** *IntAu&W 91X*
**Brotherhood,** William Rowland 1912- *Who 92*
**Brothers,** Alfred Douglas 1939- *AmMWSc 92*

**Brothers,** Constance Forsyth 1931- *WhoAmP 91*
**Brothers,** Dean Anderson 1944- *WhoAmP 91*
**Brothers,** Edith 1936- *WhoBlA 92*
**Brothers,** Edward Bruce 1948- *AmMWSc 92*
**Brothers,** Fletcher Arnold 1948- *WhoRel 92*
**Brothers,** Henry J., II 1957- *WhoAmL 92*
**Brothers,** Jack Anthony 1943- *WhoMW 92*
**Brothers,** John Edwin 1937- *AmMWSc 92*
**Brothers,** Joyce *LesBEnT 92, WrDr 92*
**Brothers,** Joyce Diane *WhoEnt 92*
**Brothers,** Peter Malam 1917- *Who 92*
**Brothers,** Philip Raymond 1951- *WhoWest 92*
**Brothers,** Randall 1936- *WhoAmP 91*
**Brothers,** William Henry Francis 1887-1979 *RelLAm 91*
**Brotherson,** Donald E 1932- *AmMWSc 92*
**Brotherson,** Eric 1911-1989 *ConTFT 9*
**Brotherson,** Jack De Von 1938- *WhoWest 92*
**Brotherson,** Jack DeVon 1938- *AmMWSc 92*
**Brotherston,** Gordon 1939- *WrDr 92*
**Brotherton,** Jeffrey Dale 1954- *WhoMW 92*
**Brotherton,** John Michael 1935- *Who 92*
**Brotherton,** Michael Lewis 1931- *Who 92*
**Brotherton,** Robert John 1928- *AmMWSc 92*
**Brotherton,** W T, Jr 1926- *WhoAmP 91*
**Brotherton,** Wilbur V 1922- *WhoAmP 91*
**Brotherton,** William T., Jr. 1926- *WhoAmL 92*
**Brothwick,** John Livingston Dinwiddie 1840?-1904 *BilnAmS*
**Brothwood,** John 1931- *Who 92*
**Brotman,** Carol Eileen 1955- *WhoWest 92*
**Brotman,** Jeffrey H. 1942- *WhoWest 92*
**Brotman,** Richard Dennis 1952- *WhoWest 92*
**Brotman,** Stanley Seymour 1924- *WhoAmL 92*
**Brotman,** Stuart Neil 1952- *WhoEnt 92*
**Brott,** Alexander 1915- *ConCom 92, NewAmDM, WhoEnt 92*
**Brott,** Boris 1944- *WhoEnt 92*
**Brott,** Boris 1945- *NewAmDM*
**Brott,** John Lawrence 1946- *WhoWest 92*
**Brott,** Lotte 1922- *WhoEnt 92*
**Brotzen,** Franz R 1915- *AmMWSc 92*
**Brotzman,** Donald G 1922- *WhoAmP 91*
**Brotzman,** Paul David 1946- *WhoWest 92*
**Broucek,** William Samuel 1950- *WhoFI 92*
**Broucher,** David Stuart 1944- *Who 92*
**Broude Brothers** *NewAmDM*
**Broude,** Alexander *NewAmDM*
**Broude,** John Samuel 1949- *WhoAmL 92*
**Broude,** Richard Frederick 1936- *WhoAmL 92*
**Broude,** Ronald 1941- *WhoEnt 92*
**Broudy,** Nat d1991 *NewYTBS 91*
**Brough,** Bruce Alvin 1937- *WhoWest 92*
**Brough,** Colin 1932- *Who 92*
**Brough,** Edward 1918- *Who 92*
**Brough,** H. O. 1929- *WhoRel 92, WhoWest 92*
**Brough,** Jean Marie 1942- *WhoAmP 91*
**Brough,** John Herbert 1945- *WhoWest 92*
**Brough,** Karen Tanassy 1946- *WhoWest 92*
**Brough,** Michael David 1942- *Who 92*
**Brough,** Norman R *WhoAmP 91*
**Brough,** Walter 1935- *IntMPA 92*
**Brough,** Walter John 1925- *WhoEnt 92*
**Brougham** *Who 92*
**Brougham,** Christopher John 1947- *Who 92*
**Brougham,** Glen Scott Rocky 1950- *WhoWest 92*
**Brougham,** Henry Peter 1778-1868 *DcLB 110 [port]*
**Brougham,** John 1810-1880 *BenetAL 91*
**Brougham And Vaux,** Baron 1938- *Who 92*
**Broughshane,** Baron 1903- *Who 92*
**Broughton** *Who 92*
**Broughton,** Beverly Jane 1927- *WhoFI 92, WhoMW 92*
**Broughton,** Bruce 1945- *IntMPA 92*
**Broughton,** Bruce Harold 1945- *WhoEnt 92*
**Broughton,** Carrie Longee 1879-1957 *DcNCBi 1*
**Broughton,** Charles 1911- *Who 92*
**Broughton,** Christopher Leon 1964- *WhoBlA 92*
**Broughton,** Evelyn Delves 1915- *Who 92*
**Broughton,** Geoffrey 1927- *WrDr 92*
**Broughton,** James *DrAPF 91*
**Broughton,** James 1913- *ConPo 91, WrDr 92*
**Broughton,** James Richard 1913- *IntAu&W 91*
**Broughton,** James Walter 1946- *WhoWest 92*
**Broughton,** John Renata 1947- *IntAu&W 91*
**Broughton,** Joseph Melville 1888-1949 *DcNCBi 1*
**Broughton,** Leonard 1924- *Who 92*
**Broughton,** Luke Dennis 1828-1898 *RelLAm 91*
**Broughton,** M B 1929- *AmMWSc 92*
**Broughton,** Needham Bryant 1848-1914 *DcNCBi 1*
**Broughton,** Ray Monroe 1922- *WhoFI 92, WhoWest 92*
**Broughton,** Richard Irving 1941- *WhoEnt 92*
**Broughton,** Robert Stephen 1934- *AmMWSc 92*
**Broughton,** Robert William 1936- *WhoAmP 91*
**Broughton,** Roger James 1936- *AmMWSc 92*
**Broughton,** Spencer Arthur 1926- *WhoIns 92*
**Broughton,** T. Alan *DrAPF 91*
**Broughton,** T. Alan 1936- *WrDr 92*
**Broughton,** William Albert 1914- *AmMWSc 92*
**Brouhard,** Ben Herman 1946- *WhoMW 92*
**Brouhard,** Deborah Taliaferro 1949- *WhoBlA 92*
**Brouhard,** James A. 1943- *WhoWest 92*
**Brouillard,** Robert Ernest 1915- *AmMWSc 92*
**Brouillet,** Arthur A, Jr *WhoAmP 91*
**Brouillet,** Frank B 1928- *WhoAmP 91*
**Brouillet,** Luc 1954- *AmMWSc 92*
**Brouillette,** James Gordon 1928- *WhoAmP 91*
**Brouillette,** Robert T 1947- *AmMWSc 92*
**Brouillette,** Walter 1925- *AmMWSc 92*
**Broujos,** John H. 1929- *WhoAmL 92, WhoAmP 91*
**Broumas,** John G. 1917- *IntMPA 92*
**Broumas,** Nikolaos 1916- *Who 92*
**Broumas,** Olga *DrAPF 91*
**Broumas,** Olga 1949- *ConPo 91, WrDr 92*
**Broun,** Emily *AmPeW*
**Broun,** Heywood 1888-1939 *BenetAL 91*
**Broun,** Kenneth Stanley 1939- *WhoAmL 92*
**Broun,** Lionel John Law 1927- *Who 92*
**Broun,** Paul C 1916- *WhoAmP 91*
**Broun,** Thorowgood Taylor, Jr 1923- *AmMWSc 92*
**Broun,** William LeRoy 1827-1902 *BilnAmS*
**Brouns,** Richard John 1917- *AmMWSc 92*
**Brountas,** Paul Peter 1932- *WhoAmL 92*
**Brous,** Don W 1913- *AmMWSc 92*
**Brous,** Jack 1926- *AmMWSc 92*
**Brousaard,** Allen E. 1929- *WhoAmL 92*
**Broussard,** Allen E. 1929- *WhoBlA 92, WhoWest 92*
**Broussard,** Allen Edgar 1929- *WhoAmP 91*
**Broussard,** Alston Derrick 1956- *WhoRel 92*
**Broussard,** Arnold Anthony 1947- *WhoBlA 92*
**Broussard,** Catherine Dianne 1955- *WhoBlA 92*
**Broussard,** Daniel E., Jr. 1941- *WhoAmL 92*
**Broussard,** David Harold 1947- *WhoAmP 91*
**Broussard,** Leroy 1948- *WhoBlA 92*
**Broussard,** Rose A 1925- *WhoAmP 91*
**Broussard,** Steve 1967- *WhoBlA 92*
**Broussard,** Vernon 1934- *WhoBlA 92*
**Broussard,** William Arren 1956- *WhoAmL 92*
**Brousse,** Pierre 1926- *IntWW 91*
**Brousseau,** Nancy Marie 1947- *WhoRel 92*
**Brousseau,** Nicole 1948- *AmMWSc 92*
**Brousseau,** Robert Raymond 1954- *WhoAmP 91*
**Broutman,** Lawrence Jay 1938- *AmMWSc 92*
**Brouwenstyn,** Gerarda *IntWW 91*
**Brouwer,** Arie Raymond 1935- *WhoRel 92*
**Brouwer,** Dirk 1902-1966 *FacFETw*
**Brouwer,** Leo 1939- *NewAmDM*
**Brouwer,** Luitzen Egbertus Jan 1881-1966 *FacFETw*
**Brovarnik,** Herbert Charles 1912- *WhoNob 90*
**Broverman,** Robert Lee 1931- *WhoAmP 91*
**Brovikov,** Vladimir Ignatyevich 1931- *IntWW 91*
**Browaldh,** Tore 1917- *IntWW 91, Who 92*
**Browall,** Kenneth Walter 1947- *AmMWSc 92*
**Browde,** Holly T. 1955- *WhoEnt 92*
**Browder,** Anne Elna 1935- *WhoBlA 92*
**Browder,** Catherine *DrAPF 91*
**Browder,** Earl 1891-1973 *FacFETw*
**Browder,** Earl Russell 1891-1973 *AmPolLe*
**Browder,** Edward Carmack 1909- *WhoAmP 91*
**Browder,** Felix Earl 1927- *AmMWSc 92, IntWW 91*
**Browder,** Glen 1943- *AlmAP 92 [port]*
**Browder,** James Steve 1939- *AmMWSc 92*
**Browder,** John Glen 1943- *WhoAmP 91*
**Browder,** Leon Wilfred 1940- *AmMWSc 92*
**Browder,** Lewis Eugene 1932- *AmMWSc 92*
**Browder,** Michael Heath 1951- *WhoRel 92*
**Browder,** Olin Lorraine, Jr. 1913- *WhoAmL 92*
**Browder,** William 1934- *AmMWSc 92*
**Browdy,** Craig Lawrence 1958- *AmMWSc 92*
**Browdy,** Joseph Eugene 1937- *WhoAmL 92*
**Browe,** John Harold 1915- *AmMWSc 92*
**Browell,** Edward Vern 1947- *AmMWSc 92*
**Brower,** Allen S 1926- *AmMWSc 92*
**Brower,** Charles Nelson 1935- *WhoAmL 92*
**Brower,** David Ross 1912- *WrDr 92*
**Brower,** Frank M 1921- *AmMWSc 92*
**Brower,** George David 1948- *WhoFI 92*
**Brower,** Gregory Allen 1945- *WhoMW 92*
**Brower,** Jacob Vradenberg 1844-1905 *BilnAmS*
**Brower,** James Calvin 1914- *WhoMW 92*
**Brower,** James Clinton 1934- *AmMWSc 92*
**Brower,** John Harold 1940- *AmMWSc 92*
**Brower,** John Morehead 1845-1913 *DcNCBi 1*
**Brower,** Kay Robert 1928- *AmMWSc 92*
**Brower,** Keith Lamar 1936- *AmMWSc 92*
**Brower,** Kenneth 1944- *WrDr 92*
**Brower,** Kent Everett 1946- *WhoRel 92*
**Brower,** Lincoln Pierson 1931- *AmMWSc 92*
**Brower,** Millicent *DrAPF 91*
**Brower,** Myron Riggs 1949- *WhoFI 92, WhoWest 92*
**Brower,** Robert Bruce 1951- *WhoMW 92*
**Brower,** Thomas Dudley 1924- *AmMWSc 92*
**Brower,** Thomas Patrick 1946- *WhoAmL 92*
**Brower,** William B, Jr 1922- *AmMWSc 92*
**Brown,** A. David 1942- *WhoBlA 92*
**Brown,** A Hayden, Jr 1946- *AmMWSc 92*
**Brown,** A. Sue 1946- *WhoBlA 92*
**Brown,** Abbott Louis 1943- *WhoEnt 92, WhoFI 92*
**Brown,** Abbott S. 1955- *WhoAmL 92*
**Brown,** Abner Bertrand 1942- *WhoBlA 92*
**Brown,** Acton Richard 1920- *AmMWSc 92*
**Brown,** Ada Katherine 1927- *WhoAmP 91*
**Brown,** Addison 1830-1913 *BilnAmS*
**Brown,** Agnes Marie 1933- *WhoBlA 92*
**Brown,** Alan Crawford 1956- *WhoAmL 92, WhoMW 92*
**Brown,** Alan James 1921- *Who 92*
**Brown,** Alan Morris 1963- *WhoRel 92*
**Brown,** Alan R *AmMWSc 92*
**Brown,** Alan Thomas 1928- *Who 92*
**Brown,** Alan Winthrop 1934- *Who 92*
**Brown,** Alanna Kathleen 1944- *WhoWest 92*
**Brown,** Albert C 1918- *WhoAmP 91*
**Brown,** Albert Erskine 1863-1924 *DcNCBi 1*
**Brown,** Albert Loren 1923- *AmMWSc 92*
**Brown,** Albert Peter 1913- *Who 92*
**Brown,** Alberta Mae 1932- *WhoWest 92*
**Brown,** Alex 1913- *WhoBlA 92*
**Brown,** Alex Cyril 1938- *AmMWSc 92*
**Brown,** Alexander Claude 1931- *IntWW 91*
**Brown,** Alexander Cosens Lindsay 1920- *Who 92*
**Brown,** Alexander Crosby, Jr. 1936- *WhoWest 92*
**Brown,** Alexander Douglas G. *Who 92*
**Brown,** Alfred 1931- *WhoWest 92*
**Brown,** Alfred Bruce, Jr 1920- *AmMWSc 92*
**Brown,** Alfred Edward 1916- *AmMWSc 92*
**Brown,** Alfred Ellis 1941- *AmMWSc 92*
**Brown,** Alice 1857-1948 *BenetAL 91, ScFEYrs*
**Brown,** Alice M. 1857-1948 *HanAmWH*
**Brown,** Alice Regina 1960- *BlkOlyM*
**Brown,** Alison Kay 1957- *AmMWSc 92*
**Brown,** Allen 1911- *Who 92*
**Brown,** Allen 1919- *WhoAmL 92*
**Brown,** Allyn Stephens 1916- *WhoFI 92*
**Brown,** Alvin Montero 1924- *WhoBlA 92*
**Brown,** Alyce Doss *WhoBlA 92*
**Brown,** Amos Cleophilus 1941- *WhoBlA 92, WhoRel 92*
**Brown,** Amos Peaslee 1864-1917 *BilnAmS*
**Brown,** Amy 1959- *WhoWest 92*
**Brown,** Andre L. 1966- *WhoBlA 92*
**Brown,** Andrew J. 1922- *WhoBlA 92*
**Brown,** Angela Yvette 1964- *WhoBlA 92*
**Brown,** Angeline 1931- *WhoEnt 92*
**Brown,** Ann L. 1964- *WhoBlA 92*
**Brown,** Annie Gibson 1944- *WhoBlA 92*
**Brown,** Anthony B. 1922- *WhoWest 92*
**Brown,** Anthony Layne 1961- *WhoMW 92*
**Brown,** Anthony Lemar 1957- *WhoMW 92*
**Brown,** Anthony Vincent 1961- *WhoBlA 92*
**Brown,** Anthony William Aldridge 1911- *AmMWSc 92*
**Brown,** Anthony Wynn 1961- *WhoFI 92*
**Brown,** Archibald Haworth 1938- *IntAu&W 91, Who 92, WrDr 92*
**Brown,** Archie 1911-1990 *FacFETw*
**Brown,** Archie Earl 1913- *WhoRel 92*
**Brown,** Arlen 1926- *AmMWSc 92*
**Brown,** Arlin James 1933- *AmMWSc 92*
**Brown,** Arlon Ray 1938- *WhoMW 92*
**Brown,** Arnold 1913- *Who 92*
**Brown,** Arnold 1939- *AmMWSc 92*
**Brown,** Arnold E. 1932- *WhoBlA 92*
**Brown,** Arnold Harris 1930- *WhoMW 92*
**Brown,** Arnold Lanehart, Jr 1926- *AmMWSc 92*
**Brown,** Arthru Joseph 1914- *IntWW 91*
**Brown,** Arthur 1922- *AmMWSc 92*
**Brown,** Arthur 1940- *WhoWest 92*
**Brown,** Arthur A 1915- *AmMWSc 92*
**Brown,** Arthur Carl, Jr. 1915- *WhoRel 92, WhoWest 92*
**Brown,** Arthur Charles 1929- *AmMWSc 92*
**Brown,** Arthur Durrant 1926- *Who 92*
**Brown,** Arthur Erwin 1850-1910 *BilnAmS*
**Brown,** Arthur Godfrey Kilner 1915- *Who 92*
**Brown,** Arthur I Parry 1908- *Who 92*
**Brown,** Arthur James Stephen 1906- *Who 92*
**Brown,** Arthur Joseph 1914- *Who 92*
**Brown,** Arthur Judson 1856-1963 *AmPeW*
**Brown,** Arthur Lloyd 1915- *AmMWSc 92*
**Brown,** Arthur Morton 1932- *AmMWSc 92*
**Brown,** Arthur Whitten *FacFETw*
**Brown,** Arthur William, Jr. 1939- *WhoAmL 92*
**Brown,** Arza Edward 1942- *WhoRel 92*
**Brown,** Ashmun N. 1930- *WhoRel 92*
**Brown,** Athol Earle McDonald 1905- *Who 92*
**Brown,** Aubrey Neblett, Jr. 1908- *WhoRel 92*
**Brown,** Audrey Kathleen 1923- *AmMWSc 92*
**Brown,** Austen Patrick 1940- *Who 92*
**Brown,** Austin Robert, Jr 1925- *AmMWSc 92*
**Brown,** Autry 1924- *WhoMW 92*
**Brown,** B Peter 1922- *WhoIns 92*
**Brown,** B. R. 1932- *WhoFI 92*
**Brown,** Bachman Storch, Jr 1926- *WhoAmP 91*
**Brown,** Bailey 1917- *WhoAmL 92*
**Brown,** Barbara Ann 1949- *WhoBlA 92*
**Brown,** Barbara D 1929- *WhoAmP 91*
**Brown,** Barbara Eddy 1924- *WhoAmP 91*
**Brown,** Barbara Illingworth 1924- *AmMWSc 92*
**Brown,** Barbara J. *WhoBlA 92*
**Brown,** Barbara Mahone 1944- *WhoBlA 92*
**Brown,** Barker Hastings 1910- *AmMWSc 92*
**Brown,** Barri Anne 1961- *WhoBlA 92*
**Brown,** Barron Kirkpatrick 1947- *WhoRel 92*
**Brown,** Barry *Who 92*
**Brown,** Barry 1942- *WhoEnt 92*
**Brown,** Barry Lee 1944- *AmMWSc 92*
**Brown,** Barry Stephen 1949- *AmMWSc 92*
**Brown,** Barry W 1939- *AmMWSc 92*
**Brown,** Barton 1924- *WhoFI 92*
**Brown,** Basil W 1927- *WhoAmP 91*
**Brown,** Beatrice 1917- *WhoEnt 92*
**Brown,** Beatrice S. 1950- *WhoBlA 92*
**Brown,** Bedford 1795-1870 *DcNCBi 1*
**Brown,** Ben 1941- *WhoAmP 91*
**Brown,** Benjamin G 1837-1903 *BilnAmS*
**Brown,** Benjamin Gene 1953- *BlkOlyM*
**Brown,** Benjamin Lathrop 1947- *AmMWSc 92*
**Brown,** Benjamin Leonard 1929- *WhoBlA 92*
**Brown,** Bernard E. 1925- *WrDr 92*
**Brown,** Bernard Michael 1933- *WhoEnt 92*
**Brown,** Bernice Baynes 1935- *WhoBlA 92*
**Brown,** Bernice H. 1907- *WhoBlA 92*
**Brown,** Bert Elwood 1926- *AmMWSc 92*
**Brown,** Beryl P. *Who 92*
**Brown,** Beth Elaine 1946- *WhoRel 92*
**Brown,** Bettye Jean 1955- *WhoBlA 92*
**Brown,** Bevan W, Jr 1928- *AmMWSc 92*
**Brown,** Beverly Ann 1951- *AmMWSc 92*
**Brown,** Beverly J. *DrAPF 91*
**Brown,** Billings 1920- *AmMWSc 92*
**Brown,** Blair 1948- *IntMPA 92*
**Brown,** Blair Alan 1948- *WhoAmP 91*
**Brown,** Blanche Lenn 1895- *WhoAmP 91*
**Brown,** Bob M 1937- *WhoAmP 91*
**Brown,** Bob Oliver 1929- *WhoMW 92*
**Brown,** Bobby 1954- *WhoBlA 92*
**Brown,** Bobby 1966- *WhoBlA 92*
**Brown,** Bobby 1969- *CurBio 91 [port], WhoEnt 92*

**Brown,** Bobby Wayne 1955- *WhoAmL 92*
**Brown,** Bonnie Jeffreys 1941- *WhoRel 92*
**Brown,** Bonnie Louise 1942- *WhoAmP 91*
**Brown,** Bonnie Maryetta 1953- *WhoAmL 92*
**Brown,** Booker T. 1950- *WhoBlA 92*
**Brown,** Bowman 1941- *WhoAmL 92*
**Brown,** Boyd Zanet 1930- *WhoWest 92*
**Brown,** Bradford E 1938- *AmMWSc 92*
**Brown,** Brewster Warren 1947- *WhoAmP 91*
**Brown,** Brian 1934- *Who 92*
**Brown,** Bruce 1931- *WhoFI 92*
**Brown,** Bruce Allen 1948- *WhoAmL 92*
**Brown,** Bruce Claire 1944- *AmMWSc 92*
**Brown,** Bruce Elliot 1930- *AmMWSc 92*
**Brown,** Bruce Lide 1923- *WhoAmP 91*
**Brown,** Bruce Macdonald 1930- *Who 92*
**Brown,** Bruce Ritchie 1936- *WhoRel 92*
**Brown,** Bruce Stilwell 1945- *AmMWSc 92*
**Brown,** Bruce Willard 1927- *AmMWSc 92*
**Brown,** Bryan 1947- *IntMPA 92*
**Brown,** Buck 1936- *WhoBlA 92*
**Brown,** Buck F 1932- *AmMWSc 92*
**Brown,** Burnell V. 1925- *WhoBlA 92*
**Brown,** Burton Primrose 1917- *AmMWSc 92*
**Brown,** Buster Jack 1944- *WhoAmP 91*
**Brown,** Byrd R. 1929- *WhoBlA 92*
**Brown,** Byron William 1958- *WhoBlA 92*
**Brown,** Byron William, Jr 1930- *AmMWSc 92, WhoWest 92*
**Brown,** C. Christopher 1960- *WhoRel 92*
**Brown,** C E 1938- *WhoIns 92*
**Brown,** C N 1858?-1902 *BiInAmS*
**Brown,** C Stuart *WhoAmP 91*
**Brown,** Calvin Anderson, Jr. 1931- *WhoBlA 92*
**Brown,** Calvin Scott 1859-1936 *DcNCBi 1*
**Brown,** Capability 1715-1783 *BlkwCEP*
**Brown,** Carl Anthony 1930- *WhoBlA 92*
**Brown,** Carl Dee 1919- *AmMWSc 92*
**Brown,** Carl Henry 1932- *WhoMW 92*
**Brown,** Carl Williamson 1944- *WhoWest 92*
**Brown,** Carol Ann 1952- *WhoBlA 92*
**Brown,** Carol Dunn 1941- *WhoMW 92*
**Brown,** Carol R. 1933- *WhoEnt 92*
**Brown,** Carol Sue 1950- *WhoRel 92*
**Brown,** Carolyn M. 1948- *WhoBlA 92*
**Brown,** Carolyn Smith 1946- *WhoWest 92*
**Brown,** Carroll Elizabeth 1942- *WhoBlA 92*
**Brown,** Carter *Who 92*
**Brown,** Cathie 1944- *WhoWest 92*
**Brown,** Cecil *DrAPF 91*
**Brown,** Cecil Kenneth 1900-1957 *DcNCBi 1*
**Brown,** Cecil M. 1943- *WhoBlA 92*
**Brown,** Cedric Harold 1935- *Who 92*
**Brown,** Cedric Wilfred George E. *Who 92*
**Brown,** Channing T 1929- *WhoAmP 91*
**Brown,** Charles 1939- *BlkOlyM*
**Brown,** Charles 1951- *WhoAmP 91*
**Brown,** Charles Allan 1944- *AmMWSc 92*
**Brown,** Charles Brockden 1771-1810 *BenetAL 91*
**Brown,** Charles D. 1960- *WhoAmL 92*
**Brown,** Charles Dargie 1927- *Who 92*
**Brown,** Charles Earl 1919- *WhoAmL 92*
**Brown,** Charles Edward 1948- *WhoBlA 92*
**Brown,** Charles Eric 1946- *AmMWSc 92*
**Brown,** Charles Frederick Richmond 1902- *Who 92*
**Brown,** Charles G, III 1950- *WhoAmP 91*
**Brown,** Charles Henry 1847?-1901 *BiInAmS*
**Brown,** Charles Henry 1929- *WhoRel 92*
**Brown,** Charles Irving 1932- *WhoWest 92*
**Brown,** Charles Julian, Jr 1932- *AmMWSc 92*
**Brown,** Charles L 1920- *AmMWSc 92*
**Brown,** Charles Moseley 1943- *AmMWSc 92*
**Brown,** Charles Myers 1927- *AmMWSc 92*
**Brown,** Charles Nelson 1941- *AmMWSc 92*
**Brown,** Charles Quentin 1928- *AmMWSc 92*
**Brown,** Charles S 1920- *AmMWSc 92*
**Brown,** Charles Sumner 1937- *WhoBlA 92*
**Brown,** Charles Thomas 1928- *AmMWSc 92*
**Brown,** Charles Vertis, Jr 1943- *WhoAmP 91*
**Brown,** Charlie 1938- *WhoAmP 91, WhoBlA 92*
**Brown,** Charlotte Hawkins 1883-1961 *DcNCBi 1, NotBlAW 92 [port]*
**Brown,** Charnele *WhoEnt 92*
**Brown,** Chauncey I., Jr. 1928- *WhoBlA 92*
**Brown,** Chester Harvey, Jr *AmMWSc 92*
**Brown,** Chet, Jr. 1938- *WhoWest 92*
**Brown,** Chris 1961- *WhoBlA 92*
**Brown,** Chris A 1962- *WhoIns 92*
**Brown,** Christina Hambley *Who 92*
**Brown,** Christopher 1938- *Who 92*
**Brown,** Christopher 1943- *ConCom 92*
**Brown,** Christopher C. 1938- *WhoBlA 92*
**Brown,** Christopher David 1944- *Who 92*
**Brown,** Christopher Scott 1958- *WhoFI 92*
**Brown,** Christopher W 1938- *AmMWSc 92*
**Brown,** Christy 1932-1981 *FacFETw*
**Brown,** Cindy 1965- *BlkOlyM*
**Brown,** Clancy 1958- *IntMPA 92*
**Brown,** Clarence 1890-1987 *FacFETw, IntDcF 2-2 [port]*
**Brown,** Clarence J 1927- *WhoAmP 91*
**Brown,** Clarence William 1933- *WhoBlA 92*
**Brown,** Clarice Ernestine 1929- *WhoBlA 92*
**Brown,** Clark Anthony 1951- *WhoRel 92*
**Brown,** Clark S. *WhoBlA 92*
**Brown,** Clark Samuel 1911- *WhoAmP 91*
**Brown,** Clark Tait 1935- *WhoWest 92*
**Brown,** Claude *DrAPF 91*
**Brown,** Claude 1937- *Au&Arts 7 [port], BenetAL 91, BlkLC [port]*
**Brown,** Claudell, Jr. 1949- *WhoBlA 92*
**Brown,** Clay Jonathan 1958- *WhoRel 92*
**Brown,** Cliff *WhoAmP 91*
**Brown,** Clifford 1930-1956 *FacFETw, NewAmDM*
**Brown,** Clifford Anthony 1951- *WhoBlA 92*
**Brown,** Clifford Edward 1947- *WhoMW 92*
**Brown,** Clifford Wilton 1920- *WhoAmL 92*
**Brown,** Clifton George 1959- *WhoBlA 92*
**Brown,** Colin Bertram 1929- *AmMWSc 92*
**Brown,** Colin Wegand 1949- *WhoAmL 92, WhoFI 92*
**Brown,** Colon Robert 1953- *WhoMW 92, WhoRel 92*
**Brown,** Conella Coulter 1925- *WhoBlA 92*
**Brown,** Connell Jean 1924- *AmMWSc 92*
**Brown,** Connie Yates 1947- *WhoFI 92*
**Brown,** Constance Charlene 1939- *WhoBlA 92*
**Brown,** Constance M. 1953- *WhoFI 92*
**Brown,** Constance Young 1933- *WhoBlA 92*
**Brown,** Corrick *WhoEnt 92*
**Brown,** Corrine 1946- *WhoAmP 91*
**Brown,** Costello L. 1942- *WhoBlA 92*
**Brown,** Courtney Coleridge 1924- *WhoBlA 92*
**Brown,** Craig Vincent 1943- *WhoBlA 92*
**Brown,** Curtis Carnegie, Jr. 1951- *WhoBlA 92*
**Brown,** Cynthia Ann 1945- *AmMWSc 92*
**Brown,** Cyril H. 1931-1990 *WhoBlA 92N*
**Brown,** Cyril James 1904- *Who 92*
**Brown,** Cyril Maxwell Palmer 1914- *Who 92*
**Brown,** D. Joan *WhoBlA 92*
**Brown,** Dale Francis 1956- *WhoWest 92*
**Brown,** Dale Gordon 1944- *AmMWSc 92*
**Brown,** Dale H 1922- *AmMWSc 92*
**Brown,** Dale Marius *AmMWSc 92*
**Brown,** Dale Patrick 1947- *WhoMW 92*
**Brown,** Dale Robert 1967- *WhoWest 92*
**Brown,** Dale W 1926- *IntAu&W 91, WrDr 92*
**Brown,** Dale Weaver 1926- *WhoRel 92*
**Brown,** Dallas C., Jr. 1932- *WhoBlA 92*
**Brown,** Daniel 1946- *WhoFI 92, WhoMW 92*
**Brown,** Daniel A. 1940- *WhoRel 92*
**Brown,** Daniel Joseph 1941- *AmMWSc 92*
**Brown,** Daniel Mason 1939- *AmMWSc 92*
**Brown,** Daniel McGillivray 1923- *IntWW 91, Who 92*
**Brown,** Daniel Warren 1930- *WhoWest 92*
**Brown,** Darrell Houston 1952- *WhoRel 92*
**Brown,** Darrell Quentin 1932- *AmMWSc 92*
**Brown,** Darryl Newton 1944- *WhoAmP 91*
**Brown,** Dave 1948- *WhoAmP 91*
**Brown,** Dave Steven 1953- *WhoBlA 92*
**Brown,** David 1904- *IntWW 91, Who 92*
**Brown,** David 1916- *IntMPA 92*
**Brown,** David Anthony 1936- *Who 92*
**Brown,** David Arthur 1929- *IntWW 91*
**Brown,** David Chester 1942- *AmMWSc 92*
**Brown,** David Clifford 1929- *Who 92*
**Brown,** David Clifford 1938- *WhoRel 92, WhoWest 92*
**Brown,** David E 1947- *AmMWSc 92*
**Brown,** David Edward 1909- *AmMWSc 92*
**Brown,** David Emerson 1926- *WhoAmP 91*
**Brown,** David Eugene 1938- *WhoBlA 92*
**Brown,** David Francis 1935- *AmMWSc 92*
**Brown,** David Frederick 1928- *AmMWSc 92*
**Brown,** David G 1943- *AmMWSc 92*
**Brown,** David George Boyd *WhoEnt 92*
**Brown,** David Hazzard 1925- *AmMWSc 92*
**Brown,** David John Bowes 1925- *Who 92*
**Brown,** David K. *Who 92*
**Brown,** David K 1936- *WhoAmP 91*
**Brown,** David Lee 1947- *WhoAmL 92*
**Brown,** David Lyle 1943- *AmMWSc 92*
**Brown,** David Lynn 1949- *WhoRel 92*
**Brown,** David Michael 1953- *WhoRel 92*
**Brown,** David Millard 1918- *WhoAmP 91*
**Brown,** David Mitchell 1935- *AmMWSc 92*
**Brown,** David P 1934- *AmMWSc 92*
**Brown,** David Randolph 1923- *AmMWSc 92*
**Brown,** David Robert 1954- *AmMWSc 92*
**Brown,** David Ronald 1939- *WhoAmL 92*
**Brown,** David Rupert 1934- *WhoFI 92, WhoMW 92*
**Brown,** David Smith 1944- *AmMWSc 92*
**Brown,** David T 1936- *AmMWSc 92*
**Brown,** David Vincent 1958- *WhoRel 92*
**Brown,** David William 1948- *Who 92*
**Brown,** David Worthington 1927- *Who 92*
**Brown,** Dawn LaRue 1948- *AmMWSc 92*
**Brown,** Dean 1927- *WhoAmL 92*
**Brown,** Dean E. *WhoRel 92*
**Brown,** Dean Naomi 1944- *WhoWest 92*
**Brown,** Dean Raymond *AmMWSc 92*
**Brown,** Deborah 1929- *TwCPaSc*
**Brown,** Deborah Elizabeth 1952- *WhoEnt 92*
**Brown,** Debra Wood 1951- *WhoAmP 91*
**Brown,** Debria M. 1936- *WhoBlA 92*
**Brown,** Dee 1908- *TwCWW 91, WrDr 92*
**Brown,** Dee 1968- *WhoBlA 92*
**Brown,** Delores Elaine 1945- *WhoBlA 92*
**Brown,** Deloris A. *WhoBlA 92*
**Brown,** Delos D 1933- *AmMWSc 92*
**Brown,** Deloss 1941- *WhoEnt 92*
**Brown,** Delwin 1935- *ConAu 135*
**Brown,** Denise Lebreton *Who 92*
**Brown,** Denise Sharon 1957- *WhoBlA 92*
**Brown,** Dennis L 1948- *WhoAmP 91*
**Brown,** Dennis Ray 1954- *WhoRel 92*
**Brown,** Dennis Snowden 1954- *WhoBlA 92*
**Brown,** Dennis William 1957- *WhoMW 92*
**Brown,** Dennison Robert 1934- *AmMWSc 92*
**Brown,** Denys Downing 1918- *Who 92*
**Brown,** Derrick H. *Who 92*
**Brown,** Diana *DrAPF 91*
**Brown,** Diana 1928- *IntAu&W 91*
**Brown,** Diana Johnson 1951- *WhoBlA 92*
**Brown,** Dick Terrell 1944- *WhoAmL 92*
**Brown,** Donald A 1916- *AmMWSc 92*
**Brown,** Donald D 1931- *AmMWSc 92*
**Brown,** Donald David 1931- *IntWW 91*
**Brown,** Donald Doyle, Jr. 1946- *WhoAmL 92*
**Brown,** Donald Frederick Mackenzie 1919- *AmMWSc 92*
**Brown,** Donald James, Jr. 1948- *WhoAmL 92*
**Brown,** Donald James, Jr. 1955- *WhoFI 92*
**Brown,** Donald Jerould 1926- *AmMWSc 92, WhoWest 92*
**Brown,** Donald John 1933- *AmMWSc 92*
**Brown,** Donald M 1920- *AmMWSc 92*
**Brown,** Donald R., Sr. 1939- *WhoBlA 92*
**Brown,** Donald Ray 1932- *WhoRel 92*
**Brown,** Donald Ray 1935- *WhoMW 92*
**Brown,** Donald Robert 1925- *WhoMW 92*
**Brown,** Donald S. 1928- *IntWW 91*
**Brown,** Doreen Leah Hurwitz 1927- *WhoFI 92*
**Brown,** Doretta Hosley 1917- *WhoMW 92*
**Brown,** Doris Jean 1953- *WhoEnt 92, WhoMW 92*
**Brown,** Dorothy 1919- *NotBlAW 92*
**Brown,** Dorothy Lavania 1919- *WhoBlA 92*
**Brown,** Dorothy Lynne 1947- *WhoRel 92*
**Brown,** Douglas 1917- *Who 92*
**Brown,** Douglas 1931- *Who 92*
**Brown,** Douglas Edward 1926- *AmMWSc 92*
**Brown,** Douglas Fletcher 1934- *AmMWSc 92*
**Brown,** Douglas Kenneth 1964- *WhoRel 92*
**Brown,** Douglas Leo 1937- *WhoRel 92*
**Brown,** Douglas Marshall 1955- *WhoWest 92*
**Brown,** Douglas Richard 1942- *AmMWSc 92*
**Brown,** Duane 1918- *AmMWSc 92*
**Brown,** Dudley Earl, Jr 1928- *WhoAmP 91*
**Brown,** Duncan Fraser 1921- *WhoFI 92*
**Brown,** Dwayne Marc 1962- *WhoBlA 92*
**Brown,** E. Lynn 1936- *WhoRel 92*
**Brown,** Earl Eugene, Jr. 1942- *WhoMW 92*
**Brown,** Earl Ivan, II 1917- *AmMWSc 92*
**Brown,** Earl Richard 1952- *WhoBlA 92*
**Brown,** Earle 1926- *NewAmDM, WhoEnt 92*
**Brown,** Earle, Jr 1926- *ConCom 92*
**Brown,** Earle Palmer 1922- *WhoFI 92*
**Brown,** Earlene Dennis 1935-1983 *BlkOlyM*
**Brown,** Eddie C. 1940- *WhoBlA 92*
**Brown,** Edgar Henry, Jr 1926- *AmMWSc 92*
**Brown,** Edmond 1924- *AmMWSc 92*
**Brown,** Edmund G, Jr 1938- *FacFETw*
**Brown,** Edmund Gerald 1905- *IntWW 91*
**Brown,** Edmund Gerald, Jr. 1938- *IntWW 91, NewYTBS 91 [port], Who 92, WhoAmP 91, WhoWest 92*
**Brown,** Edmund Hosmer 1920- *AmMWSc 92*
**Brown,** Edward Herriot, Jr 1926- *AmMWSc 92*
**Brown,** Edward James 1937- *WhoFI 92*
**Brown,** Edward James 1948- *AmMWSc 92*
**Brown,** Edward Joseph d1991 *Who 92N*
**Brown,** Edward Lee 1948- *WhoRel 92*
**Brown,** Edward Lynn 1936- *WhoBlA 92*
**Brown,** Edward Martin 1933- *AmMWSc 92*
**Brown,** Edward Sherman 1940- *WhoFI 92*
**Brown,** Edward Stanton, III 1949- *WhoEnt 92*
**Brown,** Edwin C., Jr. 1935- *WhoBlA 92*
**Brown,** Edwin Eugene, Jr. 1956- *WhoRel 92*
**Brown,** Edwin Pierce 1903-1972 *DcNCBi 1*
**Brown,** Edwin Thomas 1938- *Who 92*
**Brown,** Edwin Wilson, Jr 1926- *AmMWSc 92*
**Brown,** Effie Mayhan Jones 1922- *WhoBlA 92*
**Brown,** Egbert Ethelred 1875-1956 *RelLAm 91*
**Brown,** Eleanor Moore 1936- *AmMWSc 92*
**Brown,** Eleanor Stockstrom McMillen d1991 *NewYTBS 91 [port]*
**Brown,** Elisabeth Potts 1939- *ConAu 133*
**Brown,** Elise Ann Brandenburger 1928- *AmMWSc 92*
**Brown,** Elizabeth *DrAPF 91*
**Brown,** Elizabeth Crichton *WhoAmP 91*
**Brown,** Ellen 1912- *AmMWSc 92*
**Brown,** Ellen Rochelle 1949- *WhoBlA 92*
**Brown,** Ellen Ruth 1947- *AmMWSc 92*
**Brown,** Ellis Vincent 1908- *AmMWSc 92*
**Brown,** Ellsworth Howard 1943- *WhoMW 92*
**Brown,** Elmer Burrell 1926- *AmMWSc 92*
**Brown,** Elmer Burrell, Jr. 1926- *WhoMW 92*
**Brown,** Elona M 1917- *WhoAmP 91*
**Brown,** Emily Freeman 1956- *WhoEnt 92*
**Brown,** Emmett Earl 1932- *WhoBlA 92*
**Brown,** Eric 1950- *AmMWSc 92*
**Brown,** Eric 1960- *TwCSFW 91*
**Brown,** Eric David 1953- *WhoEnt 92*
**Brown,** Eric Herbert 1922- *Who 92*
**Brown,** Eric Melrose 1919- *Who 92*
**Brown,** Eric Reeder 1925- *AmMWSc 92*
**Brown,** Eric Richard 1942- *AmMWSc 92*
**Brown,** Ernest Calvin 1941- *WhoBlA 92*
**Brown,** Ernest Henry Phelps 1906- *IntWW 91, Who 92*
**Brown,** Esther Marie 1923- *AmMWSc 92*
**Brown,** Evelyn 1930- *WhoBlA 92*
**Brown,** Evelyn Drewery 1935- *WhoBlA 92*
**Brown,** Everett W 1912- *WhoAmP 91*
**Brown,** Ewart F., Jr. 1946- *WhoBlA 92*
**Brown,** F. Reed 1960- *WhoEnt 92*
**Brown,** Fannie E. Garrett 1924- *WhoBlA 92*
**Brown,** Farrell Blenn 1934- *AmMWSc 92*
**Brown,** Fielding 1924- *AmMWSc 92*
**Brown,** Firman Hewitt, Jr. 1926- *WhoEnt 92*
**Brown,** Flavy Buster 1928- *WhoRel 92*
**Brown,** Floyd A. 1930- *WhoBlA 92*
**Brown,** Forbes Taylor 1934- *AmMWSc 92*
**Brown,** Fountaine Christine 1923- *AmMWSc 92*
**Brown,** Franchot A. 1943- *WhoBlA 92*
**Brown,** Francis C 1830-1900 *BiInAmS*
**Brown,** Francis H., III 1959- *WhoAmL 92*
**Brown,** Frank 1935- *WhoBlA 92*
**Brown,** Frank, Jr. 1942- *WhoMW 92*
**Brown,** Frank Beverly, IV 1945- *WhoAmL 92*
**Brown,** Frank Clyde 1870-1943 *DcNCBi 1*
**Brown,** Frank Malloy 1950- *WhoMW 92*
**Brown,** Frank Markham 1930- *AmMWSc 92*
**Brown,** Frank Mustard 1931- *WhoRel 92*
**Brown,** Fred 1925- *IntWW 91, Who 92*
**Brown,** Fred H *ScFEYrs*
**Brown,** Fred R 1912- *AmMWSc 92*
**Brown,** Freddiemae Eugenia 1928- *WhoBlA 92*
**Brown,** Frederic Emil 1943- *WhoAmP 91*
**Brown,** Frederic Milton 1946- *WhoAmP 91*
**Brown,** Frederick 1851-1941 *TwCPaSc*
**Brown,** Frederick Calvin 1924- *AmMWSc 92*
**Brown,** Frederick G. 1932- *WrDr 92*
**Brown,** Frederick H 1927- *WhoIns 92*
**Brown,** Frederick Harold 1927- *WhoFI 92*
**Brown,** Frederick Herbert Stanley 1910- *Who 92*
**Brown,** Frederick Lee 1940- *WhoMW 92*
**Brown,** Frederick Wilhelm 1955- *WhoEnt 92*
**Brown,** Fredric 1906-1972 *TwCSFW 91*
**Brown,** Freezell, Jr. 1957- *WhoMW 92, WhoRel 92*

**Brown,** G Steven 1947- WhoAmP 91
**Brown,** Gardner Russell, Mrs. WhoFI 92
**Brown,** Garrett Edward, Jr. 1943- WhoAmL 92
**Brown,** Garry Leslie 1942- AmMWSc 92
**Brown,** Gary S 1940- AmMWSc 92
**Brown,** Gary W. 1944- WhoBlA 92
**Brown,** Gates 1939- WhoBlA 92
**Brown,** Gavin 1942- IntWW 91
**Brown,** Gene Monte 1926- AmMWSc 92
**Brown,** Geoffrey E. Who 92
**Brown,** Geoffrey Harold 1930- Who 92
**Brown,** Geoffrey William 1950- WhoWest 92
**Brown,** Georg Stanford 1943- IntMPA 92
**Brown,** George, Jr. 1942- WhoRel 92
**Brown,** George Arthur 1922- Who 92
**Brown,** George D, Jr 1931- AmMWSc 92
**Brown,** George Douglas RfGEnL 91
**Brown,** George E., Jr. 1920- AlmAP 92 [port]
**Brown,** George Earl 1906- AmMWSc 92
**Brown,** George Edward, Jr 1920- WhoAmP 91, WhoWest 92
**Brown,** George Frederick William 1908- Who 92
**Brown,** George Hardin 1931- WhoWest 92
**Brown,** George Henry, Jr. 1939- WhoBlA 92
**Brown,** George Houston 1916- WhoBlA 92
**Brown,** George Hubbard 1850-1926 DcNCBi 1
**Brown,** George L. 1926- WhoBlA 92
**Brown,** George Lincoln 1921- AmMWSc 92
**Brown,** George Mackay 1921- ConNov 91, ConPo 91, RfGEnL 91, Who 92, WrDr 92
**Brown,** George Malcolm 1925- IntWW 91, Who 92
**Brown,** George Marshall 1921- AmMWSc 92
**Brown,** George Martin 1919- AmMWSc 92
**Brown,** George McKay 1921- IntAu&W 91
**Brown,** George Milton 1948- WhoAmP 91
**Brown,** George Noel 1942- Who 92
**Brown,** George Philip 1920- WhoBlA 92
**Brown,** George S 1918-1978 FacFETw
**Brown,** George Stephen 1945- AmMWSc 92, WhoWest 92
**Brown,** George Thomas 1869-1913 DcNCBi 1
**Brown,** George W. 1871-1950 DcNCBi 1
**Brown,** George Wallace 1939- AmMWSc 92
**Brown,** George Willard, Jr 1924- AmMWSc 92
**Brown,** George William 1917- AmMWSc 92
**Brown,** George William 1930- Who 92
**Brown,** Georgia 1933- ConTFT 9
**Brown,** Georgia R. WhoBlA 92
**Brown,** Georgia W. 1934- WhoBlA 92
**Brown,** Gerald E 1926- AmMWSc 92
**Brown,** Gerald Eugene 1949- WhoRel 92
**Brown,** Gerald Lee 1935- WhoAmL 92
**Brown,** Gerald Leonard 1936- AmMWSc 92
**Brown,** Gerald Richard 1937- AmMWSc 92
**Brown,** Gerviece Hortense 1940- WhoWest 92
**Brown,** Gilbert David, III 1949- WhoBlA 92
**Brown,** Gilbert J 1948- AmMWSc 92
**Brown,** Gilbert Morris 1947- AmMWSc 92
**Brown,** Gillian 1923- Who 92
**Brown,** Gillian 1937- Who 92
**Brown,** Glen Francis 1911- AmMWSc 92
**Brown,** Glenda Ann Walters 1937- WhoEnt 92
**Brown,** Glenn A AmMWSc 92
**Brown,** Glenn Arthur 1953- WhoBlA 92
**Brown,** Glenn E 1943- WhoAmP 91
**Brown,** Glenn Halstead 1915- AmMWSc 92
**Brown,** Glenn Lamar 1923- AmMWSc 92
**Brown,** Glenn R 1930- AmMWSc 92
**Brown,** Glenn Willard 1918- WhoBlA 92
**Brown,** Glenn William, Jr. 1955- WhoAmL 92, WhoFI 92
**Brown,** Gloria Campos 1954- WhoHisp 92
**Brown,** Godfrey Norman 1926- Who 92
**Brown,** Goold 1791-1857 BenetAL 91
**Brown,** Gordon Who 92, WhoAmP 91
**Brown,** Gordon Edgar, Jr 1943- AmMWSc 92
**Brown,** Gordon Elliott 1936- AmMWSc 92
**Brown,** Gordon Manley 1933- AmMWSc 92
**Brown,** Gordon S AmMWSc 92
**Brown,** Grady 1944- WhoAmP 91
**Brown,** Graham 1924- ConTFT 9
**Brown,** Grant C WhoAmP 91
**Brown,** Graydon L 1924- AmMWSc 92
**Brown,** Greggory Lee 1953- WhoBlA 92
**Brown,** Gregory Gaynor 1948- AmMWSc 92
**Brown,** Gregory Neil 1938- AmMWSc 92
**Brown,** Guendoline 1936- AmMWSc 92
**Brown,** H. Dennis 1944- WhoWest 92
**Brown,** H. Rap 1943- WhoBlA 92
**Brown,** H. William 1933- WhoWest 92
**Brown,** H. William 1938- WhoFI 92
**Brown,** Hallie 1845?-1949 NotBlAW 92 [port]
**Brown,** Hamilton 1786-1870 DcNCBi 1
**Brown,** Hamilton Allen 1837-1917 DcNCBi 1
**Brown,** Hank 1940- AlmAP 92 [port], IntWW 91, WhoAmP 91, WhoWest 92
**Brown,** Hannah M. 1939- WhoBlA 92
**Brown,** Harlan James 1933- WhoFI 92
**Brown,** Harley Procter 1921- AmMWSc 92
**Brown,** Harold 1917- AmMWSc 92
**Brown,** Harold 1927- AmMWSc 92, IntWW 91, Who 92, WhoAmP 91
**Brown,** Harold Arthur Neville 1914- Who 92
**Brown,** Harold Berger, Jr. 1940- WhoRel 92
**Brown,** Harold C, Jr 1932- WhoAmP 91
**Brown,** Harold David 1940- AmMWSc 92
**Brown,** Harold Hubley 1926- AmMWSc 92
**Brown,** Harold James 1911- Who 92
**Brown,** Harold Mack, Jr 1936- AmMWSc 92
**Brown,** Harold Probert 1908- AmMWSc 92
**Brown,** Harold Victor 1918- AmMWSc 92
**Brown,** Harold Vivian 1945- Who 92
**Brown,** Harriet DrAPF 91
**Brown,** Harriett Baltimore 1917- WhoBlA 92
**Brown,** Harrison 1917-1986 FacFETw
**Brown,** Harrison D. 1846-1940 RelLAm 91
**Brown,** Harry 1917-1986 BenetAL 91
**Brown,** Harry Allen 1925- AmMWSc 92
**Brown,** Harry Benjamin 1913- AmMWSc 92
**Brown,** Harry Darrow 1925- AmMWSc 92
**Brown,** Harry Lester 1924- AmMWSc 92, WhoWest 92
**Brown,** Hazel Evelyn 1940- WhoBlA 92
**Brown,** Headley Adolphus IntWW 91
**Brown,** Helen Avis 1934- WhoAmP 91
**Brown,** Helen Bennett 1902- AmMWSc 92
**Brown,** Helen Gurley IntWW 91
**Brown,** Helen Gurley 1922- BenetAL 91, FacFETw, WrDr 92
**Brown,** Henry 1899- IntMPA 92
**Brown,** Henry 1920- AmMWSc 92
**Brown,** Henry Alfred 1846-1929 DcNCBi 1
**Brown,** Henry B 1836-1913 FacFETw
**Brown,** Henry Clay 1948- AmMWSc 92
**Brown,** Henry Clay, III 1919- AmMWSc 92
**Brown,** Henry E, Jr 1935- WhoAmP 91
**Brown,** Henry H. WhoBlA 92
**Brown,** Henry Harrison 1840-1918 RelLAm 91
**Brown,** Henry Phelps Who 92
**Brown,** Henry Phelps 1906- IntAu&W 91, WrDr 92
**Brown,** Henry Seawell 1930- AmMWSc 92
**Brown,** Henry Thomas C. Who 92
**Brown,** Herbert 1930- AmMWSc 92
**Brown,** Herbert Allen 1940- AmMWSc 92
**Brown,** Herbert C. 1912- WrDr 92
**Brown,** Herbert Charles 1912- AmMWSc 92, FacFETw, IntWW 91, Who 92, WhoMW 92, WhoNob 90
**Brown,** Herbert Ensign AmMWSc 92
**Brown,** Herbert Eugene 1915- AmMWSc 92
**Brown,** Herbert R. 1940- WhoBlA 92
**Brown,** Herbert Russell 1931- WhoAmL 92, WhoAmP 91, WhoMW 92
**Brown,** Herman 1922- WhoBlA 92
**Brown,** Herman 1928- WhoRel 92
**Brown,** Herman Cubbage 1925- WhoAmP 91
**Brown,** Hermione Kopp 1915- WhoWest 92
**Brown,** Hezekiah 1923- WhoBlA 92
**Brown,** Himan 1910- IntMPA 92
**Brown,** Hobson, Jr. 1942- WhoFI 92
**Brown,** Homer E 1909- AmMWSc 92
**Brown,** Horace Dean 1919- AmMWSc 92
**Brown,** Howard 1916- AmMWSc 92
**Brown,** Howard Bernard 1924- WhoFI 92
**Brown,** Howard C. 1901- IntMPA 92
**Brown,** Howard Howland, Jr 1934- AmMWSc 92
**Brown,** Howard James 1907- WhoRel 92
**Brown,** Howard Mayer 1930- Who 92, WhoEnt 92, WhoMW 92, WrDr 92
**Brown,** Howard S 1921- AmMWSc 92
**Brown,** Hoyt C. 1920- WhoBlA 92
**Brown,** Hubert 1943- FacFETw
**Brown,** Hugh Boycott 1909- TwCPaSc
**Brown,** Hugh Dunbar 1919- Who 92
**Brown,** Hugh Keith 1945- AmMWSc 92
**Brown,** Hugh Needham 1928- AmMWSc 92
**Brown,** I. B. WhoRel 92
**Brown,** Ian David 1932- AmMWSc 92
**Brown,** Ian James Morris 1945- Who 92
**Brown,** Ian McLaren 1935- AmMWSc 92
**Brown,** Ian Ross 1943- AmMWSc 92
**Brown,** Iona 1941- WhoEnt 92, WhoWest 92
**Brown,** Ira Bernard 1927- WhoFI 92
**Brown,** Ira Charles 1916- AmMWSc 92
**Brown,** Irma Hunter 1939- WhoAmP 91
**Brown,** Irma Jean 1948- WhoBlA 92
**Brown,** Irmel Nelson 1912- AmMWSc 92
**Brown,** J. Aaron WhoEnt 92
**Brown,** J. Curtis 1943- WhoMW 92
**Brown,** J David 1957- AmMWSc 92
**Brown,** J Douglas 1898-1986 FacFETw
**Brown,** J E 1940- WhoAmP 91
**Brown,** J H U 1918- AmMWSc 92
**Brown,** J Martin 1941- AmMWSc 92
**Brown,** J. Norman 1954- WhoAmL 92
**Brown,** J.P.S. 1930- TwCWW 91, WrDr 92
**Brown,** J. Quantin WhoBlA 92
**Brown,** J.W. DrAPF 91
**Brown,** J Willcox 1915- WhoAmP 91
**Brown,** Jack 1929- Who 92
**Brown,** Jack A WhoAmP 91
**Brown,** Jack Chapler 1919- WhoFI 92
**Brown,** Jack H. 1939- WhoFI 92, WhoWest 92
**Brown,** Jack Harold Upton 1918- AmMWSc 92
**Brown,** Jack Stanley 1929- AmMWSc 92
**Brown,** Jacqueline D. 1957- WhoBlA 92
**Brown,** James DrAPF 91, LesBEnT 92
**Brown,** James 1863-1943 TwCPaSc
**Brown,** James 1909-1983 ConAu 135
**Brown,** James 1925- Who 92
**Brown,** James 1928- FacFETw, IntWW 91, News 91 [port], Who 92, WhoEnt 92
**Brown,** James 1933?- NewAmDM
**Brown,** James 1934- WhoBlA 92
**Brown,** James Alexander 1914- Who 92
**Brown,** James Anthony 1932- WhoEnt 92
**Brown,** James Barrow 1932- WhoRel 92
**Brown,** James Barry 1937- Who 92
**Brown,** James Benton 1945- WhoAmL 92
**Brown,** James C 1936- WhoAmP 91
**Brown,** James Carrington, III 1939- WhoWest 92
**Brown,** James Carson 1948- WhoAmL 92
**Brown,** James Chandler 1947- WhoWest 92
**Brown,** James Channing 1944- WhoFI 92
**Brown,** James Curtiss 1921- WhoAmL 92
**Brown,** James Douglas 1934- AmMWSc 92
**Brown,** James E. 1923- WhoBlA 92
**Brown,** James Earle 1950- WhoFI 92
**Brown,** James Edward 1939- WhoAmP 91
**Brown,** James Edward 1945- AmMWSc 92
**Brown,** James Edward 1949- WhoFI 92
**Brown,** James Elmer 1927- WhoAmP 91
**Brown,** James Franklin 1957- WhoRel 92
**Brown,** James Frederick 1941- WhoFI 92
**Brown,** James Frederick 1943- WhoEnt 92
**Brown,** James Goldie 1901- ScFEYrs
**Brown,** James Gordon 1951- IntWW 91, Who 92
**Brown,** James H. 1935- WhoBlA 92
**Brown,** James Harmon 1949- WhoEnt 92
**Brown,** James Harold 1931- AmMWSc 92
**Brown,** James Harold 1961- WhoWest 92
**Brown,** James Harvey 1924- WhoBlA 92
**Brown,** James Harvey 1940- WhoAmP 91
**Brown,** James Hemphill 1942- AmMWSc 92
**Brown,** James Henry, Jr 1934- AmMWSc 92
**Brown,** James Hyatt 1937- WhoAmP 91
**Brown,** James I. 1908- WrDr 92
**Brown,** James Isaac 1908- IntAu&W 91
**Brown,** James Joseph 1944- WhoAmL 92
**Brown,** James K 1945- AmMWSc 92
**Brown,** James Kerr 1938- AmMWSc 92
**Brown,** James Louis 1933- WhoEnt 92
**Brown,** James Marion 1952- WhoBlA 92
**Brown,** James Marston 1950- WhoWest 92
**Brown,** James Melton 1925- AmMWSc 92
**Brown,** James Michael 1955- AmMWSc 92
**Brown,** James Monroe 1928- WhoAmP 91, WhoBlA 92
**Brown,** James Nathaniel 1936- FacFETw
**Brown,** James Richard 1931- AmMWSc 92
**Brown,** James Robert 1955- WhoMW 92
**Brown,** James Roy 1923- AmMWSc 92
**Brown,** James Russell 1932- AmMWSc 92
**Brown,** James Scott 1945- WhoAmL 92
**Brown,** James T, Jr 1939- AmMWSc 92
**Brown,** James Thompson, Jr. 1935- WhoFI 92
**Brown,** James Walker, Jr 1930- AmMWSc 92
**Brown,** James Ward 1934- AmMWSc 92
**Brown,** James Wilcox 1948- WhoAmL 92
**Brown,** James William 1944- WhoFI 92
**Brown,** Jamie 1945- IntAu&W 91
**Brown,** J'Amy Maroney 1945- WhoWest 92
**Brown,** Jan W 1942- WhoAmP 91
**Brown,** Janice 1935- WhoWest 92
**Brown,** Jarvis Howard 1937- AmMWSc 92
**Brown,** Jason Rosch 1963- WhoAmL 92
**Brown,** Jasper C., Jr. 1946- WhoBlA 92
**Brown,** Jay Clark 1942- AmMWSc 92
**Brown,** Jay Wright 1945- WhoFI 92
**Brown,** Jean Rae 1956- WhoAmL 92
**Brown,** Jeanette Snyder 1925- AmMWSc 92
**Brown,** Jefferson W. Z. 1942- WhoAmL 92
**Brown,** Jeffrey 1946- WhoAmL 92
**Brown,** Jeffrey Allen 1954- WhoMW 92
**Brown,** Jeffrey D. WhoEnt 92
**Brown,** Jeffrey Hale 1953- WhoEnt 92
**Brown,** Jeffrey LaMonte 1961- WhoRel 92
**Brown,** Jeffrey LeMonte 1961- WhoBlA 92
**Brown,** Jeffrey M 1962- WhoAmP 91
**Brown,** Jeffrey Randall 1955- WhoWest 92
**Brown,** Jennavon Lee 1947- WhoRel 92
**Brown,** Jennifer Elizabeth 1973- WhoEnt 92
**Brown,** Jeremy James 1954- WhoIns 92
**Brown,** Jerome Engel 1924- AmMWSc 92
**Brown,** Jerram L 1930- AmMWSc 92
**Brown,** Jerrold Stanley 1953- WhoAmL 92
**Brown,** Jerry Who 92
**Brown,** Jerry 1936- AmMWSc 92
**Brown,** Jerry 1938- WhoWest 92
**Brown,** Jerry Duane 1934- WhoRel 92
**Brown,** Jerry L 1935- AmMWSc 92
**Brown,** Jerry William 1925- AmMWSc 92
**Brown,** Jesse J, Jr 1939- AmMWSc 92
**Brown,** Jewelle Harbin 1921- WhoAmP 91
**Brown,** Jim 1936- ConTFT 9, IntMPA 92, WhoBlA 92, WhoEnt 92
**Brown,** Jim J. 1941- WhoRel 92
**Brown,** Joan Heller 1946- AmMWSc 92
**Brown,** Joan P. WhoBlA 92
**Brown,** Joanne Carlson 1953- WhoRel 92
**Brown,** Joe 1930- Who 92
**Brown,** Joe 1932- WhoAmP 91
**Brown,** Joe B. 1930- WhoAmL 92
**Brown,** Joe Blackburn 1940- WhoAmL 92
**Brown,** Joe Ellis 1933- WhoAmP 91
**Brown,** Joe Ned, Jr 1947- AmMWSc 92
**Brown,** Joeanna Hurston 1939- WhoBlA 92
**Brown,** Joel Edward 1937- AmMWSc 92
**Brown,** Joel Robert 1962- WhoAmL 92
**Brown,** Joel W 1964- WhoAmP 91
**Brown,** John 1735-1788 BlkwCEP
**Brown,** John 1738-1812 DcNCBi 1
**Brown,** John 1772-1845 DcNCBi 1
**Brown,** John 1800-1859 BenetAL 91, RComAH
**Brown,** John 1923- Who 92
**Brown,** John 1931- Who 92
**Brown,** John Andrew 1945- WhoBlA 92
**Brown,** John Angus 1925- AmMWSc 92
**Brown,** John Arnesby 1866-1955 TwCPaSc
**Brown,** John B. Who 92
**Brown,** John Baker, Jr. 1947- WhoBlA 92
**Brown,** John Boyer 1924- AmMWSc 92
**Brown,** John C. 1921- WhoIns 92
**Brown,** John C 1952- WhoAmP 91
**Brown,** John C., Jr. 1939- WhoBlA 92
**Brown,** John Callaway 1928- WhoFI 92
**Brown,** John Canvin 1938- IntWW 91
**Brown,** John Carter 1934- Who 92
**Brown,** John Clifford 1943- AmMWSc 92
**Brown,** John Douglas Keith 1913- Who 92
**Brown,** John Edward Who 92
**Brown,** John Edward 1930- WhoRel 92
**Brown,** John Edward 1939- WhoMW 92
**Brown,** John Evans 1827-1895 DcNCBi 1
**Brown,** John Francis, Jr 1926- AmMWSc 92
**Brown,** John Francis Seccombe d1989 Who 92N
**Brown,** John Fred 1941- WhoFI 92
**Brown,** John Gilbert Newton 1916- IntWW 91, Who 92
**Brown,** John Henry 1924- AmMWSc 92
**Brown,** John J. 1946- WhoMW 92
**Brown,** John Joseph 1931- IntWW 91
**Brown,** John L 1952- WhoAmP 91
**Brown,** John Lawrence, Jr 1925- AmMWSc 92
**Brown,** John Lott 1924- AmMWSc 92
**Brown,** John M AmMWSc 92
**Brown,** John Mason 1900-1969 BenetAL 91
**Brown,** John Michael 1929- Who 92
**Brown,** John Mitchell, Sr. 1929- WhoBlA 92
**Brown,** John Ollis 1922- WhoBlA 92
**Brown,** John Ollis Langfuld, Jr. 1946- WhoWest 92
**Brown,** John Otis, III 1948- WhoMW 92
**Brown,** John Pairman 1923- WhoRel 92
**Brown,** John Robert 1909- WhoAmL 92
**Brown,** John Robert 1935- WhoFI 92
**Brown,** John Robert 1948- WhoRel 92
**Brown,** John Russell 1923- IntAu&W 91, Who 92, WrDr 92
**Brown,** John Scott 1930- WhoBlA 92
**Brown,** John Thomas 1948- WhoAmL 92
**Brown,** John Walter 1918- WhoAmP 91
**Brown,** John Walter 1939- WhoAmP 91
**Brown,** John Wayne 1949- WhoAmL 92
**Brown,** John Wesley 1925- AmMWSc 92
**Brown,** John Wesley 1933- AmMWSc 92

**Brown,** John William 1913- *WhoAmP 91, WhoFI 92*
**Brown,** John Y, Jr 1933- *WhoAmP 91*
**Brown,** John Young 1858 1921 *ScFEYrs*
**Brown,** Johnnie Edward 1962- *WhoAmL 92*
**Brown,** Johnny Mac *WhoBlA 92*
**Brown,** Jonathan 1939- *WrDr 92*
**Brown,** Jonathan 1955- *TwCPaSc*
**Brown,** Joseph 1733-1785 *BiInAmS*
**Brown,** Joseph A. 1926- *WhoAmL 92*
**Brown,** Joseph Bernard 1948- *WhoAmL 92*
**Brown,** Joseph Clifton 1908- *WhoBlA 92*
**Brown,** Joseph Davidson, Sr. 1929- *WhoBlA 92*
**Brown,** Joseph E 1951- *WhoAmP 91*
**Brown,** Joseph Lawler 1921- *Who 92*
**Brown,** Joseph M 1928- *AmMWSc 92*
**Brown,** Joseph Ross 1920- *AmMWSc 92*
**Brown,** Joseph Samuel 1943- *WhoBlA 92*
**Brown,** Joseph Simon, Jr. 1907- *WhoFI 92*
**Brown,** Joseph Theodore 1924- *WhoFI 92*
**Brown,** Joshua Robert Calloway 1915- *AmMWSc 92*
**Brown,** Joyce 1937- *WhoBlA 92*
**Brown,** Joyce Aline 1938- *WhoEnt 92*
**Brown,** Joyce F. 1946- *WhoBlA 92*
**Brown,** Judi 1961- *BlkOlyM*
**Brown,** Judith Adele 1944- *AmMWSc 92*
**Brown,** Judith Ellen 1950- *WhoWest 92*
**Brown,** Judy 1944- *WhoEnt 92*
**Brown,** Judy Lynne 1960- *WhoMW 92*
**Brown,** Julie 1958- *ConTFT 9*
**Brown,** Julie M 1935- *WhoAmP 91*
**Brown,** Julius 1915- *AmMWSc 92*
**Brown,** Julius J. 1907- *WhoBlA 92*
**Brown,** Julius Ray 1940- *WhoBlA 92*
**Brown,** June Gibbs 1933- *WhoAmP 91*
**Brown,** June P. *Who 92*
**Brown,** Jurutha 1950- *WhoBlA 92*
**Brown,** Justine Thomas 1938- *WhoBlA 92*
**Brown,** Karen *WhoEnt 92*
**Brown,** Karen F. 1951- *WhoBlA 92*
**Brown,** Karen Kay 1944- *AmMWSc 92, WhoMW 92*
**Brown,** Karen Mary 1951- *WhoMW 92*
**Brown,** Karl Leslie 1925- *AmMWSc 92*
**Brown,** Kathie 1947- *WhoMW 92*
**Brown,** Kathleen *WhoAmP 91, WhoWest 92*
**Brown,** Kay *WhoAmP 91*
**Brown,** Kay 1903- *ReelWom*
**Brown,** Keith 1933- *WhoEnt 92*
**Brown,** Keith 1947- *TwCPaSc*
**Brown,** Keith Charles 1942- *AmMWSc 92*
**Brown,** Keith H 1939- *AmMWSc 92*
**Brown,** Keith Jeffery 1950- *WhoFI 92*
**Brown,** Keith Lapham 1925- *IntWW 91, WhoAmP 91*
**Brown,** Keith Spalding 1913- *WhoAmP 91*
**Brown,** Kenneth C 1923- *WhoAmP 91*
**Brown,** Kenneth Charles 1952- *WhoFI 92*
**Brown,** Kenneth Edward 1946- *WhoBlA 92*
**Brown,** Kenneth H. *DrAPF 91*
**Brown,** Kenneth H. 1936- *WrDr 92*
**Brown,** Kenneth Henry 1939- *AmMWSc 92*
**Brown,** Kenneth Howard 1936- *WhoEnt 92*
**Brown,** Kenneth Howard 1942- *AmMWSc 92*
**Brown,** Kenneth Lee 1936- *WhoAmP 91*
**Brown,** Kenneth Michael 1948- *AmMWSc 92*
**Brown,** Kenneth Ray 1946- *WhoRel 92*
**Brown,** Kenneth S. 1919- *WhoBlA 92*
**Brown,** Kenneth Stephen 1929- *AmMWSc 92*
**Brown,** Kenneth Stephen 1949- *AmMWSc 92*
**Brown,** Kenneth Taylor 1922- *AmMWSc 92*
**Brown,** Kermit 1939?- *ConTFT 9*
**Brown,** Kermit Earl 1923- *AmMWSc 92*
**Brown,** Keturah *WhoRel 92*
**Brown,** Kevin 1959- *WhoAmP 91*
**Brown,** Kevin Gerald 1961- *WhoRel 92*
**Brown,** Kevin Matthew 1954- *WhoMW 92*
**Brown,** Kevin Michael 1948- *WhoFI 92*
**Brown,** Killock 1856-1934 *TwCPaSc*
**Brown,** Kyle Nelson 1958- *WhoAmL 92*
**Brown,** L C 1937- *AmMWSc 92*
**Brown,** L Carlton 1915- *AmMWSc 92*
**Brown,** L. David *WhoRel 92*
**Brown,** L. Dean 1920- *IntWW 91*
**Brown,** L Ed 1937- *WhoAmP 91*
**Brown,** Lana M *WhoAmP 91*
**Brown,** Lanita *WhoBlA 92*
**Brown,** LaRita Early Dawn Ma-Ka-Re 1937- *WhoFI 92*
**Brown,** Larry 1951- *ConAu 134*
**Brown,** Larry Patrick 1942- *AmMWSc 92*
**Brown,** Larry Robert 1946- *AmMWSc 92*
**Brown,** Larry T. 1947- *WhoBlA 92*
**Brown,** Lauren Evans 1939- *AmMWSc 92*
**Brown,** Laurence Ambrose 1907- *Who 92*
**Brown,** Laurence David 1926- *WhoMW 92, WhoRel 92*
**Brown,** Laurie Lizbeth 1946- *AmMWSc 92*
**Brown,** Laurie Mark 1923- *AmMWSc 92*
**Brown,** Lawrence 1907-1988 *NewAmDM*
**Brown,** Lawrence D 1940- *AmMWSc 92*
**Brown,** Lawrence E 1914- *AmMWSc 92*
**Brown,** Lawrence E. 1947- *WhoBlA 92*
**Brown,** Lawrence G 1943- *AmMWSc 92*
**Brown,** Lawrence Ira 1931- *WhoAmL 92*
**Brown,** Lawrence M., Sr. 1927-1989 *WhoBlA 92N*
**Brown,** Lawrence Michael 1936- *IntWW 91, Who 92*
**Brown,** Lawrence Milton 1927- *AmMWSc 92*
**Brown,** Lawrence Raymond, Jr. 1928- *WhoAmL 92*
**Brown,** Lawrence S, Jr 1949- *AmMWSc 92*
**Brown,** Leander A. 1959- *WhoBlA 92*
**Brown,** Leanna 1935- *WhoAmP 91*
**Brown,** Lee F 1929- *AmMWSc 92*
**Brown,** Lee P 1937- *ConBlB 1 [port]*
**Brown,** Lee Patrick 1937- *WhoBlA 92*
**Brown,** Lee R. 1949- *WhoRel 92*
**Brown,** Lee Roy, Jr 1926- *AmMWSc 92*
**Brown,** Leland 1914- *IntAu&W 91, WrDr 92*
**Brown,** Leland R 1928- *WhoAmP 91*
**Brown,** Leland Ralph 1922- *AmMWSc 92*
**Brown,** Leo d1991 *NewYTBS 91*
**Brown,** Leo C., Jr. 1942- *WhoBlA 92*
**Brown,** Leo Dale 1948- *AmMWSc 92*
**Brown,** Leon Frank 1952- *WhoEnt 92*
**Brown,** Leon Sylvester 1965- *WhoMW 92*
**Brown,** Leonard D 1930- *AmMWSc 92*
**Brown,** Leonard Franklin, Jr 1928- *AmMWSc 92*
**Brown,** LeRoy 1936- *WhoBlA 92*
**Brown,** Leroy Bradford 1929- *WhoBlA 92*
**Brown,** Leroy J. H. 1912- *WhoBlA 92*
**Brown,** LeRoy Ronald 1949- *WhoBlA 92*
**Brown,** Leroy Thomas 1922- *WhoBlA 92*
**Brown,** Les 1926- *WhoWest 92*
**Brown,** Les 1928- *WhoEnt 92*
**Brown,** Leslie 1902- *Who 92*
**Brown,** Leslie F. *Who 92*
**Brown,** Leslie Wilfrid 1912- *Who 92*
**Brown,** Lester J. 1942- *WhoBlA 92*
**Brown,** Lester R 1934- *AmMWSc 92*
**Brown,** Lester Raymond 1912- *WhoEnt 92*
**Brown,** Letitia 1915-1976 *NotBlAW 92*
**Brown,** Lettie June 1927- *WhoAmP 91*
**Brown,** Lewis Clare 1928- *WhoEnt 92*
**Brown,** Lewis Frank 1929- *WhoBlA 92, WhoWest 92*
**Brown,** Lewis Marvin 1950- *AmMWSc 92*
**Brown,** Lewis Nathan 1953- *WhoAmL 92*
**Brown,** Lewis Raymond 1930- *AmMWSc 92*
**Brown,** Lewis W 1921- *WhoAmP 91*
**Brown,** Lillian Eriksen 1921- *WhoWest 92*
**Brown,** Linda A. *DrAPF 91*
**Brown,** Linda Jenkins 1946- *WhoBlA 92*
**Brown,** Linda Rose 1945- *AmMWSc 92*
**Brown,** LindaJean *DrAPF 91*
**Brown,** Lindsay Dietrich 1929- *AmMWSc 92*
**Brown,** Linfield Cutter 1942- *AmMWSc 92*
**Brown,** Lionel Neville 1923- *Who 92*
**Brown,** Llewellyn Don 1945- *WhoBlA 92*
**Brown,** Lloyd 1938- *WhoBlA 92*
**Brown,** Lloyd George 1944- *WhoFI 92*
**Brown,** Lloyd Leonard 1927- *AmMWSc 92*
**Brown,** Lloyd Odom, Sr. 1928- *WhoBlA 92*
**Brown,** Lloyd Robert 1924- *AmMWSc 92, WhoMW 92*
**Brown,** Lois Heffington 1940- *WhoFI 92*
**Brown,** Lois Luaine 1931- *WhoMW 92*
**Brown,** Lomas, Jr. 1963- *WhoBlA 92*
**Brown,** Loretta Ann Port 1945- *AmMWSc 92*
**Brown,** Louis 1929- *AmMWSc 92*
**Brown,** Louis M. 1909- *WhoAmL 92*
**Brown,** Louis Milton 1939- *WhoRel 92*
**Brown,** Louis Sylvester 1930- *WhoBlA 92*
**Brown,** Louise M. 1959- *WhoAmL 92*
**Brown,** Loverne W. *DrAPF 91*
**Brown,** Lowell Henry 1929- *WhoRel 92*
**Brown,** Lowell Kent 1939- *WhoFI 92*
**Brown,** Lowell Severt 1934- *AmMWSc 92*
**Brown,** Luther Park 1951- *AmMWSc 92*
**Brown,** Lyn Stephen 1952- *WhoRel 92*
**Brown,** Lynette Joy 1954- *WhoRel 92*
**Brown,** Lynette Ralya 1926- *WhoMW 92*
**Brown,** Lynn Ranney 1928- *AmMWSc 92*
**Brown,** Lynn William 1950- *WhoAmL 92*
**Brown,** Lynne Brendel 1956- *WhoMW 92*
**Brown,** M. Editha *WhoRel 92*
**Brown,** Mabel Estle 1907- *WhoMW 92*
**Brown,** Malcolm *Who 92*
**Brown,** Malcolm Hamrick 1929- *WhoEnt 92*
**Brown,** Malcolm McCleod 1931- *WhoBlA 92*
**Brown,** Marc 1946- *ConAu 36NR, WrDr 92*
**Brown,** Marcia 1918- *WrDr 92*
**Brown,** Marcus Leland 1951- *WhoRel 92*
**Brown,** Margaret Ann 1954- *WhoMW 92*
**Brown,** Margaret Au 1956- *WhoFI 92*
**Brown,** Margaret deBeers 1943- *WhoAmL 92, WhoFI 92*
**Brown,** Margaret Helen 1934- *WhoRel 92*
**Brown,** Margaret Ruth Anderson 1944- *WhoAmP 91*
**Brown,** Margaret Wise 1910-1952 *BenetAL 91*
**Brown,** Margery Wheeler *WhoBlA 92*
**Brown,** Margrethe B. J. *WhoRel 92*
**Brown,** Marie Jenkins 1909- *AmMWSc 92*
**Brown,** Marion Patricia 1927- *Who 92*
**Brown,** Mark 1925- *AmMWSc 92*
**Brown,** Mark H 1900- *IntAu&W 91*
**Brown,** Mark Ransom 1959- *WhoFI 92, WhoWest 92*
**Brown,** Mark S 1951- *WhoAmP 91*
**Brown,** Mark Steven 1955- *WhoWest 92*
**Brown,** Mark Thomas 1956- *WhoWest 92*
**Brown,** Mark Wendell 1953- *AmMWSc 92*
**Brown,** Marsha J. 1949- *WhoBlA 92*
**Brown,** Marshall Carson 1918- *WhoBlA 92*
**Brown,** Martha Hursey *WhoBlA 92*
**Brown,** Martha Taylor 1922- *WhoAmP 91*
**Brown,** Martin M 1916- *WhoIns 92*
**Brown,** Marva Y. 1936- *WhoBlA 92*
**Brown,** Marvin Lee 1933- *WhoRel 92*
**Brown,** Marvin Ross 1947- *AmMWSc 92*
**Brown,** Mary 1847-1935 *BiDBrF 2*
**Brown,** Mary Boykin 1942- *WhoBlA 92*
**Brown,** Mary C 1935- *WhoAmP 91*
**Brown,** Mary Carolyn 1934- *WhoAmP 91*
**Brown,** Mary Elizabeth 1932- *WhoBlA 92*
**Brown,** Mary Katherine 1948- *WhoBlA 92*
**Brown,** Mary Lee 1923- *WhoBlA 92*
**Brown,** Mary Ward 1917- *ConAu 133*
**Brown,** Mattie R. 1901- *WhoBlA 92*
**Brown,** Maurice Vertner 1908- *AmMWSc 92*
**Brown,** Max *Who 92*
**Brown,** Max Louis 1936- *AmMWSc 92*
**Brown,** Maxine J. Childress 1943- *WhoBlA 92*
**Brown,** Melissa Kern 1959- *WhoAmL 92*
**Brown,** Melissa Rose 1957- *WhoFI 92*
**Brown,** Melvin Edward *DrAPF 91*
**Brown,** Melvin F. 1935- *WhoFI 92, WhoMW 92*
**Brown,** Melvin Floyd 1943- *WhoRel 92*
**Brown,** Melvin Henry 1919- *AmMWSc 92*
**Brown,** Melvin R 1938- *WhoAmP 91*
**Brown,** Meredith M. 1940- *WhoAmL 92*
**Brown,** Merle *WhoAmP 91*
**Brown,** Merlyn Louis 1954- *WhoAmP 91*
**Brown,** Merton F 1935- *AmMWSc 92*
**Brown,** Mervyn 1923- *IntWW 91, Who 92*
**Brown,** Meyer 1910- *AmMWSc 92*
**Brown,** Michael *DcNCBi 1, Who 92*
**Brown,** Michael 1931- *Who 92*
**Brown,** Michael 1939- *AmMWSc 92*
**Brown,** Michael 1947- *AmMWSc 92*
**Brown,** Michael Angel *WhoHisp 92*
**Brown,** Michael Bruce 1949- *WhoRel 92*
**Brown,** Michael David 1948- *WhoFI 92*
**Brown,** Michael David 1951- *WhoMW 92*
**Brown,** Michael David 1958- *WhoFI 92*
**Brown,** Michael DeWayne 1954- *WhoAmL 92, WhoBlA 92*
**Brown,** Michael Douglas 1948- *WrDr 92*
**Brown,** Michael Eugene 1952- *WhoAmL 92*
**Brown,** Michael Hoover 1957- *WhoFI 92*
**Brown,** Michael John Douglas 1936- *Who 92*
**Brown,** Michael L. 1958- *WhoMW 92*
**Brown,** Michael Rene Warneford 1915- *Who 92*
**Brown,** Michael Richard 1959- *WhoMW 92, WhoRel 92*
**Brown,** Michael Russell 1951- *Who 92*
**Brown,** Michael S 1941- *AmMWSc 92*
**Brown,** Michael Steven 1950- *WhoFI 92*
**Brown,** Michael Stuart 1941- *IntWW 91, Who 92, WhoNob 90*
**Brown,** Michael Wayne 1955- *WhoEnt 92*
**Brown,** Milbert Orlando 1956- *WhoBlA 92*
**Brown,** Milton 1903-1936 *NewAmDM*
**Brown,** Milton F. 1943- *WhoBlA 92*
**Brown,** Morgan Cornelius 1916- *WhoBlA 92*
**Brown,** Morris 1951- *WhoMW 92*
**Brown,** Morris Jonathan 1951- *Who 92*
**Brown,** Morse L. 1943- *WhoBlA 92*
**Brown,** Mortimer 1874-1966 *TwCPaSc*
**Brown,** Mortimer 1924- *WhoBlA 92*
**Brown,** Morton 1931- *AmMWSc 92*
**Brown,** Moses 1738-1836 *AmPeW*
**Brown,** Murray 1929- *WrDr 92*
**Brown,** Murray Allison 1927- *AmMWSc 92*
**Brown,** Myrtle Laurestine 1926- *AmMWSc 92*
**Brown,** Nacio Herb 1896-1964 *NewAmDM*
**Brown,** Nancy Cofield 1932- *WhoBlA 92*
**Brown,** Nancy Diane 1961- *WhoWest 92*
**Brown,** Nancy J 1943- *AmMWSc 92*
**Brown,** Nancy Joyce 1942- *WhoAmP 91*
**Brown,** Nancy Newman 1951- *WhoAmL 92*
**Brown,** Neal B 1938- *AmMWSc 92*
**Brown,** Neal Curtis 1939- *AmMWSc 92*
**Brown,** Neil Dallas 1938- *TwCPaSc*
**Brown,** Neil Harry 1940- *AmMWSc 92*
**Brown,** Neil W. 1938- *WhoRel 92*
**Brown,** Nicholas Hugh 1950- *Who 92*
**Brown,** Nigel Andrew 1953- *AmMWSc 92*
**Brown,** Noah, Jr. 1925- *WhoBlA 92*
**Brown,** Norman 1921- *AmMWSc 92*
**Brown,** Norman 1942- *TwCPaSc*
**Brown,** Norman E. 1935- *WhoBlA 92*
**Brown,** Norman James 1942- *WhoFI 92*
**Brown,** Norman L *WhoIns 92*
**Brown,** Norman Louis 1923- *AmMWSc 92*
**Brown,** Norman Wesley 1931- *WhoFI 92*
**Brown,** Ogden, Jr. 1927- *WhoWest 92*
**Brown,** Ola M. 1941- *WhoBlA 92*
**Brown,** Olen Ray 1935- *AmMWSc 92*
**Brown,** Oliver Leonard Inman 1911- *AmMWSc 92*
**Brown,** Oliver Monroe 1944- *AmMWSc 92*
**Brown,** Olivia *WhoBlA 92*
**Brown,** Olympia 1835-1926 *HanAmWH, RelLAm 91*
**Brown,** Oral Lee 1945- *WhoBlA 92*
**Brown,** Oren Lathrop *WhoEnt 92*
**Brown,** Otha N., Jr. 1931- *WhoBlA 92*
**Brown,** Otha Nathaniel, Jr 1931- *WhoAmP 91*
**Brown,** Otto G 1925- *AmMWSc 92*
**Brown,** Owsley, II 1942- *WhoEnt 92, WhoFI 92*
**Brown,** Palmer 1919- *WrDr 92*
**Brown,** Pamela 1924- *IntAu&W 91*
**Brown,** Pat Crawford 1929- *WhoEnt 92*
**Brown,** Patricia *Who 92*
**Brown,** Patricia B 1939- *WhoAmP 91*
**Brown,** Patricia Irene *WhoAmL 92*
**Brown,** Patricia Leonard 1950- *WhoAmL 92*
**Brown,** Patricia Lynn 1928- *AmMWSc 92*
**Brown,** Patricia Stocking 1942- *AmMWSc 92*
**Brown,** Patrick *Who 92*
**Brown,** Patrick Michael 1938- *AmMWSc 92*
**Brown,** Paul d1991 *NewYTBS 91 [port]*
**Brown,** Paul 1908-1991 *News 92-1*
**Brown,** Paul, Jr. 1926- *WhoBlA 92*
**Brown,** Paul Alan 1963- *WhoEnt 92*
**Brown,** Paul B 1942- *AmMWSc 92*
**Brown,** Paul D. 1901- *WhoBlA 92*
**Brown,** Paul David 1953- *WhoAmL 92*
**Brown,** Paul E. *WhoMW 92*
**Brown,** Paul E. X. 1910- *WhoBlA 92*
**Brown,** Paul Edmondson 1915- *WhoAmL 92, WhoMW 92*
**Brown,** Paul Edmund 1916- *AmMWSc 92*
**Brown,** Paul Fremont 1921- *WhoWest 92*
**Brown,** Paul Joseph 1924- *AmMWSc 92*
**Brown,** Paul L. 1919- *WhoBlA 92*
**Brown,** Paul Lawson 1918- *AmMWSc 92*
**Brown,** Paul Lopez 1919- *AmMWSc 92*
**Brown,** Paul Neeley 1926- *WhoAmL 92*
**Brown,** Paul Neil 1942- *WhoAmP 91*
**Brown,** Paul R. 1954- *WhoRel 92*
**Brown,** Paul Sherman 1921- *WhoAmL 92*
**Brown,** Paul Truett 1954- *WhoAmL 92*
**Brown,** Paul Wayne 1935- *AmMWSc 92*
**Brown,** Paul Wayne 1944- *WhoMW 92*
**Brown,** Paul Wheeler 1936- *AmMWSc 92*
**Brown,** Paul William 1948- *WhoRel 92*
**Brown,** Paul Woodrow 1919- *AmMWSc 92*
**Brown,** Perry Clendenin 1955- *WhoRel 92*
**Brown,** Peter *Who 92*
**Brown,** Peter 1935- *WrDr 92*
**Brown,** Peter 1938- *AmMWSc 92*
**Brown,** Peter Douglas 1925- *WrDr 92*
**Brown,** Peter Edward 1960- *WhoAmL 92*
**Brown,** Peter Harrison 1943- *WhoWest 92*
**Brown,** Peter L. 1935- *WhoEnt 92*
**Brown,** Peter Manson 1933- *WhoEnt 92, WhoWest 92*
**Brown,** Peter Marshall 1859-1913 *DcNCBi 1*
**Brown,** Peter Megargee 1922- *WhoAmL 92*
**Brown,** Peter Robert Lamont 1935- *Who 92*
**Brown,** Peter Wilfred Henry 1941- *Who 92*
**Brown,** Philip 1958- *TwCPaSc*
**Brown,** Philip 1962- *BlkOlyM*
**Brown,** Philip Anthony Russell 1924- *Who 92*
**Brown,** Philip Edward 1952- *AmMWSc 92*
**Brown,** Philip Rayfield, III 1917- *WhoBlA 92*
**Brown,** Phillip Edward 1927- *WhoAmL 92*
**Brown,** Phillip Stephen 1936- *WhoMW 92*
**Brown,** Phyllis R 1924- *AmMWSc 92*
**Brown,** Polly Sarah 1952- *WhoWest 92*
**Brown,** Preston Condrey 1926- *WhoRel 92*
**Brown,** R A S 1934- *AmMWSc 92*
**Brown,** R. H. 1940- *WrDr 92*
**Brown,** R. Jess, Sr. 1912-1989 *WhoBlA 92N*
**Brown,** Ralph 1928- *TwCPaSc, Who 92*
**Brown,** Ralph 1931- *Who 92*
**Brown,** Ralph H. 1919- *WhoBlA 92*
**Brown,** Ralph James 1944- *WhoFI 92*

**Brown,** Ralph Kilner 1909- *Who 92*
**Brown,** Ralph R 1944- *WhoAmP 91*
**Brown,** Randall Emory 1917- *AmMWSc 92, WhoWest 92*
**Brown,** Ray 1926- *NewAmDM*
**Brown,** Ray, Mrs. *Who 92*
**Brown,** Ray Kent 1924- *AmMWSc 92*
**Brown,** Raymond *Who 92*
**Brown,** Raymond 1928- *Who 92*
**Brown,** Raymond Bryan 1923-1977 *ConAu 133*
**Brown,** Raymond Edward 1928- *WhoRel 92*
**Brown,** Raymond Frederick d1991 *Who 92N*
**Brown,** Raymond George 1924- *WrDr 92*
**Brown,** Raymond Madison 1949- *WhoBlA 92*
**Brown,** Raymond Russell 1926- *AmMWSc 92*
**Brown,** Rayner 1912- *WhoEnt 92*
**Brown,** Rebecca *DrAPF 91, IntAu&W 91*
**Brown,** Rebecca Ruth 1963- *WhoEnt 92*
**Brown,** Reginald DeWayne 1952- *WhoWest 92*
**Brown,** Reginald Royce, Sr. 1946- *WhoBlA 92*
**Brown,** Rex Bennett 1935- *WhoMW 92*
**Brown,** Rhoderick Edmiston, Jr 1953- *AmMWSc 92*
**Brown,** Richard 1924- *WhoRel 92*
**Brown,** Richard 1927- *WhoBlA 92*
**Brown,** Richard Alger 1905- *WhoBlA 92*
**Brown,** Richard Arthur *WhoAmP 91*
**Brown,** Richard Blaine 1951- *WhoMW 92*
**Brown,** Richard C. *WhoRel 92*
**Brown,** Richard Dean 1941- *AmMWSc 92*
**Brown,** Richard Don 1940- *AmMWSc 92*
**Brown,** Richard Earl 1922- *WhoBlA 92*
**Brown,** Richard Elmo 1937- *WhoMW 92*
**Brown,** Richard Emery 1929- *AmMWSc 92*
**Brown,** Richard Eric 1951- *WhoAmL 92*
**Brown,** Richard George Bolney 1935- *AmMWSc 92*
**Brown,** Richard Harland 1921- *AmMWSc 92*
**Brown,** Richard Harris 1947- *WhoFI 92, WhoMW 92*
**Brown,** Richard Julian Challis 1936- *AmMWSc 92*
**Brown,** Richard K 1917- *AmMWSc 92*
**Brown,** Richard Kettel 1928- *AmMWSc 92*
**Brown,** Richard Kevin 1956- *WhoAmL 92*
**Brown,** Richard L 1938- *WhoIns 92*
**Brown,** Richard L 1964- *AmMWSc 92*
**Brown,** Richard Laurence 1962- *WhoEnt 92, WhoFI 92*
**Brown,** Richard Lawrence 1932- *WhoAmL 92, WhoMW 92*
**Brown,** Richard Leland 1912- *AmMWSc 92*
**Brown,** Richard M. 1940- *WhoBlA 92*
**Brown,** Richard M. 1942- *WhoWest 92*
**Brown,** Richard Malcolm, Jr 1939- *AmMWSc 92*
**Brown,** Richard Martin 1937- *AmMWSc 92*
**Brown,** Richard Maurice 1924- *AmMWSc 92*
**Brown,** Richard McPike 1926- *AmMWSc 92*
**Brown,** Richard Osborne 1930- *WhoBlA 92*
**Brown,** Richard Searl 1946- *WhoAmL 92*
**Brown,** Rita Mae *DrAPF 91*
**Brown,** Rita Mae 1944- *BenetAL 91, ConAu 35NR, ConNov 91, HanAmWH, IntAu&W 91, WrDr 92*
**Brown,** Robert 1908- *IntWW 91, Who 92*
**Brown,** Robert 1931- *WhoFI 92*
**Brown,** Robert 1941- *AmMWSc 92*
**Brown,** Robert 1943- *Who 92*
**Brown,** Robert 1949- *WhoAmL 92*
**Brown,** Robert, Jr. 1936- *WhoBlA 92*
**Brown,** Robert A 1951- *AmMWSc 92*
**Brown,** Robert Alan 1927- *AmMWSc 92*
**Brown,** Robert Alan 1934- *AmMWSc 92*
**Brown,** Robert Alan 1943- *AmMWSc 92*
**Brown,** Robert B 1955- *WhoAmP 91*
**Brown,** Robert Bruce 1938- *AmMWSc 92*
**Brown,** Robert Burnett 1942- *Who 92*
**Brown,** Robert C. *Who 92*
**Brown,** Robert Calfee 1951- *WhoAmL 92*
**Brown,** Robert Calvin 1933- *AmMWSc 92*
**Brown,** Robert Cecil 1928- *WhoAmL 92*
**Brown,** Robert Cephas, Sr. 1925- *WhoBlA 92*
**Brown,** Robert Charles 1954- *WhoAmL 92*
**Brown,** Robert Crofton 1921- *Who 92*
**Brown,** Robert Dale 1917- *WhoAmP 91*
**Brown,** Robert Dale 1945- *AmMWSc 92*
**Brown,** Robert Dillon 1933- *AmMWSc 92*
**Brown,** Robert Don 1942- *AmMWSc 92*
**Brown,** Robert Durry 1965- *WhoFI 92*
**Brown,** Robert Edward *DrAPF 91*
**Brown,** Robert Epps 1956- *WhoRel 92*
**Brown,** Robert Eugene 1925- *AmMWSc 92*
**Brown,** Robert Freeman 1935- *AmMWSc 92, WhoWest 92*
**Brown,** Robert G. 1923- *WrDr 92*
**Brown,** Robert George 1937- *AmMWSc 92*
**Brown,** Robert Getman 1917- *AmMWSc 92*
**Brown,** Robert Glencairn 1930- *Who 92*
**Brown,** Robert Glenn 1938- *AmMWSc 92*
**Brown,** Robert Goodell 1923- *AmMWSc 92*
**Brown,** Robert Hanbury 1916- *FacFETw, IntWW 91, Who 92*
**Brown,** Robert Harrison 1938- *AmMWSc 92*
**Brown,** Robert Henry 1915- *WhoWest 92*
**Brown,** Robert Henry 1926- *WhoAmP 91*
**Brown,** Robert J., III 1919- *WhoBlA 92*
**Brown,** Robert James 1935- *WhoIns 92*
**Brown,** Robert James Sidford 1924- *AmMWSc 92*
**Brown,** Robert Joe 1935- *WhoBlA 92*
**Brown,** Robert John 1935- *WhoAmP 91*
**Brown,** Robert Joseph 1929- *WhoAmP 91*
**Brown,** Robert Joseph 1947- *WhoAmP 91*
**Brown,** Robert L *WhoAmP 91*
**Brown,** Robert L. 1921- *WrDr 92*
**Brown,** Robert Laurence 1953- *WhoFI 92*
**Brown,** Robert Lee 1908- *AmMWSc 92*
**Brown,** Robert Lee 1932- *AmMWSc 92*
**Brown,** Robert Lee 1936- *AmMWSc 92*
**Brown,** Robert Lee 1947- *WhoBlA 92*
**Brown,** Robert Lee 1960- *WhoBlA 92*
**Brown,** Robert Lewis 1956- *WhoFI 92*
**Brown,** Robert Lindsay 1959- *WhoRel 92*
**Brown,** Robert McAfee 1920- *IntWW 91, WhoRel 92, WrDr 92*
**Brown,** Robert Melbourne 1924- *AmMWSc 92*
**Brown,** Robert Michael 1929- *WhoAmL 92*
**Brown,** Robert Ordway 1917- *AmMWSc 92*
**Brown,** Robert Raymond 1922- *AmMWSc 92*
**Brown,** Robert Raymond 1936- *Who 92*
**Brown,** Robert Reginald 1923- *AmMWSc 92*
**Brown,** Robert Ross Buchanan 1909- *Who 92*
**Brown,** Robert Saville 1914- *Who 92*
**Brown,** Robert Stanley 1946- *AmMWSc 92*
**Brown,** Robert Stephen 1938- *AmMWSc 92*
**Brown,** Robert Theodore 1931- *AmMWSc 92*
**Brown,** Robert Thorson 1923- *AmMWSc 92*
**Brown,** Robert Wade 1933- *AmMWSc 92*
**Brown,** Robert Walker, Jr. 1960- *WhoAmL 92*
**Brown,** Robert Wayne 1923- *AmMWSc 92*
**Brown,** Robert Wayne 1942- *WhoAmL 92*
**Brown,** Robert William 1941- *AmMWSc 92*
**Brown,** Robert Zanes 1926- *AmMWSc 92*
**Brown,** Robin R. *WhoBlA 92*
**Brown,** Roderick 1952- *WhoBlA 92*
**Brown,** Rodger Alan 1937- *AmMWSc 92*
**Brown,** Rodger L., Jr. 1955- *WhoBlA 92*
**Brown,** Rodney Duvall, III 1931- *AmMWSc 92*
**Brown,** Rodney Jay 1948- *WhoWest 92*
**Brown,** Rodney Morgan 1949- *WhoEnt 92*
**Brown,** Rodney W. *WhoBlA 92*
**Brown,** Roger Alan 1948- *WhoAmL 92*
**Brown,** Roger E 1920- *AmMWSc 92*
**Brown,** Roger William 1925- *IntWW 91, WrDr 92*
**Brown,** Roger William 1940- *WhoMW 92*
**Brown,** Roland George MacCormack 1924- *Who 92*
**Brown,** Roland O. 1929- *WhoBlA 92*
**Brown,** Ron 1961- *BlkOlyM, WhoBlA 92*
**Brown,** Ronald *Who 92*
**Brown,** Ronald 1900- *WhoFI 92*
**Brown,** Ronald 1930- *WhoFI 92*
**Brown,** Ronald 1940- *Who 92*
**Brown,** Ronald Alan 1936- *AmMWSc 92*
**Brown,** Ronald Drayton 1927- *IntWW 91*
**Brown,** Ronald Edward 1952- *WhoBlA 92*
**Brown,** Ronald Franklin 1940- *AmMWSc 92*
**Brown,** Ronald Gerald 1949- *WhoMW 92*
**Brown,** Ronald H. 1941- *IntWW 91, WhoAmP 91, WhoBlA 92*
**Brown,** Ronald Harmon 1941- *WhoAmL 92*
**Brown,** Ronald Harold 1935- *AmMWSc 92*
**Brown,** Ronald Malcolm 1938- *WhoWest 92*
**Brown,** Ronald Osborne 1941- *WhoFI 92*
**Brown,** Ronald Paul 1938- *WhoBlA 92*
**Brown,** Ronald Travis 1955- *WhoRel 92*
**Brown,** Ronald William 1917- *Who 92*
**Brown,** Ronald William 1921- *Who 92*
**Brown,** Roosevelt H., Jr. 1932- *WhoBlA 92*
**Brown,** Roscoe C., Jr. 1922- *WhoBlA 92*
**Brown,** Rosel George 1926- *TwCSFW 91*
**Brown,** Rosellen *DrAPF 91*
**Brown,** Rosellen 1939- *WrDr 92*
**Brown,** Ross Duncan, Jr 1935- *AmMWSc 92*
**Brown,** Rowine Hayes 1913- *WhoAmL 92*
**Brown,** Roy 1948- *TwCPaSc*
**Brown,** Roy Dudley 1916- *Who 92*
**Brown,** Roy Hershel 1924- *WhoBlA 92*
**Brown,** Roy Melton 1878-1962 *DcNCBi 1*
**Brown,** Roy S. F. *Who 92*
**Brown,** Ruby Edmonia 1943- *WhoBlA 92*
**Brown,** Rubye Golsby 1923- *WhoAmP 91, WhoBlA 92*
**Brown,** Russell *Who 92*
**Brown,** Russell Ellsworth 1943- *WhoFI 92*
**Brown,** Russell G 1958- *WhoAmP 91*
**Brown,** Russell M 1929- *WhoAmP 91*
**Brown,** Russell Vedder 1925- *AmMWSc 92*
**Brown,** Sally 1923- *WhoRel 92*
**Brown,** Samuel 1769-1830 *BiInAmS*
**Brown,** Samuel Allen 1951- *WhoAmP 91*
**Brown,** Samuel Franklin, Jr. 1921- *WhoBlA 92*
**Brown,** Samuel Heffner 1933- *AmMWSc 92*
**Brown,** Samuel Joseph, Jr. 1941- *WhoFI 92*
**Brown,** Sandra 1944- *AmMWSc 92*
**Brown,** Sandra 1948- *WrDr 92*
**Brown,** Sandra Jean 1936- *WhoFI 92*
**Brown,** Sandra Marie 1958- *WhoEnt 92, WhoFI 92*
**Brown,** Sanford Donald 1952- *WhoAmL 92*
**Brown,** Sanford Webster 1957- *WhoRel 92*
**Brown,** Sara Lou 1942- *WhoFI 92*
**Brown,** Sarah E. 1936- *WhoAmL 92*
**Brown,** Sarah Elizabeth 1943- *Who 92*
**Brown,** Sarah S 1932- *WhoAmP 91*
**Brown,** Scott McLean 1945- *WhoAmL 92*
**Brown,** Seth Nikolai 1959- *WhoEnt 92*
**Brown,** Seward Ralph 1920- *AmMWSc 92*
**Brown,** Sharon Gail 1941- *WhoFI 92, WhoMW 92*
**Brown,** Sharon Hancock 1958- *WhoWest 92*
**Brown,** Sharon Hendrickson 1944- *WhoEnt 92*
**Brown,** Sharon Lu 1954- *WhoEnt 92*
**Brown,** Sharon Marjorie Revels 1938- *WhoBlA 92*
**Brown,** Sheldon 1915- *AmMWSc 92*
**Brown,** Sherman Daniel 1929- *AmMWSc 92*
**Brown,** Sherman L. 1943- *WhoBlA 92*
**Brown,** Sherrod Campbell 1952- *WhoAmP 91*
**Brown,** Shirley Ann Vining *WhoBlA 92*
**Brown,** Shirley Anne 1955- *WhoWest 92*
**Brown,** Sidonie Dossin 1947- *WhoMW 92*
**Brown,** Simon Denis 1937- *Who 92*
**Brown,** Simon F. 1952- *WhoBlA 92*
**Brown,** Stacye Monique 1966- *WhoFI 92*
**Brown,** Stanley *Who 92*
**Brown,** Stanley Alfred 1943- *AmMWSc 92*
**Brown,** Stanley Donovan 1933- *WhoBlA 92*
**Brown,** Stanley Gordon 1939- *AmMWSc 92*
**Brown,** Stanley Kingsford 1938- *WhoWest 92*
**Brown,** Stanley Monty 1943- *AmMWSc 92*
**Brown,** Stephanie Diane 1944- *WhoWest 92*
**Brown,** Stephen *Who 92*
**Brown,** Stephen 1924- *Who 92*
**Brown,** Stephen Clawson 1941- *AmMWSc 92*
**Brown,** Stephen David Reid 1945- *Who 92*
**Brown,** Stephen Francis 1933- *WhoRel 92*
**Brown,** Stephen H. 1927- *WhoBlA 92*
**Brown,** Stephen Jeffery 1944- *WhoFI 92*
**Brown,** Stephen Joseph 1957- *WhoEnt 92*
**Brown,** Stephen L 1937- *AmMWSc 92*
**Brown,** Stephen Landesman 1938- *WhoFI 92*
**Brown,** Stephen Phillip 1941- *WhoAmL 92*
**Brown,** Stephen Robert 1939- *WhoFI 92*
**Brown,** Stephen Smiley 1952- *WhoAmL 92*
**Brown,** Sterling 1901-1989 *AfrAmW, BlkLC [port]*
**Brown,** Sterling A. 1901-1989 *BenetAL 91*
**Brown,** Sterling Allen 1901-1989 *FacFETw*
**Brown,** Steve 1960- *WhoBlA 92*
**Brown,** Steven Brien 1952- *WhoWest 92*
**Brown,** Steven Ford *DrAPF 91*
**Brown,** Steven Jeffrey 1955- *WhoFI 92*
**Brown,** Steven Kent 1949- *WhoRel 92*
**Brown,** Steven Lee 1955- *WhoRel 92*
**Brown,** Steven M. 1950- *WhoRel 92*
**Brown,** Steven Michael 1944- *AmMWSc 92, WhoMW 92*
**Brown,** Steven Odell 1951- *WhoFI 92*
**Brown,** Steven Spencer 1948- *WhoAmL 92*
**Brown,** Steven Wesley 1955- *WhoMW 92*
**Brown,** Steven William 1954- *WhoAmL 92*
**Brown,** Stewart 1951- *ConAu 135*
**Brown,** Stewart Anglin 1925- *AmMWSc 92*
**Brown,** Stewart Cliff 1928- *AmMWSc 92*
**Brown,** Stuart Christopher 1950- *Who 92*
**Brown,** Stuart Gerry 1912-1991 *ConAu 135*
**Brown,** Stuart Houston 1941- *AmMWSc 92*
**Brown,** Stuart Irwin 1933- *AmMWSc 92*
**Brown,** Sue 1945- *TwCPaSc*
**Brown,** T. Alan 1939- *WhoAmL 92*
**Brown,** Talmage Thurman, Jr 1939- *AmMWSc 92*
**Brown,** Terence 1944- *IntAu&W 91, WrDr 92*
**Brown,** Teresa E 1953- *WhoAmP 91*
**Brown,** Terrence Neal 1954- *WhoRel 92*
**Brown,** Terry Wayne 1950- *WhoAmP 91*
**Brown,** Theodore Cecil 1907- *AmMWSc 92*
**Brown,** Theodore D 1944- *AmMWSc 92*
**Brown,** Theodore E, Jr 1960- *WhoAmP 91*
**Brown,** Theodore Gates, Jr 1920- *AmMWSc 92*
**Brown,** Theodore Lawrence 1928- *AmMWSc 92, WhoMW 92*
**Brown,** Theodore M 1925- *IntAu&W 91, WrDr 92*
**Brown,** Theophile Waldorf 1925- *WhoBlA 92*
**Brown,** Theresa Elizabeth 1959- *WhoMW 92*
**Brown,** Thomas 1744-1811 *DcNCBi 1*
**Brown,** Thomas 1915- *Who 92*
**Brown,** Thomas 1949- *WhoFI 92, WhoMW 92*
**Brown,** Thomas Allan 1942- *WhoIns 92*
**Brown,** Thomas Allen *AmMWSc 92*
**Brown,** Thomas C., Jr. 1945- *WhoAmL 92*
**Brown,** Thomas Charles 1948- *WhoFI 92*
**Brown,** Thomas Edison, Jr. 1952- *WhoBlA 92*
**Brown,** Thomas Edward 1925- *AmMWSc 92*
**Brown,** Thomas Elzie, Jr 1929- *WhoAmP 91*
**Brown,** Thomas Harold 1930- *WhoWest 92*
**Brown,** Thomas Orvin 1932- *WhoMW 92*
**Brown,** Thomas Philip, III 1931- *WhoAmL 92*
**Brown,** Thomas Walter Falconer 1901- *Who 92*
**Brown,** Tilmon F. 1945- *WhoBlA 92*
**Brown,** Timothy Donell 1966- *WhoBlA 92*
**Brown,** Timothy L 1940- *WhoIns 92*
**Brown,** Tina 1953- *IntWW 91, News 92-1 [port], Who 92, WhoFI 92*
**Brown,** Tod David 1936- *WhoRel 92, WhoWest 92*
**Brown,** Todd Hamilton 1960- *WhoWest 92*
**Brown,** Tom 1663-1704 *RfGEnL 91*
**Brown,** Tom, Jr 1950- *IntAu&W 91*
**Brown,** Tom C 1933- *WhoAmP 91*
**Brown,** Tommie Florence 1934- *WhoBlA 92*
**Brown,** Tony 1933- *WhoBlA 92*
**Brown,** Tony 1957- *WhoEnt 92*
**Brown,** Tony 1960- *WhoBlA 92*
**Brown,** Tony Ersic 1946- *WhoEnt 92*
**Brown,** Tony Ray 1939- *AmMWSc 92*
**Brown,** Totlee D. *WhoBlA 92*
**Brown,** Truman Roscoe 1918- *AmMWSc 92*
**Brown,** Tyrone *LesBEnT 92*
**Brown,** Tyrone W. 1940- *WhoBlA 92*
**Brown,** Verne R 1935- *AmMWSc 92*
**Brown,** Vernon E. 1943- *WhoBlA 92*
**Brown,** Victor Lee 1914- *WhoRel 92*
**Brown,** Vinson 1912- *WrDr 92*
**Brown,** Virdin C 1941- *WhoAmP 91*
**Brown,** Virgil E., Jr. *WhoBlA 92*
**Brown,** Virgil Jackson 1944- *WhoRel 92*
**Brown,** Virginia Mae d1991 *NewYTBS 91*
**Brown,** Virginia Mae 1923-1991 *CurBio 91N*
**Brown,** Virginia Ruth *AmMWSc 92*
**Brown,** Vivian *Who 92*
**Brown,** W Virgil 1938- *AmMWSc 92*
**Brown,** Wade H. 1940- *WhoWest 92*
**Brown,** Walter Creighton 1913- *AmMWSc 92*
**Brown,** Walter E. 1931- *WhoBlA 92*
**Brown,** Walter Eric 1918- *AmMWSc 92*
**Brown,** Walter Franklin 1952- *WhoWest 92*
**Brown,** Walter Frederick 1926- *WhoAmP 91, WhoWest 92*
**Brown,** Walter John 1928- *AmMWSc 92*
**Brown,** Walter Lyons 1924- *AmMWSc 92*
**Brown,** Walter Redvers John 1925- *AmMWSc 92*
**Brown,** Walter V 1915- *WhoAmP 91*
**Brown,** Wanda Lois 1922- *AmMWSc 92*
**Brown,** Wanda Marie 1945- *WhoWest 92*
**Brown,** Warren Aloysius 1948- *WhoBlA 92*
**Brown,** Warren Henry, Jr. 1905- *WhoBlA 92*
**Brown,** Warren Shelburne, Jr 1944- *AmMWSc 92, WhoWest 92*

**Brown,** Webster Clay 1923-1989 *WhoBlA 92N*
**Brown,** Weir Messick 1914- *WhoFI 92*
**Brown,** Weldon Grant 1908- *AmMWSc 92*
**Brown,** Wendell Blane 1945- *WhoAmP 91*
**Brown,** Wendell Howard 1947- *WhoFI 92*
**Brown,** Wendell Stimpson 1943- *AmMWSc 92*
**Brown,** Wesley *DrAPF 91*
**Brown,** Wesley Anthony 1927- *WhoBlA 92*
**Brown,** Wesley Dean 1945- *WhoMW 92*
**Brown,** Wesley Ernest 1907- *WhoAmL 92, WhoMW 92*
**Brown,** Wilbur K 1932- *AmMWSc 92*
**Brown,** Will C. 1905- *TwCWW 91*
**Brown,** Willard A., Jr. 1931- *WhoFI 92, WhoMW 92*
**Brown,** Willard Andrew 1921- *AmMWSc 92*
**Brown,** Willard L. 1911- *WhoBlA 92*
**Brown,** Willet Henry *IntMPA 92*
**Brown,** Willet Henry 1905- *WhoEnt 92*
**Brown,** William 1929- *IntMPA 92, Who 92*
**Brown,** William, Jr. 1935- *WhoBlA 92*
**Brown,** William A 1930- *WhoAmP 91*
**Brown,** William A. 1957- *WhoAmL 92*
**Brown,** William Adams 1865-1943 *RelLAm 91*
**Brown,** William Albert Gallatin 1830-1906 *DcNCBi 1*
**Brown,** William Anderson 1929- *AmMWSc 92*
**Brown,** William Arnold 1933- *AmMWSc 92*
**Brown,** William Arthur 1945- *Who 92*
**Brown,** William Augustin 1932- *AmMWSc 92*
**Brown,** William B. P. *Who 92*
**Brown,** William Bernard 1936- *AmMWSc 92*
**Brown,** William Boyd 1939- *WhoAmL 92*
**Brown,** William Carl 1958- *WhoAmL 92*
**Brown,** William Charles Langdon 1931- *IntWW 91, Who 92*
**Brown,** William Christopher 1928- *Who 92*
**Brown,** William Clayton 1953- *WhoAmL 92*
**Brown,** William Crawford 1925- *WhoBlA 92*
**Brown,** William Crews 1920- *WhoBlA 92*
**Brown,** William E 1923- *AmMWSc 92*
**Brown,** William E 1933- *AmMWSc 92*
**Brown,** William E 1945- *AmMWSc 92*
**Brown,** William Eden T. *Who 92*
**Brown,** William Edwin 1934- *WhoWest 92*
**Brown,** William F. 1900- *WhoBlA 92*
**Brown,** William Ferdinand 1928- *WhoEnt 92*
**Brown,** William Forster *ScFEYrs*
**Brown,** William G 1938- *AmMWSc 92*
**Brown,** William George 1853-1920 *BiInAmS*
**Brown,** William Glanville 1907- *Who 92*
**Brown,** William H. 1929- *WhoBlA 92*
**Brown,** William H. 1935- *WhoBlA 92*
**Brown,** William H., III 1928- *WhoBlA 92*
**Brown,** William H., Jr. *WhoFI 92*
**Brown,** William Hedrick 1933- *AmMWSc 92*
**Brown,** William Henry 1932- *AmMWSc 92*
**Brown,** William Henry 1942- *AmMWSc 92*
**Brown,** William Hill 1765-1793 *BenetAL 91, DcNCBi 1*
**Brown,** William Hill, III 1928- *WhoAmL 92*
**Brown,** William Holmes 1929- *WhoAmP 91*
**Brown,** William J *AmMWSc 92*
**Brown,** William J. 1917- *WhoBlA 92*
**Brown,** William Jann 1919- *AmMWSc 92*
**Brown,** William John 1920- *WhoRel 92*
**Brown,** William John 1940- *AmMWSc 92*
**Brown,** William L. 1922- *WhoFI 92*
**Brown,** William Lacy d1991 *NewYTBS 91*
**Brown,** William Lacy 1913- *AmMWSc 92*
**Brown,** William Lacy 1913-1991 *IntWW 91, -91N*
**Brown,** William Lee Lyons, Jr. 1936- *WhoFI 92*
**Brown,** William Lewis 1928- *AmMWSc 92*
**Brown,** William Louis, Jr 1922- *AmMWSc 92*
**Brown,** William M 1932- *AmMWSc 92*
**Brown,** William M 1942- *WhoIns 92*
**Brown,** William Martyn 1914- *Who 92*
**Brown,** William McKinley, Jr. 1926- *WhoBlA 92*
**Brown,** William Melvin, Jr. 1934- *WhoBlA 92*
**Brown,** William Montgomery 1855-1937 *RelLAm 91*
**Brown,** William Oliver, Jr. 1952- *WhoFI 92*
**Brown,** William Oscar 1915- *WhoWest 92*
**Brown,** William Patrick 1945- *WhoFI 92, WhoWest 92*
**Brown,** William R 1939- *WhoIns 92*
**Brown,** William Randall 1913- *AmMWSc 92*
**Brown,** William Rocky, III 1955- *WhoBlA 92*
**Brown,** William Roy 1945- *AmMWSc 92*
**Brown,** William Samuel, Jr 1940- *AmMWSc 92*
**Brown,** William Stanley 1935- *AmMWSc 92*
**Brown,** William T. 1929- *WhoBlA 92*
**Brown,** William T. 1947- *WhoBlA 92*
**Brown,** William Wells 1816-1884 *BenetAL 91, BlkLC [port], DramC 1 [port]*
**Brown,** Willie *WhoBlA 92*
**Brown,** Willie B 1940- *WhoAmP 91, WhoBlA 92*
**Brown,** Willie L. 1932- *WhoBlA 92*
**Brown,** Willie L, Jr 1934- *WhoAmP 91, WhoBlA 92*
**Brown,** Willie Lewis, Jr. 1934- *WhoWest 92*
**Brown,** Willis, Jr. 1924- *WhoBlA 92*
**Brown,** Willis Donald 1929- *WhoAmP 91*
**Brown,** Willis Noel 1940- *WhoRel 92*
**Brown,** Winfred James 1926- *WhoRel 92*
**Brown,** Winton 1912- *AmMWSc 92*
**Brown,** Wood, III 1936- *WhoAmL 92*
**Brown,** Woodrow Martin 1944- *WhoAmP 91*
**Brown,** Yvonne Margaret Rose 1940- *WhoWest 92*
**Brown,** Zack Bernard 1946- *WhoBlA 92*
**Brown,** Zane Eric 1957- *WhoEnt 92*
**Brown-Ankrom,** Nancy Eynon 1932- *WhoMW 92*
**Brown-Francisco,** Teresa Elaine 1960- *WhoBlA 92*
**Brown-Knable,** Bobbie Margaret 1936- *WhoBlA 92*
**Brown Leatherberry,** Thomas Henry 1930- *WhoEnt 92*
**Brown-Nash,** JoAhn Weaver 1935- *WhoBlA 92*
**Brown Preston,** Mary Oliver 1953- *WhoEnt 92*
**Brown-Sequard,** C E 1866?-1896 *BiInAmS*
**Brown-Sequard,** Charles-Edouard 1817-1894 *BiInAmS*
**Brown-Wright,** Marjorie 1935- *WhoBlA 92*
**Brownawell,** Woodrow Dale 1942- *AmMWSc 92*
**Browne** *Who 92*
**Browne and Nolan** *DcLB 106*
**Browne,** Alan Lampe 1944- *AmMWSc 92, WhoMW 92*
**Browne,** Aldis Jerome, Jr. 1912- *WhoFI 92, WhoMW 92*
**Browne,** Andrew Harold 1923- *Who 92*
**Browne,** Anthony 1946- *ConAu 36NR, WrDr 92*
**Browne,** Anthony Arthur Duncan M. *Who 92*
**Browne,** Bernard Peter Francis K. *Who 92*
**Browne,** Carole Lynn 1950- *AmMWSc 92*
**Browne,** Charles Duncan Alfred 1922- *Who 92*
**Browne,** Charles Farrar *BenetAL 91*
**Browne,** Charles Idol 1922- *AmMWSc 92*
**Browne,** Colin Lanfear 1928- *AmMWSc 92*
**Browne,** Coral 1913-1991 *CurBio 91N, NewYTBS 91 [port]*
**Browne,** Coral Edith d1991 *Who 92N*
**Browne,** Cornelius Payne 1923- *AmMWSc 92, WhoMW 92*
**Browne,** Daniel Jay 1804-1867 *BiInAmS*
**Browne,** David A. 1931- *WhoBlA 92*
**Browne,** David Henry 1864-1917 *BiInAmS*
**Browne,** Denis George *Who 92*
**Browne,** Desmond John Michael 1947- *Who 92*
**Browne,** Dik *SmATA 67 [port]*
**Browne,** Douglas Townsend 1942- *AmMWSc 92*
**Browne,** Edward Michael 1910- *Who 92*
**Browne,** Edward Tankard, Jr 1926- *AmMWSc 92*
**Browne,** Ernest C., Jr. 1925- *WhoBlA 92*
**Browne,** Francis C 1830?-1900 *BiInAmS*
**Browne,** G. Morgan 1935- *WhoFI 92*
**Browne,** Gerald Austin *WrDr 92*
**Browne,** Gillian Brenda B. *Who 92*
**Browne,** H Monroe 1917- *WhoAmP 91*
**Browne,** Harry *WrDr 92*
**Browne,** Harry 1933- *WrDr 92*
**Browne,** Henry 1918- *WrDr 92*
**Browne,** Howard 1908- *IntAu&W 91, WrDr 92*
**Browne,** J. Ross 1821-1875 *BenetAL 91*
**Browne,** Jackson *WhoEnt 92*
**Browne,** Jackson 1949- *NewAmDM*
**Browne,** James Broach 1935- *WhoAmL 92*
**Browne,** James Clayton 1935- *AmMWSc 92*
**Browne,** James Lowrie 1947- *WhoRel 92*
**Browne,** Jeffrey Francis 1944- *WhoAmL 92, WhoFI 92*
**Browne,** John Ernest Douglas Delavalette 1938- *Who 92*
**Browne,** John Mwalimu 1939- *AmMWSc 92*
**Browne,** John Philip Ravenscroft 1937- *Who 92*
**Browne,** Joseph Peter 1929- *WhoWest 92*
**Browne,** Kathleen 1905- *TwCPaSc*
**Browne,** Kristi Lynn 1963- *WhoAmL 92*
**Browne,** Lee F. 1922- *WhoBlA 92*
**Browne,** Leslie 1957- *WhoEnt 92*
**Browne,** Mervyn Ernest 1916- *Who 92*
**Browne,** Michael *Who 92*
**Browne,** Michael Dennis *DrAPF 91*
**Browne,** Michael Dennis 1940- *ConPo 91, WrDr 92*
**Browne,** Michael Edwin 1930- *AmMWSc 92*
**Browne,** Michael Joseph Dennis 1940- *IntAu&W 91*
**Browne,** Michael Leon 1946- *WhoAmL 92*
**Browne,** Moyra 1918- *Who 92*
**Browne,** Patrick 1907- *Who 92*
**Browne,** Percy Basil 1923- *Who 92*
**Browne,** Peter 1766?-1833 *DcNCBi 1*
**Browne,** Peter Arrell 1782-1860 *BiInAmS*
**Browne,** Peter K. *Who 92*
**Browne,** Porter Emerson *ScFEYrs A*
**Browne,** Ray Broadus 1922- *WhoMW 92*
**Browne,** Richard Arthur Allan 1917-1989 *SmATA 67 [port]*
**Browne,** Robert Glenn 1951- *AmMWSc 92*
**Browne,** Robert McCormick 1926- *WhoWest 92*
**Browne,** Robert Span 1924- *WhoBlA 92, WhoFI 92*
**Browne,** Robert William M. *Who 92*
**Browne,** Ronald K 1934- *AmMWSc 92*
**Browne,** Roscoe Lee 1925- *IntMPA 92, WhoBlA 92*
**Browne,** Sally Jane *WhoFI 92*
**Browne,** Sheila Ewing 1949- *AmMWSc 92*
**Browne,** Sheila Jeanne 1924- *Who 92*
**Browne,** Stanhope Stryker 1931- *WhoAmL 92*
**Browne,** Steven Emery 1950- *WhoEnt 92, WhoWest 92*
**Browne,** Thomas 1605-1682 *RfGEnL 91*
**Browne,** Thomas Alexander *RfGEnL 91*
**Browne,** Vee F. 1956- *WhoEnt 92*
**Browne,** Vincent J. 1917- *WhoBlA 92*
**Browne,** Vincent Jefferson, Jr. 1953- *WhoBlA 92*
**Browne,** Vivian E. 1929- *WhoBlA 92*
**Browne,** W H 1915- *AmMWSc 92*
**Browne,** William 1590?-1645? *RfGEnL 91*
**Browne,** William Garl, Jr. 1823-1894 *DcNCBi 1*
**Browne,** William Samuel 1932- *WhoAmP 91*
**Browne-Cave,** Robert C. *Who 92*
**Browne Miller,** Angela 1952- *ConAu 135*
**Browne-Wilkinson,** Nicolas Christopher H. 1930- *IntWW 91, Who 92*
**Brownell,** Anna Gale 1942- *AmMWSc 92*
**Brownell,** Barry Clayton 1922- *WhoFI 92*
**Brownell,** Edwin Rowland 1924- *WhoFI 92*
**Brownell,** Frank Herbert, III 1922- *AmMWSc 92*
**Brownell,** George H 1938- *AmMWSc 92*
**Brownell,** George L 1923- *AmMWSc 92*
**Brownell,** Gordon Lee 1922- *AmMWSc 92*
**Brownell,** Henry Howard 1820-1872 *BenetAL 91*
**Brownell,** Herbert 1904- *IntWW 91, WhoAmP 91*
**Brownell,** James Richard 1932- *AmMWSc 92*
**Brownell,** John Howard 1942- *AmMWSc 92*
**Brownell,** John T 1836-1886 *BiInAmS*
**Brownell,** Kate 1842- *EncAmaz 91*
**Brownell,** Melvin Russell 1925- *WhoMW 92*
**Brownell,** Philip Harry 1947- *AmMWSc 92*
**Brownell,** R M 1930- *AmMWSc 92*
**Brownell,** Robert Harrie 1938- *WhoMW 92*
**Brownell,** Robert Leo, Jr 1943- *AmMWSc 92*
**Brownell,** Samuel Miller d1990 *IntWW 91N*
**Brownell,** Samuel Miller 1900-1990 *CurBio 91N*
**Brownell,** Thomas F *WhoAmP 91*
**Brownell,** W. C. 1851-1928 *BenetAL 91*
**Brownell,** Walter Abner 1838-1904 *BiInAmS*
**Brownell,** Wayne E 1918- *AmMWSc 92*
**Brownell,** William Edward 1942- *AmMWSc 92*
**Browner,** Joey Matthew 1960- *WhoBlA 92*
**Browner,** Robert Herman 1943- *AmMWSc 92*
**Browner,** Ross 1954- *WhoBlA 92*
**Brownfield,** Charles William 1941- *WhoAmL 92*
**Brownfield,** Katherine Annette 1956- *WhoMW 92*
**Brownhill,** Bud H. 1941- *WhoWest 92*
**Brownie,** Alexander C 1931- *AmMWSc 92*
**Browning,** Amy Katherine 1882-1970 *TwCPaSc*
**Browning,** Carol Dan 1960- *WhoAmL 92*
**Browning,** Cecile' Lieux 1943- *WhoMW 92*
**Browning,** Charles Benton 1931- *AmMWSc 92*
**Browning,** Chauncey H, Jr 1934- *WhoAmP 91*
**Browning,** Christopher Corwin 1956- *WhoAmL 92*
**Browning,** Christopher R. 1944- *WrDr 92*
**Browning,** Colin Arrott 1935- *WhoFI 92*
**Browning,** Craig *TwCSFW 91*
**Browning,** Daniel Dwight 1921- *AmMWSc 92*
**Browning,** David Gunter 1937- *AmMWSc 92*
**Browning,** David Peter 1927- *Who 92*
**Browning,** David Stuart 1939- *WhoAmL 92, WhoFI 92*
**Browning,** Deborah Lea 1955- *WhoAmL 92*
**Browning,** Dixie Burrus 1930- *WrDr 92*
**Browning,** Don 1934- *WrDr 92*
**Browning,** Don Spencer 1934- *WhoRel 92*
**Browning,** Edmond L. 1929- *IntWW 91*
**Browning,** Edmond Lee *WhoRel 92*
**Browning,** Edmond Lee 1929- *Who 92*
**Browning,** Edmond Lee 1930- *RelLAm 91*
**Browning,** Edward T 1939- *AmMWSc 92*
**Browning,** Elizabeth Barrett 1806-1861 *CnDBLB 4 [port], RfGEnL 91*
**Browning,** Francesca Alsing 1905- *WhoEnt 92*
**Browning,** Frank W 1937- *WhoIns 92*
**Browning,** Galen B 1923- *WhoAmP 91*
**Browning,** George Victor 1942- *Who 92*
**Browning,** Grainger 1917- *WhoBlA 92*
**Browning,** Guston Hassell 1926- *WhoRel 92*
**Browning,** Horace Lawrence, Jr 1932- *AmMWSc 92*
**Browning,** Ian Andrew 1941- *Who 92*
**Browning,** Iben d1991 *NewYTBS 91*
**Browning,** James Louis, Jr. 1932- *WhoAmL 92*
**Browning,** James R *WhoAmP 91*
**Browning,** James Robert 1918- *WhoAmL 92*
**Browning,** Jesse Harrison 1935- *WhoWest 92*
**Browning,** Joe Leon 1925- *AmMWSc 92*
**Browning,** John 1933- *NewAmDM*
**Browning,** John Artie 1923- *AmMWSc 92*
**Browning,** John Moses 1855-1926 *FacFETw*
**Browning,** Kaye 1933- *WhoAmP 91*
**Browning,** Keith Anthony 1938- *IntWW 91, Who 92*
**Browning,** Kirk *LesBEnT 92*
**Browning,** Kirk 1921- *IntMPA 92*
**Browning,** Michael Gorry *WhoMW 92, WhoWest 92*
**Browning,** Peter *Who 92*
**Browning,** Peter Crane 1941- *WhoFI 92*
**Browning,** R. Stephen 1940- *WhoFI 92*
**Browning,** Reba Smith 1926- *WhoFI 92*
**Browning,** Rex Alan 1930- *Who 92*
**Browning,** Richard 1952- *WhoAmP 91*
**Browning,** Robert 1812-1889 *CnDBLB 4 [port], RfGEnL 91*
**Browning,** Robert 1914- *IntAu&W 91, IntWW 91, Who 92, WrDr 92*
**Browning,** Robert Lynn 1924- *WhoRel 92*
**Browning,** Robert Mark 1955- *WhoWest 92*
**Browning,** Ronald Anthony 1940- *AmMWSc 92*
**Browning,** Rufus Putnam 1934- *IntAu&W 91*
**Browning,** Sarah Louise 1952- *WhoAmP 91*
**Browning,** Scott David 1931- *WhoRel 92*
**Browning,** Sterry *TwCWW 91*
**Browning,** Tod 1880-1962 *IntDcF 2-2 [port]*
**Browning,** Tod 1882-1962 *FacFETw*
**Browning,** Wilfrid 1918- *WrDr 92*
**Browning,** Wilfrid Robert Francis 1918- *Who 92*
**Browning,** William Blaine 1953- *WhoRel 92*
**Browning,** William Docker 1931- *WhoAmL 92, WhoWest 92*
**Brownjohn,** Alan 1931- *ConPo 91, IntAu&W 91, WrDr 92*
**Brownjohn,** John Nevil Maxwell *IntAu&W 91*
**Brownlee,** Christene 1955- *WhoAmP 91*
**Brownlee,** Donald E 1943- *AmMWSc 92*
**Brownlee,** George 1911- *IntWW 91, Who 92*
**Brownlee,** George Gow 1942- *Who 92*
**Brownlee,** Geraldine Daniels *WhoBlA 92*
**Brownlee,** Jack M. 1940- *WhoBlA 92*
**Brownlee,** Judith Marilyn 1940- *WhoRel 92*

**Brownlee**, Lester Harrison-Pierce 1915- *WhoBlA 92*
**Brownlee**, Paula Pimlott 1934- *AmMWSc 92*
**Brownlee**, Robert Hammel 1951- *WhoAmL 92*
**Brownlee**, Robert Rex 1924- *AmMWSc 92*
**Brownlee**, Vivian Aplin 1946- *WhoBlA 92*
**Brownlee**, Wilson Elliot, Jr. 1941- *WhoWest 92*
**Brownlee**, Wyatt China 1909- *WhoBlA 92*
**Brownley**, Edwin Allen, Jr. 1948- *WhoFI 92*
**Brownlie**, Albert Dempster 1932- *IntWW 91, Who 92*
**Brownlie**, Deborah Louise 1955- *WhoAmP 91*
**Brownlie**, Ian 1932- *IntWW 91, Who 92, WrDr 92*
**Brownlow** *Who 92*
**Brownlow**, Baron *Who 92*
**Brownlow**, Arthur Hume 1933- *AmMWSc 92*
**Brownlow**, Bertrand 1929- *Who 92*
**Brownlow**, James Hilton 1925- *Who 92*
**Brownlow**, Kevin 1938- *IntAu&W 91, IntMPA 92, IntWW 91, SmATA 65, Who 92, WrDr 92*
**Brownlow**, Roger W 1922- *AmMWSc 92*
**Brownlow**, William Gannaway 1805-1877 *BenetAL 91*
**Brownlow**, William Stephen 1921- *Who 92*
**Brownmiller**, Susan 1935- *ConAu 35NR, WrDr 92*
**Brownridge**, J. Paul 1945- *WhoBlA 92*
**Brownrigg**, Nicholas 1932- *Who 92*
**Brownrigg**, Philip Henry Akerman 1911- *Who 92*
**Brownrigg**, S. F. 1937- *WhoEnt 92*
**Brownscheidle**, Carol Mary 1946- *AmMWSc 92*
**Brownscombe**, Eugene Russell 1906- *AmMWSc 92*
**Brownson**, Charles *DrAPF 91*
**Brownson**, Orestes Augustus 1803-1876 *BenetAL 91*
**Brownson**, Robert Henry 1925- *AmMWSc 92*
**Brownson**, William Clarence 1928- *WhoRel 92*
**Brownstein**, Barbara L 1931- *AmMWSc 92*
**Brownstein**, Harris Allen 1958- *WhoFI 92*
**Brownstein**, Karen Osney 1944- *IntAu&W 91*
**Brownstein**, Kenneth Robert 1936- *AmMWSc 92*
**Brownstein**, Michael *DrAPF 91*
**Brownstein**, Michael 1943- *ConPo 91, WrDr 92*
**Brownstein**, Michael Jay 1943- *AmMWSc 92*
**Brownstein**, Philip Nathan 1917- *WhoAmL 92, WhoFI 92*
**Brownstein**, Ronald Jay 1958- *WhoWest 92*
**Brownstein**, Sydney Kenneth 1931- *AmMWSc 92*
**Brownstein-Santiago**, Cheryl *WhoHisp 92*
**Brownstone**, Hugh Michael 1957- *WhoFI 92*
**Brownstone**, Yehoshua Shieky 1929- *AmMWSc 92*
**Brownsword**, Harold 1885-1961 *TwCPaSc*
**Brownwood**, David Owen 1935- *WhoAmL 92, WhoFI 92*
**Browse**, Lillian Gertrude *Who 92*
**Browse**, Nicholas 1954- *WhoEnt 92*
**Browse**, Norman Leslie 1931- *Who 92*
**Browzin**, Boris S 1912- *AmMWSc 92*
**Broxbourne**, Baron 1910- *Who 92*
**Broxmeyer**, Hal Edward 1944- *AmMWSc 92, WhoMW 92*
**Broxon**, Mildred Downey 1944- *IntAu&W 91, TwCSFW 91, WrDr 92*
**Broxton**, David Edward 1952- *AmMWSc 92*
**Broydrick**, Bill B 1948- *WhoAmP 91*
**Broyhill**, James T 1927- *WhoAmP 91*
**Broyhill**, Linda Sharon 1951- *WhoAmL 92*
**Broyles**, Arthur Augustus 1923- *AmMWSc 92*
**Broyles**, Carter D 1924- *AmMWSc 92*
**Broyles**, Marie Irene 1950- *WhoMW 92*
**Broyles**, Robert 1933- *WhoEnt 92*
**Broyles**, Robert Herman 1943- *AmMWSc 92*
**Broyles**, William Dodson, Jr. 1944- *IntWW 91*
**Broyles-Williams**, Maxine *WhoBlA 92*
**Broz-Tito**, Josip *DcAmImH*
**Brozek**, Richard Carl 1953- *WhoFI 92*
**Brozen**, Yale 1917- *WhoMW 92*
**Brualdi**, Richard Anthony 1939- *AmMWSc 92*
**Brubach**, Holly Beth 1953- *WhoEnt 92*
**Brubacher**, Elaine Schnitker *AmMWSc 92*
**Brubaker**, Burton D 1935- *AmMWSc 92*
**Brubaker**, Carl H, Jr 1925- *AmMWSc 92*
**Brubaker**, Crawford Francis, Jr. 1924- *WhoWest 92*
**Brubaker**, George Randell 1939- *AmMWSc 92*
**Brubaker**, Harold J 1946- *WhoAmP 91*
**Brubaker**, Inara Mencis 1938- *AmMWSc 92*
**Brubaker**, James Clark 1947- *WhoMW 92*
**Brubaker**, James D. 1937- *IntMPA 92*
**Brubaker**, James Edward 1935- *WhoFI 92*
**Brubaker**, Karen Sue 1953- *WhoFI 92*
**Brubaker**, Kenton Kaylor 1932- *AmMWSc 92*
**Brubaker**, Lauren Edgar 1914- *WhoRel 92*
**Brubaker**, Leonard Hathaway 1934- *AmMWSc 92*
**Brubaker**, Merlin L 1922- *AmMWSc 92*
**Brubaker**, Paul Eugene, II 1934- *AmMWSc 92*
**Brubaker**, Peter P. 1946- *WhoEnt 92*
**Brubaker**, Robert Loring 1947- *WhoAmL 92*
**Brubaker**, Robert Robinson 1933- *AmMWSc 92*
**Brubaker**, Ruth 1959- *WhoWest 92*
**Brubaker**, Stephen Craig 1957- *WhoEnt 92*
**Brubaker**, Thomas Allen 1935- *AmMWSc 92*
**Brubaker-Sarak**, Brenda Marie 1960- *WhoFI 92*
**Brubeck**, Dave 1920- *FacFETw, NewAmDM*
**Brubeck**, David Warren 1920- *IntWW 91, Who 92, WhoEnt 92*
**Brubeck**, William H. 1920- *IntWW 91*
**Brucat**, Philip John 1956- *AmMWSc 92*
**Bruccoli**, Matthew J. 1931- *WrDr 92*
**Bruce** *Who 92*
**Bruce**, Lord 1961- *Who 92*
**Bruce**, Adam Todd d1887 *BiInAmS*
**Bruce**, Agnes Marie 1910- *WhoAmP 91*
**Bruce**, Alan Kenneth 1927- *AmMWSc 92*
**Bruce**, Alexander Robson 1907- *Who 92*
**Bruce**, Anne 1927- *TwCPaSc*
**Bruce**, Archibald 1777-1818 *BiInAmS*
**Bruce**, Arthur Atkinson 1895- *Who 92*
**Bruce**, Beverly Joan 1927- *WhoAmP 91*
**Bruce**, Bill Ed 1950- *WhoEnt 92*
**Bruce**, Blanche K 1841-1898 *RComAH*
**Bruce**, Blanche Kelso 1841-1898 *AmPolLe*
**Bruce**, Brenda 1922- *ConTFT 9, IntMPA 92*
**Bruce**, Cameron Kevin 1962- *WhoWest 92*
**Bruce**, Carl Vernon, Jr. 1940- *WhoEnt 92*
**Bruce**, Carol 1954- *WhoWest 92*
**Bruce**, Carol Pitt 1941- *WhoBlA 92*
**Bruce**, Catherine Wolfe 1816-1900 *BiInAmS*
**Bruce**, Charles 1906-1971 *BenetAL 91*
**Bruce**, Charles J 1953- *WhoIns 92*
**Bruce**, Charles Robert 1925- *AmMWSc 92*
**Bruce**, Charles Wikoff 1937- *AmMWSc 92*
**Bruce**, Christopher 1945- *Who 92*
**Bruce**, Danny Monroe 1950- *WhoAmP 91*
**Bruce**, David *IntAu&W 91X*
**Bruce**, David 1855-1931 *FacFETw*
**Bruce**, David 1927- *Who 92*
**Bruce**, David Lionel 1933- *AmMWSc 92*
**Bruce**, David Stewart 1939- *AmMWSc 92, WhoMW 92*
**Bruce**, Debra M. *DrAPF 91*
**Bruce**, Dickson Davies, Jr. 1946- *WrDr 92*
**Bruce**, E Ivan, Jr 1917- *AmMWSc 92*
**Bruce**, Estel Edward 1938- *WhoAmL 92*
**Bruce**, Francis Michael Ian *Who 92*
**Bruce**, Frederick Fyvie d1990 *IntWW 91N, Who 92N*
**Bruce**, Frederick Fyvie 1910- *IntAu&W 91*
**Bruce**, George 1909- *ConPo 91, IntAu&W 91, WrDr 92*
**Bruce**, George John Done 1930- *Who 92*
**Bruce**, George Walter, Jr. 1958- *WhoMW 92*
**Bruce**, Hervey 1952- *Who 92*
**Bruce**, Ian Cameron 1947- *Who 92*
**Bruce**, Ian Waugh 1945- *Who 92*
**Bruce**, Jackson Martin, Jr. 1931- *WhoAmL 92*
**Bruce**, Jackson Miller 1942- *WhoAmL 92*
**Bruce**, James C. 1929- *WhoBlA 92*
**Bruce**, James Donald 1936- *AmMWSc 92*
**Bruce**, James Edmond 1927- *WhoAmP 91*
**Bruce**, James Edward 1947- *WhoWest 92*
**Bruce**, John Allen 1934- *WhoWest 92*
**Bruce**, John Anthony 1931- *WhoWest 92*
**Bruce**, John Goodall, Jr 1927- *AmMWSc 92*
**Bruce**, John Irvin 1927- *AmMWSc 92*
**Bruce**, John Irvin 1929- *WhoBlA 92*
**Bruce**, Josephine Beall 18--?-1923 *NotBlAW 92 [port]*
**Bruce**, Katharine Fenn 1925- *WhoAmP 91*
**Bruce**, Kenneth E. 1921- *WhoBlA 92*
**Bruce**, Kim Barry 1948- *AmMWSc 92*
**Bruce**, Lennart *DrAPF 91*
**Bruce**, Lennart 1919- *IntAu&W 91, WrDr 92*
**Bruce**, Lenny 1925-1966 *FacFETw*
**Bruce**, Malcolm Gray 1944- *Who 92*
**Bruce**, Marion 1912- *WhoAmP 91*
**Bruce**, Martha Elena Aguilar 1946- *WhoHisp 92*
**Bruce**, Mary 1895-1990 *AnObit 1990*
**Bruce**, Michael 1943- *WhoFI 92*
**Bruce**, Michael Gregory 1957- *WhoEnt 92*
**Bruce**, Michael Ian 1926- *Who 92*
**Bruce**, Michael Stewart Rae *Who 92*
**Bruce**, Muriel *ScFEYrs*
**Bruce**, Paul Love 1933- *WhoAmP 91*
**Bruce**, Preston, Jr. 1936- *WhoBlA 92*
**Bruce**, Richard Conrad 1936- *AmMWSc 92*
**Bruce**, Robert Arthur 1916- *AmMWSc 92*
**Bruce**, Robert Cecil 1950- *WhoWest 92*
**Bruce**, Robert Nigel 1907- *Who 92*
**Bruce**, Robert Nolan, Jr 1930- *AmMWSc 92*
**Bruce**, Robert Rockwell 1944- *WhoAmL 92*
**Bruce**, Robert Russell 1926- *AmMWSc 92*
**Bruce**, Rufus Elbridge, Jr 1926- *AmMWSc 92*
**Bruce**, Stephen Robert 1950- *WhoAmL 92*
**Bruce**, Terry L. 1944- *AlmAP 92 [port], WhoAmP 91, WhoMW 92*
**Bruce**, William David 1928- *WhoIns 92*
**Bruce-Gardner**, Douglas 1917- *Who 92*
**Bruce-Gardyne**, Lord 1930-1990 *AnObit 1990*
**Bruce Lockhart**, Logie 1921- *Who 92*
**Bruce Lockhart**, Robin 1920- *WrDr 92*
**Bruce-Mitford**, Rupert Leo Scott 1914- *IntWW 91, Who 92*
**Bruce-Novoa** *DrAPF 91*
**Bruce-Novoa**, Juan 1944- *WhoHisp 92*
**Bruce of Donington**, Baron 1912- *Who 92*
**Bruch**, John C, Jr 1940- *AmMWSc 92*
**Bruch**, Ludwig Walter 1940- *AmMWSc 92*
**Bruch**, Max 1838-1920 *NewAmDM*
**Bruch**, Thomas James 1959- *WhoFI 92*
**Bruchac**, Joseph 1942- *IntAu&W 91, WrDr 92*
**Bruchac**, Joseph E. *DrAPF 91*
**Bruchal**, Richard Symeon 1937- *WhoAmP 91*
**Bruchard**, Charles E. 1951- *WhoRel 92*
**Bruchesi**, Jean 1901- *IntWW 91*
**Bruchovsky**, Nicholas 1936- *AmMWSc 92*
**Bruck**, Connie Jane 1946- *WhoFI 92*
**Bruck**, Daniel Stephen 1956- *WhoEnt 92*
**Bruck**, David Lewis 1933- *AmMWSc 92*
**Bruck**, Erika 1908- *AmMWSc 92*
**Bruck**, George 1904- *AmMWSc 92*
**Bruck**, Hermann Alexander 1905- *IntWW 91, Who 92*
**Bruck**, Jaen Francois Julien 1918- *IntWW 91*
**Bruck**, Richard Hubert 1914- *AmMWSc 92*
**Bruck**, Robert Ian 1952- *AmMWSc 92*
**Bruck**, Rodney L 1945- *WhoIns 92*
**Bruck**, Stephen Desiderius 1927- *AmMWSc 92*
**Brucken**, Robert Matthew 1934- *WhoAmL 92*
**Bruckenstein**, Stanley 1927- *AmMWSc 92*
**Brucker**, Andrew Gerald 1943- *WhoAmL 92*
**Brucker**, Edward Byerly 1931- *AmMWSc 92*
**Brucker**, Johann Jakob 1696-1770 *BlkwCEP*
**Brucker**, Paul Charles 1931- *AmMWSc 92*
**Bruckerhoff**, Vernon E 1944- *WhoAmP 91*
**Bruckheimer**, Jerry *IntMPA 92, WhoEnt 92*
**Bruckman**, Betty *WhoAmP 91*
**Bruckmann**, Gerhart 1932- *IntWW 91*
**Bruckner**, Adam Peter 1943- *AmMWSc 92*
**Bruckner**, Andrew M 1932- *AmMWSc 92*
**Bruckner**, Anton 1824-1896 *NewAmDM*
**Bruckner**, Christine 1921- *IntWW 91*
**Bruckner**, David Alan 1941- *AmMWSc 92*
**Bruckner**, Ferdinand 1891-1958 *EncTR 91, LiExTwC*
**Bruckner**, James Victor 1944- *AmMWSc 92*
**Bruckner**, Lawrence Adam 1940- *AmMWSc 92*
**Bruckner**, Robert Joseph 1921- *AmMWSc 92*
**Bruckner**, Wilhelm 1884-1954 *EncTR 91*
**Bruckner**, Willa Cohen 1954- *WhoAmL 92*
**Bruckner**, William J. 1944- *WhoAmL 92*
**Bruckstein**, Ludovic 1920- *IntAu&W 91*
**Brudenell-Bruce** *Who 92*
**Bruder**, Gary A. 1954- *WhoAmL 92*
**Bruder**, Gerald 1936- *WhoFI 92*
**Bruder**, Jospeh Albert 1938- *AmMWSc 92*
**Bruder**, Judith *DrAPF 91*
**Bruder**, Ronald B. 1948- *WhoFI 92*
**Bruderlin**, Beat Dominik 1955- *WhoWest 92*
**Brudner**, Harvey Jerome 1931- *AmMWSc 92*
**Brudno**, Barbara 1941- *WhoAmL 92*
**Brue**, Stanley Leonard 1945- *WhoFI 92*
**Brueck**, Steven Roy Julien 1944- *AmMWSc 92*
**Brueckner**, Guenter Erich 1934- *AmMWSc 92*
**Brueckner**, Hannes Kurt 1940- *AmMWSc 92*
**Brueckner**, Jan Keith 1950- *WhoFI 92, WhoMW 92*
**Brueckner**, Keith Allan 1924- *AmMWSc 92, IntWW 91*
**Brueckner**, Robert Davis 1935- *WhoFI 92*
**Bruegel**, David Robert 1953- *WhoAmL 92*
**Brueggeman**, Charles Joseph 1931- *WhoFI 92*
**Brueggeman**, James Alan 1938- *WhoMW 92*
**Brueggemann**, Dale Alan 1949- *WhoRel 92*
**Brueggemeier**, Robert Wayne 1950- *AmMWSc 92*
**Brueggen**, Frans 1934- *NewAmDM*
**Bruegman**, Gary Richard 1946- *WhoMW 92*
**Bruehl**, George William 1919- *AmMWSc 92*
**Bruehl**, Heidi d1991 *NewYTBS 91*
**Bruel**, Jean-Marc Andre 1936- *IntWW 91*
**Bruemmer**, Fred 1929- *WrDr 92*
**Bruen**, David D 1929- *WhoAmP 91*
**Bruen**, James A. 1943- *WhoAmL 92*
**Bruen**, Ru 1940- *TwCPaSc*
**Bruenderman**, Katherine R. 1945- *WhoAmL 92*
**Bruening**, George 1938- *AmMWSc 92*
**Bruening**, James Theodore 1949- *AmMWSc 92*
**Bruening**, Richard Patrick 1939- *WhoAmL 92*
**Bruenner**, Frederick Herman 1920- *WhoAmL 92*
**Bruenner**, Rolf Sylvester 1921- *AmMWSc 92*
**Bruere**, Martha S Bensley 1879-1953 *ScFEYrs*
**Brues**, Alice Mossie 1913- *AmMWSc 92*
**Brues**, Austin 1906- *AmMWSc 92*
**Bruesch**, Simon Rulin 1914- *AmMWSc 92*
**Bruesewitz**, Terry Blake 1941- *WhoAmL 92*
**Brueske**, Charles H 1937- *AmMWSc 92*
**Brueske**, Patrick Jeremy 1964- *WhoRel 92*
**Bruess**, David Lincoln 1961- *WhoRel 92*
**Bruetman**, Martin Edgardo 1932- *AmMWSc 92*
**Bruey**, Alfred J. *DrAPF 91*
**Bruff**, Harold Hastings 1944- *WhoAmL 92*
**Bruford**, Marjorie 1902-1958 *TwCPaSc*
**Brufsky**, Allen David 1939- *WhoAmL 92*
**Brugaletta**, John J. *DrAPF 91*
**Brugam**, Richard Blair 1946- *AmMWSc 92*
**Brugel**, Edward William 1948- *WhoWest 92*
**Brugere**, Melvin John, III 1950- *WhoMW 92*
**Brugge**, John F 1937- *AmMWSc 92*
**Bruggeman**, Douglas L. 1960- *WhoFI 92*
**Bruggeman**, Gordon Arthur 1933- *AmMWSc 92*
**Bruggeman**, Lewis LeRoy 1941- *WhoWest 92*
**Bruggeman**, Terrance John 1946- *WhoFI 92*
**Bruggen**, Frans 1934- *Who 92, WhoEnt 92*
**Brugger**, Ernst 1914- *IntWW 91*
**Brugger**, John Edward 1923- *AmMWSc 92*
**Brugger**, Paul Raymond 1942- *WhoWest 92*
**Brugger**, Robert Melvin 1929- *AmMWSc 92*
**Brugger**, Thomas C 1927- *AmMWSc 92*
**Bruggink**, Eric G. 1949- *WhoAmL 92*
**Brugh**, Max, Jr 1938- *AmMWSc 92*
**Brugman**, Winnie 1945- *WhoEnt 92*
**Brugmans**, Hendrik 1906- *IntWW 91*
**Bruhn**, Erik 1928-1986 *FacFETw*
**Bruhn**, Gary David 1954- *WhoAmL 92*
**Bruhn**, H D 1907- *AmMWSc 92*
**Bruhn**, Hans-Juergen 1940- *WhoFI 92*
**Bruhn**, John G 1934- *AmMWSc 92*
**Bruhweiler**, Frederick Carlton, Jr 1946- *AmMWSc 92*
**Bruice**, Thomas Charles 1925- *AmMWSc 92*
**Bruin**, Barbara 1957- *WhoAmL 92*
**Bruin**, John *IntAu&W 91X, WrDr 92*
**Bruin**, John 1924- *WhoBlA 92*
**Bruin**, Linda Lou 1938- *WhoAmL 92*
**Bruington**, John Edward 1947- *WhoRel 92*
**Bruins**, Elton John 1927- *WhoRel 92*
**Bruins**, Paul F 1905- *AmMWSc 92*
**Bruinvels**, Peter Nigel Edward 1950- *Who 92*
**Brukner**, Ira Beryl *DrAPF 91*
**Bruley**, Duane Frederick 1933- *AmMWSc 92*
**Brulez**, Mary Anne 1949- *WhoMW 92*
**Bruller**, Jean 1902-1991 *ConAu 134, NewYTBS 91*
**Bruller**, Jean Marcel *IntWW 91*

**Brullo**, Robert Angelo 1948- *WhoMW 92*
**Brulls**, Christian *ConAu 35NR*
**Brulon**, Angelique *EncAmaz 91*
**Brulotte**, Gaetan 1945- *IntAu&W 91*
**Brulte**, Jim *WhoAmP 91*
**Brum**, Brenda Kay 1954- *WhoAmP 91*
**Brumage**, William Harry 1923- *AmMWSc 92*
**Brumaghim**, Paul 1926- *WhoMW 92*
**Brumback**, Arthur Marion 1869-1916 *BiInAmS*
**Brumback**, Charles Tiedtke 1928- *WhoFI 92, WhoMW 92*
**Brumbaugh**, David Scott 1940- *WhoWest 92*
**Brumbaugh**, Donald Verwey 1952- *AmMWSc 92*
**Brumbaugh**, Joe H 1930- *AmMWSc 92*
**Brumbaugh**, John 1935- *AmMWSc 92*
**Brumbaugh**, John A., Jr. 1927- *WhoFI 92*
**Brumbaugh**, John Maynard 1927- *WhoAmL 92*
**Brumbaugh**, Philip 1932- *AmMWSc 92*
**Brumbaugh**, Robert Dan, Jr. *WhoFI 92*
**Brumbaugh**, Robert S. 1918- *WrDr 92*
**Brumberg**, Bruce Samuel 1959- *WhoFI 92*
**Brumberger**, Harry 1926- *AmMWSc 92*
**Brumby**, Colin 1933- *ConCom 92*
**Brumby**, Richard Trapier 1804-1875 *BiInAmS*
**Brumby**, Sewell 1952- *WhoAmL 92*
**Brumel**, Antoine 1460?-1525? *NewAmDM*
**Brumel**, Valeriy Nikolaevich 1942- *SovUnBD*
**Brumer**, Milton 1902- *AmMWSc 92*
**Brumer**, Paul William 1945- *AmMWSc 92*
**Brumfield**, Ana Maria 1957- *WhoEnt 92*
**Brumfit**, Christopher John 1940- *Who 92*
**Brumidi**, Constantino 1805-1880 *DcAmImH*
**Brumit**, J. Scott 1949- *WhoEnt 92*
**Brumleve**, Stanley John 1924- *AmMWSc 92*
**Brumley**, David Lee 1949- *WhoFI 92*
**Brumley**, George H. 1940- *WhoMW 92*
**Brumm**, Douglas B 1940- *AmMWSc 92*
**Brumm**, James Leslie Hart 1962- *WhoRel 92*
**Brummel**, Douglas John 1964- *WhoRel 92*
**Brummel**, Fred B *WhoAmP 91*
**Brummel**, Mark Joseph 1933- *WhoMW 92, WhoRel 92*
**Brummel**, Steven William 1946- *WhoWest 92*
**Brummels**, J.V. *DrAPF 91*
**Brummer**, Chauncey Eugene 1948- *WhoBlA 92*
**Brummer**, Johannes J 1921- *AmMWSc 92*
**Brummer**, Richard H 1942- *WhoAmP 91*
**Brummer**, Robert Craig 1945- *WhoFI 92*
**Brummet**, Colin 1943- *WhoIns 92*
**Brummet**, John *DrAPF 91*
**Brummett**, Anna Ruth 1924- *AmMWSc 92*
**Brummett**, Claudia Mae 1927- *WhoAmP 91*
**Brummett**, Robert E 1934- *AmMWSc 92*
**Brummett**, Robert Eddie 1934- *WhoWest 92*
**Brummett**, Terry Lee 1967- *WhoMW 92*
**Brummond**, David Joseph 1950- *WhoAmL 92*
**Brummond**, Dewey Otto 1925- *AmMWSc 92*
**Brumsickle**, Bill *WhoAmP 91*
**Brumund**, William Frank 1942- *AmMWSc 92*
**Brun**, Herbert 1918- *NewAmDM, WhoEnt 92*
**Brun**, Judy Kay *WhoMW 92, WhoWest 92*
**Brun**, Kim Eric 1947- *WhoWest 92*
**Brun**, Margaret Ann Charlene 1945- *WhoWest 92*
**Brun**, Milivoj Konstantin 1948- *AmMWSc 92*
**Brun**, Roy L 1953- *WhoAmP 91*
**Brun**, William Alexander 1925- *AmMWSc 92*
**Bruna**, Dick 1927- *ConAu 36NR, Who 92*
**Brunacini**, Alan Vincent 1937- *WhoWest 92*
**Brunda**, Michael J 1950- *AmMWSc 92*
**Brundage**, Arthur Lain 1927- *AmMWSc 92*
**Brundage**, Donald Keith 1913- *AmMWSc 92*
**Brundage**, Howard Denton 1923- *IntWW 91*
**Brundage**, James A. 1929- *WrDr 92*
**Brundage**, James Arthur 1929- *IntAu&W 91, WhoMW 92*
**Brunden**, Kurt Russell 1958- *AmMWSc 92*
**Brunden**, Marshall Nils 1934- *AmMWSc 92*
**Brundidge**, Carl Irwin 1955- *WhoAmL 92*
**Brundidge**, Kenneth Cloud 1927- *AmMWSc 92*
**Brundidge**, Nancy Corinne 1920- *WhoBlA 92*
**Brundin**, Brian Jon 1939- *WhoAmL 92, WhoWest 92*
**Brundin**, Clark Lannerdahl 1931- *IntWW 91, Who 92*
**Brundit**, Reginald G. 1883-1960 *TwCPaSc*
**Brundtland**, Gro Harlem 1939- *IntWW 91*
**Brundy**, Stanley Dwayne 1967- *WhoBlA 92*
**Brune**, Goldie Esther 1912- *WhoAmP 91*
**Brune**, James N 1934- *AmMWSc 92*
**Brune**, Lester Hugo 1926- *WhoMW 92*
**Brune**, Stephen Wayne 1952- *WhoFI 92*
**Bruneau**, Bill 1948- *WhoWest 92*
**Bruneau**, Charles Emile, Jr 1942- *WhoAmP 91*
**Bruneau**, Leslie Herbert 1928- *AmMWSc 92*
**Bruneau**, William Joseph, Jr. 1947- *WhoRel 92*
**Bruneaux**, Debra Louise 1953- *WhoEnt 92*
**Brunei**, Sultan of *IntWW 91, Who 92*
**Brunel**, Dean Curtis 1940- *WhoAmL 92*
**Brunel**, Pierre 1931- *AmMWSc 92*
**Brunell**, Geoffrey 1945- *TwCPaSc*
**Brunell**, Gloria Florette 1925- *AmMWSc 92*
**Brunell**, Karl 1922- *AmMWSc 92*
**Brunell**, Philip Alfred 1931- *AmMWSc 92*
**Brunelle**, Eugene John, Jr 1932- *AmMWSc 92*
**Brunelle**, Paul-Edouard 1936- *AmMWSc 92*
**Brunelle**, Richard Leon 1937- *AmMWSc 92*
**Brunelle**, Thomas E 1935- *AmMWSc 92*
**Brunelli**, Louis Jean *WhoEnt 92*
**Brunello**, Rosanne 1960- *WhoWest 92*
**Brunengraber**, Henri 1940- *AmMWSc 92*
**Brunenkant**, Jon Lodwick 1950- *WhoAmL 92*
**Bruner**, Barbara Stephenson 1931- *AmMWSc 92*
**Bruner**, Charles Hughes 1948- *WhoAmP 91*
**Bruner**, Dorsey William 1906- *AmMWSc 92*
**Bruner**, Harry Davis 1911- *AmMWSc 92*
**Bruner**, James Dowden 1864-1945 *DcNCBi 1*
**Bruner**, James Ernest 1952- *WhoEnt 92*
**Bruner**, Jeffrey Marc 1946- *WhoMW 92*
**Bruner**, Jerome S. 1915- *WrDr 92*
**Bruner**, Jerome Seymour 1915- *IntWW 91, Who 92*
**Bruner**, John Joseph 1817-1890 *DcNCBi 1*
**Bruner**, Laman Harmon, Jr. 1917- *WhoRel 92*
**Bruner**, Leon James 1931- *AmMWSc 92*
**Bruner**, Leonard Bretz, Jr 1921- *AmMWSc 92*
**Bruner**, Mabel D 1916- *WhoAmP 91*
**Bruner**, Madelin Eve 1938- *WhoEnt 92*
**Bruner**, Marilyn E 1934- *AmMWSc 92*
**Bruner**, Millie *WhoAmP 91*
**Bruner**, Nancy Skyles 1937- *WhoWest 92*
**Bruner**, Paul Daniel 1952- *WhoAmL 92*
**Bruner**, Philip Lane 1939- *WhoAmL 92*
**Bruner**, Stephen C. 1941- *WhoAmL 92*
**Bruner**, Tom 1945- *WhoEnt 92*
**Bruner**, Van B., Jr. 1931- *WhoBlA 92*
**Bruner**, Vincent Michael 1957- *WhoAmP 91*
**Bruner**, William Evans, II 1949- *WhoMW 92*
**Brunet**, Jacques 1901-1990 *IntWW 91, -91N*
**Brunet**, Marta 1897-1967 *SpAmWW*
**Brunet**, Pierre 1902-1991 *NewYTBS 91 [port]*
**Brunett**, Emery W 1927- *AmMWSc 92*
**Brunetta**, Renato 1950- *IntWW 91*
**Brunette**, Donald Maxwell 1944- *AmMWSc 92*
**Brunetti**, Frank Leo 1949- *WhoAmL 92*
**Brunetti**, Melvin T *WhoAmP 91*
**Brunetti**, Melvin T. 1933- *WhoAmL 92*
**Brunetti**, Wayne Henry 1942- *WhoFI 92*
**Brunfield**, Bruce Alton 1962- *WhoFI 92*
**Brungardt**, Helen Ruth 1931- *WhoRel 92, WhoWest 92*
**Brungardt**, Wayne Michael 1941- *WhoMW 92*
**Brungot**, Catherine V 1922- *WhoAmP 91*
**Brungot**, George Oliver Robert 1923- *WhoFI 92*
**Brungraber**, Robert J 1929- *AmMWSc 92*
**Brungs**, Robert Anthony 1931- *AmMWSc 92, WhoMW 92, WhoRel 92*
**Brungs**, William Aloysius 1932- *AmMWSc 92*
**Brunhart**, Hans 1945- *IntWW 91*
**Brunhes**, Jean 1869-1930 *FacFETw*
**Brunhild of Austrasia** d613 *EncAmaz 91*
**Bruni**, John Richard 1951- *WhoWest 92*
**Bruni**, Lev Aleksandrovich 1894-1948 *SovUnBD*
**Bruni-Sakraischik**, Claudio Alberico 1926- *IntWW 91*
**Bruning**, Donald Francis 1942- *AmMWSc 92*
**Bruning**, Heinrich 1885-1970 *EncTR 91 [port], FacFETw*
**Bruning**, Richard R. *IntMPA 92*
**Brunings**, Karl John 1913- *AmMWSc 92*
**Brunjes**, A S 1906- *AmMWSc 92*
**Brunjes**, Peter Crawford 1953- *AmMWSc 92*
**Brunk**, Clifford Franklin 1940- *AmMWSc 92*
**Brunk**, George E., III 1939- *WhoRel 92*
**Brunk**, Gunter William 1934- *WhoFI 92*
**Brunk**, Hugh Daniel 1919- *AmMWSc 92*
**Brunk**, William Edward 1928- *AmMWSc 92*
**Brunkan**, Walter Leo 1930- *WhoRel 92*
**Brunkard**, Kathleen Marie 1953- *AmMWSc 92*
**Brunke**, Karen J 1952- *AmMWSc 92*
**Brunken**, Gerald Walter, Sr. 1938- *WhoMW 92*
**Brunn**, David Kevin 1956- *WhoWest 92*
**Brunner**, Carl Alan 1934- *AmMWSc 92*
**Brunner**, Charlotte 1948- *AmMWSc 92*
**Brunner**, David Derstine 1938- *WhoRel 92*
**Brunner**, David Lee 1953- *WhoEnt 92*
**Brunner**, Earl Chester, Jr. 1924- *WhoWest 92*
**Brunner**, Edward A 1929- *AmMWSc 92*
**Brunner**, Emil 1889-1966 *FacFETw*
**Brunner**, Franz Von Sales *DcAmImH*
**Brunner**, Gail Ann 1953- *WhoAmL 92*
**Brunner**, Gordon Francis 1938- *AmMWSc 92, WhoFI 92*
**Brunner**, Guido 1930- *IntWW 91, Who 92*
**Brunner**, Jay Robert 1918- *AmMWSc 92*
**Brunner**, John 1934- *TwCSFW 91, WrDr 92*
**Brunner**, John Henry Kilian 1927- *Who 92*
**Brunner**, John Kilian Houston 1934- *IntAu&W 91*
**Brunner**, Ludwig 1954- *WhoEnt 92*
**Brunner**, Marguerite Ashworth 1913- *WrDr 92*
**Brunner**, Mary Martinez 1945- *WhoMW 92*
**Brunner**, Mathias J 1922- *AmMWSc 92*
**Brunner**, Michael 1943- *AmMWSc 92*
**Brunner**, Robert Francis 1938- *WhoEnt 92, WhoWest 92*
**Brunner**, Robert Lee 1945- *AmMWSc 92*
**Brunner**, Stephen James 1952- *WhoFI 92*
**Brunni**, Conni M. 1961- *WhoWest 92*
**Brunning**, David Wilfrid 1943- *Who 92*
**Brunning**, Richard Dale 1932- *AmMWSc 92*
**Brunnow**, Franz Friedrich Ernst 1821-1891 *BiInAmS*
**Bruno**, Anthony 1947- *WhoEnt 92*
**Bruno**, Charles Frank 1936- *AmMWSc 92*
**Bruno**, David Joseph 1951- *AmMWSc 92*
**Bruno**, Frank A. 1962- *WhoEnt 92*
**Bruno**, Frank Alan 1955- *WhoMW 92*
**Bruno**, Frank Eugene 1945- *WhoEnt 92*
**Bruno**, Frank Michael 1955- *WhoWest 92*
**Bruno**, George C 1942- *WhoAmP 91*
**Bruno**, Grace Angelia 1935- *WhoFI 92*
**Bruno**, Harold Robinson, III 1960- *WhoAmL 92*
**Bruno**, Joseph L 1929- *WhoAmP 91*
**Bruno**, Judyth Ann 1944- *WhoWest 92*
**Bruno**, Kevin Joseph 1958- *WhoAmL 92*
**Bruno**, Kim G. 1955- *WhoAmL 92*
**Bruno**, Louis Leonard, Jr. 1947- *WhoFI 92*
**Bruno**, Mauro Adamauro 1933- *WhoEnt 92*
**Bruno**, Merle Sanford 1939- *AmMWSc 92*
**Bruno**, Michael 1932- *IntWW 91*
**Bruno**, Michael B. 1948- *WhoBlA 92*
**Bruno**, Michael Stephen 1958- *AmMWSc 92*
**Bruno**, Nicholas Joseph 1938- *WhoFI 92*
**Bruno**, Ronald C 1946- *AmMWSc 92*
**Bruno**, Ronald G. *WhoFI 92*
**Bruno**, Stephen Francis 1948- *AmMWSc 92*
**Bruno**, Teresa Puckett 1961- *WhoAmL 92*
**Bruno**, Thomas J 1954- *AmMWSc 92*
**Bruno**, Vincent James 1933- *WhoAmP 91*
**Bruns**, Billy Lee 1925- *WhoMW 92*
**Bruns**, Charles Alan 1930- *AmMWSc 92*
**Bruns**, Danny Lee 1949- *WhoFI 92*
**Bruns**, David Eugene *AmMWSc 92*
**Bruns**, Donald Gene 1952- *AmMWSc 92*
**Bruns**, Herbert Arnold 1950- *AmMWSc 92*
**Bruns**, Lester George 1933- *AmMWSc 92*
**Bruns**, Mark Robert 1952- *WhoMW 92*
**Bruns**, Mark William 1963- *WhoWest 92*
**Bruns**, Nicolaus, Jr. 1926- *WhoAmL 92*
**Bruns**, Patricia Jane 1925- *WhoAmP 91*
**Bruns**, Paul Donald 1914- *AmMWSc 92*
**Bruns**, Paul Eric 1915- *AmMWSc 92*
**Bruns**, Peter John 1942- *AmMWSc 92*
**Bruns**, Robert Frederick *AmMWSc 92*
**Bruns**, Roy Edward 1941- *AmMWSc 92*
**Bruns**, William John, Jr. 1935- *WhoFI 92, WrDr 92*
**Brunschwig**, Bruce Samuel 1944- *AmMWSc 92*
**Brunsdale**, Anne E *WhoAmP 91*
**Brunsdale**, Mitzi Louisa Mallarian 1939- *WhoMW 92*
**Brunsden**, Denys 1936- *Who 92*
**Brunsdon**, Norman Keith 1930- *Who 92*
**Brunsen**, William Henry 1940- *WhoWest 92*
**Brunser**, Oscar 1935- *AmMWSc 92*
**Brunski**, John Beyer 1949- *AmMWSc 92*
**Brunskill**, Gregg John 1941- *AmMWSc 92*
**Brunskill**, Ronald William 1929- *IntAu&W 91, Who 92, WrDr 92*
**Brunson**, Clayton 1921- *AmMWSc 92*
**Brunson**, Debora Bradley 1952- *WhoBlA 92*
**Brunson**, Donald Ellard 1946- *WhoFI 92*
**Brunson**, Dorothy 1938- *ConBlB 1 [port]*
**Brunson**, Dorothy E. 1938- *WhoEnt 92*
**Brunson**, Dorothy Edwards 1938- *WhoBlA 92*
**Brunson**, Hugh Ellis 1927- *WhoAmL 92*
**Brunson**, Jack E 1956- *WhoIns 92*
**Brunson**, Jack Rushing 1928- *WhoIns 92*
**Brunson**, John Soles 1934- *WhoFI 92*
**Brunson**, John Taylor 1940- *AmMWSc 92*
**Brunson**, Royal Bruce 1914- *AmMWSc 92*
**Brunsting**, Elmer H 1921- *AmMWSc 92*
**Brunsvig**, Per 1917- *IntWW 91*
**Brunsvold**, Brian Garrett 1938- *WhoAmL 92*
**Brunsvold**, Joel Dean 1942- *WhoAmP 91*
**Brunt**, Peter Astbury 1917- *IntWW 91, Who 92*
**Brunt**, Peter William 1936- *Who 92*
**Brunt**, Samuel, Captain *ScFEYrs*
**Brunt**, Samuel Jay 1961- *WhoBlA 92*
**Bruntisfield**, Baron 1899- *Who 92*
**Brunton**, Edward Francis Lauder 1916- *Who 92*
**Brunton**, George Delbert 1924- *AmMWSc 92*
**Brunton**, Gordon 1921- *Who 92*
**Brunton**, Gordon Charles 1921- *IntWW 91*
**Brunton**, Lauder *Who 92*
**Brunton**, Laurence 1947- *AmMWSc 92*
**Brunton**, Mary 1778-1818 *RfGEnL 91*
**Brunton**, Paul D 1944- *WhoAmP 91*
**Brunvand**, Dana Kari 1964- *WhoWest 92*
**Brupbacher**, Frederick Arnold, II 1954- *WhoFI 92*
**Brus**, Louis Eugene 1943- *AmMWSc 92*
**Brus**, Wlodzimierz 1921- *IntWW 91, Who 92*
**Brusca**, Frank Xavier 1956- *WhoEnt 92*
**Brusca**, Gary J 1939- *AmMWSc 92*
**Brusca**, Richard Charles 1945- *AmMWSc 92*
**Brusca**, Robert Andrew 1950- *WhoFI 92*
**Bruscantini**, Sesto 1919- *NewAmDM*
**Bruscke**, Mark Karl 1951- *WhoFI 92*
**Brusenback**, Robert A 1927- *AmMWSc 92*
**Brusewitz**, Gerald Henry 1942- *AmMWSc 92*
**Brusewitz**, Gunnar 1924- *IntAu&W 91*
**Brush**, Alan Howard 1934- *AmMWSc 92*
**Brush**, B Joseph, Jr *WhoAmP 91*
**Brush**, Charles Benjamin 1848-1897 *BiInAmS*
**Brush**, David Elden 1950- *WhoEnt 92, WhoFI 92, WhoWest 92*
**Brush**, Duane Carter 1950- *WhoRel 92*
**Brush**, F Robert 1929- *AmMWSc 92*
**Brush**, George Jarvis 1831-1912 *BiInAmS*
**Brush**, Grace Somers 1931- *AmMWSc 92*
**Brush**, James S 1929- *AmMWSc 92*
**Brush**, John 1912- *AmMWSc 92*
**Brush**, Katharine 1902-1952 *BenetAL 91*
**Brush**, Louis Frederick 1946- *WhoAmL 92*
**Brush**, Lucien M, Jr 1929- *AmMWSc 92*
**Brush**, Miriam Kelly 1915- *AmMWSc 92*
**Brush**, Ruth Damaris *WhoEnt 92*
**Brush**, Sally Anderson 1934- *WhoMW 92*
**Brush**, Stephen George *AmMWSc 92*
**Brush**, Thomas *DrAPF 91*
**Brushaber**, George Karl 1938- *WhoRel 92*
**Brushwyler**, Lawrence Ronald 1936- *WhoRel 92*
**Brusie**, James Powers 1918- *AmMWSc 92*
**Brusiloff**, Paul David *WhoEnt 92*
**Brusilow**, Anshel 1928- *NewAmDM, WhoEnt 92*
**Brusilow**, Saul W 1927- *AmMWSc 92*
**Bruski**, Betty Jean 1927- *WhoAmP 91*
**Bruski**, Paul Steven 1949- *WhoMW 92*
**Bruskin Grisha**, Brouskine Grigori 1945- *IntWW 91*
**Brusko**, Marlene Guimond 1940- *WhoMW 92*
**Bruso**, Robert Arthur 1939- *WhoRel 92*
**Brussard**, Peter Frans 1938- *AmMWSc 92*
**Brusse**, James A. 1934- *WhoHisp 92*
**Brussel**, Morton Kremen 1929- *AmMWSc 92*
**Brussof**, Valery *ScFEYrs*
**Brust**, David 1935- *WhoWest 92*
**Brust**, David Philip 1934- *AmMWSc 92*
**Brust**, Harry Francis 1914- *AmMWSc 92*

**Brust,** Leo 1916- *WhoRel 92*
**Brust,** Manfred 1923- *AmMWSc 92*
**Brust,** Reinhart A 1934- *AmMWSc 92*
**Brust,** Susan Melinda 1951- *WhoFI 92*
**Brustad,** Orin Daniel 1941- *WhoAmL 92*
**Brustad,** Tor 1926- *IntWW 91*
**Brustad,** Wesley O. 1943- *WhoWest 92*
**Brustein,** Abram Isaac 1946- *WhoFI 92*
**Brustein,** Robert 1927- *IntWW 91, WrDr 92*
**Brustein,** Robert Sanford 1927- *WhoEnt 92*
**Brustman,** Jayson Allan 1957- *WhoAmL 92*
**Brustowicz,** Paul M 1944- *WhoIns 92*
**Brusven,** Merlyn Ardel 1937- *AmMWSc 92*
**Brutcher,** Frederick Vincent, Jr 1922- *AmMWSc 92*
**Brutents,** Karen Nersesovich 1924- *IntWW 91*
**Brutlag,** Douglas Lee 1946- *AmMWSc 92*
**Bruton,** Bertram A. 1931- *WhoBlA 92*
**Bruton,** Dorothy Virginia 1945- *WhoRel 92*
**Bruton,** Eric 1915- *IntAu&W 91, WrDr 92*
**Bruton,** John 1947- *Who 92*
**Bruton,** John Fletcher 1861-1946 *DcNCBi 1*
**Bruton,** John Gerard 1947- *IntWW 91*
**Bruton,** John Macaulay 1937- *WhoFI 92*
**Bruton,** Margo Olwen 1951- *WhoEnt 92*
**Bruton,** Marvin Dwayne 1945- *WhoAmP 91*
**Bruton,** O. Grant 1931- *WhoAmL 92*
**Brutosky,** Mary Veronica 1932- *WhoWest 92*
**Brutsaert,** Wilfried 1934- *AmMWSc 92*
**Brutten,** Gene J 1928- *AmMWSc 92, WhoMW 92*
**Brutus,** Dennis 1924- *BlkLC [port], ConAu 14AS [port], ConPo 91, IntWW 91, LiExTwC, WrDr 92*
**Brutus,** Dennis Vincent 1924- *IntAu&W 91, WhoBlA 92*
**Brutvan,** Donald Richard 1924- *AmMWSc 92*
**Bruvold,** Kathleen Parker *WhoAmL 92*
**Bruyas,** Alfred 1801-1873 *ThHEIm [port]*
**Bruyere,** Andre 1912- *DcTwDes*
**Bruyere,** Harold Joseph, Jr. 1947- *WhoWest 92*
**Bruynzeel,** Chris John 1966- *WhoRel 92*
**Bry,** Edith d1991 *NewYTBS 91*
**Bry,** Jeffrey Allen 1949- *WhoMW 92*
**Bry,** Laura Felicia 1961- *WhoEnt 92*
**Bryan,** Adelbert M 1943- *WhoAmP 91, WhoBlA 92*
**Bryan,** Albert Hugh 1874-1920 *BiInAmS*
**Bryan,** Alice Ricca 1940- *WhoWest 92*
**Bryan,** Alonzo Jay 1917- *WhoWest 92*
**Bryan,** Arthur 1923- *IntWW 91, Who 92*
**Bryan,** Ashley Monroe 1917- *AmMWSc 92*
**Bryan,** Barry Richard 1930- *WhoAmL 92*
**Bryan,** Billy Bird 1921- *AmMWSc 92*
**Bryan,** C Clark 1910- *WhoIns 92*
**Bryan,** C.D.B. *DrAPF 91, SourALJ*
**Bryan,** Cardis William, Jr. 1938- *WhoMW 92, WhoRel 92*
**Bryan,** Carl Eddington 1917- *AmMWSc 92*
**Bryan,** Carter Byrd 1945- *WhoIns 92*
**Bryan,** Charles Englert 1946- *WhoAmL 92*
**Bryan,** Charles F 1937- *AmMWSc 92*
**Bryan,** Charles Shepard 1865-1956 *DcNCBi 1*
**Bryan,** Christopher F 1951- *AmMWSc 92*
**Bryan,** Clarice 1923- *WhoBlA 92*
**Bryan,** Clifton A 1930- *WhoAmP 91*
**Bryan,** Curtis *WhoBlA 92*
**Bryan,** David A 1946- *AmMWSc 92*
**Bryan,** David Barclay 1933- *WhoAmL 92*
**Bryan,** David Everett, Jr. 1947- *WhoBlA 92*
**Bryan,** David Tennant 1906- *WhoFI 92*
**Bryan,** Dora 1923- *WhoEnt 92*
**Bryan,** Dora 1924- *IntMPA 92, Who 92*
**Bryan,** Edward H 1924- *AmMWSc 92*
**Bryan,** Elizabeth Letson 1874-1919 *BiInAmS*
**Bryan,** Eugene Francis 1937- *WhoFI 92*
**Bryan,** Flize A. *WhoBlA 92*
**Bryan,** Ford R. 1912- *ConAu 134*
**Bryan,** Francis Lee, III 1951- *WhoFI 92*
**Bryan,** Frank Leon 1930- *AmMWSc 92*
**Bryan,** George 1731-1791 *BlkwEAR*
**Bryan,** George Terrell 1932- *AmMWSc 92*
**Bryan,** George Thomas 1930- *AmMWSc 92*
**Bryan,** Gerald Jackson 1921- *Who 92*
**Bryan,** Gordon Henry 1915- *AmMWSc 92*
**Bryan,** Gordon Redman, Jr. 1928- *WhoWest 92*
**Bryan,** Harris Leden, Sr 1935- *WhoAmP 91*
**Bryan,** Harrison 1923- *WrDr 92*
**Bryan,** Hayden Gitt 1945- *WhoAmP 91*
**Bryan,** Henry H. d1835 *DcNCBi 1*
**Bryan,** Henry Ravenscroft 1836-1919 *DcNCBi 1*
**Bryan,** Herbert Harris 1932- *AmMWSc 92*
**Bryan,** Hob 1952- *WhoAmP 91*
**Bryan,** Horace Alden 1928- *AmMWSc 92*
**Bryan,** Howard F 1942- *WhoAmP 91*
**Bryan,** Jacob F, IV 1943- *WhoIns 92*
**Bryan,** James Augustus 1839-1923 *DcNCBi 1*
**Bryan,** James Bevan 1926- *AmMWSc 92*
**Bryan,** James Bicknell 1947- *WhoMW 92*
**Bryan,** James Clarence 1923- *AmMWSc 92*
**Bryan,** James E, Jr 1948- *WhoAmP 91*
**Bryan,** James West 1805-1864 *DcNCBi 1*
**Bryan,** Jean Marie Wehmueller 1964- *WhoMW 92*
**Bryan,** Jesse A. 1939- *WhoBlA 92*
**Bryan,** Joan Carr 1944- *WhoRel 92*
**Bryan,** John Henry 1936- *IntWW 91, WhoFI 92, WhoMW 92*
**Bryan,** John Henry Donald 1926- *AmMWSc 92*
**Bryan,** John Herritage 1798-1870 *DcNCBi 1*
**Bryan,** John Kent 1936- *AmMWSc 92*
**Bryan,** John L. 1949- *WhoAmL 92*
**Bryan,** John Rodney 1953- *WhoWest 92*
**Bryan,** John Stewart, III 1938- *WhoFI 92*
**Bryan,** John Wesley 1942- *WhoEnt 92*
**Bryan,** Joseph *AmMWSc 92*
**Bryan,** Joseph Hunter 1782-1840 *DcNCBi 1*
**Bryan,** Joseph Shepard 1894-1974 *DcNCBi 1*
**Bryan,** Joseph Shepard, Jr. 1922- *WhoAmL 92, WhoFI 92*
**Bryan,** Kirk 1929- *AmMWSc 92*
**Bryan,** L L 1920- *WhoAmP 91*
**Bryan,** Lawrence Dow 1945- *WhoMW 92*
**Bryan,** Margaret 1929- *Who 92*
**Bryan,** Marsha Lynne 1946- *WhoMW 92*
**Bryan,** Mildred Gott *WhoAmL 92*
**Bryan,** Monk 1914- *WhoRel 92*
**Bryan,** Morgan 1671-1763 *DcNCBi 1*
**Bryan,** Nathan 1748-1798 *DcNCBi 1*
**Bryan,** Norman E. 1947- *WhoMW 92*
**Bryan,** Paul 1913- *Who 92*
**Bryan,** Paul Robey, Jr. *WhoEnt 92*
**Bryan,** Philip R. *WhoRel 92*
**Bryan,** Philip Steven 1944- *AmMWSc 92*
**Bryan,** Richard H. 1937- *AlmAP 92 [port], IntWW 91, WhoAmP 91, WhoWest 92*
**Bryan,** Richard Ray 1932- *WhoFI 92*
**Bryan,** Robert Fessler 1913- *WhoFI 92*
**Bryan,** Robert Finlay 1933- *AmMWSc 92*
**Bryan,** Robert H 1924- *AmMWSc 92*
**Bryan,** Robert J. 1934- *WhoAmL 92, WhoWest 92*
**Bryan,** Robert Neff 1939- *AmMWSc 92*
**Bryan,** Robert Patrick 1926- *Who 92*
**Bryan,** Ronald Arthur 1932- *AmMWSc 92*
**Bryan,** Roy *DrAPF 91*
**Bryan,** Samuel 1726?-1798 *DcNCBi 1*
**Bryan,** Sara E 1922- *AmMWSc 92*
**Bryan,** Scott Roydeen 1959- *WhoMW 92*
**Bryan,** Sharon Ann 1941- *WhoWest 92*
**Bryan,** Thomas Lynn 1935- *WhoAmL 92*
**Bryan,** Thomas T 1925- *AmMWSc 92*
**Bryan,** Thornton Embry 1927- *AmMWSc 92*
**Bryan,** Washington 1853-1927 *DcNCBi 1*
**Bryan,** Wayne Clarence 1934- *WhoFI 92*
**Bryan,** Wilbur Lowell 1921- *AmMWSc 92*
**Bryan,** Wilfred Bottrill 1932- *AmMWSc 92*
**Bryan,** William 1733?-1780 *DcNCBi 1*
**Bryan,** William Jennings 1860-1925 *AmPeW, AmPolLe [port], BenetAL 91, FacFETw, RComAH, RelLAm 91*
**Bryan,** William L 1928- *AmMWSc 92*
**Bryan,** William Phelan 1930- *AmMWSc 92*
**Bryan,** William Shepard 1827-1906 *DcNCBi 1*
**Bryan,** William Wright d1991 *NewYTBS 91*
**Bryan,** Wright 1905-1991 *ConAu 133*
**Bryans,** Alexander 1921- *AmMWSc 92*
**Bryans,** Anne 1909- *Who 92*
**Bryans,** Charles Iverson, Jr 1919- *AmMWSc 92*
**Bryans,** John Thomas 1924- *AmMWSc 92*
**Bryans,** Richard W. 1931- *WhoAmL 92*
**Bryans,** Richard Waldron, Jr. 1955- *WhoEnt 92*
**Bryans,** Robin H 1928- *IntAu&W 91*
**Bryans,** Tom 1920- *Who 92*
**Bryans,** Trabue Daley 1952- *AmMWSc 92*
**Bryanston,** Hilary 1951- *TwCPaSc*
**Bryant,** Alan Christopher 1923- *Who 92*
**Bryant,** Alan Willard, Jr. 1940- *WhoFI 92, WhoWest 92*
**Bryant,** Andrea Pair 1942- *WhoBlA 92*
**Bryant,** Anthony 1963- *WhoBlA 92*
**Bryant,** Anxious E. 1938- *WhoBlA 92*
**Bryant,** Archer Goodney 1949- *WhoWest 92*
**Bryant,** Arthur H. 1954- *WhoAmL 92*
**Bryant,** Arthur L 1934- *WhoIns 92*
**Bryant,** Barbara Everitt 1926- *AmMWSc 92*
**Bryant,** Barty Wyatt 1952- *WhoEnt 92*
**Bryant,** Ben S 1923- *AmMWSc 92*
**Bryant,** Benjamin 1905- *Who 92*
**Bryant,** Betty Jane 1926- *WhoMW 92*
**Bryant,** Beverley Brown 1942- *WhoAmP 91*
**Bryant,** Billy Finney 1922- *AmMWSc 92*
**Bryant,** Britain Hamilton 1940- *WhoAmP 91*
**Bryant,** Bruce Hazelton 1930- *AmMWSc 92*
**Bryant,** Carol Lee 1946- *WhoWest 92*
**Bryant,** Castell Vaughn *WhoBlA 92*
**Bryant,** Cecil Farris 1914- *WhoAmP 91*
**Bryant,** Celia Mae Small 1913- *WhoEnt 92*
**Bryant,** Christopher *Who 92*
**Bryant,** Clarence 1928- *WhoBlA 92*
**Bryant,** Clarence W. 1931- *WhoBlA 92*
**Bryant,** Clovis *WhoAmP 91*
**Bryant,** Connie L. 1936- *WhoBlA 92*
**Bryant,** Cunningham C. 1921- *WhoBlA 92*
**Bryant,** David 1951- *WhoAmL 92*
**Bryant,** David John 1931- *Who 92*
**Bryant,** David Michael Arton 1942- *Who 92*
**Bryant,** David Steve 1921- *WhoEnt 92*
**Bryant,** David Thompson 1924- *WhoAmL 92*
**Bryant,** Delores Hall E. 1935- *WhoBlA 92*
**Bryant,** Demetrius Edward 1956- *WhoRel 92*
**Bryant,** Denis William 1918- *Who 92*
**Bryant,** Derek Thomas 1933- *Who 92*
**Bryant,** Don Estes 1917- *WhoWest 92*
**Bryant,** Donald G 1927- *AmMWSc 92*
**Bryant,** Donald L., Jr. 1942- *WhoFI 92*
**Bryant,** Donald Loudon 1908- *WhoFI 92*
**Bryant,** Donnie L. 1942- *WhoBlA 92*
**Bryant,** Dorothy 1930- *IntAu&W 91, WrDr 92*
**Bryant,** Douglas Wallace 1913- *IntWW 91*
**Bryant,** Edward *DrAPF 91*
**Bryant,** Edward 1945- *TwCSFW 91, WrDr 92*
**Bryant,** Edward Clark 1915- *AmMWSc 92*
**Bryant,** Edward Joe, III 1947- *WhoBlA 92*
**Bryant,** Edwin 1805-1869 *BenetAL 91*
**Bryant,** Ernest Atherton 1931- *AmMWSc 92*
**Bryant,** Faye B. 1937- *WhoBlA 92*
**Bryant,** Felice *WhoEnt 92*
**Bryant,** Flossie Byrd 1907- *WhoAmP 91*
**Bryant,** Gary Allen 1951- *WhoAmL 92*
**Bryant,** Gary David 1949- *WhoAmL 92*
**Bryant,** Gary Jones 1942- *WhoRel 92*
**Bryant,** Gay 1945- *WrDr 92*
**Bryant,** George Macon 1926- *AmMWSc 92*
**Bryant,** Gerald C. 1954- *WhoEnt 92*
**Bryant,** Glenn D 1918- *AmMWSc 92*
**Bryant,** Glenn E *WhoAmP 91*
**Bryant,** Greyham Frank 1931- *Who 92*
**Bryant,** Henry 1820-1867 *BiInAmS*
**Bryant,** Henry C. 1915- *WhoBlA 92*
**Bryant,** Henry Edward Cowan 1873-1967 *DcNCBi 1*
**Bryant,** Howard Carnes 1933- *AmMWSc 92*
**Bryant,** Howard Sewall 1928- *AmMWSc 92*
**Bryant,** Hubert Hale 1931- *WhoBlA 92*
**Bryant,** Hurley Douglas, Jr. 1944- *WhoWest 92*
**Bryant,** Ira Houston, III 1942- *WhoAmL 92*
**Bryant,** Isaac Rutledge 1914- *WhoBlA 92*
**Bryant,** James Bruce 1961- *WhoAmL 92*
**Bryant,** James W. 1922- *WhoBlA 92*
**Bryant,** Janice Elaine 1950- *WhoFI 92*
**Bryant,** Jeff Dwight 1960- *WhoBlA 92*
**Bryant,** Jenkins, Jr *WhoAmP 91, WhoBlA 92*
**Bryant,** Jerome Benjamin 1916- *WhoBlA 92*
**Bryant,** Jerri Lynn Saunders 1961- *WhoAmL 92*
**Bryant,** Jerry Doyle 1947- *WhoAmP 91*
**Bryant,** Jesse A. 1922- *WhoBlA 92*
**Bryant,** Jo Elizabeth 1937- *WhoAmP 91*
**Bryant,** John 1947- *AlmAP 92 [port]*
**Bryant,** John Bradbury 1947- *WhoFI 92*
**Bryant,** John Frederick 1955- *WhoEnt 92*
**Bryant,** John H 1920- *AmMWSc 92*
**Bryant,** John Harland 1925- *AmMWSc 92*
**Bryant,** John Logan 1940- *AmMWSc 92*
**Bryant,** John Richard 1943- *WhoBlA 92*
**Bryant,** John Wiley 1947- *WhoAmP 91*
**Bryant,** John William, Jr 1957- *WhoAmP 91*
**Bryant,** Joseph Allen, Jr 1919- *IntAu&W 91, WrDr 92*
**Bryant,** Joseph Decatur 1845-1914 *BiInAmS*
**Bryant,** Judith Marie 1942- *Who 92*
**Bryant,** Karen Worstell 1942- *WhoFI 92*
**Bryant,** Kelvin LeRoy 1960- *WhoBlA 92*
**Bryant,** Lawrence E, Jr 1936- *AmMWSc 92*
**Bryant,** Lester R. 1930- *WhoMW 92*
**Bryant,** Lester Richard 1930- *AmMWSc 92*
**Bryant,** Louise 1885-1936 *LiExTwC*
**Bryant,** Louise 1887-1936 *HanAmWH*
**Bryant,** Marcus David 1924- *WhoRel 92*
**Bryant,** Mark 1965- *WhoBlA 92*
**Bryant,** Mark Joseph Lee 1961- *WhoAmL 92*
**Bryant,** Marvin Pierce 1925- *AmMWSc 92*
**Bryant,** Michael 1928- *IntWW 91*
**Bryant,** Michael 1940- *WhoRel 92*
**Bryant,** Michael David 1951- *AmMWSc 92*
**Bryant,** Michael Dennis 1928- *Who 92*
**Bryant,** N. Z., Jr. 1949- *WhoMW 92*
**Bryant,** Nancy Troskowski 1953- *WhoFI 92*
**Bryant,** Napoleon Adebola, Jr. 1929- *WhoBlA 92*
**Bryant,** Noel F. 1945- *WhoAmL 92*
**Bryant,** Patricia Sand 1940- *AmMWSc 92*
**Bryant,** Paul James 1929- *AmMWSc 92*
**Bryant,** Peter *TwCSFW 91*
**Bryant,** Peter Elwood *Who 92*
**Bryant,** Peter George Francis 1932- *Who 92*
**Bryant,** Peter James *AmMWSc 92*
**Bryant,** Preston 1938- *WhoBlA 92*
**Bryant,** R. Kelly, Jr. 1917- *WhoBlA 92*
**Bryant,** Ralph Clement 1913- *AmMWSc 92*
**Bryant,** Rebecca Smith 1955- *AmMWSc 92*
**Bryant,** Regina Lynn 1950- *WhoBlA 92*
**Bryant,** Rhys 1936- *AmMWSc 92*
**Bryant,** Richard Charles 1908- *Who 92*
**Bryant,** Robert E. 1910- *WhoBlA 92*
**Bryant,** Robert Edward 1931- *WhoBlA 92*
**Bryant,** Robert Emory 1942- *AmMWSc 92*
**Bryant,** Robert George 1943- *AmMWSc 92*
**Bryant,** Robert Harry 1925- *IntAu&W 91, WhoRel 92, WrDr 92*
**Bryant,** Robert L 1928- *AmMWSc 92*
**Bryant,** Robert Monroe 1966- *WhoFI 92*
**Bryant,** Robert Wesley *AmMWSc 92*
**Bryant,** Robert William 1925- *AmMWSc 92*
**Bryant,** Rosalyn 1956- *BlkOlyM*
**Bryant,** Roy 1923- *WhoRel 92*
**Bryant,** Shirley Hills 1924- *AmMWSc 92*
**Bryant,** Stephen G 1951- *AmMWSc 92*
**Bryant,** Steven Harry 1946- *WhoWest 92*
**Bryant,** Susan Victoria 1943- *AmMWSc 92*
**Bryant,** Sylvia Leigh 1947- *IntAu&W 91*
**Bryant,** T. J. 1934- *WhoBlA 92*
**Bryant,** Taimie L. 1953- *WhoAmL 92*
**Bryant,** Teresena Wise 1940- *WhoBlA 92*
**Bryant,** Thomas 1938- *Who 92*
**Bryant,** Thomas Edward 1936- *AmMWSc 92, IntWW 91*
**Bryant,** Timothy Paul 1961- *WhoRel 92*
**Bryant,** Vaughn Motley, Jr 1940- *AmMWSc 92*
**Bryant,** Wayne R. 1947- *WhoBlA 92*
**Bryant,** Wayne Richard 1947- *WhoAmP 91*
**Bryant,** Willa Coward 1919- *WhoBlA 92*
**Bryant,** William Arnett, Jr. 1942- *WhoBlA 92*
**Bryant,** William B. 1911- *WhoAmL 92*
**Bryant,** William Benson 1911- *WhoBlA 92*
**Bryant,** William Cullen 1794-1878 *BenetAL 91*
**Bryant,** William Cullen 1951- *WhoBlA 92*
**Bryant,** William Henry, Jr. 1963- *WhoBlA 92*
**Bryant,** William Jesse 1935- *WhoBlA 92*
**Bryant,** William M *WhoAmP 91*
**Bryant,** William R, Jr 1938- *WhoAmP 91*
**Bryant,** William Richards 1930- *AmMWSc 92*
**Bryant,** William Stanley 1943- *AmMWSc 92*
**Bryant,** Winston 1938- *WhoAmL 92, WhoAmP 91*
**Bryant-Greenwood,** Gillian Doreen 1942- *AmMWSc 92*
**Bryant-Mitchell,** Ruth Harriet 1943- *WhoBlA 92*
**Bryant-Reid,** Johanne 1949- *WhoBlA 92*
**Bryars,** Donald Leonard 1929- *Who 92*
**Bryars,** Gavin 1943- *ConCom 92, IntWW 91*
**Bryars,** John Desmond 1928- *Who 92*
**Bryce** *Who 92*
**Bryce,** Gabe Robb 1921- *Who 92*
**Bryce,** Gale Rex 1939- *AmMWSc 92*
**Bryce,** Gordon *Who 92*
**Bryce,** Gordon 1943- *TwCPaSc*
**Bryce,** Herrington J. *WhoBlA 92*
**Bryce,** Hugh Glendinning 1917- *AmMWSc 92*
**Bryce,** Jabez Leslie *Who 92*
**Bryce,** James *BenetAL 91*
**Bryce,** Ken 1956- *TwCPaSc*
**Bryce,** Lloyd 1851-1917 *ScFEYrs*
**Bryce,** William Delf 1932- *WhoAmL 92*

**Bryce,** William Gordon 1913- Who 92
**Bryce-Laporte,** Roy Simon 1933- WhoBlA 92
**Bryce-Smith,** Derek 1926- Who 92
**Brychel,** Rudolph Myron 1934- WhoWest 92
**Bryden,** David John 1943- Who 92
**Bryden,** Harry Leonard 1946- AmMWSc 92
**Bryden,** John 1943- ConAu 134
**Bryden,** John Heilner 1920- AmMWSc 92
**Bryden,** Robert Richmond 1916- AmMWSc 92
**Bryden,** Wayne A 1955- AmMWSc 92
**Bryden,** William Campbell Rough 1942- Who 92
**Brydges,** Harold A 1858-1939 ScFEYrs
**Brydges,** Louis Worthington, Sr. 1932- WhoAmL 92
**Brydges,** Samuel Egerton 1762-1837 DcLB 107 [port]
**Brydon,** Harold Wesley 1923- WhoFI 92, WhoWest 92
**Brydon,** James Emerson 1928- AmMWSc 92
**Brydon,** Ruth Vickery 1930- WhoWest 92
**Bryer,** Anthony Applemore Mornington 1937- Who 92
**Bryers,** William John 1955- WhoAmL 92
**Bryggman,** Larry 1938- ConTFT 9
**Bryman,** Douglas Andrew 1945- AmMWSc 92
**Bryman,** Jeff Philip 1956- WhoAmL 92
**Brymer,** Jack 1915- IntWW 91, Who 92
**Bryn-Julson,** Phyllis 1945- NewAmDM
**Brynd,** Scott Richard 1954- WhoEnt 92
**Brynelson,** Floyd A. 1914- WhoAmL 92
**Bryner,** Charles Leslie 1914- AmMWSc 92
**Bryner,** John C 1931- AmMWSc 92
**Bryner,** John Henry 1924- AmMWSc 92
**Bryner,** Joseph S 1920- AmMWSc 92
**Bryngdahl,** Olof 1933- AmMWSc 92
**Bryngelson,** Jim 1941- WhoWest 92
**Bryngil,** Judith Anne 1958- WhoAmL 92
**Brynielsson,** Harry Anders Bertil 1914- IntWW 91
**Brynildson,** Oscar Marius 1916- AmMWSc 92
**Bryning,** Frank 1907- TwCSFW 91
**Brynjolfsson,** Ari 1926- AmMWSc 92
**Brynn,** Edward P 1942- WhoAmP 91
**Brynner,** Yul 1915-1985 FacFETw
**Bryon,** Kathleen 1922- IntMPA 92
**Brysac,** Shareen Blair WhoEnt 92
**Brysk,** Miriam Mason 1935- AmMWSc 92
**Bryson,** Arthur E, Jr 1925- AmMWSc 92
**Bryson,** Arthur Joseph 1946- WhoAmL 92
**Bryson,** Bruce Alan Randy 1946- WhoWest 92
**Bryson,** Dorothy Printup 1894- WhoWest 92
**Bryson,** Dyan Carol 1956- WhoBlA 92
**Bryson,** Gary Spath 1943- WhoEnt 92, WhoFI 92
**Bryson,** George Gardner 1935- AmMWSc 92
**Bryson,** James Graeme 1913- Who 92
**Bryson,** John 1923- ConAu 133
**Bryson,** John E. 1943- WhoFI 92
**Bryson,** Joseph Raleigh 1893-1953 DcNCBi 1
**Bryson,** Julie Ann 1956- WhoMW 92
**Bryson,** Lindsay 1925- Who 92
**Bryson,** Lindsay Sutherland 1925- IntWW 91
**Bryson,** Marion Ritchie 1927- AmMWSc 92
**Bryson,** Melvin Joseph 1916- AmMWSc 92
**Bryson,** Ralph J. 1922- WhoBlA 92
**Bryson,** Reid Allen 1920- AmMWSc 92, WhoMW 92
**Bryson,** Rick Neeley 1957- WhoAmL 92
**Bryson,** Seymour L. 1937- WhoBlA 92
**Bryson,** Thomas Allan 1944- AmMWSc 92
**Bryson,** W. Hamilton 1941- ConAu 36NR
**Bryson,** William Shields 1946- WhoEnt 92
**Bryson,** Winfred Octavus, Jr. 1915- WhoBlA 92
**Brytczuk,** Gary Albert 1947- WhoFI 92
**Brytczuk,** Walter L 1907- AmMWSc 92
**Bryukhanov,** Nikolay Pavlovich 1878-1942 SovUnBD
**Bryusov,** Valeriy Yakovlevich 1873-1924 SovUnBD
**Bryusov,** Valery 1873-1924 TwCSFW 91A
**Bryusov,** Valery Yakovlevich 1873-1924 FacFETw
**Brzana,** Stanislaus Joseph 1917- WhoRel 92
**Brzenk,** Ronald Michael 1949- AmMWSc 92
**Brzezinski,** Zbigniew 1928- WhoAmP 91, WrDr 92
**Brzezinski,** Zbigniew K. 1928- IntWW 91
**Brzezinski,** Zbigniew Kazimierz 1928- AmPolLe
**Brzozowski,** Janusz Antoni 1935- AmMWSc 92
**Brzustowski,** Thomas Anthony 1937- AmMWSc 92
**Brzycki,** James Joseph 1952- WhoFI 92, WhoMW 92
**Bschorr,** Paul Joseph 1941- WhoAmL 92
**Bu He** 1926- IntWW 91
**Bu,** Charles Qiyue 1958- WhoMW 92
**Bua,** Nicholas John 1925- WhoAmL 92, WhoMW 92
**Buaia,** Fam 1939- WhoRel 92
**Buanann** EncAmaz 91
**Buatta,** Mario 1935- CurBio 91 [port]
**Bub,** Alexander David 1949- WhoMW 92
**Bubalo,** Gregory Joe 1955- WhoAmL 92
**Bubar,** John Stephen 1929- AmMWSc 92
**Bubash,** James Edward 1945- WhoMW 92
**Bubb,** Brian David 1962- WhoWest 92
**Bubb,** David Lester 1958- WhoRel 92
**Bubb,** Harry Geiple 1924- WhoWest 92
**Bubba,** Joseph L 1938- WhoAmP 91
**Bube,** Richard H. 1927- WrDr 92
**Bube,** Richard Howard 1927- AmMWSc 92
**Bubeck,** Robert Clayton 1937- AmMWSc 92
**Bubeck,** Roy R 1946- WhoIns 92
**Bubel,** Hans Curt 1925- AmMWSc 92
**Bubenzer,** Gary Dean 1940- AmMWSc 92
**Buber,** Martin 1878-1965 FacFETw [port], LiExTwC
**Bubka,** Sergey 1964- IntWW 91, SovUnBD
**Bublitz,** Clark 1927- AmMWSc 92
**Bublitz,** Donald Edward 1935- AmMWSc 92
**Bublitz,** Larry Elmer 1941- WhoMW 92
**Bublitz,** Walter John, Jr 1920- AmMWSc 92
**Bubnic,** Anne Marie 1949- WhoWest 92
**Bubnov,** Andrei Sergeyevich 1883-1940? FacFETw
**Bubnov,** Andrey Sergeevich 1883-1940 SovUnBD
**Bubulka,** Grace Marie 1951- WhoWest 92
**Buc,** Nancy Lillian 1944- WhoAmL 92
**Bucalossi,** Pietro 1905- IntWW 91
**Bucard,** Marcel 1895-1946 BiDExR
**Bucareli y Ursua,** Antonio Maria de 1717-1779 HisDSpE
**Bucaro,** Kathleen Therese 1959- WhoMW 92
**Buccafusco,** Jerry Joseph 1949- AmMWSc 92
**Buccella,** William Victor 1943- WhoAmL 92, WhoFI 92
**Bucchi,** Ronald A. 1955- WhoFI 92
**Bucchieri,** Peter Charles 1955- WhoFI 92
**Bucci,** Anthony J 1925- WhoAmP 91
**Bucci,** Elaine Theresa 1957- WhoAmP 91
**Bucci,** Enrico 1932- AmMWSc 92
**Bucci,** Maurizio 1923- IntWW 91
**Bucci,** Robert James 1941- AmMWSc 92
**Bucci,** Thomas WhoAmP 91
**Bucci,** Thomas Joseph 1934- AmMWSc 92
**Buccieri,** M. Elaine 1960- WhoAmL 92
**Buccigrossi,** David Eric 1956- WhoWest 92
**Buccino,** Alphonse 1931- AmMWSc 92
**Buccino,** Ernest John, Jr. 1945- WhoAmL 92
**Buccino,** Salvatore George 1933- AmMWSc 92
**Buccleuch,** Duke of 1923- Who 92
**Bucco,** Martin 1929- WhoWest 92
**Buccola,** Steven Thomas 1944- AmMWSc 92
**Bucerius,** Gerd 1906- IntWW 91
**Buch,** Eva-Maria 1921-1943 EncTR 91
**Buch,** Rene Augusto 1925- WhoHisp 92
**Buch,** Walter 1883-1946 BiDExR
**Buch,** Walter 1883-1949 EncTR 91 [port]
**Bucha,** Edward Richard 1954- WhoFI 92
**Buchachenko,** Anatoliy Leonidovich 1935- IntWW 91
**Buchal,** Robert Norman 1930- AmMWSc 92
**Buchalter,** Stuart David 1937- WhoFI 92
**Buchan** Who 92
**Buchan,** Earl of 1930- Who 92
**Buchan,** David 1939- IntAu&W 91
**Buchan,** Eric Ancrum 1907- Who 92
**Buchan,** George Colin 1927- AmMWSc 92
**Buchan,** Hamish Noble 1944- WhoFI 92
**Buchan,** James Ellis, Jr. 1951- WhoAmL 92, WhoRel 92
**Buchan,** Janey 1926- Who 92
**Buchan,** John 1873-1940 ScFEYrs
**Buchan,** John 1875-1940 FacFETw, RfGEnL 91, TwCLC 41 [port]
**Buchan,** John 1912- Who 92
**Buchan,** Norman 1922-1990 AnObit 1990
**Buchan,** Norman Findlay d1990 Who 92N
**Buchan,** Stevenson 1907- Who 92
**Buchan,** Thomas Johnston Who 92
**Buchan,** Tom 1931- ConPo 91, IntAu&W 91, WrDr 92
**Buchan-Hepburn,** Ninian 1922- Who 92
**Buchan of Auchmacoy,** David William S 1929- Who 92
**Buchanan,** Alexander Stanley 1953- WhoAmL 92
**Buchanan,** Andrew George 1937- Who 92
**Buchanan,** Angela Marie 1948- WhoAmP 91
**Buchanan,** Beverly Anne 1946- WhoWest 92
**Buchanan,** Bob Branch 1937- AmMWSc 92
**Buchanan,** Brenda J. WhoFI 92
**Buchanan,** Bruce G 1940- AmMWSc 92
**Buchanan,** Bryce John 1965- WhoWest 92
**Buchanan,** Charles Alexander James L. Who 92
**Buchanan,** Charles Duffy 1950- WhoAmL 92
**Buchanan,** Charles Franklin 1936- WhoAmP 91
**Buchanan,** Charlotte Stark WhoAmL 92
**Buchanan,** Christine Elizabeth 1946- AmMWSc 92
**Buchanan,** Colin 1907- Who 92
**Buchanan,** Colin 1934- WrDr 92
**Buchanan,** Colin Douglas 1907- IntWW 91
**Buchanan,** Colin Ogilvie 1934- Who 92
**Buchanan,** Colin Ogilvie 1936- IntAu&W 91
**Buchanan,** David 1944- WhoFI 92
**Buchanan,** David Bradley 1938- WhoMW 92
**Buchanan,** David Hamilton 1942- AmMWSc 92
**Buchanan,** David Roy 1953- WhoAmL 92
**Buchanan,** David Royal 1934- AmMWSc 92
**Buchanan,** David Shane 1953- AmMWSc 92
**Buchanan,** Dennis Who 92
**Buchanan,** Ed Buck 1948- WhoEnt 92
**Buchanan,** Edison Cherrington 1954- WhoFI 92
**Buchanan,** Edward A. 1937- WhoMW 92
**Buchanan,** Edward Bracy, Jr 1927- AmMWSc 92
**Buchanan,** George Dale 1928- AmMWSc 92
**Buchanan,** George Duncan Who 92
**Buchanan,** George Duncan 1935- IntWW 91
**Buchanan,** George R 1939- AmMWSc 92
**Buchanan,** Gerald Wallace 1943- AmMWSc 92
**Buchanan,** Harry Eugene 1898-1974 DcNCBi 1
**Buchanan,** Hayle 1925- AmMWSc 92
**Buchanan,** Hubert A 1905- IntAu&W 91
**Buchanan,** Hugh 1958- TwCPaSc
**Buchanan,** Isobel 1954- IntWW 91
**Buchanan,** Isobel Wilson 1954- Who 92
**Buchanan,** J Robert 1928- AmMWSc 92, IntWW 91
**Buchanan,** J. Vincent Marino 1951- WhoAmL 92
**Buchanan,** J W WhoAmP 91
**Buchanan,** Jack Evon 1934- WhoWest 92
**Buchanan,** James 1791-1868 AmPolLe [port], BenetAL 91, RComAH
**Buchanan,** James J. 1925- WrDr 92
**Buchanan,** James M. 1919- WrDr 92
**Buchanan,** James McGill 1919- IntWW 91, Who 92, WhoFI 92, WhoNob 90
**Buchanan,** James Wesley 1937- AmMWSc 92
**Buchanan,** John WhoAmP 91
**Buchanan,** John Brett 1949- WhoMW 92
**Buchanan,** John Chalkley 1911- WhoAmP 91
**Buchanan,** John David 1916- Who 92
**Buchanan,** John Donald 1927- AmMWSc 92
**Buchanan,** John Hall, Jr 1928- WhoAmP 91
**Buchanan,** John Machlin 1917- AmMWSc 92, IntWW 91
**Buchanan,** John MacLennan 1931- IntWW 91, WhoAmL 92
**Buchanan,** Jonet Marie 1959- WhoEnt 92
**Buchanan,** Lovell 1949- WhoEnt 92
**Buchanan,** Marie WrDr 92
**Buchanan,** Marie 1922- IntAu&W 91
**Buchanan,** Mary Estill 1934- WhoAmP 91
**Buchanan,** Michael A 1949- WhoAmP 91
**Buchanan,** Minor Ferris 1951- WhoAmL 92
**Buchanan,** Otis 1951- WhoBlA 92
**Buchanan,** Patrick J. LesBEnT 92
**Buchanan,** Patrick Joseph 1938- IntWW 91, WhoAmP 91
**Buchanan,** Paul D 1938- WhoAmP 91
**Buchanan,** Paul Murray 1931- WhoAmL 92
**Buchanan,** Peter 1925- Who 92
**Buchanan,** Peter Townley 1934- WhoFI 92
**Buchanan,** Ranald Dennis 1932- Who 92
**Buchanan,** Randall John 1930- WhoEnt 92
**Buchanan,** Ray Allen 1947- WhoRel 92
**Buchanan,** Relva Chester 1936- AmMWSc 92
**Buchanan,** Richard 1912- Who 92
**Buchanan,** Richard Lee 1947- WhoAmL 92
**Buchanan,** Roberdeau 1839-1916 BiInAmS
**Buchanan,** Robert Alexander 1932- AmMWSc 92
**Buchanan,** Robert Angus 1930- Who 92, WrDr 92
**Buchanan,** Robert Eugene, Jr. 1956- WhoRel 92
**Buchanan,** Robert Fulton 1955- WhoFI 92
**Buchanan,** Robert Lester 1946- AmMWSc 92
**Buchanan,** Robert Martin 1951- AmMWSc 92
**Buchanan,** Robert McLeod 1932- WhoAmL 92
**Buchanan,** Robert Michael 1953- WhoMW 92
**Buchanan,** Robert Rhinehart, Jr. 1951- WhoRel 92
**Buchanan,** Robert Williams 1848-1901 ScFEYrs
**Buchanan,** Robert Wilson 1930- Who 92
**Buchanan,** Ronald James 1938- AmMWSc 92
**Buchanan,** Ronald Leslie 1937- AmMWSc 92
**Buchanan,** Ronnie Joe 1944- AmMWSc 92
**Buchanan,** Russell Allen 1928- AmMWSc 92
**Buchanan,** Sonny 1934- WhoEnt 92
**Buchanan,** Teri Bailey 1946- WhoFI 92
**Buchanan,** Thomas Joseph 1929- AmMWSc 92
**Buchanan,** William Hobart, Jr. 1937- WhoAmL 92, WhoFI 92
**Buchanan,** William Jennings 1948- WhoAmL 92
**Buchanan,** William Murray 1935- WhoMW 92
**Buchanan,** William Russell 1957- WhoWest 92
**Buchanan-Crosbie,** Anne 1919- TwCPaSc
**Buchanan-Davidson,** Dorothy Jean 1925- AmMWSc 92
**Buchanan-Dunlop,** Richard 1919- Who 92
**Buchanan-Jardine,** A. R. J. Who 92
**Buchanan-Smith,** Alick Laidlaw d1991 Who 92N
**Buchanan-Smith,** Jock Gordon 1940- AmMWSc 92
**Buchberg,** Harry 1917- AmMWSc 92
**Buchbinder,** Darrell Bruce 1946- WhoAmL 92
**Buchbinder,** Jonathan 1960- WhoFI 92
**Buchbinder-Green,** Barbara Joyce 1944- WhoMW 92
**Buchdahl,** Gerd 1914- WrDr 92
**Bucheger,** Ronald R. 1948- WhoWest 92
**Bucheister,** Patt 1942- WrDr 92
**Buchel,** Johannes A 1926- AmMWSc 92
**Buchele,** W F 1920- AmMWSc 92
**Buchele,** Wesley Fisher 1920- WhoMW 92
**Buchenau,** George William 1932- AmMWSc 92
**Buchenholz,** Jane Jacobs 1918- WhoAmP 91
**Bucher,** Francois 1927- WrDr 92
**Bucher,** George Scott 1942- WhoIns 92
**Bucher,** John Henry 1939- AmMWSc 92
**Bucher,** Nancy L R 1913- AmMWSc 92
**Bucher,** Otto Norman 1933- WhoRel 92
**Bucher,** Ronald E. 1959- WhoAmL 92
**Bucher,** T T Nelson 1919- AmMWSc 92
**Buchert,** Thomas Vincent 1946- WhoMW 92
**Buchheim,** H Paul 1947- AmMWSc 92
**Buchheim,** Lothar-Gunther 1918- IntWW 91
**Buchheit,** Richard D 1924- AmMWSc 92
**Buchholz,** Allan C 1940- AmMWSc 92
**Buchholz,** Carolyn Leigh 1955- WhoAmL 92
**Buchholz,** David Louis 1936- WhoFI 92
**Buchholz,** Donald Alden 1929- WhoFI 92
**Buchholz,** Horst 1933- IntMPA 92
**Buchholz,** James Joseph 1947- WhoRel 92
**Buchholz,** Jeffrey Carl 1947- AmMWSc 92, WhoFI 92
**Buchholz,** R Alan AmMWSc 92
**Buchholz,** Robert Henry 1924- AmMWSc 92
**Buchholz,** Scot Alan 1959- WhoFI 92
**Buchholz,** William Edward 1942- WhoMW 92
**Buchholz,** William James 1945- WhoFI 92
**Buchholz Shaw,** Donna Marie 1950- AmMWSc 92
**Buchi,** George 1921- AmMWSc 92
**Buchi,** George H. 1921- IntWW 91
**Buchignani,** Leo Joseph, Jr. 1954- WhoAmL 92
**Buchin,** Irving D 1920- AmMWSc 92
**Buchin,** Stanley Ira 1931- WhoFI 92
**Buchinski,** Michael J. 1957- WhoEnt 92
**Buchla,** Donald 1937- NewAmDM

**Buchler,** Edward Raymond 1942- *AmMWSc 92*
**Buchler,** Jean-Robert 1942- *AmMWSc 92*
**Buchler,** Justus d1991 *NewYTBS 91 [port]*
**Buchler,** Justus 1914-1991 *ConAu 134*
**Buchma,** Amvrozy Maksimilyanovich 1891-1957 *SovUnBD*
**Buchman,** Elwood 1923- *AmMWSc 92*
**Buchman,** Frank 1878-1961 *FacFETw*
**Buchman,** Frank Nathan Daniel 1878-1961 *RelLAm 91*
**Buchman,** Kenneth William 1956- *WhoAmL 92*
**Buchman,** Lorne M. *WhoEnt 92*
**Buchman,** Marion *DrAPF 91*
**Buchman,** Matthew Lieber 1958- *WhoWest 92*
**Buchman,** Russell 1947- *AmMWSc 92*
**Buchman,** Seth Barry 1955- *WhoAmL 92*
**Buchmann,** Alan Paul 1934- *WhoAmL 92, WhoAmP 91*
**Buchmann,** George Allen 1920- *WhoAmL 92*
**Buchmeyer,** Jerry 1933- *WhoAmL 92*
**Buchner,** Eduard 1860-1917 *FacFETw, WhoNob 90*
**Buchner,** James 1932- *WhoFI 92*
**Buchner,** Morgan M, Jr 1939- *AmMWSc 92*
**Buchner,** Stephen Peter 1945- *AmMWSc 92*
**Bucholtz,** Alan Howard 1937- *WhoAmL 92*
**Bucholtz,** Dennis Lee 1951- *AmMWSc 92*
**Buchsbaum,** David Alvin 1929- *AmMWSc 92*
**Buchsbaum,** Gershon 1949- *AmMWSc 92*
**Buchsbaum,** Herbert Joseph 1934- *AmMWSc 92*
**Buchsbaum,** Monte Stuart 1940- *AmMWSc 92*
**Buchsbaum,** Peter A. 1945- *WhoAmL 92*
**Buchsbaum,** Ralph 1907- *AmMWSc 92*
**Buchsbaum,** Solomon J. 1929- *IntWW 91*
**Buchsbaum,** Solomon Jan 1929- *AmMWSc 92, WhoFI 92*
**Buchsieb,** Walter Charles 1929- *WhoMW 92*
**Bucht,** Gunnar 1927- *ConCom 92*
**Buchta,** John C 1927- *AmMWSc 92*
**Buchta,** Raymond Charles 1942- *AmMWSc 92*
**Buchtel,** Henry Augustus, IV 1942- *AmMWSc 92*
**Buchthal,** David C 1943- *AmMWSc 92*
**Buchthal,** Fritz 1907- *IntWW 91*
**Buchthal,** Hugh H. 1909- *IntWW 91*
**Buchthal,** Hugo 1909- *Who 92*
**Buchwald,** Art 1925- *IntAu&W 91, IntWW 91, Who 92, WrDr 92*
**Buchwald,** Caryl Edward 1937- *AmMWSc 92*
**Buchwald,** Don David 1944- *WhoAmL 92*
**Buchwald,** Elias 1924- *WhoFI 92*
**Buchwald,** Emilie *DrAPF 91*
**Buchwald,** Henry 1932- *AmMWSc 92, WhoMW 92*
**Buchwald,** Jennifer S 1930- *AmMWSc 92*
**Buchwald,** Joseph 1917- *WhoEnt 92*
**Buchwald,** Lee E. 1958- *WhoFI 92*
**Buchwald,** Martyn Jerel 1942- *WhoEnt 92*
**Buchwald,** Naomi Reice 1944- *WhoAmL 92*
**Buchwald,** Nathaniel Avrom 1925- *AmMWSc 92*
**Buchy,** G James 1940- *WhoAmP 91*
**Bucio,** Paz Guadalupe 1942- *WhoHisp 92*
**Buck,** Albert Charles 1910- *Who 92*
**Buck,** Alfred A 1921- *AmMWSc 92*
**Buck,** Antony 1928- *Who 92*
**Buck,** Carl John 1929- *AmMWSc 92*
**Buck,** Carol Whitlow 1925- *AmMWSc 92*
**Buck,** Carolyn E. Burrel *WhoWest 92*
**Buck,** Charles 1915- *AmMWSc 92*
**Buck,** Charles Elon 1919- *AmMWSc 92*
**Buck,** Charles Frank 1920- *AmMWSc 92*
**Buck,** Christian Brevoort Zabriskie 1914- *WhoFI 92, WhoWest 92*
**Buck,** Clayton Arthur 1937- *AmMWSc 92*
**Buck,** David Homer 1920- *AmMWSc 92*
**Buck,** Douglas L 1931- *AmMWSc 92*
**Buck,** Dudley 1839-1909 *NewAmDM*
**Buck,** Earl Chris 1947- *WhoMW 92*
**Buck,** Earl Wayne 1939- *WhoMW 92*
**Buck,** Ernest Mauro 1930- *AmMWSc 92*
**Buck,** F A Mackinnon 1920- *AmMWSc 92*
**Buck,** Frank 1884-1950 *BenetAL 91*
**Buck,** Frank F 1943- *WhoAmP 91*
**Buck,** Fred A 1945- *WhoIns 92*
**Buck,** George Sumner, Jr 1914- *AmMWSc 92*
**Buck,** Griffith J 1915- *AmMWSc 92*
**Buck,** Gurdon Hall 1936- *WhoAmL 92*
**Buck,** Harry M. 1921- *WrDr 92*
**Buck,** Ivory M., Jr. 1928- *WhoBlA 92*
**Buck,** Jack *LesBEnT 92, WhoMW 92*
**Buck,** James R 1930- *AmMWSc 92*
**Buck,** Jean Coberg 1935- *AmMWSc 92*
**Buck,** John Bonner 1912- *AmMWSc 92*
**Buck,** John David 1935- *AmMWSc 92*
**Buck,** John Henry 1912- *AmMWSc 92*
**Buck,** Judith Brooks 1949- *WhoBlA 92*
**Buck,** Jules 1917- *IntMPA 92*
**Buck,** Keith Taylor 1940- *AmMWSc 92*
**Buck,** Lawrence Richard 1953- *WhoWest 92*
**Buck,** Leffert Lefferts 1837-1909 *BiInAmS*
**Buck,** Linda Dee 1946- *WhoWest 92*
**Buck,** Linda Susan 1949- *WhoAmL 92*
**Buck,** Lynn *DrAPF 91*
**Buck,** Margaret Waring 1910- *WrDr 92*
**Buck,** Marion Gilmour 1936- *AmMWSc 92*
**Buck,** Martin John 1951- *WhoMW 92*
**Buck,** Natalie Smith 1923- *WhoWest 92*
**Buck,** Otto 1933- *AmMWSc 92*
**Buck,** Paul 1927- *AmMWSc 92*
**Buck,** Pearl 1892-1973 *BenetAL 91, FacFETw [port]*
**Buck,** Pearl Comfort Sydenstricker 1892-1973 *AmPeW, WhoNob 90*
**Buck,** Pearl S 1892-1973 *ConAu 34NR*
**Buck,** Raymond Wilbur, Jr 1919- *AmMWSc 92*
**Buck,** Richard Clay 1962- *WhoFI 92*
**Buck,** Richard F 1921- *AmMWSc 92*
**Buck,** Richard Pierson 1929- *AmMWSc 92*
**Buck,** Robert Crawforth 1923- *AmMWSc 92*
**Buck,** Robert Creighton 1920- *AmMWSc 92*
**Buck,** Robert Edward 1912- *AmMWSc 92*
**Buck,** Robert Follette 1917- *IntWW 91*
**Buck,** Samuel Jay 1835-1918 *BiInAmS*
**Buck,** Stephen Henderson 1947- *AmMWSc 92*
**Buck,** Steven Wayne 1952- *WhoMW 92*
**Buck,** Thomas 1949- *WhoEnt 92*
**Buck,** Thomas Bryant, III 1938- *WhoAmP 91*
**Buck,** Thomas M 1920- *AmMWSc 92*
**Buck,** Thomas Randolph 1930- *WhoAmL 92*
**Buck,** Vernon Ashley, Jr. 1920- *WhoBlA 92*
**Buck,** Vince 1968- *WhoBlA 92*
**Buck,** Walter Hellier 1943- *WhoFI 92*
**Buck,** Warren Howard 1942- *AmMWSc 92*
**Buck,** Warren Louis 1921- *AmMWSc 92*
**Buck,** Warren W, III 1946- *AmMWSc 92*
**Buck,** William Boyd 1933- *AmMWSc 92*
**Buck,** William R 1950- *AmMWSc 92*
**Buckalew,** Louis Walter 1944- *AmMWSc 92*
**Buckalew,** Vardaman M, Jr 1933- *AmMWSc 92*
**Buckardt,** Everett L. *WhoMW 92*
**Buckardt,** Henry Lloyd 1904- *AmMWSc 92*
**Buckaway,** William Allen, Jr. 1934- *WhoAmL 92*
**Buckbee,** Albert W, II 1939- *WhoIns 92*
**Bucke,** Charles 1781-1846 *DcLB 110*
**Bucke,** Richard Maurice 1837-1902 *BenetAL 91*
**Buckel,** John Joseph 1951- *WhoRel 92*
**Buckelew,** Albert Rhoades, Jr 1942- *AmMWSc 92*
**Buckelew,** Joseph Earl 1929- *WhoAmP 91*
**Buckelew,** Thomas Paul 1943- *AmMWSc 92*
**Bucker,** Homer Park, Jr 1933- *AmMWSc 92*
**Buckeridge,** Anthony 1912- *WrDr 92*
**Buckeridge,** Anthony Malcolm 1912- *IntAu&W 91*
**Buckeye,** Donald Andrew 1930- *AmMWSc 92*
**Buckhalter,** Emerson R. 1954- *WhoBlA 92*
**Buckham,** James *ScFEYrs*
**Buckham,** James A 1925- *AmMWSc 92*
**Buckhanan,** Dorothy Wilson 1958- *WhoBlA 92*
**Buckholts,** Claudia *DrAPF 91*
**Buckholtz,** James Donnell 1935- *AmMWSc 92*
**Buckhouse,** John Chapple 1944- *AmMWSc 92*
**Buckhout,** Robert 1935-1990 *ConAu 133*
**Buckhoy,** Leroy 1938- *WhoFI 92*
**Buckhurst,** Lord 1979- *Who 92*
**Bucki,** Carl Leo 1953- *WhoAmL 92*
**Buckingham,** Archdeacon of *Who 92*
**Buckingham,** Area Bishop of 1928- *Who 92*
**Buckingham,** Duke of 1628-1687 *RfGEnL 91*
**Buckingham,** Alfred Carmichael 1931- *AmMWSc 92*
**Buckingham,** Amyand David 1930- *IntWW 91, Who 92*
**Buckingham,** Charles Herbert 1950- *WhoFI 92*
**Buckingham,** David Cowan 1951- *WhoAmL 92*
**Buckingham,** Edwin John, III 1947- *WhoAmL 92*
**Buckingham,** Hugh Fletcher 1932- *Who 92*
**Buckingham,** Kerry Joe 1951- *WhoMW 92*
**Buckingham,** Michael John 1943- *WhoWest 92*
**Buckingham,** Nancy *WrDr 92*
**Buckingham,** Richard Arthur 1911- *Who 92*
**Buckingham,** Vivian Leona 1925- *WhoAmP 91*
**Buckingham,** W Bruce 1955- *WhoAmP 91*
**Buckingham,** William Thomas 1921- *AmMWSc 92, WhoMW 92*
**Buckinghamshire,** Earl of 1944- *Who 92*
**Buckland,** Raymond 1934- *RelLAm 91*
**Buckland,** Roger Basil 1942- *AmMWSc 92*
**Buckland,** Ronald John Denys Eden 1920- *Who 92*
**Buckland,** Ross 1942- *Who 92*
**Buckland-Wright,** John 1897-1954 *TwCPaSc*
**Buckle,** Christopher Richard 1916- *Who 92*
**Buckle,** Denys Herbert Vintcent 1902- *Who 92*
**Buckle,** Edward Gilbert 1926- *Who 92*
**Buckle,** Richard *Who 92*
**Buckle,** Richard 1916- *IntWW 91, WrDr 92*
**Buckle,** Rodney 1945- *WhoEnt 92*
**Buckle,** Wayne Ford 1916- *WhoAmP 91*
**Buckler,** Ernest 1908-1984 *BenetAL 91, FacFETw*
**Buckler,** Ernest Jack 1914- *AmMWSc 92*
**Buckler,** Sheldon A 1931- *AmMWSc 92, WhoFI 92*
**Buckles,** Marjorie Fox 1922- *AmMWSc 92*
**Buckles,** Robert Edwin 1917- *AmMWSc 92*
**Buckles,** Robert Howard 1932- *WhoFI 92*
**Buckley** *Who 92*
**Buckley,** Agnes O'Connell 1931- *WhoAmP 91*
**Buckley,** Anna Patricia 1924- *WhoAmP 91*
**Buckley,** Anthony James Henthorne 1934- *Who 92*
**Buckley,** Betty 1947- *IntMPA 92*
**Buckley,** C Fitzgerald, III 1918- *WhoAmP 91*
**Buckley,** Cecelia Anne 1940- *WhoAmP 91*
**Buckley,** Charles Edward 1929- *AmMWSc 92*
**Buckley,** Charles Robinson, III 1942- *WhoAmL 92*
**Buckley,** Christopher *DrAPF 91*
**Buckley,** Christopher Henry, Jr. 1940- *WhoAmL 92*
**Buckley,** Conk, Jr. 1941- *WhoFI 92*
**Buckley,** Dale Eliot 1936- *AmMWSc 92*
**Buckley,** Denys 1906- *Who 92*
**Buckley,** Donald 1955- *IntMPA 92*
**Buckley,** Edward Harland 1931- *AmMWSc 92*
**Buckley,** Eric Joseph 1920- *Who 92*
**Buckley,** Ernest Robertson 1872-1912 *BiInAmS*
**Buckley,** Esther Gonzalez-Arroyo 1948- *WhoAmP 91, WhoHisp 92*
**Buckley,** Eugene Kenyon 1928- *WhoAmL 92*
**Buckley,** Francis Joseph 1928- *IntAu&W 91, WhoRel 92, WrDr 92*
**Buckley,** Fred Thomas 1951- *AmMWSc 92*
**Buckley,** Frederick Jean 1923- *WhoAmL 92*
**Buckley,** G. Brady, III 1960- *WhoFI 92*
**Buckley,** Gail Lumet 1937- *WhoBlA 92*
**Buckley,** George Eric 1916- *Who 92*
**Buckley,** George James d1991 *Who 92N*
**Buckley,** Ginny 1953- *WhoEnt 92*
**Buckley,** Glenn R 1943- *AmMWSc 92*
**Buckley,** Helen Ann 1926- *WhoAmL 92*
**Buckley,** Hilda Mayer 1948- *WhoMW 92*
**Buckley,** Horace Lawson 1941- *WhoAmP 91*
**Buckley,** J.B. 1937- *TwCPaSc*
**Buckley,** James 1923- *FacFETw*
**Buckley,** James 1944- *Who 92*
**Buckley,** James Arthur 1917- *Who 92*
**Buckley,** James L 1923- *WhoAmP 91*
**Buckley,** James Lane 1923- *IntWW 91, WhoAmL 92*
**Buckley,** James Monroe 1836-1920 *RelLAm 91*
**Buckley,** James Thomas 1942- *AmMWSc 92*
**Buckley,** James W. 1933- *WhoWest 92*
**Buckley,** Jay Selleck, Jr 1924- *AmMWSc 92*
**Buckley,** Jeremiah Stephen 1944- *WhoAmL 92*
**Buckley,** John 1913- *Who 92*
**Buckley,** John Dennis 1928- *AmMWSc 92*
**Buckley,** John Joseph 1929- *WhoAmP 91*
**Buckley,** John Joseph 1930- *WhoMW 92*
**Buckley,** John Joseph, Jr. 1944- *WhoMW 92*
**Buckley,** John P. 1967- *WhoRel 92*
**Buckley,** Joseph Edward, Jr. 1945- *WhoAmL 92*
**Buckley,** Joseph J 1922- *AmMWSc 92*
**Buckley,** Joseph Paul 1924- *AmMWSc 92*
**Buckley,** Joseph Thaddeus 1937- *AmMWSc 92*
**Buckley,** Joseph W. 1943- *WhoFI 92*
**Buckley,** Kenneth 1904- *Who 92*
**Buckley,** Kevin Joseph 1957- *WhoAmL 92*
**Buckley,** Martin Christopher Burton 1936- *Who 92*
**Buckley,** Michael Edward 1950- *WhoAmL 92*
**Buckley,** Michael Francis 1943- *WhoAmL 92*
**Buckley,** Michael Sydney 1939- *Who 92*
**Buckley,** Nancy Margaret 1924- *AmMWSc 92*
**Buckley,** Page Scott 1918- *AmMWSc 92*
**Buckley,** Paul Richard 1935- *WhoFI 92*
**Buckley,** Peter d1991 *NewYTBS 91*
**Buckley,** Peter 1938-1991 *ConAu 134*
**Buckley,** R Russ 1939- *AmMWSc 92*
**Buckley,** Ralph Eugene 1931- *WhoRel 92*
**Buckley,** Raymond Carl, II 1959- *WhoAmP 91*
**Buckley,** Rebecca Hatcher 1933- *AmMWSc 92*
**Buckley,** Richard 1928- *Who 92*
**Buckley,** Richard Bennett 1942- *WhoFI 92*
**Buckley,** Richard Edward 1953- *WhoEnt 92*
**Buckley,** Roger 1939- *Who 92*
**Buckley,** Samuel Botsford 1809-1884 *BiInAmS*
**Buckley,** Sheridan John 1930- *WhoMW 92*
**Buckley,** Stephen 1944- *IntWW 91, TwCPaSc*
**Buckley,** Thomas 1932- *WrDr 92*
**Buckley,** Timothy Andrew 1950- *WhoEnt 92*
**Buckley,** Trevor 1938- *Who 92*
**Buckley,** William Edwin 1937- *WhoIns 92*
**Buckley,** William F, Jr 1925- *FacFETw, RComAH, WrDr 92*
**Buckley,** William Frank, Jr. 1925- *IntWW 91, WhoAmP 91*
**Buckley,** William Kemmis 1921- *Who 92*
**Buckley,** William Randolph 1957- *WhoWest 92*
**Bucklin,** Dennis Arthur 1949- *WhoWest 92*
**Bucklin,** Donald Thomas 1938- *WhoAmL 92*
**Bucklin,** Leonard Herbert 1933- *WhoAmL 92, WhoMW 92*
**Bucklin,** Louis Pierre 1928- *WhoWest 92*
**Bucklin,** Patricia Kerr 1954- *WhoAmL 92*
**Bucklin,** Robert van Zandt 1916- *AmMWSc 92*
**Bucklo,** Elaine Edwards 1944- *WhoAmL 92*
**Buckman,** Alvin Bruce 1941- *AmMWSc 92*
**Buckman,** H H *ScFEYrs*
**Buckman,** Harley Royal 1907- *WhoFI 92*
**Buckman,** James F. *WhoWest 92*
**Buckman,** Peter 1941- *WrDr 92*
**Buckman,** Repha Joan 1942- *WhoEnt 92*
**Buckman,** Repha Joan Glenn 1942- *IntAu&W 91*
**Buckman,** Thomas Richard 1923- *WhoEnt 92*
**Buckman,** William Gordon 1934- *AmMWSc 92*
**Buckmaster** *Who 92*
**Buckmaster,** Viscount 1921- *Who 92*
**Buckmaster,** Cuthbert Harold Septimus 1903- *Who 92*
**Buckmaster,** Harvey Allen 1929- *AmMWSc 92*
**Buckmaster,** John David 1941- *AmMWSc 92*
**Buckmaster,** Maurice James 1902- *Who 92*
**Buckminster,** Joseph Stevens 1784-1812 *BenetAL 91*
**Buckmire,** Reginald Eugene 1938- *AmMWSc 92*
**Bucknall,** Barbara Jane 1933- *WrDr 92*
**Bucknam,** Deborah Jane 1946- *WhoAmL 92*
**Bucknam,** Robert Campbell 1940- *AmMWSc 92*
**Bucknell,** Larry Alan 1950- *WhoRel 92*
**Buckner,** Carl Kenneth *AmMWSc 92*
**Buckner,** Charles Henry 1928- *AmMWSc 92*
**Buckner,** David Lee 1948- *AmMWSc 92*
**Buckner,** Edwin R. 1914- *WhoBlA 92*
**Buckner,** Gail M 1950- *WhoAmP 91*
**Buckner,** Iris Bernell 1952- *WhoBlA 92*
**Buckner,** James L. 1934- *WhoBlA 92*
**Buckner,** James Stewart 1942- *AmMWSc 92*
**Buckner,** Linda Iverson 1950- *WhoFI 92*
**Buckner,** Mary Alice 1948- *WhoBlA 92*
**Buckner,** Milt 1915-1977 *NewAmDM*
**Buckner,** Ralph Gupton 1921- *AmMWSc 92*
**Buckner,** Regina Elizabeth 1948- *WhoFI 92*
**Buckner,** Richard Lee 1947- *AmMWSc 92*

**Buckner**, Robert H. 1906- *IntMPA 92*
**Buckner**, Sally *DrAPF 91*
**Buckner**, William Pat, Jr. 1929- *WhoBlA 92*
**Buckner**, William Quinn 1954- *BlkOlyM*
**Buckner Bright**, Rose Laminack 1945- *WhoMW 92*
**Buckney**, Edward L. 1929- *WhoBlA 92*
**Buckout**, William A 1846-1912 *BiInAmS*
**Buckson**, Toni Yvonne 1949- *WhoBlA 92*
**Buckstein**, Mark 1939- *IntWW 91*
**Buckstein**, Mark Aaron 1939- *WhoAmL 92, WhoFI 92*
**Buckstone**, John Baldwin 1802-1879 *RfGEnL 91*
**Buckton**, Raymond William 1922- *Who 92*
**Buckvar**, Felice *DrAPF 91*
**Buckwald**, Stephen Charles 1954- *WhoEnt 92*
**Buckwalter**, Gary Lee 1934- *AmMWSc 92*
**Buckwalter**, Joseph Addison 1920- *AmMWSc 92*
**Buckwalter**, Tracy Vere, Jr 1918- *AmMWSc 92*
**Buckwell**, Allan Edgar 1947- *Who 92*
**Buckwheat Zydeco** 1947?- *ConMus 6 [port]*
**Buckwold**, Sidney Joshua 1919- *AmMWSc 92*
**Buckworth**, Gerald Allan 1940- *WhoAmP 91*
**Buco**, Stephen W 1943- *WhoAmP 91*
**Bucovaz**, Edsel Tony 1928- *AmMWSc 92*
**Bucuzzo**, Estelle Lemire 1927- *WhoFI 92*
**Bucy**, J Fred 1928- *AmMWSc 92*
**Bucy**, Paul Clancy 1904- *AmMWSc 92*
**Bucy**, Richard Snowden 1935- *AmMWSc 92*
**Buczacki**, Stefan Tadeusz 1945- *IntAu&W 91*
**Buczak**, Douglas Chester 1949- *WhoFI 92, WhoMW 92*
**Buczko**, Thaddeus 1926- *WhoAmP 91*
**Buczkowski**, Arthur Walter 1930- *WhoEnt 92*
**Buda**, Fred C. 1935- *WhoEnt 92*
**Budagher**, John A 1946- *WhoAmP 91*
**Budai**, John David 1952- *AmMWSc 92*
**Budak**, Mary Kay *WhoAmP 91*
**Budantseyev**, Sergei Fedorovich 1896-1938? *FacFETw*
**Budapest**, Zsuzsanna E. 1940- *RelLAm 91*
**Budapest**, Zsuzsanna Emese 1940- *WhoWest 92*
**Buday**, Paul Vincent 1931- *AmMWSc 92*
**Budbill**, David *DrAPF 91*
**Budbill**, David 1940- *ConPo 91, WrDr 92*
**Budd**, Alan Peter 1937- *IntWW 91, Who 92*
**Budd**, Bernard Wilfred 1912- *Who 92*
**Budd**, Colin Richard 1945- *Who 92*
**Budd**, Dan S 1927- *WhoAmP 91*
**Budd**, David 1927-1991 *NewYTBS 91*
**Budd**, David Glenn 1934- *WhoAmL 92*
**Budd**, Donald Dean 1944- *WhoRel 92*
**Budd**, Edward H 1933- *WhoIns 92*
**Budd**, Edward Hey 1933- *WhoFI 92*
**Budd**, Geoffrey Colin 1935- *AmMWSc 92*
**Budd**, Harold 1936- *ConCom 92*
**Budd**, Hugh Christopher *Who 92*
**Budd**, Jim *WhoMW 92*
**Budd**, John H 1938- *WhoIns 92*
**Budd**, Joseph Lancaster 1835-1904 *BiInAmS*
**Budd**, Karen Jean 1957- *WhoAmL 92*
**Budd**, Leonard H. 1933- *WhoRel 92*
**Budd**, Mary Beth *WhoEnt 92*
**Budd**, Mavis *IntAu&W 91*
**Budd**, Rachel 1960- *TwCPaSc*
**Budd**, Robert Wesley 1956- *WhoWest 92*
**Budd**, Thomas d1698 *BenetAL 91*
**Budd**, Thomas Wayne 1946- *AmMWSc 92*
**Budd**, Timothy Alan 1955- *WhoWest 92*
**Budd**, Wayne A. *WhoAmL 92*
**Budd**, William Karl 1955- *WhoAmL 92*
**Budde**, Mary Laurence 1929- *AmMWSc 92*
**Budde**, Paul Bernard 1926- *AmMWSc 92*
**Budde**, William L 1934- *AmMWSc 92*
**Buddee**, Paul Edgar 1913- *IntAu&W 91, WrDr 92*
**Budden**, James Thomas 1941- *WhoFI 92*
**Budden**, Julian Medforth 1924- *Who 92*
**Budden**, Kenneth George 1915- *IntWW 91, Who 92*
**Buddenberg**, Hellmuth 1924- *IntWW 91*
**Buddenbohm**, Harold William 1959- *WhoWest 92*
**Buddenbohn**, Robert W 1929- *WhoIns 92*
**Buddenhagen**, Ivan William 1930- *AmMWSc 92*
**Budding**, Antonius Jacob 1922- *AmMWSc 92*
**Bude**, George James 1937- *WhoAmL 92*
**Budelman**, Robert Burns, Jr. 1937- *WhoAmL 92*
**Buden**, Rosemary V 1931- *AmMWSc 92*
**Budenny**, Semen Mikhaylovich 1883-1973 *SovUnBD*
**Budenny**, Semyon Mikhailovich 1883-1973 *FacFETw*
**Budenstein**, Paul Philip 1928- *AmMWSc 92*
**Budenz**, Julia *DrAPF 91*
**Buderer**, Melvin Charles 1941- *AmMWSc 92*
**Budge**, Don 1915- *FacFETw [port]*
**Budge**, Donald 1915- *IntWW 91*
**Budge**, Hamer Harold 1910- *WhoAmP 91*
**Budge**, Hamilton Whithed 1928- *WhoAmL 92*
**Budge**, Ian 1936- *IntAu&W 91, WrDr 92*
**Budge**, Reed William 1921- *WhoAmP 91*
**Budge**, Wallace Don 1933- *AmMWSc 92*
**Budgen**, Nicholas William 1937- *Who 92*
**Budgor**, Aaron Bernard 1948- *AmMWSc 92*
**Budiansky**, Bernard 1925- *AmMWSc 92*
**Budic**, Patrick Robert 1968- *WhoEnt 92*
**Budick**, Burton 1938- *AmMWSc 92*
**Budig**, Gene Arthur 1939- *WhoMW 92*
**Budil**, Edward Joseph, Jr. 1930- *WhoMW 92*
**Budin**, Beverly R. 1945- *WhoAmL 92*
**Budinger**, Charles Jude 1940- *WhoFI 92*
**Budinger**, Thomas Francis 1932- *AmMWSc 92*
**Budinski**, Kenneth Gerard 1939- *AmMWSc 92*
**Budke**, Clifford Charles 1932- *AmMWSc 92, WhoMW 92*
**Budkevics**, Girts Janis 1952- *WhoFI 92*
**Budler**, Melitta Mary 1952- *WhoMW 92*
**Budnick**, Ernest Joseph 1948- *WhoEnt 92, WhoFI 92*
**Budnick**, Joseph Ignatius 1929- *AmMWSc 92*
**Budnitz**, Arron Edward 1949- *WhoAmL 92*
**Budnitz**, Mark Elliott 1944- *WhoAmL 92*
**Budnitz**, Robert Jay 1940- *AmMWSc 92*
**Budny**, James Charles 1948- *WhoMW 92*
**Budny**, Robert Vierling 1942- *AmMWSc 92*
**Budow**, Leonard Norman 1956- *WhoAmL 92*
**Budowski**, Gerardo 1925- *AmMWSc 92, IntWW 91*
**Budrys**, Algis 1931- *ConAu 14AS [port], IntAu&W 91, TwCSFW 91, WrDr 92*
**Budrys**, Rimgaudas S 1925- *AmMWSc 92*
**Budson**, Susan B. 1943- *WhoAmL 92*
**Budy**, Andrea Hollander *DrAPF 91*
**Budyak**, James Thomas 1957- *WhoFI 92*
**Budyka**, Aleksandr Dmitrievich 1927- *IntWW 91*
**Budzak**, Kathryn Sue 1940- *WhoMW 92*
**Budzilovich**, Gleb Nicholas 1923- *AmMWSc 92*
**Budzinski**, James Edward 1953- *WhoWest 92*
**Budzinski**, Walter Valerian 1937- *AmMWSc 92*
**Budzinsky**, Armin Alexander 1942- *WhoFI 92*
**Bue**, Carl Olaf, Jr. 1922- *WhoAmL 92*
**Buech**, Richard Reed 1940- *AmMWSc 92*
**Bueche**, Frederick Joseph 1923- *AmMWSc 92*
**Bueche**, Wendell F. 1930- *IntWW 91*
**Buechel**, William Benjamin 1926- *WhoAmL 92*
**Buecheler**, Richard Gordon 1948- *WhoFI 92*
**Buechlein**, Daniel Mark 1938- *WhoRel 92*
**Buechler**, Jean Ann 1945- *WhoEnt 92, WhoMW 92*
**Buechner**, Carl Frederick 1926- *WhoRel 92*
**Buechner**, Frederick *DrAPF 91*
**Buechner**, Frederick 1926- *BenetAL 91, ConNov 91, WrDr 92*
**Buechner**, John William 1940- *WhoAmP 91*
**Buechner**, Margaret 1922- *WhoEnt 92*
**Buechner**, Robert William 1947- *WhoAmL 92*
**Buege**, Dennis Richard 1945- *AmMWSc 92*
**Buehler**, Charles John 1943- *WhoMW 92*
**Buehler**, Edwin Vernon 1929- *AmMWSc 92*
**Buehler**, J Frank 1919- *WhoAmP 91*
**Buehler**, Robert Joseph 1925- *AmMWSc 92*
**Buehler**, Thomas Lee 1948- *WhoAmL 92*
**Buehlmeier**, Harry Scott 1949- *WhoEnt 92*
**Buehnau**, Ludwig *ConAu 36NR*
**Buehrig**, Gordon M. 1904-1990 *DcTwDes*
**Buehrig**, James Otto, Jr. 1954- *WhoFI 92*
**Buehrig**, Marga *WhoRel 92*
**Buehring**, Gertrude Case 1940- *AmMWSc 92, WhoWest 92*
**Buel**, James Wes 1937- *WhoWest 92*
**Buel**, Jesse 1778-1839 *BiInAmS*
**Buel**, Richard David 1964- *WhoEnt 92*
**Bueler**, William Merwin 1934- *WrDr 92*
**Buell**, Carmen D *WhoAmP 91*
**Buell**, David Syme 1956- *WhoEnt 92*
**Buell**, Duncan Alan 1950- *AmMWSc 92*
**Buell**, Frederick 1942- *WrDr 92*
**Buell**, Frederick Henderson *DrAPF 91*
**Buell**, Frederick Henderson 1942- *IntAu&W 91*
**Buell**, Garrett Karl 1955- *WhoAmL 92*
**Buell**, Glen R 1931- *AmMWSc 92*
**Buell**, Guy Vaughn 1943- *WhoWest 92*
**Buell**, Kim James 1953- *WhoFI 92*
**Buell**, Lawrence Lee 1934- *WhoAmP 91*
**Buell**, Raymond Leslie 1896-1946 *AmPeW*
**Buell**, Robert C 1931- *WhoAmP 91*
**Buell**, Rodd Russell 1946- *WhoAmL 92*
**Buell**, Thomas Allan 1931- *WhoFI 92*
**Buell**, Victor P. 1914- *WrDr 92*
**Buelow**, Albert Henry 1934- *WhoRel 92*
**Buelow**, Edward Heller, Jr 1940- *WhoAmP 91*
**Buelow**, Frederick H 1929- *AmMWSc 92*
**Bueltel**, Joseph Anthony 1961- *WhoAmL 92*
**Buenger**, Barbara Copeland 1948- *WhoMW 92*
**Buening**, Gerald Matthew 1940- *AmMWSc 92*
**Bueno**, Antonio De Padua Jose Maria 1942- *Who 92*
**Buergel**, Bruno Hans 1875-1948 *ScFEYrs*
**Buerger**, David Bernard 1909- *WhoAmL 92*
**Buerger**, David Charles 1949- *WhoEnt 92*
**Buerger**, Jim 1940- *WhoAmP 91*
**Buerk**, Michael Duncan 1946- *Who 92*
**Buerkle**, Stephen Vincent 1951- *WhoFI 92*
**Buero-Vallejo**, Antonio 1916- *IntAu&W 91, IntWW 91*
**Bueschel**, David Alan 1942- *WhoFI 92*
**Buescher**, Brent J 1940- *AmMWSc 92*
**Buescher**, Daniel Marvin 1939- *WhoAmL 92*
**Buescher**, Kathleen Eleanor 1949- *WhoFI 92*
**Buescher**, Thomas Paul 1949- *WhoMW 92*
**Buesking**, Clarence W 1919- *AmMWSc 92*
**Buesser**, Frederick Gustavus, III 1941- *WhoAmL 92*
**Buestrin**, Mary F 1939- *WhoAmP 91*
**Buetens**, Eric D. 1953- *WhoAmL 92*
**Buetow**, Dennis Edward 1932- *AmMWSc 92*
**Buettner**, Carol Ann 1948- *WhoAmP 91*
**Buettner**, Garry Richard 1945- *AmMWSc 92*
**Buettner**, Harlan Dale 1957- *WhoRel 92*
**Buettner**, Joyce Margueritte 1937- *WhoAmP 91*
**Buettner**, Mark Roland 1949- *AmMWSc 92*
**Buettner**, Michael Lewis 1957- *WhoFI 92*
**Bufalini**, David Anthony 1952- *WhoAmL 92*
**Bufe**, Charles Glenn 1938- *AmMWSc 92*
**Buff**, Conrad 1886-1975 *ConAu 135*
**Buff**, Frank Paul 1924- *AmMWSc 92*
**Buff**, Gayle Helene 1951- *WhoFI 92*
**Buff**, Iva Moore 1932- *WhoEnt 92*
**Buff**, Mary 1890-1970 *ConAu 135*
**Buffalo Bird Woman** 1839-1929 *RelLAm 91*
**Buffaloe**, Neal Dollison 1924- *AmMWSc 92*
**Buffarini-Guidi**, Guido 1895-1945 *BiDExR*
**Buffenstein**, Allan S. 1940- *WhoAmL 92*
**Buffet**, Bernard 1928- *FacFETw, IntWW 91, Who 92*
**Buffett**, George D *WhoAmP 91*
**Buffett**, Jimmy 1946- *WhoEnt 92*
**Buffett**, Rita Frances 1917- *AmMWSc 92*
**Buffett**, Warren Edward 1930- *WhoFI 92, WhoMW 92*
**Buffington**, Andrew 1938- *AmMWSc 92*
**Buffington**, Bill J. 1938- *WhoMW 92*
**Buffington**, Edwin Conger 1920- *AmMWSc 92*
**Buffington**, F S 1916- *AmMWSc 92*
**Buffington**, Gary Lee Roy 1946- *WhoFI 92*
**Buffington**, J Larry 1953- *WhoAmP 91*
**Buffington**, John Douglas 1941- *AmMWSc 92*
**Buffington**, Linda Brice 1936- *WhoWest 92*
**Buffkins**, Archie Lee 1934- *WhoEnt 92*
**Buffler**, Charles Rogers 1934- *AmMWSc 92*
**Buffler**, Patricia Ann Happ 1938- *AmMWSc 92*
**Buffler**, Richard Thurman 1937- *AmMWSc 92*
**Buffon**, Charles Edward 1939- *WhoAmL 92*
**Buffon**, Georges-Louis Leclerc, comte de 1707-1788 *BlkwCEP*
**Buffone**, Charles Joseph 1919- *WhoAmP 91*
**Buffone**, Ida Paulette 1964- *WhoEnt 92*
**Buffong**, Eric Arnold 1951- *WhoBlA 92*
**Bufford**, Edward Eugene 1935- *WhoBlA 92*
**Bufford**, Samuel L. 1943- *WhoAmL 92, WhoWest 92*
**Buffum**, C Emery 1910- *AmMWSc 92*
**Buffum**, Donald C 1918- *AmMWSc 92*
**Buffum**, William Burnside 1921- *IntWW 91*
**Bufis**, Paul *DrAPF 91*
**Bufka**, John Andrew 1958- *WhoMW 92*
**Bufkin**, Billy George 1946- *AmMWSc 92*
**Buford**, Floyd Moye, Jr. 1957- *WhoAmL 92, WhoAmP 91*
**Buford**, Jack William 1912- *WhoFI 92, WhoWest 92*
**Buford**, James Henry 1944- *WhoBlA 92*
**Buford**, Kenneth L. 1917- *WhoBlA 92*
**Buford**, Robert Paschal 1939- *WhoRel 92*
**Buford**, Robert Pegram 1925- *WhoAmL 92*
**Buford**, Ronetta Marie 1946- *WhoMW 92*
**Buford**, Sharnia 1939- *WhoBlA 92*
**Buford**, Tom 1949- *WhoAmP 91*
**Buford**, William Holmes 1954- *Who 92*
**Buford**, William P. 1936- *WhoBlA 92*
**Bufton**, Sydney Osborne 1908- *Who 92*
**Bugaev**, B.N. *SovUnBD*
**Bugaj**, Tomasz *WhoEnt 92*
**Bugatti**, Carlo 1856-1940 *DcTwDes*
**Bugatti**, Ettore 1881-1947 *DcTwDes, FacFETw*
**Bugatti**, Jean 1909-1939 *DcTwDes, FacFETw*
**Bugatto**, B John 1934- *WhoAmP 91*
**Bugayev**, Boris Pavlovich 1923- *IntWW 91*
**Bugbee**, Victoria Jean 1951- *WhoEnt 92*
**Bugden**, Sue 1950- *WhoEnt 92*
**Bugeja**, Michael J. *DrAPF 91*
**Bugel**, Joe 1940- *WhoWest 92*
**Bugen**, David Henry 1948- *WhoFI 92*
**Bugenhagen**, Thomas Gordon 1932- *AmMWSc 92*
**Bugental**, James F. T. 1915- *WrDr 92*
**Bugg**, Charles Basil 1942- *WhoRel 92*
**Bugg**, Charles Edward 1941- *AmMWSc 92*
**Bugg**, George Wendell 1935- *WhoBlA 92*
**Bugg**, James Nelson 1904- *WhoBlA 92*
**Bugg**, June Moore 1919- *WhoAmP 91*
**Bugg**, Mayme Carol 1945- *WhoBlA 92*
**Bugg**, Randy 1951- *WhoEnt 92*
**Bugg**, Robert 1941- *WhoAmP 91, WhoBlA 92*
**Bugg**, Rod 1946- *TwCPaSc*
**Bugg**, Sterling L 1920- *AmMWSc 92*
**Bugg**, William J 1939- *WhoIns 92*
**Bugg**, William Joseph, Jr. 1939- *WhoFI 92*
**Bugg**, William Maurice 1931- *AmMWSc 92*
**Buggage**, Cynthia Marie 1958- *WhoBlA 92*
**Bugge**, Lawrence John 1936- *WhoAmL 92*
**Bugge Fougner**, Else 1944- *IntWW 91*
**Buggey**, Lesley JoAnne 1938- *WhoMW 92*
**Buggie**, Frederick Denman 1929- *WhoFI 92*
**Buggs**, Charles Wesley 1906- *AmMWSc 92, WhoBlA 92*
**Buggs**, George *DrAPF 91*
**Buggs**, James 1925- *WhoBlA 92*
**Bugher**, Mark *WhoMW 92*
**Bugher**, Mark D *WhoAmP 91*
**Bugielski**, Robert J 1947- *WhoAmP 91*
**Bugin**, Harry 1929- *WhoEnt 92*
**Bugli**, Ralph William 1913- *WhoFI 92*
**Bugliarello**, George 1927- *AmMWSc 92*
**Bugnolo**, Dimitri Spartaco 1929- *AmMWSc 92*
**Bugosh**, John 1924- *AmMWSc 92*
**Bugotu**, Francis 1937- *Who 92*
**Buhac**, Ivo 1926- *AmMWSc 92*
**Buhaina**, Abdullah Ibn 1919-1990 *WhoBlA 92N*
**Buhari**, Muhammadu 1942- *IntWW 91*
**Buhechaolu** 1928- *IntWW 91*
**Buhks**, Ephraim 1949- *AmMWSc 92*
**Buhl**, Allen Edwin 1947- *AmMWSc 92*
**Buhl**, Carolyn 1939- *WhoMW 92*
**Buhl**, David 1936- *AmMWSc 92*
**Buhl**, Lloyd Frank 1918- *WhoAmP 91*
**Buhl**, Robert Carl 1931- *WhoFI 92*
**Buhl**, Robert Frank 1922- *AmMWSc 92*
**Buhle**, Emmett Loren 1918- *AmMWSc 92*
**Buhler**, Charlotte M 1893-1974 *WomPsyc*
**Buhler**, Donald Raymond 1925- *AmMWSc 92*
**Buhler**, Gregory Wallace 1949- *WhoAmL 92*
**Buhler**, Jane Ellen 1954- *WhoMW 92*
**Buhler**, Jill Lorie 1945- *WhoWest 92*
**Buhler**, Joan Elizabeth 1961- *WhoAmL 92*
**Buhler**, Karl L 1879-1963 *FacFETw*
**Buhler**, Lynn Bledsoe 1949- *WhoAmL 92*
**Buhler**, Michael 1940- *TwCPaSc*
**Buhler**, Phillip Arthur 1962- *WhoFI 92*
**Buhler**, Richard Gerhard 1946- *WhoRel 92*
**Buhler**, Robert 1916-1989 *TwCPaSc*
**Buhler**, Winfried 1929- *IntWW 91*
**Buhlman**, Robert Andrew 1964- *WhoAmL 92*
**Buhlmann**, Michael Richard 1960- *WhoWest 92*
**Buhner**, Byron Bevis 1950- *WhoMW 92*

**Buhr,** Florence D 1933- *WhoAmP 91*
**Buhr,** Glenn 1930- *WhoAmP 91*
**Buhr,** Joseph Lee 1948- *WhoEnt 92*
**Buhr,** Robert K *AmMWSc 92*
**Buhr,** Rosemary Elizabeth 1933- *WhoMW 92*
**Buhrig,** Marga 1915- *DcEcMov*
**Buhrman,** Dorothy Carol 1951- *WhoEnt 92*
**Buhrman,** Robert Alan 1945- *AmMWSc 92*
**Buhrow,** William Carl 1934- *WhoRel 92*
**Buhse,** Howard Edward, Jr 1934- *AmMWSc 92*
**Buhsmer,** Charles P 1937- *AmMWSc 92*
**Bui,** Khoi Tien 1937- *WhoEnt 92*
**Bui,** Nhon Van 1948- *WhoMW 92*
**Bui,** Tien Dai 1945- *AmMWSc 92*
**Bui,** Tien Rung 1935- *AmMWSc 92*
**Buick,** David Dunbar 1854-1929 *FacFETw*
**Buidang,** George *WhoWest 92*
**Buie,** Aubrey William, Jr. 1942- *WhoRel 92*
**Buie,** Becky Ruth Lineberger 1941- *WhoRel 92*
**Buie,** Bennett Frank 1910- *AmMWSc 92*
**Buie,** Elissa Pauline 1960- *WhoFI 92*
**Buie,** James Randall 1953- *WhoWest 92*
**Buie,** Sampson, Jr. 1929- *WhoBlA 92*
**Buie,** T Dan 1941- *WhoAmP 91*
**Buie,** Tammy Kotsonaros 1965- *WhoAmL 92*
**Buijnsters,** Piet J. 1933- *IntWW 91*
**Buikema,** Arthur L, Jr 1941- *AmMWSc 92*
**Buikstra,** Jane Ellen 1945- *AmMWSc 92*
**Buira,** Ariel 1940- *IntWW 91*
**Buis,** Otto J 1931- *AmMWSc 92*
**Buis,** Patricia Frances 1953- *AmMWSc 92*
**Buis,** Thomas Paul 1952- *WhoAmP 91*
**Buisson,** Ferdinand Edouard 1841-1932 *WhoNob 90*
**Buist,** Aline Sonia 1940- *AmMWSc 92*
**Buist,** John Latto Farquharson 1930- *Who 92*
**Buist,** Neil R M 1932- *AmMWSc 92*
**Buitenhuis,** Peter M. 1925- *WrDr 92*
**Buiter,** Willem Hendrik 1949- *Who 92*
**Buiteweg,** Johannes Arnold 1926- *WhoFI 92*
**Buiting,** Francis P 1924- *AmMWSc 92*
**Buitrago,** Fanny 1940- *SpAmWW*
**Buitrago,** Rudy G. 1951- *WhoHisp 92*
**Buitrago,** Walter 1935- *WhoHisp 92*
**Buividas,** Anthony John 1953- *WhoFI 92*
**Bujak,** Zbigniew 1954- *IntWW 91*
**Bujake,** John Edward, Jr 1933- *AmMWSc 92*
**Bujanda,** Moises Arturo 1958- *WhoHisp 92*
**Bujold,** Genevieve *WhoEnt 92*
**Bujold,** Genevieve 1942- *IntMPA 92*
**Bujold,** Lois McMaster 1949- *TwCSFW 91*
**Bujones,** Fernando 1955- *IntWW 91, WhoHisp 92*
**Bujones,** Fernando Calleiro 1955- *WhoEnt 92*
**Bukacek,** Richard F 1927- *AmMWSc 92*
**Bukalski,** Peter Julian 1941- *WhoEnt 92*
**Bukantz,** Samuel Charles 1911- *AmMWSc 92*
**Bukar,** Margaret Witty 1950- *WhoMW 92*
**Buker,** Robert Joseph 1930- *AmMWSc 92*
**Buketoff,** Igor 1915- *WhoEnt 92*
**Bukhari,** Ahmad Iqbal 1943- *AmMWSc 92*
**Bukharin,** Nikolai Ivanovich 1888-1938 *FacFETw*
**Bukharin,** Nikolay Ivanovich 1888-1938 *SovUnBD*
**Buki,** Dennis Gabor 1945- *WhoAmL 92*
**Bukiet,** Melvin Jules *DrAPF 91*
**Bukovac,** Martin 1929- *IntWW 91*
**Bukovac,** Martin John 1929- *AmMWSc 92*
**Bukovnik,** Gary A. 1947- *WhoWest 92*
**Bukovsan,** Laura A 1940- *AmMWSc 92*
**Bukovsan,** William 1929- *AmMWSc 92*
**Bukovsky,** Vladimir 1942- *IntWW 91, LiExTwC*
**Bukovsky,** Vladimir Konstantinovich 1942- *SovUnBD*
**Bukowiecki,** Angeline Bernadette 1937- *WhoRel 92*
**Bukowski,** Charles *DrAPF 91*
**Bukowski,** Charles 1920- *BenetAL 91, ConNov 91, ConPo 91, FacFETw, IntAu&W 91, WrDr 92*
**Bukowski,** Gary L 1951- *WhoAmP 91*
**Bukowski,** Horst Norbert 1960- *WhoHisp 92*
**Bukowski,** Richard William 1947- *AmMWSc 92*
**Bukrey,** Richard Robert 1941- *AmMWSc 92*
**Bukry,** John David 1941- *AmMWSc 92*
**Bula,** Irmina 1926- *WhoRel 92*
**Bula,** Raymond J 1927- *AmMWSc 92*
**Bulani,** Walter 1928- *AmMWSc 92*
**Bulas,** Romuald 1922- *AmMWSc 92*
**Bulatovic,** Miodrag d1991 *NewYTBS 91*
**Bulatovic,** Miodrag 1930-1991 *ConAu 133*
**Bulatovic,** Moidrag 1930-1991 *IntWW 91, -91N*
**Bulatovic,** Vukoje 1927- *IntWW 91*
**Bulbank,** Israel 1934- *WhoHisp 92*
**Bulbenko,** George Fedir 1927- *AmMWSc 92*
**Bulbring,** Edith *IntWW 91N*
**Bulbring,** Edith 1903-1990 *AnObit 1990*
**Buldakov,** Gennadiy Nikonorich 1924- *IntWW 91*
**Buldrini,** George James *WhoAmL 92*
**Bulen,** Lawrence Keith 1926- *WhoAmP 91*
**Buley,** Joseph Roland 1939- *WhoWest 92*
**Bulfield,** Peter William 1930- *Who 92*
**Bulfinch,** Charles 1763-1844 *BenetAL 91*
**Bulfinch,** Thomas 1796-1867 *BenetAL 91*
**Bulgakov,** Mikhail 1891-1940 *TwCSFW 91A*
**Bulgakov,** Mikhail Afanas'evich 1891-1940 *SovUnBD*
**Bulgakov,** Mikhail Afanasievich 1891-1940 *ScFEYrs*
**Bulgakov,** Mikhail Afanasyevich 1891-1940 *FacFETw*
**Bulgakov,** Sergei Nikolayevich 1871-1944 *FacFETw*
**Bulgakov,** Sergius 1871-1944 *DcEcMov*
**Bulganin,** Nikolai 1895-1975 *FacFETw*
**Bulganin,** Nikolay Aleksandrovich 1895-1975 *SovUnBD*
**Bulger,** Anthony Clare 1912- *Who 92*
**Bulger,** Lucille O. 1912- *WhoBlA 92*
**Bulger,** Robert J. 1915- *WhoAmL 92*
**Bulger,** Roger James 1933- *AmMWSc 92, IntWW 91*
**Bulger,** Ruth Ellen 1936- *AmMWSc 92*
**Bulger,** Tom *WhoAmP 91*
**Bulger,** William M *WhoAmP 91*
**Bulger,** William Thomas 1927- *WhoMW 92*
**Bulgren,** William Gerald 1937- *AmMWSc 92, WhoMW 92*
**Bulgrin,** Vernon Carl 1923- *AmMWSc 92*
**Bulich,** Anthony Andrew 1944- *AmMWSc 92*
**Bulin,** Rene Henri 1920- *IntWW 91*
**Bulitt,** Patricia Ann 1949- *WhoWest 92*
**Bulkeley,** Gershom 1636-1713 *BiInAmS*
**Bulkeley,** Richard H. D. W. *Who 92*
**Bulkeley,** William M. 1950- *ConAu 135*
**Bulkin,** Bernard Joseph 1942- *AmMWSc 92*
**Bulkley,** George 1917- *AmMWSc 92*
**Bulkley,** Jonathan William 1938- *AmMWSc 92*
**Bulkley,** Ross Vivian 1927- *AmMWSc 92*
**Bulkowski,** David Allen 1963- *WhoRel 92*
**Bulkowski,** John Edmund 1942- *AmMWSc 92*
**Bull,** Adam 1965- *TwCPaSc*
**Bull,** Alice Louise 1924- *AmMWSc 92*
**Bull,** Angela 1936- *WrDr 92*
**Bull,** Angela Mary 1936- *IntAu&W 91*
**Bull,** Anthony 1908- *Who 92*
**Bull,** Benjamin Francis Wyman 1950- *WhoAmL 92*
**Bull,** Brian S 1937- *AmMWSc 92*
**Bull,** Brian Stanley 1937- *WhoFI 92*
**Bull,** Charles Stedman 1845-1911 *BiInAmS*
**Bull,** Colin Bruce Bradley 1928- *AmMWSc 92*
**Bull,** Coralee Kitchings *WhoAmP 91*
**Bull,** Daniel Newell 1939- *AmMWSc 92*
**Bull,** David Lee 1947- *WhoMW 92*
**Bull,** Don Lee 1929- *AmMWSc 92*
**Bull,** Ephraim Wales 1806-1895 *BiInAmS*
**Bull,** Everett L, Jr 1949- *AmMWSc 92*
**Bull,** George Anthony 1929- *Who 92*
**Bull,** John 1562?-1628 *NewAmDM*
**Bull,** John Michael 1934- *Who 92*
**Bull,** John Prince 1917- *Who 92*
**Bull,** Kenneth Winson 1930- *WhoAmP 91*
**Bull,** Leonard Seth 1941- *AmMWSc 92*
**Bull,** Mary Jane 1945- *WhoMW 92*
**Bull,** Megan Patricia 1922- *Who 92*
**Bull,** Odd 1907- *IntWW 91*
**Bull,** Ole 1810-1880 *NewAmDM*
**Bull,** Oliver Richard Silvester 1930- *Who 92*
**Bull,** Richard *Who 92*
**Bull,** Richard C 1934- *AmMWSc 92*
**Bull,** Richard Sutton, Jr. 1926- *WhoMW 92*
**Bull,** Roger John 1940- *Who 92*
**Bull,** Sandy 1941- *WhoEnt 92*
**Bull,** Simeon 1934- *Who 92*
**Bull,** Stanley R 1941- *AmMWSc 92*
**Bull,** Storm 1856-1907 *BiInAmS*
**Bull,** Thomas Henry 1949- *WhoEnt 92*
**Bull,** Tony Raymond 1934- *Who 92*
**Bull,** W Rex 1929- *AmMWSc 92*
**Bull,** Walter 1902- *Who 92*
**Bull,** William Benham 1930- *AmMWSc 92*
**Bull,** William Earnest 1933- *AmMWSc 92*
**Bull,** William Tillinghast 1849-1909 *BiInAmS*
**Bulla,** Ben F. 1920- *WhoFI 92*
**Bulla,** Clyde Robert 1914- *IntAu&W 91, WrDr 92*
**Bulla,** Lee Austin, Jr 1941- *AmMWSc 92*
**Bullard,** Bill 1948- *WhoAmP 91*
**Bullard,** Clark W 1944- *AmMWSc 92*
**Bullard,** Clark Wesley 1944- *WhoMW 92*
**Bullard,** Denys Gradwell 1912- *Who 92*
**Bullard,** Edward A., Jr. 1947- *WhoBlA 92*
**Bullard,** Edward Crisp 1907-1980 *FacFETw*
**Bullard,** Edward Payson, IV 1935- *WhoFI 92*
**Bullard,** Edwin Roscoe, Jr 1921- *AmMWSc 92*
**Bullard,** Ervin Trowbridge 1920- *AmMWSc 92*
**Bullard,** Fred Mason 1901- *AmMWSc 92*
**Bullard,** George Woodrow, Jr. 1950- *WhoRel 92*
**Bullard,** Gilda 1927- *WhoWest 92*
**Bullard,** Giles 1926- *Who 92*
**Bullard,** Giles Lionel 1926- *IntWW 91*
**Bullard,** Helen 1902- *WrDr 92*
**Bullard,** Herbert Todd 1961- *WhoAmL 92, WhoFI 92*
**Bullard,** John Kilburn 1947- *WhoAmP 91*
**Bullard,** John Moore 1932- *WhoRel 92*
**Bullard,** Julian 1928- *IntWW 91, Who 92*
**Bullard,** Kevin Lee 1956- *WhoRel 92*
**Bullard,** Lawrence Edward 1943- *WhoRel 92*
**Bullard,** Lyman Greenleaf, Jr. 1955- *WhoAmL 92*
**Bullard,** Mary Ellen 1926- *WhoRel 92*
**Bullard,** Matt *WhoBlA 92*
**Bullard,** Paul 1918- *TwCPaSc*
**Bullard,** Perry 1942- *WhoAmP 91*
**Bullard,** Richard Forrest 1937- *WhoWest 92*
**Bullard,** Rockwood Wilde, III 1944- *WhoMW 92*
**Bullard,** Roger Aubrey 1937- *WhoRel 92*
**Bullard,** Thais Jeanne *WhoWest 92*
**Bullard,** Thomas 1944- *ConTFT 9*
**Bullard,** Truman Robert 1939- *AmMWSc 92*
**Bullard,** Willis Clare, Jr 1943- *WhoAmP 91*
**Bullard,** Willis Gale 1940- *WhoWest 92*
**Bullas,** Leonard Raymond 1929- *AmMWSc 92*
**Bullen Bear** *WrDr 92*
**Bullen,** Allan Graham Robert 1936- *AmMWSc 92*
**Bullen,** Frederick Hamilton 1915- *WhoAmL 92*
**Bullen,** Keith Edward 1906-1976 *FacFETw*
**Bullen,** Peter Southcott 1928- *AmMWSc 92*
**Bullen,** Reginald 1920- *Who 92*
**Bullen,** William Alexander *Who 92*
**Buller** *Who 92*
**Buller,** Alan Wade 1954- *WhoEnt 92*
**Buller,** Arthur John 1923- *IntWW 91, Who 92*
**Buller,** Clarence S 1932- *AmMWSc 92*
**Buller,** Herman 1923- *IntAu&W 91*
**Buller,** Herman 1927- *WrDr 92*
**Buller,** James Harlan 1944- *WhoMW 92*
**Buller,** John 1927- *ConCom 92*
**Buller,** Norman Eugene 1927- *WhoMW 92*
**Bullerman,** Lloyd Bernard 1939- *AmMWSc 92, WhoMW 92*
**Bullers,** Ronald Alfred 1931- *Who 92*
**Bullett,** Audrey Kathryn 1937- *WhoAmP 91, WhoBlA 92*
**Bullett,** David B 1938- *WhoIns 92*
**Bullett,** Vicky 1967- *BlkOlyM*
**Bullimore,** John Wallace MacGregor 1945- *Who 92*
**Bullington,** James Richard 1940- *WhoAmP 91*
**Bullington,** John Orville 1942- *WhoFI 92*
**Bullins,** Ed 1935- *BenetAL 91, BlkLC [port], WhoBlA 92, WrDr 92*
**Bullio,** Priscilla Faye 1954- *WhoMW 92*
**Bullis,** George LeRoy 1922- *AmMWSc 92*
**Bullis,** Harvey Raymond, Jr 1924- *AmMWSc 92*
**Bullis,** Jerald *DrAPF 91*
**Bullis,** William Murray 1930- *AmMWSc 92*
**Bullitt,** James Bell 1874-1964 *DcNCBi 1*
**Bullmore,** Edward 1933- *TwCPaSc*
**Bullmore,** John Jeremy David 1929- *Who 92*
**Bulloch,** John 1928- *ConAu 134*
**Bullock** *Who 92*
**Bullock,** Baron 1914- *IntWW 91, Who 92*
**Bullock,** Lord 1914- *WrDr 92*
**Bullock,** Bob 1929- *WhoAmP 91*
**Bullock,** Byron Swanson 1955- *WhoBlA 92*
**Bullock,** Charles 1826-1900 *BiInAmS*
**Bullock,** Clifton Vernice 1928- *WhoBlA 92, WhoRel 92*
**Bullock,** Donald Melvin 1933- *WhoRel 92*
**Bullock,** Donald Wayne 1947- *WhoWest 92*
**Bullock,** Edward Anthony Watson 1926- *Who 92*
**Bullock,** Elbert L. 1934- *WhoBlA 92*
**Bullock,** Francis Jeremiah 1937- *AmMWSc 92*
**Bullock,** Frank William, Jr. 1938- *WhoAmL 92*
**Bullock,** George Daniel 1942- *WhoAmP 91*
**Bullock,** Graham Lambert 1935- *AmMWSc 92*
**Bullock,** H. Ridgely 1934- *WhoFI 92*
**Bullock,** Harvey Reade 1921- *WhoEnt 92*
**Bullock,** Hugh 1898- *Who 92*
**Bullock,** J Bruce 1940- *AmMWSc 92*
**Bullock,** J. Jerome 1948- *WhoBlA 92*
**Bullock,** James 1926- *WhoBlA 92*
**Bullock,** James Robert 1916- *WhoAmL 92*
**Bullock,** John 1932- *AmMWSc 92*
**Bullock,** John 1933- *Who 92*
**Bullock,** Jonathan S, IV 1942- *AmMWSc 92*
**Bullock,** Joseph Daniel 1942- *WhoMW 92*
**Bullock,** Joseph Moses 1891- *WhoBlA 92*
**Bullock,** Kathryn Rice 1945- *AmMWSc 92*
**Bullock,** Kenneth C 1918- *AmMWSc 92*
**Bullock,** Leslie Patricia 1936- *AmMWSc 92*
**Bullock,** Mark Alfred 1945- *WhoMW 92*
**Bullock,** Michael 1918- *ConPo 91, WrDr 92*
**Bullock,** Michael Hale 1918- *IntAu&W 91*
**Bullock,** Peter Bradley 1934- *WhoFI 92*
**Bullock,** R Morris 1957- *AmMWSc 92*
**Bullock,** Richard Henry Watson 1920- *Who 92*
**Bullock,** Richard Melvin 1918- *AmMWSc 92*
**Bullock,** Robert 1828-1905 *DcNCBi 1*
**Bullock,** Robert Crossley 1924- *AmMWSc 92*
**Bullock,** Robert Foster 1934- *WhoFI 92*
**Bullock,** Robert Haydon, Jr. 1945- *WhoRel 92*
**Bullock,** Robert M, III 1937- *AmMWSc 92*
**Bullock,** Ronald Elvin 1934- *AmMWSc 92*
**Bullock,** Samuel Carey 1921- *WhoBlA 92*
**Bullock,** Theodore 1928- *WhoBlA 92*
**Bullock,** Theodore Holmes 1915- *AmMWSc 92, IntWW 91*
**Bullock,** Thomas Abbott 1922- *WhoFI 92*
**Bullock,** Thomas Edward, Jr 1938- *AmMWSc 92*
**Bullock,** Thurman Ruthe 1947- *WhoBlA 92*
**Bullock,** Ward Ervin, Jr 1931- *AmMWSc 92*
**Bullock,** Wilbur Lewis 1922- *AmMWSc 92*
**Bullock,** William H. 1927- *WhoRel 92*
**Bullock,** William Horace 1919- *WhoBlA 92*
**Bulloff,** Aaron Harley 1948- *WhoAmL 92*
**Bulloff,** Jack John 1914- *AmMWSc 92*
**Bullough,** Donald Auberon 1928- *Who 92*
**Bullough,** John Frank 1928- *WhoEnt 92*
**Bullough,** Robert V., Jr. 1949- *ConAu 135*
**Bullough,** Ronald 1931- *Who 92*
**Bullough,** Vern L 1928- *AmMWSc 92, IntAu&W 91, WrDr 92*
**Bullough,** William Sydney 1914- *Who 92*
**Bullrich,** Silvina 1915- *SpAmWW*
**Bullus,** Eric 1906- *Who 92*
**Bullus,** Eric E. 1906- *WrDr 92*
**Bulman,** Aaron E. *DrAPF 91*
**Bulman,** William Patrick 1925- *WhoFI 92*
**Bulmer,** Esmond *Who 92*
**Bulmer,** Gerald 1920- *Who 92*
**Bulmer,** Glenn Stuart 1931- *AmMWSc 92*
**Bulmer,** Henry Kenneth 1921- *IntAu&W 91*
**Bulmer,** James Esmond 1935- *Who 92*
**Bulmer,** Kenneth *IntAu&W 91X, WrDr 92*
**Bulmer,** Kenneth 1921- *TwCSFW 91*
**Bulmer,** Peter R. 1959- *WhoAmL 92*
**Bulmer,** Thomas Sanderson d1898 *BiInAmS*
**Bulmer,** William Edward 1958- *WhoFI 92*
**Bulmer-Thomas,** Ivor *IntWW 91*
**Bulmer-Thomas,** Ivor 1905- *Who 92, WrDr 92*
**Bulosan,** Carlos 1913-1956 *BenetAL 91*
**Bulovic,** Danica 1937- *WhoFI 92*
**Bulow,** Frank Joseph 1941- *AmMWSc 92*
**Bulow,** Hans Von 1830-1894 *NewAmDM*
**Bulpin,** Thomas Victor 1918- *IntAu&W 91*
**Bulpitt,** Cecil Arthur Charles 1919- *Who 92*
**Buls,** Bruce B 1930- *WhoAmP 91*
**Bulson,** David Eric 1953- *WhoAmL 92*
**Bulteel,** Christopher Harris 1921- *Who 92*
**Bultema,** Harry J. R. 1936- *WhoRel 92*
**Bultman,** John D 1924- *AmMWSc 92*
**Bultmann,** Rudolf 1884-1976 *FacFETw*
**Bultmann,** William Arnold 1922- *WhoWest 92*
**Bululu,** Lunda *IntWW 91*
**Bulusu,** Suryanarayana 1927- *AmMWSc 92*

**Bulwer-Lytton,** Edward 1803-1873 RfGEnL 91, ScFEYrs
**Bulwinkle,** Alfred Lee 1883-1950 DcNCBi 1
**Bulzacchelli,** John G. 1939- WhoFI 92
**Bulzacchelli,** Victor F. 1958- WhoFI 92
**Bumanglag,** Alejandro Guira 1950- WhoWest 92
**Bumbleburg,** Joseph Theodore 1937- WhoAmL 92
**Bumbry,** George Nordlinger 1922- WhoBlA 92
**Bumbry,** Grace 1937- IntWW 91, NewAmDM, Who 92, WhoEnt 92
**Bumbry,** Grace Ann 1937- NotBlAW 92 [port], WhoBlA 92
**Bumby,** Richard Thomas AmMWSc 92
**Bumcrot,** Robert J 1936- AmMWSc 92
**Bumer,** Charles Theodore 1923- WhoAmL 92
**Bumgardner,** Carl Lee 1925- AmMWSc 92
**Bumgardner,** David Webster, Jr 1921- WhoAmP 91
**Bumgardner,** Donna Lee Arrington 1950- WhoAmL 92
**Bumgardner,** Larry G. 1957- WhoWest 92
**Bumgardner,** Thomas Arthur 1942- WhoMW 92
**Bumgarner,** Gary Dale 1938- WhoAmP 91
**Bumgarner,** James McNabb 1919- WhoAmL 92
**Bumiller,** Donald Robert 1955- WhoAmL 92
**Bumke,** Erwin 1874-1945 EncTR 91
**Bump,** Charles Kilbourne 1907- AmMWSc 92
**Bump,** Larry J. 1939- WhoFI 92
**Bump,** Mark William 1956- WhoAmL 92
**Bump,** Suzanne 1956- WhoAmP 91
**Bump,** William E. 1958- WhoAmL 92
**Bumpass,** Frances Webb 1819-1898 DcNCBi 1
**Bumpers,** Dale 1925- AlmAP 92 [port]
**Bumpers,** Dale L 1925- WhoAmP 91
**Bumpers,** Dale Leon 1925- IntWW 91
**Bumphus,** Walter Gayle 1948- WhoBlA 92
**Bumpus,** Francis Merlin 1922- AmMWSc 92
**Bumpus,** Frederick J 1929- WhoIns 92
**Bumpus,** Jerry DrAPF 91
**Bumpus,** John 1929- WhoAmP 91
**Bumpus,** John Arthur 1948- AmMWSc 92
**Bumstead,** Dawn D. 1965- WhoRel 92
**Bumstead,** Henry Andrews 1870-1920 BiInAmS
**Bumstead,** James Walter 1958- WhoFI 92
**Bumsted,** J. M. 1938- WrDr 92
**Bunaes,** Bard E 1935- WhoIns 92
**Bunag,** Ruben David 1931- AmMWSc 92
**Bunbury** Who 92
**Bunbury,** Bishop of 1932- Who 92
**Bunbury,** David Leslie 1933- AmMWSc 92
**Bunbury,** Michael Who 92
**Bunbury,** Michael 1946- Who 92
**Bunbury,** Richard David Michael 1927- Who 92
**Bunce,** Elizabeth Thompson 1915- AmMWSc 92
**Bunce,** George Edwin 1932- AmMWSc 92
**Bunce,** Gerry Michael AmMWSc 92
**Bunce,** James Arthur 1949- AmMWSc 92
**Bunce,** Michael John 1935- Who 92
**Bunce,** Nigel James 1943- AmMWSc 92
**Bunce,** Oliver Bell 1828-1890 BenetAL 91
**Bunce,** Paul Leslie 1916- AmMWSc 92
**Bunce,** Stanley Chalmers 1917- AmMWSc 92
**Buncel,** Erwin 1931- AmMWSc 92
**Bunch,** Albert William 1933- WhoRel 92
**Bunch,** Austin 1918- Who 92
**Bunch,** Barbara J 1952- WhoAmP 91
**Bunch,** Charlotte 1944- IntAu&W 91
**Bunch,** David R TwCSFW 91
**Bunch,** David William 1936- AmMWSc 92
**Bunch,** Fred R 1952- WhoAmP 91
**Bunch,** Harry Dean 1915- AmMWSc 92
**Bunch,** James R 1940- AmMWSc 92
**Bunch,** Phillip Carter 1946- AmMWSc 92
**Bunch,** Richard Addison 1940- WhoRel 92
**Bunch,** Robert Maxwell 1953- AmMWSc 92
**Bunch,** Theodore Eugene 1936- AmMWSc 92
**Bunch,** Wilbur Lyle 1925- AmMWSc 92
**Bunch,** William Franklin 1935- WhoEnt 92
**Bunch,** Wilton Herbert 1935- AmMWSc 92
**Bunche,** Ralph 1904-1971 FacFETw, RComAH
**Bunche,** Ralph Johnson 1904-1971 AmPeW, WhoNob 90
**Buncher,** Alan 1946- WhoMW 92
**Buncher,** Charles Ralph 1938- AmMWSc 92
**Buncher,** James Edward 1936- WhoFI 92
**Bunchman,** Herbert Harry, II 1942- WhoWest 92
**Buncombe,** Edward 1742-1778 DcNCBi 1
**Bund,** Karlheinz 1925- IntWW 91
**Bunda,** Robert 1947- WhoAmP 91
**Bunde,** Carl Albert 1907- AmMWSc 92
**Bunde,** Daryl E 1937- AmMWSc 92
**Bundesen,** Faye Stimers 1932- WhoWest 92
**Bundles,** A'Lelia Perry 1952- WhoBlA 92
**Bundschuh,** George A W 1933- WhoIns 92
**Bundschuh,** George August William 1933- WhoFI 92
**Bundschuh,** James Edward 1941- AmMWSc 92
**Bundschuh,** Marjorie Gurevitz 1952- WhoWest 92
**Bundu,** Abass 1948- IntWW 91
**Bundy,** Blakely Fetridge 1944- WhoMW 92
**Bundy,** Bonita Marie 1948- AmMWSc 92
**Bundy,** David Dale 1948- WhoRel 92
**Bundy,** David Hollister 1947- WhoAmL 92
**Bundy,** Francis P 1910- AmMWSc 92
**Bundy,** Gordon Leonard 1942- AmMWSc 92
**Bundy,** Hallie Flowers 1925- AmMWSc 92
**Bundy,** James Lomax 1920- WhoBlA 92
**Bundy,** Kirk Jon 1947- AmMWSc 92
**Bundy,** Larry Gene 1943- AmMWSc 92
**Bundy,** McGeorge 1919- AmPolLe, FacFETw, IntWW 91, Who 92
**Bundy,** Nathan Hollister 1927- WhoFI 92
**Bundy,** Robert W 1924- AmMWSc 92
**Bundy,** Roy Elton 1924- AmMWSc 92
**Bundy,** Stephen M. 1951- WhoAmL 92
**Bundy,** Wayne Miley 1924- AmMWSc 92
**Bundy,** William d1692 DcNCBi 1
**Bundy,** William Francis 1946- WhoWest 92
**Bundy,** William P 1917- WhoAmP 91
**Bundy,** William Putnam 1917- IntWW 91
**Bunford,** John Farrant 1901- Who 92
**Bungaard,** Ernest 1920- WhoEnt 92
**Bungay,** Henry Robert, III 1928- AmMWSc 92
**Bungay,** Peter M 1941- AmMWSc 92
**Bunge,** Carlos Federico 1941- AmMWSc 92
**Bunge,** David Bruce 1955- WhoFI 92
**Bunge,** David Paul 1937- WhoEnt 92
**Bunge,** Jonathan Gunn 1936- WhoMW 92
**Bunge,** Marcia JoAnn 1954- WhoRel 92
**Bunge,** Mario Augusto 1919- AmMWSc 92
**Bunge,** Mary Bartlett 1931- AmMWSc 92
**Bunge,** Nancy Liddell 1942- WhoMW 92
**Bunge,** Richard Paul 1932- AmMWSc 92
**Bunge,** Wilfred Franklin 1931- WhoRel 92
**Bunge,** William Ronald 1934- WhoAmP 91
**Bunger,** James Walter 1945- AmMWSc 92
**Bunger,** Rolf 1941- AmMWSc 92
**Bungeroth,** William Martin, Jr. 1946- WhoWest 92
**Bungey,** John Henry 1944- WrDr 92
**Bungey,** Michael 1940- IntWW 91, Who 92
**Bungo,** Michael William 1950- AmMWSc 92
**Bunich,** Pavel Grigorevich 1929- IntWW 91, SovUnBD
**Bunick,** Gerard John 1947- AmMWSc 92
**Bunim,** Mary-Ellis 1946- WhoEnt 92
**Bunin,** Ivan 1870-1953 FacFETw
**Bunin,** Ivan Alexeievich 1870-1953 WhoNob 90
**Bunin,** Ivan Alexeyevitch 1870-1953 LiExTwC
**Bunitsky,** Victor Nicholas, Jr. WhoAmL 92
**Buniva,** Brian Lawrence 1950- WhoAmL 92
**Bunker,** Albert Rowland 1913- Who 92
**Bunker,** Bruce Alan 1952- AmMWSc 92
**Bunker,** Chang 1811-1874 DcNCBi 1
**Bunker,** Eng 1811-1874 DcNCBi 1
**Bunker,** Ira S ScFEYrs
**Bunker,** James Edward 1936- AmMWSc 92
**Bunker,** John Birkbeck 1926- WhoFI 92
**Bunker,** John Philip 1920- AmMWSc 92
**Bunker,** Merle E 1923- AmMWSc 92
**Bunker,** Norene Rae 1931- WhoAmP 91
**Bunker,** Rick Shane 1963- WhoFI 92
**Bunkley,** Lonnie R. 1932- WhoBlA 92
**Bunn,** Benjamin Hickman 1844-1907 DcNCBi 1
**Bunn,** Charles Nixon 1926- WhoFI 92, WhoWest 92
**Bunn,** Clive Leighton 1945- AmMWSc 92
**Bunn,** Dorothy Irons 1948- WhoWest 92
**Bunn,** Douglas Henry David 1928- Who 92
**Bunn,** Edward Ted 1928- WhoMW 92
**Bunn,** George 1925- WhoAmP 91
**Bunn,** George Regan, Jr. 1940- WhoAmL 92
**Bunn,** Henry Gaston 1838-1908 DcNCBi 1
**Bunn,** Howard Franklin 1935- AmMWSc 92
**Bunn,** James 1956- WhoAmP 91
**Bunn,** Joe M 1932- AmMWSc 92
**Bunn,** John D. 1959- WhoRel 92
**Bunn,** Paul A, Jr 1945- AmMWSc 92
**Bunn,** Robert Burgess 1933- WhoAmL 92
**Bunn,** Stan 1946- WhoAmP 91
**Bunn,** Warren J. 1914- WhoBlA 92
**Bunn,** William Bernice, III 1952- AmMWSc 92
**Bunnag,** Marut 1925- IntWW 91
**Bunnage,** Avis 1923-1990 AnObit 1990
**Bunnell,** Don Carlos 1930- WhoRel 92
**Bunnell,** Frederick Lindsley 1942- AmMWSc 92
**Bunnell,** Omar B 1912- WhoAmP 91
**Bunnell,** Ron Dale 1945- WhoWest 92
**Bunner,** Alan Newton 1938- AmMWSc 92
**Bunner,** H. C. 1855-1896 BenetAL 91
**Bunner,** Patricia Andrea 1953- WhoAmL 92
**Bunner,** William Keck 1949- WhoAmL 92
**Bunnett,** Joseph Frederick 1921- AmMWSc 92
**Bunney,** Benjamin Stephenson 1938- AmMWSc 92
**Bunney,** William E 1930- AmMWSc 92
**Bunning,** Erwin 1906- IntWW 91
**Bunning,** Jack 1954- WhoEnt 92
**Bunning,** James P 1931- WhoAmP 91
**Bunning,** Jim 1931- AlmAP 92 [port]
**Bunshaft,** Gordon d1990 IntWW 91N
**Bunshaft,** Gordon 1909- DcTwDes
**Bunshaft,** Gordon 1909-1990 AnObit 1990, FacFETw, News 91
**Bunshah,** Rointan F 1927- AmMWSc 92
**Bunster,** Don Alvaro 1920- Who 92
**Bunt,** James Richard 1941- WhoFI 92
**Bunt,** Raymond, Jr 1944- WhoAmP 91
**Bunte,** Doris 1933- WhoAmP 91, WhoBlA 92
**Buntele,** Richard Arthur 1938- WhoAmL 92
**Bunten,** William Wallace 1930- WhoAmP 91
**Buntin,** Stephen George 1954- WhoWest 92
**Buntinas,** Martin George 1941- AmMWSc 92, WhoMW 92
**Bunting,** A. E. WrDr 92
**Bunting,** Arthur Hugh 1917- Who 92
**Bunting,** Basil 1900- IntAu&W 91
**Bunting,** Basil 1900-1985 FacFETw, RfGEnL 91
**Bunting,** Brian Talbot 1932- AmMWSc 92
**Bunting,** Bruce Gordon 1948- AmMWSc 92
**Bunting,** Christopher David 1944- AmMWSc 92
**Bunting,** David Cuyp 1940- WhoWest 92
**Bunting,** Dewey Lee, II 1932- AmMWSc 92
**Bunting,** Eve 1928- WrDr 92
**Bunting,** George H, Jr 1944- WhoAmP 91
**Bunting,** Glenn Forbes 1956- WhoWest 92
**Bunting,** Jackie Ondra 1938- AmMWSc 92
**Bunting,** John 1918- IntWW 91, Who 92
**Bunting,** John Reginald 1916- Who 92
**Bunting,** John William 1943- AmMWSc 92
**Bunting,** Martin Brian 1934- Who 92
**Bunting,** Robert L. 1946- WhoFI 92
**Bunting,** Roger Kent 1935- AmMWSc 92
**Buntley,** George Jule 1924- AmMWSc 92
**Buntline,** Ned BenetAL 91
**Bunton,** Clifford A 1920- AmMWSc 92
**Bunton,** George Louis 1920- Who 92
**Bunton,** Henry Clay 1903- WhoBlA 92
**Bunton,** Lucius Desha, III 1924- WhoAmL 92
**Buntrock,** Dean Lewis WhoFI 92, WhoMW 92
**Buntrock,** Robert Edward 1940- AmMWSc 92
**Bunuel,** Luis 1900-1983 FacFETw, IntDcF 2-2 [port]
**Bunyan,** Ellen Lackey Spotz 1921- AmMWSc 92
**Bunyan,** John 1628-1688 CnDBLB 2 [port], RfGEnL 91
**Bunyan,** Peter John 1936- Who 92
**Bunyard,** Robert Sidney 1930- Who 92
**Bunyon,** Ronald S. 1935- WhoBlA 92
**Bunzel,** David Lee 1955- WhoWest 92
**Bunzel,** John Harvey 1924- WhoWest 92
**Buol,** Stanley Walter 1934- AmMWSc 92
**Buonaguro,** Anthony Roger 1946- WhoAmL 92
**Buonamici,** Rino 1929- AmMWSc 92
**Buonanni,** Brian Francis 1945- WhoFI 92
**Buonanno,** Christopher Paul 1952- WhoAmP 91
**Buongiorno,** Joseph 1944- AmMWSc 92
**Buoni,** Frederick Buell 1934- AmMWSc 92
**Buoni,** John J 1943- AmMWSc 92
**Buono,** John 1963- WhoFI 92
**Buono,** John Arthur 1947- AmMWSc 92
**Buono,** Ronald Michael 1946- WhoFI 92
**Buonocore,** Michelina DrAPF 91
**Buonocore,** Thomas Anthony 1958- WhoAmL 92
**Buonomo,** Frances Catherine 1955- AmMWSc 92
**Buonopane,** Ralph A 1938- AmMWSc 92
**Buoscio,** Angelo Arthur 1938- WhoAmL 92
**Bupp,** Lamar Paul 1921- AmMWSc 92
**Bupp,** Water TwCSFW 91
**Bur,** Anthony J 1935- AmMWSc 92
**Burack,** Elmer H. 1927- WrDr 92
**Burack,** Elmer Howard 1927- IntAu&W 91
**Burack,** Michael Leonard 1942- WhoAmL 92
**Burack,** Sylvia Kamerman 1916- IntAu&W 91
**Burack,** Walter Richard AmMWSc 92
**Buraczynski,** Anthony C 1908- WhoAmP 91
**Burak,** Howard Paul 1934- WhoAmL 92
**Burak,** Larry Stephen 1960- WhoFI 92
**Burakow,** Nicholas 1949- WhoFI 92
**Burandt,** Gary Edward 1943- WhoFI 92
**Burandt,** Steven Lee 1954- WhoMW 92
**Buranelli,** Vincent 1919- WrDr 92
**Buranelli,** Vincent John 1919- IntAu&W 91
**Burani,** Sergio 1946- WhoFI 92
**Buras,** Edmund Maurice 1921- AmMWSc 92
**Buras,** Nathan 1921- AmMWSc 92, WhoWest 92
**Buratti,** Bonnie J AmMWSc 92
**Burba,** Aleksandras DcAmImH
**Burba,** John Vytautas 1926- AmMWSc 92
**Burbach,** Daniel Joseph 1960- WhoMW 92
**Burbage,** Eleanor Claire 1951- WhoAmP 91
**Burbage,** Joseph James 1914- AmMWSc 92
**Burbanck,** Madeline Palmer 1914- AmMWSc 92
**Burbanck,** William Dudley 1913- AmMWSc 92
**Burbank,** Jim DrAPF 91
**Burbank,** John Emerson 1872-1919 BiInAmS
**Burbank,** John Thorn 1939- WhoEnt 92, WhoMW 92
**Burbank,** Luther 1849-1926 FacFETw [port]
**Burbank,** Nathan C, Jr 1916- AmMWSc 92
**Burbank,** Stephen Bradner 1947- WhoAmL 92
**Burbeck,** Allan Beal 1882-1920 BiInAmS
**Burbeck,** Christina Anderson 1948- AmMWSc 92
**Burbidge,** Eleanor Margaret Who 92
**Burbidge,** Eleanor Margaret 1919- AmMWSc 92
**Burbidge,** Eleanor Margaret 1922- FacFETw
**Burbidge,** Eleanor Margaret Peachey 1948- IntWW 91
**Burbidge,** Geoffrey 1925- AmMWSc 92, FacFETw, IntWW 91, Who 92, WhoWest 92
**Burbidge,** Herbert 1904- Who 92
**Burbidge,** Keith A 1920- WhoAmP 91
**Burbidge,** Margaret Who 92
**Burbridge,** John Paul 1932- Who 92
**Burbridge,** Stephen Nigel 1934- Who 92
**Burbury,** Stanley Charles 1909- Who 92
**Burbutis,** Paul Philip 1927- AmMWSc 92
**Burch,** Benjamin Clay 1948- AmMWSc 92
**Burch,** Brian Douglas 1963- WhoMW 92
**Burch,** Charles William, Sr. 1959- WhoFI 92
**Burch,** Claire DrAPF 91
**Burch,** Claire 1925- WhoWest 92
**Burch,** Claire R 1925- IntAu&W 91
**Burch,** Clark Wayne 1907- AmMWSc 92
**Burch,** Craig Alan 1954- WhoFI 92
**Burch,** Curtis Eugene, Jr. 1945- WhoEnt 92
**Burch,** D Russell 1941- WhoIns 92
**Burch,** David Stewart 1926- AmMWSc 92
**Burch,** Dean d1991 LesBEnT 92
**Burch,** Dean 1927- IntWW 91, WhoAmP 91
**Burch,** Dean 1927-1991 NewYTBS 91 [port]
**Burch,** Derek George 1933- AmMWSc 92
**Burch,** Elizabeth WhoAmP 91
**Burch,** Geoffrey d1990 Who 92N
**Burch,** George Nelson Blair 1921- AmMWSc 92
**Burch,** Harold Dee 1928- WhoMW 92
**Burch,** Helen Bulbrook 1906- AmMWSc 92
**Burch,** James D. 1943- WhoFI 92
**Burch,** James Leo 1942- AmMWSc 92
**Burch,** Jerry W 1945- WhoAmP 91
**Burch,** John Bayard 1929- AmMWSc 92
**Burch,** John Christopher, Jr. 1940- WhoFI 92
**Burch,** John Thomas, Jr. 1942- WhoAmL 92
**Burch,** John Walter 1925- WhoFI 92
**Burch,** Keith 1931- Who 92
**Burch,** Kevin Andre 1960- WhoFI 92, WhoMW 92

**Burch,** Mary Kappel 1957- AmMWSc 92
**Burch,** Mary Lou 1930- WhoWest 92
**Burch,** Mary Seelye 1925- WhoAmL 92
**Burch,** Michael I 1941- WhoAmP 91
**Burch,** Paul Michael 1954- WhoAmP 91
**Burch,** Philip J. 1937- WhoFI 92
**Burch,** Phillip Michael 1949- WhoMW 92
**Burch,** Reynold Edward 1910- WhoBlA 92
**Burch,** Robert 1925- WrDr 92
**Burch,** Robert Dale 1928- WhoAmL 92
**Burch,** Robert Emmett 1933- AmMWSc 92
**Burch,** Robert L WhoAmP 91
**Burch,** Robert Ray 1924- AmMWSc 92
**Burch,** Robert Ray, Jr 1956- AmMWSc 92
**Burch,** Ronald Martin 1955- AmMWSc 92
**Burch,** Stephen Kenneth 1945- WhoMW 92
**Burch,** Thaddeus Joseph 1930- AmMWSc 92
**Burch,** Thomas J 1931- WhoAmP 91
**Burch,** Voris Reagan 1930- WhoAmL 92
**Burch,** William Alva 1925- WhoAmP 91
**Burch,** William Gerald 1911- Who 92
**Burchall,** James J 1932- AmMWSc 92
**Burcham,** Donald Preston 1916- AmMWSc 92
**Burcham,** Eva Helen 1941- WhoMW 92
**Burcham,** Jeffrey Glen 1959- WhoAmL 92
**Burcham,** Paul Baker 1916- AmMWSc 92
**Burcham,** Randall Parks 1917- WhoAmL 92
**Burcham,** Thomas H 1936- WhoIns 92
**Burcham,** Thomas Herbert 1936- WhoAmL 92
**Burcham,** Wayne B. 1948- WhoEnt 92
**Burcham,** William Ernest 1913- IntWW 91, Who 92, WrDr 92
**Burchard,** Ellen Williams 1913- WhoEnt 92, WhoFI 92
**Burchard,** Hermann Georg 1934- AmMWSc 92
**Burchard,** Jeanette 1917- AmMWSc 92
**Burchard,** John Kenneth 1936- AmMWSc 92
**Burchard,** Peter 1921- SmATA 13AS [port]
**Burchard,** Robert P 1938- AmMWSc 92
**Burchard,** Roger Frank 1958- WhoFI 92
**Burchard,** Thomas Kirk 1948- WhoWest 92
**Burchardt,** Bill 1917- TwCWW 91, WrDr 92
**Burchell,** Charles R. 1946- WhoBlA 92
**Burchell,** Howard Bertram 1907- AmMWSc 92
**Burchell,** R. A. 1941- WrDr 92
**Burchenal,** Joseph Holland 1912- AmMWSc 92
**Burchett,** Alan Edward 1943- WhoAmL 92
**Burchett,** Daryl Wayne 1959- WhoRel 92
**Burchett,** Dewey Eldridge, Jr 1939- WhoAmP 91
**Burchett,** James Clark 1932- WhoRel 92
**Burchett,** O Neill J 1935- AmMWSc 92
**Burchett,** Paul Preston 1948- WhoAmP 91
**Burchett,** Sam Preston 1954- WhoAmL 92
**Burchfiel,** Burrell Clark 1934- AmMWSc 92
**Burchfiel,** James Lee 1941- AmMWSc 92
**Burchfield,** Bobby R. 1954- WhoAmL 92
**Burchfield,** Charles 1893-1967 FacFETw, ModArCr 2 [port]
**Burchfield,** Charles Frederick 1931- WhoFI 92
**Burchfield,** Harry P 1915- AmMWSc 92
**Burchfield,** James R 1924- WhoIns 92
**Burchfield,** James Ralph 1924- WhoAmL 92, WhoFI 92, WhoMW 92
**Burchfield,** Robert Shannon 1952- WhoWest 92
**Burchfield,** Robert William 1923- ConAu 35NR, IntAu&W 91, IntWW 91, Who 92, WrDr 92
**Burchfield,** Thomas Elwood 1951- AmMWSc 92
**Burchill,** Brower Rene 1938- AmMWSc 92
**Burchill,** Charles Eugene 1932- AmMWSc 92
**Burchill,** Julie 1960- ConAu 135, IntAu&W 91
**Burchill,** Thomas Francis 1942- WhoEnt 92, WhoFI 92
**Burchmore,** David Wegner 1952- WhoAmL 92
**Burchmore,** Eric 1920- Who 92
**Burciaga,** Cecilia Preciado de 1945- WhoHisp 92
**Burciaga,** Jose Antonio DrAPF 91
**Burciaga,** Jose Antonio 1940- WhoHisp 92
**Burciaga,** Juan G. 1929- WhoHisp 92
**Burciaga,** Juan Guerrero 1929- WhoAmL 92
**Burciaga,** Juan Ramon 1953- WhoHisp 92
**Burck,** Larry Harold 1945- AmMWSc 92
**Burck,** Philip John 1936- AmMWSc 92
**Burckel,** Josef 1895-1944 BiDExR, EncTR 91 [port]
**Burckel,** Robert Bruce 1939- AmMWSc 92, WhoMW 92
**Burckhardt,** Carl Jacob 1891-1974 EncTR 91 [port]
**Burckhardt,** Christoph B 1935- AmMWSc 92
**Burczyk,** Mary Elizabeth 1953- WhoFI 92, WhoWest 92
**Burd,** Francis John 1940- WhoMW 92
**Burd,** James M 1931- WhoAmP 91
**Burd,** Laurence Ira AmMWSc 92
**Burd,** Michael Sedgwick 1952- WhoFI 92
**Burdakin,** David Campbell 1955- WhoFI 92
**Burdan,** Danny Reid 1952- WhoRel 92
**Burdash,** Nicholas Michael 1941- AmMWSc 92
**Burdashaw,** John Timothy 1958- WhoRel 92
**Burdekin,** Frederick Michael 1938- Who 92
**Burdekin,** Katharine 1896-1963 TwCSFW 91
**Burdekin,** Kay 1896- ScFEYrs
**Burden** Who 92
**Burden,** Baron 1916- Who 92
**Burden,** Alan 1938- TwCPaSc
**Burden,** Derrick Frank 1918- Who 92
**Burden,** Harvey Worth 1933- AmMWSc 92
**Burden,** Hubert White 1943- AmMWSc 92
**Burden,** James Ewers 1939- WhoAmL 92, WhoFI 92
**Burden,** Jean DrAPF 91
**Burden,** Jean 1914- WrDr 92
**Burden,** Jerry Don 1944- WhoRel 92
**Burden,** Lowell Francisco 1933- WhoEnt 92
**Burden,** Pennie L. 1910- WhoBlA 92
**Burden,** Richard L AmMWSc 92
**Burden,** Stanley Lee, Jr 1939- AmMWSc 92
**Burden,** William Douglas 1898-1978 FacFETw
**Burden,** Willie James 1951- WhoBlA 92
**Burdetsky,** Ben 1928- WhoFI 92
**Burdett,** Donna 1960- WhoWest 92
**Burdett,** George Craig 1943- WhoMW 92
**Burdett,** James Richard 1934- WhoMW 92
**Burdett,** Jeremy Keith 1947- AmMWSc 92
**Burdett,** Lorenzo Worth 1916- AmMWSc 92
**Burdett,** Philip Hawley 1914- WhoEnt 92
**Burdett,** Savile 1931- Who 92
**Burdette,** Keith 1955- WhoAmP 91
**Burdette,** Lawrence R. 1929- WhoFI 92
**Burdette,** Robert J. 1844-1914 BenetAL 91
**Burdette,** Robert Soelberg 1955- WhoFI 92
**Burdette,** Walter James 1915- AmMWSc 92
**Burdette,** William James 1962- WhoFI 92
**Burdette,** Winston LesBEnT 92
**Burdg,** Donald Eugene 1929- AmMWSc 92
**Burdge,** David Newman 1931- AmMWSc 92
**Burdge,** Geoffrey Lynn 1947- AmMWSc 92
**Burdge,** Richard James, Jr. 1949- WhoWest 92
**Burdi,** Alphonse R 1935- AmMWSc 92
**Burdick,** Allan Bernard 1920- AmMWSc 92
**Burdick,** Bruce 1933- DcTwDes
**Burdick,** Charles Lalor 1892- AmMWSc 92
**Burdick,** Daniel 1915- AmMWSc 92
**Burdick,** Donald Smiley 1937- AmMWSc 92
**Burdick,** Eugene Allan 1912- WhoAmL 92
**Burdick,** Gary Lee 1952- WhoRel 92
**Burdick,** Glenn Arthur 1932- AmMWSc 92
**Burdick,** Leander W, Jr 1925- WhoAmP 91
**Burdick,** Quentin N. 1908- AlmAP 92 [port], WhoAmP 91
**Burdick,** Quentin Northrop 1908- IntWW 91, WhoMW 92
**Burdine,** Glenn D 1930- WhoAmP 91
**Burdine,** Howard William 1909- AmMWSc 92
**Burdine,** John Alton 1936- AmMWSc 92
**Burditt,** Arthur Kendall, Jr 1928- AmMWSc 92
**Burditt,** George Miller, Jr. 1922- WhoAmL 92
**Burdsall,** Harold Hugh, Jr 1940- AmMWSc 92
**Burdus,** Ann 1933- Who 92
**Burek,** Anthony John 1946- AmMWSc 92
**Burelli Rivas,** Miguel Angel 1922- IntWW 91
**Burenga,** Kenneth L. 1944- WhoFI 92
**Bures,** Donald John 1938- AmMWSc 92
**Bures,** Milan F 1932- AmMWSc 92
**Bures,** Stephen Gregg 1950- WhoMW 92
**Buresch,** Charles Edward 1947- WhoMW 92
**Buresh,** C. John 1945- WhoAmL 92
**Buresh,** James Francis 1942- WhoAmL 92
**Buresh,** Timothy Brent 1954- WhoWest 92
**Buresova,** Dagmar 1929- IntWW 91
**Burfening,** Peter J 1942- AmMWSc 92
**Burfield,** Eva IntAu&W 91X
**Burford,** Earl of 1965- Who 92
**Burford,** Arthur Edgar 1928- AmMWSc 92
**Burford,** Dorothy Wright 1903- WhoAmP 91
**Burford,** Effie Lois 1927- WhoBlA 92
**Burford,** Eleanor IntAu&W 91X, Who 92, WrDr 92
**Burford,** Hugh Jonathan 1931- AmMWSc 92
**Burford,** Janice Elizabeth 1953- WhoFI 92
**Burford,** Jeremy Michael Joseph 1942- Who 92
**Burford,** Lolah 1931- WrDr 92
**Burford,** M Gilbert 1910- AmMWSc 92
**Burford,** Neil 1958- AmMWSc 92
**Burford,** Robert F 1923- WhoAmP 91
**Burford,** Roger Lewis 1930- AmMWSc 92
**Burford,** Thomas George 1949- WhoEnt 92
**Burford,** William DrAPF 91
**Burford,** William 1927- ConPo 91, WrDr 92
**Burg,** Anton Behme 1904- AmMWSc 92
**Burg,** Barry Richard 1938- WhoWest 92
**Burg,** Dale 1942- IntAu&W 91
**Burg,** Dale Ronda 1942- WhoEnt 92
**Burg,** Gary G. 1956- WhoWest 92
**Burg,** Gerald William 1923- WhoRel 92, WhoWest 92
**Burg,** Gisela Elisabeth 1939- Who 92
**Burg,** James Allen 1941- WhoAmP 91
**Burg,** John Parker 1931- AmMWSc 92
**Burg,** Josef 1909- IntWW 91
**Burg,** Marion 1921- AmMWSc 92
**Burg,** Maurice B 1931- AmMWSc 92
**Burg,** Michael S. 1950- WhoAmL 92
**Burg,** Richard William 1932- AmMWSc 92
**Burg,** Ruth Cooper 1926- WhoAmL 92
**Burg,** William Robert 1929- AmMWSc 92
**Burgamy,** Michael Barnet 1945- WhoWest 92
**Burgan,** Cathy Denice 1953- WhoAmL 92
**Burgan,** Salih Khalil 1918- IntWW 91
**Burgard,** Horst 1929- IntWW 91
**Burgarino,** Anthony Emanuel 1948- WhoWest 92
**Burgauer,** Paul David 1926- AmMWSc 92
**Burgdoerfer,** Jerry 1958- WhoAmL 92
**Burge,** Catherine Alice 1956- WhoEnt 92
**Burge,** David Russell 1930- WhoEnt 92
**Burge,** Dennis Knight 1935- AmMWSc 92
**Burge,** Gary Mitchell 1952- WhoMW 92, WhoRel 92
**Burge,** Gregg WhoEnt 92
**Burge,** Jean C 1947- AmMWSc 92
**Burge,** Robert Ernest, Jr 1925- AmMWSc 92
**Burge,** Ronald Edgar 1932- Who 92
**Burge,** Stuart 1918- Who 92
**Burge,** Wylie D 1925- AmMWSc 92
**Burgee,** John 1933- DcTwDes, FacFETw
**Burgei,** Daniel Lynn 1950- WhoMW 92
**Burgen,** Arnold 1922- IntWW 91, Who 92
**Burgener,** Clair W 1921- WhoAmP 91
**Burgener,** Francis Andre 1942- AmMWSc 92
**Burgener,** Robert Howard 1936- WhoFI 92
**Burgeon,** G A L IntAu&W 91X
**Burger,** Alewyn Petrus 1927- IntWW 91
**Burger,** Alfred 1905- AmMWSc 92
**Burger,** Ambrose William 1923- AmMWSc 92
**Burger,** Carol J 1944- AmMWSc 92
**Burger,** Carolyn S. 1940- WhoFI 92
**Burger,** Christian P 1929- AmMWSc 92
**Burger,** Dionys 1923- AmMWSc 92
**Burger,** Edward James, Jr 1933- AmMWSc 92
**Burger,** George Vanderkarr 1927- AmMWSc 92
**Burger,** Gottfried August 1748-1794 BlkwCEP
**Burger,** Henry Robert, III 1940- AmMWSc 92
**Burger,** Joanna 1941- AmMWSc 92
**Burger,** John Edward 1946- WhoRel 92
**Burger,** Kenneth Eugene 1950- WhoRel 92
**Burger,** Leland Leonard 1917- AmMWSc 92
**Burger,** Mary Williams WhoBlA 92
**Burger,** Ray Othmar 1952- WhoMW 92
**Burger,** Richard Melton 1941- AmMWSc 92
**Burger,** Robert 1931- WrDr 92
**Burger,** Robert M 1927- AmMWSc 92
**Burger,** Warren 1907- FacFETw [port], RComAH
**Burger,** Warren Clark 1923- AmMWSc 92
**Burger,** Warren E. 1907- IntWW 91, WhoAmP 91
**Burger,** Warren Earl 1907- AmPolLe, Who 92, WhoAmL 92
**Burger,** Wilhelm 1824-1869 ThHEIm
**Burgert,** Bill E 1929- AmMWSc 92
**Burgert,** David Lee 1959- WhoAmL 92
**Burges,** Alan Who 92
**Burges,** Betty Who 92
**Burges,** Dempsey 1751-1800 DcNCBi 1
**Burges,** Norman Alan 1911- Who 92, WrDr 92
**Burges,** Rodney Lyon Travers 1914- Who 92
**Burges,** Stephen John 1944- AmMWSc 92
**Burges,** Thomas 1712-1779 DcNCBi 1
**Burges Watson,** Richard Eagleson Gordon Who 92
**Burgeson,** Noreen Theresa 1953- WhoFI 92
**Burgeson,** Robert Eugene 1945- AmMWSc 92
**Burgess,** Lord 1924- WhoBlA 92
**Burgess,** Alan 1936- TwCPaSc
**Burgess,** Ann Baker 1942- AmMWSc 92
**Burgess,** Anthony DrAPF 91
**Burgess,** Anthony 1917- CnDBLB 8 [port], ConCom 92, ConNov 91, FacFETw, IntAu&W 91, IntWW 91, LiExTwC, RfGEnL 91, TwCSFW 91, Who 92, WrDr 92
**Burgess,** Anthony Reginald Frank 1932- Who 92
**Burgess,** Averil 1938- Who 92
**Burgess,** Benjamin L., Jr. 1943- WhoAmL 92
**Burgess,** Brio DrAPF 91
**Burgess,** Bruce Howland 1950- WhoFI 92
**Burgess,** Cecil Edmund 1920- AmMWSc 92
**Burgess,** Charles 1932- WrDr 92
**Burgess,** Charles Harry 1926- WhoMW 92
**Burgess,** Clara Woodward 1918- WhoWest 92
**Burgess,** Claude Bramall 1910- Who 92
**Burgess,** Cyril Duncan 1929- Who 92
**Burgess,** D. Gene 1939- WhoRel 92
**Burgess,** David 1948- WhoAmL 92, WhoFI 92
**Burgess,** David John 1939- Who 92
**Burgess,** David Ray 1947- AmMWSc 92
**Burgess,** David Stewart 1917- WhoRel 92
**Burgess,** Dennis Lane 1953- WhoFI 92, WhoMW 92
**Burgess,** Dilys Averil Who 92
**Burgess,** Donald Wayne 1947- AmMWSc 92
**Burgess,** Dwight A. 1927- WhoBlA 92
**Burgess,** Edward 1848-1891 BiInAmS
**Burgess,** Edward 1927- Who 92
**Burgess,** Edward Meredith 1934- AmMWSc 92
**Burgess,** Edward S WhoAmP 91
**Burgess,** Forrest d1991 NewYTBS 91
**Burgess,** Fred J 1926- AmMWSc 92
**Burgess,** Gelett 1866-1951 BenetAL 91, ScFEYrs, -A
**Burgess,** Geoffrey Harold Orchard 1926- Who 92
**Burgess,** Geoffrey Kelsen 1935- Who 92
**Burgess,** George Evans, III 1946- WhoFI 92
**Burgess,** Gwendolyn Diane 1953- WhoAmL 92
**Burgess,** Hayden Fern 1946- WhoAmL 92
**Burgess,** Henry Ernest 1929- WhoWest 92
**Burgess,** Hovey Mann 1916- AmMWSc 92
**Burgess,** Hugh 1929- WhoAmP 91
**Burgess,** Ian Glencross 1931- IntWW 91
**Burgess,** Isabel Andrews WhoAmP 91
**Burgess,** Jack 1942- WhoAmP 91
**Burgess,** Jack D 1924- AmMWSc 92
**Burgess,** James Edward 1936- WhoMW 92
**Burgess,** James Harland 1929- AmMWSc 92
**Burgess,** James R., Jr. 1915- WhoBlA 92
**Burgess,** Janet Helen 1933- WhoFI 92
**Burgess,** Jeanne Llewellyn 1923- WhoFI 92
**Burgess,** John 1929- Who 92
**Burgess,** John A. 1951- WhoAmL 92
**Burgess,** John C 1923- AmMWSc 92
**Burgess,** John Edward 1930- Who 92
**Burgess,** John Herbert 1933- AmMWSc 92
**Burgess,** John Melville 1909- WhoBlA 92
**Burgess,** John Paul 1954- WhoRel 92
**Burgess,** John S 1918- AmMWSc 92
**Burgess,** John Stuart 1920- WhoAmP 91
**Burgess,** Joseph Edward 1935- WhoBlA 92
**Burgess,** Joseph James, Jr. 1924- WhoWest 92
**Burgess,** Joseph Stuart 1929- Who 92
**Burgess,** Joseph Wesley 1910- WhoWest 92
**Burgess,** Michael 1948- WhoWest 92
**Burgess,** Paul Richards 1934- AmMWSc 92
**Burgess,** Raymond L. WhoBlA 92
**Burgess,** Richard James WhoEnt 92
**Burgess,** Richard Ray 1942- AmMWSc 92
**Burgess,** Robert Charles 1959- WhoWest 92
**Burgess,** Robert E., Sr. 1937- WhoBlA 92
**Burgess,** Robert Kyle 1948- WhoAmL 92
**Burgess,** Robert Lewis 1931- AmMWSc 92
**Burgess,** Roger 1927- WhoRel 92
**Burgess,** Sally 1953- Who 92

**Burgess**, Stanley Milton 1937- *WhoRel 92*
**Burgess**, Stuart *Who 92*
**Burgess**, Teresa Lynn 1957- *AmMWSc 92*
**Burgess**, Thomas David 1947- *WhoFI 92*
**Burgess**, Thomas Edward 1923- *AmMWSc 92*
**Burgess**, Thornton W. 1874-1965 *BenetAL 91*
**Burgess**, Tony *Who 92*
**Burgess**, W. Starling 1878-1947 *DcTwDes, FacFETw*
**Burgess**, Warren E. 1932- *WrDr 92*
**Burgess**, William Henry 1917- *WhoWest 92*
**Burgess**, William Howard 1924- *AmMWSc 92*
**Burgess**, William J *WhoAmP 91*
**Burgess**, William Thomas, IV 1959- *WhoAmL 92*
**Burgess**, William Vander 1934- *WhoWest 92*
**Burgess**, Wilson Hales 1954- *AmMWSc 92*
**Burgest**, David Raymond 1943- *WhoBlA 92*
**Burget**, Franz Anthony, III 1939- *WhoWest 92*
**Burgett**, Paul Joseph *WhoBlA 92*
**Burgette**, James M. 1937- *WhoBlA 92*
**Burgevin**, Henry Andrea 1836-1865 *DcNCBi 1*
**Burgevine**, Henry Andrea 1836-1865 *DcNCBi 1*
**Burggraf**, Odus R 1929- *AmMWSc 92*
**Burggren**, Warren William 1951- *AmMWSc 92*
**Burgh**, Baron 1935- *Who 92*
**Burgh**, John 1925- *Who 92*
**Burgh**, John Charles 1925- *IntWW 91*
**Burgh**, Steven Lawrence 1950- *WhoEnt 92*
**Burghardt**, Gordon Martin 1941- *AmMWSc 92*
**Burghardt**, Robert Casey 1947- *AmMWSc 92*
**Burghardt**, Walter J. 1914- *IntWW 91*
**Burghardt**, Walter John 1914- *WhoRel 92*
**Burghart**, James H 1938- *AmMWSc 92*
**Burgheim**, Richard Allan 1933- *WhoEnt 92*
**Burghersh**, Lord 1951- *Who 92*
**Burghley**, Lord 1970- *Who 92*
**Burghley**, Rose *WrDr 92*
**Burghoff**, Gary 1943- *IntMPA 92*
**Burghoff**, Henry L 1907- *AmMWSc 92*
**Burgi**, Ernest, Jr 1924- *AmMWSc 92*
**Burgie**, Irving Louis 1924- *WhoBlA 92*
**Burgin**, George Hans 1930- *AmMWSc 92*
**Burgin**, Max Edward 1934- *WhoRel 92*
**Burgin**, Richard *DrAPF 91*
**Burgin**, Richard 1892-1981 *NewAmDM*
**Burgin**, Richard Arlen 1944- *WhoFI 92*
**Burgin**, Ruth L. W. *WhoBlA 92*
**Burgin**, Victor 1941- *IntWW 91, TwCPaSc*
**Burgin**, William Garner, Jr 1924- *WhoAmP 91*
**Burgin**, William Olin 1877-1946 *DcNCBi 1*
**Burgin**, William Townsend 1943- *WhoFI 92*
**Burginyon**, Gary Alfred 1935- *AmMWSc 92*
**Burgio**, Jane *WhoAmP 91*
**Burgison**, Raymond Merritt 1917- *AmMWSc 92*
**Burgland**, Jane Harvey 1931- *WhoAmP 91*
**Burglass**, Bruce Donald, Jr. *WhoAmL 92*
**Burgmaier**, George John 1944- *AmMWSc 92*
**Burgman**, Dierdre Ann 1948- *WhoAmL 92, WhoFI 92*
**Burgner**, Robert Louis 1919- *AmMWSc 92*
**Burgner**, Thomas Ulric 1932- *Who 92*
**Burgoa**, Benali 1956- *AmMWSc 92*
**Burgoa**, John Francis 1948- *WhoHisp 92*
**Burgon**, Geoffrey 1941- *ConCom 92, IntWW 91, Who 92*
**Burgon**, M. Kent 1936- *WhoWest 92*
**Burgos**, Fernando 1927- *WhoHisp 92*
**Burgos**, Jose d1872 *HisDSpE*
**Burgos**, Joseph 1966- *WhoHisp 92*
**Burgos**, Joseph Agner, Jr. 1945- *WhoHisp 92*
**Burgos**, Julia de 1914-1953 *SpAmWW*
**Burgos**, Luis Noel 1963- *WhoHisp 92*
**Burgos-Aguilar**, Benjamin 1941- *WhoHisp 92*
**Burgos-Sasscer**, Ruth 1931- *WhoHisp 92*
**Burgoyne**, Bruce E. 1924- *ConAu 135*
**Burgoyne**, Edward Eynon 1918- *AmMWSc 92*
**Burgoyne**, George Harvey 1939- *AmMWSc 92*
**Burgoyne**, J Albert 1914- *WhoIns 92*
**Burgoyne**, John 1722-1792 *BenetAL 91, BlkwEAR [port], RfGEnL 91*
**Burgoyne**, Peter Nicholas 1932- *AmMWSc 92*
**Burgoyne**, Robert Anthony 1956- *WhoAmL 92*
**Burgoyne**, Robert Michael 1927- *Who 92*
**Burgoyne**, Thomas H. 1855-1894 *RelLAm 91*
**Burgstahler**, Albert William 1928- *AmMWSc 92*
**Burgstahler**, Sylvan 1928- *AmMWSc 92*
**Burguiere**, Julius Edward 1958- *WhoRel 92*
**Burguieres**, John Berchman, Jr. 1945- *WhoAmL 92*
**Burguieres**, Philip Joseph 1943- *WhoFI 92*
**Burgum**, Katherine K 1915- *WhoAmP 91*
**Burgus**, Roger Cecil 1934- *AmMWSc 92*
**Burgus**, Warren Harold 1919- *AmMWSc 92*
**Burgweger**, Francis Joseph Dewes, Jr. 1942- *WhoAmL 92*
**Burgwin**, George William Bush 1787-1854 *DcNCBi 1*
**Burgwin**, John 1731-1803 *DcNCBi 1*
**Burgwin**, John Henry King 1810-1847 *DcNCBi 1*
**Burgwin**, Nathaniel Hill 1825-1898 *DcNCBi 1*
**Burgwyn**, Henry King, Jr. 1841-1863 *DcNCBi 1*
**Burgwyn**, John Fanning 1783-1864 *DcNCBi 1*
**Burgwyn**, William Hyslop Sumner 1845-1913 *DcNCBi 1*
**Burgwyn**, William Hyslop Sumner 1886-1977 *DcNCBi 1*
**Burhans**, Ralph W 1922- *AmMWSc 92*
**Burhoe**, Ralph Wendell 1911- *WhoRel 92*
**Burholt**, Dennis Robert 1942- *AmMWSc 92*
**Burhop**, Kenneth Eugene 1953- *AmMWSc 92*
**Burhouse**, Susan Marie 1946- *WhoFI 92*
**Buri**, Charles Edward 1950- *WhoAmL 92*
**Buria**, Silvia 1940- *WhoHisp 92*
**Burian**, Jarka M. 1927- *WrDr 92*
**Burian**, Richard M 1941- *AmMWSc 92*
**Burick**, Richard Joseph 1939- *AmMWSc 92*
**Burigana**, Enus A 1928- *WhoIns 92*
**Burin Des Roziers**, Etienne 1913- *IntWW 91*
**Burington**, Don William 1908- *WhoAmL 92*
**Buriok**, Gerald Michael 1943- *AmMWSc 92*
**Burish**, Thomas Gerard 1950- *AmMWSc 92*
**Burita**, Countess *EncAmaz 91*
**Burk**, Carl John 1935- *AmMWSc 92*
**Burk**, Cornelius Franklin, Jr 1933- *AmMWSc 92*
**Burk**, Creighton 1929- *AmMWSc 92*
**Burk**, David Lawrence 1929- *AmMWSc 92*
**Burk**, Donald Louis 1957- *WhoFI 92, WhoMW 92*
**Burk**, Gary Maurice 1943- *WhoFI 92*
**Burk**, Jack Andrew 1935- *WhoWest 92*
**Burk**, Lawrence G 1920- *AmMWSc 92*
**Burk**, Norman 1937- *WhoMW 92*
**Burk**, Raymond Franklin, Jr 1942- *AmMWSc 92*
**Burk**, Robert F. 1955- *ConAu 134*
**Burk**, Robert W, Jr 1939- *WhoAmP 91*
**Burka**, Maria Karpati 1948- *AmMWSc 92*
**Burka**, Mark B 1950- *WhoIns 92*
**Burka**, Robert Alan 1944- *WhoAmL 92*
**Burkacki**, Garry Shawn 1961- *WhoRel 92*
**Burkard**, Michael *DrAPF 91*
**Burkard**, Otto Michael 1908- *IntWW 91*
**Burkard**, Peter Hubert 1940- *WhoAmL 92*
**Burkart**, Burke 1933- *AmMWSc 92*
**Burkart**, Jeffrey Edward 1948- *WhoMW 92*
**Burkart**, Jordan V. 1935- *WhoWest 92*
**Burkart**, Leonard F 1920- *AmMWSc 92*
**Burkart**, Milton W 1922- *AmMWSc 92*
**Burkart**, Timothy Clement 1954- *WhoAmL 92*
**Burkat**, Leonard 1919- *WhoEnt 92*
**Burke**, Aedanus 1743-1802 *BlkwEAR*
**Burke**, Alfred 1918- *IntMPA 92*
**Burke**, Anne M. *WhoRel 92*
**Burke**, Anthony Duane 1955- *WhoMW 92*
**Burke**, Arleigh Albert 1901- *Who 92*
**Burke**, Arthur Thomas 1919- *WhoWest 92*
**Burke**, Augustin Emile 1922- *WhoRel 92*
**Burke**, Bernard Flood 1928- *AmMWSc 92, IntWW 91*
**Burke**, Billy Brown 1928- *WhoAmP 91*
**Burke**, Brian B 1958- *WhoAmP 91, WhoMW 92*
**Burke**, Brian Peter 1958- *WhoAmL 92*
**Burke**, Brian Thomas 1947- *IntWW 91, Who 92*
**Burke**, Bruce Thomas Hudson 1950- *WhoAmL 92*
**Burke**, Carol *DrAPF 91*
**Burke**, Carroll N 1929- *AmMWSc 92*
**Burke**, Christine F 1956- *WhoAmP 91*
**Burke**, Crescent Frederick 1961- *WhoMW 92*
**Burke**, Daniel *WhoAmP 91*
**Burke**, Daniel B. *LesBEnT 92 [port]*
**Burke**, Daniel Barnett 1929- *WhoEnt 92, WhoFI 92*
**Burke**, David H 1939- *AmMWSc 92*
**Burke**, David Roy 1950- *WhoEnt 92*
**Burke**, David W. *LesBEnT 92*
**Burke**, DeGrandval 1909- *WhoBlA 92*
**Burke**, Delta 1956- *IntMPA 92, WhoEnt 92*
**Burke**, Denise Williamson 1947- *WhoEnt 92*
**Burke**, Dennis Garth 1935- *AmMWSc 92*
**Burke**, Dennis Keith 1943- *AmMWSc 92*
**Burke**, Denzer 1933- *WhoBlA 92*
**Burke**, Derek Clissold 1930- *Who 92*
**Burke**, Edmond W 1935- *WhoAmP 91*
**Burke**, Edmond Wayne 1935- *WhoAmL 92, WhoWest 92*
**Burke**, Edmund 1729-1797 *BlkwCEP, BlkwEAR, RfGEnL 91*
**Burke**, Edmund C 1919- *AmMWSc 92*
**Burke**, Edmund C 1921- *AmMWSc 92*
**Burke**, Edmund R 1949- *AmMWSc 92*
**Burke**, Edmund William 1948- *WhoAmL 92, WhoFI 92*
**Burke**, Edward Aloysius 1929- *AmMWSc 92*
**Burke**, Edward Kenneth 1937- *WhoAmP 91*
**Burke**, Edward L 1943- *WhoAmP 91*
**Burke**, Edward M 1943- *WhoAmP 91*
**Burke**, Edward Walter, Jr 1924- *AmMWSc 92*
**Burke**, Emmett C. 1920- *WhoBlA 92*
**Burke**, France *DrAPF 91*
**Burke**, Frank Welsh 1920- *WhoAmP 91*
**Burke**, Frederic Gerard 1946- *WhoIns 92*
**Burke**, Gay Ann Wolesensky 1954- *WhoAmL 92*
**Burke**, Geoffrey 1913- *Who 92*
**Burke**, Gerard Patrick 1930- *WhoAmP 91*
**Burke**, Gordon B 1941- *WhoAmP 91*
**Burke**, Hanna Suss 1926- *AmMWSc 92*
**Burke**, Harold DeVere 1922- *WhoWest 92*
**Burke**, J Anthony 1937- *AmMWSc 92*
**Burke**, J E 1914- *AmMWSc 92*
**Burke**, Jack L 1949- *WhoIns 92*
**Burke**, Jacqueline Yvonne 1949- *WhoEnt 92, WhoFI 92*
**Burke**, James 1936- *IntAu&W 91, WrDr 92*
**Burke**, James 1948- *WhoAmP 91*
**Burke**, James 1956- *Who 92*
**Burke**, James David 1937- *AmMWSc 92*
**Burke**, James Donald 1939- *WhoMW 92*
**Burke**, James Edward 1931- *AmMWSc 92*
**Burke**, James Joseph 1937- *AmMWSc 92*
**Burke**, James Joseph, Jr 1931- *AmMWSc 92*
**Burke**, James Joseph, Jr. 1951- *WhoFI 92*
**Burke**, James L 1918- *AmMWSc 92*
**Burke**, James Lee 1936- *WrDr 92*
**Burke**, James Otey 1912- *AmMWSc 92*
**Burke**, James Patrick *AmMWSc 92*
**Burke**, Jane D. 1956- *WhoAmL 92*
**Burke**, Janice Marie *AmMWSc 92*
**Burke**, Jeffrey Burke 1950- *WhoFI 92*
**Burke**, Jeffrey Peter 1941- *Who 92*
**Burke**, Jerome A 1937- *WhoAmP 91*
**Burke**, John 1922- *WrDr 92*
**Burke**, John 1928- *WhoRel 92*
**Burke**, John A 1936- *AmMWSc 92*
**Burke**, John Charles 1946- *WhoWest 92*
**Burke**, John Daly 1775?-1808 *BenetAL 91*
**Burke**, John Francis 1922- *AmMWSc 92*
**Burke**, John Frederick 1922- *IntAu&W 91*
**Burke**, John James 1928- *WhoAmL 92, WhoFI 92*
**Burke**, John Kenneth 1939- *Who 92*
**Burke**, John Michael 1941- *WhoAmL 92*
**Burke**, John Michael 1946- *AmMWSc 92*
**Burke**, John P 1954- *WhoAmP 91*
**Burke**, John T 1929- *AmMWSc 92*
**Burke**, Jonathan *IntAu&W 91X, WrDr 92*
**Burke**, Joseph 1913- *Who 92*
**Burke**, Kenneth 1897- *BenetAL 91, ConPo 91, IntAu&W 91, IntWW 91*
**Burke**, Kenneth B S 1935- *AmMWSc 92*
**Burke**, Kenneth Edison 1936- *WhoRel 92*
**Burke**, Kenneth John 1939- *WhoAmL 92*
**Burke**, Kerry *Who 92*
**Burke**, Kevin Charles 1929- *AmMWSc 92*
**Burke**, Kevin Michael 1946- *WhoAmL 92, WhoAmP 91*
**Burke**, Kevin Thomas 1961- *WhoWest 92*
**Burke**, Kirkland R. 1948- *WhoBlA 92*
**Burke**, Kristin Marie 1970- *WhoEnt 92*
**Burke**, Lawrence A. *WhoRel 92*
**Burke**, Leslie Carlton 1941- *WhoRel 92*
**Burke**, Lillian W. 1917- *WhoBlA 92*
**Burke**, Lisa Gaye 1960- *WhoMW 92*
**Burke**, Logan 1933- *WhoAmP 91*
**Burke**, Margaret Ann 1961- *WhoFI 92*
**Burke**, Marjorie 1932- *WhoAmP 91*
**Burke**, Marnie Sparre 1937- *WhoRel 92*
**Burke**, Martin B 1940- *WhoAmP 91*
**Burke**, Mary Catherine 1929- *WhoAmP 91*
**Burke**, Mary Williams 1782-1869 *DcNCBi 1*
**Burke**, Michael Francis 1939- *AmMWSc 92, WhoWest 92*
**Burke**, Michael Henry 1952- *WhoAmL 92*
**Burke**, Michael John 1942- *AmMWSc 92*
**Burke**, Michele Christine *WhoEnt 92*
**Burke**, Morris 1938- *AmMWSc 92*
**Burke**, Nancy Aelishia 1933- *WhoAmP 91*
**Burke**, Olga Pickering 1946- *WhoBlA 92*
**Burke**, Owen *WrDr 92*
**Burke**, Patrick 1932- *TwCPaSc*
**Burke**, Patrick Joseph 1949- *WhoAmL 92*
**Burke**, Patrick Walton 1922- *WhoAmP 91*
**Burke**, Paul 1926- *IntMPA 92*
**Burke**, Paul Aloysius 1956- *WhoFI 92*
**Burke**, Paul E, Jr 1934- *WhoAmP 91, WhoMW 92*
**Burke**, Paul Edmund 1948- *WhoFI 92*
**Burke**, Paul J 1920- *AmMWSc 92*
**Burke**, Paul Norman 1955- *WhoMW 92*
**Burke**, Peter Michael 1948- *WhoAmL 92*
**Burke**, Peter Sibley 1946- *WhoEnt 92*
**Burke**, Philip George 1932- *IntWW 91, Who 92*
**Burke**, Ralph *ConAu 36NR, TwCSFW 91*
**Burke**, Ralph 1960- *WhoAmP 91*
**Burke**, Ray 1943- *IntWW 91*
**Burke**, Richard 1932- *IntWW 91, Who 92*
**Burke**, Richard Edward 1946- *WhoAmL 92*
**Burke**, Richard J, Jr 1940- *WhoAmP 91*
**Burke**, Richard Lerda 1925- *AmMWSc 92*
**Burke**, Robert Bertram 1942- *WhoAmL 92*
**Burke**, Robert D 1951- *AmMWSc 92*
**Burke**, Robert Dana 1954- *WhoAmL 92*
**Burke**, Robert Emmett 1934- *AmMWSc 92*
**Burke**, Robert F 1925- *AmMWSc 92*
**Burke**, Robert Harry 1945- *WhoMW 92*
**Burke**, Robert James 1934- *WhoAmP 91*
**Burke**, Robert Leslie 1957- *WhoMW 92*
**Burke**, Robert Wayne 1958- *AmMWSc 92*
**Burke**, Samuel Martin 1906- *IntWW 91*
**Burke**, Selma Hortense 1900- *NotBlAW 92, WhoBlA 92*
**Burke**, Shawn Edmund 1959- *AmMWSc 92*
**Burke**, Shawn Patrick 1958- *WhoFI 92*
**Burke**, Stephen 1970- *WhoAmP 91*
**Burke**, Stephen S 1945- *WhoIns 92*
**Burke**, Steven Douglas 1951- *AmMWSc 92*
**Burke**, Steven Francis 1952- *WhoMW 92*
**Burke**, Terence 1931- *WhoWest 92*
**Burke**, Terry 1927- *TwCPaSc*
**Burke**, Thomas 1744?-1783 *DcNCBi 1*
**Burke**, Thomas 1747-1783 *BlkwEAR*
**Burke**, Thomas 1906-1945 *TwCPaSc*
**Burke**, Thomas C 1941- *WhoIns 92*
**Burke**, Thomas Edmund 1932- *WhoAmL 92*
**Burke**, Thomas John 1947- *WhoMW 92*
**Burke**, Thomas John, Jr. 1943- *WhoRel 92*
**Burke**, Thomas Joseph 1927- *WhoMW 92*
**Burke**, Thomas Joseph 1938- *AmMWSc 92*
**Burke**, Thomas Joseph, Jr. 1941- *WhoAmL 92*
**Burke**, Thomas Kerry 1942- *IntWW 91, Who 92*
**Burke**, Thomas Michael 1956- *WhoAmL 92*
**Burke**, Thomas Raymond 1928- *WhoAmL 92*
**Burke**, Thomas Richard 1963- *WhoFI 92*
**Burke**, Timothy J 1948- *WhoAmP 91*
**Burke**, Tom 1947- *Who 92*
**Burke**, Vincent Cornelius, III 1951- *WhoAmL 92*
**Burke**, Vivian H *WhoAmP 91, WhoBlA 92*
**Burke**, Waymon Eugene 1951- *WhoAmP 91*
**Burke**, William Arthur 1939- *WhoBlA 92*
**Burke**, William Henry 1924- *AmMWSc 92*
**Burke**, William J 1935- *AmMWSc 92*
**Burke**, William James 1912- *AmMWSc 92*
**Burke**, William Joseph 1940- *AmMWSc 92*
**Burke**, William L 1941- *AmMWSc 92*
**Burke**, William Temple, Jr. 1935- *WhoAmL 92*
**Burke**, William Thomas, Jr 1924- *AmMWSc 92*
**Burke**, Yvonne Braithwaite 1932- *NotBlAW 92 [port]*
**Burke**, Yvonne Watson Brathwaite 1932- *WhoAmL 92, WhoBlA 92, WhoWest 92*
**Burke-Gaffney**, John Campion 1932- *Who 92*
**Burke-Gaffney**, Michael Anthony Bowes 1928- *Who 92*
**Burke-Sullivan**, Eileen Catherine 1949- *WhoRel 92*
**Burkee**, Irvin 1918- *WhoWest 92*
**Burkel**, William E 1938- *AmMWSc 92*
**Burkemper**, Thomas A. 1962- *WhoMW 92*
**Burken**, Ruth Marie 1956- *WhoMW 92*
**Burkert**, Nancy Ekholm 1933- *SmATA 14AS [port]*

**Burkert,** Walter 1931- *ConAu 34NR*
**Burkes,** Wayne Oliver 1929- *WhoAmP 91*
**Burket,** Gail Brook 1905- *WhoMW 92*
**Burket,** George Edward 1912- *AmMWSc 92*
**Burket,** Patricia Krise 1952- *WhoAmL 92*
**Burkett,** Albert LeRoy 1897- *WhoWest 92*
**Burkett,** Edward Eugene 1955- *WhoRel 92*
**Burkett,** Gerald Arthur 1939- *WhoEnt 92*
**Burkett,** Howard 1916- *AmMWSc 92*
**Burkett,** Joe Wylie 1945- *WhoAmL 92*
**Burkett,** Lawrence V. *WhoAmL 92*
**Burkett,** Mary Elizabeth *Who 92*
**Burkett,** Mike 1948- *WhoAmP 91*
**Burkett,** Randall Keith 1943- *WhoRel 92*
**Burkett,** William Ray, Jr. 1943- *WhoWest 92*
**Burkette,** Tyrone *WhoBlA 92*
**Burkey,** Bruce Curtiss 1938- *AmMWSc 92*
**Burkey,** Jacob Brent 1946- *WhoAmL 92*
**Burkey,** Lee Melville 1914- *WhoAmL 92, WhoMW 92*
**Burkey,** Ronald Steven 1957- *AmMWSc 92*
**Burkhalter,** Alan 1932- *AmMWSc 92*
**Burkhalter,** Barton R 1938- *AmMWSc 92*
**Burkhalter,** Jane *WhoEnt 92*
**Burkhalter,** Philip Gary 1937- *AmMWSc 92*
**Burkhammer,** Eugene Ronald 1944- *WhoRel 92*
**Burkhard,** Donald George 1918- *AmMWSc 92*
**Burkhard,** Mahlon Daniel 1923- *AmMWSc 92*
**Burkhard,** Raymond Kenneth 1924- *AmMWSc 92*
**Burkhardt,** Alan Elmer 1947- *AmMWSc 92*
**Burkhardt,** Charles Henry 1915- *WhoFI 92*
**Burkhardt,** Christian Carl 1924- *AmMWSc 92*
**Burkhardt,** Donald Malcolm 1936- *WhoAmL 92*
**Burkhardt,** Douglas A. 1947- *WhoMW 92*
**Burkhardt,** Edward Arnold 1938- *WhoFI 92, WhoMW 92*
**Burkhardt,** Francois 1936- *IntWW 91*
**Burkhardt,** James Kevin 1954- *WhoMW 92*
**Burkhardt,** Jerold Wayne 1941- *WhoWest 92*
**Burkhardt,** Kenneth J 1945- *AmMWSc 92*
**Burkhardt,** Lawrence, III 1932- *WhoFI 92*
**Burkhardt,** Peter Henry 1938- *WhoFI 92*
**Burkhardt,** Walter H *AmMWSc 92*
**Burkhart,** Betty M 1931- *WhoAmP 91*
**Burkhart,** Elizabeth Flores 1935- *WhoHisp 92*
**Burkhart,** Harold Eugene 1944- *AmMWSc 92*
**Burkhart,** John Ernest 1927- *WhoRel 92*
**Burkhart,** Kathe *DrAPF 91*
**Burkhart,** Kathryn Watterson 1942- *ConAu 34NR*
**Burkhart,** Kitsi *ConAu 34NR*
**Burkhart,** Lawrence E 1929- *AmMWSc 92*
**Burkhart,** Paul James 1956- *WhoAmL 92*
**Burkhart,** Richard Delmar 1934- *AmMWSc 92*
**Burkhart,** Richard Henry 1946- *AmMWSc 92*
**Burkhart,** Robert Dean 1945- *WhoFI 92*
**Burkhart,** Robin Lee 1952- *WhoRel 92*
**Burkhart,** Stephen 1931- *WhoAmP 91*
**Burkhart,** Susan Lynn 1950- *WhoMW 92*
**Burkhauser,** Teresa Elaine 1955- *WhoWest 92*
**Burkhead,** Martin Samuel 1933- *AmMWSc 92*
**Burkhead,** Rebecca Rose 1959- *WhoWest 92*
**Burkholder,** David Frederick 1931- *AmMWSc 92*
**Burkholder,** Donald Lyman 1927- *AmMWSc 92*
**Burkholder,** John Henry 1925- *AmMWSc 92*
**Burkholder,** Joyce Lynn 1951- *WhoWest 92*
**Burkholder,** Peter M 1933- *AmMWSc 92*
**Burkholder,** Timothy Jay 1941- *AmMWSc 92*
**Burkholder,** Wendell Eugene 1928- *AmMWSc 92*
**Burkholz,** Herbert *DrAPF 91, IntAu&W 91X*
**Burkholz,** Yvonne 1934- *WhoAmP 91*
**Burki,** Henry John 1940- *AmMWSc 92*
**Burki,** Nausherwan Khan *AmMWSc 92*
**Burkill,** John Charles 1900- *IntWW 91, Who 92*
**Burkin,** Mary 1949- *IntAu&W 91*
**Burkitt,** Denis Parsons 1911- *IntWW 91, Who 92*
**Burkitt,** Lemuel 1750-1807 *DcNCBi 1*
**Burkle,** Joseph S 1919- *AmMWSc 92*
**Burkley,** Dennis H. 1945- *WhoEnt 92*
**Burkley,** George G. d1991 *NewYTBS 91 [port]*
**Burkley,** Paul Edwin 1919- *WhoAmP 91*
**Burkley,** Richard M 1941- *AmMWSc 92*
**Burkman,** Allan Maurice 1932- *AmMWSc 92*
**Burkman,** Carol Lynn 1930- *WhoAmP 91*
**Burkman,** Ernest 1929- *AmMWSc 92*
**Burkoff,** John Michael 1948- *WhoAmL 92*
**Burks,** Ann Turner 1943- *WhoAmL 92*
**Burks,** Arthur J 1898-1974 *ScFEYrs*
**Burks,** Christian 1954- *AmMWSc 92*
**Burks,** Ellis Rena 1964- *WhoBlA 92*
**Burks,** Francis Edward, Jr. 1947- *WhoFI 92*
**Burks,** Frederick Eugene 1947- *WhoAmP 91*
**Burks,** G Edwin 1901- *AmMWSc 92*
**Burks,** J. Cooper 1919- *IntMPA 92*
**Burks,** James Kenneth 1945- *AmMWSc 92*
**Burks,** James William, Jr. 1938- *WhoBlA 92*
**Burks,** Juanita Pauline 1920- *WhoBlA 92*
**Burks,** Robert Edward 1930- *WhoRel 92*
**Burks,** Sterling Leon 1938- *AmMWSc 92*
**Burks,** Thomas F 1938- *AmMWSc 92*
**Burks,** Tommy 1940- *WhoAmP 91*
**Burkstrand,** James Michael 1946- *AmMWSc 92*
**Burkush,** Peter 1921- *WhoAmP 91*
**Burkush,** Wilfred *WhoAmP 91*
**Burkwall,** Morris Paton, Jr 1939- *AmMWSc 92*
**Burky,** Albert John 1942- *AmMWSc 92*
**Burlaga,** Leonard F 1938- *AmMWSc 92*
**Burlamaqui,** Jean-Jacques 1694-1748 *BlkwCEP*
**Burland,** Brian *DrAPF 91*
**Burland,** Brian Berkeley 1931- *IntAu&W 91*
**Burland,** Donald Maxwell 1943- *AmMWSc 92*
**Burland,** Harris 1870-1926 *ScFEYrs*
**Burland,** John Boscawen 1936- *Who 92*
**Burlant,** William Jack 1928- *AmMWSc 92*
**Burlatsky,** Fedor Mikhailovich 1927- *IntWW 91*
**Burlatsky,** Fedor Mikhaylovich 1927- *SovUnBD*
**Burleigh,** Bruce Daniel, Jr 1942- *AmMWSc 92*
**Burleigh,** Douglas 1949- *WhoFI 92*
**Burleigh,** Douglas Glen 1945- *WhoRel 92*
**Burleigh,** George Hall d1991 *Who 92N*
**Burleigh,** Harry T. 1866-1949 *NewAmDM*
**Burleigh,** Harry Thacker 1866-1949 *FacFETw*
**Burleigh,** James Reynolds 1936- *AmMWSc 92*
**Burleigh,** Joseph Gaynor 1942- *AmMWSc 92*
**Burleigh,** Judith Cushing 1934- *WhoMW 92*
**Burleigh,** Lewis Albert 1940- *WhoAmL 92*
**Burleigh,** Michael 1955- *ConAu 135*
**Burleigh,** Rita Jean 1943- *WhoWest 92*
**Burleigh,** Scott Crague 1951- *WhoFI 92*
**Burleigh,** Thomas Haydon 1911- *Who 92*
**Burleigh,** William Robert 1935- *WhoFI 92*
**Burlein,** Lester F 1905- *WhoAmP 91*
**Burleski,** Joseph Anthony, Jr. 1960- *WhoFI 92*
**Burleson,** Brant Raney 1952- *WhoMW 92*
**Burleson,** Daniel Evan 1967- *WhoRel 92*
**Burleson,** Edward 1793-1851 *DcNCBi 1*
**Burleson,** George Robert 1933- *AmMWSc 92*
**Burleson,** Helen L. 1929- *WhoBlA 92*
**Burleson,** Jane Geneva 1928- *WhoBlA 92*
**Burleson,** Karen Tripp 1955- *WhoAmL 92, WhoFI 92*
**Burleson,** Robert Odell *WhoAmP 91*
**Burleson,** Timothy Warren 1954- *WhoRel 92*
**Burleson,** William 1929- *WhoWest 92*
**Burlett,** Donald James 1949- *AmMWSc 92*
**Burlew,** Ann Kathleen 1948- *WhoBlA 92*
**Burley,** Carlton Edwin *AmMWSc 92*
**Burley,** Dale S. 1961- *WhoBlA 92*
**Burley,** David Richard 1942- *AmMWSc 92*
**Burley,** Dolores Marguerite 1933- *WhoEnt 92*
**Burley,** Gordon 1925- *AmMWSc 92*
**Burley,** J William Atkinson 1928- *AmMWSc 92*
**Burley,** Jeffery 1936- *Who 92*
**Burley,** Kathleen M 1942- *IntAu&W 91*
**Burley,** Mark Alan 1951- *WhoEnt 92*
**Burley,** Nancy 1949- *AmMWSc 92*
**Burley,** Victor 1914- *Who 92*
**Burley,** W. J. 1914- *WrDr 92*
**Burley,** William John 1914- *IntAu&W 91*
**Burlin,** Natalie Curtis 1875-1921 *BenetAL 91*
**Burlin,** Terence Eric 1931- *Who 92*
**Burling,** James P 1930- *AmMWSc 92*
**Burling,** James Sherman 1954- *WhoAmL 92*
**Burling,** Peter 1945- *WhoAmP 91*
**Burling,** Ronald William 1920- *AmMWSc 92*
**Burlingame,** Alma L 1937- *AmMWSc 92*
**Burlingame,** Anson d1991 *NewYTBS 91*
**Burlingame,** Barbara C *WhoAmP 91*
**Burlingame,** Daniel Wessels 1930- *WhoAmL 92*
**Burlingame,** John Francis 1922- *IntWW 91, WhoFI 92*
**Burlingame,** John Hunter 1933- *WhoAmL 92*
**Burlingame,** Roger 1889-1967 *BenetAL 91*
**Burlingame,** Stephen Lee 1950- *WhoAmL 92*
**Burlingham,** Richard Avery 1961- *WhoEnt 92*
**Burlington,** Earl of 1969- *Who 92*
**Burlington,** Harold 1925- *AmMWSc 92*
**Burlington,** Roy Frederick 1936- *AmMWSc 92*
**Burlison,** James David 1958- *WhoAmL 92*
**Burlitch,** James Michael *AmMWSc 92*
**Burman,** B. Don 1951- *WhoMW 92*
**Burman,** Bari Dreiband 1950- *WhoEnt 92*
**Burman,** Barry 1943- *TwCPaSc*
**Burman,** Ben Lucien 1896-1984 *BenetAL 91*
**Burman,** Charles 1908- *Who 92*
**Burman,** Edward 1947- *ConAu 134*
**Burman,** John Thomas 1934- *WhoMW 92*
**Burman,** Jose Lionel 1917- *WrDr 92*
**Burman,** Kenneth Dale 1944- *AmMWSc 92*
**Burman,** Marsha Linkwald 1949- *WhoFI 92*
**Burman,** Mary Mortensen 1930- *WhoRel 92*
**Burman,** Robert L 1933- *AmMWSc 92*
**Burman,** Stephen 1904- *Who 92*
**Burman,** Sudhir 1955- *AmMWSc 92*
**Burmeister,** Harland Reno 1929- *AmMWSc 92*
**Burmeister,** John Luther 1938- *AmMWSc 92*
**Burmeister,** Louis C 1935- *AmMWSc 92*
**Burmeister,** Robert Alfred 1939- *AmMWSc 92*
**Burmester,** Terri Lynn 1960- *WhoWest 92*
**Burn,** Adrian *Who 92*
**Burn,** Andrew Robert d1991 *Who 92N*
**Burn,** Andrew Robert 1902- *IntAu&W 91, WrDr 92*
**Burn,** Angus Maitland P. *Who 92*
**Burn,** Bryan Adrian 1945- *Who 92*
**Burn,** Gordon 1948- *IntAu&W 91*
**Burn,** Ian 1937- *AmMWSc 92*
**Burn,** Malcolm 1949- *WhoEnt 92*
**Burn,** Michael Clive 1912- *IntAu&W 91, Who 92*
**Burn,** Richard Hardy 1938- *Who 92*
**Burn,** Rodney 1899-1984 *TwCPaSc*
**Burnam,** John William 1953- *WhoMW 92*
**Burnam,** Michael Gordon 1953- *WhoMW 92*
**Burnash,** Robert John Charles 1931- *WhoWest 92*
**Burneko,** Guy Christian 1946- *WhoRel 92*
**Burnell,** Daniel Koewing 1963- *WhoMW 92*
**Burnell,** Diana Louise 1958- *WhoEnt 92*
**Burnell,** Edwin Elliott 1943- *AmMWSc 92*
**Burnell,** George Edwin 1863-1948 *RelLAm 91*
**Burnell,** James McIndoe 1921- *AmMWSc 92*
**Burnell,** Jocelyn B. *Who 92*
**Burnell,** Louis A 1928- *AmMWSc 92*
**Burnell,** Robert H 1929- *AmMWSc 92*
**Burnell,** S Jocelyn Bell 1943- *AmMWSc 92*
**Burneo,** Francisco Felipe, Jr. 1942- *WhoHisp 92*
**Burner,** Alpheus Wilson, Jr 1947- *AmMWSc 92*
**Burner,** Victor Joseph 1937- *WhoEnt 92*
**Burnes,** Carol *DrAPF 91*
**Burnes,** Donald Edward 1926- *WhoRel 92*
**Burnes,** Kennett Farrar 1943- *WhoFI 92*
**Burnes,** Linda Jane 1949- *WhoMW 92*
**Burness,** Alfred Thomas Henry 1934- *AmMWSc 92*
**Burness,** James Hubert 1949- *AmMWSc 92*
**Burnet,** Alastair *IntWW 91*
**Burnet,** Alastair 1928- *WrDr 92*
**Burnet,** David Staats 1808-1867 *AmPeW*
**Burnet,** Frank MacFarlane 1899-1985 *WhoNob 90*
**Burnet,** George 1924- *AmMWSc 92*
**Burnet,** James William Alexander 1928- *IntAu&W 91, IntWW 91, Who 92*
**Burnet,** Jean R. 1920- *WrDr 92*
**Burnet,** Macfarlane 1899-1985 *FacFETw*
**Burnet,** Pauline Ruth 1920- *Who 92*
**Burnett,** Alfred David 1937- *IntAu&W 91, WrDr 92*
**Burnett,** Angela 1955- *WhoAmL 92*
**Burnett,** Arthur Louis, Sr. 1935- *WhoBlA 92*
**Burnett,** Bescye P. 1950- *WhoBlA 92*
**Burnett,** Bill Bendyshe 1917- *IntWW 91, Who 92*
**Burnett,** Bob J 1933- *WhoAmP 91*
**Burnett,** Bobby J. 1932- *WhoRel 92*
**Burnett,** Brian 1913- *Who 92*
**Burnett,** Bruce Burton 1927- *AmMWSc 92*
**Burnett,** Bryan Reeder 1945- *AmMWSc 92*
**Burnett,** Calvin W. 1932- *WhoBlA 92*
**Burnett,** Carol 1933- *IntMPA 92*
**Burnett,** Carol 1936?- *ConMus 6 [port], WhoEnt 92*
**Burnett,** Charles *NewYTBS 91 [port]*
**Burnett,** Charles Henry 1842-1902 *BiInAmS*
**Burnett,** Charles John 1940- *Who 92*
**Burnett,** Claire Conklin 1954- *WhoEnt 92*
**Burnett,** Clyde Ray 1923- *AmMWSc 92*
**Burnett,** David Humphery 1918- *Who 92*
**Burnett,** David Lawrence 1956- *WhoBlA 92*
**Burnett,** Deborah Becher 1949- *WhoFI 92*
**Burnett,** Donald Stacy 1937- *AmMWSc 92*
**Burnett,** Eric Stephen 1924- *WhoWest 92*
**Burnett,** Frances Eliza Hodgson 1849-1924 *FacFETw*
**Burnett,** Frances Hodgson 1849-1924 *BenetAL 91, ChlLR 24 [port], RfGEnL 91*
**Burnett,** Fredrick Wayne 1944- *WhoRel 92*
**Burnett,** Hallie *DrAPF 91*
**Burnett,** Hallie Southgate 1908-1991 *CurBio 91N*
**Burnett,** Hallie Southgate 1909?-1991 *ConAu 135*
**Burnett,** Howard David 1950- *WhoAmL 92*
**Burnett,** James Curtis 1944- *WhoFI 92*
**Burnett,** James H 1917- *WhoAmP 91*
**Burnett,** James R 1925- *AmMWSc 92*
**Burnett,** James Robert 1925- *WhoFI 92*
**Burnett,** Jean Bullard 1924- *AmMWSc 92*
**Burnett,** Jerrold J 1931- *AmMWSc 92*
**Burnett,** Jim 1947- *WhoAmP 91*
**Burnett,** John 1922- *Who 92*
**Burnett,** John 1925- *IntAu&W 91, WrDr 92*
**Burnett,** John G. d1991 *NewYTBS 91*
**Burnett,** John L 1932- *AmMWSc 92*
**Burnett,** John Lambe 1934- *AmMWSc 92*
**Burnett,** John Laurence 1932- *WhoWest 92*
**Burnett,** John Nicholas 1939- *AmMWSc 92*
**Burnett,** Joseph 1820-1894 *BiInAmS*
**Burnett,** Joseph W 1933- *AmMWSc 92*
**Burnett,** Kenneth C. 1950- *WhoRel 92*
**Burnett,** Kenneth King 1935- *WhoAmL 92*
**Burnett,** Lou Gehrig 1941- *WhoAmP 91*
**Burnett,** Lowell Jay 1941- *AmMWSc 92*
**Burnett,** Luther C. 1925- *WhoBlA 92*
**Burnett,** Lynn Barkley 1948- *WhoWest 92*
**Burnett,** Mary Coghill 1907- *WhoBlA 92*
**Burnett,** Mary Parham 1956- *WhoAmL 92*
**Burnett,** Michele Marie 1956- *WhoEnt 92*
**Burnett,** Patricia Hill *WhoAmP 91*
**Burnett,** Philip Stephen 1914- *Who 92*
**Burnett,** Philip Whitworth 1908- *Who 92*
**Burnett,** Richard James 1922- *WhoAmP 91*
**Burnett,** Robert A. 1927- *WhoFI 92, WhoMW 92*
**Burnett,** Robert Clayton 1928- *WhoWest 92*
**Burnett,** Robert Walter 1944- *AmMWSc 92*
**Burnett,** Roger Macdonald 1941- *AmMWSc 92*
**Burnett,** Sam Thomas 1942- *WhoAmP 91*
**Burnett,** Sidney Obed 1924- *WhoBlA 92*
**Burnett,** St. Claire Y. *WhoRel 92*
**Burnett,** Stephen Cable 1951- *WhoMW 92*
**Burnett,** Thompson Humphrey 1941- *AmMWSc 92*
**Burnett,** Virgil 1928- *IntAu&W 91*
**Burnett,** W. R. 1899-1982 *BenetAL 91, FacFETw, TwCWW 91*
**Burnett,** Waldo Irving 1827-1854 *BiInAmS*
**Burnett,** Walter 1921- *Who 92*
**Burnett,** Whit 1899-1973 *BenetAL 91*
**Burnett,** William *DcTwDes*
**Burnett,** William Craig 1945- *AmMWSc 92*
**Burnett,** William E, Jr 1927- *WhoIns 92*
**Burnett,** Woodrow Wilson 1913- *WhoAmP 91*
**Burnett-Leys,** Alan Arbuthnott 1924- *IntAu&W 91*
**Burnett of Leys,** Baronetcy of *Who 92*
**Burnett-Stuart,** Joseph 1930- *Who 92*
**Burnette,** Ada Puryear *WhoBlA 92*
**Burnette,** Joe Edward 1918- *WhoRel 92*
**Burnette,** Kelly Frances 1966- *WhoEnt 92*
**Burnette,** Mahlon Admire, III 1946- *AmMWSc 92*
**Burnette,** Marie 1940- *WhoEnt 92*
**Burnette,** Mark Gunn 1954- *WhoAmL 92*

**Burnette**, Mary Malissa 1950- *WhoAmL 92*
**Burnette**, Ralph Edwin, Jr. 1953- *WhoAmL 92*
**Burnette**, Rand 1936- *WhoMW 92*
**Burnette**, Robert Vance 1955- *WhoWest 92*
**Burnette**, Susan Lynn 1955- *WhoAmL 92*
**Burnette**, Ward Watkins 1941- *WhoAmP 91*
**Burney**, Cecil 1923- *Who 92*
**Burney**, Charles 1726-1814 *BlkwCEP, NewAmDM*
**Burney**, Curtis Michael 1947- *AmMWSc 92*
**Burney**, Donald Eugene 1915- *AmMWSc 92*
**Burney**, Fanny 1752-1840 *BlkwCEP, RfGEnL 91*
**Burney**, Harry L., Jr. 1913- *WhoBlA 92*
**Burney**, John Michael 1952- *WhoMW 92*
**Burney**, Sayed Muzaffir Hussain 1923- *IntWW 91*
**Burney**, Victoria Kalgaard 1943- *WhoWest 92*
**Burney**, William D., Jr. 1951- *WhoBlA 92*
**Burnham**, Baron 1920- *Who 92*
**Burnham**, Alan Kent 1950- *AmMWSc 92*
**Burnham**, Anthony Gerald 1936- *Who 92*
**Burnham**, Bruce Franklin 1931- *AmMWSc 92*
**Burnham**, Bryson Paine 1917- *WhoAmL 92*
**Burnham**, Charles *TwCWW 91*
**Burnham**, Charles Grinnell 1954- *WhoEnt 92*
**Burnham**, Charles Wilson 1933- *AmMWSc 92*
**Burnham**, Christopher B 1956- *WhoAmP 91*
**Burnham**, Daniel M 1929- *WhoAmP 91*
**Burnham**, Dawn Addison 1954- *WhoAmP 91*
**Burnham**, Deborah *DrAPF 91*
**Burnham**, Donald C 1915- *AmMWSc 92*
**Burnham**, Donald Love 1922- *AmMWSc 92*
**Burnham**, Duane Lee 1942- *WhoFI 92, WhoMW 92*
**Burnham**, Dwight Comber 1922- *AmMWSc 92*
**Burnham**, Gregory *DrAPF 91*
**Burnham**, J. V. 1923- *WhoFI 92*
**Burnham**, James 1905-1987 *FacFETw*
**Burnham**, James B. 1939- *IntWW 91*
**Burnham**, Jed James 1944- *WhoFI 92*
**Burnham**, Jeffrey C 1942- *AmMWSc 92*
**Burnham**, John Chynoweth 1929- *WhoMW 92*
**Burnham**, John Ludwig 1953- *WhoEnt 92*
**Burnham**, Kenneth Donald 1922- *AmMWSc 92*
**Burnham**, Margaret Ann 1944- *WhoBlA 92*
**Burnham**, Marvin William 1925- *AmMWSc 92*
**Burnham**, Robert 1943- *WhoMW 92*
**Burnham**, Robert Bailey 1947- *WhoMW 92*
**Burnham**, Robert Danner 1944- *AmMWSc 92*
**Burnham**, Sophy 1936- *IntAu&W 91, SmATA 65*
**Burnham**, Thomas K 1927- *AmMWSc 92*
**Burnham**, William A. 1947- *WhoWest 92*
**Burnheimer**, Mark Alan 1959- *WhoAmL 92*
**Burnim**, Kalman Aaron 1928- *WhoEnt 92*
**Burnim**, Mellonee Victoria 1950- *WhoBlA 92*
**Burnim**, Mickey L. 1949- *WhoBlA 92*
**Burningham**, Haven Ralph 1918- *WhoAmP 91*
**Burningham**, John 1936- *ConAu 36NR, IntAu&W 91, WrDr 92*
**Burningham**, John Mackintosh 1936- *Who 92*
**Burningham**, Kim Richard 1936- *WhoAmP 91*
**Burningham**, Steven Dale 1949- *WhoFI 92*
**Burnison**, Boyd Edward 1934- *WhoAmL 92, WhoFI 92, WhoWest 92*
**Burnison**, Bryan Kent 1943- *AmMWSc 92*
**Burniston**, Ernest Edmund 1937- *AmMWSc 92*
**Burniston**, George Garrett 1914- *Who 92*
**Burniston**, Karen Sue 1939- *WhoMW 92*
**Burnley**, Bishop Suffragan of 1927- *Who 92*
**Burnley**, Christopher John 1936- *Who 92*
**Burnley**, James H., IV 1948- *IntWW 91*
**Burnley**, James Horace, IV 1948- *WhoAmP 91*
**Burns and Allen** *FacFETw, LesBEnT 92*
**Burns and Lambert** *DcLB 106*
**Burns and Oates** *DcLB 106*
**Burns**, Lambert and Oates *DcLB 106*
**Burns**, Oates and Washbourne *DcLB 106*
**Burns**, A Leslie 1948- *WhoAmP 91*
**Burns**, Aaron d1991 *NewYTBS 91*
**Burns**, Aaron 1922- *DcTwDes*
**Burns**, Alan *DrAPF 91*
**Burns**, Alan 1929- *ConAu 34NR, ConNov 91, IntAu&W 91, WrDr 92*
**Burns**, Alan Raymond 1936- *WhoEnt 92*
**Burns**, Alexandra Darrow 1946- *WhoWest 92*
**Burns**, Alfred Warren 1921- *WhoRel 92*
**Burns**, Allan Fielding 1936- *AmMWSc 92*
**Burns**, Andrew *Who 92*
**Burns**, Ann *WhoBlA 92*
**Burns**, Anne 1915- *Who 92*
**Burns**, Anne M 1921- *WhoAmP 91*
**Burns**, Anneliese 1965- *WhoEnt 92*
**Burns**, Arnold Irwin 1930- *WhoAmL 92*
**Burns**, Arthur F 1904-1987 *FacFETw*
**Burns**, Avon Lorraine 1952- *WhoMW 92*
**Burns**, B. Delisle 1915- *Who 92*
**Burns**, Benedict DeLisle 1915- *IntWW 91*
**Burns**, Betty X. 1926- *WhoEnt 92*
**Burns**, Bonnie 1951- *WhoEnt 92*
**Burns**, Brenda 1950- *WhoAmP 91*
**Burns**, Brian Douglas 1939- *WhoAmP 91*
**Burns**, Bruce Peter 1942- *AmMWSc 92*
**Burns**, C M 1938- *AmMWSc 92*
**Burns**, Calvin Louis 1952- *WhoBlA 92*
**Burns**, Carol 1934- *IntAu&W 91, WrDr 92*
**Burns**, Carole Jean 1961- *WhoFI 92*
**Burns**, Carroll D 1932- *WhoIns 92*
**Burns**, Cassandra Stroud 1960- *WhoAmL 92*
**Burns**, Cathy Jean 1955- *WhoRel 92*
**Burns**, Charles Thurgoode 1914- *WhoBlA 92*
**Burns**, Chester Ray 1937- *AmMWSc 92*
**Burns**, Clarence 1918- *WhoAmP 91*
**Burns**, Clarence Du 1918- *WhoBlA 92*
**Burns**, Clarica Ann 1940- *WhoEnt 92*
**Burns**, Conrad 1935- *AlmAP 92 [port]*
**Burns**, Conrad R 1935- *WhoAmP 91*
**Burns**, Conrad Ray 1935- *WhoWest 92*
**Burns**, Dan W. 1925- *WhoFI 92, WhoWest 92*
**Burns**, Daniel Hobart 1928- *WhoFI 92, WhoWest 92*
**Burns**, Daniel Robert 1955- *AmMWSc 92*
**Burns**, Dargan J. 1925- *WhoBlA 92*
**Burns**, David Allan 1937- *Who 92*
**Burns**, David Jerome 1922- *AmMWSc 92*
**Burns**, David John 1958- *WhoMW 92*
**Burns**, David W. 1923- *WhoEnt 92*
**Burns**, Denise *WhoBlA 92*
**Burns**, Denver P 1940- *AmMWSc 92*
**Burns**, Diane L. 1950- *ConAu 135*
**Burns**, Donal Joseph 1941- *AmMWSc 92*
**Burns**, Donald Carlton 1929- *WhoIns 92*
**Burns**, Donald Howard 1928- *WhoAmP 91*
**Burns**, Donald Snow 1925- *WhoWest 92*
**Burns**, Duncan Thorburn 1934- *IntWW 91*
**Burns**, Eddie Owen 1960- *WhoEnt 92*
**Burns**, Edward Eugene 1926- *AmMWSc 92*
**Burns**, Edward Francis, Jr 1931- *WhoAmP 91*
**Burns**, Edward Morton, II 1947- *WhoAmP 91*
**Burns**, Edward Robert 1939- *AmMWSc 92*
**Burns**, Eileen *WhoEnt 92*
**Burns**, Elizabeth Mary *AmMWSc 92*
**Burns**, Elizabeth Murphy 1945- *WhoEnt 92*
**Burns**, Ellen Bree 1923- *WhoAmL 92*
**Burns**, Emmett C. *WhoBlA 92*
**Burns**, Erskine John Thomas 1944- *AmMWSc 92*
**Burns**, Eugene Warren 1946- *WhoAmP 91*
**Burns**, Felton 1936- *WhoBlA 92*
**Burns**, Frank Bernard 1928- *AmMWSc 92*
**Burns**, Fred Paul 1922- *AmMWSc 92*
**Burns**, Fredric Jay 1937- *AmMWSc 92*
**Burns**, George *Who 92*
**Burns**, George 1896- *ConTFT 9, FacFETw, IntAu&W 91, IntMPA 92, IntWW 91, WhoEnt 92, WrDr 92*
**Burns**, George 1925- *AmMWSc 92*
**Burns**, George Robert 1931- *AmMWSc 92*
**Burns**, George W 1913- *AmMWSc 92*
**Burns**, Gerald 1932- *AmMWSc 92*
**Burns**, Geraldine Hamilton *WhoBlA 92*
**Burns**, Glenn Richard 1951- *WhoMW 92*
**Burns**, Grover Preston 1918- *AmMWSc 92, WhoFI 92*
**Burns**, H Donald 1946- *AmMWSc 92*
**Burns**, H. Michael 1937- *WhoMW 92*
**Burns**, Harold Wilbur 1926- *WhoAmP 91*
**Burns**, Ian Morgan 1939- *Who 92*
**Burns**, Ivan Alfred 1935- *WhoFI 92*
**Burns**, Jack Hancock 1920- *WhoWest 92*
**Burns**, Jack O'Neal 1953- *AmMWSc 92*
**Burns**, Jacqueline 1927- *WhoRel 92*
**Burns**, James 1808-1871 *DcLB 106*
**Burns**, James 1902- *Who 92*
**Burns**, James 1931- *Who 92*
**Burns**, James A. 1944- *WhoFI 92*
**Burns**, James Alan, Jr. 1955- *WhoAmL 92*
**Burns**, James Alvin 1935- *WhoWest 92*
**Burns**, James Edward 1950- *WhoAmP 91*
**Burns**, James Henderson 1921- *Who 92*
**Burns**, James MacGregor 1918- *IntAu&W 91, WrDr 92*
**Burns**, James Marcus 1939- *WhoAmP 91*
**Burns**, James Michael 1953- *WhoRel 92*
**Burns**, Jay, III 1924- *AmMWSc 92*
**Burns**, Jeff, Jr. 1950- *WhoBlA 92*
**Burns**, Jeffrey Alan 1956- *WhoAmL 92*
**Burns**, Jerry 1927- *WhoMW 92*
**Burns**, Jim 1936- *ConPo 91, IntAu&W 91, WrDr 92*
**Burns**, Jimmy 1953- *ConAu 134*
**Burns**, Joan Simpson 1927- *WrDr 92*
**Burns**, John 1858-1943 *FacFETw*
**Burns**, John 1920- *IntWW 91*
**Burns**, John Allen 1945- *AmMWSc 92*
**Burns**, John Crawford d1991 *Who 92N*
**Burns**, John E *WhoAmP 91*
**Burns**, John Francis 1901- *AmMWSc 92*
**Burns**, John Francis 1936- *WhoAmL 92, WhoMW 92*
**Burns**, John Horne 1916-1953 *BenetAL 91*
**Burns**, John Howard 1930- *AmMWSc 92*
**Burns**, John J 1920- *AmMWSc 92*
**Burns**, John Joseph, Jr 1925- *AmMWSc 92*
**Burns**, John Joseph, Jr. 1931- *WhoFI 92*
**Burns**, John Lanier 1943- *WhoRel 92*
**Burns**, John MacDougal, III 1933- *WhoAmL 92*
**Burns**, John McLauren 1932- *AmMWSc 92*
**Burns**, John Mitchell 1940- *AmMWSc 92*
**Burns**, John Richard 1951- *WhoMW 92*
**Burns**, John Thomas 1943- *AmMWSc 92*
**Burns**, John Walker *WhoWest 92*
**Burns**, Jon Perry 1957- *WhoFI 92*
**Burns**, Jonathan Gilbert 1946- *WhoRel 92*
**Burns**, Joseph A 1941- *AmMWSc 92*
**Burns**, Joseph Charles 1937- *AmMWSc 92*
**Burns**, Kathleen Anne 1944- *WhoFI 92*
**Burns**, Ken *LesBEnT 92*
**Burns**, Kenneth Franklin 1916- *AmMWSc 92*
**Burns**, Kenneth Harold 1929- *WhoAmL 92*
**Burns**, Kenneth Jones, Jr. 1926- *WhoFI 92*
**Burns**, Kenneth P. *WhoMW 92*
**Burns**, Kevin Francis Xavier 1930- *IntWW 91, Who 92*
**Burns**, Laird Allen 1960- *WhoFI 92*
**Burns**, Lawrence Aloysius, Jr. 1949- *WhoFI 92, WhoMW 92*
**Burns**, Lawrence Anthony 1940- *AmMWSc 92*
**Burns**, Leo Richard 1939- *WhoFI 92*
**Burns**, Leonard L. 1922- *WhoBlA 92*
**Burns**, Marshall Shelby, Jr. 1931- *WhoAmL 92*
**Burns**, Marvin Gerald 1930- *WhoAmL 92*
**Burns**, Mary Claude *WhoRel 92*
**Burns**, Melissa Emerson 1957- *WhoRel 92*
**Burns**, Michael 1917- *Who 92*
**Burns**, Michael 1958- *WhoAmP 91*
**Burns**, Michael J 1956- *AmMWSc 92*
**Burns**, Michael R. 1958- *WhoWest 92*
**Burns**, Milton Jerome 1965- *WhoFI 92*
**Burns**, Mitchel Anthony 1942- *WhoFI 92*
**Burns**, Moore J 1917- *AmMWSc 92*
**Burns**, Nancy A 1936- *AmMWSc 92*
**Burns**, Ned Hamilton 1932- *AmMWSc 92*
**Burns**, Olive Ann 1924-1990 *SmATA 65 [port]*
**Burns**, Ollie Hamilton 1911- *WhoBlA 92*
**Burns**, Otway, Jr. 1775-1850 *DcNCBi 1*
**Burns**, Pamela 1938- *TwCPaSc*
**Burns**, Pat Ackerman Gonia 1938- *WhoFI 92*
**Burns**, Patout, Jr. 1939- *WhoRel 92*
**Burns**, Patricia Henrietta 1934- *WhoRel 92, WhoWest 92*
**Burns**, Paul Yoder 1920- *AmMWSc 92*
**Burns**, Peter Francis 1949- *WhoAmL 92*
**Burns**, Ralph *DrAPF 91*
**Burns**, Ralph 1922- *IntMPA 92*
**Burns**, Regina Lynn 1961- *WhoBlA 92*
**Burns**, Rex 1935- *WrDr 92*
**Burns**, Rex Raul Stephen Sehler 1935- *IntAu&W 91*
**Burns**, Richard Charles 1930- *AmMWSc 92*
**Burns**, Richard James 1951- *WhoFI 92*
**Burns**, Richard Owen 1942- *WhoAmL 92*
**Burns**, Richard Price 1932- *AmMWSc 92*
**Burns**, Richard Ramsey 1946- *WhoAmL 92, WhoFI 92*
**Burns**, Robert 1759-1796 *CnDBLB 3 [port], DcLB 109 [port], RfGEnL 91*
**Burns**, Robert 1869-1941 *TwCPaSc*
**Burns**, Robert 1925- *WhoAmP 91*
**Burns**, Robert A. *DrAPF 91*
**Burns**, Robert Alexander *AmMWSc 92*
**Burns**, Robert Andrew 1943- *Who 92*
**Burns**, Robert Bob *WhoAmP 91*
**Burns**, Robert David 1929- *AmMWSc 92*
**Burns**, Robert Earle 1925- *AmMWSc 92*
**Burns**, Robert Edward 1919- *WhoMW 92*
**Burns**, Robert Edward 1953- *WhoAmL 92*
**Burns**, Robert Emmett 1918- *AmMWSc 92*
**Burns**, Robert Emmett 1933- *WhoAmL 92*
**Burns**, Robert F *WhoAmP 91*
**Burns**, Robert Grant *DrAPF 91*
**Burns**, Robert Harrison 1941- *WhoIns 92*
**Burns**, Robert L. 1937- *WhoWest 92*
**Burns**, Robert Obed 1910- *WhoWest 92*
**Burns**, Robert Patrick 1947- *WhoAmL 92*
**Burns**, Robert Wallace 1950- *WhoRel 92*
**Burns**, Robert Ward 1941- *AmMWSc 92*
**Burns**, Robin *WhoFI 92*
**Burns**, Robin 1953?- *News 91*
**Burns**, Roger George 1937- *AmMWSc 92*
**Burns**, Ronald Melvin 1942- *WhoBlA 92*
**Burns**, Russell MacBain 1926- *AmMWSc 92*
**Burns**, Sandra Kaye 1949- *WhoAmL 92, WhoFI 92*
**Burns**, Sandra Pauline 1938- *Who 92*
**Burns**, Sarah Ann 1938- *WhoBlA 92*
**Burns**, Sarah Ellen 1949- *WhoAmL 92*
**Burns**, Simon Hugh McGuigan 1952- *Who 92*
**Burns**, Stephen James 1939- *AmMWSc 92*
**Burns**, Terence 1944- *IntWW 91, Who 92*
**Burns**, Terrence Michael 1954- *WhoAmL 92*
**Burns**, Terry Dee 1956- *WhoMW 92*
**Burns**, Tex *TwCWW 91*
**Burns**, Thomas David 1921- *WhoAmL 92*
**Burns**, Thomas Donald 1956- *WhoWest 92*
**Burns**, Thomas Ferrier 1906- *Who 92*
**Burns**, Thomas Wade 1924- *AmMWSc 92, WhoMW 92*
**Burns**, Timothy Gerard 1954- *WhoEnt 92*
**Burns**, Timothy John 1949- *AmMWSc 92*
**Burns**, Tom 1913- *IntWW 91, Who 92*
**Burns**, Tommie, Jr. 1933- *WhoBlA 92*
**Burns**, Vernon D 1953- *WhoAmP 91*
**Burns**, Victor Will 1925- *AmMWSc 92*
**Burns**, W. Haywood 1940- *WhoBlA 92*
**Burns**, Walter Arthur George 1911- *Who 92*
**Burns**, Walter Noble 1872-1932 *TwCWW 91*
**Burns**, William *DrAPF 91*
**Burns**, William 1909- *Who 92*
**Burns**, William 1921-1972 *TwCPaSc*
**Burns**, William, Jr 1938- *AmMWSc 92*
**Burns**, William Chandler 1926- *AmMWSc 92*
**Burns**, William Francis 1951- *WhoAmL 92*
**Burns**, William Glenn 1949- *WhoAmL 92*
**Burns**, William O 1930- *WhoIns 92*
**Burns**, William Robert 1922- *WhoIns 92*
**Burns**, Willie Miles *WhoBlA 92*
**Burns-Bisogno**, Louisa 1936- *ConAu 134*
**Burnshaw**, Stanley *DrAPF 91*
**Burnshaw**, Stanley 1906- *ConPo 91, IntAu&W 91, WrDr 92*
**Burnside**, Brad 1952- *WhoMW 92*
**Burnside**, Burnie R. 1953- *WhoRel 92*
**Burnside**, Dudley 1912- *TwCPaSc*
**Burnside**, Edith *Who 92*
**Burnside**, Edward Blair 1937- *AmMWSc 92*
**Burnside**, Mary Beth 1943- *AmMWSc 92*
**Burnside**, Orvin C 1932- *AmMWSc 92*
**Burnside**, Phillips Brooks 1927- *AmMWSc 92*
**Burnside**, Thomas Reuben, Jr. 1938- *WhoAmL 92*
**Burnstein**, Daniel 1946- *WhoAmL 92*
**Burnstein**, Frances 1935- *WhoFI 92*
**Burnstein**, Ray A 1930- *AmMWSc 92*
**Burnstein**, Theodore 1925- *AmMWSc 92*
**Burnstock**, Geoffrey 1929- *IntWW 91, Who 92*
**Burnton**, Stanley Jeffrey 1942- *Who 92*
**Burnyeat**, Myles Fredric 1939- *IntWW 91, Who 92*
**Burokyavichus**, Mikolas Martinovich 1927- *IntWW 91*
**Burose**, Renee 1962- *WhoBlA 92*
**Burov**, Andrey Konstantinovich 1900-1957 *SovUnBD*
**Burow**, Duane Frueh 1940- *AmMWSc 92*
**Burow**, Kenneth Wayne, Jr 1946- *AmMWSc 92*
**Burpee**, David 1893-1980 *FacFETw*
**Burpo**, Robert Michael 1949- *WhoFI 92*
**Burr**, Aaron 1756-1836 *AmPolLe [port], BenetAL 91, RComAH*
**Burr**, Alexander Fuller 1931- *AmMWSc 92*
**Burr**, Anne Christian 1947- *WhoAmL 92*
**Burr**, Arthur Albert 1913- *AmMWSc 92*
**Burr**, Brooks Milo 1949- *AmMWSc 92*
**Burr**, Dan 1951- *SmATA 65*
**Burr**, Edward B 1923- *WhoIns 92*
**Burr**, George Oswald 1896- *AmMWSc 92*
**Burr**, Gray *DrAPF 91*
**Burr**, Helen Gunderson 1918- *AmMWSc 92*
**Burr**, James 1926- *TwCPaSc*
**Burr**, James Edward 1941- *WhoMW 92*
**Burr**, Jeffrey Lynn 1952- *WhoAmL 92*
**Burr**, John Green 1918- *AmMWSc 92*
**Burr**, John Roy 1933- *WhoMW 92*

**Burr**, Lawrence C. 1913- *WhoBlA 92*
**Burr**, Raymond *LesBEnT 92*
**Burr**, Raymond 1917- *ConTFT 9, IntMPA 92, WhoEnt 92*
**Burr**, Scott Allen 1964- *WhoAmL 92*
**Burr**, Theodore 1771-1822? *BiInAmS*
**Burr**, Wesley R. 1936- *WrDr 92*
**Burr**, Wesley Ray 1936- *IntAu&W 91*
**Burr**, William Wesley, Jr 1923- *AmMWSc 92*
**Burra**, Edward 1905-1976 *TwCPaSc*
**Burrage**, Jeanette Ruth 1952- *WhoAmP 91*
**Burrage**, Lawrence Minott 1925- *AmMWSc 92*
**Burrall**, Frederic H 1935- *WhoAmP 91*
**Burrell**, Barbara 1941- *WhoBlA 92*
**Burrell**, Calvin Archie 1943- *WhoRel 92*
**Burrell**, Clinton Blane 1956- *WhoBlA 92*
**Burrell**, David Bakewell 1933- *WhoMW 92, WhoRel 92*
**Burrell**, David Colin *AmMWSc 92*
**Burrell**, Derek William 1925- *Who 92*
**Burrell**, Donald Eugene 1928- *WhoAmL 92*
**Burrell**, Elliott Joseph, Jr 1929- *AmMWSc 92*
**Burrell**, Emma P. *WhoBlA 92*
**Burrell**, George Reed, Jr. 1948- *WhoBlA 92*
**Burrell**, John Raymond 1934- *Who 92*
**Burrell**, Kenneth Earl 1931- *WhoBlA 92*
**Burrell**, Lewis Percy 1936- *WhoMW 92*
**Burrell**, Louie 1873-1971 *TwCPaSc*
**Burrell**, Morris 1908- *WhoBlA 92*
**Burrell**, Peter 1905- *Who 92*
**Burrell**, Raymond *Who 92*
**Burrell**, Robert 1933- *AmMWSc 92*
**Burrell**, Robert Clifford 1947- *WhoMW 92*
**Burrell**, Sam *WhoAmP 91*
**Burrell**, Thomas J. *WhoMW 92*
**Burrell**, Thomas J. 1939- *WhoBlA 92*
**Burrell**, Thomas William 1923- *WrDr 92*
**Burrell**, Victor Gregory, Jr 1925- *AmMWSc 92*
**Burrenchobay**, Dayendranath 1919- *IntWW 91, Who 92*
**Burreson**, Eugene M 1944- *AmMWSc 92*
**Burress**, James R. 1913- *WhoBlA 92*
**Burrett**, Gordon 1921- *Who 92*
**Burri**, Betty Jane 1955- *AmMWSc 92, WhoWest 92*
**Burridge**, Alan 1921- *Who 92*
**Burridge**, Michael John 1942- *AmMWSc 92*
**Burridge**, Robert 1937- *AmMWSc 92*
**Burridge**, Robert Gardiner 1930- *WhoAmL 92*
**Burrier**, Gail Warren 1927- *WhoMW 92*
**Burrier**, Robert E 1957- *AmMWSc 92*
**Burrill**, Claude Wesley 1925- *AmMWSc 92*
**Burrill**, Melinda Jane 1947- *AmMWSc 92*
**Burrill**, Robert Meredith 1933- *AmMWSc 92*
**Burrill**, Russell Clayton 1941- *WhoRel 92*
**Burrill**, Thomas Jonathan 1839-1916 *BiInAmS*
**Burrill**, Timothy 1931- *IntMPA 92, Who 92*
**Burrington**, Ernest 1926- *IntAu&W 91, Who 92*
**Burrington**, George 1682?-1759 *DcNCBi 1*
**Burrington**, William Wesley 1961- *WhoAmL 92*
**Burris**, Bertram Ray 1950- *WhoBlA 92*
**Burris**, Bill Buchanan, Jr. 1957- *WhoFI 92*
**Burris**, Bradford 1932- *WhoMW 92*
**Burris**, Conrad Timothy 1924- *AmMWSc 92*
**Burris**, Hazel Lorene 1921- *WhoAmP 91*
**Burris**, James F 1947- *AmMWSc 92*
**Burris**, John Edward 1949- *AmMWSc 92*
**Burris**, John L. 1945- *WhoBlA 92*
**Burris**, John M 1946- *WhoAmP 91*
**Burris**, Joseph Stephen 1942- *AmMWSc 92*
**Burris**, Leslie 1922- *AmMWSc 92*
**Burris**, Martin Joe 1927- *AmMWSc 92*
**Burris**, Nathan Kevin 1954- *WhoEnt 92*
**Burris**, Robert Harza 1914- *AmMWSc 92, IntWW 91*
**Burris**, Roland W. 1937- *WhoBlA 92*
**Burris**, Roland Wallace 1937- *WhoAmL 92, WhoAmP 91, WhoMW 92*
**Burris**, Rolanda Sue 1964- *WhoMW 92*
**Burris**, Stephen Eugene 1950- *WhoRel 92*
**Burris**, Steven Michael 1952- *WhoAmL 92*
**Burris**, William Edmon 1924- *AmMWSc 92*
**Burriss**, John Hay 1946- *WhoAmP 91*
**Burriss**, Milford D 1937- *WhoAmP 91*
**Burriss**, Thomas Moffatt 1919- *WhoAmP 91*
**Burritt**, Elihu 1810-1879 *AmPeW, BenetAL 91*
**Burritt**, Elijah Hinsdale 1794-1838 *BiInAmS*
**Burroff**, Teresa Jean 1961- *WhoAmL 92*
**Burros**, Raymond Herbert 1922- *AmMWSc 92*
**Burrough**, Alan 1917- *Who 92*
**Burrough**, John Outhit Harold 1916- *Who 92*
**Burrough**, John Paul 1916- *Who 92*
**Burroughs**, Baldwin Wesley 1915- *WhoBlA 92*
**Burroughs**, Bruce Douglas 1944- *WhoEnt 92*
**Burroughs**, Edgar Rice 1875-1950 *BenetAL 91, FacFETw, ScFEYrs, TwCSFW 91, TwCWW 91*
**Burroughs**, Hugh Charles 1940- *WhoBlA 92*
**Burroughs**, John 1837-1921 *BenetAL 91*
**Burroughs**, John A, Jr 1936- *WhoAmP 91*
**Burroughs**, John Andrew, Jr. 1936- *WhoBlA 92*
**Burroughs**, Kate 1953- *WhoWest 92*
**Burroughs**, Leonard 1921- *WhoBlA 92*
**Burroughs**, Margaret Taylor 1917- *NotBlAW 92, WhoBlA 92*
**Burroughs**, Miggs 1946- *WhoEnt 92*
**Burroughs**, Nannie Helen 1879-1961 *NotBlAW 92 [port]*
**Burroughs**, Richard 1946- *AmMWSc 92*
**Burroughs**, Richard Lee 1932- *AmMWSc 92*
**Burroughs**, Robert A. 1948- *WhoBlA 92*
**Burroughs**, Robert Clark 1923- *WhoEnt 92*
**Burroughs**, Robert Howard 1937- *WhoRel 92*
**Burroughs**, Roland Arthur 1935- *WhoAmP 91*
**Burroughs**, Sarah G. 1943- *WhoBlA 92*
**Burroughs**, Shane Edward 1956- *WhoRel 92*
**Burroughs**, Todd Steven 1968- *WhoBlA 92*
**Burroughs**, William S. *DrAPF 91*
**Burroughs**, William S. 1914- *BenetAL 91, ConNov 91, FacFETw, IntAu&W 91, LiExTwC, TwCSFW 91, WrDr 92*
**Burroughs**, William Seward 1855-1898 *BiInAmS*
**Burroughs**, William Seward 1914- *IntWW 91*
**Burrous**, Stanley Emerson 1928- *AmMWSc 92*
**Burrow**, Charles C, III 1945- *WhoAmP 91*
**Burrow**, Dennis 1930- *WhoFI 92*
**Burrow**, Gerard N 1933- *AmMWSc 92*
**Burrow**, Harold 1914- *WhoFI 92, WhoWest 92*
**Burrow**, J A 1932- *IntAu&W 91, WrDr 92*
**Burrow**, John Anthony 1932- *Who 92*
**Burrow**, John Edwin 1926- *WhoEnt 92*
**Burrow**, John Halcrow 1935- *Who 92*
**Burrow**, John Wyon 1935- *IntWW 91, Who 92*
**Burrow**, Marie Brabham 1915- *WhoBlA 92*
**Burrow**, Paul David 1938- *AmMWSc 92*
**Burroway**, Janet *DrAPF 91*
**Burroway**, Janet 1936- *ConNov 91, WrDr 92*
**Burroway**, Janet Gay 1936- *IntAu&W 91*
**Burrowes**, Edmund Stanley Spencer 1906- *Who 92*
**Burrowes**, Mike 1937- *WrDr 92*
**Burrowes**, Norma Elizabeth *IntWW 91, Who 92*
**Burrows**, Adam Seth *AmMWSc 92*
**Burrows**, Benjamin 1927- *AmMWSc 92*
**Burrows**, Bernard 1910- *Who 92*
**Burrows**, Bernard Alexander Brocas 1910- *IntWW 91*
**Burrows**, Cecil J. 1922- *WhoMW 92*
**Burrows**, Clare 1938- *WhoBlA 92*
**Burrows**, Cynthia Jane 1953- *AmMWSc 92*
**Burrows**, Dallas Frederick 1928- *WhoEnt 92*
**Burrows**, E.G. *DrAPF 91*
**Burrows**, Edward William 1928- *WhoHisp 92*
**Burrows**, Elizabeth MacDonald 1930- *WhoRel 92*
**Burrows**, Elizabeth Parker 1930- *AmMWSc 92*
**Burrows**, Eva 1929- *IntWW 91, Who 92*
**Burrows**, Eva Evelyn 1929- *WhoRel 92*
**Burrows**, Fred 1925- *Who 92*
**Burrows**, George Bill 1930- *WhoAmP 91*
**Burrows**, George Edward 1935- *AmMWSc 92*
**Burrows**, George Richard 1946- *Who 92*
**Burrows**, Gordon W *WhoAmP 91*
**Burrows**, James 1940- *IntMPA 92, WhoEnt 92*
**Burrows**, Janice H. 1944- *WhoBlA 92*
**Burrows**, Jay Edward 1949- *WhoAmL 92*
**Burrows**, John 1941- *WhoEnt 92*
**Burrows**, John Alan 1945- *IntAu&W 91*
**Burrows**, John Edward 1950- *WhoFI 92*
**Burrows**, John H 1924- *IntMPA 92*
**Burrows**, Kenneth David 1941- *WhoEnt 92*
**Burrows**, Kerilyn Christine 1951- *AmMWSc 92*
**Burrows**, Lionel John 1912- *Who 92*
**Burrows**, Malcolm 1943- *Who 92*
**Burrows**, Mary McCauley 1932- *WhoAmP 91*
**Burrows**, Meade Gordon 1954- *WhoAmL 92*
**Burrows**, Michael Donald 1944- *WhoAmL 92*
**Burrows**, Michael L 1934- *AmMWSc 92*
**Burrows**, Reginald Arthur 1918- *Who 92*
**Burrows**, Richard *Who 92*
**Burrows**, Robert Beck 1907- *AmMWSc 92*
**Burrows**, Roberta *IntMPA 92*
**Burrows**, Simon Hedley *Who 92*
**Burrows**, Stuart *IntWW 91*
**Burrows**, Thomas Wesley 1943- *AmMWSc 92*
**Burrows**, Vernon Douglas 1930- *AmMWSc 92*
**Burrows**, Vinie 1928- *NotBlAW 92 [port]*
**Burrows**, Virginia Moore 1956- *WhoAmL 92*
**Burrows**, Walter Herbert 1911- *AmMWSc 92*
**Burrows**, William Dickinson 1930- *AmMWSc 92*
**Burrs**, E. Daniel 1932- *WhoMW 92*
**Burrud**, Bill d1991 *LesBEnT 92*
**Burrus**, Bob 1938- *WhoEnt 92*
**Burrus**, Charles Andrew, Jr 1927- *AmMWSc 92*
**Burrus**, Charles Sidney 1934- *AmMWSc 92*
**Burrus**, Clark 1928- *WhoBlA 92, WhoMW 92*
**Burrus**, Daniel Allen 1947- *WhoFI 92*
**Burrus**, Harry *DrAPF 91*
**Burrus**, Robert Tilden 1935- *AmMWSc 92*
**Burrus**, William Henry 1936- *WhoBlA 92*
**Burruss**, Lloyd Earl, Jr. 1957- *WhoBlA 92*
**Burry**, John Henry William 1938- *AmMWSc 92*
**Burry**, Kenneth A 1942- *AmMWSc 92*
**Burry**, Kenneth Arnold 1942- *WhoWest 92*
**Burschell**, Friedrich 1889-1970 *EncTR 91*
**Burschka**, Martin A 1952- *AmMWSc 92*
**Burse**, Delores Tate 1940- *WhoAmP 91*
**Burse**, Luther 1937- *WhoBlA 92*
**Burse**, Raymond Malcolm 1951- *WhoBlA 92*
**Burse**, Richard Luck 1936- *AmMWSc 92*
**Bursell**, Rupert David Hingston 1942- *Who 92*
**Bursey**, Charles Robert 1940- *AmMWSc 92*
**Bursey**, Joan Tesarek 1943- *AmMWSc 92*
**Bursey**, Maurice Moyer 1939- *AmMWSc 92*
**Bursh**, Talmage Poutau 1932- *AmMWSc 92*
**Bursian**, Steven John 1947- *AmMWSc 92*
**Bursk**, Christopher *DrAPF 91*
**Bursky**, Herman Aaron 1938- *WhoAmL 92*
**Bursley**, Gilbert E 1913- *WhoAmP 91*
**Bursnall**, John Treharne 1940- *AmMWSc 92*
**Burson**, Billy B, II 1949- *WhoEnt 92*
**Burson**, Byron Lynn 1940- *AmMWSc 92*
**Burson**, Charles W. *WhoAmL 92*
**Burson**, Charles W 1944- *WhoAmP 91*
**Burson**, Harold 1921- *IntWW 91, WhoFI 92*
**Burson**, Lorraine Eloise 1925- *WhoWest 92*
**Burson**, Sherman Leroy, Jr 1923- *AmMWSc 92*
**Burst**, John Frederick 1923- *AmMWSc 92, WhoMW 92*
**Burstall**, Clare 1931- *Who 92*
**Burstein**, Albert 1922- *WhoAmP 91*
**Burstein**, Beatrice S. 1915- *WhoAmL 92*
**Burstein**, Daniel Leon 1953- *WhoFI 92*
**Burstein**, David 1947- *AmMWSc 92*
**Burstein**, Elias 1917- *AmMWSc 92*
**Burstein**, Harvey 1923- *WhoAmL 92*
**Burstein**, Jack David 1945- *WhoFI 92, WhoMW 92*
**Burstein**, Karen 1942- *WhoAmP 91*
**Burstein**, Lonnie 1957- *WhoEnt 92*
**Burstein**, Richard Joel 1945- *WhoAmL 92*
**Burstein**, Rose *Who 92*
**Burstein**, Samuel Z 1935- *AmMWSc 92*
**Burstein**, Sol 1922- *AmMWSc 92*
**Burstein**, Sumner 1932- *AmMWSc 92*
**Bursten**, Bruce Edward 1954- *AmMWSc 92*
**Burstermann**, Juliette Phifer 1905- *WhoBlA 92*
**Burston**, Richard Mervin 1924- *WhoFI 92*
**Burston**, Samuel 1915- *Who 92*
**Burstone**, Charles Justin 1928- *AmMWSc 92*
**Burstyn**, Ellen 1932- *FacFETw, IntMPA 92, IntWW 91, WhoEnt 92*
**Burstyn**, Harold Lewis 1930- *AmMWSc 92, WhoAmL 92*
**Burstyn**, Mike Lawrence 1945- *WhoEnt 92*
**Bursuker**, Isia 1941- *AmMWSc 92*
**Bursztajn**, Sherry 1946- *AmMWSc 92*
**Bursztynsky**, Susan Lynn 1961- *WhoAmL 92*
**Burt**, Alice Louise 1925- *WhoIns 92*
**Burt**, Alistair James Hendrie 1955- *Who 92*
**Burt**, Alvin Miller, III 1935- *AmMWSc 92*
**Burt**, Ann Louise 1962- *WhoAmL 92*
**Burt**, Brian Aubrey 1939- *AmMWSc 92*
**Burt**, Charles Tyler 1942- *AmMWSc 92*
**Burt**, Cyril L 1883-1971 *FacFETw*
**Burt**, Cyril O 1923- *WhoAmP 91*
**Burt**, David Anthony 1960- *WhoWest 92*
**Burt**, David Arlin 1949- *WhoIns 92*
**Burt**, David Reed 1943- *AmMWSc 92*
**Burt**, Debra Lynn 1954- *WhoFI 92*
**Burt**, Donald McLain 1943- *AmMWSc 92*
**Burt**, Francis 1918- *Who 92*
**Burt**, Francis 1926- *ConCom 92*
**Burt**, Gerald Dennis 1936- *AmMWSc 92*
**Burt**, Gerald Raymond 1926- *Who 92*
**Burt**, James E. 1946- *WhoBlA 92*
**Burt**, James Kay 1934- *AmMWSc 92*
**Burt**, James Melvin 1933- *WhoFI 92*
**Burt**, Janis Mae *AmMWSc 92*
**Burt**, Jeffrey Amsterdam 1944- *WhoAmL 92*
**Burt**, John Harris 1918- *WhoRel 92*
**Burt**, Katharine 1882-1977 *TwCWW 91*
**Burt**, Katharine Newlin 1882- *BenetAL 91*
**Burt**, Laurie 1925- *TwCPaSc*
**Burt**, Linda K. 1951- *WhoFI 92, WhoMW 92*
**Burt**, Marvin Roger 1937- *WhoFI 92*
**Burt**, Maurice Edward 1921- *Who 92*
**Burt**, Michael David Brunskill 1938- *AmMWSc 92*
**Burt**, Michael Patrick 1950- *WhoMW 92*
**Burt**, Nathaniel 1913- *WrDr 92*
**Burt**, Peter Alexander 1944- *Who 92*
**Burt**, Philip Barnes 1934- *AmMWSc 92*
**Burt**, Richard 1947- *IntWW 91*
**Burt**, Richard Max 1944- *WhoAmL 92*
**Burt**, Richard R 1947- *WhoAmP 91*
**Burt**, Robert Amsterdam 1939- *IntWW 91, WhoAmL 92*
**Burt**, Robert Eugene 1926- *WhoMW 92*
**Burt**, Robert Norcross 1937- *WhoMW 92*
**Burt**, Struthers 1881-1954 *DcNCBi 1*
**Burt**, Struthers 1882-1954 *BenetAL 91*
**Burt**, Wallace Joseph, Jr. 1924- *WhoFI 92, WhoIns 92*
**Burt**, Wallace Lockwood 1948- *WhoIns 92*
**Burt**, Wayne Vincent 1917- *AmMWSc 92*
**Burt**, William Frank 1950- *WhoWest 92*
**Burt-Andrews**, Charles Beresford Eaton 1913- *Who 92*
**Burt-Andrews**, Stanley George d1990 *Who 92N*
**Burtchaell**, James Tunstead 1934- *IntWW 91, WhoMW 92, WhoRel 92, WrDr 92*
**Burte**, Harris M 1927- *AmMWSc 92*
**Burte**, Harris Merl 1927- *WhoMW 92*
**Burte**, Hermann 1879-1960 *EncTR 91*
**Burtell**, Joseph J. 1931- *WhoAmL 92*
**Burtenshaw**, Claude Junior 1918- *WhoAmP 91*
**Burti**, Christopher Louis 1950- *WhoAmL 92*
**Burtin**, Cipe Pineles d1991 *NewYTBS 91 [port]*
**Burtin**, Will 1908-1972 *DcTwDes*
**Burtis**, Carl A, Jr 1937- *AmMWSc 92*
**Burtis**, Theodore A 1922- *AmMWSc 92*
**Burtis**, Thomson 1896- *ScFEYrs*
**Burtle**, James Lindley 1919- *WhoFI 92*
**Burtle**, Paul Walter 1950- *WhoMW 92*
**Burtless**, Gary Thomas 1950- *WhoFI 92*
**Burtner**, Dale Charles 1926- *AmMWSc 92*
**Burtner**, Roger Lee 1936- *AmMWSc 92*
**Burtness**, Roger William 1925- *AmMWSc 92*
**Burtnett**, Robert Ellis 1946- *WhoFI 92*
**Burton** *Who 92*
**Burton**, Baron 1924- *Who 92*
**Burton**, Al *WhoEnt 92, WhoWest 92*
**Burton**, Alan Harvey 1952- *WhoMW 92*
**Burton**, Albert Frederick 1929- *AmMWSc 92*
**Burton**, Alexis Lucien 1922- *AmMWSc 92*
**Burton**, Alice Jean 1934- *AmMWSc 92*
**Burton**, Anthony 1934- *WrDr 92*
**Burton**, Anthony David 1937- *Who 92*
**Burton**, Anthony George Graham 1934- *IntAu&W 91, Who 92*
**Burton**, Benjamin Theodore 1919- *AmMWSc 92*
**Burton**, Bernard Leo 1932- *WhoAmL 92*
**Burton**, Bertha Edwina 1949- *WhoWest 92*
**Burton**, Betty June 1923- *WhoMW 92, WhoRel 92*
**Burton**, Beverly S d1904 *BiInAmS*
**Burton**, Calvin E. *WhoBlA 92*
**Burton**, Carlisle 1921- *Who 92*
**Burton**, Charles 1929- *TwCPaSc*
**Burton**, Charles Henning 1915- *WhoAmL 92*
**Burton**, Charles Howard, Jr. 1945- *WhoBlA 92*

**Burton,** Charles Jewell 1916- *AmMWSc 92*
**Burton,** Clifton Allen 1933- *WhoWest 92*
**Burton,** Clyde Leaon *AmMWSc 92*
**Burton,** Dan 1938- *AlmAP 92 [port]*
**Burton,** Dan L 1938- *WhoAmP 91*
**Burton,** Daniel Frederick 1915- *AmMWSc 92, WhoAmP 91*
**Burton,** Danni Elizabeth 1940- *WhoEnt 92*
**Burton,** Danny Lee 1938- *WhoMW 92*
**Burton,** Darrell Irvin 1926- *WhoMW 92*
**Burton,** David *Who 92*
**Burton,** David Harold 1947- *Who 92*
**Burton,** David Lloyd 1956- *WhoBlA 92*
**Burton,** David Norman 1941- *AmMWSc 92*
**Burton,** Dennis Thorpe 1941- *AmMWSc 92*
**Burton,** DeWitt A. *WhoRel 92*
**Burton,** Donald C. 1938- *WhoBlA 92*
**Burton,** Donald Eugene 1941- *AmMWSc 92*
**Burton,** Donald Gene 1953- *WhoWest 92*
**Burton,** Donald Joseph 1934- *AmMWSc 92*
**Burton,** Dorothy Jo *WhoFI 92*
**Burton,** Edward Lewis 1935- *WhoFI 92, WhoWest 92*
**Burton,** Erlie P. 1926- *WhoMW 92*
**Burton,** Eugene *DrAPF 91*
**Burton,** Francis George *ScFEYrs*
**Burton,** Frederick Glenn 1939- *AmMWSc 92, WhoWest 92*
**Burton,** Gabrielle *DrAPF 91*
**Burton,** Gary 1943- *NewAmDM*
**Burton,** Gary L 1945- *WhoAmP 91*
**Burton,** Gene Craig 1954- *WhoWest 92*
**Burton,** George 1916- *Who 92*
**Burton,** George Aubrey, Jr 1926- *WhoAmP 91*
**Burton,** George Dexter 1855-1918 *BiInAmS*
**Burton,** George Joseph 1919- *AmMWSc 92*
**Burton,** Gilbert W 1936- *AmMWSc 92*
**Burton,** Glenn 1940- *WhoMW 92*
**Burton,** Glenn Willard 1910- *AmMWSc 92, IntWW 91*
**Burton,** Graham Stuart 1941- *Who 92*
**Burton,** Harold 1943- *AmMWSc 92*
**Burton,** Harold H 1888-1964 *FacFETw*
**Burton,** Harry 1919- *Who 92*
**Burton,** Hester 1913- *IntAu&W 91, WrDr 92*
**Burton,** Hubert Dickson 1958- *WhoAmL 92*
**Burton,** Humphrey McGuire 1931- *Who 92*
**Burton,** Hutchins Gordon 1774?-1836 *DcNCBi 1*
**Burton,** Ian 1935- *IntWW 91*
**Burton,** Iola Brantley *WhoBlA 92*
**Burton,** Iris Grace *Who 92*
**Burton,** Iris Grace 1940- *IntAu&W 91*
**Burton,** Ivor 1923- *WrDr 92*
**Burton,** Janet Ferree 1955- *WhoEnt 92*
**Burton,** Joan E. 1945- *WhoBlA 92*
**Burton,** Joe *WhoAmP 91*
**Burton,** John 1915- *IntAu&W 91, WrDr 92*
**Burton,** John 1932- *WhoAmP 91*
**Burton,** John Allan, Jr. 1947- *WhoAmL 92*
**Burton,** John Andrew 1944- *IntAu&W 91, WrDr 92*
**Burton,** John Anthony, Jr. 1965- *WhoWest 92*
**Burton,** John Campbell 1932- *WhoFI 92*
**Burton,** John Charles 1920- *WhoAmP 91*
**Burton,** John Frederick 1913- *WhoBlA 92*
**Burton,** John H. 1910- *WhoBlA 92*
**Burton,** John Harold Stanley 1913- *Who 92*
**Burton,** John Heslop 1938- *AmMWSc 92*
**Burton,** John Lee 1927- *WhoFI 92*
**Burton,** John Paul 1943- *WhoAmL 92, WhoWest 92*
**Burton,** John Robert 1927- *WhoMW 92*
**Burton,** John Scott 1955- *WhoAmL 92*
**Burton,** John Williams 1937- *AmMWSc 92*
**Burton,** Joseph Randolph 1951- *WhoAmL 92*
**Burton,** Juanita Sharon 1946- *WhoBlA 92*
**Burton,** Karen Poliner 1952- *AmMWSc 92*
**Burton,** Kate 1957- *IntMPA 92*
**Burton,** Keith Augustus 1963- *WhoRel 92*
**Burton,** Kenneth 1926- *IntWW 91, Who 92*
**Burton,** Kenneth Raymond 1944- *WhoWest 92*
**Burton,** Lana Doreen 1953- *WhoBlA 92*
**Burton,** Larry C 1939- *AmMWSc 92*
**Burton,** Leonard Pattillo 1918- *AmMWSc 92*
**Burton,** Leroy Melvin, Jr. 1940- *WhoBlA 92*
**Burton,** Lester Percy Joseph 1953- *AmMWSc 92*
**Burton,** Levar *WhoBlA 92*
**Burton,** Levar 1957- *IntMPA 92*
**Burton,** Levardis Robert Martyn, Jr. *WhoEnt 92A*
**Burton,** Lloyd Edward 1922- *AmMWSc 92*
**Burton,** Louis 1949- *AmMWSc 92*
**Burton,** Margaret Ann 1926- *WhoWest 92*
**Burton,** Martin Nelson 1961- *WhoAmL 92*
**Burton,** Maurice 1898- *IntAu&W 91, Who 92, WrDr 92*
**Burton,** Melvin Matthew, Jr 1929- *WhoAmP 91*
**Burton,** Michael Angelo 1956- *WhoBlA 92*
**Burton,** Michael John 1946- *Who 92*
**Burton,** Michael St Edmund 1937- *Who 92*
**Burton,** Mike 1941- *WhoAmP 91*
**Burton,** Neil Edward David d1990 *Who 92N*
**Burton,** Paul Floyd 1939- *WhoWest 92*
**Burton,** Paul Ray 1931- *AmMWSc 92*
**Burton,** Philip L. 1915- *WhoBlA 92*
**Burton,** Phillip 1926-1983 *FacFETw*
**Burton,** Ralph A 1925- *AmMWSc 92*
**Burton,** Ralph Gaines 1955- *AmMWSc 92*
**Burton,** Ralph L 1936- *AmMWSc 92*
**Burton,** Randall James 1950- *WhoAmL 92*
**Burton,** Raymond L *TwCSFW 91*
**Burton,** Richard 1861-1940 *BenetAL 91*
**Burton,** Richard 1925-1984 *FacFETw [port]*
**Burton,** Richard Greene 1936- *WhoFI 92*
**Burton,** Richard Hilary 1923- *Who 92*
**Burton,** Richard Roghaar 1941- *WhoWest 92*
**Burton,** Robert 1577-1640 *RfGEnL 91*
**Burton,** Robert 1747-1825 *DcNCBi 1*
**Burton,** Robert Clyde 1929- *AmMWSc 92*
**Burton,** Robert Dale 1960- *WhoRel 92*
**Burton,** Robert Lee 1943- *AmMWSc 92*
**Burton,** Robert Main 1927- *AmMWSc 92*
**Burton,** Roger 1946- *Who 92*
**Burton,** Ronald E. 1936- *WhoBlA 92*
**Burton,** Ronald J. 1947- *WhoBlA 92*
**Burton,** Rosemary 1951- *TwCPaSc*
**Burton,** Ross Bland 1956- *WhoRel 92*
**Burton,** Russell Rohan 1932- *AmMWSc 92*
**Burton,** Scott 1939-1989 *DcTwDes*
**Burton,** Sheril Dale 1935- *AmMWSc 92*
**Burton,** Stephanie Lynette 1961- *WhoEnt 92*
**Burton,** Sydney Harold 1916- *Who 92*
**Burton,** Theodore Allen 1935- *AmMWSc 92*
**Burton,** Theodore Elijah 1851-1929 *AmPeW*
**Burton,** Thomas *IntAu&W 91X, WrDr 92*
**Burton,** Thomas Lawson 1922- *WhoAmP 91*
**Burton,** Thomas Maxie 1941- *AmMWSc 92*
**Burton,** Tim 1958- *CurBio 91 [port], IntMPA 92*
**Burton,** Tim 1960- *ConTFT 9, WhoEnt 92*
**Burton,** Vernon James 1962- *WhoEnt 92*
**Burton,** Verona Devine 1922- *AmMWSc 92, WhoAmP 91, WhoMW 92*
**Burton,** Walter Brandon 1946- *WhoAmP 91*
**Burton,** Walter Ervin 1903- *WhoMW 92*
**Burton,** Wayne M 1944- *WhoAmP 91*
**Burton,** Wilford Moyler 1950- *WhoAmL 92*
**Burton,** Willard White 1922- *AmMWSc 92*
**Burton,** William Butler 1940- *AmMWSc 92*
**Burton,** William Evans 1804-1860 *BenetAL 91*
**Burton,** Willie Ricardo 1968- *WhoBlA 92*
**Burton,** Woody 1945- *WhoAmP 91*
**Burton-Bradley,** Burton 1914- *Who 92*
**Burton-Chadwick,** Joshua 1954- *Who 92*
**Burton-Junior,** Eva Westbrook 1944- *WhoBlA 92*
**Burton Kaplan,** Helene 1918- *WhoFI 92, WhoMW 92*
**Burton-Lyles,** Blanche 1933- *WhoBlA 92*
**Burton of Coventry,** Baroness 1904- *Who 92*
**Burton-Shannon,** Clarinda 1959- *WhoBlA 92*
**Burton-Taylor,** Alvin d1991 *Who 92N*
**Burts,** Everett C 1931- *AmMWSc 92*
**Burtschi,** Mary Pauline 1911- *WrDr 92*
**Burtt,** Ben 1948- *WhoEnt 92*
**Burtt,** Benjamin Pickering 1921- *AmMWSc 92*
**Burtt,** Edward Howland, Jr 1948- *AmMWSc 92*
**Burty,** Philippe 1820-1890 *ThHEIm*
**Burwash,** Peter Francis 1945- *WhoWest 92*
**Burwash,** Ronald Allan 1925- *AmMWSc 92*
**Burwasser,** Herman 1927- *AmMWSc 92*
**Burwell,** Bill Loren 1952- *WhoWest 92*
**Burwell,** Bryan Ellis 1955- *WhoBlA 92*
**Burwell,** Calvin C 1930- *AmMWSc 92*
**Burwell,** E Langdon *AmMWSc 92*
**Burwell,** Henry McAden 1945- *WhoAmL 92*
**Burwell,** James Robert 1929- *AmMWSc 92*
**Burwell,** Margaret Anna Robertson *DcNCBi 1*
**Burwell,** Martin *DrAPF 91*
**Burwell,** Rex *DrAPF 91*
**Burwell,** Robert Armistead 1802-1895 *DcNCBi 1*
**Burwell,** Robert L., Jr. 1912- *IntWW 91*
**Burwell,** Robert Lemmon, Jr 1912- *AmMWSc 92*
**Burwell,** Robin Anderson 1956- *WhoEnt 92*
**Burwell,** Wayne Gregory 1933- *AmMWSc 92*
**Burwell,** William David, Jr. 1942- *WhoBlA 92*
**Burwen,** Susan Jo 1946- *AmMWSc 92*
**Burwitz,** Nils 1940- *IntWW 91*
**Bury,** David Alfred 1933- *WhoRel 92*
**Bury,** John 1925- *Who 92*
**Bury,** John Patrick Tuer 1908- *IntAu&W 91*
**Bury,** Lindsay Claude Neils 1939- *Who 92*
**Bury,** Michael Oswell 1922- *Who 92*
**Bury,** Morley 1919- *TwCPaSc*
**Bury,** Pol 1922- *WorArt 1980*
**Bury,** Shirley Joan 1925- *Who 92*
**Bury,** Thomas Malcolm Grahame 1918- *Who 92*
**Burzynski,** Denny Keith 1948- *WhoWest 92*
**Burzynski,** J Bradley *WhoAmP 91*
**Burzynski,** Norbert J 1929- *AmMWSc 92*
**Burzynski,** Peter Raymond 1948- *WhoMW 92*
**Burzynski,** Stanislaw Rajmund 1943- *AmMWSc 92*
**Bus,** James Stanley 1949- *AmMWSc 92*
**Busath,** Kevin Warren 1954- *WhoMW 92*
**Busbee,** Charles Manly 1845-1909 *DcNCBi 1*
**Busbee,** Fabius Haywood 1848-1908 *DcNCBi 1*
**Busbee,** George D 1927- *WhoAmP 91*
**Busbee,** Jacques 1870-1947 *DcNCBi 1*
**Busbee,** Juliana Royster 1876-1962 *DcNCBi 1*
**Busbee,** Kline Daniel, Jr. 1933- *WhoAmL 92*
**Busbee,** Maury Judson 1947- *WhoAmP 91*
**Busbee,** Shirlee 1941- *IntAu&W 91, WrDr 92*
**Busbey,** Douglas Earle 1948- *WhoAmL 92*
**Busbey,** Louisa Kay 1954- *WhoEnt 92*
**Busbice,** Wayne Evon 1929- *WhoEnt 92*
**Busboom,** Larry D. 1942- *WhoWest 92*
**Busboom,** Patricia Gail 1936- *WhoAmP 91*
**Busbridge,** A W *ScFEYrs*
**Busby,** David 1926- *WhoAmL 92*
**Busby,** Edward Oliver 1926- *AmMWSc 92*
**Busby,** Everett C. *WhoBlA 92*
**Busby,** F M 1921- *IntAu&W 91, TwCSFW 91, WrDr 92*
**Busby,** George 1926- *TwCPaSc*
**Busby,** Gerald 1935- *WhoEnt 92*
**Busby,** Hubbard Taylor, Jr 1941- *AmMWSc 92*
**Busby,** Jheryl *WhoBlA 92, WhoEnt 92*
**Busby,** John 1928- *TwCPaSc*
**Busby,** Matt 1909- *IntWW 91*
**Busby,** Matthew 1909- *Who 92*
**Busby,** Robert Clark 1940- *AmMWSc 92*
**Busby,** Roger 1941- *IntAu&W 91, WrDr 92*
**Busby,** V. Eugene 1937- *WhoBlA 92*
**Busby,** William Fisher, Jr 1939- *AmMWSc 92*
**Buscaglia,** Leo 1924- *SmATA 65 [port]*
**Buscaglia,** Leo F. *SmATA 65*
**Buscaglia,** Leo F. 1924- *WrDr 92*
**Buscaglia,** Marta Carmen 1953- *WhoHisp 92*
**Buscemi,** Peter 1950- *WhoAmL 92*
**Buscemi,** Philip Augustus 1926- *AmMWSc 92*
**Busch,** Adolf 1891-1952 *NewAmDM*
**Busch,** Allan Julius, Jr. 1942- *WhoMW 92*
**Busch,** Arthur Allen 1954- *WhoAmL 92*
**Busch,** Arthur Winston 1926- *AmMWSc 92*
**Busch,** August Adolphus, III 1937- *WhoFI 92, WhoMW 92*
**Busch,** August Anheuser, Jr 1899-1989 *FacFETw*
**Busch,** Briton Cooper 1936- *ConAu 36NR, WrDr 92*
**Busch,** Charles Gardner 1939- *WhoWest 92*
**Busch,** Christine 1947- *WhoEnt 92*
**Busch,** Constantinus Albertus Maria 1937- *Who 92*
**Busch,** Corey *WhoWest 92*
**Busch,** Daniel Adolph 1912- *AmMWSc 92*
**Busch,** Daryle Hadley 1928- *AmMWSc 92*
**Busch,** Eberhard 1937- *WhoRel 92*
**Busch,** Ernst 1885-1945 *EncTR 91 [port]*
**Busch,** Frederick *DrAPF 91*
**Busch,** Frederick 1941- *BenetAL 91, ConNov 91, WrDr 92*
**Busch,** Frederick Carl 1873-1914 *BiInAmS*
**Busch,** Frederick Matthew 1941- *WhoEnt 92*
**Busch,** Fritz 1890-1951 *NewAmDM*
**Busch,** George Jacob *AmMWSc 92*
**Busch,** H. Donald 1935- *IntMPA 92*
**Busch,** Harris 1923- *AmMWSc 92*
**Busch,** J. Mark 1960- *WhoMW 92*
**Busch,** J Michael 1946- *WhoAmP 91*
**Busch,** Joseph Sherman 1927- *AmMWSc 92*
**Busch,** Joyce Ida 1934- *WhoWest 92*
**Busch,** Kenneth Louis 1953- *AmMWSc 92*
**Busch,** Kenneth Walter 1944- *AmMWSc 92*
**Busch,** Lloyd Victor 1918- *AmMWSc 92*
**Busch,** Marc Allen 1953- *WhoWest 92*
**Busch,** Marianna Anderson 1943- *AmMWSc 92*
**Busch,** Michael 1947- *WhoAmP 91*
**Busch,** Niven d1991 *NewYTBS 91*
**Busch,** Niven 1903- *BenetAL 91, TwCWW 91, WrDr 92*
**Busch,** Niven 1903-1991 *ConAu 135, WhoEnt 92*
**Busch,** Noel Henry 1940- *WhoFI 92*
**Busch,** Randall William 1946- *WhoMW 92*
**Busch,** Robert Edward 1924- *AmMWSc 92*
**Busch,** Robert Henry 1937- *AmMWSc 92, WhoMW 92*
**Busch,** Rolf Trygue 1920- *IntWW 91*
**Busch,** Rolf Trygve 1920- *Who 92*
**Busch,** Thomas Anthony 1947- *WhoEnt 92*
**Busch,** Tyrone Glen 1948- *WhoWest 92*
**Buschbach,** Thomas Charles 1923- *AmMWSc 92*
**Busche,** Robert M 1926- *AmMWSc 92*
**Buschert,** Robert Cecil 1924- *AmMWSc 92*
**Buschke,** Herman 1932- *AmMWSc 92*
**Buschmann,** Donald Gene 1951- *WhoEnt 92*
**Buschmann,** MaryBeth Tank 1942- *AmMWSc 92*
**Buschmann,** Robert J 1942- *AmMWSc 92*
**Buschmann,** Siegfried 1937- *WhoFI 92, WhoMW 92*
**Buscombe,** William 1918- *AmMWSc 92*
**Buse,** John Frederick 1921- *AmMWSc 92*
**Buse,** Margaret Lynn 1948- *WhoWest 92*
**Buse,** Maria F Gordon 1927- *AmMWSc 92*
**Buse,** Reuben Charles 1932- *AmMWSc 92*
**Buseck,** Peter R 1935- *AmMWSc 92*
**Busek,** Erhard 1941- *IntWW 91*
**Buselt,** Clara Irene 1921- *WhoMW 92, WhoRel 92*
**Busemann,** Adolf 1901- *AmMWSc 92*
**Busemann,** Adolf 1901-1986 *FacFETw*
**Busenberg,** Eurybiades 1939- *AmMWSc 92*
**Busenberg,** Stavros Nicholas 1941- *AmMWSc 92, WhoWest 92*
**Buser,** Kenneth Rene 1925- *AmMWSc 92*
**Buser,** Mary Paul 1928- *AmMWSc 92*
**Buser,** Paul Joseph 1947- *WhoAmP 91*
**Buser,** Sue 1949- *WhoAmL 92*
**Buser,** Walter Emil 1926- *IntWW 91*
**Busey,** Gary 1944- *IntMPA 92, WhoEnt 92*
**Busey,** George Brian 1953- *WhoAmL 92*
**Busey,** James B *WhoAmP 91*
**Busey,** James Buchanan, IV 1932- *WhoFI 92*
**Busey,** Richard Hoover 1919- *AmMWSc 92*
**Busey,** Stephen Donald 1944- *WhoAmL 92*
**Busfield,** Roger Melvil, Jr. 1926- *WhoFI 92*
**Busfield,** Timothy 1957- *IntMPA 92, WhoEnt 92*
**Bush,** Alan 1900- *ConCom 92, IntWW 91, Who 92*
**Bush,** Alfred Lerner 1919- *AmMWSc 92*
**Bush,** Alvin C 1924- *WhoAmP 91*
**Bush,** Anita 1883-1974 *NotBlAW 92 [port]*
**Bush,** Ann 1939- *WhoBlA 92*
**Bush,** Barbara Pierce 1925- *IntWW 91*
**Bush,** Barney *DrAPF 91*
**Bush,** Barry 1938- *WrDr 92*
**Bush,** Bernard Joseph, Jr. 1934- *WhoRel 92*
**Bush,** Billie Voss 1914- *WhoAmP 91*
**Bush,** Bryan 1936- *Who 92*
**Bush,** C Allen 1938- *AmMWSc 92*
**Bush,** Charles Edward 1938- *AmMWSc 92*
**Bush,** Charles Jay 1935- *WhoRel 92*
**Bush,** Charles Vernon 1939- *WhoBlA 92*
**Bush,** David Clair 1922- *AmMWSc 92*
**Bush,** David E 1952- *AmMWSc 92*
**Bush,** David Graves 1922- *AmMWSc 92*
**Bush,** Don E 1923- *WhoAmP 91*
**Bush,** Dorothy 1916- *WhoAmP 91*
**Bush,** Dorothy Vredenburgh 1916- *IntWW 91*
**Bush,** Dorothy Vredenburgh 1916-1991 *NewYTBS 91 [port]*
**Bush,** Duncan 1946- *IntAu&W 91*
**Bush,** Eugene Nyle 1952- *WhoMW 92*
**Bush,** F. Donald 1946- *WhoMW 92*
**Bush,** Francis M 1933- *AmMWSc 92*
**Bush,** Frederick Morris 1949- *WhoAmP 91*

**Bush**, Gage *WhoEnt 92*
**Bush**, Gary Graham 1950- *AmMWSc 92, WhoWest 92*
**Bush**, Gary Robert 1948- *WhoWest 92*
**Bush**, Geoffrey 1920- *ConCom 92, IntWW 91*
**Bush**, Geoffrey Hubert 1942- *Who 92*
**Bush**, George 1796-1859 *AmPeW*
**Bush**, George 1924- *BenetAL 91, FacFETw [port], RComAH*
**Bush**, George Clark 1930- *AmMWSc 92*
**Bush**, George Edward 1937- *AmMWSc 92*
**Bush**, George F 1909- *AmMWSc 92*
**Bush**, George Herbert Walker 1924- *AmPolLe [port], IntWW 91, Who 92, WhoAmP 91*
**Bush**, George Ray 1938- *WhoIns 92*
**Bush**, Glenn W 1933- *AmMWSc 92*
**Bush**, Graeme Webster 1950- *WhoAmL 92*
**Bush**, Guy L 1929- *AmMWSc 92*
**Bush**, Harry 1883-1957 *TwCPaSc*
**Bush**, James Michael 1955- *WhoWest 92*
**Bush**, Janel Marie 1949- *WhoAmL 92*
**Bush**, John 1914- *Who 92*
**Bush**, John Benjamin 1956- *WhoAmL 92*
**Bush**, John William 1950- *WhoMW 92*
**Bush**, Judy Lynn 1938- *WhoRel 92*
**Bush**, June Lee 1942- *WhoWest 92*
**Bush**, Karen Jean 1943- *AmMWSc 92*
**Bush**, Kate *IntWW 91*
**Bush**, L. Russ 1944- *WhoRel 92*
**Bush**, Lenoris 1949- *WhoBlA 92*
**Bush**, Leon F 1924- *AmMWSc 92*
**Bush**, Linville John 1928- *AmMWSc 92*
**Bush**, Lowell Palmer 1939- *AmMWSc 92*
**Bush**, Mark Stuart 1960- *WhoRel 92*
**Bush**, Martin H. 1930- *WrDr 92*
**Bush**, Mary *DrAPF 91*
**Bush**, Mary K. 1948- *WhoBlA 92*
**Bush**, Maurice E 1936- *AmMWSc 92*
**Bush**, Millie 1987?- *News 92-1 [port]*
**Bush**, Nathaniel 1949- *WhoBlA 92*
**Bush**, Norman 1929- *AmMWSc 92*
**Bush**, Peter John 1924- *Who 92*
**Bush**, Randall Bruce 1953- *WhoRel 92*
**Bush**, Raymond George 1952- *WhoAmL 92*
**Bush**, Raymond Sydney 1931- *AmMWSc 92*
**Bush**, Richard Norman 1951- *WhoAmL 92*
**Bush**, Richard Wayne 1934- *AmMWSc 92*
**Bush**, Robert Bradford 1953- *WhoAmL 92*
**Bush**, Robert G., III 1936- *WhoAmL 92, WhoAmP 91*
**Bush**, Ronald L. 1946- *WhoWest 92*
**Bush**, Roy *DrAPF 91*
**Bush**, Roy Sidney 1946- *AmMWSc 92*
**Bush**, S H 1920- *AmMWSc 92*
**Bush**, Sarah Lillian 1920- *WhoWest 92*
**Bush**, Sargent, Jr. 1937- *WhoMW 92*
**Bush**, Stan M. 1953- *WhoWest 92*
**Bush**, Stanley Giltner 1928- *WhoWest 92*
**Bush**, Stephanie R 1953- *WhoAmP 91*
**Bush**, Stewart Fowler 1941- *AmMWSc 92*
**Bush**, Susan Ensign Hilles 1933- *IntAu&W 91*
**Bush**, T. W. *WhoBlA 92*
**Bush**, Thomas Norman 1947- *WhoAmL 92*
**Bush**, Tom 1948- *WhoAmP 91*
**Bush**, Vannevar 1890-1974 *FacFETw*
**Bush**, Vernon Louis 1930- *WhoWest 92*
**Bush**, Warren V. d1991 *NewYTBS 91*
**Bush**, Warren Van Ness 1931- *AmMWSc 92*
**Bush**, William E *WhoAmP 91*
**Bush**, William Edward 1959- *WhoRel 92*
**Bush**, William Merritt 1941- *WhoAmL 92*
**Busha**, Gary C. *DrAPF 91*
**Bushaw**, Donald 1926- *AmMWSc 92*
**Bushby**, Frederick Henry 1924- *Who 92*
**Bushe**, Fred 1931- *TwCPaSc*
**Bushe**, Frederick Joseph William 1939- *Who 92*
**Bushee**, Eleanor Jane 1922- *WhoMW 92*
**Bushehri**, Ali 1957- *WhoWest 92*
**Bushell**, Agnes 1949- *ConAu 135*
**Bushell**, John Christopher Wyndowe 1919- *IntWW 91, Who 92*
**Bushell**, Raymond 1910- *WrDr 92*
**Bushey**, A Scott 1930- *WhoIns 92*
**Bushey**, Albert Henry 1911- *AmMWSc 92*
**Bushey**, Dean Franklin 1950- *AmMWSc 92*
**Bushey**, Gerald Blair 1950- *WhoIns 92*
**Bushey**, Gordon Lake 1922- *AmMWSc 92*
**Bushey**, Leonel H 1922- *WhoAmP 91*
**Bushey**, Michelle Marie 1960- *AmMWSc 92*
**Bushing**, Jan *WhoAmP 91*
**Bushinsky**, David Allen 1949- *AmMWSc 92*
**Bushkin**, Yuri 1949- *AmMWSc 92*
**Bushmaker**, Sandra Jean 1947- *WhoAmL 92*
**Bushman**, Edwin Francis Arthur 1919- *WhoWest 92*
**Bushman**, Jess Richard 1921- *AmMWSc 92*
**Bushman**, John Branson 1926- *AmMWSc 92*
**Bushman**, Naomi *DrAPF 91*
**Bushman**, Richard Lyman 1931- *WrDr 92*
**Bushmann**, Eugene G *WhoAmP 91*
**Bushnell**, Alexander Lynn 1911- *Who 92*
**Bushnell**, Asa Smith 1925- *WhoWest 92*
**Bushnell**, Bill 1937- *WhoEnt 92, WhoWest 92*
**Bushnell**, Catharine 1950- *WhoFI 92*
**Bushnell**, David 1742?-1824 *BiInAmS*
**Bushnell**, David L 1929- *AmMWSc 92*
**Bushnell**, Gene Raymond 1938- *WhoAmL 92, WhoMW 92*
**Bushnell**, George Edward, III 1952- *WhoAmL 92*
**Bushnell**, George Edward, Jr. 1924- *WhoAmL 92*
**Bushnell**, Gordon William 1936- *AmMWSc 92*
**Bushnell**, Horace 1802-1876 *BenetAL 91*
**Bushnell**, James Judson 1934- *AmMWSc 92*
**Bushnell**, John Alden 1933- *WhoAmP 91*
**Bushnell**, John Horace 1925- *AmMWSc 92*
**Bushnell**, Kent O 1929- *AmMWSc 92*
**Bushnell**, Mary B 1932- *WhoAmP 91*
**Bushnell**, Richard 1926- *WhoAmL 92*
**Bushnell**, Robert Hempstead 1924- *AmMWSc 92*
**Bushnell**, Roderick Paul 1944- *WhoWest 92*
**Bushnell**, William Rodgers 1931- *AmMWSc 92, WhoMW 92*
**Bushno**, Joan G 1931- *IntAu&W 91*
**Bushong**, Jerold Ward 1935- *AmMWSc 92*
**Bushong**, Stewart Carlyle 1936- *AmMWSc 92*
**Bushre**, Peter Alvin 1943- *WhoFI 92*
**Bushuk**, Walter 1929- *AmMWSc 92*
**Bushuyev**, Konstantin D 1914-1978 *FacFETw*
**Bushweller**, Charles Hackett 1939- *AmMWSc 92*
**Bushyeager**, Peter *DrAPF 91*
**Busia**, Kofi 1913-1978 *FacFETw*
**Busick**, Charles Philip 1928- *WhoWest 92*
**Busick**, Denzel Rex 1945- *WhoAmL 92, WhoMW 92*
**Busick**, Robert James 1950- *WhoMW 92*
**Busig**, Rick Harold 1952- *WhoWest 92*
**Busignies**, Henri Gaston 1905-1981 *FacFETw*
**Busigo**, George Charles 1933- *WhoHisp 92*
**Busing**, William Richard 1923- *AmMWSc 92*
**Businger**, John Arnold 1945- *WhoAmP 91*
**Businger**, Joost Alois 1924- *AmMWSc 92*
**Busk**, Douglas Laird d1990 *Who 92N*
**Busk**, Grant Curtis, Jr 1949- *AmMWSc 92*
**Busk**, Leslie Francis Harry 1937- *Who 92*
**Buske**, Norman L 1943- *AmMWSc 92*
**Busker**, Gary Leon 1946- *WhoAmL 92*
**Buskey**, J L *WhoAmP 91*
**Buskey**, James E *WhoAmP 91, WhoBlA 92*
**Buskey**, John *WhoBlA 92*
**Buskirk**, Elsworth Robert 1925- *AmMWSc 92*
**Buskirk**, Fred Ramon 1928- *AmMWSc 92*
**Buskirk**, Phyllis Richardson 1930- *WhoFI 92, WhoMW 92*
**Buskirk**, Ruth Elizabeth 1944- *AmMWSc 92*
**Buslaev**, Yuri A. 1929- *IntWW 91*
**Buslig**, Bela Stephen 1938- *AmMWSc 92*
**Buslik**, Arthur J 1933- *AmMWSc 92*
**Busnaina**, Ahmed A 1953- *AmMWSc 92*
**Busner**, Philip H. 1927- *WhoAmL 92*
**Busnois**, Antoine 1430?-1492 *NewAmDM*
**Busoni**, Ferruccio 1866-1924 *NewAmDM*
**Busoni**, Ferruccio B 1866-1924 *FacFETw*
**Busquin**, Philippe 1941- *IntWW 91*
**Buss**, Barbara Ann 1932- *Who 92*
**Buss**, Daryl Dean 1945- *AmMWSc 92*
**Buss**, David R 1939- *AmMWSc 92*
**Buss**, David Richard 1939- *WhoMW 92*
**Buss**, Dennis Darcy 1942- *AmMWSc 92*
**Buss**, Dietrich G. 1939- *WhoWest 92*
**Buss**, Edward George 1921- *AmMWSc 92*
**Buss**, Glenn Richard 1940- *AmMWSc 92*
**Buss**, Jack Theodore 1943- *AmMWSc 92*
**Buss**, Jerry Hatten *WhoWest 92*
**Buss**, Leo William 1953- *AmMWSc 92*
**Buss**, Marie Louise 1900- *WhoAmP 91*
**Buss**, Samuel Rudolph 1957- *WhoWest 92*
**Buss**, William Charles 1938- *AmMWSc 92*
**Bussard**, Stephen Vince 1964- *WhoWest 92*
**Bussart**, Ford Thomas 1945- *WhoAmP 91*
**Busse**, Ewald William 1917- *AmMWSc 92*
**Busse**, Felix 1940- *IntWW 91*
**Busse**, Friedrich Hermann 1936- *AmMWSc 92*
**Busse**, Kent Vernon 1943- *WhoEnt 92*
**Busse**, Leonard Wayne 1938- *WhoWest 92*
**Busse**, Richard Paul 1950- *WhoRel 92*
**Busse**, Robert Franklyn 1937- *AmMWSc 92*
**Busse**, Robert L. 1928- *WhoMW 92*
**Bussel**, Daniel Jay 1960- *WhoAmL 92*
**Bussell**, Bertram 1923- *AmMWSc 92*
**Bussell**, Sally Carney 1958- *WhoAmL 92*
**Bussell**, William Harrison 1923- *AmMWSc 92*
**Busselle**, Rebecca 1941- *ConAu 135*
**Bussema**, Kenneth Edward 1949- *WhoMW 92*
**Bussert**, Jack Francis 1922- *AmMWSc 92*
**Bussert**, John Robert 1956- *WhoMW 92*
**Bussey**, Arthur Howard *AmMWSc 92*
**Bussey**, Charles David 1933- *WhoBlA 92*
**Bussey**, George Davis 1949- *WhoWest 92*
**Bussey**, Howard Emerson 1917- *AmMWSc 92*
**Bussey**, Joani Sarkiss 1960- *WhoFI 92*
**Bussey**, Reuben T. 1943- *WhoBlA 92*
**Bussgang**, J J 1925- *AmMWSc 92*
**Bussian**, Alfred Erich 1933- *AmMWSc 92*
**Bussie**, Victor 1919- *WhoAmP 91*
**Bussiere**, William Allan 1948- *WhoEnt 92*
**Bussing**, Mary Agnes 1938- *WhoAmP 91*
**Bussinger**, Robert E. 1932- *WhoWest 92*
**Bussman**, Donald Herbert 1925- *WhoMW 92*
**Bussman**, John W 1924- *AmMWSc 92*
**Bussmann**, Harry Theodore, III 1948- *WhoMW 92*
**Bussone**, David Eben 1947- *WhoFI 92*
**Bussotti**, Sylvano 1931- *ConCom 92, NewAmDM*
**Bussy**, Patricia Jean 1923- *WhoWest 92*
**Busta**, Francis Fredrick 1935- *AmMWSc 92*
**Bustad**, Leo Kenneth 1920- *AmMWSc 92*
**Bustamante**, Albert G. 1935- *AlmAP 92 [port], WhoAmP 91, WhoHisp 92*
**Bustamante**, Alexander 1884-1977 *FacFETw [port]*
**Bustamante**, Arturo 1944- *WhoHisp 92*
**Bustamante**, Carlos Maria de 1774-1848 *HisDSpE*
**Bustamante**, Cody Antonio 1955- *WhoHisp 92*
**Bustamante**, David Anthony 1954- *WhoHisp 92*
**Bustamante**, J. W. Andre 1961- *WhoBlA 92*
**Bustamante**, John H. 1929- *WhoBlA 92*
**Bustamante**, Leonard Eliecer 1938- *WhoHisp 92*
**Bustamante**, Ricardo 1962- *WhoHisp 92*
**Bustamante**, Richard *WhoEnt 92*
**Bustamante**, Roberto J. 1946- *WhoHisp 92*
**Bustamante**, Valentin M., Sr. 1931- *WhoHisp 92*
**Bustamante**, Z. Sonali 1958- *WhoBlA 92*
**Bustamante Carlos Inca**, Calixto *HisDSpE*
**Bustamante y Guerra**, Jose de *HisDSpE*
**Bustamate y Rivero**, Jose Luis 1894-1989 *FacFETw*
**Bustamente**, Cecilia *WhoHisp 92*
**Bustard**, Clarke 1950- *WhoEnt 92*
**Bustard**, Thomas Stratton 1934- *AmMWSc 92*
**Bustead**, Ronald Lorima, Jr 1930- *AmMWSc 92*
**Busteed**, Robert Charles 1907- *AmMWSc 92*
**Bustelo Y Garcia Del Real**, Carlos 1936- *IntWW 91*
**Buster**, Jim *WhoAmP 91*
**Busterud**, John Armand 1921- *WhoAmL 92*
**Bustillo**, Eloy 1951- *WhoHisp 92*
**Bustillo**, Oscar, Jr. *WhoHisp 92*
**Bustillos**, Herbert P., Jr. 1937- *WhoHisp 92*
**Bustin**, Beverly Miner 1936- *WhoAmP 91*
**Bustin**, Michael 1937- *AmMWSc 92*
**Bustin**, Robert Marc 1952- *AmMWSc 92*
**Busto**, Rafael Pedro 1939- *WhoHisp 92*
**Bustos**, Aida *WhoHisp 92*
**Bustos Domecq**, Honorio *IntAu&W 91X*
**Bustos-Valdes**, Sergio Enrique 1932- *AmMWSc 92*
**Busuttil**, James Joseph 1958- *WhoAmL 92*
**Busvine**, James Ronald 1912- *Who 92, WrDr 92*
**Buswell**, James Oliver 1946- *NewAmDM, WhoEnt 92*
**Buswell**, Robert Evans, Jr. 1953- *WhoRel 92*
**Busygin**, Mikhail Ivanovich 1948- *IntWW 91*
**Busza**, Wit 1940- *AmMWSc 92*
**Buta**, Paul Charles 1962- *WhoFI 92*
**Butch**, William Louis 1932- *WhoIns 92*
**Butcharev**, Vera *EncAmaz 91*
**Butchart**, Wayne M. 1915- *WhoRel 92*
**Butchbaker**, Allen F 1935- *AmMWSc 92*
**Butcher**, Anthony John 1934- *Who 92*
**Butcher**, Brian T 1940- *AmMWSc 92*
**Butcher**, Bruce Cameron 1947- *WhoAmL 92*
**Butcher**, Connie Joan 1960- *WhoAmL 92*
**Butcher**, David John 1948- *IntWW 91*
**Butcher**, Fred Ray 1943- *AmMWSc 92*
**Butcher**, Goler Teal 1925- *WhoBlA 92*
**Butcher**, Grace *DrAPF 91*
**Butcher**, Harvey Raymond, III 1947- *AmMWSc 92*
**Butcher**, Henry Clay, IV 1933- *AmMWSc 92*
**Butcher**, Howard, III d1991 *NewYTBS 91*
**Butcher**, Jack Robert 1941- *WhoWest 92*
**Butcher**, James R *WhoAmP 91*
**Butcher**, John Charles 1933- *IntWW 91*
**Butcher**, John Edward 1923- *AmMWSc 92*
**Butcher**, John Patrick *Who 92*
**Butcher**, Jonathan 1941- *WhoFI 92*
**Butcher**, Larry L 1940- *AmMWSc 92*
**Butcher**, Philip 1918- *WhoBlA 92*
**Butcher**, Raymond John 1945- *AmMWSc 92*
**Butcher**, Reginald William 1930- *AmMWSc 92*
**Butcher**, Richard James 1926- *Who 92*
**Butcher**, Roy Lovell 1930- *AmMWSc 92*
**Butcher**, Samuel Shipp 1936- *AmMWSc 92*
**Butcher**, Susan 1954- *CurBio 91 [port], News 91 [port]*
**Butcher**, Thomas Kennedy 1914- *WrDr 92*
**Butcher**, Willard Carlisle 1926- *IntWW 91, Who 92*
**Butchino**, Edward Charles, Jr. 1947- *WhoFI 92*
**Butchman**, Alan A 1938- *WhoAmP 91*
**Bute**, Marquess of 1933- *Who 92*
**Bute**, Mary Ellen 1909- *ReelWom [port]*
**Buteau**, L J 1932- *AmMWSc 92*
**Butel**, Janet Susan 1941- *AmMWSc 92*
**Butenandt**, Adolf 1903- *EncTR 91 [port], Who 92*
**Butenandt**, Adolf Friedrich Johann 1903- *FacFETw, IntWW 91*
**Butenandt**, Adolf Friedrick Johann 1903- *WhoNob 90*
**Butenko**, Constantine 1918- *WhoAmP 91*
**Butensky**, Avram 1933- *WhoEnt 92*
**Butensky**, Irwin 1936- *AmMWSc 92*
**Butensky**, Martin Samuel 1937- *AmMWSc 92*
**Butera**, Constance Diane 1936- *WhoAmL 92*
**Butera**, Richard Anthony 1934- *AmMWSc 92*
**Butera**, Robert James 1935- *WhoAmP 91*
**Buteyn**, Donald Peter 1924- *WhoRel 92*
**Buth**, Carl Eugene 1940- *AmMWSc 92*
**Buth**, Donald George 1949- *AmMWSc 92*
**Buth**, Martin D 1917- *WhoAmP 91*
**Buthelezi**, Manas 1935- *IntWW 91*
**Buthelezi**, Mangosuthu Gatsha 1928- *FacFETw, IntWW 91, NewYTBS 91 [port]*
**Buthod**, Mary Clare 1945- *WhoRel 92*
**Butigan**, William Clay 1957- *WhoAmL 92*
**Butki**, Arnold 1935- *WhoFI 92*
**Butkiewicz**, Edward Thomas 1935- *AmMWSc 92*
**Butkov**, Eugene 1928- *AmMWSc 92*
**Butkovitz**, Alan L 1952- *WhoAmP 91*
**Butkow**, Alan Lee 1947- *WhoFI 92*
**Butkus**, Antanas 1918- *AmMWSc 92*
**Butkus**, Dick 1942- *WhoEnt 92*
**Butland**, Gilbert J. 1910- *WrDr 92*
**Butland**, Gilbert James 1910- *IntAu&W 91*
**Butland**, Jeffrey H *WhoAmP 91*
**Butler** *Who 92*
**Butler**, Adam 1931- *Who 92*
**Butler**, Alan 1940- *IntWW 91*
**Butler**, Aldis Perrin 1913- *WhoWest 92*
**Butler**, Allan Geoffrey Roy 1933- *Who 92*
**Butler**, Andrew Pickens 1796-1857 *AmPolLe*
**Butler**, Ann Benedict 1945- *AmMWSc 92*
**Butler**, Annette G. 1944- *WhoBlA 92*
**Butler**, Anthony John 1945- *Who 92*
**Butler**, Arthur 1918- *TwCPaSc*
**Butler**, Arthur Bates, III 1944- *WhoAmL 92*
**Butler**, Arthur Hamilton d1991 *Who 92N*
**Butler**, Arthur Maurice 1947- *WhoWest 92*
**Butler**, Arthur P 1908- *AmMWSc 92*
**Butler**, Arthur William 1929- *Who 92*
**Butler**, Audrey Maude Beman 1936- *Who 92*
**Butler**, B. Janelle 1949- *WhoBlA 92*
**Butler**, Basil Richard Ryland 1930- *IntWW 91, Who 92*
**Butler**, Benjamin Franklin 1818-1893 *AmPolLe*
**Butler**, Benjamin Willard 1933- *WhoBlA 92*
**Butler**, Bernard Francis 1937- *WhoMW 92*
**Butler**, Bill *ConAu 133, -135*
**Butler**, Blaine R, Jr 1925- *AmMWSc 92*
**Butler**, Broadus Nathaniel 1920- *WhoBlA 92*
**Butler**, Bruce David 1953- *AmMWSc 92*

**Butler,** Byron C 1918- *AmMWSc 92*
**Butler,** Byron Clinton 1918- *WhoWest 92*
**Butler,** Calvin Charles 1937- *AmMWSc 92*
**Butler,** Cass C. 1956- *WhoAmL 92*
**Butler,** Charles David 1936- *WhoFI 92*
**Butler,** Charles H. 1925- *WhoBlA 92*
**Butler,** Charles Morgan 1929- *AmMWSc 92*
**Butler,** Charles Thomas 1932- *AmMWSc 92*
**Butler,** Charles W. 1922- *WhoBlA 92*
**Butler,** Charles William 1922- *WhoRel 92*
**Butler,** Christopher David 1942- *Who 92*
**Butler,** Christopher John 1950- *Who 92*
**Butler,** Claire Draper 1928- *WhoIns 92*
**Butler,** Clary Kent 1948- *WhoBlA 92*
**Butler,** Clifford 1922- *Who 92*
**Butler,** Clifford Charles 1922- *IntWW 91*
**Butler,** Colin G. 1913- *WrDr 92*
**Butler,** Colin Gasking 1913- *IntWW 91, Who 92*
**Butler,** Cynthia Calibani 1959- *WhoAmL 92*
**Butler,** David *Who 92*
**Butler,** David 1924- *IntAu&W 91, WrDr 92*
**Butler,** David 1936- *Who 92*
**Butler,** David Dalrymple 1927- *WhoEnt 92*
**Butler,** David Edgeworth 1924- *Who 92*
**Butler,** David Jeffery 1939- *WhoMW 92*
**Butler,** Daws d1988 *LesBEnT 92*
**Butler,** Debra Sue 1955- *WhoMW 92*
**Butler,** Denis J *WhoAmP 91*
**Butler,** Denis William Langford 1926- *Who 92*
**Butler,** Denver 1938- *WhoAmP 91*
**Butler,** Dolores J. 1930- *WhoRel 92*
**Butler,** Don 1960- *AmMWSc 92*
**Butler,** Donald Edward 1946- *WhoRel 92*
**Butler,** Donald Eugene 1933- *AmMWSc 92, WhoMW 92*
**Butler,** Donald J 1925- *AmMWSc 92*
**Butler,** Donald K. 1944- *WhoAmL 92*
**Butler,** Dorothy 1925- *ConAu 133, WrDr 92*
**Butler,** Douglas 1948- *WhoWest 92*
**Butler,** Douglas Neve 1936- *AmMWSc 92*
**Butler,** Douthard Roosevelt 1934- *WhoBlA 92*
**Butler,** Dwain Kent 1946- *AmMWSc 92*
**Butler,** E. Bruce 1939- *WhoAmL 92*
**Butler,** Edward Clive Barber 1904- *Who 92*
**Butler,** Edward Eugene 1919- *AmMWSc 92, WhoWest 92*
**Butler,** Edward Franklyn 1937- *WhoAmL 92*
**Butler,** Edward Lee 1945- *WhoRel 92*
**Butler,** Eliot Andrew 1926- *AmMWSc 92*
**Butler,** Elizabeth Maire 1948- *WhoAmL 92*
**Butler,** Elizabeth Randolph 1954- *WhoAmL 92*
**Butler,** Ellis Parker 1869-1937 *BenetAL 91, ScFEYrs*
**Butler,** Eric Scott 1907- *Who 92*
**Butler,** Ernest Daniel 1913- *WhoBlA 92*
**Butler,** Eugene Thaddeus, Jr. 1922- *WhoBlA 92*
**Butler,** Eula M. 1927- *WhoBlA 92*
**Butler,** Frances Anne *BenetAL 91*
**Butler,** Frederick Douglas 1942- *WhoBlA 92*
**Butler,** Frederick Edward Robin 1938- *IntWW 91, Who 92*
**Butler,** Frederick Guy 1918- *IntAu&W 91, IntWW 91*
**Butler,** G 1927- *AmMWSc 92*
**Butler,** Gary Frank 1954- *WhoAmL 92*
**Butler,** Gary Lee 1934- *WhoAmP 91*
**Butler,** George 1904- *Who 92*
**Butler,** George Andrews 1928- *WhoFI 92*
**Butler,** George Bergen 1916- *AmMWSc 92*
**Butler,** George Daniel, Jr 1923- *AmMWSc 92*
**Butler,** George Washington, Jr. 1944- *WhoAmL 92*
**Butler,** George William P. *Who 92*
**Butler,** Gerald Norman 1930- *Who 92*
**Butler,** Geraldine Heiskell *WhoEnt 92*
**Butler,** Gertrude I 1922- *WhoAmP 91*
**Butler,** Gilbert W 1941- *AmMWSc 92*
**Butler,** Gordon Cecil 1913- *AmMWSc 92*
**Butler,** Graham Wesley 1928- *IntWW 91*
**Butler,** Guy 1918- *ConPo 91, RfGEnL 91, WrDr 92*
**Butler,** Gwen Elisabeth 1945- *WhoEnt 92*
**Butler,** Gwendoline 1922- *IntAu&W 91, WrDr 92*
**Butler,** Harold S 1931- *AmMWSc 92*
**Butler,** Harry 1916- *AmMWSc 92*
**Butler,** Henry Nolde 1954- *WhoFI 92*
**Butler,** Herbert I 1914- *AmMWSc 92*
**Butler,** Hew Dacres George 1922- *Who 92*
**Butler,** Homer L. 1934- *WhoBlA 92*
**Butler,** Howard Gardner 1960- *WhoAmL 92*
**Butler,** Howard W 1916- *AmMWSc 92*
**Butler,** Hugh Alan 1952- *WhoAmP 91*
**Butler,** Hugh C 1925- *AmMWSc 92*
**Butler,** Ian Geoffrey 1925- *Who 92*
**Butler,** Ian Sydney 1939- *AmMWSc 92*
**Butler,** Iris Mary 1905- *WrDr 92*
**Butler,** Ivan 1909- *IntAu&W 91, WrDr 92*
**Butler,** Ivan Scott 1962- *WhoFI 92*
**Butler,** Ivory Ernest, Jr. 1928- *WhoFI 92*
**Butler,** J. Ray 1923- *WhoBlA 92*
**Butler,** Jack 1944- *WrDr 92*
**Butler,** Jack F 1933- *AmMWSc 92*
**Butler,** Jackie Dean 1931- *AmMWSc 92*
**Butler,** James *Who 92*
**Butler,** James 1931- *TwCPaSc*
**Butler,** James Anthony 1955- *WhoMW 92*
**Butler,** James Bryan, Jr. 1959- *WhoFI 92*
**Butler,** James Edward 1955- *WhoMW 92*
**Butler,** James Ehrich 1944- *AmMWSc 92*
**Butler,** James Hansel 1936- *AmMWSc 92*
**Butler,** James Henry 1931- *WhoFI 92*
**Butler,** James Hunter 1942- *WhoEnt 92*
**Butler,** James Johnson 1926- *AmMWSc 92*
**Butler,** James Keith 1926- *AmMWSc 92*
**Butler,** James Lee 1927- *AmMWSc 92*
**Butler,** James Martin 1948- *WhoMW 92*
**Butler,** James Newton 1934- *AmMWSc 92*
**Butler,** James Patrick 1957- *WhoRel 92, WhoWest 92*
**Butler,** James Preston 1945- *AmMWSc 92*
**Butler,** James Robert 1930- *AmMWSc 92*
**Butler,** James Robertson, Jr. 1946- *WhoAmL 92, WhoFI 92*
**Butler,** James Walter 1931- *Who 92*
**Butler,** James William 1920- *WhoMW 92*
**Butler,** Jean Rouverol 1916- *WhoEnt 92*
**Butler,** Jeffrey Daniel 1963- *WhoFI 92*
**Butler,** Jeffrey Sheridan 1939- *WhoWest 92*
**Butler,** Jerome M. 1944- *WhoBlA 92*
**Butler,** Jerry *WhoEnt 92*
**Butler,** Jerry 1939- *WhoBlA 92*
**Butler,** Jerry Frank 1938- *AmMWSc 92*
**Butler,** Jerry O'Dell 1957- *WhoBlA 92*
**Butler,** Jesse Houston 1929- *WhoAmL 92*
**Butler,** Jesse Lee 1953- *WhoFI 92*
**Butler,** Jim Glen 1950- *WhoRel 92*
**Butler,** John d1786 *DcNCBi 1*
**Butler,** John 1923- *AmMWSc 92*
**Butler,** John 1948- *TwCPaSc*
**Butler,** John A. 1932- *WhoFI 92*
**Butler,** John Ben, Jr 1923- *AmMWSc 92*
**Butler,** John Benson 1938- *WhoFI 92*
**Butler,** John C 1941- *AmMWSc 92*
**Butler,** John Carleton 1954- *WhoEnt 92*
**Butler,** John Donald 1910- *WhoBlA 92*
**Butler,** John E 1938- *AmMWSc 92*
**Butler,** John Earl 1918- *AmMWSc 92*
**Butler,** John Edward 1938- *AmMWSc 92*
**Butler,** John Eric 1962- *WhoEnt 92*
**Butler,** John F 1932- *AmMWSc 92*
**Butler,** John Francis 1954- *WhoWest 92*
**Butler,** John Gordon 1942- *WhoBlA 92*
**Butler,** John Joseph 1920- *AmMWSc 92*
**Butler,** John L., Jr. 1931- *WhoEnt 92*
**Butler,** John Linton 1943- *WhoAmP 91*
**Butler,** John Louis 1934- *AmMWSc 92*
**Butler,** John Mann 1917- *AmMWSc 92*
**Butler,** John Manton 1909- *Who 92*
**Butler,** John Michael 1959- *WhoAmL 92*
**Butler,** John Michael, II 1969- *WhoWest 92*
**Butler,** John Musgrave 1928- *WhoFI 92*
**Butler,** John Nathaniel 1932- *WhoBlA 92*
**Butler,** John Nicholas 1942- *Who 92*
**Butler,** John O. 1926- *WhoBlA 92*
**Butler,** John Paul 1935- *WhoFI 92*
**Butler,** John Scott 1950- *WhoFI 92*
**Butler,** John Sibley 1947- *WhoBlA 92*
**Butler,** Johnnella E. 1947- *WhoBlA 92*
**Butler,** Jon 1940- *ConAu 134, WrDr 92*
**Butler,** Jon Terry 1943- *AmMWSc 92*
**Butler,** Joseph 1692-1752 *BlkwCEP*
**Butler,** Joseph T 1932- *IntAu&W 91, WrDr 92*
**Butler,** Josephine deNatale 1911- *WhoEnt 92*
**Butler,** Joyce M. 1941- *WhoBlA 92*
**Butler,** Joyce Shore *Who 92*
**Butler,** Karl Douglas, Sr 1910- *AmMWSc 92*
**Butler,** Katharine Gorrell 1925- *AmMWSc 92*
**Butler,** Keith A *WhoAmP 91*
**Butler,** Keith Andre 1955- *WhoBlA 92*
**Butler,** Keith Stephenson 1917- *Who 92*
**Butler,** Keith Winston 1941- *AmMWSc 92*
**Butler,** Kenneth David 1930- *WhoWest 92*
**Butler,** Kenneth Van 1934- *WhoAmL 92*
**Butler,** Kent Alan 1958- *WhoWest 92*
**Butler,** Kern 1936- *WhoMW 92*
**Butler,** Kevin Gregory 1962- *WhoMW 92*
**Butler,** Larry G 1933- *AmMWSc 92*
**Butler,** Laurie Jeanne 1959- *WhoMW 92*
**Butler,** Leslie Ann 1945- *WhoWest 92*
**Butler,** Lewis Clark 1923- *AmMWSc 92*
**Butler,** Lillian Catherine *AmMWSc 92*
**Butler,** Lillian Catherine 1919- *WhoWest 92*
**Butler,** Lillian Ida 1910- *AmMWSc 92*
**Butler,** Linda 1943- *AmMWSc 92*
**Butler,** Lorenza Phillips, Jr. 1960- *WhoBlA 92*
**Butler,** Loretta M. *WhoBlA 92*
**Butler,** Louis Peter 1953- *AmMWSc 92*
**Butler,** Manley Caldwell 1925- *WhoAmP 91*
**Butler,** Margaret *WrDr 92*
**Butler,** Margaret K 1924- *AmMWSc 92*
**Butler,** Marie Joseph 1860-1940 *RelLAm 91*
**Butler,** Marilyn 1937- *IntAu&W 91, WrDr 92*
**Butler,** Marilyn Speers 1937- *Who 92*
**Butler,** Marion 1863-1938 *DcNCBi 1*
**Butler,** Marjorie Johnson 1911- *WhoBlA 92*
**Butler,** Martin 1960- *ConCom 92*
**Butler,** Martin J *WhoAmP 91*
**Butler,** Martyn Don 1939- *WhoAmP 91*
**Butler,** Max R. 1912- *WhoBlA 92*
**Butler,** Melford Daniel 1940- *WhoMW 92*
**Butler,** Michael *Who 92*
**Butler,** Michael 1927- *Who 92*
**Butler,** Michael Alfred 1943- *AmMWSc 92*
**Butler,** Michael Dacres 1927- *IntWW 91*
**Butler,** Michael Eugene 1950- *WhoBlA 92*
**Butler,** Michael Howard 1936- *Who 92*
**Butler,** Morse Rodney 1914- *WhoWest 92*
**Butler,** Nathan *IntAu&W 91X, WrDr 92*
**Butler,** Neil A. 1927- *WhoBlA 92*
**Butler,** Neville Roy 1920- *Who 92*
**Butler,** Newman N 1914- *WhoAmP 91*
**Butler,** Nicholas M 1862-1947 *FacFETw*
**Butler,** Nicholas Murray 1862-1947 *AmPeW, BenetAL 91, WhoNob 90*
**Butler,** Nick *Who 92*
**Butler,** Norman John Terence 1946- *Who 92*
**Butler,** Octavia E. 1947- *IntAu&W 91, NotBlAW 92, TwCSFW 91, WhoBlA 92, WrDr 92*
**Butler,** Ogbourne Duke, Jr 1918- *AmMWSc 92*
**Butler,** Oliver Richard 1941- *WhoBlA 92*
**Butler,** Patrick *WrDr 92*
**Butler,** Patrick Hampton 1933- *WhoBlA 92*
**Butler,** Paul 1947- *TwCPaSc*
**Butler,** Percy James 1929- *Who 92*
**Butler,** Peter J. 1935- *WhoAmL 92*
**Butler,** Philip Alan 1914- *AmMWSc 92*
**Butler,** Pierce 1866-1939 *FacFETw*
**Butler,** Pinkney L. 1948- *WhoBlA 92*
**Butler,** R M 1927- *AmMWSc 92*
**Butler,** Ralph David 1931- *WhoAmL 92*
**Butler,** Randall Edward 1954- *WhoAmL 92*
**Butler,** Raymond Leonard 1956- *WhoBlA 92*
**Butler,** Rebecca Batts *WhoBlA 92*
**Butler,** Reginald 1913-1981 *TwCPaSc*
**Butler,** Reginald Michael 1928- *Who 92*
**Butler,** Rex Lamont 1951- *WhoAmL 92, WhoWest 92*
**Butler,** Richard *ConAu 34NR*
**Butler,** Richard 1925- *IntAu&W 91*
**Butler,** Richard 1929- *Who 92*
**Butler,** Richard Austen 1902-1982 *FacFETw*
**Butler,** Richard C, Jr 1937- *WhoAmP 91*
**Butler,** Richard Edmund 1926- *IntWW 91, Who 92*
**Butler,** Richard Gordon 1943- *AmMWSc 92*
**Butler,** Richard Lincoln 1941- *WhoFI 92*
**Butler,** Richard Noel 1942- *IntWW 91*
**Butler,** Rick Landes 1956- *WhoMW 92*
**Butler,** Robert Allan 1923- *AmMWSc 92*
**Butler,** Robert Brian 1949- *WhoEnt 92*
**Butler,** Robert Calvin 1959- *WhoBlA 92*
**Butler,** Robert Franklin 1946- *AmMWSc 92*
**Butler,** Robert John 1936- *WhoRel 92*
**Butler,** Robert Leonard 1931- *WhoFI 92*
**Butler,** Robert Miller 1946- *WhoRel 92*
**Butler,** Robert Neil 1927- *AmMWSc 92*
**Butler,** Robert Olen *DrAPF 91*
**Butler,** Robin *IntWW 91, Who 92*
**Butler,** Rohan D'Olier 1917- *IntAu&W 91, Who 92*
**Butler,** Ronald George 1951- *AmMWSc 92*
**Butler,** Roy 1949- *WhoBlA 92*
**Butler,** Samuel 1612-1680 *LitC 16 [port]*
**Butler,** Samuel 1613?-1680 *RfGEnL 91*
**Butler,** Samuel 1835-1902 *CnDBLB 5 [port], RfGEnL 91, ScFEYrs, TwCSFW 91*
**Butler,** Samuel Coles 1930- *WhoAmL 92*
**Butler,** Selena Sloan 1872?-1964 *NotBlAW 92*
**Butler,** Sheneather 1960- *WhoAmP 91*
**Butler,** Shirley Elaine 1949- *WhoMW 92*
**Butler,** Stanley S 1916- *AmMWSc 92*
**Butler,** Thelma Jean 1933- *WhoAmP 91*
**Butler,** Thomas Arthur 1919- *AmMWSc 92*
**Butler,** Thomas Belden 1806-1873 *BiInAmS*
**Butler,** Thomas Daniel 1938- *AmMWSc 92*
**Butler,** Thomas Frederick *Who 92*
**Butler,** Thomas Michael 1948- *AmMWSc 92*
**Butler,** Thomas Pierce 1910- *Who 92*
**Butler,** Thomas Sean 1955- *WhoAmL 92*
**Butler,** Thomas W 1938- *AmMWSc 92*
**Butler,** Thomas Wayne 1944- *WhoAmP 91*
**Butler,** Thorne Gordon 1948- *WhoMW 92*
**Butler,** Velma Sydney 1902- *WhoBlA 92*
**Butler,** Vincent 1933- *TwCPaSc*
**Butler,** Vincent Arthur 1952- *WhoAmL 92, WhoFI 92*
**Butler,** Vincent Frederick 1933- *Who 92*
**Butler,** Vincent Paul, Jr 1929- *AmMWSc 92*
**Butler,** Vivian *ConAu 135*
**Butler,** Walter Cassius 1910- *AmMWSc 92*
**Butler,** Walter John 1936- *AmMWSc 92*
**Butler,** Washington Roosevelt, Jr. 1933- *WhoBlA 92*
**Butler,** Wendell Harding 1924- *WhoBlA 92*
**Butler,** William *ConAu 135, DcNCBi 1*
**Butler,** William Albert 1922- *AmMWSc 92*
**Butler,** William Allen 1825-1902 *BenetAL 91*
**Butler,** William Barkley 1943- *AmMWSc 92*
**Butler,** William E. 1929- *WhoMW 92*
**Butler,** William Elliott 1939- *Who 92*
**Butler,** William H 1943- *AmMWSc 92*
**Butler,** William Howard 1928- *WhoEnt 92*
**Butler,** William Huxford 1934-1977 *ConAu 133*
**Butler,** William Joseph 1924- *WhoAmL 92*
**Butler,** William Joseph 1934- *IntWW 91*
**Butler,** William T 1932- *AmMWSc 92*
**Butler,** William Thomas 1935- *AmMWSc 92*
**Butler,** William Vivian 1927- *ConAu 135*
**Butler-Hamilton,** Melba 1954- *WhoBlA 92*
**Butler-Sloss,** Elizabeth 1933- *IntWW 91, Who 92*
**Butler-Sloss,** Joseph William Alexander 1926- *Who 92*
**Butlin,** Martin 1929- *IntAu&W 91, WrDr 92*
**Butlin,** Martin Richard Fletcher 1929- *IntWW 91, Who 92*
**Butlin,** Phil Pearson 1929- *WhoIns 92*
**Butlin,** Robin Alan 1938- *Who 92*
**Butlin,** Ron 1949- *ConPo 91, IntAu&W 91, WrDr 92*
**Butman,** Bryan Timothy 1952- *AmMWSc 92*
**Butman,** Harry Raymond 1904- *WhoRel 92, WhoWest 92*
**Butner,** Henry Wolff 1875-1937 *DcNCBi 1*
**Butor,** Michel 1926- *FacFETw, GuFrLit 1, IntWW 91*
**Butow,** Robert J. C. 1924- *WrDr 92*
**Butow,** Robert Joseph Charles 1924- *WhoWest 92*
**Butow,** Ronald A 1936- *AmMWSc 92*
**Butrimovitz,** Gerald Paul *WhoFI 92, WhoWest 92*
**Butros,** Albert Jamil 1934- *IntWW 91, Who 92*
**Butros,** Frank A. 1944- *WhoMW 92*
**Butrum,** Hillous Buel 1928- *WhoEnt 92*
**Butrum,** Ritva Rauanheimo 1927- *AmMWSc 92*
**Butsch,** Don *WhoAmP 91*
**Butsch,** Richard 1943- *ConAu 135*
**Butsch,** Robert Stearns 1914- *AmMWSc 92*
**Butscher,** Edward *DrAPF 91*
**Butsikares,** Socrates K. 1923-1991 *NewYTBS 91 [port]*
**Butson,** Alton Thomas 1926- *AmMWSc 92*
**Butt,** Alfred Kenneth 1908- *Who 92*
**Butt,** Billy Arthur 1931- *AmMWSc 92*
**Butt,** Edward Thomas, Jr. 1947- *WhoAmL 92*
**Butt,** Geoffrey Frank 1943- *Who 92*
**Butt,** Howard Edward d1991 *NewYTBS 91*
**Butt,** Hugh Roland *AmMWSc 92*
**Butt,** John B 1935- *AmMWSc 92*
**Butt,** Kenneth *Who 92*
**Butt,** Michael Acton 1942- *IntWW 91, Who 92*
**Butt,** Peter Doane 1929- *WhoIns 92*
**Butt,** Richard Bevan 1943- *Who 92*
**Buttaci,** Sal St. John *DrAPF 91*
**Buttar,** Harpal Singh 1939- *AmMWSc 92*
**Buttchen,** Terry Gerard 1958- *WhoWest 92*
**Butte,** Anthony Jeffrey 1951- *WhoFI 92*
**Buttemer,** William Ashley 1947- *AmMWSc 92*
**Buttenwieser,** Lawrence Benjamin 1932- *WhoAmL 92*
**Buttenwieser,** Paul 1938- *ConAu 35NR*
**Butter,** David Henry 1920- *Who 92*
**Butter,** John Henry 1916- *Who 92*
**Butter,** Neil 1933- *Who 92*

**Butter,** Peter Herbert 1921- *IntAu&W 91, Who 92, WrDr 92*
**Butter,** Peter Joseph Michael 1932- *Who 92*
**Butter,** Stephen Allan 1937- *AmMWSc 92*
**Butterbaugh,** Jerry Kent 1946- *WhoMW 92*
**Butterfield** *Who 92*
**Butterfield,** Baron 1920- *IntWW 91, Who 92*
**Butterfield,** Alexander P. 1926- *IntWW 91*
**Butterfield,** Anthony Swindt 1931- *WhoWest 92*
**Butterfield,** Billy 1917-1988 *NewAmDM*
**Butterfield,** Charles Harris 1911- *Who 92*
**Butterfield,** David Allan 1946- *AmMWSc 92*
**Butterfield,** Don 1923- *WhoBlA 92*
**Butterfield,** Earle James 1949- *AmMWSc 92*
**Butterfield,** James D. 1960- *WhoRel 92*
**Butterfield,** John 1920- *WrDr 92*
**Butterfield,** John Michael 1926- *Who 92*
**Butterfield,** Lindsay Philip 1869-1948 *DcTwDes*
**Butterfield,** R. Keith 1941- *WhoFI 92*
**Butterfield,** Roger 1907-1981 *CurBio 91N*
**Butterfield,** Veloy Hansen, Jr 1942- *AmMWSc 92*
**Butterfield,** William H. 1910- *WrDr 92*
**Butterfill,** John Valentine 1941- *Who 92*
**Butterfoss,** Edwin Johnson 1955- *WhoAmL 92*
**Butterick,** Brian *DrAPF 91*
**Butterly,** Sean C *WhoAmP 91*
**Buttermore,** Daniel L. 1955- *WhoMW 92*
**Buttermore,** Rodney Everett 1950- *WhoAmL 92*
**Butters,** Christopher *DrAPF 91*
**Butters,** Dorothy Gilman *IntAu&W 91X, WrDr 92*
**Butters,** John Patrick 1933- *WhoFI 92*
**Butterss,** Robert Leopold 1931- *Who 92*
**Butterworth** *Who 92*
**Butterworth,** Baron 1918- *Who 92*
**Butterworth,** Alan Randolph 1952- *WhoAmL 92*
**Butterworth,** Bernard Bert 1923- *AmMWSc 92*
**Butterworth,** Byron Edwin 1941- *AmMWSc 92*
**Butterworth,** Charles E, Jr 1923- *AmMWSc 92*
**Butterworth,** Darrell David 1950- *WhoRel 92*
**Butterworth,** Edward Joseph 1951- *WhoRel 92*
**Butterworth,** Edward Livingston 1914- *WhoFI 92, WhoWest 92*
**Butterworth,** Eric 1916- *RelLAm 91*
**Butterworth,** Francis M 1935- *AmMWSc 92*
**Butterworth,** George 1885-1916 *FacFETw*
**Butterworth,** George A M 1935- *AmMWSc 92*
**Butterworth,** George Neville 1911- *IntWW 91, Who 92*
**Butterworth,** Henry 1926- *Who 92*
**Butterworth,** Ian 1930- *IntWW 91, Who 92*
**Butterworth,** Jane Rogers Fitch 1937- *WhoMW 92*
**Butterworth,** John 1945- *TwCPaSc*
**Butterworth,** Neville *Who 92*
**Butterworth,** Oliver 1915- *IntAu&W 91, WrDr 92*
**Butterworth,** Oliver 1915-1990 *SmATA 66*
**Butterworth,** Robert A. 1942- *WhoAmL 92, WhoAmP 91*
**Butterworth,** Robert Roman 1946- *WhoFI 92, WhoWest 92*
**Butterworth,** Thomas Austin 1944- *AmMWSc 92*
**Buttery,** James Franklin, Jr. 1954- *WhoAmL 92*
**Buttery,** Janet Louise 1953- *WhoEnt 92*
**Buttfield,** Nancy 1912- *Who 92*
**Buttgen,** Joseph Chris 1955- *WhoRel 92*
**Buttigieg,** Joseph Stanley 1944- *WhoMW 92*
**Buttiker,** Markus 1950- *AmMWSc 92*
**Buttinger,** Richard Walter 1932- *WhoRel 92*
**Buttitta,** Anthony 1907- *IntAu&W 91*
**Buttitta,** Ignazio 1899- *DcLB 114*
**Buttitta,** Patricia Anne 1950- *WhoEnt 92*
**Buttitta,** Tony 1907- *WrDr 92*
**Buttke,** Thomas Martin 1952- *AmMWSc 92*
**Buttlaire,** Daniel Howard 1941- *AmMWSc 92*
**Buttlar,** Rudolph O 1934- *AmMWSc 92*
**Buttle,** Eileen 1937- *Who 92*
**Buttner,** F H 1920- *AmMWSc 92*
**Buttolph,** David 1902- *IntMPA 92*
**Button,** Arthur Daniel d1991 *Who 92N*
**Button,** Don K 1933- *AmMWSc 92*
**Button,** Glenn Marshall 1958- *WhoWest 92*
**Button,** Henry George 1913- *Who 92*
**Button,** James Clarence 1957- *WhoFI 92*
**Button,** John 1932- *IntWW 91*
**Button,** Kenneth J. 1948- *WrDr 92*
**Button,** Kenneth Rodman 1946- *WhoFI 92*
**Button,** Marian Lucille 1930- *WhoAmP 91*
**Button,** Richard Totten 1929- *FacFETw, WhoEnt 92*
**Button-Shafer,** Janice 1931- *AmMWSc 92*
**Buttons,** Red *LesBEnT 92*
**Buttons,** Red 1919- *IntMPA 92*
**Buttram,** James Alan 1953- *WhoFI 92*
**Buttram,** James David 1941- *WhoMW 92, WhoRel 92*
**Buttram,** Pat 1917?- *ConTFT 9*
**Buttress,** Donald Reeve 1932- *Who 92*
**Buttrey,** Benton Wilson 1919- *AmMWSc 92*
**Buttrey,** Donald Wayne 1935- *WhoAmL 92*
**Buttrey,** Douglas Norton *IntAu&W 91, WrDr 92*
**Buttrey,** Theodore Vern 1929- *Who 92*
**Buttrick,** David Gardner 1927- *WhoRel 92*
**Buttrick,** George Arthur 1892-1980 *RelLAm 91*
**Buttrill,** Sidney Eugene, Jr 1944- *AmMWSc 92*
**Butts,** Arthur Edward 1947- *WhoFI 92*
**Butts,** Calvin O., III *NewYTBS 91 [port]*
**Butts,** Carlyle A. 1935- *WhoBlA 92*
**Butts,** Charles Lewis 1942- *WhoAmP 91*
**Butts,** Cyril William, Jr. 1954- *WhoAmL 92*
**Butts,** David 1932- *AmMWSc 92*
**Butts,** David Lester 1953- *WhoRel 92*
**Butts,** Edward Eugene 1938- *WhoIns 92*
**Butts,** Hubert S 1923- *AmMWSc 92*
**Butts,** Hugh F. 1926- *WhoBlA 92*
**Butts,** James A 1950- *BlkOlyM*
**Butts,** Jeffrey A 1947- *AmMWSc 92*
**Butts,** Marion Stevenson, Jr. 1966- *WhoBlA 92*
**Butts,** Robert Ransdell 1946- *WhoAmL 92*
**Butts,** S. L. *WhoRel 92*
**Butts,** W.E. *DrAPF 91*
**Butts,** William Cunningham 1942- *AmMWSc 92*
**Butts,** William Lester 1931- *AmMWSc 92*
**Butts,** Wilson Henry 1932- *WhoBlA 92*
**Butz,** Andrew 1931- *AmMWSc 92*
**Butz,** Donald Josef 1958- *AmMWSc 92, WhoMW 92*
**Butz,** Earl 1909- *IntWW 91*
**Butz,** Earl L. 1909- *WhoMW 92*
**Butz,** Earl Lauer 1909- *WhoAmP 91*
**Butz,** Geneva Mae 1944- *WhoRel 92*
**Butz,** Robert Frederick 1949- *AmMWSc 92*
**Butzer,** Karl W *AmMWSc 92*
**Butzer,** Karl W. 1934- *WrDr 92*
**Butziger,** Robert Anton 1937- *WhoRel 92*
**Butzner,** John Decker, Jr. 1917- *WhoAmL 92*
**Butzow,** James J 1935- *AmMWSc 92*
**Buurman,** Clarence Harold 1915- *AmMWSc 92*
**Buxbaum,** David Charles 1933- *WhoAmL 92*
**Buxbaum,** James M. *IntMPA 92*
**Buxbaum,** Joel N 1938- *AmMWSc 92*
**Buxbaum,** Martin 1912- *WrDr 92*
**Buxbaum,** Martin 1912-1991 *ConAu 134*
**Buxbaum,** Martin David 1912- *IntAu&W 91*
**Buxbaum,** Richard M. 1930- *WhoAmL 92*
**Buxtehude,** Dietrich 1637?-1707 *NewAmDM*
**Buxton** *Who 92*
**Buxton,** Adrian Clarence 1925- *Who 92*
**Buxton,** Andrew Robert Fowell 1939- *IntWW 91, Who 92*
**Buxton,** Charles Ingraham, II 1924- *WhoIns 92*
**Buxton,** Charles Michael 1946- *WhoAmL 92*
**Buxton,** David Roden 1910- *WrDr 92*
**Buxton,** Dwayne Revere 1939- *AmMWSc 92*
**Buxton,** Frank *LesBEnT 92*
**Buxton,** Georgia B 1929- *WhoAmP 91*
**Buxton,** Iain Laurie Offord 1950- *AmMWSc 92*
**Buxton,** Jarvis 1820-1902 *DcNCBi 1*
**Buxton,** Jay A 1919- *AmMWSc 92*
**Buxton,** John 1912- *IntAu&W 91*
**Buxton,** John Cameron 1852-1917 *DcNCBi 1*
**Buxton,** John Noel 1933- *Who 92*
**Buxton,** Neil Keith 1940- *Who 92*
**Buxton,** Paul William Jex 1925- *Who 92*
**Buxton,** Ralph Potts 1826-1900 *DcNCBi 1*
**Buxton,** Raymond Naylor 1915- *Who 92*
**Buxton,** Richard Joseph 1938- *Who 92*
**Buxton,** Richard Millard 1948- *WhoWest 92*
**Buxton,** Ronald Carlile 1923- *Who 92*
**Buxton,** Thomas Fowell Victor 1925- *Who 92*
**Buxton,** Winslow H. *WhoMW 92*
**Buxton,** Zane Kelly 1946- *WhoRel 92*
**Buxton of Alsa,** Baron 1918- *Who 92*
**Buya,** Wallace J 1925- *WhoIns 92*
**Buyck,** Mark Wilson, Jr. 1934- *WhoAmL 92*
**Buydos,** Geary Stephan 1950- *WhoEnt 92, WhoWest 92*
**Buyers,** John William Amerman 1928- *WhoFI 92, WhoWest 92*
**Buyers,** Thomas Bartlett 1926- *Who 92*
**Buyers,** William James Leslie 1937- *AmMWSc 92*
**Buyniski,** Joseph P 1941- *AmMWSc 92*
**Buyoya,** Pierre 1949- *IntWW 91*
**Buys,** Clifford Richards 1923- *WhoFI 92*
**Buyse,** Emile Jules 1927- *WhoEnt 92*
**Buyse,** Leone *WhoEnt 92*
**Buyske,** Donald Albert 1927- *AmMWSc 92*
**Buysse,** James T 1955- *WhoIns 92*
**Buzacott,** J A 1937- *AmMWSc 92*
**Buzard,** James Albert 1927- *AmMWSc 92*
**Buzard,** Kurt Andre 1953- *WhoWest 92*
**Buzas,** Martin A 1934- *AmMWSc 92*
**Buzatu,** Gheorghe 1939- *IntWW 91*
**Buzbee,** Billy Lewis 1936- *AmMWSc 92*
**Buzbee,** Kenneth V 1937- *WhoAmP 91*
**Buzen,** Jeffrey Peter 1943- *AmMWSc 92*
**Buziak,** Frank T 1947- *WhoIns 92*
**Buzin,** Carolyn Hattox *AmMWSc 92*
**Buzina,** Ratko 1920- *AmMWSc 92*
**Buzitis,** Betty Jean 1933- *WhoRel 92*
**Buznego,** Angel *WhoHisp 92*
**Buzo,** Alexander 1944- *WrDr 92*
**Buzo,** Alexander John 1944- *IntAu&W 91*
**Buzogany,** Robert John 1942- *WhoMW 92*
**Buzoianu,** Catalina 1938- *IntWW 91*
**Buzolich,** Robert Allan 1951- *WhoFI 92*
**Buzunis,** Constantine Dino 1958- *WhoAmL 92, WhoWest 92*
**Buzydlowski,** Frank P 1954- *WhoAmP 91*
**Buzyna,** George 1938- *AmMWSc 92*
**Buzzard,** Anthony 1935- *Who 92*
**Buzzard,** Anthony Farquhar 1935- *WhoRel 92*
**Buzzard,** Steven Ray 1946- *WhoAmL 92*
**Buzzati,** Dino 1906-1972 *TwCSFW 91A*
**Buzzell,** Donald Warren 1920- *WhoAmP 91*
**Buzzell,** John Gibson 1922- *AmMWSc 92*
**Buzzell,** Richard Irving 1929- *AmMWSc 92*
**Buzzelli,** Donald Edward 1936- *AmMWSc 92*
**Buzzelli,** Edward S 1939- *AmMWSc 92*
**Buzzelli,** Elizabeth Kane *DrAPF 91*
**Buzzelli,** Laurence Francis 1943- *WhoAmL 92, WhoMW 92*
**Buzzi,** Ruth 1936- *WhoEnt 92*
**Buzzi,** Ruth 1939- *IntMPA 92*
**Bwakira,** Melchior 1937- *IntWW 91*
**Byalik,** Chaim Nachman 1873-1934 *FacFETw*
**Byall,** Elliott Bruce 1940- *AmMWSc 92*
**Byalynitsky-Birulya,** Vitol'd Kaetanovich 1897-1957 *SovUnBD*
**Byam,** Milton S. 1922- *WhoBlA 92*
**Byam,** Seward Groves, Jr. 1928- *WhoFI 92*
**Byam-Baldwin,** Carmen Sylvia *WhoRel 92*
**Byam Shaw,** James 1903- *Who 92*
**Byam Shaw,** Nicholas Glencairn 1934- *IntWW 91, Who 92*
**Byambasuren,** Dashiin 1942- *IntWW 91*
**Byar,** David Peery 1938- *AmMWSc 92*
**Byard,** James Leonard 1941- *AmMWSc 92*
**Byard,** John Arthur, Jr. 1922- *WhoBlA 92*
**Byard,** Pamela Joy 1951- *AmMWSc 92*
**Byars,** Betsy 1928- *ConAu 36NR, IntAu&W 91, WrDr 92*
**Byars,** Edward F 1925- *AmMWSc 92*
**Byars,** Keith 1963- *WhoBlA 92*
**Byars,** Ronald Preston 1937- *WhoRel 92*
**Byas,** Don 1912-1972 *NewAmDM*
**Byas,** Thomas Haywood 1922- *WhoBlA 92*
**Byas,** Ulysses 1924- *WhoBlA 92*
**Byas,** William Herbert 1932- *WhoBlA 92*
**Byatt,** A S *FacFETw, NewYTBS 91 [port]*
**Byatt,** A. S. 1936- *ConLC 65 [port], ConNov 91, CurBio 91 [port], WrDr 92*
**Byatt,** Antonia Susan 1936- *IntAu&W 91, IntWW 91, Who 92*
**Byatt,** Hugh Campbell 1927- *IntWW 91, Who 92*
**Byatt,** Ian Charles Rayner 1932- *IntWW 91, Who 92*
**Byatt,** Pamela Hilda 1916- *AmMWSc 92*
**Byatt,** Ronald Archer Campbell 1930- *IntWW 91, Who 92*
**Bybee,** Edward Joseph 1944- *WhoAmP 91*
**Bybee,** Shannon Larmer, Jr. 1938- *WhoAmL 92*
**Bychkov,** Aleksey Mikhailovich 1928- *IntWW 91*
**Bychkov,** Aleksey Mikhaylovich 1928- *SovUnBD*
**Bychkov,** Semyon 1952- *IntWW 91*
**Byck,** Robert 1933- *AmMWSc 92*
**Bydal,** Bruce A 1937- *AmMWSc 92*
**Bydalek,** David Allen 1943- *WhoWest 92*
**Bydalek,** Thomas Joseph 1935- *AmMWSc 92*
**Bye,** Beryl 1926- *WrDr 92*
**Bye,** James Edward 1930- *WhoAmL 92*
**Bye,** Reed *DrAPF 91*
**Bye,** Roseanne Marie 1946- *WhoWest 92*
**Byer,** Diana 1946- *WhoEnt 92*
**Byer,** Kathryn Stripling *DrAPF 91*
**Byer,** Norman Ellis 1940- *AmMWSc 92*
**Byer,** Philip Howard 1948- *AmMWSc 92*
**Byer,** Robert L 1942- *AmMWSc 92*
**Byerley,** Lauri Olson 1957- *AmMWSc 92*
**Byerly,** Don Wayne 1933- *AmMWSc 92*
**Byerly,** Gary Ray 1948- *AmMWSc 92*
**Byerly,** Paul Robertson, Jr 1922- *AmMWSc 92*
**Byerly,** Perry Edward 1926- *AmMWSc 92*
**Byerly,** Rex R *WhoAmP 91*
**Byerrum,** Richard Uglow 1920- *AmMWSc 92*
**Byers,** Benjamin Rowe 1936- *AmMWSc 92*
**Byers,** Breck Edward 1939- *AmMWSc 92*
**Byers,** Charles Harry 1940- *AmMWSc 92*
**Byers,** Charles Wesley 1946- *AmMWSc 92*
**Byers,** Floyd Michael 1947- *AmMWSc 92*
**Byers,** Francis Robert 1920- *WhoAmP 91*
**Byers,** Frank Milton, Jr 1916- *AmMWSc 92*
**Byers,** Fred Custer, Jr. 1955- *WhoAmL 92*
**Byers,** Gary William 1948- *WhoRel 92*
**Byers,** George William 1923- *AmMWSc 92*
**Byers,** Harold Hill 1928- *WhoRel 92*
**Byers,** Harold Ralph 1944- *WhoEnt 92*
**Byers,** Horace 1906- *WrDr 92*
**Byers,** Horace Robert 1906- *AmMWSc 92, IntWW 91*
**Byers,** J Donald, Jr. 1947- *WhoRel 92*
**Byers,** John A. *WhoRel 92*
**Byers,** John Bruce 1952- *WhoRel 92*
**Byers,** John Kaye 1930- *WhoAmL 92*
**Byers,** John Robert 1937- *AmMWSc 92*
**Byers,** Joseph Murray 1944- *WhoMW 92*
**Byers,** L Eugene *WhoAmP 91*
**Byers,** Larry Douglas 1947- *AmMWSc 92*
**Byers,** Laurence Primm 1921- *WhoRel 92*
**Byers,** Lawrence Wallace 1916- *AmMWSc 92*
**Byers,** Marianne 1941- *WhoBlA 92*
**Byers,** Maurice 1917- *Who 92*
**Byers,** Maurice Hearne 1917- *IntWW 91*
**Byers,** Nina 1930- *AmMWSc 92*
**Byers,** Paul Duncan 1922- *Who 92*
**Byers,** Paul Heed 1943- *WhoEnt 92*
**Byers,** R Lee 1935- *AmMWSc 92*
**Byers,** Robert Allan 1936- *AmMWSc 92*
**Byers,** Roland O 1919- *AmMWSc 92*
**Byers,** Ronald Elner 1936- *AmMWSc 92*
**Byers,** Sanford Oscar 1918- *AmMWSc 92*
**Byers,** Stanley A 1931- *AmMWSc 92*
**Byers,** Thomas Jones 1935- *AmMWSc 92*
**Byers,** Timothy Todd 1959- *WhoFI 92*
**Byers,** Vera Steinberger 1942- *AmMWSc 92*
**Byers,** Walter 1922- *WhoMW 92*
**Byers,** Walter Hayden 1914- *AmMWSc 92*
**Byers Brown,** Betty 1927- *WrDr 92*
**Byfield,** John Eric 1936- *AmMWSc 92*
**Byford,** Lawrence 1925- *Who 92*
**Byford,** William Heath 1817-1890 *BiInAmS*
**Bygraves,** Max 1922- *IntMPA 92*
**Bygraves,** Max Walter 1922- *Who 92*
**Byington,** Keith H 1935- *AmMWSc 92*
**Byington,** Mary 1918- *WhoAmP 91*
**Byington,** S. John *WhoAmL 92*
**Byington,** Samuel Jospeh, III 1948- *WhoMW 92*
**Byington,** Spring d1971 *LesBEnT 92*
**Byk,** Curtis Lee 1955- *WhoEnt 92*
**Bykau,** Vasil' 1924- *SovUnBD*
**Byker,** Gary 1920- *WhoAmP 91*
**Bykerk,** Cecil Dale 1944- *WhoMW 92*
**Bykhovsky,** Arkadi Gregory 1943- *WhoFI 92*
**Bykofsky,** Seth Darryl 1956- *WhoAmL 92*
**Bykov,** Valeriy Alekseyevich 1938- *IntWW 91*
**Bykov,** Vasiliy Vladimirovich 1924- *SovUnBD*
**Bykov,** Vasily Vladimirovich 1924- *IntWW 91*
**Bykova,** Yelizaveta Ivanovna 1913- *FacFETw*
**Bykovsky,** Valery 1934- *FacFETw*
**Bykowski,** Anthony 1945- *WhoAmL 92*
**Byland,** Peter *WhoMW 92*
**Bylander,** Dag Christer 1954- *WhoMW 92*
**Byler,** David Michael 1945- *AmMWSc 92*
**Byler,** Gary Clarence 1957- *WhoAmP 91*
**Byler,** Robert Harris, Jr. 1930- *WhoMW 92*
**Byler,** Thomas Ward 1957- *WhoMW 92*
**Byles,** Daniel William 1923- *WhoAmL 92*
**Byles,** Joan Montgomery *DrAPF 91*
**Byles,** Mary Josephine 1913- *WhoRel 92*
**Byles,** Mather 1707-1788 *BenetAL 91*

**Byles**, Peter Henry 1931- *AmMWSc 92*
**Byles**, Robert Valmore 1937- *WhoAmP 91*
**Bylinski**, Janusz 1952- *IntWW 91*
**Bylinsky**, Gene 1930- *WrDr 92*
**Bylinsky**, Gene Michael 1930- *IntAu&W 91*
**Bylund**, David Bruce 1946- *AmMWSc 92*
**Bynam**, Sawyer Lee, III 1933- *WhoBlA 92*
**Byner**, Earnest Alexander 1962- *WhoBlA 92*
**Bynes**, Frank Howard, Jr. 1950- *WhoBlA 92*
**Byng** *Who 92*
**Byng-Lucas**, Caroline d1967 *TwCPaSc*
**Bynner**, Edwin Lassetter 1842-1893 *BenetAL 91, ScFEYrs*
**Bynner**, Witter 1881-1968 *BenetAL 91*
**Bynoe**, Hilda Louisa 1921- *Who 92*
**Bynoe**, John Garvey 1926- *WhoBlA 92*
**Bynoe**, Peter C. B. 1951- *WhoBlA 92*
**Bynoe**, Peter Charles Bernard 1951- *WhoMW 92, WhoWest 92*
**Bynum**, Barbara S 1936- *AmMWSc 92*
**Bynum**, Horace Charles, Sr. 1916- *WhoBlA 92*
**Bynum**, Jesse Atherton 1797-1868 *DcNCBi 1*
**Bynum**, Kevin Murry 1950- *WhoMW 92*
**Bynum**, Raleigh Wesley 1936- *WhoBlA 92*
**Bynum**, T E 1939- *AmMWSc 92*
**Bynum**, Valerie Callymore 1942- *WhoBlA 92*
**Bynum**, William Lee 1936- *AmMWSc 92*
**Bynum**, William Preston 1820-1909 *DcNCBi 1*
**Bynum**, William Preston, II 1861-1926 *DcNCBi 1*
**Byram**, Gary Bruce 1952- *WhoMW 92*
**Byram**, George Wayne 1938- *AmMWSc 92*
**Byram**, Stanley Harold 1906- *WhoAmP 91*
**Byrd**, Albert Alexander 1927- *WhoBlA 92*
**Byrd**, Alma *WhoAmP 91*
**Byrd**, Andrew Wayne 1954- *WhoFI 92*
**Byrd**, Anne Gee 1938- *WhoEnt 92*
**Byrd**, Arthur Ray 1947- *WhoWest 92*
**Byrd**, Arthur W. 1943- *WhoBlA 92*
**Byrd**, Benjamin Franklin, Jr 1918- *AmMWSc 92*
**Byrd**, Bobby *DrAPF 91*
**Byrd**, C Don 1940- *WhoIns 92*
**Byrd**, Camolia Alcorn *WhoBlA 92*
**Byrd**, Caruth C. 1941- *IntMPA 92*
**Byrd**, Charles Everett 1909- *WhoRel 92*
**Byrd**, Corine Williams 1946- *WhoBlA 92*
**Byrd**, Dan R 1944- *WhoAmP 91*
**Byrd**, Daniel Madison, III 1940- *AmMWSc 92*
**Byrd**, Daryl Glynn 1954- *WhoFI 92*
**Byrd**, David Lamar 1922- *AmMWSc 92*
**Byrd**, David Shelton 1930- *AmMWSc 92*
**Byrd**, Don *DrAPF 91*
**Byrd**, Donald 1932- *NewAmDM*
**Byrd**, Earl William, Jr 1946- *AmMWSc 92*
**Byrd**, Edward Travis 1946- *WhoAmP 91*
**Byrd**, Edwin R. 1920- *WhoBlA 92*
**Byrd**, Enola 1927- *WhoAmP 91*
**Byrd**, Frederick E. 1918- *WhoBlA 92*
**Byrd**, Frederick Wayne 1948-1990 *WhoBlA 92N*
**Byrd**, George Edward 1941- *WhoBlA 92*
**Byrd**, Gill Arnette 1961- *WhoBlA 92*
**Byrd**, Glenn Nelson 1922- *WhoRel 92*
**Byrd**, Grant Travis 1962- *WhoRel 92*
**Byrd**, Gwendolyn Pauline 1943- *WhoRel 92*
**Byrd**, Harold W *WhoAmP 91*
**Byrd**, Harriett Elizabeth 1926- *WhoAmP 91, WhoBlA 92*
**Byrd**, Harry F 1887-1966 *FacFETw*
**Byrd**, Harry Flood, Jr. 1914- *IntWW 91, WhoAmP 91*
**Byrd**, Helen P. 1943- *WhoBlA 92*
**Byrd**, Isaac, Jr. 1952- *WhoBlA 92*
**Byrd**, Isaac Burlin 1925- *AmMWSc 92*
**Byrd**, J Rogers 1931- *AmMWSc 92*
**Byrd**, James Dotson 1932- *AmMWSc 92*
**Byrd**, James W. 1925- *WhoBlA 92*
**Byrd**, James William 1936- *AmMWSc 92*
**Byrd**, Jan G 1942- *WhoAmP 91*
**Byrd**, Jerry Stewart 1935- *WhoBlA 92*
**Byrd**, Joann Kathleen 1943- *WhoWest 92*
**Byrd**, John *IntMPA 92*
**Byrd**, Jonathan Eugene 1952- *WhoFI 92*
**Byrd**, Joseph Keys 1953- *WhoBlA 92*
**Byrd**, Katie W. *WhoBlA 92*
**Byrd**, Kenneth Alfred 1940- *AmMWSc 92*
**Byrd**, Larry Donald 1936- *AmMWSc 92*
**Byrd**, Linward Tonnett 1921- *WhoAmL 92*
**Byrd**, Lloyd G *AmMWSc 92*
**Byrd**, Lumus, Jr. 1942- *WhoBlA 92*
**Byrd**, Manford, Jr. 1928- *WhoBlA 92*
**Byrd**, Marc Robert 1954- *WhoFI 92, WhoWest 92*
**Byrd**, Mary Elaine 1953- *WhoRel 92*
**Byrd**, Max 1942- *WrDr 92*
**Byrd**, Mitchell Agee 1928- *AmMWSc 92*
**Byrd**, Nellie J. 1924- *WhoBlA 92*
**Byrd**, Norman Robert 1921- *AmMWSc 92*
**Byrd**, Odell Richard, Jr 1944- *IntAu&W 91*
**Byrd**, Otto Lee 1946- *WhoWest 92*
**Byrd**, Percy L. 1937- *WhoBlA 92*
**Byrd**, Richard Dowell 1933- *AmMWSc 92*
**Byrd**, Richard E. 1888-1957 *BenetAL 91*
**Byrd**, Richard Evelyn 1888-1957 *FacFETw*
**Byrd**, Richard Gregory 1958- *WhoAmL 92*
**Byrd**, Robert C. *NewYTBS 91*
**Byrd**, Robert C. 1917- *AlmAP 92 [port], IntWW 91, WhoAmP 91*
**Byrd**, Robert Lee 1949- *WhoAmP 91*
**Byrd**, Roger C 1954- *WhoAmP 91*
**Byrd**, Ronald Dallas 1934- *WhoWest 92*
**Byrd**, Samuel Armanie, Jr. 1908-1955 *DcNCBi 1*
**Byrd**, Sherman Clifton 1928- *WhoBlA 92*
**Byrd**, Stephen Fred 1928- *WhoFI 92*
**Byrd**, Taylor 1940- *WhoBlA 92*
**Byrd**, Vernon R. *WhoRel 92*
**Byrd**, W. Michael 1943- *WhoBlA 92*
**Byrd**, Wilbert Preston 1926- *AmMWSc 92*
**Byrd**, William 1543?-1623 *NewAmDM*
**Byrd**, William 1674-1744 *BenetAL 91*
**Byrd**, William, II 1674-1744 *BiInAmS*
**Byrd**, William Floyd 1943- *WhoAmP 91*
**Byrd-Tillman**, Jacqueline Pearl 1946- *WhoAmL 92*
**Byrds**, The *FacFETw*
**Byrge**, Charles Webster, II 1962- *WhoFI 92*
**Byrge**, Duane Paul 1949- *WhoEnt 92*
**Byrkit**, Donald Raymond 1933- *AmMWSc 92*
**Byrn**, Ernest Edward 1924- *AmMWSc 92*
**Byrn**, Stephen R. 1944- *WhoMW 92*
**Byrn**, Stephen Robert 1944- *AmMWSc 92*
**Byrne**, Allan Dean 1930- *WhoRel 92*
**Byrne**, Barbara Jean McManamy 1941- *AmMWSc 92*
**Byrne**, Brendan Thomas 1924- *WhoAmP 91*
**Byrne**, Bruce Campbell 1945- *AmMWSc 92*
**Byrne**, Clarence 1903- *Who 92*
**Byrne**, Daniel Francis 1943- *WhoAmL 92*
**Byrne**, David 1952- *IntMPA 92, IntWW 91, WhoEnt 92*
**Byrne**, David Andrew 1961- *WhoAmL 92*
**Byrne**, David Dan 1942- *WhoMW 92*
**Byrne**, Dennis Joseph 1940- *WhoFI 92*
**Byrne**, Donn *BenetAL 91*
**Byrne**, Donn E. *WrDr 92*
**Byrne**, Douglas Norman 1924- *Who 92*
**Byrne**, Edward *DrAPF 91*
**Byrne**, Francis Patrick 1913- *AmMWSc 92*
**Byrne**, Gabriel *IntWW 91*
**Byrne**, Gabriel 1950- *IntMPA 92*
**Byrne**, George D 1933- *AmMWSc 92*
**Byrne**, George Melvin 1933- *WhoWest 92*
**Byrne**, Gerard Anthony 1944- *WhoEnt 92*
**Byrne**, Harry J. 1921- *WhoRel 92*
**Byrne**, J Gerald 1930- *AmMWSc 92*
**Byrne**, James 1948- *TwCPaSc*
**Byrne**, James Joseph 1908- *WhoRel 92*
**Byrne**, James Thomas, Jr. 1939- *WhoFI 92*
**Byrne**, Jane 1934- *WhoAmP 91*
**Byrne**, Jeffrey Edward 1939- *AmMWSc 92*
**Byrne**, Jerome Camillus 1925- *WhoAmL 92*
**Byrne**, John 1825-1902 *BiInAmS*
**Byrne**, John 1940- *IntAu&W 91, TwCPaSc, WrDr 92*
**Byrne**, John Howard *AmMWSc 92*
**Byrne**, John Joseph 1916- *AmMWSc 92*
**Byrne**, John Joseph 1925- *WhoAmL 92*
**Byrne**, John Joseph, Jr. 1932- *WhoFI 92*
**Byrne**, John Keyes *Who 92*
**Byrne**, John Maxwell 1933- *AmMWSc 92*
**Byrne**, John P. 1936- *WhoIns 92*
**Byrne**, John Richard 1926- *AmMWSc 92*
**Byrne**, John V. 1928- *IntWW 91*
**Byrne**, John Vincent 1928- *AmMWSc 92, WhoWest 92*
**Byrne**, K. Maple *WhoEnt 92*
**Byrne**, Kathleen A 1936- *WhoAmP 91*
**Byrne**, Kevin J 1944- *AmMWSc 92*
**Byrne**, Kevin M 1948- *AmMWSc 92*
**Byrne**, Kevin O. *DrAPF 91*
**Byrne**, Kevin Thomas 1939- *WhoAmL 92*
**Byrne**, Leslie Larkin 1946- *WhoAmP 91*
**Byrne**, Martha 1969- *WhoEnt 92*
**Byrne**, Michael Francis 1955- *WhoFI 92*
**Byrne**, Michael Joseph 1928- *WhoFI 92, WhoMW 92*
**Byrne**, Michael Joseph, Jr. 1952- *WhoMW 92*
**Byrne**, Nelson 1937- *AmMWSc 92*
**Byrne**, Noel Thomas 1943- *WhoFI 92, WhoWest 92*
**Byrne**, Olivia Sherrill 1957- *WhoAmL 92*
**Byrne**, Patrick Edward, II 1952- *WhoAmP 91*
**Byrne**, Patrick James 1949- *WhoFI 92*
**Byrne**, Patrick Michael 1952- *WhoFI 92*
**Byrne**, Paul Laurence 1932- *Who 92*
**Byrne**, Peggy 1949- *WhoAmP 91*
**Byrne**, Peter M 1936- *AmMWSc 92*
**Byrne**, Philip Matthew 1940- *WhoFI 92*
**Byrne**, Robert 1930- *ConAu 35NR, WrDr 92*
**Byrne**, Robert Howard 1941- *AmMWSc 92*
**Byrne**, Robert James 1953- *WhoFI 92*
**Byrne**, Robert John 1932- *AmMWSc 92*
**Byrne**, Robert William 1958- *WhoAmL 92*
**Byrne**, Terence Niall 1942- *Who 92*
**Byrne**, William Matthew, Jr. 1930- *WhoAmL 92*
**Byrnes**, Edd 1933- *IntMPA 92*
**Byrnes**, Eugene William 1933- *AmMWSc 92*
**Byrnes**, Frederick, Jr. *DrAPF 91*
**Byrnes**, James F 1879-1972 *FacFETw*
**Byrnes**, James Francis 1879-1972 *AmPolLe*
**Byrnes**, James Lawrence 1952- *WhoAmP 91*
**Byrnes**, John Carroll 1939- *WhoAmP 91*
**Byrnes**, Michael Clinton 1946- *WhoWest 92*
**Byrnes**, Michael Francis 1957- *WhoMW 92*
**Byrnes**, Michael William 1944- *WhoFI 92*
**Byrnes**, Robert Francis 1917- *WrDr 92*
**Byrnes**, Thomas Anthony 1943- *WhoRel 92*
**Byrnes**, Thomas H, Jr *WhoAmP 91*
**Byrnes**, William Joseph 1940- *WhoAmL 92, WhoEnt 92*
**Byrnes**, William Richard 1924- *AmMWSc 92*
**Byrns**, Allan Mark 1937- *WhoEnt 92*
**Byrns**, Joseph Wellington 1869-1936 *AmPolLe*
**Byrom**, John 1692-1763 *RfGEnL 91*
**Byrom**, Peter Craig 1927- *Who 92*
**Byron**, Baron 1950- *Who 92*
**Byron**, Lord 1788-1824 *DcLB 110 [port], RfGEnL 91*
**Byron**, Beverly B. 1932- *AlmAP 92 [port], WhoAmP 91*
**Byron**, Cheryl *DrAPF 91*
**Byron**, Don *WhoEnt 92*
**Byron**, George Gordon, Lord 1788-1824 *CnDBLB 3 [port]*
**Byron**, Gilbert *DrAPF 91*
**Byron**, Gilbert 1903-1991 *ConAu 134*
**Byron**, H.J. 1835-1884 *RfGEnL 91*
**Byron**, Jeffrey 1955- *WhoEnt 92*
**Byron**, John W 1861-1895 *BiInAmS*
**Byron**, Joseph Winston 1930- *AmMWSc 92*
**Byron**, Richard J 1938- *WhoIns 92*
**Byron**, Rita Ellen Cooney *WhoMW 92*
**Byron**, Robert Welton 1925- *WhoFI 92*
**Byron**, Stuart *DrAPF 91*
**Byron**, Thomas E. 1949- *WhoRel 92*
**Byron**, Thomas P *ScFEYrs*
**Byrt**, Edwin Andrew 1932- *WrDr 92*
**Byrt**, John 1929- *Who 92*
**Byrtus**, Joe Robert 1914- *WhoAmP 91*
**Byrum**, David Lawrence 1948- *WhoWest 92*
**Byrum**, Dianne 1954- *WhoAmP 91*
**Byrum**, John 1947- *IntMPA 92*
**Byrum**, Judith Miriam 1943- *WhoFI 92, WhoMW 92*
**Byrum**, Mark White, Jr. 1955- *WhoAmL 92*
**Byrum**, Marni Elaine 1955- *WhoAmL 92*
**Byrum**, Reginald Dale 1961- *WhoRel 92*
**Byrum**, Ronald Lane, Jr. 1968- *WhoRel 92*
**Bystedt**, Gosta 1929- *IntWW 91*
**Bystroff**, Roman Ivan 1931- *AmMWSc 92*
**Bystryn**, Jean-Claude 1938- *AmMWSc 92*
**Byun**, Wha Kyung *WhoEnt 92*
**Byvik**, Charles Edward 1940- *AmMWSc 92*
**Bywater**, Anthony Colin 1948- *AmMWSc 92*
**Bywater**, David Llewellyn 1937- *Who 92*
**Bywaters**, Eric George Lapthorne 1910- *Who 92*
**Byzantine**, Julian Sarkis 1945- *IntWW 91*
**Byzewski**, Mark T. 1960- *WhoWest 92*
**Bzdula**, Wayne Barry 1951- *WhoFI 92*
**Bzoch**, Kenneth R 1927- *AmMWSc 92*
**Bzoch**, Ronald Charles 1930- *AmMWSc 92*
**Bzoskie**, James Steven 1949- *WhoRel 92*

# C

**C de Baca,** Celeste M. 1957- *WhoHisp 92*
**C. de Baca,** Frances 1937- *WhoFI 92*
**C de Baca,** Richard 1939- *WhoHisp 92*
**C. William,** Byrne 1945- *WhoWest 92*
**Caan,** James *NewYTBS 91 [port]*
**Caan,** James 1939- *IntWW 91*
**Caan,** James 1940- *IntMPA 92, WhoEnt 92*
**Cababe,** Louise Diana 1944- *WhoRel 92*
**Caballe,** Montserrat *IntWW 91*
**Caballe,** Montserrat 1933- *NewAmDM, Who 92, WhoEnt 92*
**Caballero,** Alfredo A. *WhoHisp 92*
**Caballero,** Anna Marie 1954- *WhoHisp 92*
**Caballero,** Eddie *WhoHisp 92*
**Caballero,** Eduardo *WhoHisp 92*
**Caballero,** Pedro Juan 1786- *HisDSpE*
**Caballero,** Raymond C. 1942- *WhoHisp 92*
**Caballero,** Raymond Cesar 1942- *WhoAmL 92*
**Caballero,** Roberto 1958- *WhoHisp 92*
**Caballero,** Santiago 1936- *WhoHisp 92*
**Caballero,** Servando 1942- *WhoHisp 92*
**Caballero Bonald,** Jose Manuel 1926- *DcLB 108 [port]*
**Caballero Calderon,** Eduardo 1910- *IntWW 91*
**Caballero de la Torre,** Jose Agustin 1771-1835 *HisDSpE*
**Caballero y Gongora,** Antonio 1723-1796 *HisDSpE*
**Cabalquinto,** Luis *DrAPF 91*
**Caban,** Beatriz L. 1962- *WhoHisp 92*
**Caban,** Delia 1957- *WhoHisp 92*
**Caban,** Juan Pedro, Jr. 1931- *WhoHisp 92*
**Caban,** Luis A. 1939- *WhoHisp 92*
**Caban Davila,** Luis E *WhoAmP 91*
**Cabana,** Aldee 1935- *AmMWSc 92*
**Cabana,** Veneracion Garganta 1942- *AmMWSc 92*
**Cabanas,** Humberto 1947- *WhoHisp 92*
**Cabanas,** Lazaro V. 1956- *WhoHisp 92*
**Cabaner** 1832-1881 *ThHEIm*
**Cabanes,** William Ralph, Jr 1932- *AmMWSc 92*
**Cabanilla,** Raquel Blancaflor 1916- *WhoRel 92*
**Cabanillas DeLlanos DeLaMata,** Mercedes *IntWW 91*
**Cabanillas Gallas,** Pio d1991 *NewYTBS 91*
**Cabanillas Gallas,** Pio 1923- *IntWW 91*
**Cabanis,** Jose 1922- *IntAu&W 91, IntWW 91*
**Cabanis,** Pierre-Jean-Georges 1757-1808 *BlkwCEP*
**Cabaniss,** Mark Gold 1960- *WhoEnt 92*
**Cabaniss,** W J, Jr 1938- *WhoAmP 91*
**Cabannes,** Jean 1925- *IntWW 91*
**Cabansag,** Vicente Dacanay, Jr. 1942- *WhoMW 92*
**Cabanya,** Mary Louise 1947- *WhoWest 92*
**Cabarrus,** Stephen 1754-1808 *DcNCBi 1*
**Cabasso,** Israel 1942- *AmMWSc 92*
**Cabasso,** Victor Jack 1915- *AmMWSc 92*
**Cabauy,** Henry 1936- *WhoEnt 92*
**Cabbell,** Edward Joseph 1946- *WhoBlA 92*
**Cabbiness,** Dale Keith 1937- *AmMWSc 92*
**Cabe,** Gloria Burford 1941- *WhoAmP 91*
**Cabe,** John 1752-1818 *DcNCBi 1*
**Cabe,** Robert D. 1942- *WhoAmL 92*
**Cabeceiras,** James 1930- *WrDr 92*
**Cabeen,** Samuel Kirkland 1931- *AmMWSc 92*
**Cabell,** James Branch 1879-1958 *BenetAL 91, FacFETw*
**Cabell,** James Lawrence 1813-1889 *BiInAmS*
**Cabell,** Polly *ScFEYrs*
**Cabello,** Aida *WhoHisp 92*
**Cabello,** Marco V. 1960- *WhoHisp 92*
**Cabello,** Robert 1950- *WhoHisp 92*
**Cabello de Carbonera,** Mercedes 1845-1909 *SpAmWW*
**Cabello y Mesa,** Francisco Antonio 1764-1814 *HisDSpE*
**Cabet,** Etienne 1788-1856 *BenetAL 91*
**Cabeza de Vaca,** Alvar Nunez 1490?-1556 *HisDSpE*
**Cabeza de Vaca,** Alvar Nunez 1490?-1557? *BenetAL 91*
**Cabezas,** Heriberto, Jr. 1952- *WhoHisp 92*
**Cabezas,** Rafael 1937- *WhoHisp 92*
**Cabezon,** Antonio de 1510-1566 *NewAmDM*
**Cabezut,** Alejandro 1962- *WhoHisp 92*
**Cabezut-Ortiz,** Delores J. 1948- *WhoHisp 92*
**Cabib,** Enrico 1925- *AmMWSc 92*
**Cabieles,** Lucy 1924- *WhoHisp 92*
**Cabieles Irahola,** Lucy 1924- *WhoWest 92*
**Cabigayan,** Nelida *EncAmaz 91*
**Cable,** Charles Allen 1932- *AmMWSc 92*
**Cable,** George Washington 1844-1925 *BenetAL 91*
**Cable,** Gregory Duane 1955- *WhoMW 92*
**Cable,** Howard Reid 1920- *WhoEnt 92*
**Cable,** James 1920- *Who 92*
**Cable,** Joe Wood 1931- *AmMWSc 92*
**Cable,** Kenneth *WhoRel 92*
**Cable,** Kenneth A. *WhoRel 92*
**Cable,** Kenneth Duane 1935- *WhoMW 92*
**Cable,** Laura Lynn 1962- *WhoMW 92*
**Cable,** Peter George 1936- *AmMWSc 92*
**Cable,** Raymond Millard 1909- *AmMWSc 92*
**Cable,** Richard Albert 1950- *WhoWest 92*
**Cable-Alexander,** Patrick 1936- *Who 92*
**Cabo,** Federico *WhoHisp 92*
**Caborn,** Richard George 1943- *Who 92*
**Cabot,** Charles Codman, Jr. 1930- *WhoAmL 92*
**Cabot,** Hugh, III 1930- *WhoWest 92*
**Cabot,** John 1450-1498 *BenetAL 91*
**Cabot,** John Boit, II 1946- *AmMWSc 92*
**Cabot,** John G. L. 1934- *WhoFI 92*
**Cabot,** Laurie 1933- *RelLAm 91*
**Cabot,** Louis Wellington 1921- *WhoFI 92*
**Cabot,** Myles Clayton 1948- *AmMWSc 92*
**Cabot,** Paul Codman 1898- *IntWW 91*
**Cabot,** Samuel 1850-1906 *BiInAmS*
**Cabot,** Samuel, Jr 1815-1885 *BiInAmS*
**Cabot,** Sebastian 1484-1557 *HisDSpE*
**Caboto,** Giovanni 1450-1498 *BenetAL 91*
**Cabou,** Daniel 1929- *IntWW 91*
**Cabouat,** Jean-Pierre Noel 1921- *IntWW 91*
**Cabral,** Alfredo Lopes 1946- *IntWW 91*
**Cabral,** Antonio F *WhoAmP 91*
**Cabral,** Bernardo Joseph 1944- *WhoAmL 92*
**Cabral,** Darien 1949- *WhoWest 92*
**Cabral,** Evelyn Amelia 1939- *WhoWest 92*
**Cabral,** Guy Antony 1938- *AmMWSc 92*
**Cabral,** Luis de Almeida 1931- *IntWW 91*
**Cabral,** Olga *DrAPF 91*
**Cabral,** Ramon 1956- *WhoHisp 92*
**Cabranes,** Jose A. 1940- *WhoHisp 92*
**Cabranes,** Jose Alberto 1940- *WhoAmL 92*
**Cabrera,** Angelina *WhoAmP 91, WhoHisp 92*
**Cabrera,** Blas 1946- *AmMWSc 92*
**Cabrera,** Charles R. 1944- *WhoHisp 92*
**Cabrera,** Edelberto Jose 1944- *AmMWSc 92*
**Cabrera,** Eduardo *WhoHisp 92*
**Cabrera,** Eloise J. 1932- *WhoBlA 92*
**Cabrera,** Francisco 1966- *WhoHisp 92*
**Cabrera,** Francisco Torres *WhoAmP 91*
**Cabrera,** George Albert 1946- *WhoHisp 92*
**Cabrera,** Gilda 1949- *WhoHisp 92*
**Cabrera,** Jeronimo Luis de 1528-1574 *HisDSpE*
**Cabrera,** Jose Antonio 1768-1820 *HisDSpE*
**Cabrera,** Jose R *WhoAmP 91*
**Cabrera,** Lucio L., Sr. *WhoHisp 92*
**Cabrera,** Lydia d1991 *NewYTBS 91*
**Cabrera,** Lydia 1900- *SpAmWW*
**Cabrera,** Lydia 1900-1991 *WhoHisp 92N*
**Cabrera,** Nestor L. 1957- *WhoHisp 92*
**Cabrera,** Pablo 1931- *WhoEnt 92*
**Cabrera,** Raimundo 1852-1923 *HisDSpE*
**Cabrera,** Richard Anthony 1941- *WhoHisp 92*
**Cabrera,** Rosa Maria 1918- *WhoHisp 92*
**Cabrera-Baukus,** Maria B. 1954- *WhoHisp 92*
**Cabrera Infante,** Guillermo 1929- *BenetAL 91, DcLB 113 [port], IntWW 91, LiExTwC*
**Cabri,** Louis J 1934- *AmMWSc 92*
**Cabrillo,** Juan Rodriguez 149-?-1543 *HisDSpE*
**Cabrinety,** Patricia Ann Butler 1932- *IntAu&W 91*
**Cabrinety,** Patricia Butler 1932- *WhoFI 92*
**Cabrini,** Frances Xavier 1850-1917 *DcAmImH, HanAmWH, RelLAm 91*
**Caccamo,** Leonard P. 1922- *WhoMW 92*
**Caccamo,** Pedro 1936- *WhoHisp 92*
**Caccia,** Baron d1990 *IntWW 91N, Who 92N*
**Caccia,** Lord 1905-1990 *AnObit 1990*
**Caccia,** Harold 1905-1990 *CurBio 91N*
**Cacciamani,** Eugene Richard, Jr *AmMWSc 92*
**Cacciatore,** Ronald Keith 1937- *WhoFI 92*
**Cacciatore,** Vera 1911- *IntAu&W 91, WrDr 92*
**Cacciavillan,** Agostino 1926- *WhoRel 92*
**Caccini,** Francesca 1587-1640? *NewAmDM*
**Caccini,** Giulio 1545?-1618 *NewAmDM*
**Cacciolfi,** William Peter, Jr. 1960- *WhoMW 92*
**Cacciotti,** Joseph John, Jr. 1954- *WhoEnt 92*
**Cacella,** Arthur Ferreira 1920- *AmMWSc 92*
**Caceres,** Adrian *WhoRel 92*
**Caceres,** Cesar A 1927- *AmMWSc 92*
**Caceres,** German Gustavo 1954- *WhoEnt 92*
**Caceres,** John 1909- *WhoHisp 92*
**Caceres,** Virginia *WhoHisp 92*
**Caceres Contreras,** Carlos 1940- *IntWW 91*
**Cachapero,** Emilya *DrAPF 91*
**Cacharel,** Jean 1932- *IntWW 91*
**Cachelin,** Francy 1923- *Who 92*
**Cacheris,** James C. 1933- *WhoAmL 92*
**Cacheris,** Plato 1929- *WhoAmL 92*
**Cachia,** Pierre 1921- *WrDr 92*
**Cachola,** Romy Munoz 1938- *WhoAmP 91*
**Cacia,** Paul Scott 1956- *WhoEnt 92*
**Cacicedo,** Paul 1927- *WhoHisp 92*
**Cacioppo,** John T 1951- *AmMWSc 92*
**Cacioppo,** John Terrance 1951- *WhoMW 92*
**Cacioppo,** Peter Thomas 1947- *WhoWest 92*
**Cacopardo,** Marco 1969- *NewYTBS 91 [port]*
**Cacoyannis,** Michael 1922- *IntMPA 92, IntWW 91, Who 92*
**Cacoyannis,** Michael 1927- *IntDcF 2-2 [port]*
**Cada,** Glenn Francis 1949- *AmMWSc 92*
**Cada,** Ronald Lee 1944- *AmMWSc 92*
**Cadagan,** Dan John, III 1949- *WhoAmL 92*
**Cadaval,** Olivia 1943- *WhoHisp 92*
**Cadbury,** Adrian *Who 92*
**Cadbury,** Adrian 1929- *IntWW 91*
**Cadbury,** Belinda 1939- *TwCPaSc*
**Cadbury,** Dominic *Who 92*
**Cadbury,** George Adrian 1929- *Who 92*
**Cadbury,** George Woodall 1907- *Who 92*
**Cadbury,** Henry Joel 1883-1974 *AmPeW, RelLAm 91*
**Cadbury,** Kenneth Hotham d1991 *Who 92N*
**Cadbury,** Nicholas Dominic 1940- *Who 92*
**Cadbury,** Peter 1918- *Who 92*
**Cadbury-Brown,** Henry Thomas 1913- *IntWW 91, Who 92*
**Cadd,** Gary Genoris 1953- *WhoWest 92*
**Caddell,** Joan Louise 1927- *AmMWSc 92*
**Caddell,** Michael Jon 1941- *WhoAmL 92*
**Caddell,** William Joseph 1939- *WhoMW 92*
**Cadden,** Joan *WhoAmP 91*
**Cadden,** Tom Thomas Scott 1923- *WhoMW 92*
**Caddick,** Kathleen 1937- *TwCPaSc*
**Caddoe,** Sean *DrAPF 91*
**Caddy,** John *DrAPF 91*
**Caddy,** Michael Douglas 1938- *WhoAmL 92*
**Caddy,** Peter 1917- *RelLAm 91*
**Caddy,** Thomas John 1952- *WhoWest 92*
**Cade,** Alfred Jackal 1931- *WhoBlA 92*
**Cade,** Harold Edward 1929- *WhoBlA 92*
**Cade,** Henry d1991 *WhoBlA 92N*
**Cade,** Jack Carlton 1948- *WhoFI 92, WhoWest 92*
**Cade,** James Robert 1927- *AmMWSc 92*
**Cade,** John A 1929- *WhoAmP 91*
**Cade,** Lillian Ferrara *WhoAmP 91*
**Cade,** Robin *IntAu&W 91X, WrDr 92*
**Cade,** Ruth Ann 1937- *AmMWSc 92*
**Cade,** Thomas Grant 1941- *WhoWest 92*
**Cade,** Thomas Joseph 1928- *AmMWSc 92*
**Cade,** Tommories 1961- *WhoBlA 92*
**Cade,** Toni 1939- *WhoBlA 92*
**Cade,** Valarie Swain 1952- *WhoBlA 92*
**Cade,** Walter, III *WhoBlA 92*
**Cade,** William Henry 1946- *AmMWSc 92*
**Cadell,** Colin Simson 1905- *Who 92*

**Cadell,** Elizabeth 1903- *IntAu&W 91*
**Cadell,** Francis Campbell Boileau 1883-1937 *TwCPaSc*
**Cadell,** John 1929- *Who 92*
**Cadell,** Patrick Moubray 1941- *Who 92*
**Cadell,** Simon 1950- *ConTFT 9*
**Cadena,** Carlos C. *WhoHisp 92*
**Cadena,** Emilio E., II 1964- *WhoHisp 92*
**Cadena,** Guadalupe, Jr. 1966- *WhoHisp 92*
**Cadena,** Patricia Elizabeth 1966- *WhoEnt 92*
**Cadena,** Val, Sr. 1929- *WhoHisp 92*
**Cadenas,** Rafael 1920- *ConSpAP*
**Cadenas,** Ricardo A. 1953- *WhoHisp 92*
**Cadenhead,** David Allan 1930- *AmMWSc 92*
**Cadenhead,** William 1934- *TwCPaSc*
**Cades,** Julius Russell 1904- *WhoAmL 92*
**Cadet,** Gardy 1955- *AmMWSc 92*
**Cadieux,** Dennis Barry 1936- *WhoRel 92*
**Cadieux,** Leo 1908- *Who 92*
**Cadieux,** Pierre H. 1948- *IntWW 91, WhoFI 92*
**Cadigan,** Patrick Joseph 1936- *WhoAmL 92*
**Cadigan,** Robert Allen 1918- *AmMWSc 92*
**Cadilla,** Manuel Alberto 1912- *WhoHisp 92*
**Cadillac,** Antoine de la Mothe 1658-1730 *BenetAL 91*
**Cadle,** Dean *DrAPF 91*
**Cadle,** Farris W. 1952- *ConAu 135*
**Cadle,** Richard Dunbar 1914- *AmMWSc 92*
**Cadle,** Steven Howard 1946- *AmMWSc 92*
**Cadman** *Who 92*
**Cadman,** Baron 1938- *Who 92*
**Cadman,** Charles 1881-1946 *NewAmDM*
**Cadman,** Charles Wakefield 1881-1946 *BenetAL 91*
**Cadman,** Edward 1918- *Who 92*
**Cadman,** Edwin Clarence 1945- *AmMWSc 92*
**Cadman,** Samuel Parkes 1864-1936 *RelLAm 91*
**Cadman,** Theodore W 1940- *AmMWSc 92*
**Cadman,** Wilson Kennedy 1927- *WhoFI 92, WhoMW 92*
**Cadmus,** Craig William 1951- *WhoFI 92*
**Cadmus,** Robert R 1914- *AmMWSc 92*
**Cadmus,** Robert Randall, Jr 1946- *AmMWSc 92*
**Cadnum,** Michael *DrAPF 91*
**Cadogan** *Who 92*
**Cadogan,** Earl 1914- *Who 92*
**Cadogan,** Edward John Patrick 1939- *WhoWest 92*
**Cadogan,** John 1930- *Who 92*
**Cadogan,** John Ivan George 1930- *IntWW 91*
**Cadogan,** Kevin Denis 1939- *AmMWSc 92*
**Cadogan,** Mary 1928- *IntAu&W 91, WrDr 92*
**Cadogan,** Peter William 1921- *Who 92*
**Cadogan,** W P 1919- *AmMWSc 92*
**Cadoret,** Remi Jere 1928- *AmMWSc 92*
**Cadoria,** Sherian Grace 1940- *WhoBlA 92*
**Cadot,** Andrew Allinson 1945- *WhoAmL 92*
**Cadotte,** John Edward 1925- *AmMWSc 92*
**Cadovius,** Poul 1911- *DcTwDes*
**Cadow,** Stanton Lee 1956- *WhoAmP 91*
**Cadwalader,** George Lyell 1919- *WhoAmL 92*
**Cadwalader,** Thomas 1707?-1779 *BiInAmS*
**Cadwallader,** Donald Elton 1931- *AmMWSc 92*
**Cadwallader,** Douglas Stephen 1944- *WhoRel 92*
**Cadwallader,** Eva Hauel 1933- *WhoRel 92*
**Cadwallader,** Fay Margaret 1964- *WhoWest 92*
**Cadwallader,** Howard George 1919- *Who 92*
**Cadwallader,** James Kerrick 1927- *WhoAmP 91*
**Cadwallader,** John 1902- *Who 92*
**Cadwell,** David Robert 1934- *WhoAmL 92, WhoWest 92*
**Cady,** Blake 1930- *AmMWSc 92*
**Cady,** Duane Lynn 1946- *WhoMW 92*
**Cady,** Edwin H. 1917- *WrDr 92*
**Cady,** Foster Bernard 1931- *AmMWSc 92*
**Cady,** Frank *DrAPF 91*
**Cady,** Frank 1915- *ConTFT 9*
**Cady,** George Hamilton 1906- *AmMWSc 92*
**Cady,** Harriet Emilie 1848-1941 *RelLAm 91*
**Cady,** Howard Hamilton 1931- *AmMWSc 92*
**Cady,** Jack *DrAPF 91*
**Cady,** Jack 1932- *IntAu&W 91*
**Cady,** John Gilbert 1914- *AmMWSc 92*
**Cady,** K Bingham 1936- *AmMWSc 92*
**Cady,** Lee, Jr 1927- *AmMWSc 92*
**Cady,** Louis Byron 1955- *WhoMW 92*
**Cady,** Philip Dale 1933- *AmMWSc 92*
**Cady,** Stephanie Gordon 1947- *WhoWest 92*
**Cady,** Thomas Chapman 1935- *WhoAmL 92*
**Cady,** Wallace Martin 1912- *AmMWSc 92*
**Cadzow,** Dorothy Forrest 1916- *WhoEnt 92*
**Cadzow,** James A 1936- *AmMWSc 92*
**Caecilian** d345? *EncEarC*
**Caedmon** *ClMLC 7*
**Caen,** Herb 1916- *WhoWest 92*
**Caenepeel,** Christopher Leon 1942- *AmMWSc 92*
**Caeria** *EncAmaz 91*
**Caesar,** Anthony Douglass 1924- *Who 92*
**Caesar,** Berel 1927- *WhoAmL 92*
**Caesar,** Carol Ann 1945- *WhoWest 92*
**Caesar,** Harry 1928- *WhoBlA 92*
**Caesar,** Irving 1895- *IntMPA 92, Who 92*
**Caesar,** Lois 1922- *WhoBlA 92*
**Caesar,** Neil Benjamin 1957- *WhoAmL 92*
**Caesar,** Philip D 1917- *AmMWSc 92*
**Caesar,** Shirley *WhoBlA 92*
**Caesar,** Shirley 1938- *NotBlAW 92, RelLAm 91*
**Caesar,** Sid *LesBEnT 92*
**Caesar,** Sid 1922- *ConTFT 9, FacFETw, IntMPA 92, WhoEnt 92*
**Caesarius of Arles** 469?-542 *EncEarC*
**Caetano,** Marcello 1906-1980 *FacFETw*
**Caetano,** Marcelo Jose das Neves Alves 1906-1980 *BiDExR*
**Cafarelli,** Enzo Donald 1942- *AmMWSc 92*
**Cafaro,** Albert 1948- *WhoEnt 92*
**Cafasso,** Fred A 1930- *AmMWSc 92*
**Caffarelli** 1710-1783 *NewAmDM*
**Caffarelli,** Joseph J. 1945- *WhoFI 92*
**Caffarelli,** Luis Angel 1948- *AmMWSc 92*
**Caffee,** Lorren Dale 1947- *WhoAmL 92*
**Caffee,** Marcus Pat 1948- *WhoFI 92*
**Cafferata,** Patricia Dillon 1940- *WhoAmP 91*
**Cafferty,** Michael Angelo 1927- *Who 92*
**Cafferty,** Pastora San Juan 1940- *WhoHisp 92*
**Caffey,** Horace Rouse 1929- *AmMWSc 92*
**Caffey,** James E 1934- *AmMWSc 92*
**Caffey,** William Ballard, Jr. 1941- *WhoRel 92*
**Caffin,** Albert Edward 1902- *Who 92*
**Caffin,** Arthur Crawford 1910- *Who 92*
**Caffrey,** Andrew Augustine 1920- *WhoAmL 92*
**Caffrey,** Augustine Joseph 1948- *WhoWest 92*
**Caffrey,** James Louis 1946- *AmMWSc 92*
**Caffrey,** John Gordon 1922- *WhoWest 92*
**Caffrey,** Margaret M. 1947- *ConAu 135*
**Caffrey,** Robert E 1920- *AmMWSc 92*
**Cafiero,** Eugene A. 1926- *WhoFI 92*
**Cafiero,** James S 1928- *WhoAmP 91*
**Cafiero,** Renee Vera 1943- *WhoAmP 91*
**Caflisch,** Edward George 1925- *AmMWSc 92*
**Caflisch,** George Barrett 1952- *AmMWSc 92*
**Caflisch,** Robert Galen 1956- *AmMWSc 92*
**Caflisch,** Russel Edward 1954- *AmMWSc 92, WhoWest 92*
**Cafritz,** Peggy Cooper 1947- *WhoBlA 92, WhoEnt 92*
**Cafruny,** Edward Joseph 1924- *AmMWSc 92*
**Caftori,** Netiva 1949- *WhoMW 92*
**Cagan,** Laird Quincy 1958- *WhoWest 92*
**Cagan,** Phillip 1927- *WrDr 92*
**Cagan,** Robert H 1938- *AmMWSc 92*
**Cagan,** Scott Lawrence 1963- *WhoAmL 92*
**Cagatay,** Mustafa 1937- *IntWW 91*
**Cage,** John *DrAPF 91*
**Cage,** John 1912- *BenetAL 91, ConCom 92, IntWW 91, NewAmDM, RComAH, WhoEnt 92, WrDr 92*
**Cage,** John Milton 1912- *FacFETw*
**Cage,** Michael Jerome 1962- *WhoBlA 92*
**Cage,** Nicholas 1965- *WhoEnt 92*
**Cage,** Nicolas 1964- *IntMPA 92, IntWW 91, News 91 [port]*
**Cagel,** Nate *WhoHisp 92*
**Caggiano,** Joseph Anthony, Jr 1938- *AmMWSc 92*
**Caggiano,** Michael Vincent 1936- *WhoFI 92*
**Cagiati,** Andrea 1922- *IntWW 91, Who 92*
**Cagin,** Charles Richard 1949- *WhoMW 92*
**Caglayangil,** Ihsan Sabri 1908- *IntWW 91*
**Cagle,** Fredric William, Jr 1924- *AmMWSc 92*
**Cagle,** Johnny *WhoAmP 91*
**Cagle,** Roy Francis 1938- *WhoAmP 91*
**Cagle,** Terry Dee 1955- *WhoRel 92*
**Cagle,** William Rea 1933- *WhoMW 92*
**Caglione,** John Paul, Jr. 1957- *WhoEnt 92*
**Caglioti,** Vincenzo 1902- *IntWW 91*
**Cagney,** James 1899-1986 *FacFETw [port]*
**Cagney,** Nanette Heath 1957- *WhoAmL 92*
**Caguiat,** Carlos J. 1937- *WhoHisp 92*
**Cahalan,** Donald 1912- *WhoWest 92*
**Cahan,** Abraham *SourALJ*
**Cahan,** Abraham 1860-1951 *BenetAL 91, DcAmImH*
**Cahan,** Judith E. 1951- *WhoAmL 92*
**Cahen,** Alfred 1929- *IntWW 91*
**Cahen,** Raymond Winston 1943- *WhoEnt 92*
**Cahill,** Charles L 1933- *AmMWSc 92*
**Cahill,** Clyde S. 1923- *WhoAmL 92*
**Cahill,** Clyde S., Jr. 1923- *WhoBlA 92*
**Cahill,** David Leonard 1940- *WhoMW 92*
**Cahill,** Donald R *WhoIns 92*
**Cahill,** George Francis 1925- *WhoFI 92*
**Cahill,** George Francis, Jr 1927- *AmMWSc 92*
**Cahill,** Gerald Morey 1954- *WhoFI 92*
**Cahill,** Glen Thomas 1958- *WhoFI 92*
**Cahill,** James David 1924- *WhoAmL 92, WhoMW 92*
**Cahill,** John Conway 1930- *Who 92*
**Cahill,** John William, Jr. 1960- *WhoFI 92*
**Cahill,** Jones F 1920- *AmMWSc 92*
**Cahill,** Kevin M 1936- *AmMWSc 92*
**Cahill,** Kevin Richard 1949- *WhoMW 92*
**Cahill,** Laurence James, Jr 1924- *AmMWSc 92*
**Cahill,** Lisa Sowle 1948- *WhoRel 92*
**Cahill,** Mary Frances 1965- *WhoAmP 91*
**Cahill,** Michael Leo 1928- *Who 92*
**Cahill,** Mike *IntAu&W 91X*
**Cahill,** Neil 1923- *WhoFI 92, WhoMW 92*
**Cahill,** Pamela L 1953- *WhoAmP 91*
**Cahill,** Patricia Deal 1947- *WhoEnt 92, WhoMW 92*
**Cahill,** Paul A 1959- *AmMWSc 92*
**Cahill,** Richard Frederick 1953- *WhoWest 92*
**Cahill,** Richard William 1931- *AmMWSc 92*
**Cahill,** Rosalie Marie 1923- *WhoRel 92*
**Cahill,** Stephen N 1946- *WhoAmP 91*
**Cahill,** Steven James 1948- *WhoAmL 92*
**Cahill,** Teresa Mary 1944- *IntWW 91, Who 92*
**Cahill,** Thomas A 1937- *AmMWSc 92*
**Cahill,** Thomas J. 1935- *WhoIns 92*
**Cahill,** Vern Richard 1918- *AmMWSc 92*
**Cahill,** Virginia Arnoldy 1942- *WhoAmL 92*
**Cahill,** William Joseph, Jr. 1923- *WhoFI 92*
**Cahill,** William Peter 1953- *WhoAmP 91*
**Cahill,** William Ronald 1951- *WhoWest 92*
**Cahillane,** Sean Francis 1951- *WhoAmP 91*
**Cahilly,** D. Bruce 1939- *WhoAmL 92*
**Cahina** *EncAmaz 91*
**Cahir,** John Joseph 1933- *AmMWSc 92*
**Cahir,** Thomas S 1952- *WhoAmP 91*
**Cahlan,** John Forest 1957- *WhoAmL 92*
**Cahn,** Albert Jonas 1924- *Who 92*
**Cahn,** Arno 1923- *AmMWSc 92*
**Cahn,** Christopher Lawrence 1966- *WhoFI 92*
**Cahn,** David Stephen 1940- *AmMWSc 92*
**Cahn,** Edward N. 1933- *WhoAmL 92*
**Cahn,** Jean Camper d1991 *NewYTBS 91 [port]*
**Cahn,** Jean Camper 1935-1991 *WhoBlA 92N*
**Cahn,** Jeffrey Barton 1943- *WhoAmL 92*
**Cahn,** John W 1928- *AmMWSc 92*
**Cahn,** Julius Hofeller 1919- *AmMWSc 92*
**Cahn,** Miriam Epstein 1943- *WhoAmL 92*
**Cahn,** Phyllis Hofstein 1928- *AmMWSc 92*
**Cahn,** Richard Caleb 1932- *WhoAmL 92*
**Cahn,** Robert Nathan 1944- *AmMWSc 92*
**Cahn,** Robert Wolfgang 1924- *Who 92*
**Cahn,** Sammy 1913- *FacFETw, IntMPA 92, WhoEnt 92*
**Cahn,** Stanley Eric Ollendorff 1939- *WhoFI 92*
**Cahnmann,** Hans Julius 1906- *AmMWSc 92*
**Cahoo,** Kenneth James 1954- *WhoEnt 92*
**Cahoon,** Garth Arthur 1924- *AmMWSc 92*
**Cahoon,** Howard C, Jr *WhoAmP 91*
**Cahoon,** John C 1863-1891 *BiInAmS*
**Cahoon,** John Raymond 1939- *AmMWSc 92*
**Cahoon,** Mary Odile 1929- *AmMWSc 92*
**Cahoon,** Peter T. 1953- *WhoAmL 92*
**Cahouet,** Frank Vondell 1932- *WhoFI 92*
**Cahoy,** Roger Paul 1927- *AmMWSc 92*
**Cahusac,** Louis de 1706-1759 *BlkwCEP*
**Cai Cheng** *IntWW 91*
**Cai Ninglin** *IntWW 91*
**Cai Qi-jiao** 1918- *LiExTwC*
**Cai Qijiao** 1918- *IntWW 91*
**Cai Ruo-Hong** 1910- *IntWW 91*
**Cai Zaidu** *IntWW 91*
**Cai,** Camilla 1940- *WhoMW 92*
**Cai,** Francis Fuchun 1958- *WhoFI 92*
**Cai,** Jin-yi 1961- *AmMWSc 92*
**Cai,** Khiem Van 1954- *WhoWest 92*
**Caicedo,** Claudia 1955- *WhoHisp 92*
**Caicedo,** Eduardo 1945- *WhoHisp 92*
**Caicedo,** Harry 1928- *WhoHisp 92*
**Caid,** Ahmed Ould 193-?- *HisDSpE*
**Caidin,** Martin 1927- *TwCSFW 91, WrDr 92*
**Caidin,** Martin Karl von Strasser 1927- *IntAu&W 91*
**Caillard,** Anthony 1927- *Who 92*
**Caillat,** Claude 1918- *Who 92*
**Caillaux,** Joseph 1863-1944 *FacFETw*
**Caille,** Alain Emeril 1945- *AmMWSc 92*
**Caille,** Andre 1943- *WhoFI 92*
**Caille,** Gilles 1935- *AmMWSc 92*
**Cailleau,** Relda 1909- *AmMWSc 92*
**Caillebotte,** Gustave 1848-1894 *ThHEIm*
**Caillier,** James Allen 1940- *WhoBlA 92*
**Cailliet,** Gregor Michel 1943- *AmMWSc 92*
**Caillou,** Alan 1914- *IntAu&W 91, WrDr 92*
**Caillouet,** Charles W, Jr 1937- *AmMWSc 92*
**Cain** *Who 92*
**Cain,** Bernest 1949- *WhoAmP 91*
**Cain,** Bob *LesBEnT 92*
**Cain,** Brian Patrick 1961- *WhoAmL 92*
**Cain,** Carl, Jr 1931- *AmMWSc 92*
**Cain,** Carl Cecil 1934- *BlkOlyM*
**Cain,** Charles Alan 1943- *AmMWSc 92*
**Cain,** Charles Columbus 1915- *AmMWSc 92*
**Cain,** Charles Eugene 1932- *AmMWSc 92*
**Cain,** Clifford Chalmers 1950- *WhoMW 92, WhoRel 92*
**Cain,** Cyric William, Jr *WhoAmP 91*
**Cain,** David H 1947- *WhoAmP 91*
**Cain,** Dennis Francis 1930- *AmMWSc 92*
**Cain,** Douglas Mylchreest 1938- *WhoAmL 92*
**Cain,** Edney *Who 92*
**Cain,** Edney 1924- *IntWW 91*
**Cain,** Edward 1916- *Who 92*
**Cain,** Frank 1930- *WhoBlA 92*
**Cain,** Frank Edward, Jr. 1924- *WhoBlA 92*
**Cain,** Gary M 1943- *WhoIns 92*
**Cain,** George D 1940- *AmMWSc 92*
**Cain,** George Lee, Jr 1934- *AmMWSc 92*
**Cain,** George M. 1943- *WhoBlA 92*
**Cain,** George M A *ScFEYrs*
**Cain,** George Robert T. *Who 92*
**Cain,** Gerry Ronald 1961- *WhoBlA 92*
**Cain,** Gloria 1941- *WhoRel 92*
**Cain,** Gordon 1947- *TwCPaSc*
**Cain,** Guy A, Jr *WhoAmP 91*
**Cain,** Henry Edney 1924- *Who 92*
**Cain,** Henry Wayne *WhoAmP 91*
**Cain,** Herbert R., Jr. 1916- *WhoBlA 92*
**Cain,** Herman 1945- *WhoBlA 92*
**Cain,** J Allan 1935- *AmMWSc 92*
**Cain,** James Clarence 1913- *AmMWSc 92*
**Cain,** James David 1938- *WhoAmP 91*
**Cain,** James M. 1892-1977 *BenetAL 91, ConAu 34NR, FacFETw*
**Cain,** James Michael 1955- *WhoAmL 92*
**Cain,** James Nelson 1930- *WhoEnt 92*
**Cain,** James Thomas 1942- *AmMWSc 92*
**Cain,** Jerome Richard 1947- *AmMWSc 92*
**Cain,** Joe Jack 1929- *WhoEnt 92*
**Cain,** John 1931- *IntWW 91, Who 92*
**Cain,** John Clifford 1924- *Who 92*
**Cain,** John Manford 1932- *AmMWSc 92*
**Cain,** Johnnie M. 1940- *WhoBlA 92*
**Cain,** Joseph Carter, III 1930- *AmMWSc 92*
**Cain,** Laurence Sutherland 1946- *AmMWSc 92*
**Cain,** Lawrence D. 1944- *WhoMW 92*
**Cain,** Lester James, Jr. 1937- *WhoBlA 92*
**Cain,** Louis Perkins, III 1941- *WhoFI 92*
**Cain,** Madeline Ann 1949- *WhoAmP 91*
**Cain,** Margaret 1946- *WhoIns 92*
**Cain,** Michael 1933- *FacFETw*
**Cain,** Michael Scott *DrAPF 91*
**Cain,** Michele Marie 1962- *WhoMW 92*
**Cain,** Patricia A. 1945- *WhoAmL 92*
**Cain,** Patricia Jean 1931- *WhoFI 92, WhoWest 92*
**Cain,** Richard Wilson 1926- *WhoRel 92*
**Cain,** Robert Gaynor 1951- *WhoAmL 92*
**Cain,** Robert R. 1944- *WhoBlA 92*
**Cain,** Ruth *WhoMW 92*
**Cain,** Ruth Rodney 1935- *WhoAmP 91*
**Cain,** Simon Lawrence 1927- *WhoBlA 92*
**Cain,** Stanley A 1902- *AmMWSc 92*
**Cain,** Stanley Robert 1954- *WhoMW 92*
**Cain,** Stephen Malcolm 1928- *AmMWSc 92*
**Cain,** Thecla *WhoRel 92*
**Cain,** Thomas G 1938- *WhoAmP 91*
**Cain,** Thomas William 1935- *Who 92*
**Cain,** Vernon Wesley 1947- *WhoMW 92*
**Cain,** Virginia Hartigan 1922- *WhoAmP 91, WhoWest 92*
**Cain,** Waldo 1921- *WhoBlA 92*
**Cain,** William 1847-1930 *DcNCBi 1*
**Cain,** William 1931- *ConTFT 9*
**Cain,** William Aaron 1939- *AmMWSc 92*
**Cain,** William F 1937- *AmMWSc 92*
**Cain,** William Howard 1949- *WhoMW 92*

**Caine**, Carol Whitacre 1925- *WhoWest 92*
**Caine**, Drury Sullivan, III 1932- *AmMWSc 92*
**Caine**, Emma Harriet *Who 92*
**Caine**, Geoffrey *SmATA 66*
**Caine**, Howard 1926- *WhoEnt 92*
**Caine**, John 1934- *IntAu&W 91*
**Caine**, Lawrence Patrick 1930- *WhoEnt 92*
**Caine**, Marco 1923- *IntWW 91*
**Caine**, Mark *IntAu&W 91X*
**Caine**, Michael 1927- *Who 92*
**Caine**, Michael 1933- *IntMPA 92, IntWW 91, Who 92, WhoEnt 92*
**Caine**, Michael Harris 1927- *IntWW 91*
**Caine**, Osmund 1914- *TwCPaSc*
**Caine**, Shulamith Wechter *DrAPF 91*
**Caine**, Stanley Paul 1940- *WhoMW 92*
**Caine**, Stephen Howard 1941- *WhoFI 92, WhoWest 92*
**Caine**, Sydney d1991 *IntWW 91N, Who 92N*
**Caine**, T Nelson 1939- *AmMWSc 92*
**Caine**, William 1872?-1925 *ScFEYrs*
**Caine**, William and Fairbairn, John *ScFEYrs*
**Caines**, Eric 1936- *Who 92*
**Caines**, Jeannette 19--?- *ChILR 24 [port]*
**Caines**, John 1933- *Who 92*
**Caines**, Kenneth L.D. *WhoWest 92*
**Caines**, Thomas R. 1953- *WhoEnt 92*
**Cains**, Gerald A. 1932- *TwCPaSc*
**Caird**, Donald Arthur Richard *Who 92*
**Caird**, Donald Arthur Richard 1925- *IntWW 91, WhoRel 92*
**Caird**, Janet 1913- *IntAu&W 91, WrDr 92*
**Caird**, John Allyn 1947- *AmMWSc 92*
**Caird**, John Newport 1948- *Who 92*
**Caird**, William Douglas Sime 1917- *Who 92*
**Cairncross**, Alexander 1911- *WrDr 92*
**Cairncross**, Alexander Kirkland 1911- *IntAu&W 91, IntWW 91, Who 92*
**Cairncross**, Allan 1936- *AmMWSc 92*
**Cairncross**, Frances Anne 1944- *IntAu&W 91, Who 92*
**Cairncross**, Neil Francis 1920- *Who 92*
**Cairns** *Who 92*
**Cairns**, Earl 1939- *Who 92*
**Cairns**, Cecilia 1944- *TwCPaSc*
**Cairns**, Charles Wallace 1934- *WhoMW 92*
**Cairns**, David Adam 1926- *IntWW 91*
**Cairns**, David Allen 1946- *WhoFI 92*
**Cairns**, Diane Patricia 1957- *WhoWest 92*
**Cairns**, Earle E. 1910- *WrDr 92*
**Cairns**, Elaine Joy 1942- *WhoWest 92*
**Cairns**, Elton James 1932- *AmMWSc 92*
**Cairns**, Geoffrey Crerar 1926- *Who 92*
**Cairns**, H. Alan C. 1930- *IntWW 91*
**Cairns**, Hugh John Forster 1922- *IntWW 91, Who 92*
**Cairns**, James Ford 1914- *IntWW 91, Who 92*
**Cairns**, James George Hamilton Dickson 1920- *Who 92*
**Cairns**, Jeffrey Peter 1954- *WhoAmL 92*
**Cairns**, John, Jr 1923- *AmMWSc 92*
**Cairns**, John B. 1941- *WhoAmL 92, WhoFI 92*
**Cairns**, John Mackay 1912- *AmMWSc 92*
**Cairns**, John Simpson 1862-1895 *DcNCBi 1*
**Cairns**, Joyce 1947- *TwCPaSc*
**Cairns**, Marion G 1928- *WhoAmP 91*
**Cairns**, Raymond Eldon, Jr. 1932- *WhoFI 92*
**Cairns**, Scott *DrAPF 91*
**Cairns**, Shirley Ann 1937- *WhoWest 92*
**Cairns**, Stephen Douglas 1949- *AmMWSc 92*
**Cairns**, Theodore L 1914- *AmMWSc 92*
**Cairns**, Theodore Lesueur 1914- *IntWW 91*
**Cairns**, Thomas W 1931- *AmMWSc 92*
**Cairns**, Tom 1952- *ConTFT 9*
**Cairns**, William Louis 1942- *AmMWSc 92*
**Cais**, Rudolf Edmund 1947- *AmMWSc 92*
**Caisley**, William T. 1939- *WhoAmL 92*
**Caison**, Thelma Jann 1950- *WhoBlA 92*
**Caisse**, Albert Leo 1950- *WhoAmP 91*
**Caisse**, Susan Ann *WhoAmP 91*
**Caisson**, Joel Thomas 1934- *WhoAmP 91*
**Caithamer**, Claire S 1955- *WhoIns 92*
**Caithness**, Archdeacon of *Who 92*
**Caithness**, Earl 1948- *Who 92*
**Cajero**, Carmen *WhoAmP 91, WhoHisp 92*
**Cajero**, Meg Huntington *WhoWest 92*
**Cajigal**, Joseph A. 1953- *WhoFI 92*
**Cajthaml**, Michael Joseph 1955- *WhoFI 92*
**Cakebread**, Steven Robert 1946- *WhoRel 92*
**Cakmak**, Ahmet Sefik 1934- *AmMWSc 92*
**Cal**, Luis Jesus 1943- *WhoHisp 92*
**Cala**, John Joseph 1960- *WhoWest 92*
**Calabi**, Eugenio 1923- *AmMWSc 92*
**Calabi**, Lorenzo 1922- *AmMWSc 92*
**Calabi**, Ornella *AmMWSc 92*
**Calabia**, Dawn Tennant 1941- *WhoAmP 91*
**Calabrese**, Alphonse Francis Xavier 1923- *WhoRel 92*
**Calabrese**, Anthony 1937- *AmMWSc 92*
**Calabrese**, Arnold Joseph 1960- *WhoAmL 92*
**Calabrese**, Carmelo 1929- *AmMWSc 92*
**Calabrese**, Diane M 1949- *AmMWSc 92*
**Calabrese**, Joseph C *AmMWSc 92*
**Calabrese**, Marta Perez 1950- *WhoHisp 92*
**Calabrese**, Philip G 1941- *AmMWSc 92*
**Calabrese**, Richard Joseph 1942- *WhoMW 92*
**Calabrese**, Ronald Lewis 1947- *AmMWSc 92*
**Calabrese**, Rosalie Sue 1938- *WhoEnt 92*
**Calabrese**, Sylvia M 1934- *WhoAmP 91*
**Calabresi**, Guido 1932- *WhoAmL 92*
**Calabresi**, Paul 1907- *AmMWSc 92*
**Calabresi**, Paul 1930- *AmMWSc 92*
**Calabretta**, Marti 1940- *WhoAmP 91*
**Calafati**, Peter Gabe 1957- *WhoFI 92*
**Calafell**, Dag O., II 1952- *WhoMW 92*
**Calagna**, Stephen Lee 1952- *WhoRel 92*
**Calahan**, Donald A 1935- *AmMWSc 92*
**Calamari**, Andrew M. 1918- *WhoAmL 92*
**Calamari**, John Daniel 1921- *WhoAmL 92*
**Calamari**, Timothy A, Jr 1936- *AmMWSc 92*
**Calame**, Gerald Paul 1930- *AmMWSc 92*
**Calame**, Kathryn Lee 1940- *AmMWSc 92*
**Calamity Jane** d1903 *EncAmaz 91*
**Calamity Jane** 1852?-1903 *BenetAL 91*
**Calan**, Pierre 1911- *IntWW 91*
**Calancha**, Antonio de la 1584-1654 *HisDSpE*
**Calandra**, Dale 1954- *WhoEnt 92*
**Calandra**, Joseph Carl 1917- *AmMWSc 92*
**Calapai**, Delia *WhoEnt 92*
**Calarca** d1607 *HisDSpE*
**Calarco**, Natale Joseph 1938- *WhoMW 92*
**Calarco**, Patricia G *AmMWSc 92*
**Calarco**, Rod 1947- *WhoEnt 92*
**Calarese**, Norma Carr 1939- *WhoAmL 92*
**Calaresu**, Franco Romano 1931- *AmMWSc 92*
**Calavan**, Edmond Clair 1913- *AmMWSc 92*
**Calawa**, Leon, Jr 1929- *WhoAmP 91*
**Calaway**, Dennis Louis 1960- *WhoFI 92*
**Calazans De Magalhaes**, Camillo 1928- *IntWW 91*
**Calbert**, Harold Edward 1918- *AmMWSc 92*
**Calbert**, Roosevelt 1931- *WhoBlA 92*
**Calbert**, William Edward 1918- *WhoBlA 92, WhoRel 92*
**Calbo**, Leonard Joseph 1941- *AmMWSc 92*
**Calcagni**, Joseph 1956- *WhoFI 92*
**Calcagnie**, Kevin Frank 1955- *WhoAmL 92*
**Calcagno**, Anne *DrAPF 91*
**Calcagno**, Philip Louis 1918- *AmMWSc 92*
**Calcamuggio**, Larry Glenn 1951- *WhoMW 92*
**Calcaterra**, Lynette Grala 1948- *WhoHisp 92*
**Calcaterra**, Robert John 1942- *AmMWSc 92*
**Calcote**, Alan Dean 1933- *WhoRel 92*
**Calcote**, Hartwell Forrest 1920- *AmMWSc 92*
**Calcott**, Peter Howard 1948- *WhoMW 92*
**Calcutt**, David 1930- *Who 92*
**Calcutt**, David Charles 1930- *IntWW 91*
**Calcutt**, Harry 1918- *WhoMW 92*
**Calcutta**, Archbishop of 1926- *Who 92*
**Calcutta**, Bishop of 1934- *Who 92*
**Caldara**, Antonio 1670?-1736 *NewAmDM*
**Caldarazzo**, Richard Joseph 1948- *WhoAmL 92*
**Caldas**, Francisco Jose de 1770-1816 *HisDSpE*
**Caldecote**, Viscount 1917- *IntWW 91, Who 92*
**Caldecott**, John Andrew d1990 *IntWW 91N*
**Caldecott**, Jon 1924- *TwCPaSc*
**Caldecott**, Moyra 1927- *IntAu&W 91*
**Caldecott**, Randolph 1846-1886 *BenetAL 91*
**Caldecott**, Richard S 1924- *AmMWSc 92*
**Caldeira**, Carl Anthony 1948- *WhoMW 92*
**Caldeira**, Gregory Anthony 1951- *WhoMW 92*
**Calden**, Gertrude Beckwith 1909- *WhoAmP 91*
**Calder and Boyars** *DcLB 112*
**Calder**, Alexander 1898-1976 *DcTwDes, FacFETw, ModArCr 2 [port], RComAH*
**Calder**, Alexander, Jr. d1991 *NewYTBS 91*
**Calder**, Angus 1942- *IntAu&W 91, WrDr 92*
**Calder**, Bruce 1925- *WhoAmP 91*
**Calder**, Clarence Andrew 1937- *AmMWSc 92, WhoWest 92*
**Calder**, Dale Ralph 1941- *AmMWSc 92*
**Calder**, Elisabeth Nicole 1938- *Who 92*
**Calder**, Iain Wilson 1939- *WhoFI 92*
**Calder**, John *DcLB 112*
**Calder**, John 1927- *ConAu 133*
**Calder**, John Archer 1942- *AmMWSc 92*
**Calder**, John Mackenzie 1927- *IntWW 91, Who 92*
**Calder**, Julian Richard 1941- *Who 92*
**Calder**, Kent Eyring 1948- *WhoFI 92*
**Calder**, Nigel 1931- *WrDr 92*
**Calder**, Nigel David Ritchie 1931- *IntAu&W 91, Who 92*
**Calder**, Peter N 1938- *AmMWSc 92*
**Calder**, Robert Mac 1932- *WhoWest 92*
**Calder**, William Alexander, III 1934- *AmMWSc 92*
**Calder-Marshall**, Arthur 1908- *Who 92, WrDr 92*
**Caldera**, Louis Edward 1956- *WhoAmL 92, WhoHisp 92*
**Caldera Rodriguez**, Rafael 1916- *IntWW 91*
**Calderazzo**, Joseph N., Jr. 1960- *WhoHisp 92*
**Calderin**, Carolina *WhoHisp 92*
**Calderin**, Roberto Antonio 1952- *WhoHisp 92*
**Calderon**, Alberto Pedro 1920- *AmMWSc 92, IntWW 91, WhoHisp 92*
**Calderon**, Alejandro A. 1963- *WhoHisp 92*
**Calderon**, Arnulfo Subia 1922- *WhoHisp 92*
**Calderon**, Calixto P. 1939- *WhoHisp 92*
**Calderon**, Calixto Pedro 1939- *AmMWSc 92*
**Calderon**, Cesar A., Jr. 1944- *WhoHisp 92*
**Calderon**, Charles 1950- *WhoHisp 92*
**Calderon**, Charles M 1950- *WhoAmP 91*
**Calderon**, Edith M. 1962- *WhoHisp 92*
**Calderon**, Ernesto 1928- *WhoHisp 92*
**Calderon**, Eulalio, Jr. 1932- *WhoHisp 92*
**Calderon**, Ivan 1962- *WhoBlA 92, WhoHisp 92*
**Calderon**, Jack 1929- *WhoHisp 92*
**Calderon**, Joseph 1915- *WhoAmL 92, WhoEnt 92*
**Calderon**, Juan A. 1938- *WhoHisp 92*
**Calderon**, Larry A. 1950- *WhoHisp 92*
**Calderon**, Margarita Espino *WhoHisp 92*
**Calderon**, Nissim 1933- *AmMWSc 92*
**Calderon**, Raul Morales 1954- *WhoAmL 92*
**Calderon**, Roberto R. *DrAPF 91*
**Calderon**, Rosa Margarita 1952- *WhoHisp 92*
**Calderon**, Rossie 1951- *WhoHisp 92*
**Calderon**, Sandra Socorro 1963- *WhoHisp 92*
**Calderon**, William Frank 1865-1943 *TwCPaSc*
**Calderon-Bartolomei**, Jose Manuel 1952- *WhoHisp 92*
**Calderon-Burris**, Enna 1951- *WhoHisp 92*
**Calderon Fournier**, Rafael Angel 1949- *IntWW 91*
**Calderon-Gomez**, Miguel 1950- *BlkOlyM*
**Calderon Rodriguez**, Elsie *WhoAmP 91, WhoHisp 92*
**Calderon Woodruff**, Irma E. 1951- *WhoHisp 92*
**Calderone**, Joseph Daniel 1948- *WhoRel 92*
**Calderone**, Julius G 1928- *AmMWSc 92*
**Calderone**, Richard Arthur 1942- *AmMWSc 92*
**Calderwood**, Donald Hugh 1931- *WhoRel 92*
**Calderwood**, James Albert 1941- *WhoAmL 92*
**Calderwood**, James Lee 1930- *IntAu&W 91, WrDr 92*
**Calderwood**, Keith Wright 1924- *AmMWSc 92*
**Calderwood**, Robert 1932- *Who 92*
**Calderwood**, Robert Charles 1901- *WhoRel 92*
**Calderwood**, William Arthur 1941- *WhoWest 92*
**Caldicott**, Helen Broinowski 1938- *AmPeW*
**Caldini**, Paolo *AmMWSc 92*
**Caldito**, Gloria C 1944- *AmMWSc 92*
**Caldow**, William James 1919- *Who 92*
**Caldwell**, Adrian Bernard 1966- *WhoBlA 92*
**Caldwell**, Allan Blair 1929- *WhoFI 92*
**Caldwell**, Augustus George 1923- *AmMWSc 92*
**Caldwell**, Benjamin 1937- *WhoBlA 92*
**Caldwell**, Bessie Ellis 1917- *WhoBlA 92*
**Caldwell**, Carlyle Gordon 1914- *AmMWSc 92*
**Caldwell**, Catherine Carolyn Di Nardo 1938- *WhoFI 92*
**Caldwell**, Charles 1772-1853 *BiInAmS, DcNCBi 1*
**Caldwell**, Christopher Sterling 1942- *AmMWSc 92*
**Caldwell**, Courtney Lynn 1948- *WhoAmL 92, WhoWest 92*
**Caldwell**, Dabney Withers 1927- *AmMWSc 92*
**Caldwell**, Dale Gilbert 1960- *WhoFI 92*
**Caldwell**, Daniel R 1936- *AmMWSc 92*
**Caldwell**, David 1725-1824 *DcNCBi 1*
**Caldwell**, David Bruce 1956- *WhoEnt 92*
**Caldwell**, David Franklin 1791-1867 *DcNCBi 1*
**Caldwell**, David Franklin 1814-1898 *DcNCBi 1*
**Caldwell**, David Keller 1928- *AmMWSc 92*
**Caldwell**, David Knox 1960- *WhoEnt 92*
**Caldwell**, David Orville 1925- *AmMWSc 92*
**Caldwell**, Dick *Who 92*
**Caldwell**, Donald R. 1946- *WhoFI 92*
**Caldwell**, Douglas Ray 1936- *AmMWSc 92*
**Caldwell**, Edward George 1941- *Who 92*
**Caldwell**, Edward Sabiston 1928- *WhoRel 92*
**Caldwell**, Edwin L., Jr. 1935- *WhoBlA 92*
**Caldwell**, Elvin R. 1919- *WhoBlA 92*
**Caldwell**, Elwood F 1923- *AmMWSc 92*
**Caldwell**, Eric Dick 1909- *Who 92*
**Caldwell**, Erskine 1903- *FacFETw [port], IntAu&W 91*
**Caldwell**, Erskine 1903-1987 *BenetAL 91*
**Caldwell**, Esly Samuel, II 1938- *WhoBlA 92*
**Caldwell**, Eugene Wilson 1870-1918 *BiInAmS*
**Caldwell**, Excetral Kerwin 1957- *WhoAmL 92*
**Caldwell**, Frank 1921- *WhoBlA 92*
**Caldwell**, Frank Griffiths 1921- *Who 92*
**Caldwell**, Franklin D. 1934- *WhoRel 92*
**Caldwell**, Fred T, Jr 1925- *AmMWSc 92*
**Caldwell**, George Chapman 1834-1907 *BiInAmS*
**Caldwell**, George Theron, Sr. 1939- *WhoBlA 92*
**Caldwell**, Gladys Emanuel *WhoBlA 92*
**Caldwell**, Glyn Gordon 1934- *AmMWSc 92*
**Caldwell**, Greene Washington 1806-1864 *DcNCBi 1*
**Caldwell**, Howard Bryant 1944- *WhoWest 92*
**Caldwell**, J Edward 1927- *WhoAmP 91*
**Caldwell**, J J, Jr 1915- *AmMWSc 92*
**Caldwell**, James E. 1930- *WhoBlA 92*
**Caldwell**, James Wiley 1923- *WhoAmL 92*
**Caldwell**, Joe Louis 1941- *BlkOlyM*
**Caldwell**, John Bernard 1926- *IntWW 91, Who 92*
**Caldwell**, John Edward 1937- *WhoBlA 92*
**Caldwell**, John James 1933- *WhoWest 92*
**Caldwell**, John James 1944- *AmMWSc 92*
**Caldwell**, John R 1918- *AmMWSc 92*
**Caldwell**, John Thomas 1937- *AmMWSc 92*
**Caldwell**, John William 1943- *WhoRel 92*
**Caldwell**, Johnnie L 1922- *WhoAmP 91*
**Caldwell**, Joni 1948- *WhoWest 92*
**Caldwell**, Joseph 1773-1835 *BiInAmS, DcNCBi 1*
**Caldwell**, Joseph Pearson 1808-1853 *DcNCBi 1*
**Caldwell**, Joseph Pearson 1853-1911 *DcNCBi 1*
**Caldwell**, Judy Carol 1946- *WhoFI 92*
**Caldwell**, Justin *DrAPF 91*
**Caldwell**, Karin D *AmMWSc 92*
**Caldwell**, Keesha Maria 1948- *WhoBlA 92*
**Caldwell**, Kristina Peterson 1964- *WhoWest 92*
**Caldwell**, L. Scott *WhoEnt 92*
**Caldwell**, Larry D 1932- *AmMWSc 92*
**Caldwell**, Lewis A. H. 1905- *WhoBlA 92*
**Caldwell**, M. Milford 1928- *WhoBlA 92*
**Caldwell**, Marion Milford, Jr. 1952- *WhoBlA 92*
**Caldwell**, Martyn Mathews 1941- *AmMWSc 92*
**Caldwell**, Melba Carstarphen 1921- *AmMWSc 92*
**Caldwell**, Michael D 1943- *AmMWSc 92*
**Caldwell**, Patty Jean Grosskopf 1937- *WhoMW 92*
**Caldwell**, Paul Willis, Jr. 1930- *WhoWest 92*
**Caldwell**, Paulette M. 1944- *WhoAmL 92*
**Caldwell**, Peter Derek 1940- *WhoWest 92*
**Caldwell**, Philip 1920- *IntWW 91, Who 92, WhoFI 92*
**Caldwell**, Price *DrAPF 91*
**Caldwell**, Ravin, Jr. 1963- *WhoBlA 92*
**Caldwell**, Robert Allen 1940- *WhoMW 92*
**Caldwell**, Robert John 1949- *WhoWest 92*
**Caldwell**, Robert L. 1933- *WhoIns 92*
**Caldwell**, Robert William 1942- *AmMWSc 92*
**Caldwell**, Rodney K. 1937- *WhoAmL 92*

**Caldwell,** Roger Lee 1938- *AmMWSc 92*
**Caldwell,** Rossie Juanita Brower 1917- *WhoBlA 92*
**Caldwell,** Samuel Craig 1919- *AmMWSc 92*
**Caldwell,** Sandra Ishmael 1948- *WhoBlA 92*
**Caldwell,** Sarah 1924- *NewAmDM, WhoEnt 92*
**Caldwell,** Sloan Daniel 1943- *AmMWSc 92*
**Caldwell,** Stephen E 1946- *AmMWSc 92*
**Caldwell,** Stratton F. *DrAPF 91*
**Caldwell,** Taylor 1900-1985 *BenetAL 91, FacFETw*
**Caldwell,** Terry 1947- *WhoEnt 92*
**Caldwell,** Thomas Howell, Jr. 1934- *WhoFI 92*
**Caldwell,** Thomas Michael 1946- *WhoWest 92*
**Caldwell,** Tod Robinson 1818-1874 *DcNCBi 1*
**Caldwell,** Wallace Everett 1890-1961 *DcNCBi 1*
**Caldwell,** Walter Edward 1941- *WhoWest 92*
**Caldwell,** Wayne Eugene 1923- *WhoRel 92*
**Caldwell,** Wendy Jean 1966- *WhoRel 92*
**Caldwell,** Wiley North 1927- *WhoFI 92, WhoMW 92*
**Caldwell,** Will M. 1925- *WhoFI 92*
**Caldwell,** William Gerald 1934- *WhoRel 92*
**Caldwell,** William Glen Elliot 1932- *AmMWSc 92*
**Caldwell,** William Mackay, III 1922- *WhoWest 92*
**Caldwell,** William V 1917- *AmMWSc 92*
**Caldwell,** William Wilson 1925- *WhoAmL 92*
**Caldwell,** Zoe 1933- *WhoEnt 92*
**Caldwell-Bono,** Deborah Suzanne 1953- *WhoAmL 92*
**Caldwell-Lee,** Laurie Neilson 1947- *WhoAmL 92*
**Caldwell-Moore,** Patrick *Who 92*
**Caldwell Swisher,** Rozella Kathrine 1908- *WhoBlA 92*
**Cale,** Albert Duncan, Jr 1928- *AmMWSc 92*
**Cale,** Bernard Jerome 1948- *WhoFI 92*
**Cale,** Charles Griffin 1940- *WhoAmL 92*
**Cale,** David *DrAPF 91*
**Cale,** William Graham, Jr 1947- *AmMWSc 92*
**Cale,** William Robert 1913- *AmMWSc 92*
**Caledon,** Earl of 1955- *Who 92*
**Caledonia,** Bishop of 1937- *Who 92*
**Caledonia,** George Ernest 1941- *AmMWSc 92*
**Calef,** Robert 1648-1719 *BenetAL 91*
**Calegari,** Maria 1957- *WhoEnt 92*
**Calehuff,** Girard Lester 1925- *AmMWSc 92*
**Calek,** Robert Edward, Jr. 1954- *WhoMW 92*
**Calendar,** Lauren *WhoAmP 91*
**Calendar,** Richard 1940- *AmMWSc 92*
**Calendine,** Richard Harley 1939- *WhoMW 92*
**Calero,** Ramon *WhoHisp 92*
**Calesnick,** Benjamin 1915- *AmMWSc 92*
**Calestino,** Karen Joan 1952- *WhoFI 92*
**Caley,** Wendell J, Jr 1928- *AmMWSc 92*
**Calfa,** Marian 1946- *IntWW 91*
**Calfano,** Albert J 1945- *WhoIns 92*
**Calfee,** David Walker 1921- *WhoWest 92*
**Calfee,** Peter Haas 1950- *WhoFI 92*
**Calfee,** William Lewis 1917- *WhoAmL 92, WhoFI 92*
**Calfo,** Cathryn Cathy 1957- *WhoAmP 91*
**Calgary,** Bishop of 1933- *Who 92*
**Calhoon,** Donald Alan 1950- *AmMWSc 92*
**Calhoon,** Ed Latta 1922- *WhoAmP 91*
**Calhoon,** Jeffrey David 1950- *WhoEnt 92*
**Calhoon,** Robert Ellsworth 1938- *AmMWSc 92*
**Calhoon,** Stephen Wallace, Jr 1930- *AmMWSc 92*
**Calhoun,** Bertram Allen 1925- *AmMWSc 92*
**Calhoun,** Calvin L 1927- *AmMWSc 92*
**Calhoun,** Calvin Lee 1927- *WhoBlA 92*
**Calhoun,** Carol Victoria 1953- *WhoAmL 92*
**Calhoun,** Cecelia C. 1922- *WhoBlA 92*
**Calhoun,** Chad *TwCWW 91*
**Calhoun,** Clayne Marsh 1950- *WhoAmL 92*
**Calhoun,** Credell 1945- *WhoAmP 91*
**Calhoun,** David H 1942- *AmMWSc 92*
**Calhoun,** David Van 1956- *WhoRel 92*
**Calhoun,** Donald Eugene, Jr. 1926- *WhoAmL 92*
**Calhoun,** Dorothy Eunice 1936- *WhoBlA 92*
**Calhoun,** Douglas Alan 1951- *WhoRel 92*
**Calhoun,** Ellsworth L 1928- *WhoIns 92*
**Calhoun,** Eric A. 1950- *WhoBlA 92*
**Calhoun,** Frank Gilbert 1939- *AmMWSc 92*
**Calhoun,** Fred Steverson 1947- *WhoBlA 92*
**Calhoun,** Gordon James 1953- *WhoAmL 92, WhoWest 92*
**Calhoun,** Jack Johnson, Jr. 1938- *WhoBlA 92*
**Calhoun,** Jason Harris 1956- *WhoAmL 92*
**Calhoun,** Jerry L 1943- *WhoAmP 91*
**Calhoun,** John 1937- *WhoBlA 92*
**Calhoun,** John Bumpass 1917- *AmMWSc 92*
**Calhoun,** John C. 1782-1850 *BenetAL 91, RComAH*
**Calhoun,** John C, Jr 1917- *AmMWSc 92*
**Calhoun,** John Caldwell 1782-1850 *AmPolLe [port]*
**Calhoun,** John Cozart 1937- *WhoFI 92*
**Calhoun,** John Curtis 1963- *WhoEnt 92*
**Calhoun,** John H. *WhoAmL 92*
**Calhoun,** Joshua Wesley 1956- *WhoBlA 92*
**Calhoun,** Lee A. 1947- *WhoBlA 92*
**Calhoun,** Lee Quency 1933- *BlkOlyM*
**Calhoun,** Lillian Scott *WhoBlA 92, WhoMW 92*
**Calhoun,** Madeleine S. Abler 1961- *WhoEnt 92*
**Calhoun,** Millard Clayton 1935- *AmMWSc 92*
**Calhoun,** Nancy 1944- *WhoAmP 91*
**Calhoun,** Noah Robert 1921- *AmMWSc 92, WhoBlA 92*
**Calhoun,** Paul, III 1938- *WhoRel 92*
**Calhoun,** Ralph Vernon, Jr 1949- *AmMWSc 92*
**Calhoun,** Richard Carl 1943- *WhoMW 92*
**Calhoun,** Richard J. 1926- *WrDr 92*
**Calhoun,** Robert *WhoAmP 91*
**Calhoun,** Robert Kier 1942- *WhoAmL 92*
**Calhoun,** Rory 1922- *ConTFT 9, IntMPA 92*
**Calhoun,** Sally J. 1955- *WhoAmL 92*
**Calhoun,** Shirley Meacham 1927- *WhoAmP 91*
**Calhoun,** Thomas 1932- *WhoBlA 92*
**Calhoun,** V O, Jr 1951- *WhoAmP 91*
**Calhoun,** Vern Thomas 1960- *WhoEnt 92*
**Calhoun,** Wes *TwCWW 91, WrDr 92*
**Calhoun,** Wheeler, Jr 1916- *AmMWSc 92*
**Calhoun,** William Michael 1952- *WhoRel 92*
**Calhoun-Senghor,** Keith 1955- *WhoAmL 92*
**Calian,** Carnegie Samuel 1933- *WhoRel 92, WrDr 92*
**Calicuchima** d1553 *HisDSpE*
**Caliendo,** G. D. 1941- *WhoAmL 92*
**Caliestro,** Jacques Andre, III 1945- *WhoEnt 92*
**Calif,** Ruth 1922- *ConAu 134, SmATA 67 [port]*
**Califano,** Joseph A, Jr 1931- *IntAu&W 91, WhoAmP 91, WrDr 92*
**Califano,** Joseph Anthony, Jr. 1931- *IntWW 91, WhoAmL 92*
**Califano,** Mark Gerard 1962- *WhoAmL 92*
**Califia,** Pat *DrAPF 91*
**Califia,** Pat 1954- *ConAu 133*
**Califice,** Alfred 1916- *IntWW 91*
**Caligari,** Peter Douglas Savaria 1949- *Who 92*
**Caligiuri,** Joseph Frank 1928- *AmMWSc 92, WhoFI 92*
**Caligiuri,** Robert Domenic 1951- *AmMWSc 92*
**Caliguiri,** Lawrence Anthony 1933- *AmMWSc 92*
**Calika,** Omer Hursit 1918- *WhoFI 92*
**Calille,** Albert 1951- *WhoAmL 92*
**Calingaert,** Peter 1931- *AmMWSc 92*
**Calinger,** Ronald Steve 1942- *AmMWSc 92*
**Calinger,** Walter M *WhoAmP 91*
**Calinoiu,** Nicolae 1926- *IntWW 91*
**Calio,** Anthony John 1929- *AmMWSc 92, WhoAmP 91*
**Calise,** Nicholas James 1941- *WhoAmL 92*
**Calise,** Ronald Jan 1948- *WhoFI 92*
**Calisher,** Charles Henry 1936- *AmMWSc 92*
**Calisher,** Hortense *DrAPF 91*
**Calisher,** Hortense 1911- *BenetAL 91, ConNov 91, IntWW 91, WrDr 92*
**Calitri,** Charles *DrAPF 91*
**Calivas,** Alkiviadis *WhoRel 92*
**Calkin,** Melvin Gilbert 1936- *AmMWSc 92*
**Calkin,** Parker E 1933- *AmMWSc 92*
**Calkins,** Benjamin 1956- *WhoAmL 92*
**Calkins,** Carrol Otto 1937- *AmMWSc 92*
**Calkins,** Catherine E *AmMWSc 92*
**Calkins,** Charles Richard 1921- *AmMWSc 92*
**Calkins,** Harmon Eldred 1912- *AmMWSc 92*
**Calkins,** Harold LeRoy 1920- *WhoRel 92*
**Calkins,** Jean *DrAPF 91*
**Calkins,** Jerry Milan 1942- *WhoWest 92*
**Calkins,** John 1926- *AmMWSc 92*
**Calkins,** John Thiers 1925- *WhoAmP 91*
**Calkins,** Judith Moritz 1942- *WhoFI 92*
**Calkins,** Keith Gordon 1958- *WhoMW 92*
**Calkins,** Marilyn Ruth 1939- *WhoRel 92*
**Calkins,** Mary Whiton 1863-1930 *FacFETw, WomPsyc*
**Calkins,** Ralph Nelson 1926- *WhoFI 92*
**Calkins,** Russel Crosby 1921- *AmMWSc 92*
**Calkins,** William Graham 1926- *AmMWSc 92*
**Calkins,** William Harold 1918- *AmMWSc 92*
**Call,** Arthur Deerin 1869-1941 *AmPeW*
**Call,** Barbara Jo 1960- *WhoAmL 92*
**Call,** Craig M 1948- *WhoAmP 91*
**Call,** Dwight Vincent 1934- *WhoWest 92*
**Call,** Edward *WhoEnt 92*
**Call,** Edward Prior 1926- *AmMWSc 92*
**Call,** Gene 1944- *WhoAmP 91*
**Call,** John E *WhoAmP 91*
**Call,** John Sealey, Jr. 1925- *WhoAmL 92*
**Call,** Joseph Rudd 1950- *WhoWest 92*
**Call,** Justin David 1923- *AmMWSc 92*
**Call,** Merlin Wendell 1931- *WhoWest 92*
**Call,** Patrick Joseph 1949- *AmMWSc 92*
**Call,** Ralph Ivan 1945- *WhoFI 92, WhoMW 92*
**Call,** Reginald Lessey 1926- *AmMWSc 92*
**Call,** Reuel *WhoWest 92*
**Call,** Richard C. 1930- *WhoFI 92*
**Call,** Richard Ellsworth 1856-1917 *BiInAmS*
**Call,** Richard William 1924- *WhoFI 92, WhoWest 92*
**Call,** Robert E. 1934- *WhoRel 92*
**Call,** Robert W. 1945- *WhoFI 92*
**Call,** Scott Joseph 1963- *WhoWest 92*
**Calladine,** Christopher Reuben 1935- *IntWW 91, Who 92*
**Callaghan** *Who 92*
**Callaghan,** Allan 1903- *Who 92*
**Callaghan,** Barry 1937- *ConPo 91, WrDr 92*
**Callaghan,** Bede 1912- *Who 92*
**Callaghan,** Brendan Alphonsus 1948- *Who 92*
**Callaghan,** Catherine A. *DrAPF 91*
**Callaghan,** Desmond Noble 1915- *Who 92*
**Callaghan,** Edward Terence 1948- *WhoEnt 92*
**Callaghan,** James 1912- *FacFETw*
**Callaghan,** James 1927- *Who 92*
**Callaghan,** Morley d1990 *IntWW 91N*
**Callaghan,** Morley 1903- *BenetAL 91, IntAu&W 91*
**Callaghan,** Morley 1903-1990 *AnObit 1990, ConLC 65 [port], LiExTwC, RfGEnL 91*
**Callaghan,** Morley Edward 1903-1990 *FacFETw*
**Callaghan,** Owen Hugh 1927- *AmMWSc 92*
**Callaghan,** Robert J 1926- *WhoAmP 91*
**Callaghan,** Robert Michael 1958- *WhoEnt 92*
**Callaghan,** William M. d1991 *NewYTBS 91 [port]*
**Callaghan,** William Stuart 1945- *WhoAmP 91*
**Callaghan Of Cardiff,** Baron 1912- *IntWW 91, Who 92*
**Callaham,** Mac A 1936- *AmMWSc 92*
**Callaham,** Robert Zina 1927- *AmMWSc 92*
**Callahan,** Adelina Pena 1935- *WhoHisp 92*
**Callahan,** Bobbie Yolanda 1949- *WhoAmL 92*
**Callahan,** Charles, III 1949- *WhoFI 92*
**Callahan,** Charles Edmund, Jr. 1951- *WhoEnt 92*
**Callahan,** Christine H *WhoAmP 91*
**Callahan,** Clarence Arthur 1943- *AmMWSc 92*
**Callahan,** Daniel 1930- *AmMWSc 92, WrDr 92*
**Callahan,** Daniel J *WhoAmP 91*
**Callahan,** Daniel John 1930- *WhoFI 92*
**Callahan,** David 1947- *WhoMW 92*
**Callahan,** Dennis M 1942- *WhoAmP 91*
**Callahan,** Era Eugene 1933- *WhoAmP 91*
**Callahan,** Gerald William 1936- *WhoAmL 92*
**Callahan,** H. L. 1932- *AlmAP 92 [port], WhoAmP 91*
**Callahan,** Harry 1912- *DcTwDes*
**Callahan,** Harry M. 1912- *IntWW 91*
**Callahan,** Hugh James 1940- *AmMWSc 92*
**Callahan,** James Louis 1926- *AmMWSc 92*
**Callahan,** James P 1939- *WhoAmP 91*
**Callahan,** James Patrick 1942- *WhoEnt 92*
**Callahan,** James Richard 1951- *WhoAmL 92*
**Callahan,** James Thomas 1945- *AmMWSc 92*
**Callahan,** Jeffrey Edwin 1943- *AmMWSc 92*
**Callahan,** John *TwCWW 91*
**Callahan,** John Edward 1941- *AmMWSc 92*
**Callahan,** John F. 1912- *WrDr 92*
**Callahan,** John Joseph 1925- *AmMWSc 92*
**Callahan,** John Martin 1943- *WhoEnt 92*
**Callahan,** John William 1942- *AmMWSc 92*
**Callahan,** John William 1947- *WhoAmL 92*
**Callahan,** Joseph Thomas 1922- *AmMWSc 92*
**Callahan,** Kemper Leroy 1929- *AmMWSc 92*
**Callahan,** Kenneth Paul 1943- *AmMWSc 92*
**Callahan,** Leslie G, Jr 1923- *AmMWSc 92*
**Callahan,** Lloyd Milton 1934- *AmMWSc 92*
**Callahan,** Marilyn Ann 1940- *WhoMW 92*
**Callahan,** Marilyn Joy 1934- *WhoWest 92*
**Callahan,** Mary Vincent 1922- *AmMWSc 92*
**Callahan,** Michael Thomas 1948- *WhoAmL 92*
**Callahan,** Nelson J. *WrDr 92*
**Callahan,** Nelson James 1927- *WhoRel 92*
**Callahan,** North 1908- *IntAu&W 91, WrDr 92*
**Callahan,** Patrick Michael 1947- *WhoAmL 92*
**Callahan,** Philip Serna 1923- *AmMWSc 92*
**Callahan,** Richard A. 1941- *WhoWest 92*
**Callahan,** Richard J. 1941- *WhoFI 92*
**Callahan,** Richard James 1928- *WhoFI 92*
**Callahan,** Robert Edward 1949- *WhoAmL 92*
**Callahan,** Robert F., Jr. *WhoEnt 92*
**Callahan,** Robert J *WhoAmP 91*
**Callahan,** Robert J. 1930- *WhoAmL 92*
**Callahan,** Samuel P. 1924- *WhoBlA 92*
**Callahan,** Steven P 1952- *IntAu&W 91*
**Callahan,** Thomas Dennis 1952- *WhoIns 92*
**Callahan,** Thomas William 1925- *AmMWSc 92*
**Callahan,** Vincent Francis, Jr 1931- *WhoAmP 91*
**Callahan,** William *IntAu&W 91X, TwCSFW 91*
**Callahan-Compton,** Joan 1948- *WhoWest 92*
**Callahan-Compton,** Joan Rea 1948- *AmMWSc 92*
**Callam,** Daniel 1935- *WhoRel 92*
**Callam,** Edward *TwCPaSc*
**Callan,** Curtis 1942- *AmMWSc 92*
**Callan,** Edwin Joseph 1922- *AmMWSc 92*
**Callan,** Harold Garnet 1917- *IntWW 91, Who 92*
**Callan,** Herbert Quentin 1922- *WhoAmP 91*
**Callan,** Ivan Roy 1942- *Who 92*
**Callan,** Jamie *DrAPF 91*
**Callan,** Michael 1925- *Who 92*
**Callan,** Michael 1935- *IntMPA 92*
**Callan,** Terrence A. 1939- *WhoAmL 92*
**Callanan,** Jane Elizabeth 1926- *AmMWSc 92*
**Callanan,** Kathleen Joan 1940- *WhoMW 92*
**Callanan,** Margaret Joan 1926- *AmMWSc 92*
**Calland,** Diana Baker 1935- *WhoEnt 92*
**Calland,** Ruth 1963- *TwCPaSc*
**Callander,** Kay Eileen Paisley 1938- *WhoMW 92*
**Callander,** Robert John 1931- *WhoFI 92*
**Callantine,** Merritt Reece 1936- *AmMWSc 92*
**Callard,** Eric John 1913- *Who 92*
**Callard,** Gloria Vincz 1938- *AmMWSc 92*
**Callard,** Jack 1913- *IntWW 91*
**Callard,** Maurice 1912- *WrDr 92*
**Callas,** Gerald 1932- *AmMWSc 92*
**Callas,** John Peter 1950- *WhoEnt 92*
**Callas,** Maria 1923-1977 *NewAmDM*
**Callas,** Maria 1924-1977 *FacFETw [port]*
**Callas,** Michael G 1921- *WhoAmP 91*
**Callas,** Peter G *WhoAmP 91*
**Callas,** Theo *IntAu&W 91X, WrDr 92*
**Callaway,** Betty *Who 92*
**Callaway,** Charles Franklin 1933- *WhoMW 92*
**Callaway,** Clifford Wayne 1941- *AmMWSc 92*
**Callaway,** David Henry, Jr. 1912- *WhoFI 92*
**Callaway,** Dwight W. 1932- *WhoBlA 92*
**Callaway,** Enoch, III 1924- *AmMWSc 92*
**Callaway,** Frank 1919- *Who 92*
**Callaway,** Henry Abbott, III 1958- *WhoAmL 92*
**Callaway,** Howard H. 1927- *IntWW 91*
**Callaway,** Howard Hollis 1927- *WhoAmP 91, WhoWest 92*
**Callaway,** Jasper Lamar 1911- *AmMWSc 92*
**Callaway,** Joseph 1931- *AmMWSc 92*

**Callaway**, Karen Alice 1946- *WhoMW 92*
**Callaway**, Kathy *DrAPF 91*
**Callaway**, Louis Marshall, Jr. 1939- *WhoBlA 92*
**Callaway**, Paul Frederick, Jr. 1951- *WhoFI 92*
**Callaway**, Richard Earl 1951- *WhoMW 92*
**Callaway-Fittall**, Betty Daphne 1928- *Who 92*
**Callcott**, Thomas Anderson 1937- *AmMWSc 92*
**Calle**, Carlos Ignacio 1945- *AmMWSc 92*
**Calle**, Luz Marina 1947- *AmMWSc 92, WhoHisp 92*
**Calleja del Rey**, Felix Maria 1759-1828 *HisDSpE*
**Callejas**, Manuel Mancia, Jr. 1933- *WhoHisp 92*
**Callejas**, Marlene Theresa 1957- *WhoHisp 92*
**Callejas**, Rafael *IntWW 91*
**Callen**, Craig Randall 1950- *WhoAmL 92*
**Callen**, Earl Robert 1925- *AmMWSc 92*
**Callen**, Herbert Bernard 1919- *AmMWSc 92*
**Callen**, James Donald 1941- *AmMWSc 92*
**Callen**, Jerry, Jr *WhoAmP 91*
**Callen**, John Holmes, Jr. 1932- *WhoFI 92*
**Callen**, Joseph Edward 1920- *AmMWSc 92*
**Callen**, Lon Edward 1929- *WhoWest 92*
**Callenbach**, Ernest 1929- *TwCSFW 91, WrDr 92*
**Callenbach**, John Anton 1908- *AmMWSc 92*
**Callendar**, Malcolm *WhoAmP 91*
**Callender**, Carl O. 1936- *WhoBlA 92*
**Callender**, Clive Orville 1936- *WhoBlA 92*
**Callender**, Jonathan Ferris 1944- *AmMWSc 92*
**Callender**, Leroy R. 1932- *WhoBlA 92*
**Callender**, Lucinda R. 1957- *WhoBlA 92*
**Callender**, Maurice Henry 1916- *Who 92*
**Callender**, Ralph A. 1932- *WhoBlA 92*
**Callender**, Robert 1932- *TwCPaSc*
**Callender**, Valerie Dawn 1960- *WhoBlA 92*
**Callender**, Wade Lee 1926- *AmMWSc 92*
**Callender**, Wilfred A. 1929- *WhoBlA 92*
**Callens**, Earl Eugene, Jr 1940- *AmMWSc 92*
**Caller**, Maxwell Marshall 1951- *Who 92*
**Callerame**, Joseph 1950- *AmMWSc 92*
**Calleros**, Charles R. 1953- *WhoHisp 92*
**Callery**, Patrick Stephen 1944- *AmMWSc 92*
**Calles**, Plutarco Elias 1877-1945 *FacFETw*
**Calles**, Rosa Maria 1949- *WhoHisp 92*
**Callewaert**, Denis Marc 1947- *AmMWSc 92, WhoMW 92*
**Calley**, Henry 1914- *Who 92*
**Calley**, John 1930- *IntMPA 92, WhoEnt 92*
**Calley**, William L *FacFETw*
**Calleya**, Octav 1942- *WhoEnt 92*
**Callias**, Nina de 1844-1884 *ThHEIm*
**Callicott**, Clint 1948- *WhoAmP 91*
**Callicott**, J. Baird 1941- *ConAu 135*
**Callier**, Barry Luke 1940- *WhoEnt 92*
**Callier**, Frank Maria 1942- *AmMWSc 92*
**Callier**, M. Alice *WhoRel 92*
**Callies**, David Lee 1943- *WhoAmL 92*
**Calligan**, Michael Edward 1945- *WhoAmL 92*
**Callighan**, Phillip Edward 1951- *WhoMW 92*
**Callihan**, Alfred Dixon 1908- *AmMWSc 92*
**Callihan**, C Michael 1947- *WhoAmP 91, WhoWest 92*
**Callihan**, Clayton D 1919- *AmMWSc 92*
**Callihan**, Dixon 1908- *AmMWSc 92*
**Callihan**, Robert Harold 1933- *AmMWSc 92*
**Callil**, Carmen Therese 1938- *IntWW 91, Who 92*
**Callimachos**, Panos Demetrios 1879-1963 *RelLAm 91*
**Callinan**, Bernard 1913- *Who 92*
**Callinan**, Bernard J. 1913- *WrDr 92*
**Callirgos**, Judy Ann 1959- *WhoEnt 92*
**Callis**, Bruce *WhoIns 92*
**Callis**, Bruce 1939- *WhoAmP 91*
**Callis**, Clayton Fowler 1923- *AmMWSc 92*
**Callis**, James Bertram 1943- *AmMWSc 92*
**Callis**, Jerry Jackson 1926- *AmMWSc 92*
**Callis**, John Benton 1828-1898 *DcNCBi 1*
**Callis**, Patrik Robert 1938- *AmMWSc 92*
**Callison**, Brian 1934- *IntAu&W 91, WrDr 92*
**Callison**, George 1940- *AmMWSc 92*
**Callison**, James W. 1928- *WhoAmL 92, WhoFI 92*
**Callison**, Nancy Fowler 1931- *WhoWest 92*
**Callison**, Russell James 1954- *WhoAmL 92*
**Callison**, Scott Dale 1961- *WhoMW 92*
**Calliste**, Gerald Carlton, Jr. 1965- *WhoEnt 92*
**Callister**, Louis Henry, Jr. 1935- *WhoWest 92*
**Callister**, Marion Jones 1921- *WhoAmL 92, WhoWest 92*
**Callister**, Matthew Q 1955- *WhoAmP 91*
**Callister**, Susan Price 1945- *WhoAmL 92*
**Callistus I** *EncEarC*
**Callman**, Clive Vernon 1927- *Who 92*
**Callner**, Bruce Warren 1948- *WhoAmL 92*
**Callner**, Marty 1946- *WhoEnt 92*
**Callner**, Robert Mark 1951- *WhoEnt 92*
**Callon**, Colin J. 1932- *TwCPaSc*
**Callow**, Allan Dana 1916- *AmMWSc 92*
**Callow**, Henry William 1926- *Who 92*
**Callow**, Keith McLean 1925- *WhoAmL 92, WhoAmP 91, WhoWest 92*
**Callow**, Philip 1924- *ConNov 91, IntAu&W 91, WrDr 92*
**Callow**, Simon 1949- *IntMPA 92*
**Callow**, Simon Philip Hugh 1949- *IntWW 91*
**Callow**, Simon Phillip Hugh 1949- *Who 92*
**Callow**, Thomas Edward 1954- *WhoAmL 92*
**Callow**, William Grant 1921- *WhoAmL 92, WhoAmP 91, WhoMW 92*
**Calloway**, Blanche 1902-1973 *NotBlAW 92*
**Calloway**, Cab 1907- *ConMus 6 [port], FacFETw, NewAmDM*
**Calloway**, Cab, III 1907- *WhoBlA 92*
**Calloway**, Colin G. 1953- *ConAu 135*
**Calloway**, Curtis A. 1939- *WhoBlA 92*
**Calloway**, D. Wayne 1935- *WhoFI 92*
**Calloway**, David Karl 1947- *WhoEnt 92*
**Calloway**, DeVerne Lee 1916- *WhoAmP 91, WhoBlA 92*
**Calloway**, Doris Howes 1923- *AmMWSc 92*
**Calloway**, E Dean 1924- *AmMWSc 92*
**Calloway**, Ernest 1909-1989 *WhoBlA 92N*
**Calloway**, James 1806-1878 *DcNCBi 1*
**Calloway**, Jean Mitchener 1923- *AmMWSc 92, WhoMW 92*
**Calloway**, Rick *WhoBlA 92*
**Callstrom**, Matthew Raymond 1960- *WhoMW 92*
**Callum**, Agnes Kane 1925- *WhoBlA 92*
**Callum**, Myles 1934- *IntAu&W 91, WhoEnt 92*
**Callwood**, June 1924- *IntAu&W 91, IntWW 91, WrDr 92*
**Calman**, Carl Hubert 1925- *WhoMW 92*
**Calman**, Kenneth Charles 1941- *Who 92*
**Calman**, Mel 1931- *IntAu&W 91, Who 92*
**Calmenson**, Stephanie Lyn *IntAu&W 91*
**Calmes**, Christian 1913- *IntWW 91*
**Calmes**, Richard Allen 1932- *WhoMW 92*
**Calmon De Sa**, Angelo *IntWW 91*
**Calnan**, Charles Dermod 1917- *Who 92*
**Calnan**, James Stanislaus 1916- *Who 92*
**Calne**, Donald Brian 1936- *AmMWSc 92*
**Calne**, Roy 1930- *Who 92*
**Calne**, Roy Yorke 1930- *IntWW 91*
**Calne And Calstone**, Viscount 1970- *Who 92*
**Calnek**, Bruce Wixson 1932- *AmMWSc 92*
**Calo**, Joseph Manuel 1944- *AmMWSc 92*
**Calogero**, Pascal Frank, Jr. 1931- *WhoAmL 92, WhoAmP 91*
**Calomee**, Annie E. 1910- *WhoBlA 92*
**Calouri**, Theodore Lawrence 1941- *WhoAmP 91*
**Calovski**, Mitko 1930- *IntWW 91, Who 92*
**Calow**, Jane 1953- *TwCPaSc*
**Calpin**, Martin J 1934- *WhoIns 92*
**Calpouzos**, Lucas 1927- *AmMWSc 92*
**Cals**, Adolphe-Felix 1810-1880 *ThHEIm*
**Caltagirone**, Leopoldo Enrique 1927- *AmMWSc 92*
**Caltagirone**, Thomas Richard 1942- *WhoAmP 91*
**Calthorpe** *Who 92*
**Calthorpe**, Baron 1927- *Who 92*
**Calton**, Judy Bamberger 1952- *WhoAmL 92*
**Caltrider**, Paul Gene 1935- *AmMWSc 92*
**Calub**, Alfonso deGuzman 1938- *AmMWSc 92*
**Calusdian**, Richard Frank 1935- *AmMWSc 92*
**Calvani**, Terry 1947- *WhoAmL 92, WhoAmP 91*
**Calvanico**, Nickolas Joseph 1936- *AmMWSc 92*
**Calvanico**, Thomas Paul 1955- *WhoAmL 92*
**Calvaruso**, Michael A. 1955- *WhoEnt 92*
**Calve**, Emma 1858-1942 *NewAmDM*
**Calve de Roquer**, Emma 1858-1942 *NewAmDM*
**Calvelli**, Theresa A *AmMWSc 92*
**Calvello**, Angelo Anthony 1956- *WhoFI 92, WhoMW 92*
**Calver**, James Lewis 1913- *AmMWSc 92*
**Calverley**, Baron 1946- *Who 92*
**Calverley**, Charles Stuart 1831-1884 *RfGEnL 91*
**Calverley**, John Robert 1932- *AmMWSc 92*
**Calvert**, Allen Fisher 1927- *AmMWSc 92*
**Calvert**, Ann 1935- *WhoAmP 91*
**Calvert**, Barbara Adamson 1926- *Who 92*
**Calvert**, Cynthia Thomas 1960- *WhoAmL 92*
**Calvert**, Dale 1937- *WhoIns 92*
**Calvert**, David Victor 1934- *AmMWSc 92*
**Calvert**, Denis *Who 92*
**Calvert**, Florence Irene 1912- *Who 92*
**Calvert**, George Henry 1803-1889 *BenetAL 91*
**Calvert**, Henry Reginald 1904- *Who 92*
**Calvert**, Jack George 1923- *AmMWSc 92*
**Calvert**, James Bowles 1935- *AmMWSc 92*
**Calvert**, Jay Gregory 1959- *AmMWSc 92*
**Calvert**, Jay H., Jr. 1945- *WhoAmL 92*
**Calvert**, Jeffrey Robert 1960- *WhoAmL 92*
**Calvert**, Jody Lee 1961- *WhoRel 92*
**Calvert**, Jon Channing 1941- *AmMWSc 92*
**Calvert**, Kenneth Elsworth 1928- *WhoAmP 91*
**Calvert**, Laura *DrAPF 91*
**Calvert**, Louis Victor Denis 1924- *Who 92*
**Calvert**, Mary *IntAu&W 91X, WrDr 92*
**Calvert**, Melanie A. 1954- *WhoAmL 92*
**Calvert**, Norman Hilton 1925- *Who 92*
**Calvert**, Oscar Hugh 1918- *AmMWSc 92*
**Calvert**, Patricia Joyce 1931- *IntAu&W 91*
**Calvert**, Peter 1936- *WrDr 92*
**Calvert**, Peter Anthony Richard 1936- *IntAu&W 91*
**Calvert**, Phyllis 1915- *Who 92*
**Calvert**, Ralph Lowell 1910- *AmMWSc 92*
**Calvert**, Richard John 1955- *AmMWSc 92*
**Calvert**, Robert Lyle, Jr. 1966- *WhoMW 92*
**Calvert**, Sam Vernon 1950- *WhoAmL 92*
**Calvert**, Thomas W 1936- *AmMWSc 92*
**Calvert**, Walter Randolph 1958- *WhoAmL 92*
**Calvert**, William Leonard 1943- *WhoMW 92*
**Calvert-Smith**, David 1945- *Who 92*
**Calverton**, V. F. 1900-1940 *BenetAL 91*
**Calvet**, Cesar E. *WhoHisp 92*
**Calvet**, Corinne 1925- *IntMPA 92, WhoEnt 92*
**Calvet**, Jacques 1931- *IntWW 91, Who 92*
**Calvet**, James P 1945- *AmMWSc 92*
**Calvey**, Brian J. 1949- *WhoAmL 92*
**Calvey**, Faye Lorraine 1943- *WhoAmL 92*
**Calvillo**, David Neal 1960- *WhoHisp 92*
**Calvillo**, Evelyn Ruiz 1943- *WhoHisp 92*
**Calvin**, Clyde Lacey 1934- *AmMWSc 92*
**Calvin**, Darrell Somerset 1940- *WhoEnt 92*
**Calvin**, Donald Lee 1931- *WhoFI 92*
**Calvin**, Dorothy Ver Strate 1929- *WhoFI 92, WhoWest 92*
**Calvin**, Earl David 1934- *WhoBlA 92*
**Calvin**, Harold I 1936- *AmMWSc 92*
**Calvin**, Henry *WrDr 92*
**Calvin**, Larry Nelson 1946- *WhoRel 92*
**Calvin**, Lyle D 1923- *AmMWSc 92*
**Calvin**, Matthews 1938- *WhoEnt 92*
**Calvin**, Melvin 1911- *AmMWSc 92, FacFETw, IntWW 91, Who 92, WhoNob 90, WhoWest 92, WrDr 92*
**Calvin**, Michael Byron *WhoBlA 92*
**Calvin**, Samuel 1840-1911 *BiInAmS*
**Calvin**, Stafford Richard 1931- *WhoMW 92*
**Calvin**, Virginia Brown 1945- *WhoBlA 92*
**Calvin**, William H. 1939- *WrDr 92*
**Calvin**, William Howard 1939- *AmMWSc 92*
**Calvin**, Willie J. 1913- *WhoBlA 92*
**Calvino**, Italo 1923-1985 *FacFETw, TwCSFW 91A*
**Calvino**, Italo 1923-1988 *LiExTwC*
**Calvo**, Alberto 1957- *WhoHisp 92*
**Calvo**, Carlos Rafael 1965- *WhoEnt 92*
**Calvo**, David Jaime 1934- *WhoRel 92*
**Calvo**, Edward M *WhoAmP 91*
**Calvo**, Francisco Omar 1948- *WhoHisp 92*
**Calvo**, J. Manuel 1949- *WhoHisp 92*
**Calvo**, Julian S 1939- *WhoAmP 91*
**Calvo**, Manuel Frank 1922- *WhoHisp 92*
**Calvo**, Paul McDonald *WhoAmP 91*
**Calvo**, Roberto Q. *Who 92*
**Calvo-Roth**, Fortuna 1934- *WhoHisp 92*
**Calvo-Sotelo**, Joaquin 1905- *IntWW 91*
**Calvo-Sotelo Bustelo**, Leopoldo 1926- *IntWW 91*
**Calvocoressi**, Peter 1912- *IntAu&W 91, IntWW 91, Who 92, WrDr 92*
**Calvocoressi**, Richard Edward Ion 1951- *Who 92*
**Calys**, Emanuel G 1933- *AmMWSc 92*
**Calzabigi**, Raniero 1714-1795 *BlkwCEP*
**Calzada**, Edelmira C. 1930- *WhoHisp 92*
**Calzada**, Humberto 1944- *WhoHisp 92*
**Calzonetti**, Frank J 1949- *AmMWSc 92*
**Cam**, Theodore Victor 1928- *WhoBlA 92*
**Camacci**, Michael A. 1951- *WhoMW 92*
**Camacho**, Alvro Manuel 1927- *AmMWSc 92*
**Camacho**, Antonio Muna *WhoAmP 91*
**Camacho**, Blanca Ester 1956- *WhoEnt 92*
**Camacho**, Enrique *WhoHisp 92*
**Camacho**, Ernest M. 1944- *WhoHisp 92*
**Camacho**, Francisco *WhoAmP 91*
**Camacho**, Hector 1967- *WhoHisp 92*
**Camacho**, Henry Francis 1930- *WhoFI 92*
**Camacho**, James, Jr. 1956- *WhoHisp 92*
**Camacho**, Marco Antonio 1960- *WhoHisp 92*
**Camacho**, Ralph Alberto 1954- *WhoHisp 92*
**Camacho**, Robert Gregory 1953- *WhoHisp 92*
**Camacho**, Salvador 1942- *WhoHisp 92*
**Camacho**, Tomas Aguon 1933- *WhoRel 92, WhoWest 92*
**Camacho-Gingerich**, Alina Luisa 1947- *WhoHisp 92*
**Camadona**, Juan *WhoHisp 92*
**Camandari**, Manuel Talamas 1917- *WhoRel 92*
**Camara Laye** *LiExTwC*
**Camara**, Assan Musa 1923- *IntWW 91*
**Camara**, Helder Pessoa 1909- *IntWW 91*
**Camarata**, Martin Louis 1934- *WhoWest 92*
**Camarda**, Harry Salvatore 1938- *AmMWSc 92*
**Camarena**, Edward 1938- *WhoHisp 92*
**Camarena Badia**, Vicente 1941- *IntWW 91*
**Camargo**, Francis Javier 1929- *WhoHisp 92*
**Camargo**, Hernando Dominguez *HisDSpE*
**Camargo**, Martin Joseph 1950- *WhoHisp 92*
**Camargo**, Sergio de 1930- *IntWW 91*
**Camargosilva**, Marcos A. 1958- *WhoEnt 92*
**Camarillo**, Albert Michael 1948- *WhoHisp 92*
**Camarillo**, Teresa 1943- *WhoHisp 92*
**Camas**, Marianne Theresa 1954- *WhoEnt 92*
**Cambeiro**, Arturo B. 1932- *WhoHisp 92*
**Cambel**, Ali B 1923- *AmMWSc 92*
**Cambell**, Dennis Royle Farquharson 1907- *Who 92*
**Cambers**, Philip William 1957- *WhoRel 92*
**Cambey**, Leslie Alan 1934- *AmMWSc 92*
**Cambi**, Joseph Armand 1957- *WhoFI 92*
**Cambie**, Richard Conrad 1931- *IntWW 91*
**Cambier**, John C 1948- *AmMWSc 92*
**Cambitoglou**, Alexander *IntWW 91*
**Camblin**, Ron E. 1954- *WhoRel 92*
**Cambon brothers** *FacFETw*
**Cambon**, Jules 1845-1935 *FacFETw*
**Cambon**, Paul 1843-1924 *FacFETw*
**Cambosos**, Bruce Michael 1941- *WhoBlA 92*
**Cambour**, Virginia Staples 1943- *WhoEnt 92*
**Cambreleng**, Churchill Caldom 1786-1862 *DcNCBi 1*
**Cambreling**, Sylvain 1948- *IntWW 91*
**Cambreling**, Sylvian 1948- *WhoEnt 92*
**Cambrice**, Robert Louis 1947- *WhoAmL 92*
**Cambridge**, Alan John 1925- *Who 92*
**Cambridge**, Sydney John Guy 1928- *Who 92*
**Cambridge**, William G. 1931- *WhoAmL 92, WhoMW 92*
**Camburn**, Marvin E 1938- *AmMWSc 92*
**Camden** *BlkwEAR*
**Camden**, Marquess 1930- *Who 92*
**Camden**, John 1925- *IntWW 91, Who 92*
**Camdessus**, Jean-Michel 1933- *IntWW 91*
**Camdessus**, Michel 1933- *Who 92*
**Came**, Paul E 1937- *AmMWSc 92*
**Camenzind**, Mark J 1956- *AmMWSc 92, WhoWest 92*
**Cameo**, Michael Wayne 1948- *WhoFI 92*
**Camera**, Michael J 1954- *WhoAmP 91*
**Camerano**, Fabio Giorgio 1961- *WhoFI 92*
**Camerini**, Mario 1895-1981 *IntDcF 2-2*
**Camerini-Otero**, Rafael Daniel 1947- *AmMWSc 92*
**Camerino**, Steven Victor 1958- *WhoAmL 92*
**Camerius**, James Walter 1939- *WhoMW 92*
**Camerman**, Arthur 1939- *AmMWSc 92*
**Camerman**, Norman 1939- *AmMWSc 92*
**Camero**, Arthur Anthony 1947- *AmMWSc 92*
**Cameron** *Who 92*
**Cameron**, Lord 1900- *Who 92*
**Cameron**, Alan Douglas Edward 1938- *Who 92*
**Cameron**, Alastair Graham Walter 1925- *AmMWSc 92*
**Cameron**, Alexander *ConAu 134*
**Cameron**, Alexander d1781 *DcNCBi 1*
**Cameron**, Alexander Menzies 1930- *AmMWSc 92*
**Cameron**, Allan John 1917- *Who 92*

**Cameron,** Allan Williams 1938- *WhoAmP 91*
**Cameron,** Averil Millicent 1940- *IntWW 91, Who 92*
**Cameron,** Barry Winston 1940- *AmMWSc 92*
**Cameron,** Bennehan 1854-1925 *DcNCBi 1*
**Cameron,** Bert 1959- *BlkOlyM*
**Cameron,** Brett *IntAu&W 91X*
**Cameron,** Bruce 1913-1979 *ConAu 133*
**Cameron,** Bruce Francis 1934- *AmMWSc 92*
**Cameron,** Cara Ebert 1946- *WhoEnt 92*
**Cameron,** Carey 1952- *ConAu 135*
**Cameron,** Carey Marbut 1935- *WhoAmL 92*
**Cameron,** Charles D *ScFEYrs*
**Cameron,** Clive Bremner 1921- *Who 92*
**Cameron,** Clyde Robert 1913- *IntWW 91*
**Cameron,** Colin Campbell 1927- *WhoWest 92*
**Cameron,** Cordon Donald 1950- *WhoEnt 92*
**Cameron,** D Y *IntAu&W 91X*
**Cameron,** David George 1947- *AmMWSc 92*
**Cameron,** David Glen 1934- *AmMWSc 92*
**Cameron,** David Young 1865-1945 *TwCPaSc*
**Cameron,** Deborah 1958- *IntAu&W 91*
**Cameron,** Don Frank 1947- *AmMWSc 92*
**Cameron,** Donald Forbes 1920- *AmMWSc 92*
**Cameron,** Douglas Ewan 1941- *AmMWSc 92*
**Cameron,** Douglas George 1917- *AmMWSc 92*
**Cameron,** Duncan 1777-1853 *DcNCBi 1*
**Cameron,** Duncan Ferguson 1930- *WhoWest 92*
**Cameron,** Duncan MacLean, Jr 1931- *AmMWSc 92*
**Cameron,** Edward Alan 1938- *AmMWSc 92*
**Cameron,** Edward Alexander 1907- *AmMWSc 92*
**Cameron,** Edward Madison, III 1933- *WhoIns 92*
**Cameron,** Eleanor 1912- *IntAu&W 91, WrDr 92*
**Cameron,** Ellen *Who 92*
**Cameron,** Elsa Sue 1939- *WhoWest 92*
**Cameron,** Eric 1936- *TwCPaSc*
**Cameron,** Eugene Foster 1945- *WhoWest 92*
**Cameron,** Eugene Nathan 1910- *AmMWSc 92*
**Cameron,** Eustace John 1913- *Who 92*
**Cameron,** Ewen Donald 1926- *Who 92*
**Cameron,** Francis 1927- *Who 92*
**Cameron,** George Edmund 1911- *Who 92*
**Cameron,** Gordon Roy 1899-1966 *FacFETw*
**Cameron,** Gordon Stewart 1916- *TwCPaSc, Who 92*
**Cameron,** Guy E 1958- *WhoAmP 91*
**Cameron,** Guy Neil 1942- *AmMWSc 92*
**Cameron,** H Ronald 1929- *AmMWSc 92*
**Cameron,** Howard K., Jr. 1930- *WhoBlA 92*
**Cameron,** Ian *IntAu&W 91X, WrDr 92*
**Cameron,** Ian Alexander 1938- *Who 92*
**Cameron,** Ian Rennell 1936- *Who 92*
**Cameron,** Irvine R 1919- *AmMWSc 92*
**Cameron,** Ivan Lee 1934- *AmMWSc 92*
**Cameron,** J A 1929- *AmMWSc 92*
**Cameron,** J. Stephen 1944- *WhoMW 92*
**Cameron,** Jack Lyndon 1961- *WhoBlA 92*
**Cameron,** James 1911-1985 *FacFETw*
**Cameron,** James 1954- *IntMPA 92*
**Cameron,** James Clark 1905- *Who 92*
**Cameron,** James Duke 1925- *WhoAmL 92, WhoAmP 91, WhoWest 92*
**Cameron,** James Malcolm 1930- *Who 92*
**Cameron,** James Munro 1910- *Who 92, WrDr 92*
**Cameron,** James N 1944- *AmMWSc 92*
**Cameron,** James Wagner 1913- *AmMWSc 92*
**Cameron,** Joanna *IntMPA 92, WhoEnt 92*
**Cameron,** John *Who 92*
**Cameron,** John 1939- *AmMWSc 92*
**Cameron,** John Adams 1788-1838 *DcNCBi 1*
**Cameron,** John Alastair 1938- *Who 92*
**Cameron,** John Alexander 1936- *AmMWSc 92*
**Cameron,** John Bell 1939- *Who 92*
**Cameron,** John Charles Finlay 1928- *Who 92*
**Cameron,** John Clifford 1946- *WhoAmL 92*
**Cameron,** John E. 1932- *WhoBlA 92*
**Cameron,** John Robinson 1936- *Who 92*
**Cameron,** John Roderick 1922- *AmMWSc 92*
**Cameron,** John Stanley 1952- *AmMWSc 92*
**Cameron,** John Taylor *Who 92*
**Cameron,** John Watson 1901- *Who 92*
**Cameron,** Joseph A. 1942- *WhoBlA 92*
**Cameron,** Joseph Marion 1922- *AmMWSc 92*
**Cameron,** Judith Elaine Moellering 1943- *WhoWest 92*
**Cameron,** Judith Lynne 1945- *WhoWest 92*
**Cameron,** Julie *WrDr 92*
**Cameron,** Ken 1913- *WhoAmL 92*
**Cameron,** Kenneth 1922- *IntWW 91, Who 92*
**Cameron,** Kim Sterling 1946- *WhoMW 92*
**Cameron,** Kirk 1970- *IntMPA 92*
**Cameron,** Krystol Cornell 1961- *WhoEnt 92*
**Cameron,** Lawrence Michael 1959- *WhoRel 92*
**Cameron,** Lenore Hopewell 1945- *WhoBlA 92*
**Cameron,** Lewis 1935- *Who 92*
**Cameron,** Lorna *IntAu&W 91X*
**Cameron,** Lou 1924- *TwCWW 91, WrDr 92*
**Cameron,** Louis McDuffy 1935- *AmMWSc 92*
**Cameron,** Margaret Davis 1920- *AmMWSc 92*
**Cameron,** Marvin Glen 1953- *WhoRel 92*
**Cameron,** Mary Evelyn 1944- *WhoBlA 92*
**Cameron,** Nicholas Allen 1939- *WhoFI 92*
**Cameron,** Norman 1905-1953 *RfGEnL 91*
**Cameron,** Paul Archibald, Jr. 1931- *WhoFI 92*
**Cameron,** Paul Carrington 1808-1891 *DcNCBi 1*
**Cameron,** Peter Alfred Gordon 1930- *WhoFI 92*
**Cameron,** Peter Duncanson 1952- *IntWW 91*
**Cameron,** Prudence Lanegran 1934- *WhoAmP 91*
**Cameron,** Randolph W. *WhoBlA 92*
**Cameron,** Richard Irwin 1941- *WhoFI 92*
**Cameron,** Richfield J 1921- *WhoIns 92*
**Cameron,** Robert Alan 1926- *AmMWSc 92*
**Cameron,** Robert Horton 1908- *AmMWSc 92*
**Cameron,** Rondo 1925- *WrDr 92*
**Cameron,** Rosaline Briskin *WhoEnt 92*
**Cameron,** Ross G 1949- *AmMWSc 92*
**Cameron,** Roy 1929- *AmMWSc 92*
**Cameron,** Roy Eugene 1929- *WhoFI 92, WhoWest 92*
**Cameron,** Roy James 1923- *IntWW 91, Who 92*
**Cameron,** Sam Archie 1943-1988 *WhoBlA 92N*
**Cameron,** Sheila Morag Clark 1934- *Who 92*
**Cameron,** Silver Donald 1937- *IntAu&W 91, WrDr 92*
**Cameron,** Simon 1799-1889 *AmPolLe*
**Cameron,** Stuart Gordon 1924- *Who 92*
**Cameron,** T Stanley 1942- *AmMWSc 92*
**Cameron,** Ulysses 1930- *WhoBlA 92*
**Cameron,** Wilburn Macio, Jr. *WhoBlA 92*
**Cameron,** William Duncan 1925- *WhoFI 92*
**Cameron,** William Edward 1950- *AmMWSc 92*
**Cameron,** William Wright 1941- *WhoWest 92*
**Cameron,** Winifred Sawtell 1918- *AmMWSc 92*
**Cameron Of Lochbroom,** Baron 1931- *IntWW 91, Who 92*
**Cameron of Lochiel,** Donald 1910- *Who 92*
**Cameron-Ramsay-Fairfax-Lucy** *Who 92*
**Cameron Watt,** Donald 1928- *IntAu&W 91, IntWW 91, Who 92, WrDr 92*
**Cami,** Foto 1925- *IntWW 91*
**Camic,** David Edward 1954- *WhoAmL 92*
**Camic,** Paul Marc 1955- *WhoMW 92*
**Camiel,** Peter J. d1991 *NewYTBS 91*
**Camien,** Merrill Nelson 1920- *AmMWSc 92*
**Camiener,** Gerald Walter 1932- *AmMWSc 92*
**Camilion,** Oscar Hector 1930- *IntWW 91*
**Camilleri,** Charles 1931- *ConCom 92, IntWW 91*
**Camilleri,** Victor 1942- *Who 92*
**Camillo,** Victor Peter 1945- *AmMWSc 92*
**Camilo,** Michel 1954- *WhoHisp 92*
**Camin,** Baldwin Albert 1940- *WhoRel 92*
**Caminetti,** Anthony 1854-1923 *DcAmImH*
**Caming,** H. W. William 1919- *WhoAmL 92*
**Caminiti,** Donald Angelo *WhoAmL 92*
**Caminos,** Maria A. Caminos 1941- *WhoHisp 92*
**Camisi,** Domenick J. 1947- *WhoFI 92*
**Camiz,** Sergio 1946- *AmMWSc 92*
**Camm,** A John 1947- *Who 92*
**Camm,** Beatrice *TwCPaSc*
**Camma,** Philip 1923- *WhoFI 92, WhoMW 92*
**Cammack,** Charles Lee, Jr. 1954- *WhoBlA 92*
**Cammaker,** Sheldon Ira 1939- *WhoAmL 92*
**Cammalleri,** Joseph Anthony 1935- *WhoWest 92*
**Cammann,** Helmuth Carl 1927- *IntWW 91*
**Cammarata,** John 1922- *AmMWSc 92*
**Cammarata,** Joseph 1958- *WhoAmL 92*
**Cammarata,** Peter S 1920- *AmMWSc 92*
**Cammell,** John Ernest 1932- *Who 92*
**Cammen,** Leon Matthew 1949- *AmMWSc 92*
**Camner,** Howard *DrAPF 91*
**Camougis,** George 1930- *AmMWSc 92*
**Camoys,** Baron 1940- *IntWW 91, Who 92*
**Camp,** Albert T 1920- *AmMWSc 92*
**Camp,** Alida Diane 1955- *WhoAmL 92*
**Camp,** Bennie Joe 1927- *AmMWSc 92*
**Camp,** Billy Joe 1938- *WhoAmP 91*
**Camp,** Carolyn Hopkins 1939- *WhoEnt 92*
**Camp,** Colleen 1953- *IntMPA 92*
**Camp,** Cordelia 1884-1973 *DcNCBi 1*
**Camp,** Dave 1953- *AlmAP 92 [port], WhoMW 92*
**Camp,** David Conrad 1934- *AmMWSc 92*
**Camp,** David Lee 1953- *WhoAmP 91*
**Camp,** David Thomas 1937- *AmMWSc 92, WhoMW 92*
**Camp,** Earl D 1918- *AmMWSc 92*
**Camp,** Eldridge Kimbel 1915- *AmMWSc 92*
**Camp,** Frank A, III 1947- *AmMWSc 92*
**Camp,** Frederick William 1934- *AmMWSc 92*
**Camp,** George 1926- *WhoAmP 91*
**Camp,** Greg Alan 1960- *WhoWest 92*
**Camp,** Haney Bolon 1938- *AmMWSc 92*
**Camp,** Herbert Latimer 1939- *WhoAmL 92*
**Camp,** Herbert V, Jr 1935- *WhoAmP 91*
**Camp,** Jack Tarpley, Jr. 1943- *WhoAmL 92*
**Camp,** James *DrAPF 91*
**Camp,** Jeffery Bruce *Who 92*
**Camp,** Jeffery Bruce 1923- *IntWW 91*
**Camp,** Jeffrey 1923- *TwCPaSc*
**Camp,** Jimmy D. 1954- *WhoRel 92*
**Camp,** Joe 1939- *IntMPA 92*
**Camp,** John 1939- *WhoAmP 91*
**Camp,** John Michael Francis 1915- *IntAu&W 91*
**Camp,** Joseph Shelton, Jr. 1939- *WhoEnt 92*
**Camp,** Kimberly Noreen 1956- *WhoBlA 92*
**Camp,** Lewis F., Jr. *WhoAmL 92*
**Camp,** Mark Jeffrey 1947- *AmMWSc 92*
**Camp,** Marva Jo 1961- *WhoAmL 92, WhoBlA 92*
**Camp,** Max Wayne 1935- *WhoEnt 92*
**Camp,** Pamela Jean 1954- *AmMWSc 92*
**Camp,** Paul R 1919- *AmMWSc 92*
**Camp,** Robert Gounod, Sr. 1915- *WhoWest 92*
**Camp,** Ronald Lee 1944- *AmMWSc 92*
**Camp,** Ronnie Wayne 1943- *AmMWSc 92*
**Camp,** Russell R 1941- *AmMWSc 92*
**Camp,** Sokari Douglas 1958- *TwCPaSc*
**Camp,** Thomas Edward 1929- *WhoRel 92*
**Camp,** William C *WhoAmP 91, WhoWest 92*
**Camp,** William Newton Alexander 1926- *Who 92*
**Campagna,** Richard Vincent 1952- *WhoAmL 92*
**Campagne,** Thomas Elmer 1950- *WhoAmL 92*
**Campagnola,** Gino *IntMPA 92*
**Campagnoni,** Anthony Thomas 1941- *AmMWSc 92*
**Campaigne,** Ernest Edwin 1914- *AmMWSc 92, WhoMW 92*
**Campana,** Ana Isabel 1934- *WhoFI 92*
**Campana,** Dino 1885-1932 *DcLB 114 [port], FacFETw*
**Campana,** Joseph E. 1952- *WhoFI 92, WhoMW 92*
**Campana,** Michael Emerson 1948- *WhoWest 92*
**Campana,** Richard John 1918- *AmMWSc 92*
**Campanella,** Americo 1922- *WhoAmP 91*
**Campanella,** Joseph 1927- *WhoEnt 92*
**Campanella,** Migdalia Cavazos 1961- *WhoHisp 92*
**Campanella,** Roy 1921- *FacFETw [port]*
**Campanella,** Roy, Sr. 1921- *WhoBlA 92*
**Campanella,** Samuel Joseph 1926- *AmMWSc 92*
**Campanella,** Tom *IntMPA 92*
**Campanella,** Tommaso 1568-1639 *ScFEYrs*
**Campanelli,** John A 1918- *WhoAmP 91*
**Campaneris,** Bert 1942- *WhoHisp 92*
**Campanini,** Cleofonte 1860-1919 *NewAmDM*
**Campany,** Andrew Daniel 1956- *WhoWest 92*
**Camparo,** James Charles 1956- *AmMWSc 92*
**Campbell** *Who 92*
**Campbell,** Ada Marie 1920- *AmMWSc 92*
**Campbell,** Alan 1919- *Who 92*
**Campbell,** Alan 1944- *AmMWSc 92*
**Campbell,** Alan Hugh 1919- *IntWW 91*
**Campbell,** Alan Richard William 1937- *WhoRel 92*
**Campbell,** Alex 1932- *TwCPaSc*
**Campbell,** Alexander 1788-1866 *AmPeW*
**Campbell,** Alexander Bradshaw 1933- *IntWW 91, Who 92*
**Campbell,** Alexander Buchanan 1914- *Who 92*
**Campbell,** Alexander Colin 1908- *Who 92*
**Campbell,** Alexander Elmslie 1929- *Who 92*
**Campbell,** Alice del Campillo 1928- *AmMWSc 92*
**Campbell,** Alie Michael *WhoEnt 92*
**Campbell,** Alistair 1925- *ConPo 91, RfGEnL 91, WrDr 92*
**Campbell,** Alistair Te Ariki 1925- *IntAu&W 91*
**Campbell,** Alister Bruce 1948- *WhoWest 92*
**Campbell,** Allan Adams, Jr. 1945- *WhoAmL 92*
**Campbell,** Allan Barrie 1923- *AmMWSc 92*
**Campbell,** Allan McCulloch 1929- *AmMWSc 92, IntWW 91*
**Campbell,** Alma Porter 1948- *WhoBlA 92*
**Campbell,** Andrew Edward 1962- *WhoMW 92*
**Campbell,** Andrew Garrett 1960- *WhoWest 92*
**Campbell,** Andrew Prescott 1965- *WhoMW 92*
**Campbell,** Andrew Robert 1954- *WhoWest 92*
**Campbell,** Anthony *Who 92*
**Campbell,** Antoine LaMont 1954- *WhoRel 92*
**Campbell,** Archibald 1914- *Who 92*
**Campbell,** Arthur B 1943- *AmMWSc 92*
**Campbell,** Arthur Carlyle 1894-1977 *DcNCBi 1*
**Campbell,** Arthur McLure 1932- *Who 92*
**Campbell,** Arthur Ree 1943- *WhoBlA 92*
**Campbell,** Arthur Waldron 1944- *WhoWest 92*
**Campbell,** Barbara Ellen 1926- *WhoRel 92*
**Campbell,** Barbara J *WhoAmP 91*
**Campbell,** Barbara Seim 1932- *WhoAmP 91*
**Campbell,** Barry Keith 1947- *WhoAmP 91*
**Campbell,** Bartley 1843-1888 *BenetAL 91*
**Campbell,** Beatrice Murphy 1908- *WhoBlA 92*
**Campbell,** Ben D 1947- *WhoAmP 91*
**Campbell,** Ben Henry 1948- *WhoMW 92*
**Campbell,** Ben Nighthorse *NewYTBS 91 [port]*
**Campbell,** Ben Nighthorse 1933- *AlmAP 92 [port], WhoAmP 91, WhoWest 92*
**Campbell,** Benedict James 1927- *AmMWSc 92*
**Campbell,** Bernerd Eugene 1938- *AmMWSc 92, WhoMW 92*
**Campbell,** Bertrand Charles 1941- *WhoAmP 91*
**Campbell,** Blanch 1941- *WhoBlA 92*
**Campbell,** Bobby Lamar 1949- *WhoBlA 92*
**Campbell,** Bonita Jean 1943- *AmMWSc 92*
**Campbell,** Bonnalie Oetting 1933- *AmMWSc 92*
**Campbell,** Bonnie 1948- *WhoAmP 91*
**Campbell,** Bonnie Jean 1948- *WhoAmL 92, WhoMW 92*
**Campbell,** Brenda C. 1957- *WhoRel 92*
**Campbell,** Bruce, Jr 1931- *AmMWSc 92*
**Campbell,** Bruce Carleton 1949- *AmMWSc 92*
**Campbell,** Bruce Henry 1940- *AmMWSc 92*
**Campbell,** Bud 1938- *WhoAmP 91*
**Campbell,** Byron *WhoAmP 91*
**Campbell,** C K 1927- *AmMWSc 92*
**Campbell,** Calvin C. 1924- *WhoBlA 92*
**Campbell,** Carl Merritt, III 1960- *WhoFI 92*
**Campbell,** Carl Walter 1929- *AmMWSc 92*
**Campbell,** Carlos, Sr. 1946- *WhoBlA 92*
**Campbell,** Carlos Boyd Godfrey 1934- *AmMWSc 92*
**Campbell,** Carlos C 1937- *WhoAmP 91*
**Campbell,** Carlos Cardozo 1937- *WhoBlA 92*
**Campbell,** Caroline Krause 1926- *WhoFI 92*
**Campbell,** Carolyn Milburn 1961- *WhoAmL 92*
**Campbell,** Carrol Nunn 1952- *WhoBlA 92*
**Campbell,** Carroll A., Jr. 1940- *AlmAP 92 [port]*

**Campbell,** Carroll Ashmore 1940- *IntWW 91*
**Campbell,** Carroll Ashmore, Jr 1940- *WhoAmP 91*
**Campbell,** Catherine Chase 1905- *AmMWSc 92*
**Campbell,** Catherine Mary 1956- *WhoEnt 92*
**Campbell,** Chalen J. 1937- *WhoRel 92*
**Campbell,** Charlene Marie 1949- *WhoEnt 92*
**Campbell,** Charles Alton 1944- *WhoFI 92*
**Campbell,** Charles Edgar 1921- *AmMWSc 92*
**Campbell,** Charles Edward 1942- *WhoAmL 92*
**Campbell,** Charles Edwin 1942- *AmMWSc 92*
**Campbell,** Charles Everett 1933- *WhoBlA 92*
**Campbell,** Charles J 1915- *AmMWSc 92*
**Campbell,** Charles Peter 1926- *Who 92*
**Campbell,** Charlotte Catherine 1914- *AmMWSc 92*
**Campbell,** Cheryl 1949- *Who 92*
**Campbell,** Cheryl Nichols 1948- *WhoMW 92*
**Campbell,** Christopher 1908- *TwCPaSc*
**Campbell,** Christopher 1952- *WhoEnt 92*
**Campbell,** Christopher James 1936- *Who 92*
**Campbell,** Clair Gilliland 1961- *WhoAmL 92*
**Campbell,** Clarence L, Jr 1921- *AmMWSc 92*
**Campbell,** Clarence Southerland 1905-1977 *FacFETw*
**Campbell,** Clement, Jr 1930- *AmMWSc 92*
**Campbell,** Cliff *TwCWW 91*
**Campbell,** Clifford 1892- *Who 92*
**Campbell,** Clifford Clarence 1892- *IntWW 91*
**Campbell,** Clifford V 1921- *WhoAmP 91*
**Campbell,** Clifton *TwCPaSc*
**Campbell,** Clyde Del 1930- *AmMWSc 92*
**Campbell,** Clyde Harvey, Jr. 1928- *WhoFI 92*
**Campbell,** Colin *Who 92*
**Campbell,** Colin 1927- *AmMWSc 92*
**Campbell,** Colin Dearborn 1917- *WhoFI 92*
**Campbell,** Colin Francis 1951- *WhoAmL 92*
**Campbell,** Colin Herald 1911- *WhoWest 92*
**Campbell,** Colin Judson 1962- *WhoEnt 92*
**Campbell,** Colin Kydd 1927- *IntWW 91*
**Campbell,** Colin Malcolm 1953- *Who 92*
**Campbell,** Colin Moffat 1925- *Who 92*
**Campbell,** Colin Murray 1944- *IntWW 91, Who 92*
**Campbell,** Courtney Lee 1957- *WhoAmL 92*
**Campbell,** Craig Bartlett 1938- *WhoAmP 91*
**Campbell,** Craig Eaton 1952- *WhoWest 92*
**Campbell,** Cynthia Ann 1960- *WhoRel 92*
**Campbell,** Dan Norvell 1928- *AmMWSc 92*
**Campbell,** David Brian 1957- *WhoAmP 91*
**Campbell,** David Charles *WhoFI 92*
**Campbell,** David Gwynne 1930- *WhoFI 92*
**Campbell,** David John G. *Who 92*
**Campbell,** David Kelly 1944- *AmMWSc 92*
**Campbell,** David Lee 1955- *WhoAmL 92*
**Campbell,** David Lloyd 1941- *WhoRel 92*
**Campbell,** David Owen 1927- *AmMWSc 92*
**Campbell,** David Paul 1944- *AmMWSc 92*
**Campbell,** David White 1945- *WhoFI 92*
**Campbell,** Dawson Allen 1912- *WhoWest 92*
**Campbell,** Demarest Lindsay *WhoEnt 92, WhoWest 92*
**Campbell,** Denise St. Peter 1959- *WhoWest 92*
**Campbell,** Dennis George 1949- *WhoFI 92*
**Campbell,** Dennis Marion 1945- *WhoRel 92*
**Campbell,** Dennis Miles 1952- *WhoFI 92*
**Campbell,** Diana Butt 1943- *WhoAmL 92*
**Campbell,** Dick C. 1903- *WhoBlA 92*
**Campbell,** Doak Sheridan 1945- *WhoAmP 91*
**Campbell,** Don 1922-1991 *ConAu 135*
**Campbell,** Donald 1930- *Who 92*
**Campbell,** Donald 1940- *ConPo 91, IntAu&W 91, WrDr 92*
**Campbell,** Donald A 1922- *WhoAmP 91*
**Campbell,** Donald Bruce 1942- *AmMWSc 92*
**Campbell,** Donald Edward 1928- *AmMWSc 92*
**Campbell,** Donald Fisher 1909- *WhoRel 92*
**Campbell,** Donald Graham 1925- *WhoFI 92*
**Campbell,** Donald K. 1926- *WhoRel 92*
**Campbell,** Donald L 1940- *AmMWSc 92*
**Campbell,** Donald le Strange 1919- *Who 92*
**Campbell,** Donald Malcolm 1921-1967 *FacFETw*
**Campbell,** Donald Perry 1951- *WhoRel 92*
**Campbell,** Donald R 1930- *AmMWSc 92*
**Campbell,** Douglas 1896-1990 *FacFETw*
**Campbell,** Douglas Argyle 1929- *WhoFI 92, WhoWest 92*
**Campbell,** Douglas G. *DrAPF 91*
**Campbell,** Douglas Michael 1943- *AmMWSc 92, WhoWest 92*
**Campbell,** Douglass 1919- *WhoFI 92*
**Campbell,** Duncan 1935- *Who 92*
**Campbell,** Dwayne Louis 1944- *WhoRel 92*
**Campbell,** E. Alexander 1927- *WhoBlA 92*
**Campbell,** Earl Christian 1955- *WhoBlA 92*
**Campbell,** Earl William *AmMWSc 92*
**Campbell,** Edward Adolph 1936- *WhoMW 92*
**Campbell,** Edward Charles 1913- *AmMWSc 92*
**Campbell,** Edward Clinton 1929- *WhoFI 92*
**Campbell,** Edward Fay, Jr. 1932- *WhoRel 92*
**Campbell,** Edward J *AmMWSc 92*
**Campbell,** Edward J Moran 1925- *AmMWSc 92*
**Campbell,** Edward L. 1950- *WhoAmL 92*
**Campbell,** Edwin Stewart 1926- *AmMWSc 92*
**Campbell,** Elden Jerome 1968- *WhoBlA 92*
**Campbell,** Emmett Earle 1927- *WhoBlA 92*
**Campbell,** Emory Shaw 1941- *WhoBlA 92*
**Campbell,** Eunice M 1920- *WhoAmP 91*
**Campbell,** Everett O. 1934- *WhoBlA 92*
**Campbell,** Ewing *DrAPF 91*
**Campbell,** Farquhard 1730?-1808 *DcNCBi 1*
**Campbell,** Fergus William 1924- *IntWW 91, Who 92*
**Campbell,** Ferrell Rulon 1937- *AmMWSc 92*
**Campbell,** Finley Alexander 1927- *AmMWSc 92, IntWW 91*
**Campbell,** Foster L, Jr 1947- *WhoAmP 91*
**Campbell,** Francis James 1924- *AmMWSc 92*
**Campbell,** Francis Stuart *WrDr 92*
**Campbell,** Frank Ross 1936- *WhoRel 92*
**Campbell,** Franklin Carter 1958- *WhoMW 92*
**Campbell,** Franklyn D. 1947- *WhoBlA 92*
**Campbell,** Frederick Hollister 1923- *WhoWest 92*
**Campbell,** G. S. 1940- *WrDr 92*
**Campbell,** Gary Homer *AmMWSc 92*
**Campbell,** Gary Lloyd 1951- *WhoBlA 92*
**Campbell,** Gary Martin 1932- *WhoWest 92*
**Campbell,** Gary Thomas 1946- *AmMWSc 92*
**Campbell,** Gaylon Sanford 1940- *AmMWSc 92, WhoWest 92*
**Campbell,** Gene *WhoAmP 91*
**Campbell,** George 1719-1796 *BlkwCEP*
**Campbell,** George 1916- *ConPo 91*
**Campbell,** George 1917- *TwCPaSc*
**Campbell,** George, Jr. 1945- *WhoBlA 92*
**Campbell,** George Anthony 1952- *WhoAmP 91*
**Campbell,** George Emerson 1932- *WhoAmL 92, WhoFI 92*
**Campbell,** George Lynn 1944-1988 *WhoBlA 92N*
**Campbell,** George Melvin 1929- *AmMWSc 92*
**Campbell,** George S 1926- *AmMWSc 92*
**Campbell,** George W 1922- *WhoAmP 91*
**Campbell,** George Washington, Jr 1919- *AmMWSc 92*
**Campbell,** Gerald Allan 1946- *AmMWSc 92*
**Campbell,** Gertrude M. 1923- *WhoBlA 92*
**Campbell,** Gilbert Godfrey 1920- *WhoBlA 92*
**Campbell,** Gilbert Sadler 1924- *AmMWSc 92*
**Campbell,** Glen 1936- *IntMPA 92, WhoEnt 92*
**Campbell,** Gordon Muir 1948- *WhoWest 92*
**Campbell,** Graham F. 1939- *WhoBlA 92*
**Campbell,** Graham Gordon 1924- *Who 92*
**Campbell,** Graham Hays 1936- *AmMWSc 92*
**Campbell,** Graham Le Mesurier 1941- *AmMWSc 92*
**Campbell,** Gregory August 1941- *AmMWSc 92*
**Campbell,** Gregory Ray 1955- *WhoWest 92*
**Campbell,** Grover R 1954- *WhoAmP 91*
**Campbell,** Guy 1910- *Who 92*
**Campbell,** H R 1929- *WhoAmP 91*
**Campbell,** Hallock Cowles 1910- *AmMWSc 92*
**Campbell,** Hamish Manus 1905- *Who 92*
**Campbell,** Harold Alexander 1909- *AmMWSc 92*
**Campbell,** Harold Edward 1915- *Who 92*
**Campbell,** Harry Woodson 1946- *WhoWest 92*
**Campbell,** Helen Jean *WhoEnt 92*
**Campbell,** Henry *TwCPaSc*
**Campbell,** Hugh 1916- *Who 92*
**Campbell,** Hugh Hall 1944- *Who 92*
**Campbell,** Iain Malcolm 1940- *AmMWSc 92*
**Campbell,** Ian 1926- *Who 92*
**Campbell,** Ian 1942- *IntAu&W 91, WrDr 92*
**Campbell,** Ian Barclay 1916- *WrDr 92*
**Campbell,** Ian Burns 1938- *Who 92*
**Campbell,** Ian David 1945- *WhoEnt 92, WhoWest 92*
**Campbell,** Ian Dugald 1916- *Who 92*
**Campbell,** Ian James 1923- *Who 92*
**Campbell,** Ian Macdonald 1922- *Who 92*
**Campbell,** Ian McIvor, Mrs. *Who 92*
**Campbell,** Ian Robert 1920- *Who 92*
**Campbell,** Ian Ross 1900- *Who 92*
**Campbell,** Ian Tofts 1923- *Who 92*
**Campbell,** Ila Jean 1949- *WhoWest 92*
**Campbell,** Irene Elizabeth 1937- *WhoAmL 92*
**Campbell,** J. Cameron 1943- *WhoFI 92*
**Campbell,** Jack Dee 1928- *WhoFI 92*
**Campbell,** Jack James Ramsay 1918- *AmMWSc 92*
**Campbell,** James 1700?-1780 *DcNCBi 1*
**Campbell,** James 1907- *AmMWSc 92*
**Campbell,** James 1935- *Who 92*
**Campbell,** James A. 1920-1982 *WhoBlA 92N*
**Campbell,** James A 1928- *AmMWSc 92*
**Campbell,** James Alexander 1913- *AmMWSc 92*
**Campbell,** James Archibald 1862-1934 *DcNCBi 1*
**Campbell,** James Arthur 1916- *AmMWSc 92*
**Campbell,** James Arthur 1924- *WhoMW 92*
**Campbell,** James B 1939- *AmMWSc 92*
**Campbell,** James Edward 1917- *AmMWSc 92*
**Campbell,** James Edward 1961- *WhoWest 92*
**Campbell,** James Franklin 1941- *AmMWSc 92*
**Campbell,** James Fulton 1932- *AmMWSc 92*
**Campbell,** James Howard, Jr. 1958- *WhoFI 92*
**Campbell,** James Hugh 1926- *Who 92*
**Campbell,** James L 1924- *AmMWSc 92*
**Campbell,** James Lawrence 1928- *WhoEnt 92*
**Campbell,** James Marshall 1942- *WhoAmP 91*
**Campbell,** James Nicoll 1930- *AmMWSc 92*
**Campbell,** James Otis 1955- *WhoFI 92*
**Campbell,** James Robert 1942- *WhoFI 92*
**Campbell,** James Stewart 1923- *AmMWSc 92*
**Campbell,** James W *WhoAmP 91*
**Campbell,** James W. 1945- *WhoBlA 92*
**Campbell,** James Wayne 1932- *AmMWSc 92*
**Campbell,** Jane Louise 1953- *WhoAmP 91*
**Campbell,** Jean 1925- *WhoFI 92*
**Campbell,** Jeffrey Dean 1955- *WhoMW 92*
**Campbell,** Jeptha Edward, Jr 1923- *AmMWSc 92*
**Campbell,** Joan 1929- *WhoFI 92*
**Campbell,** Joan Brown *WhoRel 92*
**Campbell,** Joe Bill 1943- *WhoAmL 92*
**Campbell,** John 1653-1728 *BenetAL 91*
**Campbell,** John 1700?-1781 *DcNCBi 1*
**Campbell,** John 1705-1782 *BlkwEAR*
**Campbell,** John 1934- *WhoAmP 91*
**Campbell,** John 1947- *ConAu 35NR*
**Campbell,** John Alexander 1940- *AmMWSc 92*
**Campbell,** John Arthur 1930- *AmMWSc 92*
**Campbell,** John Bryan 1933- *AmMWSc 92*
**Campbell,** John C 1920- *AmMWSc 92*
**Campbell,** John Charles 1867-1919 *BenetAL 91, DcNCBi 1*
**Campbell,** John Coleman 1935- *WhoEnt 92*
**Campbell,** John Davies 1921- *Who 92*
**Campbell,** John Douglas 1943- *WhoRel 92*
**Campbell,** John Duncan 1923- *AmMWSc 92*
**Campbell,** John Frank 1947- *WhoWest 92*
**Campbell,** John H 1847-1897 *BiInAmS*
**Campbell,** John Harl 1944- *WhoAmL 92*
**Campbell,** John Howard 1949- *WhoRel 92*
**Campbell,** John Howland 1938- *AmMWSc 92*
**Campbell,** John Hyde 1947- *AmMWSc 92*
**Campbell,** John Jette 1947- *WhoFI 92*
**Campbell,** John L. 1906- *Who 92*
**Campbell,** John Lyle 1818-1886 *BiInAmS*
**Campbell,** John Lyle 1827-1904 *BiInAmS*
**Campbell,** John Malcolm 1947- *IntAu&W 91*
**Campbell,** John Morgan 1947- *WhoFI 92*
**Campbell,** John Morgan, Sr 1922- *AmMWSc 92*
**Campbell,** John Palmer 1923- *WhoAmP 91*
**Campbell,** John Pendleton 1863-1918 *BiInAmS*
**Campbell,** John Quentin 1939- *Who 92*
**Campbell,** John R 1933- *AmMWSc 92*
**Campbell,** John Raymond 1944- *AmMWSc 92*
**Campbell,** John Richard 1932- *AmMWSc 92*
**Campbell,** John Slater 1944- *WhoAmL 92*
**Campbell,** John TenBrook 1833-1911 *BiInAmS*
**Campbell,** John Tucker 1912- *WhoAmP 91*
**Campbell,** John W 1910-1971 *ConAu 34NR*
**Campbell,** John W, Jr 1910-1971 *TwCSFW 91*
**Campbell,** Joseph 1904-1987 *BenetAL 91, ConLC 69 [port], FacFETw*
**Campbell,** Joseph Albert, III 1953- *WhoEnt 92*
**Campbell,** Joyce *WhoRel 92*
**Campbell,** Joyce Berney 1936- *WhoEnt 92*
**Campbell,** Judith 1914- *IntAu&W 91, WrDr 92*
**Campbell,** Judith Lowe 1946- *WhoMW 92*
**Campbell,** Judith Lynn 1943- *AmMWSc 92*
**Campbell,** Juliet Jeanne d'Auvergne 1935- *IntWW 91, Who 92*
**Campbell,** Karen *IntAu&W 91X, WrDr 92*
**Campbell,** Katherine Ann 1949- *WhoWest 92*
**Campbell,** Katherine Smith 1943- *AmMWSc 92*
**Campbell,** Kathleen Mary 1948- *WhoAmL 92*
**Campbell,** Ken Patrick 1959- *WhoMW 92*
**Campbell,** Kenneth Archibald 1936- *Who 92*
**Campbell,** Kenneth B *AmMWSc 92*
**Campbell,** Kenneth Eugene, Jr 1943- *AmMWSc 92*
**Campbell,** Kenneth Lyle 1948- *AmMWSc 92*
**Campbell,** Kenneth Nielsen 1905- *AmMWSc 92*
**Campbell,** Kenneth Wilford 1942- *AmMWSc 92*
**Campbell,** Kevin Peter 1952- *AmMWSc 92*
**Campbell,** Kevin Richard 1956- *WhoAmL 92*
**Campbell,** Kirby I 1933- *AmMWSc 92*
**Campbell,** Lachlan Ross 1932- *WhoFI 92*
**Campbell,** Larry Enoch 1938- *AmMWSc 92*
**Campbell,** Larry L 1931- *WhoAmP 91*
**Campbell,** Larry N 1946- *AmMWSc 92*
**Campbell,** Laughlin Andrew 1942- *WhoWest 92*
**Campbell,** Laurence Jamieson 1927- *Who 92*
**Campbell,** Laurence Joseph 1937- *AmMWSc 92*
**Campbell,** Lawrence Pike 1922- *WhoFI 92*
**Campbell,** Leila 1911- *Who 92*
**Campbell,** Leslie Hartwell 1892-1970 *DcNCBi 1*
**Campbell,** Levin H *WhoAmP 91*
**Campbell,** Levin Hicks 1927- *WhoAmL 92*
**Campbell,** Linzy Leon 1927- *AmMWSc 92*
**Campbell,** Lois Jeannette 1923- *AmMWSc 92*
**Campbell,** Louis Lorne 1928- *AmMWSc 92*
**Campbell,** Lucie Eddie 1885-1963 *NewAmDM*
**Campbell,** Lucien Benton 1942- *WhoAmL 92*
**Campbell,** Lucinda Solomon 1925- *WhoAmP 91*
**Campbell,** M. Douglas, Jr. 1962- *WhoAmL 92*
**Campbell,** M L *ScFEYrs*
**Campbell,** Malcolm 1885-1949 *FacFETw*
**Campbell,** Malcolm John 1937- *AmMWSc 92*
**Campbell,** Margie 1954- *WhoBlA 92*
**Campbell,** Maria Bouchelle 1944- *WhoAmL 92*
**Campbell,** Maria Dolores Delgado 1943- *WhoHisp 92*
**Campbell,** Marilyn R 1932- *WhoAmP 91*
**Campbell,** Marion 1948- *ConNov 91*

**Campbell**, Mark Gerald 1948- *WhoMW 92*
**Campbell**, Martin James 1965- *WhoWest 92*
**Campbell**, Marty *DrAPF 91*
**Campbell**, Mary Allison 1937- *WhoBlA 92*
**Campbell**, Mary Belle *DrAPF 91*
**Campbell**, Mary Beth 1952- *WhoAmL 92*
**Campbell**, Mary Delois 1940- *WhoBlA 92*
**Campbell**, Mary Kathleen 1944- *WhoFI 92, WhoWest 92*
**Campbell**, Mary Kathryn 1939- *AmMWSc 92*
**Campbell**, Mary Schmidt 1947- *WhoBlA 92*
**Campbell**, Marybelle Schmitt 1923- *WhoAmP 91*
**Campbell**, Matthew 1907- *Who 92*
**Campbell**, Maura *WhoRel 92*
**Campbell**, Menzies *Who 92*
**Campbell**, Michael David 1941- *AmMWSc 92*
**Campbell**, Michael Edward 1947- *WhoFI 92*
**Campbell**, Michael Floyd 1942- *AmMWSc 92, WhoMW 92*
**Campbell**, Michael Lee 1958- *WhoWest 92*
**Campbell**, Michael Leonard 1945- *WhoAmL 92, WhoMW 92*
**Campbell**, Milton 1933- *WhoBlA 92*
**Campbell**, Milton Gray 1934- *BlkOlyM*
**Campbell**, Milton Hugh 1928- *AmMWSc 92*
**Campbell**, Naomi 1970- *ConBlB 1 [port]*
**Campbell**, Neil John 1925- *AmMWSc 92*
**Campbell**, Newton Allen 1928- *WhoFI 92*
**Campbell**, Niall 1925- *Who 92*
**Campbell**, Niall Gordon 1941- *Who 92*
**Campbell**, Norman *LesBEnT 92*
**Campbell**, Norman E Ross 1920- *AmMWSc 92*
**Campbell**, Olive 1822- *BenetAL 91*
**Campbell**, Olive Dame 1882-1954 *DcNCBi 1*
**Campbell**, Orland 1942- *WhoAmP 91*
**Campbell**, Otis, Jr. 1953- *WhoBlA 92*
**Campbell**, Otis Levy 1935- *WhoBlA 92*
**Campbell**, Patricia J 1930- *ConAu 35NR*
**Campbell**, Patton 1926- *WhoEnt 92*
**Campbell**, Patty *ConAu 35NR*
**Campbell**, Paul Barton 1930- *WhoAmL 92*
**Campbell**, Paul Gilbert 1925- *AmMWSc 92*
**Campbell**, Paul N. 1923- *WrDr 92*
**Campbell**, Paula Marie 1943- *WhoAmP 91*
**Campbell**, Paulina Yager 1927- *WhoAmP 91*
**Campbell**, Peter *Who 92*
**Campbell**, Peter 1926- *WrDr 92*
**Campbell**, Peter 1931- *TwCPaSc*
**Campbell**, Peter Hallock 1940- *AmMWSc 92*
**Campbell**, Peter Nelson 1921- *Who 92*
**Campbell**, Peter Walter 1926- *Who 92*
**Campbell**, Phil 1928- *WhoFI 92*
**Campbell**, Phillip Craig 1952- *WhoRel 92*
**Campbell**, Pollyann S. 1949- *WhoAmL 92*
**Campbell**, Priscilla Ann 1940- *AmMWSc 92*
**Campbell**, Quentin *Who 92*
**Campbell**, R. Nelson 1964- *WhoFI 92*
**Campbell**, Ralph Edmund 1927- *AmMWSc 92*
**Campbell**, Ramsey 1946- *IntAu&W 91, WrDr 92*
**Campbell**, Randy Linn 1953- *WhoAmP 91*
**Campbell**, Ray *WhoAmP 91*
**Campbell**, Ray Worthy 1955- *WhoAmL 92*
**Campbell**, Raymond Earl 1941- *AmMWSc 92*
**Campbell**, Reginald Lawrence 1943- *WhoWest 92*
**Campbell**, Richard Alden 1926- *WhoWest 92*
**Campbell**, Richard Bruce 1947- *WhoAmL 92*
**Campbell**, Richard Dana 1939- *AmMWSc 92*
**Campbell**, Richard Evens 1928- *WhoMW 92*
**Campbell**, Richard H, Jr 1920- *WhoAmP 91*
**Campbell**, Richard M 1930- *AmMWSc 92*
**Campbell**, Richard P. 1947- *WhoAmL 92*
**Campbell**, Riley Keith 1941- *WhoWest 92*
**Campbell**, Robert 1926- *WrDr 92*
**Campbell**, Robert 1927- *WrDr 92*
**Campbell**, Robert 1929- *Who 92*
**Campbell**, Robert A 1924- *AmMWSc 92*
**Campbell**, Robert Charles 1924- *WhoRel 92*
**Campbell**, Robert Craig, III 1942- *WhoAmL 92*
**Campbell**, Robert Fishburne 1858-1947 *DcNCBi 1*
**Campbell**, Robert Gordon 1922- *WhoEnt 92*
**Campbell**, Robert H. 1937- *WhoFI 92*
**Campbell**, Robert H. 1948- *WhoAmL 92, WhoFI 92*
**Campbell**, Robert J 1937- *WhoAmP 91*
**Campbell**, Robert Louis 1925- *AmMWSc 92*
**Campbell**, Robert M *WhoAmP 91*
**Campbell**, Robert Maurice 1922- *IntMPA 92*
**Campbell**, Robert Noe 1929- *AmMWSc 92*
**Campbell**, Robert Terry 1932- *AmMWSc 92*
**Campbell**, Robert Walter 1934- *WhoFI 92*
**Campbell**, Robert Wayne 1940- *AmMWSc 92*
**Campbell**, Robert William Duncan 1951- *WhoEnt 92*
**Campbell**, Robin Auchinbreck 1922- *Who 92*
**Campbell**, Roderick Samuel Fisher 1924- *IntWW 91*
**Campbell**, Rogers Edward, III 1951- *WhoBlA 92*
**Campbell**, Roland Ramon 1932- *WhoFI 92*
**Campbell**, Ronald 1943- *Who 92*
**Campbell**, Ronald Bruce 1946- *WhoMW 92*
**Campbell**, Ronald Francis Boyd 1912- *Who 92*
**Campbell**, Ronald Hugh 1924- *IntWW 91*
**Campbell**, Ronald Kent 1934- *WhoAmP 91*
**Campbell**, Ronald Michael 1957- *WhoRel 92*
**Campbell**, Ronald Wayne 1919- *AmMWSc 92*
**Campbell**, Ross 1916- *Who 92*
**Campbell**, Ross 1918- *Who 92*
**Campbell**, Roy 1901-1957 *FacFETw, LiExTwC, RfGEnL 91*
**Campbell**, Russell Bruce 1952- *WhoMW 92*
**Campbell**, Russell Harper 1928- *AmMWSc 92*
**Campbell**, Samuel d1790? *DcNCBi 1*
**Campbell**, Samuel George 1961- *WhoFI 92*
**Campbell**, Samuel Gordon 1933- *AmMWSc 92*
**Campbell**, Sandra J *WhoAmP 91*
**Campbell**, Scott 1924- *TwCPaSc*
**Campbell**, Scott G. 1950- *WhoAmL 92*
**Campbell**, Scott Robert 1946- *WhoFI 92*
**Campbell**, Sean P 1952- *WhoAmP 91*
**Campbell**, Selaura Joy 1944- *WhoAmL 92, WhoFI 92*
**Campbell**, Shirley Ann *WhoAmP 91*
**Campbell**, Stephen La Vern 1945- *AmMWSc 92*
**Campbell**, Steven 1953- *TwCPaSc*
**Campbell**, Steven MacMillan 1953- *IntWW 91*
**Campbell**, Stewart John 1947- *AmMWSc 92*
**Campbell**, Susan L 1956- *WhoIns 92*
**Campbell**, Suzann Kay 1943- *AmMWSc 92*
**Campbell**, Sylvan Lloyd 1931- *WhoBlA 92*
**Campbell**, Sylvester Briscoe 1938- *WhoEnt 92*
**Campbell**, Thomas *BenetAL 91*
**Campbell**, Thomas 1777-1844 *RfGEnL 91*
**Campbell**, Thomas C. *Who 92*
**Campbell**, Thomas Colin 1934- *AmMWSc 92*
**Campbell**, Thomas Cooper 1932- *AmMWSc 92*
**Campbell**, Thomas Douglas 1951- *WhoAmL 92*
**Campbell**, Thomas Hodgen 1924- *AmMWSc 92*
**Campbell**, Thomas Humphreys, III 1932- *WhoAmP 91*
**Campbell**, Thomas J. 1952- *WhoAmL 92, WhoWest 92*
**Campbell**, Thomas R, Jr 1940- *WhoAmP 91*
**Campbell**, Thomas W. 1957- *WhoBlA 92*
**Campbell**, Tom 1952- *AlmAP 92 [port], WhoAmP 91*
**Campbell**, Tonie 1960- *BlkOlyM*
**Campbell**, Tony 1962- *WhoBlA 92*
**Campbell**, Travis Austin 1943- *AmMWSc 92*
**Campbell**, Truman F 1928- *WhoAmP 91*
**Campbell**, Virginia Gwen Rush 1939- *WhoFI 92*
**Campbell**, Virginia Wiley 1937- *AmMWSc 92*
**Campbell**, W M 1915- *AmMWSc 92*
**Campbell**, Wallace G, Jr 1930- *AmMWSc 92*
**Campbell**, Wallace Hall 1926- *AmMWSc 92*
**Campbell**, Wallace J. 1910- *ConAu 135*
**Campbell**, Walter 1921- *Who 92*
**Campbell**, Walter Benjamin 1921- *IntWW 91*
**Campbell**, Walter Menzies 1941- *Who 92*
**Campbell**, Walter Stanley 1887-1957 *BenetAL 91*
**Campbell**, Warren Adams 1936- *AmMWSc 92*
**Campbell**, Warren Elwood 1931- *AmMWSc 92*
**Campbell**, Wendell J. 1927- *WhoBlA 92*
**Campbell**, Wesley Allen Douglas 1945- *WhoMW 92*
**Campbell**, Wesley Glenn 1924- *WhoWest 92*
**Campbell**, Wilbur Harold 1945- *AmMWSc 92*
**Campbell**, Wilfred 1861-1918 *BenetAL 91*
**Campbell**, Will Davis 1924- *RelLAm 91*
**Campbell**, William *IntMPA 92*
**Campbell**, William 1906- *AmMWSc 92*
**Campbell**, William 1935- *WhoAmP 91*
**Campbell**, William Andrew 1906- *AmMWSc 92*
**Campbell**, William Anthony 1936- *Who 92*
**Campbell**, William B 1935- *AmMWSc 92*
**Campbell**, William Bryson 1947- *AmMWSc 92*
**Campbell**, William Cecil 1930- *AmMWSc 92*
**Campbell**, William Earl 1965- *WhoBlA 92*
**Campbell**, William Edward 1927- *WhoMW 92*
**Campbell**, William Edward 1946- *WhoFI 92*
**Campbell**, William Edward March *BenetAL 91*
**Campbell**, William Frank 1928- *AmMWSc 92*
**Campbell**, William Gant 1941- *WhoAmL 92*
**Campbell**, William Howard 1942- *AmMWSc 92*
**Campbell**, William Hughes 1956- *WhoFI 92*
**Campbell**, William J *AmMWSc 92*
**Campbell**, William Jackson 1929- *AmMWSc 92*
**Campbell**, William Joseph 1926- *AmMWSc 92*
**Campbell**, William M 1934- *AmMWSc 92*
**Campbell**, William P 1913- *WhoAmP 91*
**Campbell**, William Steen 1919- *WhoFI 92*
**Campbell**, William Tait 1912- *Who 92*
**Campbell**, William Vernon 1924- *AmMWSc 92*
**Campbell**, Willis Preston 1945- *WhoWest 92*
**Campbell**, Woodrow Wilson, Jr. 1944- *WhoAmL 92*
**Campbell-Bannerman**, Henry 1836-1908 *FacFETw*
**Campbell-Bell**, Dorothy Kathryn 1955- *WhoEnt 92*
**Campbell-Gray** *Who 92*
**Campbell-Gray**, Iona 1962- *TwCPaSc*
**Campbell-Johnson**, Alan 1913- *Who 92*
**Campbell-Johnston**, Michael Alexander N 1931- *Who 92*
**Campbell of Airds**, Lorne Maclaine d1991 *Who 92N*
**Campbell of Alloway**, Baron 1917- *Who 92*
**Campbell Of Croy**, Baron 1921- *IntWW 91, Who 92*
**Campbell Of Eskan**, Baron 1912- *IntWW 91, Who 92*
**Campbell of Succoth**, Ilay 1927- *Who 92*
**Campbell Orde**, Alan Colin 1898- *Who 92*
**Campbell-Orde**, John A. *Who 92*
**Campbell-Preston**, Frances 1918- *Who 92*
**Campbell-Preston of Ardchattan**, Robert M 1909- *Who 92*
**Campbell-Savours**, Dale Norman 1943- *Who 92*
**Campbell-White**, Annette Jane 1947- *WhoFI 92*
**Campbell Williams**, Lucie 1885-1962 *NotBlAW 92*
**Campden**, Viscount 1950- *Who 92*
**Campeanu**, Radu Ioan 1949- *AmMWSc 92*
**Campeau**, Robert 1924- *WhoFI 92*
**Campen**, Philippus Canisius Maria van 1911- *IntWW 91*
**Campenot**, Robert Barry 1946- *AmMWSc 92*
**Camper**, Diane G. 1948- *WhoBlA 92*
**Camper**, John Emory Toussaint 1894- *WhoBlA 92*
**Camper**, John Jacob 1943- *WhoMW 92*
**Camper**, John Saxton 1929- *WhoWest 92*
**Camper**, Nyal Dwight 1939- *AmMWSc 92*
**Camper**, Peter 1722-1789 *BlkwCEP*
**Campfield**, Regis William 1942- *WhoAmL 92*
**Camphausen**, Fred Howard 1933- *WhoWest 92*
**Camphor**, Michael Gerard *WhoBlA 92*
**Campillo**, Anthony Joseph 1942- *AmMWSc 92*
**Campion**, Daniel *DrAPF 91*
**Campion**, Harry 1905- *Who 92*
**Campion**, James J 1939- *AmMWSc 92*
**Campion**, Jane *News 91 [port]*
**Campion**, Oliver 1928- *TwCPaSc*
**Campion**, Owen Francis 1940- *WhoRel 92*
**Campion**, Patricia Marie 1947- *WhoFI 92*
**Campion**, Peter James 1926- *Who 92*
**Campion**, Sidney 1891- *TwCPaSc*
**Campion**, Thomas 1567-1620 *CnDBLB 1, NewAmDM, RfGEnL 91*
**Campion**, Thomas Francis 1935- *WhoAmL 92*
**Campisi**, Louis Sebastian 1935- *AmMWSc 92*
**Camplin**, Leonard *WhoEnt 92*
**Campling**, C H R 1922- *AmMWSc 92*
**Campling**, Christopher Russell 1925- *Who 92, WrDr 92*
**Campling**, Elizabeth 1948- *WrDr 92*
**Campman**, Marie Katherine 1917- *WhoAmP 91*
**Campo**, Manuel 1932-1991 *WhoHisp 92N*
**Campo**, Robert D 1930- *AmMWSc 92*
**Campo**, Terry Thomas 1957- *WhoAmP 91*
**Campoamer**, Diana *WhoHisp 92*
**Campobasso**, Eleanor M 1922- *WhoAmP 91*
**Campobello**, Nellie 1900- *SpAmWW*
**Campolattaro**, Alfonso 1933- *AmMWSc 92*
**Campoli**, Alfredo d1991 *Who 92N*
**Campomanes**, Pedro Rodriguez *HisDSpE*
**Campomanes**, Pedro Rodriguez, conde de 1723-1803 *BlkwCEP*
**Camponeschi**, Eugene Thomas, Jr 1955- *AmMWSc 92*
**Campora**, Hector J 1909-1980 *FacFETw*
**Campora**, Mario 1930- *Who 92*
**Camporesi**, Enrico M *AmMWSc 92*
**Campos**, Christophe Lucien 1938- *Who 92*
**Campos**, Eduardo Javier, Sr. 1949- *WhoHisp 92*
**Campos**, Elizabeth Marie 1955- *WhoHisp 92*
**Campos**, Gloria 1954- *WhoHisp 92*
**Campos**, Joaquin Paul, III 1962- *WhoWest 92*
**Campos**, Julieta 1932- *SpAmWW*
**Campos**, Leonard Peter 1932- *WhoWest 92*
**Campos**, Pete 1953- *WhoAmP 91, WhoHisp 92*
**Campos**, Porfirio, Jr. 1941- *WhoHisp 92*
**Campos**, R. Yvonne 1948- *WhoHisp 92*
**Campos**, Rafael 1935- *WhoHisp 92*
**Campos**, Robert 1938- *WhoHisp 92*
**Campos**, Roberto de Oliveira 1917- *Who 92*
**Campos**, Roberto de Oliviera *IntWW 91*
**Campos**, Rodolfo Estuardo 1967- *WhoHisp 92*
**Campos**, Santiago E. 1926- *WhoAmL 92, WhoHisp 92*
**Campos**, Victor Manuel 1942- *WhoHisp 92*
**Campoy**, Sylvia *WhoHisp 92*
**Campra**, Andre 1660-1744 *NewAmDM*
**Campra**, Frances L. 1940- *WhoWest 92*
**Camps**, Jeffrey Lowell 1954- *WhoFI 92*
**Camps**, Luis 1928- *SmATA 66 [port]*
**Camps**, William Anthony 1910- *Who 92*
**Campton**, David 1924- *IntAu&W 91, WrDr 92*
**Campusano**, Silvestre 1966- *WhoHisp 92*
**Camras**, Marvin 1916- *AmMWSc 92*
**Camrass**, David 1939- *TwCPaSc*
**Camrose**, Viscount 1909- *Who 92*
**Camu**, Pierre 1923- *IntWW 91*
**Camurati**, Mireya B. 1934- *WhoHisp 92*
**Camus**, Albert 1913-1960 *ConLC 69 [port], DramC 2 [port], FacFETw [port], GuFrLit 1, ShSCr 9 [port], WhoNob 90*
**Camus**, Edward Poland 1932- *WhoAmL 92*
**Camus**, Raoul Francois 1930- *WhoEnt 92*
**Camwell Ness**, Barbara Lynne 1957- *WhoEnt 92*
**Canaan**, Lee 1931- *WhoEnt 92*
**Canada**, Metropolitan of *Who 92*
**Canada**, Primate of *Who 92*
**Canada**, Primate of All *Who 92*
**Canada**, Andrew Joseph, Jr 1939- *WhoAmP 91*
**Canada**, Benjamin Oleander 1945- *WhoBlA 92*
**Canada**, Bud 1925- *WhoAmP 91*
**Canada**, Cournal 1939- *WhoMW 92*
**Canada**, Ron L. 1949- *WhoMW 92*
**Canaday**, Doris Charlene 1932- *WhoFI 92*
**Canaday**, Marvin Cleveland 1954- *WhoRel 92*
**Canady**, Alexa 1950- *NotBlAW 92*
**Canady**, Alexa I. 1950- *WhoBlA 92*
**Canady**, Blanton Thandreus 1948- *WhoBlA 92*
**Canady**, Charles T 1954- *WhoAmP 91*
**Canady**, Herman G., Jr. *WhoBlA 92*
**Canady**, Hortense Golden 1927- *WhoBlA 92*
**Canady**, Ozrie Young 1940- *WhoMW 92*
**Canady**, William James 1924- *AmMWSc 92*
**Canady-Davis**, Alexa 1950- *WhoBlA 92*

**Canakes**, Stephen George 1950- WhoFI 92
**Canal**, Marguerite 1890-1978 NewAmDM
**Canal-Frederick**, Ghislaine R 1933- AmMWSc 92
**Canale**, Raymond Patrick 1941- AmMWSc 92
**Canale-Parola**, Ercole 1929- AmMWSc 92
**Canales**, Adolph WhoHisp 92
**Canales**, H. Paul WhoHisp 92
**Canales**, Judith Ann 1962- WhoHisp 92
**Canales**, Manuel WhoHisp 92
**Canales**, Maria Cristina 1949- WhoHisp 92
**Canales**, Martin A., Jr. WhoHisp 92
**Canales**, Oscar Mario 1939- WhoHisp 92
**Canales**, Terry A. WhoHisp 92
**Canaletto Canale**, Giovanni Antonio 1697-1768 BlkwCEP
**Canan**, Janine DrAPF 91
**Canan**, Penelope 1946- WhoWest 92
**Canapary**, Herbert C 1932- WhoIns 92
**Canardo**, Hernando Vicente 1957- WhoFI 92
**Canaris**, Wilhelm 1887-1945 EncTR 91 [port], FacFETw
**Canaris**, Wilhelm Franz 1887-1945 BiDExR
**Canary**, John J 1925- AmMWSc 92
**Canary**, Nancy Halliday 1941- WhoAmL 92
**Canary**, Thomas Lynch, Jr. 1959- WhoAmL 92
**Canas**, Alberto J. 1953- WhoHisp 92
**Canas**, Angel 1939- WhoHisp 92
**Canas**, Antonio Jose 1785-1845 HisDSpE
**Canas**, Richard Leon 1941- WhoHisp 92
**Canatsey**, Sandy 1940- WhoAmP 91
**Canavan**, Dennis Andrew 1942- Who 92
**Canavan**, Ellen M 1941- WhoAmP 91
**Canavan**, Robert I 1927- AmMWSc 92
**Canavan**, Thomas Gerard 1953- WhoEnt 92
**Canavan**, Vincent Joseph 1946- Who 92
**Canawati**, Hanna N 1938- AmMWSc 92
**Canaway**, Bill IntAu&W 91X
**Canaway**, W H 1925- IntAu&W 91
**Canberra And Goulburn**, Bishop of 1934- Who 92
**Canby**, Henry Seidel 1878-1961 BenetAL 91
**Canby**, Vincent 1924- IntMPA 92, WhoEnt 92
**Canby**, William C, Jr WhoAmP 91
**Canby**, William Cameron, Jr. 1931- WhoAmL 92, WhoWest 92
**Cancel**, Adrian R. 1946- WhoHisp 92
**Cancel**, Luis R. WhoHisp 92
**Canchiani**, Celia 1949- WhoHisp 92
**Canchola**, Acencion 1934- WhoHisp 92
**Canchola**, Joe Paul 1935- WhoHisp 92
**Canchola**, Jose L. WhoHisp 92
**Canchola**, Joseph Paul, Jr. 1954- WhoHisp 92
**Canchola**, Samuel Victor 1944- WhoHisp 92
**Cancio**, Angela Maria 1955- WhoAmL 92
**Cancio**, Norma Gloria 1961- WhoHisp 92
**Cancro**, Michael P 1949- AmMWSc 92
**Cancro**, Robert 1932- AmMWSc 92
**Candace** EncAmaz 91
**Candace Amanirenas** EncAmaz 91
**Candace Shenakdahkete** EncAmaz 91
**Candal**, Francisco Javier 1952- WhoHisp 92
**Candal**, Luis Fernando 1944- WhoAmL 92
**Candales de Lopez**, Maria D. 1930- WhoHisp 92
**Candau**, Eugenie 1938- WhoWest 92
**Cande**, W Zacheus 1945- AmMWSc 92
**Candea**, Virgil 1927- IntWW 91
**Candee**, Marshall Greene 1915- WhoAmL 92
**Candee**, Michael A. 1954- WhoEnt 92
**Candela**, Felix 1910- IntWW 91
**Candela**, Hilario Francisco 1934- WhoHisp 92
**Candela Outerino**, Felix 1910- Who 92
**Candelaria**, Cordelia Chavez 1943- WhoHisp 92
**Candelaria**, John 1953- WhoHisp 92
**Candelaria**, Michael Richard 1955- WhoHisp 92
**Candelaria**, Nash DrAPF 91
**Candelaria**, Nash 1928- WhoHisp 92
**Candelario**, Eva Nydia 1954- WhoHisp 92
**Candelario**, John S. 1916- WhoHisp 92
**Candelario**, Nilda 1947- WhoHisp 92
**Candelas**, Graciela C 1922- AmMWSc 92
**Cander**, Leon 1926- AmMWSc 92
**Candia**, Oscar A 1935- AmMWSc 92
**Candia**, Ruben Araiza 1938- WhoHisp 92
**Candido**, Edward Peter Mario 1946- AmMWSc 92
**Candilis**, Georges 1913- IntWW 91
**Candilis**, Wray O. 1927- WrDr 92
**Candland**, Douglas Keith 1934- WrDr 92
**Candland**, Shelby Victor 1924- WhoWest 92
**Candler**, Asa Griggs 1851-1929 FacFETw
**Candler**, James Nall, Jr. 1943- WhoAmL 92
**Candler**, Warren Akin 1857-1941 RelLAm 91
**Candlin**, Christopher Noel 1940- Who 92
**Candlin**, Frances Ann 1945- WhoWest 92
**Candlish**, Malcolm 1935- WhoMW 92
**Candlish**, Thomas Tait 1926- Who 92
**Candon**, John C WhoAmP 91
**Candon**, Mary Eva 1950- WhoAmL 92, WhoAmP 91
**Candon**, Patrick James 1908- WhoAmP 91
**Candon**, Thomas Henry WhoAmP 91
**Candris**, Laura A. 1955- WhoAmL 92
**Candy**, Edward 1925- IntAu&W 91, WrDr 92
**Candy**, J C 1929- AmMWSc 92
**Candy**, John 1950- IntMPA 92
**Candy**, John Franklin 1950- WhoEnt 92
**Cane**, David Earl 1944- AmMWSc 92
**Cane**, Louis Paul Joseph 1943- IntWW 91
**Cane**, Mark A 1944- AmMWSc 92
**Cane**, Melville 1879-1980 BenetAL 91
**Cane**, R. Thomas 1939- WhoAmL 92
**Cane**, Violet Rosina 1916- Who 92
**Canel**, Fausto 1939- WhoHisp 92
**Canellakis**, Evangelo S 1922- AmMWSc 92
**Canellakis**, Martin 1942- WhoEnt 92
**Canellakis**, Zoe Nakos 1927- AmMWSc 92
**Canellas**, Dionisio J., IV 1935- WhoHisp 92
**Canellos**, George P 1934- AmMWSc 92
**Canellos**, Peter Constantine 1944- WhoAmL 92
**Canelstein**, David Howard 1952- WhoEnt 92
**Canepa**, Adolfo John 1940- IntWW 91
**Canepa**, John Charles 1930- WhoMW 92
**Canepa**, Mario Alfredo 1932- WhoHisp 92
**Canepa**, Richard Thomas 1946- WhoMW 92
**Canessa**, Francesco 1927- WhoEnt 92
**Canestrari**, Ronald J WhoAmP 91
**Canestri**, Giovanni 1918- IntWW 91, WhoRel 92
**Canet**, Lawrence George 1910- Who 92
**Canete**, Alfredo 1942- IntWW 91
**Canetti**, Elias 1905- FacFETw, IntWW 91, LiExTwC, Who 92, WhoNob 90
**Canfarotta**, Thomas William 1952- WhoFI 92
**Canfield**, Alyce IntMPA 92
**Canfield**, Austin F., Jr. 1930- WhoAmL 92
**Canfield**, Brian A. 1938- WhoWest 92
**Canfield**, Carl Rex, Jr 1923- AmMWSc 92
**Canfield**, Craig Jennings 1932- AmMWSc 92
**Canfield**, Dorothy BenetAL 91
**Canfield**, Earl Rodney 1949- AmMWSc 92
**Canfield**, Earle Lloyd 1918- AmMWSc 92
**Canfield**, Francis Xavier 1920- WhoRel 92
**Canfield**, Grant Wellington, Jr. 1923- WhoFI 92, WhoWest 92
**Canfield**, James Howard 1930- AmMWSc 92
**Canfield**, Jimmie Gilliam DrAPF 91
**Canfield**, Karen Bonander 1961- WhoFI 92
**Canfield**, Mark Floyd 1963- WhoEnt 92
**Canfield**, Richard Charles 1937- AmMWSc 92
**Canfield**, Robert Charles 1922- AmMWSc 92
**Canfield**, Robert Cleo 1938- WhoAmL 92
**Canfield**, Robert E 1931- AmMWSc 92
**Canfield**, Terry Lee 1955- WhoRel 92
**Canfield**, William H 1920- AmMWSc 92
**Canfora**, Phillip H., Sr. 1950- WhoMW 92
**Cangemi**, Joseph P. 1936- IntWW 91
**Cangiamila**, Brion M 1962- WhoAmP 91
**Canham**, Bryan Frederick 1920- Who 92
**Canham**, Charles Howard 1962- WhoEnt 92
**Canham**, John Edward 1924- AmMWSc 92
**Canham**, Paul George 1933- Who 92
**Canham**, Peter Who 92
**Canham**, Peter Bennett 1941- AmMWSc 92
**Canham**, Richard Gordon 1928- AmMWSc 92
**Canidia** EncAmaz 91
**Caniff**, Milton A. 1907-1988 BenetAL 91
**Canin**, Ethan 1960- ConAu 135
**Canin**, Martin WhoEnt 92
**Canin**, Stuart Victor 1926- WhoEnt 92
**Canino**, Glorisa J. 1946- WhoHisp 92
**Canino**, Ian WhoHisp 92
**Canino**, Roberto A. WhoHisp 92
**Canino**, Victor Manuel, Jr. 1940- WhoHisp 92
**Canion**, Joseph Rod 1945- WhoFI 92
**Caniparoli**, Val William 1951- WhoEnt 92
**Canis**, Wayne F 1939- AmMWSc 92
**Canizales**, Orlando WhoHisp 92
**Canizalez**, Thomas Manuel 1957- WhoHisp 92
**Canizares**, Claude Roger 1945- AmMWSc 92
**Canizares**, Orlando 1910- AmMWSc 92
**Canizares Poey**, Rafael 1950- BlkOlyM
**Canizarro**, Vincent, Jr. DrAPF 91
**Canjar**, Patricia McWade 1932- WhoMW 92
**Canlas**, Lourdes S. WhoFI 92
**Cann**, Charles Richard 1937- Who 92
**Cann**, John Rusweiler 1920- AmMWSc 92
**Cann**, Johnson Robin 1937- Who 92
**Cann**, Malcolm Calvin 1924- AmMWSc 92
**Cann**, Michael Charles 1947- AmMWSc 92
**Cann**, William Francis 1922- WhoAmL 92
**Cann**, William Hopson 1916- WhoWest 92
**Cannadine**, David 1950- WrDr 92
**Cannady**, Alonzo James 1947- WhoBlA 92
**Cannady**, Edward Wyatt, Jr. 1906- WhoWest 92
**Cannaliato**, Vincent, Jr. 1941- WhoFI 92
**Cannan**, Denis 1919- IntAu&W 91, Who 92, WrDr 92
**Cannan**, Edward Alexander Capparis 1920- Who 92
**Cannan**, Thomas Hannah, Jr. 1934- WhoEnt 92
**Cannarozzi-Harris**, Kathleen Marie 1955- WhoEnt 92
**Cannell**, Charles Frederick 1913- WhoMW 92
**Cannell**, David Skipwith 1943- AmMWSc 92
**Cannell**, Glen H 1919- AmMWSc 92
**Cannell**, John Redferne 1937- WhoAmL 92
**Cannell**, Robert Quirk 1937- Who 92
**Cannell**, Stephen J. LesBEnT 92
**Cannell**, Stephen J. 1942- IntMPA 92
**Cannell**, Stephen Joseph 1941- WhoEnt 92
**Cannella**, John Matthew 1908- WhoAmL 92
**Cannella**, Sal WhoAmP 91
**Cannestra**, Kenneth W. WhoWest 92
**Canney**, Carroll E 1945- WhoAmP 91
**Canney**, Donald James 1930- WhoAmP 91
**Canney**, Frank Cogswell 1920- AmMWSc 92
**Canney**, Michael 1923- TwCPaSc
**Canning** Who 92
**Canning**, John Anthony, Jr. 1944- WhoMW 92
**Canning**, John Raymond 1939- WhoWest 92
**Canning**, T F 1927- AmMWSc 92
**Canning**, William Matthew 1921- WhoMW 92
**Cannistra**, Philip 1954- WhoEnt 92
**Cannizzaro**, Linda A 1953- AmMWSc 92
**Cannizzaro**, Paul Peter 1925- WhoFI 92
**Cannon**, Abraham Hoagland 1859-1896 RelLAm 91
**Cannon**, Alberry Charles 1936- WhoRel 92
**Cannon**, Albert 1921- AmMWSc 92
**Cannon**, Aleta 1942- WhoBlA 92
**Cannon**, Allen Eudelle 1920- WhoEnt 92
**Cannon**, Annie Jump 1863-1941 FacFETw
**Cannon**, Barbara E. M. 1936- WhoBlA 92
**Cannon**, Bettie 1922- IntAu&W 91
**Cannon**, Buddy 1947- WhoEnt 92
**Cannon**, Calvin Curtis 1952- WhoBlA 92
**Cannon**, Charles Albert 1892-1971 DcNCBi 1
**Cannon**, Charles Earl 1946- WhoBlA 92
**Cannon**, Charles James 1800-1860 BenetAL 91
**Cannon**, Chris J. 1954- WhoWest 92
**Cannon**, Christopher John 1954- WhoAmL 92, WhoWest 92
**Cannon**, Christopher John 1961- WhoRel 92
**Cannon**, Clinton Croxall 1958- WhoFI 92
**Cannon**, Craig Lee 1955- WhoEnt 92
**Cannon**, Curt IntAu&W 91X
**Cannon**, Daniel Humphreys 1923- WhoMW 92
**Cannon**, Daniel Willard 1920- WhoAmL 92, WhoFI 92
**Cannon**, David Joseph 1933- WhoAmL 92
**Cannon**, David Price 1946- WhoEnt 92
**Cannon**, Davita Louise 1949- WhoBlA 92
**Cannon**, Dickson Y 1935- AmMWSc 92
**Cannon**, Donald Charles 1934- AmMWSc 92
**Cannon**, Donnie E. 1929- WhoBlA 92
**Cannon**, Douglas Robert 1954- WhoFI 92
**Cannon**, Dyan 1937- IntMPA 92, WhoEnt 92
**Cannon**, Edith H. 1940- WhoBlA 92
**Cannon**, Elton Molock 1920- WhoBlA 92
**Cannon**, Eugene Nathaniel 1944- WhoBlA 92
**Cannon**, Franklin Jenne 1859-1933 RelLAm 91
**Cannon**, Garland 1924- WrDr 92
**Cannon**, Gary Curtis 1951- WhoAmL 92
**Cannon**, Geoffrey John 1940- IntAu&W 91
**Cannon**, George Quayle 1827-1901 RelLAm 91
**Cannon**, Glenn Albert 1940- AmMWSc 92
**Cannon**, H. LeRoy 1916- WhoBlA 92
**Cannon**, Heather Symmes 1944- WhoMW 92
**Cannon**, Helen Leighton 1911- AmMWSc 92
**Cannon**, Helen Virginia Graham 1913- WhoFI 92
**Cannon**, Howard S 1926- AmMWSc 92
**Cannon**, Howard Walter WhoAmP 91
**Cannon**, Hugh 1931- WhoAmP 91
**Cannon**, Ilvi Joe 1937- WhoAmP 91
**Cannon**, James, III 1892-1960 DcNCBi 1
**Cannon**, James, Jr 1864-1944 FacFETw
**Cannon**, James Anthony 1938- WhoFI 92
**Cannon**, James Edwin 1941- WhoAmL 92
**Cannon**, James W. 1927- WhoWest 92
**Cannon**, James Washington, Jr. 1951- WhoAmL 92
**Cannon**, James Welden 1943- WhoWest 92
**Cannon**, James William 1852-1921 DcNCBi 1
**Cannon**, Janet DrAPF 91
**Cannon**, Jerry Allam 1931- WhoFI 92
**Cannon**, Jerry Wayne 1942- AmMWSc 92
**Cannon**, John 1930- WhoFI 92
**Cannon**, John, III 1954- WhoAmL 92
**Cannon**, John Ashton 1926- Who 92
**Cannon**, John Burns 1948- AmMWSc 92
**Cannon**, John Francis 1940- AmMWSc 92
**Cannon**, John Francis Michael 1930- Who 92
**Cannon**, John Kemper 1932- WhoAmL 92
**Cannon**, John N 1927- AmMWSc 92
**Cannon**, John Rozier 1938- AmMWSc 92
**Cannon**, Jonathan H WhoAmP 91
**Cannon**, Joseph G 1926- AmMWSc 92
**Cannon**, Joseph Gurney 1836-1926 AmPolLe, DcNCBi 1, FacFETw
**Cannon**, Joseph Nevel 1942- WhoBlA 92
**Cannon**, Katie Geneva 1950- WhoBlA 92
**Cannon**, Kim Decker 1948- WhoAmL 92
**Cannon**, Lawrence Orson 1935- AmMWSc 92
**Cannon**, LeGrand, Jr. 1899-1979 BenetAL 91
**Cannon**, Lynne Marple 1955- WhoFI 92
**Cannon**, M Dale 1921- AmMWSc 92
**Cannon**, Marvin Samuel 1940- AmMWSc 92
**Cannon**, Melissa DrAPF 91
**Cannon**, Michael Lee 1940- WhoEnt 92
**Cannon**, Newton 1781-1841 DcNCBi 1
**Cannon**, Orson Silver 1908- AmMWSc 92
**Cannon**, Patrick Francis 1938- WhoMW 92
**Cannon**, Patrick Joseph 1947- AmMWSc 92
**Cannon**, Paul L., Jr. 1934- WhoBlA 92
**Cannon**, Paul Lewis 1956- WhoAmL 92
**Cannon**, Peter 1932- AmMWSc 92
**Cannon**, Peter John 1953- WhoMW 92
**Cannon**, Philip Jan 1940- AmMWSc 92
**Cannon**, Ralph S, Jr 1910- AmMWSc 92
**Cannon**, Raymond Joseph, Jr AmMWSc 92
**Cannon**, Reuben 1946- WhoBlA 92
**Cannon**, Richard Walter 1923- Who 92
**Cannon**, Robert Carl 1945- WhoAmL 92
**Cannon**, Robert H, Jr 1923- AmMWSc 92
**Cannon**, Robert L 1939- AmMWSc 92
**Cannon**, Robert Lester 1942- WhoRel 92
**Cannon**, Robert Wareing 1957- WhoAmL 92
**Cannon**, Robert Young 1917- AmMWSc 92
**Cannon**, Ronald Clarence 1952- WhoEnt 92
**Cannon**, Ruth Louise Coltrane 1891-1965 DcNCBi 1
**Cannon**, Sherri Dettmer 1958- WhoWest 92
**Cannon**, Steve DrAPF 91
**Cannon**, Thomas 1945- Who 92
**Cannon**, Thomas Quentin 1906- WhoAmP 91
**Cannon**, Walter Bradford 1871-1945 FacFETw
**Cannon**, Walton Wayne 1918- AmMWSc 92
**Cannon**, William 1937- IntMPA 92
**Cannon**, William Charles 1926- AmMWSc 92
**Cannon**, William Nathaniel 1927- AmMWSc 92
**Cannon**, William Nelson, Jr 1932- AmMWSc 92
**Cannon**, William Ragsdale 1916- WhoRel 92
**Cannon-Brookes**, Peter 1938- Who 92
**Cannonito**, Frank Benjamin 1926- AmMWSc 92
**Canny**, Nicholas Patrick 1944- IntWW 91
**Cano**, Francis Robert 1944- AmMWSc 92
**Cano**, Gilbert Lucero 1932- AmMWSc 92
**Cano**, Jamie 1953- WhoHisp 92
**Cano**, Kristin Maria 1951- WhoAmL 92

**Cano,** Marine, Jr. 1954- *WhoHisp 92*
**Cano,** Mario Stephen 1953- *WhoAmL 92*
**Cano,** Michael Dennis 1956- *WhoHisp 92*
**Cano,** Olivia Dean 1934- *WhoHisp 92*
**Cano,** Orlando Marquez 1957- *WhoHisp 92*
**Cano,** Rey Edward 1959- *WhoWest 92*
**Cano-Montenegro,** Miguel Federico 1938- *WhoHisp 92*
**Canoff,** Karen Huston 1954- *WhoAmL 92*
**Canoles,** Leroy Thomas, Jr. 1925- *WhoAmL 92*
**Canolty,** Nancy Lemmon 1942- *AmMWSc 92*
**Canon,** Robert Morris 1941- *WhoEnt 92*
**Canon,** Roy Frank 1942- *AmMWSc 92*
**Canon,** William Ward 1930- *WhoAmP 91*
**Canonaco,** Anthony Joseph 1966- *WhoMW 92*
**Canonchet** d1676 *BenetAL 91*
**Canonero,** Milena *ConTFT 9*
**Canonico,** Domenic Andrew 1930- *AmMWSc 92*
**Canonico,** Peter Guy 1942- *AmMWSc 92*
**Canonne,** Persephone 1932- *AmMWSc 92*
**Canopari,** Gerald Eugene 1944- *WhoFI 92*
**Canova,** Antonio 1757-1822 *BlkwCEP*
**Canova,** Diana 1952- *IntMPA 92*
**Canova-Davis,** Eleanor 1938- *WhoWest 92*
**Canovan,** Margaret Evelyn 1939- *WrDr 92*
**Canovas Del Castillo,** Antonio 1828-1897 *HisDSpE*
**Canright,** James Edward 1920- *AmMWSc 92*
**Cansdale,** George Soper 1909- *Who 92*
**Canseco,** Jose 1964- *CurBio 91 [port], WhoHisp 92, WhoWest 92*
**Canseco,** Jose Santiago 1958- *WhoHisp 92*
**Canson,** Fannie Joanna 1926- *WhoBlA 92*
**Canson,** Virna M. 1921- *WhoBlA 92*
**Cant,** Harry William Macphail 1921- *Who 92*
**Cant,** James 1911-1982 *TwCPaSc*
**Cant,** Robert 1915- *Who 92*
**Cantacuzene,** Jean Michel 1933- *IntWW 91*
**Cantacuzino,** Sherban 1928- *Who 92*
**Cantalapiedra,** Benito *WhoHisp 92*
**Cantalupo,** Charles 1951- *IntAu&W 91*
**Cantarella,** Francesco Paguin 1932- *WhoFI 92*
**Cantarella,** Marcia Y. 1946- *WhoBlA 92*
**Cantarelli,** Giuseppe Eugenio 1952- *WhoEnt 92*
**Cante,** Charles John 1941- *AmMWSc 92*
**Cantelli,** Guido 1920-1956 *FacFETw, NewAmDM*
**Cantelo,** William Wesley 1926- *AmMWSc 92*
**Canteloube,** Joseph 1879-1957 *NewAmDM*
**Canteloube de Calaret,** Joseph 1879-1957 *NewAmDM*
**Cantenot,** Jean 1919- *IntWW 91*
**Canter,** David Victor 1944- *Who 92*
**Canter,** Deborah Dean 1950- *WhoMW 92*
**Canter,** Herbert Milford 1925- *WhoAmL 92*
**Canter,** Larry Wayne 1939- *AmMWSc 92*
**Canter,** Marc Aaron 1957- *WhoEnt 92*
**Canter,** Nathan H 1942- *AmMWSc 92*
**Canter,** Neil M 1956- *AmMWSc 92*
**Canter,** Stanley Stanton 1933- *WhoEnt 92, WhoWest 92*
**Canter,** Stephen Edward 1945- *WhoFI 92*
**Canter,** William M. 1948- *WhoEnt 92*
**Canterac,** Jose 1775-1835 *HisDSpE*
**Canterbery,** E. Ray 1935- *WhoFI 92*
**Canterbury,** Archbishop of *IntWW 91*
**Canterbury,** Archbishop of 1935- *Who 92*
**Canterbury,** Archdeacon of *Who 92*
**Canterbury,** Dean of *Who 92*
**Canterbury,** Hugh Franklin, Sr. 1930- *WhoRel 92*
**Canterino,** Peter John 1920- *AmMWSc 92*
**Canterna,** Ronald William 1946- *AmMWSc 92*
**Cantero,** Araceli M. 1944- *WhoHisp 92*
**Cantilli,** Edmund Joseph 1927- *AmMWSc 92*
**Cantillo,** Edgardo J. 1946- *WhoHisp 92*
**Cantilo,** Patrick Herrera 1954- *WhoAmL 92*
**Cantin,** Gilles 1927- *AmMWSc 92*
**Cantin,** Marc 1933- *AmMWSc 92*
**Cantino,** Edward Charles 1921- *AmMWSc 92*
**Cantino,** Philip Douglas 1948- *AmMWSc 92, WhoMW 92*
**Cantlay,** George Thomson 1907- *Who 92*
**Cantley,** Joseph 1910- *Who 92*
**Cantley,** Lewis Clayton 1949- *AmMWSc 92*
**Cantliffe,** Daniel James 1943- *AmMWSc 92*
**Cantlin,** Richard Anthony 1946- *WhoAmL 92*
**Cantlon,** John Edward 1921- *AmMWSc 92*
**Canto,** Orlando J. *WhoHisp 92*
**Canton,** Arthur H. *IntMPA 92*
**Canton,** Douglas 1931- *WhoAmP 91*
**Canton,** Douglas E. 1931- *WhoBlA 92*
**Canton,** Mari *WhoFI 92*
**Canton,** Mark *NewYTBS 91 [port]*
**Canton,** Mark 1949- *IntMPA 92*
**Canton,** Peter Joseph 1947- *WhoMW 92*
**Cantoni,** Giampiero Carlo 1939- *IntWW 91*
**Cantoni,** Giulio L 1915- *AmMWSc 92, IntWW 91*
**Cantoni,** Marie Lucille 1930- *WhoEnt 92*
**Cantor,** Alan Bruce 1948- *WhoFI 92*
**Cantor,** Austin H 1942- *AmMWSc 92*
**Cantor,** Charles R. 1942- *IntWW 91*
**Cantor,** Charles Robert 1942- *AmMWSc 92, WhoWest 92*
**Cantor,** David Geoffrey 1935- *AmMWSc 92*
**Cantor,** David Milton 1952- *AmMWSc 92*
**Cantor,** David S 1956- *AmMWSc 92*
**Cantor,** Eddie d1964 *LesBEnT 92*
**Cantor,** Eddie 1892-1964 *FacFETw, NewAmDM*
**Cantor,** Eli *DrAPF 91*
**Cantor,** Ena D 1920- *AmMWSc 92*
**Cantor,** Geoffrey 1943- *ConAu 135*
**Cantor,** Harvey 1942- *AmMWSc 92*
**Cantor,** Herbert I. 1935- *WhoAmL 92*
**Cantor,** Irvin Victor 1953- *WhoAmL 92*
**Cantor,** Irwin 1924- *WhoAmL 92*
**Cantor,** Kenneth P 1941- *AmMWSc 92*
**Cantor,** Mark Henry 1953- *WhoAmL 92*
**Cantor,** Marvin H 1935- *AmMWSc 92*
**Cantor,** Melvyn Leon 1942- *WhoAmL 92*
**Cantor,** Paul 1927- *WhoEnt 92*
**Cantor,** Robert Frank 1943- *WhoWest 92*
**Cantor,** Samuel C. 1919- *WhoAmL 92, WhoIns 92*
**Cantor,** Stanley 1929- *AmMWSc 92*
**Cantor,** Stefanie Dara 1956- *WhoAmL 92*
**Cantor,** Steven Gary 1960- *WhoFI 92*
**Cantow,** Manfred Josef Richard 1926- *AmMWSc 92*
**Cantral,** Kimberly Ann 1962- *WhoMW 92*
**Cantrall,** Irving James 1909- *AmMWSc 92, WhoMW 92*
**Cantrell,** Almos Calvin 1932- *WhoRel 92*
**Cantrell,** Charles Leonard 1948- *WhoAmL 92*
**Cantrell,** Cyrus D, III 1940- *AmMWSc 92*
**Cantrell,** Elmer J 1929- *WhoAmP 91*
**Cantrell,** Elroy Taylor 1943- *AmMWSc 92*
**Cantrell,** Forrest Daniel 1938- *WhoBlA 92*
**Cantrell,** Grady Leon 1936- *AmMWSc 92*
**Cantrell,** James Cecil 1931- *AmMWSc 92*
**Cantrell,** James Herbert 1949- *WhoFI 92*
**Cantrell,** James Marcus 1959- *WhoEnt 92*
**Cantrell,** John H 1943- *AmMWSc 92*
**Cantrell,** John Leonard 1939- *AmMWSc 92*
**Cantrell,** John Roland 1888-1968 *DcNCBi 1*
**Cantrell,** Joseph Sires 1932- *AmMWSc 92, WhoMW 92*
**Can'trell,** Karen S. 1953- *WhoWest 92*
**Cantrell,** Lana 1943- *WhoEnt 92*
**Cantrell,** Lana Corrine 1953- *WhoEnt 92*
**Cantrell,** Thomas Samuel 1938- *AmMWSc 92*
**Cantrell,** William Allen 1920- *AmMWSc 92*
**Cantrell,** William Fletcher 1916- *AmMWSc 92*
**Cantrelle,** Joseph, Sr. 1951- *WhoWest 92*
**Cantril,** Hadley 1906-1969 *ScFEYrs*
**Cantril,** Hadley, Gaudet, H & Herzog, H *ScFEYrs*
**Cantrill,** James Egbert 1933- *AmMWSc 92*
**Cantu,** Antonio Arnoldo 1941- *AmMWSc 92*
**Cantu,** Charlie 1954- *WhoHisp 92*
**Cantu,** David Oscar 1956- *WhoHisp 92*
**Cantu,** Emilio *WhoAmP 91, WhoHisp 92*
**Cantu,** George E. 1935- *WhoHisp 92*
**Cantu,** Gilbert, Jr. 1946- *WhoHisp 92*
**Cantu,** Juan Blanco 1947- *WhoHisp 92*
**Cantu,** Juan M. 1955- *WhoHisp 92*
**Cantu,** Norma V. *WhoHisp 92*
**Cantu,** Oralia E. 1933- *WhoHisp 92*
**Cantu,** Ricardo M. *WhoHisp 92*
**Cantu,** Richard Rene 1939- *WhoHisp 92*
**Cantu,** Rodolfo *WhoHisp 92*
**Cantus,** Jane Scott 1965- *WhoWest 92*
**Cantwell,** Dennis Michael 1943- *WhoFI 92*
**Cantwell,** Don 1935- *WhoEnt 92*
**Cantwell,** Edward N, Jr 1927- *AmMWSc 92*
**Cantwell,** Frederick Francis 1941- *AmMWSc 92*
**Cantwell,** John Christopher 1936- *AmMWSc 92, WhoMW 92*
**Cantwell,** Kathleen Gordon 1945- *WhoBlA 92*
**Cantwell,** Lawrence Michael 1953- *WhoIns 92*
**Cantwell,** Maria *WhoAmP 91*
**Cantwell,** Richard E. 1943- *WhoRel 92*
**Cantwell,** Robert *DrAPF 91*
**Cantwell,** Robert E. 1908-1978 *BenetAL 91*
**Cantwell,** William Frederick 1924- *WhoMW 92*
**Cantwell,** William Patterson 1921- *WhoAmL 92*
**Canty,** Brian George John 1931- *Who 92*
**Canty,** Carrie Rebecca 1927- *WhoRel 92*
**Canty,** George 1931- *WhoBlA 92*
**Canty,** Gerald Edward 1931- *WhoMW 92*
**Canty,** Henrietta Mathis *WhoAmP 91*
**Canty,** Miriam Monroe 1916- *WhoBlA 92*
**Canty,** Otis Andrew 1934- *WhoBlA 92*
**Canty,** Ralph Waldo 1945- *WhoBlA 92*
**Canuck,** Abe *IntAu&W 91X, TwCWW 91*
**Canup,** Larry Dale 1955- *WhoMW 92*
**Canvin,** David T 1931- *AmMWSc 92*
**Canziani,** Estella Louisa Michaela 1887-1964 *TwCPaSc*
**Canzoneri,** Matthew B. *WhoFI 92*
**Canzoneri,** Robert *DrAPF 91*
**Canzonier,** Walter J 1936- *AmMWSc 92*
**Cao Keqiang** *IntWW 91*
**Cao Tianqin** 1920- *IntWW 91*
**Cao Yu** 1910- *IntWW 91*
**Cao Yuanxin** *IntWW 91*
**Cao,** Diansheng 1962- *WhoWest 92*
**Cao,** Hengchu 1962- *AmMWSc 92*
**Cao,** Thai-Hai 1954- *WhoWest 92*
**Cao,** Than Van 1932- *WhoFI 92, WhoWest 92*
**Caonabo** *HisDSpE*
**Caouette,** Aurelia 1833-1905 *RelLAm 91*
**Caouette,** Cathrine Reddy 1935- *WhoAmP 91*
**Caouette,** John Bernard 1944- *WhoFI 92*
**Capa,** Cornell 1918- *FacFETw*
**Capa,** Robert 1913-1954 *FacFETw*
**Capablanca,** Fernando Aquiles 1944- *WhoFI 92*
**Capalbo,** Carmen Charles 1925- *WhoEnt 92*
**Capaldi,** Anthony C. 1939- *WhoFI 92*
**Capaldi,** Dante James 1957- *AmMWSc 92*
**Capaldi,** Eugene Carmen 1937- *AmMWSc 92*
**Capaldo,** Guy 1950- *WhoMW 92*
**Capalino,** Marco Steven 1960- *WhoMW 92*
**Capani,** Peter Michael 1951- *WhoFI 92*
**Capasso,** Federico 1949- *AmMWSc 92*
**Capco,** David G *AmMWSc 92*
**Cape,** Arthur Tregoning 1904- *AmMWSc 92*
**Cape,** Donald Paul Montagu Stewart 1923- *Who 92*
**Cape,** John Anthony 1929- *AmMWSc 92*
**Cape,** Jonathan 1879-1960 *DcLB 112 [port]*
**Cape,** Judith *IntAu&W 91X, WrDr 92*
**Cape,** Ronald Elliot 1932- *AmMWSc 92*
**Cape,** Safford 1906-1973 *NewAmDM*
**Cape,** Timothy Frederick 1915- *Who 92*
**Cape Town,** Archbishop of 1931- *Who 92*
**Cape Town,** Bishops Suffragan of *Who 92*
**Capecce,** Victor P. 1950- *WhoEnt 92*
**Capecchi,** Mario Renato 1937- *AmMWSc 92*
**Capecelatro,** Mark John 1948- *WhoAmL 92*
**Capehart,** Barney Lee 1940- *AmMWSc 92*
**Capehart,** Homer Earl, Jr. 1922- *WhoAmL 92*
**Capehart,** Johnnie Lawrence 1947- *WhoBlA 92*
**Capek,** Karel 1890-1938 *DramC 1 [port], FacFETw, ScFEYrs, TwCSFW 91A*
**Capek,** Radan 1931- *AmMWSc 92*
**Capel,** Charles Edward 1922- *AmMWSc 92*
**Capel,** Felton Jeffrey 1927- *WhoBlA 92*
**Capel,** Wallace 1915- *WhoBlA 92*
**Capel Cure,** Nigel 1908- *Who 92*
**Capell** *Who 92*
**Capella,** David John 1949- *WhoFI 92*
**Capellan,** Angel 1942- *WhoHisp 92*
**Capelle,** Russell B. 1917- *WrDr 92*
**Capelouto,** Gary David 1954- *WhoEnt 92*
**Capen,** Charles Chabert 1936- *AmMWSc 92*
**Capen,** Charles Franklin, Jr 1926- *AmMWSc 92*
**Capen,** Ronald L 1942- *AmMWSc 92*
**Capen,** Samuel Billings 1842-1914 *AmPeW*
**Capen,** Victor Lawrence 1943- *WhoFI 92*
**Capener,** Regner Alvin 1942- *WhoRel 92, WhoWest 92*
**Caperon,** John 1929- *AmMWSc 92*
**Capers,** Eliza Virginia 1925- *WhoBlA 92*
**Capers,** Evelyn Lorraine 1925- *AmMWSc 92*
**Caperton,** Albert Franklin 1936- *WhoMW 92*
**Caperton,** Dee K 1943- *WhoAmP 91*
**Caperton,** Gaston 1940- *AlmAP 92 [port], WhoAmP 91*
**Caperton,** George Coble 1950- *WhoAmL 92*
**Caperton,** Kent Allen 1949- *WhoAmP 91*
**Caperton,** Richard Walton 1948- *WhoFI 92*
**Capes,** Bernard 1870?-1918 *ScFEYrs*
**Capetola,** Robert Joseph 1949- *AmMWSc 92*
**Capey,** Montague Martin 1933- *Who 92*
**Capezza,** Joseph C 1955- *WhoIns 92*
**Capice,** Philip *LesBEnT 92*
**Capice,** Philip Charles 1931- *WhoEnt 92*
**Capiel-Collin,** Susan 1952- *WhoWest 92*
**Capineri,** Joseph A 1929- *WhoAmP 91*
**Capistran,** Eleno Pete, III 1958- *WhoHisp 92*
**Capitan,** William H. 1933- *WrDr 92*
**Capitel,** Irving Sheldon 1941- *WhoAmL 92*
**Capizzi,** John A 1954- *WhoIns 92*
**Capizzi,** Michael Robert 1939- *WhoAmL 92*
**Capizzi,** Robert L 1938- *AmMWSc 92*
**Caplan,** Lord 1929- *Who 92*
**Caplan,** Arnold I 1942- *AmMWSc 92*
**Caplan,** Arthur L. 1950- *WrDr 92*
**Caplan,** Aubrey G 1923- *AmMWSc 92, WhoFI 92*
**Caplan,** Coren 1944- *IntAu&W 91*
**Caplan,** Daniel 1915- *Who 92*
**Caplan,** Daniel Bennett 1937- *AmMWSc 92*
**Caplan,** Donald 1917- *AmMWSc 92*
**Caplan,** Edwin Harvey 1926- *WhoWest 92*
**Caplan,** Frank 1919- *WhoWest 92*
**Caplan,** John Alan 1945- *WhoWest 92*
**Caplan,** John D 1926- *AmMWSc 92*
**Caplan,** Jonathan Michael 1951- *Who 92*
**Caplan,** Joyce F 1933- *WhoAmP 91*
**Caplan,** Lawrence Allen 1958- *WhoAmL 92*
**Caplan,** Lazarus David 1940- *WhoFI 92*
**Caplan,** Leonard 1909- *Who 92*
**Caplan,** Louis James 1937- *WhoMW 92*
**Caplan,** Louis Robert 1936- *AmMWSc 92*
**Caplan,** Mark Jeffrey 1950- *WhoAmL 92*
**Caplan,** Marsha *WhoRel 92*
**Caplan,** Michael Irwin 1956- *WhoEnt 92*
**Caplan,** Milton Irving 1933- *WhoAmP 91*
**Caplan,** Paul E 1924- *AmMWSc 92*
**Caplan,** Paula Joan 1947- *AmMWSc 92*
**Caplan,** Philip Isaac *Who 92*
**Caplan,** Philip Judah 1927- *AmMWSc 92*
**Caplan,** Richard Melvin 1929- *AmMWSc 92*
**Caplan,** Yale Howard 1941- *AmMWSc 92*
**Caplat,** Moran Victor Hingston 1916- *Who 92*
**Caple,** Gerald 1935- *AmMWSc 92*
**Caple,** Ronald 1937- *AmMWSc 92*
**Caples,** Richard James 1949- *WhoEnt 92*
**Caplet,** Andre 1878-1925 *NewAmDM*
**Caplin,** Arnold Stewart 1929- *WhoEnt 92*
**Caplin,** Barbara Ellen 1954- *WhoEnt 92*
**Caplin,** Lee 1946- *WhoEnt 92*
**Caplin,** Michael Andrew 1951- *WhoEnt 92*
**Caplin,** Mortimer M. 1916- *IntWW 91*
**Caplin,** Mortimer Maxwell 1916- *WhoAmL 92*
**Caplinger,** Paula Ruth 1948- *WhoWest 92*
**Caplis,** Michael E 1938- *AmMWSc 92*
**Caplis,** Michael Edward 1938- *WhoMW 92*
**Caplis,** Stephen Bennett 1947- *WhoAmL 92*
**Caplow,** Michael 1935- *AmMWSc 92*
**Capo,** Helena Frances 1959- *WhoEnt 92*
**Capo,** Manuel *WhoHisp 92*
**Capo-Chichi,** Gratien Tonakpon 1938- *IntWW 91*
**Capobianco,** Daniel Lauro 1962- *WhoMW 92*
**Capobianco,** Michael F 1931- *AmMWSc 92*
**Capobianco,** Tito 1931- *NewAmDM, WhoEnt 92*
**Capodieci,** Gregor 1947- *WhoFI 92*
**Capolarello,** Joe R. 1961- *WhoEnt 92*
**Capon,** Brian 1931- *AmMWSc 92*
**Capon,** Edmund 1940- *WrDr 92*
**Capon,** Paul 1912-1969 *TwCSFW 91*
**Capone,** Al 1899-1947 *FacFETw [port]*
**Capone,** Douglas George 1950- *AmMWSc 92*
**Capone,** James J 1945- *AmMWSc 92*
**Caponegro,** Ernest Mark 1957- *WhoFI 92*
**Caponetti,** James Dante 1932- *AmMWSc 92*
**Caponio,** Joseph Francis 1926- *AmMWSc 92*
**Caporale,** Charles Michael 1950- *WhoIns 92*
**Caporale,** D. Nick 1928- *WhoAmL 92, WhoAmP 91, WhoMW 92*
**Caporale,** Lynn Helena 1947- *AmMWSc 92*
**Caporali,** Ronald Van 1936- *AmMWSc 92*
**Caporaso,** Fredric 1947- *AmMWSc 92, WhoWest 92*
**Caporello-Szykman,** Corradina *WhoEnt 92*

**Capote,** Luciano Caridad 1926- *WhoHisp 92*
**Capote,** Maria Romero 1935- *WhoHisp 92*
**Capote,** Truman 1924- *SourALJ*
**Capote,** Truman 1924-1984 *BenetAL 91, FacFETw*
**Capozzi,** Anthony Patrick 1945- *WhoAmP 91*
**Capozzi,** Louis Joseph, Jr. 1961- *WhoAmL 92*
**Capozzoli,** Jeanne Johnson 1940- *WhoAmP 91*
**Capp,** Al 1909-1979 *BenetAL 91, FacFETw*
**Capp,** Bernard 1943- *WrDr 92*
**Capp,** Grayson L 1936- *AmMWSc 92*
**Capp,** Michael Paul 1930- *AmMWSc 92*
**Capp,** Walter B 1933- *AmMWSc 92*
**Cappa,** Dominic Michael 1952- *WhoFI 92*
**Cappa,** Donald 1930- *WhoWest 92*
**Cappabianca,** Italo S 1936- *WhoAmP 91*
**Cappallo,** Roger James 1949- *AmMWSc 92*
**Capparelli,** Ralph C 1924- *WhoAmP 91*
**Cappas,** Alberto O., Jr. 1946- *WhoHisp 92*
**Cappas,** Alberto Oscar *DrAPF 91*
**Cappas,** C 1926- *AmMWSc 92*
**Cappel,** C Robert 1942- *AmMWSc 92*
**Cappel,** Constance 1936- *WhoWest 92*
**Cappelen,** Andreas Zeier 1915- *IntWW 91*
**Cappell,** Joe Frederick 1927- *WhoAmP 91*
**Cappell,** Sylvain Edward 1946- *AmMWSc 92*
**Cappelletti,** Mauro 1927- *WhoAmL 92*
**Cappelletti,** Norma Leone *WhoAmP 91*
**Cappellini,** Raymond Adolph 1926- *AmMWSc 92*
**Cappello,** A. Barry 1942- *WhoAmL 92*
**Cappello,** Carmelo 1912- *IntWW 91*
**Cappello,** Juan C. *WhoHisp 92*
**Cappello,** Richard 1949- *WhoRel 92*
**Cappello,** Rosemary *DrAPF 91*
**Capper,** Edmund Michael Hubert 1908- *Who 92*
**Cappitella,** Mauro John 1934- *WhoFI 92*
**Cappo,** Bruce Michael 1960- *WhoMW 92*
**Cappo,** Louis Cesare 1919- *WhoRel 92*
**Cappon,** Andre Alfred 1948- *WhoFI 92*
**Cappon,** Daniel 1921- *WrDr 92*
**Cappone,** Norberto 1952- *WhoEnt 92*
**Capponi,** Paul Henry 1960- *WhoFI 92*
**Capps,** Anthony Thomas *WhoWest 92*
**Capps,** Ben 1922- *WrDr 92*
**Capps,** Benjamin 1922- *TwCWW 91*
**Capps,** Charles Wilson, Jr 1925- *WhoAmP 91*
**Capps,** David Bridgman 1925- *AmMWSc 92*
**Capps,** Gilmer N 1932- *WhoAmP 91*
**Capps,** James Leigh, II 1956- *WhoAmL 92*
**Capps,** John Paul 1934- *WhoAmP 91*
**Capps,** Kenneth P. 1939- *WhoFI 92*
**Capps,** Richard H 1928- *AmMWSc 92*
**Capps,** Richard Huntley 1928- *WhoMW 92*
**Capps,** Robert VanBuren 1938- *WhoRel 92*
**Capps,** Thomas Edward 1935- *WhoFI 92*
**Capps,** Walter Holden 1934- *WhoRel 92*
**Cappucci,** Dario Ted, Jr 1941- *AmMWSc 92*
**Cappuccilli,** Piero 1929- *IntWW 91, NewAmDM*
**Cappuccio,** Charlene A. 1951- *WhoEnt 92*
**Cappuyns,** Hendrik Frans Ferdinand 1913- *IntWW 91*
**Cappy,** Ralph J 1943- *WhoAmP 91*
**Cappy,** Ralph Joseph 1943- *WhoAmL 92*
**Capra,** Carlo 1938- *IntWW 91*
**Capra,** Frank d1991 *Who 92N*
**Capra,** Frank 1897- *BenetAL 91, IntDcF 2-2 [port]*
**Capra,** Frank 1897-1985 *FacFETw*
**Capra,** Frank 1897-1991 *ConAu 135, ConTFT 9, CurBio 91N, NewYTBS 91 [port], News 92-2*
**Capra,** Frank, Jr. *IntMPA 92*
**Capra,** Frank R. 1897- *IntWW 91*
**Capra,** J Donald 1937- *AmMWSc 92*
**Capranica,** Robert R 1931- *AmMWSc 92*
**Capretta,** Patrick J. 1929-1982 *ConAu 135*
**Capretta,** Umberto 1922- *AmMWSc 92*
**Capri,** Anton Zizi 1938- *AmMWSc 92*
**Capria,** Nicola 1932- *IntWW 91*
**Capriati,** Jennifer 1976- *News 91 [port]*
**Caprio,** Frank Thomas 1966- *WhoAmP 91*
**Caprio,** Giuseppe 1914- *IntWW 91*
**Caprio,** James R 1939- *AmMWSc 92*
**Caprio,** John Theodore 1945- *AmMWSc 92*
**Caprio,** Joseph Giuseppe 1914- *WhoRel 92*
**Caprio,** Joseph Michael 1923- *AmMWSc 92*
**Caprio,** Linda Geralyn 1962- *WhoEnt 92*
**Caprio-Stilwell,** Julie Ann 1963- *WhoEnt 92*
**Caprioglio,** Carl John 1964- *WhoEnt 92*
**Caprioglio,** Giovanni 1932- *AmMWSc 92*
**Caprioli,** Richard Michael 1943- *AmMWSc 92*
**Capriotti,** Eugene Raymond 1937- *AmMWSc 92*
**Capron,** Alexander Morgan 1944- *AmMWSc 92, IntWW 91*
**Capron,** Christopher 1935- *Who 92*
**Capron,** Harold H. 1944- *WhoEnt 92*
**Capsalis,** Barbara Damon 1943- *WhoFI 92*
**Capshaw,** Kate *WhoEnt 92*
**Capshaw,** Kate 1953- *IntMPA 92*
**Capshaw,** Tom Dean 1936- *WhoAmL 92, WhoMW 92*
**Capshaw,** Walter L d1915 *BiInAmS*
**Capstack,** Ernest 1930- *AmMWSc 92*
**Capstick,** Brian Eric 1927- *Who 92*
**Capstick,** Charles William 1934- *Who 92*
**Capstick,** John Anthony 1939- *WhoFI 92*
**Captain Beefheart** 1941- *NewAmDM*
**Capucine** 1923?-1990 *AnObit 1990*
**Capucine** 1933-1990 *FacFETw*
**Capucine** 1935?-1990 *ConTFT 9*
**Caputi,** Anthony 1924- *WrDr 92*
**Caputi,** Roger William 1935- *AmMWSc 92*
**Caputo,** Bruce 1943- *WhoAmP 91*
**Caputo,** Dante 1943- *IntWW 91*
**Caputo,** David Armand 1943- *WhoMW 92*
**Caputo,** Joseph Anthony 1940- *AmMWSc 92*
**Caputo,** Lucio 1935- *WhoFI 92*
**Caputo,** Nicholas *WhoAmP 91*
**Caputo,** Philip Joseph 1941- *IntAu&W 91*
**Caputo,** Richard Paul 1931- *WhoAmL 92*
**Capuzzo,** Judith M 1947- *AmMWSc 92*
**Capwell,** Robert J 1940- *AmMWSc 92*
**Cara,** Irene 1959- *IntMPA 92, WhoEnt 92*
**Caraballo,** Jose 1932- *WhoRel 92*
**Caraballo,** Jose Noel 1955- *WhoHisp 92*
**Caraballo,** Luis Benito 1954- *WhoHisp 92*
**Caraballo,** Manuel De J. 1936- *WhoHisp 92*
**Caraballo-Oramas,** Jose A. 1961- *WhoHisp 92*
**Carabateas,** Philip M 1930- *AmMWSc 92*
**Carabello,** Vincent J. 1942- *WhoEnt 92*
**Carabillo,** Joseph Anthony 1946- *WhoAmL 92, WhoIns 92*
**Caracalla** 188-217 *EncEarC*
**Caracciola,** Joseph John 1915- *WhoAmP 91*
**Caracena,** Fernando 1936- *AmMWSc 92*
**Caraco,** Thomas Benjamin 1946- *AmMWSc 92*
**Caradon,** Baron d1990 *IntWW 91N*
**Caradon,** Lord 1907-1990 *AnObit 1990, FacFETw*
**Caradus,** Selwyn Ross 1935- *AmMWSc 92*
**Caraher,** Brian Gregory 1951- *WhoMW 92*
**Caraher,** James H. 1950- *WhoEnt 92*
**Caram,** Dorothy Farrington 1933- *WhoHisp 92*
**Caram,** Hugo Simon 1945- *AmMWSc 92*
**Caramanlis,** Constantine 1907- *FacFETw*
**Caramello,** Anne Olszewski 1951- *WhoEnt 92*
**Caramitru,** Ion 1942- *IntWW 91*
**Caranci,** Anthony Benjamin, Jr 1930- *WhoAmP 91*
**Caranci,** Paul Francis 1955- *WhoAmP 91*
**Caranfa,** Patrick L 1943- *WhoIns 92*
**Carapella,** S C, Jr 1923- *AmMWSc 92*
**Carapellotti,** Paul Remeo 1921- *WhoMW 92*
**Caras,** Constantine George 1938- *WhoFI 92*
**Caras,** Gus J 1929- *AmMWSc 92*
**Caras,** Roger A. 1928- *WrDr 92*
**Caras,** Roger Andrew 1928- *IntAu&W 91*
**Carassa,** Francesco 1922- *AmMWSc 92*
**Carasso,** Alfred Samuel 1939- *AmMWSc 92*
**Caravia,** Manuel A. *WhoHisp 92*
**Caraway,** Wendell Thomas 1920- *AmMWSc 92*
**Caraway,** Yolanda H 1950- *WhoAmP 91, WhoBlA 92*
**Caray,** Harry Christopher 1919- *WhoMW 92*
**Carazo Odio,** Rodrigo 1926- *IntWW 91*
**Carb,** Evan Daniel 1960- *WhoAmL 92*
**Carbajal,** Bernard Gonzales, III 1933- *AmMWSc 92*
**Carbajal,** Michael 1968- *WhoHisp 92*
**Carballo,** Julio R. 1946- *WhoHisp 92*
**Carballo,** Pedro Pablo 1953- *WhoMW 92*
**Carballosa,** Evis L. *WhoRel 92*
**Carbary,** James F 1951- *AmMWSc 92*
**Carbaugh,** John Edward, Jr. 1945- *WhoAmL 92*
**Carberry,** Deirdre *WhoEnt 92*
**Carberry,** Edward Andrew 1941- *AmMWSc 92*
**Carberry,** Glenn Thomas 1955- *WhoAmP 91*
**Carberry,** James John 1925- *AmMWSc 92*
**Carberry,** John J. 1904- *WhoMW 92*
**Carberry,** John Joseph 1904- *RelLAm 91*
**Carberry,** Judith B 1936- *AmMWSc 92*
**Carbery,** Baron 1920- *Who 92*
**Carbery,** Michael Thomas 1958- *WhoFI 92*
**Carbery,** Thomas Francis 1925- *Who 92*
**Carbiener,** Wayne Alan 1936- *AmMWSc 92*
**Carbine,** James Edmond 1945- *WhoAmL 92*
**Carbine,** Sharon 1950- *WhoAmL 92*
**Carbno,** William Clifford 1930- *AmMWSc 92*
**Carbon,** John Anthony 1931- *AmMWSc 92*
**Carbon,** Max W 1922- *AmMWSc 92*
**Carbonaro,** Paul Anthony 1951- *WhoAmL 92*
**Carbone,** Gabriel 1927- *AmMWSc 92*
**Carbone,** James A. 1952- *WhoFI 92*
**Carbone,** John Vito 1922- *AmMWSc 92*
**Carbone,** Leslie Ann 1964- *WhoHisp 92*
**Carbone,** Nicholas R 1936- *WhoAmP 91*
**Carbone,** Paul P 1931- *AmMWSc 92*
**Carbone,** Richard Edward 1944- *AmMWSc 92*
**Carbone,** Robert James 1930- *AmMWSc 92*
**Carbonell,** Jaime Guillermo 1953- *AmMWSc 92*
**Carbonell,** Joseph Fernando 1936- *WhoHisp 92*
**Carbonell,** Nestor *WhoHisp 92*
**Carbonell,** Robert Joseph 1927- *AmMWSc 92*
**Carbonell,** William Leycester Rouse 1912- *Who 92*
**Carboni,** Joan M *AmMWSc 92*
**Carboni,** Richard *DrAPF 91*
**Carboni,** Rudolph A 1922- *AmMWSc 92*
**Carbonin,** Stefano 1960- *WhoFI 92*
**Carbutt,** John 1832-1905 *BiInAmS*
**Carcani,** Adil 1922- *IntWW 91*
**Carchman,** Richard A *AmMWSc 92*
**Carcieri,** Anthony J *WhoAmP 91*
**Card,** Andrew Hill, Jr 1947- *WhoAmP 91*
**Card,** Claudia Falconer 1940- *WhoMW 92*
**Card,** James Willard 1941- *WhoFI 92*
**Card,** Kenneth D 1937- *AmMWSc 92*
**Card,** Larry J 1950- *WhoIns 92*
**Card,** Orson Scott 1951- *IntAu&W 91, TwCSFW 91, WrDr 92*
**Card,** Roger John 1947- *AmMWSc 92*
**Card,** Walter D. 1934- *WhoFI 92*
**Card,** Wilbur Wade 1873-1948 *DcNCBi 1*
**Cardalena,** Peter Paul, Jr. 1943- *WhoAmL 92*
**Cardamone,** Richard J *WhoAmP 91*
**Cardamone,** Richard J. 1925- *WhoAmL 92*
**Cardarelli,** Joseph *DrAPF 91*
**Cardarelli,** Joseph S 1944- *AmMWSc 92*
**Cardarelli,** Nathan Frank 1931- *WhoMW 92*
**Cardarelli,** Vincenzo 1887-1959 *DcLB 114 [port]*
**Carde,** Ring Richard Tomlinson 1943- *AmMWSc 92*
**Cardeilhac,** Paul T *AmMWSc 92*
**Cardell,** Robert Ridley, Jr 1931- *AmMWSc 92*
**Cardelli,** James Allen *AmMWSc 92*
**Cardellino,** Donna 1958- *WhoEnt 92*
**Cardello,** Armand Vincent 1949- *AmMWSc 92*
**Carden,** Allen 1949- *WhoRel 92*
**Carden,** Arnold Eugene 1930- *AmMWSc 92*
**Carden,** Brian Eugene 1958- *WhoFI 92*
**Carden,** Derrick Charles 1921- *Who 92*
**Carden,** Graham Stephen 1935- *Who 92*
**Carden,** Henry 1908- *Who 92*
**Carden,** Joan Maralyn *IntWW 91*
**Carden,** John Craven 1926- *Who 92*
**Carden,** Joy C. 1932- *WhoWest 92*
**Carden,** Richard John Derek 1943- *Who 92*
**Carden,** Stephen *Who 92*
**Carden,** Thomas Ray *WhoWest 92*
**Cardenal,** Ernesto 1925- *ConSpAP*
**Cardenas,** Anthony *WhoHisp 92*
**Cardenas,** Bernardino de 1579-1668 *HisDSpE*
**Cardenas,** Carlos Guillermo 1941- *AmMWSc 92*
**Cardenas,** Deborah Ileana 1962- *WhoHisp 92*
**Cardenas,** Gerardo Felipe 1962- *WhoHisp 92*
**Cardenas,** Henry *WhoHisp 92*
**Cardenas,** Jose A. 1930- *WhoHisp 92*
**Cardenas,** Judith Frances 1961- *WhoHisp 92*
**Cardenas,** Leo Elias 1935- *WhoHisp 92*
**Cardenas,** Lucy R. 1945- *WhoHisp 92*
**Cardenas,** Luis *WhoHisp 92*
**Cardenas,** Manuel 1942- *AmMWSc 92*
**Cardenas,** Maria de la Luz Rodriguez 1945- *WhoHisp 92*
**Cardenas,** Maria Elena 1939- *WhoHisp 92*
**Cardenas,** Mario J. 1925- *WhoHisp 92*
**Cardenas,** Mike 1955- *WhoHisp 92*
**Cardenas,** Nick 1940- *WhoHisp 92*
**Cardenas,** Norma Yvette 1944- *WhoHisp 92*
**Cardenas,** Patricia Lorain Hicks 1939- *WhoMW 92*
**Cardenas,** Rafael 1949- *WhoHisp 92*
**Cardenas,** Raul 1937- *WhoHisp 92*
**Cardenas,** Raul R, Jr 1929- *AmMWSc 92, WhoHisp 92*
**Cardenas,** Raymond *WhoHisp 92*
**Cardenas,** Renato E. *WhoHisp 92*
**Cardenas,** Rene 1928- *WhoWest 92*
**Cardenas,** Rene F. 1933- *WhoHisp 92*
**Cardenas,** Rene Fernando 1933- *WhoFI 92*
**Cardenas,** Robert Isaac 1936- *WhoHisp 92*
**Cardenas,** Robert Leon 1920- *WhoHisp 92*
**Cardenas,** Rudolfo Robert, Jr 1949- *WhoAmP 91*
**Cardenas-Escovar,** Alberto 1917- *WhoHisp 92*
**Cardenas-Jaffe,** Veronica 1947- *WhoHisp 92*
**Cardenes,** Andres Jorge 1957- *WhoEnt 92*
**Cardente,** Alfred W 1925- *WhoAmP 91*
**Carder,** David Ross 1940- *AmMWSc 92*
**Carder,** Kendall L 1942- *AmMWSc 92*
**Carder,** Larry William 1958- *WhoWest 92*
**Carder,** Leigh *TwCWW 91*
**Carder,** Malcolm 1936- *TwCPaSc*
**Cardew,** Cornelius 1936-1981 *NewAmDM*
**Cardiasmenos,** Apostle George *AmMWSc 92*
**Cardiello,** Natalie Lutz 1960- *WhoAmL 92*
**Cardiff,** Archbishop of 1929- *Who 92*
**Cardiff,** Gladys H. *DrAPF 91*
**Cardiff,** Jack 1914- *IntMPA 92, IntWW 91, Who 92*
**Cardiff,** Robert Darrell 1935- *AmMWSc 92*
**Cardigan,** Earl of 1952- *Who 92*
**Cardillo,** Clement John 1925- *WhoRel 92*
**Cardillo,** Frances M 1932- *AmMWSc 92*
**Cardillo,** Joe *DrAPF 91*
**Cardillo,** John Pollara 1942- *WhoAmL 92*
**Cardillo,** Mark J 1943- *AmMWSc 92*
**Cardin,** Benjamin L. 1943- *AlmAP 92 [port]*
**Cardin,** Benjamin Louis 1943- *WhoAmL 92, WhoAmP 91*
**Cardin,** Charles Edward 1929- *WhoAmL 92*
**Cardin,** Pierre 1922- *DcTwDes, FacFETw, IntWW 91, Who 92*
**Cardin,** Shoshana Shoubin 1926- *WhoRel 92*
**Cardin,** Tommie Sullivan 1961- *WhoAmL 92, WhoAmP 91*
**Cardinal,** Claus 1943- *WhoIns 92*
**Cardinal,** Douglas Joseph 1934- *IntWW 91*
**Cardinal,** John Robert 1943- *AmMWSc 92*
**Cardinal,** Michael Scott 1968- *WhoEnt 92*
**Cardinal,** Roger 1940- *IntAu&W 91, WrDr 92*
**Cardinale,** Claudia 1938- *IntWW 91*
**Cardinale,** Claudia 1939- *IntMPA 92*
**Cardinale,** George Joseph 1936- *AmMWSc 92*
**Cardinale,** Gerald 1934- *WhoAmP 91*
**Cardine,** G Joseph *WhoAmP 91*
**Cardine,** Godfrey Joseph 1924- *WhoAmL 92, WhoWest 92*
**Cardinet,** George Hugh, III 1934- *AmMWSc 92*
**Cardis,** Angeline Baird 1943- *AmMWSc 92*
**Cardle,** Maria Joan Pastuszek 1959- *WhoWest 92*
**Cardman,** Lawrence Santo 1944- *AmMWSc 92*
**Cardner,** David V 1935- *AmMWSc 92*
**Cardon,** Bartley Lowell 1940- *AmMWSc 92*
**Cardon,** Marriner Paul 1932- *WhoAmL 92*
**Cardon,** Samuel Zelig 1918- *AmMWSc 92*
**Cardona,** Carlos J., Jr. 1940- *WhoHisp 92*
**Cardona,** Fernando 1935- *WhoHisp 92*
**Cardona,** Florencia Bisenta de Casillas M *WhoEnt 92*
**Cardona,** Gilbert Tommy 1938- *WhoHisp 92*
**Cardona,** Manuel 1934- *AmMWSc 92*
**Cardona-Hine,** Alvaro *DrAPF 91*
**Cardone,** James Joseph, Jr. 1948- *WhoRel 92*
**Cardoso,** Dinora C. 1959- *WhoHisp 92*
**Cardoso,** Sergio Steiner 1927- *AmMWSc 92*
**Cardoso E Cunha,** Antonio Jose 1933- *IntWW 91*
**Cardoso E Cunha,** Antonio Jose Baptista 1934- *Who 92*
**Cardoza,** Anne de Sola 1941- *WhoEnt 92*
**Cardoza,** Jose Alfredo 1953- *WhoHisp 92*
**Cardoza,** Marvin Edmund 1913- *WhoWest 92*
**Cardoza,** Raul John 1944- *WhoHisp 92*
**Cardoza,** Robert J. *WhoHisp 92*
**Cardozo,** Benjamin 1870-1938 *RComAH*
**Cardozo,** Benjamin N 1870-1938 *FacFETw*

**Cardozo,** Benjamin Nathan 1870-1938 *AmPolLe, BenetAL 91*
**Cardozo,** Michael A. 1941- *WhoAmL 92*
**Cardozo,** Michael Hart 1910- *WhoAmL 92*
**Cardozo,** Michael Hart, V 1940- *WhoAmP 91*
**Cardozo,** Richard Nunez 1936- *WhoMW 92*
**Cardross,** Lord 1960- *Who 92*
**Carducci,** Giosue 1835-1907 *FacFETw*
**Carducci,** Giosue Alessandro Guiseppe 1835-1907 *WhoNob 90*
**Cardullo,** Joseph P 1945- *WhoAmP 91*
**Cardus,** David 1922- *AmMWSc 92*
**Cardwell,** Alvin Boyd 1902- *AmMWSc 92*
**Cardwell,** David Earl 1951- *WhoAmL 92*
**Cardwell,** David Michael 1949- *AmMWSc 92*
**Cardwell,** Donald Stephen Lowell 1919- *IntWW 91*
**Cardwell,** Gerald Douglas 1949- *WhoMW 92*
**Cardwell,** Joe Thomas 1922- *AmMWSc 92*
**Cardwell,** John James 1931- *IntWW 91*
**Cardwell,** Michael Dexter 1950- *WhoWest 92*
**Cardwell,** Paul H 1912- *AmMWSc 92*
**Cardwell,** Vernon Bruce 1936- *AmMWSc 92*
**Cardwell,** William Thomas, Jr 1917- *AmMWSc 92*
**Cardy,** John Lawrence 1947- *Who 92*
**Carelli,** Gabor Paul 1915- *WhoEnt 92*
**Carelli,** Mario Domenico *AmMWSc 92*
**Caren,** Linda Davis 1941- *AmMWSc 92*
**Caren,** Robert Poston 1932- *AmMWSc 92*
**Cares,** William Ronald 1941- *AmMWSc 92*
**Caress,** Edward Alan 1936- *AmMWSc 92*
**Caret,** Robert Laurent 1947- *AmMWSc 92*
**Caretti,** Richard Louis 1953- *WhoFI 92, WhoMW 92*
**Caretto,** Albert A, Jr 1928- *AmMWSc 92*
**Carew,** Baron 1905- *Who 92*
**Carew,** Colin A. 1943- *WhoBlA 92*
**Carew,** David P 1928- *AmMWSc 92*
**Carew,** Henry *ScFEYrs*
**Carew,** James L 1945- *AmMWSc 92*
**Carew,** Jan 1925- *BenetAL 91, IntAu&W 91, LiExTwC, WrDr 92*
**Carew,** John Francis 1937- *AmMWSc 92*
**Carew,** Keggie 1957- *TwCPaSc*
**Carew,** Lyndon Belmont, Jr 1932- *AmMWSc 92*
**Carew,** Rivers 1935- *Who 92, WrDr 92*
**Carew,** Rodney Cline 1945- *WhoBlA 92*
**Carew,** Thomas 1594?-1640 *RfGEnL 91*
**Carew,** Thomas Edward 1943- *AmMWSc 92*
**Carew,** Topper 1943- *WhoBlA 92*
**Carew,** William James d1990 *Who 92N*
**Carew Pole,** John 1902- *Who 92*
**Carew Pole,** Richard 1938- *Who 92*
**Carey,** Addison, Jr. 1933- *WhoBlA 92*
**Carey,** Alban M. 1906- *Who 92*
**Carey,** Alfred W, Jr 1924- *AmMWSc 92*
**Carey,** Andrew Galbraith, Jr 1932- *AmMWSc 92*
**Carey,** Andrew John, III 1943- *WhoAmP 91*
**Carey,** Archibald James, Jr. 1908-1981 *WhoBlA 92N*
**Carey,** Audrey L. 1937- *WhoBlA 92*
**Carey,** Barbara I 1946- *WhoIns 92*
**Carey,** Bernard Joseph 1941- *AmMWSc 92*
**Carey,** Carnice 1945- *WhoBlA 92*
**Carey,** Charles *ScFEYrs*
**Carey,** Charles Edward 1953- *WhoAmL 92*
**Carey,** Charles John 1933- *Who 92*
**Carey,** Christopher Edwin 1958- *WhoAmL 92*
**Carey,** Christopher James 1956- *WhoAmL 92*
**Carey,** Claire Lamar 1943- *WhoBlA 92*
**Carey,** Conan Jerome 1936- *Who 92*
**Carey,** Cynthia 1947- *AmMWSc 92*
**Carey,** D. M. M. 1917- *Who 92*
**Carey,** Daniel Douglas 1963- *WhoMW 92*
**Carey,** David Crockett 1939- *AmMWSc 92*
**Carey,** David Marsden, Jr. 1954- *WhoEnt 92, WhoFI 92*
**Carey,** de Vic Graham 1940- *Who 92*
**Carey,** Edward Marshel, Jr. 1942- *WhoFI 92, WhoMW 92*
**Carey,** Ernestine Gilbreth *WrDr 92*
**Carey,** Francis Arthur 1937- *AmMWSc 92*
**Carey,** Francis G 1931- *AmMWSc 92*
**Carey,** Gary 1938- *ConAu 34NR*
**Carey,** Geoffrey R. B. 1961- *WhoFI 92*
**Carey,** George 1935- *CurBio 91 [port], FacFETw*
**Carey,** George Leonard *Who 92*
**Carey,** George Leonard 1935- *IntWW 91, WhoRel 92*
**Carey,** Gerald E 1937- *WhoIns 92*
**Carey,** Godfrey Mohun Cecil 1941- *Who 92*
**Carey,** Graham Francis 1944- *AmMWSc 92*
**Carey,** Harmon Roderick 1936- *WhoBlA 92*
**Carey,** Harry, Jr. 1921- *IntMPA 92*
**Carey,** Henry 1687?-1743 *RfGEnL 91*
**Carey,** Howard H. 1937- *WhoBlA 92*
**Carey,** Hugh L 1919- *WhoAmP 91*
**Carey,** Hugh Leo 1919- *Who 92*
**Carey,** James Joseph 1939- *WhoAmP 91*
**Carey,** James William 1945- *WhoBlA 92*
**Carey,** Jane Quellmalz 1952- *WhoFI 92*
**Carey,** Jean Lebeis 1943- *WhoFI 92*
**Carey,** Jennifer Davis 1956- *WhoBlA 92*
**Carey,** John 1797?-1880 *BiInAmS*
**Carey,** John 1934- *ConAu 35NR, IntAu&W 91, IntWW 91, Who 92, WrDr 92*
**Carey,** John Andrew 1949- *WhoFI 92*
**Carey,** John Hugh 1947- *AmMWSc 92*
**Carey,** John J 1928- *WhoIns 92*
**Carey,** John Joseph 1911- *AmMWSc 92*
**Carey,** John Leo 1920- *WhoAmL 92*
**Carey,** John Michael 1951- *WhoAmL 92*
**Carey,** John Patrick 1963- *WhoEnt 92*
**Carey,** Joseph Kuhn 1957- *ConAu 135*
**Carey,** Julian *TwCSFW 91*
**Carey,** Kathryn Ann 1949- *WhoFI 92, WhoWest 92*
**Carey,** Larry Campbell 1933- *AmMWSc 92*
**Carey,** Linda Marie 1962- *WhoRel 92*
**Carey,** Macdonald 1913- *IntMPA 92, WhoEnt 92*
**Carey,** Marcia J. 1941- *WhoWest 92*
**Carey,** Margaret Hatfield 1953- *WhoFI 92*
**Carey,** Mariah *WhoEnt 92, WhoHisp 92*
**Carey,** Mariah 1970?- *ConMus 6 [port], News 91 [port], -91-3 [port]*
**Carey,** Marsha Clifton 1951- *WhoAmL 92*
**Carey,** Martin Conrad 1939- *AmMWSc 92*
**Carey,** Mathew 1760-1839 *BenetAL 91, BlkwEAR*
**Carey,** Matthew 1760-1839 *DcAmImH*
**Carey,** Michael Andrew 1954- *WhoMW 92*
**Carey,** Michael Dean 1946- *AmMWSc 92*
**Carey,** Milburn Ernest 1912- *WhoEnt 92*
**Carey,** Milton Gales 1926- *WhoBlA 92*
**Carey,** Nancy Sue 1942- *WhoAmP 91*
**Carey,** Naomi Ruth 1930- *WhoMW 92*
**Carey,** Omer L. 1929- *WhoWest 92*
**Carey,** Patricia M. *WhoBlA 92*
**Carey,** Paul L 1923- *AmMWSc 92*
**Carey,** Paul Richard 1945- *AmMWSc 92*
**Carey,** Pearl M. *WhoBlA 92*
**Carey,** Peter 1943- *ConNov 91, IntWW 91, WrDr 92*
**Carey,** Peter Philip 1943- *IntAu&W 91, Who 92*
**Carey,** Peter Willoughby 1923- *IntWW 91, Who 92*
**Carey,** Phil 1925- *IntMPA 92*
**Carey,** Phillip 1942- *WhoBlA 92*
**Carey,** Raymond Giddens, Jr. 1944- *WhoAmL 92*
**Carey,** Richard Edward 1957- *WhoWest 92*
**Carey,** Robert E. 1920- *WhoAmL 92*
**Carey,** Ronald R 1936- *NewYTBS 91 [port]*
**Carey,** Steve *DrAPF 91*
**Carey,** Thomas Cornelius 1947- *WhoAmL 92*
**Carey,** Thomas Devore 1931- *WhoEnt 92*
**Carey,** Thomas E *AmMWSc 92*
**Carey,** Tobe 1942- *WhoEnt 92*
**Carey,** V George 1928- *WhoAmP 91*
**Carey,** William Arthur 1920- *WhoAmP 91*
**Carey,** William Bacon 1926- *AmMWSc 92*
**Carey,** William Craig 1942- *WhoAmL 92*
**Carey,** William Daniel 1916- *AmMWSc 92*
**Carey,** William Polk 1930- *WhoFI 92*
**Carey Evans,** David Lloyd 1925- *Who 92*
**Carey-Foster,** George Arthur 1907- *Who 92*
**Carey Jones,** Norman Stewart 1911- *Who 92*
**Carfagno,** Daniel Gaetano 1935- *AmMWSc 92*
**Carfagno,** Salvatore P 1925- *AmMWSc 92*
**Carfax,** Catherine *IntAu&W 91X, WrDr 92*
**Carfolite,** David Warren 1954- *WhoEnt 92*
**Carfora,** Carmel Henry 1878-1958 *RelLAm 91*
**Cargas,** Harry James 1932- *IntAu&W 91*
**Cargerman,** Alan William 1945- *WhoAmL 92*
**Cargile,** C. B., Jr. 1926- *WhoBlA 92*
**Cargile,** David L 1946- *WhoIns 92*
**Cargile,** Michael Edward 1942- *WhoMW 92*
**Cargile,** William, III *WhoBlA 92*
**Cargill,** B F 1922- *AmMWSc 92*
**Cargill,** G Slade, III 1943- *AmMWSc 92*
**Cargill,** Gilbert Allen 1916- *WhoBlA 92*
**Cargill,** Robert Lee, Jr 1934- *AmMWSc 92*
**Cargill,** Robert Mason 1948- *WhoAmL 92*
**Cargill,** Sandra Morris 1953- *WhoBlA 92*
**Cargiulo,** Ralph J 1935- *WhoIns 92*
**Cargo,** David Garrett 1924- *AmMWSc 92*
**Cargo,** Gerald Thomas 1930- *AmMWSc 92*
**Cargo,** William Abram 1947- *WhoRel 92*
**Carhart,** Henry Smith 1844-1920 *BiInAmS*
**Carhart,** Richard Alan 1939- *AmMWSc 92*
**Carhart,** Vera Margaret 1928- *WhoAmP 91*
**Carico,** James Edwin 1937- *AmMWSc 92*
**Caridas,** Evangeline Chris 1950- *WhoFI 92*
**Carignan,** Jean 1916- *NewAmDM*
**Carignan,** Shanda Mulford Heiser 1950- *WhoRel 92*
**Carignon,** Alain 1949- *IntWW 91*
**Carillo,** Gilberto *BlkOlyM*
**Carillo,** Michael A. 1951- *WhoHisp 92*
**Carim,** Hatim Mohamed 1946- *AmMWSc 92*
**Carine,** James 1934- *Who 92*
**Carington** *Who 92*
**Carioba,** John 1929- *WhoEnt 92*
**Cariou,** Len 1939- *IntMPA 92*
**Cariou,** Len Joseph 1939- *WhoEnt 92*
**Caris,** Barry M. 1939- *WhoMW 92*
**Carisch,** George 1935- *IntMPA 92*
**Carisella,** P. J. 1922- *ConAu 134*
**Carissimi,** Giacomo 1605-1674 *NewAmDM*
**Carithers,** Jeanine Rutherford 1933- *AmMWSc 92*
**Carithers,** Robert Prentice 1950- *WhoAmL 92*
**Carkeet,** David *DrAPF 91*
**Carkeet,** David 1946- *WhoMW 92, WrDr 92*
**Carl XVI Gustaf** 1946- *IntWW 91*
**Carl,** Angela Reeves 1949- *WhoMW 92*
**Carl,** Barbara Balling 1950- *WhoAmL 92*
**Carl,** Beverly May 1932- *WhoAmL 92*
**Carl,** Douglas 1951- *WhoAmP 91*
**Carl,** Earl Lawrence 1919- *WhoBlA 92*
**Carl,** Edward Lee 1945- *WhoRel 92*
**Carl,** James Dudley 1935- *AmMWSc 92*
**Carl,** Janet A 1948- *WhoAmP 91*
**Carl,** Matthew John 1957- *WhoAmL 92*
**Carl,** Philip Louis 1939- *AmMWSc 92*
**Carl,** Robert E. 1927- *WhoFI 92*
**Carl,** Tommie Ewert 1921- *WhoEnt 92*
**Carl,** William Crane 1865-1936 *NewAmDM*
**Carlan,** Alan J 1930- *AmMWSc 92*
**Carlan,** Audrey M *AmMWSc 92*
**Carlander,** John Robert 1943- *WhoWest 92*
**Carlander,** Kenneth Dixon 1915- *AmMWSc 92*
**Carlberg,** Carl Ernfried 1889-1962 *BiDExR*
**Carlberg,** David Marvin 1934- *AmMWSc 92*
**Carlberg,** James Edwin 1950- *WhoAmL 92*
**Carlberg,** Karen Ann 1949- *AmMWSc 92*
**Carle,** Eric 1929- *IntAu&W 91, SmATA 65 [port], WrDr 92*
**Carle,** Glenn Clifford 1936- *AmMWSc 92*
**Carle,** Harry Lloyd 1927- *WhoWest 92*
**Carle,** Kenneth Roberts 1929- *AmMWSc 92*
**Carle,** Lawrence Jerry 1946- *WhoMW 92*
**Carlebach,** Shlomo 1926- *RelLAm 91*
**Carlee,** Christopher Lothrop 1955- *WhoMW 92*
**Carlee,** Jan Lothrop 1952- *WhoEnt 92*
**Carlen,** Peter Louis 1943- *AmMWSc 92*
**Carleon,** A. *WrDr 92*
**Carleone,** Joseph 1946- *AmMWSc 92, WhoWest 92*
**Carless,** Hugh Michael 1925- *Who 92*
**Carless,** John Edward 1922- *Who 92*
**Carleton,** Blondel Henry 1904- *AmMWSc 92*
**Carleton,** Bruce Alan 1947- *WhoMW 92*
**Carleton,** Bukk Griffith 1909- *WhoFI 92*
**Carleton,** Gordon Robert 1955- *WhoEnt 92*
**Carleton,** Guy 1724-1808 *BlkwEAR*
**Carleton,** Henry Guy 1856-1910 *BenetAL 91*
**Carleton,** Herbert Ruck 1928- *AmMWSc 92*
**Carleton,** John, Mrs. *Who 92*
**Carleton,** John Lowndes 1925- *WhoWest 92*
**Carleton,** Joseph G, Jr 1945- *WhoAmP 91*
**Carleton,** Mark Thomas 1935- *WrDr 92*
**Carleton,** Nathaniel Phillips 1929- *AmMWSc 92*
**Carleton,** Paul Hunter 1948- *WhoMW 92*
**Carleton,** Richard Allyn 1931- *AmMWSc 92*
**Carleton,** Will 1845-1912 *BenetAL 91*
**Carleton,** William 1794-1869 *RfGEnL 91*
**Carleton,** William Peter, Jr. 1932- *WhoMW 92*
**Carleton-Smith,** Michael Edward 1931- *Who 92*
**Carley,** Charles Team, Jr 1932- *AmMWSc 92*
**Carley,** David Don 1935- *AmMWSc 92*
**Carley,** Harold Edwin 1942- *AmMWSc 92*
**Carley,** James F 1923- *AmMWSc 92*
**Carley,** John Blythe 1934- *WhoWest 92*
**Carley,** John Halliday 1941- *WhoAmP 91*
**Carley,** Kurt 1962- *WhoEnt 92*
**Carley,** Robert Joseph 1930- *WhoAmP 91*
**Carley,** Thomas Gerald 1935- *AmMWSc 92*
**Carli,** Guido 1914- *IntWW 91*
**Carli-Rubbi,** Giovanni Rinaldo 1720-1795 *BlkwCEP*
**Carlier,** Anthony Neil 1937- *Who 92*
**Carlile,** Alexander Charles 1948- *Who 92*
**Carlile,** Edward Wilson 1915- *Who 92*
**Carlile,** Henry *DrAPF 91*
**Carlile,** Keith Smith 1928- *WhoRel 92*
**Carlile,** Richard 1790-1843 *DcLB 110 [port]*
**Carlile,** Robert Elliot 1933- *AmMWSc 92*
**Carlile,** Robert Leslie 1924- *WhoMW 92*
**Carlile,** Robert Nichols 1929- *AmMWSc 92*
**Carlile,** Thomas 1924- *IntWW 91, Who 92*
**Carlill,** John Hildred 1925- *Who 92*
**Carlill,** Stephen Hope 1902- *Who 92*
**Carlin,** Benedict 1911- *WhoFI 92*
**Carlin,** Charles Herrick 1939- *AmMWSc 92*
**Carlin,** Charles Stephen 1943- *WhoRel 92*
**Carlin,** Clair Myron 1947- *WhoAmL 92, WhoMW 92*
**Carlin,** Daniel Allan 1947- *WhoEnt 92*
**Carlin,** David Robert, Jr 1938- *WhoAmP 91*
**Carlin,** Deborah Lynn 1956- *WhoMW 92*
**Carlin,** Donald Walter 1934- *WhoAmL 92*
**Carlin,** George 1937- *IntMPA 92*
**Carlin,** George Denis 1937- *WhoEnt 92*
**Carlin,** Herbert J 1917- *AmMWSc 92*
**Carlin,** John David 1962- *WhoAmL 92*
**Carlin,** John William 1940- *IntWW 91, WhoAmP 91*
**Carlin,** Melissa Joann 1949- *WhoHisp 92*
**Carlin,** Paul Victor 1945- *WhoAmL 92*
**Carlin,** Philip R. 1928- *WhoAmL 92*
**Carlin,** Richard Lewis 1935- *AmMWSc 92*
**Carlin,** Robert Burnell 1916- *AmMWSc 92*
**Carlin,** Ronald D 1946- *AmMWSc 92*
**Carlin,** Roy H. 1939- *WhoAmL 92*
**Carlin,** Sean Michael 1958- *WhoAmL 92*
**Carlin,** Sidney Alan 1925- *WhoEnt 92*
**Carlin,** Steve *LesBEnT 92*
**Carlin,** Thomas A. d1991 *NewYTBS 91*
**Carline,** George 1855-1920 *TwCPaSc*
**Carline,** Hilda 1889-1950 *TwCPaSc [port]*
**Carline,** Nancy 1909- *TwCPaSc*
**Carline,** Richard 1896-1980 *TwCPaSc*
**Carline,** Sydney 1888-1929 *TwCPaSc*
**Carline,** William Ralph 1910- *WhoBlA 92*
**Carling,** Francis 1945- *WhoAmL 92*
**Carling,** George 1852- *ScFEYrs*
**Carling,** Richard Junius 1937- *WhoAmP 91*
**Carlini,** James 1954- *WhoFI 92*
**Carlino,** Guy Thomas 1928- *WhoFI 92*
**Carlino,** Lewis John 1932- *IntAu&W 91, IntMPA 92, WrDr 92*
**Carlisle** *Who 92*
**Carlisle,** Archdeacon of *Who 92*
**Carlisle,** Bishop of 1932- *Who 92*
**Carlisle,** Dean of *Who 92*
**Carlisle,** Earl of 1923- *Who 92*
**Carlisle,** Brian Apcar 1919- *Who 92*
**Carlisle,** D M *IntAu&W 91X*
**Carlisle,** David Brez 1926- *AmMWSc 92*
**Carlisle,** Donald 1919- *AmMWSc 92*
**Carlisle,** Edith M 1922- *AmMWSc 92*
**Carlisle,** Fionna 1954- *TwCPaSc*
**Carlisle,** Gene Ozelle 1939- *AmMWSc 92*
**Carlisle,** Harry J *AmMWSc 92*
**Carlisle,** Henry *DrAPF 91*
**Carlisle,** Hugh Bernard Harwood 1937- *Who 92*
**Carlisle,** James Patton 1946- *WhoRel 92*
**Carlisle,** John Griffin 1835-1910 *AmPolLe*
**Carlisle,** John Michael 1929- *Who 92*
**Carlisle,** John Reid 1942- *WhoAmP 91*
**Carlisle,** John Russell 1942- *Who 92*
**Carlisle,** Kay Susan 1945- *AmMWSc 92*
**Carlisle,** Kenneth Melville 1941- *Who 92*
**Carlisle,** Kitty 1915- *WhoEnt 92*
**Carlisle,** Lilburn Wayne 1936- *WhoAmP 91*
**Carlisle,** Margo Duer Black *WhoAmP 91*
**Carlisle,** Maurice Eugene, Jr. 1933- *WhoFI 92*
**Carlisle,** Michael *Who 92*
**Carlisle,** Patricia Kinley 1949- *WhoFI 92*
**Carlisle,** Randall Dean 1956- *WhoFI 92*
**Carlisle,** Richard Kenneth 1950- *WhoMW 92*
**Carlisle,** Ronald Dwight 1940- *WhoAmP 91*
**Carlisle,** Thomas John *DrAPF 91*
**Carlisle,** Thomas John 1913- *WhoRel 92*
**Carlisle,** Vervene *WhoAmP 91*
**Carlisle,** Victor Walter 1922- *AmMWSc 92*
**Carlisle,** Ward 1951- *WhoEnt 92*

**Carlisle**, Waylon Arnold 1937- *WhoRel 92*
**Carlisle Of Bucklow**, Baron 1929- *IntWW 91, Who 92*
**Carlitz**, Leonard 1907- *AmMWSc 92*
**Carlitz**, Robert D 1945- *AmMWSc 92*
**Carll**, John Franklin 1828-1904 *BiInAmS*
**Carlo**, Michael 1945- *TwCPaSc*
**Carlo**, Nelson *WhoBlA 92*
**Carlo**, Nelson 1938- *WhoHisp 92, WhoMW 92*
**Carlo**, Waldemar Alberto 1952- *AmMWSc 92*
**Carlock**, John Timothy 1951- *AmMWSc 92*
**Carlock**, Jon Thompson 1964- *WhoRel 92*
**Carlock**, Mahlon Waldo 1926- *WhoMW 92*
**Carlomagno**, Stephen Guido 1948- *WhoMW 92*
**Carlon**, Ancel R 1940- *WhoAmP 91*
**Carlon**, Hugh Robert 1934- *AmMWSc 92*
**Carlone**, Robert Leo 1948- *AmMWSc 92*
**Carlos**, John 1945- *WhoBlA 92*
**Carlos**, John Wesley 1945- *BlkOlyM [port]*
**Carlos**, Laurie *DrAPF 91*
**Carlos**, Thomas Peter 1939- *WhoAmL 92*
**Carlos**, Wendy 1939- *NewAmDM*
**Carlos**, William Edward 1949- *AmMWSc 92*
**Carlotti**, Ronald John 1942- *AmMWSc 92*
**Carlotti**, Stephen Jon 1942- *WhoAmL 92*
**Carlow**, Viscount 1965- *Who 92*
**Carlozzi**, Carlo, Jr. 1958- *WhoFI 92*
**Carlozzo**, Ben John 1953- *WhoMW 92*
**Carlquist**, Sherwin 1930- *AmMWSc 92*
**Carls**, Jon Roland 1954- *WhoMW 92*
**Carls**, Kenneth Raymond 1947- *WhoMW 92*
**Carls**, Ralph A 1938- *AmMWSc 92*
**Carlsen**, Edward 1940- *WhoFI 92*
**Carlsen**, G. Robert 1917- *WrDr 92*
**Carlsen**, Richard Chester 1940- *AmMWSc 92*
**Carlson**, A Bruce 1937- *AmMWSc 92*
**Carlson**, Alan Douglas 1951- *WhoAmL 92*
**Carlson**, Albert Dewayne, Jr 1930- *AmMWSc 92*
**Carlson**, Allan David 1939- *AmMWSc 92*
**Carlson**, Andrew R. 1934- *WrDr 92*
**Carlson**, Anita Lynne 1952- *WhoMW 92*
**Carlson**, Arne H. 1934- *AlmAP 92 [port], WhoAmP 91*
**Carlson**, Arne Helge 1934- *WhoMW 92*
**Carlson**, Arthur, Jr 1922- *AmMWSc 92*
**Carlson**, Arthur Stephen 1919- *AmMWSc 92*
**Carlson**, Beecey 1931- *WhoEnt 92*
**Carlson**, Bernice Wells 1910- *WrDr 92*
**Carlson**, Bille Chandler 1924- *AmMWSc 92, WhoMW 92*
**Carlson**, Bradley Lee 1951- *WhoWest 92*
**Carlson**, Brian Jay 1956- *WhoMW 92*
**Carlson**, Bruce Arne 1946- *AmMWSc 92*
**Carlson**, Bruce Lyman 1938- *WhoRel 92*
**Carlson**, Bruce Martin 1938- *AmMWSc 92*
**Carlson**, Carl E 1922- *AmMWSc 92*
**Carlson**, Carl J. d1991 *NewYTBS 91*
**Carlson**, Charles A. 1933- *WhoFI 92*
**Carlson**, Charles Long 1917- *WhoWest 92*
**Carlson**, Charles Merton 1934- *AmMWSc 92*
**Carlson**, Charles Richard 1944- *WhoMW 92*
**Carlson**, Charles Wendell 1921- *AmMWSc 92*
**Carlson**, Clarence Albert, Jr 1937- *AmMWSc 92*
**Carlson**, Clarence Boyden 1935- *WhoMW 92*
**Carlson**, Clinton E 1942- *AmMWSc 92*
**Carlson**, Curtis Eugene 1942- *WhoWest 92*
**Carlson**, Curtis Keith 1946- *WhoEnt 92*
**Carlson**, Curtis LeRoy 1914- *WhoFI 92, WhoMW 92*
**Carlson**, Curtis Raymond 1945- *AmMWSc 92*
**Carlson**, Dale Alan 1959- *WhoAmL 92*
**Carlson**, Dale Arvid 1925- *AmMWSc 92*
**Carlson**, Dale Lynn 1946- *WhoAmL 92*
**Carlson**, Dana Peter 1931- *AmMWSc 92*
**Carlson**, Darryl Dean 1938- *WhoWest 92*
**Carlson**, David Arthur 1940- *AmMWSc 92*
**Carlson**, David Emil 1942- *AmMWSc 92*
**Carlson**, David George 1959- *WhoAmL 92*
**Carlson**, David Hilding 1936- *AmMWSc 92*
**Carlson**, David L 1936- *AmMWSc 92*
**Carlson**, David Martin 1940- *WhoFI 92*
**Carlson**, David Sten 1948- *AmMWSc 92*
**Carlson**, Dennis Arthur 1946- *WhoMW 92*
**Carlson**, Dennis Nobel 1946- *WhoRel 92*
**Carlson**, Dianne Elizabeth 1958- *WhoAmL 92*
**Carlson**, Don 1929- *WhoAmP 91*
**Carlson**, Don Marvin 1931- *AmMWSc 92*
**Carlson**, Donna Jean 1938- *WhoAmP 91*
**Carlson**, Douglas *DrAPF 91*
**Carlson**, Douglas W 1930- *AmMWSc 92*
**Carlson**, Douglas W 1939- *WhoAmP 91*
**Carlson**, Drew E 1948- *AmMWSc 92*
**Carlson**, Edgar A 1929- *WhoAmP 91*
**Carlson**, Edward H 1932- *AmMWSc 92*
**Carlson**, Edwin Theodore 1946- *WhoFI 92*
**Carlson**, Elof Axel 1931- *AmMWSc 92*
**Carlson**, Emil Herbert 1929- *AmMWSc 92*
**Carlson**, Eric Dungan 1929- *AmMWSc 92*
**Carlson**, Eric Theodore 1922- *AmMWSc 92*
**Carlson**, Ernest Howard 1933- *AmMWSc 92*
**Carlson**, F Roy, Jr 1944- *AmMWSc 92*
**Carlson**, Francis Dewey 1921- *AmMWSc 92*
**Carlson**, Frederick Paul 1938- *AmMWSc 92*
**Carlson**, Gary 1928- *AmMWSc 92, WhoFI 92*
**Carlson**, Gary Alden 1941- *AmMWSc 92*
**Carlson**, Gary B. 1952- *WhoWest 92*
**Carlson**, Gary Lee 1954- *WhoEnt 92, WhoWest 92*
**Carlson**, Gary P 1943- *AmMWSc 92*
**Carlson**, Gary Wayne 1944- *AmMWSc 92*
**Carlson**, George A 1947- *AmMWSc 92*
**Carlson**, Gerald Eugene 1932- *AmMWSc 92*
**Carlson**, Gerald M 1941- *AmMWSc 92*
**Carlson**, Gerald Michael 1946- *AmMWSc 92*
**Carlson**, Gerald Wesley 1947- *WhoMW 92*
**Carlson**, Glenn Richard 1945- *AmMWSc 92*
**Carlson**, Gordon Andrew 1917- *AmMWSc 92*
**Carlson**, Gunnar Carl, Jr. 1939- *WhoWest 92*
**Carlson**, Guy Raymond 1918- *WhoMW 92, WhoRel 92*
**Carlson**, H Maurice 1916- *AmMWSc 92*
**Carlson**, Harold C R 1908- *AmMWSc 92*
**Carlson**, Harold Ernest 1943- *AmMWSc 92*
**Carlson**, Harry William 1924- *AmMWSc 92*
**Carlson**, Herb *WhoAmP 91*
**Carlson**, Herbert Christian, Jr 1937- *AmMWSc 92*
**Carlson**, Irving Theodore 1926- *AmMWSc 92*
**Carlson**, James Andrew 1946- *AmMWSc 92*
**Carlson**, James C 1928- *AmMWSc 92*
**Carlson**, James Gordon 1908- *AmMWSc 92*
**Carlson**, James H 1935- *AmMWSc 92*
**Carlson**, James Leslie 1932- *WhoRel 92*
**Carlson**, James Reynold 1948- *AmMWSc 92*
**Carlson**, James Roy 1939- *AmMWSc 92*
**Carlson**, James Wayne 1955- *WhoMW 92*
**Carlson**, Jane Elizabeth 1918- *WhoEnt 92*
**Carlson**, Janet Lynn 1952- *AmMWSc 92*
**Carlson**, Joan *WhoAmP 91*
**Carlson**, John Bernard 1926- *AmMWSc 92*
**Carlson**, John F. 1938- *WhoFI 92*
**Carlson**, John Godfrey, Jr. 1926- *WhoFI 92*
**Carlson**, John Gregory 1941- *AmMWSc 92*
**Carlson**, John Henry 1945- *WhoAmL 92, WhoFI 92*
**Carlson**, John W 1940- *AmMWSc 92*
**Carlson**, Jon Frederick 1940- *AmMWSc 92*
**Carlson**, Jon Olaf 1942- *WhoEnt 92*
**Carlson**, Karen Lou *WhoWest 92*
**Carlson**, Karin Anne 1961- *WhoEnt 92*
**Carlson**, Katherine *DrAPF 91*
**Carlson**, Keith Douglas 1933- *AmMWSc 92*
**Carlson**, Keith J 1938- *AmMWSc 92*
**Carlson**, Kenneth George 1949- *WhoMW 92*
**Carlson**, Kenneth Theodore 1921- *AmMWSc 92*
**Carlson**, Kermit Howard 1913- *AmMWSc 92*
**Carlson**, Kit *DrAPF 91*
**Carlson**, Kristin Rowe 1940- *AmMWSc 92*
**Carlson**, Lawrence Evan 1944- *AmMWSc 92*
**Carlson**, Lee Arnold 1939- *AmMWSc 92*
**Carlson**, LeRoy Theodore Sheridan, Sr. 1916- *WhoMW 92*
**Carlson**, Lester William 1933- *AmMWSc 92*
**Carlson**, Lewis John 1924- *AmMWSc 92*
**Carlson**, Loraine 1923- *WrDr 92*
**Carlson**, Loren Dale 1943- *WhoFI 92*
**Carlson**, Lyndon Richard 1940- *WhoAmP 91*
**Carlson**, Margaret Allyn 1951- *WhoEnt 92*
**Carlson**, Margaret Ellen 1955- *WhoWest 92*
**Carlson**, Marian B 1952- *AmMWSc 92*
**Carlson**, Marvin Albert 1935- *WhoEnt 92*
**Carlson**, Marvin Paul 1935- *AmMWSc 92*
**Carlson**, Mary Ann 1944- *WhoAmP 91*
**Carlson**, Merle Thomas 1932- *WhoAmP 91*
**Carlson**, Merle Winslow 1942- *AmMWSc 92*
**Carlson**, Nancy Lee 1950- *WhoWest 92*
**Carlson**, Natalie S. 1906- *BenetAL 91*
**Carlson**, Natalie Savage 1906- *SmATA 68 [port], WrDr 92*
**Carlson**, Norman A 1933- *WhoAmP 91*
**Carlson**, Norman Arthur 1939- *AmMWSc 92*
**Carlson**, Norman Wesley 1958- *WhoMW 92*
**Carlson**, Orville James 1944- *WhoFI 92*
**Carlson**, Oscar Norman 1920- *AmMWSc 92, WhoMW 92*
**Carlson**, P. M. *ConAu 36NR*
**Carlson**, Patricia M. 1940- *ConAu 36NR*
**Carlson**, Paul C. 1951- *WhoFI 92*
**Carlson**, Paul Edwin 1944- *WhoWest 92*
**Carlson**, Paul Roland 1933- *AmMWSc 92*
**Carlson**, Peter Michael 1947- *WhoMW 92*
**Carlson**, Philip R 1931- *AmMWSc 92*
**Carlson**, Ralph William, Jr. 1936- *WhoWest 92*
**Carlson**, Randy Eugene 1948- *WhoMW 92*
**Carlson**, Ria Marie 1961- *WhoWest 92*
**Carlson**, Richard Carl 1942- *WhoFI 92*
**Carlson**, Richard Eugene 1940- *AmMWSc 92*
**Carlson**, Richard Frederick 1936- *AmMWSc 92*
**Carlson**, Richard Gregory 1949- *WhoMW 92*
**Carlson**, Richard M 1925- *AmMWSc 92*
**Carlson**, Richard Merrill 1925- *WhoWest 92*
**Carlson**, Richard Oscar 1926- *AmMWSc 92*
**Carlson**, Richard P 1939- *AmMWSc 92*
**Carlson**, Richard Paul 1945- *WhoRel 92*
**Carlson**, Richard Raymond 1923- *AmMWSc 92*
**Carlson**, Richard Walter 1954- *AmMWSc 92*
**Carlson**, Richard Warner 1941- *WhoAmP 91*
**Carlson**, Robert Bruce 1938- *AmMWSc 92*
**Carlson**, Robert Codner 1939- *WhoFI 92, WhoWest 92*
**Carlson**, Robert E. 1930- *WhoAmL 92*
**Carlson**, Robert E. 1936- *WhoIns 92*
**Carlson**, Robert Ernest 1924- *WhoWest 92*
**Carlson**, Robert G 1928- *AmMWSc 92*
**Carlson**, Robert Gideon 1938- *AmMWSc 92*
**Carlson**, Robert J. 1929- *IntWW 91*
**Carlson**, Robert James 1944- *WhoRel 92*
**Carlson**, Robert Joel 1932- *WhoMW 92*
**Carlson**, Robert Kenneth 1928- *AmMWSc 92*
**Carlson**, Robert L 1924- *AmMWSc 92*
**Carlson**, Robert Leonard 1932- *AmMWSc 92*
**Carlson**, Robert M 1940- *AmMWSc 92*
**Carlson**, Robert Marvin 1932- *AmMWSc 92*
**Carlson**, Roger 1937- *AmMWSc 92*
**Carlson**, Roger Allan 1932- *WhoFI 92, WhoMW 92*
**Carlson**, Roger Charles 1937- *WhoIns 92*
**Carlson**, Roger David 1946- *WhoWest 92*
**Carlson**, Roger Dean 1953- *WhoMW 92*
**Carlson**, Roland David 1933- *WhoMW 92*
**Carlson**, Rolland Sigfrid 1932- *WhoFI 92*
**Carlson**, Ron *DrAPF 91*
**Carlson**, Ron 1934- *WrDr 92*
**Carlson**, Ron 1947- *WrDr 92*
**Carlson**, Ronald 1936- *TwCPaSc*
**Carlson**, Ronald Frank 1947- *IntAu&W 91, WhoWest 92*
**Carlson**, Ronald L. 1934- *ConAu 35NR*
**Carlson**, Ronald Lee 1934- *WhoAmL 92*
**Carlson**, Ronald Scott 1958- *WhoMW 92*
**Carlson**, Roy W 1900- *AmMWSc 92*
**Carlson**, Sarah *WhoAmP 91*
**Carlson**, Scott Alexander 1955- *WhoFI 92*
**Carlson**, Scott Norman 1962- *WhoAmL 92*
**Carlson**, Stanley David 1934- *AmMWSc 92*
**Carlson**, Stanley L 1937- *AmMWSc 92*
**Carlson**, Stephen Curtis 1951- *WhoAmL 92*
**Carlson**, Stephen Thomas 1945- *WhoAmP 91*
**Carlson**, Steve 1943- *WhoEnt 92*
**Carlson**, Steven Edward 1952- *WhoAmL 92*
**Carlson**, Terrance L. 1953- *WhoAmL 92*
**Carlson**, Thomas Arthur 1928- *AmMWSc 92*
**Carlson**, Thomas J 1953- *WhoAmP 91*
**Carlson**, Thomas Joseph 1953- *WhoAmL 92, WhoMW 92*
**Carlson**, Thomas L. 1938- *WhoIns 92*
**Carlson**, Toby Nahum 1936- *AmMWSc 92*
**Carlson**, Walter Carl 1953- *WhoAmL 92*
**Carlson**, Wayne C 1945- *AmMWSc 92*
**Carlson**, Wayne Harold 1944- *WhoRel 92*
**Carlson**, Wayne R 1940- *AmMWSc 92*
**Carlson**, William Dwight 1928- *AmMWSc 92*
**Carlson**, William Theodore 1933- *AmMWSc 92*
**Carlson-Gardner**, Denise Ann 1959- *WhoEnt 92*
**Carlsson**, Bo A.V. 1942- *WhoMW 92*
**Carlsson**, David James 1940- *AmMWSc 92*
**Carlsson**, Erik 1924- *AmMWSc 92*
**Carlsson**, Ingvar Gosta 1934- *IntWW 91*
**Carlsson**, Roine 1937- *IntWW 91*
**Carlstead**, Edward Meredith 1925- *AmMWSc 92*
**Carlsten**, John Lennart 1947- *AmMWSc 92*
**Carlston**, Richard Charles 1929- *WhoFI 92*
**Carlstone**, Darry Scott 1939- *AmMWSc 92*
**Carlstrom**, David John 1945- *WhoEnt 92*
**Carlstrom**, R. William 1944- *WhoWest 92*
**Carlton**, Viscount 1980- *Who 92*
**Carlton**, Alfred Pershing, Jr. 1947- *WhoAmL 92*
**Carlton**, Amy 1961- *WhoMW 92*
**Carlton**, Bruce Charles 1935- *AmMWSc 92*
**Carlton**, David 1938- *WrDr 92*
**Carlton**, Donald James 1947- *WhoMW 92*
**Carlton**, Donald Morrill 1937- *AmMWSc 92*
**Carlton**, Donna G 1941- *WhoAmP 91*
**Carlton**, Fran 1936- *WhoAmP 91*
**Carlton**, Graham Cullen *WhoEnt 92*
**Carlton**, James Theodore 1948- *AmMWSc 92*
**Carlton**, Jay *ConAu 135*
**Carlton**, John Jeffries 1951- *WhoEnt 92*
**Carlton**, John Wayne 1946- *WhoRel 92*
**Carlton**, Michael Will 1936- *WhoMW 92*
**Carlton**, Pamela Gean 1954- *WhoBlA 92*
**Carlton**, Peter Lynn 1931- *AmMWSc 92*
**Carlton**, Richard 1919- *IntMPA 92*
**Carlton**, Richard Anthony 1951- *WhoWest 92*
**Carlton**, Richard Walter 1942- *AmMWSc 92*
**Carlton**, Robert Austin 1927- *AmMWSc 92*
**Carlton**, Robert L. 1918- *WhoMW 92*
**Carlton**, Terry Scott 1939- *AmMWSc 92, WhoMW 92*
**Carlton**, Thomas A, Jr 1927- *AmMWSc 92*
**Carlton**, William Herbert 1940- *AmMWSc 92*
**Carlton**, William Walter 1929- *AmMWSc 92*
**Carlucci**, Angelo Francis 1931- *AmMWSc 92*
**Carlucci**, Frank Charles 1930- *IntWW 91*
**Carlucci**, Frank Vito 1948- *AmMWSc 92*
**Carlucci**, Joseph Paul 1942- *WhoAmL 92*
**Carluccio**, Frank 1919- *AmMWSc 92*
**Carluccio**, Leeds Mario 1936- *AmMWSc 92*
**Carlyle**, Frank Ertel 1897-1960 *DcNCBi 1*
**Carlyle**, Irving Edward 1896-1971 *DcNCBi 1*
**Carlyle**, Jack Webster 1933- *AmMWSc 92*
**Carlyle**, Joan Hildred 1931- *IntWW 91, Who 92*
**Carlyle**, John Bethune 1859-1911 *DcNCBi 1*
**Carlyle**, John Bethune, Jr. 1901-1951 *DcNCBi 1*
**Carlyle**, Thomas 1795-1881 *CnDBLB 3 [port], RfGEnL 91*
**Carlyon**, Candace Cay 1961- *WhoAmL 92*
**Carlzon**, Jan 1941- *IntWW 91*
**Carlzon**, Jan Gosta 1941- *WhoFI 92*
**Carmack**, Comer Aston, Jr. 1932- *WhoFI 92*
**Carmack**, Daniel Fieser 1926- *WhoAmL 92*
**Carmack**, David English 1938- *WhoAmL 92*
**Carmack**, Donald Gene 1932- *WhoAmP 91*
**Carmack**, Marvin 1913- *AmMWSc 92, WhoMW 92*
**Carmalt**, Churchill 1866-1905 *BiInAmS*
**Carman**, Albert 1833-1917 *RelLAm 91*
**Carman**, Bliss 1861-1929 *BenetAL 91, RfGEnL 91*
**Carman**, Charles Jerry 1938- *AmMWSc 92, WhoMW 92*
**Carman**, David Neale 1944- *WhoFI 92*
**Carman**, Ed Bradley 1955- *WhoRel 92*
**Carman**, Edwin G. 1951- *WhoBlA 92*
**Carman**, Ernest Day *WhoAmL 92*
**Carman**, Gary Michael 1949- *WhoAmL 92*
**Carman**, George Alfred 1929- *Who 92*
**Carman**, George Martin 1950- *AmMWSc 92*
**Carman**, Glenn Elwin 1914- *AmMWSc 92*
**Carman**, Gregory W 1937- *WhoAmP 91*
**Carman**, Gregory Wright 1937- *WhoAmL 92*
**Carman**, Howard Smith, Jr 1959- *AmMWSc 92*

**Carman,** James Craig 1941- *WhoAmL 92*
**Carman,** Laura Junge 1952- *WhoAmL 92*
**Carman,** Max Fleming, Jr 1924- *AmMWSc 92*
**Carman,** Michael Dennis 1938- *WhoWest 92*
**Carman,** Philip Douglas 1916- *AmMWSc 92*
**Carman,** Phillip 1944- *WhoEnt 92*
**Carman,** Robert Lincoln, Jr 1941- *AmMWSc 92*
**Carman,** William Young 1909- *IntAu&W 91, WrDr 92*
**Carmean,** Jerry Richard 1938- *WhoEnt 92*
**Carmean,** Willard Handy 1922- *AmMWSc 92*
**Carmel,** Ralph 1940- *AmMWSc 92*
**Carmeli,** Moshe 1933- *AmMWSc 92*
**Carmen,** Elaine 1939- *AmMWSc 92*
**Carmen,** Gerald P 1930- *WhoAmP 91*
**Carmen,** Julie 1960- *WhoHisp 92*
**Carmen,** Marilyn *DrAPF 91*
**Carmen,** Marilyn Elain 1941- *IntAu&W 91*
**Carmer,** Carl 1893-1976 *BenetAL 91*
**Carmer,** Samuel Grant 1932- *AmMWSc 92*
**Carmi,** Shlomo 1937- *AmMWSc 92*
**Carmichael** *Who 92*
**Carmichael,** Anne Gaye 1961- *WhoMW 92*
**Carmichael,** Benjamin G. 1938- *WhoBlA 92*
**Carmichael,** Bill 1933- *WhoAmP 91*
**Carmichael,** Carole A. 1950- *WhoBlA 92*
**Carmichael,** Catherine McIntosh 1925- *Who 92*
**Carmichael,** Charles Elmore, Jr 1923- *WhoAmP 91*
**Carmichael,** Charles Wesley 1919- *WhoFI 92, WhoMW 92*
**Carmichael,** Clifford Lee 1914- *WhoRel 92*
**Carmichael,** David James 1936- *AmMWSc 92*
**Carmichael,** David William G. C. *Who 92*
**Carmichael,** Donald C 1933- *AmMWSc 92*
**Carmichael,** Donald Scott 1912- *WhoFI 92*
**Carmichael,** Dorothy S 1925- *WhoAmP 91*
**Carmichael,** Fred Walker 1924- *IntAu&W 91*
**Carmichael,** Gilbert Ellzey 1927- *WhoAmP 91*
**Carmichael,** Gregory Richard 1952- *AmMWSc 92*
**Carmichael,** Halbert Hart 1937- *AmMWSc 92*
**Carmichael,** Hoagy 1899-1981 *FacFETw, NewAmDM*
**Carmichael,** Howard John 1950- *AmMWSc 92*
**Carmichael,** Ian 1920- *IntMPA 92, Who 92*
**Carmichael,** Ian Stuart 1930- *AmMWSc 92*
**Carmichael,** J W, Jr 1940- *AmMWSc 92*
**Carmichael,** Joe William 1928- *WhoFI 92, WhoMW 92*
**Carmichael,** Joel 1915- *IntAu&W 91, WrDr 92*
**Carmichael,** John 1910- *Who 92*
**Carmichael,** Kay *Who 92*
**Carmichael,** Keith Stanley 1929- *Who 92*
**Carmichael,** Lawrence Ray 1958- *WhoAmL 92, WhoAmP 91*
**Carmichael,** Lee Harold 1949- *WhoBlA 92*
**Carmichael,** Leland E 1930- *AmMWSc 92*
**Carmichael,** Leonard Lawrence 1952- *WhoMW 92*
**Carmichael,** Marc 1950- *WhoAmP 91*
**Carmichael,** Margaret Susan 1923- *WhoRel 92*
**Carmichael,** Peter 1933- *Who 92*
**Carmichael,** Ralph Harry 1923- *AmMWSc 92*
**Carmichael,** Richard Dudley 1942- *AmMWSc 92*
**Carmichael,** Robert Stewart 1942- *AmMWSc 92*
**Carmichael,** Robert William 1958- *WhoFI 92*
**Carmichael,** Ronald L 1921- *AmMWSc 92*
**Carmichael,** Stephen Webb 1945- *AmMWSc 92*
**Carmichael,** Stokely *DcAmImH*
**Carmichael,** Stokely 1941- *FacFETw, WhoBlA 92*
**Carmichael,** Wayne William 1947- *AmMWSc 92*
**Carmichael,** William Donald, Jr. 1900-1961 *DcNCBi 1*
**Carmichael,** William Donald, Sr. 1873-1959 *DcNCBi 1*
**Carmichael of Kelvingrove,** Baron 1921- *Who 92*
**Carmichel,** Alexander Campbell, IV 1949- *WhoRel 92*
**Carmine,** Curtis Alan *WhoMW 92*
**Carmines,** Alvin Allison, Jr. 1936- *WhoRel 92*
**Carmines,** Pamela Kay 1955- *AmMWSc 92*
**Carmody,** George Edward 1931- *WhoFI 92*
**Carmody,** George R 1938- *AmMWSc 92*
**Carmody,** James Albert 1945- *WhoAmL 92*
**Carmody,** Richard Patrick 1942- *WhoAmL 92*
**Carmody,** Robert Edward 1942- *WhoFI 92*
**Carmody,** Tim 1946- *WhoAmP 91*
**Carmody,** Timothy James 1946- *WhoAmL 92*
**Carmody,** Victor Wallace, Jr. 1945- *WhoAmL 92*
**Carmon,** Angela Ingram 1962- *WhoAmL 92*
**Carmon,** Haggai 1944- *WhoAmL 92*
**Carmona,** Benhur 1960- *WhoHisp 92*
**Carmona,** Jose Antonio 1960- *WhoHisp 92*
**Carmona,** Rene A 1947- *AmMWSc 92*
**Carmona,** Richard Henry 1949- *WhoHisp 92*
**Carmona,** Roel Guerra 1935- *WhoHisp 92*
**Carmony,** Donald Duane 1935- *AmMWSc 92*
**Carmony,** Kevin Brackett 1959- *WhoWest 92*
**Carmouche,** L N 1916- *AmMWSc 92*
**Carmoy,** Guy de 1907- *IntWW 91*
**Carn,** Andrew James 1950- *WhoAmP 91*
**Carnac** *Who 92*
**Carnahan,** Brice 1933- *AmMWSc 92*
**Carnahan,** Chalon Lucius 1933- *AmMWSc 92*
**Carnahan,** Clarence Earl 1935- *WhoIns 92*
**Carnahan,** Frank Chadwick 1951- *WhoAmL 92*
**Carnahan,** George Richard 1935- *WhoMW 92*
**Carnahan,** James Claude 1943- *AmMWSc 92*
**Carnahan,** James Elliot 1920- *AmMWSc 92*
**Carnahan,** John Hillis 1929- *WhoAmP 91*
**Carnahan,** John Russell 1958- *WhoAmP 91*
**Carnahan,** Jon Winston 1955- *AmMWSc 92*
**Carnahan,** Laurie Schober 1963- *WhoAmL 92*
**Carnahan,** Lew Wallace 1946- *WhoAmL 92*
**Carnahan,** Marvin R. 1941- *WhoMW 92*
**Carnahan,** Mel 1934- *WhoAmP 91*
**Carnahan,** Mel Eugene 1934- *WhoMW 92*
**Carnahan,** Michael William 1946- *WhoAmL 92*
**Carnahan,** Robert D 1931- *AmMWSc 92*
**Carnahan,** Robert Edward 1925- *AmMWSc 92*
**Carnahan,** Robert Narvell 1928- *WhoAmL 92*
**Carnahan,** Wanda Edwina 1929- *WhoAmP 91*
**Carnall,** Geoffrey Douglas 1927- *WrDr 92*
**Carnall,** William Thomas 1927- *AmMWSc 92*
**Carnap,** Rudolf 1891-1970 *FacFETw*
**Carnarvon,** Earl of 1924- *Who 92*
**Carnase,** Thomas Paul 1939- *WhoEnt 92*
**Carnathan,** Gilbert William 1951- *WhoWest 92*
**Carne,** James Power 1906-1986 *FacFETw*
**Carne,** Marcel 1906- *IntWW 91*
**Carne,** Marcel 1909?- *FacFETw, IntDcF 2-2 [port]*
**Carne,** Stuart John 1926- *Who 92*
**Carnecchia,** Baldo M., Jr. 1947- *WhoAmL 92*
**Carnegie** *Who 92*
**Carnegie,** Andrew 1835-1919 *AmPeW, BenetAL 91, RComAH*
**Carnegie,** Andrew 1950- *TwCPaSc*
**Carnegie,** Dale 1888-1955 *BenetAL 91, FacFETw*
**Carnegie,** Jack Gardiner 1958- *WhoAmL 92*
**Carnegie,** Lawrence Gales Lonnie 1944- *WhoEnt 92*
**Carnegie,** Mary Elizabeth 1916- *NotBlAW 92 [port]*
**Carnegie,** Randolph David 1952- *WhoBlA 92*
**Carnegie,** Robin 1926- *Who 92*
**Carnegie,** Roderick 1932- *Who 92*
**Carnegie,** Roderick Howard 1932- *IntWW 91*
**Carnegie,** Sacha 1920- *WrDr 92*
**Carnegy of Lour,** Baroness 1925- *Who 92*
**Carnell,** Edward John 1919-1967 *RelLAm 91*
**Carnell,** Frederick James d1902 *BiInAmS*
**Carnell,** Geoffrey Gordon 1918- *Who 92*
**Carnell,** Lougenia Littlejohn 1947- *WhoBlA 92*
**Carnell,** Marion P 1928- *WhoAmP 91*
**Carnelley,** Desmond 1929- *Who 92*
**Carner,** Charles Robert, Jr. 1957- *WhoEnt 92*
**Carner,** William John 1948- *WhoFI 92*
**Carnero,** Guillermo 1947- *DcLB 108 [port]*
**Carnes,** Anthony Peter 1957- *WhoEnt 92*
**Carnes,** Bruce Alfred 1950- *AmMWSc 92*
**Carnes,** David Lee, Jr 1946- *AmMWSc 92*
**Carnes,** James Edward 1939- *AmMWSc 92*
**Carnes,** Jay Russell 1964- *WhoWest 92*
**Carnes,** Joseph John 1917- *AmMWSc 92*
**Carnes,** Mark Alan 1960- *WhoFI 92*
**Carnes,** Walter Rosamond 1922- *AmMWSc 92*
**Carnes,** William Henry 1909- *AmMWSc 92*
**Carnesale,** Albert 1936- *AmMWSc 92*
**Carnesoltas,** Ana-Maria 1948- *WhoAmL 92*
**Carnett,** Mark Christian 1965- *WhoMW 92*
**Carnevale,** Anthony, Jr *WhoAmP 91*
**Carnevale,** Anthony P. 1946- *ConAu 135*
**Carnevale,** Ted Anthony 1957- *WhoFI 92*
**Carney,** Alfonso Linwood, Jr. 1949- *WhoBlA 92*
**Carney,** Art *LesBEnT 92*
**Carney,** Art 1918- *IntMPA 92*
**Carney,** Arthur William Matthew 1918- *WhoEnt 92*
**Carney,** Bruce William 1946- *AmMWSc 92*
**Carney,** Callie I. 1934- *WhoBlA 92*
**Carney,** D J 1921- *AmMWSc 92*
**Carney,** Daniel Joseph 1942- *WhoEnt 92*
**Carney,** Darrell Howard 1948- *AmMWSc 92*
**Carney,** David 1925- *IntWW 91*
**Carney,** David E. 1966- *WhoFI 92*
**Carney,** Deborah Leah Turner 1952- *WhoAmL 92*
**Carney,** Devon Edwards 1959- *WhoEnt 92*
**Carney,** Edward J 1929- *AmMWSc 92*
**Carney,** Eliza Macaulay 1937- *WhoAmP 91*
**Carney,** Frank Thomas 1956- *WhoEnt 92, WhoFI 92*
**Carney,** Fred 1914- *IntMPA 92*
**Carney,** G. Daniel 1937- *WhoAmL 92*
**Carney,** Gordon C 1934- *AmMWSc 92*
**Carney,** Gregory John 1946- *WhoFI 92*
**Carney,** Harry 1910-1974 *NewAmDM*
**Carney,** Heath Joseph 1955- *WhoWest 92*
**Carney,** J.W., Jr. 1952- *WhoAmL 92*
**Carney,** James F. *Who 92*
**Carney,** Jean Kathryn 1948- *WhoMW 92*
**Carney,** Jeffrey Dean 1967- *WhoEnt 92*
**Carney,** John Michael 1947- *AmMWSc 92*
**Carney,** Joseph Buckingham 1928- *WhoAmL 92*
**Carney,** Joseph E 1945- *WhoIns 92*
**Carney,** Kathleen L. 1947- *WhoMW 92*
**Carney,** Kay 1933- *WhoEnt 92*
**Carney,** Kim 1925- *WhoFI 92*
**Carney,** Larry Brady 1948- *WhoMW 92*
**Carney,** Lester 1934- *BlkOlyM*
**Carney,** Margaret 1941- *WhoRel 92*
**Carney,** Michael 1937- *Who 92, WhoEnt 92*
**Carney,** Pat 1928- *WhoAmP 91*
**Carney,** Patricia 1935- *IntWW 91*
**Carney,** Phillita Toyia 1952- *WhoFI 92*
**Carney,** Richard William James 1934- *AmMWSc 92*
**Carney,** Robert Arthur 1937- *WhoFI 92*
**Carney,** Robert B. 1895-1990 *AnObit 1990*
**Carney,** Robert Bostwick 1895-1990 *FacFETw*
**Carney,** Robert Gibson 1914- *AmMWSc 92*
**Carney,** Robert Matthew 1928- *WhoBlA 92*
**Carney,** Robert Spencer 1945- *AmMWSc 92*
**Carney,** Ronald Eugene 1943- *WhoMW 92*
**Carney,** Rose Agnes *AmMWSc 92*
**Carney,** Russell Neil 1950- *WhoMW 92*
**Carney,** Stephen Wright 1762-1811 *DcNCBi 1*
**Carney,** Thomas 1953- *WhoAmP 91*
**Carney,** Thomas E *WhoAmP 91*
**Carney,** Thomas Joseph 1934- *WhoAmP 91*
**Carney,** Thomas Mellis 1942- *WhoAmL 92*
**Carney,** William John 1937- *WhoAmL 92*
**Carney,** William Patrick 1938- *AmMWSc 92*
**Carney,** William Ray 1940- *WhoAmL 92*
**Carney-DeBord,** Nancy Hallidae 1958- *WhoMW 92*
**Carnicero,** Jorge E. 1921- *WhoHisp 92*
**Carnicke,** Sharon Marie 1949- *WhoEnt 92*
**Carnicom,** Gene E. 1944- *WhoWest 92*
**Carniglia,** Stephen C 1922- *AmMWSc 92*
**Carnine,** Albert J. 1943- *WhoRel 92*
**Carnine,** Douglas Wayne 1947- *WhoWest 92*
**Carnine,** Roy Leland 1949- *WhoAmL 92*
**Carnley,** Peter Frederick *Who 92*
**Carnley,** Peter Frederick 1937- *IntWW 91, WrDr 92*
**Carnley,** Samuel Fleetwood 1918- *WhoAmL 92*
**Carnochan,** John Low, Jr. 1918- *WhoFI 92*
**Carnochan,** W. B. 1930- *WrDr 92*
**Carnock,** Baron 1920- *Who 92*
**Carnogursky,** Jan 1944- *IntWW 91*
**Carnovsky,** Morris 1897- *CurBio 91 [port], FacFETw*
**Carnow,** Bertram Warren 1922- *AmMWSc 92*
**Carns,** Jim *WhoAmP 91*
**Carns,** W H 1912- *WhoIns 92*
**Carnwath,** Andrew Hunter 1909- *Who 92*
**Carnwath,** Robert John Anderson 1945- *Who 92*
**Caro,** Anthony 1924- *IntWW 91, TwCPaSc, Who 92*
**Caro,** Cesar M. 1954- *WhoHisp 92*
**Caro,** Charles Crawford 1946- *WhoFI 92*
**Caro,** David Edmund 1922- *IntWW 91, Who 92*
**Caro,** Doris A. 1946- *WhoHisp 92*
**Caro,** Eugenio, Sr. *WhoHisp 92*
**Caro,** Joseph James 1942- *WhoWest 92*
**Caro,** Lucien G 1928- *AmMWSc 92*
**Caro,** Mike 1944- *WhoWest 92*
**Caro,** Rafael *WhoAmP 91*
**Caro,** Rafael 1952- *WhoHisp 92*
**Caro,** Robert A. *WrDr 92*
**Caro,** Robert A. 1936- *WhoHisp 92*
**Caro,** Warren 1907- *WhoEnt 92*
**Caroff,** Lawrence John 1941- *AmMWSc 92*
**Carol II** 1893-1953 *FacFETw*
**Carol,** Sister *Who 92*
**Carol,** Bill J *IntAu&W 91X, WrDr 92*
**Carolan,** Geraldine Patricia 1957- *WhoAmL 92*
**Carolan,** James Anthony 1953- *WhoAmL 92*
**Carolan,** Richard James 1961- *WhoAmL 92*
**Carolin,** Peter Burns 1936- *Who 92*
**Carolin,** Valentine Mott, Jr 1918- *AmMWSc 92*
**Caroline,** J. C. 1933- *WhoBlA 92*
**Carollo,** James Paul 1946- *WhoIns 92*
**Carolus-Duran,** Emile-Auguste 1838-1917 *ThHEIm [port]*
**Carome,** Edward F 1927- *AmMWSc 92*
**Carome,** Patrick Joseph 1957- *WhoAmL 92*
**Caron,** Aimery Pierre 1930- *AmMWSc 92*
**Caron,** Cynthia Ann 1960- *WhoFI 92*
**Caron,** David Dennis 1952- *WhoAmL 92*
**Caron,** Dewey Maurice 1942- *AmMWSc 92*
**Caron,** E Louis 1922- *AmMWSc 92*
**Caron,** Glenn Gordon *LesBEnT 92*
**Caron,** Leslie 1931- *IntMPA 92, Who 92, WhoEnt 92*
**Caron,** Leslie Clair Margaret 1931- *IntWW 91*
**Caron,** Maurice Lawrence, Jr 1945- *WhoAmP 91*
**Caron,** Michael 1960- *WhoAmP 91*
**Caron,** Paul Eugene 1955- *WhoAmP 91*
**Caron,** Paul R 1934- *AmMWSc 92*
**Caron,** Richard Edward 1950- *AmMWSc 92*
**Caron,** Richard John 1954- *AmMWSc 92*
**Caron,** Ronald Jacques *WhoMW 92*
**Caron,** Wilfred Rene 1931- *WhoAmL 92*
**Carona,** John 1955- *WhoAmP 91*
**Carondelet,** Luis Francisco Hector 1748-1807 *HisDSpE*
**Carone,** Frank 1927- *AmMWSc 92*
**Carone,** Patricia 1943- *WhoAmP 91*
**Caronis,** George John 1933- *WhoFI 92*
**Caronite,** Salvatore Charles 1935- *WhoMW 92*
**Caroselli,** Patricia Ann 1954- *WhoEnt 92*
**Caroselli,** Remus Francis 1916- *AmMWSc 92*
**Caroselli,** Robert Anthony *AmMWSc 92*
**Caroselli,** William R. 1941- *WhoAmL 92*
**Carossa,** Hans 1878-1956 *EncTR 91 [port]*
**Carothers,** A. J. 1931- *WhoEnt 92*
**Carothers,** Chuck 1957- *WhoRel 92*
**Carothers,** Josiah S Robins, Jr 1938- *WhoAmP 91*
**Carothers,** Neil, III 1919- *WhoAmP 91*
**Carothers,** Otto M 1930- *AmMWSc 92*
**Carothers,** Robert L. *DrAPF 91*
**Carothers,** Steven Warren 1943- *AmMWSc 92*
**Carothers,** Wallace Hume 1896-1937 *FacFETw*
**Carothers,** William Douglas, Jr. 1937- *WhoAmL 92*
**Carothers,** Zane Bland 1924- *AmMWSc 92*
**Carovale,** Mark J. 1951- *WhoEnt 92*
**Carovillano,** Robert L 1932- *AmMWSc 92*
**Carow,** John 1913- *AmMWSc 92*
**Carozza,** Davy Angelo 1926- *WhoRel 92*
**Carozza,** Gerald Nicholas, Jr. 1960- *WhoAmL 92*
**Carozzi,** Albert Victor 1925- *AmMWSc 92*
**Carozzolo,** Shirley Jean 1935- *WhoRel 92*
**Carp,** E. Wayne 1946- *WhoWest 92*
**Carp,** Gerald 1924- *AmMWSc 92*
**Carp,** Richard Irvin 1934- *AmMWSc 92*

**Carp,** Richard Lawrence 1926- *WhoAmL 92*
**Carp,** Richard Merchant 1949- *WhoRel 92*
**Carpanini,** David 1946- *TwCPaSc*
**Carpanini,** Jane 1949- *TwCPaSc*
**Carparelli,** Russell E. 1948- *WhoAmL 92*
**Carpel,** Kenneth Richard 1947- *WhoFI 92*
**Carpenito,** Eleanor Frances 1934- *WhoAmP 91*
**Carpenito,** James William 1956- *WhoAmP 91*
**Carpentaria,** Bishop of 1940- *Who 92*
**Carpenter** *ConAu 133, Who 92*
**Carpenter,** The Little *DcNCBi 1*
**Carpenter,** Adelaide Trowbridge Clark 1944- *AmMWSc 92*
**Carpenter,** Alden B 1936- *AmMWSc 92*
**Carpenter,** Allan 1917- *IntAu&W 91, WrDr 92*
**Carpenter,** Alvin Rauso 1942- *WhoFI 92*
**Carpenter,** Ann M. 1934- *WhoBlA 92*
**Carpenter,** Anna-Mary 1916- *AmMWSc 92*
**Carpenter,** Arthur James 1931- *WhoAmP 91*
**Carpenter,** Barry Keith 1949- *AmMWSc 92*
**Carpenter,** Benjamin H 1921- *AmMWSc 92*
**Carpenter,** Bill *WhoAmP 91*
**Carpenter,** Bogdana 1941- *ConAu 135*
**Carpenter,** Bogdana Maria Magdalena 1941- *WhoMW 92*
**Carpenter,** Brent Peter 1959- *WhoAmL 92*
**Carpenter,** Brian Wells 1956- *WhoFI 92*
**Carpenter,** Bruce H 1932- *AmMWSc 92, WhoFI 92*
**Carpenter,** C. Donald, Jr. 1933- *WhoFI 92*
**Carpenter,** C LeRoy 1915- *AmMWSc 92*
**Carpenter,** Carl, Jr 1935- *WhoAmP 91*
**Carpenter,** Carleton 1926- *IntMPA 92*
**Carpenter,** Carolyn Virus 1940- *AmMWSc 92*
**Carpenter,** Charles *WhoRel 92*
**Carpenter,** Charles C J 1931- *AmMWSc 92*
**Carpenter,** Charles Congden 1921- *AmMWSc 92*
**Carpenter,** Charles Curtiss 1961- *WhoEnt 92*
**Carpenter,** Charles Elford, Jr. 1944- *WhoAmL 92*
**Carpenter,** Charles Francis 1957- *WhoAmL 92*
**Carpenter,** Charles H 1908- *AmMWSc 92*
**Carpenter,** Charles Loren, Jr. 1947- *WhoAmL 92*
**Carpenter,** Charles Patten 1910- *AmMWSc 92*
**Carpenter,** Charlton Henry 1937- *WhoAmL 92*
**Carpenter,** Clarence E., Jr. 1941- *WhoBlA 92*
**Carpenter,** D. A. 1946- *ConAu 134*
**Carpenter,** Dante K *WhoAmP 91*
**Carpenter,** Darwin R., Jr. 1947- *WhoFI 92*
**Carpenter,** David Allan 1951- *WhoAmL 92*
**Carpenter,** David J. d1991 *NewYTBS 91*
**Carpenter,** David L *WhoAmP 91*
**Carpenter,** David O 1937- *AmMWSc 92*
**Carpenter,** David R 1939- *WhoIns 92*
**Carpenter,** David Roland 1939- *WhoFI 92, WhoWest 92*
**Carpenter,** David William 1950- *WhoAmL 92*
**Carpenter,** Deborah Joan 1958- *WhoAmL 92*
**Carpenter,** Delma Rae, Jr 1928- *AmMWSc 92*
**Carpenter,** Dennis D. 1954- *WhoRel 92*
**Carpenter,** Dewey Kenneth 1928- *AmMWSc 92*
**Carpenter,** Don *DrAPF 91*
**Carpenter,** Donald Blodgett 1916- *WhoWest 92*
**Carpenter,** Donald Gilbert 1927- *AmMWSc 92*
**Carpenter,** Dorothy F 1933- *WhoAmP 91*
**Carpenter,** Dudley Saltonstall 1944- *WhoEnt 92*
**Carpenter,** Dwight William 1936- *AmMWSc 92*
**Carpenter,** Ed *WhoAmP 91*
**Carpenter,** Edmund Mogford 1941- *WhoFI 92*
**Carpenter,** Edward 1844-1929 *BiDBrF 2*
**Carpenter,** Edward Childs 1872-1950 *BenetAL 91*
**Carpenter,** Edward Frederick 1910- *Who 92*
**Carpenter,** Edward J 1942- *AmMWSc 92*
**Carpenter,** Edwin David 1932- *AmMWSc 92*
**Carpenter,** Esther 1903- *AmMWSc 92*
**Carpenter,** Frances Lynn 1944- *AmMWSc 92*
**Carpenter,** Francis J *WhoAmP 91*
**Carpenter,** Frank Charles, Jr. 1917- *WhoWest 92*
**Carpenter,** Frank G 1920- *AmMWSc 92*
**Carpenter,** Frank Grant 1923- *AmMWSc 92*
**Carpenter,** Frank Morton 1902- *AmMWSc 92*
**Carpenter,** Frank Robert 1946- *WhoRel 92*
**Carpenter,** Franklin Reuben 1848-1910 *BiInAmS*
**Carpenter,** Frederic I. *ConAu 134*
**Carpenter,** Frederic I. 1903- *WrDr 92*
**Carpenter,** Frederic Ives d1991 *NewYTBS 91*
**Carpenter,** Frederic Ives 1903-1991 *ConAu 134*
**Carpenter,** Frederick Charles 1920- *Who 92*
**Carpenter,** Gail Alexandra 1948- *AmMWSc 92*
**Carpenter,** Gary Grant 1929- *AmMWSc 92*
**Carpenter,** Gene Blakely 1922- *AmMWSc 92*
**Carpenter,** Geoffrey Congden 1960- *WhoWest 92*
**Carpenter,** George Frederick 1917- *Who 92*
**Carpenter,** George Washington 1802-1860 *BiInAmS*
**Carpenter,** Grace Herring 1935- *WhoFI 92*
**Carpenter,** Graham Frederick 1944- *AmMWSc 92*
**Carpenter,** Graham John Charles 1939- *AmMWSc 92*
**Carpenter,** Harry C 1921- *AmMWSc 92*
**Carpenter,** Harry James 1901- *Who 92*
**Carpenter,** Harry Leonard 1925- *Who 92*
**Carpenter,** Howard Grant, Jr. 1939- *WhoAmL 92, WhoFI 92*
**Carpenter,** Howard Ralph 1919- *WhoEnt 92*
**Carpenter,** Hoyle Dameron 1909- *WhoEnt 92*
**Carpenter,** Humphrey 1946- *IntAu&W 91, WrDr 92*
**Carpenter,** Humphrey William Bouverie 1946- *Who 92*
**Carpenter,** Irvin Watson, Jr 1923- *AmMWSc 92*
**Carpenter,** Isaac M. 1920- *WhoEnt 92*
**Carpenter,** Jack William 1925- *AmMWSc 92*
**Carpenter,** James Allen 1936- *WhoRel 92*
**Carpenter,** James E 1921- *AmMWSc 92*
**Carpenter,** James E 1932- *AmMWSc 92*
**Carpenter,** James Edward 1946- *AmMWSc 92*
**Carpenter,** James F. 1926- *WhoWest 92*
**Carpenter,** James Franklin 1923- *AmMWSc 92*
**Carpenter,** James L, Jr 1925- *AmMWSc 92*
**Carpenter,** James Russell 1927- *WhoAmP 91*
**Carpenter,** James Willard 1935- *WhoFI 92*
**Carpenter,** James William 1935- *AmMWSc 92*
**Carpenter,** James Woodford 1922- *AmMWSc 92*
**Carpenter,** John *DrAPF 91, Who 92*
**Carpenter,** John 1921- *TwCPaSc*
**Carpenter,** John 1948- *ConAu 134, IntDcF 2-2, IntMPA 92*
**Carpenter,** John Alden 1876-1951 *FacFETw, NewAmDM*
**Carpenter,** John C 1930- *WhoAmP 91*
**Carpenter,** John Everett 1923- *WhoWest 92*
**Carpenter,** John Harold 1929- *AmMWSc 92*
**Carpenter,** John Howard 1948- *IntWW 91*
**Carpenter,** John Jo *TwCWW 91*
**Carpenter,** John Loring 1948- *WhoRel 92*
**Carpenter,** John Marland 1935- *AmMWSc 92*
**Carpenter,** John Richard 1938- *AmMWSc 92*
**Carpenter,** Joseph, II 1937- *WhoBlA 92*
**Carpenter,** Kenneth Halsey 1939- *AmMWSc 92*
**Carpenter,** Kenneth John 1923- *AmMWSc 92*
**Carpenter,** Kenneth Russell 1955- *WhoMW 92*
**Carpenter,** Kent Heisley 1938- *AmMWSc 92*
**Carpenter,** Kent Richard 1942- *WhoWest 92*
**Carpenter,** Kevin Starr 1954- *WhoAmL 92*
**Carpenter,** Kirk Duane 1950- *WhoAmP 91*
**Carpenter,** Lawrence Michael 1961- *WhoWest 92*
**Carpenter,** Leslie Arthur 1927- *IntWW 91, Who 92*
**Carpenter,** Lewis 1928- *WhoBlA 92*
**Carpenter,** Louise *Who 92*
**Carpenter,** Lucas *DrAPF 91*
**Carpenter,** Lucas 1947- *IntAu&W 91*
**Carpenter,** Lynn Allen 1943- *AmMWSc 92*
**Carpenter,** M. Rick 1950- *WhoRel 92*
**Carpenter,** Malcolm Breckenridge 1921- *AmMWSc 92*
**Carpenter,** Martha Stahr 1920- *AmMWSc 92*
**Carpenter,** Mary-Chapin 1958?- *ConMus 6 [port]*
**Carpenter,** Mary Laure 1953- *WhoMW 92*
**Carpenter,** Mary Pitynski 1926- *AmMWSc 92*
**Carpenter,** Michael Alan 1947- *WhoFI 92*
**Carpenter,** Michael E. 1947- *WhoAmL 92*
**Carpenter,** Michael Eugene 1947- *WhoAmP 91*
**Carpenter,** Michael James 1943- *WhoRel 92*
**Carpenter,** Michael Kevin 1954- *AmMWSc 92*
**Carpenter,** Morley *TwCSFW 91*
**Carpenter,** Nan Cooke 1912- *WrDr 92*
**Carpenter,** Nancy Jane 1946- *AmMWSc 92*
**Carpenter,** Patricia 1923- *WhoEnt 92*
**Carpenter,** Paul Gershom 1914- *AmMWSc 92*
**Carpenter,** Paul Leonard 1920- *WhoAmL 92*
**Carpenter,** Paul Samuel 1956- *WhoFI 92*
**Carpenter,** Peter Rockefeller 1939- *WhoWest 92*
**Carpenter,** Philip John 1957- *AmMWSc 92*
**Carpenter,** Phyllis Marie Rosenau 1926- *WhoMW 92*
**Carpenter,** Randle Burt 1939- *WhoAmL 92*
**Carpenter,** Ray Warren 1934- *AmMWSc 92, WhoWest 92*
**Carpenter,** Raymon T 1929- *AmMWSc 92*
**Carpenter,** Richard A 1926- *AmMWSc 92*
**Carpenter,** Richard Lynn 1946- *WhoEnt 92*
**Carpenter,** Richard M. 1927- *WhoMW 92*
**Carpenter,** Richard M 1943- *AmMWSc 92*
**Carpenter,** Richard Norris 1937- *WhoAmL 92*
**Carpenter,** Robert C 1924- *WhoAmP 91*
**Carpenter,** Robert Halstead 1914- *AmMWSc 92*
**Carpenter,** Robert James, Jr 1945- *AmMWSc 92*
**Carpenter,** Robert L. 1927- *IntMPA 92*
**Carpenter,** Robert Leland 1942- *AmMWSc 92*
**Carpenter,** Robert Raymond 1933- *AmMWSc 92*
**Carpenter,** Roger Edwin 1935- *AmMWSc 92*
**Carpenter,** Roland LeRoy 1926- *AmMWSc 92*
**Carpenter,** Rolla Clinton 1852-1919 *BiInAmS*
**Carpenter,** Roy *AmMWSc 92*
**Carpenter,** Russell LeGrand d1991 *NewYTBS 91*
**Carpenter,** Sammy 1928- *AmMWSc 92*
**Carpenter,** Scott 1925- *FacFETw*
**Carpenter,** Stanley Barton 1937- *AmMWSc 92*
**Carpenter,** Stanley John 1936- *AmMWSc 92*
**Carpenter,** Stanley Waterman 1921- *WhoFI 92*
**Carpenter,** Stephen Russell 1952- *AmMWSc 92*
**Carpenter,** Steve Haycock 1938- *AmMWSc 92*
**Carpenter,** Stuart Gordon 1931- *AmMWSc 92*
**Carpenter,** Sunny Lynne 1950- *WhoWest 92*
**Carpenter,** Susan Karen 1951- *WhoAmL 92*
**Carpenter,** Thomas J 1927- *AmMWSc 92*
**Carpenter,** Thomas Roberts, Jr. 1955- *WhoRel 92*
**Carpenter,** Timothy W 1960- *WhoAmP 91*
**Carpenter,** Torrey C 1922- *WhoAmP 91*
**Carpenter,** Victor Harry John 1921- *Who 92*
**Carpenter,** Vivian L. 1952- *WhoBlA 92*
**Carpenter,** Walter Juliand Grant 1939- *WhoRel 92*
**Carpenter,** Will Dockery 1930- *AmMWSc 92*
**Carpenter,** William *DrAPF 91*
**Carpenter,** William Arthur, II 1965- *WhoBlA 92*
**Carpenter,** William C., Jr. 1951- *WhoAmL 92*
**Carpenter,** William Graham 1931- *AmMWSc 92*
**Carpenter,** William John 1927- *AmMWSc 92*
**Carpenter,** William Marbury 1811-1848 *BiInAmS*
**Carpenter,** William Randolph, Jr. 1932- *WhoAmL 92*
**Carpenter,** Willis Vincent 1929- *WhoAmL 92*
**Carpenter,** Zerle Leon 1935- *AmMWSc 92*
**Carpentier,** Alejo 1904-1980 *BenetAL 91, DcLB 113 [port], LiExTwC*
**Carpentier,** Jean Claude Gabriel 1926- *IntWW 91*
**Carpentier,** Robert George 1929- *AmMWSc 92*
**Carper,** Diane Clements 1945- *WhoFI 92*
**Carper,** Freda Smith 1953- *WhoFI 92*
**Carper,** Gloria G. 1930- *WhoBlA 92*
**Carper,** Thomas R. 1947- *AlmAP 92 [port], WhoAmP 91*
**Carper,** William G, Jr 1946- *WhoAmP 91*
**Carper,** William Robert 1935- *AmMWSc 92*
**Carpino,** Christine Marie 1952- *WhoMW 92*
**Carpino,** Francesco 1905- *IntWW 91, WhoRel 92*
**Carpino,** Louis A 1927- *AmMWSc 92*
**Carpio,** Julio Fernando 1947- *WhoHisp 92*
**Carpio,** Virginia Ann 1939- *WhoHisp 92*
**Carpocrates** *EncEarC*
**Carpousis-Seifert,** Pamela 1949- *WhoEnt 92*
**Carpreau,** Henri 1923- *TwCPaSc*
**Carr** *Who 92*
**Carr,** Albert A 1930- *AmMWSc 92*
**Carr,** Albert Raymond 1919- *IntWW 91, Who 92*
**Carr,** Allan *WhoEnt 92, WhoWest 92*
**Carr,** Allan 1939- *IntMPA 92*
**Carr,** Andrew Ramey 1964- *WhoMW 92*
**Carr,** Anne Elizabeth 1934- *WhoRel 92*
**Carr,** Antoine Labotte 1961- *WhoBlA 92*
**Carr,** Arthur Wesley 1941- *Who 92*
**Carr,** Audri Joan 1936- *WhoMW 92*
**Carr,** Benjamin 1768-1831 *NewAmDM*
**Carr,** Billie J 1928- *WhoAmP 91*
**Carr,** Bob 1943- *AlmAP 92 [port]*
**Carr,** Bonnie Jean 1947- *WhoMW 92*
**Carr,** Bruce R *AmMWSc 92*
**Carr,** Calvin Johnson 1960- *WhoRel 92*
**Carr,** Carolyn Kehlor 1948- *WhoMW 92*
**Carr,** Carolyn Sue Dean 1943- *WhoRel 92*
**Carr,** Cassandra Colvin 1944- *WhoFI 92*
**Carr,** Catharine *IntAu&W 91X*
**Carr,** Charles Jelleff 1910- *AmMWSc 92*
**Carr,** Charles Louis 1930- *WhoRel 92*
**Carr,** Charles Robert 1920- *WhoAmP 91*
**Carr,** Charles William 1917- *AmMWSc 92*
**Carr,** Christopher 1944- *Who 92*
**Carr,** Christopher C. 1950- *WhoAmL 92*
**Carr,** Clara B. 1948- *WhoBlA 92*
**Carr,** Clide Isom 1920- *AmMWSc 92*
**Carr,** Cynthia 1953- *WhoAmL 92*
**Carr,** Dan *DrAPF 91*
**Carr,** Dana Michael 1960- *WhoFI 92*
**Carr,** Daniel Floyd 1959- *WhoAmP 91*
**Carr,** Daniel Oscar 1934- *AmMWSc 92*
**Carr,** David 1915-1968 *TwCPaSc*
**Carr,** David 1944- *TwCPaSc*
**Carr,** David Harvey 1928- *AmMWSc 92*
**Carr,** David Turner 1914- *AmMWSc 92*
**Carr,** Davis Haden 1940- *WhoAmL 92*
**Carr,** Denis John 1915- *Who 92*
**Carr,** Dodd S 1925- *AmMWSc 92*
**Carr,** Doleen Pellett 1950- *WhoMW 92*
**Carr,** Donald Bryce 1926- *Who 92*
**Carr,** Donald Dean 1931- *AmMWSc 92*
**Carr,** Duane Tucker 1932- *AmMWSc 92*
**Carr,** Edward 1892-1982 *FacFETw*
**Carr,** Edward Albert, Jr 1922- *AmMWSc 92*
**Carr,** Edward Frank 1920- *AmMWSc 92*
**Carr,** Edward Gary 1947- *AmMWSc 92*
**Carr,** Edward Mark 1918- *AmMWSc 92*
**Carr,** Edwin 1926- *ConCom 92*
**Carr,** Elias 1839-1900 *DcNCBi 1*
**Carr,** Emily 1871-1945 *BenetAL 91*
**Carr,** Eric d1991 *NewYTBS 91*
**Carr,** Eric Francis 1919- *Who 92*
**Carr,** Ezra Slocum 1819-1894 *BiInAmS*
**Carr,** Francis *ScFEYrs*
**Carr,** Frank George Griffith d1991 *Who 92N*
**Carr,** Fred K 1942- *AmMWSc 92*
**Carr,** Gary 1954- *WhoRel 92*
**Carr,** Gary Thomas 1946- *WhoMW 92*
**Carr,** George Francis, Jr. 1939- *WhoAmL 92*
**Carr,** George Leroy 1927- *AmMWSc 92*
**Carr,** Gerald Dwayne 1945- *AmMWSc 92*
**Carr,** Gerald Paul 1932- *AmMWSc 92, IntWW 91*
**Carr,** Glyn *Who 92*
**Carr,** Glyn 1908- *IntAu&W 91, WrDr 92*
**Carr,** Harold Noflet 1921- *WhoFI 92*
**Carr,** Harry Elwood 1932- *WhoRel 92*
**Carr,** Henry 1894-1970 *TwCPaSc*
**Carr,** Henry 1942- *BlkOlyM*
**Carr,** Herman Yaggi 1924- *AmMWSc 92*
**Carr,** Howard Earl 1915- *AmMWSc 92*
**Carr,** Howard Ernest 1908- *WhoFI 92*
**Carr,** Hubert Franklin 1920- *WhoAmL 92*
**Carr,** Ian *AmMWSc 92*

**Carr,** J. L. 1912- ConNov 91, IntAu&W 91, WrDr 92
**Carr,** Jack 1948- IntWW 91
**Carr,** Jack A 1920- AmMWSc 92
**Carr,** Jacquelyn Carney 1956- WhoWest 92
**Carr,** James David 1938- AmMWSc 92
**Carr,** James Drew 1935- WhoAmP 91
**Carr,** James Michael 1950- WhoAmL 92
**Carr,** James Ozborn 1869-1949 DcNCBi 1
**Carr,** James Patrick 1950- WhoAmL 92
**Carr,** James Russell 1957- AmMWSc 92
**Carr,** James T 1937- WhoIns 92
**Carr,** James W, Jr 1921- AmMWSc 92
**Carr,** Jan 1943- AmMWSc 92
**Carr,** Jay D. WhoRel 92
**Carr,** Jay Phillip 1936- WhoEnt 92
**Carr,** Jayge 1940- TwCSFW 91, WrDr 92
**Carr,** Jerome Brian 1938- AmMWSc 92
**Carr,** Jess 1930- IntAu&W 91, WrDr 92
**Carr,** Jesse Metteau, III 1952- WhoAmL 92
**Carr,** Jo Crisler 1926- IntAu&W 91
**Carr,** John B 1937- AmMWSc 92
**Carr,** John Darcy B. Who 92
**Carr,** John Dickson 1906-1977 BenetAL 91, FacFETw
**Carr,** John F. 1932- WhoRel 92
**Carr,** John Lyle, Jr. 1946- WhoAmL 92
**Carr,** John Mark 1953- WhoRel 92
**Carr,** John P 1945- WhoIns 92
**Carr,** John Roger 1927- Who 92
**Carr,** John Weber, III 1923- AmMWSc 92
**Carr,** John Wesley 1945- WhoFI 92
**Carr,** Julian Lanier, Jr. 1946- WhoMW 92
**Carr,** Julian Shakespeare 1845-1924 DcNCBi 1
**Carr,** Kenneth 1955- BlkOlyM
**Carr,** Kenneth Monroe 1925- WhoAmP 91, WhoFI 92
**Carr,** Kenny 1955- WhoBlA 92
**Carr,** Larry L. 1939- WhoMW 92
**Carr,** Laurence A 1942- AmMWSc 92
**Carr,** Lawrence Edward, Jr. 1923- WhoAmL 92
**Carr,** Lawrence George 1920- Who 92
**Carr,** Lawrence John 1939- AmMWSc 92
**Carr,** Lenford 1938- WhoBlA 92
**Carr,** Leonard G. 1902- WhoBlA 92
**Carr,** M Robert 1943- WhoAmP 91, WhoMW 92
**Carr,** Margaret 1935- IntAu&W 91, WrDr 92
**Carr,** Martin d1987 LesBEnT 92
**Carr,** Martin 1932- IntMPA 92
**Carr,** Mary Elizabeth 1925- WhoRel 92
**Carr,** Mary Lois 1948- WhoFI 92
**Carr,** Maurice Chapman 1937- Who 92
**Carr,** Meg Brady 1949- AmMWSc 92
**Carr,** Michael 1946- Who 92
**Carr,** Michael H 1935- AmMWSc 92
**Carr,** Michael John 1946- AmMWSc 92
**Carr,** Nate 1960- BlkOlyM
**Carr,** Noly Cruz 1940- WhoWest 92
**Carr,** Norine Joyce 1937- WhoRel 92
**Carr,** Norman L 1924- AmMWSc 92
**Carr,** Norman Robert 1928- WhoEnt 92
**Carr,** Norman Stewart 1936- WhoAmL 92
**Carr,** Oscar Clark, III 1951- WhoAmL 92
**Carr,** Pat DrAPF 91
**Carr,** Pat 1932- IntAu&W 91
**Carr,** Patrick E. 1922- WhoAmL 92
**Carr,** Paul Henry 1935- AmMWSc 92
**Carr,** Paula McBee 1948- WhoMW 92
**Carr,** Percy L. 1941- WhoBlA 92
**Carr,** Peter Derek 1930- Who 92
**Carr,** Peter William 1944- AmMWSc 92
**Carr,** Philippa IntAu&W 91X, Who 92, WrDr 92
**Carr,** Phyllis Anne 1935- WhoAmP 91
**Carr,** Pressley Rodney 1930- WhoBlA 92
**Carr,** Ralph W 1946- AmMWSc 92
**Carr,** Raymond Who 92
**Carr,** Raymond 1919- WrDr 92
**Carr,** Richard Dean 1929- AmMWSc 92
**Carr,** Richard Gordon Granville 1953- WhoFI 92
**Carr,** Richard J AmMWSc 92
**Carr,** Richard Lloyd 1937- WhoWest 92
**Carr,** Robert Charles 1946- AmMWSc 92
**Carr,** Robert Eugene 1958- WhoMW 92
**Carr,** Robert H 1935- AmMWSc 92
**Carr,** Robert J 1931- AmMWSc 92
**Carr,** Robert Leroy 1929- WhoMW 92
**Carr,** Robert Leroy 1940- AmMWSc 92
**Carr,** Robert Locke 1930- WhoFI 92, WhoWest 92
**Carr,** Robert M 1937- WhoAmP 91
**Carr,** Robert Spencer 1909- ScFEYrs
**Carr,** Robert Stuart 1946- WhoAmL 92
**Carr,** Robert Wilson, Jr 1934- AmMWSc 92
**Carr,** Roberta WrDr 92
**Carr,** Robyn IntAu&W 91
**Carr,** Robyn 1951- WrDr 92
**Carr,** Roderich Marion 1956- WhoBlA 92
**Carr,** Roger Byington 1936- AmMWSc 92
**Carr,** Roger Vaughan 1937- IntAu&W 91
**Carr,** Ronald E 1932- AmMWSc 92
**Carr,** Ronald Gene 1946- WhoAmL 92
**Carr,** Ronald Irving 1935- AmMWSc 92
**Carr,** Russell L K 1926- AmMWSc 92
**Carr,** Ruth Anne 1947- WhoAmL 92
**Carr,** Sandra Jean Irons 1940- WhoBlA 92
**Carr,** Scott Bligh 1934- AmMWSc 92
**Carr,** Stephen Howard 1942- AmMWSc 92, WhoMW 92
**Carr,** Susan Price 1946- WhoAmL 92
**Carr,** Terry 1937- IntAu&W 91
**Carr,** Terry 1937-1987 TwCSFW 91
**Carr,** Thomas Deaderick 1917- AmMWSc 92
**Carr,** Thomas Eldridge 1953- WhoAmL 92
**Carr,** Thomas Ernest Ashdown 1915- Who 92
**Carr,** Thomas Michael 1953- WhoMW 92
**Carr,** Tom 1909- TwCPaSc
**Carr,** Tommy Russell 1946- AmMWSc 92
**Carr,** Vikki WhoEnt 92
**Carr,** Vikki 1940- WhoHisp 92
**Carr,** Virgil H. WhoBlA 92
**Carr,** Virginia McMillan 1944- AmMWSc 92
**Carr,** Virginia Spencer 1929- DcLB 111 [port]
**Carr,** Walter James, Jr 1918- AmMWSc 92
**Carr,** Willard Zeller, Jr. 1927- IntWW 91, WhoAmL 92
**Carr,** William Compton 1918- Who 92
**Carr,** William George 1901- WrDr 92
**Carr,** William Henry A. 1924- WhoFI 92, WhoMW 92
**Carr,** William N 1936- AmMWSc 92
**Carr,** William Pitts 1947- WhoAmP 91
**Carr-Ellison,** Ralph 1925- Who 92
**Carr-Gomm,** Richard Culling 1922- Who 92
**Carr-Hamilton,** Jacqueline Diane 1951- WhoRel 92
**Carr Linford,** Alan 1926- Who 92
**Carr Of Hadley,** Baron 1916- IntWW 91, Who 92
**Carra,** Carlo 1881-1966 FacFETw
**Carrabine,** John Anthony 1928- AmMWSc 92
**Carrad,** David Clayton 1944- WhoFI 92
**Carradine,** Beverly 1848-1919 RelLAm 91
**Carradine,** David 1936- IntMPA 92, WhoEnt 92
**Carradine,** Keith 1949- CurBio 91 [port], IntMPA 92
**Carradine,** Keith Ian 1949- WhoEnt 92
**Carradine,** Robert 1954- IntMPA 92
**Carradine,** William Radell, Jr 1941- AmMWSc 92
**Carrado,** Kathleen Anne 1960- AmMWSc 92
**Carragher,** Audrey A WhoAmP 91
**Carragher,** Mary Alice 1960- WhoAmL 92, WhoMW 92
**Carraher,** Charles E. 1941- ConAu 135
**Carraher,** Charles Eugene, Jr 1941- AmMWSc 92
**Carraher,** Charles Jacob, Jr. 1922- WhoMW 92
**Carraher,** Daniel Peter 1953- WhoFI 92
**Carral,** Anselmo WhoRel 92
**Carrano,** Anthony Vito 1942- AmMWSc 92
**Carrano,** Richard Alfred 1940- AmMWSc 92
**Carrano,** Salvatore Andrew 1915- AmMWSc 92
**Carranza,** Andres 1951- WhoRel 92
**Carranza,** Eduardo 1913-1985 ConSpAP
**Carranza,** Roque Guillermo 1919- IntWW 91
**Carrara,** Arthur Alfonso 1914- WhoEnt 92
**Carrara,** Paul Edward 1947- AmMWSc 92
**Carraro,** Franco 1939- IntWW 91
**Carraro,** Joseph J WhoAmP 91
**Carras,** George Peter 1950- WhoRel 92
**Carrasco,** Alejandro 1962- WhoHisp 92
**Carrasco,** Carlos 1948- WhoHisp 92
**Carrasco,** Cecilia Carmina 1966- WhoHisp 92
**Carrasco,** Connie M. WhoHisp 92
**Carrasco,** David 1944- WhoHisp 92
**Carrasco,** David L. 1919-1990 WhoHisp 92N
**Carrasco,** Emma J. WhoHisp 92
**Carrasco,** Gilbert Paul 1953- WhoAmL 92
**Carrasco,** Hector R. 1948- WhoHisp 92
**Carrasco,** Julian WhoHisp 92
**Carrasco,** Lourdes 1947- WhoHisp 92
**Carrasco,** Mario 1945- WhoHisp 92
**Carrasco,** Michael M 1951- WhoAmP 91
**Carrasco,** Robert Anthony 1966- WhoHisp 92
**Carrasco,** Virginia 1958- WhoHisp 92
**Carrasco Briceno,** Bartolome 1918- WhoRel 92
**Carrasquer,** Gaspar 1925- AmMWSc 92
**Carrasquillo,** Angela L. 1941- WhoHisp 92
**Carrasquillo,** Arnaldo 1937- AmMWSc 92
**Carrasquillo,** Frank WhoHisp 92
**Carrasquillo,** M. M. 1952- WhoHisp 92
**Carratala,** Jose Manuel de 1781-1854 HisDSpE
**Carraway,** Coralie Anne Carothers AmMWSc 92
**Carraway,** Kermit Lee 1940- AmMWSc 92
**Carreathers,** Kevin R. 1957- WhoBlA 92
**Carreau,** Pierre 1939- AmMWSc 92
**Carregal,** Enrique Jose Alvarez 1932- AmMWSc 92
**Carreira,** Lionel Andrade 1944- AmMWSc 92
**Carreiro,** Anthony David 1954- WhoEnt 92
**Carreker,** Alphonso 1962- WhoBlA 92
**Carreker,** R P, Jr 1925- AmMWSc 92
**Carreker,** William, Jr. 1936- WhoBlA 92
**Carrel,** Alexis 1873-1944 FacFETw, WhoNob 90
**Carrel,** Frederic ScFEYrs
**Carrel,** James Elliott 1944- AmMWSc 92
**Carrel,** Mark TwCWW 91
**Carrel,** Philip 1915- Who 92
**Carrel,** Wendy Jane WhoEnt 92
**Carrell,** Bobby 1938- WhoAmP 91
**Carrell,** Daniel Allan 1941- WhoAmL 92
**Carrell,** Robin Wayne 1936- IntWW 91, Who 92
**Carrell,** Terry Eugene 1938- WhoFI 92, WhoMW 92
**Carrell,** Thomas Tyrone WhoAmP 91
**Carren,** David Bennett 1952- WhoEnt 92
**Carreno,** Eufronio Roman 1941- WhoHisp 92
**Carreno,** Jose R. 1930- WhoHisp 92
**Carreno,** Mark WhoHisp 92
**Carreno,** Richard D. J. 1946- WhoHisp 92
**Carreon,** Jesus V. 1945- WhoHisp 92
**Carrera,** Arturo 1948- ConSpAP
**Carrera,** Barbara WhoEnt 92
**Carrera,** Barbara 1945- IntMPA 92
**Carrera,** Barbara 1951- WhoHisp 92
**Carrera,** Jose Luis 1932- WhoHisp 92
**Carrera,** Maria-Cecilia 1954- WhoHisp 92
**Carrera,** Victor Manuel 1954- WhoAmL 92
**Carrera Andrade,** Jorge 1903-1978 BenetAL 91
**Carrera Verdugo,** Jose Miguel 1786-1821 HisDSpE
**Carreras,** James 1909-1990 AnObit 1990
**Carreras,** Jose 1946- FacFETw, NewAmDM
**Carreras,** Jose 1947- IntWW 91
**Carreras,** Leonardo Alfredo 1920- WhoHisp 92
**Carreras,** Ricardo Luis 1949- BlkOlyM
**Carrere,** Charles Scott 1937- WhoAmL 92
**Carrere D'Encausse,** Helene IntWW 91
**Carrero,** Jaime 1931- WhoHisp 92
**Carret,** Philip Lord 1896- WhoFI 92
**Carretta,** Albert Aloysius 1907- WhoAmL 92
**Carrey,** Neil 1942- WhoAmL 92, WhoWest 92
**Carrick,** Earl of 1931- Who 92
**Carrick,** Alexander 1882-1966 TwCPaSc
**Carrick,** B Cramton 1913- WhoIns 92
**Carrick,** Benjamin Lane 1958- WhoFI 92
**Carrick,** Edward Who 92, WrDr 92
**Carrick,** John 1918- Who 92
**Carrick,** John Lee 1886-1972 DcNCBi 1
**Carrick,** John Leslie 1918- IntWW 91
**Carrick,** Kathleen Michele 1950- WhoAmL 92
**Carrick,** Lee 1943- AmMWSc 92
**Carrick,** Malcolm 1945- IntAu&W 91, WrDr 92
**Carrick,** Roger John 1937- Who 92
**Carrick,** Thomas Welsh 1914- Who 92
**Carrick,** Wayne Lee 1927- AmMWSc 92
**Carrick-Schreiber,** Charles Raphael 1961- WhoRel 92
**Carrico,** Christine Kathryn 1950- AmMWSc 92
**Carrico,** Harry L 1916- WhoAmP 91
**Carrico,** Harry Lee 1916- WhoAmL 92
**Carrico,** Robert Joseph 1938- AmMWSc 92
**Carrie,** Jacques DrAPF 91
**Carrier,** Bernard 1929- WhoAmP 91
**Carrier,** Clara L. DeGay 1939- WhoBlA 92
**Carrier,** Constance DrAPF 91
**Carrier,** Constance 1908- WrDr 92
**Carrier,** Estelle Stacy 1913- WhoAmP 91
**Carrier,** George Francis 1918- AmMWSc 92, IntWW 91
**Carrier,** Gerald Burton 1927- AmMWSc 92
**Carrier,** Glass Bowling, Jr. 1931- WhoFI 92
**Carrier,** Herve 1921- IntWW 91, WhoRel 92
**Carrier,** Joseph Aaron 1919- WhoEnt 92
**Carrier,** Judith Ann 1942- WhoEnt 92
**Carrier,** Kathryn Earlene 1945- WhoWest 92
**Carrier,** Linda Susan 1954- WhoFI 92
**Carrier,** Mark 1965- WhoBlA 92
**Carrier,** Steven Theodore 1938- AmMWSc 92
**Carrier,** W David, III 1943- AmMWSc 92
**Carrier,** Warren DrAPF 91
**Carrier,** Warren 1918- IntAu&W 91, WrDr 92
**Carriere,** Jean Paul Jacques 1932- IntWW 91
**Carriere,** Rita Margaret 1930- AmMWSc 92
**Carriere,** Serge AmMWSc 92
**Carrigan,** Andrew G. DrAPF 91
**Carrigan,** Charles Roger 1949- AmMWSc 92
**Carrigan,** Henry Lowell, Jr. 1954- WhoMW 92
**Carrigan,** Jim Richard 1929- WhoAmL 92, WhoWest 92
**Carrigan,** JoAnn 1933- WhoMW 92
**Carrigan,** John Lionel 1948- WhoWest 92
**Carrigan,** John Richard 1948- WhoAmL 92
**Carrigan,** Richard Alfred 1906- AmMWSc 92
**Carrigan,** Richard Alfred, Jr 1932- AmMWSc 92
**Carrigg,** James A. 1933- WhoFI 92
**Carriker,** Melbourne Romaine 1915- AmMWSc 92
**Carriker,** Robert Charles 1940- WhoWest 92
**Carriker,** Roy C 1937- AmMWSc 92
**Carriker,** Russell Lloyd 1932- WhoFI 92
**Carriker,** Steve Alan 1950- WhoAmP 91
**Carril,** Peter J. 1931- WhoHisp 92
**Carrillo,** Arsenio WhoHisp 92
**Carrillo,** Carlos Gilberto WhoHisp 92
**Carrillo,** Carmen 1943- WhoHisp 92
**Carrillo,** Charles Michael 1956- WhoHisp 92
**Carrillo,** Eduardo L. 1937- WhoHisp 92
**Carrillo,** Efrain de la Cerda 1953- WhoHisp 92
**Carrillo,** Federico Martinez 1937- WhoHisp 92
**Carrillo,** Fred Anthony 1946- WhoHisp 92
**Carrillo,** George WhoHisp 92
**Carrillo,** Gilberto 1926- WhoWest 92
**Carrillo,** Joe M., Jr. 1927- WhoHisp 92
**Carrillo,** Jose Arturo 1944- WhoHisp 92
**Carrillo,** Juan Carlos WhoHisp 92
**Carrillo,** Julian 1875-1965 NewAmDM
**Carrillo,** Ken 1958- WhoHisp 92
**Carrillo,** Lawrence W. 1920- WrDr 92
**Carrillo,** Michael Anthony 1960- WhoHisp 92
**Carrillo,** Miguel Angel 1964- WhoHisp 92
**Carrillo,** Raul Armando, Jr. 1962- WhoAmL 92
**Carrillo,** Ray WhoHisp 92
**Carrillo,** Robert S. 1932- WhoHisp 92
**Carrillo,** Santiago 1915- IntWW 91
**Carrillo-Beron,** Carmen 1943- WhoHisp 92
**Carrillo-Trujillo,** Julian 1875-1965 NewAmDM
**Carrington,** Baron 1919- IntWW 91, Who 92
**Carrington,** Alan 1934- IntWW 91, Who 92
**Carrington,** Christine H. 1941- WhoBlA 92
**Carrington,** Colin Edward George 1936- Who 92
**Carrington,** Donald P. 1907- TwCPaSc
**Carrington,** Dora 1893-1932 TwCPaSc
**Carrington,** G.A. TwCWW 91
**Carrington,** George Lunsford 1893-1972 DcNCBi 1
**Carrington,** Glenda DrAPF 91
**Carrington,** Grant DrAPF 91
**Carrington,** James 1904- WhoBlA 92
**Carrington,** James Donald 1933- WhoRel 92
**Carrington,** Jerrold Bruce 1957- WhoFI 92
**Carrington,** Joanna 1931- TwCPaSc
**Carrington,** Laura Stock 1946- WhoAmP 91
**Carrington,** Leonora 1917- LiExTwC
**Carrington,** Marsha Solomon 1954- WhoAmP 91
**Carrington,** Matthew Hadrian Marshall 1947- Who 92
**Carrington,** McKen Vincent 1949- WhoAmL 92
**Carrington,** Michael Davis 1938- WhoMW 92
**Carrington,** Paul DeWitt 1931- WhoAmL 92, WrDr 92
**Carrington,** Roy WhoEnt 92
**Carrington,** Samuel Richard 1930- WhoMW 92
**Carrington,** Shirley Stancil Rice 1934- WhoRel 92
**Carrington,** Sylvia 1960- WhoEnt 92
**Carrington,** Terri Lyne 1965- WhoBlA 92
**Carrington,** Thomas Jack 1929- AmMWSc 92
**Carrington,** Tucker 1927- AmMWSc 92
**Carrio de la Vandera,** Alonso HisDSpE

**Carrion,** Audrey J. Sylvia 1958- *WhoAmL 92*
**Carrion,** Daniel Edward 1958- *WhoHisp 92*
**Carrion,** Richard L. *WhoHisp 92*
**Carrion,** Teresita Milagros 1964- *WhoHisp 92*
**Carrisi,** Albano Ottavio *WhoEnt 92*
**Carriveau,** Michael Jon 1956- *WhoMW 92*
**Carrizal,** Ernesto, Jr. 1933- *WhoHisp 92*
**Carro,** John 1927- *WhoHisp 92*
**Carro,** John Placid 1920- *WhoHisp 92*
**Carro,** Jorge L. 1924- *WhoHisp 92*
**Carro,** Jorge Luis 1924- *WhoAmL 92*
**Carro,** Paul Russell d1991 *NewYTBS 91*
**Carrock,** Frederick E 1931- *AmMWSc 92*
**Carrol,** Charles Gordon 1935- *Who 92*
**Carrol,** Raoul Lord 1950- *WhoBlA 92*
**Carroll,** Adorna Occhialini 1952- *WhoFI 92*
**Carroll,** Aidan M. *WhoRel 92*
**Carroll,** Alan G *AmMWSc 92*
**Carroll,** Alice Marie 1950- *WhoEnt 92*
**Carroll,** Andy 1935- *WhoEnt 92*
**Carroll,** Annie Haywood 1904- *WhoBlA 92*
**Carroll,** Anthony Joseph 1951- *WhoAmL 92*
**Carroll,** Arthur Paul 1942- *AmMWSc 92*
**Carroll,** Benajah Harvey 1843-1914 *RelLAm 91*
**Carroll,** Benjamin Franklin, Jr. 1932- *WhoRel 92*
**Carroll,** Bernard James 1940- *AmMWSc 92*
**Carroll,** Beverly A. 1946- *WhoBlA 92*
**Carroll,** Bonnie 1941- *WhoEnt 92*
**Carroll,** C. Edward 1923- *WrDr 92*
**Carroll,** Carroll d1991 *LesBEnT 92, NewYTBS 91*
**Carroll,** Carroll 1902-1991 *ConAu 133*
**Carroll,** Cecil Earl 1925- *WhoRel 92*
**Carroll,** Charlene O. 1950- *WhoBlA 92*
**Carroll,** Charles 1737-1832 *BlkwEAR*
**Carroll,** Charles Geiger 1875-1916 *BiInAmS*
**Carroll,** Charles H. 1910- *WhoBlA 92*
**Carroll,** Charles Michael 1921- *WhoEnt 92*
**Carroll,** Charles William Desmond 1919- *Who 92*
**Carroll,** Christiana Marie 1962- *WhoEnt 92*
**Carroll,** Clark Edward 1938- *AmMWSc 92*
**Carroll,** Clifford Andrew 1906- *WhoRel 92*
**Carroll,** Constance Marie 1945- *WhoBlA 92*
**Carroll,** Dana 1943- *AmMWSc 92, WhoWest 92*
**Carroll,** Danford Frederic 1948- *WhoAmL 92*
**Carroll,** Daniel Thomas 1934- *WhoRel 92*
**Carroll,** David H. *WhoEnt 92*
**Carroll,** David Joseph 1979- *WhoEnt 92*
**Carroll,** David Todd 1959- *WhoWest 92*
**Carroll,** Dennis D. 1947- *WhoAmL 92*
**Carroll,** Dennis Patrick 1941- *AmMWSc 92*
**Carroll,** Derek Raymond 1919- *Who 92*
**Carroll,** Diahann 1935- *IntMPA 92, NotBlAW 92, WhoBlA 92, WhoEnt 92*
**Carroll,** Don Eugene 1942- *WhoEnt 92*
**Carroll,** Donal Shemus Allingham 1927- *IntWW 91*
**Carroll,** Donnell Philip 1950- *WhoAmP 91*
**Carroll,** Douglas James 1949- *WhoAmL 92*
**Carroll,** Dudley Dewitt 1885-1971 *DcNCBi 1*
**Carroll,** Earl Hamblin 1925- *WhoAmL 92, WhoWest 92*
**Carroll,** Edith B 1930- *WhoAmP 91*
**Carroll,** Edward Elmer 1930- *AmMWSc 92*
**Carroll,** Edward Gonzalez 1910- *WhoBlA 92*
**Carroll,** Edward James, Jr 1945- *AmMWSc 92*
**Carroll,** Edward Joseph 1949- *WhoMW 92*
**Carroll,** Edward Major 1916- *WhoBlA 92*
**Carroll,** Edward Perry 1934- *WhoEnt 92*
**Carroll,** Elizabeth *ConAu 135, WrDr 92*
**Carroll,** Eustace Seth *ScFEYrs*
**Carroll,** Evelyn Fae 1951- *WhoFI 92*
**Carroll,** F Ivy 1935- *AmMWSc 92*
**Carroll,** Felix Alvin, Jr 1947- *AmMWSc 92*
**Carroll,** Floyd Dale 1914- *AmMWSc 92*
**Carroll,** Francis P. *WhoRel 92*
**Carroll,** Francis W 1932- *AmMWSc 92*
**Carroll,** Frank J. 1947- *WhoAmL 92*
**Carroll,** Frank Richard 1947- *WhoWest 92*
**Carroll,** George Arthur 1919- *WhoAmP 91*
**Carroll,** George C 1940- *AmMWSc 92*
**Carroll,** George D. 1923- *WhoBlA 92*
**Carroll,** George Hattersley 1940- *WhoWest 92*
**Carroll,** Gerald V 1921- *AmMWSc 92*
**Carroll,** Gladys Hasty 1904- *BenetAL 91, WrDr 92*
**Carroll,** Gordon 1928- *IntMPA 92*
**Carroll,** Harry Milton 1925-1987 *WhoBlA 92N*
**Carroll,** Harvey Franklin 1939- *AmMWSc 92*
**Carroll,** Howard W. *WhoRel 92*
**Carroll,** Howard William 1942- *WhoAmP 91*
**Carroll,** J Gregory 1948- *AmMWSc 92*
**Carroll,** J. Speed 1936- *WhoAmL 92*
**Carroll,** Jackson Walker 1932- *WhoRel 92*
**Carroll,** James 1854-1907 *BiInAmS*
**Carroll,** James 1943- *WrDr 92*
**Carroll,** James Barr 1929- *AmMWSc 92*
**Carroll,** James Francis 1929- *WhoWest 92*
**Carroll,** James Joseph 1935- *AmMWSc 92*
**Carroll,** James Kevin 1945- *WhoAmL 92*
**Carroll,** James Larry 1946- *WhoEnt 92*
**Carroll,** James S. 1945- *WhoBlA 92*
**Carroll,** Jane Skelley 1956- *WhoAmL 92*
**Carroll,** Janet 1940- *WhoEnt 92*
**Carroll,** Jeffrey William 1959- *WhoWest 92*
**Carroll,** Jim *DrAPF 91*
**Carroll,** Joanne H 1931- *WhoAmP 91*
**Carroll,** Joe Barry 1958- *WhoBlA 92*
**Carroll,** Joel 1924- *WhoWest 92*
**Carroll,** John 1735-1815 *BenetAL 91*
**Carroll,** John 1943- *WhoAmP 91*
**Carroll,** John Bissell 1916- *IntWW 91*
**Carroll,** John Edward 1934- *Who 92*
**Carroll,** John Francis 1957- *WhoAmL 92*
**Carroll,** John H *WhoAmP 91*
**Carroll,** John H. 1946- *WhoFI 92*
**Carroll,** John Howard 1927- *WhoMW 92*
**Carroll,** John Millar 1925- *AmMWSc 92*
**Carroll,** John Richard, Jr. 1963- *WhoMW 92*
**Carroll,** John S 1929- *WhoAmP 91*
**Carroll,** John T, III 1960- *AmMWSc 92, WhoMW 92*
**Carroll,** John Terrance 1942- *AmMWSc 92*
**Carroll,** John Timothy 1954- *WhoRel 92*
**Carroll,** Joseph F. 1910-1991 *CurBio 91N, NewYTBS 91 [port]*
**Carroll,** Juanitaelizabeth P. 1954- *WhoBlA 92*
**Carroll,** Julian Morton 1931- *IntWW 91, WhoAmL 92, WhoAmP 91*
**Carroll,** Kenneth Girard 1914- *AmMWSc 92*
**Carroll,** Kenneth Kitchener 1923- *AmMWSc 92, IntWW 91*
**Carroll,** Lawrence W. 1923- *WhoBlA 92*
**Carroll,** Lawrence William, III 1950- *WhoBlA 92*
**Carroll,** Lee Francis 1937- *AmMWSc 92*
**Carroll,** Lewis 1832-1898 *CnDBLB 4 [port], RfGEnL 91*
**Carroll,** Linda B. 1961- *WhoAmL 92*
**Carroll,** Lucy Ellen 1946- *WhoEnt 92*
**Carroll,** Margaret Kelly 1956- *WhoMW 92*
**Carroll,** Martin *IntAu&W 91X, WrDr 92*
**Carroll,** Mary Ann 1947- *WhoRel 92*
**Carroll,** Mary Beth 1944- *WhoEnt 92*
**Carroll,** Mary Teresa *WhoRel 92*
**Carroll,** Maura *WhoAmP 91*
**Carroll,** Michael Adrian 1946- *WhoEnt 92*
**Carroll,** Michael Allen 1960- *WhoMW 92*
**Carroll,** Michael M 1936- *AmMWSc 92*
**Carroll,** Michele Mary 1957- *WhoWest 92*
**Carroll,** Molly Patricia 1957- *WhoMW 92*
**Carroll,** Pat 1927- *IntMPA 92*
**Carroll,** Patricia Whitehead 1954- *WhoFI 92*
**Carroll,** Patrick D 1941- *WhoAmP 91*
**Carroll,** Paul *DrAPF 91*
**Carroll,** Paul 1927- *ConPo 91, IntAu&W 91, WrDr 92*
**Carroll,** Paul Treat 1943- *AmMWSc 92*
**Carroll,** Paul Vincent 1900-1968 *RfGEnL 91*
**Carroll,** Paula Marie 1933- *WhoFI 92, WhoWest 92*
**Carroll,** Philip Joseph 1937- *WhoFI 92*
**Carroll,** Raoul Lord 1950- *WhoAmL 92, WhoAmP 91*
**Carroll,** Raymond 1924- *IntAu&W 91*
**Carroll,** Raymond James 1949- *AmMWSc 92*
**Carroll,** Rebecca Lois 1952- *WhoEnt 92*
**Carroll,** Rhoda *DrAPF 91*
**Carroll,** Richard Ellis 1955- *WhoEnt 92, WhoRel 92*
**Carroll,** Robert *WrDr 92*
**Carroll,** Robert 1933- *WhoIns 92*
**Carroll,** Robert Alan 1935- *WhoWest 92*
**Carroll,** Robert Baker 1921- *AmMWSc 92*
**Carroll,** Robert Buck 1940- *AmMWSc 92*
**Carroll,** Robert F. 1931- *WhoBlA 92*
**Carroll,** Robert Graham 1954- *AmMWSc 92*
**Carroll,** Robert J 1928- *AmMWSc 92*
**Carroll,** Robert Lynn 1938- *AmMWSc 92*
**Carroll,** Robert Owen, Jr. 1958- *WhoAmL 92*
**Carroll,** Robert Wayne 1930- *AmMWSc 92*
**Carroll,** Robert William 1938- *AmMWSc 92*
**Carroll,** Rosemary Frances 1935- *WhoAmL 92, WhoMW 92*
**Carroll,** Sally G. *WhoBlA 92*
**Carroll,** Samuel Edwin 1928- *AmMWSc 92*
**Carroll,** Steven R 1956- *WhoAmP 91*
**Carroll,** Terence Patrick 1948- *Who 92*
**Carroll,** Theresa Avelline 1947- *WhoFI 92*
**Carroll,** Thomas F. 1941- *WhoIns 92*
**Carroll,** Thomas Joseph 1912- *AmMWSc 92*
**Carroll,** Thomas Joseph 1941- *WhoFI 92*
**Carroll,** Thomas Lawrence, Jr. 1931- *WhoEnt 92*
**Carroll,** Thomas William 1932- *AmMWSc 92*
**Carroll,** Victoria Susan 1950- *WhoMW 92*
**Carroll,** Vinnette *WhoBlA 92*
**Carroll,** William 1936- *WhoBlA 92*
**Carroll,** William J 1923- *AmMWSc 92*
**Carroll,** William Joseph 1943- *WhoAmP 91*
**Carroll,** William Kenneth 1927- *WhoMW 92*
**Carroll,** William M. 1932- *WhoFI 92*
**Carroll-Smith,** Elisabeth Nicole Eliane 1937- *WhoEnt 92*
**Carron,** Neal Jay 1941- *AmMWSc 92*
**Carrott,** John Arden 1947- *WhoFI 92, WhoWest 92*
**Carrow,** Robert Duane 1934- *WhoAmL 92*
**Carrozza,** John Henry 1944- *AmMWSc 92*
**Carruth,** Betty Ruth *AmMWSc 92*
**Carruth,** Hayden *DrAPF 91*
**Carruth,** Hayden 1862-1932 *ScFEYrs*
**Carruth,** Hayden 1921- *BenetAL 91, ConPo 91, WrDr 92*
**Carruth,** James Harrison 1807-1896 *BiInAmS*
**Carruth,** James Harvey 1938- *AmMWSc 92*
**Carruth,** Theodore Raymond 1941- *WhoRel 92*
**Carruth,** Willis Lee 1909- *AmMWSc 92*
**Carruthers,** Alwyn Guy 1925- *Who 92*
**Carruthers,** Bill *LesBEnT 92*
**Carruthers,** Christopher 1909- *AmMWSc 92*
**Carruthers,** Colin Malcolm 1931- *Who 92*
**Carruthers,** Derek 1935- *TwCPaSc*
**Carruthers,** Garrey E 1939- *WhoAmP 91*
**Carruthers,** Garrey Edward 1939- *IntWW 91, WhoWest 92*
**Carruthers,** George 1917- *Who 92*
**Carruthers,** George Robert 1939- *WhoBlA 92*
**Carruthers,** James Edwin 1928- *Who 92*
**Carruthers,** Jimmy 1929-1990 *AnObit 1990, FacFETw*
**Carruthers,** John Robert 1935- *AmMWSc 92*
**Carruthers,** Kent 1949- *WhoFI 92*
**Carruthers,** Lucy Marston 1937- *AmMWSc 92*
**Carruthers,** Norman Harry 1935- *Who 92*
**Carruthers,** Peter A 1935- *AmMWSc 92*
**Carruthers,** Philip C 1953- *WhoAmP 91*
**Carruthers,** Raymond Ingalls 1951- *AmMWSc 92*
**Carruthers,** Robert 1921- *IntWW 91*
**Carruthers,** Robert 1925- *TwCPaSc*
**Carruthers,** Roderick William 1933- *WhoWest 92*
**Carruthers,** Samuel George 1945- *AmMWSc 92*
**Carruthers,** Thomas Neely, Jr. 1928- *WhoAmL 92*
**Carruthers,** Walter Edward Royden 1938- *WhoEnt 92*
**Carruthers,** William Buttrick 1929- *Who 92*
**Carry Back** 1958-1983 *FacFETw*
**Carry,** Helen Ward *WhoBlA 92*
**Carry,** Myrtle Louise 1914- *WhoEnt 92*
**Carry,** Tim Sean 1958- *WhoEnt 92*
**Carryer,** Haddon McCutchen 1914- *AmMWSc 92, WhoMW 92*
**Carryl,** Charles Edward 1841-1920 *BenetAL 91*
**Carryl,** Guy Wetmore 1873-1904 *BenetAL 91*
**Cars,** The *NewAmDM*
**Carsberg,** Bryan 1939- *IntWW 91, Who 92*
**Carsch,** Ruth Elizabeth 1945- *WhoFI 92*
**Carse,** Henry H 1918- *WhoAmP 91*
**Carsell,** Carolyn Kay 1938- *WhoMW 92*
**Carselle,** John Paul 1961- *WhoMW 92*
**Carsello,** Carmen Joseph 1915- *WhoMW 92*
**Carsey,** Marcia Lee Peterson 1944- *WhoEnt 92*
**Carsey-Werner** *LesBEnT 92*
**Carski,** Theodore Robert 1930- *AmMWSc 92*
**Carsola,** Alfred James 1919- *AmMWSc 92*
**Carson,** Albert Gus, IV 1960- *WhoEnt 92*
**Carson,** Anthony Bruce 1940- *WhoRel 92*
**Carson,** Benjamin 1951- *ConBlB 1 [port]*
**Carson,** Benjamin Solomon, Sr. 1951- *WhoBlA 92*
**Carson,** Bobb 1943- *AmMWSc 92*
**Carson,** Bonnie L Bachert 1940- *AmMWSc 92*
**Carson,** Charles R. 1945- *WhoFI 92*
**Carson,** Chester Carrol 1918- *AmMWSc 92*
**Carson,** Christopher Leonard 1940- *WhoAmL 92*
**Carson,** Ciaran 1948- *WrDr 92*
**Carson,** Ciaran Gerard 1948- *IntAu&W 91*
**Carson,** Curtis C., Jr. 1920- *WhoBlA 92*
**Carson,** Daniel Douglas 1953- *AmMWSc 92*
**Carson,** Dave *WhoAmP 91, WhoEnt 92*
**Carson,** Dennis A 1946- *AmMWSc 92*
**Carson,** Donald Duane 1942- *WhoFI 92*
**Carson,** Dwight Keith 1951- *WhoBlA 92*
**Carson,** Eben 1951- *WhoRel 92*
**Carson,** Edward Henry 1854-1935 *FacFETw*
**Carson,** Edward Mansfield 1929- *IntWW 91, WhoWest 92*
**Carson,** Eugene Watson, Jr 1939- *AmMWSc 92*
**Carson,** Fiddlin' John 1868-1949 *NewAmDM*
**Carson,** Frederick Wallace 1940- *AmMWSc 92*
**Carson,** Gayle Norma 1938- *WhoFI 92*
**Carson,** George John 1936- *WhoAmL 92*
**Carson,** George Stephen 1948- *AmMWSc 92*
**Carson,** Gordon B 1911- *AmMWSc 92*
**Carson,** Hampton L. 1914- *IntWW 91*
**Carson,** Hampton Lawrence 1914- *AmMWSc 92*
**Carson,** Hank *TwCWW 91*
**Carson,** Harry Donald 1953- *WhoBlA 92*
**Carson,** Herbert L. 1929- *WrDr 92*
**Carson,** Herbert Lee 1929- *WhoMW 92*
**Carson,** Irma 1935- *WhoBlA 92*
**Carson,** James Donald 1929- *WhoRel 92*
**Carson,** James Matthew 1944- *WhoWest 92*
**Carson,** Jeannie *IntMPA 92*
**Carson,** John 1934- *Who 92*
**Carson,** John Little 1945- *WhoRel 92*
**Carson,** John William 1944- *AmMWSc 92*
**Carson,** Johnny *LesBEnT 92 [port]*
**Carson,** Johnny 1925- *FacFETw, IntMPA 92, IntWW 91, WhoEnt 92*
**Carson,** Johnny Lee 1949- *AmMWSc 92*
**Carson,** Joseph 1808-1876 *BiInAmS*
**Carson,** Josephine *DrAPF 91*
**Carson,** Julia M *WhoAmP 91*
**Carson,** Julia M. 1938- *WhoBlA 92*
**Carson,** Keith Alan 1952- *AmMWSc 92*
**Carson,** Kenneth A. *WhoAmL 92*
**Carson,** Kit 1809-1868 *BenetAL 91*
**Carson,** L. Turner 1924- *WhoAmL 92*
**Carson,** Leta Nelle 1937- *WhoEnt 92*
**Carson,** Lillian Gershenson 1933- *WhoWest 92*
**Carson,** Loftus C. 1923-1989 *WhoBlA 92N*
**Carson,** Loftus C., II 1946- *WhoAmL 92*
**Carson,** Lois Montgomery 1931- *WhoBlA 92*
**Carson,** Marvin Wayne 1955- *WhoWest 92*
**Carson,** Paul Langford 1942- *AmMWSc 92*
**Carson,** Paul Llewellyn 1919- *AmMWSc 92*
**Carson,** Rachel 1885-1964 *HanAmWH*
**Carson,** Rachel 1904-1964 *BenetAL 91*
**Carson,** Rachel 1907-1964 *FacFETw, RComAH*
**Carson,** Rachel Louise 1907-1964 *ConAu 35NR*
**Carson,** Ralph S 1922- *AmMWSc 92*
**Carson,** Regina Edwards *WhoFI 92*
**Carson,** Regina M. Edwards 1946- *WhoBlA 92*
**Carson,** Richard McKee 1912- *WhoMW 92*
**Carson,** Richard Taylor, Jr. 1955- *WhoFI 92*
**Carson,** Robert Andrew Glendinning 1918- *Who 92*
**Carson,** Robert Cleland 1924- *AmMWSc 92, WhoMW 92*
**Carson,** Robert James, III *AmMWSc 92*
**Carson,** Robert John 1924- *Who 92*
**Carson,** Robert John 1935- *WhoAmL 92*
**Carson,** Robert Taylor 1919- *TwCPaSc*
**Carson,** Samuel Price 1798-1838 *DcNCBi 1*
**Carson,** Steven 1925- *AmMWSc 92*
**Carson,** Steven Douglas 1951- *AmMWSc 92*
**Carson,** Timothy Joseph 1949- *WhoAmP 91*
**Carson,** Virginia Gottschall *WhoWest 92*
**Carson,** Virginia Rosalie Gottschall *AmMWSc 92*
**Carson,** Wallace P, Jr 1934- *WhoAmP 91*

**Carson,** Wallace Preston, Jr. 1934- *WhoAmL 92, WhoWest 92*
**Carson,** Warren Jason, Jr. 1953- *WhoBlA 92*
**Carson,** William Charles 1924- *WhoFI 92*
**Carson,** William Hunter 1942- *IntWW 91*
**Carson,** William Hunter Fisher 1942- *Who 92*
**Carson,** Willis E. 1912-1989 *WhoBlA 92N*
**Carsrud,** Alan Lee 1946- *WhoWest 92*
**Carstairs,** Charles Young 1910- *Who 92*
**Carstairs,** George Morrison d1991 *Who 92N*
**Carstairs,** George Morrison 1916-1991 *IntWW 91, -91N*
**Carstea,** Dumitru 1930- *AmMWSc 92*
**Carstedt,** William Douglas 1938- *WhoAmL 92*
**Carsten,** Arland L 1930- *AmMWSc 92*
**Carsten,** Calvin F 1915- *WhoAmP 91*
**Carsten,** Francis Ludwig 1911- *Who 92, WrDr 92*
**Carsten,** Mary E 1922- *AmMWSc 92*
**Carstens,** Allan Matlock 1939- *AmMWSc 92*
**Carstens,** Earl E 1950- *AmMWSc 92*
**Carstens,** Eric Bruce *AmMWSc 92*
**Carstens,** John C 1937- *AmMWSc 92*
**Carstens,** Karl 1914- *IntWW 91, Who 92*
**Carstensen,** Bob 1931- *WhoMW 92*
**Carstensen,** Edwin L 1919- *AmMWSc 92*
**Carstensen,** Jens T 1926- *AmMWSc 92*
**Carstensen,** Marilyn Joyce 1938- *WhoAmP 91*
**Carstensen,** Peter C. 1942- *WhoAmL 92*
**Carstensen,** Roger 1920- *WrDr 92*
**Carstensen,** Roger Norwood 1920- *WhoRel 92*
**Carstetter,** David Wilson 1937- *WhoAmL 92*
**Carswell,** Allan Ian 1933- *AmMWSc 92*
**Carswell,** Gloria Nadine Sherman 1951- *WhoBlA 92*
**Carswell,** John 1931- *TwCPaSc*
**Carswell,** John Patrick 1918- *IntAu&W 91, Who 92, WrDr 92*
**Carswell,** Robert 1928- *WhoAmL 92, WhoAmP 91*
**Carswell,** Robert 1934- *Who 92*
**Carswell,** Robert Dean 1940- *WhoAmL 92*
**Carswell,** Thomas W., Jr. 1949- *WhoBlA 92*
**Cart,** Eldred Nolen, Jr 1934- *AmMWSc 92*
**Cart,** Pauline Harmon 1914- *WhoRel 92*
**Cartagena,** Luis A. 1946- *WhoHisp 92*
**Cartagena,** Roberto A. 1947- *WhoHisp 92*
**Cartan,** Elie Joseph 1869-1951 *FacFETw*
**Cartan,** Henri Paul 1904- *IntWW 91*
**Cartan-Hansen,** Joan Kathleen 1961- *WhoAmP 91*
**Cartano,** Tony 1944- *IntAu&W 91*
**Carte,** George Wayne 1940- *WhoWest 92*
**Carte,** Richard D'Oyly 1844-1901 *NewAmDM*
**Cartee,** Gary Lane 1954- *WhoAmL 92*
**Cartee,** Thomas Edward, Jr. 1960- *WhoFI 92*
**Cartelli,** Mary Anne *DrAPF 91*
**Cartellieri,** Ulrich 1937- *IntWW 91*
**Carten,** Francis Noel 1935- *WhoAmL 92*
**Carten,** Thomas Francis 1942- *WhoEnt 92*
**Carter** *Who 92*
**Carter,** Baron 1932- *Who 92*
**Carter Family,** The *NewAmDM*
**Carter,** Alden R. *DrAPF 91*
**Carter,** Alden R. 1947- *ConAu 135, SmATA 67 [port]*
**Carter,** Allen D. 1947- *WhoBlA 92*
**Carter,** Alphonse H. 1928- *WhoBlA 92*
**Carter,** Ambrose Wayne 1948- *WhoRel 92*
**Carter,** Andrew 1943- *Who 92*
**Carter,** Angela 1940- *ConAu 36NR, ConNov 91, FacFETw, IntAu&W 91, IntWW 91, SmATA 66 [port], TwCSFW 91, Who 92, WrDr 92*
**Carter,** Anne Cohen 1919- *AmMWSc 92*
**Carter,** Annette Wheeler *WhoAmP 91*
**Carter,** Anthony 1960- *WhoBlA 92*
**Carter,** Arlington W., Jr. 1933- *WhoBlA 92*
**Carter,** Arnold Gary 1936- *WhoMW 92*
**Carter,** Arnold Nick 1929- *WhoEnt 92*
**Carter,** Arthur 1916- *WhoAmP 91*
**Carter,** Arthur Michael 1940- *WhoBlA 92*
**Carter,** Ashley Hale 1924- *AmMWSc 92*
**Carter,** Ashton Baldwin 1954- *AmMWSc 92*
**Carter,** Augustus Harry 1949- *WhoEnt 92*
**Carter,** B.A.R. 1909- *TwCPaSc*
**Carter,** Barbara Lillian 1942- *WhoBlA 92*
**Carter,** Barrie J 1944- *AmMWSc 92*
**Carter,** Barry Edward 1942- *WhoAmL 92*
**Carter,** Bennett Lester 1907- *WhoEnt 92*
**Carter,** Benny 1907- *NewAmDM*
**Carter,** Bernard 1920- *TwCPaSc*
**Carter,** Bernard Thomas 1920- *Who 92*
**Carter,** Betty 1927- *WhoBlA 92*
**Carter,** Betty 1929- *NotBlAW 92*
**Carter,** Betty 1930- *ConMus 6 [port], NewAmDM*
**Carter,** Bill G 1928- *WhoAmP 91*
**Carter,** Billy L. *WhoBlA 92*
**Carter,** Blanche Nelson 1907- *WhoBlA 92*
**Carter,** Brandon 1942- *IntWW 91, Who 92*
**Carter,** Bruce *IntAu&W 91X, Who 92, WrDr 92*
**Carter,** Bruce D *WhoAmP 91*
**Carter,** Calvin W. 1934- *WhoIns 92*
**Carter,** Cameron Augustus 1961- *WhoRel 92*
**Carter,** Carl Anthony 1964- *WhoBlA 92*
**Carter,** Carol Sue 1944- *AmMWSc 92*
**Carter,** Carolyn McCraw 1932- *WhoBlA 92*
**Carter,** Carolyn Sue 1959- *AmMWSc 92*
**Carter,** Charleata A 1960- *AmMWSc 92*
**Carter,** Charles 1919- *Who 92, WrDr 92*
**Carter,** Charles Conrad 1924- *AmMWSc 92*
**Carter,** Charles Douglas 1946- *WhoMW 92*
**Carter,** Charles Edward 1919- *AmMWSc 92*
**Carter,** Charles Edward 1925- *WhoBlA 92*
**Carter,** Charles Frederick 1919- *IntWW 91*
**Carter,** Charles Michael 1943- *WhoBlA 92*
**Carter,** Charles Williams, Jr 1945- *AmMWSc 92*
**Carter,** Charlotte *DrAPF 91*
**Carter,** Charlotte 1943- *AmMWSc 92*
**Carter,** Chester C. 1921- *WhoBlA 92*
**Carter,** Chickering 1865-1922 *ScFEYrs*
**Carter,** Cindy 1961- *WhoMW 92*
**Carter,** Claude Daniel 1932- *WhoAmP 91*
**Carter,** Clint Earl 1941- *AmMWSc 92*
**Carter,** Connie Bernice 1943- *WhoWest 92*
**Carter,** Curtis William 1927- *WhoAmP 91*
**Carter,** Daisy 1931- *WhoBlA 92*
**Carter,** Daniel Paul 1948- *WhoAmL 92*
**Carter,** Darline Louretha 1933- *WhoBlA 92*
**Carter,** David *Who 92*
**Carter,** David Craig 1940- *Who 92*
**Carter,** David Edward 1942- *WhoEnt 92*
**Carter,** David G., Sr. 1942- *WhoBlA 92*
**Carter,** David J. 1934- *WhoWest 92*
**Carter,** David L 1933- *AmMWSc 92*
**Carter,** David LaVere 1933- *AmMWSc 92*
**Carter,** David Martin 1936- *AmMWSc 92*
**Carter,** David Miller 1830-1879 *DcNCBi 1*
**Carter,** David Southard 1926- *AmMWSc 92*
**Carter,** Derrick 1906- *Who 92*
**Carter,** Dexter Anthony 1967- *WhoBlA 92*
**Carter,** Dian Jean 1952- *WhoRel 92*
**Carter,** Dixie *WhoEnt 92*
**Carter,** Dixie 1939- *IntMPA 92*
**Carter,** Don 1928- *WhoAmP 91*
**Carter,** Don E 1926- *AmMWSc 92*
**Carter,** Don Gray 1953- *WhoAmL 92*
**Carter,** Dorothy Ethel Fleming 1928- *Who 92*
**Carter,** Dorval Ronald 1935- *WhoBlA 92*
**Carter,** Douglas 1911- *Who 92*
**Carter,** Douglas Brian 1958- *WhoRel 92*
**Carter,** Earl Thomas 1922- *AmMWSc 92*
**Carter,** Edward Albert 1945- *AmMWSc 92*
**Carter,** Edward Earl 1939- *WhoBlA 92*
**Carter,** Edward William 1911- *WhoWest 92*
**Carter,** Edwin Charles 1931- *WhoFI 92*
**Carter,** Elizabeth 1717-1806 *BlkwCEP, DcLB 109 [port]*
**Carter,** Ellin *DrAPF 91*
**Carter,** Elliot, Jr 1908- *FacFETw*
**Carter,** Elliott 1908- *ConCom 92, NewAmDM, Who 92*
**Carter,** Elliott Cook, Jr. 1908- *IntWW 91, WhoEnt 92*
**Carter,** Elmer Buzby 1930- *AmMWSc 92*
**Carter,** Eloise 1945- *AmMWSc 92*
**Carter,** Eloise B 1950- *AmMWSc 92*
**Carter,** Emily Ann 1960- *AmMWSc 92, WhoWest 92*
**Carter,** Enrique Delano 1945- *WhoBlA 92*
**Carter,** Eric Bairstow 1912- *Who 92*
**Carter,** Eric Stephen 1923- *Who 92*
**Carter,** Eunice Hunton 1899-1970 *NotBlAW 92*
**Carter,** Eva Meador 1921- *WhoAmP 91*
**Carter,** Everett 1919- *WrDr 92*
**Carter,** Fairie Lyn 1926- *AmMWSc 92*
**Carter,** Felicity 1906- *WrDr 92*
**Carter,** Forrest 1925-1979 *TwCWW 91*
**Carter,** Frances Monet 1923- *WrDr 92*
**Carter,** Frances Tunnell *IntAu&W 91, WrDr 92*
**Carter,** Francis Graves 1912-1960 *DcNCBi 1*
**Carter,** Francis Jackson 1899- *Who 92*
**Carter,** Francis Mark 1947- *WhoFI 92*
**Carter,** Frank Ernest Lovell 1909- *Who 92*
**Carter,** Fred 1945- *WhoBlA 92*
**Carter,** Frederick 1885-1967 *TwCPaSc*
**Carter,** Frederick Brian 1933- *Who 92*
**Carter,** Frederick J 1929- *AmMWSc 92*
**Carter,** G Clifford 1945- *AmMWSc 92*
**Carter,** Gary Lee 1939- *WhoWest 92*
**Carter,** Gene 1935- *WhoAmL 92*
**Carter,** Gene Raymond 1939- *WhoBlA 92*
**Carter,** Gene Stratton 1926- *WhoRel 92*
**Carter,** Geoffrey Norton 1944- *WhoBlA 92*
**Carter,** George Dennis 1947- *WhoRel 92*
**Carter,** George Emmitt, Jr 1946- *AmMWSc 92*
**Carter,** George H 1916- *AmMWSc 92*
**Carter,** George Henry, IV 1955- *WhoWest 92*
**Carter,** George Kent 1935- *WhoFI 92*
**Carter,** Georgian L. 1939- *WhoRel 92*
**Carter,** Gerald Emmett 1912- *IntWW 91, RelLAm 91, Who 92, WhoRel 92*
**Carter,** Geraldine Faye 1943- *WhoMW 92*
**Carter,** Gesina C 1939- *AmMWSc 92*
**Carter,** Gilbert Lino 1945- *WhoBlA 92*
**Carter,** Giles Frederick 1930- *AmMWSc 92, WhoMW 92*
**Carter,** Glenn Douglas 1940- *WhoMW 92*
**Carter,** Glenn Thomas 1934- *WhoAmL 92*
**Carter,** Godfrey James 1919- *Who 92*
**Carter,** Gwendolen M. d1991 *NewYTBS 91*
**Carter,** Gwendolen M. 1906-1991 *ConAu 133*
**Carter,** Gwendolen Margaret 1906- *IntAu&W 91*
**Carter,** Gwendolyn Burns 1932- *WhoBlA 92*
**Carter,** Hanson 1932- *WhoAmP 91*
**Carter,** Harley Willis 1927- *WhoAmP 91*
**Carter,** Harlon B. d1991 *NewYTBS 91 [port]*
**Carter,** Harold 1925- *WrDr 92*
**Carter,** Harold Lloyd *WhoMW 92*
**Carter,** Harriet LaShun 1963- *WhoBlA 92*
**Carter,** Harry Hart 1921- *AmMWSc 92*
**Carter,** Harvey 1938- *WhoAmP 91*
**Carter,** Harvey Pate 1927- *AmMWSc 92*
**Carter,** Hazo William, Jr. *WhoBlA 92*
**Carter,** Henry Lee 1935- *WhoAmP 91*
**Carter,** Herbert Byron, III 1962- *WhoAmL 92*
**Carter,** Herbert E. 1919- *WhoBlA 92*
**Carter,** Herbert Edmund 1910- *AmMWSc 92, IntWW 91*
**Carter,** Herbert Randal 1960- *WhoRel 92*
**Carter,** Hodding, III *FacFETw, LesBEnT 92*
**Carter,** Hodding, III 1935- *WhoEnt 92*
**Carter,** Horace Sanders, Jr. 1943- *WhoAmL 92*
**Carter,** Howard 1873-1939 *FacFETw*
**Carter,** Howard 1938- *TwCPaSc*
**Carter,** Howard Julian 1936- *WhoRel 92*
**Carter,** Howard Payne 1921- *AmMWSc 92, WhoBlA 92*
**Carter,** Hubert Kennon 1941- *AmMWSc 92*
**Carter,** J. B., Jr. 1937- *WhoBlA 92*
**Carter,** Jack 1923- *IntMPA 92*
**Carter,** Jack Franklin 1919- *AmMWSc 92*
**Carter,** Jack Lee 1929- *AmMWSc 92*
**Carter,** James 1944- *WhoBlA 92*
**Carter,** James Alfred 1941- *WhoAmL 92*
**Carter,** James Clarence 1927- *AmMWSc 92*
**Carter,** James Earl, Jr. 1924- *AmPolLe [port], Who 92*
**Carter,** James Earl, Jr. 1943- *WhoBlA 92*
**Carter,** James Edward 1929- *AmMWSc 92*
**Carter,** James Edward 1935- *WhoRel 92*
**Carter,** James Edward, III 1938- *WhoBlA 92*
**Carter,** James Edward, Jr. 1906- *WhoBlA 92*
**Carter,** James Evan 1941- *AmMWSc 92*
**Carter,** James H. 1935- *WhoAmL 92, WhoAmP 91, WhoMW 92*
**Carter,** James Hal, Jr. 1943- *WhoAmL 92*
**Carter,** James Harrison, II 1945- *AmMWSc 92*
**Carter,** James Harvey 1934- *WhoBlA 92*
**Carter,** James L. 1933- *WhoBlA 92*
**Carter,** James Lawrence 1945- *WhoMW 92*
**Carter,** James M 1921- *AmMWSc 92*
**Carter,** James Madison Gore 1843-1919 *BiInAmS*
**Carter,** James McCord 1952- *WhoEnt 92*
**Carter,** James Norman *Who 92*
**Carter,** James P. *WhoBlA 92*
**Carter,** James Paul 1940- *WhoRel 92*
**Carter,** James R *AmMWSc 92*
**Carter,** James Richard 1953- *AmMWSc 92*
**Carter,** James Woodford, Jr. 1943- *WhoAmL 92*
**Carter,** Jandra D. 1948- *WhoBlA 92*
**Carter,** Jane *Who 92*
**Carter,** Jane Foster 1927- *WhoAmP 91, WhoWest 92*
**Carter,** Janice Joene 1948- *WhoWest 92*
**Carter,** Jared *DrAPF 91*
**Carter,** Jefferson *DrAPF 91*
**Carter,** Jeffrey W. 1963- *WhoMW 92*
**Carter,** Jesse Lee, Sr. 1926- *WhoBlA 92*
**Carter,** Jimmy *WrDr 92*
**Carter,** Jimmy 1924- *BenetAL 91, FacFETw [port], IntWW 91, RComAH, WhoAmP 91*
**Carter,** Joan Elizabeth 1937- *WhoBlA 92*
**Carter,** Joann Bell 1943- *WhoRel 92*
**Carter,** JoAnne Williams 1935- *WhoBlA 92*
**Carter,** John *WhoAmP 91*
**Carter,** John d1991 *NewYTBS 91 [port]*
**Carter,** John 1737-1781 *DcNCBi 1*
**Carter,** John 1919- *IntWW 91, Who 92*
**Carter,** John 1921- *Who 92*
**Carter,** John 1942- *TwCPaSc*
**Carter,** John B. d1991 *NewYTBS 91 [port]*
**Carter,** John C H 1925- *AmMWSc 92*
**Carter,** John Coles 1920- *WhoAmL 92*
**Carter,** John Crowley 1932- *WhoRel 92*
**Carter,** John Dale 1944- *WhoMW 92*
**Carter,** John Douglas 1946- *WhoAmL 92, WhoFI 92*
**Carter,** John H. 1948- *WhoBlA 92*
**Carter,** John Haas 1930- *AmMWSc 92*
**Carter,** John Lemuel, Jr 1920- *AmMWSc 92*
**Carter,** John Lyman 1934- *AmMWSc 92*
**Carter,** John Mack 1928- *WhoFI 92*
**Carter,** John Newton 1921- *AmMWSc 92*
**Carter,** John Paul 1930- *AmMWSc 92*
**Carter,** John Paul, Jr 1951- *AmMWSc 92*
**Carter,** John R. 1941- *WhoBlA 92*
**Carter,** John Robert 1917- *AmMWSc 92*
**Carter,** John Ross 1938- *WhoRel 92*
**Carter,** John T. 1921- *WrDr 92*
**Carter,** John Timothy 1944- *Who 92*
**Carter,** John Vernon 1940- *AmMWSc 92*
**Carter,** Joseph 1918- *WhoAmP 91*
**Carter,** Joseph 1960- *WhoBlA 92*
**Carter,** Joseph, Jr. 1927- *WhoBlA 92*
**Carter,** Joseph Carlyle, Jr. 1927- *WhoAmL 92*
**Carter,** Joseph Gaylord 1947- *AmMWSc 92*
**Carter,** Joy Eaton 1923- *WhoWest 92*
**Carter,** Judy L. 1942- *WhoBlA 92*
**Carter,** Judy Sharon 1951- *WhoBlA 92*
**Carter,** Julia H *AmMWSc 92*
**Carter,** Karen Louise 1953- *WhoMW 92*
**Carter,** Karl W., Jr. *DrAPF 91*
**Carter,** Keith Derwin 1955- *WhoMW 92*
**Carter,** Kelly Elizabeth 1962- *WhoBlA 92*
**Carter,** Kenneth 1914- *AmMWSc 92*
**Carter,** Kenneth 1928- *TwCPaSc*
**Carter,** Kenneth Gregory 1959- *WhoBlA 92*
**Carter,** Kenneth Harper, Jr. 1957- *WhoRel 92*
**Carter,** Kenneth Nolon 1925- *AmMWSc 92*
**Carter,** Kirk A. 1961- *WhoAmL 92*
**Carter,** Lamore Joseph 1925- *WhoBlA 92*
**Carter,** Landon 1760-1800 *DcNCBi 1*
**Carter,** Lark P. 1930- *WhoWest 92*
**Carter,** Lark Poland 1930- *AmMWSc 92*
**Carter,** Larry Alexander 1940- *WhoFI 92, WhoWest 92*
**Carter,** Larry Ernest 1941- *WhoWest 92*
**Carter,** Larry Michael 1949- *WhoMW 92*
**Carter,** Lawrence 1942- *WhoBlA 92*
**Carter,** Lawrence E., Sr. 1941- *WhoBlA 92*
**Carter,** Lawrence Robert 1936- *WhoBlA 92*
**Carter,** Lee 1917- *AmMWSc 92, WhoMW 92*
**Carter,** Leland LaVelle 1937- *AmMWSc 92*
**Carter,** Lemorie, Jr. 1944- *WhoBlA 92*
**Carter,** Lenora 1941- *WhoBlA 92*
**Carter,** Leo F 1939- *AmMWSc 92*
**Carter,** Lewis Winston 1920- *WhoBlA 92*
**Carter,** Lin 1930-1988 *TwCSFW 91*
**Carter,** Linda G 1949- *AmMWSc 92*
**Carter,** Linda Susan 1950- *WhoEnt 92*
**Carter,** Lisa Renee 1966- *WhoWest 92*
**Carter,** Lisle Carleton, Jr. 1925- *WhoBlA 92*
**Carter,** Loren Sheldon 1939- *AmMWSc 92*
**Carter,** Lynda *IntMPA 92, WhoEnt 92*
**Carter,** Lynda Cordoba *WhoHisp 92*
**Carter,** Manley Lanier, Jr. d1991 *NewYTBS 91*
**Carter,** Manson Hildreth 1923- *WhoFI 92*
**Carter,** Margaret Louise 1935- *WhoAmP 91, WhoBlA 92*
**Carter,** Marian Elizabeth 1935- *WhoAmP 91*
**Carter,** Marion Elizabeth *WhoBlA 92*
**Carter,** Marlene C 1945- *WhoAmP 91*
**Carter,** Marshall Nichols 1940- *WhoFI 92*
**Carter,** Marshall Sylvester 1909- *IntWW 91*
**Carter,** Martin 1927- *ConPo 91, WrDr 92*
**Carter,** Martin Joseph 1930- *WhoBlA 92*
**Carter,** Mary *DrAPF 91*
**Carter,** Mary Arkley *IntAu&W 91*
**Carter,** Mary Eddie 1925- *AmMWSc 92*
**Carter,** Mary Kathleen 1922- *AmMWSc 92*
**Carter,** Mary Louise 1937- *WhoBlA 92*
**Carter,** Mary Missy 1942- *WhoFI 92*

**Carter**, Mason Carlton 1933- *AmMWSc 92*
**Carter**, Matthew 1938- *DcTwDes*
**Carter**, Matthew Gamaliel 1913- *WhoBlA 92*
**Carter**, Maybelle 1909-1978 *FacFETw*
**Carter**, Melvin Whitsett 1941- *WhoWest 92*
**Carter**, Melvin Winsor 1928- *AmMWSc 92*
**Carter**, Michael 1960- *BlkOlyM, WhoBlA 92*
**Carter**, Michael Ray 1953- *WhoWest 92*
**Carter**, Michael Robert 1944- *WhoEnt 92*
**Carter**, Michael Scott 1961- *WhoAmL 92*
**Carter**, Milton O., Sr. 1912- *WhoBlA 92*
**Carter**, Morrison Gray, Jr. 1952- *WhoWest 92*
**Carter**, Nanette Carolyn 1954- *WhoBlA 92*
**Carter**, Nell 1948- *ConMus 7 [port], IntMPA 92, WhoBlA 92, WhoEnt 92*
**Carter**, Nevada *TwCWW 91*
**Carter**, Neville Louis 1934- *AmMWSc 92*
**Carter**, Nick *ConAu 35NR, IntAu&W 91X, SmATA 67, WrDr 92*
**Carter**, Ora Williams 1925- *WhoBlA 92*
**Carter**, Orwin Lee 1942- *AmMWSc 92*
**Carter**, Oscar Charles Sumner 1857-1917 *BiInAmS*
**Carter**, Oscar Earl, Jr. 1922- *WhoBlA 92*
**Carter**, Parvin Salmassie 1948- *WhoMW 92*
**Carter**, Patrick Francis 1947- *WhoAmP 91*
**Carter**, Patrick Henry, Jr. 1939- *WhoBlA 92*
**Carter**, Paul Bearnson 1918- *AmMWSc 92*
**Carter**, Paul Dennis 1950- *WhoRel 92*
**Carter**, Paul Richard 1922- *AmMWSc 92*
**Carter**, Paul Thomas 1922- *WhoAmP 91*
**Carter**, Paula J *WhoAmP 91*
**Carter**, Peers Lee 1916- *Who 92*
**Carter**, Percy A., Jr. 1929- *WhoBlA 92*
**Carter**, Perry W. 1960- *WhoBlA 92*
**Carter**, Peter 1929- *IntAu&W 91, WrDr 92*
**Carter**, Peter Basil 1921- *Who 92*
**Carter**, Peter Greer 1937- *WhoWest 92*
**Carter**, Philip Brian 1945- *AmMWSc 92*
**Carter**, Philip David 1927- *Who 92*
**Carter**, Philip W., Jr. 1941- *WhoBlA 92*
**Carter**, R Owen, Jr 1915- *AmMWSc 92*
**Carter**, Ray Morgan 1941- *WhoAmP 91*
**Carter**, Raymond Gene, Sr. 1936- *WhoBlA 92*
**Carter**, Raymond John 1935- *Who 92*
**Carter**, Rex Lyle 1925- *WhoAmP 91*
**Carter**, Richard Bert 1916- *WhoRel 92, WhoWest 92*
**Carter**, Richard Cleon, III 1956- *WhoMW 92*
**Carter**, Richard Duane *WhoFI 92*
**Carter**, Richard Gerald, Jr 1947- *WhoAmP 91*
**Carter**, Richard John 1941- *AmMWSc 92*
**Carter**, Richard P 1915- *AmMWSc 92*
**Carter**, Richard Thomas 1936- *AmMWSc 92*
**Carter**, Robert Alfred Copsey 1910- *Who 92*
**Carter**, Robert Cornelius 1917- *WhoAmP 91*
**Carter**, Robert Eldred 1923- *AmMWSc 92*
**Carter**, Robert Emerson 1920- *AmMWSc 92*
**Carter**, Robert Everett 1937- *AmMWSc 92*
**Carter**, Robert Felton 1935- *WhoRel 92*
**Carter**, Robert Henry, III 1941- *WhoBlA 92*
**Carter**, Robert L 1918- *AmMWSc 92*
**Carter**, Robert Lee 1917- *WhoBlA 92*
**Carter**, Robert Lee 1954- *WhoMW 92*
**Carter**, Robert Philip, Sr. 1946- *WhoAmL 92*
**Carter**, Robert S 1925- *WhoAmP 91*
**Carter**, Robert Sague 1925- *AmMWSc 92*
**Carter**, Robert T. 1938- *WhoBlA 92*
**Carter**, Robert Thompson 1937- *WhoBlA 92*
**Carter**, Robert William Bernard 1913- *Who 92*
**Carter**, Roberta Eccleston *WhoWest 92*
**Carter**, Rodney 1957- *WhoFI 92*
**Carter**, Rodney Carl 1964- *WhoBlA 92*
**Carter**, Roland 1924- *Who 92*
**Carter**, Romelia Mae 1934- *WhoBlA 92*
**Carter**, Ron 1937- *NewAmDM*
**Carter**, Ronald 1937- *WhoEnt 92*
**Carter**, Ronald David 1927- *Who 92*
**Carter**, Ronald Louis 1926- *Who 92*
**Carter**, Ronald M. 1934- *WhoMW 92*
**Carter**, Ronnie Eugene 1937- *WhoRel 92*
**Carter**, Rosalynn 1927- *WrDr 92*
**Carter**, Roy McCain 1930- *WhoEnt 92*
**Carter**, Rubin 1952- *WhoBlA 92*
**Carter**, Rufus Earl 1938- *WhoRel 92*
**Carter**, Ruth Durley 1922- *WhoBlA 92*
**Carter**, Sally Jo Hamrick 1929- *WhoAmP 91*
**Carter**, Sam Allen, Jr. 1962- *WhoAmL 92*
**Carter**, Samuel Emmanuel 1919- *WhoRel 92*
**Carter**, Sandra Ruth 1945- *WhoMW 92*
**Carter**, Scott Hays 1960- *WhoAmL 92*
**Carter**, Sean Alexandre 1963- *WhoFI 92*
**Carter**, Shannan Louise 1953- *WhoAmL 92*
**Carter**, Shari Elaine *DrAPF 91*
**Carter**, Shirley *NewAmDM*
**Carter**, Stefan A 1928- *AmMWSc 92*
**Carter**, Stephen 1949- *TwCPaSc*
**Carter**, Stephen Edward 1954- *WhoAmL 92*
**Carter**, Stephen James 1941- *WhoRel 92*
**Carter**, Stephen Keith 1937- *AmMWSc 92*
**Carter**, Stephen Lisle *WhoAmL 92*
**Carter**, Susan D 1949- *WhoAmP 91*
**Carter**, Susan Miller 1952- *WhoMW 92*
**Carter**, Susan Montgomery *WhoEnt 92*
**Carter**, Theodore R., III 1954- *WhoAmL 92*
**Carter**, Theodore Ulysses 1931- *WhoBlA 92*
**Carter**, Thomas *ConTFT 9, LesBEnT 92, WhoEnt 92*
**Carter**, Thomas Allen 1935- *WhoBlA 92*
**Carter**, Thomas Barton 1949- *WhoAmL 92*
**Carter**, Thomas Earl 1947- *ConAu 133*
**Carter**, Thomas Edward, Jr 1953- *AmMWSc 92*
**Carter**, Thomas F. d1991 *NewYTBS 91 [port]*
**Carter**, Thomas Floyd, Jr. 1927- *WhoBlA 92*
**Carter**, Thomas Heyward, Jr. 1946- *WhoAmL 92*
**Carter**, Thomas Smith, Jr. 1921- *WhoFI 92, WhoMW 92*
**Carter**, Timothy *Who 92*
**Carter**, Timothy Howard 1944- *AmMWSc 92*
**Carter**, Tom *ConAu 133*
**Carter**, Tommy 1934- *WhoAmP 91*
**Carter**, Tony 1943- *TwCPaSc*
**Carter**, Tremlett *ScFEYrs*
**Carter**, Vivian Leone 1941- *WhoMW 92*
**Carter**, W. Minor 1940- *WhoIns 92*
**Carter**, Walter Hansbrough, Jr 1941- *AmMWSc 92*
**Carter**, Walter Horace 1921- *IntAu&W 91*
**Carter**, Warrick L. 1942- *WhoBlA 92*
**Carter**, Wendell Patrick 1966- *WhoBlA 92*
**Carter**, Weptanomah Washington 1937- *WhoBlA 92*
**Carter**, Wesley Byrd 1942- *WhoBlA 92*
**Carter**, Wilf 1904- *NewAmDM*
**Carter**, Wilford 1947- *WhoAmP 91*
**Carter**, Wilfred 1912- *Who 92*
**Carter**, Will J. *WhoBlA 92*
**Carter**, William 1863-1939 *TwCPaSc*
**Carter**, William Alfred 1935- *AmMWSc 92*
**Carter**, William Beverly, III 1947- *WhoBlA 92*
**Carter**, William Caswell 1917- *AmMWSc 92*
**Carter**, William Douglas 1926- *AmMWSc 92*
**Carter**, William Eugene 1939- *AmMWSc 92*
**Carter**, William G *AmMWSc 92*
**Carter**, William Glenn 1960- *WhoRel 92*
**Carter**, William Harold 1938- *AmMWSc 92*
**Carter**, William Hodding, III 1935- *WhoAmP 91*
**Carter**, William Hodding, Jr 1907-1972 *FacFETw*
**Carter**, William Joseph 1949- *WhoAmL 92*
**Carter**, William Lacy 1925- *WhoAmP 91*
**Carter**, William Nicholas 1912- *Who 92*
**Carter**, William Oscar 1905- *Who 92*
**Carter**, William Thomas, Jr. 1944- *WhoBlA 92*
**Carter**, William Walton 1921- *AmMWSc 92*
**Carter**, Willie A. 1909- *WhoBlA 92*
**Carter**, Willie Lee 1946- *WhoMW 92*
**Carter**, Wilmoth Annette *WhoBlA 92*
**Carter**, Yvonne P. 1939- *WhoBlA 92*
**Carter Brooks**, Elizabeth 1867-1951 *NotBlAW 92*
**Carter-Clayton**, Connie Lynn 1956- *WhoFI 92*
**Carter-Jones**, Lewis 1920- *Who 92*
**Carter-Ruck**, Peter Frederick 1914- *Who 92*
**Carter-Su**, Christin 1950- *AmMWSc 92*
**Carteret**, Peter 1641- *DcNCBi 1*
**Carterette**, Edward Calvin Hayes 1921- *AmMWSc 92*
**Cartey**, Wilfred G. O. 1931- *WhoBlA 92*
**Carthan**, Eddie James 1949- *WhoBlA 92*
**Carthen**, Billy Burton 1950- *WhoFI 92*
**Carthon**, Maurice 1961- *WhoBlA 92*
**Cartier**, Brian Evans 1950- *WhoFI 92*
**Cartier**, Carol Jean McMaster 1954- *WhoWest 92*
**Cartier**, George Thomas 1924- *AmMWSc 92*
**Cartier**, Jacques 1494?-1557? *BenetAL 91*
**Cartier**, Jean Jacques 1927- *AmMWSc 92*
**Cartier**, Marie *DrAPF 91*
**Cartier**, Peter G *AmMWSc 92*
**Cartier**, Rudolph 1908- *Who 92*
**Cartier**, Thomas Nicholas 1950- *WhoMW 92*
**Cartier-Bresson**, Henri 1908- *DcTwDes, FacFETw, IntWW 91, ModArCr 2 [port], Who 92*
**Cartimandua** d57? *EncAmaz 91*
**Cartland**, Barbara *IntAu&W 91, Who 92, WrDr 92*
**Cartland**, Barbara 1901- *ConAu 34NR, IntWW 91*
**Cartland**, Barbara Hamilton 1901- *FacFETw*
**Cartland**, George 1912- *Who 92*
**Cartledge**, Bryan 1931- *Who 92*
**Cartledge**, Bryan George 1931- *IntWW 91*
**Cartledge**, Frank 1938- *AmMWSc 92*
**Cartledge**, Raymond Eugene 1929- *WhoFI 92*
**Cartlidge**, Arthur J. 1942- *WhoBlA 92*
**Cartlidge**, William *IntMPA 92*
**Cartmel**, Hilary 1958- *TwCPaSc*
**Cartmell**, Alan D. 1956- *WhoWest 92*
**Cartmell**, Elizabeth Bayley 1957- *WhoFI 92*
**Cartmell**, Robert Root 1921- *AmMWSc 92*
**Cartmill**, Charles David 1946- *WhoEnt 92*
**Cartmill**, Cleve 1908-1964 *TwCSFW 91*
**Cartmill**, Matt *AmMWSc 92*
**Carto**, Willis Allison 1926- *WhoFI 92*
**Cartoceti**, Robert John 1957- *WhoAmL 92*
**Carton**, Charles Allan 1920- *AmMWSc 92*
**Carton**, Edwin Beck 1927- *AmMWSc 92*
**Cartrett**, Peter 1641- *DcNCBi 1*
**Carttiss**, Michael Reginald Harry 1938- *Who 92*
**Cartun**, Lois B. 1933- *WhoMW 92*
**Cartwright**, Andrew J. 1835-1903 *DcNCBi 1*
**Cartwright**, Aubrey Lee, Jr 1952- *AmMWSc 92*
**Cartwright**, Bill 1957- *WhoBlA 92*
**Cartwright**, Brian Grant 1947- *WhoAmL 92*
**Cartwright**, Carole B. 1940- *WhoBlA 92*
**Cartwright**, David Chapman 1937- *AmMWSc 92*
**Cartwright**, David Edgar 1926- *Who 92*
**Cartwright**, Edward David 1920- *Who 92*
**Cartwright**, Frederick *Who 92*
**Cartwright**, George Charles 1927- *WhoIns 92*
**Cartwright**, Harry 1919- *Who 92*
**Cartwright**, Hugh Manning *AmMWSc 92*
**Cartwright**, James Elgin 1943- *WhoBlA 92*
**Cartwright**, John Cameron 1933- *Who 92*
**Cartwright**, Keros 1934- *AmMWSc 92, WhoMW 92*
**Cartwright**, Lenora T. 1936-1989 *WhoBlA 92N*
**Cartwright**, Lucette *TwCPaSc*
**Cartwright**, Marguerite Dorsey *WhoBlA 92*
**Cartwright**, Mary Lucy 1900- *IntWW 91, Who 92*
**Cartwright**, Myron Roger 1919- *WhoMW 92*
**Cartwright**, Peter 1785-1872 *BenetAL 91*
**Cartwright**, Philip Crawford 1946- *WhoFI 92, WhoWest 92*
**Cartwright**, Phillip August 1953- *WhoFI 92, WhoMW 92*
**Cartwright**, Reg 1938- *TwCPaSc*
**Cartwright**, Richard Fox 1913- *Who 92*
**Cartwright**, Robert Eugene, II 1956- *WhoWest 92*
**Cartwright**, Samuel Adolphus 1793-1863 *BiInAmS*
**Cartwright**, Silvia 1943- *Who 92*
**Cartwright**, Thomas Campbell 1924- *AmMWSc 92*
**Cartwright**, Thomas Joseph 1949- *WhoMW 92*
**Cartwright**, Veronica 1949- *IntMPA 92*
**Cartwright**, William 1611-1643 *RfGEnL 91*
**Cartwright**, William Frederick 1906- *Who 92*
**Cartwright Sharp**, Michael *Who 92*
**Carty**, Arthur John 1940- *AmMWSc 92*
**Carty**, Daniel T 1935- *AmMWSc 92*
**Carty**, John Joseph 1861-1932 *FacFETw*
**Carty**, John Lydon 1945- *WhoFI 92*
**Carty**, John Wesley 1923- *WhoFI 92, WhoMW 92*
**Carty**, Paul Vernon 1954- *WhoAmL 92*
**Carty**, Raymond Wesley 1956- *WhoMW 92*
**Carty**, Thomas F 1918- *WhoAmP 91*
**Carty-Bennia**, Denise S. 1947- *WhoBlA 92*
**Caru**, Roy 1955- *WhoAmP 91*
**Carubelli**, Raoul 1929- *AmMWSc 92*
**Caruccio**, Frank Thomas 1935- *AmMWSc 92*
**Carufel**, Joan Patricia 1935- *WhoEnt 92*
**Carulla**, Juan Emiliano 1888-1968 *BiDExR*
**Caruolo**, Edward Vitangelo 1931- *AmMWSc 92*
**Caruolo**, George D 1952- *WhoAmP 91*
**Carus**, Louis Revell 1927- *Who 92*
**Carus**, Marianne 1928- *IntAu&W 91*
**Carus**, Paul 1852-1919 *BenetAL 91, BiInAmS, RelLAm 91*
**Carus**, Roderick 1944- *Who 92*
**Carusillo**, Bruce Edward 1955- *WhoFI 92*
**Carusillo**, Joan Gloria 1931- *WhoRel 92*
**Caruso**, Anthony Robert 1960- *WhoAmL 92*
**Caruso**, Charles Michael 1950- *WhoAmL 92*
**Caruso**, Christopher L *WhoAmP 91*
**Caruso**, Daniel F *WhoAmP 91*
**Caruso**, David John 1959- *WhoFI 92*
**Caruso**, Donato 1942- *WhoAmL 92*
**Caruso**, Enrico 1873-1921 *FacFETw [port], NewAmDM*
**Caruso**, Frank Lawrence 1949- *AmMWSc 92*
**Caruso**, Frank San Carlo 1936- *AmMWSc 92*
**Caruso**, John Anthony 1907- *WrDr 92*
**Caruso**, June Marie 1963- *WhoEnt 92*
**Caruso**, Mark J 1957- *WhoAmP 91*
**Caruso**, Mark John 1957- *WhoAmL 92*
**Caruso**, Nicholas Dominic 1957- *WhoFI 92*
**Caruso**, Paul Douglas 1958- *WhoAmL 92*
**Caruso**, Peter Daniel 1953- *WhoFI 92*
**Caruso**, Rocco Andrew 1964- *WhoEnt 92*
**Caruso**, Sebastian Charles 1926- *AmMWSc 92*
**Caruthers**, Barbara Sue Apgar 1943- *WhoMW 92*
**Caruthers**, Edward J, Jr 1945- *BlkOlyM*
**Caruthers**, Eli Washington 1793-1865 *DcNCBi 1*
**Caruthers**, John Quincy 1913- *AmMWSc 92*
**Caruthers**, Marvin Harry 1940- *AmMWSc 92*
**Caruthers**, Patricia Wayne 1939- *WhoBlA 92*
**Caruthers**, William Alexander 1800-1846 *BenetAL 91*
**Carva**, George *WhoHisp 92*
**Carvajal**, Carlos Konrad 1931- *WhoEnt 92*
**Carvajal**, Fernando 1913- *AmMWSc 92*
**Carvajal**, Fernando David 1944- *AmMWSc 92*
**Carvajal**, Francisco 1468- *HisDSpE*
**Carvajal**, Gaspar de 1504-1584 *HisDSpE*
**Carvajal**, Pedro Segundo 1963- *WhoEnt 92*
**Carvajal Prado**, Patricio 1916- *IntWW 91*
**Carvalho**, Angelina C A 1938- *AmMWSc 92*
**Carvalho**, Bryan 1942- *TwCPaSc*
**Carvalho**, Eleazar de 1912- *NewAmDM*
**Carvalho**, Emilio Julio Miguel de 1933- *WhoRel 92*
**Carvalho**, Niedja Mangueira 1956- *WhoEnt 92*
**Carvalho**, Sebastiao Jose de *BlkwCEP*
**Carvallo**, Jorge N. 1945- *WhoHisp 92*
**Carvallo y Goyeneche**, Vicente 1742-1816 *HisDSpE*
**Carvel**, Elbert Nostrand 1910- *WhoAmP 91*
**Carvel**, Tom 1906-1990 *FacFETw*
**Carvell**, Kenneth Llewellyn 1925- *AmMWSc 92*
**Carvelli**, John Joseph, Jr. 1962- *WhoWest 92*
**Carver** *Who 92*
**Carver**, Baron 1915- *IntWW 91, Who 92*
**Carver**, Charles E, Jr 1922- *AmMWSc 92*
**Carver**, Charles Mark 1960- *WhoAmL 92*
**Carver**, Charles Ray 1929- *WhoFI 92*
**Carver**, Dave *IntAu&W 91X, TwCWW 91, WrDr 92*
**Carver**, David Bruce 1960- *WhoRel 92*
**Carver**, David Harold 1930- *AmMWSc 92*
**Carver**, Eugene Arthur 1944- *AmMWSc 92*
**Carver**, Frank Gould 1928- *WhoRel 92, WhoWest 92*
**Carver**, Gary Paul 1942- *AmMWSc 92*
**Carver**, George Washington 1864-1943 *FacFETw [port], RComAH*
**Carver**, Jack Ecton 1932- *WhoEnt 92*
**Carver**, James 1916- *Who 92*
**Carver**, James 1932- *WhoMW 92*
**Carver**, James Clark 1945- *AmMWSc 92*
**Carver**, Jeffrey A. *DrAPF 91*
**Carver**, John Guill 1924- *AmMWSc 92*
**Carver**, John Henry 1926- *IntWW 91*
**Carver**, Jonathan 1710-1780 *BenetAL 91*
**Carver**, Keith Ross 1940- *AmMWSc 92*
**Carver**, Loyce Cleo 1918- *WhoRel 92*
**Carver**, Martin Gregory 1948- *WhoFI 92*
**Carver**, Michael 1915- *WrDr 92*
**Carver**, Michael Bruce 1941- *AmMWSc 92*
**Carver**, Michael Joseph 1923- *AmMWSc 92*

**Carver,** Norman Francis, Jr. 1928- *WrDr 92*
**Carver,** O T 1924- *AmMWSc 92*
**Carver,** Patricia Anne 1950- *WhoBlA 92*
**Carver,** Raymond 1938- *IntAu&W 91*
**Carver,** Raymond 1938-1988 *BenetAL 91, ConAu 34NR, FacFETw, ShSCr 8 [port], TwCWW 91*
**Carver,** Richard E 1937- *WhoAmP 91*
**Carver,** Robert E 1931- *AmMWSc 92*
**Carver,** Steve 1945- *IntMPA 92*
**Carver,** Terrell 1946- *ConAu 133*
**Carver,** W. Edmund 1928- *WhoRel 92*
**Carver,** William Louie 1939- *WhoRel 92*
**Carvey,** Dana 1955- *IntMPA 92*
**Carvill,** Patrick 1943- *Who 92*
**Cary** *Who 92*
**Cary,** Alice 1820-1871 *BenetAL 91*
**Cary,** Alice Dugged d1941 *NotBlAW 92*
**Cary,** Annie Louise 1841-1921 *NewAmDM*
**Cary,** Arlene D. 1930- *WhoMW 92*
**Cary,** Arthur Simmons 1925- *AmMWSc 92*
**Cary,** Carl *DrAPF 91*
**Cary,** Diana Serra 1918- *WhoEnt 92*
**Cary,** Elton Mikell 1929- *WhoFI 92*
**Cary,** Emily Pritchard *DrAPF 91*
**Cary,** Howard Bradford 1920- *AmMWSc 92*
**Cary,** James Donald 1919- *IntAu&W 91*
**Cary,** Jeffrey Patrick 1967- *WhoEnt 92*
**Cary,** Joyce 1888-1957 *CnDBLB 6 [port], FacFETw, RfGEnL 91*
**Cary,** Jud *IntAu&W 91X, WrDr 92*
**Cary,** Julian *TwCSFW 91*
**Cary,** Kevin E. 1955- *WhoEnt 92*
**Cary,** Lorene 1956- *ConAu 135*
**Cary,** Lowell *WhoRel 92*
**Cary,** Phillip H d1916 *BiInAmS*
**Cary,** Phoebe 1824-1871 *BenetAL 91*
**Cary,** Reby *WhoAmP 91*
**Cary,** Reby 1920- *WhoBlA 92*
**Cary,** Richard 1909- *IntAu&W 91*
**Cary,** Richard Durant 1916- *WhoEnt 92*
**Cary,** Roger Hugh 1926- *Who 92*
**Cary,** Ruth Margaret 1917- *WhoAmP 91*
**Cary,** Thomas d1720? *DcNCBi 1*
**Cary,** William David 1945- *WhoWest 92*
**Cary,** William Sterling 1927- *WhoBlA 92, WhoRel 92*
**Caryer,** Emerson Lee 1917- *WhoIns 92*
**Caryll,** Ivan 1861-1921 *NewAmDM*
**Casa-Debeljevic,** Lisa Della *IntWW 91*
**Casabella,** Philip A 1933- *AmMWSc 92*
**Casabon-Sanchez,** Luis 1931- *WhoHisp 92*
**Casad,** Burton M 1933- *AmMWSc 92*
**Casad,** Robert Clair 1929- *WhoAmL 92*
**Casada,** Sarah M *WhoAmP 91*
**Casadaban,** Malcolm John 1949- *AmMWSc 92, WhoMW 92*
**Casadesus,** Gaby *FacFETw*
**Casadesus,** Gaby 1901- *NewAmDM*
**Casadesus,** Jean 1927-1972 *NewAmDM*
**Casadesus,** Jean Claude 1935- *IntWW 91*
**Casadesus,** Penelope Ann 1940- *WhoEnt 92*
**Casadesus,** Robert 1899-1972 *NewAmDM*
**Casadesus,** Robert 1899-1973 *FacFETw*
**Casado,** Andrew Richard 1950- *WhoHisp 92*
**Casado,** Frank d1990 *WhoHisp 92N*
**Casado,** Gustavo E. 1935- *WhoHisp 92*
**Casado-Baena,** Mateo 1937- *WhoHisp 92*
**Casady,** Alfred Jackson 1916- *AmMWSc 92*
**Casagrande,** Daniel Joseph 1945- *AmMWSc 92*
**Casagrande,** Leo 1903- *AmMWSc 92*
**Casal,** Julian Del 1863-1893 *HisDSpE*
**Casale,** Alfred Paul 1955- *WhoRel 92*
**Casale,** Anthony J 1947- *WhoAmP 91*
**Casale,** Francis Joseph 1947- *WhoRel 92*
**Casale,** George N. 1947- *WhoIns 92*
**Casale,** Joseph Vincent 1935- *WhoFI 92*
**Casaletto,** Paul James 1957- *WhoMW 92*
**Casali,** Liberty 1911- *AmMWSc 92*
**Casalino,** Mikal Rebecca 1946- *WhoWest 92*
**Casalone,** Carlo D. *Who 92*
**Casals,** Jordi 1911- *AmMWSc 92*
**Casals,** Pablo 1876-1973 *FacFETw [port], NewAmDM*
**Casamajor,** Paul 1831-1887 *BiInAmS*
**Casamento,** Tina Marie 1964- *WhoEnt 92*
**Casanas,** Alejandro 1954- *BlkOlyM*
**Casani,** John R 1932- *AmMWSc 92*
**Casanova,** Alicia A. 1955- *WhoHisp 92*
**Casanova,** Alicia L. 1937- *WhoHisp 92*
**Casanova,** Arthur E. 1933- *WhoHisp 92*
**Casanova,** Georgina M. 1961- *WhoHisp 92*
**Casanova,** Giovanni Giacomo 1725-1798 *ScFEYrs*
**Casanova,** Giovanni Jacopo 1725-1798 *BlkwCEP*
**Casanova,** Hector L. 1941- *WhoHisp 92*
**Casanova,** Jose Manuel 1930- *WhoHisp 92*
**Casanova,** Joseph 1931- *AmMWSc 92*
**Casanova,** Paul *WhoHisp 92*
**Casanova,** Ronald Joaquin 1949- *WhoHisp 92*
**Casares,** Maria 1922- *IntWW 91*
**Casares,** Paul Lee 1955- *WhoHisp 92*
**Casarett,** Alison Provoost 1930- *AmMWSc 92*
**Casarett,** George William 1920- *AmMWSc 92*
**Casarez,** Rosendo, Jr. 1943- *WhoHisp 92*
**Casarez,** Rosendo, Sr. 1910- *WhoHisp 92*
**Casarez,** Rueben C. 1953- *WhoHisp 92*
**Casarez,** Sylvia Jimenez 1954- *WhoHisp 92*
**Casaroli,** Agostino 1914- *IntWW 91, WhoRel 92*
**Casas,** Bartolome de las *HisDSpE*
**Casas,** Eduardo 1961- *WhoHisp 92*
**Casas,** Mayra 1952- *WhoHisp 92*
**Casas,** Melesio, III 1929- *WhoHisp 92*
**Casas,** Myrna 1934- *WhoHisp 92*
**Casas,** Roberto 1931- *WhoAmP 91, WhoHisp 92*
**Casasent,** David P 1942- *AmMWSc 92*
**Casassa,** Edward Francis 1924- *AmMWSc 92*
**Casassa,** Ethel Zaiser 1924- *AmMWSc 92*
**Casassa,** Michael Paul 1956- *AmMWSc 92*
**Casavant,** Dominique Paul 1930- *WhoAmP 91*
**Casavant,** Lucille M 1935- *WhoAmP 91*
**Casazza,** John Andrew 1924- *AmMWSc 92*
**Casberg,** John Martin 1934- *AmMWSc 92*
**Cascarano,** Joseph 1928- *AmMWSc 92*
**Casci,** Mauro Carlo 1950- *WhoAmL 92*
**Casciano,** Daniel Anthony 1941- *AmMWSc 92*
**Casciato,** Georgia Greanias 1958- *WhoMW 92*
**Cascieri,** Margaret Anne 1951- *AmMWSc 92*
**Cascino,** Anthony Elmo, Jr. 1948- *WhoAmL 92, WhoMW 92*
**Cascio,** Michael Joseph 1950- *WhoEnt 92*
**Cascio,** Wayne Francis 1946- *WhoWest 92*
**Casciola,** Steven George 1948- *WhoWest 92*
**Cascone,** Jeanette L. 1918- *WhoBlA 92*
**Cascos,** Carlos Humberto 1952- *WhoHisp 92*
**Case,** Albert Avion d1990 *Who 92N*
**Case,** Anthea Fiendley 1945- *Who 92*
**Case,** Arthur M. 1950- *WhoBlA 92*
**Case,** Bill *ConAu 133*
**Case,** Cindee 1967- *WhoRel 92*
**Case,** Clinton Meredith 1940- *AmMWSc 92*
**Case,** Clyde Willard, Jr. *WhoFI 92*
**Case,** Daniel Hibbard, III 1957- *WhoFI 92*
**Case,** David 1937- *WrDr 92*
**Case,** David Andrew 1948- *AmMWSc 92*
**Case,** David Leon 1948- *WhoAmL 92*
**Case,** Denis Stephen 1944- *AmMWSc 92*
**Case,** Douglas Manning 1947- *WhoAmL 92, WhoFI 92, WhoMW 92*
**Case,** Douglas Nelson 1954- *WhoWest 92*
**Case,** Edmund Charles 1950- *WhoAmL 92*
**Case,** Edward William 1958- *WhoAmL 92*
**Case,** Everett Needham 1901- *IntWW 91*
**Case,** Franklin D. 1932- *WhoMW 92*
**Case,** Hadley 1909- *WhoFI 92*
**Case,** Hank 1938- *WhoMW 92*
**Case,** Humphrey John 1918- *Who 92*
**Case,** James B 1928- *AmMWSc 92*
**Case,** James Cale 1958- *WhoFI 92*
**Case,** James Edward 1933- *AmMWSc 92*
**Case,** James Frederick 1926- *AmMWSc 92*
**Case,** James Hughson 1928- *AmMWSc 92*
**Case,** Jane McFarling 1955- *WhoRel 92*
**Case,** John *DrAPF 91*
**Case,** John Philip 1952- *WhoMW 92*
**Case,** John William 1942- *AmMWSc 92*
**Case,** Karen Ann 1944- *WhoAmL 92*
**Case,** Kenneth E 1944- *AmMWSc 92*
**Case,** Kenneth Myron 1923- *AmMWSc 92*
**Case,** Lee Owen, Jr. 1925- *WhoWest 92*
**Case,** Linda Ray 1938- *WhoAmP 91*
**Case,** Lloyd Allen 1943- *AmMWSc 92*
**Case,** Margaret A 1938- *WhoAmP 91*
**Case,** Marvin Theodore 1934- *AmMWSc 92*
**Case,** Mary Elizabeth 1925- *AmMWSc 92*
**Case,** Max *WhoAmP 91*
**Case,** Mervin R 1956- *WhoAmP 91*
**Case,** Michael James 1959- *WhoAmL 92, WhoAmP 91*
**Case,** Norman Mondell 1917- *AmMWSc 92*
**Case,** Richard Vere Essex 1904- *Who 92*
**Case,** Robbie 1944- *WhoWest 92*
**Case,** Robert B 1920- *AmMWSc 92*
**Case,** Robert Oliver 1935- *AmMWSc 92*
**Case,** Robert Ormond 1895- *TwCWW 91*
**Case,** Ronald Mark 1940- *AmMWSc 92, WhoMW 92*
**Case,** Shirley Jackson 1872-1947 *RelLAm 91*
**Case,** Stephen H. 1942- *WhoAmL 92, WhoFI 92*
**Case,** Stephen Shevlin 1943- *WhoAmL 92*
**Case,** Steve Wayne 1957- *WhoRel 92*
**Case,** Steven Charles 1951- *WhoRel 92*
**Case,** Steven Thomas 1949- *AmMWSc 92*
**Case,** Sylvester Quezada 1941- *WhoRel 92*
**Case,** Ted Joseph 1947- *AmMWSc 92*
**Case,** Ted. S. 1951- *WhoWest 92*
**Case,** Theodore Willard 1920- *ConAu 133*
**Case,** Thomas Louis 1947- *WhoAmL 92*
**Case,** Verna Miller 1948- *AmMWSc 92*
**Case,** Vernon Wesley 1935- *AmMWSc 92*
**Case,** Weldon Wood 1921- *WhoFI 92*
**Case,** Willard Erastus 1857-1918 *BiInAmS*
**Case,** William Bleicher 1941- *AmMWSc 92*
**Case-Winters,** Anna *WhoRel 92*
**Casebeer,** Edwin Frank, Jr. 1933- *WhoMW 92*
**Casebier,** Lindy 1960- *WhoAmP 91*
**Casei,** Nedda *WhoEnt 92*
**Casel,** Mary Lynn 1943- *WhoFI 92*
**Casella,** Alexander Joseph 1939- *AmMWSc 92*
**Casella,** Alfredo 1883-1947 *NewAmDM*
**Casella,** Clarence J 1929- *AmMWSc 92*
**Casella,** Donna 1945- *WhoEnt 92*
**Casella,** John Francis 1944- *AmMWSc 92*
**Casella,** Lynn Francisco 1940- *WhoWest 92*
**Casella,** Peter Fiore 1922- *WhoAmL 92*
**Casella,** Russell Carl 1929- *AmMWSc 92*
**Casellas,** Gilbert F. 1952- *WhoHisp 92*
**Caselli,** Robert E *WhoAmP 91*
**Casely-Hayford,** J.E. 1866-1930 *BlkLC [port]*
**Caseman,** A Bert 1922- *AmMWSc 92*
**Casement,** Donald Hulbert 1929- *WhoMW 92*
**Casement,** Roger 1864-1916 *FacFETw*
**Casemore,** Robert 1915- *ConAu 35NR*
**Caseria,** Carol Shuler 1919- *WhoWest 92*
**Caserio,** Marjorie C 1929- *AmMWSc 92*
**Caserio,** Marjorie Constance 1929- *WhoWest 92*
**Caserio,** Martin J 1916- *AmMWSc 92*
**Casey,** A. Marline 1931- *WhoWest 92*
**Casey,** Adria Catala 1934- *AmMWSc 92*
**Casey,** Albert V. 1920- *IntWW 91*
**Casey,** Albert Vincent 1920- *WhoFI 92*
**Casey,** Barbara Ann 1951- *WhoAmP 91*
**Casey,** Barbara Ann Perea 1951- *WhoHisp 92*
**Casey,** Bernard Joseph 1942- *WhoAmL 92*
**Casey,** Bernie 1939- *IntMPA 92*
**Casey,** Carey Walden, Sr. 1955- *WhoBlA 92*
**Casey,** Carol A 1953- *AmMWSc 92*
**Casey,** Charles P 1942- *AmMWSc 92*
**Casey,** Clare Ellen 1950- *AmMWSc 92*
**Casey,** Clifton G. 1924- *WhoBlA 92*
**Casey,** Colleen Sue 1956- *WhoAmL 92*
**Casey,** Dan 1938- *WhoAmP 91*
**Casey,** Daniel Arthur 1956- *WhoAmL 92*
**Casey,** Daniel Edward 1947- *AmMWSc 92*
**Casey,** Daniel F. *WhoRel 92*
**Casey,** Daniel Joseph 1935- *WhoRel 92*
**Casey,** Daniel Patrick 1950- *WhoAmL 92*
**Casey,** Deb *DrAPF 91*
**Casey,** Debora De Vore 1964- *WhoRel 92*
**Casey,** Eamonn *Who 92*
**Casey,** Eamonn 1927- *IntWW 91*
**Casey,** Edmund C. *WhoBlA 92*
**Casey,** Edward John 1953- *WhoRel 92*
**Casey,** Ethel Laughlin 1926- *WhoEnt 92*
**Casey,** Frank Leslie 1935- *WhoBlA 92*
**Casey,** George Edward, Jr. 1946- *WhoFI 92*
**Casey,** Gerard William 1942- *WhoAmL 92*
**Casey,** H Craig, Jr 1934- *AmMWSc 92*
**Casey,** Harold W 1932- *AmMWSc 92*
**Casey,** Horace Craig, Jr 1934- *AmMWSc 92*
**Casey,** James 1949- *AmMWSc 92*
**Casey,** James Broadus 1935- *WhoEnt 92*
**Casey,** James G, Sr 1917- *WhoAmP 91*
**Casey,** James M 1949- *WhoAmP 91*
**Casey,** James Michael 1964- *WhoFI 92*
**Casey,** James Patrick 1915- *AmMWSc 92*
**Casey,** Janice Marie 1954- *WhoFI 92*
**Casey,** John *DrAPF 91, WhoAmP 91*
**Casey,** John 1939- *BenetAL 91, WrDr 92*
**Casey,** John Edward, Jr 1930- *AmMWSc 92*
**Casey,** John Thayer 1931- *WhoWest 92*
**Casey,** Joseph Edward 1913- *WhoAmP 91*
**Casey,** Joseph F. 1914- *WhoBlA 92*
**Casey,** Joseph T. 1931- *WhoFI 92*
**Casey,** Kenneth L 1935- *AmMWSc 92*
**Casey,** Kevin 1940- *WrDr 92*
**Casey,** Kevin Robert 1957- *WhoAmL 92*
**Casey,** Lawrence W 1949- *WhoAmP 91*
**Casey,** Maria Terese 1963- *WhoAmL 92*
**Casey,** Mark Evan 1954- *WhoWest 92*
**Casey,** Matthew Scott 1963- *WhoWest 92*
**Casey,** Maureen Therese 1953- *WhoAmL 92*
**Casey,** Maurice Eugene 1923- *Who 92*
**Casey,** Michael *DrAPF 91*
**Casey,** Michael 1947- *WrDr 92*
**Casey,** Michael Andrew 1955- *WhoAmL 92*
**Casey,** Michael Bernard 1928- *IntWW 91, Who 92*
**Casey,** Michael Harrington 1947- *WhoWest 92*
**Casey,** Michael Vince 1927- *Who 92*
**Casey,** Murray Joseph 1936- *WhoMW 92*
**Casey,** Patricia Carolyn 1936- *WhoWest 92*
**Casey,** Patrick Anthony 1944- *WhoAmL 92*
**Casey,** Patrick Jon 1943- *WhoAmL 92*
**Casey,** Patrick Joseph 1913- *Who 92*
**Casey,** Patrick Joseph 1947- *WhoAmL 92*
**Casey,** Paul C 1961- *WhoAmP 91*
**Casey,** Peter Michael 1966- *WhoFI 92*
**Casey,** Phillip Earl 1942- *WhoFI 92*
**Casey,** Raymond 1917- *Who 92*
**Casey,** Raymond Richard 1935- *WhoFI 92, WhoMW 92*
**Casey,** Richard Delos 1952- *WhoAmL 92*
**Casey,** Robert Francis 1959- *WhoMW 92*
**Casey,** Robert J. 1890-1962 *BenetAL 91*
**Casey,** Robert P. 1932- *AlmAP 92 [port], IntWW 91, WhoAmP 91*
**Casey,** Ronald Dwain 1952- *WhoAmL 92*
**Casey,** Stella 1924- *Who 92*
**Casey,** Stephen Joseph 1941- *WhoRel 92*
**Casey,** Steven C 1952- *WhoAmP 91*
**Casey,** Thomas A 1931- *WhoAmP 91*
**Casey,** Thomas J. 1952- *WhoAmL 92*
**Casey,** Thomas Lincoln 1831-1896 *BiInAmS*
**Casey,** Thomas Warren 1942- *WhoEnt 92*
**Casey,** Timothy Frank 1947- *WhoRel 92*
**Casey,** Timothy John 1951- *WhoAmP 91*
**Casey,** Timothy M 1949- *AmMWSc 92*
**Casey,** William J. d1987 *NewYTBS 91 [port]*
**Casey,** William Joseph 1913-1987 *AmPolLe*
**Casey,** William R, Jr 1944- *WhoAmP 91*
**Casey,** William Robert 1959- *WhoFI 92*
**Casey,** Willis A. *WhoWest 92*
**Cash,** Alan Sherwin 1938- *WhoMW 92*
**Cash,** Anthony 1933- *WrDr 92*
**Cash,** Anthony Earl 1948- *WhoMW 92*
**Cash,** Arlene Marie 1955- *WhoBlA 92*
**Cash,** Bettye Joyce 1936- *WhoBlA 92*
**Cash,** Dewey Byron 1930- *AmMWSc 92*
**Cash,** Floyd Lee 1926- *AmMWSc 92*
**Cash,** Gerald 1917- *Who 92*
**Cash,** Gerald Christopher 1917- *IntWW 91*
**Cash,** Grace Savannah 1915- *IntAu&W 91*
**Cash,** James Ireland, Jr. 1947- *WhoBlA 92*
**Cash,** Johnny 1932- *NewAmDM, WhoEnt 92*
**Cash,** Johnny D. H. 1932- *IntWW 91*
**Cash,** Joseph L. 1941- *WhoIns 92*
**Cash,** June Carter 1929- *ConMus 6 [port], WhoEnt 92*
**Cash,** Pamela J. 1948- *WhoBlA 92*
**Cash,** Pat 1965- *IntWW 91*
**Cash,** Rick Gordon 1947- *WhoRel 92*
**Cash,** Robert Clyde 1951- *WhoMW 92*
**Cash,** Robert Joseph 1955- *WhoAmL 92*
**Cash,** Rosalind *WhoEnt 92*
**Cash,** Rosalind 1938- *IntMPA 92*
**Cash,** Rosanne 1955- *CurBio 91 [port], WhoEnt 92*
**Cash,** Rowley Vincent 1917- *AmMWSc 92*
**Cash,** Roy Don 1942- *WhoWest 92*
**Cash,** Susan Patricia 1956- *WhoEnt 92*
**Cash,** Tedd Delane 1938- *WhoMW 92*
**Cash,** Wilbur Joseph 1900-1941 *DcNCBi 1*
**Cash,** William Davis 1930- *AmMWSc 92*
**Cash,** William L., Jr. 1915- *WhoBlA 92*
**Cash,** William Nigel Paul 1940- *Who 92*
**Cash-Rhodes,** Winifred E. *WhoBlA 92*
**Cashatt,** Charles Alvin 1929- *WhoWest 92*
**Cashdollar,** Kenneth Leroy 1947- *AmMWSc 92*
**Cashel,** Martha Frances 1955- *WhoMW 92*
**Cashel,** Michael 1937- *AmMWSc 92*
**Cashel,** Thomas William 1930- *WhoAmL 92*
**Cashel And Emly,** Archbishop of *Who 92*
**Cashel And Ossory,** Bishop of 1926- *Who 92*
**Cashen,** John F 1937- *AmMWSc 92*
**Cashill,** Thomas J 1931- *WhoAmP 91*
**Cashin,** Bonnie 1915- *DcTwDes*
**Cashin,** Edward Archibald 1905- *WhoFI 92*
**Cashin,** Francis Joseph 1924- *WhoFI 92*
**Cashin,** Kenneth D 1921- *AmMWSc 92*
**Cashion,** Marvin J. 1945- *WhoIns 92*
**Cashion,** Peter Joseph 1940- *AmMWSc 92*
**Cashman,** Charles William, III 1951- *WhoRel 92*
**Cashman,** David *DrAPF 91*
**Cashman,** Donald P. 1955- *WhoRel 92*
**Cashman,** Edmund Joseph, Jr. 1936- *WhoFI 92*
**Cashman,** George Donald 1927- *WhoFI 92*
**Cashman,** John Anthony 1950- *WhoAmP 91*

**Cashman**, John Prescott 1930- *Who 92*
**Cashman**, John Richard 1954- *WhoWest 92*
**Cashman**, Michael Richard 1926- *WhoWest 92*
**Cashman**, Michael W, Sr. 1949- *WhoIns 92*
**Cashmore**, John David 1951- *WhoFI 92*
**Cashmore**, Roger John 1944- *Who 92*
**Cashorali**, Peter *DrAPF 91*
**Cashwell**, Gaston Barnabas 1860-1916 *RelLAm 91*
**Casiano**, Americo *DrAPF 91*
**Casiano**, Americo, Jr. 1951- *WhoHisp 92*
**Casiano**, Luz Nereida 1950- *WhoHisp 92*
**Casiano**, Manuel A., Jr. 1931- *WhoHisp 92*
**Casiano Vargas**, Ulises 1933- *WhoRel 92*
**Casida**, John Edward 1929- *AmMWSc 92*
**Casida**, Lester Earl, Jr 1928- *AmMWSc 92*
**Casillas**, Edmund Rene 1938- *AmMWSc 92*
**Casillas**, Lucius 1926- *WhoHisp 92*
**Casillas**, Mark 1953- *WhoAmL 92*
**Casimir**, Hendrik Brugt Gerhard 1909- *FacFETw, IntWW 91*
**Casimiro**, Jorge L. 1953- *WhoHisp 92*
**Casimiro**, Luis *WhoHisp 92*
**Casinelli**, Joseph L 1937- *WhoAmP 91*
**Casino**, Bruce John 1953- *WhoAmL 92*
**Casjens**, Sherwood Reid 1945- *AmMWSc 92*
**Casken**, John 1949- *ConCom 92*
**Caskey**, Albert Leroy 1931- *AmMWSc 92*
**Caskey**, Charles Thomas 1938- *AmMWSc 92*
**Caskey**, George R, Jr 1928- *AmMWSc 92*
**Caskey**, Harold Leroy 1938- *WhoAmP 91, WhoMW 92*
**Caskey**, Jerry Allan 1938- *AmMWSc 92*
**Caskey**, Joseph Fredick 1932- *WhoFI 92*
**Caskey**, Michael Conway 1950- *AmMWSc 92*
**Caskie**, William Wirt 1945- *WhoWest 92*
**Caslavska**, Vera 1942- *IntWW 91*
**Caslavska**, Vera Barbara 1934- *AmMWSc 92*
**Caslavsky**, Jaroslav Ladislav 1928- *AmMWSc 92*
**Casler**, David Robert 1920- *AmMWSc 92*
**Casler**, Michael Darwin 1954- *AmMWSc 92*
**Caslon**, William 1692-1766 *BlkwCEP*
**Casner**, Bruce Morgan 1949- *WhoAmP 91*
**Caso**, Louis Victor 1924- *AmMWSc 92*
**Caso**, Marguerite Miriam 1919- *AmMWSc 92*
**Caso**, Ralph George 1917- *WhoAmP 91*
**Casola**, Armand Ralph 1918- *AmMWSc 92*
**Casolari**, Richard Bruno 1949- *WhoMW 92*
**Cason**, David, Jr 1923- *WhoAmP 91, WhoBlA 92*
**Cason**, Dee Marie *WhoRel 92*
**Cason**, Gary Carlton 1943- *WhoAmP 91*
**Cason**, James, Jr 1912- *AmMWSc 92*
**Cason**, James Landreth, III 1941- *WhoEnt 92*
**Cason**, James Lee 1922- *AmMWSc 92*
**Cason**, Joseph L. 1939- *WhoBlA 92*
**Cason**, June Macnabb 1930- *WhoEnt 92*
**Cason**, Marilynn Jean 1943- *WhoAmL 92, WhoBlA 92*
**Cason**, Neal M 1938- *AmMWSc 92*
**Cason**, Udell, Jr. 1940- *WhoBlA 92*
**Casona**, Alejandro 1905-1965 *LiExTwC*
**Casoria**, Giuseppe 1908- *IntWW 91, WhoRel 92*
**Casorla**, Rodrigo Chaves 1950- *WhoWest 92*
**Caspar**, George J., III 1933- *WhoFI 92*
**Caspari**, Ernst Wolfgang 1909- *AmMWSc 92*
**Caspari**, Max Edward 1923- *AmMWSc 92*
**Casparian**, Gregory *ScFEYrs*
**Caspary**, Donald M 1943- *AmMWSc 92*
**Caspary**, Vera 1904-1987 *BenetAL 91*
**Casper**, Barry Michael 1939- *AmMWSc 92*
**Casper**, David 1949- *WhoMW 92*
**Casper**, Eric Michael 1959- *WhoAmL 92*
**Casper**, Gerhard 1937- *WhoAmL 92*
**Casper**, John Matthew 1946- *AmMWSc 92*
**Casper**, Leonard 1923- *WrDr 92*
**Casper**, Richard H. 1950- *WhoAmL 92*
**Casper**, Robert J. 1943- *WhoFI 92, WhoIns 92*
**Casper**, Stewart Michael 1953- *WhoAmL 92*
**Casper**, William Earl 1931- *IntWW 91*
**Caspers**, Hubert Henri 1929- *AmMWSc 92*
**Caspers**, Mary Lou *AmMWSc 92*
**Caspersen**, Finn Michael Westby 1941- *WhoFI 92*
**Caspersen**, Sven Lars 1935- *IntWW 91*
**Casperson**, Lee Wendel 1944- *AmMWSc 92*
**Caspersson**, Torbjorn Oskar 1910- *FacFETw*
**Caspi**, Eliahu 1913- *AmMWSc 92*
**Caspi**, Rachel R *AmMWSc 92*
**Caspy**, Barbara Jane 1945- *WhoWest 92*
**Cass**, April Lorraine 1957- *WhoEnt 92*
**Cass**, Carol E 1942- *AmMWSc 92*
**Cass**, David D 1938- *AmMWSc 92*
**Cass**, Edward Geoffrey 1916- *Who 92*
**Cass**, Frederick Garlington 1942- *WhoAmL 92*
**Cass**, Geoffrey Arthur 1932- *IntWW 91, Who 92*
**Cass**, George Frank 1939- *WhoIns 92*
**Cass**, Glen R 1947- *AmMWSc 92*
**Cass**, Joan E *IntAu&W 91, WrDr 92*
**Cass**, John 1909- *Who 92*
**Cass**, John 1925- *Who 92*
**Cass**, Lewis 1782-1866 *AmPolLe*
**Cass**, Melnea 1896-1978 *NotBlAW 92*
**Cass**, Millard 1916- *WhoAmL 92*
**Cass**, Peggy 1924- *IntMPA 92*
**Cass**, Penny Sue 1945- *WhoMW 92*
**Cass**, Robert Michael 1945- *WhoAmL 92*
**Cass**, Ronald Andrew 1949- *WhoAmL 92*
**Cass**, Thomas Robert 1936- *AmMWSc 92*
**Cass**, Willard Warn, Jr. 1930- *WhoAmL 92*
**Cass**, William F *WhoAmP 91*
**Cass**, Zoe *WrDr 92*
**Cassab**, Judy 1920- *IntWW 91*
**Cassady**, Ann R 1927- *WhoAmP 91*
**Cassady**, Carolyn 1923- *ConAu 133*
**Cassady**, Claude *TwCWW 91*
**Cassady**, George 1934- *AmMWSc 92*
**Cassady**, George Edward, III 1958- *WhoAmL 92*
**Cassady**, John Mac 1938- *AmMWSc 92*
**Cassady**, Joseph Rudolph, III 1959- *WhoEnt 92, WhoMW 92*
**Cassady**, Kenneth Edward 1948- *WhoMW 92*
**Cassady**, Neal 1926-1968 *BenetAL 91*
**Cassady**, Neely *WhoAmP 91*
**Cassagne**, Gilbert Michael 1956- *WhoFI 92*
**Cassandre**, A.M. 1901-1968 *DcTwDes*
**Cassanego**, Michael John 1950- *WhoIns 92*
**Cassanelli**, Emilio 1955- *WhoFI 92*
**Cassanova**, Robert Anthony 1942- *AmMWSc 92*
**Cassar**, Francis Felix Anthony 1934- *Who 92*
**Cassar**, Jon Francis 1958- *WhoEnt 92*
**Cassar**, Joseph 1918- *IntWW 91*
**Cassard**, Daniel W 1923- *AmMWSc 92*
**Cassatt**, Mary 1844-1926 *RComAH, ThHEIm [port]*
**Cassatt**, Mary 1845-1926 *FacFETw*
**Cassatt**, Mary Stevenson 1844-1926 *HanAmWH*
**Cassavetes**, John 1929-1989 *BenetAL 91, FacFETw, IntDcF 2-2 [port]*
**Casseday**, John Herbert 1934- *AmMWSc 92*
**Casseday**, S A d1860 *BiInAmS*
**Cassedy**, Edward S, Jr 1927- *AmMWSc 92*
**Cassedy**, James H. 1919- *WrDr 92*
**Cassedy**, Sylvia 1930-1989 *ChlLR 26 [port]*
**Cassel** *Who 92*
**Cassel**, Alvin I. *IntMPA 92*
**Cassel**, D Keith 1940- *AmMWSc 92*
**Cassel**, David Giske 1939- *AmMWSc 92*
**Cassel**, David Wayne 1936- *AmMWSc 92*
**Cassel**, Harold 1916- *Who 92*
**Cassel**, Herbert William 1931- *WhoRel 92*
**Cassel**, J Frank 1916- *AmMWSc 92*
**Cassel**, Jean-Pierre 1932- *IntMPA 92, IntWW 91*
**Cassel**, John Elden 1934- *WhoFI 92*
**Cassel**, Marwin Shepard 1925- *WhoAmL 92*
**Cassel**, Russell N 1911- *AmMWSc 92, WrDr 92*
**Cassel**, Seymour 1937- *ConTFT 9, WhoEnt 92*
**Cassel**, Seymour 1938- *IntMPA 92*
**Cassel**, Timothy Felix Harold 1942- *Who 92*
**Cassel**, Walter 1910- *NewAmDM*
**Cassel**, Walter 1920- *WhoEnt 92*
**Cassel**, William Alwein 1924- *AmMWSc 92*
**Casseldine**, Nigel 1947- *TwCPaSc*
**Cassell**, Petter and Galpin *DcLB 106*
**Cassell**, Anthony K. 1941- *WhoMW 92*
**Cassell**, Eric J 1928- *AmMWSc 92*
**Cassell**, Eugene Alan 1934- *AmMWSc 92*
**Cassell**, Frank 1930- *Who 92*
**Cassell**, Frank Hyde 1916- *WhoMW 92*
**Cassell**, Gail Houston 1946- *AmMWSc 92*
**Cassell**, Joan 1929- *ConAu 135*
**Cassell**, John 1817-1865 *DcLB 106 [port]*
**Cassella**, Mark Crowley 1953- *WhoEnt 92*
**Cassells**, Cyrus *DrAPF 91*
**Cassells**, Cyrus Curtis 1957- *IntAu&W 91*
**Casselman**, Barry *DrAPF 91*
**Casselman**, John Malcolm 1940- *AmMWSc 92*
**Casselman**, Warren Gottlieb Bruce 1921- *AmMWSc 92*
**Casselman**, William E., II 1941- *WhoAmL 92*
**Cassels**, Alan 1929- *WrDr 92*
**Cassels**, James 1907- *IntWW 91, Who 92*
**Cassels**, James Macdonald 1924- *IntWW 91, Who 92*
**Cassels**, John 1928- *Who 92*
**Cassels**, John William Scott 1922- *IntWW 91, Who 92*
**Cassels**, Peter 1949- *IntWW 91*
**Cassels**, Simon 1928- *Who 92*
**Cassels-Brown**, Alastair Kennedy 1927- *WhoEnt 92*
**Cassen**, Patrick Michael 1940- *AmMWSc 92*
**Cassen**, Robert Harvey 1935- *Who 92*
**Cassen**, Thomas Joseph *AmMWSc 92*
**Cassens**, Daniel Lee 1946- *AmMWSc 92*
**Cassens**, Nicholas, Jr. 1948- *WhoWest 92*
**Cassens**, Patrick 1938- *AmMWSc 92*
**Cassens**, Robert G 1937- *AmMWSc 92*
**Casserberg**, Bo R 1941- *AmMWSc 92*
**Casserley**, Julian Victor Langmead 1909-1978 *ConAu 133*
**Casserly**, James Lund 1951- *WhoAmL 92*
**Cassette**, Robert Louis, Sr 1928- *WhoAmP 91*
**Cassian**, John 365?-433? *EncEarC*
**Cassian**, Nina 1924- *LiExTwC*
**Cassidi**, Desmond 1925- *Who 92*
**Cassidy**, Adrian Clyde 1916- *WhoFI 92*
**Cassidy**, Alan Francis 1942- *WhoEnt 92*
**Cassidy**, Bryan Michael Deece 1934- *Who 92*
**Cassidy**, Carl Eugene 1924- *AmMWSc 92*
**Cassidy**, Charles Michael Ardagh 1936- *IntWW 91*
**Cassidy**, Charles Philip 1937- *WhoWest 92*
**Cassidy**, Christine *DrAPF 91*
**Cassidy**, Daniel C. 1937- *WhoAmL 92*
**Cassidy**, David 1950- *IntMPA 92*
**Cassidy**, David Bruce 1950- *WhoEnt 92*
**Cassidy**, Donald Lawrence 1933- *WhoWest 92*
**Cassidy**, Ed. 1954- *WhoWest 92*
**Cassidy**, Edward *Who 92*
**Cassidy**, Edward Idris 1924- *WhoRel 92*
**Cassidy**, Esther Christmas 1933- *AmMWSc 92*
**Cassidy**, Eugene Patrick 1940- *WhoMW 92*
**Cassidy**, Frederic Gomes 1907- *WrDr 92*
**Cassidy**, George Henry 1942- *Who 92*
**Cassidy**, Guy Morrow 1955- *WhoMW 92*
**Cassidy**, Harold Gomes 1906- *AmMWSc 92*
**Cassidy**, Herbert 1935- *Who 92*
**Cassidy**, Idris Edward 1924- *Who 92*
**Cassidy**, Jack Edward 1952- *WhoFI 92*
**Cassidy**, James Edward 1928- *AmMWSc 92*
**Cassidy**, James Joseph 1916- *WhoFI 92*
**Cassidy**, James Mark 1942- *WhoFI 92, WhoMW 92*
**Cassidy**, James Patrick 1925- *WhoRel 92*
**Cassidy**, James T 1930- *AmMWSc 92*
**Cassidy**, Joanna 1944- *IntMPA 92*
**Cassidy**, John 1928- *ConAu 35NR*
**Cassidy**, John Harold 1925- *WhoAmL 92*
**Cassidy**, John J 1930- *AmMWSc 92*
**Cassidy**, John Lemont 1934- *WhoMW 92*
**Cassidy**, John Robert 1933- *WhoWest 92*
**Cassidy**, Joseph *Who 92*
**Cassidy**, Kevin John 1950- *WhoMW 92*
**Cassidy**, Laurence Patrick 1950- *IntAu&W 91*
**Cassidy**, Lee M 1933- *WhoAmP 91*
**Cassidy**, Marie Mullaney *AmMWSc 92*
**Cassidy**, Michael 1936- *WrDr 92*
**Cassidy**, Michael Edward 1955- *WhoAmP 91*
**Cassidy**, Michael Stanley 1938- *WhoFI 92*
**Cassidy**, Patrick 1961- *IntMPA 92*
**Cassidy**, Patrick Edward 1937- *AmMWSc 92*
**Cassidy**, Richard Arthur 1944- *WhoWest 92*
**Cassidy**, Richard Murray 1944- *AmMWSc 92*
**Cassidy**, Robert Joseph 1930- *WhoFI 92*
**Cassidy**, Robert Valentine 1930- *WhoAmP 91*
**Cassidy**, Sam H 1950- *WhoAmP 91*
**Cassidy**, Shaun 1958- *IntMPA 92*
**Cassidy**, Sheila Anne 1937- *IntWW 91, Who 92*
**Cassidy**, Suzanne Bletterman 1944- *AmMWSc 92*
**Cassidy**, Thomas Philip 1960- *WhoWest 92*
**Cassidy**, Tom d1991 *NewYTBS 91 [port]*
**Cassidy**, William Arthur 1928- *AmMWSc 92*
**Cassidy**, William Dunnigan, III 1941- *WhoFI 92*
**Cassidy**, William F 1908- *AmMWSc 92*
**Cassie**, Robert MacGregor 1935- *AmMWSc 92*
**Cassiers**, Juan 1931- *IntWW 91*
**Cassill**, Kay *DrAPF 91*
**Cassill**, R.V. *DrAPF 91*
**Cassill**, R. V. 1919- *BenetAL 91, ConNov 91, WrDr 92*
**Cassill**, Ronald Verlin *IntAu&W 91*
**Cassillis**, Earl of 1956- *Who 92*
**Cassilly**, Richard 1927- *IntWW 91, NewAmDM, Who 92, WhoEnt 92*
**Cassils**, Peter *IntAu&W 91X*
**Cassim**, Joseph Yusuf Khan 1924- *AmMWSc 92*
**Cassimatis**, Emanuel Andrew 1926- *WhoAmL 92*
**Cassin**, James Richard 1933- *WhoMW 92*
**Cassin**, John 1813-1869 *BiInAmS*
**Cassin**, Joseph M 1928- *AmMWSc 92*
**Cassin**, Maxine *DrAPF 91*
**Cassin**, Rene 1887-1976 *FacFETw*
**Cassin**, Rene-Samuel 1887-1976 *WhoNob 90*
**Cassin**, Sidney 1928- *AmMWSc 92*
**Cassin**, William Bourke 1931- *WhoAmL 92, WhoFI 92*
**Cassina**, Cesare 1909- *DcTwDes*
**Cassinelli**, Joseph Patrick 1940- *AmMWSc 92*
**Cassiodorus** 485?-580? *EncEarC*
**Cassirer**, Ernst 1874-1945 *EncTR 91 [port], FacFETw, LiExTwC*
**Cassirer**, Henry R. 1911- *IntWW 91*
**Cassirer**, Reinhold, Mrs. *Who 92*
**Cassis**, Glenn Albert 1951- *WhoBlA 92*
**Cassity**, Joe, Jr. 1943- *WhoAmL 92*
**Cassity**, Turner *DrAPF 91*
**Cassity**, Turner 1929- *WrDr 92*
**Cassius** *IntAu&W 91X*
**Cassman**, Marvin 1936- *AmMWSc 92*
**Cassola**, Charles A 1913- *AmMWSc 92*
**Cassola**, Robert Louis 1941- *AmMWSc 92, WhoMW 92*
**Casson**, Frederick Michael 1925- *Who 92*
**Casson**, Hugh 1910- *TwCPaSc, Who 92, WrDr 92*
**Casson**, Hugh Maxwell 1910- *ConAu 36NR, IntWW 91, SmATA 65 [port]*
**Casson**, Luella Howard 1935-1985 *WhoBlA 92N*
**Casson**, Margaret MacDonald 1913- *Who 92*
**Casson**, Mark Christopher 1945- *Who 92*
**Casson**, Michael *Who 92*
**Casson**, Richard Frederick 1939- *WhoAmL 92, WhoFI 92*
**Cassoni**, Vittorio 1942- *IntWW 91*
**Casstevens**, Bill 1928- *WhoAmP 91*
**Casstevens**, Bill J. 1928- *WhoMW 92*
**Casstevens**, Thomas William 1937- *WhoMW 92, WrDr 92*
**Cassyd**, Syd 1908- *WhoEnt 92*
**Cast**, Anita Hursh 1939- *WhoMW 92*
**Castagna**, Michael 1927- *AmMWSc 92*
**Castagna**, William John 1924- *WhoAmL 92*
**Castagnary**, Jules 1830-1888 *ThHEIm*
**Castagnetta**, Grace Sharp 1912- *WhoEnt 92*
**Castagnetto**, Perry Michael 1959- *WhoWest 92*
**Castagnoli**, Neal, Jr 1936- *AmMWSc 92*
**Castaing**, Raimond Bernard Rene 1921- *IntWW 91*
**Castaldi**, Thomas Edward 1939- *WhoFI 92, WhoMW 92*
**Castaldo**, John N. 1956- *WhoEnt 92*
**Castaldo**, Joseph 1927- *NewAmDM*
**Castaneda**, Aldo R. 1930- *WhoHisp 92*
**Castaneda**, Aldo Ricardo 1930- *AmMWSc 92*
**Castaneda**, Blas 1949- *WhoHisp 92*
**Castaneda**, Carlos 1925?- *FacFETw, WhoHisp 92*
**Castaneda**, Carlos 1931- *BenetAL 91, WrDr 92*
**Castaneda**, James Agustin 1933- *WhoHisp 92*
**Castaneda**, Jorge 1921- *IntWW 91*
**Castaneda**, Martha *WhoHisp 92*
**Castaneda**, Octavio Emilio, Jr. 1960- *WhoHisp 92*
**Castaneda**, Omar S. *DrAPF 91*
**Castaneda**, Omar S. 1954- *ConAu 135*
**Castaneda**, Omar Sigfrido 1954- *WhoWest 92*
**Castaneda**, Oswaldo 1944- *WhoHisp 92*
**Castaneda**, Roberto Rudolph 1956- *WhoFI 92*
**Castaneira Colon**, Rafael 1936- *WhoAmP 91, WhoHisp 92*
**Castaner**, David 1934- *AmMWSc 92*
**Castaner**, Juan Antonio 1949- *WhoFI 92*
**Castanera**, Esther Goossen 1920- *AmMWSc 92*
**Castania**, Michael Frank 1950- *WhoEnt 92*
**Castano**, Gregory Joseph 1929- *WhoAmL 92*

**Castano,** John Roman 1926- *AmMWSc 92*
**Castanuela,** Elio *WhoHisp 92*
**Castanuela,** Mary Helen 1950- *WhoHisp 92*
**Castater,** Robert Dewitt 1922- *AmMWSc 92*
**Castberg,** Eileen Sue 1946- *WhoWest 92*
**Castedo,** Elena 1937- *ConLC 65 [port], WhoHisp 92*
**Casteel,** Rose M 1932- *WhoAmP 91*
**Casteen,** John T., III 1943- *IntWW 91*
**Castel,** John Christopher 1954- *WhoFI 92*
**Castel,** Moshe 1909-1991 *NewYTBS 91*
**Castel,** P. Kevin 1950- *WhoAmL 92*
**Castele,** Theodore John 1928- *WhoMW 92*
**Castelein,** John Donald 1948- *WhoRel 92*
**Castelfranco,** Paul Alexander 1921- *AmMWSc 92*
**Castell,** Adrian George 1935- *AmMWSc 92*
**Castell,** Donald O 1935- *AmMWSc 92*
**Castell,** George Coventry 1936- *WhoEnt 92*
**Castell,** John Daniel 1943- *AmMWSc 92*
**Castella,** Frank Robert 1936- *AmMWSc 92*
**Castellan,** Gilbert William 1924- *AmMWSc 92*
**Castellan,** Norman J 1912- *AmMWSc 92*
**Castellana,** Frank Sebastian 1942- *AmMWSc 92*
**Castellani,** Renato 1913-1985 *IntDcF 2-2*
**Castellani,** Robert Joseph 1941- *WhoAmL 92*
**Castellani,** Victor 1947- *WhoWest 92*
**Castellano,** Daniel Anthony 1951- *WhoFI 92*
**Castellano,** Joe Cruz, Jr. 1944- *WhoHisp 92*
**Castellano,** Michael Angelo 1956- *WhoWest 92*
**Castellano,** Salvatore Mario 1925- *AmMWSc 92*
**Castellanos,** Diego Antonio 1933- *WhoHisp 92*
**Castellanos,** Jesus Antonio 1942- *WhoHisp 92*
**Castellanos,** Juan de 1522-1607 *HisDSpE*
**Castellanos,** Julio Jesus 1910- *WhoFI 92*
**Castellanos,** Laura 1965- *WhoHisp 92*
**Castellanos,** Ricardo C. 1945- *WhoHisp 92*
**Castellanos,** Robert J. 1940- *WhoHisp 92*
**Castellanos,** Rosario 1925-1974 *ConLC 66, ConSpAP, DcLB 113 [port], SpAmWW*
**Castellanos,** Theodora 1940- *WhoHisp 92*
**Castellaw,** Earlene Johnson 1928- *WhoRel 92*
**Castelli,** Juan Jose 1764-1812 *HisDSpE*
**Castelli,** Leo 1907- *IntWW 91*
**Castelli,** Vittorio 1934- *AmMWSc 92*
**Castelli,** Walter Andrew 1929- *AmMWSc 92*
**Castelli,** William Peter 1931- *AmMWSc 92*
**Castellini,** William McGregor 1928- *WhoAmP 91*
**Castellino,** Francis Joseph 1943- *AmMWSc 92*
**Castellion,** Alan William 1934- *AmMWSc 92*
**Castello,** Hugo Martinez 1914- *WhoHisp 92*
**Castello,** John Donald 1952- *AmMWSc 92*
**Castello,** John Edward 1944- *WhoFI 92*
**Castelloe,** Raleigh Roosevelt, Jr. 1939- *WhoRel 92*
**Castellon,** Michael Cary 1961- *WhoAmL 92*
**Castellot,** John J, Jr *AmMWSc 92*
**Castellucci,** Nicholas Thomas 1940- *WhoWest 92*
**Castellucci,** Vincent F 1940- *AmMWSc 92*
**Castelnuovo-Tedesco,** Mario 1895-1968 *FacFETw, NewAmDM*
**Castelnuovo-Tedesco,** Pietro 1925- *AmMWSc 92*
**Castelo,** Joseph 1945- *WhoAmP 91*
**Casten,** Richard Francis 1941- *AmMWSc 92*
**Casten,** Richard G 1943- *AmMWSc 92*
**Castenell,** Louis Anthony 1947- *WhoMW 92*
**Castenell,** Louis Anthony, Jr. 1947- *WhoBlA 92*
**Castenholz,** Richard William 1931- *AmMWSc 92*
**Castenschiold,** Rene 1923- *AmMWSc 92*
**Castenson,** Roger R 1943- *AmMWSc 92*
**Caster,** Caroleigh Tuitt 1947- *WhoBlA 92*
**Caster,** Kenneth Edward 1908- *AmMWSc 92*
**Caster,** William Oviatt 1919- *AmMWSc 92*
**Casterline,** William Hale, Jr. 1951- *WhoAmL 92*
**Casterlow,** Carolyn B. 1948- *WhoBlA 92*
**Castetter,** Gregory Keeler 1935- *WhoMW 92*
**Castiel,** Janet Ellen 1954- *WhoEnt 92*
**Castier,** Jules *ScFEYrs*
**Castiglioni,** Achille 1918- *DcTwDes*
**Castiglioni,** Livio 1911-1979 *DcTwDes*
**Castiglioni,** Luigi 1757-1832 *DcAmImH*
**Castiglioni,** Niccolo 1932- *NewAmDM*
**Castiglioni,** Piergiacomo 1913-1968 *DcTwDes*
**Castignetti,** Domenic 1951- *AmMWSc 92*
**Castile,** Rand 1938- *WhoWest 92*
**Castile,** Robert G 1947- *AmMWSc 92*
**Castilla,** Rene *WhoHisp 92*
**Castille,** Armand 1943- *WhoAmP 91*
**Castillo,** Madre 1671-1742 *SpAmWW*
**Castillo,** Alba N. 1945- *WhoHisp 92*
**Castillo,** Alvaro 1960- *WhoHisp 92*
**Castillo,** Amelia *WhoHisp 92*
**Castillo,** Ana *DrAPF 91*
**Castillo,** Ana 1953- *WhoHisp 92*
**Castillo,** Angel, Jr. 1946- *WhoAmL 92*
**Castillo,** Beatriz V. 1954- *WhoHisp 92*
**Castillo,** Brenda Victoria 1962- *WhoHisp 92*
**Castillo,** C. Thomas *WhoHisp 92*
**Castillo,** Carmen 1958- *WhoHisp 92*
**Castillo,** Craig Michael 1967- *WhoHisp 92, WhoMW 92*
**Castillo,** Dennis Angelo 1958- *WhoRel 92*
**Castillo,** Diane M. 1952- *WhoHisp 92*
**Castillo,** Eduardo A. *WhoHisp 92*
**Castillo,** Estela 1965- *WhoHisp 92*
**Castillo,** Evelyn C. 1958- *WhoHisp 92*
**Castillo,** Florencio de 1778-1834 *HisDSpE*
**Castillo,** Francisca Josefa de la C. de 1671-1742 *SpAmWW*
**Castillo,** Franklin H. 1943- *WhoHisp 92*
**Castillo,** Gabriel Alejandro 1962- *WhoHisp 92*
**Castillo,** Gloria J. 1954- *WhoHisp 92*
**Castillo,** Hal Stephen 1947- *WhoAmL 92*
**Castillo,** Helen M. 1936- *WhoHisp 92*
**Castillo,** Javier M. 1967- *WhoHisp 92*
**Castillo,** John G. 1951- *WhoHisp 92*
**Castillo,** John Roy 1948- *WhoAmL 92, WhoHisp 92, WhoMW 92*
**Castillo,** Jose G. *WhoHisp 92*
**Castillo,** Jose Ramon 1934- *WhoHisp 92*
**Castillo,** Joseph A 1933- *WhoAmP 91, WhoHisp 92*
**Castillo,** Leonel Javier 1939- *WhoAmP 91, WhoHisp 92*
**Castillo,** Lucy Narvaez 1943- *WhoFI 92*
**Castillo,** Manuel H. 1949- *WhoHisp 92*
**Castillo,** Mary 1947- *WhoHisp 92*
**Castillo,** Mary Helen *WhoHisp 92*
**Castillo,** Max *WhoHisp 92*
**Castillo,** Michael Jay 1949- *WhoHisp 92*
**Castillo,** Michel Xavier Janicot del 1933- *IntWW 91*
**Castillo,** Miguel A. 1954- *WhoHisp 92*
**Castillo,** Nilda 1956- *WhoHisp 92*
**Castillo,** Osvaldo J. *WhoHisp 92*
**Castillo,** Pedro Antonio 1926- *WhoHisp 92*
**Castillo,** Rafael C. 1950- *WhoHisp 92*
**Castillo,** Ramona 1928- *WhoHisp 92*
**Castillo,** Ricardo Orlando 1948- *WhoHisp 92*
**Castillo,** Richard Cesar 1949- *WhoHisp 92*
**Castillo,** Robert Charles 1952- *WhoHisp 92*
**Castillo,** Rudolph Innocent 1927- *Who 92*
**Castillo,** Santos 1942- *WhoHisp 92*
**Castillo,** Steven David 1944- *WhoHisp 92*
**Castillo,** Tony 1963- *WhoHisp 92*
**Castillo,** Victor Rodriguez 1945- *WhoHisp 92*
**Castillo Andraca y Tamayo,** Francisco del 1716-1770 *HisDSpE*
**Castillo Arriola,** Eduardo 1914- *IntWW 91*
**Castillo Lara,** Rosalio Jose 1922- *IntWW 91, WhoRel 92*
**Castillo Morales,** Carlos Manuel 1928- *IntWW 91*
**Castillo-Quinones,** Isabel 1953- *WhoHisp 92*
**Castillo-Speed,** Lillian 1949- *WhoHisp 92*
**Castillo Toledo Guevara Nino y Rojas,** F 1671-1742 *SpAmWW*
**Castillo-Tovar,** Maria-Lourdes 1950- *WhoHisp 92*
**Castillo y Guevara,** Francisca Josefa 1671-1742 *SpAmWW*
**Castillo y Guevara,** Francisca Josefa de 1671-1742 *HisDSpE*
**Castle** *Who 92*
**Castle,** Alan Lee 1950- *WhoEnt 92*
**Castle,** Alfred 1948- *WhoWest 92*
**Castle,** Barbara Anne 1911- *FacFETw*
**Castle,** Bruce Edward 1958- *WhoAmL 92*
**Castle,** Carlyle Fairfax 1955- *WhoRel 92*
**Castle,** Charles 1939- *IntAu&W 91*
**Castle,** Christian Lancelot *WhoAmL 92, WhoEnt 92, WhoWest 92*
**Castle,** Elowyn 1940- *WhoEnt 92*
**Castle,** Enid 1936- *Who 92*
**Castle,** Frederick Ted *DrAPF 91*
**Castle,** George Samuel Peter 1939- *AmMWSc 92*
**Castle,** Howard Blaine 1935- *WhoRel 92*
**Castle,** Irene 1893-1969 *FacFETw*
**Castle,** James 1946- *TwCPaSc*
**Castle,** John Edwards 1919- *AmMWSc 92*
**Castle,** John Granville, Jr 1924- *AmMWSc 92*
**Castle,** Karen G 1948- *AmMWSc 92*
**Castle,** Keith L. *WhoBlA 92*
**Castle,** Manford C 1942- *AmMWSc 92*
**Castle,** Michael N. 1939- *AlmAP 92 [port], IntWW 91*
**Castle,** Michael Newbold 1939- *WhoAmP 91*
**Castle,** Nick 1947- *IntMPA 92*
**Castle,** Peter Myer 1940- *AmMWSc 92*
**Castle,** Philip 1929- *TwCPaSc*
**Castle,** Raymond Nielson 1916- *AmMWSc 92*
**Castle,** Robert Marvin 1920- *WhoAmP 91*
**Castle,** Robert O 1926- *AmMWSc 92*
**Castle,** Stephen Neil 1952- *WhoFI 92*
**Castle,** Vernon 1887-1918 *FacFETw*
**Castle,** Vernon Charles 1931- *WhoEnt 92, WhoFI 92*
**Castle,** Walter H. 1905- *IntMPA 92*
**Castle,** Wendell 1932- *DcTwDes*
**Castle,** William Bosworth d1990 *IntWW 91N*
**Castle,** William Bosworth 1897- *AmMWSc 92*
**Castle Of Blackburn,** Baroness 1910- *IntWW 91, Who 92*
**Castle Stewart,** Earl 1928- *Who 92*
**Castleberry,** Arline Alrick 1919- *WhoWest 92*
**Castleberry,** Donald Grant 1929- *WhoAmP 91*
**Castleberry,** Edward J. 1928- *WhoBlA 92*
**Castleberry,** George E 1918- *AmMWSc 92*
**Castleberry,** Kelly L 1926- *WhoAmP 91*
**Castleberry,** Leo Alexander 1931- *WhoEnt 92*
**Castleberry,** Rhebena Taylor 1917- *WhoBlA 92*
**Castleberry,** Ron M 1941- *AmMWSc 92*
**Castlemaine,** Baron 1943- *Who 92*
**Castleman,** Albert Welford, Jr 1936- *AmMWSc 92*
**Castleman,** Charles 1941- *NewAmDM*
**Castleman,** Charles Martin 1941- *WhoEnt 92*
**Castleman,** Christopher Norman Anthony 1941- *IntWW 91, Who 92*
**Castleman,** Dick 1926- *WhoAmP 91*
**Castleman,** Elise Marie 1925- *WhoBlA 92*
**Castleman,** L S 1918- *AmMWSc 92*
**Castlemon,** Harry *BenetAL 91*
**Castlereagh,** Viscount 1972- *Who 92*
**Castlereagh,** Edith Helen Vale-Tempest 1879-1959 *BiDBrF 2*
**Castles,** James Joseph, Jr 1940- *AmMWSc 92*
**Castles,** John William 1947- *WhoFI 92*
**Castles,** Thomas R 1937- *AmMWSc 92*
**Castleton,** David J. 1954- *WhoAmL 92*
**Castleton,** Kenneth Bitner 1903- *AmMWSc 92*
**Castner,** Edward Richard 1950- *WhoEnt 92*
**Castner,** Hamilton Young 1859-1899 *BiInAmS*
**Castner,** James Lee 1954- *AmMWSc 92*
**Castner,** Theodore Grant, Jr 1930- *AmMWSc 92*
**Casto,** Clyde Christy 1912- *AmMWSc 92*
**Casto,** Robert Clayton *DrAPF 91*
**Casto,** Robert Clayton 1932- *IntAu&W 91*
**Caston,** Geoffrey 1926- *IntWW 91*
**Caston,** Geoffrey Kemp 1926- *Who 92*
**Caston,** J Douglas 1932- *AmMWSc 92*
**Caston,** Ralph Henry 1915- *AmMWSc 92*
**Castonguay,** Alexander Nelson 1956- *WhoEnt 92*
**Castonguay,** Richard Norman 1939- *AmMWSc 92*
**Castonguay,** Thomas T 1909- *AmMWSc 92*
**Castor,** Betty 1941- *WhoAmP 91*
**Castor,** C. William, Jr. 1925- *WhoMW 92*
**Castor,** Cecil William 1925- *AmMWSc 92*
**Castor,** John I 1943- *AmMWSc 92*
**Castor,** LaRoy Northrop 1924- *AmMWSc 92*
**Castor,** Richard Gilbert 1927- *WhoIns 92*
**Castor,** Wilbur Wright 1932- *WhoWest 92*
**Castor,** William Stuart, Jr 1926- *AmMWSc 92*
**Castore,** Glen M *AmMWSc 92*
**Castorena y Ursua,** Juan Ignacio de 1668-1733 *HisDSpE*
**Castracane,** V Daniel 1940- *AmMWSc 92*
**Castranova,** Vincent 1949- *AmMWSc 92*
**Castree,** Samuel John, Jr. 1961- *WhoAmL 92*
**Castric,** Peter Allen 1938- *AmMWSc 92*
**Castrillon,** Jose P A 1926- *AmMWSc 92*
**Castrillon,** Uriel 1961- *WhoRel 92*
**Castro,** Albert Joseph 1916- *AmMWSc 92*
**Castro,** Alberto 1933- *AmMWSc 92*
**Castro,** Alfonso 1950- *WhoHisp 92*
**Castro,** Alfonso H. Peter, III 1955- *WhoHisp 92*
**Castro,** Alfred A 1932- *AmMWSc 92, WhoHisp 92*
**Castro,** Amado Alejandro 1924- *IntWW 91*
**Castro,** Anthony J 1930- *AmMWSc 92*
**Castro,** Bernard 1904-1991 *NewYTBS 91 [port]*
**Castro,** Bill 1931- *WhoHisp 92*
**Castro,** C. Elizabeth 1950- *WhoHisp 92*
**Castro,** Carlos Arturo, Sr. 1954- *WhoHisp 92*
**Castro,** Celia 1949- *WhoHisp 92*
**Castro,** Charles E 1931- *AmMWSc 92*
**Castro,** David 1947- *WhoHisp 92*
**Castro,** Emilio 1927- *DcEcMov*
**Castro,** Emilio Enrique 1927- *Who 92*
**Castro,** Ernesto 1967- *WhoHisp 92*
**Castro,** Fernando A. 1952- *WhoHisp 92*
**Castro,** Fidel *IntWW 91*
**Castro,** Fidel 1926- *FacFETw [port], News 91 [port]*
**Castro,** George 1939- *AmMWSc 92, WhoHisp 92*
**Castro,** George A 1936- *WhoAmP 91*
**Castro,** Gilbert Anthony 1939- *AmMWSc 92*
**Castro,** Gonzalo *AmMWSc 92*
**Castro,** Irma *WhoHisp 92*
**Castro,** Jaime 1943- *WhoHisp 92*
**Castro,** Jan Garden *DrAPF 91*
**Castro,** John Gonzales 1935- *WhoRel 92*
**Castro,** John M. 1951- *WhoHisp 92*
**Castro,** Jose Alfredo 1930- *WhoHisp 92*
**Castro,** Joseph Armand 1927- *WhoEnt 92, WhoWest 92*
**Castro,** Leonard Edward 1934- *WhoAmL 92, WhoWest 92*
**Castro,** Lillian 1954- *WhoHisp 92*
**Castro,** Loretta Faith 1930- *WhoEnt 92*
**Castro,** Manuel Francisco 1946- *WhoHisp 92*
**Castro,** Maria del Rosario 1947- *WhoHisp 92*
**Castro,** Mario Humberto 1934- *WhoHisp 92*
**Castro,** Max Jose 1951- *WhoHisp 92*
**Castro,** Michael *DrAPF 91*
**Castro,** Michael 1945- *WhoHisp 92*
**Castro,** Mike *WhoHisp 92*
**Castro,** Peter 1943- *AmMWSc 92, WhoHisp 92*
**Castro,** Peter S 1926- *AmMWSc 92*
**Castro,** Rafaela Gonzales 1943- *WhoHisp 92*
**Castro,** Raul *IntWW 91*
**Castro,** Raul H. 1916- *WhoHisp 92*
**Castro,** Raul Hector 1916- *WhoAmP 91*
**Castro,** Richard T. 1946-1991 *WhoHisp 92N*
**Castro,** Rick R. 1938- *WhoHisp 92*
**Castro,** Rodolfo H. 1942- *WhoHisp 92*
**Castro,** Tanja Hendrickson 1959- *WhoAmL 92*
**Castro,** Thomas *WhoHisp 92*
**Castro,** Thomas Henry 1954- *WhoAmP 91*
**Castro,** Walter Ernest 1934- *AmMWSc 92*
**Castro-Blanco,** David *WhoHisp 92*
**Castro de DeLaRosa,** Maria Guadalupe 1944- *WhoHisp 92*
**Castro-Gomez,** Margaret 1959- *WhoHisp 92*
**Castro Jijon,** Ramon 1915- *IntWW 91*
**Castro-Klaren,** Sara 1942- *WhoHisp 92*
**Castro Marchand,** Hector 1942- *WhoAmP 91*
**Castro Ruiz,** Manuel 1918- *WhoRel 92*
**Castro Ruz,** Fidel 1927- *IntWW 91*
**Castro Ruz,** Raul 1931- *IntWW 91*
**Castroleal,** Alicia 1945- *WhoHisp 92*
**Castronis,** John Michael 1948- *WhoRel 92*
**Castronovo,** David 1945- *ConAu 35NR*
**Castronovo,** Frank Paul, Jr 1940- *AmMWSc 92*
**Castronovo,** Michael Louis 1963- *WhoFI 92*
**Castroviejo,** Ramon 1904-1987 *FacFETw*
**Castrovinci,** Philip J. 1961- *WhoAmL 92*
**Castrucci,** George E. *WhoEnt 92*
**Castruccio,** Peter Adalbert 1925- *AmMWSc 92*
**Casty,** Alan Howard 1929- *WrDr 92*
**Casudi** 1945- *WhoEnt 92*
**Casullo,** Joanne M. *DrAPF 91*
**Casurella,** Anthony 1946- *WhoRel 92*
**Casuso,** Jose A. 1932- *WhoHisp 92*
**Caswell,** Adam Gerard 1958- *WhoAmL 92*
**Caswell,** Albert, Jr 1931- *WhoAmP 91*
**Caswell,** Alexis 1799-1877 *BiInAmS*
**Caswell,** Anthony H 1940- *AmMWSc 92*
**Caswell,** Benjamin 1737-1791 *DcNCBi 1*
**Caswell,** Catheryne Willis 1917- *WhoBlA 92*
**Caswell,** Donald *DrAPF 91*

**Caswell**, Dorothy Ann Cottrell 1938- *WhoEnt 92*
**Caswell**, Gregory K 1947- *AmMWSc 92*
**Caswell**, Hal 1949- *AmMWSc 92*
**Caswell**, Herbert Hall, Jr 1923- *AmMWSc 92*
**Caswell**, Hollis Leland 1931- *WhoFI 92*
**Caswell**, Jeffry Claxton 1959- *WhoFI 92*
**Caswell**, John Henry 1846-1909 *BiInAmS*
**Caswell**, John N 1920- *AmMWSc 92*
**Caswell**, Lyman Ray 1928- *AmMWSc 92*
**Caswell**, Martin 1733-1789? *DcNCBi 1*
**Caswell**, Randall Smith 1924- *AmMWSc 92*
**Caswell**, Richard 1685-1755 *DcNCBi 1*
**Caswell**, Richard 1729-1789 *DcNCBi 1*
**Caswell**, Robert Little 1918- *AmMWSc 92*
**Caswell**, William 1754-1785 *DcNCBi 1*
**Catabelle**, Jean-Marie Henri 1941- *WhoFI 92*
**Catacalos**, Rosemary 1944- *WhoHisp 92*
**Catacosinos**, Paul Anthony 1933- *AmMWSc 92*
**Catacosinos**, William James 1930- *WhoFI 92*
**Catala**, Mario E., II 1942- *WhoHisp 92*
**Catala**, Rafael *DrAPF 91*
**Catala**, Rafael Enrique 1942- *IntAu&W 91, WhoHisp 92*
**Catalan Uriel**, Jose 1944- *WhoWest 92*
**Cataland**, James Ronald 1944- *WhoFI 92*
**Catalani**, Alfredo 1854-1893 *NewAmDM*
**Catalano**, Anthony William 1947- *AmMWSc 92*
**Catalano**, Carl Philip 1953- *WhoEnt 92*
**Catalano**, Carlos Enrique 1954- *WhoHisp 92*
**Catalano**, Dennis Michael 1956- *WhoWest 92*
**Catalano**, Frank 1951- *WhoWest 92*
**Catalano**, Gene *WhoHisp 92*
**Catalano**, Gerald 1949- *WhoFI 92, WhoMW 92*
**Catalano**, John George 1950- *WhoWest 92*
**Catalano**, Raymond Anthony 1938- *AmMWSc 92*
**Catalano**, Stephen 1952- *ConAu 135*
**Cataldi**, Horace A 1918- *AmMWSc 92*
**Cataldo**, Charles Eugene 1927- *AmMWSc 92*
**Cataldo**, Chet William 1955- *WhoRel 92*
**Cataldo**, Dominic Anthony 1942- *AmMWSc 92*
**Cataldo**, Frank A. 1951- *WhoEnt 92*
**Cataldo**, Joseph C 1937- *AmMWSc 92*
**Catalfo**, Alfred, Jr. 1920- *WhoAmL 92, WhoFI 92*
**Catalfomo**, Philip 1931- *AmMWSc 92*
**Catallo**, Clarence Guerrino, Jr. 1940- *WhoFI 92*
**Catalon**, Virginia Keel 1925- *WhoAmP 91*
**Catalona**, William John 1942- *AmMWSc 92*
**Catanach**, J.N. *DrAPF 91*
**Catanach**, Leo D 1931- *WhoAmP 91*
**Catanach**, Wallace M, Jr 1930- *AmMWSc 92*
**Catanese**, Adrienne Marie 1959- *WhoAmL 92*
**Catanese**, Carmen Anthony 1942- *AmMWSc 92*
**Catania**, Frank 1941- *WhoAmP 91*
**Catania**, Peter J 1942- *AmMWSc 92*
**Catania**, Susan Kmetty 1941- *WhoAmP 91*
**Catanzano**, Frank Alexander 1947- *WhoFI 92*
**Catanzarite**, Catherine Marie 1925- *WhoAmP 91*
**Catanzaro**, Edward John 1933- *AmMWSc 92*
**Catanzaro**, Marci-lee 1941- *WhoWest 92*
**Catanzaro**, Tony *WhoEnt 92*
**Catapane**, Edward John 1951- *AmMWSc 92*
**Catapano**, Joseph John 1935- *WhoFI 92*
**Catapano**, Thomas F 1949- *WhoAmP 91, WhoHisp 92*
**Catchen**, Gary Lee 1950- *AmMWSc 92*
**Catcheside**, David Guthrie 1907- *IntWW 91, Who 92*
**Catching**, Jerome Peter 1926- *WhoEnt 92*
**Catchings**, Howard Douglas 1939- *WhoBlA 92*
**Catchings**, Robert Merritt, III 1942- *AmMWSc 92*
**Catchings**, Walter J. 1933- *WhoBlA 92*
**Catchings**, Yvonne Parks *WhoBlA 92*
**Catchmaid**, George d1667 *DcNCBi 1*
**Catchmaie**, George d1667 *DcNCBi 1*
**Catchmeyd**, George d1667 *DcNCBi 1*
**Catchpole**, Hubert Ralph 1906- *AmMWSc 92*
**Catchpole**, Margaret 1762-1819 *EncAmaz 91*
**Catchpole**, Nancy Mona 1929- *Who 92*
**Catchpole**, W. Park 1918- *WhoAmL 92*
**Cate**, Byron Lee 1942- *WhoAmP 91*
**Cate**, Charles Thomas 1945- *WhoRel 92*
**Cate**, Curtis 1924- *WrDr 92*
**Cate**, Floyd Mills 1917- *WhoWest 92*
**Cate**, Fred Harrison 1963- *WhoAmL 92*
**Cate**, James Richard, Jr *AmMWSc 92*
**Cate**, John Ordway 1933- *WhoWest 92*
**Cate**, Milton A *WhoAmP 91*
**Cate**, Patrick O'Hair 1940- *WhoRel 92*
**Cate**, Robert Bancroft 1924- *AmMWSc 92*
**Cate**, Robert Louis 1932- *WhoRel 92*
**Cate**, Rodney Lee 1950- *AmMWSc 92*
**Cate**, Thomas Randolph 1935- *AmMWSc 92*
**Cate**, Tom 1956- *WhoAmP 91*
**Cate**, William Burke 1924- *WhoRel 92*
**Cateforis**, Vasily C 1939- *AmMWSc 92*
**Catell**, Robert Barry 1937- *WhoFI 92*
**Catenhusen**, John 1909- *AmMWSc 92*
**Cater**, Alice Ruth Wallace 1935- *WhoFI 92*
**Cater**, Anna L. 1933- *WhoBlA 92*
**Cater**, Antony John E. *Who 92*
**Cater**, Douglass 1923- *IntWW 91, Who 92, WrDr 92*
**Cater**, Earle David 1934- *AmMWSc 92*
**Cater**, Frank Sydney 1934- *AmMWSc 92*
**Cater**, Jack 1922- *IntWW 91, Who 92*
**Cater**, James Thomas 1948- *WhoFI 92*
**Cater**, John Robert 1919- *Who 92*
**Cater**, Wilhelmenia Mitchell 1933- *WhoMW 92*
**Caterson**, Bruce 1947- *AmMWSc 92*
**Cates**, Charles Bradley 1950- *WhoAmP 91*
**Cates**, Charles Fletcher 1872-1947 *DcNCBi 1*
**Cates**, David Marshall 1922- *AmMWSc 92*
**Cates**, Ed *DrAPF 91*
**Cates**, Geoffrey William 1923- *AmMWSc 92*
**Cates**, Gilbert *LesBEnT 92*
**Cates**, Gilbert 1934- *IntMPA 92, WhoEnt 92*
**Cates**, James William 1944- *WhoAmP 91*
**Cates**, Jo A. 1958- *ConAu 134*
**Cates**, Joseph *LesBEnT 92*
**Cates**, Joseph 1924- *IntMPA 92, WhoEnt 92*
**Cates**, Lindley A 1932- *AmMWSc 92*
**Cates**, Lynn Wallace 1943- *WhoEnt 92*
**Cates**, Marshall L 1942- *AmMWSc 92*
**Cates**, Phillip Keith 1958- *WhoRel 92*
**Cates**, Phoebe 1963- *IntMPA 92*
**Cates**, Phoebe 1964- *WhoEnt 92*
**Cates**, Sidney Hayward, III 1931- *WhoBlA 92*
**Cates**, Thomas Bradley 1955- *WhoAmL 92*
**Cates**, Vernon E 1931- *AmMWSc 92*
**Catesby**, Mark 1679?-1749 *BenetAL 91*
**Catesby**, Mark 1683-1749 *BiInAmS, DcNCBi 1*
**Cateura**, Linda Brandi 1924- *ConAu 135*
**Catford**, Robin 1923- *Who 92*
**Cathala**, Thierry Gerard 1925- *IntWW 91*
**Cathcart** *Who 92*
**Cathcart**, Earl 1919- *Who 92*
**Cathcart**, David Arthur 1940- *WhoAmL 92*
**Cathcart**, George LeBlanc 1947- *WhoWest 92*
**Cathcart**, George W. 1910- *WhoBlA 92*
**Cathcart**, Helen *IntAu&W 91, WrDr 92*
**Cathcart**, James B 1917- *AmMWSc 92, WhoWest 92*
**Cathcart**, John Almon 1916- *AmMWSc 92*
**Cathcart**, John Varn 1923- *AmMWSc 92*
**Cathcart**, Kevin James 1939- *IntWW 91*
**Cathcart**, Marilyn Sue 1944- *WhoMW 92*
**Cathcart**, Martha K 1951- *AmMWSc 92*
**Cathcart**, Mary R *WhoAmP 91*
**Cathcart**, Richard C 1944- *WhoAmP 91*
**Cathcart**, William 1710?-1773 *DcNCBi 1*
**Cather**, James Newton 1931- *AmMWSc 92, WhoMW 92*
**Cather**, Kathleen Anne 1955- *WhoMW 92*
**Cather**, Willa 1873-1947 *BenetAL 91, HanAmWH, ModAWWr, RComAH, TwCWW 91*
**Cather**, Willa 1876-1947 *FacFETw [port]*
**Cather**, Willa Sibert 1876-1947 *DcAmImH*
**Catherine II** 1729-1796 *BlkwCEP*
**Catherine de Clermont** *EncAmaz 91*
**Catherine**, Saint *EncAmaz 91*
**Catherine the Great** 1729-1796 *BlkwCEP, EncAmaz 91*
**Catherwood**, Cummins, Jr. 1942- *WhoFI 92*
**Catherwood**, Frederick 1925- *IntAu&W 91, IntWW 91, Who 92, WrDr 92*
**Catherwood**, Herbert Sidney Elliott 1929- *Who 92*
**Catherwood**, Mary 1847-1902 *BenetAL 91*
**Cathey**, Dean Edward 1946- *WhoWest 92*
**Cathey**, George Leonidas 1822-1923 *DcNCBi 1*
**Cathey**, Hugh Charles 1950- *WhoFI 92*
**Cathey**, Jimmie Joe 1941- *AmMWSc 92*
**Cathey**, LeConte 1923- *AmMWSc 92*
**Cathey**, Sharon Sue Rinn 1940- *WhoWest 92*
**Cathey**, Wade Thomas, Jr 1937- *AmMWSc 92*
**Cathey**, William Blair 1954- *WhoFI 92*
**Cathey**, William Newton 1939- *AmMWSc 92*
**Cathles**, Lawrence MacLagan, III 1943- *AmMWSc 92*
**Cathou**, Renata Egone 1935- *AmMWSc 92*
**Catignani**, George Louis 1943- *AmMWSc 92*
**Catizone**, Richard Alan 1946- *WhoEnt 92*
**Catjakis**, Athan 1931- *WhoAmP 91*
**Catledge**, Terry Dewayne 1963- *WhoBlA 92*
**Catlett**, Duane Stewart 1940- *AmMWSc 92*
**Catlett**, Elizabeth 1915- *NotBlAW 92 [port]*
**Catlett**, Elizabeth 1919?- *ConBlB 2 [port], WhoBlA 92*
**Catlett**, Mary Jo 1938- *WhoEnt 92*
**Catlett**, Robert Bishop 1952- *WhoFI 92, WhoMW 92*
**Catlett**, Sid 1910-1951 *NewAmDM*
**Catlin**, A B *WhoAmP 91*
**Catlin**, Alan *DrAPF 91*
**Catlin**, Avery 1924- *AmMWSc 92*
**Catlin**, B Wesley 1917- *AmMWSc 92*
**Catlin**, Charles Albert 1849-1916 *BiInAmS*
**Catlin**, Don Hardt *AmMWSc 92*
**Catlin**, Don Robert *ScFEYrs*
**Catlin**, Donald E 1936- *AmMWSc 92*
**Catlin**, Francis I 1925- *AmMWSc 92*
**Catlin**, George 1796-1872 *BenetAL 91, BiInAmS*
**Catlin**, John Anthony 1947- *Who 92*
**Catlin**, Peter Bostwick 1930- *AmMWSc 92*
**Catlin**, Robert A. 1940- *WhoBlA 92*
**Catlin**, William Arthur 1941- *WhoMW 92*
**Catling**, Brian 1948- *TwCPaSc*
**Catling**, Darrel *TwCPaSc*
**Catling**, Hector William 1924- *Who 92*
**Catling**, Paul Miles 1947- *AmMWSc 92*
**Catling**, Richard 1912- *Who 92*
**Catlow**, Charles Richard Arthur 1947- *Who 92*
**Cato**, Arnott Samuel 1912- *Who 92*
**Cato**, Benjamin Ralph, Jr 1925- *AmMWSc 92*
**Cato**, Bette M 1924- *WhoAmP 91*
**Cato**, Brian Hudson 1928- *Who 92*
**Cato**, Harry F 1958- *WhoAmP 91*
**Cato**, Milton 1915- *Who 92*
**Cato**, Nancy 1917- *WrDr 92*
**Cato**, Robert Milton 1915- *IntWW 91*
**Catoe**, Samuel George 1946- *WhoRel 92*
**Caton**, Charles Allen 1937- *WhoWest 92*
**Caton**, Jerald A 1949- *AmMWSc 92*
**Caton**, John Dean 1812-1895 *BiInAmS*
**Caton**, Kathleen Lynn *WhoEnt 92*
**Caton**, Kenneth Lloyd 1943- *WhoRel 92*
**Caton**, Randall Hubert 1942- *AmMWSc 92*
**Caton**, Robert Luther 1937- *AmMWSc 92*
**Caton**, Roy Dudley, Jr 1930- *AmMWSc 92*
**Caton-Jones**, Michael 1958- *IntWW 91*
**Catoni**, Pedro Miguel 1957- *WhoHisp 92*
**Cator**, Silvio 1900- *BlkOlyM*
**Catovsky**, Julia Margaret *Who 92*
**Catrambone**, Eugene Dominic 1926- *WhoWest 92*
**Catrambone**, Joseph Anthony, Sr 1924- *AmMWSc 92*
**Catravas**, George Nicholas 1916- *AmMWSc 92*
**Catravas**, John D 1950- *AmMWSc 92*
**Catrett**, John Thomas, III 1947- *WhoRel 92, WhoWest 92*
**Catrillo**, Charles J *WhoAmP 91*
**Catron**, Delbert Dean 1929- *WhoMW 92*
**Catron**, William G. 1945- *WhoAmL 92, WhoEnt 92*
**Catsiff**, Ephraim Herman *AmMWSc 92*
**Catsimpoolas**, Nicholas 1931- *AmMWSc 92*
**Catt**, Carrie Chapman 1859-1947 *AmPeW, HanAmWH, RComAH*
**Catt**, Kevin John 1932- *AmMWSc 92*
**Catt**, Michael Cameron 1952- *WhoRel 92*
**Catt**, Neal Emery 1943- *WhoMW 92*
**Cattan**, Henry 1906- *IntAu&W 91, WrDr 92*
**Cattanach**, Bruce MacIntosh 1932- *IntWW 91, Who 92*
**Cattanach**, Helen 1920- *Who 92*
**Cattaneo**, Jacquelyn Annette Kammerer 1944- *WhoWest 92*
**Cattaneo**, John Leo 1944- *WhoWest 92*
**Cattaneo**, L E 1920- *AmMWSc 92*
**Cattaneo**, Michael S. 1948- *WhoMW 92*
**Cattani**, Eduardo 1946- *AmMWSc 92*
**Cattani**, Maryellen B. 1943- *WhoAmL 92, WhoFI 92*
**Cattano**, Benjamin Nunzio, Sr. 1931- *WhoFI 92*
**Cattell**, George Harold Bernard 1920- *Who 92*
**Cattell**, Raymond Bernard 1905- *IntAu&W 91, WrDr 92*
**Cattell**, William Ashburner 1863-1920 *BiInAmS*
**Catterall**, James F 1949- *AmMWSc 92*
**Catterall**, John Ashley 1928- *Who 92*
**Catterall**, John Stewart 1939- *Who 92*
**Catterall**, Peter 1961- *ConAu 134*
**Catterall**, William A 1940- *AmMWSc 92*
**Catterall**, William E 1920- *AmMWSc 92*
**Cattermole**, Joan Eileen *Who 92*
**Cattermole**, Lancelot Harry Mosse 1898- *Who 92*
**Cattermole**, Richard A. *WhoRel 92*
**Catterson**, Allen Duane 1929- *AmMWSc 92*
**Catterton**, Marianne Rose 1922- *WhoWest 92*
**Cattin**, Carlo Donat d1991 *NewYTBS 91*
**Cattle Kate** 1862?-1888 *EncAmaz 91*
**Catto** *Who 92*
**Catto**, Baron 1923- *IntWW 91, Who 92*
**Catto**, Henry E 1930- *WhoAmP 91*
**Catto**, Henry Edward 1930- *IntWW 91, Who 92*
**Catto**, Peter James 1943- *AmMWSc 92*
**Catto**, William James 1957- *WhoAmL 92*
**Cattoi**, Robert Louis 1926- *WhoFI 92*
**Cattolico**, Rose Ann 1943- *AmMWSc 92*
**Catton**, Bruce 1899-1978 *BenetAL 91, FacFETw*
**Catton**, Ivan 1934- *AmMWSc 92*
**Cattrall**, Kim 1956- *IntMPA 92*
**Cattrell**, Louise 1957- *TwCPaSc*
**Catts**, Elmer Paul 1930- *AmMWSc 92*
**Catucci**, Paul Frank 1956- *WhoRel 92*
**Catudal**, Honore 1944- *IntAu&W 91*
**Catudal**, Honore, Jr. 1944- *WrDr 92*
**Catura**, Richard Clarence 1935- *AmMWSc 92*
**Catuzzi**, J. P., Jr. 1938- *WhoAmL 92*
**Catz**, Boris 1923- *AmMWSc 92, WhoWest 92*
**Catz**, Charlotte Schifra *AmMWSc 92*
**Catz**, Jerome 1932- *AmMWSc 92*
**Cau**, Jean 1925- *IntWW 91*
**Cauas**, Jorge *IntWW 91*
**Cauble**, John Russell, Jr. 1957- *WhoWest 92*
**Caucau**, Isireli M. *WhoRel 92*
**Caudel**, Gary Dewayne 1949- *WhoEnt 92*
**Caudell**, James A 1929- *WhoAmP 91*
**Caudill**, Franklin Terrell 1945- *WhoAmL 92*
**Caudill**, Harry M. 1922-1990 *ConAu 133*
**Caudill**, James Mason 1950- *WhoWest 92*
**Caudill**, Reggie Jackson 1949- *AmMWSc 92*
**Caudill**, Terry Lee 1947- *WhoWest 92*
**Caudill**, Tom Holden 1945- *WhoMW 92*
**Caudill**, William Howard 1951- *WhoAmL 92*
**Caudle**, Ben Hall 1923- *AmMWSc 92*
**Caudle**, Danny Dearl 1937- *AmMWSc 92*
**Caudle**, Theron Lamar 1904-1969 *DcNCBi 1*
**Caudle**, William Brandon, II 1942- *WhoAmP 91*
**Caudron**, John Armand 1944- *WhoWest 92*
**Caudwell**, Sarah *WrDr 92*
**Caughey**, David Alan 1944- *AmMWSc 92*
**Caughey**, George Herbert 1953- *WhoWest 92*
**Caughey**, John Lyon, Jr 1904- *AmMWSc 92*
**Caughey**, Thomas Harcourt Clarke 1911- *Who 92*
**Caughey**, Thomas Kirk 1927- *AmMWSc 92*
**Caughey**, Winslow Spaulding 1926- *AmMWSc 92*
**Caughlan**, Charles Norris 1915- *AmMWSc 92*
**Caughlan**, Georgeanne Robertson 1916- *AmMWSc 92, WhoWest 92*
**Caughlan**, John Arthur 1921- *AmMWSc 92*
**Caughlin**, Ian 1948- *TwCPaSc*
**Caughlin**, Stephenie Jane 1948- *WhoFI 92, WhoWest 92*
**Caughran**, William Hermann, Jr. 1956- *WhoAmL 92*
**Caul**, Jean Frances 1915- *AmMWSc 92*
**Caulcott**, Thomas Holt 1927- *Who 92*
**Caulder**, Jerry Dale 1942- *AmMWSc 92*
**Caulder**, Mary Mezzanotte 1953- *WhoFI 92*
**Cauldwell**, Frank *IntAu&W 91X, WrDr 92*
**Cauley**, James Robert 1952- *WhoAmL 92*
**Caulfeild** *Who 92*
**Caulfield**, Barbara Ann 1947- *WhoAmL 92*
**Caulfield**, Bernard 1914- *Who 92*
**Caulfield**, Daniel Francis 1935- *AmMWSc 92*
**Caulfield**, Henry John 1936- *AmMWSc 92*
**Caulfield**, Ian George 1942- *Who 92*
**Caulfield**, James 1728-1799 *BlkwCEP*
**Caulfield**, James Benjamin 1927- *AmMWSc 92*

**Caulfield,** Jerome Joseph 1949- *WhoAmL 92*
**Caulfield,** Joan d1991 *NewYTBS 91 [port]*
**Caulfield,** Joan 1922-1991 *CurBio 91N, News 92-1*
**Caulfield,** Joan 1943- *WhoMW 92*
**Caulfield,** John P 1944- *AmMWSc 92*
**Caulfield,** Mark Francis 1958- *WhoFI 92*
**Caulfield,** Maxwell 1959- *IntMPA 92*
**Caulfield,** Patrick 1936- *IntWW 91, TwCPaSc, Who 92*
**Caulfield,** Sharon Elizabeth 1956- *WhoAmL 92*
**Caulk,** David Allen 1950- *AmMWSc 92*
**Caulk,** Wallace G, Jr 1941- *WhoAmP 91*
**Caulley,** Thomas Scott 1952- *WhoRel 92*
**Caulton,** M 1925- *AmMWSc 92*
**Cauna,** Nikolajs 1914- *AmMWSc 92*
**Caupolican** d1558 *HisDSpE*
**Causa,** Alfredo G 1928- *AmMWSc 92*
**Causer,** William Sydney 1876-1958 *TwCPaSc*
**Causey,** Ardee 1915- *AmMWSc 92*
**Causey,** C. Harry 1942- *WhoRel 92*
**Causey,** Calvin Gerald 1930- *WhoRel 92*
**Causey,** G Donald 1926- *AmMWSc 92*
**Causey,** Gerald David 1934- *WhoRel 92*
**Causey,** Gilbert 1907- *Who 92, WrDr 92*
**Causey,** James Robert 1956- *WhoFI 92*
**Causey,** John Norman 1952- *WhoRel 92*
**Causey,** John Paul, Jr. 1943- *WhoAmL 92*
**Causey,** Marion Edward, II 1947- *WhoRel 92*
**Causey,** Miles Keith 1940- *AmMWSc 92*
**Causey,** Richard Wayne 1935- *WhoRel 92*
**Causey,** William McLain 1938- *AmMWSc 92*
**Causley,** Charles 1917- *ConAu 35NR, ConPo 91, IntAu&W 91, SmATA 66 [port], WrDr 92*
**Causley,** Charles Stanley 1917- *IntWW 91, Who 92*
**Causse,** Jean-Pierre 1926- *IntWW 91*
**Caust-Ellenbogen,** Sanford Nathan 1954- *WhoAmL 92*
**Causwell,** Duane 1968- *WhoBlA 92*
**Caute,** David 1936- *ConNov 91, IntAu&W 91, IntWW 91, Who 92, WrDr 92*
**Cauthen,** Charles Edward, Jr. 1931- *WhoFI 92*
**Cauthen,** Cheryl G. 1957- *WhoBlA 92*
**Cauthen,** E. Larry 1930- *WhoIns 92*
**Cauthen,** Henry J. *LesBEnT 92*
**Cauthen,** Irby Bruce, Jr. 1919- *WrDr 92*
**Cauthen,** Kenneth 1930- *WrDr 92*
**Cauthen,** Richard L. 1944- *WhoBlA 92*
**Cauthen,** Sally Eugenia 1932- *AmMWSc 92*
**Cauthen,** Steve 1960- *FacFETw*
**Cauthron,** Robin J. 1950- *WhoAmL 92*
**Cautis,** C Victor 1946- *AmMWSc 92*
**Cautley,** Patricia Woodward 1914- *WhoMW 92*
**Cauttero,** George Anthony 1951- *WhoEnt 92*
**Cava,** Michael Patrick 1926- *AmMWSc 92*
**Cavaco Silva,** Anibal 1939- *CurBio 91 [port], IntWW 91*
**Cavafy,** Constantine 1863-1933 *FacFETw*
**Cavafy,** Constantine P. 1863-1933 *LiExTwC*
**Cavagna,** Giancarlo Antonio 1938- *AmMWSc 92*
**Cavalaris,** John Constantine 1962- *WhoFI 92*
**Cavalcanti,** Alberto 1897-1982 *IntDcF 2-2 [port]*
**Cavalcanti,** Edward L. 1963- *WhoHisp 92*
**Cavalcanti,** Giacomo 1952- *IntWW 91*
**Cavalero,** George N. d1991 *NewYTBS 91*
**Cavalier,** Darlene D. 1961- *WhoEnt 92*
**Cavalier,** John F 1947- *AmMWSc 92*
**Cavaliere,** Alphonse Ralph 1937- *AmMWSc 92*
**Cavalieri,** Anthony Joseph, II 1951- *AmMWSc 92*
**Cavalieri,** Donald Joseph 1942- *AmMWSc 92*
**Cavalieri,** Emilio de' 1550?-1602 *NewAmDM*
**Cavalieri,** Ercole Luigi 1937- *AmMWSc 92*
**Cavalieri,** Grace *DrAPF 91*
**Cavalieri,** Ralph R 1932- *AmMWSc 92*
**Cavalieri,** Vivian L. 1956- *WhoAmL 92*
**Cavaliero,** Roderick 1928- *Who 92*
**Cavallaro,** Augustine L. *WhoHisp 92*
**Cavallaro,** Joseph John 1932- *AmMWSc 92*
**Cavallaro,** Mary Caroline 1932- *AmMWSc 92*
**Cavallera,** Charles 1909- *Who 92*
**Cavallero,** Hazel Helen 1913- *WhoWest 92*
**Cavallero,** Ugo 1880-1943 *FacFETw*
**Cavalli,** Pier Francesco 1602-1676 *NewAmDM*
**Cavalli-Sforza,** Luigi Luca 1922- *AmMWSc 92, FacFETw, WhoWest 92*
**Cavallito,** Chester John 1915- *AmMWSc 92*
**Cavallo,** Carol 1954- *WhoEnt 92*
**Cavallo,** Diana *DrAPF 91*
**Cavallo,** Diana 1931- *WrDr 92*
**Cavallo,** Domingo Felipe 1946- *IntWW 91*
**Cavallo,** Joseph Charles, Jr. 1944- *WhoRel 92*
**Cavallo,** Michael William 1949- *WhoFI 92*
**Cavallon,** Juan de *HisDSpE*
**Cavan,** Earl of 1944- *Who 92*
**Cavan,** Ruth Shonle 1896- *WomSoc*
**Cavanagh,** Carroll John 1943- *WhoFI 92*
**Cavanagh,** Denis 1923- *AmMWSc 92*
**Cavanagh,** Edward Dean 1949- *WhoAmL 92*
**Cavanagh,** Harrison Dwight 1940- *AmMWSc 92*
**Cavanagh,** Jeffrey 1948- *WhoMW 92*
**Cavanagh,** John Bryan 1914- *Who 92*
**Cavanagh,** John Charles 1932- *WhoWest 92*
**Cavanagh,** John Joseph, Jr 1942- *WhoAmP 91*
**Cavanagh,** Karen Marie 1941- *WhoRel 92*
**Cavanagh,** Kit 1667-1739 *EncAmaz 91*
**Cavanagh,** Mary Jo 1956- *WhoRel 92*
**Cavanagh,** Michael F *WhoAmP 91*
**Cavanagh,** Michael Francis 1940- *WhoAmL 92, WhoMW 92*
**Cavanagh,** Peter R 1947- *AmMWSc 92*
**Cavanagh,** Richard Edward 1946- *WhoFI 92*
**Cavanagh,** Richard Roy 1950- *AmMWSc 92*
**Cavanagh,** Timothy D 1938- *AmMWSc 92*
**Cavanah,** Frances 1899-1982 *ConAu 133*
**Cavanah,** Lloyd 1919- *AmMWSc 92*
**Cavanaugh,** Andrew *IntMPA 92*
**Cavanaugh,** Evelyn Beatrice 1940- *WhoAmL 92*
**Cavanaugh,** James Richard 1934- *AmMWSc 92*
**Cavanaugh,** John Daniel 1938- *WhoEnt 92*
**Cavanaugh,** John G. 1936- *WhoIns 92*
**Cavanaugh,** John J, III 1945- *WhoAmP 91*
**Cavanaugh,** John Joseph, Jr. 1936- *WhoAmL 92*
**Cavanaugh,** John Lance 1957- *WhoMW 92*
**Cavanaugh,** Ken Matthew, III 1959- *WhoWest 92*
**Cavanaugh,** Lee Earl 1951- *WhoFI 92*
**Cavanaugh,** Michael *ConTFT 9*
**Cavanaugh,** Patricia L. 1954- *WhoMW 92*
**Cavanaugh,** Robert J 1942- *AmMWSc 92*
**Cavanaugh,** Vontros Eugene 1928- *WhoRel 92*
**Cavani,** Liliana *ReelWom*
**Cavani,** Liliana 1937- *IntMPA 92*
**Cavanna,** Betty 1909- *IntAu&W 91, WrDr 92*
**Cavaretta,** Alfred S 1944- *AmMWSc 92*
**Cavasso,** Cam 1950- *WhoAmP 91*
**Cavazos,** Ben 1950- *WhoHisp 92*
**Cavazos,** Eddie 1942- *WhoAmP 91, WhoHisp 92*
**Cavazos,** Henry J. *WhoHisp 92*
**Cavazos,** Irma Estella 1964- *WhoHisp 92*
**Cavazos,** Joel *WhoHisp 92*
**Cavazos,** Lauro F. 1927- *WhoHisp 92*
**Cavazos,** Lauro Fred 1927- *AmMWSc 92, IntWW 91, WhoAmP 91*
**Cavazos,** Miguel A., Jr. 1943- *WhoHisp 92*
**Cavazos,** Rosa I. 1954- *WhoHisp 92*
**Cavazza,** Fabio Luca 1927- *WhoFI 92*
**Cavazzoni,** Girolamo 1510-1565? *NewAmDM*
**Cavazzoni,** Marco Antonio 1490?-1570 *NewAmDM*
**Cave,** Alexander James Edward 1900- *Who 92*
**Cave,** Alfred Earl 1940- *WhoBlA 92*
**Cave,** Charles 1927- *Who 92*
**Cave,** Charles Philip H. *Who 92*
**Cave,** Claude Bertrand 1910- *WhoBlA 92*
**Cave,** Emma *WrDr 92*
**Cave,** George Harold, III 1957- *WhoAmL 92*
**Cave,** Herbert G. 1922- *WhoBlA 92*
**Cave,** John Arthur 1915- *Who 92*
**Cave,** Mac Donald 1939- *AmMWSc 92*
**Cave,** Perstein Ronald 1947- *WhoBlA 92*
**Cave,** Shannon Daily 1949- *WhoAmP 91*
**Cave,** Terence Christopher 1938- *Who 92*
**Cave,** Vernal G. *WhoBlA 92*
**Cave,** William 1637-1713 *EncEarC*
**Cave,** William Thompson 1917- *AmMWSc 92*
**Cave-Browne-Cave,** Robert 1929- *Who 92*
**Cavedo,** Bradley Brent 1955- *WhoAmL 92, WhoAmP 91*
**Cavell,** Edith 1865-1915 *FacFETw [port]*
**Cavell,** John Kingsmill 1916- *Who 92*
**Cavell,** Ronald George 1938- *AmMWSc 92*
**Caven,** James David 1943- *WhoAmL 92*
**Cavenagh,** Winifred *WrDr 92*
**Cavenagh,** Winifred Elizabeth *Who 92*
**Cavenagh-Mainwaring,** Maurice Kildare 1908- *Who 92*
**Cavender,** James C 1936- *AmMWSc 92*
**Cavender,** James Vere, Jr 1922- *AmMWSc 92*
**Cavender,** Michael Charles 1954- *WhoEnt 92*
**Cavender,** Patricia Lee 1950- *AmMWSc 92*
**Cavendish** *Who 92*
**Cavendish,** Elizabeth 1926- *Who 92*
**Cavendish,** Margaret 1623?-1673? *RfGEnL 91*
**Cavendish,** Peter Boucher 1925- *Who 92*
**Cavendish,** Richard 1930- *IntAu&W 91, WrDr 92*
**Cavendish of Furness,** Baron 1941- *Who 92*
**Cavenee,** Charles James 1958- *WhoAmL 92*
**Caveney,** Stanley 1945- *AmMWSc 92*
**Caveney,** William John 1944- *WhoFI 92*
**Cavens,** Sharon Sue 1942- *WhoBlA 92*
**Caveny,** Leonard Hugh 1934- *AmMWSc 92*
**Caver,** Carmen C. Murphy 1915- *WhoBlA 92*
**Caverly,** Charles Solomon 1856-1918 *BiInAmS*
**Cavers,** Paul Brethen 1938- *AmMWSc 92*
**Cavert,** Henry Mead 1922- *AmMWSc 92*
**Cavert,** Samuel McCrea 1888-1976 *RelLAm 91*
**Cavert,** Twila Lytton d1991 *NewYTBS 91*
**Caves,** Carlton Morris 1950- *AmMWSc 92*
**Caves,** Richard Earl 1931- *WrDr 92*
**Caves,** Thomas Courtney 1940- *AmMWSc 92*
**Cavett,** Dick *LesBEnT 92*
**Cavett,** Dick 1936- *WhoEnt 92*
**Cavett,** Dick 1937- *IntMPA 92*
**Cavey,** Michael John 1946- *AmMWSc 92*
**Cavicchio,** Daniel Joseph, Jr. 1944- *WhoFI 92*
**Caviedes,** Juan Del Valle y 1652?-1697 *HisDSpE*
**Cavill,** Ronald William 1944- *WhoFI 92*
**Cavin,** Alonzo C. 1939- *WhoBlA 92*
**Cavin,** Clark 1939- *WhoAmL 92*
**Cavin,** Edward Scott 1953- *WhoFI 92*
**Cavin,** William Pinckney 1925- *AmMWSc 92*
**Caviness,** Bobby Forrester 1940- *AmMWSc 92*
**Caviness,** E. Theophilus 1928- *WhoBlA 92*
**Caviness,** Lorraine F. 1914- *WhoBlA 92*
**Caviness,** Verne Strudwick, Jr 1934- *AmMWSc 92*
**Cavins,** William Robert 1953- *WhoRel 92*
**Cavis,** Ella *DrAPF 91*
**Caviston,** William Michael 1928- *WhoAmL 92*
**Cavitch,** Zolman 1925- *WhoAmL 92*
**Cavitt,** Bruce Edward 1945- *WhoAmL 92*
**Cavitt,** Ross N. 1961- *WhoEnt 92*
**Cavitt,** Stanley Bruce 1934- *AmMWSc 92*
**Cavnar,** Samuel Melmon 1925- *WhoAmP 91, WhoWest 92*
**Cavolina,** Larry Andrew 1949- *WhoEnt 92*
**Cavonius,** Carl Richard 1932- *AmMWSc 92*
**Cavoukian,** Raffi 1948- *SmATA 68 [port]*
**Cawdor,** Earl 1932- *Who 92*
**Cawein,** Madison 1865-1914 *BenetAL 91*
**Cawein,** Madison Julius 1926- *AmMWSc 92*
**Cawley** *Who 92*
**Cawley,** Baron 1913- *Who 92*
**Cawley,** Charles 1907- *Who 92*
**Cawley,** Edward Philip 1912- *AmMWSc 92*
**Cawley,** Edward T 1931- *AmMWSc 92*
**Cawley,** Evonne Fay 1951- *IntWW 91*
**Cawley,** Gaynor 1941- *WhoAmP 91*
**Cawley,** James Hughes 1945- *WhoAmL 92*
**Cawley,** John Arnold, Jr. 1943- *WhoAmL 92*
**Cawley,** John Joseph 1932- *AmMWSc 92*
**Cawley,** Leo Patrick 1922- *AmMWSc 92*
**Cawley,** Robert 1936- *AmMWSc 92*
**Cawley,** Robert Hugh 1924- *Who 92*
**Cawley,** Robert Lucian 1934- *WhoAmP 91*
**Cawley,** William Arthur 1925- *AmMWSc 92*
**Cawley,** Winifred 1915- *WrDr 92*
**Cawood,** Albert McLaurin 1939- *WhoMW 92*
**Cawood,** James Clement, Jr. 1936- *WhoAmL 92*
**Cawood,** James Scott 1956- *WhoFI 92*
**Cawood,** Stephen Carl 1943- *WhoAmP 91*
**Caws,** Mary Ann 1933- *IntAu&W 91, WrDr 92*
**Caws,** Peter 1931- *WrDr 92*
**Caws,** Richard Byron 1927- *Who 92*
**Cawson,** Roderick Anthony 1921- *Who 92*
**Cawthern,** Beth Anne 1956- *WhoMW 92*
**Cawthorn,** Robert Elston 1935- *WhoFI 92*
**Cawthorne,** Dennis Otto 1940- *WhoAmP 91*
**Cawthorne,** Hugh William Howarth 1939- *WhoAmL 92*
**Cawthorne,** Kenneth Clifford 1936- *WhoFI 92*
**Cawthra,** Arthur James 1911- *Who 92*
**Cawthra,** David Wilkinson 1943- *Who 92*
**Cawthra,** Hermon 1886- *TwCPaSc*
**Caxton,** William 1421?-1491 *LitC 17 [port]*
**Cayabyab,** Louise Martha 1962- *WhoMW 92*
**Cayatte,** Andre 1909-1989 *IntDcF 2-2 [port]*
**Cayce,** Charles Thomas 1942- *RelLAm 91*
**Cayce,** Edgar 1877-1945 *RelLAm 91*
**Cayce,** Hugh Lynn 1907-1982 *ConAu 34NR, RelLAm 91*
**Cayce,** W. H. *WhoRel 92*
**Cayea,** Donald Joseph 1948- *WhoAmL 92*
**Cayen,** Mitchell Ness 1938- *AmMWSc 92*
**Cayetano,** Benjamin J. 1939- *WhoHisp 92*
**Cayetano,** Benjamin Jerome 1939- *WhoAmP 91, WhoWest 92*
**Cayford,** Afton Herbert 1929- *AmMWSc 92*
**Cayford,** Florence Evelyn 1897- *Who 92*
**Caygill,** David Francis 1948- *IntWW 91, Who 92*
**Cayle** *DrAPF 91*
**Cayle,** Theodore 1928- *AmMWSc 92*
**Cayley,** Digby 1944- *Who 92*
**Cayley,** Henry Douglas d1991 *Who 92N*
**Caylor,** Chester A. 1933- *WhoRel 92*
**Caylor,** Florence Byrens 1910- *WhoEnt 92*
**Caylus,** Anne-Claude-Philippe, comte de 1692-1765 *BlkwCEP*
**Cayne,** James E. 1934- *WhoFI 92*
**Cayou,** Nontsizi Kirton 1937- *WhoBlA 92*
**Cayrol,** Jean 1911- *IntWW 91*
**Cayrol,** Roland 1941- *IntWW 91*
**Cayton,** Andrew Robert Lee 1954- *IntAu&W 91*
**Cayton,** Mary Evelyn 1926- *WhoRel 92*
**Caywood,** David Mikel 1962- *WhoRel 92*
**Caywood,** Paul 1921- *WhoEnt 92*
**Caywood,** Stanley William, Jr 1924- *AmMWSc 92*
**Caywood,** Thomas E 1919- *AmMWSc 92*
**Caywood,** Thomas Elias 1919- *WhoMW 92*
**Cayzer** *Who 92*
**Cayzer,** Baron 1910- *IntWW 91, Who 92*
**Cayzer,** James Arthur 1931- *Who 92*
**Cazalet,** Edward 1936- *Who 92*
**Cazalet,** Peter 1929- *IntWW 91, Who 92*
**Cazalet-Keir,** Thelma 1899-1989 *BiDBrF 2*
**Cazares,** Carlos A. *WhoHisp 92*
**Cazares,** Roger 1941- *WhoHisp 92*
**Cazares,** Roy B. *WhoHisp 92*
**Cazaubon,** Maurice Samuel, Jr. 1941- *WhoAmL 92*
**Cazavan,** Larry O. 1945- *WhoEnt 92*
**Cazden,** Norman 1914-1980 *NewAmDM*
**Cazeau,** Charles J 1931- *AmMWSc 92, SmATA 65 [port]*
**Cazeaux,** Isabelle Anne Marie 1926- *WhoEnt 92*
**Cazel,** Hugh Allen 1923- *WhoFI 92*
**Cazenave,** Noel Anthony 1948- *WhoBlA 92*
**Cazeneuve,** Jean 1915- *IntWW 91*
**Cazenove,** Christopher 1945- *IntMPA 92*
**Cazenove,** Christopher de Lerisson 1945- *IntWW 91*
**Cazet,** Denys 1938- *WrDr 92*
**Cazier,** Barry James 1943- *WhoWest 92*
**Cazier,** Gail Allan 1931- *WhoWest 92*
**Cazier,** Mont Adelbert 1911- *AmMWSc 92*
**Cazier,** Stanford 1930- *WhoWest 92*
**Cazin,** John, Jr 1929- *AmMWSc 92*
**Ce,** Marco 1925- *WhoRel 92*
**Ceasar,** Gerald P 1940- *AmMWSc 92*
**Ceasar,** Mitchell 1954- *WhoAmL 92*
**Cease,** Jane Hardy 1936- *WhoAmP 91, WhoWest 92*
**Cease,** Ron 1931- *WhoAmP 91*
**Ceausescu,** Nicolae 1918-1989 *FacFETw*
**Ceballos,** Cedric Z. 1969- *WhoBlA 92*
**Ceballos,** Marta 1950- *WhoAmL 92*
**Ceballos,** Pedro de 1715-1778 *HisDSpE*
**Ceballos,** Ricardo 1930- *AmMWSc 92*
**Ceballos Ordonez,** Luz Priscila *IntWW 91*
**Cebertowicz,** Janina 1953- *TwCPaSc*
**Cebollero,** Carlos 1927- *WhoIns 92*
**Cebra,** John Joseph 1934- *AmMWSc 92*
**Cebrian,** Teresa del Carmen 1960- *WhoHisp 92*
**Cebrian Echarri,** Juan Luis 1944- *IntWW 91*
**Cebuc,** Alexandru 1932- *IntWW 91*
**Cebulash,** Mel 1937- *WrDr 92*
**Cebull,** Stanley Edward 1934- *AmMWSc 92*
**Ceccato,** Aldo 1934- *IntWW 91, NewAmDM, WhoEnt 92*
**Cecchetti,** Stephen Giovanni 1956- *WhoFI 92, WhoMW 92*
**Cecchi,** Joseph Leonard 1947- *AmMWSc 92*
**Cecchi,** Robert Lee d1991 *NewYTBS 91*

**Cech**, Carol Martinson 1947- AmMWSc 92
**Cech**, Joseph Harold 1951- WhoMW 92
**Cech**, Joseph Jerome, Jr 1943- AmMWSc 92
**Cech**, Robert E 1924- AmMWSc 92
**Cech**, Thomas Robert 1947- AmMWSc 92, IntWW 91, WhoNob 90, WhoWest 92
**Ceci**, Jesse Arthur 1924- WhoEnt 92
**Ceci**, Louis J. 1927- WhoAmL 92, WhoAmP 91, WhoMW 92
**Cecil** Who 92
**Cecil**, Christopher Henry Amherst 1965- WhoFI 92
**Cecil**, David 1902-1986 ConAu 34NR, FacFETw
**Cecil**, David, Lord ConAu 34NR
**Cecil**, David Rolf 1935- AmMWSc 92
**Cecil**, Dorcas Ann 1945- WhoMW 92
**Cecil**, Earl Ivan 1946- WhoRel 92
**Cecil**, Edgar Algernon Robert Gascoyne 1864-1958 WhoNob 90
**Cecil**, Elmer James 1922- WhoAmP 91
**Cecil**, Helene Carter 1933- AmMWSc 92
**Cecil**, Henry Richard Amherst 1943- Who 92
**Cecil**, Nigel Amherst 1925- Who 92
**Cecil**, Richard DrAPF 91
**Cecil**, Robert 1864-1958 FacFETw
**Cecil**, Robert 1913- Who 92
**Cecil**, Rose 1956- TwCPaSc
**Cecil**, Sam Reber 1916- AmMWSc 92
**Cecil**, Stephen Don 1958- WhoRel 92
**Cecil**, Thomas E 1945- AmMWSc 92
**Cecil**, Vander Bethea 1947- WhoEnt 92
**Cecile**, Michael Peter 1946- AmMWSc 92
**Cecire**, Robert Clyde 1940- WhoRel 92
**Cecutti**, Edward Valentino 1931- WhoMW 92
**Cedain Zhoma** 1937- IntWW 91
**Cedar**, Frank James 1945- AmMWSc 92
**Cedar**, Paul Arnold 1938- WhoMW 92, WhoRel 92
**Cedarbaum**, Miriam Goldman 1929- WhoAmL 92
**Cedarleaf**, John Lennart 1915- WhoRel 92
**Cedarleaf**, John Nevins 1943- WhoRel 92
**Cedeno**, Andujar 1969- WhoHisp 92
**Cedeno**, Cesar 1951- WhoHisp 92
**Cedeno**, Cesar 1957- WhoBlA 92
**Cedeno**, Manuel 1781-1821 HisDSpE
**Ceder**, Jack G 1933- AmMWSc 92
**Cederbaum**, Eugene E. 1942- WhoAmL 92
**Cederberg**, James W 1939- AmMWSc 92
**Cederberg**, John Edwin 1943- WhoFI 92
**Cedergren**, Robert J 1939- AmMWSc 92
**Cederholm**, David Tither 1945- WhoFI 92
**Cedering**, Siv DrAPF 91
**Cedillo**, Arnulfo 1951- WhoHisp 92
**Cedoline**, Anthony John 1942- WhoWest 92
**Cedrone**, Louis Robert, Jr. 1923- WhoEnt 92
**Ceely**, Robert Paige 1930- WhoEnt 92
**Cefalo**, Michael Joseph 1940- WhoAmP 91
**Cefis**, Eugenio 1921- IntWW 91
**Cefkin**, J Leo 1916- WhoAmP 91
**Cegielka**, Francis 1908- WrDr 92
**Cegielka**, Francis Anthony 1908- IntAu&W 91
**Ceglio**, Natale Mauro 1944- AmMWSc 92
**Ceglowski**, Walter Stanley 1932- AmMWSc 92
**Ceithaml**, Joseph James 1916- AmMWSc 92
**Cejas**, Paul L. 1943- WhoHisp 92
**Cejka**, Oliver John, Jr. 1950- WhoAmL 92
**Cela**, Camilo Jose 1916- IntAu&W 91, IntWW 91, WhoNob 90
**Celac**, Sergiu 1939- Who 92
**Celan**, Paul 1920-1970 FacFETw, LiExTwC
**Celander**, Evelyn Faun 1926- AmMWSc 92
**Celauro**, Francis L AmMWSc 92
**Celaya**, Carlos S. 1946- WhoHisp 92
**Celaya**, Frank WhoAmP 91, WhoHisp 92
**Celaya**, Gabriel 1911-1991 DcLB 108 [port], NewYTBS 91
**Celaya**, Mary Susan 1962- WhoHisp 92
**Celaya**, Oscar WhoHisp 92
**Celebrezze**, Anthony J., Jr. 1941- WhoAmL 92, WhoAmP 91
**Celebrezze**, Frank D 1928- WhoAmP 91
**Celebrezze**, James P 1938- WhoAmP 91
**Celecia**, Frank John 1946- WhoWest 92
**Celedonia**, Baila Handelman 1945- WhoAmL 92
**Celender**, Ivy M 1935- AmMWSc 92
**Celentano**, Francis Michael 1928- WhoWest 92
**Celentano**, Mark Edward 1963- WhoEnt 92
**Celentino**, Luciano 1940- IntMPA 92
**Celentino**, Theodore 1938- WhoFI 92
**Celesia**, Gastone G 1933- AmMWSc 92
**Celesk**, Roger A 1949- AmMWSc 92
**Celeste**, Richard F. 1937- IntWW 91, WhoAmP 91
**Celeste**, Theodore Samuel 1945- WhoAmP 91, WhoEnt 92
**Celestin**, Papa 1884-1954 NewAmDM
**Celestin**, Robert Adrien 1959- WhoEnt 92
**Celestin**, Toussaint A. 1930- WhoBlA 92
**Celestine I** EncEarC
**Celestius** EncEarC
**Celiano**, Alfred 1928- AmMWSc 92
**Celibidache**, Sergiu 1912- FacFETw, IntWW 91, NewAmDM, Who 92, WhoEnt 92
**Celier**, Pierre 1917- IntWW 91
**Celik**, Hasan Ali AmMWSc 92
**Celine**, Louis-Ferdinand 1894-1961 BiDExR, FacFETw, GuFrLit 1, LiExTwC
**Celinski**, Olgierd J Z 1922- AmMWSc 92
**Celio**, Nello 1914- IntWW 91
**Celis**, Manuel 1944- WhoWest 92
**Celis**, Roberto T F 1930- AmMWSc 92
**Celizic**, Mike 1948- ConAu 135
**Cell**, Edward Charles 1928- IntAu&W 91, WhoMW 92, WrDr 92
**Cella**, Carl Edward 1941- WhoAmP 91
**Cella**, Frank J 1939- WhoIns 92
**Cella**, John Anthony 1926- WhoWest 92
**Cella**, Richard Joseph, Jr 1942- AmMWSc 92
**Cellan-Jones**, James 1931- IntMPA 92
**Cellan-Jones**, James Gwynne 1931- WhoEnt 92
**Cellarius**, Richard Andrew 1937- AmMWSc 92
**Celler**, Emanuel 1888-1981 DcAmImH, FacFETw
**Celler**, George K 1947- AmMWSc 92
**Celli**, Kenneth Dana 1956- WhoWest 92
**Celli**, Vittorio 1936- AmMWSc 92
**Celliers**, Peter Joubert 1920- WhoFI 92
**Cellucci**, Argeo Paul 1948- WhoAmP 91
**Celmaster**, William Noah 1950- AmMWSc 92
**Celmer**, Walter Daniel 1925- AmMWSc 92
**Celmins**, Aivars Karlis Richards 1927- AmMWSc 92
**Celmins**, Gustavs 1899-1968 BiDExR
**Celniker**, Susan Elizabeth 1954- AmMWSc 92
**Celona**, John Anthony 1953- WhoAmP 91
**Celotta**, Robert James 1943- AmMWSc 92
**Celovsky**, Joseph James 1926- WhoAmP 91
**Celsi**, Dick 1933- WhoAmP 91
**Celsius**, Anders 1701-1744 BlkwCEP
**Celsor**, Billy Frank 1924- WhoAmP 91
**Celsus** EncEarC
**Cember**, Herman 1924- AmMWSc 92
**Cembrola**, Robert John 1949- AmMWSc 92
**Cena**, Emily Geilker 1961- WhoAmL 92
**Cenac**, Winston Francis 1925- IntWW 91
**Cenarrusa**, Pete T. 1917- WhoHisp 92, WhoWest 92
**Cenarrusa**, Peter Thomas 1917- WhoAmP 91
**Cence**, Robert J 1930- AmMWSc 92
**Cenci**, Harry Joseph 1930- AmMWSc 92
**Cendali**, Dale Margaret 1959- WhoAmL 92
**Cendes**, Zoltan Joseph 1946- AmMWSc 92
**Cendrars**, Blaise ConAu 36NR
**Cendrars**, Blaise 1887-1961 FacFETw, GuFrLit 1
**Cenedella**, Richard J 1939- AmMWSc 92
**Cenerini**, Frank Joseph 1944- WhoAmP 91
**Cengel**, John Anthony 1936- AmMWSc 92
**Cengeloglu**, Yilmaz 1966- AmMWSc 92
**Ceniceros**, Joseph F. WhoHisp 92
**Ceniceros**, Kay WhoHisp 92
**Cenkl**, Bohumil 1934- AmMWSc 92
**Cenkner**, William 1930- WhoRel 92
**Cenkowski**, Stefan 1950- AmMWSc 92
**Censits**, Richard John 1937- WhoFI 92
**Censky**, Peter John 1949- WhoMW 92
**Centeio**, Jose Couto 1960- WhoAmL 92
**Centennius**, Ralph ScFEYrs
**Centeno**, Herbert Elliott 1948- WhoHisp 92
**Centeno**, Jesse 1950- WhoMW 92
**Centeno**, Martha Aixchel 1960- WhoHisp 92
**Centeno**, Miguel Angel 1957- WhoHisp 92
**Center**, Charles R. 1958- WhoAmL 92
**Center**, Elizabeth M 1928- AmMWSc 92
**Center**, Robert E 1935- AmMWSc 92
**Center**, Sharon Anne 1949- AmMWSc 92
**Centers**, Louise Claudena WhoMW 92
**Centgraf**, Damian Louis 1957- WhoEnt 92
**Centifanto**, Ysolina M 1928- AmMWSc 92
**Centkowski**, Mark 1950- WhoEnt 92
**Centlivre**, Susanna 1669?-1723 RfGEnL 91
**Centlivre**, Susannah 1667?-1723 BlkwCEP
**Centner**, Charles William 1915- WhoAmL 92, WhoMW 92
**Centner**, Rosemary Louise 1926- AmMWSc 92
**Centner**, Terence J. WhoAmL 92
**Centofanti**, Louis F 1943- AmMWSc 92
**Centola**, Grace Marie 1951- AmMWSc 92
**Centonze**, Victoria E 1958- AmMWSc 92
**Centorino**, James Joseph 1923- AmMWSc 92
**Central Africa**, Archbishop of 1935- Who 92
**Centrella**, Albert J. 1957- WhoEnt 92
**Century**, Bernard 1928- AmMWSc 92
**Cenzer**, Douglas 1947- AmMWSc 92
**Cepeda**, Joseph C. 1948- WhoHisp 92
**Cepeda**, Joseph Cherubini 1948- AmMWSc 92
**Cepeda**, Orlando Manuel Pennes 1937- WhoHisp 92
**Cepeda Garcia**, Samuel WhoAmP 91, WhoHisp 92
**Ceperley**, David Matthew 1949- AmMWSc 92
**Ceponis**, Michael John 1916- AmMWSc 92
**Ceppos**, Jerome Merle 1946- WhoFI 92, WhoWest 92
**Ceprini**, Mario Q 1925- AmMWSc 92
**Cera**, Jack WhoAmP 91
**Cera**, Lee M 1950- AmMWSc 92
**Cerami**, Anthony 1940- AmMWSc 92
**Cerankowski**, Leon Dennis 1940- AmMWSc 92
**Cerankowski**, Rosa Milagros 1949- WhoHisp 92
**Cerasano**, Susan 1953- WhoEnt 92
**Cerasoli**, Robert Angelo 1947- WhoAmP 91
**Ceraul**, David James 1955- WhoAmL 92
**Cerbon-Solorzano**, Jorge 1930- AmMWSc 92
**Cerbulis**, Janis 1913- AmMWSc 92
**Cerce**, Timothy Paul 1958- WhoRel 92
**Cercone**, Nicholas Joseph 1946- AmMWSc 92
**Cerda**, David 1927- WhoHisp 92
**Cerda**, Ernestine Castro 1943- WhoHisp 92
**Cerda**, James J 1930- AmMWSc 92
**Cerda**, Martin G. 1964- WhoHisp 92
**Cere**, Ronald Carl 1947- WhoMW 92
**Cerefice**, Steven A 1943- AmMWSc 92
**Cereghino**, James Joseph 1937- AmMWSc 92
**Cereijo**, Manuel Ramon 1938- WhoHisp 92
**Ceresia**, Richard David 1952- WhoAmL 92
**Cerezo**, Carmen Consuelo 1940- WhoAmL 92
**Cerezo Arevalo**, Mario Vinicio 1942- IntWW 91
**Cerf**, Alan Robert 1924- WhoFI 92
**Cerf**, Bennett 1898-1971 BenetAL 91, FacFETw
**Cerf**, Vinton Gray 1943- AmMWSc 92
**Cergol**, Gregory Gerard 1959- WhoEnt 92
**Cerha**, Friedrich 1926- ConCom 92, NewAmDM
**Ceriani**, Gary James 1947- WhoAmL 92
**Ceriello**, Vincent Ralph 1937- WhoFI 92
**Cerimele**, Benito Joseph 1936- AmMWSc 92, WhoFI 92
**Cerini**, Costantino Peter 1931- AmMWSc 92
**Cerini**, Kenneth Russell 1964- WhoFI 92
**Cerinthus** EncEarC
**Cerkanowicz**, Anthony Edward 1941- AmMWSc 92
**Cerkas**, Michael William 1956- WhoMW 92
**Cerklewski**, Florian Lee 1949- AmMWSc 92
**Cermak**, J E 1922- AmMWSc 92
**Cermak**, John Frank, Jr. 1956- WhoAmL 92
**Cerna**, Enrique Santiago 1953- WhoHisp 92
**Cerna-Plata**, Angela 1941- WhoHisp 92
**Cernak**, Keith Patrick 1954- WhoWest 92
**Cernan**, Eugene 1934- FacFETw
**Cernansky**, Nicholas P 1946- AmMWSc 92
**Cernek**, Jeffrey T. 1958- WhoAmL 92
**Cernera**, Anthony Joseph 1950- WhoRel 92
**Cerney**, James V 1914- IntAu&W 91
**Cerni**, Todd Andrew 1947- AmMWSc 92
**Cernica**, John N 1932- AmMWSc 92
**Cerniglia**, Mark Andrew 1954- WhoRel 92
**Cernik**, Oldrich 1921- FacFETw, IntWW 91
**Cernosek**, Stanley Frank, Jr 1940- AmMWSc 92
**Cernovitch**, Nicholas 1929- WhoEnt 92
**Cernuda**, Luis 1902-1963 LiExTwC
**Cernuda**, Luis 1904-1963 FacFETw
**Cernuda**, Ramon WhoHisp 92
**Cernuschi**, Felix 1908- AmMWSc 92
**Cerny**, Frank J 1946- AmMWSc 92
**Cerny**, Joseph, III 1936- AmMWSc 92
**Cerny**, Joseph Charles 1930- AmMWSc 92, WhoMW 92
**Cerny**, Laurence Charles 1929- AmMWSc 92
**Cerny**, Louis Thomas 1942- WhoFI 92
**Cerny**, Pavel 1946- WhoEnt 92
**Cerny**, William F, Jr WhoAmP 91
**Ceroke**, Clarence John 1921- WhoMW 92
**Cerone**, James Francis 1938- WhoMW 92
**Cerone**, Michael Anthony, Jr. 1955- WhoAmL 92
**Cerra**, Ramona Gail 1940- WhoAmP 91
**Cerra**, Robert Frank 1955- AmMWSc 92
**Cerratto**, Fernando 1939- WhoHisp 92
**Cerreta**, Kenneth Vincent 1942- AmMWSc 92
**Cerretto**, Michael Patrick 1940- WhoRel 92
**Cerria**, Philip Michael 1934- WhoAmP 91
**Cerrina**, Francesco 1948- AmMWSc 92
**Cerrito**, Oratio Alfonso 1911- WhoFI 92, WhoWest 92
**Cerro**, Ramon Luis 1941- AmMWSc 92
**Cerrone**, Jean-Baptiste d1991 NewYTBS 91
**Cerroni**, Rose E 1930- AmMWSc 92
**Cerruto**, Oscar 1912-1981 ConSpAP
**Certilman**, Steven Andrew WhoAmL 92
**Certon**, Pierre 1510?-1572 NewAmDM
**Cerullo**, Alfred C, III WhoAmP 91
**Cerullo**, Morris 1931- RelLAm 91, WhoRel 92
**Cerussi**, Michael Anthony, Jr. 1949- WhoAmL 92
**Cervantes**, Alfonso 1937- WhoHisp 92
**Cervantes**, David Michael 1955- WhoHisp 92
**Cervantes**, Donald E. WhoHisp 92
**Cervantes**, Evelio 1937- WhoHisp 92
**Cervantes**, Francisco 1938- ConSpAP
**Cervantes**, James V. DrAPF 91
**Cervantes**, Jorge Alberto 1961- WhoHisp 92
**Cervantes**, Joseph M. 1950- WhoHisp 92
**Cervantes**, Lorna Dee DrAPF 91
**Cervantes**, Lorna Dee 1954- WhoHisp 92
**Cervantes**, Magdalena WhoHisp 92
**Cervantes**, Miguel R. 1938- WhoHisp 92
**Cervantes**, Olivia WhoHisp 92
**Cervantes**, Richard E. WhoHisp 92
**Cervantes**, Salvador A. 1948- WhoHisp 92
**Cervantes de Salazar**, Francisco 1514-1575 HisDSpE
**Cervantes Sahagun**, Miguel 1959- WhoHisp 92
**Cervantez**, Pedro 1915- WhoHisp 92
**Cervella**, Albert Thomas 1935- WhoRel 92
**Cervene**, Richard T. 1927- WhoMW 92
**Cervenka**, Jaroslav 1933- AmMWSc 92
**Cervenka**, William Joseph 1931- WhoAmP 91
**Cerveny**, Caroline Jeanne 1943- WhoMW 92, WhoRel 92
**Cerveny**, Frank Stanley 1933- WhoRel 92
**Cerveny**, Thelma Jannette 1949- AmMWSc 92
**Cervi**, Dennis Paul 1943- WhoEnt 92
**Cervilla**, Constance Marlene 1951- WhoMW 92
**Cervone**, Anthony Louis 1962- WhoAmL 92
**Cervoni**, Peter 1931- AmMWSc 92
**Cervoni**, Robert Angelo 1953- WhoFI 92
**Cerwonka**, Robert Henry 1931- AmMWSc 92
**Cerwonka**, Ronald Paul 1933- WhoFI 92
**Cesaire**, Aime 1913- BenetAL 91, BlkLC [port], GuFrLit 1, LiExTwC
**Cesaire**, Aime Ferdinand 1913- FacFETw
**Cesaire**, Aime Fernand 1913- IntWW 91
**Cesar**, Francisco d1538 HisDSpE
**Cesarano**, Gregory Morgen 1946- WhoAmL 92
**Cesari**, Lamberto 1910- AmMWSc 92
**Cesario**, Robert Charles 1941- WhoMW 92
**Cesario**, Robert James 1951- WhoEnt 92
**Cescas**, Michel Pierre 1936- AmMWSc 92
**Cesena**, Alma WhoHisp 92
**Cespedes**, Carlos Manuel de 1819-1874 HisDSpE
**Cespedes**, Rogelio Miguel 1943- WhoHisp 92
**Cess**, Robert D 1933- AmMWSc 92
**Cessar**, Richard J 1928- WhoAmP 91
**Cessna**, Clyde Vernon 1879-1954 FacFETw
**Cessna**, Jay Bertram 1950- WhoAmP 91
**Cessna**, Lawrence C, Jr 1939- AmMWSc 92
**Cestari**, Constance G 1931- WhoAmP 91
**Cestero**, Herman J., Jr. 1941- WhoHisp 92
**Cesti**, Antonio 1623-1669 NewAmDM
**Ceszkowski**, Daniel David 1954- WhoFI 92
**Cetas**, Thomas Charles 1941- WhoWest 92
**Cetron**, Marvin J 1930- AmMWSc 92
**Cevallos**, Francisco Javier 1956- WhoHisp 92
**Cevallos**, Ramon Yuri 1963- WhoHisp 92
**Cevallos**, Victor Hugo 1949- WhoHisp 92
**Cevallos**, William Hernan 1932- AmMWSc 92

**Cevasco,** Albert Anthony 1940- *AmMWSc 92*
**Cevasco,** G. A. 1924- *WrDr 92*
**Ceverha,** Bill 1936- *WhoAmP 91*
**Cewang Jigmei** 1945- *IntWW 91*
**Ceylan,** Tamer 1952- *WhoMW 92*
**Ceynar,** Marvin Emil 1934- *WhoMW 92, WhoRel 92*
**Ceyrac,** Francois 1912- *IntWW 91*
**Ceysson,** Bernard 1939- *IntWW 91*
**Cezairliyan,** Ared 1934- *AmMWSc 92*
**Cezanne,** Paul 1839-1906 *ThHElm [port]*
**Cezelli,** Constance de *EncAmaz 91*
**Cha,** Dae Yang 1936- *AmMWSc 92*
**Cha,** Liang-Chien 1905- *IntWW 91*
**Cha,** Sungman 1928- *AmMWSc 92*
**Chaar,** Alfonso Lopez 1938- *WhoAmP 91*
**Chabai,** Albert John 1929- *AmMWSc 92*
**Chaban,** Lawrence Richard 1955- *WhoAmL 92*
**Chaban-Delmas,** Jacques Michel Pierre 1915- *IntWW 91*
**Chaban-Delmas,** Jacques Pierre Michel 1915- *Who 92*
**Chabaud,** Andre 1921- *IntWW 91*
**Chaberek,** Ed *DrAPF 91*
**Chabert,** Jos 1933- *IntWW 91*
**Chabert,** Leonard J 1932- *WhoAmP 91*
**Chabler,** Allan Jerome 1935- *WhoAmL 92*
**Chabner,** Bruce A *AmMWSc 92*
**Chabon,** Michael 1965- *WrDr 92*
**Chabot,** Benoit 1956- *AmMWSc 92*
**Chabot,** Brian F 1943- *AmMWSc 92*
**Chabot,** Elliot Charles 1955- *WhoAmL 92*
**Chabot,** Herbert L. 1931- *WhoAmL 92*
**Chabot,** Philip Louis, Jr. 1951- *WhoAmL 92, WhoFI 92*
**Chabot-Fence,** Dene 1932- *WhoWest 92*
**Chabran,** Richard 1950- *WhoHisp 92*
**Chabre,** Virgil *DrAPF 91*
**Chabreck,** Robert Henry 1933- *AmMWSc 92*
**Chabrier,** Emmanuel 1841-1894 *NewAmDM*
**Chabries,** Douglas M 1942- *AmMWSc 92*
**Chabrol,** Claude 1930- *FacFETw, IntDcF 2-2 [port], IntMPA 92, IntWW 91*
**Chabrow,** Penn Benjamin 1939- *WhoAmL 92*
**Chabukiani,** Vakhtang Mikhaylovich 1910- *SovUnBD*
**Chace,** Alden Buffington, Jr 1939- *AmMWSc 92*
**Chace,** Elizabeth Buffum 1806-1899 *AmPeW*
**Chace,** Fenner Albert, Jr 1908- *AmMWSc 92*
**Chace,** Frederic Mason 1906- *AmMWSc 92*
**Chace,** Isobel 1934- *WrDr 92*
**Chace,** Milton A 1934- *AmMWSc 92*
**Chace,** Nathan Ward 1940- *WhoAmL 92*
**Chace,** Rick Frederic 1945- *WhoEnt 92*
**Chacholiades,** Miltiades 1937- *WhoFI 92*
**Chackerian,** Charles, Jr 1935- *AmMWSc 92*
**Chackes,** Kenneth Michael 1949- *WhoAmL 92*
**Chacko,** George Kuttickal 1930- *AmMWSc 92, WhoFI 92*
**Chacko,** George Kutty 1933- *AmMWSc 92*
**Chacko,** Mathew Chethipurackal 1932- *WhoRel 92*
**Chacko,** Rosy J *AmMWSc 92*
**Chacko,** Samuel K 1942- *AmMWSc 92*
**Chacksfield,** Bernard 1913- *Who 92*
**Chacon,** Alicia *WhoHisp 92*
**Chacon,** Carlos R. 1959- *WhoHisp 92*
**Chacon,** Edilia Loretto 1938- *WhoWest 92*
**Chacon,** George 1953- *WhoHisp 92*
**Chacon,** Peter R. 1925- *WhoHisp 92*
**Chacon,** Peter Robert 1925- *WhoAmP 91*
**Chacon,** Rafael Van Severen 1931- *AmMWSc 92*
**Chacon,** Raul 1956- *WhoHisp 92*
**Chada,** Sharon Lynne Wachtel 1960- *WhoWest 92*
**Chadabe,** Joel 1938- *ConCom 92, NewAmDM*
**Chadbourn,** James Harmon 1853-1913 *DcNCBi 1*
**Chadbourne,** James Francis, III 1950- *WhoFI 92*
**Chadde,** Frank Ernest 1929- *AmMWSc 92*
**Chaddock,** Dennis Hilliar 1908- *Who 92*
**Chaddock,** Jack B 1924- *AmMWSc 92*
**Chaddock,** Richard E 1916- *AmMWSc 92*
**Chadenet,** Bernard 1915- *IntWW 91*
**Chader,** Gerald Joseph 1937- *AmMWSc 92*
**Chadha,** Indrajit Singh 1933- *IntWW 91*
**Chadha,** Kailash Chandra 1943- *AmMWSc 92*
**Chadi,** James D 1947- *AmMWSc 92*
**Chadick,** Gary Robert 1961- *WhoAmL 92*
**Chadick,** Stan R 1941- *AmMWSc 92*
**Chadirji,** Rifat Kamil 1926- *IntWW 91*
**Chadli,** Bendjedid 1929- *CurBio 91 [port], IntWW 91*
**Chadwell,** James Russell, Jr. 1948- *WhoFI 92*
**Chadwell,** Kurt Brian 1965- *WhoWest 92*
**Chadwell,** Susie 1940- *WhoFI 92*
**Chadwick,** Arthur Vorce 1943- *AmMWSc 92*
**Chadwick,** Bill 1915- *FacFETw*
**Chadwick,** Bruce Albert 1940- *WhoWest 92*
**Chadwick,** Bruce Michael 1946- *WhoAmL 92*
**Chadwick,** Charles McKenzie 1932- *Who 92*
**Chadwick,** Daniel Duane 1936- *WhoMW 92*
**Chadwick,** David Henry 1918- *AmMWSc 92*
**Chadwick,** Derek James 1948- *Who 92*
**Chadwick,** Don 1936- *DcTwDes*
**Chadwick,** Duane G 1925- *AmMWSc 92*
**Chadwick,** George 1854-1931 *NewAmDM*
**Chadwick,** George Brierley 1931- *AmMWSc 92*
**Chadwick,** George F 1930- *AmMWSc 92*
**Chadwick,** Gerald William St John 1915- *Who 92*
**Chadwick,** Graham Charles 1923- *Who 92*
**Chadwick,** Harold King 1930- *AmMWSc 92*
**Chadwick,** Helen 1953- *TwCPaSc*
**Chadwick,** Henry 1920- *IntWW 91, Who 92, WrDr 92*
**Chadwick,** Ina B. *DrAPF 91*
**Chadwick,** J Scot 1953- *WhoAmP 91*
**Chadwick,** James 1891-1974 *FacFETw, WhoNob 90*
**Chadwick,** John *Who 92*
**Chadwick,** John 1915- *WrDr 92*
**Chadwick,** John 1920- *IntWW 91, Who 92, WrDr 92*
**Chadwick,** John Edwin 1957- *WhoMW 92*
**Chadwick,** John Murray 1941- *Who 92*
**Chadwick,** Joseph *TwCWW 91*
**Chadwick,** Joshua Kenneth B. *Who 92*
**Chadwick,** June Stephens *AmMWSc 92*
**Chadwick,** Lester *SmATA 67*
**Chadwick,** Lynn 1914- *FacFETw, TwCPaSc*
**Chadwick,** Lynn Russell 1914- *IntWW 91, Who 92*
**Chadwick,** Michael Stephan 1951- *WhoFI 92*
**Chadwick,** Nanette Elizabeth 1959- *AmMWSc 92*
**Chadwick,** Oliver 1942- *TwCPaSc*
**Chadwick,** Owen *Who 92*
**Chadwick,** Owen 1916- *IntAu&W 91, IntWW 91, WrDr 92*
**Chadwick,** Peter 1931- *IntWW 91, Who 92*
**Chadwick,** Richard Simeon 1941- *AmMWSc 92*
**Chadwick,** Robert 1924- *WhoAmL 92*
**Chadwick,** Robert Aull 1929- *AmMWSc 92*
**Chadwick,** Robert Everard 1916- *Who 92*
**Chadwick,** Roger Parks 1963- *WhoWest 92*
**Chadwick,** Ronald Paul 1935- *WhoRel 92*
**Chadwick,** Sharon Stevens 1951- *WhoWest 92*
**Chadwick,** Wallace Lacy 1897- *AmMWSc 92*
**Chadwick,** William Frank Percival d1991 *Who 92N*
**Chadwick,** William Owen 1916- *Who 92*
**Chadwick-Jones,** John Knighton 1928- *Who 92*
**Chadwyck-Healey,** Charles 1940- *Who 92*
**Chae,** Chi-Bom 1940- *AmMWSc 92*
**Chae,** Kun 1944- *AmMWSc 92*
**Chae,** Soo Bong 1939- *AmMWSc 92*
**Chae,** Yong Suk 1930- *AmMWSc 92*
**Chae,** Yoon Kwon 1932- *WhoRel 92*
**Chae,** Young C 1932- *AmMWSc 92*
**Chaet,** Alfred Bernard 1927- *AmMWSc 92*
**Chafe,** Wallace L. 1927- *WrDr 92*
**Chafee,** John H. 1922- *AlmAP 92 [port], IntWW 91*
**Chafee,** John Hubbard 1922- *WhoAmP 91*
**Chafee,** Zechariah, Jr 1885-1957 *FacFETw*
**Chafer,** Lewis Sperry 1871-1952 *RelLAm 91*
**Chafetz,** Harry 1929- *AmMWSc 92*
**Chafetz,** Lester 1929- *AmMWSc 92*
**Chafetz,** Marc Edward 1953- *WhoAmL 92*
**Chafetz,** Morris Edward 1924- *AmMWSc 92*
**Chaffee,** Eleanor 1934- *AmMWSc 92*
**Chaffee,** Esther Ridenour *WhoRel 92*
**Chaffee,** Jerome Norton 1938- *WhoMW 92*
**Chaffee,** Maurice A 1937- *AmMWSc 92*
**Chaffee,** Maurice Ahlborn 1937- *WhoWest 92*
**Chaffee,** Paul Charles 1947- *WhoMW 92*
**Chaffee,** Roger 1935-1967 *FacFETw*
**Chaffee,** Rowand R J 1925- *AmMWSc 92*
**Chaffers,** James A. 1941- *WhoBlA 92*
**Chaffetz,** Hammond Edward 1907- *WhoAmL 92*
**Chaffey,** Charles Elswood 1941- *AmMWSc 92*
**Chaffin,** B W 1927- *WhoIns 92*
**Chaffin,** Charlie Cole 1938- *WhoAmP 91*
**Chaffin,** Don B 1939- *AmMWSc 92*
**Chaffin,** James B. *TwCWW 91*
**Chaffin,** John Craig 1955- *WhoRel 92*
**Chaffin,** Julie Eileen 1959- *WhoAmL 92*
**Chaffin,** Kenny Allen 1953- *WhoWest 92*
**Chaffin,** Roger James 1941- *AmMWSc 92*
**Chaffin,** Tommy L 1943- *AmMWSc 92*
**Chaffin-Kash,** Lillie D. *DrAPF 91*
**Chafin,** Eugene Wilder 1852-1920 *AmPolLe*
**Chafin,** H Truman 1945- *WhoAmP 91*
**Chafin,** John Michael 1950- *WhoAmP 91*
**Chafouleas,** James G 1948- *AmMWSc 92*
**Chagall,** David 1930- *IntAu&W 91*
**Chagall,** Marc 1887-1985 *FacFETw, ModArCr 2 [port], SovUnBD*
**Chaganti,** Raju Sreerama Kamalasana 1933- *AmMWSc 92*
**Chagas,** Carlos 1910- *IntWW 91*
**Chagnon,** Andre 1932- *AmMWSc 92*
**Chagnon,** Jean Yves 1934- *AmMWSc 92*
**Chagnon,** Paul Robert 1929- *AmMWSc 92*
**Chagnon,** Raymond Joseph 1954- *WhoAmP 91*
**Chagnon,** Yvette L *WhoAmP 91*
**Chagula,** Wilbert K. 1926- *IntWW 91*
**Chahine,** Moustafa Toufic 1935- *AmMWSc 92*
**Chahine,** Youssef 1926- *IntDcF 2-2, IntWW 91*
**Chai Shufan** 1905- *IntWW 91*
**Chai Zemin** 1915- *IntWW 91*
**Chai,** An-Ti 1939- *AmMWSc 92*
**Chai,** Chen Kang 1916- *AmMWSc 92*
**Chai,** Hyman 1920- *AmMWSc 92*
**Chai,** Winchung A 1939- *AmMWSc 92*
**Chaib,** Elie *WhoEnt 92*
**Chaides,** Rudy L. 1931- *WhoHisp 92*
**Chaiken,** Barry Paul 1956- *WhoFI 92*
**Chaiken,** Irwin M 1942- *AmMWSc 92*
**Chaiken,** Jan Michael 1939- *AmMWSc 92*
**Chaiken,** Paul W. 1949- *WhoAmL 92*
**Chaiken,** Robert Francis 1928- *AmMWSc 92*
**Chaikin,** Nancy *DrAPF 91*
**Chaikin,** Paul Michael 1945- *AmMWSc 92*
**Chaikin,** Philip 1948- *AmMWSc 92*
**Chaikin,** Saul William 1921- *AmMWSc 92*
**Chaikin,** Sol C. d1991 *NewYTBS 91 [port]*
**Chaikin,** Sol C. 1918-1991 *CurBio 91N*
**Chaikin,** William E. 1919- *IntMPA 92*
**Chailakhyan,** Mikhail Khristoforovich 1902- *IntWW 91*
**Chaille,** Stanford Emerson 1830-1911 *BiInAmS*
**Chailly,** Luciano 1920- *ConCom 92*
**Chailly,** Riccardo 1953- *CurBio 91 [port], IntWW 91, WhoEnt 92*
**Chaim,** Robert Alex 1947- *WhoWest 92*
**Chaimowicz,** Marc Camille 1945- *TwCPaSc*
**Chain,** Ernst Boris 1906-1979 *FacFETw, WhoNob 90*
**Chain,** Larry 1959- *WhoEnt 92*
**Chair,** Somerset de *Who 92*
**Chaires,** Jonathan Bradford 1950- *AmMWSc 92*
**Chairez,** Jesus 1953- *WhoHisp 92*
**Chais,** Pamela Herbert *DrAPF 91*
**Chaisson,** Eric Joseph 1946- *AmMWSc 92*
**Chait,** Arnold 1930- *AmMWSc 92*
**Chait,** Edward Martin 1942- *AmMWSc 92*
**Chait,** Helen Sporn 1914- *WhoAmL 92*
**Chait,** Robert Harlan 1954- *WhoMW 92*
**Chaitman,** Helen Davis 1941- *WhoAmL 92*
**Chaiyabhat,** Win 1950- *WhoMW 92*
**Chakaipa,** Patrick *Who 92*
**Chakaipa,** Patrick Fani 1932- *IntWW 91, WhoRel 92*
**Chakansky,** Michael I. 1951- *WhoAmL 92*
**Chakeres,** Michael H. *IntMPA 92*
**Chakerian,** Gulbank Donald 1933- *AmMWSc 92*
**Chakiris,** George 1934- *IntMPA 92*
**Chakkalakal,** Dennis Abraham 1939- *AmMWSc 92*
**Chakko,** Mathew K 1934- *AmMWSc 92*
**Chakko,** Sarah 1905-1954 *DcEcMov [port]*
**Chaklader,** Asoke Chandra Das 1930- *AmMWSc 92*
**Chako,** Nicholas 1910- *AmMWSc 92*
**Chakovsky,** Aleksandr Borisovich 1913- *IntWW 91, SovUnBD*
**Chakrabarti,** Chuni Lal 1920- *AmMWSc 92*
**Chakrabarti,** Paritosh M 1940- *AmMWSc 92*
**Chakrabarti,** Siba Gopal 1923- *AmMWSc 92*
**Chakrabarti,** Subrata K 1941- *AmMWSc 92*
**Chakrabarti,** Supriya 1953- *AmMWSc 92*
**Chakrabarty,** Ananda Mohan 1938- *AmMWSc 92*
**Chakrabarty,** Manoj R 1933- *AmMWSc 92*
**Chakraborty,** Jyotsna 1934- *AmMWSc 92*
**Chakraborty,** Ranajit 1946- *AmMWSc 92*
**Chakraburtty,** Kalpana *AmMWSc 92*
**Chakravarthy,** Balaji Srinivasan 1947- *WhoFI 92*
**Chakravarthy,** Srinivasaraghavan 1953- *AmMWSc 92, WhoMW 92*
**Chakravarti Rajagopalachari** 1878-1972 *FacFETw*
**Chakravarti,** Kalidas *AmMWSc 92*
**Chakravartty,** Iswar C 1935- *AmMWSc 92*
**Chakravarty,** Indranil 1954- *AmMWSc 92*
**Chakravarty,** Sukhamoy d1990 *IntWW 91N*
**Chakravorty,** S K 1922- *AmMWSc 92*
**Chakrin,** Lawrence William 1938- *AmMWSc 92*
**Chalabi,** A Fattah 1924- *AmMWSc 92*
**Chalandon,** Albin Paul Henri 1920- *IntWW 91*
**Chalberg-Plunkett,** Sherri Linell 1960- *WhoMW 92*
**Chaldecott,** John Anthony 1916- *Who 92*
**Chaleff,** Carl Thomas 1945- *WhoFI 92*
**Chalenski,** Arthur Abdon, Jr. 1943- *WhoAmL 92*
**Chalfant,** Edward Cole 1937- *WhoRel 92*
**Chalfant,** Richard Bruce 1929- *AmMWSc 92*
**Chalfie,** Martin *AmMWSc 92*
**Chalfin,** Norman Leonard 1913- *WhoWest 92*
**Chalfont,** Baron 1919- *IntWW 91, Who 92*
**Chalfont,** Lord 1919- *WrDr 92*
**Chalfont,** Alun Arthur Gwynne Jones 1919- *IntAu&W 91*
**Chalgren,** Steve Dwayne 1940- *AmMWSc 92*
**Chaliapin** *SovUnBD*
**Chaliapin,** Feodor 1873-1938 *FacFETw [port]*
**Chaliapin,** Fyodor 1873-1938 *NewAmDM*
**Chalid,** Idham *IntWW 91*
**Chalidze,** Lisa Leah 1958- *WhoAmL 92*
**Chalidze,** Valeriy Nikolayevich 1938- *IntWW 91*
**Chalif,** Seymour Hunt 1927- *WhoAmL 92*
**Chalifoux,** Alice E. 1908- *WhoEnt 92*
**Chalifoux,** Richard George 1959- *WhoAmL 92*
**Chalik,** Barbara *WhoMW 92*
**Chalk,** Gordon 1913- *Who 92*
**Chalk,** John 1922- *AmMWSc 92*
**Chalk,** Martyn 1945- *TwCPaSc*
**Chalk,** Richard E, Jr 1952- *WhoAmP 91*
**Chalk,** Russell Jay 1956- *WhoAmL 92*
**Chalk,** Warren *DcTwDes*
**Chalker,** Jack Bridger 1918- *TwCPaSc*
**Chalker,** Jack L 1944- *IntAu&W 91, TwCSFW 91, WrDr 92*
**Chalker,** James Eugene 1927- *WhoAmP 91*
**Chalker,** Kenneth Wayne 1949- *WhoMW 92, WhoRel 92*
**Chalker,** Lynda 1942- *Who 92*
**Chalker,** Mary Anne 1929- *WhoHisp 92*
**Chalker,** Ronald Franklin 1957- *WhoAmL 92*
**Chalkley,** Brian 1948- *TwCPaSc*
**Chalkley,** David Walter 1915- *Who 92*
**Chalkley,** G Roger 1939- *AmMWSc 92*
**Chalkley,** Roger 1931- *AmMWSc 92*
**Chalkley,** Thomas 1675-1741 *BenetAL 91*
**Challe,** Maurice 1905-1979 *FacFETw*
**Challem,** Jack Joseph 1950- *WhoWest 92*
**Challen,** Michael Boyd 1932- *Who 92*
**Challender,** Stuart d1991 *NewYTBS 91*
**Challenger,** James Edgar, Jr. 1956- *WhoMW 92*
**Challenger,** Michael 1942- *TwCPaSc*
**Challenor,** Herschelle 1938- *WhoBlA 92*
**Challens,** Wallace John 1915- *Who 92*
**Challice,** Cyril Eugene 1926- *AmMWSc 92*
**Challice,** Kenneth *WrDr 92*
**Challifour,** John Lee 1939- *AmMWSc 92*
**Challinor,** David 1920- *AmMWSc 92*
**Challis,** Anthony Arthur Leonard 1921- *IntWW 91, Who 92*
**Challis,** Bill 1904- *NewAmDM*
**Challis,** George *TwCWW 91*
**Challis,** John 1907-1974 *NewAmDM*
**Challis,** Margaret Joan 1917- *Who 92*
**Challis,** Simon *WrDr 92*
**Challoner,** David Reynolds 1935- *AmMWSc 92*
**Chally,** Elizabeth Lorraine Neal 1958- *WhoWest 92*
**Chalmers,** Bruce 1907- *AmMWSc 92*
**Chalmers,** Floyd Sherman 1898- *IntWW 91*
**Chalmers,** Franklin Stevens, Jr. 1928- *WhoFI 92*
**Chalmers,** Geoffrey Teale 1935- *WhoFI 92*
**Chalmers,** George Everett N. 1905- *IntWW 91*

**Chalmers,** Ian Pender 1939- *Who 92*
**Chalmers,** Jacqueline Louise 1952- *WhoWest 92*
**Chalmers,** John Harvey, Jr 1940- *AmMWSc 92*
**Chalmers,** Joseph Stephen 1938- *AmMWSc 92*
**Chalmers,** Laurie MacPherson 1950- *WhoAmP 91*
**Chalmers,** Lionel 1715-1777 *BiInAmS*
**Chalmers,** Mary 1927- *SmATA 14AS [port], WrDr 92*
**Chalmers,** Mary Eilleen 1927- *IntAu&W 91*
**Chalmers,** Neil Robert 1942- *IntWW 91, Who 92*
**Chalmers,** Patrick Edward Bruce 1939- *Who 92*
**Chalmers,** Robert Anton 1930- *AmMWSc 92*
**Chalmers,** Stephen 1880-1935 *ScFEYrs*
**Chalmers,** Thelma Faye 1947- *WhoBlA 92*
**Chalmers,** Thomas Clark 1917- *AmMWSc 92*
**Chalmers,** Thomas Wightman 1913- *Who 92*
**Chalmers,** William 1905- *AmMWSc 92*
**Chalmers,** William Gordon 1922- *Who 92*
**Chalmot,** Guillaume Louis Jacques de *BiInAmS*
**Chaloff,** Serge 1923-1957 *NewAmDM*
**Chalokwu,** Christopher Iloba 1952- *AmMWSc 92*
**Chalon,** Jon *WrDr 92*
**Chaloner** *Who 92*
**Chaloner,** John *IntAu&W 91, WrDr 92*
**Chaloner,** John Armstrong 1862-1935 *DcNCBi 1*
**Chaloner,** William Gilbert 1928- *IntWW 91, Who 92*
**Chalos,** P Pete 1927- *WhoAmP 91*
**Chaloud,** J Hoyt 1920- *AmMWSc 92*
**Chaloult,** Douglas P 1932- *WhoIns 92*
**Chaloupka,** Frank Joseph 1962- *WhoFI 92*
**Chaloux,** Maurice Eugene 1951- *WhoAmP 91*
**Chalpin,** Lila *DrAPF 91*
**Chalquest,** Richard Ross 1929- *AmMWSc 92*
**Chalstrom,** Polly Jo 1962- *WhoMW 92*
**Chalsty,** John Steele 1933- *WhoFI 92*
**Chalupa,** Leo M 1945- *AmMWSc 92*
**Chalupa,** William Victor 1937- *AmMWSc 92*
**Chalupnik,** James Dvorak 1930- *AmMWSc 92*
**Chaly,** Nathalie 1950- *AmMWSc 92*
**Chamant,** Jean 1913- *IntWW 91*
**Chamberlain,** A R 1929- *AmMWSc 92*
**Chamberlain,** Adrian Ramond 1929- *WhoWest 92*
**Chamberlain,** Alexander Francis 1865-1914 *BiInAmS*
**Chamberlain,** Austen 1863-1937 *FacFETw*
**Chamberlain,** Barbara Kaye Greene 1962- *WhoAmP 91*
**Chamberlain,** Ben Cletus 1950- *WhoFI 92*
**Chamberlain,** Brenda 1912-1971 *TwCPaSc*
**Chamberlain,** Carol Moore 1946- *WhoRel 92*
**Chamberlain,** Charles Calvin 1920- *AmMWSc 92*
**Chamberlain,** Charles Craig 1933- *AmMWSc 92*
**Chamberlain,** Charles E 1917- *WhoAmP 91*
**Chamberlain,** Christopher 1918- *TwCPaSc*
**Chamberlain,** Craig Stanley 1947- *AmMWSc 92*
**Chamberlain,** David Harold 1944- *WhoFI 92*
**Chamberlain,** David Leroy, Jr 1917- *AmMWSc 92*
**Chamberlain,** David M. 1943- *WhoWest 92*
**Chamberlain,** David Morrow 1946- *WhoRel 92*
**Chamberlain,** Dilworth Woolley 1933- *AmMWSc 92*
**Chamberlain,** Donald F 1914- *AmMWSc 92*
**Chamberlain,** Donald William 1905- *AmMWSc 92*
**Chamberlain,** Douglas W 1942- *WhoAmP 91*
**Chamberlain,** Elaine Rollwagen *DrAPF 91*
**Chamberlain,** Erling William 1934- *AmMWSc 92*
**Chamberlain,** Ernest Henry 1915- *WhoRel 92*
**Chamberlain,** G. Hope Summerell 1870-1960 *DcNCBi 1*
**Chamberlain,** Gary Lee 1938- *WhoRel 92*
**Chamberlain,** Geoffrey Victor Price 1930- *Who 92*
**Chamberlain,** George Agnew 1879-1966 *BenetAL 91*
**Chamberlain,** George Digby 1898- *Who 92*
**Chamberlain,** George Philip 1905- *Who 92*
**Chamberlain,** George Richard 1935- *IntWW 91*
**Chamberlain,** Helen Wacker 1926- *WhoAmP 91*
**Chamberlain,** Houston Stewart 1855-1927 *BiDExR, EncTR 91 [port], FacFETw*
**Chamberlain,** Jack G 1933- *AmMWSc 92*
**Chamberlain,** James Luther 1925- *AmMWSc 92*
**Chamberlain,** Jerome Patton 1929- *WhoEnt 92*
**Chamberlain,** John 1923- *AmMWSc 92*
**Chamberlain,** Joseph Austen 1863-1937 *EncTR 91 [port], WhoNob 90*
**Chamberlain,** Joseph Miles 1923- *AmMWSc 92, WhoMW 92*
**Chamberlain,** Joseph Redington 1861-1926 *DcNCBi 1*
**Chamberlain,** Joseph Wyan 1928- *AmMWSc 92, IntWW 91*
**Chamberlain,** Kent Clair *DrAPF 91*
**Chamberlain,** Kevin John 1942- *Who 92*
**Chamberlain,** Leslie Neville 1939- *Who 92*
**Chamberlain,** Marisha *DrAPF 91*
**Chamberlain,** Mark Douglas 1961- *WhoFI 92*
**Chamberlain,** Mark Steven 1954- *WhoRel 92*
**Chamberlain,** Mary 1947- *WrDr 92*
**Chamberlain,** Maurice 1934- *TwCPaSc*
**Chamberlain,** Michael Aubrey 1939- *Who 92*
**Chamberlain,** Neville *Who 92*
**Chamberlain,** Neville 1869-1940 *EncTR 91 [port], FacFETw [port]*
**Chamberlain,** Nugent Francis 1916- *AmMWSc 92*
**Chamberlain,** Owen 1920- *AmMWSc 92, FacFETw, IntWW 91, Who 92, WhoNob 90, WhoWest 92*
**Chamberlain,** Peter Edwin 1939- *Who 92*
**Chamberlain,** Phyllis Ione 1938- *AmMWSc 92*
**Chamberlain,** Reca Rene 1961- *WhoAmL 92*
**Chamberlain,** Reginald Roderic 1901- *Who 92*
**Chamberlain,** Richard *LesBEnT 92*
**Chamberlain,** Richard 1914- *Who 92*
**Chamberlain,** Richard 1935- *IntMPA 92, WhoEnt 92*
**Chamberlain,** Richard Gene 1938- *WhoAmP 91*
**Chamberlain,** Robert Glenn 1939- *AmMWSc 92*
**Chamberlain,** Roderick *Who 92*
**Chamberlain,** Ronald Lee 1941- *WhoFI 92*
**Chamberlain,** Roy William 1916- *AmMWSc 92*
**Chamberlain,** S G 1941- *AmMWSc 92*
**Chamberlain,** Scott B. 1954- *WhoAmL 92*
**Chamberlain,** Stuart Hay, Jr. 1943- *WhoEnt 92*
**Chamberlain,** Theodore *IntAu&W 91X*
**Chamberlain,** Theodore Klock 1930- *AmMWSc 92*
**Chamberlain,** Thomas Taber, Jr. 1945- *WhoAmL 92*
**Chamberlain,** Thomas Wilson, Sr 1923- *WhoAmP 91*
**Chamberlain,** Trevor 1933- *TwCPaSc*
**Chamberlain,** Virgil Ralph 1916- *WhoWest 92*
**Chamberlain,** Walter 1936- *TwCPaSc*
**Chamberlain,** Willard Thomas 1928- *WhoFI 92*
**Chamberlain,** William Edwin, Jr. 1951- *WhoWest 92*
**Chamberlain,** William Maynard 1938- *AmMWSc 92*
**Chamberlain,** William Richard Frank 1925- *Who 92*
**Chamberlain,** Wilt 1936- *FacFETw [port]*
**Chamberlain,** Wilt Norman 1936- *WhoBlA 92*
**Chamberlain-Garrington,** Elsie Dorothea d1991 *Who 92N*
**Chamberland,** Bertrand Leo 1934- *AmMWSc 92*
**Chamberlen,** Nicholas Hugh 1939- *Who 92*
**Chamberlin,** Benjamin B 1831-1888 *BiInAmS*
**Chamberlin,** Donald L 1935- *WhoAmP 91*
**Chamberlin,** Earl Martin 1914- *AmMWSc 92*
**Chamberlin,** Edward Mark 1958- *WhoWest 92*
**Chamberlin,** Edwin Phillip 1941- *AmMWSc 92*
**Chamberlin,** Elizabeth Stevens 1955- *WhoAmL 92*
**Chamberlin,** Eugene Keith 1916- *WhoWest 92*
**Chamberlin,** Harrie Rogers 1920- *AmMWSc 92*
**Chamberlin,** Herbert Charles 1932- *WhoRel 92*
**Chamberlin,** Howard Allen 1921- *AmMWSc 92*
**Chamberlin,** James C 1912- *WhoAmP 91*
**Chamberlin,** John MacMullen 1935- *AmMWSc 92*
**Chamberlin,** Mary 1914- *WrDr 92*
**Chamberlin,** Mary Ellen 1935- *WhoAmP 91*
**Chamberlin,** Michael John 1937- *AmMWSc 92*
**Chamberlin,** Michael Meade *WhoAmL 92*
**Chamberlin,** Pamela Ann 1958- *WhoAmL 92*
**Chamberlin,** Ralph Vary 1956- *AmMWSc 92*
**Chamberlin,** Richard Eliot 1923- *AmMWSc 92*
**Chamberlin,** Robert Joseph 1929- *WhoWest 92*
**Chamberlin,** Sandra L. 1960- *WhoFI 92*
**Chamberlin,** Thomas Chrowder 1843-1928 *FacFETw*
**Chamberlin,** Ward B., Jr. *LesBEnT 92*
**Chamberlin,** William Bricker, III 1943- *AmMWSc 92*
**Chambers,** Aidan 1934- *IntAu&W 91, WrDr 92*
**Chambers,** Alan Brent 1948- *WhoEnt 92*
**Chambers,** Alex A. 1934- *WhoBlA 92*
**Chambers,** Alfred Hayes 1914- *AmMWSc 92*
**Chambers,** Andrew David 1943- *Who 92*
**Chambers,** Ann Franklin 1948- *AmMWSc 92*
**Chambers,** Anne 1949- *IntAu&W 91*
**Chambers,** Barbara Mae Fromm 1940- *AmMWSc 92*
**Chambers,** Beverly Zivitski 1952- *WhoEnt 92*
**Chambers,** Carl Ellis 1946- *WhoEnt 92*
**Chambers,** Carolyn Silva 1931- *WhoWest 92*
**Chambers,** Catharine E. *WrDr 92*
**Chambers,** Charles MacKay 1941- *AmMWSc 92, WhoFI 92*
**Chambers,** Clarice Lorraine 1938- *WhoBlA 92*
**Chambers,** Clytia Montllor 1922- *WhoWest 92*
**Chambers,** Colin 1950- *ConAu 134*
**Chambers,** Craig Van 1953- *WhoRel 92*
**Chambers,** Curtis Allen 1924- *WhoRel 92*
**Chambers,** David L., III 1940- *WhoAmL 92*
**Chambers,** Derrell Lynn 1934- *AmMWSc 92*
**Chambers,** Donald A 1936- *AmMWSc 92*
**Chambers,** Donald C. 1936- *WhoBlA 92*
**Chambers,** Doris Foster 1929- *WhoBlA 92*
**Chambers,** Dorothy Rose 1941- *WhoWest 92*
**Chambers,** Douglas Robert 1929- *Who 92*
**Chambers,** Doyle 1918- *AmMWSc 92*
**Chambers,** Earl Denton 1925- *WhoIns 92*
**Chambers,** Edward Lucas 1917- *AmMWSc 92*
**Chambers,** Elizabeth 1916- *WhoRel 92*
**Chambers,** Ephraim 1680?-1740 *BlkwCEP*
**Chambers,** Ernest *WhoAmP 91*
**Chambers,** Esther Marie 1942- *WhoWest 92*
**Chambers,** Everett 1926- *IntMPA 92*
**Chambers,** F. Clayton 1960- *WhoFI 92*
**Chambers,** Frank Warman 1948- *AmMWSc 92*
**Chambers,** Fredrick 1928- *WhoBlA 92*
**Chambers,** Gary Lee 1953- *WhoAmL 92*
**Chambers,** George *DrAPF 91*
**Chambers,** George Michael 1928- *IntWW 91, Who 92*
**Chambers,** Harry, Jr. 1956- *WhoBlA 92*
**Chambers,** Harry Heyworth 1926- *Who 92*
**Chambers,** Howard Wayne 1939- *AmMWSc 92*
**Chambers,** James 1948- *WhoEnt 92*
**Chambers,** James Q 1938- *AmMWSc 92*
**Chambers,** James R. 1915- *WhoBlA 92*
**Chambers,** James Richard 1914- *AmMWSc 92*
**Chambers,** James Robert 1942- *AmMWSc 92*
**Chambers,** James Vernon 1935- *AmMWSc 92, WhoMW 92*
**Chambers,** Janice E 1947- *AmMWSc 92*
**Chambers,** Jimmie Joe 1951- *WhoRel 92*
**Chambers,** John McKinley 1941- *AmMWSc 92*
**Chambers,** John William 1929- *AmMWSc 92*
**Chambers,** Jonathan Goetz 1955- *WhoWest 92*
**Chambers,** Julius 1850-1920 *ScFEYrs*
**Chambers,** Julius LeVonne 1936- *WhoBlA 92*
**Chambers,** Kate *WrDr 92*
**Chambers,** Kathleen Camille 1947- *AmMWSc 92*
**Chambers,** Kenton Lee 1929- *AmMWSc 92*
**Chambers,** Larry William 1946- *AmMWSc 92*
**Chambers,** Lee Mason 1936- *AmMWSc 92*
**Chambers,** Leigh Ross 1932- *IntWW 91*
**Chambers,** Lenoir 1891-1970 *DcNCBi 1*
**Chambers,** Linda *WhoAmP 91*
**Chambers,** Lois Irene 1935- *WhoFI 92, WhoWest 92*
**Chambers,** Madrith Bennett 1935- *WhoBlA 92*
**Chambers,** Margaret Warner 1959- *WhoAmL 92*
**Chambers,** Mary Peyton 1931- *WhoAmP 91*
**Chambers,** Maxwell 1780-1855 *DcNCBi 1*
**Chambers,** Michael Joseph 1944- *WhoMW 92*
**Chambers,** Nicholas Mordaunt 1944- *Who 92*
**Chambers,** Olivia Marie 1942- *WhoBlA 92*
**Chambers,** Ollie F. 1943- *WhoMW 92*
**Chambers,** Pamela S. 1961- *WhoBlA 92*
**Chambers,** Peter 1924- *WrDr 92*
**Chambers,** Peter R. 1953- *WhoWest 92*
**Chambers,** R 1802-1871 *DcLB 106 [port]*
**Chambers,** R 1917- *IntAu&W 91*
**Chambers,** Ralph Arnold 1933- *AmMWSc 92*
**Chambers,** Ray Benjamin 1940- *WhoAmP 91*
**Chambers,** Richard 1923- *AmMWSc 92*
**Chambers,** Richard Lee 1947- *AmMWSc 92*
**Chambers,** Robert Alexander H. *Who 92*
**Chambers,** Robert Arthur 1946- *WhoEnt 92*
**Chambers,** Robert Ben 1949- *WhoRel 92*
**Chambers,** Robert C 1952- *WhoAmP 91*
**Chambers,** Robert Eugene 1910- *WhoAmP 91*
**Chambers,** Robert Guy 1924- *Who 92*
**Chambers,** Robert J 1930- *AmMWSc 92*
**Chambers,** Robert Rood 1923- *AmMWSc 92*
**Chambers,** Robert W. 1865-1933 *BenetAL 91, ScFEYrs, TwCLC 41 [port]*
**Chambers,** Robert Warner 1924- *AmMWSc 92*
**Chambers,** Robert William 1943- *WhoFI 92*
**Chambers,** Roberta Nadine 1924- *WhoEnt 92*
**Chambers,** Russell Raymond 1948- *WhoEnt 92*
**Chambers,** Ruth-Marie Frances 1953- *WhoBlA 92*
**Chambers,** Stephen 1960- *TwCPaSc*
**Chambers,** Stephen L. 1956- *WhoWest 92*
**Chambers,** Thomas Doane 1959- *WhoWest 92*
**Chambers,** Timothy Lachlan 1946- *Who 92*
**Chambers,** Vactor Tousey 1830-1883 *BiInAmS*
**Chambers,** Vaughan Crandall 1925- *AmMWSc 92*
**Chambers,** Virgina Ellen 1927- *WhoWest 92*
**Chambers,** Virginia Anne 1931- *WhoEnt 92*
**Chambers,** W 1800-1883 *DcLB 106 [port]*
**Chambers,** Wendy Mae 1953- *WhoEnt 92*
**Chambers,** Whittaker *FacFETw*
**Chambers,** Wilbert Franklin 1923- *AmMWSc 92*
**Chambers,** William 1723-1796 *BlkwCEP*
**Chambers,** William Douglas 1945- *WhoMW 92*
**Chambers,** William Edward 1933- *AmMWSc 92*
**Chambers,** William Everett 1931- *WhoMW 92*
**Chambers,** William Hyland 1922- *AmMWSc 92*
**Chambers,** YJean S. 1921- *WhoBlA 92*
**Chambers-Meyers,** Tressa 1942- *WhoWest 92*
**Chamblee,** Andrea Ellen 1961- *WhoAmL 92*
**Chamblee,** Carl 1933- *WhoAmP 91*
**Chamblee,** Cebron Daniel 1928- *WhoAmP 91*
**Chamblee,** Douglas Scales 1921- *AmMWSc 92*
**Chamblee,** John James, Jr. 1949- *WhoAmL 92*
**Chambless,** Thomas Sidney 1943- *WhoAmP 91*
**Chamblin,** Steven Kyle 1959- *WhoRel 92*
**Chambliss,** Carlson Rollin 1941- *AmMWSc 92*
**Chambliss,** Chris 1948- *WhoBlA 92*
**Chambliss,** Glenn Hilton 1942- *AmMWSc 92, WhoMW 92*
**Chambliss,** Ida Belle 1935- *WhoBlA 92*
**Chambliss,** Joe Preston 1947- *WhoFI 92*
**Chambliss,** Keith Wayne 1926- *AmMWSc 92*

**Chambliss**, Oyette Lavaughn 1936- *AmMWSc 92*
**Chambonnieres**, Jacques Champion 1601?-1672 *NewAmDM*
**Chambre**, Paul L 1918- *AmMWSc 92*
**Chameides**, Steven B. 1946- *WhoAmL 92*
**Chameides**, William Lloyd 1949- *AmMWSc 92*
**Chamfort**, Sebastien-Roch-Nicolas 1741-1794 *BlkwCEP*
**Chamier**, Anthony Edward Deschamps 1935- *Who 92*
**Chaminade**, Cecile 1857-1944 *FacFETw, NewAmDM*
**Chamis**, Alice Yanosko *AmMWSc 92*
**Chamis**, Christos Constantinos 1930- *AmMWSc 92*
**Chamness**, Rodney Allen 1961- *WhoAmL 92*
**Chamorro**, Violeta Barrios de *IntWW 91*
**Chamorro**, Violeta Barrios de 1930- *FacFETw*
**Chamot**, Dennis 1943- *AmMWSc 92*
**Chamoun**, Camille Nimer 1900-1987 *FacFETw*
**Chamoux**, Francois *IntWW 91*
**Chamoy**, Lewis 1946- *WhoMW 92*
**Champ**, Norman Barnard, Jr 1928- *WhoAmP 91, WhoFI 92*
**Champ**, Stanley Gordon 1919- *WhoWest 92*
**Champa**, Rudolph Allen 1945- *WhoWest 92*
**Champagne**, Andree 1939- *IntWW 91*
**Champagne**, Claude 1891-1965 *NewAmDM*
**Champagne**, Claude P 1953- *AmMWSc 92*
**Champagne**, Gayle Lynn 1950- *WhoMW 92*
**Champagne**, Jocelyne D 1942- *WhoAmP 91*
**Champagne**, John *DrAPF 91*
**Champagne**, Norman E 1941- *WhoAmP 91*
**Champagne**, Paul Ernest 1946- *AmMWSc 92*
**Champagne**, Richard L 1926- *WhoAmP 91*
**Champe**, Pamela Chambers 1945- *AmMWSc 92*
**Champe**, Sewell Preston 1932- *AmMWSc 92*
**Champeny**, Susan Jean 1957- *WhoEnt 92*
**Champernowne**, David 1912- *WrDr 92*
**Champernowne**, David Gawen 1912- *Who 92*
**Champfleury** 1821-1889 *GuFrLit 1*
**Champfleury**, Jules Husson 1821-1889 *ThHEIm*
**Champie**, Ellmore Alfred 1916- *WhoWest 92*
**Champine**, Dennis *WhoAmP 91*
**Champine**, George Allen 1934- *AmMWSc 92*
**Champion**, Andrew 1966- *TwCPaSc*
**Champion**, Gower 1919-1980 *FacFETw*
**Champion**, Hale 1922- *WhoAmP 91*
**Champion**, Jacques *NewAmDM*
**Champion**, James A. 1947- *WhoBlA 92*
**Champion**, Jerrye G. 1940- *WhoBlA 92*
**Champion**, Jesse 1927- *WhoBlA 92*
**Champion**, John C. 1923- *IntMPA 92*
**Champion**, John Carr 1923- *WhoEnt 92*
**Champion**, John Stuart 1921- *Who 92*
**Champion**, Kenneth Stanley Warner 1923- *AmMWSc 92*
**Champion**, Larry S. 1932- *WrDr 92*
**Champion**, Larry Stephen 1932- *IntAu&W 91*
**Champion**, Marge *FacFETw*
**Champion**, Marge 1923- *IntMPA 92, WhoEnt 92, WhoWest 92*
**Champion**, Paul Morris 1946- *AmMWSc 92*
**Champion**, Richard Gordon 1931- *WhoRel 92*
**Champion**, Tempii Bridgene 1961- *WhoBlA 92*
**Champion**, William 1930- *AmMWSc 92*
**Champkin**, Peter 1918- *WrDr 92*
**Champlain**, Samuel de 1567?-1635 *BenetAL 91*
**Champlin**, Arthur Kingsley 1938- *AmMWSc 92*
**Champlin**, Charles Davenport 1926- *IntAu&W 91, WhoEnt 92*
**Champlin**, Joseph M. 1930- *WrDr 92*
**Champlin**, Keith S 1930- *AmMWSc 92*
**Champlin**, Robert L 1930- *AmMWSc 92*
**Champlin**, Tim 1937- *TwCWW 91, WrDr 92*
**Champlin**, William G 1923- *AmMWSc 92*
**Champness**, Clifford Harry 1926- *AmMWSc 92*
**Champness**, R. J. 1933- *WhoFI 92*
**Champney**, Don 1927- *WhoMW 92*
**Champney**, William Scott 1943- *AmMWSc 92*
**Champoux**, Michael Francis 1962- *WhoAmP 91*
**Chamson**, Andre 1900-1983 *GuFrLit 1*
**Chan**, Agnes Isabel 1917- *WhoAmP 91*
**Chan**, Albert Sun Chi 1950- *AmMWSc 92*
**Chan**, Allen Fong 1957- *WhoWest 92*
**Chan**, Anthony Kaikwong 1954- *WhoEnt 92*
**Chan**, Arthur Wing Kay 1941- *AmMWSc 92*
**Chan**, Bertram Kim Cheong 1937- *AmMWSc 92*
**Chan**, Bock G 1935- *AmMWSc 92*
**Chan**, Carlyle Hung-lun 1949- *WhoMW 92*
**Chan**, Chiu Yeung 1941- *AmMWSc 92*
**Chan**, Cho-chak John 1943- *Who 92*
**Chan**, Chun Kin 1953- *AmMWSc 92*
**Chan**, Chung 1956- *WhoFI 92*
**Chan**, Curtis Joseph 1953- *WhoEnt 92*
**Chan**, Daniel Chung-Yin 1948- *WhoAmL 92*
**Chan**, Daniel Wan-Yui 1949- *AmMWSc 92*
**Chan**, David S 1940- *AmMWSc 92*
**Chan**, Eddie Chin Sun 1931- *AmMWSc 92*
**Chan**, Edward Ming 1957- *WhoMW 92*
**Chan**, Eliza Y. *WhoEnt 92*
**Chan**, Florentius 1953- *WhoWest 92*
**Chan**, Gary Mannerstedt 1947- *AmMWSc 92*
**Chan**, Hak-Foon 1942- *AmMWSc 92*
**Chan**, Harvey Thomas, Jr 1940- *AmMWSc 92*
**Chan**, Heng Chee 1942- *IntWW 91*
**Chan**, Jack-Kang 1950- *AmMWSc 92*
**Chan**, Jackie 1955?- *ConTFT 9*
**Chan**, James C 1937- *AmMWSc 92*
**Chan**, James C M 1937- *AmMWSc 92*
**Chan**, Jean B 1937- *AmMWSc 92*
**Chan**, Jeffery Paul *DrAPF 91*
**Chan**, Jerry Kum Nam 1960- *WhoWest 92*
**Chan**, John Yeuk-hon 1947- *AmMWSc 92*
**Chan**, Julius 1939- *IntWW 91, Who 92*
**Chan**, Ka-Kong *AmMWSc 92*
**Chan**, Kai Chiu 1934- *AmMWSc 92*
**Chan**, Kenneth Kin-Hing 1940- *AmMWSc 92*
**Chan**, Kwing Lam 1949- *AmMWSc 92*
**Chan**, Kwok-chi Dominic 1946- *AmMWSc 92*
**Chan**, Kwoklong Roland 1933- *AmMWSc 92*
**Chan**, Lai Kow 1940- *AmMWSc 92*
**Chan**, Laurence Kwong-fai 1947- *AmMWSc 92*
**Chan**, Lawrence Chin Bong 1942- *AmMWSc 92*
**Chan**, Lee-Nien Lillian 1941- *AmMWSc 92*
**Chan**, Loren Briggs 1943- *WhoWest 92*
**Chan**, Mabel M 1948- *AmMWSc 92*
**Chan**, Maureen Gillen 1939- *AmMWSc 92*
**Chan**, Michael Chiu-Hon 1961- *WhoWest 92*
**Chan**, Moses Hung-Wai 1946- *AmMWSc 92*
**Chan**, Nai Keong 1931- *Who 92*
**Chan**, Nolan Garrett 1937- *WhoWest 92*
**Chan**, Paul C 1936- *AmMWSc 92*
**Chan**, Peter Sinchun 1938- *AmMWSc 92*
**Chan**, Peter Wing Kwong 1949- *WhoWest 92*
**Chan**, Phillip C 1928- *AmMWSc 92*
**Chan**, Ping-Kwong 1949- *AmMWSc 92*
**Chan**, Po Chuen 1935- *AmMWSc 92*
**Chan**, Pui-Kwong *AmMWSc 92*
**Chan**, Raymond Kai-Chow 1933- *AmMWSc 92*
**Chan**, Richard Y. D. 1954- *WhoWest 92*
**Chan**, Robin Yau-Hing 1932- *WhoFI 92*
**Chan**, Sai-Kit 1941- *AmMWSc 92*
**Chan**, Samuel H P 1941- *AmMWSc 92*
**Chan**, Sek Kwan 1944- *AmMWSc 92*
**Chan**, Sham-Yuen *AmMWSc 92*
**Chan**, Shi-Kit 1960- *WhoMW 92*
**Chan**, Shih Hung 1943- *AmMWSc 92*
**Chan**, Shu Fun 1939- *AmMWSc 92*
**Chan**, Shu-Gar 1927- *AmMWSc 92*
**Chan**, Shu-Park 1929- *AmMWSc 92*
**Chan**, Shung Kai 1935- *AmMWSc 92*
**Chan**, Silas Cheng-Yi 1940- *WhoRel 92*
**Chan**, Siu-Kee 1936- *AmMWSc 92*
**Chan**, Stephen 1942- *AmMWSc 92*
**Chan**, Sunney Ignatius 1936- *AmMWSc 92*
**Chan**, Tak-Hang 1941- *AmMWSc 92*
**Chan**, Tat-Hung 1951- *AmMWSc 92*
**Chan**, Teh-Sheng *AmMWSc 92*
**Chan**, Tim Tin 1937- *WhoWest 92*
**Chan**, Timothy M 1939- *AmMWSc 92*
**Chan**, Tony Chi-Hung 1954- *WhoWest 92*
**Chan**, Vincent Sikhung 1949- *AmMWSc 92*
**Chan**, W Y 1932- *AmMWSc 92*
**Chan**, Wah Chun 1934- *AmMWSc 92*
**Chan**, Wai-Yee 1950- *AmMWSc 92*
**Chan**, William Hsiao-Lien 1939- *WhoFI 92*
**Chan**, Wing Cheng Raymond 1936- *AmMWSc 92*
**Chan**, Yat Yung 1936- *AmMWSc 92*
**Chan**, Yick-Kwong 1935- *AmMWSc 92*
**Chan**, Yun Lai 1941- *AmMWSc 92*
**Chan**, Yupo *AmMWSc 92*
**Chanak**, Adam George Steven 1954- *WhoAmL 92*
**Chanan**, Michael 1946- *WrDr 92*
**Chanana**, Arjun Dev 1930- *AmMWSc 92*
**Chanani**, Madhu Sudan 1952- *WhoWest 92*
**Chance**, Britton 1913- *AmMWSc 92, FacFETw, IntWW 91*
**Chance**, Charles 1936- *WhoIns 92*
**Chance**, Charles Jackson 1914- *AmMWSc 92*
**Chance**, Dudley Raymond 1916- *Who 92*
**Chance**, George A, Jr 1918- *WhoAmP 91*
**Chance**, Hugh E. 1911- *WhoRel 92*
**Chance**, James Bradley 1954- *WhoRel 92*
**Chance**, James William 1938- *WhoFI 92*
**Chance**, Jane *DrAPF 91*
**Chance**, Janet 1885-1953 *BiDBrF 2*
**Chance**, Jean Carver 1938- *WhoAmP 91*
**Chance**, Jeremy 1926- *Who 92*
**Chance**, John T. *ConAu 134*
**Chance**, Kelly Van 1947- *AmMWSc 92*
**Chance**, Kenneth Bernard 1953- *AmMWSc 92, WhoBlA 92*
**Chance**, Michael Spencer 1938- *Who 92*
**Chance**, Robert L 1924- *AmMWSc 92*
**Chance**, Ronald E 1934- *AmMWSc 92*
**Chance**, Ronald Richard 1947- *AmMWSc 92*
**Chance**, Stephen *IntAu&W 91X, WrDr 92*
**Chance**, William Claudius, Sr. 1880-1970 *DcNCBi 1*
**Chancellor**, Alexander Surtees 1940- *IntAu&W 91, IntWW 91, Who 92*
**Chancellor**, Carl Eugene 1929- *WhoBlA 92*
**Chancellor**, Christopher John 1904-1989 *FacFETw*
**Chancellor**, J W 1876- *ScFEYrs*
**Chancellor**, John *LesBEnT 92 [port]*
**Chancellor**, John 1927- *IntAu&W 91, IntMPA 92, IntWW 91, WrDr 92*
**Chancellor**, Robert Tearle 1936- *WhoEnt 92*
**Chancey**, C Ray 1914- *WhoAmP 91*
**Chancey**, Dudley H. *WhoRel 92*
**Chancey**, Edmund d1677? *DcNCBi 1*
**Chancy**, Edmund d1677? *DcNCBi 1*
**Chand Bibi** *EncAmaz 91*
**Chand**, Naresh *AmMWSc 92*
**Chand**, Naresh 1951- *AmMWSc 92*
**Chanda**, Alec 1962- *TwCPaSc*
**Chandan**, Harish Chandra *AmMWSc 92*
**Chandan**, Ramesh Chandra 1934- *AmMWSc 92, WhoMW 92*
**Chandavarkar**, Anand Gopalkrishna 1925- *WhoFI 92*
**Chandavimol**, Abhai 1908- *IntWW 91*
**Chander**, Jagdish 1933- *AmMWSc 92*
**Chander**, Satish 1937- *AmMWSc 92*
**Chandernagor**, Andre 1921- *IntWW 91*
**Chandler**, A. B. 1898-1991 *CurBio 91N, NewYTBS 91 [port]*
**Chandler**, A Bertram 1912-1984 *TwCSFW 91*
**Chandler**, A Bleakley 1926- *AmMWSc 92*
**Chandler**, A. Lee 1922- *WhoAmL 92, WhoAmP 91*
**Chandler**, Adele Rico 1923- *WhoHisp 92*
**Chandler**, Albert Benjamin 1898- *FacFETw*
**Chandler**, Albert Morrell 1932- *AmMWSc 92*
**Chandler**, Alfred D., Jr. 1918- *WrDr 92*
**Chandler**, Allen Eugene 1935- *WhoBlA 92*
**Chandler**, Alton H. 1942- *WhoBlA 92*
**Chandler**, Arthur Cecil, Jr 1933- *AmMWSc 92*
**Chandler**, Brian Keith 1960- *WhoRel 92*
**Chandler**, Bruce Frederick 1926- *WhoWest 92*
**Chandler**, Burton 1934- *WhoAmL 92*
**Chandler**, Caleb J 1943- *WhoAmP 91*
**Chandler**, Carl Davis, Jr 1944- *AmMWSc 92*
**Chandler**, Carmen Ramos 1963- *WhoHisp 92*
**Chandler**, Chan 1960- *WhoEnt 92*
**Chandler**, Charles H 1918- *AmMWSc 92*
**Chandler**, Charles Henry 1840-1912 *BiInAmS*
**Chandler**, Charles Howard 1935- *WhoRel 92*
**Chandler**, Chris 1951- *WhoAmP 91*
**Chandler**, Clay Morris 1927- *AmMWSc 92*
**Chandler**, Colby H. 1925- *IntWW 91*
**Chandler**, Colin 1939- *Who 92*
**Chandler**, Colston 1939- *AmMWSc 92*
**Chandler**, Dana C., Jr. 1941- *WhoBlA 92*
**Chandler**, David 1934- *IntAu&W 91, WrDr 92*
**Chandler**, David 1944- *AmMWSc 92*
**Chandler**, Dean Wesley 1944- *AmMWSc 92*
**Chandler**, Debra Janet 1957- *WhoEnt 92*
**Chandler**, Dennis Courtland 1893- *WhoBlA 92*
**Chandler**, Denvil Ford, II 1954- *WhoEnt 92*
**Chandler**, Donald Ernest 1925- *AmMWSc 92*
**Chandler**, Donald Stewart 1949- *AmMWSc 92*
**Chandler**, Dorothy Buffum *WhoWest 92*
**Chandler**, Douglas Edwin 1945- *AmMWSc 92, WhoWest 92*
**Chandler**, Earle W 1913- *WhoAmP 91*
**Chandler**, Ed 1950- *WhoEnt 92*
**Chandler**, Edward William 1953- *WhoWest 92*
**Chandler**, Edwin George 1914- *Who 92*
**Chandler**, Edwin Russell 1932- *WhoRel 92*
**Chandler**, Effie L. 1927- *WhoBlA 92*
**Chandler**, Eileen 1904- *TwCPaSc*
**Chandler**, Everett A. 1926- *WhoBlA 92*
**Chandler**, Francis Woodrow, Jr 1943- *AmMWSc 92*
**Chandler**, Frank *WrDr 92*
**Chandler**, Frederick William 1938- *AmMWSc 92*
**Chandler**, Gary *WhoAmP 91*
**Chandler**, Gene Giles 1947- *WhoAmP 91*
**Chandler**, Geoffrey 1922- *Who 92*
**Chandler**, George 1915- *IntAu&W 91, IntWW 91, Who 92, WrDr 92*
**Chandler**, George Francis, III 1940- *WhoAmL 92*
**Chandler**, Harold R. 1941- *WhoBlA 92*
**Chandler**, Horace W 1927- *AmMWSc 92*
**Chandler**, J. King, III *WhoBlA 92*
**Chandler**, J Ryan 1923- *AmMWSc 92*
**Chandler**, James A 1931- *WhoAmP 91*
**Chandler**, James Barton 1922- *IntWW 91, WhoMW 92*
**Chandler**, James Harry, III 1950- *AmMWSc 92*
**Chandler**, James Michael 1943- *AmMWSc 92*
**Chandler**, James P. 1938- *WhoBlA 92*
**Chandler**, Janet Carncross *DrAPF 91*
**Chandler**, Jasper S 1911- *AmMWSc 92*
**Chandler**, Jerry LeRoy 1940- *AmMWSc 92*
**Chandler**, John Brandon, Jr. 1939- *WhoAmL 92*
**Chandler**, John C. 1946- *WhoWest 92*
**Chandler**, John Edward 1927- *WhoRel 92*
**Chandler**, John Edward 1941- *AmMWSc 92*
**Chandler**, John P a, Jr 1911- *WhoAmP 91*
**Chandler**, John Preston 1961- *WhoRel 92*
**Chandler**, Joyce A. *DrAPF 91*
**Chandler**, Karyln Dorothy 1943- *WhoFI 92*
**Chandler**, Kent, Jr. 1920- *WhoAmL 92*
**Chandler**, Kristian 1948- *WhoWest 92*
**Chandler**, Lawrence Bradford, Jr. 1942- *WhoAmL 92*
**Chandler**, Louis 1922- *AmMWSc 92*
**Chandler**, Malcolm Arthur 1923- *WhoAmL 92*
**Chandler**, Margaret K. d1991 *NewYTBS 91*
**Chandler**, Mark *WrDr 92*
**Chandler**, Mark Joseph 1956- *WhoWest 92*
**Chandler**, Mittie Olion 1949- *WhoBlA 92*
**Chandler**, Nancy Ann 1933- *WhoAmP 91*
**Chandler**, Otis 1927- *IntAu&W 91, IntWW 91, WhoWest 92*
**Chandler**, Raymond 1888-1959 *BenetAL 91, FacFETw*
**Chandler**, Reginald Frank 1941- *AmMWSc 92*
**Chandler**, Rex W 1937- *WhoAmP 91*
**Chandler**, Richard Edward 1937- *AmMWSc 92*
**Chandler**, Robert *LesBEnT 92*
**Chandler**, Robert Flint, Jr 1907- *AmMWSc 92*
**Chandler**, Robert Leslie 1948- *WhoFI 92*
**Chandler**, Robert Walter 1932- *AmMWSc 92*
**Chandler**, Rod 1942- *AlmAP 92 [port]*
**Chandler**, Rod Dennis 1942- *WhoAmP 91, WhoWest 92*
**Chandler**, Roger Eugene 1934- *AmMWSc 92*
**Chandler**, Ronald Jay 1949- *WhoAmL 92*
**Chandler**, Rory Wayne 1959- *WhoBlA 92*
**Chandler**, S. Bernard 1921- *WrDr 92*
**Chandler**, Sandra 1955- *WhoEnt 92*
**Chandler**, Seth Carlo 1846-1913 *BiInAmS*
**Chandler**, Stephen James 1949- *WhoFI 92*
**Chandler**, Tertius 1915- *WhoWest 92, WrDr 92*
**Chandler**, Theodore Alan 1949- *WhoBlA 92*
**Chandler**, Theodore Arthur 1932- *WhoMW 92*
**Chandler**, Thomas Franklin 1947- *WhoWest 92*
**Chandler**, Thomas Henderson 1824?-1895 *BiInAmS*
**Chandler**, Tom *DrAPF 91*
**Chandler**, Tony John 1928- *Who 92*

**Chandler,** Wallace Lee 1926- *WhoFI 92*
**Chandler,** Wesley Sandy 1956- *WhoBlA 92*
**Chandler,** William David 1940- *AmMWSc 92*
**Chandler,** William Everett 1943- *WhoFI 92*
**Chandler,** William Henry 1841-1906 *BiInAmS*
**Chandler,** William Knox 1933- *AmMWSc 92*
**Chandler,** Willis Thomas 1923- *AmMWSc 92*
**Chandley,** Katherine Ragsdale 1937- *WhoAmP 91*
**Chandley,** Peter Warren 1934- *Who 92*
**Chandonnet,** Ann Fox *DrAPF 91*
**Chandonnet,** Ann Fox 1943- *WhoWest 92*
**Chandos,** Viscount 1953- *Who 92*
**Chandos,** Fay *ConAu 34NR*
**Chandos-Pole,** John 1909- *Who 92*
**Chandos-Pole,** John Walkelyne 1913- *Who 92*
**Chandra,** Abhijit 1957- *AmMWSc 92, WhoWest 92*
**Chandra,** Avinash 1931- *IntWW 91*
**Chandra,** Dhanesh 1944- *AmMWSc 92*
**Chandra,** G Ram 1933- *AmMWSc 92*
**Chandra,** Grish 1939- *AmMWSc 92*
**Chandra,** Jagdish 1935- *AmMWSc 92*
**Chandra,** Kailash 1938- *AmMWSc 92*
**Chandra,** Pradeep 1944- *AmMWSc 92*
**Chandra,** Purna 1929- *AmMWSc 92*
**Chandra,** Ramesh 1925- *IntWW 91*
**Chandra,** Satish 1917- *IntWW 91*
**Chandra,** Suresh 1939- *AmMWSc 92*
**Chandra,** Sushil 1931- *AmMWSc 92*
**Chandra Shekhar,** N. L. 1927- *IntWW 91*
**Chandrachud,** Yeshwant Vishnu 1920- *IntWW 91, Who 92*
**Chandramouli,** Ramamurti 1947- *WhoWest 92*
**Chandran,** Joshua Russell 1918- *DcEcMov*
**Chandran,** Krishnan Bala 1944- *AmMWSc 92*
**Chandran,** Satish Raman 1938- *AmMWSc 92*
**Chandran,** V Ravi 1955- *AmMWSc 92*
**Chandrasekaran,** Balakrishnan 1942- *AmMWSc 92*
**Chandrasekaran,** Perinkolam Raman 1949- *WhoFI 92*
**Chandrasekaran,** Santosh Kumar *AmMWSc 92*
**Chandrasekhar,** B S 1928- *AmMWSc 92*
**Chandrasekhar,** Bhagwat Subrahmanya 1945- *IntWW 91*
**Chandrasekhar,** Prasanna 1957- *AmMWSc 92*
**Chandrasekhar,** S *AmMWSc 92*
**Chandrasekhar,** Sivaramakrishna 1930- *IntWW 91, Who 92*
**Chandrasekhar,** Sripati 1918- *IntWW 91*
**Chandrasekhar,** Subrahmanyan 1910- *AmMWSc 92, FacFETw, IntWW 91, Who 92, WhoMW 92, WhoNob 90, WrDr 92*
**Chandrasekharan,** Komaravolu 1920- *IntWW 91*
**Chandrashekar,** Muthu 1947- *AmMWSc 92*
**Chandross,** Edwin A 1934- *AmMWSc 92*
**Chandross,** Ronald Jay 1935- *AmMWSc 92*
**Chandy,** Kanianthra Thomas 1913- *IntWW 91*
**Chanel,** Gabrielle 1883-1971 *DcTwDes, FacFETw [port]*
**Chanen,** Franklin Allen 1933- *WhoAmL 92*
**Chanen,** Steven Robert 1953- *WhoAmL 92, WhoEnt 92*
**Chanes,** Jerome Alan 1943- *WhoRel 92*
**Chaney,** Albert Andrew 1954- *WhoRel 92*
**Chaney,** Albion Henry 1921- *WhoRel 92*
**Chaney,** Allan Harold 1923- *AmMWSc 92*
**Chaney,** Campbell Kent 1959- *WhoFI 92*
**Chaney,** Charles Lester 1930- *AmMWSc 92*
**Chaney,** Dale Rex 1955- *WhoEnt 92*
**Chaney,** David Webb 1915- *AmMWSc 92*
**Chaney,** Don 1946- *WhoBlA 92*
**Chaney,** Frederick 1914- *Who 92*
**Chaney,** Frederick Bennett 1936- *WhoWest 92*
**Chaney,** Frederick Michael 1941- *IntWW 91*
**Chaney,** George L 1930- *AmMWSc 92*
**Chaney,** J M *ScFEYrs*
**Chaney,** Jill 1932- *WrDr 92*
**Chaney,** John *WhoBlA 92*
**Chaney,** Lenore *ScFEYrs*
**Chaney,** Lon 1883-1930 *FacFETw [port]*
**Chaney,** Robert Bruce, Jr 1932- *AmMWSc 92*
**Chaney,** Robert Eugene 1957- *WhoFI 92*
**Chaney,** Robert Galen 1913- *WhoRel 92*
**Chaney,** Robert Wayne 1947- *WhoMW 92*
**Chaney,** Robin W 1938- *AmMWSc 92*
**Chaney,** Stephen Gifford 1944- *AmMWSc 92*
**Chaney,** William R 1941- *AmMWSc 92*
**Chaney-LeBlanc,** Michelle Marie 1950- *WhoEnt 92*
**Chang Chieh** *ConAu 133*
**Chang Chien** *ConAu 133*
**Chang Chongxuan** 1931- *IntWW 91*
**Chang Do Yung** 1923- *IntWW 91*
**Chang Feng-Hsu** 1928- *IntWW 91*
**Chang Jiong** 1917- *IntWW 91*
**Chang King-Yuh** 1937- *IntWW 91*
**Chang Lifu** 1912- *IntWW 91*
**Chang Shana** 1931- *IntWW 91*
**Chang Shuhong** 1905- *IntWW 91*
**Chang Xiangyu** 1921- *IntWW 91*
**Chang,** Albert Yen 1936- *AmMWSc 92*
**Chang,** Alfred Tieh-Chun 1942- *AmMWSc 92*
**Chang,** Amos Ih-Tiao 1916- *WhoMW 92*
**Chang,** Amy Y *AmMWSc 92*
**Chang,** Anthony Kai Ung 1944- *WhoAmP 91, WhoWest 92*
**Chang,** Betty *AmMWSc 92*
**Chang,** Bomshik 1931- *AmMWSc 92*
**Chang,** Bunwoo Bertram 1947- *AmMWSc 92*
**Chang,** C Hsiung 1956- *AmMWSc 92*
**Chang,** C. Yul 1934- *WhoFI 92*
**Chang,** Catherine Teh-Lin *AmMWSc 92*
**Chang,** Chae Han Joseph 1929- *AmMWSc 92*
**Chang,** Charles Hung 1924- *AmMWSc 92*
**Chang,** Charles Shing 1940- *WhoWest 92*
**Chang,** Charles Yu-Chun 1941- *AmMWSc 92*
**Chang,** Chawnshang 1955- *WhoMW 92*
**Chang,** Chen Chung 1927- *AmMWSc 92*
**Chang,** Chi 1944- *AmMWSc 92*
**Chang,** Chi Hsiung *AmMWSc 92*
**Chang,** Chi Kwong 1947- *AmMWSc 92*
**Chang,** Chia-Cheng 1939- *AmMWSc 92*
**Chang,** Chieh Chien 1913- *AmMWSc 92*
**Chang,** Chih-Pei 1945- *AmMWSc 92*
**Chang,** Chin-An 1943- *AmMWSc 92*
**Chang,** Chin-Chuan 1925- *AmMWSc 92*
**Chang,** Chin-Hai *AmMWSc 92*
**Chang,** Chin Hao 1926- *AmMWSc 92*
**Chang,** Chin Hsiung 1939- *AmMWSc 92*
**Chang,** Ching-Jen 1941- *AmMWSc 92*
**Chang,** Ching-Jer 1942- *AmMWSc 92*
**Chang,** Ching Ming 1935- *AmMWSc 92*
**Chang,** Ching Shung 1947- *AmMWSc 92*
**Chang,** Chiu-Cheng 1940- *WhoFI 92*
**Chang,** Chong-Hwan 1950- *AmMWSc 92, WhoMW 92*
**Chang,** Christine 1946- *WhoFI 92*
**Chang,** Christopher Teh-Min 1936- *AmMWSc 92*
**Chang,** Chu Huai 1917- *AmMWSc 92*
**Chang,** Chuan Chung 1938- *AmMWSc 92*
**Chang,** Chun-Yen 1937- *AmMWSc 92*
**Chang,** Clifford Wah Jun 1938- *AmMWSc 92*
**Chang,** Daniel P Y 1947- *AmMWSc 92*
**Chang,** David Bing Jue 1935- *AmMWSc 92*
**Chang,** David Wen-Wei 1929- *WhoMW 92*
**Chang,** Deborah Sook 1960- *WhoAmL 92, WhoFI 92*
**Chang,** Debra Wei Kuan 1952- *WhoEnt 92*
**Chang,** Diana *DrAPF 91*
**Chang,** Ding 1940- *AmMWSc 92*
**Chang,** Donald Choy 1942- *AmMWSc 92*
**Chang,** Donald Mark 1927- *WhoWest 92*
**Chang,** Eddie Li 1948- *AmMWSc 92*
**Chang,** Edward Shi Tou 1940- *AmMWSc 92*
**Chang,** Eileen 1920- *LiExTwC*
**Chang,** Elfreda Te-Hsin 1935- *AmMWSc 92*
**Chang,** Elizabeth B 1942- *AmMWSc 92*
**Chang,** Eppie Sheng 1946- *AmMWSc 92*
**Chang,** Ernest Sun-Mei 1950- *AmMWSc 92*
**Chang,** Fa Yan 1932- *AmMWSc 92*
**Chang,** Frank Keng 1922- *AmMWSc 92*
**Chang,** Frank N *AmMWSc 92*
**Chang,** Franklin 1942- *AmMWSc 92, WhoWest 92*
**Chang,** Franklin Shih Chuan 1915- *AmMWSc 92*
**Chang,** Freddy Wilfred Lennox 1935- *AmMWSc 92*
**Chang,** Frederic Chewming 1905- *AmMWSc 92*
**Chang,** George Chunyi 1935- *AmMWSc 92*
**Chang,** George Washington 1942- *AmMWSc 92*
**Chang,** H K 1940- *AmMWSc 92*
**Chang,** Hai-Won 1929- *AmMWSc 92*
**Chang,** Henry 1944- *AmMWSc 92*
**Chang,** Herbert Yu-Pang 1937- *AmMWSc 92*
**Chang,** Hou-Min 1938- *AmMWSc 92*
**Chang,** Howard 1939- *AmMWSc 92*
**Chang,** Howard How Chung 1922- *AmMWSc 92*
**Chang,** Hsien-Hsin 1942- *AmMWSc 92*
**Chang,** Hsu 1932- *AmMWSc 92*
**Chang,** I-Dee 1922- *AmMWSc 92*
**Chang,** I-Lok 1943- *AmMWSc 92*
**Chang,** Ifay F 1942- *AmMWSc 92*
**Chang,** In-Kook 1943- *AmMWSc 92*
**Chang,** Jack Che-Man 1941- *AmMWSc 92*
**Chang,** Jae Chan 1941- *AmMWSc 92*
**Chang,** James C 1930- *AmMWSc 92*
**Chang,** James H. 1942- *WhoAmL 92*
**Chang,** Jaw-Kang 1942- *AmMWSc 92*
**Chang,** Jeffrey 1963- *WhoWest 92*
**Chang,** Jeffrey C F 1928- *AmMWSc 92*
**Chang,** Jeffrey Peh-I 1917- *AmMWSc 92*
**Chang,** Jen-Shih 1947- *AmMWSc 92*
**Chang,** Jennie C C 1951- *AmMWSc 92*
**Chang,** Jerry L 1947- *WhoAmP 91*
**Chang,** Jhy-Jiun 1944- *AmMWSc 92, WhoMW 92*
**Chang,** John H 1937- *AmMWSc 92*
**Chang,** Joseph Yoon 1952- *AmMWSc 92*
**Chang,** Joseph Yung 1932- *AmMWSc 92*
**Chang,** Juang-Chi 1936- *AmMWSc 92*
**Chang,** Jun Hsin *AmMWSc 92*
**Chang,** Jung-Ching 1939- *AmMWSc 92*
**Chang,** K. Laurence 1922- *WhoMW 92*
**Chang,** Kang-Tsung 1943- *WhoWest 92*
**Chang,** Kaung-Jain 1945- *AmMWSc 92*
**Chang,** Kenneth Shueh-Shen 1929- *AmMWSc 92*
**Chang,** Kuang-Chou 1949- *AmMWSc 92*
**Chang,** Kuo Wei 1938- *AmMWSc 92*
**Chang,** Kwai Sing 1921- *WhoRel 92*
**Chang,** Kwang-chih 1931- *IntWW 91*
**Chang,** Kwang-Poo 1942- *AmMWSc 92, WhoMW 92*
**Chang,** Kwen-Jen *AmMWSc 92*
**Chang,** L L 1936- *AmMWSc 92*
**Chang,** Lay Nam 1943- *AmMWSc 92*
**Chang,** Lena 1938- *AmMWSc 92*
**Chang,** Leroy L *AmMWSc 92*
**Chang,** Lois Leilani 1955- *WhoWest 92*
**Chang,** Louis Wai-Wah 1944- *AmMWSc 92*
**Chang,** Lucy Ming-Shih 1942- *AmMWSc 92*
**Chang,** Luke Li-Yu 1935- *AmMWSc 92*
**Chang,** M.C. d1991 *NewYTBS 91 [port]*
**Chang,** Mei Ling 1915- *AmMWSc 92*
**Chang,** Min Chueh 1908- *AmMWSc 92, FacFETw*
**Chang,** Ming-Houng 1947- *AmMWSc 92*
**Chang,** Mingteh 1939- *AmMWSc 92*
**Chang,** Morris 1931- *AmMWSc 92*
**Chang,** Mou-Hsiung 1944- *AmMWSc 92*
**Chang,** Ngee Pong 1940- *AmMWSc 92*
**Chang,** Pauline Kimm 1926- *AmMWSc 92*
**Chang,** Pei Kung 1936- *AmMWSc 92*
**Chang,** Pei Wen 1923- *AmMWSc 92*
**Chang,** Peter Asha, Jr. 1937- *WhoAmL 92*
**Chang,** Ping 1960- *AmMWSc 92*
**Chang,** Potter Chien-Tien 1934- *AmMWSc 92*
**Chang,** Raymond 1939- *AmMWSc 92*
**Chang,** Raymond S L 1943- *AmMWSc 92*
**Chang,** Ren-Fang 1938- *AmMWSc 92*
**Chang,** Richard C 1918- *AmMWSc 92*
**Chang,** Richard Kounai 1940- *AmMWSc 92*
**Chang,** Robert Shihman 1922- *AmMWSc 92, WhoWest 92*
**Chang,** Robert Timothy 1958- *WhoFI 92*
**Chang,** Robin 1951- *AmMWSc 92*
**Chang,** Rodney Eiu Joon 1945- *WhoWest 92*
**Chang,** S.J. 1949- *WhoFI 92*
**Chang,** Sam Hsien-Cheng 1946- *WhoAmL 92*
**Chang,** Sarah 1980- *ConMus 7 [port]*
**Chang,** Shao-chien 1930- *AmMWSc 92*
**Chang,** Shari Yamamoto 1958- *WhoFI 92*
**Chang,** Shau-Jin 1937- *AmMWSc 92*
**Chang,** Sheldon S L 1920- *AmMWSc 92*
**Chang,** Sheng-Yen 1930- *WhoRel 92*
**Chang,** Shi Kuo 1944- *AmMWSc 92*
**Chang,** Shih-Ger 1941- *AmMWSc 92*
**Chang,** Shih-Ming Li 1959- *WhoEnt 92*
**Chang,** Shih-Yung 1938- *AmMWSc 92*
**Chang,** Shu-Pei 1922- *AmMWSc 92*
**Chang,** Shu-Sing 1935- *AmMWSc 92*
**Chang,** Simon H 1930- *AmMWSc 92*
**Chang,** Stephen Szu Shiang 1918- *AmMWSc 92*
**Chang,** Sun-Yung Alice 1948- *AmMWSc 92*
**Chang,** T-Y 1937- *AmMWSc 92*
**Chang,** Ta-kuang 1955- *WhoAmL 92*
**Chang,** Ta-Min *AmMWSc 92*
**Chang,** Ta-Yuan 1945- *AmMWSc 92*
**Chang,** Tai Ming 1938- *AmMWSc 92*
**Chang,** Tai Yup 1933- *AmMWSc 92*
**Chang,** Tao-Yuan 1937- *AmMWSc 92*
**Chang,** Te Wen 1920- *AmMWSc 92*
**Chang,** Ted T 1935- *AmMWSc 92*
**Chang,** Theodore Chien-Hsin 1926- *WhoMW 92*
**Chang,** Thomas Ming Swi 1933- *AmMWSc 92*
**Chang,** Tien-Chien Ted 1954- *WhoMW 92*
**Chang,** Tien-ding 1921- *AmMWSc 92*
**Chang,** Tien-Lin 1943- *AmMWSc 92*
**Chang,** Tien Sun 1931- *AmMWSc 92*
**Chang,** Timothy Scott 1925- *AmMWSc 92, WhoMW 92*
**Chang,** Tsong-How 1929- *AmMWSc 92*
**Chang,** Tsu-Shuan 1950- *WhoWest 92*
**Chang,** Victor Hugh 1953- *WhoMW 92*
**Chang,** Wen-Hsuan 1926- *AmMWSc 92*
**Chang,** Wilbert Douglas *WhoWest 92*
**Chang,** William S C 1931- *AmMWSc 92*
**Chang,** William Wei-Lien 1933- *AmMWSc 92*
**Chang,** William Y B 1948- *AmMWSc 92*
**Chang,** Y Austin *AmMWSc 92*
**Chang,** Yao Teh *AmMWSc 92*
**Chang,** Yau-Wai David 1961- *WhoWest 92*
**Chang,** Yew Chun 1941- *AmMWSc 92*
**Chang,** Yi-Cheng 1943- *WhoFI 92*
**Chang,** Yi-Han 1933- *AmMWSc 92*
**Chang,** Yia-Chung *AmMWSc 92*
**Chang,** Yiwei *WhoAmL 92*
**Chang,** Yoon Il 1942- *AmMWSc 92*
**Chang,** Yung-Feng 1935- *AmMWSc 92*
**Chang-Diaz,** Franklin Ramon 1950- *WhoHisp 92*
**Chang-Him,** French Kitchener *Who 92, WhoRel 92*
**Chang-Him,** French Kitchener 1938- *IntWW 91*
**Chang-Mota,** Roberto 1935- *WhoFI 92*
**Chang-Rodriguez,** Eugenio 1926- *WhoHisp 92*
**Changeux,** Jean-Pierre 1936- *ConAu 134, IntWW 91*
**Changnon,** Chris 1963- *WhoMW 92*
**Changnon,** Stanley A, Jr 1928- *AmMWSc 92*
**Changnon,** Stanley Alcide, Jr 1928- *AmMWSc 92*
**Chango,** Clovr *DrAPF 91*
**Chanick,** Richard Alan 1953- *WhoWest 92*
**Chanin,** Leah Farb 1929- *WhoAmL 92*
**Chanin,** Lorne Maxwell 1927- *AmMWSc 92*
**Chanin,** Robert Howard 1934- *WhoAmL 92*
**Chanlett,** Emil T 1915- *AmMWSc 92*
**Chanley,** Jacob David 1918- *AmMWSc 92*
**Chanmugam,** Ganesar 1939- *AmMWSc 92*
**Channel,** Lawrence Edwin 1927- *AmMWSc 92*
**Channell,** Eula L. 1928- *WhoBlA 92*
**Channell,** Robert Bennie 1924- *AmMWSc 92*
**Channels,** Mark Evan 1953- *WhoFI 92*
**Channick,** Herbert S. 1929- *WhoMW 92*
**Channin,** Donald Jones 1942- *AmMWSc 92*
**Channing,** Carol 1921- *IntMPA 92, IntWW 91*
**Channing,** Carol 1923- *ConMus 6 [port], WhoEnt 92*
**Channing,** Edward 1856-1931 *FacFETw*
**Channing,** Edward Tyrrell 1790-1856 *BenetAL 91*
**Channing,** Steven A. 1940- *WrDr 92*
**Channing,** Stockard *WhoEnt 92*
**Channing,** Stockard 1944- *CurBio 91 [port], IntMPA 92*
**Channing,** Stockard 1946?- *News 91 [port], -91-3 [port]*
**Channing,** William Ellery 1780-1842 *AmPeW, BenetAL 91*
**Channing,** William Ellery 1818-1901 *BenetAL 91*
**Channing,** William Henry 1810-1884 *AmPeW, BenetAL 91*
**Channon,** Derek French 1939- *Who 92*
**Channon,** Paul 1935- *Who 92*
**Channon,** Paul Guinness 1935- *IntWW 91*
**Channon,** Stephen R 1947- *AmMWSc 92*
**Chanock,** Robert Merritt 1924- *AmMWSc 92*
**Chanover,** Pierre E. *DrAPF 91*
**Chanowitz,** Michael Stephen 1943- *AmMWSc 92*
**Chanson,** Samuel T *AmMWSc 92*
**Chansy,** Edmund d1677? *DcNCBi 1*
**Chant,** Davis Ryan 1938- *WhoFI 92*
**Chant,** Donald A 1928- *AmMWSc 92*
**Chantell,** Charles J 1931- *AmMWSc 92*
**Chantels,** The *NewAmDM*
**Chantikian,** Kosrof *DrAPF 91*
**Chantres,** Gerald Robert 1942- *WhoFI 92*
**Chantrey,** Melvyn 1945- *TwCPaSc*
**Chantry,** George William 1933- *Who 92*
**Chantry,** William Amdor 1924- *AmMWSc 92*
**Chanute,** Octave 1832-1910 *BiInAmS*
**Chao Chi-kang** 1931- *LiExTwC*
**Chao Yao-Tung** 1915- *IntWW 91*
**Chao,** B T 1918- *AmMWSc 92*
**Chao,** Chih Hsu 1939- *WhoWest 92*
**Chao,** Chong-Yun 1930- *AmMWSc 92*

**Chao,** Eddy Lee 1952- *WhoWest 92*
**Chao,** Edward Ching-Te 1919- *AmMWSc 92*
**Chao,** Elaine L *WhoAmP 91, WhoFI 92*
**Chao,** Fu-chuan 1919- *AmMWSc 92*
**Chao,** James Min-Tzu 1940- *WhoFI 92, WhoWest 92*
**Chao,** Jia-Arng 1941- *AmMWSc 92*
**Chao,** Jing 1924- *AmMWSc 92*
**Chao,** Jowett 1915- *AmMWSc 92*
**Chao,** Julie 1940- *AmMWSc 92*
**Chao,** Kwang Chu 1925- *AmMWSc 92, WhoMW 92*
**Chao,** Lee 1939- *AmMWSc 92*
**Chao,** Mou Shu 1924- *AmMWSc 92*
**Chao,** Raul Edward 1939- *AmMWSc 92*
**Chao,** Sherman S 1947- *AmMWSc 92*
**Chao,** Tai Siang 1919- *AmMWSc 92*
**Chao,** Tsun Tien 1918- *AmMWSc 92*
**Chao,** Yu-Sheng 1945- *AmMWSc 92*
**Chao,** Yuh J 1953- *AmMWSc 92*
**Chapa,** Alfonso 1930- *WhoHisp 92*
**Chapa,** Amancio Jose, Jr. 1946- *WhoHisp 92*
**Chapa,** Armando 1944- *WhoHisp 92*
**Chapa,** Arthur *WhoHisp 92*
**Chapa,** Carmen 1947- *WhoHisp 92*
**Chapa,** Elia Kay 1960- *WhoHisp 92*
**Chapa,** Joseph S. 1948- *WhoHisp 92*
**Chapa,** Judy J. 1957- *WhoHisp 92*
**Chapa,** Ramon, Jr. 1958- *WhoHisp 92*
**Chapa,** Raul Roberto 1948- *WhoHisp 92*
**Chapa,** Rodolfo Chino 1958- *WhoHisp 92*
**Chapa-Guzman,** Hugo Gerardo 1953- *WhoHisp 92*
**Chaparas,** Sotiros D 1929- *AmMWSc 92*
**Chaparro,** Carmen 1947- *WhoHisp 92*
**Chaparro,** Jose L. 1955- *WhoHisp 92*
**Chaparro,** Luis *WhoHisp 92*
**Chaparro,** Luis F. 1947- *WhoHisp 92*
**Chaparro,** Reynaldo *WhoHisp 92*
**Chapas,** Richard Bernard 1945- *AmMWSc 92*
**Chapatwala,** Kirit D *AmMWSc 92*
**Chapayev,** Vasily Ivanovich 1887-1919 *FacFETw*
**Chapaygin,** Alexei Pavlovich 1870-1937 *FacFETw*
**Chapdelaine,** Roland Joseph 1946- *WhoWest 92*
**Chapel,** Alain 1937-1990 *AnObit 1990*
**Chapel,** Alain Germain Gustave d1990 *IntWW 91N*
**Chapel,** Charles Sidney 1941- *WhoAmL 92*
**Chapel,** James L 1920- *AmMWSc 92*
**Chapel,** Raymond Eugene 1921- *AmMWSc 92*
**Chapel,** Robert Clyde 1945- *WhoEnt 92*
**Chapelain-Midy,** Roger 1904- *IntWW 91*
**Chapelle,** Anthony Earl 1954- *WhoBlA 92*
**Chapelli,** Armando C., Jr. *WhoHisp 92*
**Chapello,** Craig Alan 1956- *WhoAmL 92*
**Chaperon,** Edward Alfred 1930- *AmMWSc 92*
**Chapey,** Paul Lucien 1944- *WhoFI 92*
**Chapian,** Grieg Hovsep 1913- *WhoWest 92*
**Chapin,** Alice Earle *ScFEYrs*
**Chapin,** Charles Edward 1932- *AmMWSc 92*
**Chapin,** David Lambert 1948- *AmMWSc 92*
**Chapin,** Diana Derby 1942- *WhoAmP 91*
**Chapin,** Doug *IntMPA 92*
**Chapin,** Douglas McCall 1940- *AmMWSc 92*
**Chapin,** Douglas Scott 1922- *AmMWSc 92*
**Chapin,** Earl Cone 1919- *AmMWSc 92*
**Chapin,** Edward William, Jr 1943- *AmMWSc 92*
**Chapin,** Ernest K *ScFEYrs*
**Chapin,** F Stuart, III 1944- *AmMWSc 92*
**Chapin,** F. Stuart, Jr. 1916- *WrDr 92*
**Chapin,** Harry 1942-1981 *ConMus 6 [port]*
**Chapin,** Henry J 1908- *AmMWSc 92*
**Chapin,** Howard B *WhoAmP 91*
**Chapin,** James Chris 1940- *WhoAmL 92*
**Chapin,** Joan Beggs 1929- *AmMWSc 92*
**Chapin,** John Carsten 1920- *WhoAmP 91*
**Chapin,** John Ladner 1916- *AmMWSc 92*
**Chapin,** John Nettleton, Jr. 1933- *WhoFI 92*
**Chapin,** Mary Real 1953- *WhoAmL 92*
**Chapin,** Melville 1918- *WhoAmL 92*
**Chapin,** Ned 1927- *WhoFI 92*
**Chapin,** Schuyler Garrison 1923- *IntWW 91, WhoEnt 92*
**Chapin,** Shelley 1953- *WhoRel 92*
**Chapin,** Theodore Steinway 1950- *WhoEnt 92*
**Chapin,** Tuck Ralston 1928- *WhoAmL 92*
**Chaplais,** Pierre Theophile Victorien M 1920- *Who 92*
**Chapler,** Christopher Keith 1940- *AmMWSc 92*
**Chaplin,** Ansel Burt 1931- *WhoAmL 92*
**Chaplin,** Arthur Hugh 1905- *IntWW 91, Who 92*
**Chaplin,** Bob 1947- *TwCPaSc*
**Chaplin,** Boris Nikolaevich 1931- *IntWW 91*
**Chaplin,** Charles 1889-1977 *IntDcF 2-2 [port]*
**Chaplin,** Charles S 1911- *IntMPA 92*
**Chaplin,** Charlie 1889-1977 *BenetAL 91, EncTR 91 [port], FacFETw [port], LiExTwC, RComAH*
**Chaplin,** David Dunbar 1952- *WhoMW 92*
**Chaplin,** Frank S 1910- *AmMWSc 92*
**Chaplin,** George 1914- *WhoWest 92*
**Chaplin,** Geraldine 1944- *ConTFT 9, IntMPA 92, IntWW 91, WhoEnt 92*
**Chaplin,** Hugh, Jr 1923- *AmMWSc 92*
**Chaplin,** James Ferris 1920- *AmMWSc 92*
**Chaplin,** James Patrick 1919- *WrDr 92*
**Chaplin,** Jim 1944- *WhoAmP 91*
**Chaplin,** John Cyril 1926- *Who 92*
**Chaplin,** Lita Grey 1908- *WhoEnt 92*
**Chaplin,** Malcolm Hilbery *Who 92*
**Chaplin,** Michael H 1943- *AmMWSc 92*
**Chaplin,** Norman John 1918- *AmMWSc 92*
**Chaplin,** Oona O'Neill d1991 *NewYTBS 91 [port]*
**Chaplin,** Robert Lee, Jr 1923- *AmMWSc 92*
**Chaplin,** Saul 1912- *IntMPA 92*
**Chaplin,** Stephen 1934- *TwCPaSc*
**Chaplin,** Sybil Judith 1939- *Who 92*
**Chapline,** George Frederick, Jr 1942- *AmMWSc 92*
**Chaplock,** Sharon Kayne 1948- *WhoMW 92*
**Chapman** *Who 92*
**Chapman and Hall** *DcLB 106*
**Chapman Brothers** *DcLB 106*
**Chapman,** Alan J 1925- *AmMWSc 92*
**Chapman,** Alan T 1929- *AmMWSc 92*
**Chapman,** Albert Lee 1933- *AmMWSc 92*
**Chapman,** Alger Baldwin 1931- *WhoFI 92*
**Chapman,** Alice Mariah 1947- *WhoBlA 92*
**Chapman,** Allen *SmATA 67*
**Chapman,** Allen Floyd 1930- *WhoFI 92*
**Chapman,** Alvah Herman, Jr. 1921- *WhoFI 92*
**Chapman,** Alvan Wentworth 1809-1899 *BiInAmS*
**Chapman,** Amy R 1962- *WhoAmP 91*
**Chapman,** Angela Mary 1940- *Who 92*
**Chapman,** Anthea *TwCPaSc*
**Chapman,** Arthur Barclay 1908- *AmMWSc 92*
**Chapman,** Arthur Owen 1913- *AmMWSc 92*
**Chapman,** Audrey Bridgeforth 1941- *WhoBlA 92*
**Chapman,** Ben *Who 92*
**Chapman,** Bill 1955- *WhoEnt 92*
**Chapman,** Bobbie 1947- *TwCPaSc*
**Chapman,** Brian Richard 1946- *AmMWSc 92*
**Chapman,** Brian Timothy 1955- *WhoMW 92*
**Chapman,** C. Alan 1949- *WhoIns 92*
**Chapman,** Carl Edward 1959- *WhoEnt 92*
**Chapman,** Carl H. 1915-1987 *ConAu 133*
**Chapman,** Carl Joseph 1939- *AmMWSc 92*
**Chapman,** Carleton Abramson 1911- *AmMWSc 92*
**Chapman,** Carleton Burke 1915- *AmMWSc 92*
**Chapman,** Carolyn 1942- *WhoWest 92*
**Chapman,** Charles Cyril Staplee 1936- *Who 92*
**Chapman,** Charles F. 1947- *WhoBlA 92*
**Chapman,** Charles Hickerson, Jr 1920- *WhoAmP 91*
**Chapman,** Charles Taylor, Jr. 1955- *WhoRel 92*
**Chapman,** Christopher Hugh 1945- *Who 92*
**Chapman,** Clark Russell 1945- *AmMWSc 92*
**Chapman,** Cleveland M. *WhoBlA 92*
**Chapman,** Clinton W *WhoAmP 91*
**Chapman,** Conrad Daniel 1933- *WhoAmL 92, WhoMW 92*
**Chapman,** Craig Bruce 1958- *WhoRel 92*
**Chapman,** Cyril Donald 1920- *Who 92*
**Chapman,** Dan G. 1939- *WhoRel 92*
**Chapman,** Daniel Ahmling *Who 92*
**Chapman,** David 1941- *Who 92*
**Chapman,** David Anthony 1949- *WhoBlA 92*
**Chapman,** David Eley 1938- *WhoEnt 92*
**Chapman,** David J 1939- *AmMWSc 92*
**Chapman,** David MacLean 1935- *AmMWSc 92*
**Chapman,** David N. 1953- *WhoMW 92*
**Chapman,** Dean R 1922- *AmMWSc 92*
**Chapman,** Dennis 1927- *IntWW 91, Who 92*
**Chapman,** Derek D 1932- *AmMWSc 92*
**Chapman,** Diana Cecelia 1954- *WhoBlA 92*
**Chapman,** Dorothy Hilton 1934- *WhoBlA 92*
**Chapman,** Douglas George 1920- *AmMWSc 92*
**Chapman,** Douglas Wilfred 1921- *AmMWSc 92*
**Chapman,** E Gary 1935- *WhoAmP 91*
**Chapman,** Elaine Grace 1956- *WhoWest 92*
**Chapman,** Elizabeth 1919- *IntAu&W 91, WrDr 92*
**Chapman,** Elizabeth Nina 1947- *WhoRel 92*
**Chapman,** Eugenia Sheldon 1923- *WhoAmP 91*
**Chapman,** Fern Schumer 1954- *WhoMW 92*
**Chapman,** Floyd Barton 1911- *AmMWSc 92*
**Chapman,** Frances Elizabeth Clausen 1920- *WhoMW 92*
**Chapman,** Francis Ian 1925- *Who 92*
**Chapman,** Frank 1942- *WhoBlA 92*
**Chapman,** Frederick John 1939- *Who 92*
**Chapman,** Garth 1917- *Who 92*
**Chapman,** Gary Adair 1937- *AmMWSc 92*
**Chapman,** Gary Allen 1938- *AmMWSc 92*
**Chapman,** Gary Levi 1946- *WhoRel 92*
**Chapman,** Gary Theodore 1934- *AmMWSc 92*
**Chapman,** Geoffrey Lloyd 1928- *Who 92*
**Chapman,** George 1559?-1634 *RfGEnL 91*
**Chapman,** George 1908- *TwCPaSc*
**Chapman,** George 1927- *Who 92*
**Chapman,** George Bunker 1925- *AmMWSc 92*
**Chapman,** George David 1940- *AmMWSc 92*
**Chapman,** George Wallace, Jr. 1940- *WhoBlA 92*
**Chapman,** Gilbert Bryant, II 1935- *WhoBlA 92*
**Chapman,** Graham 1941-1989 *ConAu 35NR*
**Chapman,** Harry A, Jr 1936- *WhoAmP 91*
**Chapman,** Henry Cadwalader 1845-1909 *BiInAmS*
**Chapman,** Herbert L, Jr 1923- *AmMWSc 92*
**Chapman,** Hugh McMaster 1932- *WhoFI 92*
**Chapman,** Ian *Who 92*
**Chapman,** Ian 1925- *IntWW 91*
**Chapman,** Ian M. *WhoRel 92*
**Chapman,** J. Dudley 1928- *WrDr 92*
**Chapman,** Jacqueline Sue 1935- *AmMWSc 92*
**Chapman,** James Blaine 1884-1947 *RelLAm 91*
**Chapman,** James Claude 1931- *WhoFI 92, WhoMW 92*
**Chapman,** James David 1938- *WhoWest 92*
**Chapman,** James Edward 1927- *WhoAmL 92*
**Chapman,** James Keith 1940- *Who 92*
**Chapman,** Janet Carter Goodrich 1922- *WhoFI 92*
**Chapman,** Janet Warner 1962- *WhoRel 92*
**Chapman,** Jeff Crawford 1940- *WhoFI 92*
**Chapman,** Jerome Ian 1939- *WhoAmL 92*
**Chapman,** Jim 1945- *WhoAmP 91*
**Chapman,** Jim, Jr. 1945- *AlmAP 92 [port]*
**Chapman,** Joe Alexander 1919- *AmMWSc 92*
**Chapman,** John *BenetAL 91*
**Chapman,** John 1821-1894 *DcLB 106 [port]*
**Chapman,** John Donald 1941- *AmMWSc 92*
**Chapman,** John E 1931- *AmMWSc 92*
**Chapman,** John Edward 1962- *WhoMW 92*
**Chapman,** John Forrest d1991 *NewYTBS 91*
**Chapman,** John Franklin, Jr 1945- *AmMWSc 92*
**Chapman,** John Henry Benjamin 1899- *Who 92*
**Chapman,** John Jay 1862-1933 *BenetAL 91*
**Chapman,** John Judson 1918- *AmMWSc 92*
**Chapman,** John S 1908- *AmMWSc 92*
**Chapman,** John Sherwood 1936- *WhoAmP 91*
**Chapman,** John Wilbur 1859-1918 *RelLAm 91*
**Chapman,** Joseph Alan 1942- *AmMWSc 92*
**Chapman,** Joseph Conrad, Jr. 1937- *WhoBlA 92*
**Chapman,** Judith-Anne Williams 1949- *AmMWSc 92*
**Chapman,** Judith L 1941- *WhoAmP 91*
**Chapman,** Julius *WhoBlA 92*
**Chapman,** Karen Louise 1954- *WhoAmL 92*
**Chapman,** Kathleen Halloran 1937- *WhoAmP 91*
**Chapman,** Kathleen Violet 1903- *Who 92*
**Chapman,** Kenneth Reginald 1924- *AmMWSc 92*
**Chapman,** Kent M 1928- *AmMWSc 92*
**Chapman,** Lamar Christopher, III 1953- *WhoMW 92*
**Chapman,** Larry Arthur 1946- *WhoMW 92*
**Chapman,** Laura *DrAPF 91*
**Chapman,** Laurel Israel 1950- *WhoFI 92*
**Chapman,** Lee *WrDr 92*
**Chapman,** Lee Manuel 1932- *WhoBlA 92*
**Chapman,** Lemmie Jerry 1934- *WhoFI 92*
**Chapman,** Leslie Charles 1919- *Who 92*
**Chapman,** Lloyd William 1938- *AmMWSc 92*
**Chapman,** Lonny Leonard 1920- *WhoEnt 92*
**Chapman,** Loring 1929- *WhoWest 92*
**Chapman,** Loring Frederick 1929- *AmMWSc 92*
**Chapman,** Marguerite 1918- *WhoEnt 92*
**Chapman,** Maria Weston 1806-1865 *BenetAL 91*
**Chapman,** Maria Weston 1806-1885 *AmPeW, PorAmW [port]*
**Chapman,** Mark Fenger 1934- *Who 92*
**Chapman,** Marshall 1949- *WhoEnt 92*
**Chapman,** Martha Lynn 1962- *WhoEnt 92*
**Chapman,** Martin Odes 1922-1982 *WhoBlA 92N*
**Chapman,** Max 1911- *TwCPaSc*
**Chapman,** Melvin 1928- *WhoBlA 92*
**Chapman,** Michael 1935- *IntMPA 92*
**Chapman,** Michael Beverley 1959- *WhoEnt 92*
**Chapman,** Michael Ray 1951- *WhoRel 92*
**Chapman,** Michael Robin 1939- *Who 92*
**Chapman,** Miles Dean 1963- *WhoMW 92*
**Chapman,** Nathaniel 1780-1853 *BiInAmS*
**Chapman,** Norman Bellamy 1916- *Who 92*
**Chapman,** Orville Lamar 1932- *AmMWSc 92, IntWW 91*
**Chapman,** Paula Anne 1960- *WhoFI 92, WhoMW 92*
**Chapman,** Peter *WhoEnt 92*
**Chapman,** Peter Herbert 1953- *WhoFI 92*
**Chapman,** Peter John 1936- *AmMWSc 92*
**Chapman,** Philip Russell 1935- *WhoEnt 92*
**Chapman,** R Keith 1916- *AmMWSc 92*
**Chapman,** Ramona Marie 1945- *AmMWSc 92*
**Chapman,** Randy 1953- *WhoEnt 92*
**Chapman,** Ray LaVar *AmMWSc 92*
**Chapman,** Reid Gillis 1920- *WhoEnt 92*
**Chapman,** Richard 1951- *TwCPaSc*
**Chapman,** Richard A. 1937- *ConAu 133*
**Chapman,** Richard Alexander 1932- *AmMWSc 92*
**Chapman,** Richard D 1911-1978 *FacFETw*
**Chapman,** Richard David 1928- *AmMWSc 92*
**Chapman,** Richard Leroy 1932- *WhoFI 92, WhoWest 92*
**Chapman,** Robert 1933- *TwCPaSc*
**Chapman,** Robert 1937- *WrDr 92*
**Chapman,** Robert Dale 1955- *AmMWSc 92*
**Chapman,** Robert DeWitt 1937- *AmMWSc 92*
**Chapman,** Robert Earl, Jr 1941- *AmMWSc 92*
**Chapman,** Robert F 1926- *WhoAmP 91*
**Chapman,** Robert Foster 1926- *WhoAmL 92*
**Chapman,** Robert Galbraith 1926- *WhoWest 92*
**Chapman,** Robert Hett 1771-1833 *DcNCBi 1*
**Chapman,** Robert Hollister 1868-1920 *BiInAmS*
**Chapman,** Robert L. *WhoRel 92*
**Chapman,** Robert L., Sr. 1923- *WhoBlA 92*
**Chapman,** Robert Lane 1933- *WhoWest 92*
**Chapman,** Robert Lee 1926- *WhoRel 92*
**Chapman,** Robert Mills 1918- *AmMWSc 92*
**Chapman,** Robert Pringle 1926- *AmMWSc 92*
**Chapman,** Roger Charles 1936- *AmMWSc 92*
**Chapman,** Roger Stevens, Jr. 1927- *WhoFI 92*
**Chapman,** Ronald Thomas 1933- *WhoEnt 92*
**Chapman,** Ross Alexander 1913- *AmMWSc 92*
**Chapman,** Rosyln C. 1956- *WhoBlA 92*
**Chapman,** Roy de Courcy 1936- *Who 92*
**Chapman,** Roy John 1936- *Who 92*
**Chapman,** Russell Leonard 1946- *AmMWSc 92*
**Chapman,** S E *ScFEYrs*
**Chapman,** Sally 1946- *AmMWSc 92*
**Chapman,** Samuel Greeley 1929- *WrDr 92*
**Chapman,** Samuel Milton 1920- *WhoBlA 92*
**Chapman,** Sharon Jeanette 1949- *WhoBlA 92*
**Chapman,** Sharon K 1939- *AmMWSc 92*

**Chapman,** Silas Stacy, III 1954- *WhoAmL 92*
**Chapman,** Stanley David 1935- *IntAu&W 91, WrDr 92*
**Chapman,** Stephen d1991 *Who 92N*
**Chapman,** Stephen James 1954- *WhoMW 92*
**Chapman,** Stephen R 1936- *AmMWSc 92*
**Chapman,** Steven Dale 1951- *WhoMW 92*
**Chapman,** Susan *DrAPF 91*
**Chapman,** Sydney 1888-1970 *FacFETw*
**Chapman,** Sydney Brookes 1935- *Who 92*
**Chapman,** Thomas F. *WhoIns 92*
**Chapman,** Thomas Woodring 1940- *AmMWSc 92*
**Chapman,** Toby Marshall 1938- *AmMWSc 92*
**Chapman,** Tracy 1964- *WhoBlA 92, WhoEnt 92*
**Chapman,** Verne M 1938- *AmMWSc 92*
**Chapman,** Walker *ConAu 36NR*
**Chapman,** Walter *WrDr 92*
**Chapman,** Warren Howe 1925- *AmMWSc 92*
**Chapman,** Wes *WhoEnt 92*
**Chapman,** William *WhoEnt 92*
**Chapman,** William Edward 1945- *AmMWSc 92*
**Chapman,** William Frank 1944- *AmMWSc 92*
**Chapman,** William Talbert 1944- *WhoBlA 92*
**Chapman,** Willie Lasco, Jr 1928- *AmMWSc 92*
**Chapman,** Willie R. 1942- *WhoBlA 92*
**Chapman-Mortimer,** William Charles 1907- *IntAu&W 91*
**Chapman Nyaho,** Daniel Ahmling 1909- *IntWW 91, Who 92*
**Chapnick,** Barry M *AmMWSc 92*
**Chapone,** Hester 1727-1801 *BlkwCEP*
**Chapoton,** John E 1936- *WhoAmP 91*
**Chapoton,** John Edgar 1936- *WhoAmL 92, WhoFI 92*
**Chappano,** Perry Michael 1961- *WhoAmL 92, WhoMW 92*
**Chappars,** Timothy Stephen 1952- *WhoAmL 92*
**Chappe-Garcia,** Pedro 1943- *BlkOlyM*
**Chappel,** Clifford 1925- *AmMWSc 92*
**Chappel,** Scott Carlton 1950- *AmMWSc 92*
**Chappelear,** David C 1931- *AmMWSc 92*
**Chappelear,** Harold E. 1938- *WhoFI 92*
**Chappelear,** Stephen Eric 1952- *WhoAmL 92*
**Chappell,** Bonnie Dell 1927- *WhoRel 92*
**Chappell,** Charles Franklin 1927- *AmMWSc 92*
**Chappell,** Charles Richard 1943- *AmMWSc 92*
**Chappell,** Clovis Gillham, Jr. 1911- *WhoAmL 92*
**Chappell,** Colon 1909- *WhoAmP 91*
**Chappell,** Danny Michael 1956- *WhoAmL 92*
**Chappell,** David Wellington 1940- *WhoRel 92, WhoWest 92*
**Chappell,** Dorothy Field 1947- *AmMWSc 92*
**Chappell,** Duncan 1939- *WhoWest 92*
**Chappell,** Elizabeth 1927- *AmMWSc 92*
**Chappell,** Emma Carolyn 1941- *WhoBlA 92*
**Chappell,** Fred *DrAPF 91*
**Chappell,** George S. *BenetAL 91*
**Chappell,** Gregory Stephen 1948- *IntWW 91*
**Chappell,** Guy Lee Monty 1940- *AmMWSc 92*
**Chappell,** Jeffrey 1952- *WhoEnt 92*
**Chappell,** John Charles 1935- *WhoAmL 92*
**Chappell,** John Francis 1936- *WhoFI 92*
**Chappell,** John Franklin 1948- *WhoEnt 92*
**Chappell,** Mark Allen 1951- *AmMWSc 92*
**Chappell,** Michael James 1946- *WhoBlA 92*
**Chappell,** Milton Leroy 1951- *WhoAmL 92*
**Chappell,** Mollie *IntAu&W 91, WrDr 92*
**Chappell,** Philip 1929- *Who 92*
**Chappell,** Richard Lee 1938- *AmMWSc 92*
**Chappell,** Roy M. 1932- *WhoRel 92*
**Chappell,** Ruth Rax 1932- *WhoBlA 92*
**Chappell,** Samuel Estelle 1931- *AmMWSc 92*
**Chappell,** Stephen Randall 1948- *WhoAmL 92*
**Chappell,** Wade Millard 1946- *WhoRel 92*
**Chappell,** Warren d1991 *NewYTBS 91 [port]*
**Chappell,** Warren 1904-1991 *ConAu 134, SmATA 67, -68 [port]*
**Chappell,** Willard Ray 1938- *AmMWSc 92*
**Chappell,** William 1908- *Who 92*
**Chappelle,** Daniel Eugene 1933- *AmMWSc 92*
**Chappelle,** Emmett W 1925- *AmMWSc 92*
**Chappelle,** Thomas Oscar, Sr. *WhoBlA 92*
**Chappelle,** Thomas W 1918- *AmMWSc 92*
**Chappellet,** Cyril d1991 *NewYTBS 91*
**Chappelow,** Cecil Clendis, III 1948- *AmMWSc 92*
**Chappelow,** Cecil Clendis, Jr 1928- *AmMWSc 92*
**Chappie,** Alice A. 1942- *WhoMW 92*
**Chappie,** Gene A 1920- *WhoAmP 91*
**Chapple** *Who 92*
**Chapple,** Baron 1921- *Who 92*
**Chapple,** Christopher 1954- *WhoRel 92*
**Chapple,** John 1931- *IntWW 91, Who 92*
**Chapple,** John Alfred Victor 1928- *IntAu&W 91, WrDr 92*
**Chapple,** John Hunt 1928- *WhoRel 92*
**Chapple,** Paul James 1933- *AmMWSc 92, WhoMW 92*
**Chapple,** Steve *DrAPF 91*
**Chapple,** Thomas Leslie 1947- *WhoAmL 92*
**Chapple,** William Dismore 1936- *AmMWSc 92*
**Chapple,** Wreford G. d1991 *NewYTBS 91*
**Chapple Camacho,** Marie Christine 1960- *WhoHisp 92*
**Chaptal,** Jean Antoine 1756-1832 *BlkwCEP*
**Chapuis,** Glen Edward 1953- *WhoMW 92*
**Chapus,** Edmond F. d1991 *NewYTBS 91*
**Chaput,** Charles J. 1944- *WhoMW 92, WhoRel 92*
**Chaput,** Christopher Joseph 1960- *WhoAmL 92*
**Chaput,** Raymond Leo 1940- *AmMWSc 92*
**Char,** Daniel Scott 1960- *WhoAmL 92*
**Char,** Donald F B 1925- *AmMWSc 92*
**Char,** Patricia Helen 1952- *WhoAmL 92*
**Char,** Rene 1907-1988 *FacFETw, GuFrLit 1*
**Char,** Richard Jay 1959- *WhoAmL 92*
**Char,** Vernon Fook Leong 1934- *WhoAmL 92*
**Char,** Walter F 1920- *AmMWSc 92*
**Charache,** Patricia 1929- *AmMWSc 92*
**Charache,** Samuel 1930- *AmMWSc 92*
**Characklis,** William Gregory 1941- *AmMWSc 92*
**Charalambopoulos,** Yannis 1919- *IntWW 91*
**Charalambou,** Sotikaris 1947- *TwCPaSc*
**Charap,** Stanley H 1932- *AmMWSc 92*
**Charbeneau,** Gerald T 1925- *AmMWSc 92*
**Charbeneau,** Randall Jay 1950- *AmMWSc 92*
**Charbeneau,** Travis *DrAPF 91*
**Charboneau,** David George 1954- *WhoMW 92*
**Charboneau,** Elaine M 1936- *WhoAmP 91*
**Charbonneau,** Henry 1913-1982 *BiDExR*
**Charbonneau,** Hubert 1936- *IntWW 91*
**Charbonneau,** Larry Francis 1939- *AmMWSc 92*
**Charbonneau,** Louis 1924- *IntAu&W 91, TwCSFW 91, WrDr 92*
**Charbonneau,** Louis Henry *TwCWW 91*
**Charbonneau,** Ralph Gray 1929- *WhoFI 92, WhoWest 92*
**Charbonneau,** Rhona Mae 1928- *WhoAmP 91*
**Charbonneau,** Robert 1911-1966 *FacFETw*
**Charbonnel,** Jean 1927- *IntWW 91*
**Charbonnet,** Louis, III *WhoAmP 91*
**Charbonnet,** Louis, III 1939- *WhoBlA 92*
**Charbonnier,** Francis Marcel 1927- *AmMWSc 92*
**Charbonnier,** Volker 1939- *WhoFI 92*
**Chard,** Dorothy Doreen 1916- *IntAu&W 91*
**Chard,** Judy 1916- *WrDr 92*
**Chard,** Nancy I 1933- *WhoAmP 91*
**Chard,** Timothy 1937- *Who 92*
**Chardin,** Jean Baptiste Simeon 1699-1779 *BlkwCEP*
**Chardon,** Phoebe A 1933- *WhoAmP 91*
**Chardoul,** Paul Nicholas 1939- *WhoMW 92*
**Chareau,** Pierre 1883-1950 *DcTwDes, FacFETw*
**Charest,** Philip George 1930- *WhoMW 92*
**Charest,** Pierre M 1953- *AmMWSc 92*
**Charette,** Robert L 1923- *WhoAmP 91*
**Charewicz,** David Michael 1932- *WhoMW 92*
**Chargaff,** Erwin 1905- *AmMWSc 92, FacFETw, IntWW 91*
**Charging Elk,** Edward 1944- *WhoAmP 91*
**Chargois,** Jenelle M. 1949- *WhoBlA 92*
**Chari,** Nallan C 1931- *AmMWSc 92*
**Charing Cross,** Archdeacon of *Who 92*
**Charis,** Sister 1948- *WhoBlA 92*
**Charisse,** Cyd 1921- *IntMPA 92*
**Charisse,** Cyd 1923- *WhoEnt 92*
**Charity,** Lawrence Everett 1935- *WhoBlA 92*
**Charity,** Ruth Harvey *WhoBlA 92*
**Charkes,** N David 1931- *AmMWSc 92*
**Charkey,** Lowell William *AmMWSc 92*
**Charkham,** Jonathan Philip 1930- *Who 92*
**Charkiewicz,** Mitchell Michael, Jr. 1946- *WhoFI 92*
**Charkin,** Richard Denis Paul 1949- *Who 92*
**Charkoudian,** Arppie 1925- *WhoAmP 91*
**Charkoudian,** John Charles 1941- *AmMWSc 92*
**Charland,** Gary George 1957- *WhoAmL 92*
**Charlang,** Gisela Wohlrab 1938- *AmMWSc 92*
**Charlap,** E. Paul d1991 *NewYTBS 91*
**Charlap,** Leonard Stanton 1938- *AmMWSc 92*
**Charlebois,** Robert 1945- *NewAmDM*
**Charlemont,** Earl of *BlkwCEP*
**Charlemont,** Viscount 1934- *Who 92*
**Charles** 1903-1983 *FacFETw*
**Charles** 1948- *FacFETw [port]*
**Charles I** *HisDSpE*
**Charles I** 1887-1922 *FacFETw*
**Charles II** 1661-1700 *HisDSpE*
**Charles III** 1716-1788 *BlkwCEP, HisDSpE*
**Charles IV** 1748-1819 *HisDSpE*
**Charles V** 1500-1558 *HisDSpE*
**Charles XII** 1682-1718 *BlkwCEP*
**Charles,** Adrian Owen 1926- *Who 92*
**Charles,** Alfred W. 1931- *WhoAmL 92*
**Charles,** Anita *WrDr 92*
**Charles,** Anne 1941- *WhoAmP 91*
**Charles,** Anthony Harold d1990 *Who 92N*
**Charles,** Arthur William Hessin 1948- *Who 92*
**Charles,** Bernard L. 1927- *WhoBlA 92*
**Charles,** Bernard Leopold 1929- *Who 92*
**Charles,** Bertram 1918- *WhoEnt 92*
**Charles,** Caroline 1942- *IntWW 91*
**Charles,** Christopher Donald 1956- *WhoFI 92*
**Charles,** Doreen Alicia 1960- *WhoBlA 92*
**Charles,** E. Otis 1926- *WhoRel 92*
**Charles,** Edgar Davidson, Jr 1943- *AmMWSc 92*
**Charles,** Eugenia *Who 92*
**Charles,** Eugenia 1919- *IntWW 91*
**Charles,** Fred Lemar 1872-1911 *BiInAmS*
**Charles,** George William 1915- *AmMWSc 92*
**Charles,** Gerda *ConNov 91*
**Charles,** Glen *WhoEnt 92*
**Charles,** Hampton *WrDr 92*
**Charles,** Harry 1957- *WhoAmL 92*
**Charles,** Harry Krewson, Jr 1944- *AmMWSc 92*
**Charles,** Henry *WrDr 92*
**Charles,** Horatio Nathan 1952- *WhoMW 92*
**Charles,** Jack 1923- *Who 92*
**Charles,** James Anthony 1926- *Who 92*
**Charles,** John A. 1951- *WhoHisp 92*
**Charles,** Joseph 1908- *Who 92*
**Charles,** Joseph, Jr 1944- *WhoAmP 91*
**Charles,** Joseph C. 1941- *WhoBlA 92*
**Charles,** Les *WhoEnt 92*
**Charles,** Leslie Stanley Francis 1917- *Who 92*
**Charles,** Lewis 1945- *WhoBlA 92*
**Charles,** Louis *SmATA 67*
**Charles,** Lucile Marie Hoerr 1903-1965 *DcNCBi 1*
**Charles,** Lyn Ellen 1951- *WhoFI 92*
**Charles,** Maria 1929- *IntMPA 92*
**Charles,** Mary Eugenia 1919- *Who 92*
**Charles,** Mary Louise 1922- *WhoWest 92*
**Charles,** Michael Edward 1935- *AmMWSc 92*
**Charles,** Michael Geoffrey A. *Who 92*
**Charles,** Nicholas *WrDr 92*
**Charles,** Nicholas J. *SmATA 68*
**Charles,** Nick 1946- *WhoEnt 92*
**Charles,** Pearnel 1936- *IntWW 91*
**Charles,** R J 1925- *AmMWSc 92*
**Charles,** Ray 1918- *WhoEnt 92*
**Charles,** Ray 1930- *FacFETw, IntWW 91, NewAmDM, WhoBlA 92, WhoEnt 92*
**Charles,** Rex Stephen 1953- *WhoRel 92*
**Charles,** Robert Bruce 1960- *WhoAmL 92*
**Charles,** Robert Wilson 1945- *AmMWSc 92*
**Charles,** Roderick Edward 1927- *WhoBlA 92*
**Charles,** Roland Scott 1947- *WhoWest 92*
**Charles,** Searle F 1923- *IntAu&W 91*
**Charles,** Serge Elie 1941- *IntWW 91*
**Charles,** Steven Gale 1952- *WhoMW 92*
**Charles,** Sydney Anicetus *WhoRel 92*
**Charles,** Teddy 1928- *NewAmDM*
**Charles,** Theresa *ConAu 34NR*
**Charles,** Walter 1945- *WhoEnt 92*
**Charles,** William Michael 1951- *WhoMW 92*
**Charles-Burrows-Charles** *LesBEnT 92*
**Charles-Roux,** Edmonde 1920- *IntWW 91*
**Charleson,** Ian 1949-1990 *AnObit 1990*
**Charleston,** Craig Williams 1953- *WhoFI 92*
**Charleston,** Gomez, Jr. 1950- *WhoBlA 92*
**Charleston,** Robert Jesse 1916- *Who 92, WrDr 92*
**Charlesworth,** Arthur Leonard 1927- *Who 92*
**Charlesworth,** Brian 1945- *AmMWSc 92, Who 92*
**Charlesworth,** Clifford E. 1931-1991 *NewYTBS 91*
**Charlesworth,** Henry A K 1931- *AmMWSc 92*
**Charlesworth,** James Hamilton 1940- *WhoRel 92*
**Charlesworth,** Peter James 1944- *Who 92*
**Charlesworth,** Rita Susbauer 1950- *WhoWest 92*
**Charlesworth,** Robert K 1923- *AmMWSc 92*
**Charlesworth,** Stanley 1920- *Who 92*
**Charlet,** Laurence Dean 1946- *AmMWSc 92*
**Charlevoix,** Pierre Francois Xavier de 1682-1761 *BlkwCEP*
**Charley,** Philip J 1921- *AmMWSc 92*
**Charley,** Philip James 1921- *WhoFI 92*
**Charlier,** Roger Henri 1921- *AmMWSc 92, IntAu&W 91, WrDr 92*
**Charlip,** Remy 1929- *IntAu&W 91, SmATA 68 [port], WrDr 92*
**Charlish,** Dennis Norman 1918- *Who 92*
**Charlop,** Zevulun 1929- *WhoRel 92*
**Charlot,** Gaston 1904- *IntWW 91*
**Charlot,** Jean 1932- *IntWW 91*
**Charlot,** Martin 1944- *ConAu 35NR*
**Charlotte,** Countess of Derby *EncAmaz 91*
**Charlotte von Nassau-Weilburg** 1896-1985 *FacFETw*
**Charlsen,** Nadine L. 1947- *WhoEnt 92*
**Charlson,** Chauncey R, Jr 1933- *WhoIns 92*
**Charlson,** David Harvey 1947- *WhoMW 92*
**Charlson,** Michael Lloyd 1958- *WhoAmL 92*
**Charlton,** Alan 1948- *TwCPaSc*
**Charlton,** Betty Jo 1923- *WhoAmP 91*
**Charlton,** Bobby *Who 92*
**Charlton,** Bobby 1937- *WrDr 92*
**Charlton,** Charles Hayes 1940- *WhoBlA 92*
**Charlton,** Clifford Tyrone 1965- *WhoBlA 92*
**Charlton,** David Berry 1904- *AmMWSc 92*
**Charlton,** Edward John 1953- *WhoAmL 92*
**Charlton,** Evan 1904-1984 *TwCPaSc*
**Charlton,** Felicity 1913- *TwCPaSc*
**Charlton,** Ferrier 1923- *Who 92*
**Charlton,** Frederick Noel 1906- *Who 92*
**Charlton,** George 1899- *TwCPaSc*
**Charlton,** Gordon Randolph 1937- *AmMWSc 92*
**Charlton,** Gordon Taliaferro, Jr. 1923- *WhoRel 92*
**Charlton,** Graham *Who 92*
**Charlton,** Graham 1928- *Who 92*
**Charlton,** Harvey Johnson 1934- *AmMWSc 92*
**Charlton,** Hilda 1910-1988 *RelLAm 91*
**Charlton,** Jack Fields 1928- *WhoBlA 92*
**Charlton,** James Leslie 1942- *AmMWSc 92*
**Charlton,** John *WrDr 92*
**Charlton,** John 1935- *Who 92*
**Charlton,** John Frederick, III 1944- *WhoRel 92*
**Charlton,** John Kipp 1937- *WhoWest 92*
**Charlton,** Kenneth 1925- *Who 92*
**Charlton,** Mervyn 1945- *TwCPaSc*
**Charlton,** Philip 1930- *Who 92*
**Charlton,** Robert 1937- *FacFETw, IntWW 91, Who 92*
**Charlton,** Robert William 1929- *IntWW 91*
**Charlton,** Thomas Alfred Graham 1913- *Who 92*
**Charlton,** Thomas Malcolm 1923- *Who 92, WrDr 92*
**Charlwood,** D. E. 1915- *WrDr 92*
**Charm,** Stanley E 1926- *AmMWSc 92*
**Charmbury,** H Beecher 1914- *AmMWSc 92*
**Charme,** Stuart Zane 1951- *WhoRel 92*
**Charmot,** Guy 1914- *IntWW 91*
**Charnas,** Douglas William 1953- *WhoAmL 92*
**Charnas,** Fran Elka *WhoEnt 92*
**Charnas,** Michael 1947- *WhoMW 92*
**Charnas,** Suzy McKee *DrAPF 91*
**Charnas,** Suzy McKee 1939- *IntAu&W 91, TwCSFW 91, WrDr 92*
**Charnay,** John Bruce 1949- *WhoWest 92*
**Charneco,** Jerry Charles 1947- *WhoHisp 92*
**Charnes,** Abraham 1917- *AmMWSc 92*
**Charney,** Dennis S 1951- *AmMWSc 92*
**Charney,** Elliot 1922- *AmMWSc 92*
**Charney,** Evan *AmMWSc 92*
**Charney,** Jonathan Isa 1943- *WhoAmL 92*
**Charney,** Louise Verrette 1931- *WhoEnt 92*
**Charney,** Martha R 1942- *AmMWSc 92*

**Charney**, Maurice Myron 1929- *WhoEnt 92*
**Charney**, Michael 1911- *AmMWSc 92*
**Charney**, Miriam *WhoEnt 92*
**Charney**, Nicolas Herman 1941- *WhoEnt 92*
**Charney**, Philip 1939- *WhoWest 92*
**Charney**, Scott Jason 1954- *WhoAmL 92*
**Charney**, Susan Elizabeth 1958- *WhoEnt 92*
**Charney**, William 1918- *AmMWSc 92*
**Charnin**, Martin *LesBEnT 92*
**Charnin**, Martin 1934- *WhoEnt 92*
**Charnley**, Clare 1949- *TwCPaSc*
**Charnley**, Donn 1928- *WhoAmP 91*
**Charnley**, John 1922- *Who 92*
**Charnock**, Henry 1920- *IntWW 91, Who 92*
**Charnoff**, Deborah Bernstein 1953- *WhoAmL 92*
**Charny**, Israel 1931- *WrDr 92*
**Charo**, Robin Alta 1958- *WhoAmL 92*
**Charobee**, Danny David 1950- *WhoWest 92*
**Charola**, Asuncion Elena 1942- *AmMWSc 92*
**Charon**, Lourdes 1956- *WhoHisp 92*
**Charon**, Nyles William 1943- *AmMWSc 92*
**Charoux**, Siegfried 1896- *TwCPaSc*
**Charp**, Solomon 1920- *AmMWSc 92*
**Charpentier**, Georges 1846-1905 *ThHEIm*
**Charpentier**, Gustav 1860-1956 *FacFETw*
**Charpentier**, Gustave 1860-1956 *NewAmDM*
**Charpentier**, Marc-Antoine 1650?-1704 *NewAmDM*
**Charpie**, Robert Alan 1925- *AmMWSc 92*
**Charrad**, Mounira *WhoFI 92*
**Charren**, Peggy *LesBEnT 92*
**Charren**, Peggy 1928- *WhoEnt 92*
**Charrier**, Michael Edward 1945- *WhoFI 92*
**Charriere**, Isabelle de 1740-1805 *FrenWW*
**Charriere**, Isobel van Tuyll 1740-1805 *BlkwCEP*
**Charron**, Estelle Irma 1928- *WhoRel 92*
**Charron**, Martin 1960- *AmMWSc 92*
**Charron**, Robert R *WhoAmP 91*
**Charron**, William C. 1938- *WhoMW 92*
**Charroppin**, Charles M d1915 *BiInAmS*
**Charrow**, Robert Phillip 1944- *WhoFI 92*
**Charry**, Michael Ronald 1933- *WhoEnt 92*
**Charry Lara**, Fernando 1920- *ConSpAP*
**Chartener**, Robert Victor 1958- *WhoFI 92*
**Charteris** *Who 92*
**Charteris**, Leslie 1907- *IntAu&W 91, IntWW 91, Who 92, WrDr 92*
**Charteris**, Leslie C *FacFETw*
**Charteris of Amisfield**, Baron 1913- *Who 92*
**Charters**, Ann 1936- *ConAu 34NR, WrDr 92*
**Charters**, Cynthia Grace 1949- *WhoWest 92*
**Charters**, Samuel 1929- *ConAu 34NR, WrDr 92*
**Charters**, Samuel Barclay 1929- *IntAu&W 91*
**Chartier**, Janellen Olsen 1951- *WhoMW 92*
**Chartier**, Myron Raymond 1938- *WhoMW 92, WhoRel 92*
**Chartier**, Normand L. 1945- *SmATA 66 [port]*
**Chartier**, Vernon L 1939- *AmMWSc 92*
**Chartier**, Vernon Lee 1939- *WhoWest 92*
**Chartock**, Michael Andrew 1943- *AmMWSc 92*
**Chartoff**, Melanie Barbara *WhoEnt 92*
**Chartoff**, Robert 1933- *IntMPA 92*
**Chartoff**, Robert Irwin *WhoEnt 92*
**Charton**, George N., Jr. 1923- *WhoBlA 92*
**Charton**, Marvin 1931- *AmMWSc 92*
**Chartrand**, Bernard Francis 1925- *WhoAmP 91*
**Chartrand**, Gary 1936- *AmMWSc 92*
**Chartrand**, Gary Theodore 1936- *WhoMW 92*
**Chartrand**, Mark Ray, III 1943- *AmMWSc 92*
**Chartrand**, Robert Lee 1928- *AmMWSc 92*
**Chartres**, Bruce A 1939- *AmMWSc 92*
**Charusathira**, Prapas 1912- *IntWW 91*
**Charvat**, F R 1931- *AmMWSc 92*
**Charvat**, Iris 1940- *AmMWSc 92*
**Charvet**, Richard Christopher Larkins 1936- *Who 92*
**Charvonia**, David Alan 1929- *AmMWSc 92*
**Charwat**, Andrew F 1925- *AmMWSc 92*
**Charyk**, Joseph Vincent 1920- *AmMWSc 92, IntWW 91*
**Charyn**, Jerome *DrAPF 91*
**Charyn**, Jerome 1937- *ConNov 91, IntAu&W 91, WrDr 92*
**Charyulu**, Komanduri K N 1924- *AmMWSc 92*
**Chasalow**, Fred I 1942- *AmMWSc 92*
**Chasalow**, Ivan G 1930- *AmMWSc 92*
**Chasanow**, Howard Stuart 1937- *WhoAmP 91*
**Chasar**, Dwight William 1943- *WhoMW 92*
**Chase**, Adam *TwCSFW 91*
**Chase**, Alan Lewis 1947- *WhoRel 92*
**Chase**, Alston Hurd 1906- *WrDr 92*
**Chase**, Andrew J 1916- *AmMWSc 92*
**Chase**, Ann Renee 1954- *AmMWSc 92*
**Chase**, Arleen Ruth 1945- *AmMWSc 92*
**Chase**, Arnett C. 1940- *WhoBlA 92*
**Chase**, Arthur E *WhoAmP 91*
**Chase**, Blanche Mary 1948- *WhoEnt 92*
**Chase**, Borden 1900-1971 *TwCWW 91*
**Chase**, Brandon *IntMPA 92*
**Chase**, Charles Elroy, Jr 1929- *AmMWSc 92*
**Chase**, Charles Jonathan 1959- *WhoWest 92*
**Chase**, Chevy *LesBEnT 92*
**Chase**, Chevy 1943- *ConTFT 9, IntWW 91, WhoEnt 92*
**Chase**, Chevy 1944- *IntMPA 92*
**Chase**, Clement Grasham 1944- *AmMWSc 92*
**Chase**, Cochrane 1932- *WhoFI 92*
**Chase**, Curtis Alden, Jr 1936- *AmMWSc 92*
**Chase**, Cyril Charles 1917- *WhoAmP 91*
**Chase**, David Bruce 1949- *AmMWSc 92*
**Chase**, David Marion 1930- *AmMWSc 92*
**Chase**, Donald Jacob 1944- *WhoEnt 92*
**Chase**, Edna Woolman 1877-1957 *BenetAL 91*
**Chase**, Edward 1940- *WhoFI 92*
**Chase**, Elaine R. 1949- *ConAu 36NR*
**Chase**, Elaine Raco *DrAPF 91*
**Chase**, Elaine Raco 1949- *IntAu&W 91, WrDr 92*
**Chase**, Emily *SmATA 68*
**Chase**, Fred Leroy 1914- *AmMWSc 92*
**Chase**, Gary Andrew 1945- *AmMWSc 92*
**Chase**, Gary Dale 1942- *WhoEnt 92*
**Chase**, Gene Barry 1943- *AmMWSc 92*
**Chase**, Gerald Roy 1938- *AmMWSc 92*
**Chase**, Grafton D 1921- *AmMWSc 92*
**Chase**, Harry Woodburn 1883-1955 *DcNCBi 1*
**Chase**, Helen Christina 1917- *AmMWSc 92*
**Chase**, Helen Louise 1943- *WhoFI 92*
**Chase**, Howard Edwin 1936- *WhoAmL 92*
**Chase**, Howard Marion 1938- *WhoMW 92*
**Chase**, Ilka 1905-1978 *BenetAL 91*
**Chase**, Ivan Dmitri 1943- *AmMWSc 92*
**Chase**, J Vincent 1949- *WhoAmP 91*
**Chase**, James *WhoBlA 92*
**Chase**, James Edward 1943- *WhoWest 92*
**Chase**, James Staton 1932- *WhoAmP 91*
**Chase**, Jay Benton 1940- *AmMWSc 92*
**Chase**, Joan *ConAu 134*
**Chase**, John David 1920- *AmMWSc 92*
**Chase**, John Donald 1935- *AmMWSc 92*
**Chase**, John S. 1925- *WhoBlA 92*
**Chase**, John William 1944- *AmMWSc 92*
**Chase**, Judith Helfer 1939- *WhoWest 92*
**Chase**, Keith William 1953- *WhoRel 92*
**Chase**, Larry Eugene 1943- *AmMWSc 92*
**Chase**, Larry J. 1945- *WhoWest 92*
**Chase**, Laurence F 1915- *WhoAmP 91*
**Chase**, Lawrence Arthur, Jr 1948- *WhoAmP 91*
**Chase**, Linda Arville 1953- *WhoEnt 92*
**Chase**, Lloyd Fremont, Jr 1931- *AmMWSc 92*
**Chase**, Lloyd Lee 1939- *AmMWSc 92*
**Chase**, Loriene Eck 1934- *WhoWest 92*
**Chase**, Louisa 1951- *WorArt 1980 [port]*
**Chase**, Lucia 1897-1986 *FacFETw*
**Chase**, Lyndon *WrDr 92*
**Chase**, Margaret S 1944- *WhoAmP 91*
**Chase**, Mary 1907-1981 *DramC 1 [port]*
**Chase**, Mary Coyle 1907-1981 *BenetAL 91*
**Chase**, Mary Ellen 1887-1973 *BenetAL 91*
**Chase**, Mary Jane 1938- *WhoAmP 91*
**Chase**, Melody Ann Schobert 1953- *WhoMW 92*
**Chase**, Merrill Wallace 1905- *AmMWSc 92*
**Chase**, Michael 1915- *TwCPaSc*
**Chase**, Morris 1918- *WhoFI 92*
**Chase**, Naomi Feigelson *DrAPF 91*
**Chase**, Norman Bradford 1924- *WhoAmP 91*
**Chase**, Norman E 1926- *AmMWSc 92*
**Chase**, Oscar Gottfried *WhoAmL 92*
**Chase**, Pliny Earle 1820-1886 *BiInAmS*
**Chase**, Randolph Montieth, Jr 1928- *AmMWSc 92*
**Chase**, Richard Barth 1939- *WhoWest 92*
**Chase**, Richard L 1933- *AmMWSc 92*
**Chase**, Richard Lyle 1945- *AmMWSc 92*
**Chase**, Richard V., Jr. 1914-1962 *BenetAL 91*
**Chase**, Robert A 1923- *AmMWSc 92*
**Chase**, Robert Arthur 1923- *IntWW 91*
**Chase**, Robert John 1943- *Who 92*
**Chase**, Robert L 1926- *AmMWSc 92*
**Chase**, Robert M 1944- *WhoAmP 91*
**Chase**, Robert Silmon, Jr 1930- *AmMWSc 92*
**Chase**, Roger Robert 1928- *Who 92*
**Chase**, Ronald 1940- *AmMWSc 92*
**Chase**, Russell C 1907- *WhoAmP 91*
**Chase**, Salmon Portland 1808-1873 *AmPolLe [port]*
**Chase**, Samuel 1741-1811 *AmPolLe, BlkwEAR*
**Chase**, Samuel Brown 1932- *WhoFI 92*
**Chase**, Sherret Spaulding 1918- *AmMWSc 92*
**Chase**, Stanley *IntMPA 92*
**Chase**, Stephanie R. 1953- *WhoEnt 92*
**Chase**, Steven Alan 1946- *WhoAmL 92*
**Chase**, Stuart 1888- *BenetAL 91*
**Chase**, Stuart 1888-1985 *FacFETw*
**Chase**, Theodore, Jr 1938- *AmMWSc 92, WhoAmP 91*
**Chase**, Thomas Newell 1932- *AmMWSc 92*
**Chase**, Thomas Richard 1954- *AmMWSc 92*
**Chase**, Thornton 1847-1912 *RelLAm 91*
**Chase**, Vernon Lindsay 1920- *AmMWSc 92*
**Chase**, William Arthur 1878-1944 *TwCPaSc*
**Chase**, William C 1895-1986 *FacFETw*
**Chase**, William E. 1931- *WhoAmL 92*
**Chase**, William Henry 1927- *AmMWSc 92*
**Chase**, William Robert 1951- *WhoEnt 92*
**Chase-Riboud**, Barbara *LiExTwC*
**Chase-Riboud**, Barbara 1939- *NotBlAW 92*
**Chase-Riboud**, Barbara DeWayne 1939- *WhoBlA 92*
**Chaseman**, Joel *LesBEnT 92*
**Chaseman**, Joel 1926- *WhoEnt 92*
**Chasens**, Abram I 1912- *AmMWSc 92*
**Chaset**, Alan Jay 1946- *WhoAmL 92*
**Chasey**, Jacqueline *WhoAmL 92*
**Chasin**, Helen *DrAPF 91*
**Chasin**, Lawrence Allen 1941- *AmMWSc 92*
**Chasin**, Mark 1942- *AmMWSc 92*
**Chasin**, Werner David 1932- *AmMWSc 92*
**Chasins**, Abram 1903-1987 *NewAmDM*
**Chasis**, Herbert 1905- *AmMWSc 92*
**Chasman**, Chellis 1932- *AmMWSc 92*
**Chasman**, David 1925- *IntMPA 92*
**Chasnoff**, Joel 1936- *WhoAmP 91*
**Chasnoff**, Jules 1927- *WhoAmL 92*
**Chason**, Jacob Leon 1915- *AmMWSc 92*
**Chass**, Jacob 1926- *AmMWSc 92*
**Chassan**, Jacob Bernard 1916- *AmMWSc 92*
**Chasse**, Richard D 1924- *WhoAmP 91*
**Chasson**, Robert Lee 1919- *AmMWSc 92*
**Chassy**, Bruce Matthew 1942- *AmMWSc 92*
**Chastagner**, Gary A 1948- *AmMWSc 92*
**Chastain**, Benjamin Burton 1936- *AmMWSc 92*
**Chastain**, Jane Steppe 1943- *WhoEnt 92*
**Chastain**, Margaret *WhoEnt 92*
**Chastain**, Marian Faulkner 1922- *AmMWSc 92*
**Chastain**, Randall Meads 1945- *WhoAmL 92*
**Chastain**, Thomas *WrDr 92*
**Chastain**, Vicki *WhoAmP 91*
**Chastant**, Harold P 1923- *WhoIns 92*
**Chasteen**, John Ray 1955- *WhoRel 92*
**Chasteen**, Norman Dennis 1941- *AmMWSc 92*
**Chastel**, Andre d1990 *IntWW 91N*
**Chastel**, Andre 1912-1990 *AnObit 1990*
**Chastellux**, Francois Jean de 1734-1788 *BenetAL 91*
**Chastine**, Ronald Freeman 1940- *WhoRel 92*
**Chaszeyka**, Michael A 1920- *AmMWSc 92*
**Chaszeyka**, Michael Andrew 1920- *WhoMW 92*
**Chatain**, Robert *DrAPF 91*
**Chataway**, Christopher John 1931- *IntWW 91, Who 92*
**Chateau**, Francois Michel 1956- *WhoAmL 92*
**Chateaubriand**, Francois Rene, Vicomte de 1768-1848 *BenetAL 91, GuFrLit 1*
**Chateaubriant**, Alphonse de 1877-1951 *BiDExR*
**Chateauneuf**, John Edward 1957- *AmMWSc 92*
**Chatelain**, Jack Ellis 1922- *AmMWSc 92*
**Chatelet**, Gabrielle Emilie, marquise du 1706-1749 *BlkwCEP*
**Chatenet**, Pierre 1917- *IntWW 91*
**Chatenever**, Alfred 1916- *AmMWSc 92*
**Chater**, Anthony Philip John *Who 92*
**Chater**, Anthony Philip John 1929- *IntAu&W 91*
**Chater**, Nancy 1915- *Who 92*
**Chater**, Shirley S *AmMWSc 92*
**Chatfield** *Who 92*
**Chatfield**, Baron 1917- *Who 92*
**Chatfield**, Cheryl Ann 1946- *WhoFI 92, WhoWest 92*
**Chatfield**, Dale Alton 1947- *AmMWSc 92*
**Chatfield**, Donald Franklin 1935- *WhoMW 92, WhoRel 92*
**Chatfield**, E. Charles 1934- *WrDr 92*
**Chatfield**, Gail L 1933- *WhoAmP 91*
**Chatfield**, Hale *DrAPF 91*
**Chatfield**, Joan 1932- *WhoRel 92, WhoWest 92*
**Chatfield**, John A 1943- *AmMWSc 92*
**Chatfield**, John Freeman 1929- *Who 92*
**Chatfield**, John Norville 1941- *WhoWest 92*
**Chatfield**, Robert Harmon 1947- *WhoMW 92*
**Chatham** *BlkwEAR*
**Chatham**, Earl of *BlkwCEP*
**Chatham**, Alexander 1834-1920 *DcNCBi 1*
**Chatham**, Gerald Wilborn, Sr. 1944- *WhoAmL 92*
**Chatham**, Hugh Gwyn 1864-1929 *DcNCBi 1*
**Chatham**, Larry *IntAu&W 91X, TwCWW 91*
**Chatham**, Richard Thurmond 1896-1957 *DcNCBi 1*
**Chatham**, Russell 1939- *WhoWest 92*
**Chatichai**, Choonhavan 1922- *FacFETw*
**Chatigny**, Mark A 1920- *AmMWSc 92*
**Chatland**, Harold 1911- *AmMWSc 92*
**Chatlow**, Michael 1944- *TwCPaSc*
**Chatman**, Alex 1943- *WhoBlA 92*
**Chatman**, Anna Lee 1919- *WhoBlA 92*
**Chatman**, Donald Leveritt 1934- *WhoBlA 92*
**Chatman**, Jacob L. 1938- *WhoBlA 92*
**Chatman**, Jennifer Anna 1959- *WhoMW 92*
**Chatman**, Melvin E. 1933- *WhoBlA 92*
**Chatman**, Seymour 1928- *WrDr 92*
**Chatman-Royce**, Edgar Truitt 1924- *WhoRel 92*
**Chatmon**, Linda Carol 1951- *WhoBlA 92*
**Chato**, David Joseph 1958- *WhoMW 92*
**Chato**, John C 1929- *AmMWSc 92*
**Chato**, John Clark 1929- *WhoMW 92*
**Chatoff**, Michael Alan 1946- *WhoAmL 92*
**Chatroo**, Arthur Jay 1946- *WhoAmL 92, WhoFI 92, WhoMW 92*
**Chatt**, Allen Barrett 1949- *AmMWSc 92*
**Chatt**, Amares *AmMWSc 92*
**Chatt**, Joseph 1914- *IntWW 91, Who 92*
**Chattaway**, William 1927- *TwCPaSc*
**Chatten**, Harold Raymond Percy *Who 92*
**Chatten**, Leslie George 1920- *AmMWSc 92*
**Chatterjee**, Amiya K. 1938- *WhoMW 92*
**Chatterjee**, Bandana 1951- *AmMWSc 92*
**Chatterjee**, Bijoy Gopal 1937- *WhoWest 92*
**Chatterjee**, Lois Jordan 1940- *WhoBlA 92*
**Chatterjee**, Nando Kumar 1938- *AmMWSc 92*
**Chatterjee**, Pranab 1936- *WhoMW 92*
**Chatterjee**, Pronoy Kumar 1936- *AmMWSc 92*
**Chatterjee**, Ramananda 1936- *AmMWSc 92*
**Chatterjee**, Samprit 1938- *AmMWSc 92*
**Chatterjee**, Sankar 1943- *AmMWSc 92*
**Chatterjee**, Satya Narayan 1934- *AmMWSc 92*
**Chatterjee**, Satya Saran 1922- *Who 92*
**Chatterjee**, Subroto 1947- *AmMWSc 92*
**Chatterjee**, Sunil Kumar 1940- *AmMWSc 92*
**Chatterji**, Debajyoti 1944- *AmMWSc 92*
**Chatterley**, James Philip 1923- *WhoMW 92*
**Chatterton**, Brian Douglas Eyre 1943- *AmMWSc 92*
**Chatterton**, C V 1918- *WhoAmP 91*
**Chatterton**, Karen Smith 1951- *WhoEnt 92*
**Chatterton**, Norman Jerry 1939- *AmMWSc 92*
**Chatterton**, Robert Treat, Jr 1935- *AmMWSc 92*
**Chatterton**, Thomas 1752-1770 *BlkwCEP, DcLB 109 [port], RfGEnL 91*
**Chatterton**, Wayne Joseph 1962- *WhoMW 92*
**Chatterton**, William Alonzo 1926- *WhoAmL 92*
**Chattha**, Mohinder Singh 1940- *AmMWSc 92*
**Chattin**, Gilbert Marshall 1914- *WhoFI 92*
**Chatto and Windus** *DcLB 106*
**Chatto**, Beth 1923- *Who 92*
**Chattoraj**, Sati Charan 1934- *AmMWSc 92*
**Chattoraj**, Shib Charan 1924- *WhoMW 92*
**Chatty**, Habib 1916-1991 *IntWW 91, -91N*
**Chaturvedi**, Arvind Kumar 1947- *AmMWSc 92*
**Chaturvedi**, Mahesh Chandra 1940- *AmMWSc 92*
**Chaturvedi**, Ram Prakash 1931- *AmMWSc 92*

**Chaturvedi**, Rama Kant 1933- *AmMWSc 92*
**Chatwin**, Bruce 1940-1989 *FacFETw*
**Chatwin**, Michael 1943- *TwCPaSc*
**Chaty**, John Culver 1925- *AmMWSc 92*
**Chatzidakis**, Manos 1925- *IntWW 91*
**Chau**, Alfred Shun-Yuen 1941- *AmMWSc 92*
**Chau**, Cheuk-Kin 1941- *AmMWSc 92*
**Chau**, Hin Fai 1964- *AmMWSc 92, WhoMW 92*
**Chau**, Ling-Lie 1939- *AmMWSc 92*
**Chau**, Michael Ming-Kee 1947- *AmMWSc 92*
**Chau**, Thuy Thanh 1944- *AmMWSc 92*
**Chau**, Vincent 1952- *AmMWSc 92*
**Chau**, Wai-Yin 1939- *AmMWSc 92*
**Chau**, Yiu-Kee 1927- *AmMWSc 92*
**Chaubal**, Madhukar Gajanan 1930- *AmMWSc 92*
**Chaubal**, Pinakin Chintamani 1957- *WhoMW 92*
**Chaubey**, Mahendra 1948- *AmMWSc 92*
**Chaucer**, Geoffrey 1340?-1400 *CnDBLB 1 [port], LitC 17 [port], RfGEnL 91*
**Chaudhari**, Anshumali 1947- *AmMWSc 92*
**Chaudhari**, Bipin Bhudharlal 1935- *AmMWSc 92*
**Chaudhari**, Praveen 1937- *AmMWSc 92*
**Chaudhary**, Amarsingh Bhilabhai 1941- *IntWW 91*
**Chaudhary**, Rabindra Kumar *AmMWSc 92*
**Chaudhri**, Amin Qamar 1942- *IntMPA 92, WhoEnt 92*
**Chaudhri**, Safee U 1944- *AmMWSc 92*
**Chaudhry**, G Rasul 1948- *AmMWSc 92*
**Chaudhry**, M. Hanif *WhoWest 92*
**Chaudhuri**, Haridas 1913-1975 *RelLAm 91*
**Chaudhuri**, Kirti Narayan 1934- *Who 92*
**Chaudhuri**, Naranarain 1916- *IntWW 91*
**Chaudhuri**, Nirad C. 1897- *LiExTwC*
**Chaudhuri**, Nirad Chandra 1897- *Who 92*
**Chaudhuri**, Tapan K 1944- *AmMWSc 92*
**Chaudhuri**, Tuhin 1942- *AmMWSc 92*
**Chaudry**, Irshad Hussain 1945- *AmMWSc 92*
**Chauffe**, Leroy 1936- *AmMWSc 92*
**Chaufournier**, Roger 1924- *IntWW 91*
**Chauhan**, Joseph Hirendra 1922- *WhoFI 92*
**Chauhan**, Ved P S 1953- *AmMWSc 92*
**Chauls**, Robert Nathan 1942- *WhoEnt 92*
**Chauncey**, Beatrice Arlene *WhoEnt 92*
**Chauncey**, Minion Kenneth 1946- *WhoBlA 92*
**Chauncey**, Robert Ernest 1941- *WhoFI 92*
**Chauncey**, Tom Webster, II 1947- *WhoAmL 92, WhoWest 92*
**Chauncy**, Charles 1705-1787 *BenetAL 91*
**Chaunu**, Pierre 1923- *IntWW 91*
**Chaus**, Bernard d1991 *NewYTBS 91*
**Chaushian**, Levon 1946- *ConCom 92*
**Chaussee**, John Barry 1960- *WhoAmL 92*
**Chausson**, Ernest 1855-1899 *NewAmDM*
**Chauteau-Gay**, Madame de *EncAmaz 91*
**Chauveaux**, Billie 1925- *WhoAmP 91*
**Chauvenet**, Regis 1842-1920 *BiInAmS*
**Chauvenet**, William 1820-1870 *BiInAmS*
**Chauvin**, Leonard Stanley, Jr. 1935- *WhoAmL 92*
**Chauvin**, Louis 1881-1908 *NewAmDM*
**Chauvin**, Richard Lucien 1949- *WhoWest 92*
**Chauvin**, Robert S 1920- *AmMWSc 92*
**Chauvire**, Yvette 1917- *IntWW 91, Who 92*
**Chavan**, Shankarrao Bhaorao 1920- *IntWW 91*
**Chavannes**, Albert 1836-1903 *ScFEYrs*
**Chavarria**, Adam, Jr. 1949- *WhoHisp 92*
**Chavarria**, Dolores Esparza 1952- *WhoFI 92*
**Chavarria**, Doroteo *WhoHisp 92*
**Chavarria**, Ernest M., Jr. 1955- *WhoHisp 92*
**Chavarria**, Ernest Montes, Jr. 1955- *WhoFI 92*
**Chavarria**, Fernando 1952- *WhoHisp 92*
**Chavarria**, Hector Manuel 1934- *WhoHisp 92*
**Chavarria**, Jesus *WhoHisp 92*
**Chavarria**, Oscar 1947- *WhoHisp 92*
**Chavarria**, Phil 1929- *WhoHisp 92*
**Chavarria Chairez**, Rebecca 1956- *WhoHisp 92*
**Chavas**, John Joseph, Jr. 1939- *WhoMW 92*
**Chavasse**, Christopher Patrick Grant 1928- *Who 92*
**Chave**, Alan Dana 1953- *AmMWSc 92*
**Chave**, Charles Trudeau 1905- *AmMWSc 92*
**Chave**, Keith Ernest 1928- *AmMWSc 92*
**Chavel**, Francois M 1946- *WhoIns 92*
**Chavel**, Isaac 1939- *AmMWSc 92*
**Chaves**, Cristobal de 1533-1629 *HisDSpE*
**Chaves**, Jose A 1941- *WhoIns 92*
**Chaves**, Lloyd Zamora, Jr. 1948- *WhoHisp 92*
**Chaves**, Manuel 1945- *IntWW 91*
**Chaves**, Melvin *WhoHisp 92*
**Chaves**, Nufrio de 1518-1568 *HisDSpE*
**Chaves-Carballo**, Enrique 1936- *WhoHisp 92*
**Chaves De Mendonca**, Antonio Aureliano 1929- *IntWW 91*
**Chavez**, Abel Max 1951- *WhoHisp 92*
**Chavez**, Abraham 1927- *WhoHisp 92*
**Chavez**, Abraham, Jr. 1927- *WhoEnt 92*
**Chavez**, Albert Blas 1952- *WhoWest 92*
**Chavez**, Alice Diaz 1956- *WhoHisp 92*
**Chavez**, Andrew 1939- *WhoHisp 92*
**Chavez**, Angelico 1910- *WhoHisp 92*
**Chavez**, Anita *WhoHisp 92*
**Chavez**, Benjamin Anthony *WhoHisp 92*
**Chavez**, Bernadette Louise 1947- *WhoHisp 92*
**Chavez**, Bernadette Marie 1955- *WhoHisp 92*
**Chavez**, Carlos 1899-1978 *FacFETw, NewAmDM*
**Chavez**, Carmela B. 1950- *WhoHisp 92*
**Chavez**, Carmen L. 1955- *WhoHisp 92*
**Chavez**, Ceasar 1927- *WhoAmP 91*
**Chavez**, Cesar 1927- *FacFETw [port], RComAH*
**Chavez**, Cesar Estrada 1927- *WhoHisp 92, WhoWest 92*
**Chavez**, Cesar Tizoc 1952- *WhoHisp 92*
**Chavez**, Cynthia 1967- *WhoHisp 92*
**Chavez**, Darlene 1950- *WhoHisp 92*
**Chavez**, Denise Elia 1948- *WhoEnt 92, WhoHisp 92*
**Chavez**, Dennis C *WhoAmP 91, WhoHisp 92*
**Chavez**, Dennis M. 1954- *WhoHisp 92*
**Chavez**, Don Antonio 1950- *WhoHisp 92*
**Chavez**, Eduardo Arcenio 1917- *WhoHisp 92*
**Chavez**, Edward John 1943- *WhoHisp 92*
**Chavez**, Edward L. 1963- *WhoHisp 92, WhoWest 92*
**Chavez**, Elaine Juanita 1964- *WhoHisp 92*
**Chavez**, Elida *WhoHisp 92*
**Chavez**, Eliverio 1940- *WhoHisp 92*
**Chavez**, Ernest L. 1949- *WhoHisp 92*
**Chavez**, Fabian 1924- *WhoHisp 92*
**Chavez**, Felix P. 1933- *WhoHisp 92*
**Chavez**, Frank 1929- *WhoHisp 92*
**Chavez**, Frank Norman 1941- *WhoAmL 92*
**Chavez**, Gabriel Anthony 1955- *WhoHisp 92*
**Chavez**, Genovevo Teodoro 1945- *WhoHisp 92*
**Chavez**, Gilbert Espinoza 1932- *WhoRel 92, WhoWest 92*
**Chavez**, Helen Pappas 1925- *WhoAmP 91*
**Chavez**, Ida Lillian 1944- *WhoHisp 92*
**Chavez**, Isidro Ontiveros 1948- *WhoHisp 92*
**Chavez**, Joe Robert 1958- *WhoHisp 92*
**Chavez**, John *WhoHisp 92*
**Chavez**, John Anthony 1955- *WhoAmL 92*
**Chavez**, John G. *WhoHisp 92*
**Chavez**, John I. E. 1949- *WhoHisp 92*
**Chavez**, John J. 1935- *WhoHisp 92*
**Chavez**, John Montoya 1952- *WhoHisp 92*
**Chavez**, John S. *WhoHisp 92*
**Chavez**, Joseph Arnold 1939- *WhoHisp 92*
**Chavez**, Joseph Philip 1946- *WhoRel 92*
**Chavez**, Julio Cesar *WhoHisp 92*
**Chavez**, Julio Cesar 1923- *WhoEnt 92*
**Chavez**, Larry Sterling 1948- *WhoHisp 92*
**Chavez**, Linda *WhoHisp 92*
**Chavez**, Linda 1947- *WhoHisp 92*
**Chavez**, Luis 1953- *WhoHisp 92*
**Chavez**, Manuel C. *WhoHisp 92*
**Chavez**, Manuel Camacho, Sr. 1930- *WhoHisp 92*
**Chavez**, Maria D. 1939- *WhoHisp 92*
**Chavez**, Mariano, Jr. *WhoHisp 92*
**Chavez**, Martin J 1952- *WhoAmP 91*
**Chavez**, Martin Joseph 1952- *WhoHisp 92*
**Chavez**, Mary 1952- *WhoHisp 92*
**Chavez**, Mary B. 1925- *WhoHisp 92*
**Chavez**, Mauro 1947- *WhoHisp 92*
**Chavez**, Melchor 1934- *WhoAmP 91*
**Chavez**, Melesio Romo 1935- *WhoHisp 92*
**Chavez**, Michael Mendez 1959- *WhoHisp 92*
**Chavez**, Octavio Vega 1939- *WhoHisp 92*
**Chavez**, Pablo R. 1935- *WhoHisp 92*
**Chavez**, Patricia L. 1954- *WhoHisp 92*
**Chavez**, Ray 1950- *WhoHisp 92*
**Chavez**, Raymond M. 1947- *WhoHisp 92*
**Chavez**, Richard G. *WhoHisp 92*
**Chavez**, Richard J. 1946- *WhoHisp 92*
**Chavez**, Richard Ralph 1943- *WhoRel 92*
**Chavez**, Rodolfo Lucas 1950- *WhoHisp 92*
**Chavez**, Sonny *WhoHisp 92*
**Chavez**, Thomas McCroskey 1965- *WhoFI 92*
**Chavez**, Tibo J. *WhoHisp 92*
**Chavez**, Tito David 1947- *WhoAmP 91, WhoHisp 92*
**Chavez**, Tony, Jr. 1939- *WhoHisp 92*
**Chavez**, Tony A. 1931- *WhoHisp 92*
**Chavez**, Trinidad Jose, Jr. 1937- *WhoHisp 92*
**Chavez**, Victor B. 1945- *WhoHisp 92*
**Chavez**, Victoria Marie 1933- *WhoHisp 92*
**Chavez**, William Xavier, Jr. 1955- *WhoHisp 92*
**Chavez Ahner**, Yolanda 1937- *WhoHisp 92*
**Chavez-Andonegui**, Carlos E. 1946- *WhoHisp 92*
**Chavez-Cornish**, Patricia Marie 1951- *WhoHisp 92*
**Chavez Kelley**, Christina L. G. 1953- *WhoHisp 92*
**Chavez-Mendez**, Ricardo 1953- *WhoHisp 92*
**Chavez-Thompson**, Linda *WhoHisp 92*
**Chavez-Vasquez**, Gloria *WhoHisp 92*
**Chavez y Ramirez**, Carlos 1899-1978 *NewAmDM*
**Chaviano**, Hugo 1952- *WhoHisp 92*
**Chavin**, Walter 1925- *AmMWSc 92*
**Chavis**, Benjamin Franklin, Jr. 1948- *WhoBlA 92*
**Chavis**, John 1763?-1838 *DcNCBi 1*
**Chavis**, Theodore R. 1922- *WhoBlA 92*
**Chavis-Butler**, Grace Lee 1916- *WhoWest 92*
**Chavous**, Barney Lewis 1951- *WhoBlA 92*
**Chavunduka**, Gordon Lloyd 1931- *IntWW 91*
**Chaw**, Sau Yee Sally 1963- *WhoFI 92*
**Chawla**, Krishan Kumar 1942- *WhoFI 92*
**Chawla**, Mangal Dass 1932- *AmMWSc 92*
**Chawner**, William Donald 1903- *AmMWSc 92*
**Chayama**, Yukihiko 1947- *WhoFI 92*
**Chayanne** 1969- *WhoHisp 92*
**Chayanov**, Aleksandr Vasil'evich 1888-1939 *SovUnBD*
**Chayefsky**, Paddy d1981 *LesBEnT 92*
**Chayefsky**, Paddy 1923-1981 *BenetAL 91*
**Chayes**, Abram 1922- *IntWW 91, WhoAmL 92*
**Chayevsky**, Paddy 1923-1981 *FacFETw*
**Chaykin**, Robert Leroy 1944- *WhoWest 92*
**Chaykin**, Sterling 1929- *AmMWSc 92*
**Chaykov**, Iosif Moiseevich 1888-1979 *SovUnBD*
**Chaykovsky**, Boris Aleksandrovich 1925- *SovUnBD*
**Chaykovsky**, Michael 1934- *AmMWSc 92*
**Chaynes**, Charles 1925- *ConCom 92*
**Chaytor**, George Reginald 1912- *Who 92*
**Chazanoff**, Daniel 1923- *WhoEnt 92*
**Chazen**, Melvin Leonard 1933- *WhoWest 92*
**Chazin**, Alan Howard 1946- *WhoEnt 92*
**Chazotte**, Brad Nelson 1954- *AmMWSc 92*
**Chazov**, Yevgeniy Ivanovich 1929- *SovUnBD*
**Chazov**, Yevgeny 1929- *IntWW 91*
**Che Peiqin** *IntWW 91*
**Che**, Christopher Nji 1962- *WhoFI 92*
**Che**, Stanley Chia-Lin 1946- *AmMWSc 92*
**Cheadle**, Eric 1908- *Who 92*
**Cheadle**, Vernon Irvin 1910- *AmMWSc 92*
**Cheal**, Beryl Irene 1935- *WhoWest 92*
**Cheal**, MaryLou 1926- *AmMWSc 92*
**Cheap Trick** *NewAmDM*
**Cheatham**, Adolphus A. 1905- *WhoBlA 92*
**Cheatham**, Betty L. 1940- *WhoBlA 92*
**Cheatham**, Bruce Allan 1946- *WhoAmL 92*
**Cheatham**, Charlotte *DrAPF 91*
**Cheatham**, Daniel E. 1949- *WhoFI 92*
**Cheatham**, David G 1951- *WhoAmP 91*
**Cheatham**, Della M. 1920- *WhoBlA 92*
**Cheatham**, Doc 1905- *NewAmDM*
**Cheatham**, Eugene Calvin, III 1945- *WhoFI 92*
**Cheatham**, Frank S., Jr. 1924- *WhoAmL 92*
**Cheatham**, Gary Lynn 1953- *WhoRel 92*
**Cheatham**, Henry Boles 1943- *WhoBlA 92*
**Cheatham**, Henry Plummer 1857-1935 *DcNCBi 1*
**Cheatham**, John B, Jr 1924- *AmMWSc 92*
**Cheatham**, John Bryan 1896- *WhoAmP 91*
**Cheatham**, Karyn Follis *DrAPF 91*
**Cheatham**, Linda Moye 1948- *WhoBlA 92*
**Cheatham**, Robert Gary 1926- *AmMWSc 92*
**Cheatham**, Robert William 1938- *WhoAmL 92*
**Cheatham**, Roy E. 1941- *WhoBlA 92*
**Cheatham**, Thomas J 1944- *AmMWSc 92*
**Cheatham**, William Joseph *AmMWSc 92*
**Cheatwood**, Earl 1928- *WhoAmP 91*
**Cheavens**, Frank 1905- *WrDr 92*
**Cheavens**, Thomas Henry 1930- *AmMWSc 92*
**Chebrikov**, Viktor Mikhailovich 1923- *IntWW 91*
**Chebrikov**, Viktor Mikhaylovich 1923- *SovUnBD*
**Checa**, Eduardo 1959- *WhoFI 92*
**Checa**, Feliciano 1779-1846 *HisDSpE*
**Checchi**, Alfred A. 1948- *WhoFI 92*
**Checchi**, Vincent Victor 1918- *WhoFI 92*
**Checchia**, Anthony Phillip 1930- *WhoEnt 92*
**Chechik**, Boris 1931- *AmMWSc 92*
**Check**, Irene J 1946- *AmMWSc 92*
**Checkel**, M David 1954- *AmMWSc 92*
**Checker**, Chubby 1941- *ConMus 7 [port], NewAmDM, WhoBlA 92*
**Checketts**, David 1930- *Who 92*
**Checketts**, Guy Tresham 1927- *Who 92*
**Checketts**, Keith Thomas 1935- *WhoWest 92*
**Checkland**, Michael *LesBEnT 92*
**Checkland**, Michael 1936- *IntWW 91, Who 92*
**Checkoway**, Robert 1951- *WhoAmL 92*
**Checole**, Kassahun 1947- *WhoBlA 92*
**Checota**, Joseph W 1939- *WhoAmP 91*
**Chedgy**, David George 1939- *WhoFI 92*
**Chediak**, Christopher Veach 1957- *WhoAmL 92*
**Chediak**, Natalio 1909- *WhoHisp 92*
**Chedid**, Andree 1920- *FrenWW, IntWW 91*
**Chedid**, John G. 1923- *WhoRel 92, WhoWest 92*
**Chedlow**, Barry William 1921- *Who 92*
**Chee**, Percival Hon Yin 1936- *WhoWest 92*
**Cheech** 1946- *WhoEnt 92*
**Cheek**, David Lynn 1963- *WhoFI 92*
**Cheek**, Dennis William 1955- *WhoRel 92*
**Cheek**, Donald Kato 1930- *WhoBlA 92*
**Cheek**, Donna Marie 1963- *WhoBlA 92*
**Cheek**, Emerson, III 1944- *WhoAmL 92*
**Cheek**, Jack Thomas, Jr. 1934- *WhoFI 92*
**Cheek**, James Edward 1932- *IntWW 91, WhoBlA 92*
**Cheek**, James Richard 1936- *WhoAmP 91*
**Cheek**, King Virgil, Jr. 1937- *WhoBlA 92*
**Cheek**, Malcolm 1950- *WhoMW 92*
**Cheek**, Nicholas Byron 1952- *WhoRel 92*
**Cheek**, Randy Michael 1952- *WhoRel 92*
**Cheek**, Robert Benjamin, III 1931- *WhoBlA 92*
**Cheek**, Will T 1943- *WhoAmP 91*
**Cheeke**, Peter Robert 1941- *AmMWSc 92*
**Cheeks**, Carl L. 1937- *WhoBlA 92*
**Cheeks**, Darryl Lamont 1968- *WhoBlA 92*
**Cheeks**, Donald E *WhoAmP 91*
**Cheeks**, Maurice Edward 1956- *WhoBlA 92*
**Cheeley**, Joseph Elbert, III 1955- *WhoAmL 92*
**Cheely**, Daniel Joseph 1949- *WhoAmL 92*
**Cheema**, Mohindar Singh 1929- *AmMWSc 92*
**Cheema**, Zafarullah K 1934- *AmMWSc 92*
**Cheer**, Clair James 1937- *AmMWSc 92*
**Cheerath**, Ram Mohan 1959- *WhoAmL 92*
**Cheese**, Bernard 1925- *TwCPaSc*
**Cheese**, Chloe 1952- *TwCPaSc*
**Cheese**, Pauline Staten *WhoBlA 92*
**Cheeseborough**, Chandra 1959- *BlkOlyM*
**Cheeseman**, Douglas Taylor, Jr. 1937- *WhoWest 92*
**Cheeseman**, Harold 1915- *TwCPaSc*
**Cheeseman**, Ian Clifford 1926- *Who 92*
**Cheeseman**, Stephen Carl 1944- *WhoAmL 92*
**Cheeseman**, Valerie Christine 1949- *WhoFI 92*
**Cheeseman**, William John 1943- *WhoAmL 92*
**Cheesman**, Benbow Palmer, Jr. 1942- *WhoAmL 92*
**Cheesman**, John Michael 1943- *WhoRel 92*
**Cheesman**, Kerry Lee 1954- *WhoMW 92*
**Cheesman**, Timothy Matlack 1853-1919 *BiInAmS*
**Cheetham**, Alan Herbert 1928- *AmMWSc 92*
**Cheetham**, Anthony John Valerian 1943- *IntWW 91, Who 92*
**Cheetham**, Anthony Kevin 1946- *Who 92*
**Cheetham**, Francis William 1928- *Who 92*
**Cheetham**, James 1772-1810 *BenetAL 91*
**Cheetham**, John Frederick Thomas 1919- *Who 92*
**Cheetham**, Juliet 1939- *Who 92*
**Cheetham**, Nicolas 1910- *Who 92*
**Cheetham**, Ronald D 1943- *AmMWSc 92*
**Cheevasit**, Kriengsak 1954- *WhoFI 92*
**Cheever**, Allen 1932- *AmMWSc 92*
**Cheever**, Byron William 1841-1888 *BiInAmS*
**Cheever**, Dan J. 1955- *WhoWest 92*
**Cheever**, David Williams 1831-1915 *BiInAmS*
**Cheever**, Ezekiel 1615?-1708 *BenetAL 91*
**Cheever**, Herbert Edward, Jr 1938- *WhoAmP 91*

Cheever, John 1912-1982 BenetAL 91, FacFETw
Cheever, Kenneth Lee 1939- WhoMW 92
Cheever, Susan 1943- WrDr 92
Cheevers, William Harold 1918- Who 92
Cheevers, William Phillip 1941- AmMWSc 92
Chefetz, Jeffrey M. 1950- WhoWest 92
Chegini, Nasser AmMWSc 92
Cheh, Albert Mei-Chu 1947- AmMWSc 92
Cheh, Huk Yuk 1939- AmMWSc 92, WhoFI 92
Chehovin, Richard John 1957- WhoFI 92
Chein, Orin Nathaniel 1943- AmMWSc 92
Cheirrett, Peggy Ann 1948- WhoFI 92, WhoWest 92
Cheitlin, Melvin Donald 1929- AmMWSc 92
Chekanauskas, Vitautas Algirdo 1930- IntWW 91
Chekarin, Yevgeniv Mikhailovich 1924- IntWW 91
Cheke, Dudley John 1912- Who 92
Chekhov, Anton 1860-1904 FacFETw [port]
Chelapati, Chunduri V 1933- AmMWSc 92
Chelberg, Bruce Stanley 1934- WhoFI 92
Chelemer, Harold 1928- AmMWSc 92
Chelette, Ricky Paul 1962- WhoRel 92
Chelf, Carl P. 1937- WrDr 92
Cheli, Giovanni 1918- IntWW 91
Cheli, Ronald Peter 1952- WhoAmL 92
Chelidonis EncAmaz 91
Chelidze, Otar Silovanovich 1925- IntWW 91
Chelikowsky, James Robert 1948- AmMWSc 92
Chelius, James Robert 1943- WhoFI 92
Chell, Beverly C. 1942- WhoAmL 92
Chell, Edward 1958- TwCPaSc
Chellappa, Ramalingam 1953- AmMWSc 92
Chellew, Norman Raymond 1917- AmMWSc 92
Chellgren, Paul Wilbur 1943- WhoFI 92
Chellis, Sharon Lee Hayes 1943- WhoAmP 91
Chello, Paul Larson 1942- AmMWSc 92
Chelmer, Baron 1914- Who 92
Chelmsford, Bishop of 1930- Who 92
Chelmsford, Provost of Who 92
Chelmsford, Viscount 1931- Who 92
Chelomey, Vladimir Nikolaevich 1914-1984 SovUnBD
Chelsea, Viscount 1937- Who 92
Chelsi, Lawrence George 1920- WhoEnt 92
Chelstrom, Marilyn Ann WhoMW 92
Cheltenham, Archdeacon of Who 92
Chelton, Dudley B 1928- AmMWSc 92
Chelton, John IntAu&W 91X, WrDr 92
Chelton, Lewis William Leonard 1934- Who 92
Chemers, Robert Marc 1951- WhoAmL 92
Chemetov, Paul 1928- IntWW 91
Chen Ailian 1939- IntWW 91
Chen Baichen 1908- IntWW 91
Chen Bangzhu 1934- IntWW 91
Chen Biao 1923- IntWW 91
Chen Bin 1919- IntWW 91
Chen Boda 1905-1989 FacFETw
Chen Chi-Lu 1923- IntWW 91
Chen Dun 1928- IntWW 91
Chen Fang 1957- IntWW 91
Chen Gang 1935- IntWW 91
Chen Guangyi 1933- IntWW 91
Chen Guodong 1911- IntWW 91
Chen Hanseng 1897- IntWW 91
Chen Heqiao 1914- IntWW 91
Chen Huangmei 1913- IntWW 91
Chen Huiguang 1939- IntWW 91
Chen Jingrun 1933- IntWW 91
Chen Junsheng 1927- IntWW 91
Chen Kaige LiExTwC
Chen Kaige 1952- IntDcF 2-2
Chen Kaige 1954- IntWW 91
Chen Lei 1917- IntWW 91
Chen Li-An 1937- IntWW 91
Chen Luzhi IntWW 91
Chen Mingyi 1917- IntWW 91
Chen Mingyuan 1941- IntWW 91
Chen Minzhang 1931- IntWW 91
Chen Muhua 1920- IntWW 91
Chen Peiqiu 1922- IntWW 91
Chen Pixian 1916- IntWW 91
Ch'en Po-ta 1905-1989 FacFETw
Chen Puru 1918- IntWW 91
Chen Rongti 1919- IntWW 91
Chen Shaowu IntWW 91
Chen Shixu 1947- IntWW 91
Chen Shuliang 1911- IntWW 91
Chen Shunli 1917- IntWW 91
Chen Shupeng 1920- IntWW 91
Chen Songlu IntWW 91
Chen Suzhi 1931- IntWW 91
Chen Weiqiang 1958- IntWW 91
Chen Xieyang 1939- IntWW 91
Chen Xilian 1915- IntWW 91
Chen Xinren 1915- IntWW 91
Chen Xitong 1930- IntWW 91
Chen Yi 1953- ConCom 92, IntWW 91
Chen Ying 1919- IntWW 91
Chen Yonggui 1913-1986 FacFETw
Chen Yun 1905- IntWW 91
Chen Zaidao 1909- IntWW 91
Chen Zhaobo 1927- IntWW 91
Chen Zhaoyuan 1918- IntWW 91, Who 92
Chen Zhongjing 1915- IntWW 91
Chen Zhongwei 1929- IntWW 91
Chen Zongji 1922- IntWW 91
Chen Zuohuang 1947- IntWW 91
Chen Zuolin IntWW 91
Chen, Albert Tsu-Fu 1937- AmMWSc 92
Chen, Alice Tung-Hua 1949- AmMWSc 92
Chen, An-Ban 1942- AmMWSc 92
Chen, Andrew Tat-Leng 1938- AmMWSc 92
Chen, Anne Chi 1962- AmMWSc 92
Chen, Anthony Bartheolomew AmMWSc 92
Chen, Anthony Hing 1945- AmMWSc 92
Chen, Arthur Chih-Mei 1939- AmMWSc 92
Chen, Audrey Wen-Yin 1959- WhoAmL 92
Chen, B H 1933- AmMWSc 92
Chen, B T AmMWSc 92
Chen, Bang-Yen 1943- AmMWSc 92, WhoMW 92
Chen, Basilio 1953- WhoWest 92
Chen, Benjamin P P 1955- AmMWSc 92
Chen, Benjamin Yun-Hai 1951- AmMWSc 92
Chen, Bill Shun-Zer 1941- WhoFI 92
Chen, C W 1922- AmMWSc 92
Chen, Carl W 1936- AmMWSc 92
Chen, Carolyn 1965- WhoEnt 92
Chen, Catherine S H AmMWSc 92
Chen, Chang-Hwei 1941- AmMWSc 92
Chen, Chao-Hsing Stanley 1933- AmMWSc 92
Chen, Chao Ling 1937- AmMWSc 92
Chen, Char-Nie 1938- IntWW 91
Chen, Charles Chin-Tse 1929- AmMWSc 92
Chen, Charles Shin-Yang 1934- AmMWSc 92
Chen, Chen Ho 1929- AmMWSc 92
Chen, Chen-Tung Arthur 1949- AmMWSc 92
Chen, Cheng Hsuan 1946- AmMWSc 92
Chen, Cheng-Lin 1929- AmMWSc 92
Chen, Cheng-lung 1931- AmMWSc 92
Chen, Chi-Hau 1937- AmMWSc 92
Chen, Chi-Po 1940- AmMWSc 92
Chen, Chi-Tsong 1936- AmMWSc 92
Chen, Chi-yun 1933- WhoWest 92
Chen, Chia Hwa AmMWSc 92
Chen, Chiadao 1913- AmMWSc 92
Chen, Chin Hsin 1943- AmMWSc 92
Chen, Chin-Lin 1937- AmMWSc 92
Chen, Ching-chih 1937- AmMWSc 92
Chen, Ching-Jen 1936- AmMWSc 92, WhoMW 92
Chen, Ching-Ling Chu 1948- AmMWSc 92
Chen, Ching-Nien 1945- AmMWSc 92
Chen, Chiou Shiun 1938- AmMWSc 92
Chen, Chong Maw AmMWSc 92
Chen, Chuan Fang 1932- AmMWSc 92
Chen, Chuan Ju 1947- AmMWSc 92
Chen, Chung-Ho 1937- AmMWSc 92
Chen, Chung-Hsuan 1948- AmMWSc 92
Chen, Chung Wei 1921- AmMWSc 92
Chen, Cindy Chei-Jen 1953- AmMWSc 92
Chen, Cyndi Shiou-hua 1951- WhoMW 92
Chen, David J 1944- AmMWSc 92
Chen, Davidson Tah-Chuen 1942- AmMWSc 92
Chen, Di 1929- AmMWSc 92
Chen, Edward Chuck-Ming 1937- AmMWSc 92
Chen, Edwin Hung-Teh 1934- AmMWSc 92
Chen, Er-Ping 1944- AmMWSc 92
Chen, Erh-Chun 1934- AmMWSc 92
Chen, Fang Shang 1928- AmMWSc 92
Chen, Felix Kuo-Hung 1943- WhoWest 92
Chen, Fengshan Frank 1956- WhoMW 92
Chen, Francis F 1929- AmMWSc 92, WhoWest 92
Chen, Francis Hap-Kwong 1948- AmMWSc 92
Chen, Franklin M 1946- AmMWSc 92
Chen, Fred Fen Chuan 1934- AmMWSc 92
Chen, Fu-Tai Albert 1944- AmMWSc 92
Chen, Goong 1950- AmMWSc 92
Chen, Gui-Qiang 1962- WhoMW 92
Chen, H R 1929- AmMWSc 92
Chen, Han-Ping 1949- WhoWest 92
Chen, Hao-Chia 1935- AmMWSc 92
Chen, Harry Wu-Shiong 1937- AmMWSc 92
Chen, Henry Lowe 1940- AmMWSc 92
Chen, Ho-Hong H. H. 1933- WhoFI 92
Chen, Ho Sou 1932- AmMWSc 92
Chen, Hoffman Hor-Fu 1941- AmMWSc 92
Chen, Hollis C 1935- AmMWSc 92
Chen, Hollis Ching 1935- WhoMW 92
Chen, Hsien-Jen James 1931- AmMWSc 92
Chen, Hsing-Hen 1947- AmMWSc 92
Chen, Hsuan 1936- AmMWSc 92
Chen, Hubert Jan-Peing 1942- AmMWSc 92
Chen, I-Wen 1934- AmMWSc 92
Chen, Inan 1933- AmMWSc 92
Chen, Isaac I H 1929- AmMWSc 92
Chen, Jack Cheng-Kai 1966- WhoFI 92
Chen, James Che Wen 1930- AmMWSc 92
Chen, James L 1914- AmMWSc 92
Chen, James Pai-Fun 1929- AmMWSc 92
Chen, James Ralph 1939- AmMWSc 92
Chen, Jiann-Shin 1943- AmMWSc 92
Chen, Jin 1967- WhoFI 92
Chen, Jo-hsi 1938- LiExTwC
Chen, John Chun-Chien 1934- AmMWSc 92
Chen, Joseph Cheng Yih 1933- AmMWSc 92
Chen, Joseph H 1931- AmMWSc 92
Chen, Joseph Ke-Chou 1936- AmMWSc 92
Chen, Joseph T. 1925- WrDr 92
Chen, Juei-Teng 1938- AmMWSc 92
Chen, Juh Wah 1928- AmMWSc 92
Chen, Kan 1928- AmMWSc 92
Chen, Kao 1919- AmMWSc 92
Chen, Keddy T. 1961- WhoWest 92
Chen, Kenneth Yat-Yi 1941- AmMWSc 92
Chen, Kok-Choo 1947- WhoFI 92
Chen, Kuang Chung 1954- WhoFI 92
Chen, Kun-Mu 1933- AmMWSc 92
Chen, Kuo-Tsai 1923- AmMWSc 92
Chen, Kwan-Yu 1930- AmMWSc 92
Chen, L T 1938- AmMWSc 92
Chen, Lawrence Chien-Ming 1933- AmMWSc 92
Chen, Lily Ching-Chun 1946- AmMWSc 92
Chen, Linda Li-Yueh Huang 1937- AmMWSc 92
Chen, Liu 1946- AmMWSc 92
Chen, Lo-Chai 1939- AmMWSc 92
Chen, Lung-chu 1935- WhoAmL 92
Chen, Madeleine Mimi WhoWest 92
Chen, Maynard Ming-Liang 1950- AmMWSc 92
Chen, Michael Chia-Chao 1947- AmMWSc 92
Chen, Michael Ming 1932- AmMWSc 92
Chen, Michael S K 1941- AmMWSc 92
Chen, Michael Yu-Men 1941- AmMWSc 92
Chen, Min 1960- WhoMW 92
Chen, Min-Shih 1942- AmMWSc 92
Chen, Ming Chih 1920- AmMWSc 92
Chen, Ming M 1919- AmMWSc 92
Chen, Ming Sheng 1941- AmMWSc 92
Chen, Mo-Shing 1931- AmMWSc 92
Chen, Nai-Fu 1950- WhoWest 92
Chen, Nai Y 1926- AmMWSc 92
Chen, Ning Hsing 1918- AmMWSc 92
Chen, Pei-Li 1958- WhoMW 92
Chen, Peter 1941- AmMWSc 92
Chen, Peter Pin-Shan AmMWSc 92
Chen, Peter Wei-Teh 1942- WhoWest 92
Chen, Philip Minkang 1944- WhoAmL 92, WhoFI 92
Chen, Philip Stanley, Jr 1932- AmMWSc 92
Chen, Pi-Fuay 1930- AmMWSc 92
Chen, Ping-Fan 1917- AmMWSc 92
Chen, Priscilla B AmMWSc 92
Chen, Raymond F 1933- AmMWSc 92
Chen, Robert Chia-Hua 1946- AmMWSc 92
Chen, Robert Long Wen 1925- AmMWSc 92
Chen, Rong Yaw 1933- AmMWSc 92
Ch'en, Shang-Yi 1910- AmMWSc 92
Chen, Shao Lin 1918- AmMWSc 92
Chen, Shaw-Horng 1948- AmMWSc 92
Chen, Shepley S 1938- AmMWSc 92
Chen, Shi-Han 1936- AmMWSc 92
Chen, Shih-Fong 1949- AmMWSc 92
Chen, Shiou-Shan 1938- AmMWSc 92
Chen, Shuhchung Steve 1950- AmMWSc 92
Chen, Sow-Hsin 1935- AmMWSc 92
Chen, Sow-Yeh 1939- AmMWSc 92
Chen, Stanley Shiao-Hsiung 1937- AmMWSc 92
Chen, Stephen P K 1942- AmMWSc 92
Chen, Stephen Shi-Hua 1939- AmMWSc 92
Chen, Steve S 1944- AmMWSc 92
Chen, Su-shing 1939- AmMWSc 92
Chen, Sung Jen 1939- AmMWSc 92
Chen, T R AmMWSc 92
Chen, T Y 1923- AmMWSc 92
Chen, Ta-Shen 1932- AmMWSc 92
Chen, Tar Timothy 1945- AmMWSc 92, WhoRel 92
Chen, Theodore Tien Yiu 1946- WhoWest 92
Chen, Theresa S 1944- AmMWSc 92
Chen, Thomas Pei-Fan 1943- WhoFI 92
Chen, Thomas Shih-Nien 1936- AmMWSc 92
Chen, Thomas Tien 1947- AmMWSc 92
Chen, Tien Chi 1928- AmMWSc 92
Chen, Timothy Shieh-Sheng 1949- AmMWSc 92
Chen, Tsai Hwa 1923- AmMWSc 92
Chen, Tsang Jan 1934- AmMWSc 92
Chen, Tseh-An 1928- AmMWSc 92
Chen, Tsong Meng 1935- AmMWSc 92
Chen, Tsong-Ming 1934- AmMWSc 92
Chen, Tu 1935- AmMWSc 92
Chen, Tuan Wu 1936- AmMWSc 92
Chen, Tung-Shan 1939- AmMWSc 92
Chen, Victor John 1952- AmMWSc 92
Chen, W K 1936- AmMWSc 92
Chen, Wai-Fah 1936- AmMWSc 92
Chen, Wayne H 1922- AmMWSc 92
Chen, Wen-Chi 1955- WhoWest 92
Chen, Wen Fu 1942- WhoMW 92
Chen, Wen-Pin 1956- WhoMW 92
Chen, Wen Sherng AmMWSc 92
Chen, Wenpeng AmMWSc 92
Chen, Wesley 1954- WhoAmL 92
Chen, William Kwo-Wei 1928- AmMWSc 92
Chen, Winston Win-Hower 1942- AmMWSc 92
Chen, Yang-Jen 1947- AmMWSc 92
Chen, Yi-Der 1940- AmMWSc 92
Chen, Yih-Wen 1948- AmMWSc 92
Chen, Ying-Chih 1948- AmMWSc 92
Chen, Yok 1931- AmMWSc 92
Chen, Young Chang 1935- AmMWSc 92
Chen, Yu 1921- AmMWSc 92
Chen, Yu Why 1910- AmMWSc 92
Chen, Yuan-tsung 1932- SmATA 65
Chen, Yudong 1961- AmMWSc 92
Chen, Yuh-Ching 1930- AmMWSc 92
Chen, Yuki Y. Kuo 1930- WhoFI 92
Chen, Yung-Lin 1952- WhoWest 92
Chen, Yung Ming 1935- AmMWSc 92
Chen, Zuohuang 1947- WhoEnt 92, WhoMW 92
Chen-Tsai, Charlotte Hsiao-yu AmMWSc 92
Chenault, James Stouffer 1923- WhoAmL 92
Chenault, Kenneth 1952- WhoBlA 92
Chenault, Myron Maurice 1949- WhoBlA 92
Chenault, William J. 1928- WhoBlA 92
Chenaux, Henry Eliot 1947- WhoHisp 92
Chenea, Paul F 1918- AmMWSc 92
Chenery, Hollis 1918- WrDr 92
Chenery, Hollis Burnley 1918- IntWW 91
Chenery, Peter James 1946- Who 92
Chenevert, Phillip Joseph 1948- WhoBlA 92
Chenevert, Robert 1947- AmMWSc 92
Chenevey, Paul Robert 1938- WhoEnt 92
Cheney, Albert Nelson 1849-1901 BiInAmS
Cheney, Amy March NewAmDM
Cheney, B Vernon 1936- AmMWSc 92
Cheney, Brainard 1900- IntAu&W 91
Cheney, Carl D 1934- AmMWSc 92
Cheney, Charles Brooker 1912- AmMWSc 92
Cheney, Charles Edward 1836-1916 RelLAm 91
Cheney, Clarissa M 1946- AmMWSc 92
Cheney, Darwin L 1940- AmMWSc 92
Cheney, Dick 1941- NewYTBS 91 [port], News 91 [port], -91-3 [port], WhoWest 92
Cheney, Elliott Ward 1929- AmMWSc 92
Cheney, Eric Swenson 1934- AmMWSc 92
Cheney, Frederick Wyman 1935- AmMWSc 92
Cheney, Horace Bellatti 1913- AmMWSc 92
Cheney, James A 1927- AmMWSc 92
Cheney, Jeffrey Paul 1956- WhoFI 92
Cheney, John Vance 1848-1922 BenetAL 91
Cheney, Lynne Ann 1941- WhoAmP 91
Cheney, Margaret 1955- AmMWSc 92
Cheney, Monroe G 1919- AmMWSc 92
Cheney, Paul David 1947- AmMWSc 92
Cheney, Peter A 1942- WhoIns 92
Cheney, Richard B. 1941- IntWW 91
Cheney, Richard Bruce 1941- Who 92, WhoAmP 91
Cheney, Richard Eugene 1921- WhoFI 92
Cheney, Richard P 1937- WhoAmP 91
Cheney, Simeon Pease 1818-1890 NewAmDM
Cheng Jianxin 1962- IntWW 91
Cheng Lianchang 1931- IntWW 91
Cheng Mian 1933- IntWW 91
Cheng Shifa 1921- IntWW 91
Cheng Shu-Ren 1942- IntWW 91
Cheng Yanan 1936- IntWW 91
Cheng Zihua 1905-1991 IntWW 91

**Cheng,** Alexander H-D 1952- *AmMWSc 92*
**Cheng,** Andrew Francis 1951- *AmMWSc 92*
**Cheng,** Ben 1953- *WhoFI 92*
**Cheng,** Cheng-Yin 1930- *AmMWSc 92*
**Cheng,** Chia-Chung 1925- *AmMWSc 92*
**Cheng,** Chiang-Shuei 1935- *AmMWSc 92*
**Cheng,** Chin-Chuan 1936- *WhoMW 92*
**Cheng,** Chu-Liang 1954- *WhoWest 92*
**Cheng,** Chuen Hon 1950- *AmMWSc 92*
**Cheng,** Chung-Chieh *AmMWSc 92*
**Cheng,** David 1941- *AmMWSc 92*
**Cheng,** David H 1920- *AmMWSc 92*
**Cheng,** David H S *AmMWSc 92*
**Cheng,** David Keun 1918- *AmMWSc 92*
**Cheng,** Edward Teh-Chang 1946- *AmMWSc 92*
**Cheng,** Francis Sheng-Hsiung *AmMWSc 92*
**Cheng,** Frank Hsieh Fu 1923- *AmMWSc 92*
**Cheng,** Franklin Yih 1936- *AmMWSc 92*
**Cheng,** Fred Tun-Jen 1953- *WhoWest 92*
**Cheng,** Fu-Ding 1943- *WhoWest 92*
**Cheng,** George Chiwo 1928- *AmMWSc 92*
**Cheng,** H K 1923- *AmMWSc 92*
**Cheng,** Hazel Pei-Ling *AmMWSc 92*
**Cheng,** Herbert S 1929- *AmMWSc 92*
**Cheng,** Herbert Su-Yuen 1929- *WhoMW 92*
**Cheng,** Hsien *AmMWSc 92*
**Cheng,** Hsien Hua 1935- *AmMWSc 92*
**Cheng,** Hung-Yuan 1950- *AmMWSc 92*
**Cheng,** Hwei-Hsien 1932- *AmMWSc 92*
**Cheng,** J. Chester 1926- *WrDr 92*
**Cheng,** Kang 1946- *AmMWSc 92*
**Cheng,** Keh-Yung 1946- *WhoMW 92*
**Cheng,** Kimberly Ming-Tak 1948- *AmMWSc 92*
**Cheng,** Kuang Liu 1919- *AmMWSc 92*
**Cheng,** Kuang Lu 1919- *AmMWSc 92*
**Cheng,** Kuo-Joan 1940- *AmMWSc 92*
**Cheng,** Kwok-Tsang 1950- *AmMWSc 92*
**Cheng,** Lanna 1941- *AmMWSc 92*
**Cheng,** Lawrence Kar-Hiu 1947- *AmMWSc 92*
**Cheng,** Lester 1944- *AmMWSc 92*
**Cheng,** Linda Yi Hsien 1958- *WhoAmL 92*
**Cheng,** Paul Hung-Chiao 1930- *WhoFI 92*
**Cheng,** Paul J T 1935- *AmMWSc 92*
**Cheng,** Pi-Wan 1943- *AmMWSc 92*
**Cheng,** Ping *AmMWSc 92*
**Cheng,** Ralph T 1938- *AmMWSc 92*
**Cheng,** Richard M H *AmMWSc 92*
**Cheng,** Samson 1934- *WhoFI 92*
**Cheng,** Shang I 1920- *AmMWSc 92*
**Cheng,** Sheue-yann 1939- *AmMWSc 92*
**Cheng,** Shu-Sing 1923- *AmMWSc 92*
**Cheng,** Shun 1919- *AmMWSc 92*
**Cheng,** Sin-I 1921- *AmMWSc 92*
**Cheng,** Sze-Chuh 1921- *AmMWSc 92*
**Cheng,** Ta-Pei *AmMWSc 92*
**Cheng,** Thomas Clement 1930- *AmMWSc 92*
**Cheng,** Tsen-Chung 1944- *AmMWSc 92*
**Cheng,** Tsu-yu 1916- *IntAu&W 91*
**Cheng,** Tsung O 1925- *AmMWSc 92*
**Cheng,** Tu-chen *AmMWSc 92*
**Cheng,** William J P 1915- *AmMWSc 92*
**Cheng,** Wu-Chieh 1922- *AmMWSc 92*
**Cheng,** Yean Fu 1924- *AmMWSc 92*
**Cheng,** Yih-Shyun Edmond 1944- *AmMWSc 92*
**Cheng,** Yung-Chi 1944- *AmMWSc 92*
**Cheng,** Yung-Sung 1947- *AmMWSc 92*
**Cheng,** Zihua 1905-1991 *IntWW 91N*
**Cheng-Chung,** John Baptist *WhoRel 92*
**Cheng-Guajardo,** Miguel A. 1943- *WhoHisp 92*
**Cheng-Wu,** Fei 1914- *TwCPaSc*
**Chengalath,** Rama *AmMWSc 92*
**Cheniae,** George Maurice 1928- *AmMWSc 92*
**Chenicek,** Albert George 1913- *AmMWSc 92*
**Chenier,** Clifton 1925-1987 *ConMus 6 [port]*
**Chenier,** Philip John 1943- *AmMWSc 92*
**Chennault,** Anna Chan 1925- *WhoAmP 91, WhoEnt 92*
**Chennault,** Madelyn 1934- *WhoBlA 92*
**Chennevieres-Pointel,** C-P, Marquis de 1820-1899 *ThHEIm*
**Chenot,** Bernard 1909- *IntWW 91*
**Chenot,** Charles Frederic 1938- *AmMWSc 92*
**Chenoweth,** Carol Kathryn 1928- *WhoAmP 91*
**Chenoweth,** Christopher Evan 1957- *WhoAmL 92*
**Chenoweth,** Darrel Lee 1941- *AmMWSc 92*
**Chenoweth,** Dennis Edwin 1944- *AmMWSc 92*
**Chenoweth,** Elizabeth Rearick Wineland 1933- *WhoMW 92*
**Chenoweth,** James Merl 1924- *AmMWSc 92*
**Chenoweth,** Joe Elling 1936- *WhoMW 92*
**Chenoweth,** Maynard Burton 1917- *AmMWSc 92*
**Chenoweth,** Philip Andrew 1919- *AmMWSc 92*
**Chenoweth,** R D 1926- *AmMWSc 92*
**Chenoweth,** Wanda L *AmMWSc 92*
**Chenoweth,** William Harwick 1961- *WhoFI 92*
**Chenoweth,** William Lyman 1928- *AmMWSc 92, WhoWest 92*
**Chenowith,** Lonnie Lynn 1959- *WhoRel 92*
**Chentoff,** Polia 1896-1933 *TwCPaSc*
**Chenzira,** Ayoka *ReelWom*
**Cheo,** Bernard Ru-Shao 1930- *AmMWSc 92*
**Cheo,** Li-hsiang Aria S *AmMWSc 92*
**Cheo,** Peter K 1930- *AmMWSc 92*
**Chepenik,** Kenneth Paul 1938- *AmMWSc 92*
**Chepiga,** Michael Joseph 1948- *WhoAmL 92*
**Chepiga,** Pamela Rogers 1949- *WhoAmL 92*
**Chepko-Sade,** Bonita Diane 1948- *AmMWSc 92*
**Cher** *IntWW 91, LesBEnT 92*
**Cher** 1946- *ConTFT 9, CurBio 91 [port], IntMPA 92, WhoEnt 92*
**Cher,** Mark 1932- *AmMWSc 92*
**Cheramie,** Mildred 1928- *WhoRel 92*
**Cheraskin,** Emanuel 1916- *AmMWSc 92*
**Cherayil,** George Devassia 1929- *AmMWSc 92*
**Cherbas,** Peter Thomas 1946- *AmMWSc 92*
**Cherberg,** John Andrew 1910- *WhoAmP 91*
**Cherches,** Peter *DrAPF 91*
**Cherchiglia,** Dean Kenneth 1956- *WhoAmL 92*
**Chercover,** Murray *LesBEnT 92*
**Chercover,** Murray 1929- *WhoEnt 92, WhoFI 92*
**Chereau,** Patrice 1944- *IntWW 91*
**Cherelle-Caruth,** Boni 1958- *WhoWest 92*
**Cheremisinoff,** Paul N 1929- *AmMWSc 92*
**Cheremnykh,** Mikhail Mikhaylovich 1890-1962 *SovUnBD*
**Cheren,** Robert M. 1947- *IntMPA 92*
**Cherenack,** Paul Francis 1942- *AmMWSc 92*
**Cherenkov,** Pavel Alekseyevich 1904- *FacFETw, WhoNob 90*
**Cherenkov,** Pavel Alexeevich 1904- *Who 92*
**Cherenzia,** Bradley James 1931- *WhoMW 92*
**Cherepanov,** Ivan Mikhailovich 1929- *IntWW 91*
**Cherepnin** *NewAmDM*
**Chereskin,** Alvin 1928- *WhoFI 92*
**Cherewka,** Michael 1955- *WhoAmL 92*
**Cherian,** M George 1941- *AmMWSc 92*
**Cherian,** Sebastian K 1938- *AmMWSc 92*
**Cherif,** Safwat El- 1933- *IntWW 91*
**Cherin,** Paul 1934- *AmMWSc 92*
**Cherin,** Stephen J. 1962- *WhoWest 92*
**Cheris,** Samuel David 1945- *WhoAmL 92*
**Cheriton,** David Ross 1951- *AmMWSc 92*
**Cherkasky,** Martin 1911- *AmMWSc 92*
**Cherkasov,** Nikolay Konstantinovich 1903-1966 *SovUnBD*
**Cherkassky,** Shura 1911- *IntWW 91, NewAmDM, Who 92*
**Cherkes,** Martin 1946- *WhoMW 92*
**Cherkeziya,** Otari Yevtikhevich 1933- *IntWW 91*
**Cherkin,** Arthur 1913- *AmMWSc 92*
**Cherkofsky,** Saul Carl 1942- *AmMWSc 92*
**Cherlin,** George Yale 1924- *AmMWSc 92*
**Chermack,** Cy 1929- *IntMPA 92*
**Chermack,** Eugene E A 1934- *AmMWSc 92*
**Chermak,** Cy *LesBEnT 92*
**Chermayeff,** Ivan 1932- *DcTwDes, WhoEnt 92*
**Chermayeff,** Serge 1900- *DcTwDes, IntWW 91, Who 92*
**Chermont,** Jayme Sloan 1903- *Who 92*
**Cherms,** Frank Llewellyn, Jr 1930- *AmMWSc 92*
**Chern,** Ming-Fen Myra 1946- *AmMWSc 92*
**Chern,** Shiing-Shen 1911- *AmMWSc 92, IntWW 91*
**Chern,** Wen Shyong 1941- *AmMWSc 92*
**Cherna,** John C 1921- *AmMWSc 92*
**Chernaik,** Judith *DrAPF 91*
**Chernak,** Jerald Lee 1942- *WhoEnt 92*
**Chernak,** Jess 1928- *AmMWSc 92*
**Chernavin,** Vladimir Nikolaevich 1928- *SovUnBD*
**Chernavin,** Vladimir Nikolayevich 1928- *IntWW 91*
**Chernenko,** John G 1924- *WhoAmP 91*
**Chernenko,** Konstantin 1911-1985 *FacFETw*
**Chernenko,** Konstantin Ustinovich 1911-1985 *SovUnBD*
**Cherner,** Anne *DrAPF 91*
**Chernesky,** Max Alexander 1938- *AmMWSc 92*
**Chernesky,** Richard John 1939- *WhoAmL 92*
**Cherney,** Andrew Knox 1947- *WhoAmL 92*
**Cherney,** James Alan 1948- *WhoAmL 92*
**Cherniack,** Helen Wessel 1911- *WhoMW 92*
**Cherniack,** Neil S 1931- *AmMWSc 92*
**Cherniack,** Reuben Mitchell 1924- *AmMWSc 92*
**Cherniak,** Eugene Anthony 1930- *AmMWSc 92*
**Cherniak,** Robert 1936- *AmMWSc 92*
**Cherniavsky,** Ellen Abelson 1947- *AmMWSc 92*
**Cherniavsky,** Fyodor Andre 1953- *WhoEnt 92*
**Cherniavsky,** John Charles 1947- *AmMWSc 92*
**Cherniawski,** Anthony Michael 1950- *WhoFI 92, WhoMW 92*
**Chernichaw,** Mark 1946- *WhoEnt 92*
**Chernick,** Michael Ross 1947- *AmMWSc 92*
**Chernick,** Sidney Samuel 1921- *AmMWSc 92*
**Chernick,** Victor 1935- *AmMWSc 92*
**Chernick,** Warren Sanford 1929- *AmMWSc 92*
**Chernikhov,** Yakov Georgievich 1889-1951 *SovUnBD*
**Chernin,** Eli 1924- *AmMWSc 92*
**Chernin,** Peter *WhoEnt 92*
**Chernin,** Russell Scott 1957- *WhoAmL 92*
**Chernish,** Stanley Michael 1924- *WhoMW 92*
**Cherniss,** David Alan 1954- *WhoAmL 92*
**Chernock,** Warren Philip 1926- *AmMWSc 92*
**Chernoff,** Amoz Immanuel 1923- *AmMWSc 92*
**Chernoff,** Donald Alan 1952- *AmMWSc 92, WhoMW 92*
**Chernoff,** Ellen Ann Goldman 1952- *AmMWSc 92*
**Chernoff,** Herman 1923- *AmMWSc 92, IntWW 91*
**Chernoff,** Larry E. 1951- *WhoEnt 92*
**Chernoff,** Maxine *DrAPF 91*
**Chernoff,** Maxine 1952- *WhoMW 92*
**Chernoff,** Paul Robert 1942- *AmMWSc 92*
**Chernoff,** Robert 1922- *WhoRel 92*
**Chernoff,** Sanford *DrAPF 91*
**Chernoff,** Sheryl Stern 1954- *WhoAmL 92*
**Chernomyrdin,** Viktor Stepanovich 1938- *IntWW 91*
**Chernosky,** Edwin Jasper 1914- *AmMWSc 92*
**Chernov,** Mikhail Aleksandrovich 1891-1938 *SovUnBD*
**Chernova,** Tanja *EncAmaz 91*
**Chernow,** Eli Isaac 1939- *WhoAmL 92*
**Chernow,** Fred 1932- *AmMWSc 92*
**Chernow,** Jay Howard 1935- *WhoEnt 92*
**Chernow,** Jeffrey Scott 1951- *WhoAmL 92*
**Chernow,** Joseph Michael 1939- *WhoFI 92*
**Cherny,** Aleksey Klementevich 1921- *IntWW 91*
**Cherny,** David Edward 1957- *WhoAmL 92*
**Cherny,** Gorimir Gorimirovich 1923- *IntWW 91*
**Cherny,** Walter B 1926- *AmMWSc 92, WhoWest 92*
**Chernyaev,** Anatoliy Sergeevich 1921- *SovUnBD*
**Chernyakhovsky,** Ivan Danilovich 1906-1945 *SovUnBD*
**Chernyakov,** Yuriy Nikolayevich 1918- *IntWW 91*
**Chernyayev,** Anatoly Sergeyevich 1921- *IntWW 91*
**Chernyshev,** Nikolay Mikhaylovich 1886-1973 *SovUnBD*
**Cherot,** Nicholas Maurice 1947- *WhoBlA 92*
**Cherpack,** John, Jr. 1910- *WhoEnt 92*
**Cherrick,** Henry M 1939- *AmMWSc 92*
**Cherrington,** Alan Douglas *AmMWSc 92*
**Cherrington,** Blake Edward 1937- *AmMWSc 92*
**Cherrito,** Joseph Anthony Michael 1965- *WhoMW 92*
**Cherry,** Andrew Jackson 1927- *WhoBlA 92*
**Cherry,** Annie Moore 1891-1976 *DcNCBi 1*
**Cherry,** Bridget Katherine 1941- *Who 92*
**Cherry,** Cassandra Brabble 1947- *WhoBlA 92*
**Cherry,** Charles Conrad 1937- *WhoRel 92, WrDr 92*
**Cherry,** Charles William 1928- *WhoBlA 92*
**Cherry,** Colin 1931- *Who 92*
**Cherry,** Deron Leigh 1959- *WhoBlA 92*
**Cherry,** Don 1936- *NewAmDM*
**Cherry,** Donald E. 1936- *WhoBlA 92*
**Cherry,** Donald Gordon 1942- *WhoAmL 92*
**Cherry,** Donald Stephen 1943- *AmMWSc 92*
**Cherry,** Edward Earl, Sr. 1926- *WhoBlA 92*
**Cherry,** Edward Taylor 1941- *AmMWSc 92*
**Cherry,** Eric Leroy 1952- *WhoMW 92*
**Cherry,** Flora Finch *AmMWSc 92*
**Cherry,** Gloria Barry 1935- *WhoAmL 92*
**Cherry,** Gordon Emanuel 1931- *Who 92*
**Cherry,** James Donald 1930- *AmMWSc 92*
**Cherry,** Jerry Arthur 1942- *AmMWSc 92*
**Cherry,** Jesse Theodore 1931- *AmMWSc 92*
**Cherry,** Jim Marion, Jr. 1939- *WhoFI 92*
**Cherry,** Joe H 1934- *AmMWSc 92*
**Cherry,** John 1942- *Who 92*
**Cherry,** John D, Jr 1951- *WhoAmP 91*
**Cherry,** John Mitchell 1937- *Who 92*
**Cherry,** John Paul 1941- *AmMWSc 92*
**Cherry,** John Thomas 1951- *WhoWest 92*
**Cherry,** Joseph Blount 1816?-1882 *DcNCBi 1*
**Cherry,** Kelly *DrAPF 91, IntAu&W 91, WhoMW 92, WrDr 92*
**Cherry,** Lee Otis 1944- *WhoBlA 92, WhoWest 92*
**Cherry,** Leonard Victor 1923- *AmMWSc 92*
**Cherry,** Linda Z 1951- *WhoAmP 91*
**Cherry,** Mark Stuart 1957- *WhoAmL 92*
**Cherry,** Muriel Elizabeth 1947- *WhoFI 92*
**Cherry,** Philip 1931- *WhoEnt 92*
**Cherry,** Robert Gregg 1891-1957 *DcNCBi 1*
**Cherry,** Robert Lee 1941- *WhoBlA 92*
**Cherry,** Robert Steven, III 1951- *WhoMW 92*
**Cherry,** Ronald Lee 1934- *WhoAmL 92*
**Cherry,** S 1928- *AmMWSc 92*
**Cherry,** Theodore W. 1932- *WhoBlA 92*
**Cherry,** Warren W. 1942-1990 *WhoBlA 92N*
**Cherry,** Wendell d1991 *NewYTBS 91*
**Cherry,** William Bailey 1916- *AmMWSc 92*
**Cherry,** William Henry 1919- *AmMWSc 92*
**Cherry,** William Walton 1806-1845 *DcNCBi 1*
**Cherryh,** C J 1942- *IntAu&W 91, TwCSFW 91, WrDr 92*
**Cherryhomes,** John Earl 1948- *WhoEnt 92*
**Cherryman,** A E *IntAu&W 91X*
**Cherryman,** John Richard 1932- *Who 92*
**Chertkoff,** Marvin Joseph 1930- *AmMWSc 92*
**Chertock,** George 1914- *AmMWSc 92*
**Chertok,** Haim 1938- *IntAu&W 91*
**Chertok,** Harvey 1932- *IntMPA 92*
**Chertok,** Jack *LesBEnT 92*
**Chertok,** Jack 1906- *IntMPA 92*
**Chertok,** Robert Joseph 1935- *AmMWSc 92*
**Chertow,** Bernard 1919- *AmMWSc 92*
**Cherubini,** Lillian M Williams 1916- *WhoAmP 91*
**Cherubini,** Luigi 1760-1842 *NewAmDM*
**Cherundolo,** John Charles 1948- *WhoAmL 92*
**Chervenick,** Paul A 1932- *AmMWSc 92*
**Chervenkov,** Vulko 1900-1980 *FacFETw*
**Chervin,** Joseph 1937- *WhoAmL 92*
**Chervitz,** David Howard 1958- *WhoAmL 92*
**Chervonenko,** Stepan Vasil'evich 1915- *SovUnBD*
**Chervonenko,** Stepan Vasiliyevich 1915- *IntWW 91*
**Cherwin,** Joel Ira 1942- *WhoAmL 92*
**Chery,** Donald Luke, Jr 1937- *AmMWSc 92*
**Cheryan,** Munir 1946- *AmMWSc 92*
**Chesbro,** Bruce W *AmMWSc 92*
**Chesbro,** George C. 1940- *WrDr 92*
**Chesbro,** Ray T 1925- *WhoAmP 91*
**Chesbro,** Vern 1925- *WhoAmP 91*
**Chesbro,** William Ronald 1928- *AmMWSc 92*
**Chesebrough,** Harry E 1909- *AmMWSc 92*
**Cheselden,** William 1688-1752 *BlkwCEP*
**Chesemore,** David Lee 1939- *AmMWSc 92*
**Chesen,** Eli S. 1944- *WrDr 92*
**Chesham,** Baron 1941- *Who 92*
**Chesham,** Henry *IntAu&W 91X*
**Chesham,** Sallie *WrDr 92*
**Chesher,** A.W. 1895-1972 *TwCPaSc*
**Chesher,** Kim 1955- *IntAu&W 91*
**Cheshier,** Joffre Paul 1961- *WhoMW 92, WhoRel 92*
**Cheshire** *Who 92*
**Cheshire,** Baron 1917- *Who 92*
**Cheshire,** Geoffrey Leonard 1917- *IntWW 91*
**Cheshire,** Giff 1905- *TwCWW 91*

**Cheshire,** Joseph Blount 1814-1899 *DcNCBi 1*
**Cheshire,** Joseph Blount, Jr. 1850-1932 *DcNCBi 1*
**Cheshire,** Molly Patterson 1961- *WhoEnt 92*
**Cheshire,** Sandra Kay 1958- *WhoAmL 92*
**Chesick,** John Polk 1933- *AmMWSc 92*
**Chesky,** Edward Joseph 1926- *WhoFI 92*
**Chesky,** Jeffrey Alan 1946- *AmMWSc 92, WhoMW 92*
**Chesler,** David Alan *AmMWSc 92*
**Chesler,** Stanley Richard 1947- *WhoAmL 92*
**Chesley,** Leon Carey 1908- *AmMWSc 92*
**Chesley,** Phyllis Dickerson 1956- *WhoFI 92*
**Chesley,** Roger T., Sr. 1959- *WhoBlA 92*
**Chesley,** Roger Thomas 1959- *WhoMW 92*
**Chesley,** Stanley Morris 1936- *WhoAmL 92, WhoMW 92*
**Cheslik,** Julie Marie 1960- *WhoAmL 92*
**Chesman,** Andrea 1952- *ConAu 135*
**Chesne,** Steven Todd 1960- *WhoEnt 92*
**Chesneau,** Ernest 1833-1898 *ThHEIm*
**Chesner,** Robert W. 1940- *WhoIns 92*
**Chesney,** Ann *ConAu 135*
**Chesney,** Charles Frederic *AmMWSc 92*
**Chesney,** George Tomkyns 1830-1895 *ScFEYrs*
**Chesney,** Marion 1936- *WrDr 92*
**Chesney,** Russell Wallace 1941- *AmMWSc 92*
**Chesney,** Weatherby *ScFEYrs, TwCSFW 91*
**Chesnieres,** Virginie d1873 *EncAmaz 91*
**Chesnik,** Earl 1934- *WhoAmP 91*
**Chesnin,** Leon 1919- *AmMWSc 92*
**Chesnut,** Carol Fitting 1937- *WhoWest 92*
**Chesnut,** Donald Blair 1932- *AmMWSc 92*
**Chesnut,** Donald R, Jr 1948- *AmMWSc 92*
**Chesnut,** Dwayne A 1936- *AmMWSc 92*
**Chesnut,** Franklin Gilmore 1919- *WhoRel 92*
**Chesnut,** Kelli Elizabeth 1962- *WhoMW 92*
**Chesnut,** Mary Boykin 1823-1886 *BenetAL 91, HanAmWH*
**Chesnut,** Robert W *AmMWSc 92*
**Chesnut,** Thomas Lloyd 1942- *AmMWSc 92*
**Chesnut,** Walter G 1928- *AmMWSc 92*
**Chesnutt,** Charles W 1858-1932 *AfrAmW, BenetAL 91, BlkLC [port]*
**Chesnutt,** Charles Waddell 1858-1932 *DcNCBi 1*
**Cheson,** Bruce David 1946- *AmMWSc 92*
**Chesrow,** Cathleen Gwen 1947- *IntAu&W 91*
**Chess,** Karin V T 1939- *AmMWSc 92*
**Chess,** Leonard 1943- *AmMWSc 92*
**Chess,** Robert Hubert 1930-1981 *WhoBlA 92N*
**Chess,** Sammie, Jr. 1934- *WhoBlA 92*
**Chess,** Stanley David 1947- *WhoAmL 92*
**Chessells,** Arthur David 1941- *Who 92*
**Chesser,** Jeffrey L. 1942- *WhoEnt 92*
**Chesser,** Joe Max 1948- *WhoRel 92*
**Chesser,** Kerry Royce 1956- *WhoFI 92*
**Chesser,** Nancy Jean 1946- *AmMWSc 92*
**Chesser,** Roger Moreton 1945- *WhoEnt 92*
**Chesser,** William LaGrand 1940- *WhoWest 92*
**Chessey,** Joseph J, Jr 1948- *WhoAmP 91*
**Chessher,** Danny Edward 1953- *WhoEnt 92*
**Chesshire,** Geoffrey S 1958- *AmMWSc 92*
**Chesshyre,** Hubert 1940- *Who 92*
**Chessick,** Richard D 1931- *AmMWSc 92*
**Chessin,** Henry 1919- *AmMWSc 92*
**Chessin,** Hyman 1920- *AmMWSc 92*
**Chessin,** Meyer 1921- *AmMWSc 92*
**Chessman,** Caryl d1960 *FacFETw*
**Chessman,** Daniel 1787-1839 *AmPeW*
**Chesson,** Eugene, Jr 1928- *AmMWSc 92*
**Chesson,** Peter Leith 1952- *AmMWSc 92*
**Chestang,** Leon Wilbert 1937- *WhoBlA 92*
**Chesteen,** Richard Dallas 1939- *WhoAmP 91*
**Chester,** Archdeacon of *Who 92*
**Chester,** Bishop of 1930- *Who 92*
**Chester,** Dean of *Who 92*
**Chester,** Albert Huntington 1843-1903 *BiInAmS*
**Chester,** Alexander Jeffrey 1950- *AmMWSc 92*
**Chester,** Alfred 1928-1971 *LiExTwC*
**Chester,** Arthur Noble 1940- *AmMWSc 92*
**Chester,** Arthur Warren 1940- *AmMWSc 92*
**Chester,** Brent 1942- *AmMWSc 92*
**Chester,** Clarence Lucian 1915- *WhoWest 92*
**Chester,** Clive Ronald 1930- *AmMWSc 92*
**Chester,** Daniel Leon 1943- *AmMWSc 92*
**Chester,** Edward Howard 1931- *AmMWSc 92*
**Chester,** Edward M 1912- *AmMWSc 92*
**Chester,** Geoffrey 1951- *WhoAmL 92*
**Chester,** George Randolph 1869-1924 *BenetAL 91*
**Chester,** Giraud *LesBEnT 92*
**Chester,** Giraud 1922- *WhoEnt 92*
**Chester,** Hawley Thomas, III 1944- *WhoEnt 92*
**Chester,** Joseph A., Sr. 1914- *WhoBlA 92*
**Chester,** Laura *DrAPF 91*
**Chester,** Lewis Alexander 1937- *IntAu&W 91*
**Chester,** Marvin 1930- *AmMWSc 92, WhoWest 92*
**Chester,** Peter *WrDr 92*
**Chester,** Peter Francis 1929- *Who 92*
**Chester,** Ray 1955- *WhoAmL 92*
**Chester,** Roberta *DrAPF 91*
**Chester,** Russell Gilbert, Jr. 1947- *WhoMW 92*
**Chester,** Sharon Rose 1942- *WhoWest 92*
**Chester,** Stephanie Ann 1951- *WhoAmL 92, WhoMW 92*
**Chester,** Theodore Edward d1991 *Who 92N*
**Chester,** Timothy J. *WhoMW 92*
**Chester Jones,** Ian 1916- *Who 92*
**Chesterfield,** Archdeacon of *Who 92*
**Chesterfield,** Arthur Desborough d1991 *Who 92N*
**Chesterfield,** Diane 1943- *TwCPaSc*
**Chesterfield,** Philip D Stanhope, Earl of 1694-1773 *BlkwCEP*
**Chesterfield,** Rhydonia Ruth Epperson 1919- *WhoFI 92, WhoWest 92*
**Chesterman,** Jack 1938- *TwCPaSc*
**Chesterman,** Ross 1909- *Who 92*
**Chesterman,** William *TwCPaSc*
**Chesters,** Alan David *Who 92*
**Chesters,** Charles Geddes Coull 1904- *Who 92*
**Chesters,** Graham 1944- *WrDr 92*
**Chesters,** John Hugh 1906- *IntWW 91, Who 92*
**Chesterton,** Arthur Keith 1899-1973 *BiDExR*
**Chesterton,** David 1939- *Who 92*
**Chesterton,** Elizabeth 1915- *Who 92*
**Chesterton,** G. K. 1874-1936 *CnDBLB 6 [port], FacFETw, RfGEnL 91*
**Chesterton,** Gilbert Keith 1874-1936 *ScFEYrs*
**Chesterton,** Oliver 1913- *Who 92*
**Chestnut,** Alphonse F 1917- *AmMWSc 92*
**Chestnut,** Cynthia Moore 1949- *WhoAmP 91*
**Chestnut,** Dennis Earl 1947- *WhoBlA 92*
**Chestnut,** Edwin, Sr. 1924- *WhoBlA 92*
**Chestnut,** H 1917- *AmMWSc 92*
**Cheston,** Charles 1882-1960 *TwCPaSc*
**Cheston,** Charles Edward 1911- *AmMWSc 92*
**Cheston,** Evelyn 1875-1929 *TwCPaSc*
**Cheston,** Sheila Carol 1958- *WhoAmL 92*
**Cheston,** Warren Bruce 1926- *AmMWSc 92*
**Chesworth,** Donald O. *WhoAmL 92*
**Chesworth,** Donald Piers d1991 *Who 92N*
**Chesworth,** George Arthur 1930- *Who 92*
**Chesworth,** Robert Hadden 1929- *AmMWSc 92*
**Chetsanga,** Christopher J 1935- *AmMWSc 92*
**Chettle,** Alvin Basil, Jr. 1937- *WhoAmL 92*
**Chettle,** Henry 1560?-1607? *RfGEnL 91*
**Chetty,** Veerappa Karuppan 1938- *WhoFI 92*
**Chetverikov,** Sergey Sergeevich 1880-1959 *SovUnBD*
**Chetwin,** Grace *WrDr 92*
**Chetwode** *Who 92*
**Chetwode,** Baron 1937- *Who 92*
**Chetwode,** R D *ScFEYrs*
**Chetwood,** Clifford 1928- *Who 92*
**Chetwyn,** Robert 1933- *Who 92*
**Chetwynd** *Who 92*
**Chetwynd,** Viscount 1935- *Who 92*
**Chetwynd,** Arthur 1913- *Who 92*
**Chetwynd,** Lionel *WhoEnt 92, WhoWest 92*
**Chetwynd,** Lionel 1940- *IntMPA 92*
**Chetwynd-Talbot** *Who 92*
**Chetwynd-Talbot,** Richard Michael Arthur *Who 92*
**Cheung,** Harry 1931- *AmMWSc 92*
**Cheung,** Harry Michael 1957- *WhoMW 92*
**Cheung,** Herbert Chiu-Ching 1933- *AmMWSc 92*
**Cheung,** Hou Tak 1950- *AmMWSc 92*
**Cheung,** Jeffrey Tai-Kin 1946- *AmMWSc 92*
**Cheung,** John Yan-Poon 1950- *AmMWSc 92*
**Cheung,** Lim H *AmMWSc 92*
**Cheung,** Mo-Tsing Miranda 1942- *AmMWSc 92*
**Cheung,** Oswald 1922- *Who 92*
**Cheung,** Paul James 1942- *AmMWSc 92*
**Cheung,** Peter Pak Lun 1939- *AmMWSc 92*
**Cheung,** Shiu Ming 1942- *AmMWSc 92*
**Cheung,** Wai Yiu 1933- *AmMWSc 92*
**Cheuse,** Alan 1940- *WrDr 92*
**Chevalier,** Howard L 1931- *AmMWSc 92*
**Chevalier,** Louis 1911- *ConAu 35NR, IntWW 91*
**Chevalier,** Maurice 1888-1972 *ConMus 6 [port], FacFETw*
**Chevalier,** Peggy *AmMWSc 92*
**Chevalier,** Peter Andrew 1940- *AmMWSc 92*
**Chevalier,** Robert Louis 1946- *AmMWSc 92*
**Chevalier,** Roger 1922- *IntWW 91*
**Chevalier,** Roger Alan 1949- *AmMWSc 92*
**Chevalier,** Samuel Fletcher 1934- *WhoFI 92*
**Chevallaz,** Georges-Andre 1915- *IntWW 91*
**Chevallier,** Annette 1944- *TwCPaSc*
**Chevat,** Edith *DrAPF 91*
**Cheveallier,** J. Clint 1943- *WhoRel 92*
**Cheveley,** Stephen William d1991 *Who 92N*
**Chevenement,** Jean-Pierre 1939- *IntWW 91*
**Cheves,** Langdon 1776-1857 *AmPolLe*
**Chevigny,** Hector 1904-1965 *BenetAL 91*
**Chevigny,** Paul Graves 1935- *WhoAmL 92*
**Cheville,** Norman F 1934- *AmMWSc 92*
**Chevin,** Nathaniel d1720? *DcNCBi 1*
**Chevis,** Cheryl Ann 1947- *WhoAmL 92*
**Chevone,** Boris Ivan 1943- *AmMWSc 92*
**Chevray,** Rene 1937- *AmMWSc 92*
**Chevreul,** Eugene 1786-1889 *ThHEIm*
**Chevrier,** Lionel 1903-1987 *FacFETw*
**Chevrillon,** Olivier 1929- *IntWW 91*
**Chevska,** Maria 1948- *TwCPaSc*
**Chew,** Allen F. 1924- *WrDr 92*
**Chew,** Bettye L. 1940- *WhoBlA 92*
**Chew,** Catherine S 1942- *AmMWSc 92*
**Chew,** Frances Sze-Ling 1948- *AmMWSc 92*
**Chew,** Frank 1916- *AmMWSc 92*
**Chew,** Geoffrey Foucar 1924- *AmMWSc 92, IntWW 91*
**Chew,** Gregory Steven 1950- *WhoEnt 92*
**Chew,** Hemming 1933- *AmMWSc 92*
**Chew,** Herman W *AmMWSc 92*
**Chew,** Ju-Nam 1923- *AmMWSc 92*
**Chew,** Ka-Wing 1957- *WhoWest 92*
**Chew,** Kenneth 1915- *Who 92*
**Chew,** Kenneth Kendall 1933- *AmMWSc 92*
**Chew,** Linda Ann 1962- *WhoFI 92*
**Chew,** Linda Lee 1941- *WhoWest 92*
**Chew,** Robert L. 1935- *WhoBlA 92*
**Chew,** Robert Marshall 1923- *AmMWSc 92*
**Chew,** Victor 1923- *AmMWSc 92*
**Chew,** Weng Cho 1953- *AmMWSc 92*
**Chew,** William Hubert, Jr 1933- *AmMWSc 92*
**Chew,** Woodrow W 1913- *AmMWSc 92*
**Chewning,** Emily Blair *DrAPF 91*
**Chewton,** Viscount 1940- *Who 92*
**Chey,** George S. 1930- *WhoFI 92*
**Cheydleur,** Benjamin Frederic 1912- *AmMWSc 92*
**Cheyette,** Herbert Basil 1928- *WhoEnt 92*
**Cheyfitz,** Eric *DrAPF 91*
**Cheyne,** George 1671-1743 *BlkwCEP*
**Cheyne,** Ian 1895-1955 *TwCPaSc*
**Cheyne,** Joseph 1914- *Who 92*
**Cheyney,** Curtis Paul, III 1942- *WhoAmL 92*
**Cheyney,** Thomas Edward, Jr. 1957- *WhoRel 92*
**Cheyney-Coker,** Syl 1945- *ConPo 91, WrDr 92*
**Cheysson,** Claude 1920- *IntWW 91, Who 92*
**Chezem,** Curtis Gordon 1924- *AmMWSc 92*
**Chhabildas,** Lalit Chandra 1945- *WhoWest 92*
**Chhabra,** Rajendra S 1939- *AmMWSc 92*
**Chhatwal,** Surbir Jit Singh 1931- *IntWW 91*
**Chheda,** Girish B 1934- *AmMWSc 92*
**Chi Biqing** 1920- *IntWW 91*
**Chi Haotian** 1929- *IntWW 91*
**Chi,** Benjamin E 1933- *AmMWSc 92*
**Chi,** Chang Hwi 1934- *WhoWest 92*
**Chi,** Chao Shu 1936- *AmMWSc 92*
**Chi,** Che 1949- *AmMWSc 92*
**Chi,** Cheng-Ching 1939- *AmMWSc 92*
**Chi,** David Shyh-Wei 1943- *AmMWSc 92*
**Chi,** Donald Nan-Hua 1939- *AmMWSc 92*
**Chi,** Donna Sherman 1954- *WhoWest 92*
**Chi,** John Wen Hua 1934- *AmMWSc 92*
**Chi,** L K 1933- *AmMWSc 92*
**Chi,** Lois Wong *AmMWSc 92*
**Chi,** Michael *AmMWSc 92*
**Chi,** Minn-Shong 1940- *AmMWSc 92*
**Chi,** Myung Sun 1940- *AmMWSc 92*
**Chi,** Robin Lai-Ping 1958- *WhoFI 92*
**Chia,** E Henry 1940- *AmMWSc 92*
**Chia,** Fu-Shiang 1931- *AmMWSc 92, WhoWest 92*
**Chia,** Mantak 1944- *RelLAm 91*
**Chia,** Pei-Yuan 1939- *WhoFI 92*
**Chia,** Sandro 1946- *WorArt 1980 [port]*
**Chiabai,** Jennifer Lynn 1962- *WhoMW 92*
**Chiacchierini,** Richard Philip 1943- *AmMWSc 92*
**Chiado,** Michael Eugene 1956- *WhoEnt 92*
**Chiakulas,** John James 1915- *AmMWSc 92*
**Chialastri,** Joseph Robert 1960- *WhoFI 92*
**Chianelli,** Russell Robert 1944- *AmMWSc 92*
**Chiang Ch'ing** 1914- *EncAmaz 91*
**Chiang Ch'ing** 1914-1991 *FacFETw*
**Chiang Hsiao-wu** d1991 *NewYTBS 91*
**Chiang Kai-shek** 1887-1975 *FacFETw [port]*
**Chiang Kai-Shek,** Madame *IntWW 91, Who 92*
**Chiang,** Albert Chin-Liang 1937- *WhoWest 92*
**Chiang,** Anne 1942- *AmMWSc 92*
**Chiang,** Bin-Yea *AmMWSc 92*
**Chiang,** Chao-Wang 1925- *AmMWSc 92*
**Chiang,** Chin Long 1916- *AmMWSc 92*
**Chiang,** Chwan K 1943- *AmMWSc 92*
**Chiang,** Donald C 1931- *AmMWSc 92*
**Chiang,** Fay *DrAPF 91*
**Chiang,** Fu-Pen 1936- *AmMWSc 92*
**Chiang,** George C 1931- *AmMWSc 92*
**Chiang,** Han-Shing 1929- *AmMWSc 92*
**Chiang,** Huai C 1915- *AmMWSc 92*
**Chiang,** Joseph Fei 1939- *AmMWSc 92*
**Chiang,** Kwen-Sheng 1939- *AmMWSc 92*
**Chiang,** Martin Kuang Ping 1933- *WhoWest 92*
**Chiang,** Morgan S 1926- *AmMWSc 92*
**Chiang,** Peter K 1941- *AmMWSc 92*
**Chiang,** S H 1929- *AmMWSc 92*
**Chiang,** Samuel Edward 1959- *WhoRel 92*
**Chiang,** Soong Tao 1937- *AmMWSc 92*
**Chiang,** Tai-Chang 1949- *AmMWSc 92*
**Chiang,** Thomas Chi-Nan 1945- *WhoFI 92*
**Chiang,** Thomas M 1940- *AmMWSc 92*
**Chiang,** Tze I 1923- *AmMWSc 92*
**Chiang,** Yuen-Sheng 1936- *AmMWSc 92*
**Chiao,** Jen Wei *AmMWSc 92*
**Chiao,** Raymond Yu 1940- *AmMWSc 92*
**Chiao,** Wen Bin 1948- *AmMWSc 92*
**Chiao,** Yu-Chih 1949- *AmMWSc 92*
**Chiappelli,** Francesco 1953- *WhoWest 92*
**Chiapperino,** Frank Anthony 1952- *WhoRel 92*
**Chiappetti,** Thomas More 1949- *WhoFI 92*
**Chiappinelli,** Vincent A 1951- *AmMWSc 92*
**Chiapuris,** Camilla Eva 1933- *WhoEnt 92*
**Chiara,** Frank Joseph, Jr. 1937- *WhoAmL 92*
**Chiara,** John Carmen 1949- *WhoRel 92*
**Chiara,** Maria 1939- *IntWW 91*
**Chiaramonte,** Andrew 1943- *WhoEnt 92*
**Chiaramonte,** Nicola 1905-1972 *LiExTwC*
**Chiarappa,** Luigi 1925- *AmMWSc 92*
**Chiarchiaro,** Frank John 1945- *WhoAmL 92*
**Chiarelli,** Joseph 1946- *WhoFI 92*
**Chiarello,** Donald Frederick 1940- *WhoAmL 92*
**Chiarkas,** Nicholas L. *WhoAmL 92*
**Chiaro,** A. William 1928- *WhoFI 92*
**Chiarodo,** Andrew 1934- *AmMWSc 92*
**Chiarucci,** Vincent A. 1929- *WhoMW 92*
**Chiasson,** Donat *Who 92*
**Chiasson,** Donat 1930- *WhoRel 92*
**Chiasson,** Leo Patrick 1918- *AmMWSc 92*
**Chiasson,** Robert Breton 1925- *AmMWSc 92, WhoWest 92*
**Chiat,** Jay 1931- *WhoFI 92*
**Chiaureli,** Mikhail Edisherovich 1894-1974 *SovUnBD*
**Chiaverini,** John Edward 1924- *WhoFI 92*
**Chiazze,** Leonard, Jr 1934- *AmMWSc 92*
**Chiba,** Kazuo 1925- *Who 92*
**Chiba,** Mikio 1929- *AmMWSc 92*
**Chibeau,** Edmond *DrAPF 91*
**Chibeau,** Edmond Victor 1947- *WhoEnt 92*
**Chibesakunda,** Lombe Phyllis 1944- *IntWW 91*
**Chibnall,** Marjorie McCallum 1915- *Who 92, WrDr 92*
**Chibnik,** Sheldon 1925- *AmMWSc 92*
**Chiburdanidze,** Mariya Grigorevna 1961- *IntWW 91*
**Chiburdanidze,** Maya 1961- *SovUnBD*
**Chiburis,** Edward Frank 1933- *AmMWSc 92*
**Chiburis,** Edward Frank, Jr. 1956- *WhoEnt 92*
**Chibuzo,** Gregory Anenonu 1943- *AmMWSc 92*
**Chicago** *NewAmDM*
**Chicago Seven** *RComAH*
**Chicago,** Judy 1939- *HanAmWH, WorArt 1980 [port]*

**Chicherin,** Georgiy Vasil'evich 1872-1936 *SovUnBD*
**Chichester** *Who 92*
**Chichester,** Archdeacon of *Who 92*
**Chichester,** Bishop of 1915- *Who 92*
**Chichester,** Dean of *Who 92*
**Chichester,** Earl of 1944- *Who 92*
**Chichester,** Viscount 1990- *Who 92*
**Chichester,** Clinton Oscar 1925- *AmMWSc 92*
**Chichester,** Donald Wallace 1933- *WhoRel 92*
**Chichester,** Francis 1901-1972 *FacFETw*
**Chichester,** John 1916- *Who 92*
**Chichester,** John H 1937- *WhoAmP 91*
**Chichester,** Lyle Franklin 1931- *AmMWSc 92*
**Chichester,** Susan Mary 1936- *WhoWest 92*
**Chichester,** Suzy M C 1949- *WhoAmP 91*
**Chichester-Clark** *Who 92*
**Chichester-Clark,** Robert 1928- *Who 92*
**Chichetto,** James William *DrAPF 91*
**Chichibabin,** Aleksey Yevgen'evich 1871-1945 *SovUnBD*
**Chick,** Geoffrey Parker Hyde 1944- *WhoWest 92*
**Chick,** James P, Jr 1947- *WhoIns 92*
**Chick,** John Stephen 1935- *Who 92*
**Chick,** Terrence Charles 1947- *WhoFI 92*
**Chick,** Thomas Wesley 1940- *AmMWSc 92*
**Chickering,** John White 1831-1913 *BiInAmS*
**Chickering,** Jonas 1797-1853 *NewAmDM*
**Chickos,** James S 1941- *AmMWSc 92*
**Chicks,** Charles Hampton 1930- *AmMWSc 92, WhoWest 92*
**Chico,** Raymundo Jose 1930- *AmMWSc 92*
**Chicoine,** Luc 1929- *AmMWSc 92*
**Chicoine,** Roland A 1922- *WhoAmP 91*
**Chicoine,** Roland Alvin 1922- *WhoMW 92*
**Chicorel,** Ralph 1930- *WhoEnt 92*
**Chicoye,** Etzer 1926- *AmMWSc 92, WhoBIA 92*
**Chida,** Junaid Hasan 1956- *WhoAmL 92*
**Chidambaranathan,** Sornampillai 1930- *WhoFI 92*
**Chidambaraswamy,** Jayanthi 1927- *AmMWSc 92*
**Chiddix,** Max Eugene 1918- *AmMWSc 92*
**Chidester,** Glen Alan 1957- *WhoAmL 92*
**Chidley,** Douglas Joseph 1946- *WhoMW 92*
**Chidsey,** Christopher E 1957- *AmMWSc 92*
**Chidsey,** Jane Louise 1908- *AmMWSc 92*
**Chiecchi,** Dino *WhoHisp 92*
**Chief Earth Woman** *EncAmaz 91*
**Chief Joseph** *RComAH*
**Chieffalo,** Mario Victor 1934- *WhoWest 92*
**Chieftains,** The *ConMus 7 [port], FacFETw*
**Chien,** Andrew Andai 1964- *AmMWSc 92*
**Chien,** Chia-Ling 1942- *AmMWSc 92*
**Chien,** Chih-Yung 1939- *AmMWSc 92*
**Chien,** Fredrick Foo 1935- *IntWW 91*
**Chien,** Henry H 1935- *AmMWSc 92*
**Chien,** James C W 1929- *AmMWSc 92*
**Chien,** Kuei-Ru 1945- *WhoFI 92, WhoWest 92*
**Chien,** Luther C 1923- *AmMWSc 92*
**Chien,** Norbert Wei 1955- *WhoWest 92*
**Chien,** Ping-Lu 1928- *AmMWSc 92*
**Chien,** Robert Chun 1929- *IntWW 91*
**Chien,** Sen Hsiung 1941- *AmMWSc 92*
**Chien,** Shu 1931- *AmMWSc 92*
**Chien,** Sze-Foo 1929- *AmMWSc 92*
**Chien,** Victor 1948- *AmMWSc 92*
**Chien,** Yi-Tzuu 1938- *AmMWSc 92*
**Chien,** Yie W 1938- *AmMWSc 92*
**Chiene,** John 1937- *Who 92*
**Chiepe,** Gaositwe Keagakwa Tibe *IntWW 91*
**Chiepe,** Gaositwe Keagakwa Tibe 1922- *Who 92*
**Chierchia,** Madeline Carmella 1943- *WhoFI 92*
**Chieri,** P A 1905- *AmMWSc 92*
**Chieri,** Pericle Adriano C. 1905- *WhoFI 92*
**Chierici,** George J 1926- *AmMWSc 92*
**Chiesi,** Lanier Joseph 1953- *WhoMW 92*
**Chifley,** Benedict 1885-1951 *FacFETw*
**Chiga,** Masahiro 1925- *AmMWSc 92*
**Chigbu,** Gibson Chuks 1956- *WhoBIA 92*
**Chigier,** Norman 1933- *AmMWSc 92*
**Chignell,** Colin Francis 1938- *AmMWSc 92*
**Chignell,** Derek Alan 1943- *AmMWSc 92*
**Chigounis,** Evans *DrAPF 91*
**Chih,** Chung-Ying 1916- *AmMWSc 92*
**Ch'ih,** John Juwei 1933- *AmMWSc 92*
**Chihara,** Carol Joyce 1941- *AmMWSc 92*
**Chihara,** Paul 1938- *NewAmDM*
**Chihara,** Theodore Seio 1929- *AmMWSc 92*
**Chihorek,** John Paul 1943- *WhoFI 92*
**Chik,** Sabbaruddin 1941- *IntWW 91*
**Chikada,** Tadashi 1919- *IntMPA 92*
**Chikalla,** Thomas D 1935- *AmMWSc 92*
**Chikalla,** Thomas David 1935- *WhoWest 92*
**Chikane,** Frank 1951- *IntWW 91*
**Chikaraishi,** Dona M 1947- *AmMWSc 92*
**Chiketa,** Stephen Cletus 1942- *Who 92*
**Chikh,** Slimane 1940- *IntWW 91*
**Chikin,** Valentin Vasilevich 1932- *IntWW 91*
**Chiko,** Arthur Wesley 1938- *AmMWSc 92*
**Chikosi,** Davidson 1961- *WhoRel 92*
**Chikousky,** Fred 1958- *WhoAmL 92*
**Chikvaidze,** Alexander Davidovich 1932- *IntWW 91*
**Chila,** Anthony George 1937- *WhoMW 92*
**Chiladze,** Tamaz Ivanovich 1931- *IntWW 91*
**Chilcot,** John Anthony 1939- *Who 92*
**Chilcote,** David Bonnell 1958- *WhoFI 92*
**Chilcote,** David Owen 1931- *AmMWSc 92*
**Chilcote,** Max Eli 1917- *AmMWSc 92*
**Chilcote,** Ronald H. 1935- *WrDr 92*
**Chilcote,** Samuel Day, Jr. 1937- *WhoFI 92*
**Chilcote,** William W 1918- *AmMWSc 92*
**Chilcott,** Timothy Bruce 1958- *WhoWest 92*
**Child,** Mrs. *SmATA 67 [port]*
**Child,** Arthur James Edward 1910- *WhoFI 92*
**Child,** Barbara Ann 1938- *WhoAmL 92*
**Child,** Charles Gardner, III d1991 *NewYTBS 91*
**Child,** Charles Gardner, III 1908- *AmMWSc 92*
**Child,** Charles Judson, Jr. 1923- *WhoRel 92*
**Child,** Charles T 1867?-1902 *BiInAmS*
**Child,** Christopher Thomas 1920- *Who 92*
**Child,** Clifton James 1912- *Who 92*
**Child,** Coles John Jeremy 1944- *Who 92*
**Child,** Denis Marsden 1926- *Who 92*
**Child,** Edward T 1930- *AmMWSc 92*
**Child,** Francis d1792 *DcNCBi 1*
**Child,** Francis J. 1825-1896 *BenetAL 91*
**Child,** Frank Malcolm 1931- *AmMWSc 92*
**Child,** Harry Ray 1928- *AmMWSc 92*
**Child,** Jeffrey James 1936- *AmMWSc 92*
**Child,** Jeremy *Who 92*
**Child,** John Sowden, Jr. 1944- *WhoAmL 92, WhoFI 92*
**Child,** Joseph Alan 1959- *WhoRel 92*
**Child,** Julia 1912- *WrDr 92*
**Child,** Julia McWilliams 1912- *WhoEnt 92*
**Child,** L. Maria *SmATA 67 [port]*
**Child,** Lydia Maria 1802-1880 *BenetAL 91, RComAH, SmATA 67 [port]*
**Child,** Lydia Maria 1802-1888 *DcAmImH*
**Child,** Lydia Maria Francis 1802-1880 *AmPeW, HanAmWH*
**Child,** Mark Sheard 1937- *Who 92*
**Child,** Mary 1959- *WhoFI 92*
**Child,** Philip 1898-1978 *BenetAL 91*
**Child,** Proctor Louis 1925- *AmMWSc 92*
**Child,** Ralph Grassing 1919- *AmMWSc 92*
**Child,** Richard Blyth 1943- *WhoAmL 92*
**Child,** St. John 1936- *TwCPaSc*
**Child,** Thomas *DcNCBi 1*
**Child Villiers** *Who 92*
**Childe,** David Cyril 1963- *WhoFI 92*
**Childers,** Donald Gene 1935- *AmMWSc 92*
**Childers,** Donnell C 1932- *WhoAmP 91*
**Childers,** Elsie Trusty 1924- *WhoEnt 92*
**Childers,** Erasmus Roy 1925- *WhoAmP 91*
**Childers,** Eugene M 1938- *WhoAmP 91*
**Childers,** Joanne *DrAPF 91*
**Childers,** John Charles 1950- *WhoAmL 92*
**Childers,** John Henry 1930- *WhoFI 92, WhoMW 92*
**Childers,** John Scott 1946- *WhoMW 92*
**Childers,** Kathryn Clark 1947- *WhoEnt 92*
**Childers,** Kevin Robert 1954- *WhoMW 92*
**Childers,** L Doyle 1944- *WhoAmP 91*
**Childers,** Norman Franklin 1910- *AmMWSc 92*
**Childers,** Phil 1949- *WhoAmP 91*
**Childers,** Ray Fleetwood 1945- *AmMWSc 92*
**Childers,** Richard Lee 1930- *AmMWSc 92*
**Childers,** Robert L 1918- *WhoAmP 91*
**Childers,** Robert Lee 1936- *AmMWSc 92*
**Childers,** Robert Wayne 1937- *AmMWSc 92*
**Childers,** Roderick W 1931- *AmMWSc 92*
**Childers,** Steven Roger 1950- *AmMWSc 92*
**Childers,** Susan Lynn Bohn 1948- *WhoMW 92*
**Childers,** Suzanne Michele 1953- *WhoEnt 92*
**Childers,** Terry L. 1952- *WhoBIA 92*
**Childers,** Terry Lee 1948- *WhoMW 92*
**Childers,** Walter Robert 1916- *AmMWSc 92*
**Childers,** Wyon Dale 1933- *WhoAmP 91*
**Childre,** Aubrey Mitchell 1948- *WhoAmP 91*
**Childress,** Albert Franklin 1963- *WhoAmL 92*
**Childress,** Alice *DrAPF 91*
**Childress,** Alice 1920- *Au&Arts 8 [port], BlkLC [port], IntAu&W 91, NotBlAW 92, WhoBIA 92, WhoEnt 92, WrDr 92*
**Childress,** Barry Lee 1941- *WhoMW 92*
**Childress,** Carol Sue 1948- *WhoRel 92*
**Childress,** Denver Ray 1937- *AmMWSc 92*
**Childress,** Dudley Stephen 1934- *AmMWSc 92*
**Childress,** Evelyn Tutt 1926- *AmMWSc 92*
**Childress,** James Franklin 1940- *WhoRel 92*
**Childress,** James J 1942- *AmMWSc 92*
**Childress,** John S 1932- *WhoIns 92, WhoMW 92*
**Childress,** Mark 1957- *ConAu 134, WrDr 92*
**Childress,** Otis Steele, Jr 1936- *AmMWSc 92*
**Childress,** Scott Julius 1926- *AmMWSc 92*
**Childress,** Steven Alan 1959- *WhoAmL 92*
**Childress,** William 1933- *ConAu 34NR*
**Childress,** William Stephen 1934- *AmMWSc 92*
**Childs,** Barney 1926- *ConCom 92, NewAmDM*
**Childs,** Barton 1916- *AmMWSc 92*
**Childs,** Brevard Springs 1923- *WhoRel 92*
**Childs,** Casey Christoper Robert 1954- *WhoEnt 92*
**Childs,** David 1933- *WrDr 92*
**Childs,** David Haslam 1933- *IntAu&W 91*
**Childs,** Diana M 1947- *WhoIns 92*
**Childs,** Donald Ray 1930- *AmMWSc 92*
**Childs,** Ellen Marie 1942- *WhoFI 92*
**Childs,** Francine C. *WhoBIA 92*
**Childs,** Gary Lee 1959- *WhoRel 92*
**Childs,** George Douglas 1957- *WhoFI 92*
**Childs,** Gerald 1961- *WhoFI 92*
**Childs,** Gerald Lee 1938- *WhoMW 92*
**Childs,** Gordon Bliss 1927- *WhoEnt 92*
**Childs,** Holly H 1942- *WhoAmP 91*
**Childs,** Hymen 1938- *WhoEnt 92*
**Childs,** Jack Douglas 1954- *WhoFI 92*
**Childs,** James Fielding Lewis 1910- *AmMWSc 92*
**Childs,** James Henry 1938- *WhoAmP 91*
**Childs,** James William 1935- *WhoAmL 92*
**Childs,** John David 1939- *WhoFI 92, WhoWest 92*
**Childs,** John Farnsworth 1909- *WhoFI 92*
**Childs,** John Oakley 1932- *WhoFI 92*
**Childs,** Josie Brown 1926- *WhoAmP 91*
**Childs,** Josie L. *WhoBIA 92*
**Childs,** Joy 1951- *WhoBIA 92*
**Childs,** Lindsay Nathan 1940- *AmMWSc 92*
**Childs,** Marian Tolbert 1925- *AmMWSc 92, WhoWest 92*
**Childs,** Marquis 1903-1990 *AnObit 1990*
**Childs,** Marquis W. 1903-1990 *BenetAL 91*
**Childs,** Marquis William d1990 *IntWW 91N*
**Childs,** Mary Jane 1936- *WhoMW 92*
**Childs,** Morris E 1923- *AmMWSc 92*
**Childs,** Oliver Bernard, Sr. 1933- *WhoBIA 92*
**Childs,** Orlo E 1914- *AmMWSc 92*
**Childs,** Ralph 1946- *WhoEnt 92*
**Childs,** Richard B. 1937- *IntMPA 92*
**Childs,** Robert Peter, Jr. 1957- *WhoFI 92*
**Childs,** Ronald Frank 1939- *AmMWSc 92*
**Childs,** S Bart 1938- *AmMWSc 92*
**Childs,** T Allen, Jr 1920- *WhoAmP 91*
**Childs,** Theodore Francis 1921- *WhoBIA 92*
**Childs,** William Henry 1907- *AmMWSc 92*
**Childs,** William Henry 1941- *AmMWSc 92*
**Childs,** William Jeffries 1926- *AmMWSc 92*
**Childs,** William Ves 1935- *AmMWSc 92*
**Childs,** Winston 1931- *WhoBIA 92*
**Childs,** Wylie J 1922- *AmMWSc 92*
**Chile,** Bishop of 1935- *Who 92*
**Chilenskas,** Albert Andrew 1927- *AmMWSc 92*
**Chiles,** Fran *WhoAmP 91*
**Chiles,** Harry Frazier 1953- *WhoAmL 92*
**Chiles,** John G, Jr 1933- *WhoAmP 91*
**Chiles,** John Houser 1928- *WhoAmL 92*
**Chiles,** Lawton 1930- *AlmAP 92 [port]*
**Chiles,** Lawton M., Jr. *NewYTBS 91*
**Chiles,** Lawton Mainor 1930- *IntWW 91*
**Chiles,** Lawton Mainor, Jr 1930- *WhoAmP 91*
**Chiles,** Linden *ConTFT 9*
**Chiles,** Lois Cleveland *WhoEnt 92*
**Chiles,** Stephen Michael 1942- *WhoAmL 92*
**Chilgreen,** Donald Ray 1939- *AmMWSc 92*
**Chilgren,** John Douglas 1943- *AmMWSc 92*
**Chilian,** William M *AmMWSc 92*
**Chilingarian,** George V 1929- *AmMWSc 92*
**Chilingirian,** Levon 1948- *IntWW 91*
**Chilivis,** Nickolas Peter 1931- *WhoAmL 92*
**Chilla,** Mildred J. 1932- *WhoMW 92*
**Chillida Juantegui,** Eduardo 1924- *IntWW 91*
**Chilsen,** Walter John 1923- *WhoAmP 91*
**Chilson,** Olin Hatfield 1903- *WhoWest 92*
**Chilson,** Oscar P 1932- *AmMWSc 92*
**Chilson,** Rob 1945- *TwCSFW 91*
**Chilson,** Robert 1945- *WrDr 92*
**Chilston,** Viscount 1946- *Who 92*
**Chilstrom,** Herbert Walfred 1931- *RelLAm 91, WhoRel 92*
**Chilton,** A B 1918- *AmMWSc 92*
**Chilton,** Bruce David 1949- *WhoRel 92*
**Chilton,** Bruce L 1935- *AmMWSc 92*
**Chilton,** Charles 1917- *TwCSFW 91*
**Chilton,** Claude Lysias 1917- *WhoRel 92*
**Chilton,** David Lee 1954- *WhoRel 92*
**Chilton,** Edward *Who 92*
**Chilton,** Frederick Oliver 1905- *Who 92*
**Chilton,** George 1767?-1836? *BiInAmS*
**Chilton,** Horace Thomas 1923- *WhoFI 92*
**Chilton,** James Renwick 1809?-1863 *BiInAmS*
**Chilton,** John Morgan 1921- *AmMWSc 92*
**Chilton,** Mary-Dell Matchett 1939- *AmMWSc 92*
**Chilton,** Michael 1934- *TwCPaSc*
**Chilton,** Neal Warwick 1921- *AmMWSc 92*
**Chilton,** Ronald Hanley 1935- *WhoEnt 92*
**Chilton,** William David 1954- *WhoMW 92*
**Chilton,** William Scott 1933- *AmMWSc 92*
**Chilver** *Who 92*
**Chilver,** Baron 1926- *IntWW 91, Who 92*
**Chilver,** Brian Outram 1933- *Who 92*
**Chilver,** Elizabeth Millicent 1914- *Who 92*
**Chilver,** Peter 1933- *IntAu&W 91, WrDr 92*
**Chilvers,** Robert Merritt 1942- *WhoAmL 92*
**Chilwell,** Muir Fitzherbert 1924- *Who 92*
**Chimenti,** Dale Everett 1946- *AmMWSc 92*
**Chimenti,** Frank A 1939- *AmMWSc 92*
**Chimera,** Cathy 1959- *WhoAmL 92*
**Chimes,** Daniel 1921- *AmMWSc 92*
**Chimet,** Iordan 1924- *IntAu&W 91*
**Chimoskey,** John Edward 1937- *AmMWSc 92*
**Chimples,** George 1924- *WhoAmL 92, WhoFI 92*
**Chimuka,** Augustine Namakube 1938- *IntWW 91*
**Chimy,** Jerome Isidore 1919- *WhoRel 92, WhoWest 92*
**Chin Iee Chong** 1921- *IntWW 91*
**Ch'in Liang-yu** d1668 *EncAmaz 91*
**Chin,** Byong Han 1934- *AmMWSc 92*
**Chin,** Charles L D 1923- *AmMWSc 92*
**Chin,** Christine F. 1964- *WhoWest 92*
**Chin,** Cynthia *WhoEnt 92*
**Chin,** David *AmMWSc 92*
**Chin,** Der-Tau 1939- *AmMWSc 92*
**Chin,** Edward 1926- *AmMWSc 92*
**Chin,** Elizabeth Mae 1938- *IntMPA 92*
**Chin,** Frank *DrAPF 91*
**Chin,** Gilbert Yukyu 1934- *AmMWSc 92*
**Chin,** Hong Woo 1935- *AmMWSc 92, WhoMW 92*
**Chin,** Hsiao-Ling M 1947- *AmMWSc 92*
**Chin,** James Ying 1953- *WhoFI 92*
**Chin,** Jane Elizabeth Heng 1933- *AmMWSc 92*
**Chin,** Jin H 1928- *AmMWSc 92*
**Chin,** Kenneth 1950- *WhoFI 92*
**Chin,** Lincoln *AmMWSc 92*
**Chin,** Llewellyn Philip 1957- *WhoAmL 92*
**Chin,** Marilyn *DrAPF 91*
**Chin,** Marjorie Scarlett 1941- *WhoWest 92*
**Chin,** Maw-Rong 1951- *AmMWSc 92*
**Ch'in,** Michael Kuo-hsing 1921- *WhoFI 92*
**Chin,** Nee Fong 1959- *WhoAmL 92*
**Chin,** NeeOo Wong 1955- *WhoMW 92*
**Chin,** Robert Allen 1950- *AmMWSc 92, WhoFI 92*
**Chin,** Ruth Lew 1954- *WhoMW 92*
**Chin,** See Leang 1942- *AmMWSc 92*
**Chin,** Sue SooneMarian *WhoWest 92*
**Chin,** Susan Wong 1946- *WhoWest 92*
**Chin,** Sylvia Fung 1949- *WhoAmL 92*
**Chin,** Tom Doon Yuen 1922- *AmMWSc 92*
**Chin,** Wanda Won 1952- *WhoWest 92*
**Chin,** William W 1947- *AmMWSc 92*
**Chin,** Yu-Ren 1938- *AmMWSc 92*
**Chin A Sen,** Hendrik Rudolf 1934- *IntWW 91*
**Chin-Bing,** Stanley Arthur 1942- *AmMWSc 92*

**Chin-Caplan,** Sylvia 1955- *WhoAmL 92*
**Chin-Lee,** Cynthia Denise 1958- *WhoAmP 91*
**Chin-Tsung-Chien,** John *WhoRel 92*
**Chinard,** Francis Pierre 1918- *AmMWSc 92*
**Chinaud,** Roger Michel 1934- *IntWW 91*
**Chincarini,** Guido Ludovico 1938- *AmMWSc 92*
**Chindamo,** Michael Leonard 1949- *WhoFI 92*
**Chinea-Varela,** Migdia *WhoEnt 92*
**Chinery,** Michael 1938- *IntAu&W 91, WrDr 92*
**Ching,** Andy Kwok-yee 1956- *WhoRel 92*
**Ching,** Chauncey T K 1940- *AmMWSc 92*
**Ching,** Chiang *WhoEnt 92*
**Ching,** Donald D H 1926- *WhoAmP 91*
**Ching,** Eric San Hing 1951- *WhoWest 92*
**Ching,** Francis F. T. 1930- *WhoWest 92*
**Ching,** Fred Yet-Fan 1957- *WhoWest 92*
**Ching,** Henry 1933- *Who 92*
**Ching,** Hilda 1934- *AmMWSc 92*
**Ching,** Hsi Kai *EncAmaz 91*
**Ching,** Jason Kwock Sung 1940- *AmMWSc 92*
**Ching,** Julia 1934- *WhoRel 92*
**Ching,** Laureen *DrAPF 91*
**Ching,** Lawrence Lin Tai 1920- *WhoFI 92*
**Ching,** Louis Michael 1956- *WhoAmL 92*
**Ching,** Melvin Chung Hing 1935- *AmMWSc 92, WhoMW 92*
**Ching,** Patrick Douglas 1957- *WhoFI 92*
**Ching,** Stefanie W. 1966- *WhoWest 92*
**Ching,** Stephen Wing-Fook 1936- *AmMWSc 92*
**Ching,** Ta Yen 1947- *AmMWSc 92*
**Ching,** Te May 1923- *AmMWSc 92*
**Ching,** Wai-Yim 1945- *AmMWSc 92*
**Chinh,** Trong 1908-1988 *FacFETw*
**Chinich,** Jesse 1921- *IntMPA 92*
**Chinich,** Michael *IntMPA 92*
**Chiniquy,** Charles Paschal Telespore 1809-1899 *RelLAm 91*
**Chinitz,** Wallace 1935- *AmMWSc 92*
**Chinmayananda,** Swami 1916- *RelLAm 91*
**Chinmoy,** Sri *DrAPF 91*
**Chinmoy,** Sri 1931- *RelLAm 91, WhoEnt 92*
**Chinn,** Clarence Edward 1925- *AmMWSc 92*
**Chinn,** Herman Isaac 1913- *AmMWSc 92*
**Chinn,** John Clarence 1938- *WhoBlA 92*
**Chinn,** Leland Jew 1924- *AmMWSc 92, WhoWest 92*
**Chinn,** May Edward 1896-1980 *NotBlAW 92*
**Chinn,** Menzie David 1961- *WhoFI 92*
**Chinn,** Phyllis Zweig 1941- *AmMWSc 92, WhoWest 92*
**Chinn,** Rex Arlyn 1935- *WhoMW 92*
**Chinn,** Robert Dudley 1949- *WhoIns 92*
**Chinn,** Roberta Naomi 1955- *WhoWest 92*
**Chinn,** Stanley H F 1914- *AmMWSc 92*
**Chinn,** Thomas Wayne 1909- *WhoWest 92*
**Chinn,** Trevor 1935- *Who 92*
**Chinnappa,** Kuppanda Muthayya 1914- *IntWW 91*
**Chinnery,** Derek 1925- *Who 92*
**Chinnery,** Michael Alistair 1933- *AmMWSc 92*
**Chinnici,** Joseph Patrick 1945- *WhoRel 92*
**Chinnici,** Joseph Peter 1943- *AmMWSc 92*
**Chinnici,** Joseph W 1919- *WhoAmP 91*
**Chinowsky,** Alan Eric 1954- *WhoMW 92*
**Chinowsky,** William 1929- *AmMWSc 92*
**Chinoy,** Helen Krich 1922- *WhoEnt 92*
**Chinoy,** Kathy 1944- *WhoAmP 91*
**Chintreuil,** Antoine 1814-1873 *ThHEIm*
**Chio,** E Hang 1948- *AmMWSc 92*
**Chiocca,** Allan R 1954- *WhoAmP 91*
**Chiodo,** Pilar Taboada 1961- *WhoFI 92*
**Chioffi,** Donald J 1944- *WhoAmP 91*
**Chioffi,** Nancy 1942- *WhoAmP 91*
**Chiogioji,** Melvin Hiroaki 1939- *AmMWSc 92*
**Chiola,** Vincent 1922- *AmMWSc 92*
**Chiolis,** Mark Joseph 1959- *WhoEnt 92, WhoWest 92*
**Chiomaca** *EncAmaz 91*
**Chiona,** James *Who 92, WhoRel 92*
**Chiotti,** Premo 1911- *AmMWSc 92*
**Chiou,** C 1924- *AmMWSc 92*
**Chiou,** Cary T 1940- *AmMWSc 92*
**Chiou,** George Chung-Yih 1934- *AmMWSc 92*
**Chiou,** Minshon Jebb 1951- *AmMWSc 92*
**Chiou,** Wen-An 1948- *AmMWSc 92*
**Chiou,** Win Loung 1938- *AmMWSc 92*
**Chipasula,** Frank Mkalawile 1949- *LiExTwC*
**Chipault,** Jacques Robert 1914- *AmMWSc 92*
**Chiphangwi,** S. D. *WhoRel 92*
**Chipimo,** Elias Marko 1931- *Who 92*
**Chipkin,** Robert Gerald 1945- *WhoFI 92*
**Chipley,** Benjamin Ned 1935- *WhoRel 92*
**Chipley,** Robert MacNeill 1939- *AmMWSc 92*
**Chiplin,** Brian 1945- *WrDr 92*
**Chipman,** Bruce Lewis 1946- *WrDr 92*
**Chipman,** Charles Joseph 1931- *WhoRel 92*
**Chipman,** David Mayer 1940- *AmMWSc 92*
**Chipman,** De Witt C *ScFEYrs*
**Chipman,** Donald 1928- *WrDr 92*
**Chipman,** Eugene Nelson, Sr. 1927- *WhoAmL 92*
**Chipman,** Gary Russell 1943- *AmMWSc 92*
**Chipman,** James Thomas 1952- *WhoMW 92*
**Chipman,** John Somerset 1926- *WhoMW 92*
**Chipman,** Luzene Stanley 1798-1886 *DcNCBi 1*
**Chipman,** Marion Walter 1920- *WhoAmL 92*
**Chipman,** R A 1912- *AmMWSc 92*
**Chipman,** Richard Manning, Jr. 1806-1893 *AmPeW*
**Chipman,** Robert K 1931- *AmMWSc 92*
**Chipman,** Wilmon B 1932- *AmMWSc 92*
**Chipp,** David Allan 1927- *IntAu&W 91, IntWW 91, Who 92*
**Chipp,** Donald Leslie 1925- *IntWW 91*
**Chipperfield,** Geoffrey Howes 1933- *Who 92*
**Chipperfield,** Jimmy 1912-1990 *AnObit 1990*
**Chippindale,** Christopher Ralph 1951- *Who 92*
**Chiquoine,** A Duncan 1926- *AmMWSc 92*
**Chirac,** Jacques 1932- *FacFETw*
**Chirac,** Jacques Rene 1932- *IntWW 91, Who 92*
**Chirarochana,** Sitthi 1920- *IntWW 91*
**Chirau,** Jeremiah 1923-1985 *FacFETw*
**Chirdon,** Paul F. 1943- *WhoWest 92*
**Chirelstein,** Marvin A. 1928- *WhoAmL 92*
**Chirica,** Andrei *IntWW 91*
**Chirichigno,** John Francis 1959- *WhoFI 92*
**Chirico,** Giorgio de 1888-1978 *FacFETw, ModArCr 2 [port]*
**Chirico,** Peter Francis 1927- *WhoRel 92*
**Chirigos,** Michael Anthony 1924- *AmMWSc 92*
**Chirikjian,** Jack G 1940- *AmMWSc 92*
**Chirinko,** Robert S. 1953- *WhoFI 92, WhoMW 92*
**Chirisa,** Farai Jonah 1940- *WhoRel 92*
**Chirkov,** Boris Petrovich 1901-1982 *SovUnBD*
**Chirlian,** Paul M 1931- *AmMWSc 92*
**Chisari,** Francis Vincent 1942- *AmMWSc 92*
**Chiscon,** J Alfred 1933- *AmMWSc 92*
**Chiscon,** Martha Oakley 1935- *AmMWSc 92*
**Chisholm,** A.M. 1872-1960 *TwCWW 91*
**Chisholm,** Alexander James 1941- *AmMWSc 92*
**Chisholm,** Alexander William John 1922- *Who 92*
**Chisholm,** Archibald Hugh Tennent 1902- *Who 92*
**Chisholm,** Clarence Edward 1949- *WhoBlA 92*
**Chisholm,** David R 1923- *AmMWSc 92*
**Chisholm,** Donald Alexander 1927- *IntWW 91*
**Chisholm,** Donald Alexander 1936- *AmMWSc 92*
**Chisholm,** Donald E 1938- *WhoIns 92*
**Chisholm,** Donald William 1953- *WhoWest 92*
**Chisholm,** Douglas Blanchard 1943- *AmMWSc 92*
**Chisholm,** Frank Anderson 1910- *WhoFI 92*
**Chisholm,** Geoffrey D. 1931- *IntWW 91*
**Chisholm,** Geoffrey Duncan 1931- *Who 92*
**Chisholm,** George Nickolaus 1936- *WhoMW 92*
**Chisholm,** James Joseph 1936- *AmMWSc 92*
**Chisholm,** John Alexander Raymond 1946- *Who 92*
**Chisholm,** Joseph Carrel, Jr. 1935- *WhoBlA 92*
**Chisholm,** June Faye 1949- *WhoBlA 92*
**Chisholm,** Malcolm Harold 1945- *AmMWSc 92, Who 92*
**Chisholm,** Matt 1919-1983 *TwCWW 91*
**Chisholm,** Michael 1931- *WrDr 92*
**Chisholm,** Michael Donald Inglis 1931- *Who 92*
**Chisholm,** Reginald Constantine 1934- *WhoBlA 92*
**Chisholm,** Roderick Aeneas 1911- *Who 92*
**Chisholm,** Sallie Watson 1947- *AmMWSc 92*
**Chisholm,** Samuel Jackson 1942- *WhoBlA 92*
**Chisholm,** Shirley *DcAmImH*
**Chisholm,** Shirley 1924- *ConBlB 2 [port], FacFETw, HanAmWH, NotBlAW 92 [port], WhoBlA 92*
**Chisholm,** Shirley Anita 1924- *WhoAmP 91*
**Chisholm,** Shirley Anita St. Hill 1924- *AmPolLe [port]*
**Chisholm,** Tom Shepherd 1941- *WhoWest 92*
**Chisholm,** Tommy 1941- *WhoFI 92*
**Chisholm,** Walter Samuel 1926- *WhoRel 92*
**Chisholm,** William DeWayne 1924- *WhoFI 92, WhoRel 92*
**Chishti,** Athar Husain 1957- *AmMWSc 92*
**Chisler,** John Adam 1937- *AmMWSc 92*
**Chislett,** Derek Victor 1929- *Who 92*
**Chism,** Grady William, III 1946- *AmMWSc 92*
**Chism,** Harolyn B. 1941- *WhoBlA 92*
**Chism,** James Arthur 1933- *WhoFI 92, WhoMW 92*
**Chism-Peace,** Yvonne *DrAPF 91*
**Chisman,** James Allen 1935- *AmMWSc 92*
**Chisnell,** Janice Hoffman 1960- *WhoAmL 92*
**Chisnell,** John Gilbert, Sr. 1938- *WhoRel 92*
**Chisolm,** Grace Butler *WhoBlA 92*
**Chisolm,** Guy M *AmMWSc 92*
**Chisolm,** James Julian, Jr 1921- *AmMWSc 92*
**Chissano,** Joaquim 1939- *FacFETw, IntWW 91*
**Chissell,** Herbert Garland 1922- *WhoBlA 92*
**Chissell,** Joan Olive *WrDr 92*
**Chissell,** Joan Olive 1919- *IntAu&W 91*
**Chisum,** Gloria Twine 1930- *WhoBlA 92*
**Chisum,** Warren D 1938- *WhoAmP 91*
**Chiswell,** Peter *Who 92*
**Chiswell,** Peter Irvine 1930- *Who 92*
**Chiswik,** Haim H 1915- *AmMWSc 92*
**Chitaley,** Shyamala D 1918- *AmMWSc 92*
**Chitanava,** Nodari Amrosievich 1935- *IntWW 91, SovUnBD*
**Chitgopekar,** Sharad Shankarrao 1938- *AmMWSc 92*
**Chitham,** Edward 1932- *WrDr 92*
**Chitham,** Edward Harry Gordon 1932- *IntAu&W 91*
**Chitharanjan,** D 1940- *AmMWSc 92*
**Chitnis** *Who 92*
**Chitnis,** Baron 1936- *Who 92*
**Chittenden,** David H 1935- *AmMWSc 92*
**Chittenden,** Hiram Martin 1858-1917 *BiInAmS*
**Chittenden,** Mark Eustace, Jr 1939- *AmMWSc 92*
**Chittenden,** William A 1927- *AmMWSc 92*
**Chittenden-Bascom,** Cathleen 1962- *WhoRel 92*
**Chittick,** Arden Boone 1936- *WhoWest 92*
**Chittick,** Donald Ernest 1932- *AmMWSc 92*
**Chittick,** K A 1903- *AmMWSc 92*
**Chittim,** Richard Leigh 1915- *AmMWSc 92*
**Chittister,** Joan D. 1936- *IntWW 91*
**Chittock,** John Dudley 1928- *IntAu&W 91*
**Chittolini,** Giorgio 1940- *IntWW 91*
**Chitty,** Alison Jill 1948- *Who 92*
**Chitty,** Anthony 1931- *Who 92*
**Chitty,** Beryl 1917- *Who 92*
**Chitty,** Dennis Hubert 1912- *AmMWSc 92*
**Chitty,** Mae Elizabeth 1928- *WhoBlA 92*
**Chitty,** Monte L. 1961- *WhoRel 92*
**Chitty,** Susan 1929- *IntAu&W 91, WrDr 92*
**Chitty,** Susan Elspeth 1929- *Who 92*
**Chitty,** Thomas *WrDr 92*
**Chitty,** Thomas 1926- *IntAu&W 91*
**Chitty,** Thomas Willes 1926- *IntWW 91, Who 92*
**Chitvira,** Thongyod *IntWW 91*
**Chitwood,** David Joseph 1950- *AmMWSc 92*
**Chitwood,** Howard 1932- *AmMWSc 92*
**Chitwood,** James Leroy 1943- *AmMWSc 92*
**Ch'iu Chin** *EncAmaz 91*
**Chiu Chuang-Huan** 1925- *IntWW 91*
**Chiu,** Arthur Nang Lick 1929- *AmMWSc 92*
**Chiu,** Chao-Lin 1934- *AmMWSc 92*
**Chiu,** Charles Bin 1940- *AmMWSc 92*
**Chiu,** Ching Ching *AmMWSc 92*
**Chiu,** Chu Jeng 1934- *AmMWSc 92*
**Chiu,** Hong-Yee 1932- *AmMWSc 92*
**Chiu,** Huei-Huang 1930- *AmMWSc 92*
**Chiu,** Hungdah 1936- *IntAu&W 91, WrDr 92*
**Chiu,** Jen 1924- *AmMWSc 92*
**Chiu,** Jen-Fu 1940- *AmMWSc 92*
**Chiu,** John Shih-Yao 1928- *AmMWSc 92*
**Chiu,** Kirts C 1933- *AmMWSc 92*
**Chiu,** Lian-Hwang 1935- *WhoMW 92*
**Chiu,** Lue-Yung Chow 1931- *AmMWSc 92*
**Chiu,** Martin Thomas 1964- *WhoWest 92*
**Chiu,** Peter Ching-Tai 1944- *WhoRel 92*
**Chiu,** Peter Jiunn-Shyong 1942- *AmMWSc 92*
**Chiu,** Peter Yee-Chew 1948- *WhoWest 92*
**Chiu,** Samuel Shin-Wai 1951- *WhoWest 92*
**Chiu,** Shing-Yan 1952- *WhoMW 92*
**Chiu,** Tai-Woo 1944- *AmMWSc 92*
**Chiu,** Tak-Ming 1949- *AmMWSc 92*
**Chiu,** Thomas T 1933- *AmMWSc 92*
**Chiu,** Tien-Heng 1953- *AmMWSc 92*
**Chiu,** Tin-Ho 1942- *AmMWSc 92*
**Chiu,** Tony Man-Kuen *AmMWSc 92*
**Chiu,** Tsao Yi 1925- *AmMWSc 92*
**Chiu,** Victor *AmMWSc 92*
**Chiu,** Wan-Cheng 1919- *AmMWSc 92*
**Chiu,** Yam-Tsi 1940- *AmMWSc 92*
**Chiu,** Yih-Ping 1933- *AmMWSc 92*
**Chiu,** Ying-Nan 1933- *AmMWSc 92*
**Chiueh,** Chuang Chin 1943- *AmMWSc 92*
**Chiulli,** Angelo Joseph *AmMWSc 92*
**Chiusano,** Thomas Charles 1947- *WhoEnt 92*
**Chivas,** Silvia 1954- *BlkOlyM*
**Chivers,** Hugh John 1932- *AmMWSc 92*
**Chivers,** James Leeds 1939- *WhoAmL 92*
**Chivers,** Thomas Holley 1809-1858 *BenetAL 91*
**Chivian,** Eric Seth 1942- *AmMWSc 92*
**Chivian,** Jay Simon 1931- *AmMWSc 92*
**Chivis,** Martin Lewis 1952- *WhoBlA 92*
**Chivukula,** Ramamohana Rao 1933- *AmMWSc 92*
**Chiykowski,** Lloyd Nicholas 1929- *AmMWSc 92*
**Chizaki,** Usaburo 1919- *IntWW 91*
**Chizek,** Jerry 1936- *WhoAmP 91*
**Chizhov,** Ludvig Aleksandrovich 1936- *IntWW 91*
**Chizinsky,** Walter 1926- *AmMWSc 92*
**Chizmadia,** Stephen Mark 1950- *WhoAmL 92, WhoFI 92*
**Chizmar,** Nancy L 1936- *WhoAmP 91*
**Chizzonite,** Richard A *AmMWSc 92*
**Chkheidze,** Revaz Davidovich 1924- *IntWW 91*
**Chkhikvadze,** Ramaz 1928- *IntWW 91*
**Chlanda,** Frederick P 1943- *AmMWSc 92*
**Chlapek,** Marvin *WhoRel 92*
**Chlapowski,** Francis Joseph 1944- *AmMWSc 92*
**Chlebowski,** Jan F 1943- *AmMWSc 92*
**Chlebowy,** William Louis 1959- *WhoFI 92*
**Chloris** *EncAmaz 91*
**Chlouber,** Kenneth Wayne 1939- *WhoAmP 91*
**Chlubna,** David John 1953- *WhoMW 92*
**Chlystek,** David Bryant 1958- *WhoMW 92*
**Chmell,** Samuel Jay 1952- *WhoMW 92*
**Chmiel,** Joseph Anthony, Jr. 1959- *WhoFI 92*
**Chmiel,** Kenneth Walter 1944- *WhoWest 92*
**Chmielewska,** Joanna 1932- *IntAu&W 91*
**Chmielewski,** Florian 1927- *WhoAmP 91*
**Chmielinski,** Edward Alexander 1925- *WhoFI 92*
**Chmura-Meyer,** Carol A 1939- *AmMWSc 92*
**Chmurny,** Alan Bruce 1944- *AmMWSc 92*
**Chmurny,** Gwendolyn Neal 1937- *AmMWSc 92*
**Chmurny,** William Wayne 1941- *WhoMW 92*
**Chnoupek,** Bohuslav 1925- *IntWW 91*
**Cho,** Alfred Chih-Fang 1921- *AmMWSc 92*
**Cho,** Alfred Y 1937- *AmMWSc 92*
**Cho,** Arthur Kenji 1928- *AmMWSc 92*
**Cho,** Byong Kwon 1944- *AmMWSc 92*
**Cho,** Byung-Ryul 1926- *AmMWSc 92*
**Cho,** Cheng T 1937- *AmMWSc 92*
**Cho,** Chung Won 1931- *AmMWSc 92*
**Cho,** Daniel Dowoong 1956- *WhoAmL 92*
**Cho,** David Dong-Jin 1924- *WhoRel 92*
**Cho,** Eun-Sook 1940- *AmMWSc 92*
**Cho,** Han-Ru 1945- *AmMWSc 92*
**Cho,** Kiyoko Takeda 1917- *IntWW 91*
**Cho,** Kon Ho 1937- *AmMWSc 92*
**Cho,** Peck 1956- *WhoMW 92*
**Cho,** Ramaswamy 1934- *IntWW 91*
**Cho,** Sang Ha 1936- *AmMWSc 92*
**Cho,** Soung Moo 1937- *AmMWSc 92*
**Cho,** Sung Yoon 1928- *WhoAmL 92*
**Cho,** Tai Yong 1943- *WhoAmL 92*
**Cho,** Yongock 1935- *AmMWSc 92*
**Cho,** Young-chung 1940- *AmMWSc 92*
**Cho,** Young Won 1931- *AmMWSc 92*
**Cho-Chung,** Yoon Sang 1932- *AmMWSc 92*
**Choate,** Alan G. 1939- *WhoAmL 92*
**Choate,** Alec Herbert 1915- *IntAu&W 91*
**Choate,** Edward Lee 1951- *WhoAmL 92*
**Choate,** Emily Teresa 1953- *WhoEnt 92*
**Choate,** Eugene 1936- *WhoIns 92*
**Choate,** Jerry D 1938- *WhoIns 92*
**Choate,** Jerry Ronald 1943- *AmMWSc 92*
**Choate,** John Irvan *WhoEnt 92*
**Choate,** John Richard 1946- *WhoFI 92*

**Choate**, Mitchell Kent 1960- WhoRel 92
**Choate**, Ralph J 1947- WhoAmP 91
**Choate**, William Clay 1934- AmMWSc 92
**Choban**, Nick Mitchell 1957- WhoEnt 92
**Chobanian**, Aram V 1929- AmMWSc 92
**Chobot**, John Charles 1948- WhoAmL 92
**Chobotar**, Bill 1934- AmMWSc 92
**Chock**, Clifford Yet-Chong 1951- WhoWest 92
**Chock**, David Poileng 1943- AmMWSc 92
**Chock**, Ernest Phaynan 1937- AmMWSc 92
**Chock**, Jan Sun-Lum 1944- AmMWSc 92
**Chock**, Jay Richard 1955- WhoAmL 92
**Chock**, Margaret Irvine 1944- AmMWSc 92
**Chock**, P Boon 1939- AmMWSc 92
**Chock**, Stephen Kan Leong 1955- WhoRel 92
**Chocquet**, Victor 1821-1891 ThHEIm [port]
**Chodera**, Jerry 1947- WhoWest 92
**Chodes**, John Jay 1939- IntAu&W 91
**Chodor**, Kathleen DrAPF 91
**Chodorkoff**, Bernard 1925- WhoMW 92
**Chodorow**, Marvin 1913- AmMWSc 92, IntWW 91
**Chodorow**, Nancy 1944- WrDr 92
**Chodos**, Alan A 1943- AmMWSc 92
**Chodos**, Arthur A 1922- AmMWSc 92
**Chodos**, Gabriel WhoEnt 92
**Chodos**, Robert Bruno 1918- AmMWSc 92
**Chodos**, Robert Irwin 1947- WhoRel 92
**Chodos**, Steven Leslie 1943- AmMWSc 92
**Chodosh**, Sanford 1928- AmMWSc 92
**Chodroff**, Saul 1914- AmMWSc 92
**Choe**, Byung-Kil 1933- AmMWSc 92
**Choe**, H. Amy 1966- WhoFI 92
**Choe**, Hyung Tae 1927- AmMWSc 92, WhoMW 92
**Choe**, Joseph Jong Kook 1961- WhoWest 92
**Choe**, Victor Hee Seung 1963- WhoRel 92
**Choe**, Won-Gil 1932- WhoEnt 92, WhoFI 92, WhoWest 92
**Choguill**, Harold Samuel 1907- AmMWSc 92, WhoMW 92
**Choi Kyu-Hah** 1919- IntWW 91
**Choi**, Byung Chang 1940- AmMWSc 92
**Choi**, Byung Ho 1928- AmMWSc 92
**Choi**, Chan-Young 1926- WhoRel 92
**Choi**, Duk-In 1936- AmMWSc 92
**Choi**, Eun Kwan 1946- WhoFI 92
**Choi**, Jake Hyunggab 1963- WhoMW 92
**Choi**, Kwan-Yiu Calvin 1954- AmMWSc 92
**Choi**, Kyu-Yong 1953- AmMWSc 92
**Choi**, Kyung Kook 1946- AmMWSc 92
**Choi**, Man-Duen 1945- AmMWSc 92, IntWW 91
**Choi**, Nung Won 1931- AmMWSc 92
**Choi**, Paul Soo-Woong 1943- WhoWest 92
**Choi**, Sang-il 1931- AmMWSc 92
**Choi**, Seungmook 1952- WhoMW 92
**Choi**, Sook Y 1938- AmMWSc 92
**Choi**, Stephen U S 1942- AmMWSc 92
**Choi**, Sung Chil 1930- AmMWSc 92
**Choi**, Sunu 1916- IntWW 91
**Choi**, Tai-Soon 1935- AmMWSc 92
**Choi**, Thomas Sungsoo 1958- WhoRel 92
**Choi**, Won Kil 1943- AmMWSc 92
**Choi**, Ye-Chin 1929- AmMWSc 92
**Choi**, Yong Chun 1935- AmMWSc 92
**Choi**, Yong Sung 1936- AmMWSc 92
**Choike**, James Richard 1942- AmMWSc 92
**Choiseul**, Etienne-Francois de 1719-1785 HisDSpE
**Chojnacka**, Elisabeth 1939- IntWW 91
**Chojnacki**, Julian Edward John 1953- WhoEnt 92
**Chojnacki**, Paul Ervin 1950- WhoMW 92
**Chojnowska-Liskiewicz**, Krystyna 1936- IntWW 91
**Choksi**, Jal R 1932- AmMWSc 92
**Cholak**, Jacob 1900- AmMWSc 92
**Cholakis**, Constantine George 1930- WhoAmL 92
**Choldin**, Harvey M. 1939- WhoMW 92
**Cholerton**, Frederick Arthur 1917- Who 92
**Cholette**, A 1918- AmMWSc 92
**Cholette**, Paul Edward 1955- WhoMW 92
**Cholick**, Fred Andrew 1950- AmMWSc 92
**Cholis**, Thomas Joseph, Jr. 1946- WhoFI 92
**Chollet**, Deborah 1950- WhoFI 92
**Chollet**, Raymond 1946- AmMWSc 92
**Cholmeley**, John Adye 1902- Who 92
**Cholmeley**, Montague 1935- Who 92
**Cholmondeley** Who 92
**Cholmondeley**, Marquess of 1960- Who 92
**Cholmondeley**, Paula H. J. 1947- WhoBlA 92
**Cholmondeley Clarke**, Marshal Butler 1919- Who 92
**Cholodowski**, Antonia Marie 1932- WhoRel 92
**Choltitz**, Dietrich von 1894-1966 EncTR 91 [port]
**Cholvin**, Neal R 1928- AmMWSc 92
**Choma**, John, Jr 1941- AmMWSc 92
**Chomchalow**, Narong 1935- AmMWSc 92
**Chomeau**, David D 1937- WhoIns 92
**Chomica**, John 1937 WhoIns 92
**Chompff**, Alfred J 1930- AmMWSc 92
**Chomsky**, Jack Steven 1955- WhoRel 92
**Chomsky**, Marvin J. LesBEnT 92
**Chomsky**, Marvin J. 1929- IntMPA 92, WhoEnt 92
**Chomsky**, Natt B. 1953- WhoEnt 92
**Chomsky**, Noam 1928- AmMWSc 92, AmPeW, FacFETw, IntWW 91, Who 92, WrDr 92
**Chon**, Choon Taik 1946- AmMWSc 92
**Chona**, Mainza 1930- IntWW 91
**Chonacky**, Norman J 1939- AmMWSc 92
**Chong Sok-Mo** 1929- IntWW 91
**Chong**, Aaron Barton 1956- WhoWest 92
**Chong**, Anson 1938- WhoAmP 91
**Chong**, Berni Patricia 1945- AmMWSc 92
**Chong**, Calvin 1943- AmMWSc 92
**Chong**, Clyde Hok Heen 1933- AmMWSc 92, WhoMW 92
**Chong**, Dianne 1949- WhoMW 92
**Chong**, Gerald H. W. 1940- WhoWest 92
**Chong**, Howard, Jr 1942- WhoAmP 91
**Chong**, James York 1944- AmMWSc 92
**Chong**, Joshua Anthony 1943- AmMWSc 92
**Chong**, Ken Pin 1942- AmMWSc 92
**Chong**, Ping DrAPF 91
**Chong**, Rae Dawn 1962- IntMPA 92
**Chong**, Richard David 1946- WhoWest 92
**Chong**, Shuang-Ling 1943- AmMWSc 92
**Chong**, Shui-Fong 1954- WhoEnt 92
**Chong**, Thomas 1938- WhoEnt 92
**Chong**, Tommy 1938- IntMPA 92
**Chongwe**, Rodger Masauso Alivas 1940- IntWW 91
**Chonko**, Lorraine N 1936- WhoAmP 91
**Choo**, Samuel Kam-Chee 1916- WhoRel 92
**Choo**, Thin-Meiw 1947- AmMWSc 92
**Choo**, Vincent Ki Seng 1952- WhoWest 92
**Choo**, Yeow Ming 1953- WhoAmL 92
**Chookaszian**, Dennis Haig 1943- WhoFI 92, WhoIns 92
**Chooluck**, Leon 1920- IntMPA 92, WhoEnt 92
**Choong**, Elvin T 1932- AmMWSc 92
**Choong**, Hsia Shaw-Lwan 1945- AmMWSc 92
**Choonhavan**, Chatichai 1922- IntWW 91
**Chope**, Christopher Robert 1947- Who 92
**Choper**, Jesse Herbert 1935- WhoAmL 92
**Chopin**, Fryderyk 1810-1849 NewAmDM
**Chopin**, Kate 1850-1904 ModAWWr
**Chopin**, Kate 1851-1904 BenetAL 91, ShSCr 8 [port]
**Chopin**, L. Frank 1942- WhoAmL 92
**Chopin**, Susan Gardiner 1947- WhoAmL 92
**Chopko**, Mark E. 1953- WhoRel 92
**Choppin**, Gregory Robert 1927- AmMWSc 92
**Choppin**, Purnell Whittington 1929- AmMWSc 92, IntWW 91
**Chopra**, Anil K 1941- AmMWSc 92
**Chopra**, Baldeo K 1942- AmMWSc 92
**Chopra**, Dev Raj 1930- AmMWSc 92
**Chopra**, Dharam Pal 1944- AmMWSc 92
**Chopra**, Dharam-Vir 1930- AmMWSc 92
**Chopra**, Inder Jit 1939- AmMWSc 92
**Chopra**, Joginder Gurbux 1932- AmMWSc 92
**Chopra**, Joyce ReelWom [port]
**Chopra**, Naiter Mohan 1923- AmMWSc 92
**Chopra**, Sudhir Kumar 1949- WhoMW 92
**Choquet**, Gustave Alfred Arthur 1915- IntWW 91
**Choquette**, Adrienne 1915-1973 BenetAL 91
**Choquette**, Dave WhoAmP 91
**Choquette**, Philip Wheeler 1930- AmMWSc 92
**Choquette**, Robert 1905- BenetAL 91
**Chorafas**, Dimitris N. 1926- WrDr 92
**Chorengel**, Bernd WhoMW 92
**Chorin**, Alexandre J 1938- AmMWSc 92
**Chorley** Who 92
**Chorley**, Baron 1930- IntWW 91, Who 92
**Chorley**, Francis Kenneth 1926- Who 92
**Chorley**, Harold d1990 Who 92N
**Chorley**, Richard J. 1927- WrDr 92
**Chorley**, Richard John 1927- Who 92
**Chorlton**, David DrAPF 91
**Chorlton**, Graham 1953- TwCPaSc
**Chormann**, Richard F. 1937- WhoFI 92
**Chornock**, Orestes 1883-1977 RelLAm 91
**Chornovil**, Vyacheslav Maksymovych 1937- SovUnBD
**Chorny**, Ammos 1961- WhoRel 92
**Chorpenning**, Frank Winslow 1913- AmMWSc 92
**Chorpita**, Fred Michael 1940- WhoIns 92
**Chortyk**, Orestes Timothy 1935- AmMWSc 92
**Chorvat**, Robert John 1942- AmMWSc 92
**Chory**, James Allan 1955- WhoEnt 92
**Chorzempa**, Daniel Walter 1944- IntWW 91
**Chorzempa**, Marie Andree 1926- WhoRel 92
**Chosy**, John Eugene 1948- WhoAmL 92
**Chotard**, Yvon 1921- IntWW 91
**Chotiner**, Kenneth Lee 1937- WhoAmL 92, WhoWest 92
**Chottiner**, Lawrence R. 1949- WhoRel 92
**Chou En-lai** 1898-1976 FacFETw [port]
**Chou Wen-chung** 1923- ConCom 92, NewAmDM
**Chou Yang** FacFETw
**Chou**, Chen-Lin 1943- AmMWSc 92
**Chou**, Ching 1941- AmMWSc 92
**Chou**, Ching-Chung 1932- AmMWSc 92
**Chou**, Chung-Chi 1936- AmMWSc 92
**Chou**, Chung-Kwang 1946- AmMWSc 92
**Chou**, Chung-Kwang 1947- WhoWest 92
**Chou**, David Yuan Pin 1922- AmMWSc 92
**Chou**, Dorthy T C T 1940- AmMWSc 92
**Chou**, Erwin C. 1952- WhoFI 92
**Chou**, Frank Fu 1931- WhoMW 92
**Chou**, Iih-Nan 1943- AmMWSc 92
**Chou**, James C S 1920- AmMWSc 92
**Chou**, Janice Y AmMWSc 92
**Chou**, Jordan Quan Ban 1941- AmMWSc 92
**Chou**, Kuo Chen 1938- AmMWSc 92, WhoMW 92
**Chou**, Larry I-Hui 1936- AmMWSc 92
**Chou**, Libby Wang AmMWSc 92
**Chou**, Mark 1910- WhoFI 92
**Chou**, Mei-In Melissa Liu 1947- AmMWSc 92
**Chou**, Nelson Shih-Toon 1935- AmMWSc 92
**Chou**, Pei Chi 1924- AmMWSc 92, WhoFI 92
**Chou**, Shelley Nien-Chun 1924- AmMWSc 92
**Chou**, Shyan-Yih 1941- AmMWSc 92
**Chou**, T T 1934- AmMWSc 92
**Chou**, Ting-Chao 1938- AmMWSc 92
**Chou**, Tsai-Chia Peter 1959- AmMWSc 92
**Chou**, Tsong-Wen 1933- AmMWSc 92
**Chou**, Tsu-Wei 1940- AmMWSc 92
**Chou**, Tzi Shan 1942- AmMWSc 92
**Chou**, Wen-chung 1923- WhoEnt 92
**Chou**, Wushow 1939- AmMWSc 92
**Chou**, Y T 1924- AmMWSc 92
**Chou**, Yue Hong 1952- WhoWest 92
**Chou**, Yungnien John AmMWSc 92
**Choudary**, Jasti Bhaskararao 1933- AmMWSc 92
**Choudary**, Prabhakara Velagapudi 1948- AmMWSc 92
**Choudhary**, Manoj Kumar 1952- AmMWSc 92
**Choudhury**, Abdul Barkat Ataul Ghani Khan 1927- IntWW 91
**Choudhury**, Abdul Latif 1933- AmMWSc 92
**Choudhury**, Deo C 1926- AmMWSc 92
**Choudhury**, Humayan Rasheed 1928- IntWW 91
**Choudhury**, Malay Roy 1939- ConAu 14AS [port]
**Choudhury**, P Roy 1930- AmMWSc 92
**Chouffot**, Geoffrey Charles Who 92
**Choufi**, Hammoud el- 1935- IntWW 91
**Chouinard**, Guy 1944- AmMWSc 92
**Chouinard**, Leo George, II 1949- AmMWSc 92
**Chouinard**, Paul Lewellyn 1945- WhoFI 92
**Chouinard**, Richard J. 1932- WhoIns 92
**Choukas**, Nicholas C 1923- AmMWSc 92
**Choukas-Bradley**, James Richard 1950- WhoAmL 92
**Choun**, Robert Joseph, Jr. 1948- WhoRel 92
**Chovan**, James Peter 1948- AmMWSc 92
**Chovanes**, Eugene 1926- WhoAmL 92
**Chover**, Joshua 1928- AmMWSc 92
**Chovet**, Abraham 1704-1790 BiInAmS
**Chovitz**, Bernard H 1924- AmMWSc 92
**Chovnick**, Arthur 1927- AmMWSc 92
**Chow Shu-Kai** 1913- IntWW 91
**Chow**, Alfred Wen-Jen 1924- AmMWSc 92
**Chow**, Andrew S. 1963- WhoFI 92
**Chow**, Arthur 1936- AmMWSc 92
**Chow**, Brian G 1941- AmMWSc 92
**Chow**, Bryant 1936- AmMWSc 92
**Chow**, Chao K 1928- AmMWSc 92
**Chow**, Che Chung 1935- AmMWSc 92
**Chow**, Chee Yan 1955- WhoFI 92
**Chow**, Chi-Ming 1931- WhoMW 92
**Chow**, Ching Kuang 1940- AmMWSc 92
**Chow**, Chuen-Yen 1932- AmMWSc 92
**Chow**, David Kimkwong 1947- WhoFI 92
**Chow**, Donna Arlene 1941- AmMWSc 92
**Chow**, Edna 1960- WhoWest 92
**Chow**, Franklin Szu-Chien 1956- WhoWest 92
**Chow**, George Sheung-Kwan 1948- WhoFI 92
**Chow**, Ida AmMWSc 92
**Chow**, Kao Liang 1918- AmMWSc 92
**Chow**, Laurence Chung-Lung 1943- AmMWSc 92
**Chow**, Leonard Yew Tong 1940- WhoFI 92
**Chow**, Louise Tsi 1943- AmMWSc 92
**Chow**, Martin Mei-Ta 1956- WhoRel 92
**Chow**, Pao Liu 1936- AmMWSc 92
**Chow**, Paul C 1926- AmMWSc 92
**Chow**, Paul Chuan-Juin 1926- WhoWest 92
**Chow**, Raymond 1927- IntMPA 92
**Chow**, Richard H 1924- AmMWSc 92
**Chow**, Rita K 1926- AmMWSc 92
**Chow**, Shin-Kien 1935- AmMWSc 92
**Chow**, Stanley M. 1951- WhoAmL 92
**Chow**, Stephen Yee 1952- WhoAmL 92, WhoFI 92
**Chow**, Tai-Low 1937- AmMWSc 92
**Chow**, Tat-Sing Paul 1953- AmMWSc 92
**Chow**, Thien Lien 1944- AmMWSc 92
**Chow**, Tony Nging-Tung 1953- WhoMW 92
**Chow**, Tsaihwa James 1924- AmMWSc 92
**Chow**, Tseng Yeh 1921- AmMWSc 92
**Chow**, Tsu Ling 1915- AmMWSc 92
**Chow**, Tsu-Sen 1939- AmMWSc 92
**Chow**, Wen Lung 1924- AmMWSc 92
**Chow**, Wen Mou 1919- AmMWSc 92
**Chow**, Weng Wah 1948- AmMWSc 92
**Chow**, Winston 1946- WhoFI 92, WhoWest 92
**Chow**, Yuan Lang 1929- AmMWSc 92
**Chow**, Yuan Shih 1924- AmMWSc 92
**Chow**, Yung Leonard 1936- AmMWSc 92
**Chow**, Yutze 1927- AmMWSc 92
**Chow-Kai**, Juan 1963- WhoHisp 92
**Chowdhry**, Uma 1947- AmMWSc 92
**Chowdhuri**, Pritindra 1927- AmMWSc 92
**Chowdhury**, Abdur Rahim 1953- WhoFI 92
**Chowdhury**, Abul Fazal Mohammad A. 1915- IntWW 91
**Chowdhury**, Debabrata 1962- WhoWest 92
**Chowdhury**, Dipak Kumar 1936- AmMWSc 92, WhoMW 92
**Chowdhury**, Ikbalur Rashid 1939- AmMWSc 92
**Chowdhury**, Mizanur Rahman 1928- IntWW 91
**Chowdhury**, Mridula 1938- AmMWSc 92
**Chowdhury**, Parimal 1940- AmMWSc 92
**Chowdhury**, Paul Gopal 1949- TwCPaSc
**Chowdhury**, Ruhul Ambia 1942- WhoMW 92
**Chowdhury**, Salahuddin Quader 1949- IntWW 91
**Chown**, Edward Holton 1932- AmMWSc 92
**Chowne**, Gerard 1875-1917 TwCPaSc
**Chowning**, Frank Edmond WhoBlA 92
**Chowning**, John M. 1934- NewAmDM
**Chowning**, Vonne Stout 1943- WhoAmP 91
**Chowrashi**, Prokash K AmMWSc 92
**Choy**, Christine ReelWom
**Choy**, Daniel S J 1926- AmMWSc 92
**Choy**, Herbert Young Cho 1916- WhoAmL 92
**Choy**, Patrick C 1944- AmMWSc 92
**Choy**, Wai Nang 1946- AmMWSc 92, WhoWest 92
**Choy**, Wilbur Wong Yan 1918- WhoRel 92
**Choyke**, Phyllis May Ford 1921- IntAu&W 91, WhoFI 92, WhoMW 92
**Choyke**, Wolfgang Justus 1926- AmMWSc 92
**Chraibi**, Driss 1926- IntWW 91
**Chrambach**, Andreas C 1927- AmMWSc 92
**Chramostova**, Vlasta 1926- IntWW 91
**Chrapliwy**, Peter Stanley 1923- AmMWSc 92
**Chraplyvy**, Andrew R 1950- AmMWSc 92
**Chrein**, Maxine 1950- WhoEnt 92
**Chrenko**, Richard Michael 1930- AmMWSc 92
**Chrepta**, Stephen John 1921- AmMWSc 92
**Chrest**, James H 1938- WhoAmP 91
**Chrestenson**, Hubert Edwin 1927- AmMWSc 92
**Chretien**, Gladys M. WhoBlA 92
**Chretien**, Jean 1934- Who 92
**Chretien**, Jean-Loup 1938- FacFETw
**Chretien**, Joseph Jacques Jean 1934- IntWW 91
**Chretien**, Marc A 1954- WhoAmP 91
**Chretien**, Max 1924- AmMWSc 92
**Chretien**, Michel 1936- AmMWSc 92
**Chrey**, Kristine Ann 1951- WhoAmL 92
**Chrichlow**, Livingston L. 1925- WhoBlA 92
**Chrichlow**, Mary L. 1927- WhoBlA 92
**Chrien**, Robert Edward 1930- AmMWSc 92
**Chrien**, Robert Edward 1954- WhoWest 92
**Chrimes**, Henry Bertram 1915- Who 92

**Chris**, Harry Joseph 1938- *WhoFI 92*
**Chrisman**, Arthur Bowie 1889-1953 *BenetAL 91*
**Chrisman**, Charles Bowles 1921- *WhoIns 92*
**Chrisman**, Charles Larry 1941- *AmMWSc 92*
**Chrisman**, James Joseph 1954- *WhoFI 92*
**Chrisman**, Noel Judson 1940- *AmMWSc 92*
**Chrisope**, Terry Alan 1947- *WhoMW 92*
**Chrispeels**, Maarten Jan 1938- *AmMWSc 92*
**Chrispens**, Pamela Bartos 1960- *WhoFI 92*
**Chriss**, Terry Michael 1945- *AmMWSc 92*
**Chriss**, Timothy D. A. 1950- *WhoAmL 92*
**Chrissis**, James W 1953- *AmMWSc 92*
**Christ** *EncEarC [port]*
**Christ**, Adolph Ervin 1929- *AmMWSc 92*
**Christ**, Carl Finley 1923- *WhoFI 92*
**Christ**, Chris Steve 1936- *WhoAmL 92*
**Christ**, Daryl Dean 1942- *AmMWSc 92*
**Christ**, Donald Clough 1935- *WhoAmL 92*
**Christ**, Henry I 1915- *IntAu&W 91, WrDr 92*
**Christ**, John Ernest 1946- *AmMWSc 92*
**Christ**, Peter George 1938- *WhoEnt 92*
**Christ**, Ronald 1936- *WrDr 92*
**Christ**, Susann Temmee 1944- *WhoMW 92*
**Christ**, Vincent B. 1931- *WhoMW 92*
**Christ Church**, Bishop of 1943- *Who 92*
**Christ Church Dublin**, Dean of *Who 92*
**Christ Church Oxford**, Dean of *Who 92*
**Christadoss**, Premkumar 1950- *AmMWSc 92*
**Christakos**, Sylvia *AmMWSc 92*
**Christaldi**, Brian 1940- *WhoAmL 92*
**Christe**, Karl Otto 1936- *AmMWSc 92*
**Christel**, Diane Jennifer 1961- *WhoAmL 92*
**Christell**, Roy Ernest 1952- *WhoRel 92*
**Christen**, David Kent 1945- *AmMWSc 92*
**Christenberry**, George Andrew 1915- *AmMWSc 92*
**Christenbury**, Edward Samuel 1941- *WhoFI 92*
**Christensen**, A Kent 1927- *AmMWSc 92*
**Christensen**, Albert Kent 1927- *WhoMW 92*
**Christensen**, Albert Sherman 1905- *WhoAmL 92, WhoWest 92*
**Christensen**, Allen Clare 1935- *AmMWSc 92, WhoWest 92*
**Christensen**, Allen Thomas 1952- *WhoAmL 92*
**Christensen**, Andrew Brent 1940- *AmMWSc 92*
**Christensen**, Arnold 1936- *WhoAmP 91, WhoWest 92*
**Christensen**, Arthur Roy 1937- *WhoRel 92*
**Christensen**, Axel W. 1881-1955 *NewAmDM*
**Christensen**, Barbara Ann 1963- *WhoAmL 92*
**Christensen**, Barbara Jean 1951- *WhoAmP 91*
**Christensen**, Benjamin 1879-1959 *IntDcF 2-2 [port]*
**Christensen**, Bent Aksel 1928- *AmMWSc 92*
**Christensen**, Bert Einar 1904- *AmMWSc 92*
**Christensen**, Bruce L. *LesBEnT 92*
**Christensen**, Bruce LeRoy 1943- *WhoEnt 92, WhoFI 92*
**Christensen**, Burgess Nyles 1940- *AmMWSc 92*
**Christensen**, Burke Arthur 1945- *WhoIns 92*
**Christensen**, Burton Grant 1930- *AmMWSc 92, WhoFI 92*
**Christensen**, C. Lewis 1936- *WhoFI 92*
**Christensen**, Caroline 1936- *WhoWest 92*
**Christensen**, Charles Brophy 1948- *WhoAmL 92*
**Christensen**, Charles Neil 1924- *WhoMW 92*
**Christensen**, Charles Richard 1938- *AmMWSc 92*
**Christensen**, Chris Edward 1953- *WhoEnt 92*
**Christensen**, Christian Martin 1946- *AmMWSc 92*
**Christensen**, Clark G 1943- *AmMWSc 92*
**Christensen**, Craig C. 1956- *WhoFI 92*
**Christensen**, Craig Mitchell 1932- *AmMWSc 92*
**Christensen**, Dean Lee 1949- *WhoMW 92*
**Christensen**, Dennis Lee 1938- *WhoEnt 92*
**Christensen**, Dirk Glen 1956- *WhoAmL 92*
**Christensen**, Don M. 1929- *WhoFI 92*
**Christensen**, Donn Wayne 1941- *WhoWest 92*
**Christensen**, Douglas Allen 1939- *AmMWSc 92*
**Christensen**, Duane Lee 1938- *WhoRel 92*
**Christensen**, Edward Richards 1924- *AmMWSc 92*
**Christensen**, Eric Herbert 1923- *Who 92*
**Christensen**, Erik Regnar 1943- *AmMWSc 92*
**Christensen**, Erleen J. *DrAPF 91*
**Christensen**, Erma H 1909- *WhoAmP 91*
**Christensen**, George Curtis *AmMWSc 92*
**Christensen**, George Manford 1920- *WhoAmP 91*
**Christensen**, Gerald M 1928- *AmMWSc 92*
**Christensen**, Gustav Amstrup 1947- *WhoFI 92*
**Christensen**, Gwen Joyner 1930- *WhoRel 92*
**Christensen**, Hal 1935- *WhoAmP 91*
**Christensen**, Halvor Niels 1915- *AmMWSc 92*
**Christensen**, Henry, III 1944- *WhoAmL 92*
**Christensen**, Homer Cobb 1940- *WhoRel 92*
**Christensen**, Howard Anthony 1928- *AmMWSc 92*
**Christensen**, Howard Dix 1940- *AmMWSc 92*
**Christensen**, J. A. 1927- *WrDr 92*
**Christensen**, James 1932- *AmMWSc 92*
**Christensen**, James Henry 1942- *AmMWSc 92, WhoMW 92*
**Christensen**, James Roger 1925- *AmMWSc 92*
**Christensen**, Jens 1921- *IntWW 91, Who 92*
**Christensen**, Joan K *WhoAmP 91*
**Christensen**, John 1908- *AmMWSc 92*
**Christensen**, John Michel 1951- *WhoWest 92*
**Christensen**, Kai 1916- *IntWW 91*
**Christensen**, Karen Kay 1947- *WhoAmL 92*
**Christensen**, Kenner Allen 1943- *AmMWSc 92*
**Christensen**, Kent Twedt 1935- *WhoWest 92*
**Christensen**, Larry Wayne 1943- *AmMWSc 92*
**Christensen**, Lora Lynn 1951- *WhoEnt 92*
**Christensen**, Lydell Lee 1934- *WhoFI 92*
**Christensen**, Margaret Jane 1938- *WhoMW 92*
**Christensen**, Mark Newell 1930- *AmMWSc 92*
**Christensen**, Martha 1932- *AmMWSc 92*
**Christensen**, Marvin Nelson 1927- *WhoMW 92*
**Christensen**, Mary Lucas 1937- *AmMWSc 92*
**Christensen**, N A 1903- *AmMWSc 92*
**Christensen**, Nadia *DrAPF 91*
**Christensen**, Ned Jay 1929- *AmMWSc 92*
**Christensen**, Nikolas Ivan 1937- *AmMWSc 92*
**Christensen**, Norman Leroy, Jr 1946- *AmMWSc 92*
**Christensen**, Odin Dale 1947- *AmMWSc 92*
**Christensen**, Patricia Anne Watkins 1947- *WhoAmL 92*
**Christensen**, Paul *DrAPF 91, WhoRel 92*
**Christensen**, Paul 1943- *WrDr 92*
**Christensen**, Paul Gordon 1948- *WhoMW 92*
**Christensen**, Ralph C 1939- *AmMWSc 92*
**Christensen**, Ray Richards 1922- *WhoAmL 92*
**Christensen**, Raymond A 1922- *WhoAmP 91*
**Christensen**, Reginald Bernard 1923- *WhoMW 92*
**Christensen**, Richard G 1938- *AmMWSc 92*
**Christensen**, Richard Monson 1932- *AmMWSc 92*
**Christensen**, Robert A. 1940- *WhoAmL 92*
**Christensen**, Robert Lee 1929- *AmMWSc 92*
**Christensen**, Robert Wayne, Jr. 1948- *WhoWest 92*
**Christensen**, S H 1915- *AmMWSc 92*
**Christensen**, Sally H 1935- *WhoAmP 91*
**Christensen**, Stanley Howard 1935- *AmMWSc 92*
**Christensen**, Steven Brent 1959- *WhoWest 92*
**Christensen**, Thomas Frank 1956- *WhoAmL 92*
**Christensen**, Thomas Gash 1944- *AmMWSc 92*
**Christensen**, Thomas Gordon Steffen 1923- *WhoAmL 92*
**Christensen**, Tom 1925- *WhoAmP 91*
**Christensen**, William E. 1927- *WhoMW 92*
**Christensen**, William James 1955- *WhoMW 92*
**Christenson**, Alfred Mandt 1943- *WhoRel 92*
**Christenson**, Andrew Lewis 1950- *WhoWest 92*
**Christenson**, Bernard Wyman 1938- *WhoAmP 91*
**Christenson**, Charles Elroy 1942- *WhoWest 92*
**Christenson**, Charles O 1936- *AmMWSc 92*
**Christenson**, Donald Robert 1937- *AmMWSc 92*
**Christenson**, Gordon A. 1932- *WhoAmL 92*
**Christenson**, James Andreas 1914- *WhoFI 92*
**Christenson**, Le Roy Howard 1948- *WhoMW 92*
**Christenson**, LeRoy H. 1948- *WhoIns 92*
**Christenson**, Lisa 1956- *AmMWSc 92*
**Christenson**, Paul John 1921- *AmMWSc 92*
**Christenson**, Philip A 1948- *AmMWSc 92*
**Christenson**, Philip L 1947- *WhoAmP 91*
**Christenson**, Richard Harry 1943- *WhoFI 92*
**Christenson**, Robert Lawrence 1953- *WhoFI 92*
**Christenson**, Roger Morris 1919- *AmMWSc 92*
**Christesen**, C. B. 1911- *WrDr 92*
**Christesen**, Clement Byrne 1911- *IntWW 91*
**Christgau**, John *DrAPF 91*
**Christgau**, Robert Thomas 1942- *WhoEnt 92*
**Christgau**, Victor Laurence August d1991 *NewYTBS 91 [port]*
**Christhilf**, John Harwood 1946- *WhoFI 92*
**Christiaanse**, Jan Hendrikus 1932- *IntWW 91*
**Christiaens**, B F Chris 1940- *WhoAmP 91*
**Christiaens**, Chris 1940- *WhoWest 92*
**Christian X** 1870-1947 *FacFETw*
**Christian**, Lady Bruce *EncAmaz 91*
**Christian**, Almeric L. 1919- *WhoBlA 92*
**Christian**, Ann Seger 1954- *WhoWest 92*
**Christian**, Betty Jo 1936- *WhoAmL 92, WhoAmP 91*
**Christian**, Bobby 1911- *WhoEnt 92*
**Christian**, Carol Cathay 1923- *IntAu&W 91, WrDr 92*
**Christian**, Carol Pendergast 1948- *WhoFI 92*
**Christian**, Charles Donald 1930- *AmMWSc 92*
**Christian**, Charles L 1926- *AmMWSc 92*
**Christian**, Charlie 1919-1942 *NewAmDM*
**Christian**, Clarence Wendol 1927- *WhoAmP 91*
**Christian**, Clifford Stuart 1907- *Who 92*
**Christian**, Cora LeEthel 1947- *WhoBlA 92*
**Christian**, Curtis Gilbert 1917- *AmMWSc 92*
**Christian**, David C 1948- *WhoAmP 91*
**Christian**, David Ralph 1952- *WhoAmP 91*
**Christian**, Dolly Lewis *WhoBlA 92*
**Christian**, Donald Jacobs 1951- *WhoWest 92*
**Christian**, Donald Paul 1949- *AmMWSc 92*
**Christian**, Edith Ann 1950- *WhoAmL 92*
**Christian**, Edward Kieren 1944- *WhoEnt 92, WhoFI 92, WhoMW 92*
**Christian**, Emory Denise Tate 1957- *WhoAmL 92*
**Christian**, Francis Joseph 1942- *WhoRel 92*
**Christian**, Frederick *WrDr 92*
**Christian**, Frederick Ade 1937- *AmMWSc 92*
**Christian**, Frederick H. 1931- *TwCWW 91*
**Christian**, Gail P. 1940- *WhoBlA 92*
**Christian**, Gary Dale 1937- *AmMWSc 92*
**Christian**, Gary Irvin 1951- *WhoAmL 92*
**Christian**, Geraldine Ashley McConnell 1929- *WhoBlA 92*
**Christian**, Howard J 1923- *AmMWSc 92*
**Christian**, Hugh 1943- *WhoEnt 92*
**Christian**, J. C., Jr. 1957- *WhoRel 92*
**Christian**, James A 1935- *AmMWSc 92*
**Christian**, James M 1948- *WhoAmP 91*
**Christian**, Jeffrey Mark 1955- *WhoFI 92*
**Christian**, Jerald Cronis 1933- *WhoBlA 92*
**Christian**, Jerry Dale 1937- *AmMWSc 92*
**Christian**, Joe Clark 1934- *AmMWSc 92*
**Christian**, John *IntAu&W 91X, WrDr 92*
**Christian**, John B *AmMWSc 92*
**Christian**, John Catlett, Jr. 1929- *WhoAmL 92*
**Christian**, John Jermyn 1917- *AmMWSc 92*
**Christian**, John L. 1940- *WhoBlA 92*
**Christian**, John Wyrill 1926- *IntWW 91, Who 92, WrDr 92*
**Christian**, Joseph Ralph 1920- *AmMWSc 92*
**Christian**, Kenneth Edward 1935- *WhoMW 92*
**Christian**, Larry Omar 1936- *AmMWSc 92*
**Christian**, Lauren L 1936- *AmMWSc 92*
**Christian**, Linda 1924- *IntMPA 92*
**Christian**, Lynda Gregorian 1938- *WhoAmL 92*
**Christian**, Mae Armster 1934- *WhoBlA 92*
**Christian**, Mark Robert 1965- *WhoRel 92*
**Christian**, Mary Blount 1933- *IntAu&W 91, WrDr 92*
**Christian**, Mary Nordean 1944- *WhoWest 92*
**Christian**, Mary Taylor 1924- *WhoAmP 91*
**Christian**, Patricia Lane Holmes 1953- *WhoRel 92*
**Christian**, Paul Jackson 1920- *AmMWSc 92*
**Christian**, Reginald Frank 1924- *Who 92*
**Christian**, Robert Roland 1924- *AmMWSc 92*
**Christian**, Robert Vernon, Jr 1919- *AmMWSc 92*
**Christian**, Roland Carl 1938- *WhoWest 92*
**Christian**, Ross Edgar 1925- *AmMWSc 92*
**Christian**, Roy Cloberry 1914- *IntAu&W 91, WrDr 92*
**Christian**, Samuel Terry 1937- *AmMWSc 92*
**Christian**, Sherril Duane 1931- *AmMWSc 92*
**Christian**, Spencer 1947- *WhoBlA 92*
**Christian**, Suzanne Hall 1935- *WhoFI 92, WhoWest 92*
**Christian**, Terry James 1956- *WhoEnt 92*
**Christian**, Theresa 1917- *WhoBlA 92*
**Christian**, Wayne Gillespie 1918- *AmMWSc 92*
**Christian**, William Joseph 1960- *WhoEnt 92*
**Christian**, William Richardson 1950- *WhoWest 92*
**Christian**, Wolfgang C 1949- *AmMWSc 92*
**Christian**, Yolanda 1957- *TwCPaSc*
**Christian-Green**, Donna-Marie 1945- *WhoBlA 92*
**Christian-Jaque** 1904- *IntDcF 2-2 [port]*
**Christiano**, John G 1917- *AmMWSc 92*
**Christiano**, Paul P 1942- *AmMWSc 92*
**Christians**, Charles J 1934- *AmMWSc 92*
**Christians**, Charles John 1934- *WhoMW 92*
**Christians**, F. Wilhelm 1922- *IntWW 91*
**Christiansen**, Alan Keith 1946- *WhoMW 92*
**Christiansen**, Alfred W 1940- *AmMWSc 92*
**Christiansen**, Andrew Perry 1953- *WhoAmP 91*
**Christiansen**, Cheryl L. 1945- *WhoWest 92*
**Christiansen**, David Ernest 1937- *AmMWSc 92*
**Christiansen**, Donald Barry 1939- *WhoFI 92*
**Christiansen**, Donald David 1927- *AmMWSc 92*
**Christiansen**, E A 1928- *AmMWSc 92*
**Christiansen**, E B 1910- *AmMWSc 92*
**Christiansen**, Eric H 1953- *AmMWSc 92*
**Christiansen**, F. Melius 1871-1955 *NewAmDM*
**Christiansen**, Francis Wyman 1912- *AmMWSc 92*
**Christiansen**, Friedrich 1879-1972 *EncTR 91*
**Christiansen**, H J 1930- *WhoAmP 91*
**Christiansen**, J E 1905- *AmMWSc 92*
**Christiansen**, James Brackney 1911- *AmMWSc 92*
**Christiansen**, Jeffrey Dean 1956- *WhoWest 92*
**Christiansen**, Jerald N 1931- *AmMWSc 92*
**Christiansen**, John V 1927- *AmMWSc 92*
**Christiansen**, Jon Peter 1950- *WhoAmL 92*
**Christiansen**, Joyce L. Soelberg 1924- *WhoWest 92*
**Christiansen**, Kenneth Allen 1924- *AmMWSc 92*
**Christiansen**, Marjorie Miner 1922- *AmMWSc 92*
**Christiansen**, Mark D. 1955- *WhoAmL 92*
**Christiansen**, Meryl Naeve 1925- *AmMWSc 92*
**Christiansen**, Patricia Ann 1949- *WhoEnt 92*
**Christiansen**, Paul Arthur 1932- *AmMWSc 92*
**Christiansen**, Raymond Stephan 1950- *WhoMW 92*
**Christiansen**, Richard Dean 1931- *WhoEnt 92, WhoMW 92*
**Christiansen**, Richard Louis 1935- *AmMWSc 92*
**Christiansen**, Robert George 1924- *AmMWSc 92*
**Christiansen**, Robert Lorenz 1935- *AmMWSc 92, WhoWest 92*

**Christiansen**, Robert M 1924- *AmMWSc 92*
**Christiansen**, Robert W. *IntMPA 92*
**Christiansen**, Robert W., & Rosenberg, R. *LesBEnT 92*
**Christiansen**, Rupert 1954- *ConAu 135*
**Christiansen**, Sarah Lee 1944- *WhoMW 92*
**Christiansen**, Steven Maurice 1948- *WhoEnt 92*
**Christiansen**, Walter Henry 1934- *AmMWSc 92*
**Christiansen**, Wayne Arthur *AmMWSc 92*
**Christiansen**, Wilbur Norman 1913- *IntWW 91*
**Christianson**, Alan 1909- *Who 92*
**Christianson**, Clinton Curtis 1928- *AmMWSc 92*
**Christianson**, Conrad Johan, Jr. 1935- *WhoRel 92*
**Christianson**, Deann, Jr 1941- *AmMWSc 92*
**Christianson**, Donald Duane 1931- *AmMWSc 92*
**Christianson**, Floyd Kenneth 1917- *WhoMW 92*
**Christianson**, George 1917- *AmMWSc 92*
**Christianson**, George 1920- *WhoAmP 91*
**Christianson**, James Duane 1952- *WhoMW 92*
**Christianson**, Karen Maria Anna 1949- *WhoAmL 92*
**Christianson**, Lee 1940- *AmMWSc 92*
**Christianson**, Michael Lee 1950- *AmMWSc 92*
**Christianson**, Roger Allen 1943- *WhoAmP 91*
**Christianson**, Roger Gordon 1947- *WhoWest 92*
**Christianson**, Stanley David 1931- *WhoMW 92*
**Christianson**, T Loren *WhoAmP 91*
**Christianssen**, Kenneth Gordon 1931- *WhoAmL 92*
**Christie**, A. B. 1909- *WrDr 92*
**Christie**, Agatha 1890-1976 *CnDBLB 6 [port], FacFETw, RfGEnL 91, ScFEYrs*
**Christie**, Andrew, Jr 1943- *WhoAmP 91*
**Christie**, Andrew D *WhoAmP 91*
**Christie**, Andrew Dobbie 1922- *WhoAmL 92*
**Christie**, Ann 1939- *TwCPaSc*
**Christie**, Ann Philippa *Who 92*
**Christie**, Bertram Rodney 1933- *AmMWSc 92*
**Christie**, Campbell 1937- *Who 92*
**Christie**, Charles Henry 1924- *Who 92*
**Christie**, Charles Valk 1950- *WhoWest 92*
**Christie**, David George 1930- *WhoFI 92*
**Christie**, George 1934- *Who 92*
**Christie**, George Custis 1934- *WhoAmL 92*
**Christie**, George Foster 1937- *WhoAmL 92*
**Christie**, George Nicholas 1924- *WhoFI 92*
**Christie**, George William Langham 1934- *IntWW 91*
**Christie**, Hans Frederick 1933- *WhoWest 92*
**Christie**, Herbert 1933- *Who 92*
**Christie**, Howard J 1912- *IntMPA 92*
**Christie**, Ian 1919- *WrDr 92*
**Christie**, Ian Ralph 1919- *IntAu&W 91, IntWW 91, Who 92*
**Christie**, James 1840-1911 *BiInAmS*
**Christie**, James Elder 1847-1914 *TwCPaSc*
**Christie**, John Arthur Kingsley 1915- *Who 92*
**Christie**, John Belford Wilson 1914- *Who 92*
**Christie**, John McDougall 1931- *AmMWSc 92*
**Christie**, John Rankin 1918- *Who 92*
**Christie**, John Reginald Halliday d1953 *FacFETw*
**Christie**, Joseph Herman 1937- *AmMWSc 92*
**Christie**, Joseph J. 1940- *WhoMW 92*
**Christie**, Julie 1940?- *ConTFT 9, FacFETw, Who 92, WhoEnt 92*
**Christie**, Julie 1941- *IntMPA 92*
**Christie**, Julie Frances 1940- *IntWW 91*
**Christie**, Les John 1947- *WhoRel 92*
**Christie**, Linford 1960- *BlkOlyM, IntWW 91*
**Christie**, Mary Anne 1934- *WhoAmP 91*
**Christie**, Michael Allen 1952- *AmMWSc 92*
**Christie**, Paul C. *WhoRel 92*
**Christie**, Peter Allan 1940- *AmMWSc 92*
**Christie**, Phillip 1961- *AmMWSc 92*
**Christie**, Robert Alexander 1937- *WhoWest 92*
**Christie**, Robert Lusk 1936- *WhoRel 92*
**Christie**, Robert William 1923- *AmMWSc 92*
**Christie**, Scott Graham 1953- *WhoFI 92*
**Christie**, Tessa 1941- *TwCPaSc*
**Christie**, Thomas J 1942- *WhoAmP 91*
**Christie**, Tod Stephens 1958- *WhoFI 92*
**Christie**, Vernon 1909- *Who 92*
**Christie**, Walter Scott 1922- *WhoFI 92, WhoMW 92*
**Christie**, Warner Howard 1929- *AmMWSc 92*
**Christie**, William 1913- *Who 92*
**Christie**, William 1944- *NewAmDM*
**Christie**, William James 1932- *Who 92*
**Christie-Murray**, David 1913- *WrDr 92*
**Christie-Murray**, David Hugh Arthur 1913- *IntAu&W 91*
**Christina**, Queen of Sweden 1626-1689 *EncAmaz 91*
**Christina**, Martha *DrAPF 91*
**Christina-Marie** *DrAPF 91*
**Christine de Pizan** 1365?-1430? *FrenWW*
**Christine**, Robert Lee 1952- *WhoEnt 92*
**Christine**, Virginia 1920- *IntMPA 92*
**Christine**, Virginia Feld 1920- *WhoEnt 92*
**Christison**, Philip 1893- *Who 92*
**Christl**, Donald Joseph 1941- *WhoAmL 92*
**Christlieb**, Albert Richard 1935- *AmMWSc 92*
**Christman**, Arthur Castner, Jr 1922- *AmMWSc 92*
**Christman**, Bruce Lee 1955- *WhoAmL 92*
**Christman**, David R 1923- *AmMWSc 92*
**Christman**, Edward Arthur 1943- *AmMWSc 92*
**Christman**, Elizabeth *DrAPF 91*
**Christman**, Helen Dorothy Nelson 1922- *WhoWest 92*
**Christman**, Judith Kershaw 1941- *AmMWSc 92*
**Christman**, Luther P 1915- *AmMWSc 92*
**Christman**, Luther Parmalee 1915- *IntWW 91*
**Christman**, Quentin E *WhoAmP 91*
**Christman**, Robert Adam 1924- *AmMWSc 92*
**Christman**, Russell Fabrique 1936- *AmMWSc 92*
**Christman**, Steven Philip 1945- *AmMWSc 92*
**Christmas**, Arthur Napier 1913- *Who 92*
**Christmas**, Elizabeth Harris 1953- *WhoAmL 92*
**Christmas**, Ellsworth P 1935- *AmMWSc 92*
**Christmas**, Joyce 1939- *WrDr 92*
**Christmas**, Linda 1943- *IntAu&W 91*
**Christmas**, R.A. *DrAPF 91*
**Christmas**, Robert H. 1941- *WhoBlA 92*
**Christmas**, William 1753?-1811 *DcNCBi 1*
**Christner**, David Lee 1949- *WhoMW 92*
**Christner**, James Edward *AmMWSc 92*
**Christner**, Robert Edward 1934- *WhoMW 92*
**Christner**, Theodore Carroll 1932- *WhoMW 92*
**Christo** 1935- *FacFETw, IntWW 91*
**Christodoulou**, Anastasios 1932- *IntWW 91, Who 92*
**Christodoulou**, Aris Peter 1939- *WhoFI 92*
**Christodoulou**, Efthymios 1932- *IntWW 91*
**Christofas**, Kenneth 1917- *IntWW 91, Who 92*
**Christoff**, Boris 1918- *NewAmDM*
**Christoff**, Boris 1919- *IntWW 91, Who 92*
**Christoffersen**, Donald John 1934- *AmMWSc 92*
**Christoffersen**, Jon Michael 1942- *WhoWest 92*
**Christoffersen**, Ralph Earl 1937- *AmMWSc 92*
**Christofferson**, Eric 1939- *AmMWSc 92*
**Christofferson**, Glen Davis 1931- *AmMWSc 92*
**Christofides**, Andrew 1946- *TwCPaSc*
**Christol**, Carl Quimby 1913- *WhoAmL 92*
**Christolon**, Warren Kenneth *WhoAmL 92*
**Christoph**, Francis Theodore, Jr 1943- *AmMWSc 92*
**Christoph**, Greg Robert 1949- *AmMWSc 92*
**Christoph**, James B. 1928- *WrDr 92*
**Christoph**, James Bernard 1928- *IntAu&W 91*
**Christoph**, Susan Catherine 1960- *WhoFI 92*
**Christopher**, Alexander George 1941- *WhoFI 92, WhoMW 92*
**Christopher**, Alta 1942- *WhoEnt 92*
**Christopher**, Andre Lamone 1965- *WhoEnt 92*
**Christopher**, Ann 1947- *Who 92*
**Christopher**, Anthony Martin Grosvenor 1925- *Who 92*
**Christopher**, Charles Benson 1958- *WhoAmL 92*
**Christopher**, Colin Alfred 1932- *Who 92*
**Christopher**, Daniel Roy 1947- *WhoAmL 92*
**Christopher**, Dennis 1955- *IntMPA 92*
**Christopher**, Diana *WrDr 92*
**Christopher**, Edgar Earl *ScFEYrs*
**Christopher**, Frank E. 1952- *WhoWest 92*
**Christopher**, Gaylaird Wiley 1951- *WhoWest 92*
**Christopher**, Gregory Theodore 1958- *WhoRel 92*
**Christopher**, Huw 1945- *WhoRel 92*
**Christopher**, James Alexander 1938- *WhoRel 92*
**Christopher**, Jhon Frank 1949- *WhoEnt 92*
**Christopher**, John 1922- *IntAu&W 91, TwCSFW 91, WrDr 92*
**Christopher**, John 1923- *AmMWSc 92*
**Christopher**, John A. 1941- *WhoBlA 92*
**Christopher**, John Anthony 1924- *Who 92*
**Christopher**, Jordan 1941- *IntMPA 92*
**Christopher**, M Ronald 1941- *WhoAmP 91*
**Christopher**, Matt 1917- *ConAu 36NR*
**Christopher**, Matt F. 1917- *WrDr 92*
**Christopher**, Matthew F 1917- *IntAu&W 91*
**Christopher**, Nancy B 1942- *WhoAmP 91*
**Christopher**, Nicholas *DrAPF 91*
**Christopher**, R. Patrick 1950- *WhoWest 92*
**Christopher**, Richard Douglas 1953- *WhoAmP 91*
**Christopher**, Robert Paul 1932- *AmMWSc 92*
**Christopher**, Russell Lewis 1930- *WhoEnt 92*
**Christopher**, Sharon A. Brown 1944- *WhoMW 92, WhoRel 92*
**Christopher**, Steve 1953- *WhoEnt 92*
**Christopher**, Steven Duane 1958- *WhoAmL 92*
**Christopher**, Steven Lee 1956- *WhoRel 92*
**Christopher**, Thomas Weldon 1917- *WhoAmL 92*
**Christopher**, Warren 1925- *WhoAmL 92, WhoAmP 91*
**Christopher**, William *WhoEnt 92*
**Christopher**, William Garth 1940- *WhoAmL 92*
**Christophersen**, Dale Bjorn 1940- *WhoWest 92*
**Christophersen**, Henning 1939- *IntWW 91, Who 92*
**Christophersen**, Paul 1911- *IntAu&W 91, WrDr 92*
**Christopherson**, Christine Young 1950- *WhoAmP 91*
**Christopherson**, Derman 1915- *Who 92*
**Christopherson**, Derman Guy 1915- *IntWW 91*
**Christopherson**, Harald Fairbairn 1920- *Who 92*
**Christopherson**, John 1921- *TwCPaSc*
**Christopherson**, Myrvin Frederick 1939- *WhoMW 92*
**Christopherson**, Romola Carol Andrea 1939- *Who 92*
**Christopherson**, Violet Margaret 1922- *WhoRel 92*
**Christopherson**, William Martin 1916- *AmMWSc 92*
**Christophides**, Andreas Nicolaou 1937- *IntWW 91*
**Christophides**, Takis 1931- *IntWW 91*
**Christophorou**, Loucas Georgiou 1937- *AmMWSc 92*
**Christou**, George 1953- *AmMWSc 92*
**Christov**, Dragan Spirov 1934- *WhoFI 92*
**Christowe**, Margaret Wooters *WhoAmP 91*
**Christowe**, Stoyan 1898- *BenetAL 91*
**Christy**, Alfred Lawrence 1945- *AmMWSc 92*
**Christy**, C Dana 1913- *WhoAmP 91*
**Christy**, David 1820-1868? *BiInAmS*
**Christy**, Edwin P. 1815-1862 *BenetAL 91*
**Christy**, Edwin Pearce 1815-1862 *NewAmDM*
**Christy**, Gary Christopher 1948- *WhoAmL 92*
**Christy**, James T. 1936- *WhoRel 92*
**Christy**, James Walter 1938- *AmMWSc 92*
**Christy**, John Gilray 1932- *WhoFI 92*
**Christy**, John Harlan 1937- *AmMWSc 92*
**Christy**, John Wick 1927- *WhoRel 92*
**Christy**, June 1925-1990 *AnObit 1990*
**Christy**, Kaign Noel 1958- *WhoAmL 92*
**Christy**, Nicholas Pierson 1923- *AmMWSc 92*
**Christy**, Perry T 1941- *WhoAmP 91*
**Christy**, Perry Thomas 1941- *WhoAmL 92*
**Christy**, Robert Allen 1956- *WhoFI 92*
**Christy**, Robert Frederick 1916- *AmMWSc 92*
**Christy**, Robert Wentworth 1922- *AmMWSc 92*
**Christy**, Samuel Benedict 1853-1914 *BiInAmS*
**Christy**, Thomas Burns 1927- *WhoFI 92*
**Christy**, Thomas Patrick 1943- *WhoWest 92*
**Christy**, William O 1907- *AmMWSc 92*
**Christy's Minstrels** *NewAmDM*
**Chriszt**, James Robert 1956- *WhoAmL 92*
**Chritton**, George A. 1933- *WhoEnt 92*
**Chrodielde** *EncAmaz 91*
**Chromey**, Fred Carl 1918- *AmMWSc 92*
**Chromow**, Sheri P. 1946- *WhoAmL 92*
**Chrones**, James 1925- *AmMWSc 92*
**Chronic**, John 1921- *AmMWSc 92*
**Chronicle**, William 1755-1780 *DcNCBi 1*
**Chronin**, Ann 1950- *TwCPaSc*
**Chronister**, Eric Lee 1958- *WhoWest 92*
**Chronister**, Harry B 1922- *WhoAmP 91*
**Chronister**, Robert Blair 1942- *AmMWSc 92*
**Chronister**, Rochelle Beach 1939- *WhoAmP 91*
**Chrysant**, Steven George 1934- *AmMWSc 92*
**Chrysippus of Cappadocia** d478? *EncEarC*
**Chrysler**, Walter P 1875-1940 *FacFETw*
**Chrysochoos**, John 1934- *AmMWSc 92*
**Chrysostom**, Brother 1863-1917 *BiInAmS*
**Chrysostomos**, Archbishop 1927- *WhoRel 92*
**Chrysostomos of Oreoi**, Bishop 1945- *WhoRel 92*
**Chrysoulakis**, Gennadios 1924- *WhoRel 92*
**Chryss**, George 1941- *WhoFI 92*
**Chryssa** 1933- *IntWW 91*
**Chryssafopoulos**, Hanka Wanda Sobczak *AmMWSc 92*
**Chryssafopoulos**, Nicholas 1919- *AmMWSc 92*
**Chryssanthou**, Christodoulos 1935- *IntWW 91*
**Chryssanthou**, Chryssanthos 1925- *AmMWSc 92*
**Chryssis**, George Christopher 1947- *WhoFI 92*
**Chryssostomidis**, Chryssostomos 1942- *AmMWSc 92*
**Chryst**, Gary 1949- *WhoEnt 92*
**Chrystie**, Thomas Ludlow 1933- *WhoFI 92*
**Chrystos** *DrAPF 91*
**Chrzan-Seelig**, Patricia Ann 1954- *WhoFI 92*
**Chrzanowski**, Adam 1932- *AmMWSc 92*
**Chrzanowski**, Thomas Henry 1952- *AmMWSc 92*
**Chrzanowski**, Wieslaw Marian 1923- *IntWW 91*
**Chu Fu-Sung** 1915- *IntWW 91*
**Chu Huy Man** 1920- *IntWW 91*
**Chu Jiang** 1917- *IntWW 91*
**Chu Teh** 1886-1976 *FacFETw*
**Chu**, Arthur 1916-1979 *ConAu 133*
**Chu**, Benjamin Peng-Nien 1932- *AmMWSc 92*
**Chu**, Boa-Teh 1924- *AmMWSc 92*
**Chu**, C. F. *WhoRel 92*
**Chu**, Chang-Chi 1933- *AmMWSc 92*
**Chu**, Chauncey C 1924- *AmMWSc 92*
**Chu**, Chi-Ming 1917- *IntWW 91*
**Chu**, Chia-Kun 1927- *AmMWSc 92*
**Chu**, Chieh 1922- *AmMWSc 92*
**Chu**, Ching-Wu 1941- *AmMWSc 92*
**Chu**, Chun-Lung 1950- *AmMWSc 92*
**Chu**, Chung K 1941- *AmMWSc 92*
**Chu**, Chung-Yu Chester 1950- *AmMWSc 92*
**Chu**, Daniel Tim-Wo *AmMWSc 92*
**Chu**, David S C 1944- *WhoAmP 91*
**Chu**, Doris Wai-Hing 1941- *WhoEnt 92*
**Chu**, Elizabeth Wann 1921- *AmMWSc 92*
**Chu**, Ernest Hsiao-Ying 1927- *AmMWSc 92*
**Chu**, Florence Chien-Hwa 1918- *AmMWSc 92*
**Chu**, Franklin Janen 1955- *WhoFI 92*
**Chu**, Fun Sun 1933- *AmMWSc 92*
**Chu**, George Hao 1939- *WhoWest 92*
**Chu**, Horn Dean 1933- *AmMWSc 92*
**Chu**, Hsien-Kun 1947- *AmMWSc 92*
**Chu**, Irwin Y E 1937- *AmMWSc 92*
**Chu**, J Chuan 1919- *AmMWSc 92*
**Chu**, Jen-Yih 1940- *AmMWSc 92*
**Chu**, Johnson Chin Sheng 1918- *WhoMW 92*
**Chu**, Joseph Yung-Chang 1940- *AmMWSc 92*
**Chu**, Ju Chin 1919- *AmMWSc 92*
**Chu**, Judy May 1953- *WhoWest 92*
**Chu**, Kai-Ching 1944- *AmMWSc 92*
**Chu**, Keh-Cheng 1933- *AmMWSc 92*
**Chu**, Kuang-Han 1919- *AmMWSc 92*
**Chu**, Kwo Ray 1942- *AmMWSc 92*
**Chu**, Louis 1915-1970 *BenetAL 91*
**Chu**, Mamerto Loarca 1933- *AmMWSc 92*
**Chu**, Nori Yaw-Chyuan 1939- *AmMWSc 92*
**Chu**, Paul Ching-Wu 1941- *AmMWSc 92*
**Chu**, Pe-Cheng 1944- *AmMWSc 92*
**Chu**, Roderick Gong-Wah 1949- *WhoFI 92*
**Chu**, Sherwood Cheng-Wu 1937- *AmMWSc 92*
**Chu**, Shih I 1943- *AmMWSc 92, WhoMW 92*
**Chu**, Shirley Shan-Chi 1929- *AmMWSc 92*
**Chu**, Shu-Heh W *AmMWSc 92*
**Chu**, Sou Yie 1942- *AmMWSc 92*

**Chu,** Steven 1948- *AmMWSc 92*
**Chu,** Sung Gun *AmMWSc 92*
**Chu,** Sung Nee George 1947- *AmMWSc 92*
**Chu,** Ta-Shing 1934- *AmMWSc 92*
**Chu,** Tak-Kin 1938- *AmMWSc 92*
**Chu,** Ting Li 1924- *AmMWSc 92*
**Chu,** Tony Yeling 1936- *WhoWest 92*
**Chu,** Tsann Ming 1938- *AmMWSc 92*
**Chu,** Victor Fu Hua 1918- *AmMWSc 92*
**Chu,** Vincent H K 1918- *AmMWSc 92*
**Chu,** W. R. *ConAu 133*
**Chu,** Wei-Kan 1940- *AmMWSc 92*
**Chu,** Wesley W 1936- *AmMWSc 92*
**Chu,** William Tongil 1934- *AmMWSc 92*
**Chu,** Wing Tin 1935- *AmMWSc 92*
**Chu,** Yung Yee 1933- *AmMWSc 92*
**Chua Sian Chin** 1934- *IntWW 91*
**Chua,** Balvin H-L 1946- *AmMWSc 92*
**Chua,** Kian Eng 1935- *AmMWSc 92*
**Chua,** Leon O 1936- *AmMWSc 92*
**Chua,** Nam-Hai 1944- *Who 92*
**Chua,** Tommy Dy 1955- *WhoFI 92*
**Chuan Leekpai** 1938- *IntWW 91*
**Chuan,** Raymond Lu-Po 1924- *AmMWSc 92*
**Chuang,** De-Maw 1942- *AmMWSc 92*
**Chuang,** Hanson Yii-Kuan 1935- *AmMWSc 92*
**Chuang,** Harold Hwa-Ming 1941- *WhoFI 92*
**Chuang,** Henry Ning 1937- *AmMWSc 92*
**Chuang,** Kuei 1926- *AmMWSc 92*
**Chuang,** Kuen-Puo 1933- *AmMWSc 92*
**Chuang,** Ronald Yan-Li 1940- *AmMWSc 92*
**Chuang,** Strong Chieu-Hsiung 1939- *AmMWSc 92*
**Chuang,** Tsan Iang 1933- *AmMWSc 92*
**Chuang,** Tung Jung 1940- *WhoWest 92*
**Chuang,** Tze-jer 1943- *AmMWSc 92*
**Chubar',** Vlas Yakovlevich 1891-1939 *SovUnBD*
**Chubb** *Who 92*
**Chubb,** Anthony Gerald Trelawny 1928- *Who 92*
**Chubb,** Charles F, Jr 1920- *AmMWSc 92*
**Chubb,** Curtis Evans 1945- *AmMWSc 92*
**Chubb,** Elmer *ConAu 133*
**Chubb,** Francis Learmonth 1913- *AmMWSc 92*
**Chubb,** Frederick Basil 1921- *IntWW 91, Who 92*
**Chubb,** Gerald Patrick 1941- *WhoMW 92*
**Chubb,** John Oliver 1920- *Who 92*
**Chubb,** Louise B. 1927- *WhoBlA 92*
**Chubb,** Percy, III 1934- *WhoFI 92, WhoIns 92*
**Chubb,** Scott Robinson 1953- *AmMWSc 92*
**Chubb,** Talbot Albert 1923- *AmMWSc 92*
**Chubb,** Thomas Caldecot 1899-1972 *BenetAL 91*
**Chubb,** Walston 1923- *AmMWSc 92*
**Chubbuck,** Chris d1974 *LesBEnT 92*
**Chuber,** Stewart 1930- *AmMWSc 92*
**Chuchel,** Paul B *WhoIns 92*
**Chuck,** Walter Goonsun 1920- *WhoAmL 92, WhoFI 92, WhoWest 92*
**Chuckrow,** Vicki G 1941- *AmMWSc 92*
**Chucks,** Jerry 1957- *WhoBlA 92*
**Chudacoff,** Bruce Gary 1956- *WhoEnt 92*
**Chudakov,** Aleksandr Yevgeniyevich 1921- *IntWW 91*
**Chudin,** Vitaliy Ivanovich 1929- *IntWW 91*
**Chudnovsky,** Gregory V 1952- *AmMWSc 92*
**Chudobiak,** Walter James 1942- *WhoFI 92*
**Chudwin,** David S 1950- *AmMWSc 92*
**Chudzinski,** Mark Adam 1956- *WhoAmL 92*
**Chueh,** Chun Fei 1932- *AmMWSc 92*
**Chuey,** Carl F 1944- *AmMWSc 92*
**Chuey,** Carl Francis 1944- *WhoMW 92*
**Chugh,** Ashok Kumar 1942- *AmMWSc 92*
**Chugh,** Ram L. 1935- *WhoFI 92*
**Chugh,** Yoginder Paul 1940- *AmMWSc 92*
**Chuhran,** Linda 1949- *WhoMW 92*
**Chui,** Charles Kam-Tai 1940- *AmMWSc 92*
**Chui,** David H K 1939- *AmMWSc 92*
**Chui,** Siu-Tat 1949- *AmMWSc 92*
**Chuikov,** Vasily Ivanovich 1900-1982 *FacFETw*
**Chuiza,** Baltazara *EncAmaz 91*
**Chukarin,** Viktor Ivanovich 1921- *SovUnBD*
**Chukhontsev,** Oleg Grigor'evich 1938- *SovUnBD*
**Chukhrai,** Grigoriy Naumovich 1921- *IntWW 91*
**Chukovskaya,** Lidiya Korneevna 1907- *SovUnBD*
**Chukovskaya,** Linda Korneyeva 1907- *IntWW 91*
**Chukovsky,** Korney Ivanovich 1882-1969 *SovUnBD*
**Chukwueke,** Gerald Ndudi 1957- *WhoBlA 92*
**Chulack,** Peter G, Sr 1945- *WhoAmP 91*
**Chulasapya,** Dawee 1914- *IntWW 91*
**Chulay,** Frank Joseph 1921- *WhoMW 92*
**Chulick,** Eugene Thomas 1944- *AmMWSc 92*
**Chulski,** Thomas 1921- *AmMWSc 92*
**Chum,** Helena Li 1946- *AmMWSc 92*
**Chumacero,** Ali 1918- *ConSpAP*
**Chumakov,** Mikhail Petrovich 1909- *IntWW 91*
**Chumas,** Henry John 1933- *Who 92*
**Chumbley,** Robert Edward 1954- *WhoEnt 92*
**Chumlea,** William Cameron 1947- *AmMWSc 92*
**Chumley,** Norris Jewett 1956- *WhoEnt 92, WhoFI 92*
**Chumney,** Carol *WhoAmP 91*
**Chumney,** Vern Franklin 1936- *WhoAmL 92*
**Chun Doo-Hwan** 1931- *IntWW 91*
**Chun,** Alexander Hing Chinn 1928- *AmMWSc 92*
**Chun,** Alvin 1950- *WhoWest 92*
**Chun,** Byungkyu 1928- *AmMWSc 92*
**Chun,** Edward Hing Loy 1930- *AmMWSc 92*
**Chun,** Jerrold Yeu-Quong 1948- *WhoAmP 91, WhoWest 92*
**Chun,** Kee Won *AmMWSc 92*
**Chun,** Lowell Koon Wa 1944- *WhoWest 92*
**Chun,** Michael Sing Fong 1944- *WhoWest 92*
**Chun,** Myung K 1932- *AmMWSc 92*
**Chun,** Paul Kwai Tung 1922- *WhoFI 92*
**Chun,** Paul W 1928- *AmMWSc 92*
**Chun,** Raymond Wai Mun 1926- *AmMWSc 92, WhoMW 92*
**Chun,** Se-Choong 1929- *WhoFI 92*
**Chun,** Sun Woong 1934- *AmMWSc 92*
**Chun,** Suzanne 1961- *WhoAmP 91*
**Chun,** Wendy Sau Wan 1951- *WhoWest 92*
**Chunder,** Pratap Chandra 1919- *IntWW 91*
**Chung Il Kwon** 1917- *IntWW 91*
**Chung Shih-Yi** 1914- *IntWW 91*
**Chung,** Albert Edward 1936- *AmMWSc 92*
**Chung,** Andrew Paul 1958- *WhoFI 92*
**Chung,** Arthur 1918- *IntWW 91*
**Chung,** Benjamin T *AmMWSc 92*
**Chung,** Chin Sik 1924- *AmMWSc 92*
**Chung,** Choong Wha 1918- *AmMWSc 92*
**Chung,** Connie *LesBEnT 92 [port]*
**Chung,** Connie 1946- *ConTFT 9, IntMPA 92*
**Chung,** Dae Hyun 1934- *AmMWSc 92*
**Chung,** David Yih 1936- *AmMWSc 92*
**Chung,** Deborah Duen Ling 1952- *AmMWSc 92*
**Chung,** Do Sup 1935- *AmMWSc 92*
**Chung,** Ed Baik 1928- *AmMWSc 92*
**Chung,** Eunyong *AmMWSc 92*
**Chung,** Frank H 1930- *AmMWSc 92*
**Chung,** Harrison Paul 1951- *WhoAmL 92*
**Chung,** Ho 1938- *AmMWSc 92*
**Chung,** Hui-Ying 1927- *AmMWSc 92*
**Chung,** Hyung Chan 1931- *WhoFI 92*
**Chung,** Jay Hoon 1947- *WhoWest 92*
**Chung,** Jing Yan 1939- *AmMWSc 92*
**Chung,** Jiwhey 1936- *AmMWSc 92*
**Chung,** Jung Git 1922- *WhoFI 92*
**Chung,** Kai Lai 1917- *AmMWSc 92*
**Chung,** Kuk Soo 1935- *AmMWSc 92*
**Chung,** Kyung-Wha 1948- *IntWW 91, Who 92*
**Chung,** Kyung Won 1938- *AmMWSc 92*
**Chung,** Myung-Whun 1953- *IntWW 91*
**Chung,** Okkyung Kim 1936- *AmMWSc 92*
**Chung,** Paul M 1929- *AmMWSc 92*
**Chung,** Riley M *AmMWSc 92*
**Chung,** Ronald Aloysius 1936- *AmMWSc 92*
**Chung,** Samuel Sunwhee 1947- *WhoMW 92*
**Chung,** Shana Kim 1960- *WhoAmL 92*
**Chung,** Shiau-Ta 1934- *AmMWSc 92*
**Chung,** Stephen *AmMWSc 92*
**Chung,** Stewart 1956- *WhoWest 92*
**Chung,** Sue Fawn 1944- *WhoWest 92*
**Chung,** Suh Urk 1936- *AmMWSc 92*
**Chung,** Sze-yuen 1917- *IntWW 91, Who 92*
**Chung,** Tchang-Il 1932- *WhoFI 92*
**Chung,** Ting-Horng 1945- *AmMWSc 92*
**Chung,** Tze-Chiang 1953- *AmMWSc 92*
**Chung,** Victor 1940- *AmMWSc 92*
**Chung,** Yip-Wah *AmMWSc 92*
**Chung,** Young Sup 1937- *AmMWSc 92*
**Chung,** YounKook Peter 1956- *WhoFI 92*
**Chung,** Yun C 1956- *AmMWSc 92*
**Chungviwatanant,** Smith 1959- *WhoFI 92*
**Chunn,** Gregory Wade 1965- *WhoWest 92*
**Chunn,** Jay Carrington, II 1938- *WhoBlA 92*
**Chunovich,** Larry Walter 1942- *WhoAmP 91*
**Chunprapaph,** Boonmee 1938- *WhoMW 92*
**Chuong,** Cheng-Ming 1952- *AmMWSc 92*
**Chupka,** William Andrew 1923- *AmMWSc 92*
**Chupp,** Edward Lowell 1927- *AmMWSc 92*
**Chupp,** Timothy E 1954- *AmMWSc 92*
**Chur,** Daniel Eric 1956- *WhoAmL 92*
**Chur-Ogura,** Lois Leilani 1955- *WhoWest 92*
**Chura,** David *DrAPF 91*
**Churbanov,** Yuriy Mikhailovich 1930- *IntWW 91*
**Churbuck,** David Chatfield 1958- *WhoFI 92*
**Church,** Alonzo 1903- *AmMWSc 92, WhoWest 92*
**Church,** Avery Grenfell 1937- *IntAu&W 91*
**Church,** Benjamin 1639-1718 *BenetAL 91*
**Church,** Benjamin, III 1734-1776? *BenetAL 91*
**Church,** Brooks Davis 1918- *AmMWSc 92*
**Church,** Charles Alexander, Jr 1932- *AmMWSc 92*
**Church,** Charles Henry 1929- *AmMWSc 92*
**Church,** Dale Walker 1939- *WhoAmL 92*
**Church,** David Arthur 1939- *AmMWSc 92*
**Church,** David Calvin 1925- *AmMWSc 92*
**Church,** Eugene Lent 1925- *AmMWSc 92*
**Church,** F. Forrester 1948- *ConAu 133*
**Church,** Frank 1924-1984 *FacFETw*
**Church,** Frank Forrester 1948- *WhoRel 92*
**Church,** George Earl 1835-1910 *BiInAmS*
**Church,** George Lyle 1903- *AmMWSc 92*
**Church,** Gilbert Wells 1934- *WhoAmL 92*
**Church,** Ian David 1941- *Who 92*
**Church,** Irene Zaboly 1947- *WhoMW 92*
**Church,** James Anthony *Who 92*
**Church,** Jay Kay 1927- *WhoMW 92*
**Church,** John Adams 1843-1917 *BiInAmS*
**Church,** John Armistead 1937- *AmMWSc 92*
**Church,** John Carver 1929- *Who 92*
**Church,** John I. *DrAPF 91*
**Church,** John Phillips 1934- *AmMWSc 92*
**Church,** John Trammell 1917- *WhoAmP 91, WhoFI 92*
**Church,** Joseph August 1946- *AmMWSc 92*
**Church,** Julia Frances 1963- *WhoAmL 92*
**Church,** Katherine 1910- *TwCPaSc*
**Church,** Kathleen *AmMWSc 92*
**Church,** Larry B 1939- *AmMWSc 92*
**Church,** Lloyd Eugene 1919- *AmMWSc 92*
**Church,** Lorene Kemmerer 1929- *WhoWest 92*
**Church,** Margaret Ruth 1960- *WhoFI 92*
**Church,** Marshall Robbins 1948- *AmMWSc 92*
**Church,** Philip Throop 1931- *AmMWSc 92*
**Church,** Randolph Warner, Jr. 1934- *WhoAmL 92*
**Church,** Richard Lee *AmMWSc 92*
**Church,** Robert 1932- *IntAu&W 91*
**Church,** Robert Bertram 1937- *AmMWSc 92*
**Church,** Robert Fitz 1930- *AmMWSc 92*
**Church,** Robert Frederick 1953- *WhoAmL 92*
**Church,** Robert T., Sr. 1909- *WhoBlA 92*
**Church,** Ronald James H. *Who 92*
**Church,** Ronald L 1930- *AmMWSc 92*
**Church,** Ruth Ellen d1991 *NewYTBS 91*
**Church,** Ruth Ellen 1910?-1991 *ConAu 135*
**Church,** Ruth Joan 1927- *WhoAmP 91*
**Church,** Stanley Eugene 1943- *AmMWSc 92*
**Church,** Sterling Ray 1942- *WhoWest 92*
**Church,** Steven Morgan 1947- *WhoRel 92*
**Church,** Thomas 1673-1748 *BenetAL 91*
**Church,** Tony 1930- *Who 92, WhoEnt 92*
**Church,** William Richard 1936- *AmMWSc 92*
**Church,** William Robert 1959- *WhoMW 92*
**Churcher,** Charles Stephen 1928- *AmMWSc 92*
**Churcher,** John Bryan 1905- *Who 92*
**Churchhouse,** Robert Francis 1927- *Who 92*
**Churchill** *Who 92*
**Churchill,** Viscount 1934- *Who 92*
**Churchill,** Algernon Coolidge 1937- *AmMWSc 92*
**Churchill,** Allen Delos 1921- *WhoAmL 92*
**Churchill,** Caryl 1938- *IntWW 91, RfGEnL 91, WrDr 92*
**Churchill,** Charles 1731-1764 *DcLB 109 [port]*
**Churchill,** Charles 1732-1764 *RfGEnL 91*
**Churchill,** Constance Louise 1941- *AmMWSc 92*
**Churchill,** Daniel Wayne 1947- *WhoFI 92*
**Churchill,** David Charles 1958- *WhoRel 92*
**Churchill,** David James 1945- *WhoAmP 91*
**Churchill,** Dewey Ross, Jr 1926- *AmMWSc 92*
**Churchill,** Diana 1913- *Who 92*
**Churchill,** Don W 1930- *AmMWSc 92*
**Churchill,** E. Richard 1937- *WrDr 92*
**Churchill,** Elizabeth *IntAu&W 91X, WrDr 92*
**Churchill,** Frederick Charles 1940- *AmMWSc 92*
**Churchill,** Geoffrey Barker 1950- *AmMWSc 92*
**Churchill,** Helen Mar 1907- *AmMWSc 92*
**Churchill,** John Alvord 1920- *AmMWSc 92*
**Churchill,** John George Spencer 1909- *Who 92*
**Churchill,** John Spencer 1909- *TwCPaSc*
**Churchill,** Joseph Lacy 1944- *WhoAmL 92*
**Churchill,** Lynn 1947- *AmMWSc 92*
**Churchill,** Melvyn Rowen 1940- *AmMWSc 92*
**Churchill,** Michael 1939- *WhoAmL 92*
**Churchill,** Naomi Davis 1950- *WhoAmL 92*
**Churchill,** Odette Maria Celine *IntWW 91*
**Churchill,** Paul Clayton 1941- *AmMWSc 92*
**Churchill,** Ralph John 1944- *AmMWSc 92*
**Churchill,** Robert W 1947- *WhoAmP 91*
**Churchill,** Stuart W 1920- *AmMWSc 92*
**Churchill,** Thomas *DrAPF 91*
**Churchill,** Thomas John 1961- *WhoEnt 92, WhoMW 92*
**Churchill,** Trevor Anthony John 1941- *WhoEnt 92*
**Churchill,** Ward 1947- *ConAu 135*
**Churchill,** William 1859-1920 *BiInAmS*
**Churchill,** William DeLee 1919- *WhoWest 92*
**Churchill,** William Lloyd 1929- *WhoAmP 91*
**Churchill,** William Wilberforce 1867-1910 *BiInAmS*
**Churchill,** Winston 1871-1947 *BenetAL 91, FacFETw*
**Churchill,** Winston 1874-1965 *CnDBLB 5 [port], EncTR 91 [port], TwCPaSc*
**Churchill,** Winston Leonard Spencer 1874-1965 *FacFETw [port], WhoNob 90*
**Churchill,** Winston Spencer 1940- *Who 92*
**Churchland,** Paul M. 1942- *WrDr 92*
**Churchman,** David Alan 1938- *WhoWest 92*
**Churchman,** John 1753-1805 *BiInAmS*
**Churchward,** L. G. 1919- *WrDr 92*
**Churchwell,** Caesar Alfred 1932- *WhoBlA 92*
**Churchwell,** Charles Darrett 1926- *WhoBlA 92*
**Churchwell,** Edward Bruce 1940- *AmMWSc 92*
**Churchyard,** Thomas 1520-1604 *RfGEnL 91*
**Churg,** Jacob 1910- *AmMWSc 92*
**Churgin,** Michael Jay 1948- *WhoAmL 92*
**Churikova,** Inna Mikhailovna 1943- *IntWW 91*
**Churkin,** Michael, Jr 1932- *AmMWSc 92*
**Churnside,** James H 1951- *AmMWSc 92*
**Churston,** Baron d1991 *Who 92N*
**Churston,** Baron 1934- *Who 92*
**Churton,** E. d1885 *DcLB 106*
**Churton,** William d1767 *DcNCBi 1*
**Churus,** Nicholas H. 1958- *WhoEnt 92*
**Chused,** Richard Harris 1943- *WhoAmL 92*
**Chused,** Thomas Morton 1940- *AmMWSc 92*
**Chusid,** Eugene G. 1963- *WhoFI 92*
**Chusid,** Joseph George 1914- *AmMWSc 92*
**Chusid,** Michael Joseph 1944- *AmMWSc 92*
**Chute,** Carolyn 1947- *WrDr 92*
**Chute,** Harold LeRoy 1921- *WhoFI 92*
**Chute,** Marchette 1909- *Who 92, WrDr 92*
**Chute,** Marchette G. 1909- *BenetAL 91*
**Chute,** Robert Maurice 1926- *AmMWSc 92, IntWW 91*
**Chutjian,** Ara 1941- *AmMWSc 92*
**Chutkow,** Jerry Grant 1933- *AmMWSc 92*
**Chuykov,** Semen Afanas'evich 1902- *SovUnBD*
**Chuykov,** Vasiliy Ivanovich 1900-1982 *SovUnBD*
**Chvala,** Charles Joseph 1954- *WhoAmP 91*
**Chvapil,** Milos 1928- *AmMWSc 92*
**Chwalek,** Bernadine Elisabeth 1955- *WhoAmL 92*
**Chwang,** Allen Tse-Yung 1944- *AmMWSc 92*
**Chwast,** Seymour 1931- *DcTwDes, WhoEnt 92*
**Chwat,** John Steven 1950- *WhoAmP 91*
**Chydenius,** Anders 1729-1803 *BlkwCEP*
**Chyi,** Lindgren Lin 1941- *WhoMW 92*
**Chylek,** Petr 1937- *AmMWSc 92*

**Chynoweth**, Alan Gerald 1927- *AmMWSc 92, IntWW 91*
**Chynoweth**, David Boyd 1940- *Who 92*
**Chynoweth**, Neville James 1922- *Who 92*
**Chytil**, Frank 1924- *AmMWSc 92*
**Chytilova**, Vera 1929- *IntDcF 2-2*
**Chyu**, Ming-Chien *AmMWSc 92*
**Chyung**, Chi Han 1933- *WhoFI 92*
**Chyung**, Dong Hak 1937- *AmMWSc 92, WhoMW 92*
**Chyung**, Kenneth 1936- *AmMWSc 92*
**Ci Yungui** 1931- *IntWW 91*
**Cia**, Manuel Lopez 1937- *WhoHisp 92*
**Ciabattari**, Jane *DrAPF 91*
**Cialdella**, Cataldo 1926- *AmMWSc 92*
**Cialella**, Carmen Michael 1925- *AmMWSc 92*
**Ciamaga**, Gustav 1930- *NewAmDM*
**Ciampa**, George Richard 1945- *WhoAmL 92*
**Ciampa**, Vincent Paul *WhoAmP 91*
**Ciampi**, Carlo Azeglio 1920- *IntWW 91*
**Ciancanelli**, Eugene Vincent 1939- *AmMWSc 92*
**Cianchettini**, Veronica Rosalia 1779-1833 *NewAmDM*
**Cianci**, Vincent Albert 1941- *WhoAmP 91*
**Ciancio**, Sebastian Gene 1937- *AmMWSc 92*
**Cianciolo**, Rosemary *WhoRel 92*
**Ciancolo**, George J *AmMWSc 92*
**Cianetti**, Tullio 1899-1976 *BiDExR*
**Ciangio**, Donna Lenore 1949- *WhoRel 92*
**Ciani**, Suzanne Elizabeth 1946- *WhoEnt 92*
**Ciano**, Galeazzo 1903-1944 *BiDExR, EncTR 91 [port], FacFETw*
**Ciantra**, Nicholas Cesare 1963- *WhoEnt 92*
**Ciappenelli**, Donald John 1943- *AmMWSc 92*
**Ciappi**, Mario Luigi 1909- *IntWW 91, WhoRel 92*
**Ciaramitaro**, David A 1946- *AmMWSc 92*
**Ciaramitaro**, Nick 1951- *WhoAmP 91*
**Ciardi**, John 1916- *IntAu&W 91*
**Ciardi**, John 1916-1986 *BenetAL 91, SmATA 65 [port]*
**Ciardi**, John Anthony 1916-1986 *FacFETw*
**Ciarlone**, Alfred Edward 1932- *AmMWSc 92*
**Ciarlone**, Anthony Michael 1929- *WhoAmP 91*
**Ciarrocchi**, Jerome William 1921- *WhoRel 92*
**Ciattei**, James Nicholas 1957- *WhoEnt 92*
**Ciatteo**, Carmen Thomas 1921- *WhoMW 92*
**Ciavola**, Louise Arlene 1933- *WhoMW 92*
**Ciavola**, Rex George 1931- *WhoFI 92*
**Ciavolella**, Massimo 1942- *ConAu 135*
**Cibber**, Colley 1671-1757 *RfGEnL 91*
**Cibes**, William Joseph, Jr 1943- *WhoAmP 91*
**Cibik**, Rosemarie E. *WhoRel 92*
**Cibils**, Luis Angel 1927- *AmMWSc 92*
**Cibula**, Adam Burt 1934- *AmMWSc 92*
**Cibula**, William Ganley 1932- *AmMWSc 92*
**Cibulka**, Frank 1923- *AmMWSc 92*
**Cibulsky**, Robert John 1946- *AmMWSc 92*
**Ciccarelli**, Roger N 1934- *AmMWSc 92*
**Ciccarelli**, Salvatore 1941- *WhoAmP 91*
**Cicchetti**, Mark Anthony 1956- *WhoFI 92*
**Cicciarelli**, James Carl 1947- *WhoWest 92*
**Ciccolella**, Anthony 1959- *WhoEnt 92*
**Ciccolella**, Joseph A 1909- *AmMWSc 92*
**Ciccone**, Madonna Louise Veronica 1958- *WhoEnt 92*
**Ciccone**, Patrick Edwin 1944- *AmMWSc 92*
**Ciccone**, Richard 1940- *WhoMW 92*
**Cicconi**, James William 1952- *WhoAmP 91*
**Ciccotelli**, Teresa T. *WhoAmL 92*
**Cicellis**, Kay 1926- *WrDr 92*
**Cicero**, Frank, Jr. 1935- *WhoAmL 92*
**Cicero**, Theodore James 1942- *AmMWSc 92*
**Cicerone**, Carol Mitsuko 1943- *AmMWSc 92*
**Cicerone**, Ralph John 1943- *AmMWSc 92*
**Cicet**, Donald James 1940- *WhoAmL 92, WhoFI 92*
**Cichelli**, Mario T 1920- *AmMWSc 92*
**Cichello**, Samuel Joseph 1931- *WhoFI 92*
**Cichoke**, Anthony Joseph, Jr. 1931- *WhoWest 92*
**Cichon**, Joanne M 1959- *WhoIns 92*
**Cichowski**, Robert Stanley 1942- *AmMWSc 92*
**Cicilline**, Stephen E 1942- *WhoAmP 91*
**Cico**, Carol Elaine 1942- *WhoMW 92*
**Ciconia**, Johannes 1370?-1411 *NewAmDM*
**Cid**, A. Louis 1923- *WhoHisp 92*
**Cid Perez**, Jose 1906- *WhoHisp 92*
**Cidre**, Cynthia 1957- *WhoHisp 92*
**Ciechanover**, Joseph 1933- *WhoAmL 92, WhoFI 92*
**Cieminski**, Leo John 1916- *WhoMW 92*
**Ciemniewski**, Jerzy 1939- *IntWW 91*
**Cienek**, Raymond Paul 1948- *WhoFI 92*
**Cieplak**, Jan d1926 *SovUnBD*
**Cier**, H E 1912- *AmMWSc 92*
**Ciereszko**, Leon Stanley, Sr 1917- *AmMWSc 92*
**Ciernia**, James Richard 1933- *WhoWest 92*
**Cieslewski**, Peter Henry 1955- *WhoRel 92*
**Cieslinski**, L. John *DrAPF 91*
**Ciesniewski**, Anthony Richard 1945- *WhoEnt 92*
**Cieszewski**, Sandra Josephine 1941- *WhoMW 92*
**Cieza de Leon**, Pedro 1518-1560 *HisDSpE*
**Cifaldi**, Gerald James 1947- *WhoFI 92*
**Ciffone**, Stephen E. 1953- *WhoEnt 92*
**Cifone**, Maria Ann 1945- *AmMWSc 92*
**Cifonelli**, Joseph Anthony 1916- *AmMWSc 92*
**Cifra**, Antonio 1584-1629 *NewAmDM*
**Ciftan**, Mikael 1935- *AmMWSc 92*
**Cifuentes**, Luis Arturo 1956- *WhoHisp 92*
**Cihlar**, Frank Phillip 1943- *WhoAmL 92*
**Cihlarz**, Wolfgang 1954- *IntWW 91*
**Cihonski**, John Leo 1948- *AmMWSc 92*
**Cilea**, Francesco 1866-1950 *NewAmDM*
**Cilento**, Diane 1934- *IntMPA 92*
**Ciletti**, James *DrAPF 91*
**Ciletti**, James Anthony 1943- *WhoEnt 92*
**Cilke**, Robert Henry 1941- *WhoRel 92*
**Cillie**, Petrus Johannes 1917- *IntWW 91*
**Cillino**, Susan Norman 1955- *WhoWest 92*
**Cillo**, Paul A 1953- *WhoAmP 91*
**Cimarosa**, Domenico 1749-1801 *BlkwCEP, NewAmDM*
**Cimbala**, Michele *AmMWSc 92*
**Cimberg**, Robert Lawrence 1944- *AmMWSc 92*
**Ciment**, Jill *DrAPF 91*
**Ciment**, Melvyn 1941- *AmMWSc 92*
**Ciminello**, Emanuel, Jr. *WhoHisp 92*
**Cimini**, Anthony J 1922- *WhoAmP 91*
**Cimini**, Leonard Joseph, Jr 1956- *AmMWSc 92*
**Cimini**, Sally Griffith 1957- *WhoAmL 92*
**Cimino**, Anthony John 1947- *WhoAmP 91*
**Cimino**, Frank Joseph 1947- *WhoAmL 92*
**Cimino**, Michael 1940- *IntDcF 2-2 [port]*
**Cimino**, Michael 1943- *IntAu&W 91, IntMPA 92, IntWW 91, WrDr 92*
**Cimino**, Michael 1948- *WhoEnt 92*
**Cimino**, Ralph Liebert 1918- *WhoRel 92*
**Cimino**, Richard Angelo 1929- *WhoEnt 92, WhoWest 92*
**Cimino**, Richard Dennis 1947- *WhoAmL 92*
**Cimino**, Salvatore P 1933- *WhoAmP 91*
**Cimino**, Thomas 1935- *WhoIns 92*
**Cimo**, JoAnn Belmonte 1949- *WhoMW 92*
**Cimochowicz**, Diane Marie 1955- *WhoWest 92*
**Cimonetti**, William J 1931- *WhoAmP 91*
**Cina**, Colin 1943- *TwCPaSc*
**Cinabro**, Robert Henry 1948- *WhoAmL 92*
**Cinader**, Bernhard 1919- *AmMWSc 92, IntWW 91*
**Cinader**, Robert A. d1982 *LesBEnT 92*
**Cinadr**, Bernard F 1933- *AmMWSc 92*
**Cinat**, Laura Jean 1967- *WhoMW 92*
**Cinciotta**, Linda Ann 1943- *WhoAmL 92*
**Cincotta**, Joseph John 1931- *AmMWSc 92*
**Cinelli**, Ferdinando Oreste Federico 1916- *WhoMW 92*
**Cinelli**, Giovanna M. 1959- *WhoAmL 92*
**Cink**, Calvin Lee 1947- *AmMWSc 92*
**Cink**, James Henry 1959- *WhoMW 92*
**Cinlar**, Erhan 1941- *AmMWSc 92*
**Cino**, Paul Michael 1946- *AmMWSc 92*
**Cinotti**, Alfonse A 1923- *AmMWSc 92*
**Cinotti**, Jeffrey William 1965- *WhoEnt 92*
**Cinotti**, William Ralph 1926- *AmMWSc 92*
**Cinque**, Andrew Anthony 1960- *WhoEnt 92*
**Cinquina**, Carmela Louise 1936- *AmMWSc 92*
**Cintas**, Michael Douglas 1948- *WhoWest 92*
**Cinti**, David A 1962- *WhoIns 92*
**Cinti**, Dominick Louis 1939- *AmMWSc 92*
**Cintron**, Angel *WhoAmP 91*
**Cintron**, Benigno, Jr. 1955- *WhoHisp 92*
**Cintron**, Carmen Delia 1939- *WhoRel 92*
**Cintron**, Charles 1936- *AmMWSc 92*
**Cintron**, Conchita *EncAmaz 91*
**Cintron**, Emma V. 1926- *WhoHisp 92*
**Cintron**, Guillermo B 1942- *AmMWSc 92*
**Cintron**, Martin 1948- *WhoHisp 92*
**Cintron**, Nitza Margarita *WhoHisp 92*
**Cintron**, Victor Manuel 1949- *WhoWest 92*
**Cintron-Budet**, Nancy *WhoHisp 92*
**Cintron-Garcia**, Angel *WhoHisp 92*
**Ciochon**, Russell Lynn 1948- *AmMWSc 92*
**Cioffi**, Frank Louis 1951- *WhoWest 92*
**Cioffi**, Michael Lawrence 1953- *WhoAmL 92*
**Cioffi**, Paul Peter 1896- *AmMWSc 92*
**Cioffi-Revilla**, Claudio 1951- *WhoWest 92*
**Ciolino**, Laura Ann 1961- *WhoMW 92*
**Cion**, Judith Ann 1943- *WhoAmL 92*
**Cionca**, John Richard 1946- *WhoRel 92*
**Cionco**, Ronald Martin 1934- *AmMWSc 92*
**Cioran**, E. M. 1911- *LiExTwC*
**Ciosek**, Carl Peter, Jr 1943- *AmMWSc 92*
**Ciosek**, Stanislaw 1939- *IntWW 91*
**Cioslowski**, Jerzy 1963- *AmMWSc 92*
**Cipa**, Walter Johannes 1928- *IntWW 91*
**Cipale**, Joseph Michael 1958- *WhoWest 92*
**Ciparick**, Carmen Beauchamp *WhoHisp 92*
**Cipau**, Gabriel R 1941- *AmMWSc 92*
**Cipera**, John Dominik 1923- *AmMWSc 92*
**Cipes**, Arianne Ulmer *IntMPA 92*
**Cipes**, Bret 1909- *WhoEnt 92*
**Cipes**, Jay H. *IntMPA 92*
**Cipinko**, Scott J. 1960- *WhoAmL 92*
**Cipolla**, Carlo M 1922- *IntAu&W 91, WrDr 92*
**Cipolla**, John William, Jr 1942- *AmMWSc 92*
**Cipolla**, Roland Horace, II 1947- *WhoWest 92*
**Cipolla**, Sam J 1940- *AmMWSc 92*
**Cipollone**, Anthony Dominic 1939- *WhoAmL 92*
**Ciporin**, Leone Louise 1960- *WhoAmL 92*
**Cipriani**, Cipriano 1923- *AmMWSc 92*
**Cipriani**, Harriet Emily *WhoAmP 91*
**Cipriano**, Irene P. 1942- *WhoHisp 92*
**Cipriano**, Leonard Francis 1938- *AmMWSc 92*
**Cipriano**, Patricia Ann 1946- *WhoWest 92*
**Cipriano**, Ramon John *AmMWSc 92*
**Ciprios**, George 1931- *AmMWSc 92*
**Ciraldi**, Anthony F 1918- *WhoAmP 91*
**Circeo**, Louis Joseph, Jr 1934- *AmMWSc 92*
**Circle**, Lilias Wagner 1928- *WhoMW 92*
**Circo**, Dennis Paul 1947- *WhoMW 92*
**Cirella**, Daniel George 1943- *WhoEnt 92*
**Cirese**, Eugenio 1884-1955 *DcLB 114*
**Ciresi**, Michael Vincent 1946- *WhoAmL 92*
**Ciriacks**, Jean Lorraine 1925- *WhoAmP 91*
**Ciriacks**, John A 1936- *AmMWSc 92*
**Ciriacks**, Kenneth W 1938- *AmMWSc 92*
**Ciriacy**, Edward W 1924- *AmMWSc 92*
**Ciriani**, Henri 1936- *IntWW 91*
**Ciricillo**, Samuel F 1920- *AmMWSc 92*
**Ciriello**, John 1950- *AmMWSc 92*
**Cirillo**, J. Richard, Jr. 1946- *WhoFI 92, WhoMW 92*
**Cirillo**, John M. 1956- *WhoEnt 92*
**Cirillo**, Nancy *WhoEnt 92*
**Cirillo**, Vincent Paul 1925- *AmMWSc 92*
**Cirino**, Jerry C. 1951- *WhoMW 92*
**Cirino**, Leonard John *DrAPF 91*
**Cirker**, Hayward 1917- *IntWW 91*
**Cirone**, Anthony James 1941- *WhoEnt 92*
**Cirou**, Joseph Philip 1943- *WhoRel 92*
**Ciruelas**, Dominador Benedicto 1940- *WhoFI 92, WhoMW 92*
**Ciruli**, Floyd 1946- *WhoAmP 91*
**Ciry**, Michel 1919- *IntWW 91*
**Cis**, Mark Michael 1950- *WhoIns 92*
**Cisar**, Timothy Richard 1957- *WhoAmL 92*
**Cisco**, Ronald Ray 1940- *WhoMW 92*
**Cisin**, Ira Hubert 1919- *AmMWSc 92*
**Cisky**, Jon *WhoAmP 91*
**Cisky**, Jon Ayres 1941- *WhoMW 92*
**Cisler**, Dennis Keith 1949- *WhoIns 92*
**Cisler**, Walker L 1897- *AmMWSc 92*
**Cisne**, John Luther 1947- *AmMWSc 92*
**Cisneros**, Antonio 1942- *ConSpAP*
**Cisneros**, Arnoldo 1951- *WhoHisp 92*
**Cisneros**, Baltasar Hidalgo de 1775-1829 *HisDSpE*
**Cisneros**, Carlos R *WhoAmP 91, WhoHisp 92*
**Cisneros**, Connie P. *WhoHisp 92*
**Cisneros**, Eleonora de 1878-1934 *NewAmDM*
**Cisneros**, Evelyn 1955- *WhoEnt 92, WhoHisp 92*
**Cisneros**, Frank G. *WhoHisp 92*
**Cisneros**, Henry Gabriel 1947- *WhoAmP 91, WhoHisp 92*
**Cisneros**, James M. 1951- *WhoHisp 92*
**Cisneros**, Joe Alvarado 1935- *WhoHisp 92*
**Cisneros**, Rafael 1934- *WhoHisp 92*
**Cisneros**, Sandra *DrAPF 91*
**Cisneros**, Sandra 1954- *ConLC 69 [port], WhoHisp 92*
**Cisneros Betancourt**, Salvador 1828-1914 *HisDSpE*
**Cisse**, Jeanne Martin 1926- *IntWW 91*
**Cissell**, James Charles 1940- *WhoAmL 92*
**Cissoko**, Alioune Badara 1952- *WhoBlA 92*
**Cissoko**, Filifing 1936- *IntWW 91*
**Cist**, Jacob 1782-1825 *BiInAmS*
**Cistaro**, Anthony Michael 1963- *WhoEnt 92*
**Ciszek**, Ted F 1942- *AmMWSc 92*
**Ciszewski**, Bohdan 1922- *IntWW 91*
**Citation** 1945-1970 *FacFETw*
**Citino**, David *DrAPF 91*
**Citrin**, Jeffery B. 1958- *WhoFI 92*
**Citrin**, Willie 1947- *WhoWest 92*
**Citrine** *Who 92*
**Citrine**, Baron 1914- *Who 92*
**Citro**, Angelo T *WhoAmP 91*
**Citrola**, Rosemary Nicolina 1958- *WhoEnt 92*
**Citron**, Beatrice Sally 1929- *WhoAmL 92*
**Citron**, Christiane Hyde 1949- *WhoAmL 92*
**Citron**, David S 1920- *AmMWSc 92*
**Citron**, Irvin Meyer 1924- *AmMWSc 92*
**Citron**, Joel David 1941- *AmMWSc 92*
**Citron**, M. Sloane 1956- *WhoWest 92*
**Citron**, Michelle 1948- *WhoEnt 92*
**Citron**, Minna 1896-1991 *NewYTBS 91*
**Citron**, Richard Stefan 1953- *WhoEnt 92*
**Citron**, Stephen J 1933- *AmMWSc 92*
**Ciuba**, Lynne Parkhurst 1953- *WhoAmL 92*
**Ciucu**, George d1990 *IntWW 91N*
**Ciufolini**, Marco A 1956- *AmMWSc 92*
**Ciuha**, Joze 1924- *IntWW 91*
**Ciula**, Richard Paul 1933- *AmMWSc 92*
**Ciulei**, Liviu 1923- *IntWW 91*
**Civan**, Mortimer M 1934- *AmMWSc 92*
**Civardi**, Ernesto 1906- *WhoRel 92*
**Civasaqui**, Jose 1916- *IntAu&W 91*
**Civelli**, Oliver 1949- *AmMWSc 92*
**Civen**, Morton 1929- *AmMWSc 92*
**Civera**, Mario J, Jr 1946- *WhoAmP 91*
**Civiak**, Robert L 1947- *AmMWSc 92*
**Civiletti**, Benjamin R. 1935- *IntWW 91*
**Civin**, Paul 1919- *AmMWSc 92*
**Civitelli**, Roberto 1955- *WhoMW 92*
**Cixous**, Helene 1937- *FrenWW, IntAu&W 91, IntWW 91*
**Cizek**, David John 1959- *WhoMW 92*
**Cizek**, Eric Paul 1926- *WhoFI 92*
**Cizek**, Louis Joseph 1916- *AmMWSc 92*
**Cizik**, Robert 1931- *IntWW 91, WhoFI 92*
**Cizmar**, Paula L 1949- *IntAu&W 91*
**Cizza**, John Anthony 1952- *WhoMW 92*
**Claassen**, E J, Jr 1920- *AmMWSc 92*
**Claassen**, John Carl 1949- *WhoEnt 92*
**Claassen**, Richard Strong 1922- *AmMWSc 92*
**Claassen**, Walter Marshall 1943- *WhoMW 92*
**Clabaugh**, Elmer Eugene, Jr. 1927- *WhoAmL 92, WhoFI 92*
**Clabaugh**, Henry Edward Doyle 1942- *WhoMW 92*
**Clabaugh**, Stephen Edmund 1918- *AmMWSc 92*
**Clack**, Charles Gilbert 1937- *WhoAmP 91*
**Clack**, Doris H. 1928- *WhoBlA 92*
**Clack**, Floyd 1940- *WhoAmP 91, WhoBlA 92*
**Clack**, Leigh Langston 1956- *WhoAmL 92*
**Clack**, R. C. 1938- *WhoBlA 92*
**Cladis**, John Baros 1922- *AmMWSc 92*
**Cladis**, Patricia Elizabeth Ruth 1937- *AmMWSc 92*
**Cladpole**, Jim *IntAu&W 91X*
**Claerbaut**, Rhonda Renee *WhoMW 92*
**Claerbout**, Jon F *AmMWSc 92*
**Claes**, Daniel John 1931- *WhoFI 92, WhoWest 92*
**Claes**, Willy 1938- *IntWW 91*
**Claeson**, Tord Claes 1938- *IntWW 91*
**Claessens**, Pierre 1939- *AmMWSc 92*
**Claff**, Chester Eliot, Jr 1928- *AmMWSc 92*
**Claff**, Warren L. 1911- *WhoAmL 92*
**Clafin**, Lola White *DrAPF 91*
**Claflin**, Alice J 1932- *AmMWSc 92*
**Claflin**, Arthur Cary 1950- *WhoAmL 92*
**Claflin**, Jeffrey 1953- *WhoEnt 92*
**Claflin**, Robert Malden 1921- *AmMWSc 92*
**Claflin**, Tom O 1939- *AmMWSc 92*
**Clagett**, Brice McAdoo 1933- *WhoAmL 92*
**Clagett**, Carl Owen *AmMWSc 92*
**Clagett**, Donald Carl 1939- *AmMWSc 92*
**Clagett**, Robert P *AmMWSc 92*
**Claggett**, William Nathaniel 1951- *WhoFI 92*
**Clague**, David A 1948- *AmMWSc 92*
**Clague**, Joan 1931- *Who 92*
**Clague**, William Donald 1920- *AmMWSc 92*
**Claiborne**, C Clair 1952- *AmMWSc 92*
**Claiborne**, Craig 1920- *WrDr 92*
**Claiborne**, Earl Ramsey 1921- *WhoBlA 92*
**Claiborne**, H C 1921- *AmMWSc 92*
**Claiborne**, Herbert Augustine, III 1955- *WhoAmL 92*
**Claiborne**, Lewis T, Jr 1935- *AmMWSc 92*
**Claiborne**, Liz 1929- *WhoFI 92*
**Claiborne**, Lloyd R. 1936- *WhoBlA 92*
**Claiborne**, Richard Alan 1955- *WhoMW 92*

**Claiborne,** Sybil *DrAPF 91*
**Claiborne,** Vernal 1946- *WhoBlA 92*
**Clair,** Areatha G. 1931- *WhoBlA 92*
**Clair,** John Joseph 1956- *WhoMW 92, WhoRel 92*
**Clair,** Joseph Alexander, III 1931- *WhoFI 92*
**Clair,** Louis Serge 1940- *IntWW 91*
**Clair,** Matthew Wesley, Sr. 1865-1943 *RelLAm 91*
**Clair,** Rene 1898-1981 *FacFETw, IntDcF 2-2 [port]*
**Clair,** Robert Thomas 1955- *WhoFI 92*
**Clair,** Theodore Nat 1929- *WhoWest 92*
**Clairault,** Alexis Claude 1713-1765 *BlkwCEP*
**Clairaut,** Alexis Claude 1713-1765 *BlkwCEP*
**Clairbuschae,** William Felton 1951- *WhoEnt 92*
**Claire,** Anne Marie Arancibia 1948- *WhoWest 92*
**Claire,** Fred *WhoWest 92*
**Claire,** Janet 1950- *WhoEnt 92*
**Claire,** Thomas Andrew 1951- *WhoFI 92*
**Claire,** William *DrAPF 91*
**Clairmonte,** Christopher 1932- *TwCPaSc*
**Claisse,** Fernand 1923- *AmMWSc 92*
**Claitor,** L Carroll 1918- *AmMWSc 92*
**Clamageran,** Alice Germaine Suzanne 1906- *Who 92*
**Claman,** Henry Neumann 1930- *AmMWSc 92*
**Clamann,** H Peter 1939- *AmMWSc 92*
**Clambey,** Gary Kenneth 1945- *AmMWSc 92*
**Clamme,** Marvin Leslie 1953- *WhoEnt 92*
**Clampett,** Bob d1984 *LesBEnT 92*
**Clampitt,** Amy *DrAPF 91*
**Clampitt,** Amy 1920- *BenetAL 91, ConPo 91, WrDr 92*
**Clanagan,** Mazzetta Price 1920- *WhoBlA 92*
**Clancarty,** Earl of 1911- *Who 92*
**Clancey,** Delores Ann 1930- *WhoIns 92*
**Clanchy,** Joan Lesley 1939- *Who 92*
**Clancy Brothers** *FacFETw*
**Clancy,** Daniel Francis 1918- *WhoMW 92*
**Clancy,** Donna L 1943- *WhoIns 92*
**Clancy,** Edward Bede *Who 92*
**Clancy,** Edward Bede 1923- *IntWW 91, WhoRel 92*
**Clancy,** Edward J, Jr *WhoAmP 91*
**Clancy,** Edward Philbrook 1913- *AmMWSc 92*
**Clancy,** James Richard 1935- *WhoMW 92*
**Clancy,** John 1922- *AmMWSc 92*
**Clancy,** John F *WhoAmP 91*
**Clancy,** John Patrick 1942- *WhoFI 92*
**Clancy,** Joseph Patrick Thomas 1928- *IntAu&W 91*
**Clancy,** Laurence James 1942- *IntAu&W 91*
**Clancy,** Laurie 1942- *WrDr 92*
**Clancy,** Madeline *WhoRel 92*
**Clancy,** Magalene Aldoshia 1938- *WhoBlA 92*
**Clancy,** Raymond Edward 1926- *WhoWest 92*
**Clancy,** Richard L 1933- *AmMWSc 92*
**Clancy,** Sam 1958- *WhoBlA 92*
**Clancy,** Thomas H. 1923- *WrDr 92*
**Clancy,** Thomas Hanley 1923- *WhoRel 92*
**Clancy,** Thomas L, Jr 1947- *IntAu&W 91*
**Clancy,** Tom 1923-1990 *AnObit 1990, FacFETw*
**Clancy,** Tom 1947- *BenetAL 91, WrDr 92*
**Clandinin,** Donald Robert 1914- *AmMWSc 92*
**Clandinin,** Michael Thomas 1949- *AmMWSc 92*
**Clanfield,** Viscount 1976- *Who 92*
**Clanmorris,** Baron 1937- *Who 92*
**Clanton,** David Albert 1944- *WhoAmP 91*
**Clanton,** Donald Cather 1926- *AmMWSc 92*
**Clanton,** Donald Henry 1926- *AmMWSc 92*
**Clanton,** Earl Spencer, III 1919- *WhoBlA 92N*
**Clanton,** Lemuel Jacque 1931- *WhoBlA 92*
**Clanton,** Randolph J. 1944- *WhoBlA 92*
**Clanton,** Thomas L 1949- *AmMWSc 92*
**Clanton,** Thomas Lindsay 1949- *WhoMW 92*
**Clanwilliam,** Earl of 1919- *Who 92*
**Clap,** Thomas 1703-1767 *BiInAmS*
**Clapcott,** Helen 1952- *TwCPaSc*
**Clapham,** Arthur Roy d1990 *Who 92N*
**Clapham,** Arthur Roy 1904-1990 *ConAu 133*
**Clapham,** Brian Ralph 1913- *Who 92*
**Clapham,** Christopher 1941- *WrDr 92*
**Clapham,** John 1908- *IntAu&W 91, WrDr 92*
**Clapham,** Michael 1912- *Who 92*
**Clapham,** Michael John Sinclair 1912- *IntWW 91*
**Clapham,** Peter 1924- *TwCPaSc*
**Clapham,** Peter Brian 1940- *Who 92*
**Claplanhoo,** Edward E 1928- *WhoAmP 91*
**Clapman,** Peter C 1936- *WhoIns 92*
**Clapman,** Peter Carlyle 1936- *WhoAmL 92, WhoFI 92*
**Clapp,** Allen Linville 1943- *WhoFI 92*
**Clapp,** Asahel 1792-1862 *BiInAmS*
**Clapp,** C Edward 1930- *AmMWSc 92*
**Clapp,** Carol Shlifer 1947- *WhoAmL 92*
**Clapp,** Charles E., II 1923- *WhoAmL 92*
**Clapp,** Charles H 1948- *AmMWSc 92*
**Clapp,** Elinor J 1925- *WhoAmP 91*
**Clapp,** Harold Eugene 1943- *WhoMW 92*
**Clapp,** James Hargett 1951- *WhoAmL 92*
**Clapp,** James R 1931- *AmMWSc 92*
**Clapp,** John Garland, Jr 1936- *AmMWSc 92*
**Clapp,** John McMahon 1944- *WhoFI 92*
**Clapp,** Joseph Mark 1936- *WhoMW 92*
**Clapp,** Kenneth Wayne 1948- *WhoRel 92*
**Clapp,** Laurel Rebecca 1944- *WhoAmL 92*
**Clapp,** Leallyn Burr 1913- *AmMWSc 92*
**Clapp,** Lloyd *WhoAmP 91*
**Clapp,** Margaret Ann 1954- *WhoRel 92*
**Clapp,** Michael Cecil 1932- *Who 92*
**Clapp,** Neal K 1928- *AmMWSc 92*
**Clapp,** Patricia 1912- *IntAu&W 91, WrDr 92*
**Clapp,** Philip Charles 1935- *AmMWSc 92*
**Clapp,** Richard Crowell 1915- *AmMWSc 92*
**Clapp,** Richard Gardner 1911- *AmMWSc 92*
**Clapp,** Roger Edge 1919- *AmMWSc 92*
**Clapp,** Roger Williams, Jr 1929- *AmMWSc 92*
**Clapp,** Stephen Henry 1939- *WhoEnt 92*
**Clapp,** Thomas Wright 1937- *AmMWSc 92*
**Clapp,** Wayne George 1950- *WhoRel 92*
**Clapp,** William Lee 1943- *AmMWSc 92*
**Clappe,** Louise Amelia Knapp Smith 1819-1906 *BenetAL 91*
**Clapper,** David Lee 1945- *AmMWSc 92*
**Clapper,** Gregory Scott 1951- *WhoRel 92*
**Clapper,** Muir 1913- *AmMWSc 92*
**Clapper,** Thomas Wayne 1915- *AmMWSc 92*
**Clappier,** Bernard 1913- *IntWW 91*
**Clapprood,** Marjorie A O'Neill *WhoAmP 91*
**Claps,** Nicholas John 1946- *WhoFI 92*
**Clapshaw,** Patric Arnold 1937- *AmMWSc 92*
**Clapton,** Eric 1945- *FacFETw, IntWW 91, NewAmDM, WhoEnt 92*
**Clardy,** George L 1927- *WhoAmP 91*
**Clardy,** Jon Christel 1943- *AmMWSc 92*
**Clardy,** LeRoy 1910- *AmMWSc 92*
**Clardy,** Virginia Mae 1923- *WhoAmP 91*
**Clardy,** William J. 1935- *WhoBlA 92*
**Clare** *Who 92*
**Clare,** Ada *BenetAL 91*
**Clare,** Anthony Ward 1942- *Who 92*
**Clare,** David Ross 1925- *IntWW 91*
**Clare,** Debra A *AmMWSc 92*
**Clare,** Elizabeth *IntAu&W 91X*
**Clare,** Ellen *IntAu&W 91X, WrDr 92*
**Clare,** George 1920- *WrDr 92*
**Clare,** George 1930- *WhoFI 92*
**Clare,** Helen *IntAu&W 91X, WrDr 92*
**Clare,** Herbert Mitchell N. *Who 92*
**Clare,** John 1793-1864 *RfGEnL 91*
**Clare,** Kenneth Guilford 1918- *WhoFI 92*
**Clare,** Samantha *ConAu 135*
**Clare,** Stephen 1958- *TwCPaSc*
**Clare,** Stewart 1913- *AmMWSc 92*
**Clarebrough,** Leo Michael 1924- *IntWW 91*
**Claremon,** Neil *DrAPF 91*
**Clarenbach,** David E 1953- *WhoAmP 91*
**Clarenburg,** Rudolf 1931- *AmMWSc 92*
**Clarence,** Daniel Jerome 1959- *WhoFI 92*
**Clarendon,** Earl of 1933- *Who 92*
**Clarens,** Angel *WhoHisp 92*
**Clareson,** Thomas 1926- *ScFEYrs*
**Clareson,** Thomas Dean 1926- *IntAu&W 91*
**Claretie,** Jules 1840-1913 *ThHEIm*
**Clarey,** Alison A. 1947- *WhoMW 92*
**Clarey,** John Robert 1942- *WhoFI 92*
**Clarfelt,** Jack Gerald 1914- *Who 92*
**Claridge,** E L 1917- *AmMWSc 92*
**Claridge,** Michael Frederick 1934- *Who 92*
**Claridge,** Richard Allen 1932- *AmMWSc 92*
**Claridge,** Robert Harold 1947- *WhoAmL 92*
**Clarie,** T. Emmet 1913- *WhoAmL 92*
**Claringbull,** Frank d1990 *Who 92N*
**Clark** *Who 92*
**Clark,** A Gavin 1938- *AmMWSc 92*
**Clark,** Admont Halsey 1888-1918 *BiInAmS*
**Clark,** Alan Barthwell 1936- *WhoWest 92*
**Clark,** Alan Benjamin 1946- *WhoAmL 92*
**Clark,** Alan Charles *Who 92*
**Clark,** Alan Curtis 1944- *AmMWSc 92*
**Clark,** Alan Fred 1936- *AmMWSc 92*
**Clark,** Alan Kenneth McKenzie 1928- *Who 92*
**Clark,** Alan Richard 1939- *Who 92*
**Clark,** Albert William 1922- *Who 92*
**Clark,** Alfred *ScFEYrs*
**Clark,** Alfred 1909- *AmMWSc 92*
**Clark,** Alfred, Jr 1936- *AmMWSc 92*
**Clark,** Alfred James 1933- *AmMWSc 92*
**Clark,** Alistair Campbell 1933- *Who 92*
**Clark,** Allan H 1935- *AmMWSc 92*
**Clark,** Allen Keith 1933- *AmMWSc 92*
**Clark,** Allen LeRoy 1938- *AmMWSc 92*
**Clark,** Allen Varden 1941- *AmMWSc 92*
**Clark,** Alonzo Howard 1850-1918 *BiInAmS*
**Clark,** Alton Harold 1939- *AmMWSc 92*
**Clark,** Alvan 1804-1887 *BiInAmS*
**Clark,** Alvan Graham 1832-1897 *BiInAmS*
**Clark,** Alvin John 1933- *AmMWSc 92*
**Clark,** Ameera H. 1919- *WhoBlA 92*
**Clark,** Andrew Eric 1963- *WhoFI 92*
**Clark,** Andrew Galen 1954- *AmMWSc 92*
**Clark,** Ann Nolan 1896- *IntAu&W 91*
**Clark,** Anthony 1942- *TwCPaSc*
**Clark,** Anthony Howard 1951- *WhoEnt 92*
**Clark,** Anthony Warner 1951- *WhoAmL 92*
**Clark,** Armin Lee 1928- *AmMWSc 92*
**Clark,** Arnold Franklin 1916- *AmMWSc 92*
**Clark,** Arnold M 1916- *AmMWSc 92*
**Clark,** Arthur Brodie 1935- *WhoFI 92*
**Clark,** Arthur Edward 1932- *AmMWSc 92*
**Clark,** Arthur Joseph, Jr. 1921- *WhoWest 92*
**Clark,** Augusta Alexander *WhoAmP 91*
**Clark,** Augusta Alexander 1932- *WhoBlA 92*
**Clark,** Badger *TwCWW 91*
**Clark,** Badger 1883-1957 *BenetAL 91*
**Clark,** Barbara *WhoAmP 91*
**Clark,** Barbara M 1939- *WhoAmP 91*
**Clark,** Barry Gillespie 1938- *AmMWSc 92*
**Clark,** Benjamin Cates, Jr *AmMWSc 92*
**Clark,** Benjamin F. 1910- *WhoBlA 92*
**Clark,** Benton C 1937- *AmMWSc 92*
**Clark,** Bernard Francis, Jr. 1956- *WhoAmL 92*
**Clark,** Bertha Smith 1943- *WhoBlA 92*
**Clark,** Beth 1914- *WhoRel 92*
**Clark,** Bettie I. 1927- *WhoBlA 92*
**Clark,** Betty Elizabeth 1928- *WhoAmP 91*
**Clark,** Betty Jean 1920- *WhoAmP 91*
**Clark,** Betty Jean 1944- *WhoAmP 91*
**Clark,** Beverly A *WhoAmP 91*
**Clark,** Beverly Jean 1939- *WhoAmL 92*
**Clark,** Bill 1944- *WhoAmP 91*
**Clark,** Bill 1946- *WhoAmP 91*
**Clark,** Bill Pat 1939- *AmMWSc 92*
**Clark,** Billy Pat 1939- *WhoFI 92*
**Clark,** Bob 1941- *IntMPA 92*
**Clark,** Brian 1932- *WrDr 92*
**Clark,** Brian D 1956- *WhoAmP 91*
**Clark,** Brian Robert 1932- *IntAu&W 91, Who 92*
**Clark,** Brian Thomas 1951- *WhoWest 92*
**Clark,** Bruce 1918- *IntAu&W 91, WrDr 92*
**Clark,** Bruce 1958- *WhoBlA 92*
**Clark,** Bruce R 1941- *AmMWSc 92*
**Clark,** Bryan Lewis 1964- *WhoWest 92*
**Clark,** Burnill Fred 1941- *WhoEnt 92, WhoWest 92*
**Clark,** Burr, Jr 1924- *AmMWSc 92*
**Clark,** C C 1928- *AmMWSc 92*
**Clark,** C Elmer 1921- *AmMWSc 92*
**Clark,** C Ray 1939- *WhoAmP 91*
**Clark,** C. Scott *IntWW 91*
**Clark,** C Scott 1938- *AmMWSc 92*
**Clark,** Caesar A. W. 1914- *WhoBlA 92*
**Clark,** Caleb Morgan 1945- *WhoWest 92*
**Clark,** Candy *IntMPA 92, WhoEnt 92*
**Clark,** Carl Arthur 1911- *WhoMW 92*
**Clark,** Carl Cyrus 1924- *AmMWSc 92*
**Clark,** Carl Heritage 1925- *AmMWSc 92*
**Clark,** Carleton Earl 1942- *WhoFI 92*
**Clark,** Carolyn Cochran 1941- *WhoAmL 92*
**Clark,** Charles 1925- *WhoAmL 92, WhoAmP 91*
**Clark,** Charles Anthony 1940- *Who 92*
**Clark,** Charles Austin 1915- *AmMWSc 92*
**Clark,** Charles Cauthen 1829-1911 *DcNCBi 1*
**Clark,** Charles Champ, Sr 1926- *WhoAmP 91*
**Clark,** Charles Christopher 1943- *AmMWSc 92*
**Clark,** Charles David Lawson 1933- *Who 92*
**Clark,** Charles E. 1929- *WrDr 92*
**Clark,** Charles Edward 1921- *WhoAmL 92*
**Clark,** Charles Edward 1923- *AmMWSc 92*
**Clark,** Charles Edward 1947- *WhoAmL 92*
**Clark,** Charles Heber 1847-1915 *BenetAL 91*
**Clark,** Charles Joseph 1939- *IntWW 91, Who 92, WhoWest 92*
**Clark,** Charles Kittredge 1906- *AmMWSc 92*
**Clark,** Charles Lester 1917- *AmMWSc 92*
**Clark,** Charles Malcolm, Jr 1938- *AmMWSc 92*
**Clark,** Charles Manning Hope 1915- *IntWW 91*
**Clark,** Charles Richard 1947- *AmMWSc 92*
**Clark,** Charles Roger 1957- *WhoWest 92*
**Clark,** Charles Stone 1954- *WhoFI 92*
**Clark,** Charles Sutter 1927- *WhoWest 92*
**Clark,** Charles Warfield 1917- *WhoBlA 92*
**Clark,** Charles Winthrop 1952- *AmMWSc 92*
**Clark,** Chester William 1906- *AmMWSc 92*
**Clark,** Christine Philpot 1937- *WhoBlA 92*
**Clark,** Christopher Alan 1949- *AmMWSc 92*
**Clark,** Christopher Harvey 1946- *Who 92*
**Clark,** Christophor David 1951- *IntAu&W 91*
**Clark,** Clarence Bendenson, Jr. 1943- *WhoBlA 92*
**Clark,** Clarence Floyd 1912- *AmMWSc 92*
**Clark,** Claude 1915- *WhoWest 92*
**Clark,** Claude Lockhart 1945- *WhoBlA 92*
**Clark,** Clayton 1912- *AmMWSc 92*
**Clark,** Clifton Bob 1927- *AmMWSc 92*
**Clark,** Colin 1918- *Who 92*
**Clark,** Colin Whitcomb 1931- *AmMWSc 92*
**Clark,** Connie *AmMWSc 92*
**Clark,** Craig G. 1949- *WhoWest 92*
**Clark,** Crosman Jay 1925- *AmMWSc 92*
**Clark,** Curt *IntAu&W 91X, WrDr 92*
**Clark,** D L *AmMWSc 92*
**Clark,** Dale Allen 1922- *AmMWSc 92*
**Clark,** Dane 1915- *IntMPA 92*
**Clark,** Daniel 1953- *WhoAmL 92*
**Clark,** Daniel Cooper 1948- *WhoRel 92*
**Clark,** Daniel F 1954- *WhoAmP 91*
**Clark,** Dave 1913- *WhoBlA 92*
**Clark,** David *WrDr 92*
**Clark,** David 1877-1955 *DcNCBi 1*
**Clark,** David 1939- *Who 92*
**Clark,** David, Sr 1922- *WhoAmP 91*
**Clark,** David A 1943- *AmMWSc 92*
**Clark,** David Barrett 1913- *AmMWSc 92*
**Clark,** David Beatson 1933- *Who 92*
**Clark,** David Delano 1924- *AmMWSc 92*
**Clark,** David Edward 1946- *AmMWSc 92*
**Clark,** David Ellsworth 1922- *AmMWSc 92*
**Clark,** David Eugene 1957- *WhoMW 92*
**Clark,** David Gillis 1933- *WhoWest 92*
**Clark,** David John 1947- *Who 92*
**Clark,** David Lee 1939- *AmMWSc 92*
**Clark,** David Lee 1942- *AmMWSc 92*
**Clark,** David Lee 1959- *WhoEnt 92*
**Clark,** David Leigh 1931- *AmMWSc 92*
**Clark,** David M 1947- *AmMWSc 92*
**Clark,** David Neil 1953- *AmMWSc 92, WhoWest 92*
**Clark,** David Ridgley 1920- *IntAu&W 91, WrDr 92*
**Clark,** David Robert 1953- *WhoAmL 92*
**Clark,** David Scott 1944- *WhoAmL 92*
**Clark,** David Sedgefield 1929- *AmMWSc 92*
**Clark,** David Thurmond 1925- *AmMWSc 92*
**Clark,** David Wright 1948- *WhoAmL 92*
**Clark,** Dayle Meritt 1933- *WhoFI 92*
**Clark,** Denis 1943- *Who 92*
**Clark,** Dennis Lee 1947- *WhoRel 92*
**Clark,** Dennis Richard 1944- *AmMWSc 92*
**Clark,** Derek John 1929- *Who 92*
**Clark,** Desmond *Who 92*
**Clark,** Dewey P 1934- *WhoIns 92*
**Clark,** Dick *LesBEnT 92 [port]*
**Clark,** Dick 1929- *FacFETw, IntMPA 92, WhoEnt 92*
**Clark,** Dick Clarence 1928- *IntWW 91*
**Clark,** Diddo Ruth 1950- *WhoAmL 92*
**Clark,** Donald Cameron 1931- *WhoFI 92, WhoMW 92*
**Clark,** Donald Eldon 1936- *AmMWSc 92*
**Clark,** Donald James 1957- *WhoRel 92*
**Clark,** Donald Lewis 1926- *WhoRel 92*
**Clark,** Donald Lewis 1935- *WhoBlA 92*
**Clark,** Donald Lyndon 1920- *AmMWSc 92*
**Clark,** Donald M 1923- *WhoAmP 91*
**Clark,** Donald Ray, Jr 1940- *AmMWSc 92*
**Clark,** Donald Rowlee 1925- *WhoWest 92*
**Clark,** Donna Jean 1940- *WhoMW 92*
**Clark,** Donna Marie 1954- *WhoMW 92*
**Clark,** Douglas 1919- *IntAu&W 91, WrDr 92*
**Clark,** Douglas Alan 1958- *WhoMW 92*
**Clark,** Douglas Henderson 1917- *Who 92*
**Clark,** Douglas Kenneth 1947- *WhoWest 92*
**Clark,** Douglas L. 1935- *WhoBlA 92*
**Clark,** Douglas Napier 1944- *AmMWSc 92*
**Clark,** Douglas O. 1936- *WhoMW 92*

**Clark,** Douglas Paul 1960- *WhoMW 92*
**Clark,** Duncan C. 1952- *IntMPA 92*
**Clark,** Duncan William 1910- *AmMWSc 92*
**Clark,** Dwight DeLong 1934- *WhoWest 92*
**Clark,** Earnest Hubert, Jr. 1926- *WhoWest 92*
**Clark,** Edgar Sanderford 1933- *WhoFI 92, WhoWest 92*
**Clark,** Edward 1926- *WhoBlA 92*
**Clark,** Edward Alan 1947- *WhoWest 92*
**Clark,** Edward Aloysius 1934- *AmMWSc 92*
**Clark,** Edward Depriest, Sr. 1930- *WhoBlA 92*
**Clark,** Edward E 1930- *WhoAmP 91*
**Clark,** Edward Maurice 1920- *AmMWSc 92*
**Clark,** Edward Shannon 1930- *AmMWSc 92*
**Clark,** Edythe Audrey 1929- *WhoWest 92*
**Clark,** Eleanor *DrAPF 91*
**Clark,** Eleanor 1913- *BenetAL 91, ConNov 91, IntAu&W 91, WrDr 92*
**Clark,** Elijah *DcNCBi 1*
**Clark,** Elmer Talmage 1886-1966 *DcNCBi 1, RelLAm 91*
**Clark,** Eloise Elizabeth 1931- *AmMWSc 92*
**Clark,** Elvira R. 1948- *WhoEnt 92*
**Clark,** Emory Eugene 1931- *WhoFI 92*
**Clark,** Eric 1937- *IntAu&W 91, WrDr 92*
**Clark,** Eric Charles 1951- *WhoAmP 91*
**Clark,** Eugene T 1947- *WhoAmP 91*
**Clark,** Eugene Walter 1915- *WhoAmP 91*
**Clark,** Eugenie 1922- *AmMWSc 92*
**Clark,** Evelyn Genevieve 1922- *AmMWSc 92*
**Clark,** Ezekail Louis 1912- *AmMWSc 92, WhoWest 92*
**Clark,** Faye Louise 1936- *WhoEnt 92*
**Clark,** Findlay *Who 92*
**Clark,** Flora Mae 1933- *AmMWSc 92*
**Clark,** Forrester A, Jr 1934- *WhoAmP 91*
**Clark,** Francis 1924- *Who 92*
**Clark,** Francis Edward 1851-1927 *RelLAm 91*
**Clark,** Francis John 1933- *AmMWSc 92*
**Clark,** Francis Leo 1920- *Who 92*
**Clark,** Frank Eugene 1919- *AmMWSc 92*
**Clark,** Frank S 1933- *AmMWSc 92*
**Clark,** Fred 1930- *WhoFI 92*
**Clark,** G. Peter 1948- *WhoAmL 92*
**Clark,** G. Russell 1904-1991 *NewYTBS 91 [port]*
**Clark,** Gary C. 1962- *WhoBlA 92*
**Clark,** Gary Edwin 1939- *AmMWSc 92*
**Clark,** Gary Kenneth 1936- *WhoRel 92, WhoWest 92*
**Clark,** Gary Michael 1951- *WhoFI 92*
**Clark,** Gaylord Parsons 1856-1907 *BiInAmS*
**Clark,** Gene d1991 *NewYTBS 91*
**Clark,** Geoffrey 1946- *WhoFI 92*
**Clark,** Geoffrey D. *DrAPF 91*
**Clark,** George 1905- *AmMWSc 92*
**Clark,** George 1927- *WhoMW 92*
**Clark,** George Alexander 1927- *WhoMW 92*
**Clark,** George Alfred, Jr 1936- *AmMWSc 92*
**Clark,** George Anthony d1991 *Who 92N*
**Clark,** George Archibald 1864-1918 *BiInAmS*
**Clark,** George Bassett 1827-1891 *BiInAmS*
**Clark,** George C 1930- *AmMWSc 92*
**Clark,** George L 1941- *WhoAmP 91*
**Clark,** George M, Jr 1947- *WhoIns 92*
**Clark,** George Richmond, II 1938- *AmMWSc 92*
**Clark,** George Rogers 1752-1818 *BenetAL 91, BlkwEAR*
**Clark,** George Whipple 1928- *AmMWSc 92, IntWW 91*
**Clark,** Georgianna Mae Georgi 1940- *WhoEnt 92*
**Clark,** Gerald 1933- *Who 92*
**Clark,** Gerald Edmondson 1935- *Who 92*
**Clark,** Gerald L 1938- *WhoIns 92*
**Clark,** Gil Ronald 1961- *WhoEnt 92*
**Clark,** Glen Edward 1943- *WhoWest 92*
**Clark,** Glen W 1931- *AmMWSc 92*
**Clark,** Glenn 1882-1956 *RelLAm 91*
**Clark,** Gordon Haddon 1902-1985 *RelLAm 91*
**Clark,** Gordon Meredith 1934- *AmMWSc 92*
**Clark,** Gordon Murray 1925- *AmMWSc 92*
**Clark,** Grady Wayne 1922- *AmMWSc 92*
**Clark,** Grahame *Who 92*
**Clark,** Grahame 1907- *WrDr 92*
**Clark,** Granville E., Sr. 1927- *WhoBlA 92*
**Clark,** Gregor Munro 1946- *Who 92*
**Clark,** Grenville 1882-1967 *AmPeW*
**Clark,** Greydon 1943- *IntMPA 92*
**Clark,** H B 1928- *AmMWSc 92*
**Clark,** Harlan Eugene 1941- *AmMWSc 92*
**Clark,** Harold Arthur 1910- *AmMWSc 92*
**Clark,** Harold Eugene 1906- *AmMWSc 92*
**Clark,** Harry W. 1946- *WhoBlA 92*
**Clark,** Helen 1950- *IntWW 91*
**Clark,** Helen Elizabeth 1950- *Who 92*
**Clark,** Henry Benjamin, Jr. 1915- *WhoWest 92*
**Clark,** Henry James 1826-1873 *BiInAmS*
**Clark,** Henry Maitland 1929- *Who 92*
**Clark,** Henry Ogden 1944- *WhoMW 92*
**Clark,** Henry Selby 1809-1869 *DcNCBi 1*
**Clark,** Henry Toole 1808-1874 *DcNCBi 1*
**Clark,** Henry Wallace 1926- *Who 92*
**Clark,** Herbert Edward 1945- *WhoAmP 91*
**Clark,** Herbert Mottram 1918- *AmMWSc 92*
**Clark,** Herman 1942- *WhoAmL 92, WhoAmP 91*
**Clark,** Hilary J *IntMPA 92*
**Clark,** Hilton Bancroft 1943- *WhoAmP 91*
**Clark,** Howard Charles 1929- *AmMWSc 92, IntWW 91*
**Clark,** Howard Charles, Jr 1937- *AmMWSc 92*
**Clark,** Howard Garmany 1928- *AmMWSc 92*
**Clark,** Howard Longstreth 1916- *IntWW 91*
**Clark,** Howell R 1926- *AmMWSc 92*
**Clark,** Hugh 1914- *AmMWSc 92*
**Clark,** Hugh Kidder 1918- *AmMWSc 92*
**Clark,** I Crane *ScFEYrs*
**Clark,** Ian Robertson 1939- *IntWW 91, Who 92*
**Clark,** Irwin 1918- *AmMWSc 92*
**Clark,** J B 1924- *AmMWSc 92*
**Clark,** J. C. D. 1951- *WrDr 92*
**Clark,** J Desmond 1916- *AmMWSc 92, WrDr 92*
**Clark,** J E *WhoAmP 91*
**Clark,** J Edwin 1933- *AmMWSc 92*
**Clark,** Jack 1932- *WhoFI 92*
**Clark,** James Alan 1950- *AmMWSc 92*
**Clark,** James Allen 1948- *WhoAmL 92*
**Clark,** James Beauchamp 1850-1921 *AmPolLe, FacFETw*
**Clark,** James Bennett 1923- *AmMWSc 92*
**Clark,** James Derrell 1937- *AmMWSc 92*
**Clark,** James Donald 1918- *AmMWSc 92*
**Clark,** James Edward 1926- *AmMWSc 92*
**Clark,** James Enes 1943- *WhoWest 92*
**Clark,** James Ernest 1942- *WhoRel 92*
**Clark,** James H 1952- *WhoAmP 91*
**Clark,** James Hamel 1960- *WhoEnt 92*
**Clark,** James Henry 1932- *AmMWSc 92*
**Clark,** James Irving, Jr. 1936- *WhoBlA 92*
**Clark,** James Joseph 1954- *WhoAmL 92*
**Clark,** James Kendall 1948- *WhoAmL 92*
**Clark,** James Leonard 1923- *Who 92*
**Clark,** James McAdam 1916- *Who 92*
**Clark,** James Michael 1938- *AmMWSc 92*
**Clark,** James N. 1934- *WhoBlA 92*
**Clark,** James Norman 1932- *WhoIns 92, WhoMW 92*
**Clark,** James Orie, II 1950- *AmMWSc 92, WhoWest 92*
**Clark,** James Richard 1946- *WhoAmL 92*
**Clark,** James Richard 1951- *AmMWSc 92*
**Clark,** James S *WhoAmP 91*
**Clark,** James Samuel 1957- *AmMWSc 92*
**Clark,** James West 1779-1843 *DcNCBi 1*
**Clark,** James William 1924- *AmMWSc 92*
**Clark,** James Willis 1944- *WhoAmL 92*
**Clark,** Janet Eileen 1940- *WhoWest 92*
**Clark,** Janet Lee 1952- *WhoMW 92*
**Clark,** Jean *DrAPF 91*
**Clark,** Jean Manson 1902- *TwCPaSc*
**Clark,** Jeff Ray 1947- *WhoFI 92*
**Clark,** Jeffrey Raphiel 1953- *WhoFI 92*
**Clark,** Jeffry Russell 1950- *WhoWest 92*
**Clark,** Jere Walton 1922- *WhoFI 92*
**Clark,** Jerold R. 1954- *WhoEnt 92*
**Clark,** Jerome Bayard 1882-1959 *DcNCBi 1*
**Clark,** Jerry 1944- *WhoAmP 91*
**Clark,** Jerry Dale 1955- *WhoRel 92*
**Clark,** Jerry Norton 1941- *WhoFI 92*
**Clark,** Jesse B., III 1925- *WhoBlA 92*
**Clark,** Jessie 1960- *WhoBlA 92*
**Clark,** Jimmy Dorral 1939- *AmMWSc 92*
**Clark,** Jimmy E. 1934- *WhoBlA 92*
**Clark,** Jimmy Howard 1941- *AmMWSc 92, WhoMW 92*
**Clark,** Joan *ConAu 134, SmATA 65*
**Clark,** Joe *Who 92*
**Clark,** Joe 1939- *ConBlB 1 [port], FacFETw, WhoWest 92*
**Clark,** Joe Louis 1939- *WhoBlA 92*
**Clark,** John 1766-1832 *DcNCBi 1*
**Clark,** John 1926- *Who 92*
**Clark,** John 1943- *TwCPaSc*
**Clark,** John A 1923- *AmMWSc 92*
**Clark,** John A. 1926- *IntWW 91*
**Clark,** John Arthur 1920- *WhoAmL 92*
**Clark,** John Bates 1847-1938 *AmPeW*
**Clark,** John Benton 1942- *WhoAmL 92*
**Clark,** John Cosmo 1897-1967 *TwCPaSc*
**Clark,** John Desmond 1916- *IntWW 91, Who 92*
**Clark,** John Douglas d1991 *Who 92N*
**Clark,** John Edward 1932- *Who 92*
**Clark,** John Elwood 1931- *WhoAmP 91, WhoWest 92*
**Clark,** John F 1920- *AmMWSc 92*
**Clark,** John Foster 1950- *WhoAmL 92*
**Clark,** John Graham, III 1950- *WhoAmL 92*
**Clark,** John Grahame 1907- *Who 92*
**Clark,** John Grahame Douglas 1907- *IntWW 91*
**Clark,** John Harlan 1948- *AmMWSc 92*
**Clark,** John Holley, III 1918- *WhoAmL 92*
**Clark,** John Howard 1946- *WhoAmP 91*
**Clark,** John Ives 1958- *WhoAmP 91*
**Clark,** John Jefferson 1922- *AmMWSc 92*
**Clark,** John Joseph 1954- *WhoBlA 92*
**Clark,** John L. 1907- *IntMPA 92*
**Clark,** John Magruder, Jr 1932- *AmMWSc 92*
**Clark,** John Nathaniel 1831?-1903 *BiInAmS*
**Clark,** John Paul 1940- *WhoAmP 91*
**Clark,** John Pepper 1935- *BlkLC [port], ConPo 91, IntAu&W 91, RfGEnL 91, WrDr 92*
**Clark,** John Peter, III 1942- *AmMWSc 92, WhoMW 92*
**Clark,** John R 1911- *AmMWSc 92*
**Clark,** John R 1918- *AmMWSc 92*
**Clark,** John R. 1930- *WrDr 92*
**Clark,** John Richard 1930- *IntAu&W 91*
**Clark,** John Robert 1955- *WhoAmP 91*
**Clark,** John S. *Who 92*
**Clark,** John W 1922- *AmMWSc 92*
**Clark,** John Walter 1935- *AmMWSc 92*
**Clark,** John Washington 1887-1969 *DcNCBi 1*
**Clark,** John Whitcomb 1918- *AmMWSc 92*
**Clark,** Jon D 1946- *AmMWSc 92*
**Clark,** Jonathan Charles Douglas 1951- *IntAu&W 91, IntWW 91*
**Clark,** Jonathan Huntington 1955- *WhoFI 92*
**Clark,** Joseph *IntWW 91*
**Clark,** Joseph E 1935- *AmMWSc 92*
**Clark,** Joseph S. 1901-1990 *AnObit 1990*
**Clark,** Joseph Talmage 1941- *WhoAmL 92*
**Clark,** Judith Wells 1943- *WhoEnt 92*
**Clark,** Judy 1949- *TwCPaSc*
**Clark,** Julian Joseph 1935- *AmMWSc 92*
**Clark,** June *Who 92*
**Clark,** Karen *WhoAmP 91*
**Clark,** Karen Heath 1944- *WhoAmL 92*
**Clark,** Karen Lynne 1964- *WhoEnt 92*
**Clark,** Katherine Antoinette 1952- *WhoMW 92*
**Clark,** Kathleen Ann 1951- *WhoWest 92*
**Clark,** Kelly 1957- *WhoAmP 91*
**Clark,** Kenneth 1899- *IntMPA 92*
**Clark,** Kenneth 1903- *FacFETw*
**Clark,** Kenneth 1903-1983 *ConAu 36NR*
**Clark,** Kenneth B 1914- *FacFETw*
**Clark,** Kenneth Bancroft 1914- *IntWW 91, WhoBlA 92, WrDr 92*
**Clark,** Kenneth Courtright 1919- *AmMWSc 92*
**Clark,** Kenneth Edward 1945- *AmMWSc 92*
**Clark,** Kenneth Frederick 1933- *AmMWSc 92*
**Clark,** Kenneth James 1922- *Who 92*
**Clark,** Kenneth R 1947- *WhoAmP 91*
**Clark,** Kenneth William 1960- *WhoMW 92*
**Clark,** Kerry Bruce 1945- *AmMWSc 92*
**Clark,** Kevin Cronin 1960- *WhoFI 92*
**Clark,** Kevin M. 1955- *WhoMW 92*
**Clark,** Kim Bryce 1949- *WhoFI 92*
**Clark,** Kim Delon 1959- *WhoWest 92*
**Clark,** Kristy Louise 1949- *WhoWest 92*
**Clark,** L.D. *DrAPF 91*
**Clark,** L G 1924- *AmMWSc 92*
**Clark,** La Verne Harrell 1929- *WrDr 92*
**Clark,** Laron Jefferson, Jr. 1937- *WhoBlA 92*
**Clark,** Larry 1945- *WhoAmP 91*
**Clark,** Larry P 1936- *AmMWSc 92*
**Clark,** Laurie Jane 1951- *WhoAmL 92*
**Clark,** LaVerne Harrell *DrAPF 91*
**Clark,** LaWanna Gibbs 1941- *WhoBlA 92*
**Clark,** Lawrence M., Sr. 1934- *WhoBlA 92*
**Clark,** Leif Michael 1947- *WhoAmL 92*
**Clark,** Leigh Bruce 1934- *AmMWSc 92*
**Clark,** Leland Charles, Jr 1918- *AmMWSc 92*
**Clark,** Leo *Who 92*
**Clark,** Leon Henry 1941- *WhoBlA 92*
**Clark,** Leon Stanley 1930- *WhoBlA 92*
**Clark,** Leonard Weslorn, Jr. 1942- *WhoBlA 92*
**Clark,** LeRoy D. 1917- *WhoBlA 92*
**Clark,** Leslie Joseph 1914- *Who 92*
**Clark,** Lewis Gaylord 1808-1873 *BenetAL 91*
**Clark,** Ligia 1920- *IntWW 91*
**Clark,** Lincoln Dufton 1923- *AmMWSc 92*
**Clark,** Llewellyn Evans 1932- *AmMWSc 92*
**Clark,** Lloyd 1923- *WhoWest 92*
**Clark,** Lloyd Allen 1932- *AmMWSc 92*
**Clark,** Lloyd Douglas 1940- *AmMWSc 92*
**Clark,** Lonnie Paul 1943- *WhoAmP 91*
**Clark,** Louie Max *WhoAmP 91*
**Clark,** Louis James 1940- *WhoBlA 92*
**Clark,** Louis Morris, Jr. 1931- *WhoFI 92*
**Clark,** Loyal Frances 1958- *WhoWest 92*
**Clark,** Luther Johnson 1941- *Who 92*
**Clark,** Lynda Margaret *Who 92*
**Clark,** Lynn C. 1947- *WhoIns 92*
**Clark,** M Rita 1915- *WhoAmP 91*
**Clark,** Major 1917- *WhoBlA 92*
**Clark,** Major L., III 1946- *WhoBlA 92*
**Clark,** Malcolm 1931- *Who 92*
**Clark,** Malcolm Aiken 1905- *Who 92*
**Clark,** Malcolm Gray 1947- *WhoRel 92*
**Clark,** Malcolm John Roy 1944- *AmMWSc 92*
**Clark,** Malcolm Mallory 1931- *AmMWSc 92*
**Clark,** Mamie 1917-1983 *FacFETw*
**Clark,** Mamie Phipps 1917-1983 *WhoBlA 92N, WomPsyc*
**Clark,** Manning 1915-1991 *ConAu 134*
**Clark,** Margaret 1949- *WhoRel 92*
**Clark,** Margaret Goff 1913- *WrDr 92*
**Clark,** Margaret June 1941- *Who 92*
**Clark,** Margaret Pruitt 1946- *WhoAmP 91*
**Clark,** Marilyn Greene 1957- *WhoEnt 92*
**Clark,** Mario Sean 1954- *WhoBlA 92*
**Clark,** Mark 1896-1984 *FacFETw*
**Clark,** Mark Ross 1951- *WhoEnt 92*
**Clark,** Martha F 1942- *WhoAmP 91*
**Clark,** Martin Elliott 1945- *WhoMW 92*
**Clark,** Martin Fillmore, Jr. 1959- *WhoAmL 92*
**Clark,** Martin Ralph *AmMWSc 92*
**Clark,** Mary Eleanor 1927- *AmMWSc 92*
**Clark,** Mary Elizabeth 1954- *AmMWSc 92*
**Clark,** Mary Higgins 1929- *ConAu 36NR, IntAu&W 91, WrDr 92*
**Clark,** Mary Jane 1925- *AmMWSc 92*
**Clark,** Mary Jane 1948- *WhoFI 92*
**Clark,** Mary T. *WrDr 92*
**Clark,** Mary Twibill *IntAu&W 91*
**Clark,** Matt 1936- *IntMPA 92*
**Clark,** Matthew Harvey 1937- *WhoRel 92*
**Clark,** Matthew Mashuri 1952- *WhoFI 92*
**Clark,** Maurice Coates 1921- *WhoRel 92*
**Clark,** Mavis Thorpe *IntAu&W 91, WrDr 92*
**Clark,** Maxine 1949- *WhoFI 92*
**Clark,** Maxine Marjorie 1924- *WhoFI 92*
**Clark,** Mayree Carroll 1957- *WhoFI 92*
**Clark,** Melville, Jr 1921- *AmMWSc 92*
**Clark,** Merle *WrDr 92*
**Clark,** Mervin Leslie 1921- *AmMWSc 92*
**Clark,** Michael *DrAPF 91*
**Clark,** Michael 1918-1990 *TwCPaSc*
**Clark,** Michael 1935- *Who 92*
**Clark,** Michael George 1956- *WhoWest 92*
**Clark,** Michael Jay 1945- *WhoAmP 91*
**Clark,** Michael Olin 1943- *WhoFI 92*
**Clark,** Michael Wayne 1952- *AmMWSc 92*
**Clark,** Michael William 1927- *IntWW 91, Who 92*
**Clark,** Micheal Dale 1954- *WhoWest 92*
**Clark,** Michele d1972 *LesBEnT 92*
**Clark,** Michele A. 1954- *WhoEnt 92*
**Clark,** Michele Arleen 1954- *WhoBlA 92*
**Clark,** Mildred E. 1936- *WhoBlA 92*
**Clark,** Morris Shandell 1945- *WhoBlA 92*
**Clark,** Nancy Barnes 1939- *AmMWSc 92*
**Clark,** Nancy Randall 1938- *WhoAmP 91*
**Clark,** Naomi *DrAPF 91*
**Clark,** Nathan Edward 1940- *AmMWSc 92*
**Clark,** Neil Rex 1929- *IntWW 91*
**Clark,** Neil Scott 1953- *WhoMW 92*
**Clark,** Nelson T. 1940- *WhoMW 92*
**Clark,** Neri Anthony 1918- *AmMWSc 92*
**Clark,** Nigel Norman 1958- *AmMWSc 92*
**Clark,** Noble Baxter 1938- *WhoEnt 92*
**Clark,** Norman 1913- *TwCPaSc*
**Clark,** Odis Morrison 1944- *WhoRel 92*
**Clark,** Oswald William Hugh 1917- *Who 92*
**Clark,** Pamela Morris 1937- *WhoAmP 91*
**Clark,** Pat English 1940- *WhoAmL 92*
**Clark,** Patricia *DrAPF 91*
**Clark,** Patricia Ann Andre 1938- *AmMWSc 92*
**Clark,** Patricia Denise 1921- *IntAu&W 91*
**Clark,** Patricia Guy 1951- *WhoFI 92*
**Clark,** Patricia Jean 1951- *WhoAmP 91*
**Clark,** Paul 1932- *WhoAmP 91*
**Clark,** Paul Alan 1943- *WhoFI 92*
**Clark,** Paul Derek 1939- *Who 92*
**Clark,** Paul Enoch 1905- *AmMWSc 92*
**Clark,** Paul G. d1991 *NewYTBS 91*
**Clark,** Paul Newton 1947- *WhoMW 92*
**Clark,** Paul Nicholas Rowntree 1940- *Who 92*
**Clark,** Paul Sleman 1942- *WhoAmP 91*
**Clark,** Paul Thomas 1954- *WhoAmL 92*
**Clark,** Peggy 1915- *WhoEnt 92*
**Clark,** Peter David 1952- *AmMWSc 92*
**Clark,** Peter O 1938- *AmMWSc 92*

**Clark,** Petula 1932- *IntMPA 92*
**Clark,** Petula 1934- *IntWW 91, Who 92*
**Clark,** Philip Lindsey 1889- *TwCPaSc*
**Clark,** Philip Maclean 1929- *WhoMW 92*
**Clark,** R. Bradbury 1924- *WhoAmL 92, WhoFI 92, WhoWest 92*
**Clark,** R. Thomas 1951- *WhoAmL 92*
**Clark,** Ralph B 1933- *AmMWSc 92*
**Clark,** Ralph Leigh 1908- *AmMWSc 92*
**Clark,** Ralph M 1926- *AmMWSc 92*
**Clark,** Ralph O 1912- *AmMWSc 92*
**Clark,** Ramsey *NewYTBS 91*
**Clark,** Ramsey 1927- *FacFETw, IntWW 91, Who 92, WhoAmP 91*
**Clark,** Randall Livingston 1943- *WhoFI 92*
**Clark,** Randolph A. 1939- *WhoBlA 92*
**Clark,** Raymond Loyd 1935- *AmMWSc 92*
**Clark,** Raymond Oakes 1944- *WhoWest 92*
**Clark,** Reginald Harold 1928- *AmMWSc 92*
**Clark,** Rex L 1941- *AmMWSc 92*
**Clark,** Richard Alan 1953- *WhoWest 92*
**Clark,** Richard Bennett 1920- *AmMWSc 92*
**Clark,** Richard Charles 1935- *ConAu 133*
**Clark,** Richard Clarence 1928- *WhoAmP 91*
**Clark,** Richard David 1934- *Who 92*
**Clark,** Richard James 1935- *AmMWSc 92*
**Clark,** Richard James 1945- *WhoWest 92*
**Clark,** Richard McCourt 1937- *WhoAmL 92*
**Clark,** Richard R 1943- *WhoAmP 91*
**Clark,** Richard Stanley 1955- *WhoRel 92*
**Clark,** Richard W. 1954- *WhoRel 92*
**Clark,** Richard Ward 1938- *WhoWest 92*
**Clark,** Ricky Merle 1955- *WhoAmP 91*
**Clark,** Robert 1911- *WrDr 92*
**Clark,** Robert 1924- *Who 92*
**Clark,** Robert 1933- *AmMWSc 92*
**Clark,** Robert 1951- *TwCPaSc*
**Clark,** Robert A 1942- *AmMWSc 92*
**Clark,** Robert Alfred 1908- *AmMWSc 92*
**Clark,** Robert Alfred 1924- *AmMWSc 92*
**Clark,** Robert Anthony 1924- *IntWW 91*
**Clark,** Robert Arthur 1923- *AmMWSc 92*
**Clark,** Robert Beck 1941- *AmMWSc 92*
**Clark,** Robert Bernard 1923- *Who 92*
**Clark,** Robert Brewster 1927- *WhoAmP 91*
**Clark,** Robert C 1942- *WhoAmP 91*
**Clark,** Robert Charles 1944- *WhoAmL 92*
**Clark,** Robert Edward Holmes 1947- *AmMWSc 92*
**Clark,** Robert Eugene 1931- *WhoRel 92*
**Clark,** Robert G. 1929- *WhoBlA 92*
**Clark,** Robert George, Jr 1929- *WhoAmP 91*
**Clark,** Robert H 1921- *AmMWSc 92*
**Clark,** Robert Henry, Jr. 1941- *WhoFI 92*
**Clark,** Robert James Vodden 1907- *Who 92*
**Clark,** Robert M., Jr. 1948- *WhoAmL 92, WhoAmP 91*
**Clark,** Robert Newhall 1925- *AmMWSc 92*
**Clark,** Robert Paul 1935- *AmMWSc 92*
**Clark,** Robert Phillips 1921- *IntAu&W 91*
**Clark,** Robert Stokes 1954- *WhoAmL 92*
**Clark,** Robert W *WhoAmP 91*
**Clark,** Robert Wesley 1946- *WhoMW 92*
**Clark,** Robert William 1942- *WhoFI 92*
**Clark,** Roberta Humphrey 1942- *WhoAmL 92*
**Clark,** Robin Jon Hawes 1935- *Who 92*
**Clark,** Roger Alan 1946- *AmMWSc 92*
**Clark,** Roger Arthur 1932- *WhoAmL 92*
**Clark,** Roger William 1942- *AmMWSc 92*
**Clark,** Roland Everett 1933- *WhoMW 92*
**Clark,** Ronald C. 1935- *WhoBlA 92*
**Clark,** Ronald David 1938- *AmMWSc 92*
**Clark,** Ronald Duane 1938- *AmMWSc 92*
**Clark,** Ronald George 1928- *Who 92*
**Clark,** Ronald Harry 1904- *WrDr 92*
**Clark,** Ronald Jay 1960- *WhoAmL 92*
**Clark,** Ronald Jene 1932- *AmMWSc 92*
**Clark,** Ronald Joseph 1951- *WhoFI 92*
**Clark,** Ronald Keith 1941- *AmMWSc 92*
**Clark,** Ronald Rogers 1935- *AmMWSc 92*
**Clark,** Rosalind K. 1943- *WhoBlA 92*
**Clark,** Ross Alan 1960- *WhoRel 92*
**Clark,** Ross Bert, II 1932- *WhoAmL 92*
**Clark,** Ross Godfrey 1949- *WhoEnt 92, WhoWest 92*
**Clark,** Roy 1933- *NewAmDM, WhoEnt 92*
**Clark,** Russell Gentry 1925- *WhoAmL 92, WhoMW 92*
**Clark,** Russell Norman 1921- *AmMWSc 92*
**Clark,** Ruth 1942- *WhoBlA 92*
**Clark,** Sally Newbert 1934- *WhoWest 92*
**Clark,** Sam *WhoAmP 91*
**Clark,** Sam Lillard, Jr 1926- *AmMWSc 92*
**Clark,** Samuel Findlay 1909- *Who 92*
**Clark,** Samuel Friend 1914- *AmMWSc 92*
**Clark,** Samuel Kelly 1924- *AmMWSc 92*
**Clark,** Sandra Helen Becker 1938- *AmMWSc 92*
**Clark,** Sandra Marie 1942- *WhoFI 92*
**Clark,** Sanza Barbara 1940- *WhoBlA 92*
**Clark,** Savanna M. Vaughn 1927- *WhoBlA 92*
**Clark,** Scott Allen 1940- *WhoMW 92*
**Clark,** Septima 1898-1987 *NotBlAW 92 [port]*
**Clark,** Septima Poinsette 1891-1987 *FacFETw*
**Clark,** Shannon Lisa 1962- *WhoEnt 92*
**Clark,** Sharon Kay 1946- *WhoAmP 91*
**Clark,** Sheila Wheatley 1948- *WhoBlA 92*
**Clark,** Sheldon Ray 1953- *WhoMW 92*
**Clark,** Sheree Lee 1956- *WhoEnt 92*
**Clark,** Shirley Lorraine 1936- *WhoBlA 92*
**Clark,** Sidney Gilbert 1930- *AmMWSc 92*
**Clark,** Stanley Joe 1931- *AmMWSc 92*
**Clark,** Stanley McDeed 1944- *WhoAmL 92*
**Clark,** Stanley Preston 1917- *AmMWSc 92*
**Clark,** Stanley Ross 1937- *AmMWSc 92*
**Clark,** Stephen Darrough 1945- *AmMWSc 92*
**Clark,** Stephen Howard 1940- *AmMWSc 92*
**Clark,** Stephen Morrieson 1950- *WhoRel 92*
**Clark,** Stephen P 1923- *WhoAmP 91*
**Clark,** Stephen R. *DrAPF 91, WhoAmL 92*
**Clark,** Stephen Russell 1949- *WhoAmP 91*
**Clark,** Sterling 1940- *WhoEnt 92*
**Clark,** Steven English 1950- *WhoAmP 91*
**Clark,** Steven Grange 1948- *WhoEnt 92*
**Clark,** Steven Marston 1947- *WhoEnt 92, WhoWest 92*
**Clark,** Susan 1940- *IntMPA 92*
**Clark,** Susan 1944- *WhoEnt 92*
**Clark,** Susan Kathleen 1961- *WhoEnt 92*
**Clark,** Susan Matthews 1950- *WhoMW 92*
**Clark,** Sydney P, Jr 1929- *AmMWSc 92*
**Clark,** T K 1930- *AmMWSc 92*
**Clark,** Tama Myers *WhoBlA 92*
**Clark,** Terence 1934- *Who 92*
**Clark,** Teresa Marie 1961- *WhoFI 92*
**Clark,** Terry Allen 1960- *WhoAmL 92*
**Clark,** Terry N. 1940- *WrDr 92*
**Clark,** Theodore Lee 1907- *WhoBlA 92*
**Clark,** Theresa Tierney 1959- *WhoFI 92*
**Clark,** Thomas 1741-1792 *DcNCBi 1*
**Clark,** Thomas 1916- *Who 92*
**Clark,** Thomas 1926- *WhoAmP 91*
**Clark,** Thomas A *WhoAmP 91*
**Clark,** Thomas Alan 1938- *AmMWSc 92*
**Clark,** Thomas Alonzo 1920- *WhoAmL 92*
**Clark,** Thomas Arvid 1939- *AmMWSc 92*
**Clark,** Thomas Bertram, Sr. 1943- *WhoFI 92*
**Clark,** Thomas H. 1893- *IntWW 91*
**Clark,** Thomas Henry 1893- *AmMWSc 92*
**Clark,** Thomas Johnson 1953- *WhoFI 92*
**Clark,** Thomas Joseph 1926- *WhoWest 92*
**Clark,** Thomas March 1812-1903 *ScFEYrs*
**Clark,** Thomas Ryan 1925- *WhoWest 92*
**Clark,** Thomas Sullivan 1947- *WhoWest 92*
**Clark,** Thorne McKenzie 1889-1971 *DcNCBi 1*
**Clark,** Timothy John Hayes 1935- *Who 92*
**Clark,** Timothy Ross 1952- *WhoEnt 92*
**Clark,** Tom *DrAPF 91*
**Clark,** Tom 1941- *ConPo 91, WrDr 92*
**Clark,** Tom C 1899-1977 *FacFETw*
**Clark,** Tony *Who 92*
**Clark,** Trevor H 1909- *AmMWSc 92*
**Clark,** VeVe A. 1944- *WhoBlA 92*
**Clark,** Victor Joseph 1930- *WhoRel 92*
**Clark,** Vincent W. 1950- *WhoBlA 92*
**Clark,** Virginia 1928- *AmMWSc 92*
**Clark,** Virginia Lee 1945- *AmMWSc 92*
**Clark,** W Murray *WhoAmP 91*
**Clark,** Wallace *Who 92*
**Clark,** Wallace Henderson, Jr 1924- *AmMWSc 92*
**Clark,** Wallace Lee 1944- *AmMWSc 92*
**Clark,** Wallace Thomas, III 1953- *AmMWSc 92, WhoWest 92*
**Clark,** Walter Ernest 1916- *AmMWSc 92*
**Clark,** Walter H. 1928- *WhoBlA 92*
**Clark,** Walter Leighton, III 1921- *AmMWSc 92*
**Clark,** Walter McKenzie 1846-1924 *DcNCBi 1*
**Clark,** Walter van Tilburg 1909-1971 *BenetAL 91, TwCWW 91*
**Clark,** Warren, Jr 1936- *WhoAmP 91*
**Clark,** Wayne Elden 1943- *AmMWSc 92*
**Clark,** Wayne Timothy 1948- *WhoFI 92*
**Clark,** Wesley Gleason 1933- *AmMWSc 92*
**Clark,** Wesley Glenn 1929- *WhoRel 92*
**Clark,** Wilburn O 1938- *AmMWSc 92*
**Clark,** Wiliam B 1924- *WhoIns 92*
**Clark,** Will 1964- *WhoWest 92*
**Clark,** William 1770-1838 *BenetAL 91*
**Clark,** William 1917- *Who 92*
**Clark,** William 1937- *WhoBlA 92*
**Clark,** William, Jr 1930- *WhoAmP 91*
**Clark,** William A 1937- *WhoAmP 91*
**Clark,** William A 1958- *WhoAmP 91*
**Clark,** William Alan Thomas 1948- *AmMWSc 92*
**Clark,** William Alfred 1928- *WhoAmL 92*
**Clark,** William Arthur 1954- *WhoAmL 92*
**Clark,** William B 1917- *AmMWSc 92*
**Clark,** William Bullock 1860-1917 *BiInAmS*
**Clark,** William Burton, IV 1947- *AmMWSc 92*
**Clark,** William C 1901- *AmMWSc 92*
**Clark,** William Cummin 1948- *AmMWSc 92*
**Clark,** William David 1954- *WhoAmP 91*
**Clark,** William Dean 1936- *AmMWSc 92*
**Clark,** William Dennis 1948- *AmMWSc 92*
**Clark,** William E *WhoAmP 91*
**Clark,** William Edwin 1934- *AmMWSc 92*
**Clark,** William Elgan, Jr. 1948- *WhoBlA 92*
**Clark,** William Frederick 1941- *WhoAmL 92*
**Clark,** William G 1924- *WhoAmP 91*
**Clark,** William G 1933- *WhoIns 92*
**Clark,** William George 1924- *WhoAmL 92, WhoMW 92*
**Clark,** William Gilbert 1930- *AmMWSc 92*
**Clark,** William Greer 1945- *AmMWSc 92*
**Clark,** William Hilton 1944- *AmMWSc 92*
**Clark,** William Howard, Jr. 1951- *WhoAmL 92, WhoFI 92*
**Clark,** William J 1923- *WhoIns 92*
**Clark,** William James 1923- *WhoFI 92*
**Clark,** William Jesse 1923- *AmMWSc 92*
**Clark,** William Kemp 1925- *AmMWSc 92*
**Clark,** William Lee 1950- *WhoMW 92*
**Clark,** William Melvin, Jr 1922- *AmMWSc 92*
**Clark,** William Merle, Jr 1937- *AmMWSc 92*
**Clark,** William Noble 1921- *WhoAmP 91*
**Clark,** William Northington 1941- *WhoAmL 92*
**Clark,** William P. 1931- *IntWW 91, Who 92*
**Clark,** William R 1938- *AmMWSc 92*
**Clark,** William Richard 1949- *AmMWSc 92*
**Clark,** William Robert, Jr. 1951- *WhoAmL 92*
**Clark,** William Smith 1826-1886 *BiInAmS*
**Clark,** Willis Gaylord 1808-1841 *BenetAL 91*
**Clark,** Winston Craig 1949- *AmMWSc 92*
**Clark,** Worley H., Jr. 1932- *WhoMW 92*
**Clark,** Xenos 1853-1889 *BiInAmS*
**Clark-Cole,** Brian Howard 1956- *WhoAmL 92*
**Clark-Eddington,** Paul *Who 92*
**Clark-Gates,** Brenda *WhoBlA 92*
**Clark Hutchison** *Who 92*
**Clark-Kennedy,** A. E. *ConAu 134*
**Clark-Kennedy,** Archibald Edmund 1893-1985 *ConAu 134*
**Clark of Herriotshall,** Arthur Melville 1895- *IntAu&W 91*
**Clark-Thomas,** Eleanor M. 1938- *WhoBlA 92*
**Clarke,** Aidan 1933- *IntWW 91*
**Clarke,** Alan 1935-1990 *AnObit 1990*
**Clarke,** Alan Douglas Benson 1922- *Who 92*
**Clarke,** Alan R 1938- *AmMWSc 92*
**Clarke,** Alexander Mallory 1936- *AmMWSc 92*
**Clarke,** Allan James 1949- *AmMWSc 92*
**Clarke,** Allen *Who 92*
**Clarke,** Allen Bruce 1927- *AmMWSc 92*
**Clarke,** Allen Richard 1957- *WhoAmL 92*
**Clarke,** Alyce Griffin *WhoAmP 91*
**Clarke,** Alyce Griffin 1939- *WhoBlA 92*
**Clarke,** Angela Webb 1932- *WhoBlA 92*
**Clarke,** Ann Neistadt 1946- *AmMWSc 92*
**Clarke,** Anna 1919- *IntAu&W 91, WrDr 92*
**Clarke,** Anthony John 1955- *AmMWSc 92*
**Clarke,** Anthony Peter 1943- *Who 92*
**Clarke,** Arther C 1917- *IntAu&W 91*
**Clarke,** Arthur C. 1917- *ConNov 91, FacFETw, LiExTwC, TwCSFW 91, WrDr 92*
**Clarke,** Arthur Charles 1917- *IntWW 91, Who 92*
**Clarke,** Arthur Grenfell 1906- *Who 92*
**Clarke,** Arthur S. 1923- *Who 92*
**Clarke,** Ashley *Who 92*
**Clarke,** Austin 1896-1974 *FacFETw, RfGEnL 91*
**Clarke,** Austin 1934- *BlkLC [port]*
**Clarke,** Austin Ardinel Chesterfield 1934- *IntAu&W 91*
**Clarke,** Austin C. 1934- *BenetAL 91, ConNov 91, LiExTwC, WrDr 92*
**Clarke,** Benjamin Franklin 1831-1908 *BiInAmS*
**Clarke,** Benjamin L *AmMWSc 92*
**Clarke,** Benjamin Louis 1944- *WhoBlA 92*
**Clarke,** Bernard *Who 92*
**Clarke,** Bobby 1949- *WhoMW 92*
**Clarke,** Brenda 1926- *IntAu&W 91, WrDr 92*
**Clarke,** Brian 1953- *IntWW 91, TwCPaSc*
**Clarke,** Bruce Leslie 1942- *AmMWSc 92*
**Clarke,** Bryan Campbell 1932- *IntWW 91, Who 92*
**Clarke,** C J *WhoIns 92*
**Clarke,** C Langton 1857-1936 *ScFEYrs*
**Clarke,** Carolyn Carpenter 1937- *WhoRel 92*
**Clarke,** Catherine Therese 1960- *WhoAmL 92*
**Clarke,** Charles Fenton 1916- *WhoAmL 92*
**Clarke,** Charles Mansfield Tobias 1939- *Who 92*
**Clarke,** Charles Patrick 1948- *WhoWest 92*
**Clarke,** Cheryl *DrAPF 91*
**Clarke,** Christopher Michael 1952- *Who 92*
**Clarke,** Christopher Simon Courtenay S 1947- *Who 92*
**Clarke,** Clifford Montreville 1925- *WhoFI 92*
**Clarke,** Cora Huidekoper 1851-1916 *BiInAmS*
**Clarke,** Cyril 1907- *WrDr 92*
**Clarke,** Cyril Alfred Allen 1910- *Who 92*
**Clarke,** Cyril Astley 1907- *FacFETw, IntWW 91, Who 92*
**Clarke,** David A 1943- *WhoAmP 91*
**Clarke,** David Beach 1947- *WhoAmL 92*
**Clarke,** David Clive 1942- *Who 92*
**Clarke,** David E *AmMWSc 92*
**Clarke,** David H. 1941- *WhoFI 92*
**Clarke,** David Harrison 1930- *AmMWSc 92*
**Clarke,** David Stuart 1942- *Who 92*
**Clarke,** David William 1948- *WhoFI 92*
**Clarke,** Denis 1952- *TwCPaSc*
**Clarke,** Derrick Harry 1919- *WrDr 92*
**Clarke,** Dini Vernon 1923- *WhoEnt 92*
**Clarke,** Donald Dudley 1930- *AmMWSc 92, WhoBlA 92*
**Clarke,** Donald Harrison, Jr. 1949- *WhoAmL 92*
**Clarke,** Donald Roberts 1933- *Who 92*
**Clarke,** Dorothy Clotelle 1908- *WrDr 92*
**Clarke,** Dorothy Hoff 1943- *WhoAmL 92*
**Clarke,** Duane Grookett 1918- *AmMWSc 92*
**Clarke,** Edith 1883-1959 *FacFETw*
**Clarke,** Edward Nielsen 1925- *AmMWSc 92*
**Clarke,** Edward Owen, Jr. 1929- *WhoAmL 92*
**Clarke,** Edwin Kent *Who 92*
**Clarke,** Edwin Kent 1932- *WhoRel 92*
**Clarke,** Edwin Richards, III 1946- *WhoMW 92*
**Clarke,** Edwin Sisterson 1919- *IntWW 91, Who 92*
**Clarke,** Eleanora Norwood 1927- *WhoBlA 92*
**Clarke,** Elijah 1733-1799 *DcNCBi 1*
**Clarke,** Elizabeth Bleckly 1915- *Who 92*
**Clarke,** Ellis 1917- *Who 92*
**Clarke,** Ellis Emmanuel Innocent 1917- *IntWW 91*
**Clarke,** Errol Moncrieffe 1953- *WhoFI 92*
**Clarke,** Eugene H., Jr. 1920- *WhoBlA 92*
**Clarke,** Everee Jimerson 1926- *WhoBlA 92*
**Clarke,** Fletcher James 1942- *WhoBlA 92*
**Clarke,** Francis 1945- *AmMWSc 92*
**Clarke,** Francis Devereux 1849-1913 *DcNCBi 1*
**Clarke,** Francis H *ScFEYrs*
**Clarke,** Frank 1921- *WhoWest 92*
**Clarke,** Frank Eldridge 1913- *AmMWSc 92*
**Clarke,** Frank Henderson 1927- *AmMWSc 92*
**Clarke,** Frederic B, III 1942- *AmMWSc 92*
**Clarke,** Frederick 1928- *Who 92*
**Clarke,** Frederick James 1915- *AmMWSc 92*
**Clarke,** Garry K C 1941- *AmMWSc 92*
**Clarke,** Gary Anthony 1946- *AmMWSc 92*
**Clarke,** Geoffrey 1924- *IntWW 91, TwCPaSc, Who 92*
**Clarke,** George 1915- *AmMWSc 92*
**Clarke,** George A 1933- *AmMWSc 92*
**Clarke,** George Arthur 1918- *WhoAmL 92*
**Clarke,** George Herbert 1873-1953 *BenetAL 91*
**Clarke,** Gillian 1937- *ConPo 91, WrDr 92*
**Clarke,** Gordon 1931- *WhoRel 92*
**Clarke,** Graeme Wilber 1934- *IntWW 91*
**Clarke,** Graham Neil 1956- *Who 92*
**Clarke,** Gregory Ray 1942- *WhoWest 92*
**Clarke,** Greta Fields *WhoBlA 92*
**Clarke,** Guy Hamilton 1910- *Who 92*
**Clarke,** H Harrison 1902- *IntAu&W 91, WrDr 92*
**Clarke,** Hansen 1957- *WhoAmP 91*
**Clarke,** Harold G, Jr 1927- *WhoAmP 91*

**Clarke,** Harold Gravely 1927- *WhoAmL 92*
**Clarke,** Helen 1939- *Who 92*
**Clarke,** Henry Ashley 1903- *IntWW 91, Who 92*
**Clarke,** Henry Benwell 1950- *Who 92*
**Clarke,** Henry Leland 1907- *NewAmDM, WhoEnt 92*
**Clarke,** Henry Louis 1908- *WhoBlA 92*
**Clarke,** Hilton Swift 1909- *Who 92*
**Clarke,** Hugh Vincent 1919- *IntAu&W 91, WrDr 92*
**Clarke,** Irene Fortune Irwin 1903- *IntWW 91*
**Clarke,** J. Calvitt, Jr. 1920- *WhoAmL 92*
**Clarke,** Jack Frederick 1936- *WhoWest 92*
**Clarke,** James 1927- *AmMWSc 92*
**Clarke,** James Alexander 1924- *WhoBlA 92*
**Clarke,** James Freeman 1810-1888 *BenetAL 91, RelLAm 91*
**Clarke,** James Harold 1945- *AmMWSc 92*
**Clarke,** James McClure 1917- *WhoAmP 91*
**Clarke,** James Newton 1948- *AmMWSc 92*
**Clarke,** James Samuel 1921- *Who 92*
**Clarke,** Jeff 1935- *TwCPaSc*
**Clarke,** Jennifer Ann 1959- *WhoMW 92*
**Clarke,** Jeremiah 1674?-1707 *NewAmDM*
**Clarke,** Joan L. 1920- *WrDr 92*
**Clarke,** Joan Lorraine 1920- *IntAu&W 91*
**Clarke,** John *DrAPF 91*
**Clarke,** John 1609-1676 *BenetAL 91*
**Clarke,** John 1942- *AmMWSc 92, IntWW 91, Who 92*
**Clarke,** John Bernard 1934- *Who 92*
**Clarke,** John F 1939- *AmMWSc 92*
**Clarke,** John Frederick 1927- *Who 92*
**Clarke,** John Frederick Gates 1905- *AmMWSc 92*
**Clarke,** John Frederick Gates, Jr 1933- *AmMWSc 92*
**Clarke,** John H 1857-1945 *FacFETw*
**Clarke,** John Henrik 1915- *WhoBlA 92*
**Clarke,** John Hessin 1857-1945 *AmPeW*
**Clarke,** John Innes 1929- *Who 92*
**Clarke,** John Kevin Aloysius 1931- *IntWW 91*
**Clarke,** John Mills 1949- *AmMWSc 92*
**Clarke,** John Neil 1934- *IntWW 91, Who 92*
**Clarke,** John Patrick 1930- *WhoMW 92*
**Clarke,** John Ross 1941- *AmMWSc 92*
**Clarke,** John Terrel 1952- *WhoMW 92*
**Clarke,** Jonathan 1930- *Who 92*
**Clarke,** Joseph H 1927- *AmMWSc 92*
**Clarke,** Joseph Lance 1941- *WhoBlA 92*
**Clarke,** Joy Adele 1937- *WhoBlA 92*
**Clarke,** Kenneth 1940- *Who 92*
**Clarke,** Kenneth Harry 1940- *IntWW 91*
**Clarke,** Kenneth Kingsley 1924- *AmMWSc 92, WhoFI 92*
**Clarke,** Kenny 1914-1985 *FacFETw, NewAmDM*
**Clarke,** Kim Annette 1954- *WhoEnt 92*
**Clarke,** Laurie 1934- *IntMPA 92*
**Clarke,** Leon Edison 1949- *WhoBlA 92*
**Clarke,** LeRoy P. 1938- *WhoBlA 92*
**Clarke,** Lilian A 1915- *AmMWSc 92*
**Clarke,** Linda Dumas 1944- *WhoAmP 91*
**Clarke,** Lindsay *IntAu&W 91*
**Clarke,** Lindsay 1939- *WrDr 92*
**Clarke,** Lori A 1947- *AmMWSc 92*
**Clarke,** Lucien Gill 1921- *AmMWSc 92*
**Clarke,** MacDonald 1798-1842 *BenetAL 91*
**Clarke,** Malcolm *WhoEnt 92*
**Clarke,** Malcolm Roy 1930- *IntWW 91, Who 92*
**Clarke,** Marcus 1846-1881 *RfGEnL 91*
**Clarke,** Margaret Burnett *AmMWSc 92*
**Clarke,** Marshal Butler C. *Who 92*
**Clarke,** Martha 1944- *WhoEnt 92*
**Clarke,** Martin Lowther 1909- *Who 92, WrDr 92*
**Clarke,** Mary 1923- *IntAu&W 91, Who 92, WrDr 92*
**Clarke,** Mary Bayard Devereux 1827-1886 *DcNCBi 1*
**Clarke,** Mary Stetson 1911- *WrDr 92*
**Clarke,** Matthew Gerard *Who 92*
**Clarke,** Mercer Kaye 1944- *WhoAmL 92*
**Clarke,** Michael F 1942- *WhoIns 92*
**Clarke,** Michael Gilbert 1944- *Who 92*
**Clarke,** Michael J 1946- *AmMWSc 92*
**Clarke,** Milton Charles 1929- *WhoAmL 92*
**Clarke,** Neil *Who 92*
**Clarke,** Neil 1937- *WhoAmP 91*
**Clarke,** Norman 1916- *Who 92*
**Clarke,** Norman Eley 1930- *Who 92*
**Clarke,** Norman Ellsworth, III 1953- *WhoMW 92*
**Clarke,** Oscar Withers 1919- *WhoMW 92*
**Clarke,** P Joseph 1933- *WhoAmP 91*
**Clarke,** Pamela Jones 1945- *WhoFI 92*
**Clarke,** Pat 1940- *TwCPaSc*
**Clarke,** Patricia Hannah 1919- *IntWW 91, Who 92*
**Clarke,** Pauline *IntAu&W 91X*
**Clarke,** Pauline 1921- *WrDr 92*
**Clarke,** Percy *ScFEYrs*
**Clarke,** Peter 1922- *Who 92*
**Clarke,** Peter 1936- *WhoWest 92*
**Clarke,** Peter 1951- *TwCPaSc*
**Clarke,** Peter Cecil 1927- *Who 92*
**Clarke,** Peter Frederick 1942- *Who 92, WrDr 92*
**Clarke,** Peter James 1934- *Who 92*
**Clarke,** Priscilla 1960- *WhoBlA 92*
**Clarke,** Raymond 1950- *WhoBlA 92*
**Clarke,** Raymond Dennis 1946- *AmMWSc 92*
**Clarke,** Raymonde Alexis 1926- *WhoAmL 92*
**Clarke,** Richard *TwCWW 91*
**Clarke,** Richard Alan 1930- *WhoFI 92, WhoWest 92*
**Clarke,** Richard Penfield 1919- *AmMWSc 92*
**Clarke,** Richard V. 1927- *WhoBlA 92*
**Clarke,** Rita-Lou 1934- *WhoRel 92*
**Clarke,** Robert C. 1929- *IntWW 91*
**Clarke,** Robert Cyril 1929- *Who 92*
**Clarke,** Robert Earle 1949- *WhoMW 92*
**Clarke,** Robert Emmett 1906- *WhoWest 92*
**Clarke,** Robert Francis 1919- *AmMWSc 92*
**Clarke,** Robert LaGrone 1917- *AmMWSc 92*
**Clarke,** Robert Lee 1922- *AmMWSc 92*
**Clarke,** Robert Logan 1942- *WhoAmP 91, WhoFI 92*
**Clarke,** Robert Sydney 1935- *Who 92*
**Clarke,** Robert Travis 1937- *AmMWSc 92*
**Clarke,** Robin Mitchell 1917- *Who 92*
**Clarke,** Rockne Wayne 1949- *WhoAmP 91*
**Clarke,** Roger Eric 1939- *Who 92*
**Clarke,** Roger Howard 1943- *Who 92*
**Clarke,** Ronald 1941- *IntAu&W 91*
**Clarke,** Roy 1947- *AmMWSc 92*
**Clarke,** Roy Slayton, Jr 1925- *AmMWSc 92*
**Clarke,** Rupert William John 1919- *Who 92*
**Clarke,** Samuel 1675-1729 *BlkwCEP*
**Clarke,** Samuel Harrison 1903- *Who 92*
**Clarke,** Samuel Laurence Harrison 1929- *Who 92*
**Clarke,** Shirley 1925- *IntDcF 2-2, ReelWom [port]*
**Clarke,** Stanley George 1914- *Who 92*
**Clarke,** Stanley Marvin 1951- *WhoBlA 92*
**Clarke,** Stella Rosemary 1932- *Who 92*
**Clarke,** Stephen Emil 1955- *WhoFI 92*
**Clarke,** Steven Donald 1948- *AmMWSc 92*
**Clarke,** Steven Gerard 1949- *AmMWSc 92*
**Clarke,** T E B 1907-1989 *FacFETw*
**Clarke,** Terence Hugh 1904- *Who 92*
**Clarke,** Terence Michael 1937- *WhoFI 92*
**Clarke,** Theodore Henson 1923- *WhoBlA 92*
**Clarke,** Thomas 1941- *Who 92*
**Clarke,** Thomas Arthur 1940- *AmMWSc 92*
**Clarke,** Thomas Crawford 1932- *WhoFI 92*
**Clarke,** Thomas Curtis 1827-1901 *BiInAmS*
**Clarke,** Thomas Ernest Bennett 1907- *IntAu&W 91*
**Clarke,** Thomas Lowe 1948- *AmMWSc 92*
**Clarke,** Thomas P. 1917- *WhoBlA 92*
**Clarke,** Thomas Roy 1940- *AmMWSc 92*
**Clarke,** Tobias *Who 92*
**Clarke,** Tom 1918- *Who 92*
**Clarke,** Urana 1902- *WhoWest 92*
**Clarke,** Vaughn Anthony 1953- *WhoFI 92*
**Clarke,** Velma Greene 1930- *WhoBlA 92*
**Clarke,** W T W 1920- *AmMWSc 92*
**Clarke,** Wilbur Bancroft 1929- *AmMWSc 92*
**Clarke,** William Decker 1925- *WhoBlA 92*
**Clarke,** William J 1937- *WhoIns 92*
**Clarke,** William John 1819-1886 *DcNCBi 1*
**Clarke,** William M 1922- *ConAu 34NR*
**Clarke,** William Malpas 1922- *Who 92*
**Clarke,** William Newton 1841-1912 *RelLAm 91*
**Clarke,** Wilton E L 1942- *AmMWSc 92*
**Clarke Hall,** Denis 1910- *Who 92*
**Clarke-Hall,** Edna 1879-1979 *TwCPaSc*
**Clarke-Smith,** Q. H. 1963- *WhoEnt 92*
**Clarkin,** John Francis 1936- *WhoFI 92*
**Clarkson,** Alan Geoffrey 1934- *Who 92*
**Clarkson,** Allen Boykin, Jr 1943- *AmMWSc 92*
**Clarkson,** Andrew MacBeth 1937- *WhoFI 92*
**Clarkson,** Barbara Moore *DrAPF 91*
**Clarkson,** Bayard D 1926- *AmMWSc 92*
**Clarkson,** Brian Leonard 1930- *Who 92*
**Clarkson,** C Jack 1930- *WhoAmP 91*
**Clarkson,** David M 1927- *WhoAmP 91*
**Clarkson,** Derek Joshua 1929- *Who 92*
**Clarkson,** E. Margaret 1915- *WrDr 92*
**Clarkson,** Ewan 1929- *IntAu&W 91, WrDr 92*
**Clarkson,** Geoffrey Peniston Elliott 1934- *Who 92*
**Clarkson,** Gerald Dawson 1939- *Who 92*
**Clarkson,** Helen *IntAu&W 91X, WrDr 92*
**Clarkson,** Heriot 1863-1942 *DcNCBi 1*
**Clarkson,** J F *IntAu&W 91X, WrDr 92*
**Clarkson,** Jack 1906-1986 *TwCPaSc*
**Clarkson,** Jack E 1936- *AmMWSc 92*
**Clarkson,** Kenneth Wright 1942- *WhoFI 92*
**Clarkson,** Lawrence William 1938- *WhoWest 92*
**Clarkson,** Mark H 1917- *AmMWSc 92*
**Clarkson,** Ormand *TwCWW 91*
**Clarkson,** Pamela 1946- *TwCPaSc*
**Clarkson,** Patrick Robert James 1949- *Who 92*
**Clarkson,** Paul R 1935- *WhoIns 92*
**Clarkson,** Paul Sumpter 1928- *WhoAmP 91*
**Clarkson,** Peter David 1945- *Who 92*
**Clarkson,** Robert Breck 1943- *AmMWSc 92*
**Clarkson,** Roy Burdette 1926- *AmMWSc 92*
**Clarkson,** Ted Hamby 1958- *WhoAmL 92*
**Clarkson,** Thomas Boston 1931- *AmMWSc 92*
**Clarkson,** Thomas William 1932- *AmMWSc 92, IntWW 91*
**Clarkson,** William Morris 1954- *WhoMW 92*
**Clarno,** Beverly A 1936- *WhoAmP 91*
**Clarren,** Sterling Keith 1947- *WhoWest 92*
**Clarricoats,** Peter John Bell 1932- *Who 92*
**Clary,** Alexia Barbara 1954- *WhoFI 92*
**Clary,** Bobby Leland 1938- *AmMWSc 92*
**Clary,** Bradley Grayson 1950- *WhoAmL 92*
**Clary,** Bruce Maxfield 1939- *WhoRel 92*
**Clary,** Glenn Warren 1955- *WhoAmP 91*
**Clary,** John d1825 *DcNCBi 1*
**Clary,** John Quinn, Jr. 1946- *WhoFI 92*
**Clary,** Keith Uhl 1921- *WhoMW 92*
**Clary,** Richard Wayland 1953- *WhoAmL 92*
**Clary,** Robert 1926- *WhoEnt 92*
**Clary,** Ronald Gordon 1940- *WhoFI 92*
**Clary,** Rosalie Brandon Stanton 1928- *WhoFI 92, WhoMW 92*
**Clary,** Sydney Ann 1948- *IntAu&W 91*
**Clary,** Warren Powell 1936- *AmMWSc 92, WhoWest 92*
**Clary,** William Victor 1946- *WhoRel 92*
**Clase,** Howard John 1938- *AmMWSc 92*
**Clasen,** George Henry 1916- *WhoAmP 91*
**Clasen,** Raymond Adolph 1926- *AmMWSc 92*
**Clash,** The *NewAmDM*
**Claspill,** James Louis 1946- *WhoFI 92, WhoMW 92*
**Class,** Calvin Miller 1924- *AmMWSc 92*
**Class,** Heinrich 1868-1953 *BiDExR, EncTR 91*
**Class,** Jay Bernard 1928- *AmMWSc 92*
**Class,** Loretta Mina 1913- *WhoAmP 91*
**Class-Rivera,** Ana Nydia 1951- *WhoHisp 92*
**Classen,** Henry Ward 1959- *WhoAmL 92*
**Classen,** James Stark 1935- *WhoFI 92*
**Clator,** Irvin Garrett 1941- *AmMWSc 92*
**Clatsoff,** William Adam 1940- *WhoFI 92*
**Clatterbaugh,** Barbara Ann 1944- *WhoAmP 91*
**Clatworthy,** Robert 1928- *IntWW 91, TwCPaSc, Who 92*
**Clatworthy,** Willard Hubert 1915- *AmMWSc 92*
**Clauberg,** Carl 1898-1957 *EncTR 91 [port]*
**Claude de Sermisy** *NewAmDM*
**Claude,** Albert 1898- *FacFETw*
**Claude,** Albert 1898-1983 *WhoNob 90*
**Claude,** Georges 1870-1960 *FacFETw*
**Claude,** Philippa 1936- *AmMWSc 92*
**Claude,** Richard Pierre 1934- *IntAu&W 91, WrDr 92*
**Claudel,** Paul 1868-1955 *GuFrLit 1*
**Claudel,** Paul 1888-1955 *FacFETw*
**Claudia Quintas** *EncAmaz 91*
**Claudianus Mamertus** 425?-474 *EncEarC*
**Claudio,** Pete 1956- *WhoHisp 92*
**Claudio-Homs,** Rafael 1945- *WhoFI 92*
**Claudius** 10BC-54AD *EncEarC*
**Claudius Claudianus** d404? *EncEarC*
**Claudius,** Hermann 1898-1980 *EncTR 91*
**Claudon,** Jean-Louis Rene 1950- *WhoFI 92*
**Claudson,** T T 1933- *AmMWSc 92*
**Clauer,** Allan Henry 1936- *AmMWSc 92*
**Clauer,** C Robert, Jr 1948- *AmMWSc 92*
**Claughton,** Richard *AmPeW*
**Claus,** Alfons Jozef 1932- *AmMWSc 92*
**Claus,** Clyde Robert 1931- *WhoFI 92*
**Claus,** Gary Robert 1952- *WhoFI 92*
**Claus,** George William 1936- *AmMWSc 92*
**Claus,** Richard Otto 1951- *AmMWSc 92*
**Claus,** Thomas Harrison 1943- *AmMWSc 92*
**Claus-Walker,** Jacqueline Lucy 1915- *AmMWSc 92*
**Clausel,** Nancy Karen 1948- *WhoRel 92, WhoWest 92*
**Clausen,** Alden Winship 1923- *IntWW 91, Who 92, WhoWest 92*
**Clausen,** Alf Heiberg 1941- *WhoEnt 92*
**Clausen,** Bret Mark 1958- *WhoWest 92*
**Clausen,** Chris Anthony 1940- *AmMWSc 92*
**Clausen,** Don H 1923- *WhoAmP 91*
**Clausen,** Edgar Clemens 1951- *AmMWSc 92*
**Clausen,** Eric Neil 1943- *AmMWSc 92*
**Clausen,** Fritz 1893-1947 *BiDExR*
**Clausen,** George 1852-1944 *TwCPaSc*
**Clausen,** Hans Peter 1928- *IntWW 91*
**Clausen,** J Earl 1873-1937 *ScFEYrs*
**Clausen,** Jan *DrAPF 91*
**Clausen,** John A. 1914- *IntWW 91*
**Clausen,** Peter A d1991 *NewYTBS 91*
**Clausen,** Thomas G *WhoAmP 91*
**Clausen,** William E 1938- *AmMWSc 92*
**Clauser,** Donald Roberdeau 1941- *WhoEnt 92*
**Clauser,** Francis Hettinger 1913- *AmMWSc 92*
**Clauser,** John Anthony 1938- *WhoEnt 92*
**Clauser,** John Francis 1942- *AmMWSc 92*
**Clauser,** Milton John 1940- *AmMWSc 92*
**Clauser,** Suzanne Phillips 1929- *WhoEnt 92*
**Clausing,** A M 1936- *AmMWSc 92*
**Clausing,** Arthur M. 1936- *WhoMW 92*
**Clausing,** John Maurice 1934- *WhoRel 92*
**Clausnitzer,** Dale A 1951- *WhoAmP 91*
**Clauson,** Peter A 1955- *WhoIns 92*
**Clauson,** Sharyn Ferne 1946- *WhoFI 92*
**Clauson,** W W 1926- *AmMWSc 92*
**Clauss,** Charles J 1925- *WhoIns 92*
**Clauss,** Eliot Reid 1952- *WhoAmL 92*
**Clauss,** Ludwig Ferdinand 1892-1974 *EncTR 91*
**Clauss,** Peter Otto 1936- *WhoAmL 92*
**Clauss,** Roy H 1923- *AmMWSc 92*
**Claussen,** Bonnie Addison, II 1942- *WhoWest 92*
**Claussen,** Dane Sherman 1963- *WhoMW 92*
**Claussen,** Dennis Lee 1941- *AmMWSc 92*
**Claussen,** Howard Boyd 1946- *WhoFI 92*
**Claussen,** Karen *DrAPF 91*
**Claussen,** Mark J 1952- *AmMWSc 92*
**Claussen,** Ronald Vernon 1938- *WhoWest 92*
**Claussen,** Russell George 1934- *WhoRel 92*
**Clausz,** John Clay 1940- *AmMWSc 92*
**Clavan,** Walter 1921- *AmMWSc 92*
**Clave,** Antoni 1913- *IntWW 91*
**Claveau,** Rosario 1924- *AmMWSc 92*
**Clavel,** Bernard 1923- *IntWW 91*
**Clavell,** James *IntAu&W 91, Who 92*
**Clavell,** James 1924- *IntWW 91, WhoEnt 92, WrDr 92*
**Clavell,** James 1925- *ConNov 91*
**Clavenna,** LeRoy Russell 1943- *AmMWSc 92*
**Claver,** Pedro 1580-1654 *HisDSpE*
**Claver,** Robert Earl 1928- *WhoEnt 92*
**Claveria,** Ramon Cayetano 1942- *WhoEnt 92*
**Claverie,** Melvin Juice 1960- *WhoEnt 92*
**Clavers,** Mary *BenetAL 91*
**Clavier,** Anthony Forbes Moreton 1940- *RelLAm 91*
**Clavijero,** Francisco Javier 1731-1787 *HisDSpE*
**Clawges,** Russell Maxwell, Jr. 1950- *WhoAmL 92*
**Clawson,** Albert J 1924- *AmMWSc 92*
**Clawson,** Arthur Emory 1953- *WhoRel 92*
**Clawson,** Candace Lee 1961- *WhoMW 92*
**Clawson,** David Kay 1927- *AmMWSc 92*
**Clawson,** Delwin Morgan 1914- *WhoAmP 91*
**Clawson,** Florence Elizabeth 1921- *WhoAmP 91*
**Clawson,** Harry Quintard Moore 1924- *WhoFI 92*
**Clawson,** John Thomas 1945- *WhoAmP 91*
**Clawson,** Kim Roger 1953- *WhoMW 92*
**Clawson,** Michael Scott 1958- *WhoAmL 92*
**Clawson,** Raymond Walden 1906- *WhoFI 92, WhoWest 92*
**Clawson,** Robert Charles 1929- *AmMWSc 92*
**Clawson,** Rodger Vernon 1944- *WhoEnt 92*
**Clax,** Freda Marie 1959- *WhoEnt 92*
**Claxton,** Charles Robert 1903- *Who 92*
**Claxton,** Edward Burton, III 1956- *WhoAmL 92*
**Claxton,** John Francis d1991 *Who 92N*
**Claxton,** Larry Davis 1946- *AmMWSc 92*

**Claxton**, Patrick Fisher 1915- *Who 92*
**Claxton**, Philander Priestley 1862-1957 *DcNCBi 1*
**Claxton**, Richard Allen 1931- *WhoAmL 92*
**Clay**, Alberta Z *WhoAmP 91*
**Clay**, Alison *TwCWW 91*
**Clay**, Andrew Dice 1958- *News 91 [port]*
**Clay**, Bill, Jr 1956- *WhoAmP 91*
**Clay**, Camille Alfreda 1946- *WhoBlA 92*
**Clay**, Cassius *RComAH*
**Clay**, Cassius Marcellus 1942- *WhoBlA 92*
**Clay**, Charles Commander *WhoAmP 91*
**Clay**, Charles Kenneth 1964- *WhoFI 92*
**Clay**, Clarence Samuel 1923- *AmMWSc 92*
**Clay**, Cliff *WhoBlA 92*
**Clay**, Donald Owen, Jr. 1959- *WhoRel 92*
**Clay**, Emery Donald, III 1959- *WhoWest 92*
**Clay**, Eric Lee 1948- *WhoBlA 92*
**Clay**, Forrest Pierce, Jr 1927- *AmMWSc 92*
**Clay**, George A 1938- *AmMWSc 92*
**Clay**, George H 1941- *WhoAmP 91*
**Clay**, George R. *DrAPF 91*
**Clay**, H P *ScFEYrs*
**Clay**, Harold R. 1936- *WhoBlA 92*
**Clay**, Harris Aubrey 1911- *WhoFI 92*
**Clay**, Henry 1777-1852 *AmPolLe [port], BenetAL 91, RComAH*
**Clay**, Henry Carroll, Jr. 1928- *WhoBlA 92*
**Clay**, Henry Jones 1915- *WhoAmL 92*
**Clay**, James Andrew 1947- *WhoMW 92*
**Clay**, James Franklin 1911- *WhoAmL 92*
**Clay**, James Jordan, Jr. 1962- *WhoMW 92*
**Clay**, James Ray 1938- *AmMWSc 92*
**Clay**, Jasper R. 1933- *WhoAmL 92*
**Clay**, John Ernest 1921- *WhoAmL 92*
**Clay**, John Lionel 1918- *Who 92*
**Clay**, John Martin 1927- *IntWW 91, Who 92*
**Clay**, John Paul 1910- *AmMWSc 92*
**Clay**, Lucius D 1897-1978 *FacFETw*
**Clay**, Marie 1926- *Who 92*
**Clay**, Mary Ellen 1940- *AmMWSc 92*
**Clay**, Michael M 1920- *AmMWSc 92*
**Clay**, Michelle Catherine 1958- *WhoAmL 92*
**Clay**, Nathaniel, Jr. 1943- *WhoBlA 92*
**Clay**, Nicholas 1946- *WhoEnt 92*
**Clay**, Orson C. 1930- *WhoFI 92, WhoIns 92*
**Clay**, Philip G 1952- *WhoIns 92*
**Clay**, Reuben Anderson, Jr. 1938- *WhoBlA 92*
**Clay**, Richard 1940- *Who 92*
**Clay**, Robert Alan 1946- *Who 92*
**Clay**, Ross Collins 1908- *WhoBlA 92*
**Clay**, Rudolph 1935- *WhoBlA 92*
**Clay**, Stanley Bennett 1950- *WhoBlA 92*
**Clay**, Theodore Roosevelt, Jr. 1931- *WhoBlA 92*
**Clay**, Timothy Byron 1955- *WhoBlA 92*
**Clay**, Trevor 1936- *Who 92*
**Clay**, William 1931- *AlmAP 92 [port]*
**Clay**, William A. L. 1899- *WhoBlA 92*
**Clay**, William L. 1931- *WhoBlA 92*
**Clay**, William Lacy 1931- *WhoAmP 91, WhoMW 92*
**Clay**, William Lacy, Jr. 1956- *WhoBlA 92*
**Clay**, William Robert 1932- *WhoFI 92*
**Clay**, William Roger 1919- *WhoBlA 92*
**Clay**, Willie B. 1929- *WhoBlA 92*
**Claybaker**, Beth 1930- *WhoAmP 91*
**Claybaker**, Paul Mark 1962- *WhoMW 92*
**Claybaugh**, Glenn Alan 1927- *AmMWSc 92*
**Claybaugh**, William Robert, II 1949- *WhoWest 92*
**Clayberg**, Carl Dudley 1931- *AmMWSc 92*
**Clayborn**, Ray Dewayne 1955- *WhoBlA 92*
**Clayborn**, Wilma W. *WhoBlA 92*
**Clayborne**, Oneal 1940- *WhoAmP 91, WhoBlA 92*
**Claybourn**, Colleen Talmadge 1934- *WhoRel 92*
**Claybourne**, Doug 1947- *IntMPA 92*
**Claybourne**, Edward P. 1927- *WhoBlA 92*
**Claybrook**, James Russell 1936- *AmMWSc 92*
**Clayburgh**, Bennie James 1924- *WhoAmP 91*
**Clayburgh**, Jill 1944- *IntMPA 92, IntWW 91, WhoEnt 92*
**Clayburgh**, Richard Scott *WhoAmP 91*
**Claycomb**, Cecil Keith 1920- *AmMWSc 92*
**Claycomb**, William Creighton 1942- *AmMWSc 92*
**Claydon**, Geoffrey Bernard 1930- *Who 92*
**Claye**, Charlene Marette 1945- *WhoBlA 92*
**Clayman**, Bruce Philip 1942- *AmMWSc 92*
**Clayman**, David 1933- *WhoRel 92*
**Clayman**, David 1934- *Who 92*
**Clayman**, Jacob d1991 *NewYTBS 91 [port]*
**Clayman**, Lewis 1947- *WhoMW 92*
**Clayman**, Michelle R. 1953- *WhoFI 92*
**Claypole**, Edith Jane 1870-1915 *BiInAmS*
**Claypole**, Edward Waller 1835-1901 *BiInAmS*
**Claypole**, Eugene 1938- *WhoAmP 91*
**Claypool**, George Edwin 1939- *AmMWSc 92*
**Claypool**, John Rowan, IV 1930- *WhoRel 92*
**Claypool**, Lawrence Leonard 1907- *AmMWSc 92*
**Claypool**, William, III *WhoMW 92*
**Claypool Miner**, Jane 1933- *IntAu&W 91*
**Claypoole**, Susan L. 1950- *WhoAmL 92*
**Clayson**, Christopher William 1903- *Who 92*
**Clayton**, Allen Lee 1951- *WhoRel 92*
**Clayton**, Anthony Broxholme 1940- *AmMWSc 92*
**Clayton**, Barbara 1922- *Who 92*
**Clayton**, Bernard Miles, Jr. 1953- *WhoFI 92*
**Clayton**, Billy Wayne 1928- *WhoAmP 91*
**Clayton**, Bruce David 1947- *WhoMW 92*
**Clayton**, Buck d1991 *NewYTBS 91 [port]*
**Clayton**, Buck 1911- *NewAmDM*
**Clayton**, Byron Cordell 1957- *WhoMW 92*
**Clayton**, C. Guy 1936- *WrDr 92*
**Clayton**, Charles M. 1889- *WhoBlA 92*
**Clayton**, Cheryl Ann 1949- *WhoEnt 92*
**Clayton**, Christopher John 1958- *WhoEnt 92*
**Clayton**, Claude Feemster, Jr 1948- *WhoAmP 91*
**Clayton**, Clive Robert 1949- *AmMWSc 92*
**Clayton**, Constance *WhoBlA 92*
**Clayton**, Constance 1927?- *ConBlB 1 [port]*
**Clayton**, Constance E *NewYTBS 91 [port]*
**Clayton**, Dale Leonard 1939- *AmMWSc 92*
**Clayton**, David 1936- *Who 92*
**Clayton**, David Walton *AmMWSc 92*
**Clayton**, Donald Delbert 1935- *AmMWSc 92*
**Clayton**, Eugene Duane 1923- *AmMWSc 92*
**Clayton**, Evelyn Williams 1951- *WhoFI 92*
**Clayton**, Frances Elizabeth 1922- *AmMWSc 92*
**Clayton**, Fred Ralph, Jr 1940- *AmMWSc 92*
**Clayton**, Frederick William 1913- *Who 92*
**Clayton**, Gareth 1914- *Who 92*
**Clayton**, Gary Paige 1947- *WhoWest 92*
**Clayton**, George 1922- *Who 92*
**Clayton**, Glen Talmadge 1929- *AmMWSc 92*
**Clayton**, Ina Smiley 1924- *WhoBlA 92*
**Clayton**, J T 1924- *AmMWSc 92*
**Clayton**, Jack 1921- *IntDcF 2-2 [port], IntMPA 92, IntWW 91, Who 92*
**Clayton**, James Henry 1944- *WhoBlA 92*
**Clayton**, James Wallace 1933- *AmMWSc 92*
**Clayton**, Janet Theresa 1955- *WhoBlA 92*
**Clayton**, Jay *DrAPF 91*
**Clayton**, Joe Edward 1932- *AmMWSc 92*
**Clayton**, John 1694-1773 *BiInAmS*
**Clayton**, John Charles 1924- *AmMWSc 92*
**Clayton**, John J. *DrAPF 91*
**Clayton**, John J. 1917- *WhoEnt 92*
**Clayton**, John Mark 1945- *AmMWSc 92*
**Clayton**, John Middleton 1796-1856 *AmPolLe*
**Clayton**, John Pilkington 1921- *Who 92*
**Clayton**, John Wesley, Jr 1924- *AmMWSc 92*
**Clayton**, Jonathan Alan 1937- *WhoFI 92*
**Clayton**, Kathleen R. 1952- *WhoBlA 92*
**Clayton**, Keith Martin 1928- *Who 92*
**Clayton**, Kelvin C. 1935- *WhoWest 92*
**Clayton**, Kirk Marshall 1947- *WhoWest 92*
**Clayton**, Laura Ancelina 1960- *WhoAmL 92, WhoBlA 92*
**Clayton**, Lawrence Dean 1957- *WhoWest 92*
**Clayton**, Lloyd E. 1921- *WhoBlA 92*
**Clayton**, Lucie *Who 92*
**Clayton**, Margaret Ann 1941- *Who 92*
**Clayton**, Mark Gregory 1961- *WhoBlA 92*
**Clayton**, Matthew Arthur 1958- *WhoEnt 92*
**Clayton**, Matthew D. 1941- *WhoBlA 92*
**Clayton**, Mayme Agnew 1923- *WhoBlA 92*
**Clayton**, Michael Aylwin 1934- *Who 92*
**Clayton**, Michael Thomas Emilius 1917- *Who 92*
**Clayton**, Minnie H. *WhoBlA 92*
**Clayton**, Neal 1913- *AmMWSc 92*
**Clayton**, Paula Jean 1934- *AmMWSc 92*
**Clayton**, Randy Joe 1954- *WhoFI 92*
**Clayton**, Raymond Brazenor 1925- *AmMWSc 92*
**Clayton**, Richard Henry Michael *IntAu&W 91*
**Clayton**, Richard Henry Michael 1907- *Who 92*
**Clayton**, Richard Reese 1938- *WhoFI 92*
**Clayton**, Robert 1915- *Who 92*
**Clayton**, Robert Allen 1922- *AmMWSc 92*
**Clayton**, Robert James 1915- *IntWW 91*
**Clayton**, Robert L. 1938- *WhoBlA 92*
**Clayton**, Robert Louis 1934- *WhoBlA 92*
**Clayton**, Robert Norman 1930- *AmMWSc 92, IntWW 91, Who 92*
**Clayton**, Roderick Keener 1922- *AmMWSc 92*
**Clayton**, Sally Lynn 1946- *WhoAmL 92*
**Clayton**, Stanley James 1919- *Who 92*
**Clayton**, Theaoseus T. 1930- *WhoBlA 92*
**Clayton**, William Alexander, Jr. 1946- *WhoWest 92*
**Clayton**, William Howard 1927- *AmMWSc 92*
**Clayton**, Willie Burke, Jr. 1922- *WhoBlA 92*
**Clayton**, Xernona 1930- *WhoBlA 92, WhoEnt 92*
**Clayton-Hill**, Kelli 1965- *WhoWest 92*
**Clayton-Hopkins**, Judith Ann 1939- *AmMWSc 92*
**Claytor**, Charles E. 1936- *WhoBlA 92*
**Claytor**, Thomas Nelson 1949- *AmMWSc 92*
**Claytor**, W Graham, Jr 1912- *WhoAmP 91*
**Claytor**, William Graham, Jr. 1912- *WhoFI 92*
**Clazie**, Ronald N 1938- *AmMWSc 92*
**Cleage**, Albert B., Jr. 1911- *WhoBlA 92*
**Cleall**, Charles 1927- *Who 92, WrDr 92*
**Cleall**, John Frederick 1934- *AmMWSc 92*
**Clear**, John Michael 1948- *WhoAmL 92, WhoMW 92*
**Cleare**, Henry Murray 1928- *AmMWSc 92*
**Cleare**, John S. 1936- *WrDr 92*
**Cleare**, John Silvey 1936- *IntAu&W 91*
**Clearfield**, Abraham 1927- *AmMWSc 92*
**Cleary**, Audrey *WhoAmP 91*
**Cleary**, Beverly 1916- *ConAu 36NR, WrDr 92*
**Cleary**, Beverly Atlee 1916- *IntAu&W 91*
**Cleary**, Christine 1948- *WhoAmL 92*
**Cleary**, David Laurence 1941- *WhoAmL 92*
**Cleary**, Denis Mackrow 1907- *Who 92*
**Cleary**, Edward Louis 1929- *WhoRel 92*
**Cleary**, Florence Damon 1896-1982 *ConAu 133*
**Cleary**, James Charles, Jr. 1921- *WhoEnt 92*
**Cleary**, James Joseph, Jr. 1949- *WhoAmL 92*
**Cleary**, James William 1926- *AmMWSc 92*
**Cleary**, Jon 1917- *ConNov 91, IntAu&W 91, WrDr 92*
**Cleary**, Jon Stephen 1917- *IntWW 91, Who 92*
**Cleary**, Joseph Francis d1991 *Who 92N*
**Cleary**, Joseph Jackson 1902- *Who 92*
**Cleary**, Lisa Elaine 1958- *WhoAmL 92*
**Cleary**, Margot Phoebe 1948- *AmMWSc 92*
**Cleary**, Martin Joseph 1935- *WhoFI 92*
**Cleary**, Michael 1950- *AmMWSc 92*
**Cleary**, Michael E 1947- *AmMWSc 92*
**Cleary**, Michael J. *WhoRel 92*
**Cleary**, Patricia Anne 1954- *WhoAmL 92*
**Cleary**, Patrick James 1929- *WhoAmP 91*
**Cleary**, Patrick John 1955- *WhoAmL 92*
**Cleary**, Paul Patrick 1941- *AmMWSc 92*
**Cleary**, Philip Edward 1947- *WhoAmL 92*
**Cleary**, Polly Chase *DrAPF 91*
**Cleary**, Raymond P. 1939- *WhoFI 92*
**Cleary**, Richard Simon 1956- *WhoAmL 92*
**Cleary**, Robert Emmet 1937- *WhoMW 92*
**Cleary**, Shirley Jean 1942- *WhoWest 92*
**Cleary**, Stephen Francis 1936- *AmMWSc 92*
**Cleary**, Suzanne *DrAPF 91*
**Cleary**, Theresa Anne 1935- *WhoMW 92*
**Cleary**, Timothy Finbar 1925- *WhoAmP 91*
**Cleary**, Timothy Joseph 1942- *AmMWSc 92*
**Cleary**, William James 1943- *AmMWSc 92*
**Cleary**, William Joseph, Jr. 1942- *WhoFI 92, WhoWest 92*
**Cleasby**, John Leroy 1928- *AmMWSc 92*
**Cleasby**, Thomas Wood Ingram 1920- *Who 92*
**Cleator**, Iain Morrison 1939- *AmMWSc 92*
**Cleave**, Robert Randall 1963- *WhoWest 92*
**Cleaveland**, Parker 1780-1858 *BiInAmS*
**Cleavelin**, Leonard Robert 1957- *WhoAmL 92, WhoMW 92*
**Cleaver**, A V d1977 *FacFETw*
**Cleaver**, Alan Richard 1952- *IntWW 91*
**Cleaver**, Anthony Brian 1938- *IntWW 91, Who 92*
**Cleaver**, Charles E 1938- *AmMWSc 92*
**Cleaver**, Eldridge 1935- *BenetAL 91, BlkLC [port], FacFETw, LiExTwC, WhoBlA 92, WrDr 92*
**Cleaver**, Emanuel, II *WhoMW 92*
**Cleaver**, Emanuel, II 1944- *WhoBlA 92*
**Cleaver**, Frank L 1925- *AmMWSc 92*
**Cleaver**, James 1911- *TwCPaSc*
**Cleaver**, James Edward 1938- *AmMWSc 92, WhoWest 92*
**Cleaver**, Leonard Harry 1909- *Who 92*
**Cleaver**, Lucy Templeton 1929- *WhoRel 92*
**Cleaver**, Peter 1919- *Who 92*
**Cleaver**, Vera 1919- *WrDr 92*
**Cleaver**, William Benjamin 1921- *Who 92*
**Cleaver**, William Lehn 1949- *WhoAmL 92*
**Cleaves**, Emery Taylor 1936- *AmMWSc 92*
**Cleaves**, Mark Andrew 1960- *WhoAmL 92*
**Clebnik**, Sherman Michael 1943- *AmMWSc 92*
**Clebsch**, Alfred, Jr 1921- *AmMWSc 92*
**Clebsch**, Edward Ernst Cooper 1929- *AmMWSc 92*
**Clecak**, Dvera Vivian Bozman 1944- *WhoWest 92*
**Clecak**, Peter 1938- *WrDr 92*
**Cleckley**, Betty J. *WhoBlA 92*
**Cledwyn Of Penrhos**, Baron 1916- *IntWW 91, Who 92*
**Cleek**, Given Wood 1916- *AmMWSc 92*
**Cleeland**, Charles Samuel 1938- *AmMWSc 92*
**Cleere**, Henry Forester 1926- *Who 92*
**Cleese**, John 1939- *ConAu 35NR, IntAu&W 91, IntMPA 92, WrDr 92*
**Cleese**, John Marwood 1939- *IntWW 91, Who 92, WhoEnt 92*
**Cleeton**, David Lawrence 1952- *WhoMW 92*
**Cleeton**, Roger Earl 1949- *WhoRel 92*
**Cleeve**, Brian 1921- *WrDr 92*
**Cleeve**, Brian Talbot 1921- *IntAu&W 91*
**Cleeves**, Ann 1954- *WrDr 92*
**Clegg**, Albert Lawrence 1931- *WhoRel 92*
**Clegg**, Bert E. 1943- *WhoFI 92*
**Clegg**, Brian George Herbert 1921- *Who 92*
**Clegg**, Edward John 1925- *Who 92*
**Clegg**, Frederick Wingfield 1944- *AmMWSc 92*
**Clegg**, Hugh Armstrong 1920- *Who 92*
**Clegg**, J. David 1933- *TwCPaSc*
**Clegg**, James S 1933- *AmMWSc 92*
**Clegg**, John 1909- *IntAu&W 91, WrDr 92*
**Clegg**, John C 1927- *AmMWSc 92*
**Clegg**, John Cardwell 1927- *WhoWest 92*
**Clegg**, Legrand H., II 1944- *WhoBlA 92*
**Clegg**, Michael Tran 1941- *AmMWSc 92*
**Clegg**, Moses Tran 1876-1918 *BiInAmS*
**Clegg**, Philip Charles 1942- *Who 92*
**Clegg**, Richard Ninian Barwick 1938- *Who 92*
**Clegg**, Robert Edward 1914- *AmMWSc 92*
**Clegg**, Roger Burton 1955- *WhoAmL 92*
**Clegg**, Ronald Anthony 1937- *Who 92*
**Clegg**, Thomas Boykin 1940- *AmMWSc 92*
**Clegg**, Walter 1920- *Who 92*
**Clegg**, William 1949- *Who 92*
**Clegg-Hill** *Who 92*
**Cleghorn**, Everett Knight, Jr. 1936- *WhoWest 92*
**Cleghorn**, John E. 1941- *IntWW 91*
**Cleghorn**, Robert Allen 1904- *AmMWSc 92*
**Cleghorn**, Sarah N. 1876-1959 *BenetAL 91*
**Cleghorn**, Sarah Norcliffe 1876-1959 *AmPeW*
**Clein**, A. Michael 1937- *WhoAmL 92*
**Clelan**, Douglas Richard 1951- *WhoFI 92*
**Cleland**, Charles Frederick 1939- *AmMWSc 92*
**Cleland**, Edward Gordon 1949- *WhoAmL 92*
**Cleland**, Franklin Andrew 1928- *AmMWSc 92*
**Cleland**, George Horace 1921- *AmMWSc 92*
**Cleland**, John 1710?-1789 *RfGEnL 91*
**Cleland**, John Gregory 1946- *AmMWSc 92*
**Cleland**, John W 1921- *AmMWSc 92*
**Cleland**, Joseph Maxwell 1942- *WhoAmP 91*
**Cleland**, Laurence Lynn 1939- *AmMWSc 92*
**Cleland**, Rachel 1906- *Who 92*
**Cleland**, Robert E 1932- *AmMWSc 92*
**Cleland**, Robert Lindbergh 1927- *AmMWSc 92*
**Cleland**, Wilfred Earl 1937- *AmMWSc 92*
**Cleland**, William Paton 1912- *Who 92*
**Cleland**, William Wallace 1930- *AmMWSc 92, WhoMW 92*
**Clelia** *EncAmaz 91*
**Clelland**, David Gordon 1943- *Who 92*
**Clelland**, Richard Cook 1921- *AmMWSc 92*
**Clem**, Alan L. 1929- *WrDr 92*
**Clem**, Casey Galyean 1954- *WhoFI 92*
**Clem**, Chester 1937- *WhoAmP 91*
**Clem**, Elizabeth Ann Stumpf 1945- *WhoEnt 92*
**Clem**, John R 1938- *AmMWSc 92*
**Clem**, John Richard 1938- *WhoMW 92*
**Clem**, Lane William 1944- *WhoWest 92*
**Clem**, Lester William 1934- *AmMWSc 92*
**Clem**, Steve 1942- *WhoMW 92*

**Clemans**, George Burtis 1938- *AmMWSc 92*
**Clemans**, Kermit Grover 1921- *AmMWSc 92*
**Clemans**, Stephen D 1939- *AmMWSc 92*
**Clemeau**, Carol *DrAPF 91*
**Clemen**, John Douglas 1944- *WhoAmL 92*
**Clemen**, Wolfgang H 1909- *IntAu&W 91*
**Clemence**, Barbara Ann 1927- *WhoMW 92*
**Clemence**, Gerald Maurice 1908-1974 *FacFETw*
**Clemence**, Samuel Patton 1939- *AmMWSc 92*
**Clemenceau**, Georges 1841-1929 *EncTR 91 [port], FacFETw [port], ThHElm [port]*
**Clemency**, Charles V 1929- *AmMWSc 92*
**Clemendor**, Anthony A., IV 1961- *WhoBlA 92*
**Clemendor**, Anthony Arnold 1933- *WhoBlA 92*
**Clemens**, Alvin Honey 1937- *WhoFI 92*
**Clemens**, Breckenridge 1829?-1867 *BiInAmS*
**Clemens**, Brian 1931- *IntMPA 92*
**Clemens**, Brian Keith 1967- *WhoMW 92*
**Clemens**, Bruce Montgomery 1953- *AmMWSc 92*
**Clemens**, Carl Frederick 1924- *AmMWSc 92*
**Clemens**, Charles Herbert 1939- *AmMWSc 92*
**Clemens**, Clive Carruthers 1924- *Who 92*
**Clemens**, Cyril 1902- *BenetAL 91*
**Clemens**, Daniel Theodore 1959- *AmMWSc 92*
**Clemens**, David Allen 1941- *WhoRel 92*
**Clemens**, David Allen 1959- *WhoMW 92*
**Clemens**, David Henry 1931- *AmMWSc 92*
**Clemens**, Donald Faull 1929- *AmMWSc 92*
**Clemens**, Earl L. 1925- *WhoMW 92*
**Clemens**, Edgar Thomas 1938- *AmMWSc 92*
**Clemens**, Frank Joseph 1940- *WhoAmL 92*
**Clemens**, Howard Paul 1923- *AmMWSc 92*
**Clemens**, Jacobus 1510?-1556? *NewAmDM*
**Clemens**, James Allen 1941- *AmMWSc 92*
**Clemens**, Jeremiah 1814-1865 *BenetAL 91*
**Clemens**, Jon K 1938- *AmMWSc 92*
**Clemens**, Lawrence Martin 1937- *AmMWSc 92*
**Clemens**, Michael Keith 1947- *WhoFI 92*
**Clemens**, Michael Terrence 1950- *WhoMW 92*
**Clemens**, Richard Glenn 1940- *WhoAmL 92*
**Clemens**, Robert Jay 1957- *AmMWSc 92*
**Clemens**, Roger *NewYTBS 91 [port]*
**Clemens**, Roger 1962- *News 91 [port]*
**Clemens**, Samuel *RComAH*
**Clemens**, Samuel Langhorne *BenetAL 91, TwCSFW 91*
**Clemens**, Samuel Langhorne 1835-1910 *ConAu 135*
**Clemens**, Scott William 1949- *WhoWest 92*
**Clemens**, Stanley Ray 1941- *AmMWSc 92*
**Clemens**, Stephanie *WhoEnt 92*
**Clemens**, T. Pat 1944- *WhoFI 92, WhoMW 92*
**Clemens**, Walter C., Jr. 1933- *WrDr 92*
**Clemens**, William Alvin 1932- *AmMWSc 92*
**Clemens non Papa**, Jacobus 1510?-1556? *NewAmDM*
**Clement** *AmPeW*
**Clement XIV** 1705-1774 *BlkwCEP*
**Clement of Alexandria** 160?-215 *EncEarC*
**Clement of Rome** *EncEarC*
**Clement**, The Most Reverent Bishop *WhoRel 92*
**Clement**, Allan M, III 1955- *WhoIns 92*
**Clement**, Arthur John Howard, III 1934- *WhoAmP 91*
**Clement**, Bob 1943- *AlmAP 92 [port], WhoAmP 91*
**Clement**, Christine Mary *AmMWSc 92*
**Clement**, D B *WhoAmP 91*
**Clement**, Dale Eugene 1933- *WhoFI 92*
**Clement**, Daniel Roy, III 1943- *WhoFI 92*
**Clement**, David James 1930- *Who 92*
**Clement**, David Morris 1911- *Who 92*
**Clement**, Donald D 1929- *WhoIns 92*
**Clement**, Duncan 1917- *AmMWSc 92*
**Clement**, Frank Harold 1941- *WhoFI 92*
**Clement**, Gerald Edwin 1935- *AmMWSc 92*
**Clement**, Hal 1922- *IntAu&W 91, TwCSFW 91, WrDr 92*
**Clement**, John 1932- *IntWW 91, Who 92, WhoFI 92*
**Clement**, John Edward Simpson 1934- *WhoRel 92*
**Clement**, John Handel 1920- *Who 92*
**Clement**, John Reid, Jr 1921- *AmMWSc 92*
**Clement**, Joseph D 1928- *AmMWSc 92*
**Clement**, Josephine Dobbs 1918- *WhoBlA 92*
**Clement**, Loran T 1946- *AmMWSc 92*
**Clement**, Maurice James Young 1938- *AmMWSc 92*
**Clement**, Patricia Ellen 1955- *WhoRel 92*
**Clement**, Rene 1913- *IntDcF 2-2 [port], IntWW 91, Who 92*
**Clement**, Richard 1937- *IntAu&W 91, Who 92*
**Clement**, Robert Alton 1929- *AmMWSc 92*
**Clement**, Robert Lebby, Jr. 1928- *WhoAmL 92*
**Clement**, Rutledge Carter, Jr. 1943- *WhoAmL 92*
**Clement**, Stephen LeRoy 1944- *AmMWSc 92*
**Clement**, Thomas Earl 1932- *WhoAmL 92*
**Clement**, Walter Hough 1931- *WhoWest 92*
**Clement**, Whittington Whiteside 1947- *WhoAmP 91*
**Clement**, William A. 1912- *WhoBlA 92*
**Clement**, William A., Jr. 1943- *WhoBlA 92*
**Clement**, William Glenn 1931- *AmMWSc 92*
**Clement**, William H 1931- *AmMWSc 92*
**Clement**, William Madison, Jr 1928- *AmMWSc 92*
**Clemente**, Carmine Domenic 1928- *AmMWSc 92, IntWW 91*
**Clemente**, Francesco 1952- *News 92-2 [port], WorArt 1980 [port]*
**Clemente**, Henry Joseph 1941- *WhoFI 92*
**Clemente**, Holly Anne *WhoFI 92*
**Clemente**, Mark Andrew 1951- *WhoAmL 92*
**Clemente**, Patrocinio Ablola 1941- *WhoWest 92*
**Clemente**, Robert Stephen 1956- *WhoAmL 92*
**Clemente**, Roberto 1934-1972 *FacFETw*
**Clemente**, Vince *DrAPF 91*
**Clementi**, Aldo 1925- *ConCom 92*
**Clementi**, Francois Antoine 1910-1982 *BiDExR*
**Clementi**, Muzio 1752-1832 *NewAmDM*
**Clements**, Alan William 1928- *Who 92*
**Clements**, Andrew Joseph 1950- *Who 92*
**Clements**, Arthur L *DrAPF 91*
**Clements**, Arthur L. 1932- *WrDr 92*
**Clements**, Bernadette Stone 1943- *WhoEnt 92*
**Clements**, Bob 1946- *WhoEnt 92*
**Clements**, Boots E. 1945- *WhoEnt 92*
**Clements**, Brant Alistari Bruce 1957- *WhoRel 92*
**Clements**, Brian Matthew 1946- *WhoFI 92*
**Clements**, Bruce 1931- *WrDr 92*
**Clements**, Bruce W 1942- *WhoIns 92*
**Clements**, Burie Webster 1927- *AmMWSc 92*
**Clements**, Colin 1894-1948 *BenetAL 91*
**Clements**, Douglas John 1949- *WhoMW 92*
**Clements**, Edward Earl 1955- *WhoEnt 92*
**Clements**, Eric Lee 1963- *WhoRel 92*
**Clements**, Francis E 1917- *WhoAmP 91*
**Clements**, George 1932- *ConBlB 2 [port]*
**Clements**, George Francis 1931- *AmMWSc 92, WhoWest 92*
**Clements**, George H. 1932- *WhoBlA 92*
**Clements**, Gerald F *WhoAmP 91*
**Clements**, Gregory Leland 1949- *AmMWSc 92*
**Clements**, John Allen 1923- *AmMWSc 92*
**Clements**, John B 1929- *AmMWSc 92*
**Clements**, John Brian 1928- *WhoEnt 92*
**Clements**, John Robert 1950- *WhoWest 92*
**Clements**, Julia *Who 92*
**Clements**, Kenneth John 1905- *Who 92*
**Clements**, Lewis Frederick, Jr. 1961- *WhoEnt 92*
**Clements**, Linda L 1945- *AmMWSc 92*
**Clements**, Otis 1926- *WhoEnt 92*
**Clements**, Reginald Montgomery 1940- *AmMWSc 92*
**Clements**, Richard Harry 1928- *Who 92*
**Clements**, Robert 1912- *WrDr 92*
**Clements**, Ronald Ernest 1929- *Who 92*
**Clements**, S L, Jr 1928- *WhoAmP 91*
**Clements**, S. Patrick 1957- *WhoFI 92*
**Clements**, Shirley Ann 1935- *WhoAmP 91*
**Clements**, Thomas 1898- *AmMWSc 92*
**Clements**, Walter H. 1928- *WhoBlA 92*
**Clements**, Walter Samuel 1949- *WhoMW 92*
**Clements**, Wayne Irwin 1931- *AmMWSc 92*
**Clements**, William Earl 1942- *AmMWSc 92*
**Clements**, William Howard 1908- *WhoAmP 91*
**Clements**, William Lewis, Jr. 1952- *WhoRel 92*
**Clements**, William P, Jr 1917- *WhoAmP 91*
**Clements**, William Perry, Jr. 1917- *IntWW 91*
**Clementson**, Gerhardt C 1917- *AmMWSc 92*
**Clementz**, David Michael 1945- *AmMWSc 92*
**Clemet**, Kristin 1957- *IntWW 91*
**Clemetson**, Charles Alan Blake 1923- *AmMWSc 92*
**Cleminshaw**, Clarence Higbee 1902-1985 *ConAu 134*
**Cleminshaw**, John Douglas 1958- *WhoMW 92*
**Cleminson**, James 1921- *Who 92*
**Cleminson**, James Arnold Stacey 1921- *IntWW 91*
**Clemits**, John Henry 1934- *Who 92*
**Clemitson**, Ivor Malcolm 1931- *Who 92*
**Clemm**, Lester V *WhoAmP 91*
**Clemm**, Virginia 1822-1847 *BenetAL 91*
**Clemmens**, Raymond Leopold 1922- *AmMWSc 92*
**Clemmesen**, Johannes 1908- *IntWW 91*
**Clemmons**, Clifford R. *WhoBlA 92*
**Clemmons**, David Roberts 1947- *AmMWSc 92*
**Clemmons**, Francois *DrAPF 91*
**Clemmons**, Ithiel *WhoRel 92*
**Clemmons**, Jackson Joshua Walter 1923- *AmMWSc 92, WhoBlA 92*
**Clemmons**, Jane Goodrich 1934- *WhoRel 92*
**Clemmons**, John B 1918- *AmMWSc 92*
**Clemmons**, Roger M 1949- *AmMWSc 92*
**Clemmons**, William Baylus, Jr. 1957- *WhoAmL 92*
**Clemo**, Jack *IntAu&W 91X*
**Clemo**, Jack 1916- *ConPo 91, WrDr 92*
**Clemo**, Reginald John 1916- *IntAu&W 91*
**Clemoes**, Peter Alan Martin 1920- *Who 92*
**Clemon**, U. W. 1943- *WhoAmL 92, WhoAmP 91, WhoBlA 92*
**Clemons**, Billy 1949- *WhoAmP 91*
**Clemons**, Clarence 1942- *ConMus 7 [port]*
**Clemons**, Eric K *AmMWSc 92*
**Clemons**, Flenor 1921- *WhoBlA 92*
**Clemons**, Frankie D. 1931- *WhoWest 92*
**Clemons**, Gerald Randolph 1956- *WhoEnt 92*
**Clemons**, Howard Leslie 1956- *WhoAmL 92*
**Clemons**, Jane 1946- *WhoAmP 91*
**Clemons**, John Gregory 1954- *WhoBlA 92*
**Clemons**, Michael L. 1955- *WhoBlA 92*
**Clemons**, Russell Edward 1930- *AmMWSc 92*
**Clemons**, Scott 1960- *WhoAmP 91*
**Clemons**, Thomasina 1938- *WhoBlA 92*
**Clemow**, Brian 1944- *WhoAmL 92*
**Clemson**, Harry C 1934- *AmMWSc 92*
**Clemson**, Thomas Green 1807-1888 *BiInAmS*
**Clench**, Mary Heimerdinger 1932- *AmMWSc 92*
**Clendenen**, Brian 1946- *WhoWest 92*
**Clendenen**, Leigh Ann 1964- *WhoMW 92*
**Clendenin**, James Edwin 1939- *AmMWSc 92*
**Clendenin**, John L. 1934- *WhoFI 92*
**Clendenin**, Martha Anne 1944- *AmMWSc 92*
**Clendening**, John Albert 1932- *AmMWSc 92*
**Clendeninn**, Neil J. 1949- *WhoBlA 92*
**Clendenning**, Lester M 1933- *AmMWSc 92*
**Clendenning**, William Edmund 1931- *AmMWSc 92*
**Clendenon**, Nancy Ruth 1933- *AmMWSc 92*
**Clendinen**, James Augustus d1991 *NewYTBS 91*
**Clendinning**, Robert Andrew 1931- *AmMWSc 92*
**Clenney**, Brent B. 1963- *WhoEnt 92*
**Cleobury**, Nicholas Randall 1950- *IntWW 91, Who 92*
**Cleobury**, Stephen John 1948- *Who 92*
**Cleopatra** d308?BC *EncAmaz 91*
**Cleopatra I** *EncAmaz 91*
**Cleopatra II** d173BC *EncAmaz 91*
**Cleopatra III** d81BC *EncAmaz 91*
**Cleopatra VII**, Queen of Egypt 69BC-30BC *EncAmaz 91*
**Cleopatra V**, Selene 129?BC-69BC *EncAmaz 91*
**Cleopatra VI**, Tryphaena d50?BC *EncAmaz 91*
**Clerambault**, Louis-Nicolas 1676-1749 *NewAmDM*
**Clercq**, Willy De 1927- *IntWW 91*
**Clerico**, John Anthony 1941- *WhoFI 92*
**Clerides**, Glavkos John 1919- *IntWW 91*
**Clerk of Penicuik**, John Dutton 1917- *Who 92*
**Clerke**, John Edward Longueville 1913- *Who 92*
**Clermont**, Kevin Michael 1945- *WhoAmL 92*
**Clermont**, Volna 1924- *WhoBlA 92*
**Clermont**, Yves Wilfred 1926- *AmMWSc 92*
**Clermont**, Yves Wilfrid 1926- *IntWW 91*
**Clesceri**, Lenore Stanke 1935- *AmMWSc 92*
**Clesceri**, Nicholas Louis 1936- *AmMWSc 92*
**Cleva**, Fausto 1902-1971 *NewAmDM*
**Cleve**, George 1936- *WhoEnt 92, WhoWest 92*
**Cleve**, John *TwCSFW 91*
**Cleveland**, Archdeacon of *Who 92*
**Cleveland**, Aaron 1744-1815 *AmPeW*
**Cleveland**, Alfred W. 1930- *WhoEnt 92*
**Cleveland**, Benjamin 1738-1806 *DcNCBi 1*
**Cleveland**, Bruce Taylor 1937- *AmMWSc 92*
**Cleveland**, Carl Service, Jr. 1918- *WhoWest 92*
**Cleveland**, Charles Douglas 1927- *WhoAmL 92*
**Cleveland**, Clyde 1935- *WhoAmP 91, WhoBlA 92*
**Cleveland**, Connie L 1960- *WhoAmP 91*
**Cleveland**, Cromwell Cook, Jr. 1948- *WhoRel 92*
**Cleveland**, David Martin, Jr 1920- *WhoAmP 91*
**Cleveland**, Don W 1950- *AmMWSc 92*
**Cleveland**, Donald Edward 1928- *AmMWSc 92*
**Cleveland**, Gerald Lloyd 1931- *WhoWest 92*
**Cleveland**, Granville E. 1937- *WhoBlA 92*
**Cleveland**, Gregor George 1948- *AmMWSc 92*
**Cleveland**, Grover 1837-1908 *BenetAL 91, RComAH*
**Cleveland**, Hal L. 1953- *WhoEnt 92*
**Cleveland**, Harlan 1918- *IntWW 91, Who 92, WhoAmP 91, WrDr 92*
**Cleveland**, Hattye M. 1911- *WhoBlA 92*
**Cleveland**, Hilary Paterson 1927- *WhoAmP 91*
**Cleveland**, James 1931-1991 *CurBio 91N, NewYTBS 91, WhoBlA 92N*
**Cleveland**, James 1932?-1991 *News 91, -91-3*
**Cleveland**, James C 1920- *WhoAmP 91*
**Cleveland**, James L. 1932-1991 *NewAmDM*
**Cleveland**, James Perry 1942- *AmMWSc 92*
**Cleveland**, Jim *TwCWW 91*
**Cleveland**, Jimmy 1926- *NewAmDM*
**Cleveland**, John *IntAu&W 91X, WrDr 92*
**Cleveland**, John 1613?-1658 *RfGEnL 91*
**Cleveland**, John H 1932- *AmMWSc 92*
**Cleveland**, John J *WhoAmP 91*
**Cleveland**, John Paul 1970- *WhoRel 92*
**Cleveland**, John Warren 1956- *WhoFI 92*
**Cleveland**, Laurence F 1905- *AmMWSc 92*
**Cleveland**, Leslie 1921- *WrDr 92*
**Cleveland**, M Duke *WhoAmP 91*
**Cleveland**, Merrill L 1928- *AmMWSc 92*
**Cleveland**, Michael James 1944- *WhoFI 92, WhoMW 92*
**Cleveland**, Paul Matthews 1931- *IntWW 91, WhoAmP 91*
**Cleveland**, Peter Watkins 1955- *WhoAmL 92*
**Cleveland**, Ray L. 1929- *WrDr 92*
**Cleveland**, Richard Warren 1924- *AmMWSc 92*
**Cleveland**, Robert Harold 1922- *WhoMW 92*
**Cleveland**, Roger Pecke 1901- *WhoRel 92*
**Cleveland**, Stephen Grover 1837-1908 *AmPolLe [port]*
**Cleveland**, Tessie Anita Smith 1939- *WhoBlA 92*
**Cleveland**, William C 1948- *WhoAmP 91*
**Cleveland**, William Grover, Jr 1951- *AmMWSc 92*
**Cleveland**, William Swain 1943- *AmMWSc 92*
**Cleveland Hooper**, Cathy Beth 1953- *WhoEnt 92*
**Cleven**, Carol Chapman 1928- *WhoAmP 91*
**Clevenger**, Jeffrey Griswold 1949- *WhoWest 92*
**Clevenger**, Michelle Lee 1966- *WhoEnt 92*
**Clevenger**, Penelope 1940- *WhoMW 92*
**Clevenger**, Raymond C, III *WhoAmP 91*
**Clevenger**, Raymond C., III 1937- *WhoAmL 92*
**Clevenger**, Richard Lee 1931- *AmMWSc 92*
**Clevenger**, Sarah 1926- *AmMWSc 92*
**Clevenger**, Shobal Vail 1843-1920 *BiInAmS*
**Clevenger**, Timothy R. 1964- *WhoEnt 92*
**Clevenger**, William A *AmMWSc 92*
**Clever**, David Arthur 1943- *WhoMW 92*

**Clever,** Henry Lawrence 1923- *AmMWSc 92*
**Clever,** Linda Hawes *AmMWSc 92*
**Clever,** Richard Floyd 1932- *WhoMW 92*
**Cleverley Ford,** Douglas William 1914- *Who 92*
**Cleverly Ford,** D. W. *WrDr 92*
**Clevert,** Charles N., Jr. 1947- *WhoBlA 92*
**Clevert,** Charles Nelson, Jr. 1947- *WhoAmL 92*
**Clevinger,** Paul *IntAu&W 91X*
**Clewe,** Jane Elizabeth 1954- *WhoWest 92*
**Clewe,** Thomas Hailey 1925- *AmMWSc 92*
**Clewell,** David *DrAPF 91*
**Clewell,** Dayton Harris 1912- *AmMWSc 92*
**Clewell,** Don B. 1941- *WhoMW 92*
**Clewell,** Don Bert 1941- *AmMWSc 92*
**Clewell,** John Henry 1855-1922 *DcNCBi 1*
**Clewes,** Dorothy 1907- *WrDr 92*
**Clewes,** Howard Charles Vivian 1912- *IntAu&W 91*
**Clewett,** Rick *DrAPF 91*
**Clewlow,** Warren 1936- *IntWW 91*
**Clews,** Michael Arthur 1919- *Who 92*
**Clews,** William Vincent 1943- *WhoEnt 92*
**Clfford,** Debra Markowitz *WhoEnt 92*
**Cliath,** Mark Marshall 1935- *AmMWSc 92*
**Clibborn,** Donovan Harold 1917- *Who 92*
**Clibborn,** John Donovan Nelson dalla Rosa 1941- *Who 92*
**Clibborn,** Stanley Eric Francis B. *Who 92*
**Cliborn,** Dennis Elvin, Sr. 1950- *WhoRel 92*
**Cliburn,** Joseph William 1926- *AmMWSc 92*
**Cliburn,** Van *NewYTBS 91 [port]*
**Cliburn,** Van 1934- *FacFETw [port], IntWW 91, NewAmDM, Who 92, WhoEnt 92*
**Click,** David Forrest 1947- *WhoAmL 92, WhoEnt 92, WhoFI 92*
**Click,** Robert Edward 1937- *AmMWSc 92*
**Clickner,** Susan *WhoEnt 92*
**Cliett,** Charles Buren 1924- *AmMWSc 92*
**Cliett,** Otis Jay 1944- *AmMWSc 92*
**Cliff,** Barry Lee 1943- *WhoFI 92*
**Cliff,** Eugene M 1944- *AmMWSc 92*
**Cliff,** Frank Samuel 1928- *AmMWSc 92*
**Cliff,** Jimmy 1948- *WhoEnt 92*
**Cliff,** Johnnie Marie 1935- *WhoMW 92*
**Cliff,** Judith Anita 1941- *WhoRel 92*
**Cliff,** Michelle *DrAPF 91*
**Cliff,** Steven Burris 1952- *WhoFI 92*
**Cliff,** Walter Conway 1932- *WhoAmL 92*
**Cliffe,** Dan Mack 1946- *WhoFI 92*
**Cliffe,** Roger William 1947- *WhoMW 92*
**Clifford** *Who 92*
**Clifford,** Alan Frank 1919- *AmMWSc 92*
**Clifford,** Charles H. 1933- *WhoBlA 92*
**Clifford,** Clark McAdams 1906- *AmPolLe, IntWW 91, NewYTBS 91 [port], Who 92, WhoAmP 91*
**Clifford,** Derek Plint 1917- *IntAu&W 91*
**Clifford,** Dermot *Who 92*
**Clifford,** Donald Francis, Jr. 1935- *WhoAmL 92*
**Clifford,** Donald H 1925- *AmMWSc 92*
**Clifford,** Eugene Thomas 1941- *WhoAmL 92*
**Clifford,** George *WhoRel 92*
**Clifford,** George O 1924- *AmMWSc 92*
**Clifford,** Graeme *IntMPA 92*
**Clifford,** Henry Charles 1861-1947 *TwCPaSc*
**Clifford,** Howard James 1939- *AmMWSc 92*
**Clifford,** Hugh Fleming 1931- *AmMWSc 92*
**Clifford,** John Leger 1950- *WhoAmL 92*
**Clifford,** Mary Louise 1926- *WrDr 92*
**Clifford,** Maurice C. 1920- *WhoBlA 92*
**Clifford,** Paul Ingraham 1914- *WhoBlA 92*
**Clifford,** Paul Rowntree 1913- *Who 92*
**Clifford,** Peter 1925- *WhoRel 92*
**Clifford,** Ralph D. 1954- *WhoAmL 92*
**Clifford,** Robert L. 1924- *WhoAmL 92, WhoAmP 91*
**Clifford,** Robert Laning 1912- *WhoAmP 91*
**Clifford,** Robert William 1937- *WhoAmL 92, WhoAmP 91*
**Clifford,** Roger 1936- *Who 92*
**Clifford,** Sidney, Jr. 1937- *WhoAmL 92*
**Clifford,** Stephen Michael 1960- *WhoMW 92*
**Clifford,** Steven Francis 1943- *AmMWSc 92*
**Clifford,** Stewart Burnett 1929- *WhoFI 92*
**Clifford,** Sylvester 1929- *WhoMW 92*
**Clifford,** Therasa 1961- *TwCPaSc*
**Clifford,** Thomas E. 1929- *WhoBlA 92*
**Clifford,** Thomas John 1921- *WhoMW 92*
**Clifford,** Thomas Robert 1957- *WhoEnt 92*
**Clifford,** Timothy Peter Plint 1946- *Who 92*
**Clifford,** Walter Howard 1912- *WhoWest 92*
**Clifford,** Walter Jess 1944- *WhoWest 92*
**Clifford,** William Henry Morton 1909- *Who 92*
**Clifford of Chudleigh,** Baron 1948- *Who 92*
**Clifford-Turner,** Raymond 1906- *Who 92*
**Cliffton,** Michael Duane 1952- *AmMWSc 92*
**Clift,** Charles Kenneth 1938- *WhoRel 92*
**Clift,** David Brian 1962- *WhoRel 92*
**Clift,** G W 1952- *IntAu&W 91*
**Clift,** Joseph William 1938- *WhoBlA 92*
**Clift,** Montgomery 1920-1966 *FacFETw*
**Clift,** Richard Dennis 1933- *IntWW 91, Who 92*
**Clift,** Roland 1942- *Who 92*
**Clift,** Wallace Bruce 1926- *WhoRel 92*
**Clift,** Wallace Bruce, Jr. 1926- *WhoWest 92*
**Clift,** William Orrin 1914- *AmMWSc 92*
**Clifton,** Bishop of 1925- *Who 92*
**Clifton,** Lord 1968- *Who 92*
**Clifton,** Brian John 1937- *AmMWSc 92*
**Clifton,** Chester V., Jr. d1991 *NewYTBS 91 [port]*
**Clifton,** David Geyer 1924- *AmMWSc 92*
**Clifton,** David S, Jr 1943- *AmMWSc 92*
**Clifton,** David Samuel, Jr. 1943- *WhoFI 92*
**Clifton,** Donald F 1917- *AmMWSc 92*
**Clifton,** Donald K. 1946- *WhoWest 92*
**Clifton,** Dorothy May 1922- *WhoAmP 91*
**Clifton,** Henry, Jr. 1909- *WhoAmL 92*
**Clifton,** Hugh Edward 1934- *AmMWSc 92*
**Clifton,** Ivery Dwight 1943- *WhoBlA 92*
**Clifton,** James Albert 1923- *AmMWSc 92, IntWW 91*
**Clifton,** John M., Jr. 1937- *WhoAmL 92*
**Clifton,** Kelly Hardenbrook 1927- *AmMWSc 92*
**Clifton,** Linda J. *DrAPF 91*
**Clifton,** Linda J 1940- *IntAu&W 91*
**Clifton,** Lucille *DrAPF 91*
**Clifton,** Lucille 1936- *BenetAL 91, BlkLC, ConLC 66 [port], ConPo 91, WhoBlA 92, WrDr 92*
**Clifton,** Mark 1906-1963 *TwCSFW 91*
**Clifton,** Merritt *DrAPF 91*
**Clifton,** Michael Crawford 1948- *WhoRel 92*
**Clifton,** Michael Edward 1949- *WhoWest 92*
**Clifton,** Oliver Lee *TwCWW 91*
**Clifton,** Peter Thomas 1911- *Who 92*
**Clifton,** Robert Blaine 1937- *WhoWest 92*
**Clifton,** Rodney James 1937- *AmMWSc 92*
**Clifton,** William John *NewAmDM*
**Cligrow,** Edward Thomas, Jr. 1934- *WhoMW 92*
**Clikas,** Steve *WhoAmP 91*
**Clikeman,** Franklyn Miles 1933- *AmMWSc 92*
**Climaco,** Vicente Mariano 1950- *WhoRel 92*
**Climenhaga,** Joel *DrAPF 91*
**Climenhaga,** John Leroy 1916- *AmMWSc 92*
**Climenko,** Hyman 1875-1920 *BiInAmS*
**Climent,** Silvia 1940- *WhoHisp 92*
**Climmons,** Willie Mathew 1923- *WhoBlA 92*
**Clinard,** Frank Welch, Jr 1933- *AmMWSc 92, WhoAmP 91*
**Clinard,** Joseph Hiram, Jr. 1938- *WhoFI 92*
**Clinard,** Robert Noel 1946- *WhoAmL 92*
**Clinard,** Turner N. 1917-1981 *ConAu 135*
**Clinch,** David John 1937- *Who 92*
**Clinch,** Duncan Lamont 1787-1849 *DcNCBi 1*
**Clinch,** John 1934- *TwCPaSc*
**Clinch,** Joseph John, Jr. 1754-1795 *DcNCBi 1*
**Cline,** Andrew Haley 1951- *WhoAmL 92*
**Cline,** Billy H. 1927- *WhoRel 92*
**Cline,** Bryan M. 1959- *WhoWest 92*
**Cline,** Carl F 1928- *AmMWSc 92*
**Cline,** Charles *DrAPF 91*
**Cline,** Charles William 1937- *WhoMW 92*
**Cline,** David E. 1932- *WhoMW 92*
**Cline,** Douglas 1934- *AmMWSc 92*
**Cline,** Edward Terry 1914- *AmMWSc 92*
**Cline,** Eileen Tate 1935- *WhoBlA 92, WhoEnt 92*
**Cline,** Fred Albert, Jr. 1929- *WhoWest 92*
**Cline,** George Bruce 1936- *AmMWSc 92*
**Cline,** George Thomas, Jr. 1928- *WhoMW 92*
**Cline,** Harold Edwin 1930- *WhoRel 92*
**Cline,** Harvey Ellis 1940- *AmMWSc 92*
**Cline,** J F 1917- *AmMWSc 92*
**Cline,** Jack Henry 1927- *AmMWSc 92*
**Cline,** James E 1931- *AmMWSc 92*
**Cline,** James Edward 1913- *AmMWSc 92*
**Cline,** James Ralph, Jr. 1928- *WhoRel 92*
**Cline,** Jane Lynn 1956- *WhoAmP 91*
**Cline,** Judy Ann 1952- *WhoFI 92*
**Cline,** Judy Elizabeth 1944- *WhoAmP 91*
**Cline,** Kenneth Charles 1948- *AmMWSc 92*
**Cline,** Lee Williamson 1944- *WhoAmL 92*
**Cline,** Leonard 1893-1929 *ScFEYrs*
**Cline,** Lowell Eugene 1935- *WhoAmP 91*
**Cline,** Marlin George 1909- *AmMWSc 92*
**Cline,** Michael Castle 1945- *AmMWSc 92*
**Cline,** Michael Robert 1949- *WhoAmL 92*
**Cline,** Morris George 1931- *AmMWSc 92*
**Cline,** Patsy 1932-1963 *NewAmDM*
**Cline,** Paul Charles 1933- *WhoAmP 91*
**Cline,** Platt Herrick 1911- *WhoWest 92*
**Cline,** Randall Eugene 1931- *AmMWSc 92*
**Cline,** Ray S. 1918- *ConAu 133*
**Cline,** Richard Allen 1955- *WhoAmL 92*
**Cline,** Richard Gordon 1935- *WhoFI 92, WhoMW 92*
**Cline,** Richard Lee 1942- *WhoAmL 92*
**Cline,** Richard Lee 1950- *WhoMW 92, WhoRel 92*
**Cline,** Robert *DrAPF 91*
**Cline,** Robert Corde 1933- *WhoAmP 91*
**Cline,** Robert Stanley 1937- *WhoFI 92, WhoWest 92*
**Cline,** Roy Lee 1937- *WhoFI 92*
**Cline,** Russell Brian 1959- *WhoWest 92*
**Cline,** Sylvia Good 1928- *AmMWSc 92*
**Cline,** Thomas L 1932- *AmMWSc 92*
**Cline,** Thomas Warren 1946- *AmMWSc 92*
**Cline,** Tilford R 1939- *AmMWSc 92*
**Cline,** Tilford Robert 1939- *WhoMW 92*
**Cline,** Todd Wakefield 1964- *WhoAmL 92*
**Cline,** Warren Kent 1921- *AmMWSc 92*
**Cline,** William H, Jr 1940- *AmMWSc 92*
**Cline,** Wilson Ettason 1914- *WhoAmL 92, WhoWest 92*
**Clinebell,** Howard J., Jr. 1922- *WrDr 92*
**Clineschmidt,** Bradley Van 1941- *AmMWSc 92*
**Clingan,** Forest Melrose 1918- *WhoFI 92*
**Clingan,** Lee 1921- *WhoAmP 91*
**Clingan,** Wanda Jacqueline 1928- *WhoMW 92, WhoRel 92*
**Clinger,** William F., Jr. 1929- *AlmAP 92 [port]*
**Clinger,** William Floyd, Jr 1929- *WhoAmP 91*
**Clingerman,** Edgar Allen, Sr. 1934- *WhoFI 92*
**Clingerman,** John R 1931- *WhoAmP 91*
**Clingham,** Leonard F, Jr 1938- *WhoAmP 91*
**Clingham,** Leonard Francis 1958- *WhoAmL 92*
**Clingman,** Evan Earl 1925- *WhoIns 92*
**Clingman,** Thomas Lanier 1812-1897 *DcNCBi 1*
**Clingman,** William Herbert, Jr 1929- *AmMWSc 92, WhoFI 92*
**Clinkscales,** Jerry A. 1933- *WhoBlA 92*
**Clinkscales,** John William, Jr. 1925- *WhoBlA 92*
**Clinnick,** Mansfield 1922- *AmMWSc 92*
**Clinton** *Who 92*
**Clinton,** Baron 1934- *Who 92*
**Clinton,** Alan 1931- *Who 92*
**Clinton,** Bill 1946- *AlmAP 92 [port], IntWW 91, News 92-1 [port], WhoAmL 92, WhoAmP 91*
**Clinton,** Bruce Allan 1937- *AmMWSc 92*
**Clinton,** Charles A *WhoIns 92*
**Clinton,** DeWitt *DrAPF 91*
**Clinton,** DeWitt 1769-1828 *AmPolLe, BiInAmS*
**Clinton,** Dirk *ConAu 36NR*
**Clinton,** Dorothy Louise Randle 1925- *IntAu&W 91*
**Clinton,** Edward Joseph 1959- *WhoAmL 92*
**Clinton,** Edward Xavier 1930- *WhoAmL 92*
**Clinton,** F. G. *WrDr 92*
**Clinton,** Gail M 1946- *AmMWSc 92*
**Clinton,** George 1739-1812 *AmPolLe, BenetAL 91, BlkwEAR*
**Clinton,** George 1940- *NewAmDM*
**Clinton,** George 1941- *ConMus 7 [port]*
**Clinton,** George William 1807-1885 *BiInAmS*
**Clinton,** Henry 1730-1795 *BlkwEAR*
**Clinton,** Henry 1738?-1795 *BenetAL 91*
**Clinton,** Hillary Rodham 1947- *WhoAmL 92*
**Clinton,** Jeff *IntAu&W 91X, TwCWW 91, WrDr 92*
**Clinton,** John Hart 1905- *WhoWest 92*
**Clinton,** John Philip Martin 1935- *WhoFI 92*
**Clinton,** Kathie Anne Troudt *WhoAmL 92*
**Clinton,** Lloyd Dewitt 1946- *WhoMW 92*
**Clinton,** Nancy Jean 1951- *WhoEnt 92*
**Clinton,** Raymond Otto 1918- *AmMWSc 92*
**Clinton,** Richard 1721-1796 *DcNCBi 1*
**Clinton,** Richard M. 1941- *WhoAmL 92*
**Clinton,** Stephen Michael 1944- *WhoRel 92*
**Clinton,** Stephen William 1950- *WhoFI 92*
**Clinton,** Thomas Leonard 1916- *WhoAmL 92*
**Clinton,** Thomas R. 1909-1991 *WhoBlA 92N*
**Clinton,** William J 1946- *NewYTBS 91 [port]*
**Clinton,** William L 1930- *AmMWSc 92*
**Clinton-Davis** *Who 92*
**Clinton-Davis,** Baron 1928- *IntWW 91, Who 92*
**Clipp,** Roger W. d1979 *LesBEnT 92*
**Clipper,** Milton Clifton, Jr. 1948- *WhoBlA 92*
**Clippinger,** Frank Warren, Jr 1925- *AmMWSc 92*
**Clipsham,** Robert Charles 1955- *WhoWest 92*
**Clise,** Ronald Leo 1923- *AmMWSc 92*
**Clitherall,** James 1740?-1804? *DcNCBi 1*
**Clithero,** Monte Paul 1953- *WhoAmL 92*
**Clithero,** Paul Harvey 1952- *WhoEnt 92*
**Clithero,** William Maurice 1936- *WhoWest 92*
**Clitheroe,** Baron 1929- *Who 92*
**Clitheroe,** H John 1935- *AmMWSc 92*
**Clive,** Viscount 1952- *Who 92*
**Clive,** Dennis *TwCSFW 91*
**Clive,** Eric McCredie 1938- *Who 92*
**Clive,** John 1924- *WrDr 92*
**Clive,** Nigel David 1917- *Who 92*
**Clive,** William *IntAu&W 91X*
**Cliver,** Dean Otis 1935- *AmMWSc 92*
**Cloake,** John 1924- *ConAu 133*
**Cloake,** John Cecil 1924- *Who 92*
**Clock,** Herbert and Boetzel, Eric *ScFEYrs*
**Clocksin,** Donald E 1944- *WhoAmP 91*
**Clode,** Frances 1903- *Who 92*
**Clodfelter,** Jesse 1804- *DcNCBi 1*
**Clodius,** Albert Howard 1911- *WhoWest 92*
**Clodman,** Jo Mira 1954- *WhoFI 92*
**Cloete,** Johan 1957- *ConCom 92*
**Clogher,** Bishop of 1934- *Who 92*
**Clogher,** Bishop of 1936- *Who 92*
**Clogston,** Albert McCavour 1917- *AmMWSc 92*
**Cloherty,** Thomas Patrick 1948- *WhoRel 92*
**Cloke,** Paul LeRoy 1929- *AmMWSc 92*
**Cloke,** Richard *DrAPF 91*
**Clompus,** Bradley *DrAPF 91*
**Clonch,** L Dale 1944- *WhoAmP 91*
**Clonch,** Leslie Allen, Jr. 1961- *WhoFI 92*
**Cloney,** Richard Alan 1930- *AmMWSc 92*
**Cloney,** Robert Dennis 1927- *AmMWSc 92*
**Cloney,** Terence J. 1953- *WhoAmL 92*
**Cloninger,** Claude Robert 1944- *AmMWSc 92*
**Cloninger,** Larry H. 1945- *WhoMW 92*
**Clopine,** Gordon Alan 1936- *WhoWest 92*
**Clopine,** Sandra Lou 1936- *WhoRel 92*
**Clopper,** Edward N. 1879-1953 *DcAmImH*
**Clopper,** Herschel 1941- *AmMWSc 92*
**Clopton,** Abner Wentworth 1784-1833 *DcNCBi 1*
**Cloran,** John James 1958- *WhoAmL 92*
**Clore,** Frank Caldin 1942- *WhoRel 92*
**Clore,** Lawrence H. 1944- *WhoAmL 92*
**Clore,** Leon *IntMPA 92*
**Clore,** Walter Joseph 1911- *AmMWSc 92*
**Clos,** Charles *WrDr 92*
**Close,** Allyn David 1962- *WhoFI 92*
**Close,** Charles M 1927- *AmMWSc 92*
**Close,** David Matzen 1942- *AmMWSc 92*
**Close,** David Palmer 1915- *WhoAmL 92*
**Close,** Donald Alan 1946- *AmMWSc 92*
**Close,** Donald Pembroke 1920- *WhoFI 92*
**Close,** Elmer Harry 1937- *WhoAmP 91, WhoEnt 92, WhoFI 92*
**Close,** Glenn 1947- *ConTFT 9, IntMPA 92, IntWW 91, WhoEnt 92*
**Close,** Melvin Dilkes, Jr 1934- *WhoAmP 91*
**Close,** Perry 1921- *AmMWSc 92*
**Close,** R N 1923- *AmMWSc 92*
**Close,** Reginald Arthur 1909- *WrDr 92*
**Close,** Richard Charles 1949- *Who 92*
**Close,** Richard Thomas 1934- *AmMWSc 92*
**Close,** Roy Edwin 1920- *Who 92*
**Closen,** Michael Lee 1949- *WhoAmL 92*
**Closets,** Francois de 1933- *IntWW 91*
**Closier,** Zoe 1850?-1920? *ThHEIm [port]*
**Closmann,** Philip Joseph 1925- *AmMWSc 92*
**Closs,** Gerhard Ludwig 1928- *AmMWSc 92*
**Closser,** Charles Ervin, Jr. 1942- *WhoEnt 92*
**Closser,** Patrick Denton 1945- *WhoRel 92*
**Closson,** John Eugene, Jr. 1947- *WhoWest 92*
**Closson,** Kay L. *DrAPF 91*
**Closson,** Linda Marlene 1963- *WhoFI 92*
**Closson,** William Deane 1934- *AmMWSc 92*
**Closure,** Vanilla Threats 1946- *WhoBlA 92*
**Clotfelter,** Beryl E. 1926- *WrDr 92*
**Clotfelter,** Beryl Edward 1926- *AmMWSc 92*

**Clotfelter**, Charles T. 1947- *WhoFI 92*
**Clotfelter**, Virgil Jackson, Jr. 1954- *WhoRel 92*
**Clothey**, Frederick Wilson 1936- *WhoRel 92*
**Clothier**, Cecil 1919- *Who 92*
**Clothier**, Galen Edward 1933- *AmMWSc 92*
**Clothier**, Peter *DrAPF 91*
**Clothier**, Robert Frederic 1925- *AmMWSc 92*
**Clotilda** 470?-545 *EncEarC*
**Cloud**, Bruce Benjamin, Sr. 1920- *WhoFI 92*
**Cloud**, Clara Martha 1949- *WhoMW 92*
**Cloud**, Gary Lee 1937- *AmMWSc 92*
**Cloud**, Jack Leslie 1925- *WhoMW 92*
**Cloud**, James Merle 1947- *WhoWest 92*
**Cloud**, Joseph 1770-1845 *BiInAmS*
**Cloud**, Joseph George 1944- *AmMWSc 92*
**Cloud**, Preston d1991 *NewYTBS 91*
**Cloud**, Preston 1912- *AmMWSc 92*
**Cloud**, Preston 1912-1991 *ConAu 133, IntWW 91, -91N*
**Cloud**, Sanford, Jr. 1944- *WhoBlA 92*
**Cloud**, Sharon Lee 1948- *WhoAmL 92*
**Cloud**, Stephen R 1949- *WhoAmP 91*
**Cloud**, W. Eric 1946- *WhoBlA 92*
**Cloud**, William K 1910- *AmMWSc 92*
**Cloud**, William Max 1923- *AmMWSc 92*
**Clouden**, LaVerne C. 1933- *WhoBlA 92*
**Cloudsley-Thompson**, John 1921- *WrDr 92*
**Cloudsley-Thompson**, John Leonard 1921- *IntAu&W 91, IntWW 91, Who 92*
**Cloues**, Edward Blanchard, II 1947- *WhoAmL 92*
**Clough**, Alan *Who 92*
**Clough**, Anson W 1936- *WhoIns 92*
**Clough**, Arthur Hugh 1819-1861 *RfGEnL 91*
**Clough**, Brenda Wang 1955- *IntAu&W 91*
**Clough**, Charles Elmer 1930- *WhoFI 92*
**Clough**, David Alan 1955- *WhoAmL 92*
**Clough**, David Edwards 1946- *AmMWSc 92*
**Clough**, Francis Bowman 1924- *AmMWSc 92*
**Clough**, Fred M *ScFEYrs*
**Clough**, G Wayne *AmMWSc 92*
**Clough**, Gordon 1934- *Who 92*
**Clough**, John Alan 1924- *Who 92*
**Clough**, John Wendell 1942- *AmMWSc 92*
**Clough**, Philip Gerard 1924- *Who 92*
**Clough**, Prunella 1919- *TwCPaSc, Who 92*
**Clough**, Ray William 1920- *AmMWSc 92*
**Clough**, Ray William, Jr. 1920- *IntWW 91*
**Clough**, Richard H 1922- *AmMWSc 92*
**Clough**, Robert Ragan 1942- *AmMWSc 92*
**Clough**, Roger Lee 1949- *AmMWSc 92*
**Clough**, Shepard Anthony 1931- *AmMWSc 92*
**Clough**, Stuart Benjamin 1937- *AmMWSc 92*
**Clough**, Stuart Chandler 1943- *AmMWSc 92*
**Clough**, Thomas Collingwood 1903- *TwCPaSc*
**Clough**, Wendy Glasgow 1942- *AmMWSc 92*
**Clougherty**, Dennis Paul *WhoWest 92*
**Clouse**, Bill 1952- *WhoAmP 91*
**Clouse**, Bonnidell 1928- *WhoRel 92*
**Clouse**, James Robert, Jr. 1930- *WhoAmL 92*
**Clouse**, John Daniel 1925- *WhoAmL 92, WhoFI 92, WhoMW 92*
**Clouse**, Karen L. 1961- *WhoAmL 92*
**Clouse**, Robert Gordon 1931- *IntAu&W 91, WhoRel 92, WrDr 92*
**Clouse**, Robert Wilburn 1937- *WhoFI 92*
**Clouser**, E. Randall 1957- *WhoMW 92*
**Clouser**, James Brady 1935- *WhoEnt 92, WhoMW 92*
**Clouser**, Michael Allen 1963- *WhoWest 92*
**Clouser**, William Sands 1921- *AmMWSc 92*
**Clousher**, Fred Eugene 1941- *WhoEnt 92*
**Clouston**, J Storer 1870-1944 *ScFEYrs*
**Clout**, Hugh Donald 1944- *ConAu 34NR*
**Clouthier**, Dennis James 1950- *AmMWSc 92*
**Cloutier**, Ardis Lucille 1930- *WhoMW 92*
**Cloutier**, Conrad Francois 1948- *AmMWSc 92*
**Cloutier**, David *DrAPF 91*
**Cloutier**, Gilles G. 1928- *IntWW 91*
**Cloutier**, Gilles Georges 1928- *AmMWSc 92*
**Cloutier**, James Robert 1947- *AmMWSc 92*
**Cloutier**, Leonce 1928- *AmMWSc 92*
**Cloutier**, Paul Andrew 1943- *AmMWSc 92*
**Cloutier**, Raymond Arthur 1938- *WhoAmL 92*
**Cloutier**, Roger Joseph 1930- *AmMWSc 92*
**Cloutier**, Sylvain 1929- *IntWW 91*
**Cloutier**, Wayne Roger 1943- *WhoFI 92*
**Cloutier**, William Joseph 1949- *WhoMW 92, WhoRel 92*
**Cloutman**, Edward Bradbury, III 1945- *WhoAmL 92*
**Cloutman**, Geoffrey William 1920- *Who 92*
**Cloutman**, Lawrence Dean 1944- *AmMWSc 92*
**Clouzot**, Henri-Georges 1907-1977 *IntDcF 2-2 [port]*
**Clover**, Frank M. 1940- *WhoMW 92*
**Clover**, Marian *DrAPF 91*
**Clover**, Philip Thornton 1935- *WhoFI 92*
**Clover**, Richmond Bennett 1943- *AmMWSc 92*
**Clover**, Robert Gordon 1911- *Who 92*
**Clover**, William John, Jr 1944- *AmMWSc 92*
**Clovis** 466?-511 *EncEarC*
**Clovis**, Albert L. 1935- *WhoAmL 92*
**Clovis**, Donna L. *DrAPF 91*
**Clovis**, James S 1937- *AmMWSc 92*
**Clovis**, Jesse Franklin 1921- *AmMWSc 92*
**Clow**, Barbara Hand 1943- *ConAu 133*
**Clow**, Gordon Henry 1942- *WhoFI 92*
**Clow**, Timothy James 1960- *WhoAmL 92*
**Clower**, Dan Fredric 1928- *AmMWSc 92*
**Clowers**, Churby Conrad, Jr 1934- *AmMWSc 92*
**Clowers**, Myles Leonard 1944- *WhoWest 92*
**Clowes**, A. W. 1931- *Who 92*
**Clowes**, Alexander Whitehill 1946- *WhoWest 92*
**Clowes**, Garth Anthony 1926- *WhoWest 92*
**Clowes**, George Henry Alexander, Jr *AmMWSc 92*
**Clowes**, Henry 1911- *Who 92*
**Clowes**, Ronald Martin 1942- *AmMWSc 92*
**Clowes**, Royston Courtenay 1921- *AmMWSc 92*
**Clowes**, W Laird and Burgoyne, Alan H *ScFEYrs*
**Clowes**, William Laird 1856-1905 *ScFEYrs*
**Clowney**, Audrey E. 1961- *WhoBlA 92*
**Cloyd**, Grover David 1918- *AmMWSc 92*
**Cloyd**, James C, III 1948- *AmMWSc 92*
**Cloyd**, Thomas Earl 1944- *WhoEnt 92*
**Clubb**, Bruce Edwin 1931- *WhoAmL 92*
**Clubb**, Henry Steven 1827-1921 *AmPeW*
**Clubb**, O Edmund 1901-1989 *FacFETw*
**Clubbe**, John L. E. 1938- *WrDr 92*
**Clubbe**, John Louis Edwin 1938- *IntAu&W 91*
**Clube**, Victor 1934- *WrDr 92*
**Clucas**, Kenneth 1921- *Who 92*
**Cluett**, Shelagh 1947- *TwCPaSc*
**Cluff**, Algy 1940- *IntWW 91*
**Cluff**, Carwin Brent 1935- *AmMWSc 92*
**Cluff**, Edward Fuller 1928- *AmMWSc 92*
**Cluff**, John Gordon 1940- *Who 92*
**Cluff**, Leighton Eggertsen 1923- *AmMWSc 92, IntWW 91*
**Cluff**, Lloyd Sterling 1933- *AmMWSc 92*
**Cluff**, Robert Murri 1953- *AmMWSc 92*
**Clug**, A. Stephen 1929- *IntMPA 92*
**Clulo**, Paul Jacques 1939- *WhoAmL 92*
**Clum**, James Avery 1937- *AmMWSc 92*
**Clump**, Curtis William 1923- *AmMWSc 92*
**Clune**, Henry W. *DrAPF 91*
**Clune**, Henry W. 1890- *BenetAL 91*
**Clune**, Joseph Henry 1914- *WhoRel 92*
**Clune**, Robert Bell 1920- *WhoRel 92*
**Cluney**, John Charles 1948- *WhoRel 92*
**Clunie**, Thomas John 1940- *AmMWSc 92*
**Clurman**, Harold 1901-1980 *BenetAL 91, FacFETw*
**Clurman**, Judith Sue 1953- *WhoEnt 92*
**Cluse**, Kenny Joseph 1945- *WhoBlA 92*
**Cluse**, Susan Marie 1959- *WhoWest 92*
**Cluskey**, Frank 1930- *Who 92*
**Cluster**, Richard *DrAPF 91*
**Clute**, Donna Lee 1964- *WhoRel 92*
**Clute**, John E. 1934- *WhoAmL 92, WhoFI 92*
**Clute**, Judith 1942- *TwCPaSc*
**Clute**, Robert Eugene, Jr. 1953- *WhoAmL 92*
**Clute**, Steve 1948- *WhoAmP 91*
**Clute**, William Thomas 1941- *WhoMW 92*
**Clutha**, Janet Paterson Frame 1924- *ConAu 36NR*
**Cluthe**, E. *DrAPF 91*
**Clutter**, B Allen 1942- *WhoAmP 91*
**Clutter**, Mary Elizabeth *AmMWSc 92*
**Clutter**, Roderick William 1933- *WhoMW 92*
**Clutter**, Russell Eugene 1939- *WhoAmP 91*
**Clutterbuck**, David Granville 1913- *Who 92*
**Clutterbuck**, Edmund Harry Michael d1991 *Who 92N*
**Clutterbuck**, Richard 1917- *WrDr 92*
**Clutterbuck**, Richard Lewis 1917- *IntAu&W 91, Who 92*
**Clutterham**, David Robert 1922- *AmMWSc 92*
**Clutton**, Rafe Henry 1929- *Who 92*
**Clutton-Brock**, Alan 1904-1976 *TwCPaSc*
**Clutton-Brock**, Arthur Guy 1906- *Who 92*
**Clutton-Brock**, Guy 1906- *IntWW 91*
**Clutton-Brock**, Timothy Hugh 1946- *Who 92*
**Cluver**, Claus 1932- *WhoMW 92*
**Cluxton**, David H 1943- *AmMWSc 92*
**Cluysenaar**, Anne 1936- *ConPo 91, IntAu&W 91, WrDr 92*
**Cluytens**, Andre 1905-1967 *NewAmDM*
**Cluzel**, Jean 1923- *IntWW 91*
**Clwyd**, Baron 1935- *Who 92*
**Clwyd**, Ann 1937- *Who 92*
**Clyborne**, H Howell, Jr 1953- *WhoAmP 91*
**Clyburn**, James E. 1940- *WhoBlA 92*
**Clyburn**, John B. 1942- *WhoBlA 92*
**Clyburn**, Luther Linn 1942- *WhoMW 92*
**Clyde**, Lord 1932- *Who 92*
**Clyde**, Calvin G 1924- *AmMWSc 92*
**Clyde**, David Neil 1934- *WhoAmL 92*
**Clyde**, Elmore Louis 1929- *WhoRel 92*
**Clyde**, Larry Forbes 1941- *WhoFI 92*
**Clyde**, Maggie 1952- *TwCPaSc*
**Clyde**, Wallace Alexander, Jr 1929- *AmMWSc 92*
**Clyder**, Thomas John 1953- *WhoMW 92*
**Clydesdale**, Edward Thomas 1960- *WhoEnt 92*
**Clydesdale**, Fergus Macdonald 1937- *AmMWSc 92*
**Clydesmuir**, Baron 1917- *Who 92*
**Clymer**, Arthur Benjamin 1920- *AmMWSc 92*
**Clymer**, Brian William 1947- *WhoFI 92*
**Clymer**, Eleanor 1906- *WrDr 92*
**Clymer**, Eleanor Lowenton 1906- *IntAu&W 91*
**Clymer**, Lewis W. 1910- *WhoBlA 92*
**Clymer**, Paul I 1937- *WhoAmP 91*
**Clymer**, Wayne Kenton 1917- *WhoRel 92*
**Clyne**, James W 1933- *WhoIns 92*
**Clyne**, John Rennel 1926- *WhoBlA 92*
**Clyne**, Michael George 1939- *IntWW 91*
**CmejLa**, Howard Edward 1926- *AmMWSc 92*
**Cmich**, Stanley A *WhoAmP 91*
**Coachman**, Alice 1923- *BlkOlyM, NotBlAW 92*
**Coachman**, Lawrence Keyes 1926- *AmMWSc 92*
**Coachman**, Winfred Charles 1927- *WhoBlA 92*
**Coad**, Brian William 1946- *AmMWSc 92*
**Coad**, Kermit *DrAPF 91*
**Coad**, Michele Marie 1949- *WhoAmL 92*
**Coady**, Aubrey William Burleton 1915- *Who 92*
**Coady**, Larry B 1933- *AmMWSc 92*
**Coady**, William Francis 1940- *WhoFI 92*
**Coage**, Allen James 1943- *BlkOlyM*
**Coaker**, A William 1927- *AmMWSc 92*
**Coaker**, George Mack 1927- *WhoRel 92*
**Coakley**, Charles Seymour 1914- *AmMWSc 92*
**Coakley**, George Washington 1814-1893 *BiInAmS*
**Coakley**, James Alexander, Jr 1946- *AmMWSc 92*
**Coakley**, John Phillip 1940- *AmMWSc 92*
**Coakley**, Mary Lewis *IntAu&W 91*
**Coakley**, Mary Lewis 1907- *WrDr 92*
**Coakley**, Mary Peter *AmMWSc 92*
**Coakley**, William Leo *DrAPF 91*
**Coakley**, William Thomas 1946- *WhoFI 92*
**Coale**, Ansley J 1917- *AmMWSc 92*
**Coale**, Edward Hodge 1920- *WhoFI 92*
**Coale**, J. Matthew 1959- *WhoEnt 92*
**Coales**, John Flavell 1907- *IntWW 91, Who 92*
**Coalson**, Jacqueline Jones 1938- *AmMWSc 92*
**Coalson**, Robert Ellis 1928- *AmMWSc 92*
**Coalter**, Milton J, Jr. 1949- *WhoRel 92*
**Coan**, Eugene Victor 1943- *AmMWSc 92*
**Coan**, John O, III 1953- *WhoAmP 91*
**Coan**, Richard W. 1928- *WrDr 92*
**Coan**, Richard Welton 1928- *IntAu&W 91*
**Coan**, Stephen B 1921- *AmMWSc 92*
**Coan**, Titus 1801-1882 *BiInAmS*
**Coane**, James B. 1948- *WhoEnt 92*
**Coar**, David H. 1943- *WhoAmL 92*
**Coar**, Richard J 1921- *AmMWSc 92*
**Coart**, John Craddock 1940- *WhoAmL 92*
**Coartney**, James S 1938- *AmMWSc 92*
**Coase**, Ronald H. 1910- *NewYTBS 91 [port]*
**Coase**, Ronald Harry 1910- *WhoMW 92*
**Coash**, John Russell 1922- *AmMWSc 92*
**Coash**, William Louis 1931- *WhoAmL 92*
**Coasters**, The *NewAmDM*
**Coaston**, Shirley Ann Dumas 1939- *WhoBlA 92*
**Coate**, Lester Edwin 1936- *WhoWest 92*
**Coates**, Albert 1882-1953 *NewAmDM*
**Coates**, Anne V. *IntMPA 92*
**Coates**, Anthony George 1936- *AmMWSc 92*
**Coates**, Anthony Robert M. *Who 92*
**Coates**, Arthur Donwell 1928- *AmMWSc 92*
**Coates**, Austin 1922- *WrDr 92*
**Coates**, Cecil Gray 1931- *WhoRel 92*
**Coates**, Clarence L, Jr 1923- *AmMWSc 92*
**Coates**, David Randall 1942- *Who 92*
**Coates**, Donald Allen 1938- *AmMWSc 92*
**Coates**, Donald Denison 1935- *WhoEnt 92*
**Coates**, Donald Robert 1922- *AmMWSc 92*
**Coates**, Doreen 1912- *WrDr 92*
**Coates**, Dudley James 1946- *Who 92*
**Coates**, Edward Malcolm, III 1966- *WhoFI 92*
**Coates**, Ernest 1916- *Who 92*
**Coates**, Frederick 1916- *Who 92*
**Coates**, Frederick Ross 1933- *WhoAmL 92*
**Coates**, Gary Joseph 1947- *AmMWSc 92*
**Coates**, Geoffrey Edward 1917- *AmMWSc 92, Who 92*
**Coates**, George *TwCPaSc*
**Coates**, Glenn Richard 1923- *WhoAmL 92*
**Coates**, James Richard 1935- *Who 92*
**Coates**, Janice E. 1942- *WhoBlA 92*
**Coates**, Jesse 1908- *AmMWSc 92*
**Coates**, John Francis 1922- *Who 92*
**Coates**, John Henry 1945- *IntWW 91, Who 92*
**Coates**, John Robert 1961- *WhoFI 92*
**Coates**, Joseph Francis 1929- *AmMWSc 92*
**Coates**, Ken 1930- *WrDr 92*
**Coates**, Kenneth 1956- *WrDr 92*
**Coates**, Kenneth Sidney 1930- *Who 92*
**Coates**, Michael Arthur 1924- *Who 92*
**Coates**, Norman 1931- *WhoFI 92*
**Coates**, Patrick Devereux d1990 *Who 92N*
**Coates**, Paul Douglas 1956- *WhoAmL 92*
**Coates**, R J 1922- *AmMWSc 92*
**Coates**, Ralph L 1934- *AmMWSc 92*
**Coates**, Reginald Charles 1920- *Who 92*
**Coates**, Reynell 1802-1886 *BiInAmS*
**Coates**, Robert C. 1928- *IntWW 91*
**Coates**, Robert C. 1937- *ConAu 134*
**Coates**, Robert Crawford 1937- *WhoAmL 92*
**Coates**, Robert M. 1897-1973 *BenetAL 91, ScFEYrs*
**Coates**, Robert Mercer 1938- *AmMWSc 92*
**Coates**, Ross Alexander 1932- *WhoWest 92*
**Coates**, Sean Steven 1968- *WhoWest 92*
**Coates**, Sheila *WrDr 92*
**Coates**, Shelby L. 1931- *WhoBlA 92*
**Coates**, Tom 1941- *TwCPaSc*
**Coates**, Wayne Evan 1947- *WhoWest 92*
**Coates**, Wells 1895-1958 *DcTwDes, FacFETw*
**Coatie**, Robert Mason 1945- *WhoBlA 92*
**Coats**, Alastair Francis Stuart 1921- *Who 92*
**Coats**, Alfred Bob *WhoFI 92*
**Coats**, Alfred Cornell 1936- *AmMWSc 92*
**Coats**, Arthur William 1930- *WhoRel 92*
**Coats**, Daniel R. 1943- *AlmAP 92 [port], WhoAmP 91, WhoMW 92*
**Coats**, David Jervis 1924- *IntWW 91*
**Coats**, Douglas James 1933- *WhoIns 92*
**Coats**, George W. 1936- *WrDr 92*
**Coats**, James O *WhoAmP 91*
**Coats**, Joel Robert 1948- *AmMWSc 92*
**Coats**, Keith Hal 1934- *AmMWSc 92*
**Coats**, Peggy Ruth 1952- *WhoWest 92*
**Coats**, Richard Lee 1936- *AmMWSc 92*
**Coats**, Robert Roy 1910- *AmMWSc 92*
**Coats**, William David 1924- *Who 92*
**Coats**, William Sloan, III 1950- *WhoAmL 92*
**Coatsworth**, Elizabeth 1893- *BenetAL 91*
**Coaxum**, Callie B. 1930- *WhoBlA 92*
**Coaxum**, Henry L., Jr. 1951- *WhoBlA 92*
**Cobalt**, Martin *SmATA 68*
**Cobau**, John Reed 1934- *WhoAmL 92*
**Cobb**, Amelie Suberbielle 1941- *WhoAmP 91*
**Cobb**, Arnett Cleophus 1918-1989 *FacFETw*
**Cobb**, Beatrice 1888-1959 *DcNCBi 1*
**Cobb**, Brian Eric 1945- *WhoEnt 92*
**Cobb**, Calvin Hayes, Jr. 1924- *WhoAmL 92*
**Cobb**, Carolus M 1922- *AmMWSc 92*
**Cobb**, Carolyn Jane 1943- *WhoEnt 92*
**Cobb**, Charles E. 1916- *WhoBlA 92*
**Cobb**, Charles E, Jr 1936- *WhoAmP 91*
**Cobb**, Charles Madison 1940- *AmMWSc 92*
**Cobb**, Clinton Levering 1842-1879 *DcNCBi 1*
**Cobb**, Collier 1862-1934 *DcNCBi 1*
**Cobb**, Cynthia Joan 1959- *WhoBlA 92*
**Cobb**, Donald D 1943- *AmMWSc 92*
**Cobb**, Elizabeth *WhoRel 92*
**Cobb**, Emerson Gillmore 1907- *AmMWSc 92*
**Cobb**, Ethel Washington 1925- *WhoBlA 92*

**Cobb,** Fields White, Jr 1932- AmMWSc 92
**Cobb,** Frederick Ross AmMWSc 92
**Cobb,** Garry Wilbert 1957- WhoBlA 92
**Cobb,** Glenn Wayne 1936- AmMWSc 92
**Cobb,** Grover C. d1975 LesBEnT 92
**Cobb,** Grover Cleveland, Jr 1935- AmMWSc 92
**Cobb,** Harold 1941- WhoBlA 92
**Cobb,** Henry Nichols 1926- Who 92
**Cobb,** Henry Stephen 1926- Who 92
**Cobb,** Howell 1772-1818 DcNCBi 1
**Cobb,** Howell 1815-1868 AmPolLe
**Cobb,** Howell 1922- WhoAmL 92
**Cobb,** Irvin S. 1876-1944 BenetAL 91
**Cobb,** J. WhoRel 92
**Cobb,** James C 1948- AmMWSc 92
**Cobb,** James Gurley 1947- WhoRel 92
**Cobb,** James Temple, Jr 1938- AmMWSc 92
**Cobb,** Jewel Plummer 1924- AmMWSc 92, NotBlAW 92 [port], WhoBlA 92, WhoWest 92
**Cobb,** John 1946- TwCPaSc
**Cobb,** John 1954- WhoAmP 91
**Cobb,** John Blackwell 1857-1923 DcNCBi 1
**Cobb,** John Boswell, Jr. 1925- RelLAm 91, WhoRel 92, WhoWest 92
**Cobb,** John Candler 1919- AmMWSc 92
**Cobb,** John Hunter, Jr. 1953- WhoBlA 92
**Cobb,** John Iverson 1938- AmMWSc 92
**Cobb,** Joseph B. 1819-1858 BenetAL 91
**Cobb,** Katrina Crawford 1960- WhoEnt 92
**Cobb,** Katrina Kees 1947- WhoWest 92
**Cobb,** Laurence A WhoAmP 91
**Cobb,** Loren 1948- AmMWSc 92
**Cobb,** Lucy Maria 1877-1969 DcNCBi 1
**Cobb,** Marck Redell 1948- WhoMW 92
**Cobb,** Nathaniel E. 1939- WhoBlA 92
**Cobb,** Needham Bryan 1836-1905 DcNCBi 1
**Cobb,** Owens Taylor, Jr. 1933- WhoAmL 92
**Cobb,** Patrick Dale 1952- WhoFI 92
**Cobb,** Raymond Lynn 1929- AmMWSc 92
**Cobb,** Raymond William 1957- WhoAmL 92
**Cobb,** Reginald John 1968- WhoBlA 92
**Cobb,** Richard 1917- WrDr 92
**Cobb,** Richard Charles 1917- IntWW 91, Who 92
**Cobb,** Robert Edward 1946- WhoEnt 92
**Cobb,** Ronald Lavell 1948- WhoAmP 91
**Cobb,** Rowena Noelani Blake 1939- WhoWest 92
**Cobb,** Roy Lampkin, Jr. 1934- WhoWest 92
**Cobb,** Sam Burton, Jr. 1927- WhoAmL 92
**Cobb,** Sharon A. 1953- WhoAmL 92
**Cobb,** Sharon Yvonne 1950- WhoEnt 92
**Cobb,** Shirley Ann 1936- WhoFI 92, WhoWest 92
**Cobb,** Stephen Archibald 1944- WhoAmP 91
**Cobb,** Stephen Henry 1942- WhoAmP 91
**Cobb,** Sue McCourt 1937- WhoAmL 92
**Cobb,** Susan Asmus 1955- WhoAmP 91
**Cobb,** Sylvanus, Jr. 1821-1887 BenetAL 91
**Cobb,** Terri R. 1934- WhoEnt 92
**Cobb,** Thelma M. WhoBlA 92
**Cobb,** Thomas DrAPF 91
**Cobb,** Thomas Berry 1939- AmMWSc 92
**Cobb,** Thomas Charles 1930- WhoWest 92
**Cobb,** Timothy Humphry 1909- Who 92
**Cobb,** Timothy Lee 1948- WhoWest 92
**Cobb,** Ty 1886-1961 FacFETw [port]
**Cobb,** Vicki 1938- IntAu&W 91, WrDr 92
**Cobb,** W. Montague 1904-1990 WhoBlA 92N
**Cobb,** Weldon J ScFEYrs
**Cobb,** William DrAPF 91
**Cobb,** William Montague 1904- AmMWSc 92
**Cobb,** William Thompson 1942- AmMWSc 92
**Cobban,** James 1910- Who 92
**Cobban,** James MacLaren 1849-1903 ScFEYrs
**Cobban,** William Aubrey 1916- AmMWSc 92, WhoWest 92
**Cobbe,** James Hamilton 1946- WhoFI 92
**Cobbe,** Thomas James 1918- AmMWSc 92
**Cobbett,** David John 1928- Who 92
**Cobbett,** Richard IntAu&W 91X
**Cobbett,** William 1763-1835 BenetAL 91, DcLB 107 [port], RfGEnL 91
**Cobbin,** Gloria Constance 1939- WhoAmP 91, WhoBlA 92
**Cobbin,** W. Frank, Jr. 1947- WhoBlA 92
**Cobbing,** Bob 1920- ConPo 91, IntAu&W 91, WrDr 92
**Cobble,** James Wikle 1926- AmMWSc 92
**Cobble,** Milan Houston 1922- AmMWSc 92
**Cobbold** Who 92
**Cobbold,** Baron 1937- Who 92
**Cobbold,** David 1919- Who 92
**Cobbold,** Patrick Mark 1934- Who 92
**Cobbold,** R S C 1931- AmMWSc 92
**Cobbold,** Richard Francis 1942- Who 92
**Cobbs,** David E. 1940- WhoBlA 92
**Cobbs,** Hartzell James 1942- WhoWest 92
**Cobbs,** John Lewis d1991 NewYTBS 91
**Cobbs,** Price Mashaw 1928- WhoBlA 92
**Cobbs,** Susie Ann 1924- WhoBlA 92
**Cobbs,** Winston H. B., Jr. 1955- WhoBlA 92
**Cobe,** Lori 1957- WhoEnt 92
**Cobe,** Sandy 1928- IntMPA 92, WhoEnt 92
**Cobe,** Sharyon Reis IntMPA 92
**Coben,** Marion 1922- WhoEnt 92
**Coberly,** Camden Arthur 1922- AmMWSc 92, WhoMW 92
**Cobern,** Martin E 1946- AmMWSc 92
**Cobert,** Robert William 1924- WhoWest 92
**Cobey,** William W, Jr 1939- WhoAmP 91
**Cobham,** Viscount 1943- Who 92
**Cobham,** Michael John 1927- Who 92
**Cobham,** William Emanuel, Jr. 1944- WhoEnt 92
**Cobian,** Miguelina 1947- BlkOlyM
**Cobianchi,** Thomas Theodore 1941- WhoWest 92
**Coble,** Anna Jane 1936- AmMWSc 92
**Coble,** Anne McKay 1957- WhoEnt 92
**Coble,** Harold Dean 1943- AmMWSc 92
**Coble,** Howard 1931- AlmAP 92 [port]
**Coble,** John Howard 1931- WhoAmP 91
**Coble,** Paul Ishler 1926- WhoMW 92
**Coble,** R L 1928- AmMWSc 92
**Coble,** William Carroll 1958- WhoFI 92
**Coblentz,** Donald Richard 1948- WhoAmL 92
**Coblentz,** Gaston 1918- WhoFI 92
**Coblentz,** Stanton A 1896-1982 TwCSFW 91
**Coblentz,** William Weber 1873-1962 FacFETw
**Coblenz,** Walter IntMPA 92
**Cobler,** John George 1918- AmMWSc 92
**Coblitz,** Gary Richard 1953- WhoFI 92
**Cobo,** Juan Cristobal 1963- WhoEnt 92
**Cobo Borda,** Juan Gustavo 1948- ConSpAP
**Cobos,** Ruben 1911- ConAu 135
**Coburn,** Alvin Langdon 1882-1966 FacFETw
**Coburn,** Andrew DrAPF 91
**Coburn,** Andrew 1932- ConAu 36NR, IntAu&W 91, WrDr 92
**Coburn,** Corbett Benjamin, Jr 1940- AmMWSc 92
**Coburn,** David Allen 1934- WhoAmP 91
**Coburn,** Donald Lee 1938- WhoEnt 92
**Coburn,** Donald Stephen 1939- WhoAmP 91
**Coburn,** Everett Robert 1915- AmMWSc 92
**Coburn,** Frank Emerson 1912- AmMWSc 92
**Coburn,** Horace Hunter 1922- AmMWSc 92
**Coburn,** Jack Wesley 1932- AmMWSc 92, WhoWest 92
**Coburn,** James 1928- IntMPA 92, IntWW 91, WhoEnt 92A
**Coburn,** James Edward 1945- WhoMW 92
**Coburn,** James LeRoy 1933- WhoMW 92
**Coburn,** Joel Thomas 1955- AmMWSc 92
**Coburn,** John 1925- IntWW 91
**Coburn,** John Bowen 1914- WhoRel 92
**Coburn,** John Wyllie 1933- AmMWSc 92
**Coburn,** Kathleen 1905- Who 92
**Coburn,** Kathleen 1905-1991 ConAu 135
**Coburn,** L.J. TwCWW 91, WrDr 92
**Coburn,** Lewis Alan 1940- AmMWSc 92
**Coburn,** Marjorie Foster 1939- WhoWest 92
**Coburn,** Michael Doyle 1939- AmMWSc 92
**Coburn,** Nesbitt Ellison 1947- WhoMW 92
**Coburn,** Richard Karl 1920- AmMWSc 92
**Coburn,** Robert A 1938- AmMWSc 92
**Coburn,** Robert Leonard 1929- WhoMW 92
**Coburn,** Ronald F 1931- AmMWSc 92
**Coburn,** Stephen Putnam 1936- AmMWSc 92
**Coburn,** Theodore James 1926- AmMWSc 92
**Coburn,** Thomas Bowen 1944- WhoRel 92
**Coburn,** Tom C WhoAmP 91
**Coburn,** Walt 1889-1971 TwCWW 91
**Coburn,** William Carl, Jr 1926- AmMWSc 92
**Coby,** William Francis 1948- WhoWest 92
**Coca,** Imogene LesBEnT 92
**Coca,** Imogene 1908- ConTFT 9, IntMPA 92
**Coca,** Joella Rosemary 1954- WhoHisp 92
**Cocadiz,** Norval Tardecilla 1943- WhoMW 92
**Cocanougher,** Arthur Benton 1938- WhoFI 92
**Cocanougher,** George Truett 1941- WhoRel 92
**Cocanower,** R D 1920- AmMWSc 92
**Cocca,** M A 1925- AmMWSc 92
**Coccagna,** Edmund G. 1938- WhoFI 92
**Cocchi,** John 1939- IntMPA 92
**Cocchiarella,** Vicki Marshall 1949- WhoAmP 91
**Cocciolone,** Vincent Scott 1964- WhoEnt 92
**Cocco,** Jacqueline M WhoAmP 91
**Coccodrilli,** Gus D, Jr 1945- AmMWSc 92
**Coccoli Palsho,** Dorothea 1947- WhoFI 92
**Coceani,** Flavio 1937- AmMWSc 92
**Coch,** Nicholas Kyros 1938- AmMWSc 92
**Cocheo,** John Frank 1944- WhoAmL 92
**Cochis,** Thomas 1936- AmMWSc 92
**Cochkanoff,** O 1926- AmMWSc 92
**Cochran,** Allan Chester 1942- AmMWSc 92
**Cochran,** Andrew Aaron 1919- AmMWSc 92
**Cochran,** Anne Westfall 1954- WhoWest 92
**Cochran,** Billy Juan 1933- AmMWSc 92
**Cochran,** Charles Norman 1925- AmMWSc 92
**Cochran,** Dale M 1928- WhoAmP 91
**Cochran,** Dale Raymond 1952- WhoWest 92
**Cochran,** David L 1929- AmMWSc 92
**Cochran,** David Lee AmMWSc 92
**Cochran,** Deborah Rand 1939- WhoAmP 91
**Cochran,** Donald Gordon 1927- AmMWSc 92
**Cochran,** Donald Roy Francis 1926- AmMWSc 92
**Cochran,** Donnie L. 1954- WhoBlA 92
**Cochran,** Earl V. 1922- WhoFI 92
**Cochran,** Eddie 1938-1960 NewAmDM
**Cochran,** Edward G. 1953- WhoBlA 92
**Cochran,** George Calloway, III 1932- WhoAmL 92, WhoFI 92
**Cochran,** George Thomas 1938- AmMWSc 92
**Cochran,** George Van Brunt 1932- AmMWSc 92
**Cochran,** Harry Young WhoAmP 91
**Cochran,** Henry Douglas, Jr 1943- AmMWSc 92
**Cochran,** Herschel J. 1928-1987 WhoBlA 92N
**Cochran,** Jackie 1906?-1980 FacFETw
**Cochran,** Jacqueline d1980 HanAmWH
**Cochran,** Jacqueline Louise 1953- WhoFI 92
**Cochran,** James 1761-1817 DcNCBi 1
**Cochran,** James Alan 1936- AmMWSc 92
**Cochran,** James David, Jr. 1951- WhoBlA 92
**Cochran,** Jeff IntAu&W 91X, TwCWW 91, WrDr 92
**Cochran,** Jeffery Keith 1952- AmMWSc 92
**Cochran,** John Charles 1935- AmMWSc 92
**Cochran,** John Euell, Jr 1944- AmMWSc 92
**Cochran,** John Francis 1930- AmMWSc 92
**Cochran,** John M., III 1941- WhoAmL 92
**Cochran,** John Robert 1937- WhoMW 92
**Cochran,** John Rodney 1920- AmMWSc 92
**Cochran,** Johnnie L., Jr. 1937- WhoBlA 92
**Cochran,** Joseph Edward, II 1952- WhoFI 92
**Cochran,** Joseph Wesley 1954- WhoAmL 92
**Cochran,** Kenneth William 1923- AmMWSc 92, WhoMW 92
**Cochran,** Kent Hays 1949- WhoRel 92
**Cochran,** Leonard DrAPF 91
**Cochran,** Lewis Wellington 1915- AmMWSc 92
**Cochran,** Mary Miriam 1963- WhoEnt 92
**Cochran,** Patrick Holmes 1937- AmMWSc 92
**Cochran,** Paul Terry 1938- AmMWSc 92
**Cochran,** Rebecca Sue 1959- WhoFI 92
**Cochran,** Robert Allen 1942- WhoMW 92
**Cochran,** Robert G. 1944- WhoAmL 92
**Cochran,** Robert Glenn 1919- AmMWSc 92
**Cochran,** S. Thomas 1950- WhoBlA 92
**Cochran,** Scott Coryell 1960- WhoEnt 92
**Cochran,** Stephen G 1947- AmMWSc 92
**Cochran,** Stephen Grey 1947- WhoAmL 92
**Cochran,** Thad 1937- AlmAP 92 [port], IntWW 91, WhoAmP 91
**Cochran,** Thomas 1902- WrDr 92
**Cochran,** Thomas B 1940- AmMWSc 92
**Cochran,** Thomas Howard 1940- AmMWSc 92
**Cochran,** Todd S. 1920- WhoBlA 92
**Cochran,** Verlan Leyerl 1938- AmMWSc 92
**Cochran,** William 1922- IntWW 91, Who 92
**Cochran,** William C 1934- WhoAmP 91
**Cochran,** William Ronald 1940- AmMWSc 92
**Cochrane** Who 92
**Cochrane,** Lord 1991- Who 92
**Cochrane,** Alexander 1802-1865 BiInAmS
**Cochrane,** Alexander, Jr 1840-1919 BiInAmS
**Cochrane,** Betsy Lane WhoAmP 91
**Cochrane,** Bradford Fleming 1956- WhoEnt 92
**Cochrane,** Cameron 1933- Who 92
**Cochrane,** Chappelle Cecil 1913- AmMWSc 92
**Cochrane,** Charles Martel 1956- WhoAmL 92
**Cochrane,** Christopher Duncan 1938- Who 92
**Cochrane,** David Earle 1944- AmMWSc 92
**Cochrane,** Francis Douglas 1920- WhoAmL 92
**Cochrane,** Grizel EncAmaz 91
**Cochrane,** Hector 1940- AmMWSc 92
**Cochrane,** John Campbell 1929- WhoAmP 91
**Cochrane,** Kevin Samuel 1956- WhoEnt 92
**Cochrane,** Marc 1946- Who 92
**Cochrane,** Michael David 1948- WhoEnt 92
**Cochrane,** Peggy 1926- WrDr 92
**Cochrane,** Richard James Christopher 1945- WhoRel 92
**Cochrane,** Robert H. 1924- WhoRel 92
**Cochrane,** Robert Lowe 1931- AmMWSc 92
**Cochrane,** Robert W 1940- AmMWSc 92
**Cochrane,** Shirley Graves DrAPF 91
**Cochrane,** Stephen TwCPaSc
**Cochrane,** Steven G. 1952- WhoFI 92
**Cochrane,** William 1926- AmMWSc 92
**Cochrane,** William McWhorter 1917- WhoAmP 91
**Cochrane of Cults,** Baron 1926- Who 92
**Cochrum,** Arthur L 1925- AmMWSc 92
**Cochrun,** John Wesley 1918- WhoFI 92, WhoWest 92
**Cocivera,** Michael 1937- AmMWSc 92
**Cock,** Lorne M 1932- AmMWSc 92
**Cockburn,** Alden G., Jr. 1947- WhoBlA 92
**Cockburn,** Alexander 1941- WrDr 92
**Cockburn,** Catharine 1679-1749 BlkwCEP
**Cockburn,** Cliff J. 1963- WhoRel 92
**Cockburn,** Eve Gillian 1924- WhoMW 92
**Cockburn,** Forrester 1934- Who 92
**Cockburn,** John 1925- Who 92
**Cockburn,** Robert 1909- IntWW 91, Who 92
**Cockburn,** Sarah Caudwell IntAu&W 91
**Cockburn,** William 1943- Who 92
**Cockburn-Campbell,** Thomas 1918- Who 92
**Cockcroft,** George P. 1932- WhoEnt 92
**Cockcroft,** Janet Rosemary 1916- Who 92
**Cockcroft,** John Douglas 1897-1967 FacFETw, WhoNob 90
**Cockcroft,** John Hoyle 1934- IntAu&W 91, Who 92
**Cockcroft,** Wilfred 1923- Who 92
**Cocke,** John 1925- AmMWSc 92
**Cocke,** Norman Atwater 1884-1974 DcNCBi 1
**Cockell,** Michael Henry 1933- Who 92
**Cocker,** Douglas 1945- TwCPaSc
**Cocker,** Joe 1944- WhoEnt 92
**Cockeram,** Eric 1924- Who 92
**Cockerell,** Christopher 1910- IntWW 91, Who 92
**Cockerell,** Gary Lee 1945- AmMWSc 92
**Cockerham,** C. Clark 1921- IntWW 91
**Cockerham,** Columbus Clark 1921- AmMWSc 92
**Cockerham,** Gloria Ross 1953- WhoBlA 92
**Cockerham,** Haven Earl 1947- WhoBlA 92
**Cockerham,** Kirby Lee, Jr. 1926- WhoWest 92
**Cockerham,** Lorris G 1935- AmMWSc 92
**Cockerill,** Geoffrey Fairfax 1922- Who 92
**Cockerline,** Alan Wesley 1926- AmMWSc 92
**Cockerton,** John Clifford Penn 1927- Who 92
**Cockett,** Abraham Timothy K 1928- AmMWSc 92
**Cockett,** Frank Bernard 1916- Who 92
**Cockett,** Geoffrey Howard 1926- Who 92
**Cockett,** Mary 1915- IntAu&W 91, WrDr 92
**Cockfield** Who 92
**Cockfield,** Baron 1916- IntWW 91, Who 92
**Cockin,** George Eyles Irwin 1908- Who 92
**Cocking,** Edward Charles Daniel 1931- IntWW 91, Who 92
**Cocking,** W Dean 1940- AmMWSc 92
**Cockley,** David Hoyt 1944- WhoMW 92
**Cocklin,** Anna Wallace 1923- WhoAmP 91
**Cockman,** Richard Lee 1949- WhoRel 92
**Cockram,** George 1861-1950 TwCPaSc
**Cockram,** John 1908- Who 92
**Cockrell,** Cathy DrAPF 91

Cockrell, Edwin Lynn 1959- WhoMW 92
Cockrell, Frank Boyd, II 1948- WhoEnt 92, WhoWest 92
Cockrell, Lila WhoAmP 91
Cockrell, Marian 1909- WrDr 92
Cockrell, Mechera Ann 1953- WhoBlA 92
Cockrell, Michael Kevin 1957- WhoEnt 92
Cockrell, Richard Carter 1925- WhoAmL 92
Cockrell, Robert Alexander 1909- AmMWSc 92
Cockrell, Ronald Spencer 1938- AmMWSc 92
Cockrell, William Foster, Jr. 1944- WhoAmL 92
Cockrem, Michael Charles Milner 1959- WhoMW 92
Cockrill, Ann Teresa 1953- WhoAmL 92
Cockrill, Maurice 1936- TwCPaSc
Cockrum, Elmer Lendell 1920- AmMWSc 92
Cockrum, Richard Henry 1950- AmMWSc 92
Cockrum, Robert Barrett 1947- WhoMW 92
Cockrum, William Monroe, III 1937- WhoFI 92, WhoWest 92
Cocks Who 92
Cocks, Anna Gwenllian S. Who 92
Cocks, Francis William 1913- Who 92
Cocks, Franklin H 1941- AmMWSc 92
Cocks, Freda Mary 1915- Who 92
Cocks, Gary Thomas 1943- AmMWSc 92
Cocks, George Gosson 1919- AmMWSc 92
Cocks, Leonard Robert Morrison 1938- Who 92
Cocks, Robin Who 92
Cocks Of Hartcliffe, Baron 1929- IntWW 91, Who 92
Cockshaw, Alan 1937- Who 92
Cockshut, A. O. J. 1927- WrDr 92
Cockshut, Gillian Elise Who 92
Cockshutt, E P 1929- AmMWSc 92
Cockwell, Jack Lynn 1941- WhoFI 92
Coco, Mark Steven 1952- WhoAmL 92
Coco, Richard Alan 1952- WhoFI 92
Coco, Samuel Barbin 1927- WhoFI 92
Cocolas, George Harry 1929- AmMWSc 92
Cocoris, George Michael 1939- WhoRel 92
Cocozza, Anthony J 1950- WhoIns 92
Cocozzoli, Gary Richard 1951- WhoMW 92
Cocteau, Jean 1889-1963 GuFrLit 1, IntDcF 2-2 [port]
Cocteau, Jean 1891-1963 FacFETw
Coda-Wagener, Shaw Bradley 1959- WhoFI 92
Codd, Edgar Frank 1923- AmMWSc 92
Codd, John Edward 1936- AmMWSc 92
Codd, Ronald Geoffrey 1932- Who 92
Codding, Edward George 1942- AmMWSc 92
Codding, George A., Jr. 1923- WrDr 92
Codding, George Arthur, Jr 1923- IntAu&W 91, WhoWest 92
Codding, Penelope Wixson 1946- AmMWSc 92
Coddington, Earl Alexander 1920- AmMWSc 92
Coddington, Iqbal Jwaideh 1935- WhoWest 92
Code, Arthur Dodd 1923- AmMWSc 92
Code, Charles Frederick 1910- AmMWSc 92
Coden, Michael H 1947- AmMWSc 92
Coden, Michael Henri 1947- WhoFI 92
Coder, S. Maxwell 1902- WrDr 92
Coder, Samuel Maxwell 1902- IntAu&W 91, WhoRel 92
Coderre, Elaine A 1947- WhoAmP 91
Coderre, Jeffrey Albert 1953- AmMWSc 92
Codey, Richard J 1946- WhoAmP 91
Codikow, Stacy E. 1962- WhoEnt 92
Codina, Armando Mario 1946- WhoHisp 92
Codington, John F 1920- AmMWSc 92
Codispoti, Gregory Mark 1951- WhoMW 92
Codispoti, Louis Anthony 1940- AmMWSc 92
Codreanu, Corneliu Zelea 1899-1938 BiDExR, EncTR 91 [port]
Codrescu, Andrei DrAPF 91
Codrescu, Andrei 1946- ConAu 34NR, LiExTwC, WrDr 92
Codrington, Isabel TwCPaSc
Codrington, John Ernest Fleetwood 1919- Who 92
Codrington, Robert Smith 1925- AmMWSc 92
Codrington, Simon 1923- Who 92
Codrington, William 1934- Who 92
Codron, Michael Victor 1930- Who 92
Cody, Al TwCWW 91
Cody, Buffalo Bill 1846-1917 RComAH
Cody, D Thane 1932- AmMWSc 92
Cody, Dorothy A 1935- WhoAmP 91
Cody, George Dewey 1930- AmMWSc 92
Cody, Henry Leroy 1922- WhoBlA 92
Cody, Iron Eyes 1915- WhoEnt 92
Cody, James IntAu&W 91X
Cody, James Marion DrAPF 91
Cody, James R. WrDr 92
Cody, Jess TwCWW 91
Cody, John TwCWW 91
Cody, John Patrick 1907-1982 RelLAm 91
Cody, John T 1949- AmMWSc 92
Cody, Judith DrAPF 91
Cody, Liza 1944- WrDr 92
Cody, Martin Leonard 1941- AmMWSc 92
Cody, Michael Albert 1934- WhoWest 92
Cody, Nancy Cosgrove 1954- WhoAmL 92
Cody, Peter Sebastian 1962- WhoFI 92
Cody, Regina Jacqueline 1943- AmMWSc 92
Cody, Reynolds M 1929- AmMWSc 92
Cody, Stetson TwCWW 91
Cody, Terence Edward 1938- AmMWSc 92
Cody, Thomas G 1929- WhoAmP 91
Cody, Thomas Gerald 1941- WhoAmL 92, WhoFI 92
Cody, Vivian 1943- AmMWSc 92
Cody, W J Michael 1936- WhoAmP 91
Cody, Walt IntAu&W 91X, TwCWW 91
Cody, Wayne Livingston 1959- AmMWSc 92
Cody, William Frederick 1846-1917 BenetAL 91
Cody, William James 1922- AmMWSc 92
Cody, William L. 1934- WhoBlA 92
Cody, Wilmer S WhoAmP 91
Coe, Beresford 1919- AmMWSc 92
Coe, Bernice WhoEnt 92
Coe, Carol Arnetta 1947- WhoAmP 91
Coe, Charles Francis 1890- BenetAL 91
Coe, Charles Gardner 1950- AmMWSc 92
Coe, Cynthia Wesson 1955- WhoEnt 92
Coe, Denis Walter 1929- Who 92
Coe, Edward Harold, Jr 1926- AmMWSc 92
Coe, Elmon Lee 1931- AmMWSc 92
Coe, Fred d1979 LesBEnT 92
Coe, Fredric Lawrence 1936- AmMWSc 92
Coe, George Albert 1862-1951 RelLAm 91
Coe, Gerald Edwin 1922- AmMWSc 92
Coe, Gordon Randolph 1933- AmMWSc 92
Coe, Henry H R 1946- WhoAmP 91
Coe, Howard Sheldon 1888-1918 BilnAmS
Coe, Ilse G. 1911- WhoAmL 92
Coe, Jo-Anne L 1933- WhoAmP 91
Coe, John Emmons 1931- AmMWSc 92
Coe, John William 1924- WhoMW 92
Coe, Jonathan 1961- ConAu 133
Coe, Kenneth Loren 1927- AmMWSc 92
Coe, Linda Marlene Wolfe 1941- WhoMW 92
Coe, Lisa Ann 1960- WhoMW 92
Coe, Margaret Louise Shaw 1917- WhoWest 92
Coe, Marvin Parnick 1931- WhoFI 92
Coe, Michael 1929- WrDr 92
Coe, Michael Douglas 1929- AmMWSc 92
Coe, Richard Hanson 1920- AmMWSc 92
Coe, Richard N 1923- IntAu&W 91
Coe, Robert H, Jr 1950- WhoAmP 91
Coe, Robert Milton 1931- WhoEnt 92
Coe, Robert Stephen 1939- AmMWSc 92
Coe, Robert William 1927- WhoAmP 91
Coe, Roger Norman 1935- WhoAmL 92
Coe, Sebastian Newbold 1956- IntWW 91, Who 92
Coe, Sue 1951- TwCPaSc
Coe, Sue 1952- WorArt 1980 [port]
Coe, Tucker IntAu&W 91X, WrDr 92
Coe, William C. 1930- WrDr 92
Coe, William Charles 1930- IntAu&W 91
Coe, William Jerome 1935- WhoWest 92
Coelho, Anthony Mendes, Jr 1947- AmMWSc 92, WhoFI 92
Coelho, Joseph Richard 1946- WhoRel 92
Coelho, Peter J. 1921- WhoBlA 92
Coelho, Tony 1942- IntWW 91, WhoAmP 91, WhoWest 92
Coeme, Guy 1946- IntWW 91
Coen, Ethan 1958- IntAu&W 91, IntMPA 92, News 92-1 [port], WhoEnt 92
Coen, Gerald Marvin 1939- AmMWSc 92
Coen, Guido IntMPA 92
Coen, Joel 1955- IntAu&W 91, IntMPA 92, News 92-1 [port], WhoEnt 92
Coen, Lodewijk Karel Celina 1952- WhoEnt 92
Coen, Massimo 1918- Who 92
Coen, Rena Neumann 1925- IntAu&W 91, WrDr 92
Coen, Victoria Lynn 1954- WhoWest 92
Coerper, Milo George 1925- WhoAmL 92
Coerr, Eleanor 1922- SmATA 67 [port]
Coerr, Eleanor Beatrice 1922- IntAu&W 91, WrDr 92
Coes, Donald Vinton 1943- WhoFI 92
Coester, Fritz 1921- AmMWSc 92
Coetsee, Hendrik Jacobus 1931- IntWW 91
Coetzee, J.M. 1940- ConLC 66 [port], ConNov 91, FacFETw, WrDr 92
Coetzee, Johannes Francois 1924- AmMWSc 92
Coetzee, John M 1940- IntAu&W 91, IntWW 91, Who 92
Coetzer, William Bedford d1989 IntWW 91N
Coey, John Michael David 1945- IntWW 91
Cofer, Berdette Henry WhoWest 92
Cofer, Daniel Baxter AmMWSc 92
Cofer, Harland E, Jr 1922- AmMWSc 92
Cofer, James Henry 1925- WhoBlA 92
Cofer, Judith Ortiz DrAPF 91
Cofer, Judith Ortiz 1952- WhoHisp 92, WrDr 92
Cofer, Michael Lynn 1960- WhoBlA 92
Coffee, Gale Furman 1939- WhoEnt 92
Coffee, Gary 1956- WhoAmP 91
Coffee, John Collins, Jr. 1944- WhoAmL 92
Coffee, Lawrence Winston 1929- WhoBlA 92
Coffee, Lenore 1900-1984 ReelWom
Coffee, Melvin Arnold 1934- WhoAmL 92
Coffee, Richard J WhoAmP 91
Coffee, Robert Dodd 1920- AmMWSc 92
Coffee, Virginia Claire 1920- WhoMW 92
Coffeen, W W 1914- AmMWSc 92
Coffen, Richard Wayne 1941- WhoRel 92
Coffer, David Edwin 1913- Who 92
Coffey, Barbara J. 1931- WhoBlA 92
Coffey, Bert WhoAmP 91
Coffey, Brian ConAu 36NR, LiExTwC, WrDr 92
Coffey, Charles William, II 1949- AmMWSc 92
Coffey, David L 1932- WhoAmP 91
Coffey, David Roy 1941- Who 92
Coffey, Dennis James 1940- WhoMW 92
Coffey, Dewitt, Jr 1935- AmMWSc 92
Coffey, Donald Straley 1932- AmMWSc 92
Coffey, Gilbert Haven, Jr. 1926- WhoBlA 92
Coffey, Henry Joseph, Jr. 1952- WhoFI 92
Coffey, Jack Franklin 1928- WhoRel 92
Coffey, James Cecil, Jr 1938- AmMWSc 92
Coffey, James Robert 1942- WhoIns 92
Coffey, John J WhoAmP 91
Coffey, John Joseph 1940- AmMWSc 92
Coffey, John L WhoAmP 91
Coffey, John Lawrence 1926- WhoEnt 92
Coffey, John Louis 1922- WhoAmL 92
Coffey, John P. 1941- WhoMW 92
Coffey, John William 1937- AmMWSc 92
Coffey, Kathryn Robinson WhoWest 92
Coffey, Kelly Ann 1954- WhoMW 92
Coffey, Kendall Brindley 1952- WhoAmL 92
Coffey, Larry Bruce 1940- WhoAmL 92
Coffey, Marilyn DrAPF 91
Coffey, Marvin Dale 1930- AmMWSc 92
Coffey, Michael Desmond 1928- WhoAmP 91
Coffey, Richard WhoBlA 92
Coffey, Ronald Gibson 1936- AmMWSc 92
Coffey, Sean O 1950- WhoAmP 91
Coffey, Shelby, III IntWW 91
Coffey, Terry D. 1964- WhoEnt 92
Coffey, Thomas IntWW 91
Coffey, Thomas William 1959- WhoAmL 92
Coffey, Timothy 1941- AmMWSc 92
Coffey, Virginia Mae 1929- WhoAmP 91
Coffey, William L. 1924- WhoBlA 92
Coffield, Conrad Eugene 1930- WhoAmL 92
Coffill, Marjorie Louise 1917- WhoWest 92
Coffin, Addison 1822-1897 DcNCBi 1
Coffin, Audress Marie 1949- WhoFI 92
Coffin, Bertha Louise 1919- WhoFI 92, WhoMW 92
Coffin, Charles Carleton 1823-1896 BenetAL 91
Coffin, Cyril Edwin 1919- Who 92
Coffin, David L 1913- AmMWSc 92
Coffin, David R. 1918- WrDr 92
Coffin, David R. 1954- WhoWest 92
Coffin, Dwight Clay 1938- WhoFI 92
Coffin, Frances Dunkle AmMWSc 92
Coffin, Frank Morey 1919- IntWW 91, WhoAmL 92
Coffin, Harold Garth 1938- AmMWSc 92
Coffin, Harold Glen 1926- AmMWSc 92
Coffin, Harold Walter 1908- WhoWest 92
Coffin, Henry S 1877-1954 FacFETw
Coffin, Henry Sloane, Sr. 1877-1954 RelLAm 91
Coffin, James Henry 1806-1873 BilnAmS
Coffin, James Robert 1942- WhoAmP 91, WhoHisp 92
Coffin, John Huntington Crane 1815-1890 BilnAmS
Coffin, John Miller 1944- AmMWSc 92
Coffin, Laurence Haines 1933- AmMWSc 92
Coffin, Levi 1789-1877 DcNCBi 1
Coffin, Louis F, Jr 1917- AmMWSc 92
Coffin, Lyn DrAPF 91
Coffin, Oscar Jackson 1887-1956 DcNCBi 1
Coffin, Perley Andrews 1908- AmMWSc 92
Coffin, Philip Milton, III WhoAmL 92
Coffin, Richard Keith 1940- WhoAmL 92
Coffin, Robert P. Tristram 1892-1955 BenetAL 91
Coffin, Robert Parker 1917- WhoMW 92
Coffin, Roy Riddell 1932- WhoRel 92
Coffin, Selden Jennings 1838-1915 BilnAmS
Coffin, Tristram 1912- IntAu&W 91, WrDr 92
Coffin, Tristram Potter 1922- WrDr 92
Coffin, Violet B 1920- WhoAmP 91
Coffin, William Sloane, Jr. 1924- AmPeW, FacFETw
Coffinas, George Gustav 1958- WhoAmL 92
Coffinger, Maralin Katharyne 1935- WhoWest 92
Coffino, Philip 1942- AmMWSc 92
Coffman, Barbara Frances 1907- WrDr 92
Coffman, Barry Preston 1947- WhoEnt 92
Coffman, Charles Benjamin 1941- AmMWSc 92
Coffman, Charles Vernon 1935- AmMWSc 92
Coffman, Dallas Whitney 1957- WhoFI 92
Coffman, Edward G, Jr 1934- AmMWSc 92
Coffman, Edward M. 1929- WrDr 92
Coffman, Gary L. 1949- WhoWest 92
Coffman, Glen Earl 1943- WhoFI 92
Coffman, Harold H 1915- AmMWSc 92
Coffman, Harry Thomas 1910- WhoAmL 92
Coffman, Hugh Marshall 1948- WhoAmP 91
Coffman, James Bruce 1925- AmMWSc 92
Coffman, James Raymond 1946- WhoRel 92
Coffman, Jay D 1928- AmMWSc 92
Coffman, John S. 1848-1899 AmPeW
Coffman, John Samuel 1848-1899 RelLAm 91
Coffman, John W 1931- AmMWSc 92
Coffman, Kenneth Morrow 1921- WhoMW 92
Coffman, Mark Anthony 1966- WhoRel 92
Coffman, Mike 1955- WhoAmP 91
Coffman, Moody Lee 1925- AmMWSc 92
Coffman, Orene Burton 1938- WhoFI 92
Coffman, Phillip Hudson 1936- WhoMW 92
Coffman, Ralph Eugene, Jr. 1951- WhoFI 92
Coffman, Robert Edgar 1931- AmMWSc 92
Coffman, Steven DrAPF 91
Coffman, Virginia 1914- IntAu&W 91, WrDr 92
Coffman, Ward Denver, III 1953- WhoAmL 92
Coffman, William Eugene 1913- WhoMW 92
Coffman, William Page 1942- AmMWSc 92
Coffman, William Thomas 1940- WhoAmL 92
Coffou, Sara Jane WhoFI 92
Coffrin, Albert Wheeler 1919- WhoAmL 92
Coffy, Robert 1920- WhoRel 92
Cofield, Elizabeth Bias 1920- WhoBlA 92
Cofield, Howard John 1926- WhoAmL 92
Cofield, James E., Jr. 1945- WhoBlA 92
Cofield, Philip Thomas 1951- WhoWest 92
Cofoid, Paul Brian 1945- WhoMW 92
Cofrancesco, Anthony J 1910- AmMWSc 92
Cogan, Adrian Ilie 1946- AmMWSc 92
Cogan, David Glendenning 1908- AmMWSc 92
Cogan, David Joseph 1923- WhoEnt 92
Cogan, Edward J 1925- AmMWSc 92
Cogan, Harold Louis 1931- AmMWSc 92
Cogan, Jerry Albert, Jr 1935- AmMWSc 92
Cogan, John Francis, Jr. 1926- WhoAmL 92
Cogan, Mark Charles 1956- WhoAmL 92
Cogan, Marshall S. 1937- WhoFI 92
Cogan, Martin AmMWSc 92
Cogan, Mordechai 1939- WhoRel 92
Cogan, Robert David 1930- WhoEnt 92
Cogan, Wade Emerson 1949- WhoMW 92
Cogbill, Bell A 1909- AmMWSc 92
Cogburn, Max Oliver 1927- WhoAmL 92
Cogburn, Robert Francis 1944- AmMWSc 92
Cogburn, Robert Ray 1935- AmMWSc 92
Cogdell, D Parthenia 1938- WhoAmP 91
Cogdell, Parthenia D. 1938- WhoBlA 92

**Cogdell**, Richard 1724-1787 *DcNCBi 1*
**Cogdell**, Thomas James 1934- *AmMWSc 92*
**Cogen**, William Maurice 1909- *AmMWSc 92*
**Coger**, Rick 1940- *WhoMW 92*
**Coggan**, Baron 1909- *IntWW 91, Who 92*
**Coggan**, Lord 1909- *WrDr 92*
**Coggan**, Donald 1909- *FacFETw*
**Coggan**, Frederick Donald 1909- *WhoRel 92*
**Coggeshall**, Bruce Amsden 1941- *WhoAmL 92*
**Coggeshall**, Janice Reddig 1935- *WhoAmP 91*
**Coggeshall**, Norman David 1916- *AmMWSc 92, WhoFI 92*
**Coggeshall**, Richard E 1932- *AmMWSc 92*
**Coggeshall**, Rosanne *DrAPF 91*
**Coggin**, Charlotte Joan 1928- *WhoWest 92*
**Coggin**, Frank E *WhoAmP 91*
**Coggin**, Joseph Hiram 1938- *AmMWSc 92*
**Coggin**, Philip A. 1917- *WrDr 92*
**Coggin**, Walter Arthur 1916- *WhoRel 92*
**Coggins**, Charles William, Jr 1930- *AmMWSc 92*
**Coggins**, George Miller, Jr. 1939- *WhoFI 92*
**Coggins**, Jack B. 1914- *WrDr 92*
**Coggins**, James Ray 1947- *AmMWSc 92*
**Coggins**, John Thomas 1945- *WhoMW 92*
**Coggins**, Leroy 1932- *AmMWSc 92*
**Coggins**, Paul E 1951- *IntAu&W 91*
**Coggins**, Paul Edward 1951- *WhoAmL 92*
**Coggleshall**, William Turner 1824-1867 *BenetAL 91*
**Coggon**, Philip 1942- *AmMWSc 92*
**Coggs**, G Spencer 1949- *WhoAmP 91*
**Coggs**, Granville Coleridge 1925- *WhoBlA 92*
**Coggs**, Marcia P 1928- *WhoAmP 91*
**Coggs-Jones**, Elizabeth Monette 1956- *WhoAmP 91*
**Coggshall**, Gene *DrAPF 91*
**Coghill**, Egerton James Nevill Tobias 1930- *Who 92*
**Coghill**, John B 1925- *WhoAmP 91*
**Coghill**, John Bruce 1925- *WhoWest 92*
**Coghill**, William Thomas, Jr. 1927- *WhoAmL 92*
**Coghlan**, Anne Eveline 1927- *AmMWSc 92*
**Coghlan**, David B 1920- *AmMWSc 92*
**Coghlan**, Frank Edward, Jr. 1916- *WhoEnt 92*
**Coghlan**, Matthew Edward 1962- *WhoAmL 92*
**Cogley**, Allen C 1940- *AmMWSc 92*
**Cogley**, Gary James 1937- *WhoEnt 92*
**Coglianese**, James Anthony 1960- *WhoMW 92*
**Cogliano**, Joseph Albert 1930- *AmMWSc 92*
**Cogman**, Frederick Walter 1913- *Who 92*
**Cogsville**, Donald J. 1937- *WhoBlA 92*
**Cogswell**, Fred 1917- *ConPo 91, IntAu&W 91, WrDr 92*
**Cogswell**, Gary Laverne 1942- *WhoFI 92*
**Cogswell**, George Wallace 1923- *AmMWSc 92*
**Cogswell**, Howard Lyman 1915- *AmMWSc 92*
**Cogswell**, Howard Winwood, Jr 1923- *AmMWSc 92*
**Cogswell**, Joseph Green 1786-1871 *BiInAmS*
**Cogswell**, Robert Elzy 1939- *WhoRel 92*
**Cogswell**, Theodore R 1918- *TwCSFW 91*
**Cohalan**, Peter Fox 1938- *WhoAmL 92, WhoAmP 91*
**Cohan**, Anthony Robert 1939- *IntAu&W 91*
**Cohan**, Christopher Scott 1952- *AmMWSc 92*
**Cohan**, George M. 1878-1942 *BenetAL 91, FacFETw [port], NewAmDM*
**Cohan**, Leon Sumner 1929- *WhoAmL 92, WhoFI 92*
**Cohan**, Martin 1932- *WhoEnt 92*
**Cohan**, Robert Paul 1925- *IntWW 91, Who 92*
**Cohan**, Tony *DrAPF 91*
**Cohart**, Edward Maurice 1909- *AmMWSc 92*
**Cohee**, George Vincent 1907- *AmMWSc 92*
**Cohen** *Who 92*
**Cohen**, Aaron 1931- *AmMWSc 92*
**Cohen**, Abraham Bernard 1922- *AmMWSc 92*
**Cohen**, Adolph Irvin 1924- *AmMWSc 92*
**Cohen**, Alan Barry 1943- *WhoMW 92*
**Cohen**, Alan Geoffrey 1958- *WhoAmL 92*
**Cohen**, Alan Jay 1956- *WhoWest 92*
**Cohen**, Alan Mathew 1943- *AmMWSc 92*
**Cohen**, Alan P. 1957- *WhoEnt 92*
**Cohen**, Alan Samuel 1961- *WhoEnt 92*
**Cohen**, Alan Seymour 1926- *AmMWSc 92*
**Cohen**, Albert 1929- *WhoEnt 92*
**Cohen**, Albert Diamond 1914- *WhoFI 92*
**Cohen**, Alberto 1932- *WhoMW 92*
**Cohen**, Alex 1931- *AmMWSc 92*
**Cohen**, Alexander *LesBEnT 92*
**Cohen**, Alexander H. 1920- *IntWW 91, WhoEnt 92*
**Cohen**, Alfred 1920- *TwCPaSc*
**Cohen**, Alfred M *AmMWSc 92*
**Cohen**, Alice Eve *DrAPF 91*
**Cohen**, Allan Richard 1947- *WhoEnt 92*
**Cohen**, Allen Barry 1939- *AmMWSc 92*
**Cohen**, Allen Irving 1932- *AmMWSc 92*
**Cohen**, Alonzo Clifford, Jr 1911- *AmMWSc 92*
**Cohen**, Alvin Jerome 1918- *AmMWSc 92*
**Cohen**, Amaziah VanBuren 1916- *WhoBlA 92*
**Cohen**, Andrew 1955- *ConAu 135*
**Cohen**, Andrew Scott 1954- *AmMWSc 92*
**Cohen**, Anna 1924- *AmMWSc 92*
**Cohen**, Anne Carolyn Constant 1935- *AmMWSc 92*
**Cohen**, Anthea 1913- *WrDr 92*
**Cohen**, Armond E. 1909- *WhoRel 92*
**Cohen**, Arnold A 1914- *AmMWSc 92*
**Cohen**, Arnold Norman 1949- *WhoWest 92*
**Cohen**, Arnold P. 1948- *WhoAmL 92*
**Cohen**, Arthur *Who 92*
**Cohen**, Arthur Abram 1917- *WhoAmL 92*
**Cohen**, Arthur David 1942- *AmMWSc 92*
**Cohen**, Arthur Leroy 1916- *AmMWSc 92*
**Cohen**, Arthur William 1922- *WhoEnt 92*
**Cohen**, Avis Hope 1941- *AmMWSc 92*
**Cohen**, Avram Nathan 1933- *WhoAmL 92*
**Cohen**, Avrum Isaac 1941- *WhoMW 92, WhoWest 92*
**Cohen**, Barbara 1932- *WrDr 92*
**Cohen**, Barry George 1930- *AmMWSc 92*
**Cohen**, Benjamin Jerry 1937- *WhoFI 92*
**Cohen**, Benjamin R 1942- *WhoAmP 91*
**Cohen**, Benjamin Victor 1894-1983 *FacFETw*
**Cohen**, Bennett J 1925- *AmMWSc 92*
**Cohen**, Bernard 1926- *WrDr 92*
**Cohen**, Bernard 1929- *AmMWSc 92*
**Cohen**, Bernard 1933- *IntWW 91, TwCPaSc*
**Cohen**, Bernard Allan 1946- *AmMWSc 92*
**Cohen**, Bernard Barrie 1944- *WhoAmL 92*
**Cohen**, Bernard Lande 1902- *WrDr 92*
**Cohen**, Bernard Leonard 1924- *AmMWSc 92*
**Cohen**, Bernard S 1934- *WhoAmP 91*
**Cohen**, Bernard Woolf 1933- *Who 92*
**Cohen**, Bernice Hirschhorn 1924- *AmMWSc 92*
**Cohen**, Betty *Who 92*
**Cohen**, Beverly Singer 1933- *AmMWSc 92*
**Cohen**, Bruce Ira 1948- *AmMWSc 92*
**Cohen**, Bruce Lewis 1961- *WhoEnt 92*
**Cohen**, Bruce Preston 1940- *WhoAmL 92*
**Cohen**, Burton 1950- *WhoAmP 91*
**Cohen**, Burton D 1926- *AmMWSc 92*
**Cohen**, Burton David 1940- *WhoFI 92*
**Cohen**, Carl 1920- *AmMWSc 92*
**Cohen**, Carl Alexander 1952- *WhoEnt 92*
**Cohen**, Carl M 1946- *AmMWSc 92*
**Cohen**, Carolyn 1929- *AmMWSc 92*
**Cohen**, Cary 1935- *WhoEnt 92*
**Cohen**, Cheryl Diane Durda 1947- *WhoMW 92*
**Cohen**, Clarence B 1925- *AmMWSc 92*
**Cohen**, Cynthia Marylyn 1945- *WhoAmL 92*
**Cohen**, Daniel 1936- *Au&Arts 7 [port], IntAu&W 91*
**Cohen**, Daniel Isaac Aryeh 1946- *AmMWSc 92*
**Cohen**, Daniel Morris 1930- *AmMWSc 92*
**Cohen**, David *AmMWSc 92*
**Cohen**, David 1956- *WhoFI 92*
**Cohen**, David Alan 1963- *WhoFI 92*
**Cohen**, David B 1947- *WhoAmP 91*
**Cohen**, David Harris 1938- *AmMWSc 92*
**Cohen**, David Norman 1938- *WhoAmP 91*
**Cohen**, David Walter 1926- *AmMWSc 92*
**Cohen**, David Warren 1940- *AmMWSc 92*
**Cohen**, Dean Brian 1959- *WhoWest 92*
**Cohen**, Donald 1920- *AmMWSc 92*
**Cohen**, Donald J 1940- *AmMWSc 92*
**Cohen**, Donald Sussman 1934- *AmMWSc 92*
**Cohen**, E Richard 1922- *AmMWSc 92*
**Cohen**, Edgar A, Jr 1938- *AmMWSc 92*
**Cohen**, Edmund Stephen 1946- *WhoAmL 92*
**Cohen**, Edward 1912- *IntWW 91, Who 92*
**Cohen**, Edward 1921- *AmMWSc 92, WhoFI 92*
**Cohen**, Edward Arthur 1936- *WhoAmL 92*
**Cohen**, Edward Barth 1949- *WhoAmL 92*
**Cohen**, Edward David 1937- *AmMWSc 92*
**Cohen**, Edward Herschel 1938- *WhoAmL 92*
**Cohen**, Edward Hirsch 1947- *AmMWSc 92*
**Cohen**, Edward M. 1936- *ConTFT 9, WhoEnt 92*
**Cohen**, Edward Morton 1936- *AmMWSc 92*
**Cohen**, Edward P 1932- *AmMWSc 92*
**Cohen**, Edward Richard 1944- *WhoWest 92*
**Cohen**, Edwin 1924- *AmMWSc 92*
**Cohen**, Edwin 1934- *AmMWSc 92*
**Cohen**, Edwin Robert 1939- *WhoFI 92, WhoMW 92*
**Cohen**, Edwin Samuel 1914- *WhoAmL 92*
**Cohen**, Elaine 1946- *AmMWSc 92*
**Cohen**, Elaine L. 1939- *WhoWest 92*
**Cohen**, Elias 1920- *AmMWSc 92*
**Cohen**, Elizabeth A. 1954- *WhoEnt 92*
**Cohen**, Elliott 1930- *AmMWSc 92*
**Cohen**, Ellis A. 1945- *IntMPA 92*
**Cohen**, Ellis N 1919- *AmMWSc 92*
**Cohen**, Eric Martin 1955- *WhoAmL 92*
**Cohen**, Esther *DrAPF 91*
**Cohen**, Eugene Joseph 1918- *WhoRel 92*
**Cohen**, Eve 1940- *WhoFI 92*
**Cohen**, Ezechiel Godert David 1923- *AmMWSc 92*
**Cohen**, Ezra H. 1942- *WhoAmL 92*
**Cohen**, Felix Asher 1943- *WhoAmL 92*
**Cohen**, Florence d1991 *NewYTBS 91*
**Cohen**, Florence Emery 1944- *WhoFI 92*
**Cohen**, Flossie 1925- *AmMWSc 92*
**Cohen**, Fran Beroukhim *WhoMW 92*
**Cohen**, Frank Burton 1927- *WhoFI 92*
**Cohen**, Fred 1958- *WhoEnt 92*
**Cohen**, Fred Howard 1948- *WhoAmL 92*
**Cohen**, Fred Lewis 1948- *WhoFI 92*
**Cohen**, Fred M. *LesBEnT 92*
**Cohen**, Frederick 1935- *WhoAmL 92*
**Cohen**, Fredric Sumner 1935- *AmMWSc 92*
**Cohen**, Gabriel Murrel 1908- *WhoMW 92*
**Cohen**, Gary Dale 1951- *WhoAmL 92*
**Cohen**, Gary Dee 1952- *WhoAmL 92, WhoMW 92*
**Cohen**, Gary H 1934- *AmMWSc 92*
**Cohen**, Gary Ormond 1937- *WhoAmL 92*
**Cohen**, Gary S. 1948- *WhoAmL 92*
**Cohen**, Geoffrey Merrill 1954- *WhoEnt 92*
**Cohen**, George Cormack 1909- *Who 92*
**Cohen**, George Leon 1930- *WhoAmL 92*
**Cohen**, George Lester 1939- *AmMWSc 92*
**Cohen**, Gerald *DrAPF 91*
**Cohen**, Gerald 1930- *AmMWSc 92*
**Cohen**, Gerald Allan 1941- *IntWW 91, Who 92*
**Cohen**, Gerald H 1922- *AmMWSc 92*
**Cohen**, Gerald Stanley 1926- *AmMWSc 92*
**Cohen**, Geraldine H 1942- *AmMWSc 92*
**Cohen**, Gerda 1925- *TwCPaSc*
**Cohen**, Gerson D. d1991 *NewYTBS 91 [port]*
**Cohen**, Gerson H 1939- *AmMWSc 92*
**Cohen**, Glenn Milton 1943- *AmMWSc 92*
**Cohen**, Gloria 1930- *AmMWSc 92*
**Cohen**, Gloria Ernestine 1942- *WhoFI 92*
**Cohen**, Gordon Mark 1948- *AmMWSc 92*
**Cohen**, Gordon S. 1937- *WhoFI 92*
**Cohen**, Harley 1933- *AmMWSc 92*
**Cohen**, Harold 1928- *TwCPaSc*
**Cohen**, Harold Jeffrey 1947- *WhoAmL 92*
**Cohen**, Harold Karl 1915- *AmMWSc 92*
**Cohen**, Harold P 1924- *AmMWSc 92*
**Cohen**, Harry 1916- *AmMWSc 92*
**Cohen**, Harry 1949- *Who 92*
**Cohen**, Harvey Jay 1940- *AmMWSc 92*
**Cohen**, Haskell 1920- *AmMWSc 92*
**Cohen**, Helen Degen 1934- *IntAu&W 91*
**Cohen**, Henry 1933- *WrDr 92*
**Cohen**, Henry Rodgin 1944- *WhoAmL 92*
**Cohen**, Herbert Daniel 1937- *AmMWSc 92*
**Cohen**, Herman 1915- *AmMWSc 92*
**Cohen**, Herman 1932- *WhoAmP 91*
**Cohen**, Herman Jacob 1922- *AmMWSc 92*
**Cohen**, Hirsh G 1925- *AmMWSc 92*
**Cohen**, Howard David 1940- *AmMWSc 92*
**Cohen**, Howard Joseph 1928- *AmMWSc 92*
**Cohen**, Howard Lionel 1940- *AmMWSc 92*
**Cohen**, Howard Marvin 1926- *WhoAmL 92*
**Cohen**, Howard Melvin 1936- *AmMWSc 92*
**Cohen**, Howard Robert 1942- *WhoWest 92*
**Cohen**, Hyman L 1919- *AmMWSc 92*
**Cohen**, I Bernard 1914- *AmMWSc 92*
**Cohen**, I Kelman 1935- *AmMWSc 92*
**Cohen**, Ira *DrAPF 91*
**Cohen**, Ira Alan 1950- *WhoMW 92*
**Cohen**, Ira D. 1951- *WhoFI 92*
**Cohen**, Ira M 1937- *AmMWSc 92*
**Cohen**, Irving Allan 1944- *AmMWSc 92*
**Cohen**, Irving David 1945- *AmMWSc 92*
**Cohen**, Irwin 1924- *AmMWSc 92, WhoMW 92*
**Cohen**, Irwin 1936- *WhoFI 92*
**Cohen**, Irwin A 1939- *AmMWSc 92*
**Cohen**, Irwin R. 1924- *IntMPA 92*
**Cohen**, Irwin Robert 1924- *WhoEnt 92*
**Cohen**, Isaac 1936- *AmMWSc 92*
**Cohen**, Isidore Leonard 1922- *WhoEnt 92*
**Cohen**, Ivor Harold 1931- *Who 92*
**Cohen**, J B 1932- *AmMWSc 92*
**Cohen**, J Craig 1950- *AmMWSc 92*
**Cohen**, Jack 1937- *AmMWSc 92*
**Cohen**, Jack Sidney 1938- *AmMWSc 92*
**Cohen**, Jacob *WhoRel 92*
**Cohen**, Jacob Isaac 1941- *AmMWSc 92*
**Cohen**, James R. 1951- *WhoAmL 92*
**Cohen**, James Samuel 1946- *AmMWSc 92*
**Cohen**, Janet 1940- *IntAu&W 91*
**Cohen**, Jay 1956- *WhoAmL 92*
**Cohen**, Jay Allen 1951- *WhoAmL 92*
**Cohen**, Jay Loring 1953- *WhoAmL 92*
**Cohen**, Jay O 1930- *AmMWSc 92*
**Cohen**, Jeffrey 1950- *WhoRel 92*
**Cohen**, Jeffrey M 1940- *AmMWSc 92*
**Cohen**, Jeffrey Marc 1963- *WhoAmL 92*
**Cohen**, Jeffrey Michael 1940- *WhoAmL 92*
**Cohen**, Jeremy Patrick 1960- *WhoAmL 92*
**Cohen**, Jerome Alan 1930- *WhoAmL 92*
**Cohen**, Jerome Bernard 1932- *WhoMW 92*
**Cohen**, Jerome D. 1936- *WhoEnt 92*
**Cohen**, Joel C. *WhoEnt 92*
**Cohen**, Joel Ephraim 1944- *AmMWSc 92*
**Cohen**, Joel J. 1938- *WhoAmL 92, WhoFI 92*
**Cohen**, Joel M 1941- *AmMWSc 92*
**Cohen**, Joel Mark 1946- *WhoAmL 92*
**Cohen**, Joel Ralph 1926- *AmMWSc 92*
**Cohen**, Joel Seymour 1941- *AmMWSc 92*
**Cohen**, John David 1946- *AmMWSc 92*
**Cohen**, Jon Stephan 1943- *WhoAmL 92*
**Cohen**, Jonathan *DrAPF 91*
**Cohen**, Jonathan 1915- *AmMWSc 92*
**Cohen**, Jonathan Brewer 1944- *AmMWSc 92*
**Cohen**, Jordan J 1934- *AmMWSc 92*
**Cohen**, Jose, Sr. 1938- *WhoHisp 92*
**Cohen**, Joyce E 1937- *WhoAmP 91, WhoWest 92*
**Cohen**, Judith Beth *DrAPF 91*
**Cohen**, Judith Gamora 1946- *AmMWSc 92*
**Cohen**, Judith Helen Berliner 1942- *WhoAmL 92*
**Cohen**, Judith Lynne 1951- *WhoFI 92*
**Cohen**, Jules 1931- *AmMWSc 92*
**Cohen**, Jules Bernard 1933- *AmMWSc 92*
**Cohen**, Julius 1926- *AmMWSc 92*
**Cohen**, Julius Jay 1923- *AmMWSc 92*
**Cohen**, Karl 1913- *AmMWSc 92*
**Cohen**, Keith *DrAPF 91*
**Cohen**, Kenneth Louis 1952- *WhoRel 92*
**Cohen**, Kenneth R. 1954- *WhoAmL 92*
**Cohen**, Kenneth Samuel 1937- *AmMWSc 92*
**Cohen**, Larry 1938- *IntDcF 2-2*
**Cohen**, Larry 1947- *IntMPA 92*
**Cohen**, Larry William 1936- *AmMWSc 92*
**Cohen**, Laurence Joel 1932- *WhoAmL 92*
**Cohen**, Laurence Jonathan 1923- *IntWW 91, Who 92, WrDr 92*
**Cohen**, Lawrence 1926- *AmMWSc 92*
**Cohen**, Lawrence Baruch 1939- *AmMWSc 92*
**Cohen**, Lawrence David 1933- *WhoAmP 91*
**Cohen**, Lawrence Mark *AmMWSc 92*
**Cohen**, Lawrence Sorel 1933- *AmMWSc 92*
**Cohen**, Leonard 1925- *WhoWest 92*
**Cohen**, Leonard 1934- *ConNov 91, ConPo 91, IntAu&W 91, WrDr 92*
**Cohen**, Leonard 1943- *BenetAL 91*
**Cohen**, Leonard A 1939- *AmMWSc 92*
**Cohen**, Leonard Arlin 1924- *AmMWSc 92*
**Cohen**, Leonard David 1932- *AmMWSc 92*
**Cohen**, Leonard George 1941- *AmMWSc 92*
**Cohen**, Leonard Harold Lionel 1922- *Who 92*
**Cohen**, Leonard Harvey 1925- *AmMWSc 92*
**Cohen**, Leslie 1923- *AmMWSc 92*
**Cohen**, Lewis H 1937- *AmMWSc 92*
**Cohen**, Lloyd Robert 1947- *WhoAmL 92*
**Cohen**, Lois K *AmMWSc 92*
**Cohen**, Lois Wolk 1934- *WhoFI 92*
**Cohen**, Louis d1991 *NewYTBS 91 [port]*
**Cohen**, Louis 1925- *Who 92*
**Cohen**, Louis 1928- *AmMWSc 92, WhoMW 92*
**Cohen**, Louis Arthur 1926- *AmMWSc 92*
**Cohen**, Maimon Moses 1935- *AmMWSc 92*
**Cohen**, Malcolm Stuart 1942- *WhoMW 92*
**Cohen**, Marc *DrAPF 91*
**Cohen**, Marc Singman 1950- *AmMWSc 92*
**Cohen**, Margo Nita Panush 1940- *AmMWSc 92*
**Cohen**, Marion D. *DrAPF 91*
**Cohen**, Mark B 1949- *WhoAmP 91*
**Cohen**, Mark Herbert 1932- *WhoEnt 92*
**Cohen**, Mark N. 1947- *WhoFI 92*
**Cohen**, Mark Nathan 1943- *ConAu 135*
**Cohen**, Marlene Lois 1945- *AmMWSc 92*
**Cohen**, Marlene Zichi 1951- *WhoWest 92*
**Cohen**, Marsha A 1952- *WhoIns 92*

**Cohen,** Marshall Harris 1926- *AmMWSc 92*
**Cohen,** Martin 1932- *WhoEnt 92*
**Cohen,** Martin Gilbert 1938- *AmMWSc 92*
**Cohen,** Martin Joseph 1921- *AmMWSc 92*
**Cohen,** Martin O 1940- *AmMWSc 92*
**Cohen,** Martin William 1935- *AmMWSc 92*
**Cohen,** Marty *DrAPF 91*
**Cohen,** Marvin *DrAPF 91*
**Cohen,** Marvin Lou 1935- *AmMWSc 92, IntWW 91*
**Cohen,** Marvin Morris 1940- *AmMWSc 92*
**Cohen,** Marvin S 1931- *WhoAmP 91*
**Cohen,** Mary Ann 1943- *WhoAmL 92*
**Cohen,** Matt 1942- *ConNov 91, IntAu&W 91, WrDr 92*
**Cohen,** Matthew Lawrence 1954- *WhoEnt 92*
**Cohen,** Max Mark 1939- *WhoWest 92*
**Cohen,** Maxwell 1910- *IntAu&W 91, WrDr 92*
**Cohen,** Maynard 1920- *AmMWSc 92*
**Cohen,** Melanie Rovner 1944- *WhoAmL 92*
**Cohen,** Melvin Joseph 1928- *AmMWSc 92*
**Cohen,** Melvyn Douglas 1943- *WhoFI 92*
**Cohen,** Merrill 1926- *AmMWSc 92*
**Cohen,** Michael 1930- *AmMWSc 92*
**Cohen,** Michael Alan 1946- *AmMWSc 92*
**Cohen,** Michael Antony 1940- *Who 92*
**Cohen,** Michael Ben 1954- *WhoAmL 92*
**Cohen,** Michael I *AmMWSc 92*
**Cohen,** Michael Paul 1947- *AmMWSc 92*
**Cohen,** Michael Peter 1944- *WhoWest 92*
**Cohen,** Michele Frances 1959- *WhoAmL 92*
**Cohen,** Miles Jon 1941- *WhoMW 92*
**Cohen,** Milton d1991 *NewYTBS 91*
**Cohen,** Milton E. *IntMPA 92*
**Cohen,** Mitchell S 1930- *AmMWSc 92*
**Cohen,** Monroe W 1940- *AmMWSc 92*
**Cohen,** Montague 1925- *AmMWSc 92*
**Cohen,** Mordaunt 1916- *Who 92*
**Cohen,** Morrel Herman 1927- *AmMWSc 92*
**Cohen,** Morris 1911- *AmMWSc 92, IntWW 91*
**Cohen,** Morris 1921- *AmMWSc 92*
**Cohen,** Morris Leo 1927- *WhoAmL 92*
**Cohen,** Morton Allan 1935- *WhoFI 92*
**Cohen,** Morton Irving 1923- *AmMWSc 92*
**Cohen,** Morton N. 1921- *WrDr 92*
**Cohen,** Morton Norton 1921- *IntAu&W 91*
**Cohen,** Moses E *AmMWSc 92*
**Cohen,** Murray Samuel 1925- *AmMWSc 92*
**Cohen,** Myrella 1927- *Who 92*
**Cohen,** Myron Leslie 1934- *AmMWSc 92*
**Cohen,** Myron S 1950- *AmMWSc 92*
**Cohen,** Nadine Dale 1949- *AmMWSc 92*
**Cohen,** Naomi Kurnitsky 1941- *WhoAmP 91*
**Cohen,** Natalie Shulman 1938- *AmMWSc 92, WhoWest 92*
**Cohen,** Nathan 1919- *WhoAmL 92*
**Cohen,** Nathan 1962- *TwCPaSc*
**Cohen,** Nathan Leslie 1908- *Who 92*
**Cohen,** Nathan Wolf 1919- *AmMWSc 92*
**Cohen,** Nathaniel Arthur 1898- *Who 92*
**Cohen,** Neil M *WhoAmP 91*
**Cohen,** Nelson Craig 1947- *WhoAmL 92*
**Cohen,** Nicholas 1938- *AmMWSc 92*
**Cohen,** Noal 1937- *AmMWSc 92*
**Cohen,** Noel Lee 1930- *AmMWSc 92*
**Cohen,** Norman 1936- *AmMWSc 92*
**Cohen,** Norman 1938- *AmMWSc 92*
**Cohen,** Norman Ian *WhoEnt 92*
**Cohen,** Octavus Roy 1891-1959 *BenetAL 91*
**Cohen,** Paul 1912- *AmMWSc 92*
**Cohen,** Paul Frederick 1944- *WhoWest 92*
**Cohen,** Paul Joseph 1934- *AmMWSc 92*
**Cohen,** Paul S 1939- *AmMWSc 92*
**Cohen,** Peter Sachary 1931- *IntAu&W 91*
**Cohen,** Peter Zachary 1931- *WrDr 92*
**Cohen,** Philip 1931- *AmMWSc 92*
**Cohen,** Philip 1945- *Who 92*
**Cohen,** Philip Francis 1911- *WhoAmL 92*
**Cohen,** Philip Gary 1950- *WhoAmL 92*
**Cohen,** Philip Ira 1948- *AmMWSc 92*
**Cohen,** Philip Pacy 1908- *AmMWSc 92, IntWW 91*
**Cohen,** Phyllis Joanne 1935- *WhoMW 92*
**Cohen,** Pinya 1935- *AmMWSc 92*
**Cohen,** Raquel E. 1922- *WhoHisp 92*
**Cohen,** Raymond 1923- *AmMWSc 92*
**Cohen,** Richard 1955- *WhoAmL 92*
**Cohen,** Richard Henry Lionel 1907- *Who 92*
**Cohen,** Richard J 1949- *WhoAmP 91*
**Cohen,** Richard Lawrence 1922- *AmMWSc 92*
**Cohen,** Richard Lewis 1936- *AmMWSc 92*
**Cohen,** Richard M 1946- *AmMWSc 92*
**Cohen,** Richard Neil 1953- *WhoAmL 92*
**Cohen,** Richard Paul 1945- *WhoAmL 92*
**Cohen,** Richard Steven 1942- *WhoFI 92*
**Cohen,** Richard Stockman 1937- *WhoAmL 92*
**Cohen,** Rob 1949- *IntMPA 92*
**Cohen,** Robert *DrAPF 91*
**Cohen,** Robert 1924- *AmMWSc 92*
**Cohen,** Robert 1938- *ConAu 34NR*
**Cohen,** Robert 1957- *WhoAmL 92*
**Cohen,** Robert 1959- *IntWW 91*
**Cohen,** Robert Avram 1929- *WhoAmL 92*
**Cohen,** Robert B. *IntMPA 92*
**Cohen,** Robert Bernard 1933- *WhoAmL 92*
**Cohen,** Robert Bruce 1959- *WhoFI 92*
**Cohen,** Robert Donald 1933- *Who 92*
**Cohen,** Robert Edward 1947- *AmMWSc 92*
**Cohen,** Robert Elliot 1953- *AmMWSc 92*
**Cohen,** Robert Jay 1942- *AmMWSc 92*
**Cohen,** Robert L. 1936- *WhoEnt 92*
**Cohen,** Robert Martin 1946- *AmMWSc 92*
**Cohen,** Robert Roy 1939- *AmMWSc 92*
**Cohen,** Robert Sonne 1923- *AmMWSc 92*
**Cohen,** Robert Stephan 1939- *WhoAmL 92*
**Cohen,** Robert Stephen 1938- *WhoEnt 92, WhoWest 92*
**Cohen,** Robin 1944- *ConAu 134*
**Cohen,** Rochelle Sandra 1945- *AmMWSc 92*
**Cohen,** Roger D H 1938- *AmMWSc 92*
**Cohen,** Ronald Eli 1937- *WhoEnt 92*
**Cohen,** Ronald Hoffman 1913- *WhoAmL 92*
**Cohen,** Ronald Jay 1948- *WhoAmL 92*
**Cohen,** Ronald Marc 1951- *WhoAmL 92*
**Cohen,** Ronald R H 1947- *AmMWSc 92*
**Cohen,** Ruth Christman 1955- *WhoMW 92*
**Cohen,** Ruth Louisa d1991 *Who 92N*
**Cohen,** Samuel Alan 1947- *AmMWSc 92*
**Cohen,** Samuel H 1938- *AmMWSc 92*
**Cohen,** Samuel Israel 1933- *WhoFI 92, WhoRel 92*
**Cohen,** Samuel J. d1991 *NewYTBS 91*
**Cohen,** Samuel Monroe 1946- *AmMWSc 92, WhoMW 92*
**Cohen,** Sanford Barry 1956- *WhoEnt 92*
**Cohen,** Sanford I 1928- *AmMWSc 92*
**Cohen,** Sanford Ned 1935- *AmMWSc 92*
**Cohen,** Saul 1925- *WrDr 92*
**Cohen,** Saul 1927- *WhoAmL 92, WhoEnt 92*
**Cohen,** Saul G 1916- *AmMWSc 92*
**Cohen,** Saul Israel 1926- *AmMWSc 92*
**Cohen,** Saul Louis 1913- *AmMWSc 92*
**Cohen,** Saul Mark 1924- *AmMWSc 92*
**Cohen,** Selma Jeanne 1920- *WhoEnt 92, WrDr 92*
**Cohen,** Seymour 1917- *WhoAmL 92*
**Cohen,** Seymour I. 1931- *WhoAmL 92, WhoWest 92*
**Cohen,** Seymour Jay 1922- *WhoRel 92*
**Cohen,** Seymour Stanley 1917- *AmMWSc 92, FacFETw, IntWW 91*
**Cohen,** Sheldon A 1947- *AmMWSc 92*
**Cohen,** Sheldon Gilbert 1918- *AmMWSc 92*
**Cohen,** Sheldon H 1934- *AmMWSc 92*
**Cohen,** Sheldon Irwin 1937- *WhoAmL 92*
**Cohen,** Sheldon P. *WhoAmL 92*
**Cohen,** Sheldon Stanley 1927- *WhoAmL 92*
**Cohen,** Sidney 1913- *AmMWSc 92*
**Cohen,** Sidney 1928- *AmMWSc 92*
**Cohen,** Simon S. 1909- *WhoAmL 92*
**Cohen,** Stanley 1922- *AmMWSc 92, IntWW 91, Who 92, WhoNob 90*
**Cohen,** Stanley 1927- *AmMWSc 92, Who 92*
**Cohen,** Stanley 1928- *ConAu 34NR*
**Cohen,** Stanley 1935- *IntWW 91*
**Cohen,** Stanley 1937- *AmMWSc 92, IntWW 91*
**Cohen,** Stanley 1942- *Who 92*
**Cohen,** Stanley Alvin *AmMWSc 92*
**Cohen,** Stanley I. *DrAPF 91*
**Cohen,** Stanley I 1928- *IntAu&W 91, WrDr 92*
**Cohen,** Stanley Norman 1935- *AmMWSc 92, WhoWest 92*
**Cohen,** Stephen F 1938- *ConAu 35NR, IntAu&W 91, WrDr 92*
**Cohen,** Stephen Howard 1938- *WhoAmL 92*
**Cohen,** Stephen Ira 1944- *WhoAmL 92*
**Cohen,** Stephen Ira 1949- *WhoAmP 91*
**Cohen,** Stephen Lawrence 1948- *WhoFI 92*
**Cohen,** Stephen Marshall 1929- *WhoWest 92*
**Cohen,** Stephen Martin 1957- *WhoAmL 92*
**Cohen,** Stephen Robert 1928- *AmMWSc 92*
**Cohen,** Steven 1947- *WhoEnt 92*
**Cohen,** Steven Charles 1947- *AmMWSc 92*
**Cohen,** Steven Donald 1942- *AmMWSc 92*
**Cohen,** Steven Martin 1950- *WhoRel 92*
**Cohen,** Stewart 1953- *WhoEnt 92*
**Cohen,** Stuart Kenneth 1960- *WhoAmL 92*
**Cohen,** Susan 1938- *IntAu&W 91*
**Cohen,** Susan Gloria 1952- *WhoWest 92*
**Cohen,** Sydney 1921- *IntWW 91, Who 92*
**Cohen,** Theodore 1929- *AmMWSc 92*
**Cohen,** Tobe Michael 1960- *WhoFI 92*
**Cohen,** Vincent H. 1936- *WhoBlA 92*
**Cohen,** Wallace M. 1908- *WhoAmL 92*
**Cohen,** William 1931- *AmMWSc 92*
**Cohen,** William 1933- *WhoAmL 92*
**Cohen,** William Benjamin 1941- *WrDr 92*
**Cohen,** William C 1933- *AmMWSc 92*
**Cohen,** William David 1928- *AmMWSc 92*
**Cohen,** William Jay 1950- *WhoAmL 92*
**Cohen,** William S. 1940- *AlmAP 92 [port], IntWW 91, WhoAmP 91*
**Cohen,** Yeruham d1991 *NewYTBS 91*
**Cohen-Albrecht,** Patricia Rebeca 1957- *WhoHisp 92*
**Cohick,** A Doyle, Jr 1939- *AmMWSc 92*
**Cohill,** Maurice Blanchard, Jr. 1929- *WhoAmL 92*
**Cohl,** Izora Corpman *DrAPF 91*
**Cohlan,** Sidney Quex 1915- *AmMWSc 92*
**Cohlberg,** Jeffrey Allan 1943- *AmMWSc 92*
**Cohn,** Al 1925-1988 *NewAmDM*
**Cohn,** Alan Jeffrey 1964- *WhoFI 92*
**Cohn,** Allen Howard 1955- *WhoEnt 92*
**Cohn,** Andrew Howard 1945- *WhoAmL 92*
**Cohn,** Arthur 1910- *NewAmDM*
**Cohn,** Barry S. 1954- *WhoWest 92*
**Cohn,** Bruce 1931- *WhoEnt 92*
**Cohn,** Charles Erwin 1931- *AmMWSc 92*
**Cohn,** Daniel Howard 1955- *WhoWest 92*
**Cohn,** Daniel Ross 1943- *AmMWSc 92*
**Cohn,** David L 1943- *AmMWSc 92*
**Cohn,** David L. 1953- *WhoEnt 92*
**Cohn,** David Maxwell 1953- *WhoAmL 92*
**Cohn,** David Stephen 1945- *WhoAmL 92*
**Cohn,** David Valor 1926- *AmMWSc 92*
**Cohn,** Deirdre Arline *AmMWSc 92*
**Cohn,** Don Stephen 1950- *WhoAmL 92*
**Cohn,** Edward Paul 1948- *WhoRel 92*
**Cohn,** Ellen Rassas 1953- *AmMWSc 92*
**Cohn,** Ernst M 1920- *AmMWSc 92*
**Cohn,** George I 1921- *AmMWSc 92*
**Cohn,** Gerald Edward 1943- *AmMWSc 92*
**Cohn,** Haim 1911- *IntWW 91*
**Cohn,** Hans Otto 1927- *AmMWSc 92*
**Cohn,** Harry 1891-1958 *FacFETw*
**Cohn,** Harvey 1923- *AmMWSc 92*
**Cohn,** Herbert B. 1912- *WhoAmL 92*
**Cohn,** Hillel 1938- *WhoRel 92*
**Cohn,** Howard T 1929- *WhoIns 92*
**Cohn,** Isidore, Jr 1921- *AmMWSc 92*
**Cohn,** J Gunther 1911- *AmMWSc 92*
**Cohn,** Jack 1932- *AmMWSc 92*
**Cohn,** James Myron 1928- *WhoEnt 92*
**Cohn,** Jay Binswanger 1922- *AmMWSc 92*
**Cohn,** Jay Norman 1930- *AmMWSc 92*
**Cohn,** Jim *DrAPF 91*
**Cohn,** John J. 1941- *WhoHisp 92*
**Cohn,** Kim 1939- *AmMWSc 92*
**Cohn,** Lawrence H 1937- *AmMWSc 92*
**Cohn,** Lawrence Steven 1945- *WhoWest 92*
**Cohn,** Leopold 1862-1937 *RelLAm 91*
**Cohn,** Leslie 1943- *AmMWSc 92*
**Cohn,** Lucile 1924- *WhoMW 92*
**Cohn,** Major Lloyd 1927- *AmMWSc 92*
**Cohn,** Mark Barry 1947- *WhoAmL 92*
**Cohn,** Martin David 1925- *WhoAmL 92*
**Cohn,** Mildred 1913- *AmMWSc 92, IntWW 91*
**Cohn,** Milton Herbert, Jr. 1948- *WhoWest 92*
**Cohn,** Nathan 1907- *AmMWSc 92*
**Cohn,** Nathan 1918- *WhoAmL 92*
**Cohn,** Norman 1915- *IntWW 91, Who 92, WrDr 92*
**Cohn,** Norman Stanley 1930- *AmMWSc 92*
**Cohn,** Paul Daniel 1936- *AmMWSc 92*
**Cohn,** Paul David 1962- *WhoFI 92*
**Cohn,** Paul Moritz 1924- *IntWW 91, Who 92*
**Cohn,** Peter Frank 1939- *AmMWSc 92*
**Cohn,** Richard Moses 1919- *AmMWSc 92*
**Cohn,** Richard Steven 1956- *WhoEnt 92*
**Cohn,** Robert 1909- *AmMWSc 92*
**Cohn,** Robert 1920- *IntMPA 92*
**Cohn,** Robert 1922- *WhoFI 92*
**Cohn,** Robert Greer 1921- *WhoWest 92*
**Cohn,** Robert M 1941- *AmMWSc 92*
**Cohn,** Ronald Dennis 1942- *WhoAmL 92*
**Cohn,** Roy 1927-1986 *FacFETw*
**Cohn,** Ruby 1922- *IntAu&W 91*
**Cohn,** Sam 1929- *WhoEnt 92*
**Cohn,** Seymour B 1920- *AmMWSc 92*
**Cohn,** Sherman Louis 1932- *WhoAmL 92*
**Cohn,** Sidney Arthur 1918- *AmMWSc 92*
**Cohn,** Stanley Howard 1926- *AmMWSc 92*
**Cohn,** Stanton Harry 1920- *AmMWSc 92*
**Cohn,** Theodore E 1941- *AmMWSc 92*
**Cohn,** Victor Hugo 1930- *AmMWSc 92*
**Cohn,** Waldo E 1910- *AmMWSc 92*
**Cohn,** William McDougal 1937- *WhoMW 92*
**Cohn,** Zanvil A 1926- *AmMWSc 92*
**Cohn-Sfetcu,** Sorin 1944- *AmMWSc 92*
**Cohoe,** Grey *DrAPF 91*
**Cohoon,** Dennis M 1953- *WhoAmP 91*
**Cohrs,** William Henry, Jr. 1927- *WhoMW 92*
**Cohrssen,** John Joseph 1939- *WhoAmL 92*
**Coia,** Raymond Christopher 1961- *WhoAmL 92*
**Coia,** Theodore N 1947- *WhoIns 92*
**Coico,** Richard F *AmMWSc 92*
**Coigney,** Martha Wadsworth 1933- *WhoEnt 92*
**Coil,** Henry Wilson, Jr 1932- *WhoAmP 91*
**Coil,** William Herschell 1925- *AmMWSc 92*
**Coile,** Russell Cleven 1917- *AmMWSc 92*
**Coiley,** John Arthur 1932- *Who 92*
**Coiner,** Miles Warren, Jr. 1938- *WhoEnt 92*
**Coing,** Helmut 1912- *IntWW 91*
**Cointat,** Michel 1921- *IntWW 91*
**Coish,** Harold Roy 1918- *AmMWSc 92*
**Coit,** Michele Vivian 1954- *WhoEnt 92*
**Coit,** R. Ken 1943- *WhoWest 92*
**Cokayne** *Who 92*
**Cokayne,** Aston 1608?-1684 *RfGEnL 91*
**Coke** *Who 92*
**Coke,** Viscount 1936- *Who 92*
**Coke,** C Eugene *AmMWSc 92*
**Coke,** Charles Michael 1943- *WhoEnt 92*
**Coke,** Chauncey Eugene *WhoFI 92*
**Coke,** Dorothy 1897-1979 *TwCPaSc*
**Coke,** James Logan 1933- *AmMWSc 92*
**Coke,** Marguerite 1950- *WhoEnt 92*
**Coke,** Octavius 1840-1895 *DcNCBi 1*
**Cokelet,** Edward Davis 1947- *AmMWSc 92*
**Cokelet,** Giles R 1932- *AmMWSc 92*
**Coken,** Richard Allen 1947- *WhoEnt 92*
**Coker,** Charlotte Noel 1930- *WhoAmP 91*
**Coker,** David *WhoRel 92*
**Coker,** Earl Howard, Jr 1934- *AmMWSc 92*
**Coker,** Harold L 1929- *WhoAmP 91*
**Coker,** Henry Benjamin, III 1951- *WhoFI 92*
**Coker,** Lynda *WhoAmP 91*
**Coker,** Peter 1926- *TwCPaSc*
**Coker,** Peter Godfrey 1926- *IntWW 91, Who 92*
**Coker,** Robert Ervin 1876-1967 *DcNCBi 1*
**Coker,** Robert Hilton 1947- *WhoFI 92*
**Coker,** Samuel Terry 1926- *AmMWSc 92*
**Coker,** William Chambers 1872-1953 *DcNCBi 1*
**Coker,** William Rory 1939- *AmMWSc 92*
**Cokinos,** Dimitrios *AmMWSc 92*
**Colacci,** Mario 1910-1968 *ConAu 135*
**Colacurcio,** Daniel V 1948- *WhoIns 92*
**Colafella,** Nick A 1939- *WhoAmP 91*
**Colagiovanni,** Joseph Alfred, Jr. 1956- *WhoAmL 92*
**Colagiovanni,** Richard Francis 1949- *WhoEnt 92*
**Colahan,** Patrick Timothy 1948- *AmMWSc 92*
**Colahan,** Peter DuMont 1956- *WhoFI 92*
**Colahan,** Timothy John 1958- *WhoAmL 92*
**Colahan,** William Edward d1991 *Who 92N*
**Colaianni,** Joseph Vincent 1935- *WhoAmL 92*
**Colaizzi,** John Louis 1938- *AmMWSc 92*
**Colaizzo,** Anthony L 1930- *WhoAmP 91*
**Colakovic,** Bozidar 1931- *IntWW 91*
**Colamarino,** Leonard James 1951- *WhoAmL 92*
**Colan,** Owen Richard 1922- *WhoAmL 92*
**Colan,** Thomas Robert 1955- *WhoFI 92*
**Colander,** Valerie Nieman *DrAPF 91*
**Colandrea,** Thomas Richard 1938- *WhoWest 92*
**Colaner,** Robert Lee 1953- *WhoMW 92, WhoRel 92*
**Colangelo,** Jerry John 1939- *WhoWest 92*
**Colangelo,** Robert d1991 *NewYTBS 91 [port]*
**Colani,** Luigi 1928- *DcTwDes, FacFETw*
**Colantuono,** Thomas 1951- *WhoAmP 91*
**Colao,** Anthony F *WhoIns 92*
**Colapietro,** Bruno 1935- *WhoAmL 92*
**Colarossi,** Steven A. 1964- *WhoAmL 92*
**Colas,** Antonio E 1928- *AmMWSc 92*
**Colas,** Antonio Espada 1928- *WhoHisp 92*
**Colasanti,** Brenda Karen 1945- *AmMWSc 92*
**Colavita,** Anthony Joseph 1935- *WhoAmP 91*
**Colaw,** Emerson S. *WhoRel 92*
**Colaw,** Nathan Rene 1941- *WhoRel 92*
**Colbeck,** Maurice 1925- *ConAu 34NR, IntAu&W 91, WrDr 92*
**Colbeck,** Samuel C 1940- *AmMWSc 92*
**Colbeck-Welch,** Edward Lawrence 1914- *Who 92*
**Colberg,** Thomas Pearsall 1948- *WhoFI 92*
**Colbert,** Alison *DrAPF 91*
**Colbert,** Annette Darcia 1959- *WhoFI 92*

**Colbert**, Benjamin James 1942- *WhoBlA 92*
**Colbert**, Charles 1919- *AmMWSc 92*
**Colbert**, Claudette 1903- *IntMPA 92, IntWW 91, Who 92, WhoEnt 92*
**Colbert**, Edwin Harris 1905- *AmMWSc 92, IntWW 91, WrDr 92*
**Colbert**, Ernest, Sr. 1916- *WhoBlA 92*
**Colbert**, George Clifford 1949- *WhoBlA 92*
**Colbert**, Judith Alane 1960- *WhoAmL 92*
**Colbert**, Lester Lum, Jr. 1934- *WhoFI 92*
**Colbert**, Margot Mink 1935- *WhoEnt 92*
**Colbert**, Marvin J 1923- *AmMWSc 92*
**Colbert**, Olga 1959- *WhoWest 92*
**Colbert**, Paul 1949- *WhoAmP 91*
**Colbert**, Richard A. 1942- *WhoRel 92*
**Colbert**, Robert Reed, Jr. 1949- *WhoFI 92*
**Colbert**, Thelma Quince 1949- *WhoBlA 92*
**Colbert**, Thomas Albert 1935- *WhoMW 92*
**Colbert**, Virgis W. 1939- *WhoBlA 92*
**Colbert**, Virgis William 1939- *WhoFI 92*
**Colbert**, William Barry 1947- *WhoMW 92*
**Colbeth**, Richard Stanley 1938- *WhoRel 92*
**Colborn**, Gene Louis 1935- *AmMWSc 92*
**Colborn**, Nigel 1944- *IntAu&W 91*
**Colborne**, William George 1926- *AmMWSc 92*
**Colbourn**, Charles Joseph 1953- *AmMWSc 92*
**Colbow**, Konrad 1935- *AmMWSc 92*
**Colburn**, Burnham Standish 1872-1959 *DcNCBi 1*
**Colburn**, C William 1939- *WhoAmP 91*
**Colburn**, Charles Buford 1923- *AmMWSc 92*
**Colburn**, David Dunton 1958- *WhoFI 92*
**Colburn**, Gene Lewis 1932- *WhoFI 92, WhoWest 92*
**Colburn**, Harold L, Jr 1925- *WhoAmP 91*
**Colburn**, Ivan Paul 1927- *AmMWSc 92*
**Colburn**, James Allan 1942- *WhoAmL 92*
**Colburn**, Larry B 1944- *WhoIns 92*
**Colburn**, Mickey 1929- *WhoAmP 91*
**Colburn**, Nancy Hall 1941- *AmMWSc 92*
**Colburn**, Paul Leroy 1948- *WhoWest 92*
**Colburn**, Ralph Jonathan 1916- *WhoRel 92, WhoWest 92*
**Colburn**, Richard F 1950- *WhoAmP 91*
**Colburn**, Theodore R 1939- *AmMWSc 92*
**Colburn**, W W d1899 *BiInAmS*
**Colburn**, Warren 1793-1833 *BiInAmS*
**Colburn**, Wayne Alan 1947- *AmMWSc 92*
**Colburn**, Zerah 1804-1839 *BiInAmS*
**Colby**, Bainbridge 1869-1950 *AmPolLe*
**Colby**, Barbara Diane 1932- *WhoWest 92*
**Colby**, Bruce Redfearn 1934- *WhoMW 92*
**Colby**, Charles Edwards 1855-1897 *BiInAmS*
**Colby**, David Anthony 1946- *AmMWSc 92*
**Colby**, Edward Eugene 1929- *AmMWSc 92*
**Colby**, Everett 1874-1943 *AmPeW*
**Colby**, Frank Gerhardt 1915- *AmMWSc 92*
**Colby**, Fred Ralph 1948- *WhoEnt 92*
**Colby**, George Vincent, Jr 1931- *AmMWSc 92*
**Colby**, Howard David 1944- *AmMWSc 92*
**Colby**, Jean 1907- *IntAu&W 91*
**Colby**, Jean Poindexter 1907- *WrDr 92*
**Colby**, Joan *DrAPF 91*
**Colby**, Kenneth Mark 1920- *WhoWest 92*
**Colby**, Kenneth P, Sr 1908- *WhoIns 92*
**Colby**, Mark Steven 1949- *WhoEnt 92*
**Colby**, Neal D., Jr. *WhoRel 92*
**Colby**, Peter J 1933- *AmMWSc 92*
**Colby**, Richard H 1939- *AmMWSc 92*
**Colby**, Robert Lester 1941- *WhoWest 92*
**Colby**, Ronald *IntMPA 92*
**Colby**, Virginia Little 1917- *WhoRel 92*
**Colby**, William Egan 1920- *IntWW 91, WhoAmL 92, WhoAmP 91*
**Colby**, William Michael 1942- *WhoAmL 92*
**Colchado**, Jose D., Jr. 1946- *WhoHisp 92*
**Colchester**, Archdeacon of *Who 92*
**Colchester**, Area Bishop of 1929- *Who 92*
**Colchester**, Halsey Sparrowe 1918- *Who 92*
**Colchester**, Nicholas Benedick Sparrowe 1946- *Who 92*
**Colchester**, Trevor Charles 1909- *Who 92*
**Colchie**, Elizabeth Schneider *ConAu 36NR*
**Colclaser**, Robert Gerald 1933- *AmMWSc 92*
**Colcord**, Elmer Danforth 1895- *WhoRel 92*
**Colcord**, Herbert Nathaniel, III 1951- *WhoFI 92*
**Colcord**, J E 1922- *AmMWSc 92*
**Colcord**, Joanna Carver 1883-1960 *HanAmWH*
**Colcord**, Lincoln 1883-1947 *BenetAL 91*
**Colcord**, Linda Miller 1953- *WhoEnt 92*
**Colcord**, Ray, III 1949- *WhoEnt 92*
**Colden**, Cadwallader 1688-1776 *BenetAL 91, BiInAmS*
**Colden**, Jane 1724-1766 *BiInAmS*
**Coldren**, Clarke L 1926- *AmMWSc 92*
**Coldren**, John 1944- *WhoAmP 91*
**Coldrick**, Albert Percival 1913- *Who 92*
**Coldsmith**, Don 1926- *TwCWW 91, WrDr 92*
**Coldstream**, George 1907- *Who 92*
**Coldstream**, John Nicolas 1927- *Who 92*
**Coldstream**, William 1908-1987 *TwCPaSc*
**Coldwell**, David F. C. 1923-1973 *ConAu 134*
**Coldwell**, Joan 1936- *IntAu&W 91*
**Coldwell**, Robert Lynn 1941- *AmMWSc 92*
**Coldwell**, Timothy Earl 1958- *WhoMW 92*
**Coldwells**, Alan Alfred 1930- *Who 92*
**Cole** *Who 92*
**Cole**, Aaron Hodgman 1856-1913 *BiInAmS*
**Cole**, Adolph 1923- *WhoBlA 92*
**Cole**, Adrian Christopher Synnot 1949- *IntAu&W 91*
**Cole**, Alan James 1956- *WhoMW 92*
**Cole**, Alexander Colin 1922- *Who 92*
**Cole**, Anthony F. 1955- *WhoEnt 92*
**Cole**, Arthur 1942- *WhoBlA 92*
**Cole**, Avean Wayne 1934- *AmMWSc 92*
**Cole**, Barbara Ruth 1941- *AmMWSc 92*
**Cole**, Barry 1936- *ConNov 91, IntAu&W 91, WrDr 92*
**Cole**, Barry Charles *AmMWSc 92*
**Cole**, Bebette *WrDr 92*
**Cole**, Benjamin Theodore 1921- *AmMWSc 92*
**Cole**, Bert L 1910- *WhoAmP 91*
**Cole**, Bob 1863-1911 *NewAmDM*
**Cole**, Boris Norman 1924- *Who 92*
**Cole**, Brian J 1943- *AmMWSc 92*
**Cole**, Bruce 1938- *WrDr 92*
**Cole**, Bruce Kasner 1939- *WhoRel 92*
**Cole**, C Vernon 1922- *AmMWSc 92*
**Cole**, Carlos Lane 1958- *WhoRel 92*
**Cole**, Carolyn Jo 1943- *WhoFI 92*
**Cole**, Cathy Joyce 1953- *WhoWest 92*
**Cole**, Charles *ScFEYrs*
**Cole**, Charles Dewey, Jr. 1952- *WhoAmL 92*
**Cole**, Charles E. 1927- *WhoAmL 92, WhoAmP 91, WhoWest 92*
**Cole**, Charles F, Jr 1926- *AmMWSc 92*
**Cole**, Charles Franklyn 1928- *AmMWSc 92*
**Cole**, Charles N 1946- *AmMWSc 92*
**Cole**, Charles Ralph 1942- *AmMWSc 92*
**Cole**, Charles Zhivaga 1957- *WhoBlA 92*
**Cole**, Clarence Russell 1918- *AmMWSc 92*
**Cole**, Claude Neville David 1928- *Who 92*
**Cole**, Clifford Adair 1915- *WhoRel 92*
**Cole**, Colin *Who 92*
**Cole**, Colin 1922- *IntWW 91*
**Cole**, Cozy 1909-1981 *NewAmDM*
**Cole**, Curtis, Jr. 1953- *WhoBlA 92*
**Cole**, Curtis Allen 1946- *WhoAmL 92*
**Cole**, Cyrus *ScFEYrs*
**Cole**, Dale Warren 1931- *AmMWSc 92*
**Cole**, David *Who 92*
**Cole**, David 1920- *Who 92*
**Cole**, David 1945- *WhoWest 92*
**Cole**, David A 1937- *WhoAmP 91*
**Cole**, David Christopher 1962- *WhoRel 92*
**Cole**, David Douglas 1958- *WhoAmL 92*
**Cole**, David Edward 1937- *AmMWSc 92, WhoMW 92*
**Cole**, David F 1933- *AmMWSc 92*
**Cole**, David Le Roy 1939- *AmMWSc 92*
**Cole**, David Lee 1947- *WhoIns 92*
**Cole**, David Winslow 1947- *WhoWest 92*
**Cole**, Dayton Thomas 1954- *WhoAmL 92*
**Cole**, Dean Allen 1952- *WhoWest 92*
**Cole**, Diana Barajon 1938- *WhoWest 92*
**Cole**, Donald Charles 1937- *WhoAmP 91*
**Cole**, Donald Willard 1920- *WhoRel 92*
**Cole**, Dorthy Gattin 1933- *WhoAmP 91*
**Cole**, Douglas L 1947- *AmMWSc 92*
**Cole**, Douglas Leon 1947- *WhoMW 92*
**Cole**, E.R. *DrAPF 91*
**Cole**, E. R. 1930- *WrDr 92*
**Cole**, Edmond Ray 1928- *AmMWSc 92*
**Cole**, Edmund Keith 1919- *WrDr 92*
**Cole**, Edward Anthony 1932- *AmMWSc 92*
**Cole**, Edward Isaac, Jr 1959- *AmMWSc 92*
**Cole**, Edward L 1944- *WhoAmP 91*
**Cole**, Edyth Bryant *WhoBlA 92*
**Cole**, Eileen Marie Lucy 1924- *Who 92*
**Cole**, Elsa Kircher 1949- *WhoAmL 92*
**Cole**, Elsie Vera 1885-1968 *TwCPaSc*
**Cole**, Eric Stuart 1906- *Who 92*
**Cole**, Eugene Roger 1930- *IntAu&W 91, WhoMW 92*
**Cole**, Evelyn 1910- *AmMWSc 92*
**Cole**, Florence M 1917- *WhoAmP 91*
**Cole**, Francis Bernard, Jr. 1933- *WhoRel 92*
**Cole**, Francis Talmage 1925- *AmMWSc 92*
**Cole**, Frank *Who 92*
**Cole**, Frank Maurice 1935- *WhoWest 92*
**Cole**, Franklin Ruggles 1925- *AmMWSc 92*
**Cole**, G Rolland 1925- *AmMWSc 92*
**Cole**, Garry Thomas 1941- *AmMWSc 92*
**Cole**, Gary *IntMPA 92*
**Cole**, Geoffrey Alexander 1963- *WhoIns 92*
**Cole**, George 1925- *ConTFT 9, IntMPA 92, Who 92*
**Cole**, George Christopher 1929- *AmMWSc 92*
**Cole**, George David 1925- *AmMWSc 92*
**Cole**, George Francis 1918- *Who 92*
**Cole**, George Luis 1957- *WhoFI 92*
**Cole**, George Stuart 1955- *WhoAmL 92*
**Cole**, George William 1933- *AmMWSc 92*
**Cole**, Gerald Ainsworth 1917- *AmMWSc 92*
**Cole**, Gerald Alan 1931- *AmMWSc 92*
**Cole**, Gerald Sidney 1936- *AmMWSc 92, WhoMW 92*
**Cole**, Glen David 1933- *WhoRel 92*
**Cole**, Grace *WhoAmP 91*
**Cole**, Gretchen Bornor 1927- *WhoMW 92*
**Cole**, Hank *TwCWW 91*
**Cole**, Harold David 1940- *WhoMW 92*
**Cole**, Harold S 1916- *AmMWSc 92*
**Cole**, Harry A *WhoAmP 91*
**Cole**, Harry A. 1921- *WhoBlA 92*
**Cole**, Harvey M 1920- *AmMWSc 92*
**Cole**, Helen 1922- *WhoAmP 91*
**Cole**, Henderson 1924- *AmMWSc 92*
**Cole**, Henry George 1875-1957 *TwCPaSc*
**Cole**, Herbert, Jr 1933- *AmMWSc 92*
**Cole**, Howard Chandler 1934- *WhoMW 92*
**Cole**, Humphrey John Douglas 1928- *Who 92*
**Cole**, Jack 1943- *WhoEnt 92, WhoWest 92*
**Cole**, Jack Robert 1929- *AmMWSc 92*
**Cole**, Jack Westley 1920- *AmMWSc 92*
**Cole**, Jackson *TwCWW 91*
**Cole**, Jacques Pierre 1926- *IntAu&W 91*
**Cole**, James A 1939- *AmMWSc 92*
**Cole**, James Channing 1948- *AmMWSc 92*
**Cole**, James Edward 1940- *AmMWSc 92*
**Cole**, James M *WhoAmP 91*
**Cole**, James O. 1941- *WhoBlA 92*
**Cole**, James S. *Who 92*
**Cole**, James Webb, Jr 1910- *AmMWSc 92*
**Cole**, Janet 1922- *WhoEnt 92*
**Cole**, Jeffrey Clark 1966- *WhoMW 92*
**Cole**, Jeffrey Joseph 1954- *WhoAmL 92*
**Cole**, Jerome Foster 1940- *AmMWSc 92*
**Cole**, Jerry Joe 1938- *AmMWSc 92*
**Cole**, Joanna 1944- *ConAu 36NR*
**Cole**, Joe Clinton 1938- *WhoWest 92*
**Cole**, John Daniel 1952- *WhoEnt 92*
**Cole**, John Donald 1949- *WhoIns 92*
**Cole**, John E, III 1942- *AmMWSc 92*
**Cole**, John L., Jr. 1928- *WhoBlA 92*
**Cole**, John Morrison 1927- *IntAu&W 91, Who 92*
**Cole**, John Oliver 1915- *AmMWSc 92*
**Cole**, John Peter 1928- *Who 92*
**Cole**, John Pope, Jr. 1930- *WhoAmL 92*
**Cole**, John Rufus, Jr 1938- *AmMWSc 92*
**Cole**, John Vicat 1903- *TwCPaSc*
**Cole**, Johnnetta Betsch 1936- *NotBlAW 92 [port], WhoBlA 92*
**Cole**, Jon A 1939- *AmMWSc 92*
**Cole**, Jonathan 1942- *WrDr 92*
**Cole**, Jonathan Jay 1953- *AmMWSc 92*
**Cole**, Joseph Derham 1952- *WhoAmP 91*
**Cole**, Joseph Edmund 1915- *WhoMW 92*
**Cole**, Joseph H. 1913- *WhoBlA 92*
**Cole**, Julian D 1925- *AmMWSc 92*
**Cole**, Karen Kay 1956- *WhoAmL 92*
**Cole**, Kathleen Ann 1946- *WhoMW 92*
**Cole**, Kay *ConAu 134*
**Cole**, Keith David 1929- *IntWW 91*
**Cole**, Kenneth A 1938- *WhoAmP 91*
**Cole**, Kenneth Bridges, Jr. 1959- *WhoAmL 92*
**Cole**, Kenneth J 1936- *WhoAmP 91*
**Cole**, Kenneth Merle, III 1946- *WhoAmP 91*
**Cole**, Kevin 1962- *WhoEnt 92*
**Cole**, Kevin O'Neill 1949- *WhoWest 92*
**Cole**, Kris W. 1957- *WhoEnt 92*
**Cole**, Laramee *TwCWW 91*
**Cole**, Larry King 1939- *AmMWSc 92*
**Cole**, Larry Lee 1941- *AmMWSc 92*
**Cole**, Larry S 1906- *AmMWSc 92*
**Cole**, Lawrence Frederick 1947- *WhoRel 92*
**Cole**, Lee Arthur 1953- *AmMWSc 92*
**Cole**, Leslie 1910- *TwCPaSc*
**Cole**, Lewis George 1931- *WhoAmL 92*
**Cole**, Louise Marie 1952- *WhoFI 92*
**Cole**, Luther Francis 1925- *WhoAmL 92, WhoAmP 91*
**Cole**, Maceola Louise 1934- *WhoBlA 92*
**Cole**, Madison Brooks, Jr 1940- *AmMWSc 92*
**Cole**, Malcolm Stanley 1936- *WhoEnt 92*
**Cole**, Malvin 1933- *WhoWest 92*
**Cole**, Michael Allen 1943- *AmMWSc 92*
**Cole**, Michael L. 1945- *WhoWest 92*
**Cole**, Milton Walter 1942- *AmMWSc 92*
**Cole**, Monica M. 1922- *Who 92*
**Cole**, Morton S 1929- *AmMWSc 92*
**Cole**, Murray Lee 1922- *WhoFI 92*
**Cole**, Nancy 1902- *AmMWSc 92*
**Cole**, Nancy Berkey 1936- *WhoEnt 92*
**Cole**, Nat d1965 *LesBEnT 92*
**Cole**, Nat 1917-1965 *NewAmDM*
**Cole**, Nat 1919-1965 *FacFETw [port]*
**Cole**, Natalie 1950- *CurBio 91 [port], WhoBlA 92*
**Cole**, Natalie Maria 1950- *WhoEnt 92*
**Cole**, Noel Andy 1949- *AmMWSc 92*
**Cole**, Nyla J 1925- *AmMWSc 92*
**Cole**, Patricia A. 1940- *WhoBlA 92*
**Cole**, Patricia Ann 1953- *WhoFI 92*
**Cole**, Patricia Ellen 1944- *AmMWSc 92*
**Cole**, Perry James 1957- *WhoFI 92*
**Cole**, Peter Geoffrey 1945- *Who 92*
**Cole**, Phillip Allen 1940- *WhoAmL 92*
**Cole**, Phyllis M 1945- *WhoAmP 91*
**Cole**, Ralph *WhoAmP 91*
**Cole**, Ralph A 1915- *WhoAmP 91*
**Cole**, Ralph Davis, Jr. 1914- *WhoAmL 92*
**Cole**, Ralph I 1905- *AmMWSc 92*
**Cole**, Randal Hudie 1908- *AmMWSc 92*
**Cole**, Randall Knight 1912- *AmMWSc 92*
**Cole**, Randel F. 1950- *WhoEnt 92*
**Cole**, Rebecca J. 1846-1922 *NotBlAW 92*
**Cole**, Rex Vicat 1870-1940 *TwCPaSc*
**Cole**, Richard *DrAPF 91, WrDr 92*
**Cole**, Richard 1924- *AmMWSc 92*
**Cole**, Richard A. 1951- *WhoAmL 92*
**Cole**, Richard Allen 1942- *AmMWSc 92*
**Cole**, Richard Charles 1950- *WhoAmL 92*
**Cole**, Richard Garfield 1926- *WhoEnt 92, WhoFI 92*
**Cole**, Richard George 1948- *WhoWest 92*
**Cole**, Richard H 1930- *AmMWSc 92*
**Cole**, Richard Henry 1926- *WhoFI 92*
**Cole**, Richard P. 1948- *WhoAmL 92*
**Cole**, Richard Raymond Buxton 1937- *Who 92*
**Cole**, Robert *TwCWW 91*
**Cole**, Robert 1928- *AmMWSc 92*
**Cole**, Robert Bates 1911- *WhoAmL 92*
**Cole**, Robert Benjamin 1956- *WhoEnt 92*
**Cole**, Robert H. 1931- *WhoAmL 92*
**Cole**, Robert Hugh 1914- *AmMWSc 92*
**Cole**, Robert J. 1925- *ConAu 133*
**Cole**, Robert Kleiv 1928- *AmMWSc 92*
**Cole**, Robert Stephen 1943- *AmMWSc 92*
**Cole**, Robert Stephen, Jr. 1951- *WhoFI 92*
**Cole**, Robert Templeman 1918- *Who 92*
**Cole**, Robert Theodore 1932- *WhoAmL 92*
**Cole**, Robert Virgil 1937- *WhoWest 92*
**Cole**, Robert W *ScFEYrs*
**Cole**, Robert William 1926- *Who 92*
**Cole**, Robin 1955- *WhoBlA 92*
**Cole**, Roger David 1924- *AmMWSc 92*
**Cole**, Roger M 1934- *AmMWSc 92*
**Cole**, Ronald Berkeley 1913- *Who 92*
**Cole**, Rossetter Gleason 1866-1952 *NewAmDM*
**Cole**, Samuel Thornton 1932- *WhoIns 92*
**Cole**, Sheila R. 1939- *WrDr 92*
**Cole**, Stacey W 1921- *WhoAmP 91*
**Cole**, Stephen H 1942- *AmMWSc 92*
**Cole**, Stephen Salisbury 1950- *WhoFI 92*
**Cole**, Stephen William 1813-1889 *DcNCBi 1*
**Cole**, Steve Paul 1952- *WhoWest 92*
**Cole**, Steven Patrick 1960- *WhoAmL 92*
**Cole**, Susan Jane 1949- *WhoAmL 92*
**Cole**, Terrence 1953- *ConAu 135*
**Cole**, Terri Lynn 1951- *WhoWest 92*
**Cole**, Terry 1931- *AmMWSc 92*
**Cole**, Terry Paul 1945- *WhoAmL 92*
**Cole**, Theodore John 1953- *WhoMW 92*
**Cole**, Thomas 1801-1848 *BenetAL 91*
**Cole**, Thomas A 1936- *AmMWSc 92*
**Cole**, Thomas Amor 1948- *WhoAmL 92*
**Cole**, Thomas E 1933- *WhoAmP 91*
**Cole**, Thomas Earle 1922- *AmMWSc 92*
**Cole**, Thomas Ernest 1951- *AmMWSc 92*
**Cole**, Thomas Winston, Jr 1941- *AmMWSc 92, WhoBlA 92*
**Cole**, Thomas Winston, Sr. 1915- *WhoBlA 92*
**Cole**, Tom 1949- *WhoAmP 91*
**Cole**, Tom C 1937- *WhoAmP 91*
**Cole**, Versa V *AmMWSc 92*
**Cole**, Vinson *WhoEnt 92*
**Cole**, Wallace Bartz 1928- *WhoRel 92*
**Cole**, Walter Earl 1921- *AmMWSc 92*
**Cole**, Walter Eckle 1928- *AmMWSc 92*
**Cole**, Wayne 1913- *AmMWSc 92*
**Cole**, Wayne S. 1922- *WrDr 92*
**Cole**, Wayne Stanley 1922- *IntAu&W 91*
**Cole**, Wilbur Vose 1913- *AmMWSc 92*
**Cole**, Willard Glover 1906-1965 *DcNCBi 1*
**Cole**, William *DrAPF 91, Who 92*
**Cole**, William 1919- *IntAu&W 91, WrDr 92*
**Cole**, William Charles 1909- *Who 92*
**Cole**, William Francis 1955- *WhoFI 92*
**Cole**, William James 1948- *WhoAmP 91*
**Cole**, William Owen 1931- *WhoRel 92*
**Cole**, William Russell 1928- *WhoIns 92*
**Cole**, William Scott 1902- *Who 92*
**Cole**, Yvonne 1953- *TwCPaSc*
**Cole-Hamilton**, Arthur Richard 1935- *Who 92*
**Cole-Hamilton**, John 1899- *Who 92*
**Cole Vazquez**, Benjamin *WhoAmP 91*

**Colebrook,** George, Jr. 1942- *WhoBlA 92*
**Colebrook,** Joan *DrAPF 91*
**Colebrook,** Joan d1991 *NewYTBS 91*
**Colebrook,** Lawrence David 1930- *AmMWSc 92*
**Colebrook,** Philip Victor Charles 1924- *Who 92*
**Coleburt,** James Russell 1920- *WrDr 92*
**Coleby,** Anthony Laurie 1935- *Who 92*
**Colecchi,** Stephen 1954- *WhoAmL 92*
**Coleclough,** Peter Cecil 1917- *Who 92*
**Colegate,** Isabel 1931- *ConNov 91, WrDr 92*
**Colegate,** Isabel Diana 1931- *IntAu&W 91, Who 92*
**Colegate,** Raymond 1927- *Who 92*
**Colegrove,** Forrest Donald 1929- *AmMWSc 92*
**Colella,** Donald Francis *AmMWSc 92*
**Colella,** Roberto 1935- *AmMWSc 92*
**Colello,** Alan R. 1949- *WhoFI 92*
**Colello,** Daniel R 1948- *WhoIns 92*
**Coleman,** A. D. 1943- *WrDr 92*
**Coleman,** Alan Brouse 1929- *WhoWest 92*
**Coleman,** Albert *WhoEnt 92*
**Coleman,** Albert John 1918- *AmMWSc 92*
**Coleman,** Alice Mary 1923- *Who 92*
**Coleman,** Allen Markley 1949- *WhoMW 92*
**Coleman,** Alyce Marie 1911- *WhoAmP 91*
**Coleman,** Andrew Lee 1960- *WhoBlA 92*
**Coleman,** Anna M 1913- *AmMWSc 92*
**Coleman,** Annette Wilbois 1934- *AmMWSc 92*
**Coleman,** Arlene Florence 1926- *WhoWest 92*
**Coleman,** Arthur *DrAPF 91*
**Coleman,** Arthur H. 1920- *WhoBlA 92*
**Coleman,** Arthur Percy 1922- *Who 92*
**Coleman,** Audrey Rachelle 1934- *WhoBlA 92*
**Coleman,** Avant Patrick 1936- *WhoBlA 92*
**Coleman,** Barbara Lee Weinstein 1948- *WhoWest 92*
**Coleman,** Barbara Sims 1932- *WhoBlA 92*
**Coleman,** Ben Carl 1927- *WhoBlA 92N*
**Coleman,** Bernard 1928- *Who 92*
**Coleman,** Bernard David 1930- *AmMWSc 92*
**Coleman,** Bernell 1929- *AmMWSc 92*
**Coleman,** Bessie 1893-1926 *NotBlAW 92*
**Coleman,** Bessie 1896-1926 *HanAmWH*
**Coleman,** Bryan Douglas 1948- *WhoAmL 92, WhoFI 92*
**Coleman,** Buck *TwCWW 91*
**Coleman,** Caesar David 1919- *WhoBlA 92*
**Coleman,** Carolyn 1952- *WhoAmP 91*
**Coleman,** Cecil R. 1934- *WhoBlA 92*
**Coleman,** Charles Clyde 1937- *AmMWSc 92*
**Coleman,** Charles Franklin 1917- *AmMWSc 92*
**Coleman,** Charles Mosby 1925- *AmMWSc 92*
**Coleman,** Charles W 1932- *WhoAmP 91*
**Coleman,** Clarence d1918 *BiInAmS*
**Coleman,** Clarence William 1909- *WhoFI 92, WhoMW 92*
**Coleman,** Claude M. 1940- *WhoBlA 92*
**Coleman,** Clinton R. *WhoRel 92*
**Coleman,** Columbus E., Jr. 1948- *WhoBlA 92*
**Coleman,** Courtney 1930- *AmMWSc 92*
**Coleman,** Cy 1929- *NewAmDM, WhoEnt 92*
**Coleman,** Dabney *LesBEnT 92*
**Coleman,** Dabney 1932- *IntMPA 92*
**Coleman,** Dabney W. 1932- *WhoEnt 92*
**Coleman,** Dave Allen 1959- *WhoEnt 92*
**Coleman,** David Cecil 1937- *WhoFI 92*
**Coleman,** David Cowan 1938- *AmMWSc 92*
**Coleman,** David Dennis, II 1957- *WhoEnt 92*
**Coleman,** David Manley 1948- *AmMWSc 92*
**Coleman,** David Michael 1942- *WhoRel 92*
**Coleman,** Deborah Ann 1951- *WhoAmL 92*
**Coleman,** Derrick 1967- *WhoBlA 92*
**Coleman,** Don Edwin 1928- *WhoBlA 92*
**Coleman,** Donald Alvin 1952- *WhoBlA 92*
**Coleman,** Donald Brooks 1934- *AmMWSc 92*
**Coleman,** Donald Cuthbert 1920- *IntWW 91, Who 92*
**Coleman,** Donald Lee 1936- *WhoWest 92*
**Coleman,** Donald Richard d1991 *Who 92N*
**Coleman,** Donna 1949- *WhoAmP 91*
**Coleman,** E. Thomas 1943- *AlmAP 92 [port], WhoAmP 91, WhoMW 92*
**Coleman,** Edward J. 1957- *WhoAmL 92*
**Coleman,** Edward M *WhoAmP 91*
**Coleman,** Edwin Leon, II 1932- *WhoBlA 92*
**Coleman,** Elijah 1924- *WhoAmP 91*
**Coleman,** Elizabeth Sheppard *WhoBlA 92*
**Coleman,** Emily R. 1947- *ConAu 135*
**Coleman,** Emmett 1938- *WhoBlA 92*
**Coleman,** Eric Dean 1951- *WhoAmP 91, WhoBlA 92*
**Coleman,** Everod A. 1920- *WhoBlA 92*
**Coleman,** Frankie Lynn 1950- *WhoBlA 92*
**Coleman,** Gary 1968- *IntMPA 92, WhoBlA 92*
**Coleman,** Geoffry N 1946- *AmMWSc 92*
**Coleman,** George Edward 1935- *WhoBlA 92, WhoEnt 92*
**Coleman,** George Hunt 1928- *AmMWSc 92*
**Coleman,** George Michael 1953- *WhoMW 92*
**Coleman,** George W 1900- *AmMWSc 92*
**Coleman,** George Willard 1912- *WhoFI 92*
**Coleman,** Gerald Christopher 1939- *WhoFI 92*
**Coleman,** Gilbert Irving 1940- *WhoBlA 92*
**Coleman,** Gilbert P 1866- *ScFEYrs*
**Coleman,** Gilbert Robey 1955- *WhoFI 92*
**Coleman,** Gloria Jean 1952- *WhoMW 92*
**Coleman,** Greg Jerome 1954- *WhoBlA 92*
**Coleman,** Harry A. *WhoBlA 92*
**Coleman,** Harry Theodore 1943- *WhoBlA 92*
**Coleman,** Herman W. 1939- *WhoBlA 92*
**Coleman,** Horace *DrAPF 91*
**Coleman,** Howard S 1917- *AmMWSc 92*
**Coleman,** Hume Field 1938- *WhoAmL 92*
**Coleman,** Hurley J., Jr. 1953- *WhoBlA 92*
**Coleman,** Isobel Mary *Who 92*
**Coleman,** J. P. 1914-1991 *CurBio 91N*
**Coleman,** J Tom, Jr 1928- *WhoAmP 91*
**Coleman,** Jack L, Jr 1953- *WhoAmP 91*
**Coleman,** James *DrAPF 91*
**Coleman,** James 1926- *WrDr 92*
**Coleman,** James A. 1921- *WrDr 92*
**Coleman,** James Andrew 1921- *AmMWSc 92*
**Coleman,** James Edward 1928- *AmMWSc 92*
**Coleman,** James Edwin, Jr. 1923- *WhoAmL 92*
**Coleman,** James Howard, Jr. 1909- *WhoAmL 92*
**Coleman,** James J 1950- *AmMWSc 92*
**Coleman,** James Julian 1915- *WhoAmL 92*
**Coleman,** James Julian, Jr. 1941- *WhoAmL 92, WhoFI 92*
**Coleman,** James Malcolm 1935- *AmMWSc 92*
**Coleman,** James P. d1991 *NewYTBS 91 [port]*
**Coleman,** James R 1937- *AmMWSc 92*
**Coleman,** James Regis 1946- *WhoMW 92*
**Coleman,** James Roland 1946- *AmMWSc 92*
**Coleman,** James Samuel 1926- *IntWW 91*
**Coleman,** James Stafford 1928- *AmMWSc 92*
**Coleman,** Jane Candia *DrAPF 91*
**Coleman,** Jane Dwight Dexter 1942- *WhoEnt 92*
**Coleman,** Jason Gill 1961- *WhoEnt 92*
**Coleman,** Jean Ellen *WhoBlA 92*
**Coleman,** Jean Stapleton 1925- *WhoAmP 91*
**Coleman,** Jeffrey Peters 1959- *WhoAmL 92*
**Coleman,** Joel Gregory 1957- *WhoFI 92*
**Coleman,** John 1956- *TwCPaSc*
**Coleman,** John B. 1929- *WhoBlA 92*
**Coleman,** John Dee 1932- *AmMWSc 92*
**Coleman,** John Ennis 1930- *Who 92*
**Coleman,** John Everett, Jr. 1957- *WhoFI 92*
**Coleman,** John Franklin 1939- *AmMWSc 92*
**Coleman,** John H. 1928- *WhoBlA 92*
**Coleman,** John Howard 1925- *AmMWSc 92*
**Coleman,** John Michael 1949- *WhoAmL 92, WhoFI 92*
**Coleman,** John Russell 1933- *AmMWSc 92*
**Coleman,** Johnnie 1920?- *RelLAm 91*
**Coleman,** Jonathan Strickland 1960- *WhoAmL 92*
**Coleman,** Joseph E *WhoAmP 91*
**Coleman,** Joseph E. 1922- *WhoBlA 92*
**Coleman,** Joseph Emory 1930- *AmMWSc 92*
**Coleman,** Jules L. 1947- *WhoAmL 92*
**Coleman,** Jules Victor 1907- *AmMWSc 92*
**Coleman,** Kenneth L. 1942- *WhoBlA 92*
**Coleman,** Kenneth William 1930- *WhoFI 92*
**Coleman,** Lamar William 1934- *AmMWSc 92, WhoFI 92*
**Coleman,** Larry DeMurr 1933- *WhoMW 92*
**Coleman,** Lawrence Bruce 1948- *AmMWSc 92*
**Coleman,** Lemon, Jr. 1935- *WhoBlA 92*
**Coleman,** Leslie Charles 1926- *AmMWSc 92*
**Coleman,** Lester Earl 1930- *AmMWSc 92, WhoFI 92, WhoMW 92*
**Coleman,** Lester F 1922- *AmMWSc 92*
**Coleman,** Lewis Waldo 1942- *WhoFI 92*
**Coleman,** Loren 1947- *ConAu 133*
**Coleman,** Louis H. 1943- *WhoBlA 92*
**Coleman,** Malcolm Graham, II 1957- *WhoEnt 92*
**Coleman,** Malcolm James, Jr. 1947- *WhoEnt 92*
**Coleman,** Marcia Lepri *AmMWSc 92*
**Coleman,** Marian M. 1948- *WhoBlA 92*
**Coleman,** Marilyn A 1946- *AmMWSc 92*
**Coleman,** Marion Leslie 1925- *WhoFI 92*
**Coleman,** Mark Warren 1957- *WhoAmL 92*
**Coleman,** Mary Ann *DrAPF 91*
**Coleman,** Mary Ann 1928- *IntAu&W 91*
**Coleman,** Mary Channing 1883-1947 *DcNCBi 1*
**Coleman,** Mary Sue 1943- *AmMWSc 92*
**Coleman,** Mattison Barr 1934- *WhoWest 92*
**Coleman,** Melvin D. 1948- *WhoBlA 92*
**Coleman,** Michael Andrew 1950- *WhoRel 92*
**Coleman,** Michael B. 1946- *WhoWest 92*
**Coleman,** Michael Murray 1938- *AmMWSc 92*
**Coleman,** Monte 1957- *WhoBlA 92*
**Coleman,** Morton 1939- *AmMWSc 92*
**Coleman,** Nancy 1917- *IntMPA 92*
**Coleman,** Nancy Catherine 1912- *WhoEnt 92*
**Coleman,** Nancy Pees 1955- *AmMWSc 92*
**Coleman,** Neil Lloyd 1930- *AmMWSc 92*
**Coleman,** Norman Arthur 1923- *WhoFI 92*
**Coleman,** Norman P, Jr 1942- *AmMWSc 92*
**Coleman,** Ornette 1930- *FacFETw, NewAmDM, WhoBlA 92, WhoEnt 92*
**Coleman,** Otto Harvey 1905- *AmMWSc 92*
**Coleman,** P D 1918- *AmMWSc 92*
**Coleman,** Patricia Joanne 1941- *WhoEnt 92*
**Coleman,** Patricia M 1948- *WhoIns 92*
**Coleman,** Patrick Louis *AmMWSc 92*
**Coleman,** Paul David 1927- *AmMWSc 92*
**Coleman,** Paul Jerome, Jr 1932- *AmMWSc 92, WhoFI 92*
**Coleman,** Paul Timothy 1951- *WhoAmL 92*
**Coleman,** Peter Everard *Who 92*
**Coleman,** Peter Stephen 1938- *AmMWSc 92*
**Coleman,** Peter Tali 1919- *WhoAmP 91, WhoWest 92*
**Coleman,** Philip Hoxie 1933- *AmMWSc 92*
**Coleman,** Philip Lynn 1944- *AmMWSc 92*
**Coleman,** Ralph Edward 1943- *AmMWSc 92*
**Coleman,** Ralph Orval, Jr 1931- *AmMWSc 92*
**Coleman,** Raymond Cato 1918- *WhoBlA 92*
**Coleman,** Raymond James 1923- *ConAu 36NR*
**Coleman,** Richard *DrAPF 91*
**Coleman,** Richard Daly 1932- *WhoIns 92*
**Coleman,** Richard Walter 1922- *AmMWSc 92, WhoMW 92*
**Coleman,** Richard William 1935- *WhoAmL 92*
**Coleman,** Rita Denise 1959- *WhoAmL 92*
**Coleman,** Robert A. 1932- *WhoBlA 92*
**Coleman,** Robert Dennis 1944- *WhoMW 92*
**Coleman,** Robert E 1921- *AmMWSc 92*
**Coleman,** Robert E 1928- *ConAu 35NR*
**Coleman,** Robert Earl, Jr. 1961- *WhoBlA 92*
**Coleman,** Robert F. 1944- *WhoAmL 92*
**Coleman,** Robert George Gilbert 1929- *Who 92*
**Coleman,** Robert Griffin 1923- *AmMWSc 92*
**Coleman,** Robert J 1941- *AmMWSc 92*
**Coleman,** Robert John 1943- *Who 92*
**Coleman,** Robert Lee 1929- *WhoAmL 92, WhoMW 92*
**Coleman,** Robert Marshall 1925- *AmMWSc 92*
**Coleman,** Robert Trent 1936- *WhoWest 92*
**Coleman,** Robert Vincent 1930- *AmMWSc 92*
**Coleman,** Robert Winston 1942- *WhoAmL 92*
**Coleman,** Roderick Flynn 1958- *WhoAmL 92*
**Coleman,** Rodney Albert 1938- *WhoBlA 92*
**Coleman,** Roger Dixon 1915- *WhoWest 92*
**Coleman,** Roger W. 1929- *WhoFI 92, WhoWest 92*
**Coleman,** Ronald D. 1941- *AlmAP 92 [port], WhoAmP 91*
**Coleman,** Ronald Frederick 1931- *Who 92*
**Coleman,** Ronald Gerald 1944- *WhoBlA 92*
**Coleman,** Ronald K. 1934- *WhoBlA 92*
**Coleman,** Ronald L. 1959- *WhoFI 92*
**Coleman,** Ronald Leon 1934- *AmMWSc 92*
**Coleman,** Roy Everett 1942- *WhoMW 92*
**Coleman,** Rudolph W. 1929- *WhoBlA 92*
**Coleman,** Ruth M. 1917- *WhoBlA 92*
**Coleman,** Samuel Melville 1961- *WhoAmL 92*
**Coleman,** Shalom 1918- *WhoRel 92*
**Coleman,** Sherri Ann 1957- *WhoMW 92*
**Coleman,** Shirley *WhoAmP 91*
**Coleman,** Sidney 1937- *IntWW 91*
**Coleman,** Sidney Richard 1937- *AmMWSc 92*
**Coleman,** Sinclair B. 1946- *WhoBlA 92*
**Coleman,** Stephen Dennis 1953- *WhoFI 92*
**Coleman,** Steven Eugene 1955- *WhoRel 92*
**Coleman,** Sylvia Ethel 1933- *AmMWSc 92*
**Coleman,** T. Rupert 1908- *WhoRel 92*
**Coleman,** Ted 1953- *WhoWest 92*
**Coleman,** Terry 1931- *IntAu&W 91, IntWW 91, Who 92, WrDr 92*
**Coleman,** Terry L 1943- *WhoAmP 91*
**Coleman,** Terry Lee 1959- *WhoRel 92*
**Coleman,** Thaddeus Charles 1837-1895 *DcNCBi 1*
**Coleman,** Theo Houghton 1921- *AmMWSc 92*
**Coleman,** Thomas Charles 1932- *WhoAmL 92*
**Coleman,** Thomas D *WhoAmP 91*
**Coleman,** Thomas George *AmMWSc 92*
**Coleman,** Thomas J. 1950- *IntMPA 92*
**Coleman,** Thomas Loyd 1947- *WhoAmP 91*
**Coleman,** Timothy John 1958- *WhoAmL 92*
**Coleman,** Verna *ConAu 134*
**Coleman,** Vicki Doree 1950- *WhoBlA 92*
**Coleman,** Vincent Maurice 1961- *WhoBlA 92*
**Coleman,** Virginia Flood 1945- *WhoAmL 92*
**Coleman,** W L d1904 *BiInAmS*
**Coleman,** Wanda *DrAPF 91*
**Coleman,** Wanda 1946- *WhoBlA 92*
**Coleman,** Warren B. 1932- *WhoBlA 92*
**Coleman,** Warren Clay 1849-1904 *DcNCBi 1*
**Coleman,** Warren Kent 1945- *AmMWSc 92*
**Coleman,** Wayne Dudley 1927- *WhoMW 92*
**Coleman,** Wendell Lawrence 1946- *WhoAmP 91*
**Coleman,** William Carleton, Jr 1925- *WhoAmP 91, WhoFI 92*
**Coleman,** William Fletcher 1944- *AmMWSc 92*
**Coleman,** William Gilbert 1951- *WhoWest 92*
**Coleman,** William Gilmore, Jr 1942- *AmMWSc 92*
**Coleman,** William H 1937- *AmMWSc 92*
**Coleman,** William Lewis 1942- *WhoWest 92*
**Coleman,** William Matthew 1922- *WhoAmP 91*
**Coleman,** William Robert 1916- *WhoWest 92*
**Coleman,** William Robert 1917- *Who 92*
**Coleman,** William T., Jr. 1920- *WhoBlA 92*
**Coleman,** William Thaddeus, Jr. 1920- *WhoAmL 92*
**Coleman,** William Thomas 1938- *WhoAmL 92*
**Coleman,** Winson 1905- *WhoBlA 92*
**Coleman,** Wisdom F. 1944- *WhoBlA 92*
**Coleman-Beattie,** Brenda Kay 1960- *WhoFI 92*
**Coleman-Burns,** Patricia Wendolyn 1947- *WhoBlA 92*
**Colemon,** Johnnie *WhoBlA 92*
**Colen,** Alan Hugh 1939- *AmMWSc 92*
**Colen,** Frederick Haas 1947- *WhoAmL 92*
**Coler,** Joel H. 1931- *IntMPA 92*
**Coler,** Myron Abraham 1913- *AmMWSc 92*
**Coler,** Robert A 1928- *AmMWSc 92*
**Coleraine,** Baron 1931- *Who 92*
**Coleridge** *Who 92*
**Coleridge,** Baron 1937- *Who 92*
**Coleridge,** Clarence Nicholas 1930- *WhoRel 92*
**Coleridge,** David Ean 1932- *IntWW 91, Who 92*
**Coleridge,** Geraldine Margaret 1948- *Who 92*
**Coleridge,** John *TwCSFW 91*
**Coleridge,** Marguerite Georgina 1916- *Who 92*
**Coleridge,** Nicholas David 1957- *IntAu&W 91, Who 92*

**Coleridge,** Samuel Taylor 1772-1834 *BlkwCEP, CnDBLB 3 [port], DcLB 107 [port], RfGEnL 91*
**Coleridge,** Sara 1802-1852 *NinCLC 31 [port]*
**Coleridge-Taylor,** Samuel 1875-1912 *NewAmDM*
**Coles,** Anna Bailey 1925- *AmMWSc 92, WhoBlA 92*
**Coles,** Anna L. Bailey 1925- *IntWW 91*
**Coles,** Arthur John 1937- *Who 92*
**Coles,** Bimbo 1968- *WhoBlA 92*
**Coles,** Bruce *Who 92*
**Coles,** Bryan Randell 1926- *Who 92*
**Coles,** Darnell 1962- *WhoBlA 92*
**Coles,** David John *Who 92*
**Coles,** Don 1928- *ConPo 91, WrDr 92*
**Coles,** Donald 1924- *AmMWSc 92*
**Coles,** Donald Langdon 1928- *IntAu&W 91*
**Coles,** Dwight Ross 1952- *WhoWest 92*
**Coles,** Embert Harvey, Jr 1923- *AmMWSc 92*
**Coles,** Eric Scott 1965- *WhoEnt 92*
**Coles,** Gerald James Kay 1933- *Who 92*
**Coles,** Graham 1948- *WhoEnt 92*
**Coles,** Ian Ronald 1956- *WhoAmL 92*
**Coles,** James Reed *WhoAmP 91*
**Coles,** James Stacy 1913- *AmMWSc 92*
**Coles,** Janis *ConAu 135*
**Coles,** Joan M. 1947- *ConAu 133*
**Coles,** John *Who 92*
**Coles,** John Edward 1951- *WhoBlA 92*
**Coles,** John M 1930- *ConAu 34NR*
**Coles,** John Morton 1930- *IntAu&W 91, IntWW 91, Who 92, WrDr 92*
**Coles,** Joseph C. 1902- *WhoBlA 92*
**Coles,** Joseph Carlyle, Jr. 1926- *WhoBlA 92*
**Coles,** Kenneth George 1926- *Who 92*
**Coles,** Leslie Stephen 1941- *WhoWest 92*
**Coles,** Lorraine McClellan 1929- *WhoMW 92*
**Coles,** Mabel Irene *Who 92*
**Coles,** Norman 1914- *Who 92*
**Coles,** Norman Bruce 1937- *Who 92*
**Coles,** Richard Warren 1939- *AmMWSc 92*
**Coles,** Robert 1929- *AmMWSc 92, IntAu&W 91, WrDr 92*
**Coles,** Robert Martin 1929- *IntWW 91*
**Coles,** Robert Traynham 1929- *WhoBlA 92*
**Coles,** Stephen Lee 1944- *AmMWSc 92*
**Coles,** Susan 1952- *TwCPaSc*
**Coles,** Vernell 1968- *BlkOlyM*
**Coles,** William Jeffrey 1929- *AmMWSc 92*
**Colescott,** Robert H. 1925- *WorArt 1980*
**Coleshill,** Archdeacon of *Who 92*
**Coleson,** Joseph Edward 1947- *WhoRel 92, WhoWest 92*
**Colestah** *EncAmaz 91*
**Coletta,** James Paul 1954- *WhoAmP 91*
**Coletta,** Ralph John 1921- *WhoAmL 92*
**Colette** 1873-1954 *FacFETw, FrenWW*
**Colette,** Sidonie-Gabrielle 1873-1954 *GuFrLit 1*
**Coletti,** John Anthony 1952- *WhoAmL 92*
**Coletti,** Paul Anthony 1958- *WhoAmL 92*
**Coley,** Caroline Rita 1962- *WhoEnt 92*
**Coley,** Donald Lee 1953- *WhoBlA 92*
**Coley,** Esther B. 1915- *WhoBlA 92*
**Coley,** Franklin Luke, Jr. 1958- *WhoAmL 92*
**Coley,** Gerald Sydney 1914- *WhoBlA 92*
**Coley,** H Turner, Jr 1942- *WhoIns 92*
**Coley,** Henry D. 1819?-1887 *DcNCBi 1*
**Coley,** Philip B. 1952- *WhoEnt 92*
**Coley,** Robert Bernard 1951- *WhoFI 92*
**Coley,** Ronald Frank 1941- *AmMWSc 92*
**Colfax,** Schuyler 1823-1885 *AmPolLe*
**Colfin,** Bruce Elliott 1951- *WhoAmL 92, WhoEnt 92*
**Colflesh,** Trudy Patterson 1939- *WhoRel 92*
**Colford,** Robert Wade 1949- *WhoEnt 92*
**Colfox,** John 1924- *Who 92*
**Colgan,** Charles Joseph 1926- *WhoAmP 91*
**Colgan,** Michael Anthony 1950- *IntWW 91*
**Colgan,** Michael Byrley 1948- *WhoAmL 92*
**Colgan,** Samuel Hezlett 1945- *Who 92*
**Colgate,** Samuel Oran 1933- *AmMWSc 92*
**Colgate,** Stirling Auchincloss 1925- *AmMWSc 92*
**Colglazier,** Merle Lee 1920- *AmMWSc 92*
**Colglazier,** Patrick V 1950- *WhoAmP 91*
**Colgrain,** Baron 1920- *Who 92*
**Colgrass,** Michael Charles 1932- *NewAmDM, WhoEnt 92*
**Colgren,** Richard Dean 1961- *WhoWest 92*
**Colgrove,** Steven Gray 1953- *AmMWSc 92*
**Colgrove,** Thomas Michael 1930- *WhoMW 92*
**Colhapp,** Barbara Jones 1935- *WhoAmP 91*
**Colhoun,** John 1913- *Who 92*
**Colhour,** Donald Bruce 1946- *WhoEnt 92*
**Coli,** G J, Jr 1921- *AmMWSc 92*
**Colicchio,** Roy E. 1931- *WhoAmL 92*
**Colicelli,** Elena Jeanmarie 1950- *AmMWSc 92*
**Coligan,** John E 1944- *AmMWSc 92*
**Colihan,** James Charles 1953- *WhoAmL 92*
**Colijn,** Geert Jan 1946- *WhoFI 92*
**Colilla,** William 1938- *AmMWSc 92*
**Colin,** George H. *WhoBlA 92*
**Colin,** Gerald Fitzmaurice 1913- *Who 92*
**Colin,** Lawrence 1931- *AmMWSc 92*
**Colin,** Margaret *IntMPA 92*
**Colin,** Oswaldo Roberto 1924- *IntWW 91*
**Colin,** Ralph *LesBEnT 92*
**Colin,** Ralph Frederick, Jr. 1933- *WhoEnt 92*
**Colin,** Todd Berger 1963- *WhoMW 92*
**Colingsworth,** Donald Rudolph 1912- *AmMWSc 92*
**Colinvaux,** Paul Alfred 1930- *AmMWSc 92*
**Colish,** Marcia Lillian 1937- *WhoMW 92, WrDr 92*
**Colista,** Feliciano Philip, Jr. 1933- *WhoAmL 92*
**Coliver,** Norman 1918- *WhoAmL 92*
**Coll,** Alberto Raoul 1955- *WhoAmL 92*
**Coll,** Colleen *WhoAmP 91*
**Coll,** David C 1933- *AmMWSc 92*
**Coll,** Elizabeth Anne Loosemore E. *Who 92*
**Coll,** Gary Albert 1957- *WhoEnt 92*
**Coll,** Hans 1929- *AmMWSc 92*
**Coll,** Ivonne *WhoHisp 92*
**Coll,** John Peter, Jr. 1943- *WhoAmL 92*
**Coll,** Max 1932- *WhoAmP 91*
**Coll,** Norman Alan 1940- *WhoAmL 92*
**Coll,** Richard Joseph 1952- *WhoAmL 92*
**Coll Blasini,** Nestor 1931- *Who 92*
**Colla,** Marcel 1943- *IntWW 91*
**Colla,** Richard A. 1936- *WhoEnt 92*
**Colla,** Virginia Covert 1937- *WhoWest 92*
**Collado,** Efrain 1953- *WhoEnt 92*
**Collado,** Francisco 1951- *WhoHisp 92*
**Collamore,** Joanne 1950- *WhoFI 92*
**Collamore,** Thomas Jones 1959- *WhoAmP 91*
**Collander,** Ruth Emily 1918- *WhoEnt 92*
**Collard,** Douglas Reginald 1916- *Who 92*
**Collard,** Eugene Albert 1915- *WhoRel 92*
**Collard,** Harold Rieth 1932- *AmMWSc 92*
**Collard,** Jean Philippe 1948- *IntWW 91*
**Collaro,** Andrew *WhoAmP 91*
**Collas,** Juan Garduno, Jr. 1932- *WhoAmL 92*
**Collat,** Justin White 1928- *AmMWSc 92*
**Collazo,** Denice M. 1953- *WhoFI 92*
**Collazo,** Enrique 1848-1921 *HisDSpE*
**Collazo,** Francisco Jose 1931- *WhoHisp 92*
**Collazo,** Frank, Jr 1931- *WhoAmP 91, WhoHisp 92*
**Collazo,** Joe Manuel 1945- *WhoHisp 92*
**Collazo,** Jose Antonio 1943- *WhoHisp 92*
**Collazo,** Salvador 1948- *WhoHisp 92*
**Colle,** Ronald 1946- *AmMWSc 92*
**Colledge,** Charles Hopson 1911- *WhoEnt 92*
**Colledge,** Malcolm 1939- *WrDr 92*
**Collee,** John Gerald 1929- *Who 92*
**Colleli,** Frank Edward 1953- *WhoEnt 92*
**Colleluori,** Anthony John 1959- *WhoAmL 92*
**Collen,** John 1954- *WhoAmL 92*
**Collen,** Morris F 1913- *AmMWSc 92*
**Collender,** Andrew Robert 1946- *Who 92*
**Collens,** Lewis Morton 1938- *WhoAmL 92, WhoMW 92*
**Coller,** Barry Spencer 1945- *AmMWSc 92*
**Colleran,** Bill *IntMPA 92*
**Colleran,** Kevin 1941- *WhoAmL 92*
**Colles,** Christopher 1738-1816 *BiInAmS*
**Collet,** Bernt Johan 1941- *IntWW 91*
**Collet,** John Abraham *DcNCBi 1*
**Collet,** Ruth 1909- *TwCPaSc*
**Collett,** Christopher 1931- *Who 92*
**Collett,** D. Walter 1954- *WhoRel 92*
**Collett,** David Mark 1952- *WhoRel 92*
**Collett,** Edward 1934- *AmMWSc 92*
**Collett,** Ian 1953- *Who 92*
**Collett,** John 1828-1899 *BiInAmS*
**Collett,** John Abraham *DcNCBi 1*
**Collett,** Merrill Judson 1914- *WhoWest 92*
**Collett,** Wayne Curtis 1949- *BlkOlyM*
**Collette,** Bruce Baden 1934- *AmMWSc 92*
**Collette,** Charles T. 1944- *WhoAmL 92*
**Collette,** John Wilfred 1933- *AmMWSc 92*
**Colletti,** Daniel Alon 1954- *WhoRel 92*
**Colletti,** Paul Joseph 1939- *WhoAmL 92*
**Colley,** Ann Daniel 1950- *WhoWest 92*
**Colley,** Bryan 1934- *Who 92*
**Colley,** Daniel George 1943- *AmMWSc 92*
**Colley,** Ian Harris 1922- *Who 92*
**Colley,** John Austin 1931- *WhoMW 92*
**Colley,** Kenneth 1937- *ConTFT 9*
**Colley,** Mark Douglas 1955- *WhoAmL 92*
**Colley,** Michael F 1936- *WhoAmP 91*
**Colley,** Nathaniel S., Jr. 1956- *WhoBlA 92*
**Colley,** Nathaniel Sextus, Jr. 1956- *WhoEnt 92*
**Colley,** Paul Sims 1924- *WhoAmL 92*
**Colley,** Peter Michael 1949- *WhoWest 92*
**Colley,** William W. 1847-1909 *RelLAm 91*
**Colli,** Bart Joseph 1948- *WhoAmL 92*
**Colliander,** Douglas C 1943- *WhoIns 92*
**Collias,** Elsie Cole 1920- *AmMWSc 92*
**Collias,** Eugene Evans 1925- *AmMWSc 92*
**Collias,** Nicholas Elias 1914- *AmMWSc 92*
**Collie,** Alexander Conn 1913- *Who 92*
**Collie,** John, Jr. 1934- *WhoMW 92*
**Collie,** Kathryn Kaye 1952- *WhoAmL 92*
**Collie,** Kelsey E. 1935- *WhoBlA 92*
**Collie,** Kelsey Eugene 1935- *WhoEnt 92*
**Collier** *Who 92*
**Collier,** Albert 1921- *WhoAmP 91*
**Collier,** Albert, III 1926- *WhoBlA 92*
**Collier,** Alice Elizabeth 1927- *WhoMW 92*
**Collier,** Andrew James 1923- *Who 92*
**Collier,** Andrew John 1939- *Who 92*
**Collier,** Boyd David 1937- *AmMWSc 92*
**Collier,** Brian 1940- *AmMWSc 92*
**Collier,** Calvin Joseph 1942- *WhoAmP 91*
**Collier,** Clarence Marie *WhoBlA 92*
**Collier,** Clarence Robert 1919- *AmMWSc 92*
**Collier,** Curtis Newton 1933- *WhoRel 92*
**Collier,** Donald Lynn 1958- *WhoWest 92*
**Collier,** Donald W 1920- *AmMWSc 92*
**Collier,** Donald Walter 1920- *WhoMW 92*
**Collier,** Elizabeth Jane 1954- *WhoRel 92*
**Collier,** Eugenia W. 1928- *WhoBlA 92*
**Collier,** Francis Nash, Jr 1917- *AmMWSc 92*
**Collier,** Gaylan Jane 1924- *WhoEnt 92*
**Collier,** Gerald 1930- *AmMWSc 92*
**Collier,** Gerrit S 1918- *WhoIns 92*
**Collier,** Gilman Frederick 1929- *WhoEnt 92*
**Collier,** Graham 1937- *WrDr 92*
**Collier,** H. M., Jr. 1916- *WhoBlA 92*
**Collier,** Herbert Bruce 1905- *AmMWSc 92*
**Collier,** Herman Edward, Jr 1927- *AmMWSc 92*
**Collier,** Jack Reed 1926- *AmMWSc 92*
**Collier,** James Bryan 1944- *AmMWSc 92*
**Collier,** James Lincoln 1928- *WrDr 92*
**Collier,** James Warren 1940- *WhoAmL 92*
**Collier,** Jane *WrDr 92*
**Collier,** Jesse Wilton 1914- *AmMWSc 92*
**Collier,** John 1850-1934 *TwCPaSc*
**Collier,** John 1884-1968 *BenetAL 91*
**Collier,** John 1901-1980 *FacFETw, ScFEYrs*
**Collier,** John Gordon 1935- *Who 92*
**Collier,** John Robert 1939- *AmMWSc 92*
**Collier,** Julia Marie 1949- *WhoBlA 92*
**Collier,** Kenneth 1910- *WrDr 92*
**Collier,** Kenneth Gerald 1910- *Who 92*
**Collier,** Lelia Anne 1958- *WhoAmL 92*
**Collier,** Lesley Faye 1947- *IntWW 91, Who 92*
**Collier,** Leslie Harold 1921- *Who 92*
**Collier,** Louis Malcolm 1919- *WhoBlA 92*
**Collier,** Lucille Ann *WhoEnt 92*
**Collier,** Manning Gary 1951- *AmMWSc 92*
**Collier,** Marjorie McCann *AmMWSc 92*
**Collier,** Marsha Ann 1950- *WhoWest 92*
**Collier,** Mary 1689?-1759? *BlkwCEP*
**Collier,** Matthew S 1957- *WhoAmP 91*
**Collier,** Matthew Samuel 1957- *WhoMW 92*
**Collier,** Melvin Lowell 1934- *AmMWSc 92*
**Collier,** Michael *DrAPF 91*
**Collier,** Michael William 1964- *WhoWest 92*
**Collier,** Nathan Morris 1924- *WhoEnt 92, WhoMW 92*
**Collier,** Peter 1835-1896 *BiInAmS*
**Collier,** Peter 1939- *IntAu&W 91, WrDr 92*
**Collier,** Richard 1924- *WrDr 92*
**Collier,** Richard Bangs 1918- *WhoWest 92*
**Collier,** Richard Hughesdon 1924- *IntAu&W 91*
**Collier,** Robert Jacob 1926- *AmMWSc 92*
**Collier,** Robert John 1938- *AmMWSc 92*
**Collier,** Robert Joseph 1947- *AmMWSc 92*
**Collier,** Robert Steven 1952- *WhoEnt 92*
**Collier,** Roger Malcolm 1950- *WhoRel 92*
**Collier,** Shirley Lucille 1933- *WhoAmP 91*
**Collier,** Steven Edward 1952- *WhoFI 92*
**Collier,** Susan S 1939- *AmMWSc 92*
**Collier,** Tom W. 1948- *WhoEnt 92*
**Collier,** Torrence Junis 1932- *WhoBlA 92*
**Collier,** Troy 1941- *WhoBlA 92*
**Collier,** Wayne Frederick 1954- *WhoAmL 92*
**Collier,** William H 1926- *WhoAmP 91*
**Collier,** William Thayer 1928- *WhoEnt 92*
**Collier,** Willye 1922- *WhoBlA 92*
**Collier,** Zena *DrAPF 91*
**Collier,** Zena 1926- *WrDr 92*
**Collier-Thomas,** Bettye *WhoBlA 92*
**Collier-Wright,** John Hurrell 1915- *Who 92*
**Colligan,** Elsa *DrAPF 91*
**Colligan,** George Austin 1928- *AmMWSc 92*
**Colligan,** John Clifford 1906- *Who 92*
**Colligan,** John Joseph 1937- *AmMWSc 92*
**Colligan,** Michael F. 1943- *WhoAmL 92*
**Collin,** Alonzo 1837-1918 *BiInAmS*
**Collin,** C.F. 1890-1937 *TwCPaSc*
**Collin,** Geoffrey de Egglesfield 1921- *Who 92*
**Collin,** Jack 1945- *Who 92*
**Collin,** Jean 1924- *IntWW 91*
**Collin,** Marion 1928- *WrDr 92*
**Collin,** Michel 1905-1974 *RelLAm 91*
**Collin,** Pierre-Paul 1920- *AmMWSc 92*
**Collin,** Reginald *IntMPA 92*
**Collin,** Robert E 1928- *AmMWSc 92*
**Collin,** Thomas James 1949- *WhoAmL 92*
**Collin,** William Kent 1938- *AmMWSc 92*
**Colling,** Cecilia Gail 1949- *WhoAmP 91*
**Colling,** Dennis Robert 1947- *WhoAmP 91*
**Colling,** James Oliver 1923- *Who 92*
**Collingbourne,** Stephen 1943- *TwCPaSc*
**Collinge,** Gail Joan 1941- *WhoWest 92*
**Collingridge,** Jean Mary 1923- *Who 92*
**Collings,** Celeste Louise 1948- *WhoWest 92*
**Collings,** David 1949- *TwCPaSc*
**Collings,** Edward William 1930- *AmMWSc 92*
**Collings,** I. J. *WrDr 92*
**Collings,** Juliet Jeanne d'Auvergne *Who 92*
**Collings,** Michael 1947- *WrDr 92*
**Collings,** Michael R. *DrAPF 91*
**Collings,** Peter John 1947- *AmMWSc 92*
**Collingswood,** Frederick *WrDr 92*
**Collingsworth,** Ann Taylor 1933- *WhoAmP 91*
**Collingsworth,** Joe B. 1952- *WhoRel 92*
**Collingwood,** Charles d1985 *LesBEnT 92*
**Collingwood,** Francis 1834-1911 *BiInAmS*
**Collingwood,** Harry 1851-1922 *ScFEYrs*
**Collingwood,** John Gildas 1917- *Who 92*
**Collins,** Adrian Anthony 1937- *WhoAmL 92*
**Collins,** Aliki Karipidou 1958- *AmMWSc 92*
**Collins,** Allan Clifford 1942- *AmMWSc 92*
**Collins,** Allan Meakin 1937- *AmMWSc 92*
**Collins,** Allan Wayne 1934- *WhoWest 92*
**Collins,** Alva LeRoy, Jr 1940- *AmMWSc 92*
**Collins,** Andre 1968- *WhoBlA 92*
**Collins,** Andrew David 1942- *Who 92*
**Collins,** Anita Marguerite 1947- *AmMWSc 92*
**Collins,** Anthony 1676-1729 *BlkwCEP*
**Collins,** Arlee Gene 1927- *AmMWSc 92*
**Collins,** Arlene Rycombel 1940- *AmMWSc 92*
**Collins,** Arthur 1911- *Who 92*
**Collins,** Arthur John 1931- *Who 92*
**Collins,** Barbara Anne 1935- *WhoRel 92*
**Collins,** Barbara Jane 1929- *AmMWSc 92*
**Collins,** Barbara-Rose 1939- *AlmAP 92 [port], WhoAmP 91, WhoBlA 92, WhoMW 92*
**Collins,** Barry 1941- *WrDr 92*
**Collins,** Basil Eugene Sinclair 1923- *IntWW 91, Who 92*
**Collins,** Bernice Elaine 1957- *WhoBlA 92*
**Collins,** Bert 1934- *WhoBlA 92, WhoIns 92*
**Collins,** Billy *DrAPF 91*
**Collins,** Bonietha Inez 1961- *WhoBlA 92*
**Collins,** Brendan Kennedy 1964- *WhoAmL 92*
**Collins,** Cardiss 1931- *AlmAP 92 [port], NotBlAW 92 [port], WhoAmP 91, WhoBlA 92, WhoMW 92*
**Collins,** Carl Baxter, Jr 1940- *AmMWSc 92*
**Collins,** Carol Desormeau 1954- *AmMWSc 92*
**Collins,** Carol Hollingworth 1931- *AmMWSc 92*
**Collins,** Carolyn Jane 1942- *AmMWSc 92*
**Collins,** Carter Compton 1925- *AmMWSc 92*
**Collins,** Carter H. 1928- *WhoBlA 92*
**Collins,** Carvel 1912- *IntAu&W 91*
**Collins,** Cecil 1908-1989 *TwCPaSc*
**Collins,** Charles David 1949- *WhoFI 92*
**Collins,** Charles Miller 1947- *WhoBlA 92, WhoWest 92*
**Collins,** Charles Thompson 1938- *AmMWSc 92*
**Collins,** Christopher Carl 1950- *WhoFI 92*
**Collins,** Clair Joseph 1915- *AmMWSc 92*
**Collins,** Clifford B 1916- *AmMWSc 92*
**Collins,** Clifford Jacob, III 1947- *WhoBlA 92*
**Collins,** Constance Renee Wilson 1932- *WhoBlA 92*
**Collins,** Corene 1948- *WhoBlA 92*
**Collins,** Cornelia Faye 1963- *WhoBlA 92*
**Collins,** Craig Allan 1959- *WhoMW 92*
**Collins,** Craig L. 1931- *WhoAmL 92*
**Collins,** Curtis Allan 1940- *AmMWSc 92, WhoWest 92*
**Collins,** Cynthia Joan 1958- *WhoFI 92*

**Collins,** Daisy G. 1937- *WhoBlA 92*
**Collins,** Damon L. 1966- *WhoEnt 92*
**Collins,** Dana Jon 1956- *WhoMW 92*
**Collins,** Dane H. 1961- *WhoWest 92*
**Collins,** Daniel A. 1916- *WhoBlA 92*
**Collins,** Daniel Francis 1942- *WhoAmL 92, WhoFI 92*
**Collins,** Daniel G. 1930- *WhoAmL 92*
**Collins,** David Albert Charles 1952- *AmMWSc 92*
**Collins,** David Browning 1922- *WhoRel 92*
**Collins,** David Harvey 1951- *WhoRel 92*
**Collins,** David R. 1940- *WrDr 92*
**Collins,** David Raymond 1940- *WhoMW 92*
**Collins,** Dean Robert 1935- *AmMWSc 92*
**Collins,** Delwood C 1937- *AmMWSc 92*
**Collins,** Dennis Glenn 1944- *WhoMW 92*
**Collins,** Desmond H 1938- *AmMWSc 92*
**Collins,** Don Cary 1951- *WhoAmL 92*
**Collins,** Don Desmond 1934- *AmMWSc 92*
**Collins,** Donald F *WhoAmP 91*
**Collins,** Donald Lamar 1929- *WhoAmP 91*
**Collins,** Donald Ogden 1934- *WhoAmL 92*
**Collins,** Dorothy Lee 1932- *WhoBlA 92*
**Collins,** Douglas Patrick, Jr. 1961- *WhoEnt 92*
**Collins,** Earlean *WhoAmP 91*
**Collins,** Edward A 1928- *AmMWSc 92*
**Collins,** Edwin Bruce 1921- *AmMWSc 92*
**Collins,** Eileen Louise 1942- *WhoFI 92*
**Collins,** Eileen Mary 1933- *WhoMW 92*
**Collins,** Elizabeth 1905- *TwCPaSc*
**Collins,** Elliott 1943- *WhoBlA 92*
**Collins,** Elliott Joel 1919- *AmMWSc 92*
**Collins,** Elsie *WhoBlA 92*
**Collins,** Eric Lee 1963- *WhoMW 92*
**Collins,** F. Donald *WhoRel 92*
**Collins,** F R 1926- *AmMWSc 92*
**Collins,** Francis *WhoMW 92*
**Collins,** Francis Allen 1931- *AmMWSc 92*
**Collins,** Francis James 1933- *WhoAmP 91*
**Collins,** Francis Sellers 1950- *AmMWSc 92*
**Collins,** Frank 1938- *TwCPaSc*
**Collins,** Frank Charles 1911- *AmMWSc 92*
**Collins,** Frank Charles, Jr. 1927- *WhoFI 92*
**Collins,** Frank Gibson 1938- *AmMWSc 92*
**Collins,** Frank Miles 1928- *AmMWSc 92*
**Collins,** Frank Shipley 1848-1920 *BiInAmS*
**Collins,** Frank William, Jr 1945- *AmMWSc 92*
**Collins,** Franklyn 1929- *AmMWSc 92*
**Collins,** Frederick Clinton 1941- *AmMWSc 92*
**Collins,** Galen Franklin 1927- *AmMWSc 92*
**Collins,** Gary 1938- *IntMPA 92*
**Collins,** Gary Brent 1940- *AmMWSc 92*
**Collins,** Gary Scott 1944- *AmMWSc 92*
**Collins,** Gary Willis 1958- *WhoFI 92*
**Collins,** Gene *WhoAmP 91*
**Collins,** George Briggs 1906- *AmMWSc 92*
**Collins,** George Edward 1880-1968 *TwCPaSc*
**Collins,** George Edwin 1928- *AmMWSc 92*
**Collins,** George H 1927- *AmMWSc 92*
**Collins,** George John 1953- *WhoMW 92*
**Collins,** George Joseph *WhoFI 92*
**Collins,** George Timothy 1943- *WhoWest 92*
**Collins,** George W, II 1937- *AmMWSc 92*
**Collins,** George William, II 1937- *WhoMW 92*
**Collins,** George William, Jr. 1951- *WhoAmL 92*
**Collins,** Gerard *Who 92*
**Collins,** Gerry 1938- *IntWW 91*
**Collins,** Gilbert 1890- *ScFEYrs*
**Collins,** Glenn Burton 1939- *AmMWSc 92*
**Collins,** Gordon Dent 1924- *WhoEnt 92*
**Collins,** Gordon Geoffrey 1958- *WhoBlA 92*
**Collins,** Grover 1945- *WhoFI 92*
**Collins,** H Douglas 1928- *AmMWSc 92*
**Collins,** Hal *LesBEnT 92*
**Collins,** Hannah 1956- *TwCPaSc*
**Collins,** Harold R. 1915- *WrDr 92*
**Collins,** Harry David 1931- *WhoFI 92*
**Collins,** Harvey Arnold 1927- *WhoMW 92*
**Collins,** Henry A 1932- *AmMWSc 92*
**Collins,** Henry Edward 1903- *Who 92*
**Collins,** Henry Edward 1937- *WhoMW 92*
**Collins,** Heron Sherwood 1922- *AmMWSc 92*
**Collins,** Hollie L 1938- *AmMWSc 92*
**Collins,** Horace Clayton 1950- *WhoEnt 92*
**Collins,** Horace Rutter 1930- *AmMWSc 92*
**Collins,** Hubert 1936- *WhoAmP 91*
**Collins,** Hubert Michael 1939- *WhoFI 92*
**Collins,** Hunt *IntAu&W 91X, TwCSFW 91, WrDr 92*
**Collins,** Hyacinth Roxane 1948- *WhoBlA 92*
**Collins,** J. Barclay, II 1944- *WhoAmL 92*
**Collins,** J Lawton 1896-1987 *FacFETw*
**Collins,** J. Michael 1935- *WhoEnt 92*
**Collins,** Jack 1943- *WhoAmP 91*
**Collins,** Jack A 1929- *AmMWSc 92*
**Collins,** Jackie *IntAu&W 91, IntWW 91, WrDr 92*
**Collins,** James Arthur 1926- *WhoFI 92, WhoWest 92*
**Collins,** James Douglas 1931- *WhoBlA 92*
**Collins,** James Francis 1942- *AmMWSc 92, WhoWest 92*
**Collins,** James Francis 1943- *WhoAmL 92, WhoMW 92*
**Collins,** James Gerard 1938- *Who 92*
**Collins,** James H. 1946- *WhoBlA 92*
**Collins,** James Ian 1937- *AmMWSc 92*
**Collins,** James Joseph 1947- *AmMWSc 92*
**Collins,** James Lee 1945- *IntAu&W 91*
**Collins,** James Malcolm 1938- *AmMWSc 92*
**Collins,** James Patrick 1947- *WhoWest 92*
**Collins,** James Paul 1947- *AmMWSc 92*
**Collins,** James Paul, Jr. 1945- *WhoAmL 92*
**Collins,** James R *AmMWSc 92*
**Collins,** James Slade, II 1937- *WhoAmL 92*
**Collins,** James William 1942- *WhoAmL 92*
**Collins,** Jan 1943- *WhoAmP 91*
**Collins,** Janet 1917- *NotBlAW 92, WhoBlA 92*
**Collins,** Jeffery Allen 1944- *AmMWSc 92*
**Collins,** Jeffrey Hamilton 1930- *Who 92*
**Collins,** Jeffrey Jay 1945- *AmMWSc 92*
**Collins,** Jenny Galloway *DrAPF 91*
**Collins,** Jeremiah C. 1929- *WhoAmL 92*
**Collins,** Jerry Allan 1936- *WhoFI 92*
**Collins,** Jerry C 1941- *AmMWSc 92*
**Collins,** Jerry Dale 1943- *AmMWSc 92*
**Collins,** Jerry Holman 1939- *WhoMW 92*
**Collins,** Jimmie Lee 1934- *AmMWSc 92*
**Collins,** Jimmy Harold 1948- *AmMWSc 92*
**Collins,** Joan *LesBEnT 92*
**Collins,** Joan 1933- *IntAu&W 91, IntMPA 92, IntWW 91, WrDr 92*
**Collins,** Joan Henrietta 1933- *WhoEnt 92*
**Collins,** Joann Ruth *WhoBlA 92*
**Collins,** Joanne Kay 1951- *WhoMW 92*
**Collins,** Joanne Marcella 1935- *WhoAmP 91, WhoBlA 92*
**Collins,** John A 1929- *AmMWSc 92*
**Collins,** John Alexander 1941- *Who 92*
**Collins,** John Barrett 1949- *AmMWSc 92*
**Collins,** John Clements 1949- *AmMWSc 92*
**Collins,** John Dennis 1938- *WhoFI 92*
**Collins,** John Eliot 1950- *WhoEnt 92*
**Collins,** John Ernest Harley 1923- *Who 92*
**Collins,** John Henry 1942- *AmMWSc 92*
**Collins,** John J. d1991 *NewYTBS 91*
**Collins,** John Joseph 1936- *WhoWest 92*
**Collins,** John Martin 1929- *Who 92*
**Collins,** John Morris 1931- *Who 92*
**Collins,** John Patrick 1939- *WhoAmL 92*
**Collins,** John Patrick 1942- *WhoFI 92*
**Collins,** John Richard 1961- *WhoFI 92*
**Collins,** John Roger 1941- *WhoFI 92*
**Collins,** John Wendler 1930- *WhoWest 92*
**Collins,** Johnnie B 1943- *AmMWSc 92*
**Collins,** Jon David 1935- *AmMWSc 92*
**Collins,** Joseph Charles, Jr 1931- *AmMWSc 92*
**Collins,** Joseph Clinton d1991 *Who 92N*
**Collins,** Joseph V. 1936- *WhoFI 92*
**Collins,** Joseph William 1839-1904 *BiInAmS*
**Collins,** Josiah, II 1763-1839 *DcNCBi 1*
**Collins,** Josiah, III 1808-1863 *DcNCBi 1*
**Collins,** Josiah, Sr. 1735-1819 *DcNCBi 1*
**Collins,** Judy 1939- *FacFETw, NewAmDM*
**Collins,** Judy Marjorie 1939- *WhoEnt 92*
**Collins,** Kathleen *DrAPF 91*
**Collins,** Kathleen 1942-1988 *ReelWom [port]*
**Collins,** Kathleen Elizabeth 1951- *WhoFI 92*
**Collins,** Kenneth Darlingston 1939- *Who 92*
**Collins,** Kenneth Elmer 1926- *AmMWSc 92*
**Collins,** Kenneth James 1937- *WhoAmP 91*
**Collins,** Kenneth L. 1933- *WhoBlA 92*
**Collins,** Kevin Heath 1955- *WhoAmL 92*
**Collins,** Kevin Philip 1950- *WhoFI 92*
**Collins,** Larry 1929- *IntAu&W 91, IntWW 91, WrDr 92*
**Collins,** Larry Wayne 1941- *WhoMW 92*
**Collins,** LaVerne Francis 1946- *WhoBlA 92*
**Collins,** LaVerne Vines 1947- *WhoBlA 92*
**Collins,** Lenora W. 1925- *WhoBlA 92*
**Collins,** LeRoy d1991 *LesBEnT 92, NewYTBS 91 [port]*
**Collins,** Leroy 1909-1991 *CurBio 91N*
**Collins,** Leroy Anthony, Jr. 1950- *WhoBlA 92*
**Collins,** Lesley Elizabeth *Who 92*
**Collins,** Limone C. 1921- *WhoBlA 92*
**Collins,** Lora Suzanne 1935- *WhoAmL 92*
**Collins,** Lorence Gene 1931- *AmMWSc 92*
**Collins,** Lou 1936- *WhoFI 92*
**Collins,** Mac *WhoAmP 91*
**Collins,** Malcolm Frank 1935- *AmMWSc 92*
**Collins,** Margaret Andree Marie 1949- *IntAu&W 91*
**Collins,** Margaret Elizabeth 1927- *Who 92*
**Collins,** Mark Gregory 1960- *WhoMW 92*
**Collins,** Martha *DrAPF 91*
**Collins,** Martha 1940- *IntAu&W 91*
**Collins,** Martha Layne 1936- *IntWW 91, WhoAmP 91*
**Collins,** Martin *Who 92*
**Collins,** Marva 1936- *NotBlAW 92 [port], WrDr 92*
**Collins,** Marva Delores Nettles 1936- *WhoBlA 92*
**Collins,** Mary Alice 1937- *WhoMW 92*
**Collins,** Mary Ann 1953- *WhoAmL 92*
**Collins,** Mary Elizabeth 1953- *AmMWSc 92, WhoAmL 92*
**Collins,** Mary Ellen 1949- *WhoMW 92*
**Collins,** Mary Ellen Kennedy 1939- *WhoMW 92*
**Collins,** Mary Jane 1940- *AmMWSc 92*
**Collins,** Mary Lynne Perille 1949- *AmMWSc 92*
**Collins,** Mary Margaret 1932- *WhoAmP 91*
**Collins,** Matthew Conley 1957- *WhoEnt 92*
**Collins,** Maurice A. 1936- *WhoBlA 92*
**Collins,** Max Allan 1948- *IntAu&W 91, WrDr 92*
**Collins,** Michael *IntAu&W 91X, WrDr 92*
**Collins,** Michael 1890-1922 *FacFETw*
**Collins,** Michael 1930- *FacFETw, IntWW 91, Who 92*
**Collins,** Michael 1951- *AmMWSc 92*
**Collins,** Michael A 1955- *WhoAmP 91*
**Collins,** Michael Albert 1942- *AmMWSc 92*
**Collins,** Michael Brendan 1932- *Who 92*
**Collins,** Michael Crain 1942- *WhoWest 92*
**Collins,** Michael Edward 1938- *WhoRel 92*
**Collins,** Michael Eugene 1955- *WhoRel 92*
**Collins,** Michael Geoffrey 1948- *Who 92*
**Collins,** Michael J 1940- *WhoAmP 91*
**Collins,** Michael John 1944- *WhoMW 92*
**Collins,** Michael John 1962- *Who 92*
**Collins,** Michael Lee, Sr. 1952- *WhoRel 92*
**Collins,** Michael Patrick 1964- *WhoMW 92*
**Collins,** Michael Sean 1951- *WhoWest 92*
**Collins,** Moira Ann 1942- *WhoMW 92*
**Collins,** Mordecai 1785-1864 *DcNCBi 1*
**Collins,** Nancy Marksberry 1953- *WhoAmL 92*
**Collins,** Neil Adam 1947- *Who 92*
**Collins,** Niamh 1956- *TwCPaSc*
**Collins,** Nicholas Clark 1946- *AmMWSc 92*
**Collins,** Nicolas B. 1954- *WhoEnt 92*
**Collins,** Nina *Who 92*
**Collins,** Norman Edward, Jr 1940- *AmMWSc 92*
**Collins,** O David 1945- *WhoAmP 91*
**Collins,** O'Neil Ray 1931- *AmMWSc 92*
**Collins,** Otis Grant 1919- *WhoBlA 92*
**Collins,** Patricia Hill 1948- *WhoBlA 92*
**Collins,** Patrick W. 1929- *WhoWest 92*
**Collins,** Patrick Winchester 1936- *WhoRel 92*
**Collins,** Paul 1936- *WhoBlA 92*
**Collins,** Paul Everett 1917- *AmMWSc 92*
**Collins,** Paul John 1936- *WhoFI 92*
**Collins,** Paul L. 1931- *WhoBlA 92*
**Collins,** Paul V. 1918- *WhoBlA 92*
**Collins,** Paul Waddell 1940- *AmMWSc 92*
**Collins,** Pauline 1940- *IntMPA 92, IntWW 91, Who 92*
**Collins,** Peter G. 1935- *Who 92*
**Collins,** Peter Spencer 1930- *Who 92*
**Collins,** Peter Xavier 1942- *WhoEnt 92*
**Collins,** Phil *WhoEnt 92*
**Collins,** Phil 1951- *IntWW 91*
**Collins,** Philip 1951- *Who 92*
**Collins,** Philip Arthur William 1923- *IntAu&W 91, Who 92, WrDr 92*
**Collins,** Philip Reilly 1921- *WhoAmL 92*
**Collins,** Ralph Porter 1927- *AmMWSc 92*
**Collins,** Ray *WhoAmP 91*
**Collins,** Ray Michael 1954- *WhoAmL 92*
**Collins,** Raymond V, Jr 1942- *WhoAmP 91*
**Collins,** Reid *LesBEnT 92*
**Collins,** Richard d1991 *NewYTBS 91*
**Collins,** Richard Andrew 1924- *AmMWSc 92*
**Collins,** Richard Arlen 1930- *AmMWSc 92*
**Collins,** Richard Cornelius 1941- *AmMWSc 92*
**Collins,** Richard Francis 1938- *AmMWSc 92, WhoMW 92*
**Collins,** Richard Lapointe 1938- *AmMWSc 92*
**Collins,** Richard Lee 1927- *WhoEnt 92*
**Collins,** Richard Stratton 1929- *WhoAmL 92, WhoMW 92*
**Collins,** Richard William 1930- *WhoAmL 92*
**Collins,** Robert C 1942- *AmMWSc 92*
**Collins,** Robert Frederick 1931- *WhoAmL 92, WhoBlA 92*
**Collins,** Robert Giffen 1964- *WhoFI 92*
**Collins,** Robert H. 1934- *WhoBlA 92*
**Collins,** Robert James 1928- *AmMWSc 92*
**Collins,** Robert Joseph 1923- *AmMWSc 92*
**Collins,** Robert O. 1933- *WrDr 92*
**Collins,** Robert Oakley 1933- *IntAu&W 91*
**Collins,** Ronald William 1936- *AmMWSc 92*
**Collins,** Rosecrain 1929- *WhoBlA 92*
**Collins,** Royal Eugene 1925- *AmMWSc 92*
**Collins,** Russell Brent 1956- *WhoEnt 92*
**Collins,** Russell Lewis 1928- *AmMWSc 92*
**Collins,** Samuel Wilson, Jr 1923- *WhoAmP 91*
**Collins,** Scott Edward 1963- *WhoAmL 92*
**Collins,** Seward B. 1899-1952 *BiDExR*
**Collins,** Stephen 1927- *AmMWSc 92*
**Collins,** Stephen 1947- *IntMPA 92, WhoEnt 92*
**Collins,** Stephen Patrick 1958- *WhoFI 92*
**Collins,** Steve Michael 1947- *AmMWSc 92*
**Collins,** Steven M. 1952- *WhoAmL 92*
**Collins,** Stuart Verdun 1916- *Who 92*
**Collins,** Sylva Heghinian 1948- *AmMWSc 92*
**Collins,** Sylvia Durnell 1934- *WhoBlA 92*
**Collins,** Terence Bernard 1927- *Who 92*
**Collins,** Terrence James 1952- *AmMWSc 92*
**Collins,** Terrence Lee 1942- *WhoWest 92*
**Collins,** Tessil John 1952- *WhoBlA 92*
**Collins,** Theodicia Deborah 1959- *WhoBlA 92*
**Collins,** Theodore John 1936- *WhoAmL 92*
**Collins,** Thomas Asa 1921- *WhoRel 92*
**Collins,** Thomas C 1936- *AmMWSc 92*
**Collins,** Thomas Frederick James 1905- *Who 92*
**Collins,** Thomas Henry 1961- *WhoRel 92*
**Collins,** Thomas Joseph, Jr. 1936- *WhoFI 92*
**Collins,** Thomas Merrigan 1926- *WhoEnt 92, WhoFI 92*
**Collins,** Thomas Michael 1934- *WhoFI 92*
**Collins,** Thomas William 1926- *WhoMW 92*
**Collins,** Tom *RfGEnL 91*
**Collins,** Tom 1962- *WhoEnt 92*
**Collins,** Tomothy Clark 1956- *WhoFI 92*
**Collins,** Travis Murray 1959- *WhoRel 92*
**Collins,** Truman Edward 1919- *WhoRel 92*
**Collins,** Tucker *AmMWSc 92*
**Collins,** V Max 1922- *WhoAmP 91*
**Collins,** Vernon Kirkpatrick 1917- *AmMWSc 92*
**Collins,** Vernon O. 1947- *WhoWest 92*
**Collins,** Vincent J 1914- *AmMWSc 92*
**Collins,** Vincent Peter 1947- *AmMWSc 92*
**Collins,** Virginia M 1937- *WhoAmP 91*
**Collins,** Walter Marshall 1917- *AmMWSc 92*
**Collins,** Walter Stowe 1926- *WhoEnt 92*
**Collins,** Warren Eugene 1947- *AmMWSc 92, WhoBlA 92*
**Collins,** Wayne Dale 1951- *WhoAmL 92*
**Collins,** Whitfield James 1918- *WhoAmL 92*
**Collins,** Wilkie 1824-1889 *CnDBLB 4 [port], RfGEnL 91*
**Collins,** William d1709? *DcNCBi 1*
**Collins,** William 1721-1759 *DcLB 109 [port], RfGEnL 91*
**Collins,** William, Jr. 1924- *WhoBlA 92*
**Collins,** William Arthur 1935- *WhoAmP 91*
**Collins,** William Beck 1926- *AmMWSc 92*
**Collins,** William Daniel, Jr 1932- *WhoAmP 91*
**Collins,** William Edgar 1935- *AmMWSc 92*
**Collins,** William Edward 1932- *AmMWSc 92*
**Collins,** William Erle 1929- *AmMWSc 92*
**Collins,** William F 1918- *AmMWSc 92*
**Collins,** William Francis, Jr 1924- *AmMWSc 92*
**Collins,** William Henry 1930- *AmMWSc 92*
**Collins,** William Janson 1929- *Who 92*
**Collins,** William John 1934- *AmMWSc 92*
**Collins,** William Keelan 1914- *WhoBlA 92*
**Collins,** William Kerr 1931- *AmMWSc 92*
**Collins,** William Leroy 1942- *WhoWest 92*
**Collins,** William Lewis 1954- *WhoAmL 92*
**Collins,** William Thomas 1922- *AmMWSc 92*
**Collins,** Zaccheus 1764-1831 *BiInAmS*
**Collins-Bondon,** Carolyn R. 1949- *WhoBlA 92*
**Collins-Eaglin,** Jan Theresa 1950- *WhoBlA 92*

**Collins-Grant,** Earlean WhoBlA 92
**Collins-Reid,** LaVerne Francis 1946- WhoBlA 92
**Collins-Williams,** Cecil 1918- AmMWSc 92
**Collinson,** Charles William 1923- AmMWSc 92
**Collinson,** Dale Stanley 1938- WhoAmL 92
**Collinson,** James W 1938- AmMWSc 92
**Collinson,** Laurence 1925- IntAu&W 91
**Collinson,** Patrick 1929- IntWW 91, Who 92
**Collinson,** Roger 1936- IntAu&W 91, WrDr 92
**Collipp,** Bruce Garfield 1929- AmMWSc 92
**Collipp,** Platon Jack 1932- AmMWSc 92
**Collis,** Kay Lynn 1958- WhoFI 92
**Collis,** Louise 1925- WrDr 92
**Collis,** Louise Edith 1925- IntAu&W 91
**Collis,** Maurice 1889-1973 TwCPaSc
**Collis,** Ronald Thomas 1920- AmMWSc 92
**Collison** Who 92
**Collison,** Baron 1909- Who 92
**Collison,** Clarence H 1945- AmMWSc 92
**Collison,** Diane Wittrock 1939- WhoFI 92
**Collison,** J. Daniel 1943- WhoMW 92
**Collisson,** Ellen Whited 1946- AmMWSc 92
**Collister,** Alfred James 1869-1964 TwCPaSc
**Collister,** Earl Harold 1923- AmMWSc 92
**Collman,** James Paddock 1932- AmMWSc 92, IntWW 91
**Collmer,** Russell Cravener 1924- WhoFI 92, WhoWest 92
**Colloff,** Roger David 1946- WhoEnt 92
**Collom,** Jack DrAPF 91
**Collomb,** Bertrand Pierre 1942- WhoFI 92
**Collomb,** Bertrand Pierre Charles 1942- IntWW 91
**Colloms,** Brenda 1919- IntAu&W 91, WrDr 92
**Collons,** Rodger Duane 1935- WhoAmL 92
**Collopy,** Bernard James 1927- WhoWest 92
**Collopy,** Daniel Richard 1954- WhoAmL 92
**Collopy,** William Thomas 1930- WhoMW 92
**Collor De Mello,** Fernando 1949- IntWW 91
**Colloton,** John W 1931- AmMWSc 92
**Colloton,** John William 1931- WhoMW 92
**Colloton,** Patrick G 1942- WhoIns 92
**Collum,** David Boshart 1955- AmMWSc 92
**Collum,** Hugh Robert 1940- IntWW 91
**Collumb,** Peter John 1942- WhoFI 92
**Collura,** John 1948- AmMWSc 92
**Collyear,** John 1927- Who 92
**Collyear,** John Gowen 1927- IntWW 91
**Collyer,** Bud d1979 LesBEnT 92
**Collyer,** Michael 1942- WhoAmL 92
**Collymore,** Edward L. 1938- WhoBlA 92
**Collymore,** Walter Arthur 1933- WhoBlA 92
**Colman,** Baron 1928- IntWW 91
**Colman,** Alec d1991 Who 92N
**Colman,** Anthony David 1938- Who 92
**Colman,** Anthony John 1943- Who 92
**Colman,** Benjamin 1673-1747 BenetAL 91, BiInAmS
**Colman,** Brian 1933- AmMWSc 92
**Colman,** David Russell 1949- AmMWSc 92
**Colman,** David Stacy 1906- Who 92
**Colman,** E Adrian M 1930- IntAu&W 91, WrDr 92
**Colman,** Edward Brof 1952- WhoEnt 92
**Colman,** Fraser Macdonald 1925- IntWW 91
**Colman,** George 1732-1794 RfGEnL 91
**Colman,** George 1762-1836 RfGEnL 91
**Colman,** Henry 1923- WhoEnt 92
**Colman,** Hila SmATA 14AS [port], WrDr 92
**Colman,** John Edward 1923- IntAu&W 91, WrDr 92
**Colman,** Martin 1941- AmMWSc 92
**Colman,** Michael 1928- Who 92
**Colman,** Neville 1945- AmMWSc 92
**Colman,** Richard Thomas 1935- WhoAmL 92
**Colman,** Robert W 1935- AmMWSc 92
**Colman,** Roberta F 1938- AmMWSc 92
**Colman,** Samuel 1933- WhoAmP 91
**Colman,** Steven Michael 1949- AmMWSc 92
**Colman,** Timothy James Alan 1929- Who 92
**Colman,** Warren 1944- SmATA 67 [port]
**Colman,** Warren David 1944- WhoEnt 92
**Colmano,** Germille 1921- AmMWSc 92
**Colmano,** Marino Giovanni Augusto 1948- WhoEnt 92
**Colmant,** Andrew Robert 1931- WhoAmL 92
**Colmenares,** Carlos Adolfo 1932- AmMWSc 92
**Colmenares,** Margarita Hortensia 1957- WhoHisp 92
**Colmer,** John 1921- ConAu 34NR
**Colmer,** John Anthony 1921- IntAu&W 91, IntWW 91, WrDr 92
**Coln,** William Alexander, III 1942- WhoWest 92
**Colnbrook,** Baron 1922- IntWW 91, Who 92
**Colocolo** 1515?-1561 HisDSpE
**Colodny,** Charles Stewart 1950- WhoMW 92
**Colodny,** Edwin Irving 1926- WhoFI 92
**Colodny,** Paul Charles 1930- AmMWSc 92
**Colom,** Vilma M. 1954- WhoHisp 92
**Coloma,** Eduardo I. 1948- WhoHisp 92
**Colomb,** Patrick Louis 1922- WhoAmL 92
**Colombani,** Paul Michael 1951- AmMWSc 92
**Colombant,** Denis Georges 1942- AmMWSc 92
**Colombini,** Marco 1948- AmMWSc 92
**Colombini,** Victor Domenic 1924- AmMWSc 92
**Colombo,** Metropolitan Archbishop of 1932- Who 92
**Colombo,** Emilio 1920- IntWW 91, Who 92
**Colombo,** Frank V. 1956- WhoFI 92
**Colombo,** Frederick J. 1916- WhoAmL 92, WhoMW 92
**Colombo,** Furio Marco 1931- IntAu&W 91, WhoFI 92
**Colombo,** Gino R 1939- WhoAmP 91
**Colombo,** Giovanni 1902- IntWW 91, WhoRel 92
**Colombo,** Joe 1930-1971 DcTwDes
**Colombo,** John Robert 1936- ConPo 91, IntAu&W 91, IntWW 91, WrDr 92
**Colombo,** Louis Robert 1925- WhoAmP 91
**Colombo,** Marco 1957- WhoEnt 92
**Colombo,** Umberto 1927- IntWW 91
**Colombo,** Vittorino 1925- IntWW 91
**Colomer Viadel,** Vicente 1946- IntWW 91
**Colominas,** Kathleen Adele 1948- ConAu 134
**Colon,** Alex 1941- WhoEnt 92
**Colon,** Alicia V. 1944- WhoHisp 92
**Colon,** Anthony Ezequiel 1955- WhoHisp 92
**Colon,** Denise Cassandra 1952- WhoFI 92
**Colon,** Diego L. 1943- WhoHisp 92
**Colon,** Frazier Paige 1934- AmMWSc 92
**Colon,** Gilberto 1963- WhoHisp 92
**Colon,** Gustavo Alberto 1938- WhoHisp 92
**Colon,** Israel 1940- WhoHisp 92
**Colon,** Jac Agustin 1942- WhoRel 92
**Colon,** James Anthony 1943- WhoRel 92
**Colon,** Joseph Q. 1930- WhoHisp 92
**Colon,** Julio Ismael 1928- AmMWSc 92
**Colon,** Leonardo, Jr. 1958- WhoHisp 92
**Colon,** Maria Caridad 1958- BlkOlyM
**Colon,** Matilde Cristina 1942- WhoHisp 92
**Colon,** Miriam 1945- WhoHisp 92
**Colon,** Nelson 1960- WhoHisp 92
**Colon,** Nicholas, Jr. 1909- WhoHisp 92
**Colon,** Oscar A. 1937- WhoHisp 92
**Colon,** Ramiro Luis, Jr. 1936- WhoHisp 92
**Colon,** Richard J. WhoHisp 92
**Colon,** Samuel Alberto 1950- WhoHisp 92
**Colon,** Vilma Estrella 1945- WhoHisp 92
**Colon,** William Ralph 1930- WhoHisp 92
**Colon,** Willie 1950- WhoHisp 92
**Colon Alvarado,** Carlos WhoHisp 92
**Colon-Arroyo,** David 1950- WhoHisp 92
**Colon-Carlo,** Ileana M WhoAmP 91
**Colon-Navarro,** Fernando 1952- WhoAmL 92
**Colon-Pacheco,** Rico Butch 1927- WhoHisp 92
**Colona,** Stanley Maurice 1962- WhoMW 92
**Colonel,** Sheri Lynn 1955- WhoFI 92
**Coloney,** Wayne Herndon 1925- WhoFI 92
**Colonias,** John S 1928- AmMWSc 92
**Colonna,** Edouard 1862-1948 DcTwDes
**Colonna,** Ralph Joseph, Jr. 1937- WhoWest 92
**Colonna,** Robert Angelo 1936- WhoWest 92
**Colonna,** Rocco J WhoAmP 91
**Colonna,** William Mark 1956- WhoMW 92
**Colonne,** Edouard 1838-1910 NewAmDM
**Colonnier,** Marc 1930- AmMWSc 92
**Colony-Cokely,** Pamela 1947- AmMWSc 92
**Colorado,** Antonio J 1939- WhoAmP 91, WhoHisp 92
**Colosimo,** Mary Lynn Sukurs 1950- WhoMW 92
**Colosimo,** Murray Bernard 1944- WhoEnt 92
**Colosimo,** Robert 1929- WhoFI 92
**Colotka,** Peter 1925- IntWW 91
**Colovos,** George 1932- AmMWSc 92
**Colp,** John Lewis AmMWSc 92
**Colpa,** Johannes Pieter 1926- AmMWSc 92
**Colpron,** Merlyn Dallas 1933- WhoFI 92, WhoWest 92
**Colquhoun,** Andrew John 1949- Who 92
**Colquhoun,** Cyril 1903- Who 92
**Colquhoun,** David 1936- Who 92
**Colquhoun,** Donald John 1932- AmMWSc 92
**Colquhoun,** Frank 1909- Who 92
**Colquhoun,** Ithell 1906-1988 TwCPaSc
**Colquhoun,** Keith 1933- IntAu&W 91
**Colquhoun,** Keith 1937- WrDr 92
**Colquhoun,** Maureen Morfydd 1928- Who 92
**Colquhoun,** Peter Jeffrey 1956- WhoMW 92
**Colquhoun,** Robert 1914-1962 TwCPaSc
**Colquhoun of Luss,** Ivar 1916- Who 92
**Colquitt,** Landon Augustus 1919- AmMWSc 92
**Colsky,** Andrew Evan 1964- WhoAmL 92
**Colson,** Bill TwCWW 91
**Colson,** Charles W. 1931- WrDr 92
**Colson,** Charles Wendell 1931- WhoRel 92
**Colson,** Donald F. 1939- WhoEnt 92
**Colson,** Earl M. 1930- WhoAmL 92
**Colson,** Elizabeth 1917- WrDr 92
**Colson,** Elizabeth F 1917- AmMWSc 92, IntAu&W 91
**Colson,** Elizabeth Florence 1917- IntWW 91
**Colson,** Harold Roy 1876-1913 BiInAmS
**Colson,** John Francis 1933- WhoEnt 92
**Colson,** Joseph S., Jr. 1947- WhoBlA 92
**Colson,** Laramie TwCWW 91
**Colson,** Steven Douglas 1941- AmMWSc 92
**Colston,** Colin Charles 1937- Who 92
**Colston,** Freddie C. 1936- WhoBlA 92
**Colston,** Michael 1932- Who 92
**Colston,** Monroe James 1933- WhoBlA 92
**Colt,** Clem IntAu&W 91X, TwCWW 91, WrDr 92
**Colt,** Edward 1936- Who 92
**Colt,** James D 1932- WhoAmP 91
**Colt,** Marshall IntMPA 92
**Colt,** Zandra WrDr 92
**Coltelli,** Laura Rauch 1958- WhoAmL 92
**Colten,** Harvey Radin 1939- AmMWSc 92, WhoMW 92
**Colten,** Jerrold Lewis 1925- WhoMW 92
**Colten,** Oscar A 1912- AmMWSc 92
**Colter,** Cyrus 1910- ConNov 91, WrDr 92
**Colter,** Cyrus J. 1910- WhoBlA 92
**Colter,** John Sparby 1922- AmMWSc 92
**Colter,** Shayne IntAu&W 91X, TwCWW 91
**Colter,** Steve 1962- WhoBlA 92
**Coltharp,** Forrest Lee 1933- AmMWSc 92
**Coltharp,** George B 1928- AmMWSc 92
**Coltharp,** Lurline H. 1913- WrDr 92
**Colthup,** Norman Bertram 1924- AmMWSc 92
**Colthurst,** Richard La Touche 1928- Who 92
**Coltman,** Charles Arthur, Jr 1930- AmMWSc 92
**Coltman,** Edward Jeremiah 1948- WhoEnt 92
**Coltman,** John Wesley 1915- AmMWSc 92
**Coltman,** Leycester 1938- Who 92
**Coltman,** Ralph Read, Jr 1924- AmMWSc 92
**Coltman,** Will IntAu&W 91X, TwCWW 91
**Colton,** Arlan Miller 1955- WhoWest 92
**Colton,** Buel Preston 1852-1906 BiInAmS
**Colton,** Clarence Eugene 1914- IntAu&W 91, WrDr 92
**Colton,** Clark Kenneth 1941- AmMWSc 92
**Colton,** David L 1943- AmMWSc 92
**Colton,** Ed Lynn, Jr. 1951- WhoEnt 92
**Colton,** Edward H. 1938- WhoWest 92
**Colton,** Elizabeth Avery 1872-1924 DcNCBi 1
**Colton,** Ervin 1927- AmMWSc 92
**Colton,** Frank Benjamin 1923- AmMWSc 92
**Colton,** Frank G 1939- WhoAmP 91
**Colton,** Henry Elliott 1836-1892 DcNCBi 1
**Colton,** James WrDr 92
**Colton,** James Dale 1945- AmMWSc 92
**Colton,** Joel 1918- IntAu&W 91, WrDr 92
**Colton,** John 1889?-1946 BenetAL 91
**Colton,** John Patrick, Jr 1938- WhoAmP 91
**Colton,** Jonathan Stuart 1959- AmMWSc 92
**Colton,** Kendrew H. 1955- WhoAmL 92
**Colton,** Lawrence Mark 1949- WhoMW 92
**Colton,** Marie W WhoAmP 91
**Colton,** Milo WhoAmP 91
**Colton,** Richard David 1961- WhoMW 92
**Colton,** Richard J 1950- AmMWSc 92
**Colton,** Roberta Ann 1957- WhoAmL 92
**Colton,** Roger Burnham 1924- AmMWSc 92
**Colton,** Roy Charles 1941- WhoFI 92, WhoWest 92
**Colton,** Simeon 1785-1868 DcNCBi 1
**Colton,** Sterling Don 1929- WhoAmL 92, WhoFI 92
**Colton,** Victor Robert 1930- WhoFI 92, WhoMW 92
**Colton,** Walter 1797-1851 BenetAL 91
**Coltrane,** Alice Turiya 1937- WhoBlA 92
**Coltrane,** Daniel Branson 1842-1937 DcNCBi 1
**Coltrane,** John 1926-1967 FacFETw [port], NewAmDM
**Coltrane,** John William 1926-1967 DcNCBi 1
**Coltrane,** Robbie 1950- IntMPA 92
**Coltrin-Brink,** Jeanie Dawn 1949- WhoAmL 92
**Colucci,** Anthony Joseph 1957- WhoWest 92
**Colucci,** Anthony Joseph, III 1958- WhoAmL 92
**Colucci,** Anthony Vito 1938- AmMWSc 92
**Colucci,** Joseph M 1937- AmMWSc 92
**Colum,** Mary 1880?-1957 BenetAL 91
**Colum,** Padraic 1881-1972 BenetAL 91, ConAu 35NR, FacFETw, RfGEnL 91
**Columb,** P H 1831-1899 ScFEYrs
**Columb,** P H, Maurice, J F, Maude, F N ScFEYrs
**Columba** 521?-597? EncEarC
**Columbanus** d615 EncEarC
**Columbo,** John Arthur 1951- WhoWest 92
**Columbus,** Bartholomew 1451?- HisDSpE
**Columbus,** Chris 1959- IntMPA 92
**Columbus,** Chris Joseph 1958- WhoEnt 92
**Columbus,** Christopher 1451-1506 BenetAL 91, HisDSpE, NewYTBS 91 [port]
**Columbus,** Diego 1480-1526 HisDSpE
**Columbus,** Judy Lee 1939- WhoFI 92
**Columbus,** Robert Howard 1952- WhoFI 92
**Columbus,** Thomas Michael 1944- WhoMW 92
**Colvard,** Dean Wallace 1913- AmMWSc 92
**Colvard,** Landon, Sr 1921- WhoAmP 91
**Colvard,** Michael David 1954- WhoMW 92
**Colver,** C Phillip 1935- AmMWSc 92, WhoWest 92
**Colvert,** Kenneth Ronald 1942- WhoRel 92
**Colville** Who 92
**Colville,** Master of 1959- Who 92
**Colville,** John 1915-1987 FacFETw
**Colville,** Margaret 1918- Who 92
**Colville,** Robert E. 1935- WhoAmL 92
**Colville,** Wilberforce Juvenal 1859?-1917 RelLAm 91
**Colville of Culross,** Viscount 1933- Who 92
**Colvin,** Alonza James 1931- WhoBlA 92
**Colvin,** Andrew James 1947- Who 92
**Colvin,** Burton Houston 1916- AmMWSc 92
**Colvin,** Clair Ivan 1927- AmMWSc 92
**Colvin,** Dallas Verne 1937- AmMWSc 92
**Colvin,** David 1931- Who 92
**Colvin,** David Hugh 1941- Who 92
**Colvin,** Donald Andrew 1915- WhoWest 92
**Colvin,** Edwin A 1927- WhoAmP 91
**Colvin,** Ernest J. 1935- WhoBlA 92
**Colvin,** Gary Lee 1940- WhoRel 92
**Colvin,** Gary Robert 1956- WhoWest 92
**Colvin,** Greta Wilmoth 1962- WhoEnt 92
**Colvin,** H. M. 1919- WrDr 92
**Colvin,** Harry Walter, Jr 1921- AmMWSc 92
**Colvin,** Herbert, Jr. 1923- WhoEnt 92
**Colvin,** Howard Allen 1953- AmMWSc 92
**Colvin,** Howard Montagu 1919- IntAu&W 91, IntWW 91, Who 92
**Colvin,** James TwCSFW 91
**Colvin,** John Alexander 1950- WhoRel 92
**Colvin,** John Horace Ragnar 1922- Who 92
**Colvin,** John O. 1946- WhoAmL 92
**Colvin,** Lloyd Dayton 1915- WhoWest 92
**Colvin,** Mark Alan 1959- WhoEnt 92
**Colvin,** Michael Keith Beale 1932- Who 92
**Colvin,** Robert B 1942- AmMWSc 92
**Colvin,** Sherrill William 1938- WhoAmL 92
**Colvin,** Thomas Stuart 1947- AmMWSc 92
**Colvin,** Thurman Jack 1925- WhoFI 92
**Colvin,** William E. 1930- WhoBlA 92
**Colvis,** John Paris 1946- AmMWSc 92, WhoWest 92
**Colwell,** Carlton H WhoAmP 91
**Colwell,** Gene Thomas 1937- AmMWSc 92
**Colwell,** Jack Harold 1931- AmMWSc 92
**Colwell,** James Lee 1926- WhoWest 92
**Colwell,** Jane B. 1952- WhoEnt 92
**Colwell,** John Amory 1928- AmMWSc 92

**Colwell,** John McKenna 1948- *WhoEnt 92*
**Colwell,** Joseph F 1929- *AmMWSc 92*
**Colwell,** Richard James 1930- *WhoEnt 92*
**Colwell,** Rita R 1934- *AmMWSc 92*
**Colwell,** Robbie Elena 1956- *WhoAmP 91*
**Colwell,** Robert Knight 1943- *AmMWSc 92*
**Colwell,** Robert Neil 1918- *AmMWSc 92*
**Colwell,** Steven Michael 1954- *WhoRel 92*
**Colwell,** William Maxwell 1931- *AmMWSc 92*
**Colwell,** William Tracy 1934- *AmMWSc 92*
**Colwick,** Rex Floyd 1922- *AmMWSc 92*
**Colwill,** Jack M 1932- *AmMWSc 92*
**Colwin,** Arthur Lentz 1911- *AmMWSc 92*
**Colwin,** Laura Hunter 1911- *AmMWSc 92*
**Colwin,** Laurie 1944- *WrDr 92*
**Colwyn,** Baron 1942- *Who 92*
**Colyer,** Dale Keith 1931- *WhoFI 92*
**Colyer,** Henry D 1920- *WhoAmP 91*
**Colyer,** John Stuart 1935- *Who 92*
**Colyer,** Kirk Klein 1956- *WhoAmP 91*
**Colyer,** Sheryl Lynn 1959- *WhoBlA 92*
**Colyer-Fergusson,** James Herbert Hamilton 1917- *Who 92*
**Colyton,** Baron 1902- *Who 92*
**Coma,** Agim 1958- *WhoEnt 92*
**Comai-Fuerherm,** Karen 1946- *AmMWSc 92*
**Coman,** Dale Rex 1906- *AmMWSc 92*
**Coman,** Ion 1926- *IntWW 91*
**Comaneci,** Nadia 1961- *FacFETw, IntWW 91*
**Comanor,** William S. 1937- *WhoFI 92*
**Comans,** Raymond 1930- *WhoAmP 91*
**Comas Bacardi,** Adolfo T. 1944- *WhoHisp 92*
**Comay,** Sholom D. d1991 *NewYTBS 91 [port]*
**Comba,** Paul Gustavo 1926- *AmMWSc 92*
**Combas,** Robert 1957- *WorArt 1980 [port]*
**Combe,** David Alfred 1942- *WhoAmL 92*
**Combe,** Gordon Desmond 1917- *WrDr 92*
**Combe,** Ivan DeBlois 1911- *WhoFI 92*
**Combe,** John Clifford, Jr. 1939- *WhoAmL 92*
**Combe,** William 1742-1823 *RfGEnL 91*
**Combee,** Byron R 1947- *WhoAmP 91*
**Comber,** Anthony James 1927- *Who 92*
**Comber,** Neil M. 1951- *WhoHisp 92*
**Comber,** Thomas Francis, III 1927- *WhoAmL 92*
**Comberford,** Nicholas d1673 *DcNCBi 1*
**Combermere,** Viscount 1929- *Who 92*
**Combes,** Burton 1927- *AmMWSc 92*
**Combest,** Larry 1945- *AlmAP 92 [port]*
**Combest,** Larry Ed 1945- *WhoAmP 91*
**Combie,** Joan D 1946- *AmMWSc 92*
**Combie,** Joan Diane 1946- *WhoWest 92*
**Combier,** Elizabeth Irene 1949- *WhoEnt 92*
**Combitsis,** Constantine 1932- *WhoRel 92*
**Combopiano,** Charles Angelo 1935- *WhoEnt 92*
**Combs,** Alan B 1939- *AmMWSc 92*
**Combs,** Austin Olin 1917- *WhoFI 92*
**Combs,** Bert T. d1991 *NewYTBS 91 [port]*
**Combs,** Bert Thomas 1911- *WhoAmP 91*
**Combs,** Clarence Murphy 1925- *AmMWSc 92*
**Combs,** Creed Jeffery 1960- *WhoEnt 92*
**Combs,** Curtis Floyd 1959- *WhoRel 92*
**Combs,** Dan Jack *WhoAmP 91*
**Combs,** Delia 1941- *WhoAmP 91*
**Combs,** Don E 1934- *WhoIns 92*
**Combs,** Gene Donald 1926- *WhoAmP 91*
**Combs,** George Ernest 1927- *AmMWSc 92*
**Combs,** Gerald Fuson 1920- *AmMWSc 92*
**Combs,** Gerald Fuson, Jr 1947- *AmMWSc 92*
**Combs,** Ira, Jr. 1958- *WhoMW 92, WhoRel 92*
**Combs,** James Everett 1941- *WhoMW 92*
**Combs,** Janet Louise 1959- *WhoFI 92*
**Combs,** Julia Carolyn 1950- *WhoEnt 92*
**Combs,** Julius V. 1931- *WhoBlA 92*
**Combs,** Kermit Stephen, Jr. 1941- *WhoRel 92*
**Combs,** Leon Lamar, III 1938- *AmMWSc 92*
**Combs,** Linda Jones 1948- *WhoFI 92*
**Combs,** Maxine *DrAPF 91*
**Combs,** Melvin, Jr. 1941- *WhoAmL 92*
**Combs,** Mike 1947- *WhoAmP 91*
**Combs,** Philip Dee 1947- *WhoRel 92*
**Combs,** Raymond E 1932- *WhoAmP 91*
**Combs,** Robert Glade 1930- *AmMWSc 92*
**Combs,** Robert L, Jr 1928- *AmMWSc 92*
**Combs,** Ronald S. 1950- *WhoFI 92*
**Combs,** Sylvester Lawrence 1925- *WhoBlA 92*
**Combs,** Thomas Neal 1942- *IntWW 91*
**Combs,** Timothy Lee 1947- *WhoAmP 91*
**Combs,** Tram *DrAPF 91*
**Combs,** Willa R. 1925- *WhoBlA 92*
**Combs,** William Henry, III 1949- *WhoAmL 92, WhoWest 92*
**Combs,** Willis 1916- *Who 92*
**Comden and Green** *FacFETw*
**Comden,** Betty 1919- *FacFETw, IntMPA 92, WhoEnt 92*
**Comeau,** Andre I 1945- *AmMWSc 92*
**Comeau,** Jack Francis 1955- *WhoEnt 92*
**Comeau,** Louis Roland 1941- *WhoFI 92*
**Comeau,** Michael Gerard 1956- *WhoAmL 92*
**Comeau,** Roger William 1933- *AmMWSc 92*
**Comeford,** John J 1928- *AmMWSc 92*
**Comeford,** Lorrie Lynn 1962- *AmMWSc 92*
**Comeforo,** Jay E 1922- *AmMWSc 92*
**Comegys,** Daphne D. 1932- *WhoBlA 92*
**Comegys,** Walker Brockton 1929- *WhoAmL 92*
**Comelin,** Jean-Paul 1936- *WhoEnt 92*
**Comencini,** Luigi 1916- *ConTFT 9, IntDcF 2-2 [port]*
**Comer,** David J 1939- *AmMWSc 92*
**Comer,** James P. 1934- *CurBio 91 [port]*
**Comer,** James Pierpont 1934- *AmMWSc 92, WhoBlA 92*
**Comer,** Jeffrey Melvin 1961- *WhoMW 92*
**Comer,** John Fletcher, Jr. 1946- *WhoRel 92*
**Comer,** Jonathan 1921- *WhoBlA 92*
**Comer,** Joseph John 1920- *AmMWSc 92*
**Comer,** M Margaret 1942- *AmMWSc 92*
**Comer,** Marian Wilson 1938- *WhoBlA 92*
**Comer,** Norman David 1935- *WhoBlA 92*
**Comer,** Russell Wayne 1959- *WhoFI 92*
**Comer,** Stephen Daniel 1941- *AmMWSc 92*
**Comer,** Troy Tillman 1938- *WhoMW 92*
**Comer,** William Joseph 1935- *WhoAmP 91*
**Comer,** William Timmey 1936- *AmMWSc 92*
**Comer,** Zeke 1938- *WhoBlA 92*
**Comerford,** George Emory 1928- *WhoAmP 91*
**Comerford,** Jonell Duda 1949- *WhoMW 92*
**Comerford,** Leo P, Jr 1947- *AmMWSc 92*
**Comerford,** Leo Paul, Jr. 1947- *WhoMW 92*
**Comerford,** Matthias F 1925- *AmMWSc 92*
**Comes,** Richard Durward 1931- *AmMWSc 92*
**Comes,** Robert George 1931- *WhoWest 92*
**Comet,** Catherine *WhoEnt 92*
**Comey,** Dale R 1941- *WhoIns 92*
**Comey,** James H. *DrAPF 91*
**Comfort,** Alex 1920- *ConPo 91, IntAu&W 91, WrDr 92*
**Comfort,** Alexander 1920- *AmMWSc 92, IntWW 91, Who 92*
**Comfort,** Anthony Francis 1920- *Who 92*
**Comfort,** Charles Fraser 1900- *Who 92*
**Comfort,** Dennis L. 1952- *WhoWest 92*
**Comfort,** George Augustus 1963- *WhoMW 92*
**Comfort,** Iris Tracy *IntAu&W 91*
**Comfort,** Jeffrey Charles 1959- *WhoFI 92*
**Comfort,** Joseph Robert 1940- *AmMWSc 92*
**Comfort,** Mary Boynton 1945- *WhoWest 92*
**Comfort,** Montgomery *IntAu&W 91X*
**Comfort,** Nemo Robert 1932- *WhoBlA 92*
**Comfort,** Nicholas Alfred Fenner 1946- *IntAu&W 91*
**Comfort,** Patrick Connell 1930- *WhoAmL 92, WhoWest 92*
**Comfort,** Richard E. 1937- *WhoFI 92*
**Comfort,** Robert Dennis 1950- *WhoAmL 92*
**Comfort,** Will Levington 1878-1932 *BenetAL 91, TwCWW 91*
**Comfort,** Will Levington 1931- *WhoWest 92*
**Comfort,** William Michael 1934- *WhoRel 92*
**Comfort,** William Wistar 1933- *AmMWSc 92*
**Comfrey,** Kathleen Marie 1951- *WhoAmL 92*
**Comi,** Girolamo 1890-1968 *DcLB 114*
**Comi,** Paul 1932- *WhoEnt 92*
**Comings,** David Edward 1935- *AmMWSc 92*
**Comings,** Edward Walter 1908- *AmMWSc 92*
**Comini,** Alessandra 1934- *IntAu&W 91, WrDr 92*
**Comini,** Diane Sparks 1947- *WhoMW 92*
**Cominos,** Achilles Zachariah 1911- *WhoFI 92*
**Comins,** Neil Francis 1951- *AmMWSc 92*
**Cominsky,** Lynn Ruth 1953- *AmMWSc 92*
**Cominsky,** Nell Catherine 1920- *AmMWSc 92*
**Comis,** Donald J *WhoIns 92*
**Comis,** Gerald C 1948- *WhoIns 92*
**Comis,** Robert Leo 1945- *AmMWSc 92*
**Comisar,** Chris Farah-Lynn 1952- *WhoMW 92*
**Comiskey,** Anne Terese 1941- *WhoRel 92*
**Comiskey,** Brendan 1935- *IntWW 91*
**Comiskey,** Michael Peter 1948- *WhoAmL 92*
**Comisky,** Marvin 1918- *WhoAmL 92*
**Comiso,** Josefino Cacas 1940- *AmMWSc 92*
**Comissiona,** Sergiu 1928- *NewAmDM, WhoEnt 92, WhoWest 92*
**Comito,** Frank Alfred 1939- *WhoAmL 92*
**Comito,** Richard Le 1939- *WhoAmP 91*
**Comizzoli,** Robert Benedict 1940- *AmMWSc 92*
**Comley,** Peter Nigel 1951- *AmMWSc 92*
**Comly,** Hunter Hall 1919- *AmMWSc 92*
**Comly,** James B 1936- *AmMWSc 92*
**Comm,** Dorothy Belle Minchin 1929- *WhoWest 92*
**Commack,** William Earl 1929- *WhoFI 92, WhoIns 92*
**Commager,** Henry Steele 1902- *BenetAL 91, IntWW 91, Who 92, WrDr 92*
**Commarato,** Michael A 1940- *AmMWSc 92*
**Commer,** Eric Alan 1955- *WhoAmL 92*
**Commerford,** John D 1929- *AmMWSc 92*
**Commins,** Dorothy Berliner d1991 *NewYTBS 91*
**Commins,** Eugene David 1932- *AmMWSc 92*
**Commire,** Anne *WhoEnt 92*
**Commiso,** Rocco B. 1949- *WhoFI 92*
**Commissiong,** John Wesley 1944- *AmMWSc 92*
**Commisso,** Italia Ann 1953- *WhoEnt 92*
**Commito,** John Angelo 1949- *AmMWSc 92*
**Commodian** *EncEarC*
**Commodores,** The *NewAmDM*
**Common,** Robert Haddon 1907- *AmMWSc 92*
**Commoner,** Barry 1917- *AmMWSc 92, IntWW 91, WrDr 92*
**Commons,** Donald William 1951- *WhoAmL 92*
**Commons,** John Rogers 1862-1945 *DcAmImH*
**Comninou,** Maria 1947- *AmMWSc 92*
**Como,** Perry *LesBEnT 92*
**Como,** Perry 1912- *IntMPA 92*
**Como,** Perry 1913- *WhoEnt 92*
**Comodeca,** James Albert 1962- *WhoAmL 92*
**Comotto,** Jeffrey John 1957- *WhoMW 92*
**Comp,** Philip Cinnamon 1945- *AmMWSc 92*
**Compaan,** Alvin Dell 1943- *AmMWSc 92, WhoMW 92*
**Compagna,** Robert A 1918- *WhoAmP 91*
**Compagnet,** Alex *WhoHisp 92*
**Compagni,** Frederick George, Sr 1923- *WhoAmP 91*
**Compagnon,** Antoine Marcel Thomas 1950- *IntWW 91*
**Compagnone,** Nick Peter 1952- *WhoRel 92*
**Companion,** Audrey 1932- *AmMWSc 92*
**Compans,** Richard W 1940- *AmMWSc 92*
**Compaore,** Blaise *IntWW 91*
**Compaore,** Jean-Marie *WhoRel 92*
**Comparin,** Robert A 1928- *AmMWSc 92*
**Comper,** Francis Anthony 1945- *IntWW 91*
**Compere,** Edgar Lattimore 1917- *AmMWSc 92*
**Compere,** Edward L, Jr 1927- *AmMWSc 92*
**Compere,** Loyset 1445?-1518 *NewAmDM*
**Compfort,** Marjorie Lenore *DrAPF 91*
**Compher,** Marvin Keen, Jr 1942- *AmMWSc 92*
**Compo,** Lawrence Judd 1955- *WhoFI 92*
**Compo,** Susan 1955- *ConAu 134*
**Compretta,** Joseph Patrick 1945- *WhoAmP 91*
**Comprone,** Joseph J 1943- *ConAu 35NR*
**Compston,** Alastair *Who 92*
**Compston,** Christopher Dean 1940- *Who 92*
**Compston,** David Alastair 1948- *Who 92*
**Compston,** Peter 1915- *Who 92*
**Compston,** William 1931- *Who 92*
**Compton** *Who 92*
**Compton,** Earl 1973- *Who 92*
**Compton,** A Christian 1929- *WhoAmP 91*
**Compton,** Alfred George 1835-1913 *BiInAmS*
**Compton,** Allen T. 1938- *WhoAmL 92, WhoAmP 91, WhoWest 92*
**Compton,** Arthur Holly 1892-1962 *FacFETw, WhoNob 90*
**Compton,** Asbury Christian 1929- *WhoAmL 92*
**Compton,** Burt 1951- *WhoEnt 92*
**Compton,** D G 1930- *IntAu&W 91, TwCSFW 91, WrDr 92*
**Compton,** Dale L 1935- *AmMWSc 92*
**Compton,** Dale Leonard 1935- *WhoFI 92*
**Compton,** David Bruce 1952- *WhoMW 92*
**Compton,** Denis 1918- *WrDr 92*
**Compton,** Denis Charles Scott 1918- *FacFETw, IntWW 91, Who 92*
**Compton,** Duane W 1918- *WhoAmP 91*
**Compton,** Edmund 1906- *Who 92*
**Compton,** Ell Dee 1916- *AmMWSc 92*
**Compton,** Erlinda Rae 1947- *WhoHisp 92*
**Compton,** Francis Snow *BenetAL 91*
**Compton,** George Wade 1946- *WhoAmP 91*
**Compton,** Gregory Alan 1960- *WhoAmL 92*
**Compton,** Guy *IntAu&W 91X, WrDr 92*
**Compton,** Holly Kay 1967- *WhoEnt 92*
**Compton,** J. Paul, Jr. 1963- *WhoAmL 92*
**Compton,** James V. 1928- *WrDr 92*
**Compton,** James W. 1939- *WhoBlA 92*
**Compton,** John George Melvin 1926- *IntWW 91, Who 92*
**Compton,** John S 1958- *AmMWSc 92*
**Compton,** Joyce 1907- *IntMPA 92*
**Compton,** Leslie Ellwyn 1943- *AmMWSc 92*
**Compton,** Linda *WhoRel 92*
**Compton,** Mary Pearl 1930- *WhoAmP 91*
**Compton,** Michael Graeme 1927- *Who 92*
**Compton,** Oliver Cecil 1903- *AmMWSc 92*
**Compton,** Ralph Theodore, Jr 1935- *AmMWSc 92*
**Compton,** Richard Wesley 1925- *WhoAmP 91*
**Compton,** Robert Bruce 1944- *WhoRel 92*
**Compton,** Robert Edward John 1922- *Who 92*
**Compton,** Robert Norman 1938- *AmMWSc 92*
**Compton,** Robert Ross 1922- *AmMWSc 92*
**Compton,** Roger Ellsworth 1932- *WhoMW 92, WhoRel 92*
**Compton,** Ronald E. 1933- *WhoFI 92*
**Compton,** Ronald Edward 1933- *WhoIns 92*
**Compton,** Ronald Eugene 1946- *WhoMW 92*
**Compton,** Thomas Lee 1942- *AmMWSc 92*
**Compton,** W. Dale 1929- *WhoMW 92*
**Compton,** Walter Dale 1929- *AmMWSc 92*
**Compton,** William A 1927- *AmMWSc 92*
**Compton,** William Thomas 1945- *WhoFI 92*
**Compton-Burnett,** I. 1884-1969 *RfGEnL 91*
**Compton-Burnett,** Ivy 1884-1969 *FacFETw*
**Compton Miller,** John 1900- *Who 92*
**Comras,** Jay 1934- *WhoEnt 92, WhoFI 92*
**Comrie,** Peter 1924- *Who 92*
**Comstock,** Anne 1951- *WhoWest 92*
**Comstock,** Anthony 1844-1915 *BenetAL 91*
**Comstock,** Christine Mason 1942- *WhoMW 92*
**Comstock,** Cyrus Ballou 1831-1910 *BiInAmS*
**Comstock,** Dale Robert 1934- *AmMWSc 92, WhoWest 92*
**Comstock,** Donald W. 1928- *WhoFI 92*
**Comstock,** Frank Gould *ScFEYrs*
**Comstock,** Gary Lynn 1954- *WhoRel 92*
**Comstock,** George Wills 1915- *AmMWSc 92*
**Comstock,** Jack Charles 1943- *AmMWSc 92*
**Comstock,** James Patrick 1957- *WhoAmL 92*
**Comstock,** Mark Bond 1954- *WhoAmL 92*
**Comstock,** Rebecca Ann 1950- *WhoAmL 92*
**Comstock,** Robert Francis 1936- *WhoAmL 92*
**Comstock,** Theodore Bryant 1849-1915 *BiInAmS*
**Comstock,** Verne Edward 1919- *AmMWSc 92*
**Comtois,** Mary Elizabeth *WhoEnt 92, WhoWest 92*
**Comtois,** Pierre V. 1955- *WhoEnt 92*
**Comuntzis,** Chris 1950- *WhoAmL 92*
**Comvalius,** Nadia Hortense 1926- *WhoBlA 92*
**Comyn,** James 1921- *Who 92*
**Comyns,** Jacqueline Roberta 1943- *Who 92*
**Conable,** Barber B. 1922- *IntWW 91*
**Conable,** Barber B., Jr. 1922- *WhoFI 92*
**Conaboy,** Richard Paul 1925- *WhoAmL 92*
**Conacher,** Desmond John 1918- *IntWW 91*
**Conahan,** Walter Charles 1927- *WhoAmP 91*
**Conan,** Robert James, Jr 1924- *AmMWSc 92*
**Conan Doyle,** Arthur 1859-1930 *CnDBLB 5 [port]*
**Conan Doyle,** Jean 1912- *Who 92*
**Conant,** Allah B., Jr. 1939- *WhoAmL 92*
**Conant,** Curtis Terry *AmMWSc 92*
**Conant,** Dale Holdrege 1939- *AmMWSc 92*

Conant, Floyd Sanford 1914- AmMWSc 92
Conant, Francis Paine 1926- AmMWSc 92
Conant, Franklin Story 1870?-1897 BiInAmS
Conant, James Bryant 1893-1978 FacFETw
Conant, Joan 1943- WhoAmP 91
Conant, John 1923- Who 92
Conant, John Lund 1954- WhoMW 92
Conant, Levi Leonard 1857-1916 BiInAmS
Conant, Louis Cowles 1902- AmMWSc 92
Conant, Ralph W. 1926- WrDr 92
Conant, Robert Henry 1916- AmMWSc 92
Conant, Robert Scott 1928- WhoEnt 92
Conant, Roger 1909- AmMWSc 92
Conant, Roger C 1938- AmMWSc 92
Conant, Steven George 1949- WhoMW 92
Conard, Alfred Fletcher 1911- WhoAmL 92
Conard, Arlyn Mark 1948- WhoRel 92
Conard, Brad DrAPF 91
Conard, George P 1919- AmMWSc 92
Conard, Gordon Joseph 1939- AmMWSc 92
Conard, Robert Allen 1913- AmMWSc 92
Conard, William Thomas 1958- WhoAmL 92
Conarko, Jeanne Marie 1946- WhoEnt 92
Conary, David Arlan 1937- WhoFI 92
Conaway, Alexander Gordon 1951- WhoFI 92
Conaway, Charles William 1943- AmMWSc 92
Conaway, Howard Herschel 1940- AmMWSc 92
Conaway, Jeff 1950- IntMPA 92
Conaway, Mary Ann 1940- WhoMW 92
Conaway, Mary Ward Prindle 1943- WhoBlA 92
Conboy, Kenneth 1938- WhoAmL 92
Conboy, Patrick M 1944- WhoAmP 91
Conca, Romeo John 1926- AmMWSc 92
Concannon, Brian Eugene WhoAmL 92
Concannon, Donald O 1927- WhoAmP 91
Concannon, John Dennis 1930- Who 92
Concannon, Joseph N 1920- AmMWSc 92
Concannon, Kevin William 1940- WhoWest 92
Concannon, Richard James 1933- WhoAmL 92
Concannon, Terence Patrick d1990 Who 92N
Concepcion, Dave 1948- WhoHisp 92
Concepcion, David Ismael 1948- WhoBlA 92
Concepcion Baez, Arcadio WhoAmP 91, WhoHisp 92
Concepcion Valdes, Diego Gabriel de HisDSpE
Concevitch, Bill Byron 1958- WhoFI 92
Concha, Joseph L. DrAPF 91
Conchon, Georges d1990 IntWW 91N
Concia, Suzanne Vazzana 1961- WhoFI 92
Conciatori, Anthony Bernard 1916- AmMWSc 92
Concolorcorvo HisDSpE
Concordia, Charles 1908- AmMWSc 92
Concus, Paul 1933- AmMWSc 92, WhoWest 92
Condas, Thomas Michael, Sr. 1957- WhoAmL 92
Conde, Alice 1946- WhoHisp 92
Conde, Anselmo 1944- WhoHisp 92
Conde, Carlos D. 1936- WhoHisp 92
Conde, Carmen 1901- DcLB 108 [port]
Conde, Emilia WhoHisp 92
Conde, Rita IntMPA 92
Condell, William John, Jr 1927- AmMWSc 92
Condell, Yvonne C 1931- AmMWSc 92
Condello, Dana Joseph 1948- WhoWest 92
Condello, Victor F d1991 NewYTBS 91
Condeni, Joseph Anthony 1956- WhoAmL 92
Conder, Charles 1868-1909 TwCPaSc
Conder, George Anthony 1950- AmMWSc 92
Conder, Harold Lee 1945- AmMWSc 92
Conder, James Richard WhoAmP 91
Condict, Edgar Rhodes 1940- WhoFI 92
Condie, Kent Carl 1936- AmMWSc 92
Condike, George Francis 1916- AmMWSc 92
Condillac, Etienne Bonnot de 1714-1780 BlkwCEP
Condit, Carl W. 1914- WrDr 92
Condit, Gary A. WhoWest 92
Condit, Gary A. 1948- AlmAP 92 [port]
Condit, Gary Adrian 1948- WhoAmP 91
Condit, Linda Faulkner 1947- WhoFI 92
Condit, Paul Brainard 1943- AmMWSc 92
Condit, Paul Carr 1914- AmMWSc 92
Condit, Philip M 1941- AmMWSc 92
Condit, Ralph Howell 1929- AmMWSc 92, WhoWest 92
Conditt, Marion Witherspoon 1928- WhoRel 92
Condliffe, Peter George 1922- AmMWSc 92
Condo, Albert Carman, Jr 1924- AmMWSc 92
Condo, George T 1934- AmMWSc 92
Condo, Tony M. 1949- WhoEnt 92
Condodemetraky, George 1936- WhoAmP 91
Condon, Breen O'Malley 1944- WhoAmL 92
Condon, Chris J 1922- IntMPA 92
Condon, Dean Francis 1962- WhoRel 92
Condon, Denis David 1910- Who 92
Condon, Donald Stephen 1930- WhoFI 92
Condon, Eddie 1905-1973 NewAmDM
Condon, Edward John, Jr. 1940- WhoFI 92
Condon, Francis Edward 1919- AmMWSc 92
Condon, James Benton 1940- AmMWSc 92
Condon, James Justin 1945- AmMWSc 92
Condon, Lawrence Michael 1944- WhoMW 92
Condon, Lester P 1922- WhoAmP 91
Condon, Margaret Jean DrAPF 91
Condon, Mark William 1957- WhoWest 92
Condon, Michael Edward 1945- AmMWSc 92
Condon, Richard 1915- BenetAL 91, ConNov 91, IntAu&W 91, WrDr 92
Condon, Richard Thomas 1915- IntWW 91, WhoEnt 92
Condon, Robert Edward 1929- AmMWSc 92
Condon, Thomas 1822-1907 BiInAmS
Condorcanqui, Jose Gabriel HisDSpE
Condorcet, Jean-Antoine-N.C., marquis de 1743-1794 BlkwCEP
Condouris, George Anthony 1925- AmMWSc 92
Condra, Allen Lee 1950- WhoAmL 92
Condran, Cynthia Marie 1953- WhoEnt 92
Condrate, Robert Adam 1938- AmMWSc 92
Condray, Ben Rogers 1925- AmMWSc 92
Condrell, William Kenneth 1926- WhoAmL 92
Condry, Dorothea DrAPF 91
Condry, Robert Stewart 1941- WhoMW 92
Condry, William 1918- WrDr 92
Condry, William Moreton 1918- IntAu&W 91
Cone, Carl B. 1916- WrDr 92
Cone, Ceasar 1859-1917 DcNCBi 1
Cone, Cecil Wayne 1937- WhoBlA 92
Cone, Clarence Donald, Jr 1931- AmMWSc 92
Cone, Conrad 1939- AmMWSc 92
Cone, David NewYTBS 91 [port]
Cone, Donald R 1921- AmMWSc 92
Cone, Edward Christopher 1937- WhoFI 92
Cone, Edward Jackson 1942- AmMWSc 92
Cone, Edward T. 1917- NewAmDM
Cone, Edward Toner 1917- WhoEnt 92
Cone, Edwin Earl 1916- WhoWest 92
Cone, Helen Bess 1906- WhoMW 92
Cone, James H. 1938- WhoBlA 92
Cone, James Hal 1938- RelLAm 91, WhoRel 92
Cone, Juanita Fletcher 1947- WhoBlA 92
Cone, June Elizabeth 1918- WhoWest 92
Cone, Laura Weil 1888-1970 DcNCBi 1
Cone, Lawrence Arthur 1928- WhoWest 92
Cone, Martha Caroline 1933- WhoEnt 92
Cone, Michael McKay 1947- AmMWSc 92
Cone, Molly Zelda 1918- IntAu&W 91
Cone, Moses Herman 1857-1908 DcNCBi 1
Cone, Richard Allen 1936- AmMWSc 92
Cone, Robert Edward 1943- AmMWSc 92
Cone, Sydney M., III 1930- WhoAmL 92
Cone, Thomas E, Jr 1915- AmMWSc 92
Cone, William Frederick 1947- WhoEnt 92
Cone, Wyatt Wayne 1934- AmMWSc 92
Conejo, Mary Lynn 1951- WhoHisp 92
Conerly, William Booth 1952- WhoFI 92
Coney, Hydia Lutrice 1963- WhoBlA 92
Coney, Loraine Chapell 1935- WhoBlA 92
Coney, Michael G 1932- TwCSFW 91, WrDr 92
Coney, Michael Greatrex 1932- IntAu&W 91
Coney, Peter James AmMWSc 92
Coneyrs, Sue Ann 1942- WhoFI 92
Confalone, Pat N 1945- AmMWSc 92
Confer, Anthony Wayne 1947- AmMWSc 92
Confer, Gregory Lee 1954- AmMWSc 92
Confer, John L 1940- AmMWSc 92
Conford, Ellen 1942- IntAu&W 91, SmATA 68 [port], WrDr 92
Conforti, Evandro 1947- AmMWSc 92
Conforti, Michael Peter 1945- WhoMW 92
Congalton, Christopher William 1946- WhoAmL 92
Congar, Yves 1904- DcEcMov [port], IntWW 91
Congdon, Charles C 1920- AmMWSc 92
Congdon, Ernest Arnold 1866-1917 BiInAmS
Congdon, Gayla Cooper 1954- WhoRel 92
Congdon, Jay Stewart 1951- WhoEnt 92
Congdon, Justin Daniel 1941- AmMWSc 92
Congdon, Kirby DrAPF 91
Congdon, Richard Allen 1949- WhoAmP 91
Congdon, Rita Isabel 1948- WhoHisp 92
Congdon, Roger Douglass 1918- WhoRel 92, WhoWest 92
Congel, Frank Joseph 1943- AmMWSc 92
Conger, Alan Douglas 1917- AmMWSc 92
Conger, Bob Vernon 1938- AmMWSc 92
Conger, Dean D. 1927- WhoEnt 92
Conger, Eric Davis 1946- WhoEnt 92
Conger, Harry Calvin 1931- WhoFI 92, WhoWest 92
Conger, Harry M 1930- AmMWSc 92
Conger, Harry Milton 1930- WhoFI 92, WhoWest 92
Conger, John 1921- WrDr 92
Conger, John Janeway 1921- AmMWSc 92
Conger, Joseph Harold, III 1948- WhoEnt 92
Conger, Kyril Bailey 1913- AmMWSc 92
Conger, Robert Kay 1947- WhoWest 92
Conger, Robert Perrigo 1922- AmMWSc 92
Conger, William Lawrence 1937- AmMWSc 92
Congleton, Baron 1930- Who 92
Congleton, James Lee 1942- AmMWSc 92
Congleton, Joseph Patrick 1947- WhoAmL 92
Congleton, William C. 1935- WhoBlA 92
Congo, Sonia Who 92
Congram, John Douglas 1937- WhoRel 92
Congreve, Ambrose 1907- Who 92
Congreve, Mario Ricardo 1957- WhoEnt 92, WhoWest 92
Congreve, Willard J. 1921-1979 ConAu 134
Congreve, William 1670-1729 BlkwCEP, CnDBLB 2 [port], DramC 2 [port], RfGEnL 91
Conhagen, Alfred 1897- WhoFI 92
Coni, Peter Richard Carstairs 1935- Who 92
Conibear, Shirley Ann 1946- AmMWSc 92, WhoMW 92
Conidi, Daniel Joseph 1957- WhoMW 92
Coniff, John Harold 1952- WhoWest 92
Conigland, Edward 1819-1877 DcNCBi 1
Conigliaro, Peter James 1942- AmMWSc 92
Conigliaro, Tony 1945-1990 AnObit 1990
Coniglio, John Giglio 1919- AmMWSc 92
Conine, James William 1926- AmMWSc 92
Conine, Merland Junior 1936- WhoAmP 91
Coningsby, Thomas Arthur Charles 1933- Who 92
Conino, Joseph Aloysius 1920- WhoAmL 92
Coniston, Ed IntAu&W 91X, TwCWW 91
Conkel, Robert Dale 1936- WhoAmL 92
Conkel, Terrence Emerson 1951- WhoAmL 92
Conkey, Sharyn Yanoshak 1945- WhoWest 92
Conkie, William R 1932- AmMWSc 92
Conkin, James E 1924- AmMWSc 92
Conkin, Robert A 1920- AmMWSc 92
Conkle, D. Steven DrAPF 91
Conkle, Daniel Oliver 1953- WhoAmL 92
Conkle, Harold Nicholas 1950- WhoMW 92
Conklin, Charles D 1938- WhoIns 92
Conklin, Daniel George 1943- WhoRel 92
Conklin, Deborah Lynn 1950- WhoRel 92
Conklin, Donald Ransford 1936- WhoFI 92
Conklin, Douglas Edgar 1942- AmMWSc 92
Conklin, Gayle Underwood 1948- WhoAmP 91
Conklin, George William 1908- WhoAmP 91
Conklin, Gerald Thomas 1935- WhoIns 92
Conklin, Glenn Ernest 1929- AmMWSc 92
Conklin, Groff 1904-1968 ScFEYrs
Conklin, Hal Harold Edwin 1945- WhoWest 92
Conklin, Howard Lawrence 1943- WhoAmL 92
Conklin, James Byron, Jr 1937- AmMWSc 92
Conklin, John Douglas, Sr 1933- AmMWSc 92
Conklin, John E. 1943- WrDr 92
Conklin, John Evan 1943- IntAu&W 91
Conklin, John Roger 1933- WhoFI 92
Conklin, R N 1921- AmMWSc 92
Conklin, Richard Allan 1939- WhoFI 92
Conklin, Richard James 1930- WhoAmP 91
Conklin, Richard Louis 1923- AmMWSc 92
Conklin, Robert Eugene 1930- WhoMW 92
Conklin, Thomas J. 1946- WhoFI 92
Conklin, William Augustus 1837-1913 BiInAmS
Conkling, Grace Hazard 1878-1958 BenetAL 91
Conkling, Hilda 1910- BenetAL 91
Conkling, Roscoe 1829-1888 AmPolLe
Conlan, Bernard 1923- Who 92
Conlan, James 1923- AmMWSc 92
Conlan, John B, Jr 1930- WhoAmP 91
Conlee, Robert Keith 1942- AmMWSc 92
Conley, Blair J WhoAmP 91
Conley, Carl Edward 1938- WhoRel 92
Conley, Charles S. 1921- WhoBlA 92
Conley, Darlene Ann WhoEnt 92
Conley, Diana Jean Montenaro 1953- WhoMW 92
Conley, Elizabeth-Lucy Carter 1919- WhoBlA 92
Conley, Elizabeth Simona 1942- WhoAmL 92, WhoWest 92
Conley, Emmitt Jerome 1922- WhoBlA 92
Conley, Francis Raymond 1916- AmMWSc 92
Conley, George Emery 1933- WhoAmL 92
Conley, Gerard P, Jr 1930- WhoAmP 91
Conley, H Dean 1946- WhoAmP 91
Conley, Harry Lee, Jr 1935- AmMWSc 92
Conley, Harry V 1927- WhoAmP 91
Conley, Herbert A. 1942- WhoBlA 92
Conley, Jack Michael 1943- AmMWSc 92
Conley, James Franklin 1931- AmMWSc 92
Conley, James Monroe 1915- WhoBlA 92
Conley, James Sylvester, Jr. 1942- WhoBlA 92
Conley, John A. 1928- WhoBlA 92
Conley, Karyne 1953- WhoAmP 91
Conley, Mariita Arosemena 1951- WhoHisp 92
Conley, Martha Richards 1947- WhoBlA 92
Conley, Mike 1962- BlkOlyM
Conley, Raymond K, Jr WhoAmP 91
Conley, Robert Eugene 1936- WhoAmP 91
Conley, Robert J. DrAPF 91
Conley, Robert J 1929- WhoAmP 91
Conley, Robert J 1940- ConAu 34NR, TwCWW 91, WrDr 92
Conley, Robert T 1931- AmMWSc 92
Conley, Sarah Ann 1942- WhoMW 92
Conley, Thomas Anthony 1954- WhoRel 92
Conley, Tom Clark 1943- WhoMW 92
Conley, Toni DrAPF 91
Conley, Veronica Lucey 1919- AmMWSc 92
Conley, Weld E 1911- AmMWSc 92
Conley, William Thompson 1952- WhoMW 92
Conley, Zeb Bristol, Jr. 1936- WhoWest 92
Conlin, Bernard Joseph 1935- AmMWSc 92
Conlin, Karen Jo 1942- WhoEnt 92
Conlin, Roxanne Barton 1944- WhoAmP 91
Conlin, William Richard, II 1913- WhoWest 92
Conlisk, Jean T. Kavanaugh 1934- WhoMW 92
Conlon, Donald Robert 1931- WhoAmP 91
Conlon, James WhoAmP 91
Conlon, James 1950- IntWW 91, NewAmDM
Conlon, James Joseph 1950- WhoEnt 92
Conlon, Joseph R WhoIns 92
Conlon, Michael William 1946- WhoAmL 92
Conlon, Peter John, Jr. 1951- WhoFI 92
Conlon, Suzanne B. 1939- WhoAmL 92, WhoMW 92
Conlon, Walter 1947- WhoAmP 91
Conly, Frank ScFEYrs
Conly, Frank 1930- WhoIns 92
Conly, John F 1933- AmMWSc 92
Conly, Michael Frederick 1945- WhoMW 92
Conmy, Patrick A. 1934- WhoAmL 92, WhoMW 92
Conn, Anita Ruth 1927- WhoAmP 91
Conn, Arthur L 1913- AmMWSc 92
Conn, Carol 1952- WhoEnt 92
Conn, Charles William 1902- RelLAm 91
Conn, Didi 1951- ConTFT 9
Conn, Edward 1918- Who 92
Conn, Eric Edward 1923- AmMWSc 92
Conn, Hadley Lewis, Jr 1921- AmMWSc 92
Conn, Harold O 1930- AmMWSc 92
Conn, Herbert William 1859-1917 BiInAmS
Conn, James Frederick 1924- AmMWSc 92
Conn, James Stephen 1945- WhoRel 92
Conn, Jerome W 1907- AmMWSc 92, IntWW 91

**Conn,** John Farquhar Christie 1903- *Who 92*
**Conn,** P Michael 1949- *AmMWSc 92*
**Conn,** Paul Harding, Jr. 1955- *WhoFI 92*
**Conn,** Paul Joseph 1940- *AmMWSc 92*
**Conn,** Paul Kohler 1929- *AmMWSc 92*
**Conn,** Philip Wesley 1942- *WhoMW 92*
**Conn,** Rex Boland 1927- *AmMWSc 92*
**Conn,** Richard Leslie 1947- *AmMWSc 92*
**Conn,** Robert A. 1926- *IntMPA 92*
**Conn,** Robert Henry 1925- *WhoAmP 91*
**Conn,** Robert William 1942- *AmMWSc 92*
**Conn,** Ross Edward 1913- *WhoAmP 91*
**Conn,** Roy 1931- *TwCPaSc*
**Conn,** Sandra Jean 1944- *WhoMW 92*
**Conn,** Stewart 1936- *ConPo 91, IntAu&W 91, WrDr 92*
**Conn,** Walter Eugene 1940- *WhoRel 92*
**Conn,** Walter Jennings 1922- *WhoAmP 91*
**Connair,** Pierce F 1926- *WhoAmP 91*
**Connally,** C. Ellen 1945- *WhoBlA 92*
**Connally,** John B 1917- *FacFETw*
**Connally,** John Bowden 1917- *Who 92*
**Connally,** John Bowden, Jr. 1917- *IntWW 91*
**Connally,** Thomas 1877-1963 *FacFETw*
**Connamacher,** Robert Henle 1933- *AmMWSc 92*
**Connar,** Richard Grigsby 1920- *AmMWSc 92*
**Connard,** Philip 1876-1958 *TwCPaSc*
**Connare,** William Graham 1911- *WhoRel 92*
**Connaughton,** Michael Edward 1946- *WhoMW 92*
**Connecorte** *DcNCBi 1*
**Conneffe,** James F d1910 *BiInAmS*
**Connell,** Alastair McCrae 1929- *AmMWSc 92*
**Connell,** Brian Reginald 1916- *IntAu&W 91, WrDr 92*
**Connell,** Cameron 1944- *WhoBlA 92*
**Connell,** Carolyn Joanne *AmMWSc 92*
**Connell,** Charles Percy 1902- *Who 92*
**Connell,** David R 1950- *WhoAmP 91*
**Connell,** David Wayne 1957- *WhoMW 92*
**Connell,** Desmond *Who 92, WhoRel 92*
**Connell,** Elizabeth *IntWW 91*
**Connell,** Eugene C 1954- *WhoIns 92*
**Connell,** Evan *DrAPF 91*
**Connell,** Evan S. 1924- *Au&Arts 7 [port]*
**Connell,** Evan S., Jr. 1924- *BenetAL 91, ConNov 91, WrDr 92*
**Connell,** Foster Gladwin 1938- *WhoRel 92*
**Connell,** Francis Joseph, III 1946- *WhoAmL 92*
**Connell,** George Edward 1930- *AmMWSc 92, IntWW 91, Who 92*
**Connell,** George Herman, Jr. 1944- *WhoAmL 92*
**Connell,** Gordon 1923- *WhoEnt 92*
**Connell,** Grover 1918- *WhoFI 92*
**Connell,** Jack 1919- *WhoAmP 91*
**Connell,** Jack 1961- *WhoRel 92*
**Connell,** James Joseph, Jr. 1928- *WhoWest 92*
**Connell,** Jerome F, Sr *WhoAmP 91*
**Connell,** John Jeffrey 1927- *Who 92*
**Connell,** John MacFarlane 1924- *Who 92*
**Connell,** John Morris 1911- *Who 92*
**Connell,** Joseph H 1923- *AmMWSc 92*
**Connell,** Kathleen 1937- *WhoAmP 91*
**Connell,** Kathy *WhoEnt 92*
**Connell,** Lawrence Emmett, Jr. 1946- *WhoMW 92*
**Connell,** Mark Steven 1951- *WhoAmL 92*
**Connell,** Michael Bryan 1939- *Who 92*
**Connell,** Michael James 1958- *WhoEnt 92*
**Connell,** Ninette *Who 92*
**Connell,** Philip Francis 1924- *WhoFI 92*
**Connell,** Philip Henry 1921- *IntWW 91, Who 92*
**Connell,** Richard 1893-1949 *BenetAL 91*
**Connell,** Richard Allen 1929- *AmMWSc 92*
**Connell,** Wallace James, Jr. 1945- *WhoMW 92*
**Connell,** Walter Ford 1906- *AmMWSc 92*
**Connell,** William 1916- *WrDr 92*
**Connell,** William D. 1955- *WhoAmL 92*
**Connell,** William Francis 1938- *WhoFI 92*
**Connell-Smith,** Gordon Edward 1917- *Who 92*
**Connell-Tatum,** Elizabeth Bishop 1925- *AmMWSc 92*
**Connellan,** Leo *DrAPF 91*
**Connellee-Clay,** Barbara 1929- *WhoWest 92*
**Connelly,** Betty Fees 1924- *WhoRel 92*
**Connelly,** Brian Robert 1935- *WhoAmP 91*
**Connelly,** Carolyn Thomas 1941- *AmMWSc 92*
**Connelly,** Charles Michael 1938- *WhoAmL 92*
**Connelly,** Clarence Morley 1916- *AmMWSc 92*
**Connelly,** Claudia Ausdal 1959- *WhoAmL 92*
**Connelly,** Colin Charles 1956- *WhoAmL 92*
**Connelly,** David Barry 1940- *WhoAmP 91*
**Connelly,** David O'Brien 1952- *WhoEnt 92*
**Connelly,** Donald Patrick 1942- *AmMWSc 92, WhoMW 92*
**Connelly,** Elizabeth Ann *WhoAmP 91*
**Connelly,** George William 1945- *WhoAmL 92*
**Connelly,** J Alvin 1942- *AmMWSc 92*
**Connelly,** Joe Turner 1926- *WhoAmP 91*
**Connelly,** John Dooley 1946- *WhoMW 92*
**Connelly,** John Francis 1905- *IntWW 91*
**Connelly,** John Joseph, Jr 1925- *AmMWSc 92*
**Connelly,** Karon Kay 1949- *WhoAmL 92*
**Connelly,** Kimberly Ann 1961- *WhoAmL 92*
**Connelly,** Kyran William 1941- *WhoEnt 92*
**Connelly,** Lewis Branch Sutton 1950- *WhoAmL 92*
**Connelly,** Lloyd G 1945- *WhoAmP 91*
**Connelly,** Marc 1890-1980 *BenetAL 91*
**Connelly,** Mary Ellen *WhoAmP 91*
**Connelly,** Michael Robert 1947- *WhoAmP 91*
**Connelly,** Michele *DrAPF 91*
**Connelly,** Paul V. 1923- *IntMPA 92*
**Connelly,** R Terry 1946- *WhoAmP 91*
**Connelly,** Rebecca Buehler 1963- *WhoAmL 92*
**Connelly,** Thomas George 1945- *AmMWSc 92*
**Connelly,** Thomas John 1925- *Who 92*
**Connelly,** Thomas Joseph 1940- *WhoAmL 92*
**Connelly,** Timothy Joseph 1959- *WhoFI 92*
**Connelly,** William Joseph 1931- *WhoFI 92*
**Connelly,** William Joseph 1954- *WhoAmL 92*
**Conner,** Albert Z 1921- *AmMWSc 92*
**Conner,** Andrew Jackson 1860-1931 *DcNCBi 1*
**Conner,** Brenda Jean *AmMWSc 92*
**Conner,** Bruce 1933- *IntDcF 2-2*
**Conner,** Charles M. 1925- *IntMPA 92*
**Conner,** David Emory 1950- *WhoRel 92*
**Conner,** David John 1947- *Who 92*
**Conner,** Donn Brian 1939- *WhoFI 92*
**Conner,** Doyle E 1928- *WhoAmP 91*
**Conner,** Finis 1943- *WhoFI 92*
**Conner,** Fred L. 1909- *WhoAmL 92*
**Conner,** Gail Patricia 1948- *WhoBlA 92*
**Conner,** George William 1935- *AmMWSc 92*
**Conner,** H. Clinton 1937- *WhoMW 92*
**Conner,** Harry W. 1929- *WhoMW 92*
**Conner,** Howard Emmett 1930- *AmMWSc 92*
**Conner,** Hubert Andrew 1909- *WhoMW 92*
**Conner,** Jack Michael 1935- *AmMWSc 92*
**Conner,** Janie 1959- *WhoEnt 92*
**Conner,** Jerry Power 1927- *AmMWSc 92*
**Conner,** Laban Calvin 1936- *WhoBlA 92*
**Conner,** Leland Lavon 1930- *WhoMW 92*
**Conner,** Lester Allen 1959- *WhoBlA 92*
**Conner,** Linda Adcock 1959- *WhoEnt 92*
**Conner,** Lindsay Andrew 1956- *WhoAmL 92*
**Conner,** Lucy Shull 1938- *WhoBlA 92*
**Conner,** Marcia Lynne 1958- *WhoBlA 92*
**Conner,** Maurice Wayne 1938- *WhoMW 92*
**Conner,** Patrick 1947- *WrDr 92*
**Conner,** Paul H 1925- *WhoAmP 91*
**Conner,** Phillip Lee 1953- *WhoAmL 92*
**Conner,** Pierre Euclide, Jr 1932- *AmMWSc 92*
**Conner,** Prudence Ophelia 1963- *WhoAmL 92*
**Conner,** Rearden d1991 *Who 92N*
**Conner,** Rearden 1907- *WrDr 92*
**Conner,** Richard Lee 1939- *WhoWest 92*
**Conner,** Robert Louis 1927- *AmMWSc 92*
**Conner,** Ronald Parks 1945- *WhoRel 92*
**Conner,** Stewart Edmund 1941- *WhoAmL 92*
**Conner,** Victor Randal 1953- *WhoRel 92*
**Conner,** Virginia S. 1950- *WhoHisp 92*
**Conner,** Warren Wesley 1932- *WhoAmL 92*
**Conner,** William Curtis 1920- *WhoAmL 92*
**Conner,** William Guy 1952- *WhoMW 92*
**Connerney,** John E P 1950- *AmMWSc 92*
**Conners,** Carmen Keith 1933- *AmMWSc 92*
**Conners,** Gary Hamilton 1936- *AmMWSc 92*
**Conners,** John B 1945- *WhoIns 92*
**Conners,** John Brendan 1945- *WhoFI 92*
**Conners,** Kenneth Wray 1909- *WrDr 92*
**Conners,** Maynard Gilbert 1918- *WhoAmP 91*
**Conners,** Richard J 1910- *WhoAmP 91*
**Connery,** Gloria Jean 1951- *WhoRel 92*
**Connery,** Sean 1929- *FacFETw*
**Connery,** Sean 1930- *IntMPA 92, IntWW 91, Who 92, WhoEnt 92*
**Connett,** William C 1939- *AmMWSc 92*
**Conney,** Allan Howard 1930- *AmMWSc 92*
**Connick,** C. Milo *WrDr 92*
**Connick,** Charles Milo 1917- *WhoRel 92*
**Connick,** Harry 1926- *WhoAmL 92*
**Connick,** Harry, Jr. *NewYTBS 91 [port]*
**Connick,** Harry, Jr. 1967- *IntMPA 92, News 91 [port]*
**Connick,** Harry, Jr. 1968- *WhoEnt 92*
**Connick,** Robert Elwell 1917- *AmMWSc 92, IntWW 91*
**Connick,** William Joseph, Jr 1939- *AmMWSc 92*
**Conniff,** Ray 1916- *NewAmDM, WhoEnt 92*
**Connington,** J J 1880-1947 *ScFEYrs*
**Connole,** William Roger d1991 *NewYTBS 91*
**Connolly,** Cyril 1903-1974 *FacFETw, RfGEnL 91*
**Connolly,** Denis Joseph 1938- *AmMWSc 92*
**Connolly,** Edward G *WhoAmP 91*
**Connolly,** Edward Joseph 1936- *WhoAmP 91*
**Connolly,** Edward Thomas 1935- *Who 92*
**Connolly,** Elma Troutman 1931- *WhoFI 92*
**Connolly,** Geraldine *DrAPF 91*
**Connolly,** Grace *WhoAmP 91*
**Connolly,** J. Joseph 1948- *WhoAmL 92*
**Connolly,** J. Wray 1934- *WhoFI 92*
**Connolly,** James 1870-1916 *FacFETw*
**Connolly,** James B. 1868?-1957 *BenetAL 91*
**Connolly,** James D 1943- *AmMWSc 92*
**Connolly,** James L 1948- *AmMWSc 92*
**Connolly,** Janet Claire Whitty 1936- *WhoAmP 91*
**Connolly,** John Charles 1953- *AmMWSc 92*
**Connolly,** John E 1923- *AmMWSc 92*
**Connolly,** John Earle 1923- *WhoWest 92*
**Connolly,** John Francis 1936- *AmMWSc 92*
**Connolly,** John Francis 1948- *AmMWSc 92*
**Connolly,** John Irving, Jr 1936- *AmMWSc 92*
**Connolly,** John Stephen 1936- *AmMWSc 92*
**Connolly,** John W 1936- *AmMWSc 92*
**Connolly,** John William Domville 1938- *AmMWSc 92*
**Connolly,** Joseph Anthony *AmMWSc 92*
**Connolly,** Joseph M *WhoAmP 91*
**Connolly,** K. Thomas 1940- *WhoAmL 92*
**Connolly,** Kenneth Scott 1965- *WhoRel 92*
**Connolly,** Kevin Michael 1952- *AmMWSc 92*
**Connolly,** L. William 1923- *WhoAmL 92*
**Connolly,** Laurence E, Jr *WhoAmP 91*
**Connolly,** Martin F. 1949- *WhoEnt 92*
**Connolly,** Matthew Bernard, Jr. 1941- *WhoMW 92*
**Connolly,** Maureen Catherine 1934-1969 *FacFETw*
**Connolly,** Michael Francis 1962- *WhoAmL 92*
**Connolly,** Michael Ignatius 1956- *WhoMW 92*
**Connolly,** Michael Joseph 1947- *WhoAmP 91*
**Connolly,** Michael W 1945- *WhoAmP 91*
**Connolly,** Michaela 1945- *WhoRel 92*
**Connolly,** Paul *WrDr 92*
**Connolly,** Peter 1935- *IntAu&W 91, WrDr 92*
**Connolly,** Peter Dominic 1949- *WhoFI 92*
**Connolly,** Phyllis Fern 1929- *WhoAmP 91*
**Connolly,** Ray *IntAu&W 91, WrDr 92*
**Connolly,** Steve James 1919- *WhoWest 92*
**Connolly,** Thomas B 1963- *WhoAmP 91*
**Connolly,** Thomas Edward 1942- *WhoAmL 92, WhoFI 92*
**Connolly,** Thomas Joseph 1922- *WhoRel 92, WhoWest 92*
**Connolly,** Thomas Joseph 1957- *WhoAmL 92*
**Connolly,** Walter Curtis 1922- *AmMWSc 92*
**Connolly-O'Neill,** Barrie Jane 1943- *WhoWest 92*
**Connor,** Bishop of 1926- *Who 92*
**Connor,** Brian Nichols 1946- *WhoRel 92*
**Connor,** Cecil Martin 1945- *WhoMW 92*
**Connor,** Daniel Henry 1928- *AmMWSc 92*
**Connor,** Daniel S 1938- *AmMWSc 92*
**Connor,** David John 1953- *WhoMW 92*
**Connor,** David Thomas 1939- *AmMWSc 92*
**Connor,** Dolores L. 1950- *WhoHisp 92*
**Connor,** Dolores Lillie 1950- *WhoBlA 92*
**Connor,** Donald W 1923- *AmMWSc 92*
**Connor,** Frank Field 1932- *AmMWSc 92*
**Connor,** Gary Edward 1948- *WhoWest 92*
**Connor,** George C., Jr. 1921- *WhoBlA 92*
**Connor,** George Whitfield 1872-1938 *DcNCBi 1*
**Connor,** Georgia Kathleen 1949- *WhoEnt 92*
**Connor,** Gerald Raymond 1946- *WhoFI 92*
**Connor,** Henry Groves 1852-1924 *DcNCBi 1*
**Connor,** Henry William 1793-1866 *DcNCBi 1*
**Connor,** James A 1936- *WhoAmP 91*
**Connor,** James D 1926- *AmMWSc 92*
**Connor,** James Edward, Jr 1924- *AmMWSc 92*
**Connor,** James Edward, Jr 1948- *WhoAmP 91*
**Connor,** James Michael 1951- *Who 92*
**Connor,** James Richard 1928- *WhoMW 92*
**Connor,** James Russell 1940- *WhoBlA 92*
**Connor,** Jeffery Scott 1954- *WhoMW 92*
**Connor,** Jeremy George 1938- *Who 92*
**Connor,** John Arthur 1940- *AmMWSc 92*
**Connor,** John D 1933- *AmMWSc 92*
**Connor,** John Gregory 1955- *WhoAmL 92*
**Connor,** John Michael 1938- *AmMWSc 92*
**Connor,** John Murray 1943- *WhoFI 92, WhoMW 92*
**Connor,** John Thomas, Jr. 1941- *WhoAmL 92, WhoFI 92*
**Connor,** John William 1930- *WhoWest 92*
**Connor,** Jon James 1932- *AmMWSc 92*
**Connor,** Joseph Andrew 1952- *WhoFI 92*
**Connor,** Joseph E. 1931- *IntWW 91, WhoFI 92*
**Connor,** Joseph Gerard, Jr 1936- *AmMWSc 92*
**Connor,** Joseph Patrick, III 1953- *WhoAmL 92*
**Connor,** Keith 1957- *BlkOlyM*
**Connor,** Kenneth *IntMPA 92*
**Connor,** Kenneth Wilson 1919- *WhoMW 92*
**Connor,** Kevin *IntAu&W 91X*
**Connor,** Kevin 1959- *WhoMW 92*
**Connor,** Laurence Davis 1938- *WhoAmL 92*
**Connor,** Lawrence John 1945- *AmMWSc 92*
**Connor,** Martin 1945- *WhoAmP 91*
**Connor,** Ralph *BenetAL 91*
**Connor,** Ralph 1860-1937 *TwCWW 91*
**Connor,** Ralph 1907- *AmMWSc 92*
**Connor,** Robert Dickson 1922- *AmMWSc 92*
**Connor,** Robert Digges Wimberly 1878-1950 *DcNCBi 1*
**Connor,** Robert Joseph 1927- *WhoAmP 91*
**Connor,** Robert Patrick 1948- *WhoEnt 92*
**Connor,** Robert Thomas 1938- *WhoAmP 91*
**Connor,** Roger David 1939- *Who 92*
**Connor,** Roger George 1926- *WhoAmP 91*
**Connor,** Sidney G 1947- *AmMWSc 92*
**Connor,** Terence Gregory 1942- *WhoAmL 92*
**Connor,** Thomas Byrne 1921- *AmMWSc 92*
**Connor,** Thomas Gene 1938- *WhoFI 92*
**Connor,** Thomas Maxwell, Sr 1924- *WhoAmP 91*
**Connor,** Tony *DrAPF 91*
**Connor,** Tony 1930- *ConPo 91, IntAu&W 91, WrDr 92*
**Connor,** Ulysses J., Jr. 1948- *WhoBlA 92*
**Connor,** William Elliott 1921- *AmMWSc 92*
**Connor,** William Gorden 1936- *AmMWSc 92*
**Connor,** William Keith 1931- *AmMWSc 92*
**Connor-Bey,** Brenda *DrAPF 91*
**Connors,** Alfred F, Jr 1950- *AmMWSc 92*
**Connors,** Andree *DrAPF 91*
**Connors,** Bruton 1931- *WrDr 92*
**Connors,** Carol Ekern 1953- *WhoAmP 91*
**Connors,** Christopher J 1956- *WhoAmP 91*
**Connors,** Chuck 1921- *IntMPA 92*
**Connors,** Chuck Kevin Joseph 1921- *WhoEnt 92*
**Connors,** Don 1945- *WhoEnt 92*
**Connors,** Donald R 1928- *AmMWSc 92*
**Connors,** Dorsey *WhoMW 92*
**Connors,** Edward Joseph 1929- *WhoMW 92*
**Connors,** Eugene Kenneth 1946- *WhoAmL 92*
**Connors,** Frank Joseph 1944- *WhoAmL 92*
**Connors,** Henry Joseph 1931- *WhoAmP 91*
**Connors,** Hollis Gay 1912- *WhoAmP 91*
**Connors,** James Patrick 1952- *WhoAmL 92*
**Connors,** James Scott 1952- *FacFETw, IntWW 91*
**Connors,** James T. 1935- *WhoFI 92*
**Connors,** John H *WhoAmP 91*
**Connors,** John Henry 1929- *WhoAmP 91*
**Connors,** John Michael *AmMWSc 92*

**Connors,** John Patrick, Jr. 1956- *WhoAmL 92*
**Connors,** Joseph Aloysius, III 1946- *WhoAmL 92*
**Connors,** Joseph Conlin 1948- *WhoAmL 92*
**Connors,** Kenneth A 1932- *AmMWSc 92*
**Connors,** Kevin Gerard 1961- *WhoFI 92, WhoWest 92*
**Connors,** Kevin Joseph 1955- *WhoAmL 92*
**Connors,** Kevin Philip 1961- *WhoWest 92*
**Connors,** Leonard T, Jr 1929- *WhoAmP 91*
**Connors,** Michael *ConTFT 9*
**Connors,** Mike 1925- *ConTFT 9, IntMPA 92, WhoEnt 92*
**Connors,** Natalie Ann *AmMWSc 92*
**Connors,** Philip Irving 1937- *AmMWSc 92*
**Connors,** Robert Edward 1945- *AmMWSc 92*
**Connors,** Robert Leo 1940- *WhoFI 92*
**Connors,** Stephen Wilfred 1918- *WhoAmL 92*
**Connors,** Thomas H. 1959- *WhoAmL 92*
**Connors,** Thomas P, Sr *WhoAmP 91*
**Connors,** Touch *ConTFT 9*
**Connors,** William Matthew 1921- *AmMWSc 92*
**Connuck,** Paul Dennis 1951- *WhoAmL 92*
**Conoby,** Joseph Francis 1930- *WhoFI 92*
**Conole,** Clement Vincent 1908- *WhoFI 92*
**Conole,** Richard Clement 1936- *WhoFI 92*
**Conoley,** Gillian *DrAPF 91*
**Conoley,** Gillian Flavia 1955- *IntAu&W 91*
**Conolly,** John R 1936- *AmMWSc 92*
**Conolly,** Yvonne Cecile 1939- *Who 92*
**Conolly-Carew** *Who 92*
**Conom,** Tom Peter 1949- *WhoAmL 92*
**Conombo,** Joseph Issoufou 1917- *IntWW 91*
**Conomos,** Tasso John 1938- *AmMWSc 92*
**Conomy,** John Paul 1938- *AmMWSc 92*
**Conon** d250? *EncEarC*
**Conoscenti,** Thomas C. 1945- *WhoFI 92*
**Conot,** Robert E 1929- *IntAu&W 91, WrDr 92*
**Conour,** William Frederick 1947- *WhoAmL 92*
**Conover,** Brooks William, III 1959- *WhoAmL 92*
**Conover,** C. Allan 1938- *WhoWest 92*
**Conover,** Charles Albert 1934- *AmMWSc 92*
**Conover,** Clyde S 1916- *AmMWSc 92*
**Conover,** Frederic King 1933- *WhoAmL 92*
**Conover,** James H 1942- *AmMWSc 92*
**Conover,** John Hoagland 1916- *AmMWSc 92*
**Conover,** Lloyd Hillyard 1923- *AmMWSc 92*
**Conover,** Max *WhoAmP 91*
**Conover,** Michael Robert 1951- *AmMWSc 92*
**Conover,** Raymond Arthur 1950- *WhoEnt 92*
**Conover,** Robert A *WhoIns 92*
**Conover,** Robert Warren 1937- *WhoWest 92*
**Conover,** Roger L. *DrAPF 91*
**Conover,** Thomas Ellsworth 1931- *AmMWSc 92*
**Conover,** William Garrett 1925- *WhoAmL 92*
**Conover,** William Jay 1936- *AmMWSc 92*
**Conover,** Woodrow Wilson 1947- *AmMWSc 92*
**Conquest,** Loveday Loyce 1948- *AmMWSc 92*
**Conquest,** Ned 1931- *WrDr 92*
**Conquest,** Robert 1917- *ConPo 91, IntAu&W 91, Who 92, WrDr 92*
**Conrad,** Albert G 1902- *AmMWSc 92*
**Conrad,** Allen Lawrence 1940- *WhoAmP 91*
**Conrad,** Arnold Spencer 1942- *WhoRel 92*
**Conrad,** Barnaby 1922- *BenetAL 91*
**Conrad,** Bruce 1943- *AmMWSc 92*
**Conrad,** Carl Eugene 1931- *WhoMW 92*
**Conrad,** Charles 1930- *FacFETw*
**Conrad,** Charles W. 1947- *WhoEnt 92*
**Conrad,** Christian *WhoEnt 92*
**Conrad,** Daniel Harper *AmMWSc 92*
**Conrad,** David K. 1956- *WhoAmL 92*
**Conrad,** David Paul 1946- *WhoFI 92*
**Conrad,** Diethelm 1933- *WhoRel 92*
**Conrad,** Donald Glover 1930- *IntWW 91*
**Conrad,** Earle Wilson 1943- *WhoFI 92*
**Conrad,** Edna Jones 1925- *WhoMW 92*
**Conrad,** Edward Ezra 1927- *AmMWSc 92*
**Conrad,** Emmett J. 1923- *WhoBlA 92*
**Conrad,** Eugene Anthony 1927- *AmMWSc 92*
**Conrad,** Flavius Leslie, Jr. 1920- *WhoRel 92*
**Conrad,** Franklin 1921- *AmMWSc 92*
**Conrad,** Gary Warren 1941- *AmMWSc 92, WhoMW 92*
**Conrad,** Geoffrey Wentworth 1947- *WhoMW 92*
**Conrad,** Hal *ConAu 134*
**Conrad,** Hans 1922- *AmMWSc 92*
**Conrad,** Harold d1991 *NewYTBS 91*
**Conrad,** Harold 1911-1991 *ConAu 134*
**Conrad,** Harold August 1928- *WhoMW 92, WhoRel 92*
**Conrad,** Harry Edward 1929- *AmMWSc 92*
**Conrad,** Harry Russell 1925- *AmMWSc 92*
**Conrad,** Herbert M 1927- *AmMWSc 92*
**Conrad,** James Watson, Jr. 1958- *WhoAmL 92*
**Conrad,** John R. 1915- *WhoMW 92*
**Conrad,** John Regis 1955- *WhoAmL 92*
**Conrad,** John Rudolph 1947- *AmMWSc 92*
**Conrad,** John Wilfred 1935- *WhoWest 92*
**Conrad,** Joseph 1856-1924 *ScFEYrs*
**Conrad,** Joseph 1857-1924 *CnDBLB 5 [port], FacFETw [port], LiExTwC, RfGEnL 91, ShSCr 9 [port], TwCLC 43 [port]*
**Conrad,** Joseph and Hueffer, Ford Madox *ScFEYrs*
**Conrad,** Joseph H 1926- *AmMWSc 92*
**Conrad,** Joseph M., Jr. 1936- *WhoBlA 92*
**Conrad,** Juana Carol 1939- *WhoRel 92*
**Conrad,** Kelley Allen 1941- *WhoMW 92*
**Conrad,** Kent 1948- *AlmAP 92 [port], IntWW 91, WhoAmP 91, WhoMW 92*
**Conrad,** Larry A *WhoAmP 91*
**Conrad,** Larry Wayne 1961- *WhoRel 92*
**Conrad,** Laurie Margaret 1946- *WhoEnt 92*
**Conrad,** Lola Irene 1943- *WhoRel 92*
**Conrad,** Loretta Jane 1934- *WhoMW 92*
**Conrad,** Lori Lynn 1963- *WhoMW 92*
**Conrad,** Malcolm Alvin 1927- *AmMWSc 92*
**Conrad,** Marcel E 1928- *AmMWSc 92*
**Conrad,** Marian Rideout *WhoAmP 91*
**Conrad,** Michael 1941- *AmMWSc 92*
**Conrad,** Pam 1947- *ConAu 36NR, WrDr 92*
**Conrad,** Paul 1921- *AmMWSc 92*
**Conrad,** Paul Edward 1956- *WhoAmL 92*
**Conrad,** Paul Francis 1924- *WhoWest 92*
**Conrad,** Peter 1948- *WrDr 92*
**Conrad,** Phillip Gordon 1957- *WhoAmL 92*
**Conrad,** Robert 1935- *IntMPA 92, WhoEnt 92*
**Conrad,** Robert Dean 1923- *AmMWSc 92*
**Conrad,** Robert Taylor 1810-1858 *BenetAL 91*
**Conrad,** Sally 1941- *WhoAmP 91*
**Conrad,** Shane *WhoEnt 92*
**Conrad,** Solomon White 1779-1831 *BiInAmS*
**Conrad,** Terry Lee 1954- *WhoFI 92*
**Conrad,** Timothy Abbott 1803-1877 *BiInAmS*
**Conrad,** Trude Lois 1923- *WhoRel 92*
**Conrad,** Walter Edmund 1920- *AmMWSc 92*
**Conrad,** William 1920- *IntMPA 92*
**Conrad,** William *LesBEnT 92*
**Conrad,** William 1920- *WhoEnt 92*
**Conrad,** Winthrop Brown, Jr. 1945- *WhoAmL 92*
**Conrades,** George Henry 1939- *WhoFI 92*
**Conradi,** Mark Stephen 1952- *AmMWSc 92*
**Conradi,** Peter J. 1945- *ConAu 133*
**Conrads,** Robert John 1947- *WhoFI 92*
**Conradt,** Jerome F. 1948- *WhoMW 92*
**Conrady,** James Louis 1933- *WhoWest 92*
**Conran,** Anthony 1931- *ConPo 91, IntAu&W 91, WrDr 92*
**Conran,** Elizabeth Margaret 1939- *Who 92*
**Conran,** Jasper Alexander Thirlby 1959- *IntWW 91, Who 92*
**Conran,** Joseph Palmer 1945- *WhoAmL 92*
**Conran,** Shirley 1932- *IntAu&W 91, WrDr 92*
**Conran,** Shirley Ida 1932- *IntWW 91, Who 92*
**Conran,** Terence 1931- *DcTwDes, FacFETw, Who 92*
**Conran,** Terence Orby 1931- *IntWW 91*
**Conrardy,** Daniel Michael 1954- *WhoWest 92*
**Conrath,** Barney Jay 1935- *AmMWSc 92*
**Conrey,** Bert L 1920- *AmMWSc 92*
**Conrey,** Theron Albert 1948- *WhoRel 92*
**Conroe,** Mark Gustav 1958- *WhoWest 92*
**Conrow,** Kenneth 1933- *AmMWSc 92*
**Conroy,** Al *TwCWW 91*
**Conroy,** Charles J. 1953- *WhoAmL 92*
**Conroy,** Charles William 1927- *AmMWSc 92*
**Conroy,** David Jerome 1929- *WhoAmL 92*
**Conroy,** Harry 1943- *Who 92*
**Conroy,** Jack *SmATA 65*
**Conroy,** Jack 1899- *BenetAL 91, FacFETw*
**Conroy,** James D 1933- *AmMWSc 92*
**Conroy,** James Strickler 1931- *AmMWSc 92*
**Conroy,** Janet M 1931- *WhoAmP 91*
**Conroy,** Jim *TwCWW 91*
**Conroy,** Joe *WhoAmP 91*
**Conroy,** John Wesley 1899-1990 *SmATA 65*
**Conroy,** Kenneth Clement 1927- *WhoMW 92*
**Conroy,** Lawrence Edward 1926- *AmMWSc 92*
**Conroy,** Mary A *WhoAmP 91*
**Conroy,** Michael J. 1946- *WhoMW 92*
**Conroy,** Pat 1945- *Au&Arts 8 [port], WrDr 92*
**Conroy,** Stephen 1964- *TwCPaSc*
**Conroy,** Thomas 1924- *IntMPA 92*
**Conroy,** Thomas Francis 1938- *WhoFI 92*
**Conroy,** Thomas Hyde 1922- *WhoMW 92*
**Conroy,** Thomas Joseph 1956- *WhoFI 92*
**Conroy,** Thomas R 1934- *WhoAmP 91*
**Conroy,** Williams Eugene 1933- *WhoIns 92*
**Conry,** Thomas Francis 1942- *AmMWSc 92*
**Cons,** Derek 1928- *Who 92*
**Cons,** Emma 1838-1912 *BiDBrF 2*
**Cons,** Jean Marie Abele 1934- *AmMWSc 92*
**Cons,** Richard *WhoHisp 92*
**Consag,** Fernando *DcAmImH*
**Consagra,** Pietro 1920- *IntWW 91*
**Consalvi,** Simon Alberto 1929- *IntWW 91*
**Conser,** John Hugh, II 1941- *WhoWest 92*
**Considine,** David D 1939- *WhoAmP 91*
**Considine,** Frank William 1921- *WhoFI 92*
**Considine,** Steven Thomas 1960- *WhoFI 92*
**Considine,** Terry 1947- *WhoAmP 91*
**Considine,** Timothy James 1953- *WhoFI 92*
**Consigli,** Richard Albert 1931- *AmMWSc 92*
**Consoli,** John F *WhoAmP 91*
**Consoli,** Marc-Antonio 1941- *WhoEnt 92*
**Consolo,** V. James 1959- *WhoMW 92*
**Consroe,** Paul F 1942- *AmMWSc 92*
**Constable,** Archibald *DcLB 112*
**Constable,** Edward Thomas 1930- *WhoAmL 92*
**Constable,** Frank Challice 1846-1937 *ScFEYrs*
**Constable,** Henry 1562-1613 *RfGEnL 91*
**Constable,** James Harris 1942- *AmMWSc 92*
**Constable,** John 1936- *Who 92*
**Constable,** Martin 1961- *TwCPaSc*
**Constable,** Robert Frederick S. *Who 92*
**Constable,** Robert L 1942- *AmMWSc 92*
**Constable,** Robert Thomas 1940- *WhoMW 92*
**Constable,** Trevor James 1925- *IntAu&W 91*
**Constance,** Diana 1934- *TwCPaSc*
**Constance,** Eugene Roy 1937- *WhoHisp 92*
**Constance,** John Anthony 1942- *WhoFI 92*
**Constance,** Lincoln 1909- *AmMWSc 92*
**Constancio,** Vitor 1943- *IntWW 91*
**Constans** 323?-350 *EncEarC*
**Constant,** Antony 1916- *Who 92*
**Constant,** Benjamin 1767-1830 *BlkwCEP*
**Constant,** Christopher Andrew 1966- *WhoRel 92*
**Constant,** Clinton 1912- *AmMWSc 92, IntAu&W 91, WhoFI 92, WhoWest 92*
**Constant,** Frank Woodbridge 1904- *AmMWSc 92*
**Constant,** Jan *ConAu 135*
**Constant,** Marc Duncan 1941- *AmMWSc 92*
**Constant,** Marius 1925- *NewAmDM, WhoEnt 92*
**Constant,** Paul C, Jr 1922- *AmMWSc 92*
**Constant,** Paule 1944- *IntWW 91*
**Constant,** Richard Michael 1954- *WhoEnt 92*
**Constant,** Stephen 1931- *WrDr 92*
**Constant de Rebecque,** Benjamin 1767-1830 *BlkwCEP*
**Constant De Rebecque,** Henri-Benjamin 1767-1830 *GuFrLit 1*
**Constantelos,** Demetrios J. 1927- *WrDr 92*
**Constantelos,** Demetrios John 1927- *WhoRel 92*
**Constantin,** Roysell Joseph 1939- *AmMWSc 92*
**Constantine** *Who 92*
**Constantine I** 1868-1923 *FacFETw*
**Constantine II** 1940- *FacFETw*
**Constantine XII** 1940- *IntWW 91*
**Constantine The Great** 285?-337 *EncEarC [port]*
**Constantine,** Clement *WhoRel 92*
**Constantine,** David 1944- *ConPo 91, WrDr 92*
**Constantine,** Dennis Stephan 1948- *WhoEnt 92*
**Constantine,** Denny G 1925- *AmMWSc 92*
**Constantine,** Dorothy 1937- *WhoEnt 92*
**Constantine,** George Harmon, Jr 1936- *AmMWSc 92*
**Constantine,** Herbert Patrick 1929- *AmMWSc 92*
**Constantine,** Hugh 1908- *Who 92*
**Constantine,** Jan Friedman 1948- *WhoAmL 92*
**Constantine,** Jay Winfred 1926- *AmMWSc 92*
**Constantine,** K C *IntAu&W 91, WrDr 92*
**Constantine,** Michael 1927- *WhoEnt 92*
**Constantine,** Murray *TwCSFW 91*
**Constantine,** Storm 1956- *TwCSFW 91*
**Constantine,** Virginia *WhoAmP 91*
**Constantine of Stanmore,** Baron *Who 92*
**Constantine-Paton,** Martha 1947- *AmMWSc 92*
**Constantineau,** Constance Juliette 1937- *WhoWest 92*
**Constantinescu,** Gheorghe M. 1932- *WhoMW 92*
**Constantini,** Louis Orlando 1948- *WhoFI 92*
**Constantinides,** Christos T 1931- *AmMWSc 92*
**Constantinides,** Dinos Demetrios 1929- *WhoEnt 92*
**Constantinides,** George Michael 1947- *WhoFI 92*
**Constantinides,** Panayiotis Pericleous 1953- *AmMWSc 92*
**Constantinides,** Paris 1919- *AmMWSc 92*
**Constantinides,** Spiros Minas 1932- *AmMWSc 92*
**Constantino,** William, Jr *WhoAmP 91*
**Constantinou,** Andreas I 1951- *AmMWSc 92*
**Constantinou,** Michalakis 1955- *AmMWSc 92*
**Constantinou,** Stavros Theophilos 1951- *WhoMW 92*
**Constantius II** 317-361 *EncEarC*
**Constantius I Chlorus** 250?-306 *EncEarC [port]*
**Constantopoulos,** George 1923- *AmMWSc 92*
**Constantz,** George Doran 1947- *AmMWSc 92*
**Constiner,** Merle 1902-1979 *TwCWW 91*
**Conston,** Henry Siegismund 1928- *WhoAmL 92*
**Consul,** Prem Chandra 1923- *AmMWSc 92*
**Conta,** Barbara Saunders *AmMWSc 92*
**Conta,** Bart J 1914- *AmMWSc 92*
**Contamine,** Claude Maurice 1929- *IntWW 91*
**Contamine,** Philippe 1932- *IntWW 91*
**Contandriopoulos,** Andre-Pierre 1943- *AmMWSc 92*
**Contant,** Alexis 1858-1918 *NewAmDM*
**Contarino,** John Leonardo 1966- *WhoEnt 92*
**Contario,** John Joseph 1944- *AmMWSc 92*
**Conte,** Arthur 1920- *IntWW 91*
**Conte,** Courtney Brennan 1956- *WhoEnt 92*
**Conte,** Frank Philip 1929- *AmMWSc 92*
**Conte,** James D 1959- *WhoAmP 91*
**Conte,** John *IntMPA 92*
**Conte,** John Salvatore 1932- *AmMWSc 92*
**Conte,** Lansana *IntWW 91*
**Conte,** Lou 1942- *WhoEnt 92*
**Conte,** Maryanne Micchelli 1959- *WhoEnt 92*
**Conte,** Rafael 1925- *WhoHisp 92*
**Conte,** Samuel D 1917- *AmMWSc 92*
**Conte,** Silvio O. d1991 *NewYTBS 91 [port]*
**Contee,** Carolyn Ann 1945- *WhoBlA 92*
**Conteh,** Abdulai Osman 1945- *IntWW 91*
**Contento,** Isobel 1940- *AmMWSc 92*
**Contesse,** Juan Pablo 1952- *WhoHisp 92*
**Conti,** Adam Jerome 1949- *WhoAmL 92*
**Conti,** Ann Patricia 1933- *WhoAmP 91*
**Conti,** Bill 1942- *IntMPA 92, WhoEnt 92*
**Conti,** Carl Joseph 1937- *WhoFI 92*
**Conti,** Daniel Joseph 1949- *WhoWest 92*
**Conti,** David Victor 1939- *WhoAmP 91*
**Conti,** Edmund *DrAPF 91*
**Conti,** Isabella 1942- *WhoFI 92*
**Conti,** James J 1930- *AmMWSc 92*
**Conti,** Joy Flowers 1948- *WhoAmL 92*
**Conti,** Leonardo 1900-1945 *EncTR 91 [port]*
**Conti,** Louis Thomas Moore 1949- *WhoAmL 92*
**Conti,** Mario Giuseppe 1934- *IntWW 91*
**Conti,** Mario Joseph *Who 92*
**Conti,** Paul Louis 1945- *WhoMW 92*
**Conti,** Peter Lino, Jr. 1955- *WhoEnt 92*
**Conti,** Peter Selby 1934- *AmMWSc 92*
**Conti,** Samuel F 1931- *AmMWSc 92*
**Conti,** Tom *IntWW 91*
**Conti,** Tom 1941- *IntMPA 92, WhoEnt 92*
**Conti,** Tom 1942- *Who 92*
**Conti,** Vincent R 1943- *AmMWSc 92*
**Contie,** Leroy John, Jr. 1920- *WhoAmL 92, WhoMW 92*
**Contillo,** Paul J 1929- *WhoAmP 91*
**Contino,** Vincent Nicholas 1952- *WhoFI 92, WhoMW 92*
**Conto,** Aristides 1931- *WhoWest 92*

**Contogeorgis,** George 1912- *Who 92*
**Contogouris,** Andreas P 1931- *AmMWSc 92*
**Contois,** David Ely 1928- *AmMWSc 92*
**Contois,** Joy Faith 1943- *WhoRel 92*
**Contopoulos,** George 1928- *AmMWSc 92*
**Contorinis,** Joseph 1964- *WhoWest 92*
**Contos,** Paul Anthony 1926- *WhoWest 92*
**Contoski,** Victor *DrAPF 91*
**Contractor,** Dinshaw N 1933- *AmMWSc 92*
**Contractor,** Farok 1946- *WhoFI 92*
**Contrera,** Beba *WhoHisp 92*
**Contrera,** Joseph Fabian 1938- *AmMWSc 92*
**Contreras,** Abraham 1965- *WhoHisp 92*
**Contreras,** Adela Marie 1960- *WhoHisp 92*
**Contreras,** Benigno, Jr. 1941- *WhoHisp 92*
**Contreras,** Carl Toby 1957- *WhoHisp 92*
**Contreras,** Carlos 1942- *WhoHisp 92*
**Contreras,** Carlos Arturo 1922- *WhoHisp 92*
**Contreras,** Don L. 1962- *WhoHisp 92*
**Contreras,** Esther Cajahuaringa 1962- *WhoHisp 92*
**Contreras,** Fernando, Jr. 1950- *WhoHisp 92*
**Contreras,** Frank R. 1942- *WhoHisp 92*
**Contreras,** Hiram *WhoHisp 92*
**Contreras,** James *WhoHisp 92*
**Contreras,** Joe W. *WhoHisp 92*
**Contreras,** Jose Antonio 1953- *WhoHisp 92*
**Contreras,** Luis A. 1952- *WhoHisp 92*
**Contreras,** Matias Ricardo 1946- *WhoHisp 92*
**Contreras,** Patricia Cristina 1956- *AmMWSc 92*
**Contreras,** Raoul Lowery 1941- *WhoHisp 92*
**Contreras,** Thomas Jose 1945- *AmMWSc 92, WhoHisp 92*
**Contreras,** Vincent John 1943- *WhoHisp 92*
**Contreras-Sweet,** Maria *WhoHisp 92*
**Contreras-Velasquez,** Simon Rafael 1956- *WhoHisp 92*
**Controulis,** John 1919- *AmMWSc 92*
**Converse,** Alvin O 1932- *AmMWSc 92*
**Converse,** C. M. 1935- *WhoEnt 92*
**Converse,** Frank *ScFEYrs*
**Converse,** Frank 1938- *ConTFT 9, IntMPA 92*
**Converse,** Frederick 1871-1940 *NewAmDM*
**Converse,** Harriet Maxwell 1836-1903 *BiInAmS*
**Converse,** James Clarence 1942- *AmMWSc 92*
**Converse,** Kenneth E 1930- *WhoAmP 91*
**Converse,** Philip E 1928- *IntAu&W 91, IntWW 91, WrDr 92*
**Converse,** Richard Hugo 1925- *AmMWSc 92*
**Converse,** Rob Roy McGregor 1917- *WhoAmP 91*
**Convertino,** Victor Anthony 1949- *AmMWSc 92*
**Convery,** F Richard 1932- *AmMWSc 92*
**Convery,** John Aloysius 1955- *WhoAmL 92*
**Convery,** Patrick George 1953- *WhoMW 92*
**Convery,** Robert James 1931- *AmMWSc 92*
**Convery,** Samuel V *WhoAmP 91*
**Convey,** Edward Michael 1939- *AmMWSc 92*
**Convey,** Frances 1956- *TwCPaSc*
**Convey,** John 1910- *AmMWSc 92*
**Convis,** Charles Lester, Jr. 1954- *WhoWest 92*
**Conviser,** Richard James 1938- *WhoFI 92, WhoMW 92*
**Convisser,** Martin 1932- *WhoAmP 91*
**Convy,** Bert d1991 *NewYTBS 91 [port]*
**Convy,** Bert 1934?-1991 *News 92-1*
**Conway,** Alan 1920- *WrDr 92*
**Conway,** Brian Evans 1927- *AmMWSc 92*
**Conway,** Carol Ann 1937- *WhoEnt 92*
**Conway,** Casey Anthony 1953- *WhoFI 92*
**Conway,** Celine *WrDr 92*
**Conway,** Charles D. 1947- *WhoFI 92*
**Conway,** Daniel Edward 1941- *WhoMW 92*
**Conway,** David 1939- *IntAu&W 91, WrDr 92*
**Conway,** David Martin 1935- *Who 92*
**Conway,** Denis L. 1946- *WhoFI 92*
**Conway,** Dennis David 1936- *WhoAmL 92*
**Conway,** Derek Leslie 1953- *Who 92*
**Conway,** Dominic J. *Who 92*
**Conway,** Dwight Colbur 1930- *AmMWSc 92*
**Conway,** E. Virgil 1929- *WhoFI 92*
**Conway,** Edward Daire, III 1937- *AmMWSc 92*
**Conway,** Edwin Michael 1934- *WhoRel 92*
**Conway,** Eugene Francis 1950- *WhoFI 92*
**Conway,** Frank Harrison 1913- *WhoAmL 92, WhoAmP 91*
**Conway,** French Hoge 1918- *WhoAmL 92*
**Conway,** Gary 1939- *IntMPA 92*
**Conway,** Gene Farris 1928- *AmMWSc 92*
**Conway,** Gerald A 1947- *WhoAmP 91*
**Conway,** Gerald Allen 1947- *WhoMW 92*
**Conway,** Gordon Richard 1938- *Who 92*
**Conway,** H D 1917- *AmMWSc 92*
**Conway,** Hertsell S 1914- *AmMWSc 92*
**Conway,** Hollis 1967- *BlkOlyM*
**Conway,** James Francis 1932- *WhoAmP 91*
**Conway,** James Joseph 1929- *AmMWSc 92*
**Conway,** James Stephen 1930- *WhoAmP 91*
**Conway,** Jeff 1948- *WhoAmP 91*
**Conway,** Jill Ker 1934- *CurBio 91 [port]*
**Conway,** John *TwCWW 91*
**Conway,** John Bell 1936- *AmMWSc 92*
**Conway,** John Bligh 1939- *AmMWSc 92*
**Conway,** John E. 1934- *WhoAmL 92, WhoWest 92*
**Conway,** John George, Jr 1922- *AmMWSc 92*
**Conway,** John Horton *IntWW 91, Who 92*
**Conway,** John Richard 1943- *AmMWSc 92*
**Conway,** John Thomas 1924- *WhoFI 92*
**Conway,** Joseph C, Jr 1939- *AmMWSc 92*
**Conway,** Joseph P. 1930- *WhoAmL 92*
**Conway,** Katherine 1867-1950 *BiDBrF 2*
**Conway,** Kathleen M. 1940- *WhoAmL 92*
**Conway,** Kenneth Edward 1943- *AmMWSc 92*
**Conway,** Kenneth Edwin 1934- *WhoMW 92*
**Conway,** Kevin 1942- *IntMPA 92, WhoEnt 92*
**Conway,** Kevin John 1951- *WhoAmL 92*
**Conway,** Louis Earl 1933- *WhoAmL 92*
**Conway,** Lynda Diane 1951- *WhoRel 92*
**Conway,** Lynn Ann 1938- *AmMWSc 92*
**Conway,** Mark Allyn 1957- *WhoMW 92*
**Conway,** Martin *Who 92*
**Conway,** Michael A 1947- *WhoIns 92*
**Conway,** Michael Campion 1946- *WhoEnt 92*
**Conway,** Michael Francis 1954- *WhoFI 92, WhoMW 92*
**Conway,** Michael J. 1945- *WhoWest 92*
**Conway,** Moncure D. 1832-1907 *BenetAL 91*
**Conway,** Morna Helen 1945- *WhoFI 92*
**Conway,** Neil James, III 1950- *WhoAmL 92, WhoMW 92*
**Conway,** Norman H 1942- *WhoAmP 91*
**Conway,** Paul Gary 1952- *AmMWSc 92*
**Conway,** Peter P 1936- *WhoIns 92*
**Conway,** Richard A 1931- *AmMWSc 92*
**Conway,** Richard Walter 1931- *AmMWSc 92*
**Conway,** Robert *WhoAmP 91*
**Conway,** Robert George, Jr. 1951- *WhoAmL 92*
**Conway,** Sari Elizabeth 1951- *Who 92*
**Conway,** Thomas F *WhoAmP 91*
**Conway,** Thomas William 1931- *AmMWSc 92*
**Conway,** Tim *LesBEnT 92*
**Conway,** Tim 1933- *IntMPA 92, WhoEnt 92*
**Conway,** Tina Marie *DrAPF 91*
**Conway,** Todd Avery 1967- *WhoEnt 92*
**Conway,** Tony *WhoEnt 92*
**Conway,** Troy *WrDr 92*
**Conway,** Wallace Xavier, Sr. 1920- *WhoBlA 92*
**Conway,** Walter Donald 1931- *AmMWSc 92*
**Conway,** William Michael 1949- *WhoAmL 92*
**Conway,** William Scott 1943- *AmMWSc 92*
**Conway de Macario,** Everly 1939- *AmMWSc 92*
**Conway Morris,** Simon 1951- *Who 92*
**Conwell,** Esther Marly 1922- *AmMWSc 92*
**Conwell,** Russell H. 1843-1925 *BenetAL 91*
**Conwell,** Russell Herman 1843-1925 *RelLAm 91*
**Conwill,** Giles A. 1944- *WhoBlA 92*
**Conyers,** Charles L. 1927- *WhoBlA 92*
**Conyers,** Emery Swinford 1939- *AmMWSc 92*
**Conyers,** James E. 1932- *WhoBlA 92*
**Conyers,** John, Jr. 1929- *AlmAP 92 [port], WhoAmP 91, WhoBlA 92, WhoMW 92*
**Conyers,** Nathan G. 1932- *WhoBlA 92*
**Conyne,** Richard Francis 1919- *AmMWSc 92*
**Conyne,** Robert Karlton 1944- *WhoMW 92*
**Conyngham** *Who 92*
**Conyngham,** Marquess 1924- *Who 92*
**Conyngham,** Barry 1944- *ConCom 92*
**Conzani,** Barbara Anne 1953- *WhoFI 92*
**Conzelman,** James Ken 1953- *WhoAmP 91*
**Conzett,** Homer Eugene 1920- *AmMWSc 92*
**Coobar,** Abdulmegid 1909- *IntWW 91*
**Cooch,** Frederick Graham 1928- *AmMWSc 92*
**Cooder,** Ry 1947- *WhoEnt 92*
**Coodley,** Eugene Leon 1920- *AmMWSc 92*
**Coogan,** Alan H 1929- *AmMWSc 92*
**Coogan,** Charles H, Jr 1908- *AmMWSc 92*
**Coogan,** Charles Owen 1932- *WhoMW 92*
**Coogan,** Daniel 1915-1980 *ConAu 134*
**Coogan,** Jackie 1914-1984 *FacFETw*
**Coogan,** Keith 1970- *IntMPA 92*
**Coogan,** Philip Shields 1938- *AmMWSc 92*
**Coogan,** Robert Arthur William 1929- *Who 92*
**Coogle,** Joseph Moore, Jr. 1933- *WhoFI 92*
**Coohill,** Thomas Patrick 1941- *AmMWSc 92*
**Cooil,** Bruce James 1914- *AmMWSc 92*
**Cook,** A Grace *BiInAmS*
**Cook,** Addison Gilbert 1933- *AmMWSc 92*
**Cook,** Alan 1922- *Who 92, WrDr 92*
**Cook,** Alan Frederick 1939- *AmMWSc 92*
**Cook,** Alan Hugh 1922- *IntWW 91*
**Cook,** Albert *DrAPF 91*
**Cook,** Albert 1925- *WrDr 92*
**Cook,** Albert John 1842-1916 *BiInAmS*
**Cook,** Albert Moore 1943- *AmMWSc 92*
**Cook,** Albert Thomas Thornton, Jr. 1940- *WhoFI 92, WhoWest 92*
**Cook,** Albert William 1922- *AmMWSc 92*
**Cook,** Alexander Burns 1924- *WhoMW 92*
**Cook,** Alfred Melville 1912- *Who 92*
**Cook,** Allan Fairchild, II 1922- *AmMWSc 92*
**Cook,** Ancel Eugene 1909- *AmMWSc 92*
**Cook,** Ann *Who 92*
**Cook,** Anthony Lacquise 1967- *WhoBlA 92*
**Cook,** Arthur Thompson 1923- *Who 92*
**Cook,** August Joseph 1926- *WhoAmL 92*
**Cook,** Barbara 1927- *NewAmDM*
**Cook,** Barnett C 1923- *AmMWSc 92*
**Cook,** Barrie 1929- *TwCPaSc*
**Cook,** Benjamin Jacob 1930- *AmMWSc 92*
**Cook,** Beryl 1926- *IntWW 91, TwCPaSc*
**Cook,** Beryl Frances 1926- *Who 92*
**Cook,** Beverly Susan 1957- *WhoAmP 91*
**Cook,** Bill 1896-1986 *FacFETw*
**Cook,** Billy Dean 1935- *AmMWSc 92*
**Cook,** Bob 1961- *ConAu 134*
**Cook,** Bobby Ray 1946- *WhoRel 92*
**Cook,** Bradford Eastman 1948- *WhoAmL 92*
**Cook,** Brian Francis 1933- *Who 92*
**Cook,** Brian Hartley K. *Who 92*
**Cook,** Brian Rayner 1945- *IntWW 91*
**Cook,** Bruce, Sr *WhoAmP 91*
**Cook,** Bruce Alan 1929- *WhoFI 92*
**Cook,** Bruce Edward, I 1944- *WhoFI 92*
**Cook,** Bruce William 1952- *WhoEnt 92*
**Cook,** Bryson Leitch 1948- *WhoAmL 92*
**Cook,** Camille Wright *WhoAmL 92*
**Cook,** Carl Edward 1952- *WhoRel 92*
**Cook,** Charles d1991 *NewYTBS 91*
**Cook,** Charles A. 1946- *WhoBlA 92*
**Cook,** Charles Alfred George 1913- *Who 92*
**Cook,** Charles Alston 1848-1916 *DcNCBi 1*
**Cook,** Charles Conway 1917- *WhoBlA 92*
**Cook,** Charles Davenport 1919- *AmMWSc 92*
**Cook,** Charles David 1935- *WhoAmP 91*
**Cook,** Charles Emerson 1926- *AmMWSc 92*
**Cook,** Charles F, Jr 1932- *AmMWSc 92*
**Cook,** Charles Falk 1928- *AmMWSc 92*
**Cook,** Charles Francis 1941- *WhoFI 92*
**Cook,** Charles Garland 1959- *AmMWSc 92*
**Cook,** Charles J 1923- *AmMWSc 92*
**Cook,** Charles Lowell 1927- *WhoRel 92*
**Cook,** Charles S 1938- *AmMWSc 92*
**Cook,** Charles Wayne 1914- *AmMWSc 92*
**Cook,** Charles William 1927- *AmMWSc 92*
**Cook,** Chris 1945- *WrDr 92*
**Cook,** Christopher 1959- *TwCPaSc*
**Cook,** Christopher Piers 1945- *IntAu&W 91*
**Cook,** Christopher Wymondham Rayner H 1938- *Who 92*
**Cook,** Clarence Edgar 1936- *AmMWSc 92*
**Cook,** Clarence Harlan 1925- *AmMWSc 92*
**Cook,** Clarence Sharp 1918- *AmMWSc 92*
**Cook,** Claude 1936- *WhoRel 92*
**Cook,** Clayton Henry 1912- *WhoAmP 91*
**Cook,** Cleland V 1933- *AmMWSc 92*
**Cook,** Coralie 18--?-1942 *NotBlAW 92 [port]*
**Cook,** Daniel Eugene 1957- *WhoMW 92*
**Cook,** David 1940- *ConNov 91, IntAu&W 91, WrDr 92*
**Cook,** David 1957- *TwCPaSc*
**Cook,** David Alastair 1942- *AmMWSc 92*
**Cook,** David Allan 1940- *AmMWSc 92*
**Cook,** David Bruce 1957- *WhoWest 92*
**Cook,** David E. 1940- *WhoMW 92*
**Cook,** David Edgar 1940- *AmMWSc 92*
**Cook,** David Edwin 1935- *AmMWSc 92*
**Cook,** David George 1937- *WhoFI 92*
**Cook,** David Greenfield 1941- *AmMWSc 92*
**Cook,** David Jerome 1957- *WhoMW 92*
**Cook,** David Lee 1952- *WhoAmL 92*
**Cook,** David Marsden 1938- *AmMWSc 92*
**Cook,** David Marvin 1953- *WhoAmL 92*
**Cook,** David Robert 1952- *AmMWSc 92, WhoMW 92*
**Cook,** David Russell 1922- *AmMWSc 92*
**Cook,** David Somerville 1944- *Who 92*
**Cook,** David Wallace 1962- *WhoAmL 92*
**Cook,** David Wilson 1939- *AmMWSc 92*
**Cook,** Delores Woodrum 1933- *WhoAmP 91*
**Cook,** Derek Edward 1931- *Who 92*
**Cook,** Desmond C 1949- *AmMWSc 92*
**Cook,** Don 1920- *IntAu&W 91, WrDr 92*
**Cook,** Donald Bowker 1917- *AmMWSc 92*
**Cook,** Donald E. 1928- *WhoWest 92*
**Cook,** Donald J 1920- *AmMWSc 92*
**Cook,** Donald Jack 1915- *AmMWSc 92*
**Cook,** Donald Latimer 1916- *AmMWSc 92*
**Cook,** Donald Lawrence 1940- *WhoAmL 92*
**Cook,** Donald Ray 1943- *WhoRel 92*
**Cook,** Doris Jean 1934- *WhoAmP 91*
**Cook,** Dorothy Mary *IntAu&W 91*
**Cook,** Douglas John 1944- *WhoRel 92*
**Cook,** Douglas Neilson 1929- *WhoEnt 92*
**Cook,** Dwight Ray 1951- *WhoAmL 92*
**Cook,** Earl Ferguson 1920- *AmMWSc 92*
**Cook,** Ebenezer 1672?-1732 *BenetAL 91*
**Cook,** Ebenezer Wake 1843-1926 *TwCPaSc*
**Cook,** Edward Hahn, II 1958- *WhoFI 92*
**Cook,** Edward Hoopes, Jr 1929- *AmMWSc 92*
**Cook,** Edwin Francis 1918- *AmMWSc 92*
**Cook,** Elisha, Jr. 1907- *IntMPA 92*
**Cook,** Elizabeth Anne 1926- *AmMWSc 92*
**Cook,** Elizabeth G. 1960- *WhoBlA 92*
**Cook,** Elizabeth Wilbanks 1956- *WhoAmL 92*
**Cook,** Ellsworth Barrett 1916- *AmMWSc 92*
**Cook,** Elton Straus 1909- *AmMWSc 92*
**Cook,** Ernest Ewart 1926- *AmMWSc 92*
**Cook,** Eugene A 1938- *WhoAmP 91*
**Cook,** Eugene Augustus 1938- *WhoAmL 92*
**Cook,** Everett L 1927- *AmMWSc 92*
**Cook,** Evin Lee 1918- *AmMWSc 92*
**Cook,** Fannie 1893-1949 *BenetAL 91*
**Cook,** Fielder *LesBEnT 92, WhoEnt 92*
**Cook,** Fielder 1923- *IntMPA 92*
**Cook,** Frances D 1945- *WhoAmP 91*
**Cook,** Francis 1935- *Who 92*
**Cook,** Francis John Granville 1913- *Who 92*
**Cook,** Frank Patrick 1920- *Who 92*
**Cook,** Frank Robert, Jr. 1923- *WhoBlA 92*
**Cook,** Frankland Shaw 1921- *AmMWSc 92*
**Cook,** Fred D 1921- *AmMWSc 92*
**Cook,** Fred Harrison, III 1952- *WhoBlA 92*
**Cook,** Freda Maxine 1928- *WhoWest 92*
**Cook,** Frederick 1865-1940 *FacFETw*
**Cook,** Frederick Ahrens 1950- *AmMWSc 92*
**Cook,** Frederick Lee 1940- *AmMWSc 92*
**Cook,** Frederick William *WhoRel 92*
**Cook,** G. Bradford 1937- *IntWW 91*
**Cook,** Garry David 1953- *WhoRel 92*
**Cook,** Gary Dean 1947- *WhoAmP 91*
**Cook,** Gary Dennis 1951- *WhoWest 92*
**Cook,** Gary L *WhoAmP 91*
**Cook,** Geoffrey *DrAPF 91*
**Cook,** George A 1944- *AmMWSc 92*
**Cook,** George Cram 1873-1924 *BenetAL 91*
**Cook,** George David 1925- *Who 92*
**Cook,** George Edward 1938- *AmMWSc 92*
**Cook,** George Hammell 1818-1889 *BiInAmS*
**Cook,** George Patrick 1947- *WhoAmL 92*
**Cook,** George Steveni L. *Who 92*
**Cook,** Georgia Mae 1929- *WhoAmP 91*
**Cook,** Gerald 1937- *AmMWSc 92*
**Cook,** Glen 1944- *IntAu&W 91, TwCSFW 91, WrDr 92*
**Cook,** Glen Andre 1954- *WhoAmL 92*
**Cook,** Glenn Melvin 1935- *AmMWSc 92*
**Cook,** Gordon Charles 1932- *IntWW 91*
**Cook,** Gordon Smith 1914- *AmMWSc 92*
**Cook,** Haney Judaea 1926- *WhoBlA 92*
**Cook,** Harland Keith 1913- *WhoMW 92*
**Cook,** Harold Andrew 1941- *AmMWSc 92*
**Cook,** Harold Dale 1924- *WhoAmL 92*
**Cook,** Harold J. 1946- *WhoBlA 92*
**Cook,** Harold James 1926- *Who 92*
**Cook,** Harold Rodney 1944- *WhoFI 92*
**Cook,** Harry Clayton, Jr. 1935- *WhoAmL 92*

**Cook,** Harry E, III 1935- *AmMWSc 92*
**Cook,** Harry Edgar 1939- *AmMWSc 92*
**Cook,** Henry George 1906- *Who 92*
**Cook,** Henry Home 1918- *Who 92*
**Cook,** Henry Lee, Sr. 1939- *WhoBlA 92*
**Cook,** Howard 1933- *AmMWSc 92*
**Cook,** J. Rowland 1942- *WhoAmL 92*
**Cook,** Jack E 1931- *AmMWSc 92*
**Cook,** James *DcAmImH*
**Cook,** James 1728-1779 *BenetAL 91, BlkwCEP*
**Cook,** James 1926- *WhoEnt 92*
**Cook,** James Arthur *AmMWSc 92*
**Cook,** James Arthur 1920- *AmMWSc 92*
**Cook,** James Dennis 1936- *AmMWSc 92*
**Cook,** James E. 1925- *WhoBlA 92*
**Cook,** James Edward 1963- *WhoAmP 91*
**Cook,** James Ellsworth 1923- *AmMWSc 92*
**Cook,** James H, Jr 1937- *AmMWSc 92*
**Cook,** James Harry 1959- *WhoAmL 92*
**Cook,** James Ivan 1925- *WhoRel 92*
**Cook,** James L 1946- *AmMWSc 92*
**Cook,** James Lee 1955- *WhoAmP 91*
**Cook,** James Marion 1941- *AmMWSc 92*
**Cook,** James Minton 1945- *AmMWSc 92*
**Cook,** James P. 1863-1928 *DcNCBi 1*
**Cook,** James Richard 1929- *AmMWSc 92*
**Cook,** James Robert 1941- *AmMWSc 92*
**Cook,** James William Dunbar 1921- *Who 92*
**Cook,** Jan 1939- *WhoEnt 92*
**Cook,** Jan 1955- *WhoAmP 91*
**Cook,** Jean M. 1948- *WhoMW 92*
**Cook,** Jeffery L 1952- *WhoAmP 91*
**Cook,** Jeffrey 1934- *WrDr 92*
**Cook,** John 1926- *Who 92*
**Cook,** John 1944- *WhoAmP 91*
**Cook,** John Alvin 1952- *WhoFI 92*
**Cook,** John Barry 1940- *Who 92*
**Cook,** John Carey 1917- *AmMWSc 92*
**Cook,** John Edward E. *Who 92*
**Cook,** John Jimerson 1944- *WhoFI 92*
**Cook,** John Keith 1935- *WhoRel 92*
**Cook,** John Manuel 1910- *IntWW 91, Who 92*
**Cook,** John P 1924- *AmMWSc 92*
**Cook,** John Philip 1947- *WhoFI 92*
**Cook,** John R 1943- *WhoIns 92*
**Cook,** John Samuel 1927- *AmMWSc 92*
**Cook,** John William 1946- *AmMWSc 92*
**Cook,** Joseph 1838-1901 *BiInAmS*
**Cook,** Joseph 1917- *Who 92*
**Cook,** Joseph Marion 1924- *AmMWSc 92, WhoMW 92*
**Cook,** Joyce Mitchell 1933- *WhoBlA 92*
**Cook,** Julian Abele, Jr. 1930- *WhoAmL 92, WhoBlA 92, WhoMW 92*
**Cook,** Karmen *DrAPF 91*
**Cook,** Kathleen Thomas 1960- *WhoMW 92*
**Cook,** Kelsey Donald 1952- *AmMWSc 92*
**Cook,** Kenneth Emery 1928- *AmMWSc 92*
**Cook,** Kenneth L 1934- *WhoIns 92*
**Cook,** Kenneth Lorimer 1915- *AmMWSc 92*
**Cook,** Kenneth Marlin 1920- *AmMWSc 92*
**Cook,** Kenneth R 1931- *AmMWSc 92*
**Cook,** Kenneth Totman 1950- *WhoAmL 92*
**Cook,** Kevin Bernhard 1966- *WhoMW 92*
**Cook,** Kwenam David 1922- *IntMPA 92*
**Cook,** L Scott 1948- *AmMWSc 92*
**Cook,** Ladda Banks 1935- *WhoBlA 92*
**Cook,** Lawrence C 1925- *AmMWSc 92*
**Cook,** Lawrence John 1949- *WhoMW 92*
**Cook,** LeAnn Cecilia 1950- *WhoAmL 92*
**Cook,** Leonard 1924- *AmMWSc 92*
**Cook,** LeRoy Franklin, Jr 1931- *AmMWSc 92*
**Cook,** Leslie Alan 1954- *WhoFI 92*
**Cook,** Leslie G 1914- *AmMWSc 92*
**Cook,** Lisa Ann 1960- *WhoAmP 91*
**Cook,** Lisle M 1936- *WhoAmP 91*
**Cook,** Liz *DrAPF 91*
**Cook,** Lloyd E, Sr 1928- *WhoAmP 91*
**Cook,** Lodwrick M. 1928- *IntWW 91*
**Cook,** Lodwrick Monroe 1928- *WhoFI 92, WhoWest 92*
**Cook,** Lyle Edwards 1918- *WhoWest 92*
**Cook,** Lyn *WrDr 92*
**Cook,** Lynette Rene 1961- *WhoWest 92*
**Cook,** Lynn *IntAu&W 91X*
**Cook,** Margaret E. 1960- *WhoMW 92*
**Cook,** Marie Mildred 1939- *AmMWSc 92*
**Cook,** Mark 1942- *WrDr 92*
**Cook,** Mark Eric 1956- *AmMWSc 92*
**Cook,** Marsha Eichenberg 1943- *WhoRel 92*
**Cook,** Mary Louise 1933- *WhoAmP 91*
**Cook,** Mary Murray 1936- *WhoBlA 92*
**Cook,** Mary Rozella 1936- *AmMWSc 92*
**Cook,** Mattie 1921- *WhoBlA 92*
**Cook,** Maurice Gayle 1932- *AmMWSc 92*
**Cook,** Melville *Who 92*
**Cook,** Melvin Alonzo 1911- *AmMWSc 92*
**Cook,** Melvin Garfield 1940- *WhoWest 92*
**Cook,** Merrill Alonzo 1946- *WhoAmP 91*
**Cook,** Michael 1933- *IntAu&W 91, WrDr 92*
**Cook,** Michael Anthony 1956- *WhoFI 92*
**Cook,** Michael Arnold 1944- *AmMWSc 92*
**Cook,** Michael David 1953- *WhoWest 92*
**Cook,** Michael Harry 1947- *WhoAmL 92*
**Cook,** Michael John 1930- *Who 92*
**Cook,** Michael Lewis 1944- *WhoAmL 92*
**Cook,** Michael Lyles 1946- *WhoEnt 92*
**Cook,** Michael Miller 1945- *AmMWSc 92*
**Cook,** Michael Wayne 1945- *WhoMW 92*
**Cook,** Nancy W 1936- *WhoAmP 91*
**Cook,** Nathan Henry 1925- *AmMWSc 92*
**Cook,** Nathan Howard 1939- *AmMWSc 92, WhoBlA 92*
**Cook,** Neville G W *AmMWSc 92*
**Cook,** Noel Robert 1937- *WhoFI 92*
**Cook,** Norma Baker *WhoFI 92*
**Cook,** Norman Charles 1906- *Who 92*
**Cook,** Norman Edgar 1920- *IntAu&W 91, Who 92*
**Cook,** Oscar d1952 *ScFEYrs*
**Cook,** Pat *Who 92*
**Cook,** Paul *DrAPF 91*
**Cook,** Paul Derek 1934- *Who 92*
**Cook,** Paul Fabyan 1946- *AmMWSc 92*
**Cook,** Paul J. 1942- *WhoEnt 92*
**Cook,** Paul L. 1925- *WhoMW 92*
**Cook,** Paul Laverne 1925- *AmMWSc 92*
**Cook,** Paul M. *WhoWest 92*
**Cook,** Paul M 1924- *AmMWSc 92*
**Cook,** Paul Pakes, Jr 1927- *AmMWSc 92*
**Cook,** Peter *DcTwDes*
**Cook,** Peter 1937- *FacFETw, IntMPA 92*
**Cook,** Peter 1943- *IntWW 91*
**Cook,** Peter Edward 1937- *IntAu&W 91, IntWW 91, Who 92*
**Cook,** Peter John 1938- *Who 92*
**Cook,** Petronelle Marguerite Mary 1925- *IntAu&W 91*
**Cook,** Philip 1925- *WhoAmL 92*
**Cook,** Philip J. 1946- *ConAu 133*
**Cook,** Philip Jackson 1946- *WhoFI 92*
**Cook,** Philip James 1960- *WhoEnt 92*
**Cook,** Philip W 1936- *AmMWSc 92*
**Cook,** Ralph D. 1934- *WhoWest 92*
**Cook,** Ralph Richard 1939- *WhoMW 92*
**Cook,** Ray 1947- *WhoMW 92*
**Cook,** Ray Lewis 1904- *AmMWSc 92*
**Cook,** Reginald 1918- *Who 92*
**Cook,** Richard *IntMPA 92*
**Cook,** Richard 1947- *TwCPaSc*
**Cook,** Richard Alfred 1942- *AmMWSc 92*
**Cook,** Richard Arthur 1908- *Who 92*
**Cook,** Richard James 1947- *AmMWSc 92*
**Cook,** Richard Kaufman 1910- *AmMWSc 92*
**Cook,** Richard Sherrard 1921- *AmMWSc 92*
**Cook,** Robert Andrew d1991 *NewYTBS 91 [port]*
**Cook,** Robert Andrew 1912-1991 *ConAu 133*
**Cook,** Robert Bigham, Jr 1944- *AmMWSc 92*
**Cook,** Robert Bruce, Jr. 1943- *WhoRel 92*
**Cook,** Robert Crossland 1947- *AmMWSc 92*
**Cook,** Robert D 1936- *AmMWSc 92*
**Cook,** Robert Douglas 1941- *AmMWSc 92*
**Cook,** Robert Edward 1925- *WhoFI 92*
**Cook,** Robert Edward 1927- *AmMWSc 92*
**Cook,** Robert Edward 1946- *AmMWSc 92*
**Cook,** Robert Finlayson 1946- *IntWW 91, Who 92*
**Cook,** Robert Francis Leonard 1939- *Who 92*
**Cook,** Robert H. 1937- *WhoMW 92*
**Cook,** Robert Harry 1941- *AmMWSc 92*
**Cook,** Robert James 1937- *AmMWSc 92*
**Cook,** Robert James 1950- *AmMWSc 92*
**Cook,** Robert John 1951- *WhoMW 92*
**Cook,** Robert Joseph 1937- *WhoAmP 91*
**Cook,** Robert Lee 1936- *AmMWSc 92*
**Cook,** Robert Manuel 1909- *IntWW 91, Who 92*
**Cook,** Robert Merold 1930- *AmMWSc 92*
**Cook,** Robert Neal 1940- *AmMWSc 92*
**Cook,** Robert Nevin 1912- *WhoAmL 92*
**Cook,** Robert Patterson 1947- *AmMWSc 92*
**Cook,** Robert Sewell 1929- *AmMWSc 92*
**Cook,** Robert Thomas 1937- *AmMWSc 92*
**Cook,** Robert William 1955- *WhoFI 92*
**Cook,** Robin *Who 92*
**Cook,** Robin 1931- *IntAu&W 91, WrDr 92*
**Cook,** Rodney Mims 1924- *WhoAmP 91*
**Cook,** Roger 1949- *WhoAmL 92*
**Cook,** Ron *WhoAmP 91*
**Cook,** Ronald Dean 1963- *WhoAmL 92, WhoFI 92*
**Cook,** Ronald Frank 1939- *AmMWSc 92*
**Cook,** Ronald J. *WhoRel 92*
**Cook,** Roy *ConAu 36NR*
**Cook,** Rufus 1936- *WhoBlA 92*
**Cook,** Russell Lynn 1954- *WhoRel 92*
**Cook,** Ruth E 1929- *WhoAmP 91*
**Cook,** Sallie Bell 1936- *WhoAmP 91*
**Cook,** Samuel DuBois 1928- *WhoBlA 92*
**Cook,** Samuel Ronald, Jr. 1945- *WhoAmL 92*
**Cook,** Sharon Evonne 1941- *WhoWest 92*
**Cook,** Shirl Eldon 1918- *AmMWSc 92*
**Cook,** Smalley Mike 1939- *WhoBlA 92*
**Cook,** Staley Albright 1895-1966 *DcNCBi 1*
**Cook,** Stanley 1922- *ConPo 91, IntAu&W 91, WrDr 92*
**Cook,** Stanley Joseph 1935- *WhoWest 92*
**Cook,** Stanton Arnold 1929- *AmMWSc 92*
**Cook,** Stanton R. 1925- *IntWW 91, WhoMW 92*
**Cook,** Stephen Arthur 1939- *AmMWSc 92, IntWW 91*
**Cook,** Stephen Champlin 1915- *WhoWest 92*
**Cook,** Stephen Hubbard 1960- *WhoAmL 92*
**Cook,** Stephen L 1941- *WhoAmP 91*
**Cook,** Stephen Ramond 1955- *WhoAmL 92*
**Cook,** Steven R. 1955- *WhoFI 92*
**Cook,** Stuart D 1936- *AmMWSc 92*
**Cook,** Sue 1951- *WhoMW 92*
**Cook,** Theodore Davis 1924- *AmMWSc 92*
**Cook,** Thomas Bratton, Jr 1926- *AmMWSc 92*
**Cook,** Thomas Charles 1938- *WhoAmP 91*
**Cook,** Thomas M 1931- *AmMWSc 92*
**Cook,** Thurlow Adrean 1939- *AmMWSc 92*
**Cook,** Timothy Lind 1958- *WhoEnt 92*
**Cook,** Timothy M. d1991 *NewYTBS 91*
**Cook,** Valerie 1953- *WhoAmP 91*
**Cook,** Vernice Wilhelmina Barnes 1919- *WhoBlA 92*
**Cook,** Vernon F 1927- *WhoAmP 91*
**Cook,** Victor 1929- *AmMWSc 92, WhoWest 92*
**Cook,** Victor Joseph, Jr. 1938- *WhoFI 92*
**Cook,** Vivian E *WhoAmP 91*
**Cook,** W W 1867-1933 *ScFEYrs*
**Cook,** Wallace Jeffery 1932- *WhoBlA 92*
**Cook,** Warren Ayer 1900- *AmMWSc 92, WhoMW 92*
**Cook,** Warren Lawrence 1925- *WrDr 92*
**Cook,** Wayne Robert 1953- *WhoEnt 92*
**Cook,** Wendell Sherwood 1916- *AmMWSc 92*
**Cook,** Will 1921-1964 *TwCWW 91*
**Cook,** Will Marion 1869-1944 *NewAmDM*
**Cook,** William A 1925- *WhoAmP 91*
**Cook,** William Birkett 1931- *Who 92*
**Cook,** William Boyd 1918- *AmMWSc 92*
**Cook,** William John 1929- *AmMWSc 92*
**Cook,** William Joseph 1949- *AmMWSc 92*
**Cook,** William Leslie, Jr. 1949- *WhoAmL 92*
**Cook,** William R, Jr 1927- *AmMWSc 92*
**Cook,** William Robert 1928- *WhoRel 92, WhoWest 92*
**Cook,** William Robert 1930- *AmMWSc 92*
**Cook,** William Wallace 1867-1933 *TwCWW 91*
**Cook,** William Wilburt 1933- *WhoBlA 92*
**Cook,** Yvonne Gober *WhoAmP 91*
**Cook,** Yvonne Macon 1936- *WhoBlA 92*
**Cook-Ioannidis,** Leslie Pamela 1946- *AmMWSc 92*
**Cook-Lynn,** Elizabeth *DrAPF 91*
**Cook-Lynn,** Elizabeth 1930- *ConAu 133*
**Cooke,** Alexander Hamilton 1941- *WhoAmL 92*
**Cooke,** Alexander Macdougall 1899- *Who 92*
**Cooke,** Alfred Alistair 1908- *WhoEnt 92*
**Cooke,** Alistair *LesBEnT 92 [port]*
**Cooke,** Alistair 1908- *BenetAL 91, ConAu 34NR, FacFETw, IntAu&W 91, IntMPA 92, IntWW 91, Who 92, WrDr 92*
**Cooke,** Ann *ConAu 36NR*
**Cooke,** Anna L. *WhoBlA 92*
**Cooke,** Annette Mary 1946- *WhoAmP 91*
**Cooke,** Anson Richard 1926- *AmMWSc 92*
**Cooke,** Anthony John 1927- *Who 92*
**Cooke,** Arnold 1906- *ConCom 92*
**Cooke,** Arthur *TwCSFW 91*
**Cooke,** Audre Pinny 1923- *WhoAmP 91*
**Cooke,** Bernard 1922- *WrDr 92*
**Cooke,** Bernard J. 1922- *ConAu 34NR*
**Cooke,** Brian 1935- *Who 92*
**Cooke,** Brian Ernest Dudley 1920- *Who 92*
**Cooke,** Cecil d1991 *Who 92N*
**Cooke,** Charles C 1916- *AmMWSc 92*
**Cooke,** Charles Fletcher F. *Who 92*
**Cooke,** Charles Mather 1844-1920 *DcNCBi 1*
**Cooke,** Charles Robert 1929- *AmMWSc 92*
**Cooke,** Cynthia Felicity Joan 1919- *Who 92*
**Cooke,** David 1935- *Who 92*
**Cooke,** David Frederick 1948- *WhoMW 92*
**Cooke,** David Wayne 1947- *AmMWSc 92*
**Cooke,** Dean William 1931- *AmMWSc 92*
**Cooke,** Derry Douglas 1937- *AmMWSc 92*
**Cooke,** Edward Francis, Jr. 1953- *WhoFI 92*
**Cooke,** Elbert Ronald, III 1963- *WhoRel 92*
**Cooke,** Francis W 1934- *AmMWSc 92*
**Cooke,** Fred 1936- *AmMWSc 92*
**Cooke,** G. Dennis 1937- *WhoMW 92*
**Cooke,** George Dennis 1937- *AmMWSc 92*
**Cooke,** George Venables 1918- *Who 92*
**Cooke,** George William 1916- *IntWW 91, Who 92*
**Cooke,** Gilbert Andrew 1923- *Who 92*
**Cooke,** Gloria Dedrick 1932- *WhoMW 92*
**Cooke,** Gwendolyn J 1943- *WhoAmP 91*
**Cooke,** Harlan Walter 1936- *WhoRel 92*
**Cooke,** Helen Joan 1943- *AmMWSc 92*
**Cooke,** Henry Charles 1913- *AmMWSc 92*
**Cooke,** Herbert Basil Sutton 1915- *AmMWSc 92, IntWW 91*
**Cooke,** Holland 1950- *WhoEnt 92*
**Cooke,** Ian McLean 1933- *AmMWSc 92*
**Cooke,** J David 1939- *AmMWSc 92*
**Cooke,** J Esten 1830-1886 *ScFEYrs*
**Cooke,** Jack Kent 1912- *WhoWest 92*
**Cooke,** Jacob E 1924- *ConAu 34NR*
**Cooke,** Jacob Ernest 1924- *WrDr 92*
**Cooke,** James Alan 1962- *WhoMW 92*
**Cooke,** James Allen 1948- *WhoWest 92*
**Cooke,** James Barry 1915- *AmMWSc 92*
**Cooke,** James Louis 1929- *AmMWSc 92*
**Cooke,** James Robert 1939- *AmMWSc 92*
**Cooke,** James Wallace 1812-1869 *DcNCBi 1*
**Cooke,** Jean 1927- *TwCPaSc [port]*
**Cooke,** Jean Esme Oregon 1927- *IntWW 91, Who 92*
**Cooke,** Jeffrey Allen 1945- *WhoAmL 92*
**Cooke,** Jeremy Lionel 1949- *Who 92*
**Cooke,** Jim 1950- *WhoEnt 92*
**Cooke,** John Arthur 1943- *Who 92*
**Cooke,** John Byrne 1940- *WhoEnt 92*
**Cooke,** John Cooper 1939- *AmMWSc 92*
**Cooke,** John Esten 1830-1886 *BenetAL 91*
**Cooke,** John Estes *ConAu 133*
**Cooke,** John Franklin 1946- *WhoIns 92*
**Cooke,** John Nigel Carlyle 1922- *Who 92*
**Cooke,** John Rogers 1833-1891 *DcNCBi 1*
**Cooke,** Joseph *Who 92*
**Cooke,** Josiah Parsons, Jr 1827-1894 *BiInAmS*
**Cooke,** Karen *WhoAmP 91*
**Cooke,** Kenneth *Who 92*
**Cooke,** Kenneth Lloyd 1925- *AmMWSc 92*
**Cooke,** Lawrence Henry 1914- *WhoAmL 92*
**Cooke,** Lee 1944- *WhoAmP 91*
**Cooke,** Lloyd M. 1916- *WhoBlA 92*
**Cooke,** Lloyd Miller 1916- *AmMWSc 92*
**Cooke,** Lot Howell 1952- *WhoAmL 92*
**Cooke,** Manning Patrick, Jr 1941- *AmMWSc 92*
**Cooke,** Marian Goppert 1923- *WhoWest 92*
**Cooke,** Mark Grisham 1954- *WhoRel 92*
**Cooke,** Marvin Lee 1947- *WhoRel 92*
**Cooke,** Michael Thomas 1963- *WhoAmL 92*
**Cooke,** Nellie 1948- *WhoBlA 92*
**Cooke,** Norman E 1922- *AmMWSc 92*
**Cooke,** Patrick Joseph *Who 92*
**Cooke,** Paul Phillips 1917- *WhoBlA 92*
**Cooke,** Peter *Who 92*
**Cooke,** Peter Hayman 1943- *AmMWSc 92*
**Cooke,** Peter Maurice 1927- *Who 92*
**Cooke,** Philip Pendleton 1816-1850 *BenetAL 91*
**Cooke,** Philip St. George 1809-1895 *BenetAL 91*
**Cooke,** Randle Henry 1930- *Who 92*
**Cooke,** Richard A 1954- *AmMWSc 92*
**Cooke,** Richard Kenneth 1917- *Who 92*
**Cooke,** Robert Clark *AmMWSc 92*
**Cooke,** Robert E 1920- *AmMWSc 92*
**Cooke,** Robert Phillip 1936- *WhoMW 92*
**Cooke,** Robert Sanderson 1944- *AmMWSc 92*
**Cooke,** Robert Wayne 1927- *WhoRel 92*
**Cooke,** Robin 1926- *Who 92*
**Cooke,** Robin Brunskill 1926- *IntWW 91*
**Cooke,** Roger 1940- *AmMWSc 92*
**Cooke,** Roger Anthony 1948- *WhoAmL 92*
**Cooke,** Roger Arnold 1939- *Who 92*
**Cooke,** Roger Lee 1942- *AmMWSc 92*
**Cooke,** Roger Malcolm 1945- *Who 92*
**Cooke,** Ron Charles 1947- *AmMWSc 92*
**Cooke,** Ronald Urwick 1941- *Who 92*
**Cooke,** Rose Terry 1827-1892 *BenetAL 91*
**Cooke,** Roy 1930- *Who 92*
**Cooke,** Sam 1935-1964 *NewAmDM*
**Cooke,** Samuel Leonard 1931- *AmMWSc 92*
**Cooke,** Stephen DeWitt 1953- *WhoAmL 92*
**Cooke,** Susan Marie 1945- *WhoAmL 92*
**Cooke,** T Derek V 1938- *AmMWSc 92*
**Cooke,** Terence J. 1921-1983 *RelLAm 91*
**Cooke,** Theodore Frederic 1913- *AmMWSc 92*
**Cooke,** Thomas Fitzpatrick 1911- *Who 92*

**Cooke**, Thomas H., Jr. 1929- WhoBlA 92
**Cooke**, Thornton, II 1928- WhoIns 92
**Cooke**, Victor Alexander 1920- Who 92
**Cooke**, Wells Woodbridge 1858-1916 BiInAmS
**Cooke**, Wilce L 1939- WhoAmP 91, WhoBlA 92
**Cooke**, Wilhelmina Reuben 1946- WhoBlA 92
**Cooke**, William 1942- IntAu&W 91, WrDr 92
**Cooke**, William Branson 1927- WhoBlA 92
**Cooke**, William Bridge 1908- AmMWSc 92
**Cooke**, William Dewey 1811-1885 DcNCBi 1
**Cooke**, William Donald 1918- AmMWSc 92
**Cooke**, William Peter 1932- Who 92
**Cooke**, William Peyton, Jr 1934- AmMWSc 92
**Cooke-Priest**, Colin Herbert Dickinson 1939- Who 92
**Cookman**, Aubrey Oliver 1913- WhoAmP 91
**Cooks**, Johnie Earl 1958- WhoBlA 92
**Cooks**, Stoney 1943- WhoBlA 92
**Cooksey**, Bobby Joe 1942- WhoRel 92
**Cooksey**, Danny 1975- WhoEnt 92
**Cooksey**, David James Scott 1940- Who 92
**Cooksey**, Donald Arthur 1955- WhoWest 92
**Cooksey**, Frank C 1933- WhoAmP 91
**Cooksey**, John Charles 1941- WhoAmP 91
**Cooksey**, May Louise Greville 1878-1943 TwCPaSc
**Cooksley**, Clarence Harrington d1991 Who 92N
**Cookson**, Alan Howard 1939- AmMWSc 92
**Cookson**, Catherine 1906- IntAu&W 91, IntWW 91, WrDr 92
**Cookson**, Catherine Ann 1906- Who 92
**Cookson**, Francis Bernard 1928- AmMWSc 92
**Cookson**, Jane 1939- WhoFI 92
**Cookson**, John T, Jr 1939- AmMWSc 92
**Cookson**, Michael John Blencowe 1927- Who 92
**Cookson**, Patricia Kay 1953- WhoAmL 92
**Cookson**, Peter 1913-1990 ConTFT 9
**Cookson**, Richard Clive 1922- IntWW 91, Who 92
**Cookson**, Roland Antony 1908- Who 92
**Cool**, Bingham Mercur 1918- AmMWSc 92
**Cool**, James Kevin 1959- WhoMW 92
**Cool**, Raymond Dean 1902- AmMWSc 92
**Cool**, Terrill A 1936- AmMWSc 92
**Coolahan**, John Carroll 1932- WhoAmP 91
**Coolbaugh**, Ronald Charles 1944- AmMWSc 92, WhoMW 92
**Coolbirth**, Ina Donna 1842-1928 BenetAL 91
**Coolbroth**, Frederick James 1951- WhoAmL 92
**Cooledge**, Richard Calvin 1943- WhoAmL 92
**Coolehan**, Daniel W. 1933- WhoWest 92
**Cooler**, Frederick William 1930- AmMWSc 92
**Cooley**, Adrian B, Jr 1928- AmMWSc 92
**Cooley**, Alan 1920- Who 92
**Cooley**, Albert Marvin 1908- AmMWSc 92
**Cooley**, Andrew Scott 1950- WhoWest 92
**Cooley**, David Lewis 1959- WhoWest 92
**Cooley**, Denton Arthur 1920- AmMWSc 92, IntWW 91
**Cooley**, Duane Stuart 1923- AmMWSc 92
**Cooley**, Edward H. 1922- WhoWest 92
**Cooley**, Harold Dunbar 1897-1974 DcNCBi 1
**Cooley**, Howard Dager 1934- WhoMW 92
**Cooley**, James F. 1926- WhoBlA 92
**Cooley**, James Franklin 1926- WhoRel 92
**Cooley**, James Hollis 1930- AmMWSc 92
**Cooley**, James Howard 1955- WhoRel 92
**Cooley**, James William 1926- AmMWSc 92
**Cooley**, John Dibrell 1963- WhoRel 92
**Cooley**, Keith Winston 1945- WhoMW 92
**Cooley**, Leland Frederick 1909- WhoWest 92
**Cooley**, Leroy Clark 1833-1916 BiInAmS
**Cooley**, Loralee Coleman 1943- WhoEnt 92
**Cooley**, Marie Szpiruk 1935- WhoFI 92
**Cooley**, Nathan J. 1924- WhoBlA 92
**Cooley**, Nelson Reede 1920- AmMWSc 92
**Cooley**, Peter DrAPF 91
**Cooley**, Richard Lewis 1940- AmMWSc 92
**Cooley**, Richard Pierce 1923- WhoWest 92
**Cooley**, Robert Earl 1930- WhoRel 92
**Cooley**, Robert Lee 1927- AmMWSc 92
**Cooley**, Spade 1910-1969 NewAmDM
**Cooley**, Steve 1947- WhoAmP 91
**Cooley**, Stone Deavours 1922- AmMWSc 92
**Cooley**, Thomas 1824-1898 RComAH
**Cooley**, Vanessa Lynne 1952- WhoBlA 92
**Cooley**, Wendy 1948- WhoAmL 92
**Cooley**, Wendy 1950- WhoAmP 91
**Cooley**, William C 1924- AmMWSc 92
**Cooley**, William Edward 1930- AmMWSc 92, WhoMW 92
**Cooley**, William Emory, Jr. 1941- WhoMW 92
**Cooley**, William Leslie 1946- WhoWest 92
**Cooley**, Wils LaHugh 1942- AmMWSc 92
**Coolidge**, Archibald Cary 1866-1928 AmPeW
**Coolidge**, Ardath Anders 1919- AmMWSc 92
**Coolidge**, Calvin 1872-1933 AmPolLe [port], BenetAL 91, FacFETw [port], RComAH
**Coolidge**, Clark DrAPF 91
**Coolidge**, Clark 1939- ConPo 91, IntAu&W 91, WrDr 92
**Coolidge**, Dane 1873-1940 TwCWW 91
**Coolidge**, Edwin Channing 1925- AmMWSc 92
**Coolidge**, Elizabeth Sprague 1864-1953 NewAmDM
**Coolidge**, Jacqueline Gunn 1958- WhoMW 92
**Coolidge**, Martha ReelWom
**Coolidge**, Martha 1946- IntMPA 92, WhoEnt 92
**Coolidge**, Mary Elizabeth Burroughs R. 1860-1945 WomSoc
**Coolidge**, Olivia 1908- WrDr 92
**Coolidge**, Olivia Ensor 1908- IntAu&W 91
**Coolidge**, Rita 1945- WhoEnt 92
**Coolidge**, Robert Tytus 1933- WhoRel 92
**Coolidge**, Susan BenetAL 91
**Coolidge**, Thomas B AmMWSc 92
**Coolidge**, William D 1873-1975 FacFETw
**Cooling**, Joyce Concetta WhoEnt 92
**Coolley**, Ronald B. 1946- WhoAmL 92
**Coolman**, Timothy Allen 1959- WhoMW 92
**Cools**, Andre 1927- IntWW 91
**Cools-Lartigue**, Louis 1905- Who 92
**Coombe**, George William, Jr. 1925- IntWW 91, WhoFI 92
**Coombe**, Gerald Hugh 1925- Who 92
**Coombe**, John Davis 1946- WhoAmL 92
**Coombe**, Michael Rew 1930- Who 92
**Coombe**, Richard Irwin 1942- WhoAmP 91
**Coombes**, Charles Allan 1934- AmMWSc 92
**Coombes**, Keva Christopher 1949- Who 92
**Coombes**, Terri Lee 1954- WhoAmP 91
**Coombs**, Anthony Michael Vincent 1952- Who 92
**Coombs**, Bertha I. 1961- WhoHisp 92
**Coombs**, Camilla H 1944- WhoAmP 91
**Coombs**, C'Ceal Phelps WhoWest 92
**Coombs**, Charles I. 1914- ConAu 36NR
**Coombs**, Chick ConAu 36NR
**Coombs**, Derek Michael 1937- Who 92
**Coombs**, Douglas Saxon 1924- IntWW 91
**Coombs**, Douglas Stafford 1924- Who 92
**Coombs**, Fletcher 1924- WhoBlA 92
**Coombs**, Gary Brian 1948- WhoWest 92
**Coombs**, Harry James 1935- WhoBlA 92
**Coombs**, Herbert Cole 1906- IntWW 91, Who 92
**Coombs**, Howard A 1906- AmMWSc 92
**Coombs**, Jim Le 1964- WhoWest 92
**Coombs**, Margery Chalifoux 1945- AmMWSc 92
**Coombs**, Orde WhoBlA 92
**Coombs**, Patricia WrDr 92
**Coombs**, Patricia 1926- IntAu&W 91
**Coombs**, Peter Bertram 1928- Who 92
**Coombs**, Peter Michael 1940- WhoWest 92
**Coombs**, Peter Richard 1951- WhoAmP 91
**Coombs**, Philip 1915- WrDr 92
**Coombs**, Philip H. 1915- IntWW 91
**Coombs**, Robert Mowbray 1951- WhoFI 92
**Coombs**, Robert Royston Amos 1921- IntWW 91, Who 92
**Coombs**, Robert Victor 1937- AmMWSc 92
**Coombs**, Simon Christopher 1947- Who 92
**Coombs**, William, Jr 1924- AmMWSc 92
**Coombs**, William Elmer 1911- WhoAmL 92, WhoAmP 91, WhoWest 92
**Coomer**, Joe DrAPF 91
**Coomer**, Joe 1958- WrDr 92
**Coomer**, Joyce Mae 1954- WhoEnt 92
**Coomer**, Kenneth H. 1953- WhoRel 92
**Coomes**, Edward Arthur 1909- AmMWSc 92
**Coomes**, Marguerite Wilton AmMWSc 92
**Coomes**, Richard Merril 1939- AmMWSc 92
**Coon**, Carleton S, Jr 1927- WhoAmP 91
**Coon**, Charles Lee 1868-1927 DcNCBi 1
**Coon**, Craig Nelson 1944- AmMWSc 92
**Coon**, Darryl Douglas 1941- AmMWSc 92
**Coon**, David Gordon 1952- WhoAmL 92
**Coon**, Gary M 1964- WhoAmP 91
**Coon**, J Frederick 1951- WhoIns 92
**Coon**, James Huntington 1914- AmMWSc 92
**Coon**, Jane A 1929- WhoAmP 91
**Coon**, Judith Arlene 1945- WhoEnt 92
**Coon**, Julian Barham 1939- AmMWSc 92
**Coon**, Julius Mosher 1910- AmMWSc 92
**Coon**, Ken WhoAmP 91
**Coon**, Lewis Hulbert 1925- AmMWSc 92
**Coon**, Marion Gene 1950- WhoRel 92
**Coon**, Minor J 1921- AmMWSc 92
**Coon**, Minor Jesser 1921- IntWW 91
**Coon**, Robert L AmMWSc 92
**Coon**, Robert William 1920- AmMWSc 92
**Coon**, Sidney Alan 1942- AmMWSc 92
**Coon**, Susan Louise 1952- WhoEnt 92
**Coon**, William Warner 1925- AmMWSc 92
**Coonce**, Harry B 1938- AmMWSc 92
**Coonelly**, Francis Xavier 1960- WhoAmL 92
**Coonen**, Karen Passler 1959- WhoEnt 92
**Cooner**, James Joseph 1939- WhoFI 92
**Cooney**, Charles Leland 1944- AmMWSc 92
**Cooney**, Daniel Timothy 1954- WhoMW 92
**Cooney**, David Francis 1954- WhoAmL 92
**Cooney**, David Ogden 1939- AmMWSc 92
**Cooney**, Ellen DrAPF 91
**Cooney**, Gary James 1960- WhoAmL 92
**Cooney**, George A., Jr. 1942- WhoAmL 92
**Cooney**, James E. d1991 NewYTBS 91
**Cooney**, Joan Ganz LesBEnT 92
**Cooney**, Joan Ganz 1929- IntMPA 92, WhoEnt 92
**Cooney**, John Anthony 1922- AmMWSc 92
**Cooney**, John Gerard 1952- WhoAmL 92
**Cooney**, John Gordon 1930- WhoAmL 92
**Cooney**, John Gordon, Jr. 1959- WhoAmL 92
**Cooney**, John Leo 1928- AmMWSc 92
**Cooney**, John Richardson 1942- WhoAmL 92
**Cooney**, Joseph Jude 1934- AmMWSc 92
**Cooney**, Leighton H, Jr 1944- WhoAmP 91
**Cooney**, Leslie Larkin 1949- WhoAmL 92
**Cooney**, Lynn Futch 1961- WhoAmL 92
**Cooney**, Marion Kathleen 1920- AmMWSc 92
**Cooney**, Michael Rodman 1954- WhoAmP 91
**Cooney**, Mike 1954- WhoWest 92
**Cooney**, Miriam Patrick 1925- AmMWSc 92
**Cooney**, Patrick 1931- IntWW 91
**Cooney**, Patrick Ronald 1934- WhoMW 92, WhoRel 92
**Cooney**, Ray 1932- IntAu&W 91, WrDr 92
**Cooney**, Raymond George Alfred 1932- Who 92
**Cooney**, Robert John 1934- WhoAmL 92
**Cooney**, Rory 1952- ConMus 6 [port]
**Cooney**, Thomas O. 1944- WhoAmL 92
**Cooney**, Timothy J, Jr WhoAmP 91
**Cooney**, Vern Maurice 1937- WhoWest 92
**Cooney**, William J. 1929- WhoAmL 92
**Cooney**, William Joseph 1937- WhoAmL 92
**Cooney**, Wilson Charles 1934- WhoIns 92
**Coonley**, Thomas Paul 1942- WhoFI 92
**Coons**, Edwin Thaine 1943- WhoFI 92
**Coons**, Eldo Jess, Jr. 1924- WhoFI 92
**Coons**, Fred F 1923- AmMWSc 92
**Coons**, Harold Meredith 1911- WhoAmP 91
**Coons**, John E. 1929- WhoAmL 92
**Coons**, John Max 1945- WhoWest 92
**Coons**, Lewis Bennion 1938- AmMWSc 92
**Coons**, Marion McDowell 1915- WhoFI 92
**Coons**, William Dean 1959- WhoFI 92
**Coonts**, Stephen 1946- ConAu 133
**Coontz**, Morris Stephen 1946- WhoAmL 92
**Coontz**, Stephanie Jean 1944- WhoWest 92
**Coony**, Thomas M WhoAmP 91
**Coop**, Eddie Paul 1946- WhoAmP 91
**Coop**, Louise C 1913- WhoAmP 91
**Coop**, Maurice 1907- Who 92
**Coope**, John Arthur Robert 1931- AmMWSc 92
**Cooper** Who 92
**Cooper**, Aaron David 1928- AmMWSc 92
**Cooper**, Alan Who 92
**Cooper**, Alan John 1942- WhoAmL 92
**Cooper**, Albert, Sr. 1934- WhoBlA 92
**Cooper**, Albert Samuel 1905- Who 92
**Cooper**, Alcie Lee, Jr. 1939- WhoFI 92
**Cooper**, Alfred Donald 1946- WhoAmL 92
**Cooper**, Alfred Egerton 1883-1974 TwCPaSc
**Cooper**, Alfred J 1913- AmMWSc 92
**Cooper**, Alfred R, Jr 1924- AmMWSc 92
**Cooper**, Alfred William Madison 1932- AmMWSc 92
**Cooper**, Alice 1945- NewAmDM
**Cooper**, Alice 1948- WhoEnt 92
**Cooper**, Allen D 1942- AmMWSc 92
**Cooper**, Almeta E. 1950- WhoBlA 92
**Cooper**, Andrew Ramsden 1902- Who 92
**Cooper**, Anna J. 1858?-1964 NotBlAW 92 [port]
**Cooper**, Anne 1935- WhoAmP 91
**Cooper**, Arthur Joseph L 1946- AmMWSc 92
**Cooper**, Arthur Wells 1931- AmMWSc 92
**Cooper**, Augusta Mosley 1903- WhoBlA 92
**Cooper**, Austin 1890- TwCPaSc
**Cooper**, Austin Morris 1959- WhoWest 92
**Cooper**, B Anne WhoIns 92
**Cooper**, Barbara Jean WhoBlA 92
**Cooper**, Ben 1933- IntMPA 92
**Cooper**, Benjamin Stubbs 1941- AmMWSc 92
**Cooper**, Bernard DrAPF 91
**Cooper**, Bernard 1951- ConAu 134
**Cooper**, Bernard A 1928- AmMWSc 92
**Cooper**, Bernard Richard 1936- AmMWSc 92
**Cooper**, Beryl Phyllis 1927- Who 92
**Cooper**, Bill WhoAmP 91
**Cooper**, Bobbie Morgan 1913- WhoWest 92
**Cooper**, Bobby G. 1938- WhoBlA 92
**Cooper**, Bonnie Sue 1934- WhoAmP 91
**Cooper**, Brian 1919- WrDr 92
**Cooper**, Brian Newman 1919- IntAu&W 91
**Cooper**, Brown 1957- WhoEnt 92
**Cooper**, Bryan 1932- IntAu&W 91, WrDr 92
**Cooper**, Candace D. 1948- WhoBlA 92
**Cooper**, Candace Lucretia 1961- WhoBlA 92
**Cooper**, Carl 1919- AmMWSc 92
**Cooper**, Carol Ann 1940- WhoMW 92
**Cooper**, Carolyn Kraemer DrAPF 91
**Cooper**, Cary Lynn 1940- Who 92
**Cooper**, Cary Wayne 1939- AmMWSc 92
**Cooper**, Cecil 1922- AmMWSc 92
**Cooper**, Cecil 1949- WhoBlA 92
**Cooper**, Charles 1926- WhoEnt 92
**Cooper**, Charles Burleigh 1920- AmMWSc 92
**Cooper**, Charles Dewey 1924- AmMWSc 92
**Cooper**, Charles F 1924- AmMWSc 92, WhoWest 92
**Cooper**, Charles G. 1928- WhoFI 92
**Cooper**, Charles Justin 1952- WhoAmL 92
**Cooper**, Charles Kneeland, III 1953- WhoFI 92
**Cooper**, Charles Neilson 1935- WhoAmL 92
**Cooper**, Charles Richard 1946- WhoEnt 92
**Cooper**, Charles W. 1929- WhoBlA 92
**Cooper**, Charles William, Jr. 1931- WhoRel 92
**Cooper**, Christopher 1942- WrDr 92
**Cooper**, Clarence 1942- WhoBlA 92
**Cooper**, Clement Theodore 1930- WhoBlA 92
**Cooper**, Clifford Warren 1954- WhoFI 92
**Cooper**, Clive V. 1945- WhoWest 92
**Cooper**, Clyde James, Jr. 1931- WhoAmL 92
**Cooper**, Colin Symons 1926- IntAu&W 91, WrDr 92
**Cooper**, Constance Deloris WhoBlA 92
**Cooper**, Constance Marie 1952- WhoBlA 92
**Cooper**, Courtney Ryley 1886-1940 BenetAL 91, TwCWW 91
**Cooper**, Curt S. 1951- WhoMW 92
**Cooper**, Curtis V. WhoBlA 92
**Cooper**, Cynthia 1963- BlkOlyM
**Cooper**, Dale A 1958- AmMWSc 92
**Cooper**, Dan 1901-1965 DcTwDes
**Cooper**, Daneen Ravenell 1958- WhoBlA 92
**Cooper**, Daniel T 1961- WhoAmP 91
**Cooper**, Daniel Thomas 1964- WhoWest 92
**Cooper**, Darren Eugene 1960- WhoWest 92
**Cooper**, David WhoAmP 91
**Cooper**, David 1931-1986 FacFETw
**Cooper**, David 1952- TwCPaSc
**Cooper**, David B 1933- AmMWSc 92
**Cooper**, David Gordon 1947- AmMWSc 92
**Cooper**, David Samuel 1955- WhoAmL 92
**Cooper**, David Young 1847-1920 DcNCBi 1
**Cooper**, David Young 1924- AmMWSc 92
**Cooper**, Dean Fletcher 1954- WhoAmL 92
**Cooper**, Debra Lyn 1958- WhoMW 92
**Cooper**, Denise Marie 1956- WhoAmL 92
**Cooper**, Dennis 1953- ConAu 133
**Cooper**, Dennis R. 1952- WhoMW 92
**Cooper**, Derek 1925- WrDr 92
**Cooper**, Derek MacDonald 1925- IntAu&W 91, Who 92
**Cooper**, Dermot M F AmMWSc 92
**Cooper**, Diana 1892-1986 FacFETw
**Cooper**, Diane WhoRel 92

**Cooper,** Dolores G 1922- *WhoAmP 91*
**Cooper,** Dominic 1944- *IntAu&W 91, WrDr 92*
**Cooper,** Dona Hanks 1950- *WhoEnt 92*
**Cooper,** Donald Arthur 1930- *Who 92*
**Cooper,** Donald Edward 1952- *AmMWSc 92*
**Cooper,** Donald Russell 1917- *AmMWSc 92*
**Cooper,** Douglas 1911-1984 *FacFETw*
**Cooper,** Douglas Elhoff 1912- *AmMWSc 92*
**Cooper,** Douglas W 1942- *AmMWSc 92*
**Cooper,** Drucilla Hawkins 1950- *WhoBlA 92*
**Cooper,** Duane H 1923- *AmMWSc 92*
**Cooper,** Duff 1890-1954 *EncTR 91*
**Cooper,** Earl, II 1944- *WhoBlA 92*
**Cooper,** Earl Dana 1926- *AmMWSc 92*
**Cooper,** Edgar Mauney 1922- *WhoRel 92*
**Cooper,** Edmund 1926-1982 *TwCSFW 91*
**Cooper,** Edward L., Sr. *WhoBlA 92*
**Cooper,** Edward Sawyer 1926- *WhoBlA 92*
**Cooper,** Edwin Lowell 1936- *AmMWSc 92*
**Cooper,** Eileen 1953- *TwCPaSc*
**Cooper,** Elaine Janice 1937- *WhoMW 92*
**Cooper,** Elbert Nathan 1928- *WhoFI 92*
**Cooper,** Ellis 1921- *WhoRel 92*
**Cooper,** Elmer James 1920- *AmMWSc 92*
**Cooper,** Emerson Amenhotep 1924- *AmMWSc 92*
**Cooper,** Emmett E., Jr. 1921- *WhoBlA 92*
**Cooper,** Ernest, Jr. 1941- *WhoBlA 92*
**Cooper,** Ethel Thomas 1919- *WhoBlA 92*
**Cooper,** Eugene Perry 1915- *AmMWSc 92*
**Cooper,** Evelyn Kaye 1941- *WhoBlA 92*
**Cooper,** Farobag Homi 1957- *WhoEnt 92*
**Cooper,** Frank *BenetAL 91*
**Cooper,** Frank 1922- *Who 92*
**Cooper,** Franklin Seaney 1908- *AmMWSc 92*
**Cooper,** Frederick Eansor 1942- *WhoAmP 91*
**Cooper,** Frederick Howard Michael C. *Who 92*
**Cooper,** Frederick Michael 1944- *AmMWSc 92*
**Cooper,** Garrett 1904- *AmMWSc 92*
**Cooper,** Gary 1901-1961 *FacFETw*
**Cooper,** Gary Allan 1947- *WhoAmL 92*
**Cooper,** Gary Pettus 1933- *AmMWSc 92*
**Cooper,** Gary T. 1948- *WhoBlA 92*
**Cooper,** Geoffrey 1907- *Who 92*
**Cooper,** Geoffrey Kenneth 1949- *AmMWSc 92*
**Cooper,** Geoffrey Mitchell 1948- *AmMWSc 92*
**Cooper,** George 1925- *Who 92*
**Cooper,** George, IV 1942- *AmMWSc 92*
**Cooper,** George A. 1915- *Who 92*
**Cooper,** George Daniel 1923- *WhoWest 92*
**Cooper,** George Edward 1915- *Who 92*
**Cooper,** George Emery 1916- *AmMWSc 92*
**Cooper,** George Everett 1945- *AmMWSc 92*
**Cooper,** George Raymond 1916- *AmMWSc 92*
**Cooper,** George S 1914- *AmMWSc 92*
**Cooper,** George William 1928- *AmMWSc 92*
**Cooper,** George Wilson 1927- *WhoAmL 92*
**Cooper,** Gerald Rice 1914- *AmMWSc 92*
**Cooper,** Glenn Adair, Jr 1931- *AmMWSc 92*
**Cooper,** Gordon 1927- *FacFETw*
**Cooper,** Gordon Mayo 1925- *WhoFI 92*
**Cooper,** Gordon R., II 1941- *WhoBlA 92*
**Cooper,** Gregory Lee 1965- *WhoMW 92*
**Cooper,** Gustav Arthur 1902- *AmMWSc 92*
**Cooper,** Hal 1923- *IntMPA 92, WhoEnt 92*
**Cooper,** Hal Dean 1934- *WhoAmL 92*
**Cooper,** Helen *DrAPF 91*
**Cooper,** Henry *WrDr 92*
**Cooper,** Henry 1934- *Who 92*
**Cooper,** Henry Franklyn, Jr 1936- *AmMWSc 92*
**Cooper,** Henry S. F., Jr. *SmATA 65*
**Cooper,** Henry Spotswood Fenimore, Jr. 1933- *SmATA 65*
**Cooper,** Herbert A 1938- *AmMWSc 92*
**Cooper,** Homer Chassell 1923- *WhoAmP 91*
**Cooper,** Howard Gordon 1927- *AmMWSc 92*
**Cooper,** Howard K 1934- *AmMWSc 92*
**Cooper,** Hugh Adair 1937- *WhoRel 92*
**Cooper,** Ilene *SmATA 66*
**Cooper,** Imogen 1949- *IntWW 91, Who 92*
**Cooper,** Iris N. 1942- *WhoBlA 92*
**Cooper,** Irma Julian 1912- *WhoBlA 92*
**Cooper,** Irmgard M. 1946- *WhoBlA 92*
**Cooper,** Irving Ben 1902- *WhoAmL 92*
**Cooper,** Irving L. 1930- *WhoAmL 92*
**Cooper,** Irving S 1922-1985 *FacFETw*
**Cooper,** Irving Steiger 1882-1935 *RelLAm 91*
**Cooper,** J. California *WhoBlA 92*
**Cooper,** Jack Loring 1925- *AmMWSc 92*
**Cooper,** Jack Ross 1924- *AmMWSc 92*
**Cooper,** Jackie *LesBEnT 92*
**Cooper,** Jackie 1922- *ConAu 133, IntMPA 92, WhoEnt 92*
**Cooper,** James Alfred 1942- *AmMWSc 92*
**Cooper,** James Burgess 1954- *AmMWSc 92*
**Cooper,** James Erwin 1933- *AmMWSc 92*
**Cooper,** James Fenimore 1789-1851 *BenetAL 91, RComAH, ScFEYrs*
**Cooper,** James Graham 1830-1902 *BiInAmS*
**Cooper,** James Hayes Shofner 1954- *WhoAmP 91*
**Cooper,** James J 1924- *WhoAmP 91*
**Cooper,** James M, Jr. 1941- *WhoIns 92*
**Cooper,** James Randall 1960- *WhoWest 92*
**Cooper,** James William 1943- *AmMWSc 92*
**Cooper,** Jane *DrAPF 91*
**Cooper,** Jane 1924- *ConPo 91, WrDr 92*
**Cooper,** Jane Elizabeth 1937- *AmMWSc 92*
**Cooper,** Jane Todd *DrAPF 91*
**Cooper,** Janis Campbell 1947- *WhoMW 92*
**Cooper,** Jean Campbell 1905- *IntAu&W 91*
**Cooper,** Jean Saralee 1946- *WhoAmP 91*
**Cooper,** Jeanette Irene 1939- *WhoRel 92*
**Cooper,** Jeffery Bernard *WhoRel 92*
**Cooper,** Jeffrey 1950- *WhoAmL 92*
**Cooper,** Jeremy 1946- *WrDr 92*
**Cooper,** Jerome Gary 1936- *WhoAmP 91, WhoBlA 92*
**Cooper,** Jerry Ronald 1941- *WhoRel 92*
**Cooper,** Jerry W 1948- *WhoAmP 91*
**Cooper,** Jilly 1937- *IntAu&W 91, Who 92, WrDr 92*
**Cooper,** Jim 1954- *AlmAP 92 [port]*
**Cooper,** Joan Davies 1914- *Who 92*
**Cooper,** John 1922- *AmMWSc 92*
**Cooper,** John 1937- *AmMWSc 92*
**Cooper,** John Allen Dicks 1918- *AmMWSc 92, IntWW 91*
**Cooper,** John Arnold 1917- *WhoFI 92, WhoMW 92*
**Cooper,** John C, Jr 1936- *AmMWSc 92*
**Cooper,** John Charles *DrAPF 91*
**Cooper,** John Daniel 1949- *WhoRel 92*
**Cooper,** John Downey 1849-1921 *DcNCBi 1*
**Cooper,** John Joseph 1924- *WhoAmL 92*
**Cooper,** John Leslie 1933- *Who 92*
**Cooper,** John Milton 1940- *WrDr 92*
**Cooper,** John Montgomery 1881-1949 *FacFETw*
**Cooper,** John Neale 1938- *AmMWSc 92*
**Cooper,** John Niessink 1914- *AmMWSc 92*
**Cooper,** John Paul *WhoRel 92*
**Cooper,** John Philip 1923- *IntWW 91, Who 92*
**Cooper,** John Raymond 1931- *AmMWSc 92*
**Cooper,** John Robert 1940- *WhoFI 92*
**Cooper,** John Sherman 1901-1991 *CurBio 91N, NewYTBS 91 [port]*
**Cooper,** John Spencer 1933- *Who 92*
**Cooper,** John Wesley 1946- *AmMWSc 92*
**Cooper,** Jon Hugh 1940- *WhoEnt 92, WhoWest 92*
**Cooper,** Joseph *WhoBlA 92*
**Cooper,** Joseph 1912- *IntWW 91, Who 92*
**Cooper,** Joseph E 1921- *AmMWSc 92*
**Cooper,** Josephine H. 1936- *WhoBlA 92*
**Cooper,** Judith *DrAPF 91*
**Cooper,** Judson Merri 1931- *WhoAmP 91*
**Cooper,** Julius, Jr. 1944- *WhoBlA 92*
**Cooper,** Kathleen Bell 1945- *WhoFI 92*
**Cooper,** Keith Edward 1922- *AmMWSc 92*
**Cooper,** Keith Raymond 1951- *AmMWSc 92*
**Cooper,** Kelsy Brown 1898- *WhoBlA 92*
**Cooper,** Kenneth Dean 1943- *WhoWest 92*
**Cooper,** Kenneth Ernest 1903- *Who 92*
**Cooper,** Kenneth H *IntAu&W 91*
**Cooper,** Kenneth H. 1931- *ConAu 134*
**Cooper,** Kenneth James 1954- *WhoAmL 92*
**Cooper,** Kenneth Reginald 1931- *IntWW 91, Who 92*
**Cooper,** Kenneth Robert 1942- *WhoRel 92*
**Cooper,** Kenneth Willard 1912- *AmMWSc 92*
**Cooper,** Kent *DrAPF 91*
**Cooper,** Kent 1880-1965 *FacFETw*
**Cooper,** Kent Lynn 1945- *WhoWest 92*
**Cooper,** LaMoyne Mason 1931- *WhoBlA 92*
**Cooper,** Larry B. 1946- *WhoBlA 92*
**Cooper,** Larry Clark 1942- *WhoFI 92*
**Cooper,** Larry Russell 1934- *AmMWSc 92*
**Cooper,** Larry S. 1957- *WhoWest 92*
**Cooper,** Laurie A. 1952- *WhoAmL 92*
**Cooper,** Lawrence Allen 1948- *WhoAmL 92*
**Cooper,** Lee E., Jr. 1960- *WhoRel 92*
**Cooper,** Lee Pelham 1926- *WrDr 92*
**Cooper,** Leon N 1930- *AmMWSc 92, IntWW 91, Who 92, WhoFI 92*
**Cooper,** Leon Neil 1930- *FacFETw, WhoNob 90*
**Cooper,** Leonard Marvin 1931- *WhoAmL 92*
**Cooper,** Leslie Francis 1949- *WhoRel 92*
**Cooper,** Lettice 1897- *ConNov 91, IntAu&W 91, WrDr 92*
**Cooper,** Linda G. 1954- *WhoBlA 92*
**Cooper,** Lisa Ivy 1961- *WhoAmL 92*
**Cooper,** Lois Louise 1931- *WhoBlA 92*
**Cooper,** Louis Jacques B. *Who 92*
**Cooper,** Louis Zucker 1931- *AmMWSc 92*
**Cooper,** Lynn Dale 1932- *WhoRel 92*
**Cooper,** M. Scott 1950- *WhoAmL 92*
**Cooper,** M. Truman *DrAPF 91*
**Cooper,** Margaret Hardesty 1944- *AmMWSc 92*
**Cooper,** Margaret Jean Drummond 1922- *Who 92*
**Cooper,** Marilyn *WhoEnt 92*
**Cooper,** Marilyn P. 1943- *WhoMW 92*
**Cooper,** Martha Rose 1956- *WhoAmL 92*
**Cooper,** Martin 1928- *AmMWSc 92*
**Cooper,** Martin David 1945- *AmMWSc 92*
**Cooper,** Martin Jacob 1939- *AmMWSc 92*
**Cooper,** Mary Adrienne 1927- *WhoFI 92*
**Cooper,** Mary Anderson 1938- *WhoRel 92*
**Cooper,** Mary Weis 1942- *AmMWSc 92*
**Cooper,** Matthew N. 1914- *WhoBlA 92*
**Cooper,** Maudine R. 1941- *WhoBlA 92*
**Cooper,** Maurice Zealot 1908- *AmMWSc 92*
**Cooper,** Max Dale 1933- *AmMWSc 92*
**Cooper,** Melvin Wayne 1943- *AmMWSc 92*
**Cooper,** Merrill Pittman 1921- *WhoBlA 92*
**Cooper,** Michael *DrAPF 91*
**Cooper,** Michael Anthony 1936- *WhoAmL 92*
**Cooper,** Michael Edward 1945- *WhoAmL 92*
**Cooper,** Michael Gary 1954- *WhoBlA 92*
**Cooper,** Michael Jerome 1956- *WhoBlA 92*
**Cooper,** Miki Jean 1943- *WhoAmP 91*
**Cooper,** Miles Robert 1933- *AmMWSc 92*
**Cooper,** Milford J 1920- *WhoAmP 91*
**Cooper,** Morris Davidson 1943- *AmMWSc 92*
**Cooper,** Myles 1735-1785 *BenetAL 91*
**Cooper,** Neil R 1934- *AmMWSc 92*
**Cooper,** Nigel Cookson 1929- *Who 92*
**Cooper,** Norman George 1942- *WhoAmL 92*
**Cooper,** Norman John 1950- *AmMWSc 92*
**Cooper,** Norman S 1920- *AmMWSc 92*
**Cooper,** Patrick Graham Astley 1918- *Who 92*
**Cooper,** Paul 1926- *ConAu 34NR*
**Cooper,** Paul W 1929- *AmMWSc 92*
**Cooper,** Paulette 1945- *IntAu&W 91*
**Cooper,** Peggy Lou 1933- *WhoRel 92*
**Cooper,** Peter 1791-1883 *BenetAL 91, BiInAmS*
**Cooper,** Peter B 1936- *AmMWSc 92*
**Cooper,** Peter D 1940- *WhoIns 92*
**Cooper,** Philip John 1929- *Who 92*
**Cooper,** Phillip P. 1947- *WhoMW 92*
**Cooper,** R Belvin 1923- *WhoIns 92*
**Cooper,** R. John, III 1942- *WhoAmL 92, WhoFI 92*
**Cooper,** R S 1932- *AmMWSc 92*
**Cooper,** Ralph Sherman 1931- *AmMWSc 92*
**Cooper,** Raymond David 1927- *AmMWSc 92*
**Cooper,** Reginald Rudyard 1932- *AmMWSc 92*
**Cooper,** Reid F 1955- *AmMWSc 92*
**Cooper,** Richard 1934- *Who 92*
**Cooper,** Richard Alan 1953- *WhoMW 92*
**Cooper,** Richard Craig 1941- *WhoAmL 92*
**Cooper,** Richard Earl 1947- *WhoAmL 92*
**Cooper,** Richard Grant 1934- *AmMWSc 92*
**Cooper,** Richard H. 1940- *WhoFI 92*
**Cooper,** Richard Kent 1937- *AmMWSc 92, WhoWest 92*
**Cooper,** Richard Lee 1932- *AmMWSc 92*
**Cooper,** Richard Newell 1934- *IntAu&W 91, WhoAmP 91, WhoFI 92, WrDr 92*
**Cooper,** Richard Wayne, Sr. 1940- *WhoFI 92, WhoMW 92*
**Cooper,** Robert Arthur, Jr 1932- *AmMWSc 92*
**Cooper,** Robert Chauncey 1928- *AmMWSc 92*
**Cooper,** Robert Elbert 1920- *WhoAmL 92, WhoAmP 91*
**Cooper,** Robert Francis 1947- *Who 92*
**Cooper,** Robert George 1936- *Who 92*
**Cooper,** Robert James 1929- *WhoMW 92*
**Cooper,** Robert Michael 1939- *AmMWSc 92*
**Cooper,** Robin D G 1938- *AmMWSc 92*
**Cooper,** Roger Harvey 1941- *WhoFI 92*
**Cooper,** Roger M 1944- *WhoAmP 91*
**Cooper,** Ronald Cecil Macleod 1931- *Who 92*
**Cooper,** Ronald Stephen 1945- *WhoAmL 92*
**Cooper,** Ronda Fern 1943- *AmMWSc 92*
**Cooper,** Ronnie Edward 1948- *WhoMW 92*
**Cooper,** Roy Asberry, III 1957- *WhoAmP 91*
**Cooper,** Russell *Who 92*
**Cooper,** Russell Jacob, III 1956- *WhoWest 92*
**Cooper,** Samuel 1914- *WhoAmL 92*
**Cooper,** Samuel H., Jr. 1955- *WhoBlA 92*
**Cooper,** Sandra Kay 1950- *WhoMW 92*
**Cooper,** Saul 1934- *WhoEnt 92*
**Cooper,** Shari Marcele 1968- *WhoEnt 92*
**Cooper,** Sheldon *IntMPA 92, WhoMW 92*
**Cooper,** Sheldon Mark 1942- *AmMWSc 92*
**Cooper,** Shirley Fields 1943- *WhoAmP 91*
**Cooper,** Sidney G. *Who 92*
**Cooper,** Sidney Pool 1919- *Who 92*
**Cooper,** Simon Christie 1936- *Who 92*
**Cooper,** Sophie *ConAu 36NR*
**Cooper,** Stephanie R. 1944- *WhoAmL 92*
**Cooper,** Stephen 1937- *AmMWSc 92*
**Cooper,** Stephen Allen 1946- *AmMWSc 92*
**Cooper,** Stephen C. 1944- *WhoAmL 92, WhoAmP 91*
**Cooper,** Stephen Douglas 1950- *WhoEnt 92*
**Cooper,** Stephen Herbert 1939- *WhoAmL 92*
**Cooper,** Stephen Robert 1957- *WhoWest 92*
**Cooper,** Steven Jon 1941- *WhoWest 92*
**Cooper,** Stoney 1918-1977 *NewAmDM*
**Cooper,** Stuart L 1941- *AmMWSc 92*
**Cooper,** Susan 1935- *IntAu&W 91, TwCSFW 91, WrDr 92*
**Cooper,** Susan Fenimore 1813-1894 *BenetAL 91*
**Cooper,** Susie 1902- *Who 92*
**Cooper,** Syretha C. 1930- *WhoBlA 92*
**Cooper,** Terence Alfred 1941- *AmMWSc 92*
**Cooper,** Terrance G 1942- *AmMWSc 92*
**Cooper,** Theo Russell 1941- *Who 92*
**Cooper,** Theodore 1928- *AmMWSc 92, WhoFI 92, WhoMW 92*
**Cooper,** Thomas 1759-1839 *BenetAL 91, BiInAmS*
**Cooper,** Thomas D 1932- *AmMWSc 92*
**Cooper,** Thomas Edward 1943- *AmMWSc 92*
**Cooper,** Tommye 1938- *AmMWSc 92*
**Cooper,** Valerie Antionette 1961- *WhoBlA 92*
**Cooper,** Virgil David 1949- *WhoRel 92*
**Cooper,** W E 1924- *AmMWSc 92*
**Cooper,** Wallace J. 1926- *WhoFI 92*
**Cooper,** Wallace LeGrand 1951- *WhoRel 92*
**Cooper,** Walter 1928- *AmMWSc 92, WhoBlA 92*
**Cooper,** Warren Ernest 1933- *IntWW 91, Who 92*
**Cooper,** Wayne 1956- *WhoBlA 92*
**Cooper,** Wendy 1919- *WrDr 92*
**Cooper,** Wendy E 1950- *WhoIns 92*
**Cooper,** Wendy Fein 1946- *WhoAmL 92*
**Cooper,** Whina 1895- *Who 92*
**Cooper,** William 1754-1809 *BenetAL 91*
**Cooper,** William 1797-1864 *BiInAmS*
**Cooper,** William 1910- *ConNov 91, FacFETw, Who 92, WrDr 92*
**Cooper,** William 1955- *Who 92*
**Cooper,** William Allen 1943- *WhoMW 92*
**Cooper,** William Anderson 1927- *AmMWSc 92*
**Cooper,** William B. 1956- *WhoBlA 92*
**Cooper,** William Cecil 1909- *AmMWSc 92*
**Cooper,** William Clark 1912- *AmMWSc 92, WhoWest 92*
**Cooper,** William E 1938- *AmMWSc 92*
**Cooper,** William Edward 1942- *AmMWSc 92*
**Cooper,** William Frank 1921- *Who 92*
**Cooper,** William Harry Summerfield Hoff 1910- *IntAu&W 91*
**Cooper,** William Hugh Alan 1909- *Who 92*
**Cooper,** William Hurlbert 1924- *WhoAmP 91*
**Cooper,** William James 1945- *AmMWSc 92*
**Cooper,** William Lewis 1944- *WhoAmL 92*
**Cooper,** William M. *Who 92, WhoBlA 92*
**Cooper,** William S 1935- *AmMWSc 92*
**Cooper,** William Secord 1935- *WhoWest 92*
**Cooper,** William Wager 1914- *WhoFI 92*
**Cooper,** William Wailes 1941- *AmMWSc 92, WhoFI 92*
**Cooper,** Wilson Wayne 1942- *AmMWSc 92*
**Cooper,** Winston Lawrence 1946- *WhoBlA 92*
**Cooper-Avrick,** Anita Beverly *WhoEnt 92*
**Cooper-Fratrik,** Julie *DrAPF 91*
**Cooper-Lewter,** Nicholas Charles 1948- *WhoBlA 92*

**Cooperman,** Alvin IntMPA 92, LesBEnT 92, WhoEnt 92
**Cooperman,** Barry S 1941- AmMWSc 92
**Cooperman,** Hasye WrDr 92
**Cooperman,** Hasye 1909- IntAu&W 91
**Cooperman,** Jack M 1921- AmMWSc 92
**Cooperman,** Leon G. 1943- WhoFI 92
**Cooperrider,** Donald Elmer 1914- AmMWSc 92
**Cooperrider,** Tom Smith 1927- AmMWSc 92, WhoMW 92
**Coopersmith,** Bernard Ira 1914- WhoMW 92
**Coopersmith,** Esther Lipsen WhoAmP 91
**Coopersmith,** Fredric S. WhoFI 92
**Coopersmith,** Henry Joseph WhoAmL 92
**Coopersmith,** Jeffrey Alan 1946- WhoMW 92
**Coopersmith,** Jerome 1925- WhoEnt 92
**Coopersmith,** Judy 1933- WhoEnt 92
**Coopersmith,** Michael Henry 1936- AmMWSc 92
**Coopersmith,** Stanley 1926-1979 ConAu 133
**Cooperstein,** Claire DrAPF 91
**Cooperstein,** Foster Jay 1948- WhoAmL 92
**Cooperstein,** Paul Andrew 1953- WhoAmL 92
**Cooperstein,** Raymond 1924- AmMWSc 92
**Cooperstein,** Sherwin Jerome 1923- AmMWSc 92
**Cooperstein,** Theodore Mark 1963- WhoAmL 92
**Cooperstock,** Fred Isaac 1940- AmMWSc 92
**Cooprider,** R. Scott 1961- WhoFI 92
**Coor,** James DcNCBi 1
**Coor,** Lattie Finch 1936- IntWW 91, WhoWest 92
**Coor,** Thomas 1922- AmMWSc 92
**Cooray,** Anura 1936- Who 92
**Coordsen,** George WhoAmP 91
**Coore,** David Hilton 1925- IntWW 91
**Coorey,** Chandana Aelian 1921- IntWW 91
**Coors,** Jeffrey H. 1945- WhoWest 92
**Coors,** Joseph LesBEnT 92
**Coors,** Joseph 1917- WhoWest 92
**Coors,** Peter Hanson 1946- WhoWest 92
**Coors,** William K. 1916- WhoWest 92
**Coorts,** Gerald Duane 1932- AmMWSc 92
**Coote,** Christopher 1928- Who 92
**Coote,** Denis Richard 1945- AmMWSc 92
**Coote,** John Haven 1937- Who 92
**Coote,** John Oldham 1921- Who 92
**Coote,** Roderic Norman 1915- Who 92
**Coote,** William DcAmImH
**Cooter,** Dale A. 1948- WhoAmL 92
**Cooter,** John Adams 1939- WhoFI 92
**Cooter,** Robert 1945- WhoAmL 92
**Coots,** Alonzo Freeman 1927- AmMWSc 92
**Coots,** Billy Edward 1939- WhoRel 92
**Coots,** Daniel Jay 1951- WhoFI 92
**Coots,** Edwin Davis 1944- WhoAmL 92
**Coots,** Robert Herman 1928- AmMWSc 92
**Coovelis,** Mark DrAPF 91
**Coover,** Harry Wesley, Jr 1919- AmMWSc 92
**Coover,** James Burrell 1925- WhoEnt 92
**Coover,** Robert DrAPF 91
**Coover,** Robert 1932- BenetAL 91, ConNov 91, CurBio 91 [port], IntAu&W 91, WrDr 92
**Coox,** Alvin D. 1924- WrDr 92
**Copage,** Marc Diego 1962- WhoBlA 92
**Copaken,** Robert R. 1939- WhoFI 92
**Copanas,** Thomas M. 1944- WhoFI 92
**Copani,** Anthony Frank 1957- WhoAmL 92
**Copans,** Kenneth Gary 1946- WhoFI 92
**Copas,** Ronnie 1932- TwCPaSc
**Copas,** Virgil 1915- Who 92
**Cope,** Alfred Haines 1912- WhoFI 92
**Cope,** Arthur 1857-1940 TwCPaSc
**Cope,** Charles Dudley 1943- WhoAmP 91
**Cope,** Charles S 1928- AmMWSc 92
**Cope,** David DrAPF 91
**Cope,** David 1948- WrDr 92
**Cope,** David Franklin 1912- AmMWSc 92
**Cope,** David Robert 1944- Who 92
**Cope,** David Robert 1946- Who 92
**Cope,** Donald Lloyd 1936- WhoBlA 92
**Cope,** Edward Drinker 1840-1897 BiInAmS
**Cope,** F Wolverson 1909- Who 92
**Cope,** Frederick Oliver 1946- AmMWSc 92, WhoMW 92
**Cope,** Jack 1913- ConNov 91, LiExTwC, WrDr 92
**Cope,** Jack Robert Knox 1913- IntAu&W 91
**Cope,** Jackson I 1925- ConAu 34NR, WrDr 92
**Cope,** James Francis 1907- Who 92
**Cope,** Joe L. 1953- WhoAmL 92
**Cope,** John 1937- Who 92
**Cope,** John Robert 1942- WhoAmL 92
**Cope,** John Thomas, Jr 1921- AmMWSc 92
**Cope,** Laurence Brian 1951- WhoFI 92
**Cope,** Maclachlan Alan Carl S. Who 92
**Cope,** Nancy Elizabeth 1952- WhoWest 92
**Cope,** O. Lamar 1938- WhoRel 92
**Cope,** Oliver 1902- AmMWSc 92
**Cope,** Oliver Brewern 1916- AmMWSc 92
**Cope,** Oswald James 1934- AmMWSc 92
**Cope,** Shelby Ann 1962- WhoFI 92
**Cope,** Thom K. 1948- WhoAmL 92
**Cope,** Virgil W 1943- AmMWSc 92
**Cope,** Wendy 1945- ConPo 91, WrDr 92
**Cope,** Wendy Mary 1945- Who 92
**Cope,** Will Allen 1922- AmMWSc 92
**Cope,** William Robert 1942- WhoAmL 92
**Copeau,** Jacques 1879-1949 FacFETw
**Copek,** Peter Joseph 1945- WhoWest 92
**Copel,** Ken 1962- WhoEnt 92
**Copelan,** John Jefferson, Jr. 1951- WhoAmL 92
**Copeland,** Ann DrAPF 91
**Copeland,** Ann 1932- WrDr 92
**Copeland,** Arthur Herbert, Jr 1926- AmMWSc 92
**Copeland,** Barry Bernard 1957- WhoBlA 92
**Copeland,** Betty Marable 1946- WhoBlA 92
**Copeland,** Billy Joe 1936- AmMWSc 92
**Copeland,** Bradley Ellsworth 1921- AmMWSc 92
**Copeland,** Charles Wesley, Jr 1932- AmMWSc 92
**Copeland,** David Anthony 1942- AmMWSc 92
**Copeland,** David Y, III 1931- WhoAmP 91
**Copeland,** Donald Eugene 1912- AmMWSc 92
**Copeland,** Douglas Allen 1956- WhoAmL 92
**Copeland,** Douglas Wallace, Jr 1952- WhoAmP 91
**Copeland,** Edmund Sargent 1936- AmMWSc 92
**Copeland,** Edward Jerome 1933- WhoAmL 92
**Copeland,** Edwin 1916- WrDr 92
**Copeland,** Edwin Luther 1916- IntAu&W 91
**Copeland,** Elaine Johnson 1943- WhoBlA 92
**Copeland,** Emily America 1918- WhoBlA 92
**Copeland,** Floyd Dean 1939- WhoAmL 92
**Copeland,** Fred E 1932- WhoAmP 91
**Copeland,** Frederick Cleveland 1912- AmMWSc 92
**Copeland,** Gary Earl 1940- AmMWSc 92
**Copeland,** George d1991 NewYTBS 91
**Copeland,** Helen M. DrAPF 91
**Copeland,** Henry Jefferson, Jr. 1936- WhoMW 92
**Copeland,** Howard Edgar 1944- WhoAmP 91
**Copeland,** James Clinton 1937- AmMWSc 92
**Copeland,** James Lewis 1931- AmMWSc 92
**Copeland,** James William 1943- WhoMW 92
**Copeland,** Joan Miller WhoEnt 92
**Copeland,** John Alexander 1941- AmMWSc 92
**Copeland,** Joseph Conrad 1944- WhoMW 92
**Copeland,** Joyanne Winifred Who 92
**Copeland,** Kathleen 1915- WhoBlA 92
**Copeland,** Keith Lamont 1946- WhoEnt 92
**Copeland,** Kenneth 1937- RelLAm 91
**Copeland,** Kenneth Edward 1962- WhoRel 92, WhoWest 92
**Copeland,** Kevon 1953- WhoBlA 92
**Copeland,** Leon L. 1945- WhoBlA 92
**Copeland,** Leon Troy 1942- WhoAmP 91
**Copeland,** Leticia Salvatierra 1962- WhoHisp 92
**Copeland,** Mary Shawn 1947- WhoBlA 92
**Copeland,** Miles 1916?-1991 ConAu 133
**Copeland,** Miles, Sr. d1991 NewYTBS 91
**Copeland,** Miles Alexander 1934- AmMWSc 92
**Copeland,** Milton Harold 1935- WhoAmL 92
**Copeland,** Murray John 1928- AmMWSc 92
**Copeland,** Oliver Perry 1816- DcNCBi 1
**Copeland,** Phillips Jerome 1921- WhoWest 92
**Copeland,** Ray 1926- WhoBlA 92
**Copeland,** Richard Franklin 1938- AmMWSc 92
**Copeland,** Robert B 1938- AmMWSc 92
**Copeland,** Robert M. 1943- WhoBlA 92
**Copeland,** Robert Marshall 1945- WhoEnt 92
**Copeland,** Robert Tayloe 1947- WhoAmL 92
**Copeland,** Ross H. 1930-1980 ConAu 133
**Copeland,** Tatiana Brandt WhoFI 92
**Copeland,** Terrilyn Denise 1954- WhoBlA 92
**Copeland,** Thomas Earl WhoFI 92
**Copeland,** Thompson Preston 1921- AmMWSc 92
**Copeland,** Vicki Renae 1959- WhoAmL 92
**Copeland,** William D 1934- AmMWSc 92
**Copeland,** William Henry 1920- WhoMW 92
**Copelin,** Harry B 1918- AmMWSc 92
**Copelin,** Sherman 1943- WhoAmP 91
**Copelin,** Sherman Nathaniel, Jr. 1943- WhoBlA 92
**Copello,** Angelo Gene 1959- WhoWest 92
**Copeman,** Constance Gertrude 1864-1953 TwCPaSc
**Copeman,** George Henry 1922- WrDr 92
**Copeman,** Harold Arthur 1918- Who 92
**Copeman,** Robert James 1942- AmMWSc 92
**Copen,** John Leslie 1945- WhoFI 92
**Copenbarger,** Lloyd Gaylord 1941- WhoAmL 92
**Copenhaver,** Charles Leonard, III 1944- WhoAmL 92
**Copenhaver,** John Harrison, Jr 1922- AmMWSc 92
**Copenhaver,** John Thomas, Jr. 1925- WhoAmL 92
**Copenhaver,** Marion Lamson 1925- WhoAmP 91
**Copenhaver,** Thomas Wesley 1945- AmMWSc 92
**Coperario,** John NewAmDM
**Copertino,** John 1928- WhoAmL 92
**Copes,** Frederick Albert 1937- AmMWSc 92
**Copes,** Parzival 1924- AmMWSc 92
**Copes,** Ronald Adrian 1941- WhoBlA 92
**Copi,** Irving M. 1917- WrDr 92
**Copi,** Irving Marmer 1917- IntAu&W 91, WhoWest 92
**Copisarow,** Alcon 1920- Who 92
**Copithorne,** Maurice Danby 1931- IntWW 91
**Coplan,** Daniel Jonathan 1955- WhoEnt 92
**Coplan,** Michael Alan 1938- AmMWSc 92
**Coplan,** Myron J 1922- AmMWSc 92
**Copland,** Aaron d1990 IntWW 91N, Who 92N
**Copland,** Aaron 1900-1990 AnObit 1990, BenetAL 91, ConAu 133, ConCom 92, CurBio 91N, FacFETw, NewAmDM, News 91, RComAH
**Copland,** Charles McAlester 1910- Who 92
**Cople,** William James, III 1955- WhoAmL 92
**Copleston,** Ernest Reginald 1909- Who 92
**Copleston,** Frederick Charles 1907- IntAu&W 91, IntWW 91, Who 92, WrDr 92
**Coplestone-Boughey,** John Fenton 1912- Who 92
**Copley,** Alfred Lewin 1910- AmMWSc 92
**Copley,** David C. WhoWest 92
**Copley,** Edward Alvin 1936- WhoAmL 92
**Copley,** Helen Kinney 1922- WhoWest 92
**Copley,** John 1875-1950 TwCPaSc
**Copley,** John 1933- Who 92
**Copley,** John Singleton 1738-1815 RComAH
**Copley,** Lawrence Gordon 1939- AmMWSc 92
**Copley,** Rita Louise 1924- WhoAmP 91
**Coplien,** James O 1954- AmMWSc 92
**Coplin,** David Louis 1945- AmMWSc 92
**Copman,** Louis 1934- WhoWest 92
**Copnall,** Edward Bainbridge 1903-1973 TwCPaSc
**Copnall,** Frank 1870-1949 TwCPaSc
**Copnall,** John 1928- TwCPaSc
**Copnall,** Teresa Norah 1882-1972 TwCPaSc
**Copp,** Albert Nils 1937- AmMWSc 92
**Copp,** Darrell John Barkwell 1922- Who 92
**Copp,** Douglas Harold 1915- AmMWSc 92
**Copp,** Earle Morse, III 1955- WhoEnt 92
**Copp,** Harold 1915- IntWW 91, Who 92
**Copp,** James 1913- IntAu&W 91
**Copp,** Jim WrDr 92
**Copp,** Terry 1938- ConAu 134
**Coppa,** Frank John 1937- WrDr 92
**Coppa,** Nicholas V 1955- AmMWSc 92
**Coppage,** William Eugene 1934- AmMWSc 92
**Coppard,** A.E. 1878-1957 RfGEnL 91
**Coppe,** Albert 1911- IntWW 91
**Coppedge,** Arthur L. 1938- WhoBlA 92
**Coppel,** Alfred DrAPF 91
**Coppel,** Alfred 1921- TwCSFW 91, WrDr 92
**Coppel,** Claude Peter 1932- AmMWSc 92
**Coppel,** Harry Charles 1918- AmMWSc 92
**Coppel,** Lawrence David 1944- WhoAmL 92
**Coppel,** Ronald Lewis 1933- IntWW 91
**Coppen,** Alec James 1923- IntWW 91, Who 92
**Coppenger,** Claude Jackson 1927- AmMWSc 92
**Coppens,** Alan Berchard 1936- AmMWSc 92
**Coppens,** Philip 1930- AmMWSc 92
**Coppens,** Yves 1934- IntWW 91
**Copper,** Basil 1924- ConAu 133, WrDr 92
**Copper,** Joe 1928- WhoAmP 91
**Copper,** John A 1934- AmMWSc 92
**Copper,** Paul 1940- AmMWSc 92
**Copperfield,** David 1956- WhoEnt 92
**Coppersmith,** Don 1950- AmMWSc 92
**Coppersmith,** Frederick Martin 1947- AmMWSc 92
**Copperud,** Roy H. 1915- WrDr 92
**Copperud,** Roy Herman d1991 NewYTBS 91
**Coppet,** Louis Casimir de 1841-1911 BiInAmS
**Coppi,** Bruno 1935- AmMWSc 92
**Coppi,** Robin Ellen 1957- WhoWest 92
**Coppick,** Glendon Cleon 1926- WhoRel 92
**Coppieters,** Emmanuel 1925- IntWW 91
**Coppin,** Ann Stacy 1944- WhoWest 92
**Coppin,** Charles Arthur 1941- AmMWSc 92
**Coppin,** Fanny Jackson 1837-1913 NotBlAW 92 [port]
**Coppin,** Fanny Muriel Jackson 1837-1913 RelLAm 91
**Coppin,** Levi Jenkins 1848-1924 RelLAm 91
**Coppinger,** John F. WhoRel 92
**Coppinger,** Raymond Parke 1937- AmMWSc 92
**Copple,** Robert Francis 1955- WhoAmL 92
**Copple,** Ronald Lloyd 1945- WhoWest 92
**Copplestone,** Frank Henry 1925- Who 92
**Coppoc,** Gordon Lloyd 1939- AmMWSc 92
**Coppoc,** William Joseph 1913- AmMWSc 92
**Coppock,** Ada Gregory 1960- WhoEnt 92
**Coppock,** Carl Edward 1932- AmMWSc 92
**Coppock,** David Arthur 1931- Who 92
**Coppock,** Donald Leslie 1947- AmMWSc 92
**Coppock,** Glenn E 1924- AmMWSc 92
**Coppock,** John Terence 1921- IntWW 91, Who 92
**Coppock,** Richard Miles 1938- WhoWest 92
**Coppock,** Robert Walter 1942- AmMWSc 92
**Coppola,** Alan Carl 1947- WhoWest 92
**Coppola,** Carmine d1991 NewYTBS 91 [port]
**Coppola,** Carmine 1910-1991 News 91
**Coppola,** Elia Domenico 1941- AmMWSc 92
**Coppola,** Francesco 1878-1959 BiDExR
**Coppola,** Francis Ford 1939- BenetAL 91, CurBio 91 [port], FacFETw, IntDcF 2-2 [port], IntMPA 92, IntWW 91, Who 92, WhoEnt 92, WhoWest 92
**Coppola,** Patrick Paul 1917- AmMWSc 92
**Coppolechia,** Yillian Castro 1948- WhoHisp 92
**Coppolillo,** Henry P 1926- AmMWSc 92
**Coppridge,** William Maurice 1893-1959 DcNCBi 1
**Copps,** Lonnie Jacobs 1959- WhoAmL 92
**Copps,** Michael Joseph 1940- WhoAmP 91
**Copra,** Richard Edward 1948- WhoWest 92
**Coprario,** John 1580?-1626? NewAmDM
**Copsetta,** Norman George 1932- WhoAmL 92
**Copson,** David Arthur 1918- AmMWSc 92
**Copson,** Harry Rollason 1908- AmMWSc 92
**Copulsky,** William 1922- AmMWSc 92
**Copway,** George BenetAL 91
**Coquillet,** Daniel William 1856-1911 BiInAmS
**Coquillette,** William Hollis 1949- WhoAmL 92
**Coquillette-Dean,** Daniel Robert 1944- WhoAmL 92
**Cora,** George F. WhoRel 92
**Cora,** Joey 1965- WhoHisp 92
**Corace,** Joseph Russell 1953- WhoFI 92
**Corak,** William Sydney 1922- AmMWSc 92
**Corales,** Miguel Patricio 1944- WhoHisp 92
**Coram,** Donald Sidney 1945- AmMWSc 92
**Coram,** Edward Clinton 1947- WhoFI 92
**Coran,** Arnold Gerald 1938- AmMWSc 92
**Coran,** Aubert Y 1932- AmMWSc 92
**Coraor,** George Robert 1924- AmMWSc 92
**Corash,** Richard 1938- WhoAmL 92
**Coray,** Carla Winn 1925- WhoAmP 91

**Coray**, Hans 1907- DcTwDes
**Coray**, Jeffrey Warren 1958- WhoWest 92
**Corazza**, Paul Joseph 1954- WhoMW 92
**Corazzini**, Sergio 1886-1907 DcLB 114 [port]
**Corballis**, Michael Charles 1936- IntWW 91
**Corbally**, John Edward 1924- IntWW 91
**Corbato**, Charles Edward 1932- AmMWSc 92
**Corbato**, Fernando Jose 1926- AmMWSc 92
**Corbeels**, Roger 1936- AmMWSc 92
**Corbeil**, Lynette B 1938- AmMWSc 92
**Corben**, Albert Edward 1923- Who 92
**Corben**, Beverly Byrd 1926- IntAu&W 91
**Corben**, Herbert Charles 1914- AmMWSc 92
**Corber**, Brian Lee 1952- WhoEnt 92
**Corber**, Robert Jack, I 1926- WhoAmL 92, WhoFI 92
**Corbet**, Donald Lee 1959- WhoEnt 92, WhoMW 92
**Corbet**, Freda 1900- Who 92
**Corbet**, Gordon Barclay 1933- Who 92
**Corbet**, John 1911- Who 92
**Corbet**, Leo Frank, Jr 1936- WhoAmP 91
**Corbett** Who 92
**Corbett**, Alan 1943- WhoEnt 92
**Corbett**, Chan TwCSFW 91
**Corbett**, Charles Eric Who 92
**Corbett**, Dennis Dale 1944- WhoMW 92
**Corbett**, Dennis Paul 1953- WhoAmL 92
**Corbett**, Doris R. 1947- WhoBlA 92
**Corbett**, Edmund V. WrDr 92
**Corbett**, Edward P. J. 1919- WrDr 92
**Corbett**, Edward Patrick Joseph 1919- WhoMW 92
**Corbett**, Elizabeth Frances 1887-1981 BenetAL 91
**Corbett**, Gail Rushford 1936- AmMWSc 92
**Corbett**, Glenn 1929?- ConTFT 9
**Corbett**, Gordon Leroy 1920- WhoRel 92
**Corbett**, H. Stewart 1935- WhoEnt 92
**Corbett**, Hugh Askew 1916- Who 92
**Corbett**, Jack Elliott 1920- WhoFI 92
**Corbett**, James Daniel 1949- WhoAmP 91
**Corbett**, James John 1940- AmMWSc 92
**Corbett**, James Michael 1927- WhoIns 92
**Corbett**, James Murray 1938- AmMWSc 92
**Corbett**, James William 1928- AmMWSc 92
**Corbett**, Jerry G 1917- WhoAmP 91
**Corbett**, John Dudley 1926- AmMWSc 92
**Corbett**, John Frank 1935- AmMWSc 92
**Corbett**, John Patrick 1916- Who 92
**Corbett**, Jules John 1919- AmMWSc 92, WhoMW 92
**Corbett**, Keith Bernard, Sr. 1956- WhoFI 92
**Corbett**, Kenneth S 1957- WhoAmP 91
**Corbett**, Kevin Patrick 1956- WhoWest 92
**Corbett**, Laurence Paul 1920- WhoAmL 92
**Corbett**, Leon H., Jr. 1937- WhoAmL 92
**Corbett**, M Kenneth 1927- AmMWSc 92
**Corbett**, Michael Dennis 1944- AmMWSc 92
**Corbett**, Michael Derrik 1929- WhoFI 92
**Corbett**, Michael McGregor 1923- Who 92
**Corbett**, Peter Edgar 1920- Who 92
**Corbett**, Richard 1582-1635 RfGEnL 91
**Corbett**, Richard Tewhill 1951- WhoAmL 92
**Corbett**, Robert B 1917- AmMWSc 92
**Corbett**, Robert Edward 1923- IntWW 91
**Corbett**, Robert G 1935- AmMWSc 92
**Corbett**, Robert John Swan 1940- Who 92
**Corbett**, Robin 1933- Who 92
**Corbett**, Ron J 1960- WhoAmP 91
**Corbett**, Ronald Balfour 1930- Who 92
**Corbett**, Scott 1913- WrDr 92
**Corbett**, Shirley Anne Tugwell 1936- WhoAmP 91
**Corbett**, Steven Bradley, Sr. 1959- WhoRel 92
**Corbett**, Thomas Hughes 1938- AmMWSc 92
**Corbett**, Thomas Wingett, Jr. 1949- WhoAmL 92
**Corbett**, Uvedale 1909- Who 92
**Corbett**, W. J. 1938- WrDr 92
**Corbett**, Warren Lee 1944- WhoAmL 92
**Corbett**, William DrAPF 91
**Corbett**, William Arnold 1947- WhoFI 92
**Corbett**, William Lynnwood 1927- WhoRel 92
**Corbett**, William Thomas, Jr. 1960- WhoAmL 92
**Corbett Ashby**, Margery Irene 1882-1981 BiDBrF 2
**Corbett-Winder**, John Lyon d1990 Who 92N
**Corbie**, Leo A. WhoBlA 92
**Corbiere**, Tristan 1845-1875 GuFrLit 1
**Corbin**, Alan 1934- AmMWSc 92
**Corbin**, Alice BenetAL 91
**Corbin**, Angela Lenore 1958- WhoBlA 92
**Corbin**, Barry IntMPA 92
**Corbin**, Carl Edward 1937- WhoFI 92
**Corbin**, Charles Paul 1943- WhoEnt 92
**Corbin**, Christine Marie 1947- WhoMW 92
**Corbin**, Claire 1913- WrDr 92
**Corbin**, David R 1943- WhoAmP 91
**Corbin**, Donald Louis 1938- WhoAmP 91
**Corbin**, Evelyn D. 1923- WhoBlA 92
**Corbin**, Francis d1767 DcNCBi 1
**Corbin**, Frederick Thomas 1929- AmMWSc 92
**Corbin**, Gary George 1941- WhoAmP 91
**Corbin**, Herbert Leonard 1940- WhoFI 92
**Corbin**, Jack David 1941- AmMWSc 92
**Corbin**, James Edward 1921- AmMWSc 92
**Corbin**, James Lee 1935- AmMWSc 92
**Corbin**, Kendall Brooks 1907- AmMWSc 92
**Corbin**, Kendall Wallace 1939- AmMWSc 92
**Corbin**, Krestine Margaret 1937- WhoFI 92, WhoWest 92
**Corbin**, Margaret Cochran 1751-1800? BlkwEAR, EncAmaz 91
**Corbin**, Maurice Haig Alleyne 1916- Who 92
**Corbin**, Michael TwCSFW 91
**Corbin**, Michael H 1949- AmMWSc 92
**Corbin**, Patrick WhoEnt 92
**Corbin**, Paul Alan 1956- WhoMW 92
**Corbin**, Raymond Monroe 1917- WhoEnt 92
**Corbin**, Raymond Pierre Louis 1907- IntWW 91
**Corbin**, Robert K 1928- WhoAmP 91
**Corbin**, Robert Keith 1928- WhoAmL 92, WhoWest 92
**Corbin**, Robert Lyle 1922- WhoAmP 91
**Corbin**, Ronald Eugene 1942- WhoRel 92
**Corbin**, Sol Neil 1927- WhoAmL 92
**Corbin**, Steven DrAPF 91
**Corbin**, Thomas Elbert 1940- AmMWSc 92
**Corbin**, Tyrone Kennedy 1962- WhoBlA 92
**Corbin**, William ConAu 36NR
**Corbitt**, David Leroy 1895-1967 DcNCBi 1
**Corbitt**, John H. 1941- WhoBlA 92
**Corbitt**, Maurice R 1931- AmMWSc 92
**Corbitt**, Richard Johnson 1873-1961 DcNCBi 1
**Corbo**, Vincent James 1943- AmMWSc 92
**Corboy**, James McNally 1940- WhoFI 92, WhoWest 92
**Corboy**, Philip Harnett 1924- WhoAmL 92, WhoMW 92
**Corbridge**, James Noel, Jr. 1934- WhoWest 92
**Corbusier** DcTwDes
**Corby**, Brian 1929- IntWW 91, Who 92
**Corby**, Donald G 1934- AmMWSc 92
**Corby**, Ellen 1913- ConTFT 9
**Corby**, Francis Michael, Jr. 1944- WhoFI 92
**Corby**, George Arthur 1917- Who 92
**Corbyn**, Jeremy Bernard 1949- Who 92
**Corchado**, Alfredo 1960- WhoHisp 92
**Corchado y Juarbe**, Manuel M. 1840-1884 HisDSpE
**Corcoran**, Andrew Patrick, Jr. 1948- WhoAmL 92
**Corcoran**, Ann M. 1939- WhoEnt 92
**Corcoran**, Barbara DrAPF 91
**Corcoran**, Barbara 1911- WrDr 92
**Corcoran**, Barbara Asenath 1911- IntAu&W 91
**Corcoran**, Brian Christopher 1957- WhoAmL 92
**Corcoran**, C. Timothy, III 1945- WhoAmL 92
**Corcoran**, Eugene Francis 1916- AmMWSc 92
**Corcoran**, George Bartlett, III 1948- AmMWSc 92
**Corcoran**, Gertrude B. 1923- WrDr 92
**Corcoran**, Gregory Michael 1961- WhoMW 92
**Corcoran**, James Desmond 1928- Who 92
**Corcoran**, James Martin, Jr. 1932- WhoAmL 92
**Corcoran**, John Joseph 1920- WhoAmL 92
**Corcoran**, John W 1924- AmMWSc 92
**Corcoran**, John William 1927- AmMWSc 92
**Corcoran**, Joseph V 1925- WhoAmP 91
**Corcoran**, Marjorie 1950- AmMWSc 92
**Corcoran**, Mary Ritzel 1928- AmMWSc 92
**Corcoran**, Maureen Elizabeth 1944- WhoAmL 92
**Corcoran**, Neil 1948- ConAu 135
**Corcoran**, Robert Joseph 1929- WhoFI 92
**Corcoran**, Thomas G 1900-1981 FacFETw
**Corcoran**, Thomas Joseph 1922- WhoAmP 91
**Corcoran**, Timothy R 1950- WhoAmP 91
**Corcoran**, Tom 1939- WhoAmP 91
**Corcoran**, Vincent John 1934- AmMWSc 92
**Corcoran**, William P 1922- AmMWSc 92
**Corcos**, Alain Francois 1925- AmMWSc 92
**Corcos**, Gilles M 1926- AmMWSc 92
**Corcos**, Lucille 1908-1973 ConAu 134
**Corcuera Cuesta**, Jose Luis 1945- IntWW 91
**Cord**, Alex 1933?- ConTFT 9, IntMPA 92, WhoEnt 92
**Cord**, Barry 1913- IntAu&W 91
**Cord**, Barry 1913-1983 TwCWW 91
**Corda**, Mike 1921- WhoEnt 92
**Cordano**, Angel AmMWSc 92
**Corday**, Barbara 1944- IntMPA 92
**Corddry**, Paul Imlay 1936- WhoFI 92
**Cordea**, James Nicholas 1937- AmMWSc 92
**Cordeiro**, Joseph Who 92
**Cordeiro**, Joseph 1918- IntWW 91, WhoRel 92
**Cordel**, Virginia Ann 1927- WhoAmP 91
**Cordell**, Alexander 1914- IntAu&W 91, WrDr 92
**Cordell**, Bruce Monteith 1949- AmMWSc 92
**Cordell**, Cathleen 1915- WhoEnt 92
**Cordell**, Francis Merritt 1932- AmMWSc 92
**Cordell**, Geoffrey Alan 1946- AmMWSc 92
**Cordell**, Joe B. 1927- WhoFI 92
**Cordell**, La Doris Hazzard 1949- WhoBlA 92
**Cordell**, LaDoris Hazzard 1949- WhoAmL 92
**Cordell**, Michael Bragg 1946- WhoFI 92
**Cordell**, Richard William 1939- AmMWSc 92
**Cordell**, Robert James 1917- AmMWSc 92
**Cordell**, Steven Mark 1955- WhoMW 92
**Corden**, Malcolm Ernest 1927- AmMWSc 92
**Corden**, Pierce Stephen 1941- AmMWSc 92
**Corden**, Warner Max 1927- IntWW 91, WhoFI 92, WrDr 92
**Corder**, Clinton Nicholas 1941- AmMWSc 92
**Corderi**, Victoria Marta 1957- WhoHisp 92
**Corderman**, John Printz 1942- WhoAmP 91
**Cordero**, Angel Tomas, Jr. 1942- WhoHisp 92
**Cordero**, Brenda Sue 1967- WhoHisp 92
**Cordero**, Carlos WhoHisp 92
**Cordero**, Edward C. WhoHisp 92
**Cordero**, Fausto 1954- WhoHisp 92
**Cordero**, James E. WhoHisp 92
**Cordero**, Joseph A. 1953- WhoHisp 92
**Cordero**, Julio 1923- AmMWSc 92
**Cordero**, Rafael WhoAmP 91
**Cordero**, Ronald Anthony 1940- WhoHisp 92
**Cordero**, Roque 1917- ConCom 92, NewAmDM, WhoHisp 92
**Cordero**, Sylvia D. 1959- WhoHisp 92
**Cordero de Noriega**, Diane C. 1943- WhoHisp 92
**Cordero Jimenez**, Carlos O. 1948- WhoHisp 92
**Cordero-Santiago**, Rafael 1942- WhoHisp 92
**Cordero-Spampinato**, Sylvia D. 1959- WhoHisp 92
**Corderoy**, Graham Thomas 1931- Who 92
**Cordery**, Robert Arthur 1952- AmMWSc 92
**Cordery**, Sara Brown 1920- WhoBlA 92
**Cordes**, Alexander Charles 1925- WhoAmL 92
**Cordes**, Arthur Wallace 1934- AmMWSc 92
**Cordes**, Carroll Lloyd 1938- AmMWSc 92
**Cordes**, Craig M 1944- AmMWSc 92
**Cordes**, Donald Ormond 1930- AmMWSc 92
**Cordes**, Eugene H 1936- AmMWSc 92
**Cordes**, Herman Fredrick 1927- AmMWSc 92
**Cordes**, James F. 1940- WhoWest 92
**Cordes**, Mary Kenrick 1933- WhoMW 92
**Cordes**, William Charles 1929- AmMWSc 92
**Cordey**, Frederic 1854-1911 ThHEIm
**Cordiano**, Dean Martin 1952- WhoAmL 92
**Cordier**, Andrew Wellington 1901-1975 AmPeW
**Cordier**, Baude NewAmDM
**Cordier**, Mary Hurlbut 1930- WhoMW 92
**Cordiner**, James B, Jr 1915- AmMWSc 92
**Cordiner**, William Lawson 1935- Who 92
**Cording**, Edward J AmMWSc 92
**Cordingley**, John Edward 1916- Who 92
**Cordingly**, David 1938- WrDr 92
**Cordingly**, David Michael Bradley 1938- Who 92
**Cordingly**, Richard Henry 1931- AmMWSc 92
**Cordis**, Maria 1929- WhoRel 92
**Cordle**, John Howard 1912- Who 92
**Cordle**, Kenneth Edwin, Jr. 1964- WhoRel 92
**Cordle**, William Lance 1959- WhoRel 92
**Cordoba**, Becky Abbate 1956- WhoHisp 92
**Cordoba**, Jose IntWW 91
**Cordoba**, Jose Maria 1799-1829 HisDSpE
**Cordoba**, Mariano 1924- WhoHisp 92
**Cordoba**, Matias de 1750-1828 HisDSpE
**Cordoba**, Pedro de 1482-1521 HisDSpE
**Cordobes**, Roland Esteban 1938- WhoHisp 92
**Cordon**, Martin 1928- AmMWSc 92
**Cordon**, Norman 1904-1964 DcNCBi 1
**Cordon-Cardo**, Carlos 1957- AmMWSc 92
**Cordoni**, Barbara Keene 1933- WhoMW 92
**Cordova**, Carlos D. 1954- WhoHisp 92
**Cordova**, Fabian D. 1931- WhoHisp 92
**Cordova**, France Anne-Dominic 1947- AmMWSc 92
**Cordova**, Francisco Ray 1963- WhoHisp 92
**Cordova**, J. Gustavo 1949- WhoHisp 92
**Cordova**, John Lawrence 1948- WhoHisp 92
**Cordova**, Johnny Amezquita 1946- WhoHisp 92
**Cordova**, Kandy 1936- WhoHisp 92
**Cordova**, Kathryn M. 1947- WhoHisp 92
**Cordova**, Linda L. 1957- WhoHisp 92
**Cordova**, Manuel 1949- WhoHisp 92
**Cordova**, Mark Allan 1956- WhoHisp 92
**Cordova**, Moses E. WhoHisp 92
**Cordova**, Ralph Aguirre 1933- WhoHisp 92
**Cordova**, Renaldo C. 1947- WhoBlA 92
**Cordova**, Sam 1932- WhoHisp 92
**Cordova**, Victor WhoHisp 92
**Cordova**, Vincent Frank 1936- AmMWSc 92
**Cordova**, William 1930- WhoHisp 92
**Cordova-Salinas**, Maria Asuncion AmMWSc 92
**Cordoves**, Margarita 1947- WhoHisp 92
**Cordovez**, Diego 1935- IntWW 91
**Cordovi**, Marcel A 1915- AmMWSc 92
**Cordray**, Richard Adams 1959- WhoAmP 91
**Cordrey**, Pauline Shockley 1927- WhoAmP 91
**Cordrey**, Richard Stephen 1933- WhoAmP 91
**Cords**, Carl Ernest, Jr 1933- AmMWSc 92
**Cords**, Donald Philip 1940- AmMWSc 92
**Cordts**, Richard Henry, Jr 1934- AmMWSc 92
**Corduneanu**, Constantin C 1928- AmMWSc 92
**Cordy**, Donald R 1913- AmMWSc 92
**Cordy**, Timothy Soames 1949- Who 92
**Core**, Earl Lemley 1902- AmMWSc 92
**Core**, Edward K WhoAmP 91
**Core**, Harold Addison 1920- AmMWSc 92
**Core**, Jesse F 1913- AmMWSc 92
**Core**, Marguerite M. 1954- WhoEnt 92
**Corea**, Chick 1941- ConMus 6 [port], FacFETw [port], NewAmDM, WhoEnt 92
**Corea**, Gamani 1925- IntWW 91
**Corell**, Robert Walden 1934- AmMWSc 92
**Corella**, John C. WhoHisp 92
**Corelli**, Arcangelo 1653-1713 NewAmDM
**Corelli**, Franco IntWW 91
**Corelli**, Franco 1921- NewAmDM
**Corelli**, Franco 1923- FacFETw
**Corelli**, John C 1930- AmMWSc 92
**Corelli**, John Charles 1930- AmMWSc 92
**Corelli**, Marie 1855-1924 RfGEnL 91, ScFEYrs
**Coren**, Alan 1928- IntAu&W 91
**Coren**, Alan 1938- IntWW 91, Who 92, WrDr 92
**Coren**, Arthur 1933- WhoFI 92
**Coren**, Richard L 1932- AmMWSc 92
**Coret**, Irving Allen 1920- AmMWSc 92
**Corey**, Albert Eugene 1928- AmMWSc 92
**Corey**, Arthur Thomas 1919- AmMWSc 92
**Corey**, Barry Martin 1942- WhoAmL 92
**Corey**, Brian E 1947- AmMWSc 92
**Corey**, Clark L 1921- AmMWSc 92
**Corey**, Elias James 1928- AmMWSc 92, FacFETw, IntWW 91, WhoNob 90
**Corey**, Esther Marie 1927- WhoRel 92
**Corey**, Eugene R 1935- AmMWSc 92
**Corey**, Gilbert 1923- AmMWSc 92
**Corey**, Giles d1692 BenetAL 91
**Corey**, Harold Scott 1919- AmMWSc 92
**Corey**, Irene 1925- WhoEnt 92
**Corey**, Jeff 1914- IntMPA 92, WhoEnt 92
**Corey**, Jo WhoEnt 92
**Corey**, John Charles 1938- AmMWSc 92
**Corey**, Joyce Yagla 1938- AmMWSc 92
**Corey**, Kenneth Edward 1938- AmMWSc 92

Corey, Leroy Dale 1942- WhoAmP 91
Corey, Marion Willson 1932- AmMWSc 92
Corey, Mark 1958- WhoFI 92
Corey, Paul 1903- BenetAL 91, WrDr 92
Corey, Paul Frederick 1950- AmMWSc 92
Corey, Raye W. 1941- WhoFI 92
Corey, Richard Boardman 1927- AmMWSc 92
Corey, Sharon Eva 1945- AmMWSc 92
Corey, Stephen DrAPF 91
Corey, Stuart Merton 1933- WhoRel 92
Corey, Victor Brewer 1915- AmMWSc 92
Corey, Virgil E WhoAmP 91
Corfield, Frederick 1915- Who 92
Corfield, Frederick Vernon 1915- IntWW 91
Corfield, Kenneth 1924- Who 92
Corfield, Kenneth George 1924- IntWW 91
Corfield, Peter William Reginald 1937- AmMWSc 92
Corfield, Timothy Lynn 1943- WhoWest 92
Corfman, Caris 1955- WhoEnt 92
Corfman, Philip Albert 1926- AmMWSc 92
Corfu, Haim 1921- IntWW 91
Cori, Carl Ferdinand 1896-1984 FacFETw, WhoNob 90
Cori, Gerty Theresa Radnitz 1896-1957 FacFETw, WhoNob 90
Cori, Osvaldo d1987 IntWW 91N
Coria, Jose Conrado 1952- AmMWSc 92
Coriaty, George Michael 1933- WhoRel 92
Coriden, Michael Warner 1948- WhoAmL 92
Coriell, Kathleen Patricia 1935- AmMWSc 92
Coriell, Lewis L 1911- AmMWSc 92
Coriell, Sam Ray 1935- AmMWSc 92
Corigliano, John 1938- ConCom 92, NewAmDM
Corigliano, John Paul 1938- WhoEnt 92
Corinaldesi, Ernesto 1923- AmMWSc 92
Corinaldi, Austin 1921- WhoBlA 92
Corio, Angela Marie 1964- WhoEnt 92
Coriolanus WrDr 92
Coris, Leonard M. 1940- WhoFI 92
Corish, Joseph Patrick 1961- WhoAmL 92
Corish, Patrick Joseph 1921- IntWW 91
Cork, Cloyne And Ross, Bishop of 1930- Who 92
Cork, Bruce 1915- AmMWSc 92
Cork, Donald Burl 1949- WhoMW 92
Cork, Douglas J 1950- AmMWSc 92
Cork, Holly A 1966- WhoAmP 91
Cork, Howard Dean 1942- WhoRel 92
Cork, Kenneth 1913- IntWW 91, Who 92
Cork, Larry Donald 1942- WhoMW 92
Cork, Linda K Collins 1936- AmMWSc 92
Cork, Patrick Carlyle 1958- WhoAmL 92
Cork, Richard 1947- WrDr 92
Cork, Roger William 1947- Who 92
Cork And Orrery, Earl of 1910- Who 92
Corke, Charles Thomas 1921- AmMWSc 92
Corker, William Russell 1949- WhoAmL 92
Corkern, Walter Harold 1939- AmMWSc 92
Corkery, Christopher Jane DrAPF 91
Corkery, Michael 1926- Who 92
Corkery, Neil A 1940- WhoAmP 91
Corkin, Suzanne Hammond 1937- AmMWSc 92
Corkle, Joseph Patrick 1951- WhoAmP 91
Corkum, Kenneth C 1930- AmMWSc 92
Corle, Edwin 1906-1956 BenetAL 91, TwCWW 91
Corless, Joseph Michael James 1944- AmMWSc 92
Corlett, Clive William 1938- Who 92
Corlett, Ewan Christian Brew 1923- Who 92
Corlett, Gerald Lingham 1925- Who 92
Corlett, Mabel Isobel 1939- AmMWSc 92
Corlett, Michael Philip 1937- AmMWSc 92
Corlett, William 1938- IntAu&W 91, WrDr 92
Corlette, Edith 1942- WhoBlA 92
Corlew, John Gordon 1943- WhoAmL 92
Corley, Anthony 1923- ConAu 34NR
Corley, Charles Calhoun, Jr 1927- AmMWSc 92
Corley, Ernest IntAu&W 91X, WrDr 92
Corley, Glyn Jackson 1916- AmMWSc 92
Corley, John Bryson 1913- AmMWSc 92
Corley, Kenneth 1908- Who 92
Corley, Leslie M. 1946- WhoFI 92
Corley, Michael Early Ferrand 1909- Who 92
Corley, Pat 1930- WhoEnt 92
Corley, Peter Maurice Sinclair 1933- Who 92
Corley, Ralph Randall 1941- WhoFI 92
Corley, Robert Keith 1955- WhoRel 92
Corley, Roger David 1933- Who 92
Corley, Ronald Bruce 1948- AmMWSc 92
Corley, Thomas Anthony Buchanan 1923- IntAu&W 91, WrDr 92
Corley, Tom Edward 1921- AmMWSc 92
Corley, William Gene 1935- AmMWSc 92
Corley-Saunders, Angela Rose 1947- WhoBlA 92
Corley Smith, Gerard Thomas 1909- Who 92
Corliss, Charles Howard 1919- AmMWSc 92
Corliss, Clark Edward 1919- AmMWSc 92
Corliss, Douglas Ralph 1930- WhoWest 92
Corliss, Edith Lou Rovner 1920- AmMWSc 92
Corliss, George Henry 1817-1888 BiInAmS
Corliss, Harry Percival 1886?-1918 BiInAmS
Corliss, John Burt 1936- AmMWSc 92
Corliss, John Ozro 1922- AmMWSc 92
Corliss, Lester Myron 1919- AmMWSc 92
Corliss, Richard Nelson 1944- WhoEnt 92
Cormack, Allan MacLeod 1924- AmMWSc 92, FacFETw, IntWW 91, Who 92, WhoNob 90
Cormack, George Douglas 1933- AmMWSc 92
Cormack, James Frederick 1927- AmMWSc 92
Cormack, John 1922- Who 92
Cormack, Magnus 1906- Who 92
Cormack, Margaret Lawson 1912- ConAu 35NR
Cormack, Patrick 1939- WrDr 92
Cormack, Patrick Thomas 1939- Who 92
Cormack, Robert George Hall 1904- AmMWSc 92
Cormack, Robert Linklater Burke 1935- Who 92
Cormack, William Macintosh 1941- WhoWest 92
Corman, Avery 1935- IntAu&W 91
Corman, Cid 1924- BenetAL 91, ConPo 91, IntAu&W 91, WrDr 92
Corman, Emmett Gary 1930- AmMWSc 92
Corman, Eugene Harold 1927- WhoEnt 92
Corman, Gene 1927- ConTFT 9, IntMPA 92
Corman, Jacob Doyle, Jr 1932- WhoAmP 91
Corman, James Allen 1952- WhoAmL 92
Corman, Julie Ann 1942- WhoEnt 92
Corman, Rebecca Davis 1935- WhoAmP 91
Corman, Roger 1926- FacFETw, IntDcF 2-2
Corman, Roger William 1926- IntMPA 92, IntWW 91, WhoEnt 92
Cormanick, Rosa-Maria 1946- WhoMW 92
Cormany, Michael 1951- ConAu 135
Cormie, Donald Mercer 1922- WhoWest 92
Cormier, Alan Dennis 1945- AmMWSc 92
Cormier, Bruno M 1919- AmMWSc 92
Cormier, Lawrence J. 1927- WhoBlA 92
Cormier, Mark Stephen 1960- WhoWest 92
Cormier, Milton Joseph 1926- AmMWSc 92
Cormier, Randal 1930- AmMWSc 92
Cormier, Reginald Albert 1930- AmMWSc 92
Cormier, Robert 1925- IntAu&W 91, WrDr 92
Cormier, Romae Joseph 1928- AmMWSc 92, WhoMW 92
Cormier, Rufus, Jr. 1948- WhoBlA 92
Cormier, Thomas Michael 1947- AmMWSc 92
Cormon, Fernand 1845-1924 ThHEIm
Corn, Alfred DrAPF 91
Corn, Alfred 1943- BenetAL 91, ConPo 91, IntAu&W 91, WrDr 92
Corn, Gary Richard 1946- WhoFI 92
Corn, Herman 1921- AmMWSc 92
Corn, Ira George, Jr. 1921-1982 ConAu 35NR
Corn, Joseph Edward, Jr. 1932- WhoEnt 92
Corn, Morton 1933- AmMWSc 92
Corn, Robert Bowden 1952- WhoAmP 91
Corn, Stephen Leslie 1944- WhoAmL 92
Corna, Mark Steven 1949- WhoFI 92
Cornaby, Kay Sterling 1936- WhoAmL 92, WhoAmP 91, WhoWest 92
Cornacchio, Joseph V 1934- AmMWSc 92
Cornatzer, William Eugene 1918- AmMWSc 92
Cornberg, Sol, Mrs. Who 92
Cornblath, Marvin 1925- AmMWSc 92
Cornblatt, Alan Jack 1936- WhoAmL 92
Cornbleet, James Sanford 1953- WhoFI 92
Corne, Ray Garrison 1952- WhoAmL 92
Cornea, Doina 1926- IntWW 91
Corneal, Jon Stephen 1946- WhoEnt 92
Corneil, Ernest Ray 1932- AmMWSc 92
Corneil, Hampton Gaskill 1914- WhoMW 92
Corneille IntWW 91
Corneille, Barrett J. 1955- WhoAmL 92
Cornejo, Daniel 1946- WhoHisp 92
Cornejo, Jeffrey Martin 1959- WhoHisp 92
Cornejo, John Francis 1962- WhoEnt 92
Cornejo-Polar, Antonio 1936- WhoHisp 92
Cornelia EncAmaz 91
Cornelio, Albert C 1930- WhoIns 92
Cornelis, Francois 1949- IntWW 91
Cornelison, Carole Jane 1946- WhoBlA 92
Cornelison, Charles Owen 1945- WhoAmL 92
Cornelison, Richard Dan 1942- WhoFI 92
Cornelissen, Michael Adriaan 1943- WhoFI 92
Cornelissen Guillaume, Germaine G 1949- AmMWSc 92
Cornelius EncEarC
Cornelius, Archie J 1931- AmMWSc 92
Cornelius, Billy Dean 1939- AmMWSc 92
Cornelius, Charles Edward 1927- AmMWSc 92
Cornelius, Charles LeSueur, Jr. 1915- WhoAmL 92
Cornelius, David Frederick 1932- Who 92
Cornelius, David Joseph 1939- WhoAmP 91
Cornelius, Don 1937- WhoBlA 92
Cornelius, E B 1918- AmMWSc 92
Cornelius, Helen Lorene 1941- WhoEnt 92
Cornelius, James Alfred 1936- WhoFI 92
Cornelius, James Russell 1953- WhoAmL 92
Cornelius, Karla Marie 1945- WhoFI 92
Cornelius, Larry Max 1943- AmMWSc 92
Cornelius, Marion Edna 1930- WhoWest 92
Cornelius, Peter 1824-1874 NewAmDM
Cornelius, Richard Dean 1947- AmMWSc 92
Cornelius, Robert Nelson, Jr. 1928- WhoBlA 92
Cornelius, Russell Martin 1939- WhoAmL 92
Cornelius, Steven Gregory 1951- AmMWSc 92
Cornelius, Steven Joel 1948- WhoMW 92
Cornelius, Ulysses S., Sr. 1913- WhoBlA 92
Cornelius, Walter Felix 1922- WhoAmL 92
Cornelius, William Joseph 1927- WhoAmL 92
Cornelius, William Milton 1936- WhoBlA 92
Corneliussen, Roger DuWayne 1931- AmMWSc 92
Cornell, Alan 1929- AmMWSc 92
Cornell, C Allin 1938- AmMWSc 92
Cornell, Creighton N 1933- AmMWSc 92
Cornell, David 1925- AmMWSc 92
Cornell, David Allan 1937- AmMWSc 92
Cornell, David Roger 1944- WhoMW 92
Cornell, Donald Gilmore 1931- AmMWSc 92
Cornell, Ellie 1963- WhoEnt 92
Cornell, George Vincent, III 1956- WhoAmL 92
Cornell, Howard Vernon 1947- AmMWSc 92
Cornell, James Mark 1953- WhoRel 92
Cornell, James Morris 1937- AmMWSc 92
Cornell, James S 1947- AmMWSc 92
Cornell, John 1941- IntMPA 92
Cornell, John Alston 1922- AmMWSc 92, WhoFI 92
Cornell, John Andrew 1941- AmMWSc 92
Cornell, John Christopher 1952- WhoEnt 92
Cornell, John Robert 1943- WhoAmL 92
Cornell, Joseph 1903-1972 FacFETw, ModArCr 2 [port]
Cornell, Julien 1910- AmPeW
Cornell, Katherine 1893-1974 FacFETw
Cornell, Kenneth Lee 1945- WhoAmL 92
Cornell, Neal William 1937- AmMWSc 92
Cornell, Richard Farnham 1952- WhoAmL 92
Cornell, Richard Garth 1930- AmMWSc 92
Cornell, Robert John 1919- WhoAmP 91
Cornell, Robert Joseph 1940- AmMWSc 92
Cornell, Roy W 1943- WhoAmP 91
Cornell, Samuel 1730-1781 DcNCBi 1
Cornell, Samuel Douglas 1915- AmMWSc 92
Cornell, Samuel Douglas, III 1946- WhoWest 92
Cornell, Stephen Watson 1942- AmMWSc 92
Cornell, Theodore Elmer 1949- WhoAmL 92
Cornell, Vincent Joseph 1951- WhoRel 92
Cornell, W A 1921- AmMWSc 92
Cornell, Ward MacLaurin 1924- Who 92
Cornell, William Ainsworth, Jr 1952- WhoAmP 91
Cornell, William Crowninshield 1941- AmMWSc 92
Cornell-Bell, Ann Hall AmMWSc 92
Cornelsen, Linda Sue 1951- WhoRel 92
Cornelsen, Paul Frederick 1923- WhoFI 92, WhoMW 92
Cornelsen, Rufus 1914- WhoRel 92
Cornely, Paul B. 1906- WhoBlA 92
Cornely, Paul Bertau 1906- AmMWSc 92
Corner, Edred John Henry 1906- FacFETw, IntWW 91, Who 92
Corner, Frank Henry 1920- Who 92
Corner, Harold Leroy 1934- WhoFI 92
Corner, James Oliver 1917- AmMWSc 92
Corner, Mark Adrian 1953- WhoRel 92
Corner, Philip 1924- Who 92
Corner, Thomas James 1960- WhoMW 92
Corner, Thomas Richard 1940- AmMWSc 92
Corness, Colin Ross 1931- IntWW 91, Who 92
Cornet, I I 1912- AmMWSc 92
Cornetet, Wendell Hillis, Jr 1923- AmMWSc 92
Cornett, Laureen Elizabeth 1946- WhoWest 92
Cornett, Lawrence Eugene 1951- AmMWSc 92
Cornett, R. Orin 1913- WrDr 92
Cornett, Richard Orin 1913- AmMWSc 92
Cornette, James L 1935- AmMWSc 92
Cornfeld, David 1926- AmMWSc 92
Cornfeld, Richard Steven 1950- WhoAmL 92
Cornfeld, Stuart IntMPA 92
Cornfield, Darlene 1953- WhoAmP 91
Cornfield, Hubert 1929- WhoEnt 92
Cornford, Clifford 1918- Who 92
Cornford, Eain M 1942- AmMWSc 92
Cornford, James Peters 1935- Who 92
Cornforth, Clarence Michael 1940- AmMWSc 92
Cornforth, John 1917- Who 92
Cornforth, John Warcup 1917- FacFETw, IntWW 91, WhoNob 90
Corngold, Noel Robert David 1929- AmMWSc 92
Corngold, Stanley 1934- WrDr 92
Cornhill, John Fredrick 1949- AmMWSc 92
Cornie, James Allen 1937- AmMWSc 92
Cornillon, Pierre 1935- IntWW 91
Cornilsen, Bahne Carl 1945- AmMWSc 92
Corning, Joy 1932- WhoAmP 91
Corning, Joy Cole 1932- WhoMW 92
Corning, Mary Elizabeth 1925- AmMWSc 92
Corning, Nicholas F. 1945- WhoAmL 92
Corning, Roland Shelton 1943- WhoAmP 91
Cornish, Betty W. 1936- WhoBlA 92
Cornish, F TwCSFW 91
Cornish, Francis Who 92
Cornish, Jack Bertram 1918- Who 92
Cornish, James Easton 1939- Who 92
Cornish, Jeannette Carter 1946- WhoAmL 92, WhoBlA 92
Cornish, Kurtis George 1942- AmMWSc 92
Cornish, Larry Martin 1946- WhoWest 92
Cornish, Louis Craig 1870-1950 RelLAm 91
Cornish, Robert Francis 1942- Who 92
Cornish, Sam 1935- ConPo 91, IntAu&W 91, WrDr 92
Cornish, William Herbert 1906- Who 92
Cornish, William Rodolph 1937- IntWW 91, Who 92
Cornman, Ivor 1914- AmMWSc 92
Cornman, Susan Bambi 1956- WhoAmL 92
Corno, Charles Joseph, Jr. 1946- WhoRel 92
Cornock, Archibald Rae 1920- Who 92
Cornock, Charles Gordon 1935- Who 92
Cornock, Dana Wolf 1956- WhoEnt 92
Cornoni-Huntley, Joan Claire 1931- AmMWSc 92
Cornplanter BenetAL 91
Cornsweet, Tom Norman 1929- AmMWSc 92
Cornwall, Archdeacon of Who 92
Cornwall, Claude Cyril, Jr. 1934- WhoFI 92
Cornwall, Henry Bedinger 1844-1917 BiInAmS
Cornwall, Ian Wolfran 1909- Who 92
Cornwall, John Michael 1934- AmMWSc 92, WhoWest 92
Cornwall, Kent Neeley 1954- WhoWest 92
Cornwall, Shirley M. 1918- WhoBlA 92
Cornwall-Legh Who 92
Cornwallis Who 92
Cornwallis, Baron 1921- Who 92
Cornwallis, Charles 1738-1805 BenetAL 91, BlkwEAR [port]
Cornwell, Anita R. DrAPF 91
Cornwell, Bernard IntAu&W 91
Cornwell, Bernard 1944- WrDr 92

**Cornwell**, Charles Daniel 1924- *AmMWSc 92*
**Cornwell**, David George 1927- *AmMWSc 92*
**Cornwell**, David John Moore 1931- *IntAu&W 91, IntWW 91, Who 92*
**Cornwell**, Edward Eugene, III 1956- *WhoBlA 92*
**Cornwell**, John *IntAu&W 91*
**Cornwell**, John Calhoun 1944- *AmMWSc 92*
**Cornwell**, John Fenimore 1941- *WhoMW 92*
**Cornwell**, Larry Wilmer 1941- *AmMWSc 92*
**Cornwell**, Mary Ramona 1933- *WhoAmP 91*
**Cornwell**, Patricia Daniels 1956- *ConAu 134*
**Cornwell**, Roger Eliot 1922- *Who 92*
**Cornwell**, W. Don 1948- *WhoBlA 92*
**Cornwell**, William David 1960- *WhoBlA 92*
**Cornwell**, William John 1959- *WhoAmL 92*
**Cornyn**, John *WhoAmP 91*
**Cornyn**, John Eugene 1906- *WhoFI 92, WhoMW 92*
**Cornyn**, John Eugene, III 1945- *WhoWest 92*
**Cornyn**, John Joseph 1944- *AmMWSc 92*
**Coro**, Alicia Camacho 1937- *WhoHisp 92*
**Corona**, Barry N. *WhoHisp 92*
**Corona**, Bert N. 1918- *WhoHisp 92*
**Corona**, Catherine 1956- *WhoEnt 92*
**Corona**, Henry *WhoHisp 92*
**Corona**, Richard Patrick 1962- *WhoHisp 92*
**Coronado**, Apolonio, Jr. 1935- *WhoHisp 92*
**Coronado**, Beatriz 1960- *WhoHisp 92*
**Coronado**, Elaine Marie 1959- *WhoHisp 92*
**Coronado**, Francisco Vasquez de 1510?-1554 *BenetAL 91, HisDSpE*
**Coronado**, Gil 1936- *WhoHisp 92*
**Coronado**, Jose 1950- *WhoHisp 92*
**Coronado**, Jose R. 1932- *WhoHisp 92*
**Coronado**, Juan Vasquez de 1523-1565 *HisDSpE*
**Coronado**, Leopoldo Angel 1942- *WhoHisp 92*
**Coronado**, Santiago Sybert 1951- *WhoAmL 92*
**Coronado**, Shirley Jeanne 1948- *WhoFI 92*
**Coronado-Greeley**, Adela 1934- *WhoHisp 92*
**Coronas**, Jose J. 1942- *WhoHisp 92*
**Coronel**, Francisco Faustino 1948- *WhoHisp 92, WhoWest 92*
**Coronel**, Gustavo Rafael 1933- *WhoFI 92*
**Coronel De Palma**, Luis 1925- *IntWW 91*
**Coroniti**, Ferdinand Vincent 1943- *AmMWSc 92*
**Cororan**, Robert J *WhoAmP 91*
**Corot**, Camille 1796-1875 *ThHEIm [port]*
**Corotis**, Ross Barry 1945- *AmMWSc 92*
**Corpe**, William Albert 1924- *AmMWSc 92*
**Corpening**, Wayne 1914- *WhoAmP 91*
**Corpi**, Lucha 1945- *WhoHisp 92*
**Corpman**, Izora *DrAPF 91*
**Corprew**, Charles Sumner, Jr. 1929- *WhoBlA 92*
**Corpstein**, Pete *WhoAmP 91*
**Corpus**, Alfonso 1940- *WhoHisp 92*
**Corpuz**, Teresa Agrifina 1951- *WhoWest 92*
**Corr**, Chris 1963- *WhoAmP 91*
**Corr**, Edwin Gharst 1934- *IntWW 91, WhoAmP 91*
**Corr**, Kelly 1948- *WhoAmL 92*
**Corr**, Mary Ann *WhoRel 92*
**Corr**, Robert Mark 1948- *WhoMW 92*
**Corrada**, Baltasar 1935- *WhoAmP 91*
**Corrada**, Roberto Leon 1960- *WhoAmL 92*
**Corrada-Bertsch**, Aida 1958- *WhoHisp 92*
**Corradadel Rio**, Alvaro 1942- *WhoRel 92*
**Corradini**, Enrico 1865-1931 *BiDExR, EncTR 91*
**Corradino**, Robert Anthony 1938- *AmMWSc 92*
**Corrado**, Ernest Joseph 1926- *WhoAmL 92*
**Corrado**, Fred 1940- *WhoFI 92*
**Corral**, Edward Anthony 1931- *WhoHisp 92*
**Corral**, Wilfrido Howard 1950- *WhoHisp 92*
**Corralejo**, Robert A. 1935- *WhoHisp 92*
**Corrales**, Frank N. 1939- *WhoHisp 92*
**Corrales**, Hector P. 1953- *WhoHisp 92*
**Corrales**, Jose 1937- *WhoHisp 92*
**Corrales**, Oralia Lillie 1940- *WhoHisp 92*
**Corrales**, Pat 1941- *WhoHisp 92*
**Corrales**, Scott Fidel 1963- *WhoHisp 92*
**Corrallo**, Mark Lyman 1957- *WhoAmL 92*
**Correa**, Charles M. 1930- *IntWW 91*
**Correa**, Charles Mark 1930- *Who 92*
**Correa**, Emilio *BlkOlyM*
**Correa**, Galo Arturo, Sr. 1944- *WhoHisp 92*
**Correa**, Gustavo H. *WhoHisp 92*
**Correa**, Hernan Dario 1960- *WhoWest 92*
**Correa**, Jose Ramon 1929- *WhoHisp 92*
**Correa**, Victor M. 1935- *WhoHisp 92*
**Correa**, Yamil 1943- *WhoRel 92*
**Correa Do Lago**, Antonio 1918- *IntWW 91*
**Correa-Perez**, Margarita *WhoHisp 92*
**Corredor**, Livia Margarita 1960- *WhoAmL 92*
**Correia**, Alberto Abrantes 1956- *WhoFI 92*
**Correia**, John Arthur 1945- *AmMWSc 92*
**Correia**, John F *WhoAmP 91*
**Correia**, John Sidney 1937- *AmMWSc 92*
**Correia**, Kathaleen Marie 1965- *WhoEnt 92*
**Correia**, Linda Mercedes 1955- *WhoHisp 92*
**Correia**, Maria Almira 1946- *AmMWSc 92*
**Correia**, Robert 1939- *WhoAmP 91*
**Correia-Afonso**, John 1924- *WhoRel 92*
**Correll**, Joanna Rae 1948- *WhoAmL 92*
**Correll**, Noble Otto, Jr. 1920- *WhoWest 92*
**Correll**, Patrick Gerald 1955- *WhoRel 92*
**Correll**, Philip Kent 1954- *WhoAmL 92*
**Correll**, Ruth A 1915- *WhoAmP 91*
**Corren**, Grace *IntAu&W 91X, TwCSFW 91, WrDr 92*
**Co-rens**, Karl Erich 1864-1933 *FacFETw*
**Correnti**, Mario *ConAu 133*
**Corretjer**, Juan Antonio 1908-1985 *WhoHisp 92N*
**Corretti**, Gilberto *DcTwDes*
**Correy**, Lee *TwCSFW 91, WrDr 92*
**Correze**, Jacques 1912-1991 *NewYTBS 91 [port]*
**Corri**, Adrienne 1933- *IntMPA 92*
**Corrie**, Craig Royal *WhoIns 92*
**Corrie**, John Alexander 1935- *Who 92*
**Corrie**, W. Rodney 1919- *Who 92*
**Corriel**, Michele *DrAPF 91*
**Corriere**, Joseph N, Jr 1937- *AmMWSc 92*
**Corrigall**, Don Joseph 1929- *WhoMW 92*
**Corrigan**, Charles Lawrence 1936- *WhoRel 92*
**Corrigan**, Daniel Gerard 1957- *WhoFI 92*
**Corrigan**, Dennis Arthur 1951- *AmMWSc 92*
**Corrigan**, E. Gerald 1941- *IntWW 91, WhoFI 92*
**Corrigan**, James John, Jr 1935- *AmMWSc 92*
**Corrigan**, John Joseph 1929- *AmMWSc 92*
**Corrigan**, John Raymond 1919- *AmMWSc 92*
**Corrigan**, Judith Ann 1937- *WhoRel 92*
**Corrigan**, Kevin Edward 1956- *WhoEnt 92*
**Corrigan**, Lynda Dyann 1949- *WhoAmL 92*
**Corrigan**, Mairead 1944- *FacFETw [port], WhoNob 90*
**Corrigan**, Margaret Mary *Who 92*
**Corrigan**, Mary Kathryn 1930- *WhoWest 92*
**Corrigan**, Maura Denise 1948- *WhoAmL 92*
**Corrigan**, Patricia Ouimette 1930- *WhoAmP 91*
**Corrigan**, Paul G., Jr. *DrAPF 91*
**Corrigan**, Robert Anthony 1935- *WhoWest 92*
**Corrigan**, Robert W 1927- *IntAu&W 91, WrDr 92*
**Corrigan**, Thomas C 1938- *WhoAmP 91*
**Corrigan**, Thomas Stephen 1932- *Who 92*
**Corrigan**, William Thomas 1921- *WhoEnt 92*
**Corrigan-Maguire**, Mairead 1944- *IntWW 91, Who 92*
**Corrin**, Darwin Brent 1949- *WhoMW 92*
**Corrin**, John Bowes 1922- *Who 92*
**Corrin**, John William 1932- *Who 92*
**Corrin**, Malcolm L. 1924- *WhoBlA 92*
**Corrington**, Joyce Hooper 1936- *WhoEnt 92*
**Corripio**, Armando Benito 1941- *AmMWSc 92*
**Corripio Ahumada**, Ernesto 1919- *IntWW 91, WhoRel 92*
**Corris**, Peter 1942- *ConAu 135, IntAu&W 91, WrDr 92*
**Corriveau**, Armand Gerard 1945- *AmMWSc 92*
**Corroon**, Robert F 1922- *WhoIns 92*
**Corrozi**, Philip J 1933- *WhoAmP 91*
**Corruccini**, Linton Reid 1944- *AmMWSc 92*
**Corruccini**, Robert Spencer 1949- *AmMWSc 92, WhoMW 92*
**Corry** *Who 92*
**Corry**, Viscount 1985- *Who 92*
**Corry**, Andrew F 1922- *AmMWSc 92*
**Corry**, Carl *WhoEnt 92*
**Corry**, Charles Albert 1932- *WhoFI 92*
**Corry**, John Adams 1931- *WhoAmL 92*
**Corry**, Kathryn Mary 1948- *WhoWest 92*
**Corry**, Patricia A. 1944- *WhoBlA 92*
**Corry**, Thomas M 1926- *AmMWSc 92*
**Corry**, William 1924- *Who 92*
**Corsar**, Mary Drummond 1927- *Who 92*
**Corsaro**, Frank Andrew 1924- *IntWW 91, WhoEnt 92*
**Corsaro**, Robert Dominic 1944- *AmMWSc 92*
**Corse**, Joseph Walters 1913- *AmMWSc 92*
**Corsello**, Lily Joann 1953- *WhoRel 92*
**Corseri**, Gary Steven *DrAPF 91*
**Corsi**, Edward 1896-1965 *DcAmImH*
**Corsi**, Philip Donald 1928- *WhoAmL 92*
**Corsiglia**, George Richard 1935- *WhoAmL 92*
**Corsini**, A 1934- *AmMWSc 92*
**Corsini**, Dennis Lee 1942- *AmMWSc 92*
**Corskie**, John Campbell *WhoAmP 91*
**Corso**, Frank Mitchell 1928- *WhoAmL 92*
**Corso**, Gregory *DrAPF 91*
**Corso**, Gregory 1930- *BenetAL 91, ConPo 91, WrDr 92*
**Corso**, Thomas David 1960- *WhoMW 92*
**Corson**, Dale R. 1914- *IntWW 91*
**Corson**, Dale Raymond 1914- *AmMWSc 92*
**Corson**, David Allan 1951- *WhoRel 92*
**Corson**, Don Edward 1956- *WhoAmL 92*
**Corson**, George Edwin, Jr 1940- *AmMWSc 92*
**Corson**, Harry Herbert 1931- *AmMWSc 92*
**Corson**, J. Jay, IV 1935- *WhoAmL 92*
**Corson**, Joseph Mackie 1924- *AmMWSc 92*
**Corson**, Maurice S. 1933- *WhoRel 92*
**Corson**, Richard *IntAu&W 91, WrDr 92*
**Corson**, Samuel Abraham 1909- *AmMWSc 92*
**Corson**, Thomas Harold 1927- *WhoFI 92, WhoMW 92*
**Corstange**, Engel 1923- *WhoAmP 91*
**Corsten**, Severin 1920- *IntWW 91*
**Corstvet**, Richard E 1928- *AmMWSc 92*
**Cort**, Bud 1950- *IntMPA 92*
**Cort**, Bud 1951- *WhoEnt 92*
**Cort**, Robert W. *IntMPA 92*
**Cort**, Susannah 1957- *AmMWSc 92*
**Cort**, Van *TwCWW 91*
**Cort**, Winifred Mitchell *AmMWSc 92*
**Cortada**, James W. 1946- *ConAu 133*
**Cortada**, Rafael L. 1934- *IntWW 91*
**Cortada**, Rafael Leon 1934- *WhoBlA 92, WhoHisp 92*
**Cortazar**, Julio 1914-1984 *BenetAL 91, DcLB 113 [port], FacFETw, LiExTwC*
**Cortazar Sanz**, Rene 1953- *IntWW 91*
**Cortazzi**, Hugh 1924- *IntWW 91, Who 92*
**Corte**, Arthur B 1934- *WhoAmP 91*
**Corte**, Lawrence Julius 1954- *WhoAmL 92*
**Corteen**, Craig *IntAu&W 91X*
**Corteen**, Wes *IntAu&W 91X, TwCWW 91*
**Cortelyou**, John R. 1914- *WhoMW 92*
**Cortes**, Antonio 1956- *WhoHisp 92*
**Cortes**, Carlos Eliseo 1934- *WhoHisp 92*
**Cortes**, Freddy G. 1941- *WhoHisp 92*
**Cortes**, Gary Hoffman 1939- *WhoHisp 92*
**Cortes**, Hernan 1485-1547 *HisDSpE*
**Cortes**, Hernando 1485-1547 *BenetAL 91*
**Cortes**, Martin *HisDSpE*
**Cortes**, Martin 1532?- *HisDSpE*
**Cortes**, Pedro Juan 1949- *WhoHisp 92*
**Cortes**, Ramiro 1933-1984 *NewAmDM*
**Cortes**, William Antony 1947- *WhoHisp 92*
**Cortes**, William Patrick 1955- *WhoAmL 92, WhoFI 92*
**Cortes Candelaria**, Doris Janice 1956- *WhoHisp 92*
**Cortes-Hwang**, Adriana *WhoHisp 92*
**Cortese**, Alfred William, Jr. 1937- *WhoAmL 92*
**Cortese**, Dominic L 1932- *WhoAmP 91*
**Cortese**, Joseph Samuel, II 1955- *WhoAmL 92*
**Cortese**, Ramona Ann 1940- *WhoAmP 91*
**Cortese**, Valentina 1925- *IntMPA 92*
**Cortesi**, Gaetano 1912- *IntWW 91*
**Cortez**, Angela Denise 1964- *WhoHisp 92*
**Cortez**, Angelina Guadalupe 1949- *WhoHisp 92*
**Cortez**, Carlos Alfredo 1923- *WhoHisp 92*
**Cortez**, Frank T. 1950- *WhoHisp 92*
**Cortez**, Gilbert Diaz, Sr. 1942- *WhoHisp 92*
**Cortez**, Hernando 1485-1547 *BenetAL 91*
**Cortez**, Hernando Ventura 1964- *WhoEnt 92*
**Cortez**, Jayne *DrAPF 91*
**Cortez**, Jayne 1936- *WhoBlA 92*
**Cortez**, Johnny J. 1950- *WhoHisp 92*
**Cortez**, Louis M. *WhoHisp 92*
**Cortez**, Luis Abran 1935- *WhoAmP 91*
**Cortez**, Manuel J. 1939- *WhoHisp 92*
**Cortez**, Stanley 1908- *IntMPA 92*
**Cortez-Gentner**, Celia M. 1964- *WhoHisp 92*
**Corth**, Richard 1925- *AmMWSc 92*
**Corti**, Thomas George 1955- *WhoMW 92*
**Cortina**, Raquel 1946- *WhoHisp 92*
**Cortina**, Rodolfo Jose 1946- *WhoHisp 92*
**Cortina Mauri**, Pedro 1908- *IntWW 91*
**Cortina y Mauri**, Pedro 1908- *HisDSpE*
**Cortner**, Jean A 1930- *AmMWSc 92*
**Cortner**, Melvin Lloyd 1942- *WhoMW 92*
**Cortner**, Scott Alan 1955- *WhoMW 92*
**Cortor**, Eldzier 1916- *WhoBlA 92*
**Cortot**, Alfred 1877-1962 *FacFETw, NewAmDM*
**Cortright**, Edgar Maurice 1923- *AmMWSc 92*
**Cortright**, Inga Ann 1949- *WhoWest 92*
**Corty**, Claude 1924- *AmMWSc 92*
**Corujo Collazo**, Juan *WhoAmP 91*
**Corum**, Beverly Ann 1936- *WhoAmP 91*
**Corum**, James Frederic 1943- *AmMWSc 92*
**Corum**, Raymond Keith 1947- *WhoRel 92*
**Corvalan**, Maria Celia 1949- *WhoEnt 92*
**Corvedale**, Viscount 1973- *Who 92*
**Corvino**, Alfredo Alfonso 1916- *WhoEnt 92*
**Corvo**, Baron *LiExTwC, RfGEnL 91*
**Corwin**, Brent Edwin 1951- *WhoAmL 92*
**Corwin**, Bruce Conrad 1940- *IntMPA 92*
**Corwin**, Bruce James 1947- *WhoWest 92*
**Corwin**, Gilbert 1921- *AmMWSc 92*
**Corwin**, H E 1919- *AmMWSc 92*
**Corwin**, Harold G, Jr 1943- *AmMWSc 92*
**Corwin**, Harry O 1938- *AmMWSc 92*
**Corwin**, Jack B. 1951- *WhoWest 92*
**Corwin**, James Blade 1948- *WhoWest 92*
**Corwin**, Jeffrey Todd 1951- *AmMWSc 92*
**Corwin**, Laurence Martin 1929- *AmMWSc 92*
**Corwin**, Lawrence Jay 1943- *AmMWSc 92*
**Corwin**, Norman *LesBEnT 92*
**Corwin**, Norman 1910- *BenetAL 91, IntMPA 92, IntWW 91, WhoEnt 92, WrDr 92*
**Corwin**, Philip Seth 1950- *WhoAmL 92, WhoFI 92*
**Corwin**, Sherman Phillip 1917- *WhoAmL 92*
**Corwin**, Thomas Lewis 1947- *AmMWSc 92*
**Cory**, Charles Raymond 1922- *Who 92*
**Cory**, Charles Robinson 1955- *WhoEnt 92, WhoFI 92*
**Cory**, Clinton James Donald d1991 *Who 92N*
**Cory**, Desmond *IntAu&W 91X, WrDr 92*
**Cory**, Donald 1937- *Who 92*
**Cory**, Jerre Viera 1949- *WhoMW 92*
**Cory**, John 1928- *Who 92*
**Cory**, Joseph G 1937- *AmMWSc 92*
**Cory**, Michael 1941- *AmMWSc 92*
**Cory**, Paul R 1926- *WhoIns 92*
**Cory**, Raymond *Who 92*
**Cory**, Robert Mackenzie 1943- *AmMWSc 92*
**Cory**, Timothy Robert 1961- *WhoMW 92*
**Cory**, William Eugene 1927- *AmMWSc 92*
**Cory-Slechta**, Deborah Ann 1950- *AmMWSc 92*
**Cory-Wright**, Richard 1944- *Who 92*
**Coryell**, Daniel Carl 1951- *WhoRel 92*
**Coryell**, Janet L. 1955- *ConAu 135*
**Coryell**, John Russell 1848?-1924 *BenetAL 91*
**Coryell**, Larry 1943- *WhoEnt 92*
**Coryell**, Margaret E 1913- *AmMWSc 92*
**Coryn**, James J. 1932- *WhoAmL 92*
**Corzine**, Vernon Dale 1933- *WhoRel 92*
**Corzo**, Humberto 1935- *WhoHisp 92*
**Corzo**, Miguel Angel 1942- *WhoHisp 92*
**Cosa**, Juan de la d1510 *HisDSpE*
**Cosand**, Walter Allen 1950- *WhoWest 92*
**Cosar**, Ahmet 1952- *WhoFI 92*
**Cosby**, Bill *LesBEnT 92 [port], SmATA 66 [port]*
**Cosby**, Bill 1937- *ConTFT 9, FacFETw, IntAu&W 91, WhoEnt 92, WrDr 92*
**Cosby**, Bill 1938- *IntMPA 92*
**Cosby**, Camille 1945- *NotBlAW 92*
**Cosby**, Camille Olivia Hanks 1945- *WhoBlA 92*
**Cosby**, Dabney 1779?-1862 *DcNCBi 1*
**Cosby**, James C. *WhoBlA 92*
**Cosby**, Jane Whykoff Royster 1929- *WhoRel 92*
**Cosby**, Lynwood Anthony 1928- *AmMWSc 92*
**Cosby**, Michael Ray 1950- *WhoRel 92*
**Cosby**, William Francis, Jr 1949- *WhoAmP 91*
**Cosby**, William Henry 1937- *WhoBlA 92*
**Cosby**, William Henry, Jr. 1937- *SmATA 66 [port]*
**Coscarelli**, Don 1954- *WhoEnt 92*
**Coscarelli**, Waldimero 1926- *AmMWSc 92*
**Coscia**, Anthony Thomas 1928- *AmMWSc 92*
**Coscia**, Carmine James 1935- *AmMWSc 92*
**Coscina**, Donald Victor 1943- *AmMWSc 92*
**Cose**, Ellis 1951- *WhoBlA 92*
**Cosell**, Howard *LesBEnT 92*
**Cosell**, Howard 1920- *IntMPA 92*
**Cosens**, Kenneth W 1915- *AmMWSc 92*

**Cosentino,** Robert J. 1954- *WhoAmL 92*
**Cosenza,** Arthur George 1924- *WhoEnt 92*
**Cosenza,** Vincent John 1962- *WhoFI 92*
**Coser,** Lewis A. 1913- *WrDr 92*
**Coser,** Rose Laub 1916- *WomSoc*
**Cosford,** William Clark 1946- *WhoEnt 92*
**Cosgarea,** Andrew, Jr 1934- *AmMWSc 92*
**Cosgrave,** Liam 1920- *IntWW 91, Who 92*
**Cosgrave,** Patrick 1941- *IntAu&W 91, WrDr 92*
**Cosgrave,** Patrick John 1941- *Who 92*
**Cosgriff,** Thomas Michael 1945- *AmMWSc 92*
**Cosgrove,** Cameron 1957- *WhoWest 92*
**Cosgrove,** Clifford James 1927- *AmMWSc 92*
**Cosgrove,** Daniel Joseph 1952- *AmMWSc 92*
**Cosgrove,** David R. 1957- *WhoAmL 92*
**Cosgrove,** Elly 1930- *WhoMW 92*
**Cosgrove,** Gerald Edward 1920- *AmMWSc 92*
**Cosgrove,** Hazel Josephine *Who 92*
**Cosgrove,** Howard Edward, Jr. 1943- *WhoFI 92*
**Cosgrove,** James 1939- *TwCPaSc*
**Cosgrove,** James Francis 1929- *AmMWSc 92*
**Cosgrove,** John 1945- *WhoFI 92*
**Cosgrove,** John Francis 1949- *WhoAmP 91*
**Cosgrove,** John Joseph 1935- *WhoEnt 92*
**Cosgrove,** Kathleen Ann 1958- *WhoFI 92*
**Cosgrove,** Stanley Leonard 1926- *AmMWSc 92*
**Cosgrove,** William Burnham 1920- *AmMWSc 92*
**Cosgrove,** William Jerome 1909- *WhoFI 92*
**Cosh,** John Morton 1924- *WhoWest 92*
**Coshburn,** Henry S., Jr. 1936- *WhoBlA 92*
**Cosimano,** Thomas Francis 1951- *WhoFI 92*
**Coskran,** Kathleen *DrAPF 91*
**Cosler,** Steven Douglas 1955- *WhoMW 92*
**Coslett,** Franklin *WhoAmP 91*
**Cosman,** Bard Clifford 1963- *AmMWSc 92, WhoWest 92*
**Cosman,** David John 1954- *AmMWSc 92*
**Cosman,** Milein 1922- *TwCPaSc*
**Cosmas and Damian** *EncEarC*
**Cosmas Indicopleustes** *EncEarC*
**Cosmas Melodos** d760? *EncEarC*
**Cosmas Vestitor** *EncEarC*
**Cosmas,** Stephen Constantine 1943- *WhoMW 92*
**Cosmatos,** George Pan *IntMPA 92*
**Cosmides,** George James 1926- *AmMWSc 92*
**Cosmos,** Ethel 1923- *AmMWSc 92*
**Cosmos,** Jean 1923- *IntWW 91*
**Cosner,** Wendell E 1929- *WhoAmP 91*
**Cosper,** Andrea Verbie *WhoMW 92*
**Cosper,** David Russell 1942- *AmMWSc 92, WhoMW 92*
**Cosper,** Paula 1947- *AmMWSc 92*
**Cosper,** Sammie Wayne 1933- *AmMWSc 92*
**Cospolich,** James D 1944- *AmMWSc 92*
**Coss,** John Edward 1947- *WhoMW 92*
**Coss,** Raymond Lee 1956- *WhoAmL 92*
**Coss,** Ronald Allen 1947- *AmMWSc 92*
**Coss,** Sharon Elizabeth 1950- *WhoWest 92*
**Cossa,** Dominic Frank 1935- *WhoEnt 92*
**Cossack,** Zafrallah Taha 1948- *AmMWSc 92*
**Cossairt,** Jack Donald 1948- *AmMWSc 92*
**Cossar,** George Payne 1907- *WhoAmP 91*
**Cosse,** R. Paul 1956- *WhoFI 92*
**Cosseboom,** Michael John 1963- *WhoFI 92*
**Cosserat,** Kay 1947- *Who 92*
**Cossette,** Bill Roger 1955- *WhoMW 92*
**Cossette,** Pierre *WhoEnt 92*
**Cossey,** James Edwin 1947- *WhoRel 92*
**Cossham,** Christopher Hugh 1929- *Who 92*
**Cossi,** Olga *SmATA 67 [port]*
**Cossiga,** Francesco 1928- *IntWW 91*
**Cossins,** Edwin Albert 1937- *AmMWSc 92, IntWW 91*
**Cossitt,** James Henry 1957- *WhoAmL 92*
**Cossitt,** Jan 1950- *WhoRel 92*
**Cosslett,** Vernon Ellis d1990 *IntWW 91N, Who 92N*
**Cossons,** Neil 1939- *IntWW 91, Who 92*
**Cossotto,** Fiorenza 1935- *NewAmDM*
**Cossutta,** Carlo 1932- *IntWW 91*
**Cossutta,** Renee Claire 1955- *WhoWest 92*
**Cost,** J L 1920- *AmMWSc 92*
**Cost,** James R 1928- *AmMWSc 92*
**Cost,** Thomas Lee 1937- *AmMWSc 92*
**Costa,** Anthony Paul 1961- *WhoHisp 92*
**Costa,** Antonio Maria 1941- *IntWW 91*
**Costa,** Catherine A 1926- *WhoAmP 91*
**Costa,** Clarence 1947- *WhoEnt 92*
**Costa,** Daniel Louis 1948- *AmMWSc 92*
**Costa,** Daniel Paul 1952- *AmMWSc 92*
**Costa,** Erminio 1924- *AmMWSc 92*
**Costa,** Frank J. *WhoHisp 92*
**Costa,** Frank N 1945- *WhoAmP 91*
**Costa,** Gustavo 1930- *WhoWest 92*
**Costa,** James Manuel 1952- *WhoAmP 91*
**Costa,** John 1922- *WhoEnt 92*
**Costa,** John Emil 1947- *AmMWSc 92*
**Costa,** Lorenzo F 1931- *AmMWSc 92*
**Costa,** Lucio 1902- *IntWW 91*
**Costa,** Luis *WhoHisp 92*
**Costa,** Manuel Pinto da 1937- *IntWW 91*
**Costa,** Marithelma 1955- *WhoHisp 92*
**Costa,** Max 1952- *AmMWSc 92*
**Costa,** Patricia Ann 1953- *WhoEnt 92*
**Costa,** Paul T, Jr 1942- *AmMWSc 92*
**Costa,** Ralph Charles 1956- *WhoHisp 92*
**Costa,** Raymond Lincoln, Jr 1948- *AmMWSc 92*
**Costa,** Rebecca Dazai 1955- *WhoWest 92*
**Costa,** Santo Joseph 1945- *WhoAmL 92*
**Costa,** Sequeria 1929- *WhoEnt 92*
**Costa,** William Thomas, Jr 1932- *WhoAmP 91*
**Costa Ferreira,** Jose d1991 *NewYTBS 91*
**Costa-Gavras** 1933- *FacFETw*
**Costa-Gavras,** Constantin 1933- *IntDcF 2-2 [port], IntMPA 92*
**Costa-Gavras,** Kostantinos 1933- *IntWW 91*
**Costa Mendez,** Nicanor 1922- *IntWW 91*
**Costabile,** Fred 1952- *WhoFI 92*
**Costache,** George Ioan 1943- *AmMWSc 92*
**Costain,** Cecil Clifford 1922- *AmMWSc 92*
**Costain,** John Kendall 1929- *AmMWSc 92*
**Costain,** Noel Leslie 1914- *Who 92*
**Costain,** Peter John 1938- *Who 92*
**Costain,** Thomas 1885-1965 *BenetAL 91*
**Costakis,** George 1912-1990 *AnObit 1990, SovUnBD*
**Costales,** Federico *WhoHisp 92*
**Costamagna,** Carlo 1881-1965 *BiDExR*
**Costantini,** Dominique 1889-1986 *BiDExR*
**Costantino,** Marc Shaw 1945- *AmMWSc 92*
**Costantino,** Raymond Scott 1963- *WhoAmL 92*
**Costantino,** Robert Francis 1941- *AmMWSc 92*
**Costanza,** Albert James 1917- *AmMWSc 92*
**Costanza,** David Joseph 1954- *WhoEnt 92*
**Costanza,** Gerald Francis 1944- *WhoFI 92*
**Costanza,** Mary E 1937- *AmMWSc 92*
**Costanza,** Michael Charles *AmMWSc 92*
**Costanza,** Robert 1950- *AmMWSc 92*
**Costanzi,** Edwin J. B. *Who 92*
**Costanzi,** John J 1936- *AmMWSc 92*
**Costanzo,** Gerald *DrAPF 91*
**Costanzo,** Linda Schupper 1947- *AmMWSc 92*
**Costanzo,** Marie Allen 1957- *WhoRel 92*
**Costanzo,** Richard Michael 1947- *AmMWSc 92*
**Costar,** Norman 1909- *Who 92*
**Costas,** Bob *LesBEnT 92 [port]*
**Costas,** Peter Louis 1931- *WhoAmL 92*
**Costas,** William 1929- *WhoAmP 91*
**Costea,** Ileana 1947- *WhoWest 92*
**Costea,** Nicolas V 1927- *AmMWSc 92*
**Costeley,** Guillaume 1530?-1606 *NewAmDM*
**Costello,** Andrew Jackson 1939- *WhoRel 92*
**Costello,** Catherine E 1943- *AmMWSc 92*
**Costello,** Christopher Hollet 1913- *AmMWSc 92*
**Costello,** Daniel Brian 1950- *WhoAmL 92*
**Costello,** Daniel Walter 1930- *WhoFI 92, WhoWest 92*
**Costello,** Debbie W. 1953- *WhoEnt 92*
**Costello,** Donald F 1934- *AmMWSc 92*
**Costello,** Donald Francis 1936- *WhoMW 92*
**Costello,** Donald Paul 1931- *WhoMW 92*
**Costello,** Elvis 1954- *WhoEnt 92*
**Costello,** Elvis 1955- *FacFETw, NewAmDM*
**Costello,** Ernest F, Jr 1923- *AmMWSc 92*
**Costello,** Gary Ewing 1940- *WhoWest 92*
**Costello,** Gordon John 1921- *Who 92*
**Costello,** Herman T 1920- *WhoAmP 91*
**Costello,** Jerry F. *WhoMW 92*
**Costello,** Jerry F. 1949- *AlmAP 92 [port], WhoAmP 91*
**Costello,** John Edmond 1943- *WhoEnt 92*
**Costello,** John H., III 1947- *WhoFI 92, WhoMW 92*
**Costello,** John William 1947- *WhoAmL 92*
**Costello,** Joseph Mark, III 1940- *WhoEnt 92*
**Costello,** Joseph Michael 1925- *WhoAmL 92*
**Costello,** Kenneth William 1948- *WhoMW 92*
**Costello,** Lou *FacFETw*
**Costello,** Mark *DrAPF 91*
**Costello,** Michael John 1966- *WhoFI 92*
**Costello,** Nicholas J *WhoAmP 91*
**Costello,** P F *TwCSFW 91*
**Costello,** Philip Neill, Jr 1930- *WhoAmP 91*
**Costello,** Richard Gray 1938- *AmMWSc 92*
**Costello,** Sharon Yevonne 1944- *WhoWest 92*
**Costello,** Steven Patrick 1958- *WhoWest 92*
**Costello,** Susan Joan 1963- *WhoAmL 92*
**Costello,** Thomas Joseph 1929- *WhoRel 92*
**Costello,** Thomas Patrick 1931- *WhoFI 92, WhoMW 92*
**Costello,** Thomas Walter 1945- *WhoAmP 91*
**Costello,** Walter James 1945- *AmMWSc 92*
**Costello,** William James 1932- *AmMWSc 92*
**Costen,** Melva Wilson 1933- *WhoBlA 92*
**Costenbader,** Charles Michael 1935- *WhoAmL 92, WhoFI 92*
**Coster,** Dirk 1889-1950 *FacFETw*
**Coster,** Joseph Constant *AmMWSc 92*
**Costerton,** J William F 1934- *AmMWSc 92*
**Costes,** Nicholas Constantine 1926- *AmMWSc 92*
**Costich,** Emmett Rand 1921- *AmMWSc 92*
**Costigan,** Daniel M. 1929- *WrDr 92*
**Costigan,** Daniel Michael 1929- *IntAu&W 91*
**Costigan,** Edward John 1914- *WhoFI 92*
**Costigan,** James *LesBEnT 92*
**Costigan,** John Mark 1942- *WhoAmL 92*
**Costigan,** Kelley A. 1964- *WhoEnt 92*
**Costigan,** Ken 1934- *ConTFT 9, WhoEnt 92*
**Costikyan,** Andrew Mihran 1922- *WhoEnt 92*
**Costill,** David Lee 1936- *AmMWSc 92*
**Costin,** Anatol 1926- *AmMWSc 92*
**Costin Guest,** Janet Rae 1961- *WhoWest 92*
**Costine,** John Mark 1954- *WhoAmL 92*
**Costle,** Douglas Michael 1939- *WhoAmL 92*
**Costley,** Bill *ConAu 35NR, DrAPF 91*
**Costley,** Bill 1942- *WrDr 92*
**Costley,** Gary E 1943- *AmMWSc 92*
**Costley,** Gary Edward 1943- *WhoFI 92*
**Costley,** William K, Jr. 1942- *ConAu 35NR*
**Costlow,** John DeForest 1927- *AmMWSc 92*
**Costlow,** Mark Enoch 1942- *AmMWSc 92*
**Costlow,** Richard Dale 1925- *AmMWSc 92*
**Costner,** Kevin 1955- *ConTFT 9, IntMPA 92, IntWW 91, WhoEnt 92*
**Costoff,** Allen 1935- *AmMWSc 92*
**Coston,** Bessie Ruth 1916- *WhoBlA 92*
**Coston,** Henry Georges 1910- *BiDExR*
**Coston,** James Dennis 1954- *WhoEnt 92*
**Coston,** Julia Ringwood *NotBlAW 92*
**Coston,** Tullos Oswell 1905- *AmMWSc 92*
**Coston,** William Dean 1950- *WhoAmL 92*
**Costonis,** John J. 1937- *WhoAmL 92*
**Costos,** Robert Wayne 1946- *WhoFI 92*
**Costrell,** Louis 1915- *AmMWSc 92*
**Cosulich,** Donna Bernice 1918- *AmMWSc 92*
**Cosway,** Harry F 1932- *AmMWSc 92*
**Cot,** Jean-Pierre 1937- *IntWW 91*
**Cot,** Pierre Donatien Alphonse 1911- *Who 92*
**Cota,** Harold Maurice 1936- *AmMWSc 92, WhoWest 92*
**Cota-Robles,** Eugene H 1926- *AmMWSc 92*
**Cota-Robles,** Eugene Henry 1926- *WhoHisp 92*
**Cotabish,** Harry N 1916- *AmMWSc 92*
**Cotanch,** Patricia Holleran 1945- *AmMWSc 92*
**Cotanch,** Stephen Robert 1947- *AmMWSc 92*
**Cotchett,** Joseph Winters 1939- *WhoAmL 92*
**Cote,** Constance D 1927- *WhoAmP 91*
**Cote,** David E 1960- *WhoAmP 91*
**Cote,** Denise 1946- *WhoAmL 92*
**Cote,** Jennifer Wanty 1954- *WhoAmL 92*
**Cote,** John P. 1956- *WhoEnt 92*
**Cote,** Joseph Leo 1914- *WhoAmP 91*
**Cote,** Louis J 1921- *AmMWSc 92*
**Cote,** Lucien Joseph 1928- *AmMWSc 92*
**Cote,** Michael Joseph 1950- *WhoFI 92*
**Cote,** Michel *IntWW 91*
**Cote,** Patricia L 1926- *WhoAmP 91*
**Cote,** Philip Norman 1942- *AmMWSc 92*
**Cote,** Ralph Warren 1927- *WhoWest 92*
**Cote,** Richard Thomas 1947- *WhoWest 92*
**Cote,** Roger Albert 1928- *AmMWSc 92*
**Cote,** Wilfred Arthur, Jr 1924- *AmMWSc 92*
**Coteanu,** Ion 1920- *IntWW 91*
**Cotellessa,** Robert F 1923- *AmMWSc 92*
**Cotera,** Augustus S, Jr 1931- *AmMWSc 92*
**Cotera,** Martha P. 1938- *WhoHisp 92*
**Cotes,** Peter *Who 92, WrDr 92*
**Cotes,** Peter 1912- *IntAu&W 91*
**Cotes,** Roger 1682-1716 *BlkwCEP*
**Cotharn,** Preston Sigmunde, Sr. 1925- *WhoBlA 92*
**Cothen,** Grady Coulter, Jr. 1946- *WhoAmL 92*
**Cothern,** Charles Richard 1937- *AmMWSc 92*
**Cothorn,** Marguerite Esters 1909- *WhoBlA 92*
**Cothran,** Elaynne Beverly 1949- *WhoAmL 92*
**Cothran,** Terrell Eugene 1946- *WhoRel 92*
**Cothran,** Tilman Christopher 1918- *WhoBlA 92*
**Cothran,** Warren Roderic 1938- *AmMWSc 92*
**Cotill,** John Atrill T. *Who 92*
**Cotilla,** Adolfo Jose, Jr. 1953- *WhoHisp 92*
**Cotlar,** Morton 1928- *WhoFI 92*
**Cotman,** Carl Wayne 1940- *AmMWSc 92*
**Cotman,** Henry Earl 1943- *WhoBlA 92*
**Cotman,** Ivan Louis 1940- *WhoBlA 92*
**Cotner,** Howard Paul 1925- *WhoAmP 91*
**Cotner,** James Bryan, Jr 1959- *AmMWSc 92*
**Cotner,** John M. 1945- *WhoAmL 92*
**Cotner,** Mercedes R 1905- *WhoAmP 91*
**Cotner,** Robert Eugene 1946- *WhoRel 92*
**Coto,** Juan Carlos 1966- *WhoHisp 92*
**Cotov,** Paula Robin 1961- *WhoRel 92*
**Cotran,** Ramzi S 1932- *AmMWSc 92*
**Cotrubas,** Ileana *Who 92, WhoEnt 92*
**Cotrubas,** Ileana 1939- *IntWW 91, NewAmDM*
**Cotruvo,** Joseph Alfred 1942- *AmMWSc 92*
**Cotsonas,** Nicholas John, Jr 1919- *AmMWSc 92*
**Cott,** Jerry Mason 1946- *AmMWSc 92*
**Cott,** Jonathan *DrAPF 91*
**Cott,** Nancy F. 1945- *WrDr 92*
**Cott,** Ted d1973 *LesBEnT 92*
**Cott Rosario,** Hector Manuel 1950- *WhoHisp 92*
**Cotta,** Michele 1937- *IntWW 91*
**Cottafavi,** Luigi 1917- *IntWW 91*
**Cottam,** Bradley Scott 1958- *WhoWest 92*
**Cottam,** Gene Larry 1940- *AmMWSc 92*
**Cottam,** Grant 1918- *AmMWSc 92*
**Cottam,** Harold 1938- *Who 92*
**Cotteleer,** Michael Alexander 1944- *WhoMW 92*
**Cottell,** Philip L 1941- *AmMWSc 92*
**Cotten,** Bruce 1873-1954 *DcNCBi 1*
**Cotten,** Elizabeth 1892-1987 *NotBlAW 92 [port]*
**Cotten,** Elizabeth 1893-1987 *NewAmDM*
**Cotten,** Elizabeth Brownrigg Henderson 1875-1975 *DcNCBi 1*
**Cotten,** George Richard 1929- *AmMWSc 92*
**Cotten,** Joseph *IntWW 91, WhoEnt 92*
**Cotten,** Joseph 1905- *IntMPA 92*
**Cotten,** Larry Evans 1949- *WhoAmL 92*
**Cotten,** Lyman Atkinson 1874-1926 *DcNCBi 1*
**Cotten,** Robert Randolph 1839-1928 *DcNCBi 1*
**Cotten,** Sallie Swepson Sims Southall 1846-1929 *DcNCBi 1*
**Cotten,** Samuel R *WhoAmP 91*
**Cotten,** Samuel Richard 1946- *WhoWest 92*
**Cottenham,** Earl of 1948- *Who 92*
**Cotter,** Berchmans Paul, Jr. 1937- *WhoAmL 92*
**Cotter,** David James 1932- *AmMWSc 92*
**Cotter,** Delaval James Alfred 1911- *Who 92*
**Cotter,** Donald James 1930- *AmMWSc 92*
**Cotter,** Donald R. d1991 *NewYTBS 91*
**Cotter,** Douglas Adrian 1943- *AmMWSc 92*
**Cotter,** Edward 1936- *AmMWSc 92*
**Cotter,** Edward F 1910- *AmMWSc 92*
**Cotter,** Gary William 1947- *WhoFI 92*
**Cotter,** H Barton 1940- *WhoIns 92*
**Cotter,** James Finn *DrAPF 91*
**Cotter,** James Finn 1929- *IntAu&W 91, WrDr 92*
**Cotter,** James Michael 1942- *WhoAmL 92, WhoFI 92*
**Cotter,** Jeffrey Lee 1946- *WhoRel 92*
**Cotter,** John d1991 *NewYTBS 91*
**Cotter,** John Catlin 1950- *WhoWest 92*
**Cotter,** Joseph Seamon, Sr. 1861-1949 *BlkLC [port]*
**Cotter,** Lawrence Raffety 1933- *WhoWest 92*
**Cotter,** Martha Ann 1943- *AmMWSc 92*
**Cotter,** Mary Louise 1947- *WhoEnt 92*
**Cotter,** Maurice Joseph 1933- *AmMWSc 92*
**Cotter,** Richard 1943- *AmMWSc 92*
**Cotter,** Richard Vern 1930- *WhoFI 92*
**Cotter,** Robert James 1930- *AmMWSc 92*
**Cotter,** Robert James 1943- *AmMWSc 92*
**Cotter,** Susan M 1943- *AmMWSc 92*
**Cotter,** Vincent Paul 1927- *WhoFI 92*

**Cotter,** William Bryan, Jr 1926- *AmMWSc 92*
**Cotterell,** Geoffrey 1919- *Who 92, WrDr 92*
**Cotterell,** John 1935- *Who 92*
**Cotterill,** David Lee 1937- *WhoFI 92*
**Cotterill,** Kenneth William 1921- *Who 92*
**Cotterill,** Rodney Michael John 1933- *IntWW 91*
**Cotterill,** Ronald Wayne 1948- *WhoFI 92*
**Cotterill,** Sarah *DrAPF 91*
**Cottesloe,** Baron 1900- *IntWW 91, Who 92*
**Cottey,** Jack 1939- *WhoAmP 91*
**Cottham,** George William 1944- *Who 92*
**Cotti,** Flavio 1939- *IntWW 91*
**Cottier,** Joseph G C 1874?-1897 *BiInAmS*
**Cottin,** Sophie 1770-1807 *FrenWW*
**Cottine,** Bertram Robert 1947- *WhoAmP 91*
**Cotting,** James Charles 1933- *IntWW 91, WhoFI 92, WhoMW 92*
**Cotting,** John Ruggles 1778-1867 *BiInAmS*
**Cottingham,** James Garry 1927- *AmMWSc 92*
**Cottingham,** John 1943- *ConAu 133*
**Cottingham,** John Allen 1954- *WhoAmL 92*
**Cottingham,** Richard Allan 1934- *WhoMW 92*
**Cottingham,** Richard Sumner 1941- *WhoFI 92*
**Cottingham,** Robert 1935- *IntWW 91*
**Cottingham,** Stephen Kent 1951- *WhoFI 92*
**Cottingham,** Susan Marie 1950- *WhoWest 92*
**Cottingham,** William Brooks 1933- *WhoMW 92*
**Cottingham,** William Bryan, Jr. 1946- *WhoEnt 92*
**Cottle,** Craig Hansen 1943- *WhoWest 92*
**Cottle,** L Glen 1915- *WhoAmP 91*
**Cottle,** Merva Kathryn Warren 1928- *AmMWSc 92*
**Cottle,** Richard W 1934- *AmMWSc 92*
**Cottle,** Thomas J. 1937- *WrDr 92*
**Cottle,** Walter Henry 1921- *AmMWSc 92*
**Cotto,** Antonio, II 1939- *WhoHisp 92*
**Cotto,** Henry 1961- *WhoHisp 92*
**Cotto,** Irving 1954- *WhoRel 92*
**Cottom,** Melvin C 1924- *AmMWSc 92*
**Cotton** *Who 92*
**Cotton Pickers** *NewAmDM*
**Cotton,** Alan 1936- *TwCPaSc*
**Cotton,** Albert E. 1939- *WhoBlA 92*
**Cotton,** Bernard Edward 1920- *Who 92*
**Cotton,** Charles 1630-1687 *RfGEnL 91*
**Cotton,** Chester Christie 1939- *WhoWest 92*
**Cotton,** Christopher P. *Who 92*
**Cotton,** Diana Rosemary 1941- *Who 92*
**Cotton,** Eugene T 1924- *WhoIns 92*
**Cotton,** Fran Edward 1948- *IntWW 91*
**Cotton,** Frank Albert 1930- *AmMWSc 92, IntWW 91*
**Cotton,** Frank Ethridge, Jr 1923- *AmMWSc 92*
**Cotton,** Garner 1923- *WhoBlA 92*
**Cotton,** Henry Egerton 1929- *Who 92*
**Cotton,** Herbert Louis 1940- *WhoWest 92*
**Cotton,** Howard Evan 1958- *WhoAmL 92*
**Cotton,** Ira Walter 1945- *AmMWSc 92*
**Cotton,** James 1739-1785 *DcNCBi 1*
**Cotton,** Jerry Lee 1939- *WhoRel 92*
**Cotton,** Joe Walter 1926- *WhoEnt 92*
**Cotton,** John *TwCSFW 91*
**Cotton,** John 1584-1652 *BenetAL 91*
**Cotton,** John 1925- *ConPo 91, IntAu&W 91, WrDr 92*
**Cotton,** John Anthony 1926- *Who 92*
**Cotton,** John Edward 1924- *AmMWSc 92*
**Cotton,** John Richard 1909- *Who 92*
**Cotton,** John Robert 1950- *WhoAmL 92*
**Cotton,** Joseph Aaron 1919- *WhoEnt 92*
**Cotton,** Kathleen Laura 1940- *WhoFI 92*
**Cotton,** Leonard Thomas 1922- *Who 92*
**Cotton,** Marcus Glenn 1966- *WhoBlA 92*
**Cotton,** Mary Elizabeth 1945- *WhoAmP 91*
**Cotton,** Oliver 1944- *ConTFT 9*
**Cotton,** Richard 1944- *WhoAmL 92*
**Cotton,** Robert Anthony 1965- *WhoFI 92*
**Cotton,** Robert Carrington 1915- *IntWW 91, Who 92*
**Cotton,** Robert Henry 1914- *AmMWSc 92*
**Cotton,** Robert Thomas 1919- *WhoMW 92*
**Cotton,** Ronald Woodrow 1945- *WhoEnt 92*
**Cotton,** Ruffen Henry, Jr. 1943- *WhoFI 92*
**Cotton,** Therese Marie *AmMWSc 92*
**Cotton,** William Frederick 1928- *IntWW 91, Who 92*
**Cotton,** William Reuben 1940- *AmMWSc 92*
**Cotton,** William Robert 1931- *AmMWSc 92*
**Cotton,** Wyatt Daniel 1943- *AmMWSc 92*
**Cottone,** James Anthony 1947- *AmMWSc 92*
**Cottone,** Peter Joseph 1952- *WhoMW 92*
**Cottony,** Herman Vladimir 1909- *AmMWSc 92*
**Cottrell,** Alan 1919- *IntWW 91, Who 92, WrDr 92*
**Cottrell,** Alan Howard 1919- *FacFETw*
**Cottrell,** Bryce Arthur Murray 1931- *Who 92*
**Cottrell,** Comer J. 1931- *WhoBlA 92*
**Cottrell,** David Lee 1951- *WhoEnt 92*
**Cottrell,** David Milton 1951- *WhoEnt 92*
**Cottrell,** Donald Peery 1902- *IntWW 91*
**Cottrell,** G. Walton 1939- *WhoFI 92*
**Cottrell,** Ian William 1943- *AmMWSc 92*
**Cottrell,** Mary-Patricia Tross 1934- *WhoFI 92*
**Cottrell,** Philip Edgar 1933- *WhoMW 92*
**Cottrell,** Richard John 1943- *Who 92*
**Cottrell,** Roger Leslie Anderton 1940- *AmMWSc 92*
**Cottrell,** Roy 1939- *AmMWSc 92*
**Cottrell,** Stephen F 1943- *AmMWSc 92*
**Cottrell,** Thomas S 1934- *AmMWSc 92*
**Cottrell,** Wendell Lynn 1941- *WhoWest 92*
**Cottrell,** William Barber 1924- *AmMWSc 92*
**Cottrol,** Robert James 1949- *WhoAmL 92, WhoBlA 92*
**Cotts,** Arthur C 1922- *AmMWSc 92*
**Cotts,** Crichton Mitchell 1903- *Who 92*
**Cotts,** Cynthia *DrAPF 91*
**Cotts,** David Bryan 1954- *AmMWSc 92*
**Cotts,** Patricia Metzger 1953- *AmMWSc 92*
**Cotts,** Robert Milo 1927- *AmMWSc 92*
**Cotty,** Val Francis 1926- *AmMWSc 92*
**Coty,** Francois 1874-1934 *BiDExR*
**Coty,** William Allen 1948- *AmMWSc 92*
**Couch,** Barbara H 1926- *WhoAmP 91*
**Couch,** Charles Edward 1944- *WhoRel 92*
**Couch,** Christopher 1946- *TwCPaSc*
**Couch,** George Walter, III 1947- *WhoWest 92*
**Couch,** Houston Brown 1924- *AmMWSc 92*
**Couch,** Jack Gary 1936- *AmMWSc 92*
**Couch,** James Russell 1909- *AmMWSc 92*
**Couch,** James Russell, Jr 1939- *AmMWSc 92*
**Couch,** John Alexander 1938- *AmMWSc 92*
**Couch,** John Charles 1939- *WhoFI 92*
**Couch,** John Nathaniel 1896- *AmMWSc 92*
**Couch,** Leon Worthington, II 1941- *AmMWSc 92*
**Couch,** Leslie Franklin 1930- *WhoAmL 92*
**Couch,** Margaret Wheland 1941- *AmMWSc 92*
**Couch,** Nena Louise 1950- *WhoMW 92*
**Couch,** Richard W 1931- *AmMWSc 92*
**Couch,** Richard Wesley 1937- *AmMWSc 92*
**Couch,** Robert Barnard 1930- *AmMWSc 92*
**Couch,** Robert Franklin 1947- *WhoWest 92*
**Couch,** Terry Lee 1944- *AmMWSc 92*
**Couch,** Thomas Emmett 1938- *WhoFI 92*
**Couche,** Robert 1918- *WhoBlA 92*
**Couche,** Ruby S. 1919- *WhoBlA 92*
**Couchell,** Gus Perry 1939- *AmMWSc 92*
**Couchman,** James C 1929- *AmMWSc 92*
**Couchman,** James Randall 1942- *Who 92*
**Couchman,** Jeffrey *DrAPF 91*
**Couchman,** Martin 1947- *Who 92*
**Couchman,** Peter Robert 1947- *AmMWSc 92*
**Couchot,** Lise King *DrAPF 91*
**Coucouvanis,** Dimitri N 1940- *AmMWSc 92*
**Coucouzis,** Demetrios A. 1911- *WhoRel 92*
**Coudriet,** Charles Edward 1946- *WhoFI 92*
**Coudron,** Thomas A 1951- *AmMWSc 92*
**Coues,** Elliott 1842-1899 *BiInAmS*
**Couey,** Duane Emerson 1924- *WhoRel 92*
**Couey,** H Melvin 1926- *AmMWSc 92*
**Coufal,** Hans-Jurgen 1945- *AmMWSc 92, WhoWest 92*
**Cougar,** John 1951- *WhoEnt 92*
**Couger,** J Daniel 1929- *AmMWSc 92*
**Coughanowr,** D R 1928- *AmMWSc 92*
**Coughenour,** Clyde Irvin, Sr. 1933- *WhoAmL 92*
**Coughenour,** John Clare 1941- *WhoAmL 92*
**Coughenour,** Michael B 1952- *AmMWSc 92*
**Coughenour,** Robert Allen 1931- *WhoRel 92*
**Coughlan,** Basil Joseph, II 1940- *WhoFI 92*
**Coughlan,** Gary Patrick 1944- *WhoFI 92*
**Coughlan,** Jeffrey Lee 1959- *WhoWest 92*
**Coughlan,** Kenneth Lewis 1940- *WhoAmL 92*
**Coughlan,** Robert 1914- *WrDr 92*
**Coughlin,** Barring 1913- *WhoAmL 92*
**Coughlin,** Charles E 1891-1979 *FacFETw, RComAH*
**Coughlin,** Charles Edward 1891-1979 *BiDExR, RelLAm 91*
**Coughlin,** Colleen 1962- *WhoAmL 92*
**Coughlin,** Cornelius Edward 1927- *WhoFI 92*
**Coughlin,** David Michael 1960- *WhoEnt 92*
**Coughlin,** Francis Raymond, Jr. 1927- *WhoAmL 92*
**Coughlin,** James Robert 1946- *AmMWSc 92*
**Coughlin,** Lawrence 1929- *AlmAP 92 [port]*
**Coughlin,** Mary Samuel 1868-1959 *HanAmWH*
**Coughlin,** Maureen Elizabeth 1956- *WhoRel 92*
**Coughlin,** Peter Lutz 1945- *WhoEnt 92*
**Coughlin,** R Lawrence *WhoAmP 91*
**Coughlin,** Raymond Francis 1943- *AmMWSc 92*
**Coughlin,** Robert William 1934- *AmMWSc 92*
**Coughlin,** Timothy Lee 1959- *WhoAmL 92*
**Coughlin,** Walter J. 1961- *WhoFI 92*
**Coughran,** William Marvin, Jr 1953- *AmMWSc 92*
**Couillard,** Pierre 1928- *AmMWSc 92*
**Coull,** Alexander 1931- *Who 92*
**Coull,** Bruce Charles 1942- *AmMWSc 92*
**Coull,** John Taylor 1934- *Who 92*
**Coulman,** G A 1930- *AmMWSc 92*
**Coulomb,** Charles Augustin de 1736-1806 *BlkwCEP*
**Coulomb,** Jean 1904- *IntWW 91*
**Coulombe,** Harry N 1939- *AmMWSc 92*
**Coulombe,** Henry W 1935- *WhoAmP 91*
**Coulombe,** Louis Joseph 1920- *AmMWSc 92*
**Coulombe,** Yvonne 1938- *WhoAmP 91*
**Coulombe-Saint-Marcoux,** Micheline *NewAmDM*
**Coulon,** Burnel Elton 1929- *WhoBlA 92*
**Coulondre,** Robert 1885-1959 *EncTR 91*
**Coulsfield,** Lord 1934- *Who 92*
**Coulshed,** Frances 1904- *Who 92*
**Coulson,** Alan Stewart 1941- *WhoWest 92*
**Coulson,** Ann Margaret 1935- *Who 92*
**Coulson,** Charles Alfred 1910-1974 *FacFETw*
**Coulson,** Dale Robert 1938- *AmMWSc 92*
**Coulson,** J Philip 1949- *WhoIns 92*
**Coulson,** Jack Richard 1931- *AmMWSc 92*
**Coulson,** James Michael 1927- *Who 92*
**Coulson,** Jesse Edward 1940- *WhoRel 92*
**Coulson,** John Eltringham 1909- *IntWW 91, Who 92*
**Coulson,** John H A 1906- *IntAu&W 91, WrDr 92*
**Coulson,** Juanita 1933- *TwCSFW 91, WrDr 92*
**Coulson,** Juanita Ruth 1933- *IntAu&W 91*
**Coulson,** Kinsell Leroy 1916- *AmMWSc 92*
**Coulson,** Larry Vernon 1943- *AmMWSc 92*
**Coulson,** Michael *Who 92*
**Coulson,** Norman M. *WhoWest 92*
**Coulson,** Patricia Bunker 1942- *AmMWSc 92*
**Coulson,** Richard *AmMWSc 92*
**Coulson,** Richard L 1943- *AmMWSc 92*
**Coulson,** Robert 1924- *ConAu 36NR, WhoAmL 92, WhoFI 92*
**Coulson,** Robert 1928- *TwCSFW 91, WrDr 92*
**Coulson,** Robert N 1943- *AmMWSc 92*
**Coulson,** Robert Stratton 1928- *IntAu&W 91*
**Coulson,** Roland Armstrong 1915- *AmMWSc 92*
**Coulson,** Walter F 1926- *AmMWSc 92*
**Coulson,** William Roy 1949- *WhoAmL 92*
**Coulson-Thomas,** Colin Joseph 1949- *IntWW 91*
**Coulston,** Mary Lou 1938- *AmMWSc 92*
**Coultass,** Clive 1931- *Who 92*
**Coulter,** Amy Renee 1962- *WhoMW 92*
**Coulter,** Andrew 1958- *WhoWest 92*
**Coulter,** Borden McKee 1917- *WhoFI 92*
**Coulter,** Byron Leonard 1941- *AmMWSc 92*
**Coulter,** Charles L 1933- *AmMWSc 92*
**Coulter,** Claude Alton 1936- *AmMWSc 92*
**Coulter,** Deborah Ann 1952- *WhoFI 92*
**Coulter,** Dwight Bernard 1935- *AmMWSc 92*
**Coulter,** Elizabeth Jackson 1919- *AmMWSc 92*
**Coulter,** Glenn Hartman 1947- *AmMWSc 92*
**Coulter,** Henry W 1927- *AmMWSc 92*
**Coulter,** Herbert David, Jr 1939- *AmMWSc 92*
**Coulter,** Jack B. 1923- *WhoAmL 92*
**Coulter,** James B *AmMWSc 92*
**Coulter,** Joe Dan 1944- *AmMWSc 92*
**Coulter,** John 1888-1980 *BenetAL 91*
**Coulter,** Lowell Vernon 1913- *AmMWSc 92*
**Coulter,** Malcolm Wilford 1920- *AmMWSc 92*
**Coulter,** Michael 1937- *TwCPaSc*
**Coulter,** Murray W 1932- *AmMWSc 92*
**Coulter,** Neal Stanley 1944- *AmMWSc 92*
**Coulter,** Norman Arthur, Jr 1920- *AmMWSc 92*
**Coulter,** Paul David 1938- *AmMWSc 92*
**Coulter,** Philip W 1938- *AmMWSc 92*
**Coulter,** Richard Lincoln 1945- *AmMWSc 92*
**Coulter,** Stephen 1914- *IntAu&W 91, WrDr 92*
**Coulter,** Steven Arthur 1947- *WhoAmP 91*
**Coulter,** Wallace H *AmMWSc 92*
**Coulter,** William Laurence 1941- *WhoMW 92*
**Coulter,** William Robert 1930- *WhoRel 92*
**Coulthard,** Colin Weal 1921- *Who 92*
**Coulthard,** Jean 1908- *NewAmDM*
**Coulthard,** John Joseph 1935- *WhoFI 92*
**Coulthard,** William Henderson 1913- *Who 92*
**Coulton,** Martha Jean Glasscoe 1927- *WhoMW 92*
**Coulton,** Nicholas Guy 1940- *Who 92*
**Counce,** Elmer Wylie 1921- *WhoAmP 91*
**Counce,** Sheila Jean 1927- *AmMWSc 92*
**Council,** Arthur 1755-1777 *DcNCBi 1*
**Council,** Carl C. 1895-1964 *DcNCBi 1*
**Council,** Commodore Thomas, Sr. 1886-1960 *DcNCBi 1*
**Council,** John Pickett 1855-1929 *DcNCBi 1*
**Council,** Marion Earl 1929- *AmMWSc 92*
**Council Austin,** Mary H. 1953- *WhoRel 92*
**Councill,** James Paul, Jr 1921- *WhoAmP 91*
**Councill,** Richard J 1923- *AmMWSc 92*
**Councill,** Warren Parker 1947- *WhoAmP 91*
**Counelis,** James Steve 1927- *WhoWest 92*
**Counihan,** Gene W 1941- *WhoAmP 91*
**Counsell,** Hazel Rosemary 1931- *Who 92*
**Counsell,** Lee Albert 1923- *WhoMW 92*
**Counsell,** Melanie 1964- *TwCPaSc*
**Counsell,** Nicola 1963- *TwCPaSc*
**Counsell,** Paul Hayward 1926- *Who 92*
**Counsell,** Raymond Ernest 1930- *AmMWSc 92*
**Counselman,** Charles C, Jr. 1916- *WhoIns 92*
**Counselman,** Charles Claude, III 1943- *AmMWSc 92*
**Counselman,** Mary Elizabeth *DrAPF 91*
**Count,** Earl W. 1899- *WrDr 92*
**Count,** Earl Wendel 1899- *IntAu&W 91*
**Counte,** Michael Alan 1946- *WhoMW 92*
**Countee,** Thomas Hilaire, Jr. 1939- *WhoBlA 92*
**Counter,** Fred T 1934- *WhoAmP 91*
**Counter,** Frederick T, Jr 1934- *AmMWSc 92*
**Counter,** James Nicholas, III 1940- *WhoWest 92*
**Counter,** Janice Elaine 1943- *WhoAmP 91*
**Country Gentlemen, The** *ConMus 7 [port]*
**Country Joe and the Fish** *NewAmDM*
**Countryman,** David Wayne 1943- *AmMWSc 92*
**Countryman,** Gary Lee 1939- *WhoFI 92, WhoIns 92*
**Countryman,** Gratia Alta 1866-1953 *HanAmWH*
**Countryman,** John R 1933- *WhoAmP 91*
**Countryman,** John Woods 1944- *WhoAmP 91*
**Countryman,** Louis William 1941- *WhoRel 92*
**Countryman,** Michael 1955- *ConTFT 9*
**Countryman,** Thomas Arthur 1957- *WhoAmL 92*
**Countryman,** Vern 1917- *WhoAmL 92, WrDr 92*
**Countrymen,** Christopher Charles 1955- *WhoWest 92*
**Counts,** David 1936- *WhoAmP 91*
**Counts,** David Francis 1948- *AmMWSc 92*
**Counts,** George S 1889-1974 *DcAmImH*
**Counts,** George W 1935- *AmMWSc 92, WhoBlA 92*
**Counts,** Jon Milton 1937- *AmMWSc 92*
**Counts,** Wayne Boyd 1936- *AmMWSc 92*
**Coupe,** James Warnick 1949- *WhoAmL 92*
**Coupee,** Francis 1775-1814 *DcNCBi 1*
**Couper,** Alastair Dougal 1931- *Who 92*
**Couper,** David Courtland 1938- *WhoMW 92*
**Couper,** Heather Anita 1949- *Who 92*
**Couper,** J. M. 1914- *WrDr 92*
**Couper,** James Hamilton 1794-1866 *BiInAmS*
**Couper,** James R 1925- *AmMWSc 92*
**Couper,** John Mill 1914- *IntAu&W 91*
**Couper,** Nicholas 1945- *Who 92*
**Couper,** William 1947- *WhoFI 92*

Couperin, Francois 1668-1733 NewAmDM
Couperin, Louis 1626?-1661 NewAmDM
Couperus, Molleurus 1906- AmMWSc 92
Coupet, Joseph 1937- AmMWSc 92
Coupland, Rex Ernest 1924- Who 92
Coupland, Robert Thomas 1920- AmMWSc 92
Courage, James 1903-1963 RfGEnL 91
Courage, Richard Hubert 1915- Who 92
Courage, Walter James 1940- Who 92
Courant, Ernest D. 1920- IntWW 91
Courant, Ernest David 1920- AmMWSc 92
Courant, Hans Wolfgang Julius 1924- AmMWSc 92
Courbet, Gustave 1819-1877 ThHEIm
Courcel, Baron de 1912- Who 92
Courcel, Geoffroy Chodron de 1912- IntWW 91
Courchaine, Robert Michael 1955- WhoMW 92
Courchene, Thomas Joseph 1940- IntWW 91
Courchene, William Leon 1926- AmMWSc 92
Courchesne, Eric 1949- AmMWSc 92
Courcy Who 92
Couri, Daniel 1930- AmMWSc 92
Couric, Katherine 1957- News 91 [port]
Courlander, Harold 1908- IntAu&W 91
Cournand, Andre F. 1895-1988 WhoNob 90
Cournand, Andre Frederic 1895-1988 FacFETw
Cournos, John 1881-1966 BenetAL 91
Courreges, Andre 1923- DcTwDes, IntWW 91
Coursen, Bradner Wood 1929- AmMWSc 92
Coursen, Christopher Dennison 1948- WhoAmL 92, WhoFI 92
Coursen, David Linn 1923- AmMWSc 92
Coursen, H.R. DrAPF 91
Courser, Lori Ann 1956- WhoWest 92
Coursey, Bert Marcel 1942- AmMWSc 92
Coursey, Marcha Lyn 1955- WhoEnt 92
Courson, David Merle 1947- WhoRel 92
Courson, Donald Clair 1944- WhoAmL 92
Courson, Gardner Greene 1948- WhoAmL 92
Courson, John Edward 1944- WhoAmP 91
Court, Anita 1930- AmMWSc 92
Court, Arnold 1914- AmMWSc 92, WhoWest 92
Court, Charles 1911- Who 92
Court, Charles Walter Michael 1911- IntWW 91
Court, Donald 1912- Who 92
Court, John Christian 1942- WhoMW 92
Court, Leonard 1947- WhoAmL 92
Court, Margaret 1942- IntWW 91
Court, Wesli DrAPF 91
Court, William Arthur 1943- AmMWSc 92
Court de Gebelin, Antoine 1725-1784 BlkwCEP
Courtauld, Christopher 1934- Who 92
Courtauld, Samuel 1876-1947 FacFETw
Courtaway, Thomas Lewis 1950- WhoFI 92
Courtemanche, Jack WhoAmP 91
Courtenay Who 92
Courtenay, Lord 1942- Who 92
Courtenay, Edward Henry 1803-1853 BiInAmS
Courtenay, Margaret Carolyn 1923- WhoEnt 92
Courtenay, Thomas Daniel 1937- Who 92
Courtenay, Tom 1937- IntMPA 92, IntWW 91
Courtenay, Walter Rowe, Jr 1933- AmMWSc 92
Courteney, Luke Theophilus 1846-1929 ScFEYrs
Courter, Gay 1944- IntAu&W 91, WrDr 92
Courter, James Andrew 1936- WhoFI 92
Courter, James Andrew 1941- NewYTBS 91 [port], WhoAmP 91
Courter, R W 1935- AmMWSc 92
Courter, Stacy Gene 1943- WhoMW 92
Courthion, Pierre-Barthelemy 1902- IntWW 91
Courtland, Jerome 1926- IntMPA 92
Courtnage, Lee Edmund 1932- WhoMW 92
Courtnage, Michael Stewart 1946- WhoAmL 92
Courtney, Caroline 1920- WrDr 92
Courtney, Cassandra Hill 1949- WhoBlA 92
Courtney, Charles Hill 1947- AmMWSc 92
Courtney, David Michael 1941- WhoAmP 91
Courtney, Edward 1932- Who 92
Courtney, Esau WhoRel 92
Courtney, Gerald Denning 1953- WhoEnt 92
Courtney, Gladys 1930- AmMWSc 92
Courtney, Gwendoline WrDr 92
Courtney, Howard Perry 1911- WhoRel 92
Courtney, James Edmond 1931- WhoFI 92
Courtney, James Robert 1936- WhoAmP 91
Courtney, John Charles 1938- AmMWSc 92
Courtney, Joseph D 1953- WhoAmP 91
Courtney, Kathleen D'Olier 1878-1974 BiDBrF 2
Courtney, Kenneth Oliver 1906- AmMWSc 92
Courtney, Kenneth Randall 1944- AmMWSc 92
Courtney, Nicholas Piers 1944- IntAu&W 91
Courtney, Peter 1943- WhoAmP 91
Courtney, Richard Augustus 1953- WhoAmL 92
Courtney, Richard J 1941- AmMWSc 92
Courtney, Richard James 1941- AmMWSc 92
Courtney, Roger Graham 1946- Who 92
Courtney, Ronald Stanley 1957- WhoAmL 92
Courtney, Stephen Alexander 1957- WhoBlA 92
Courtney, Thomas Hugh 1938- AmMWSc 92
Courtney, Victoria Black 1943- WhoWest 92
Courtney, Wayne C 1909- WhoAmP 91
Courtney, Welby Gillette 1925- AmMWSc 92
Courtney, William Henry, III 1948- AmMWSc 92
Courtney-Greene, Laura Ann 1962- WhoEnt 92
Courtney-Pratt, Jeofry Stuart 1920- AmMWSc 92
Courtot, Martha DrAPF 91
Courtot, Philippe Frederic 1944- WhoWest 92
Courtown, Earl of 1954- Who 92
Courtright, Hernando Patrick 1956- WhoEnt 92
Courtright, James Ben 1941- AmMWSc 92
Courtright, Ken 1935- WhoEnt 92
Courtright, Lee Flippen 1947- WhoFI 92
Courtright, Morris, Jr 1930- WhoAmP 91
Courtright, Paul Barber 1942- WhoRel 92
Courts, Barbara Jane 1931- WhoMW 92
Courts, Daniel William 1800-1883 DcNCBi 1
Courville, Jacques 1935- AmMWSc 92
Coury, Arthur Joseph 1940- AmMWSc 92
Coury, Michael WhoRel 92
Coury, Michael Joseph 1951- WhoMW 92
Couse, Philip Edward 1936- Who 92
Couser, Raymond Dowell 1931- AmMWSc 92
Couser, Thomas Donald 1946- WhoRel 92
Couser, William Griffith 1939- AmMWSc 92
Cousin, Maribeth Anne 1949- AmMWSc 92, WhoMW 92
Cousin, Philip R. 1933- WhoBlA 92, WhoRel 92
Cousin, Rebecca Elizabeth 1932- WhoMW 92
Cousineau, Gilles H 1932- AmMWSc 92
Cousineau, R. David WhoRel 92
Cousino, Paul James 1941- WhoMW 92
Cousins, Althea L. 1932- WhoBlA 92
Cousins, Brian Harry 1933- Who 92
Cousins, David 1942- Who 92
Cousins, Frank 1904-1986 FacFETw
Cousins, James Mackay 1944- Who 92
Cousins, James R., Jr. 1906- WhoBlA 92
Cousins, John Peter 1931- Who 92
Cousins, Linda DrAPF 91
Cousins, Margaret 1905- IntAu&W 91, WrDr 92
Cousins, Michael 1938- DcTwDes
Cousins, Morison 1934- DcTwDes
Cousins, Norman d1990 IntWW 91N, Who 92N
Cousins, Norman 1912-1990 AmPeW, CurBio 91N
Cousins, Norman 1915-1990 AnObit 1990, BenetAL 91, FacFETw
Cousins, Norman Leonard 1944- WhoAmL 92
Cousins, Peter Edward 1928- WrDr 92
Cousins, Philip 1923- Who 92
Cousins, Richard Francis 1955- WhoWest 92
Cousins, Robert John 1941- AmMWSc 92
Cousins, William, Jr. 1927- WhoBlA 92
Cousins, William Joseph 1917- WhoAmL 92
Cousteau, Jacques-Yves LesBEnT 92 [port]
Cousteau, Jacques-Yves 1910- AmMWSc 92, FacFETw [port], IntMPA 92, IntWW 91, Who 92
Cousteau, Pierre-Antoine 1906-1958 BiDExR
Cousy, Bob 1928- FacFETw
Coutanche, Michael 1720?-1762? DcNCBi 1
Coutant, Charles Coe 1938- AmMWSc 92
Coutard, Raoul 1924- IntMPA 92, IntWW 91
Coutchie, Pamela Ann AmMWSc 92
Couthouy, Joseph Pitty 1808-1864 BiInAmS
Coutinho, Antonio Alba Rosa 1926- IntWW 91
Coutinho, Claude Bernard 1931- AmMWSc 92
Coutinho, Graca 1949- TwCPaSc
Coutinho, John AmMWSc 92
Couto, Walter 1932- AmMWSc 92
Coutsoheras, Yannis 1904- IntWW 91
Coutts Who 92
Coutts, Frederick Lee 1899-1986 ConAu 36NR
Coutts, Gordon Who 92
Coutts, Herbert 1944- Who 92
Coutts, Ian Dewar 1927- Who 92
Coutts, John Archibald 1909- Who 92
Coutts, John Russell 1936- WhoFI 92
Coutts, John Wallace 1923- AmMWSc 92
Coutts, Robert Francis 1941- WhoWest 92
Coutts, Ronald Thomson 1931- AmMWSc 92, IntWW 91
Coutts, Thomas Gordon 1933- Who 92
Coutu, Charles Arthur 1927- WhoRel 92
Coutu, Ronald Charles 1951- WhoAmL 92
Coutu-Melka, Nancy Grace 1953- WhoFI 92
Couture, Cheri JoEllen 1959- WhoFI 92
Couture, Daniel Archie 1945- WhoAmP 91
Couture, Guillaume 1851-1915 NewAmDM
Couture, Jean Desire 1913- IntWW 91
Couture, Jean Guy 1929- WhoRel 92
Couture, Josaphat Michel 1949- AmMWSc 92
Couture, Maurice 1926- WhoRel 92
Couture, Roger 1930- AmMWSc 92
Couture, Ronald David 1944- WhoEnt 92
Couture, Thomas 1815-1879 ThHEIm
Couturier, Gordon W 1942- AmMWSc 92
Couturier, Guy 1929- WhoRel 92
Couturier, Paul-Irenee 1881-1953 DcEcMov
Couturier, Ronald Lee 1949- WhoFI 92
Couve De Murville, Maurice 1907- IntWW 91, Who 92
Couve De Murville, Maurice Noel Leon Who 92
Couve De Murville, Maurice Noel Leon 1929- IntWW 91
Couvent, Marie Bernard 1757?-1837 NotBlAW 92
Couvillion, David Irvin 1934- WhoAmL 92
Couvillion, John Lee 1941- AmMWSc 92
Couvillon, Malcolm Joseph 1931- WhoEnt 92
Couzens, Kenneth 1925- IntWW 91, Who 92
Couzin, Sharon 1943- WhoEnt 92
Couzyn, Jeni 1942- ConPo 91, IntAu&W 91, WrDr 92
Cova, Dario R 1928- AmMWSc 92
Covacevich, Anthony 1954- WhoFI 92
Covacevich, Thomas 1915- Who 92
Covaliu, Bradut 1924- IntWW 91
Covalt, Genevieve 1919- WhoEnt 92
Covalt, Robert Byron 1931- WhoFI 92
Covalt-Dunning, Dorothy 1937- AmMWSc 92
Covan, DeForest W. 1917- WhoBlA 92
CoVan, Jack Phillip 1912- AmMWSc 92
Covarrubias, Miguel 1905-1958 BenetAL 91
Covarrubias, Patricia Olivia 1951- WhoWest 92
Covatta, Anthony Gallo, Jr. 1944- WhoAmL 92
Covault, Donald O 1926- AmMWSc 92
Covel, Mitchel Dale 1917- AmMWSc 92
Coveleski, Stan 1890-1984 FacFETw
Covell, Charles VanOrden, Jr 1935- AmMWSc 92
Covell, David Gene 1949- AmMWSc 92
Covell, James Wachob 1936- AmMWSc 92
Covell, Richard Bertram 1929- WhoFI 92
Covell, Roger David 1931- IntWW 91
Covello, Alfred B WhoAmP 91
Covello, Alfred Vincent 1933- WhoAmL 92
Covello, Leonard 1887-1982 DcAmImH
Coven, Edwina Olwyn 1921- Who 92
Coven, Frank 1910- Who 92
Coveney, James 1920- IntWW 91, Who 92
Coveney, Maurice John 1933- WhoRel 92
Coveney, Michael William 1948- Who 92
Coveney, Raymond Martin, Jr 1942- AmMWSc 92
Coventry Who 92
Coventry, Archdeacon of Who 92
Coventry, Bishop of 1930- Who 92
Coventry, Earl of 1934- Who 92
Coventry, Provost of Who 92
Coventry, Brian Keith 1965- WhoFI 92
Coventry, Frederick Halford 1905- TwCPaSc
Coventry, John Seton 1915- IntWW 91, Who 92
Coventry, Mark Bingham 1913- AmMWSc 92
Cover, Arthur Byron 1950- TwCSFW 91, WrDr 92
Cover, E. McIntosh 1933- WhoAmL 92
Cover, Franklin Edward 1928- WhoEnt 92
Cover, Herbert Lee 1921- AmMWSc 92
Cover, Margaret Peery 1927- WhoAmP 91
Cover, Paul Willard 1924- WhoMW 92
Cover, Ralph A 1943- AmMWSc 92
Cover, Richard Edward 1926- AmMWSc 92
Cover, Thomas Merrill 1938- AmMWSc 92
Coverdale, Gabriela 1963- WhoHisp 92
Coverdale, Glen Eugene 1930- WhoFI 92
Coverdale, Henry Standish ScFEYrs
Coverdale, Herbert Linwood 1940- WhoBlA 92
Coverdale, John Foy 1940- WhoAmL 92
Coverdell, Paul D 1939- WhoAmP 91
Coveri, Enrico 1952- IntWW 91
Covert, Eugene Edzards 1926- AmMWSc 92
Covert, Richard Perry 1928- WhoFI 92
Covert, Roger A 1929- AmMWSc 92
Covey, Curtis Charles 1951- AmMWSc 92
Covey, David L. 1945- WhoEnt 92
Covey, Debra Renee 1958- WhoMW 92
Covey, Douglas Floyd 1945- AmMWSc 92
Covey, Frank Michael, Jr. 1932- WhoAmL 92, WhoFI 92
Covey, Harold D 1930- WhoIns 92
Covey, Harold Dean 1930- WhoFI 92
Covey, Irene Mabel 1931- AmMWSc 92
Covey, Ronald Perrin, Jr 1929- AmMWSc 92
Covey, Rupert Alden 1929- AmMWSc 92
Covey, Stephen Merrill Richards 1962- WhoFI 92, WhoWest 92
Covey, William Danny 1940- AmMWSc 92
Covey, Winton Guy, Jr 1929- AmMWSc 92
Coviello, Frank Joseph 1940- WhoAmL 92
Coviello, Vincent F., Jr. 1940- WhoWest 92
Coville, Bruce Farrington 1950- IntAu&W 91
Covin, David L. 1940- WhoBlA 92
Covina, Gina DrAPF 91
Covington, Almerritt Virgal 1950- WhoEnt 92
Covington, Ann K WhoAmP 91
Covington, Ann K. 1942- WhoAmL 92, WhoMW 92
Covington, Dean 1916- WhoAmP 91
Covington, George Morse 1942- WhoAmL 92
Covington, H. Douglas 1935- WhoBlA 92
Covington, James Arthur 1927- WhoBlA 92
Covington, James W. 1917- WrDr 92
Covington, John Ewbank 1946- WhoRel 92
Covington, John Ryland 1936- WhoBlA 92
Covington, Kim Ann 1964- WhoBlA 92
Covington, M. Stanley 1937- WhoBlA 92
Covington, Marlow Stanley 1937- WhoAmL 92
Covington, Nicholas 1929- Who 92
Covington, Patricia Ann 1946- WhoMW 92
Covington, Robert Newman 1936- WhoAmL 92
Covington, Suzanne 1949- WhoAmL 92
Covington, Vicki 1952- ConAu 133
Covington, Willa Alma Greene 1902- WhoBlA 92
Covington-Kent, Dawna Marie 1948- WhoMW 92
Covino, Benjamin Gene 1930- AmMWSc 92
Covino, Joseph, Jr. 1954- WhoWest 92
Covino, Michael DrAPF 91
Covino, Paul Francis Xavier 1958- WhoRel 92
Covitch, Michael J 1949- AmMWSc 92
Cowan, Alan Who 92
Cowan, Alan 1942- AmMWSc 92
Cowan, Andrew Glenn 1951- WhoEnt 92
Cowan, Archibald B 1915- AmMWSc 92
Cowan, Charles Donald 1923- Who 92
Cowan, Colin Hunter 1920- Who 92
Cowan, Daniel Francis 1934- AmMWSc 92
Cowan, Darrel Sidney 1945- AmMWSc 92
Cowan, David J 1936- AmMWSc 92
Cowan, David Lawrence 1936- AmMWSc 92
Cowan, David Prime AmMWSc 92
Cowan, Donald D 1938- AmMWSc 92
Cowan, Donovan Frankland 1919- IntAu&W 91
Cowan, Dwaine O 1935- AmMWSc 92
Cowan, Edward 1944- WrDr 92
Cowan, Elliot Paul 1955- AmMWSc 92

Cowan, Eric Ward 1957- WhoAmL 92
Cowan, Eugene Woodville 1920- AmMWSc 92
Cowan, F Brian M 1938- AmMWSc 92
Cowan, Frank 1844-1905 ScFEYrs
Cowan, Frederic J 1945- WhoAmP 91
Cowan, Frederic Joseph 1945- WhoAmL 92
Cowan, Frederick Fletcher, Jr 1933- AmMWSc 92
Cowan, Frederick Pierce 1906- AmMWSc 92
Cowan, Garry Ian McTaggart 1940- AmMWSc 92
Cowan, Gary Lawrence 1934- WhoFI 92
Cowan, George A 1920- AmMWSc 92
Cowan, George Arthur 1920- WhoFI 92
Cowan, Gordon 1933- IntAu&W 91, WrDr 92
Cowan, Grant S. 1959- WhoAmL 92
Cowan, Henry 1919- WrDr 92
Cowan, Henry Jacob 1919- IntAu&W 91
Cowan, Homer H, Jr. 1923- WhoIns 92
Cowan, Homer Harvey, Jr. 1923- WhoAmL 92
Cowan, Ian Borthwick d1990 Who 92N
Cowan, Ian Borthwick 1932- IntAu&W 91
Cowan, Ian Borthwick 1932-1990 ConAu 133
Cowan, Ian McTaggart 1910- AmMWSc 92
Cowan, Jack David 1933- AmMWSc 92
Cowan, James 1870-1943 ScFEYrs
Cowan, James Alan 1923- Who 92
Cowan, James C. 1927- WrDr 92
Cowan, James Edington 1930- WhoWest 92
Cowan, James R. 1919- WhoBlA 92
Cowan, James Robertson 1919- Who 92
Cowan, James W 1930- AmMWSc 92
Cowan, Jeremy Who 92
Cowan, Jerry Louis 1927- WhoAmL 92, WhoMW 92
Cowan, Joel Harvey 1936- WhoAmP 91
Cowan, John 1943- AmMWSc 92
Cowan, John Arthur 1921- AmMWSc 92
Cowan, John C 1911- AmMWSc 92
Cowan, John D, Jr 1918- AmMWSc 92
Cowan, John James 1948- AmMWSc 92
Cowan, John Joseph 1932- WhoAmL 92
Cowan, Larine Yvonne 1949- WhoBlA 92
Cowan, Lionel David 1929- Who 92
Cowan, Louis G. d1976 LesBEnT 92
Cowan, Maynard, Jr 1925- AmMWSc 92
Cowan, Michael John Julian 1952- WhoFI 92
Cowan, Paul Earl 1946- WhoAmP 91
Cowan, Peter 1914- ConNov 91, IntAu&W 91, WrDr 92
Cowan, Raymond 1914- AmMWSc 92
Cowan, Richard Sumner 1921- AmMWSc 92
Cowan, Robert 1932- Who 92
Cowan, Robert Duane 1919- AmMWSc 92
Cowan, Robert Lee 1920- AmMWSc 92
Cowan, Rosalie 1912- WhoAmP 91
Cowan, Ross C 1928- WhoIns 92
Cowan, Russell 1912- AmMWSc 92
Cowan, Stuart Marshall 1932- WhoWest 92
Cowan, Ted M 1940- WhoAmP 91
Cowan, Theodore IntMPA 92
Cowan, Thomas F, Sr 1927- WhoAmP 91
Cowan, Tom Keith 1916- WrDr 92
Cowan, W Maxwell 1931- AmMWSc 92
Cowan, W R 1942- AmMWSc 92
Cowan, Wallace Edgar 1924- WhoAmL 92
Cowan, Warren J. IntMPA 92
Cowan, William Allen 1920- AmMWSc 92
Cowan, William Graham 1919- Who 92
Cowan, William Maxwell 1931- IntWW 91, Who 92
Cowans, Alvin Jeffrey 1955- WhoBlA 92
Coward, David Hand 1934- AmMWSc 92
Coward, David John 1917- Who 92
Coward, James Kenderdine 1938- AmMWSc 92
Coward, Jasper Earl 1932- WhoBlA 92
Coward, Joe Edwin 1938- AmMWSc 92
Coward, John 1937- Who 92
Coward, John Stephen 1937- Who 92
Coward, Michael David 1940- WhoFI 92
Coward, Nathan A 1927- AmMWSc 92
Coward, Noel 1899-1973 CnDBLB 6 [port], ConAu 35NR, FacFETw [port], LiExTwC, NewAmDM, RfGEnL 91
Coward, Onida Lavoneia 1964- WhoBlA 92
Coward, Richard Edgar 1927- Who 92
Coward, Stuart Jess 1936- AmMWSc 92
Cowart, Jack 1945- WrDr 92
Cowart, Jim Cash 1951- WhoFI 92, WhoWest 92
Cowart, Thomas David 1953- WhoAmL 92
Cowart, Vincent WhoEnt 92
Cowasjee, Saros IntAu&W 91
Cowasjee, Saros 1931- WrDr 92
Cowburn, David 1945- AmMWSc 92
Cowburn, Norman 1920- Who 92
Cowden, Clark Douglas 1961- WhoRel 92
Cowden, Jere Lee 1947- WhoFI 92
Cowden, John P. LesBEnT 92
Cowden, John William 1945- WhoAmL 92
Cowden, Michael E. 1951- WhoBlA 92
Cowden, Robert Hapgood 1934- WhoEnt 92
Cowden, Robert Laughlin 1933- WhoEnt 92
Cowden, Ronald Reed 1931- AmMWSc 92
Cowderoy, Brenda 1925- Who 92
Cowdery, Robert Douglas 1926- WhoMW 92
Cowdray, Viscount 1910- IntWW 91, Who 92
Cowdrey, Colin Who 92
Cowdrey, Colin 1932- IntWW 91, WrDr 92
Cowdrey, Eric John 1945- AmMWSc 92
Cowdrey, Herbert Edward John 1926- Who 92
Cowdrey, Michael Colin 1932- Who 92
Cowdry, Rex William 1947- AmMWSc 92
Cowe, Collin 1917- Who 92
Cowell, Aaron Dale, Jr. 1962- WhoAmL 92
Cowell, Bruce Craig 1937- AmMWSc 92
Cowell, Catherine 1921- WhoBlA 92
Cowell, Ernest Saul 1927- WhoWest 92
Cowell, Frank A. ConAu 135
Cowell, Henry 1897-1965 NewAmDM
Cowell, James Leo 1944- AmMWSc 92
Cowell, John Richard 1933- Who 92
Cowell, Marion Aubrey, Jr. 1934- WhoAmL 92
Cowell, Raymond 1937- Who 92
Cowell, Ronald James 1941- WhoRel 92
Cowell, Ronald Raymond 1946- WhoAmP 91
Cowell, Stanley A. 1941- WhoBlA 92
Cowell, Stephanie Amy DrAPF 91
Cowell, Wayne Russell 1926- AmMWSc 92
Cowell, Wilburn James 1940- WhoRel 92
Cowen, Bruce David 1953- WhoFI 92
Cowen, Carl Claudius 1924- WhoMW 92
Cowen, Carl Claudius, Jr 1945- AmMWSc 92
Cowen, David 1907- AmMWSc 92
Cowen, Donald Eugene 1918- WhoWest 92
Cowen, Edward S. 1936- WhoAmL 92
Cowen, Eugene Sherman 1925- WhoEnt 92
Cowen, Eve ConAu 34NR
Cowen, Frances 1915- IntAu&W 91, WrDr 92
Cowen, Jerry Arnold 1924- AmMWSc 92
Cowen, Martin Harvey 1941- WhoAmL 92
Cowen, Richard 1940- AmMWSc 92
Cowen, Richard Albert 1934- WhoMW 92
Cowen, Robert, III 1956- WhoEnt 92
Cowen, Robert E. 1930- WhoAmL 92, WhoAmP 91
Cowen, Robert Henry 1915- WhoAmL 92
Cowen, Ron 1944- WrDr 92
Cowen, Roy Chadwell, Jr. 1930- WhoMW 92
Cowen, William Frank 1945- AmMWSc 92
Cowen, Wilson 1905- WhoAmL 92
Cowen, Zelman 1919- IntAu&W 91, IntWW 91, Who 92, WrDr 92
Cowenhoven, Garret Peter 1941- WhoAmP 91
Cowens, Alfred Edward, Jr. 1951- WhoBlA 92
Cowett, Everett R 1935- AmMWSc 92
Cowett, Richard Michael 1942- AmMWSc 92
Cowey, Alan 1935- Who 92
Cowey, Bernard Turing Vionnee 1911- Who 92
Cowger, Marilyn L 1931- AmMWSc 92
Cowgill, Bryan 1927- Who 92
Cowgill, Robert Lee, III 1947- WhoFI 92
Cowgill, Robert Warren 1920- AmMWSc 92
Cowgill, Ursula Moser 1927- AmMWSc 92, WhoMW 92
Cowherd, Chatten, Jr 1939- AmMWSc 92
Cowherd, Edwin Russell 1921- WhoFI 92
Cowhey, Gregory Joseph 1961- WhoFI 92
Cowie, Lord 1926- Who 92
Cowie, Alexander 1896- BenetAL 91
Cowie, Bruce Edgar 1938- WhoEnt 92
Cowie, Edward 1943- ConCom 92
Cowie, Hamilton Russell 1931- IntAu&W 91, WrDr 92
Cowie, James 1886-1956 TwCPaSc
Cowie, Lennox Lauchlan 1950- AmMWSc 92
Cowie, Leonard Wallace 1919- IntAu&W 91, WrDr 92
Cowie, Martin 1947- AmMWSc 92
Cowie, Mervyn 1909- WrDr 92
Cowie, Mervyn Hugh 1909- IntAu&W 91, Who 92
Cowie, Peter Duff 1939- WhoEnt 92
Cowie, William Lorn Kerr Who 92
Cowin, Stephen Corteen 1934- AmMWSc 92
Cowing, Sheila DrAPF 91
Cowl, Jane 1884-1950 FacFETw
Cowles, Calvin Josiah 1821-1907 DcNCBi 1
Cowles, Charles Holden 1875-1957 DcNCBi 1
Cowles, Chauncey D 1911- WhoIns 92
Cowles, Chauncey Deming 1911- WhoFI 92
Cowles, David Lyle 1955- AmMWSc 92
Cowles, David William 1954- WhoWest 92
Cowles, Edward 1837-1919 BiInAmS
Cowles, Edward J 1918- AmMWSc 92
Cowles, Edward Terry 1953- WhoFI 92
Cowles, Eugene Hutchinson 1855-1892 BiInAmS
Cowles, Fleur IntAu&W 91, WrDr 92
Cowles, Frederick Oliver 1937- WhoAmL 92
Cowles, Harold Andrews 1924- AmMWSc 92
Cowles, Henry Chandler 1869-1939 FacFETw
Cowles, Henry Clay 1842-1914 DcNCBi 1
Cowles, James Arthur 1952- WhoRel 92
Cowles, Joe Richard 1941- AmMWSc 92
Cowles, John, Jr. 1929- IntWW 91
Cowles, John Richard 1945- AmMWSc 92
Cowles, Josiah 1791-1873 DcNCBi 1
Cowles, Lenny John 1951- WhoEnt 92
Cowles, Mary Ellen 1925- WhoEnt 92
Cowles, Robert L, III 1950- WhoAmP 91
Cowles, William Henry Harrison 1840-1901 DcNCBi 1
Cowles, William Hutchinson, III 1932- WhoWest 92
Cowles, William Warren 1934- AmMWSc 92
Cowley, Earl 1934- Who 92
Cowley, Abraham 1618-1667 RfGEnL 91
Cowley, Alan H. IntWW 91
Cowley, Alan H 1934- AmMWSc 92
Cowley, Alan Herbert 1934- Who 92
Cowley, Allen Wilson, Jr 1940- AmMWSc 92
Cowley, Anne Pyne 1938- AmMWSc 92
Cowley, Benjamin D, Jr 1956- AmMWSc 92
Cowley, Charles Ramsay 1934- AmMWSc 92
Cowley, Colin Patrick 1902- Who 92
Cowley, Gerald Taylor 1931- AmMWSc 92
Cowley, Gil Henry, Jr. 1941- WhoEnt 92
Cowley, Hannah 1743-1809 RfGEnL 91
Cowley, John Cain 1918- Who 92
Cowley, John Guise 1905- Who 92
Cowley, John Maxwell 1923- AmMWSc 92, IntWW 91, Who 92
Cowley, John W 1946- WhoIns 92
Cowley, Joseph DrAPF 91
Cowley, Kenneth Martin 1912- Who 92
Cowley, Malcolm 1898- IntAu&W 91
Cowley, Malcolm 1898-1989 BenetAL 91, FacFETw, LiExTwC
Cowley, R. Adams d1991 NewYTBS 91
Cowley, Roger A. 1939- IntWW 91
Cowley, Roger Arthur 1939- Who 92
Cowley, Samuel Parkinsan 1934- WhoAmL 92
Cowley, Thomas Gladman 1938- AmMWSc 92
Cowley, William Austin 1931- WhoRel 92
Cowlin, Dorothy 1911- IntAu&W 91
Cowlin, Henry Lawrence 1924- WhoAmL 92
Cowling, Ellis Brevier 1932- AmMWSc 92
Cowling, Gareth Who 92
Cowling, Maurice John 1926- Who 92
Cowling, Randal Keith 1957- WhoRel 92
Cowling, Thomas d1990 IntWW 91N
Cowling, Thomas Gareth 1944- Who 92
Cowling, Vincent Frederick 1918- AmMWSc 92
Cowlishaw, John David 1938- AmMWSc 92
Cowlishaw, Mary Lou 1932- WhoAmP 91
Cowman, Richard Ammon 1938- AmMWSc 92
Cowman, William Henry 1910- WhoAmP 91
Cownie, John Bowler 1940- WhoFI 92
Cowper, Frank Cadogan 1877-1958 TwCPaSc
Cowper, George 1921- AmMWSc 92
Cowper, George Richard 1930- AmMWSc 92
Cowper, Richard WrDr 92
Cowper, Richard 1926- TwCSFW 91
Cowper, Stephen Cambreleng 1938- WhoWest 92
Cowper, Steve Cambreleng 1938- IntWW 91, WhoAmP 91
Cowper, William 1731-1800 DcLB 109 [port], RfGEnL 91
Cowperthwaite, David Jarvis 1921- Who 92
Cowperthwaite, John James 1915- Who 92
Cowperthwaite, Michael 1932- AmMWSc 92
Cowsar, Donald Roy 1942- AmMWSc 92
Cowser, Danny Lee 1948- WhoAmL 92
Cowser, Kenneth Emery 1926- AmMWSc 92
Cowser, Robert DrAPF 91
Cowsik, Ramanath 1940- AmMWSc 92
Cowtan, Frank Willoughby John 1920- Who 92
Cox Who 92
Cox, Baroness 1937- Who 92
Cox, A B 1893-1970 ScFEYrs
Cox, Aaron J 1941- AmMWSc 92
Cox, Alan George 1936- Who 92
Cox, Alan Seaforth 1915- Who 92
Cox, Albert Edward 1916- Who 92
Cox, Albert Edward 1935- WhoRel 92
Cox, Albert Lyman 1883-1965 DcNCBi 1
Cox, Alex 1954- IntMPA 92
Cox, Alfred Bertram 1902- WrDr 92
Cox, Alison Lesley 1962- WhoFI 92
Cox, Alister Stransom 1934- Who 92
Cox, Allan J. 1937- WhoMW 92
Cox, Alva Irwin, Jr. 1925- WhoEnt 92
Cox, Alvin Joseph, Jr 1907- AmMWSc 92
Cox, Andrew Chadwick 1936- AmMWSc 92
Cox, Andrew Hood 1917- WhoAmL 92
Cox, Andrew Paul, Jr. 1937- WhoFI 92
Cox, Ann Bruger AmMWSc 92
Cox, Anthony Who 92
Cox, Anthony Robert 1938- Who 92
Cox, Anthony Wakefield 1915- Who 92
Cox, Archibald 1912- FacFETw, IntWW 91, Who 92, WhoAmP 91, WrDr 92
Cox, Archibald, Jr. 1940- Who 92, WhoFI 92
Cox, Arlie E. 1928- WhoMW 92
Cox, Arthur Dean 1961- WhoBlA 92
Cox, Arthur George Ernest S. Who 92
Cox, Arthur James, Sr. 1943- WhoBlA 92
Cox, Arthur Nelson 1927- AmMWSc 92, WhoWest 92
Cox, B 1931- AmMWSc 92
Cox, Benjamin Vincent 1934- AmMWSc 92
Cox, Beverley Lenore 1929- AmMWSc 92
Cox, Bradley Burton 1941- AmMWSc 92
Cox, Brian Who 92
Cox, Brian 1931- AmMWSc 92
Cox, Brian 1946- ConTFT 9
Cox, Brian Dennis 1946- Who 92
Cox, Brian Escott 1932- Who 92
Cox, Brian Martyn 1939- AmMWSc 92
Cox, Bruce Baldwin 1931- WhoEnt 92
Cox, C. Christopher 1952- AlmAP 92 [port]
Cox, Carol DrAPF 91
Cox, Carolyn Gleaton 1933- WhoEnt 92
Cox, Cathleen Ruth 1948- AmMWSc 92
Cox, Chapman Beecher 1940- WhoAmL 92, WhoAmP 91
Cox, Charles Anthony 1957- WhoMW 92
Cox, Charles Brian 1928- IntAu&W 91, Who 92, WrDr 92
Cox, Charles C. 1945- WhoAmL 92
Cox, Charles Donald 1918- AmMWSc 92
Cox, Charles Finney 1846-1912 BiInAmS
Cox, Charles Philip 1919- AmMWSc 92
Cox, Charles Russell 1957- WhoAmL 92
Cox, Charles Shipley 1922- AmMWSc 92
Cox, Cheryl Craft 1948- WhoEnt 92
Cox, Christopher 1952- WhoAmP 91, WhoWest 92
Cox, Christopher Barry 1931- Who 92, WrDr 92
Cox, Christopher Sherman 1964- WhoEnt 92
Cox, Clair Edward, II 1933- AmMWSc 92
Cox, Clifford Ernest 1942- WhoFI 92
Cox, Corine 1944- WhoBlA 92
Cox, Courteney 1964- IntMPA 92
Cox, Cyrus W 1924- AmMWSc 92
Cox, Dallas Wendell, Jr. 1943- WhoAmL 92
Cox, Daniel G. WhoRel 92
Cox, Daniel Thomas 1946- WhoIns 92
Cox, David 1924- IntWW 91, Who 92
Cox, David Arnold 1937- WhoEnt 92
Cox, David Austin 1955- WhoAmL 92
Cox, David Buchtel 1927- AmMWSc 92
Cox, David Carson 1937- WhoMW 92
Cox, David Dundas 1933- IntAu&W 91
Cox, David Ernest 1934- AmMWSc 92
Cox, David Frame 1931- AmMWSc 92
Cox, David Jackson 1934- AmMWSc 92, WhoMW 92
Cox, David M. 1956- WhoAmL 92
Cox, David S 1942- WhoIns 92
Cox, David W 1951- WhoAmP 91
Cox, Dennis Dean 1950- AmMWSc 92
Cox, Dennis George 1914- Who 92
Cox, Dennis Henry 1925- AmMWSc 92
Cox, Dennis Purver 1929- AmMWSc 92
Cox, Diane Wilson 1937- AmMWSc 92
Cox, Doak Carey 1917- AmMWSc 92
Cox, Donald Clyde 1937- AmMWSc 92
Cox, Donald Cody 1936- AmMWSc 92
Cox, Donald David 1926- AmMWSc 92

Cox, Douglas Charles 1944- WhoWest 92
Cox, DuBois V. 1950- WhoBlA 92
Cox, Dudley 1929- AmMWSc 92
Cox, E. Albert 1876-1955 TwCPaSc
Cox, Ed DrAPF 91
Cox, Edmond Rudolph, Jr 1932- AmMWSc 92
Cox, Edward Who 92
Cox, Edward Charles 1937- AmMWSc 92
Cox, Edwin, III 1931- AmMWSc 92
Cox, Eldon Weston 1939- WhoRel 92
Cox, Elenor R AmMWSc 92
Cox, Emmett R WhoAmP 91
Cox, Emmett Ripley 1935- WhoAmL 92
Cox, Erle 1873-1950 ScFEYrs, TwCSFW 91
Cox, Ernest Gordon 1906- IntWW 91, Who 92
Cox, Euola Wilson WhoBlA 92
Cox, Francis Augustus 1885-1978 DcNCBi 1
Cox, Fred Ward, Jr 1914- AmMWSc 92
Cox, Frederick Eugene 1938- AmMWSc 92
Cox, Frederick Russell 1932- AmMWSc 92
Cox, Garen 1951- WhoAmL 92
Cox, Garry Richard 1935- WhoMW 92
Cox, Gary Evans 1937- WhoWest 92
Cox, Gene Spracher 1921- AmMWSc 92, WhoMW 92
Cox, Geoffrey 1910- Who 92, WrDr 92
Cox, Geoffrey Sandford 1910- IntAu&W 91
Cox, George Elton 1931- AmMWSc 92
Cox, George Sherwood 1963- WhoRel 92
Cox, George Stanley 1946- AmMWSc 92
Cox, George Trenchard Who 92
Cox, George W 1935- AmMWSc 92
Cox, George Warren 1960- AmMWSc 92
Cox, George Wyatt 1935- WhoWest 92
Cox, Georgetta Manning 1947- WhoBlA 92
Cox, Gerald Wayne 1943- WhoAmP 91
Cox, Geraldine Anne Vang 1944- AmMWSc 92
Cox, Gertrude Mary 1900-1978 DcNCBi 1
Cox, Gladys M 1911- WhoAmP 91
Cox, Glenda Evonne 1937- WhoAmL 92
Cox, Glenn A. 1929- IntWW 91
Cox, Glenn Andrew, Jr. 1929- WhoFI 92
Cox, Gordon Who 92
Cox, Gordon F N 1948- AmMWSc 92
Cox, Graham Campbell 1932- IntWW 91
Cox, Gregory Richardson 1948- WhoAmP 91
Cox, H C 1927- AmMWSc 92
Cox, Hannibal Maceo, Jr. 1923- WhoBlA 92
Cox, Hardin Charles 1928- WhoAmP 91
Cox, Harvey 1929- WrDr 92
Cox, Harvey G 1929- FacFETw
Cox, Harvey Gallagher 1929- WhoRel 92
Cox, Harvey Gallagher, Jr. 1929- RelLAm 91
Cox, Headley Morris, Jr. 1916- WhoAmL 92
Cox, Henry Miot 1907- AmMWSc 92
Cox, Henry Reid 1956- WhoAmL 92
Cox, Herald Rea 1907- AmMWSc 92
Cox, Hiden Toy 1917- AmMWSc 92
Cox, Hollace Lawton, Jr 1935- AmMWSc 92
Cox, Horace B. T. Who 92
Cox, Hugh Ronald 1939- WhoRel 92
Cox, Ida 1889-1967 NewAmDM
Cox, Ida 1896-1967 NotBlAW 92
Cox, Ivan William Robert 1950- WhoRel 92
Cox, J. Arthur 1940- WhoRel 92
Cox, J E 1935- AmMWSc 92
Cox, J. Ray 1925- WhoAmL 92
Cox, Jacob Dolson 1828-1900 BiInAmS
Cox, James 1928- Who 92
Cox, James Allan 1941- AmMWSc 92
Cox, James Alphonso 1920-1988 WhoBlA 92N
Cox, James Anthony 1924- Who 92
Cox, James Carl, Jr. 1919- WhoFI 92
Cox, James D. 1943- WhoAmL 92
Cox, James DeWitt 1940- WhoWest 92
Cox, James L. 1922- WhoBlA 92
Cox, James Lee 1938- AmMWSc 92
Cox, James Lester, Jr 1942- AmMWSc 92
Cox, James Middleton 1870-1957 AmPolLe, FacFETw
Cox, James Reed, Jr 1932- AmMWSc 92
Cox, James Steven 1958- WhoAmP 91
Cox, James Talley 1921- WhoAmL 92
Cox, James William 1923- WhoRel 92
Cox, Jeffery WhoAmP 91
Cox, Jeffrey Lorentz 1951- WhoFI 92
Cox, Jeffrey Ray 1962- WhoAmL 92
Cox, Jennie Palmero 1940- WhoAmP 91
Cox, Jerome R, Jr 1925- AmMWSc 92
Cox, Jerry Marshall 1947- WhoFI 92
Cox, Jesse L. 1946- WhoBlA 92
Cox, Joe Bruce 1939- WhoAmL 92
Cox, John WhoAmP 91
Cox, John 1935- Who 92
Cox, John B. 1932- WhoRel 92
Cox, John Colin Leslie 1933- Who 92
Cox, John David 1954- AmMWSc 92
Cox, John E 1923- AmMWSc 92
Cox, John F WhoAmP 91
Cox, John Frederick 1955- WhoWest 92
Cox, John Henry 1941- WhoRel 92
Cox, John Horace 1944- WhoRel 92
Cox, John Jay, Jr 1929- AmMWSc 92
Cox, John Jeffrey 1954- WhoAmP 91
Cox, John Layton 1943- AmMWSc 92
Cox, John Michael Holland 1928- Who 92
Cox, John Samuel 1959- WhoRel 92
Cox, John Theodore 1950- AmMWSc 92
Cox, John W., Jr. 1947- AlmAP 92 [port], WhoMW 92
Cox, John Wesley 1929- WhoBlA 92
Cox, John William d1990 Who 92N
Cox, John William 1928- AmMWSc 92
Cox, Jonathan Elwood 1856-1932 DcNCBi 1
Cox, Joseph John 1845-1903 DcNCBi 1
Cox, Joseph King 1950- WhoAmL 92
Cox, Joseph Lawrence 1932- WhoAmL 92
Cox, Joseph Mason Andrew 1930- WhoBlA 92
Cox, Joseph Merrells, II 1949- WhoFI 92
Cox, Joseph Robert 1934- AmMWSc 92
Cox, Joseph W ScFEYrs
Cox, Joseph William 1937- WhoWest 92
Cox, Julius Grady 1926- AmMWSc 92
Cox, K. K., Jr. 1951- WhoRel 92
Cox, Kathryn Honaker 1924- WhoRel 92
Cox, Keith Gordon 1933- Who 92
Cox, Kenneth A. LesBEnT 92
Cox, Kenneth Roger 1928- WhoAmP 91
Cox, Kevin C. 1949- WhoBlA 92
Cox, Kevin Creuzot 1949- WhoAmP 91
Cox, Kevin Robert 1939- IntAu&W 91, WhoMW 92, WrDr 92
Cox, Lawrence Edward 1944- AmMWSc 92
Cox, Lawrence Henry 1947- AmMWSc 92
Cox, Leonard Hearst, Jr. 1948- WhoEnt 92
Cox, Lewis Calvin 1924- WhoAmL 92
Cox, Lionel Audley 1916- AmMWSc 92
Cox, Loren Charles 1938- WhoAmP 91
Cox, Lota Clare 1942- WhoMW 92
Cox, M Kirkland 1957- WhoAmP 91
Cox, M. Maurice 1951- WhoBlA 92
Cox, Malcolm AmMWSc 92
Cox, Marjorie Herrmann 1918- WhoAmP 91
Cox, Mark DrAPF 91
Cox, Marshall 1932- WhoAmL 92
Cox, Martha 1908- AmMWSc 92
Cox, Marvin Melvin, Jr. 1953- WhoFI 92
Cox, Mary Anthony WhoEnt 92
Cox, Mary E 1937- AmMWSc 92
Cox, Mary Linda 1946- WhoMW 92
Cox, Mencea Ethereal 1906- Who 92
Cox, Merrill Anthony 1952- WhoAmP 91
Cox, Mervyn Kay 1936- WhoWest 92
Cox, Michael 1941- AmMWSc 92
Cox, Michael Lee 1964- WhoWest 92
Cox, Michael Matthew 1952- AmMWSc 92
Cox, Milton D 1939- AmMWSc 92
Cox, Myron Keith 1926- WhoMW 92
Cox, Neil D 1932- AmMWSc 92
Cox, Nelson Anthony 1943- AmMWSc 92
Cox, Norman Ernest 1921- Who 92
Cox, Oliver Jasper 1920- Who 92
Cox, Otis Edward 1941- WhoAmP 91
Cox, Otis Graham, Jr. 1941- WhoBlA 92
Cox, P. Thomas 1930- WhoWest 92
Cox, Palmer 1840-1924 BenetAL 91, ChlLR 24 [port]
Cox, Parker Graham 1913- AmMWSc 92
Cox, Patricia Ann 1931- Who 92
Cox, Patricia Anne Who 92
Cox, Paul 1940- IntWW 91
Cox, Paul Alan 1953- AmMWSc 92
Cox, Paul L. 1946- WhoAmL 92
Cox, Paul William 1957- Who 92
Cox, Peter Arthur 1922- Who 92
Cox, Peter Denzil John H. Who 92
Cox, Peter Richmond 1914- Who 92
Cox, Philip 1922- Who 92
Cox, Prentiss Gwendolyn 1932- AmMWSc 92
Cox, Randy 1947- WhoEnt 92
Cox, Randy Carter 1960- WhoRel 92
Cox, Ray 1943- AmMWSc 92
Cox, Ray Ellis 1946- WhoMW 92
Cox, Raybon Edward 1937- WhoMW 92
Cox, Raymond H 1936- AmMWSc 92
Cox, Raymond Whitten, III 1949- WhoWest 92
Cox, Richard 1931- IntAu&W 91, WrDr 92
Cox, Richard Charles 1920- Who 92
Cox, Richard Harvey 1943- AmMWSc 92
Cox, Richard Horton 1920- AmMWSc 92, WhoFI 92
Cox, Richard Joseph 1929- WhoEnt 92
Cox, Robert De Lafayette 1934- WhoHisp 92
Cox, Robert Harold 1937- AmMWSc 92
Cox, Robert L. 1933- WhoBlA 92
Cox, Robert M., Jr. 1945- WhoMW 92
Cox, Robert O 1917- WhoAmP 91
Cox, Robert Sayre, Jr 1925- AmMWSc 92
Cox, Robert Winifred 1937- WhoAmL 92
Cox, Rody Powell 1926- AmMWSc 92
Cox, Roger 1936- WrDr 92
Cox, Roger Charles 1941- Who 92
Cox, Roger L. 1931- ConAu 135
Cox, Ronald d1991 Who 92N
Cox, Ronald Baker 1943- AmMWSc 92
Cox, Ronald Wayne 1942- WhoMW 92
Cox, Ronnie 1952- WhoBlA 92
Cox, Ronny 1938- IntMPA 92
Cox, Rowland, Jr 1871?-1916 BiInAmS
Cox, Roy Arthur 1925- Who 92
Cox, Roy Vernone WhoEnt 92
Cox, Sandra Hicks 1939- WhoBlA 92
Cox, Stanley Brian 1949- WhoAmP 91
Cox, Stephen Angus ScFEYrs
Cox, Stephen James 1946- Who 92
Cox, Stephen Joseph 1946- IntWW 91
Cox, Stephen Kent 1940- AmMWSc 92
Cox, Steven B. 1950- WhoFI 92
Cox, Steven Thomas 1960- WhoMW 92
Cox, Sue Green 1940- WhoAmP 91
Cox, Susan Hanna 1953- WhoMW 92
Cox, Taylor H., Sr. 1926- WhoBlA 92
Cox, Terrence Guy 1956- WhoFI 92
Cox, Thomas C 1950- AmMWSc 92
Cox, Thomas J, Jr 1935- WhoAmP 91
Cox, Thomas Michael 1930- Who 92
Cox, Thomas Reginald 1951- WhoFI 92
Cox, Timothy M. 1957- WhoRel 92
Cox, Trenchard 1905- IntWW 91, Who 92
Cox, Ulysses Orange 1864-1920 BiInAmS
Cox, Velma Jean 1933- WhoAmP 91
Cox, Vicki Allane 1955- WhoAmL 92
Cox, Wally d1973 LesBEnT 92
Cox, Warren E. 1936- WhoBlA 92
Cox, Wendell 1914- WhoBlA 92
Cox, William 1901- IntAu&W 91
Cox, William Albert, Jr. 1927- WhoRel 92
Cox, William Argus 1959- WhoRel 92
Cox, William Donald, Jr. 1957- WhoAmL 92
Cox, William Edward 1944- AmMWSc 92
Cox, William Harvey, Jr 1942- WhoAmP 91
Cox, William Jackson 1921- WhoRel 92
Cox, William Martin 1922- WhoAmL 92
Cox, William Miles 1943- WhoMW 92
Cox, William R. 1901-1988 TwCWW 91
Cox, William Ruffin 1832-1919 DcNCBi 1
Cox, William Trevor Who 92, WrDr 92
Cox, Winston H. 1941- WhoEnt 92
Cox-Brakefield, Cathy Ann 1960- WhoAmL 92
Cox-Murphy, Sarah JoAnn 1933- WhoAmP 91
Cox-Pursley, Carol Sue 1951- WhoFI 92
Cox-Rawles, Rani 1927- WhoBlA 92
Coxe, Eckley Brinton 1839-1895 BiInAmS
Coxe, Franklin 1839-1903 DcNCBi 1
Coxe, G. Caliman 1908- WhoBlA 92
Coxe, John Redman 1773-1864 BiInAmS
Coxe, Louis DrAPF 91
Coxe, Louis 1918- ConPo 91, IntAu&W 91, WrDr 92
Coxe, Louis O. 1918- BenetAL 91
Coxe, William, Jr 1762-1831 BiInAmS
Coxe, William Haddon 1920- WhoBlA 92
Coxeter, Harold Scott MacDonald 1907- AmMWSc 92, IntWW 91, Who 92, WrDr 92
Coxhead, George Leavell 1920- WhoAmP 91
Coxon, John Anthony 1943- AmMWSc 92
Coxon, Raymond 1896- TwCPaSc
Coy, A. Wayne d1957 LesBEnT 92
Coy, Charles Russell 1926- WhoAmP 91
Coy, Daniel Charles 1963- AmMWSc 92
Coy, David DrAPF 91
Coy, David Howard 1944- AmMWSc 92
Coy, George Somerville 1943- WhoAmP 91
Coy, Jeffrey Wayne 1951- WhoAmP 91
Coy, John T. 1939- WhoBlA 92
Coy, Richard Eugene 1925- AmMWSc 92
Coy, Willard Jene 1955- WhoRel 92
Coye, Robert Dudley 1924- AmMWSc 92
Coyer, Gabriel-Francois 1707-1782 BlkwCEP
Coyer, James A AmMWSc 92
Coyer, Philip Exton 1948- AmMWSc 92
Coyier, Duane L 1926- AmMWSc 92
Coykendall, Alan Littlefield 1937- AmMWSc 92
Coyle, Bernard Andrew 1934- AmMWSc 92
Coyle, Beverly 1946- ConAu 133
Coyle, Catherine Louise 1952- AmMWSc 92
Coyle, Dennis Patrick 1938- WhoAmL 92
Coyle, Edward John 1956- AmMWSc 92
Coyle, Eurfron Gwynne Who 92
Coyle, Frederick Alexander 1942- AmMWSc 92
Coyle, Gerard Joseph 1946- WhoFI 92
Coyle, Grace Longwell 1892-1962 HanAmWH
Coyle, Grady Ellis 1946- WhoRel 92
Coyle, Harry Michael 1927- AmMWSc 92
Coyle, James Edwin, Jr. 1945- WhoEnt 92
Coyle, John Patrick 1935- WhoFI 92
Coyle, Joseph T 1943- AmMWSc 92
Coyle, Marie Bridget 1935- AmMWSc 92
Coyle, Martin Adolphus, Jr. 1941- WhoAmL 92, WhoFI 92, WhoMW 92
Coyle, Mary Dee 1916- WhoBlA 92
Coyle, Michael Lee 1944- WhoAmL 92
Coyle, Patrick Otis 1960- WhoRel 92
Coyle, Peter 1939- AmMWSc 92
Coyle, Richard Jay 1948- WhoFI 92
Coyle, Robert Everett 1930- WhoAmL 92, WhoWest 92
Coyle, Thomas Davidson 1931- AmMWSc 92
Coyle, William Robert 1928- WhoEnt 92
Coyne, Brian D 1959- WhoAmP 91
Coyne, Charles Cole 1948- WhoAmL 92
Coyne, Colleen Ann 1959- WhoAmL 92
Coyne, Daniel William 1946- WhoAmL 92
Coyne, Dermot P 1929- AmMWSc 92
Coyne, Donald Gerald 1936- AmMWSc 92
Coyne, Edward James, Jr 1953- AmMWSc 92
Coyne, Frank J. 1948- WhoAmL 92
Coyne, George Vincent 1933- AmMWSc 92
Coyne, James E 1925- AmMWSc 92
Coyne, James Elliott 1910- Who 92
Coyne, James K 1946- WhoAmP 91
Coyne, James O 1928- WhoIns 92
Coyne, John Martin 1916- WhoAmP 91
Coyne, Joseph E. 1918-1978 ConAu 134
Coyne, M. Jeanne 1926- WhoAmL 92, WhoAmP 91, WhoMW 92
Coyne, Mary Downey 1938- AmMWSc 92
Coyne, Patrick Ivan 1944- AmMWSc 92, WhoMW 92
Coyne, Patrick Joseph 1956- WhoAmL 92
Coyne, Raymond Francis 1950- WhoMW 92
Coyne, Richard Dale 1940- WhoWest 92
Coyne, Robert Patrick 1961- WhoAmL 92
Coyne, Terrance Charles 1946- WhoFI 92
Coyne, Thomas Joseph 1933- WhoMW 92
Coyne, William J. 1936- AlmAP 92 [port]
Coyne, William Joseph 1936- WhoAmP 91
Coyner, Eugene Casper 1918- AmMWSc 92
Coyote, Peter 1942- IntMPA 92
Coyote, The 1954- WhoEnt 92
Coyro, William Frederick, Jr. 1943- WhoHisp 92
Cozad, George Carmon 1927- AmMWSc 92
Cozad, James W. 1927- WhoFI 92, WhoMW 92
Cozad, James William 1927- IntWW 91
Cozad, John Condon 1944- WhoAmL 92
Cozart, John 1928- WhoBlA 92
Cozen, Stephen Allen 1939- WhoAmL 92
Cozens, Barbara 1906- Who 92
Cozens, Henry Iliffe 1904- Who 92
Cozens, John Robert 1752-1797 BlkwCEP
Cozens, Richard 1952- WhoWest 92
Cozens, Robert William 1927- Who 92
Cozens, Thomas Joseph 1958- WhoFI 92
Cozine, Ann 1941- WhoAmP 91
Cozmo-Th'-Mystik DrAPF 91
Cozort, Amber Lynne 1963- WhoMW 92
Cozort, Wayne 1931- WhoAmP 91
Cozzarelli, Francis A 1933- AmMWSc 92
Cozzarelli, Nicholas Robert 1938- AmMWSc 92
Cozzens, Frederick S. 1818-1869 BenetAL 91
Cozzens, Issachar 1780-1865 BiInAmS
Cozzens, James Gould 1903-1978 BenetAL 91, FacFETw
Cozzens, Robert Bruce, Jr. 1949- WhoAmL 92
Cozzens, Robert F 1941- AmMWSc 92
Cozzi, Joanne WhoRel 92
Cozzi, Nicholas Vito 1953- WhoMW 92
Cozzolino, Salvatore James 1924- WhoFI 92
Cprek, Kent Gordon 1953- WhoAmL 92
Craane, Janine Lee 1961- WhoHisp 92
Crabb, Allan Edward 1933- WhoMW 92
Crabb, Barbara Brandriff 1939- WhoAmL 92
Crabb, David William 1953- WhoMW 92
Crabb, Delbert Elmo 1916- WhoAmP 91
Crabb, Frederick Hugh Wright 1915- Who 92
Crabb, Gerald Allen 1949- WhoRel 92
Crabb, Henry Stuart Malcolm 1922- WrDr 92
Crabb, Kenneth Wayne 1950- WhoMW 92
Crabb, Robert James 1949- WhoWest 92
Crabb, Robert Talmage, III 1945- WhoEnt 92
Crabb, Tony William 1933- Who 92
Crabbe, Buster 1907-1983 FacFETw
Crabbe, George 1754-1832 RfGEnL 91

**Crabbe**, Kenneth Herbert Martineau 1916- Who 92
**Crabbe**, Pauline 1914- Who 92
**Crabbe**, Pierre 1928- AmMWSc 92
**Crabbe**, Reginald James Williams 1909- Who 92
**Crabbe**, Samuel Azu 1918- IntWW 91
**Crabbie**, Christopher Donald 1946- Who 92
**Crabbie**, Veronica 1910- Who 92
**Crabbs**, Roger Alan 1928- WhoWest 92
**Crabill**, Edward Vaughn 1930- AmMWSc 92
**Crable**, Dallas Eugene 1927- WhoBlA 92
**Crable**, Deborah J. 1957- WhoBlA 92
**Crable**, George Francis 1922- AmMWSc 92
**Crable**, John Vincent 1923- AmMWSc 92
**Crabs**, Donald Benjamin 1926- WhoEnt 92, WhoWest 92
**Crabtree**, Arthur Bamford 1910- WhoRel 92
**Crabtree**, Burnie R WhoAmP 91
**Crabtree**, David Emerson 1927- WhoAmL 92
**Crabtree**, David Melvin 1945- AmMWSc 92
**Crabtree**, Davida Foy 1944- WhoRel 92
**Crabtree**, Derek Thomas 1930- Who 92
**Crabtree**, Douglas Everett 1938- AmMWSc 92
**Crabtree**, Frank Dee 1932- WhoMW 92
**Crabtree**, Garvin 1929- AmMWSc 92
**Crabtree**, George William 1944- AmMWSc 92
**Crabtree**, Gerald Winston 1941- AmMWSc 92
**Crabtree**, Jack 1938- TwCPaSc
**Crabtree**, Jack Turner 1936- WhoAmL 92
**Crabtree**, James Bruce 1918- AmMWSc 92
**Crabtree**, John David 1947- WhoMW 92
**Crabtree**, Jonathan 1934- Who 92
**Crabtree**, Keith Alan 1952- WhoFI 92
**Crabtree**, Koby Takayashi 1934- AmMWSc 92, WhoMW 92
**Crabtree**, Lewis Frederick 1924- Who 92
**Crabtree**, Ray S 1935- WhoIns 92
**Crabtree**, Robert Dee 1935- WhoRel 92
**Crabtree**, Robert Eugene 1934- WhoMW 92
**Crabtree**, Robert H 1948- AmMWSc 92
**Crabtree**, Ross Edward 1932- AmMWSc 92
**Crabtree**, Samuel William 1950- WhoMW 92, WhoRel 92
**Crabtree**, Simon Who 92
**Crace**, Jim 1946- ConAu 135, ConNov 91
**Crace**, Joseph Brent 1954- WhoAmL 92
**Cracium**, John Odie 1944- WhoMW 92
**Cracknell**, Basil Edward 1925- WrDr 92
**Cracknell**, Malcolm Thomas 1943- Who 92
**Cracknell**, Martin 1929- Who 92
**Cracraft**, Joel Lester 1942- AmMWSc 92
**Cracraft**, John Michael 1933- WhoFI 92
**Cracraft**, Mary Miller 1946- WhoAmL 92, WhoFI 92
**Cracroft**, Peter Dicken 1907- Who 92
**Cracroft**, Stephen Glen 1949- WhoFI 92
**Craddick**, Donald Lee 1932- WhoAmP 91
**Craddick**, Jan O'Neil 1933- WhoEnt 92
**Craddick**, Thomas Russell 1943- WhoAmP 91
**Craddock**, Aleck 1924- Who 92
**Craddock**, Billy Wayne 1940- WhoEnt 92
**Craddock**, Charles Egbert BenetAL 91
**Craddock**, Elysse Margaret 1944- AmMWSc 92
**Craddock**, Garnet Roy 1926- AmMWSc 92
**Craddock**, J Campbell 1930- AmMWSc 92
**Craddock**, James Richard 1921- WhoRel 92
**Craddock**, John Harvey 1936- AmMWSc 92
**Craddock**, Kenneth Julius Holt 1910-1989 TwCPaSc
**Craddock**, Michael Kevin 1936- AmMWSc 92
**Craddock**, Robert Glen 1931- WhoAmP 91
**Craddock**, Shirley Anne 1934- WhoAmP 91
**Cradduck**, Trevor David AmMWSc 92
**Cradock**, John Anthony 1921- Who 92
**Cradock**, Percy 1923- IntWW 91, Who 92
**Cradock-Hartopp**, J. E. Who 92
**Crady**, George 1931- WhoAmP 91
**Crady**, Shannon Louise 1962- WhoRel 92
**Craft**, David William 1952- WhoAmL 92
**Craft**, E. Carrie 1928- WhoBlA 92
**Craft**, Ellen 1826?-1897? NotBlAW 92 [port]
**Craft**, George Arthur 1916- AmMWSc 92
**Craft**, Guy Calvin 1929- WhoBlA 92
**Craft**, Harold Dumont, Jr 1938- AmMWSc 92
**Craft**, Ian Logan 1937- Who 92
**Craft**, James Allan 1952- WhoAmL 92
**Craft**, John Edward 1943- WhoEnt 92, WhoWest 92
**Craft**, K. Y. SmATA 65 [port]
**Craft**, Kinuko SmATA 65 [port]
**Craft**, Kinuko Y 1940- SmATA 65 [port]
**Craft**, Mary Ellen 1946- WhoMW 92
**Craft**, Maurice 1932- Who 92
**Craft**, Richard Howard 1944- WhoRel 92
**Craft**, Robbie Wright 1951- WhoWest 92
**Craft**, Robert 1923- IntAu&W 91, NewAmDM, WrDr 92
**Craft**, Robert Homan, Jr. 1939- WhoAmL 92
**Craft**, Robert Merrill 1958- WhoAmL 92
**Craft**, Rolf V 1937- WhoAmP 91
**Craft**, Ruth 1935- ConAu 133
**Craft**, Sally-Ann Roberts 1953- WhoBlA 92
**Craft**, Thomas J., Sr. 1924- WhoBlA 92
**Craft**, Thomas Jacob, Sr 1924- AmMWSc 92
**Crafton**, Donald Clayton 1947- WhoEnt 92, WhoMW 92
**Crafton**, Paul A 1923- AmMWSc 92
**Crafton-Masterson**, Adrienne 1926- WhoFI 92
**Crafts**, James Mason 1839-1917 BiInAmS
**Crafts**, Roger Conant 1911- AmMWSc 92
**Crafts**, William 1787-1826 BenetAL 91
**Crager**, Teddy Jack 1925- WhoEnt 92
**Cragg**, Albert Kenneth 1913- DcEcMov, Who 92
**Cragg**, Anthony Douglas 1949- IntWW 91
**Cragg**, Anthony John 1943- Who 92
**Cragg**, Donald George Lynn 1933- WhoRel 92
**Cragg**, Ernest E 1927- WhoIns 92
**Cragg**, Gordon Mitchell 1936- AmMWSc 92
**Cragg**, James Birkett 1910- Who 92
**Cragg**, Kenneth Who 92
**Cragg**, Kenneth 1913- WrDr 92
**Cragg**, Tony 1949- TwCPaSc, WorArt 1980
**Craggs**, James Wilkinson 1920- Who 92
**Craggs**, John Drummond 1915- Who 92
**Craggs**, Robert F 1937- AmMWSc 92
**Craghead**, James Douglas 1950- WhoWest 92
**Cragin**, Charles Langmaid 1943- WhoAmL 92, WhoAmP 91
**Cragin**, Edwin Bradford 1859-1918 BiInAmS
**Cragle**, Raymond George 1926- AmMWSc 92
**Crago**, Sylvia S AmMWSc 92
**Crago**, Thomas Howard 1907- IntAu&W 91, WrDr 92
**Cragoe**, Arthur Clement 1927- WhoIns 92
**Cragoe**, Douglas Arthur 1952- WhoEnt 92
**Cragoe**, Edward Jethro, Jr 1917- AmMWSc 92
**Cragon**, Harvey George 1929- AmMWSc 92
**Cragun**, Calvin 1940- WhoWest 92
**Cragwall**, J S, Jr 1919- AmMWSc 92
**Crahan**, Elizabeth Schmidt 1913- WhoWest 92
**Craib**, Douglas Duncan Simpson 1914- Who 92
**Craib**, Ian 1945- WrDr 92
**Craib**, James F 1913- AmMWSc 92
**Craig** Who 92
**Craig**, A.A. ConAu 34NR
**Craig**, Alan Daniel 1935- AmMWSc 92
**Craig**, Alan Knowlton 1930- AmMWSc 92
**Craig**, Albert Burchfield, Jr 1924- AmMWSc 92
**Craig**, Albert James 1924- Who 92
**Craig**, Albert Morrison 1943- AmMWSc 92
**Craig**, Alexander ScFEYrs
**Craig**, Alisa IntAu&W 91X, WrDr 92
**Craig**, Andrew Billings, III 1931- WhoMW 92
**Craig**, Anna Maynard 1944- WhoFI 92
**Craig**, Arnold Charles 1933- AmMWSc 92
**Craig**, Barbara Denise 1915- Who 92
**Craig**, Barbara Hinkson 1942- ConAu 135
**Craig**, Barry Gordon 1941- WhoAmL 92
**Craig**, Benjamin Hogan, Jr. 1921- WhoFI 92
**Craig**, Brent Maurice 1963- WhoAmL 92
**Craig**, Brian TwCSFW 91, WrDr 92
**Craig**, Bruce Lance 1949- WhoAmP 91
**Craig**, Burton Mackay 1918- AmMWSc 92
**Craig**, Catherine Lee 1951- AmMWSc 92
**Craig**, Charles 1920- Who 92
**Craig**, Charles Grant 1957- WhoEnt 92
**Craig**, Charles Hilan ScFEYrs
**Craig**, Charles Robert 1936- AmMWSc 92
**Craig**, Charles Samuel 1943- WhoFI 92
**Craig**, Cheryl Allen 1947- WhoBlA 92
**Craig**, Christopher John Sinclair 1941- Who 92
**Craig**, Claude Burgess 1946- WhoBlA 92
**Craig**, Claude Burgess, Sr 1946- WhoAmP 91
**Craig**, Colin ScFEYrs
**Craig**, Dana Michael 1950- WhoMW 92
**Craig**, Daniel Robert 1957- WhoRel 92
**Craig**, David WrDr 92
**Craig**, David Brownrigg 1929- IntWW 91
**Craig**, David Clarke 1955- WhoFI 92
**Craig**, David Howard 1951- WhoRel 92
**Craig**, David Irvin 1849-1925 DcNCBi 1
**Craig**, David Parker 1919- IntWW 91, Who 92
**Craig**, David R WhoAmP 91
**Craig**, David W. 1925- WhoAmL 92
**Craig**, Dexter Hildreth 1924- AmMWSc 92
**Craig**, Donald Spence 1923- AmMWSc 92
**Craig**, Donald Wiley 1912- WhoMW 92
**Craig**, Douglas 1916- Who 92
**Craig**, Douglas Abercrombie M 1939- AmMWSc 92
**Craig**, Douglas Harold 1954- WhoEnt 92
**Craig**, Edith 1869-1947 BiDBrF 2
**Craig**, Edith G 1869-1947 FacFETw
**Craig**, Edward Anthony 1905- Who 92, WrDr 92
**Craig**, Edward Charles 1949- WhoWest 92
**Craig**, Edward Gordon 1872-1966 TwCPaSc
**Craig**, Edward J 1924- AmMWSc 92
**Craig**, Edward M, Jr 1950- WhoAmP 91
**Craig**, Elaine Hartung 1932- WhoAmL 92
**Craig**, Elizabeth Anne 1946- AmMWSc 92
**Craig**, Ellen Walker 1906- WhoBlA 92
**Craig**, Elson L. 1933- WhoBlA 92
**Craig**, Emma Jeanelle Patton WhoBlA 92
**Craig**, Francis Northrop 1911- AmMWSc 92
**Craig**, Frederick A. 1933- WhoBlA 92
**Craig**, Gail Heidbreder 1941- WhoWest 92
**Craig**, George Black 1921- AmMWSc 92
**Craig**, George Brownlee, Jr 1930- AmMWSc 92, IntWW 91, WhoMW 92
**Craig**, George Charles Graham 1946- Who 92
**Craig**, George Dennis 1936- WhoFI 92
**Craig**, Gordon 1872-1966 FacFETw
**Craig**, Gordon 1913- WrDr 92
**Craig**, Harmon 1926- AmMWSc 92
**Craig**, Hurshel Eugene 1932- WhoMW 92
**Craig**, James Who 92
**Craig**, James 1744-1795 BlkwCEP
**Craig**, James Clifford, Jr 1936- AmMWSc 92
**Craig**, James I 1942- AmMWSc 92
**Craig**, James Kent 1955- WhoAmL 92
**Craig**, James L. 1949- WhoMW 92
**Craig**, James Morrison 1916- AmMWSc 92
**Craig**, James Oscar 1927- Who 92
**Craig**, James Porter, Jr 1926- AmMWSc 92
**Craig**, James Robert 1913- WhoMW 92
**Craig**, James Roland 1940- AmMWSc 92
**Craig**, James Verne 1924- AmMWSc 92
**Craig**, James William 1921- AmMWSc 92
**Craig**, Jerry Wayne 1946- WhoMW 92
**Craig**, John 1864-1912 BiInAmS
**Craig**, John Charles 1946- WhoMW 92
**Craig**, John Cymerman 1920- AmMWSc 92
**Craig**, John Egwin 1932- Who 92
**Craig**, John Frank 1945- AmMWSc 92
**Craig**, John Frazer 1943- Who 92
**Craig**, John Horace 1942- AmMWSc 92
**Craig**, John James 1950- WhoRel 92
**Craig**, John Merrill 1913- AmMWSc 92
**Craig**, John Philip 1923- AmMWSc 92
**Craig**, John Robert 1947- WhoMW 92
**Craig**, John Tucker 1926- WhoFI 92
**Craig**, Jonathan IntAu&W 91X
**Craig**, Judith 1937- WhoRel 92
**Craig**, Kenneth Denton 1937- AmMWSc 92
**Craig**, Kenneth P 1944- WhoAmP 91
**Craig**, Larry 1945- AlmAP 92 [port]
**Craig**, Larry Edwin 1945- IntWW 91, WhoAmP 91, WhoWest 92
**Craig**, Lawrance B., III WhoAmL 92
**Craig**, Lexie Ferrell 1921- WhoWest 92
**Craig**, Lillian WhoEnt 92
**Craig**, Locke 1860-1924 DcNCBi 1
**Craig**, Louis Elwood 1921- AmMWSc 92
**Craig**, Lyman Creighton 1906-1974 FacFETw
**Craig**, M. F. ConAu 133, SmATA 65
**Craig**, M. S. ConAu 133, SmATA 65
**Craig**, Malcolm McDearmid 1937- IntAu&W 91
**Craig**, Marion James, III 1950- WhoAmL 92
**Craig**, Mary ConAu 133, SmATA 65
**Craig**, Mary 1928- IntWW 91
**Craig**, Mary Ann 1947- WhoEnt 92
**Craig**, Mary Francis 1927- IntAu&W 91
**Craig**, Mary S. ConAu 133, SmATA 65
**Craig**, Mary Shura 1923-1991 ConAu 133, SmATA 65
**Craig**, Maxwell Davidson 1931- Who 92
**Craig**, Mayadelle Dell 1937- WhoWest 92
**Craig**, Michael 1928- IntWW 91
**Craig**, Michael 1929- IntMPA 92
**Craig**, Moses d1913 BiInAmS
**Craig**, Nessly Coile 1942- AmMWSc 92
**Craig**, Norman 1920- Who 92
**Craig**, Norman Castleman 1931- AmMWSc 92
**Craig**, Oscar Who 92
**Craig**, P James 1925- WhoIns 92
**Craig**, Patricia 1943- WrDr 92
**Craig**, Paul Alfred 1957- WhoMW 92
**Craig**, Paul N 1921- AmMWSc 92
**Craig**, Paul Palmer 1933- AmMWSc 92
**Craig**, Peter Harry 1929- AmMWSc 92
**Craig**, Peter John 1959- WhoAmL 92
**Craig**, Plezzy Harbor, Jr 1937- WhoAmP 91
**Craig**, Raymond Allen 1920- AmMWSc 92
**Craig**, Raymond S 1917- AmMWSc 92
**Craig**, Rhonda Patricia 1953- WhoBlA 92
**Craig**, Richard 1915- WhoBlA 92
**Craig**, Richard 1937- AmMWSc 92
**Craig**, Richard Anderson 1936- AmMWSc 92
**Craig**, Richard Ansel 1922- AmMWSc 92
**Craig**, Richard Gary 1949- AmMWSc 92, WhoMW 92
**Craig**, Robert 1917- IntWW 91, Who 92
**Craig**, Robert Bruce 1944- AmMWSc 92
**Craig**, Robert Charles 1921- WrDr 92
**Craig**, Robert Emmet 1933- WhoAmP 91
**Craig**, Robert George 1923- AmMWSc 92
**Craig**, Robert Lee, Jr. 1950- WhoAmL 92
**Craig**, Robert Wallace 1924- WhoWest 92
**Craig**, Roger Lee 1930- WhoWest 92
**Craig**, Roger Timothy 1960- WhoBlA 92, WhoWest 92
**Craig**, Roy Phillip 1924- AmMWSc 92
**Craig**, Sandra Noel 1954- WhoAmL 92
**Craig**, Stanley Francis 1952- WhoRel 92
**Craig**, Stanley Harold 1909- AmMWSc 92
**Craig**, Starlett Russell 1947- WhoBlA 92
**Craig**, Stephen Wright 1932- WhoWest 92
**Craig**, Stuart N. 1942- WhoEnt 92
**Craig**, Susan Walker AmMWSc 92
**Craig**, Syndey Pollock, III 1945- AmMWSc 92
**Craig**, Thomas 1855-1900 BiInAmS
**Craig**, Thomas Rae 1906- Who 92
**Craig**, Timothy DrAPF 91
**Craig**, Vicki Rene 1957- WhoAmL 92
**Craig**, Wilfred Stuart 1916- AmMWSc 92
**Craig**, William 1924- IntWW 91, Who 92
**Craig**, William Emerson 1942- WhoAmL 92
**Craig**, William Warren 1935- AmMWSc 92
**Craig**, Winston John 1947- AmMWSc 92
**Craig-Cooper**, Michael 1936- Who 92
**Craig-Martin**, Michael 1941- TwCPaSc
**Craig-McFeely**, Elizabeth Sarah Ann 1927- Who 92
**Craig of Radley**, Baron 1929- Who 92
**Craig-Rudd**, Joan 1931- WhoBlA 92
**Craigavon**, Viscount 1944- Who 92
**Craige**, Ernest 1918- AmMWSc 92
**Craige**, Francis Burton 1811-1875 DcNCBi 1
**Craige**, Kerr 1843-1904 DcNCBi 1
**Craigen**, Desmond Seaward 1916- Who 92
**Craigen**, James Mark 1938- Who 92
**Craighead**, Alexander 1707-1766 DcNCBi 1
**Craighead**, Betty Jo 1932- WhoAmP 91
**Craighead**, David Caperton 1931- WhoAmP 91
**Craighead**, Frank Cooper, Jr. 1916- WhoWest 92
**Craighead**, John Edward 1930- AmMWSc 92
**Craighead**, John J 1916- AmMWSc 92
**Craighead**, Robert Lincoln, Jr. 1941- WhoMW 92
**Craighead**, Wendel Lee 1936- WhoEnt 92, WhoMW 92
**Craighill**, William Price 1833-1909 BiInAmS
**Craigie**, Edward Horne 1894- AmMWSc 92
**Craigie**, Frederick Charles 1949- WhoMW 92
**Craigie**, Hamilton ScFEYrs
**Craigie**, Hugh Brechin 1908- Who 92
**Craigie**, John Hubert 1887- Who 92
**Craigmiles**, Julian Pryor 1921- AmMWSc 92
**Craigmyle**, Baron 1923- Who 92
**Craigo**, Gordon Earl 1951- WhoMW 92
**Craigo**, Oshel 1937- WhoAmP 91
**Craigton**, Baron 1904- Who 92
**Craigwell**, Hadyn H. 1907- WhoBlA 92
**Craik**, Mrs. RfGEnL 91
**Craik**, Charles S 1954- AmMWSc 92
**Craik**, Duncan Robert Steele 1916- Who 92
**Craik**, Eva Lee 1919- AmMWSc 92
**Craik**, Fergus Ian Muirden 1935- IntWW 91
**Craik**, Philip Lee 1952- WhoEnt 92
**Craik**, Roger George 1940- Who 92
**Craik**, T. W. 1927- WrDr 92

**Craik,** Thomas Wallace 1927- *IntAu&W 91*
**Craik,** Wendy Ann 1934- *IntAu&W 91, WrDr 92*
**Crain,** Billy Ray 1929- *WhoAmP 91*
**Crain,** Charles Anthony 1931- *WhoWest 92*
**Crain,** Cullen Malone 1920- *AmMWSc 92*
**Crain,** Donald Lee 1933- *AmMWSc 92*
**Crain,** Floyd Harrell 1929- *WhoAmP 91*
**Crain,** Gayla Campbell 1950- *WhoAmL 92*
**Crain,** Gladys Armour 1924- *WhoAmP 91*
**Crain,** James Arnold 1952- *WhoRel 92*
**Crain,** James Harry 1951- *WhoRel 92*
**Crain,** Jeanne 1925- *IntMPA 92*
**Crain,** Rance *WhoFI 92, WhoMW 92*
**Crain,** Richard Cullen 1951- *AmMWSc 92*
**Crain,** Richard Willson 1931- *WhoWest 92*
**Crain,** Richard Willson, Jr 1931- *AmMWSc 92*
**Crain,** Stanley M 1923- *AmMWSc 92*
**Crain,** Steven Anthony 1961- *WhoMW 92*
**Crain,** William Rathbone, Jr 1944- *AmMWSc 92*
**Crain,** Willie E 1942- *WhoAmP 91*
**Craine,** Elliott Maurice 1924- *AmMWSc 92*
**Craine,** Lloyd Bernard 1921- *AmMWSc 92*
**Crainz,** Franco 1913- *IntWW 91*
**Craker,** Lyle E 1941- *AmMWSc 92*
**Craker,** Wendel Dean 1929- *WhoRel 92*
**Crall,** James Monroe 1914- *AmMWSc 92*
**Cralley,** John Clement 1932- *AmMWSc 92*
**Cram,** Alastair Lorimer 1909- *Who 92*
**Cram,** Donald James 1919- *AmMWSc 92, FacFETw, IntWW 91, Who 92, WhoNob 90, WhoWest 92*
**Cram,** Douglas M. *WhoAmL 92*
**Cram,** John Robert 1929- *WhoWest 92*
**Cram,** Leighton Scott 1942- *AmMWSc 92*
**Cram,** Ralph Adams 1863-1942 *DcTwDes, FacFETw*
**Cram,** Thomas Jefferson 1807?-1883 *BiInAmS*
**Cram,** William Thomas 1927- *AmMWSc 92*
**Cramb,** G. Stanley 1949- *WhoAmL 92*
**Cramblett,** Henry G 1929- *AmMWSc 92*
**Cramer,** Alice Carver *DrAPF 91*
**Cramer,** Archie Barrett 1909- *AmMWSc 92*
**Cramer,** Arden Lee 1960- *WhoMW 92*
**Cramer,** Browning 1944- *WhoEnt 92*
**Cramer,** Bud *WhoAmP 91*
**Cramer,** Calvin O 1926- *AmMWSc 92*
**Cramer,** Carl Frederick 1922- *AmMWSc 92*
**Cramer,** Carmen *DrAPF 91*
**Cramer,** Curtis Albert 1939- *WhoFI 92*
**Cramer,** David Alan 1925- *AmMWSc 92*
**Cramer,** Donald V 1941- *AmMWSc 92*
**Cramer,** Douglas S. *IntMPA 92, LesBEnT 92*
**Cramer,** Douglas Schoolfield *WhoEnt 92, WhoWest 92*
**Cramer,** Edward Morton 1925- *WhoAmL 92, WhoEnt 92*
**Cramer,** Eva Brown 1944- *AmMWSc 92*
**Cramer,** Friedrich D. 1923- *IntWW 91*
**Cramer,** George Bennett 1903- *WhoFI 92*
**Cramer,** Gerald d1991 *NewYTBS 91*
**Cramer,** Gisela Turck 1934- *AmMWSc 92*
**Cramer,** Harold 1927- *WhoAmL 92*
**Cramer,** Harrison Emery 1919- *AmMWSc 92*
**Cramer,** Howard Ross 1925- *AmMWSc 92*
**Cramer,** James D 1937- *AmMWSc 92*
**Cramer,** Jan 1928- *IntWW 91*
**Cramer,** Jane Harris 1942- *AmMWSc 92*
**Cramer,** Jeffrey Allen 1951- *WhoAmL 92*
**Cramer,** Joe J., Jr. *WhoBlA 92*
**Cramer,** John 1896- *Who 92*
**Cramer,** John Allen 1943- *AmMWSc 92*
**Cramer,** John Gleason 1934- *AmMWSc 92*
**Cramer,** John McNaight 1941- *WhoAmL 92*
**Cramer,** John Wesley 1928- *AmMWSc 92*
**Cramer,** Joseph Benjamin 1914- *AmMWSc 92*
**Cramer,** Lee H. 1945- *WhoFI 92*
**Cramer,** Malinda Elliott 1844-1906 *RelLAm 91*
**Cramer,** Mark Robert 1959- *WhoAmL 92*
**Cramer,** Michael Brown 1938- *AmMWSc 92*
**Cramer,** Michael William 1924- *WhoFI 92, WhoMW 92*
**Cramer,** Owen Carver 1941- *WhoWest 92*
**Cramer,** Richard 1913- *AmMWSc 92*
**Cramer,** Richard Ben *SourALJ*
**Cramer,** Robert E. 1947- *AlmAP 92 [port]*
**Cramer,** Roger Earl 1943- *AmMWSc 92*
**Cramer,** Rosalind Faber 1935- *WhoEnt 92*
**Cramer,** Sanford Wendell, III 1948- *WhoWest 92*
**Cramer,** Stanley H. 1933- *WrDr 92*
**Cramer,** Steven Edward 1945- *WhoWest 92*
**Cramer,** Stuart Warren 1868-1940 *DcNCBi 1*
**Cramer,** Walter 1886-1944 *EncTR 91*
**Cramer,** Wesley A. 1953- *WhoAmL 92*
**Cramer,** William Anthony 1938- *AmMWSc 92*
**Cramer,** William C 1922- *WhoAmP 91*
**Cramer,** William Smith 1914- *AmMWSc 92*
**Cramm,** Gottfried von 1909-1976 *EncTR 91 [port]*
**Cramond,** Ronald Duncan 1927- *Who 92*
**Cramond,** William Alexander 1920- *IntWW 91, Who 92*
**Cramp,** John Franklin 1923- *WhoAmL 92*
**Cramp,** Rosemary Jean 1929- *Who 92*
**Crampton,** Arthur Edward Sean 1918- *Who 92*
**Crampton,** Betty 1922- *WhoAmP 91*
**Crampton,** Charles Albert 1858-1915 *BiInAmS*
**Crampton,** George H 1926- *AmMWSc 92*
**Crampton,** Helen *WrDr 92*
**Crampton,** James Mylan 1923- *AmMWSc 92*
**Crampton,** Janet Wert 1934- *AmMWSc 92*
**Crampton,** John Vernon 1930- *WhoFI 92*
**Crampton,** Peter Duncan 1932- *Who 92*
**Crampton,** Sean 1918- *TwCPaSc*
**Crampton,** Stuart J B 1936- *AmMWSc 92*
**Crampton,** Theodore Henry Miller 1926- *AmMWSc 92*
**Crampton Smith,** Alex *Who 92*
**Cramton,** Charles Davis 1955- *WhoAmL 92*
**Cramton,** Roger Conant 1929- *WhoAmL 92*
**Cramton,** Thomas James 1938- *AmMWSc 92*
**Cran,** James Douglas 1944- *Who 92*
**Cran,** Mark Dyson Gordon 1948- *Who 92*
**Cranados Navedo,** Jose 1946- *WhoAmP 91*
**Cranberg,** Lawrence 1917- *AmMWSc 92*
**Cranborne,** Viscount 1946- *Who 92*
**Cranbrook,** Earl of 1933- *Who 92*
**Cranch,** Christopher Pearse 1813-1892 *BenetAL 91*
**Cranch,** Edmund Titus 1922- *AmMWSc 92*
**Cranch,** Harold Covert 1911- *WhoRel 92*
**Crandall,** Arthur Jared 1939- *AmMWSc 92*
**Crandall,** Charles Lee 1850-1917 *BiInAmS*
**Crandall,** Dana Irving 1915- *AmMWSc 92*
**Crandall,** David Hugh 1942- *AmMWSc 92*
**Crandall,** David L 1952- *AmMWSc 92*
**Crandall,** Edward D 1938- *AmMWSc 92*
**Crandall,** Elbert Williams 1920- *AmMWSc 92*
**Crandall,** Ira Carlton 1931- *AmMWSc 92*
**Crandall,** Jack Kenneth 1937- *AmMWSc 92*
**Crandall,** John L 1927- *WhoIns 92*
**Crandall,** John Lou 1920- *AmMWSc 92*
**Crandall,** John Lynn 1927- *WhoFI 92*
**Crandall,** John R 1914- *AmMWSc 92*
**Crandall,** Lee W 1913- *AmMWSc 92*
**Crandall,** Loree Yoko 1964- *WhoWest 92*
**Crandall,** Michael Grain 1940- *AmMWSc 92*
**Crandall,** Nancy 1940- *WhoAmP 91*
**Crandall,** Nelson David, III 1954- *WhoAmL 92*
**Crandall,** Norma *WrDr 92*
**Crandall,** Paul Herbert 1923- *AmMWSc 92*
**Crandall,** Philip Glen 1948- *AmMWSc 92*
**Crandall,** Prudence 1803-1890 *RComAH*
**Crandall,** Prudence 1804-1889 *HanAmWH*
**Crandall,** Richard B 1928- *AmMWSc 92*
**Crandall,** Robert Earl 1917- *WhoWest 92*
**Crandall,** Robert L 1935- *News 92-1 [port]*
**Crandall,** Robert Lloyd 1935- *IntWW 91, WhoFI 92*
**Crandall,** Stephen H 1920- *AmMWSc 92*
**Crandall,** Vern Jay 1939- *WhoWest 92*
**Crandall,** Walter Ellis 1916- *AmMWSc 92*
**Crandall,** William B 1921- *AmMWSc 92*
**Crandall Hollick,** Julian Bernard Hugh 1947- *WhoEnt 92*
**Crandall-Stotler,** Barbara Jean 1942- *AmMWSc 92*
**Crandell,** Dwight Raymond 1923- *AmMWSc 92*
**Crandell,** Dwight Samuel 1943- *WhoMW 92*
**Crandell,** George Frank 1932- *AmMWSc 92*
**Crandell,** John Underhill d1991 *NewYTBS 91*
**Crandell,** Judith Speizer *DrAPF 91*
**Crandell,** Kenneth James 1957- *WhoFI 92*
**Crandell,** Kevin Scott 1955- *WhoAmL 92*
**Crandell,** Merrell Edward 1938- *AmMWSc 92*
**Crandell,** Robert Allen 1924- *AmMWSc 92*
**Crandell,** Walter Bain 1911- *AmMWSc 92*
**Crandlemere,** Robert Wayne 1947- *AmMWSc 92*
**Crane,** Anatole 1933- *AmMWSc 92*
**Crane,** Angus Edgar 1955- *WhoAmL 92*
**Crane,** August Reynolds 1908- *AmMWSc 92*
**Crane,** Barry d1985 *FacFETw*
**Crane,** Benjamin Field 1929- *WhoAmL 92*
**Crane,** Bruce 1909- *WhoAmP 91*
**Crane,** Bruce Alan 1947- *WhoWest 92*
**Crane,** Burton *DrAPF 91*
**Crane,** Carl 1939- *WhoAmP 91*
**Crane,** Carol Jacobson 1944- *WhoMW 92*
**Crane,** Caroline 1930- *WrDr 92*
**Crane,** Charles Arthur 1938- *WhoWest 92*
**Crane,** Charles Edward 1950- *WhoRel 92*
**Crane,** Charles Russell 1928- *AmMWSc 92*
**Crane,** Ernest F 1921- *WhoAmP 91*
**Crane,** Faye 1947- *WhoMW 92*
**Crane,** Fenwick James 1923- *WhoIns 92*
**Crane,** Francis Roger 1910- *Who 92*
**Crane,** Frank 1861-1928 *BenetAL 91*
**Crane,** Frederick Loring 1925- *AmMWSc 92*
**Crane,** Geoffrey David 1934- *Who 92*
**Crane,** George Thomas 1928- *AmMWSc 92*
**Crane,** Gerald William 1938- *WhoFI 92*
**Crane,** Gregory Scott 1955- *WhoRel 92*
**Crane,** Hart 1899-1932 *BenetAL 91, FacFETw, PoeCrit 3 [port]*
**Crane,** Henrietta Page *WhoAmP 91*
**Crane,** Hewitt David 1927- *AmMWSc 92*
**Crane,** Horace Richard 1907- *AmMWSc 92, IntWW 91*
**Crane,** James 1921- *Who 92*
**Crane,** Joseph Leland 1935- *AmMWSc 92*
**Crane,** Jules M, Jr 1928- *AmMWSc 92*
**Crane,** Julian Coburn 1918- *AmMWSc 92*
**Crane,** Langdon Teachout, Jr 1930- *AmMWSc 92*
**Crane,** Laura Jane 1941- *AmMWSc 92*
**Crane,** Lee Stanley 1915- *AmMWSc 92*
**Crane,** Leo Stanley 1915- *WhoFI 92*
**Crane,** Les *LesBEnT 92*
**Crane,** Linda Patricia 1961- *WhoEnt 92*
**Crane,** Louis Arthur 1922- *WhoAmL 92*
**Crane,** Margaret Ann 1940- *WhoMW 92*
**Crane,** Mitchell Gregory 1947- *WhoAmL 92*
**Crane,** Nathalia 1913- *BenetAL 91*
**Crane,** Patrick Conrad 1948- *AmMWSc 92, WhoWest 92*
**Crane,** Paul Levi 1925- *AmMWSc 92*
**Crane,** Peter Francis 1940- *Who 92*
**Crane,** Philip M. 1930- *AlmAP 92 [port]*
**Crane,** Philip Miller 1930- *WhoAmP 91, WhoMW 92*
**Crane,** Philippe 1943- *AmMWSc 92*
**Crane,** Rea Babcock 1942- *WhoFI 92*
**Crane,** Richard 1944- *WrDr 92*
**Crane,** Richard Arthur 1944- *IntAu&W 91*
**Crane,** Robert *TwCWW 91*
**Crane,** Robert Kellogg 1919- *AmMWSc 92*
**Crane,** Robert Kendall 1935- *AmMWSc 92*
**Crane,** Robert Q 1926- *WhoAmP 91*
**Crane,** Roger *Who 92*
**Crane,** Roger L 1933- *AmMWSc 92*
**Crane,** Ron 1948- *WhoAmP 91*
**Crane,** Sara W 1951- *AmMWSc 92*
**Crane,** Sheldon Cyr 1918- *AmMWSc 92*
**Crane,** Stephen *SourALJ*
**Crane,** Stephen 1871-1900 *BenetAL 91, RComAH*
**Crane,** Stephen Gerson *WhoAmL 92*
**Crane,** Steven 1959- *WhoWest 92*
**Crane,** Susan Jill 1959- *WhoAmL 92*
**Crane,** Walter 1845-1915 *DcTwDes*
**Crane,** William Ward *ScFEYrs*
**Cranefield,** Paul Frederic 1925- *AmMWSc 92*
**Craney,** Stephen Harold 1944- *WhoFI 92*
**Cranfield,** Charles Ernest Burland 1915- *IntWW 91, Who 92, WrDr 92*
**Cranford,** Eula Forrest 1923- *WhoFI 92*
**Cranford,** Jack Allen 1939- *AmMWSc 92*
**Cranford,** Kenneth Alan 1952- *WhoEnt 92*
**Cranford,** Page Deronde 1935- *WhoAmL 92, WhoFI 92*
**Cranford,** Robert Henry 1935- *AmMWSc 92*
**Cranford,** Sharon Hill 1946- *WhoBlA 92*
**Cranford,** William B 1920- *AmMWSc 92*
**Crang,** Richard Francis Earl 1936- *AmMWSc 92*
**Crangle,** Joseph F 1932- *WhoAmP 91*
**Crangle,** Robert D. 1943- *WhoAmL 92*
**Crank,** Charles Edward, Jr. 1923- *WhoRel 92*
**Crank,** Robert Neil 1938- *WhoRel 92*
**Cranko,** John 1927-1973 *FacFETw*
**Crankshaw,** John Hamilton 1914- *WhoFI 92*
**Cranley,** Viscount 1967- *Who 92*
**Cranmer,** Charles N. 1953- *WhoFI 92*
**Cranmer,** Philip 1918- *Who 92*
**Cranmer,** Thomas William 1951- *WhoAmL 92*
**Crannell,** Carol Jo Argus 1938- *AmMWSc 92*
**Crannell,** Hall L 1936- *AmMWSc 92*
**Crannell,** Kenneth Charles, Sr. 1934- *WhoEnt 92*
**Crannell,** Melvin Y, Jr 1948- *WhoIns 92*
**Cranney,** Marilyn Kanrek 1949- *WhoAmL 92*
**Cranny,** Charles Joseph 1935- *WhoMW 92*
**Crano,** John Carl 1935- *AmMWSc 92*
**Cranston,** Alan 1914- *AlmAP 92 [port], IntWW 91, WhoWest 92*
**Cranston,** Alan MacGregor 1914- *WhoAmP 91*
**Cranston,** Frederick Pitkin, Jr 1922- *AmMWSc 92*
**Cranston,** Howard Stephen 1937- *WhoAmL 92, WhoFI 92, WhoWest 92*
**Cranston,** Jeffrey Scott 1961- *WhoRel 92*
**Cranston,** John Montgomery 1909- *WhoAmL 92*
**Cranston,** Joseph William, Jr 1944- *AmMWSc 92*
**Cranston,** Mary B. 1947- *WhoAmL 92*
**Cranston,** Maurice 1920- *IntWW 91, Who 92, WrDr 92*
**Cranston,** Monroe G. 1915- *WhoBlA 92*
**Cranston,** R. M. 1949- *WhoAmL 92*
**Cranston,** William Ian 1928- *Who 92*
**Crants,** Doctor Robert, Jr. 1944- *WhoFI 92*
**Cranwell,** Charles Richard 1942- *WhoAmP 91*
**Cranworth,** Baron 1940- *Who 92*
**Crapo,** Henry Howland 1932- *AmMWSc 92*
**Crapo,** John Jennings 1937- *WhoAmP 91*
**Crapo,** Michael Dean 1951- *WhoAmP 91, WhoWest 92*
**Crapo,** Patti Lee Dayton 1953- *WhoEnt 92*
**Crapo,** Richley H. 1943- *WhoWest 92*
**Crapo,** Sheila Anne 1951- *WhoWest 92*
**Crapo,** Terry LaVelle 1939- *WhoAmP 91*
**Crapper,** Donald Raymond 1932- *AmMWSc 92*
**Crapser,** William *DrAPF 91*
**Crapsey,** Adelaide 1878-1914 *BenetAL 91*
**Crapsey,** Algernon Sidney 1847-1927 *RelLAm 91*
**Crapuchettes,** Paul W 1917- *AmMWSc 92*
**Crary,** Albert Paddock 1911- *AmMWSc 92*
**Crary,** Miner Dunham, Jr. 1920- *WhoAmL 92*
**Crary,** Selden Bronson 1949- *AmMWSc 92*
**Crary,** William Frederick, II 1954- *WhoAmL 92*
**Cras,** Patrick 1958- *AmMWSc 92*
**Crase,** Douglas *DrAPF 91*
**Crasemann,** Bernd 1922- *AmMWSc 92*
**Crashaw,** Richard 1612?-1649 *RfGEnL 91*
**Craske,** Margaret 1892-1990 *AnObit 1990*
**Crass,** Maurice Frederick, III 1934- *AmMWSc 92*
**Crassaris,** Leonidas George 1935- *WhoFI 92*
**Crast,** Leonard Bruce, Jr 1936- *AmMWSc 92*
**Craston,** Colin 1922- *Who 92*
**Craswell,** Ellen 1932- *WhoAmP 91*
**Craswell,** Janet L. 1962- *WhoFI 92*
**Craswell,** Keith J 1936- *AmMWSc 92*
**Crater,** Judge *FacFETw*
**Crater,** Horace William 1942- *AmMWSc 92*
**Cratesipolis,** Queen of Sicyon *EncAmaz 91*
**Crathorne,** Baron 1939- *Who 92*
**Cratin,** Paul David 1929- *AmMWSc 92*
**Cratty,** Bryant J. 1929- *WrDr 92*
**Cratty,** Leland Earl, Jr 1930- *AmMWSc 92*
**Cratty,** Mabel 1868-1928 *RelLAm 91*
**Craufurd,** Robert 1937- *Who 92*
**Cravalho,** Ernest G 1939- *AmMWSc 92*
**Craven** *Who 92*
**Craven,** Archdeacon of *Who 92*
**Craven,** Earl of 1989- *Who 92*
**Craven,** Anthony Britton 1938- *WhoAmL 92*
**Craven,** Braxton 1822-1882 *DcNCBi 1*
**Craven,** Bryan Maxwell 1932- *AmMWSc 92*
**Craven,** Claude Jackson 1908- *AmMWSc 92*
**Craven,** Daniel Hartman 1910- *IntWW 91*
**Craven,** David Leigh 1953- *WhoAmL 92*
**Craven,** Donald Edward 1944- *AmMWSc 92*
**Craven,** Donald Neil 1924- *WhoFI 92*
**Craven,** Edward d1991 *NewYTBS 91*
**Craven,** Gemma 1950- *IntMPA 92*
**Craven,** George W. 1951- *WhoAmL 92*
**Craven,** Homer Henry, Jr. 1925- *WhoFI 92, WhoWest 92*
**Craven,** James d1755 *DcNCBi 1*
**Craven,** James Braxton, III 1942- *WhoAmL 92*
**Craven,** James J, Jr *WhoAmP 91*
**Craven,** James M *WhoAmP 91*
**Craven,** John Anthony 1940- *IntWW 91, Who 92*

**Craven,** John P 1924- *AmMWSc 92*
**Craven,** Michael David 1956- *WhoMW 92*
**Craven,** Patricia A 1944- *AmMWSc 92*
**Craven,** Paul John, Jr. 1934- *WhoRel 92*
**Craven,** Robert Edward 1916- *Who 92*
**Craven,** T. A. M. *LesBEnT 92*
**Craven,** Wes 1939- *IntDcF 2-2*
**Craven,** Wes 1949- *IntMPA 92*
**Craven,** William A 1921- *WhoAmP 91*
**Cravens,** Gwyneth *DrAPF 91*
**Cravens,** Hartley Dodge 1935- *WhoIns 92*
**Cravens,** Kathryn d1991 *NewYTBS 91*
**Cravens,** Malcolm 1907- *WhoIns 92*
**Cravens,** Thirkield Ellis, Jr. 1932- *WhoBlA 92*
**Cravens,** William Windsor 1914- *AmMWSc 92*
**Craver,** Bennie Dale 1950- *WhoRel 92*
**Craver,** Charles Bradford 1944- *WhoAmL 92*
**Craver,** Clara Diddle 1924- *AmMWSc 92, WhoMW 92*
**Craver,** James Bernard 1943- *WhoAmL 92*
**Craver,** John Kenneth 1915- *AmMWSc 92, WhoMW 92*
**Cravey,** Charles Edward 1951- *WhoRel 92*
**Cravez,** Glenn Edward 1957- *WhoAmL 92*
**Cravioto,** Humberto 1924- *AmMWSc 92*
**Cravitz,** Leo 1918- *AmMWSc 92*
**Craw,** Albert 1850-1908 *BiInAmS*
**Craw,** Freeman *WhoEnt 92*
**Craw,** William Jarvis 1830-1897 *BiInAmS*
**Crawe,** Ithamar B 1794-1847 *BiInAmS*
**Crawfis,** Robert P. 1950- *WhoWest 92*
**Crawford,** Earl of 1927- *Who 92*
**Crawford,** Adair 1748-1795 *BlkwCEP*
**Crawford,** Alan 1943- *WrDr 92*
**Crawford,** Alvin Clegg 1932- *WhoWest 92*
**Crawford,** Andrew Charles 1949- *Who 92*
**Crawford,** Barbara Hopkins *WhoBlA 92*
**Crawford,** Barrett Lynn 1951- *WhoAmL 92*
**Crawford,** Barry Steele 1946- *WhoRel 92*
**Crawford,** Betty Marilyn 1948- *WhoBlA 92*
**Crawford,** Bo *WhoAmP 91*
**Crawford,** Bob 1948- *WhoAmP 91*
**Crawford,** Bryce, Jr 1914- *AmMWSc 92, IntWW 91*
**Crawford,** Burnett Hayden 1922- *WhoAmL 92*
**Crawford,** Carl M. 1932- *WhoBlA 92*
**Crawford,** Carol Forsyth 1911- *WhoAmP 91*
**Crawford,** Carol Tallman 1943- *WhoAmL 92*
**Crawford,** Charles L. 1929- *WhoBlA 92*
**Crawford,** Christina 1939- *WrDr 92*
**Crawford,** Clan, Jr. 1927- *WhoAmL 92*
**Crawford,** Clifford Smeed 1932- *AmMWSc 92*
**Crawford,** Cranford L., Jr. 1940- *WhoBlA 92*
**Crawford,** Crayton McCants 1926- *AmMWSc 92*
**Crawford,** Curtis Scott 1960- *WhoFI 92*
**Crawford,** Dan Reavis 1941- *WhoRel 92*
**Crawford,** Daniel J 1935- *AmMWSc 92*
**Crawford,** Daniel John 1942- *AmMWSc 92*
**Crawford,** David *ConAu 134*
**Crawford,** David 1941- *WhoBlA 92*
**Crawford,** David Carl 1939- *WhoFI 92*
**Crawford,** David Lee 1935- *AmMWSc 92*
**Crawford,** David Livingstone 1931- *AmMWSc 92*
**Crawford,** Dawn Constance 1919- *WhoEnt 92*
**Crawford,** Dean *DrAPF 91*
**Crawford,** Deborah Collins 1947- *WhoBlA 92*
**Crawford,** Desiree White 1953- *WhoAmP 91*
**Crawford,** Dewey Byers 1941- *WhoAmL 92*
**Crawford,** Dewitt Charles, Sr 1923- *WhoAmP 91*
**Crawford,** Dick *WhoAmP 91*
**Crawford,** Dock D., Jr. 1899-1988 *WhoBlA 92N*
**Crawford,** Donald Dunn 1968- *WhoMW 92*
**Crawford,** Donald Lee 1947- *AmMWSc 92*
**Crawford,** Donald W 1928- *AmMWSc 92*
**Crawford,** Douglas *Who 92*
**Crawford,** Duane Austin 1929- *AmMWSc 92*
**Crawford,** Edward Hamon 1925- *WhoIns 92*
**Crawford,** Edwin Ethelbert, Jr. 1935- *WhoWest 92*
**Crawford,** Ella Mae 1932- *WhoBlA 92*
**Crawford,** Eric Winthrop 1945- *WhoFI 92*
**Crawford,** Eugene Carson, Jr 1931- *AmMWSc 92*
**Crawford,** Evelyn Carlene 1931- *WhoAmP 91*
**Crawford,** F. Marion 1854-1909 *BenetAL 91*
**Crawford,** Florence Louise 1872-1936 *RelLAm 91*
**Crawford,** Frank Stevens, Jr 1923- *AmMWSc 92*
**Crawford,** Frederick 1931- *Who 92*
**Crawford,** Frederick William 1931- *AmMWSc 92, IntWW 91*
**Crawford,** G. Mike 1940- *WhoFI 92*
**Crawford,** George Douglas 1939- *Who 92*
**Crawford,** George Hunter 1911- *Who 92*
**Crawford,** George Oswald 1902- *Who 92*
**Crawford,** George Truett 1936- *WhoWest 92*
**Crawford,** George William 1906- *AmMWSc 92*
**Crawford,** George Wolf 1922- *AmMWSc 92*
**Crawford,** Gerald James Browning 1926- *AmMWSc 92*
**Crawford,** Gerald Wayne 1949- *WhoAmP 91*
**Crawford,** Gladys P 1927- *AmMWSc 92*
**Crawford,** H R 1939- *WhoAmP 91*
**Crawford,** Hasely 1950- *BlkOlyM*
**Crawford,** Hazle R. 1939- *WhoBlA 92*
**Crawford,** Hewlette Spencer, Jr 1931- *AmMWSc 92*
**Crawford,** Homer 1916- *WhoAmL 92, WhoFI 92*
**Crawford,** Howard 1947- *WhoAmP 91*
**Crawford,** Hugh Adam 1898-1982 *TwCPaSc*
**Crawford,** Iain 1938- *Who 92*
**Crawford,** Irving Pope 1930- *AmMWSc 92*
**Crawford,** Isaac Benjamin 1948- *WhoRel 92*
**Crawford,** Isaac Lyle 1942- *AmMWSc 92*
**Crawford,** Isabell C *ScFEYrs*
**Crawford,** Isabella Valancy 1850-1887 *RfGEnL 91*
**Crawford,** Isabella Valaney 1850-1887 *BenetAL 91*
**Crawford,** Jack, Jr. *DrAPF 91*
**Crawford,** Jacob Wendell 1942- *WhoBlA 92*
**Crawford,** James *WhoAmP 91*
**Crawford,** James Dalton 1919- *AmMWSc 92*
**Crawford,** James E. 1934- *WhoAmL 92*
**Crawford,** James Ellis, III 1945- *WhoMW 92*
**Crawford,** James Gordon 1929- *AmMWSc 92*
**Crawford,** James Joseph L 1931- *AmMWSc 92*
**Crawford,** James Richard 1948- *Who 92*
**Crawford,** James Thomas 1925- *WhoEnt 92*
**Crawford,** James W, Jr 1937- *WhoAmP 91*
**Crawford,** James Weldon 1927- *AmMWSc 92*
**Crawford,** James Wesley 1942- *WhoBlA 92*
**Crawford,** James Winfield 1936- *WhoRel 92*
**Crawford,** James Worthington 1944- *AmMWSc 92*
**Crawford,** Janet Kathryn 1939- *WhoMW 92*
**Crawford,** Jayne Suzanne 1958- *WhoBlA 92*
**Crawford,** Jean Andre 1941- *WhoMW 92*
**Crawford,** Jean Veghte 1919- *AmMWSc 92*
**Crawford,** Jerry Lee 1935- *WhoFI 92*
**Crawford,** Jerry LeRoy 1934- *WhoEnt 92, WhoWest 92*
**Crawford,** Joan 1906-1977 *FacFETw*
**Crawford,** Joanna 1942- *WhoEnt 92*
**Crawford,** John Arthur 1946- *AmMWSc 92*
**Crawford,** John Charlton 1931- *WhoEnt 92*
**Crawford,** John Clark 1935- *AmMWSc 92*
**Crawford,** John David *AmMWSc 92*
**Crawford,** John Douglas 1920- *AmMWSc 92*
**Crawford,** John Emerson 1943- *WhoWest 92*
**Crawford,** John Gilliand 1946- *WhoAmP 91*
**Crawford,** John Joseph 1948- *WhoFI 92*
**Crawford,** John Michael 1938- *Who 92*
**Crawford,** John Okerson 1949- *AmMWSc 92*
**Crawford,** John Richard 1932- *WrDr 92*
**Crawford,** John S 1921- *AmMWSc 92*
**Crawford,** John T *WhoIns 92*
**Crawford,** John Wallace 1847-1917 *BenetAL 91*
**Crawford,** Joyce Catherine Holmes 1918- *WhoWest 92*
**Crawford,** Keith Edward 1953- *WhoFI 92*
**Crawford,** Kelly Griffith 1951- *WhoEnt 92*
**Crawford,** Lawrence Douglas 1949- *WhoAmP 91, WhoBlA 92*
**Crawford,** Leonidas Wakefield 1842-1908 *DcNCBi 1*
**Crawford,** Lester M 1938- *AmMWSc 92*
**Crawford,** Lester Mills, Jr. 1938- *WhoFI 92*
**Crawford,** Linda *DrAPF 91*
**Crawford,** Linda Sibery 1947- *WhoAmL 92*
**Crawford,** Lionel Vivian 1932- *Who 92*
**Crawford,** Lloyd V 1923- *AmMWSc 92*
**Crawford,** Lloyd W 1928- *AmMWSc 92*
**Crawford,** Lucy A 1947- *WhoIns 92*
**Crawford,** Marc *DrAPF 91*
**Crawford,** Margaret Ward 1937- *WhoBlA 92*
**Crawford,** Maria Luisa Buse 1939- *AmMWSc 92*
**Crawford,** Mark Alan 1956- *WhoEnt 92*
**Crawford,** Martelia Theresa 1956- *WhoAmL 92*
**Crawford,** Martin 1934- *AmMWSc 92*
**Crawford,** Mary Caroline 1874-1932 *BenetAL 91*
**Crawford,** Mary Greer *WhoBlA 92*
**Crawford,** Max *DrAPF 91*
**Crawford,** Michael 1942- *IntMPA 92, IntWW 91, Who 92*
**Crawford,** Michael Anthony 1955- *WhoFI 92*
**Crawford,** Michael David 1964- *WhoRel 92*
**Crawford,** Michael Hewson 1939- *IntWW 91, Who 92*
**Crawford,** Michael Howard 1943- *AmMWSc 92*
**Crawford,** Michael Karl 1954- *AmMWSc 92*
**Crawford,** Morris Lee Jackson 1933- *AmMWSc 92*
**Crawford,** Muriel C. *WhoBlA 92*
**Crawford,** Muriel Laura *WhoAmL 92*
**Crawford,** Myron Lloyd 1938- *AmMWSc 92, WhoWest 92*
**Crawford,** Narvel J, Jr 1929- *WhoAmP 91*
**Crawford,** Natalie Wilson 1939- *WhoWest 92*
**Crawford,** Nathaniel, Jr. 1951- *WhoBlA 92*
**Crawford,** Nicholas Charles 1942- *AmMWSc 92*
**Crawford,** Norman Holmes 1935- *AmMWSc 92*
**Crawford,** Oakley H 1938- *AmMWSc 92*
**Crawford,** Patricia A 1928- *WhoAmP 91*
**Crawford,** Paul B 1921- *AmMWSc 92*
**Crawford,** Paul Douglas 1952- *WhoRel 92*
**Crawford,** Paul Vincent 1933- *AmMWSc 92*
**Crawford,** Peter John 1930- *Who 92*
**Crawford,** Philip Stanley 1944- *WhoWest 92*
**Crawford,** Purdy *WhoFI 92*
**Crawford,** Raymon Edward 1939- *WhoBlA 92*
**Crawford,** Raymond Maxwell, Jr 1933- *AmMWSc 92*
**Crawford,** Richard Bradway 1933- *AmMWSc 92*
**Crawford,** Richard Clark 1953- *WhoMW 92*
**Crawford,** Richard Dwight 1947- *AmMWSc 92*
**Crawford,** Richard Eben, Jr. 1930- *WhoWest 92*
**Crawford,** Richard H 1923- *AmMWSc 92*
**Crawford,** Richard Haygood, Jr 1954- *AmMWSc 92*
**Crawford,** Richard L 1951- *WhoAmP 91*
**Crawford,** Richard Whittier 1936- *AmMWSc 92*
**Crawford,** Robert *IntAu&W 91X, WrDr 92*
**Crawford,** Robert Dean 1936- *WhoMW 92*
**Crawford,** Robert Field 1930- *AmMWSc 92*
**Crawford,** Robert Franklin 1951- *WhoRel 92*
**Crawford,** Robert Gammie 1924- *Who 92*
**Crawford,** Robert George 1943- *WhoAmL 92*
**Crawford,** Robert James 1929- *AmMWSc 92*
**Crawford,** Robert Norman 1923- *Who 92*
**Crawford,** Robert R 1944- *AmMWSc 92*
**Crawford,** Robert Stewart 1913- *Who 92*
**Crawford,** Robert William Kenneth 1945- *Who 92*
**Crawford,** Roger Brentley 1951- *WhoFI 92*
**Crawford,** Ronald L 1947- *AmMWSc 92*
**Crawford,** Ronald Lyle 1947- *AmMWSc 92, WhoWest 92*
**Crawford,** Roy Douglas 1933- *AmMWSc 92*
**Crawford,** Roy Edgington, III 1938- *WhoAmL 92*
**Crawford,** Roy Kent 1941- *AmMWSc 92*
**Crawford,** Russell 1939- *WhoAmP 91*
**Crawford,** Ruth 1901-1953 *NewAmDM*
**Crawford,** Samuel D. 1936- *WhoBlA 92*
**Crawford,** Sarah Carter 1938- *WhoEnt 92*
**Crawford,** Scott Lee 1955- *WhoFI 92*
**Crawford,** Stanley *DrAPF 91*
**Crawford,** Stanley Everett 1924- *AmMWSc 92*
**Crawford,** Susan Jean 1947- *WhoAmL 92*
**Crawford,** Susan Young *AmMWSc 92*
**Crawford,** Tad *DrAPF 91*
**Crawford,** Tad 1946- *ConAu 133*
**Crawford,** Theodore 1911- *Who 92*
**Crawford,** Theron Clark *ScFEYrs*
**Crawford,** Thomas 1920- *IntAu&W 91*
**Crawford,** Thomas Charles 1945- *AmMWSc 92*
**Crawford,** Thomas H 1931- *AmMWSc 92*
**Crawford,** Thomas James *WhoAmP 91*
**Crawford,** Thomas Michael 1928- *AmMWSc 92*
**Crawford,** Timothy Patrick 1948- *WhoAmL 92*
**Crawford,** Todd V 1931- *AmMWSc 92*
**Crawford,** Tom *DrAPF 91*
**Crawford,** Van Hale 1946- *AmMWSc 92*
**Crawford,** Vanella Alise 1947- *WhoBlA 92*
**Crawford,** Vanessa Reese 1952- *WhoBlA 92*
**Crawford,** Vernon 1919- *AmMWSc 92*
**Crawford,** Wayne Halburton, Jr. 1927- *WhoWest 92*
**Crawford,** William 1638?-1700? *DcNCBi 1*
**Crawford,** William 1907- *Who 92*
**Crawford,** William A 1936- *WhoAmP 91, WhoBlA 92*
**Crawford,** William Arthur 1935- *AmMWSc 92*
**Crawford,** William Avery 1915- *IntWW 91*
**Crawford,** William David 1945- *WhoFI 92*
**Crawford,** William Hamilton Raymund 1936- *Who 92*
**Crawford,** William Harris 1772-1834 *AmPolLe*
**Crawford,** William Howard, Jr 1937- *AmMWSc 92*
**Crawford,** William Rex 1928- *WhoAmP 91*
**Crawford,** William S *WhoAmP 91*
**Crawford,** William Stanley Hayes 1918- *AmMWSc 92*
**Crawford,** William Thomas 1856-1913 *DcNCBi 1*
**Crawford,** William Walsh 1927- *WhoAmL 92*
**Crawford-Brown,** Douglas John 1953- *AmMWSc 92*
**Crawford-Mason,** Clare Wootten 1936- *WhoEnt 92*
**Crawford Seeger,** Ruth 1901-1953 *NewAmDM*
**Crawhall,** Joseph 1861-1913 *TwCPaSc*
**Crawley,** A. Bruce 1946- *WhoBlA 92*
**Crawley,** Aidan 1908- *WrDr 92*
**Crawley,** Aidan Merivale 1908- *Who 92*
**Crawley,** Bettye Jean 1955- *WhoBlA 92*
**Crawley,** Beverly Ann 1940- *WhoRel 92*
**Crawley,** Charles William 1899- *Who 92*
**Crawley,** Christine Mary 1950- *Who 92*
**Crawley,** Darline 1941- *WhoBlA 92*
**Crawley,** David *Who 92*
**Crawley,** Desmond John Chetwode 1917- *Who 92*
**Crawley,** Edward Francis 1954- *AmMWSc 92*
**Crawley,** Frederick William 1926- *IntWW 91, Who 92*
**Crawley,** George Claudius 1934- *WhoBlA 92*
**Crawley,** Gerard Marcus 1938- *AmMWSc 92*
**Crawley,** Gregory Daryl 1962- *WhoFI 92*
**Crawley,** Harriet 1948- *ConAu 134*
**Crawley,** Jacqueline N 1950- *AmMWSc 92*
**Crawley,** James Winston, Jr 1947- *AmMWSc 92*
**Crawley,** John *WhoAmP 91*
**Crawley,** John Cecil 1909- *Who 92*
**Crawley,** John Maurice 1933- *Who 92*
**Crawley,** Lantz Stephen 1944- *AmMWSc 92*
**Crawley,** Oscar Lewis 1942- *WhoBlA 92*
**Crawley,** Thomas Michael 1963- *WhoMW 92*
**Crawley,** Willie Gene 1945- *WhoMW 92*
**Crawley-Boevey,** Thomas 1928- *Who 92*
**Crawmer,** Daryl E 1949- *AmMWSc 92*
**Crawshaw,** Baron 1933- *Who 92*
**Crawshaw,** Craig Frederick 1947- *WhoRel 92*
**Crawshaw,** Daniel d1991 *Who 92N*
**Crawshaw,** Larry Ingram 1942- *AmMWSc 92*
**Crawshaw,** Ralph 1921- *IntWW 91, WhoWest 92*
**Crawshaw,** Ralph Shelton 1921- *AmMWSc 92*
**Crawshay,** Elisabeth Mary Boyd 1927- *Who 92*
**Crawshay,** William 1920- *Who 92*
**Craxi,** Benedetto 1934- *FacFETw*
**Craxi,** Bettino 1934- *IntWW 91*
**Craxton,** Antony 1918- *Who 92*
**Craxton,** John 1922- *TwCPaSc*
**Craxton,** Robert Stephen 1949- *AmMWSc 92*
**Cray,** Barbara A. 1954- *WhoAmL 92*
**Cray,** Edward 1933- *WrDr 92*

**Cray**, Robert 1953- *WhoBlA 92, WhoEnt 92*
**Cray**, William, Sr. 1726-1778 *DcNCBi 1*
**Craycraft**, Allie V *WhoAmP 91*
**Crayder**, Teresa *WrDr 92*
**Crayne**, Larry Randolph 1942- *WhoAmL 92*
**Crayon**, Geoffrey *BenetAL 91*
**Craythorne**, N W Brian 1931- *AmMWSc 92*
**Crayton**, Billy Gene 1931- *WhoMW 92*
**Crayton**, James Edward 1943- *WhoBlA 92*
**Crayton**, Philip Hastings 1928- *AmMWSc 92*
**Crayton**, Samuel S. 1916- *WhoBlA 92*
**Craze**, Steven Lee 1950- *WhoFI 92*
**Crazy Horse** 1842?-1877 *RComAH*
**Crazy Horse** 1849?-1877 *BenetAL 91*
**Creadick**, Wayne Samuel, Jr. 1962- *WhoFI 92*
**Creagan**, Robert Joseph 1919- *AmMWSc 92*
**Creager**, Charles Bicknell 1924- *AmMWSc 92*
**Creager**, Clara 1930- *WrDr 92*
**Creager**, Clifford Raymond 1937- *WhoWest 92*
**Creager**, Joan Guynn 1932- *AmMWSc 92*
**Creager**, Joe Scott 1929- *AmMWSc 92*
**Creagh**, Kilner Rupert B *Who 92*
**Creagh-Deyter**, Linda T 1941- *AmMWSc 92*
**Creal**, Julie Ann 1964- *WhoAmL 92*
**Creal**, Theresa Marie 1975- *WhoEnt 92*
**Cream** *NewAmDM*
**Cream**, Arnold 1914- *WhoBlA 92*
**Creamer**, Brian 1926- *Who 92*
**Creamer**, Bruce Cunningham 1941- *WhoMW 92*
**Creamer**, Dennis Brian 1951- *WhoWest 92*
**Creamer**, James Edward, Jr 1958- *WhoAmP 91*
**Creamer**, James Larry 1954- *WhoRel 92*
**Creamer**, Robert Allan 1941- *WhoAmL 92*
**Creamer**, Robert W. 1922- *WrDr 92*
**Crean**, Daniel Joseph 1963- *WhoWest 92*
**Crean**, Frank 1916- *IntWW 91, Who 92*
**Crean**, Gerald Philip, Jr 1936- *WhoAmP 91*
**Crean**, Geraldine L *AmMWSc 92*
**Crean**, John C. 1925- *WhoWest 92*
**Crean**, Mark Dennis 1951- *WhoWest 92*
**Crean**, Robert d1974 *LesBEnT 92*
**Crean**, Simon 1949- *IntWW 91*
**Crean**, William Francis 1931- *WhoEnt 92*
**Creany**, Cathleen Annette 1950- *WhoEnt 92*
**Creary**, Ludlow Barrington 1930- *WhoBlA 92*
**Creasey**, Beverly Ann 1946- *WhoEnt 92*
**Creasey**, John 1908-1973 *TwCSFW 91*
**Creasey**, Savill Cyrus 1917- *AmMWSc 92*
**Creasey**, William Alfred 1933- *AmMWSc 92*
**Creasia**, Donald Anthony 1937- *AmMWSc 92*
**Creasman**, James Craig 1957- *WhoRel 92*
**Creasman**, William Paul 1952- *WhoAmL 92, WhoFI 92*
**Creason**, Gary Wayne 1948- *WhoFI 92*
**Creason**, Norwood A 1918- *WhoAmP 91*
**Creason**, Timothy T. 1959- *WhoMW 92*
**Creasy**, Leonard Richard 1912- *Who 92*
**Creasy**, Leroy L 1938- *AmMWSc 92*
**Creasy**, William Russel 1958- *AmMWSc 92*
**Creath**, Katherine 1958- *WhoWest 92*
**Creaven**, Patrick Joseph 1933- *AmMWSc 92*
**Crebbin**, Anthony Micek 1952- *WhoAmL 92*
**Crebbin**, Kenneth Clive 1924- *AmMWSc 92*
**Creber**, Frank 1959- *TwCPaSc*
**Crebillon**, Claude-Prosper Jolyot de 1707-1777 *BlkwCEP*
**Crecco**, Marion *WhoAmP 91*
**Crecelius**, Eric A 1945- *AmMWSc 92*
**Crecelius**, Robert Lee 1922- *AmMWSc 92*
**Crecelius**, Sylvia Ann 1942- *WhoFI 92*
**Crecely**, Roger William 1942- *AmMWSc 92*
**Crechales**, Anthony George 1926- *WhoEnt 92*
**Crecine**, John Patrick 1939- *WhoFI 92*
**Crecquillon**, Thomas 1500?-1557 *NewAmDM*
**Crecy**, Jeanne *WrDr 92*
**Crede**, Brian H. 1952- *WhoEnt 92*
**Crede**, Robert H 1915- *AmMWSc 92*
**Crede**, Robert Henry 1915- *WhoWest 92*
**Crediton**, Bishop Suffragan of 1928- *Who 92*
**Creditt**, Thelma Cobb 1902- *WhoBlA 92*
**Cree**, Allan 1910- *AmMWSc 92*
**Cree**, Gerald Hilary 1905- *Who 92*
**Cree**, Janet 1910- *TwCPaSc*
**Creech**, Barry Lynn 1960- *WhoAmL 92*
**Creech**, Billy James 1943- *WhoAmP 91*
**Creech**, Hugh John 1910- *AmMWSc 92*
**Creech**, Oscar, Jr. 1916-1967 *DcNCBi 1*
**Creech**, Richard Hearne 1940- *AmMWSc 92*
**Creech**, Roy G 1935- *AmMWSc 92*
**Creech**, Wendy E. 1969- *WhoEnt 92*
**Creech**, William Ayden 1925- *WhoAmP 91*
**Creecy**, Charles Melvin 1920- *WhoAmP 91*
**Creecy**, Rachel Alice 1950- *WhoRel 92*
**Creecy**, Richard Benbury 1813-1908 *DcNCBi 1*
**Creed**, David 1943- *AmMWSc 92*
**Creed**, Joel *TwCWW 91*
**Creed**, John Bradley 1957- *WhoRel 92*
**Creed**, John Henry 1940- *WhoWest 92*
**Creed**, Susan Lynn 1950- *WhoMW 92*
**Creedence Clearwater Revival** *FacFETw, NewAmDM*
**Creedon**, John J. 1924- *IntWW 91, WhoFI 92*
**Creedon**, Michael C 1946- *WhoAmP 91*
**Creeggan**, Jack Burnett 1902- *Who 92*
**Creek**, Jefferson Louis 1945- *AmMWSc 92*
**Creek**, Kim E *AmMWSc 92*
**Creek**, Malcolm Lars 1931- *IntWW 91, Who 92*
**Creek**, Robert Omer 1928- *AmMWSc 92*
**Creekmore**, David Dickason 1942- *WhoAmL 92*
**Creekmore**, Frederick Hillary 1937- *WhoAmP 91*
**Creekmore**, Hubert 1907-1966 *BenetAL 91*
**Creekmore**, Marion V, Jr *WhoAmP 91*
**Creel**, Austin Bowman 1929- *WhoRel 92*
**Creel**, David Russel 1949- *WhoFI 92*
**Creel**, Donnell Joseph 1942- *AmMWSc 92*
**Creel**, George 1876-1953 *AmPolLe*
**Creel**, George Edward 1876-1953 *FacFETw*
**Creel**, Gordon C 1926- *AmMWSc 92*
**Creel**, Michael Allen 1953- *WhoFI 92*
**Creel**, Roger E 1933- *WhoIns 92*
**Creel**, Ronald Joseph 1938- *WhoAmP 91*
**Creeley**, Bobbie *DrAPF 91*
**Creeley**, Robert *DrAPF 91*
**Creeley**, Robert 1926- *BenetAL 91, ConPo 91, FacFETw, WrDr 92*
**Creeley**, Robert White 1926- *IntAu&W 91, IntWW 91*
**Creely**, Gene Francis, II 1957- *WhoAmL 92*
**Creely**, Robert Scott 1926- *AmMWSc 92*
**Creenan**, Katherine Heras 1945- *WhoAmL 92*
**Creese**, Diane Dobson 1962- *WhoMW 92*
**Creese**, Ian N 1949- *AmMWSc 92*
**Creese**, Nigel Arthur Holloway 1927- *Who 92*
**Creese**, Thomas Morton 1934- *AmMWSc 92, WhoMW 92*
**Creese**, Wesley William 1959- *WhoFI 92*
**Creevey**, Caroline Alathea Stickney 1843-1920 *BiInAmS*
**Creffield**, Dennis 1931- *TwCPaSc*
**Cregan**, David 1931- *IntAu&W 91, WrDr 92*
**Cregan**, John B 1930- *WhoIns 92*
**Creger**, Clarence R 1934- *AmMWSc 92*
**Creger**, Paul LeRoy 1930- *AmMWSc 92*
**Cregg**, Hugh Anthony, III 1951- *WhoEnt 92*
**Cregger**, David C 1949- *WhoIns 92*
**Cregor**, John Marshall, Jr. 1945- *WhoWest 92*
**Crehan**, Joseph Edward 1938- *WhoAmL 92*
**Crehan**, Matthew Joseph 1936- *WhoAmL 92*
**Crehore**, Charles Aaron 1946- *WhoAmL 92*
**Creightmore**, Peter Beauchamp 1928- *Who 92*
**Creighton**, Alan Joseph 1936- *Who 92*
**Creighton**, Charlie Scattergood 1926- *AmMWSc 92*
**Creighton**, Don *WrDr 92*
**Creighton**, Donald John 1946- *AmMWSc 92*
**Creighton**, Donald L 1932- *AmMWSc 92*
**Creighton**, Douglas George 1923- *WhoWest 92*
**Creighton**, Gale Russell 1957- *WhoFI 92*
**Creighton**, Harold Digby Fitzgerald 1927- *Who 92*
**Creighton**, Harriet Baldwin 1909- *AmMWSc 92*
**Creighton**, John Rogers 1935- *AmMWSc 92*
**Creighton**, John W., Jr. 1932- *WhoFI 92, WhoWest 92*
**Creighton**, Phillip David 1945- *AmMWSc 92*
**Creighton**, Stephen Mark 1920- *AmMWSc 92*
**Creighton**, Thomas Edwin 1940- *AmMWSc 92*
**Creighton**, Tom 1927- *WhoAmP 91*
**Creighton-Zollar**, Ann 1946- *WhoBlA 92*
**Creim**, William Benjamin 1954- *WhoAmL 92*
**Creinin**, Howard Lee 1942- *AmMWSc 92*
**Crelin**, Edmund Slocum 1923- *AmMWSc 92*
**Crelling**, John Crawford 1941- *AmMWSc 92*
**Creme**, Benjamin 1922- *RelLAm 91*
**Cremeans**, James L. 1939- *WhoRel 92*
**Cremens**, Walter Samuel 1926- *AmMWSc 92*
**Cremer**, Fritz 1906- *IntWW 91*
**Cremer**, Leon Earl 1945- *WhoAmL 92*
**Cremer**, Natalie E 1919- *AmMWSc 92*
**Cremer**, Richard Eldon 1928- *WhoFI 92*
**Cremer**, Sheldon E 1935- *AmMWSc 92*
**Cremer**, Victoriano 1909?- *DcLB 108 [port]*
**Cremer**, William Randal 1828-1908 *WhoNob 90*
**Cremers**, Clifford J 1933- *AmMWSc 92*
**Cremin**, John Patrick 1944- *WhoAmL 92*
**Cremin**, Lawrence 1925- *WrDr 92*
**Cremin**, Lawrence Arthur d1990 *IntWW 91N*
**Cremins**, James Smyth 1921- *WhoAmL 92*
**Cremins**, James Smyth, Sr 1921- *WhoAmP 91*
**Cremins**, William Carroll 1957- *WhoAmL 92, WhoFI 92*
**Cremins**, William Daniel 1939- *WhoAmL 92*
**Cremona**, John Joseph 1918- *IntWW 91, Who 92*
**Crenna**, James Alan 1950- *WhoFI 92*
**Crenna**, Richard 1927- *IntMPA 92, WhoEnt 92*
**Crenne**, Helisenne de 1510?-1560? *FrenWW*
**Crennel**, Romeo A. 1947- *WhoBlA 92*
**Crenner**, James *DrAPF 91*
**Crenney**, Lynne Nordenberg 1949- *WhoAmL 92*
**Crenshaw**, Ander 1944- *WhoAmP 91*
**Crenshaw**, D. Kerry 1941- *WhoAmL 92*
**Crenshaw**, David Brooks 1945- *AmMWSc 92*
**Crenshaw**, Gordon Lee 1922- *WhoFI 92*
**Crenshaw**, Henry Carlton 1929- *WhoRel 92*
**Crenshaw**, James L. 1934- *ConAu 34NR, WrDr 92*
**Crenshaw**, James Lee 1934- *WhoRel 92*
**Crenshaw**, Jessica Agusta 1955- *WhoWest 92*
**Crenshaw**, John Walden, Jr 1923- *AmMWSc 92*
**Crenshaw**, Kimberle Williams 1959- *WhoAmL 92*
**Crenshaw**, Miles Aubrey 1932- *AmMWSc 92*
**Crenshaw**, Paul L 1933- *AmMWSc 92*
**Crenshaw**, Phillip Tennyson 1942- *WhoAmL 92*
**Crenshaw**, Reginald Anthony 1956- *WhoBlA 92*
**Crenshaw**, Ronald Willis 1940- *WhoBlA 92*
**Crenshaw**, Ronnie Ray 1936- *AmMWSc 92*
**Crenshaw**, Waverly David, Jr. 1956- *WhoBlA 92*
**Crentz**, William Luther 1910- *AmMWSc 92*
**Creole Jazz Band** *NewAmDM*
**Crepas**, Kenneth J. 1946- *WhoMW 92*
**Crepeau**, Michel Edouard Jean 1930- *IntWW 91*
**Crepeau**, Paul-Andre 1926- *IntWW 91*
**Crepet**, William Louis 1946- *AmMWSc 92*
**Crepin**, Jean-Albert-Emile 1908- *IntWW 91*
**Creppel**, Claire Binet 1936- *WhoFI 92*
**Crerar**, David Alexander 1945- *AmMWSc 92*
**Crescas**, Hasdai 1340?-1412? *DcLB 115*
**Crescitelli**, Frederick 1909- *AmMWSc 92*
**Creshevsky**, Noah 1945- *NewAmDM*
**Cresimore**, James Leonard 1928- *WhoAmP 91*
**Creskoff**, Ellen Ann Hodd 1943- *IntAu&W 91*
**Creson**, Thomas Kyle, Jr 1931- *WhoAmP 91*
**Crespi**, Henry Lewis 1926- *AmMWSc 92*
**Crespi**, James *Who 92*
**Crespi**, Juan 1721-1782 *BenetAL 91*
**Crespi**, Michael Albert 1946- *WhoAmP 91*
**Crespin**, George Ernest 1936- *WhoHisp 92*
**Crespin**, Leslie Ann 1947- *WhoWest 92*
**Crespin**, Regine *Who 92, WhoEnt 92*
**Crespin**, Regine 1927- *IntWW 91, NewAmDM*
**Crespo**, Jorge H 1944- *AmMWSc 92*
**Crespo**, Rafael Agapito 1938- *WhoHisp 92*
**Crespo**, Robert A. 1931- *WhoHisp 92*
**Crespy**, David Allison 1960- *WhoEnt 92*
**Cress**, Anne Elizabeth 1952- *AmMWSc 92*
**Cress**, Charles Edwin 1934- *AmMWSc 92*
**Cress**, Charles R. 1942- *WhoWest 92*
**Cress**, Daniel Hugg 1944- *AmMWSc 92*
**Cress**, Daniel William 1959- *WhoFI 92*
**Cressey**, Roger F 1930- *AmMWSc 92*
**Cressie**, Noel A C 1950- *AmMWSc 92*
**Cressman**, George Parmley 1919- *AmMWSc 92*
**Cressman**, William Arthur 1941- *AmMWSc 92*
**Cresson**, Edith 1934- *CurBio 91 [port], IntWW 91, NewYTBS 91, News 92-1 [port], Who 92*
**Cressor**, Paul Bartholomew, III 1943- *WhoMW 92*
**Cresswell**, Amos Samuel 1926- *Who 92*
**Cresswell**, B F *ScFEYrs*
**Cresswell**, Christopher Frederick 1933- *IntWW 91*
**Cresswell**, Helen 1934- *IntAu&W 91, Who 92*
**Cresswell**, Helen 1936- *WrDr 92*
**Cresswell**, Jasmine Rosemary 1941- *IntAu&W 91*
**Cresswell**, Lyell 1944- *ConCom 92*
**Cresswell**, Michael William 1937- *AmMWSc 92*
**Cresswell**, Peter 1944- *Who 92*
**Cresswell**, Peter 1945- *AmMWSc 92*
**Cressy**, Charles Lee 1943- *WhoMW 92*
**Cressy**, Ellen M 1917- *WhoAmP 91*
**Creston**, Paul 1906-1985 *NewAmDM*
**Creswell**, Barbara Marie 1951- *WhoMW 92*
**Creswell**, Brooke 1942- *WhoEnt 92*
**Creswell**, Donald Creston *WhoFI 92, WhoWest 92*
**Creswell**, Dorothy Anne 1943- *WhoFI 92*
**Creswell**, Isaiah T., Jr. 1938- *WhoBlA 92*
**Creswell**, Jack Norman 1913- *Who 92*
**Creswell**, Norman Bruce 1954- *WhoRel 92*
**Cret**, Paul Philippe 1876-1945 *DcTwDes, FacFETw*
**Cretara**, Domenic Anthony 1946- *WhoWest 92*
**Creteau**, Richard Wilfrid *WhoAmP 91*
**Cretin**, Shan 1946- *AmMWSc 92*
**Cretney**, Gary Philip 1957- *WhoMW 92*
**Cretney**, Stephen Michael 1936- *IntWW 91, Who 92*
**Creutz**, Carl Eugene 1947- *AmMWSc 92*
**Creutz**, Carol 1944- *AmMWSc 92*
**Creutz**, Edward 1913- *AmMWSc 92*
**Creutz**, Edward Chester 1913- *IntWW 91*
**Creutz**, Gustaf Philip 1731-1785 *BlkwCEP*
**Creutz**, Michael John 1944- *AmMWSc 92*
**Creutzmann**, Harry F 1943- *WhoIns 92*
**Creuzot**, Percy P. 1924- *WhoBlA 92*
**Crevasse**, Gary A 1934- *AmMWSc 92*
**Crevecoeur**, Michel-Guillaume Jean de 1735-1813 *BlkwEAR, DcAmImH*
**Crevecoeur**, St. John de 1735-1813 *BenetAL 91*
**Creveling**, Cyrus Robbins 1930- *AmMWSc 92*
**Crevelt**, Dwight Eugene 1957- *WhoFI 92*
**Crew**, Edward Dixon 1917- *Who 92*
**Crew**, Geoffrey B 1956- *AmMWSc 92*
**Crew**, John Edwin 1930- *AmMWSc 92*
**Crew**, John L., Sr. 1926- *WhoBlA 92*
**Crew**, Judson 1917- *IntAu&W 91*
**Crew**, Louie *DrAPF 91*
**Crew**, Louie 1936- *IntAu&W 91, WrDr 92*
**Crew**, Malcolm Charles 1927- *AmMWSc 92*
**Crew**, Spencer R. 1949- *WhoBlA 92*
**Crewe**, Albert V. 1927- *Who 92*
**Crewe**, Albert Victor 1927- *AmMWSc 92, IntWW 91*
**Crewe**, Candida 1964- *ConAu 135*
**Crewe**, Ivor Martin 1945- *Who 92*
**Crewe**, Jennifer *DrAPF 91*
**Crewe**, Nancy Moe 1939- *WhoMW 92*
**Crewe**, Quentin Hugh 1926- *Who 92*
**Crews**, Albert E 1932- *WhoIns 92*
**Crews**, Anita L 1952- *AmMWSc 92*
**Crews**, Clarence Leo 1929- *WhoRel 92*
**Crews**, David Pafford 1947- *AmMWSc 92*
**Crews**, David Paul 1954- *WhoEnt 92*
**Crews**, Donald 1930- *WhoBlA 92*
**Crews**, Donald Roy 1943- *WhoAmL 92*
**Crews**, Frederick C. 1933- *WrDr 92*
**Crews**, Fulton T 1950- *AmMWSc 92*
**Crews**, Grasty, II 1927- *WhoAmL 92*
**Crews**, Harry *DrAPF 91*
**Crews**, Harry 1935- *BenetAL 91, ConNov 91, WrDr 92*
**Crews**, John Eric 1946- *WhoFI 92, WhoMW 92*
**Crews**, Judson *DrAPF 91*
**Crews**, Judson 1917- *ConAu 14AS [port], ConPo 91, WrDr 92*
**Crews**, Phillip 1943- *AmMWSc 92*
**Crews**, Robert Wayne 1919- *AmMWSc 92*
**Crews**, Sandra Joanne 1961- *WhoRel 92*
**Crews**, William Edwin 1944- *WhoAmL 92*
**Crews**, William Hunter 1932- *WhoBlA 92*
**Crews**, William Odell, Jr. 1936- *WhoRel 92, WhoWest 92*

**Crews,** William Sylvester 1947- WhoBlA 92
**Crewse,** Doyle Gene 1930- WhoRel 92
**Crewse,** Leonard Lee 1934- WhoFI 92
**Crewson,** Wendy Jane 1959- WhoEnt 92
**Cribari,** Stephen Jon 1947- WhoAmL 92
**Cribb,** Herbert Joseph 1892-1967 TwCPaSc
**Cribb,** Juanita Sanders 1950- WhoBlA 92
**Cribb,** Peter Henry 1918- Who 92
**Cribb,** Troy Kenneth, Jr WhoAmP 91
**Cribben,** Larry Dean 1940- AmMWSc 92
**Cribbet,** John Edward 1918- WhoMW 92
**Cribbins,** Paul Day 1927- AmMWSc 92
**Cribbs,** Joe Stanier 1958- WhoBlA 92
**Cribbs,** Larry Luker 1955- WhoAmP 91
**Cribbs,** Theo 1915- WhoAmP 91
**Cribbs,** Theo, Sr. 1916- WhoBlA 92
**Cribbs,** Williams Charles 1927- WhoBlA 92
**Crichton** Who 92
**Crichton,** Viscount 1971- Who 92
**Crichton,** Andrew Maitland-Makgill- 1910- Who 92
**Crichton,** Charles 1910- IntDcF 2-2 [port], IntMPA 92
**Crichton,** Charles Ainslie 1910- Who 92
**Crichton,** David 1931- AmMWSc 92
**Crichton,** David George 1914- Who 92
**Crichton,** Edward Maitland-Makgill- 1916- Who 92
**Crichton,** Jack Alston 1916- WhoAmP 91
**Crichton,** James Dunlop 1907- IntAu&W 91
**Crichton,** Kyle 1896-1960 BenetAL 91
**Crichton,** Michael 1942- FacFETw, IntAu&W 91, IntMPA 92, TwCSFW 91, WrDr 92
**Crichton,** Nicholas 1943- Who 92
**Crichton,** Richard John Vesey 1916- Who 92
**Crichton,** Ronald Henry 1913- IntAu&W 91
**Crichton-Brown,** Robert 1919- IntWW 91, Who 92
**Crichton-Miller,** Donald 1906- Who 92
**Crichton-Stuart** Who 92
**Crick,** Alan John Pitts 1913- Who 92
**Crick,** Bernard 1929- Who 92, WrDr 92
**Crick,** Donald Herbert 1916- IntAu&W 91, WrDr 92
**Crick,** F. H. C. 1916- WrDr 92
**Crick,** Francis Harry Compton 1916- AmMWSc 92, FacFETw, IntWW 91, Who 92, WhoNob 90, WhoWest 92
**Crick,** R. Pitts 1917- Who 92
**Crick,** Rex Edward 1943- AmMWSc 92
**Crick,** Ronald Pitts 1917- IntWW 91
**Crickenberger,** Lawrence Jay 1951- WhoAmL 92
**Crickhowell,** Baron 1934- IntWW 91, Who 92
**Crickmay,** John Rackstrow 1914- Who 92
**Criddle,** Joan D 1935- IntAu&W 91
**Criddle,** Kay Edward 1950- WhoFI 92
**Criddle,** Richard S 1936- AmMWSc 92
**Criden,** Mark Alan 1952- WhoAmL 92
**Crider,** Bill 1941- TwCWW 91, WrDr 92
**Crider,** Edward S., III 1921- WhoBlA 92
**Crider,** Fretwell Goer 1923- AmMWSc 92
**Crider,** Hoyt 1924- WhoWest 92
**Crider,** Karen Koch 1945- WhoAmL 92
**Crider,** Melody Ann 1955- WhoRel 92
**Crider,** Robert Agustine 1935- WhoMW 92
**Cridge,** Alfred Denton d1904? ScFEYrs
**Cridge,** Edward 1817-1913 RelLAm 91
**Criel,** Laura Victoria 1933- WhoWest 92
**Cright,** Lotess Priestley 1931- WhoBlA 92
**Crighton,** David George 1942- Who 92
**Crighton,** John Clark 1903- WrDr 92
**Crigler,** John F, Jr 1919- AmMWSc 92
**Crigman,** David Ian 1945- Who 92
**Crihfield,** John Brevard 1952- WhoMW 92
**Criley,** Bruce 1939- AmMWSc 92
**Crill,** Peter 1925- Who 92
**Crill,** Wayne Elmo AmMWSc 92
**Crilly,** Eugene Richard 1923- WhoWest 92
**Crim,** Alonzo A. 1928- WhoBlA 92
**Crim,** F Fleming 1947- AmMWSc 92
**Crim,** Gary Allen 1949- AmMWSc 92
**Crim,** Joe William 1945- AmMWSc 92
**Crim,** Keith Renn 1924- WhoRel 92
**Crim,** Kenneth Jacob 1918- WhoMW 92
**Crim,** Kevin L WhoAmP 91
**Crim,** Linda Kay 1947- WhoMW 92
**Crim,** Loretta Grace 1930- WhoMW 92
**Crim,** Rodney 1957- WhoBlA 92
**Crim,** Sterling Cromwell 1927- AmMWSc 92
**Criminale,** William Oliver, Jr 1933- AmMWSc 92
**Crimmins,** John Blaine 1951- WhoRel 92
**Crimmins,** Michael Thomas 1954- AmMWSc 92
**Crimmins,** Sean Thomas 1945- WhoAmL 92
**Crimmins,** Timothy Francis 1939- AmMWSc 92
**Crine,** Jean-Pierre C 1944- AmMWSc 92
**Criner,** Clyde 1952- WhoBlA 92
**Criner-Woods,** Joyce Verdello 1943- WhoBlA 92
**Crinion,** Gregory Paul 1959- WhoAmL 92
**Crinkley,** Richmond Dillard 1940- WhoEnt 92
**Crinnion,** David Martin 1949- WhoMW 92
**Crino,** David Samuel 1959- WhoFI 92
**Cripe,** Bonnie Sue 1949- WhoMW 92
**Crippen,** Bruce D 1932- WhoAmP 91
**Crippen,** Gordon Marvin 1945- AmMWSc 92
**Crippen,** Harley 1861-1910 FacFETw
**Crippen,** Ralph Edward 1933- WhoAmP 91
**Crippen,** Raymond Charles 1917- AmMWSc 92
**Crippen,** Robert 1937- FacFETw
**Crippens,** David L. 1942- WhoBlA 92
**Crippens,** David Lee 1942- WhoWest 92
**Crippin,** Harry Trevor 1929- Who 92
**Cripps** Who 92
**Cripps,** Anthony L. Who 92
**Cripps,** Derek J 1928- AmMWSc 92
**Cripps,** Harry Norman 1925- AmMWSc 92
**Cripps,** Humphrey 1915- Who 92
**Cripps,** John Stafford 1912- Who 92
**Cripps,** Joy Beaudette 1923- IntAu&W 91
**Cripps,** Matthew Anthony Leonard 1913- Who 92
**Cripps,** Stafford 1889-1952 FacFETw
**Criqui,** Don LesBEnT 92
**Crisafio,** Anthony J. 1953- WhoEnt 92
**Crisafulli,** Frank, Jr. 1940- WhoIns 92
**Crisalli,** Joel R 1948- WhoIns 92
**Crisan,** Susana WhoHisp 92
**Crisci,** John C 1938- WhoIns 92
**Crisci,** Pat Devita 1931- WhoMW 92
**Criscoe,** Arthur Hugh 1939- WhoRel 92
**Criscuolo,** Anthony Thomas 1937- IntAu&W 91, WrDr 92
**Criscuolo,** Dominic 1908- AmMWSc 92
**Criscuolo,** Wendy Laura 1949- WhoWest 92
**Crisham,** Thomas Michael 1939- WhoAmL 92
**Crisler,** Charles Robert 1948- WhoEnt 92
**Crisler,** Joseph Presley 1922- AmMWSc 92
**Crisler,** Richard Carleton 1907- WhoFI 92
**Crisley,** Francis Daniel 1926- AmMWSc 92
**Crisman,** Mary Frances Borden 1919- WhoWest 92
**Criso,** John Peter 1961- WhoFI 92
**Crisp,** Arthur Hamilton 1930- Who 92
**Crisp,** Carl Eugene 1931- AmMWSc 92
**Crisp,** Charles Frederick 1845-1896 AmPolLe
**Crisp,** David Brian 1957- WhoMW 92
**Crisp,** Laurence WhoAmP 91
**Crisp,** Lucy Cherry 1899-1977 DcNCBi 1
**Crisp,** Michael Dennis 1942- AmMWSc 92
**Crisp,** Nelson Blount 1938- WhoAmL 92
**Crisp,** Peter 1925- Who 92
**Crisp,** Robert Carl, Jr. 1947- WhoBlA 92
**Crisp,** Robert M, Jr 1940- AmMWSc 92
**Crisp,** Thomas Mitchell, Jr 1939- AmMWSc 92
**Crisp,** Tony WrDr 92
**Crispe,** Pamela Lesler 1949- WhoAmP 91
**Crispell,** Kenneth Raymond 1916- AmMWSc 92
**Crispens,** Charles Gangloff, Jr 1930- AmMWSc 92
**Crispi,** Michele Marie 1962- WhoAmL 92
**Crispin,** Craig Alan 1951- WhoAmL 92
**Crispin,** James Hewes 1915- WhoFI 92, WhoWest 92
**Crispin,** Mark Reed 1956- WhoWest 92
**Crispin,** Robert W 1946- WhoIns 92
**Crispin,** Robert William 1946- WhoFI 92
**Crispina** d304 EncEarC
**Crispino,** Jerry L 1930- WhoAmP 91
**Crispo,** John 1933- WrDr 92
**Crispo,** Richard Charles 1945- WhoWest 92
**Criss,** A V, III 1954- WhoAmP 91
**Criss,** Cecil M 1934- AmMWSc 92
**Criss,** Darlene June 1931- WhoMW 92
**Criss,** Darrell E 1921- AmMWSc 92
**Criss,** Diane Ramsey 1941- WhoRel 92
**Criss,** John W 1941- AmMWSc 92
**Criss,** Lloyd W, Jr 1941- WhoAmP 91
**Criss,** Thomas Benjamin 1949- AmMWSc 92
**Criss,** Wayne Eldon 1940- AmMWSc 92
**Crissman,** Harry Allen 1935- AmMWSc 92
**Crissman,** Jack Kenneth, Jr 1944- AmMWSc 92
**Crissman,** John Matthews 1935- AmMWSc 92
**Crissman,** Judith Anne 1942- AmMWSc 92
**Crisswell,** R W ScFEYrs
**Crist,** Buckley, Jr 1941- AmMWSc 92
**Crist,** Charles Joseph, Jr. 1956- WhoEnt 92
**Crist,** DeLanson Ross 1940- AmMWSc 92
**Crist,** John Benjamin 1941- AmMWSc 92
**Crist,** Judith 1922- IntMPA 92, WrDr 92
**Crist,** Judith Klein 1922- WhoEnt 92
**Crist,** Le Roy 1930- WhoMW 92
**Crist,** Lewis R. 1935- WhoMW 92
**Crist,** Richard Lee 1961- WhoFI 92
**Cristaldi,** Franco 1924- IntMPA 92
**Cristelli,** Jose Gottardi WhoRel 92
**Cristiani,** Alfredo 1948?- IntWW 91
**Cristiani,** Therese Stridde 1948- WhoMW 92
**Cristiano,** Marilyn Jean 1954- WhoWest 92
**Cristini,** Angela 1948- AmMWSc 92
**Cristobal,** Adrian L 1921- WhoAmP 91
**Cristofalo,** Vincent Joseph 1933- AmMWSc 92
**Cristofer,** Michael 1945- WhoEnt 92
**Cristofer,** Michael 1946- IntAu&W 91, WrDr 92
**Cristofori,** Bartolommeo 1655-1731 NewAmDM
**Cristol,** Stanley Jerome 1916- AmMWSc 92, IntWW 91
**Criswell,** Arthurine Denton 1953- WhoBlA 92
**Criswell,** Bennie Sue 1942- AmMWSc 92
**Criswell,** Charles Harrison 1943- WhoFI 92, WhoMW 92
**Criswell,** David Russell 1941- AmMWSc 92
**Criswell,** E. G. 1940- WhoRel 92
**Criswell,** Kimberly Ann 1957- WhoFI 92, WhoWest 92
**Criswell,** Marvin Eugene 1942- AmMWSc 92
**Criswell,** Paul Lindsay 1954- WhoAmL 92
**Criswell,** Wallie Amos 1909- RelLAm 91
**Critchett,** Ian 1920- Who 92
**Critchfield,** Charles Louis 1910- AmMWSc 92
**Critchfield,** Richard 1931- IntAu&W 91, WrDr 92
**Critchfield,** William Burke 1923- AmMWSc 92
**Critchley,** John William d1910 BiInAmS
**Critchley,** Julian 1930- IntAu&W 91
**Critchley,** Julian Michael Gordon 1930- Who 92
**Critchley,** Macdonald 1900- Who 92
**Critchley,** Philip 1931- Who 92
**Critchley,** T. A. 1919-1991 ConAu 134
**Critchley,** Thomas Alan d1991 Who 92N
**Critchley,** Thomas Alan 1919- IntAu&W 91, WrDr 92
**Critchley,** Thomas Kingston 1916- IntWW 91
**Critchley,** Tom 1928- Who 92
**Critchlow,** Burtis Vaughn 1927- AmMWSc 92
**Critchlow,** Charles Howard 1950- WhoAmL 92
**Critchlow,** D 1932- AmMWSc 92
**Crite,** Allan Rohan 1910- WhoBlA 92
**Critelli,** Lylea May Dodson 1956- WhoAmL 92
**Critelli,** Paul Joseph 1949- WhoMW 92
**Crites,** John Lee 1923- AmMWSc 92
**Crites,** Joseph Allen 1943- WhoMW 92
**Crites,** Richard Don 1943- WhoAmL 92
**Crites,** Richard Ray 1952- WhoFI 92, WhoWest 92
**Crites,** Stephen Decatur 1931- WhoRel 92
**Critoph,** E 1929- AmMWSc 92
**Crits,** George J 1922- AmMWSc 92
**Critser,** Jean Anne 1956- WhoAmP 91
**Crittenberger,** Willis D 1890-1980 FacFETw
**Crittenden,** Alden La Rue 1920- AmMWSc 92
**Crittenden,** Charles Christopher 1902-1969 DcNCBi 1
**Crittenden,** Eugene Casson, Jr 1914- AmMWSc 92
**Crittenden,** Eugene Dwight, Jr. 1927- WhoFI 92
**Crittenden,** James N. 1931- WhoAmL 92
**Crittenden,** John Charles 1949- AmMWSc 92
**Crittenden,** John Jordan 1787-1863 AmPolLe
**Crittenden,** Lyman Butler 1926- AmMWSc 92
**Crittenden,** Ray Ryland 1931- AmMWSc 92
**Crittenden,** Rebecca Slover 1936- AmMWSc 92
**Crittenden,** Richard James 1930- AmMWSc 92
**Crittenden,** Steven Alan 1961- WhoAmL 92
**Crittenden,** Toya Cynthia 1958- IntAu&W 91
**Crittenden,** William 1908- WhoRel 92
**Crittendon,** Laura D. WhoHisp 92
**Crittenton,** Charles Nelson 1833-1909 DcAmImH
**Critz,** Boyd Ridley, III 1941- WhoAmL 92
**Critz,** Jerry B 1934- AmMWSc 92
**Critzer,** Rex Laird 1947- WhoIns 92
**Critzer,** William Ernest 1934- WhoFI 92
**Crivelli,** Joseph Xavier 1960- WhoFI 92
**Crivello,** Jack Evans, II 1967- WhoWest 92
**Crivello,** James V 1940- AmMWSc 92
**Croak,** Francis R. 1929- WhoAmL 92
**Croan,** Robert James 1937- WhoEnt 92
**Croan,** Thomas Malcolm 1932- Who 92
**Croat,** John Joseph 1943- AmMWSc 92
**Croat,** Thomas Bernard 1938- AmMWSc 92, WhoMW 92
**Crober,** Donald Curtis 1939- AmMWSc 92
**Crocco,** Denis Michael 1963- WhoAmL 92
**Croce,** Arlene Louise 1934- WhoEnt 92
**Croce,** Benedetto 1866-1952 FacFETw
**Croce,** Carlo Maria 1944- AmMWSc 92
**Croce,** Giovanni 1557?-1609 NewAmDM
**Croce,** Louis J 1921- AmMWSc 92
**Croche,** Monsieur NewAmDM
**Crochiere,** Ronald E 1945- AmMWSc 92
**Crock,** Stan 1950- ConAu 134
**Crockatt,** Allan 1923- Who 92
**Crocker,** Albert Rudolph 1914- WhoFI 92
**Crocker,** Allen Carrol 1925- AmMWSc 92
**Crocker,** Burton B 1920- AmMWSc 92
**Crocker,** Chester A 1941- WhoAmP 91
**Crocker,** Chester Arthur 1941- IntWW 91
**Crocker,** Clinton C. 1928- WhoBlA 92
**Crocker,** Cyril L. 1918- WhoBlA 92
**Crocker,** Daniel Bryan 1967- WhoWest 92
**Crocker,** Deborah Ann 1956- WhoMW 92
**Crocker,** Denton Winslow 1919- AmMWSc 92
**Crocker,** Diane Winston 1926- AmMWSc 92
**Crocker,** Edward 1948- WhoAmP 91
**Crocker,** Freeman 1941- WhoEnt 92
**Crocker,** Iain Hay 1928- AmMWSc 92
**Crocker,** J. A. Frazer, Jr. 1935- WhoRel 92, WhoWest 92
**Crocker,** John Lawrence 1944- WhoAmL 92
**Crocker,** Kenneth Franklin 1950- WhoWest 92
**Crocker,** Lenley Eugene 1926- WhoWest 92
**Crocker,** Lester G. 1912- WrDr 92
**Crocker,** Lucretia 1829-1886 BiInAmS
**Crocker,** Malcolm John 1938- WhoFI 92
**Crocker,** Michael Pue 1918- WhoAmL 92
**Crocker,** Peter Vernon 1926- Who 92
**Crocker,** Ray Dean 1949- WhoEnt 92
**Crocker,** Ryan WhoAmP 91
**Crocker,** Saone Baron 1943- WhoAmL 92
**Crocker,** Sylvia Fleming 1933- WhoWest 92
**Crocker,** Thomas Dunstan 1936- WhoFI 92
**Crocker,** Thomas Edward 1949- WhoAmL 92
**Crocker,** Thomas Timothy 1920- AmMWSc 92
**Crocker,** Tillman Hans 1956- WhoWest 92
**Crocker,** Walter 1902- Who 92, WrDr 92
**Crocker,** Wayne Marcus 1956- WhoBlA 92
**Crocket,** David Scott 1931- AmMWSc 92
**Crocket,** James Harvie 1932- AmMWSc 92
**Crockett,** Allen Bruce 1944- AmMWSc 92
**Crockett,** Andrew Duncan 1943- Who 92
**Crockett,** Christine Holmes WhoRel 92
**Crockett,** David James 1942- AmMWSc 92
**Crockett,** Davy 1786-1836 BenetAL 91, RComAH
**Crockett,** Delores Loraine 1947- WhoBlA 92
**Crockett,** Edward D., Jr. 1937- WhoBlA 92
**Crockett,** George Ephriam 1940- WhoMW 92
**Crockett,** George W., III 1938- WhoBlA 92
**Crockett,** George William, III 1938- WhoAmL 92
**Crockett,** George William, Jr 1909- WhoAmP 91, WhoBlA 92
**Crockett,** Gwendolyn B. 1932- WhoBlA 92
**Crockett,** James Edwin 1924- WhoMW 92
**Crockett,** James Grover, III 1937- WhoEnt 92
**Crockett,** Jerry J 1928- AmMWSc 92
**Crockett,** Mary Lou 1938- WhoWest 92
**Crockett,** Phyllis D. 1950- WhoBlA 92
**Crockett,** Richard Boyd 1944- WhoAmL 92
**Crockett,** Rita Louise 1957- BlkOlyM
**Crockett,** Theo Neill 1946- WhoFI 92
**Crockett,** Ulysses-Atum 1938- WhoBlA 92
**Crockett-Dickerman,** Margaret Williams 1918- WhoRel 92
**Crockett-Gallo,** Barbara 1920- WhoEnt 92
**Crockett-Smith,** D.L. DrAPF 91
**Crockford,** Allen Lepard 1897- Who 92
**Crockin,** Susan Lee 1954- WhoAmL 92
**Crocombe,** Ronald Gordon 1929- IntAu&W 91, WrDr 92
**Croctogino,** Reinhold Hermann 1942- AmMWSc 92

**Croes**, John James Robertson 1834-1906 *BiInAmS*
**Crofford**, Helen Lois 1932- *WhoWest 92*
**Crofford**, Oscar Bledsoe 1930- *AmMWSc 92*
**Crofoot**, Alan 1929-1979 *NewAmDM*
**Croft** *Who 92*
**Croft**, Baron 1916- *Who 92*
**Croft**, Alfred Russell 1896- *AmMWSc 92*
**Croft**, Barbara Yoder 1940- *AmMWSc 92*
**Croft**, Bruce 1952- *AmMWSc 92*
**Croft**, Charles Clayton 1914- *AmMWSc 92*
**Croft**, Charles Palmer 1943- *WhoEnt 92*
**Croft**, David Legh 1937- *Who 92*
**Croft**, George Thomas 1926- *AmMWSc 92*
**Croft**, Ira T. 1926- *WhoBlA 92*
**Croft**, John 1923- *Who 92*
**Croft**, John Archibald Radcliffe d1990 *Who 92N*
**Croft**, John Houghton 1962- *WhoFI 92*
**Croft**, Leland Chancy 1937- *WhoAmP 91*
**Croft**, Noel Andrew Cotton 1906- *Who 92*
**Croft**, Owen 1932- *Who 92*
**Croft**, Paul Douglas 1937- *AmMWSc 92*
**Croft**, Roy Henry Francis 1936- *Who 92*
**Croft**, Stanley Edward 1917- *Who 92*
**Croft**, Thomas 1959- *Who 92*
**Croft**, Thomas A 1931- *AmMWSc 92*
**Croft**, Thomas Stone 1938- *AmMWSc 92*
**Croft**, Walter Lawrence 1935- *AmMWSc 92*
**Croft**, Wardell C. *WhoBlA 92*
**Croft**, William Joseph 1926- *AmMWSc 92*
**Crofton** *Who 92*
**Crofton**, Baron 1951- *Who 92*
**Crofton**, Denis Hayes 1908- *Who 92*
**Crofton**, Hugh Dennis *Who 92*
**Crofton**, John 1912- *Who 92*
**Crofton**, Malby 1923- *Who 92*
**Crofts**, Antony R 1940- *AmMWSc 92*
**Crofts**, Geoffrey 1924- *AmMWSc 92*
**Crofts**, Inez Altman *WhoEnt 92*
**Crofut**, William Elmer 1934- *WhoEnt 92*
**Croghan**, Robert Emmett 1929- *WhoMW 92*
**Crognale**, Corey V. 1954- *WhoAmL 92*
**Croham**, Baron 1917- *IntWW 91, Who 92*
**Crohn**, Frank T 1924- *WhoIns 92*
**Crois**, John Henry 1946- *WhoMW 92*
**Croissier**, Luis Carlos 1950- *IntWW 91*
**Croizat**, Pierre D 1940- *WhoIns 92*
**Croke**, Edward John 1935- *AmMWSc 92*
**Croke**, Thomas Michael, IV 1952- *WhoAmL 92*
**Croker**, Byron P 1945- *AmMWSc 92*
**Croker**, Edgar Alfred 1924- *Who 92*
**Croker**, John Wilson 1780-1857 *DcLB 110 [port]*
**Croker**, Robert Arthur 1932- *AmMWSc 92*
**Croley**, Russell Lowell, Jr. 1951- *WhoAmL 92*
**Croley**, Thomas Edgar 1940- *AmMWSc 92*
**Croll**, David Arnold 1900- *Who 92*
**Croll**, Elizabeth J. *WrDr 92*
**Croll**, Ian Murray 1929- *AmMWSc 92*
**Croll**, James George Arthur 1943- *Who 92*
**Croll**, Robert Frederick 1934- *WhoFI 92, WhoMW 92*
**Croly**, Henry Gray 1910- *Who 92*
**Cromar**, Kevin Craig 1953- *WhoAmP 91*
**Cromartie**, Earl of 1948- *Who 92*
**Cromartie**, Eric Ross 1955- *WhoAmL 92*
**Cromartie**, Ernest W., II *WhoBlA 92*
**Cromartie**, Eugene Rufus 1936- *WhoBlA 92*
**Cromartie**, Thomas Houston 1946- *AmMWSc 92*
**Cromartie**, William James 1913- *AmMWSc 92*
**Cromartie**, William James, Jr 1947- *AmMWSc 92*
**Cromarty**, Arthur Martin 1919- *WhoAmL 92*
**Crombaugh**, Hallie 1949- *WhoBlA 92*
**Crombet**, Flor 1851-1895 *HisDSpE*
**Crombie**, Alistair Cameron 1915- *IntAu&W 91, Who 92, WrDr 92*
**Crombie**, David Edward 1936- *IntWW 91*
**Crombie**, Douglass D 1924- *AmMWSc 92*
**Crombie**, Leslie 1923- *IntWW 91, Who 92*
**Crome**, Dale John 1948- *WhoFI 92*
**Cromeans**, Theresa L. 1943- *WhoWest 92*
**Cromeenes**, James Richard 1934- *WhoAmP 91*
**Cromer**, Earl 1918-1991 *IntWW 91N*
**Cromer**, Earl of d1991 *Who 92N*
**Cromer**, Earl of 1918-1991 *CurBio 91N, IntWW 91*
**Cromer**, Earl of 1946- *Who 92*
**Cromer**, Alan H 1935- *AmMWSc 92*
**Cromer**, Benjamin Dean 1954- *WhoEnt 92*
**Cromer**, Charles L 1939- *WhoAmP 91*
**Cromer**, Don Tiffany 1923- *AmMWSc 92*
**Cromer**, Ella Mae 1916- *WhoAmP 91*
**Cromer**, James L, Jr 1963- *WhoAmP 91*
**Cromer**, Jerry Haltiwanger 1935- *AmMWSc 92*
**Cromer**, John A 1938- *AmMWSc 92*
**Cromer**, Robert John 1949- *WhoFI 92*
**Cromie**, Judith Elaine 1943- *WhoIns 92*
**Cromie**, Robert 1856-1907 *ScFEYrs, TwCSFW 91*
**Cromie**, Stanley *IntAu&W 91X*
**Cromley**, Brent Reed 1941- *WhoAmL 92, WhoAmP 91, WhoWest 92*
**Cromley**, Jon Lowell 1934- *WhoAmL 92, WhoFI 92, WhoMW 92*
**Cromley**, Leroy Hewitt 1918- *WhoAmP 91*
**Crompton**, Alfred W 1927- *AmMWSc 92*
**Crompton**, Arnold 1914- *WhoRel 92, WhoWest 92*
**Crompton**, Charles Edward 1922- *AmMWSc 92*
**Crompton**, Dan 1941- *Who 92*
**Crompton**, David William Thomasson 1937- *AmMWSc 92*
**Crompton**, Gareth 1937- *Who 92*
**Crompton**, Ian William 1936- *Who 92*
**Crompton**, Louis 1925- *WrDr 92*
**Crompton**, Roy Hartley 1921- *Who 92*
**Cromroy**, Harvey Leonard 1930- *AmMWSc 92*
**Cromwell**, Baron 1960- *Who 92*
**Cromwell**, Adelaide M. 1919- *WhoBlA 92*
**Cromwell**, Florence S 1922- *AmMWSc 92*
**Cromwell**, Gary Leon 1938- *AmMWSc 92*
**Cromwell**, Harvey 1907-1977 *ConAu 134*
**Cromwell**, John 1887-1979 *IntDcF 2-2*
**Cromwell**, John Clark 1939- *WhoFI 92*
**Cromwell**, Leslie 1924- *AmMWSc 92*
**Cromwell**, Margaret M. 1933- *WhoBlA 92*
**Cromwell**, Norman Henry 1913- *AmMWSc 92*
**Cromwell**, Otelia 1874-1972 *NotBlAW 92*
**Cromwell**, Robert Joseph 1956- *WhoRel 92*
**Cromwell**, Roger James Kissel 1931- *WhoFI 92*
**Cron**, John B. 1923- *IntMPA 92*
**Cron**, Maurice G *WhoAmP 91*
**Cronan**, Irene M 1936- *WhoAmP 91*
**Cronan**, John Emerson, Jr 1942- *AmMWSc 92*
**Cronan**, Philip Francis 1941- *WhoFI 92*
**Cronan**, Thomas Leo, III 1959- *WhoAmL 92*
**Cronan**, Timothy Michael 1953- *WhoAmL 92*
**Cronauer**, Donald 1936- *AmMWSc 92*
**Cronbach**, Abraham 1882-1965 *AmPeW*
**Cronberg**, Chris 1948- *WhoAmP 91*
**Crone**, Alla Marguerite 1923- *IntAu&W 91*
**Crone**, Anthony Joseph 1947- *AmMWSc 92*
**Crone**, Christian 1926- *IntWW 91*
**Crone**, John Rossman 1933- *WhoFI 92*
**Crone**, Lawrence John 1935- *AmMWSc 92*
**Crone**, Moira *DrAPF 91*
**Crone**, Philip Dean 1931- *WhoAmP 91*
**Crone**, Richard Allan 1947- *WhoWest 92*
**Crone**, Thomas Frederick 1958- *WhoFI 92*
**Cronemeyer**, Donald Charles 1925- *AmMWSc 92*
**Cronenberg**, August William 1944- *AmMWSc 92*
**Cronenberg**, David 1943- *IntDcF 2-2 [port], IntMPA 92, IntWW 91*
**Cronenberger**, Jo Helen 1939- *AmMWSc 92*
**Cronenwett**, William Treadwell 1932- *AmMWSc 92*
**Cronenworth**, Charles Douglas 1921- *WhoFI 92*
**Croner**, Fred B., Jr. 1929- *WhoAmL 92*
**Croney**, J. Kenneth 1942- *WhoAmL 92*
**Cronheim**, Georg Erich 1906- *AmMWSc 92*
**Cronholm**, Lois S 1930- *AmMWSc 92*
**Cronic**, David William 1960- *WhoRel 92*
**Cronin**, A J 1896-1981 *FacFETw*
**Cronin**, Anthony *IntAu&W 91*
**Cronin**, Anthony 1923- *IntWW 91*
**Cronin**, Anthony 1926- *WrDr 92*
**Cronin**, Anthony 1928- *ConPo 91*
**Cronin**, Bernard Koopmann 1917- *WhoMW 92*
**Cronin**, Dan 1959- *WhoAmP 91*
**Cronin**, Daniel Anthony 1927- *WhoRel 92*
**Cronin**, James Lawrence, Jr 1919- *AmMWSc 92*
**Cronin**, James Watson 1931- *AmMWSc 92, FacFETw, IntWW 91, WhoMW 92, WhoNob 90*
**Cronin**, Jane Smiley 1922- *AmMWSc 92*
**Cronin**, Joe A 1934- *WhoAmP 91*
**Cronin**, John Read 1937- *AmMWSc 92*
**Cronin**, Joseph Edward 1906-1984 *FacFETw*
**Cronin**, Kathleen Anne 1933- *WhoFI 92*
**Cronin**, Lewis Eugene 1917- *AmMWSc 92*
**Cronin**, Mark Joseph 1956- *WhoFI 92*
**Cronin**, Michael John 1949- *AmMWSc 92*
**Cronin**, Michael Thomas Ignatius 1924- *AmMWSc 92*
**Cronin**, Paul William 1938- *WhoAmP 91, WhoFI 92*
**Cronin**, Thomas E 1940- *WhoAmP 91*
**Cronin**, Thomas Francis, Jr. 1939- *WhoFI 92*
**Cronin**, Thomas Joseph 1943- *WhoMW 92, WhoRel 92*
**Cronin**, Thomas Mark 1950- *AmMWSc 92*
**Cronin**, Thomas Wells 1945- *AmMWSc 92*
**Cronin**, Timothy H 1939- *AmMWSc 92*
**Cronin**, Vincent Archibald Patric 1924- *IntAu&W 91*
**Cronin**, Vincent Archibald Patrick 1924- *Who 92*
**Cronin-Golomb**, Mark *AmMWSc 92*
**Cronk**, Alfred E 1915- *AmMWSc 92*
**Cronk**, Ann S. 1928- *WhoRel 92*
**Cronk**, Christine Elizabeth 1944- *AmMWSc 92*
**Cronk**, Daniel Thompson 1953- *WhoAmL 92*
**Cronk**, Judith Picard 1949- *WhoEnt 92*
**Cronk**, Mildred Schiefelbein 1909- *WhoWest 92*
**Cronk**, Ted Clifford 1946- *AmMWSc 92*
**Cronk**, William Henry 1928- *WhoEnt 92*
**Cronkhite**, Leonard Wolsey, Jr. 1919- *IntWW 91*
**Cronkhite**, Leonard Woolsey, Jr 1919- *AmMWSc 92*
**Cronkite**, Donald Lee 1944- *AmMWSc 92*
**Cronkite**, Eugene Pitcher 1914- *AmMWSc 92, IntWW 91*
**Cronkite**, Walter *LesBEnT 92 [port]*
**Cronkite**, Walter 1916- *FacFETw [port], IntMPA 92, WrDr 92*
**Cronkite**, Walter Leland, Jr. 1916- *IntWW 91*
**Cronkleton**, Thomas Eugene 1928- *WhoWest 92*
**Cronkright**, Walter Allyn, Jr 1931- *AmMWSc 92*
**Cronn**, Dagmar Rais 1946- *AmMWSc 92*
**Cronne**, Henry Alfred d1990 *Who 92N*
**Cronon**, William 1954- *WrDr 92*
**Cronquist**, Arthur John 1919- *AmMWSc 92*
**Cronshaw**, James 1933- *AmMWSc 92*
**Cronshaw**, Mark Bernard 1954- *WhoFI 92*
**Cronson**, Harry Marvin 1937- *AmMWSc 92*
**Cronvich**, James A 1914- *AmMWSc 92*
**Cronvich**, Lester Louis 1916- *AmMWSc 92*
**Cronyn**, Hume 1911- *IntMPA 92, IntWW 91, WhoEnt 92*
**Cronyn**, Marshall William 1919- *AmMWSc 92*
**Cronyn**, Tandy 1945- *ConTFT 9*
**Crook** *Who 92*
**Crook**, Baron 1926- *Who 92*
**Crook**, Arthur Charles William 1912- *Who 92*
**Crook**, Charles Samuel, III 1944- *WhoAmL 92*
**Crook**, Colin 1942- *Who 92*
**Crook**, Donald Martin 1947- *WhoAmL 92*
**Crook**, Edward 1929- *BlkOlyM*
**Crook**, Frances Rachel 1952- *Who 92*
**Crook**, Gaines Morton 1923- *WhoWest 92*
**Crook**, J. Mitchell 1952- *WhoFI 92*
**Crook**, James Cooper 1923- *Who 92*
**Crook**, James Jeffery 1938- *WhoAmL 92*
**Crook**, James Richard 1935- *AmMWSc 92*
**Crook**, John Anthony 1921- *Who 92*
**Crook**, John Robert 1947- *WhoAmL 92*
**Crook**, Joseph Mordaunt 1937- *IntAu&W 91, Who 92, WrDr 92*
**Crook**, Joseph Raymond 1936- *AmMWSc 92*
**Crook**, Kenneth Roy 1920- *Who 92*
**Crook**, Maxfield Doyle 1936- *WhoEnt 92*
**Crook**, Norris Clinton 1923- *WhoRel 92*
**Crook**, P.J. 1945- *TwCPaSc*
**Crook**, Paul Edwin 1915- *Who 92*
**Crook**, Philip George 1925- *AmMWSc 92*
**Crook**, Robert Lacey 1929- *WhoAmP 91*
**Crook**, Sean Paul 1953- *WhoWest 92*
**Crook**, Shawn Hill 1963- *WhoAmL 92*
**Crook**, Stephen Richard 1963- *WhoMW 92*
**Crook**, Tressa Helen 1956- *WhoMW 92*
**Crook**, Troy Norman 1928- *WhoFI 92*
**Crook**, Verle D. 1928- *WhoWest 92*
**Crook**, W. Edwin 1941- *WhoEnt 92*
**Crooke**, James Stratton *WhoFI 92*
**Crooke**, James Stratton 1928- *AmMWSc 92*
**Crooke**, Philip Schuyler 1944- *AmMWSc 92*
**Crooke**, Robert C *AmMWSc 92*
**Crooke**, Stanley T 1945- *AmMWSc 92*
**Crooke**, Stanley Thomas 1945- *WhoFI 92*
**Crookenden**, George Wayet Derek 1920- *Who 92*
**Crookenden**, Napier 1915- *Who 92*
**Crooker**, Barbara *DrAPF 91*
**Crooker**, John H., Jr. 1914- *WhoAmL 92*
**Crooker**, Nancy Uss 1944- *AmMWSc 92*
**Crooker**, Peter Peirce 1937- *AmMWSc 92*
**Crooks**, Carol Yvonne 1967- *WhoMW 92*
**Crooks**, Charmaine 1961- *BlkOlyM*
**Crooks**, David Manson 1931- *Who 92*
**Crooks**, George Chapman 1905- *AmMWSc 92*
**Crooks**, Glenna Marie 1950- *WhoAmP 91*
**Crooks**, John A. 1936- *WhoWest 92*
**Crooks**, John Robert Megaw 1914- *Who 92*
**Crooks**, Lewis M. *Who 92*
**Crooks**, Michael John Chamberlain 1930- *AmMWSc 92*
**Crooks**, Neil Patrick 1938- *WhoAmL 92*
**Crooks**, Peter Anthony 1942- *AmMWSc 92*
**Crooks**, Richard Lee 1954- *WhoMW 92*
**Crooks**, Stephen Lawrence 1957- *AmMWSc 92*
**Crooks**, William Howard, Jr. 1949- *WhoFI 92*
**Crookshank**, Herman Robert 1916- *AmMWSc 92*
**Crookshanks**, Betty Dorsey 1944- *WhoAmP 91, WhoEnt 92*
**Crookston**, J A 1919- *AmMWSc 92*
**Crookston**, Marie Cutbush 1920- *AmMWSc 92*
**Crookston**, Reid B 1939- *AmMWSc 92*
**Croom**, Frederick Hailey 1941- *AmMWSc 92*
**Croom**, Hardy Bryan 1797-1837 *DcNCBi 1*
**Croom**, Hardy Bryan 1798-1837 *BiInAmS*
**Croom**, Henrietta Brown 1940- *AmMWSc 92*
**Croom**, Herman Lee 1909- *WhoRel 92*
**Croom**, John Henry, III 1932- *WhoFI 92*
**Croom**, Sam Gaston, Jr. 1930- *WhoAmL 92*
**Croom**, Warren James, Jr 1950- *AmMWSc 92*
**Croom**, William 1772-1829 *DcNCBi 1*
**Croom-Johnson**, David Powell 1914- *Who 92*
**Croom-Johnson**, Henry Powell 1910- *Who 92*
**Croome**, Lewis 1907- *Who 92*
**Cropp**, Dwight Sheffery 1939- *WhoBlA 92*
**Cropp**, Frederick William, III 1932- *AmMWSc 92*
**Cropp**, Gerd J A 1930- *AmMWSc 92*
**Cropper**, James Anthony 1938- *Who 92*
**Cropper**, Peter John 1927- *Who 92*
**Cropper**, Rebecca Lynn 1957- *WhoMW 92*
**Cropper**, Walter H. 1919- *WhoAmL 92*
**Cropper**, Walter V 1917- *AmMWSc 92*
**Cropper**, Wendell Parker 1951- *AmMWSc 92*
**Cropper**, William A. 1939- *WhoFI 92*
**Cropsey**, Alan L 1952- *WhoAmP 91*
**Cropsey**, Harmon 1917- *WhoAmP 91*
**Crory**, Elizabeth Lupien *WhoAmP 91*
**Cros**, Charles 1842-1888 *GuFrLit 1*
**Crosa**, Michael L. 1942- *WhoHisp 92*
**Crosbie**, Edwin Alexander 1921- *AmMWSc 92*
**Crosbie**, John Carnell 1931- *IntWW 91, Who 92, WhoFI 92*
**Crosbie**, William 1915- *TwCPaSc, Who 92*
**Crosby**, Stills, Nash and Young *FacFETw*
**Crosby**, Stills and Nash *NewAmDM*
**Crosby**, Alan Hubert 1922- *AmMWSc 92*
**Crosby**, Alfred W., Jr. 1931- *WrDr 92*
**Crosby**, Archie R 1924- *WhoAmP 91*
**Crosby**, Benjamin Gratz 1936- *WhoFI 92*
**Crosby**, Bing d1978 *LesBEnT 92*
**Crosby**, Bing 1901-1977 *FacFETw [port]*
**Crosby**, Bing 1903?-1977 *ConMus 6 [port]*
**Crosby**, Bing 1904-1977 *NewAmDM*
**Crosby**, Bob 1913- *IntMPA 92, NewAmDM*
**Crosby**, Caresse 1892-1970 *LiExTwC*
**Crosby**, Cathy Lee *IntMPA 92*
**Crosby**, Clement 1958- *TwCPaSc*
**Crosby**, Daniel Earl 1956- *WhoRel 92*
**Crosby**, David *WhoEnt 92*
**Crosby**, David S 1938- *AmMWSc 92*
**Crosby**, Dennis M. d1991 *NewYTBS 91*
**Crosby**, Donald Allen 1932- *WhoRel 92, WhoWest 92*
**Crosby**, Donald Gibson 1928- *AmMWSc 92*
**Crosby**, Edward Harold 1859-1934 *ScFEYrs*
**Crosby**, Edward Warren 1932- *WhoBlA 92*
**Crosby**, Edwin Andrew 1924- *AmMWSc 92*
**Crosby**, Emory Spear 1928- *AmMWSc 92*
**Crosby**, Ernest Howard 1856-1907 *AmPeW, ScFEYrs*
**Crosby**, Fanny 1820-1915 *RelLAm 91*
**Crosby**, Faye J. 1947- *ConAu 36NR*
**Crosby**, Frances Jane 1820-1915 *BenetAL 91*
**Crosby**, Fred McClellen 1928- *WhoBlA 92*
**Crosby**, G. Brent 1939- *WhoWest 92*
**Crosby**, Gayle Marcella *AmMWSc 92*
**Crosby**, George M 1916- *WhoAmP 91*
**Crosby**, Glenn Arthur 1928- *AmMWSc 92*
**Crosby**, Gordon E, Jr 1920- *WhoIns 92*
**Crosby**, Guy Alexander 1942- *AmMWSc 92*
**Crosby**, Harry 1897-1929 *FacFETw*

**Crosby,** Harry 1898-1929 *LiExTwC*
**Crosby,** Harry C. *WrDr 92*
**Crosby,** Harry C, Jr *TwCSFW 91*
**Crosby,** Howard J., Jr. d1991 *NewYTBS 91*
**Crosby,** Jackie *ConAu 133*
**Crosby,** Jacqueline Garton 1961- *ConAu 133*
**Crosby,** Jane A 1920- *WhoAmP 91*
**Crosby,** Joan Carew 1934- *WhoEnt 92*
**Crosby,** John 1912- *WrDr 92*
**Crosby,** John 1912-1991 *ConAu 135, NewYTBS 91 [port]*
**Crosby,** John 1926- *NewAmDM*
**Crosby,** John Bartlett 1947- *WhoAmL 92*
**Crosby,** John C. 1912-1991 *CurBio 91N*
**Crosby,** John Campbell 1912- *IntAu&W 91, IntWW 91*
**Crosby,** John Griffith 1943- *WhoFI 92*
**Crosby,** John O'Hea 1926- *WhoEnt 92, WhoWest 92*
**Crosby,** Kathryn 1933- *IntMPA 92*
**Crosby,** Kathryn Grandstaff 1933- *WhoEnt 92*
**Crosby,** LaVon K 1924- *WhoAmP 91*
**Crosby,** LaVon Kehoe Stuart 1924- *WhoMW 92*
**Crosby,** Lon Owen 1945- *AmMWSc 92*
**Crosby,** Marshall Robert 1943- *AmMWSc 92*
**Crosby,** Mary 1959- *IntMPA 92*
**Crosby,** Michael Hugh 1940- *WhoRel 92*
**Crosby,** Norman Lawrence 1927- *WhoEnt 92*
**Crosby,** Oscar Terry 1861-1947 *AmPeW*
**Crosby,** Peter Alan 1945- *WhoFI 92*
**Crosby,** Robert Berkey 1911- *WhoAmL 92, WhoAmP 91*
**Crosby,** Robert Davis 1938- *WhoWest 92*
**Crosby,** Robert Lewis 1932- *WhoAmL 92*
**Crosby,** Robert Woodruff 1940- *WhoMW 92*
**Crosby,** Susan 1945- *WhoAmP 91*
**Crosby,** Theo 1925- *ConAu 133, DcTwDes, Who 92*
**Crosby,** Thomas Anthony 1947- *WhoEnt 92*
**Crosby,** Thomas Manville, Jr. 1938- *WhoAmL 92, WhoFI 92*
**Crosby,** Tom, Jr 1928- *WhoAmP 91*
**Crosby,** Warren Melville 1931- *AmMWSc 92*
**Crosby,** William Duncan, Jr. 1943- *WhoAmL 92, WhoAmP 91*
**Crosby,** William Holmes, Jr 1914- *AmMWSc 92*
**Crosby-Langley,** Loretta 1957- *WhoBlA 92*
**Crose,** Lester Alton 1912- *WhoRel 92*
**Crosen,** Robert Glenn, Jr 1931- *WhoIns 92*
**Crosfield,** Philip 1924- *Who 92*
**Croshaw,** Glenn R 1950- *WhoAmP 91*
**Crosier,** Billy M 1938- *WhoIns 92*
**Croslan,** John Arthur 1939- *WhoBlA 92*
**Crosland,** Anthony 1918-1977 *FacFETw*
**Crosland,** Margaret *WrDr 92*
**Crosland,** Margaret McQueen *IntAu&W 91*
**Crosland,** Maurice P. 1931- *WrDr 92*
**Crosland,** Philip Crawford 1943- *WhoFI 92*
**Crosland,** Susan Barnes *Who 92*
**Crosley,** David Risdon 1941- *AmMWSc 92*
**Crosman,** Gregory Paul 1950- *WhoEnt 92*
**Cross** *Who 92*
**Cross,** Viscont 1920- *Who 92*
**Cross,** Alexander Dennis 1932- *AmMWSc 92*
**Cross,** Alexander Galbraith 1908- *Who 92*
**Cross,** Alexander Urquhart 1906- *Who 92*
**Cross,** Alison 1950- *WhoEnt 92*
**Cross,** Amanda *WrDr 92*
**Cross,** Anthony Glenn 1936- *IntAu&W 91, Who 92, WrDr 92*
**Cross,** Austin Devon 1928- *WhoBlA 92*
**Cross,** Barry 1925- *IntWW 91, Who 92*
**Cross,** Ben 1947- *IntMPA 92*
**Cross,** Betty Jean 1946- *WhoBlA 92*
**Cross,** Beverley 1931- *IntAu&W 91, Who 92, WrDr 92*
**Cross,** Bonham E. Elwood *WhoMW 92*
**Cross,** Brenda *IntAu&W 91X, WrDr 92*
**Cross,** Carla Jean 1941- *WhoWest 92*
**Cross,** Carroll Edward 1935- *AmMWSc 92*
**Cross,** Charles Frederick 1855-1935 *FacFETw*
**Cross,** Charles Kenneth 1927- *AmMWSc 92*
**Cross,** Chester Joseph 1931- *WhoAmL 92*
**Cross,** Christopher 1951- *WhoEnt 92*
**Cross,** Christopher Charles 1952- *WhoAmL 92*
**Cross,** Claire 1932- *WrDr 92*
**Cross,** Clark Irwin 1913- *AmMWSc 92*
**Cross,** Clifford Thomas 1920- *Who 92*
**Cross,** Clinton Ferguson 1939- *WhoAmL 92*
**Cross,** Clyde Cleveland 1918- *WhoAmL 92*
**Cross,** Craig Travis 1951- *WhoFI 92*
**Cross,** David *WrDr 92*
**Cross,** David Ralston 1928- *AmMWSc 92*
**Cross,** Dennis Gerald 1945- *WhoAmL 92*
**Cross,** Dennis Ward 1943- *WhoFI 92*
**Cross,** Dolores E. 1938- *WhoBlA 92*
**Cross,** Dolores Evelyn 1938- *Who 92, WhoMW 92*
**Cross,** Donald Melvin 1935- *WhoAmP 91*
**Cross,** Dorothy 1956- *TwCPaSc*
**Cross,** Earle Albright, Jr 1925- *AmMWSc 92*
**Cross,** Edward F 1908- *AmMWSc 92*
**Cross,** Elmo Garnett, Jr 1942- *WhoAmP 91*
**Cross,** Elsa 1946- *ConSpAP*
**Cross,** Ernest James, Jr 1930- *AmMWSc 92*
**Cross,** Frank Bernard 1925- *AmMWSc 92*
**Cross,** Frank Leslie 1900-1968 *EncEarC*
**Cross,** George Alan Martin 1942- *AmMWSc 92, IntWW 91, Who 92*
**Cross,** George Elliot 1928- *AmMWSc 92*
**Cross,** George L 1905- *IntWW 91*
**Cross,** Gerald Howard 1933- *AmMWSc 92*
**Cross,** Gillian 1945- *WrDr 92*
**Cross,** Gillian Clare 1945- *IntAu&W 91*
**Cross,** Glenn Laban 1941- *WhoFI 92, WhoWest 92*
**Cross,** Haman, II 1949- *WhoRel 92*
**Cross,** Haman, Jr. 1949- *WhoBlA 92*
**Cross,** Hannah Margaret 1908- *Who 92*
**Cross,** Hardy 1885-1959 *FacFETw*
**Cross,** Harold Dick 1930- *AmMWSc 92*
**Cross,** Herbert James 1934- *WhoWest 92*
**Cross,** Hiram Russell 1944- *AmMWSc 92*
**Cross,** Ian 1925- *ConNov 91*
**Cross,** Irvie Keil 1917- *WhoRel 92*
**Cross,** J. Bruce 1949- *WhoAmL 92*
**Cross,** Jack 1926- *WhoBlA 92*
**Cross,** James *WrDr 92*
**Cross,** James Paul 1954- *WhoWest 92*
**Cross,** James Richard 1921- *Who 92*
**Cross,** James Thomas 1924- *AmMWSc 92*
**Cross,** Jane Ellen 1961- *WhoAmL 92*
**Cross,** Jayne Roberta 1953- *WhoFI 92*
**Cross,** Jeremy Ladd 1939- *WhoFI 92*
**Cross,** Jerry 1941- *WhoAmP 91*
**Cross,** Joan 1900- *Who 92*
**Cross,** John Keir 1914-1967 *TwCSFW 91*
**Cross,** John Milton 1915- *AmMWSc 92*
**Cross,** John Parson 1950- *AmMWSc 92*
**Cross,** John S. d1976 *LesBEnT 92*
**Cross,** John William 1947- *AmMWSc 92*
**Cross,** Jon Byron 1937- *AmMWSc 92*
**Cross,** June Victoria 1954- *WhoBlA 92, WhoEnt 92*
**Cross,** K. Patricia 1926- *IntWW 91, WhoWest 92, WrDr 92*
**Cross,** Kathleen Johnston 1952- *WhoFI 92*
**Cross,** Kenneth 1911- *Who 92*
**Cross,** Kenneth William d1990 *Who 92N*
**Cross,** Laura Elizabeth *WhoFI 92*
**Cross,** Lee Alan 1934- *AmMWSc 92*
**Cross,** Leland Briggs, Jr. 1930- *WhoAmL 92, WhoMW 92*
**Cross,** Leslie Eric 1923- *AmMWSc 92*
**Cross,** Margaret Natalie *Who 92*
**Cross,** Mary Harrington 1943- *WhoRel 92*
**Cross,** Michael Aduron 1944- *WhoAmP 91*
**Cross,** Mike W. 1960- *WhoRel 92*
**Cross,** Milton H. 1942- *WhoAmL 92*
**Cross,** Paul Edward 1948- *WhoWest 92*
**Cross,** Polton *TwCSFW 91, TwCWW 91*
**Cross,** Ralph Donald 1931- *AmMWSc 92*
**Cross,** Ralph Emerson 1910- *AmMWSc 92*
**Cross,** Ralph Herbert, III 1938- *AmMWSc 92*
**Cross,** Raymond 1948- *WhoAmL 92*
**Cross,** Richard James 1915- *AmMWSc 92*
**Cross,** Richard K. 1940- *WrDr 92*
**Cross,** Richard Lester 1943- *AmMWSc 92*
**Cross,** Robert Craigie 1911- *Who 92*
**Cross,** Robert Edward 1942- *AmMWSc 92*
**Cross,** Robert Franklin 1924- *AmMWSc 92*
**Cross,** Robert Leonard 1929- *WhoAmL 92*
**Cross,** Robert Roy 1935- *WhoIns 92*
**Cross,** Robert Wesley 1949- *WhoEnt 92*
**Cross,** Robert William 1937- *WhoFI 92*
**Cross,** Roger David 1947- *WhoAmP 91*
**Cross,** Ronald 1929- *WhoEnt 92*
**Cross,** Ronald Allan 1931- *AmMWSc 92*
**Cross,** Samuel S. 1919- *WhoAmL 92*
**Cross,** Stephen P 1938- *AmMWSc 92*
**Cross,** Steven Jasper 1954- *WhoFI 92*
**Cross,** Thomas B. 1949- *WrDr 92*
**Cross,** Thomas Gary 1947- *WhoFI 92*
**Cross,** Timothy Albert 1953- *AmMWSc 92*
**Cross,** Timothy Aureal 1946- *AmMWSc 92*
**Cross,** Tom 1931- *TwCPaSc*
**Cross,** Tom Peete 1879-1951 *DcNCBi 1*
**Cross,** Travis 1927- *WhoWest 92*
**Cross,** Victor *IntAu&W 91X, WrDr 92*
**Cross,** Virginia Rose 1950- *AmMWSc 92*
**Cross,** Wilbur 1918- *WrDr 92*
**Cross,** Wilbur L. 1862-1948 *BenetAL 91*
**Cross,** Wilbur Lucius 1862-1948 *FacFETw*
**Cross,** William 1936- *WhoAmP 91*
**Cross,** William Dennis 1940- *WhoAmL 92*
**Cross,** William Henley 1928- *AmMWSc 92*
**Cross,** William Howard 1946- *WhoBlA 92*
**Cross,** William Lee 1936- *WhoIns 92*
**Cross,** William Redmond 1959- *WhoFI 92*
**Crossan,** Donald Franklin 1926- *AmMWSc 92*
**Crossan,** G. D. 1950- *WrDr 92*
**Crossan,** Thomas Morrow 1819-1865 *DcNCBi 1*
**Crosse,** Gordon 1937- *ConCom 92, Who 92*
**Crosse,** St. George Idris Bryon 1939- *WhoBlA 92*
**Crossen,** Forest *DrAPF 91*
**Crossen,** Gary Charles 1951- *WhoAmL 92*
**Crossen,** Henry Morgan 1922- *WhoFI 92*
**Crosser,** Orrin Kingsbery 1929- *AmMWSc 92*
**Crossett,** Robert Nelson 1938- *Who 92*
**Crossfield,** A Scott 1921- *AmMWSc 92*
**Crossfield,** Scott 1921- *FacFETw*
**Crossin,** John William 1947- *WhoRel 92*
**Crossland,** Anthony 1931- *Who 92*
**Crossland,** Bernard 1923- *IntWW 91, Who 92*
**Crossland,** Harriet Kent 1902- *WhoWest 92*
**Crossland,** Ivan, Sr. *WhoHisp 92*
**Crossland,** Leonard 1914- *IntWW 91, Who 92*
**Crossland,** Peter Nelson 1937- *WhoAmP 91*
**Crossland,** Richard James 1943- *WhoFI 92*
**Crossland,** Ronald Arthur 1920- *Who 92*
**Crossley** *Who 92*
**Crossley,** Archibald M 1896-1985 *FacFETw*
**Crossley,** Celia Draper 1948- *WhoMW 92*
**Crossley,** Charles R., II 1938- *WhoBlA 92*
**Crossley,** David John 1944- *AmMWSc 92*
**Crossley,** DeRyee Ashton, Jr 1927- *AmMWSc 92*
**Crossley,** F R Erskine 1915- *AmMWSc 92*
**Crossley,** Frank Alphonso 1925- *AmMWSc 92, WhoBlA 92*
**Crossley,** Geoffrey Allan 1920- *Who 92*
**Crossley,** Gertrude Comilla 1925- *WhoAmP 91*
**Crossley,** Harry 1918- *Who 92*
**Crossley,** Nicholas John 1962- *Who 92*
**Crossley,** Patricia Kay 1953- *WhoAmL 92*
**Crossley,** Paul Christopher Richard 1944- *Who 92, WhoEnt 92*
**Crossley,** Peter Anthony 1939- *AmMWSc 92*
**Crossley,** Ralph John 1933- *Who 92*
**Crossley,** Vales, III 1957- *WhoEnt 92*
**Crossley-Holland,** Kevin 1941- *ConPo 91, WrDr 92*
**Crossley-Holland,** Kevin John William 1941- *IntAu&W 91, Who 92*
**Crosslin,** Evelyn Stocking 1919- *WhoBlA 92*
**Crossman,** David W 1946- *AmMWSc 92*
**Crossman,** Edwin John 1929- *AmMWSc 92*
**Crossman,** John Sherman 1943- *WhoWest 92*
**Crossman,** Kenneth Charles 1933- *WhoRel 92*
**Crossmon,** Germain Charles 1905- *AmMWSc 92*
**Crossner,** Kenneth Alan 1946- *AmMWSc 92*
**Crosson,** Albert J. 1934- *WhoWest 92*
**Crosson,** John Albert 1961- *WhoWest 92*
**Crosson,** Robert *DrAPF 91*
**Crosson,** Robert Scott 1938- *AmMWSc 92*
**Crossway,** Anne 1953- *WhoWest 92*
**Crosswhite,** Carol D 1940- *AmMWSc 92*
**Crosswhite,** F Joe 1929- *AmMWSc 92*
**Crosswhite,** Frank Samuel 1940- *AmMWSc 92*
**Crosswhite,** Henry Milton, Jr 1919- *AmMWSc 92*
**Crosswhite,** Vernon David 1955- *WhoWest 92*
**Crosthwait,** Timothy Leland 1915- *Who 92*
**Crosthwaite,** John Leslie 1940- *AmMWSc 92*
**Crotch,** George Robert 1842-1874 *BiInAmS*
**Crotch,** William 1775-1847 *NewAmDM*
**Croteau,** Denis 1932- *WhoWest 92*
**Croteau,** Rodney 1945- *AmMWSc 92*
**Crothers,** Donald M 1937- *AmMWSc 92*
**Crothers,** Rachel 1878-1958 *BenetAL 91, FacFETw*
**Crothers,** Samuel McChord 1857-1927 *BenetAL 91*
**Crotts,** Stephen Michael 1950- *WhoRel 92*
**Crotty,** Edward J 1923- *WhoAmP 91*
**Crotty,** Edward John 1923- *WhoAmP 91*
**Crotty,** Leo William 1927- *WhoFI 92*
**Crotty,** Richard Thomas 1948- *WhoAmP 91*
**Crotty,** Robert Bell 1951- *WhoAmL 92*
**Crotty,** William Joseph 1922- *AmMWSc 92*
**Crotwell,** James M 1940- *WhoIns 92*
**Crotzer,** Herbert W *ScFEYrs*
**Crouch,** Andrae 1942- *WhoBlA 92*
**Crouch,** Anthony Lee 1957- *WhoRel 92*
**Crouch,** Austin 1870-1957 *RelLAm 91*
**Crouch,** Billy G 1930- *AmMWSc 92*
**Crouch,** Colin John 1944- *Who 92*
**Crouch,** David 1919- *Who 92*
**Crouch,** Eduard Clyde *AmMWSc 92*
**Crouch,** Gary L. 1941- *WhoFI 92*
**Crouch,** Glenn LeRoy 1929- *AmMWSc 92*
**Crouch,** H Chester 1871-1903 *BiInAmS*
**Crouch,** James E. 1948- *WhoMW 92*
**Crouch,** James Ellis 1952- *WhoAmL 92*
**Crouch,** James Ensign 1908- *AmMWSc 92*
**Crouch,** Joyce K 1935- *WhoAmP 91*
**Crouch,** Leon 1928- *WhoRel 92*
**Crouch,** Madge Louise 1919- *AmMWSc 92*
**Crouch,** Marcus 1913- *IntAu&W 91*
**Crouch,** Marcus S. 1913- *WrDr 92*
**Crouch,** Marshall Fox 1920- *AmMWSc 92*
**Crouch,** Martha Louise 1951- *AmMWSc 92*
**Crouch,** Norman Albert 1940- *AmMWSc 92*
**Crouch,** Paul Franklin 1934- *WhoEnt 92, WhoFI 92, WhoRel 92*
**Crouch,** Robert Allen 1955- *WhoBlA 92*
**Crouch,** Robert Andrew 1959- *WhoRel 92*
**Crouch,** Robert J 1939- *AmMWSc 92*
**Crouch,** Robert P, Jr 1948- *WhoAmP 91*
**Crouch,** Roger Keith 1940- *AmMWSc 92*
**Crouch,** Ronald Gene, Sr. 1952- *WhoRel 92*
**Crouch,** Stanley *DrAPF 91*
**Crouch,** Stanley Ross 1940- *AmMWSc 92*
**Crouch,** Thomas Gene 1933- *WhoAmP 91*
**Crouch,** W. Eugene 1945- *WhoRel 92*
**Crouch,** William Henry 1928- *WhoRel 92*
**Crouchett,** Lawrence Paul 1922- *WhoBlA 92*
**Crough,** Daniel Francis 1936- *WhoAmL 92, WhoFI 92*
**Crounse,** Nathan Norman 1917- *AmMWSc 92*
**Crounse,** Robert Griffith 1931- *AmMWSc 92*
**Crousaz,** Jean-Pierre de 1663-1750 *BlkwCEP*
**Crouse,** Dale McClish 1941- *AmMWSc 92*
**Crouse,** David Austin 1944- *AmMWSc 92*
**Crouse,** David J, Jr 1920- *AmMWSc 92*
**Crouse,** Farrell R. 1963- *WhoAmL 92*
**Crouse,** Gail 1923- *AmMWSc 92*
**Crouse,** Gray F 1949- *AmMWSc 92*
**Crouse,** Helen Virginia *AmMWSc 92*
**Crouse,** Jeanne M. 1956- *WhoAmL 92*
**Crouse,** Joseph Robert 1946- *WhoAmL 92*
**Crouse,** Lawrence William 1955- *WhoAmL 92*
**Crouse,** Lindsay 1948- *IntMPA 92, WhoEnt 92*
**Crouse,** Philip Charles 1951- *AmMWSc 92*
**Crouse,** Russel 1893-1966 *BenetAL 91*
**Crouse,** Stephen Gary 1955- *WhoRel 92*
**Crouse,** Terry Edwin 1954- *WhoRel 92*
**Crouse,** William Arnold, Jr. 1939- *WhoRel 92*
**Crouse,** William Charles 1944- *WhoRel 92*
**Croushore,** Bruce Joseph 1947- *WhoAmL 92*
**Crout,** John J 1937- *WhoIns 92*
**Crout,** John Richard 1929- *AmMWSc 92*
**Crouter,** Richard Earl 1937- *WhoRel 92*
**Crouthamel,** Carl Eugene 1920- *AmMWSc 92*
**Crouthamel,** Steven John 1945- *WhoWest 92*
**Crouthamel,** William Guy 1942- *AmMWSc 92*
**Crouther,** Betty Jean 1950- *WhoBlA 92*
**Crouther,** Betty M. 1931- *WhoBlA 92*
**Crouther,** Melvin S., Jr. 1926- *WhoBlA 92*
**Crouzet,** Francois Marie-Joseph 1922- *IntWW 91*
**Crovetti,** Aldo Joseph 1930- *AmMWSc 92*
**Crovitz,** Louis Gordon 1958- *WhoFI 92*
**Crow,** Allan Brian 1953- *WhoAmP 91*
**Crow,** Bill 1927- *WhoEnt 92*
**Crow,** Bobby C *WhoAmP 91*
**Crow,** Carl A, Jr 1951- *WhoAmP 91*
**Crow,** Charles Delmar 1945- *WhoFI 92*
**Crow,** Charles Lloyd 1940- *WhoMW 92*
**Crow,** Dolores J *WhoAmP 91*
**Crow,** Edwin Lee 1939- *AmMWSc 92*
**Crow,** Edwin Louis 1916- *AmMWSc 92, WhoWest 92*
**Crow,** Frank Warren 1951- *AmMWSc 92*
**Crow,** Franklin Romig 1917- *AmMWSc 92*
**Crow,** Fredrick Walter 1954- *WhoAmL 92*
**Crow,** Garrett Eugene 1942- *AmMWSc 92*
**Crow,** Hershal Hilliar, Jr 1935- *WhoAmP 91*
**Crow,** Hiawatha Moore 1907- *WhoBlA 92*

**Crow,** Hilary Stephen 1934- *Who 92*
**Crow,** Jack Emerson 1939- *AmMWSc 92*
**Crow,** James F. 1916- *IntWW 91*
**Crow,** James Franklin 1916- *AmMWSc 92*
**Crow,** Jerald Donald 1941- *WhoAmL 92*
**Crow,** John H 1942- *AmMWSc 92*
**Crow,** John W. 1937- *IntWW 91*
**Crow,** Lynne Campbell Smith 1942- *WhoFI 92*
**Crow,** Mary *DrAPF 91*
**Crow,** Michael J. 1955- *WhoAmL 92*
**Crow,** Nancy Rebecca 1948- *WhoAmL 92*
**Crow,** Nedra Ann *WhoWest 92*
**Crow,** Neil Byrne 1927- *WhoWest 92*
**Crow,** Olen Dean 1944- *WhoMW 92*
**Crow,** Paul Abernathy, Jr. 1931- *WhoMW 92, WhoRel 92*
**Crow,** Robin Clyde 1943- *WhoAmL 92*
**Crow,** Sam Alfred 1926- *WhoAmL 92, WhoMW 92*
**Crow,** Stephen Monroe 1949- *WhoMW 92*
**Crow,** Terry Tom 1931- *AmMWSc 92*
**Crow,** Timothy John 1938- *Who 92*
**Crow,** Todd William 1945- *WhoEnt 92*
**Crowden,** Graham 1922- *ConTFT 9*
**Crowden,** James Gee Pascoe 1927- *Who 92*
**Crowder,** Barbara Lynn 1956- *WhoAmL 92, WhoMW 92*
**Crowder,** Bonnie Walton 1916- *WhoEnt 92*
**Crowder,** Charles Harper, Jr 1927- *WhoAmP 91*
**Crowder,** Constance Rankin 1952- *WhoEnt 92*
**Crowder,** David Lester 1941- *WhoWest 92*
**Crowder,** Elizabeth *WhoEnt 92*
**Crowder,** Enoch Herbert 1859-1932 *FacFETw*
**Crowder,** F. Petre 1919- *Who 92*
**Crowder,** Gene Autrey 1936- *AmMWSc 92*
**Crowder,** Larry A 1942- *AmMWSc 92*
**Crowder,** Larry Bryant 1950- *AmMWSc 92*
**Crowder,** Norman Harry 1926- *Who 92*
**Crowder,** Robert McKnight 1944- *WhoAmP 91*
**Crowdus,** Gary Alan 1945- *WhoEnt 92*
**Crowdy,** Joseph Porter 1923- *Who 92*
**Crowdy,** William Saunders 1847-1908 *RelLAm 91*
**Crowe,** Arlene Joyce 1931- *AmMWSc 92*
**Crowe,** Brian Lee 1938- *Who 92*
**Crowe,** Cameron Macmillan 1931- *AmMWSc 92*
**Crowe,** Cecily *IntAu&W 91*
**Crowe,** Cecily Bentley *WrDr 92*
**Crowe,** Christopher 1928- *AmMWSc 92*
**Crowe,** David Burns 1930- *AmMWSc 92*
**Crowe,** Dennis Timothy, Jr 1946- *AmMWSc 92*
**Crowe,** Dewey E, II 1947- *WhoAmP 91*
**Crowe,** Donald Warren 1927- *AmMWSc 92*
**Crowe,** George Joseph 1921- *AmMWSc 92*
**Crowe,** Gerald Patrick 1930- *Who 92*
**Crowe,** James Joseph 1935- *WhoFI 92*
**Crowe,** James Quell 1949- *WhoFI 92*
**Crowe,** John *IntAu&W 91X, WrDr 92*
**Crowe,** John H 1943- *AmMWSc 92*
**Crowe,** John T. 1938- *WhoAmL 92, WhoFI 92, WhoWest 92*
**Crowe,** Kenneth Morse 1926- *AmMWSc 92*
**Crowe,** Matthew James 1957- *WhoFI 92*
**Crowe,** Norma Jean 1938- *WhoAmP 91*
**Crowe,** Patrick J 1944- *WhoIns 92*
**Crowe,** Philip Anthony 1936- *Who 92*
**Crowe,** Ralph Vernon d1990 *Who 92N*
**Crowe,** Richard Godfrey, Jr 1944- *AmMWSc 92*
**Crowe,** Robert William 1924- *WhoAmL 92*
**Crowe,** Sylvia 1901- *Who 92*
**Crowe,** Thaddeus Lawson 1960- *WhoEnt 92*
**Crowe,** Thomas Joseph 1964- *WhoFI 92*
**Crowe,** Thomas Kealey 1957- *WhoAmL 92*
**Crowe,** Tonya *WhoEnt 92*
**Crowe,** William J, Jr 1925- *WhoAmP 91*
**Crowe,** William James, Jr. 1925- *IntWW 91*
**Crowel,** Kenneth Glen 1933- *WhoMW 92*
**Crowell,** Bernard G. 1930- *WhoBlA 92*
**Crowell,** Clara 1944- *WhoMW 92*
**Crowell,** Clarence Robert 1928- *AmMWSc 92*
**Crowell,** Dianne Eldert 1937- *WhoEnt 92*
**Crowell,** Donald Rex 1943- *WhoAmP 91*
**Crowell,** Edwin Patrick 1934- *AmMWSc 92*
**Crowell,** Elizabeth Ann 1939- *WhoAmP 91*
**Crowell,** Frances Elisabeth 1875-1950 *HanAmWH*
**Crowell,** Gilbert Earl 1952- *WhoRel 92*
**Crowell,** Hamblin Howes 1913- *AmMWSc 92*
**Crowell,** James Foster 1848-1915 *BiInAmS*
**Crowell,** John 1780-1846 *DcNCBi 1*
**Crowell,** John B, Jr 1930- *WhoAmP 91*
**Crowell,** John Chambers 1917- *AmMWSc 92*
**Crowell,** John Franklin 1857-1931 *DcNCBi 1*
**Crowell,** John Marshall 1942- *AmMWSc 92*
**Crowell,** Julian 1934- *AmMWSc 92*
**Crowell,** Kenneth Earl 1957- *WhoFI 92*
**Crowell,** Kenneth L 1933- *AmMWSc 92*
**Crowell,** Larry Gene 1941- *WhoAmL 92*
**Crowell,** Merton Howard 1932- *AmMWSc 92*
**Crowell,** Norman H 1873- *ScFEYrs*
**Crowell,** Peter Martin 1943- *WhoEnt 92*
**Crowell,** Richard Henry 1928- *AmMWSc 92*
**Crowell,** Richard Lane 1930- *AmMWSc 92*
**Crowell,** Robert Lamson 1945- *WhoAmL 92, WhoAmP 91*
**Crowell,** Robert Merrill 1921- *AmMWSc 92*
**Crowell,** Rodney J. 1950- *WhoEnt 92*
**Crowell,** Sears, Jr 1909- *AmMWSc 92*
**Crowell,** Thomas Irving 1921- *AmMWSc 92*
**Crowell,** Wayne Allen 1940- *AmMWSc 92*
**Crowell-Moustafa,** Julia J. 1923- *WhoBlA 92*
**CroweTipton,** Vaughn Eric 1962- *WhoRel 92*
**Crowfoot,** Anthony Bernard 1936- *Who 92*
**Crowhurst,** Viscount 1983- *Who 92*
**Crowl,** Philip A. 1914-1991 *ConAu 134*
**Crowl,** Richard Bern 1931- *WhoFI 92*
**Crowl,** Robert Harold 1925- *AmMWSc 92*
**Crowle,** Alfred John 1930- *AmMWSc 92*
**Crowle,** Sandi Jean 1963- *WhoEnt 92*
**Crowley,** Aleister 1875-1947 *FacFETw*
**Crowley,** Aleister Edward 1875-1947 *RelLAm 91*
**Crowley,** Carol Dee 1931- *IntAu&W 91*
**Crowley,** Christina 1945- *WhoEnt 92, WhoWest 92*
**Crowley,** David James 1942- *WhoAmL 92*
**Crowley,** David Joseph 1934- *WhoWest 92*
**Crowley,** Diane 1939- *ConAu 135*
**Crowley,** Don W *WhoAmP 91*
**Crowley,** Eileen Lopez 1949- *WhoHisp 92*
**Crowley,** Ellen 1916- *WhoAmP 91*
**Crowley,** Frederic Charles 1944- *WhoAmL 92, WhoAmP 91*
**Crowley,** George Clement 1916- *Who 92*
**Crowley,** Graham 1950- *TwCPaSc*
**Crowley,** Hank 1918- *WhoAmP 91*
**Crowley,** James Farrell 1946- *WhoFI 92*
**Crowley,** James M 1942- *WhoIns 92*
**Crowley,** James M 1949- *AmMWSc 92*
**Crowley,** James Patrick 1943- *AmMWSc 92*
**Crowley,** James Worthington 1930- *WhoAmL 92*
**Crowley,** John 1941- *Who 92*
**Crowley,** John 1942- *SmATA 65 [port], TwCSFW 91, WrDr 92*
**Crowley,** John Crane 1919- *WhoWest 92*
**Crowley,** John Desmond 1938- *Who 92*
**Crowley,** John J, Jr 1928- *WhoAmP 91*
**Crowley,** John James 1946- *AmMWSc 92*
**Crowley,** John Ward 1938- *WhoAmL 92*
**Crowley,** Joseph 1962- *WhoAmP 91*
**Crowley,** Joseph Michael 1940- *AmMWSc 92*
**Crowley,** Joseph Neil 1933- *WhoWest 92*
**Crowley,** Joseph R. 1915- *WhoRel 92*
**Crowley,** Lawrence Grandjean 1919- *AmMWSc 92*
**Crowley,** Leonard James 1921- *WhoRel 92*
**Crowley,** Leonard Vincent 1926- *AmMWSc 92*
**Crowley,** Maria Elena Perez *WhoHisp 92*
**Crowley,** Mart 1935- *WrDr 92*
**Crowley,** Mary V 1919- *WhoAmP 91*
**Crowley,** Michael Summers 1928- *AmMWSc 92*
**Crowley,** Nathaniel J, Sr *WhoAmP 91*
**Crowley,** Neely Dowall 1950- *WhoFI 92*
**Crowley,** Niall 1926- *Who 92*
**Crowley,** Pat 1938- *WhoEnt 92*
**Crowley,** Patrick Arthur 1941- *AmMWSc 92*
**Crowley,** Patrick C. 1951- *WhoEnt 92*
**Crowley,** Paul William 1949- *WhoAmP 91*
**Crowley,** Philip Haney 1946- *AmMWSc 92*
**Crowley,** Stephen Richard 1950- *WhoMW 92*
**Crowley,** Thomas Henry 1924- *AmMWSc 92*
**Crowley,** Thomas M 1935- *WhoAmP 91*
**Crowley,** Timothy Charles 1948- *WhoFI 92*
**Crowley,** William F *WhoIns 92*
**Crowley,** William Francis, Jr 1943- *AmMWSc 92*
**Crowley,** William Robert 1948- *AmMWSc 92*
**Crowley-Milling,** Denis 1919- *Who 92*
**Crowley-Milling,** Michael Crowley 1917- *Who 92*
**Crown,** David Allan 1928- *IntAu&W 91, WrDr 92*
**Crown,** Henry 1896-1990 *AnObit 1990*
**Crown,** Lester 1925- *WhoFI 92, WhoMW 92*
**Crowne,** John 1641?-1712? *RfGEnL 91*
**Crownfield,** David Ring 1930- *WhoMW 92, WhoRel 92*
**Crownover,** Richard McCranie 1936- *AmMWSc 92*
**Crowson,** Charles Neville 1919- *AmMWSc 92*
**Crowson,** Dan Michael 1953- *WhoWest 92*
**Crowson,** Daniel Alford 1945- *WhoAmL 92*
**Crowson,** Henry L 1927- *AmMWSc 92*
**Crowson,** James Lawrence 1938- *WhoAmL 92*
**Crowson,** P. S. 1913- *WrDr 92*
**Crowson,** Richard Borman 1929- *Who 92*
**Crowston,** Wallace Bruce Stewart 1934- *WhoFI 92*
**Crowther,** C Richard 1924- *AmMWSc 92*
**Crowther,** Clarence Edward 1929- *WhoRel 92*
**Crowther,** Derek *Who 92*
**Crowther,** Eric 1924- *Who 92*
**Crowther,** Harold Francis 1920- *WrDr 92*
**Crowther,** James Earl 1930- *WhoAmL 92*
**Crowther,** Leslie *IntMPA 92*
**Crowther,** Michael 1946- *TwCPaSc*
**Crowther,** Robert Hamblett 1925- *AmMWSc 92, WhoFI 92*
**Crowther,** Stanley 1925- *Who 92*
**Crowther,** Thomas Rowland 1937- *Who 92*
**Crowther,** William Ronald Hilton 1941- *Who 92*
**Crowther-Hunt,** Norman Crowther 1920-1987 *ConAu 133*
**Croxall,** Willard 1910- *AmMWSc 92*
**Croxdale,** Judith Gerow 1941- *AmMWSc 92*
**Croxford,** Lynne Louise 1947- *WhoFI 92*
**Croxon,** Raymond Patrick Austin 1928- *Who 92*
**Croxton,** C. A. 1945- *WrDr 92*
**Croxton,** Charles 1958- *WhoEnt 92*
**Croxton,** Frank Cutshaw 1907- *AmMWSc 92*
**Croxton,** Frederick E. d1991 *NewYTBS 91*
**Croxton,** Frederick E. 1899-1991 *ConAu 133*
**Croxton-Smith,** Claude 1901- *Who 92*
**Croy,** Daniel Albert 1951- *WhoRel 92*
**Croy,** Homer 1883-1965 *BenetAL 91*
**Croy,** Lavoy I 1930- *AmMWSc 92*
**Croy,** Sandra Lee 1950- *WhoFI 92*
**Croydon,** Archdeacon of *Who 92*
**Croydon,** Bishop Suffragan of 1936- *Who 92*
**Croydon,** John Edward Kenneth 1929- *Who 92*
**Crozaz,** Ghislaine M 1939- *AmMWSc 92*
**Crozier,** Andrew 1943- *ConPo 91, WrDr 92*
**Crozier,** Arthur Alger 1856-1899 *BiInAmS*
**Crozier,** Brian 1918- *WrDr 92*
**Crozier,** Brian Rossiter 1918- *IntAu&W 91, IntWW 91, Who 92*
**Crozier,** Edgar Daryl 1939- *AmMWSc 92*
**Crozier,** Eric John 1914- *Who 92*
**Crozier,** Lorna 1948- *ConPo 91, WrDr 92*
**Crozier,** Lorna Jean 1948- *IntAu&W 91*
**Crozier,** Mike 1943- *WhoAmP 91*
**Crozier,** William 1897-1930 *TwCPaSc*
**Crozier,** William 1930- *TwCPaSc*
**Crozier,** William Marshall, Jr. 1932- *WhoFI 92*
**Cruce,** Doug 1947- *WhoAmP 91*
**Cruce,** William L R 1942- *AmMWSc 92*
**Cruddace,** Raymond Gibson 1936- *AmMWSc 92*
**Cruddas,** Thomas Rennison 1921- *Who 92*
**Cruden,** David Milne 1942- *AmMWSc 92*
**Cruden,** John, Jr. d1786? *DcNCBi 1*
**Cruden,** John Charles 1946- *WhoAmL 92*
**Cruden,** Robert William 1936- *AmMWSc 92, WhoMW 92*
**Crudup,** Gwendolyn M. 1961- *WhoBlA 92*
**Crudup,** Josiah 1791-1872 *DcNCBi 1*
**Crudup,** W. *WhoRel 92*
**Crudup,** Warren George, Sr. 1923- *WhoRel 92*
**Crue,** Benjamin Lane, Jr. 1925- *WhoWest 92*
**Cruea,** Dudley 1956- *WhoAmP 91*
**Cruea,** Edmond D. *IntMPA 92*
**Cruel,** Ronnie 1957- *WhoRel 92*
**Cruess,** Leigh Saunders 1958- *WhoFI 92*
**Cruess,** Richard Leigh 1929- *AmMWSc 92*
**Cruess,** Susan Andrews 1957- *WhoFI 92*
**Cruft,** Edgar Frank 1933- *WhoFI 92*
**Cruft,** John Herbert 1914- *Who 92*
**Cruger,** F. Christopher 1935- *WhoMW 92*
**Cruice,** William James 1937- *AmMWSc 92*
**Cruickshank,** Alexander Middleton 1919- *AmMWSc 92*
**Cruickshank,** Alistair Ronald 1944- *Who 92*
**Cruickshank,** Donald Gordon 1942- *Who 92*
**Cruickshank,** Durward William John 1924- *IntWW 91, Who 92*
**Cruickshank,** Eric Kennedy 1914- *Who 92*
**Cruickshank,** Herbert James 1912- *Who 92*
**Cruickshank,** John 1924- *Who 92, WrDr 92*
**Cruickshank,** John Alexander 1920- *Who 92*
**Cruickshank,** Michael James 1929- *AmMWSc 92, WhoWest 92*
**Cruickshank,** P A 1929- *AmMWSc 92*
**Cruikshank,** Dale Paul 1939- *AmMWSc 92*
**Cruikshank,** David C 1946- *WhoIns 92*
**Cruikshank,** Donald Burgoyne, Jr 1939- *AmMWSc 92, WhoMW 92*
**Cruikshank,** Margaret Mordecai Jones 1878-1955 *DcNCBi 1*
**Cruikshank,** Thomas Henry 1931- *WhoFI 92*
**Cruise,** Donald Richard 1934- *AmMWSc 92*
**Cruise,** James E 1925- *AmMWSc 92*
**Cruise,** Julianne Marie 1962- *WhoAmL 92*
**Cruise,** R David 1956- *WhoAmP 91*
**Cruise,** Tom 1962- *ConTFT 9, IntMPA 92, IntWW 91, WhoEnt 92*
**Cruise,** Warren Michael 1939- *WhoBlA 92*
**Cruise,** Yvette *WhoEnt 92*
**Crull,** Timm F. 1931- *WhoWest 92*
**Crum,** Albert B. 1931- *WhoBlA 92*
**Crum,** Alfreda Foster 1953- *WhoRel 92*
**Crum,** Edward Hibbert 1940- *AmMWSc 92*
**Crum,** Floyd M 1922- *AmMWSc 92*
**Crum,** Gary Robert 1942- *WhoFI 92*
**Crum,** George Francis, Jr. 1926- *WhoEnt 92*
**Crum,** Glen F 1925- *AmMWSc 92*
**Crum,** Howard Alvin 1922- *AmMWSc 92*
**Crum,** James Davidson 1930- *AmMWSc 92*
**Crum,** James Francis 1934- *WhoMW 92*
**Crum,** James Louis 1940- *WhoEnt 92*
**Crum,** John Bradford 1952- *WhoWest 92*
**Crum,** John Kistler 1936- *AmMWSc 92, WhoFI 92*
**Crum,** Lawrence Arthur 1941- *AmMWSc 92*
**Crum,** Ralph G 1930- *AmMWSc 92*
**Crumb,** Candace Hertneky 1940- *WhoWest 92*
**Crumb,** George 1929- *FacFETw, IntWW 91, NewAmDM*
**Crumb,** George Henry 1929- *ConCom 92, WhoEnt 92*
**Crumb,** Glenn Howard 1927- *AmMWSc 92*
**Crumb,** Stephen Franklin 1920- *AmMWSc 92*
**Crumbaker,** Don E *WhoAmP 91*
**Crumbley,** Alex *WhoAmP 91*
**Crumbley,** R. Alex 1942- *WhoAmL 92*
**Crumbly,** Douglas Garner 1962- *WhoRel 92*
**Crumbly,** John Quantock 1916- *WhoRel 92*
**Crume,** Enyeart Charles, Jr 1931- *AmMWSc 92*
**Crumes,** William Edward 1914- *WhoRel 92*
**Crumley,** James *DrAPF 91*
**Crumley,** James 1939- *TwCWW 91, WrDr 92*
**Crumley,** James Robert, Jr. 1925- *WhoRel 92*
**Crumley,** John Walter 1944- *WhoAmL 92*
**Crumm,** David Mark 1955- *WhoRel 92*
**Crummell,** Alexander 1819-1898 *RelLAm 91*
**Crummett,** Warren B 1922- *AmMWSc 92*
**Crummy,** Andrew B 1930- *AmMWSc 92*
**Crummy,** Pressley Lee 1906- *AmMWSc 92*
**Crump,** Anne Goodwin 1962- *WhoAmL 92*
**Crump,** Arthel Eugene 1947- *WhoBlA 92*
**Crump,** Barry 1935- *IntAu&W 91, WrDr 92*
**Crump,** Charles H. *DrAPF 91*
**Crump,** Dewey G 1946- *WhoAmP 91*
**Crump,** Earl Alexander 1900-1960 *DcNCBi 1*
**Crump,** Francis Jefferson, III 1942- *WhoAmL 92*
**Crump,** Gerald Franklin 1935- *WhoAmL 92, WhoWest 92*
**Crump,** Gwyn Norman, Sr. 1932- *WhoWest 92*
**Crump,** Janice Renae 1947- *WhoBlA 92*
**Crump,** Jesse Franklin 1927- *AmMWSc 92*
**Crump,** John C, III 1940- *AmMWSc 92*
**Crump,** John William 1932- *AmMWSc 92*
**Crump,** Julianne Juanita 1950- *WhoWest 92*

**Crump,** Kenny Sherman 1939- *AmMWSc 92*
**Crump,** Malcolm Hart 1926- *AmMWSc 92*
**Crump,** Martha Lynn 1946- *AmMWSc 92*
**Crump,** Maurice 1908- *Who 92*
**Crump,** Nathaniel L., Sr. 1920- *WhoBlA 92*
**Crump,** Ronald Cordell 1951- *WhoAmL 92*
**Crump,** Stuart Faulkner 1921- *AmMWSc 92*
**Crump,** Susan Waite 1947- *WhoAmL 92*
**Crump,** Terry Richard 1946- *WhoFI 92*
**Crump,** Wayne F 1950- *WhoAmP 91*
**Crump,** Wilbert S. *WhoBlA 92*
**Crump,** William Henry Howes 1903- *Who 92*
**Crump,** William L. 1920- *WhoBlA 92*
**Crump,** William Maurice Esplen *Who 92*
**Crump,** William Wade 1926- *WhoWest 92*
**Crumpacker,** David Wilson 1929- *AmMWSc 92*
**Crumpecker,** Bradbury Robinson 1950- *WhoFI 92*
**Crumpler,** Ambrose Blackman 1863-1952 *RelLAm 91*
**Crumpler,** Thomas Bigelow 1909- *AmMWSc 92*
**Crumplin,** Colin 1946- *TwCPaSc*
**Crumpton,** Evelyn 1924- *WhoWest 92*
**Crumpton,** Michael Joseph 1929- *IntWW 91, Who 92*
**Crumrine,** David Shafer 1944- *AmMWSc 92, WhoMW 92*
**Crupper,** Clay 1935- *WhoAmP 91*
**Crusa,** Michael Charles 1947- *WhoWest 92*
**Crusberg,** Theodore Clifford 1941- *AmMWSc 92*
**Cruse,** Allan Baird 1941- *WhoWest 92*
**Cruse,** Carl Max 1936- *AmMWSc 92*
**Cruse,** Charles Plummer 1914- *WhoBlA 92*
**Cruse,** David C. *DrAPF 91*
**Cruse,** Denton W. 1944- *WhoWest 92*
**Cruse,** Fredrich James 1947- *WhoAmL 92*
**Cruse,** Harold Wright 1916- *WhoBlA 92*
**Cruse,** Irma Russell 1911- *IntAu&W 91*
**Cruse,** Julius Major, Jr 1937- *AmMWSc 92*
**Cruse,** Leonard Arthur 1941- *WhoAmL 92*
**Cruse,** Peggy *WhoAmP 91*
**Cruse,** Rex Beach, Jr. 1941- *WhoFI 92*
**Cruse,** Richard M 1950- *AmMWSc 92*
**Cruse,** Robert Ridgely 1920- *AmMWSc 92*
**Cruser,** Stephen Alan 1942- *AmMWSc 92*
**Crusoe,** Edwin *DrAPF 91*
**Crusoe,** James Michael 1956- *WhoRel 92*
**Crusto,** Mitchell Ferdinand 1953- *WhoBlA 92*
**Crutcher,** Betty Neal 1949- *WhoBlA 92*
**Crutcher,** Chris 1946- *ConAu 36NR*
**Crutcher,** Edward Torrence 1920- *WhoBlA 92*
**Crutcher,** Gabriel *WhoRel 92*
**Crutcher,** Harold L 1913- *AmMWSc 92*
**Crutcher,** Harold Trabue, Jr. 1938- *WhoMW 92*
**Crutcher,** Harry, III 1938- *WhoAmP 91*
**Crutcher,** John William 1916- *WhoAmP 91, WhoFI 92*
**Crutcher,** Keith A 1953- *AmMWSc 92*
**Crutcher,** Richard Metcalf 1945- *AmMWSc 92*
**Crutcher,** Ronald Andrew 1947- *WhoBlA 92*
**Crutcher,** Ronald James 1954- *WhoAmP 91*
**Crutchfield,** Alexander R., Jr. 1958- *WhoWest 92*
**Crutchfield,** Charlie 1928- *AmMWSc 92*
**Crutchfield,** Edward Elliott, Jr. 1941- *WhoFI 92*
**Crutchfield,** Inez *WhoAmP 91*
**Crutchfield,** James N. 1947- *WhoBlA 92*
**Crutchfield,** James Patrick 1955- *WhoWest 92*
**Crutchfield,** Marvin Mack 1934- *AmMWSc 92, WhoMW 92*
**Crutchfield,** Sabrina Dames 1957- *WhoBlA 92*
**Crutchfield,** Susan Ellis 1940- *WhoBlA 92*
**Crutchfield,** Will *WhoEnt 92*
**Crutchfield,** William Ward 1928- *WhoAmP 91*
**Crutchfield-Baker,** Verdenia 1958- *WhoBlA 92*
**Crutchley,** Brooke 1907- *Who 92*
**Crutchley,** Donald Osborne 1927- *WhoAmP 91*
**Crute,** Beverly Jean *WhoRel 92*
**Cruthers,** James 1924- *Who 92*
**Cruthers,** Larry Randall 1945- *AmMWSc 92*
**Cruthird,** J. Robert Lee 1944- *WhoBlA 92*
**Cruthird,** Robert Lee 1944- *WhoMW 92*
**Cruthirds,** Elizabeth Rennix 1952- *WhoEnt 92*
**Crutsinger,** Robert Keane 1930- *WhoFI 92*
**Cruttwell,** Geraldine *Who 92*
**Cruttwell,** Hugh 1918- *Who 92*
**Cruyff,** Johan 1947- *FacFETw*
**Cruz,** Abraham 1949- *WhoHisp 92*
**Cruz,** Albert Raymond 1933- *WhoHisp 92*
**Cruz,** Alexander 1941- *AmMWSc 92*
**Cruz,** Amada Lourdes 1961- *WhoHisp 92*
**Cruz,** Anatolio Benedicto, Jr 1933- *AmMWSc 92*
**Cruz,** Antonio L. *WhoHisp 92*
**Cruz,** Aurelio R. 1934- *WhoHisp 92*
**Cruz,** B. Roberto 1941- *WhoHisp 92*
**Cruz,** Ben Ruben 1918- *WhoHisp 92*
**Cruz,** Benjamin J *WhoAmP 91*
**Cruz,** Benjamin Joseph Franquez 1951- *WhoAmL 92*
**Cruz,** Carlos 1940- *AmMWSc 92, WhoHisp 92*
**Cruz,** Celia *WhoHisp 92*
**Cruz,** Daniel 1941- *WhoHisp 92*
**Cruz,** Daniel Louis 1951- *WhoHisp 92*
**Cruz,** David Ramirez 1961- *WhoRel 92*
**Cruz,** Emilio 1938- *WhoBlA 92*
**Cruz,** Erasmo, Sr. 1940- *WhoHisp 92*
**Cruz,** Felix Miguel 1958- *WhoHisp 92*
**Cruz,** Gilbert R. 1929- *WhoHisp 92*
**Cruz,** Gregory A. *WhoHisp 92*
**Cruz,** Iluminado Angeles 1936- *WhoBlA 92*
**Cruz,** Joaquim Carvalho 1963- *BlkOlyM [port]*
**Cruz,** John F *WhoAmP 91*
**Cruz,** John Frank 1936- *WhoHisp 92*
**Cruz,** Jose B, Jr 1932- *AmMWSc 92*
**Cruz,** Joseph *WhoHisp 92*
**Cruz,** Juan Sanjurjo 1924- *WhoHisp 92*
**Cruz,** Juana Ines de la 1648-1695 *BenetAL 91*
**Cruz,** Juana Ines de la 1651-1695 *HisDSpE*
**Cruz,** Julia Margarita 1948- *WhoHisp 92*
**Cruz,** Julio C 1934- *AmMWSc 92*
**Cruz,** Mamerto Manahan, Jr 1918- *AmMWSc 92*
**Cruz,** Maria 1961- *WhoRel 92*
**Cruz,** Maximo Leonardo 1939- *WhoHisp 92*
**Cruz,** Michael J. 1952- *WhoHisp 92*
**Cruz,** Migdalia 1958- *WhoHisp 92*
**Cruz,** Phillip 1955- *WhoHisp 92*
**Cruz,** Raymond 1953- *WhoHisp 92*
**Cruz,** Renee 1960- *WhoEnt 92*
**Cruz,** Ruben 1956- *WhoHisp 92*
**Cruz,** Secundino 1938- *WhoHisp 92*
**Cruz,** Silvia 1959- *WhoHisp 92*
**Cruz,** Tim R. 1959- *WhoHisp 92*
**Cruz,** Victor Hernandez 1949- *ConPo 91, WhoHisp 92, WrDr 92*
**Cruz,** Vincent, Jr. 1957- *WhoAmL 92*
**Cruz,** Virgil 1929- *WhoBlA 92*
**Cruz,** Wilfredo *WhoHisp 92*
**Cruz,** Willie *WhoHisp 92*
**Cruz-Aponte,** Ramon Aristides 1927- *WhoHisp 92*
**Cruz-Diez,** Carlos 1923- *IntWW 91*
**Cruz-Emeric,** Jorge A. 1951- *WhoHisp 92*
**Cruz-Rodriguez,** Escolastico 1931- *WhoHisp 92*
**Cruz Rodriguez,** Roberto *WhoAmP 91*
**Cruz-Romo,** Gilda *WhoEnt 92, WhoHisp 92*
**Cruz-Uribe,** Eugene David 1952- *WhoWest 92*
**Cruz-Velez,** David F 1951- *WhoAmP 91*
**Cruz-Velez,** David Francisco 1951- *WhoHisp 92*
**Cruzado,** George *WhoHisp 92*
**Cruzan,** Earl 1913- *WhoRel 92*
**Cruzan,** John 1942- *AmMWSc 92*
**Cruzan,** Lee Ann 1957- *WhoMW 92*
**Cruzan,** Nancy 1957?-1990 *News 91, -91-3*
**Cruzat,** Edward Pedro 1926- *WhoBlA 92*
**Cruzat,** Gwendolyn S. *WhoBlA 92*
**Cruze,** Deborah Kaye 1957- *WhoWest 92*
**Cruze,** James 1884-1942 *IntDcF 2-2 [port]*
**Cruze,** John Joseph 1943- *WhoAmL 92*
**Cruzeiro,** Maria-Manuela da Silva Nunes R 1934- *IntWW 91*
**Cruzkatz,** Ida Maria *DrAPF 91*
**Crvenkovski,** Krste 1921- *IntWW 91*
**Crwys-Williams,** David Owen 1940- *Who 92*
**Cryan,** Kenneth Jarvis 1954- *WhoFI 92*
**Cryans,** Andrew William 1947- *WhoRel 92*
**Cryberg,** Richard Lee 1941- *AmMWSc 92, WhoMW 92*
**Cryer,** Colin Walker 1935- *AmMWSc 92*
**Cryer,** Dennis Robert 1944- *AmMWSc 92*
**Cryer,** Jon 1965- *IntMPA 92, WhoEnt 92*
**Cryer,** Jonathan D 1939- *AmMWSc 92*
**Cryer,** Linkston T. 1933- *WhoBlA 92*
**Cryer,** Philip Eugene 1940- *AmMWSc 92*
**Cryer,** Robert 1934- *Who 92*
**Cryer,** Rodger Earl 1940- *WhoWest 92*
**Crynes,** Billy Lee 1938- *AmMWSc 92*
**Crystal,** Billy 1947- *IntMPA 92, IntWW 91, WhoEnt 92*
**Crystal,** David 1941- *IntAu&W 91, Who 92, WrDr 92*
**Crystal,** Eleanor *WhoRel 92*
**Crystal,** George Jeffrey 1948- *AmMWSc 92*
**Crystal,** James William 1937- *WhoFI 92*
**Crystal,** Jonathan Andrew 1943- *WhoFI 92*
**Crystal,** Lester *LesBEnT 92*
**Crystal,** Maxwell Melvin 1924- *AmMWSc 92*
**Crystal,** Michael 1948- *Who 92*
**Crystal,** Paul 1955- *WhoEnt 92*
**Crystal,** Ronald George 1941- *AmMWSc 92*
**Crystal,** Vearl Charles 1919- *WhoAmP 91*
**Crystall,** Joseph N. 1922- *WhoEnt 92*
**Csaky,** A. S. *WhoEnt 92*
**Csaky,** Susan Dischka 1926- *WhoAmL 92*
**Csaky,** Tihamer Zoltan 1915- *AmMWSc 92*
**Csallany,** Agnes Saari 1932- *AmMWSc 92*
**Csanady,** Gabriel Tibor 1925- *AmMWSc 92*
**Csanyi-Salcedo,** Zoltan F. 1964- *WhoHisp 92*
**Csaplar,** Kenneth Androvett 1956- *WhoFI 92*
**Csaszar,** Akos 1924- *IntWW 91*
**Csavinszky,** Peter John 1931- *AmMWSc 92*
**Csehak,** Judit 1940- *IntWW 91*
**Csejka,** David Andrew 1935- *AmMWSc 92*
**Csejtey,** Bela, Jr 1934- *AmMWSc 92*
**Csendes,** Ernest 1926- *AmMWSc 92, WhoFI 92, WhoWest 92*
**Csermely,** Thomas J 1931- *AmMWSc 92*
**Cserna,** Eugene George 1920- *AmMWSc 92*
**Cserr,** Helen F 1937- *AmMWSc 92*
**C'Shiva,** Oya *WhoBlA 92*
**Csicsery,** Sigmund Maria 1929- *AmMWSc 92*
**Csikos-Nagy,** Bela 1915- *IntWW 91*
**Csikszentmiha'lyi,** Miha'ly 1934- *IntWW 91*
**Csiky,** Stanford Allan 1947- *WhoMW 92*
**Csokor,** Franz Theodor 1885-1969 *LiExTwC*
**Csonka,** Paul L 1938- *AmMWSc 92*
**Csorgo,** Miklos 1932- *AmMWSc 92*
**Cua,** Antonio S. 1932- *IntAu&W 91, WrDr 92*
**Cuadra,** Carlos A 1925- *AmMWSc 92*
**Cuadra,** Julio C. 1946- *WhoHisp 92*
**Cuadra,** Pablo Antonio 1912- *ConSpAP*
**Cuadra Landrove,** Angel 1931- *LiExTwC*
**Cuadrado,** John J. *WhoHisp 92*
**Cuadros,** Alvaro Julio 1926- *WhoHisp 92*
**Cuany,** Robin Louis 1926- *AmMWSc 92*
**Cuarenta,** Jayne Stephanie 1959- *WhoHisp 92*
**Cuaron,** Alicia Valladolid 1939- *WhoHisp 92*
**Cuaron,** Marco A. 1944- *WhoHisp 92*
**Cuartas,** Francisco Ignacio 1939- *WhoHisp 92*
**Cuatrecasas,** Jose 1903- *AmMWSc 92*
**Cuatrecasas,** Pedro 1936- *AmMWSc 92, WhoHisp 92*
**Cuatrecasas,** Pedro Martin 1936- *IntWW 91*
**Cuauhtemoc** d1525 *HisDSpE*
**Cuba,** Jill Anne 1963- *WhoAmL 92*
**Cubar,** John Charles 1952- *WhoAmL 92*
**Cubas,** Jose M. *WhoHisp 92*
**Cubberley,** Adrian H 1918- *AmMWSc 92*
**Cubberley,** Ellwood Patterson 1868-1941 *DcAmImH*
**Cubberley,** Virginia 1946- *AmMWSc 92*
**Cubbon,** Brian 1928- *Who 92*
**Cubbon,** John Hamilton 1911- *Who 92*
**Cubeiro,** Emilio *DrAPF 91*
**Cubena** 1941- *WhoHisp 92*
**Cubeta,** Michael John, Jr 1951- *WhoAmP 91*
**Cubeta,** Paul 1925- *WrDr 92*
**Cubeta,** Philip B. 1949- *WhoFI 92*
**Cubicciotti,** Daniel David 1921- *AmMWSc 92*
**Cubides,** Carlos 1931- *WhoHisp 92*
**Cubie,** George 1943- *Who 92*
**Cubillas,** Teofilo 1949- *WhoHisp 92*
**Cubillos,** Robert Hernan 1957- *WhoRel 92*
**Cubillos Sallato,** Hernan 1936- *IntWW 91*
**Cubin,** Barbara L 1946- *WhoAmP 91*
**Cubine,** Margaret Virginia 1919- *WhoRel 92*
**Cubita,** Peter Naylor 1957- *WhoAmL 92*
**Cubitt** *Who 92*
**Cubitt,** Hugh 1928- *Who 92*
**Cubitt,** James 1914- *TwCPaSc*
**Cubitto,** Robert J. 1950- *WhoAmL 92*
**Cucci,** Anthony *WhoAmP 91*
**Cucci,** Cesare Eleuterio 1925- *AmMWSc 92*
**Cucci,** Edward Arnold 1944- *WhoMW 92*
**Cucco,** Ulisse P. 1929- *WhoMW 92*
**Cuchens,** Marvin A 1948- *AmMWSc 92*
**Cucin,** Robert Louis 1946- *WhoAmL 92*
**Cucina,** Vincent Robert 1936- *WhoWest 92*
**Cuckney,** John 1925- *Who 92*
**Cuckney,** John Graham 1925- *IntWW 91*
**Cucu,** Vasile 1927- *IntWW 91*
**Cuculo,** John Anthony 1924- *AmMWSc 92*
**Cudaback,** David Dill 1929- *AmMWSc 92*
**Cudaback,** Jim D 1938- *WhoAmP 91*
**Cudahy,** Richard D. 1926- *WhoAmL 92, WhoAmP 91*
**Cuddihy,** Micky 1952- *TwCPaSc*
**Cuddihy,** Robert Vincent, Jr. 1959- *WhoFI 92*
**Cuddon,** J. A. 1928- *WrDr 92*
**Cuddon,** John Anthony Bowden 1928- *IntAu&W 91*
**Cuddy,** C. Emery 1943- *WhoAmL 92*
**Cuddy,** David Warren 1952- *WhoAmP 91*
**Cuddy,** William Francis, Jr. 1949- *WhoRel 92*
**Cude,** Bobby Lee 1925- *WhoEnt 92*
**Cude,** Joe E 1939- *AmMWSc 92*
**Cude,** Willis Augustus, Jr 1922- *AmMWSc 92*
**Cuden,** Craig Thomas 1957- *WhoAmL 92*
**Cuderman,** Jerry Ferdinand 1935- *AmMWSc 92*
**Cudjoe,** Selwyn Reginald 1943- *WhoBlA 92*
**Cudkowicz,** Leon 1923- *WhoMW 92*
**Cudlipp** *Who 92*
**Cudlipp,** Baron 1913- *IntWW 91, Who 92*
**Cudlipp,** Michael John 1934- *Who 92*
**Cudlipp,** Reginald 1910- *Who 92*
**Cudmore,** Dana 1954- *ConAu 134*
**Cudmore,** Laurence E. *WhoMW 92*
**Cudney,** Gerald Edward 1941- *WhoRel 92*
**Cudnowski,** David Peter 1959- *WhoAmL 92*
**Cudworth,** Allen L. 1929- *WhoFI 92*
**Cudworth,** Clair William 1942- *WhoMW 92*
**Cudworth,** Jack 1930- *TwCPaSc*
**Cudworth,** Kyle McCabe 1947- *AmMWSc 92, WhoMW 92*
**Cudworth,** Nick 1947- *TwCPaSc*
**Cue,** Berkeley Wendell, Jr 1947- *AmMWSc 92*
**Cue,** Nelson 1941- *AmMWSc 92*
**Cuebas-Incle,** Esteban Luis 1955- *WhoHisp 92*
**Cuelho,** Art, Jr. *DrAPF 91*
**Cuellar,** Alfredo 1946- *WhoHisp 92*
**Cuellar,** Benjamin 1942- *WhoHisp 92*
**Cuellar,** Enrique Roberto 1955- *WhoHisp 92*
**Cuellar,** Evelio *WhoHisp 92*
**Cuellar,** Fernando Daniel 1941- *WhoHisp 92*
**Cuellar,** Gilbert, Jr. *WhoHisp 92*
**Cuellar,** Henry 1955- *WhoAmP 91*
**Cuellar,** Jose B. 1941- *WhoHisp 92*
**Cuellar,** Luis E. 1962- *WhoHisp 92*
**Cuellar,** Luis Loretto, Jr. 1956- *WhoMW 92*
**Cuellar,** Michael J. 1956- *WhoHisp 92*
**Cuellar,** Mike 1937- *WhoHisp 92*
**Cuellar,** Orlando 1934- *AmMWSc 92, WhoHisp 92*
**Cuellar,** Raul David 1951- *WhoMW 92*
**Cuellar,** Renato 1927- *WhoAmP 91, WhoHisp 92*
**Cuellar,** Robert 1949- *WhoHisp 92*
**Cuellar,** Robert Aleman 1939- *WhoFI 92*
**Cuellar,** Salvador M., Jr. 1949- *WhoHisp 92*
**Cuello,** Jose *WhoHisp 92*
**Cuenca,** Peter Nicolas 1943- *WhoHisp 92*
**Cuenod,** Hugues 1902- *NewAmDM, Who 92*
**Cuenod,** Ronald Pillot, Jr. 1958- *WhoFI 92*
**Cuenz,** Caspar d1752 *BlkwCEP*
**Cuesta,** Yolanda *WhoHisp 92*
**Cuestas,** David *WhoHisp 92*
**Cuestas,** Felix Vincent 1934- *WhoRel 92*
**Cueto,** Cipriano, Jr 1923- *AmMWSc 92*
**Cueto,** Jose Manuel 1924- *WhoHisp 92*
**Cueto,** Luis M. 1931- *WhoHisp 92*
**Cuevas,** Betty 1953- *WhoHisp 92*
**Cuevas,** Carlos 1941- *WhoHisp 92*
**Cuevas,** Carlos M. 1951- *WhoHisp 92*
**Cuevas,** David 1947- *WhoHisp 92*
**Cuevas,** Helen 1952- *WhoHisp 92*
**Cuevas,** Hipolito 1966- *WhoHisp 92*
**Cuevas,** Jose, Jr. *WhoHisp 92*
**Cuevas,** Jose Luis 1934- *IntWW 91*
**Cuevas,** Joseph B. 1942- *WhoHisp 92*
**Cuevas,** Rosemary 1958- *WhoAmL 92*
**Cuevas Cancino,** Francisco 1921- *IntWW 91, Who 92*
**Cuff,** David J 1933- *AmMWSc 92*
**Cuff,** George Wayne 1923- *WhoBlA 92*
**Cuffari,** Richard 1925-1978 *SmATA 66 [port]*
**Cuffe,** Paul 1759-1817 *RComAH*
**Cuffe,** Stafford Sigesmund 1949- *WhoMW 92*
**Cuffee,** Jeffrey Townsend 1928-1987 *WhoBlA 92N*
**Cuffey,** Kenneth Hugh 1956- *WhoRel 92*
**Cuffey,** Roger James 1939- *AmMWSc 92*
**Cuffin,** B Neil 1941- *AmMWSc 92*

**Cugat,** Xavier 1900-1990 *AnObit 1990, CurBio 91N, FacFETw, NewAmDM, News 91*
**Cugell,** David Wolf 1923- *AmMWSc 92*
**Cuhtahlatah** *EncAmaz 91*
**Cui Junzhi** *IntWW 91*
**Cui Naifu** 1928- *IntWW 91*
**Cui Yueli** 1920- *IntWW 91*
**Cui,** Cesar Antonovich 1835-1918 *NewAmDM*
**Cuiffo,** Frank Wayne 1943- *WhoAmL 92*
**Cuil De Stratclut,** Alecsandr A. 1931- *WhoFI 92*
**Cuitlahuac** 1476-1520 *HisDSpE*
**Cujec,** Bibijana Dobovisek 1926- *AmMWSc 92*
**Cukier,** Robert Isaac 1944- *AmMWSc 92*
**Cukierski,** Matthew John 1958- *WhoWest 92*
**Cuko,** Lenka 1938- *IntWW 91*
**Cukor,** George d1983 *LesBEnT 92*
**Cukor,** George 1899-1983 *FacFETw, IntDcF 2-2 [port]*
**Cukor,** Peter 1936- *AmMWSc 92*
**Cukuras,** Valdemar Michael 1915- *WhoRel 92*
**Culberg,** Paul S. 1942- *IntMPA 92*
**Culberson,** Charles Henry 1943- *AmMWSc 92*
**Culberson,** Chicita Frances 1931- *AmMWSc 92*
**Culberson,** Dan 1941- *WhoEnt 92*
**Culberson,** David Christopher 1961- *WhoRel 92*
**Culberson,** Guy, Jr. 1930- *WhoRel 92*
**Culberson,** James Lee 1941- *AmMWSc 92*
**Culberson,** John 1956- *WhoAmP 91*
**Culberson,** Oran L 1921- *AmMWSc 92*
**Culberson,** William Louis 1929- *AmMWSc 92*
**Culbert,** Bill 1935- *TwCPaSc*
**Culbert,** John Robert 1914- *AmMWSc 92*
**Culbert,** John Taylor 1955- *WhoMW 92*
**Culbert,** Patrick 1948- *WhoAmP 91*
**Culbertson,** Billy Muriel 1929- *AmMWSc 92, WhoMW 92*
**Culbertson,** Clyde Gray 1906- *AmMWSc 92*
**Culbertson,** Edwin Charles 1950- *AmMWSc 92*
**Culbertson,** Ely 1891-1955 *AmPeW*
**Culbertson,** Frances Mitchell 1921- *WhoMW 92*
**Culbertson,** George Edward 1937- *AmMWSc 92*
**Culbertson,** James Thomas 1911- *WhoWest 92*
**Culbertson,** John Mathew 1921- *WhoMW 92*
**Culbertson,** Mark H. 1960- *WhoEnt 92*
**Culbertson,** Marvin Criddle, Jr. 1927- *WhoRel 92*
**Culbertson,** Matthew 1967- *WhoRel 92*
**Culbertson,** Philip Edgar 1925- *WhoFI 92*
**Culbertson,** Philip Leroy 1944- *WhoRel 92*
**Culbertson,** Townley Payne 1929- *AmMWSc 92*
**Culbertson,** William 1905-1971 *RelLAm 91*
**Culbertson,** William Loren 1949- *WhoMW 92*
**Culbertson,** William Richardson 1916- *AmMWSc 92*
**Culbreath,** Joshua 1932- *BlkOlyM*
**Culbreath,** Tongila M. 1959- *WhoBlA 92*
**Culbreth,** Judith Elizabeth 1943- *AmMWSc 92*
**Culbreth,** Ronnie *WhoAmP 91*
**Culham,** Michael John 1933- *Who 92*
**Culhane,** James Edward 1941- *WhoAmL 92*
**Culhane,** John Leonard *Who 92*
**Culhane,** John William 1934- *WhoEnt 92*
**Culhane,** Rosalind *Who 92*
**Culhane,** Shamus 1908- *WhoEnt 92*
**Culick,** Fred E C 1933- *AmMWSc 92*
**Culkin,** Cynthia Ann 1955- *WhoWest 92*
**Culkin,** Macaulay 1980- *IntMPA 92, NewYTBS 91 [port], News 91 [port], -91-3 [port]*
**Cull,** Chris Alan 1947- *WhoWest 92*
**Cullan,** David J. 1940- *WhoAmL 92*
**Cullan,** David James 1940- *WhoAmP 91*
**Cullati,** Arthur G *AmMWSc 92*
**Cullberg,** Brigit Ragnhild 1908- *IntWW 91*
**Cullearn,** David 1941- *TwCPaSc*
**Cullen,** Lord 1935- *Who 92*
**Cullen,** Abbey Boyd, Jr 1915- *AmMWSc 92*
**Cullen,** Alexander Lamb 1920- *AmMWSc 92, IntWW 91, Who 92*
**Cullen,** Bill d1990 *LesBEnT 92*
**Cullen,** Bill 1920-1990 *AnObit 1990*
**Cullen,** Bruce F 1940- *AmMWSc 92*
**Cullen,** Charles G 1932- *AmMWSc 92*
**Cullen,** Christopher Terrence 1958- *WhoWest 92*
**Cullen,** Countee 1903-1946 *BenetAL 91, BlkLC [port], FacFETw, LiExTwC*
**Cullen,** Daniel Edward 1942- *AmMWSc 92, WhoFI 92*
**Cullen,** David A *WhoAmP 91*
**Cullen,** Douglas *Who 92*
**Cullen,** E.J. *DrAPF 91*
**Cullen,** Edward John 1926- *Who 92*
**Cullen,** Glenn Wherry 1931- *AmMWSc 92*
**Cullen,** Gordon *Who 92*
**Cullen,** Harry Patrick, II 1949- *WhoRel 92*
**Cullen,** Helen Frances 1919- *AmMWSc 92*
**Cullen,** Jack Sydney George Bud 1927- *IntWW 91*
**Cullen,** James D. 1925- *WhoAmL 92*
**Cullen,** James Donald 1947- *WhoAmL 92*
**Cullen,** James Patrick 1944- *WhoFI 92*
**Cullen,** James Reynolds 1900- *Who 92*
**Cullen,** James Robert 1936- *AmMWSc 92*
**Cullen,** James Thaddeus, Jr. 1935- *WhoEnt 92*
**Cullen,** James V. 1938- *IntMPA 92*
**Cullen,** Jeffrey Paul 1951- *WhoFI 92*
**Cullen,** John *Who 92*
**Cullen,** John Knox 1936- *AmMWSc 92*
**Cullen,** Jonna Lynne 1941- *WhoAmP 91*
**Cullen,** Joseph Warren 1936- *AmMWSc 92*
**Cullen,** Marion Permilla 1931- *AmMWSc 92*
**Cullen,** Michael John 1945- *IntWW 91*
**Cullen,** Michael Joseph 1945- *AmMWSc 92*
**Cullen,** Mike 1927- *WhoAmP 91*
**Cullen,** Patrick 1949- *TwCPaSc*
**Cullen,** Paula Bramsen *DrAPF 91*
**Cullen,** Randolph Fenton 1955- *WhoRel 92*
**Cullen,** Raymond 1913- *Who 92*
**Cullen,** Robert 1949- *ConAu 134*
**Cullen,** Robert John 1949- *WhoWest 92*
**Cullen,** Stephen Leonard, Jr. 1940- *WhoFI 92*
**Cullen,** Susan Elizabeth 1944- *AmMWSc 92*
**Cullen,** Terence Lindsay Graham 1930- *Who 92*
**Cullen,** Terrance Michael 1953- *WhoAmL 92*
**Cullen,** Theodore John 1928- *AmMWSc 92*
**Cullen,** Thomas d1689 *DcNCBi 1*
**Cullen,** Thomas Francis, Jr. 1949- *WhoAmL 92*
**Cullen,** Thomas Gordon 1914- *Who 92*
**Cullen,** Thomas M 1935- *AmMWSc 92*
**Cullen,** Timothy F 1944- *WhoAmP 91*
**Cullen,** William *WhoRel 92*
**Cullen,** William 1710-1790 *BlkwCEP*
**Cullen,** William, Jr. *DrAPF 91*
**Cullen,** William Charles 1919- *AmMWSc 92*
**Cullen,** William P 1954- *WhoIns 92*
**Cullen,** William Robert 1933- *AmMWSc 92*
**Cullen of Ashbourne,** Baron 1912- *Who 92*
**Cullenberg,** Ronald James 1946- *WhoAmL 92*
**Cullenberg,** Stephen Eugene 1953- *WhoWest 92*
**Cullenbine,** Roy d1991 *NewYTBS 91*
**Culler,** David Ethan 1959- *WhoWest 92*
**Culler,** Donald Merrill 1929- *AmMWSc 92*
**Culler,** F L, Jr 1923- *AmMWSc 92*
**Culler,** George F. 1956- *WhoFI 92*
**Culler,** Jonathan Dwight 1944- *WrDr 92*
**Cullerne-Brown,** Matthew 1956- *TwCPaSc*
**Cullers,** Randy Lee 1944- *WhoEnt 92*
**Cullers,** Robert Lee 1937- *AmMWSc 92*
**Cullers,** Samuel James *WhoBlA 92*
**Cullers,** Vincent T. *WhoBlA 92*
**Cullers-Delp,** Carolyn 1961- *WhoMW 92*
**Cullerton,** John James 1948- *WhoAmP 91*
**Cullerton,** Thomas W 1924- *WhoAmP 91*
**Culley,** Benjamin Hays 1913- *AmMWSc 92*
**Culley,** Dudley Dean, Jr 1937- *AmMWSc 92*
**Culley,** John Henry 1947- *WhoAmL 92*
**Culley,** Peter William 1943- *WhoAmL 92*
**Cullimore,** Charles Augustine Kaye 1933- *Who 92*
**Cullimore,** Colin Stuart 1931- *Who 92*
**Cullimore,** Denis Roy 1936- *AmMWSc 92*
**Cullimore,** Michael 1936- *TwCPaSc*
**Cullina,** William Michael 1921- *WhoAmL 92*
**Cullinan,** Alice Rae 1939- *WhoRel 92*
**Cullinan,** Brendan Peter 1927- *IntWW 91*
**Cullinan,** Charlotte 1959- *TwCPaSc*
**Cullinan,** Edward Horder 1931- *IntWW 91, Who 92*
**Cullinan,** Elizabeth *DrAPF 91*
**Cullinan,** Harry T, Jr 1938- *AmMWSc 92*
**Cullinane,** Charles Justin 1947- *WhoFI 92*
**Cullinane,** Thomas Paul 1942- *AmMWSc 92*
**Cullingford,** Eric Coome Maynard 1910- *Who 92*
**Cullingford,** Guy 1907- *WrDr 92*
**Cullingworth,** Barry 1929- *Who 92*
**Cullingworth,** J. Barry 1929- *WrDr 92*
**Cullins,** James Thomas 1930- *WhoAmP 91*
**Cullis,** Charles 1833-1892 *RelLAm 91*
**Cullis,** Charles Fowler 1922- *Who 92*
**Cullis,** Christopher Ashley 1945- *AmMWSc 92, WhoMW 92*
**Cullis,** Michael Fowler 1914- *Who 92*
**Cullis,** Pieter Rutter 1946- *AmMWSc 92*
**Cullison,** Arthur Edison 1914- *AmMWSc 92*
**Cullison,** Robert Virl 1936- *WhoAmP 91*
**Cullison,** William Lester 1931- *AmMWSc 92*
**Culliton,** Edward Milton 1906- *Who 92*
**Culliton,** Joseph Anthony 1948- *WhoEnt 92*
**Cullman,** Joseph Frederick, III 1912- *IntWW 91*
**Cullmann,** Oscar 1902- *DcEcMov, IntWW 91*
**Cullom,** Willis Richard 1867-1963 *DcNCBi 1*
**Cullum,** Jane Kehoe *AmMWSc 92*
**Cullum,** John 1930- *IntMPA 92*
**Cullum,** Leo Aloysius 1942- *WhoEnt 92*
**Cullum,** Malford Eugene 1951- *AmMWSc 92*
**Cullum,** Ridgewell 1867-1943 *TwCWW 91*
**Cullum,** Robert Francis 1932- *WhoRel 92*
**Cully,** Iris Virginia 1914- *WhoRel 92*
**Culmann,** Herbert Ernst 1921- *IntWW 91*
**Culme-Seymour,** Michael *Who 92*
**Culp,** Archie W 1931- *AmMWSc 92*
**Culp,** Arlie Franklin, Jr 1926- *WhoAmP 91*
**Culp,** Bobbie A 1947- *WhoAmP 91*
**Culp,** Carl Lester 1922- *WhoAmP 91*
**Culp,** Donald Allen 1938- *WhoAmL 92*
**Culp,** Donna Lea 1959- *WhoRel 92*
**Culp,** Frederick Lynn 1927- *AmMWSc 92*
**Culp,** Gary 1940- *WhoWest 92*
**Culp,** J Leah Nile 1939- *WhoAmL 92*
**Culp,** James David 1951- *WhoAmL 92*
**Culp,** Joe Bill 1938- *WhoEnt 92*
**Culp,** Joe Carl 1933- *WhoFI 92*
**Culp,** John H. 1907- *TwCWW 91, WrDr 92*
**Culp,** Kathy Kay 1961- *WhoMW 92*
**Culp,** Kenneth, Jr 1936- *WhoAmP 91*
**Culp,** Lloyd Anthony 1942- *AmMWSc 92*
**Culp,** Lyle Delane 1951- *WhoRel 92*
**Culp,** Mildred Louise 1949- *WhoFI 92, WhoWest 92*
**Culp,** Paula Newell 1941- *WhoEnt 92*
**Culp,** Robert 1930- *IntMPA 92, WhoEnt 92*
**Culp,** Robert D 1938- *AmMWSc 92*
**Culp,** Sandra Kay 1938- *WhoAmP 91*
**Culp,** Timothy A. 1958- *WhoRel 92*
**Culp,** William Reid, Jr. 1953- *WhoAmL 92*
**Culpeper,** Frances 1634-1690 *DcNCBi 1*
**Culpeper,** John 1633?-1692? *DcNCBi 1*
**Culpeper,** John 1764-1841 *DcNCBi 1*
**Culpepper,** Betty M. 1941- *WhoBlA 92*
**Culpepper,** Bobby L 1941- *WhoAmP 91*
**Culpepper,** David Charles 1946- *WhoAmL 92*
**Culpepper,** Dellie L. 1941- *WhoBlA 92*
**Culpepper,** George Bryant 1947- *WhoAmP 91*
**Culpepper,** John 1764-1841 *DcNCBi 1*
**Culpepper,** Lucy Nell 1951- *WhoBlA 92*
**Culpepper,** Robert Sammon 1927- *WhoWest 92*
**Culpepper,** Roy M 1947- *AmMWSc 92*
**Culshaw,** John Douglas 1927- *Who 92*
**Culter,** John Dougherty 1937- *WhoMW 92*
**Culton,** Paul Melvin 1932- *WhoWest 92*
**Culvahouse,** Arthur Boggess, Jr. 1948- *WhoAmL 92*
**Culvahouse,** Jack Wayne 1929- *AmMWSc 92*
**Culver,** Barbara Ann 1950- *WhoMW 92*
**Culver,** Barbara Green 1926- *WhoAmL 92, WhoAmP 91*
**Culver,** Bob Ed 1934- *WhoAmP 91*
**Culver,** Charles George 1937- *AmMWSc 92*
**Culver,** David Alan 1945- *AmMWSc 92*
**Culver,** David Clair 1944- *AmMWSc 92*
**Culver,** David M. 1924- *IntWW 91*
**Culver,** James F 1921- *AmMWSc 92*
**Culver,** John Andrew 1963- *WhoAmL 92*
**Culver,** John Blaine 1938- *WhoRel 92*
**Culver,** John C. 1932- *IntWW 91*
**Culver,** John Handy, III 1959- *WhoAmL 92*
**Culver,** Kenneth Earl 1956- *WhoWest 92*
**Culver,** Marjorie *DrAPF 91*
**Culver,** Maurice Edwin 1915- *WhoRel 92*
**Culver,** Rhonda 1960- *WhoBlA 92*
**Culver,** Richard S 1937- *AmMWSc 92*
**Culver,** Robert Elroy 1926- *WhoMW 92*
**Culver,** Roger Bruce 1940- *AmMWSc 92*
**Culver,** Roger Michael 1963- *WhoFI 92*
**Culver,** Timothy J *IntAu&W 91X, WrDr 92*
**Culver,** William Howard 1927- *AmMWSc 92*
**Culverwell,** Howard Glendon 1911- *WhoWest 92*
**Culverwell,** Ronald LeRoy 1936- *WhoFI 92*
**Culverwell,** Rosemary Jean 1934- *WhoMW 92*
**Culyer,** A. J. 1942- *WrDr 92*
**Culyer,** Anthony John 1942- *Who 92*
**Cumber,** John Alfred d1991 *Who 92N*
**Cumber,** Victoria Lillian 1920- *WhoBlA 92*
**Cumberbatch,** Ellis 1934- *AmMWSc 92*
**Cumberland,** Kenneth Brailey 1913- *IntAu&W 91, IntWW 91*
**Cumberland,** Richard 1732-1811 *RfGEnL 91*
**Cumberland,** William Edwin 1938- *WhoAmL 92*
**Cumberland,** William Glen 1948- *AmMWSc 92*
**Cumberlege** *Who 92*
**Cumberlege,** Baroness 1943- *Who 92*
**Cumberlege,** Marcus 1938- *ConPo 91, WrDr 92*
**Cumberlege,** Marcus Crossley 1938- *IntAu&W 91*
**Cumbey,** Constance Elizabeth 1944- *WhoMW 92*
**Cumbie,** Billy Glenn 1930- *AmMWSc 92*
**Cumbo,** Kattie M. *DrAPF 91*
**Cumbo,** Marion William 1899-1990 *WhoBlA 92N*
**Cumbrae,** Provost of *Who 92*
**Cumby,** George Edward 1956- *WhoBlA 92*
**Cuming,** Alexander 1690?-1775 *BiInAmS*
**Cuming,** Donald Runyon 1929- *WhoIns 92*
**Cuming,** Fred 1930- *TwCPaSc*
**Cuming,** Frederick George Rees 1930- *IntWW 91, Who 92*
**Cumings,** Anne Flower 1942- *WhoAmL 92*
**Cumiskey,** Mike 1940- *TwCPaSc*
**Cummer,** Jeffrey Alan 1957- *WhoFI 92*
**Cummerow,** Robert Leggett 1915- *AmMWSc 92*
**Cummin,** Alfred Samuel 1924- *AmMWSc 92, WhoFI 92, WhoMW 92*
**Cumming** *Who 92*
**Cumming,** Alan 1932- *Who 92*
**Cumming,** Bruce Gordon 1925- *AmMWSc 92*
**Cumming,** David 1943- *WhoAmL 92*
**Cumming,** Diana 1929- *TwCPaSc*
**Cumming,** George Anderson, Jr. 1942- *WhoAmL 92*
**Cumming,** George Leslie 1930- *AmMWSc 92*
**Cumming,** Glen Edward 1936- *WhoMW 92*
**Cumming,** James 1922- *TwCPaSc*
**Cumming,** James B 1928- *AmMWSc 92*
**Cumming,** Leslie Merrill 1925- *AmMWSc 92*
**Cumming,** Patricia *DrAPF 91*
**Cumming,** Peter 1951- *IntAu&W 91*
**Cumming,** Primrose 1915- *WrDr 92*
**Cumming,** Richard Jackson 1928- *WhoEnt 92*
**Cumming,** Robert *DrAPF 91*
**Cumming,** Robert 1945- *SmATA 65*
**Cumming,** Thomas Alexander 1937- *WhoFI 92, WhoWest 92*
**Cumming,** Valerie Lynn 1946- *Who 92*
**Cumming,** Virgil H 1945- *WhoIns 92*
**Cumming,** William 1724-1797? *DcNCBi 1*
**Cumming-Bruce,** Roualeyn Hovell-Thurlow- 1912- *Who 92*
**Cummings,** Albert R. 1940- *WhoBlA 92*
**Cummings,** Ann 1933- *WhoAmP 91*
**Cummings,** Barton 1946- *WhoEnt 92, WhoWest 92*
**Cummings,** Bill *WhoAmP 91*
**Cummings,** Bob d1990 *LesBEnT 92*
**Cummings,** Bob 1910-1990 *AnObit 1990*
**Cummings,** Brian Alfred 1961- *WhoWest 92*
**Cummings,** Cary, III 1949- *WhoBlA 92*
**Cummings,** Charles Arnold 1930- *AmMWSc 92*
**Cummings,** Charles Edward 1931- *WhoBlA 92*
**Cummings,** Charles Rogers 1930- *WhoAmL 92*
**Cummings,** Cimena McCane 1945- *WhoBlA 92*
**Cummings,** Clara Eaton 1855-1906 *BiInAmS*
**Cummings,** Constance *Who 92, WhoEnt 92*
**Cummings,** Constance 1910- *IntMPA 92, IntWW 91*
**Cummings,** Darold Bernard 1944- *WhoWest 92*
**Cummings,** Darrell William 1960- *WhoRel 92*
**Cummings,** David 1932- *AmMWSc 92, WhoWest 92*
**Cummings,** David K 1941- *WhoIns 92*
**Cummings,** Dennis Paul 1940- *AmMWSc 92*
**Cummings,** Diana K. 1943- *WhoEnt 92*

**Cummings**, Donald James 1941- *WhoFI 92*
**Cummings**, Donald Joseph 1930- *AmMWSc 92*
**Cummings**, Donald Wayne 1935- *WhoWest 92*
**Cummings**, Donna Louise 1944- *WhoBlA 92*
**Cummings**, E. E. 1894-1962 *BenetAL 91, ConLC 68 [port], FacFETw, LiExTwC, RComAH*
**Cummings**, E. Emerson 1917- *WhoBlA 92*
**Cummings**, Edmund George 1928- *AmMWSc 92*
**Cummings**, Edward 1861-1926 *RelLAm 91*
**Cummings**, Edward J., Jr. 1942- *WhoAmL 92*
**Cummings**, Elijah E 1951- *WhoAmP 91*
**Cummings**, Erwin Karl 1954- *WhoMW 92*
**Cummings**, Frances McArthur 1941- *WhoBlA 92*
**Cummings**, Frank 1929- *WhoAmL 92*
**Cummings**, Frank C. *WhoHisp 92*
**Cummings**, Frank C. 1929- *WhoRel 92*
**Cummings**, Frank Edson 1940- *AmMWSc 92*
**Cummings**, Frederick W 1931- *AmMWSc 92*
**Cummings**, George August 1927- *AmMWSc 92*
**Cummings**, George F. Davis 1955- *WhoWest 92*
**Cummings**, George H 1913- *AmMWSc 92*
**Cummings**, George W., III 1955- *WhoFI 92*
**Cummings**, Gregg Alex 1963- *WhoWest 92*
**Cummings**, J B d1896 *BilnAmS*
**Cummings**, Jack 1925- *TwCWW 91, WrDr 92*
**Cummings**, James Alexander 1952- *WhoRel 92*
**Cummings**, James C., Jr. 1929- *WhoBlA 92*
**Cummings**, John Albert 1931- *AmMWSc 92*
**Cummings**, John Francis 1936- *AmMWSc 92*
**Cummings**, John Patrick 1933- *AmMWSc 92*
**Cummings**, John Rhodes 1926- *AmMWSc 92*
**Cummings**, John Scott 1943- *Who 92*
**Cummings**, Josephine Anna 1949- *WhoEnt 92*
**Cummings**, Katina 1956- *WhoAmP 91*
**Cummings**, Kevin Bryan 1967- *WhoRel 92*
**Cummings**, Larry Jean 1937- *AmMWSc 92*
**Cummings**, Martha Clark *DrAPF 91*
**Cummings**, Martin Marc 1920- *AmMWSc 92*
**Cummings**, Merilyn Lloy 1939- *WhoMW 92*
**Cummings**, Michael R 1941- *AmMWSc 92*
**Cummings**, Milton C., Jr. 1933- *WrDr 92*
**Cummings**, Nancy Boucot 1927- *AmMWSc 92*
**Cummings**, Nicholas Andrew 1924- *WhoWest 92*
**Cummings**, Norman Allen 1935- *AmMWSc 92*
**Cummings**, Pat 1950- *SmATA 13AS [port]*
**Cummings**, Pat Marie 1950- *WhoBlA 92*
**Cummings**, Peter Thomas 1954- *AmMWSc 92*
**Cummings**, Quinn 1967- *WhoEnt 92*
**Cummings**, Ralph W. 1911- *IntWW 91*
**Cummings**, Ralph Waldo, Jr 1938- *AmMWSc 92*
**Cummings**, Randall Ray 1956- *WhoFI 92*
**Cummings**, Ray 1887-1957 *ScFEYrs, TwCSFW 91*
**Cummings**, Richard J. 1932- *WhoMW 92*
**Cummings**, Robert 1908-1990 *FacFETw*
**Cummings**, Robert 1910?-1990 *CurBio 91N*
**Cummings**, Roberta Spikes 1944- *WhoBlA 92*
**Cummings**, Ronald John 1933- *WhoMW 92*
**Cummings**, Russell Mark 1955- *WhoWest 92*
**Cummings**, Sam R. 1944- *WhoAmL 92*
**Cummings**, Sandy 1913- *IntMPA 92*
**Cummings**, Spangler 1936- *WhoWest 92*
**Cummings**, Stephen Emery 1955- *WhoFI 92*
**Cummings**, Stephen Thomas 1954- *WhoAmL 92*
**Cummings**, Sue Carol 1941- *AmMWSc 92*
**Cummings**, Terry 1961- *WhoBlA 92*
**Cummings**, Theresa Faith *WhoBlA 92*
**Cummings**, Thomas Fulton 1925- *AmMWSc 92*
**Cummings**, Walter J *WhoAmP 91*
**Cummings**, Walter J. 1916- *WhoAmL 92, WhoMW 92*
**Cummings**, William Charles 1932- *AmMWSc 92*
**Cummings**, William Robert, Jr. 1937- *WhoMW 92*
**Cummings**, Willis Nelson 1894- *WhoBlA 92*
**Cummins**, Alvin J 1919- *AmMWSc 92*
**Cummins**, Cecil Stratford 1918- *AmMWSc 92*
**Cummins**, Charles Fitch, Jr. 1939- *WhoAmL 92*
**Cummins**, David Gray 1936- *AmMWSc 92*
**Cummins**, Emery John 1937- *WhoWest 92*
**Cummins**, Ernie Lee 1921- *AmMWSc 92*
**Cummins**, Evelyn Freeman 1904- *WhoFI 92*
**Cummins**, Frank 1924- *Who 92*
**Cummins**, George David 1822-1876 *RelLAm 91*
**Cummins**, Gus 1943- *TwCPaSc*
**Cummins**, Harle Oren *ScFEYrs*
**Cummins**, Herman Z 1933- *AmMWSc 92*
**Cummins**, Jack D 1939- *AmMWSc 92*
**Cummins**, James *DrAPF 91*
**Cummins**, James E. 1943- *WhoMW 92*
**Cummins**, James Nelson 1925- *AmMWSc 92*
**Cummins**, John Frances 1939- *AmMWSc 92*
**Cummins**, John Stephen 1928- *WhoRel 92, WhoWest 92*
**Cummins**, Joseph E 1933- *AmMWSc 92*
**Cummins**, Kenneth Burdette 1911- *AmMWSc 92, WhoMW 92*
**Cummins**, Kenneth Copeland 1943- *WhoAmL 92*
**Cummins**, Kenneth William 1933- *AmMWSc 92*
**Cummins**, Larry Bill 1941- *AmMWSc 92*
**Cummins**, Maria Susanna 1827-1866 *BenetAL 91*
**Cummins**, Nancyellen Heckeroth 1948- *WhoWest 92*
**Cummins**, Paul Zach, II 1936- *WhoFI 92*
**Cummins**, Peggy 1925- *IntMPA 92*
**Cummins**, Richard L 1929- *AmMWSc 92*
**Cummins**, Richard Williamson 1920- *AmMWSc 92*
**Cummins**, Stewart Edward 1932- *AmMWSc 92, WhoMW 92*
**Cummins**, W Raymond 1944- *AmMWSc 92*
**Cummins**, Walter *DrAPF 91*
**Cummins**, William Lee 1947- *WhoRel 92*
**Cummiskey**, Charles 1924- *AmMWSc 92*
**Cummiskey**, Chris *WhoAmP 91*
**Cummiskey**, John William 1917- *WhoAmL 92*
**Cumpian**, Carlos *DrAPF 91, WhoHisp 92*
**Cunard**, Grace 1893-1967 *ReelWom [port]*
**Cunard**, Jeffrey Paul 1955- *WhoAmL 92*
**Cunat**, Ronald Frank 1934- *WhoMW 92*
**Cunconan-Lahr**, Robin Lynn 1960- *WhoAmL 92*
**Cundall and Addey** *DcLB 106*
**Cundall**, Charles 1890-1971 *TwCPaSc*
**Cundall**, David Langdon 1945- *AmMWSc 92*
**Cundall**, Donald R 1925- *WhoAmP 91*
**Cundall**, Joseph 1818-1895 *DcLB 106 [port]*
**Cundell**, Nora L.M. 1889-1948 *TwCPaSc*
**Cundiff**, Carl Copeland 1941- *WhoAmP 91*
**Cundiff**, John Howard *WhoBlA 92*
**Cundiff**, Larry Verl 1939- *AmMWSc 92*
**Cundiff**, Milford Mel Fields 1936- *AmMWSc 92*
**Cundiff**, Robert Hall 1922- *AmMWSc 92*
**Cundiff**, Victoria Anne 1955- *WhoAmL 92*
**Cundy**, Kenneth Raymond 1929- *AmMWSc 92*
**Cuneo**, Dennis Clifford 1950- *WhoAmL 92, WhoWest 92*
**Cuneo**, Donald Lane 1944- *WhoAmL 92*
**Cuneo**, John Frank 1945- *WhoFI 92*
**Cuneo**, Terence Tenison 1907- *Who 92*
**Cuney Hare**, Maud 1874-1936 *NotBlAW 92*
**Cunha**, Burke A 1942- *AmMWSc 92*
**Cunha**, Ireneu da Silva 1930- *WhoRel 92*
**Cunha**, John Henry, Jr. 1950- *WhoAmL 92*
**Cunha**, Juan 1910-1985 *ConSpAP*
**Cunha**, Mark Geoffrey 1955- *WhoAmL 92*
**Cunha**, Tony Joseph 1916- *AmMWSc 92*
**Cunhal**, Alvaro 1913- *IntWW 91*
**Cunia**, Tiberius 1926- *AmMWSc 92*
**Cunico**, Robert Frederick 1941- *AmMWSc 92*
**Cunill**, Ana Maria 1965- *WhoFI 92*
**Cunill**, Buenaventura Cesar 1935- *WhoHisp 92*
**Cuninghame**, John Christopher Foggo M. *Who 92*
**Cuninghame**, William Henry F. *Who 92*
**Cunliffe** *Who 92*
**Cunliffe**, Baron 1932- *Who 92*
**Cunliffe**, Barrington Windsor 1939- *Who 92*
**Cunliffe**, Barry 1939- *IntAu&W 91, WrDr 92*
**Cunliffe**, Christopher Joseph 1916- *Who 92*
**Cunliffe**, David *LesBEnT 92*
**Cunliffe**, David Ellis 1957- *Who 92*
**Cunliffe**, John 1933- *WrDr 92*
**Cunliffe**, Lawrence Francis 1929- *Who 92*
**Cunliffe**, Marcus 1922- *IntAu&W 91*
**Cunliffe**, Marcus 1922-1990 *AnObit 1990, SmATA 66*
**Cunliffe**, Peter Whalley 1926- *Who 92*
**Cunliffe**, Robert Lionel Brooke d1990 *Who 92N*
**Cunliffe**, Stella Vivian 1917- *Who 92*
**Cunliffe**, Thomas Alfred 1905- *Who 92*
**Cunliffe-Jones**, Hubert d1991 *Who 92N*
**Cunliffe-Lister** *Who 92*
**Cunliffe-Owen**, Hugo Dudley 1966- *Who 92*
**Cunnane**, James Joseph 1938- *WhoFI 92*
**Cunnane**, Joseph 1913- *Who 92*
**Cunnane**, Patricia S. 1946- *WhoWest 92*
**Cunnane**, Stephen C 1952- *AmMWSc 92*
**Cunnea**, William M 1927- *AmMWSc 92*
**Cunniff**, Patricia A 1938- *AmMWSc 92*
**Cunniff**, Patrick F 1933- *AmMWSc 92*
**Cunning**, Carol 1954- *WhoEnt 92*
**Cunning**, Joe David 1936- *AmMWSc 92*
**Cunningham**, Agnes 1923- *WhoRel 92*
**Cunningham**, Alexander Alan 1926- *Who 92*
**Cunningham**, Alfred Joe 1928- *WhoAmP 91*
**Cunningham**, Alice Jeanne 1937- *AmMWSc 92*
**Cunningham**, Ann d1647 *EncAmaz 91*
**Cunningham**, Arthur H. 1928- *WhoBlA 92*
**Cunningham**, Bennie Lee 1954- *WhoBlA 92*
**Cunningham**, Blenna A. 1946- *WhoBlA 92*
**Cunningham**, Bruce Arthur 1940- *AmMWSc 92*
**Cunningham**, Bryce A 1932- *AmMWSc 92*
**Cunningham**, Carol Clem 1938- *AmMWSc 92*
**Cunningham**, Carrie Katherine Richards 1877-1948 *AmPeW*
**Cunningham**, Cathy *WrDr 92*
**Cunningham**, Charles 1906- *Who 92*
**Cunningham**, Charles Baker, III 1941- *WhoFI 92*
**Cunningham**, Charles G 1940- *AmMWSc 92*
**Cunningham**, Charles Henry 1913- *AmMWSc 92, WhoMW 92*
**Cunningham**, Chet 1928- *TwCWW 91, WrDr 92*
**Cunningham**, Clarence Marion 1920- *AmMWSc 92*
**Cunningham**, Clark Edward 1934- *WhoMW 92*
**Cunningham**, Courtney 1962- *WhoBlA 92*
**Cunningham**, Dale Michael 1942- *WhoMW 92*
**Cunningham**, David 1924- *Who 92*
**Cunningham**, David A 1937- *AmMWSc 92*
**Cunningham**, David S., Jr. 1935- *WhoBlA 92*
**Cunningham**, David Scott 1961- *WhoRel 92*
**Cunningham**, Deborah Ann 1959- *WhoFI 92*
**Cunningham**, Dennis Dean 1939- *AmMWSc 92*
**Cunningham**, Dorothy J 1927- *AmMWSc 92*
**Cunningham**, Duane Lamar 1937- *WhoWest 92*
**Cunningham**, E. Brice 1931- *WhoBlA 92*
**Cunningham**, E. V. *WrDr 92*
**Cunningham**, Earlene Brown 1930- *AmMWSc 92*
**Cunningham**, Edward Patrick 1934- *IntWW 91*
**Cunningham**, Edward Preston, Jr. 1945- *WhoFI 92*
**Cunningham**, Ellen 1940- *WhoMW 92*
**Cunningham**, Ellen M 1940- *AmMWSc 92*
**Cunningham**, Eric DuPont 1957- *WhoFI 92*
**Cunningham**, Ernest 1936- *WhoAmP 91*
**Cunningham**, Erskine 1955- *WhoBlA 92*
**Cunningham**, Eugene 1896-1957 *TwCWW 91*
**Cunningham**, Evelyn 1936- *WhoAmP 91*
**Cunningham**, F. Malcolm 1927- *WhoBlA 92*
**Cunningham**, Fay Lavere 1922- *AmMWSc 92*
**Cunningham**, Floyd Mitchell 1931- *AmMWSc 92*
**Cunningham**, Frances Patricia 1937- *WhoRel 92*
**Cunningham**, Franklin E 1927- *AmMWSc 92*
**Cunningham**, Frederic, Jr 1921- *AmMWSc 92*
**Cunningham**, Frederick William 1902- *AmMWSc 92*
**Cunningham**, Gary Allen 1940- *WhoAmL 92*
**Cunningham**, George 1931- *Who 92*
**Cunningham**, George John 1906- *Who 92*
**Cunningham**, George Lewis, Jr 1923- *AmMWSc 92*
**Cunningham**, Glenn 1909-1988 *FacFETw*
**Cunningham**, Glenn C 1912- *WhoAmP 91*
**Cunningham**, Glenn Dale 1943- *WhoAmP 91, WhoBlA 92*
**Cunningham**, Glenn N 1940- *AmMWSc 92*
**Cunningham**, Glenn R 1940- *AmMWSc 92*
**Cunningham**, Gordon Rowe 1922- *AmMWSc 92*
**Cunningham**, Gregg Lee 1947- *WhoAmP 91*
**Cunningham**, H. Duane 1953- *WhoFI 92*
**Cunningham**, Harry Blair 1907- *IntWW 91*
**Cunningham**, Harry N, Jr 1935- *AmMWSc 92*
**Cunningham**, Howard 1942- *AmMWSc 92*
**Cunningham**, Hubert D. 1956- *WhoRel 92*
**Cunningham**, Hugh 1921- *Who 92*
**Cunningham**, Hugh Meredith 1927- *AmMWSc 92*
**Cunningham**, Imogen 1883-1976 *FacFETw*
**Cunningham**, J. V. 1911-1985 *BenetAL 91*
**Cunningham**, James Calvin 1947- *WhoAmL 92*
**Cunningham**, James Gordon 1940- *AmMWSc 92*
**Cunningham**, James J. 1938- *WhoBlA 92*
**Cunningham**, James Patrick 1950- *WhoAmL 92*
**Cunningham**, James Patrick 1956- *WhoFI 92, WhoMW 92*
**Cunningham**, James R. *WhoRel 92*
**Cunningham**, James V. 1923- *ConAu 135*
**Cunningham**, Jean Ann 1951- *WhoMW 92*
**Cunningham**, Jean Wooden 1946- *WhoAmP 91*
**Cunningham**, Jeffrey Milton 1952- *WhoFI 92*
**Cunningham**, Jere Pearson, Jr. 1943- *WhoEnt 92*
**Cunningham**, Jerome 1945- *WhoEnt 92*
**Cunningham**, Jerry Glenn 1941- *WhoAmP 91*
**Cunningham**, Jim *ConAu 135*
**Cunningham**, Joel L 1944- *AmMWSc 92*
**Cunningham**, John 1729-1773 *RfGEnL 91*
**Cunningham**, John 1917- *Who 92*
**Cunningham**, John 1926- *TwCPaSc*
**Cunningham**, John 1927- *AmMWSc 92*
**Cunningham**, John A. 1939- *IntWW 91, Who 92*
**Cunningham**, John Castel 1942- *AmMWSc 92*
**Cunningham**, John E 1931- *AmMWSc 92*
**Cunningham**, John Edward 1920- *AmMWSc 92*
**Cunningham**, John F. 1941- *WhoBlA 92*
**Cunningham**, John James *AmMWSc 92*
**Cunningham**, John Waldo 1932- *WhoEnt 92*
**Cunningham**, John Wilson 1820-1889 *DcNCBi 1*
**Cunningham**, Jordan Daniel 1951- *WhoAmL 92*
**Cunningham**, Joseph F 1924- *WhoAmP 91*
**Cunningham**, Joseph Francis 1935- *WhoAmL 92*
**Cunningham**, Joseph Leonard 1937- *WhoRel 92*
**Cunningham**, Judy Marie 1944- *WhoAmL 92*
**Cunningham**, Julia 1916- *ConAu 36NR*
**Cunningham**, Julia W. 1916- *WrDr 92*
**Cunningham**, Julie Margaret *AmMWSc 92*
**Cunningham**, Keith Allen 1922- *WhoAmL 92*
**Cunningham**, Kevin Frederick 1938- *WhoAmL 92*
**Cunningham**, Kirk B 1943- *WhoIns 92*
**Cunningham**, Laura *DrAPF 91*
**Cunningham**, Laura 1947- *WhoEnt 92*
**Cunningham**, Lawrence David 1936- *WhoRel 92*
**Cunningham**, Lawrence Springer 1935- *WhoRel 92*
**Cunningham**, Leon William 1927- *AmMWSc 92*
**Cunningham**, Loren Duane 1935- *WhoRel 92*
**Cunningham**, Louis Ernest 1951- *WhoBlA 92*
**Cunningham**, Madeleine White 1946- *AmMWSc 92*
**Cunningham**, Madonna Marie 1933- *WhoRel 92*
**Cunningham**, Margaret 1915- *WhoBlA 92*
**Cunningham**, Marion *NewYTBS 91 [port]*
**Cunningham**, Marion 1922- *WrDr 92*
**Cunningham**, Mark Eric 1962- *WhoMW 92*
**Cunningham**, Mary Elizabeth 1931- *AmMWSc 92*
**Cunningham**, Matthew Zachary 1961- *WhoEnt 92*
**Cunningham**, Merce *WhoEnt 92*
**Cunningham**, Merce 1919- *FacFETw, IntWW 91, Who 92*

**Cunningham,** Michael 1947- *WhoMW 92*
**Cunningham,** Michael Gerald 1937- *WhoMW 92*
**Cunningham,** Michael Paul 1943- *AmMWSc 92*
**Cunningham,** Murrell Thomas 1933- *WhoRel 92*
**Cunningham,** Newlin Buchanan 1917- *AmMWSc 92*
**Cunningham,** Noel B. 1944- *WhoAmL 92*
**Cunningham,** Patricia Rogers 1961- *WhoAmL 92*
**Cunningham,** Patrick Joseph, III 1950- *WhoMW 92*
**Cunningham,** Paul Bernard 1943- *WhoWest 92*
**Cunningham,** Paul George 1937- *WhoRel 92*
**Cunningham,** Paul Johnston 1928- *WhoAmP 91*
**Cunningham,** Paul Raymond Goldwyn 1949- *WhoBlA 92*
**Cunningham,** Paul Thomas 1936- *AmMWSc 92*
**Cunningham,** Pierce Edward 1934- *WhoAmL 92*
**Cunningham,** Ralph Eugene, Jr. 1927- *WhoAmL 92*
**Cunningham,** Ralph Sanford 1940- *WhoFI 92*
**Cunningham,** Randall 1963- *CurBio 91 [port], WhoBlA 92*
**Cunningham,** Randy 1941- *AlmAP 92 [port], WhoAmP 91, WhoWest 92*
**Cunningham,** Raymond Clement 1931- *WhoFI 92*
**Cunningham,** Richard G 1921- *AmMWSc 92*
**Cunningham,** Richard H G 1944- *WhoAmP 91*
**Cunningham,** Richard Preston 1948- *AmMWSc 92*
**Cunningham,** Richard T. 1918- *WhoBlA 92*
**Cunningham,** Robert Ashley 1923- *AmMWSc 92*
**Cunningham,** Robert Cyril 1914- *WhoRel 92*
**Cunningham,** Robert D. *WhoAmL 92*
**Cunningham,** Robert Elwin 1929- *AmMWSc 92, WhoMW 92*
**Cunningham,** Robert James 1942- *WhoAmL 92*
**Cunningham,** Robert Kerr 1923- *Who 92*
**Cunningham,** Robert Kuhlman, Sr 1922- *WhoAmP 91*
**Cunningham,** Robert Lester 1929- *AmMWSc 92*
**Cunningham,** Robert M 1919- *AmMWSc 92*
**Cunningham,** Robert Shannon, Jr. 1958- *WhoBlA 92*
**Cunningham,** Robert Stephen 1942- *AmMWSc 92, WhoWest 92*
**Cunningham,** Roger A. 1921- *WhoAmL 92*
**Cunningham,** Ron 1939- *WhoWest 92*
**Cunningham,** Ronald M. *WhoRel 92*
**Cunningham,** Rosemary Thomas 1957- *WhoFI 92*
**Cunningham,** Samuel Lewis, Jr. 1950- *WhoBlA 92*
**Cunningham,** Sean S. 1941- *IntMPA 92, WhoEnt 92*
**Cunningham,** Sheldon Arthur 1936- *WhoFI 92*
**Cunningham,** Stanley Lloyd 1938- *WhoAmL 92*
**Cunningham,** T. J. 1930- *WhoBlA 92*
**Cunningham,** Terence Thomas, III 1943- *WhoMW 92*
**Cunningham,** Thomas B 1946- *AmMWSc 92*
**Cunningham,** Thomas William 1911- *WhoRel 92*
**Cunningham,** Toby Ross 1944- *WhoEnt 92*
**Cunningham,** Tom Alan 1946 *WhoAmL 92*
**Cunningham,** Vera 1897-1955 *TwCPaSc*
**Cunningham,** Verenessa Smalls-Brantley 1949- *WhoBlA 92*
**Cunningham,** Virgil Dwayne 1930- *AmMWSc 92*
**Cunningham,** W J 1917- *AmMWSc 92*
**Cunningham,** W Pete 1929- *WhoAmP 91*
**Cunningham,** Warren P., III 1953- *WhoEnt 92*
**Cunningham,** William 1929- *WhoBlA 92*
**Cunningham,** William Allen 1945- *WhoAmL 92*
**Cunningham,** William Dean 1937- *WhoBlA 92*
**Cunningham,** William E. 1920- *WhoBlA 92*
**Cunningham,** William L. 1939- *WhoBlA 92*
**Cunningham-Jardine,** Ronald Charles 1931- *Who 92*
**Cunninghame Graham,** R.B. *RfGEnL 91*
**Cunninham-Rundles,** Charlotte 1943- *AmMWSc 92*
**Cunny,** Robert William 1924- *AmMWSc 92*
**Cuno,** Wilhelm 1876-1933 *EncTR 91 [port]*
**Cuny,** Robert Michael 1952- *AmMWSc 92*
**Cunynghame,** Andrew 1942- *Who 92*
**Cunyus,** George Marvin 1930- *WhoFI 92*
**Cuomo,** George *DrAPF 91*
**Cuomo,** George 1929- *WrDr 92*
**Cuomo,** Mario *NewYTBS 91 [port]*
**Cuomo,** Mario 1932- *News 92-2 [port], RComAH, WrDr 92*
**Cuomo,** Mario M. 1932- *AlmAP 92 [port]*
**Cuomo,** Mario Matthew 1932- *IntWW 91, Who 92, WhoAmP 91*
**Cupery,** Kenneth N 1937- *AmMWSc 92*
**Cupery,** Robert Rink 1944- *WhoWest 92*
**Cupery,** Willis Eli 1932- *AmMWSc 92*
**Cupit,** Charles R 1930- *AmMWSc 92*
**Cupit,** Danny E *WhoAmP 91*
**Cupitt,** Don 1934- *IntWW 91, Who 92*
**Cupp,** Calvin R 1924- *AmMWSc 92*
**Cupp,** Eddie Wayne 1941- *AmMWSc 92*
**Cupp,** John S., Jr. 1950- *WhoAmL 92*
**Cupp,** Joyce Ann 1950- *WhoRel 92*
**Cupp,** Mary Katherine Hyer 1932- *WhoWest 92*
**Cupp,** Paul Vernon, Jr 1942- *AmMWSc 92*
**Cupp,** Robert R 1950- *WhoAmP 91*
**Cupp,** Samuel B 1945- *WhoIns 92*
**Cuppage,** Francis Edward 1932- *AmMWSc 92*
**Cupper,** Robert 1942- *AmMWSc 92*
**Cupper,** Robert Alton 1918- *AmMWSc 92*
**Cupples,** Barrett L 1941- *AmMWSc 92*
**Cupples,** Charles d1785? *DcNCBi 1*
**Cupps,** Perry Thomas 1916- *AmMWSc 92*
**Cuppy,** B. Milton, Jr. 1933- *WhoMW 92*
**Cuppy,** Will 1884-1949 *BenetAL 91*
**Cuprak,** Peter V *WhoAmP 91*
**Cuprowski,** Paul *WhoAmP 91*
**Curato,** Randy Joseph 1958- *WhoMW 92*
**Curatola,** Robert Joseph 1963- *WhoAmL 92*
**Curatolo,** Barbara Doreen 1960- *WhoMW 92*
**Curb,** Michael *WhoAmP 91*
**Curbelo,** Silvia Maria 1955- *WhoHisp 92*
**Curbow,** Deryl Crawford 1922- *WhoAmP 91*
**Curchoe,** Carl A. 1944- *WhoFI 92*
**Curci,** Frank X. 1959- *WhoAmL 92*
**Curci,** Joseph E., II 1962- *WhoFI 92*
**Curci,** Michael C. 1925- *WhoAmL 92*
**Curcio,** Carl Anthony 1946- *WhoFI 92*
**Curcio,** Christopher Frank 1950- *WhoEnt 92, WhoWest 92*
**Curcio,** Lawrence Nicholas 1950- *AmMWSc 92*
**Curcio,** Rick Vincent 1952- *WhoAmL 92*
**Curcuru,** Felix 1947- *WhoIns 92*
**Curd,** Freed 1933- *WhoAmP 91*
**Curd,** Milton Rayburn 1928- *AmMWSc 92*
**Curd,** Philip Logan 1937- *WhoAmL 92*
**Cure,** Kenneth Graham 1924- *Who 92*
**Cureau,** Frank Raymond 1955- *WhoWest 92*
**Cureeu,** Nigel C. *Who 92*
**Cureton,** Benjamin, Jr. 1947- *WhoWest 92*
**Cureton,** Glen Lee 1938- *AmMWSc 92*
**Cureton,** John Porter 1936- *WhoBlA 92*
**Cureton,** Kirk J 1947- *AmMWSc 92*
**Cureton,** Michael 1955- *WhoBlA 92*
**Cureton,** Stewart Cleveland 1930- *WhoBlA 92*
**Cureton,** Thomas, Jr 1901- *AmMWSc 92*
**Curfew,** James V. 1946- *WhoFI 92*
**Curiale,** Salvatore R 1945- *WhoIns 92*
**Curie,** Eve 1904- *Who 92*
**Curie,** Leonardo Rodolfo 1950- *WhoHisp 92*
**Curie,** Marie 1867-1934 *FacFETw [port], WhoNob 90*
**Curie,** Pierre 1859-1906 *FacFETw, WhoNob 90*
**Curie-Cohen,** Martin Michael 1951- *AmMWSc 92*
**Curiel,** Herman F., II 1934- *WhoHisp 92*
**Curiel,** Imma Jacinta 1960- *WhoHisp 92*
**Curiel,** Tony *WhoHisp 92*
**Curiel,** Yoram 1941- *WhoWest 92*
**Curien,** Gilles 1922- *IntWW 91*
**Curien,** Hubert 1924- *IntWW 91*
**Curis,** Carlo 1923- *WhoRel 92*
**Curjel,** Caspar Robert 1931- *AmMWSc 92*
**Curkendall,** Brenda Irene 1954- *WhoFI 92*
**Curl,** Elroy Arvel 1921- *AmMWSc 92*
**Curl,** Herbert, Jr 1928- *AmMWSc 92*
**Curl,** James Stevens 1937- *IntAu&W 91, WrDr 92*
**Curl,** Mack Wade 1950- *WhoWest 92*
**Curl,** Rane L 1929- *AmMWSc 92*
**Curl,** Rane Locke 1929- *WhoMW 92*
**Curl,** Robert Floyd 1933- *AmMWSc 92*
**Curl,** Sam E *AmMWSc 92*
**Curle,** James Leonard 1925- *Who 92*
**Curle,** John 1915- *Who 92*
**Curlee,** Lane 1955- *WhoAmP 91*
**Curlee,** Neil J, Jr 1930- *AmMWSc 92*
**Curlee,** Robert C., Jr. 1935- *WhoRel 92*
**Curless,** Robert Bruce 1945- *WhoRel 92*
**Curless,** William Toole 1928- *AmMWSc 92*
**Curley,** Dennis M *AmMWSc 92*
**Curley,** Jack R. 1928- *WhoWest 92*
**Curley,** James 1796-1889 *BiInAmS*
**Curley,** James Edward 1944- *AmMWSc 92*
**Curley,** James Michael 1874-1958 *FacFETw*
**Curley,** John E., Jr. *WhoRel 92*
**Curley,** John Francis, Jr. 1939- *WhoFI 92*
**Curley,** John J. 1938- *WhoFI 92*
**Curley,** John Joseph 1948- *WhoAmL 92*
**Curley,** Jonathan Edward 1953- *WhoWest 92*
**Curley,** Lucy Alford *WhoAmP 91*
**Curley,** Michael Edward 1946- *WhoAmL 92*
**Curley,** Robert Ambrose, Jr. 1949- *WhoAmL 92*
**Curley,** Sarah Sharer *WhoWest 92*
**Curley,** Thomas *DrAPF 91*
**Curley,** Thomas J., Jr. 1957- *WhoAmL 92*
**Curley,** Walter J P *WhoAmP 91*
**Curley,** Walter Joseph Patrick, Jr. 1922- *IntWW 91*
**Curley,** Winifred H 1951- *AmMWSc 92*
**Curlin,** George Tams 1939- *AmMWSc 92*
**Curlin,** Lemuel Calvert 1913- *AmMWSc 92*
**Curling,** Audrey *IntAu&W 91*
**Curling,** Bryan William Richard 1911- *IntAu&W 91*
**Curlook,** Walter 1929- *WhoFI 92*
**Curls,** Phillip B 1942- *WhoAmP 91, WhoBlA 92*
**Curman,** Johan 1919- *IntWW 91*
**Curme,** Henry Garrett 1923- *AmMWSc 92*
**Curnen,** Edward Charles, Jr 1909- *AmMWSc 92*
**Curnen,** Mary G McCrea *AmMWSc 92*
**Curnen,** Tim 1945- *WhoEnt 92*
**Curnin,** Thomas Francis 1933- *WhoAmL 92*
**Curnow,** Allen 1911- *ConPo 91, IntAu&W 91, RfGEnL 91, WrDr 92*
**Curnow,** Elizabeth Ann Marguerite 1935- *Who 92*
**Curnow,** Frank *IntAu&W 91X, WrDr 92*
**Curnow,** Randall T *AmMWSc 92*
**Curnow,** Richard Dennis 1943- *AmMWSc 92*
**Curnow,** Thomas Allen Monro 1911- *IntAu&W 91*
**Curns,** Eileen Bohan 1927- *WhoMW 92*
**Curnutt,** Brian Joe 1962- *WhoRel 92*
**Curnutt,** Jerry Lee 1942- *AmMWSc 92*
**Curnutte,** Basil, Jr 1923- *AmMWSc 92*
**Curnutte,** John Tolliver, III 1951- *AmMWSc 92, WhoWest 92*
**Curnutte,** Mark William 1954- *WhoAmL 92*
**Curoe,** Bernadine Mary 1930- *WhoMW 92*
**Curott,** David Richard 1937- *AmMWSc 92*
**Curotto,** Ricky Joseph 1931- *WhoAmL 92, WhoFI 92, WhoWest 92*
**Curphey,** Thomas John 1934- *AmMWSc 92*
**Currah,** Jack Ellwood 1920- *AmMWSc 92*
**Currah,** Walter E 1936- *AmMWSc 92*
**Currall,** Alexander 1917- *Who 92*
**Curram,** James William Thomas 1946- *WhoMW 92*
**Curran,** Barbara A 1940- *WhoAmP 91*
**Curran,** Barbara Adell 1928- *WhoAmL 92*
**Curran,** Charles d1980 *LesBEnT 92*
**Curran,** Charles E. 1934- *IntWW 91, WhoRel 92, WrDr 92*
**Curran,** Charles Edward 1934- *RelLAm 91*
**Curran,** Charles Eschman, III 1946- *WhoFI 92*
**Curran,** Colleen 1954- *IntAu&W 91*
**Curran,** Connie 1947- *WhoMW 92*
**Curran,** Daniel Richard 1961- *WhoWest 92*
**Curran,** David James 1932- *AmMWSc 92*
**Curran,** Dennis Patrick 1953- *AmMWSc 92*
**Curran,** Donald Robert 1932- *AmMWSc 92*
**Curran,** Edward Milford 1922- *WhoWest 92*
**Curran,** Francis X. 1914- *WrDr 92*
**Curran,** Geoffrey Michael 1949- *WhoAmL 92*
**Curran,** Gerald Joseph 1939- *WhoAmP 91*
**Curran,** Harold Allen 1940- *AmMWSc 92*
**Curran,** J. Joseph, Jr. 1931- *WhoAmL 92, WhoAmP 91*
**Curran,** James J. *WhoWest 92*
**Curran,** James W 1944- *AmMWSc 92*
**Curran,** John James 1937- *WhoAmL 92*
**Curran,** John Michael 1959- *WhoAmL 92*
**Curran,** John S 1940- *AmMWSc 92*
**Curran,** Joseph Patrick 1951- *WhoAmL 92*
**Curran,** Leigh 1943- *WhoEnt 92*
**Curran,** Leo Gabriel Columbanus 1930- *Who 92*
**Curran,** Louis Jerome, Jr. 1934- *WhoEnt 92*
**Curran,** Mark Albert 1954- *WhoWest 92*
**Curran,** Maurice Francis 1931- *WhoAmL 92*
**Curran,** Michael D 1945- *WhoAmP 91*
**Curran,** Patrick Barton 1953- *WhoAmL 92*
**Curran,** Paul Saether 1960- *WhoAmL 92*
**Curran,** Philip E *WhoAmP 91*
**Curran,** Robert Crowe 1921- *Who 92*
**Curran,** Robert Kyran 1931- *AmMWSc 92*
**Curran,** Robert M 1921- *AmMWSc 92*
**Curran,** Samuel 1912- *Who 92*
**Curran,** Samuel Crowe 1912- *IntWW 91*
**Curran,** Thomas J. 1924- *WhoAmL 92*
**Curran,** Ward Schenk 1935- *WhoFI 92*
**Curran,** William James, III 1940- *WhoAmL 92*
**Curran,** William Vincent 1929- *AmMWSc 92*
**Currarino,** Guido 1920- *AmMWSc 92*
**Curras,** Margarita C. 1960- *WhoHisp 92*
**Curray,** Joseph Ross 1927- *AmMWSc 92*
**Currell,** Douglas Leo 1927- *AmMWSc 92*
**Currelley,** Lorraine Rainie *DrAPF 91*
**Curren,** Caleb *AmMWSc 92*
**Curren,** Terence Paul 1958- *WhoEnt 92*
**Currens,** Robert B., II 1956- *WhoEnt 92*
**Current,** David Harlan 1941- *AmMWSc 92*
**Current,** Gloster Bryant 1913- *WhoBlA 92*
**Current,** Jerry Hall 1935- *AmMWSc 92*
**Current,** Steven P 1950- *AmMWSc 92*
**Current,** William L 1949- *AmMWSc 92*
**Currer,** Barney *DrAPF 91*
**Curreri,** P William 1936- *AmMWSc 92*
**Currey,** Edmund Neville Vincent 1906- *Who 92*
**Currey,** Harry Lloyd Fairbridge 1925- *Who 92*
**Currey,** Mary Ellen 1945- *WhoMW 92*
**Currey,** R. N. 1907- *ConPo 91, LiExTwC, WrDr 92*
**Currey,** Richard *DrAPF 91*
**Currey,** Richard 1949- *WrDr 92*
**Currey-Wilson,** Robert Thomas 1958- *WhoAmL 92*
**Currid,** Cheryl Clarke 1950- *WhoFI 92*
**Currie,** Alastair 1921- *Who 92*
**Currie,** Austin *Who 92*
**Currie,** Barbara Flynn 1940- *WhoAmP 91*
**Currie,** Bruce LaMonte 1945- *AmMWSc 92*
**Currie,** Charles H *AmMWSc 92*
**Currie,** David Anthony 1946- *Who 92*
**Currie,** David P. 1936- *ConAu 134*
**Currie,** David Park 1936- *WhoAmL 92*
**Currie,** Donald Scott 1930- *Who 92*
**Currie,** Eddie L. 1927- *WhoBlA 92*
**Currie,** Edward Jones, Jr. 1951- *WhoAmL 92*
**Currie,** Edwina 1946- *IntAu&W 91, IntWW 91, Who 92*
**Currie,** Eileen *WhoRel 92*
**Currie,** Fergus Gardner 1931- *WhoEnt 92*
**Currie,** Frances H Light 1923- *WhoAmP 91*
**Currie,** Iain George 1936- *AmMWSc 92*
**Currie,** Jackie L. 1932- *WhoBlA 92*
**Currie,** James Barker 1948- *WhoFI 92*
**Currie,** James McGill 1941- *Who 92*
**Currie,** James Orr, Jr 1943- *AmMWSc 92*
**Currie,** John 1884?-1914 *TwCPaSc*
**Currie,** John Bickell 1922- *AmMWSc 92*
**Currie,** John Thornton 1928- *WhoFI 92*
**Currie,** Joseph Austin 1939- *Who 92*
**Currie,** Joyce Marie 1954- *WhoMW 92*
**Currie,** Julia Ruth 1944- *AmMWSc 92*
**Currie,** Ken 1960- *TwCPaSc*
**Currie,** Lloyd Arthur 1930- *AmMWSc 92*
**Currie,** Madeline Ashburn 1922- *WhoWest 92*
**Currie,** Malcolm R 1927- *AmMWSc 92*
**Currie,** Malcolm Roderick 1927- *WhoFI 92, WhoWest 92*
**Currie,** Neil 1926- *Who 92*
**Currie,** Nicholas Charles 1945- *AmMWSc 92*
**Currie,** Philip John 1949- *AmMWSc 92*
**Currie,** Piers William Edward 1913- *Who 92*
**Currie,** Robert Alexander 1905- *Who 92*
**Currie,** Robert Emil 1937- *WhoAmL 92*
**Currie,** Ronald Ian 1928- *Who 92*
**Currie,** Sondra Marie 1952- *WhoEnt 92*
**Currie,** Thomas Eswin 1926- *AmMWSc 92*
**Currie,** Ulysses 1937- *WhoAmP 91*
**Currie,** Violet Evadne *AmMWSc 92*
**Currie,** William Deems 1935- *AmMWSc 92*
**Currier & Ives** *BenetAL 91*
**Currier,** Benjamin Atkinson 1933- *WhoIns 92*
**Currier,** David P 1944- *WhoAmP 91*
**Currier,** Gene Mark 1943- *WhoAmL 92, WhoMW 92*

**Currier,** Herbert Bashford 1911- *AmMWSc 92*
**Currier,** Nathaniel 1813-1888 *BenetAL 91*
**Currier,** Raymond A, Jr *WhoAmP 91*
**Currier,** Robert David 1925- *AmMWSc 92*
**Currier,** Ruth 1926- *WhoEnt 92*
**Currier,** Thomas Curtis 1947- *AmMWSc 92*
**Currier,** William Wesley 1947- *AmMWSc 92*
**Currin,** Kimberli Joyce 1958- *WhoRel 92*
**Currin,** Margaret Person 1950- *WhoAmL 92*
**Currin,** Robert Graves, Jr. 1945- *WhoAmL 92*
**Currio,** Tyman 1851-1924 *ScFEYrs*
**Currivan,** John Daniel 1947- *WhoAmL 92, WhoFI 92, WhoMW 92*
**Currlin,** Lee *LesBEnT 92*
**Currlin,** William Egon 1945- *WhoAmP 91*
**Curro,** Frederick A 1943- *AmMWSc 92*
**Curro,** John Gillette 1942- *AmMWSc 92*
**Curry,** Alan C 1933- *WhoIns 92*
**Curry,** Alan Chester 1933- *WhoFI 92*
**Curry,** Alan Stewart 1925- *Who 92*
**Curry,** Alton Frank 1933- *WhoAmL 92*
**Curry,** Avon *IntAu&W 91X*
**Curry,** Bill Perry 1937- *AmMWSc 92*
**Curry,** Bo U 1951- *AmMWSc 92*
**Curry,** Catherine V. 1952- *WhoAmL 92*
**Curry,** Charles E. 1934- *WhoBlA 92*
**Curry,** Clarence F., Jr. 1943- *WhoBlA 92*
**Curry,** Daniel Arthur 1937- *WhoAmL 92*
**Curry,** Daniel Francis Myles 1946- *WhoWest 92*
**Curry,** David *DrAPF 91*
**Curry,** David Maurice 1944- *Who 92*
**Curry,** Dell 1964- *WhoBlA 92*
**Curry,** Donald Lawrence 1936- *AmMWSc 92*
**Curry,** Donald Robert 1943- *WhoAmL 92*
**Curry,** Everett William, Jr. 1942- *WhoRel 92*
**Curry,** Francis J 1911- *AmMWSc 92*
**Curry,** George E. 1947- *WhoBlA 92*
**Curry,** George Richard 1932- *AmMWSc 92*
**Curry,** Gladys J. 1931- *WhoBlA 92*
**Curry,** Gordon Barrett 1954- *Who 92*
**Curry,** Henry Lee, III 1943- *WhoAmP 91*
**Curry,** Herbert Leard 1930- *WhoMW 92*
**Curry,** Hiram Benjamin 1927- *AmMWSc 92*
**Curry,** Howard Millard 1924- *AmMWSc 92*
**Curry,** James Eugene 1926- *AmMWSc 92*
**Curry,** James Kenneth 1920- *AmMWSc 92*
**Curry,** James Trueman, Jr. 1936- *WhoWest 92*
**Curry,** Jane 1932- *WrDr 92*
**Curry,** Jane Louise 1932- *IntAu&W 91*
**Curry,** Jerry Ralph *WhoAmP 91*
**Curry,** Jerry Ralph 1932- *WhoBlA 92*
**Curry,** Joel Bruce 1948- *WhoRel 92*
**Curry,** John Anthony 1949- *Who 92*
**Curry,** John Arthur Hugh 1938- *Who 92*
**Curry,** John D 1938- *AmMWSc 92*
**Curry,** John Joseph, III 1940- *AmMWSc 92*
**Curry,** John Patrick 1934- *WhoFI 92, WhoMW 92*
**Curry,** Johnny Lynville 1956- *WhoAmP 91*
**Curry,** Joseph C. 1918- *WhoRel 92*
**Curry,** Judith Ann 1953- *AmMWSc 92*
**Curry,** Levy Henry 1949- *WhoBlA 92*
**Curry,** Mark Alan 1956- *WhoMW 92*
**Curry,** Mary Earle Lowry 1917- *IntAu&W 91*
**Curry,** Mary Grace 1947- *AmMWSc 92*
**Curry,** Michael Joseph 1920- *AmMWSc 92*
**Curry,** Michael Paul 1952- *WhoEnt 92*
**Curry,** Mitchell L. 1935- *WhoBlA 92*
**Curry,** Mitchell Lee 1935- *WhoRel 92*
**Curry,** Norval H 1914- *AmMWSc 92*
**Curry,** Norvelle 1930- *WhoBlA 92*
**Curry,** Pam Cavender 1948- *WhoEnt 92*
**Curry,** Peggy Simson 1911-1987 *TwCWW 91*
**Curry,** Peter *Who 92*
**Curry,** Phyllis Joan 1929- *WhoBlA 92*
**Curry,** R Bruce 1929- *AmMWSc 92*
**Curry,** Richard Charles 1937- *WhoAmP 91*
**Curry,** Richard O. 1931- *WrDr 92*
**Curry,** Richard Orr 1931- *IntAu&W 91*
**Curry,** Robert Lowell 1945- *WhoEnt 92*
**Curry,** Robert Michael 1947- *WhoEnt 92*
**Curry,** Ruth A 1931- *WhoIns 92*
**Curry,** Sadye Beatryce *WhoBlA 92*
**Curry,** Stephen H *AmMWSc 92*
**Curry,** Thomas F 1926- *AmMWSc 92*
**Curry,** Thomas Harvey 1921- *AmMWSc 92*
**Curry,** Thomas Ward 1939- *WhoMW 92*
**Curry,** Tim 1946- *IntMPA 92*
**Curry,** Tom 1900-1976 *TwCWW 91*
**Curry,** Victor Tyrone 1960- *WhoBlA 92*
**Curry,** Warren H 1924- *AmMWSc 92*
**Curry,** William E, Jr *WhoAmP 91*
**Curry,** William Hirst, III 1932- *AmMWSc 92*
**Curry,** William Thomas 1943- *WhoBlA 92*
**Cursiter,** Stanley 1887-1976 *TwCPaSc*
**Curson,** Theodore 1935- *WhoBlA 92, WhoEnt 92*
**Curt,** Gregory *AmMWSc 92*
**Curt,** Jeanne Donoghue 1941- *WhoEnt 92*
**Curteis,** Ian 1935- *WrDr 92*
**Curteis,** Ian Bayley 1935- *ConAu 36NR, IntAu&W 91, IntWW 91, Who 92*
**Curti,** Merle 1897- *BenetAL 91, IntWW 91*
**Curtice,** Jay Stephen 1928- *AmMWSc 92*
**Curtice,** Walter R 1935- *AmMWSc 92*
**Curtin,** Brian Thomas 1945- *AmMWSc 92*
**Curtin,** Charles Byron 1917- *AmMWSc 92*
**Curtin,** David Stephen 1955- *WhoWest 92*
**Curtin,** David Yarrow 1920- *AmMWSc 92, IntWW 91*
**Curtin,** Frank Michael 1951- *AmMWSc 92*
**Curtin,** Gene Lawrence 1948- *WhoFI 92*
**Curtin,** James Bernard 1929- *WhoAmL 92*
**Curtin,** James Martin 1958- *WhoEnt 92*
**Curtin,** Jane 1947- *IntMPA 92*
**Curtin,** Jane Therese 1947- *WhoEnt 92*
**Curtin,** Jeremiah 1840?-1906 *BenetAL 91, BiInAmS*
**Curtin,** John 1885-1945 *FacFETw*
**Curtin,** John T. 1921- *WhoBlA 92*
**Curtin,** John Thomas 1924- *WhoAmL 92*
**Curtin,** Kevin Gerard 1951- *WhoAmL 92*
**Curtin,** Margaret Mary 1934- *WhoAmP 91*
**Curtin,** Michael Edward 1939- *IntWW 91*
**Curtin,** Patrick Edward 1963- *WhoFI 92*
**Curtin,** Phyllis 1922- *NewAmDM*
**Curtin,** Richard B 1940- *AmMWSc 92*
**Curtin,** Richard Delmar 1963- *WhoWest 92*
**Curtin,** Robert H *AmMWSc 92*
**Curtin,** Robert William 1944- *WhoMW 92*
**Curtin,** Terrence M 1926- *AmMWSc 92*
**Curtin,** Thomas J *AmMWSc 92*
**Curtin,** Thomas Lee 1932- *WhoWest 92*
**Curtin,** Timothy John 1942- *WhoAmL 92*
**Curtin,** William Joseph 1931- *WhoAmL 92*
**Curtis,** Adam Sebastian G 1934- *AmMWSc 92*
**Curtis,** Albert Bradley, II 1957- *WhoFI 92*
**Curtis,** Allan Craig 1925- *WhoEnt 92*
**Curtis,** Alton Kenneth 1939- *WhoEnt 92*
**Curtis,** Anthony 1926- *WrDr 92*
**Curtis,** Anthony Samuel 1926- *IntAu&W 91*
**Curtis,** Blake *WhoAmP 91*
**Curtis,** Brian Albert 1936- *AmMWSc 92*
**Curtis,** Bruce Franklin 1918- *AmMWSc 92*
**Curtis,** Byrd Collins 1926- *AmMWSc 92*
**Curtis,** Carl T 1905- *WhoAmP 91*
**Curtis,** Charles 1860-1936 *AmPolLe*
**Curtis,** Charles David 1939- *Who 92*
**Curtis,** Charles Edward 1943- *WhoRel 92*
**Curtis,** Charles Elliott 1937- *AmMWSc 92*
**Curtis,** Charles R 1938- *AmMWSc 92*
**Curtis,** Charles Thach, Jr. 1951- *WhoAmL 92*
**Curtis,** Charles Whittlesey 1926- *AmMWSc 92*
**Curtis,** Clark Britten 1951- *WhoFI 92, WhoMW 92*
**Curtis,** Colin Hinton Thomson 1920- *Who 92*
**Curtis,** Connie S. 1951- *WhoFI 92*
**Curtis,** Cyril Dean 1920- *AmMWSc 92*
**Curtis,** Cyrus H K 1850-1933 *FacFETw*
**Curtis,** Dan *LesBEnT 92*
**Curtis,** Dan 1928- *IntMPA 92*
**Curtis,** Daniel M. 1928- *WhoEnt 92*
**Curtis,** David *DrAPF 91*
**Curtis,** David Eugene 1937- *WhoMW 92*
**Curtis,** David Roderick 1927- *IntWW 91, Who 92*
**Curtis,** David William 1924- *AmMWSc 92*
**Curtis,** Dianne 1949- *WhoWest 92*
**Curtis,** Dick 1928- *WhoEnt 92*
**Curtis,** Doris Malkin d1991 *NewYTBS 91*
**Curtis,** Doris Malkin 1914- *AmMWSc 92*
**Curtis,** Dwayne H 1930- *AmMWSc 92*
**Curtis,** Earl Clifton, Jr 1932- *AmMWSc 92*
**Curtis,** Edward 1838-1912 *BiInAmS*
**Curtis,** Edward Leo 1907- *Who 92*
**Curtis,** Elyse Donathan *WhoEnt 92*
**Curtis,** Emma Ghent 1860-1918 *HanAmWH*
**Curtis,** Ernest Edwin 1906- *Who 92*
**Curtis,** Frank *Who 92*
**Curtis,** Fred Allen *AmMWSc 92*
**Curtis,** Frederick Augustus, Jr 1922- *AmMWSc 92*
**Curtis,** Gary Lynn 1944- *AmMWSc 92*
**Curtis,** George Clifton 1926- *AmMWSc 92*
**Curtis,** George Darwin 1928- *AmMWSc 92*
**Curtis,** George Edward 1861-1895 *BiInAmS*
**Curtis,** George Ticknor 1812-1894 *BenetAL 91*
**Curtis,** George Warren 1936- *WhoAmL 92*
**Curtis,** George William 1824-1892 *BenetAL 91*
**Curtis,** George William 1925- *AmMWSc 92*
**Curtis,** Gerald Richard 1928- *WhoFI 92*
**Curtis,** Glen Russell 1947- *WhoAmP 91, WhoWest 92*
**Curtis,** Harry S. 1934- *WhoBlA 92*
**Curtis,** Heber Doust 1872-1942 *FacFETw*
**Curtis,** Henry Stoddard 1870-1954 *DcAmImH*
**Curtis,** Herbert John 1918- *AmMWSc 92*
**Curtis,** Huntington W 1921- *AmMWSc 92*
**Curtis,** Isaac Fisher 1950- *WhoBlA 92*
**Curtis,** Ivol I. 1908- *WhoWest 92*
**Curtis,** Jack *DrAPF 91*
**Curtis,** James L. 1922- *WhoBlA 92*
**Curtis,** James O 1923- *AmMWSc 92*
**Curtis,** James Robert, Sr. 1905- *WhoEnt 92, WhoFI 92*
**Curtis,** James Theodore 1923- *WhoAmL 92*
**Curtis,** Jamie Lee 1958- *IntMPA 92, IntWW 91, WhoEnt 92*
**Curtis,** Jean-Louis 1917- *IntWW 91*
**Curtis,** Jean Trawick *WhoBlA 92, WhoMW 92*
**Curtis,** Jeff Bain 1953- *WhoAmL 92*
**Curtis,** Jesse William, Jr. 1905- *WhoAmL 92, WhoWest 92*
**Curtis,** John Barry *Who 92*
**Curtis,** John Barry 1933- *WhoRel 92, WhoWest 92*
**Curtis,** John Edward 1946- *Who 92*
**Curtis,** John Green 1844-1913 *BiInAmS*
**Curtis,** John Henry 1920- *Who 92*
**Curtis,** John Joseph 1942- *WhoAmL 92*
**Curtis,** John Russell 1934- *AmMWSc 92*
**Curtis,** Joseph C 1930- *AmMWSc 92*
**Curtis,** Joseph F., Sr. 1916- *WhoBlA 92*
**Curtis,** Joseph Robert 1962- *WhoRel 92*
**Curtis,** Joseph W 1930- *WhoAmP 91*
**Curtis,** Josephine Monica 1903- *WhoBlA 92*
**Curtis,** Juanita Gwendolyn 1920- *WhoBlA 92*
**Curtis,** Ken d1991 *NewYTBS 91 [port]*
**Curtis,** Kenneth Merwin 1931- *WhoAmP 91*
**Curtis,** Kimberly Louise 1961- *WhoWest 92*
**Curtis,** Lawrence Andrew 1942- *AmMWSc 92*
**Curtis,** Lawrence B 1924- *AmMWSc 92*
**Curtis,** Leo *Who 92*
**Curtis,** Linda Lee *DrAPF 91*
**Curtis,** Lorenzo Jan 1935- *AmMWSc 92, WhoMW 92*
**Curtis,** Marelyn Elaine 1935- *WhoWest 92*
**Curtis,** Marie Therese Dodge 1935- *WhoWest 92*
**Curtis,** Mary C. 1953- *WhoBlA 92*
**Curtis,** Michael Howard 1920- *Who 92*
**Curtis,** Morton Landers 1921- *AmMWSc 92*
**Curtis,** Moses Ashley 1808-1872 *BiInAmS, DcNCBi 1*
**Curtis,** Myron David 1938- *AmMWSc 92*
**Curtis,** Orlie Lindsey, Jr 1934- *AmMWSc 92*
**Curtis,** Otis Freeman, Jr 1915- *AmMWSc 92*
**Curtis,** Paul Robinson 1931- *AmMWSc 92*
**Curtis,** Pauline Carsten *ScFEYrs*
**Curtis,** Penny Johnson 1957- *WhoAmL 92*
**Curtis,** Philip 1908- *Who 92*
**Curtis,** Philip C. 1907- *WorArt 1980 [port]*
**Curtis,** Philip Chadsey, Jr 1928- *AmMWSc 92, WhoWest 92*
**Curtis,** Philip Kerry 1945- *WhoAmL 92*
**Curtis,** Ralph Wendell 1936- *AmMWSc 92*
**Curtis,** Richard Herbert *Who 92*
**Curtis,** Richard Lewis *WhoRel 92*
**Curtis,** Robert Arthur 1954- *AmMWSc 92*
**Curtis,** Robert Frank 1926- *Who 92*
**Curtis,** Robert Harland 1930- *WhoFI 92, WhoWest 92*
**Curtis,** Robert Orin 1927- *AmMWSc 92*
**Curtis,** Robin Livingstone 1926- *AmMWSc 92*
**Curtis,** Ronald S 1950- *AmMWSc 92*
**Curtis,** Sharon 1951- *IntAu&W 91*
**Curtis,** Sharon Curry 1958- *WhoWest 92*
**Curtis,** Stanley Bartlett 1932- *AmMWSc 92*
**Curtis,** Stephen Douglas 1954- *WhoRel 92*
**Curtis,** Stephen P 1949- *WhoAmP 91*
**Curtis,** Stephen Russell 1948- *Who 92*
**Curtis,** Steven Alan 1954- *WhoEnt 92*
**Curtis,** Susan Julia 1945- *AmMWSc 92*
**Curtis,** Thomas B. *LesBEnT 92*
**Curtis,** Thomas B 1911- *WhoAmP 91*
**Curtis,** Thomas Bradford 1911- *WhoAmL 92*
**Curtis,** Thomas Dale 1952- *IntAu&W 91*
**Curtis,** Thomas Edwin 1927- *AmMWSc 92*
**Curtis,** Thomas Hasbrook 1941- *AmMWSc 92*
**Curtis,** Tom *TwCWW 91*
**Curtis,** Tony 1925- *ConTFT 9, IntMPA 92, IntWW 91, WhoEnt 92*
**Curtis,** Tony 1946- *ConPo 91, IntAu&W 91, WrDr 92*
**Curtis,** Veronica Anne 1948- *AmMWSc 92*
**Curtis,** Wade *IntAu&W 91X, WrDr 92*
**Curtis,** Walt *DrAPF 91*
**Curtis,** Walter Alan 1941- *IntAu&W 91*
**Curtis,** Walter W. 1913- *WhoRel 92*
**Curtis,** Wardon Allan 1867-1940 *ScFEYrs*
**Curtis,** Warren Edward 1914- *WhoAmP 91*
**Curtis,** Wendell D 1945- *AmMWSc 92*
**Curtis,** Wesley E 1918- *AmMWSc 92*
**Curtis,** Wilfred Frank 1923- *Who 92*
**Curtis,** Will *IntAu&W 91X, WrDr 92*
**Curtis,** William 1935- *Who 92*
**Curtis,** William Edgar 1914- *WhoEnt 92*
**Curtis,** William J. R. 1948- *WrDr 92*
**Curtis,** William Shepley 1915- *WhoWest 92*
**Curtis-Johnson,** Robert Steven 1960- *WhoEnt 92*
**Curtis-Raleigh,** Jean Margaret Macdonald 1933- *Who 92*
**Curtis-Smith,** Curtis O B 1941- *ConCom 92*
**Curtiss,** Allen Hiram 1845-1907 *BiInAmS*
**Curtiss,** Aubyn A *WhoAmP 91*
**Curtiss,** Charles Francis 1921- *AmMWSc 92*
**Curtiss,** Elden F. 1932- *WhoRel 92, WhoWest 92*
**Curtiss,** Glenn Hammond 1878-1930 *FacFETw*
**Curtiss,** Harriette Augusta 1856-1932 *RelLAm 91*
**Curtiss,** Howard C, Jr 1930- *AmMWSc 92*
**Curtiss,** John 1924- *Who 92*
**Curtiss,** Larry Alan 1947- *AmMWSc 92*
**Curtiss,** Linda K *AmMWSc 92*
**Curtiss,** Mina 1896-1985 *ConAu 133*
**Curtiss,** Roy, III 1934- *AmMWSc 92*
**Curtiss,** Sidney Q *WhoAmP 91*
**Curtiss,** Thomas, Jr. 1941- *WhoAmL 92*
**Curtiss,** Trumbull Cary 1940- *WhoFI 92*
**Curtius,** Julius 1877-1948 *EncTR 91 [port]*
**Curtiz,** Michael 1888-1962 *IntDcF 2-2 [port]*
**Curtman,** Charles Otto 1829-1896 *BiInAmS*
**Curtright,** Robert Eugene 1944- *WhoEnt 92, WhoMW 92*
**Curtright,** Thomas Lynn 1948- *AmMWSc 92*
**Curts,** Mark Stephen 1957- *WhoRel 92*
**Curtsinger,** Dean Carroll 1942- *WhoMW 92*
**Curtsinger,** James Webb 1950- *AmMWSc 92*
**Curty,** Judith A. 1957- *WhoMW 92*
**Curvin,** Robert 1934- *WhoBlA 92*
**Curwen,** Christopher 1929- *Who 92*
**Curwen,** David 1935- *AmMWSc 92*
**Curwen,** John 1821-1901 *BiInAmS*
**Curwood,** James Oliver 1878-1927 *BenetAL 91, TwCWW 91*
**Curwood,** Sarah T. 1916-1990 *WhoBlA 92N*
**Cury,** Ivan N. 1937- *WhoEnt 92*
**Curzan,** Myron Paul 1940- *WhoAmL 92*
**Curzio,** Elaine Mary 1947- *WhoEnt 92*
**Curzio,** Francis Xavier 1944- *WhoFI 92*
**Curzon** *Who 92*
**Curzon,** Clare *IntAu&W 91X*
**Curzon,** Clare 1922- *WrDr 92*
**Curzon,** Clifford 1907-1982 *FacFETw, NewAmDM*
**Curzon,** Daniel *DrAPF 91*
**Curzon,** George N. 1859-1925 *EncTR 91*
**Curzon,** George Nathaniel 1859-1925 *FacFETw*
**Curzon,** Leonard Henry 1912- *Who 92*
**Curzon,** Lucia *WrDr 92*
**Cusachs,** Louis Chopin 1933- *AmMWSc 92*
**Cusack,** Anne E. *DrAPF 91*
**Cusack,** Betsy Michelle 1959- *WhoMW 92*
**Cusack,** Cyril 1910- *IntMPA 92*
**Cusack,** Cyril James 1910- *IntWW 91*
**Cusack,** Gregory Daniel 1943- *WhoMW 92*
**Cusack,** Henry Vernon 1895- *Who 92*
**Cusack,** Joan 1962- *IntMPA 92*
**Cusack,** John 1966- *IntMPA 92, WhoEnt 92*
**Cusack,** John Francis 1937- *WhoAmP 91*
**Cusack,** John Thomas 1935- *WhoAmL 92*
**Cusack,** Mary Josephine 1935- *WhoAmL 92*
**Cusano,** Cristino 1941- *AmMWSc 92*
**Cusano,** Dominic A 1924- *AmMWSc 92*
**Cusanovich,** Michael A 1942- *AmMWSc 92*
**Cusanovich,** Michael Anthony 1942- *WhoWest 92*
**Cuscurida,** Michael 1926- *AmMWSc 92*
**Cusdin,** Sidney Edward Thomas 1908- *Who 92*

**Cuse,** Carlton 1959- *WhoEnt 92*
**Cusens,** Anthony Ralph 1927- *Who 92*
**Cushen,** Walter Edward 1925- *AmMWSc 92*
**Cushing,** Bruce S 1955- *AmMWSc 92*
**Cushing,** Colbert Ellis 1931- *AmMWSc 92*
**Cushing,** David H 1940- *AmMWSc 92*
**Cushing,** David Henry 1920- *IntWW 91, Who 92*
**Cushing,** Edward Fitch 1862?-1911 *BiInAmS*
**Cushing,** Edward John 1933- *AmMWSc 92*
**Cushing,** Elizabeth Anne 1963- *WhoAmL 92*
**Cushing,** Frank Hamilton 1857-1900 *BenetAL 91, BiInAmS*
**Cushing,** Harvey 1869-1939 *BenetAL 91*
**Cushing,** Harvey Williams 1869-1939 *FacFETw*
**Cushing,** Jim Michael 1942- *AmMWSc 92*
**Cushing,** John, Jr 1916- *AmMWSc 92*
**Cushing,** Jonathan Peter 1793-1835 *BiInAmS*
**Cushing,** Kenneth Mayhew 1947- *AmMWSc 92*
**Cushing,** Merchant Leroy 1910- *AmMWSc 92*
**Cushing,** Peter 1913- *ConAu 133, IntMPA 92, IntWW 91*
**Cushing,** Ralph Harvey 1922- *WhoMW 92*
**Cushing,** Richard James 1895-1970 *RelLAm 91*
**Cushing,** Robert Leavitt 1914- *AmMWSc 92*
**Cushing,** Robert Reynolds, Jr 1952- *WhoAmP 91*
**Cushing,** Steven 1948- *WhoFI 92*
**Cushing,** Vincent DePaul 1934- *WhoRel 92*
**Cushingberry,** George, Jr 1953- *WhoAmP 91, WhoBlA 92*
**Cushley,** Robert John 1936- *AmMWSc 92*
**Cushman,** Aaron D. 1924- *WhoFI 92*
**Cushman,** Dan 1909- *IntAu&W 91, TwCWW 91, WrDr 92*
**Cushman,** David Wayne 1939- *AmMWSc 92*
**Cushman,** Dawn 1953- *WhoAmL 92*
**Cushman,** Doug 1953- *SmATA 65 [port]*
**Cushman,** Earle Lynwood 1940- *WhoRel 92*
**Cushman,** Eugene Crocker 1944- *WhoAmP 91*
**Cushman,** Holbrook 1857-1895 *BiInAmS*
**Cushman,** James Butler 1936- *WhoAmL 92*
**Cushman,** John Howard 1951- *AmMWSc 92*
**Cushman,** Mark 1945- *AmMWSc 92*
**Cushman,** Michael Larry 1947- *WhoWest 92*
**Cushman,** Oris Mildred 1931- *WhoMW 92*
**Cushman,** Paul, Jr 1930- *AmMWSc 92*
**Cushman,** Pauline 1835-1893 *EncAmaz 91*
**Cushman,** Robert E, Jr 1914-1985 *FacFETw*
**Cushman,** Robert Earl 1913- *WhoRel 92*
**Cushman,** Robert Vittum 1916- *AmMWSc 92*
**Cushman,** Roger Raymond, Jr. 1933- *WhoMW 92*
**Cushman,** Samuel Wright 1941- *AmMWSc 92*
**Cushman,** Vera Charlotte Scott 1876-1946 *RelLAm 91*
**Cushman,** Vera F. 1944- *WhoBlA 92*
**Cushny,** Theodorus Van Wyck 1932- *WhoFI 92*
**Cushwa,** Joy Ellen Scarnecchia 1937- *WhoFI 92*
**Cusick,** Mary Lynn 1955- *WhoMW 92*
**Cusick,** Ralph A., Jr. 1934- *WhoFI 92*
**Cusick,** Randy Gerard 1959- *WhoFI 92, WhoWest 92*
**Cusick,** Richie Tankersley 1952- *ConAu 134, SmATA 67 [port]*
**Cusick,** Robert Erik 1964- *WhoWest 92*
**Cusick,** Thomas A. 1944- *WhoMW 92*
**Cusick,** Thomas William 1943- *AmMWSc 92*
**Cusimano,** Charles Vincent, II 1953- *WhoAmP 91*
**Cussler,** Clive 1931- *IntAu&W 91, WrDr 92*
**Cussler,** Edward Lansing *WhoMW 92*
**Cusson,** Theodore J, Sr 1936- *WhoAmP 91*
**Cust** *Who 92*
**Custance,** Michael Magnus Vere 1916- *Who 92*
**Custard,** Herman Cecil 1929- *AmMWSc 92*
**Custer,** Charles Francis 1928- *WhoAmL 92*
**Custer,** Chris Edward 1960- *WhoEnt 92*
**Custer,** Clint *TwCWW 91*
**Custer,** Elizabeth 1842-1933 *EncAmaz 91*
**Custer,** Elizabeth Bacon 1842-1933 *BenetAL 91*
**Custer,** Felipe Antonio 1954- *WhoFI 92*
**Custer,** George Armstrong 1839-1876 *BenetAL 91, RComAH*
**Custer,** George Armstrong, III d1991 *NewYTBS 91*
**Custer,** Mary Louise 1936- *WhoAmP 91*
**Custer,** Michael 1910- *AmMWSc 92*
**Custer,** Quessnal Stewart, Jr. 1931- *WhoRel 92*
**Custer,** Richard Philip 1903- *AmMWSc 92*
**Custer-Chen,** Johnnie M. 1948- *WhoBlA 92*
**Custin,** Richard Randall 1960- *WhoEnt 92*
**Custis,** Clarence A. *WhoBlA 92*
**Custis,** George Washington Parke 1781-1857 *BenetAL 91*
**Custis,** Patrick James 1921- *Who 92*
**Custis,** Ronald Alfred 1931- *Who 92*
**Custis,** Thomas K. 1948- *WhoFI 92*
**Cusumano,** James A 1942- *AmMWSc 92*
**Cusumano,** Michele *DrAPF 91*
**Cusumano,** Robert M. 1937- *WhoMW 92*
**Cutbush,** Edward 1772-1843 *BiInAmS*
**Cutbush,** James 1788-1823 *BiInAmS*
**Cutcher,** Alan David 1939- *WhoAmP 91*
**Cutchins,** Clifford Armstrong, III 1923- *WhoFI 92*
**Cutchins,** Clifford Armstrong, IV 1948- *WhoFI 92*
**Cutchins,** Ernest Charles 1922- *AmMWSc 92*
**Cutchins,** Malcolm Armstrong 1935- *AmMWSc 92*
**Cutcliffe,** Jack Alexander 1929- *AmMWSc 92*
**Cutforth,** Howard Glen 1920- *AmMWSc 92*
**Cuthbert,** Lady 1904- *Who 92*
**Cuthbert,** Alan William 1932- *IntWW 91, Who 92*
**Cuthbert,** Ian Holm *Who 92*
**Cuthbert,** Marion Vera 1896-1989 *NotBlAW 92 [port]*
**Cuthbert,** Rosalind 1951- *TwCPaSc*
**Cuthbert,** William R. 1919- *WhoFI 92*
**Cuthbertson,** Betsy Alice 1952- *WhoAmL 92*
**Cuthbertson,** Harold 1911- *Who 92*
**Cuthill,** Elizabeth 1923- *AmMWSc 92*
**Cuthill,** John R 1918- *AmMWSc 92*
**Cuthrell,** Keith Coniston, Jr. 1952- *WhoFI 92*
**Cuthrell,** Robert Eugene 1933- *AmMWSc 92*
**Cutilletta,** Thomas Paul 1943- *WhoFI 92, WhoMW 92*
**Cutillo,** Louis Sabino 1934- *WhoAmP 91*
**Cutkomp,** Laurence Kremer 1916- *AmMWSc 92*
**Cutkosky,** Richard Edwin 1928- *AmMWSc 92*
**Cutler,** Arnold Robert 1908- *WhoAmL 92, WhoFI 92*
**Cutler,** Arthur Roden 1916- *IntWW 91, Who 92*
**Cutler,** Benjamin M, II 1944- *WhoIns 92*
**Cutler,** Bruce *DrAPF 91*
**Cutler,** Cassius Chapin 1914- *AmMWSc 92*
**Cutler,** Charles 1918- *Who 92*
**Cutler,** Charles Russell 1924- *WhoAmL 92*
**Cutler,** Devorah Ann 1952- *WhoEnt 92*
**Cutler,** Donald 1943- *WhoBlA 92*
**Cutler,** Doyle O 1936- *AmMWSc 92*
**Cutler,** Edward Bayler 1935- *AmMWSc 92*
**Cutler,** Frank Allen, Jr 1920- *AmMWSc 92*
**Cutler,** Frank Charles 1949- *WhoFI 92*
**Cutler,** Goldie *WhoAmP 91*
**Cutler,** Gordon Butler, Jr 1947- *AmMWSc 92*
**Cutler,** Horace 1912- *Who 92*
**Cutler,** Horace Garnett 1932- *AmMWSc 92*
**Cutler,** Horace Walter 1912- *IntWW 91*
**Cutler,** Hugh Carson 1912- *AmMWSc 92*
**Cutler,** Irwin Herbert 1943- *WhoAmL 92*
**Cutler,** Ivor *IntAu&W 91*
**Cutler,** Ivor 1923- *Who 92, WrDr 92*
**Cutler,** Jane *DrAPF 91*
**Cutler,** Janice Zemanek 1942- *AmMWSc 92*
**Cutler,** Jay B 1930- *WhoAmP 91*
**Cutler,** Jeffrey Alan 1942- *AmMWSc 92*
**Cutler,** Jimmy Edward 1944- *AmMWSc 92*
**Cutler,** John Charles 1915- *AmMWSc 92, WhoFI 92*
**Cutler,** Kenneth Burnett 1932- *WhoAmL 92*
**Cutler,** Kenneth Ross 1920- *WhoWest 92*
**Cutler,** Leonard Samuel 1928- *AmMWSc 92*
**Cutler,** Leroy Respess 1934- *WhoRel 92*
**Cutler,** Leslie Stuart 1943- *AmMWSc 92*
**Cutler,** Lloyd Norton 1917- *WhoAmL 92*
**Cutler,** Lorraine Masters 1943- *WhoWest 92*
**Cutler,** Louise Marie 1921- *AmMWSc 92*
**Cutler,** Lynn Germain 1938- *WhoAmP 91*
**Cutler,** Manasseh 1742-1823 *BiInAmS*
**Cutler,** Mary Levin 1933- *WhoWest 92*
**Cutler,** Melvin 1923- *AmMWSc 92*
**Cutler,** Norman Barry 1942- *WhoFI 92, WhoMW 92*
**Cutler,** Norton, Jr. 1952- *WhoAmL 92*
**Cutler,** Paul 1920- *AmMWSc 92*
**Cutler,** Paul H 1926- *AmMWSc 92*
**Cutler,** Richard Bruce 1931- *WhoWest 92*
**Cutler,** Richard Gail 1935- *AmMWSc 92*
**Cutler,** Robert W P 1933- *AmMWSc 92*
**Cutler,** Robin *Who 92*
**Cutler,** Roden *IntWW 91, Who 92*
**Cutler,** Roger T 1946- *AmMWSc 92*
**Cutler,** Roland *DrAPF 91*
**Cutler,** Royal Anzly, Jr 1918- *AmMWSc 92*
**Cutler,** Stephen David 1936- *WhoFI 92*
**Cutler,** Steve Keith 1948- *WhoAmP 91*
**Cutler,** Timothy Robert 1934- *Who 92*
**Cutler,** Verne Clifton 1926- *AmMWSc 92*
**Cutler,** Walter Leon 1931- *IntWW 91*
**Cutler,** Warren Gale 1922- *AmMWSc 92*
**Cutler,** Winnifred Berg 1944- *AmMWSc 92*
**Cutliff,** John Wilson 1923- *WhoBlA 92*
**Cutlip,** Michael B 1941- *AmMWSc 92*
**Cutlip,** Randall Curry 1934- *AmMWSc 92*
**Cutlip,** William Frederick 1936- *AmMWSc 92*
**Cutnell,** John Daniel 1940- *AmMWSc 92*
**Cutress,** Charles Ernest 1921- *AmMWSc 92*
**Cutrie,** Sherri Ann 1948- *WhoFI 92*
**Cutright,** James Marr 1927- *WhoAmL 92, WhoMW 92*
**Cutright,** Paul Grant, II 1947- *WhoWest 92*
**Cutrona,** Louis J 1915- *AmMWSc 92*
**Cutrone,** Emmanuel Joseph 1938- *WhoRel 92*
**Cutrone,** Luigi Cutrone 1950- *WhoFI 92*
**Cutrono,** Tony Louis 1958- *WhoEnt 92*
**Cutsforth,** Thomas William 1953- *WhoWest 92*
**Cutshall,** Norman Hollis 1938- *AmMWSc 92*
**Cutshall,** Theodore Wayne 1928- *AmMWSc 92*
**Cutshaw,** James Michael 1950- *WhoAmL 92*
**Cutshaw,** John William, Jr. 1932- *WhoAmL 92*
**Cutshaw,** Kenneth Andrew 1953- *WhoAmL 92*
**Cutt,** Roger Alan 1936- *AmMWSc 92*
**Cutt,** Samuel Robert 1925- *Who 92*
**Cutten,** George Barton 1874-1962 *DcNCBi 1*
**Cutter,** Curtis Brooks 1959- *WhoAmL 92*
**Cutter,** Dennis Michael 1945- *WhoFI 92*
**Cutter,** Elizabeth Graham 1929- *Who 92*
**Cutter,** Ephraim 1832-1917 *BiInAmS*
**Cutter,** John Michael 1952- *WhoMW 92*
**Cutter,** Lois Jotter 1914- *AmMWSc 92*
**Cutter,** Robert Charles 1940- *WhoAmL 92*
**Cutter,** Tom *ConAu 35NR, TwCWW 91, WrDr 92*
**Cutter,** William 1937- *WhoRel 92*
**Cutting,** C Suydam 1889-1972 *FacFETw*
**Cutting,** Harold D 1929- *WhoAmP 91*
**Cutting,** Hiram Adolphus 1832-1892 *BiInAmS*
**Cutting,** Mable Goodhue 1910- *WhoAmP 91*
**Cutting,** Mary Dorothea 1943- *WhoEnt 92, WhoFI 92*
**Cutts,** Charles E 1914- *AmMWSc 92*
**Cutts,** David 1940- *AmMWSc 92*
**Cutts,** James Harry 1926- *AmMWSc 92*
**Cutts,** Janet Lynn 1954- *WhoWest 92*
**Cutts,** Richard Dominicus 1817-1883 *BiInAmS*
**Cutts,** Richard Stanley 1919- *Who 92*
**Cutts,** Robert Irving 1915- *AmMWSc 92*
**Cutts,** Simon 1944- *IntWW 91*
**Cutz,** Ernest 1942- *AmMWSc 92*
**Cuvier,** Georges Leopold 1769-1832 *BlkwCEP*
**Cuvillies,** Francois 1695-1768 *BlkwCEP*
**Cuyjet,** Aloysius Baxter 1947- *WhoBlA 92*
**Cuyjet,** Cynthia K. 1948- *WhoBlA 92*
**Cuypers,** Charles James 1949- *WhoAmL 92*
**Cuypers,** Pierre Joseph Hubert 1827-1921 *DcTwDes*
**Cuyvers,** Luc 1954- *WhoEnt 92*
**Cuza,** Alexandre C. 1857-1946 *BiDExR*
**Cuza Male,** Belkis 1942- *WhoHisp 92*
**Cuzzetto,** Charles Edward 1954- *WhoFI 92*
**Cvancara,** Alan Milton 1933- *AmMWSc 92*
**Cvancara,** Victor Alan 1937- *AmMWSc 92*
**Cvengros,** William D 1948- *WhoIns 92*
**Cvetkovic,** Nikola Berndt 1945- *WhoFI 92*
**Cwalina,** Gustav Edward 1909- *AmMWSc 92*
**Cwiakala,** Anthony Michael 1956- *WhoFI 92*
**Cwik,** Wayne S 1947- *WhoIns 92*
**Cwoenthryth** *EncAmaz 91*
**Cybriwsky,** Alex 1914- *AmMWSc 92*
**Cybulski,** Radoslaw 1924- *IntWW 91*
**Cyccone,** Louis A. 1956- *WhoMW 92*
**Cycmanick,** Carol George 1944- *WhoAmP 91*
**Cygan,** Norbert Everett 1930- *AmMWSc 92*
**Cygan,** Robert Adam 1932- *WhoMW 92*
**Cyganowski,** Carol Klimick 1949- *WhoMW 92*
**Cykler,** John Freuler 1916- *AmMWSc 92*
**Cymbala,** Robert Joseph 1937- *WhoFI 92*
**Cymbalista,** Debbie *DrAPF 91*
**Cymbler,** Murray Joel 1948- *WhoFI 92*
**Cyme** *EncAmaz 91*
**Cymerman,** Allen 1942- *AmMWSc 92*
**Cymrot,** Mark Alan 1947- *WhoAmL 92*
**Cynader,** Max Sigmund 1947- *AmMWSc 92*
**Cynane** *EncAmaz 91*
**Cynethryth** *EncAmaz 91*
**Cynewulf** *RfGEnL 91*
**Cynisca** *EncAmaz 91*
**Cynkin,** Morris Abraham 1930- *AmMWSc 92*
**Cypert,** James Dean 1934- *WhoAmP 91*
**Cypess,** Raymond Harold 1940- *AmMWSc 92*
**Cypher,** Jon 1932- *ConTFT 9*
**Cyprian** 200?-258 *EncEarC*
**Cyprian of Gaul** *EncEarC*
**Cyprus And The Gulf,** Bishop in 1930- *Who 92*
**Cyprys,** Frederick 1957- *WhoFI 92*
**Cyr,** Conrad K 1931- *WhoAmP 91*
**Cyr,** Conrad Keefe 1931- *WhoAmL 92*
**Cyr,** J. V. Raymond 1934- *WhoFI 92*
**Cyr,** W Howard 1943- *AmMWSc 92*
**Cyran,** Catherine Ann 1962- *WhoEnt 92*
**Cyrankiewicz,** Jozef 1911-1989 *FacFETw*
**Cyrano De Bergerac,** Savinien 1619-1655 *ScFEYrs*
**Cyrier,** Dennis Joseph 1954- *WhoEnt 92*
**Cyril of Alexandria** 375?-444 *EncEarC*
**Cyril of Jerusalem** d387 *EncEarC*
**Cyril of Scythopolis** *EncEarC*
**Cyrillonas** *EncEarC*
**Cyrus,** Bernard E J, Jr 1953- *WhoAmP 91*
**Cyrus,** Kenneth M. *WhoAmL 92*
**Cyrus,** Ronald R 1935- *WhoAmP 91*
**Cysyk,** Richard L 1942- *AmMWSc 92*
**Cytraus,** Aldona Ona 1947- *WhoFI 92*
**Cywinska,** Izabella 1935- *IntWW 91*
**Cywinski,** Norbert Francis 1929- *AmMWSc 92*
**Czaczkes,** Morris 1955- *WhoAmL 92*
**Czaczkes,** Shmuel Yosef 1888-1970 *WhoNob 90*
**Czajka,** James Vincent 1950- *WhoFI 92*
**Czajka-Narins,** Dorice M *AmMWSc 92*
**Czajkowski,** Eva Anna 1961- *WhoFI 92*
**Czajkowski,** Frank Henry 1936- *WhoAmL 92*
**Czamanske,** Gerald Kent 1934- *AmMWSc 92*
**Czander,** Walter Wilfred 1931- *WhoFI 92*
**Czanderna,** Alvin Warren 1930- *AmMWSc 92*
**Czapanskiy,** Karen 1947- *WhoAmL 92*
**Czaplewski,** Raymond Lawrence 1949- *WhoWest 92*
**Czapski,** Ulrich Hans 1925- *AmMWSc 92*
**Czarcinski,** Donald Paul 1947- *WhoAmP 91*
**Czarnecki,** Caroline Mary Anne 1929- *AmMWSc 92*
**Czarnecki,** Eugene Bielen 1947- *WhoEnt 92*
**Czarnecki,** Gerald Milton 1940- *WhoWest 92*
**Czarnezki,** Joseph John 1954- *WhoAmP 91, WhoMW 92*
**Czarniecki,** Myron James, III 1948- *WhoMW 92*
**Czarnik,** Anthony William 1957- *WhoMW 92*
**Czarny,** Michael Richard 1950- *AmMWSc 92*
**Czarra,** Edgar F., Jr. 1928- *WhoAmL 92*
**Czartolomny,** Piotr Antoni 1946- *WhoWest 92*
**Czartoryski,** Adam Kazimierz 1734-1823 *BlkwCEP*
**Czaykowski,** Bogdan 1937- *LiExTwC*
**Czech,** Michael Paul 1945- *AmMWSc 92*
**Czechanski,** Dennis James 1946- *WhoEnt 92*
**Czeisler,** Charles Andrew 1952- *AmMWSc 92*
**Czekalski,** Loni Raven 1948- *WhoFI 92*
**Czekanski,** Pamela Nugent 1959- *WhoFI 92*
**Czepiel,** Thomas P 1932- *AmMWSc 92*
**Czepyha,** Chester George Reinhold 1927- *AmMWSc 92*
**Czerlinski,** George Heinrich 1924- *AmMWSc 92*
**Czerniawski,** Czeslaw 1925- *IntAu&W 91*

**Czernobilsky,** Bernard 1928- *AmMWSc 92*
**Czerny,** Carl 1791-1857 *NewAmDM*
**Czeropski,** Robert S 1923- *AmMWSc 92*
**Czerwinski,** Anthony William 1934- *AmMWSc 92*
**Czerwinski,** Barbara Lynn 1954- *WhoAmP 91*
**Czerwinski,** Edmund William 1940- *AmMWSc 92*
**Czerwinski,** Edward Joseph 1929- *WhoEnt 92*
**Czeschka,** Carl Otto 1878-1960 *DcTwDes, FacFETw*
**Czibere,** Tibor 1930- *IntWW 91*
**Cziffra** *Who 92*
**Cziffra,** Georges 1921- *IntWW 91*
**Czop,** Joyce K 1945- *AmMWSc 92*
**Czuba,** Leonard J 1937- *AmMWSc 92*
**Czuba,** Margaret 1947- *AmMWSc 92*
**Czuchajowski,** Leszek Maria 1926- *WhoWest 92*
**Czuchlewski,** Stephen John 1944- *AmMWSc 92*
**Czuha,** Michael, Jr 1922- *AmMWSc 92*
**Czulowski,** Edward Joseph 1914- *WhoAmP 91*
**Czuprynski,** Charles Joseph 1953- *AmMWSc 92*
**Czury,** Craig *DrAPF 91*
**Czyrek,** Jozef 1928- *IntWW 91*
**Czyzak,** Stanley Joachim 1916- *AmMWSc 92*
**Czyzewski,** Harry 1918- *AmMWSc 92*

# D

**D.A.** *AmPeW*
**Daake,** Richard Lynn 1946- *AmMWSc 92*
**Daalder,** Hans 1928- *ConAu 133*
**Daams,** Herman 1917- *AmMWSc 92*
**Daane,** Adrian Hill 1919- *AmMWSc 92*
**Daane,** James Dewey 1918- *IntWW 91*
**Daane,** Robert A 1921- *AmMWSc 92*
**Daane,** Roderick Kaye 1931- *WhoAmL 92*
**Daar,** Jeffery J. 1957- *WhoAmL 92*
**Dabb,** Wayne C., Jr. 1946- *WhoAmL 92*
**Dabbagh,** Abdallah Tahir Al- 1939- *IntWW 91*
**Dabbar,** John Michel 1962- *WhoWest 92*
**Dabberdt,** Walter F 1942- *AmMWSc 92*
**Dabbs,** Donald Henry 1921- *AmMWSc 92*
**Dabbs,** Henry Erven 1932- *WhoBlA 92, WhoEnt 92*
**Dabbs,** John Wilson Thomas 1921- *AmMWSc 92*
**Dabbs,** Roy Andrew 1950- *WhoAmP 91*
**Daberko,** David A. 1945- *WhoFI 92, WhoMW 92*
**D'Abernon,** Edgar Vincent 1857-1941 *EncTR 91 [port]*
**Dabich,** Danica 1930- *AmMWSc 92*
**Dabich,** Eli, Jr 1939- *WhoIns 92*
**Dabill,** Phillip Alvin 1942- *WhoFI 92*
**Dabner,** Jack Duane 1930- *WhoEnt 92*
**Dabney,** Charles William 1855-1945 *DcNCBi 2*
**Dabney,** David Hodges 1927- *WhoBlA 92*
**Dabney,** Fred E, II 1937- *WhoIns 92*
**Dabney,** Joseph Earl 1929- *WrDr 92*
**Dabney,** June Bosley 1935- *WhoEnt 92*
**Dabney,** Stephanie *WhoEnt 92*
**Dabney,** Virginius 1901- *IntAu&W 91, WrDr 92*
**d'Abo,** Jennifer Mary Victoria 1945- *Who 92*
**Daboll,** Nathan 1750-1818 *BiInAmS*
**Dabora,** Eli K 1928- *AmMWSc 92*
**Daborg,** Issaka 1940- *BlkOlyM*
**Dabovic,** Sebastian *DcAmImH*
**d'Abreu,** Francis Arthur 1904- *Who 92*
**D'Abrosca,** Louis A. 1950- *WhoFI 92*
**Dabrow,** Lisa Jill 1964- *WhoEnt 92*
**Dabrowiak,** James Chester 1942- *AmMWSc 92*
**Dabrowski,** Edward John 1957- *WhoEnt 92, WhoMW 92*
**Dabydeen,** Cyril 1945- *ConAu 133, WrDr 92*
**Dabydeen,** David 1956- *ConPo 91, WrDr 92*
**Dabydeen,** David 1957- *IntAu&W 91*
**Dacca** *Who 92*
**D'Accone,** Frank Anthony 1931- *WhoEnt 92*
**Dace,** Tish 1941- *IntAu&W 91, WrDr 92*
**Dace,** Wallace 1920- *ConAu 34NR*
**Dacey,** Florence Chard *DrAPF 91*
**Dacey,** George Clement 1921- *AmMWSc 92*
**Dacey,** John Robert 1914- *AmMWSc 92*
**Dacey,** John W H 1952- *AmMWSc 92*
**Dacey,** Michael F. *WhoFI 92*
**Dacey,** Philip *DrAPF 91*
**Dacey,** Philip 1939- *ConPo 91, IntAu&W 91, WrDr 92*
**Dacheux,** Ramon F, II 1947- *AmMWSc 92*
**Dacheville,** Colette 1932- *IntWW 91*
**Dachinger,** Hugo 1908- *TwCPaSc*
**Dachinger,** Meta 1916-1983 *TwCPaSc*
**Dachis,** Jeffrey Adam 1966- *WhoEnt 92*
**Dachs,** Joshua 1956- *WhoEnt 92*
**Dacie,** John 1912- *IntWW 91, Who 92*
**Daciuk,** Myron Michael 1919- *WhoRel 92*
**Dack,** Christopher Edward Hughes 1942- *WhoAmL 92*
**Dack,** Simon 1908- *AmMWSc 92*
**Dacko,** David 1930- *FacFETw, IntWW 91*
**Dackow,** Sandra Katherine 1951- *WhoEnt 92*
**Dacombe,** William John Armstrong 1934- *Who 92*
**Da Conceicao,** Jose Telles 1931- *BlkOlyM*
**da Costa,** Harvey Lloyd 1914- *Who 92*
**daCosta,** Jacob Mendez 1833-1900 *BiInAmS*
**DaCosta,** Sandra Trim 1948- *WhoBlA 92*
**da Costa,** Sergio Correa 1919- *Who 92*
**Dacquino,** Vincent T. *DrAPF 91*
**Dacre,** Baroness 1929- *Who 92*
**Dacre,** Jack Craven *AmMWSc 92*
**Dacre of Glanton,** Baron *WrDr 92*
**Dacre Of Glanton,** Baron 1914- *IntWW 91, Who 92*
**Dacri,** Stephen Robert 1952- *WhoEnt 92*
**Da Cunha,** Antonio Brito 1925- *AmMWSc 92*
**da Cunha,** John Wilfrid 1922- *Who 92*
**Dacy,** John Francis 1949- *WhoFI 92*
**Dada,** Joseph J, III 1962- *WhoFI 92*
**Dada,** Nayyar Ali 1943- *WhoFI 92*
**D'Adamo,** Amedeo Filiberto, Jr 1929- *AmMWSc 92*
**Dadd,** Robert Frederick 1947- *WhoFI 92*
**Daddah,** Moktar Ould 1924- *IntWW 91*
**Daddario,** Emilio Quincy 1918- *WhoAmP 91*
**Daddio,** Jo-Ann Rose 1959- *WhoFI 92*
**Daddona,** Joseph S 1933- *WhoAmP 91*
**Dade,** Malcolm G., Jr. 1931- *WhoBlA 92*
**Dade,** Malcolm G., Sr. 1903-1991 *WhoBlA 92N*
**Dade,** Philip Eugene 1929- *AmMWSc 92*
**Dadisman,** Lynn Ellen 1946- *WhoWest 92*
**Dado,** Arnold Emmett 1938- *WhoWest 92*
**Dadras,** Parviz 1940- *WhoMW 92*
**Dadswell,** Michael John 1944- *AmMWSc 92*
**Dadzie,** Kenneth 1930- *IntWW 91*
**Daecke,** Sigurd Martin 1932- *WhoRel 92*
**Daeger,** Phillip James 1942- *WhoAmP 91*
**Daehler,** Mark 1934- *AmMWSc 92*
**Daehler,** Max, Jr 1934- *AmMWSc 92*
**Daehnick,** Wilfried W 1928- *AmMWSc 92*
**Daellenbach,** Charles Byron 1939- *AmMWSc 92*
**Daemen,** Jaak J K *AmMWSc 92*
**Daemen,** Jaak Joseph K. *WhoWest 92*
**Daemer,** Will *WrDr 92*
**Daenzer,** Bernard J. 1916- *WrDr 92*
**Daenzer,** Bernard John 1916- *WhoIns 92*
**Daerr,** Richard Leo, Jr. 1944- *WhoFI 92*
**Daeschner,** Charles William, Jr 1920- *AmMWSc 92*
**Daessle,** Claude 1929- *AmMWSc 92*
**D'Aeth,** Richard 1912- *Who 92*
**Daetwiler,** Richard Dale 1931- *WhoWest 92*
**Dafallah,** Gizouli 1935- *IntWW 91*
**Dafermos,** Constantine M 1941- *AmMWSc 92*
**Dafermos,** Stella 1940- *AmMWSc 92*
**Daffner,** Gregg 1954- *WhoAmL 92*
**Dafforn,** Geoffrey Alan 1944- *AmMWSc 92*
**Dafny,** Nachum 1934- *AmMWSc 92*
**Dafoe,** Willem 1955- *IntMPA 92, IntWW 91, WhoEnt 92*
**Daga,** Raman Lall 1944- *AmMWSc 92*
**Daganzo,** Carlos Francisco 1948- *AmMWSc 92*
**Dagdigian,** Paul J 1945- *AmMWSc 92*
**Dage,** Richard Cyrus *AmMWSc 92*
**Dagenais,** Camille A. 1920- *IntWW 91*
**Dagenais,** Don Frederick 1951- *WhoAmL 92*
**Dagenais,** Marcel Gilles 1935- *IntWW 91*
**Dagenhart,** Larry Jones 1932- *WhoAmL 92*
**Dager,** Fernando E. 1961- *WhoHisp 92*
**Dager,** Robert Arnold *WhoMW 92*
**Dagg,** Anne Innis 1933- *AmMWSc 92*
**Dagg,** Ian Ralph 1928- *AmMWSc 92*
**Dagg,** Steven Gregory 1959- *WhoFI 92*
**Dagger,** William Carson 1949- *WhoAmL 92*
**Daggerhart,** James Alvin, Jr 1942- *AmMWSc 92*
**Daggett,** Beverly C *WhoAmP 91*
**Daggett,** Frank Slater 1855-1920 *BiInAmS*
**Daggett,** Horace 1931- *WhoAmP 91*
**Daggett,** John P *WhoAmP 91*
**Daggett,** Robert Sherman 1930- *WhoAmL 92, WhoFI 92, WhoWest 92*
**Daggett,** Thomas Whitford, Jr. 1932- *WhoWest 92*
**Daggs,** Leon, Jr. 1941- *WhoBlA 92*
**Daggs,** LeRoy W. 1924- *WhoBlA 92*
**Daggs,** Ray Gilbert 1904- *AmMWSc 92*
**Daggy,** Tom 1915- *AmMWSc 92*
**Daghir,** Gordon Joseph 1933- *WhoAmL 92*
**Dagilaitis,** Blaise 1961- *WhoFI 92*
**Dagirmanjian,** Rose 1930- *AmMWSc 92*
**Dagley,** Stanley 1916- *AmMWSc 92*
**Dagnall,** Thompson William 1956- *TwCPaSc*
**Dagnel,** Bobby Charles 1958- *WhoRel 92*
**Dagner,** Deana Willingham 1955- *WhoAmL 92*
**D'Agostino,** Annette Marie 1962- *WhoEnt 92*
**D'Agostino,** Harry J 1931- *WhoAmP 91*
**D'Agostino,** James Samuel, Jr 1946- *WhoFI 92, WhoIns 92*
**D'Agostino,** Mae A. 1954- *WhoAmL 92*
**D'Agostino,** Marie A *AmMWSc 92*
**D'Agostino,** Paul A 1956- *AmMWSc 92*
**D'Agostino,** Ralph B 1940- *AmMWSc 92*
**D'Agostino,** Thomas C. 1940- *WhoAmL 92*
**Dagostino,** Vincent F 1926- *AmMWSc 92*
**Dagotto,** Elbio Ruben *AmMWSc 92*
**Dagover,** Lil 1897-1980 *EncTR 91 [port]*
**Dagovitz,** Leonard Irving 1923- *WhoMW 92*
**Dague,** Peter 1948- *WhoFI 92*
**Dague,** Richard R 1931- *AmMWSc 92*
**D'Aguiar,** Fred 1960- *ConPo 91, WrDr 92*
**D'Agusto,** Karen Rose 1952- *WhoAmL 92*
**Dagworthy Prew,** Wendy Ann 1950- *IntWW 91*
**Dah,** Michel Monvel 1938- *IntWW 91*
**Dahab,** Abdul-Rahman Swar al- 1934- *IntWW 91*
**Dahab,** Richard Ezra 1952- *WhoFI 92*
**Dahanayake,** Wijeyananda 1902- *IntWW 91*
**Dahar,** Eleanor William 1961- *WhoAmL 92*
**Dahdah,** Paul *WhoRel 92*
**Daher,** Georganne Victoria 1951- *WhoAmL 92*
**Dahill,** Robert T, Jr 1937- *AmMWSc 92*
**Dahir,** Carol Ann 1950- *WhoEnt 92*
**Dahiya,** Jai Bhagwan 1956- *WhoMW 92*
**Dahiya,** Raghunath S 1931- *AmMWSc 92*
**Dahiya,** Rajbir Singh 1940- *AmMWSc 92, WhoMW 92*
**Dahl,** A Orville 1910- *AmMWSc 92*
**Dahl,** Adrian Hilman 1919- *AmMWSc 92*
**Dahl,** Alan Richard 1944- *AmMWSc 92, WhoWest 92*
**Dahl,** Alton 1937- *AmMWSc 92*
**Dahl,** Arlene 1928- *IntAu&W 91, IntMPA 92, WhoEnt 92*
**Dahl,** Arthur Lyon 1942- *AmMWSc 92*
**Dahl,** Arthur Richard 1930- *AmMWSc 92*
**Dahl,** Billie Eugene 1929- *AmMWSc 92*
**Dahl,** Birgitta 1937- *IntWW 91*
**Dahl,** Bren Bennington 1954- *WhoEnt 92*
**Dahl,** Bruce Eric 1963- *WhoAmL 92*
**Dahl,** Christopher T. 1943- *WhoEnt 92*
**Dahl,** Curtis 1920- *WhoAmP 91, WrDr 92*
**Dahl,** Elmer Vernon 1921- *AmMWSc 92*
**Dahl,** Frederick Andrew 1926- *WhoMW 92*
**Dahl,** Gardar Godfrey, Jr. 1946- *WhoWest 92*
**Dahl,** Gerald LuVern 1938- *WhoMW 92*
**Dahl,** Gregory C. 1948- *WhoFI 92*
**Dahl,** Gregory L *WhoAmP 91*
**Dahl,** H. Wayne *WhoMW 92*
**Dahl,** Harry Martin 1926- *AmMWSc 92*
**Dahl,** Harry Waldemar 1927- *WhoAmL 92, WhoFI 92, WhoMW 92*
**Dahl,** Harvey A 1926- *AmMWSc 92*
**Dahl,** Henry Lawrence, Jr. 1933- *WhoFI 92*
**Dahl,** Ingolf 1912-1970 *NewAmDM*
**Dahl,** John L 1920- *WhoAmP 91*
**Dahl,** John Robert 1934- *AmMWSc 92*
**Dahl,** Klaus Joachim 1936- *AmMWSc 92*
**Dahl,** Lawrence Frederick 1929- *AmMWSc 92*
**Dahl,** Loren Silvester 1921- *WhoAmL 92, WhoWest 92*
**Dahl,** Martin Astor 1933- *WhoIns 92*
**Dahl,** Michael Stephen 1955- *WhoEnt 92*
**Dahl,** Mildred *Who 92*
**Dahl,** Murdoch Edgcumbe d1991 *Who 92N*
**Dahl,** Nancy Ann 1932- *AmMWSc 92*
**Dahl,** Norman C 1918- *AmMWSc 92*
**Dahl,** Orin I 1935- *AmMWSc 92*
**Dahl,** Per Fridtjof 1932- *AmMWSc 92*
**Dahl,** Peter Steffen 1948- *AmMWSc 92*
**Dahl,** Randy Lynn 1957- *AmMWSc 92*
**Dahl,** Roald *DrAPF 91*
**Dahl,** Roald d1990 *IntWW 91N, Who 92N*
**Dahl,** Roald 1916-1990 *AnObit 1990, ConAu 133, FacFETw, News 91, SmATA 65*
**Dahl,** Robert 1915- *WrDr 92*
**Dahl,** Robert Alan 1915- *IntWW 91*
**Dahl,** Robert Henry 1910- *Who 92*
**Dahl,** Rodney Lewis 1935- *WhoWest 92*
**Dahl,** Roy Dennis 1939- *AmMWSc 92*
**Dahl,** Steve *WhoEnt 92*

**Dahl,** Terrence Curtis 1954- *WhoWest 92*
**Dahl,** William Edward 1936- *AmMWSc 92*
**Dahlbeck,** Eva 1920- *IntWW 91*
**Dahlberg,** Albert A 1908- *AmMWSc 92*
**Dahlberg,** Albert Edward 1938- *AmMWSc 92*
**Dahlberg,** Carl Fredrick, Jr. 1936- *WhoFI 92*
**Dahlberg,** Duane Arlen 1931- *AmMWSc 92*
**Dahlberg,** Earl Dan 1948- *AmMWSc 92*
**Dahlberg,** Edward 1900-1977 *BenetAL 91, FacFETw*
**Dahlberg,** Edwin Theodore 1892-1986 *RelLAm 91*
**Dahlberg,** Elizabeth Lundquist 1918- *WhoEnt 92*
**Dahlberg,** Gilbert Edward 1933- *WhoRel 92*
**Dahlberg,** James Eric 1940- *AmMWSc 92*
**Dahlberg,** Michael Lee 1939- *AmMWSc 92*
**Dahlberg,** Richard Craig 1929- *AmMWSc 92, WhoWest 92*
**Dahlburg,** Andrew Dickens 1956- *WhoRel 92*
**Dahle,** Karen 1945- *WhoEnt 92*
**Dahle,** Leland Kenneth 1926- *AmMWSc 92*
**Dahlem,** Franz 1892-1981 *EncTR 91*
**Dahlen,** Beverly *ConPo 91, DrAPF 91, WrDr 92*
**Dahlen,** Francis Anthony, Jr 1942- *AmMWSc 92*
**Dahlen,** Gretchen Mary 1955- *WhoMW 92*
**Dahlen,** R J 1937- *AmMWSc 92*
**Dahlen,** Richard Lester 1943- *WhoAmL 92*
**Dahlen,** Roger W 1935- *AmMWSc 92*
**Dahler,** Donald Lee, Jr. 1960- *WhoEnt 92*
**Dahler,** John S 1930- *AmMWSc 92*
**Dahlerup,** Troels 1925- *IntWW 91*
**Dahlerus,** Birger 1891-1957 *EncTR 91 [port]*
**Dahlfors,** John Ragnar 1934- *IntWW 91*
**Dahlgard,** Muriel Genevieve 1920- *AmMWSc 92*
**Dahlgren,** Carl Herman Per 1929- *WhoEnt 92*
**Dahlgren,** George 1929- *AmMWSc 92*
**Dahlgren,** Richard Marc 1952- *AmMWSc 92*
**Dahlgren,** Robert Bernard 1929- *AmMWSc 92*
**Dahlgren,** Robert R 1935- *AmMWSc 92*
**Dahlie,** Hallvard 1925- *WrDr 92*
**Dahlin,** David Carl 1917- *AmMWSc 92*
**Dahlin,** Marshall Bernander 1920- *WhoEnt 92*
**Dahling,** Daniel Fred 1957- *WhoRel 92*
**Dahling,** E Gunter 1931- *WhoIns 92*
**Dahling,** Gerald Vernon 1947- *WhoAmL 92*
**Dahlke,** Walter Emil 1910- *AmMWSc 92*
**Dahlke,** Wayne Theodore 1941- *WhoFI 92*
**Dahllof,** Urban Sigurd 1928- *IntWW 91*
**Dahlman,** Barbro Elsa 1946- *WhoEnt 92*
**Dahlman,** Douglas Lee 1940- *AmMWSc 92*
**Dahlquist,** Frederick Willis 1943- *AmMWSc 92*
**Dahlquist,** Wilbur Lynn 1942- *AmMWSc 92*
**Dahlstein,** David Keith 1959- *WhoRel 92*
**Dahlsten,** Donald L 1933- *AmMWSc 92*
**Dahlsten,** Gunnar 1927- *IntWW 91*
**Dahlstrom,** Becky Joanne 1957- *WhoEnt 92*
**Dahlstrom,** Bertil Philip, Jr 1931- *AmMWSc 92*
**Dahlstrom,** Donald A 1920- *AmMWSc 92*
**Dahlstrom,** Grant Russell 1954- *WhoWest 92*
**Dahlstrom,** Norman Herbert 1931- *WhoFI 92, WhoMW 92*
**Dahm,** Alfons George 1942- *WhoFI 92*
**Dahm,** Arnold J 1932- *AmMWSc 92*
**Dahm,** Cornelius George 1908- *AmMWSc 92*
**Dahm,** Donald B 1938- *AmMWSc 92*
**Dahm,** Donald J 1941- *AmMWSc 92*
**Dahm,** Donald James 1941- *WhoRel 92*
**Dahm,** Douglas Barrett 1928- *AmMWSc 92*
**Dahm,** Karl Heinz 1935- *AmMWSc 92*
**Dahm,** Marion 1918- *WhoAmP 91*
**Dahm,** Paul Adolph 1917- *AmMWSc 92*
**Dahmane,** Razak 1950- *WhoMW 92*
**Dahmen,** Gene Davidson 1941- *WhoAmL 92*
**Dahmen,** Jerome J 1919- *AmMWSc 92*
**Dahmer,** Jeffrey L. *NewYTBS 91 [port]*
**Dahmer,** Michael D 1950- *WhoAmP 91*
**Dahms,** Arthur Robert, III 1944- *WhoFI 92*
**Dahms,** Arthur Stephen 1943- *AmMWSc 92*
**Dahms,** Thomas Edward 1942- *AmMWSc 92*
**Dahmus,** Michael E 1941- *AmMWSc 92*
**Dahn,** Carl James 1936- *WhoMW 92*
**Dahn,** Conard Curtis 1939- *AmMWSc 92*
**Dahn,** Jeffery Raymond 1957- *AmMWSc 92*
**Dahneke,** Barton Eugene 1939- *AmMWSc 92*
**Dahnke,** Richard John 1934- *WhoMW 92*
**Dahod,** Aarif Mansur 1952- *WhoFI 92*
**Dahrendorf,** Ralf 1929- *IntWW 91, Who 92, WrDr 92*
**Dahy,** Edward John 1930- *WhoWest 92*
**Dai Ailian** 1916- *IntWW 91*
**Dai Jie** *IntWW 91*
**Dai Qianding** 1925- *IntWW 91*
**Dai Suli** 1960- *IntWW 91*
**Dai,** Hai-Lung 1954- *AmMWSc 92*
**Dai,** Peter Kuang-Hsun 1934- *WhoWest 92*
**Dai,** Xue Zheng 1944- *AmMWSc 92*
**Daiber,** Franklin Carl 1919- *AmMWSc 92*
**Daiber,** Hans Joachim 1942- *IntWW 91*
**Daich,** Jon E. 1956- *WhoWest 92*
**Daiches,** David 1912- *FacFETw, IntAu&W 91, IntWW 91, Who 92, WrDr 92*
**Daiches,** Lionel Henry 1911- *Who 92*
**Daicoff,** George Ronald 1930- *AmMWSc 92*
**Daidone,** Lewis Eugene 1957- *WhoFI 92*
**Daidone,** Stephen M. 1954- *WhoFI 92*
**Daie,** Jaleh 1948- *AmMWSc 92*
**Daigger,** Glen T. 1951- *WhoWest 92*
**Daigh,** John D 1930- *AmMWSc 92*
**Daigle,** Donald J 1939- *AmMWSc 92*
**Daigle,** Ellis Joseph 1948- *WhoAmL 92*
**Daigle,** Gilfred L 1929- *WhoIns 92*
**Daigle,** Josephine Siragusa 1926- *AmMWSc 92*
**Daigle,** Marsha Ann 1946- *WhoMW 92*
**Daigle,** Paul Nelson 1938- *WhoWest 92*
**Daigle,** Robert A 1921- *WhoAmP 91*
**Daigle,** Ronald Elvin 1944- *WhoWest 92*
**Daignault,** David William 1939- *WhoWest 92*
**Daignault,** Elphege *DcAmImH*
**Daigneault,** Aubert 1932- *AmMWSc 92*
**Daigneault,** Ernest Albert 1928- *AmMWSc 92*
**Daigneault,** Gary John 1951- *WhoEnt 92*
**Daigneault,** Rejean 1941- *AmMWSc 92*
**Daigon,** Ruth *DrAPF 91*
**Daijavad,** Shahvokh 1960- *AmMWSc 92*
**Daiker,** Donald Arthur 1938- *WhoAmP 91, WhoMW 92*
**Dail,** C C *ScFEYrs*
**Dail,** Clarence Wilding 1907- *AmMWSc 92*
**Dail,** Joseph Garner, Jr. 1932- *WhoAmL 92*
**Dailacis,** Diane D 1939- *WhoIns 92*
**Dailey,** Benjamin Peter 1919- *AmMWSc 92*
**Dailey,** C L 1917- *AmMWSc 92*
**Dailey,** Charles E, III 1926- *AmMWSc 92*
**Dailey,** Coleen Hall 1955- *WhoAmL 92*
**Dailey,** Cornelius Edwin, Jr. 1959- *WhoAmL 92*
**Dailey,** Floyd Collins, Jr. 1960- *WhoAmL 92*
**Dailey,** Frank Allen 1946- *AmMWSc 92*
**Dailey,** Franklyn Edward, Jr. 1921- *WhoFI 92*
**Dailey,** Fred William 1908- *WhoWest 92*
**Dailey,** Frederick M 1945- *WhoAmP 91*
**Dailey,** George 1938- *AmMWSc 92*
**Dailey,** George Randolph 1943- *WhoIns 92*
**Dailey,** Harry A 1950- *AmMWSc 92*
**Dailey,** Irene 1920- *WhoEnt 92*
**Dailey,** Jacob Edward 1927- *WhoWest 92*
**Dailey,** James Roberts 1919- *WhoAmP 91*
**Dailey,** Janet *IntAu&W 91*
**Dailey,** Janet 1944- *TwCWW 91, WrDr 92*
**Dailey,** Joel *DrAPF 91*
**Dailey,** John William 1943- *AmMWSc 92*
**Dailey,** Joseph Patrick 1922- *AmMWSc 92*
**Dailey,** Mark W *WhoAmP 91*
**Dailey,** Mary *WhoMW 92*
**Dailey,** Mitch R 1953- *WhoAmP 91*
**Dailey,** Morris Owen *AmMWSc 92*
**Dailey,** Paul William, Jr 1937- *AmMWSc 92*
**Dailey,** Pauline F 1930- *WhoAmP 91*
**Dailey,** Peter H 1930- *WhoAmP 91*
**Dailey,** Quintin 1961- *WhoBlA 92*
**Dailey,** Robert Arthur 1945- *AmMWSc 92*
**Dailey,** Thelma *WhoBlA 92*
**Daily,** Bill 1928- *ConTFT 9*
**Daily,** Carolyn Joyce 1939- *WhoMW 92*
**Daily,** Fay Kenoyer 1911- *AmMWSc 92, WhoMW 92*
**Daily,** Frank Jerome 1942- *WhoAmL 92*
**Daily,** Fred 1945- *WhoAmP 91*
**Daily,** James Milford 1926- *WhoRel 92*
**Daily,** James W 1913- *AmMWSc 92*
**Daily,** John W 1943- *AmMWSc 92*
**Daily,** Lynn Y. 1955- *WhoHisp 92*
**Daily,** Richard W. 1945- *WhoAmL 92, WhoWest 92*
**Daily,** Sandra *WhoRel 92*
**Daily,** Susan *DrAPF 91*
**Daily,** Thomas V. 1927- *WhoRel 92*
**Daily,** Todd Eugene 1963- *WhoMW 92, WhoRel 92*
**Daily,** William Allen 1912- *AmMWSc 92, WhoMW 92*
**Dain,** Arthur John 1912- *Who 92*
**Dain,** David John Michael 1940- *Who 92*
**Dain,** Jeremy George 1941- *AmMWSc 92*
**Dain,** Joel A 1931- *AmMWSc 92*
**Dain,** Lester Carroll 1951- *WhoFI 92*
**Daines,** Darrel 1922- *WhoAmP 91*
**Daingerfield,** Elliott 1859-1932 *DcNCBi 2*
**Daintith,** Terence Charles 1942- *IntWW 91, Who 92*
**Dainton** *Who 92*
**Dainton,** Baron 1914- *IntWW 91, Who 92*
**Dainton,** Frederick 1914- *WrDr 92*
**Dainton,** Frederick Sydney 1914- *FacFETw*
**Daintrey,** Adrian 1902-1988 *TwCPaSc*
**Dainty,** Anton Michael 1942- *AmMWSc 92*
**Dainty,** Christopher 1947- *Who 92*
**Dainty,** Jack 1919- *AmMWSc 92*
**Daire,** Alberto 1967- *WhoHisp 92*
**Dairiki,** Ned Tsuneo 1936- *AmMWSc 92*
**Dairiki,** Setsuo 1922- *AmMWSc 92*
**Dairman,** Wallace M *AmMWSc 92*
**Dais,** Larry 1945- *WhoBlA 92*
**Dais,** Virginia Anne 1962- *WhoMW 92*
**Daisey,** Joan M 1941- *AmMWSc 92*
**Daisley,** Edwin Trayes, Jr. 1928- *WhoMW 92*
**Daisley,** Richard John 1930- *WhoAmP 91*
**Daitch,** Susan *DrAPF 91*
**Daitch,** Susan 1954- *IntAu&W 91*
**Daitz,** Mimi Segal 1939- *WhoEnt 92*
**D'Aiutolo,** Diane Virginia 1959- *WhoAmL 92*
**Dajani,** Adnan S 1936- *AmMWSc 92*
**Dajani,** Esam Zafer 1940- *AmMWSc 92*
**Dakay,** Alan R 1952- *WhoIns 92*
**Dake,** Charles Romyn *ScFEYrs*
**Dake,** Charles Safely, Jr. 1952- *WhoRel 92*
**Dake,** James Emmit 1925- *WhoRel 92*
**Dakers,** Lionel Frederick 1924- *Who 92*
**Dakin,** Christine Whitney 1949- *WhoEnt 92*
**Dakin,** Dorothy Danvers 1919- *Who 92*
**Dakin,** James Thomas 1945- *AmMWSc 92*
**Dakin,** John A 1852-1900 *BiInAmS*
**Dakin,** Matt Eitel 1936- *AmMWSc 92*
**Dakin,** Paul Edward 1956- *WhoRel 92*
**Dakin,** Thomas Wendell 1915- *AmMWSc 92*
**Dakos,** Minas James 1937- *WhoAmP 91*
**Dakov,** Mako 1920- *IntWW 91*
**Dakshinamurti,** Krishnamurti 1928- *AmMWSc 92*
**Dakss,** Mark Ludmer 1940- *AmMWSc 92*
**Dal,** Erik 1922- *IntWW 91*
**Daladier,** Edouard 1884-1970 *EncTR 91 [port], FacFETw*
**Dalager,** Lloyd *WhoRel 92*
**Dalai Lama** *Who 92*
**Dalai Lama** 1935- *FacFETw, WhoRel 92*
**Dalai LamaXIV** 1935- *WhoNob 90*
**Dalai Lama,** The 1935- *IntWW 91*
**Dalais,** Pierre 1929- *Who 92*
**Dalal,** Fram Rustom 1935- *AmMWSc 92*
**Dalal,** Harish Maneklal 1943- *AmMWSc 92*
**Dalal,** Maneck Ardeshir Sohrab 1918- *Who 92*
**Dalal,** Nar S 1941- *AmMWSc 92*
**Dalal,** Siddhartha Ramanlal 1948- *AmMWSc 92*
**Dalal,** Vikram 1944- *AmMWSc 92*
**Dalambakis,** Christopher A. 1960- *WhoMW 92*
**D'Alarcao,** Hugo T 1937- *AmMWSc 92*
**D'Alba,** Joel Abbott 1944- *WhoAmL 92*
**Dalbec,** Paul Euclide 1935- *AmMWSc 92*
**Dalbeck,** Richard Bruce 1929- *WhoIns 92*
**Dalbeck,** Richard Warren 1948- *WhoEnt 92*
**Dalberg,** Leonard Edwin 1925- *WhoRel 92*
**Dalberto,** Michel 1955- *IntWW 91*
**Dalby,** Claire 1944- *TwCPaSc*
**Dalby,** Frederick William 1928- *AmMWSc 92*
**Dalby,** John Mark Meredith 1938- *Who 92*
**Dalby,** Peter Lenn 1943- *AmMWSc 92*
**Dalby,** Terry David 1933- *Who 92*
**Dal Canto,** Mauro Carlo 1944- *AmMWSc 92*
**Dal Co,** Francesco 1945- *ConAu 133*
**Dalcourt,** Gerard Joseph 1927- *IntAu&W 91, WrDr 92*
**Dalcroze** *NewAmDM*
**Dale,** Alfred Stuart 1926- *WhoRel 92*
**Dale,** Alvin C 1919- *AmMWSc 92*
**Dale,** Antony 1912- *IntAu&W 91, WrDr 92*
**Dale,** Barry Gordon 1938- *Who 92*
**Dale,** Beverly A 1942- *AmMWSc 92*
**Dale,** Beverly Ann 1942- *WhoWest 92*
**Dale,** Brian 1930- *AmMWSc 92*
**Dale,** Cathy Joe 1963- *WhoEnt 92*
**Dale,** Celia Marjorie *IntAu&W 91*
**Dale,** Clamma Churita 1953- *WhoBlA 92*
**Dale,** Daryl D. 1943- *WhoRel 92*
**Dale,** David Kenneth Hay 1927- *Who 92*
**Dale,** Denver Thomas, III 1931- *WhoWest 92*
**Dale,** Douglas Keith 1924- *AmMWSc 92*
**Dale,** Edward Everett, Jr 1920- *AmMWSc 92*
**Dale,** Edwin 1933- *AmMWSc 92*
**Dale,** Edwin L, Jr 1923- *WhoAmP 91*
**Dale,** Ernest 1917- *WhoFI 92*
**Dale,** Ernest Brock 1918- *AmMWSc 92*
**Dale,** Francis Lykins 1921- *WhoWest 92*
**Dale,** George 1940- *WhoAmP 91*
**Dale,** George E. *ConAu 36NR*
**Dale,** George Leslie 1948- *AmMWSc 92*
**Dale,** Glenn H 1923- *AmMWSc 92*
**Dale,** Grover 1935- *WhoEnt 92*
**Dale,** Harvey Philip 1937- *WhoAmL 92*
**Dale,** Henry Hallett 1875-1968 *FacFETw, WhoNob 90*
**Dale,** Homer Eldon 1922- *AmMWSc 92*
**Dale,** J D 1939- *AmMWSc 92*
**Dale,** Jack Kyle 1921- *AmMWSc 92*
**Dale,** James Lowell 1922- *AmMWSc 92*
**Dale,** James Michael 1948- *WhoFI 92*
**Dale,** Jim 1935- *IntMPA 92, Who 92, WhoEnt 92*
**Dale,** John Carter 1924- *WhoFI 92*
**Dale,** John Irvin, III 1935- *AmMWSc 92*
**Dale,** John Patrick 1950- *WhoMW 92*
**Dale,** John Sorensen 1945- *WhoFI 92*
**Dale,** Joseph 1923- *WhoAmP 91*
**Dale,** Judy Ries 1944- *WhoRel 92*
**Dale,** Kenneth Ray 1948- *WhoMW 92*
**Dale,** Larry Huston 1946- *WhoFI 92*
**Dale,** Leon Andrew 1921- *WhoFI 92*
**Dale,** Leonard Alvin 1921- *WhoRel 92*
**Dale,** Leonard Alvin, Jr. 1949- *WhoRel 92*
**Dale,** Louis 1935- *WhoBlA 92*
**Dale,** Margaret Jessy 1911- *IntAu&W 91*
**Dale,** Martin Albert 1932- *WhoFI 92*
**Dale,** Norman *TwCSFW 91*
**Dale,** Peter 1938- *ConPo 91, WrDr 92*
**Dale,** Peter John 1938- *IntAu&W 91*
**Dale,** Richard 1932- *WrDr 92*
**Dale,** Richard Ray 1958- *WhoAmL 92*
**Dale,** Richard Scott 1950- *WhoFI 92*
**Dale,** Robert Alan 1938- *Who 92*
**Dale,** Robert Dennis 1940- *WhoRel 92*
**Dale,** Robert J. 1943- *WhoBlA 92*
**Dale,** Sharon R. 1955- *WhoWest 92*
**Dale,** Stanley Joseph 1948- *WhoAmL 92*
**Dale,** Suzanne *DrAPF 91*
**Dale,** Virginia House 1951- *AmMWSc 92*
**Dale,** Virginia Marie 1925- *WhoBlA 92*
**Dale,** Walter Riley 1944- *WhoMW 92*
**Dale,** Wesley John 1921- *AmMWSc 92*
**Dale,** William *WrDr 92*
**Dale,** William 1906- *Who 92*
**Dale,** William 1942- *AmMWSc 92*
**Dale,** William Andrew 1920- *AmMWSc 92*
**D'Alecy,** Louis George 1941- *AmMWSc 92*
**Dalehite,** Thomas H 1918- *AmMWSc 92*
**d'Alembert,** Jean Le Rond *BlkwCEP*
**D'Alemberte,** Talbot Sandy 1933- *WhoAmL 92*
**Dalen,** Nils Gustaf 1869-1937 *FacFETw, WhoNob 90*
**D'Aleo,** Sal 1962- *WhoEnt 92*
**Dales,** George Gus 1921- *WhoMW 92*
**Dales,** Ien 1931- *IntWW 91*
**Dales,** Richard Nigel 1942- *Who 92*
**Dales,** Samuel 1927- *AmMWSc 92*
**D'Alesandro,** Philip Anthony 1927- *AmMWSc 92*
**Daleski,** H M 1926- *IntAu&W 91, WrDr 92*
**D'Alessandro,** Daniel Anthony 1949- *WhoAmL 92*
**D'Alessandro-Bacigalupo,** Antonio 1926- *AmMWSc 92*
**D'Alessio,** Edward Patrick 1958- *WhoAmL 92*
**Daley,** Alexander Spotswood 1935- *WhoRel 92*
**Daley,** Anne Belisle 1907- *WhoAmP 91*
**Daley,** Anthony 1960- *TwCPaSc*
**Daley,** Brian C 1947- *TwCSFW 91, WrDr 92*
**Daley,** Brian Charles 1947- *IntAu&W 91*
**Daley,** Daniel H 1920- *AmMWSc 92*
**Daley,** Darryl Lee 1950- *AmMWSc 92*
**Daley,** Donald Oscar 1934- *WhoFI 92*
**Daley,** Francis Darnall, Jr. 1938- *WhoFI 92*
**Daley,** Guilbert Alfred 1923- *WhoBlA 92*
**Daley,** Harry 1901-1971 *ConAu 134*
**Daley,** Henry Owen, Jr 1936- *AmMWSc 92*
**Daley,** James Morris 1946- *WhoMW 92*
**Daley,** James U. 1946- *WhoEnt 92*
**Daley,** Jodi Goddess 1957- *WhoEnt 92*
**Daley,** John 1923- *WhoAmP 91*

**Daley,** John Alexander 1953- *WhoWest 92*
**Daley,** John P 1946- *WhoAmP 91*
**Daley,** Laurence Stephen 1936- *AmMWSc 92*
**Daley,** Paul Patrick 1941- *WhoAmL 92*
**Daley,** Peter Edmund 1943- *WhoFI 92*
**Daley,** Peter John, II 1950- *WhoAmP 91*
**Daley,** Richard 1902-1976 *RComAH*
**Daley,** Richard J 1902-1976 *FacFETw*
**Daley,** Richard Joseph 1902-1976 *AmPolLe*
**Daley,** Richard M 1942- *WhoAmP 91*
**Daley,** Richard Michael 1942- *WhoMW 92*
**Daley,** Robert *IntMPA 92*
**Daley,** Robert 1930- *IntAu&W 91, WrDr 92*
**Daley,** Stephen Dennis 1948- *ConAu 133*
**Daley,** Thelma Thomas *WhoBlA 92*
**Daley,** Victor Neil 1943- *WhoIns 92*
**Daley,** Vincent Raymond, Jr. 1940- *WhoMW 92*
**Daley,** William Thomas 1961- *WhoMW 92*
**Daley-Kauffman,** Sandra 1933- *WhoAmP 91*
**Dalferes,** Edward R., Jr. 1931- *WhoBlA 92*
**D'Alfonso,** Gina Marie 1961- *WhoAmL 92*
**D'Alfonso,** Mario Joseph 1951- *WhoAmL 92*
**Dalgarno,** Alexander 1928- *AmMWSc 92, IntWW 91, Who 92*
**Dalgety,** Ramsay Robertson 1945- *Who 92*
**Dalgleish,** Arthur E 1920- *AmMWSc 92*
**Dalgleish,** James *WrDr 92*
**Dalgleish,** James C. *TwCWW 91*
**Dalgleish,** Robert Campbell 1940- *AmMWSc 92*
**Dalglish,** Edward Russell 1913- *WrDr 92*
**Dalglish,** James Stephen 1913- *Who 92*
**Dalglish,** Kenneth 1951- *FacFETw*
**Dalgoutte,** Christopher Noel 1957- *WhoAmL 92*
**Dalhart,** Vernon 1883-1948 *NewAmDM*
**Dalhouse,** Warner Norris 1934- *WhoFI 92*
**Dalhousie,** Earl of 1914- *IntWW 91, Who 92*
**Dali,** Salvador 1904-1989 *FacFETw [port]*
**Dalia,** Frank J 1928- *AmMWSc 92*
**Dalin,** Olof von 1708-1763 *BlkwCEP*
**Daling,** Paul Leslie 1959- *WhoEnt 92*
**Dalins,** Ilmars 1927- *AmMWSc 92*
**Dalis,** Irene 1925- *WhoEnt 92, WhoWest 92*
**D'Alisa,** Rose M 1948- *AmMWSc 92*
**Dalitz,** Richard Henry 1925- *IntWW 91, Who 92, WrDr 92*
**Dalka,** Dolly 1932- *IntAu&W 91*
**Dalke,** Wayne L. 1928- *WhoMW 92*
**Dalkeith,** Earl of 1954- *Who 92*
**Dall,** Caroline Wells 1822-1912 *HanAmWH*
**Dall,** Curtis B. d1991 *NewYTBS 91*
**Dalla,** Ronald Harold 1942- *AmMWSc 92*
**Dalla Betta,** Ralph A 1945- *AmMWSc 92*
**dalla Chiesa,** Romeo 1924- *IntWW 91*
**Dalla Lana,** I G 1926- *AmMWSc 92*
**Dallam,** Richard Duncan 1925- *AmMWSc 92*
**Dallam,** Richard Franklin, II 1954- *WhoWest 92*
**Dallapiccola,** Luigi 1904-1975 *FacFETw, NewAmDM*
**Dallara,** Charles H. 1948- *IntWW 91*
**Dallas,** Daniel George 1932- *WhoMW 92*
**Dallas,** George Mifflin 1792-1864 *AmPolLe*
**Dallas,** Ruth 1919- *ConPo 91, IntAu&W 91, WrDr 92*
**Dallas,** William Moffit, Jr. 1949- *WhoAmL 92*
**Dalldorf,** Frederic Gilbert 1932- *AmMWSc 92*
**Dalle,** Francois Leon Marie-Joseph 1918- *IntWW 91*
**Dallek,** Robert 1934- *IntAu&W 91, WrDr 92*
**Dallen,** James 1943- *WhoRel 92*
**Dallenbach,** Robert Barney 1927- *WhoRel 92*
**Dalley,** Arthur Frederick, II 1948- *AmMWSc 92*
**Dalley,** Christopher Mervyn 1913- *IntWW 91, Who 92*
**Dalley,** George Albert 1941- *WhoAmP 91, WhoBlA 92*
**Dalley,** Joseph W 1918- *AmMWSc 92*
**Dalley,** Terence 1935- *TwCPaSc*
**Dallin,** Leon 1918- *WhoEnt 92*
**Dallman,** Elaine *DrAPF 91*
**Dallman,** Mary Fenner *AmMWSc 92*
**Dallman,** Paul Jerald 1939- *AmMWSc 92*
**Dallman,** Peter R 1929- *AmMWSc 92*
**Dallmeier,** Francisco 1953- *WhoHisp 92*
**Dallmeyer,** Mary Dorinda Gilmore 1952- *WhoAmL 92*
**Dallmeyer,** R David 1944- *AmMWSc 92*
**Dallos,** Andras 1921- *AmMWSc 92*
**Dallos,** Peter John 1934- *AmMWSc 92*
**Dallow,** Phyllis Florence 1924- *WhoFI 92*
**Dally,** Ann 1926- *WrDr 92*
**Dally,** Ann Gwendolen 1926- *IntAu&W 91*
**Dally,** James William 1929- *AmMWSc 92*
**Dally,** Jesse LeRoy 1923- *AmMWSc 92*
**Dalman,** G Conrad 1917- *AmMWSc 92*
**Dalman,** Gary 1936- *AmMWSc 92*
**Dalman,** Jessie Fiesselmann 1933- *WhoAmP 91*
**Dalmas,** John 1926- *IntAu&W 91*
**Dalmasso,** Agustin Pascual 1933- *AmMWSc 92*
**Dalmbert,** Robert Lorts 1930- *WhoAmL 92*
**Dalmeny,** Lord 1967- *Who 92*
**Dalmia,** Mriduhari 1941- *IntWW 91*
**Dalmia,** Vishnu Hari 1924- *IntWW 91*
**D'Aloia,** Giambattista Peter 1945- *WhoAmL 92, WhoFI 92*
**Dalpe,** Yolande 1948- *AmMWSc 92*
**Dalphin,** John Francis 1940- *AmMWSc 92*
**Dalpiaz,** Julius Anthony 1931- *WhoAmP 91*
**d'Alquen,** Gunter *EncTR 91 [port]*
**D'Alquen,** Gunter 1910- *BiDExR*
**Dalquest,** Walter Woelberg 1917- *AmMWSc 92*
**Dalrymple** *Who 92*
**Dalrymple,** Viscount 1961- *Who 92*
**Dalrymple,** Byron William 1910- *WhoEnt 92*
**Dalrymple,** David Lawrence 1940- *AmMWSc 92*
**Dalrymple,** Desmond Grant 1938- *AmMWSc 92*
**Dalrymple,** Elizabeth Barkley 1945- *WhoAmP 91*
**Dalrymple,** Gary Brent 1937- *AmMWSc 92*
**Dalrymple,** Glenn Vogt 1934- *AmMWSc 92*
**Dalrymple,** Hew Hamilton- 1926- *Who 92*
**Dalrymple,** Ina Lynn 1926- *WhoRel 92*
**Dalrymple,** Jack *WhoAmP 91*
**Dalrymple,** Jean 1902- *WrDr 92*
**Dalrymple,** Jean Van Kirk 1902- *WhoEnt 92*
**Dalrymple,** Joel McKeith 1939- *AmMWSc 92*
**Dalrymple,** John 1705?-1766 *DcNCBi 2*
**Dalrymple,** John Kern 1954- *WhoMW 92*
**Dalrymple,** Robert Anthony 1945- *AmMWSc 92*
**Dalrymple,** Ronald Howell 1943- *AmMWSc 92*
**Dalrymple,** Stephen Harris 1932- *AmMWSc 92*
**Dalrymple,** Thomas Lawrence 1921- *WhoAmL 92*
**Dalrymple-Hamilton of Bargany,** North E 1922- *Who 92*
**Dalrymple-Hay,** James Brian 1928- *Who 92*
**Dalrymple-White,** Henry Arthur Dalrymple 1917- *Who 92*
**Dalsager,** Poul 1929- *Who 92*
**Dalsager,** Poul Christian 1929- *IntWW 91*
**Dal Santo,** Diane 1949- *WhoAmL 92*
**Dalshaug,** Allan Emory 1931- *WhoWest 92*
**Dalsimer,** Susan *IntMPA 92*
**Dalterio,** Susan Linda 1949- *AmMWSc 92*
**Dalton,** Alan 1923- *Who 92*
**Dalton,** Alfred Hyam 1922- *Who 92*
**Dalton,** Augustine Ivanhoe, Jr 1942- *AmMWSc 92*
**Dalton,** Barbara J 1953- *AmMWSc 92*
**Dalton,** Charles X 1840-1912 *BiInAmS*
**Dalton,** Colin 1936- *AmMWSc 92*
**Dalton,** Daniel J 1949- *WhoAmP 91*
**Dalton,** David Robert 1936- *AmMWSc 92*
**Dalton,** Donald Francis 1961- *WhoAmL 92*
**Dalton,** Dorothy *DrAPF 91*
**Dalton,** Edwina P 1936- *WhoAmP 91*
**Dalton,** Francis Norbert *AmMWSc 92*
**Dalton,** Frank H., Jr. 1956- *WhoMW 92*
**Dalton,** G. E. 1942- *WrDr 92*
**Dalton,** G Ronald 1932- *AmMWSc 92*
**Dalton,** Geoffrey 1931- *Who 92*
**Dalton,** George 1926-1991 *ConAu 135*
**Dalton,** Harry 1928- *WhoMW 92*
**Dalton,** Harry P 1929- *AmMWSc 92*
**Dalton,** Howard Clark 1915- *AmMWSc 92*
**Dalton,** Howard Edward 1937- *WhoFI 92*
**Dalton,** Irwin 1932- *Who 92*
**Dalton,** Jack L 1931- *AmMWSc 92*
**Dalton,** James Christopher 1943- *AmMWSc 92*
**Dalton,** Jay Dean 1938- *WhoAmL 92*
**Dalton,** Jessy Kid *WrDr 92*
**Dalton,** John Call, Jr 1825-1889 *BiInAmS*
**Dalton,** John Charles 1931- *AmMWSc 92*
**Dalton,** John Thomas 1879-1966 *DcNCBi 2*
**Dalton,** Joseph Ridings 1963- *WhoEnt 92*
**Dalton,** Kenneth M. 1954- *WhoAmL 92*
**Dalton,** Kevin Michael 1955- *WhoAmL 92*
**Dalton,** Kit *TwCWW 91*
**Dalton,** Larry Raymond 1943- *AmMWSc 92*
**Dalton,** Lisa 1954- *TwCPaSc*
**Dalton,** Lonnie Gene 1934- *AmMWSc 92*
**Dalton,** Margaret Anne 1951- *WhoAmL 92*
**Dalton,** Norman 1904- *Who 92*
**Dalton,** Pamela Yvonne Werton 1943- *WhoWest 92*
**Dalton,** Patrick Daly 1922- *AmMWSc 92*
**Dalton,** Peter Gerald Fox 1914- *Who 92*
**Dalton,** Peter John 1944- *WhoFI 92*
**Dalton,** Philip Benjamin 1923- *AmMWSc 92*
**Dalton,** Phyllis Irene 1909- *WhoWest 92*
**Dalton,** Priscilla *WrDr 92*
**Dalton,** Raymond Andrew 1942- *WhoBlA 92*
**Dalton,** Roger Wayne 1936- *AmMWSc 92*
**Dalton,** Ronnie Thomas 1953- *WhoRel 92*
**Dalton,** Roque 1935-1975 *ConSpAP*
**Dalton,** Roy Bale, Jr. 1952- *WhoAmL 92*
**Dalton,** Ruth Margaret 1926- *WhoMW 92*
**Dalton,** Sammy Dale 1951- *WhoAmP 91*
**Dalton,** Timothy 1946- *IntMPA 92, IntWW 91*
**Daltrey,** Roger 1944- *IntMPA 92, WhoEnt 92*
**Daluege,** Kurt 1897-1946 *BiDExR, EncTR 91 [port]*
**Daluz,** Lucia *WhoRel 92*
**Dalva,** Robert John 1942- *WhoEnt 92*
**Dalven,** Richard 1931- *AmMWSc 92*
**Dalvi,** Ramesh R 1938- *AmMWSc 92*
**Dalwood,** Dexter 1960- *TwCPaSc*
**Dalwood,** Hubert 1924-1976 *TwCPaSc*
**Daly,** Alexander Joseph 1930- *WhoRel 92*
**Daly,** Augustin 1838-1899 *BenetAL 91*
**Daly,** Barrett Bond 1954- *WhoAmL 92*
**Daly,** Bartholomew Joseph 1929- *AmMWSc 92*
**Daly,** Brendan 1940- *IntWW 91*
**Daly,** Cahal Brendan *Who 92*
**Daly,** Cahal Brendan 1917- *IntAu&W 91, IntWW 91, WhoRel 92, WrDr 92*
**Daly,** Casey *WhoAmP 91*
**Daly,** Catherine Mary 1938- *WhoRel 92*
**Daly,** Charles Joseph 1933- *WhoMW 92*
**Daly,** Charles Patrick 1816-1899 *BiInAmS*
**Daly,** Charles Wason 1916- *WhoAmL 92*
**Daly,** Christopher 1954- *IntAu&W 91*
**Daly,** Chuck 1933- *CurBio 91 [port]*
**Daly,** Clarence M d1904 *BiInAmS*
**Daly,** Colin Henry 1940- *AmMWSc 92*
**Daly,** Daniel Francis, Jr 1939- *AmMWSc 92*
**Daly,** David DeRouen 1919- *AmMWSc 92*
**Daly,** Donald Francis 1928- *WhoFI 92*
**Daly,** Edna M 1906- *WhoAmP 91*
**Daly,** Edward H, Jr 1952- *WhoIns 92*
**Daly,** Edward J 1922-1984 *FacFETw*
**Daly,** Edward Kevin 1933- *IntWW 91*
**Daly,** Elizabeth 1878-1967 *BenetAL 91*
**Daly,** Francis Lenton 1938- *Who 92*
**Daly,** Frederica Y. 1925- *WhoBlA 92*
**Daly,** Gabriel Conor 1927- *IntWW 91*
**Daly,** Gene B 1918- *WhoAmP 91*
**Daly,** George Garman 1940- *WhoFI 92*
**Daly,** Howell Vann 1933- *AmMWSc 92*
**Daly,** James C 1938- *AmMWSc 92*
**Daly,** James Edward 1948- *AmMWSc 92*
**Daly,** James Joseph 1921- *WhoRel 92*
**Daly,** James Joseph 1935- *AmMWSc 92*
**Daly,** James Michael, III 1958- *WhoMW 92*
**Daly,** James William 1931- *AmMWSc 92*
**Daly,** Jehan 1918- *TwCPaSc*
**Daly,** Jim 1938- *IntMPA 92*
**Daly,** John *NewYTBS 91 [port]*
**Daly,** John 1914-1991 *CurBio 91N*
**Daly,** John 1937- *IntMPA 92*
**Daly,** John 1947- *AmMWSc 92*
**Daly,** John, Jr. 1914-1991 *IntWW 91, -91N*
**Daly,** John Anthony 1937- *AmMWSc 92*
**Daly,** John Augustin 1838-1899 *DcNCBi 2*
**Daly,** John B *WhoAmP 91*
**Daly,** John Charles d1991 *LesBEnT 92*
**Daly,** John Charles, Jr. 1914-1991 *NewYTBS 91 [port]*
**Daly,** John Charles Sydney 1903- *Who 92*
**Daly,** John F 1912- *AmMWSc 92*
**Daly,** John Francis 1916- *AmMWSc 92*
**Daly,** John Joseph, Jr 1926- *AmMWSc 92*
**Daly,** John M *AmMWSc 92*
**Daly,** John Matthew 1925- *AmMWSc 92*
**Daly,** John Patrick, Jr. 1959- *WhoAmL 92*
**Daly,** John Paul 1939- *WhoAmL 92*
**Daly,** John T 1938- *AmMWSc 92*
**Daly,** John W 1931- *WhoAmP 91*
**Daly,** John William 1933- *AmMWSc 92*
**Daly,** Joseph Leo 1942- *WhoAmL 92, WhoMW 92*
**Daly,** Joseph Michael 1922- *AmMWSc 92*
**Daly,** Joseph Patrick 1957- *WhoAmL 92*
**Daly,** Judith Marie 1950- *WhoFI 92*
**Daly,** Kevin Richard 1931- *AmMWSc 92*
**Daly,** Lawrence 1924- *Who 92*
**Daly,** Leo 1920- *WrDr 92*
**Daly,** Leo Arthur 1920- *IntAu&W 91*
**Daly,** Lowrie J. 1914- *WrDr 92*
**Daly,** Margaret Elizabeth 1938- *Who 92*
**Daly,** Maria Vega 1950- *WhoHisp 92*
**Daly,** Marie Maynard 1921- *AmMWSc 92, WhoBlA 92*
**Daly,** Mary 1928- *HanAmWH, WrDr 92*
**Daly,** Mary F. *WhoRel 92*
**Daly,** Maureen *IntAu&W 91, WrDr 92*
**Daly,** Michael de Burgh 1922- *Who 92*
**Daly,** Michael Francis 1931- *Who 92*
**Daly,** Nancy Jane 1932- *WhoWest 92*
**Daly,** Nicholas 1946- *ConAu 36NR*
**Daly,** Niki *ConAu 36NR*
**Daly,** Niki 1946- *IntAu&W 91*
**Daly,** Patricia Marie 1963- *WhoMW 92*
**Daly,** Patrick Joseph 1933- *AmMWSc 92*
**Daly,** Patrick William 1947- *AmMWSc 92*
**Daly,** Paul Sylvester 1934- *WhoWest 92*
**Daly,** Randall Eugene 1955- *WhoWest 92*
**Daly,** Richard *WhoRel 92*
**Daly,** Robert A. *LesBEnT 92*
**Daly,** Robert A. 1936- *IntMPA 92*
**Daly,** Robert Anthony 1936- *WhoEnt 92, WhoFI 92, WhoWest 92*
**Daly,** Robert Baylor 1948- *WhoMW 92*
**Daly,** Robert E 1937- *AmMWSc 92*
**Daly,** Robert J. 1933- *WhoRel 92*
**Daly,** Robert J, Jr 1928- *WhoAmP 91*
**Daly,** Robert Ward 1932- *AmMWSc 92*
**Daly,** Ronald Edwin 1947- *WhoBlA 92*
**Daly,** Ruth Agnes 1958- *AmMWSc 92*
**Daly,** Saralyn R. *DrAPF 91*
**Daly,** Seaton Maurice, Jr. 1945- *WhoAmL 92*
**Daly,** Simeon Philip John 1922- *WhoMW 92, WhoRel 92*
**Daly,** Thomas 1913- *Who 92*
**Daly,** Thomas A. 1871-1948 *BenetAL 91*
**Daly,** Thomas J. *WhoRel 92*
**Daly,** Timothy 1956- *IntMPA 92*
**Daly,** Tyne 1946- *IntMPA 92*
**Daly,** Tyne 1947- *WhoEnt 92*
**Daly,** Walter J 1930- *AmMWSc 92*
**Daly,** William Howard 1939- *AmMWSc 92*
**Daly,** William Joseph 1928- *WhoAmL 92*
**Dalyell,** Tam 1932- *Who 92*
**Dalzell,** Jeffrey Alexander 1956- *WhoEnt 92*
**Dalzell,** Robert Clinton 1919- *AmMWSc 92*
**Dalzell,** Steven William 1958- *WhoFI 92*
**Dalzell,** William Howard 1936- *AmMWSc 92*
**Dalzell Payne,** Henry Salusbury Legh 1929- *Who 92*
**Dalziel,** Geoffrey Albert 1912- *Who 92*
**Dalziel,** Ian William Drummond 1937- *AmMWSc 92*
**Dalziel,** Keith 1921- *Who 92*
**Dalziel,** Malcolm Stuart 1936- *Who 92*
**Dam,** Carl Peter Henrik 1895-1976 *WhoNob 90*
**Dam,** Cecil Frederick 1923- *AmMWSc 92*
**Dam,** Dwight E 1917- *WhoAmP 91*
**Dam,** Johannes Victor Van 1946- *IntAu&W 91*
**Dam,** Kenneth W. 1932- *IntWW 91, WhoAmL 92, WhoFI 92*
**Dam,** Richard 1929- *AmMWSc 92*
**Dam,** Rudy Johan 1949- *AmMWSc 92*
**Dama,** Richard 1962- *WhoEnt 92*
**Damadian,** Raymond 1936- *AmMWSc 92*
**Daman,** Ernest L 1923- *AmMWSc 92*
**Daman,** Harlan Richard 1941- *AmMWSc 92*
**Damann,** Kenneth Eugene, Jr 1944- *AmMWSc 92*
**Damas,** Leon-Gontran 1912-1978 *LiExTwC*
**Damashek,** Philip Michael 1940- *WhoAmL 92*
**Damask,** Arthur Constantine 1924- *AmMWSc 92*
**Damaska,** Mirjan Radovan 1931- *WhoAmL 92*
**Damaskus,** Charles William 1924- *AmMWSc 92, WhoMW 92*
**DaMassa,** Al John 1929- *AmMWSc 92*
**Damassa,** David Allen 1950- *AmMWSc 92*
**Damasus I** *EncEarC*
**D'Amato,** Alfonse M. *NewYTBS 91 [port]*
**D'Amato,** Alfonse M. 1937- *AlmAP 92 [port], IntWW 91, WhoAmP 91*
**D'Amato,** Anthony 1937- *WhoAmL 92*
**D'Amato,** Anthony A. 1937- *WrDr 92*
**D'Amato,** Armand P 1944- *WhoAmP 91*
**D'Amato,** Constance Joan 1933- *AmMWSc 92*
**D'Amato,** Frank Edward 1963- *WhoFI 92*
**D'Amato,** Henry Edward 1928- *AmMWSc 92*
**D'Amato,** Richard John 1940- *AmMWSc 92*
**Damaz,** Paul F. 1917- *WrDr 92*
**Dambach,** George Ernest 1942- *AmMWSc 92*
**Dambach,** Virginia Lee 1949- *WhoEnt 92*

**Damberg,** David Vern 1933- *WhoMW 92*
**Damberger,** Heinz H 1933- *AmMWSc 92, WhoMW 92*
**Dambman,** Mary Elizabeth 1935- *WhoAmP 91*
**d'Amboise,** Jacques 1934- *FacFETw*
**d'Amboise,** Jacques Joseph 1934- *WhoEnt 92*
**Damborg,** Mark J 1939- *AmMWSc 92*
**D'Ambra,** James S 1946- *WhoAmP 91*
**D'Ambra,** Michael V 1947- *WhoAmP 91*
**D'Ambrosio,** Blanche Fada Grawe 1926- *WhoWest 92*
**D'Ambrosio,** Eugene Joseph 1921- *WhoFI 92*
**D'Ambrosio,** Richard Michael 1946- *WhoFI 92*
**D'Ambrosio,** Steven M 1949- *AmMWSc 92*
**D'Ambrosio,** Ubiratan 1932- *AmMWSc 92*
**D'Ambrosio,** Vinnie-Marie *DrAPF 91*
**D'Ambrosio,** Vito 1957- *WhoEnt 92*
**D'Ambrosio,** Vito Mario 1954- *WhoFI 92*
**Dambruch,** Edward L *WhoAmP 91*
**Damdin,** Paavangiyn 1931- *IntWW 91*
**Dame,** Charles 1929- *AmMWSc 92*
**Dame,** David Allan 1931- *AmMWSc 92*
**Dame,** Enid *DrAPF 91*
**Dame,** Richard Edward 1937- *AmMWSc 92*
**Dame,** Richard Franklin 1941- *AmMWSc 92*
**Dame,** Rose A 1941- *WhoAmP 91*
**Dame,** Samuel 1917- *WhoEnt 92*
**Dame,** William Page, III 1940- *WhoFI 92*
**Damen,** Margaret May 1943- *WhoFI 92*
**Damen,** Theo C 1933- *AmMWSc 92*
**Damer** *Who 92*
**Damer,** Linda K. 1938- *WhoEnt 92, WhoMW 92*
**Damerau,** Frederick Jacob 1931- *AmMWSc 92*
**Damerell,** Derek Vivian 1921- *Who 92*
**Dameron,** Chip *DrAPF 91*
**Dameron,** Larry Wright 1949- *WhoFI 92*
**Dameron,** Tadd 1917-1965 *NewAmDM*
**Damerow,** Richard Aasen 1936- *AmMWSc 92*
**Dames,** George P 1937- *WhoAmP 91*
**Dames,** Kenneth Albert *WhoBlA 92*
**Dames,** Rob 1944- *ConAu 133*
**Dames,** Sabrina A. 1957- *WhoBlA 92*
**Damewood,** Glenn *AmMWSc 92*
**Damgaard,** Neil Christian 1952- *WhoRel 92*
**Damian,** Carol G 1939- *AmMWSc 92*
**Damian,** Raymond T 1934- *AmMWSc 92*
**Damiano,** Anthony D. 1962- *WhoAmL 92*
**Damianou,** Pantelis Andrea 1953- *WhoWest 92*
**Damianov,** Vladimir B 1938- *AmMWSc 92*
**Damich,** Edward John 1948- *WhoAmL 92*
**D'Amico,** Anthony Joseph 1951- *WhoAmL 92*
**D'Amico,** Frank Jacob, Jr. 1960- *WhoAmL 92*
**D'Amico,** John C 1936- *WhoAmP 91*
**D'Amico,** Joseph Allen 1962- *WhoAmL 92, WhoFI 92*
**D'Amico,** Michael 1936- *WhoWest 92*
**Damico,** Nicholas Peter 1937- *WhoAmL 92*
**Damico,** Nuncio Joseph 1938- *WhoAmP 91*
**D'Amico,** Salvatore J 1924- *WhoAmP 91*
**Damien of Molokai,** Father 1840-1889 *RelLAm 91*
**Damilaville,** Etienne Noel 1723-1768 *BlkwCEP*
**Damin,** David E. 1947- *WhoMW 92*
**Damisch,** Mark William 1956- *WhoAmP 91*
**Damisch,** Thomas Andrew 1960- *WhoAmL 92*
**Damjanov,** Ivan 1941- *AmMWSc 92*
**Damkaer,** David Martin 1938- *AmMWSc 92*
**Damle,** Suresh B 1935- *AmMWSc 92*
**Damm,** Charles Conrad 1924- *AmMWSc 92*
**Damm,** John Silber 1926- *WhoRel 92*
**Damm,** Walter J. d1962 *LesBEnT 92*
**Damman,** Antoni Willem Hermanus 1932- *AmMWSc 92*
**Dammann,** Gordon Edward 1945- *WhoMW 92*
**Dammann,** John Francis 1917- *AmMWSc 92*
**Dammerman,** Dennis Dean 1945- *WhoFI 92*
**Dammers,** Alfred Hounsell 1921- *Who 92*
**Dammeyer,** Rodney Foster 1940- *WhoFI 92*
**Dammin,** Gustave J. d1991 *NewYTBS 91*
**Dammin,** Gustave John 1911- *AmMWSc 92*
**Damodaran,** Kalyani Muniratnam 1938- *AmMWSc 92*
**Damon,** Dwight Hills 1931- *AmMWSc 92*
**Damon,** Edward G 1927- *AmMWSc 92*
**Damon,** Edward K 1928- *AmMWSc 92*
**Damon,** Henry Eugene 1926- *WhoAmP 91*
**Damon,** James Christian 1951- *WhoWest 92*
**Damon,** James Norman 1945- *AmMWSc 92*
**Damon,** Mark 1933- *IntMPA 92*
**Damon,** Miracyl Jane 1927- *WhoAmP 91*
**Damon,** Paul Edward 1921- *AmMWSc 92*
**Damon,** Richard Winslow 1923- *AmMWSc 92*
**Damon,** Robert A 1932- *AmMWSc 92*
**Damon,** S. Foster 1893-1971 *BenetAL 91*
**Damon,** William Emerson 1838-1911 *BiInAmS*
**Damon,** William Winchell 1943- *WhoFI 92*
**Damone,** Vic 1928- *IntMPA 92*
**Damonte,** James C 1949- *WhoIns 92*
**Damonte,** John Batista 1925- *AmMWSc 92*
**Damoose,** Carol Sweeney 1942- *WhoFI 92*
**Damore,** Leo 1929- *ConAu 35NR*
**D'Amore,** Michael Brian 1945- *AmMWSc 92*
**D'Amore,** Patricia Ann 1951- *AmMWSc 92*
**D'Amore,** Thomas J 1941- *WhoAmP 91*
**D'Amore,** Victor 1943- *WhoEnt 92*
**Damos,** Diane Lynn 1949- *AmMWSc 92*
**DaMotta,** Lorraine 1957- *WhoFI 92*
**Damour,** Frederick Windle 1940- *WhoAmL 92*
**Damour,** Paul Lawrence 1937- *AmMWSc 92*
**D'Amours,** Norman Edward 1937- *WhoAmP 91*
**Damouth,** David Earl 1937- *AmMWSc 92*
**Dampier,** Frederick Walter 1941- *AmMWSc 92*
**Damron,** Bobby Leon 1941- *AmMWSc 92*
**Damron,** Charles Hoadley 1944- *WhoAmP 91*
**Damrosch,** Frank 1859-1937 *NewAmDM*
**Damrosch,** Leopold 1832-1885 *NewAmDM*
**Damrosch,** Lori Fisler 1953- *WhoAmL 92*
**Damrosch,** Walter 1862-1950 *BenetAL 91, NewAmDM*
**Damsbo,** Ann Marie 1931- *WhoWest 92*
**Damschroder,** Gene 1922- *WhoAmP 91*
**Damsel,** Richard A. 1942- *WhoFI 92, WhoMW 92*
**Damsgaard,** Kell Marsh 1949- *WhoAmL 92*
**Damski,** Mel 1946- *IntMPA 92*
**Damsky,** Kenneth Lawrence 1946- *WhoFI 92*
**Damsky,** Robert Philip 1921- *WhoWest 92*
**Damson,** Barrie Morton 1936- *WhoFI 92*
**Damsteegt,** Don Calvin 1946- *WhoMW 92*
**Damsteegt,** Vernon Dale 1936- *AmMWSc 92*
**Damstra,** Wanda Lou 1936- *WhoAmP 91*
**Damtoft,** Walter Julius 1890-1976 *DcNCBi 2*
**Damusis,** Adolfas 1908- *AmMWSc 92*
**Damuth,** John Erwin 1942- *AmMWSc 92*
**Dan,** Fedor Ilyich 1871-1947 *FacFETw*
**Dan-Cohen,** Meir 1949- *WhoAmL 92*
**Dan Dicko,** Dankoulodo 1934- *IntWW 91*
**Dan-Salami,** Olayinka J. 1959- *WhoAmL 92*
**Dana,** Bill 1924- *ConTFT 9, IntMPA 92*
**Dana,** Charles A. 1819-1897 *BenetAL 91*
**Dana,** Charles H. *WhoMW 92*
**Dana,** Deane, Jr 1926- *WhoAmP 91*
**Dana,** Donald *WhoWest 92*
**Dana,** Frank Mitchell 1942- *WhoEnt 92*
**Dana,** Henry Wadsworth Longfellow 1881-1950 *AmPeW, BenetAL 91*
**Dana,** James Dwight 1813-1895 *BenetAL 91, BiInAmS*
**Dana,** James Freeman 1793-1827 *BiInAmS*
**Dana,** Jerilyn Denise 1949- *WhoEnt 92*
**Dana,** Lauren Elizabeth 1950- *WhoAmL 92*
**Dana,** M Terry 1943- *AmMWSc 92*
**Dana,** Malcolm Niven 1922- *AmMWSc 92*
**Dana,** Randall M. 1945- *WhoAmL 92*
**Dana,** Richard *TwCWW 91*
**Dana,** Richard Henry, Jr. 1815-1882 *BenetAL 91*
**Dana,** Richard Henry, Sr. 1787-1879 *BenetAL 91*
**Dana,** Robert *DrAPF 91*
**Dana,** Robert 1929- *ConPo 91, IntAu&W 91, WrDr 92*
**Dana,** Robert Clark 1944- *AmMWSc 92*
**Dana,** Robert Watson *AmMWSc 92*
**Dana,** Samuel Luther 1795-1868 *BiInAmS*
**Dana,** Stephen Winchester 1920- *AmMWSc 92*
**Dana,** Walter Dan 1902- *WhoEnt 92*
**Dana-Davidson,** Laoma Cook 1925- *WhoWest 92*
**Danaher,** John Anthony, III 1950- *WhoAmL 92*
**Danaher,** Kevin 1913- *WrDr 92*
**Danaher,** Mallory Millett 1939- *WhoEnt 92*
**Danahy,** Michael Hugh 1947- *WhoEnt 92*
**Danahy,** Steven Francis 1948- *WhoMW 92*
**Danahy,** Thomas Micheal 1940- *WhoWest 92*
**Danatos,** Steven Clark 1951- *WhoAmL 92*
**Danberg,** James E 1927- *AmMWSc 92*
**Danburg,** Debra 1951- *WhoAmP 91*
**Danburg,** Jerome Samuel 1940- *AmMWSc 92*
**Danby,** Gordon Thompson 1929- *AmMWSc 92*
**Danby,** James Charles 1940- *WhoAmP 91*
**Danby,** John Michael Anthony 1929- *AmMWSc 92*
**Danby,** Mary 1941- *IntAu&W 91, WrDr 92*
**D'Anca,** John Arthur 1950- *WhoMW 92*
**Dance,** Brian David 1929- *Who 92*
**Dance,** Charles 1946- *IntMPA 92, IntWW 91*
**Dance,** Daryl Cumber 1938- *WhoBlA 92*
**Dance,** David Orin 1922- *WhoFI 92*
**Dance,** Eldred Leroy 1917- *AmMWSc 92*
**Dance,** Francis Esburn Xavier 1929- *WhoWest 92*
**Dance,** Gloria Fenderson 1932- *WhoEnt 92*
**Dance,** Stanley 1910- *IntAu&W 91, WrDr 92*
**Dancer,** J.B. *TwCWW 91, WrDr 92*
**Dancewicz,** John Edward 1949- *WhoFI 92*
**Danchik,** Richard S 1943- *AmMWSc 92*
**Dancik,** Bruce Paul 1943- *AmMWSc 92*
**Dancis,** Joseph 1916- *AmMWSc 92*
**Danco,** Leon Antoine 1923- *WhoMW 92*
**D'Ancona,** Hedy 1937- *IntWW 91*
**d'Ancona,** John Edward William 1935- *Who 92*
**Dancy,** Frank Battle 1860-1922 *DcNCBi 2*
**Dancy,** John *LesBEnT 92*
**Dancy,** John Campbell, Jr. 1857-1920 *DcNCBi 2*
**Dancy,** John Christopher 1920- *Who 92*
**Dancy,** Paul Bartlett 1954- *WhoRel 92*
**Dancy,** Terence E 1925- *AmMWSc 92*
**Dancy,** William F. 1924- *WhoBlA 92*
**Dancz,** Roger Lee 1930- *WhoEnt 92*
**Dandapani,** Ramaswami 1946- *AmMWSc 92*
**Dandaron,** Bidiya 1914-1974 *SovUnBD*
**Dandavate,** Madhu 1924- *IntWW 91*
**Dandekar,** Balkrishna S 1933- *AmMWSc 92*
**Dandeneau,** Marcel 1931- *WhoAmP 91*
**D'Andrade,** Hugh Alfred 1938- *WhoFI 92*
**D'Andrea,** Glenn M. 1964- *WhoEnt 92*
**D'Andrea,** Paul Philip 1939- *WhoEnt 92*
**D'Andrea,** Robert Anthony 1933- *WhoAmP 91*
**Dandridge,** Bob 1947- *WhoBlA 92*
**Dandridge,** Cheryl 1947- *WhoAmP 91*
**Dandridge,** Dorothy 1922-1965 *NotBlAW 92*
**Dandridge,** Douglas Bates 1939- *WhoRel 92*
**Dandridge,** Raymond Emmett 1913- *WhoBlA 92*
**Dandridge,** Rita Bernice 1940- *WhoBlA 92*
**Dandrow,** Ann P *WhoAmP 91*
**Dandurand,** Joseph Paul 1956- *WhoAmL 92*
**Dandy,** Clarence L. 1939- *WhoBlA 92*
**Dandy,** James William Trevor 1929- *AmMWSc 92*
**Dandy,** Roscoe Greer 1946- *WhoBlA 92*
**Dane,** Benjamin 1933- *AmMWSc 92*
**Dane,** Beth-Ann Sandler 1958- *WhoAmL 92*
**Dane,** Charles Warren 1934- *AmMWSc 92*
**Dane,** Clemence 1888-1965 *RfGEnL 91*
**Dane,** Eva *WrDr 92*
**Dane,** Harold John, III 1956- *WhoAmL 92*
**Dane,** Mark *WrDr 92*
**Dane,** Stephen Mark 1956- *WhoAmL 92*
**Daneault,** Gabriel 1924- *WhoAmP 91*
**Danehy,** James Philip 1912- *AmMWSc 92*
**Danehy,** Thomas William 1929- *WhoAmP 91*
**Danek,** Michael Jan 1941- *WhoMW 92*
**Daneker,** Robert Milton 1938- *WhoRel 92*
**Danelius,** Hans Carl Yngve 1934- *IntWW 91*
**Danen,** Wayne C 1941- *AmMWSc 92*
**Danenberg,** Peter V 1942- *AmMWSc 92*
**Daneo-Moore,** Lolita 1929- *AmMWSc 92*
**Daner,** Paul *WrDr 92*
**Danes,** C. W. *WhoRel 92*
**Danes,** Zdenko Frankenberger 1920- *AmMWSc 92*
**Danese,** Arthur E 1922- *AmMWSc 92*
**Danesh,** Hossain B. 1938- *WhoRel 92*
**Danford,** Darl Ray 1958- *WhoAmL 92*
**Danford,** Darla E 1945- *AmMWSc 92*
**Danforth,** Arthur Edwards 1925- *WhoFI 92*
**Danforth,** David Newton 1912- *AmMWSc 92*
**Danforth,** Douglas Dewitt 1922- *IntWW 91*
**Danforth,** Jack Timothy 1946- *WhoWest 92*
**Danforth,** John C. 1936- *AlmAP 92 [port]*
**Danforth,** John Claggett 1936- *IntWW 91, NewYTBS 91 [port], WhoAmP 91, WhoMW 92*
**Danforth,** Louis Fremont 1913- *WhoFI 92*
**Danforth,** Paul M. *WrDr 92*
**Danforth,** Raymond Hewes 1944- *AmMWSc 92*
**Danforth,** Robert L. 1945- *WhoBlA 92*
**Danforth,** Samuel 1696-1777 *BiInAmS*
**Danforth,** Samuel, Jr 1740-1827 *BiInAmS*
**Danforth,** William 1928- *AmMWSc 92*
**Danforth,** William H 1926- *AmMWSc 92*
**Danforth,** William Henry 1926- *WhoMW 92*
**Dang,** Marvin S.C. 1954- *WhoAmL 92, WhoAmP 91, WhoWest 92*
**Dang,** Minh Ngoc 1958- *WhoRel 92*
**Dang,** Peter Hung-Chen 1918- *AmMWSc 92*
**Dang,** Vi Duong *AmMWSc 92*
**Dangan,** Viscount 1965- *Who 92*
**D'Angelo,** Alfred J., Jr. 1948- *WhoAmL 92*
**D'Angelo,** Beverly *WhoEnt 92*
**D'Angelo,** Beverly 1954- *IntMPA 92*
**Dangelo,** Charles H 1950- *WhoIns 92*
**D'Angelo,** Christopher Scott 1953- *WhoAmL 92*
**D'Angelo,** Gaetano 1942- *AmMWSc 92*
**D'Angelo,** Henry 1932- *AmMWSc 92*
**D'Angelo,** James Cecil 1930- *WhoWest 92*
**D'Angelo,** John Philip 1951- *AmMWSc 92*
**D'Angelo,** Joseph Francis 1930- *WhoFI 92*
**D'Angelo,** Nicola 1931- *AmMWSc 92*
**D'Angelo,** Timothy Eric 1962- *WhoWest 92*
**D'Angelo,** William P. *LesBEnT 92*
**Dangerfield,** Clint *IntAu&W 91X, TwCWW 91, WrDr 92*
**Dangerfield,** Clyde Moultrie 1915- *WhoAmP 91*
**Dangerfield,** Rodney 1921- *IntMPA 92*
**Dangerfield,** Rodney 1922- *WhoEnt 92*
**D'Angio,** Giulio J 1922- *AmMWSc 92*
**Dangle,** Richard L 1930- *AmMWSc 92*
**D'Angona,** Teresita 1937- *WhoHisp 92*
**Danheiser,** Rick Lane 1951- *AmMWSc 92*
**Danhelka,** Anthony George 1945- *WhoRel 92*
**Danhof,** Ivan Edward 1928- *AmMWSc 92*
**Daniel Press** *DcLB 106*
**Daniel,** Alfred Irwin 1934- *WhoBlA 92*
**Daniel,** Charles Dwelle, Jr 1925- *AmMWSc 92*
**Daniel,** Charles Waller 1933- *AmMWSc 92*
**Daniel,** Daniel 1890-1981 *FacFETw*
**Daniel,** Daniel S 1934- *AmMWSc 92*
**Daniel,** David James 1938- *WhoFI 92*
**Daniel,** David L. 1906- *WhoBlA 92*
**Daniel,** David Logan 1906- *WhoMW 92*
**Daniel,** Don 1948- *WhoEnt 92*
**Daniel,** Donald Clifton 1942- *AmMWSc 92*
**Daniel,** Edward Bart 1955- *WhoAmL 92*
**Daniel,** Edwin Embrey 1925- *AmMWSc 92*
**Daniel,** Eleanor A. 1940- *WhoRel 92*
**Daniel,** Eleanor Sauer 1917- *WhoFI 92*
**Daniel,** Elinor Perkins 1952- *WhoRel 92*
**Daniel,** F E 1839-1914 *ScFEYrs*
**Daniel,** Gary Wayne 1948- *WhoEnt 92, WhoWest 92*
**Daniel,** George Berkley 1951- *WhoAmP 91*
**Daniel,** George Francis 1933- *WhoRel 92*
**Daniel,** Gerald Ernest 1919- *Who 92*
**Daniel,** Goronwy Hopkin 1914- *Who 92*
**Daniel,** Griselda 1938- *WhoBlA 92*
**Daniel,** Gruffydd Huw Morgan 1939- *Who 92*
**Daniel,** Hal J 1942- *AmMWSc 92*
**Daniel,** Hardie W *IntAu&W 91*
**Daniel,** Isaac M 1933- *AmMWSc 92*
**Daniel,** J Leland 1924- *AmMWSc 92*
**Daniel,** J. Reese 1924- *WhoAmL 92*
**Daniel,** Jack *Who 92*
**Daniel,** Jack L. 1942- *WhoBlA 92*
**Daniel,** James Edward 1935- *WhoAmP 91*
**Daniel,** James Howard 1949- *WhoAmL 92*
**Daniel,** James L *AmMWSc 92*
**Daniel,** James L. 1945- *WhoBlA 92*
**Daniel,** James Richard 1940- *WhoFI 92*
**Daniel,** James Wilson 1940- *AmMWSc 92*
**Daniel,** Jean 1920- *IntWW 91*
**Daniel,** Jerry Clayton 1937- *WhoAmL 92*
**Daniel,** Jessica Henderson 1944- *WhoBlA 92*
**Daniel,** Jill Rankin 1959- *WhoRel 92*
**Daniel,** John Harrison 1915- *AmMWSc 92*
**Daniel,** John Reeves Jones 1802-1868 *DcNCBi 2*
**Daniel,** John Sagar 1942- *AmMWSc 92, IntWW 91, Who 92*
**Daniel,** John T. *DrAPF 91*
**Daniel,** Jon Cameron 1942- *AmMWSc 92*

**Daniel**, Jonathan Russell 1961- *WhoEnt 92*
**Daniel**, Joseph Car, Jr 1927- *AmMWSc 92*
**Daniel**, Joseph John 1783-1848 *DcNCBi 2*
**Daniel**, Junius 1828-1864 *DcNCBi 2*
**Daniel**, Kenneth Rule 1913- *WhoFI 92*
**Daniel**, Kenneth Wayne 1944- *AmMWSc 92*
**Daniel**, Kimberly Jay 1956- *WhoAmL 92*
**Daniel**, Larry W 1951- *AmMWSc 92*
**Daniel**, Leonard Rupert 1926- *AmMWSc 92*
**Daniel**, Levi Garland 1918- *WhoBlA 92*
**Daniel**, Louise Jane 1912- *AmMWSc 92*
**Daniel**, Mark 1954- *ConAu 133*
**Daniel**, Mary Reed *WhoBlA 92*
**Daniel**, Melvin Randolph 1942- *WhoAmL 92*
**Daniel**, Michael R 1940- *WhoAmP 91*
**Daniel**, Michael Roger 1937- *AmMWSc 92*
**Daniel**, Milton Gilroy 1946- *WhoEnt 92*
**Daniel**, Norman Alexander 1919- *Who 92*
**Daniel**, O'Dell G 1920- *AmMWSc 92*
**Daniel**, Oliver d1990 *NewYTBS 91*
**Daniel**, Paul Mason 1924- *AmMWSc 92*
**Daniel**, Pete 1938- *WrDr 92*
**Daniel**, Peter Francis 1945- *AmMWSc 92*
**Daniel**, Peter Maxwell 1910- *Who 92*
**Daniel**, Phillip T. K. 1947- *WhoBlA 92*
**Daniel**, Reginald Jack 1920- *Who 92*
**Daniel**, Richard C. 1966- *WhoHisp 92*
**Daniel**, Richard Joel 1945- *WhoFI 92*
**Daniel**, Richard Nicholas 1935- *WhoFI 92*
**Daniel**, Robert d1718 *DcNCBi 2*
**Daniel**, Robert Edwin 1906- *WhoRel 92*
**Daniel**, Robert Eugene 1938- *AmMWSc 92*
**Daniel**, Robert Michael 1947- *WhoAmL 92*
**Daniel**, Robert Thomas 1773-1840 *DcNCBi 2*
**Daniel**, Robert Williams, Jr 1936- *WhoAmP 91*
**Daniel**, Ronald Scott 1936- *AmMWSc 92*
**Daniel**, Royal Thomas, III 1956- *WhoFI 92*
**Daniel**, Sam Mordochai 1941- *AmMWSc 92*
**Daniel**, Samuel 1562?-1619? *RfGEnL 91*
**Daniel**, Sean 1951- *IntMPA 92*
**Daniel**, Simmie Childrey 1934- *WhoBlA 92*
**Daniel**, T. 1945- *WhoEnt 92*
**Daniel**, Teresa Ann 1957- *WhoAmL 92*
**Daniel**, Thomas Bruce 1926- *AmMWSc 92*
**Daniel**, Thomas Henry 1942- *AmMWSc 92*
**Daniel**, Thomas Mallon 1928- *AmMWSc 92*
**Daniel**, Thomas W, Jr 1922- *AmMWSc 92*
**Daniel**, Victor Wayne 1943- *AmMWSc 92*
**Daniel**, Walter C. 1922- *WhoBlA 92*
**Daniel**, Walter Randy 1950- *WhoAmP 91*
**Daniel**, Wayne W. 1929- *ConAu 135*
**Daniel**, Wiley Young 1946- *WhoBlA 92*
**Daniel**, William A, Jr 1914- *AmMWSc 92*
**Daniel**, William Hugh 1919- *AmMWSc 92*
**Daniel**, William Jacob 1925- *WhoAmL 92*
**Daniel**, William L 1942- *AmMWSc 92*
**Daniel**, William Louis 1942- *WhoMW 92*
**Daniel**, William Wentworth 1938- *Who 92*
**Daniel**, Wolfgang Dieter 1939- *WhoIns 92*
**Daniel**, Yuli M 1925-1988 *FacFETw*
**Daniel'**, Yuliy Markovich 1925-1988 *SovUnBD*
**Daniel-Alston**, Tracey Ann 1961- *WhoBlA 92*
**Daniel-Lesur** 1908- *NewAmDM*
**Daniel-Lesur**, J. Y. 1908- *IntWW 91*
**Daniele**, Graciela 1939- *WhoHisp 92*
**Daniele**, Ronald P 1942- *AmMWSc 92*
**Danielewski**, Tad *IntMPA 92*
**Danielewski**, Tad Z. *WhoEnt 92*
**Danieley**, Earl 1924- *AmMWSc 92*
**Danielian**, Leon 1920- *WhoEnt 92*
**Daniell**, Averell John 1903- *Who 92*
**Daniell**, David Fleeman 1954- *WhoAmL 92*
**Daniell**, Ellen 1947- *AmMWSc 92*
**Daniell**, Herman Burch 1929- *AmMWSc 92*
**Daniell**, Jeff Walter 1924- *AmMWSc 92*
**Daniell**, Peter 1909- *Who 92*
**Daniell**, Ralph Allen 1915- *Who 92*
**Daniell**, Robert F. *IntWW 91*
**Daniell**, Robert F. 1933- *WhoFI 92*
**Daniell**, Rosemary *DrAPF 91*
**Daniell**, Roy Lorentz *Who 92*
**Daniells**, William Willard 1840-1912 *BiInAmS*
**Danielou**, Jean 1905-1974 *DcEcMov, EncEarC*
**Danielpour**, David 1955- *AmMWSc 92*
**Daniels**, A. Raiford 1944- *WhoBlA 92*
**Daniels**, Alfred 1926- *TwCPaSc*
**Daniels**, Alfred Claude Wynder 1934- *WhoBlA 92*
**Daniels**, Alma U 1939- *AmMWSc 92*
**Daniels**, Anthony Hawthorne 1950- *WhoBlA 92*
**Daniels**, Anthony Wade 1956- *WhoAmL 92*
**Daniels**, Archibald Lamont 1849-1918 *BiInAmS*
**Daniels**, Bill *LesBEnT 92*
**Daniels**, Brenda Faye Austin 1951- *WhoMW 92*
**Daniels**, Carlos Ruben 1928- *WhoHisp 92*
**Daniels**, Cary 1912- *WhoAmP 91*
**Daniels**, Casandra 1957- *WhoBlA 92*
**Daniels**, Cecil Edwin, III 1961- *WhoEnt 92*
**Daniels**, Cecil Tyrone 1941- *WhoBlA 92*
**Daniels**, Charles Cleaves 1864-1951 *DcNCBi 2*
**Daniels**, Charlie 1936- *WhoEnt 92*
**Daniels**, Charlie 1937- *ConMus 6 [port]*
**Daniels**, Charlie 1939- *WhoAmP 91*
**Daniels**, Cindy Lou 1959- *WhoFI 92*
**Daniels**, Clarence A., Jr. 1949- *WhoBlA 92*
**Daniels**, Curtis A. 1941- *WhoBlA 92*
**Daniels**, David Herbert, Jr. 1941- *WhoBlA 92*
**Daniels**, David Wilder 1933- *WhoEnt 92, WhoMW 92*
**Daniels**, Deborah J. *WhoAmL 92*
**Daniels**, Diana M. *WhoAmL 92*
**Daniels**, Don Edward 1942- *WhoFI 92*
**Daniels**, Doral Lee 1925- *WhoMW 92*
**Daniels**, Doria Lynn 1951- *WhoFI 92, WhoMW 92*
**Daniels**, Dorothy 1915- *IntAu&W 91, WrDr 92*
**Daniels**, Douglas Henry 1943- *IntAu&W 91*
**Daniels**, Drew 1958- *WhoAmP 91*
**Daniels**, Eddie *WhoEnt 92*
**Daniels**, Edward William 1917- *AmMWSc 92*
**Daniels**, Elizabeth 1938- *WhoBlA 92*
**Daniels**, Elizabeth Adams 1920- *WrDr 92*
**Daniels**, Farrington 1889-1972 *FacFETw*
**Daniels**, Farrington, Jr 1918- *AmMWSc 92*
**Daniels**, Fletcher 1919- *WhoAmP 91*
**Daniels**, Frank Arthur 1858-1939 *DcNCBi 2*
**Daniels**, Fred Harris 1853-1913 *BiInAmS*
**Daniels**, Gary L 1954- *WhoAmP 91*
**Daniels**, George 1926- *Who 92*
**Daniels**, George Benjamin 1953- *WhoAmL 92*
**Daniels**, George Morris 1927- *WhoRel 92*
**Daniels**, Geraldine L. *WhoBlA 92*
**Daniels**, Geraldine L 1933- *WhoAmP 91*
**Daniels**, Gill D. 1948- *WhoBlA 92*
**Daniels**, Harold *IntMPA 92*
**Daniels**, Harold Albert 1915- *Who 92*
**Daniels**, Harvey 1936- *TwCPaSc*
**Daniels**, Henry Ellis 1912- *IntWW 91, Who 92*
**Daniels**, Howard Irwin 1930- *WhoEnt 92*
**Daniels**, Isabelle Frances 1937- *BlkOlyM*
**Daniels**, Jack 1921- *WhoAmP 91*
**Daniels**, James Bruce 1952- *WhoAmL 92*
**Daniels**, James Eliot 1941- *WhoAmL 92*
**Daniels**, James Maurice 1924- *AmMWSc 92*
**Daniels**, James Walter 1945- *WhoAmL 92*
**Daniels**, Jean E. *WhoBlA 92*
**Daniels**, Jeff *WhoEnt 92*
**Daniels**, Jeff 1955- *IntMPA 92*
**Daniels**, Jeffrey Allen 1957- *WhoAmP 91*
**Daniels**, Jeffrey Irwin 1951- *AmMWSc 92*
**Daniels**, Jerry Claude *AmMWSc 92*
**Daniels**, Jerry Franklin 1915- *WhoBlA 92*
**Daniels**, Jess Donald 1934- *AmMWSc 92*
**Daniels**, Jesse 1935- *WhoBlA 92*
**Daniels**, Jim *DrAPF 91*
**Daniels**, Jimmie Leroy 1941- *WhoRel 92*
**Daniels**, John 1936- *WhoBlA 92*
**Daniels**, John C. *WhoBlA 92*
**Daniels**, John Clifford 1936- *WhoAmP 91*
**Daniels**, John Dean 1949- *WhoEnt 92*
**Daniels**, John Draper 1939- *WhoAmL 92*
**Daniels**, John Hartley 1931- *AmMWSc 92*
**Daniels**, John Maynard 1935- *AmMWSc 92*
**Daniels**, John S. *TwCWW 91, WrDr 92*
**Daniels**, Jon Mark 1953- *WhoMW 92*
**Daniels**, Jonathan 1902-1981 *BenetAL 91*
**Daniels**, Jonathan Worth 1902-1981 *DcNCBi 2*
**Daniels**, Jordan, Jr. 1923- *WhoBlA 92*
**Daniels**, Joseph 1931- *WhoBlA 92*
**Daniels**, Josephus 1862-1948 *BenetAL 91, DcNCBi 2, FacFETw*
**Daniels**, Keith Allen *DrAPF 91*
**Daniels**, Kenneth Richard 1943- *WhoEnt 92*
**Daniels**, Kevin Lee 1961- *WhoEnt 92*
**Daniels**, Kurt R. 1954- *WhoMW 92*
**Daniels**, L B 1940- *AmMWSc 92*
**Daniels**, Laurence John 1916- *Who 92*
**Daniels**, Lee A 1942- *WhoAmP 91*
**Daniels**, Legree S 1917- *WhoAmP 91*
**Daniels**, LeGree Sylvia 1920- *WhoBlA 92*
**Daniels**, Lemuel Lee 1945- *WhoBlA 92*
**Daniels**, Lincoln, Sr. 1932- *WhoBlA 92*
**Daniels**, Lorna Theresa *WhoAmP 91*
**Daniels**, Lydia M. 1932- *WhoWest 92*
**Daniels**, M K *WhoAmP 91*
**Daniels**, Mabel Wheeler 1878-1971 *NewAmDM*
**Daniels**, Malcolm 1930- *AmMWSc 92*
**Daniels**, Mary 1937- *IntAu&W 91, WrDr 92*
**Daniels**, Mathew Paul 1944- *AmMWSc 92*
**Daniels**, Max *IntAu&W 91X, WrDr 92*
**Daniels**, Melvin J. 1944- *WhoBlA 92*
**Daniels**, Melvin R, Jr 1925- *WhoAmP 91*
**Daniels**, Michael Alan 1946- *WhoAmL 92, WhoFI 92*
**Daniels**, Michael Paul 1930- *WhoAmL 92*
**Daniels**, Mitchell Elias, Jr 1949- *WhoAmP 91*
**Daniels**, N. Caroline 1953- *WhoFI 92*
**Daniels**, Ned Eugene 1949- *WhoAmP 91*
**Daniels**, Norma L *WhoAmP 91*
**Daniels**, Norman 1913- *IntAu&W 91*
**Daniels**, Norman A. *WrDr 92*
**Daniels**, Norman Talmadge, Jr. 1956- *WhoAmL 92*
**Daniels**, Olga *WrDr 92*
**Daniels**, Patricia Ann 1940- *WhoBlA 92*
**Daniels**, Patricia D 1947- *AmMWSc 92*
**Daniels**, Paul 1938- *IntMPA 92*
**Daniels**, Peter F. 1928- *WhoBlA 92*
**Daniels**, Peter John Lovell 1934- *AmMWSc 92*
**Daniels**, Philip *WrDr 92*
**Daniels**, Philip Bliss 1928- *WhoWest 92*
**Daniels**, Quincey 1941- *BlkOlyM*
**Daniels**, Ralph 1921- *AmMWSc 92*
**Daniels**, Raymond Bryant 1925- *AmMWSc 92*
**Daniels**, Raymond D 1928- *AmMWSc 92*
**Daniels**, Rebecca Haywood 1943- *WhoBlA 92*
**Daniels**, Reginald Shiffon 1963- *WhoBlA 92*
**Daniels**, Richard Allen 1945- *WhoMW 92*
**Daniels**, Richard Bernard 1944- *WhoBlA 92*
**Daniels**, Richard D. 1931- *WhoBlA 92*
**Daniels**, Richard Martin 1942- *WhoWest 92*
**Daniels**, Robert 1926- *WrDr 92*
**Daniels**, Robert 1927- *AmMWSc 92*
**Daniels**, Robert Artie 1949- *AmMWSc 92*
**Daniels**, Robert George Reginald 1916- *Who 92*
**Daniels**, Robert Vincent 1926- *WhoAmP 91*
**Daniels**, Ron D. *WhoBlA 92*
**Daniels**, Ronald Dale 1943- *WhoEnt 92*
**Daniels**, Roy G 1928- *WhoIns 92*
**Daniels**, Ruben 1917- *WhoBlA 92*
**Daniels**, Sarah 1956- *ConAu 133, WrDr 92*
**Daniels**, Shouri *DrAPF 91*
**Daniels**, Sidney 1923- *WhoBlA 92*
**Daniels**, Stacy Leroy 1937- *AmMWSc 92*
**Daniels**, Terry Stephen 1956- *WhoMW 92*
**Daniels**, Thomas Tyler 1960- *WhoFI 92*
**Daniels**, Tricia 1961- *WhoEnt 92*
**Daniels**, Vivian Cecille 1939- *WhoRel 92*
**Daniels**, Wilbur 1923- *WhoAmL 92*
**Daniels**, William 1927- *ConTFT 9, IntMPA 92*
**Daniels**, William B. 1930- *IntWW 91*
**Daniels**, William Burton 1930- *AmMWSc 92*
**Daniels**, William Fowler, Sr 1920- *AmMWSc 92*
**Daniels**, William Orlan 1944- *WhoBlA 92*
**Daniels**, William Richard 1931- *AmMWSc 92*
**Daniels**, William Ward 1926- *AmMWSc 92*
**Daniels**, Worth B, Jr 1925- *AmMWSc 92*
**Daniels-Severs**, Anne Elizabeth 1940- *AmMWSc 92*
**Danielsen**, Albert Leroy 1934- *WhoFI 92*
**Danielson**, Charles Irvin 1931- *WhoMW 92*
**Danielson**, David Gordon 1954- *WhoAmL 92*
**Danielson**, David Murray 1929- *AmMWSc 92*
**Danielson**, Deborah Lee 1955- *WhoFI 92*
**Danielson**, Gary R. 1953- *WhoAmL 92*
**Danielson**, George Edward, Jr 1939- *AmMWSc 92*
**Danielson**, George Elmore 1915- *WhoAmP 91*
**Danielson**, Gordon Douglas 1942- *WhoWest 92*
**Danielson**, Gordon Kenneth 1931- *AmMWSc 92*
**Danielson**, Irvin Sigwald *AmMWSc 92*
**Danielson**, James Clayton 1942- *WhoWest 92*
**Danielson**, Jerry Craig 1953- *WhoAmL 92*
**Danielson**, John George Green 1953- *WhoFI 92*
**Danielson**, Judith 1951- *WhoAmP 91*
**Danielson**, Lee Robert 1946- *AmMWSc 92*
**Danielson**, Loran Leroy 1913- *AmMWSc 92*
**Danielson**, Michael Jon 1960- *WhoRel 92*
**Danielson**, Neil David 1950- *AmMWSc 92*
**Danielson**, Paul Stephen 1947- *AmMWSc 92*
**Danielson**, Robert Eldon 1922- *AmMWSc 92*
**Danielsson**, Bengt Emmerik 1921- *IntWW 91*
**Daniero**, Joseph James 1938- *WhoFI 92*
**Danies Rincones**, Enrique E. *IntWW 91*
**Daniher**, John M. 1926- *WhoWest 92*
**Danilova**, Alexandra 1906- *FacFETw, Who 92*
**Danilowski**, Wladyslaw 1902- *WhoEnt 92*
**Daninos**, Pierre 1913- *IntWW 91, Who 92*
**Danis**, Julie Marie 1955- *WhoFI 92, WhoMW 92*
**Danis**, Peter G., Jr. 1932- *WhoFI 92, WhoWest 92*
**Danis**, Peter Godfrey 1909- *AmMWSc 92*
**Danish**, Barbara *DrAPF 91*
**Danishefsky**, Isidore 1923- *AmMWSc 92*
**Danishefsky**, Samuel 1936- *AmMWSc 92*
**Danisman**, Tarhan Ahmet 1937- *WhoFI 92*
**Danitz**, Marilynn Patricia *WhoEnt 92*
**Dank**, Milton 1920- *AmMWSc 92*
**Dankanyin**, Robert John 1934- *WhoWest 92*
**Danke**, Richard John 1937- *AmMWSc 92*
**Dankel**, Thaddeus George, Jr 1942- *AmMWSc 92*
**Danker**, Frederick William 1920- *WhoRel 92*
**Danker**, William John 1914- *WhoRel 92*
**Dankert**, Pieter 1934- *Who 92*
**Dankner**, Jay Warren 1949- *WhoAmL 92*
**Danko**, Harold 1947- *WhoEnt 92*
**Danko**, Joseph Christopher 1927- *AmMWSc 92*
**Danko**, Peter 1949- *DcTwDes*
**Danks**, Alan 1914- *Who 92*
**Danks**, Dale, Jr *WhoAmP 91*
**Danks**, Hugh Victor 1943- *AmMWSc 92*
**Dankworth**, C. D., Mrs. *Who 92*
**Dankworth**, Clementina Dinah 1927- *WhoEnt 92*
**Dankworth**, John Philip William 1927- *IntWW 91, Who 92*
**Dankworth**, Johnny 1927- *NewAmDM*
**Danky**, James P. 1947- *WhoMW 92*
**Danley**, William Shurtleff 1948- *WhoAmP 91*
**Danly**, Donald Ernest 1929- *AmMWSc 92*
**Dann**, B. Michael *WhoAmL 92*
**Dann**, Brad James 1947- *WhoFI 92*
**Dann**, Colin 1943- *WrDr 92*
**Dann**, Colin Michael 1943- *IntAu&W 91*
**Dann**, Jack *DrAPF 91*
**Dann**, Jack 1945- *IntAu&W 91, TwCSFW 91, WrDr 92*
**Dann**, Jill 1929- *Who 92*
**Dann**, John Robert 1921- *AmMWSc 92*
**Dann**, Michael H. *LesBEnT 92*
**Dann**, Robert William 1914- *Who 92*
**Dann**, Rosemary Weinstein 1948- *WhoAmL 92*
**Danna**, C. S., Sr. 1927- *WhoRel 92*
**Danna**, Jon Francis 1955- *WhoAmL 92*
**Danna**, Kathleen Janet 1945- *AmMWSc 92*
**Danna**, Mark R. 1957- *WhoAmL 92*
**Danna**, Robert 1951- *WhoWest 92*
**Danna**, Sammy Richard 1934- *WhoEnt 92*
**Dannatt**, George 1915- *TwCPaSc*
**Dannatt**, Trevor 1920- *Who 92*
**Dannay**, Frederic *BenetAL 91*
**Danne**, William Herbert, Jr. 1942- *WhoAmL 92*
**Dannecker**, Theodor 1913-1945 *EncTR 91*
**Danneels**, Godfried 1933- *IntWW 91, WhoRel 92*
**Dannehy**, Joseph F *WhoAmP 91*
**Danneker**, Henry Louis 1919- *WhoAmP 91*
**Danneker**, James Anthon 1951- *WhoEnt 92*
**Danneman**, Edward Carl 1959- *WhoFI 92, WhoWest 92*
**Dannemeyer**, William E. 1929- *AlmAP 92 [port]*
**Dannemeyer**, William Edwin 1929- *WhoAmP 91, WhoWest 92*
**Dannemiller**, Edward Paul 1934- *WhoWest 92*
**Dannemiller**, Nicholas Stephen 1961- *WhoFI 92*
**Dannen**, Avrum H. 1935- *WhoAmL 92*
**Dannenberg**, Arthur Milton, Jr 1923- *AmMWSc 92*
**Dannenberg**, E M 1917- *AmMWSc 92*
**Dannenberg**, James Harry 1944- *WhoAmL 92*
**Dannenberg**, Joseph *AmMWSc 92*
**Dannenberg**, Konrad K 1912- *AmMWSc 92*
**Dannenburg**, Warren Nathaniel 1926- *AmMWSc 92*
**Danner**, Blythe 1943- *IntMPA 92*

**Danner,** Blythe Katharine 1944- *WhoEnt 92*
**Danner,** Bryant Craig 1937- *WhoAmL 92*
**Danner,** Dan Gordon 1939- *WhoRel 92*
**Danner,** David William 1956- *WhoAmL 92*
**Danner,** Dean Jay 1941- *AmMWSc 92*
**Danner,** James Seager 1957- *WhoRel 92*
**Danner,** Margaret *DrAPF 91*
**Danner,** Margaret 1915- *NotBlAW 92*
**Danner,** Margaret Essie 1915- *WhoBlA 92*
**Danner,** Pat 1934- *WhoAmP 91*
**Danner,** Patsy Ann 1934- *WhoMW 92*
**Danner,** Paul Kruger, III 1957- *WhoWest 92*
**Danner,** Richard Allen 1947- *WhoAmL 92*
**Danner,** Robert Lea, Sr. 1929- *WhoRel 92*
**Danner,** Ronald Paul 1939- *AmMWSc 92*
**Danner,** Steve *WhoAmP 91*
**Danner,** Wilbert Roosevelt 1924- *AmMWSc 92*
**D'Annessa,** A T 1933- *AmMWSc 92*
**Dannhauser,** Walter 1930- *AmMWSc 92*
**Dannheim,** Lawrence C 1934- *WhoAmP 91*
**D'Anniballe,** Priscilla Lucille 1950- *WhoFI 92*
**Dannies,** Priscilla Shaw 1945- *AmMWSc 92*
**Dannley,** Ralph Lawrence 1914- *AmMWSc 92*
**D'Annunzio,** Gabriele 1863-1938 *BiDExR, EncTR 91 [port], FacFETw*
**Dano,** Royal 1922- *IntMPA 92*
**Dano,** Sven 1922- *IntWW 91*
**da Nobrega,** Mailson Ferreira *IntWW 91*
**Danoff,** I. Michael 1940- *WhoWest 92*
**Danon,** Giuliana Maria 1957- *WhoAmL 92*
**Danon,** Ruth *DrAPF 91*
**Danos,** Michael 1922- *AmMWSc 92*
**Danos,** Robert McClure 1929- *WhoWest 92*
**Danowski,** Thomas R. 1961- *WhoWest 92*
**Dansby,** Doris 1918- *AmMWSc 92*
**Dansby,** Eunice Lillith 1927- *WhoEnt 92*
**Dansby,** Jesse L., Jr. 1942- *WhoBlA 92*
**Danse,** Ilene H Raisfeld *AmMWSc 92*
**Danser,** Bonita Kay 1949- *WhoAmL 92*
**Danser,** James W 1921- *AmMWSc 92*
**Dansereau,** Pierre 1911- *AmMWSc 92, IntWW 91*
**Dansgaard,** Willi 1922- *FacFETw*
**Danson,** Barnett Jerome *Who 92*
**Danson,** Barnett Jerome 1921- *IntWW 91*
**Danson,** Ted 1947- *IntMPA 92, WhoEnt 92*
**Dante,** Joe *IntMPA 92, WhoEnt 92*
**Dante,** Joe 1948- *IntDcF 2-2*
**Dante,** Mark F 1931- *AmMWSc 92*
**Dante,** Nicholas d1991 *NewYTBS 91*
**Dante,** Robert *DrAPF 91*
**Dante,** Ronald 1930- *WhoFI 92*
**Danter,** Albert Francis 1918- *WhoRel 92*
**Danti,** August Gabriel 1923- *AmMWSc 92*
**d'Antibes,** Germain *ConAu 35NR*
**Dantin,** Elvin J, Sr 1927- *AmMWSc 92*
**Dantin,** Maurice 1929- *WhoAmL 92*
**Dantley,** Adrian 1955- *BlkOlyM*
**Dantley,** Adrian 1956- *WhoBlA 92*
**Danto,** Arthur C. 1924- *WrDr 92*
**Danton,** Georges Jacques 1759-1794 *BlkwCEP*
**Danton,** J. Periam 1908- *IntWW 91*
**Danton,** Peter W *WhoAmP 91*
**Danton,** Ray 1931- *IntMPA 92*
**Danton,** Steve Richard 1956- *WhoEnt 92*
**D'Antoni,** Philip 1929- *IntMPA 92, WhoEnt 92*
**D'Antonio,** Gregory Douglas 1951- *WhoAmL 92*
**D'Antonio,** James Joseph 1959- *WhoAmL 92*
**D'Antonio,** Nicholas 1916- *WhoRel 92*
**D'Antonio,** Peter 1941- *AmMWSc 92*
**D'Antonio,** Thomas Samuel 1957- *WhoAmL 92*
**Dantro,** Francis James 1941- *WhoFI 92*
**Dantry,** Gerald 1944- *WhoEnt 92*
**Dantus,** Marcos 1962- *WhoWest 92*
**Dantzic,** Roy Matthew 1944- *Who 92*
**Dantzig,** Anne H 1949- *AmMWSc 92*
**Dantzig,** George Bernard 1914- *AmMWSc 92, IntWW 91, WhoWest 92*
**Dantzig,** Jonathan A 1951- *AmMWSc 92*
**Dantzig,** Rudi van 1933- *FacFETw, IntWW 91*
**Dantzker,** David Roy 1943- *AmMWSc 92*
**Dantzler,** Deryl Daugherty 1944- *WhoAmL 92*
**Dantzler,** Herman 1937- *WhoBlA 92*
**Dantzler,** Herman Lee, Jr 1945- *AmMWSc 92*
**Dantzler,** John William, Jr. 1953- *WhoAmL 92*
**Dantzler,** Rick 1956- *WhoAmP 91*
**Dantzler,** William A. 1933- *WhoRel 92*
**Dantzler,** William Hoyt 1935- *AmMWSc 92*
**Danupatampa,** Ekachai 1942- *WhoWest 92*
**Danvers,** Pete *TwCWW 91*
**Danvers-Walker,** Bob 1906-1990 *AnObit 1990*
**Danwin,** Russell John 1956- *WhoMW 92*
**Danylkiw,** John David 1949- *WhoEnt 92*
**Danyluk,** Steven 1945- *AmMWSc 92*
**Danz,** Fredric A. 1918- *IntMPA 92*
**Danza,** Tony 1951- *IntMPA 92, WhoEnt 92*
**Danzansky,** Stephen Ira 1939- *WhoAmP 91*
**Danzberger,** Alexander Harris 1932- *AmMWSc 92*
**Danzer,** Laurence Alfred 1937- *AmMWSc 92*
**Danzi,** Franz 1763-1826 *NewAmDM*
**Danzi,** Michael R. 1959- *WhoFI 92*
**Danzi,** Robert F. 1954- *WhoAmL 92*
**Danzig** *ConMus 7 [port]*
**Danzig,** Allen Edward 1956- *WhoAmL 92*
**Danzig,** Morris Juda 1925- *AmMWSc 92*
**Danzig,** Richard Jeffrey 1944- *WhoAmL 92*
**Danzig,** Robert James 1932- *WhoWest 92*
**Danzig,** Sheila Ring 1948- *WhoFI 92*
**Danzig,** William Harold 1947- *WhoFI 92*
**Danziger,** Gertrude Seelig 1919- *WhoFI 92*
**Danziger,** Jerry 1924- *WhoEnt 92*
**Danziger,** Lawrence 1932- *AmMWSc 92*
**Danziger,** Louis 1923- *WhoEnt 92*
**Danziger,** Paula 1944- *WrDr 92*
**Danziger,** Robert Falzer 1928- *WhoAmL 92*
**Danzo,** Benjamin Joseph 1941- *AmMWSc 92*
**Danzy,** LeRoy Henry 1929- *WhoBlA 92*
**Dao,** Fu Tak 1943- *AmMWSc 92*
**Dao,** Minh Quang, Sr. 1955- *WhoFI 92*
**Dao,** Thomas Ling Yuan 1921- *AmMWSc 92*
**Daoud,** Alex 1944- *WhoAmP 91*
**Daoud,** Assaad S 1923- *AmMWSc 92*
**Daoud,** George Jamil 1948- *WhoFI 92, WhoMW 92*
**Daoud,** Georges 1927- *AmMWSc 92*
**Daoud,** Mohamed 1947- *WhoFI 92*
**D'Aoust,** Brian Gilbert 1938- *AmMWSc 92*
**Daoust,** Donald Roger 1935- *AmMWSc 92*
**Daoust,** Hubert 1928- *AmMWSc 92*
**Daoust,** Joseph Patrick 1939- *WhoRel 92*
**Daoust,** Richard Alan 1948- *AmMWSc 92*
**Daoust,** Roger 1924- *AmMWSc 92*
**Dapena,** Jose *WhoAmP 91*
**Dapkus,** David Conrad 1944- *AmMWSc 92*
**Dapogny,** James 1940- *WhoEnt 92*
**D'Apolito,** Frank A. 1956- *WhoMW 92*
**Da Ponte,** Lorenzo 1749-1838 *DcAmImH, NewAmDM*
**Dapper,** John Martin 1923- *WhoEnt 92*
**Dapples,** Edward Charles 1906- *AmMWSc 92*
**D'Appolonia,** Bert Luigi 1939- *AmMWSc 92*
**D'Appolonia,** Elio 1918- *AmMWSc 92*
**DaPrato,** Frank J 1916- *WhoAmP 91*
**Dapremont,** Delmont, Jr. *WhoBlA 92*
**Dapron,** Elmer Joseph, Jr. 1925- *WhoFI 92*
**Dapson,** Richard W 1941- *AmMWSc 92*
**D'Aquila,** Barbara Jean 1955- *WhoAmL 92*
**D'Aquila,** James Anthony 1960- *WhoFI 92, WhoWest 92*
**Dar,** Mohammad Saeed 1937- *AmMWSc 92*
**Dar-Es-Salaam,** Archbishop of 1912- *Who 92*
**Darach,** Peter 1940- *TwCPaSc*
**Daraio,** Robert Reid 1955- *WhoEnt 92*
**Darany,** Michael Anthony 1946- *WhoFI 92*
**Daravingas,** George Vasilios 1934- *AmMWSc 92*
**Darawalla,** Keki N. 1937- *WrDr 92*
**D'Arbanville,** Patti 1951- *IntMPA 92*
**Darbo,** Bakary Bunja 1946- *IntWW 91*
**Darbourne,** John William Charles 1935- *Who 92*
**Darboven,** Hanne 1941- *IntWW 91*
**Darby,** Ann K. *DrAPF 91*
**Darby,** Castilla A., Jr. 1946- *WhoBlA 92*
**Darby,** Catherine *IntAu&W 91X, WrDr 92*
**Darby,** Clifford *Who 92*
**Darby,** Clifford 1909- *IntAu&W 91*
**Darby,** David G 1932- *AmMWSc 92*
**Darby,** Dennis Arnold 1944- *AmMWSc 92*
**Darby,** Edwin Wheeler 1922- *WhoFI 92*
**Darby,** Eleanor Muriel Kapp 1905- *AmMWSc 92*
**Darby,** Francis John 1920- *Who 92*
**Darby,** Harold Richard 1919- *Who 92*
**Darby,** Henry Clifford 1909- *Who 92, WrDr 92*
**Darby,** Howard Darrel 1928- *WhoAmP 91*
**Darby,** James Michael 1959- *WhoAmL 92*
**Darby,** Jay Rodney 1953- *WhoMW 92*
**Darby,** Jean 1921- *SmATA 68 [port]*
**Darby,** Jerome Sigman 1950- *WhoFI 92*
**Darby,** John 1804-1877 *BiInAmS*
**Darby,** John 1940- *IntAu&W 91, WrDr 92*
**Darby,** John Feaster 1916- *AmMWSc 92*
**Darby,** John Fletcher 1803-1882 *DcNCBi 2*
**Darby,** John Oliver Robertson 1930- *Who 92*
**Darby,** Joseph B, Jr 1925- *AmMWSc 92*
**Darby,** Joseph Raymond 1911- *AmMWSc 92*
**Darby,** Kim 1948- *IntMPA 92*
**Darby,** Michael Douglas 1944- *Who 92*
**Darby,** Michael Rucker 1945- *WhoFI 92*
**Darby,** Nicholas 1946- *AmMWSc 92*
**Darby,** Peter 1924- *Who 92*
**Darby,** Ralph Lewis 1918- *AmMWSc 92*
**Darby,** Robert Albert 1930- *AmMWSc 92*
**Darby,** Ronald 1932- *AmMWSc 92*
**D'Arby,** Terence Trent *WhoBlA 92*
**Darby,** Timothy John 1947- *WhoAmL 92*
**Darby,** Wesley Andrew 1928- *WhoRel 92, WhoWest 92*
**Darby,** William 1775-1854 *BiInAmS*
**Darby,** William Duane 1942- *WhoEnt 92*
**Darby,** William Elliott 1928- *WhoAmP 91*
**Darby,** William Jefferson 1913- *AmMWSc 92*
**Darcel,** Colin Le Q 1925- *AmMWSc 92*
**Darcey,** Terrance Michael 1950- *AmMWSc 92*
**Darchun,** Lino Auksutis 1942- *WhoFI 92*
**D'Arco,** John A, Jr 1944- *WhoAmP 91*
**Darcy,** Clare *IntAu&W 91, WrDr 92*
**Darcy,** Harold P. 1929- *WhoRel 92*
**D'Arcy,** Hugh Antoine *BenetAL 91*
**D'Arcy,** John Michael 1932- *WhoRel 92*
**Darcy,** Keith Thomas 1948- *WhoRel 92*
**D'Arcy,** Margaretta *WrDr 92*
**D'Arcy,** Margaretta 1957- *IntWW 91*
**D'Arcy,** Pamela *WrDr 92*
**D'Arcy,** Stephen Paul 1950- *WhoFI 92*
**D'Arcy,** William Gerald 1931- *AmMWSc 92*
**Darcy De Knayth,** Baroness 1938- *Who 92*
**D'Arcy Hart,** Philip Montagu *Who 92*
**Darden,** Charles R. 1911- *WhoBlA 92*
**Darden,** Christine Mann 1942- *WhoBlA 92*
**Darden,** Colgate W, III 1930- *AmMWSc 92*
**Darden,** David Putnam 1958- *WhoAmL 92*
**Darden,** Edgar Bascomb 1920- *AmMWSc 92*
**Darden,** George 1943- *AlmAP 92 [port]*
**Darden,** George H, Jr 1930- *WhoAmP 91*
**Darden,** George Harry 1934- *WhoBlA 92*
**Darden,** George W 1943- *WhoAmP 91*
**Darden,** George Washington, III 1943- *WhoAmL 92*
**Darden,** John A. 1945- *WhoAmL 92*
**Darden,** John F 1946- *WhoIns 92*
**Darden,** Joseph S., Jr. 1925- *WhoBlA 92*
**Darden,** Lindley 1945- *AmMWSc 92*
**Darden,** Margaret Furr 1937- *WhoAmP 91*
**Darden,** Mills 1799-1857 *DcNCBi 2*
**Darden,** Orlando William 1930- *WhoBlA 92*
**Darden,** Sperry Eugene 1928- *AmMWSc 92*
**Darden,** Thomas Vincent 1950- *WhoBlA 92*
**Darden,** William Abram 1836-1890 *DcNCBi 2*
**Darden,** William Boone 1925- *WhoBlA 92*
**Darden,** William H, Jr 1937- *AmMWSc 92*
**D'Ardenne,** Walter H 1932- *AmMWSc 92*
**Dardiri,** Ahmed Hamed 1919- *AmMWSc 92*
**Dardis,** John G 1928- *AmMWSc 92*
**Dardis,** Thomas 1926- *WrDr 92*
**Dardis,** Thomas A 1926- *IntAu&W 91*
**Dardoufas,** Kimon C 1916- *AmMWSc 92*
**DaRe,** Aldo *ConTFT 9*
**Dare,** Ananias *DcNCBi 2*
**Dare,** Eleanor White 1565?- *DcNCBi 2*
**Dare,** Virginia 1587- *BenetAL 91, DcNCBi 2*
**Darell,** Jeffrey 1919- *Who 92*
**Darensbourg,** Donald Jude 1941- *AmMWSc 92*
**Darensbourg,** Marcetta York 1942- *AmMWSc 92*
**Daresbury,** Baron 1928- *Who 92*
**Darety,** Paul Raymond 1962- *WhoRel 92*
**Dargan,** Edmund Spann 1805-1879 *DcNCBi 2*
**Dargan,** Olive 1869-1968 *BenetAL 91*
**Dargan,** Olive Tilford 1869-1968 *DcNCBi 2*
**Dargan,** Stephen *WhoAmP 91*
**Dargan,** Thomas J. 1943- *WhoEnt 92*
**Dargie,** William Alexander 1912- *IntWW 91, Who 92*
**Dargin,** Errol Ramone 1945- *WhoAmP 91*
**Dargomizhsky,** Alexander Sergeyevich 1813-1869 *NewAmDM*
**Darian,** Craig Charles 1955- *WhoEnt 92*
**Darida,** Clelio 1927- *IntWW 91*
**Daridan,** Jean-Henri 1906- *IntWW 91*
**Darien,** Steven Martin 1942- *WhoFI 92*
**Darin,** Frank Victor John 1930- *WhoMW 92*
**Darino,** Eduardo 1944- *WhoEnt 92, WhoHisp 92*
**Dario,** Ronald A 1937- *WhoAmP 91*
**Dario,** Ruben 1867-1916 *BenetAL 91, FacFETw*
**Darion,** Joe 1917- *WhoEnt 92*
**Dariotis,** Terrence Theodore 1946- *WhoAmL 92*
**D'Arista,** Carla A. 1956- *WhoFI 92*
**Darity,** Evangeline Royall 1927- *WhoBlA 92*
**Darity,** William A. 1924- *WhoBlA 92*
**Darity,** William Alexander 1924- *AmMWSc 92*
**Dark,** Anthony Michael B. *Who 92*
**Dark,** Daniel Herbert 1954- *WhoRel 92*
**Dark,** John *IntMPA 92*
**Dark,** Johnny *IntAu&W 91X*
**Dark,** Lawrence Jerome 1953- *WhoBlA 92*
**Dark,** T. R. 1934- *WhoMW 92*
**Darkazalli,** Ghazi 1945- *AmMWSc 92*
**Darke,** Charles B. 1937- *WhoBlA 92*
**Darke,** Geoffrey James 1929- *Who 92*
**Darke,** Marjorie 1929- *ConAu 34NR, WrDr 92*
**Darke,** Marjorie Sheila 1929- *IntAu&W 91, Who 92*
**Darke,** Nick 1948- *IntAu&W 91, WrDr 92*
**Darkes,** Anna Sue 1927- *WhoRel 92*
**Darkes,** Leroy William 1924- *WhoBlA 92*
**Darkey,** Kermit Louis 1930- *WhoWest 92*
**Darkins,** Duane Adrian 1934- *WhoBlA 92*
**Darko,** Paula A 1952- *WhoAmP 91*
**Darkow,** Grant Lyle 1928- *AmMWSc 92*
**Darlage,** Larry James 1945- *AmMWSc 92*
**Darlak,** Robert 1937- *AmMWSc 92*
**Darlan,** Francois 1881-1942 *EncTR 91 [port]*
**Darlan,** Jean Francois 1881-1942 *FacFETw*
**Darley,** Dick *IntMPA 92*
**Darley,** Ellis Fleck 1915- *AmMWSc 92*
**Darley,** Felix Octavius Carr 1822-1888 *BenetAL 91*
**Darley,** Frederic Loudon 1918- *AmMWSc 92*
**Darley,** George 1795-1846 *RfGEnL 91*
**Darling** *Who 92*
**Darling,** Baron 1919- *Who 92*
**Darling,** Alberta *WhoAmP 91*
**Darling,** Alberta Statkus 1944- *WhoMW 92*
**Darling,** Alistair Maclean 1953- *Who 92*
**Darling,** Byron Thorwell 1912- *AmMWSc 92*
**Darling,** Charles M., IV 1948- *WhoAmL 92*
**Darling,** Charles Milton 1934- *AmMWSc 92*
**Darling,** Clifford 1922- *Who 92*
**Darling,** Donald Christopher 1951- *AmMWSc 92*
**Darling,** Earl Douglas 1948- *WhoFI 92*
**Darling,** Edward Flewett *Who 92*
**Darling,** Eugene Merrill, Jr 1925- *AmMWSc 92*
**Darling,** Frank Clayton 1925- *WhoRel 92*
**Darling,** Gary Lyle 1941- *WhoFI 92*
**Darling,** George Bapst 1905- *AmMWSc 92*
**Darling,** George Curtis 1928- *WhoRel 92*
**Darling,** Gerald Ralph Auchinleck 1921- *Who 92*
**Darling,** Graham Davidson 1958- *AmMWSc 92*
**Darling,** Henry Shillington 1914- *Who 92*
**Darling,** Herbert A *WhoAmP 91*
**Darling,** Hyman Gross 1950- *WhoAmL 92*
**Darling,** J N 1876-1962 *FacFETw*
**Darling,** James Ralph 1899- *IntWW 91, Who 92*
**Darling,** John Rothburn, Jr. 1937- *WhoFI 92*
**Darling,** Kenneth 1909- *Who 92*
**Darling,** Lawrence Dean 1936- *WhoMW 92*
**Darling,** Leroy 1939- *WhoBlA 92*
**Darling,** Lois 1917- *IntAu&W 91*
**Darling,** Marilyn Stagner 1935- *AmMWSc 92*
**Darling,** Marsha Jean 1947- *WhoBlA 92*
**Darling,** Michael Harold 1955- *WhoWest 92*
**Darling,** Pamela Ann Wood 1943- *WhoRel 92*
**Darling,** Richard *WhoRel 92*
**Darling,** Robert Bruce 1958- *AmMWSc 92*
**Darling,** Robert Edward 1937- *WhoEnt 92*
**Darling,** Samuel Mills 1917- *AmMWSc 92*
**Darling,** Sandra *SmATA 67 [port]*
**Darling,** Scott Edward 1949- *WhoAmL 92, WhoWest 92*
**Darling,** Stephen Deziel 1931- *AmMWSc 92*
**Darling,** Stephen Edward 1949- *WhoAmL 92*

**Darling,** Susan 1942- *Who 92*
**Darling,** William Martindale 1934- *Who 92*
**Darlington,** Charles 1910- *Who 92*
**Darlington,** David William 1945- *WhoFI 92*
**Darlington,** Gretchen Ann Jolly 1942- *AmMWSc 92*
**Darlington,** Joyce *Who 92*
**Darlington,** Sandy *DrAPF 91*
**Darlington,** Sidney 1906- *AmMWSc 92*
**Darlington,** Stephen Mark 1952- *Who 92*
**Darlington,** William 1782-1863 *BiInAmS*
**Darlington,** William Bruce 1933- *AmMWSc 92*
**Darlow,** Julia Donovan 1941- *WhoAmL 92*
**Darman,** Richard Gordon 1943- *IntWW 91, WhoAmP 91*
**Darmojuwono,** Justin 1914- *WhoRel 92*
**Darmojuwono,** Justine 1914- *IntWW 91*
**Darmon,** Marco 1930- *IntWW 91*
**D'Armond,** William Randolph 1940- *WhoAmL 92*
**Darmstaetter,** Jay Eugene 1937- *WhoWest 92*
**Darnall,** Dennis W 1941- *AmMWSc 92*
**Darnall,** Roberta Morrow 1949- *WhoWest 92*
**Darnand,** Aime Joseph Auguste 1897-1945 *BiDExR*
**Darnas,** Clara 1956- *WhoHisp 92*
**Darnay,** Arsen *WrDr 92*
**Darnay,** Arsen 1936- *TwCSFW 91*
**Darneal,** Robert Lee *AmMWSc 92*
**Darnel,** Michael Roy 1952- *WhoMW 92*
**Darnell,** Alfred Jerome 1924- *AmMWSc 92*
**Darnell,** Catherine Margaret 1957- *WhoWest 92*
**Darnell,** Edward Buddy 1930- *WhoBlA 92*
**Darnell,** Emma Ione 1937- *WhoBlA 92*
**Darnell,** Frederick Jerome 1928- *AmMWSc 92*
**Darnell,** Gerald Thomas 1942- *WhoMW 92*
**Darnell,** James Edwin, Jr 1930- *AmMWSc 92*
**Darnell,** Regna *WrDr 92*
**Darnell,** Rezneat Milton 1924- *AmMWSc 92*
**Darnell,** Riley Carlisle 1940- *WhoAmP 91*
**Darnell,** Robert Carter 1927- *WhoWest 92*
**Darnell,** Robert William 1956- *WhoAmL 92*
**Darnell,** W H 1925- *AmMWSc 92*
**Darnell,** William Nelson 1830-1915 *DcNCBi 2*
**Darner,** L Karen *WhoAmP 91*
**Darnley,** Earl of 1941- *Who 92*
**Darnley-Thomas,** John, Mrs. *Who 92*
**Darnton,** John 1941- *IntAu&W 91*
**Darnton,** Robert 1939- *WrDr 92*
**Darnton,** Robert Choate 1939- *IntWW 91*
**Daroca,** Philip Joseph, Jr 1942- *AmMWSc 92*
**Daroff,** Robert Barry 1936- *AmMWSc 92*
**Daron,** Garman Harlow 1904- *AmMWSc 92*
**Daron,** Harlow Hoover 1930- *AmMWSc 92*
**da Rosa,** Linda Jean 1966- *WhoEnt 92*
**da Roza,** Victoria Cecilia 1945- *WhoWest 92*
**D'Arpino,** Tony *DrAPF 91*
**Darquier De Pellepoix,** Louis 1897-1980 *BiDExR*
**Darr,** Ann *DrAPF 91*
**Darr,** Carole 1942- *WhoEnt 92*
**Darr,** Edward Austin 1889-1958 *DcNCBi 2*
**Darr,** J E 1921- *AmMWSc 92*
**Darr,** John 1951- *WhoFI 92*
**Darragh,** John K. 1929- *WhoMW 92*
**Darragh,** Richard T 1931- *AmMWSc 92*
**Darrah,** James Gore 1928- *WhoWest 92*
**Darrah,** Joan *WhoAmP 91*
**Darrah,** Randal Lee 1957- *WhoMW 92*
**Darrah,** Ron Tillman 1960- *WhoFI 92*
**Darrah,** William Culp 1909- *AmMWSc 92*
**d'Arrast,** Harry d'Abbadie 1897-1968 *IntDcF 2-2*
**Darrat,** Ali Farag 1949- *WhoFI 92*
**Darre,** Richard-Walther 1895-1953 *BiDExR, EncTR 91 [port]*
**Darrell,** Betty Louise 1934- *WhoBlA 92*
**Darrell,** David Jay 1957- *WhoAmL 92*
**Darrell,** Elizabeth *WrDr 92*
**Darrell,** James Harris, II 1942- *AmMWSc 92*
**Darrell,** Lewis E. 1932- *WhoBlA 92*
**Darrell,** Norris, Jr. 1929- *WhoAmL 92*
**Darren,** James 1936- *IntMPA 92*
**Darrieux,** Danielle 1917- *IntMPA 92, IntWW 91*
**D'Arrigo,** Stephen, Jr. 1922- *WhoFI 92*
**Darrin,** David Kevin 1956- *WhoWest 92*
**Darrin,** Howard 1897- *DcTwDes*
**Darrington,** Denton C 1940- *WhoAmP 91*
**Darrow,** Clarence 1857-1938 *AmPeW, FacFETw, RComAH*
**Darrow,** Clarence Allison 1940- *WhoAmP 91*
**Darrow,** Clarence S. 1857-1938 *BenetAL 91*
**Darrow,** Danny 1937- *WhoEnt 92*
**Darrow,** Douglass Sterling 1960- *WhoFI 92*
**Darrow,** Duncan Noble 1948- *WhoFI 92*
**Darrow,** Frank William 1940- *AmMWSc 92*
**Darrow,** George F. 1924- *WhoWest 92*
**Darrow,** Henry *WhoHisp 92*
**Darrow,** Kenneth Frank 1945- *WhoAmL 92*
**Darrow,** Peter P 1919- *WhoAmP 91*
**Darrow,** Ralph Carroll 1918- *WhoMW 92*
**Darrow,** Robert A 1931- *AmMWSc 92*
**Darrow,** William Richard 1939- *WhoFI 92*
**D'Arruda,** Jose Joaquim 1942- *AmMWSc 92*
**Darsky,** Julius 1907- *WhoFI 92*
**Darsow,** William Frank 1920- *AmMWSc 92*
**Darst,** Bette-Jean *DrAPF 91*
**Darst,** Philip High 1943- *AmMWSc 92*
**Darst,** Richard B 1934- *AmMWSc 92*
**Darst,** Richard L. 1944- *WhoAmL 92*
**Darst,** Thomas Campbell 1875-1948 *DcNCBi 2*
**Dart,** Jack Calhoon 1912- *AmMWSc 92*
**Dart,** John Seward 1936- *WhoRel 92*
**Dart,** Nancy 1957- *WhoAmL 92*
**Dart,** Raymond Arthur 1893-1988 *FacFETw*
**Dart,** Sidney Leonard 1918- *AmMWSc 92*
**Dart,** Stephen Plauche 1924- *WhoAmP 91*
**Dart,** Thurston 1921-1971 *NewAmDM*
**Darter,** Jeffrey Allen 1958- *WhoEnt 92*
**Dartigue,** John 1940- *IntMPA 92, WhoEnt 92*
**Dartmouth** *BlkwEAR*
**Dartmouth,** Earl of 1924- *Who 92*
**Dartnall,** Gary 1937- *IntMPA 92, Who 92*
**Darton,** Edythe M. 1921- *WhoBlA 92*
**Daruwalla,** Keki N. 1937- *ConPo 91*
**Darvall,** Charles Roger 1906- *Who 92*
**Darvall,** Roger *Who 92*
**Darvarova,** Elmira *WhoEnt 92*
**Darvas,** Endre Peter 1946- *WhoWest 92*
**Darwen,** Baron 1938- *Who 92*
**Darwent,** Basil de Baskerville 1913- *AmMWSc 92*
**Darwent,** Frederick Charles *Who 92*
**Darwin,** Charles *RfGEnL 91*
**Darwin,** Charles 1809-1882 *EncTR 91*
**Darwin,** David 1946- *AmMWSc 92, WhoMW 92*
**Darwin,** Erasmus 1731-1802 *BlkwCEP, RfGEnL 91*
**Darwin,** Henry Galton 1929- *Who 92*
**Darwin,** James T, Jr 1933- *AmMWSc 92*
**Darwin,** John Walter 1953- *WhoEnt 92*
**Darwin,** Kenneth 1921- *Who 92*
**Darwin,** Robin 1910-1974 *TwCPaSc*
**Darwin,** Steven Peter 1949- *AmMWSc 92*
**Darwish,** Adel 1945- *ConAu 135*
**Darwish,** Mahmud 1942- *LiExTwC*
**Dary,** David 1934- *IntAu&W 91*
**Dary,** David Archie 1934- *WrDr 92*
**Daryngton,** Baron 1908- *Who 92*
**Darzynkiewicz,** Zbigniew Dzierzykraj 1936- *AmMWSc 92*
**Das,** Anadijiban 1934- *AmMWSc 92*
**Das,** Ashok Kumar 1953- *AmMWSc 92*
**Das,** Badri N 1927- *AmMWSc 92*
**Das,** D. K. 1935- *WrDr 92*
**Das,** Dipak K 1946- *AmMWSc 92*
**Das,** Gopal Dwarka 1933- *AmMWSc 92, WhoMW 92*
**Das,** Kalyan 1956- *WhoAmL 92*
**Das,** Kamal 1921- *IntAu&W 91*
**Das,** Kamala 1934- *ConPo 91, WrDr 92*
**Das,** Kamalendu 1944- *AmMWSc 92*
**Das,** Kiron Moy 1941- *AmMWSc 92*
**Das,** Lovejoy S. 1952- *WhoMW 92*
**Das,** Manjusri 1946- *AmMWSc 92*
**Das,** Mihir Kumar 1939- *AmMWSc 92*
**Das,** Mukunda B 1931- *AmMWSc 92*
**Das,** Naba Kishore 1934- *AmMWSc 92*
**Das,** Nirmal Kanti 1928- *AmMWSc 92*
**Das,** Pankaj K 1937- *AmMWSc 92*
**Das,** Paritosh Kumar 1942- *AmMWSc 92*
**Das,** Phanindramohan 1926- *AmMWSc 92*
**Das,** Prasanta 1944- *AmMWSc 92*
**Das,** Salil Kumar 1940- *AmMWSc 92*
**Das,** Saroj R *AmMWSc 92*
**Das,** Subodh Kumar 1947- *AmMWSc 92*
**Das,** Suryya Kumar *AmMWSc 92*
**Das,** T. K. 1938- *WhoFI 92*
**Das,** Tara Prasad 1932- *AmMWSc 92*
**Das Gupta,** Aaron 1943- *AmMWSc 92*
**Das Gupta,** Kamalaksha 1917- *AmMWSc 92*
**Das Gupta,** Prodosh Kusum 1912- *IntWW 91*
**Das Gupta,** Somesh 1935- *AmMWSc 92*
**Das Sarma,** Basudeb 1923- *AmMWSc 92*
**Dasari,** Ramachandra R 1932- *AmMWSc 92*
**D'Asaro,** L Arthur 1927- *AmMWSc 92*
**Dasburg,** John Harold 1944- *WhoFI 92*
**Dascalescu,** Constantin 1923- *IntWW 91*
**Dascalos,** Danielle Merrie 1960- *WhoWest 92*
**Dasch,** Cameron John 1951- *WhoMW 92*
**Dasch,** Clement Eugene 1925- *AmMWSc 92*
**Dasch,** Ernest Julius 1932- *AmMWSc 92*
**Dasch,** Gregory Alan 1948- *AmMWSc 92*
**Dasch,** James R 1956- *AmMWSc 92*
**Dasch,** Jean Muhlbaier 1950- *WhoMW 92*
**Daschbach,** Charles Clark 1948- *WhoWest 92*
**Daschbach,** James McCloskey 1932- *AmMWSc 92*
**Daschbach,** Richard Joseph 1936- *WhoAmP 91*
**Daschle,** Thomas A. 1947- *AlmAP 92 [port]*
**Daschle,** Thomas Andrew 1947- *IntWW 91, WhoAmP 91, WhoMW 92*
**Dascola,** Joseph Phillip 1945- *WhoFI 92*
**d'Ascoli,** Bernard Jacques-Henri Marc 1958- *IntWW 91*
**Dascoli,** Michael Anthony 1959- *WhoRel 92, WhoWest 92*
**Dascomb,** Harry Emerson 1916- *AmMWSc 92*
**Dasgupta,** Arijit M 1957- *AmMWSc 92*
**Dasgupta,** Asim 1951- *AmMWSc 92*
**Dasgupta,** Dipankar 1952- *WhoWest 92*
**Dasgupta,** Gautam 1946- *AmMWSc 92*
**Dasgupta,** Partha Sarathi 1942- *Who 92*
**Dasgupta,** Rathindra 1948- *AmMWSc 92*
**Dasgupta,** Sunil Priya *AmMWSc 92*
**Dash,** Harriman Harvey 1910- *AmMWSc 92*
**Dash,** Harvey Dwight 1924- *WhoWest 92*
**Dash,** Hugh M. H. 1943- *WhoBlA 92*
**Dash,** Jack 1907-1989 *FacFETw*
**Dash,** Jay Gregory 1923- *AmMWSc 92*
**Dash,** John 1933- *AmMWSc 92*
**Dash,** Julie *ReelWom*
**Dash,** Leon DeCosta, Jr. 1944- *WhoBlA 92*
**Dash,** Raymond 1932- *WhoIns 92*
**Dash,** Sanford Mark 1943- *AmMWSc 92*
**Dash,** Thomas R. d1991 *NewYTBS 91*
**Dashek,** William Vincent 1939- *AmMWSc 92*
**Dashen,** Roger Frederick 1938- *AmMWSc 92, WhoWest 92*
**Dasher,** George Franklin, Jr 1922- *AmMWSc 92*
**Dasher,** John 1914- *AmMWSc 92*
**Dasher,** Paul James 1912- *AmMWSc 92*
**Dashiell,** Thomas Ronald 1927- *AmMWSc 92*
**Dashman,** Theodore 1928- *AmMWSc 92*
**Dashner,** Peter Alan 1951- *AmMWSc 92*
**Dashow,** Kenneth R. 1958- *WhoEnt 92*
**Dashwood,** Francis 1925- *Who 92*
**Dashwood,** Richard 1950- *Who 92*
**Da Silva,** Adhemar Ferreira 1927- *BlkOlyM*
**Da Silva,** John Burke 1918- *Who 92*
**DaSilva,** Leon *ConAu 35NR*
**Da Silva,** Luis Inacio 1946- *IntWW 91*
**DaSilva,** Pat *WhoHisp 92*
**Da Silva,** Raul 1933- *IntMPA 92*
**Da Silva,** Ray 1934- *IntMPA 92*
**DaSilva,** Willard H. 1923- *WhoAmL 92*
**Dasius** *EncEarC*
**Daskam,** Edward, Jr 1920- *AmMWSc 92*
**Daskin,** W 1926- *AmMWSc 92*
**Dasler,** Adolph Richard 1933- *AmMWSc 92*
**Dasler,** Waldemar 1910- *AmMWSc 92*
**Dasmann,** Raymond Fredric 1919- *AmMWSc 92*
**Dassanowsky-Harris,** Robert *DrAPF 91*
**Dassanowsky-Harris,** Robert von 1956- *WhoWest 92*
**Dassault,** Marcel 1892-1986 *FacFETw*
**Dassault,** Serge 1925- *IntWW 91*
**Dassenko,** Pamela Marie 1955- *WhoWest 92*
**Dassenko,** Paul Edward 1951- *WhoFI 92*
**Dassin,** Jules 1911- *IntDcF 2-2, IntMPA 92, IntWW 91, WhoEnt 92*
**Dassinger,** Ernest N 1931- *WhoAmP 91*
**Dassinger,** George W. 1950- *WhoEnt 92*
**Dastin,** Robert Earl 1934- *WhoAmL 92*
**D'Astolfo,** Frank Joseph 1943- *WhoEnt 92*
**Dastugue,** Quentin D 1955- *WhoAmP 91*
**Dastur,** Ardeshir Rustom 1935- *AmMWSc 92*
**Daszkowski,** Eugeniusz Andrzej 1930- *IntAu&W 91*
**Data,** Joann L 1944- *AmMWSc 92*
**Datars,** William Ross 1932- *AmMWSc 92, IntWW 91*
**Date,** William Adrian 1908- *Who 92*
**Daterman,** Gary Edward 1939- *AmMWSc 92*
**Dathorne,** O. R. 1934- *ConNov 91, IntAu&W 91, LiExTwC, WrDr 92*
**Dati,** James Donald 1958- *WhoAmL 92*
**Datsko,** Joseph 1921- *AmMWSc 92*
**Datta,** Dilip Kumar 1939- *AmMWSc 92*
**Datta,** Naomi 1922- *Who 92*
**Datta,** Padma Rag 1927- *AmMWSc 92*
**Datta,** Prasanta 1929- *AmMWSc 92*
**Datta,** Ranajit K 1935- *AmMWSc 92*
**Datta,** Ranajit Kumar 1933- *AmMWSc 92*
**Datta,** Ratna 1943- *AmMWSc 92*
**Datta,** Samir Kumar 1936- *AmMWSc 92*
**Datta,** Subhendu Kumar 1936- *AmMWSc 92*
**Datta,** Surinder P 1933- *AmMWSc 92*
**Datta,** Syamal K 1943- *AmMWSc 92*
**Datta,** Tapan K 1939- *AmMWSc 92*
**Datta,** Timir 1947- *AmMWSc 92*
**Datta,** Vijay J 1944- *AmMWSc 92*
**Dattilo,** Nicholas C. *WhoRel 92*
**Dattner,** John William 1948- *WhoIns 92*
**D'Attorre,** Leonardo 1920- *AmMWSc 92*
**Datz,** Harold J 1938- *WhoAmP 91*
**Datz,** Sheldon 1927- *AmMWSc 92*
**Dau,** Gary John 1938- *AmMWSc 92*
**Dau,** Peter Caine 1939- *AmMWSc 92*
**Dau-Schmidt,** Kenneth Glenn 1956- *WhoFI 92*
**Daub,** Clarence Theodore, Jr 1936- *AmMWSc 92*
**Daub,** Edward E 1924- *AmMWSc 92*
**Daub,** Guido William 1950- *AmMWSc 92*
**Daub,** Harold, Jr 1941- *WhoAmP 91*
**Daub,** L Anderson 1940- *WhoAmP 91*
**Daub,** Lloyd G. 1954- *WhoMW 92*
**Daub,** Robert Lee 1952- *WhoAmL 92*
**Daube,** David 1909- *IntAu&W 91, IntWW 91, Who 92, WrDr 92*
**Dauben,** Dwight Lewis 1938- *AmMWSc 92*
**Dauben,** Joseph W 1944- *AmMWSc 92*
**Dauben,** William Garfield 1919- *AmMWSc 92, IntWW 91*
**Daubenmire,** Rexford 1909- *AmMWSc 92*
**Daubenspeck,** John Andrew 1942- *AmMWSc 92*
**Daubenspeck,** Kenneth Gene 1952- *WhoMW 92*
**Daubenton,** Louis-Jean-Marie 1716-1800 *BlkwCEP*
**Daubeny,** Hugh Alexander 1931- *AmMWSc 92*
**Daubeny De Moleyns** *Who 92*
**Dauber,** Edwin George 1953- *AmMWSc 92*
**Dauber,** Ira Mitchell 1952- *WhoWest 92*
**Dauber,** Roslyn 1953- *WhoEnt 92*
**Daubert,** Thomas Edward 1937- *AmMWSc 92*
**Daubigny,** Charles Francois 1817-1878 *ThHEIm*
**Daubin,** Scott C 1922- *AmMWSc 92*
**Daubitz,** Paul C., Jr. 1941- *WhoFI 92*
**Dauble,** Dennis Deene 1950- *AmMWSc 92*
**Daubon,** Ramon E. 1945- *WhoHisp 92*
**d'Aubuisson Arrieta,** Roberto 1943- *IntWW 91*
**Dauchot,** Paul J 1935- *AmMWSc 92*
**Daud,** Sulaiman bin Haj 1933- *IntWW 91*
**Daudet,** Alphonse 1840-1897 *GuFrLit 1, ThHEIm*
**Daudet,** Leon 1867-1942 *BiDExR, FacFETw*
**Daudet,** Leon 1868-1942 *GuFrLit 1*
**Dauenhauer,** Richard *DrAPF 91*
**Dauer,** Jerald Paul 1943- *AmMWSc 92*
**Dauer,** Thomas Gerald 1929- *WhoFI 92*
**Dauerman,** Leonard 1932- *AmMWSc 92*
**Daues,** Gregory W, Jr 1928- *AmMWSc 92*
**Daues,** Joseph Thomas 1934- *WhoMW 92*
**Dauge,** Peter 1739-1801 *DcNCBi 2*
**Daughaday,** William Hamilton 1918- *AmMWSc 92, WhoMW 92*
**Daugharty,** Harry 1939- *AmMWSc 92*
**Daughenbaugh,** Randall Jay 1948- *AmMWSc 92*
**Daugherty,** Bradley Lee 1965- *WhoBlA 92, WhoMW 92*
**Daugherty,** Carroll R 1900-1988 *FacFETw*
**Daugherty,** Charles Edward 1945- *WhoWest 92*
**Daugherty,** Daniel Lee 1960- *WhoMW 92*
**Daugherty,** David Howard 1929- *WhoAmL 92*
**Daugherty,** David M 1928- *AmMWSc 92*
**Daugherty,** Dennis Alan 1952- *WhoWest 92*
**Daugherty,** Don G 1935- *AmMWSc 92*
**Daugherty,** Douglas Andrew 1960- *WhoMW 92*
**Daugherty,** Franklin W 1927- *AmMWSc 92*
**Daugherty,** Frederick Alvin 1914- *WhoAmL 92*
**Daugherty,** Guy Wilson 1912- *AmMWSc 92*
**Daugherty,** Harry M 1860-1941 *FacFETw*
**Daugherty,** Harry Micajah 1860-1941 *AmPolLe*
**Daugherty,** James Robert 1949- *WhoWest 92*

**Daugherty**, JoAnn 1930- *WhoAmP 91*
**Daugherty**, John William 1937- *WhoMW 92*
**Daugherty**, Kenneth E 1938- *AmMWSc 92*
**Daugherty**, LeRoy Arthur 1946- *AmMWSc 92*
**Daugherty**, Lewis Sylvester 1857-1919 *BiInAmS*
**Daugherty**, M Dennis 1948- *WhoAmP 91*
**Daugherty**, Ned Arthur 1934- *AmMWSc 92*
**Daugherty**, Patricia A 1922- *AmMWSc 92*
**Daugherty**, Paul Joseph 1948- *WhoMW 92*
**Daugherty**, Richard Bernard 1915- *WhoAmL 92*
**Daugherty**, Sarah Bowyer 1949- *WhoMW 92*
**Daugherty**, Steven Joe 1947- *WhoMW 92*
**Daugherty**, William Loyd 1927- *WhoFI 92*
**Daughters**, George T, II 1938- *AmMWSc 92*
**Daughton**, Donald 1932- *WhoAmL 92*
**Daughtrey**, Anne Scott 1920- *WrDr 92*
**Daughtrey**, Martha Craig 1942- *WhoAmP 91*
**Daughtridge**, Elijah Longstreet 1863-1921 *DcNCBi 2*
**Daughtry**, Herbert Daniel 1931- *RelLAm 91, WhoBIA 92*
**Daughtry**, Kay 1923- *WhoAmP 91*
**Daughtry**, Namon Leo 1940- *WhoAmP 91*
**Daugny**, Bertrand 1925- *IntWW 91*
**D'Augusta**, Alfred M. 1941- *WhoFI 92*
**Dauksewicz**, William Joseph *WhoFI 92*
**Daul**, George Cecil 1916- *AmMWSc 92*
**d'Aulaire**, Edgar Parin 1898-1986 *SmATA 66 [port]*
**d'Aulaire**, Ingri 1904-1980 *SmATA 66 [port]*
**Daulat**, Kumar 1960- *WhoMW 92*
**Daultana**, Mumtaz Mohammad Khan 1916- *Who 92*
**Daulton**, George *ScFEYrs*
**Daum**, Charles Frederick 1946- *WhoAmP 91*
**Daum**, Donald Richard 1933- *AmMWSc 92*
**Daum**, John Bradford 1957- *WhoWest 92*
**Daum**, Sol Jacob 1933- *AmMWSc 92*
**Dauman**, Anatole 1925- *IntWW 91*
**Daumen**, Michael Patrick 1946- *WhoAmL 92*
**Daumit**, Gene Philip 1943- *AmMWSc 92*
**Dauncey**, Michael Donald Keen 1920- *Who 92*
**Dauner**, Marvin K 1927- *WhoAmP 91*
**Daunora**, Louis George 1932- *AmMWSc 92*
**Daunt**, Brian 1900- *Who 92*
**Daunt**, Jacqueline Ann 1953- *WhoAmL 92*
**Daunt**, John Gilbert 1913- *AmMWSc 92*
**Daunt**, Jon *DrAPF 91*
**Daunt**, Patrick Eldon 1925- *Who 92*
**Daunt**, Stephen Joseph 1947- *AmMWSc 92*
**Daunt**, Timothy Lewis Achilles 1935- *Who 92*
**Daunton**, Nancy Gottlieb 1942- *AmMWSc 92*
**Dauphin**, Borel C. *WhoBIA 92*
**Dauphinais**, Raymond Joseph 1925- *AmMWSc 92*
**Dauphine**, T C 1913- *AmMWSc 92*
**Dauphinee**, JoAnne Louise 1950- *WhoAmP 91*
**Dauphinee**, Thomas McCaul 1916- *AmMWSc 92*
**D'Auria**, John Michael 1939- *AmMWSc 92*
**D'Auria**, Mark 1955- *WhoEnt 92*
**D'Auria**, Thomas A 1946- *AmMWSc 92*
**D'Aurora**, James Joseph 1949- *WhoMW 92*
**Dauscher**, Kenneth R 1943- *WhoIns 92*
**Dausey**, Gary Ralph 1940- *WhoRel 92*
**Dausset**, Jean 1916- *FacFETw*
**Dausset**, Jean Baptiste Gabriel 1916- *AmMWSc 92, IntWW 91*
**Dausset**, Jean Baptiste Gabriel Joachim 1916- *Who 92, WhoNob 90*
**Daussman**, Grover Frederick 1919- *WhoFI 92*
**Dauster**, William Gary 1957- *WhoAmL 92, WhoFI 92*
**Dauterive**, Wayne Patrick 1947- *WhoFI 92*
**Dauterman**, Walter Carl 1932- *AmMWSc 92*
**Dautlick**, Joseph X 1942- *AmMWSc 92*
**Dautzenberg**, Frits Mathia 1940- *AmMWSc 92*
**Dauwalder**, Marianne 1935- *AmMWSc 92*
**Dauway**, Lois McCullough 1948- *WhoBIA 92*
**Dauzier**, Pierre Marie 1939- *IntWW 91*
**Davalos**, Carlos J. 1951- *WhoHisp 92*
**DaValt**, Dorothy B. 1914- *WhoBIA 92*
**DaValt**, Dorothy Beatrix 1914- *WhoAmP 91*
**D'Avanzo**, Charlene 1947- *AmMWSc 92*
**DaVanzo**, John Paul 1927- *AmMWSc 92*
**Davar**, Dharmendar Nath 1934- *IntWW 91*
**Davar**, K S 1923- *AmMWSc 92*
**Dave**, Alfonzo, Jr. 1945- *WhoBIA 92*
**Dave**, Bhalchandra A 1931- *AmMWSc 92*
**Dave**, Raju S 1958- *AmMWSc 92*
**Dave**, Shashi Bhaishanker 1931- *WhoWest 92*
**Davee**, Lawrence W. 1900- *IntMPA 92*
**Davee**, Linda Joan 1946- *WhoAmP 91*
**Da Vella**, Ronald Vito 1957- *WhoFI 92*
**Daven**, Sherry *WhoEnt 92*
**Davenant**, William 1606-1668 *RfGEnL 91*
**Davenport**, Alan Garnett 1932- *AmMWSc 92*
**Davenport**, Alfred Larue, Jr. 1921- *WhoWest 92*
**Davenport**, Amy 1947- *WhoAmP 91*
**Davenport**, Arthur Nigel 1928- *Who 92*
**Davenport**, Benjamin Rush *ScFEYrs*
**Davenport**, Brian John 1936- *Who 92*
**Davenport**, C. Dennis 1946- *WhoBIA 92*
**Davenport**, Calvin A. 1928- *WhoBIA 92*
**Davenport**, Calvin Armstrong 1928- *AmMWSc 92*
**Davenport**, Carolyn Wesley 1952- *WhoAmL 92*
**Davenport**, Charles B 1866-1944 *DcAmImH*
**Davenport**, Charles Benedict 1866-1944 *FacFETw*
**Davenport**, Chester C. 1940- *WhoBIA 92*
**Davenport**, David 1950- *WhoRel 92, WhoWest 92*
**Davenport**, David Anthony 1944- *WhoFI 92*
**Davenport**, David John Cecil 1934- *Who 92*
**Davenport**, David William 1952- *WhoAmL 92*
**Davenport**, Derek Alfred 1927- *AmMWSc 92*
**Davenport**, Diana *DrAPF 91*
**Davenport**, Donald Lyle 1930- *WhoFI 92, WhoMW 92*
**Davenport**, Dudley Leslie d1990 *Who 92N*
**Davenport**, Ernest H. 1917- *WhoBIA 92*
**Davenport**, Fred M 1914- *AmMWSc 92*
**Davenport**, George Edward 1833-1907 *BiInAmS*
**Davenport**, Gordon, III 1956- *WhoAmL 92*
**Davenport**, Gregory Michael 1949- *WhoBIA 92*
**Davenport**, Guy *DrAPF 91*
**Davenport**, Guy 1927- *ConNov 91, WrDr 92*
**Davenport**, Guy Ralph, Jr 1947- *WhoAmP 91*
**Davenport**, Harold Allen 1926- *WhoRel 92*
**Davenport**, Horace Alexander 1919- *WhoBIA 92*
**Davenport**, Horace Willard 1912- *AmMWSc 92*
**Davenport**, Ian 1966- *TwCPaSc*
**Davenport**, J. Lee 1935- *WhoBIA 92, WhoRel 92*
**Davenport**, James 1716-1757 *BenetAL 91*
**Davenport**, James Augustus, IV 1962- *WhoEnt 92*
**Davenport**, James Guython 1932- *WhoRel 92*
**Davenport**, James H. *WhoBIA 92*
**Davenport**, James Pearce 1917- *WhoAmL 92*
**Davenport**, James Whitman 1945- *AmMWSc 92*
**Davenport**, Janet Lee 1938- *WhoWest 92*
**Davenport**, John 1597-1670 *BenetAL 91*
**Davenport**, John 1938- *WrDr 92*
**Davenport**, John Eaton 1944- *AmMWSc 92*
**Davenport**, John Edwin 1928- *WhoAmP 91*
**Davenport**, Joseph Howard 1934- *WhoAmP 91*
**Davenport**, L. B. *WhoRel 92*
**Davenport**, LaNoue 1922- *NewAmDM*
**Davenport**, Lawrence Franklin 1944- *WhoBIA 92*
**Davenport**, Lee Losee 1915- *AmMWSc 92*
**Davenport**, Lesley 1955- *AmMWSc 92*
**Davenport**, Leslie Bryan, Jr 1928- *AmMWSc 92*
**Davenport**, Marcia 1903- *BenetAL 91, WrDr 92*
**Davenport**, Maurice Hopwood 1925- *Who 92*
**Davenport**, Mitchell Francis 1960- *WhoMW 92, WhoRel 92*
**Davenport**, Nigel *Who 92*
**Davenport**, Nigel 1928- *IntMPA 92, IntWW 91*
**Davenport**, Pamela Beaver 1948- *WhoFI 92*
**Davenport**, Paul W 1951- *AmMWSc 92*
**Davenport**, Peter Malcolm 1943- *WhoAmL 92*
**Davenport**, Roger Lee 1955- *WhoWest 92*
**Davenport**, Ronald R. 1936- *WhoBIA 92*
**Davenport**, Russell Wheeler 1849-1904 *BiInAmS*
**Davenport**, Rustin Thomas 1959- *WhoAmL 92*
**Davenport**, Thomas 1802-1851 *BiInAmS*
**Davenport**, Thomas Herbert 1933- *WhoMW 92*
**Davenport**, Thomas Lee 1947- *AmMWSc 92*
**Davenport**, Tom Forest, Jr 1930- *AmMWSc 92*
**Davenport**, W Bennett 1931- *WhoIns 92*
**Davenport**, Walter Arthur B. *Who 92*
**Davenport**, Wilbur B, Jr 1920- *AmMWSc 92*
**Davenport**, William Daniel, Jr 1947- *AmMWSc 92*
**Davenport**, William H. 1908- *WrDr 92*
**Davenport**, William Harold 1935- *WhoWest 92*
**Davenport**, William Henry 1868-1936 *DcNCBi 2*
**Davenport**, Willie D. *WhoBIA 92*
**Davenport**, Willie D 1943- *BlkOlyM*
**Davenport-Handley**, David 1919- *Who 92*
**Davenport-Hines**, Richard 1953- *ConAu 134*
**Daventry**, Viscount 1921- *Who 92*
**Daver**, Edul Mindo 1944- *WhoFI 92*
**Daverman**, Robert Jay 1941- *AmMWSc 92*
**Davern**, Cedric I 1931- *AmMWSc 92*
**Daves**, Delmer 1904-1977 *IntDcF 2-2 [port]*
**Daves**, Don Michael 1938- *WhoRel 92*
**Daves**, Donald Rae 1930- *WhoEnt 92*
**Daves**, Glenn Doyle 1915- *WhoAmP 91*
**Daves**, Glenn Doyle, Jr 1936- *AmMWSc 92*
**Daves**, Graham 1836-1902 *DcNCBi 2*
**Daves**, John 1748-1804 *DcNCBi 2*
**Daves**, Marvin Lewis 1928- *AmMWSc 92*
**Daves**, Michael Lawrence 1939- *WhoEnt 92*
**Davey**, Bernard Arthur 1919- *WhoEnt 92*
**Davey**, Bruce James 1927- *WhoFI 92*
**Davey**, Charles Bingham 1928- *AmMWSc 92*
**Davey**, David Garnet 1912- *Who 92*
**Davey**, David Herbert P. *Who 92*
**Davey**, Francis 1932- *Who 92*
**Davey**, Frank 1940- *ConPo 91, IntAu&W 91, WrDr 92*
**Davey**, Frederick Richard *AmMWSc 92*
**Davey**, Geoffrey Wallace 1924- *Who 92*
**Davey**, Gerald Leland 1930- *AmMWSc 92*
**Davey**, Gerard Paul 1949- *WhoAmL 92, WhoWest 92*
**Davey**, Grenville 1961- *TwCPaSc*
**Davey**, Idris Wyn 1917- *Who 92*
**Davey**, James R 1912- *AmMWSc 92*
**Davey**, Jocelyn *Who 92, WrDr 92*
**Davey**, John Edmund 1925- *AmMWSc 92*
**Davey**, John Trevor 1923- *Who 92*
**Davey**, Jon Colin 1938- *Who 92*
**Davey**, Jon-Mark 1953- *WhoEnt 92*
**Davey**, Keith Alfred Thomas 1920- *Who 92*
**Davey**, Kenneth George 1932- *AmMWSc 92, IntWW 91*
**Davey**, Paul Oliver 1931- *AmMWSc 92*
**Davey**, Peter 1940- *ConAu 135*
**Davey**, Peter Gordon 1935- *Who 92*
**Davey**, Peter John 1940- *Who 92*
**Davey**, Ronald William 1943- *Who 92*
**Davey**, Roy Charles 1915- *Who 92*
**Davey**, Thomas A 1954- *IntAu&W 91*
**Davey**, Trevor B 1931- *AmMWSc 92*
**Davey**, William 1917- *Who 92*
**Davey**, William George 1929- *AmMWSc 92*
**Davey**, William James 1949- *WhoAmL 92*
**Davey**, William Robert 1943- *AmMWSc 92*
**Davey**, Winthrop Newbury 1918- *AmMWSc 92*
**Davi**, Robert *ConTFT 9*
**Daviau**, Allen *WhoEnt 92*
**Daviau**, Donald George 1927- *WhoFI 92*
**Davich**, Theodore Bert 1923- *AmMWSc 92*
**David** *EncEarC, Who 92*
**David**, Baroness 1913- *Who 92*
**David of Wales** *EncEarC*
**David**, Almitra *DrAPF 91*
**David**, Andrew *ConAu 36NR*
**David**, Arthur LaCurtiss 1938- *WhoBIA 92*
**David**, Austin 1935- *WhoRel 92*
**David**, Brian Gurney d1990 *Who 92N*
**David**, Bruce Kent 1947- *WhoAmL 92*
**David**, Burke 1913- *IntAu&W 91*
**David**, Carl Wolfgang 1937- *AmMWSc 92*
**David**, Chelladurai S 1936- *AmMWSc 92*
**David**, Daniel Allen 1958- *WhoAmL 92*
**David**, Donald J 1930- *AmMWSc 92*
**David**, Edward E, Jr 1925- *AmMWSc 92*
**David**, Edward Emil, Jr. 1925- *IntWW 91*
**David**, Elizabeth *IntWW 91, Who 92, WrDr 92*
**David**, Ferdinand 1810-1873 *NewAmDM*
**David**, Florence N 1909- *AmMWSc 92*
**David**, Gary Samuel 1942- *AmMWSc 92*
**David**, George 1940- *WhoFI 92*
**David**, George F., III 1923- *WhoBIA 92*
**David**, Geraldine R. 1938- *WhoBIA 92*
**David**, Hal *WhoEnt 92*
**David**, Henry P 1923- *AmMWSc 92*
**David**, Herbert Aron 1925- *AmMWSc 92*
**David**, Irvin Louis, Sr. 1948- *WhoFI 92*
**David**, Israel A 1925- *AmMWSc 92*
**David**, Jacques Henri 1943- *IntWW 91*
**David**, Jacques-Louis 1748-1825 *BlkwCEP*
**David**, James Donald 1957- *WhoFI 92*
**David**, Jean 1921- *AmMWSc 92*
**David**, Jeffrey Joseph 1964- *WhoMW 92*
**David**, Johann Nepomuk 1895-1977 *NewAmDM*
**David**, John Dewood 1942- *AmMWSc 92*
**David**, John R 1930- *AmMWSc 92*
**David**, Julienne *EncAmaz 91*
**David**, Keith *IntMPA 92*
**David**, Keith 1956- *WhoBIA 92*
**David**, Larry Gene 1938- *AmMWSc 92*
**David**, Larry Leroy 1957- *WhoFI 92*
**David**, Lawrence T. 1930- *WhoBIA 92*
**David**, Leon Thomas 1901- *WhoAmL 92, WhoWest 92*
**David**, Lynn Allen 1948- *WhoFI 92*
**David**, Marc 1925- *Who 92*
**David**, Mark Steven 1951- *WhoWest 92*
**David**, Martha Lena Huffaker 1925- *WhoEnt 92*
**David**, Michael Paul 1951- *WhoAmP 91*
**David**, Moses M 1962- *AmMWSc 92*
**David**, Murphy Samuel 1931- *WhoMW 92*
**David**, Nat *DrAPF 91*
**David**, Neal 1950- *WhoFI 92, WhoMW 92*
**David**, Oliver Joseph 1937- *AmMWSc 92*
**David**, Peter P 1932- *AmMWSc 92*
**David**, Philip 1931- *WhoFI 92*
**David**, Pierre *IntMPA 92*
**David**, Puritz 1935- *WhoAmP 91*
**David**, Rachel Mira 1954- *WhoEnt 92*
**David**, Ray 1925- *WhoAmP 91*
**David**, Remy 1955- *WhoEnt 92*
**David**, Reuben 1928- *WhoAmL 92*
**David**, Richard 1912- *Who 92*
**David**, Robert Allan 1937- *Who 92*
**David**, Robert Jefferson 1943- *WhoAmL 92*
**David**, Robin Daniel George 1922- *Who 92*
**David**, Ronald Sigmund 1940- *WhoWest 92*
**David**, Sarah 1957- *WhoEnt 92*
**David**, Saul 1921- *IntMPA 92*
**David**, Shirley Hart 1949- *WhoAmL 92*
**David**, Stanislaus Antony 1943- *AmMWSc 92*
**David**, Tudor 1921- *Who 92*
**David**, Wayne 1957- *Who 92*
**David**, Yadin B 1945- *AmMWSc 92*
**David-Weill**, Michel 1932- *IntWW 91*
**David-Weill**, Michel Alexandre 1932- *Who 92, WhoFI 92*
**Davida**, George I 1944- *AmMWSc 92*
**Davidenkov**, Sergey Nikolaevich 1880-1961 *SovUnBD*
**Davidge**, John Beale 1768-1829 *BiInAmS*
**Davidian**, Karen Gail 1957- *WhoWest 92*
**Davidian**, Nancy McConnell 1941- *AmMWSc 92*
**Davidoff**, Frank F 1934- *AmMWSc 92*
**Davidoff**, Richard Sayles 1932- *WhoAmL 92*
**Davidoff**, Robert Alan 1934- *AmMWSc 92*
**Davidoff**, Roger 1949- *WhoEnt 92*
**Davidon**, William Cooper 1927- *AmMWSc 92*
**Davidovich**, Bella 1928- *IntWW 91, WhoEnt 92*
**Davidovich**, Bella Mikhaylovna 1928- *SovUnBD*
**Davidovits**, Joseph 1935- *AmMWSc 92*
**Davidovits**, Paul 1935- *AmMWSc 92*
**Davidovsky**, Mario 1934- *NewAmDM*
**Davidow**, Bernard 1919- *AmMWSc 92*
**Davidow**, Jeffrey 1944- *WhoAmP 91*
**Davidow**, William Henry 1935- *WhoFI 92*
**Davids**, Cary Nathan 1940- *AmMWSc 92*
**Davids**, Greg 1958- *WhoAmP 91*
**Davids**, Hollace Goodman 1947- *WhoEnt 92*
**Davids**, James Alan 1951- *WhoAmL 92*
**Davidse**, Gerrit 1942- *AmMWSc 92*
**Davidsen**, Arthur Falnes 1944- *AmMWSc 92*
**Davidsen**, Donald R *WhoAmP 91*
**Davidsmeyer**, Kay L 1953- *WhoAmP 91*
**Davidson** *Who 92*
**Davidson**, Lord 1929- *Who 92*
**Davidson**, Viscount 1928- *Who 92*
**Davidson**, A N 1930- *WhoIns 92*
**Davidson**, Adam Brevard 1808-1896 *DcNCBi 2*
**Davidson**, Alan *IntAu&W 91*

**Davidson,** Alan Eaton 1924- *Who 92, WrDr 92*
**Davidson,** Alan John 1938- *WhoAmL 92, WhoFI 92, WhoMW 92*
**Davidson,** Alexander Caldwell 1826-1897 *DcNCBi 2*
**Davidson,** Alexander Grant 1927- *AmMWSc 92*
**Davidson,** Alfred E. 1911- *IntWW 91*
**Davidson,** Alfred Edward 1911- *Who 92*
**Davidson,** Allain G., Jr. 1943- *WhoFI 92*
**Davidson,** Allen Turner 1819-1905 *DcNCBi 2*
**Davidson,** Alphonzo Lowell 1941- *WhoBlA 92*
**Davidson,** Anne Stowell 1949- *WhoAmL 92*
**Davidson,** Arnold B 1930- *AmMWSc 92*
**Davidson,** Arthur 1928- *Who 92*
**Davidson,** Arthur B. 1929- *WhoBlA 92*
**Davidson,** Arthur Turner 1923- *WhoBlA 92*
**Davidson,** Avram 1923- *TwCSFW 91, WrDr 92*
**Davidson,** Barbara Taylor 1920- *WhoMW 92*
**Davidson,** Barry Rodney 1943- *WhoAmL 92*
**Davidson,** Basil 1914- *IntAu&W 91, IntWW 91, WrDr 92*
**Davidson,** Basil Risbridger 1914- *Who 92*
**Davidson,** Ben d1991 *NewYTBS 91 [port]*
**Davidson,** Betty 1933- *AmMWSc 92*
**Davidson,** Bill 1918- *WhoEnt 92, WhoWest 92*
**Davidson,** Bonnie Jean 1941- *WhoMW 92*
**Davidson,** Bradly Lee 1955- *WhoWest 92*
**Davidson,** Brian 1909- *Who 92*
**Davidson,** Bruce M 1924- *AmMWSc 92*
**Davidson,** C Girard 1910- *WhoAmP 91*
**Davidson,** Carl B. 1933- *WhoFI 92*
**Davidson,** Carol H. 1947- *WhoWest 92*
**Davidson,** Charles H 1920- *AmMWSc 92*
**Davidson,** Charles Kemp *Who 92*
**Davidson,** Charles Mackenzie 1942- *AmMWSc 92*
**Davidson,** Charles Michael Birnie 1944- *WhoFI 92*
**Davidson,** Charles Nelson 1937- *AmMWSc 92*
**Davidson,** Charles Odell 1935- *WhoBlA 92*
**Davidson,** Charles Peter Morton 1938- *Who 92*
**Davidson,** Charles Robert 1922- *WhoBlA 92*
**Davidson,** Charles Sprecher 1910- *AmMWSc 92*
**Davidson,** Christopher 1944- *AmMWSc 92*
**Davidson,** Cliff *WhoAmP 91*
**Davidson,** Cliff Ian 1950- *AmMWSc 92*
**Davidson,** Colin Henry 1928- *AmMWSc 92*
**Davidson,** Craig J. d1991 *NewYTBS 91*
**Davidson,** Crow Girard 1910- *WhoAmL 92*
**Davidson,** Dan D. 1948- *WhoFI 92*
**Davidson,** Daniel Lee 1946- *AmMWSc 92*
**Davidson,** Darwin Ervin 1943- *AmMWSc 92*
**Davidson,** David *AmMWSc 92*
**Davidson,** David Edward, Jr 1935- *AmMWSc 92*
**Davidson,** David Francis 1923- *AmMWSc 92*
**Davidson,** David Lee 1935- *AmMWSc 92*
**Davidson,** David Robert 1948- *WhoEnt 92*
**Davidson,** Diane West 1948- *AmMWSc 92*
**Davidson,** Donald 1893-1968 *BenetAL 91*
**Davidson,** Donald 1917- *IntAu&W 91, IntWW 91, WrDr 92*
**Davidson,** Donald 1934- *AmMWSc 92*
**Davidson,** Donald H 1937- *AmMWSc 92*
**Davidson,** Donald Lee 1937- *WhoAmP 91*
**Davidson,** Donald Miner, Jr 1939- *AmMWSc 92*
**Davidson,** Donald Rae 1943- *WhoBlA 92*
**Davidson,** Donald William 1936- *AmMWSc 92*
**Davidson,** Donetta Lea 1943- *WhoAmP 91*
**Davidson,** Douglas 1931- *AmMWSc 92*
**Davidson,** Douglas A. 1936- *WhoFI 92*
**Davidson,** Earnest Jefferson 1946- *WhoBlA 92*
**Davidson,** Edward S 1939- *AmMWSc 92*
**Davidson,** Edwin Dow, Jr. 1953- *WhoWest 92*
**Davidson,** Elizabeth Beck 1908- *WhoRel 92*
**Davidson,** Elizabeth West 1942- *AmMWSc 92*
**Davidson,** Elvyn Verone 1923- *WhoBlA 92*
**Davidson,** Emily *DrAPF 91*
**Davidson,** Eric Harris 1937- *AmMWSc 92, WhoWest 92*
**Davidson,** Eric Nathan 1959- *WhoRel 92*
**Davidson,** Ernest 1921- *AmMWSc 92*
**Davidson,** Ernest Roy 1936- *AmMWSc 92, WhoMW 92*
**Davidson,** Eugene 1902- *WrDr 92*
**Davidson,** Eugene Abraham 1930- *AmMWSc 92*
**Davidson,** Eugene Arthur 1902- *IntAu&W 91*
**Davidson,** Eugene Erbert 1947- *WhoAmP 91*
**Davidson,** Ezra C., Jr. 1933- *WhoBlA 92*
**Davidson,** Francis 1905- *Who 92*
**Davidson,** Frank Geoffrey 1920- *IntAu&W 91, WrDr 92*
**Davidson,** Frank Paul 1918- *WhoAmL 92, WhoFI 92*
**Davidson,** Fred, III 1941- *WhoBlA 92*
**Davidson,** Frederic M 1941- *AmMWSc 92*
**Davidson,** Gary Edward 1959- *WhoAmL 92*
**Davidson,** George 1825-1911 *BiInAmS*
**Davidson,** George Allan 1942- *WhoAmL 92*
**Davidson,** George Thomas, Jr. 1916- *WhoRel 92*
**Davidson,** Gerald Ray 1936- *WhoRel 92*
**Davidson,** Gilbert 1934- *AmMWSc 92*
**Davidson,** Glen Harris 1941- *WhoAmL 92*
**Davidson,** Glen William 1936- *WhoRel 92*
**Davidson,** Gordon 1933- *WhoEnt 92, WhoWest 92*
**Davidson,** Grant E 1919- *AmMWSc 92*
**Davidson,** H 1921- *AmMWSc 92*
**Davidson,** Harold 1919- *AmMWSc 92*
**Davidson,** Harold French, Jr. 1920- *WhoMW 92*
**Davidson,** Harold Michael 1924- *AmMWSc 92*
**Davidson,** Harry Lee 1956- *WhoEnt 92*
**Davidson,** Harvey Leonard 1940- *WhoMW 92*
**Davidson,** Howard William 1911- *Who 92*
**Davidson,** Ian Thomas Rollo 1925- *Who 92*
**Davidson,** Ivan William Frederick 1926- *AmMWSc 92*
**Davidson,** Ivor Macaulay 1924- *Who 92*
**Davidson,** J P *AmMWSc 92*
**Davidson,** Jack Dougan 1918- *AmMWSc 92*
**Davidson,** James Alfred 1922- *Who 92*
**Davidson,** James Blaine 1923- *AmMWSc 92*
**Davidson,** James Duncan Gordon 1927- *Who 92*
**Davidson,** James Harold 1942- *WhoAmL 92*
**Davidson,** James Jonathon 1960- *WhoFI 92*
**Davidson,** James Madison, III 1930- *WhoFI 92*
**Davidson,** James Melvin 1934- *AmMWSc 92*
**Davidson,** James Patton 1928- *Who 92*
**Davidson,** James Wilson 1950- *WhoMW 92, WhoRel 92*
**Davidson,** Janet Marjorie 1941- *IntWW 91*
**Davidson,** Janet Toll 1939- *WhoAmL 92*
**Davidson,** Jeannie 1938- *WhoEnt 92*
**Davidson,** Jeffrey H. 1952- *WhoAmL 92*
**Davidson,** Jeffrey Neal 1950- *AmMWSc 92*
**Davidson,** Jeffrey P. 1951- *WrDr 92*
**Davidson,** Jessica Ursula Brown 1914- *WhoEnt 92*
**Davidson,** Jill Elaine 1962- *WhoEnt 92*
**Davidson,** Jimmy Mitchel 1942- *WhoFI 92*
**Davidson,** Jo 1883-1952 *BenetAL 91, FacFETw*
**Davidson,** Jo Ann *WhoAmP 91*
**Davidson,** John 1735-1832 *DcNCBi 2*
**Davidson,** John 1857-1909 *RfGEnL 91*
**Davidson,** John 1941- *IntMPA 92, WhoEnt 92*
**Davidson,** John A 1924- *WhoAmP 91*
**Davidson,** John Angus 1933- *AmMWSc 92*
**Davidson,** John Edwin 1937- *AmMWSc 92*
**Davidson,** John Frank 1926- *IntWW 91, Who 92*
**Davidson,** John G N 1935- *AmMWSc 92*
**Davidson,** John Henry 1942- *WhoAmL 92*
**Davidson,** John Keay, III 1922- *AmMWSc 92*
**Davidson,** John Kenneth, Sr. 1939- *WhoMW 92*
**Davidson,** John Macdonald 1926- *IntWW 91*
**Davidson,** John Richard 1929- *AmMWSc 92*
**Davidson,** John Robert 1947- *WhoMW 92*
**Davidson,** John Roderick 1937- *Who 92*
**Davidson,** John Sinclair 1956- *WhoFI 92*
**Davidson,** John Vern 1933- *WhoFI 92*
**Davidson,** Jon Paul 1959- *AmMWSc 92*
**Davidson,** Joseph Killworth 1938- *AmMWSc 92*
**Davidson,** Joseph Q., Jr. 1941- *WhoAmL 92*
**Davidson,** Juli 1960- *WhoWest 92*
**Davidson,** Julian M 1931- *AmMWSc 92*
**Davidson,** Karen Sue 1950- *WhoFI 92*
**Davidson,** Keith *Who 92*
**Davidson,** Kenneth Darrell 1967- *WhoBlA 92*
**Davidson,** Kenneth LaVern 1940- *AmMWSc 92*
**Davidson,** Kenneth Lawrence 1945- *WhoAmL 92*
**Davidson,** Kerry 1935- *WhoBlA 92*
**Davidson,** Kris 1943- *AmMWSc 92*
**Davidson,** LeRoy *WhoEnt 92*
**Davidson,** Lionel 1922- *ConNov 91, IntAu&W 91, WrDr 92*
**Davidson,** Lurlean G. 1931- *WhoBlA 92*
**Davidson,** Lyle *WhoEnt 92*
**Davidson,** Lynn Blair 1940- *AmMWSc 92*
**Davidson,** Mark Rogers 1962- *AmMWSc 92*
**Davidson,** Martin 1939- *IntMPA 92, WhoEnt 92*
**Davidson,** Mayer B 1935- *AmMWSc 92*
**Davidson,** Melvin G 1938- *AmMWSc 92*
**Davidson,** Michael *DrAPF 91*
**Davidson,** Michael 1940- *WhoAmL 92*
**Davidson,** Michael 1944- *ConPo 91, IntAu&W 91, WrDr 92*
**Davidson,** Mildred 1935- *IntAu&W 91*
**Davidson,** Neal R. 1934- *WhoRel 92*
**Davidson,** Neil William 1946- *WhoEnt 92*
**Davidson,** Norman Ralph 1916- *AmMWSc 92, IntWW 91*
**Davidson,** Pamela 1954- *ConAu 133*
**Davidson,** Paula Jo 1952- *WhoAmL 92*
**Davidson,** Peter 1942- *WhoEnt 92*
**Davidson,** Peter Brooks 1953- *WhoFI 92*
**Davidson,** Phebe *DrAPF 91*
**Davidson,** Philip Harold 1944- *WhoFI 92*
**Davidson,** Philip Michael 1950- *AmMWSc 92*
**Davidson,** Ralph Howard 1908- *AmMWSc 92*
**Davidson,** Ralph P 1927- *IntAu&W 91, IntWW 91*
**Davidson,** Richard *DrAPF 91*
**Davidson,** Richard Alan 1946- *WhoMW 92*
**Davidson,** Richard Dodge 1945- *WhoAmL 92*
**Davidson,** Richard K. 1942- *WhoFI 92*
**Davidson,** Richard Laurence 1941- *AmMWSc 92*
**Davidson,** Rick Bernard 1951- *WhoBlA 92*
**Davidson,** Robert 1769-1853 *DcNCBi 2*
**Davidson,** Robert 1927- *Who 92*
**Davidson,** Robert 1928- *Who 92*
**Davidson,** Robert Bellamy 1947- *AmMWSc 92*
**Davidson,** Robert Bruce 1945- *WhoAmL 92*
**Davidson,** Robert C 1932- *AmMWSc 92*
**Davidson,** Robert C., Jr. 1945- *WhoBlA 92*
**Davidson,** Robert James 1862-1915 *BiInAmS*
**Davidson,** Robert W 1921- *AmMWSc 92*
**Davidson,** Roger H. 1936- *WrDr 92*
**Davidson,** Ronald Crosby 1941- *AmMWSc 92*
**Davidson,** Ronald G 1933- *AmMWSc 92*
**Davidson,** Ronald Hayes 1914- *WhoAmL 92*
**Davidson,** Ross Wallace, Jr 1902- *AmMWSc 92*
**Davidson,** Roy Guy, III 1953- *WhoEnt 92*
**Davidson,** Rudolph Douglas 1941- *WhoBlA 92*
**Davidson,** Samuel James 1937- *AmMWSc 92*
**Davidson,** Sheldon Jerome 1939- *WhoWest 92*
**Davidson,** Sidney 1919- *WhoFI 92, WhoMW 92*
**Davidson,** Sinclair Melville 1922- *Who 92*
**Davidson,** Sol M. 1924- *WrDr 92*
**Davidson,** Steve Edwin 1930- *AmMWSc 92*
**Davidson,** Sylvia Audrey 1922- *WhoAmP 91*
**Davidson,** Theodore 1939- *AmMWSc 92*
**Davidson,** Theodore Fulton 1845-1931 *DcNCBi 2*
**Davidson,** Thomas 1840-1900 *BenetAL 91*
**Davidson,** Thomas James 1952- *WhoRel 92*
**Davidson,** Thomas Maxwell 1937- *WhoFI 92*
**Davidson,** Thomas Ralph 1920- *AmMWSc 92*
**Davidson,** Tom William 1952- *WhoAmL 92, WhoEnt 92*
**Davidson,** Van Michael, Jr. 1945- *WhoAmL 92*
**Davidson,** Walter Frank 1956- *WhoWest 92*
**Davidson,** Wendy Fay *AmMWSc 92*
**Davidson,** William 1778-1857 *DcNCBi 2*
**Davidson,** William George, III 1938- *WhoFI 92*
**Davidson,** William Keith 1926- *Who 92*
**Davidson,** William Lee 1746?-1781 *DcNCBi 2*
**Davidson,** William M. 1921- *WhoMW 92*
**Davidson,** William Martin 1939- *AmMWSc 92*
**Davidson,** William Scott 1952- *AmMWSc 92*
**Davidson,** William Ward, III 1940- *WhoWest 92*
**Davidson-Arnott,** Robin G D 1947- *AmMWSc 92*
**Davidson-Houston,** Aubrey Claud 1906- *Who 92*
**Davie,** Alan 1920- *IntWW 91, TwCPaSc, Who 92*
**Davie,** Antony Francis F. *Who 92*
**Davie,** Donald 1922- *ConPo 91, FacFETw, RfGEnL 91, WrDr 92*
**Davie,** Donald Alfred 1922- *IntAu&W 91, IntWW 91, Who 92*
**Davie,** Earl W 1927- *AmMWSc 92*
**Davie,** Elspeth 1919- *IntAu&W 91*
**Davie,** Ian 1924- *IntAu&W 91, WrDr 92*
**Davie,** James Ronald 1951- *AmMWSc 92*
**Davie,** Joseph Myrten 1939- *AmMWSc 92*
**Davie,** Rex *Who 92*
**Davie,** Ronald 1929- *Who 92*
**Davie,** Stephen Rex 1933- *Who 92*
**Davie,** William Raymond 1924- *AmMWSc 92*
**Davie,** William Richardson 1756-1820 *DcNCBi 2*
**Davie-Martin,** Hugh *IntAu&W 91X, WrDr 92*
**Davies** *ThHEIm, Who 92*
**Davies,** Baron 1940- *Who 92*
**Davies,** Alan 1924- *Who 92*
**Davies,** Albert John 1919- *Who 92*
**Davies,** Albert Meredith 1922- *Who 92*
**Davies,** Alfred William Michael 1921- *Who 92*
**Davies,** Alma *WhoEnt 92*
**Davies,** Alun Radcliffe 1923- *Who 92*
**Davies,** Alun Talfan 1913- *Who 92*
**Davies,** Alwyn George 1926- *Who 92*
**Davies,** Andrew 1936- *IntAu&W 91, WrDr 92*
**Davies,** Andrew Owen Evan 1936- *Who 92*
**Davies,** Andrew Wynford 1936- *Who 92*
**Davies,** Angie Michael 1934- *Who 92*
**Davies,** Anna Elbina 1937- *Who 92*
**Davies,** Anthony 1912- *Who 92*
**Davies,** Anthony 1947- *TwCPaSc*
**Davies,** Anthony Roger 1940- *Who 92*
**Davies,** Arthur d1990 *Who 92N*
**Davies,** Arthur 1906- *Who 92*
**Davies,** Arthur Beverly, III 1924- *WhoAmL 92*
**Davies,** Arthur Gordon 1917- *Who 92*
**Davies,** Audrey 1935- *TwCPaSc*
**Davies,** B. Kevill 1954- *TwCPaSc*
**Davies,** Brian Meredith *Who 92*
**Davies,** Bryan 1939- *Who 92*
**Davies,** Bryn 1932- *Who 92*
**Davies,** Caleb William 1916- *Who 92*
**Davies,** Carlyle W. *Who 92*
**Davies,** Carmel *WhoEnt 92*
**Davies,** Charles 1798-1876 *BiInAmS*
**Davies,** Christian *EncAmaz 91*
**Davies,** Christie 1941- *WrDr 92*
**Davies,** Christopher Evelyn K. *Who 92*
**Davies,** Claude Nigel 1920- *Who 92*
**Davies,** Colin 1948- *Who 92*
**Davies,** Craig Edward 1943- *AmMWSc 92*
**Davies,** Cynthia Kaye 1958- *WhoMW 92*
**Davies,** Cyril James 1923- *Who 92*
**Davies,** D K 1935- *AmMWSc 92*
**Davies,** David 1939- *Who 92*
**Davies,** David Arthur d1990 *IntWW 91N*
**Davies,** David Brian *WhoIns 92*
**Davies,** David Brian Arthur Llewellyn 1932- *Who 92*
**Davies,** David Cyril 1925- *Who 92*
**Davies,** David E. N. 1935- *IntWW 91*
**Davies,** David Evan Naunton 1935- *Who 92*
**Davies,** David Garfield 1935- *Who 92*
**Davies,** David Henry 1909- *Who 92*
**Davies,** David Herbert Mervyn 1918- *Who 92*
**Davies,** David Huw 1942- *AmMWSc 92*
**Davies,** David Hywel 1929- *Who 92*
**Davies,** David John 1940- *Who 92*
**Davies,** David John Denzil 1938- *Who 92*
**Davies,** David Joseph d1991 *Who 92N*
**Davies,** David K 1940- *AmMWSc 92*
**Davies,** David Levric 1925- *Who 92*
**Davies,** David Margerison 1923- *WrDr 92*
**Davies,** David R 1927- *AmMWSc 92*
**Davies,** David Reginald 1927- *IntWW 91*
**Davies,** David Ronald 1910- *Who 92*
**Davies,** David Roy 1932- *Who 92*
**Davies,** David Theodore Alban 1940- *Who 92*
**Davies,** Dennis Russell 1944- *NewAmDM*
**Davies,** Denzil *Who 92*
**Davies,** Dickie *Who 92*
**Davies,** Donald 1924- *Who 92*
**Davies,** Donald Harry 1938- *AmMWSc 92*
**Davies,** Donald Watts 1924- *Who 92*
**Davies,** Douglas *Who 92*
**Davies,** Douglas Mackenzie 1919- *AmMWSc 92*
**Davies,** E. T. 1903- *WrDr 92*

**Davies,** Ednyfed Hudson 1929- *Who 92*
**Davies,** Edward David 1911- *WhoWest 92*
**Davies,** Edward Hunter 1936- *Who 92*
**Davies,** Elidir 1907- *Who 92*
**Davies,** Emlyn B 1927- *AmMWSc 92*
**Davies,** Emlyn Glyndwr 1916- *Who 92*
**Davies,** Emrys 1934- *IntWW 91*
**Davies,** Emrys Thomas 1934- *Who 92*
**Davies,** Eric 1939- *AmMWSc 92*
**Davies,** Ernest Albert John d1991 *Who 92N*
**Davies,** Ernest Arthur 1926- *Who 92*
**Davies,** Eurfil Rhys 1929- *Who 92*
**Davies,** Everett J. 1945- *WhoBlA 92*
**Davies,** Frederick Herbert 1916- *IntAu&W 91*
**Davies,** Frederick T, Jr 1949- *AmMWSc 92*
**Davies,** Freeman *WhoEnt 92*
**Davies,** Gareth 1930- *Who 92*
**Davies,** Gareth 1956- *TwCPaSc*
**Davies,** Gareth Lewis 1936- *Who 92*
**Davies,** Garfield *Who 92*
**Davies,** Gavyn 1950- *Who 92*
**Davies,** Geoffrey 1942- *AmMWSc 92*
**Davies,** George Francis d1987 *Who 92N*
**Davies,** George James 1947- *WhoMW 92*
**Davies,** George Raymond 1916- *Who 92*
**Davies,** George William 1941- *Who 92*
**Davies,** Gerald 1957- *TwCPaSc*
**Davies,** Gerald Kieth 1944- *WhoFI 92*
**Davies,** Glyn Arthur Owen 1933- *Who 92*
**Davies,** Gordon 1926- *TwCPaSc*
**Davies,** Graeme John 1937- *IntWW 91, Who 92*
**Davies,** Grant William 1937- *WhoWest 92*
**Davies,** Gwen F. *Who 92*
**Davies,** Gwilym E. Hudson *Who 92*
**Davies,** Gwynne Henton 1906- *Who 92*
**Davies,** Handel *Who 92*
**Davies,** Harold William 1930- *AmMWSc 92*
**Davies,** Harry 1915- *Who 92*
**Davies,** Helen Jean Conrad 1925- *AmMWSc 92*
**Davies,** Horton 1916- *WrDr 92*
**Davies,** Horton Marlais 1916- *WhoRel 92*
**Davies,** Howard 1945?- *ConTFT 9*
**Davies,** Howard John 1951- *Who 92*
**Davies,** Howell Haydn 1927- *Who 92*
**Davies,** Hugh 1946- *TwCPaSc*
**Davies,** Hugh Llewelyn 1941- *Who 92*
**Davies,** Hugh Marlais 1948- *WhoWest 92*
**Davies,** Humphrey *Who 92*
**Davies,** Hunter *Who 92, WrDr 92*
**Davies,** Hunter 1936- *IntAu&W 91*
**Davies,** Huw Humphreys 1940- *Who 92*
**Davies,** Huw M 1951- *AmMWSc 92*
**Davies,** Hywel *Who 92*
**Davies,** Ian Hewitt 1931- *Who 92*
**Davies,** Ian Leonard 1924- *Who 92*
**Davies,** Ivor 1935- *TwCPaSc*
**Davies,** Ivor Gordon 1917- *Who 92*
**Davies,** Jack 1919- *AmMWSc 92*
**Davies,** Jack 1932- *WhoAmL 92*
**Davies,** Jack Gale Wilmot 1911- *Who 92*
**Davies,** Jack Neville Phillips 1915- *AmMWSc 92*
**Davies,** Jacob Arthur Christian 1925- *IntWW 91, Who 92*
**Davies,** Jacqueline Marie 1950- *WhoRel 92*
**Davies,** James Brian Meredith 1920- *Who 92*
**Davies,** James Frederick 1924- *AmMWSc 92*
**Davies,** James Jump 1941- *WhoFI 92*
**Davies,** Janet Mary H. *Who 92*
**Davies,** Jean *Who 92*
**Davies,** Jennifer 1950- *IntAu&W 91*
**Davies,** John *Who 92*
**Davies,** John 1569?-1626 *RfGEnL 91*
**Davies,** John 1946- *TwCPaSc*
**Davies,** John A 1931- *AmMWSc 92*
**Davies,** John Alun Emlyn 1909- *Who 92*
**Davies,** John Arthur 1927- *AmMWSc 92, IntWW 91*
**Davies,** John Brian 1932- *Who 92*
**Davies,** John Clifford 1932- *AmMWSc 92*
**Davies,** John Dudley *Who 92*
**Davies,** John Duncan 1929- *Who 92*
**Davies,** John Eugene 1839-1900 *BiInAmS*
**Davies,** John G. 1929- *WhoAmL 92*
**Davies,** John Gordon d1990 *Who 92N*
**Davies,** John Gordon 1919- *WrDr 92*
**Davies,** John Henry Vaughan 1921- *Who 92*
**Davies,** John Howard 1929- *Who 92*
**Davies,** John Howard 1939- *IntMPA 92*
**Davies,** John Howard Gay 1923- *Who 92*
**Davies,** John Irfon 1930- *Who 92*
**Davies,** John Jenkyn, III 1947- *WhoAmL 92*
**Davies,** John Kenyon 1937- *Who 92*
**Davies,** John McRoy 1958- *WhoAmP 91*
**Davies,** John Michael 1940- *Who 92*
**Davies,** John Quentin 1944- *Who 92*
**Davies,** John R. Lloyd 1913- *Who 92*
**Davies,** John S 1926- *WhoAmP 91*
**Davies,** John Thomas 1933- *Who 92*
**Davies,** John Tudor 1937- *AmMWSc 92, WhoWest 92*
**Davies,** Joseph Marie 1916- *Who 92*
**Davies,** Julian Anthony 1955- *AmMWSc 92*
**Davies,** Kate 1960- *TwCPaSc*
**Davies,** Katharyn Mary 1949- *WhoEnt 92*
**Davies,** Keith Laurence M. *Who 92*
**Davies,** Kelvin J A 1951- *AmMWSc 92*
**Davies,** Kennard Michael 1941- *AmMWSc 92*
**Davies,** Kenneth 1928- *AmMWSc 92, WhoWest 92*
**Davies,** Kenneth Arthur d1991 *Who 92N*
**Davies,** Kenneth John 1958- *WhoRel 92*
**Davies,** Kenneth Thomas Reed 1934- *AmMWSc 92*
**Davies,** L P 1914- *IntAu&W 91, TwCSFW 91*
**Davies,** Lancelot Richard B. *Who 92*
**Davies,** Lawrence A. 1930- *WhoBlA 92*
**Davies,** Lewis John 1921- *Who 92*
**Davies,** Lewis Mervyn 1922- *Who 92*
**Davies,** Linda Kay 1947- *WhoMW 92*
**Davies,** Lloyd *Who 92*
**Davies,** Lucy Myfanwy 1913- *Who 92*
**Davies,** Marcia A 1938- *AmMWSc 92*
**Davies,** Marcus John A. *Who 92*
**Davies,** Margaret 1923- *WrDr 92*
**Davies,** Marissa 1962- *TwCPaSc*
**Davies,** Martin 1936- *WrDr 92*
**Davies,** Marvin 1934- *WhoBlA 92*
**Davies,** Meredith *Who 92*
**Davies,** Merton Edward 1917- *AmMWSc 92, WhoWest 92*
**Davies,** Mervyn *Who 92*
**Davies,** Michael *Who 92*
**Davies,** Michael Scott 1955- *WhoFI 92*
**Davies,** Michael Shapland 1939- *AmMWSc 92*
**Davies,** Morgan Wynn Humphrey 1911- *Who 92*
**Davies,** Nancy *DrAPF 91*
**Davies,** Neil *Who 92*
**Davies,** Nicholas E. d1991 *NewYTBS 91*
**Davies,** Nigel *Who 92*
**Davies,** Nigel 1920- *WrDr 92*
**Davies,** Noel Anthony 1942- *Who 92*
**Davies,** Norah Olwen 1926- *Who 92*
**Davies,** Norman 1939- *WrDr 92*
**Davies,** Norman Thomas 1933- *Who 92*
**Davies,** Olwen *Who 92*
**Davies,** Oswald 1920- *Who 92*
**Davies,** P. C. W. 1946- *WrDr 92*
**Davies,** Patrick Taylor 1927- *Who 92*
**Davies,** Paul Lewis, Jr. 1930- *WhoAmL 92, WhoFI 92, WhoWest 92*
**Davies,** Paul R 1939- *WhoIns 92*
**Davies,** Percy Douglas 1921- *Who 92*
**Davies,** Peter *Who 92*
**Davies,** Peter 1897-1960 *DcLB 112 [port]*
**Davies,** Peter Douglas Royston 1936- *Who 92*
**Davies,** Peter F 1947- *AmMWSc 92*
**Davies,** Peter George 1927- *Who 92*
**Davies,** Peter J. 1937- *ConAu 135*
**Davies,** Peter John 1940- *AmMWSc 92*
**Davies,** Peter Maxwell 1934- *ConCom 92, FacFETw, IntWW 91, NewAmDM, Who 92, WhoEnt 92*
**Davies,** Peter Ronald 1938- *Who 92*
**Davies,** Philip *AmMWSc 92*
**Davies,** Philip 1953- *TwCPaSc*
**Davies,** Philip Bertram 1933- *Who 92*
**Davies,** Philip Middleton 1932- *Who 92*
**Davies,** Philip Winne *AmMWSc 92*
**Davies,** Piers Anthony David 1941- *IntAu&W 91, WrDr 92*
**Davies,** Quentin *Who 92*
**Davies,** R. R. 1938- *ConAu 135*
**Davies,** Reg 1936- *AmMWSc 92*
**Davies,** Rhys Everson 1941- *Who 92*
**Davies,** Richard 1944- *TwCPaSc*
**Davies,** Richard Arthur 1951- *WhoEnt 92*
**Davies,** Richard Edgar 1915- *AmMWSc 92*
**Davies,** Richard Glyn 1934- *AmMWSc 92*
**Davies,** Richard Harries 1916- *Who 92*
**Davies,** Richard O 1931- *AmMWSc 92*
**Davies,** Richard Oelbaum 1936- *AmMWSc 92*
**Davies,** Robert, Mrs. 1923- *WhoMW 92*
**Davies,** Robert Abel, III 1935- *WhoFI 92*
**Davies,** Robert David 1927- *Who 92*
**Davies,** Robert Dillwyn 1939- *AmMWSc 92*
**Davies,** Robert Edward 1913- *Who 92*
**Davies,** Robert Ernest 1919- *AmMWSc 92, IntWW 91, Who 92*
**Davies,** Robert Henry 1921- *Who 92*
**Davies,** Robert Rees 1938- *Who 92*
**Davies,** Robert William 1925- *IntAu&W 91, WrDr 92*
**Davies,** Robertson 1913- *BenetAL 91, ConNov 91, FacFETw, IntAu&W 91, IntWW 91, RfGEnL 91, WrDr 92*
**Davies,** Rodney Deane 1930- *Who 92*
**Davies,** Roger *Who 92*
**Davies,** Roger 1948- *AmMWSc 92*
**Davies,** Roger Oliver 1945- *Who 92*
**Davies,** Roger Peter 1919- *Who 92*
**Davies,** Ronald 1946- *Who 92*
**Davies,** Ronald Edgar 1932- *AmMWSc 92*
**Davies,** Ronald Wallace 1940- *AmMWSc 92*
**Davies,** Roy Thomas *Who 92*
**Davies,** Rupert E. 1909- *WrDr 92*
**Davies,** Rupert Eric 1909- *Who 92*
**Davies,** Ryland 1943- *IntWW 91, Who 92*
**Davies,** Sam *Who 92*
**Davies,** Siobhan *Who 92*
**Davies,** Stanley Mason 1919- *Who 92*
**Davies,** Steven A 1949- *WhoAmP 91*
**Davies,** Stuart Duncan 1906- *Who 92*
**Davies,** Sumiko 1942- *IntAu&W 91*
**Davies,** Susan 1950- *Who 92*
**Davies,** Susan Elizabeth 1933- *Who 92*
**Davies,** Terence 1945- *IntDcF 2-2 [port]*
**Davies,** Thomas D. d1991 *NewYTBS 91 [port]*
**Davies,** Thomas Glyn 1905- *Who 92*
**Davies,** Todd Richard 1961- *WhoWest 92*
**Davies,** Trevor 1940- *WhoRel 92*
**Davies,** Trevor Arthur L. *Who 92*
**Davies,** Vivian *Who 92*
**Davies,** W.H. 1871-1940 *RfGEnL 91*
**Davies,** Walter 1920- *Who 92*
**Davies,** Walter Merlin 1910- *WrDr 92*
**Davies,** Warren Lewis 1920- *AmMWSc 92*
**Davies,** Wendy Elizabeth 1942- *Who 92*
**Davies,** William Allen 1930- *WhoFI 92*
**Davies,** William James *DcNCBi 2*
**Davies,** William Llewellyn M. *Who 92*
**Davies,** William Michael Neil 1931- *Who 92*
**Davies,** William Ralph 1955- *WhoWest 92*
**Davies,** William Rhys 1932- *Who 92*
**Davies,** William Rupert R. *Who 92*
**Davies,** William Thomas Pennar 1911- *IntAu&W 91*
**Davies,** William Vivian 1947- *Who 92*
**Davies,** Zelma Ince 1930- *Who 92*
**Davies-Jones,** Robert Peter 1943- *AmMWSc 92*
**Davies-McNair,** Jane 1922- *WhoMW 92*
**Davies of Penrhys,** Baron 1913- *Who 92*
**Davies-Scourfield,** Edward Grismond B 1918- *Who 92*
**Davies Tilley,** Laura Frances 1951- *WhoAmL 92*
**Daviess,** John Howard 1923- *WhoFI 92*
**Daviess,** Steven Norman 1918- *AmMWSc 92*
**Davignon,** Charles Philias 1930- *WhoRel 92*
**Davignon,** Etienne 1932- *IntWW 91, Who 92*
**Davignon,** J Paul 1937- *AmMWSc 92*
**Davignon,** Jean 1935- *AmMWSc 92*
**D'Avignon,** Roy Joseph 1942- *WhoAmL 92*
**Davila,** Alberto 1955- *WhoHisp 92*
**Davila,** Daniel 1946- *WhoRel 92*
**Davila,** Edwin 1954- *WhoAmL 92*
**Davila,** Elisa 1944- *WhoHisp 92*
**Davila,** James R. 1960- *WhoRel 92*
**Davila,** Jose Ramon 1934- *WhoHisp 92*
**Davila,** Julio C 1921- *AmMWSc 92*
**Davila,** Manuel 1955- *WhoHisp 92*
**Davila,** Maritza 1952- *WhoHisp 92*
**Davila,** Pedro Arias *HisDSpE*
**Davila,** Robert Refugio 1932- *WhoHisp 92*
**Davila,** Ruben Allen 1956- *WhoHisp 92*
**Davila,** Sonia J. 1942- *WhoHisp 92*
**Davila,** William 1931- *WhoHisp 92*
**Davila,** William A., Jr. 1952- *WhoHisp 92*
**Davila,** William Joseph 1950- *WhoHisp 92*
**Davila,** William S. 1931- *WhoFI 92, WhoWest 92*
**Davila-Colon,** Luis R. 1952- *WhoHisp 92*
**Davila Ostolaza,** Ivan E. 1946- *WhoHisp 92*
**Davila y Fernandez De Celis,** Sancho 1905-1972 *BiDExR*
**Davin,** Dan 1913- *WrDr 92*
**Davin,** Dan 1913-1990 *AnObit 1990, RfGEnL 91*
**Davin,** Daniel 1913- *IntAu&W 91*
**Davin,** Daniel Marcus d1990 *Who 92N*
**Davin,** John William 1938- *WhoMW 92*
**Da Vinci,** Mona *DrAPF 91*
**Davinroy,** Thomas Bernard 1932- *AmMWSc 92*
**Davinson,** Donald 1932- *WrDr 92*
**Davis** *Who 92*
**Davis,** A Arthur 1928- *WhoAmP 91*
**Davis,** A Douglas 1945- *AmMWSc 92*
**Davis,** Abraham, Jr. 1923- *WhoBlA 92*
**Davis,** Abram 1926- *AmMWSc 92*
**Davis,** Adrianne 1945- *WhoBlA 92*
**Davis,** Alan *DrAPF 91*
**Davis,** Alan 1932- *AmMWSc 92*
**Davis,** Alan 1955- *AmMWSc 92*
**Davis,** Alan Lynn 1946- *AmMWSc 92*
**Davis,** Alan Richard 1950- *WhoMW 92*
**Davis,** Alan Roger M. *Who 92*
**Davis,** Alan Steven 1955- *WhoEnt 92*
**Davis,** Albert William 1938- *WhoIns 92*
**Davis,** Alexander Cochran 1920- *AmMWSc 92*
**Davis,** Alexander Jackson 1803-1892 *DcNCBi 2*
**Davis,** Alfred, IV 1945- *WhoAmP 91*
**Davis,** Alfred, Jr 1919- *AmMWSc 92*
**Davis,** Alfred C., Sr. 1938- *WhoBlA 92*
**Davis,** Alfred Lewis 1941- *WhoFI 92*
**Davis,** Algenita Scott 1950- *WhoBlA 92*
**Davis,** Alice R. 1904- *WhoBlA 92*
**Davis,** Allan *Who 92*
**Davis,** Allan Windham 1954- *WhoEnt 92*
**Davis,** Allen 1929- *WhoWest 92*
**Davis,** Allen, III 1929- *WhoEnt 92*
**Davis,** Allen F. 1931- *WrDr 92*
**Davis,** Alonzo J. 1942- *WhoBlA 92*
**Davis,** Alten Bigler 1921- *WhoWest 92*
**Davis,** Alton Thomas 1947- *WhoAmP 91*
**Davis,** Alvie Lee 1931- *AmMWSc 92*
**Davis,** Alvin Glenn 1960- *WhoBlA 92*
**Davis,** Alvin Herbert 1929- *AmMWSc 92*
**Davis,** Amos 1932- *WhoBlA 92*
**Davis,** Andrew 1944- *IntWW 91, NewAmDM*
**Davis,** Andrew Frank 1944- *Who 92, WhoEnt 92*
**Davis,** Andrew George 1956- *WhoMW 92*
**Davis,** Andrew Jackson 1826-1910 *BenetAL 91, RelLAm 91*
**Davis,** Andrew Morgan 1950- *AmMWSc 92*
**Davis,** Angela 1944- *BenetAL 91, FacFETw, HanAmWH, NotBlAW 92 [port]*
**Davis,** Angela Lucretia 1942- *WhoBlA 92*
**Davis,** Angela Y. 1944- *WrDr 92*
**Davis,** Angela Yvonne 1944- *WhoBlA 92*
**Davis,** Anita Louise 1936- *WhoBlA 92*
**Davis,** Anthony 1951- *WhoEnt 92*
**Davis,** Anthony Michael John 1939- *AmMWSc 92*
**Davis,** Anthony Ronald William James 1931- *Who 92*
**Davis,** Arnor S. 1919- *WhoBlA 92*
**Davis,** Arrie W. 1940- *WhoBlA 92*
**Davis,** Arthur 1927- *IntMPA 92*
**Davis,** Arthur, III 1942- *WhoBlA 92*
**Davis,** Arthur, III 1958- *WhoFI 92*
**Davis,** Arthur, Jr. 1933- *WhoBlA 92*
**Davis,** Arthur D. *WhoBlA 92*
**Davis,** Arthur H. 1917- *IntWW 91*
**Davis,** Arthur H, Jr 1917- *WhoAmP 91*
**Davis,** Arthur Hoey *RfGEnL 91*
**Davis,** Arthur John 1924- *IntWW 91, Who 92*
**Davis,** Arthur Paul 1904- *WhoBlA 92*
**Davis,** Arthur William 1933- *WhoRel 92*
**Davis,** Audrey Elizabeth 1957- *WhoEnt 92*
**Davis,** Barbara D. *WhoBlA 92*
**Davis,** Bart McKay 1955- *WhoAmL 92*
**Davis,** Belva 1933- *WhoBlA 92*
**Davis,** Ben Hill, Jr. 1944- *WhoEnt 92*
**Davis,** Benjamin George 1941- *WhoRel 92*
**Davis,** Benjamin Harold 1905- *AmMWSc 92*
**Davis,** Benjamin Lloyd 1961- *WhoRel 92*
**Davis,** Benjamin O., Jr. 1912- *ConAu 134, ConBlB 2 [port], FacFETw, WhoBlA 92*
**Davis,** Benjamin O, Sr 1877-1970 *FacFETw [port]*
**Davis,** Benjamin Oliver, Jr 1912- *WhoAmP 91*
**Davis,** Bennie L. 1927- *WhoBlA 92*
**Davis,** Bernard Booth 1932- *AmMWSc 92*
**Davis,** Bernard D. 1916- *IntWW 91*
**Davis,** Bernard David 1916- *AmMWSc 92*
**Davis,** Bernard Eric 1937- *AmMWSc 92*
**Davis,** Bette 1908-1989 *FacFETw, HanAmWH*
**Davis,** Betty Jean Bourbonia 1931- *WhoWest 92*
**Davis,** Bettye J. 1938- *WhoBlA 92*
**Davis,** Bettye Jean 1938- *WhoAmP 91*
**Davis,** Bill *LesBEnT 92*
**Davis,** Bill David 1937- *AmMWSc 92*
**Davis,** Billy, Jr. 1938- *WhoBlA 92*
**Davis,** Billy J 1932- *AmMWSc 92*
**Davis,** Bob *WhoBlA 92*
**Davis,** Bob 1938- *AmMWSc 92*
**Davis,** Bobbi 1924- *WhoAmP 91*
**Davis,** Bobby 1946- *WhoBlA 92*
**Davis,** Bonni Gail 1957- *WhoAmL 92*
**Davis,** Brad d1991 *NewYTBS 91 [port]*
**Davis,** Bradley B. *DrAPF 91*
**Davis,** Brenda Lightsey-Hendricks 1943- *WhoBlA 92*
**Davis,** Brent 1946- *WhoEnt 92*
**Davis,** Brian Clifton 1942- *AmMWSc 92*
**Davis,** Brian Gregory 1952- *WhoFI 92*
**Davis,** Brian Kent 1939- *AmMWSc 92*
**Davis,** Brian Michael 1937- *Who 92*
**Davis,** Brian Newton *Who 92*
**Davis,** Brian Newton 1934- *IntWW 91, WhoRel 92*
**Davis,** Brian Scott 1965- *WhoFI 92*
**Davis,** Brian William 1930- *Who 92*
**Davis,** Briant LeRoy 1936- *AmMWSc 92*
**Davis,** Britt 1913- *WhoAmP 91*
**Davis,** Brownie W. 1933- *WhoBlA 92*

Davis, Bruce Allan 1941- AmMWSc 92
Davis, Bruce Allen 1948- WhoMW 92
Davis, Bruce Hewat 1951- AmMWSc 92
Davis, Bruce Owen 1935- WhoIns 92
Davis, Bruce Tolle 1953- WhoMW 92
Davis, Bruce W 1937- AmMWSc 92
Davis, Bruce Wilson 1921- AmMWSc 92
Davis, Bryan Terence 1935- AmMWSc 92
Davis, Bryce Scott 1949- WhoAmP 91
Davis, Burke 1913- WrDr 92
Davis, Burl Edward 1935- AmMWSc 92
Davis, Burns 1931- AmMWSc 92
Davis, Burtron H 1934- AmMWSc 92
Davis, Byron Preston 1944- WhoAmL 92
Davis, C Ray 1946- WhoAmP 91
Davis, Calvin Grier 1906- WhoRel 92
Davis, Calvin Russell 1951- WhoMW 92
Davis, Carl 1936- ConTFT 9, IntMPA 92, IntWW 91, Who 92
Davis, Carl F 1919- AmMWSc 92
Davis, Carl George 1937- AmMWSc 92
Davis, Carl H. 1934- WhoEnt 92
Davis, Carl Lee 1924- AmMWSc 92
Davis, Carl Lynn 1941- WhoRel 92
Davis, Carol E. 1937- WhoMW 92
Davis, Carol Pinney 1926- WhoAmP 91
Davis, Carolyn Ann McBride 1952- WhoBlA 92
Davis, Carolyn Leigh 1936- WhoRel 92, WhoWest 92
Davis, Carrie L. Filer 1924- WhoBlA 92
Davis, Catherine Faith 1959- WhoAmL 92
Davis, Cecil Gilbert 1925- AmMWSc 92
Davis, Champion McDowell 1879-1975 DcNCBi 2
Davis, Chan 1926- TwCSFW 91
Davis, Chandler 1926- AmMWSc 92
Davis, Charles 1909- Who 92
Davis, Charles 1911- AmMWSc 92
Davis, Charles 1944- WhoBlA 92
Davis, Charles A. 1922- WhoBlA 92
Davis, Charles A 1933- AmMWSc 92
Davis, Charles Abbott 1869?-1908 BiInAmS
Davis, Charles Alan 1950- AmMWSc 92
Davis, Charles Albert 1861-1916 BiInAmS
Davis, Charles Alexander 1936- WhoBlA 92
Davis, Charles Alfred 1939- AmMWSc 92
Davis, Charles Augustus 1795-1867 BenetAL 91
Davis, Charles E. 1958- WhoEnt 92
Davis, Charles Edward AmMWSc 92
Davis, Charles Edward 1958- WhoBlA 92
Davis, Charles Edwin 1940- WhoEnt 92
Davis, Charles Freeman, Jr 1925- AmMWSc 92
Davis, Charles Gregory WhoAmP 91
Davis, Charles Hargis 1938- WhoMW 92
Davis, Charles Henry 1807-1877 BiInAmS
Davis, Charles Homer 1912- AmMWSc 92
Davis, Charles Joseph 1949- WhoAmL 92
Davis, Charles Kenneth 1945- WhoFI 92
Davis, Charles Mitchell, Jr 1925- AmMWSc 92
Davis, Charles Packard 1922- AmMWSc 92
Davis, Charles Patrick 1945- AmMWSc 92
Davis, Charles R 1945- WhoAmP 91
Davis, Charles Robert 1943- WhoRel 92
Davis, Charles Stewert 1935- AmMWSc 92
Davis, Charles Thomas, III 1939- WhoRel 92
Davis, Charles Wilburt 1952- WhoAmL 92
Davis, Charles William 1936- WhoMW 92
Davis, Charles William 1948- WhoFI 92
Davis, Charlie DrAPF 91
Davis, Charlotte L Poole 1947- WhoAmP 91
Davis, Cheri WhoAmP 91
Davis, Chester L 1923- AmMWSc 92
Davis, Chester R., Jr. 1930- WhoAmL 92
Davis, Chili 1960- WhoBlA 92
Davis, Chip WhoEnt 92
Davis, Chloe Marion 1909- Who 92
Davis, Christine R. WhoBlA 92
Davis, Christopher DrAPF 91
Davis, Christopher 1928- WrDr 92
Davis, Christopher Lee 1950- WhoAmL 92
Davis, Christopher Moody 1948- WhoEnt 92
Davis, Clarence 1939- WhoBlA 92
Davis, Clarence 1942- WhoAmP 91, WhoBlA 92
Davis, Clarence, Jr 1926- WhoAmP 91
Davis, Clarence A. 1941- WhoBlA 92
Davis, Clarence Daniel 1912- AmMWSc 92
Davis, Clarence Ephraim 1941- WhoRel 92
Davis, Clark Stanley 1950- WhoFI 92
Davis, Claud Edwin, III 1958- WhoRel 92
Davis, Claude Geoffrey 1951- AmMWSc 92
Davis, Claude Junior 1922- WhoAmL 92
Davis, Claude-Leonard 1944- WhoAmL 92, WhoFI 92
Davis, Clay 1944- WhoAmP 91
Davis, Clay Savelle, Jr. 1944- WhoAmL 92
Davis, Clifton D. 1945- WhoBlA 92
Davis, Clive Jay 1934- WhoEnt 92
Davis, Clyde Brion 1894-1962 BenetAL 91
Davis, Clyde Edward 1937- AmMWSc 92
Davis, Coleen Cockerill 1930- WhoWest 92
Davis, Colin IntMPA 92
Davis, Colin 1927- NewAmDM, Who 92
Davis, Colin Rex 1927- IntWW 91, WhoEnt 92
Davis, Constance A 1949- WhoAmP 91
Davis, Corneal A 1900- WhoAmP 91
Davis, Corneal Aaron 1900- WhoBlA 92
Davis, Courtland Harwell, Jr 1921- AmMWSc 92
Davis, Craig Brian 1938- AmMWSc 92
Davis, Craig Carlton 1919- WhoFI 92, WhoWest 92
Davis, Craig H 1935- AmMWSc 92
Davis, Craig Wilson 1949- AmMWSc 92
Davis, Curry Beach 1939- AmMWSc 92
Davis, Curtiss Owen 1945- AmMWSc 92
Davis, Cynthia D'Ascenzo 1953- WhoAmL 92
Davis, Cyprian 1930- WhoBlA 92
Davis, D Wayne 1935- AmMWSc 92
Davis, Dale Brockman 1945- WhoBlA 92
Davis, Daniel Layten 1938- AmMWSc 92
Davis, Daniel Oscar, Jr. 1932- WhoRel 92
Davis, Danny 1925- WhoEnt 92
Davis, Danny Andrew 1947- WhoRel 92
Davis, Danny K 1941- WhoAmP 91, WhoBlA 92
Davis, Darragh Jean 1955- WhoAmL 92
Davis, Darrell Lawrence 1927- AmMWSc 92
Davis, Darwin N. 1932- WhoBlA 92
Davis, David Who 92
Davis, David 1815-1886 AmPolLe
Davis, David 1920- AmMWSc 92
Davis, David 1927- AmMWSc 92
Davis, David 1941- WrDr 92
Davis, David A 1918- AmMWSc 92
Davis, David Brion 1927- IntAu&W 91, WrDr 92
Davis, David Coleman 1932- WhoRel 92
Davis, David G 1935- AmMWSc 92
Davis, David Gale 1935- AmMWSc 92
Davis, David Gerhardt 1935- WhoMW 92
Davis, David M. LesBEnT 92
Davis, David MacFarland 1926- WhoEnt 92
Davis, David Michael 1948- Who 92
Davis, David Warren 1930- AmMWSc 92
Davis, Dean Frederick 1922- AmMWSc 92
Davis, Deane Chandler d1990 IntWW 91N
Davis, Debbie McCune 1951- WhoAmP 91
Davis, Deborah Lynn 1948- WhoAmL 92
Davis, Delmont Alvin, Jr. 1935- WhoFI 92, WhoMW 92
Davis, Denice Faye 1953- WhoBlA 92
Davis, Dennis Albert 1934- WhoWest 92
Davis, Dennis Duval 1941- AmMWSc 92
Davis, Dennis M WhoAmP 91
Davis, Denny Cecil 1944- AmMWSc 92
Davis, Denyvetta 1949- WhoBlA 92
Davis, Deralyn Riles 1935- WhoAmP 91
Davis, Derek Alan 1929- Who 92
Davis, Derek Richard 1945- Who 92
Davis, Derek Russell 1914- Who 92
Davis, Dermot Renn 1928- Who 92
Davis, Devra Lee NewYTBS 91 [port]
Davis, Diane Lynn 1954- WhoBlA 92
Davis, Dianne Louise 1940- WhoMW 92
Davis, Dick 1945- ConPo 91, WrDr 92
Davis, Dick D 1933- AmMWSc 92
Davis, Dolores 1925- WhoAmP 91
Davis, Dolphin Alston 1802-1881 DcNCBi 2
Davis, Don TwCWW 91
Davis, Don Clarence 1943- WhoAmP 91
Davis, Don Paul 1950- WhoAmP 91
Davis, Don R 1924- WhoIns 92
Davis, Donald Echard 1916- AmMWSc 92
Davis, Donald Fred 1935- WhoBlA 92
Davis, Donald G. 1949- WhoAmL 92
Davis, Donald James 1929- WhoRel 92
Davis, Donald Miller 1945- AmMWSc 92
Davis, Donald R. 1932- WhoWest 92
Davis, Donald Ray 1934- AmMWSc 92
Davis, Donald Ray 1939- AmMWSc 92
Davis, Donald Robert 1941- AmMWSc 92
Davis, Donald Romain 1957- WhoEnt 92
Davis, Donald W. 1934- WhoBlA 92
Davis, Donald Walter 1920- AmMWSc 92
Davis, Donn Robert 1931- WhoFI 92
Davis, Donna 1960- WhoAmL 92
Davis, Donna P. 1947- WhoBlA 92
Davis, Donnie Bruce 1965- WhoRel 92
Davis, Doris Ann WhoBlA 92
Davis, Doris Ann 1939- WhoAmP 91
Davis, Dorothy Salisbury 1916- IntAu&W 91, WrDr 92
Davis, Douglas 1933- WrDr 92
Davis, Drexell WhoAmP 91
Davis, Duane M 1933- AmMWSc 92
Davis, Dupree Daniel 1908- WhoBlA 92
Davis, Dwight E 1944- WhoIns 92
Davis, E James 1934- AmMWSc 92
Davis, E Lawrence, III 1937- WhoAmP 91
Davis, Earl S. WhoBlA 92
Davis, Earl W. 1911- WhoBlA 92
Davis, Earle Andrew, Jr 1919- AmMWSc 92
Davis, Earon Scott 1950- WhoAmL 92
Davis, Eddy R. 1940- WhoEnt 92
Davis, Edgar Glenn 1931- AmMWSc 92, IntWW 91, WhoFI 92, WhoMW 92
Davis, Edith Pancoast 1911- WhoAmP 91
Davis, Edmond Ray 1928- WhoAmL 92
Davis, Edward 1914- WhoBlA 92
Davis, Edward 1935- WhoAmP 91, WhoBlA 92
Davis, Edward Alex 1931- AmMWSc 92
Davis, Edward Allan 1917- AmMWSc 92
Davis, Edward Bertrand 1933- WhoAmL 92
Davis, Edward D. 1904- WhoBlA 92
Davis, Edward Dewey 1933- AmMWSc 92
Davis, Edward L. 1943- WhoBlA 92
Davis, Edward Lyon 1929- AmMWSc 92
Davis, Edward Melvin 1913- AmMWSc 92
Davis, Edward Michael 1916- WhoAmP 91
Davis, Edward Nathan 1911- AmMWSc 92
Davis, Edward Shippen 1932- WhoAmL 92
Davis, Edwin Alden 1923- AmMWSc 92
Davis, Edwin Nathan 1909- AmMWSc 92
Davis, Edwin Weyerhaeuser 1895-1962 FacFETw
Davis, Elaine Carsley 1921- WhoBlA 92
Davis, Elberta Coleman 1946- WhoBlA 92
Davis, Eldon Vernon 1923- AmMWSc 92
Davis, Eldred Jack 1930- AmMWSc 92
Davis, Elizabeth Allaway 1941- AmMWSc 92
Davis, Elizabeth Lindsay 1855- NotBlAW 92
Davis, Elizabeth Young 1920- AmMWSc 92
Davis, Ellery Williams 1857-1918 BiInAmS
Davis, Ellis James 1847?-1935 ScFEYrs
Davis, Elmer d1958 LesBEnT 92
Davis, Elmer 1890-1958 BenetAL 91, FacFETw
Davis, Elmer L., Sr. 1926-1983 WhoBlA 92N
Davis, Elmo Warren 1920- AmMWSc 92
Davis, Elnathan 1922- WhoAmP 91
Davis, Elwyn H 1942- AmMWSc 92
Davis, Elwyn Herbert 1942- WhoMW 92
Davis, Emery Stephen 1940- WhoFI 92
Davis, Emily 1944- WhoIns 92
Davis, Erellon Ben 1912- WhoBlA 92
Davis, Eric Keith 1962- WhoBlA 92
Davis, Ernest Howard 1918- Who 92
Davis, Ernst Michael 1933- AmMWSc 92
Davis, Erroll Brown, Jr. 1944- WhoFI 92, WhoMW 92
Davis, Ervin 1926- WhoAmP 91
Davis, Esther Gregg 1934- WhoBlA 92
Davis, Etheldra S. 1931- WhoBlA 92
Davis, Eugene Philip 1930- WhoWest 92
Davis, Eugenia Asimakopoulos 1938- AmMWSc 92
Davis, Evan Anderson 1944- WhoAmL 92
Davis, Evelyn K. 1921- WhoBlA 92
Davis, Evelyn Marguerite Bailey WhoEnt 92, WhoMW 92
Davis, F. Benjamin WhoRel 92
Davis, Flavius Eugene, IV 1933- WhoAmL 92
Davis, Floyd Asher 1934- AmMWSc 92
Davis, France Albert 1946- WhoBlA 92
Davis, Frances Maria AmMWSc 92
Davis, Francis 1946- WrDr 92
Davis, Francis Clarke 1941- AmMWSc 92
Davis, Francis D. 1923- WhoBlA 92
Davis, Francis Kaye 1918- AmMWSc 92
Davis, Francis Keith 1928- WhoMW 92
Davis, Francis Raymond 1920- WhoRel 92
Davis, Francis W 1887-1978 FacFETw
Davis, Frank 1947- WhoBlA 92
Davis, Frank Allen 1960- WhoBlA 92
Davis, Frank Burts 1944- WhoEnt 92
Davis, Frank Derocher 1934- WhoBlA 92
Davis, Frank French 1920- AmMWSc 92
Davis, Frank I. 1919- IntMPA 92
Davis, Frank Marshall 1905-1987 BlkLC [port]
Davis, Frank W AmMWSc 92
Davis, Frank W 1936- WhoAmP 91
Davis, Franklin A 1939- AmMWSc 92
Davis, Fred 1934- WhoBlA 92
Davis, Frederic I 1937- AmMWSc 92
Davis, Frederic W 1823?-1854 BiInAmS
Davis, Frederick Athie 1938- WhoMW 92
Davis, Frederick Benjamin 1926- WhoAmL 92
Davis, Frederick D. 1935- WhoBlA 92
Davis, Frederick Newton, III 1952- WhoEnt 92
Davis, G. Reuben 1943- WhoAmL 92
Davis, Gardner Fabian 1959- WhoAmL 92
Davis, Gary 1895-1972 DcNCBi 2
Davis, Gary 1896-1972 NewAmDM
Davis, Gary Everett 1944- AmMWSc 92
Davis, Geena IntWW 91, WhoEnt 92
Davis, Geena 1957?- CurBio 91 [port], IntMPA 92, News 92-1 [port]
Davis, Gene 1945- WhoAmP 91
Davis, Gene A. 1939- WhoBlA 92
Davis, Gene Deb 1937- WhoWest 92
Davis, George DrAPF 91, WhoIns 92
Davis, George 1820-1896 DcNCBi 2
Davis, George B. 1939- WhoBlA 92
Davis, George Diament 1926- AmMWSc 92
Davis, George Edward 1928- WhoFI 92
Davis, George Francis 1926- WhoEnt 92, WhoMW 92
Davis, George H 1921- AmMWSc 92
Davis, George Herbert 1942- AmMWSc 92
Davis, George Kelso 1910- AmMWSc 92, IntWW 91
Davis, George Lee 1954- WhoEnt 92
Davis, George Morgan 1938- AmMWSc 92
Davis, George Nelson, Jr. 1936- WhoBlA 92
Davis, George Thomas 1932- AmMWSc 92
Davis, George Thomas 1933- AmMWSc 92
Davis, George W. 1914- IntMPA 92
Davis, Gerald Gordon 1937- AmMWSc 92
Davis, Gerald Holt 1942- WhoAmL 92
Davis, Gerald Titus 1932- AmMWSc 92
Davis, Gerald U WhoAmP 91
Davis, Gerry TwCSFW 91, WrDr 92
Davis, Giles Jack 1943- WhoAmL 92
Davis, Gita WrDr 92
Davis, Gladys 1937- WhoRel 92
Davis, Gleam Olivia 1956- WhoAmL 92
Davis, Glendell Kirk WhoBlA 92
Davis, Glenn 1953- WhoEnt 92
Davis, Glenn Earnest 1944- WhoRel 92
Davis, Glenn Gallery 1955- WhoMW 92
Davis, Glenn Mark-Alan 1951- WhoAmP 91
Davis, Gloria 1938- WhoAmP 91
Davis, Gloria-Jeanne 1945- WhoBlA 92
Davis, Godfrey Rupert Carless 1917- Who 92
Davis, Gordon IntAu&W 91X, WrDr 92
Davis, Gordon 1940- WhoMW 92
Davis, Gordon Wayne 1945- AmMWSc 92
Davis, Grace Montanez 1926- WhoHisp 92
Davis, Grace W WhoAmP 91
Davis, Grady D., Sr. WhoBlA 92
Davis, Graham Johnson 1925- AmMWSc 92
Davis, Grant Hopkins 1956- WhoFI 92
Davis, Grant Train 1877-1920 BiInAmS
Davis, Gray 1942- WhoAmP 91, WhoWest 92
Davis, Grayson Steven 1947- AmMWSc 92
Davis, Gregory A. 1948- WhoBlA 92
Davis, Gregory Arlen 1935- AmMWSc 92
Davis, Gregory Farrell 1949- WhoFI 92
Davis, Gregory V. 1947- WhoWest 92
Davis, Gussie 1863-1899 NewAmDM
Davis, Gussie L. BenetAL 91
Davis, Guy Donald 1952- AmMWSc 92
Davis, Guy Gaylon 1941- WhoAmP 91
Davis, Gwilym George 1857-1918 BiInAmS
Davis, H. Bernard 1945- WhoBlA 92
Davis, H.L. 1894-1960 TwCWW 91
Davis, H. L. 1896-1960 BenetAL 91
Davis, Hallowell 1896- AmMWSc 92
Davis, Hamilton E 1937- WhoAmP 91
Davis, Hamilton Seymour 1920- AmMWSc 92
Davis, Harmer E 1905- AmMWSc 92
Davis, Harold WhoRel 92
Davis, Harold Judd 1948- WhoWest 92
Davis, Harold Larue 1925- AmMWSc 92
Davis, Harold Lloyd 1930 AmMWSc 92
Davis, Harold Matthew 1946- WhoBlA 92
Davis, Harold R. 1926- WhoBlA 92
Davis, Harrell Duane 1950- WhoRel 92
Davis, Harry Ellerbe 1905-1968 DcNCBi 2
Davis, Harry Floyd 1925- AmMWSc 92
Davis, Harry I 1909- AmMWSc 92
Davis, Harry L 1921- AmMWSc 92
Davis, Harry Landa 1947- WhoAmL 92
Davis, Harry R, Jr AmMWSc 92
Davis, Harry Rex 1921- WhoMW 92
Davis, Harry Scott, Jr. 1943- WhoFI 92
Davis, Harvey Samuel 1936- AmMWSc 92
Davis, Harvey Virgil 1932- AmMWSc 92
Davis, Hayden E. WhoAmL 92
Davis, Hayne 1868-1942 AmPeW, DcNCBi 2
Davis, Helen Elizabeth Who 92
Davis, Helen Gordon WhoAmP 91
Davis, Helene DrAPF 91
Davis, Henrietta Vinton 1860-1941 NotBlAW 92
Davis, Henry Barnard, Jr. 1923- WhoAmL 92, WhoFI 92, WhoMW 92

**Davis,** Henry E., Jr. *WhoBlA 92*
**Davis,** Henry Joseph, Jr. 1950- *WhoMW 92*
**Davis,** Henry Mauzee 1902- *AmMWSc 92*
**Davis,** Henry McRay 1928- *AmMWSc 92*
**Davis,** Henry Richard 1948- *WhoFI 92*
**Davis,** Henry Werner 1936- *AmMWSc 92*
**Davis,** Herbert John 1938- *AmMWSc 92*
**Davis,** Herbert L, Jr 1935- *AmMWSc 92*
**Davis,** Herman E. 1935- *WhoBlA 92*
**Davis,** Hilda 1905- *NotBlAW 92*
**Davis,** Hiram Logan 1943- *WhoBlA 92*
**Davis,** Hope Hale *DrAPF 91, WrDr 92*
**Davis,** Horace Bancroft 1898- *WrDr 92*
**Davis,** Horace Raymond 1922- *AmMWSc 92*
**Davis,** Howard *Who 92*
**Davis,** Howard C. 1928- *WhoBlA 92*
**Davis,** Howard Edward, Jr 1956- *BlkOlyM*
**Davis,** Howard Ted 1937- *AmMWSc 92*
**Davis,** Howard Thomas, Jr. 1946- *WhoAmL 92*
**Davis,** Hubert Greenidge 1915- *AmMWSc 92*
**Davis,** Hugh Michael 1958- *AmMWSc 92*
**Davis,** Humphrey Denny 1927- *WhoAmP 91, WhoMW 92*
**Davis,** Iiona Julia 1945- *TwCPaSc*
**Davis,** Irvin 1926- *WhoEnt 92*
**Davis,** Ivor John Guest 1925- *Who 92*
**Davis,** J. Alan 1961- *WhoAmL 92*
**Davis,** J Mac 1952- *WhoAmP 91, WhoMW 92*
**Davis,** J. Madison *DrAPF 91*
**Davis,** J. Madison 1951- *ConAu 134*
**Davis,** J Mason, Jr 1935- *WhoAmP 91, WhoBlA 92*
**Davis,** J Max 1938- *WhoAmP 91*
**Davis,** Jack 1917- *WrDr 92*
**Davis,** Jack 1937- *AmMWSc 92*
**Davis,** Jack D 1935- *WhoAmP 91*
**Davis,** Jack H 1939- *AmMWSc 92*
**Davis,** Jack Leonard 1917- *IntAu&W 91*
**Davis,** Jack Rodney, Jr. 1948- *WhoWest 92*
**Davis,** Jackson Beauregard 1918- *WhoAmP 91*
**Davis,** Jacob E., II 1934- *WhoAmL 92*
**Davis,** Jacqueline Zurat 1946- *WhoEnt 92*
**Davis,** James *WhoBlA 92*
**Davis,** James 1721-1785 *DcNCBi 2*
**Davis,** James A. 1924- *WhoBlA 92*
**Davis,** James Allen 1940- *AmMWSc 92*
**Davis,** James Avery 1939- *AmMWSc 92*
**Davis,** James Casey 1937- *WhoAmL 92*
**Davis,** James Cleo 1933- *WhoMW 92*
**Davis,** James D *WhoAmP 91*
**Davis,** James F. 1943- *WhoBlA 92*
**Davis,** James Gresham 1928- *Who 92*
**Davis,** James H. 1941- *WhoBlA 92*
**Davis,** James Harold 1932- *WhoBlA 92*
**Davis,** James Harold 1937- *WhoRel 92*
**Davis,** James Harold 1939- *WhoBlA 92*
**Davis,** James Harold 1943- *WhoFI 92*
**Davis,** James Ivey *AmMWSc 92*
**Davis,** James Ivey 1937- *WhoWest 92*
**Davis,** James Keet 1940- *WhoBlA 92*
**Davis,** James Kirby 1956- *WhoAmL 92*
**Davis,** James Lee 1953- *WhoMW 92*
**Davis,** James Lloyd 1928- *WhoAmP 91*
**Davis,** James Luther 1924- *WhoWest 92*
**Davis,** James McCoy 1914- *WhoFI 92*
**Davis,** James N 1939- *AmMWSc 92*
**Davis,** James O, III 1957- *WhoAmP 91*
**Davis,** James Othello 1916- *AmMWSc 92, IntWW 91*
**Davis,** James Parker 1921- *WhoBlA 92*
**Davis,** James Robert 1929- *AmMWSc 92*
**Davis,** James Roy 1937- *WhoFI 92, WhoMW 92*
**Davis,** James Royce 1938- *AmMWSc 92*
**Davis,** James Spencer 1946- *WhoMW 92*
**Davis,** James Verlin 1935- *WhoFI 92*
**Davis,** James W. 1926- *WhoBlA 92*
**Davis,** James Wagner 1886-1955 *DcNCBi 2*
**Davis,** James Wendell 1927- *AmMWSc 92*
**Davis,** Jan Deborah 1950- *WhoRel 92*
**Davis,** Jay C 1942- *AmMWSc 92*
**Davis,** Jean E. *WhoBlA 92*
**Davis,** Jean M. 1932- *WhoBlA 92*
**Davis,** Jeff 1950- *ConTFT 9*
**Davis,** Jefferson 1808-1889 *AmPolLe [port], BenetAL 91, RComAH*
**Davis,** Jefferson B *WhoAmP 91*
**Davis,** Jefferson C 1932- *AmMWSc 92*
**Davis,** Jefferson Clark, Jr 1931- *AmMWSc 92*
**Davis,** Jeffery Lee 1956- *WhoRel 92*
**Davis,** Jeffrey Arthur 1943- *AmMWSc 92*
**Davis,** Jeffrey G. 1961- *WhoRel 92*
**Davis,** Jeffrey Ivan 1957- *WhoMW 92*
**Davis,** Jeffrey Robert 1935- *AmMWSc 92*
**Davis,** Jeffrey Stuart 1942- *WhoWest 92*
**Davis,** Jeremy Matthew 1953- *WhoWest 92*
**Davis,** Jerome 1950- *WhoBlA 92*
**Davis,** Jerry *LesBEnT 92*
**Davis,** Jerry, Jr. 1925- *WhoBlA 92*
**Davis,** Jerry Collins 1943- *AmMWSc 92*
**Davis,** Jesse F 1908- *WhoAmP 91*
**Davis,** Jim 1945- *Au&Arts 8 [port]*
**Davis,** Jimmie Dan 1940- *WhoEnt 92*
**Davis,** Jimmie H. 1902- *NewAmDM*
**Davis,** Jimmy Frank 1945- *WhoAmL 92*
**Davis,** Jimmy Henry 1948- *AmMWSc 92*
**Davis,** Jimmy Kyle 1954- *WhoAmP 91*
**Davis,** JoAn 1947- *WhoWest 92*
**Davis,** Joe W *WhoAmP 91*
**Davis,** Joel 1934- *WhoFI 92*
**Davis,** Joel Foster 1953- *WhoEnt 92*
**Davis,** Joel L *AmMWSc 92*
**Davis,** John *Who 92*
**Davis,** John 1774-1854 *BenetAL 91*
**Davis,** John Aaron, Jr. 1928- *WhoWest 92*
**Davis,** John Adams, Jr. 1944- *WhoFI 92*
**Davis,** John Albert 1935- *WhoBlA 92*
**Davis,** John Albert 1940- *WhoAmL 92*
**Davis,** John Albert, Jr 1936- *AmMWSc 92*
**Davis,** John Alexander 1960- *WhoBlA 92*
**Davis,** John Allen 1923- *Who 92*
**Davis,** John Armstrong 1950- *AmMWSc 92*
**Davis,** John Aubrey 1912- *WhoBlA 92*
**Davis,** John Christian 1958- *WhoEnt 92*
**Davis,** John Clarke 1943- *WhoMW 92*
**Davis,** John Clements 1938- *AmMWSc 92*
**Davis,** John Darelan R. *Who 92*
**Davis,** John David 1937- *WrDr 92*
**Davis,** John Dunning 1929- *AmMWSc 92*
**Davis,** John Dwelle 1928- *WhoMW 92*
**Davis,** John E d1900 *BiInAmS*
**Davis,** John Edward *WhoFI 92*
**Davis,** John Edward 1913- *WhoAmP 91*
**Davis,** John Edward, Jr 1922- *AmMWSc 92*
**Davis,** John F 1917- *AmMWSc 92*
**Davis,** John Gilbert *WrDr 92*
**Davis,** John Gilbert 1936- *Who 92*
**Davis,** John Grady, Jr 1938- *AmMWSc 92*
**Davis,** John Henry 1906- *IntWW 91*
**Davis,** John Henry, Jr 1921- *BlkOlyM*
**Davis,** John Henry Harris 1906- *Who 92*
**Davis,** John Horsley Russell 1938- *Who 92*
**Davis,** John Howard 1920- *WhoMW 92*
**Davis,** John James 1936- *WhoRel 92*
**Davis,** John Litchfield 1932- *AmMWSc 92*
**Davis,** John Louis, II 1934- *WhoRel 92*
**Davis,** John MacDougall 1914- *WhoAmL 92, WhoFI 92*
**Davis,** John Marcell 1933- *AmMWSc 92*
**Davis,** John Mark 1952- *WhoFI 92*
**Davis,** John Michael 1948- *WhoAmL 92*
**Davis,** John Michael N. *Who 92*
**Davis,** John Moulton 1938- *AmMWSc 92*
**Davis,** John Park 1944- *WhoAmL 92*
**Davis,** John R 1927- *AmMWSc 92*
**Davis,** John R, Jr 1927- *WhoAmP 91*
**Davis,** John Robert 1929- *AmMWSc 92*
**Davis,** John Robert 1951- *WhoAmP 91*
**Davis,** John Sheldon 1946- *AmMWSc 92*
**Davis,** John Staige, IV 1931- *AmMWSc 92*
**Davis,** John Stewart 1952- *AmMWSc 92*
**Davis,** John W 1873-1955 *FacFETw*
**Davis,** John W., III 1958- *WhoBlA 92*
**Davis,** John Wesley, Sr. 1934- *WhoBlA 92*
**Davis,** John Westley 1933- *WhoBlA 92*
**Davis,** John William 1873-1955 *AmPolLe*
**Davis,** Johnetta Garner 1939- *WhoBlA 92*
**Davis,** Johnny Henry 1920- *AmMWSc 92*
**Davis,** Johnny Reginald 1955- *WhoBlA 92*
**Davis,** Jolene Bryant 1942- *WhoFI 92*
**Davis,** Jon *DrAPF 91*
**Davis,** Jon Edward 1952- *IntAu&W 91*
**Davis,** Jon L. 1934- *WhoWest 92*
**Davis,** Jon Preston 1945- *AmMWSc 92*
**Davis,** Jon Stuart 1958- *WhoFI 92*
**Davis,** Jordan P. 1933- *IntMPA 92*
**Davis,** Jordan Ray 1921- *WhoAmP 91*
**Davis,** Joseph 1942- *WhoBlA 92*
**Davis,** Joseph B 1933- *AmMWSc 92*
**Davis,** Joseph Baker 1845-1920 *BiInAmS*
**Davis,** Joseph Barton 1942- *WhoAmP 91*
**Davis,** Joseph Edward 1926- *WhoWest 92*
**Davis,** Joseph Harrison 1924- *AmMWSc 92*
**Davis,** Joseph Jonathan 1828-1892 *DcNCBi 2*
**Davis,** Joseph La Roy 1932- *WhoWest 92*
**Davis,** Joseph M. 1937- *WhoBlA 92*
**Davis,** Joseph Richard 1936- *AmMWSc 92*
**Davis,** Joseph Samuel 1930- *WhoFI 92*
**Davis,** Joseph Solomon 1938- *WhoBlA 92*
**Davis,** Joyce *WhoBlA 92*
**Davis,** Judith Anne 1969- *WhoRel 92*
**Davis,** Judy *IntMPA 92*
**Davis,** Julian Mason, Jr. 1935- *WhoAmL 92*
**Davis,** June Fiksdal 1944- *WhoFI 92*
**Davis,** June Leah 1922- *WhoMW 92*
**Davis,** Junius 1845-1916 *DcNCBi 2*
**Davis,** Justina 1745-1771 *DcNCBi 2*
**Davis,** Karen 1952- *WhoIns 92*
**Davis,** Karen Jean 1952- *WhoMW 92*
**Davis,** Karen Padgett 1942- *AmMWSc 92*
**Davis,** Katharine Bement 1860-1935 *WomSoc*
**Davis,** Katharine Cleland 1907-1991 *WhoAmL 92*
**Davis,** Katherine Adams Martin 1944- *WhoRel 92*
**Davis,** Kathleen M. 1947- *WhoMW 92*
**Davis,** Kathryn Leola 1954- *WhoFI 92*
**Davis,** Kathryn Rachel Sarah Rebecca S. 1905-1979 *DcNCBi 2*
**Davis,** Kathryn Wasserman 1907- *WhoFI 92*
**Davis,** Katie Elizabeth 1936- *WhoBlA 92*
**Davis,** Kay Cullefer 1957- *WhoFI 92*
**Davis,** Keith 1918- *WrDr 92*
**Davis,** Ken 1906-1982 *ConAu 135*
**Davis,** Kenn 1932- *WrDr 92*
**Davis,** Kenneth Bruce, Jr 1940- *AmMWSc 92*
**Davis,** Kenneth Culp 1908- *WhoAmL 92*
**Davis,** Kenneth Dudley 1958- *WhoAmL 92*
**Davis,** Kenneth J. 1965- *WhoEnt 92*
**Davis,** Kenneth Joseph 1937- *AmMWSc 92*
**Davis,** Kenneth Leon 1947- *AmMWSc 92*
**Davis,** Kenneth Lloyd 1933- *WhoWest 92*
**Davis,** Kenneth Morton 1939- *WhoMW 92*
**Davis,** Kenneth Wesley 1946- *WhoRel 92*
**Davis,** Kevin L. 1957- *WhoAmL 92*
**Davis,** Kevin Wynston 1955- *WhoRel 92*
**Davis,** Kitty O'Malley 1925- *WhoEnt 92*
**Davis,** Kristin Woodford 1944- *WhoFI 92*
**Davis,** Kurt R 1962- *WhoAmP 91*
**Davis,** L. Clifford 1925- *WhoBlA 92*
**Davis,** L.J. *DrAPF 91*
**Davis,** L Wayne 1929- *AmMWSc 92*
**Davis,** Lance A 1939- *AmMWSc 92*
**Davis,** Lance Edwin 1928- *WhoFI 92, WhoWest 92*
**Davis,** Lanny Jesse 1945- *WhoAmP 91*
**Davis,** Larry Alan 1940- *AmMWSc 92*
**Davis,** Larry Allen 1950- *WhoAmL 92*
**Davis,** Larry Dean 1935- *AmMWSc 92*
**Davis,** Larry Earl 1946- *WhoBlA 92*
**Davis,** Larry Ernest 1940- *AmMWSc 92*
**Davis,** Laura Alice 1943- *WhoAmP 91*
**Davis,** Laurel Elizabeth 1956- *WhoAmL 92*
**Davis,** Laurence Laird 1915- *WhoMW 92*
**Davis,** Lavene 1918- *WhoAmP 91*
**Davis,** LaVerne Gloria 1936- *WhoBlA 92*
**Davis,** Lawrence 1945- *WhoFI 92*
**Davis,** Lawrence Arnette, Jr. 1937- *WhoBlA 92*
**Davis,** Lawrence C 1935- *WhoIns 92*
**Davis,** Lawrence Clark 1945- *AmMWSc 92*
**Davis,** Lawrence H 1929- *AmMWSc 92*
**Davis,** Lawrence Ronald 1953- *WhoEnt 92*
**Davis,** Lawrence S 1934- *AmMWSc 92*
**Davis,** Lawrence William, Jr 1930- *AmMWSc 92*
**Davis,** Lee Anna 1936- *WhoAmP 91*
**Davis,** Lee Elliott 1935- *WhoFI 92*
**Davis,** Leita R 1916- *WhoAmP 91*
**Davis,** Leland Cunningham, Jr 1922- *WhoAmP 91*
**Davis,** Lelia Kasenia 1941- *WhoBlA 92*
**Davis,** Lenwood G. 1939- *ConAu 35NR*
**Davis,** Leodis 1933- *AmMWSc 92, WhoBlA 92*
**Davis,** Leon 1933- *WhoBlA 92*
**Davis,** Leonard Ellsworth 1948- *WhoAmL 92*
**Davis,** Leonard George 1946- *AmMWSc 92*
**Davis,** Leonard Harry 1927- *WhoBlA 92*
**Davis,** Leroy *AmMWSc 92*
**Davis,** Leroy Thomas 1925- *AmMWSc 92*
**Davis,** Leslie Harold Newsom 1909- *Who 92*
**Davis,** Lester E. 1918- *WhoBlA 92*
**Davis,** Leverett, Jr 1914- *AmMWSc 92*
**Davis,** Linda Jacobs 1955- *WhoWest 92*
**Davis,** Lloyd *DrAPF 91*
**Davis,** Lloyd 1928- *WhoBlA 92*
**Davis,** Lloyd Craig 1941- *AmMWSc 92*
**Davis,** Lloyd Edward 1929- *AmMWSc 92*
**Davis,** Lockjaw 1922-1987 *NewAmDM*
**Davis,** Louis E 1918- *AmMWSc 92*
**Davis,** Louis Garland *WhoBlA 92*
**Davis,** Louis Poisson, Jr. 1919- *WhoAmL 92*
**Davis,** Lourie Irene Bell 1930- *WhoFI 92*
**Davis,** Lowell E. 1931-1989 *WhoBlA 92N*
**Davis,** Lucille H. 1936- *WhoBlA 92*
**Davis,** Luckett Vanderford 1932- *AmMWSc 92*
**Davis,** Luella B. 1940- *WhoBlA 92*
**d'Avis,** Luis M. 1944- *WhoMW 92*
**Davis,** Luther 1921- *IntMPA 92, WhoEnt 92*
**Davis,** Luther, Jr 1922- *AmMWSc 92*
**Davis,** Luther Charles 1948- *WhoBlA 92*
**Davis,** Lydia *DrAPF 91*
**Davis,** Lydia Joanna 1958- *WhoBlA 92, WhoMW 92*
**Davis,** Lynn Robert 1957- *WhoAmP 91*
**Davis,** Lynn Willes 1947- *WhoAmL 92*
**Davis,** Lynne 1933- *AmMWSc 92*
**Davis,** M. G. 1930- *WhoAmL 92*
**Davis,** Mac 1942- *IntMPA 92, WhoEnt 92*
**Davis,** Maclin Paschall, Jr. 1926- *WhoAmL 92, WhoAmP 91*
**Davis,** Madeline 1925- *Who 92*
**Davis,** Major 1931- *WhoBlA 92*
**Davis,** Malcolm Waters 1889-1970 *AmPeW*
**Davis,** Marc 1947- *AmMWSc 92*
**Davis,** Margaret *WrDr 92*
**Davis,** Margaret Bryan 1931- *AmMWSc 92*
**Davis,** Margaret Thomson *IntAu&W 91*
**Davis,** Marguerite Herr 1947- *WhoAmL 92*
**Davis,** Marianna White 1929- *WhoBlA 92*
**Davis,** Marie Hermenia 1929- *WhoEnt 92*
**Davis,** Marilyn Ann Cherry 1951- *WhoBlA 92*
**Davis,** Marilynn A. 1952- *WhoBlA 92*
**Davis,** Marion Harris 1938- *WhoBlA 92*
**Davis,** Marjorie 1936- *AmMWSc 92*
**Davis,** Marjorie Alice 1917- *WhoAmP 91*
**Davis,** Mark Bryan 1960- *WhoRel 92*
**Davis,** Mark Herbert Ainsworth 1945- *Who 92*
**Davis,** Mark Herman 1962- *WhoRel 92*
**Davis,** Mark Jefferson 1954- *WhoEnt 92*
**Davis,** Mark R. 1950- *WhoAmL 92*
**Davis,** Mark Robert 1954- *WhoAmP 91*
**Davis,** Mark Stephen 1949- *WhoAmL 92*
**Davis,** Marshall Earl 1931- *AmMWSc 92*
**Davis,** Martha Algenita Scott 1950- *WhoAmL 92*
**Davis,** Martha Frances 1957- *WhoAmL 92*
**Davis,** Martin *WhoBlA 92*
**Davis,** Martin 1928- *AmMWSc 92*
**Davis,** Martin Arnold 1930- *AmMWSc 92*
**Davis,** Martin S. *NewYTBS 91 [port]*
**Davis,** Martin S. 1927- *IntMPA 92, IntWW 91, WhoEnt 92, WhoFI 92*
**Davis,** Marty Earl 1958- *WhoAmL 92*
**Davis,** Martyn P. 1929- *WrDr 92*
**Davis,** Marva Alexis Kenon 1952- *WhoAmL 92*
**Davis,** Marvin 1925- *WhoWest 92*
**Davis,** Marvin Arnold 1937- *WhoFI 92*
**Davis,** Marvin Coolidge 1924- *WhoBlA 92*
**Davis,** Marvin Lester 1916- *AmMWSc 92*
**Davis,** Marvin Robert 1956- *WhoRel 92*
**Davis,** Mary 1866-1941 *TwCPaSc*
**Davis,** Mary Agnes Miller *WhoBlA 92, WhoMW 92*
**Davis,** Mary Duesterberg 1934- *WhoRel 92*
**Davis,** Mary Elizabeth 1957- *WhoWest 92*
**Davis,** Mary Helen 1949- *WhoMW 92*
**Davis,** Mary Lillian 1928- *WhoAmP 91*
**Davis,** Mary Wright 1918- *WhoAmP 91*
**Davis,** Matilda Laverne 1926- *WhoBlA 92*
**Davis,** Maurice 1912- *Who 92*
**Davis,** Maurice 1920- *WhoRel 92*
**Davis,** Melody *DrAPF 91*
**Davis,** Melvin Lloyd 1917- *WhoBlA 92*
**Davis,** Melwood Leonard 1925- *WhoBlA 92*
**Davis,** Mendel Jackson 1942- *WhoAmP 91*
**Davis,** Merritt McGregor 1923- *AmMWSc 92*
**Davis,** Michael 1923- *Who 92*
**Davis,** Michael 1942- *AmMWSc 92*
**Davis,** Michael 1950- *WhoAmP 91*
**Davis,** Michael Allan 1941- *AmMWSc 92*
**Davis,** Michael David 1937- *WhoEnt 92*
**Davis,** Michael E 1946- *WhoAmP 91*
**Davis,** Michael E 1952- *AmMWSc 92*
**Davis,** Michael Edward 1922- *AmMWSc 92*
**Davis,** Michael I 1936- *AmMWSc 92*
**Davis,** Michael James 1947- *WhoBlA 92*
**Davis,** Michael Jay 1947- *AmMWSc 92*
**Davis,** Michael Joseph 1956- *WhoRel 92*
**Davis,** Michael Justin 1925- *IntAu&W 91, WrDr 92*
**Davis,** Michael M 1879- *DcAmImH*
**Davis,** Michael McFarland 1919- *Who 92*
**Davis,** Michael Moore 1938- *AmMWSc 92*
**Davis,** Michael S. 1947- *WhoAmL 92*
**Davis,** Michael Scott 1946- *WhoWest 92*
**Davis,** Michael Stuart 1943- *WhoAmL 92, WhoMW 92*
**Davis,** Michael Walter 1949- *AmMWSc 92*
**Davis,** Michelle Joan 1966- *WhoFI 92*
**Davis,** Michelle Yvonne 1954- *WhoFI 92*
**Davis,** Mildred 1930- *WrDr 92*
**Davis,** Mildred 1931- *IntAu&W 91*
**Davis,** Miles 1926- *FacFETw [port], NewAmDM*
**Davis,** Miles 1926-1991 *CurBio 91N, NewYTBS 91 [port], News 92-2*
**Davis,** Miles Dewey 1926- *IntWW 91, WhoBlA 92*
**Davis,** Milford Hall 1925- *AmMWSc 92*
**Davis,** Milt 1929- *WhoBlA 92*
**Davis,** Milton *WhoAmL 92, WhoBlA 92*
**Davis,** Milton W, Jr 1923- *AmMWSc 92*
**Davis,** Mitchell, Jr. 1955- *WhoFI 92*
**Davis,** Monique *WhoAmP 91*
**Davis,** Monique Deon 1936- *WhoBlA 92*
**Davis,** Monte V 1923- *AmMWSc 92*

**Davis,** Montie Grant 1936- *AmMWSc 92*
**Davis,** Monty Dale 1966- *WhoFI 92*
**Davis,** Morgan 1950- *WhoIns 92*
**Davis,** Morris E. 1945- *WhoBlA 92*
**Davis,** Morris Schuyler 1919- *AmMWSc 92*
**Davis,** Morton David 1930- *AmMWSc 92*
**Davis,** Moshe 1916- *WhoRel 92*
**Davis,** Muller 1935- *WhoAmL 92, WhoFI 92, WhoMW 92*
**Davis,** Myrtis 1918- *AmMWSc 92*
**Davis,** Myrtle Hilliard 1926- *WhoBlA 92*
**Davis,** Myrtle V. 1930- *WhoBlA 92*
**Davis,** N. June 1940- *WhoBlA 92*
**Davis,** Nada 1920- *WhoAmP 91*
**Davis,** Nancy Taggart 1944- *AmMWSc 92*
**Davis,** Nathan Edward 1945- *WhoFI 92*
**Davis,** Nathan Smith 1817-1904 *BiInAmS*
**Davis,** Nathan Smith, Jr. 1858-1920 *BiInAmS*
**Davis,** Nathan T. 1937- *WhoBlA 92*
**Davis,** Nathan Tate 1937- *WhoEnt 92*
**Davis,** Nathanael Vining 1915- *IntWW 91, Who 92*
**Davis,** Nathaniel 1925- *IntWW 91, WhoAmP 91*
**Davis,** Neal 1952- *WhoEnt 92*
**Davis,** Neil Monas 1931- *AmMWSc 92*
**Davis,** Nigel S. 1955- *WhoBlA 92*
**Davis,** Noah Knowles 1830-1910 *BiInAmS*
**Davis,** Noel Gregson 1940- *WhoBlA 92*
**Davis,** Nolan 1942- *WhoBlA 92*
**Davis,** Norman Duane 1928- *AmMWSc 92*
**Davis,** Norman Emanuel 1941- *WhoBlA 92*
**Davis,** Norman Rodger 1943- *AmMWSc 92*
**Davis,** Norman Thomas 1927- *AmMWSc 92*
**Davis,** Oroondates 1750?-1781 *DcNCBi 2*
**Davis,** Orpha L 1923- *WhoAmP 91*
**Davis,** Orval Clifton 1920- *WhoFI 92*
**Davis,** Oscar F 1928- *AmMWSc 92*
**Davis,** Ossie 1917- *BenetAL 91, ConTFT 9, IntMPA 92, WhoBlA 92, WhoEnt 92, WrDr 92*
**Davis,** Ossie B. 1922- *WhoBlA 92*
**Davis,** Otis Crandell 1932- *BlkOlyM*
**Davis,** Otis Jay 1937- *WhoRel 92*
**Davis,** Owen 1874-1956 *BenetAL 91*
**Davis,** Owen Kent 1949- *AmMWSc 92*
**Davis,** P C 1921- *AmMWSc 92*
**Davis,** Pamela Bowes 1949- *AmMWSc 92*
**Davis,** Patricia *WhoAmP 91*
**Davis,** Patricia C. 1943- *WhoBlA 92*
**Davis,** Patricia Staunton 1945- *WhoBlA 92*
**Davis,** Patrick 1925- *WrDr 92*
**Davis,** Patrick James 1956- *WhoFI 92*
**Davis,** Patti 1952- *ConAu 134, WrDr 92*
**Davis,** Paul 1934- *ConAu 135*
**Davis,** Paul Brooks 1938- *WhoEnt 92*
**Davis,** Paul Cooper 1937- *AmMWSc 92*
**Davis,** Paul Joseph 1937- *AmMWSc 92*
**Davis,** Paul Milton 1934- *WhoRel 92*
**Davis,** Paul Milton 1938- *WhoMW 92*
**Davis,** Paul Wesley 1945- *WhoRel 92*
**Davis,** Paul William 1944- *AmMWSc 92*
**Davis,** Paula Denise 1958- *WhoEnt 92*
**Davis,** Paulina Kellogg Wright 1813-1876 *HanAmWH*
**Davis,** Pauls 1921- *AmMWSc 92*
**Davis,** Peggy Benfield 1934- *WhoAmP 91*
**Davis,** Peggy Cooper 1943- *WhoAmL 92*
**Davis,** Peggy McAlister 1950- *WhoWest 92*
**Davis,** Peter *LesBEnT 92*
**Davis,** Peter 1937- *IntMPA 92, WhoRel 92*
**Davis,** Peter Bennett 1942- *WhoFI 92*
**Davis,** Peter Frank 1937- *WhoEnt 92*
**Davis,** Peter J. 1941- *IntWW 91*
**Davis,** Peter John 1941- *Who 92*
**Davis,** Peyton Nelson 1925- *AmMWSc 92*
**Davis,** Philip 1952- *WhoRel 92*
**Davis,** Philip Edwin 1954- *WhoAmP 91*
**Davis,** Philip J 1923- *AmMWSc 92*
**Davis,** Philip K 1931- *AmMWSc 92*
**Davis,** Phillip Alton 1959- *WhoBlA 92*
**Davis,** Phillip Burton 1951- *AmMWSc 92*
**Davis,** Phillip Howard 1946- *AmMWSc 92*
**Davis,** Phyllis Burke 1931- *WhoFI 92*
**Davis,** Preston Augustus *WhoAmP 91, WhoBlA 92*
**Davis,** R E 1922- *AmMWSc 92*
**Davis,** R. H. C. 1918-1991 *ConAu 134*
**Davis,** R. Keith 1953- *WhoRel 92*
**Davis,** R L 1922- *WhoAmP 91*
**Davis,** Ralph Anderson 1917- *AmMWSc 92*
**Davis,** Ralph E. 1919- *WhoMW 92*
**Davis,** Ralph Henry Carless d1991 *Who 92N*
**Davis,** Ralph Henry Carless 1918- *WrDr 92*
**Davis,** Ralph Henry Carless 1918-1991 *IntWW 91, -91N*
**Davis,** Ralph Lanier 1921- *AmMWSc 92*
**Davis,** Randall Scott 1952- *WhoWest 92*
**Davis,** Randolph Dean 1952- *WhoRel 92*
**Davis,** Randy Lynn 1960- *WhoRel 92*
**Davis,** Raoul Andr 1931- *WhoBlA 92*
**Davis,** Ray Burt 1926- *WhoFI 92*
**Davis,** Ray Carl 1939- *WhoMW 92*
**Davis,** Raymond, Jr 1914- *AmMWSc 92, IntWW 91*
**Davis,** Raymond E 1938- *AmMWSc 92*
**Davis,** Raymond Ellis 1943- *WhoAmL 92*
**Davis,** Raymond F 1928- *AmMWSc 92*
**Davis,** Rebecca Harding 1831-1910 *BenetAL 91*
**Davis,** Reginald Francis 1951- *WhoBlA 92*
**Davis,** Renn *Who 92*
**Davis,** Reuben K. 1920- *WhoBlA 92*
**Davis,** Rex Lloyd 1929- *WhoIns 92*
**Davis,** Rhett Claude 1962- *WhoAmP 91*
**Davis,** Rhonda Sue 1967- *WhoWest 92*
**Davis,** Richard 1930- *WhoBlA 92, WhoEnt 92*
**Davis,** Richard 1943- *WhoBlA 92*
**Davis,** Richard 1957- *WhoAmP 91*
**Davis,** Richard A 1925- *AmMWSc 92*
**Davis,** Richard Albert, Jr 1937- *AmMWSc 92*
**Davis,** Richard Allmon 1946- *WhoWest 92*
**Davis,** Richard Anthony 1941- *WhoEnt 92, WhoWest 92*
**Davis,** Richard Arnold 1942- *AmMWSc 92*
**Davis,** Richard Bradley 1926- *AmMWSc 92*
**Davis,** Richard C. 1925- *WhoBlA 92*
**Davis,** Richard Calhoun 1945- *WhoWest 92*
**Davis,** Richard David 1934- *WhoFI 92*
**Davis,** Richard Ernest 1936- *WhoWest 92*
**Davis,** Richard Frank 1945- *WhoAmP 91*
**Davis,** Richard Harding *SourALJ*
**Davis,** Richard Harding 1864-1916 *BenetAL 91*
**Davis,** Richard J 1946- *WhoAmP 91*
**Davis,** Richard Joseph 1921- *WhoAmP 91*
**Davis,** Richard LaVerne 1932- *AmMWSc 92*
**Davis,** Richard O. *WhoBlA 92*
**Davis,** Richard Owen 1949- *WhoAmL 92*
**Davis,** Richard Ralph 1936- *WhoAmL 92, WhoFI 92*
**Davis,** Richard Richardson 1923- *AmMWSc 92*
**Davis,** Richard Rodney 1944- *WhoMW 92*
**Davis,** Richard Whitlock 1935- *IntAu&W 91, WrDr 92*
**Davis,** Richmond Pearson 1866-1937 *DcNCBi 2*
**Davis,** Robert 1931- *AmMWSc 92*
**Davis,** Robert A 1926- *AmMWSc 92*
**Davis,** Robert Benjamin 1926- *AmMWSc 92*
**Davis,** Robert Bernard 1935- *AmMWSc 92*
**Davis,** Robert Carlton 1944- *WhoFI 92*
**Davis,** Robert Charles 1946- *WhoMW 92*
**Davis,** Robert Charles 1959- *WhoAmL 92*
**Davis,** Robert Clay 1941- *AmMWSc 92*
**Davis,** Robert Dabney 1939- *AmMWSc 92*
**Davis,** Robert Dennis 1945- *WhoWest 92*
**Davis,** Robert E *AmMWSc 92*
**Davis,** Robert E. 1908- *WhoBlA 92*
**Davis,** Robert E. 1937- *WhoBlA 92*
**Davis,** Robert Edward 1939- *AmMWSc 92*
**Davis,** Robert Edwin 1931- *WhoFI 92*
**Davis,** Robert Elliott 1930- *AmMWSc 92*
**Davis,** Robert Eugene, Jr. 1956- *WhoFI 92*
**Davis,** Robert F 1942- *AmMWSc 92*
**Davis,** Robert Foster, Jr 1937- *AmMWSc 92*
**Davis,** Robert Gene 1932- *AmMWSc 92*
**Davis,** Robert Harry 1927- *AmMWSc 92*
**Davis,** Robert Houser 1926- *AmMWSc 92*
**Davis,** Robert James 1929- *AmMWSc 92*
**Davis,** Robert Lane 1936- *AmMWSc 92*
**Davis,** Robert Larry 1942- *WhoAmL 92*
**Davis,** Robert Lawrence 1928- *WhoAmL 92*
**Davis,** Robert Leslie 1930- *Who 92*
**Davis,** Robert Lloyd 1919- *AmMWSc 92*
**Davis,** Robert Louis 1927- *WhoAmL 92*
**Davis,** Robert Maurice 1960- *WhoMW 92*
**Davis,** Robert Nolan 1953- *WhoAmL 92*
**Davis,** Robert Paul 1926- *AmMWSc 92*
**Davis,** Robert Prunier 1929- *IntAu&W 91*
**Davis,** Robert Stephen 1954- *WhoEnt 92*
**Davis,** Robert W. 1932- *AlmAP 92 [port], WhoAmP 91*
**Davis,** Robert Wallace 1956- *WhoAmL 92*
**Davis,** Robert Wayne 1947- *WhoEnt 92, WhoWest 92*
**Davis,** Robert William 1932- *WhoMW 92*
**Davis,** Robert Wilson 1910- *AmMWSc 92*
**Davis,** Roberta LaFern 1954- *WhoMW 92*
**Davis,** Robin 1928- *TwCPaSc*
**Davis,** Robin Eden Pierre 1934- *AmMWSc 92*
**Davis,** Robin M. 1957- *WhoEnt 92*
**Davis,** Roderick Leigh *AmMWSc 92*
**Davis,** Rodney Orin 1956- *WhoWest 92*
**Davis,** Roger 1929- *AmMWSc 92*
**Davis,** Roger Alan *AmMWSc 92*
**Davis,** Roger E. *WhoAmL 92*
**Davis,** Roger Edwin 1928- *WhoAmL 92, WhoFI 92*
**Davis,** Roger H. 1923- *IntMPA 92*
**Davis,** Roland Hayes *WhoBlA 92*
**Davis,** Roman 1948- *AmMWSc 92*
**Davis,** Ron Michael 1959- *WhoWest 92*
**Davis,** Ronald Earl 1944- *WhoAmP 91*
**Davis,** Ronald Glenn 1959- *WhoRel 92*
**Davis,** Ronald Merle 1948- *WhoRel 92*
**Davis,** Ronald P. 1949- *WhoBlA 92*
**Davis,** Ronald R. 1942- *WhoBlA 92*
**Davis,** Ronald Stuart 1941- *AmMWSc 92*
**Davis,** Ronald Vernon 1947- *WhoFI 92*
**Davis,** Ronald W. 1950- *WhoBlA 92*
**Davis,** Ronald Wayne 1941- *AmMWSc 92*
**Davis,** Ronda Marie *DrAPF 91*
**Davis,** Rosemary Ormond *WhoBlA 92*
**Davis,** Rowland Hallowell 1933- *AmMWSc 92*
**Davis,** Roy Eugene 1931- *RelLAm 91*
**Davis,** Roy J. 1943- *WhoFI 92*
**Davis,** Roy Wallace *ScFEYrs*
**Davis,** Roy Walton, Jr. 1930- *WhoAmL 92*
**Davis,** Roy William 1950- *WhoRel 92*
**Davis,** Rudolph Jeffery 1964- *WhoRel 92*
**Davis,** Rupert C. H. *Who 92*
**Davis,** Russ E 1941- *AmMWSc 92*
**Davis,** Russell Price 1928- *AmMWSc 92*
**Davis,** Russell Ray 1954- *WhoRel 92*
**Davis,** Ruth Margaret 1928- *AmMWSc 92*
**Davis,** S. Kenneth 1927- *WhoRel 92*
**Davis,** Sam *ScFEYrs*
**Davis,** Sam 1850-1919 *ScFEYrs*
**Davis,** Sammi 1964- *IntMPA 92*
**Davis,** Sammy, Jr. 1925-1990 *AnObit 1990, FacFETw [port], NewAmDM, WhoBlA 92N*
**Davis,** Sammy, Jr. 1930- *WhoBlA 92*
**Davis,** Samuel Bernhard 1942- *WhoMW 92*
**Davis,** Samuel Henry, Jr 1930- *AmMWSc 92*
**Davis,** Sandra B. 1947- *WhoBlA 92*
**Davis,** Scott 1952- *WhoAmP 91*
**Davis,** Scott Jonathan 1952- *WhoAmL 92*
**Davis,** Scott Livingston 1941- *WhoFI 92*
**Davis,** Scottie Lee 1954- *WhoEnt 92*
**Davis,** Selby Brinker 1914- *AmMWSc 92*
**Davis,** Seth Richard 1954- *WhoEnt 92*
**Davis,** Sharon Eileen 1951- *WhoAmP 91*
**Davis,** Sheila Parham 1954- *WhoBlA 92*
**Davis,** Shelby Cullom 1909- *WhoFI 92*
**Davis,** Sheldon W 1951- *AmMWSc 92*
**Davis,** Shirley E. 1935- *WhoBlA 92*
**Davis,** Sid *LesBEnT 92*
**Davis,** Sidney Fant 1934- *WhoFI 92*
**Davis,** Spencer Harwood, Jr 1916- *AmMWSc 92*
**Davis,** Stanford Melvin 1941- *WhoWest 92*
**Davis,** Stanley Gannaway 1922- *AmMWSc 92*
**Davis,** Stanley Nelson 1924- *AmMWSc 92*
**Davis,** Stanley Stewart 1942- *Who 92*
**Davis,** Stanton, Jr. 1945- *WhoEnt 92*
**Davis,** Starkey D 1931- *AmMWSc 92*
**Davis,** Stephen Allen 1947- *WhoAmP 91*
**Davis,** Stephen Edward 1925- *WhoAmL 92*
**Davis,** Stephen H 1939- *AmMWSc 92*
**Davis,** Stephen Parkes 1951- *WhoAmL 92*
**Davis,** Stephen Smith 1910- *WhoBlA 92*
**Davis,** Sterling Evan 1941- *WhoEnt 92*
**Davis,** Steve 1957- *IntWW 91, Who 92*
**Davis,** Steve G. *WhoBlA 92*
**Davis,** Steven Brad 1953- *WhoRel 92*
**Davis,** Steven Jewett 1961- *WhoAmL 92*
**Davis,** Steven Lewis 1941- *AmMWSc 92*
**Davis,** Stuart George 1917- *AmMWSc 92*
**Davis,** Sue A 1954- *WhoAmP 91*
**Davis,** Sumner P *AmMWSc 92*
**Davis,** Susan Gloria 1957- *WhoMW 92*
**Davis,** Suzy 1936- *WhoWest 92*
**Davis,** Tamara Petrosian 1945- *WhoFI 92*
**Davis,** Terence Anthony Gordon 1938- *Who 92*
**Davis,** Terri M. 1947- *WhoRel 92*
**Davis,** Terry 1967- *WhoBlA 92*
**Davis,** Terry Chaffin 1932- *AmMWSc 92*
**Davis,** Terry Hunter, Jr. 1931- *WhoAmL 92*
**Davis,** Thadious M. *DrAPF 91*
**Davis,** Theodore Roosevelt 1903- *WhoRel 92*
**Davis,** Theresa Ventroy *WhoAmP 91*
**Davis,** Thomas 1761-1790? *DcNCBi 2*
**Davis,** Thomas 1917- *Who 92*
**Davis,** Thomas Alan 1940- *WhoAmL 92*
**Davis,** Thomas Arthur 1939- *AmMWSc 92*
**Davis,** Thomas Austin 1934- *AmMWSc 92*
**Davis,** Thomas Crawley, III 1945- *WhoRel 92*
**Davis,** Thomas Frederick 1804-1871 *DcNCBi 2*
**Davis,** Thomas Haydn 1939- *AmMWSc 92*
**Davis,** Thomas J. 1908- *WhoBlA 92*
**Davis,** Thomas James, Jr. 1938- *WhoAmL 92, WhoEnt 92*
**Davis,** Thomas Joseph 1946- *WhoBlA 92*
**Davis,** Thomas Mooney 1934- *AmMWSc 92*
**Davis,** Thomas Neil 1932- *AmMWSc 92*
**Davis,** Thomas Paul 1951- *WhoWest 92*
**Davis,** Thomas Pearse 1926- *AmMWSc 92*
**Davis,** Thomas Robert Alexander Harries 1917- *IntWW 91*
**Davis,** Thomas Wilders 1905- *AmMWSc 92*
**Davis,** Thomas William 1946- *AmMWSc 92*
**Davis,** Thulani *DrAPF 91*
**Davis,** Timothy Bledsoe 1952- *WhoAmL 92*
**Davis,** Timothy John 1954- *WhoEnt 92*
**Davis,** Timothy Ott 1955- *WhoAmL 92*
**Davis,** Timothy William 1959- *WhoMW 92*
**Davis,** Troy Lee 1960- *WhoWest 92*
**Davis,** Twilus *WhoBlA 92*
**Davis,** Tyrone Theophilus 1948- *WhoBlA 92*
**Davis,** V Terrell 1911- *AmMWSc 92*
**Davis,** Varina Howell 1826-1906 *PorAmW [port]*
**Davis,** Vincent 1930- *WrDr 92*
**Davis,** Virginia Eischen 1925- *AmMWSc 92*
**Davis,** W Eugene *WhoAmP 91*
**Davis,** W. Jeremy 1942- *WhoAmL 92*
**Davis,** W Kenneth 1918- *AmMWSc 92*
**Davis,** W. L. *WhoMW 92*
**Davis,** Wallace, Jr 1918- *AmMWSc 92*
**Davis,** Wallace Terry 1949- *WhoRel 92*
**Davis,** Walter 1954- *WhoBlA 92*
**Davis,** Walter, Jr. 1932-1990 *AnObit 1990*
**Davis,** Walter Bond 1930- *WhoRel 92*
**Davis,** Walter G. 1920- *WhoBlA 92*
**Davis,** Walter Gould 1851-1919 *BiInAmS*
**Davis,** Walter Jackson, Jr. 1936- *WhoBlA 92*
**Davis,** Walter Lewis 1942- *AmMWSc 92*
**Davis,** Walter Lowry, Jr 1946- *WhoAmP 91*
**Davis,** Walter Paul 1954- *BlkOlyM*
**Davis,** Walter Richard 1935- *WhoAmL 92*
**Davis,** Wanda M. 1952- *WhoBlA 92*
**Davis,** Wanda Rose 1937- *WhoWest 92*
**Davis,** Ward Benjamin 1933- *AmMWSc 92*
**Davis,** Warren B. 1947- *WhoBlA 92*
**Davis,** Warren Judson 1937- *WhoAmL 92*
**Davis,** Wayne Alton 1931- *AmMWSc 92*
**Davis,** Wayne Harry 1930- *AmMWSc 92*
**Davis,** Wayne Roderick 1951- *WhoRel 92*
**Davis,** Wendell, Jr. 1933- *WhoAmL 92*
**Davis,** Wendell Tyrone 1966- *WhoBlA 92*
**Davis,** Wesley LeRoy 1943- *WhoWest 92*
**Davis,** Wilbur Marvin 1931- *AmMWSc 92*
**Davis,** Wiley M. 1927- *WhoBlA 92*
**Davis,** Wilford Lavern 1930- *AmMWSc 92*
**Davis,** Will David 1929- *WhoAmP 91*
**Davis,** William 1933- *IntAu&W 91, Who 92, WrDr 92*
**Davis,** William Ackelson 1903- *WhoAmP 91*
**Davis,** William Albert 1934- *WhoRel 92*
**Davis,** William Allan 1921- *IntWW 91, Who 92*
**Davis,** William Allison 1942- *WhoAmL 92*
**Davis,** William Arthur 1947- *AmMWSc 92*
**Davis,** William C 1933- *AmMWSc 92*
**Davis,** William Chester 1925- *AmMWSc 92*
**Davis,** William Donald 1921- *AmMWSc 92*
**Davis,** William Doyle 1931- *WhoFI 92*
**Davis,** William Duncan, Jr 1918- *AmMWSc 92*
**Davis,** William E., Sr. 1930- *WhoBlA 92*
**Davis,** William Edwin, Jr 1936- *AmMWSc 92*
**Davis,** William Ellsmore, Jr 1927- *AmMWSc 92*
**Davis,** William Emrys 1942- *WhoRel 92*
**Davis,** William Eric 1908- *Who 92*
**Davis,** William Eugene 1936- *WhoAmL 92*
**Davis,** William F 1922- *AmMWSc 92*
**Davis,** William F 1948- *WhoAmP 91*
**Davis,** William Grenville 1929- *IntWW 91, Who 92*
**Davis,** William H. d1991 *NewYTBS 91 [port]*
**Davis,** William Hayes, Sr. 1947- *WhoBlA 92*
**Davis,** William Henry 1880-1960 *DcNCBi 2*
**Davis,** William Herbert 1919- *Who 92*
**Davis,** William Howard 1951- *WhoAmL 92*
**Davis,** William Jackson 1930- *AmMWSc 92*
**Davis,** William Jackson 1942- *AmMWSc 92*
**Davis,** William James 1940- *AmMWSc 92*
**Davis,** William L. 1933- *WhoBlA 92*
**Davis,** William Lipscomb, III 1957- *WhoFI 92*
**Davis,** William M., Jr. 1929-1990 *WhoBlA 92N*
**Davis,** William Mark 1963- *WhoRel 92*

**Davis,** William Maxie, Jr. 1932- *WhoAmL 92*
**Davis,** William Michael 1951- *WhoAmP 91*
**Davis,** William Morris 1850-1934 *FacFETw*
**Davis,** William Potter, Jr 1924- *AmMWSc 92*
**Davis,** William R. 1921- *WhoBlA 92*
**Davis,** William R 1923- *AmMWSc 92*
**Davis,** William R. 1934- *WhoBlA 92*
**Davis,** William R 1945- *WhoAmP 91*
**Davis,** William Robert 1929- *AmMWSc 92*
**Davis,** William Robert, Sr. 1949- *WhoEnt 92*
**Davis,** William S 1930- *AmMWSc 92*
**Davis,** William Selassie, Jr. 1918- *WhoBlA 92*
**Davis,** William Spencer 1925- *AmMWSc 92*
**Davis,** William Thompson 1931- *AmMWSc 92*
**Davis,** William Virgil *DrAPF 91*
**Davis,** Willie A. 1948- *WhoBlA 92*
**Davis,** Willie D. 1934- *WhoBlA 92*
**Davis,** Willie J. 1935- *WhoBlA 92*
**Davis,** Willie James 1940- *WhoBlA 92*
**Davis,** Willis H. 1937- *WhoBlA 92*
**Davis,** Yvonne 1955- *WhoAmP 91*
**Davis Anthony,** Vernice 1945- *WhoBlA 92*
**Davis-Banks,** Phyllis Eileen 1918- *WhoWest 92*
**Davis-Beckett,** Luann Ruth 1951- *WhoEnt 92*
**Davis-Cartey,** Catherine B. 1954- *WhoBlA 92*
**Davis-Gardner,** Angela *DrAPF 91*
**Davis-Goff,** Annabel *DrAPF 91*
**Davis-Goff,** Robert William *Who 92*
**Davis-McFarland,** E. Elise 1946- *WhoBlA 92*
**Davis-Rice,** Peter 1930- *Who 92*
**Davis Werland,** Janine Kay 1960- *WhoMW 92*
**Davis-Williams,** Phyllis A. 1947- *WhoBlA 92*
**Davison** *Who 92*
**Davison,** Alan Nelson 1925- *Who 92*
**Davison,** Allan John 1936- *AmMWSc 92*
**Davison,** Alvin 1868-1915 *BiInAmS*
**Davison,** Archibald T. 1883-1961 *NewAmDM*
**Davison,** Arthur Clifford Percival 1918- *Who 92*
**Davison,** Beaumont 1929- *AmMWSc 92*
**Davison,** Brian Henry 1957- *AmMWSc 92*
**Davison,** Bruce 1946- *IntMPA 92*
**Davison,** C. Hamilton 1959- *WhoFI 92*
**Davison,** Calvin 1932- *WhoAmL 92*
**Davison,** Clarke 1927- *AmMWSc 92*
**Davison,** Dale 1955- *IntMPA 92*
**Davison,** Daniel Pomeroy 1925- *WhoFI 92*
**Davison,** Dennis 1923- *IntAu&W 91, WrDr 92*
**Davison,** E J 1938- *AmMWSc 92*
**Davison,** Edward Joseph 1938- *IntWW 91*
**Davison,** Edward L. 1943- *WhoBlA 92*
**Davison,** Francis 1919-1984 *TwCPaSc*
**Davison,** Frederic E. 1917- *WhoBlA 92*
**Davison,** Frederick Corbet 1929- *AmMWSc 92*
**Davison,** Geoffrey 1927- *WrDr 92*
**Davison,** Geoffrey Joseph 1927- *IntAu&W 91*
**Davison,** Helen Irene 1926- *WhoWest 92*
**Davison,** Ian Frederic Hay 1931- *IntWW 91, Who 92*
**Davison,** J Leslie 1944- *AmMWSc 92*
**Davison,** Jeffrey Blair 1956- *WhoAmL 92*
**Davison,** John 1928- *AmMWSc 92*
**Davison,** John Blake 1946- *AmMWSc 92*
**Davison,** John Herbert 1930- *WhoEnt 92*
**Davison,** John Mason 1840-1915 *BiInAmS*
**Davison,** John Stanley 1922- *Who 92*
**Davison,** Jon 1949- *IntMPA 92*
**Davison,** Kenneth Lewis 1935- *AmMWSc 92*
**Davison,** Kyle Scott 1961- *WhoFI 92*
**Davison,** Larry Virgil 1943- *WhoMW 92*
**Davison,** Lee Walker 1937- *AmMWSc 92*
**Davison,** Luella May 1922- *WhoMW 92*
**Davison,** Mark Edward 1955- *WhoEnt 92*
**Davison,** Patrick Gary 1950- *WhoEnt 92*
**Davison,** Paul Sioussa 1955- *WhoAmL 92*
**Davison,** Peter *DrAPF 91*
**Davison,** Peter 1928- *BenetAL 91, ConPo 91, WrDr 92*
**Davison,** Peter 1948- *WhoEnt 92*
**Davison,** Peter Fitzgerald 1927- *AmMWSc 92*
**Davison,** Richard 1936- *WhoMW 92*
**Davison,** Richard Read 1926- *AmMWSc 92*
**Davison,** Robert P., Jr. 1937- *WhoAmL 92*
**Davison,** Robert Wilder 1920- *AmMWSc 92*
**Davison,** Ronald 1920- *Who 92*
**Davison,** Ronald Keith 1920- *IntWW 91*
**Davison,** Sol 1922- *AmMWSc 92*
**Davison,** Stanley *Who 92*
**Davison,** Stowell Watters 1949- *WhoFI 92*
**Davison,** Sydney George 1934- *AmMWSc 92*
**Davison,** Thomas Cornell Barringer 1948- *WhoMW 92*
**Davison,** Thomas Matthew Kerr 1939- *AmMWSc 92*
**Davison,** Walter Francis 1926- *AmMWSc 92*
**Davison,** Wilburt Cornell 1892-1972 *DcNCBi 2*
**Davison,** Wild Bill 1906-1989 *NewAmDM*
**Davisson,** Charlotte Meaker 1914- *AmMWSc 92*
**Davisson,** Clinton Joseph 1881-1958 *FacFETw, WhoNob 90*
**Davisson,** James W 1914- *AmMWSc 92*
**Davisson,** Lee David 1936- *AmMWSc 92*
**Davisson,** M T 1931- *AmMWSc 92*
**Davisson,** Mary Frances 1948- *WhoRel 92*
**Davisson,** Melvin Thomas 1931- *WhoMW 92*
**Davisson,** Muriel Trask 1941- *AmMWSc 92*
**Davisson,** Vanessa Teresa 1958- *WhoEnt 92*
**Davit,** Frank Torino 1961- *WhoFI 92*
**Davitashvili,** Leo Shiovich 1895-1977 *SovUnBD*
**Davitian,** Harry Edward 1945- *AmMWSc 92*
**Davitt,** Harry James, Jr 1939- *AmMWSc 92*
**Davitt,** Richard Michael 1939- *AmMWSc 92*
**Davitz,** J. R. *ConAu 134*
**Davitz,** Joel R. 1926- *ConAu 134*
**Davlin,** Michael C 1955- *WhoIns 92*
**Davos,** Ioannis 1918- *IntWW 91*
**Davson,** Geoffrey Leo Simon *Who 92*
**Davtian,** Vagan Armenakovich 1922- *IntWW 91*
**Davy,** Gloria 1937- *WhoBlA 92*
**Davy,** Humphrey 1778-1829 *ScFEYrs*
**Davy,** Humphrey Augustine A. *Who 92*
**Davy,** Nadine Irene 1958- *WhoAmL 92*
**Davy,** Woods 1949- *WhoWest 92*
**Davydov,** Nikolai Grigorievich 1928- *IntWW 91*
**Davydov,** Yuri Vladimirovich 1924- *IntWW 91*
**Daw,** Glen Harold 1954- *AmMWSc 92*
**Daw,** Harold Albert 1925- *AmMWSc 92*
**Daw,** Harold John 1926- *WhoAmL 92*
**Daw,** John Charles 1931- *AmMWSc 92*
**Daw,** Leila McConnell *WhoMW 92*
**Daw,** Nigel Warwick 1933- *AmMWSc 92*
**Daw,** Paul Curtis 1947- *WhoAmL 92*
**Daw,** Terry LeRoy 1955- *WhoWest 92*
**Dawahare,** Sandra Mendez 1950- *WhoAmL 92*
**Dawbarn,** Robert Hugh Mackay 1860-1915 *BiInAmS*
**Dawbarn,** Simon 1923- *Who 92*
**Dawber,** Pam *WhoEnt 92*
**Dawber,** Pam 1954- *IntMPA 92*
**Dawber,** Thomas Royle 1913- *AmMWSc 92*
**Dawburn,** Joseph Yelverton 1856-1943 *TwCPaSc*
**Dawdy,** Doris Ostrander *WhoWest 92*
**Dawe,** Albert Rolke 1916- *AmMWSc 92*
**Dawe,** Bruce 1930- *ConPo 91, WrDr 92*
**Dawe,** Donald Bruce 1930- *IntAu&W 91*
**Dawe,** Donovan Arthur 1915- *Who 92*
**Dawe,** Gerald 1952- *ConAu 36NR*
**Dawe,** Harold Joseph 1912- *AmMWSc 92*
**Dawe,** Jerry Lyle 1942- *WhoRel 92*
**Dawe,** Roger James 1941- *Who 92*
**Dawes,** Charles G. 1865-1951 *EncTR 91 [port]*
**Dawes,** Charles Gates 1865-1951 *AmPolLe, FacFETw, WhoNob 90*
**Dawes,** Clinton John 1935- *AmMWSc 92*
**Dawes,** David Haddon 1938- *AmMWSc 92*
**Dawes,** Dennis Richard 1950- *WhoRel 92*
**Dawes,** Douglas Charles 1952- *WhoWest 92*
**Dawes,** Edna *WrDr 92*
**Dawes,** Edward Naasson 1914- *WrDr 92*
**Dawes,** Edwin Alfred 1925- *Who 92*
**Dawes,** Geoffrey Sharman 1918- *IntWW 91, Who 92*
**Dawes,** John Leslie 1942- *AmMWSc 92*
**Dawes,** Michael Andrew Laureys 1951- *WhoWest 92*
**Dawes,** Peter Spencer *Who 92*
**Dawes,** William Redin, Jr 1940- *AmMWSc 92*
**Dawick,** Viscount 1961- *Who 92*
**Dawid,** Igor Bert 1935- *AmMWSc 92*
**Dawida,** Michael Mathew 1949- *WhoAmP 91*
**Dawidow,** Boguslaw 1953- *WhoEnt 92*
**Dawidowicz,** Lucy 1915-1990 *AnObit 1990*
**Dawidowicz,** Lucy S. 1915- *WrDr 92*
**Dawidowicz,** Lucy S. 1915-1990 *ConAu 133*
**Dawidowicz,** Lucy Schildkret 1915-1990 *FacFETw*
**Dawkins,** Andy 1950- *WhoAmP 91*
**Dawkins,** Cecil *DrAPF 91*
**Dawkins,** Cecil 1927- *ConAu 36NR*
**Dawkins,** Clinton Richard 1941- *Who 92*
**Dawkins,** Darryl 1957- *WhoBlA 92*
**Dawkins,** Diana Fredda 1946- *WhoEnt 92*
**Dawkins,** Donald M *WhoAmP 91*
**Dawkins,** Donald Martin 1938- *WhoAmL 92*
**Dawkins,** Douglas Alfred 1927- *Who 92*
**Dawkins,** Harrill L *WhoAmP 91*
**Dawkins,** John Sydney 1947- *IntWW 91*
**Dawkins,** Julius 1961- *WhoBlA 92*
**Dawkins,** Marvin Braxton 1955- *WhoWest 92*
**Dawkins,** Maurice Anderson 1921- *WhoAmP 91*
**Dawkins,** Michael James 1953- *WhoBlA 92*
**Dawkins,** Miller J 1925- *WhoAmP 91, WhoBlA 92*
**Dawkins,** Orville Douglas 1938- *WhoFI 92*
**Dawkins,** Richard *Who 92*
**Dawkins,** Richard 1941- *FacFETw*
**Dawkins,** Rose Marie 1936- *WhoRel 92*
**Dawkins,** Stan Barrington Bancroft 1933- *WhoBlA 92*
**Dawkins,** Wayne J. 1955- *WhoBlA 92*
**Dawkins,** William Chester, Jr 1933- *WhoAmP 91*
**Dawkins,** William Lee, Jr. 1960- *WhoAmL 92*
**Dawkins,** William Paul 1934- *AmMWSc 92*
**Dawley,** Donald Lee 1936- *WhoFI 92, WhoMW 92*
**Dawley,** Patricia K. 1937- *WhoFI 92*
**Dawn,** Deborah *WhoEnt 92*
**Dawn,** Debra 1960- *WhoAmL 92*
**Dawn,** Marva Jenine 1948- *WhoRel 92*
**Dawnay** *Who 92*
**Dawnay,** Denis 1921-1983 *TwCPaSc*
**Dawood,** Nessim Joseph 1927- *Who 92*
**Daws,** Joyce 1925- *Who 92*
**Dawson,** A J 1872-1951 *ScFEYrs*
**Dawson,** Andre Fernando 1954- *WhoMW 92*
**Dawson,** Andre Nolan 1954- *WhoBlA 92*
**Dawson,** Andrew 1965- *WhoEnt 92*
**Dawson,** Anthony 1643?-1717 *DcNCBi 2*
**Dawson,** Anthony Michael 1928- *Who 92*
**Dawson,** Archibald Keith 1937- *Who 92*
**Dawson,** Arthur Donovan 1943- *AmMWSc 92*
**Dawson,** B. W. *WhoBlA 92*
**Dawson,** Bobby 1935- *WhoEnt 92*
**Dawson,** Carol 1945- *WhoAmP 91*
**Dawson,** Carol Gene 1937- *WhoAmP 91, WhoFI 92*
**Dawson,** Carrie B. 1910- *WhoBlA 92*
**Dawson,** Chandler R 1930- *AmMWSc 92*
**Dawson,** Charles H 1916- *AmMWSc 92*
**Dawson,** Christopher A *AmMWSc 92*
**Dawson,** Coningsby 1883-1959 *BenetAL 91*
**Dawson,** D E 1925- *AmMWSc 92*
**Dawson,** Daniel Joseph 1946- *AmMWSc 92*
**Dawson,** Daryl 1933- *Who 92*
**Dawson,** David Charles 1944- *AmMWSc 92*
**Dawson,** David Fleming 1926- *AmMWSc 92*
**Dawson,** David Lynn 1942- *AmMWSc 92*
**Dawson,** David M. 1954- *WhoFI 92*
**Dawson,** David Smith 1945- *WhoEnt 92*
**Dawson,** Dennis Ray 1948- *WhoAmL 92, WhoMW 92*
**Dawson,** Donald Andrew 1937- *AmMWSc 92*
**Dawson,** Doug 1944- *WhoWest 92*
**Dawson,** Earl B 1930- *AmMWSc 92*
**Dawson,** Edward John 1935- *Who 92*
**Dawson,** Edward Joseph 1944- *WhoFI 92*
**Dawson,** Elizabeth *IntAu&W 91X, WrDr 92*
**Dawson,** Elizabeth Abbott 1924- *WhoAmP 91*
**Dawson,** Elmer A. *SmATA 67*
**Dawson,** Eric 1918- *TwCPaSc*
**Dawson,** Eric Emmanuel 1937- *WhoAmP 91*
**Dawson,** F. Lawrence 1941- *WhoFI 92*
**Dawson,** Fielding *DrAPF 91*
**Dawson,** Frank G, Jr 1925- *AmMWSc 92*
**Dawson,** George Glenn 1925- *WrDr 92*
**Dawson,** George William Percy 1927- *IntWW 91*
**Dawson,** Gladys Quinty 1924- *AmMWSc 92*
**Dawson,** Glenn V 1944- *WhoAmP 91*
**Dawson,** Glyn 1943- *AmMWSc 92*
**Dawson,** Horace Greeley, Jr. 1926- *WhoBlA 92*
**Dawson,** Horace Ray 1935- *AmMWSc 92*
**Dawson,** Howard 1953- *WhoAmL 92*
**Dawson,** Hugh Michael 1956- *Who 92*
**Dawson,** Ian David 1934- *Who 92*
**Dawson,** J. Steve 1949- *WhoAmL 92*
**Dawson,** J W 1928- *AmMWSc 92*
**Dawson,** James Ambrose 1937- *WhoFI 92*
**Dawson,** James Clifford 1941- *AmMWSc 92*
**Dawson,** James Gordon 1916- *Who 92*
**Dawson,** James Linwood 1959- *WhoBlA 92*
**Dawson,** James Poast 1954- *WhoEnt 92*
**Dawson,** James Richard 1936- *WhoMW 92*
**Dawson,** James Thomas 1947- *AmMWSc 92*
**Dawson,** Janis 1936- *ConAu 135*
**Dawson,** Jean Howard 1933- *AmMWSc 92*
**Dawson,** Jeffrey Robert 1941- *AmMWSc 92*
**Dawson,** Jennifer *ConNov 91, WrDr 92*
**Dawson,** Jennifer 1929- *IntAu&W 91*
**Dawson,** Jesse R. 1921- *WhoBlA 92*
**Dawson,** John *Who 92*
**Dawson,** John 1690?-1761? *DcNCBi 2*
**Dawson,** John 1730?-1770 *DcNCBi 2*
**Dawson,** John 1946- *WorArt 1980 [port]*
**Dawson,** John Alan 1944- *Who 92*
**Dawson,** John Alan 1946- *WhoWest 92*
**Dawson,** John David 1951- *WhoRel 92*
**Dawson,** John E 1924- *AmMWSc 92*
**Dawson,** John Frederick 1936- *AmMWSc 92*
**Dawson,** John Gilmer 1892-1966 *DcNCBi 2*
**Dawson,** John H 1921- *WhoAmP 91*
**Dawson,** John Harold 1950- *AmMWSc 92*
**Dawson,** John Leonard 1932- *Who 92*
**Dawson,** John Myrick 1930- *AmMWSc 92*
**Dawson,** John William, Jr. 1920- *WhoMW 92*
**Dawson,** John William, Jr 1944- *AmMWSc 92*
**Dawson,** Jonathan Dean 1941- *IntAu&W 91*
**Dawson,** Joseph Anthony 1956- *WhoEnt 92*
**Dawson,** Joseph Martin 1879-1973 *RelLAm 91*
**Dawson,** Joseph Peter 1940- *Who 92*
**Dawson,** Keith *Who 92*
**Dawson,** Kenneth Adrian 1958- *AmMWSc 92*
**Dawson,** Kerry J 1946- *AmMWSc 92*
**Dawson,** Lawrence 1953- *WhoWest 92*
**Dawson,** Lawrence E 1916- *AmMWSc 92*
**Dawson,** Leland Bradley 1950- *WhoWest 92*
**Dawson,** Leonard Ervin 1934- *WhoBlA 92*
**Dawson,** Lewis Edward 1933- *WhoRel 92*
**Dawson,** Lin 1959- *WhoBlA 92*
**Dawson,** Linda 1949- *WrDr 92*
**Dawson,** Lumell Herbert 1934- *WhoBlA 92*
**Dawson,** M Joan 1944- *AmMWSc 92*
**Dawson,** Marcia Ilton 1942- *AmMWSc 92*
**Dawson,** Margaret Ann *AmMWSc 92*
**Dawson,** Mark H. *WhoWest 92*
**Dawson,** Martha E. 1922- *WhoBlA 92*
**Dawson,** Martha Morgan 1908- *WhoRel 92, WhoWest 92*
**Dawson,** Mary 1931- *AmMWSc 92*
**Dawson,** Mattel, Jr. 1921- *WhoBlA 92*
**Dawson,** Maxine Virginia *WhoAmP 91*
**Dawson,** Michael *Who 92*
**Dawson,** Michael Edward 1940- *WhoWest 92*
**Dawson,** Montagu J. 1894-1973 *TwCPaSc*
**Dawson,** Murray Drayton 1925- *AmMWSc 92*
**Dawson,** Paul Alan 1954- *WhoMW 92*
**Dawson,** Peter *TwCWW 91, Who 92*
**Dawson,** Peter 1907-1957 *TwCWW 91*
**Dawson,** Peter 1929- *Who 92*
**Dawson,** Peter 1933- *Who 92*
**Dawson,** Peter Edward 1931- *WhoBlA 92*
**Dawson,** Peter Henry 1937- *AmMWSc 92*
**Dawson,** Peter J 1928- *AmMWSc 92*
**Dawson,** Peter Sanford 1939- *AmMWSc 92*
**Dawson,** Peter Stephen Shevyn 1923- *AmMWSc 92*
**Dawson,** Peter Thomas 1938- *AmMWSc 92*
**Dawson,** Rex Malcolm Chaplin 1924- *Who 92*
**Dawson,** Rhett 1943- *WhoFI 92*
**Dawson,** Richard *WhoEnt 92*
**Dawson,** Richard Leonard Goodhugh 1916- *Who 92*
**Dawson,** Richard Thomas 1945- *WhoAmL 92*
**Dawson,** Robert Edward 1918- *WhoBlA 92*
**Dawson,** Robert Harold 1935- *WhoWest 92*
**Dawson,** Robert Kent 1946- *WhoAmP 91*
**Dawson,** Robert Kevin 1953- *WhoAmL 92*
**Dawson,** Robert Louis 1936- *AmMWSc 92*
**Dawson,** Robert Oscar 1939- *WhoAmL 92*

**Dawson**, Sea-Flower White Cloud *DrAPF 91*
**Dawson**, Sidney L., Jr. 1920- *WhoBlA 92*
**Dawson**, Stephen Everette 1946- *WhoAmL 92*
**Dawson**, Steven Michael 1962- *AmMWSc 92*
**Dawson**, Theresa Marie 1959- *WhoWest 92*
**Dawson**, Thomas C 1948- *WhoAmP 91*
**Dawson**, Thomas C., II 1948- *IntWW 91*
**Dawson**, Thomas Cordner 1948- *Who 92*
**Dawson**, Thomas H. *LesBEnT 92*
**Dawson**, Thomas Larry 1934- *AmMWSc 92*
**Dawson**, Thomas Thiel 1935- *WhoMW 92*
**Dawson**, Tom Henry 1937- *WhoAmP 91*
**Dawson**, Wallace Douglas, Jr 1931- *AmMWSc 92*
**Dawson**, Walter Lloyd 1902- *Who 92*
**Dawson**, Warren Hope 1939- *WhoBlA 92*
**Dawson**, Wayne Lowell 1961- *WhoRel 92*
**Dawson**, Wilfred Kenneth 1927- *AmMWSc 92*
**Dawson**, William James, Jr. 1930- *WhoWest 92*
**Dawson**, William John Richard Geoffrey P 1926- *Who 92*
**Dawson**, William Johnston 1765-1796 *DcNCBi 2*
**Dawson**, William Levi 1898- *NewAmDM*
**Dawson**, William Levi 1899- *WhoEnt 92*
**Dawson**, William Levi 1899-1990 *WhoBlA 92N*
**Dawson**, William Ryan 1927- *AmMWSc 92*
**Dawson**, William Thomas, III 1943- *WhoAmP 91*
**Dawson**, William Woodson 1933- *AmMWSc 92*
**Dawson-Damer** *Who 92*
**Dawson-Harris**, Frances Emily 1952- *WhoWest 92*
**Dawson-Moray**, Edward Bruce 1909- *Who 92*
**Dawtry**, Alan 1915- *Who 92*
**Dax**, Frank Robert 1950- *AmMWSc 92*
**Daxon**, Thomas Edward 1947- *WhoAmP 91*
**Day**, A Grove 1904- *IntAu&W 91*
**Day**, Alan Charles Lynn 1924- *Who 92*
**Day**, Alexandra *SmATA 67 [port]*
**Day**, Ann *WhoAmP 91*
**Day**, Anne Glendenning White Parker 1926- *WhoMW 92*
**Day**, Arden Dexter 1922- *AmMWSc 92*
**Day**, Austin Goodyear 1824-1889 *BiInAmS*
**Day**, Barry Leonard 1934- *WhoFI 92*
**Day**, Bartley Fuller 1948- *WhoEnt 92*
**Day**, Benjamin Downing 1936- *AmMWSc 92*
**Day**, Benjamin H. 1925-1984 *WhoBlA 92N*
**Day**, Bernard Maurice 1928- *Who 92*
**Day**, Bill 1955- *WhoAmP 91*
**Day**, Billy Neil 1930- *AmMWSc 92*
**Day**, Bryan 1934- *TwCPaSc*
**Day**, Burnis Calvin 1940- *WhoBlA 92*
**Day**, Carl 1938- *WhoEnt 92*
**Day**, Catherine-Ann 1942- *WhoAmP 91*
**Day**, Cecil LeRoy 1922- *AmMWSc 92*
**Day**, Charles Lynn 1939- *WhoFI 92*
**Day**, Charles Roger, Jr. 1947- *WhoFI 92*
**Day**, Christian Charles 1946- *WhoAmL 92*
**Day**, Christopher Sean 1949- *WhoFI 92*
**Day**, Clarence 1901-1990 *FacFETw*
**Day**, Clarence, Jr. 1874-1935 *BenetAL 91*
**Day**, Colin Leslie 1944- *WhoFI 92*
**Day**, Connie Jo 1949- *WhoMW 92*
**Day**, D E 1936- *AmMWSc 92*
**Day**, Daniel Edgar 1913- *WhoBlA 92*
**Day**, David Allen 1924- *AmMWSc 92*
**Day**, David Fisher 1829-1900 *BiInAmS*
**Day**, David John 1932- *WhoWest 92*
**Day**, David Owen 1958- *WhoAmL 92*
**Day**, David Talbot 1859-1925 *FacFETw*
**Day**, Deforest 1941- *ConAu 134*
**Day**, Dennis Gene 1936- *WhoWest 92*
**Day**, Derek 1927- *IntWW 91, Who 92*
**Day**, Donal Forest 1943- *AmMWSc 92*
**Day**, Donald d1991 *NewYTBS 91*
**Day**, Donald 1936- *WhoBlA 92*
**Day**, Donald Joseph 1929- *WhoFI 92*
**Day**, Donald Lee 1931- *AmMWSc 92, WhoMW 92*
**Day**, Donald Morfoot 1954- *WhoWest 92*
**Day**, Donald Sheldon 1924- *WhoRel 92*
**Day**, Doris 1924- *IntMPA 92, IntWW 91, WhoEnt 92*
**Day**, Dorothy 1897-1980 *FacFETw, HanAmWH, RComAH, RelLAm 91, SourALJ*
**Day**, Dorothy May 1897-1980 *AmPeW*
**Day**, Douglas Dee 1949- *WhoRel 92*
**Day**, Douglas Henry 1943- *Who 92*
**Day**, Edgar William, Jr 1936- *AmMWSc 92*
**Day**, Edward C. 1932- *ConAu 133*
**Day**, Edward Francis, Jr. 1946- *WhoAmL 92*
**Day**, Elbert Jackson 1925- *AmMWSc 92*
**Day**, Emerson 1913- *AmMWSc 92*
**Day**, Emmett E 1915- *AmMWSc 92*
**Day**, Eric Therander 1952- *WhoBlA 92*
**Day**, Eugene Davis 1925- *AmMWSc 92*
**Day**, Fisk Holbrook 1826-1903 *BiInAmS*
**Day**, Francisco 1907- *WhoEnt 92*
**Day**, Frank Patterson, Jr 1947- *AmMWSc 92*
**Day**, Fred L 1937- *WhoAmP 91*
**Day**, Gerald W. *WhoWest 92*
**Day**, Grace Anne 1933- *WhoEnt 92*
**Day**, Graham *Who 92*
**Day**, Harold J 1929- *AmMWSc 92*
**Day**, Harry Gilbert 1906- *AmMWSc 92, WhoMW 92*
**Day**, Harvey James 1929- *AmMWSc 92*
**Day**, Helen Nevitt 1913- *WhoAmP 91*
**Day**, Herman O'Neal, Jr 1925- *AmMWSc 92*
**Day**, Holman 1865-1935 *BenetAL 91*
**Day**, Ivana Podvalova 1932- *AmMWSc 92*
**Day**, J Edward 1914- *WhoAmP 91*
**Day**, Jack Calvin 1936- *AmMWSc 92*
**Day**, Jackson Harvey 1942- *WhoRel 92*
**Day**, James *LesBEnT 92*
**Day**, James 1918- *WhoEnt 92*
**Day**, James Edward 1914- *WhoAmL 92*
**Day**, James McAdam, Jr. 1948- *WhoAmL 92, WhoFI 92*
**Day**, James Meikle 1924- *AmMWSc 92*
**Day**, Jane Maxwell 1937- *AmMWSc 92*
**Day**, Janice Eldredge 1919- *WhoWest 92*
**Day**, Jennie D 1921- *WhoAmP 91*
**Day**, Jeremiah 1773-1867 *BiInAmS*
**Day**, Jerome Michael 1955- *WhoAmL 92*
**Day**, Jerry Keith 1938- *WhoRel 92*
**Day**, Jesse Harold 1916- *AmMWSc 92*
**Day**, John 1574?-1640? *RfGEnL 91*
**Day**, John 1797-1860 *DcNCBi 2*
**Day**, John Arthur 1956- *WhoAmL 92*
**Day**, John Denton 1942- *WhoWest 92*
**Day**, John J 1937- *WhoAmP 91*
**Day**, John King 1909- *Who 92*
**Day**, John Robert 1917- *IntAu&W 91*
**Day**, John W. 1933- *IntWW 91, WhoFI 92*
**Day**, Joseph Dennis 1942- *WhoWest 92*
**Day**, Judson Graham 1933- *IntWW 91, Who 92*
**Day**, Kathleen Patricia 1947- *WhoFI 92*
**Day**, Kingsley 1951- *WhoEnt 92*
**Day**, Kyle 1959- *WhoEnt 92*
**Day**, L. B. 1944- *WhoWest 92*
**Day**, Lance Reginald 1927- *Who 92*
**Day**, Laraine *IntMPA 92*
**Day**, Lawrence Eugene 1933- *AmMWSc 92*
**Day**, Leora 1937- *WhoAmP 91*
**Day**, LeRoy E 1925- *AmMWSc 92*
**Day**, Lewis Rodman 1915- *AmMWSc 92*
**Day**, Linda Gail 1938- *WhoEnt 92*
**Day**, Loren A 1936- *AmMWSc 92*
**Day**, Lucienne 1917- *Who 92*
**Day**, Lucille *DrAPF 91*
**Day**, Lucille Elizabeth 1947- *WhoWest 92*
**Day**, Mahlon Marsh 1913- *AmMWSc 92*
**Day**, Marilyn Lee 1949- *WhoWest 92*
**Day**, Marion Clyde, Jr 1927- *AmMWSc 92*
**Day**, Mary *WhoEnt 92*
**Day**, Mary Anne 1950- *WhoAmL 92*
**Day**, Maurice Jerome 1913- *WhoFI 92*
**Day**, Melvin Sherman 1923- *WhoFI 92*
**Day**, Melvyn 1923- *TwCPaSc*
**Day**, Michael Hardy 1950- *AmMWSc 92*
**Day**, Michael Herbert 1927- *WrDr 92*
**Day**, Michael John 1933- *Who 92*
**Day**, Morris 1957- *WhoBlA 92*
**Day**, Neil McPherson 1935- *WhoFI 92*
**Day**, Nicholas Edward 1939- *Who 92*
**Day**, Noorbibi Kassam *AmMWSc 92*
**Day**, Patrick Reed 1958- *WhoAmL 92*
**Day**, Peter 1938- *Who 92*
**Day**, Peter Rodney 1928- *AmMWSc 92, IntWW 91, Who 92*
**Day**, R. Cortez *DrAPF 91*
**Day**, Reed Blachly 1930- *WhoAmL 92*
**Day**, Reuben Alexander, Jr 1915- *AmMWSc 92*
**Day**, Richard Allen 1931- *AmMWSc 92, WhoMW 92*
**Day**, Richard Earl 1929- *WhoAmL 92*
**Day**, Richard Edward 1960- *WhoWest 92*
**Day**, Richard Elledge 1939- *WhoWest 92*
**Day**, Richard H 1937- *WhoAmP 91*
**Day**, Richard Putnam 1930- *WhoIns 92*
**Day**, Richard Somers 1928- *WhoWest 92*
**Day**, Richard V. 1954- *WhoAmL 92*
**Day**, Robert *DrAPF 91*
**Day**, Robert 1922- *IntMPA 92*
**Day**, Robert J 1910- *AmMWSc 92*
**Day**, Robert James 1941- *AmMWSc 92*
**Day**, Robert Jennings 1925- *WhoMW 92*
**Day**, Robert P. 1941- *TwCWW 91, WrDr 92*
**Day**, Robert William 1924- *AmMWSc 92*
**Day**, Robert Winsor 1930- *AmMWSc 92, WhoWest 92*
**Day**, Robin 1915- *DcTwDes, Who 92*
**Day**, Robin 1923- *IntAu&W 91, IntWW 91, Who 92, WrDr 92*
**Day**, Roland B 1919- *WhoAmP 91*
**Day**, Roland Bernard 1919- *WhoAmL 92, WhoMW 92*
**Day**, Ronald Elwin 1933- *WhoFI 92*
**Day**, Ronald Richard 1934- *WhoFI 92*
**Day**, Russell R *WhoAmP 91*
**Day**, Sarah Frances 1958- *IntAu&W 91*
**Day**, Stacey B. 1927- *WrDr 92*
**Day**, Stacey Biswas 1927- *AmMWSc 92, IntAu&W 91*
**Day**, Stephen Martin 1931- *AmMWSc 92*
**Day**, Stephen Peter 1938- *Who 92*
**Day**, Stephen Richard 1948- *Who 92*
**Day**, Steven M. 1960- *WhoFI 92*
**Day**, Stuart Reid 1959- *WhoAmL 92*
**Day**, Thomas 1801?-1861? *DcNCBi 2*
**Day**, Thomas Brennock 1932- *AmMWSc 92, WhoWest 92*
**Day**, Timothy Townley 1937- *WhoWest 92*
**Day**, Walter M, Sr 1917- *WhoAmP 91*
**Day**, Walter R, Jr 1931- *AmMWSc 92*
**Day**, Wayne Allan 1955- *WhoRel 92*
**Day**, Weston S 1945- *WhoIns 92*
**Day**, William Cathcart 1857-1905 *BiInAmS*
**Day**, William Charles, Jr. 1937- *WhoBlA 92*
**Day**, William H 1934- *AmMWSc 92*
**Day**, William Rufus 1849-1923 *AmPolLe, FacFETw*
**Day**, Zed Edward, III 1940- *WhoMW 92*
**Day-Gowder**, Patricia Joan 1936- *WhoWest 92*
**Day Lewis**, C 1904-1972 *ConAu 34NR, FacFETw, RfGEnL 91*
**Day Lewis**, Daniel *FacFETw, IntWW 91*
**Day-Lewis**, Daniel 1957- *ConTFT 9, IntMPA 92*
**Day-Lewis**, Sean 1931- *Who 92*
**Day-Salvatore**, Debra-Lynn 1953- *AmMWSc 92*
**Daya Mata**, Sri 1914- *WhoRel 92*
**Daya Mata**, Sri 1914- *WhoWest 92*
**Dayal**, Rajeshwar 1909- *IntWW 91*
**Dayal**, Ramesh 1942- *AmMWSc 92*
**Dayal**, Yogeshwar 1939- *AmMWSc 92*
**Dayala**, Haji Farooq 1948- *WhoWest 92*
**Dayan**, Jason Edward 1923- *AmMWSc 92*
**Dayan**, Moshe 1915-1981 *FacFETw [port]*
**Dayan**, Rodney S. 1933- *WhoAmL 92*
**Dayananda**, Mysore Ananthamurthy 1934- *AmMWSc 92*
**Daybell**, Melvin Drew 1935- *AmMWSc 92*
**Dayday**, Henry *WhoWest 92*
**Daye**, Charles Edward 1944- *WhoBlA 92*
**Daye**, Darren 1960- *WhoBlA 92*
**Daye**, Pierre 1892-1960 *BiDExR*
**Daye**, Stephen 1594?-1668 *BenetAL 91*
**Daye**, Walter O. 1918- *WhoBlA 92*
**Dayhoff**, Edward Samuel 1925- *AmMWSc 92*
**Dayioglu**, Murat Day 1939- *WhoWest 92*
**Daykin**, Christopher David 1948- *Who 92*
**Daykin**, Robert P 1920- *AmMWSc 92*
**Daylong**, Steven George 1961- *WhoRel 92*
**Daylor**, Francis Lawrence, Jr 1932- *AmMWSc 92*
**Daymond**, Douglas Godfrey d1990 *Who 92N*
**Daynard**, Richard Alan 1943- *WhoAmL 92*
**Daynes**, Raymond Austin *AmMWSc 92*
**Dayringer**, Richard Lee 1934- *WhoRel 92*
**Days**, Drew Saunders, III 1941- *WhoAmP 91, WhoBlA 92*
**Days**, Drews S. 1941- *WhoAmL 92*
**Days**, Morgan M. 1891- *WhoBlA 92*
**Days**, Rosetta Hill *WhoBlA 92*
**Days**, Virginia Mae *WhoHisp 92*
**Dayton**, Benjamin Bonney 1914- *AmMWSc 92*
**Dayton**, Bruce Mc Lean 1934- *WhoIns 92*
**Dayton**, Bruce R 1937- *AmMWSc 92*
**Dayton**, David *DrAPF 91*
**Dayton**, Edward Risedorph 1924- *WhoWest 92*
**Dayton**, Irene *DrAPF 91*
**Dayton**, James Anthony, Jr 1937- *AmMWSc 92, WhoMW 92*
**Dayton**, Jeff 1953- *WhoEnt 92*
**Dayton**, Jonathan 1760-1824 *AmPolLe*
**Dayton**, June 1923- *WhoEnt 92*
**Dayton**, Lyman D. 1941- *IntMPA 92*
**Dayton**, Mark *WhoAmP 91*
**Dayton**, Paul K 1941- *AmMWSc 92*
**Dayton**, Peter Gustav 1926- *AmMWSc 92*
**Dayton**, Ralph McDonald 1956- *WhoMW 92*
**Dayton**, William Henry, Jr. 1957- *WhoAmL 92*
**Daywitt**, James Edward 1947- *AmMWSc 92*
**Daza**, Carlos Hernan 1931- *AmMWSc 92*
**Daza**, Pedro 1925- *IntWW 91*
**Dazey**, Charles Turner *BenetAL 91*
**Dazzo**, Frank Bryan 1948- *AmMWSc 92*
**D'Azzo**, John Joachim 1919- *AmMWSc 92, WhoMW 92*
**D'Banana**, Bebe 1951- *WhoBlA 92*
**D'Beck**, Patti 1948- *WhoEnt 92*
**DCamp**, Charles Barton 1932- *WhoEnt 92*
**DCamp**, Kathryn Acker 1956- *WhoMW 92*
**De La Soul** *ConMus 7 [port]*
**De**, Gopa Sarkar *AmMWSc 92*
**Dea**, David Young Fong 1924- *WhoMW 92*
**Dea**, Phoebe Kin-Kin 1946- *AmMWSc 92*
**Deabler**, Richard Ardell 1945- *WhoFI 92*
**DeAcetis**, William 1928- *AmMWSc 92*
**de Acha**, Rafael J. *WhoEnt 92*
**Deacon**, David A G 1953- *AmMWSc 92*
**Deacon**, James Everett 1934- *AmMWSc 92*
**Deacon**, John C. 1920- *WhoAmL 92*
**Deacon**, Keith Vivian 1935- *Who 92*
**Deacon**, Peter 1945- *TwCPaSc*
**Deacon**, Richard *WrDr 92*
**Deacon**, Richard 1949- *TwCPaSc*
**Deacon**, Robert Thomas 1944- *WhoWest 92*
**Deacon Elliott**, Robert 1914- *Who 92*
**De Acosta**, Alejandro 1941- *AmMWSc 92*
**Deacy**, Ed 1946- *WhoEnt 92*
**Deacy**, Thomas Edward, Jr. 1918- *WhoAmL 92*
**Dead Kennedys** *NewAmDM*
**Deadrich**, Paul Eddy 1925- *WhoWest 92*
**Deady**, Matthew William 1953- *AmMWSc 92*
**Deagle**, Edwin Augustus, Jr. 1937- *WhoWest 92*
**Deagon**, Ann *DrAPF 91*
**Deahl**, James Edward 1945- *IntAu&W 91*
**Deahl**, Kenneth Luvere 1943- *AmMWSc 92*
**Deahl**, Salliejean 1937- *WhoRel 92*
**Deahl**, Warren Anthony 1918- *WhoAmL 92*
**Deahl**, William Evans, Jr. 1945- *WhoRel 92*
**Deak**, Charles Karol 1928- *WhoMW 92*
**Deak**, Franklin Harry 1948- *WhoAmL 92*
**Deak**, Istvan 1926- *WrDr 92*
**Deak**, Jon 1943- *WhoEnt 92*
**Deakin**, Alfred 1856-1919 *FacFETw*
**Deakin**, Cecil Martin Fothergill 1910- *Who 92*
**Deakin**, Frederick William *Who 92*
**Deakin**, Michael 1939- *Who 92*
**Deakin**, Nicholas Dampier 1936- *Who 92*
**Deakin**, William 1913- *Who 92, WrDr 92*
**Deakins**, Eric Petro 1932- *Who 92*
**Deakins**, Warren W 1938- *WhoIns 92*
**Deaktor**, Darryl Barnett 1942- *WhoAmL 92*
**Deal**, Albert Leonard, III 1937- *AmMWSc 92*
**Deal**, Borden 1922-1985 *BenetAL 91*
**Deal**, Bruce Elmer 1927- *AmMWSc 92*
**Deal**, Carl Hosea, Jr 1919- *AmMWSc 92*
**Deal**, Don Robert 1937- *AmMWSc 92*
**Deal**, Dwight Edward 1938- *AmMWSc 92*
**Deal**, Elwyn Ernest 1936- *AmMWSc 92*
**Deal**, Ervin R *AmMWSc 92*
**Deal**, George Edgar 1920- *AmMWSc 92, WhoFI 92*
**Deal**, Glenn W, Jr 1922- *AmMWSc 92*
**Deal**, J Nathan *WhoAmP 91*
**Deal**, James Edward 1957- *WhoAmL 92*
**Deal**, Jill B. 1942- *WhoAmL 92*
**Deal**, Michael Lee 1961- *WhoRel 92*
**Deal**, Ralph Macgill 1931- *AmMWSc 92*
**Deal**, Susan Strayer *DrAPF 91*
**Deal**, Terry Dean 1948- *WhoWest 92*
**Deal**, W W 1936- *WhoAmP 91*
**Deal**, William Cecil, Jr 1936- *AmMWSc 92*
**Deal**, William E, Jr 1925- *AmMWSc 92*
**Deal**, William Thomas 1949- *WhoMW 92*
**Dealaman**, Doris W 1919- *WhoAmP 91*
**De Alba**, Marlys Ann 1956- *WhoHisp 92*
**De Alba Martinez**, Jorge 1920- *AmMWSc 92*
**De Almeida**, Antonio *IntWW 91*
**de Almeida**, Luciano P. Mendes *WhoRel 92*
**Dealtry**, Richard 1936- *Who 92*
**Dealy**, James Bond, Jr 1920- *AmMWSc 92*
**Dealy**, Janette Diane 1950- *WhoWest 92*
**Dealy**, John Edward 1930- *AmMWSc 92*
**Dealy**, John Michael 1937- *AmMWSc 92*
**Deam**, James Richard 1942- *AmMWSc 92*
**Deamer**, David Wilson, Jr 1939- *AmMWSc 92*
**Dean** *Who 92*
**Dean**, Anabel 1915- *WrDr 92*
**Dean**, Andrew Griswold 1938- *AmMWSc 92*
**Dean**, Ann 1944- *AmMWSc 92*
**Dean**, Anne *Who 92*
**Dean**, Anthony Alexander 1940- *WhoAmL 92*
**Dean**, Anthony Marion 1944- *AmMWSc 92*
**Dean**, Antony Musgrave 1921- *IntWW 91*

**Dean,** Arthur H 1898-1987 *FacFETw*
**Dean,** Arthur Paul 1924- *Who 92*
**Dean,** Basil 1888-1978 *ConAu 134*
**Dean,** Beale 1922- *WhoAmL 92*
**Dean,** Beryl 1911- *WrDr 92*
**Dean,** Bill Bryan 1948- *AmMWSc 92*
**Dean,** Bill Verlin, Jr. 1957- *WhoAmL 92*
**Dean,** Brenda 1943- *Who 92*
**Dean,** Brian L. 1955- *WhoAmL 92*
**Dean,** Britten 1935- *WhoWest 92*
**Dean,** Bruce Campbell 1958- *WhoAmL 92*
**Dean,** Burton Victor 1924- *AmMWSc 92*
**Dean,** Carol Carlson 1944- *WhoAmP 91, WhoFI 92*
**Dean,** Carolynn Leslie 1952- *WhoWest 92*
**Dean,** Catherine 1905-1983 *TwCPaSc*
**Dean,** Cecil Roy 1927- *Who 92*
**Dean,** Charles E 1898- *AmMWSc 92*
**Dean,** Charles Edgar 1929- *AmMWSc 92*
**Dean,** Charles Raymond 1923- *Who 92*
**Dean,** Christopher *FacFETw*
**Dean,** Clara Russell 1927- *WhoBlA 92*
**Dean,** Dallas, Jr 1947- *WhoAmP 91*
**Dean,** Daniel R. 1941- *WhoBlA 92*
**Dean,** David 1926- *AmMWSc 92*
**Dean,** David A 1941- *AmMWSc 92*
**Dean,** David Arnold 1929- *WhoRel 92*
**Dean,** David Campbell 1931- *AmMWSc 92*
**Dean,** David Devereaux 1952- *AmMWSc 92*
**Dean,** David Edis 1922- *Who 92*
**Dean,** David Lee 1946- *AmMWSc 92*
**Dean,** Dearest 1911- *WhoEnt 92*
**Dean,** Deborah G 1954- *WhoAmP 91*
**Dean,** Dennis Dale 1953- *WhoWest 92*
**Dean,** Dewey Hobson, Jr. 1920- *WhoFI 92*
**Dean,** Diana 1942- *TwCPaSc*
**Dean,** Diane D. 1949- *WhoBlA 92*
**Dean,** Donald E 1927- *AmMWSc 92*
**Dean,** Donald Harry 1942- *AmMWSc 92*
**Dean,** Donald L 1926- *AmMWSc 92*
**Dean,** Donald W *WhoAmP 91*
**Dean,** Donna Joyce 1947- *AmMWSc 92*
**Dean,** Douglas C *WhoAmP 91*
**Dean,** Dudley *TwCWW 91*
**Dean,** Eddie *IntMPA 92*
**Dean,** Eddie 1907- *WhoEnt 92*
**Dean,** Elizabeth 1929- *TwCPaSc*
**Dean,** Eric Walter 1906- *Who 92*
**Dean,** Ernest H 1914- *WhoAmP 91*
**Dean,** Eugene Alan 1931- *AmMWSc 92*
**Dean,** Frederick Bernard 1927- *WhoFI 92*
**Dean,** Frederick Chamberlain 1927- *AmMWSc 92*
**Dean,** Frederick Rudolph 1952- *WhoBlA 92*
**Dean,** George R 1933- *WhoAmP 91*
**Dean,** George Washington 1825-1897 *BiInAmS*
**Dean,** Graham 1951- *TwCPaSc [port]*
**Dean,** Harold 1908- *Who 92*
**Dean,** Harvey Ray 1943- *WhoFI 92*
**Dean,** Helen Barbara 1945- *WhoFI 92*
**Dean,** Helen Henrietta 1905- *WhoWest 92*
**Dean,** Henry Lamar 1938- *WhoAmP 91*
**Dean,** Herbert A 1918- *AmMWSc 92*
**Dean,** Howard B 1948- *WhoAmP 91*
**Dean,** J. Thomas 1933- *WhoAmL 92, WhoAmP 91*
**Dean,** Jack Hugh 1941- *AmMWSc 92*
**Dean,** Jack Lemuel 1925- *AmMWSc 92*
**Dean,** James 1776-1849 *BiInAmS*
**Dean,** James 1931-1955 *FacFETw*
**Dean,** James Edward 1944- *WhoBlA 92*
**Dean,** James Robert 1961- *WhoRel 92*
**Dean,** Janice Lynn 1947- *WhoEnt 92*
**Dean,** Jay Hanna 1911-1974 *FacFETw*
**Dean,** Jeffrey Jerome 1962- *WhoAmL 92*
**Dean,** Jeffrey L. 1950- *WhoMW 92*
**Dean,** Jeffrey Stewart 1939- *AmMWSc 92*
**Dean,** Jennie 1852-1913 *NotBlAW 92*
**Dean,** Jimmy 1928- *IntMPA 92*
**Dean,** John, III 1938- *FacFETw [port]*
**Dean,** John Aurie 1921- *AmMWSc 92*
**Dean,** John Gilbert 1911- *AmMWSc 92*
**Dean,** John Gunther 1926- *IntWW 91, WhoAmP 91*
**Dean,** John Mark 1936- *AmMWSc 92*
**Dean,** Johnny Lydell 1946- *WhoRel 92*
**Dean,** Jonathan 1944- *WhoAmL 92*
**Dean,** Joseph 1921- *Who 92*
**Dean,** Joseph Anthony 1941- *WhoRel 92*
**Dean,** Jurrien 1947- *AmMWSc 92*
**Dean,** Karen Ann 1961- *WhoEnt 92*
**Dean,** Katharine Mary Hope *Who 92*
**Dean,** Larry 1936- *WhoEnt 92*
**Dean,** Laura Hansen 1951- *WhoAmL 92*
**Dean,** LeAnn Faye Lindquist 1948- *WhoMW 92*
**Dean,** Margaret *TwCPaSc*
**Dean,** Margo 1927- *WhoEnt 92*
**Dean,** Mark Harrison 1958- *WhoAmL 92*
**Dean,** Martin R. 1955- *IntAu&W 91*
**Dean,** Mary Ann 1941- *WhoEnt 92*
**Dean,** Mary Elizabeth 1947- *WhoAmL 92*
**Dean,** Merrill C 1941- *IntMPA 92*
**Dean,** Michael 1938- *Who 92*
**Dean,** Michael Anthony 1942- *WhoWest 92*
**Dean,** Michael F. *WhoAmL 92*
**Dean,** Michael Kim 1966- *WhoEnt 92*
**Dean,** Morton 1935- *IntMPA 92*
**Dean,** Nathan 1934- *WhoAmP 91*
**Dean,** Nathan Wesley 1941- *AmMWSc 92*
**Dean,** Patrick 1909- *Who 92*
**Dean,** Patrick Henry 1909- *IntWW 91*
**Dean,** Paul *Who 92*
**Dean,** Paul 1933- *Who 92*
**Dean,** Peter Henry 1939- *Who 92*
**Dean,** Philip Arthur Woodworth 1943- *AmMWSc 92*
**Dean,** Phillip Hayes *WrDr 92*
**Dean,** Randoll Eric 1953- *WhoRel 92*
**Dean,** Raymond *Who 92*
**Dean,** Richard A 1935- *AmMWSc 92*
**Dean,** Richard Albert 1924- *AmMWSc 92, WhoWest 92*
**Dean,** Richard James 1945- *WhoMW 92*
**Dean,** Richard Raymond 1940- *AmMWSc 92*
**Dean,** Robert Charles, Jr 1928- *AmMWSc 92*
**Dean,** Robert Gayle 1939- *WhoEnt 92*
**Dean,** Robert George 1930- *AmMWSc 92*
**Dean,** Robert Reed 1914- *AmMWSc 92*
**Dean,** Robert Waters 1929- *AmMWSc 92*
**Dean,** Robert Yost 1921- *AmMWSc 92*
**Dean,** Ronald Glenn 1944- *WhoAmL 92*
**Dean,** Roy *Who 92*
**Dean,** Russell Scott 1964- *WhoRel 92*
**Dean,** Ruth Brigham 1947- *WhoMW 92*
**Dean,** S.F.X. *WrDr 92*
**Dean,** Sheldon Williams, Jr 1935- *AmMWSc 92*
**Dean,** Shelley *WrDr 92*
**Dean,** Stafford Roderick 1937- *IntWW 91*
**Dean,** Stanley Wayne 1934- *WhoWest 92*
**Dean,** Stephen Odell 1936- *AmMWSc 92, WhoFI 92*
**Dean,** Stephen Steve Michael 1952- *WhoEnt 92*
**Dean,** Steven Owens 1958- *WhoAmL 92*
**Dean,** Susan Thorpe *AmMWSc 92*
**Dean,** Thomas Paul *WhoEnt 92*
**Dean,** Thomas Scott 1924- *AmMWSc 92*
**Dean,** Tomlinson 1947- *WhoEnt 92*
**Dean,** Trevie Crile 1947- *WhoRel 92, WhoWest 92*
**Dean,** Vera Micheles 1903-1972 *AmPeW*
**Dean,** Vernon 1959- *WhoBlA 92*
**Dean,** Vinnie Nicholas 1929- *WhoEnt 92*
**Dean,** Vyvyan Coleman 1945- *WhoBlA 92*
**Dean,** Walter Albert 1905- *AmMWSc 92*
**Dean,** Walter E, Jr 1939- *AmMWSc 92*
**Dean,** Walter Edward, Jr. 1939- *WhoWest 92*
**Dean,** Walter Keith 1917- *AmMWSc 92*
**Dean,** Walter Lee 1928- *AmMWSc 92*
**Dean,** Walter R., Jr. 1934- *WhoBlA 92*
**Dean,** Walter Raleigh, Jr 1934- *WhoAmP 91*
**Dean,** Wanda Luther 1948- *WhoAmP 91*
**Dean,** Warren Edgell 1932- *AmMWSc 92*
**Dean,** Wayne Dickerson 1925- *WhoWest 92*
**Dean,** William C 1926- *AmMWSc 92*
**Dean,** William Denard 1937- *WhoRel 92, WrDr 92*
**Dean,** William L *AmMWSc 92*
**Dean,** William Shirley 1947- *WhoEnt 92*
**Dean,** Willie B. 1951- *WhoBlA 92*
**Dean,** Winton 1916- *Who 92*
**Dean,** Winton Basil 1916- *IntWW 91*
**Dean of Beswick,** Baron 1922- *Who 92*
**De Anda,** Arnold 1946- *WhoHisp 92*
**DeAnda,** James 1925- *WhoAmL 92*
**DeAnda,** Peter 1938- *WhoBlA 92*
**De Anda,** Raul *WhoHisp 92*
**De Andrade,** Mario Pinto 1928-1990 *FacFETw*
**De Andrea,** William L 1952- *IntAu&W 91, WrDr 92*
**Deane** *Who 92*
**Deane,** Allyson *WhoEnt 92*
**Deane,** Basil 1928- *Who 92*
**Deane,** Charles Bennett 1898-1969 *DcNCBi 2*
**Deane,** Darrell Dwight 1915- *AmMWSc 92*
**Deane,** Elaine 1958- *WhoAmL 92*
**Deane,** Frederick, Jr. 1926- *WhoFI 92*
**Deane,** James 1801-1858 *BiInAmS*
**Deane,** James Richard 1935- *WhoFI 92*
**Deane,** Morgan R. 1922- *WhoBlA 92*
**Deane,** Norman 1921- *AmMWSc 92*
**Deane,** Phyllis Mary 1918- *IntWW 91, Who 92*
**Deane,** Robert Armistead 1919- *WhoBlA 92*
**Deane,** Robert Donald 1936- *WhoAmP 91*
**Deane,** Seamus Francis 1940- *IntWW 91*
**Deane,** Silas 1737-1789 *BlkwEAR*
**Deane,** William *Who 92*
**Deane-Drummond,** Anthony 1917- *WrDr 92*
**Deane-Drummond,** Anthony John 1917- *Who 92*
**Deane-Ferrucci,** Georgia Avellis 1919- *WhoEnt 92*
**Deaner,** Jeffrey Lee 1963- *WhoRel 92*
**De Angeli,** Marguerite 1889- *IntAu&W 91*
**DeAngelis,** Aldo A 1931- *WhoAmP 91*
**DeAngelis,** Donald Lee 1944- *AmMWSc 92*
**deAngelis,** Jacqueline *DrAPF 91*
**DeAngelis,** Joseph 1946- *WhoAmP 91*
**DeAngelis,** Joseph Anthony 1955- *WhoFI 92*
**DeAngelis,** Robert Paul 1962- *WhoEnt 92*
**DeAngelis,** William Martin 1929- *WhoAmP 91*
**DeAngelo,** Ann Marie 1952- *WhoEnt 92*
**Deanhardt,** Marshall Lynn 1948- *AmMWSc 92*
**Deanin,** Rudolph D 1921- *AmMWSc 92*
**Deano,** Edward J, Jr 1952- *WhoAmP 91*
**Deanovich,** Connie *DrAPF 91*
**Deans,** David Henry 1954- *WhoWest 92*
**Deans,** Harry A 1932- *AmMWSc 92*
**Deans,** Henry Clough, Jr. 1955- *WhoEnt 92*
**Deans,** John E. 1946- *WhoAmL 92*
**Deans,** Robert Jack 1927- *AmMWSc 92*
**Deans,** Roger William 1917- *Who 92*
**Deans,** Sidney Alfred Vindin 1918- *AmMWSc 92*
**Deans,** William Anderson, III 1941- *WhoRel 92*
**De Antonio,** Emile 1920-1989 *IntDcF 2-2*
**De Aparicio,** Vibiana Chamberlin *DrAPF 91*
**Dear,** Geoffrey James 1937- *Who 92*
**Dear,** Nick 1955- *IntAu&W 91*
**Dear,** Noach 1953- *WhoAmP 91*
**Dear,** Robert E A 1933- *AmMWSc 92*
**de Aragon,** Ray John 1946- *WhoHisp 92*
**De Araugo,** Tess 1930- *ConAu 135*
**De Araugo-O'Mullane,** Tess *ConAu 135*
**De Arauho Sales,** Eugenio 1920- *WhoRel 92*
**Dearborn,** Delwyn D 1933- *AmMWSc 92*
**Dearborn,** Henry Alexander Scammell 1783-1851 *BiInAmS*
**Dearborn,** John Holmes 1933- *AmMWSc 92*
**Dearborn,** Robert Wesley 1911- *WhoAmP 91*
**de Arce,** Carmen 1952- *WhoHisp 92*
**Dearden,** Basil 1911-1971 *IntDcF 2-2*
**Dearden,** Boyd L 1943- *AmMWSc 92*
**Dearden,** Douglas Morey 1923- *AmMWSc 92*
**Dearden,** James 1949- *IntMPA 92*
**Dearden,** James Shackley 1931- *IntAu&W 91, WrDr 92*
**Dearden,** John Francis 1907-1988 *RelLAm 91*
**Dearden,** Lyle Conway 1922- *AmMWSc 92*
**Deardeuff,** Robert Paul 1961- *WhoMW 92*
**Deardorf,** David A. 1937- *WhoWest 92*
**Deardorff,** Michael Kent 1949- *WhoIns 92*
**de Arechaga,** Eduardo Jimenez *IntWW 91*
**Dearie,** John C 1940- *WhoAmP 91*
**Dearie,** Raymond J. 1944- *WhoAmL 92*
**Dearin,** Ray Dean 1941- *WhoAmP 91, WhoMW 92*
**Dearing,** Deborah Carter 1957- *WhoAmL 92*
**Dearing,** Robert M 1935- *WhoAmP 91*
**Dearing,** Ronald 1930- *Who 92*
**Dearing,** Ronald Ernest 1930- *IntWW 91*
**Dearlove,** Thomas John 1941- *AmMWSc 92*
**Dearman,** Henry Hursell 1934- *AmMWSc 92*
**Dearman,** John Edward 1931- *WhoBlA 92*
**Dearman,** Roger Allen 1947- *WhoWest 92*
**de Armas,** Frederick A. 1945- *WhoHisp 92*
**De Armas,** Jorge Benito 1931- *WhoHisp 92*
**de Armas,** Luis A. 1952- *WhoHisp 92*
**De Arment,** Roderick Allen 1948- *WhoAmL 92, WhoFI 92*
**Dearmin,** Dennis Dale 1950- *WhoRel 92*
**Dearmin,** Vauda Lewis 1947- *WhoAmP 91*
**DeArmon,** Ira Alexander, Jr 1920- *AmMWSc 92*
**DeArmon,** Shari Kathryn 1961- *WhoAmL 92*
**Dearmon,** Thomas Alfred 1937- *WhoFI 92*
**DeArmond,** M Keith 1935- *AmMWSc 92, WhoWest 92*
**Dearnley,** Christopher Hugh 1930- *IntWW 91, Who 92*
**Dearth,** Bill Edward 1946- *WhoEnt 92*
**Dearth,** Glen Herbert 1955- *WhoMW 92*
**Dearth,** James Dean 1946- *AmMWSc 92*
**Deas,** Alberta D. 1934- *WhoRel 92*
**Deas,** D. L. 1957- *WhoEnt 92*
**Deas,** Jane Ellen 1933- *AmMWSc 92*
**Deas,** Larry 1945- *WhoBlA 92*
**Deas,** Richard Ryder, III 1927- *WhoEnt 92*
**Deas,** Thomas C 1921- *AmMWSc 92*
**Deason,** Edward Joseph 1955- *WhoAmL 92*
**Deason,** Temd R 1931- *AmMWSc 92*
**Deasy,** Austin 1936- *IntWW 91*
**Deasy,** John Berchmans 1911- *WhoWest 92*
**Deasy,** John Michael 1945- *WhoAmL 92*
**Deasy,** Kevin 1953- *WhoAmL 92*
**Deasy,** Theresa 1958- *WhoFI 92*
**Deat,** Marcel 1894-1955 *BiDExR*
**Deaterla,** Michael Franklin 1952- *WhoEnt 92*
**Death,** Frank Stuart 1932- *AmMWSc 92*
**Deatherage,** Junior Lee 1940- *WhoAmP 91*
**Deatherage,** Martha Martin *WhoEnt 92*
**Deatherage,** William Vernon 1927- *WhoAmL 92*
**Deathridge,** John 1944- *ConAu 133*
**Deaton,** Bobby Charles 1936- *AmMWSc 92*
**Deaton,** Charles 1921- *WhoFI 92*
**Deaton,** Charles M 1931- *WhoAmP 91*
**Deaton,** Edmund Ike 1930- *AmMWSc 92*
**Deaton,** James Washington 1934- *AmMWSc 92*
**Deaton,** Julie Frances 1961- *WhoRel 92*
**Deaton,** Lewis Edward 1949- *AmMWSc 92*
**Deaton,** Paul Reagan 1957- *WhoRel 92*
**Deaton,** Robert Lester 1936- *WhoWest 92*
**Deaton,** Susan 1952- *WhoEnt 92*
**Deats,** Edith Potter *AmMWSc 92*
**Deats,** Paul Kindred, Jr. 1918- *WhoRel 92*
**Deats,** Richard L. 1932- *WrDr 92*
**Deats,** Richard Louis 1932- *WhoRel 92*
**Deats,** Richard Warren 1945- *WhoEnt 92*
**DeAugustino-Todd,** Loyce 1928- *WhoBlA 92*
**Deaux,** George *DrAPF 91*
**Deave,** John James 1928- *Who 92*
**Deaven,** Dennis George 1937- *AmMWSc 92*
**Deaven,** Larry Lee 1940- *AmMWSc 92*
**Deaver,** Bascom Sine, Jr 1930- *AmMWSc 92*
**Deaver,** Bobby Gray 1932- *WhoAmL 92*
**Deaver,** Franklin Kennedy 1918- *AmMWSc 92*
**Deaver,** Julie Reece 1953- *SmATA 68 [port]*
**Deaver,** Phillip Lester 1952- *WhoAmL 92, WhoFI 92, WhoWest 92*
**Deavers,** Daniel Ronald 1943- *AmMWSc 92*
**Deavin,** Stanley Gwynne 1905- *Who 92*
**De Azevedo,** Lorenco 1958- *WhoHisp 92*
**Deb,** Arun K 1936- *AmMWSc 92*
**DeBacco,** R. *DrAPF 91*
**Debacker,** Hilda Spodheim 1924- *AmMWSc 92*
**De Backer-Van Ocken,** Rika 1923- *IntWW 91*
**DeBaets,** Timothy Joseph 1949- *WhoEnt 92*
**DeBakey,** Lois *AmMWSc 92*
**DeBakey,** Michael Ellis 1908- *AmMWSc 92, IntAu&W 91, IntWW 91, Who 92, WrDr 92*
**DeBakey,** Selma *AmMWSc 92*
**Debany,** Warren Harding, Jr 1955- *AmMWSc 92*
**De Baptiste,** Richard 1831-1901 *RelLAm 91*
**De Barbadillo,** John Joseph 1942- *AmMWSc 92*
**De Barbieri,** Mary Ann 1945- *WhoEnt 92*
**DeBard,** Roger 1941- *WhoFI 92*
**DeBardelaben,** Lola Alice 1945- *WhoFI 92*
**De Bardeleben,** Arthur 1918- *WhoAmL 92*
**DeBardeleben,** John F 1937- *AmMWSc 92*
**DeBardeleben,** John Thomas, Jr. 1926- *WhoFI 92*
**DeBarger,** David Michael 1944- *WhoEnt 92*
**DeBari,** Vincent A 1946- *AmMWSc 92*
**DeBartolo,** Edward J., Sr. 1919- *WhoMW 92*
**DeBartolo,** Edward John, Jr. 1946- *WhoMW 92, WhoWest 92*
**de Bary,** Paul Ambrose 1946- *WhoAmL 92*
**de Bary,** William Theodore 1919- *WhoRel 92*
**DeBas,** Haile T *AmMWSc 92*
**Debas,** Haile T. 1937- *WhoBlA 92, WhoWest 92*
**de Basto,** Gerald Arthur 1924- *Who 92*
**De Bault,** Lawrence Edward 1941- *AmMWSc 92*
**DeBaun,** Burt 1922- *WhoAmP 91*
**DeBaun,** Robert Matthew 1924- *AmMWSc 92*
**Debbasch,** Charles 1937- *IntWW 91*
**Debbeler,** John Michael 1955- *WhoAmL 92*
**Debbie Sue** 1961- *WhoEnt 92*
**Debe,** Mark K 1947- *AmMWSc 92*
**deBear,** Richard Stephen 1933- *WhoMW 92*
**DeBeaussaert,** Kenneth Joseph 1954- *WhoAmP 91*
**de Beauvoir,** Simone 1908-1986 *FacFETw [port]*
**De Beer,** Esmond Samuel d1990 *Who 92N*

**de Beer**, Gavin Rylands 1899-1972 *FacFETw*
**De Beer**, Zacharias Johannes 1928- *IntWW 91*
**deBeers**, John S. 1914- *WhoFI 92*
**DeBell**, Arthur Gerald 1912- *AmMWSc 92*
**DeBell**, Dean Shaffer 1942- *AmMWSc 92*
**de Bellaigue**, Eric 1931- *WhoFI 92*
**de Bellaigue**, Geoffrey 1931- *Who 92*
**De Benedetti**, Carlo 1934- *IntWW 91, Who 92*
**Debenedetti**, Pablo Gaston 1953- *AmMWSc 92*
**DeBenedetti**, Sergio 1912- *AmMWSc 92*
**De Benedictis**, Dario 1918- *WhoAmL 92*
**Debenham**, Alison 1903-1967 *TwCPaSc*
**Debenham**, Gilbert Ridley 1906- *Who 92*
**Debenham**, Ray Gene 1935- *WhoWest 92*
**Debenham Taylor**, John 1920- *Who 92*
**Deber**, Charles Michael 1942- *AmMWSc 92*
**DeBerg**, Betty Ann 1953- *WhoRel 92*
**DeBerge**, Gary Alan 1947- *WhoFI 92*
**DeBernardo**, Pasquale Frank 1940- *WhoAmP 91*
**de Berniere-Smart**, Reginald Piers A 1924- *Who 92*
**de Bernieres**, Louis 1954- *ConAu 133*
**DeBerry**, David Wayne 1946- *AmMWSc 92*
**DeBerry**, Dennis Charles 1932- *WhoAmL 92*
**Deberry**, Edmund 1781?-1859 *DcNCBi 2*
**DeBerry**, Lois M 1945- *WhoAmP 91*
**DeBerry**, Lois Marie 1945- *WhoBlA 92*
**De Bethune**, Andre Jacques 1919- *AmMWSc 92*
**DeBettignies**, Charles Wayne 1958- *WhoMW 92*
**Debevec**, Paul Timothy 1946- *AmMWSc 92*
**Debevoise**, Dickinson Richards 1924- *WhoAmL 92*
**Debeyre**, Guy Edouard Pierre Albert 1911- *IntWW 91*
**De Bhaldraithe**, Tomas 1916- *IntWW 91*
**Debiak**, Ted Walter 1944- *AmMWSc 92*
**DeBias**, Domenic Anthony 1925- *AmMWSc 92*
**Debicki**, Andrew Peter 1934- *WhoMW 92*
**Debierne**, Andre Louis 1874-1949 *FacFETw*
**de Blank**, Justin Robert 1927- *Who 92*
**De Blas**, Angel Luis 1950- *AmMWSc 92*
**DeBlase**, Anthony Frank 1942- *WhoWest 92*
**De Blasio**, Michael Peter 1937- *WhoFI 92*
**DeBlasio**, Susan Leach 1948- *WhoAmL 92*
**De Blasis**, Celeste 1946- *TwCWW 91, WrDr 92*
**De Blasis**, Celeste Ninette 1946- *IntAu&W 91*
**de Blasis**, James Michael 1931- *WhoEnt 92, WhoMW 92*
**De Bleser**, Willy 1934- *IntAu&W 91*
**DeBlieck**, Norman R 1926- *WhoAmP 91*
**De Blieu**, Martha Onuferko 1954- *IntAu&W 91*
**De Blieux**, Joseph Davis 1912- *WhoAmP 91*
**de Blij**, Harm J. 1935- *WrDr 92*
**DeBlois**, Ralph Walter 1922- *AmMWSc 92*
**Debnam**, Chadwick Basil 1950- *WhoBlA 92*
**Debnam**, Marjorie Boyd 1930- *WhoBlA 92*
**Debnam**, Waldman Eras 1897-1968 *DcNCBi 2*
**Debnar**, Tracey Lynn 1967- *WhoEnt 92*
**Debnath**, Lokenath 1935- *AmMWSc 92*
**Debnath**, Sadhana 1938- *AmMWSc 92*
**Debney**, George Charles, Jr 1939- *AmMWSc 92*
**Debo**, Angie 1890-1988 *BenetAL 91*
**DeBock**, Florent Alphonse 1924- *WhoFI 92*
**de Bode**, Oleg 1956- *WhoWest 92*
**de Boer**, Anthony Peter 1918- *Who 92*
**DeBoer**, Benjamin 1911- *AmMWSc 92*
**DeBoer**, Edward Dale 1955- *AmMWSc 92*
**DeBoer**, Gerrit 1942- *AmMWSc 92*
**DeBoer**, James Ronald 1956- *WhoRel 92*
**Deboer**, Jay Wayne 1953- *WhoAmP 91*
**DeBoer**, Jelle 1934- *AmMWSc 92*
**DeBoer**, Kenneth F 1938- *AmMWSc 92*
**De Boer**, P C Tobias 1930- *AmMWSc 92*
**DeBoer**, Randall Lee 1958- *WhoMW 92*
**De Boer**, Solke Harmen 1948- *AmMWSc 92*
**de Boer**, Thymen Jan 1924- *IntWW 91*
**DeBois**, James Adolphus 1929- *WhoFI 92*
**de Boissiere**, Ralph 1907- *ConNov 91, WrDr 92*
**De Bold**, Adolfo J 1942- *AmMWSc 92*
**DeBold**, Joseph Francis 1947- *AmMWSc 92*
**De Bolt**, Donald Walter 1952- *WhoWest 92*
**DeBolt**, Edward S 1938- *WhoAmP 91*
**DeBolt**, Mark Wilson 1954- *WhoMW 92*
**DeBolt**, Virginia Faye 1941- *WhoWest 92*
**DeBon**, George A. *WhoWest 92*
**DeBona**, Bruce Todd 1945- *AmMWSc 92*
**DeBonis**, Anthony, Jr 1950- *WhoAmP 91*
**De Bonis**, Donato 1930- *IntWW 91*
**DeBonis**, Michael A 1912- *WhoAmP 91*
**De Bono**, Edward 1933- *IntAu&W 91, SmATA 66 [port], WrDr 92*
**de Bono**, Edward Francis Charles Publius 1933- *IntWW 91, Who 92*
**De Bono**, Emilio 1866-1944 *BiDExR*
**Debono**, Manuel 1936- *AmMWSc 92*
**Debons**, Albert Frank 1929- *AmMWSc 92*
**de Bont**, Otto K M 1945- *WhoIns 92*
**Deboo**, Phili B 1934- *AmMWSc 92*
**De Boor**, Carl 1937- *AmMWSc 92*
**Deborah** *EncAmaz 91*
**DeBord**, Jerry L 1943- *WhoAmP 91*
**de Bordeaux**, Gilles Thierry 1955- *WhoWest 92*
**Deborin**, Abram Moyseevich 1881-1963 *FacFETw*
**De Born**, Edith *IntAu&W 91*
**de Botton**, Gilbert 1935- *Who 92*
**Debouck**, Christine Marie 1956- *AmMWSc 92*
**DeBow**, John 1745?-1783 *DcNCBi 2*
**DeBow**, W Brad 1948- *AmMWSc 92*
**DeBra**, Daniel Brown 1930- *AmMWSc 92*
**DeBracy**, Warren 1942- *WhoBlA 92*
**Debrah**, Ebenezer Moses 1928- *IntWW 91*
**DeBrahm**, John Gerar William *BiInAmS*
**DeBrahm**, William Gerard 1717-1799? *BiInAmS*
**Debray**, Regis 1940- *IntWW 91*
**Debre**, Michel 1912- *IntWW 91*
**Debre**, Michel Jean-Pierre 1912- *Who 92*
**Debreczeny**, Paul 1932- *IntAu&W 91, WrDr 92*
**De Bremaecker**, Jean-Claude 1923- *AmMWSc 92*
**Debreu**, Gerard 1921- *AmMWSc 92, IntWW 91, Who 92, WhoFI 92, WhoNob 90, WhoWest 92, WrDr 92*
**DeBrincat**, Susan Jeanne 1943- *WhoMW 92*
**Debro**, Jesse, III 1935- *WhoAmP 91*
**Debro**, Joseph Rollins 1928- *WhoBlA 92*
**Debro**, Julius 1931- *WhoBlA 92*
**de Broca**, Philippe *IntDcF 2-2*
**De Broca**, Philippe 1933- *IntMPA 92*
**de Broglie**, Gabriel Marie Joseph Anselme 1931- *IntWW 91*
**de Broglie**, Louis Victor Pierre Raymond 1892-1987 *FacFETw*
**de Broke** *Who 92*
**Debrovner**, Steven *WhoIns 92*
**Debroy**, Chitrita *AmMWSc 92*
**Debroy**, Tarasankar 1946- *AmMWSc 92*
**DeBruin**, Kenneth Edward 1942- *AmMWSc 92*
**DeBruler**, Roger O. 1934- *WhoAmL 92, WhoAmP 91, WhoMW 92*
**DeBrunner**, Louis Earl 1935- *AmMWSc 92*
**DeBrunner**, Marjorie R 1927- *AmMWSc 92*
**Debrunner**, Peter Georg 1931- *AmMWSc 92*
**DeBrunner**, Ralph Edward 1932- *AmMWSc 92*
**DeBruycker**, Jane 1936- *WhoAmP 91*
**DeBruycker**, Roger 1936- *WhoAmP 91*
**De Bruyn**, Peter Paul Henry 1910- *AmMWSc 92*
**de Bruyne**, Dirk 1920- *IntWW 91, Who 92*
**de Bruyne**, Norman Adrian 1904- *Who 92*
**De Bruyne**, Peter 1928- *AmMWSc 92*
**Debs**, Eugene V. 1855-1926 *BenetAL 91, FacFETw [port], RComAH*
**Debs**, Eugene Victor 1855-1926 *AmPeW, AmPolLe [port]*
**Debs**, Richard A. 1930- *WhoFI 92*
**Debs**, Robert Joseph 1919- *AmMWSc 92*
**Debski**, Maryann Alberta 1952- *WhoAmL 92*
**Debu-Bridel**, Jacques 1902- *IntWW 91*
**Debuchananne**, George D 1919- *AmMWSc 92*
**Debuda**, Rudolf G 1924- *AmMWSc 92*
**De Buhr**, Larry Eugene 1948- *AmMWSc 92*
**DeBunda**, Salvatore Michael 1943- *WhoAmL 92, WhoEnt 92*
**De Bunsen**, Bernard d1990 *IntWW 91N*
**De Burgos**, Rafael Frubeck *NewAmDM*
**Debus**, Allen George 1926- *AmMWSc 92, IntAu&W 91, WrDr 92*
**Debus**, Eleanor Viola 1920- *WhoEnt 92, WhoWest 92*
**Debus**, Kurt Heinrich 1908-1983 *FacFETw*
**DeBusk**, A Gib 1927- *AmMWSc 92*
**Debusman**, Paul Marshall 1932- *WhoRel 92*
**DeBussey**, Fred Woods 1944- *WhoFI 92*
**Debussy**, Claude 1862-1918 *NewAmDM*
**Debussy**, Claude-Achille 1862-1918 *FacFETw [port]*
**De Butts**, Frederick Manus 1916- *Who 92*
**Deby**, Idriss *IntWW 91*
**Deby**, John Bedford 1931- *Who 92*
**Debye**, Nordulf Wiking Gerud 1943- *AmMWSc 92*
**Debye**, Peter Josephus Wilhelmus 1884-1966 *WhoNob 90*
**DeByle**, Norbert V 1931- *AmMWSc 92*
**De Caesar**, Gabriel 1928- *IntMPA 92*
**DeCair**, Thomas Palmer 1945- *WhoAmP 91*
**Decaminada**, Joseph P 1935- *WhoIns 92*
**de Camp**, Catherine Crook 1907- *IntAu&W 91, WrDr 92*
**DeCamp**, Clifford Lee 1958- *WhoAmL 92*
**DeCamp**, Harold Lewis 1952- *WhoRel 92*
**Decamp**, John William 1941- *WhoAmP 91*
**de Camp**, L Sprague 1907- *IntAu&W 91, TwCSFW 91, WrDr 92*
**de Camp**, L. Strague 1907- *BenetAL 91*
**DeCamp**, Mark Rutledge 1946- *AmMWSc 92*
**DeCamp**, Paul Trumbull 1915- *AmMWSc 92*
**De Camp**, Rosemary 1913- *IntMPA 92*
**DeCamp**, Rosemary Shirley 1910- *WhoEnt 92*
**De Camp**, Wilson Hamilton 1936- *AmMWSc 92*
**DeCamps**, Charles Michael 1950- *WhoAmL 92*
**De Cani**, John Stapley 1924- *AmMWSc 92*
**De Caprio**, Al *IntMPA 92*
**De Carbonnel**, Francois Eric 1946- *WhoFI 92*
**De Cardenas**, Gilbert Lorenzo 1941- *WhoHisp 92*
**de Cardi**, Beatrice Eileen 1914- *Who 92*
**DeCaria**, Michael Dee 1946- *WhoWest 92*
**Decaris**, Albert Marius Hippolyte d1988 *IntWW 91N*
**De Carli**, Carlo 1910-1971 *DcTwDes*
**DeCarlo**, Candia Susan 1958- *WhoMW 92*
**De Carlo**, Charles R 1921- *AmMWSc 92*
**DeCarlo**, Donald Thomas *WhoAmL 92*
**De Carlo**, John, Jr 1918- *AmMWSc 92*
**DeCarlo**, Michael 1960- *WhoAmL 92*
**De Carlo**, Yvonne 1922- *IntMPA 92*
**de Carmoy**, Herve Pierre 1937- *Who 92*
**DeCaro**, A. Roy 1949- *WhoAmL 92*
**DeCaro**, Thomas F 1919- *AmMWSc 92*
**DeCarolis**, Mary Ann *WhoAmL 92*
**Decas**, Charles N 1937- *WhoAmP 91*
**Decas**, George Charles 1937- *WhoAmP 91*
**de Castella**, Robert 1957- *IntWW 91*
**de Castries**, Christian de la Croix 1902-1991? *NewYTBS 91 [port]*
**DeCastro**, Arthur 1911- *AmMWSc 92*
**De Castro**, Eduardo Charpentier *WhoEnt 92A*
**De Castro**, German *WhoHisp 92*
**De Castro**, Godfrey R 1922- *WhoAmP 91*
**de Castro**, Julian Edmund 1930- *WhoAmL 92*
**De Castro**, Julio O. 1959- *WhoHisp 92*
**De Castro Font**, Jorge *WhoAmP 91*
**Decatur**, Robert A. 1924- *WhoBlA 92*
**Decatur**, Stephen 1779-1820 *BenetAL 91*
**Decaux**, Alain 1925- *IntWW 91*
**Deccio**, Alex A 1927- *WhoAmP 91*
**Decedue**, Charles Joseph 1944- *AmMWSc 92*
**Decelle**, Paul A 1921- *WhoAmP 91*
**De Celles**, Charles Edouard 1942- *WhoRel 92*
**DeCesare**, Donald Emilio 1947- *WhoFI 92*
**DeCesare**, Gary Edward 1945- *WhoAmL 92*
**DeCesare**, James Charles 1931- *WhoFI 92*
**de Cespedes**, Carlos M. *WhoHisp 92*
**DeChaine**, Dean Dennis 1936- *WhoAmL 92*
**De Chair**, Somerset 1911- *IntAu&W 91, Who 92, WrDr 92*
**DeChalmot**, Guillaume Louis Jacques d1899 *BiInAmS*
**De Champlain**, Jacques 1938- *AmMWSc 92*
**Dechant**, Virgil C. 1930- *WhoRel 92*
**Dechario**, Tony Houston 1940- *WhoEnt 92, WhoWest 92*
**de Chassiron**, Charles Richard Lucien 1948- *Who 92*
**de Chazal**, Claire Denise 1955- *WhoAmL 92*
**De Chazal**, L E Marc 1921- *AmMWSc 92*
**Dechene**, James Charles 1953- *WhoAmL 92, WhoFI 92, WhoMW 92*
**Dechene**, Lucy Irene 1950- *AmMWSc 92*
**Decher**, Rudolf 1927- *AmMWSc 92*
**Decherd**, Robert William 1951- *WhoEnt 92, WhoFI 92*
**Dechert**, Michael Salvatore Alfred 1958- *WhoFI 92*
**Dechert**, Peter 1924- *WhoWest 92*
**de Chevigny**, Robert *WhoRel 92*
**Dechter**, Bradley Graham 1956- *WhoEnt 92*
**DeCicco**, Benedict Thomas 1938- *AmMWSc 92*
**DeCicco**, Yvonne Angela 1960- *WhoMW 92*
**Decies**, Baron 1915- *Who 92*
**Decima**, Terry *WhoEnt 92*
**Decio**, Arthur Julius 1930- *WhoFI 92, WhoMW 92*
**Decius** 201-251 *EncEarC*
**Decius**, Gerald William 1942- *WhoMW 92*
**Decius**, John Courtney 1920- *AmMWSc 92*
**deCiutiis**, Alfred Charles Maria 1945- *WhoWest 92*
**de Ciutiis**, Vincent Louis 1924- *WhoWest 92*
**Deck**, Allan Figueroa 1945- *WhoHisp 92*
**Deck**, Armida Amparo 1941- *WhoHisp 92*
**Deck**, Charles Francis 1930- *AmMWSc 92*
**Deck**, Howard Joseph 1938- *AmMWSc 92*
**Deck**, James David 1930- *AmMWSc 92*
**Deck**, Joseph Charles 1936- *AmMWSc 92*
**Deck**, Joseph Francis 1907- *AmMWSc 92*
**Deck**, Robert Thomas 1935- *AmMWSc 92, WhoMW 92*
**Deck**, Ronald Joseph 1934- *AmMWSc 92*
**Deckard**, Edward Lee 1943- *AmMWSc 92*
**Deckard**, Jerry 1942- *WhoAmP 91*
**Deckard**, Loren Dean 1939- *WhoRel 92*
**Decker**, Alvin Morris, Jr 1918- *AmMWSc 92*
**Decker**, Arthur John 1941- *AmMWSc 92*
**Decker**, Bernard Martin 1904- *WhoAmL 92, WhoMW 92*
**Decker**, Bob 1922- *WhoAmP 91*
**Decker**, C David 1945- *AmMWSc 92*
**Decker**, Carl Murray 1955- *WhoWest 92*
**Decker**, Clarence Ferdinand 1925- *AmMWSc 92*
**Decker**, Clifford Earl, Jr 1941- *AmMWSc 92*
**Decker**, Dallas Burr 1939- *WhoRel 92*
**Decker**, Daniel Lorenzo 1929- *AmMWSc 92*
**Decker**, David Garrison 1917- *AmMWSc 92*
**Decker**, David Lee 1946- *WhoRel 92*
**Decker**, Donna *DrAPF 91*
**Decker**, Esther Lorraine 1919- *WhoMW 92*
**Decker**, Franz Paul *WhoEnt 92*
**Decker**, Franz-Paul 1923- *NewAmDM*
**Decker**, Fred William 1917- *AmMWSc 92*
**Decker**, George David 1955- *WhoRel 92*
**Decker**, Gloria Ann 1932- *WhoAmP 91*
**Decker**, Guy Taiho Tai 1964- *WhoFI 92*
**Decker**, James Federick 1940- *AmMWSc 92*
**Decker**, James Harrison, Jr. 1948- *WhoAmL 92*
**Decker**, James Ludlow 1923- *WhoFI 92*
**Decker**, James Thomas 1944- *WhoWest 92*
**Decker**, Jane M 1935- *AmMWSc 92*
**Decker**, Joey 1955- *WhoEnt 92*
**Decker**, John Alvin, Jr. 1935- *WhoWest 92*
**Decker**, John D 1922- *AmMWSc 92*
**Decker**, John Laws 1921- *AmMWSc 92*
**Decker**, John Louis 1946- *WhoAmL 92*
**Decker**, John P 1925- *AmMWSc 92*
**Decker**, John Peter 1915- *AmMWSc 92*
**Decker**, John Robert 1952- *WhoAmL 92*
**Decker**, John William 1948- *WhoMW 92*
**Decker**, Kurt Hans 1946- *WhoAmL 92, WhoFI 92*
**Decker**, L H 1913- *AmMWSc 92*
**Decker**, Lucile Ellen 1927- *AmMWSc 92*
**Decker**, Michael Lynn 1953- *WhoAmL 92*
**Decker**, Michael P *WhoAmP 91*
**Decker**, Peter William 1919- *WhoMW 92*
**Decker**, Quintin William 1930- *AmMWSc 92*
**Decker**, R F 1930- *AmMWSc 92*
**Decker**, Richard H 1934- *AmMWSc 92*
**Decker**, Richard Jeffrey 1959- *WhoAmL 92*
**Decker**, Richard Kelsey 1927- *WhoWest 92*
**Decker**, Robert Dean 1933- *AmMWSc 92*
**Decker**, Robert Scott 1942- *AmMWSc 92*
**Decker**, Robert Wayne 1927- *AmMWSc 92*
**Decker**, Rolan Van 1936- *AmMWSc 92*
**Decker**, Russell S *WhoAmP 91*
**Decker**, Thomas Andrew 1946- *WhoAmL 92*
**Decker**, Thomas Edwin 1950- *WhoMW 92*
**Decker**, Walter Johns 1933- *AmMWSc 92*
**Decker**, Wayne Leroy 1922- *AmMWSc 92*
**Decker**, Will 1899-1945 *EncTR 91*
**Decker**, William *DrAPF 91*
**Decker**, William 1926- *TwCWW 91, WrDr 92*
**Decker**, Winston M 1923- *AmMWSc 92*
**Decker-Rodriguez**, Patricia Anne 1956- *WhoEnt 92*
**Deckers**, Jacques 1927- *AmMWSc 92*
**Deckert**, Cheryl A 1948- *AmMWSc 92*
**Deckert**, Curtis Kenneth 1939- *AmMWSc 92, WhoWest 92*
**Deckert**, Fred W 1943- *AmMWSc 92*

Deckert, Gordon Harmon 1930- AmMWSc 92
Deckert, Harlan Kennedy, Jr. 1923- WhoWest 92
Deckert, Mary Lynne 1959- WhoMW 92
Deckker, B E L 1918- AmMWSc 92
Deckter, Louis Larry 1941- WhoAmL 92
De Clara, Roberto 1955- WhoEnt 92
DeClaris, N 1931- AmMWSc 92
DeClerck, Timothy Edward 1956- WhoAmL 92
De Clercq, Jeroom Gustaaf 1884-1942 BiDExR
De Clercq, Willy 1927- Who 92
Decles, Jon 1941- IntAu&W 91
de Clifford, Baron 1928- Who 92
DeClue, Anita WhoBlA 92
DeClue, Jim W AmMWSc 92
DeCock, Hendrick DcAmImH
DeConcini, Dennis 1937- AlmAP 92 [port], IntWW 91, WhoAmP 91, WhoWest 92
de Conte, Sieur Louis ConAu 135
DeCook, Kenneth James 1925- AmMWSc 92
Decora, Andrew Wayne 1928- AmMWSc 92
De Cordova, Denise 1957- TwCPaSc
deCordova, Fred LesBEnT 92
De Cordova, Frederick 1910- IntMPA 92
de Cordova, Frederick Timmins 1910- WhoEnt 92
deCormier-Shekerjian, Regina DrAPF 91
Decorpo, James Joseph 1942- AmMWSc 92
Decossas, Kenneth Miles 1925- AmMWSc 92
DeCosse, Jerome J 1928- AmMWSc 92
DeCosta, Edwin J 1906- AmMWSc 92
DeCosta, Herbert Alexander, Jr. 1923- WhoBlA 92
DeCosta, Peter F AmMWSc 92
DeCosta-Willis, Miriam 1934- WhoBlA 92
De Coteau, Denis WhoEnt 92
de Cotret, Robert Rene 1944- IntWW 91, WhoFI 92
de Cou, Emil WhoEnt 92
de Courcy Who 92
de Courcy, Kenneth Hugh 1909- Who 92
De Courcy, Samuel Joseph, Jr 1918- AmMWSc 92
de Courcy-Ireland, Patrick Gault 1933- Who 92
de Courcy Ling, John 1933- Who 92
DeCoursey, Donn G 1934- AmMWSc 92
DeCoursey, Russell Myles 1900- AmMWSc 92
DeCoursey, Thomas Eric 1951- WhoMW 92
DeCoursey, W J 1930- AmMWSc 92
Decourtray, Albert 1923- IntWW 91, WhoRel 92
DeCoux, Beverlee Ann 1947- WhoFI 92
Decowski, Piotr 1940- AmMWSc 92
Decraene, Denis Fredrick 1942- AmMWSc 92
De Craene, Jacques Maria 1929- WhoFI 92
DeCramer, Gary M 1944- WhoAmP 91
DeCrane, Alfred C., Jr. 1931- IntWW 91
DeCrane, Alfred Charles, Jr. 1931- WhoFI 92
DeCrane, Vincent Francis 1927- WhoMW 92
DeCredico, Mary A. 1959- ConAu 135
de Creeft, Jose 1884-1982 CurBio 91N
DeCresce, Robert Patrick 1949- WhoMW 92
de Crescentis, James DrAPF 91
De Crescentis, James 1948- IntAu&W 91
De Crescenzo, Luciano 1928- ConAu 133
De Crespigny, Philip Champion, Mrs. d1935 ScFEYrs
De Crespigny, Rafe 1936- IntAu&W 91, WrDr 92
DeCristoforo, Romeo John 1917- WrDr 92
Decroce, Alex 1936- WhoAmP 91
DeCrosta, Edward Francis, Jr 1926- AmMWSc 92
DeCrosta, Susan Elyse 1956- WhoEnt 92
Decroux, Etienne d1991 NewYTBS 91 [port]
DeCrow, Karen 1937- WrDr 92
Decrow, Sarah Moore Delano 1750?-1795 DcNCBi 2
Decter, Midge 1927- WrDr 92
De Cuir, John 1918- IntMPA 92
DeCuir, John F, Jr. 1941- IntMPA 92
Decuir, Joseph Charles 1950- WhoWest 92
Decuir, Oswald A 1940- WhoAmP 91
DeCurtis, Anthony 1951- WhoEnt 92
DeDanaan, Llyn Patterson 1942- WhoWest 92
Deddeh, Wadie Peter 1920- WhoAmP 91
Deddens, J C 1928- AmMWSc 92
Deddens, James Albert 1943- AmMWSc 92
Dedeaux, Paul J. 1937- WhoWest 92
DeDecker, Hendrik Kamiel Johannes 1915- AmMWSc 92
de Deney, Geoffrey Ivor 1931- Who 92
De Deo, Joseph E. 1936- IntWW 91
Dederer, Michael Eugene 1932- WhoFI 92
Dederer, William Bowne 1945- WhoEnt 92
Dederich-Pejovich, Susan Russell 1951- WhoEnt 92
Dederick, Robert Gogan 1929- WhoFI 92, WhoMW 92
Dedert, Steven Ray 1953- WhoMW 92
Dedeurwaerder, Jose Joseph 1932- IntWW 91, WhoFI 92
Dedeyan, Charles 1910- IntWW 91
Dedhar, Shoukat 1952- AmMWSc 92
Dedijer, Vladimir d1990 IntWW 91N, Who 92N
Dedijer, Vladimir 1914-1990 ConAu 133
Dedinas, Jonas 1929- AmMWSc 92
Dedini, Eldon Lawrence 1921- WhoEnt 92, WhoWest 92
Dedinsky, Mary Lee 1948- WhoMW 92
de Dios Unanue, Manuel 1943-1992 WhoHisp 92N
Dedman, John Raymond 1947- AmMWSc 92
Dedmon, George Leroy 1939- WhoRel 92
DeDominicis, Alex John 1935- AmMWSc 92
DeDona, Francis Alfred 1924- WhoFI 92
DeDonato, Donald Michael 1952- WhoMW 92
DeDonder, Eugene Francis 1953- WhoMW 92
Dedrick, Jay Warner 1965- WhoEnt 92
Dedrick, Kent Gentry 1923- AmMWSc 92
Dedrick, Robert L 1933- AmMWSc 92
De Duve, Christian Rene 1917- AmMWSc 92, IntWW 91
de Duve, Christian Rene Marie Joseph 1917- Who 92, WhoNob 90
Dee, David Alan 1957- WhoAmL 92
Dee, Diana 1944- AmMWSc 92
Dee, John 1938- TwCPaSc
Dee, Lisa Denise 1957- WhoEnt 92
Dee, Martha Brisco 1947- WhoMW 92
Dee, Merri 1936- WhoBlA 92
Dee, Ralph, Jr. 1961- WhoFI 92, WhoWest 92
Dee, Ruby WhoBlA 92, WhoEnt 92
Dee, Ruby 1924?- ConTFT 9, IntMPA 92, NotBlAW 92
Dee, Sandra 1942- IntMPA 92
Deebel, George Franklin 1911- WhoAmP 91
Deech, Ruth Lynn 1943- Who 92
Deed, Basil Lingard d1991 Who 92N
Deedes Who 92
Deedes, Baron 1913- IntWW 91, Who 92
Deedes, Charles Julius 1913- Who 92
Deeds, Moses Earnshaw 1932- WhoRel 92
Deeds, Robert Creigh 1958- WhoAmL 92
Deeds, William Edward 1920- AmMWSc 92
Deedwania, Prakash Chandra 1948- AmMWSc 92
Deedy, John Gerard 1923- IntAu&W 91
Deeg, Emil W 1926- AmMWSc 92
Deeg, Emil Wolfgang 1926- WhoFI 92
Deeg, Peter 1908- EncTR 91
Deegan, John Edward 1935- WhoRel 92
Deegan, Joseph William 1899- Who 92
Deegan, Linda Ann 1954- AmMWSc 92
Deegan, Michael J 1942- AmMWSc 92
Deegan, Rose Mary Groetken 1917- WhoAmP 91
Deegan, Ross Alfred 1941- AmMWSc 92
Deegear, James Otis, III 1948- WhoAmL 92
Deehan, Paul Gerard 1959- WhoAmL 92
Deehr, Charles Sterling 1936- AmMWSc 92
Deeik, Khalil George 1937- WhoFI 92
Deekens, Elizabeth Tupman 1926- WhoRel 92
Deel, Bruce Lynn 1960- WhoRel 92
Deeley, Edward Joseph 1956- WhoFI 92
Deeley, Mary Katharine 1951- WhoRel 92
Deeley, Michael 1932- IntMPA 92, Who 92
Deeley, Roger Graham 1946- AmMWSc 92
Deely, John Joseph AmMWSc 92
Deem, Harlan Lee 1930- WhoRel 92
Deem, J Frank, Jr 1928- WhoAmP 91
Deem, Mary Lease 1937- AmMWSc 92
Deem, William Brady 1939- AmMWSc 92
Deemer, Bill DrAPF 91
Deemer, Charles DrAPF 91
Deemer, Marie Nieft AmMWSc 92
Deeming, Terence James 1937- AmMWSc 92
Deems, Andrew William 1946- WhoWest 92
Deems, Barrett Bruce 1915- WhoEnt 92
Deems, Charles Force 1820-1893 DcNCBi 2
Deems, Robert Eugene 1927- AmMWSc 92
Deen, David Lewis, III 1944- WhoAmP 91
Deen, Dennis Frank 1944- AmMWSc 92
Deen, Harold E 1926- AmMWSc 92
Deen, James Robert 1944- AmMWSc 92
Deen, Jesse C 1922- WhoAmP 91
Deen, Mohamed Jamal 1955- AmMWSc 92
Deen, Robert C 1929- AmMWSc 92
Deen, Thomas B 1928- AmMWSc 92
Deen, William Murray 1947- AmMWSc 92
Deener, David R. 1920-1976 ConAu 134
Deener, Larry Colby 1950- WhoAmL 92
Deep Purple NewAmDM
Deep, Ira Washington 1927- AmMWSc 92
Deepak, Adarsh 1936- AmMWSc 92
Deer, Ada Elizabeth 1935- WhoAmP 91
Deer, Frederick 1910- Who 92
Deer, James Willis 1917- WhoAmL 92, WhoFI 92
Deer, M. J. WrDr 92
Deer, Richard Elliott 1932- WhoAmL 92
Deer, Sandra Sims 1940- WhoEnt 92
Deer, William Alexander 1910- IntWW 91, Who 92
Deere, Don U 1922- AmMWSc 92
Deerhurst, Viscount 1957- Who 92
Deering, Carl F 1959- AmMWSc 92
Deering, Fred A 1928- WhoIns 92
Deering, Fred Arthur 1928- WhoWest 92
Deering, Frederick Henry 1923- WhoAmP 91
Deering, Patrick Dennis 1956- WhoAmL 92
Deering, Reginald 1932- AmMWSc 92
Deering, Richard NewAmDM
Deering, Ronald Franklin 1929- WhoRel 92
Deering, Terry W WhoAmP 91
Deering, William Dougless 1933- AmMWSc 92
Deerson, Bruce Alan 1951- WhoFI 92
Deery, Sandy DrAPF 91
Dees, Anse 1920- WhoAmP 91
Dees, Bowen Causey 1917- IntWW 91
Dees, C. Stanley 1938- WhoAmL 92
Dees, J W 1933- AmMWSc 92
Dees, James Parker 1915- WhoRel 92
Dees, Michael Kenneth 1952- WhoAmP 91
Dees, Morris 1936- News 92-1 [port]
Dees, Morris Seligman, Jr. 1936- WhoAmL 92
Dees, Richard Lee 1955- WhoAmL 92
Dees, Rick WhoEnt 92
Dees, Robert Michael 1962- WhoAmL 92
Dees, Susan Coons 1909- AmMWSc 92
Deese, David Fred 1947- WhoEnt 92
Deese, Dawson Charles 1929- AmMWSc 92
Deese, Manuel 1941- WhoBlA 92
Deeter, Charles Raymond 1930- AmMWSc 92
Deetman, Bernard Richard 1955- WhoAmL 92
Deetman, Willem Joost 1945- IntWW 91
Deets, Gary Lee 1943- AmMWSc 92
Deets, Horace 1938- WhoFI 92
Deetz, Lawrence Edward, III 1951- AmMWSc 92
Deever, David Livingstone 1939- AmMWSc 92
Deevey, Edward Smith, Jr 1914- AmMWSc 92
Deezen, Edward Harry 1957- WhoEnt 92
DeFabis, Mike 1932- WhoFI 92
DeFacio, W Brian 1936- AmMWSc 92
DeFalaise, Louis 1945- WhoAmL 92
DeFalaise, Louis Gaylord 1945- WhoAmP 91
De Falla NewAmDM
DeFanti, David R 1932- AmMWSc 92
DeFanti, Thomas A 1948- AmMWSc 92
de Faria, Antonio Leite 1904- Who 92
de Farrell, Pauline WhoHisp 92
Defauw, Desire 1885-1960 NewAmDM
DeFazio, Lynette Stevens 1930- WhoEnt 92, WhoWest 92
De Fazio, Marjorie DrAPF 91
DeFazio, Peter A. 1947- AlmAP 92 [port], WhoAmP 91, WhoWest 92
De Fazio, Thomas Luca 1940- AmMWSc 92
Defebaugh, James Elliott 1926- WhoAmP 91
Defeis, Elizabeth Frances WhoAmL 92
DeFelice, Eugene Anthony 1927- AmMWSc 92
DeFelice, Jonathan Peter 1947- WhoRel 92
DeFelice, Joyce Henrietta 1951- WhoWest 92
De Felice, Louis John 1940- AmMWSc 92
De Felice, Sally Ann 1947- WhoWest 92
De Felitta, Frank Paul WhoEnt 92
Defenbaugh, Richard Eugene 1946- AmMWSc 92
Defendi, Vittorio 1928- AmMWSc 92
DeFeo, John Eugene 1946- WhoWest 92
DeFeo, John Joseph 1922- AmMWSc 92
DeFeo, Stephen Joseph 1960- WhoAmL 92
De Feo, Vincent Joseph 1925- AmMWSc 92
de Ferranti, Sebastian Basil Joseph Z 1927- Who 92
De Ferranti, Sebastian Ziani 1927- IntWW 91
De Ferrari, Gabriella ConLC 65 [port]
DeFerrari, Harry Austin 1937- AmMWSc 92
Deferre, Gaston 1910-1986 FacFETw
De Ferreire, Mary Elizabeth 1949- WhoHisp 92
Deffaa, Chip 1951- WhoEnt 92
Deffand, Marie de Vichy, marquise du 1697-1780 BlkwCEP
Deffenbacher, Mark Edwin 1945- WhoRel 92
Deffeyes, Kenneth Stover 1931- AmMWSc 92
De Fiebre, Conrad William 1924- AmMWSc 92
DeFigio, Daniel A 1939- AmMWSc 92
De Figueiredo, Rui J P 1929- AmMWSc 92
DeFilippi, Louis J 1949- AmMWSc 92
De Filippi, R P 1936- AmMWSc 92
DeFilippi, Walter Arthur 1926- WhoAmP 91
De Filippis, Daisy Cocco 1949- WhoHisp 92
DeFilipps, Robert Anthony 1939- AmMWSc 92
DeFino, Anthony Michael 1936- WhoAmP 91
Defino, Joseph Francis 1952- WhoAmL 92
DeFiore, Leonard F. WhoRel 92
Deflassieux, Jean Sebastien 1925- IntWW 91
Defoe, Daniel 1660?-1731 BlkwCEP, CnDBLB 2 [port], RfGEnL 91, ScFEYrs
DeFoe, Mark DrAPF 91
Defoggi, Ernest AmMWSc 92
DeFoliart, Gene Ray 1925- AmMWSc 92
de Fonblanque, John Robert 1943- Who 92
Defontenay, Charlemagne Ischir 1819-1856 ScFEYrs
de Fonville, Paul Bliss 1923- WhoWest 92
DeFoor, David Martin 1959- WhoRel 92
DeFoor, James Allison, II 1953- WhoAmL 92
DeFoor, John Allen 1961- WhoEnt 92
DeFoor, Keith Alex 1960- WhoEnt 92
Defoor, Nathan Dwight 1952- WhoEnt 92
DeFoor, W. Robert 1941- WhoRel 92
DeFord, Donald Dale 1918- AmMWSc 92
Deford, Frank 1938- IntAu&W 91, WhoEnt 92, WrDr 92
DeFord, John W 1936- AmMWSc 92
deFord, Miriam Allen 1888-1975 TwCSFW 91
De Ford, Ronald K 1902- AmMWSc 92
Deford, Sara Whitcraft 1916- IntAu&W 91
Deforest, Adamadia 1933- AmMWSc 92
De Forest, Edgar Lester WhoEnt 92, WhoWest 92
DeForest, Elbert M 1917- AmMWSc 92
DeForest, Erastus Lyman 1834-1888 BiInAmS
De Forest, John W. 1826-1906 BenetAL 91
DeForest, Lee d1961 LesBEnT 92
De Forest, Lee 1873-1961 FacFETw
DeForest, Orrin L. 1923- ConAu 134
DeForest, Peter Rupert 1941- AmMWSc 92
De Forest, Ralph Edwin 1919- AmMWSc 92
DeForest, Robert W 1848-1931 DcAmImH
De Forest, Roy 1930- WorArt 1980
DeForest, Walter Pattison, III 1944- WhoAmL 92
DeForrest, Jack M 1951- AmMWSc 92
De Fossett, William K. 1920- WhoBlA 92
DeFotis, Gary Constantine 1947- AmMWSc 92
DeFouw, David O 1945- AmMWSc 92
DeFouw, Eugene Allen 1941- WhoFI 92
DeFrance, Jon Fredric 1943- AmMWSc 92
De France, Joseph J 1909- AmMWSc 92
De Francesco, Laura 1948- AmMWSc 92
De Francia, Peter 1921- TwCPaSc
de Francia, Peter Laurent 1921- Who 92
DeFrancisco, Anne Elizabeth 1944- WhoFI 92
DeFranco, Boniface Ferdinand Leonard 1923- WhoEnt 92
DeFranco, Buddy 1923- NewAmDM
DeFranco, Ronald James 1943- AmMWSc 92
DeFrank, Joseph J 1946- AmMWSc 92
DeFrantz, Anita Luceete 1952- BlkOlyM [port]
De Frees, Madeline DrAPF 91
DeFrees, Madeline 1919- WrDr 92
De Freyne, Baron 1927- Who 92
DeFries, John Clarence 1934- AmMWSc 92
De Fuentes, Fernando 1894-1958 IntDcF 2-2 [port]

**Dega,** Mary Benedicta 1934- *WhoRel 92*
**Dega,** Wiktor 1896- *IntWW 91*
**DeGabriele,** Linda Marie 1949- *WhoMW 92*
**De Gaetani,** Jan 1933-1989 *NewAmDM*
**de Gara,** Paul F. d1991 *NewYTBS 91*
**de Garcia,** Lucia 1941- *WhoHisp 92*
**De Garcia,** Orlando Frank 1947- *WhoHisp 92*
**De Garidel,** Marc Patrick 1958- *WhoMW 92*
**DeGarmo,** Lindley Grant 1953- *WhoFI 92*
**DeGarmo,** Mark Borden *WhoEnt 92*
**Degas,** Hilaire-Germain-Edgar 1834-1917 *ThHElm [port]*
**De Gasperi,** Alcide 1881-1954 *FacFETw*
**De Gaston,** Alexis Neal *AmMWSc 92*
**De Gaulle,** Charles *EncTR 91*
**De Gaulle,** Charles 1890-1970 *FacFETw*
**Degazon,** Frederick *IntWW 91*
**De Geer,** Carl 1923- *IntWW 91*
**de Geer,** Derek Jan 1870-1960 *FacFETw*
**Degen,** Bernard John, II 1937- *WhoAmP 91*
**Degen,** Larry Robert 1954- *WhoFI 92*
**Degen,** Vladimir 1931- *AmMWSc 92*
**Degen-Cohen,** Helen *DrAPF 91*
**DeGeneste,** Henry Irving 1940- *WhoBlA 92*
**Degenfisz,** Helen *DrAPF 91*
**Degenford,** James Edward 1938- *AmMWSc 92*
**Degenhardt,** Henry W. 1910- *WrDr 92*
**Degenhardt,** Johannes Joachim 1926- *IntWW 91*
**Degenhardt,** Keith Jacob 1950- *AmMWSc 92*
**Degenhardt,** William George 1926- *AmMWSc 92*
**Degenhart,** Bernhard 1907- *IntWW 91*
**Degenkolb,** Henry John 1913- *AmMWSc 92*
**De Gennaro,** Louis D 1924- *AmMWSc 92*
**De Gennes,** Pierre-Gilles 1932- *IntWW 91*
**Degenstein,** Lester Ernest *WhoFI 92*
**De George,** Lawrence Joseph 1916- *WhoFI 92*
**DeGeorge,** Richard T. 1933- *WrDr 92*
**De George,** Richard Thomas 1933- *WhoMW 92*
**Degerstrom,** James Marvin 1933- *WhoMW 92*
**DeGeus,** Wendell Ray 1948- *WhoMW 92*
**Degges,** Ronald Joseph 1954- *WhoRel 92*
**Degginger,** Charles Francis 1950- *WhoMW 92*
**Degginger,** Edward R 1926- *AmMWSc 92*
**DeGhett,** Victor John 1942- *AmMWSc 92*
**DeGiovanni,** Jack Robert, Jr. 1960- *WhoAmL 92*
**DeGiovanni-Donnelly,** Rosalie F 1926- *AmMWSc 92*
**DeGirolami,** Umberto *AmMWSc 92*
**De Giusti,** Dominic Lawrence 1911- *AmMWSc 92*
**De Glehn,** Wilfred Gabriel 1870-1951 *TwCPaSc*
**Degling,** Donald Ewald 1928- *WhoAmL 92*
**Degnan,** John James, III 1945- *AmMWSc 92*
**Degnan,** John Michael 1948- *WhoAmL 92*
**Degnan,** Kevin John *AmMWSc 92*
**Degnan,** Leon John 1914- *WhoAmL 92*
**Degnan,** Martin J. *WhoAmL 92*
**Degner,** Gerhard Waldemar 1935- *WhoRel 92*
**De Goes,** Louis 1914- *AmMWSc 92*
**De Goff,** Victoria Joan 1945- *WhoAmL 92*
**deGolian,** George Putnam 1959- *WhoEnt 92*
**DeGonia,** Katherine Sue 1949- *WhoMW 92*
**DeGood,** Douglas Kent 1947- *WhoAmP 91*
**DeGowin,** Richard Louis 1934- *AmMWSc 92*
**De Graaf,** Adriaan M 1935- *AmMWSc 92*
**DeGraaf,** Donald Earl 1926- *AmMWSc 92*
**DeGrado,** William F 1955- *AmMWSc 92*
**De Graeff,** Allen *WrDr 92*
**DeGraff,** Arthur C, Jr 1929- *AmMWSc 92*
**DeGraff,** Benjamin Anthony 1938- *AmMWSc 92*
**De Graff,** Jacques Andre 1949- *WhoBlA 92*
**DeGraffenreidt,** Andrew 1928- *WhoBlA 92*
**DeGraffenreidt,** Kermit J. *WhoRel 92*
**De Graffenried,** Micheal *WhoMW 92*
**DeGraffenried,** William Ryan, Jr 1950- *WhoAmP 91*
**de Graft-Hanson,** J. O. 1932- *WrDr 92*
**DeGrand,** Thomas Alan 1950- *AmMWSc 92*
**DeGrandi,** Joseph Anthony 1927- *WhoAmL 92*
**DeGrandpre,** Charles Allyson 1936- *WhoAmL 92*
**De Grandpre,** Jean Louis 1929- *AmMWSc 92*
**De Grandy,** Miguel A 1958- *WhoAmP 91, WhoHisp 92*
**DeGrasse,** Robert W 1929- *AmMWSc 92*
**de Grassi,** Alex 1952- *ConMus 6 [port]*
**DeGrassi,** Leonard Rene 1928- *WhoWest 92*
**Degraw,** Joseph Irving, Jr 1933- *AmMWSc 92*
**DeGraw,** Richard G 1946- *WhoAmP 91*
**DeGraw,** William Allen 1939- *AmMWSc 92*
**De Gray,** Ronald Willoughby 1938- *AmMWSc 92*
**DeGrazia,** Emilio *DrAPF 91*
**Degrazia,** Emilio 1941- *IntAu&W 91*
**De Grazia,** Sebastian 1917- *WrDr 92*
**Degreeff,** Betty A 1936- *WhoAmP 91*
**DeGregori,** Thomas Roger 1935- *WhoFI 92*
**Degrelle,** Leon 1906- *BiDExR, EncTR 91 [port]*
**de Grey** *Who 92*
**De Grey,** Roger 1918- *IntWW 91, TwCPaSc, Who 92*
**De Groat,** William C 1938- *AmMWSc 92*
**DeGroat,** William Chesney, Jr 1938- *AmMWSc 92*
**DeGroff,** Ralph Lynn, Jr. 1936- *WhoFI 92*
**De Groot,** Albert 1945- *IntWW 91*
**DeGroot,** Doug 1951- *AmMWSc 92*
**De Groot,** Harry 1920- *WhoEnt 92*
**DeGroot,** Henry 1815-1893 *BiInAmS*
**De Groot,** John Weert, Jr 1927- *WhoAmP 91*
**De Groot,** Kenneth 1929- *WhoAmP 91*
**DeGroot,** Leslie Jacob 1928- *AmMWSc 92*
**DeGroot,** Loren Edward 1935- *WhoMW 92*
**DeGroot,** Morris H 1931- *AmMWSc 92*
**DeGroot,** Rodney Charles 1934- *AmMWSc 92*
**de Groot,** Stephen F. 1961- *WhoEnt 92*
**De Groot,** Sybil Gramlich 1928- *AmMWSc 92*
**de Groote,** Jacques 1927- *IntWW 91*
**DeGroote,** Judith *DrAPF 91*
**de Grouchy,** Robert Travis, Jr. 1953- *WhoWest 92*
**DeGrow,** Dan L 1953- *WhoAmP 91*
**DeGruccio,** Paul Michael 1947- *WhoEnt 92*
**deGruchy,** Kenneth Ackerman, Jr. 1954- *WhoEnt 92*
**de Gruchy,** Nigel Ronald Anthony 1943- *Who 92*
**De Gruttla,** Germaine Edna 1931- *WhoAmP 91*
**Degtyarev,** Vasiliy Alekseevich 1880-1949 *SovUnBD*
**DeGuere,** Philip Leonard, Jr. 1944- *WhoEnt 92*
**De Guise,** Elizabeth 1934- *IntAu&W 91*
**DeHaan,** Christel 1942- *WhoMW 92*
**De Haan,** Frank P 1934- *AmMWSc 92*
**De Haan,** Henry J 1920- *AmMWSc 92*
**Dehaan,** Martin Ralph 1891-1965 *RelLAm 91*
**DeHaan,** Robert Lawrence 1930- *AmMWSc 92*
**De Haas,** Herman 1924- *AmMWSc 92*
**De Haen,** Christoph 1940- *AmMWSc 92*
**Dehaene,** Jean-Luc 1940- *IntWW 91*
**de Hamel,** Christopher Francis Rivers 1950- *Who 92*
**de Hamel,** Joan 1924- *WrDr 92*
**Dehan,** Richard 1863?-1932 *ScFEYrs*
**De Harak,** Rudolph 1924- *DcTwDes*
**DeHart,** Arnold O'Dell 1926- *AmMWSc 92*
**DeHart,** Dan William 1951- *WhoAmP 91*
**DeHart,** Henry R. 1931- *WhoBlA 92*
**DeHart,** Michael Gerald 1950- *WhoFI 92*
**DeHart,** Panzy H. 1934- *WhoBlA 92*
**DeHart,** Robert C 1917- *AmMWSc 92*
**De Harven,** Etienne 1928- *AmMWSc 92*
**DeHaven,** Kenneth Le Moyne 1913- *WhoWest 92*
**DeHaven,** Michael Allen 1950- *WhoAmL 92*
**De Haven,** Tom *DrAPF 91*
**De Haven,** Tom 1949- *ConAu 133*
**DeHaven-Hudkins,** Diane Louise 1954- *AmMWSc 92*
**De Havilland,** Olivia 1916- *IntMPA 92*
**de Havilland,** Olivia Mary 1916- *IntWW 91, Who 92, WhoEnt 92*
**Dehaye,** Pierre 1921- *IntWW 91*
**de Heer,** Joseph 1922- *AmMWSc 92*
**Dehem,** Roger Jules 1921- *IntWW 91*
**Dehennin,** Herman 1929- *Who 92*
**Deher,** Kevin L 1952- *AmMWSc 92*
**DeHerrera,** Guillermo A 1950- *WhoAmP 91*
**DeHerrera,** Guillermo Alejandro 1950- *WhoHisp 92*
**DeHerrera,** Helen L. *WhoHisp 92*
**De Herrera,** Rick *WhoHisp 92*
**De Hertogh,** August Albert 1935- *AmMWSc 92*
**DeHetre,** J. David 1941- *WhoMW 92*
**deHeyman,** William Marquand 1933- *WhoRel 92*
**De Hirsch,** Storm *DrAPF 91*
**Dehlinger,** Peter 1917- *AmMWSc 92*
**Dehm,** Henry Christopher 1921- *AmMWSc 92*
**Dehm,** Richard Lavern 1927- *AmMWSc 92*
**Dehmelt,** Hans Georg 1922- *AmMWSc 92, IntWW 91, Who 92, WhoNob 90, WhoWest 92*
**Dehmer,** Joseph Leonard 1945- *AmMWSc 92*
**Dehmer,** Patricia Moore 1945- *AmMWSc 92*
**Dehn,** Conrad Francis 1926- *Who 92*
**Dehn,** James Theodore 1930- *AmMWSc 92*
**Dehn,** Joseph William, Jr 1928- *AmMWSc 92*
**Dehn,** Letha Arlene 1916- *WhoMW 92*
**Dehn,** Olive 1914- *WrDr 92*
**Dehn,** Rudolph A 1919- *AmMWSc 92*
**Dehne,** Edward James 1911- *AmMWSc 92*
**Dehne,** George Clark 1937- *AmMWSc 92*
**Dehnel,** Paul Augustus 1922- *AmMWSc 92*
**Dehner,** Eugene William 1914- *AmMWSc 92*
**Dehnhard,** Dietrich 1934- *AmMWSc 92*
**De Hoek,** William Richard 1955- *WhoAmL 92*
**De Hoff,** George R 1923- *AmMWSc 92*
**DeHoff,** George W 1913- *WhoAmP 91*
**DeHoff,** Paul Henry, Jr 1934- *AmMWSc 92*
**DeHoff,** Robert Thomas 1934- *AmMWSc 92*
**de Hoffmann,** Frederic 1924- *AmMWSc 92*
**DeHoffmann,** Frederic 1924-1989 *FacFETw*
**de Hoghton,** Bernard 1945- *Who 92*
**DeHollander,** William Roger 1918- *AmMWSc 92*
**De Hoop,** Adrianus Teunis 1927- *IntWW 91*
**DeHoratius,** Raphael Joseph 1942- *AmMWSc 92*
**Dehority,** Burk Allyn 1930- *AmMWSc 92*
**de Hoyos,** Angela *DrAPF 91*
**De Hoyos,** Angela 1940- *WhoHisp 92*
**de Hoyos,** David Trevino 1945- *WhoHisp 92*
**DeHoyos,** Orlando Flores 1959- *WhoHisp 92*
**Dehqani-Tafti,** Hassan Barnaba 1920- *Who 92*
**Deibel,** Robert Howard 1924- *AmMWSc 92*
**Deibel,** Rudolf 1924- *AmMWSc 92*
**Deibert,** Max Curtis 1937- *AmMWSc 92*
**Deibler,** Samuel Elwood, Jr. 1945- *WhoRel 92*
**Deichman,** Shane Daniel 1967- *WhoWest 92*
**Deichmann,** Bernhard Ernst 1935- *WhoFI 92*
**Deichmann,** Frederick William 1942- *WhoIns 92*
**Deichmann,** William Bernard 1902- *AmMWSc 92*
**Deida,** Jose Fernando 1957- *WhoRel 92*
**Deidameia** *EncAmaz 91*
**Deift,** Percy Alec 1945- *AmMWSc 92*
**Deighton,** Len 1929- *CnDBLB 8 [port], ConNov 91, FacFETw, IntAu&W 91, IntWW 91, WrDr 92*
**Deihl,** Richard Harry 1928- *WhoFI 92, WhoWest 92*
**Deikel,** Theodore *WhoEnt 92*
**Deikman,** Eugene Lawrence 1927- *WhoAmL 92*
**Deily,** Fredric H 1926- *AmMWSc 92*
**Deimer,** Lorena Ruth 1926- *IntAu&W 91*
**Deiner,** John B 1940- *WhoIns 92*
**Deines,** David 1951- *WhoEnt 92*
**Deines,** Harry J. 1909- *WhoFI 92, WhoWest 92*
**Deines,** Peter 1936- *AmMWSc 92*
**Deinet,** Adolph Joseph 1920- *AmMWSc 92*
**Deinhardt,** Carol Lucy 1946- *WhoRel 92*
**Deininger,** David G 1947- *WhoAmP 91*
**Deininger,** Robert W 1927- *AmMWSc 92*
**Deininger,** Rolf A 1934- *AmMWSc 92*
**DeIntinis,** Ranier C. *WhoEnt 92*
**Deinzer,** George William 1934- *WhoMW 92*
**Deinzer,** Max Ludwig 1937- *AmMWSc 92*
**Deiotte,** Charles Edward 1946- *WhoWest 92*
**de Irala,** Mikel *WhoHisp 92*
**Deis,** Daniel Wayne 1943- *AmMWSc 92*
**Deischer,** Claude Knauss 1903- *AmMWSc 92*
**Deisenhofer,** Johann 1943- *AmMWSc 92, Who 92, WhoNob 90*
**Deisenroth,** Clinton Wilbur 1941- *WhoWest 92*
**Deisher,** Robert William 1920- *AmMWSc 92*
**Deisley,** David Lee 1956- *WhoAmL 92*
**Deiss,** Joseph Jay 1915- *WrDr 92*
**Deiss,** William Paul, Jr 1923- *AmMWSc 92*
**Deissler,** Robert G 1921- *AmMWSc 92*
**Deissler,** Robert George 1921- *WhoMW 92*
**Deist,** Robert Paul 1928- *AmMWSc 92*
**Deister,** Michealynne A. 1946- *WhoMW 92*
**Deitch,** Arline D 1922- *AmMWSc 92*
**Deitch,** Donna *ReelWom, WhoEnt 92*
**Deitcher,** Herbert 1933- *WhoFI 92*
**Deitel,** Mervyn 1936- *AmMWSc 92*
**Deiter,** Newton Elliott 1931- *WhoWest 92*
**Deiters,** Joan A 1934- *AmMWSc 92*
**Deitrich,** L Walter 1938- *AmMWSc 92*
**Deitrich,** Richard Adam 1931- *AmMWSc 92, WhoWest 92*
**Deitrick,** John E 1940- *AmMWSc 92*
**Deitrick,** Ronald Wayne 1947- *WhoWest 92*
**Deitz,** James Gilbert 1928- *WhoRel 92*
**Deitz,** Lewis Levering 1944- *AmMWSc 92*
**Deitz,** Victor Reuel 1909- *AmMWSc 92*
**Deitz,** William Harris 1925- *AmMWSc 92*
**Deitzer,** Gerald Francis 1942- *AmMWSc 92*
**Deitzler,** Harry G. 1951- *WhoAmL 92*
**Deivanayagan,** Subramanian 1941- *AmMWSc 92*
**Deiz,** Mercedes F. *WhoHisp 92*
**Deiz,** Mercedes F. 1917- *WhoBlA 92*
**De-Ja-Gou** *Who 92*
**Dejaegher,** M Bob *WhoAmP 91*
**De Jager,** Cornelis 1921- *IntWW 91*
**De Jager,** Cornelis 1925- *IntWW 91*
**Dejaiffe,** Ernest 1912- *AmMWSc 92*
**de Janosi,** Peter Engel 1928- *WhoFI 92*
**DeJarmon,** Elva Pegues 1921- *WhoBlA 92*
**DeJarnette,** Edmund, Jr 1938- *WhoAmP 91*
**DeJarnette,** Fred Roark 1933- *AmMWSc 92*
**DeJean,** Joan 1948- *ConAu 134*
**Dejean De La Batie,** Bernard 1927- *IntWW 91*
**de Jesus,** Benjamin *WhoRel 92*
**DeJesus,** Hiram Raymon 1957- *WhoHisp 92*
**De Jesus,** Ivette 1960- *WhoHisp 92*
**de Jesus,** Jose *WhoHisp 92*
**DeJesus,** Jose 1965- *WhoHisp 92*
**De Jesus,** Sara *WhoHisp 92*
**de Jesus-Berlin,** Jenny 1947- *WhoHisp 92*
**De Jesus-Burgos,** Sylvia Teresa 1941- *WhoHisp 92*
**De Jesus-Torres,** Migdalia 1944- *WhoHisp 92*
**Dejevsky,** Nikolai James 1945- *IntAu&W 91*
**Dejid,** Bugyn 1927- *IntWW 91*
**Dejmal,** Roger Kent 1940- *AmMWSc 92*
**Dejmek,** Kazimierz 1924- *IntWW 91*
**De John,** Nicholas Anthony 1944- *WhoAmL 92, WhoMW 92*
**DeJohnette,** Jack 1942- *ConMus 7 [port], WhoEnt 92*
**Dejoie,** C. C., Jr. 1914- *WhoBlA 92*
**Dejoie,** Carolyn Barnes Milanes *WhoBlA 92*
**De Jong,** Ate Tjeerd 1953- *WhoEnt 92*
**DeJong,** Bruce Allen 1946- *WhoMW 92*
**Dejong,** Constance *DrAPF 91*
**De Jong,** David Cornel 1905-1967 *BenetAL 91*
**De Jong,** David Samuel 1951- *WhoAmL 92*
**De Jong,** Diederik Cornelis Dignus 1931- *AmMWSc 92*
**DeJong,** Donald Warren 1930- *AmMWSc 92*
**De Jong,** Gary Joel 1947- *AmMWSc 92*
**De Jong,** James A. 1941- *WhoRel 92*
**De Jong,** Jan Willem 1921- *IntWW 91*
**DeJong,** Lloyd Gerald 1917- *WhoRel 92*
**DeJong,** Meindert d1991 *NewYTBS 91*
**De Jong,** Meindert 1906- *WrDr 92*
**DeJong,** Meindert 1906-1991 *ConAu 134, -36NR, CurBio 91N, SmATA 68*
**DeJong,** Peter 1915- *WhoRel 92*
**De Jong,** Peter J 1937- *AmMWSc 92*
**de Jong,** Rudolph H 1928- *AmMWSc 92*
**DeJong,** Russell Nelson 1907- *AmMWSc 92*
**De Jong,** Wilbur Leon 1929- *WhoRel 92*
**De Jonge,** Alex 1938- *IntAu&W 91, WrDr 92*
**de Jonge,** Marinus 1925- *WhoRel 92*
**DeJongh,** Don C 1937- *AmMWSc 92*
**de Jongh,** Eduard S. 1931- *IntWW 91*
**De Jongh,** James *DrAPF 91*
**de Jongh,** James Laurence 1942- *WhoBlA 92*
**Dejonghe,** Lutgard C 1941- *AmMWSc 92*
**De Josselin De Jong,** Patrick Edward 1922- *IntWW 91*

**Dekat,** Joseph Carroll Francis 1952- *WhoFI 92*
**DeKay,** James Ellsworth 1792-1851 *BiInAmS*
**deKay,** James Tertius 1930- *WhoEnt 92*
**Dekazos,** Elias Demetrios 1920- *AmMWSc 92*
**De Keersmaeker,** Paul 1929- *IntWW 91*
**Dekel,** Eddie 1958- *WhoFI 92*
**deKieffer,** Donald Eulette 1945- *WhoAmL 92*
**De Kimpe,** Christian Robert 1937- *AmMWSc 92*
**Dekker,** Alan N 1934- *WhoIns 92*
**Dekker,** Andrew 1927- *AmMWSc 92*
**Dekker,** Carl *IntAu&W 91X, WrDr 92*
**Dekker,** Charles Abram 1920- *AmMWSc 92*
**Dekker,** David Bliss 1919- *AmMWSc 92*
**Dekker,** Eugene Earl 1927- *AmMWSc 92, WhoMW 92*
**Dekker,** George 1934- *IntAu&W 91, WrDr 92*
**Dekker,** George Gilbert 1934- *WhoWest 92*
**Dekker,** Jacob Christoph Edmond 1921- *AmMWSc 92*
**Dekker,** Lois Ann 1929- *WhoRel 92*
**Dekker,** Thomas 1572?-1632 *CnDBLB 1, RfGEnL 91*
**Dekker,** W. 1924- *IntWW 91*
**DeKlavon,** Robert Allen 1954- *WhoRel 92*
**de Klerk,** Abel Jacobus 1935- *WhoRel 92*
**de Klerk,** Albert 1917- *IntWW 91*
**De Klerk,** F W 1936- *FacFETw*
**de Klerk,** Frederik Willem 1936- *IntWW 91, Who 92*
**DeKloet,** Siwo R 1933- *AmMWSc 92*
**DeKnight,** Avel 1933- *WhoBlA 92*
**De Kock,** Carroll Wayne 1938- *AmMWSc 92*
**DeKock,** Roger Lee 1943- *AmMWSc 92, WhoMW 92*
**De Kooning,** Willem 1904- *IntWW 91, RComAH*
**de Kooning,** Willem 1904-1988 *FacFETw*
**Dekornfeld,** Thomas John 1924- *AmMWSc 92*
**De Korte,** Aart 1934- *AmMWSc 92*
**DeKorte,** John Martin 1940- *AmMWSc 92*
**De Korte,** Rudolf Willem 1936- *IntWW 91*
**De Korvin,** Andre 1935- *AmMWSc 92*
**DeKoster,** Lucas James 1918- *WhoAmL 92, WhoAmP 91*
**Dekoven,** James 1831-1879 *RelLAm 91*
**DeKoven,** Lenore *WhoEnt 92*
**De Koven,** Reginald 1859-1920 *NewAmDM*
**DeKoven,** Reginald, III 1948- *WhoFI 92*
**De Krasinski,** Joseph S 1914- *AmMWSc 92*
**DeKrey,** Duane L 1956- *WhoAmP 91*
**de Kruif,** Jack H. 1921- *WhoWest 92*
**de Kruif,** Paul 1890-1971 *BenetAL 91*
**Dekster,** Boris Veniamin 1938- *AmMWSc 92*
**Del,** Sophie 1928- *WhoEnt 92*
**Dela Cruz,** Jose Santos 1948- *WhoAmL 92*
**Dela Cruz,** Ramon M *WhoAmP 91*
**Delabarre,** Everett Merrill, Jr 1918- *AmMWSc 92*
**de la Barre de Nanteuil,** Luc 1925- *IntWW 91, Who 92*
**De la Bere,** Cameron 1933- *Who 92*
**de la Billiere,** Peter 1934- *IntWW 91, Who 92*
**De La Cancela,** Victor 1952- *WhoHisp 92*
**DeLacerda,** Fred G 1937- *AmMWSc 92*
**de la Chapelle,** Frances Passerat 1940- *WhoRel 92*
**Delacombe,** Rohan 1906- *IntWW 91, Who 92*
**Delacorte,** George T. 1893-1991 *NewYTBS 91 [port]*
**Delacorte,** George T. 1894-1991 *CurBio 91N*
**Delacote,** Jacques *IntWW 91*
**Delacour,** Jean-Paul 1930- *Who 92*
**Delacour,** Yves Jean Claude Marie 1943- *WhoFI 92*
**Delacourt-Smith of Alteryn,** Baroness 1916- *Who 92*
**Delacroix,** Ferdinand-Victor-Eugene 1798-1863 *ThHEIm*
**de la Cruz,** Carlos Manuel, Sr. 1941- *WhoHisp 92*
**De La Cruz,** Daniel F. 1941- *WhoHisp 92*
**De la Cruz,** Dimitri 1957- *WhoHisp 92*
**De La Cruz,** Jerry John 1948- *WhoHisp 92*
**De La Cruz,** Pedro 1950- *WhoHisp 92*
**De La Cruz,** Roland A. 1953- *WhoFI 92*
**De la Cruz,** Vidal F 1959- *AmMWSc 92*
**De La Cruz-Cartagena,** Luis T. 1950- *WhoHisp 92*
**de la Cruz Melendez,** Francisco 1955- *WhoHisp 92*
**de la Cuadra,** Bruce *WhoHisp 92*
**DeLaCuadra-Salcedo Fernandez DelCastillo** 1946- *IntWW 91*
**de la Cuesta,** Leonel A. 1937- *WhoHisp 92*
**Delafield,** Francis 1841-1915 *BiInAmS*
**Delafield,** Joseph 1790-1875 *BiInAmS*
**Delafons,** John 1930- *Who 92*
**De La Foret,** Louis Norman 1943- *WhoEnt 92*
**De La Fuente,** Arnoldo Romeo 1959- *WhoHisp 92*
**de la Fuente,** Javier Ramirez 1947- *WhoHisp 92*
**De La Fuente,** Rollo K 1933- *AmMWSc 92*
**de la Fuente,** Roque *WhoHisp 92*
**de la Garza,** E. 1927- *AlmAP 92 [port], WhoAmP 91*
**De la Garza,** Eddie 1952- *WhoHisp 92*
**de la Garza,** Eligio 1927- *WhoHisp 92*
**de la Garza,** Kika 1927- *WhoHisp 92*
**de la Garza,** Leonardo 1937- *WhoHisp 92*
**de la Garza,** Luis Adolfo 1943- *WhoHisp 92*
**De La Garza,** Pete 1945- *WhoHisp 92*
**De La Garza,** Rene E. 1961- *WhoHisp 92*
**de la Garza,** Rodolfo O. 1942- *WhoHisp 92*
**Delage,** Marie M 1936- *WhoAmP 91*
**Delage,** Maurice 1879-1961 *NewAmDM*
**de la Geniere,** Renaud d1990 *IntWW 91N*
**Delagi,** Edward F 1911- *AmMWSc 92*
**Delagi,** Richard Gregory *AmMWSc 92*
**de la Guard,** Theodore *BenetAL 91*
**del Aguila,** Juan Manuel 1950- *WhoHisp 92*
**De La Haba,** Gabriel Luis 1926- *AmMWSc 92*
**Delahanty,** Edward Lawrence 1942- *WhoFI 92*
**Delahanty,** Thomas Edward, II 1945- *WhoAmP 91*
**Delahay,** Paul 1921- *AmMWSc 92*
**Delahaye,** Michael 1946- *WrDr 92*
**Delahaye,** Michael John 1946- *IntAu&W 91*
**Delahayes,** Jean 1936- *AmMWSc 92*
**De La Huerga,** Jesus *AmMWSc 92*
**DeLaHunt,** Elizabeth Ann 1948- *WhoMW 92*
**DeLahunta,** Alexander 1932- *AmMWSc 92*
**Delahunty,** George 1952- *AmMWSc 92*
**Delahunty,** Joseph L 1935- *WhoAmP 91*
**De La Iglesia,** Felix Alberto 1939- *AmMWSc 92*
**DeLair,** Louis, Jr. 1947- *WhoBlA 92*
**Delaire,** Jean *ScFEYrs*
**Delakova,** Katya d1991 *NewYTBS 91*
**Delalande,** Michel Richard *NewAmDM*
**de la Lanne-Mirrlees,** Robin Ian Evelyn S *Who 92*
**Delaloye,** John Francis 1945- *WhoIns 92*
**De La Luz,** Nilsa 1946- *WhoHisp 92*
**de Lama,** George 1957- *WhoHisp 92*
**de la Madrid Hurtado,** Miguel 1934- *Who 92*
**De La Madrid Hurtado,** Miguel 1935- *IntWW 91*
**de la Mare,** Albinia Catherine 1932- *Who 92*
**de la Mare,** Arthur 1914- *IntWW 91, Who 92*
**De La Mare,** Harold Elison 1922- *AmMWSc 92*
**de la Mare,** Walter 1873-1956 *CnDBLB 6 [port], FacFETw, RfGEnL 91*
**Delamarian,** Michael, III 1953- *WhoRel 92*
**DeLamater,** Edward Doane 1912- *AmMWSc 92*
**DeLaMater,** George 1922- *AmMWSc 92*
**Delamere,** Baron 1934- *Who 92*
**Delamere,** Monita 1921- *Who 92*
**De Lamirande,** Gaston 1923- *AmMWSc 92*
**De La Moneda,** Francisco Homero 1939- *AmMWSc 92*
**de la Mora,** Juan Fernandez 1952- *WhoHisp 92*
**de la Morena,** Felipe 1927- *IntWW 91, Who 92*
**Delamuraz,** Jean-Pascal 1936- *IntWW 91*
**De Lancey,** George Byers 1940- *AmMWSc 92*
**DeLancey,** Robert Houston, Jr. 1936- *WhoRel 92*
**DeLancey,** Scott Cameron 1949- *WhoWest 92*
**Delancy,** Michael Robinson 1948- *WhoMW 92, WhoRel 92*
**DeLand,** Edward Charles 1922- *AmMWSc 92*
**DeLand,** Frank H 1921- *AmMWSc 92*
**Deland,** Margaret 1857-1945 *BenetAL 91*
**De Lane Lea,** Jacques 1931- *IntMPA 92*
**Delaney,** Andrew 1920- *WhoFI 92*
**Delaney,** Andrew John 1962- *WhoAmL 92*
**Delaney,** Bernard T 1944- *AmMWSc 92*
**Delaney,** Brian Lee 1960- *WhoAmL 92*
**Delaney,** C. Timothy 1957- *WhoAmL 92*
**DeLaney,** Charles Oliver 1925- *WhoEnt 92*
**Delaney,** Denis *WrDr 92*
**Delaney,** Edward Joseph 1953- *AmMWSc 92*
**Delaney,** Edward Norman 1927- *WhoAmL 92, WhoFI 92*
**Delaney,** Francis James Joseph 1942- *IntAu&W 91, Who 92*
**Delaney,** Harold 1919- *WhoBlA 92*
**DeLaney,** Herbert Wade, Jr. 1925- *WhoAmL 92*
**Delaney,** Howard C. 1933- *WhoBlA 92*
**Delaney,** J Dennis 1937- *WhoAmP 91*
**Delaney,** John *DrAPF 91, TwCWW 91*
**Delaney,** John Adrian 1956- *WhoAmL 92*
**Delaney,** John Martin, Jr. 1956- *WhoAmL 92*
**Delaney,** John P 1930- *AmMWSc 92*
**Delaney,** John Paul 1933- *WhoBlA 92*
**Delaney,** John White 1943- *WhoAmL 92*
**Delaney,** Joseph H 1932- *TwCSFW 91, WrDr 92*
**Delaney,** Joseph P. 1934- *WhoRel 92*
**Delaney,** Juanita Battle 1921- *WhoBlA 92*
**Delaney,** Laurel Jeanne 1954- *WhoMW 92*
**Delaney,** Lucy A. 1830?- *NotBlAW 92*
**Delaney,** Margaret Lois 1955- *AmMWSc 92*
**Delaney,** Marion Patricia 1952- *WhoWest 92*
**Delaney,** Martin Robinson 1812-1885 *BenetAL 91*
**Delaney,** Mary Murray 1913- *WrDr 92*
**Delaney,** Matthew Sylvester 1927- *WhoWest 92*
**Delaney,** Michael Brian 1957- *WhoAmL 92*
**Delaney,** Michael Eugene 1946- *WhoMW 92*
**Delaney,** Michael Patrick, Jr. 1958- *WhoAmL 92*
**Delaney,** Norman Conrad 1932- *IntAu&W 91, WrDr 92*
**Delaney,** Patrick Francis, Jr 1933- *AmMWSc 92*
**Delaney,** Philip Alfred 1928- *WhoFI 92*
**Delaney,** Richard James 1946- *WhoFI 92*
**Delaney,** Richard Michael 1936- *WhoEnt 92*
**Delaney,** Richard T 1938- *WhoIns 92*
**Delaney,** Robert 1928- *AmMWSc 92*
**Delaney,** Robert Michael 1931- *AmMWSc 92*
**Delaney,** Robert Richard, Jr. 1954- *WhoAmL 92*
**Delaney,** Robert Vernon 1936- *WhoMW 92*
**Delaney,** Robert Vincent 1934- *WhoFI 92*
**Delaney,** Robert W 1929- *WhoIns 92*
**Delaney,** Sara P. 1889-1958 *NotBlAW 92 [port]*
**Delaney,** Shelagh 1930- *WrDr 92*
**Delaney,** Shelagh 1939- *CnDBLB 8 [port], FacFETw, IntAu&W 91, Who 92*
**Delaney,** Thomas Alton 1944- *WhoEnt 92*
**Delaney,** Thomas Francis 1950- *WhoEnt 92*
**Delaney,** Willi 1947- *WhoBlA 92*
**Delaney,** William F, Jr. *WhoIns 92*
**DeLaney Adams,** Donna Marie 1952- *WhoEnt 92*
**de Lange,** Nicholas Robert Michael 1944- *WhoRel 92*
**DeLange,** Robert J 1937- *AmMWSc 92, WhoWest 92*
**DeLange,** Walter J 1931- *WhoAmP 91*
**Delanglade,** Ronald Allan 1936- *AmMWSc 92*
**Delannoy,** Jean 1908- *IntDcF 2-2, IntMPA 92*
**Delannoy,** Luc Theo 1955- *WhoFI 92*
**Delano,** Alonzo 1802?-1874 *BenetAL 91*
**Delano,** Amasa 1763-1823 *BenetAL 91*
**Delano,** Anthony 1930- *IntAu&W 91, WrDr 92*
**Delano,** Erwin 1926- *AmMWSc 92*
**Delano,** Jonathan William 1949- *WhoAmP 91*
**Delano,** Juan Carlos 1941- *Who 92*
**Delano,** Robert Barnes, Jr. 1956- *WhoAmL 92*
**Delano,** Robert F 1919- *WhoAmP 91*
**Delano Ortuzar,** Juan Carlos 1941- *IntWW 91*
**De la Noue,** Joel Jean-Louis 1938- *AmMWSc 92*
**De-La-Noy,** Michael 1934- *IntAu&W 91*
**Delansky,** James F 1934- *AmMWSc 92*
**Delany,** Clarissa Scott 1901-1927 *NotBlAW 92*
**Delany,** Dana *WhoEnt 92*
**Delany,** Henry Beard 1858-1928 *DcNCBi 2*
**Delany,** Holly Diane 1957- *WhoBlA 92*
**Delany,** Martin R 1812-1885 *RComAH*
**Delany,** Samuel R. *DrAPF 91*
**Delany,** Samuel R. 1942- *BenetAL 91, BlkLC [port], ConNov 91, IntAu&W 91, TwCSFW 91, WrDr 92*
**Delany,** Samuel Ray 1942- *WhoBlA 92*
**De Lany,** William Hurd 1943- *WhoWest 92*
**Delap,** Herbert Anthony 1944- *WhoAmL 92*
**DeLap,** James Harve 1930- *AmMWSc 92*
**DeLapa,** Judith Anne 1938- *WhoMW 92*
**de la Pena,** Fernando F. 1936- *WhoHisp 92*
**De La Pena,** Javier 1940- *IntWW 91*
**de la Pena,** Nonny 1963- *WhoHisp 92*
**De la Pena,** Ramon Serrano 1936- *AmMWSc 92*
**Delaplaine,** George Birely, Jr. 1926- *WhoFI 92*
**DeLapp,** Frank Paul 1938- *WhoMW 92*
**DeLapp,** Sim Alexander, Jr 1943- *WhoAmP 91*
**DeLapp,** Tina Davis 1946- *AmMWSc 92*
**de Lappe,** Gemze 1922- *WhoEnt 92*
**Delappe,** Irving Pierce 1915- *AmMWSc 92*
**Delaquis,** Noel 1934- *WhoRel 92, WhoWest 92*
**de Lara,** Hector G., Jr. *WhoHisp 92*
**De Lara,** Jose Garcia 1940- *WhoHisp 92*
**De Lara,** Mario, Jr. 1944- *WhoFI 92, WhoHisp 92*
**de la Ramee,** Marie Louise *RfGEnL 91*
**de la Renta,** Oscar 1932- *DcTwDes, FacFETw, IntWW 91, WhoHisp 92*
**de la Rocha,** Castulo 1948- *WhoHisp 92*
**de la Rocha,** Rosamelia T. *WhoHisp 92*
**De la Roche,** Mazo 1879-1961 *BenetAL 91, RfGEnL 91*
**DeLaRosa,** Denise Maria 1954- *WhoAmL 92*
**de Larosiere de Champfeu,** Jacques 1929- *Who 92*
**de Larosiere de Champfeu,** Jacques Martin 1929- *IntWW 91*
**De Larrocha,** Alicia *NewAmDM*
**de Larrocha,** Alicia 1923- *WhoEnt 92*
**de la Rue,** Andrew 1946- *Who 92*
**Delarue,** Jean *ConAu 133*
**Delarue,** Louis C. 1939- *WhoBlA 92*
**Delarue,** Louis Charles 1939- *WhoRel 92*
**De la Rue,** Pierre *NewAmDM*
**Delarue-Mardrus,** Lucie 1874-1945 *FrenWW*
**DeLarye-Gold,** Ann Elizabeth 1955- *WhoFI 92*
**de las Casas,** Walter Mario 1947- *WhoHisp 92*
**De Las Cuevas,** Ramon *ScFEYrs*
**de la Serna,** Marcelo 1964- *WhoWest 92*
**DeLashmet,** Gordon Bartlett 1928- *WhoFI 92*
**De La Sierra,** Angell O *AmMWSc 92*
**De Lassen,** Jan Folmer 1934- *WhoWest 92*
**De la Suaree,** Octavio E., II 1943- *WhoHisp 92*
**de la Teja,** Jesus Francisco 1956- *WhoHisp 92*
**de la Torre,** Adrian Louis 1924- *WhoHisp 92*
**de la Torre,** Cristobal 1957- *WhoHisp 92*
**de la Torre,** David Joseph 1948- *WhoHisp 92, WhoWest 92*
**de la Torre,** Homero R. 1943- *WhoHisp 92*
**De la Torre,** Jack Carlos 1937- *AmMWSc 92*
**de la Torre,** Jose Agustin Pepin 1944- *WhoHisp 92*
**de la Torre,** Jose Austin 1944- *WhoMW 92*
**De La Torre,** Julie E. 1952- *WhoHisp 92*
**De La Torre,** Lillian 1902- *IntAu&W 91, WrDr 92*
**De La Torre,** Manuel 1948- *WhoHisp 92*
**de la Torre,** Pedro Eduardo, Jr. 1951- *WhoHisp 92*
**De La Torre,** Phillip E. 1953- *WhoHisp 92*
**DeLaTorre,** Phillip Eugene 1953- *WhoMW 92*
**de la Torre,** Rolando E. 1932- *WhoHisp 92*
**De La Torre-Bukowski,** Horst Norbert 1960- *WhoHisp 92*
**de Latour,** Christopher 1947- *AmMWSc 92*
**de la Tour,** Frances 1944- *IntWW 91, Who 92*
**de Lattre,** Candace Lorraine 1950- *WhoEnt 92*
**Delattre,** Pierre *DrAPF 91*
**De Laubenfels,** David John 1925- *AmMWSc 92*
**DeLauder,** William B. *WhoBlA 92*
**DeLauer,** R D 1918- *AmMWSc 92*
**Delaughter,** Jerry L. 1944- *WhoAmL 92*
**Delaunay,** Robert 1885-1941 *FacFETw*
**Delaunay,** Sonia 1885-1979 *DcTwDes, FacFETw*
**DeLaune,** Ronald D 1943- *AmMWSc 92*
**Delauney,** Maurice Charles Jules 1919- *IntWW 91*
**De Laurentiis,** Dino 1919- *IntMPA 92, IntWW 91, WhoEnt 92*
**De Laurentiis,** Raffaella *IntMPA 92*
**DeLaurentis,** Louise Budde *DrAPF 91*
**DeLauro,** Rosa *WhoAmP 91*
**DeLauro,** Rosa L. 1943- *AlmAP 92 [port]*

**De La Varre**, Andre, Jr. 1934- *IntMPA 92*
**de la Vega**, Aurelio E. 1925- *WhoHisp 92*
**de La Vega**, Enrique Miguel, III 1935- *WhoHisp 92*
**de la Vega**, Francis Joseph 1919- *WhoHisp 92*
**De la Vergne**, Hughes Jules, II 1931- *WhoAmP 91*
**De La Vina**, Gustavo 1939- *WhoHisp 92*
**de la Vina**, Lynda Y. 1950- *WhoHisp 92*
**De La Vina**, P. R. *WhoHisp 92*
**Delaware**, Dana Lewis 1951- *AmMWSc 92*
**De La Warr**, Earl 1948- *Who 92*
**De La Warr**, Sylvia *Who 92*
**De La Warr**, Thomas West, Baron 1577-1618 *BenetAL 91*
**DeLay**, Dorothy 1917- *WhoEnt 92*
**DeLay**, Larry G. 1955- *WhoRel 92*
**DeLay**, Robert Paul 1934- *WhoMW 92*
**De Lay**, Roger Lee 1945- *AmMWSc 92*
**DeLay**, Thomas Dale 1947- *WhoAmP 91*
**DeLay**, Tom 1947- *AlmAP 92 [port]*
**DeLay**, William Raymond 1929- *WhoMW 92*
**Delaye**, Marguerite *EncAmaz 91*
**Del Balzo**, Joseph Michael 1936- *WhoFI 92*
**Delbanco**, Nicholas *DrAPF 91*
**Delbanco**, Nicholas F. 1942- *WrDr 92*
**Delbanco**, Nicholas Franklin 1942- *IntAu&W 91*
**DelBane**, Robert Francis 1948- *WhoMW 92*
**Delbecq**, Charles Jarchow 1921- *AmMWSc 92*
**Del Bel**, Elsio 1920- *AmMWSc 92*
**Del Bel**, Paul Thomas 1949- *WhoFI 92*
**Del Belso**, Richard *IntMPA 92*
**Del Bene**, Janet Elaine 1939- *AmMWSc 92*
**Del Biance**, Henry Peter, Jr. 1958- *WhoAmL 92*
**Del Bianco**, Doreen M *WhoAmP 91*
**Del Bianco**, Walter 1933- *AmMWSc 92*
**Delbridge**, Richard 1942- *Who 92*
**Delbruck**, Max 1906-1981 *FacFETw, WhoNob 90*
**del Calvo**, Alberto C. 1923- *WhoHisp 92*
**Delcamp**, Robert Mitchell 1919- *AmMWSc 92*
**Del Campillo**, Miguell J. 1960- *WhoHisp 92*
**Del Campo**, Martin Bernardelli 1922- *WhoHisp 92*
**del Castillo**, A. Martin *WhoHisp 92*
**Del Castillo**, Ines 1927- *WhoHisp 92*
**del Castillo**, Jeanne Louise Taillac 1933- *WhoFI 92*
**Del Castillo**, Jose 1920- *AmMWSc 92*
**Del Castillo**, Julio Cesar 1930- *WhoMW 92*
**Del Castillo**, Ramon R. 1949- *WhoHisp 92*
**del Castillo**, Ricardo A. 1946- *WhoHisp 92*
**Del Castillo**, Virginia Lyn Moreno 1956- *WhoHisp 92*
**Del Cerro**, Manuel 1931- *AmMWSc 92*
**Delco**, Exalton Alfonso, Jr 1929- *AmMWSc 92, WhoBlA 92*
**Delco**, Wilhelmina R. 1929- *NotBlAW 92, WhoBlA 92*
**Delco**, Wilhelmina Ruth *WhoAmP 91*
**Del Colle**, Paul Lawrence 1950- *WhoEnt 92*
**Delcomyn**, Fred 1939- *AmMWSc 92*
**Delcourt**, Paul Allen 1949- *AmMWSc 92*
**Delcroix**, Robert 1938- *WhoEnt 92*
**Delderfield**, Eric R. 1909- *WrDr 92*
**Delderfield**, Eric Raymond 1909- *IntAu&W 91*
**Delderfield**, R F 1912-1972 *FacFETw*
**Deleanu**, Aristide Alexandru-Ion 1932- *AmMWSc 92*
**Delear**, Richard Henry 1927- *WhoWest 92*
**Deledda**, Grazia 1871-1936 *FacFETw, WhoNob 90*
**De Leeuw**, Adele 1899- *IntAu&W 91*
**de Leeuw**, Frank 1930- *WhoFI 92*
**DeLeeuw**, J H 1929- *AmMWSc 92*
**Deleeuw**, Paul Joseph, Jr. 1946- *WhoMW 92*
**DeLeeuw**, Samuel Leonard 1934- *AmMWSc 92*
**De Leeuw**, Ton 1926- *IntWW 91*
**Delehant**, Joseph Henry 1950- *WhoAmL 92*
**Delehanty**, Peter Michael 1954- *WhoFI 92*
**Delehanty**, William M. 1938- *WhoMW 92*
**Delelis**, Andre 1924- *IntWW 91*
**DeLellis**, Ronald Albert *AmMWSc 92*
**De Lemos**, Carmen Loretta 1937- *AmMWSc 92*
**DeLeo**, James A 1951- *WhoAmP 91*
**DeLeo**, Robert Alfred 1950- *WhoAmP 91*
**DeLeon** 1976- *WhoBlA 92*
**de Leon**, Armando 1934- *WhoHisp 92*
**De Leon**, Armando 1956- *WhoHisp 92*
**De Leon**, Belen R., Jr. 1936- *WhoHisp 92*
**De Leon**, Cesar 1934- *WhoHisp 92*
**de Leon**, Daniel Benitz 1941- *WhoRel 92*
**de Leon**, Dennis *WhoHisp 92*
**De Leon**, Fernando 1930- *WhoHisp 92*
**de Leon**, Gloria I. 1952- *WhoHisp 92*
**DeLeon**, Ildefonso R 1947- *AmMWSc 92*
**de Leon**, John Louis 1962- *WhoAmL 92*
**DeLeon**, Jose 1960- *WhoBlA 92, WhoHisp 92*
**DeLeon**, Jose R., Jr. 1928- *WhoHisp 92*
**De Leon**, Josephine 1952- *WhoHisp 92*
**De Leon**, Leonor Rosas *WhoHisp 92*
**DeLeon**, Lupe 1952- *WhoEnt 92*
**de Leon**, Marcos 1947- *WhoHisp 92*
**De Leon**, Marita Carina 1969- *WhoHisp 92*
**De Leon**, Michael Anthony 1947- *WhoHisp 92*
**DeLeon**, Morris Jack 1941- *AmMWSc 92*
**Deleon**, Nephtali *DrAPF 91*
**de Leon**, Oscar Eduardo 1937- *WhoHisp 92*
**de Leon**, Perla Maria 1952- *WhoHisp 92*
**DeLeon**, Rafael 1959- *WhoHisp 92*
**De Leon**, Thomas Cooper 1839-1914 *BenetAL 91*
**De Leon**, Val *WhoHisp 92*
**De Leon**, Victor M 1939- *AmMWSc 92*
**de Leon**, Yolanda 1940- *WhoHisp 92*
**Deleon Guerrero**, Edward M *WhoAmP 91*
**DeLeon-Guerrero**, Lorenzo Iglesias *WhoAmP 91*
**Deleon Guerrero**, Pedro R *WhoAmP 91*
**DeLeon-Jones**, Frank A., Jr. 1937- *WhoBlA 92*
**de Leon-Lavin**, Liliana Eugenia 1965- *WhoHisp 92*
**De Leonardis**, Charles Richard 1953- *WhoEnt 92*
**De Leonardis**, Nicholas John 1929- *WhoFI 92*
**DeLeone**, Carmon 1942- *WhoEnt 92*
**Deleray**, Arthur Loyd 1936- *AmMWSc 92*
**De Lerma**, Dominique-Rene Sebastien 1928- *WhoEnt 92*
**De Lerno**, Manuel Joseph 1922- *WhoMW 92*
**Delerue**, Georges 1924- *IntMPA 92*
**Delespesse**, Guy Joseph 1941- *AmMWSc 92*
**deLeur**, Robbie Lynn 1956- *WhoWest 92*
**Deleuran**, Aage 1925- *IntWW 91*
**DeLevie**, Robert 1933- *AmMWSc 92*
**Delevoryas**, Theodore 1929- *AmMWSc 92*
**Delfim Netto**, Antonio 1928- *IntWW 91*
**Delfin**, Eliseo Dais 1925- *AmMWSc 92*
**Delfine-Lanier**, Judith Marie 1956- *WhoEnt 92*
**Delfini**, Delfo 1913- *IntWW 91*
**Delflache**, Andre P 1923- *AmMWSc 92*
**Delfont** *Who 92*
**Delfont**, Baron 1909- *IntWW 91, Who 92*
**Delfont**, Bernard 1909- *IntMPA 92*
**Del Forno**, Anton 1950- *WhoEnt 92*
**Delgadillo**, Larry 1950- *WhoHisp 92*
**Delgado**, Abelardo B 1931- *ConAu 15AS [port]*
**Delgado**, Abelardo Barrientos 1931- *WhoHisp 92*
**Delgado**, Alberto Luis 1955- *WhoHisp 92*
**Delgado**, Alex V. 1934- *WhoHisp 92*
**Delgado**, Alma I. 1954- *WhoHisp 92*
**Delgado**, Alvaro 1922- *IntWW 91*
**Delgado**, Cirilo T 1938- *WhoAmP 91*
**Delgado**, Debra Ysiano 1957- *WhoHisp 92*
**Delgado**, Diana Rose 1958- *WhoHisp 92*
**Delgado**, Douglas Anthony 1934- *WhoHisp 92*
**Delgado**, Edmundo R. 1932- *WhoHisp 92*
**Delgado**, George James 1942- *WhoHisp 92*
**Delgado**, Giovanni R. 1952- *WhoHisp 92*
**Delgado**, Gloria 1953- *WhoHisp 92*
**Delgado**, Hava Jean 1941- *WhoHisp 92*
**Delgado**, Hope Lena 1927- *WhoHisp 92*
**Delgado**, Humberto 1940- *WhoHisp 92*
**Delgado**, Isabel 1934- *WhoHisp 92*
**Delgado**, Jaime Nabor 1932- *AmMWSc 92*
**Delgado**, Jane L. 1953- *WhoHisp 92*
**Delgado**, Jose 1950- *WhoHisp 92*
**Delgado**, Jose Manuel 1927- *WhoHisp 92*
**Delgado**, Jose Matias 1767-1832 *HisDSpE*
**Delgado**, Julio Francisco 1961- *WhoFI 92*
**Delgado**, Lorenzo Vincent 1934- *WhoHisp 92*
**Delgado**, M. Conchita 1942- *WhoHisp 92*
**Delgado**, Miguel Aquiles, Jr. 1943- *WhoHisp 92*
**Delgado**, Natalia 1953- *WhoAmL 92*
**Delgado**, Olga I. 1943- *WhoHisp 92*
**Delgado**, Ramon Louis 1937- *WhoEnt 92, WhoHisp 92*
**Delgado**, Rene Torres 1947- *WhoHisp 92*
**Delgado**, Richard *WhoHisp 92*
**Delgado**, Sandra Gayle 1952- *WhoWest 92*
**Delgado**, Stephen Michael 1949- *WhoAmP 91*
**Delgado**, Vernon Thomas 1932- *WhoAmP 91*
**Delgado**, Zoraida 1965- *WhoHisp 92*
**Delgado-Baguer**, Raul 1916- *WhoHisp 92*
**Delgado-Frias**, Jose G. 1954- *WhoHisp 92*
**Delgado-Morales**, Manuel 1944- *WhoHisp 92*
**Delgado-P.**, Guillermo 1950- *WhoHisp 92*
**Delgado-Vega**, Damaris 1963- *WhoAmL 92*
**Delgass**, W Nicholas 1942- *AmMWSc 92*
**del Greco**, Francesco 1923- *AmMWSc 92*
**Del Grosso**, Vincent Alfred 1925- *AmMWSc 92*
**Del Guercio**, Louis Richard M 1929- *AmMWSc 92*
**Del Guercio**, Paolo 1935- *WhoWest 92*
**Delhaye**, Jean 1921- *IntWW 91*
**Delhi**, Archbishop of 1913- *Who 92*
**D'Elia**, Christopher Francis 1946- *AmMWSc 92*
**Delia**, Margaret Helen 1931- *WhoWest 92*
**D'Elia**, Nicholas 1959- *WhoEnt 92*
**Delia**, Sylvia 1954- *WhoEnt 92*
**Delia**, Thomas J 1935- *AmMWSc 92*
**D'Elia**, William Vincent 1948- *WhoEnt 92*
**De Libero**, Libero 1906-1981 *DcLB 114 [port]*
**Delibes**, Leo 1836-1891 *NewAmDM*
**Delibes**, Miguel 1920- *IntWW 91*
**Delight**, John David 1925- *Who 92*
**Delihas**, Nicholas 1932- *AmMWSc 92*
**Delikat**, Michael 1952- *WhoAmL 92*
**Delille**, Henriette 1813-1862 *NotBlAW 92*
**Delille**, Jacques 1738-1813 *BlkwCEP*
**DeLillo**, Don *DrAPF 91*
**De Lillo**, Don 1936- *BenetAL 91, ConNov 91, IntAu&W 91, NewYTBS 91 [port], WrDr 92*
**De Lillo**, Nicholas Joseph 1939- *AmMWSc 92*
**DeLilly**, Mayo Ralph, III 1953- *WhoBlA 92*
**De Lima**, Sigrid *DrAPF 91*
**Delimitros**, Tom H. 1940- *WhoFI 92*
**Delin**, Sylvia Kaufman 1945- *WhoAmL 92*
**deLinde**, Mark Terry 1956- *WhoEnt 92*
**Delinger**, William Galen 1939- *AmMWSc 92*
**Delinsky**, Barbara 1945- *IntAu&W 91, WrDr 92*
**De Lint**, Charles 1951- *IntAu&W 91, TwCSFW 91*
**Delis**, Luis Mariano 1957- *BlkOlyM*
**Delis Fournier**, Luis Mariano 1957- *BlkOlyM*
**De Lisi**, Charles 1941- *AmMWSc 92*
**Delisi**, Dianne W 1943- *WhoAmP 91*
**Delisi**, Donald Paul 1944- *AmMWSc 92*
**De L'Isle**, Viscount d1991 *Who 92N*
**De L'Isle**, Viscount 1909-1991 *IntWW 91, -91N*
**De L'Isle**, Viscount 1945- *Who 92*
**Delisle**, Claude 1929- *AmMWSc 92*
**de Lisle**, Everard John Robert March P 1930- *Who 92*
**DeLisle**, Mark Alan 1958- *WhoMW 92*
**DeLisle**, Peter Andrew 1949- *WhoFI 92*
**de Lisle**, Suzanne Turner 1948- *WhoAmL 92*
**De Lisser**, Herbert G. 1878-1944 *BenetAL 91*
**Delitzsch**, Friedrich 1850-1922 *EncTR 91*
**Delius**, Anthony *LiExTwC*
**Delius**, Anthony 1916- *ConPo 91, WrDr 92*
**Delius**, Frederick 1862-1934 *FacFETw, NewAmDM*
**Delivanis**, Dimitrios J. 1909- *IntWW 91*
**Delivoria-Papadopoulos**, Maria 1931- *AmMWSc 92*
**Deliyannis**, Platon Constantine 1931- *AmMWSc 92*
**DeLizza**, Joseph Francis 1954- *WhoFI 92*
**Del Junco**, Tirso *WhoAmP 91*
**del Junco**, Tirso 1925- *WhoHisp 92*
**Delk**, Ann Stevens 1942- *AmMWSc 92*
**Delk**, Fannie M. 1933- *WhoBlA 92*
**Delk**, James F., Jr. 1948- *WhoBlA 92*
**Delk**, Oliver Rahn 1948- *WhoBlA 92*
**Delk**, Russell Louis 1956- *WhoAmL 92*
**Delk**, Yvonne V. 1939- *WhoBlA 92*
**Delker**, Gerald Lee 1947- *AmMWSc 92*
**Dell**, Belinda *IntAu&W 91X*
**Dell**, Berenice V *ScFEYrs*
**Dell**, Curtis G 1924- *AmMWSc 92*
**Dell**, David Humphreys 1942- *WhoAmL 92*
**Dell**, David Michael 1931- *Who 92*
**Dell**, Edmund 1921- *IntWW 91, Who 92, WrDr 92*
**Dell**, Ernest Robert 1928- *WhoAmL 92, WhoFI 92*
**Dell**, Floyd 1887-1969 *BenetAL 91*
**Dell**, George F, Jr 1931- *AmMWSc 92*
**Dell**, George Robert 1944- *WhoWest 92*
**Dell**, Helen *WhoEnt 92*
**Dell**, J. Howard *WhoRel 92*
**Dell**, Karl Joseph 1936- *WhoWest 92*
**Dell**, M Benjamin 1919- *AmMWSc 92*
**Dell**, Miriam 1924- *Who 92*
**Dell**, Philip N 1934- *WhoIns 92*
**Dell**, Robert Sydney 1922- *Who 92*
**Dell**, Roger Marcus 1936- *AmMWSc 92*
**Dell**, Sidney 1918- *WrDr 92*
**Dell**, Tommy Ray 1937- *AmMWSc 92*
**Dell**, Willie J. 1930- *WhoBlA 92*
**Della**, George W, Jr 1943- *WhoAmP 91*
**della Casa**, Lisa 1919- *NewAmDM*
**Della Casa-Debeljevic**, Lisa *IntWW 91*
**Della-Cioppa**, Guy *LesBEnT 92*
**Della Coletta**, Brent Allen 1953- *WhoMW 92*
**Della Femina**, Jerry 1936- *WhoFI 92*
**Dellafera**, Mark Dennis 1944- *WhoFI 92*
**Della-Fera**, Mary Anne 1954- *AmMWSc 92*
**Dellaira**, Michael Richard 1949- *WhoEnt 92*
**Dellal**, Jack 1923- *Who 92*
**de Llanos**, Myrka Barbara 1965- *WhoHisp 92*
**Dellapenna**, Joseph William 1942- *WhoAmL 92*
**DellaPietra**, Stephen John 1948- *WhoEnt 92*
**Dellaria**, Joseph Fred, Jr 1956- *AmMWSc 92*
**DellaRocca**, Lenny *DrAPF 91*
**Dellarocco**, Kenneth Anthony 1952- *WhoAmL 92*
**Della Rosa**, Susann G 1950- *WhoAmP 91*
**Dellas**, Robert Dennis 1944- *WhoFI 92, WhoWest 92*
**Della Torre**, Edward 1934- *AmMWSc 92*
**Della Zoppa**, Ethel Ann 1934- *WhoFI 92*
**Delle Chiaie**, Stefano 1934- *BiDExR*
**Dellenback**, John 1918- *WhoAmP 91*
**Dellenback**, Robert Joseph 1928- *AmMWSc 92*
**Deller**, Alfred 1912-1979 *NewAmDM*
**Deller**, John J. 1931- *ConAu 134*
**Deller**, John Joseph 1931- *AmMWSc 92*
**Dell'Ergo**, Robert James 1918- *WhoAmL 92*
**Dellert**, Jean T *WhoAmP 91*
**Delleur**, Jacques W 1924- *AmMWSc 92*
**Delleur**, Jacques William 1924- *WhoMW 92*
**Delli-Pizzi**, Nancy 1953- *WhoIns 92*
**DelliBovi**, Alfred A 1946- *WhoAmP 91*
**Dellicolli**, Humbert Thomas 1944- *AmMWSc 92*
**Dellinger**, Anne Maxwell 1940- *WhoAmL 92*
**Dellinger**, Charles Wade 1949- *WhoRel 92*
**Dellinger**, David 1915- *AmPeW*
**Dellinger**, Paul 1938- *IntAu&W 91*
**Dellinger**, Richard M 1936- *WhoAmP 91*
**Dellinger**, Thomas Baynes 1926- *AmMWSc 92*
**Dellinger**, Walter Estes, III 1941- *WhoAmL 92*
**Delliquanti**, James 1963- *WhoWest 92*
**Dellis**, Deborah Ruth 1960- *WhoWest 92*
**Dellis**, Fredy Michel 1945- *WhoFI 92*
**Dellmann**, H Dieter 1931- *AmMWSc 92*
**Dello Iacono**, Paul Michael 1957- *WhoAmL 92*
**Dello Joio**, Norman 1913- *ConCom 92, NewAmDM, WhoEnt 92*
**Delloff**, Stefan T. 1942- *WhoAmL 92*
**Dell'Olio**, Louis 1948- *IntWW 91*
**Dellomo**, Frank A. 1933- *WhoFI 92*
**Dellomo**, James Robert 1940- *WhoFI 92*
**Dell'Orco**, Robert T 1942- *AmMWSc 92*
**Dell'Osso**, Louis Frank 1941- *AmMWSc 92*
**Dell'Osso**, Luino, Jr. 1939- *WhoFI 92*
**Dellow**, Jeff 1949- *TwCPaSc*
**Dellow**, John 1931- *Who 92*
**Delluc**, Louis 1890-1924 *IntDcF 2-2*
**Dellums**, Ronald 1935- *ConBlB 2 [port]*
**Dellums**, Ronald V. 1935- *AlmAP 92 [port], WhoAmP 91, WhoBlA 92, WhoWest 92*
**Delluva**, Adelaide Marie 1917- *AmMWSc 92*
**Dellwig**, Louis Field 1922- *AmMWSc 92*
**Dellwo**, Dennis Aloysius 1945- *WhoAmP 91*
**Dellwo**, Robert Dennis 1917- *WhoWest 92*
**Delmaine**, Barry *IntMPA 92*
**Delman**, Stephen Bennett 1942- *WhoAmL 92*
**Del Mar**, Norman 1919- *IntAu&W 91, WrDr 92*
**Del Mar**, Norman Rene 1919- *IntWW 91, Who 92*
**Delmar**, Vina 1905- *BenetAL 91*
**Del Martia**, Astron *TwCSFW 91*
**Delmas**, Jacques Pierre Michel C. *Who 92*
**Delmastro**, Ann Mary 1945- *AmMWSc 92*
**Delmastro**, Joseph Raymond 1940- *AmMWSc 92*
**Delmer**, Deborah P 1941- *AmMWSc 92*
**Delmerico-Isaac**, Frances E. 1918- *WhoEnt 92*
**Del Mestri**, Guido 1911- *WhoRel 92*
**Delmhorst**, Arthur McGill 1938- *WhoFI 92*
**Del Monaco**, Mario 1915-1982 *FacFETw, NewAmDM*

**Del Monte,** Carlos *WhoRel 92*
**Delmonte,** David William 1930- *AmMWSc 92*
**Delmonte,** Lilian 1928- *AmMWSc 92*
**Del Moral,** Roger 1943- *AmMWSc 92, WhoHisp 92*
**Delmore Brothers** *NewAmDM*
**Del Mundo,** Renato Santiago Thomas 1955- *WhoHisp 92*
**Del Negro,** John Thomas 1948- *WhoAmL 92*
**Delnore,** Victor Eli 1943- *AmMWSc 92*
**Deloach,** Allen *DrAPF 91*
**DeLoach,** Bernard Collins, Jr 1930- *AmMWSc 92*
**DeLoach,** Culver Jackson, Jr 1932- *AmMWSc 92*
**DeLoach,** Harris Eugene, Jr. 1944- *WhoAmL 92*
**Deloach,** Joe 1967- *BlkOlyM*
**Deloach,** John Rooker 1946- *AmMWSc 92*
**Deloach,** Michael Allen 1962- *WhoRel 92*
**DeLoach,** Robert Edgar 1939- *WhoWest 92*
**DeLoatch,** Cleveland M., Sr. 1925- *WhoBlA 92*
**DeLoatch,** Eugene *WhoBlA 92*
**DeLoatch,** Eugene M 1936- *AmMWSc 92*
**Deloatch,** Myrna Loy 1938- *WhoBlA 92*
**Delogu,** Orlando E 1937- *WhoAmP 91*
**del Olmo,** Frank P. 1948- *WhoHisp 92*
**de Lome,** Enrique Dupuy 1851-1904 *HisDSpE*
**Delon,** Alain 1935- *FacFETw, IntMPA 92, IntWW 91*
**Delon,** Anne Elisabeth 1964- *WhoFI 92*
**Deloncle,** Eugene 1890-1944 *BiDExR*
**Deloney,** Thomas 1543?-1600? *RfGEnL 91*
**DeLong,** Allyn F *AmMWSc 92*
**DeLong,** Andrew 1961- *WhoRel 92*
**De Long,** Chester Wallace 1925- *AmMWSc 92*
**DeLong,** Clarence William 1940- *WhoMW 92*
**De Long,** Dale Ray 1959- *WhoMW 92*
**Delong,** Karl Thomas 1938- *AmMWSc 92*
**DeLong,** Lance Eric 1946- *AmMWSc 92*
**DeLong,** Michael Ben 1956- *WhoRel 92*
**DeLong,** Stephen Edwin 1943- *AmMWSc 92*
**DeLong,** Terry Lee 1950- *WhoRel 92*
**De Long,** William James 1930- *WhoAmP 91*
**DeLong,** William T 1921- *AmMWSc 92*
**DeLorean,** John Z 1925- *FacFETw*
**DeLorean,** John Zachary 1925- *WhoWest 92*
**De Lorenzo,** Francesco 1938- *IntWW 91*
**DeLorenzo,** Joseph Anthony, Jr 1940- *WhoAmP 91*
**De Lorenzo,** Richard A 1939- *WhoAmP 91*
**DeLorenzo,** Robert John 1947- *AmMWSc 92*
**DeLorenzo,** Ronald Anthony 1941- *AmMWSc 92*
**DeLorey,** John Alfred 1924- *WhoFI 92*
**Delorey,** Patricia Ann 1960- *WhoAmL 92*
**De Lorge,** John Oldham 1935- *AmMWSc 92*
**Deloria,** Vine, Jr. 1933- *BenetAL 91*
**Deloria,** Vine Victor, Jr. 1933- *WhoWest 92*
**Delorit,** Richard John 1921- *AmMWSc 92*
**Delorme,** Charles DuBose, Jr. 1939- *WhoFI 92*
**Delorme,** Jean 1902- *IntWW 91*
**Delors,** Jacques 1925- *NewYTBS 91 [port]*
**Delors,** Jacques Lucien Jean 1925- *IntWW 91, Who 92*
**Delort,** Mathias William 1961- *WhoAmL 92*
**de Lory,** Peter 1948- *WhoWest 92*
**Delos,** John Bernard 1944- *AmMWSc 92*
**de Los Angeles,** Victoria *NewAmDM*
**de los Angeles,** Victoria 1923- *FacFETw, IntWW 91, Who 92, WhoEnt 92*
**de los Reyes,** Anthony 1942- *WhoHisp 92*
**De Los Reyes,** Fernando Rivera *WhoHisp 92*
**De Los Reyes,** Grizelle *WhoHisp 92*
**De Los Reyes,** Harding Robert, Jr. 1946- *WhoHisp 92*
**de los Reyes,** Ramon *WhoHisp 92*
**de los Reyes,** Raul Alberto 1953- *WhoHisp 92*
**de los Santos,** Alfredo G., Jr. 1936- *WhoHisp 92*
**de los Santos,** Luis 1966- *WhoHisp 92*
**de Lotbiniere,** Edmond *Who 92*
**Delouche,** James Curtis 1930- *AmMWSc 92*
**Deloughery,** Grace Leone Meinen *IntAu&W 91*
**Delovitch,** Terry L *AmMWSc 92*
**Delp,** Alfred 1907-1945 *EncTR 91 [port]*
**Delp,** Charles Joseph 1927- *AmMWSc 92*
**Delp,** Douglas A. 1955- *WhoRel 92*
**Delp,** George William 1929- *WhoFI 92*
**Delp,** Jeffrey Alan 1955- *WhoFI 92*
**Delp,** Michael *DrAPF 91*
**Delp,** Randy Lee 1950- *WhoRel 92*
**Delp,** Wilbur Charles, Jr. 1934- *WhoAmL 92*
**Del Papa,** Frankie Sue *WhoAmP 91*
**Del Papa,** Frankie Sue 1949- *WhoAmL 92, WhoWest 92*
**Del Pesco,** Susan Marie Carr 1946- *WhoAmL 92*
**Delphey,** William Ronald 1944- *WhoFI 92*
**Delphia,** John Maurice 1925- *AmMWSc 92*
**Delphin,** Jacques Mercier 1929- *WhoBlA 92*
**Delpierre,** David Mark 1959- *WhoAmL 92*
**Del Pinal,** Jorge Huascar 1945- *WhoHisp 92*
**Del Pino,** Carlos 1963- *WhoHisp 92*
**Del Pino,** Jerome King 1946- *WhoBlA 92*
**Delpit,** Joseph A 1940- *WhoAmP 91, WhoBlA 92*
**del Portillo,** Alvaro 1914- *IntWW 91*
**del Poza,** Ivania 1947- *WhoHisp 92*
**del Prado,** Yvette 1932- *WhoHisp 92*
**Del Prete,** John F 1927- *WhoAmP 91*
**Del Raso,** Joseph Vincent 1952- *WhoAmL 92*
**Del Razo,** Erick Silva 1967- *WhoWest 92*
**Del Regato,** Juan A 1909- *AmMWSc 92*
**del Rey,** Lester *TwCSFW 91*
**del Rey,** Lester 1915- *BenetAL 91, IntAu&W 91, TwCSFW 91, WrDr 92*
**Del Ricci,** John Anthony 1951- *WhoRel 92*
**Del Rio,** Carlos Eduardo 1928- *AmMWSc 92*
**Del Rio,** Carlos H. 1949- *WhoHisp 92*
**Del Rio,** Fernando Rene 1932- *WhoHisp 92*
**del Rio,** Israel H. 1948- *WhoHisp 92*
**Del Rio,** Joaquin 1941- *WhoHisp 92*
**Del Rio,** Luis Raul 1939- *WhoHisp 92*
**Del Rosario,** Franco R. *WhoHisp 92*
**Del Rossi,** Paul R. 1942- *IntMPA 92*
**del Russo,** Alessandra Luini 1916- *WhoAmL 92*
**Del Ruth,** Thomas Anthony 1943- *WhoEnt 92*
**Delsack,** Katherine Landey 1959- *WhoAmL 92, WhoFI 92*
**Del Santo,** Lawrence A. 1934- *WhoWest 92*
**Delsanto,** Pier Paolo 1941- *AmMWSc 92*
**Delsemme,** Armand Hubert 1918- *AmMWSc 92*
**del Solar,** Daniel 1940- *WhoWest 92*
**Delson,** Eric 1945- *AmMWSc 92*
**Delton,** Mary Helen 1946- *AmMWSc 92*
**Del Toro,** Ana I. 1950- *WhoHisp 92*
**Del Toro,** Angelo 1947- *WhoAmP 91, WhoHisp 92*
**del Toro,** Raul *WhoHisp 92*
**Del Toro,** Vincent 1923- *AmMWSc 92*
**Del Tredici,** David 1937- *ConCom 92, NewAmDM, WhoEnt 92*
**Del Tufo,** Robert J *WhoAmP 91*
**Del Tufo,** Robert J. 1933- *WhoAmL 92*
**Del Turco,** John *WhoRel 92*
**Delu,** Dahl R. 1940- *WhoEnt 92*
**de Lubac,** Henri 1896-1991 *NewYTBS 91*
**Deluc,** Jean Andre 1727-1817 *BlkwCEP*
**DeLuca,** Anthony *WhoAmP 91*
**DeLuca,** Anthony M 1937- *WhoAmP 91*
**Deluca,** Carlo J 1943- *AmMWSc 92*
**De Luca,** Chester 1927- *AmMWSc 92*
**DeLuca,** Dominick *AmMWSc 92*
**DeLuca,** Donald Carl 1936- *AmMWSc 92*
**De Luca,** Giuseppe 1876-1950 *NewAmDM*
**DeLuca,** Hector Floyd 1930- *AmMWSc 92*
**DeLuca,** Louis C *WhoAmP 91*
**De Luca,** Luigi Maria 1941- *AmMWSc 92*
**DeLuca,** Patrick John 1944- *AmMWSc 92*
**DeLuca,** Patrick Phillip 1935- *AmMWSc 92*
**DeLuca,** Paul Michael, Jr 1944- *AmMWSc 92*
**DeLuca,** Robert D 1941- *AmMWSc 92*
**DeLuca,** Ronald 1924- *WhoFI 92*
**De Luca,** Thomas George 1950- *WhoAmL 92*
**DeLucca,** Gregory James 1937- *WhoFI 92, WhoWest 92*
**DeLucca,** Leopoldo Eloy 1952- *WhoMW 92*
**Delucchi,** George Paul 1938- *WhoWest 92*
**De Lucchi,** Michele 1951- *IntWW 91*
**De Lucchi,** Michele 1952- *DcTwDes*
**De Luccia,** John Jerry 1935- *AmMWSc 92*
**DeLuce,** Richard David 1928- *WhoAmL 92*
**de Luce,** Virginia 1921- *WhoEnt 92*
**De Lucia,** Frank Charles 1943- *AmMWSc 92*
**De Lucia-Weinberg,** Diane Marie 1964- *WhoFI 92*
**de Lugo,** Ron 1930- *AlmAP 92 [port], WhoHisp 92*
**De Lugo,** Ronald 1930- *WhoAmP 91*
**Deluhery,** Patrick John 1942- *WhoAmP 91, WhoMW 92*
**DeLuise,** Dom 1933- *ConTFT 9, IntMPA 92*
**De Lukie,** Donald Adrian 1944- *WhoRel 92*
**Delumeau,** Jean 1923- *WhoRel 92*
**de Luna,** Anita 1947- *WhoRel 92*
**De Luna,** Evangelina S. 1939- *WhoHisp 92*
**De Lung,** Jane Solberger 1944- *WhoFI 92*
**Delurgio,** Esther May 1944- *WhoFI 92*
**DeLury,** Daniel Bertrand 1907- *AmMWSc 92*
**DeLustro,** Frank Anthony 1948- *AmMWSc 92*
**Delvaille,** John Paul 1931- *AmMWSc 92*
**del Valle,** Antonio M. 1954- *WhoHisp 92*
**Del Valle,** Carlos Sergio 1951- *WhoHisp 92*
**del Valle,** Eduardo N. 1961- *WhoHisp 92*
**Delvalle,** Eric Arturo 1937- *IntWW 91*
**Del Valle,** Francisco Rafael 1933- *AmMWSc 92*
**Del Valle,** Hector L. 1963- *WhoHisp 92*
**Del Valle,** Irma *DrAPF 91*
**del Valle,** John 1904- *IntMPA 92*
**Del Valle,** Jose M *WhoAmP 91, WhoHisp 92*
**Del Valle,** M. 1931- *WhoHisp 92*
**Del Valle,** Miguel 1951- *WhoAmP 91, WhoHisp 92*
**DelValle,** Raymond Stephen 1954- *WhoWest 92*
**Del Valle,** Tony 1955- *WhoHisp 92*
**Del Valle Alliende,** Jaime 1931- *IntWW 91*
**Del Valle-Jacquemain,** Jean Marie 1961- *WhoHisp 92*
**del Valle-Sepulveda,** Edwin Alberto 1962- *WhoHisp 92*
**Delvau,** Alfred 1825-1867 *ThHEIm*
**Delvaux,** Andre 1926- *IntDcF 2-2 [port]*
**Delvaux,** Paul 1897- *IntWW 91*
**Delvaux,** William Preston 1957- *WhoRel 92*
**Del Vayo,** J. Alvarez *DcAmImH*
**Delve,** Frederick 1902- *Who 92*
**Del Vecchio,** John M. 1947- *DcLB DS9 [port]*
**Del Vecchio,** Vito Gerard 1939- *AmMWSc 92*
**Delvigs,** Peter 1933- *AmMWSc 92*
**Del Villano,** Bert Charles 1943- *AmMWSc 92*
**Del Villar,** Laura 1958- *WhoHisp 92*
**Delvin,** Lord *Who 92*
**Delvin,** David George 1939- *IntAu&W 91, Who 92*
**Delvoye,** Jacques Victor 1947- *WhoFI 92*
**Delwiche,** Constant Collin 1917- *AmMWSc 92*
**Delwiche,** Eugene Albert 1917- *AmMWSc 92*
**Delyannis,** Leonidas T 1926- *WhoAmP 91*
**DeLynn,** Jane *DrAPF 91*
**Delza-Munson,** Elizabeth *WhoEnt 92*
**Delzeit,** Linda Doris 1954- *WhoWest 92*
**Delzell,** Charles F. 1920- *WrDr 92*
**Delzer,** Jeff W *WhoAmP 91*
**deMaar,** Natalie Shana 1950- *WhoWest 92*
**de Maat,** Martin 1949- *WhoEnt 92*
**de MaCarty,** Peter Charles Ridgway 1952- *WhoWest 92*
**de Madariaga,** Isabel 1919- *IntWW 91*
**De Madariaga,** Salvador 1886-1978 *FacFETw*
**Demaeyer,** Bruce R *AmMWSc 92*
**DeMaeyer,** Bruce Raymond 1938- *WhoMW 92*
**DeMaggio,** Augustus Edward 1932- *AmMWSc 92*
**Demain,** Arnold Lester 1927- *AmMWSc 92*
**De Main,** John 1944- *WhoEnt 92*
**DeMain,** Paul 1955- *WhoAmP 91*
**De Maine,** Paul Alexander Desmond 1924- *AmMWSc 92*
**DeMaio,** Donald Anthony *AmMWSc 92*
**De Maio,** Victoria Antoinette 1947- *WhoWest 92*
**de Maiziere,** Lothar 1940- *IntWW 91*
**de Maiziere,** Ulrich 1912- *IntWW 91*
**de Majo,** William Maks 1917- *Who 92*
**De Man,** Hendrik 1885-1953 *BiDExR*
**DeMan,** John Maria 1925- *AmMWSc 92*
**de Man,** Paul 1919-1983 *BenetAL 91*
**Demanche,** Edna Louise 1915- *AmMWSc 92*
**Demangone,** Dominic Donald 1949- *WhoAmP 91*
**DeMann,** Jack Frank 1933- *WhoAmP 91*
**Demapan,** Ignacio Dlg *WhoAmP 91*
**Demapan,** Juan Dlg *WhoAmP 91*
**De Mar,** David Abram 1926- *WhoMW 92*
**DeMar,** Robert E 1931- *AmMWSc 92*
**DeMaranville,** Jason E. 1961- *WhoEnt 92*
**Demaray,** Donald E. 1926- *WrDr 92*
**Demaray,** Mark Marston 1953- *WhoAmL 92*
**Demarchi,** Ernest Nicholas 1939- *WhoWest 92*
**De Marco,** F A 1921- *AmMWSc 92*
**De Marco,** Guido 1931- *IntWW 91*
**DeMarco,** John Gregory 1939- *AmMWSc 92*
**DeMarco,** John W 1951- *WhoAmP 91*
**DeMarco,** Michael 1936- *WhoAmP 91*
**DeMarco,** Nicholas 1931- *WhoEnt 92*
**DeMarco,** Ralph John 1924- *WhoFI 92, WhoWest 92*
**Demarco,** Richard 1930- *TwCPaSc, Who 92*
**DeMarco,** Roland R. 1910- *WhoFI 92*
**De Marco,** Ronald Anthony 1944- *AmMWSc 92*
**DeMarco,** Vincent 1957- *WhoAmP 91*
**De Marcus,** Jamima Powell *WhoAmP 91*
**de Mare,** Eric 1910- *Who 92*
**De Mare,** Eric Samuel 1910- *IntAu&W 91*
**Demaree,** Richard Spottswood, Jr 1942- *AmMWSc 92*
**Demaree,** Thomas L 1953- *AmMWSc 92*
**Demarest,** Gerald Gregory 1959- *WhoRel 92*
**Demarest,** Harold H, Jr 1946- *WhoAmP 91*
**Demarest,** Harold Hunt, Jr 1946- *AmMWSc 92*
**Demarest,** Jeffrey R 1946- *AmMWSc 92*
**Demarest,** Keith Thomas *AmMWSc 92*
**de Margerie,** Bernard *WhoRel 92*
**de Margerie,** Emmanuel 1924- *Who 92*
**de Margerie,** Emmanuel Jacquin 1924-1991 *NewYTBS 91*
**De Margerie,** Jean-Marie 1927- *AmMWSc 92*
**de Margitay,** Gedeon 1924- *WhoFI 92*
**DeMaria,** Anthony John 1931- *AmMWSc 92*
**De Maria,** F John 1928- *AmMWSc 92*
**DeMaria,** Joseph Angelo 1957- *WhoAmL 92*
**DeMaria,** Joseph Carminus 1947- *WhoAmL 92*
**De Maria,** Michael Joseph, III 1961- *WhoFI 92*
**Demaria,** Robert *DrAPF 91*
**DeMarinis,** Bernard Daniel 1946- *AmMWSc 92*
**DeMarinis,** John Henry 1937- *WhoRel 92*
**De Marinis,** Rick *WrDr 92*
**DeMarinis,** Rick 1934- *TwCWW 91*
**Demaris,** Ovid 1919- *IntAu&W 91, WrDr 92*
**De Maris,** Ron *DrAPF 91*
**DeMaroney,** Gary Stephen 1951- *WhoEnt 92*
**Demarque,** Pierre 1932- *AmMWSc 92*
**DeMarr,** Marcia Joy 1938- *WhoWest 92*
**DeMarr,** Ralph Elgin 1930- *AmMWSc 92*
**DeMars,** Gene 1937- *WhoAmP 91*
**DeMars,** Robert A 1930- *WhoAmP 91*
**DeMars,** Robert Ivan 1928- *AmMWSc 92*
**De Marsanich,** Augusto 1893-1973 *BiDExR*
**DeMartin,** Charles Peter 1952- *WhoAmL 92*
**DeMartini,** Edward Emile 1946- *AmMWSc 92*
**DeMartini,** Frank Thomas 1962- *WhoEnt 92*
**De Martini,** James Charles 1942- *AmMWSc 92*
**DeMartini,** John 1933- *AmMWSc 92*
**DeMartinis,** Frederick Daniel 1924- *AmMWSc 92*
**De Martino,** Ciro 1903- *IntWW 91*
**De Martino,** Francesco 1907- *IntWW 91*
**De Martino,** Lyvia 1914- *WhoEnt 92*
**DeMartino,** Ronald Nicholas 1943- *AmMWSc 92*
**Demas,** James Nicholas 1942- *AmMWSc 92*
**Demas,** William Gilbert 1929- *IntWW 91*
**DeMascio,** Robert Edward 1923- *WhoAmL 92*
**DeMasi,** Jack Bernard 1946- *WhoEnt 92*
**DeMasi,** John 1960- *WhoFI 92*
**DeMaso,** Harry A 1921- *WhoAmP 91*
**DeMason,** Darleen Audrey 1951- *AmMWSc 92*
**Demassa,** Jessie G *IntAu&W 91, WhoWest 92*
**DeMassa,** Thomas A 1937- *AmMWSc 92*
**DeMaster,** Douglas Paul 1951- *AmMWSc 92*
**De Master,** Eugene Glenn 1943- *AmMWSc 92*
**De Matos Proenca,** Joao Uva *IntWW 91*
**De Matte,** Michael L 1937- *AmMWSc 92*
**de Mauley,** Baron 1921- *Who 92*
**De Mave,** Jack F. *WhoEnt 92*
**DeMay,** John Andrew 1925- *WhoAmL 92*
**De Mayo,** Benjamin 1940- *AmMWSc 92*
**de Mayo,** Paul 1924- *IntWW 91, Who 92*
**Dembart,** Lee 1946- *ConAu 133*
**Dembe,** David 1945- *WhoAmL 92*

**Dember,** Alexis Berthold 1912- *AmMWSc 92*
**Dember,** Jean Wilkins 1930- *WhoBlA 92*
**Demberg,** Lisa I. 1957- *WhoEnt 92*
**Dembicer,** Edwin Herbert 1928- *WhoAmL 92*
**Dembicki,** Harry, Jr 1951- *AmMWSc 92*
**Dembitzer,** Herbert 1934- *AmMWSc 92*
**Dembling,** Paul Gerald 1920- *WhoAmP 91*
**Dembowski,** Hermann 1928- *WhoRel 92*
**Dembowski,** Peter Vincent 1946- *AmMWSc 92*
**Dembree,** Donn Max 1930- *WhoMW 92*
**Dembrow,** Dana Lee 1953- *WhoAmP 91*
**Dembs,** Michael Eric 1959- *WhoEnt 92*
**Dembski,** Stephen Michael 1949- *WhoEnt 92*
**Dembure,** Philip Pito 1941- *AmMWSc 92*
**Demby,** Emanuel H. 1919- *IntMPA 92*
**Demby,** James E. 1936- *WhoBlA 92*
**Demby,** William 1922- *BenetAL 91, BlkLC [port]*
**Demby,** William E., Jr. 1922- *WhoBlA 92*
**Demchenko,** Vladimir Akimovich 1920- *IntWW 91*
**de Medici-Horwitz,** Cecilia 1945- *WhoEnt 92*
**DeMedicis,** E M J A 1937- *AmMWSc 92*
**DeMeester,** Wayne 1951- *WhoFI 92*
**DeMeio,** Joseph Louis 1917- *AmMWSc 92*
**De Mejo,** Oscar 1911- *IntAu&W 91*
**Demel,** Gerald Francis 1941- *WhoWest 92*
**Demel,** Robert Joseph, Jr. 1953- *WhoWest 92*
**De Mel,** Ronnie 1925- *IntWW 91*
**Demell,** Harry A. 1951- *WhoAmL 92*
**De Mello,** Augustin *DrAPF 91*
**DeMello,** Austin Eastwood 1939- *WhoWest 92*
**De Mello,** F Paul 1927- *AmMWSc 92*
**De Mello,** W Carlos 1931- *AmMWSc 92*
**De Melo,** Eurico 1925- *IntWW 91*
**Demember,** John Raymond 1942- *AmMWSc 92*
**de Mendeng,** Gregoire Ambadiang *WhoRel 92*
**de Menezes,** Ruth *DrAPF 91*
**De Ment,** Ira 1931- *WhoAmL 92*
**DeMent,** Jack 1920- *AmMWSc 92*
**De Ment,** Jack Andrew 1920- *WhoWest 92*
**DeMent,** James Alderson, Jr 1947- *WhoAmL 92*
**Dement,** John M 1949- *AmMWSc 92*
**Dement,** William Charles 1928- *AmMWSc 92*
**Dementeva,** Raisa Fedorovna 1925- *SovUnBD*
**Dementi,** Brian Armstead 1938- *AmMWSc 92*
**De Meo,** Edgar Anthony 1942- *AmMWSc 92*
**DeMeo,** James Nicholas, Jr. 1961- *WhoFI 92*
**Demer,** John Adrian, Jr. 1947- *WhoAmL 92*
**Demeray,** Donald E 1926- *IntAu&W 91*
**Demerdash,** Nabeel A O 1943- *AmMWSc 92*
**DeMere,** McCarthy 1925- *WhoAmL 92*
**Demerec,** Milislav 1895-1966 *FacFETw*
**Demeree,** Gloria 1931- *WhoWest 92*
**Demeritte,** Edwin T. 1935- *WhoBlA 92*
**Demeritte,** Richard C. 1939- *IntWW 91*
**Demeritte,** Richard Clifford 1939- *Who 92*
**Demerjian,** Kenneth Leo 1945- *AmMWSc 92*
**de Merode,** Werner 1914- *IntWW 91*
**DeMerritt,** Steven Lee 1952- *WhoFI 92*
**Demers,** James M 1956- *WhoAmP 91*
**DeMers,** Judy L 1944- *WhoAmP 91*
**Demers,** Laurence Maurice 1938- *AmMWSc 92*
**Demers,** Patricia A *WhoAmP 91*
**Demers,** Serge *AmMWSc 92*
**Demers,** Sharon Washington 1951- *WhoAmP 91*
**Demerson,** Christopher 1942- *AmMWSc 92*
**Demes,** Dennis Thomas 1949- *WhoRel 92*
**De Mesa,** Criel 1961- *WhoFI 92*
**de Mesones,** Pedro *WhoHisp 92*
**DeMet,** Edward Michael 1949- *AmMWSc 92*
**Demet,** James Douglas 1962- *WhoAmL 92*
**Demeter,** Steven 1947- *AmMWSc 92*
**Demetillo,** Ricardo Filipino 1920- *WrDr 92*
**Demetillo,** Ricaredo 1920- *ConPo 91, IntAu&W 91*
**Demetra,** Tula Alexandra 1958- *WhoEnt 92*
**Demetracopoulos,** Anthony 1953- *WhoAmP 91*
**Demetrescu,** M 1929- *AmMWSc 92*
**Demetrescu,** Mihai Constantin 1929- *WhoWest 92*
**Demetri,** Patricia *DrAPF 91*
**Demetriades,** Sterge Theodore 1928- *AmMWSc 92*
**Demetrio,** Thomas A. 1947- *WhoAmL 92*
**Demetriou,** Charles Arthur 1941- *AmMWSc 92*
**Demetriou,** Michael 1927- *WhoFI 92*
**Demetrious,** Mary 1950- *WhoAmP 91*
**Demetz,** Hana 1928- *LiExTwC*
**Demeure de Lespaul,** Edouard Henri 1928- *Who 92*
**De Meuse,** Kenneth Paul 1952- *WhoMW 92*
**DeMeyer,** Frank R 1939- *AmMWSc 92*
**DeMeyere,** Roger 1948- *WhoMW 92*
**Demgen,** Karen Diane Klomhaus 1943- *WhoWest 92*
**Demi** *ConAu 35NR, SmATA 66*
**DeMichele,** Mark Anthony 1958- *WhoEnt 92*
**De Michele,** O. Mark 1934- *WhoFI 92, WhoWest 92*
**De Michele,** Rayner 1928- *WhoEnt 92*
**De Micheli,** Giovanni 1955- *AmMWSc 92*
**De Michelis,** Gianni 1940- *IntWW 91*
**Demichelli,** Alberto 1896-1980 *FacFETw*
**Demichev,** Petr Nilovich 1918- *SovUnBD*
**Demidova,** Alla Sergeyevna 1936- *IntWW 91*
**Demijohn,** Thom *ConAu 36NR, IntAu&W 91X, WrDr 92*
**DeMiles,** Edward 1962- *WhoEnt 92*
**D'Emilio,** John 1948- *ConAu 135*
**D'Emilio,** Sandra *WhoHisp 92*
**de Mille,** Agnes *WhoEnt 92*
**De Mille,** Agnes 1905- *BenetAL 91*
**De Mille,** Agnes 1909- *FacFETw*
**de Mille,** Agnes George *Who 92*
**De Mille,** Cecil B. 1881-1959 *BenetAL 91, FacFETw, IntDcF 2-2 [port], RComAH*
**deMille,** Cecil Blount 1881-1959 *DcNCBi 2*
**DeMille,** Darcy *WhoBlA 92*
**deMille,** Henry Churchill 1853-1893 *DcNCBi 2*
**De Mille,** James 1833-1880 *ScFEYrs*
**Demille,** Nelson 1943- *WrDr 92*
**De Mille,** Richard *DrAPF 91*
**De Mille,** Richard 1922- *IntAu&W 91, WrDr 92*
**deMille,** Valerie Cecilia 1949- *WhoBlA 92*
**De Mille,** William C 1878-1955 *ScFEYrs*
**De Mille,** William Churchill 1878-1955 *BenetAL 91, DcNCBi 2*
**DeMillo,** Richard A 1947- *AmMWSc 92*
**Deming,** Alison Hawthorne *DrAPF 91*
**Deming,** Barbara 1917-1984 *AmPeW*
**Deming,** James B. 1940- *WhoWest 92*
**Deming,** Jody W 1952- *AmMWSc 92*
**Deming,** John *DrAPF 91*
**Deming,** John Miley 1925- *AmMWSc 92*
**Deming,** Kirk *TwCWW 91*
**Deming,** Philander 1829-1915 *BenetAL 91*
**Deming,** Quentin Burritt 1919- *AmMWSc 92*
**Deming,** Robert W 1928- *AmMWSc 92*
**Deming,** Stanley Norris 1944- *AmMWSc 92*
**Deming,** Thomas Edward 1954- *WhoFI 92*
**Deming,** W. Edwards 1900- *News 92-2 [port]*
**Deming,** William Edwards *WhoFI 92*
**DeMinico,** Michael Ray 1951- *WhoAmL 92*
**De Miranda,** Paulo *AmMWSc 92*
**Demirchian,** Karen Serpovich 1932- *IntWW 91*
**Demirel,** Suleyman 1924- *FacFETw, IntWW 91*
**Demirel,** T 1924- *AmMWSc 92*
**DeMirjian,** Arto, Jr. *DrAPF 91*
**Demis,** Dermot Joseph 1929- *AmMWSc 92*
**Demise,** Phil *DrAPF 91*
**De Mita,** Luigi Ciriaco 1928- *IntWW 91*
**DeMitchell,** Terri Ann 1953- *WhoAmL 92*
**Demkovich,** Paul Andrew 1922- *AmMWSc 92*
**Demkovitz,** Russell Bernard 1949- *WhoAmP 91*
**Demling,** John William 1951- *WhoAmL 92*
**Demling,** Robert Hugh *AmMWSc 92*
**Demme,** Jonathan 1944- *IntDcF 2-2, IntMPA 92, IntWW 91, WhoEnt 92*
**Demmerle,** Alan Michael 1933- *AmMWSc 92*
**Demmi,** John David 1940- *WhoAmL 92*
**Demming,** W Edwards 1900- *AmMWSc 92*
**Demmler,** John Henry 1932- *WhoAmL 92*
**Demoff,** Marvin Alan 1942- *WhoAmL 92, WhoWest 92*
**De Moleyns** *Who 92*
**De Molina,** Raul 1959- *WhoHisp 92*
**De Monasterio,** Francisco M 1944- *AmMWSc 92*
**Demonbreun,** Thelma M. 1928- *WhoBlA 92*
**De Monchaux,** Cathy 1960- *TwCPaSc*
**de Mond,** Calvin Bernard 1955- *WhoEnt 92*
**Demond,** Joan *AmMWSc 92*
**Demond,** Walter Eugene 1947- *WhoAmL 92*
**DeMoney,** Fred William 1919- *AmMWSc 92*
**Demons,** Leona Marie 1928- *WhoBlA 92*
**DeMonsabert,** Winston Russel 1915- *AmMWSc 92*
**DeMonte,** Maria 1930- *WhoRel 92*
**de Monte-Campbell,** Alpha *WhoWest 92*
**de Montebello,** Philippe 1936- *Who 92*
**DeMontmollin,** Nina Snead 1920- *WhoAmP 91*
**de Montmorency,** Arnold 1908- *Who 92*
**DeMooy,** Cornelis Jacobus 1926- *AmMWSc 92*
**Demopoulos,** Harry Byron 1932- *AmMWSc 92*
**Demopoulos,** James Thomas 1928- *AmMWSc 92*
**Demopulos,** Harold William 1924- *WhoAmL 92*
**DeMordaunt,** Walter J. 1925- *WrDr 92*
**Demorest,** Allan Frederick 1931- *WhoMW 92*
**Demorest,** Mark Stuart 1957- *WhoAmL 92*
**Demorest,** Stephen 1949- *WhoEnt 92*
**DeMorett,** Jerome Henry 1943- *WhoMW 92*
**De Morgan,** John 1848-1920? *ScFEYrs*
**De Morgan,** William 1839-1917 *RfGEnL 91*
**De Mori,** Renato 1941- *AmMWSc 92*
**De Mornay,** Rebecca 1961- *IntMPA 92, WhoEnt 92*
**DeMort,** Carole Lyle 1942- *AmMWSc 92*
**Demos,** Albert Lincoln Aries 1939- *WhoRel 92*
**Demos,** Peter Theodore *AmMWSc 92*
**DeMoss,** John A *AmMWSc 92*
**DeMoss,** Jon W. 1947- *WhoAmL 92*
**DeMoss,** Lynn Allyn 1934- *WhoRel 92*
**Demott,** Benjamin *DrAPF 91*
**Demott,** Benjamin 1924- *WrDr 92*
**Demott,** Bobby Joe 1924- *AmMWSc 92*
**Demott,** Deborah Ann 1948- *WhoAmL 92*
**DeMott,** Howard Ephraim 1913- *AmMWSc 92*
**DeMott,** Howard Lincoln 1913- *WhoAmL 92*
**DeMott,** Lawrence Lynch 1922- *AmMWSc 92*
**DeMott,** Thomas John 1952- *WhoWest 92*
**DeMotte,** Harvey Clelland 1838-1904 *BiInAmS*
**DeMoully,** Michael Henry 1963- *WhoWest 92*
**Demoulpied,** David Sargent 1942- *WhoFI 92*
**Dempesy,** Colby Wilson 1931- *AmMWSc 92*
**Dempsey,** Andrew *Who 92*
**Dempsey,** Barry J 1938- *AmMWSc 92*
**Dempsey,** Bernard Hayden, Jr. 1942- *WhoAmL 92*
**Dempsey,** Brian S *WhoAmP 91*
**Dempsey,** Daniel Francis 1929- *AmMWSc 92*
**Dempsey,** David 1914- *WrDr 92*
**Dempsey,** David B. 1949- *WhoAmL 92*
**Dempsey,** Edward Francis 1958- *WhoEnt 92*
**Dempsey,** Edward Joseph 1943- *WhoAmL 92*
**Dempsey,** Francis Burke 1962- *WhoFI 92*
**Dempsey,** Hank *TwCSFW 91*
**Dempsey,** Ivy *DrAPF 91*
**Dempsey,** James Andrew 1942- *Who 92*
**Dempsey,** James Howard, Jr. 1916- *WhoAmL 92*
**Dempsey,** Jerry Edward 1932- *WhoFI 92*
**Dempsey,** John Anthony 1963- *WhoFI 92*
**Dempsey,** John Knowles 1936- *WhoRel 92*
**Dempsey,** John Nicholas 1923- *AmMWSc 92*
**Dempsey,** John Patrick 1953- *AmMWSc 92*
**Dempsey,** Joseph P. 1930- *WhoBlA 92*
**Dempsey,** Martin E 1921- *AmMWSc 92*
**Dempsey,** Mary Elizabeth 1928- *AmMWSc 92*
**Dempsey,** Neal, III 1941- *WhoFI 92*
**Dempsey,** Patrick 1966- *IntMPA 92*
**Dempsey,** Paul Stephen 1950- *WhoAmL 92, WhoWest 92*
**Dempsey,** Raymond Leo, Jr. 1949- *WhoEnt 92, WhoRel 92*
**Dempsey,** Robert Armstrong 1935- *WhoAmP 91*
**Dempsey,** Terry M 1932- *WhoAmP 91*
**Dempsey,** Thomas W 1931- *WhoAmP 91*
**Dempsey,** Tracy 1950- *WhoAmP 91*
**Dempsey,** Walter B 1934- *AmMWSc 92*
**Dempsey,** Wesley Hugh 1926- *AmMWSc 92*
**Dempsey,** William Harrison 1895-1984 *FacFETw*
**Dempski,** Robert E 1934- *AmMWSc 92*
**Dempster,** Arthur Jeffrey 1886-1950 *FacFETw*
**Dempster,** George 1917- *AmMWSc 92*
**Dempster,** John William Scott 1938- *Who 92*
**Dempster,** Lauramay Tinsley 1905- *AmMWSc 92*
**Dempster,** Murray Wayne 1942- *WhoRel 92*
**Dempster,** Nigel Richard Patton 1941- *IntAu&W 91, Who 92*
**Dempster,** Stuart 1936- *NewAmDM*
**Dempster,** Stuart Ross 1936- *WhoWest 92*
**Dempster,** William Fred 1940- *AmMWSc 92*
**Demsetz,** Harold 1930- *WhoFI 92*
**Demshar,** Edward Harold 1944- *WhoMW 92*
**Demski,** Eva 1944- *ConAu 135*
**Demski,** Leo Stanley 1943- *AmMWSc 92*
**De Munn,** Jeffrey 1947- *IntMPA 92*
**DeMuro,** Paul Robert 1954- *WhoAmL 92*
**Demus,** Jorg 1928- *IntWW 91, NewAmDM*
**Demus,** Leslie Margot 1950- *WhoAmL 92*
**Demus,** Otto 1902-1990 *IntWW 91, -91N*
**DeMuse,** Toni Ann 1947- *WhoAmP 91*
**DeMuth,** Alan Cornelius 1935- *WhoAmL 92, WhoWest 92*
**DeMuth,** Christopher Clay 1946- *WhoAmP 91*
**DeMuth,** George Richard 1925- *AmMWSc 92*
**Demuth,** Howard B 1928- *AmMWSc 92*
**Demuth,** John Robert 1924- *AmMWSc 92*
**Demuth,** Richard H. 1910- *IntWW 91*
**Demutsky,** Daniil Porfir'evich 1893-1954 *SovUnBD*
**Demuzio,** Vince 1941- *WhoAmP 91*
**Demy,** Jacques d1990 *IntWW 91N*
**Demy,** Jacques 1931- *ConTFT 9, IntDcF 2-2 [port]*
**Demy,** Jacques 1931-1990 *AnObit 1990, FacFETw*
**Demyanenko,** Alexander Paul Serge 1963- *WhoEnt 92*
**DeMyer,** Marian Kendall *AmMWSc 92*
**De Myer,** William Erl 1924- *AmMWSc 92*
**Dena,** Stephen Paul 1952- *WhoAmL 92*
**Den Adel,** Raymond Lee 1932- *WhoMW 92*
**DeNafio,** Teresa Louise 1957- *WhoAmP 91*
**Denahan,** Joseph Anthony 1936- *WhoFI 92*
**Denahy,** John 1922- *TwCPaSc*
**de Naray,** Andrew Thomas 1942- *WhoWest 92*
**DeNardis,** Lawrence Joseph 1938- *WhoAmP 91*
**Denaro,** Charles Thomas 1953- *WhoAmL 92*
**Denaro,** Gregory 1954- *WhoAmL 92*
**De Natale,** Andrew Peter 1950- *WhoAmL 92*
**de Natale,** Francine *WrDr 92*
**De Nault,** Kenneth J 1943- *AmMWSc 92*
**De Navarro,** Jose Francisco *DcAmImH*
**de Navarro,** Michael Antony 1944- *Who 92*
**DeNave,** Connie M. *WhoEnt 92*
**Denavit,** Jacques 1930- *AmMWSc 92*
**Denawetz,** Dan Allan 1940- *WhoMW 92*
**Denber,** Herman C B 1917- *AmMWSc 92*
**Den Besten,** Ivan Eugene 1933- *AmMWSc 92*
**Denbigh,** Earl of 1943- *Who 92*
**Denbigh,** Kenneth George 1911- *IntWW 91, Who 92, WrDr 92*
**Denbo,** James Raymond 1941- *WhoAmL 92*
**Denbo,** Jerry 1950- *WhoAmP 91*
**Denbo,** John Russell 1947- *AmMWSc 92*
**Denbow,** Carl *AmMWSc 92*
**Denbow,** Carl Herbert 1911- *WhoMW 92*
**Denbow,** Carl Jon 1944- *WhoMW 92*
**Denbow,** Donald Michael 1953- *AmMWSc 92*
**Denburg,** Jeffrey Lewis 1944- *AmMWSc 92*
**Denby,** Edwin 1870-1929 *AmPolLe*
**Denby,** Lorraine *AmMWSc 92*
**Denby,** Lyall Gordon 1923- *AmMWSc 92*
**Denby,** Patrick Morris Coventry 1920- *Who 92*
**Denby,** Peter 1929- *WhoAmL 92*
**Denby,** Philippa 1938- *TwCPaSc*
**Dence,** Michael Robert 1931- *AmMWSc 92*
**Dench,** Judi 1934- *IntMPA 92*
**Dench,** Judith Olivia 1934- *IntWW 91, Who 92*
**Denckla,** Paul Douglas 1951- *WhoEnt 92*
**Dende,** Cornelian Edmund 1915- *WhoRel 92*
**Dende,** Henry John 1918- *WhoAmP 91*
**Dendinger,** James Elmer 1943- *AmMWSc 92*
**Dendinger,** Richard Donald 1936- *AmMWSc 92*

**Dendrinos,** Dimitrios Spyros 1944- *WhoMW 92*
**Dendrou,** Stergios 1950- *AmMWSc 92*
**Dendy,** Gail Carter 1945- *WhoAmP 91*
**Dendy,** H Benson, III 1956- *WhoAmP 91*
**Dendy,** Joel Eugene, Jr 1945- *AmMWSc 92*
**Dendy,** Tometta 1932- *WhoBlA 92*
**Deneau,** Gerald Antoine 1928- *AmMWSc 92*
**Deneau,** Sidney G. *IntMPA 92*
**de Necochea,** Fernando *WhoHisp 92*
**de Necochea,** Gladys *WhoHisp 92*
**de Neef,** George Reinier 1948- *WhoWest 92*
**Deneen,** Daniel Guy 1957- *WhoAmL 92*
**DeNeen,** James Francis 1938- *WhoAmL 92*
**Deneen,** Jeffrey Gordon 1964- *WhoMW 92*
**Denegall,** John Palmer, Jr. 1959- *WhoFI 92*
**Denekas,** Milton Oliver 1918- *AmMWSc 92*
**Denell,** Robin Ernest 1942- *AmMWSc 92*
**Denelsky,** Garland 1938- *AmMWSc 92*
**Denenberg,** Herbert 1929- *WrDr 92*
**Denenberg,** Herbert S 1929- *AmMWSc 92*
**Denenberg,** Herbert Sidney 1929- *IntWW 91, WhoIns 92*
**Denenberg,** Stuart Roger 1943- *WhoWest 92*
**Denenberg,** Victor Hugo 1925- *AmMWSc 92*
**Dener,** Ron Steven 1948- *WhoEnt 92*
**Denes,** Peter B 1920- *AmMWSc 92*
**Deneselya,** Helen Antoinette 1944- *WhoMW 92*
**de Neufville,** Pierre 1924- *WhoFI 92*
**de Neufville,** Richard 1939- *WrDr 92*
**De Neufville,** Richard Lawrence 1939- *AmMWSc 92*
**DeNeui,** Joel Arthur 1941- *WhoRel 92*
**Deneuve,** Catherine 1943- *FacFETw, IntMPA 92, IntWW 91, Who 92, WhoEnt 92*
**De Nevers,** Noel Howard 1932- *AmMWSc 92*
**de Nevers,** Roy Olaf 1922- *WhoFI 92, WhoMW 92*
**den Exter Blokland,** A. Francois 1949- *WhoRel 92*
**Denford,** Keith Eugene 1946- *AmMWSc 92*
**Deng Liqun** 1914- *IntWW 91*
**Deng Xiaoping** 1904- *FacFETw [port], IntWW 91*
**Deng Yingchao** 1904- *IntWW 91*
**Deng Youmei** 1931- *IntWW 91*
**Deng Zhunjing** *IntWW 91*
**Dengler,** John Morgan 1927- *WhoEnt 92*
**Dengler,** Robert Anthony 1947- *WhoMW 92*
**Dengler,** Sandy 1939- *IntAu&W 91*
**Dengo,** Gabriel 1922- *AmMWSc 92*
**Denham,** Baron 1927- *Who 92*
**Denham,** Alice *DrAPF 91*
**Denham,** Ernest William 1922- *Who 92*
**Denham,** Henry Mangles 1897- *Who 92*
**Denham,** John 1615-1669 *RfGEnL 91*
**Denham,** Joseph Milton 1930- *AmMWSc 92*
**Denham,** Maurice 1909- *IntMPA 92, Who 92*
**Denham,** Michael Thomas 1955- *WhoRel 92*
**Denham,** Patricia Eileen Keller 1952- *WhoAmL 92*
**Denham,** Robert Edwin 1945- *WhoFI 92*
**Denham,** Seymour Vivian G. *Who 92*
**Denham,** Vernon Robert, Jr. 1948- *WhoAmL 92*
**Denham,** William Ernest, Jr. 1911- *WhoRel 92*
**Denhardt,** David Tilton 1939- *AmMWSc 92, IntWW 91*
**Den Hartog,** J P 1901- *AmMWSc 92*
**Den Herder,** Robert Edward 1954- *WhoFI 92*
**Denhof,** Miki *WhoEnt 92*
**Denhoff,** Mike Louis 1943- *WhoFI 92*
**Denholm,** Alec Stuart 1929- *AmMWSc 92*
**Denholm,** Allan *Who 92*
**Denholm,** Craig Bruce 1954- *WhoMW 92*
**Denholm,** David 1924- *WrDr 92*
**Denholm,** Elizabeth Maria *AmMWSc 92*
**Denholm,** Ian *Who 92*
**Denholm,** Ian 1927- *IntWW 91*
**Denholm,** James Allan 1936- *Who 92*
**Denholm,** John Ferguson 1927- *Who 92*
**Denholm,** Mark *TwCSFW 91*
**Denholtz,** Elaine *DrAPF 91*
**Deni,** Teresa Carr 1947- *WhoAmL 92*
**Deni,** Viktor Nikolaevich 1893-1946 *SovUnBD*
**Deniau,** Jean Francois 1928- *IntWW 91*
**Deniau,** Xavier 1923- *IntWW 91*
**Denicola,** John Albert 1955- *WhoEnt 92*
**De Nicola,** Peter Francis 1954- *WhoFI 92*
**DeNier,** Robert E 1921- *WhoAmP 91*
**Denig,** William Francis 1953- *AmMWSc 92*
**Denigan,** Susan Marie 1957- *WhoAmL 92*
**Denikin,** Anton Ivanovich 1872-1947 *FacFETw*
**Denine,** Elliot Paul 1935- *AmMWSc 92*
**Denington** *Who 92*
**Denington,** Baroness 1907- *Who 92*
**deNiord,** Chard *DrAPF 91*
**De Niro,** Robert 1943- *FacFETw, IntMPA 92, IntWW 91*
**DeNiro,** Robert 1945- *WhoEnt 92*
**Denis,** Howard A 1939- *WhoAmP 91*
**Denis,** Jean Marie Louis Ghislain 1902- *BiDExR*
**Denis,** Kathleen A 1952- *AmMWSc 92*
**Denis,** Maurice 1870-1943 *FacFETw, ThHEIm*
**Denis,** Paul 1909- *IntAu&W 91*
**De Nisco,** Stanley Gabriel 1918- *AmMWSc 92*
**Denisen,** Ervin Loren 1919- *AmMWSc 92*
**Denish,** Herbert M. *WhoWest 92*
**Denisoff,** R Serge 1939- *IntAu&W 91, WrDr 92*
**Denison** *Who 92*
**Denison,** Arthur B 1936- *AmMWSc 92*
**Denison,** Candace Elizabeth Winter *WhoAmL 92*
**Denison,** Charles 1845-1909 *BiInAmS*
**Denison,** Charles Simeon 1849-1913 *BiInAmS*
**Denison,** David 1939- *TwCPaSc*
**Denison,** Dulcie Winifred Catherine 1920- *Who 92*
**Denison,** Edward F. 1915- *WrDr 92*
**Denison,** Edward Fulton 1915- *IntAu&W 91, IntWW 91, WhoFI 92*
**Denison,** Elizabeth Ann Marguerite *Who 92*
**Denison,** Floyd G 1943- *WhoIns 92*
**Denison,** Frank Willis, Jr 1921- *AmMWSc 92*
**Denison,** Jack Thomas 1926- *AmMWSc 92*
**Denison,** James C. 1958- *WhoRel 92*
**Denison,** James Dickey 1926- *WhoEnt 92*
**Denison,** John Law 1911- *Who 92*
**Denison,** John Michael 1915- *Who 92*
**Denison,** John Scott 1918- *AmMWSc 92*
**Denison,** Joseph Carl 1944- *WhoAmL 92*
**Denison,** Mark Edwin 1960- *WhoRel 92*
**Denison,** Mary Boney 1956- *WhoAmL 92*
**Denison,** Michael *Who 92*
**Denison,** Michael 1915- *IntMPA 92, WrDr 92*
**Denison,** Robert Howland 1911- *AmMWSc 92*
**Denison,** Rodger Espy 1932- *AmMWSc 92*
**Denison,** Susan S. 1946- *WhoEnt 92*
**Denison,** Thomas Renau 1960- *WhoAmL 92*
**Denison,** William Clark 1928- *AmMWSc 92, WhoWest 92*
**Denison,** William Mason 1929- *WhoAmP 91*
**Denison,** William Neil 1929- *Who 92*
**Denison,** William Rae 1937- *WhoEnt 92*
**Denison-Pender** *Who 92*
**Denison-Smith,** Anthony Arthur 1942- *Who 92*
**Denisov,** Edison 1929- *ConCom 92, IntWW 91, NewAmDM*
**Denisov,** Edison Vasil'evich 1929- *SovUnBD*
**Denisov,** Sergey Petrovich 1937- *IntWW 91*
**Denisov,** Viktor Nikolaevich 1893-1946 *SovUnBD*
**Denisse,** Jean-Francois 1915- *IntWW 91*
**Denius,** Franklin Wofford 1925- *WhoAmL 92, WhoFI 92*
**Deniz,** Gerardo 1934- *ConSpAP*
**Denk,** Ronald H 1937- *AmMWSc 92*
**Denke,** Conrad William 1947- *WhoEnt 92*
**Denke,** Paul Herman 1916- *WhoWest 92*
**Denkensohn,** Barry David 1945- *WhoAmL 92*
**Denker,** Henry 1912- *IntAu&W 91, WhoEnt 92, WrDr 92*
**Denker,** Martin William 1943- *AmMWSc 92*
**Denko,** Charles W 1916- *AmMWSc 92*
**Denko,** John V 1923- *AmMWSc 92*
**Denktas,** Rauf R. 1924- *IntWW 91*
**Denlea,** Leo Edward, Jr. 1932- *WhoWest 92*
**Denley,** David R 1950- *AmMWSc 92*
**Denlinger,** David Landis 1945- *AmMWSc 92, WhoMW 92*
**Denlinger,** Edgar J 1939- *AmMWSc 92*
**Denlinger,** John Arthur 1941- *WhoRel 92*
**Denman** *Who 92*
**Denman,** Baron 1916- *Who 92*
**Denman,** Charles d1739 *DcNCBi 2*
**Denman,** Charles Frank 1934- *WhoAmL 92*
**Denman,** Don Curry 1946- *WhoAmP 91*
**Denman,** Donald Robert 1911- *Who 92, WrDr 92*
**Denman,** Eugene D 1928- *AmMWSc 92*
**Denman,** George Roy *Who 92*
**Denman,** Gertrude Mary 1884-1954 *BiDBrF 2*
**Denman,** Harry 1893-1976 *RelLAm 91*
**Denman,** Harry Harroun 1925- *AmMWSc 92*
**Denman,** Kathleen Anne 1955- *WhoRel 92*
**Denman,** Roy 1924- *IntWW 91, Who 92*
**Denman,** Sylvia Elaine *Who 92*
**Denmark,** Florence L 1931- *WomPsyc*
**Denmark,** Harold Anderson 1921- *AmMWSc 92*
**Denmark,** Robert Richard 1930- *WhoBlA 92*
**Denn,** Cyril Joseph 1948- *WhoFI 92, WhoMW 92*
**Denn,** Morton M 1939- *AmMWSc 92*
**Dennard,** Brazeal Wayne 1929- *WhoBlA 92*
**Dennard,** Darryl W. 1957- *WhoBlA 92*
**Dennard,** Preston Jackson 1955- *WhoBlA 92*
**Dennard,** Robert H 1932- *AmMWSc 92*
**Dennard,** Turner Harrison 1913- *WhoBlA 92*
**Dennard,** Willie James A., II 1935-1989 *WhoBlA 92N*
**Dennay,** Charles William 1935- *Who 92*
**Denne,** Christopher James Alured 1945- *Who 92*
**Denneen,** John Paul 1940- *WhoAmL 92*
**Dennehy,** Brian 1938- *CurBio 91 [port]*
**Dennehy,** Brian 1939- *IntMPA 92, WhoEnt 92*
**Dennehy,** Brian 1940- *IntWW 91*
**Dennehy,** Michael Patrick 1958- *WhoAmL 92*
**Dennen,** David W 1932- *AmMWSc 92*
**Dennen,** William Henry 1920- *AmMWSc 92*
**Denner,** Johann Christoph 1655-1707 *NewAmDM*
**Denner,** Melvin Walter 1933- *AmMWSc 92, WhoMW 92*
**Dennerlein,** Barbara 1964- *WhoEnt 92*
**Dennert,** Gunther 1939- *AmMWSc 92*
**Dennery,** Moise Waldhorn 1915- *WhoAmL 92*
**Dennery,** Phyllis Armelle 1958- *WhoBlA 92*
**Dennett,** Daniel C 1942- *ConAu 35NR*
**Dennett,** James Arthur 1934- *WhoEnt 92*
**Dennett,** Mary Coffin 1872-1947 *HanAmWH*
**Dennett,** Mary Coffin Ware 1872-1947 *AmPeW*
**Dennett,** William Harrison *ScFEYrs*
**Denney,** Al B., Jr. 1935- *WhoEnt 92*
**Denney,** Donald Berend 1927- *AmMWSc 92*
**Denney,** Donald Duane 1930- *AmMWSc 92*
**Denney,** Doris Elaine 1940- *WhoWest 92*
**Denney,** James Tyre 1930- *WhoRel 92*
**Denney,** Joseph M 1927- *AmMWSc 92*
**Denney,** Lawrence E *WhoAmP 91*
**Denney,** Lucinda Ann 1938- *WhoMW 92*
**Denney,** Richard Max 1946- *AmMWSc 92*
**Denney,** Ruell *DrAPF 91*
**Dennie,** Deborah Thomas 1939- *WhoRel 92*
**Dennie,** Joseph 1768-1812 *BenetAL 91*
**Dennin,** Joseph Francis 1943- *WhoAmL 92*
**Denning,** Baron 1899- *IntWW 91, Who 92*
**Denning,** Lord 1899- *WrDr 92*
**Denning,** Alfred Thompson 1899- *IntAu&W 91*
**Denning,** Bernadine Newsom 1930- *NotBlAW 92, WhoBlA 92*
**Denning,** Dorothy Elizabeth Robling 1945- *AmMWSc 92*
**Denning,** George Smith, Jr 1931- *AmMWSc 92*
**Denning,** Joe William 1945- *WhoBlA 92*
**Denning,** Michael Marion 1943- *WhoFI 92, WhoWest 92*
**Denning,** Peter James 1942- *AmMWSc 92*
**Denning,** Richard Smith 1940- *AmMWSc 92, WhoMW 92*
**Denning,** Robert Mark 1961- *WhoWest 92*
**Dennington,** Dudley 1927- *Who 92*
**Dennis,** Alastair Wesley 1931- *Who 92*
**Dennis,** Barbara Rodgers 1946- *WhoBlA 92*
**Dennis,** Beatrice Markley 1956- *WhoAmL 92*
**Dennis,** Bengt 1930- *IntWW 91*
**Dennis,** Bobby Dale 1949- *WhoEnt 92*
**Dennis,** Bobby Gene 1938- *WhoRel 92*
**Dennis,** C.J. 1876-1938 *RfGEnL 91*
**Dennis,** Carl *DrAPF 91*
**Dennis,** Charles Newton 1942- *WhoFI 92*
**Dennis,** Clarence 1909- *AmMWSc 92*
**Dennis,** David Thomas 1936- *AmMWSc 92*
**Dennis,** David W 1912- *WhoAmP 91*
**Dennis,** David Worth 1849-1916 *BiInAmS*
**Dennis,** Dennis Michael 1949- *WhoWest 92*
**Dennis,** Don 1930- *AmMWSc 92*
**Dennis,** Donna Frances 1942- *IntWW 91*
**Dennis,** Doris Lavelle 1928- *WhoAmP 91*
**Dennis,** Edward A 1941- *AmMWSc 92*
**Dennis,** Edward Spencer Gale, Jr. 1945- *WhoAmL 92*
**Dennis,** Emery Westervelt 1905- *AmMWSc 92*
**Dennis,** Emmet Adolphus 1939- *AmMWSc 92*
**Dennis,** Frank George, Jr 1932- *AmMWSc 92*
**Dennis,** Gary Owen 1946- *WhoRel 92*
**Dennis,** Gerald C 1947- *WhoAmP 91*
**Dennis,** Gertrude Zelma Ford 1927- *WhoBlA 92*
**Dennis,** Hugo, Jr 1936- *WhoAmP 91, WhoBlA 92*
**Dennis,** Jack Bonnell 1931- *AmMWSc 92*
**Dennis,** James Carlos 1947- *WhoBlA 92*
**Dennis,** James Devereux 1951- *WhoAmL 92*
**Dennis,** James L 1936- *WhoAmP 91*
**Dennis,** James Leon 1936- *WhoAmL 92*
**Dennis,** Jan Philip 1945- *WhoRel 92*
**Dennis,** Jeffrey 1958- *TwCPaSc*
**Dennis,** Joe *AmMWSc 92*
**Dennis,** John *Who 92*
**Dennis,** John 1657-1734 *RfGEnL 91*
**Dennis,** John 1917- *WhoAmP 91*
**Dennis,** John Davison 1937- *WhoRel 92*
**Dennis,** John Emory, Jr 1939- *AmMWSc 92*
**Dennis,** John Gordon 1920- *AmMWSc 92*
**Dennis,** John Murray 1923- *AmMWSc 92*
**Dennis,** Kent Seddens 1928- *AmMWSc 92*
**Dennis,** Lawrence 1893-1977 *BiDExR*
**Dennis,** Lyle B 1953- *WhoAmP 91*
**Dennis,** Martha Greenberg 1942- *AmMWSc 92*
**Dennis,** Martin 1851-1916 *BiInAmS*
**Dennis,** Mary *EncAmaz 91*
**Dennis,** Mary 1926- *AmMWSc 92*
**Dennis,** Maxwell Lewis 1909- *Who 92*
**Dennis,** Melvin B, Jr 1937- *AmMWSc 92*
**Dennis,** Michael Mark 1942- *IntWW 91*
**Dennis,** Nigel Forbes 1912- *IntAu&W 91*
**Dennis,** Nigel Forbes 1912-1989 *FacFETw*
**Dennis,** Patricia Ann *AmMWSc 92*
**Dennis,** Patricia Diaz 1946- *WhoAmP 91, WhoHisp 92*
**Dennis,** Patrick P 1942- *AmMWSc 92*
**Dennis,** Patsy Ann 1948- *WhoRel 92*
**Dennis,** Philip H. 1925- *WhoBlA 92*
**Dennis,** Rembert Coney 1915- *WhoAmP 91*
**Dennis,** Robert 1933- *WhoEnt 92*
**Dennis,** Robert Alan 1948- *WhoFI 92*
**Dennis,** Robert E 1920- *AmMWSc 92*
**Dennis,** Rodney Howard 1936- *WhoBlA 92*
**Dennis,** Ronald *WhoEnt 92*
**Dennis,** Russell George 1954- *WhoWest 92*
**Dennis,** Rutledge M. 1939- *WhoBlA 92*
**Dennis,** Sandy 1937- *IntMPA 92, IntWW 91, WhoEnt 92*
**Dennis,** Shirley M 1938- *WhoAmP 91, WhoBlA 92*
**Dennis,** Susana R K de *AmMWSc 92*
**Dennis,** Tom Ross 1942- *AmMWSc 92*
**Dennis,** Walter Decoster 1932- *WhoBlA 92, WhoRel 92*
**Dennis,** Warren Howard 1925- *AmMWSc 92*
**Dennis,** Wayne Allen 1941- *WhoMW 92*
**Dennis,** Wesley 1903-1966 *ConAu 135*
**Dennis,** Wilburn Dwayne 1937- *WhoRel 92*
**Dennis,** William E *AmMWSc 92*
**Dennis,** William Littleton 1950- *WhoAmL 92*
**Dennis-Jones,** Harold 1915- *IntAu&W 91, WrDr 92*
**Dennison,** Anna Nasvik *WhoWest 92*
**Dennison,** Brian Kenneth 1949- *AmMWSc 92*
**Dennison,** Byron Lee 1930- *AmMWSc 92*
**Dennison,** Caroline Dorothy 1962- *WhoAmL 92*
**Dennison,** Christabel 1884-1925 *TwCPaSc*
**Dennison,** Clifford C 1922- *AmMWSc 92*
**Dennison,** David Kee 1952- *AmMWSc 92*
**Dennison,** David Severin 1932- *AmMWSc 92*
**Dennison,** David Short, Jr 1918- *WhoAmP 91*
**Dennison,** George Marshel 1935- *WhoWest 92*
**Dennison,** John Manley 1934- *AmMWSc 92*
**Dennison,** Malcolm Gray 1924- *Who 92*
**Dennison,** Mary Elizabeth 1928- *WhoRel 92*
**Dennison,** Mervyn William 1914- *Who 92*
**Dennison,** Richard Leon 1939- *WhoEnt 92*
**Dennison,** Ronald Walton 1944- *WhoWest 92*

**Dennison,** Stanley Raymond 1912- *Who 92*
**Dennison,** Stanley Richard 1930- *Who 92*
**Denniss,** Gordon Kenneth 1915- *Who 92*
**Denniston,** Brackett Badger, III 1947- *WhoAmL 92*
**Denniston,** Dorothy L. 1944- *WhoBlA 92*
**Denniston,** Joseph Charles 1940- *AmMWSc 92*
**Denniston,** Martha Kent 1920- *WhoWest 92*
**Denniston,** Robin Alastair 1926- *IntWW 91, Who 92*
**Denniston,** Rollin H, II 1914- *AmMWSc 92*
**Denniston,** Thomas Robert 1953- *WhoAmL 92*
**Denniston,** Warren Kent, Jr. 1939- *WhoFI 92*
**Denno,** Khalil I 1933- *AmMWSc 92*
**Dennon,** Gerald Burdette 1938- *WhoFI 92*
**Denny,** Alistair 1922- *Who 92*
**Denny,** Alma *DrAPF 91*
**Denny,** Anthony Coningham de Waltham 1925- *Who 92*
**Denny,** Barry Lyttelton 1928- *Who 92*
**Denny,** Bob *WhoAmP 91*
**Denny,** Charles R., Jr. *LesBEnT 92*
**Denny,** Charles Storrow 1911- *AmMWSc 92*
**Denny,** Cleve B 1925- *AmMWSc 92*
**Denny,** Collins 1854-1943 *RelLAm 91*
**Denny,** Collins, III 1933- *WhoAmL 92*
**Denny,** Dorothy 1893-1981 *HanAmWH*
**Denny,** Dorothy Detzer *AmPeW*
**Denny,** Emery Byrd 1892-1973 *DcNCBi 2*
**Denny,** Floyd Wolfe, Jr 1923- *AmMWSc 92, IntWW 91*
**Denny,** Frederick Mathewson 1939- *WhoRel 92*
**Denny,** George Hutcheson 1928- *AmMWSc 92*
**Denny,** George Vernon, Jr. 1899-1959 *DcNCBi 2*
**Denny,** J P 1921- *AmMWSc 92*
**Denny,** John Leighton 1931- *AmMWSc 92*
**Denny,** Margaret Bertha Alice 1907- *Who 92*
**Denny,** Maurice Ray 1918- *WhoMW 92*
**Denny,** Norwyn Ephraim 1924- *Who 92*
**Denny,** Otway B., Jr. 1949- *WhoAmL 92*
**Denny,** Randal Earl 1937- *WhoRel 92*
**Denny,** Raymond A, III 1961- *WhoAmP 91*
**Denny,** Robert 1920- *ConAu 135*
**Denny,** Robyn 1930- *IntWW 91, TwCPaSc*
**Denny,** Ronald Maurice 1927- *Who 92*
**Denny,** Wayne Belding 1914- *AmMWSc 92*
**Denny,** William C, Jr 1930- *WhoAmP 91*
**Denny,** William Eric 1927- *Who 92*
**Denny,** William F 1927- *AmMWSc 92*
**Denny,** William F 1946- *AmMWSc 92*
**Denny,** William Murdoch, Jr. 1934- *WhoFI 92*
**Dennys,** Cyril George d1991 *Who 92N*
**Dennys,** Nicholas Charles Jonathan 1951- *Who 92*
**Dennys,** Rodney Onslow 1911- *Who 92*
**Deno,** Don W 1924- *AmMWSc 92*
**Deno,** Lawrence M. *WhoRel 92*
**Deno,** Norman C 1921- *AmMWSc 92*
**DeNoewer,** Michael Frank 1958- *WhoFI 92*
**Denoff,** Samuel 1928- *WhoEnt 92*
**Denomme,** Michael James 1943- *WhoFI 92*
**Denoncourt,** Peter John 1948- *WhoFI 92*
**Denoncourt,** Robert Francis 1932- *AmMWSc 92*
**Denoon,** Clarence England, Jr 1915- *AmMWSc 92*
**De Noto,** Thomas Gerald 1943- *AmMWSc 92*
**Den Ouden,** Gaylin L R 1945- *WhoAmP 91*
**Denov,** Sam 1923- *WhoEnt 92*
**DeNovio,** Susan Williams 1948- *WhoFI 92*
**Denoyer,** Arsene J. 1904- *WhoMW 92*
**DeNoyer,** John M 1926- *AmMWSc 92*
**DeNoyer,** Linda Kay *AmMWSc 92*
**Densen,** Paul M 1913- *AmMWSc 92*
**Densen-Gerber,** Judianne 1934- *WrDr 92*
**Denshaw,** Joseph Moreau 1928- *AmMWSc 92*
**Densley,** John R 1943- *AmMWSc 92*
**Denslow,** David Albert, Jr. 1942- *WhoFI 92*
**Denslow,** Sharon Phillips 1947- *SmATA 68 [port]*
**Densmore,** Edward D 1940- *WhoAmP 91*
**Densmore,** Frances 1867-1957 *BenetAL 91, FacFETw*
**Densmore,** Frederick Trent 1943- *WhoAmL 92*
**Denson,** Claudius Baker 1837-1903 *DcNCBi 2*
**Denson,** Donald D 1945- *AmMWSc 92*
**Denson,** Fred L. 1937- *WhoBlA 92*
**Denson,** John Boyd 1926- *IntWW 91, Who 92*
**Denson,** Nancy Rae 1951- *WhoWest 92*
**Denson,** William Frank, III 1943- *WhoAmL 92*
**Dent,** Anthony L 1943- *AmMWSc 92, WhoBlA 92*
**Dent,** Aubrey O. 1934- *WhoBlA 92*
**Dent,** Brian Edward 1943- *AmMWSc 92*
**Dent,** Carl Ashley 1914- *WhoBlA 92*
**Dent,** Cedric Carl 1962- *WhoBlA 92*
**Dent,** Charles W 1960- *WhoAmP 91*
**Dent,** DeWitt Ronald 1937- *WhoAmL 92*
**Dent,** Ernest DuBose, Jr. 1927- *WhoFI 92, WhoWest 92*
**Dent,** Frederick Baily 1922- *WhoAmP 91*
**Dent,** Gary Kever 1950- *WhoBlA 92*
**Dent,** Guy *ScFEYrs*
**Dent,** Harold Collett 1894- *Who 92*
**Dent,** Harry Shuler 1930- *WhoAmP 91*
**Dent,** J.M. 1849-1926 *DcLB 112 [port]*
**Dent,** J.M., and Sons *DcLB 112*
**Dent,** James 1916- *AmMWSc 92*
**Dent,** John 1923- *IntWW 91, Who 92*
**Dent,** John Nicholson 1960- *WhoMW 92*
**Dent,** Jonathan Hugh Baillie 1930- *Who 92*
**Dent,** Lester 1904-1959 *TwCSFW 91*
**Dent,** Peter Boris 1936- *AmMWSc 92*
**Dent,** Preston L. 1939- *WhoBlA 92*
**Dent,** Richard Lamar 1960- *WhoBlA 92*
**Dent,** Robin John 1929- *Who 92*
**Dent,** Ronald Henry 1913- *Who 92*
**Dent,** Sara Jamison 1922- *AmMWSc 92*
**Dent,** Stanley d1991 *Who 92N*
**Dent,** Thomas Covington 1932- *WhoBlA 92*
**Dent,** Thomas Curtis 1928- *AmMWSc 92*
**Dent,** Tom *DrAPF 91*
**Dent,** William Hunter, Jr 1936- *AmMWSc 92*
**Dentai,** Andrew G 1942- *AmMWSc 92*
**Dentel,** Steven Keith 1951- *AmMWSc 92*
**Dentice,** Thomas Santo 1939- *WhoMW 92*
**Dentinger,** John A. 1952- *WhoWest 92*
**Dentinger,** Ronald Lee 1941- *WhoEnt 92, WhoFI 92*
**Dentinger,** Stephen *TwCSFW 91*
**Dentler,** William Lee, Jr *AmMWSc 92*
**Denton** *Who 92*
**Denton,** Allen Eugene, III 1951- *WhoMW 92*
**Denton,** Arnold Eugene 1925- *AmMWSc 92*
**Denton,** Betty F 1945- *WhoAmP 91*
**Denton,** Billy Ray 1949- *WhoRel 92*
**Denton,** Bobby Eugene 1938- *WhoAmP 91*
**Denton,** Catherine Margaret Mary *Who 92*
**Denton,** Charles 1937- *Who 92*
**Denton,** Charles Mandaville 1957- *WhoAmL 92*
**Denton,** Charles Murray, II 1957- *WhoAmL 92*
**Denton,** Charles William 1951- *WhoAmL 92*
**Denton,** Daniel *BenetAL 91*
**Denton,** David Allen 1963- *WhoEnt 92*
**Denton,** David Harrison 1945- *WhoMW 92*
**Denton,** Denice Dee 1959- *AmMWSc 92*
**Denton,** Derek Ashworth 1924- *IntWW 91*
**Denton,** Douglas Guy 1945- *WhoRel 92*
**Denton,** Elwood Valentine 1912- *WhoFI 92*
**Denton,** Eric 1923- *Who 92*
**Denton,** Eric James 1923- *IntWW 91*
**Denton,** Frank Trevor 1930- *IntWW 91*
**Denton,** Herbert H., Jr. 1943-1989 *WhoBlA 92N*
**Denton,** Jeremiah A 1924- *WhoAmP 91*
**Denton,** Joan E *AmMWSc 92*
**Denton,** John G. *WhoRel 92*
**Denton,** John Grant 1929- *Who 92*
**Denton,** John Joseph 1915- *AmMWSc 92*
**Denton,** Kady MacDonald *ConAu 134, SmATA 66*
**Denton,** Karl Robert 1959- *WhoMW 92*
**Denton,** Kenneth 1932- *TwCPaSc*
**Denton,** Kevin Arthur 1949- *WhoAmL 92*
**Denton,** M Bonner 1944- *AmMWSc 92*
**Denton,** Margaret *Who 92*
**Denton,** Melinda Fay 1944- *AmMWSc 92*
**Denton,** Michael John 1956- *WhoEnt 92*
**Denton,** Ray Douglas 1937- *WhoFI 92, WhoMW 92*
**Denton,** Rena Wilson 1943- *WhoRel 92*
**Denton,** Richard T 1932- *AmMWSc 92*
**Denton,** Robert William 1944- *WhoFI 92*
**Denton,** Roger Marius 1946- *WhoAmL 92*
**Denton,** Thomas Millard 1947- *WhoRel 92*
**Denton,** Timothy Lynn 1951- *WhoAmL 92*
**Denton,** Tom Eugene 1937- *AmMWSc 92*
**Denton,** William Irwin 1917- *AmMWSc 92*
**Denton,** William Jason 1944- *WhoAmL 92*
**Denton,** William Lewis 1932- *WhoEnt 92, WhoWest 92*
**Denton of Wakefield,** Baroness *Who 92*
**Denton-Thompson,** Aubrey Gordon 1920- *Who 92*
**Dentzer,** William Thompson, Jr. 1929- *WhoFI 92*
**Denu,** Marie E 1931- *WhoAmP 91*
**DeNucci,** A Joseph 1939- *WhoAmP 91*
**De Nuccio,** David Joseph 1935- *AmMWSc 92*
**De Nuccio,** Raymond Adolph 1933- *WhoFI 92*
**Denver,** Bob 1935- *IntMPA 92*
**Denver,** Drake C *IntAu&W 91X, TwCWW 91, WrDr 92*
**Denver,** John 1943- *IntMPA 92, IntWW 91, WhoEnt 92*
**Denver,** Lee *TwCWW 91*
**Denver,** Rod *TwCWW 91*
**Denvir,** James Peter, III 1950- *WhoAmL 92*
**Denvir,** Quin Anthony 1940- *WhoAmL 92*
**DeNye,** Blaine A. 1933- *WhoBlA 92*
**Denyer,** David Alexander 1933- *WhoRel 92*
**Denyer,** Roderick Lawrence 1948- *Who 92*
**Denyes,** Helen Arliss 1922- *AmMWSc 92*
**Denys,** Edward Paul 1927- *WhoMW 92*
**Denza,** Eileen 1937- *Who 92*
**Denzel,** George Eugene 1939- *AmMWSc 92*
**Denzel,** Ken John 1940- *WhoFI 92*
**Denzien,** Ricky Gerald 1955- *WhoEnt 92*
**de Obaldia,** Rene *ConAu 133*
**Deodhar,** Sharad Dinkar 1929- *AmMWSc 92*
**De Oliveira,** Joao Carlos 1954- *BlkOlyM*
**de Olloqui,** Jose Juan 1931- *Who 92*
**Deon,** Michel 1919- *IntWW 91*
**Deon,** Richard Phillip 1956- *WhoEnt 92*
**De Onate,** Juan *DcAmImH*
**Deonier,** D L 1936- *AmMWSc 92*
**Deonier,** Richard Charles 1942- *AmMWSc 92*
**DeOrchis,** Vincent Moore 1949- *WhoAmL 92*
**Deorio,** Anthony Joseph 1945- *WhoMW 92*
**DeOrio,** David James 1959- *WhoFI 92*
**de Oriol Y Urquijo,** Antonio Maria 1913- *IntWW 91*
**Deoul,** Neal 1931- *WhoFI 92*
**de Pablo,** Luis 1930- *ConCom 92*
**De Pace,** Dennis Michael 1947- *AmMWSc 92*
**DePace,** John Gordon 1962- *WhoWest 92*
**De Paiva,** Henry Albert Rawdon 1932- *AmMWSc 92*
**DePaiva,** James Paul 1957- *WhoEnt 92*
**DePalma,** Anthony Michael 1948- *AmMWSc 92*
**De Palma,** Brian 1940- *FacFETw, IntDcF 2-2 [port], IntMPA 92, IntWW 91*
**DePalma,** Brian Russell 1940- *WhoEnt 92*
**DePalma,** James John 1927- *AmMWSc 92*
**DePalma,** Philip Anthony 1930- *AmMWSc 92*
**Depalma,** Ralph G 1931- *AmMWSc 92*
**DePalma,** Richard Louis 1955- *WhoEnt 92*
**DePamphilis,** Melvin Louis 1943- *AmMWSc 92*
**De Pangher,** John 1918- *AmMWSc 92*
**DePaola,** Dominick Philip 1942- *AmMWSc 92*
**dePaola,** Tomie 1934- *ChlLR 24 [port], IntAu&W 91, WrDr 92*
**DePaoli,** Alexander 1936- *AmMWSc 92*
**De Paoli,** Thomas Martin 1947- *WhoFI 92, WhoMW 92*
**dePaolis,** Potito Umberto 1925- *WhoFI 92, WhoWest 92*
**DePaolo,** Donald James 1951- *WhoWest 92*
**Depardieu,** Gerard 1948- *FacFETw, IntMPA 92, IntWW 91, News 91 [port], WhoEnt 92*
**Depardon,** Raymond 1942- *IntWW 91*
**DePascale,** Paul Anthony 1960- *WhoAmL 92*
**DePasco,** Ronnie Nick 1943- *WhoAmP 91*
**Depasquale,** Ed *DrAPF 91*
**DePasquale,** Jill Ann 1964- *WhoMW 92*
**de Pasquale,** Joseph 1919- *WhoEnt 92*
**De Pasquali,** Giovanni 1917- *AmMWSc 92*
**DePass,** Linval R 1948- *AmMWSc 92*
**DePass,** William Brunson, Jr 1947- *WhoAmP 91*
**DePasse,** Suzanne *LesBEnT 92, WhoEnt 92, WhoFI 92*
**de Passe,** Suzanne 1948- *WhoBlA 92*
**Depatie,** David A 1934- *AmMWSc 92*
**DePatie,** David Hudson 1930- *WhoEnt 92*
**de Patta,** Margaret 1907- *DcTwDes*
**de Paula,** Clive 1916- *Who 92*
**DePaulis,** Palmer 1945- *WhoAmP 91*
**DePaulis,** Palmer Anthony 1945- *WhoWest 92*
**DePaur,** Leonard *WhoBlA 92*
**De Paur,** Leonard 1915- *NewAmDM*
**De Pauw,** Gommar Albert 1918- *RelLAm 91, WhoRel 92*
**De Pazzi,** Ellen Eugenia 1915- *IntAu&W 91*
**DePazzo,** Louis L 1932- *WhoAmP 91*
**Depeaux,** Felix-Francois 1853-1920 *ThHEIm*
**De Peaux,** Richard Joel 1941- *WhoMW 92*
**DePecol,** Benjamin J 1951- *WhoAmP 91*
**De Pena,** Hector, Jr. *WhoHisp 92*
**De Pena,** Joan Finkle 1923- *AmMWSc 92*
**de Pena,** Rosa G 1921- *AmMWSc 92*
**de Perales,** Mirta Raya *WhoHisp 92*
**Depew,** Creighton A 1931- *AmMWSc 92*
**DePew,** Marie Kathryn 1928- *WhoWest 92*
**Depew,** Richard H. 1925- *IntMPA 92*
**Depew,** Thomas Andrew 1927- *WhoRel 92*
**Depew,** Wally *DrAPF 91*
**DePew,** William Earl 1948- *WhoWest 92*
**de Peyer,** David Charles 1934- *Who 92*
**De Peyer,** Gervase 1926- *IntWW 91, Who 92*
**DePeyster,** Frederick A 1914- *AmMWSc 92*
**De Pfyffer,** Andre 1928- *WhoFI 92*
**DePhillips,** Henry Alfred, Jr 1937- *AmMWSc 92*
**Dephillips,** Paul S 1939- *WhoIns 92*
**De Phillis,** John 1936- *AmMWSc 92*
**Dephtereos,** David L. 1954- *WhoAmL 92*
**DePillars,** Murry Norman 1938- *WhoBlA 92*
**de Pineres,** Oscar G. 1932- *WhoHisp 92*
**de Pinies,** Jaime 1918- *IntWW 91*
**DePinto,** John A 1937- *AmMWSc 92*
**DePinto,** Joseph Anthony 1951- *WhoWest 92*
**de Piro,** Alan C. H. *Who 92*
**De Planque,** Gail 1945- *AmMWSc 92*
**Depocas,** Florent 1923- *AmMWSc 92*
**DePoe,** Charles Edward 1927- *AmMWSc 92*
**Depoe,** Stephen Ronald 1959- *WhoFI 92*
**Depommier,** Pierre Henri Maurice 1925- *AmMWSc 92*
**DePonte,** Jeffrey Keoni 1955- *WhoEnt 92*
**DePoorter,** Gerald Leroy 1940- *AmMWSc 92*
**De Posada,** Joachim Arturo 1947- *WhoFI 92*
**de Posada,** Robert G. 1966- *WhoHisp 92*
**de Posadas,** Luis Maria 1927- *Who 92*
**De Pourtales,** Louis Francois *BiInAmS*
**DePoy,** Phil Eugene 1935- *AmMWSc 92*
**Depp,** Johnny 1963- *CurBio 91 [port], IntMPA 92, News 91 [port], -91-3 [port], WhoEnt 92*
**Depp,** Joseph George 1943- *AmMWSc 92*
**Depp,** Steven Christopher 1961- *WhoMW 92*
**Deppe,** Brian J. 1946- *WhoAmL 92*
**Deppe,** Henry A. 1920- *WhoFI 92*
**Deppe,** Theodore *DrAPF 91*
**Deppeler,** James Gregory 1946- *WhoFI 92*
**Depperschmidt,** Thomas Orlando 1935- *WhoFI 92*
**Deppman,** John C. 1943- *WhoAmL 92*
**DePrater,** William Arthur, III 1947- *WhoRel 92*
**De Pre,** Jean-Anne *WrDr 92*
**DePree,** John Deryck 1933- *AmMWSc 92*
**De Pree,** Willard Ames 1928- *WhoAmP 91*
**DePreist,** James Anderson 1936- *WhoBlA 92, WhoEnt 92, WhoWest 92*
**De Premonville,** Myrene Sophie Marie 1949- *IntWW 91*
**Deprez,** Luisa Stormer *WhoAmP 91*
**DePriest,** C E *WhoAmP 91*
**DePriest,** Charles David 1938- *WhoMW 92*
**DePriest,** Darryl Lawrence 1954- *WhoAmL 92, WhoBlA 92*
**DePriest,** James 1936- *NewAmDM*
**De Priest,** Mary 1945- *WhoFI 92*
**De Priest,** Oscar 1871-1951 *FacFETw*
**De Priest,** Oscar Stanton 1871-1951 *AmPolLe*
**DePriest,** Oscar Stanton, III 1920- *WhoBlA 92*
**DePrima,** Charles Raymond 1918- *AmMWSc 92*
**DePrisco,** Judith Anne 1952- *WhoAmL 92*
**DePristo,** Andrew Elliott 1951- *AmMWSc 92*
**Deprit,** Andre A M 1926- *AmMWSc 92*
**DeProspo,** Nicholas Dominick 1923- *AmMWSc 92*
**Depta,** Victor M. *DrAPF 91*
**Depte,** Larry D. 1950- *WhoBlA 92*
**DePue,** Bobbie Lee 1938- *WhoFI 92*
**DePue,** David Leonard 1939- *WhoMW 92*
**Depue,** Robert Hemphill 1931- *AmMWSc 92*
**DePue,** Wallace Earl 1932- *WhoEnt 92*
**DePuit,** Edward J 1948- *AmMWSc 92*
**Depukat,** Thaddeus Stanley 1936- *WhoMW 92*
**De Puy,** Charles Herbert 1927- *AmMWSc 92*
**Dequae,** Andre 1915- *IntWW 91*
**Dequasie,** Andrew 1929- *ConAu 35NR*

**De Quille,** Dan 1829-1898 *BenetAL 91*
**De Quincey,** Thomas 1785-1859 *CnDBLB 3 [port], DcLB 110 [port], RfGEnL 91*
**De Quiros,** Beltran *DrAPF 91*
**Der,** James J., Jr. 1959- *WhoAmL 92*
**DeRaad,** Brent Eugene 1966- *WhoWest 92*
**de Rachewiltz,** Igor 1929- *IntWW 91*
**DeRaleau,** Steven James 1951- *WhoIns 92*
**Deramore,** Baron 1911- *Who 92*
**De Ramsey,** Baron 1910- *Who 92*
**DeRamus,** Judson Davie, Jr 1945- *WhoAmP 91*
**DeRango,** Mary Laura Keul *WhoMW 92*
**Deranleau,** David A 1934- *AmMWSc 92*
**Deras,** Keith A. 1957- *WhoMW 92*
**Deratany,** Tim 1939- *WhoAmP 91*
**Deratzian,** David Loris 1962- *WhoAmL 92*
**Der-Balian,** Georges Puzant 1943- *WhoWest 92*
**Derbes,** Daniel William 1930- *WhoFI 92*
**Derbigny,** Rhoda L. 1960- *WhoBlA 92*
**Derby,** Archdeacon of *Who 92*
**Derby,** Bishop of 1928- *Who 92*
**Derby,** Earl of 1918- *Who 92*
**Derby,** Provost of *Who 92*
**Derby,** Albert 1939- *AmMWSc 92*
**Derby,** Bennett Marsh 1929- *AmMWSc 92*
**Derby,** Ernest Stephen 1938- *WhoAmL 92*
**Derby,** Eugene *ScFEYrs*
**Derby,** George Horatio 1823-1861 *BenetAL 91*
**Derby,** James Victor 1944- *AmMWSc 92*
**Derby,** Mark Garald 1965- *WhoWest 92*
**Derby,** Orville Adelbert 1851-1915 *BiInAmS*
**Derby,** Stanley Kingdon 1920- *AmMWSc 92*
**Derby,** William *WhoRel 92*
**Derbyshire,** Andrew 1923- *Who 92*
**Derbyshire,** Andrew George 1923- *IntWW 91*
**Derbyshire,** John Brian 1933- *AmMWSc 92*
**Derbyshire,** William Davis 1924- *AmMWSc 92*
**Derchin,** Dary Ingham 1941- *WhoEnt 92*
**Derchin,** Michael Wayne 1942- *WhoFI 92*
**Derck,** Gary Stephen 1958- *WhoFI 92*
**Derdenger,** Patrick 1946- *WhoAmL 92, WhoFI 92, WhoWest 92*
**Derderian,** Edmond Joseph 1942- *AmMWSc 92*
**Derdeyn,** Eugene Duncan 1929- *WhoFI 92*
**DeRea,** Philip 1942- *WhoRel 92*
**De Regniers,** Beatrice Schenk 1914- *IntAu&W 91, SmATA 68 [port], WrDr 92*
**Derek,** Bo 1956- *IntMPA 92*
**Derek,** John 1926- *IntMPA 92*
**Derek,** Nadine Jelovcic 1956- *WhoMW 92*
**DeRemer,** Russell Jay 1940- *AmMWSc 92*
**Deren,** Donald David 1949- *WhoAmL 92*
**Deren,** Maya 1917-1961 *IntDcF 2-2 [port], ReelWom [port]*
**Dereniak,** Eustace Leonard 1941- *AmMWSc 92*
**De Renobales,** Mertxe 1948- *AmMWSc 92*
**De Renzo,** Edward Clarence 1925- *AmMWSc 92*
**Derenzo,** Stephen Edward 1941- *AmMWSc 92*
**Deresienski,** Stanley Mitchell 1950- *WhoRel 92*
**Deresiewicz,** Herbert 1925- *AmMWSc 92*
**de Reszke,** Edouard 1853-1917 *NewAmDM*
**de Reszke,** Jean 1850-1925 *NewAmDM*
**Derfel-Kowalski,** Blumie Rose 1951- *WhoAmL 92*
**Derfelt,** Jerry Leroy 1953- *WhoRel 92*
**Derfer,** John Mentzer 1920- *AmMWSc 92*
**Derfler,** Gene 1924- *WhoAmP 91*
**Derfler,** Leslie 1933- *IntAu&W 91, WrDr 92*
**Dergarabedian,** Paul 1922- *AmMWSc 92*
**Derge,** David Richard 1928- *WhoAmP 91*
**Derge,** G 1909- *AmMWSc 92*
**Der Hagopian,** Zgon d1991 *NewYTBS 91*
**Derham,** Arthur Morgan 1915- *WrDr 92*
**Derham,** Brigid 1943- *TwCPaSc*
**Derham,** Peter 1925- *Who 92*
**Derham,** Richard Andrew 1940- *WhoAmP 91*
**Derham,** William 1657-1757 *BlkwCEP*
**Derheimer,** Neil Eugene 1945- *WhoMW 92*
**Der-Hovanessian,** Diana *DrAPF 91*
**Der'i,** Arye 1959- *IntWW 91*
**Deri,** Robert Joseph 1957- *AmMWSc 92*
**Deriabin,** Peter 1921- *ConAu 134*
**Derian,** Patricia Murphy *WhoAmP 91*
**Deric,** Arthur J 1926- *WhoIns 92*
**Derickson,** Jeffrey Cline 1950- *WhoWest 92*
**Derieg,** Michael E 1935- *AmMWSc 92*
**DeRienzo,** Harold 1953- *WhoAmL 92*
**Derieux,** Samuel Arthur 1926- *WhoFI 92*
**De Rijk,** Waldemar G 1945- *AmMWSc 92*
**Dering,** Richard 1580?-1630 *NewAmDM*
**Deringer,** Arved 1913- *IntWW 91*
**Deringer,** Margaret K 1915- *AmMWSc 92*
**Deriso,** Richard Bruce 1951- *AmMWSc 92*
**de Rivoyre,** Christine Berthe Claude D. 1921- *IntWW 91*
**Derkits,** Gustav 1950- *AmMWSc 92*
**Derleth,** August 1909-1971 *BenetAL 91, ScFEYrs, TwCSFW 91*
**Derleth,** August and Ganzlin, Carl W *ScFEYrs*
**Derleth,** August and Schorer, Mark *ScFEYrs*
**Derman,** Cyrus 1925- *AmMWSc 92*
**Derman,** Donald A 1933- *WhoAmP 91*
**Derman,** Samuel 1931- *AmMWSc 92*
**der Mateosian,** Edward 1914- *AmMWSc 92*
**Dermer,** Otis Clifford 1909- *AmMWSc 92*
**Dermit,** George 1925- *AmMWSc 92*
**Dermody,** Frank 1951- *WhoAmP 91*
**Dermody,** Hugh Orin 1943- *WhoEnt 92*
**Dermody,** John Daniel 1909- *WhoAmP 91*
**Dermody,** Mary Louise 1917- *WhoAmP 91*
**Dermody,** William Christian 1941- *AmMWSc 92*
**Dermota,** Anton 1910-1989 *NewAmDM*
**Dermott,** Stanley Frederick 1942- *AmMWSc 92*
**Dermott,** William 1924- *Who 92*
**Dern,** Bruce 1936- *IntMPA 92*
**Dern,** Bruce MacLeish 1936- *WhoEnt 92*
**Dern,** John, Jr. 1932- *WhoEnt 92*
**Dern,** Laura 1966- *IntMPA 92, WhoEnt 92*
**Dernehl,** Paul Herman 1878-1919 *BiInAmS*
**Dernesch,** Helga 1939- *IntWW 91*
**De Robertis,** Eduardo Diego Patricio 1913- *IntWW 91*
**DeRoburt,** Hammer 1923- *IntWW 91*
**Deroc,** Jean 1925- *WhoEnt 92*
**De Rocco,** Andrew Gabriel 1929- *AmMWSc 92*
**De Rochemont,** Louis 1899-1978 *FacFETw*
**DeRodes,** Robert P 1950- *WhoIns 92*
**de Roe Devon,** Marchioness 1934- *WhoFI 92, WhoWest 92*
**DeRoma,** Leonard James 1953- *WhoFI 92*
**Derome,** Jacques Florian 1941- *AmMWSc 92*
**De Romilly,** Jacqueline 1913- *IntWW 91*
**Deron,** Edward Michael 1945- *WhoAmL 92*
**De Roo,** Anne 1931- *IntAu&W 91, WrDr 92*
**De Roo,** Edward *DrAPF 91*
**De Roo,** Remi Joseph 1924- *WhoRel 92, WhoWest 92*
**DeRoos,** Fred Lynn 1947- *AmMWSc 92*
**deRoos,** Roger McLean 1930- *AmMWSc 92*
**de Ros,** Baron 1958- *Who 92*
**DeRosa,** Francis Dominic 1936- *WhoWest 92*
**DeRose,** Anthony Francis 1920- *AmMWSc 92*
**DeRose,** Candace Margaret 1949- *WhoAmP 91*
**De Rose,** Gerard 1918-1987 *TwCPaSc*
**De Rose,** John Patrick 1943- *WhoAmL 92*
**De Rose,** Louis John 1952- *WhoFI 92*
**De Rose,** Peter Louis 1947- *WhoAmL 92*
**DeRosett,** Armand John 1767-1859 *DcNCBi 2*
**Derosier,** Ann M 1950- *WhoAmP 91*
**DeRosier,** David J 1939- *AmMWSc 92*
**DeRoss,** Evelyn Jones 1927- *WhoAmP 91*
**De Rosset,** Armand John 1767-1859 *DcNCBi 2*
**DeRosset,** Armand John 1915- *AmMWSc 92*
**De Rosset,** Lewis Henry 1724?-1786 *DcNCBi 2*
**De Rosset,** Moses John 1726-1767 *DcNCBi 2*
**De Rosset,** Moses John 1838-1881 *DcNCBi 2*
**De Rosset,** William Lord 1832-1910 *DcNCBi 2*
**De Rosset,** William Steinle 1942- *AmMWSc 92*
**de Rosso,** Diana 1921- *WrDr 92*
**De Rosso,** H.A. 1917-1960 *TwCWW 91*
**DeRoth,** Laszlo 1941- *AmMWSc 92*
**de Rothschild** *Who 92*
**Derouin,** Lawrence Walter 1948- *WhoWest 92*
**Deroulede,** Paul Marie Joseph 1846-1914 *BiDExR*
**de Roulhac** *DcNCBi 2*
**DeRoulhac,** Joseph Harold, Jr. 1953- *WhoRel 92*
**Derounian,** Arthur d1991 *NewYTBS 91*
**Derounian,** Steven B 1918- *WhoAmP 91*
**DeRousseau,** C Jean 1947- *AmMWSc 92*
**Derow,** Matthew Arnold 1909- *AmMWSc 92*
**Derow,** Peter Alfred 1940- *WhoFI 92*
**De Rozario,** Fabian Jude 1963- *WhoMW 92*
**Derr,** Amandus John 1949- *WhoRel 92*
**Derr,** Gilbert S. 1917- *WhoBlA 92*
**Derr,** John Frederick 1936- *WhoWest 92*
**Derr,** John Sebring 1941- *AmMWSc 92*
**Derr,** John W 1941- *WhoAmP 91*
**Derr,** Kenneth T. *IntWW 91, WhoWest 92*
**Derr,** Lee E. 1948- *WhoMW 92*
**Derr,** Mark 1950- *ConAu 135*
**Derr,** Robert Frederick 1934- *AmMWSc 92*
**Derr,** Ronald Louis 1938- *AmMWSc 92*
**Derr,** Teresa Marie 1953- *WhoRel 92*
**Derr,** Thomas Burchard 1929- *WhoFI 92*
**Derr,** Thomas Sieger 1931- *WhoRel 92*
**Derr,** Vernon Ellsworth 1921- *AmMWSc 92*
**Derr,** William Frederick 1939- *AmMWSc 92*
**Derreberry,** Bryan Scott 1959- *WhoMW 92*
**Derrett,** Duncan 1922- *Who 92, WrDr 92*
**Derrick,** Butler C. 1936- *AlmAP 92 [port]*
**Derrick,** Butler Carson, Jr 1936- *WhoAmP 91*
**Derrick,** Finnis Ray 1911- *AmMWSc 92*
**Derrick,** Gary Wayne 1953- *WhoAmL 92*
**Derrick,** Irvin Hendrix 1921- *WhoRel 92*
**Derrick,** John Martin, Jr. 1940- *WhoFI 92*
**Derrick,** John Rafter 1922- *AmMWSc 92*
**Derrick,** Malcolm 1933- *AmMWSc 92*
**Derrick,** Mildred Elizabeth 1941- *AmMWSc 92*
**Derrick,** Patricia *Who 92*
**Derrick,** Paul Wayne 1947- *WhoAmP 91*
**Derrick,** Robert P 1931- *AmMWSc 92*
**Derrick,** Robert Wayne 1947- *WhoRel 92*
**Derrick,** William Dennis 1946- *WhoWest 92*
**Derrick,** William Richard 1938- *AmMWSc 92*
**Derrick,** William Sheldon 1916- *AmMWSc 92*
**Derrickson,** Charles M 1927- *AmMWSc 92*
**Derrickson,** William Borden 1940- *WhoFI 92*
**Derrico,** Ellen Mary 1963- *WhoMW 92*
**Derrico,** Georgia Santangelo 1944- *WhoFI 92*
**Derricotte,** C. Bruce 1928- *WhoBlA 92*
**Derricotte,** Eugene Andrew 1926- *WhoBlA 92*
**Derricotte,** Juliette 1897-1931 *NotBlAW 92 [port]*
**Derricotte,** Toi *DrAPF 91*
**Derrida,** Jacques 1930- *BenetAL 91, FacFETw, IntWW 91*
**Derrig,** Andrea Marie 1953- *WhoFI 92*
**Derriman,** James Parkyns 1922- *IntAu&W 91*
**Derrough,** Neil E. 1936- *WhoEnt 92*
**Derry,** Charles Dale 1941- *WhoEnt 92*
**Derry,** John 1933- *WrDr 92*
**Derry,** John Wesley 1933- *IntAu&W 91*
**Derry,** Paul X. 1930- *WhoWest 92*
**Derry,** Thomas Kingston 1905- *IntAu&W 91, Who 92, WrDr 92*
**Derry And Raphoe,** Bishop of 1931- *Who 92*
**Derryberry,** Larry Dale 1939- *WhoAmP 91*
**Derryberry,** Thomas Kelly 1959- *WhoAmP 91*
**Dersch,** John Arthur 1921- *WhoFI 92*
**Derse,** Phillip H 1920- *AmMWSc 92*
**Dersh,** Rhoda E. 1934- *WhoFI 92*
**Dershem,** Herbert L 1943- *AmMWSc 92*
**Dershem,** Stephen Michael 1954- *WhoWest 92*
**Dershimer,** George LeRoy 1927- *WhoMW 92*
**Dershowitz,** A. Menashe 1910- *WhoRel 92*
**Dershowitz,** Alan 1938?- *News 92-1 [port]*
**Dershowitz,** Alan M. 1938- *WrDr 92*
**Dershowitz,** Alan Morton 1938- *IntWW 91, WhoAmL 92*
**Dershwitz,** Mark 1955- *AmMWSc 92*
**Dersonnes,** Jacques *ConAu 35NR*
**Derstadt,** Ronald Theodore 1950- *WhoMW 92*
**Derthick,** Alan Wendell 1931- *WhoFI 92*
**Dertouzos,** Michael L *AmMWSc 92*
**DeRubertis,** Frederick R 1939- *AmMWSc 92*
**DeRubertis,** Patricia Sandra 1950- *WhoWest 92*
**Derucher,** Kenneth Noel 1949- *AmMWSc 92, WhoFI 92*
**DeRugeris,** C.K. *DrAPF 91*
**de Ruiter,** Hendrikus 1934- *IntWW 91*
**de Ruiter,** Jacob 1930- *IntWW 91*
**DeRungs,** Linda Jean 1952- *WhoEnt 92*
**Derus,** Patricia Irene 1947- *WhoMW 92*
**DeRusso,** Paul M 1931- *AmMWSc 92*
**Dervaird,** Lord 1935- *Who 92*
**Dervan,** Peter Brendan 1945- *AmMWSc 92*
**Dervartanian,** Daniel Vartan 1933- *AmMWSc 92*
**Derville,** William Cranston 1945- *WhoFI 92*
**Derwent,** Baron 1930- *Who 92*
**Derwin,** Jordan 1931- *WhoAmL 92, WhoEnt 92, WhoFI 92*
**Derwinski,** Dennis Anthony 1941- *WhoMW 92*
**Derwinski,** Edward J. 1926- *CurBio 91 [port], WhoAmP 91*
**Derwinski,** Edward Joseph 1926- *IntWW 91*
**Derx,** Donald John 1928- *Who 92*
**Dery,** Mark *DrAPF 91*
**Dery,** Tibor 1894-1977 *FacFETw*
**Der Yeghiayan,** Garbis H. 1949- *WhoWest 92*
**Der-Yeghiayan,** Samuel 1952- *WhoAmL 92*
**Derzai,** Amy Ruth 1904- *WhoAmP 91*
**Derzaw,** Richard Lawrence 1954- *WhoAmL 92*
**Derzko,** Nicholas Anthony 1940- *AmMWSc 92*
**De Sa,** Richard John 1938- *AmMWSc 92*
**de Saavedra,** Ruben d1990 *WhoHisp 92N*
**De Sabata,** Victor 1892-1967 *NewAmDM*
**De Saeger,** Jozef 1911- *IntWW 91*
**Desaguliers,** John Theophilus 1683-1744 *BlkwCEP*
**Desai** *Who 92*
**Desai,** Baron 1940- *Who 92*
**Desai,** Amrit 1932- *RelLAm 91*
**Desai,** Anita 1937- *ConNov 91, FacFETw, IntAu&W 91, Who 92, WrDr 92*
**Desai,** Bipin C 1939- *AmMWSc 92*
**Desai,** Bipin Ratilal 1935- *AmMWSc 92*
**Desai,** Boman 1950- *ConAu 134*
**Desai,** Hem 1932- *WhoFI 92*
**Desai,** Hitendra Kanaiyalal 1915- *IntWW 91*
**Desai,** Indrajit Dayalji 1932- *AmMWSc 92*
**Desai,** Kantilal Panachand 1929- *AmMWSc 92*
**Desai,** Mahendrabhai Nanubhai 1931- *IntWW 91*
**Desai,** Morarji Ranchhodji 1896- *FacFETw, IntWW 91, Who 92*
**Desai,** Mukund Ramanlal 1946- *WhoMW 92*
**Desai,** Parimal R 1936- *AmMWSc 92*
**Desai,** Pramod D 1939- *AmMWSc 92*
**Desai,** Prateen V 1936- *AmMWSc 92*
**Desai,** Rajendra C 1923- *AmMWSc 92*
**Desai,** Rashmi C 1938- *AmMWSc 92*
**Desai,** Subhash Punjalal 1951- *WhoMW 92*
**Desai,** Suresh Vithoba 1950- *WhoFI 92*
**Desailly,** Jean 1920- *IntWW 91*
**de Saint Phalle,** Pierre Claude 1948- *WhoAmL 92*
**de Saint Phalle,** Thibaut 1918- *WhoAmL 92*
**De Salva,** Salvatore Joseph 1924- *AmMWSc 92*
**DeSalvo,** Joseph Salvatore 1938- *WhoFI 92*
**DeSanctis,** Roman William 1930- *AmMWSc 92, IntWW 91*
**DeSandies,** Kenneth Andre 1948- *WhoBlA 92*
**DeSando,** Richard John 1932- *WhoMW 92*
**Desandro,** Paul 1947- *WhoEnt 92*
**Desani,** G. V. 1909- *ConNov 91, WrDr 92*
**DeSantis,** Frank Joseph, Jr. 1958- *WhoWest 92*
**DeSantis,** Gia Mavena 1965- *WhoEnt 92*
**De Santis,** Giuseppe 1917- *IntDcF 2-2 [port]*
**De Santis,** Gregory Joseph 1947- *IntMPA 92, WhoEnt 92*
**DeSantis,** John Louis 1942- *AmMWSc 92*
**DeSantis,** Joseph Daniel 1959- *WhoFI 92*
**DeSantis,** Mark Edward 1942- *AmMWSc 92*
**DeSantis,** Mark Francis 1959- *WhoFI 92*
**DeSantis,** Peter Michael 1959- *WhoFI 92*
**DeSantis,** Victor Joseph 1960- *WhoAmL 92*
**DeSantis,** Vincent P. 1916- *WrDr 92*
**DeSanto,** Daniel Frank 1930- *AmMWSc 92*
**DeSanto,** James John 1943- *WhoAmL 92*
**DeSanto,** John Anthony 1941- *AmMWSc 92*
**DeSanto,** Robert Spilka 1940- *AmMWSc 92*
**de Santos,** Robin King 1958- *WhoWest 92*
**DeSapio,** Gerard Joseph 1954- *WhoEnt 92*
**De Sapio,** Rodolfo Vittorio 1936- *AmMWSc 92*
**DeSarno,** Judith Martin 1944- *WhoAmP 91*
**DeSassure,** Charles 1961- *WhoBlA 92*
**De Saumarez,** Baron d1991 *Who 92N*
**de Saumarez,** Baron 1956- *Who 92*
**De Sausmarez,** Maurice 1915-1969 *TwCPaSc*
**De Saussure,** Gerard 1924- *AmMWSc 92*

**DeSaussure,** Richard Laurens, Jr 1917- *AmMWSc 92*
**Desautels,** Edouard Joseph 1938- *AmMWSc 92*
**de Savary,** Peter John 1944- *IntWW 91, Who 92*
**Desazars De Montgailhard,** Baron 1923- *IntWW 91*
**Des Barres,** Michael Phillip 1948- *WhoEnt 92*
**Desbordes-Valmore,** Marceline 1786-1859 *FrenWW*
**Desborough,** George A 1937- *AmMWSc 92*
**Desborough,** Sharon Lee 1935- *AmMWSc 92*
**Desboutin,** Marcellin 1823-1902 *ThHEIm*
**Descalzi,** Guillermo 1947- *WhoHisp 92*
**Descano,** Richard Thomas 1952- *WhoFI 92*
**Descans,** Roland Eugene 1923- *WhoAmP 91*
**Descarries,** Auguste 1896-1958 *NewAmDM*
**Descarries,** Laurent 1939- *AmMWSc 92*
**Descartes,** Rene 1596-1650 *BlkwCEP*
**Desch,** Cyril Henry 1874-1958 *FacFETw*
**Desch,** Stephen Conway 1939- *Who 92*
**De Schaap,** Philip 1911- *IntMPA 92*
**Deschamps,** Emile 1791-1871 *GuFrLit 1*
**Deschamps,** Georges Armand 1911- *AmMWSc 92*
**Deschamps,** Leger-Marie 1716-1774 *BlkwCEP*
**Des Champs,** William Green, Jr 1917- *WhoAmP 91*
**Deschanel,** Caleb 1944- *IntMPA 92, WhoEnt 92*
**Deschanel,** Mary Jo *WhoEnt 92*
**Deschenes,** Jules 1923- *IntWW 91*
**Deschner,** Eleanor Elizabeth 1928- *AmMWSc 92*
**Descombes,** Donald R 1932- *WhoIns 92*
**Descoteaux,** Arthur G *WhoAmP 91*
**Descoteaux,** Carol J. 1948- *WhoRel 92*
**d'Escoto,** Rodrigo *WhoHisp 92*
**D'Escoto Brockmann,** Miguel 1933- *IntWW 91*
**Descour,** Jozef Maria 1939- *WhoWest 92*
**De Sear,** Edward Marshall 1946- *WhoAmL 92*
**de Seife,** Rodolphe J.A. 1925- *WhoAmL 92*
**DeSelm,** Henry Rawie 1924- *AmMWSc 92*
**De Selms,** Roy Charles 1932- *AmMWSc 92*
**Deser,** Stanley 1931- *AmMWSc 92*
**de Serres,** Frederick Joseph 1929- *AmMWSc 92*
**De Sesa,** Michael Anthony 1927- *AmMWSc 92*
**DeSesso,** John Michael 1947- *AmMWSc 92*
**Desfontaines,** Pierre Francois Guyot 1685?-1745 *ScFEYrs*
**Desforges,** Jane Fay 1921- *AmMWSc 92*
**Deshaies,** Roger Joseph 1949- *WhoFI 92*
**Desharnais,** Robert Anthony 1955- *AmMWSc 92*
**DeShaw,** James Richard 1942- *AmMWSc 92*
**De Shay,** William Leslie 1930- *WhoRel 92*
**De Shazer,** Larry Grant 1934- *AmMWSc 92*
**DeShazo,** Mary Lynn Davison 1929- *AmMWSc 92*
**Desherow,** James Dartmouth 1940- *WhoFI 92*
**DeShetler,** Kenneth Edward 1928- *WhoIns 92*
**DeShetler,** Maureen McGlinchey 1948- *WhoAmP 91*
**DeShields,** Harrison F., Jr. 1927- *WhoBlA 92*
**Deshler,** Christine Patricia 1960- *WhoAmL 92*
**Deshmukh,** Diwakar Shankar 1936- *AmMWSc 92*
**Deshotels,** Warren Julius 1926- *AmMWSc 92*
**Deshpande,** Achyut Bhalchandra *AmMWSc 92*
**Deshpande,** Krishnanath Bhaskar 1921- *AmMWSc 92*
**Deshpande,** Narayan V 1938- *AmMWSc 92*
**Deshpande,** Nilendra Ganesh 1938- *AmMWSc 92*
**Deshpande,** Shashi 1938- *ConNov 91*
**Deshpande,** Shivajirao M 1936- *AmMWSc 92*
**De Sica,** Vittorio 1902-1974 *FacFETw, IntDcF 2-2 [port]*
**Desiderato,** Robert, Jr 1939- *AmMWSc 92*
**Desiderio,** Anthony Michael 1943- *AmMWSc 92*
**Desiderio,** Dominic Morse 1941- *AmMWSc 92*
**DeSieno,** Robert P 1933- *AmMWSc 92*
**De Siervo,** August Joseph 1940- *AmMWSc 92*
**Desilets,** Brian H 1927- *AmMWSc 92*
**DeSilva,** Alan W 1932- *AmMWSc 92*
**DeSilva,** Carl Nevin 1923- *AmMWSc 92*
**de Silva,** Colin *WhoFI 92*
**de Silva,** Desmond 1939- *Who 92*
**De Silva,** John Arthur F 1933- *AmMWSc 92*
**de Silva,** Yolanda 1933- *WhoHisp 92*
**De Simone,** Daniel V 1930- *AmMWSc 92*
**De Simone,** Livio Diego 1936- *WhoFI 92*
**De Simone,** Louis A. 1922- *WhoRel 92*
**de Simone,** Richard John 1958- *WhoAmL 92*
**De Simone,** Ronald Frank 1953- *WhoMW 92*
**Desing,** David Patrick 1963- *WhoMW 92*
**Desio,** Ardito 1897- *IntWW 91, Who 92*
**Desio,** Peter John 1938- *AmMWSc 92*
**Desiree,** Laura *WhoEnt 92*
**De Sitter,** Willem 1872-1934 *FacFETw*
**Desjardins,** Claude 1938- *AmMWSc 92*
**Desjardins,** Claude W 1950- *AmMWSc 92*
**Desjardins,** Paul Alfred 1945- *WhoFI 92*
**Desjardins,** Paul Roy 1919- *AmMWSc 92*
**Desjardins,** Raoul 1933- *AmMWSc 92, WhoFI 92*
**Desjardins,** Steven G 1958- *AmMWSc 92*
**Desjarlais,** John 1953- *ConAu 135*
**Desjarlais,** John Joseph 1953- *WhoEnt 92*
**Deskey,** Donald 1894-1989 *DcTwDes, FacFETw*
**Deskin,** William Arna 1924- *AmMWSc 92*
**Deskins,** Donald R., Jr. 1932- *WhoBlA 92*
**Deskins,** Herbert, Jr 1943- *WhoAmP 91*
**Deskins,** Wilbur Eugene 1927- *AmMWSc 92*
**Deskur,** Andrzej Maria 1924- *IntWW 91, WhoRel 92*
**Deslattes,** Richard D, Jr 1931- *AmMWSc 92*
**Deslauriers,** Roxanne Marie Lorraine 1947- *AmMWSc 92*
**Desler,** Dianne Kay 1947- *WhoAmP 91*
**Desler,** Peter 1947- *WhoAmL 92*
**Desley,** John Whitney 1925- *WhoMW 92*
**Desliu,** Dan 1927- *IntWW 91*
**Desloge,** Edward Augustine 1926- *AmMWSc 92*
**Deslongchamps,** Pierre 1938- *AmMWSc 92, IntWW 91, Who 92*
**Des Marais,** David John 1948- *AmMWSc 92*
**Desmarais,** Michael George 1948- *WhoAmL 92*
**Desmarais,** Norman Paul 1946- *WhoRel 92*
**Des Marais,** Paul 1920- *NewAmDM*
**Des Marais,** Pierre, II 1934- *WhoFI 92*
**Desmarescaux,** Philippe 1938- *WhoFI 92*
**Desmarest,** Nicolas 1725-1815 *BlkwCEP*
**Desmarets,** Nicolas 1725-1815 *BlkwCEP*
**DesMarteau,** Darryl D 1940- *AmMWSc 92*
**d'Esme,** Jean 1893-1966 *ScFEYrs*
**Desmedt,** John E. 1926- *IntWW 91*
**Desmet,** Kathleen Marie *WhoRel 92*
**De Smet,** Pierre-Jean *BenetAL 91, DcAmImH*
**Desmond,** Barry 1935- *IntWW 91*
**Desmond,** Johnny 1920-1985 *FacFETw*
**Desmond,** Mark Lawrence 1958- *WhoWest 92*
**Desmond,** Mary Elizabeth 1940- *AmMWSc 92*
**Desmond,** Murdina MacFarquhar 1916- *AmMWSc 92*
**Desmond,** Paul 1924-1977 *NewAmDM*
**Desmond,** Terry Tracy 1944- *WhoAmP 91*
**Desmond,** Timothy Justice 1946- *WhoWest 92*
**Desnick,** Robert John 1943- *AmMWSc 92*
**Desnoes,** Peter Blaise *WhoEnt 92*
**Desnos,** Robert 1900-1945 *FacFETw*
**Desnoyers,** Fernand 1826-1869 *ThHEIm*
**Desnoyers,** Jacques Edouard 1935- *AmMWSc 92*
**Deso,** Robert Edward, Jr. 1943- *WhoAmL 92*
**Desoer,** Charles A 1926- *AmMWSc 92*
**de Soet,** Jan F. A. 1925- *IntWW 91*
**De Sofi,** Oliver Julius 1929- *WhoFI 92*
**De Sola,** Carla *WhoEnt 92*
**De Sola,** Ralph 1908- *WhoWest 92*
**DeSombre,** Eugene Robert 1938- *AmMWSc 92*
**De Somer,** Pierre d1985 *IntWW 91N*
**DeSomogyi,** Aileen Ada 1911- *WhoMW 92*
**Desor,** Edouard *BiInAmS*
**Desor,** Jeannette Ann 1942- *AmMWSc 92*
**Desor,** Pierre Jean Edouard 1811-1882 *BiInAmS*
**De Soto,** Benjamin Tecumseh 1958- *WhoHisp 92*
**DeSoto,** Ernest 1954- *WhoHisp 92*
**De Soto,** Hector 1951- *WhoHisp 92*
**De Soto,** Hernando 1500?-1542 *BenetAL 91*
**Desoto,** Hisaye *DrAPF 91*
**De Soto,** Rosana *WhoHisp 92*
**de Sousa Ribas,** Abilio Rodas *WhoRel 92*
**Desoutter,** Roger 1923- *TwCPaSc*
**De Souza,** Derek Anthony 1945- *WhoFI 92*
**De Souza,** Ernest Henriques 1933- *WhoRel 92*
**de Souza,** Eunice 1940- *ConPo 91, WrDr 92*
**de Souza,** Neville Wardsworth *WhoRel 92*
**De Souza,** Robert 1921- *IntWW 91*
**DeSouza,** Ronald Kent 1940- *WhoBlA 92*
**Desowitz,** Robert 1926- *AmMWSc 92*
**Despain,** Alvin M 1938- *AmMWSc 92*
**DesPain,** Donald Holt 1959- *WhoFI 92*
**Despain,** Lewis Gail 1928- *AmMWSc 92*
**Desper,** Clyde Richard 1937- *AmMWSc 92*
**Desplan,** Claude *AmMWSc 92*
**Despol,** John Anton 1913- *WhoWest 92*
**Despommier,** Dickson 1940- *AmMWSc 92*
**Desportes,** Francois-Alexandre 1661-1743 *BlkwCEP*
**Despot,** George Joseph 1927- *WhoAmP 91*
**Despotopoulos,** Johannes 1909- *IntWW 91*
**Despres,** Leo Arthur 1932- *WhoMW 92*
**Despres,** Robert 1924- *Who 92, WhoFI 92*
**Despres,** Robert 1927- *IntWW 91*
**Despres,** Thomas A 1932- *AmMWSc 92*
**Des Prez,** Josquin *NewAmDM*
**Des Prez,** Roger Moister 1927- *AmMWSc 92*
**Desrochers,** Alan Alfred 1950- *AmMWSc 92*
**Des Rochers,** Gary Joseph 1941- *WhoWest 92*
**Desrochers,** Gerald T 1920- *WhoAmP 91*
**Des Rosiers,** Camille *WhoRel 92*
**Desrosiers,** Ronald Charles 1948- *AmMWSc 92*
**Desrosiers,** William J, Jr 1940- *WhoAmP 91*
**Dess,** G.D. *ConAu 135*
**Dess,** Howard Melvin 1929- *AmMWSc 92*
**Dessane,** Antoine 1826-1873 *NewAmDM*
**Dessaso-Gordon,** Janice Marie 1942- *WhoBlA 92*
**Dessau,** Paul 1894-1979 *NewAmDM*
**Dessau,** Randy Scot 1959- *WhoAmL 92*
**Dessauer,** Herbert Clay 1921- *AmMWSc 92*
**Dessauer,** John Hans 1905- *AmMWSc 92*
**Dessauer,** John Paul 1904- *WrDr 92*
**Dessauer,** Rolf 1926- *AmMWSc 92*
**Dessauer,** Sidney Robert 1936- *WhoWest 92*
**Dessel,** Norman F 1932- *AmMWSc 92*
**Dessem,** R. Lawrence 1951- *WhoAmL 92*
**Desser,** Edwin S. 1958- *WhoEnt 92*
**Desser,** Kenneth Barry 1940- *WhoWest 92*
**Desser,** Maxwell Milton *WhoEnt 92*
**Desser,** Sherwin S 1937- *AmMWSc 92*
**Dessin,** Carolyn Louise 1957- *WhoAmL 92*
**Dessler,** Alexander Jack 1928- *AmMWSc 92*
**Dessler,** Nahum W. 1921- *WhoRel 92*
**Dessouky,** Dessouky Ahmad 1932- *AmMWSc 92*
**Dessouky,** Ibtesam Abdel Rahman 1941- *WhoFI 92*
**Dessouky,** Mohamed Ibrahim 1926- *AmMWSc 92*
**Dessy,** Raymond Edwin 1931- *AmMWSc 92*
**d'Est,** Beatrice *EncAmaz 91*
**d'Est,** Isabella *EncAmaz 91*
**Dest,** Leonard Ralph 1949- *WhoWest 92*
**De St Jorre,** Danielle Marie-Madeleine 1941- *IntWW 91*
**De St Jorre,** Danielle Marie-Madeleine J. *Who 92*
**de St. Jorre,** John 1936- *WrDr 92*
**De St Paer,** Virginia Beth 1918- *WhoAmP 91*
**Desta,** Fisseha *IntWW 91*
**de Ste. Croix,** Geoffrey Ernest Maurice 1910- *Who 92*
**De Stefani,** Alberto 1879-1969 *BiDExR*
**De Stefanis,** Daniela Angela 1965- *WhoEnt 92*
**DeStefano,** Anthony Joseph 1949- *AmMWSc 92*
**DeStefano,** C George 1912- *WhoAmP 91*
**De Stefano,** John J *WhoIns 92*
**De Stefano,** John Joseph 1949- *WhoFI 92*
**Destephano,** Arthur John 1939- *WhoMW 92*
**DeStevens,** George 1924- *AmMWSc 92*
**Destine,** Jean-Leon 1928- *WhoBlA 92*
**Destinn,** Emmy 1878-1930 *NewAmDM*
**d'Estournelles,** Paul Henri Benjamin B 1852-1924 *WhoNob 90*
**d'Estrada,** Maria *EncAmaz 91*
**Destro,** Robert A 1950- *WhoAmP 91*
**Destro,** Robert Anthony 1950- *WhoAmL 92*
**Destry,** Vince *IntAu&W 91X, TwCWW 91*
**de Strycker,** Cecil A. J. F. J. M. 1915- *IntWW 91*
**Destutt de Tracy,** Antoine-Louis-Claude 1754-1836 *BlkwCEP*
**Desty,** Denis Henry 1923- *Who 92*
**Desu,** Manavala Mahamunulu 1931- *AmMWSc 92*
**Desu,** Seshu Babu 1955- *AmMWSc 92*
**DeSua,** Frank Crispin 1921- *AmMWSc 92*
**de Suze,** Jacques Christophe 1944- *WhoEnt 92*
**De Sylva,** Donald Perrin 1928- *AmMWSc 92*
**de Tabley,** Lord 1835-1895 *RfGEnL 91*
**De Takacsy,** Nicholas Benedict 1939- *AmMWSc 92*
**Detamore,** George Edward 1924- *WhoRel 92*
**DeTar,** DeLos Fletcher 1920- *AmMWSc 92*
**Detar,** Reed L 1932- *AmMWSc 92*
**Detels,** Roger 1936- *AmMWSc 92*
**DeTemple,** Duane William 1942- *AmMWSc 92*
**DeTemple,** Thomas Albert 1941- *AmMWSc 92*
**Detenbeck,** Robert Warren 1933- *AmMWSc 92*
**De Tennis,** Gregory Paul 1959- *WhoEnt 92*
**Deter,** D Scott 1954- *WhoAmP 91*
**Deter,** Dean A. *DrAPF 91*
**Deterding,** Curtis Lynn 1958- *WhoRel 92*
**Deterding,** Floyd Marshall 1954- *WhoAmL 92*
**Deterling,** Ralph Alden, Jr 1917- *AmMWSc 92*
**Determan,** Sara-Ann 1938- *WhoAmL 92*
**De Terra,** Noel 1933- *AmMWSc 92*
**Deters,** Arthur H 1937- *WhoIns 92*
**Deters,** Donald W 1944- *AmMWSc 92*
**Detert,** Francis Lawrence 1923- *AmMWSc 92*
**de The,** Guy Blaudin 1930- *IntWW 91*
**Dethier,** Bernard Emile 1926- *AmMWSc 92*
**de Thier,** Jacques 1900- *Who 92*
**Dethier,** Vincent G 1915- *IntAu&W 91, WrDr 92*
**Dethier,** Vincent Gaston 1915- *AmMWSc 92, IntWW 91*
**Dethlefsen,** Lyle A 1934- *AmMWSc 92*
**Dethlefsen,** Rolf 1934- *AmMWSc 92, WhoWest 92*
**DeThomasis,** Louis 1940- *WhoRel 92*
**Detig,** Robert Henry 1935- *AmMWSc 92*
**De Titta,** Arthur A. 1904- *IntMPA 92*
**DeTitta,** George Thomas 1947- *AmMWSc 92*
**Detjen,** David Wheeler 1948- *WhoAmL 92*
**Detkin,** Peter N. 1960- *WhoAmL 92*
**Detlef,** John Frank 1927- *WhoMW 92*
**Detlor,** John Sydney 1940- *WhoWest 92*
**Detmar-Pines,** Gina Louise 1949- *WhoFI 92*
**Detmer,** Lawrence McCormick 1930- *WhoMW 92*
**Detmers,** Patricia Anne 1953- *AmMWSc 92*
**Detmold,** Charles Maurice 1883-1908 *TwCPaSc*
**Detmold,** Edward Julius 1883-1957 *TwCPaSc*
**De Tocqueville,** Alexis *BenetAL 91*
**De Toledano,** Ralph *DrAPF 91*
**de Toledo,** Victoria Chapin 1956- *WhoAmL 92*
**DeToma,** Robert Paul 1944- *AmMWSc 92*
**De Tommaso,** Gabriel Louis 1934- *AmMWSc 92*
**De Tornyay,** Rheba 1926- *AmMWSc 92*
**DeToro,** Irving John 1934- *WhoFI 92*
**de Torres,** Manuel *WhoHisp 92*
**De Toth,** Andre *IntMPA 92*
**De Toth,** Andre 1910- *IntDcF 2-2*
**Detra,** Ralph W 1925- *AmMWSc 92*
**de Trafford,** Dermot Humphrey 1925- *Who 92*
**Detrano,** John Michael 1927- *WhoFI 92*
**DeTray,** Donald Ervin 1917- *AmMWSc 92*
**Detraz,** Orville R 1930- *AmMWSc 92*
**Detre,** Thomas Paul 1924- *AmMWSc 92*
**de Trevino,** Elizabeth 1904- *WrDr 92*
**De Trevino,** Elizabeth Borton 1904- *IntAu&W 91*
**Detrick,** Donald Howard 1954- *WhoRel 92*
**Detrick,** John K 1920- *AmMWSc 92*
**Detrick,** Robert Sherman 1918- *AmMWSc 92*
**Detrio,** John A 1937- *AmMWSc 92*
**De Troyer,** Andre Jules 1948- *AmMWSc 92*
**Dett,** R. Nathaniel 1882-1943 *NewAmDM*
**Dettbarn,** Wolf Dietrich 1928- *AmMWSc 92*
**Dettelbach,** Thomas Lee 1937- *WhoAmL 92*
**Dettelis,** Peter Francis 1963- *WhoWest 92*
**Detten,** Georg von 1887-1934 *EncTR 91*

**Detter,** Steven Kim 1949- WhoMW 92
**Detterman,** Robert Linwood 1931- WhoWest 92
**Dettinger,** David 1919- AmMWSc 92
**Dettinger,** Warren Walter 1954- WhoAmL 92, WhoFI 92, WhoMW 92
**Dettlaff,** Theodore Herbert 1930- WhoFI 92
**Dettman,** John Warren 1926- AmMWSc 92
**Dettmer,** Richard Alan 1952- WhoMW 92
**Dettmer,** Robert Gerhart 1931- WhoFI 92
**Dettre,** Robert Harold 1928- AmMWSc 92
**Dettweiler,** Jack Henry, Jr. 1945- WhoFI 92
**Detty,** Wendell Eugene 1922- AmMWSc 92
**Detweiler,** David Kenneth 1919- AmMWSc 92, IntWW 91
**Detweiler,** Robert 1932- WrDr 92
**Detweiler,** Robert Chester 1938- WhoWest 92
**Detweiler,** Steven Lawrence 1947- AmMWSc 92
**Detweiler,** W Kenneth 1923- AmMWSc 92
**Detwiler,** Daniel Paul 1927- AmMWSc 92
**Detwiler,** Donald Scaife 1933- WhoMW 92
**Detwiler,** Harold E 1930- WhoIns 92
**Detwiler,** John Stephen 1946- AmMWSc 92
**Detwiler,** Peter Benton 1944- AmMWSc 92
**Detwiler,** Ralph Paul 1955- WhoAmL 92
**Detwiler,** Susan Margaret 1953- WhoMW 92
**Detwiler,** Thomas C 1933- AmMWSc 92
**Detwiler,** Thomas C. 1957- WhoMW 92
**Detwyler,** Robert 1929- AmMWSc 92
**Detz,** Clifford M 1942- AmMWSc 92
**Detz,** Joan WrDr 92
**Detzer,** Dorothy 1893-1981 AmPeW
**Detzler,** Miranda Lam 1965- WhoMW 92
**Detzliffin,** Anna Sophia 1738-1776 EncAmaz 91
**Deuben,** Roger R 1938- AmMWSc 92
**Deuberry,** Laura Anne 1948- WhoMW 92
**Deubert,** Karl Heinz 1929- AmMWSc 92
**Deuble,** John H 1930- WhoIns 92
**Deuble,** John L., Jr. 1932- WhoWest 92
**Deuble,** John Lewis, Jr 1932- AmMWSc 92
**Deubler,** Earl Edward, Jr 1927- AmMWSc 92
**Deubler,** Mary Josephine 1917- AmMWSc 92
**Deubner,** Russell L 1919- AmMWSc 92
**Deuchler,** Suzanne L 1929- WhoAmP 91
**Deudon,** Charles 1832-1914 ThHEIm
**Deuel,** Douglas James 1956- WhoRel 92
**Deuel,** Frank Paul 1959- WhoEnt 92
**Deuel,** Jamieson Koby 1932- WhoFI 92
**Deuel,** M. Carolyn 1952- WhoEnt 92
**Deufel,** Robert David 1928- WhoMW 92
**D'Eugenio,** David P. 1957- WhoFI 92
**Deukmejian,** George 1928- IntWW 91, WhoAmP 91, WhoWest 92
**Deukmejian,** George, Jr. 1928- Who 92
**Deunk,** Norman Howard, Jr. 1925- WhoMW 92
**Deupi,** Carlos 1936- WhoHisp 92
**Deupree,** Jean Durley 1942- AmMWSc 92
**Deupree,** Robert G 1946- AmMWSc 92
**Deurbrouck,** Albert William 1932- AmMWSc 92
**de Urioste,** George Adolfo, IV 1955- WhoWest 92
**Deuschle,** James Konrad 1956- WhoAmL 92
**Deuschle,** Kurt W 1923- AmMWSc 92
**Deuser,** Werner Georg 1935- AmMWSc 92
**D'Eustachio,** Dominic 1904- AmMWSc 92
**D'Eustachio,** Peter 1949- AmMWSc 92
**Deuster,** Donald Eugene 1929- WhoAmP 91
**Deuster,** Ralph W 1920- AmMWSc 92
**Deutch,** Bernhard Irwin 1929- AmMWSc 92
**Deutch,** Howard IntMPA 92
**Deutch,** John 1938- IntWW 91
**Deutch,** John Mark 1938- AmMWSc 92
**Deutchman,** Ira J. 1953- IntMPA 92
**Deutchman,** Lawrence Scot 1960- IntMPA 92
**Deutekom,** Cristina 1938- IntWW 91
**Deutsch,** Andre 1917- DcLB 112 [port], IntAu&W 91, IntWW 91, Who 92
**Deutsch,** Armand S. 1913- IntMPA 92
**Deutsch,** Babette 1895-1982 BenetAL 91
**Deutsch,** Barry Joseph 1941- WhoFI 92, WhoWest 92
**Deutsch,** Carol Joan AmMWSc 92
**Deutsch,** Daniel Harold 1922- AmMWSc 92
**Deutsch,** David 1926- IntMPA 92
**Deutsch,** David Jeremiah 1945- WhoFI 92
**Deutsch,** Diana 1938- WhoEnt 92
**Deutsch,** Didier 1937- WhoEnt 92
**Deutsch,** Eberhard Paul 1897-1980 AmPeW
**Deutsch,** Edward Allen 1942- AmMWSc 92
**Deutsch,** Ernst 1890-1969 EncTR 91 [port]
**Deutsch,** Ernst Robert 1924- AmMWSc 92
**Deutsch,** Erwin 1917- IntWW 91
**Deutsch,** Frank Richard 1936- AmMWSc 92
**Deutsch,** Harold Francis 1918- AmMWSc 92
**Deutsch,** Harvey Elliot 1940- WhoAmL 92
**Deutsch,** Helen IntMPA 92
**Deutsch,** Helene 1884-1982 HanAmWH
**Deutsch,** Helene Rosenbach 1884-1982 FacFETw
**Deutsch,** Herbert Arnold 1932- WhoEnt 92
**Deutsch,** Hunting Folger 1952- WhoFI 92
**Deutsch,** Jan Ginter 1935- WhoAmL 92
**Deutsch,** Jo Ann 1946- WhoAmL 92
**Deutsch,** John Ludwig 1938- AmMWSc 92
**Deutsch,** Karl 1912- WrDr 92
**Deutsch,** Laurence Peter 1946- AmMWSc 92
**Deutsch,** Lawrence Ira 1939- WhoRel 92
**Deutsch,** Marshall Emanuel 1921- AmMWSc 92
**Deutsch,** Martin 1917- AmMWSc 92
**Deutsch,** Max 1892-1982 NewAmDM
**Deutsch,** Mike John 1920- AmMWSc 92
**Deutsch,** Nina WhoEnt 92
**Deutsch,** Peter 1957- WhoAmP 91
**Deutsch,** Robert V 1959- WhoIns 92
**Deutsch,** Robert W 1924- AmMWSc 92
**Deutsch,** S 1918- AmMWSc 92
**Deutsch,** Stanley 1930- AmMWSc 92
**Deutsch,** Stephen 1946- IntMPA 92
**Deutsch,** Stephen R 1939- WhoAmP 91
**Deutsch,** Stuart Charles 1954- WhoEnt 92
**Deutsch,** Stuart Lewis 1945- WhoAmL 92
**Deutsch,** Thomas F 1932- AmMWSc 92
**Deutsch,** Walter A 1945- AmMWSc 92
**Deutscher,** Irwin 1923- WrDr 92
**Deutscher,** Murray Paul 1941- AmMWSc 92
**Deutschman,** Archie John, Jr 1917- AmMWSc 92
**Dev,** Parvati 1946- AmMWSc 92
**Dev,** Vaithilingam Gangathara 1937- AmMWSc 92
**Dev,** Vasu 1933- AmMWSc 92
**De Valera,** Eamon 1882-1975 FacFETw [port]
**Devall,** James Lee 1941- WhoAmL 92
**de Valois,** Geoffrey Herrick 1954- WhoEnt 92
**de Valois,** Ninette 1898- IntWW 91, Who 92
**Devamata,** Sister 1867-1942 RelLAm 91
**DeVan,** Jackson H AmMWSc 92
**DeVan,** Mark Roy 1948- WhoAmL 92
**Devan Nair,** Chengara Veetil 1923- IntWW 91
**Devanandan,** Paul David 1901-1962 DcEcMov
**DeVane,** Daniel H 1945- WhoAmP 91
**Devane,** John 1954- TwCPaSc
**DeVane,** Milton Phillips 1929- WhoAmL 92
**Devane,** William 1939- IntMPA 92, WhoEnt 92
**DeVaney,** Charles Alexander 1952- WhoAmP 91
**DeVaney,** Cynthia Ann 1947- WhoFI 92, WhoMW 92
**Devaney,** Dennis Martin 1946- WhoAmP 91, WhoFI 92
**Devaney,** Donald Everett 1936- WhoWest 92
**Devaney,** Edward D, Jr 1928- WhoIns 92
**Devaney,** John Francis 1946- WhoMW 92
**Devaney,** Joseph James 1924- AmMWSc 92
**DeVaney,** Larry Washburn 1950- WhoFI 92
**Devaney,** Michael Thomas 1950- WhoFI 92
**Devantier,** Paul W. 1946- WhoRel 92
**Devany,** Joseph Aloysius 1921- WhoAmP 91
**de Varon,** Lorna Cooke 1921- WhoEnt 92
**de Varona,** Esperanza Bravo WhoHisp 92
**De Varona,** Francisco Jose 1943- WhoHisp 92
**Devarre,** Spencer H d1899 BiInAmS
**Devarso,** James F 1948- WhoIns 92
**Devas,** Anthony 1911-1958 TwCPaSc
**DeVassie,** Terry Lee 1939- WhoFI 92
**De Vaucouleurs,** Gerard Henri 1918- AmMWSc 92, IntWW 91
**De Vaughn,** Deborah A. 1955- WhoEnt 92
**DeVaughn,** Edward Raymond 1926- WhoBlA 92
**DeVaughn-Stokes,** Diane 1951- WhoEnt 92
**DeVaughn-Tidline,** Donna Michelle 1954- WhoBlA 92
**De Vaul,** Virginia C IntAu&W 91X
**DeVault,** Connie Kae 1959- WhoMW 92
**DeVault,** Don Charles 1915- AmMWSc 92
**DeVaux,** George Russell 1941- WhoFI 92
**Devaux,** Louis Armand 1907- IntWW 91
**DeVay,** James Edson 1921- AmMWSc 92
**De Veau,** Robert Eugene 1960- WhoFI 92
**DeVeau,** Ronald Edward 1944- WhoAmL 92
**De Veaux,** Alexis DrAPF 91
**DeVeber,** Jean Carole 1942- WhoAmP 91
**De Veber,** Leverett L 1929- AmMWSc 92
**De Vecchi,** Cesare Maria 1884-1959 BiDExR, EncTR 91
**DeVecchio,** Lois Lindley 1916- WhoAmP 91
**De Vedia,** Luis Alberto 1941- AmMWSc 92
**De Vegvar,** Paul Geza Neuman 1957- AmMWSc 92
**Devendorf,** David Stuart 1935- WhoFI 92
**Deveney,** James Kevin 1945- AmMWSc 92
**Devenport,** Eric Nash Who 92
**Devenport,** Martyn Herbert d1991 Who 92N
**Devens,** John Searle 1940- WhoWest 92
**Devens,** Michael William 1961- WhoWest 92
**Devens,** W George 1926- AmMWSc 92
**DeVenuto,** Frank 1928- AmMWSc 92
**Dever,** Daniel WhoRel 92
**Dever,** David Francis 1931- AmMWSc 92
**Dever,** Donald Andrew 1926- AmMWSc 92
**Dever,** Edmonde 1921- IntWW 91
**Dever,** G E Alan 1941- AmMWSc 92
**Dever,** Homer Hobart 1928- WhoRel 92
**Dever,** James Columcille 1962- WhoAmL 92
**Dever,** John E, Jr 1932- AmMWSc 92
**Dever,** Peter Kent 1960- WhoAmL 92
**Deveraux,** Jude 1947- WrDr 92
**Deveraux,** Tsenre Lisetta Pompeo 1959- WhoWest 92
**de Vere,** Anthony Charles Mayle 1930- Who 92
**De Vere,** Aubrey 1814-1902 RfGEnL 91
**De Vere,** Howard ScFEYrs
**de Vere White,** Mrs. Who 92
**de Vere White,** Terence Who 92
**Devereau,** George Michael 1937- Who 92
**Deverell,** Colville 1907- Who 92
**Deverell,** Rex Johnson 1941- IntAu&W 91
**Devereueawax,** John L., III 1953- WhoBlA 92
**Devereux** Who 92
**Devereux,** Alan Robert 1933- Who 92
**Devereux,** James P S 1903-1988 FacFETw
**Devereux,** John 1761-1844 DcNCBi 2
**Devereux,** John, Jr. 1820-1893 DcNCBi 2
**Devereux,** John Rickert 1947- WhoMW 92
**Devereux,** Lawrence Hackett 1929- WhoFI 92
**Devereux,** Owen Francis 1937- AmMWSc 92
**Devereux,** Pamela Lea 1962- WhoMW 92
**Devereux,** Richard 1956- TwCPaSc
**Devereux,** Richard Blyton 1945- AmMWSc 92
**Devereux,** Theodora Reyling 1944- AmMWSc 92
**Devereux,** Thomas Pollock 1793-1869 DcNCBi 2
**Deverin,** Thomas J 1921- WhoAmP 91
**Devers,** Darryl Trimble 1955- WhoAmL 92
**Devers,** Peter Dix 1938- WhoAmL 92
**Devers,** William Thomas 1956- WhoMW 92
**DeVerter,** Walter F 1934- WhoAmP 91
**de Vesci,** Viscount 1955- Who 92
**Devesi,** Baddeley 1941- IntWW 91, Who 92
**Devgan,** Satinderpaul Singh 1939- AmMWSc 92
**Devgun,** Jas S AmMWSc 92
**Devi,** Gayatri 1906- RelLAm 91
**Devi,** Lakshmy d1981 RelLAm 91
**De Vicenzo,** Roberto 1923- IntWW 91
**de Vichy-Chamrond,** Marie 1697-1780 FrenWW
**DeVico,** Samuel S 1931- WhoAmP 91
**Devience,** Alex, Jr. 1940- WhoAmL 92
**de Vienne,** Arnaud Guy 1947- WhoFI 92
**de Vigier,** William Alphonse 1912- Who 92
**Devigne,** Karen Cooke 1943- WhoFI 92
**DeVille,** Donald Charles 1953- WhoFI 92
**De Ville,** Harold Godfrey 1925- Who 92
**DeVillez,** Edward Joseph 1939- AmMWSc 92
**de Villiers,** Baron 1911- Who 92
**de Villiers,** Dawid Jacobus 1940- IntWW 91, Who 92
**De Villiers,** Jacob 1938- IntWW 91
**De Villiers,** Jacobus Wynand Louw 1929- IntWW 91
**De Villiers,** Willem Johannes 1921-1991 IntWW 91, -91N
**DeVillis,** Jean 1935- AmMWSc 92
**Devin,** Lee 1938- WhoEnt 92
**Devin,** Paul R 1941- WhoAmL 92
**Devin,** Ronald Boyd 1933- WhoWest 92
**Devinatz,** Allen 1922- AmMWSc 92, WhoMW 92
**Devincenti,** Juan Claudio 1934- WhoHisp 92
**de Vinck,** Jose M.G.A. 1912- WrDr 92
**Devine,** Charles Joseph, Jr 1923- AmMWSc 92
**Devine,** Daniel Edward 1951- WhoFI 92
**Devine,** Daniel Scott 1958- WhoMW 92
**Devine,** David Francis 1929- WhoIns 92
**Devine,** Donn 1929- WhoAmL 92
**DeVine,** Edmond Francis 1916- WhoAmL 92
**Devine,** Edward Thomas 1867-1948 AmPeW
**Devine,** Emily Elizabeth 1955- WhoWest 92
**Devine,** Foy Roberson 1942- WhoAmL 92
**Devine,** Grant 1944- IntWW 91, Who 92, WhoWest 92
**Devine,** Hugh James, Jr. 1938- WhoFI 92
**Devine,** John Edward 1923- AmMWSc 92
**Devine,** Joseph Who 92
**DeVine,** Lawrence 1935- WhoEnt 92
**Devine,** Lesley R 1942- WhoAmP 91
**Devine,** Marjorie M 1934- AmMWSc 92
**Devine,** Michael Buxton 1953- WhoAmL 92
**Devine,** Michael J. 1945- WhoMW 92
**Devine,** Peter Merle 1948- WhoEnt 92
**Devine,** Samuel L 1915- WhoAmP 91
**Devine,** Shane 1926- WhoAmL 92
**Devine,** T. Martin 1945- WrDr 92
**Devine,** Thomas Edward AmMWSc 92
**Deviney,** Marvin Lee, Jr 1929- AmMWSc 92, WhoFI 92
**De Vinne,** Theodore L. 1828-1914 BenetAL 91
**Devins,** Delbert Wayne 1934- AmMWSc 92
**de Virion,** Tadeusz 1926- Who 92
**de Virion,** Tadeusz Jozef 1926- IntWW 91
**de Visscher,** Francois Marie 1953- WhoFI 92
**De Vita,** John DrAPF 91
**De Vita,** Joseph Stephen 1941- WhoIns 92
**DeVita,** Vincent T, Jr 1935- AmMWSc 92
**DeVito,** Alberico WhoRel 92
**DeVito,** Albert Kenneth 1919- WhoEnt 92
**De Vito,** Betty J 1934- WhoAmP 91
**DeVito,** Carl Louis 1937- AmMWSc 92, WhoWest 92
**DeVito,** Carmen Samuel 1954- WhoFI 92
**De Vito,** Danny 1944- IntMPA 92, NewYTBS 91 [port]
**Devito,** Danny Michael 1944- WhoEnt 92
**De Vito,** Gioconda 1907- Who 92
**DeVito,** Joseph 1938- WrDr 92
**DeVito,** June Logan 1928- AmMWSc 92
**DeVito,** Raymond Peter 1952- WhoMW 92
**De Vito,** Salverino 1926- IntWW 91
**Devitt,** Edward James 1911- WhoAmL 92
**Devitt,** John Martin 1937- WhoMW 92
**Devitt,** John William 1959- WhoMW 92
**Devitt,** Thomas Gordon 1902- Who 92
**Devitt-Grasso,** Pauline Virginia 1930- WhoWest 92
**DeVitto,** Kenneth James WhoMW 92
**De Vivo,** Edward Charles 1953- WhoAmL 92
**Devletian,** Jack H 1941- AmMWSc 92
**Devletoglou,** Evangelos A. IntWW 91
**Devlin** Who 92
**Devlin,** Baron 1905- IntWW 91, Who 92
**Devlin,** Lord 1905- WrDr 92
**Devlin,** Alexander 1927- Who 92
**Devlin,** Anne 1951- WrDr 92
**Devlin,** Anne Maria 1951- IntAu&W 91
**Devlin,** Bernadette Who 92
**Devlin,** Denis LiExTwC
**Devlin,** Denis 1908-1959 FacFETw, RfGEnL 91
**Devlin,** Francis James 1943- WhoAmL 92
**Devlin,** Gerald M 1930- WhoIns 92
**Devlin,** Gerard Francis 1933- WhoAmP 91
**Devlin,** Gerry 1931- WhoAmP 91
**Devlin,** James Richard 1950- WhoAmL 92
**Devlin,** Jean Theresa 1947- WhoMW 92
**Devlin,** John F 1944- AmMWSc 92
**Devlin,** Joseph Paul 1935- AmMWSc 92
**Devlin,** Keith Michael 1933- Who 92
**Devlin,** Mary Margaret 1945- WhoAmL 92
**Devlin,** Michael Coles 1942- WhoEnt 92
**Devlin,** Michael G 1931- WhoAmP 91
**Devlin,** Michael Gerard 1947- WhoFI 92
**Devlin,** Michael Patrick 1950- WhoAmL 92
**Devlin,** Richard Gerald, Jr 1942- AmMWSc 92
**Devlin,** Robert B 1947- AmMWSc 92
**Devlin,** Robert Martin 1931- AmMWSc 92
**Devlin,** Stuart Leslie 1931- IntWW 91, Who 92
**Devlin,** Thomas J 1935- AmMWSc 92
**Devlin,** Thomas McKeown 1929- AmMWSc 92
**Devlin,** Tim 1944- Who 92
**Devlin,** Timothy Robert 1959- Who 92

**Devlin-Malm**, Karyn 1948- *WhoMW 92*
**Devner**, Jon Lawrence 1943- *WhoWest 92*
**Devnich**, D. D. *WhoRel 92*
**DeVoe**, Barbara Maines 1945- *WhoAmP 91*
**DeVoe**, Howard Josselyn 1932- *AmMWSc 92*
**DeVoe**, Irving Woodrow 1936- *AmMWSc 92*
**Devoe**, James Rollo 1928- *AmMWSc 92*
**Devoe**, Ralph Godwin 1945- *AmMWSc 92*
**Devoe**, Robert Donald 1934- *AmMWSc 92, WhoMW 92*
**DeVol**, Skip 1948- *WhoMW 92*
**DeVoll**, Ray *WhoEnt 92*
**De Volpi**, Alexander 1931- *AmMWSc 92*
**Devon**, Earl of 1916- *Who 92*
**Devon**, Wesley Scott 1939- *WhoMW 92*
**Devonish**, Arnoldo 1933- *BlkOlyM*
**Devonport**, Viscount 1944- *Who 92*
**Devons**, Samuel 1914- *AmMWSc 92, IntWW 91, Who 92*
**Devonshire**, Duke of 1920- *Who 92*
**Devonshire**, Michael Norman 1930- *Who 92*
**Devor**, Arthur William 1911- *AmMWSc 92*
**Devor**, Kenneth Arthur 1943- *AmMWSc 92*
**DeVore**, Ann G 1936- *WhoAmP 91*
**DeVore**, Daun Aline 1955- *WhoAmL 92*
**DeVore**, Galvin Fray 1949- *WhoWest 92*
**DeVore**, George Warren 1924- *AmMWSc 92*
**Devore**, Janice Gehl 1950- *WhoMW 92*
**Devore**, Jeffrey Adam 1964- *WhoAmL 92*
**Devore**, Kimberly K. 1947- *WhoFI 92, WhoMW 92*
**DeVore**, Ophelia *WhoBlA 92*
**DeVore**, Thomas Carroll 1947- *AmMWSc 92*
**De Vore**, Zeth Blevens 1931- *WhoWest 92*
**DeVorkin**, David Hyam 1944- *AmMWSc 92*
**De Vorsey**, Louis, Jr. 1929- *WrDr 92*
**Devos**, Elisabeth 1958- *WhoAmP 91*
**De Vos**, Peter Jon 1938- *WhoAmP 91*
**DeVos**, Richard Marvin 1926- *WhoFI 92*
**DeVos**, Richard Marvin, Jr. 1955- *WhoMW 92*
**DeVos**, Richard Marvin Dick, Jr. 1955- *WhoFI 92*
**DeVoss**, David Arlen 1947- *WhoWest 92*
**Devoti**, William *DrAPF 91*
**De Voto**, Bernard 1897-1955 *TwCWW 91*
**De Voto**, Bernard A. 1897-1955 *BenetAL 91*
**Devoto**, Ralph Stephen 1934- *AmMWSc 92*
**De Voto**, Terence Alan 1946- *WhoWest 92*
**Devoy**, John 1842-1928 *DcAmImH*
**Devoy**, Kimball John 1941- *WhoAmL 92*
**Devreotes**, Peter Nicholas 1948- *AmMWSc 92*
**De Vries**, Adriaan 1931- *AmMWSc 92*
**Devries**, Arthur Leland 1938- *AmMWSc 92*
**De Vries**, Bert 1938- *IntWW 91*
**De Vries**, Calvin Thomas 1921- *WhoRel 92*
**Devries**, David J 1942- *AmMWSc 92*
**De Vries**, Dawn Ann 1961- *WhoRel 92*
**de Vries**, Egbert 1901- *WhoRel 92*
**DeVries**, Frederick William 1930- *AmMWSc 92*
**DeVries**, George H 1942- *AmMWSc 92*
**DeVries**, James Howard 1932- *WhoAmL 92, WhoEnt 92*
**De Vries**, Janet Margaret 1950- *WhoRel 92*
**De Vries**, John Edward 1919- *AmMWSc 92*
**DeVries**, Judith Leigh 1945- *WhoAmP 91*
**DeVries**, K Lawrence 1933- *AmMWSc 92*
**De Vries**, Kenneth Lawrence 1933- *WhoWest 92*
**de Vries**, Margaret Garritsen 1922- *WhoFI 92*
**DeVries**, Marvin Frank 1937- *AmMWSc 92, WhoMW 92*
**De Vries**, Michiel Josias 1933- *IntWW 91*
**De Vries**, Peter *DrAPF 91*
**De Vries**, Peter 1910- *BenetAL 91, ConNov 91, IntAu&W 91, IntWW 91, Who 92, WrDr 92*
**de Vries**, Philip John 1947- *WhoRel 92*
**de Vries**, Rachel 1947- *WrDr 92*
**deVries**, Rachel Guido *DrAPF 91*
**DeVries**, Ralph Milton 1944- *AmMWSc 92*
**De Vries**, Richard N 1932- *AmMWSc 92*
**DeVries**, Robert Charles 1922- *AmMWSc 92*
**De Vries**, Robert John 1932- *WhoFI 92, WhoMW 92*
**DeVries**, Robert K. 1932- *WhoRel 92*
**DeVries**, Robert Kenneth 1940- *WhoAmL 92*
**DeVries**, Ronald Clifford 1936- *AmMWSc 92*
**DeVries**, Scott Philip 1954- *WhoAmL 92*
**Devries**, William Castle 1943- *IntWW 91*
**DeVries**, Yuan Lin *AmMWSc 92*
**De Vries-Evans**, Susanna 1935- *IntAu&W 91*
**Devrouax**, Paul S., Jr. 1942- *WhoBlA 92*
**DeVylder**, Emil Raymond 1930- *WhoWest 92*
**Dew**, Alvin Glen 1920- *WhoMW 92*
**Dew**, Hartwell Coleman 1953- *WhoIns 92*
**Dew**, John N 1922- *AmMWSc 92*
**Dew**, Leslie Robert 1914- *Who 92*
**Dew**, Robb Forman *DrAPF 91*
**Dew**, Ronald Beresford 1916- *Who 92*
**Dew**, William Calland 1916- *AmMWSc 92*
**Dew**, William Waldo, Jr. 1935- *WhoRel 92, WhoWest 92*
**de Waal**, Constant Hendrik 1931- *Who 92*
**de Waal**, Hugo Ferdinand 1935- *Who 92*
**De Waal**, Marius Theodorus 1925- *IntWW 91*
**De Waal**, Ronald Burt 1932- *WrDr 92*
**de Waal**, Victor Alexander 1929- *Who 92*
**de Waart**, Edo 1941- *IntWW 91, WhoEnt 92, WhoMW 92*
**DeWaay**, Donald Gene 1916- *WhoAmL 92*
**Dewald**, Gordon Wayne 1943- *AmMWSc 92*
**Dewald**, Horace Albert 1922- *AmMWSc 92*
**Dewald**, Howard Dean 1958- *WhoMW 92*
**Dewald**, Paul A. 1920- *WrDr 92*
**Dewald**, Paul Adolph 1920- *IntAu&W 91*
**Dewald**, Robert Reinhold 1935- *AmMWSc 92*
**Dewald**, William Guenthner 1928- *WhoFI 92*
**De Wall**, Gordon 1941- *AmMWSc 92*
**DeWall**, Karen Marie 1943- *WhoWest 92*
**DeWall**, Richard A 1926- *AmMWSc 92*
**DeWalle**, David Russell 1942- *AmMWSc 92*
**DeWames**, Roger 1931- *AmMWSc 92*
**Dewan**, Edmond M 1931- *AmMWSc 92*
**Dewan**, Shashi B 1941- *AmMWSc 92*
**Dewan**, Sunil Gabriel 1957- *WhoMW 92*
**Dewanjee**, Mrinal K 1941- *AmMWSc 92*
**Dewar** *Who 92*
**Dewar**, David Alexander 1934- *Who 92*
**Dewar**, Donald Campbell 1937- *IntWW 91, Who 92*
**Dewar**, George Duncan Hamilton 1916- *Who 92*
**Dewar**, Graeme Alexander 1951- *AmMWSc 92*
**Dewar**, Ian Stewart 1929- *Who 92*
**Dewar**, James McEwen 1943- *WhoFI 92*
**Dewar**, Michael J. 1918- *WrDr 92*
**Dewar**, Michael James Steuart 1918- *AmMWSc 92, IntWW 91, Who 92*
**Dewar**, Michael James Stewart 1918- *FacFETw*
**Dewar**, Nicholas Alan Richard 1950- *WhoFI 92*
**Dewar**, Norman Ellison 1930- *AmMWSc 92*
**Dewar**, Robert James 1923- *Who 92*
**Dewar**, Robert Leith 1944- *AmMWSc 92*
**Dewar**, Thomas 1909- *Who 92*
**de Wardener**, Hugh Edward 1915- *Who 92*
**Dewart**, Gilbert 1932- *AmMWSc 92, ConAu 135*
**Dewart**, Katherine *DrAPF 91*
**Dewart**, Leslie 1922- *WrDr 92*
**DeWaters**, Clarke 1931- *WhoIns 92*
**Dewazien**, Karl Richard 1945- *WhoWest 92*
**DewBerry**, David 1961- *WhoMW 92*
**Dewberry**, David Albert 1941- *Who 92*
**Dewberry**, Madelina Denise 1958- *WhoBlA 92*
**Dewberry**, Thomas E *WhoAmP 91*
**Dewbre**, J W 1933- *WhoIns 92*
**Dewdney**, Christopher 1951- *ConPo 91, WrDr 92*
**Dewdney**, Duncan Alexander Cox 1911- *Who 92*
**Dewdney**, John Christopher 1928- *IntAu&W 91, WrDr 92*
**Dewe**, Roderick Gorrie 1935- *Who 92*
**Dewe Mathews**, Marina Sarah *Who 92*
**de Weck**, Philippe 1919- *IntWW 91*
**De Weer**, Paul Joseph 1938- *AmMWSc 92*
**De Weerdt**, Mark Murray 1928- *IntWW 91*
**Dewees**, Andre Aaron 1939- *AmMWSc 92*
**DeWeese**, David D 1913- *AmMWSc 92*
**DeWeese**, Fenton Byrd 1949- *WhoAmL 92*
**Deweese**, Gene 1934- *IntAu&W 91, TwCSFW 91, WrDr 92*
**Deweese**, Glen S 1932- *WhoAmP 91*
**Deweese**, H William 1950- *WhoAmP 91*
**DeWeese**, James A 1925- *AmMWSc 92*
**DeWeese**, Jean *WrDr 92*
**Deweese**, John Thomas 1835-1906 *DcNCBi 2*
**Deweese**, Malcolm Leslie, Jr. 1935- *WhoWest 92*
**DeWeese**, Marion Spencer 1915- *AmMWSc 92*
**Dewell**, Michael 1931- *WhoEnt 92, WhoWest 92*
**deWerd**, Bradley John 1958- *WhoMW 92*
**DeWerd**, Larry Albert 1941- *AmMWSc 92, WhoMW 92*
**DeWerth**, Douglas William 1933- *WhoMW 92*
**De Wet**, Carel 1924- *IntWW 91, Who 92*
**De Wette**, Frederik Willem 1924- *AmMWSc 92*
**de Wetter**, Herman Peter 1920- *WhoFI 92*
**Dewey**, A.A. *DrAPF 91*
**Dewey**, Anne Elizabeth Marie 1951- *WhoAmL 92*
**Dewey**, Anthony Hugh 1921- *Who 92*
**Dewey**, Bradley, Jr 1916- *AmMWSc 92*
**Dewey**, C Forbes, Jr 1935- *AmMWSc 92*
**Dewey**, Charles 1798-1880 *DcNCBi 2*
**Dewey**, Chester 1784-1867 *BiInAmS*
**Dewey**, Craig Douglas 1950- *WhoMW 92*
**Dewey**, Dennis James 1938- *WhoAmL 92*
**Dewey**, Desmond David 1931- *WhoMW 92*
**Dewey**, Donald Henry 1918- *AmMWSc 92*
**Dewey**, Donald O 1930- *AmMWSc 92, WrDr 92*
**Dewey**, Donald William 1933- *IntAu&W 91, WhoFI 92*
**Dewey**, Douglas R 1929- *AmMWSc 92*
**Dewey**, Fred McAlpin 1939- *AmMWSc 92*
**Dewey**, George 1837-1917 *RComAH*
**Dewey**, James Edwin 1917- *AmMWSc 92*
**Dewey**, James W 1943- *AmMWSc 92*
**Dewey**, Jennifer Owings 1941- *IntAu&W 91*
**Dewey**, Joel Allen 1956- *WhoAmL 92*
**Dewey**, John 1859-1952 *AmPeW, BenetAL 91, FacFETw [port], RComAH*
**Dewey**, John Edwin 1939- *WhoAmP 91*
**Dewey**, John Frederick 1937- *AmMWSc 92, IntWW 91, Who 92*
**Dewey**, John Marks 1930- *AmMWSc 92*
**Dewey**, Kathryn G 1952- *AmMWSc 92*
**Dewey**, Maynard Merle 1932- *AmMWSc 92*
**Dewey**, Melvil 1851-1931 *BenetAL 91*
**Dewey**, Michael Lawrence 1955- *WhoMW 92*
**Dewey**, Michael Lee 1944- *WhoWest 92*
**Dewey**, Roger William 1928- *WhoWest 92*
**Dewey**, S. Dayton 1944- *WhoRel 92*
**Dewey**, Thomas B 1915- *IntAu&W 91*
**Dewey**, Thomas E 1902-1971 *FacFETw [port]*
**Dewey**, Thomas E. 1941- *WhoMW 92*
**Dewey**, Thomas Edmund 1902-1971 *AmPolLe [port]*
**Dewey**, Thomas Edmund, Jr. 1932- *WhoFI 92*
**Dewey**, Thomas Gregory 1952- *AmMWSc 92*
**Dewey**, Wade G 1927- *AmMWSc 92*
**Dewey**, William 1929- *AmMWSc 92*
**Dewey**, William Leo 1934- *AmMWSc 92*
**Dewhirst**, Glenn Eric 1966- *WhoAmP 91*
**Dewhirst**, Ian 1936- *IntAu&W 91, WrDr 92*
**Dewhirst**, Leonard Wesley 1924- *AmMWSc 92*
**Dewhurst**, Blanca Maria Peres 1944- *WhoWest 92*
**Dewhurst**, Colleen d1991 *LesBEnT 92*
**Dewhurst**, Colleen 1924-1991 *CurBio 91N, NewYTBS 91 [port], News 92-2*
**Dewhurst**, Eileen 1929- *WrDr 92*
**Dewhurst**, Eileen Mary 1929- *IntAu&W 91*
**Dewhurst**, Harold Ainslie 1924- *AmMWSc 92*
**Dewhurst**, Harry *TwCPaSc*
**Dewhurst**, John 1920- *Who 92*
**Dewhurst**, Keith 1931- *IntAu&W 91, WrDr 92*
**Dewhurst**, Peter 1944- *AmMWSc 92*
**Dewhurst**, Timothy Littleton 1920- *Who 92*
**Dewhurst**, William George 1926- *AmMWSc 92, WhoWest 92*
**Dewhurst**, Wynford 1864-1941? *TwCPaSc*
**Dewhurst**, Wynford 1868-1927 *ThHEIm*
**De Wied**, David 1925- *IntWW 91*
**DeWine**, Michael 1947- *WhoAmP 91*
**DeWine**, Paul Robert 1957- *WhoWest 92*
**DeWine**, Richard Michael 1947- *WhoMW 92*
**Dewing**, Charles Benjamin 1942- *WhoRel 92*
**Dewing**, Merlin Eugene 1934- *WhoFI 92*
**Dewing**, Rolland Lloyd 1934- *WhoMW 92*
**de Winne**, Terence Leslie 1940- *WhoEnt 92*
**de Winter**, Carl 1934- *Who 92*
**de Winton**, Michael Geoffrey 1916- *Who 92*
**DeWire**, John William 1916- *AmMWSc 92*
**Dewire**, Norman Edward 1936- *WhoMW 92, WhoRel 92*
**De Wit**, Cornelis T. 1924- *IntWW 91*
**de Wit**, Harriet 1948- *WhoMW 92*
**De Wit**, Michiel 1933- *AmMWSc 92*
**DeWit**, Roland 1930- *AmMWSc 92*
**DeWitt**, Bernard James 1917- *AmMWSc 92*
**DeWitt**, Bryce Seligman 1923- *AmMWSc 92*
**DeWitt**, Charles Benjamin, III 1952- *WhoAmL 92*
**Dewitt**, Charles W 1947- *WhoAmP 91*
**DeWitt**, Charles Wayne, Jr 1921- *AmMWSc 92*
**DeWitt**, David P 1934- *AmMWSc 92*
**DeWitt**, Edward Elbert 1946- *WhoRel 92*
**DeWitt**, Frances Marie de Jong 1939- *WhoAmP 91*
**DeWitt**, Franklin Roosevelt 1936- *WhoAmP 91, WhoBlA 92*
**DeWitt**, Gerry 1952- *WhoWest 92*
**Dewitt**, Harry Morton 1920- *WhoFI 92*
**De Witt**, Hobson Dewey 1923- *AmMWSc 92*
**Dewitt**, Hugh Edgar 1930- *AmMWSc 92*
**De Witt**, Hugh Hamilton 1933- *AmMWSc 92*
**Dewitt**, Jack Richard 1918- *WhoAmL 92*
**De Witt**, Jesse R. 1918- *WhoRel 92*
**Dewitt**, John *DrAPF 91*
**DeWitt**, John 1929- *WhoAmP 91*
**DeWitt**, John Belton 1937- *WhoWest 92*
**De Witt**, John William, Jr 1922- *AmMWSc 92*
**De Witt**, Joyce 1949- *ConTFT 9, IntMPA 92*
**DeWitt**, Larry Dale 1937- *WhoRel 92*
**DeWitt**, Linda Joan 1954- *WhoFI 92*
**DeWitt**, Richard John, Jr. 1947- *WhoAmL 92*
**De Witt**, Robert Merkle 1915- *AmMWSc 92*
**DeWitt**, Rufus B. 1915- *WhoBlA 92*
**DeWitt**, Simeon 1756-1834 *BiInAmS*
**DeWitt**, Walter Allen 1962- *WhoFI 92*
**DeWitt**, William 1939- *AmMWSc 92*
**DeWitt-Morette**, Cecile 1922- *AmMWSc 92*
**DeWitz**, Loren *WhoAmP 91*
**Dewitz**, Robert Douglas 1955- *WhoWest 92*
**Dewlen**, Al 1921- *IntAu&W 91, TwCWW 91, WrDr 92*
**De Wolf**, David Alter 1934- *AmMWSc 92*
**DeWolf**, Gordon Parker, Jr 1927- *AmMWSc 92*
**De Wolf**, Harry George 1903- *Who 92*
**DeWolf**, John T 1943- *AmMWSc 92*
**DeWolfe**, Barbara Blanchard Oakeson 1912- *AmMWSc 92*
**de Wolfe**, Elsie 1865-1950 *DcTwDes, FacFETw*
**DeWolfe**, Fred Stanley 1928- *WhoWest 92*
**deWolfe**, Geoffrey Holden 1946- *WhoAmL 92*
**DeWolfe**, George Fulton 1949- *WhoAmL 92, WhoMW 92*
**DeWolfe**, Gregory S. *WhoAmL 92*
**DeWolfe**, William Arthur 1927- *WhoRel 92*
**DeWolff**, Maurice Konrad 1941- *WhoAmL 92, WhoFI 92*
**de Woody**, Charles 1914- *WhoWest 92*
**Deworme**, Elie 1932- *IntWW 91*
**DeWoskin**, Alan Ellis 1940- *WhoAmL 92, WhoMW 92*
**De Wright**, Yvonne *WhoHisp 92*
**Dews**, Edmund 1921- *AmMWSc 92*
**Dews**, Peter 1929- *Who 92*
**Dews**, Peter Booth 1922- *AmMWSc 92, IntWW 91*
**Dewsbury**, Donald Allen 1939- *AmMWSc 92*
**DeWulf**, Kathryn Colleen 1959- *IntAu&W 91*
**de Wys**, Egbert Christiaan 1924- *WhoWest 92*
**Dewys**, William Dale 1939- *AmMWSc 92*
**Dexheimer**, David Wiley 1945- *WhoMW 92*
**Dexter**, Aaron 1750-1829 *BiInAmS*
**Dexter**, Charles Edward, Jr 1950- *WhoAmP 91*
**Dexter**, Colin 1930- *IntAu&W 91, WrDr 92*
**Dexter**, Dean Joseph 1948- *WhoAmP 91*
**Dexter**, Deborah Mary 1938- *AmMWSc 92*
**Dexter**, Edward L *WhoAmP 91*
**Dexter**, Edward Ralph 1935- *Who 92*
**Dexter**, Harold 1920- *Who 92*
**Dexter**, John *WrDr 92*
**Dexter**, John 1925-1990 *AnObit 1990, FacFETw*
**Dexter**, Joseph Ira 1962- *WhoFI 92*
**Dexter**, Lewis *AmMWSc 92*
**Dexter**, Lewis Anthony 1915- *WrDr 92*
**Dexter**, Martin *TwCWW 91*

Dexter, Pete 1943- IntAu&W 91
Dexter, Ralph Warren 1912- AmMWSc 92
Dexter, Raymond Arthur 1923- WhoWest 92
Dexter, Raymond Kent 1962- WhoFI 92
Dexter, Richard Newman 1933- AmMWSc 92
Dexter, Richard Norman 1927- AmMWSc 92
Dexter, Roland Archie 1922- WhoAmL 92
Dexter, Ross TwCWW 91, WrDr 92
Dexter, Stephen C 1942- AmMWSc 92
Dexter, Theodore Henry 1923- AmMWSc 92
Dexter, Thomas Michael 1945- Who 92
Dexter, Thomas Ray 1938- WhoEnt 92, WhoWest 92
Dexter, Timothy 1747-1806 BenetAL 91
Dexter, William Prescott 1820-1890 BiInAmS
Dextras, Mary Lou 1922- WhoRel 92
Dextraze, Jacques Alfred 1919- Who 92
Dey, Abhijit 1945- AmMWSc 92
Dey, Carol Ruth 1943- WhoFI 92, WhoWest 92
Dey, Frederic Van Rensselaer 1861-1922 ScFEYrs
Dey, Joseph C., Jr. 1907-1991 ConAu 133, NewYTBS 91 [port]
Dey, Richard Morris DrAPF 91
Dey, Robert Lewis 1928- WhoAmP 91
Dey, Sudhansu Kumar 1944- AmMWSc 92
Dey, Susan 1952- IntMPA 92, WhoEnt 92
de Yarburgh-Bateson Who 92
Deye, Armin Ulfert 1913- WhoRel 92
Deye, Donna Hanzlick 1958- WhoFI 92
Deyermond, Alan David 1932- Who 92
D'Eyncourt, Mark Gervais T. Who 92
Deyneka, Aleksandr Aleksandrovich 1889-1969 SovUnBD
Deyneka, Alexander Alexandrovich 1899-1969 FacFETw
Deyneka, Peter, Jr. 1931- WhoRel 92
Deyneka, Peter, Sr. 1898-1987 RelLAm 91
Deynes Soto, Miguel A 1936- WhoAmP 91, WhoHisp 92
Deyo, Richard Alden 1949- AmMWSc 92
Deyoe, Charles W 1933- AmMWSc 92
De Young, Cliff 1947- IntMPA 92
De Young, David Spencer 1940- AmMWSc 92
De Young, Donald Bouwman 1944- AmMWSc 92
DeYoung, Edwin Lawson 1929- AmMWSc 92
DeYoung, Jacob J 1926- AmMWSc 92
Deyrup, James Alden 1936- AmMWSc 92
Deyrup-Olsen, Ingrith Johnson 1919- AmMWSc 92
Deysach, Lawrence George 1936- AmMWSc 92
De Yurre, Victor Henry 1953- WhoHisp 92
Deza, Roberto Jose 1946- WhoHisp 92
Deza, Walter Alejandro 1948- WhoWest 92
De Zafra, Robert Lee 1932- AmMWSc 92
Dezallier d'Argenville, Antoine-Joseph 1680-1765 BlkwCEP
De Zan, Luis Antonio 1943- WhoHisp 92
de Zayas, Hector 1957- WhoHisp 92
De Zeeuw, Carl Henri 1912- AmMWSc 92
DeZeeuw, Glen Warren 1948- WhoAmP 91, WhoWest 92
Dezelsky, Thomas Leroy 1934- AmMWSc 92
Dezenberg, George John 1935- AmMWSc 92
Dezenberg, George John, Jr. 1961- WhoAmL 92
DeZinno, Benjamin Nicholas, Jr 1924- WhoAmP 91
De Zoeten, Gustaaf A 1934- AmMWSc 92
de Zwager, H. WhoRel 92
Dezza, Paolo 1901- IntWW 91, WhoRel 92
Dhabba the Cahina d705 EncAmaz 91
Dhainaut Cremer, Michel Eugene Pierre 1927- WhoFI 92
Dhaka, Archbishop of 1926- Who 92
Dhaliwal, Amrik S 1934- AmMWSc 92
Dhaliwal, Ranjit S 1930- AmMWSc 92
Dhalla, Naranjan Singh 1936- AmMWSc 92
Dhami, Kewal Singh 1933- AmMWSc 92
Dhanabalan, Suppiah 1937- IntWW 91
Dhanak, Amritlal M 1925- AmMWSc 92
Dhanjal, Avtarjeet 1939- TwCPaSc
Dhar, Bansi 1930- IntWW 91
Dhar, Sachidulal 1943- AmMWSc 92
Dharamsi, Amin N 1951- AmMWSc 92
Dharani, Lokeswarappa R 1947- AmMWSc 92
Dharia, Mohan 1925- IntWW 91
Dharmapala, Anagarika 1864-1933 RelLAm 91
Dharmasakti, Sanya 1907- IntWW 91
d'Hauterives, Arnaud Louis Alain 1933- IntWW 91
Dhavamony, Mariasusai 1925- IntAu&W 91, WrDr 92
Dhavan, Shanti Swarup 1905- Who 92
Dhenin, Geoffrey 1918- Who 92
d'Herelle, Felix 1873-1949 FacFETw
Dhesi, Nazar Singh 1923- AmMWSc 92
D'Heurle, Francois Max 1925- AmMWSc 92
Dhillon, Balbir Singh 1947- AmMWSc 92
Dhillon, Gurdial Singh 1915- IntWW 91
Dhillon, Pam S. 1938- WhoMW 92
Dhindsa, Dharam Singh 1934- AmMWSc 92
Dhindsa, K S 1932- AmMWSc 92
Dhir, Surendra Kumar 1937- AmMWSc 92
Dhir, Vijay Kumar 1943- AmMWSc 92
Dhlomo, Oscar Dumisani 1943- IntWW 91
Dho Minde EncAmaz 91
d'Holbach, Paul Henri Thiry BlkwCEP
Dhollande, Laurent R. 1960- WhoWest 92
Dhom, Robert 1919- IntWW 91
D'Hondt, John Patrick 1953- WhoEnt 92
Dhondt, Steven Thomas 1944- WhoFI 92
Dhondy, Farrukh 1944- SmATA 65, WrDr 92
Dhrangadhara, Maharaja Sriraj of Halvad- 1923- Who 92
Dhruv, Harish Ratilal 1946- WhoWest 92
Dhruv, Rohini Arvind 1950- AmMWSc 92
Dhudshia, Vallabh H 1939- AmMWSc 92
D'Hue, Robert R., Jr. 1917- WhoBlA 92
Dhurandhar, Nina 1937- AmMWSc 92
Dhurjati, Prasad S 1956- AmMWSc 92
Dhyse, Frederick George 1918- AmMWSc 92
Dia, Mamadou 1910- IntWW 91
Diabelli, Anton 1781-1858 NewAmDM
Diachun, Stephen 1912- AmMWSc 92
Diaconis, Persi 1945- AmMWSc 92
Diadocus of Photice EncEarC
Diaghilev, Serge Pavlovich 1872-1929 FacFETw [port]
Diaghilev, Sergei Pavlovich 1872-1929 NewAmDM
Diah, Burhanudin Mohamad 1917- IntWW 91
Diah, Herawati 1917- IntWW 91
Diakite, Moussa 1927- IntWW 91
Diakite, Noumou 1943- IntWW 91
Diakiwsky, Nicholas Metro 1963- WhoEnt 92
Diakow, Carol AmMWSc 92
Dial, Adolph WhoAmP 91
Dial, Donna Kay 1940- WhoMW 92, WhoRel 92
Dial, Douglas E. 1965- WhoMW 92
Dial, Eleanore Maxwell 1929- WhoMW 92
Dial, Gerald O WhoAmP 91
Dial, J. Donald, Jr 1943- WhoAmL 92
Dial, Karl Glenn 1960- WhoAmL 92
Dial, Norman Arnold 1926- AmMWSc 92
Dial, Thomas Ferron 1938- WhoAmL 92
Dial, William Allen 1943- WhoEnt 92
Dial, William Richard 1914- AmMWSc 92
Diallo 1947- WhoBlA 92
Diallo, Absa Claude 1942- IntWW 91
Dials, George Edward 1945- WhoMW 92
Diamaduros, Pete Gus 1961- WhoAmL 92
Diaman, N.A. DrAPF 91
Diamand, Peter 1913- IntWW 91, Who 92
Diamandopolus, George Th 1929- AmMWSc 92
Diamandopoulos, Peter 1928- WhoFI 92
Diamant, Aviva F. 1949- WhoAmL 92
Diamant, Lincoln 1923- IntMPA 92, WhoEnt 92, WrDr 92
Diamant, Marilyn Charlotte 1933- WhoAmP 91
Diamant, Michael Harlan 1946- WhoAmL 92, WhoFI 92
Diamante, John Matthew 1940- AmMWSc 92
Diamantis, William 1923- AmMWSc 92
Diament, Barry 1954- WhoEnt 92
Diament, Joseph WhoAmP 91
Diament, Paul 1938- AmMWSc 92
Diamond Who 92
Diamond, Baron 1907- IntWW 91, Who 92
Diamond, Abel J. 1932- IntWW 91
Diamond, Ann Cynthia 1947- WhoAmL 92
Diamond, Anthony Edward John 1929- Who 92
Diamond, Arthur Mansfield, Jr. 1953- WhoFI 92
Diamond, Aubrey Lionel 1923- Who 92
Diamond, Aviva 1953- WhoFI 92, WhoWest 92
Diamond, Bernard 1918- IntMPA 92
Diamond, Bob Reed 1937- WhoEnt 92
Diamond, Bruce I 1945- AmMWSc 92
Diamond, David 1915- ConCom 92, NewAmDM
Diamond, David J 1940- AmMWSc 92
Diamond, David Jeremy 1958- WhoEnt 92
Diamond, David Judah 1929- WhoFI 92
Diamond, David Leo 1915- WhoEnt 92
Diamond, David Louis 1964- WhoFI 92
Diamond, Deborah Beroset 1960- WhoMW 92
Diamond, Derek Robin 1933- Who 92
Diamond, Earl Louis 1928- AmMWSc 92
Diamond, Ellen 1938- ConAu 133
Diamond, Eugene Christopher 1952- WhoMW 92
Diamond, Eugene Francis 1926- WhoMW 92
Diamond, Fred Irwin 1925- AmMWSc 92
Diamond, Freda 1905- DcTwDes
Diamond, G William 1945- WhoAmP 91
Diamond, Graham DrAPF 91
Diamond, Gustave 1928- WhoAmL 92
Diamond, Harley David 1959- WhoAmL 92
Diamond, Harold George 1940- AmMWSc 92
Diamond, Harvey Jerome 1928- WhoAmP 91, WhoFI 92
Diamond, Herbert 1925- AmMWSc 92
Diamond, Howard 1928- AmMWSc 92
Diamond, I A L 1920-1988 FacFETw
Diamond, Ilana Ruth 1959- WhoFI 92
Diamond, Isidore 1920- IntAu&W 91
Diamond, Ivan 1935- AmMWSc 92
Diamond, Jack 1896-1931 FacFETw
Diamond, Jacob J 1917- AmMWSc 92
Diamond, James David 1959- WhoAmL 92
Diamond, Jared Mason 1937- AmMWSc 92, IntWW 91
Diamond, Jay Harrison 1951- WhoAmL 92
Diamond, Jeffrey B 1950- WhoAmP 91
Diamond, Jeffrey Brian 1950- WhoAmL 92
Diamond, John Nathan 1954- WhoAmP 91
Diamond, John R. 1905- WhoBlA 92
Diamond, Josef 1907- WhoAmL 92, WhoWest 92
Diamond, Joseph 1935- WhoAmL 92
Diamond, Joseph Samuel 1933- WhoFI 92
Diamond, Joshua Benamy AmMWSc 92
Diamond, Julius 1925- AmMWSc 92
Diamond, Kimberley Sue 1955- WhoFI 92
Diamond, Leila 1925- AmMWSc 92
Diamond, Linda Barbara 1943- WhoFI 92
Diamond, Louis 1940- AmMWSc 92
Diamond, Louis Klein 1902- AmMWSc 92
Diamond, Louis Stanley 1920- AmMWSc 92
Diamond, M. Jerome 1942- WhoAmL 92, WhoAmP 91
Diamond, Malcolm Luria 1924- WhoRel 92
Diamond, Marc J 1960- WhoIns 92
Diamond, Maria Sophia 1958- WhoWest 92
Diamond, Marian C 1926- AmMWSc 92
Diamond, Matthew Philip 1951- WhoEnt 92
Diamond, Michael 1942- Who 92
Diamond, Michael Alan 1950- WhoMW 92
Diamond, Milton 1934- AmMWSc 92
Diamond, Morris Isaac 1921- WhoEnt 92
Diamond, Neil 1941- IntMPA 92
Diamond, Neil Leslie 1941- WhoEnt 92
Diamond, Paul Steven 1953- WhoAmL 92
Diamond, Philip Ernest 1925- WhoAmL 92
Diamond, Ray Byford 1933- AmMWSc 92
Diamond, Raymond Thaddeus 1952- WhoAmL 92
Diamond, Renee L 1937- WhoAmP 91
Diamond, Richard Edward 1932- WhoFI 92
Diamond, Richard Lee 1931- WhoMW 92
Diamond, Richard Martin 1924- AmMWSc 92
Diamond, Richard S. 1960- WhoAmL 92
Diamond, Robert M 1949- WhoAmP 91
Diamond, Robert Michael 1948- WhoAmL 92
Diamond, Robert Stephen 1939- WhoFI 92
Diamond, Rochelle Anne 1951- WhoWest 92
Diamond, Scott Eric 1960- WhoAmL 92
Diamond, Seymour 1925- AmMWSc 92
Diamond, Shari Seidman 1947- WhoAmL 92, WhoMW 92
Diamond, Sidney 1929- AmMWSc 92
Diamond, Stanley d1991 NewYTBS 91
Diamond, Stanley 1922-1991 ConAu 134
Diamond, Stanley Jay 1927- WhoAmL 92
Diamond, Stephen Earle 1944- WhoWest 92
Diamond, Steven Elliot 1949- AmMWSc 92
Diamond, Steven Jay 1952- WhoFI 92
Diamond, Steven Samuel 1956- WhoAmL 92
Diamond, Susan Zee 1949- WhoFI 92, WhoMW 92
Diamond, Walter H. 1913- WhoFI 92
Diamondstone, Lawrence 1928- WhoFI 92
Diamonstein, Alan Arnold 1931- WhoAmP 91
Diamonstein, Barbaralee D. ConAu 35NR
Diamont, David Hunter 1946- WhoAmP 91
Diana, James Stephen 1951- WhoMW 92
Diana, John N 1930- AmMWSc 92
Diana, Leonard M 1923- AmMWSc 92
Dianalan, Jamil WhoRel 92
Diane, Mamadi 1947- WhoBlA 92
Diani, Marco Fulvio 1954- WhoMW 92
D'Ianni, James Donato 1914- AmMWSc 92
Dianzani, Ferdinando 1932- AmMWSc 92
Diaper, William 1685-1717 RfGEnL 91
Diarra, Amadou Baba 1929- IntWW 91
Dias, Antonio Rainha 1948- WhoWest 92
Dias, Felix 1931- IntWW 91
Dias, Florentino 1923- WhoEnt 92
Dias, Jerry Ray 1940- AmMWSc 92
Diasio, Richard Leonard 1937- WhoFI 92, WhoMW 92
Diasio, Robert Bart 1946- AmMWSc 92
Diassi, Patrick Andrew 1926- AmMWSc 92
Diatta, Joseph 1948- IntWW 91
DiAugustine, Richard Patrick 1942- AmMWSc 92
Diaw, Rosemary K. 1950- WhoBlA 92
Diaz, Abby Morton 1821-1904 HanAmWH, RelLAm 91
Diaz, Adrian Tio 1951- WhoHisp 92
Diaz, Albert 1930- WhoHisp 92
Diaz, Albert 1958- WhoHisp 92
Diaz, Alicia 1956- WhoHisp 92
Diaz, Alvaro E. 1956- WhoHisp 92
Diaz, Antonio R. 1935- WhoHisp 92
Diaz, Arthur Fred 1938- AmMWSc 92, WhoHisp 92
Diaz, Bo 1953-1990 WhoHisp 92N
Diaz, Carlos 1951- WhoHisp 92
Diaz, Carlos Francisco 1950- WhoHisp 92
Diaz, Carlos Manuel 1932- AmMWSc 92
Diaz, Carlos Miguel 1919- WhoHisp 92
Diaz, Christian 1955- WhoHisp 92
Diaz, Clemente 1949- WhoHisp 92
Diaz, Dalia 1946- WhoHisp 92
Diaz, David 1933- WhoHisp 92
Diaz, Edgar 1964- WhoHisp 92
Diaz, Edgardo WhoAmP 91
Diaz, Eduardo 1950- WhoHisp 92
Diaz, Eduardo Ibarzabal 1961- WhoHisp 92
Diaz, Edward John 1942- WhoHisp 92
Diaz, Elizabeth 1958- WhoHisp 92
Diaz, Fernando G 1946- AmMWSc 92, WhoHisp 92
Diaz, Frank Alex 1960- WhoHisp 92
Diaz, Frank E. 1942- WhoHisp 92
Diaz, Gerald Joseph, Jr. 1952- WhoAmL 92
Diaz, Gerardo 1939- WhoHisp 92
Diaz, Guarione M. 1941- WhoHisp 92
Diaz, Gwendolyn 1950- WhoHisp 92
Diaz, H. Joseph WhoHisp 92
Diaz, Hector L WhoAmP 91, WhoHisp 92
Diaz, Henry F. 1948- WhoHisp 92
Diaz, Henry Frank 1948- AmMWSc 92
Diaz, Herminio 1941- WhoHisp 92
Diaz, Hernando WhoHisp 92
Diaz, Ismael 1951- WhoHisp 92
Diaz, Israel 1961- WhoHisp 92
Diaz, James 1927- WhoHisp 92
Diaz, James Conrad, Sr. 1943- WhoHisp 92
Diaz, Jesus Adolfo 1954- WhoHisp 92
Diaz, Jesus Ernesto 1965- WhoHisp 92
Diaz, John 1960- WhoHisp 92
Diaz, Jorge 1944- WhoFI 92
Diaz, Jose A. 1953- WhoHisp 92
Diaz, Jose Angel 1955- WhoHisp 92
Diaz, Jose Luis 1929- IntWW 91
Diaz, Jose R. 1946- WhoHisp 92
Diaz, Jose W. WhoHisp 92
Diaz, Juan Luis 1958- WhoEnt 92
Diaz, Julio Cesar 1948- WhoHisp 92
Diaz, Justino 1940- NewAmDM, WhoEnt 92
Diaz, Kris A. 1955- WhoHisp 92
Diaz, Lawrence Lucian 1957- WhoFI 92
Diaz, Lucy Alice 1950- WhoHisp 92
Diaz, Luis A. WhoHisp 92
Diaz, Luis A 1942- AmMWSc 92
Diaz, Luis Florentino 1946- AmMWSc 92, WhoHisp 92
Diaz, Luis Wilfredo 1961- WhoMW 92
Diaz, Magna M. 1951- WhoHisp 92
Diaz, Manuel G. 1921- WhoHisp 92
Diaz, Maria Cristina 1955- WhoHisp 92
Diaz, Maria V. 1949- WhoHisp 92
Diaz, Mario WhoHisp 92
Diaz, Maximo, Jr. 1944- WhoHisp 92
Diaz, Mercedes 1938- WhoHisp 92
Diaz, Michael A. 1944- WhoHisp 92
Diaz, Michael Anthony 1956- WhoHisp 92
Diaz, Nelson A. 1947- WhoHisp 92
Diaz, Nils J. 1938- WhoHisp 92
Diaz, Nils Juan 1938- AmMWSc 92
Diaz, Octavio 1951- WhoHisp 92
Diaz, Olga WhoHisp 92
Diaz, Oliver E, Jr 1959- WhoAmP 91, WhoHisp 92

Diaz, Pedro 1949- WhoHisp 92
Diaz, Porfirio 1830-1915 FacFETw
Diaz, Rafael, Jr. 1939- WhoHisp 92
Diaz, Ramon V WhoAmP 91
Diaz, Ramon Valero 1918- WhoAmL 92, WhoWest 92
Diaz, Raul J. 1947- WhoHisp 92
Diaz, Raul Zaragoza 1953- WhoHisp 92
Diaz, Raymond Franco 1952- WhoHisp 92
Diaz, Raymond Julio 1945- WhoAmL 92
Diaz, Rene Michel 1961- WhoHisp 92
Diaz, Ricardo 1951- WhoHisp 92
Diaz, Ricardo L. 1956- WhoHisp 92
Diaz, Rita M. 1941- WhoHisp 92
Diaz, Robert 1960- WhoHisp 92
Diaz, Robert James 1946- AmMWSc 92, WhoHisp 92
Diaz, Rolando 1947- IntDcF 2-2
Diaz, Ruben 1943- WhoHisp 92
Diaz, Rudolph A. 1942- WhoHisp 92
Diaz, Steven A. 1948- WhoHisp 92
Diaz, Teo 1955- WhoHisp 92
Diaz, Victor Manuel, Jr. 1960- WhoAmL 92
Diaz, William Adams 1945- WhoHisp 92
Diaz, William Emilio 1957- WhoHisp 92
Diaz-Alemany, Daisy 1948- WhoHisp 92
Diaz-Arrastia, George Ravelo 1959- WhoAmL 92
Diaz-Azcuy, Orlando 1939- WhoFI 92, WhoWest 92
Diaz-Balart, Jose A. 1960- WhoHisp 92
Diaz-Balart, Lincoln 1954- WhoAmP 91, WhoHisp 92
Diaz-Balart, Mario 1961- WhoAmP 91, WhoHisp 92
Diaz Barcelona, Isaac Alfredo 1949- WhoEnt 92, WhoWest 92
Diaz-Blanco, Eduardo J. 1944- WhoHisp 92
Diaz-Bonilla, Eugenio Angel 1948- WhoFI 92
Diaz Bosch, Mario 1944- WhoHisp 92
Diaz-Cruz, Jorge Hatuey 1914- WhoHisp 92
Diaz Cruz, Luis Ramon 1951- WhoHisp 92
Diaz de Aldrey, Ivan 1925- WhoHisp 92
Diaz de Armendariz, Lope 1575?-1640 HisDSpE
Diaz de Armendariz, Miguel d1550 HisDSpE
Diaz de Espada y Landa, Juan Jose 1756-1832 HisDSpE
Diaz de la Pena, Narcisse Virgile 1807-1876 ThHElm
Diaz Del Castillo, Bernal 1492-1580? HisDSpE
Diaz del Castillo, Bernal 1496?-1584 BenetAL 91
Diaz de Pineda, Gonzalo d1544 HisDSpE
Diaz de Solis, Juan HisDSpE
Diaz-Duque, Ozzie Francis 1955- WhoHisp 92
Diaz-Duran, Fernando Andrade 1937- IntWW 91
Diaz-Gilbert, Miriam M. 1959- WhoHisp 92
Diaz Gomez, Ramon WhoAmP 91
Diaz Gomez, Ramon L. WhoHisp 92
Diaz-Hernandez, Jaime Miguel 1950- WhoHisp 92
Diaz-Herrera, Jorge Luis 1950- WhoHisp 92
Diaz-Jimeno, Felipe WhoHisp 92
Diaz Lane, Enriqueta WhoHisp 92
Diaz-Munoz Cerdan, Carlos Ricardo 1964- WhoEnt 92
Diaz-Oliver, Remedios 1938- WhoHisp 92
Diaz-Peterson, Rosendo 1935- WhoHisp 92
Diaz-Rousselot, Guillermo WhoHisp 92
Diaz Tirado, Miguel WhoAmP 91, WhoHisp 92
Diaz Uribe, Eduardo 1953- IntWW 91
Diaz Valcarcel, Emilio 1929- ConAu 135
Diaz Vargas, Alejandro WhoHisp 92
Diaz Vela, Luis Humberto 1953- WhoWest 92
Diaz-Velez, Felix 1942- WhoHisp 92
Diaz-Verson, Salvador, Jr. 1951- WhoFI 92, WhoHisp 92
Diaz y Perez, Elias 1933- WhoHisp 92
Diaz-Zubieta, Agustin 1936- WhoWest 92
Diba, Farah IntWW 91
DiBacco-Tusinac, Sandra Jeanette 1952- WhoMW 92
Di Bartolo, Baldassare 1926- AmMWSc 92
DiBattiste, Carol 1951- WhoAmL 92
Dibb, David Walter 1943- AmMWSc 92
Dibben, Martyn James 1943- AmMWSc 92
Dibben, Michael Alan Charles 1943- Who 92
Dibble, Cornelia TwCPaSc
Dibble, Daniel Maynard 1932- WhoAmL 92
Dibble, Francis Daniel, Jr. 1947- WhoAmL 92
Dibble, Gordon Lynch 1928- WhoFI 92
Dibble, J. Birney 1925- WrDr 92
Dibble, John Thomas 1950- AmMWSc 92
Dibble, Marjorie Veit 1928- AmMWSc 92
Dibble, Russell Kurt 1945- WhoRel 92
Dibble, William E 1930- AmMWSc 92
Dibdin, Charles 1745-1814 NewAmDM, RfGEnL 91
Dibdin, Michael 1947- IntAu&W 91
Dibela, Kingsford 1932- IntWW 91, Who 92
Dibeler, Vernon Hamilton 1918- AmMWSc 92
Di Belgiojoso, Lodovico Barbiano 1909- IntWW 91
Dibelius, Martin 1883-1947 FacFETw
Dibelius, Otto 1880-1967 DcEcMov, EncTR 91 [port]
DiBella, Eugene Peter 1928- AmMWSc 92
DiBella, William A 1944- WhoAmP 91
DiBenedetto, Anthony T 1933- AmMWSc 92
di Benedetto, Eric Frank Joseph 1965- WhoFI 92
Di Benedetto, Tony 1944- WhoEnt 92
DiBeneditto, Barbara Jean 1959- WhoEnt 92
Dibennardo, Robert 1941- AmMWSc 92
Di Berardino, Angelo 1936- ConAu 135
DiBerardino, Marie A 1926- AmMWSc 92
DiBiaggio, John 1932- WhoMW 92
Dibiaggio, John A. 1932- IntWW 91
Di Bianca-Haver, Loretta 1964- WhoEnt 92
DiBiase, Michael 1957- WhoAmL 92
Di Biase, Stephen Augustine 1952- AmMWSc 92
DiBlasi, John Peter 1955- WhoAmL 92
Di Blasi, Robert Joseph 1939- WhoWest 92
Dible, William Trotter, Jr 1925- AmMWSc 92
Dibner, Mark Douglas 1951- AmMWSc 92
Dibner, Martin DrAPF 91
Diboll, Alfred 1930- AmMWSc 92
DiBona, Charles Joseph 1932- WhoFI 92
Di Bona, Gerald F AmMWSc 92
DiBona, Peter James 1941- AmMWSc 92
Dibrienza, Stephen 1954- WhoAmP 91
diBuono, Anthony Joseph 1930- WhoFI 92
DiCamillo, Gary Thomas 1950- WhoFI 92
DiCara, Lawrence S 1949- WhoAmP 91
DiCarlo, Dominick L. 1928- WhoAmL 92, WhoAmP 91
DiCarlo, Ernest Nicholas 1936- AmMWSc 92
Di Carlo, Frederick Joseph 1918- AmMWSc 92
DiCarlo, James Anthony 1938- AmMWSc 92
DiCarlo, Mario 1922- WhoEnt 92
Dicciani, Nancy Kay 1947- AmMWSc 92
Dice, Brian Charles 1936- Who 92
Dice, Bruce Burton 1926- WhoFI 92
Dice, J Fred 1947- AmMWSc 92
Dice, John Raymond 1921- AmMWSc 92
Dice, Stanley Frost 1921- AmMWSc 92
Dicello, John Francis, Jr 1938- AmMWSc 92
Di Cenzo, Colin D 1923- AmMWSc 92
diCenzo, Colin Domenic 1923- IntWW 91
Di Certo, J J 1933- IntAu&W 91, WrDr 92
Di Cesare, Mario A 1928- IntAu&W 91, WrDr 92
Di Chiera, David 1937- WhoEnt 92, WhoWest 92
DiChiro, Michael, Jr. 1961- WhoAmL 92
Dichter, Barry Joel 1950- WhoAmL 92, WhoFI 92
Dichter, Ernest d1991 NewYTBS 91 [port]
Dichter, Ernest 1907- IntAu&W 91, IntWW 91, WrDr 92
Dichter, Mark S. 1943- WhoAmL 92
Dichter, Michael 1912- AmMWSc 92
Dichter, Misha 1945- IntWW 91, NewAmDM
Dichtl, Rudolph John 1939- AmMWSc 92
DiCiccio, Salvatore Anthony 1958- WhoWest 92
DiCicco, Mario Michael 1933- WhoRel 92
DiCicco, Nicholas Joseph, Jr. 1932- WhoMW 92
Di Cicco, Pier Giorgio 1949- ConPo 91, WrDr 92
DiCioccio, Richard A 1946- AmMWSc 92
Dick, Alan TwCPaSc
Dick, Alan David 1924- Who 92
Dick, Barclay L. 1948- WhoWest 92
Dick, Bernard 1935- WrDr 92
Dick, Bernard F 1935- IntAu&W 91
Dick, Bertram Gale 1926- AmMWSc 92
Dick, Brian Donald 1957- WhoFI 92
Dick, Charles Edward 1937- AmMWSc 92
Dick, Charles T. 1947- WhoMW 92
Dick, Curtis WhoEnt 92
Dick, David Leonard 1955- WhoAmL 92
Dick, Donald Edward 1942- AmMWSc 92
Dick, Edison Warner 1937- WhoAmL 92
Dick, Elliot C 1926- AmMWSc 92
Dick, Gavin Colquhoun 1928- Who 92
Dick, George 1914- Who 92
Dick, George Albert 1940- WhoBIA 92
Dick, George Conrad 1955- WhoFI 92
Dick, George Francis 1881-1967 FacFETw
Dick, George W 1931- AmMWSc 92
Dick, Gladys Rowena Henry 1881-1963 FacFETw
Dick, Henry Henry 1922- WhoRel 92
Dick, Henry Jonathan Biddle 1946- AmMWSc 92
Dick, Henry Marvin 1931- AmMWSc 92
Dick, James Brownlee 1919- Who 92
Dick, James Gardiner 1920- AmMWSc 92
Dick, Jerry Joel 1942- AmMWSc 92
Dick, John 1920- Who 92
Dick, John Kenneth 1913- IntWW 91, Who 92
Dick, Kay 1915- IntAu&W 91, Who 92, WrDr 92
Dick, Kenneth Anderson 1937- AmMWSc 92
Dick, Kevin Scott 1963- WhoMW 92
Dick, Macdonald, II 1941- AmMWSc 92
Dick, Nancy E 1930- WhoAmP 91, WhoWest 92
Dick, Nigel Andrew Robertson 1953- WhoEnt 92
Dick, Patricia A. 1929- WhoMW 92
Dick, Paul Wyatt 1940- IntWW 91, WhoFI 92
Dick, Philip K. 1928-1982 BenetAL 91, FacFETw, TwCSFW 91
Dick, Richard Dean 1930- AmMWSc 92
Dick, Richard Irwin 1935- AmMWSc 92
Dick, Robert B. 1942- WhoMW 92
Dick, Robert C. 1938- WrDr 92
Dick, Robert Paine 1823-1898 DcNCBi 2
Dick, Roger Mylius d1991 Who 92N
Dick, Ronald 1931- Who 92
Dick, Ronald Stewart 1934- AmMWSc 92
Dick, Sheryl Lynn 1954- WhoAmL 92
Dick, Stacy S. 1956- WhoFI 92
Dick, Stanley 1936- AmMWSc 92
Dick, William Edwin, Jr 1936- AmMWSc 92
Dick, William Reid 1879-1961 TwCPaSc
Dick-Lauder, Piers Robert Who 92
Dickamore, Henry James 1933- WhoAmP 91
Dickas, Albert Binkley 1933- AmMWSc 92
Dickason, Elvis Arnie 1919- AmMWSc 92
Dickason, Glen E 1953- WhoAmP 91
Dickberry, F. ScFEYrs
Dicke, Ferdinand Frederick 1899- AmMWSc 92
Dicke, Patricia Ann 1954- WhoAmL 92
Dicke, Robert H. 1916- IntWW 91, WrDr 92
Dicke, Robert Henry 1916- AmMWSc 92
Dickel, Friedrich 1913- IntWW 91
Dickel, Helene Ramseyer 1938- AmMWSc 92
Dicken, Craig Lee 1950- WhoEnt 92
Dicken, Michael John Charles Worwood 1935- Who 92
Dickens, Arthur Geoffrey 1910- IntAu&W 91, IntWW 91, Who 92, WrDr 92
Dickens, Brian 1937- AmMWSc 92
Dickens, Charles 1812-1870 CnDBLB 4 [port], RfGEnL 91
Dickens, Charles Henderson 1934- AmMWSc 92
Dickens, Deborah E. 1951- WhoRel 92
Dickens, Doris Lee WhoBIA 92
Dickens, Edwin Larry 1938- WhoAmP 91
Dickens, Elmer Douglas, Jr 1942- AmMWSc 92, WhoMW 92
Dickens, Geoffrey Kenneth 1931- Who 92
Dickens, George Mecom 1947- WhoRel 92
Dickens, Helen Octavia WhoBIA 92
Dickens, Jacoby 1931- WhoBIA 92
Dickens, James McCulloch York 1931- Who 92
Dickens, Justin Kirk 1931- AmMWSc 92
Dickens, Lawrence Edward 1932- AmMWSc 92
Dickens, Little Jimmy 1920- ConMus 7 [port], NewAmDM
Dickens, Monica 1915- ConNov 91, IntAu&W 91, WrDr 92
Dickens, Monica Enid 1915- IntWW 91, Who 92
Dickens, Samuel 1926- WhoBIA 92
Dickens, William Theodore 1953- WhoWest 92
Dickenson, Aubrey Fiennes T. Who 92
Dickenson, Charles Royal 1907- Who 92
Dickenson, Daniel David 1932- WhoRel 92
Dickenson, Donald Dwight 1925- AmMWSc 92
Dickenson, George-Therese DrAPF 91
Dickenson, Joseph Frank 1924- Who 92
Dickenson, Vic 1906-1984 NewAmDM
Dicker, Daniel 1929- AmMWSc 92
Dicker, Herbert 1921- WhoAmL 92
Dicker, Kate 1953- TwCPaSc
Dicker, Marvin 1933- WhoAmL 92
Dicker, Paul Edward 1925- AmMWSc 92
Dickerhoof, Dean W 1935- AmMWSc 92
Dickerman, Allen Briggs 1914- WhoFI 92
Dickerman, Charles Edward 1932- AmMWSc 92
Dickerman, David Leslie 1943- WhoRel 92
Dickerman, Herbert W 1928- AmMWSc 92
Dickerman, Richard Curtis 1934- AmMWSc 92
Dickerson, Adolphus Sumner 1914- WhoBIA 92
Dickerson, Allen Bruce 1938- WhoMW 92
Dickerson, Arthur Neal 1930- WhoIns 92
Dickerson, Bette Jeanne 1951- WhoBIA 92
Dickerson, Charlesworth Lee 1927- AmMWSc 92, WhoMW 92
Dickerson, Chester T, Jr 1939- AmMWSc 92
Dickerson, Claire Moore 1950- WhoAmL 92
Dickerson, Cynthia Rowe 1956- WhoWest 92
Dickerson, Danny Ross 1954- WhoEnt 92
Dickerson, Dennis Clark 1949- WhoBIA 92
Dickerson, Donald Robert 1925- AmMWSc 92
Dickerson, Ellis L., Jr. 1934- WhoBIA 92
Dickerson, Eric Demetric 1960- WhoBIA 92
Dickerson, Ernest NewYTBS 91
Dickerson, Ernest 1952- IntMPA 92
Dickerson, Frederick Reed 1909-1991 WhoAmL 92
Dickerson, George 1933- WhoEnt 92
Dickerson, Glenda J. 1945- WhoBIA 92
Dickerson, Gordon Edwin 1912- AmMWSc 92
Dickerson, Jaffe Dean 1950- WhoAmL 92
Dickerson, James McComas 1944- WhoFI 92
Dickerson, James Perry 1939- AmMWSc 92
Dickerson, Janet 1944- WhoBIA 92
Dickerson, L L, Jr 1918- AmMWSc 92
Dickerson, Lawrence Loton, Jr 1956- WhoAmP 91
Dickerson, Lowell Dwight 1944- WhoBIA 92
Dickerson, Matthew Ennis 1961- WhoFI 92
Dickerson, Nancy LesBEnT 92
Dickerson, Nancy Whitehead WhoEnt 92
Dickerson, Ottie J 1933- AmMWSc 92
Dickerson, Pamela Ann 1953- WhoBIA 92
Dickerson, R F 1922- AmMWSc 92
Dickerson, Richard Earl 1931- AmMWSc 92
Dickerson, Robert Clinton, II 1946- WhoAmL 92
Dickerson, Stephen L 1940- AmMWSc 92
Dickerson, Steven Lynn 1962- WhoAmL 92
Dickerson, Thomas L., Jr. 1949- WhoBIA 92
Dickerson, Thomas Pasquali 1950- WhoFI 92
Dickerson, Warner Lee 1937- WhoBIA 92
Dickerson, Willard Addison 1942- AmMWSc 92
Dickerson, William H 1925- AmMWSc 92
Dickerson, William Roy 1928- WhoWest 92
Dickert, Herman A 1903- AmMWSc 92
Dickeson, Montroville Wilson 1810-1882 BiInAmS
Dickey, Angela Renee 1957- IntAu&W 91
Dickey, Bette Ellyn 1936- WhoFI 92, WhoWest 92
Dickey, Christopher WrDr 92
Dickey, Curtis Raymond 1956- WhoBIA 92
Dickey, David Herschel 1951- WhoAmL 92
Dickey, David Jerry 1939- WhoAmP 91
Dickey, David S 1946- AmMWSc 92
Dickey, Donald Floyd 1927- WhoAmP 91
Dickey, E T 1896- AmMWSc 92
Dickey, Erma Cook 1929- WhoBIA 92
Dickey, Frank R, Jr 1918- AmMWSc 92
Dickey, Frederick Pius 1916- AmMWSc 92
Dickey, Gary Alan 1946- WhoRel 92, WhoWest 92
Dickey, George Grady 1933- WhoWest 92
Dickey, Howard Chester 1913- AmMWSc 92
Dickey, James DrAPF 91
Dickey, James 1923- BenetAL 91, ConPo 91, FacFETw, IntWW 91, WrDr 92
Dickey, James Lafayette, III 1923- IntAu&W 91
Dickey, John Christian 1957- WhoAmL 92
Dickey, John Sloan 1907-1991 CurBio 91N, NewYTBS 91
Dickey, John Sloan, Jr 1941- AmMWSc 92

Dickey, Joseph Freeman 1934- AmMWSc 92
Dickey, Joseph W 1939- AmMWSc 92
Dickey, Julia Edwards 1940- WhoMW 92
Dickey, Lloyd V. WhoBlA 92
Dickey, Louise Parke 1942- WhoEnt 92
Dickey, Lynn 1949- WhoAmP 91
Dickey, Parke Atherton 1909- AmMWSc 92
Dickey, R.P. DrAPF 91
Dickey, Richard Palmer 1935- AmMWSc 92
Dickey, Robert Marvin 1950- WhoWest 92
Dickey, Robert Shaft 1921- AmMWSc 92
Dickey, Ronald Wayne 1938- AmMWSc 92
Dickey, Samuel Stephens 1921- WhoAmL 92
Dickey, Steven Ryan 1947- WhoAmL 92
Dickey, Thomas Atherton d1991 NewYTBS 91
Dickey, Wilhelmina Kuehn 1937- WhoAmP 91
Dickey, William DrAPF 91
Dickey, William 1928- ConPo 91, IntAu&W 91, WhoWest 92, WrDr 92
Dickey, William K, Jr 1920- WhoAmP 91
Dickhoff, Walton William 1947- AmMWSc 92
Dickhoner, William Harold 1921- WhoFI 92
Dickie, Arthur William 1927- WhoRel 92
Dickie, Brian 1941- WhoEnt 92
Dickie, Brian James 1941- Who 92
Dickie, Edgar Primrose d1991 Who 92N
Dickie, Helen Aird 1913- AmMWSc 92
Dickie, John Peter 1934- AmMWSc 92
Dickie, Lawrence F. WhoAmL 92
Dickie, Lloyd M. 1926- IntWW 91
Dickie, Lloyd Merlin 1926- AmMWSc 92
Dickie, Ray Alexander 1940- AmMWSc 92
Dickieson, Alton C 1905- AmMWSc 92
Dickins, Asbury 1780-1861 DcNCBi 2
Dickins, Basil Gordon 1908- Who 92
Dickins, John 1747-1798 DcNCBi 2
Dickins, Lynne 1948- TwCPaSc
Dickins, Mark Frederick Hakon S. Who 92
Dickins, Samuel 1775?-1840 DcNCBi 2
Dickinson Who 92
Dickinson, Baron 1926- Who 92
Dickinson, Alan Charles 1940- AmMWSc 92
Dickinson, Angie 1931- IntMPA 92, WhoEnt 92
Dickinson, Anne Who 92
Dickinson, Basil Philip Harriman 1916- Who 92
Dickinson, Ben Who 92
Dickinson, Bradley William 1948- AmMWSc 92
Dickinson, Brian Henry Baron 1940- Who 92
Dickinson, Charles Cameron, III 1936- WhoRel 92
Dickinson, Christopher John 1927- IntWW 91, Who 92
Dickinson, Dale Flint 1933- AmMWSc 92
Dickinson, David 1920- AmMWSc 92
Dickinson, David Budd 1936- AmMWSc 92
Dickinson, Dean Richard 1928- AmMWSc 92
Dickinson, Donald Charles 1927- WhoWest 92
Dickinson, Douglas Kent 1949- WhoMW 92
Dickinson, Edwin Dewitt 1887-1961 AmPeW
Dickinson, Edwin John 1933- AmMWSc 92
Dickinson, Emily 1830-1886 BenetAL 91, HanAmWH, ModAWWr, RComAH
Dickinson, Fairleigh Stanton, Jr. 1919- WhoFI 92
Dickinson, Frank N 1930- AmMWSc 92
Dickinson, Gloria Harper 1947- WhoBlA 92
Dickinson, Harold 1917- Who 92
Dickinson, Harry Thomas 1939- IntAu&W 91, Who 92, WrDr 92
Dickinson, Helen Rose 1945- AmMWSc 92
Dickinson, Howard C, Jr 1936- WhoAmP 91
Dickinson, Hugh Geoffrey 1929- Who 92
Dickinson, Hugh Gordon 1944- Who 92
Dickinson, Hyett Willoughby 1859-1943 BiDBrF 2
Dickinson, James Gordon 1940- WhoFI 92
Dickinson, James M 1923- AmMWSc 92
Dickinson, Janet Mae Webster 1929- WhoWest 92
Dickinson, Jerold Thomas 1941- WhoWest 92
Dickinson, JoAnne Walton 1936- WhoFI 92
Dickinson, John 1732-1808 AmPolLe, BenetAL 91, BlkwEAR [port]
Dickinson, John Hubert Who 92
Dickinson, John Lawrence 1913- Who 92
Dickinson, John Otis 1924- AmMWSc 92
Dickinson, Jonathan BenetAL 91
Dickinson, Joshua Clifton, Jr 1916- AmMWSc 92
Dickinson, Lee George 1935- WhoWest 92
Dickinson, Leonard Charles 1941- AmMWSc 92
Dickinson, Loren Eric 1943- WhoAmP 91
Dickinson, Margaret WrDr 92
Dickinson, Martin Brownlow, Jr. 1938- WhoAmL 92
Dickinson, Maryanna WhoRel 92
Dickinson, Matthew 1780-1809 DcNCBi 2
Dickinson, Monty William 1938- WhoMW 92
Dickinson, Patric 1914- ConPo 91, IntAu&W 91, WrDr 92
Dickinson, Patric Laurence 1950- Who 92
Dickinson, Patric Thomas 1914- Who 92
Dickinson, Paul R. WhoHisp 92
Dickinson, Peter 1927- TwCSFW 91, WrDr 92
Dickinson, Peter 1934- ConCom 92, Who 92
Dickinson, Peter Charles 1939- AmMWSc 92
Dickinson, Peter Malcolm 1927- IntAu&W 91
Dickinson, Peter Malcolm de Brissac 1927- Who 92
Dickinson, Platt Ketcham 1794-1867 DcNCBi 2
Dickinson, Richard Donald Nye 1929- WhoRel 92
Dickinson, Richard Henry 1944- WhoFI 92
Dickinson, Richard Herbert 1938- WhoFI 92
Dickinson, Richard Raymond 1931- WhoFI 92
Dickinson, Rick 1953- WhoAmP 91
Dickinson, Rita Harkins 1949- WhoWest 92
Dickinson, Robert Earl 1940- AmMWSc 92, WhoWest 92
Dickinson, Samuel Benson 1912- Who 92
Dickinson, Spencer 1943- WhoAmP 91
Dickinson, Stanley Key, Jr 1931- AmMWSc 92
Dickinson, Steven John 1954- WhoAmL 92
Dickinson, Temple 1956- WhoAmL 92
Dickinson, Thorold 1903-1984 IntDcF 2-2 [port]
Dickinson, Timothy 1941- TwCPaSc
Dickinson, Victoria Ann 1951- WhoFI 92, WhoWest 92
Dickinson, Vivian Earl 1924- WhoAmP 91
Dickinson, Vivienne Anne 1931- Who 92
Dickinson, Wade 1926- AmMWSc 92
Dickinson, William Borden 1926- AmMWSc 92
Dickinson, William Clarence 1922- AmMWSc 92
Dickinson, William Joseph 1940- AmMWSc 92
Dickinson, William L. 1925- AlmAP 92 [port]
Dickinson, William Louis 1925- WhoAmP 91
Dickinson, William Michael 1930- Who 92
Dickinson, William Richard 1931- AmMWSc 92, WhoWest 92
Dickinson, William Trevor 1939- AmMWSc 92
Dickinson, Winifred Ball 1933- WhoMW 92
Dickinson-Brown, Roger DrAPF 91
Dickison, Harry Leo 1912- AmMWSc 92
Dickison, William Campbell 1941- AmMWSc 92
Dickler, Howard B 1942- AmMWSc 92
Dicklich, Ronald Robert 1951- WhoAmP 91
Dickman, Albert 1903- AmMWSc 92
Dickman, Francois M 1924- WhoAmP 91
Dickman, John Theodore 1927- AmMWSc 92
Dickman, Michael David 1940- AmMWSc 92
Dickman, Murray G 1947- WhoAmP 91
Dickman, Raymond F, Jr 1937- AmMWSc 92
Dickman, Robert Laurence 1947- AmMWSc 92
Dickman, Robert Moyer 1927- WhoWest 92
Dickman, Sherman Russell 1915- AmMWSc 92
Dickman, Steven Richard 1950- AmMWSc 92
Dickow, James Fred 1943- WhoMW 92
Dicks, Jack William 1949- WhoAmL 92
Dicks, John 1818-1881 DcLB 106
Dicks, John Barber, Jr 1926- AmMWSc 92
Dicks, John Gaudry, III 1951- WhoAmP 91
Dicks, Joseph Gary 1958- WhoAmL 92
Dicks, Marilyn June 1947- WhoFI 92
Dicks, Norm 1940- AlmAP 92 [port]
Dicks, Norman De Valois 1940- WhoWest 92
Dicks, Norman DeValois 1940- WhoAmP 91
Dicks, Randall James 1950- WhoFI 92
Dicks, Terence Patrick 1937- Who 92
Dicks, Zacharias 1728?-1809? DcNCBi 2
Dicksee, Frank 1853-1928 TwCPaSc
Dickson, Alex Dockery 1926- WhoRel 92
Dickson, Alexander Graeme 1914- Who 92
Dickson, Arthur Donald 1927- AmMWSc 92
Dickson, Arthur Richard Franklin 1913- Who 92
Dickson, Brent E. WhoMW 92
Dickson, Brent E 1941- WhoAmP 91
Dickson, Brian 1916- Who 92
Dickson, David John Scott 1947- Who 92
Dickson, David Ross 1931- AmMWSc 92
Dickson, David W. D. 1919- WhoBlA 92
Dickson, Don Robert 1925- AmMWSc 92
Dickson, Donald Harold Wauchope 1924- IntAu&W 91
Dickson, Donald Ward 1938- AmMWSc 92
Dickson, Douglas Grassel 1924- AmMWSc 92
Dickson, Douglas Howard 1942- AmMWSc 92
Dickson, Eileen Wadham Who 92
Dickson, Ella Irene 1914- WhoAmP 91
Dickson, Elsie 1923- WhoMW 92
Dickson, Frank Wilson 1922- AmMWSc 92
Dickson, Frederic Howard 1946- WhoFI 92
Dickson, George 1931- Who 92
Dickson, Gordon 1923- IntAu&W 91, WrDr 92
Dickson, Gordon R. 1923- TwCSFW 91
Dickson, Gordon Ross 1932- Who 92
Dickson, James Edward 1953- WhoFI 92
Dickson, James Francis, III 1924- AmMWSc 92
Dickson, James Gary 1943- AmMWSc 92
Dickson, James Henderson 1806-1862 DcNCBi 2
Dickson, James Lothar 1949- WhoEnt 92
Dickson, Jennifer 1936- IntWW 91, TwCPaSc, Who 92
Dickson, John DrAPF 91
Dickson, John Abernethy 1915- Who 92
Dickson, John Augustus 1795-1847 DcNCBi 2
Dickson, John B. 1909- WhoRel 92
Dickson, John H 1935- WhoAmP 91
Dickson, John R. 1930- WhoMW 92
Dickson, Joseph 1745-1825 DcNCBi 2
Dickson, Joseph Lenwood 1947- WhoFI 92
Dickson, K. A. ConAu 134
Dickson, Katharine Hayland 1904- WhoEnt 92
Dickson, Kenneth Lynn 1943- AmMWSc 92
Dickson, Kwesi A. 1929- ConAu 134
Dickson, Lance E. 1939- WhoAmL 92
Dickson, Lawrence John 1947- AmMWSc 92
Dickson, Lawrence William 1956- AmMWSc 92
Dickson, Leonard Elliot 1915- Who 92
Dickson, LeRoy David 1934- AmMWSc 92
Dickson, Lovat 1902- IntAu&W 91
Dickson, Markham Allen 1922- WhoFI 92
Dickson, Mary Ann Awerkamp 1960- WhoMW 92
Dickson, Michael Hugh 1932- AmMWSc 92
Dickson, Mora Agnes 1918- IntAu&W 91, WrDr 92
Dickson, Murray Graeme 1911- Who 92
Dickson, Naida 1916- IntAu&W 91
Dickson, Nancy Starr 1936- WhoMW 92
Dickson, Onias D., Jr. 1958- WhoBlA 92
Dickson, Patricia Stoup 1939- WhoMW 92
Dickson, Paul 1939- WrDr 92
Dickson, Peter George Muir 1929- IntWW 91, Who 92
Dickson, Ray Clark DrAPF 91
Dickson, Reginald D. 1946- WhoBlA 92
Dickson, Richard Eugene 1932- AmMWSc 92
Dickson, Richard Scott 1957- WhoRel 92
Dickson, Robert Andrew 1943- Who 92
Dickson, Robert Brent AmMWSc 92
Dickson, Robert Carl 1943- AmMWSc 92
Dickson, Robert Frank 1933- WhoMW 92
Dickson, Robert George Brian Who 92
Dickson, Robert George Brian 1916- IntWW 91
Dickson, Robert Hamish 1945- Who 92
Dickson, Robert K, Jr 1942- WhoIns 92
Dickson, Robert Lee 1932- WhoAmL 92, WhoWest 92
Dickson, Robin Ann 1946- WhoWest 92
Dickson, Rodney 1956- TwCPaSc
Dickson, Samuel Henry 1798-1872 BiInAmS
Dickson, Spencer E 1938- AmMWSc 92
Dickson, Stanley 1927- AmMWSc 92
Dickson, Stanley Wayne 1934- WhoFI 92
Dickson, Temple 1934- WhoAmP 91
Dickson, Thomas William 1960- WhoAmL 92
Dickson, Violet Penelope d1991 Who 92N
Dickson, W W WhoAmP 91
Dickson, William 1739-1820 DcNCBi 2
Dickson, William Harold, Jr. 1937- WhoRel 92
Dickson, William Morris 1924- AmMWSc 92
Dickson Mabon, Jesse Who 92
Dickstein, Jack 1925- AmMWSc 92
Dickstein, Michael Ethan 1959- WhoAmL 92
Dickstein, Sidney 1925- WhoAmL 92
DiClerico, Joseph Anthony, Jr. 1941- WhoAmL 92
Di Conza, Peter James, Jr. 1948- WhoAmL 92
DiCorleto, Paul Eugene 1951- AmMWSc 92
Di Costanzo, Frank Philip 1953- WhoFI 92
Di Credico, Mary Winifred 1942- WhoFI 92
Dicterow, Glenn Eugene 1948- WhoEnt 92
Dicterow, Harold J. 1919- WhoWest 92
Di Cuollo, C John 1935- AmMWSc 92
Dicus, Aubrey Omar, Jr. 1948- WhoAmL 92
Dicus, Brian George 1961- WhoAmL 92
Dicus, Duane A 1938- AmMWSc 92
Dicus, Stephen Howard 1948- WhoAmL 92
Di Cyan, Erwin 1918- WrDr 92
Didbin, Michael 1947- WrDr 92
Didchenko, Rostislav 1921- AmMWSc 92
Diddle, Albert W 1909- AmMWSc 92
Diddley, Bo 1928- NewAmDM, WhoBlA 92
Diderot, Denis 1713-1784 BlkwCEP
Di Diego, Caroline 1945- WhoEnt 92
Didik, Frank WhoEnt 92
DiDio, Liberato John Alphonse 1920- AmMWSc 92, WhoMW 92
Didion, James J. WhoWest 92
Didion, Joan DrAPF 91, SourALJ
Didion, Joan 1934- BenetAL 91, ConNov 91, FacFETw, IntWW 91, ModAWWr, TwCWW 91, WrDr 92
Didion, Maureen Anne 1938- WhoAmP 91
Didion, Warren F 1932- WhoIns 92
Didisheim, Paul 1927- AmMWSc 92
Didlick, Wells S. 1925- WhoBlA 92
Dido EncAmaz 91
Di Domenica, Robert Anthony 1927- WhoEnt 92
DiDomenico, Mauro, Jr 1937- AmMWSc 92
DiDonato, Greg L 1961- WhoAmP 91
Di Donato, Pietro DcAmImH
Di Donato, Pietro 1911- BenetAL 91
DiDonato, Ray 1952- WhoFI 92
Didot BlkwCEP
Didot, Firmin 1761-1836 BlkwCEP
Didot, Francois 1689-1757 BlkwCEP
Didot, Francois-Ambroise 1730-1804 BlkwCEP
Didrickson, Loleta Anderson 1941- WhoAmP 91
Didriksen, Caleb H., III 1955- WhoAmL 92
Didriksen, Jan 1917- IntWW 91
Didrikson, Mildred 1913-1956 FacFETw
Didwania, Hanuman Prasad 1935- AmMWSc 92
Didymus The Blind 313-398 EncEarC
Dieball, John Allan 1936- WhoWest 92
Diebel, Gary Richard 1959- WhoMW 92
Diebel, Robert Norman 1927- AmMWSc 92
Diebenkorn, Richard Clifford 1922- IntWW 91
Diebold, Gerald Joseph 1943- AmMWSc 92
Diebold, John 1926- IntWW 91, WrDr 92
Diebold, John Brock 1944- AmMWSc 92
Diebold, Robert Ernest 1937- AmMWSc 92
Dieck, Daniel William 1951- WhoMW 92
Dieck, Ronald Lee AmMWSc 92
Diecke, Friedrich Paul Julius 1927- AmMWSc 92
Dieckert, Julius Walter 1925- AmMWSc 92
Dieckhoff, Hans Heinrich 1884-1952 EncTR 91
Diederich, Anne Marie 1943- WhoRel 92
Diederich, Daniel Kevin 1957- WhoAmL 92
Diederich, Dennis A 1936- AmMWSc 92
Diederich, Evelyn Tomlinson 1915- WhoAmP 91

**Diederich**, Francois Nico 1952- *AmMWSc 92*
**Diederich**, John William 1929- *WhoFI 92*
**Diederichs**, Nicolaas 1903-1978 *FacFETw*
**Diedrich**, Donald Frank 1932- *AmMWSc 92*
**Diedrich**, James Loren 1925- *AmMWSc 92*
**Diedrich**, Jayne F. 1956- *WhoHisp 92*
**Diedrich**, Michael G *WhoAmP 91*
**Diedrich**, William Lawler 1923- *WhoAmL 92*
**Diedrick**, Geraldine Rose 1928- *WhoWest 92*
**Diedrick**, Regina Ann 1944- *WhoMW 92*
**Diedring**, Michael Curt 1959- *WhoAmL 92*
**Diedtrich**, Elmer *WhoAmP 91*
**Diefenbach**, Dale Alan 1933- *WhoAmL 92*
**Diefenbach**, William Stephen 1928- *WhoFI 92*
**Diefenbaker**, John G 1895-1979 *FacFETw*
**Diefenderfer**, William Martin, III 1945- *WhoFI 92*
**Diefendorf**, David *DrAPF 91*
**Diefendorf**, Russell Judd 1931- *AmMWSc 92*
**Dieffenbach**, Bruce Clark 1947- *WhoFI 92*
**Dieffenbach**, Charles Maxwell 1909- *WhoAmL 92*
**Dieffenbach**, Jon Michael 1948- *WhoEnt 92*
**Diegelmann**, Robert Frederick 1943- *AmMWSc 92*
**Diegle**, Ronald Bruce 1947- *AmMWSc 92*
**Diegnan**, Glenn Alan 1947- *AmMWSc 92*
**Diego**, Eliseo 1920- *ConSpAP*
**Diego**, Kenneth M. 1956- *WhoEnt 92*
**Diegues**, Carlos 1940- *IntDcF 2-2*
**Dieguez**, Clemente 1935- *WhoHisp 92*
**Dieguez**, Richard P. 1960- *WhoHisp 92*
**Dieguez**, Richard Peter 1960- *WhoAmL 92, WhoEnt 92*
**Diehl**, Antoni Mills 1924- *AmMWSc 92*
**Diehl**, Cynthia Barre 1933- *WhoAmP 91*
**Diehl**, Digby Robert 1940- *IntAu&W 91, WhoWest 92*
**Diehl**, Fred A 1936- *AmMWSc 92*
**Diehl**, Gary James 1952- *WhoEnt 92*
**Diehl**, Harvey 1910- *AmMWSc 92*
**Diehl**, Jackson 1956- *ConAu 135*
**Diehl**, John Bertram Stuart 1944- *Who 92*
**Diehl**, John Edwin 1929- *AmMWSc 92*
**Diehl**, Kenneth Laverne 1961- *WhoMW 92*
**Diehl**, Lauren Traynor 1955- *WhoAmL 92*
**Diehl**, Paul W 1933- *WhoAmP 91*
**Diehl**, Renee Denise 1955- *AmMWSc 92*
**Diehl**, W. W. 1916-1974 *ConAu 134*
**Diehl**, Walter Francis, Jr. 1935- *WhoAmL 92, WhoFI 92*
**Diehn**, Bodo 1934- *AmMWSc 92*
**Diehr**, Beverly Hunt 1954- *WhoAmL 92*
**Diehr**, Paula Hagedorn 1941- *AmMWSc 92*
**Diekema**, Anthony J. 1933- *WhoMW 92*
**Dieker**, Lawrence L. *WhoAmL 92*
**Diekhans**, Herbert Henry 1925- *AmMWSc 92*
**Diekhaus**, Grace M. *LesBEnT 92*
**Diekman**, John David 1943- *AmMWSc 92*
**Diekman**, Norman 1939- *DcTwDes*
**Diekmann**, Gilmore Frederick, Jr. 1946- *WhoAmL 92*
**Diekmann**, Nancy Kassak 1952- *WhoEnt 92*
**Diel**, Joseph Henry 1937- *AmMWSc 92*
**Diel**, Rolf 1922- *IntWW 91*
**Dieleman**, William W 1931- *WhoAmP 91*
**Dieleman**, William Wilbur 1931- *WhoMW 92*
**Dielman**, Ray Walter 1938- *WhoFI 92*
**Dielman**, Ronald Leroy 1946- *WhoMW 92*
**Dielman**, Terry Edward 1952- *WhoFI 92*
**Diels**, Otto Paul Herman 1876-1954 *WhoNob 90*
**Diels**, Otto Paul Hermann 1876-1954 *FacFETw*
**Diels**, Rudolf 1900-1957 *EncTR 91*
**Diem**, Carl 1882-1962 *EncTR 91 [port]*
**Diem**, Hugh E 1922- *AmMWSc 92*
**Diem**, John Edwin 1937- *AmMWSc 92*
**Diem**, Kenneth Lee 1924- *AmMWSc 92*
**Diem**, Max 1947- *AmMWSc 92*
**Diem**, Ngo Dinh 1901-1963 *FacFETw [port]*
**Diemente**, Edward Philip 1923- *WhoEnt 92*
**Diemer**, Carl John, Jr. 1938- *WhoRel 92*
**Diemer**, Edward Devlin 1933- *AmMWSc 92*
**Diemer**, Emma Lou 1927- *ConCom 92, WhoEnt 92, WhoWest 92*
**Diemer**, F P 1920- *AmMWSc 92*
**Diemer**, Marvin E 1924- *WhoAmP 91*
**Dienel**, Gerald Arthur 1945- *AmMWSc 92*
**Diener**, Betty Jane 1940- *WhoFI 92*
**Diener**, David 1915- *WhoAmL 92*
**Diener**, Robert G 1938- *AmMWSc 92*
**Diener**, Robert Max 1931- *AmMWSc 92*
**Diener**, Royce 1918- *WhoFI 92, WhoWest 92*
**Diener**, Stephen I. 1938- *WhoEnt 92*
**Diener**, Theodor Otto 1921- *AmMWSc 92, IntWW 91*
**Diener**, Urban Lowell 1921- *AmMWSc 92*
**Dienes**, George Julian 1918- *AmMWSc 92*
**Dienhart**, Mark Charles 1953- *WhoMW 92*
**Dienstbier**, Jiri 1937- *IntWW 91*
**Diepgen**, Eberhard 1941- *IntWW 91*
**Diepholz**, Daniel Ray 1964- *WhoWest 92*
**Dieppa**, Margaret *WhoHisp 92*
**Diercks**, Eileen Kay 1944- *WhoMW 92*
**Diercks**, Frederick O 1912- *AmMWSc 92*
**Diercks**, Richard A. 1941- *WhoEnt 92*
**Diercks**, Walter Elmer 1945- *WhoAmL 92*
**Dierenfeldt**, Karl Emil 1940- *AmMWSc 92*
**Dierenfield**, Richard Bruce 1922- *WrDr 92*
**Dierkers**, Joseph Andrew 1930- *WhoFI 92*
**Dierking**, Herminia D *WhoAmP 91*
**Dierks**, Merton L 1932- *WhoAmP 91*
**Dierks**, Richard Ernest 1934- *AmMWSc 92*
**Diers**, Donna Kaye 1938- *AmMWSc 92*
**Diers**, Hank H. 1931- *WhoEnt 92*
**Dierschke**, Donald Joe 1934- *AmMWSc 92*
**Dierssen**, Gunther Hans 1926- *AmMWSc 92*
**Dies**, Martin, Jr. 1901-1972 *AmPolLe*
**Dies**, Martin, Jr 1921- *WhoAmP 91*
**Diesch**, Stanley L 1925- *AmMWSc 92*
**Diesch**, Stanley La Verne 1925- *WhoMW 92*
**Diescho**, Joseph 1955- *ConAu 135*
**Diesel**, John Phillip 1926- *IntWW 91*
**Diesel**, Rudolf 1858-1913 *DcTwDes*
**Diesel**, Rudolph Christian Carl 1858-1913 *FacFETw*
**Diesem**, Charles D 1921- *AmMWSc 92*
**Diesem**, John Lawrence 1941- *WhoFI 92*
**Diesen**, Carl Edwin 1921- *AmMWSc 92*
**Diesen**, Ronald W 1931- *AmMWSc 92*
**Diesi**, Sal L 1930- *WhoAmP 91*
**Diesing**, Donald Carl 1923- *WhoMW 92*
**Dieskau**, Dietrich F. *Who 92*
**Diessen**, James Hardiman 1942- *WhoAmL 92*
**Diessner**, A W 1923- *WhoAmP 91*
**Diestel**, Joseph 1943- *AmMWSc 92*
**Diestler**, Dennis Jon 1941- *AmMWSc 92*
**Dieter**, George E, Jr 1928- *AmMWSc 92*
**Dieter**, Joseph Marshall, Jr. 1951- *WhoEnt 92*
**Dieter**, Mary 1949- *WhoRel 92*
**Dieter**, Mary Quade 1948- *WhoWest 92*
**Dieter**, Michael Phillip 1938- *AmMWSc 92*
**Dieter**, Richard Karl 1951- *AmMWSc 92*
**Dieter**, Werner H. 1929- *IntWW 91*
**Dieterich**, David Allan 1946- *AmMWSc 92*
**Dieterich**, Janet E 1943- *WhoAmP 91*
**Dieterich**, Neil *WhoAmP 91*
**Dieterich**, Robert Arthur 1939- *AmMWSc 92*
**Dieterle**, William 1893-1972 *IntDcF 2-2*
**Dietert**, Margaret Flowers 1951- *AmMWSc 92*
**Dietert**, Rodney Reynolds 1951- *AmMWSc 92*
**Diethelm**, Nancy Elizabeth 1952- *WhoWest 92*
**Diethorn**, Ward Samuel 1927- *AmMWSc 92*
**Diethrich**, Edward Bronson 1935- *WhoWest 92*
**Dietl**, Eduard 1890-1944 *EncTR 91 [port]*
**Dietlein**, Lawrence Frederick 1928- *AmMWSc 92*
**Dietmeyer**, Donald L 1932- *AmMWSc 92*
**Dietrich**, Alfred Gossett, Jr. 1942- *WhoFI 92*
**Dietrich**, George Charles 1927- *WhoFI 92, WhoMW 92*
**Dietrich**, Hermann 1879-1954 *EncTR 91*
**Dietrich**, James Robert 1944- *WhoAmP 91*
**Dietrich**, John Hassler 1878-1957 *RelLAm 91*
**Dietrich**, Josef 1892-1966 *BiDExR*
**Dietrich**, Joseph 1892-1966 *EncTR 91 [port]*
**Dietrich**, Joseph Jacob 1932- *AmMWSc 92*
**Dietrich**, Marlene 1901- *EncTR 91 [port], FacFETw [port], IntMPA 92, IntWW 91, NewAmDM*
**Dietrich**, Marlene 1904- *Who 92, WhoEnt 92*
**Dietrich**, Martin Walter 1935- *AmMWSc 92*
**Dietrich**, Otto 1897-1952 *BiDExR, EncTR 91 [port]*
**Dietrich**, Raymond Henri 1894-1980 *DcTwDes*
**Dietrich**, Raymond Henry 1894-1980 *FacFETw*
**Dietrich**, Richard Smith 1947- *WhoRel 92*
**Dietrich**, Richard Vincent 1924- *AmMWSc 92*
**Dietrich**, Robert *IntAu&W 91X, WrDr 92*
**Dietrich**, Robert Anthony 1933- *WhoMW 92*
**Dietrich**, Sarah 1961- *WhoEnt 92*
**Dietrich**, Shelby Lee 1924- *AmMWSc 92*
**Dietrich**, Suzanne Claire 1937- *WhoMW 92*
**Dietrich**, Suzanne de 1891-1981 *DcEcMov [port]*
**Dietrich**, William Alan 1951- *WhoWest 92*
**Dietrich**, William Edward 1942- *AmMWSc 92*
**Dietrich**, William Thomas 1944- *WhoMW 92*
**Dietrick**, Harry Joseph 1922- *AmMWSc 92*
**Dietsch**, Alfred John 1931- *WhoFI 92*
**Dietsch**, Steven William 1956- *WhoWest 92*
**Dietschy**, John Maurice 1932- *AmMWSc 92*
**Dietterich**, Thomas Glen 1954- *WhoWest 92*
**Dietterick**, Scott 1941- *WhoAmP 91*
**Dietz**, Albert 1908- *AmMWSc 92*
**Dietz**, Allen John *WhoMW 92*
**Dietz**, Charles Kenneth 1949- *WhoMW 92*
**Dietz**, Charlton Henry 1931- *WhoAmL 92*
**Dietz**, David 1946- *AmMWSc 92, WhoWest 92*
**Dietz**, David Allen 1948- *WhoMW 92*
**Dietz**, Dayle 1928- *WhoAmP 91*
**Dietz**, Deborah Dorothy 1949- *WhoAmP 91*
**Dietz**, Dennis C. 1949- *WhoFI 92*
**Dietz**, Edward Albert, Jr 1945- *AmMWSc 92*
**Dietz**, Frank Herbert 1940- *WhoRel 92*
**Dietz**, Frank Tobias 1920- *AmMWSc 92*
**Dietz**, George Robert 1931- *AmMWSc 92*
**Dietz**, George William, Jr 1938- *AmMWSc 92*
**Dietz**, Howard 1896-1983 *BenetAL 91*
**Dietz**, James G 1942- *WhoAmP 91*
**Dietz**, Jess Clay 1914- *AmMWSc 92*
**Dietz**, John Frederick 1944- *WhoRel 92*
**Dietz**, John R 1951- *AmMWSc 92*
**Dietz**, John W 1934- *AmMWSc 92*
**Dietz**, Mark Louis 1957- *AmMWSc 92*
**Dietz**, Michael Edward 1962- *WhoMW 92*
**Dietz**, Milton S. 1931- *WhoFI 92*
**Dietz**, Peter 1924- *ConAu 135*
**Dietz**, Richard Darby 1937- *AmMWSc 92*
**Dietz**, Robert Austin 1922- *AmMWSc 92*
**Dietz**, Robert Barron 1942- *WhoAmL 92*
**Dietz**, Robert Sinclair 1914- *AmMWSc 92*
**Dietz**, Russell Noel 1938- *AmMWSc 92*
**Dietz**, Russell Scott 1963- *WhoWest 92*
**Dietz**, Sherl M 1927- *AmMWSc 92*
**Dietz**, Stephen I 1934- *WhoIns 92*
**Dietz**, Thomas Howard 1940- *AmMWSc 92*
**Dietz**, Thomas John 1963- *AmMWSc 92*
**Dietz**, Vida Lee 1952- *WhoWest 92*
**Dietz**, William C 1919- *AmMWSc 92*
**Dietz**, William H 1944- *AmMWSc 92*
**Dietz**, Wolfgang 1921- *IntWW 91*
**Dietze**, Charles Edgar 1919- *WhoRel 92*
**Dietzen**, Christopher J. 1947- *WhoAmL 92*
**Dieudonne**, Florence Carpenter 1850- *ScFEYrs*
**Dievler**, David Harold 1929- *WhoFI 92*
**Diewert**, Virginia M 1943- *AmMWSc 92*
**Diez**, Charles F. *WhoHisp 92*
**Diez**, Gerald F. *WhoHisp 92*
**Diez**, John C 1944- *WhoAmP 91, WhoHisp 92*
**Diez**, Manny Jose 1931- *WhoEnt 92*
**Diez**, Mary Elizabeth 1944- *WhoMW 92*
**Diez**, Sherry Mae 1968- *WhoHisp 92*
**Diez de Velasco**, Manuel 1926- *IntWW 91*
**Diez-Pinto**, Migdonia Maria 1964- *WhoHisp 92*
**DiezCanseco**, Carmen Rosa 1950- *WhoHisp 92*
**DiFalco**, John Patrick 1943- *WhoAmL 92, WhoWest 92*
**DiFate**, Victor George 1943- *AmMWSc 92*
**DiFazio**, Louis T 1938- *AmMWSc 92*
**DiFeo**, Daniel Richard, Jr 1948- *AmMWSc 92*
**Diffendaffer**, Gary Lee 1946- *WhoFI 92*
**Diffendal**, Robert Francis, Jr 1940- *AmMWSc 92*
**Diffendorfer**, Ralph Eugene 1879-1951 *RelLAm 91*
**Diffin**, Charles Willard *ScFEYrs*
**Diffley**, Peter 1946- *AmMWSc 92*
**Diffley**, Thomas Joseph 1958- *WhoFI 92*
**Difford**, Winthrop Cecil 1921- *AmMWSc 92*
**Diffrient**, Niels 1928- *DcTwDes, FacFETw*
**DiFilippo**, Fernando, Jr. 1948- *WhoAmL 92*
**DiFiore**, Albert Angelo 1939- *WhoAmL 92*
**DiFiore**, Gerard Salvatore 1959- *WhoAmL 92*
**DiFoggio**, Rocco 1952- *AmMWSc 92*
**DiForio**, James P, Jr. 1951- *WhoIns 92*
**Diforio**, Robert G. 1940- *IntWW 91*
**DiFrancesco**, Donald Thomas 1944- *WhoAmP 91*
**DiFrancesco**, Loretta *AmMWSc 92*
**DiFranco**, Anthony *DrAPF 91*
**Difranco**, Julius V 1925- *AmMWSc 92*
**Di Franco**, Roland B 1936- *AmMWSc 92*
**Di Frango**, Gerald Walter 1952- *WhoFI 92*
**DiFruscia**, Anthony R. 1940- *WhoAmL 92*
**Difusa**, Pati *ConAu 133*
**DiGaetani**, John Louis 1943- *ConAu 35NR*
**DiGaetano**, Paul 1953- *WhoAmP 91*
**Di Gangi**, Frank Edward 1917- *AmMWSc 92*
**DiGaudio**, Mary Rose *AmMWSc 92*
**Digby** *Who 92*
**Digby**, Baron 1924- *Who 92*
**Digby**, Lady 1934- *Who 92*
**Digby**, Adrian 1909- *Who 92*
**Digby**, James F 1921- *AmMWSc 92*
**Digby**, James Foster 1921- *WhoWest 92*
**Digby**, James Keith 1950- *WhoAmP 91*
**Digby**, Joan 1942- *IntAu&W 91*
**Digby**, John 1938- *IntAu&W 91*
**Digby**, Lettice d1658 *EncAmaz 91*
**Digby**, Peter Saki Bassett 1921- *AmMWSc 92*
**Digby**, Richard Shuttleworth W. *Who 92*
**Digby**, Simon Wingfield 1910- *Who 92*
**Digby**, Stephen Basil W. *Who 92*
**Digenis**, George A 1935- *AmMWSc 92*
**DiGenova**, Joseph Egidio 1945- *WhoAmP 91*
**Di George**, Angelo Mario 1921- *AmMWSc 92*
**Digerness**, Stanley B 1941- *AmMWSc 92*
**Digges**, Thomas Atwood 1742-1822 *BenetAL 91*
**Diggins**, Maureen Rita 1942- *AmMWSc 92*
**Diggins**, Peter Sheehan 1938- *WhoEnt 92*
**Diggle**, James 1944- *Who 92*
**Diggle**, Philip 1956- *TwCPaSc*
**Diggs**, Annie Leporte 1848-1916 *HanAmWH*
**Diggs**, Carter Lee 1934- *AmMWSc 92, WhoFI 92*
**Diggs**, Charles Coles, Jr 1922- *WhoAmP 91*
**Diggs**, Charles Edward 1949- *WhoFI 92*
**Diggs**, Estella B. 1916- *WhoBlA 92*
**Diggs**, George Minor, Jr 1952- *AmMWSc 92*
**Diggs**, Irene 1906- *NotBlAW 92, WhoBlA 92, WomSoc*
**Diggs**, John W 1936- *AmMWSc 92*
**Diggs**, Lawrence Edward 1947- *WhoAmP 91*
**Diggs**, Natalie Virgina 1918- *WhoWest 92*
**Diggs**, Orville Sylvester, III 1956- *WhoWest 92*
**Diggs**, Roy Dalton, Jr. 1929- *WhoBlA 92*
**Diggs**, William P. 1926- *WhoBlA 92*
**Dighe**, Shrikant Vishwanath 1933- *AmMWSc 92*
**Di Giacomo**, Armand 1929- *AmMWSc 92*
**DiGiacomo**, David Robert 1952- *WhoAmL 92*
**DiGiacomo**, Michael D. 1946- *WhoFI 92*
**DiGiamarino**, Marian Eleanor 1947- *WhoFI 92*
**DiGiambattista**, James Vincent 1954- *WhoEnt 92*
**DiGiorgio**, Joseph Brun 1932- *AmMWSc 92*
**Di Giorgio**, Robert d1991 *NewYTBS 91*
**DiGiovanni**, Eleanor Elma 1944- *WhoFI 92*
**Digirolamo**, Edward Leonard 1944- *WhoFI 92*
**DiGirolamo**, Glen Francis 1961- *WhoEnt 92*
**Di Girolamo**, Rudolph Gerard 1934- *AmMWSc 92, WhoWest 92*
**Di Giulio**, Richard Thomas 1950- *AmMWSc 92*
**DiGiuseppe**, Enrico *WhoEnt 92*
**DiGiusto**, Louis Joseph, III 1945- *WhoEnt 92*
**Diglio**, Clement Anthony 1943- *AmMWSc 92*
**Digman**, Lester Aloysius 1938- *WhoFI 92, WhoMW 92*
**Digman**, Robert V 1930- *AmMWSc 92*
**Dignam**, Michael John 1931- *AmMWSc 92*
**Dignam**, Robert Joseph 1925- *WhoWest 92*
**Dignam**, William Joseph 1920- *AmMWSc 92*
**Dignan**, Albert Patrick 1920- *Who 92*
**Dignan**, Jim *WhoAmP 91*
**Dignan**, Thomas Galvin 1934- *WhoAmL 92*
**Dignan**, Thomas Gregory, Jr. 1940- *WhoAmL 92*
**Dignazio**, Eileen Kazokas 1946- *WhoRel 92*

**Digney**, James Brian 1946- *WhoIns 92*
**DiGregorio**, Gino Basilio 1966- *WhoMW 92*
**Di Gregorio**, Guerino John 1940- *AmMWSc 92*
**Dihigo**, Mario Emilio 1944- *WhoMW 92*
**Diijon**, Eddie Joseph 1942- *WhoEnt 92*
**Dillio**, Charles Carmen 1912- *AmMWSc 92*
**Dijeau**, Edward F. 1946- *WhoWest 92*
**Diji**, Augustine Ebun 1932- *WhoBlA 92*
**Dijkers**, Marcellinus P 1947- *AmMWSc 92*
**Dijkstal**, Dirk 1946- *WhoWest 92*
**Dijkstra**, Minne 1937- *IntWW 91*
**Dijoud**, Paul Charles Louis 1938- *IntWW 91*
**Dike**, Jack Andrew 1957- *WhoAmL 92*
**Dike**, Kenneth Onwuka 1917- *WhoBlA 92*
**Dike**, Mary Jane 1930- *WhoEnt 92*
**Dike**, Paul Alexander 1912- *AmMWSc 92*
**Dikelsky**, Burton E. 1945- *WhoEnt 92*
**Dikeman**, May *DrAPF 91*
**Dikeman**, Roxane Norris 1942- *AmMWSc 92*
**Dikeou**, George Demetrios 1938- *WhoAmL 92*
**Dikiy**, Aleksey Denisovich 1889-1955 *SovUnBD*
**Dikshit**, Uma Shankar 1901- *IntWW 91*
**Diksic**, Mirko 1942- *AmMWSc 92*
**Dikstein**, Shabtay 1931- *AmMWSc 92*
**Diktas**, Christos James 1955- *WhoAmL 92*
**Di Lavore**, Philip, III 1931- *AmMWSc 92*
**Dilbeck**, Charles Stevens, Jr. 1944- *WhoWest 92*
**Dilcher**, David L 1936- *AmMWSc 92*
**Dilday**, Judith Nelson 1943- *WhoBlA 92*
**Dilday**, Russell Hooper 1930- *WhoRel 92*
**Dilday**, William H., Jr. *LesBEnT 92*
**Dilday**, William Horace, Jr. 1937- *WhoBlA 92*
**Dilday**, William Horace, Jr. 1939- *WhoEnt 92*
**Di Lella**, Alexander Anthony 1929- *WhoRel 92, WrDr 92*
**Dilenschneider**, Robert 1943- *IntWW 91*
**Dilenschneider**, Robert Louis 1943- *WhoFI 92*
**Di Leo**, Joseph H. 1902- *WrDr 92*
**DiLeone**, Gilbert Robert 1935- *AmMWSc 92*
**Dileski**, Patricia Parra *WhoHisp 92*
**Dilg**, Joseph Carl 1951- *WhoAmL 92*
**Dilhorne**, Viscount 1932- *Who 92*
**Diliberto**, Helen Bratney 1920- *WhoWest 92*
**Diliberto**, John Kenneth 1954- *WhoEnt 92*
**Diliberto**, Michael Reed 1958- *WhoEnt 92*
**DiLiberto**, Richard Anthony, Jr. 1961- *WhoAmL 92*
**Diliberto**, Roy Thomas 1940- *WhoFI 92*
**DiLiddo**, Bart A 1931- *AmMWSc 92*
**DiLiddo**, Rebecca McBride 1951- *AmMWSc 92*
**DiLiello**, Leo Ralph 1932- *AmMWSc 92*
**Di Liello**, Salvatore 1958- *WhoMW 92*
**DiLieto**, Biagio *WhoAmP 91*
**Diligensky**, German Germanovich 1930- *IntWW 91, SovUnBD*
**Dilke** *Who 92*
**Dilke**, Annabel Mary 1942- *WrDr 92*
**Dilke**, Caroline 1940- *IntAu&W 91*
**Dilke**, John Fisher Wentworth 1906- *Who 92*
**Dilke**, Oswald Ashton Wentworth 1915- *WrDr 92*
**Dilks**, David 1938- *ConAu 35NR*
**Dilks**, David Neville 1938- *IntWW 91, Who 92*
**Dilks**, Park Bankert, Jr. 1928- *WhoAmL 92*
**Dill**, Aloys John 1940- *AmMWSc 92*
**Dill**, Bayard 1905- *Who 92*
**Dill**, Charles Anthony 1939- *WhoFI 92*
**Dill**, Charles William 1932- *AmMWSc 92*
**Dill**, Clarence C. d1977 *LesBEnT 92*
**Dill**, Dale Robert 1934- *AmMWSc 92*
**Dill**, David Bruce 1891- *AmMWSc 92*
**Dill**, Edward D 1941- *AmMWSc 92*
**Dill**, Ellen Renee 1949- *WhoMW 92, WhoRel 92*
**Dill**, Ellis Harold 1932- *AmMWSc 92*
**Dill**, Frederick H, Jr 1932- *AmMWSc 92*
**Dill**, Gregory Allan 1949- *WhoRel 92*
**Dill**, Joel Standish Wesley 1940- *WhoMW 92*
**Dill**, John C 1939- *AmMWSc 92*
**Dill**, Kenneth Austin 1947- *AmMWSc 92*
**Dill**, Lawrence Michael 1945- *AmMWSc 92*
**Dill**, Mary Cornelia 1923- *WhoWest 92*
**Dill**, Maurice Earl 1948- *WhoAmL 92*
**Dill**, Norman Hudson 1938- *AmMWSc 92*
**Dill**, Robert Floyd 1927- *AmMWSc 92*
**Dill**, Russell Eugene 1932- *AmMWSc 92*
**Dill**, William Allen 1918- *WhoAmL 92*
**Dillahunty**, Wilbur Harris 1928- *WhoAmL 92*
**Dillaman**, Rockwell Lane 1949- *WhoRel 92*
**Dillamore**, Ian Leslie 1938- *Who 92*
**Dillard**, Annie *DrAPF 91*
**Dillard**, Annie 1945- *BenetAL 91, FacFETw, IntWW 91, WrDr 92*
**Dillard**, Cecil R. 1906- *WhoBlA 92*
**Dillard**, Clyde Ruffin 1920- *AmMWSc 92*
**Dillard**, David Hugh 1923- *AmMWSc 92*
**Dillard**, David Wayne 1966- *WhoEnt 92*
**Dillard**, Dean Innes 1947- *WhoMW 92*
**Dillard**, Dudley d1991 *NewYTBS 91*
**Dillard**, Dudley 1913-1991 *ConAu 135*
**Dillard**, Emil L. *DrAPF 91*
**Dillard**, Emmett Urcey 1917- *AmMWSc 92*
**Dillard**, Ernest *WhoAmP 91*
**Dillard**, Gary Eugene 1938- *AmMWSc 92*
**Dillard**, George Douglas 1942- *WhoAmP 91*
**Dillard**, George Stewart, III 1958- *WhoRel 92*
**Dillard**, Harrison W 1923- *BlkOlyM [port]*
**Dillard**, Howard Lee 1946- *WhoBlA 92*
**Dillard**, Jackie Smith 1948- *WhoBlA 92*
**Dillard**, James *TwCWW 91*
**Dillard**, James Hardy, II 1933- *WhoAmP 91*
**Dillard**, James William 1948- *AmMWSc 92*
**Dillard**, Joan Helen 1951- *WhoFI 92*
**Dillard**, Joey L. 1924- *WhoBlA 92*
**Dillard**, John Gammons 1938- *AmMWSc 92*
**Dillard**, John Henry 1819-1896 *DcNCBi 2*
**Dillard**, John Martin 1945- *WhoAmL 92, WhoWest 92*
**Dillard**, John Robert 1955- *WhoAmL 92*
**Dillard**, June White 1937- *WhoBlA 92*
**Dillard**, Margaret Bleick *AmMWSc 92*
**Dillard**, Marilyn Dianne 1940- *WhoFI 92, WhoWest 92*
**Dillard**, Martin Gregory 1935- *AmMWSc 92, WhoBlA 92*
**Dillard**, Melvin Rubin 1941- *WhoBlA 92*
**Dillard**, Morris, Jr 1927- *AmMWSc 92*
**Dillard**, R.H.W. *DrAPF 91*
**Dillard**, R. H. W. 1937- *ConPo 91, IntAu&W 91, WrDr 92*
**Dillard**, Richard 1857-1928 *DcNCBi 2*
**Dillard**, Robert Garing, Jr 1931- *AmMWSc 92*
**Dillard**, Rodney Jefferson 1939- *WhoFI 92*
**Dillard**, Samuel Dewell 1913- *WhoBlA 92*
**Dillard**, Thelma Deloris 1946- *WhoBlA 92*
**Dillard**, Thelma Deloris Bivins 1946- *WhoAmP 91*
**Dillard**, Thierry Rene 1953- *WhoFI 92*
**Dillaway**, Robert Beacham 1924- *AmMWSc 92*
**Dille**, Deborah Lynn 1953- *WhoFI 92*
**Dille**, Earl Kaye 1927- *WhoFI 92*
**Dille**, John Flint, Jr. 1913- *WhoMW 92*
**Dille**, John Robert 1931- *AmMWSc 92*
**Dille**, Kenneth Leroy 1925- *AmMWSc 92*
**Dille**, Roger McCormick 1923- *AmMWSc 92*
**Dille**, Roland Paul 1924- *WhoMW 92*
**Dille**, Stephen E 1945- *WhoAmP 91*
**Dillemans**, Roger Henri 1932- *IntWW 91*
**Dillenback**, Robert G 1921- *WhoAmP 91*
**Dillenbeck**, Hadley Herman, Jr. 1964- *WhoRel 92*
**Dillenberger**, Jane *WhoRel 92*
**Dillenberger**, John 1918- *WhoRel 92, WrDr 92*
**Diller**, Barry *LesBEnT 92*
**Diller**, Barry 1942- *IntMPA 92, IntWW 91, News 91 [port], WhoEnt 92, WhoFI 92, WhoWest 92*
**Diller**, Erold Ray 1922- *AmMWSc 92*
**Diller**, Kenneth Ray 1942- *AmMWSc 92*
**Diller**, Phyllis 1917- *IntMPA 92, WhoEnt 92*
**Diller**, Thomas Eugene 1950- *AmMWSc 92*
**Diller**, Violet Marion 1914- *AmMWSc 92*
**Dillery**, Carl Edward 1930- *WhoAmP 91*
**Dillery**, Dean George 1928- *AmMWSc 92*
**Dilley**, David Ross 1934- *AmMWSc 92*
**Dilley**, James Paul 1934- *AmMWSc 92*
**Dilley**, Richard Alan 1936- *AmMWSc 92*
**Dilley**, Timothy Eugene 1958- *WhoRel 92*
**Dilley**, William G 1942- *AmMWSc 92*
**Dillier**, David Allen 1955- *WhoWest 92*
**Dillihay**, Tanya Clarkson 1958- *WhoBlA 92*
**Dillin**, John Frank, Jr 1956- *WhoWest 92*
**Dillin**, Samuel Hugh 1914- *WhoAmL 92*
**Dilling**, Elizabeth 1894-1966 *BiDExR*
**Dilling**, Elizabeth Eloise 1894-1966 *HanAmWH*
**Dilling**, Kirkpatrick Wallwick 1920- *WhoAmL 92, WhoFI 92, WhoMW 92*
**Dilling**, Wendell Lee 1936- *AmMWSc 92*
**Dillinger**, John 1903-1934 *FacFETw*
**Dillingham**, Charles, III 1942- *WhoEnt 92*
**Dillingham**, Frederick 1948- *WhoAmP 91*
**Dillingham**, Grace Voorhis 1927- *WhoRel 92*
**Dillingham**, John Allen 1939- *WhoMW 92*
**Dillingham**, William B. 1930- *WrDr 92*
**Dillingham**, William Byron 1930- *IntAu&W 91*
**Dillingham**, William Paul 1843-1923 *AmPolLe, DcAmImH*
**Dillingofski**, Mary Sue 1944- *WhoMW 92*
**Dillistone**, Frederick William 1903- *Who 92*
**Dillman**, Alan D 1946- *WhoAmP 91*
**Dillman**, Bradford 1930- *IntMPA 92, WhoEnt 92*
**Dillman**, Charles Norman 1938- *WhoRel 92*
**Dillman**, Lowell Thomas 1931- *AmMWSc 92*
**Dillman**, Richard Carl 1931- *AmMWSc 92*
**Dillman**, Robert O 1947- *AmMWSc 92*
**Dillmann**, Wolfgang H 1939- *AmMWSc 92*
**Dillner**, Anders 1951- *WhoWest 92*
**Dillon** *Who 92*
**Dillon**, Viscount 1973- *Who 92*
**Dillon**, Aubrey 1938- *WhoBlA 92*
**Dillon**, Brendan 1924- *IntWW 91*
**Dillon**, Brian *Who 92*
**Dillon**, C. Douglas *FacFETw*
**Dillon**, C. Douglas 1909- *IntWW 91, Who 92*
**Dillon**, Clarence 1882-1979 *FacFETw*
**Dillon**, David 1957- *WhoEnt 92*
**Dillon**, David Brian 1951- *WhoFI 92, WhoMW 92*
**Dillon**, Eilis 1920- *ChlLR 26 [port], WrDr 92*
**Dillon**, Ellis 1920- *IntAu&W 91*
**Dillon**, Enoch *DrAPF 91*
**Dillon**, Ernestine 1928- *WhoMW 92*
**Dillon**, Evelyn Hardin *WhoBlA 92*
**Dillon**, Francis Patrick 1937- *WhoFI 92, WhoWest 92*
**Dillon**, George 1906-1968 *BenetAL 91*
**Dillon**, George Brian 1925- *Who 92*
**Dillon**, George Chaffee 1922- *WhoFI 92, WhoWest 92*
**Dillon**, Gregory Russell 1922- *WhoFI 92, WhoWest 92*
**Dillon**, Herman George 1926- *WhoAmP 91*
**Dillon**, Howard Burton 1935- *WhoMW 92*
**Dillon**, Hugh C, Jr 1930- *AmMWSc 92*
**Dillon**, J C, Jr *WhoAmP 91*
**Dillon**, Jack Dudley 1924- *WhoFI 92*
**Dillon**, James 1950- *ConCom 92*
**Dillon**, James Joseph 1948- *WhoAmL 92*
**Dillon**, James M. 1933- *WhoFI 92*
**Dillon**, John d1991 *NewYTBS 91*
**Dillon**, John 1908- *Who 92*
**Dillon**, John Callahan 1919- *WhoFI 92*
**Dillon**, John Joseph, III 1947- *AmMWSc 92*
**Dillon**, John Thomas 1947- *AmMWSc 92*
**Dillon**, Joseph Francis, Jr 1924- *AmMWSc 92*
**Dillon**, Joseph Neil 1945- *WhoRel 92*
**Dillon**, Kathleen M. *WhoAmL 92*
**Dillon**, Kevin 1965- *IntMPA 92*
**Dillon**, Lawrence Samuel 1910- *AmMWSc 92*
**Dillon**, Marcus Lunsford, Jr 1924- *AmMWSc 92*
**Dillon**, Matt 1964- *IntMPA 92, IntWW 91, News 92-2 [port], WhoEnt 92*
**Dillon**, Max 1913- *Who 92*
**Dillon**, Melinda 1939- *IntMPA 92*
**Dillon**, Millicent G. *DrAPF 91*
**Dillon**, Oscar Wendell, Jr 1928- *AmMWSc 92*
**Dillon**, Owen C. 1934- *WhoBlA 92*
**Dillon**, Patricia Anne 1948- *WhoAmP 91*
**Dillon**, Patrick Francis *AmMWSc 92*
**Dillon**, Paul Wilson 1926- *WhoFI 92*
**Dillon**, Phillip Michael 1944- *WhoFI 92, WhoMW 92*
**Dillon**, Ray William 1954- *WhoFI 92*
**Dillon**, Raymond Donald 1925- *AmMWSc 92*
**Dillon**, Richard Thomas 1928- *AmMWSc 92*
**Dillon**, Robert Chapman 1926- *WhoRel 92*
**Dillon**, Robert Morton 1923- *AmMWSc 92, WhoFI 92*
**Dillon**, Rodney Lee 1938- *WhoAmL 92*
**Dillon**, Ronald Gay 1948- *WhoRel 92*
**Dillon**, Roy Dean 1929- *AmMWSc 92*
**Dillon**, Thomas Michael 1927- *Who 92*
**Dillon**, Thomas Ray 1948- *WhoFI 92, WhoMW 92*
**Dillon**, Valerie Vance 1930- *WhoMW 92, WhoRel 92*
**Dillon**, William Patrick 1936- *AmMWSc 92*
**Dillon**, Wilton Sterling 1923- *WrDr 92*
**Dillow**, Jean Carmen *IntMPA 92*
**Dills**, Charles E 1922- *AmMWSc 92*
**Dills**, James Carl 1954- *WhoFI 92*
**Dills**, Ralph C 1910- *WhoAmP 91*
**Dills**, William L, Jr 1945- *AmMWSc 92*
**Dillwith**, Jack W *AmMWSc 92*
**Dillwyn-Venables-Llewelyn**, John Michael *Who 92*
**Dilmino**, Michael Joseph *AmMWSc 92*
**Dilnot**, Mary 1921- *Who 92*
**DiLonardo**, Joseph A 1928- *WhoAmP 91*
**DiLorenzo**, Louis Patrick 1952- *WhoAmL 92*
**Di Loreto**, Dante Finnemore *WhoEnt 92*
**Di Loreto**, Michael J 1952- *WhoIns 92*
**Dilpare**, Armand Leon 1932- *AmMWSc 92*
**Dils**, Robert James 1919- *AmMWSc 92*
**Dilsaver**, Steven Charles 1953- *AmMWSc 92*
**Dilts**, Joseph Alstyne 1942- *AmMWSc 92*
**Dilts**, Preston Vine, Jr 1934- *AmMWSc 92*
**Dilts**, Robert Voorhees 1929- *AmMWSc 92*
**DiLucia**, Samuel James 1949- *WhoWest 92*
**DiLuglio**, Thomas Ross 1931- *WhoAmP 91*
**Di Lullo**, Charles S 1938- *WhoIns 92*
**Di Lullo**, Ralph Michael 1962- *WhoWest 92*
**Di Luzio**, Nicholas Robert 1926- *AmMWSc 92*
**Dilworth**, Benjamin Conroy 1931- *AmMWSc 92*
**Dilworth**, Grace Dorothy 1930- *WhoFI 92*
**Dilworth**, Mary Elizabeth 1950- *WhoBlA 92*
**Dilworth**, Norman 1933- *TwCPaSc*
**Dilworth**, Robert Hamilton, III 1930- *AmMWSc 92*
**Dilworth**, Robert Holden 1942- *WhoAmL 92*
**Dilworth**, Sharon 1958- *ConAu 135*
**Dilziel**, Ian Martin 1947- *Who 92*
**DiMaggio**, Anthony, III 1935- *AmMWSc 92*
**Di Maggio**, Frank Louis 1929- *AmMWSc 92*
**DiMaggio**, Joe 1914- *FacFETw [port]*
**DiMaggio**, Lou 1958- *WhoEnt 92*
**DiMaio**, Virginia Sue 1921- *WhoFI 92, WhoWest 92*
**DiManna**, David Amoss 1961- *WhoMW 92*
**DiMarco**, Anthony Joseph 1938- *WhoEnt 92*
**DiMarco**, G Robert 1927- *AmMWSc 92*
**DiMarco**, Mario Anthony 1931- *WhoAmP 91*
**Di Maria**, Donelli Joseph 1946- *AmMWSc 92*
**DiMario**, Judy *WhoAmP 91*
**Di Mario**, Patrick Joseph *AmMWSc 92*
**Di Martino**, Rita 1937- *WhoAmP 91, WhoHisp 92*
**DiMarzio**, Dante J., Jr. 1950- *WhoMW 92*
**Dimarzio**, Dennis A 1943- *WhoIns 92*
**DiMarzio**, Edmund Armand 1932- *AmMWSc 92*
**Di Mascio**, John Philip 1944- *WhoAmL 92*
**DiMasi**, Gabriel Joseph 1936- *AmMWSc 92*
**DiMasi**, Salvatore Francis 1945- *WhoAmP 91*
**DiMatteo**, Anthony J 1925- *WhoAmP 91*
**DiMatteo**, Dominick, Jr. 1918- *WhoMW 92*
**DiMatteo**, John Michael 1961- *WhoAmL 92*
**di Mauro**, Concetto d1991 *NewYTBS 91*
**DiMauro**, Salvatore 1939- *AmMWSc 92*
**Dimauro**, Theodore E 1933- *WhoAmP 91*
**Dimbath**, Merle F. 1939- *WhoFI 92*
**Dimbleby**, Bel *Who 92*
**Dimbleby**, David 1938- *IntAu&W 91, IntWW 91, Who 92*
**Dimbleby**, Jonathan 1944- *IntAu&W 91, IntWW 91, Who 92, WrDr 92*
**Dimbleby**, Josceline Rose 1943- *IntAu&W 91, Who 92*
**Dimbleby**, Richard d1965 *LesBEnT 92*
**Dimechkie**, Nadim 1919- *IntWW 91, Who 92*
**Dimeff**, John 1921- *AmMWSc 92*
**Diment**, William Horace 1927- *AmMWSc 92*
**Dimeny**, Imre 1922- *IntWW 91*
**Dimeo**, Diane *WhoEnt 92*
**Dimeo**, Steven *DrAPF 91*
**DiMeola**, Al 1954- *WhoEnt 92*
**Dimes**, Edwin Kinsley 1923- *WhoAmL 92*
**DiMicco**, Joseph Anthony 1947- *AmMWSc 92*
**DiMichele**, Leonard Vincent 1952- *AmMWSc 92*
**DiMichele**, William Anthony 1951- *AmMWSc 92*
**Dimick**, Paul Slayton 1935- *AmMWSc 92*
**Dimick**, Walter S. 1950- *WhoEnt 92*
**Di Mino**, Andre Anthony 1955- *WhoFI 92*
**Dimino**, Joseph T. 1923- *WhoRel 92*
**Dimitman**, Jerome Eugene 1920- *AmMWSc 92*

**Dimitriadis**, Andre C. 1940- *WhoFI 92*
**Dimitrijevic**, Braco 1948- *TwCPaSc*
**Dimitrios I** 1914- *IntWW 91*
**Dimitrios I** 1914-1991 *NewYTBS 91 [port]*
**Dimitriou**, Theodore 1926- *WhoFI 92*
**Dimitroff**, Edward 1927- *AmMWSc 92*
**Dimitroff**, George Ernest 1938- *AmMWSc 92*
**Dimitrov**, Georgi 1882-1949 *EncTR 91 [port], FacFETw*
**Dimitrova**, Ghena 1941- *IntWW 91*
**Dimitry**, Theodore George 1937- *WhoAmL 92*
**Dimkoff**, Graydon Woodard 1947- *WhoAmP 91*
**Dimler**, Charles Henry 1943- *WhoAmP 91*
**Dimlich**, Ruth Van Weenen *AmMWSc 92*
**Dimling**, John Arthur 1938- *WhoMW 92*
**Dimma**, William Andrew 1928- *WhoFI 92*
**Dimmel**, Donald R 1940- *AmMWSc 92*
**Dimmers**, Albert Worthington 1904- *WhoAmL 92*
**Dimmich**, Jeffrey Robert 1948- *WhoAmL 92*
**Dimmick**, Carolyn Reaber 1929- *WhoAmL 92, WhoWest 92*
**Dimmick**, John Frederick 1921- *AmMWSc 92*
**Dimmick**, Ralph W 1934- *AmMWSc 92*
**Dimmig**, Daniel Ashton 1924- *AmMWSc 92*
**Dimmitt**, Lawrence Andrew 1941- *WhoAmL 92*
**Dimmler**, D Gerd 1933- *AmMWSc 92*
**Dimmock**, John O 1936- *AmMWSc 92*
**Dimmock**, Jonathan Richard 1937- *AmMWSc 92*
**Dimmock**, Peter 1920- *IntMPA 92, Who 92*
**Dimmock**, Roger Charles 1935- *Who 92*
**Dimock**, Dirck L 1930- *AmMWSc 92*
**Dimock**, George E. 1917- *ConAu 133*
**Dimock**, Marshall E. d1991 *NewYTBS 91*
**Dimock**, Marshall Edward 1903- *IntAu&W 91, WrDr 92*
**Dimock**, Ronald Vilroy, Jr 1943- *AmMWSc 92*
**Dimock**, Susan 1847-1875 *DcNCBi 2*
**Dimon**, John Edward 1916- *WhoAmP 91*
**DiMona**, Joseph John 1959- *WhoAmL 92*
**Dimond**, Alan Theodore 1943- *WhoAmL 92*
**Dimond**, Edmunds Grey 1918- *AmMWSc 92*
**Dimond**, Harold Lloyd 1922- *AmMWSc 92*
**Dimond**, John Barnet 1929- *AmMWSc 92*
**Dimond**, Marie Therese 1916- *AmMWSc 92*
**Dimond**, Randall Lloyd 1946- *AmMWSc 92*
**Dimond**, Thomas 1916- *WhoFI 92*
**Dimont**, Penelope *IntAu&W 91X, WrDr 92*
**Dimopoullos**, George Takis 1923- *AmMWSc 92*
**Dimora**, Jimmy Carl 1955- *WhoAmP 91*
**Dimos**, Jimmy N 1938- *WhoAmP 91*
**Dimsdale**, Bernard 1912- *AmMWSc 92*
**Dimson**, Gladys Felicia *Who 92*
**DiMuzio**, Michael Thomas 1949- *AmMWSc 92*
**Din**, Gilbert C. 1932- *WhoWest 92*
**Din**, Norman C. 1954- *WhoFI 92*
**Dina**, Alexander, II 1963- *WhoEnt 92*
**Dina**, Stephen James 1943- *AmMWSc 92*
**Dinan**, Carolyn *IntAu&W 91*
**Dinan**, Donald Robert 1949- *WhoAmL 92, WhoFI 92*
**Dinan**, Frank J 1933- *AmMWSc 92*
**DiNapoli**, Constance *WhoEnt 92*
**Dinapoli**, Frederick Richard 1940- *AmMWSc 92*
**DiNapoli**, Thomas John 1943- *WhoFI 92*
**DiNapoli**, Thomas P *WhoAmP 91*
**DiNardi**, Salvatore Robert 1943- *AmMWSc 92*
**DiNardo**, Luella Kay 1948- *WhoFI 92, WhoWest 92*
**Dinbergs**, Kornelius 1925- *AmMWSc 92*
**Dince**, Robert Reuben 1924- *WhoFI 92*
**Dince**, Roy R. d1991 *NewYTBS 91*
**Dincerler**, M. Vehbi 1940- *IntWW 91*
**Dinces**, Franklin Gary 1958- *WhoAmL 92*
**Dindal**, Daniel Lee 1936- *AmMWSc 92*
**Dindo**, Kathryn Warther 1949- *WhoFI 92*
**d'Indy**, Vincent *FacFETw, NewAmDM*
**Dine**, Carol *DrAPF 91*
**Dine**, James 1935- *IntWW 91*
**Dineen**, John K. 1928- *WhoAmL 92*
**Dinegar**, Robert Hudson 1921- *AmMWSc 92*
**Dinel**, Richard Henry 1942- *WhoFI 92, WhoWest 92*
**Dinelli**, Mel d1991 *NewYTBS 91*
**DiNello**, Gilbert John 1935- *WhoAmP 91*
**Diner**, Daniel Bruce 1947- *WhoWest 92*
**Diner**, Ralph Gordon 1951- *WhoWest 92*
**Diner**, Wilma Canada 1926- *AmMWSc 92*
**Dinerman**, Beatrice 1933- *WrDr 92*
**Dinerstein**, Robert Alvin 1919- *AmMWSc 92*
**Dinerstein**, Robert Joseph 1944- *AmMWSc 92*
**Dines**, Allen I 1929- *AmMWSc 92*
**Dines**, Burton 1925- *WhoEnt 92*
**Dines**, George B. 1931- *WhoBlA 92*
**Dines**, Martin Benjamin 1943- *AmMWSc 92*
**Dines**, Peter Munn 1929- *Who 92*
**Dinescu**, Violeta 1953- *ConCom 92*
**Dinesen**, Isak 1885-1962 *FacFETw, LiExTwC*
**Diness**, Arthur M 1938- *AmMWSc 92*
**Dinetz**, Glenn Robert 1950- *WhoFI 92*
**Dinevor** *Who 92*
**Ding Cong** 1916- *IntWW 91*
**Ding Fengying** *IntWW 91*
**Ding Guangeng** 1930- *IntWW 91*
**Ding Guangxun** *WhoRel 92*
**Ding Guangxun** 1915- *IntWW 91*
**Ding Guoyu** 1931- *IntWW 91*
**Ding Hao** 1930- *IntWW 91*
**Ding Henggao** 1931- *IntWW 91*
**Ding Jieyin** 1926- *IntWW 91*
**Ding Le Tunn** *EncAmaz 91*
**Ding Ling** 1904-1986 *ConLC 68 [port], FacFETw*
**Ding Shisun** 1927- *IntWW 91*
**Ding Tingmo** *IntWW 91*
**Ding Xuesong** *IntWW 91*
**Ding Yuanhong** *IntWW 91*
**Ding**, Chen 1919- *WhoFI 92*
**Ding**, Jow-Lian 1951- *AmMWSc 92*
**Ding**, Mae Lon 1954- *WhoWest 92*
**Ding**, Victor Ding-Hai *AmMWSc 92*
**Ding-Schuler**, Erwin Oskar 1912-1945 *EncTR 91*
**Dinga**, Gustav Paul 1922- *AmMWSc 92*
**Dingell**, Christopher Dennis 1957- *WhoAmP 91*
**Dingell**, James V 1931- *AmMWSc 92*
**Dingell**, John D. 1926- *AlmAP 92 [port], WhoAmP 91*
**Dingell**, John D., Jr. *NewYTBS 91 [port]*
**Dingell**, John David, Jr. 1926- *IntWW 91, WhoMW 92*
**Dingemans**, Peter George Valentin 1935- *Who 92*
**Dinger**, Ann St Clair 1945- *AmMWSc 92*
**Dinger**, John Russell 1952- *WhoAmP 91*
**Dinger**, Marvin L 1921- *WhoAmP 91*
**Dinges**, David Francis 1949- *AmMWSc 92*
**Dinges**, Richard Allen 1945- *WhoFI 92, WhoWest 92*
**Dingle**, Albert Nelson 1916- *AmMWSc 92*
**Dingle**, Allan Douglas 1936- *AmMWSc 92*
**Dingle**, Charles H 1924- *WhoAmP 91*
**Dingle**, Edwin John 1881-1972 *RelLAm 91*
**Dingle**, Graeme 1945- *WrDr 92*
**Dingle**, John Thomas 1927- *Who 92*
**Dingle**, Raymond 1935- *AmMWSc 92*
**Dingle**, Richard Douglas Hugh 1936- *AmMWSc 92*
**Dingle**, Richard William 1918- *AmMWSc 92*
**Dingle**, Robert Balson 1926- *Who 92*
**Dingle**, Thomas Walter 1936- *AmMWSc 92*
**Dingledine**, Raymond J 1948- *AmMWSc 92*
**Dingledy**, David Peter 1919- *AmMWSc 92*
**Dingley**, Glen Martin 1961- *WhoEnt 92*
**Dingman**, Charles Wesley, II 1932- *AmMWSc 92*
**Dingman**, Douglas Wayne 1953- *AmMWSc 92*
**Dingman**, Earl Richard 1951- *WhoEnt 92*
**Dingman**, Jane Van Zandt 1931- *AmMWSc 92*
**Dingman**, Maurice J. 1914- *WhoRel 92*
**Dingman**, Michael David 1931- *WhoFI 92, WhoWest 92*
**Dingman**, Richard B 1935- *WhoAmP 91*
**Dingman**, Stanley Lawrence 1939- *AmMWSc 92*
**Dings**, Fred *DrAPF 91*
**Dingus**, Ronald Shane 1938- *AmMWSc 92*
**Dingwall**, Baroness *Who 92*
**Dingwall**, Craig David 1956- *WhoAmL 92*
**Dingwall**, John James 1907- *Who 92*
**Dingwall**, Kenneth 1938- *TwCPaSc*
**Dingwall-Smith**, Ronald Alfred 1917- *Who 92*
**Dingwell**, Everett W. 1931- *WhoWest 92*
**Dingwell**, Joyce 1912- *WrDr 92*
**Dinhofer**, Alfred D. 1930- *WrDr 92*
**Dinhut**, Patrice *WhoEnt 92*
**Dini**, Joseph Edward, Jr 1929- *WhoAmP 91*
**Dini Ahmed**, Ahmed 1932- *IntWW 91*
**Dinielli**, Philip M. 1958- *WhoFI 92*
**Dininni**, Rudolph 1926- *WhoAmP 91*
**Dinitz**, Simcha 1929- *IntWW 91*
**Dinizulu**, Yao Opare d1991 *NewYTBS 91*
**Dinkel**, Ernest 1894- *TwCPaSc*
**Dinkel**, James Richardson 1952- *WhoRel 92*
**Dinkel**, Michael 1905-1983 *TwCPaSc*
**Dinkel Keet**, Emmy G.M. 1908- *TwCPaSc*
**Dinkelspiel**, Paul Gaines 1935- *WhoFI 92, WhoWest 92*
**Dinkin**, Anthony David 1944- *Who 92*
**Dinkins**, Carol Eggert 1945- *WhoAmL 92*
**Dinkins**, David 1927- *IntWW 91, WhoAmP 91*
**Dinkins**, David N. *NewYTBS 91 [port]*
**Dinkins**, David N. 1927- *WhoBlA 92*
**Dinkins**, Gordon Scott 1956- *WhoRel 92*
**Dinkins**, Reed Leon 1938- *AmMWSc 92*
**Dinkins**, Thomas Allen, III 1946- *WhoMW 92*
**Dinkins**, William Harvey, Jr. d1991 *NewYTBS 91 [port]*
**Dinkov**, Vasily Alexandrovich 1924- *IntWW 91*
**Dinman**, Bertram David 1925- *AmMWSc 92*
**Dinneen**, Gerald Paul 1924- *AmMWSc 92*
**Dinneen**, Gerald Uel 1913- *AmMWSc 92*
**Dinner**, Alan 1944- *AmMWSc 92*
**Dinner**, Janice Marie 1957- *WhoAmL 92*
**Dinner**, Lucy H. Fried 1960- *WhoRel 92*
**Dinnerstein**, Leonard 1934- *IntAu&W 91, WrDr 92*
**Dinniman**, Andrew Eric 1944- *WhoAmP 91, WhoFI 92*
**Dinning**, James Smith 1922- *AmMWSc 92*
**Dinning**, Woodford Wyndham, Jr. 1954- *WhoAmL 92*
**Dinninger**, Donald Harry 1946- *WhoRel 92*
**Dino**, Guia 1938- *WhoEnt 92*
**Di Noia**, Joseph Augustine 1943- *WhoRel 92*
**Di Nola**, Raffaello 1912- *IntWW 91*
**Dinolfo**, Richard Henry 1948- *WhoFI 92*
**Dinos**, Nicholas 1934- *AmMWSc 92, WhoMW 92*
**DiNovis**, Stephen Edward 1953- *WhoFI 92*
**DiNovo**, Theresa Christine 1958- *WhoMW 92*
**Dinsdale**, Randall Eugene 1953- *WhoFI 92*
**Dinsdale**, Reece *ConTFT 9*
**Dinsdale**, Richard Lewis 1907- *Who 92*
**Dinse**, Gregg Ernest 1954- *AmMWSc 92*
**Dinse**, John Merrell 1925- *WhoAmL 92*
**Dinsmoor**, Kim Owen 1954- *WhoFI 92*
**Dinsmore**, Bruce Heasley 1915- *AmMWSc 92*
**Dinsmore**, Charles Earle 1947- *AmMWSc 92*
**Dinsmore**, Howard Livingstone 1921- *AmMWSc 92*
**Dinsmore**, James Jay 1942- *AmMWSc 92*
**Dinsmore**, Jonathan H 1961- *AmMWSc 92*
**Dinsmore**, Philip Wade 1942- *WhoWest 92*
**Dinstel**, Edward R 1954- *WhoIns 92*
**Dintenfass**, Mark *DrAPF 91*
**Dintenfass**, Mark 1941- *WrDr 92*
**Dinter**, Artur 1876-1948 *EncTR 91*
**Dinter Brown**, Ludmila 1949- *AmMWSc 92*
**Dintzis**, Howard Marvin 1927- *AmMWSc 92*
**Dintzis**, Renee Zlochover *AmMWSc 92*
**Dinulescu**, Horia Alexander 1941- *WhoMW 92*
**DiNunno**, Cecil Malmberg 1949- *AmMWSc 92*
**DiNunzio**, James E 1950- *AmMWSc 92*
**Dinus**, Ronald John 1940- *AmMWSc 92*
**Dinusson**, William Erling 1920- *AmMWSc 92*
**Dinwiddie**, James 1837-1907 *DcNCBi 2*
**Dinwiddie**, James Harold 1937- *WhoFI 92*
**Dinwiddie**, Joseph Gray, Jr 1922- *AmMWSc 92*
**Dinwiddy**, Thomas Lutwyche 1905- *Who 92*
**Diocletian** 240?-316 *EncEarC [port]*
**Diodore of Tarsus** d390? *EncEarC*
**Diodoros I** 1923- *WhoRel 92*
**Diogenes**, Marvin *DrAPF 91*
**DioGuardi**, John 1915-1979 *FacFETw*
**DioGuardi**, Joseph John 1940- *WhoAmP 91*
**Dioguardi**, Mark David 1956- *WhoAmP 91*
**Diokno**, Ananias Cornejo 1942- *AmMWSc 92*
**Diomede**, Matthew *DrAPF 91*
**Dion** 1939- *NewAmDM*
**Dion**, Andre R 1926- *AmMWSc 92*
**Dion**, Arnold Silva 1939- *AmMWSc 92*
**Dion**, Gerard 1912- *IntWW 91*
**Dion**, John Kenneth 1955- *WhoFI 92*
**Dion**, Philip Joseph 1944- *WhoFI 92, WhoWest 92*
**Dion**, Robert L 1932- *WhoIns 92*
**Dion**, Thomas Raymond 1946- *WhoFI 92*
**Dionisije**, Bishop 1898-1979 *RelLAm 91*
**Dionisio**, William Pasquale 1933- *WhoWest 92*
**Dionisotti-Casalone**, Carlo 1908- *Who 92*
**Dionne**, Albert J 1946- *WhoAmP 91*
**Dionne**, Arthur Francis 1937- *WhoAmL 92*
**Dionne**, Gary S 1953- *WhoAmP 91*
**Dionne**, Gerald Francis 1935- *AmMWSc 92*
**Dionne**, Jean-Claude 1935- *AmMWSc 92*
**Dionne**, Joseph Gerard 1919- *WhoRel 92*
**Dionne**, Joseph Lewis 1933- *IntWW 91, WhoFI 92*
**Dionne**, Paul R 1951- *WhoAmP 91*
**Dionne**, Peggy A. 1958- *WhoFI 92*
**Dionne**, Raymond A 1946- *AmMWSc 92*
**Dionysia** *EncAmaz 91*
**Dionysius Exiguus** *EncEarC*
**Dionysius of Alexandria** d264? *EncEarC*
**Dionysius of Corinth** *EncEarC*
**Dionysius of Rome** *EncEarC*
**Dionysius The Areopagite**, Pseudo- *EncEarC*
**Diop**, Majhemout 1922- *IntWW 91*
**Dior**, Christian 1905-1957 *DcTwDes, FacFETw*
**Dioramananda** *DrAPF 91*
**Diori**, Hamani 1916-1989 *FacFETw*
**Diorio**, Alfred Frank 1933- *AmMWSc 92*
**D'Iorio**, Antoine 1925- *AmMWSc 92, IntWW 91*
**Diorio**, Margaret *DrAPF 91*
**DiOrio**, Robert Michael 1947- *WhoAmL 92*
**Diosady**, Levente Laszlo 1943- *AmMWSc 92*
**Dioscorus** d454 *EncEarC*
**Diosy**, Andrew 1924- *AmMWSc 92*
**Diotalevi**, Robert Nicholas 1959- *WhoAmL 92*
**Diouf**, Abdou 1935- *IntWW 91*
**Diouf**, Jacques 1938- *IntWW 91*
**DiPace**, Steven B. 1948- *WhoAmL 92*
**DiPalma**, Daniel 1958- *WhoWest 92*
**Di Palma**, Joseph Alphonse 1931- *WhoWest 92*
**DiPalma**, Joseph Rupert 1916- *AmMWSc 92*
**DiPalma**, Ray *DrAPF 91*
**Di Palma**, Vera June 1931- *Who 92*
**Di Paola**, Daniel Joseph 1953- *WhoEnt 92*
**Di Paola**, Jane Walsh 1917- *AmMWSc 92*
**Di Paola**, Robert Arnold 1933- *AmMWSc 92*
**DiPaolo**, Joseph Amedeo 1924- *AmMWSc 92*
**Di Paolo**, Rocco John *AmMWSc 92*
**Di Pasquale**, Emanuel *DrAPF 91*
**DiPasquale**, Gene 1932- *AmMWSc 92*
**DiPasquale**, Maria Teresa 1954- *WhoAmL 92*
**DiPaula**, Anthony Joseph 1959- *WhoAmL 92*
**Dipboye**, Larry Keith 1939- *WhoRel 92*
**Dipboye**, Marilyn Joyce 1938- *WhoMW 92*
**DiPeri**, Philip T. 1943- *WhoFI 92*
**DiPerna**, Mary *WhoFI 92*
**DiPerna**, Paula 1949- *WhoEnt 92*
**DiPersio**, Douglas John 1958- *WhoFI 92*
**DiPesa**, Dorothy Frances 1953- *WhoFI 92*
**DiPiazza**, Michael Charles 1953- *WhoFI 92*
**DiPiero**, Robert J. 1951- *WhoEnt 92*
**Di Pietra**, Rosemary *IntMPA 92*
**DiPietro**, Anthony M, Jr 1935- *WhoAmP 91*
**DiPietro**, Carmela M 1925- *WhoAmP 91*
**Di Pietro**, David Louis 1932- *AmMWSc 92*
**DiPietro**, Dominic 1905- *WhoAmP 91*
**DiPietro**, Patrick Thomas *WhoAmL 92*
**DiPietro**, Ralph Anthony 1942- *WhoFI 92*
**Di Pietro**, Robert Joseph 1932- *WrDr 92*
**Di Pietro**, Rocco 1949- *WhoEnt 92*
**Di Pietro**, Rudolph 1931- *WhoFI 92*
**DiPietro**, Santo *WhoAmP 91*
**DiPietro**, Thomas Joseph, Jr. 1955- *WhoFI 92*
**Dipilla**, Richard Angelo 1956- *WhoEnt 92*
**DiPinto**, Joseph G 1932- *WhoAmP 91*
**Di Pippo**, Ascanio G 1932- *AmMWSc 92*
**DiPippo**, Ronald 1940- *AmMWSc 92*
**DiPirro**, Michael James 1951- *AmMWSc 92*
**DiPirro**, Richard Brian 1965- *WhoEnt 92*
**Diplock**, Anthony Tytherleigh 1935- *Who 92*
**Dipner**, Randy W 1949- *AmMWSc 92*
**Dipner**, Randy Wayne 1949- *WhoWest 92*
**Dipoko**, Mbella Sonne 1936- *LiExTwC*
**DiPolvere**, Edward John 1929- *WhoFI 92*
**Dippel**, Jack Victor 1942- *WhoMW 92*
**Dippel**, William Alan 1926- *AmMWSc 92*
**Dippell**, Ruth Virginia 1920- *AmMWSc 92*
**Dipple**, Anthony 1940- *AmMWSc 92*
**D'Ippolito**, Nancy E. S. 1950- *WhoRel 92*
**Dipprey**, Duane F 1929- *AmMWSc 92*
**Diprete**, Edward D. 1934- *IntWW 91*
**DiPrete**, Edward Daniel 1934- *WhoAmP 91*
**Di Prima**, Diane *DrAPF 91*
**di Prima**, Diane 1934- *ConPo 91, WrDr 92*
**DiPrima**, Lawrence 1910- *WhoAmP 91*

**Di Prima,** Stephanie Marie 1952- *WhoMW 92*
**Di Primo,** Marie Ann 1952- *WhoAmL 92*
**Diprisco,** Joseph *DrAPF 91*
**Dirac,** P. A. M. *ConAu 133*
**Dirac,** Paul A. M. 1902-1984 *ConAu 133*
**Dirac,** Paul Adrien Maurice 1902-1984 *FacFETw, WhoNob 90*
**Diracles,** John Michael, Jr. 1944- *WhoFI 92*
**Dirck,** Edwin L 1928- *WhoAmP 91*
**Dirckx,** John H 1938- *AmMWSc 92*
**Dire Straits** *NewAmDM*
**Director,** Stephen William 1943- *AmMWSc 92*
**Di Rienzi,** Joseph 1947- *AmMWSc 92*
**Di Rienzo,** Frederick J 1948- *WhoIns 92*
**Dirige,** Ofelia Villa 1940- *AmMWSc 92*
**Dirir,** Mogue Hassan 1937- *WhoRel 92*
**Dirk,** Jan *ScFEYrs*
**Dirks,** A Stephen 1943- *WhoAmP 91*
**Dirks,** Brinton Marlo 1920- *AmMWSc 92*
**Dirks,** David McCormick 1941- *WhoFI 92, WhoWest 92*
**Dirks,** John Herbert 1933- *AmMWSc 92*
**Dirks,** Leslie C 1936- *AmMWSc 92*
**Dirks,** Richard Allen 1937- *AmMWSc 92*
**Dirkse,** Thedford Preston 1915- *AmMWSc 92*
**Dirksen,** Christiaan 1936- *AmMWSc 92*
**Dirksen,** Ellen Roter 1929- *AmMWSc 92*
**Dirksen,** Everett 1896-1969 *FacFETw [port]*
**Dirksen,** Everett McKinley 1896-1969 *AmPolLe*
**Dirksen,** Gebhard 1929- *IntWW 91*
**Dirksen,** Herbert von 1882-1955 *EncTR 91 [port]*
**Dirksen,** Thomas Reed 1931- *AmMWSc 92*
**Dirlam,** John Philip 1943- *AmMWSc 92*
**Dirlewanger,** Oskar 1895-1945 *EncTR 91*
**Di Roberto,** Samuel Joseph 1937- *WhoFI 92*
**Dirokpa,** Balufuga *WhoRel 92*
**Diroll,** David John 1951- *WhoMW 92*
**Di Rosa,** Herve 1959- *WorArt 1980*
**Dirr,** John Charles 1949- *WhoEnt 92*
**DiRugeris,** Mark Andrew 1957- *WhoAmP 91*
**DiRuscio,** Lawrence William 1941- *WhoFI 92, WhoWest 92*
**Dirvin,** Gerald Vincent 1937- *WhoFI 92*
**D'Isa,** Frank Angelo 1921- *AmMWSc 92*
**Di Sabato,** Giovanni 1929- *AmMWSc 92*
**DiSabato,** Mary Keating Croce *WhoAmP 91*
**Disalvatore,** Julie 1966- *WhoEnt 92*
**Di Salvo,** Angelo Jesus 1944- *WhoMW 92*
**DiSalvo,** Arthur F 1932- *AmMWSc 92*
**DiSalvo,** Beverly Jane 1952- *WhoWest 92*
**DiSalvo,** Charles Richard 1948- *WhoAmL 92*
**DiSalvo,** Francis Joseph, Jr 1944- *AmMWSc 92*
**DiSalvo,** Frank Paul 1946- *WhoEnt 92*
**Di Salvo,** Joseph 1935- *AmMWSc 92*
**DiSalvo,** Mark Sebastian 1954- *WhoAmP 91*
**Di Salvo,** Nicholas Armand 1920- *AmMWSc 92*
**DiSalvo,** Thomas Joseph 1953- *WhoAmL 92*
**DiSalvo,** Walter A 1920- *AmMWSc 92*
**DiSandro,** Domenic A, III *WhoAmP 91*
**DiSandro,** Edmond A. 1932- *WhoAmL 92*
**Di Sant'Agnese,** Paul Emilio Artom 1914- *AmMWSc 92*
**DiSanti,** Alexander Donald 1958- *WhoAmL 92*
**DiSanti,** Benjamin Michael 1956- *WhoMW 92*
**DiSantis,** Linda Katherine 1946- *WhoAmL 92*
**DiSanza,** Richard Amico 1931- *WhoMW 92*
**Di Sanzo,** Carmine Pasqualino 1933- *AmMWSc 92*
**Disbrey,** William Daniel 1912- *Who 92*
**Disbrow,** Arthur Ray 1932- *WhoFI 92, WhoMW 92*
**Disbrow,** Michael Ray 1959- *WhoFI 92, WhoMW 92*
**Disbrow,** Richard Edwin 1930- *IntWW 91, WhoFI 92, WhoMW 92*
**Disbrow,** Sidney Arden, Jr. 1946- *WhoMW 92*
**DiScala,** Dominick John *WhoEnt 92*
**Disch,** Hans M. 1950- *WhoMW 92*
**Disch,** Raymond L 1932- *AmMWSc 92*
**Disch,** Thomas M. *DrAPF 91*
**Disch,** Thomas M. 1940- *ConAu 36NR, ConPo 91, IntAu&W 91, TwCSFW 91, WrDr 92*
**Disch,** Thomas Michael 1940- *WhoEnt 92*
**Disch,** Tom *ConAu 36NR*
**Discher,** Clarence August 1912- *AmMWSc 92*
**Discher,** Gerald Roger 1929- *WhoRel 92*
**Discipulus** *AmPeW*
**Disend,** Michael *DrAPF 91*
**Dishart,** Kenneth Thomas 1931- *AmMWSc 92*
**Dishart,** Stephen Kenneth 1958- *WhoEnt 92*
**Dishell,** Walter David 1939- *WhoEnt 92*
**Disher,** David Alan 1944- *WhoAmL 92*
**Disher,** Eve 1894- *TwCPaSc*
**Disher,** Spencer C., III 1957- *WhoBlA 92*
**Disheroon,** Fred Russell 1931- *WhoAmL 92*
**Dishong,** George William 1933- *WhoAmL 92*
**Dishy,** Bob *IntMPA 92*
**Disimile,** Peter John 1950- *WhoMW 92*
**DiSimone,** Rita Louise *WhoAmP 91*
**Di Simone,** Robert Nicholas 1937- *WhoMW 92*
**Disinger,** John Franklin 1930- *AmMWSc 92*
**Diskant,** Gregory L. 1948- *WhoAmL 92*
**Disko,** Mildred Anne 1927- *AmMWSc 92*
**Disley,** John Ivor 1928- *Who 92*
**d'Isly,** Georges *ConAu 35NR*
**Dismore,** Roger Eugene 1950- *WhoEnt 92*
**Dismorr,** Jessica 1885-1939 *TwCPaSc*
**Dismorr,** Michael C.S. 1951- *WhoFI 92*
**Dismuke,** Leroy 1937- *WhoBlA 92*
**Dismuke,** Mary Eunice 1942- *WhoBlA 92*
**Dismuke,** William Louis 1955- *WhoAmL 92*
**Dismukes,** Edward Brock 1927- *AmMWSc 92*
**Dismukes,** Gerard Charles 1949- *AmMWSc 92*
**Dismukes,** Robert Key 1943- *AmMWSc 92*
**Disnard,** George F 1923- *WhoAmP 91*
**Disner,** Eliot Gordon 1947- *WhoAmL 92*
**Disney,** Diane Marie *WhoFI 92*
**Disney,** Harold Vernon 1907- *Who 92*
**Disney,** Kevin Alan 1953- *WhoWest 92*
**Disney,** Michael George 1955- *WhoWest 92*
**Disney,** Ralph L 1928- *AmMWSc 92*
**Disney,** Raymond Evans 1953- *WhoEnt 92*
**Disney,** Roy E. 1930- *IntMPA 92*
**Disney,** Roy Edward 1930- *WhoEnt 92, WhoWest 92*
**Disney,** Walt d1966 *LesBEnT 92*
**Disney,** Walt 1901-1966 *BenetAL 91, FacFETw [port], RComAH*
**Dispeker,** Thea *WhoEnt 92*
**Di Spigna,** Tony 1943- *WhoEnt 92*
**DiSpirito,** Alan Angelo 1954- *AmMWSc 92*
**DiSpirito,** Robert George, Jr 1959- *WhoAmP 91*
**Disraeli,** Benjamin 1804-1881 *RfGEnL 91*
**D'Israeli,** Isaac 1766-1848 *DcLB 107 [port]*
**Diss,** Eileen 1931- *Who 92*
**Dissanayake,** Chandra *WhoWest 92*
**Disser,** Maria-Elena 1946- *WhoHisp 92*
**Dissette,** Alyce Marie 1952- *WhoEnt 92*
**Disston,** Harry 1899- *WhoAmP 91*
**Distant Eagle** 1954- *WhoRel 92*
**DiStefano,** Ana Maria 1961- *WhoHisp 92*
**Di Stefano,** Giuseppe 1921- *FacFETw, NewAmDM*
**Di Stefano,** Henry Saverio 1920- *AmMWSc 92*
**DiStefano,** Joseph John, III 1938- *AmMWSc 92*
**Distefano,** Peter Andrew 1939- *WhoFI 92, WhoWest 92*
**DiStefano,** Thomas Herman 1942- *AmMWSc 92*
**DiStefano,** Victor 1924- *AmMWSc 92*
**di Stefano Lauthe,** Alfredo 1926- *FacFETw*
**Distel,** Sacha 1933- *IntWW 91*
**Distelhorst,** Craig Tipton 1941- *WhoFI 92*
**Distelhorst,** Garis Fred 1942- *WhoMW 92*
**Disterhoft,** John Francis 1944- *AmMWSc 92*
**Distler,** Charles 1915- *WhoRel 92*
**Distler,** Hugo 1908-1942 *NewAmDM*
**Distler,** Jack, Jr 1928- *AmMWSc 92*
**Distler,** Jim T 1934- *WhoAmP 91*
**Distler,** Raymond Jewel 1930- *AmMWSc 92*
**DiTaranto,** Rocco A 1926- *AmMWSc 92*
**Ditch,** Michael Terry 1944- *WhoFI 92*
**Ditchek,** Brian Michael 1951- *AmMWSc 92*
**Ditchoff,** Pamela *DrAPF 91*
**Ditfurth,** Jutta 1951- *IntWW 91*
**Dithridge,** Betty 1920- *WhoWest 92*
**Ditka,** Michael Keller 1939- *WhoMW 92*
**Ditkowsky,** Kenneth K. 1936- *WhoAmL 92*
**Ditler,** Joseph Henry 1951- *WhoEnt 92*
**Ditlev-Simonsen,** Per 1932- *IntWW 91*
**Ditmars,** John David 1943- *AmMWSc 92, WhoMW 92*
**Ditmore,** Michael Conrad 1943- *WhoWest 92*
**Dito,** John Allen 1935- *WhoAmL 92*
**DiTolla,** Alfred W. 1926- *IntMPA 92*
**DiTrani,** Louis John *WhoAmL 92*
**D'Itri,** Frank M 1933- *AmMWSc 92*
**Ditsky,** John *DrAPF 91*
**Ditson,** Oliver *NewAmDM*
**Dittberner,** Phillip Lynn 1944- *AmMWSc 92*
**Dittenhafer,** Brian Douglas 1942- *WhoFI 92*
**Ditter,** John William, Jr. 1921- *WhoAmL 92*
**Ditterich,** Eric Keith von 1913- *WhoRel 92*
**Ditterich,** Keith 1913- *WrDr 92*
**Ditterline,** Raymond Lee 1941- *AmMWSc 92*
**Dittersdorf,** Carl Ditters von 1739-1799 *NewAmDM*
**Dittert,** Lewis William 1934- *AmMWSc 92*
**Dittes,** James Edward 1926- *WhoRel 92*
**Dittfach,** John Harland 1918- *AmMWSc 92*
**Dittman,** Deborah Ruth 1932- *WhoWest 92*
**Dittman,** Frank W 1918- *AmMWSc 92*
**Dittman,** Mark Allen 1950- *WhoMW 92*
**Dittman,** Richard Henry 1937- *AmMWSc 92*
**Dittman,** Stevan Craig 1949- *WhoAmL 92*
**Dittmann,** John Paul 1948- *AmMWSc 92*
**Dittmar,** Kurt 1891-1959 *EncTR 91*
**Dittmar,** Robert L 1931- *WhoAmP 91*
**Dittmer,** Donald Charles 1927- *AmMWSc 92*
**Dittmer,** Howard James 1910- *AmMWSc 92*
**Dittmer,** John Avery 1939- *WhoMW 92*
**Dittmer,** John Edward 1939- *AmMWSc 92*
**Dittmer,** John Mark 1959- *WhoMW 92, WhoRel 92*
**Dittmer,** Karl 1914- *AmMWSc 92*
**Dittmer,** Terrance H. 1945- *WhoAmL 92*
**Dittner,** Peter Fred 1937- *AmMWSc 92*
**Ditto,** John Kane, Jr 1944- *WhoAmP 91*
**Ditto,** Larry Dean 1940- *WhoMW 92*
**Ditton,** James *IntAu&W 91X, WrDr 92*
**Dittrich,** Raymond Joseph 1932- *WhoAmL 92*
**Dityatin,** Aleksandr 1957- *IntWW 91*
**Ditzel,** Nana 1923- *DcTwDes*
**Ditzen,** Rudolf *EncTR 91*
**Ditzler,** James 1933- *ConAu 135*
**Diuguid,** John Powell 1932- *WhoAmL 92*
**Diuguid,** Lewis Walter 1955- *WhoBlA 92*
**Diuguid,** Lincoln I. 1917- *WhoBlA 92*
**Diuguid,** Lincoln Isaiah 1917- *AmMWSc 92*
**DiUlio,** Albert Joseph 1943- *WhoMW 92, WhoRel 92*
**Divadeenam,** Mundrathi 1935- *AmMWSc 92*
**Divale,** William T. 1942- *WrDr 92*
**Diveglia,** Archie Vincent 1946- *WhoAmL 92*
**Divelbiss,** Richard Irwin 1943- *WhoMW 92*
**Diveley,** William Russell 1921- *AmMWSc 92*
**Dively,** Charles Brian 1950- *WhoMW 92*
**Dively,** Emory Kevin 1956- *WhoRel 92*
**Dively,** John A., Jr. 1958- *WhoAmL 92*
**Dively,** Richard Harold 1925- *WhoMW 92*
**Diven,** Benjamin Clinton 1919- *AmMWSc 92*
**Diven,** Warren Field 1931- *AmMWSc 92*
**Diver,** Colin S. 1943- *WhoAmL 92*
**Diver,** Leslie Charles 1899- *Who 92*
**Diver,** Richard Boyer, Jr 1951- *AmMWSc 92*
**Diverres,** Armel Hugh 1914- *Who 92*
**Divers,** Shirley Anne 1955- *WhoEnt 92*
**Divett,** Robert Thomas 1925- *AmMWSc 92*
**Divgi,** Chaitanya R 1953- *AmMWSc 92*
**Divich,** Duane G 1937- *WhoIns 92*
**Divilbiss,** James Leroy 1930- *AmMWSc 92*
**Divin,** Sheryl Ann 1958- *WhoEnt 92*
**DiVincenzo,** George D 1941- *AmMWSc 92*
**Divine,** Charles Hamman 1945- *WhoWest 92*
**Divine,** David *IntAu&W 91X*
**Divine,** James R 1939- *AmMWSc 92*
**Divine,** James Robert 1939- *WhoWest 92*
**Divine,** John Francis 1830-1909 *DcNCBi 2*
**Divine,** Major Jealous 1877?-1965 *RelLAm 91*
**Divine,** Robert A 1929- *IntAu&W 91, WrDr 92*
**Divine,** Theodore Emry 1943- *WhoWest 92*
**Diviney,** Craig David 1953- *WhoAmL 92*
**Divinsky,** Nathan Joseph 1925- *AmMWSc 92, WhoWest 92*
**DiVirgilio,** Albert V *WhoAmP 91*
**Divis,** Allan Francis 1946- *AmMWSc 92*
**Divis,** Rita W. *WhoHisp 92*
**Divis,** Roy Richard 1928- *AmMWSc 92*
**DiVita,** Merle R. 1952- *WhoFI 92*
**Divjak,** August A 1949- *AmMWSc 92*
**Divok,** Mario *DrAPF 91*
**Divok,** Mario J. 1947- *IntAu&W 91*
**Divola,** John 1949- *WhoWest 92*
**Diwan,** Bhalchandra Apparao 1937- *AmMWSc 92*
**Diwan,** Joyce Johnson 1940- *AmMWSc 92*
**Diwan,** Ravinder Mohan 1945- *AmMWSc 92*
**Diwan,** Romesh Kumar 1933- *WhoFI 92*
**Dix,** Alan Michael 1922- *Who 92*
**Dix,** Bernard Hubert 1925- *Who 92*
**Dix,** Beulah Marie 1876-1970 *ReelWom*
**Dix,** David *WhoAmP 91*
**Dix,** David Arthur 1932- *WhoAmP 91*
**Dix,** Dorothea 1802-1887 *HanAmWH, RComAH*
**Dix,** Dorothy *BenetAL 91*
**Dix,** Douglas Edward 1944- *AmMWSc 92*
**Dix,** Geoffrey Herbert 1922- *Who 92*
**Dix,** Gerald Bennett 1926- *Who 92*
**Dix,** Gregory 1901-1952 *FacFETw*
**Dix,** James Seward 1932- *AmMWSc 92*
**Dix,** Otto 1891-1969 *EncTR 91 [port], FacFETw, ModArCr 2 [port]*
**Dix,** Rollin Cumming 1936- *AmMWSc 92*
**Dix,** Victor Wilkinson *Who 92*
**Dixey,** John 1926- *Who 92*
**Dixey,** Paul 1915- *Who 92*
**Dixey,** Paul Arthur Groser 1915- *IntWW 91*
**Dixie Hummingbirds,** The *NewAmDM*
**Dixie,** George Constantine 1938- *WhoAmL 92*
**Dixit,** Ajit Suresh 1950- *AmMWSc 92*
**Dixit,** Avinash Kamalakar 1944- *Who 92*
**Dixit,** Balwant N 1933- *AmMWSc 92*
**Dixit,** Jyotindranath 1936- *IntWW 91*
**Dixit,** Madhu Sudan 1942- *AmMWSc 92*
**Dixit,** Padmakar Kashinath 1921- *AmMWSc 92*
**Dixit,** Rakesh 1958- *AmMWSc 92*
**Dixit,** Saryu N 1937- *AmMWSc 92*
**Dixit,** Sudhir S 1951- *AmMWSc 92*
**Dixon** *Who 92*
**Dixon,** Alan 1927- *WhoBlA 92*
**Dixon,** Alan J. 1927- *AlmAP 92 [port]*
**Dixon,** Alan John 1927- *IntWW 91, WhoAmP 91, WhoMW 92*
**Dixon,** Amzi Clarence 1854-1925 *DcNCBi 2, RelLAm 91*
**Dixon,** Andrew Derart 1925- *AmMWSc 92*
**Dixon,** Andrew Douglas 1958- *WhoFI 92*
**Dixon,** Anthony Philip G. *Who 92*
**Dixon,** Archibald 1802-1876 *DcNCBi 2*
**Dixon,** Arminius Gray 1870-1962 *DcNCBi 2*
**Dixon,** Arrington Liggins 1942- *WhoAmP 91, WhoBlA 92*
**Dixon,** Arthur Edward 1938- *AmMWSc 92*
**Dixon,** Barbara *IntMPA 92*
**Dixon,** Barbara Boylan 1941- *WhoEnt 92*
**Dixon,** Barry Percy 1950- *WhoRel 92*
**Dixon,** Benjamin 1939- *WhoBlA 92*
**Dixon,** Benjamin Franklin 1846-1910 *DcNCBi 2*
**Dixon,** Benjamin Rollin 1930- *WhoAmP 91*
**Dixon,** Bernard 1938- *Who 92, WrDr 92*
**Dixon,** Bernard Tunbridge 1928- *Who 92*
**Dixon,** Billy Gene 1935- *WhoMW 92*
**Dixon,** Blanche V. *WhoBlA 92*
**Dixon,** Brenda Joyce 1954- *WhoBlA 92*
**Dixon,** Brian Gilbert 1951- *AmMWSc 92*
**Dixon,** Carl Franklin 1926- *AmMWSc 92*
**Dixon,** Charles 1858-1926 *ScFEYrs*
**Dixon,** Charles 1872-1934 *TwCPaSc*
**Dixon,** Clay *WhoAmP 91*
**Dixon,** Dabney White 1949- *AmMWSc 92*
**Dixon,** David Jeremy 1939- *IntWW 91, Who 92*
**Dixon,** Dean 1915-1976 *NewAmDM*
**Dixon,** Dennis Michael 1951- *AmMWSc 92*
**Dixon,** Diane 1964- *BlkOlyM*
**Dixon,** Donald 1929- *Who 92*
**Dixon,** Donald Keith 1940- *WhoRel 92*
**Dixon,** Donald Ray *NewYTBS 91 [port]*
**Dixon,** Donna 1957- *IntMPA 92*
**Dixon,** Dorsey Murdock 1897-1968 *DcNCBi 2*
**Dixon,** Dougal 1947- *IntAu&W 91, WrDr 92*
**Dixon,** Dwight R 1919- *AmMWSc 92*
**Dixon,** Earl, Jr 1937- *AmMWSc 92*
**Dixon,** Edmond Dale 1936- *AmMWSc 92*
**Dixon,** Elisabeth Ann 1944- *AmMWSc 92*
**Dixon,** Elizabeth Delia *DcNCBi 2*
**Dixon,** Ernest H. 1952- *WhoWest 92*
**Dixon,** Ernest Thomas, Jr. 1922- *WhoBlA 92, WhoRel 92*
**Dixon,** Eula Louisa 1872-1921 *DcNCBi 2*
**Dixon,** Eustace A. 1934- *WrDr 92*
**Dixon,** Floyd Eugene 1964- *WhoBlA 92*
**Dixon,** Frank James 1920- *AmMWSc 92, IntWW 91*
**Dixon,** Franklin W. *SmATA 67*
**Dixon,** Freddie Brown, Sr. 1944- *WhoRel 92*
**Dixon,** Gayle Inez *WhoEnt 92*

**Dixon,** Gemma Barbara 1951- *WhoHisp 92*
**Dixon,** George 1933- *WhoBlA 92*
**Dixon,** George David 1936- *WhoMW 92*
**Dixon,** George Sumter, Jr 1938- *AmMWSc 92*
**Dixon,** Gerald George 1955- *WhoAmL 92*
**Dixon,** Gordon H 1930- *AmMWSc 92*
**Dixon,** Gordon Henry 1930- *IntWW 91, Who 92*
**Dixon,** Guy Holford 1902- *Who 92*
**Dixon,** Hanford 1958- *WhoBlA 92*
**Dixon,** Harry 1861-1942 *TwCPaSc*
**Dixon,** Harry Dale, Jr 1942- *WhoAmP 91*
**Dixon,** Harry Donival 1925- *WhoAmP 91*
**Dixon,** Harry S 1910- *AmMWSc 92*
**Dixon,** Helen Roberta 1927- *AmMWSc 92*
**Dixon,** Henry 1750?-1782 *DcNCBi 2*
**Dixon,** Henry Marshall 1929- *AmMWSc 92*
**Dixon,** Hortense 1926- *WhoBlA 92*
**Dixon,** Howard Briten 1903-1961 *DcNCBi 2*
**Dixon,** Hugh Woody 1825-1901 *DcNCBi 2*
**Dixon,** Irma Muse 1952- *WhoAmP 91, WhoBlA 92*
**Dixon,** Isaiah, Jr 1922- *WhoAmP 91, WhoBlA 92*
**Dixon,** Ivan N. 1931- *WhoBlA 92*
**Dixon,** J. Melvin 1939- *WhoBlA 92*
**Dixon,** Jack Edward 1943- *AmMWSc 92*
**Dixon,** Jack Richard 1925- *AmMWSc 92*
**Dixon,** Jack Shawcross 1918- *Who 92*
**Dixon,** James Anthony 1967- *WhoBlA 92*
**Dixon,** James Edward 1941- *AmMWSc 92*
**Dixon,** James Francis Peter *AmMWSc 92*
**Dixon,** James George, Jr. 1922- *WhoRel 92*
**Dixon,** James Ray 1928- *AmMWSc 92*
**Dixon,** Jean T 1949- *WhoAmP 91*
**Dixon,** Jeremiah 1733-1779 *BiInAmS*
**Dixon,** Jeremy *Who 92*
**Dixon,** Jerome Wayne 1955- *WhoAmL 92*
**Dixon,** Jerry B 1937- *WhoAmP 91*
**Dixon,** Jimmy 1943- *WhoBlA 92*
**Dixon,** Jo-Ann Conte 1942- *WhoFI 92*
**Dixon,** Joe Boris 1930- *AmMWSc 92*
**Dixon,** John Aldous 1923- *AmMWSc 92*
**Dixon,** John Allen, Jr 1920- *WhoAmP 91*
**Dixon,** John Charles 1931- *AmMWSc 92*
**Dixon,** John D 1924- *AmMWSc 92*
**Dixon,** John Douglas 1937- *AmMWSc 92*
**Dixon,** John E 1927- *AmMWSc 92*
**Dixon,** John Frederick 1949- *WhoBlA 92*
**Dixon,** John Fulton 1946- *WhoMW 92*
**Dixon,** John George d1990 *Who 92N*
**Dixon,** John Kenneth 1915- *WhoAmP 91*
**Dixon,** John Kent 1934- *AmMWSc 92*
**Dixon,** John M. 1938- *WhoBlA 92*
**Dixon,** John Michael Siddons 1928- *AmMWSc 92*
**Dixon,** John R 1930- *AmMWSc 92*
**Dixon,** John Wayne 1944- *WhoMW 92*
**Dixon,** John Wesley, Jr. 1919- *WhoRel 92*
**Dixon,** Jon Edmund 1928- *Who 92*
**Dixon,** Jonathan 1949- *Who 92*
**Dixon,** Joseph 1828-1883 *DcNCBi 2*
**Dixon,** Joseph Ardiff 1919- *AmMWSc 92*
**Dixon,** Joseph Moore 1867-1934 *DcNCBi 2*
**Dixon,** Juanita Clark 1936- *WhoAmP 91*
**Dixon,** Julian C. 1934- *AlmAP 92 [port], WhoAmP 91, WhoBlA 92*
**Dixon,** Julian Carey 1934- *WhoWest 92*
**Dixon,** Julian Thomas 1913- *AmMWSc 92*
**Dixon,** Katie Loosle 1925- *WhoAmP 91*
**Dixon,** Keith Lee 1921- *AmMWSc 92*
**Dixon,** Keith R 1940- *AmMWSc 92*
**Dixon,** Kendal Cartwright d1990 *Who 92N*
**Dixon,** Kenneth Herbert Morley 1929- *IntWW 91, Who 92*
**Dixon,** Kenneth Olin 1938- *WhoMW 92*
**Dixon,** Kenneth Randall 1942- *AmMWSc 92*
**Dixon,** Kent H. *DrAPF 91*
**Dixon,** Larry Dean 1942- *WhoAmP 91*
**Dixon,** Laurinda S 1948- *IntAu&W 91*
**Dixon,** Lawrence Paul 1938- *WhoFI 92*
**Dixon,** Leon Martin 1927- *WhoBlA 92*
**Dixon,** Linda Kay 1940- *AmMWSc 92*
**Dixon,** Louis Tennyson 1941- *WhoBlA 92*
**Dixon,** Lyle Junior 1924- *AmMWSc 92*
**Dixon,** Lynn R. 1947- *WhoWest 92*
**Dixon,** Margaret Rumer Haynes *Who 92*
**Dixon,** Mark D. 1955- *WhoMW 92*
**Dixon,** Marvin Porter 1938- *AmMWSc 92*
**Dixon,** Mary *EncAmaz 91*
**Dixon,** Melvin *DrAPF 91*
**Dixon,** Melvin 1950- *WrDr 92*
**Dixon,** Melvin Morgan 1955- *WhoWest 92*
**Dixon,** Melvin W. 1950- *WhoBlA 92*
**Dixon,** Michael John 1941- *AmMWSc 92*
**Dixon,** Michael Wayne 1942- *WhoEnt 92, WhoWest 92*
**Dixon,** Nancy Alena 1892-1973 *DcNCBi 2*
**Dixon,** Norman 1922- *WrDr 92*
**Dixon,** Norman Rex 1932- *AmMWSc 92*
**Dixon,** Paige *DrAPF 91, IntAu&W 91X, WrDr 92*
**Dixon,** Paul d1975 *LesBEnT 92*
**Dixon,** Paul King 1961- *AmMWSc 92*
**Dixon,** Peggy A 1928- *AmMWSc 92*
**Dixon,** Peter Stanley 1928- *AmMWSc 92*
**Dixon,** Peter Vibart 1932- *Who 92*
**Dixon,** Philip Edgar 1932- *WhoAmL 92*
**Dixon,** Piers 1928- *Who 92*
**Dixon,** Rex *IntAu&W 91X*
**Dixon,** Richard 1937- *WhoMW 92*
**Dixon,** Richard Clay *WhoBlA 92*
**Dixon,** Richard Dillard 1888-1952 *DcNCBi 2*
**Dixon,** Richard N 1938- *WhoAmP 91*
**Dixon,** Richard Nathaniel 1938- *WhoBlA 92*
**Dixon,** Richard Newland 1930- *IntWW 91, Who 92*
**Dixon,** Richard Watson 1833-1900 *RfGEnL 91*
**Dixon,** Richard Wayne 1936- *AmMWSc 92*
**Dixon,** Robert Clyde 1932- *AmMWSc 92*
**Dixon,** Robert J. 1936- *WhoMW 92*
**Dixon,** Robert Jerome, Jr 1931- *AmMWSc 92*
**Dixon,** Robert Leland 1940- *AmMWSc 92*
**Dixon,** Robert Louis 1936- *AmMWSc 92*
**Dixon,** Robert Scott 1954- *WhoFI 92*
**Dixon,** Rodney *WhoAmP 91*
**Dixon,** Roger 1930- *IntAu&W 91, WrDr 92*
**Dixon,** Roger L 1947- *AmMWSc 92*
**Dixon,** Roscoe 1949- *WhoBlA 92*
**Dixon,** Roscoe, Jr 1949- *WhoAmP 91*
**Dixon,** Ross 1942- *AmMWSc 92*
**Dixon,** Roy Laurence Cayley 1924- *Who 92*
**Dixon,** Ruth F. 1931- *WhoBlA 92*
**Dixon,** Samuel, Jr 1927- *AmMWSc 92*
**Dixon,** Samuel Gibson 1851-1918 *BiInAmS*
**Dixon,** Samuel Rozzell Ebenezer 1921- *WhoRel 92*
**Dixon,** Scott William 1953- *WhoAmL 92*
**Dixon,** Sharon Pratt 1944- *ConBlB 1 [port], NotBlAW 92 [port], WhoAmP 91, WhoBlA 92*
**Dixon,** Shirley Juanita 1935- *WhoFI 92*
**Dixon,** Simon 1728-1781 *DcNCBi 2*
**Dixon,** Sonny *WhoAmP 91*
**Dixon,** Stanley 1900- *Who 92*
**Dixon,** Stephen *DrAPF 91*
**Dixon,** Stephen 1936- *ConNov 91, WrDr 92*
**Dixon,** Stewart Strawn, Jr. 1964- *WhoEnt 92*
**Dixon,** Thomas 1864-1946 *BenetAL 91, ScFEYrs*
**Dixon,** Thomas, Jr. 1864-1946 *DcNCBi 2*
**Dixon,** Thomas F 1916- *FacFETw, IntWW 91*
**Dixon,** Tom L. 1932- *WhoBlA 92*
**Dixon,** Wallace Clark, Jr 1922- *AmMWSc 92*
**Dixon,** Walter Reginald *AmMWSc 92*
**Dixon,** Wheeler Winston 1950- *IntMPA 92*
**Dixon,** Wilfrid Joseph 1915- *AmMWSc 92*
**Dixon,** Willard Michael 1942- *WhoWest 92*
**Dixon,** William Brightman 1935- *AmMWSc 92*
**Dixon,** William Cornelius 1904- *WhoAmL 92*
**Dixon,** William McGregor, Jr. 1949- *WhoAmL 92*
**Dixon,** William Michael 1920- *Who 92*
**Dixon,** William R. 1925- *WhoBlA 92*
**Dixon,** William Robert 1925- *WhoEnt 92*
**Dixon,** William Rossander 1925- *AmMWSc 92*
**Dixon,** Willie James 1915- *WhoEnt 92*
**Dixon-Carroll,** Elizabeth Delia 1872-1934 *DcNCBi 2*
**Dixon-Holland,** Deborah Ellen 1957- *AmMWSc 92*
**Dixon-Ward,** Frank 1922- *Who 92*
**Dixson,** Maurice Christopher Scott 1941- *Who 92*
**Dixson,** Robert Morgan 1948- *WhoFI 92*
**DiYanni,** David 1954- *WhoRel 92*
**Diz,** Adolfo Cesar 1931- *IntWW 91*
**Dizdarevic,** Raif 1926- *IntWW 91*
**Dizenfeld,** David Glass 1949- *WhoEnt 92*
**Dizenhuz,** Israel Michael 1931- *AmMWSc 92*
**Dizenzo,** Charles 1938- *WrDr 92*
**Di Zio,** Steven F 1938- *AmMWSc 92*
**Dizmang,** Gloria Ann 1943- *WhoAmP 91*
**Djang,** Arthur H K 1925- *AmMWSc 92*
**Djanikian,** Gregory *DrAPF 91*
**D'Javid,** Ismail Faridoon 1908- *WhoWest 92*
**Djeghaba,** Mohamed 1935- *IntWW 91*
**Djemal,** Ahmed 1872-1922 *FacFETw*
**Djerassi,** Carl 1923- *AmMWSc 92, IntWW 91, WhoWest 92, WrDr 92*
**Djerassi,** Isaac 1921- *AmMWSc 92*
**Djerejian,** Edward Peter 1939- *WhoAmP 91*
**Djilas,** Milovan 1911- *FacFETw, IntWW 91*
**Djindjikhadze,** Vaya Gerontiyevich 1931- *IntWW 91*
**Djohar,** Said Ahmed *IntWW 91*
**Djokic,** Georgije 1949- *WhoRel 92*
**Djokovic,** Dragomir Z 1938- *AmMWSc 92*
**Djondo,** Koffi Gervais 1937- *IntWW 91*
**Djordjevic,** Leposava *DcAmImH*
**Djoudi,** Hocine 1930- *IntWW 91*
**Djuranovic,** Veselin 1925- *IntWW 91*
**Djurdjevic,** Robert Slobodan 1945- *WhoWest 92*
**Djuric,** Dusan 1930- *AmMWSc 92*
**Djuric,** Stevan Wakefield 1954- *AmMWSc 92*
**Djurickovic,** Draginja Branko 1940- *AmMWSc 92*
**Dlab,** Vlastimil 1932- *AmMWSc 92*
**Dlabach,** Gregory Wayne 1964- *WhoMW 92*
**Dlamini,** Bhekimpi Alpheus *IntWW 91*
**Dlamini,** Sotsha *IntWW 91*
**Dlamini,** Timothy Lutfo Lucky 1952- *IntWW 91*
**Dlott,** Dana D 1952- *AmMWSc 92*
**Dlott,** Susan Judy 1949- *WhoAmL 92*
**Dlouhy,** Vladimir 1953- *IntWW 91*
**D'Lower,** Del 1912- *WhoFI 92*
**D'Lugoff,** Arthur Joshua 1924- *WhoEnt 92*
**Dlugolecki,** Walt John 1949- *WhoFI 92*
**Dlugos,** Tim *DrAPF 91*
**Dlugoszewski,** Lucia 1931- *NewAmDM*
**Dlugoszewski,** Lucia 1934?- *ConCom 92*
**D'Luhy,** John James 1933- *WhoFI 92*
**Dmitri of Dallas,** Bishop *WhoRel 92*
**Dmitrich,** Mike 1936- *WhoAmP 91*
**Dmitriev,** Georgy 1942- *ConCom 92*
**Dmitriev,** Ivan Nikolaevich 1920- *SovUnBD*
**Dmitriev,** Ivan Nikolayevich 1920- *IntWW 91*
**Dmitriev,** Valentin Ivanovich 1927- *IntWW 91*
**Dmitriev,** Vladimir Vladimirovich 1900-1948 *SovUnBD*
**Dmowski,** Roman 1864-1939 *BiDExR*
**Dmowski,** W Paul 1937- *AmMWSc 92, WhoMW 92*
**Dmytryk,** Edward 1908- *IntDcF 2-2 [port], IntMPA 92*
**Dmytryszyn,** Myron 1924- *AmMWSc 92*
**Do Muoi** 1917- *IntWW 91*
**Do,** Robert 1960- *WhoWest 92*
**Do,** Tai Huu 1942- *WhoWest 92*
**Doa,** Vincent, Sr. *WhoHisp 92*
**Doak,** Frances Blount Renfrow 1887-1974 *DcNCBi 2*
**Doak,** George Osmore 1907- *AmMWSc 92*
**Doak,** Jerome Richard 1951- *WhoAmL 92*
**Doak,** Kenneth Worley 1916- *AmMWSc 92*
**Doak,** Robert A., Jr. 1928- *WhoFI 92*
**Doak,** Wade 1940- *WrDr 92*
**Do Amaral,** Diogo Freitas 1941- *IntWW 91*
**Do Amaral,** Luiz Henrique De Filippis 1952- *WhoWest 92*
**Doan,** Arthur Sumner, Jr 1933- *AmMWSc 92*
**Doan,** David Bentley 1926- *AmMWSc 92*
**Doan,** Eleanor Lloyd *WrDr 92*
**Doan,** Gilbert Everett, Jr. 1930- *WhoRel 92*
**Doan,** James O 1909- *WhoAmP 91*
**Doan,** Michael Frederick 1942- *WhoEnt 92*
**Doan,** Reece *TwCWW 91*
**Doan,** Xuyen Van 1949- *WhoAmL 92*
**Doane,** Anthony Wayne 1956- *WhoRel 92*
**Doane,** Benjamin Knowles 1928- *AmMWSc 92*
**Doane,** Charles Chesley 1925- *AmMWSc 92*
**Doane,** Douglas V 1918- *AmMWSc 92*
**Doane,** Elliott P 1929- *AmMWSc 92*
**Doane,** Frances Whitman 1928- *AmMWSc 92*
**Doane,** J William 1935- *AmMWSc 92*
**Doane,** John Frederick 1930- *AmMWSc 92*
**Doane,** Marshall Gordon 1937- *AmMWSc 92*
**Doane,** Michael 1952- *ConAu 135*
**Doane,** Paul Vincent 1943- *WhoAmP 91*
**Doane,** Samuel H. 1917- *WhoBlA 92*
**Doane,** Ted H 1930- *AmMWSc 92*
**Doane,** William M 1930- *AmMWSc 92*
**Doane,** Winifred Walsh 1929- *AmMWSc 92*
**Doanes-Bergin,** Sharyn F. *WhoBlA 92*
**Doar,** William Walter, Jr. 1935- *WhoAmL 92, WhoAmP 91*
**Dobay,** Donald Gene 1924- *AmMWSc 92*
**Dobb,** Barbara *WhoAmP 91*
**Dobb,** Erlam Stanley 1910- *Who 92*
**Dobbe,** Kevin R. 1958- *WhoEnt 92*
**Dobbel,** Rodger Francis 1934- *WhoWest 92*
**Dobbelstein,** Thomas Norman 1940- *AmMWSc 92*
**Dobben,** Glen D 1928- *AmMWSc 92*
**Dobbert,** Daniel Joseph 1946- *WhoMW 92*
**Dobbie,** Robert Charles 1942- *Who 92*
**Dobbin,** James Cochran 1814-1857 *DcNCBi 2*
**Dobbin,** Stanley 1929- *TwCPaSc*
**Dobbing,** John 1922- *Who 92*
**Dobbins,** Albert Greene, III 1949- *WhoBlA 92*
**Dobbins,** Alphondus Milton 1924- *WhoBlA 92*
**Dobbins,** Betty Yarborough 1926- *WhoFI 92*
**Dobbins,** Caryl Dean 1947- *WhoAmL 92, WhoMW 92*
**Dobbins,** Claude Ray 1919- *WhoRel 92*
**Dobbins,** David Ross 1941- *AmMWSc 92*
**Dobbins,** Deborah Wood 1958- *WhoAmL 92*
**Dobbins,** E Fred *WhoAmP 91*
**Dobbins,** James Gregory Hall 1943- *AmMWSc 92*
**Dobbins,** James Hamilton 1939- *WhoAmL 92*
**Dobbins,** James Talmage, Jr 1926- *AmMWSc 92*
**Dobbins,** John Potter 1914- *AmMWSc 92*
**Dobbins,** John William 1942- *WhoFI 92*
**Dobbins,** Lucille R. *WhoBlA 92*
**Dobbins,** Richard Andrew 1925- *AmMWSc 92*
**Dobbins,** Robert Joseph 1940- *AmMWSc 92*
**Dobbins,** Thomas Edward 1913- *AmMWSc 92*
**Dobbs,** Arthur 1689-1765 *DcNCBi 2*
**Dobbs,** Bernard *Who 92*
**Dobbs,** Betty Jo 1930- *WrDr 92*
**Dobbs,** David Earl 1945- *AmMWSc 92*
**Dobbs,** Denny Michael 1945- *WhoAmP 91*
**Dobbs,** Edward Brice 1729-1803 *DcNCBi 2*
**Dobbs,** Edwin Roland 1924- *Who 92*
**Dobbs,** Frank W 1932- *AmMWSc 92*
**Dobbs,** Frank Wilbur 1932- *WhoMW 92*
**Dobbs,** Gregory Allan 1946- *IntAu&W 91*
**Dobbs,** Gregory Melville 1947- *AmMWSc 92*
**Dobbs,** Guy H. 1927-1990 *WhoBlA 92N*
**Dobbs,** Harry Donald 1932- *AmMWSc 92*
**Dobbs,** James Frederick 1945- *WhoFI 92*
**Dobbs,** Jeannine *DrAPF 91*
**Dobbs,** John Wesley 1931- *WhoBlA 92*
**Dobbs,** Joseph Alfred 1914- *Who 92*
**Dobbs,** Leland George *AmMWSc 92*
**Dobbs,** Lou *LesBEnT 92*
**Dobbs,** Mattiwilda *IntWW 91, Who 92, WhoBlA 92*
**Dobbs,** Mattiwilda 1925- *NewAmDM, NotBlAW 92 [port]*
**Dobbs,** Richard 1919- *Who 92*
**Dobbs,** Robert Curry 1935- *AmMWSc 92*
**Dobbs,** Roland *Who 92*
**Dobbs,** Thomas Lawrence 1943- *AmMWSc 92*
**Dobbs,** William Bernard 1925- *Who 92*
**Dobeck,** Robert Bradley 1954- *WhoAmL 92*
**Dobeck,** Timothy G. 1961- *WhoAmL 92*
**Dobelbower,** Ralph Riddall, Jr 1940- *AmMWSc 92*
**Dobelis,** George 1940- *WhoWest 92*
**Dobell,** S.T. 1824-1874 *RfGEnL 91*
**Dobelle,** William Harvey 1941- *AmMWSc 92*
**Dobereiner,** Peter Arthur Bertram 1925- *IntAu&W 91, Who 92*
**Doberenz,** Alexander R 1936- *AmMWSc 92*
**Doberneck,** Raymond C 1932- *AmMWSc 92*
**Dobersen,** Michael J 1949- *AmMWSc 92*
**Dobes,** Ivan Rastislav 1937- *WhoFI 92*
**Dobesch,** Gerhard 1939- *IntWW 91*
**Dobi,** John Steven 1948- *AmMWSc 92*
**Dobie,** Charles Caldwell 1881-1943 *BenetAL 91*
**Dobie,** J. Frank 1888-1964 *BenetAL 91*
**Dobielinska-Eliszewska,** Teresa Katarzyna 1941- *IntWW 91*
**Dobigny,** Emma 1851-1925 *ThHEIm [port]*
**Dobin,** Edward I. 1936- *WhoAmL 92*
**Dobis,** Chester F 1942- *WhoAmP 91*
**Dobishinski,** William Michael 1951- *WhoEnt 92*
**Dobkin,** David Paul 1948- *AmMWSc 92*
**Dobkin,** James Allen 1940- *WhoAmL 92*
**Dobkin,** Sheldon 1933- *AmMWSc 92*
**Doblado,** Carlos Manuel 1950- *WhoHisp 92*
**Doble,** Denis Henry 1936- *Who 92*
**Doble,** John Frederick 1941- *Who 92*
**Dobler,** Norma Mae 1917- *WhoAmP 91*
**Doblin,** Alfred 1878-1957 *EncTR 91, FacFETw, LiExTwC*
**Doblin,** Jay 1920-1989 *DcTwDes*
**Doblin,** Stephen Alan 1945- *AmMWSc 92*
**Dobner,** Christopher Adam *DrAPF 91*

**Dobo,** Emerick Joseph 1919- *AmMWSc 92*
**Dobos,** Barbara M *WhoAmP 91*
**Dobosy,** Ronald Joseph 1946- *AmMWSc 92*
**Dobraczynski,** Jan 1910- *IntWW 91*
**Dobranski,** Bernard 1939- *WhoAmL 92*
**Dobranski,** Robert Edward 1944- *WhoRel 92*
**Dobras,** Victor Edward, II 1940- *WhoMW 92*
**Dobratz,** Carroll J 1915- *AmMWSc 92*
**Dobree,** John Hatherley 1914- *Who 92*
**Dobriansky,** Lev Eugene 1918- *WhoAmP 91*
**Dobrijevic,** Stevo 1932- *WhoMW 92*
**Dobrin,** Arthur *DrAPF 91*
**Dobrin,** Lyn 1942- *ConAu 135*
**Dobrin,** Milton Burnett 1915- *AmMWSc 92*
**Dobrin,** Philip Boone 1934- *AmMWSc 92*
**Dobrin,** Sheldon L. 1945- *WhoMW 92*
**Dobris,** Joel Charles 1940- *WhoAmL 92*
**Dobrish,** Robert Zachary 1940- *WhoAmL 92*
**Dobrogosz,** Walter Jerome 1933- *AmMWSc 92*
**Dobronravov,** Boris Georg'evich 1896-1949 *SovUnBD*
**Dobronski,** Agnes M 1925- *WhoAmP 91*
**Dobrosielski,** Marian 1923- *Who 92*
**Dobrott,** Robert D 1932- *AmMWSc 92*
**Dobrov,** Wadim 1926- *AmMWSc 92*
**Dobrovolny,** Charles George 1902- *AmMWSc 92*
**Dobrovolny,** Ernest 1912- *AmMWSc 92*
**Dobrovolny,** Jerry S 1922- *AmMWSc 92*
**Dobrovolny,** Kenneth Ray 1947- *WhoWest 92*
**Dobrovolsky,** Georgi 1928-1971 *FacFETw*
**Dobrovsky,** Josef 1753-1829 *BlkwCEP*
**Dobrovsky,** Lubos 1932- *IntWW 91*
**Dobrowolski,** James Phillip 1955- *AmMWSc 92*
**Dobrowolski,** Jerzy Adam 1931- *AmMWSc 92*
**Dobrowski,** Stanley John 1951- *WhoAmL 92*
**Dobry,** Alan 1927- *AmMWSc 92*
**Dobry,** George Leon Severyn 1918- *Who 92*
**Dobry,** Reuven 1930- *AmMWSc 92*
**Dobry,** Ricardo 1937- *AmMWSc 92*
**Dobry,** Sylvia Hearn 1938- *WhoWest 92*
**Dobrynin,** Anatoliy Fedorovich 1919- *IntWW 91, SovUnBD*
**Dobrynin,** Anatoly Fedorovich 1919- *Who 92*
**Dobson,** Alan 1928- *AmMWSc 92*
**Dobson,** Austin 1840-1921 *RfGEnL 91*
**Dobson,** Bridget McColl Hursley 1938- *WhoEnt 92, WhoFI 92, WhoWest 92*
**Dobson,** Byron Eugene 1957- *WhoBlA 92*
**Dobson,** Christopher Selby Austin 1916- *Who 92*
**Dobson,** David A 1937- *AmMWSc 92*
**Dobson,** David Stuart 1938- *Who 92*
**Dobson,** Denis 1908- *Who 92*
**Dobson,** Donald C 1926- *AmMWSc 92*
**Dobson,** Dorothy Ann 1934- *WhoBlA 92*
**Dobson,** Edward G. 1949- *WhoRel 92*
**Dobson,** Frank 1886-1963 *TwCPaSc*
**Dobson,** Frank Gordon 1940- *IntWW 91, Who 92*
**Dobson,** Gavin Richard 1951- *WhoMW 92*
**Dobson,** Gerard Ramsden 1933- *AmMWSc 92*
**Dobson,** Harold Lawrence 1921- *AmMWSc 92*
**Dobson,** Helen Sutton 1926- *WhoBlA 92*
**Dobson,** Howard Richard, Jr. 1957- *WhoFI 92*
**Dobson,** James C., Jr. 1936- *WrDr 92*
**Dobson,** James Gordon, Jr 1942- *AmMWSc 92*
**Dobson,** Julia *WrDr 92*
**Dobson,** Karen 1932- *WhoRel 92*
**Dobson,** Keith *Who 92*
**Dobson,** Kevin 1943- *IntMPA 92, WhoEnt 92*
**Dobson,** Margaret Velma 1948- *AmMWSc 92*
**Dobson,** Mark Michael 1948- *WhoAmL 92*
**Dobson,** Mary *TwCPaSc*
**Dobson,** Michael William Romsey 1952- *Who 92*
**Dobson,** Patrick John H. *Who 92*
**Dobson,** Peter N, Jr 1936- *AmMWSc 92*
**Dobson,** R. Barrie 1931- *WrDr 92*
**Dobson,** R Lowry 1919- *AmMWSc 92*
**Dobson,** Richard 1914- *Who 92*
**Dobson,** Richard Barrie 1931- *Who 92*
**Dobson,** Richard Lawrence 1928- *AmMWSc 92*
**Dobson,** Robert Albertus, III 1938- *WhoAmL 92*
**Dobson,** Rosemary 1920- *ConPo 91, RfGEnL 91, WrDr 92*
**Dobson,** Sue 1946- *IntAu&W 91, Who 92*
**Dobson,** Terrance James 1940- *WhoFI 92, WhoWest 92*
**Dobson,** Vernon Jay 1904- *WhoFI 92*
**Dobson,** William DeLafayette 1924- *WhoBlA 92*
**Dobson,** William Keith 1945- *Who 92*
**Doby,** Allen E. 1934- *WhoBlA 92*
**Doby,** Lawrence Eugene 1924- *WhoBlA 92*
**Doby,** Raymond 1923- *AmMWSc 92*
**Doby,** Tibor 1914- *AmMWSc 92*
**Dobynes,** Elizabeth 1930- *WhoBlA 92*
**Dobyns,** Brown M 1913- *AmMWSc 92*
**Dobyns,** James Robert 1926- *WhoAmP 91*
**Dobyns,** Leona Danette 1930- *AmMWSc 92*
**Dobyns,** Roy A 1931- *AmMWSc 92*
**Dobyns,** Samuel Witten 1920- *AmMWSc 92*
**Dobyns,** Stephen *DrAPF 91*
**Dobyns,** Stephen 1941- *ConPo 91, WrDr 92*
**Docherty,** Daniel Joseph 1924- *Who 92*
**Docherty,** James A 1932- *WhoAmP 91*
**Docherty,** John Joseph 1941- *AmMWSc 92*
**Docherty,** Michael 1947- *TwCPaSc*
**Docherty,** Robert Kelliehan, II 1935- *WhoRel 92*
**Dochev,** Ivan Dimitrov 1906- *BiDExR*
**Dochniak,** James M. *DrAPF 91*
**Dochterman,** William Grant 1931- *WhoEnt 92*
**Dochtermann,** Wolfram John 1930- *WhoEnt 92*
**Docken,** Adrian 1913- *AmMWSc 92*
**Docken,** Adrian Merwin 1913- *WhoMW 92*
**Dockendorf,** Denise D 1953- *WhoIns 92*
**Docker,** Ivor Colin 1925- *Who 92*
**Docker,** John Thornley 1937- *WhoRel 92*
**Dockery,** Alfred 1797-1873 *DcNCBi 2*
**Dockery,** Claudius 1865-1941 *DcNCBi 2*
**Dockery,** David Samuel 1952- *WhoRel 92*
**Dockery,** Herbert Donald 1954- *WhoFI 92*
**Dockery,** John T 1936- *AmMWSc 92*
**Dockery,** Oliver Hart 1830-1906 *DcNCBi 2*
**Dockery,** Richard L. *WhoBlA 92*
**Dockery,** Robert Gerald 1948- *WhoRel 92*
**Dockery,** Robert Wyatt 1909- *WhoBlA 92*
**Dockery,** Thomas Pleasant 1833-1898 *DcNCBi 2*
**Dockery,** Vernon Joseph 1937- *WhoMW 92*
**Dockett,** Alfred B. 1935- *WhoBlA 92*
**Dockham,** Jerry C *WhoAmP 91*
**Dockhorn,** Robert John 1934- *WhoMW 92*
**Docking,** Thomas Robert 1954- *WhoAmP 91*
**Dockley,** Peter *TwCPaSc*
**Docks,** Edward Leon 1945- *AmMWSc 92*
**Dockson,** Robert Ray 1917- *WhoWest 92*
**Dockstader,** Emmett Stanley 1923- *WhoFI 92*
**Dockstader,** Jack Lee 1936- *WhoWest 92*
**Dockter,** Allen Dale 1941- *WhoMW 92*
**Dockter,** Michael Edward 1949- *AmMWSc 92*
**Docktor,** William Jay 1951- *WhoWest 92*
**Docobo,** Richard Douglas 1956- *WhoHisp 92*
**Docter,** Charles Alfred 1931- *WhoAmP 91*
**Doctor,** Bhupendra P 1930- *AmMWSc 92*
**Doctor,** Norman J 1929- *AmMWSc 92*
**Doctor,** Vasant Manilal 1926- *AmMWSc 92*
**Doctorian,** David 1934- *WhoAmP 91*
**Doctorian,** Sam Emmanuel, Jr. 1962- *WhoWest 92*
**Doctoroff,** Martin Myles 1933- *WhoAmL 92*
**Doctorow,** E.L. *DrAPF 91*
**Doctorow,** E.L. 1931- *BenetAL 91, ConLC 65 [port], ConNov 91, FacFETw [port], TwCWW 91, WrDr 92*
**Doctorow,** Edgar Lawrence 1931- *IntAu&W 91, IntWW 91, Who 92*
**Doctrow,** Susan R 1956- *AmMWSc 92*
**Dod,** Bruce Douglas 1941- *AmMWSc 92*
**Dodabalapur,** Ananth 1963- *AmMWSc 92*
**Dodak,** Lewis 1946- *WhoMW 92*
**Dodak,** Lewis N 1946- *WhoAmP 91*
**Dodd,** Alan 1942- *TwCPaSc*
**Dodd,** Anna Bowman 1858-1929 *ScFEYrs*
**Dodd,** Arthur Edward 1931- *WrDr 92*
**Dodd,** Bernice Stephens 1943- *WhoBlA 92*
**Dodd,** Burton Freeman 1952- *WhoAmL 92*
**Dodd,** Charles Gardner 1915- *AmMWSc 92*
**Dodd,** Charles H 1884-1973 *FacFETw*
**Dodd,** Charles Harold 1884-1973 *DcEcMov*
**Dodd,** Charlie Herring 1950- *WhoRel 92*
**Dodd,** Chester Curtin, Jr 1928- *WhoAmP 91*
**Dodd,** Christopher J. 1944- *AlmAP 92 [port], IntWW 91, WhoAmP 91*
**Dodd,** Curtis Wilson 1939- *AmMWSc 92*
**Dodd,** Darol Ennis 1949- *AmMWSc 92*
**Dodd,** Ed d1991 *NewYTBS 91 [port]*
**Dodd,** Ed 1902-1991 *ConAu 134, SmATA 68*
**Dodd,** Edward Elliott 1922- *AmMWSc 92*
**Dodd,** Edward William 1936- *WhoAmP 91*
**Dodd,** Edwin Dillon 1919- *IntWW 91*
**Dodd,** Francis 1874-1949 *TwCPaSc*
**Dodd,** Frank Leslie 1919- *Who 92*
**Dodd,** Gary Wayne 1958- *WhoRel 92*
**Dodd,** Gerald Dewey, Jr 1922- *AmMWSc 92*
**Dodd,** Jack Gordon 1926- *AmMWSc 92*
**Dodd,** James C. 1923- *WhoBlA 92*
**Dodd,** James Robert 1934- *AmMWSc 92*
**Dodd,** Jimmie Dale 1931- *AmMWSc 92*
**Dodd,** Joe David 1920- *WhoFI 92, WhoWest 92*
**Dodd,** John Durrance 1917- *AmMWSc 92*
**Dodd,** John Newton 1922- *IntWW 91*
**Dodd,** John P. d1991 *NewYTBS 91*
**Dodd,** Kenneth Arthur 1931- *Who 92*
**Dodd,** Lionel G. 1940- *WhoFI 92*
**Dodd,** Lynley Stuart 1941- *WrDr 92*
**Dodd,** Martha 1908-1990 *CurBio 91N*
**Dodd,** Mary Ann 1931- *WhoEnt 92*
**Dodd,** Michael F 1938- *WhoIns 92*
**Dodd,** Monroe *WhoMW 92*
**Dodd,** Richard Arthur 1922- *AmMWSc 92*
**Dodd,** Robert 1938- *WhoAmP 91*
**Dodd,** Robert Dennis 1955- *WhoEnt 92*
**Dodd,** Robert Taylor 1936- *AmMWSc 92*
**Dodd,** Roger James 1951- *WhoFI 92*
**Dodd,** Roger Yates 1944- *AmMWSc 92*
**Dodd,** Skeeter Franklin 1937- *WhoEnt 92*
**Dodd,** Susan M. *DrAPF 91*
**Dodd,** Susan M. 1946- *WrDr 92*
**Dodd,** Thomas 1907-1971 *FacFETw*
**Dodd,** Thomas J. d1971 *LesBEnT 92*
**Dodd,** Travis Curtis 1951- *WhoRel 92*
**Dodd,** Valerie A. 1944- *ConAu 134*
**Dodd,** Walta Sue 1944- *WhoAmP 91*
**Dodd,** Wayne *DrAPF 91*
**Dodd,** Wayne D. 1930- *WrDr 92*
**Dodd,** Wendell Ray 1958- *WhoRel 92*
**Dodd,** Wilfrid E. 1923- *IntMPA 92*
**Dodd,** William Atherton 1923- *Who 92*
**Dodd,** William Edward 1869-1940 *DcNCBi 2, EncTR 91*
**Dodd,** William Ferrall 1942- *WhoRel 92*
**Dodd,** William Luther, Jr 1921- *WhoAmP 91*
**Doddapaneni,** Narayan *AmMWSc 92*
**Dodderidge,** Morris 1915- *Who 92*
**Doddridge,** Joseph 1769-1826 *BenetAL 91*
**Dodds,** Alan Robert 1951- *WhoMW 92, WhoRel 92*
**Dodds,** Alvin Franklin 1919- *AmMWSc 92*
**Dodds,** Baby 1898-1959 *NewAmDM*
**Dodds,** Brenda Kay 1961- *WhoMW 92*
**Dodds,** Claudette La Vonn 1947- *WhoEnt 92, WhoMW 92*
**Dodds,** Dale Irvin 1915- *WhoWest 92*
**Dodds,** Deborah Detchon 1943- *WhoAmL 92*
**Dodds,** Denis George 1913- *Who 92*
**Dodds,** Dinah Jane 1943- *WhoWest 92*
**Dodds,** Donald Gilbert 1925- *AmMWSc 92*
**Dodds,** Douglas Allen 1950- *WhoAmL 92*
**Dodds,** Frances Alison 1950- *WhoAmL 92*
**Dodds,** George Christopher Buchanan 1916- *Who 92*
**Dodds,** James Allan 1947- *AmMWSc 92*
**Dodds,** James Pickering 1913- *Who 92*
**Dodds,** Japheth Evans 1942- *WhoRel 92*
**Dodds,** Johnny 1892-1940 *NewAmDM*
**Dodds,** Michael Bruce 1952- *WhoAmL 92*
**Dodds,** Michael John 1950- *WhoRel 92*
**Dodds,** Nigel Alexander 1958- *Who 92*
**Dodds,** R. Harcourt 1938- *WhoBlA 92*
**Dodds,** Ralph 1928- *Who 92*
**Dodds,** Stanley A 1947- *AmMWSc 92*
**Dodds,** Wellesley Jamison 1915- *AmMWSc 92*
**Dodds-Parker,** Douglas 1909- *Who 92*
**Doddy,** Reginald Nathaniel 1952- *WhoBlA 92*
**Doderer,** George Charles 1928- *AmMWSc 92*
**Doderer,** Heimito von 1896-1966 *FacFETw*
**Doderer,** Minnette Frerichs 1923- *WhoAmP 91*
**Dodge brothers** *FacFETw*
**Dodge,** Alice Hribal *AmMWSc 92*
**Dodge,** Alonzo *DrAPF 91*
**Dodge,** Alwyn Conrad 1929- *WhoMW 92*
**Dodge,** Arthur Byron, Jr. 1923- *WhoFI 92*
**Dodge,** Arthur G, Jr 1929- *WhoAmP 91*
**Dodge,** Austin Anderson 1906- *AmMWSc 92*
**Dodge,** Bertha S. 1902- *WrDr 92*
**Dodge,** Carroll William 1895- *AmMWSc 92*
**Dodge,** Charles 1942- *NewAmDM*
**Dodge,** Charles Fremont 1924- *AmMWSc 92*
**Dodge,** Charles Keene 1844?-1918 *BiInAmS*
**Dodge,** Charles Malcolm 1942- *WhoEnt 92*
**Dodge,** Clifford F 1939- *WhoAmP 91*
**Dodge,** David Frederick 1949- *WhoRel 92*
**Dodge,** David Low 1774-1852 *AmPeW*
**Dodge,** Donald W 1928- *AmMWSc 92*
**Dodge,** Douglas Stuart 1951- *WhoWest 92*
**Dodge,** E R 1910- *AmMWSc 92*
**Dodge,** Earl Farwell 1932- *WhoAmP 91*
**Dodge,** Emerson *TwCWW 91*
**Dodge,** Emma M 1930- *WhoAmP 91*
**Dodge,** Franklin C W 1934- *AmMWSc 92*
**Dodge,** Franklin Tiffany 1936- *AmMWSc 92*
**Dodge,** Fremont *SmATA 68*
**Dodge,** Garen Edward 1957- *WhoAmL 92*
**Dodge,** Gloria Evelyn *WhoFI 92*
**Dodge,** Harold T 1924- *AmMWSc 92*
**Dodge,** Herbert Warren *ScFEYrs*
**Dodge,** Horace E 1868-1920 *FacFETw*
**Dodge,** Howard L 1869- *ScFEYrs*
**Dodge,** Jacob Richards 1823-1902 *BiInAmS*
**Dodge,** James Stanley 1939- *AmMWSc 92*
**Dodge,** John 1864-1920 *FacFETw*
**Dodge,** John V. 1909- *Who 92*
**Dodge,** John Vilas 1909- *IntAu&W 91, IntWW 91*
**Dodge,** Joseph M. 1941- *WhoAmL 92*
**Dodge,** Lawrence Burnham 1942- *WhoAmP 91*
**Dodge,** Marcia Milgrom 1955- *WhoEnt 92*
**Dodge,** Margaret *ScFEYrs*
**Dodge,** Mary Mapes 1831-1905 *BenetAL 91*
**Dodge,** Patrick William 1936- *AmMWSc 92*
**Dodge,** Peter 1926- *WrDr 92*
**Dodge,** Philip Rogers 1923- *AmMWSc 92*
**Dodge,** Raymond 1871-1942 *FacFETw*
**Dodge,** Raynal 1844- *BiInAmS*
**Dodge,** Richard Allan 1930- *WhoAmP 91*
**Dodge,** Richard E 1947- *AmMWSc 92*
**Dodge,** Richard Patrick 1932- *AmMWSc 92*
**Dodge,** Theodore A 1911- *AmMWSc 92*
**Dodge,** Theodore Ayrault 1911- *WhoFI 92, WhoWest 92*
**Dodge,** Warren Francis 1928- *AmMWSc 92*
**Dodge,** William Howard 1943- *AmMWSc 92*
**Dodge,** William R 1929- *AmMWSc 92*
**Dodgen,** Andrew Clay 1961- *WhoAmL 92*
**Dodgen,** Durward F 1931- *AmMWSc 92*
**Dodgen,** Harold Warren 1921- *AmMWSc 92*
**Dodgen,** James *WhoWest 92*
**Dodgshon,** Robert A. 1941- *WrDr 92*
**Dodgson,** Catherine 1883-1954 *TwCPaSc*
**Dodgson,** Charles Lutwidge *RfGEnL 91*
**Dodgson,** John 1890-1969 *TwCPaSc*
**Dodin,** Lev 1940- *IntWW 91*
**Dodington,** Sven Henry Marriott 1912- *AmMWSc 92*
**Dodrill,** Denver Keith 1953- *WhoRel 92*
**Dodrill,** Robert Lee, Sr 1933- *WhoAmP 91*
**Dods,** Robert Douglas 1942- *WhoAmP 91*
**Dods,** Walter Arthur, Jr. 1941- *WhoFI 92*
**Dods-Withers,** Isobelle Anne 1876-1939 *TwCPaSc*
**Dodsley,** Robert 1703-1764 *BlkwCEP, RfGEnL 91*
**Dodson** *Who 92*
**Dodson,** Angela Pearl 1951- *WhoBlA 92*
**Dodson,** B C 1924- *AmMWSc 92*
**Dodson,** Bruce J. 1937- *WhoFI 92, WhoMW 92*
**Dodson,** Catherine E. Brown 1948- *WhoAmL 92*
**Dodson,** Charles Leon, Jr 1935- *AmMWSc 92*
**Dodson,** Chester Lee 1921- *AmMWSc 92*
**Dodson,** Christopher Thomas 1964- *WhoWest 92*
**Dodson,** D. Keith 1943- *WhoFI 92*
**Dodson,** Daniel B 1918- *IntAu&W 91, WrDr 92*
**Dodson,** Daniel B. 1918-1991 *ConAu 133*
**Dodson,** Daryl Theodore 1934- *WhoEnt 92*
**Dodson,** David Scott 1942- *AmMWSc 92*
**Dodson,** Derek 1920- *Who 92*
**Dodson,** Derek Sherborne Lindsell 1920- *IntWW 91*
**Dodson,** Don Charles 1944- *WhoWest 92*
**Dodson,** Edward O 1916- *AmMWSc 92*
**Dodson,** Frank Robert 1946- *WhoWest 92*
**Dodson,** Granville M. 1910- *WhoBlA 92*
**Dodson,** Howard, Jr. 1939- *WhoBlA 92*
**Dodson,** James Robert 1961- *WhoEnt 92*
**Dodson,** Jualynne E. 1942- *WhoBlA 92*
**Dodson,** Kenneth 1907- *WrDr 92*
**Dodson,** Linda S. 1952- *WhoFI 92*
**Dodson,** Norman Elmer 1909- *AmMWSc 92*
**Dodson,** Oscar Henry 1905- *WhoMW 92*
**Dodson,** Owen 1914-1983 *BlkLC [port]*
**Dodson,** Peter 1946- *AmMWSc 92*

**Dodson,** Raymond Guerrant 1947- *WhoAmL 92*
**Dodson,** Raymond Monroe 1920- *AmMWSc 92*
**Dodson,** Richard Wolford 1915- *AmMWSc 92*
**Dodson,** Robert North *Who 92*
**Dodson,** Robin Albert 1940- *AmMWSc 92*
**Dodson,** Ronald Franklin 1942- *AmMWSc 92*
**Dodson,** Vance Hayden, Jr 1922- *AmMWSc 92*
**Dodson,** Vernon N 1923- *AmMWSc 92*
**Dodson,** Vivian M. 1934- *WhoBlA 92*
**Dodson,** William Alfred, Jr. 1950- *WhoBlA 92*
**Dodson,** William Patrick 1948- *WhoAmP 91*
**Dodsworth,** Geoffrey Hugh 1928- *Who 92*
**Dodsworth,** James Martin 1935- *Who 92*
**Dodsworth,** John Christopher S. *Who 92*
**Dodsworth,** Martin *Who 92*
**Dodwell,** Charles Reginald 1922- *IntWW 91, Who 92*
**Dodworth,** Allen Stevens 1938- *WhoWest 92*
**Dodworth,** Peter 1940- *Who 92*
**Dodzik,** Andrew John, Jr. 1947- *WhoMW 92*
**Dodziuk,** Jozef 1947- *AmMWSc 92*
**Doe,** Andrew Edwin 1928- *WhoEnt 92*
**Doe,** Bruce R 1931- *AmMWSc 92*
**Doe,** Frank Joseph 1937- *AmMWSc 92*
**Doe,** Richard P 1926- *AmMWSc 92*
**Doe,** Samuel 1952-1990 *AnObit 1990, News 91*
**Doe,** Samuel Kanyon d1990 *IntWW 91N*
**Doebber,** Thomas Winfield 1946- *AmMWSc 92*
**Doebbler,** Gerald Francis 1932- *AmMWSc 92*
**Doebrick,** Hugh Eugene 1937- *WhoAmL 92*
**Doeckel,** Robert David 1959- *WhoMW 92*
**Doede,** John Henry 1937- *AmMWSc 92*
**Doede,** Linda Walton 1937- *WhoMW 92*
**Doeden,** Gerald Ennen 1918- *AmMWSc 92*
**Doedens,** David James 1942- *AmMWSc 92*
**Doedens,** Robert John 1937- *AmMWSc 92*
**Doederlein,** Deloris *WhoAmP 91*
**Doeg,** Kenneth Albert 1931- *AmMWSc 92*
**Doege,** Theodore Charles 1928- *AmMWSc 92*
**Doehler,** Robert William 1929- *AmMWSc 92*
**Doehne,** Dorothy P *WhoAmP 91*
**Doehring,** Donald O 1935- *AmMWSc 92*
**Doelker,** Frederick Harold 1953- *WhoMW 92*
**Doell,** Donald Frederick 1936- *WhoWest 92*
**Doell,** Richard Rayman 1923- *AmMWSc 92*
**Doell,** Ruth Gertrude 1926- *AmMWSc 92*
**Doelling,** Hellmut Hans 1930- *AmMWSc 92, WhoWest 92*
**Doelling,** Ralph Peter 1936- *WhoFI 92*
**Doelp,** Florinda D. 1936- *WhoFI 92*
**Doelp,** Louis C, Jr 1928- *AmMWSc 92*
**Doemel,** William Naylor *AmMWSc 92*
**Doemling,** Donald Bernard 1930- *AmMWSc 92*
**D'Oench,** Russell Grace, Jr. 1927- *WhoFI 92*
**Doenges,** Byron Frederick 1922- *WhoFI 92*
**Doenitz,** Karl 1891-1980 *FacFETw [port]*
**Doepker,** John Frederick, Jr. 1949- *WhoMW 92*
**Doepker,** Richard DuMont 1933- *AmMWSc 92*
**Doeppner,** Thomas Walter, Jr 1951- *AmMWSc 92*
**Doerder,** F Paul 1945- *AmMWSc 92*
**Doerfel,** Ken Sue 1944- *WhoAmP 91*
**Doerfer,** John C. *LesBEnT 92*
**Doerfler,** Ronald John 1941- *WhoEnt 92, WhoFI 92*
**Doerfler,** Thomas Eugene 1937- *AmMWSc 92*
**Doerfler,** Walter Hans 1933- *AmMWSc 92*
**Doerfling,** Hank 1936- *WhoWest 92*
**Doerge,** Daniel Robert 1949- *AmMWSc 92*
**Doerges,** John E 1926- *AmMWSc 92*
**Doerhoff,** Dale Charles 1946- *WhoAmL 92*
**Doering,** Charles Henry 1935- *AmMWSc 92*
**Doering,** Charles Rogers 1956- *AmMWSc 92*
**Doering,** Eugene J 1928- *AmMWSc 92*
**Doering,** Henry Hans, III 1950- *WhoAmL 92*
**Doering,** Jeffrey Louis 1949- *AmMWSc 92, WhoMW 92*
**Doering,** Richard 1939- *WhoWest 92*
**Doering,** William von Eggers 1917- *AmMWSc 92, IntWW 91*
**Doerman,** Dale Steven 1949- *WhoEnt 92*
**Doermann,** August Henry 1918- *AmMWSc 92*
**Doermann,** Ralph Walter 1930- *WhoMW 92, WhoRel 92*
**Doerner,** Martin David 1960- *WhoWest 92*
**Doerner,** Robert Carl 1926- *AmMWSc 92*
**Doerner,** William A 1920- *AmMWSc 92*
**Doerper,** John Erwin 1943- *WhoWest 92*
**Doerr,** Edd 1930- *WhoRel 92*
**Doerr,** Harriet *DrAPF 91*
**Doerr,** Howard P. 1929- *WhoFI 92*
**Doerr,** Phillip David 1942- *AmMWSc 92*
**Doerr,** Ray E 1926- *WhoAmP 91*
**Doerr,** Robert George 1941- *AmMWSc 92*
**Doerr,** Timothy Eugene 1965- *WhoWest 92*
**Doerr,** Veronica M. *WhoEnt 92*
**Doersch,** Ronald Ernest 1935- *AmMWSc 92*
**Doerschuk,** Peter Charles 1956- *WhoMW 92*
**Doershuk,** Carl Frederick 1930- *AmMWSc 92*
**Doesburg,** Theo Van 1883-1931 *DcTwDes, FacFETw*
**Doesticks,** Q.K. *BenetAL 91*
**Doetsch,** Douglas Allen 1957- *WhoAmL 92*
**Doetsch,** Gernot Siegmar 1940- *AmMWSc 92*
**Doetsch,** Paul William 1954- *AmMWSc 92*
**Doetsch,** Raymond Nicholas 1920- *AmMWSc 92*
**Doetschman,** David Charles 1942- *AmMWSc 92*
**Doeung,** Sok T. 1936- *WhoRel 92*
**Doezema,** Ryan Edward 1942- *AmMWSc 92*
**Dogali,** Jo Marie 1949- *WhoAmL 92*
**Dogan,** Husnu 1944- *IntWW 91*
**Doggart,** George Hubert Graham 1925- *Who 92*
**Dogger,** Allen J. 1947- *WhoFI 92*
**Dogger,** James Russell 1923- *AmMWSc 92*
**Doggett,** Donald T. 1968- *WhoEnt 92*
**Doggett,** John Nelson, Jr. 1918- *WhoBlA 92, WhoMW 92, WhoRel 92*
**Doggett,** LeRoy Elsworth 1941- *AmMWSc 92*
**Doggett,** Lloyd 1946- *WhoAmL 92*
**Doggett,** Lloyd Alton, II 1946- *WhoAmP 91*
**Doggett,** Mary Lousie Wallis 1928- *WhoAmP 91*
**Doggett,** Suzanne Wightman 1958- *WhoAmL 92*
**Doggett,** Wesley Osborne 1931- *AmMWSc 92*
**Doggette,** Jackson Michael, Jr. 1957- *WhoRel 92*
**Doghramji,** Karl 1954- *AmMWSc 92*
**Dogole,** Saul Harrison 1922- *WhoAmP 91*
**Dogoloff,** Lee Israel 1939- *WhoAmP 91, WhoFI 92*
**Dogramaci,** Ihsan 1915- *IntWW 91*
**Doguzhiev,** Vitaliy Khusseynovich *IntWW 91*
**Doha,** Aminur Rahman S. *Who 92*
**Doha,** Aminur Rahman S. 1929- *IntWW 91*
**Dohany,** Julius Eugene 1926- *AmMWSc 92*
**Doheny,** Donald Aloysius 1924- *WhoAmL 92, WhoFI 92, WhoMW 92*
**Doheny,** Donald Aloysius, Jr. 1954- *WhoAmL 92*
**Doheny,** Frank P., Jr. 1940- *WhoAmL 92*
**Doherty,** Adrian Walter, Jr. 1952- *WhoFI 92*
**Doherty,** Alfred Edward 1929- *WhoWest 92*
**Doherty,** Annette Marian 1961- *WhoMW 92*
**Doherty,** Barbara 1931- *WhoRel 92*
**Doherty,** Berlie 1943- *WrDr 92*
**Doherty,** Charles V. *WhoFI 92*
**Doherty,** Daniel John 1961- *WhoFI 92*
**Doherty,** Daniel Patrick 1935- *WhoAmP 91*
**Doherty,** Edmund George 1943- *WhoMW 92*
**Doherty,** Edward J. *WhoRel 92*
**Doherty,** Edward William 1921- *WhoAmP 91*
**Doherty,** Evelyn Marie 1941- *WhoFI 92*
**Doherty,** George William 1941- *WhoWest 92*
**Doherty,** Gerald Paul, IV 1946- *WhoAmP 91*
**Doherty,** James Edward, III 1923- *AmMWSc 92*
**Doherty,** John I 1941- *WhoAmP 91*
**Doherty,** Lorraine Eileen *WhoAmP 91*
**Doherty,** Lowell Ralph 1930- *AmMWSc 92*
**Doherty,** Mary Cushing 1953- *WhoAmL 92*
**Doherty,** Niall Stephen 1949- *AmMWSc 92*
**Doherty,** Patrick William 1951- *WhoAmP 91*
**Doherty,** Paul Michael 1948- *AmMWSc 92*
**Doherty,** Peter 1913-1990 *AnObit 1990*
**Doherty,** Peter Charles 1940- *IntWW 91, Who 92*
**Doherty,** Rebecca Feeney 1952- *WhoAmL 92*
**Doherty,** Robert Christopher 1943- *WhoAmL 92*
**Doherty,** Steve 1952- *WhoAmP 91*
**Doherty,** Tom 1933- *WhoEnt 92*
**Doherty,** Walter Ernest, Jr. 1912- *WhoAmL 92*
**Doherty,** William Humphrey 1907- *AmMWSc 92*
**Dohl,** Friedhelm 1936- *ConCom 92*
**Dohlman,** Claes Henrik 1922- *AmMWSc 92*
**Dohm,** Gerald Lynis 1942- *AmMWSc 92*
**Dohmae,** Hiroshi 1941- *WhoWest 92*
**Dohmann,** Barbara *Who 92*
**Dohmen,** Frederick Hoeger 1917- *WhoFI 92, WhoMW 92*
**Dohms,** John Edward 1948- *AmMWSc 92*
**Dohna-Schlobitten,** Heinrich, Count zu 1882-1944 *EncTR 91*
**Dohnal,** William Edward 1912- *WhoFI 92*
**Dohnanyi,** Christoph von *IntWW 91*
**Dohnanyi,** Christoph von 1929- *NewAmDM*
**Dohnanyi,** Erno 1877-1960 *NewAmDM*
**Dohnanyi,** Ernst von 1877-1960 *FacFETw*
**Dohnanyi,** Hans von 1902-1945 *EncTR 91 [port]*
**Dohnanyi,** Julius S 1931- *AmMWSc 92*
**Dohnanyi,** Klaus von *IntWW 91*
**Dohner,** Donald R. 1907-1944 *DcTwDes*
**Dohoo,** Roy McGregor 1919- *AmMWSc 92*
**Dohrn,** Ruth Elaine 1930- *WhoAmP 91*
**Dohse,** Craig Clayton 1948- *WhoRel 92*
**Doi,** Kunio 1939- *AmMWSc 92*
**Doi,** Lois 1951- *WhoWest 92*
**Doi,** Mary Ellen 1933- *WhoWest 92*
**Doi,** Masayuki 1933- *WhoFI 92*
**Doi,** Nelson Kiyoshi 1922- *WhoAmP 91*
**Doi,** Roy Hiroshi 1933- *AmMWSc 92*
**Doi,** Takako 1929- *IntWW 91*
**Doida,** Stanley Y. 1944- *WhoWest 92*
**Doig,** Andrew Beveridge 1914- *Who 92*
**Doig,** Dale 1935- *WhoAmP 91*
**Doig,** Elmo H. 1927- *WhoBlA 92*
**Doig,** Ivan 1939- *TwCWW 91, WhoWest 92, WrDr 92*
**Doig,** Marion Tilton, III 1943- *AmMWSc 92*
**Doig,** Peter Muir 1911- *Who 92*
**Doig,** Ralph Herbert 1909- *Who 92*
**Doig,** Ronald 1939- *AmMWSc 92*
**Doigan,** Paul 1919- *AmMWSc 92*
**Doinas,** Stefan Augustin 1922- *IntWW 91*
**Doiron,** Theodore Danos 1948- *AmMWSc 92*
**Doisy,** Edward Adelbert 1893-1986 *WhoNob 90*
**Doje Cedain** 1924- *IntWW 91*
**Doje Cering** 1938- *IntWW 91*
**Dojny,** Richard Francis 1940- *WhoFI 92*
**Doke,** Joseph J 1863-1913 *ScFEYrs*
**Doke,** Marshall J, Jr 1934- *WhoAmP 91*
**Dokey,** Richard *DrAPF 91*
**Dokoudovsky,** Nina Ludmila 1947- *WhoEnt 92*
**Dokoupil,** Jiri Georg 1954- *WorArt 1980*
**Doktor,** Paul 1919-1989 *NewAmDM*
**Doku,** Hristo Chris 1928- *AmMWSc 92*
**Dokuchaev,** Nikolay Vasil'evich 1891-1944 *SovUnBD*
**Dokurno,** Anthony David 1957- *WhoAmL 92*
**Dolak,** Anna Elizabeth 1957- *WhoAmL 92*
**Dolak,** Terence Martin 1951- *AmMWSc 92*
**Dolan,** Anthony *DrAPF 91*
**Dolan,** Beverly Franklin 1927- *IntWW 91, WhoFI 92*
**Dolan,** Charles F. *LesBEnT 92*
**Dolan,** Charles W 1943- *AmMWSc 92*
**Dolan,** Dennis Joseph 1946- *WhoAmL 92*
**Dolan,** Desmond Daniel 1916- *AmMWSc 92*
**Dolan,** Don 1940- *WhoEnt 92*
**Dolan,** Hubert G 1927- *WhoIns 92*
**Dolan,** James Bernard 1915- *WhoEnt 92*
**Dolan,** James F 1952- *AmMWSc 92*
**Dolan,** James Francis 1930- *WhoAmL 92*
**Dolan,** James Patrick 1949- *WhoFI 92*
**Dolan,** James Vincent 1938- *WhoAmL 92, WhoFI 92*
**Dolan,** Jan C 1927- *WhoAmP 91*
**Dolan,** Jo Alene 1941- *AmMWSc 92*
**Dolan,** John E 1923- *AmMWSc 92*
**Dolan,** John Ralph 1926- *WhoFI 92*
**Dolan,** Joseph Edward 1945- *AmMWSc 92*
**Dolan,** Joseph Francis 1939- *AmMWSc 92*
**Dolan,** Joseph M 1917- *WhoAmP 91*
**Dolan,** Kenneth DeWayne *WhoMW 92*
**Dolan,** Kenneth William 1940- *AmMWSc 92*
**Dolan,** Louise Ann 1950- *AmMWSc 92*
**Dolan,** Mark Peter 1960- *WhoAmL 92*
**Dolan,** Maryanne McLorn 1924- *WhoWest 92*
**Dolan,** Michael W 1942- *WhoAmP 91*
**Dolan,** Michael William 1942- *WhoAmL 92*
**Dolan,** Mick 1951- *WhoEnt 92*
**Dolan,** Robert Glennon, Jr. 1939- *WhoFI 92*
**Dolan,** Robert Lee 1943- *WhoIns 92*
**Dolan,** Ronald Vincent 1942- *WhoFI 92*
**Dolan,** Thomas Francis 1924- *WhoAmP 91*
**Dolan,** Thomas Ironside 1927- *WhoFI 92, WhoMW 92*
**Dolan,** Thomas J 1906- *AmMWSc 92*
**Dolan,** Thomas Patrick 1936- *WhoWest 92*
**Dolan,** Timothy Martin 1957- *WhoAmL 92*
**Dolan,** William Mark 1923- *WhoWest 92*
**Dolan,** William R 1945- *WhoIns 92*
**Dolan-Baldwin,** Colleen Anne 1960- *WhoFI 92*
**Dolan-Wallace,** David Bruce 1956- *WhoMW 92*
**Dolanc,** Stane 1925- *IntWW 91*
**Dolbare,** Jeff *WhoAmP 91*
**Dolbear,** Amos Emerson 1837-1910 *BiInAmS*
**Dolbear,** Geoffrey Emerson 1941- *AmMWSc 92*
**Dolbier,** William Read, Jr 1939- *AmMWSc 92*
**Dolby,** James Louis 1926- *AmMWSc 92*
**Dolby,** James Taylor 1909-1975 *TwCPaSc*
**Dolby,** Lloyd Jay 1935- *AmMWSc 92*
**Dolby,** Ray Milton 1933- *Who 92*
**Dolch,** William Lee 1925- *AmMWSc 92*
**Dolci,** Danilo 1924- *IntWW 91, Who 92*
**Dolderer,** Alan 1958- *WhoEnt 92*
**Dole,** Bob *Who 92*
**Dole,** Charles Fletcher 1845-1927 *AmPeW*
**Dole,** Elizabeth Hanford 1936- *AmPolLe [port], IntWW 91, WhoAmP 91, WhoFI 92*
**Dole,** Hollis M 1914- *WhoAmP 91*
**Dole,** Hollis Mathews 1914- *AmMWSc 92*
**Dole,** Jim 1935- *AmMWSc 92*
**Dole,** John Anthony 1929- *Who 92*
**Dole,** Malcolm 1903- *AmMWSc 92*
**Dole,** Nathan Haskell 1852-1935 *BenetAL 91*
**Dole,** Robert 1923- *AlmAP 92 [port], IntWW 91*
**Dole,** Robert J 1923- *WhoAmP 91, WhoMW 92*
**Dole,** Robert Joseph 1923- *AmPolLe, NewYTBS 91 [port], Who 92*
**Dole,** Stephen Edward 1962- *WhoEnt 92*
**Dole,** Vincent Paul 1913- *AmMWSc 92*
**Dole,** William Paul 1947- *AmMWSc 92*
**Doleac,** Charles Bartholomew 1947- *WhoAmL 92, WhoFI 92*
**Dolecek,** Elwyn Haydn 1946- *AmMWSc 92*
**Doleman,** Christopher John 1961- *WhoBlA 92*
**Dolenko,** Allan John 1942- *AmMWSc 92*
**Dolentz,** Patricia Woitel 1945- *WhoAmL 92*
**Dolenz,** Bernard Joseph 1933- *WhoAmL 92*
**Dolenz,** Mickey 1945- *WhoEnt 92*
**Doles,** John Henry, III 1943- *AmMWSc 92*
**Doley,** Harold E, Jr 1947- *WhoAmP 91, WhoBlA 92*
**Dolezal,** Dale Francis 1936- *WhoFI 92*
**Dolezal,** Edward J *WhoAmP 91*
**Dolezal,** Vaclav J 1927- *AmMWSc 92*
**Dolezalek,** Hans 1912- *AmMWSc 92*
**Dolfini,** Joseph E 1936- *AmMWSc 92*
**Dolgen,** Jonathan L. *IntMPA 92, WhoEnt 92*
**Dolgikh,** Vladimir Ivanovich 1924- *SovUnBD*
**Dolgin,** Martin 1919- *AmMWSc 92*
**Dolgoff,** Abraham 1933- *AmMWSc 92*
**Dolgoplosk,** Boris Aleksandrovich 1905- *IntWW 91*
**Dolgorunaya,** Sophie Alexandrovna *EncAmaz 91*
**Dolgow,** Allan Bentley 1933- *WhoWest 92*
**Dolhert,** Leonard Edward 1957- *AmMWSc 92*
**Dolhinow,** Phyllis Carol 1933- *AmMWSc 92*
**Dolian,** Robert Paul 1948- *WhoAmL 92*
**Doliber,** Darrel Lee 1940- *WhoFI 92, WhoWest 92*
**Dolin,** Anton 1904-1983 *FacFETw*
**Dolin,** Lonny H. 1954- *WhoAmL 92*
**Dolin,** Mitchell F. 1956- *WhoAmL 92*
**Dolin,** Morton Irwin 1920- *AmMWSc 92*
**Dolin,** Richard 1921- *AmMWSc 92*
**Dolin,** Samuel 1917- *NewAmDM*
**Dolin,** Samuel Joseph 1917- *WhoEnt 92*

**Dolinay,** Thomas V. 1923- *WhoRel 92*
**Dolinko,** David Howard 1948- *WhoAmL 92*
**Dolinsky,** Neil Leonard 1959- *WhoMW 92*
**Doll,** Alice Mary 1921- *WhoRel 92*
**Doll,** Charles George 1898- *AmMWSc 92*
**Doll,** Eugene Carter 1921- *AmMWSc 92*
**Doll,** Henri-Georges d1991 *NewYTBS 91*
**Doll,** Jerry Dennis 1943- *AmMWSc 92*
**Doll,** Jimmie Dave 1945- *AmMWSc 92*
**Doll,** Linda A. 1942- *WhoWest 92*
**Doll,** Mary Aswell 1940- *WhoRel 92*
**Doll,** Maurice E 1952- *WhoAmP 91*
**Doll,** Richard *Who 92*
**Doll,** Richard 1912- *AmMWSc 92, IntWW 91, WrDr 92*
**Doll,** Ronald C. 1913- *WrDr 92*
**Doll,** William Richard 1912- *Who 92*
**Doll-Spreitzer,** Dorothea Helen 1936- *WhoAmP 91*
**Dollahite,** Damian Gene 1939- *WhoRel 92*
**Dollahon,** James Clifford 1930- *AmMWSc 92*
**Dollahon,** Norman Richard 1944- *AmMWSc 92*
**Dollar,** Alexander M 1921- *AmMWSc 92*
**Dollar,** David Lauren 1938- *WhoMW 92*
**Dollar,** Dennis Earl 1953- *WhoAmP 91*
**Dollar,** Dolly 1962- *WhoEnt 92*
**Dollar,** Harold Ellis 1938- *WhoWest 92*
**Dollar,** Lorrie L. 1959- *WhoAmL 92*
**Dollar,** Marek 1951- *WhoMW 92*
**Dollar,** Tim Eugene 1959- *WhoAmL 92*
**Dollard,** Christopher Brickley 1960- *WhoFI 92*
**Dollard,** John D 1937- *AmMWSc 92*
**Doller,** Mikhail Ivanovich 1889-1952 *SovUnBD*
**Dollery,** Colin 1931- *IntWW 91, Who 92*
**Dolley,** Christopher 1931- *Who 92*
**Dollezhal,** Nikolay Antonovich 1899- *IntWW 91*
**Dollfus,** Audouin 1924- *IntWW 91*
**Dollfuss,** Engelbert 1892-1934 *EncTR 91 [port], FacFETw*
**Dollhopf,** William Edward 1942- *AmMWSc 92*
**Dollimore,** David 1928- *AmMWSc 92*
**Dolling,** David Stanley 1950- *AmMWSc 92*
**Dolling,** Francis Robert 1923- *IntWW 91, Who 92*
**Dolling,** Gerald 1935- *AmMWSc 92*
**Dollinger,** Elwood Johnson 1920- *AmMWSc 92*
**Dollinger,** Irving 1905- *IntMPA 92*
**Dollinger,** Werner 1918- *IntWW 91*
**Dollitz,** Grete Franke 1924- *WhoEnt 92*
**Dolliver,** Brian Kemp 1961- *WhoFI 92*
**Dolliver,** James Morgan 1924- *WhoAmL 92, WhoAmP 91, WhoWest 92*
**Dolliver,** Robert Henry 1934- *WhoMW 92*
**Dollwet,** Helmar Hermann Adolf 1929- *AmMWSc 92*
**Dolly,** Edward Dawson 1940- *AmMWSc 92*
**Dolman,** Claude Ernest 1906- *AmMWSc 92, IntWW 91*
**Dolmatovsky,** Yevgeniy Aronovich 1915- *IntWW 91*
**Dolmatovsky,** Yevgeny Aronovich 1915- *SovUnBD*
**Dolmetsch,** Arnold 1858-1940 *NewAmDM*
**Dolmetsch,** Carl 1911- *NewAmDM*
**Dolmetsch,** Carl Frederick 1911- *IntWW 91, Who 92*
**Dolmetsch,** Mabel 1874-1963 *NewAmDM*
**Dolmon,** Louis Charles 1956- *WhoMW 92*
**Dolny,** Carmen Ruthling 1942- *WhoAmP 91*
**Dolny,** Gary Mark 1955- *AmMWSc 92*
**Dolorey,** Mary *WhoRel 92*
**Dolovich,** Jerry 1936- *AmMWSc 92*
**Dolowitz,** David Augustus 1913- *WhoWest 92*
**Dolph,** Charles Laurie 1918- *AmMWSc 92*
**Dolph,** Gary Edward 1946- *AmMWSc 92, WhoMW 92*
**Dolphin,** David Henry 1940- *AmMWSc 92*
**Dolphin,** John Michael 1923- *AmMWSc 92*
**Dolphin,** John Rutherford 1936- *WhoEnt 92*
**Dolphin,** Peter James 1947- *AmMWSc 92*
**Dolphin,** Robert Earl 1929- *AmMWSc 92*
**Dolphin,** W.K. *DrAPF 91*
**Dolphin,** Warren Dean 1940- *AmMWSc 92, WhoMW 92*
**Dolphin,** Woodrow B. 1912- *WhoBlA 92*
**Dolphy,** Eric 1928-1964 *NewAmDM*
**Dolt,** Frederick Corrance 1929- *WhoAmL 92*
**Dolton,** David John William 1928- *Who 92*
**Doluisio,** James Thomas 1935- *AmMWSc 92*
**Dolukhanova,** Zara 1918- *SovUnBD*
**Dolyak,** Frank 1927- *AmMWSc 92*
**Domagala,** John Michael 1951- *AmMWSc 92*
**Domagala,** Robert F 1929- *AmMWSc 92*
**Domagala,** Robert Fielding, Jr. 1952- *WhoFI 92*
**Domagk,** Gerhard 1895-1964 *FacFETw, WhoNob 90*
**Domaille,** Peter John 1948- *AmMWSc 92*
**Domaingue,** Jacquelyn 1950- *WhoAmP 91*
**Doman,** Elvira *AmMWSc 92*
**Doman,** Glenn 1919- *WrDr 92*
**Doman,** Glenn Joseph 1919- *IntAu&W 91*
**Doman,** Margaret Horn 1946- *WhoWest 92*
**Domanico,** Robert A 1948- *WhoIns 92*
**Domanik,** Richard Anthony 1946- *AmMWSc 92*
**Domanska,** Janina *SmATA 68 [port]*
**Domanski,** Thaddeus John 1911- *AmMWSc 92*
**Domantay,** Norlito Valdez Lito 1946- *WhoWest 92*
**Domar,** Evsey D. 1914- *IntWW 91, WrDr 92*
**Domar,** Evsey David 1914- *WhoFI 92*
**Domarkas,** Juozas 1936- *WhoEnt 92*
**Domask,** W G 1920- *AmMWSc 92*
**Domaskin,** Eleanor Elaine 1922- *WhoAmP 91*
**Domazlicky,** Bruce Raymond 1948- *WhoFI 92*
**Domb,** Alexander L. 1954- *WhoAmL 92*
**Domb,** Cyril *IntWW 91, Who 92*
**Domb,** Ellen Ruth 1946- *AmMWSc 92*
**Dombalis,** Constantine Nicholas 1925- *WhoRel 92*
**Dombek,** Curtis Michael 1958- *WhoAmL 92*
**Dombey,** Philip Louis 1948- *WhoAmL 92*
**Dombkowski,** Joseph John 1961- *WhoMW 92*
**Dombourian,** Peter Mampreh 1920- *WhoEnt 92*
**Dombro,** Roy S 1933- *AmMWSc 92*
**Dombroski,** John Richard 1941- *AmMWSc 92*
**Dombrower,** Mario 1941- *WhoWest 92*
**Dombrowski,** Bernard Joseph 1929- *WhoAmP 91*
**Dombrowski,** Bob *DrAPF 91*
**Dombrowski,** Chester John 1938- *WhoFI 92*
**Dombrowski,** Edmund Theodore 1930- *WhoAmP 91*
**Dombrowski,** Gerard *DrAPF 91*
**Dombrowski,** Joanne Marie 1946- *AmMWSc 92*
**Dombrowski,** Raymond Edward, Jr. 1954- *WhoAmL 92*
**Dome,** William Douglas 1961- *WhoMW 92*
**Domelsmith,** Linda Nell 1949- *AmMWSc 92*
**Domenchina,** Juan Jose 1898-1959 *LiExTwC*
**Domengeaux,** Jerome Eraste 1919- *WhoAmL 92*
**Domenici,** Pete 1932- *WhoWest 92*
**Domenici,** Pete V. 1932- *IntWW 91, WhoAmP 91*
**Domenici,** Peter V. 1932- *AlmAP 92 [port]*
**Domenick,** Warren Lee 1945- *WhoFI 92*
**Domeniconi,** Michael John 1946- *AmMWSc 92*
**Domer,** Floyd Ray 1931- *AmMWSc 92*
**Domer,** Judith E 1939- *AmMWSc 92*
**Domeracki,** Henry Stefan 1956- *WhoAmP 91*
**Domermuth,** Charles Henry, Jr 1928- *AmMWSc 92*
**Domes,** Barry 1951- *WhoMW 92*
**Domeshek,** S 1920- *AmMWSc 92*
**Domett,** Alfred 1811-1887 *RfGEnL 91*
**Domett,** Douglas Brian 1932- *Who 92*
**Domeyko,** Cecilia 1950- *WhoEnt 92*
**Domholdt,** Elizabeth 1958- *WhoMW 92*
**Domholdt,** Lowell Curtis 1934- *AmMWSc 92*
**Domier,** Kenneth Walter 1933- *AmMWSc 92*
**Domin,** Hilde 1912- *IntWW 91, LiExTwC*
**Dominey,** Raymond Nelson 1957- *AmMWSc 92*
**Domingo,** Francisco *WhoHisp 92*
**Domingo,** Placido 1941- *FacFETw [port], IntWW 91, NewAmDM, Who 92, WhoEnt 92*
**Domingo,** Wayne Elwin 1916- *AmMWSc 92*
**Domingos,** Henry 1934- *AmMWSc 92*
**Domingue,** Angela Inzerella 1952- *WhoAmL 92*
**Domingue,** Gerald James 1937- *AmMWSc 92*
**Dominguez,** A. M., Jr. 1943- *WhoHisp 92*
**Dominguez,** Abraham A. 1927- *WhoHisp 92*
**Dominguez,** Angel De Jesus 1950- *WhoHisp 92*
**Dominguez,** Antonio 1951- *WhoHisp 92*
**Dominguez,** Cari M. 1949- *WhoHisp 92*
**Dominguez,** Cesareo Augusto 1942- *AmMWSc 92*
**Dominguez,** Eduardo Ramiro 1953- *WhoHisp 92*
**Dominguez,** Janie C. 1939- *WhoHisp 92*
**Dominguez,** Jesus Ygnacio 1940- *WhoHisp 92*
**Dominguez,** John Christopher 1954- *WhoWest 92*
**Dominguez,** Jorge Ignacio 1945- *WhoHisp 92*
**Dominguez,** Julio P. *WhoHisp 92*
**Dominguez,** Lorenzo 1953- *WhoHisp 92*
**Dominguez,** Manuel 1960- *WhoAmL 92*
**Dominguez,** Marine 1952- *IntMPA 92*
**Dominguez,** Miguel A. 1961- *WhoHisp 92*
**Dominguez,** Patricia P *WhoAmP 91*
**Dominguez,** Peter Joseph 1956- *WhoHisp 92*
**Dominguez,** Rachel 1936- *WhoHisp 92*
**Dominguez,** Ralph, Jr. 1952- *WhoHisp 92*
**Dominguez,** Richard M. *WhoHisp 92*
**Dominguez,** Roberto 1955- *WhoHisp 92*
**Dominguez,** Ronald *WhoHisp 92*
**Dominguez,** Ruben *WhoEnt 92*
**Dominguez,** Russell Guadalupe 1960- *WhoHisp 92*
**Dominguez,** Steven 1942- *WhoHisp 92*
**Dominguez Camargo,** Hernando 1601-1659 *HisDSpE*
**Dominguez-Mayoral,** Rodrigo 1947- *WhoHisp 92*
**DoMinh,** Thap 1938- *AmMWSc 92*
**Domini,** Irene C 1933- *WhoAmP 91*
**Domini,** John A. *DrAPF 91*
**Dominian,** Jack 1929- *WrDr 92*
**Dominian,** Jacobus 1929- *IntWW 91, Who 92*
**Dominianni,** Emilio Anthony 1931- *WhoAmL 92*
**Dominianni,** Samuel James 1937- *AmMWSc 92*
**Dominic,** Irwing 1930- *WhoBlA 92, WhoMW 92*
**Dominic,** R. B. *WrDr 92*
**Dominick,** Betty Garrett 1938- *WhoAmP 91*
**Dominick,** Paul Allen 1954- *WhoAmL 92*
**Dominick,** Wayne Dennis 1946- *AmMWSc 92*
**Dominik,** Hans 1872-1945 *EncTR 91*
**Dominik,** Jack Edward 1924- *WhoAmL 92*
**Dominioni,** Angelo Maria Francesco 1932- *WhoFI 92*
**Dominique,** Daniel Roy 1918- *WhoIns 92*
**Domino,** Edward Felix 1924- *AmMWSc 92*
**Domino,** Fats 1928- *FacFETw, WhoBlA 92, WhoEnt 92*
**Domino,** Fats 1929- *NewAmDM*
**Dominy,** Beryl W 1941- *AmMWSc 92*
**Dominy,** Eric Norman 1918- *WrDr 92*
**Dominy,** Sam 1945- *WhoAmP 91*
**Domitian** 51-96 *EncEarC*
**Domitien,** Elisabeth *IntWW 91*
**Domitrovich,** Michael John 1962- *WhoEnt 92*
**Domjan,** Laszlo Karoly 1947- *WhoMW 92*
**Domke,** Charles J 1914- *AmMWSc 92*
**Domke,** Gary Edward *WhoMW 92*
**Domke,** Herbert Reuben 1919- *AmMWSc 92*
**Domke,** Michael John 1963- *WhoRel 92*
**Domm,** Patricia A. 1956- *WhoFI 92*
**Dommer,** Donald Duane 1938- *WhoWest 92*
**Dommermuth,** William P. 1925- *WrDr 92*
**Dommermuth,** William Peter *WhoMW 92*
**Dommert,** Arthur Roland 1937- *AmMWSc 92*
**Domnie,** Scott Harold 1954- *WhoWest 92*
**Domning,** Daryl Paul 1947- *AmMWSc 92*
**Domogatsky,** Vladimir Nikolaevich 1876-1939 *SovUnBD*
**Domokos,** Gabor 1933- *AmMWSc 92*
**Domokos,** Matyas 1930- *Who 92*
**Domokos,** Robert Lewis 1938- *WhoMW 92, WhoRel 92*
**Domondon,** Oscar 1924- *WhoWest 92*
**Domoto,** Hisao 1928- *IntWW 91*
**Domozych,** David S *AmMWSc 92*
**Dompke,** Norbert Frank 1920- *WhoMW 92*
**Domroese,** Kenneth Arthur 1933- *AmMWSc 92*
**Domsch,** John Francis 1941- *WhoRel 92*
**Domske,** Renny 1950- *WhoRel 92*
**Domsky,** Ira Michael 1951- *WhoWest 92*
**Domsky,** Irving Isaac 1930- *AmMWSc 92*
**Don Quichotte** *ScFEYrs*
**Don,** Carl 1915- *WhoEnt 92*
**Don Camilo,** Matilda Verdu 1916- *WhoNob 90*
**Don-Wauchope,** Roger Hamilton *Who 92*
**Donabedian,** Avedis 1919- *AmMWSc 92, IntWW 91*
**Donachie,** Matthew J, Jr 1932- *AmMWSc 92*
**Donadieu,** Joseph Martin 1943- *WhoRel 92*
**Donady,** J James 1938- *AmMWSc 92*
**Donagh,** Rita 1939- *TwCPaSc*
**Donaghey,** Tanya Marie 1966- *WhoMW 92*
**Donaghy,** Gene Allen 1955- *WhoMW 92*
**Donaghy,** James Joseph 1935- *AmMWSc 92*
**Donaghy,** Laura Ann 1968- *WhoEnt 92*
**Donaghy,** Michael 1954- *WrDr 92*
**Donaghy,** Raymond Madiford Peardon 1910- *AmMWSc 92*
**Donahey,** Gertrude Walton 1908- *WhoAmP 91*
**Donahey,** Richard Sterling, Jr. 1941- *WhoAmL 92, WhoMW 92*
**Donahoe,** Bernard Francis 1932- *WhoMW 92*
**Donahoe,** Frank J 1922- *AmMWSc 92*
**Donahoe,** J Michael 1938- *WhoAmP 91*
**Donahoe,** Jim *DrAPF 91*
**Donahoe,** John Philip 1944- *AmMWSc 92*
**Donahoe,** Teresa 1960- *WhoEnt 92*
**Donahoo,** Pat 1928- *AmMWSc 92*
**Donahoo,** Stanley Ellsworth 1933- *WhoWest 92*
**Donahue,** Barbara Lynn Sean 1956- *WhoEnt 92*
**Donahue,** Charles, Jr. 1941- *WhoAmL 92*
**Donahue,** Charles Bertrand, II 1937- *WhoAmL 92*
**Donahue,** Charlotte Mary 1954- *WhoAmL 92*
**Donahue,** Craig Richard 1951- *WhoAmL 92*
**Donahue,** D Joseph 1926- *AmMWSc 92*
**Donahue,** Dennis Donald 1940- *WhoWest 92*
**Donahue,** Donald Jordan 1924- *WhoFI 92*
**Donahue,** Douglas Aidan, Jr. 1951- *WhoFI 92*
**Donahue,** Douglas James 1924- *AmMWSc 92*
**Donahue,** Elinor 1937- *IntMPA 92*
**Donahue,** Francis M 1934- *AmMWSc 92*
**Donahue,** Hayden Hackney 1912- *AmMWSc 92*
**Donahue,** J. Thomas 1934- *WhoFI 92*
**Donahue,** Jack *DrAPF 91*
**Donahue,** Jack d1991 *NewYTBS 91*
**Donahue,** Jack 1917-1991 *ConAu 135*
**Donahue,** Jack David 1938- *AmMWSc 92*
**Donahue,** James J., Jr. 1919- *WhoWest 92*
**Donahue,** John Edward 1950- *WhoAmL 92*
**Donahue,** John F 1936- *WhoIns 92*
**Donahue,** John Lawrence, Jr. 1939- *WhoMW 92*
**Donahue,** John Michael 1952- *WhoAmL 92*
**Donahue,** Karin Victoria 1945- *WhoAmL 92*
**Donahue,** Laura Kent 1949- *WhoAmP 91*
**Donahue,** Lauri Michele 1961- *WhoWest 92*
**Donahue,** Lynn Anne 1965- *WhoEnt 92*
**Donahue,** Mary Ann *WhoEnt 92*
**Donahue,** Michael Joseph 1947- *WhoAmL 92*
**Donahue,** Phil *LesBEnT 92 [port]*
**Donahue,** Phil 1935- *IntMPA 92, WhoEnt 92*
**Donahue,** Richard C. 1942- *WhoFI 92*
**Donahue,** Robin Morrow 1955- *WhoMW 92*
**Donahue,** Roy L 1908- *ConAu 34NR*
**Donahue,** Shirley Ohnstad 1937- *WhoMW 92*
**Donahue,** Terry Lee 1946- *WhoAmP 91*
**Donahue,** Thomas Michael 1921- *AmMWSc 92, IntWW 91*
**Donahue,** Thomas Raymond 1962- *WhoFI 92*
**Donahue,** Timothy Patrick 1955- *WhoAmL 92*
**Donahue,** Troy 1937- *IntMPA 92*
**Donahue,** Walter Lawrence 1931- *WhoEnt 92*
**Donahue,** William Patrick 1958- *WhoRel 92*
**Donahue,** William T. 1943- *WhoBlA 92*
**Donald,** Alan 1931- *IntWW 91, Who 92*
**Donald,** Alastair Geoffrey 1926- *Who 92*
**Donald,** Arnold Wayne 1954- *WhoBlA 92*
**Donald,** Bernice Bouie 1951- *WhoBlA 92*
**Donald,** Craig Reid Cantlie 1914- *Who 92*
**Donald,** Dennis Scott 1939- *AmMWSc 92*
**Donald,** Elizabeth Ann 1926- *AmMWSc 92*
**Donald,** Harvey C *WhoAmP 91*
**Donald,** Ian *WhoWest 92*
**Donald,** Jack C. 1934- *WhoFI 92*
**Donald,** John 1927- *Who 92*
**Donald,** Kenneth William 1911- *Who 92*
**Donald,** Merlin Wilfred *AmMWSc 92*
**Donald,** Michael Joseph 1960- *WhoRel 92*

**Donald**, Robert Walter 1948- *WhoWest 92*
**Donald**, William 1910- *WrDr 92*
**Donald**, William David 1924- *AmMWSc 92*
**Donald**, William Waldie 1950- *AmMWSc 92*
**Donalds**, Gordon *TwCWW 91, WrDr 92*
**Donaldson** *Who 92*
**Donaldson**, Alan C 1929- *AmMWSc 92*
**Donaldson**, Alan Stuart 1958- *WhoAmL 92*
**Donaldson**, Alexander Ivan 1942- *Who 92*
**Donaldson**, Alexander MacFarland 1953- *WhoAmL 92*
**Donaldson**, Antony 1939- *TwCPaSc*
**Donaldson**, Bryna *SmATA 65*
**Donaldson**, Charles Ian 1935- *Who 92*
**Donaldson**, Charles Ian Edward 1935- *IntWW 91*
**Donaldson**, Coleman DuPont 1922- *AmMWSc 92*
**Donaldson**, Craig John 1949- *WhoAmL 92*
**Donaldson**, David Abercrombie 1916- *Who 92*
**Donaldson**, David Miller 1924- *AmMWSc 92*
**Donaldson**, David Torrance 1943- *Who 92*
**Donaldson**, Dennis C 1938- *WhoAmP 91*
**Donaldson**, Donald Jay 1940- *AmMWSc 92*
**Donaldson**, Dorothy Mary 1921- *Who 92*
**Donaldson**, Edward Enslow 1923- *AmMWSc 92*
**Donaldson**, Edward Mortlock 1912- *Who 92*
**Donaldson**, Edward Mossop 1939- *AmMWSc 92*
**Donaldson**, Erle C 1926- *AmMWSc 92*
**Donaldson**, Frances 1907- *IntAu&W 91, WrDr 92*
**Donaldson**, Frances Annesley 1907- *Who 92*
**Donaldson**, Frank W. 1921- *WhoAmL 92*
**Donaldson**, Gene Michael 1953- *WhoRel 92*
**Donaldson**, George Burney 1945- *WhoWest 92*
**Donaldson**, Gordon 1913- *IntAu&W 91, Who 92, WrDr 92*
**Donaldson**, Hamish 1936- *Who 92*
**Donaldson**, Henry A. *DcNCBi 2*
**Donaldson**, Herbert 1918- *WhoEnt 92*
**Donaldson**, Ian *Who 92*
**Donaldson**, Ian 1935- *ConAu 35NR*
**Donaldson**, Islay Murray 1921- *ConAu 135*
**Donaldson**, James A 1941- *AmMWSc 92*
**Donaldson**, James Adrian 1930- *AmMWSc 92*
**Donaldson**, James Lee, III 1957- *WhoBlA 92*
**Donaldson**, Jeff Richardson 1932- *WhoBlA 92*
**Donaldson**, Joan *LesBEnT 92*
**Donaldson**, John Allan 1933- *AmMWSc 92*
**Donaldson**, John Anthony 1938- *WhoAmL 92*
**Donaldson**, John Cecil, Jr. 1933- *WhoFI 92*
**Donaldson**, John Riley 1925- *AmMWSc 92, WhoWest 92*
**Donaldson**, John Weber 1926- *WhoAmP 91*
**Donaldson**, John William 1941- *WhoAmP 91*
**Donaldson**, Lauren Russell 1903- *AmMWSc 92*
**Donaldson**, Leon Matthew 1933- *WhoBlA 92*
**Donaldson**, Leslie Anne 1955- *WhoWest 92*
**Donaldson**, Linda Margaret 1941- *WhoAmP 91*
**Donaldson**, Marcia Jean 1925- *WhoRel 92*
**Donaldson**, Mary *Who 92*
**Donaldson**, Mary 1921- *IntWW 91*
**Donaldson**, Mary Kendrick 1937- *WhoWest 92*
**Donaldson**, Maye Howe 1923- *WhoAmP 91*
**Donaldson**, Merle Richard 1920- *AmMWSc 92*
**Donaldson**, Michael Cleaves 1939- *WhoAmP 91*
**Donaldson**, Norman 1922- *WrDr 92*
**Donaldson**, Patricia Anne *Who 92*
**Donaldson**, Ray Chute 1958- *WhoBlA 92*
**Donaldson**, Richard T. 1935- *WhoBlA 92*
**Donaldson**, Robert, Jr. 1800-1872 *DcNCBi 2*
**Donaldson**, Robert Cecil 1938- *WhoEnt 92*
**Donaldson**, Robert Huntington 1929- *WhoMW 92*
**Donaldson**, Robert M, Jr 1927- *AmMWSc 92*
**Donaldson**, Robert Paul 1941- *AmMWSc 92*
**Donaldson**, Robert Rymal 1917- *AmMWSc 92*
**Donaldson**, Roger 1945- *IntMPA 92*
**Donaldson**, Sam *LesBEnT 92 [port]*
**Donaldson**, Samuel Andrew 1934- *IntWW 91*
**Donaldson**, Scott 1928- *DcLB 111 [port], WrDr 92*
**Donaldson**, Simon Kirwan 1957- *IntWW 91, Who 92*
**Donaldson**, Stephen R. *DrAPF 91*
**Donaldson**, Stephen R. 1947- *WrDr 92*
**Donaldson**, Stephen Reeder 1947- *IntAu&W 91*
**Donaldson**, Sue Karen 1943- *AmMWSc 92*
**Donaldson**, Susan Kay 1953- *WhoAmL 92*
**Donaldson**, Terrence Lee 1946- *AmMWSc 92*
**Donaldson**, Thomas 1943- *WhoIns 92*
**Donaldson**, Timothy Baswell 1934- *Who 92*
**Donaldson**, Vernon D'Arcy 1906- *Who 92*
**Donaldson**, Virginia Henrietta 1924- *AmMWSc 92*
**Donaldson**, Virginia Lee 1950- *WhoMW 92*
**Donaldson**, W Lyle 1915- *AmMWSc 92*
**Donaldson**, Walter 1893-1947 *NewAmDM*
**Donaldson**, Wilburn Lester 1931- *WhoWest 92*
**Donaldson**, William Emmert 1931- *AmMWSc 92*
**Donaldson**, William Twitty 1927- *AmMWSc 92*
**Donaldson Of Kingsbridge**, Baron 1907- *IntWW 91, Who 92*
**Donaldson of Kingsbridge**, Lady *Who 92*
**Donaldson Of Lymington**, Baron 1920- *IntWW 91, Who 92*
**Donaldson of Lymington**, Lady *Who 92*
**Donart**, Gary B 1940- *AmMWSc 92*
**Donaruma**, L Guy 1928- *AmMWSc 92*
**do Nascimento**, Alexander 1925- *WhoRel 92*
**Do Nascimento**, Alexandre 1925- *IntWW 91*
**Donat**, Peter 1928- *ConTFT 9*
**Donat**, Peter Collingwood *WhoEnt 92*
**Donat**, Rex *WhoRel 92*
**Donat-Cattin**, Carlo 1919-1991 *IntWW 91, -91N*
**Donath**, Fred Arthur 1931- *AmMWSc 92, WhoWest 92*
**Donath**, Gary Allen 1942- *WhoFI 92*
**Donath**, Helen 1940- *IntWW 91, NewAmDM*
**Donati**, Antigono 1910- *IntWW 91*
**Donati**, Edward Joseph 1924- *AmMWSc 92*
**Donati**, Robert M 1934- *AmMWSc 92*
**Donati**, Robert Mario 1934- *WhoMW 92*
**Donato**, Alfonso A., Jr. 1950- *WhoHisp 92*
**Donato**, Alfred Virgil 1917- *WhoFI 92*
**Donato**, Alma Delia 1956- *WhoHisp 92*
**Donato**, Arthur Thomas, Jr. 1955- *WhoAmL 92*
**Donato**, Baldassare 1530?-1603 *NewAmDM*
**Donato**, Rosario Francesco 1947- *AmMWSc 92*
**Donatoni**, Franco 1927- *ConCom 92, IntWW 91, NewAmDM*
**Donatucci**, Robert C 1952- *WhoAmP 91*
**Donatucci**, Ronald Rocco 1948- *WhoAmP 91*
**Donatus The Great** d355 *EncEarC*
**Donavel**, David F. *DrAPF 91*
**Donawa**, Maria Elena 1948- *WhoBlA 92*
**Donawick**, William Joseph 1940- *AmMWSc 92*
**Donay**, Natalie d1991 *NewYTBS 91*
**Doncaster**, Archdeacon of *Who 92*
**Doncaster**, Bishop Suffragan of 1927- *Who 92*
**Donchess**, James W *WhoAmP 91*
**Donchin**, Emanuel 1935- *AmMWSc 92*
**Dondanville**, John Wallace 1937- *WhoAmL 92*
**Dondelinger**, Albert Marie Joseph 1934- *IntWW 91*
**Dondelinger**, Jean 1930- *IntWW 91, Who 92*
**Dondero**, Norman Carl 1918- *AmMWSc 92*
**Dondershine**, Frank Haskin 1931- *AmMWSc 92*
**Dondershine**, Harvey Edward 1942- *WhoWest 92*
**Dondes**, Seymour 1918- *AmMWSc 92*
**Done**, Alan Kimball 1926- *AmMWSc 92*
**Done**, Robert Stacy 1965- *WhoWest 92*
**Donefer**, Allan Hadley 1955- *WhoFI 92*
**Donefer**, Eugene 1933- *AmMWSc 92*
**Donegall**, Marquess of 1916- *Who 92*
**Donegan**, Charles Edward 1933- *WhoAmL 92, WhoBlA 92*
**Donegan**, Dorothy 1922- *NotBlAW 92*
**Donegan**, Horace W. B. 1900- *Who 92*
**Donegan**, Horace W.B. 1900-1991 *NewYTBS 91*
**Donegan**, William L 1932- *AmMWSc 92*
**Donegan**, William Laurence 1932- *WhoMW 92*
**Donehoo**, Paris Nolan 1952- *WhoRel 92*
**Donehue**, John Douglas 1928- *WhoFI 92*
**Donelan**, Clarence Warren 1924- *WhoBlA 92*
**Donelan**, James M 1951- *WhoAmP 91*
**Donelan**, Mark Anthony 1942- *AmMWSc 92*
**Donelian**, Armen 1950- *WhoEnt 92*
**Donelian**, Khatchik O. d1991 *NewYTBS 91*
**Donelon**, James J 1944- *WhoAmP 91*
**Donelson**, Angie Fields Cantrell Merritt 1914- *WhoFI 92*
**Donelson**, Irene W. 1913- *WhoWest 92*
**Donelson**, John Everett 1943- *AmMWSc 92*
**Donelson**, Kenneth LaVern 1927- *WhoWest 92*
**Donelson**, Kenneth Wilber 1910- *WhoAmL 92*
**Donen**, Joshua 1955- *WhoEnt 92*
**Donen**, Stanley 1924- *IntDcF 2-2 [port], IntMPA 92, IntWW 91, WhoEnt 92*
**Donenfeld**, Alan Paul 1957- *WhoFI 92*
**Donenfeld**, Alice Greenbaum 1938- *WhoEnt 92*
**Donenfeld**, James 1917- *WhoEnt 92*
**Doner**, Colonel Vaughn 1948- *WhoRel 92*
**Doner**, Frederick Nathan 1943- *WhoEnt 92*
**Doner**, Gary William 1951- *WhoFI 92*
**Doner**, Harvey Ervin 1938- *AmMWSc 92*
**Doner**, John Roland 1949- *WhoWest 92*
**Doner**, Landis Willard 1941- *AmMWSc 92*
**Doneraile**, Viscount 1946- *Who 92*
**Donesa**, Antonio Braganza 1935- *WhoMW 92*
**Donesley**, Brian N 1948- *WhoAmP 91*
**Doneth**, John M. 1949- *WhoFI 92*
**Donewald**, Marian 1911- *WhoMW 92*
**Doney**, Charles Conrad 1942- *WhoWest 92*
**Doney**, Devon Lyle 1934- *AmMWSc 92*
**Doney**, Judith Karen 1942- *WhoRel 92*
**Donfried**, Karl Paul 1940- *WhoRel 92*
**Dong Chuncai** d1990 *IntWW 91N*
**Dong Fureng** 1927- *IntWW 91*
**Dong Jichang** 1930- *IntWW 91*
**Dong Kejun** 1939- *IntWW 91*
**Dong Zhanlin** 1923- *IntWW 91*
**Dong Zheng** 1926- *IntWW 91*
**Dong**, Alvin Lim 1955- *WhoAmL 92*
**Dong**, Pham Van *FacFETw*
**Dong**, Qianqian *WhoAmL 92*
**Dong**, Richard Gene 1935- *AmMWSc 92*
**Dong**, Stanley B 1936- *AmMWSc 92, WhoWest 92*
**Dongalen**, Geoffrey Ombian 1937- *WhoRel 92*
**Dongarra**, Jack Joseph 1950- *AmMWSc 92*
**Donges**, Samuel Arnold 1958- *WhoWest 92*
**Dongier**, Maurice Henri 1925- *AmMWSc 92*
**Donhoff**, Marion 1909- *IntWW 91*
**Doniach**, Israel 1911- *Who 92*
**Doniach**, Sebastian 1934- *AmMWSc 92*
**Donian**, Daniel Lee 1957- *WhoEnt 92*
**Donielson**, Allen Lee 1927- *WhoAmL 92*
**Doniger**, Jay 1944- *AmMWSc 92*
**Doniger**, Walter *IntMPA 92, WhoEnt 92*
**Doniger**, Wendy 1940- *WhoRel 92*
**Donington**, Robert 1907-1990 *NewAmDM*
**Donini**, Ambrogio 1903- *IntWW 91*
**Donisch**, Valentine 1919- *AmMWSc 92*
**Donisthorpe**, Christine Ann 1932- *WhoAmP 91*
**Donitz**, Karl 1891-1980 *BiDExR, EncTR 91 [port]*
**Donivan**, Frank Forbes, Jr 1943- *AmMWSc 92*
**Donizetti**, Gaetano 1797-1848 *NewAmDM*
**Donker**, John D 1920- *AmMWSc 92*
**Donker**, Richard Bruce 1950- *WhoWest 92*
**Donkersloot**, William Martin 1947- *WhoRel 92*
**Donkin**, Alexander Sim 1922- *Who 92*
**Donkin**, Nance 1915- *IntAu&W 91, WrDr 92*
**Donkin**, Peter Langloh 1913- *Who 92*
**Donkin**, Robin Arthur 1928- *Who 92*
**Donlan**, Thomas Garrett 1945- *WhoEnt 92*
**Donleavy**, J.P. *DrAPF 91*
**Donleavy**, J. P. 1926- *BenetAL 91, ConNov 91, FacFETw, LiExTwC, WrDr 92*
**Donleavy**, James Patrick 1926- *IntAu&W 91, IntWW 91, Who 92*
**Donlevy**, John Dearden 1933- *WhoAmL 92*
**Donley**, Brian C. *WhoRel 92*
**Donley**, David Arthur 1954- *WhoAmP 91*
**Donley**, Edward 1921- *WhoFI 92*
**Donley**, Glenda Jane 1954- *WhoEnt 92*
**Donley**, John P 1939- *WhoAmP 91*
**Donley**, Judy Marie 1961- *WhoMW 92*
**Donley**, Russell Lee, III 1939- *WhoAmP 91*
**Donley**, Van E 1948- *WhoAmP 91*
**Donlon**, Mildred A 1940- *AmMWSc 92*
**Donlon**, William Christopher 1952- *WhoWest 92*
**Donn**, Bertram 1919- *AmMWSc 92*
**Donn**, Cheng 1938- *AmMWSc 92*
**Donn**, Mary Cecilia 1940- *Who 92*
**Donn-Byrne**, Brian Oswald 1889-1928 *BenetAL 91*
**Donnachie**, Alexander 1936- *Who 92*
**Donnachie**, Ian 1944- *IntAu&W 91, WrDr 92*
**Donnadieu**, Agnes 1950- *WhoEnt 92*
**Donnahoe**, Alan Stanley 1916- *WhoFI 92*
**Donnalley**, James R, Jr 1918- *AmMWSc 92*
**Donnally**, Bailey Lewis 1930- *AmMWSc 92*
**Donnan**, David Leslie 1959- *WhoAmL 92*
**Donnan**, Frederick George 1879-1956 *FacFETw*
**Donnan**, Robin C. 1966- *WhoMW 92*
**Donnan**, William W 1911- *AmMWSc 92*
**Donnay**, Gabrielle 1920- *AmMWSc 92*
**Donnay**, J. D. H. 1902- *IntWW 91*
**Donnay**, Joseph Desire Hubert 1902- *AmMWSc 92*
**Donne**, David Lucas 1925- *Who 92*
**Donne**, Gaven 1914- *Who 92*
**Donne**, John 1572-1631 *CnDBLB 1 [port], RfGEnL 91*
**Donne**, John 1921- *Who 92*
**Donne**, Maxim *IntAu&W 91X*
**Donnell**, Brenda Louise *WhoAmP 91*
**Donnell**, Brian James 1955- *WhoAmL 92*
**Donnell**, Bruce Bolton 1946- *WhoEnt 92*
**Donnell**, Dana I. 1953- *WhoMW 92*
**Donnell**, George Nino 1919- *AmMWSc 92*
**Donnell**, Harold Eugene, Jr. 1935- *WhoMW 92*
**Donnell**, Henry Denny, Jr 1935- *AmMWSc 92*
**Donnell**, James Knox 1931- *WhoRel 92*
**Donnell**, John Robert 1789-1864 *DcNCBi 2*
**Donnell**, Richard Spaight 1820-1867 *DcNCBi 2*
**Donnell**, Robert 1784-1855 *DcNCBi 2*
**Donnell**, Sandra DiBella 1944- *WhoAmP 91*
**Donnella**, Michael Andre 1954- *WhoAmL 92*
**Donnellan**, Kevin J 1957- *WhoAmP 91*
**Donnelley**, James Russell 1935- *WhoFI 92*
**Donnellon**, Edward James 1924- *WhoAmP 91*
**Donnelly**, Alan John 1957- *Who 92*
**Donnelly**, Andrea 1937- *WhoRel 92*
**Donnelly**, Austin S. *WrDr 92*
**Donnelly**, Barbara Schettler 1933- *WhoFI 92*
**Donnelly**, Brendan James 1937- *AmMWSc 92*
**Donnelly**, Brian 1945- *Who 92*
**Donnelly**, Brian J. 1946- *AlmAP 92 [port], WhoAmP 91*
**Donnelly**, Denis Philip 1937- *AmMWSc 92*
**Donnelly**, Donal 1931- *IntMPA 92, WhoEnt 92*
**Donnelly**, Edward Daniel 1919- *AmMWSc 92*
**Donnelly**, George R. *WhoHisp 92*
**Donnelly**, Grace Marie 1929- *AmMWSc 92*
**Donnelly**, Ignatius *ScFEYrs B*
**Donnelly**, Ignatius 1831-1901 *AmPolLe, BenetAL 91*
**Donnelly**, James *WhoAmP 91*
**Donnelly**, James 1931- *IntWW 91*
**Donnelly**, James Corcoran, Jr. 1946- *WhoAmL 92*
**Donnelly**, James S., Jr. 1943- *WrDr 92*
**Donnelly**, Jane *WrDr 92*
**Donnelly**, John 1914- *AmMWSc 92*
**Donnelly**, John 1941- *WhoRel 92, WhoWest 92*
**Donnelly**, John James, III 1954- *AmMWSc 92*
**Donnelly**, John Joseph 1943- *WhoAmL 92*
**Donnelly**, John Patrick 1934- *WhoRel 92*
**Donnelly**, Joseph P 1939- *AmMWSc 92*
**Donnelly**, Judith Andrea 1945- *WhoWest 92*
**Donnelly**, Kathleen 1921- *WhoRel 92*
**Donnelly**, Kenneth Gerald 1937- *AmMWSc 92*
**Donnelly**, Kevin William 1954- *WhoAmL 92*
**Donnelly**, Laura Diane 1957- *WhoEnt 92*
**Donnelly**, Marion G 1939- *WhoAmP 91*
**Donnelly**, Mary Louise 1926- *WhoRel 92*
**Donnelly**, Micky 1952- *TwCPaSc*
**Donnelly**, Patricia Vryling 1933- *AmMWSc 92*
**Donnelly**, Ralph E. 1932- *IntMPA 92*
**Donnelly**, Robert Edward 1946- *WhoEnt 92*

**Donnelly,** Robert Frederic 1958- *WhoFI 92*
**Donnelly,** Robert T 1924- *WhoAmP 91*
**Donnelly,** Robert True 1924- *WhoAmL 92*
**Donnelly,** Robert William *WhoRel 92*
**Donnelly,** Russell James 1930- *AmMWSc 92*
**Donnelly,** Samuel Joseph Michael 1934- *WhoAmL 92*
**Donnelly,** Scott Francis 1962- *WhoMW 92*
**Donnelly,** Susan *DrAPF 91*
**Donnelly,** Thomas Christopher 1956- *WhoAmL 92*
**Donnelly,** Thomas Edward, Jr 1943- *AmMWSc 92*
**Donnelly,** Thomas Henry 1928- *AmMWSc 92, WhoMW 92*
**Donnelly,** Thomas R, Jr 1939- *WhoAmP 91*
**Donnelly,** Thomas Wallace 1932- *AmMWSc 92*
**Donnelly,** Thomas William 1943- *AmMWSc 92*
**Donnelly,** Timothy C *AmMWSc 92*
**Donnelly,** William H *AmMWSc 92*
**Donnem,** Roland William 1929- *WhoAmL 92*
**Donnem,** Sarah Lund 1936- *WhoMW 92*
**Donnenfeld,** Bernard 1926- *IntMPA 92*
**Donner party,** The *BenetAL 91*
**Donner,** Andreas Matthias 1918- *IntWW 91*
**Donner,** Andrew Scott 1956- *WhoAmL 92*
**Donner,** Clive 1926- *IntMPA 92, IntWW 91*
**Donner,** David Bruce 1945- *AmMWSc 92*
**Donner,** George 1784?-1847 *DcNCBi 2*
**Donner,** Henry Jay 1944- *WhoAmL 92*
**Donner,** Jacob 1781?-1847 *DcNCBi 2*
**Donner,** Jonathan Edward 1957- *WhoAmP 91*
**Donner,** Jorn 1933- *IntDcF 2-2 [port]*
**Donner,** Jorn Johan 1933- *IntWW 91*
**Donner,** Kai Otto 1922- *IntWW 91*
**Donner,** Martin W 1920- *AmMWSc 92*
**Donner,** Neal Arvid 1942- *WhoWest 92*
**Donner,** Richard *WhoEnt 92*
**Donner,** Richard 1939- *IntMPA 92*
**Donner,** Tamsen Eustis 1801-1847 *DcNCBi 2*
**Donnermeyer,** William I, Sr 1924- *WhoAmP 91*
**Donnet,** Jean Baptiste 1923- *WhoFI 92*
**Donnewald,** James H 1925- *WhoAmP 91*
**Donnison,** David Vernon 1926- *Who 92, WrDr 92*
**Donnison,** Frank Siegfried Vernon 1898- *Who 92, WrDr 92*
**Donnison,** Kay *Who 92*
**Donnithorne,** Audrey Gladys 1922- *WrDr 92*
**Donny and Marie** *LesBEnT 92*
**Donofrio,** Gene 1953- *WhoAmL 92*
**D'Onofrio,** Mary Ann 1933- *WhoWest 92*
**D'Onofrio,** Steven John 1956- *WhoAmL 92*
**D'Onofrio,** Vincent Phillip 1960- *IntMPA 92*
**Donoghue,** Daniel James 1952- *AmMWSc 92*
**Donoghue,** Denis 1928- *IntAu&W 91, IntWW 91, Who 92, WrDr 92*
**Donoghue,** John F. 1928- *WhoRel 92*
**Donoghue,** John Francis 1950- *AmMWSc 92*
**Donoghue,** John M. 1939- *WhoAmL 92*
**Donoghue,** John P *WhoAmP 91*
**Donoghue,** John Timothy 1935- *AmMWSc 92*
**Donoghue,** Joseph F 1947- *AmMWSc 92*
**Donoghue,** Mildred R. 1929- *WrDr 92*
**Donoghue,** Ronald E. 1952- *WhoEnt 92*
**Donoghue,** Timothy R 1936- *AmMWSc 92*
**Donoghue,** William F, Jr 1921- *AmMWSc 92*
**Donoho,** Alvin Leroy 1936- *AmMWSc 92*
**Donoho,** Betty Brittain 1935- *WhoFI 92*
**Donoho,** Clive Wellington, Jr 1930- *AmMWSc 92*
**Donoho,** David Leigh 1957- *AmMWSc 92*
**Donoho,** Patrick Burnap 1951- *WhoMW 92*
**Donohoe,** Gregory Wood 1948- *WhoWest 92*
**Donohoe,** Jerome Francis 1939- *WhoAmL 92, WhoFI 92*
**Donohoe,** Peter 1953- *IntWW 91*
**Donohoe,** Peter Howard 1953- *Who 92*
**Donohue,** Carroll John 1917- *WhoFI 92, WhoMW 92*
**Donohue,** David Arthur Timothy 1937- *AmMWSc 92*
**Donohue,** Delaine R. 1931- *WhoFI 92*
**Donohue,** Edward Leon 1929- *WhoRel 92*
**Donohue,** George L. 1944- *WhoWest 92*
**Donohue,** Gerald Joseph, Jr. 1959- *WhoMW 92*
**Donohue,** Hubert Francis 1921- *WhoAmP 91*
**Donohue,** James Patrick 1950- *WhoAmL 92*
**Donohue,** John F, III 1949- *WhoIns 92*
**Donohue,** John J 1919- *AmMWSc 92*
**Donohue,** John Joseph 1923- *WhoAmP 91*
**Donohue,** John William, Jr. 1935- *WhoFI 92*
**Donohue,** Joyce Morrissey 1940- *AmMWSc 92*
**Donohue,** Marc David 1951- *AmMWSc 92*
**Donohue,** Mark Philip 1954- *WhoAmL 92*
**Donohue,** Michael Dean 1957- *WhoEnt 92*
**Donohue,** Michael Edward 1939- *WhoAmL 92*
**Donohue,** Michael Joseph *WhoAmL 92*
**Donohue,** Nicholas J. 1950- *WhoAmL 92*
**Donohue,** Richard Harney 1950- *WhoAmL 92*
**Donohue,** Robert J 1934- *AmMWSc 92*
**Donohue,** Robert Peter 1942- *WhoEnt 92*
**Donohue,** Therese Brady 1937- *WhoEnt 92*
**Donohue-Babiak,** Amy Lorraine 1961- *WhoAmL 92*
**Donohugh,** Donald Lee 1924- *WhoWest 92*
**Donoian,** Haig Cadmus 1930- *AmMWSc 92*
**Donoso,** Alvaro 1951- *IntWW 91*
**Donoso,** Jose 1924- *BenetAL 91, DcLB 113 [port], FacFETw, IntWW 91, LiExTwC*
**Donoughmore,** Earl of 1927- *Who 92*
**Donoughue** *Who 92*
**Donoughue,** Baron 1934- *Who 92*
**Donoughue,** Bernard 1934- *IntAu&W 91, WrDr 92*
**Donovan,** Allen F 1914- *AmMWSc 92*
**Donovan,** Arlene *IntMPA 92*
**Donovan,** Arrie Jan 1943- *WhoAmL 92*
**Donovan,** Arthur L *AmMWSc 92*
**Donovan,** B W *WhoAmP 91*
**Donovan,** Bernard Timothy 1940- *WhoAmP 91*
**Donovan,** Bill 1946- *WhoEnt 92*
**Donovan,** Brian Joseph 1953- *WhoFI 92*
**Donovan,** Carol A *WhoAmP 91*
**Donovan,** Charles Edward 1934- *Who 92*
**Donovan,** Charles J 1938- *WhoAmP 91*
**Donovan,** Charles Stephen 1951- *WhoAmL 92*
**Donovan,** Daniel J 1958- *WhoIns 92*
**Donovan,** Daniel Joseph 1948- *WhoMW 92*
**Donovan,** Deborah Carolyn 1951 *WhoAmL 92*
**Donovan,** Denis Laurence 1950- *WhoEnt 92*
**Donovan,** Dennis Dale 1954- *WhoRel 92*
**Donovan,** Dennis Michael 1948- *WhoWest 92*
**Donovan,** Desmond Thomas 1921- *Who 92*
**Donovan,** Diane C. *DrAPF 91*
**Donovan,** Edward Francis 1918- *AmMWSc 92*
**Donovan,** Edward Francis 1949- *WhoAmL 92*
**Donovan,** Egbert Herbert 1913- *WhoRel 92*
**Donovan,** Frances R. 1880-1965 *WomSoc*
**Donovan,** Francis X 1912- *WhoAmP 91*
**Donovan,** Gerald Alton 1925- *AmMWSc 92*
**Donovan,** Hedley 1914-1990 *AnObit 1990*
**Donovan,** Hedley Williams d1990 *IntWW 91N*
**Donovan,** Hedley Williams 1914- *IntAu&W 91*
**Donovan,** Henry B. *IntMPA 92*
**Donovan,** Herbert Alcorn, Jr. 1931- *WhoRel 92*
**Donovan,** Ian Edward 1940- *Who 92*
**Donovan,** James 1906- *AmMWSc 92*
**Donovan,** James C. *WhoRel 92*
**Donovan,** James Hubert 1923- *WhoAmP 91*
**Donovan,** James M. 1957- *WhoWest 92*
**Donovan,** Jane Fagan 1929- *WhoAmL 92*
**Donovan,** John 1919- *IntAu&W 91*
**Donovan,** John 1928- *WrDr 92*
**Donovan,** John 1957- *WhoAmL 92*
**Donovan,** John Arthur 1942- *WhoAmL 92*
**Donovan,** John Carl 1930- *WhoRel 92*
**Donovan,** John Francis 1935- *AmMWSc 92*
**Donovan,** John Joseph *AmMWSc 92*
**Donovan,** John Joseph, Jr. 1916- *WhoFI 92, WhoWest 92*
**Donovan,** John Leo 1929- *AmMWSc 92*
**Donovan,** John Richard 1917- *AmMWSc 92*
**Donovan,** John W 1929- *AmMWSc 92*
**Donovan,** Kathleen 1952- *WhoAmP 91*
**Donovan,** Laurie B 1932- *WhoAmP 91*
**Donovan,** Lawrence Perry, III 1947- *WhoWest 92*
**Donovan,** Leo F 1932- *AmMWSc 92*
**Donovan,** Margaret Mary 1911- *WhoAmP 91*
**Donovan,** Mark *TwCWW 91*
**Donovan,** Mary Frances 1935- *WhoMW 92*
**Donovan,** Maurice John 1954- *WhoAmL 92*
**Donovan,** Michael Dennis 1959- *WhoAmL 92*
**Donovan,** Michael Richard 1952- *WhoWest 92*
**Donovan,** Nancy S. 1951- *WhoFI 92*
**Donovan,** P F 1932- *AmMWSc 92*
**Donovan,** Patricia Anne 1931- *WhoAmL 92*
**Donovan,** Paul Joseph 1951- *WhoAmL 92*
**Donovan,** Paul V. 1924- *WhoRel 92*
**Donovan,** Peter Andrew 1935- *WhoAmL 92*
**Donovan,** Phoebe 1902- *TwCPaSc*
**Donovan,** R. Michael 1943- *WhoFI 92*
**Donovan,** Raymond J. 1930- *IntWW 91, WhoAmP 91*
**Donovan,** Richard C 1941- *AmMWSc 92*
**Donovan,** Richard Edward 1952- *WhoAmL 92*
**Donovan,** Richard Frank 1891-1970 *NewAmDM*
**Donovan,** Richard John 1955- *WhoAmL 92*
**Donovan,** Richard Timothy 1957- *WhoAmL 92*
**Donovan,** Robert Kent 1932- *WhoMW 92*
**Donovan,** Sandra Steranka 1942- *AmMWSc 92*
**Donovan,** Susan *DrAPF 91*
**Donovan,** Terence M 1931- *AmMWSc 92*
**Donovan,** Terrence John 1936- *AmMWSc 92*
**Donovan,** Thomas Arnold 1937- *AmMWSc 92*
**Donovan,** Thomas B. 1935- *WhoAmL 92*
**Donovan,** Thomas Joseph 1946- *WhoAmL 92*
**Donovan,** Thomas Roy 1937- *WhoFI 92, WhoMW 92*
**Donovan,** Vergene 1924- *WhoAmP 91*
**Donovan,** Walt 1926- *WhoAmP 91*
**Donovan,** Walter Edgar 1926- *WhoWest 92*
**Donovan,** William 1883-1959 *FacFETw*
**Donovan,** William Alan 1937- *WhoMW 92*
**Donovan,** William Joseph 1883-1959 *AmPolLe*
**Donovan,** William Patrick 1929- *WhoMW 92*
**Donovick,** Peter Joseph 1938- *AmMWSc 92*
**Donovick,** Richard 1911- *AmMWSc 92*
**Donovon,** Patricia J 1947- *WhoAmP 91*
**Donsker,** Monroe David 1924- *AmMWSc 92*
**Donskoi,** Mark 1901-1981 *IntDcF 2-2*
**Donskoy,** Mark Semenovich 1901-1981 *SovUnBD*
**Donson,** Cyril 1919-1986 *TwCWW 91*
**Donta,** Sam Theodore 1938- *AmMWSc 92*
**DonTigny,** Richard Louis 1931- *WhoWest 92*
**Dontsop,** Paul 1937?- *IntWW 91*
**Dontsov,** Dmytro 1883-1973 *BiDExR*
**Donze,** Jerry Lynn 1943- *WhoWest 92*
**Donzella,** Niccolo *DrAPF 91*
**Doo Kingue,** Michel 1934- *IntWW 91*
**Doob,** Joseph Leo 1910- *AmMWSc 92, IntWW 91*
**Doob,** Leonard W. 1909- *IntWW 91, WrDr 92*
**Doobie Brothers** *NewAmDM*
**Doodson,** Arthur Thomas 1890-1968 *FacFETw*
**Doody,** Alton Frederick 1934- *WhoFI 92, WhoMW 92*
**Doody,** Barbara Pettett 1938- *WhoFI 92*
**Doody,** John Edward 1925- *AmMWSc 92*
**Doody,** John Robert 1955- *WhoAmL 92*
**Doody,** Loretta Irene 1937- *WhoRel 92*
**Doody,** Louis Clarence, Jr. 1940- *WhoFI 92*
**Doody,** Margaret Anne 1939- *IntWW 91*
**Doody,** Marijo 1936- *AmMWSc 92*
**Doody,** Steven Joseph 1951- *WhoWest 92*
**Dooge,** James Clement Ignatius 1922- *IntWW 91, Who 92*
**Doohan,** James 1920- *IntMPA 92*
**Doohan,** Mary Elizabeth 1950- *WhoAmL 92*
**Dookun,** Dewoonarain 1929- *Who 92*
**Doolen,** Gary Dean 1939- *AmMWSc 92*
**Dooley,** Arthur 1929- *TwCPaSc*
**Dooley,** Calvin 1954- *AlmAP 92 [port], WhoAmP 91, WhoWest 92*
**Dooley,** Cary Dale 1963- *WhoAmL 92*
**Dooley,** Dan 1948- *WhoIns 92*
**Dooley,** David Grant 1943- *WhoRel 92*
**Dooley,** David Marlin 1952- *AmMWSc 92*
**Dooley,** Douglas Charles 1946- *AmMWSc 92*
**Dooley,** Elmo S 1924- *AmMWSc 92*
**Dooley,** George Joseph, III 1941- *AmMWSc 92*
**Dooley,** Helen Bertha 1907- *WhoWest 92*
**Dooley,** J. Gordon 1935- *WhoFI 92, WhoMW 92*
**Dooley,** James Keith 1941- *AmMWSc 92*
**Dooley,** John A 1944- *WhoAmP 91*
**Dooley,** John Raymond, Jr 1925- *AmMWSc 92*
**Dooley,** Joseph Francis 1941- *AmMWSc 92*
**Dooley,** Joseph T 1944- *WhoIns 92*
**Dooley,** Mary Agnes 1923- *WhoRel 92*
**Dooley,** Michael P. 1939- *WhoAmL 92*
**Dooley,** Paul 1928- *ConAu 133, IntMPA 92, WhoEnt 92*
**Dooley,** Rodney Keith 1956- *WhoFI 92*
**Dooley,** Tom *DcNCBi 2*
**Dooley,** Wallace T 1917- *AmMWSc 92*
**Dooley,** Wallace Troy 1917- *WhoBlA 92*
**Dooley,** William Paul 1915- *AmMWSc 92*
**Doolin,** John B. 1918- *WhoAmL 92, WhoAmP 91*
**Doolin,** Joseph 1937- *WhoRel 92*
**Doolin,** Sylva Alpha 1913- *WhoRel 92*
**Dooling,** Dorothea Matthews d1991 *NewYTBS 91*
**Doolittle,** Antionette 1810-1886 *AmPeW*
**Doolittle,** Charles Herbert, III 1939- *AmMWSc 92*
**Doolittle,** Charles Leander 1843-1919 *BiInAmS*
**Doolittle,** Donald Preston 1933- *AmMWSc 92*
**Doolittle,** Eric 1869-1920 *BiInAmS*
**Doolittle,** George Leiter 1934- *WhoFI 92*
**Doolittle,** Hilda 1886-1961 *BenetAL 91, ConAu 35NR, FacFETw, HanAmWH, LiExTwC, ModAWWr*
**Doolittle,** J S 1903- *AmMWSc 92*
**Doolittle,** James 1896- *FacFETw [port]*
**Doolittle,** James H. 1896- *IntWW 91, Who 92*
**Doolittle,** Jesse William, Jr. 1929- *WhoAmL 92*
**Doolittle,** John 1950- *WhoAmP 91*
**Doolittle,** John T. 1950- *AlmAP 92 [port]*
**Doolittle,** John Taylor 1950- *WhoWest 92*
**Doolittle,** Michael Jim 1956- *WhoAmL 92*
**Doolittle,** Richard L 1953- *AmMWSc 92*
**Doolittle,** Robert Frederick, II 1925- *AmMWSc 92*
**Doolittle,** Russell F 1931- *AmMWSc 92*
**Doolittle,** Russell Francis 1931- *WhoWest 92*
**Doolittle,** Warren Ford, III 1942- *AmMWSc 92*
**Doomes,** Earl 1943- *AmMWSc 92, WhoBlA 92*
**Dooms,** Ronald Franklin 1961- *WhoAmL 92*
**Doon,** Roger Hugh 1938- *WhoIns 92*
**Dooner,** John Joseph, Jr. 1948- *WhoFI 92*
**Dooner,** Pierton W 1844-1907? *ScFEYrs*
**Doonkeen,** William 1932- *WhoHisp 92*
**Doorenbos,** Harold E 1925- *AmMWSc 92*
**Doorenbos,** Norman John 1928- *AmMWSc 92*
**Doorhy,** Brendan F. 1966- *WhoFI 92*
**Doorley,** Thomas Lawrence, III 1944- *WhoFI 92*
**Doornenbal,** Hubert 1927- *AmMWSc 92*
**Doors,** The *FacFETw, NewAmDM*
**Doory,** Ann Marie 1954- *WhoAmP 91*
**Doory,** Robert Leonard, Jr. 1948- *WhoAmL 92*
**Dooskin,** Herbert P. 1941- *WhoFI 92*
**Dopf,** Glenn William 1953- *WhoAmL 92*
**Dopheide,** Fred J 1924- *WhoIns 92*
**Dopkin,** Mark Dregant 1943- *WhoAmL 92*
**Dopkins,** Arita Leyele 1920- *WhoMW 92, WhoRel 92*
**Dopkins,** Leonard Arnold 1929- *WhoFI 92*
**Doppelt,** Earl H. *WhoAmL 92*
**Doppler,** Franz 1821-1883 *NewAmDM*
**Doppman,** John L 1928- *AmMWSc 92*
**Dorado,** Marianne Gaertner 1956- *WhoAmL 92*
**Dorai-Raj,** Diana Glover 1938- *AmMWSc 92*
**Dorain,** Paul Brendel 1926- *AmMWSc 92*
**Doramus,** Paul G *WhoAmP 91*
**Doran,** Benjamin Thomas 1955- *WhoAmL 92*
**Doran,** Charles Edward 1928- *WhoFI 92*
**Doran,** Donald George 1929- *AmMWSc 92*
**Doran,** Donald Leo 1957- *WhoRel 92*
**Doran,** Dorothy Fitz 1934- *WhoWest 92*
**Doran,** Frank 1949- *Who 92*
**Doran,** J Christopher 1945- *AmMWSc 92*
**Doran,** James Francis 1943- *WhoFI 92*
**Doran,** John Frederick 1916- *Who 92*
**Doran,** John Walsh 1945- *AmMWSc 92*
**Doran,** Lindsay *IntMPA 92*
**Doran,** Peter Cobb 1936- *AmMWSc 92*
**Doran,** Robert Stuart 1937- *AmMWSc 92*
**Doran,** Stephen William 1956- *WhoAmP 91*
**Doran,** Thomas Frederick 1949- *WhoWest 92*
**Doran,** Thomas J, Jr 1942- *AmMWSc 92*
**Doran,** Vincent James 1917- *WhoWest 92*
**Doran,** Wayne Stuart 1937- *WhoMW 92*

**Doran,** William Alexander 1929- *WhoMW 92*
**Doran,** William Rufus 1949- *WhoMW 92*
**Dorantes,** Ruth E. 1955- *WhoHisp 92*
**Dorati,** Antal 1906-1988 *FacFETw, NewAmDM*
**Dorato,** Peter 1932- *AmMWSc 92*
**Doray,** Andrea Wesley 1956- *WhoWest 92*
**Dorazio** 1927- *IntWW 91*
**D'Orazio,** Lawrence Alexander 1934- *WhoFI 92*
**D'Orazio,** Vincent T 1929- *AmMWSc 92*
**Dorbin,** Janet B 1939- *WhoAmP 91*
**Dorcas,** William Gary 1949- *WhoFI 92*
**Dorchester,** Area Bishop of 1943- *Who 92*
**Dorchester,** John Edmund Carleton 1917- *AmMWSc 92*
**Dordal,** Margaret Smith 1954- *WhoMW 92*
**Dordick,** Herbert S 1925- *AmMWSc 92*
**Dordick,** Isadore 1911- *AmMWSc 92*
**Dordick,** Johanna 1935- *WhoEnt 92*
**Dordick,** Jonathan Seth 1959- *WhoMW 92*
**Dore,** Bonny Ellen 1947- *WhoEnt 92*
**Dore,** Fred H 1925- *WhoAmP 91*
**Dore,** Fred Hudson 1925- *WhoAmL 92, WhoWest 92*
**Dore,** Janet 1950- *WhoAmL 92*
**Dore,** Michael 1950- *WhoAmL 92*
**Dore,** Ronald Philip 1925- *ConAu 34NR, IntWW 91, Who 92*
**Dore,** Susan E *WhoAmP 91*
**Dore,** Timothy William 1963- *WhoAmL 92*
**Dore-Duffy,** Paula 1948- *AmMWSc 92*
**Doremus,** John C., Jr. 1931- *WhoFI 92*
**Doremus,** Ogden 1921- *WhoAmL 92*
**Doremus,** Robert Heward 1928- *AmMWSc 92*
**Doremus,** Robert Ogden 1824-1906 *BiInAmS*
**Doren,** Douglas James 1955- *AmMWSc 92*
**Dorenbusch,** William Edwin 1936- *AmMWSc 92*
**Dorenfeld,** Adrian C 1919- *AmMWSc 92*
**Dorenkott,** Kevin Patrick 1963- *WhoEnt 92*
**Dorer,** Casper John 1922- *AmMWSc 92*
**Dorer,** Frederic Edmund 1933- *AmMWSc 92*
**Doreski,** William *DrAPF 91*
**Doret,** Michel R. *DrAPF 91*
**Dorey,** Cheryl Kathleen 1944- *AmMWSc 92*
**Dorey,** Graham Martyn 1932- *Who 92*
**Dorf,** Barbara 1933- *TwCPaSc*
**Dorf,** Carol *DrAPF 91*
**Dorf,** Jerome 1936- *WhoFI 92*
**Dorf,** Martin Edward 1944- *AmMWSc 92*
**Dorf,** Michael C. 1964- *ConAu 135*
**Dorf,** Richard C 1933- *AmMWSc 92*
**Dorff,** David Leo 1956- *WhoMW 92*
**Dorff,** Eugene Joseph 1930- *WhoAmP 91*
**Dorff,** Philip Henri, Jr. 1949- *WhoAmL 92*
**Dorfi,** Klaus G 1942- *WhoIns 92*
**Dorfles,** Gillo 1910- *DcTwDes*
**Dorfman,** Ariel 1942- *LiExTwC*
**Dorfman,** Donald 1934- *AmMWSc 92*
**Dorfman,** Gilbert Paul 1926- *WhoFI 92*
**Dorfman,** Howard David 1928- *AmMWSc 92*
**Dorfman,** Irvin S. 1924- *IntMPA 92*
**Dorfman,** Isaiah S. 1907- *WhoFI 92*
**Dorfman,** Jay Robert 1937- *AmMWSc 92*
**Dorfman,** Joel Marvin 1951- *WhoFI 92, WhoMW 92*
**Dorfman,** John Charles 1925- *WhoAmL 92*
**Dorfman,** Joseph d1991 *NewYTBS 91*
**Dorfman,** Joseph 1904-1991 *ConAu 135*
**Dorfman,** Leon Monte 1922- *AmMWSc 92*
**Dorfman,** Leslie Joseph 1943- *AmMWSc 92*
**Dorfman,** Marc Bernard 1952- *WhoAmL 92*
**Dorfman,** Martin Stanley 1945- *WhoAmL 92*
**Dorfman,** Mitchell Joseph 1956- *WhoFI 92*
**Dorfman,** Myron Herbert 1927- *AmMWSc 92*
**Dorfman,** Robert 1916- *WhoFI 92*
**Dorfman,** Ronald F *AmMWSc 92*
**Dorfsman,** Lou 1918- *DcTwDes*
**Dorfsman,** Louis *LesBEnT 92*
**Dorfsman,** Louis 1918- *WhoEnt 92*
**Dorgan,** Byron L. 1942- *AlmAP 92 [port], WhoAmP 91*
**Dorgan,** Byron Leslie 1942- *WhoMW 92*
**Dorgan,** Charity Anne 1959- *ConAu 134*
**Dorgan,** William Joseph 1938- *AmMWSc 92*
**Dorgeres,** Henri Auguste 1897-1985 *BiDExR*
**Dorheim,** Fredrick Houge 1912- *AmMWSc 92*
**Doria,** Anthony Notarnicola 1927- *WhoAmL 92*
**Doria,** Armand 1824-1896 *ThHEIm*
**Doria,** Charles *DrAPF 91*
**Doria,** Joseph V, Jr 1946- *WhoAmP 91*
**Dorian,** William D 1921- *AmMWSc 92*
**Doriety,** Bruce 1933- *WhoAmP 91*
**Dorigo,** Werner Fritz, Jr. 1947- *WhoFI 92*
**Dorin,** Bernard Jean Robert 1929- *Who 92*
**Dorin,** Francoise Andree Renee 1928- *IntWW 91*
**Dorin,** Patrick C 1939- *ConAu 34NR*
**Dorio,** Martin Matthew 1945- *WhoFI 92, WhoMW 92*
**Dorion,** Robert Charles 1926- *WhoFI 92*
**Doriot,** Jacques 1898-1945 *BiDExR*
**Doris Ann** 1917- *WhoEnt 92*
**Doris,** Alan Sanford 1947- *WhoAmL 92*
**Doris,** Francis D *WhoAmP 91*
**Doris,** Ronald Brian 1960- *WhoFI 92*
**Dority,** Douglas H. 1938- *WhoFI 92*
**Dority,** Guy Hiram 1933- *AmMWSc 92*
**Dorival,** Bernard 1914- *IntWW 91*
**Dorkey,** Charles Edward, III 1948- *WhoAmL 92, WhoFI 92*
**Dorking,** Archdeacon of *Who 92*
**Dorking,** Suffragan Bishop of 1930- *Who 92*
**Dorko,** Ernest A 1936- *AmMWSc 92*
**Dorland,** Dodge Oatwell 1948- *WhoFI 92*
**Dorland,** Frank Norton 1914- *WhoWest 92*
**Dorland,** Henry *IntAu&W 91X*
**Dorleac,** Jean-Pierre *WhoEnt 92*
**Dorler,** Ronald *WhoAmP 91*
**Dormaar,** Johan Frederik 1930- *AmMWSc 92*
**Dorman,** Albert A. 1926- *WhoWest 92*
**Dorman,** Arthur 1926- *WhoAmP 91*
**Dorman,** Charles 1920- *Who 92*
**Dorman,** Clive Edgar 1942- *AmMWSc 92*
**Dorman,** Craig Emery 1940- *AmMWSc 92*
**Dorman,** Douglas Earl 1940- *AmMWSc 92*
**Dorman,** Frederick Finck Henry 1901- *WhoFI 92*
**Dorman,** Gary Jay 1950- *WhoFI 92*
**Dorman,** Hattie L. 1932- *WhoBlA 92*
**Dorman,** Henry 1916- *WhoAmP 91*
**Dorman,** Henry James 1928- *AmMWSc 92*
**Dorman,** James Lowell 1951- *WhoRel 92*
**Dorman,** Jeffrey Lawrence 1949- *WhoAmL 92*
**Dorman,** Jeffrey Lynn 1959- *WhoMW 92*
**Dorman,** LeRoy Myron 1938- *AmMWSc 92*
**Dorman,** Linneaus C. 1935- *WhoBlA 92*
**Dorman,** Linneaus Cuthbert 1935- *AmMWSc 92*
**Dorman,** Luke *IntAu&W 91X, TwCWW 91*
**Dorman,** Maurice Henry 1912- *IntWW 91, Who 92*
**Dorman,** Michael L 1932- *IntAu&W 91, WrDr 92*
**Dorman,** Richard Bostock 1925- *Who 92*
**Dorman,** Richard W 1948- *WhoIns 92*
**Dorman,** Robert Vincent 1949- *AmMWSc 92*
**Dorman,** Sonya 1924- *IntAu&W 91, TwCSFW 91, WrDr 92*
**Dorman-Smith,** Eric 1895-1969 *FacFETw*
**Dormand** *Who 92*
**Dormand of Easington,** Baron 1919- *Who 92*
**Dormandy,** John Adam 1937- *IntWW 91*
**Dormann,** Henry D. 1932- *WhoFI 92*
**Dormann,** Joseph James 1946- *WhoMW 92*
**Dormer** *Who 92*
**Dormer,** Baron 1914- *Who 92*
**Dormer,** James Thomas 1934- *WhoWest 92*
**Dormer,** Kenneth John 1944- *AmMWSc 92*
**Dormin,** John William 1957- *WhoAmL 92*
**Dorn,** Alfred *DrAPF 91*
**Dorn,** Charles Meeker 1927- *WhoEnt 92*
**Dorn,** Charles Richard 1933- *AmMWSc 92, WhoMW 92*
**Dorn,** Dale Steven 1955- *WhoWest 92*
**Dorn,** David W 1930- *AmMWSc 92*
**Dorn,** Dieter 1935- *IntWW 91*
**Dorn,** Dolores *WhoEnt 92*
**Dorn,** Ed 1929- *ConPo 91, IntAu&W 91, WrDr 92*
**Dorn,** Edward *DrAPF 91*
**Dorn,** Edward 1929- *BenetAL 91*
**Dorn,** Edward Harvey 1952- *WhoMW 92*
**Dorn,** Friedrich Ernst 1848-1916 *FacFETw*
**Dorn,** Gordon Lee 1937- *AmMWSc 92*
**Dorn,** James Andrew 1945- *WhoFI 92*
**Dorn,** John W 1943- *WhoAmP 91*
**Dorn,** Louis Otto 1928- *WhoRel 92*
**Dorn,** Marian Margaret 1931- *WhoWest 92*
**Dorn,** Norman Philip 1945- *WhoFI 92*
**Dorn,** Randy *WhoAmP 91*
**Dorn,** Ronald I 1958- *AmMWSc 92*
**Dorn,** Roosevelt F. 1935- *WhoAmL 92, WhoBlA 92*
**Dorn,** Wanda Faye 1945- *WhoEnt 92*
**Dorn,** William Jennings Bryan 1916- *WhoAmP 91*
**Dorn,** William S 1928- *AmMWSc 92*
**Dornan,** Robert K. 1933- *AlmAP 92 [port], WhoAmP 91*
**Dornan,** Robert Kenneth 1933- *WhoWest 92*
**d'Ornano,** Michel d1991 *NewYTBS 91*
**Dornbaum,** Neil Stephen 1956- *WhoAmL 92*
**Dornberg,** John 1931- *WrDr 92*
**Dornberg,** John Robert 1931- *IntAu&W 91*
**Dornberger,** Walter 1895-1980 *FacFETw*
**Dornbusch,** Arthur A., II 1943- *WhoAmL 92, WhoFI 92*
**Dornbusch,** Rudiger 1942- *WhoFI 92*
**Dornbusch,** Sanford Maurice 1926- *WhoWest 92*
**Dornbush,** Gary Francis 1946- *WhoFI 92*
**Dornbush,** Rhea L *AmMWSc 92*
**Dornbush,** Vicky Jean 1951- *WhoFI 92, WhoWest 92*
**Dornbush,** Vonn Kevin 1959- *WhoRel 92*
**Dorne,** Arthur 1917- *AmMWSc 92*
**Dorneman,** Robert Wayne 1949- *WhoFI 92, WhoWest 92*
**Dorner,** Douglas Bloom 1941- *WhoMW 92*
**Dorner,** Marjorie 1942- *ConAu 133*
**Dorner,** Robert Wilhelm 1924- *AmMWSc 92*
**Dornette,** Ralph Meredith 1927- *WhoRel 92, WhoWest 92*
**Dornette,** William Henry Lueders 1922- *AmMWSc 92*
**Dornette,** William Stuart 1951- *WhoAmL 92*
**Dorney,** Dennis M. *DrAPF 91*
**Dornfeld,** David Alan 1949- *AmMWSc 92*
**Dornfeld,** James Lee 1954- *WhoIns 92*
**Dornfeld,** Sharon Wicks 1952- *WhoAmL 92*
**Dornfest,** Burton S 1930- *AmMWSc 92*
**Dornheim,** John Fredrick Christian, XIX 1951- *WhoRel 92*
**Dornhoff,** Larry Lee 1942- *AmMWSc 92*
**Dornhorst,** Antony Clifford 1915- *Who 92*
**Dornier,** Claude 1884-1969 *EncTR 91 [port]*
**Dornin,** Catharine Quillen 1946- *WhoEnt 92*
**Dornin,** Christopher *DrAPF 91*
**Dorning,** John Joseph 1938- *AmMWSc 92*
**Dorning,** Michael Francis Patrick 1964- *WhoMW 92*
**Dornisch,** Loretta *WhoRel 92*
**Dornish,** Margaret Hammond 1934- *WhoRel 92*
**Dorny,** C Nelson 1937- *AmMWSc 92*
**Dorocke,** Lawrence Francis 1946- *WhoAmL 92*
**Dorodnitsyin,** Anatoliy Alekseyevich 1910- *IntWW 91*
**Doronina,** Tatyana Vasiliyevna 1933- *IntWW 91*
**Doronzo,** John Fred 1958- *WhoMW 92*
**Doroshkin,** Milton 1914- *WrDr 92*
**Doroshow,** James Halpern 1948- *AmMWSc 92*
**Doroshuk,** John *WhoRel 92*
**Doroszkiewicz,** Bazyli 1914- *IntWW 91*
**Dorotheus of Antioch** *EncEarC*
**Dorotheus of Gaza** *EncEarC*
**Dorough,** Gus Downs, Jr 1922- *AmMWSc 92*
**Dorough,** H Wyman 1936- *AmMWSc 92*
**Dorpmuller,** Julius Heinrich 1869-1945 *EncTR 91*
**Dorr,** Dolores *WhoEnt 92*
**Dorr,** Donald W 1939- *WhoAmP 91*
**Dorr,** Janet Kay 1943- *WhoAmP 91*
**Dorr,** John Van Nostrand, II 1910- *AmMWSc 92*
**Dorr,** Kathleen May 1955- *WhoAmL 92*
**Dorr,** Noel 1933- *IntWW 91, Who 92*
**Dorr,** Patrick Charles 1953- *WhoAmL 92*
**Dorr,** Robert Charles 1946- *WhoAmL 92*
**Dorr,** Robert T. 1951- *WhoWest 92*
**Dorr,** Robert William 1952- *WhoMW 92*
**Dorr,** Williams Peter 1944- *WhoAmL 92*
**Dorrance,** Sturges Dick, III 1942- *WhoEnt 92, WhoWest 92*
**Dorrance,** William Henry 1921- *AmMWSc 92*
**Dorrel,** D Gordon 1940- *AmMWSc 92*
**Dorrell,** Douglas Gordon 1940- *AmMWSc 92*
**Dorrell,** Ernest John 1915- *Who 92*
**Dorrell,** Stephen James 1952- *Who 92*
**Dorrence,** Samuel Michael 1939- *AmMWSc 92*
**Dorrian,** John *WhoAmP 91*
**Dorrian,** Patrick 1953- *TwCPaSc*
**Dorrien,** Gary J. 1952- *ConAu 135*
**Dorrien,** Gary John 1952- *WhoRel 92*
**Dorrier,** Lindsay Gordon, Jr 1943- *WhoAmP 91*
**Dorrington,** Albert 1871- *ScFEYrs*
**Dorrington,** Keith John 1939- *AmMWSc 92*
**Dorris,** Gilles Marcel 1952- *AmMWSc 92*
**Dorris,** Kenneth Lee 1935- *AmMWSc 92*
**Dorris,** Michael *NewYTBS 91 [port]*
**Dorris,** Michael 1945- *TwCWW 91, WrDr 92*
**Dorris,** Peggy Rae 1933- *AmMWSc 92*
**Dorris,** Reynold Abel d1991 *NewYTBS 91*
**Dorris,** Roy Lee 1932- *AmMWSc 92*
**Dorris,** Troy Clyde 1918- *AmMWSc 92*
**Dorris,** Wilton Howard 1930- *WhoAmP 91*
**Dorroh,** James Robert 1937- *AmMWSc 92*
**Dorros,** Irwin 1929- *AmMWSc 92*
**Dorrycott,** Joyce Whigham 1930- *WhoAmP 91*
**Dors,** Diana 1931-1984 *FacFETw*
**Dorsan,** Luc *ConAu 35NR*
**Dorsange,** Jean *ConAu 35NR*
**D'Orsay,** Laurence R *ScFEYrs*
**Dorsch,** Carole Cameron 1947- *WhoMW 92*
**Dorsch,** Daniel Brown 1957- *WhoAmL 92*
**Dorsch,** Louis H. 1947- *WhoRel 92*
**Dorsch,** Raymond Michael, III 1956- *WhoFI 92*
**Dorschner,** Kenneth Peter 1921- *AmMWSc 92*
**Dorschner,** Terry Anthony 1943- *AmMWSc 92*
**Dorschu,** Karl E 1930- *AmMWSc 92*
**Dorsen,** David Milton 1935- *WhoAmL 92*
**Dorsen,** Norman 1930- *WhoAmL 92, WrDr 92*
**Dorset,** Archdeacon of *Who 92*
**Dorset,** Earl of *RfGEnL 91*
**Dorset,** Earl of 1638-1706 *RfGEnL 91*
**Dorset,** Douglas Lewis 1942- *AmMWSc 92*
**Dorset,** Gerald *DrAPF 91*
**Dorset,** Phyllis 1924- *WrDr 92*
**Dorset,** Richard *TwCSFW 91*
**Dorsett,** Burt 1930- *WhoFI 92*
**Dorsett,** Danielle *IntAu&W 91X, WrDr 92*
**Dorsett,** Katie G 1932- *WhoAmP 91*
**Dorsett,** Katie Grays 1932- *WhoBlA 92*
**Dorsett,** Thomas A. *DrAPF 91*
**Dorsett,** Tony Drew 1954- *WhoBlA 92*
**Dorsett,** Wayne Arnold 1941- *WhoEnt 92*
**Dorsey brothers** *FacFETw*
**Dorsey,** Bob Rawls 1912- *IntWW 91*
**Dorsey,** Candas Jane 1952- *TwCSFW 91*
**Dorsey,** Carolyn Ann *WhoBlA 92*
**Dorsey,** Charles Henry, Jr. 1930- *WhoBlA 92*
**Dorsey,** Clark L, Jr 1923- *AmMWSc 92*
**Dorsey,** Clinton George 1931- *WhoBlA 92*
**Dorsey,** Denise 1953- *WhoBlA 92*
**Dorsey,** Donald Merrill 1953- *WhoEnt 92*
**Dorsey,** Edmund Stanley 1930- *WhoBlA 92*
**Dorsey,** Elbert 1941- *WhoBlA 92*
**Dorsey,** Eric Hall 1964- *WhoBlA 92*
**Dorsey,** Errol C. 1945- *WhoBlA 92*
**Dorsey,** George A. 1868-1931 *BenetAL 91*
**Dorsey,** George Francis 1942- *AmMWSc 92*
**Dorsey,** Harold Aaron 1933- *WhoBlA 92*
**Dorsey,** Herman Sherwood, Jr. 1945- *WhoBlA 92*
**Dorsey,** James Baker 1927- *WhoAmL 92*
**Dorsey,** James Owen 1848-1895 *BiInAmS*
**Dorsey,** Jeremiah Edmund 1944- *WhoFI 92*
**Dorsey,** Jimmy 1904-1957 *FacFETw, NewAmDM*
**Dorsey,** John *LesBEnT 92*
**Dorsey,** John H 1937- *WhoAmP 91*
**Dorsey,** John L. 1935- *WhoBlA 92*
**Dorsey,** John Syng 1783-1818 *BiInAmS*
**Dorsey,** Joseph A. 1932- *WhoBlA 92*
**Dorsey,** Kimberly Lynne 1965- *WhoFI 92*
**Dorsey,** L. C. 1938- *WhoBlA 92*
**Dorsey,** Leon D., Sr. 1909- *WhoBlA 92*
**Dorsey,** M. Eileen 1946- *WhoFI 92*
**Dorsey,** Marc G. 1959- *WhoAmL 92*
**Dorsey,** Mary Elizabeth 1962- *WhoAmL 92*
**Dorsey,** Norbert M. 1929- *WhoRel 92*
**Dorsey,** Peter 1922- *WhoAmL 92*
**Dorsey,** Peter Collins 1931- *WhoAmL 92*
**Dorsey,** Richard P., III 1959- *WhoAmL 92, WhoAmP 91, WhoMW 92*
**Dorsey,** Robert T 1918- *AmMWSc 92*
**Dorsey,** Thomas A. 1899- *NewAmDM*
**Dorsey,** Thomas Edward 1940- *AmMWSc 92*
**Dorsey,** Tommy 1905-1956 *FacFETw, NewAmDM*
**Dorsey,** Valerie Lynn 1961- *WhoBlA 92*
**Dorsey,** William Oscar Parks, III 1948- *WhoMW 92*
**Dorskind,** James Alan 1953- *WhoAmL 92*
**Dorsky,** David Isaac 1953- *AmMWSc 92*
**Dorso,** Dick *LesBEnT 92*
**Dorso,** John M 1943- *WhoAmP 91*
**Dorson,** William John, Jr 1936- *AmMWSc 92*
**Dorst,** Jean P. 1924- *IntWW 91*
**Dorst,** John Phillips 1926- *AmMWSc 92*
**Dorst,** Tankred 1925- *IntWW 91*
**Dort,** Wakefield, Jr 1923- *AmMWSc 92*
**Dortch,** H Wayne 1931- *WhoIns 92*

**Dortch,** Thomas Wesley, Jr. 1950- *WhoBlA 92*
**Dortch,** William Theophilus 1824-1889 *DcNCBi 2*
**Dortort,** David *LesBEnT 92*
**Dortort,** David 1916- *IntMPA 92, WhoEnt 92*
**Dorus,** Elizabeth 1940- *AmMWSc 92*
**Dorward,** Ralph C 1941- *AmMWSc 92*
**Dorward,** William 1929- *Who 92*
**Dorward-King,** Elaine Jay 1957- *AmMWSc 92*
**Dorwart,** Bonnie Brice 1942- *AmMWSc 92*
**Dorwart,** David 1948- *WhoEnt 92*
**Dorwart,** Donald Bruce 1949- *WhoAmL 92*
**Dory,** Robert Allan 1936- *AmMWSc 92*
**Dorzhiev,** Avgan 1853-1938 *SovUnBD*
**Dosa,** Anna *EncAmaz 91*
**Dosanjh,** Darshan S 1921- *AmMWSc 92*
**Dosch,** Hans-Michael 1926- *AmMWSc 92*
**Doschek,** George A 1942- *AmMWSc 92*
**Doschek,** Wardella Wolford 1944- *AmMWSc 92*
**Doscher,** Marilyn Scott 1931- *AmMWSc 92*
**Dose,** Frederick Philip, Jr. 1946- *WhoMW 92*
**Dosek,** Edwin Francis 1920- *WhoAmP 91*
**Doser,** Diane Irene 1956- *AmMWSc 92*
**Doshan,** Harold David 1941- *AmMWSc 92*
**Doshi,** Anil G 1952- *AmMWSc 92*
**Doshi,** Balkrishna Vithaldas 1927- *IntWW 91*
**Doshi,** Kokila Praful 1947- *WhoFI 92*
**Doshi,** Mahendra R 1941- *AmMWSc 92*
**Doshi,** Pankaj Champak 1953- *WhoFI 92*
**Doshi,** Vinod 1932- *IntWW 91*
**Dosier,** Larry Waddell 1944- *AmMWSc 92*
**Dositheus** *EncEarC*
**Doskocil,** William Robert 1950- *WhoRel 92*
**Doskotch,** Raymond Walter 1932- *AmMWSc 92*
**Dosland,** William Buehler 1927- *WhoAmL 92*
**Dos Passos,** John 1896-1970 *BenetAL 91, LiExTwC*
**Dos Passos,** John Roderigo 1896-1970 *FacFETw*
**Doss,** Buster 1925- *WhoEnt 92*
**Doss,** Chriss Herschel 1935- *WhoAmP 91*
**Doss,** Donna Sue 1961- *WhoFI 92*
**Doss,** Evan, Jr. 1948- *WhoBlA 92*
**Doss,** James Daniel 1939- *AmMWSc 92, WhoWest 92*
**Doss,** Juanita King 1942- *WhoBlA 92*
**Doss,** LaRoy Samuel 1936- *WhoBlA 92*
**Doss,** Lawrence Paul 1927- *WhoBlA 92*
**Doss,** Margot P. 1920- *WrDr 92*
**Doss,** Margot P 1922- *IntAu&W 91*
**Doss,** Marion Turner, Jr. 1936- *WhoAmL 92*
**Doss,** Raouf 1915- *AmMWSc 92*
**Doss,** Richard Courtland 1926- *AmMWSc 92*
**Doss,** Theresa *WhoBlA 92*
**Doss,** Thomas Wayne 1963- *WhoRel 92*
**Dossage,** Jean *ConAu 35NR*
**Dos Santos,** Alexander Jose Maria 1924- *IntWW 91*
**Dos Santos,** Alexandre Jose Maria 1924- *WhoRel 92*
**Dos Santos,** Brian Leo 1949- *WhoMW 92*
**dos Santos,** Domitilia M. *WhoFI 92*
**Dos Santos,** Errol Lionel 1890- *Who 92*
**dos Santos,** Jose Eduardo 1942- *FacFETw, IntWW 91*
**Dos Santos,** Manuel 1944- *IntWW 91*
**Dos Santos,** Marcelino 1931- *IntWW 91*
**dos Santos,** Nelson Pereira *IntDcF 2-2*
**Dosseh-Anyron,** Robert-Casimir Tonyui M. *WhoRel 92*
**Dossel,** William Edward 1920- *AmMWSc 92*
**Dosser,** Douglas George Maurice 1927- *Who 92*
**Dossetor,** John Beamish 1925- *AmMWSc 92*
**Dossett,** Benjamin Franklin 1961- *WhoEnt 92*
**Dossett,** Dennis Lee 1946- *WhoMW 92*
**Dossett,** Lawrence Sherman 1936- *WhoWest 92*
**Dossett,** Walter Brown, Jr. 1927- *WhoFI 92*
**Dossey,** John Arthur 1944- *WhoMW 92*
**Dossinger,** James Malcolm 1940- *WhoFI 92*
**Dosso,** Harry William 1932- *AmMWSc 92*
**Dossor,** Frederick d1990 *Who 92N*
**Dost,** Frank Norman 1926- *AmMWSc 92*
**Dost,** Martin Hans-Ulrich 1933- *AmMWSc 92*
**Dost,** Shah Mohammad 1929- *IntWW 91*
**Dostal,** Cyril A. *DrAPF 91*
**Dostal,** Milan Mathias 1929- *WhoAmL 92*
**Dostal,** Raymond F 1943- *WhoIns 92*
**Dostart,** Paul Joseph 1951- *WhoAmL 92, WhoWest 92*
**Doster,** George Elliott, Jr. 1962- *WhoRel 92*
**Doster,** Gregory W 1954- *WhoAmP 91*
**Doster,** Joseph Michael 1954- *AmMWSc 92*
**Doster,** June Marken 1930- *WhoRel 92*
**Dosti,** Hasan d1991 *NewYTBS 91*
**Dostoevsky,** Fyodor 1821-1881 *NinCLC 33 [port]*
**Doswell,** Charles Arthur, III 1945- *AmMWSc 92*
**Doswell,** F. Lee 1948- *WhoEnt 92*
**Doto,** Irene Louise 1922- *WhoWest 92*
**Doto,** Paul Jerome 1917- *WhoFI 92*
**Dotrice,** Roy 1925- *IntWW 91, Who 92*
**Dotrice,** Roy Louis 1929- *WhoEnt 92*
**Dotson,** Allen Clark 1938- *AmMWSc 92*
**Dotson,** Betty Lou 1930- *WhoBlA 92*
**Dotson,** Bob *ConAu 134*
**Dotson,** Bruce *WhoAmP 91*
**Dotson,** Daniel Boyd, Jr 1940- *WhoAmP 91*
**Dotson,** Donald L 1938- *WhoAmP 91*
**Dotson,** Gerald Richard 1937- *WhoWest 92*
**Dotson,** Keith Mack 1938- *WhoFI 92*
**Dotson,** Marilyn Knight 1952- *AmMWSc 92*
**Dotson,** Philip Randolph 1948- *WhoBlA 92*
**Dotson,** Robert Charles 1946- *ConAu 134, IntAu&W 91, WhoEnt 92*
**Dotson,** Rosetta Delores 1936- *WhoAmP 91*
**Dotson,** William Francis 1915- *WhoAmP 91*
**Dotson,** William S. 1911- *WhoBlA 92*
**Dotson-Williams,** Henrietta 1940- *WhoBlA 92*
**Dott,** Robert Henry, Jr 1929- *AmMWSc 92*
**Dotterer,** Donald William 1953- *WhoRel 92*
**Dotterweich,** Frank H 1905- *AmMWSc 92*
**Dotterweich,** W W 1924- *WhoIns 92*
**Dottin,** Robert P *AmMWSc 92*
**Dottin,** Robert Philip 1943- *WhoBlA 92*
**Dottin,** Roger Allen 1945- *WhoBlA 92*
**Dotts,** Donald Vern 1935- *WhoWest 92*
**Dotts,** M. Franklin 1929- *WhoRel 92*
**Dotts,** Maryann J. 1933- *WhoRel 92, WrDr 92*
**Doty,** Byron James 1947- *WhoMW 92*
**Doty,** Carolyn *DrAPF 91*
**Doty,** Coy William 1931- *AmMWSc 92*
**Doty,** David Singleton 1929- *WhoAmL 92, WhoMW 92*
**Doty,** Donald D. 1928- *WhoFI 92*
**Doty,** Douglas Howard 1948- *WhoWest 92*
**Doty,** Gene *DrAPF 91*
**Doty,** Horace Jay, Jr. 1924- *WhoWest 92*
**Doty,** J.E. 1941- *WhoWest 92*
**Doty,** James Edward 1922- *WhoRel 92*
**Doty,** James Robert 1940- *WhoAmL 92*
**Doty,** Karen I. *WhoAmL 92*
**Doty,** Linda Kay 1950- *WhoEnt 92*
**Doty,** Madeleine Zabriskie 1879-1963 *AmPeW*
**Doty,** Mark *DrAPF 91*
**Doty,** Maxwell Stanford 1916- *AmMWSc 92*
**Doty,** Michael John 1947- *WhoFI 92*
**Doty,** Mitchell Emerson 1931- *AmMWSc 92*
**Doty,** Paul Mead 1920- *AmMWSc 92, IntWW 91*
**Doty,** Richard Leroy 1944- *AmMWSc 92*
**Doty,** Robert L 1918- *AmMWSc 92*
**Doty,** Robert William 1920- *AmMWSc 92*
**Doty,** Romeo A. 1938- *WhoBlA 92*
**Doty,** Shirley L *WhoAmP 91*
**Doty,** Stephen Bruce 1938- *AmMWSc 92*
**Doty,** Stephen Edward 1952- *WhoFI 92*
**Doty,** W D'Orville 1920- *AmMWSc 92*
**Doty,** William Guy 1939- *WhoRel 92*
**Dotzenrod,** James A 1946- *WhoAmP 91*
**Dotzenrod,** Ralph Clarence 1909- *WhoAmP 91*
**Doub,** Peter 1796-1869 *DcNCBi 2*
**Doub,** Randy Davis 1955- *WhoAmP 91*
**Doub,** William Blake 1924- *AmMWSc 92*
**Doub,** William Offutt 1931- *WhoAmL 92, WhoAmP 91*
**Doubek,** Dennis Lee 1944- *AmMWSc 92*
**Doubiago,** Sharon *DrAPF 91*
**Double,** Barbara Turner 1926- *WhoAmP 91*
**Doubleday,** Abner 1819-1893 *BenetAL 91*
**Doubleday,** Charles E, Jr 1944- *AmMWSc 92*
**Doubleday,** John 1947- *TwCPaSc*
**Doubleday,** John Vincent 1947- *Who 92*
**Doubleday,** Neltje Blanchan deGraff 1865-1918 *BiInAmS*
**Doubleday,** William Alan 1951- *WhoRel 92*
**Doubrovska,** Felia 1896-1981 *FacFETw*
**Doubt,** Thomas J 1944- *AmMWSc 92*
**Doubtfire,** Dianne 1918- *IntAu&W 91, WrDr 92*
**Douce,** John Leonard 1932- *Who 92*
**Doucet,** Eddie A 1924- *WhoAmP 91*
**Doucette,** Concetta Ciccozzi *DrAPF 91*
**Doucette,** David Robert 1946- *WhoFI 92*
**Doucette,** Mary-Alyce 1924- *WhoFI 92*
**Doucette,** Richard F 1918- *WhoAmP 91*
**Douchkess,** George 1911- *WhoAmL 92*
**Doud,** Jeff *WhoEnt 92*
**Doud,** John Foster 1953- *WhoRel 92*
**Doud,** Robert Eugene 1942- *WhoRel 92*
**Doudna,** John Charles 1907- *WhoRel 92*
**Doudna,** Martin Kirk 1930- *WhoWest 92*
**Doudney,** Charles Owen 1925- *AmMWSc 92*
**Doudney,** John Ervin, Jr. 1952- *WhoMW 92*
**Doudoroff,** Peter 1913- *AmMWSc 92*
**Douds,** H James 1930- *WhoIns 92*
**Douek,** Ellis Elliot 1934- *Who 92*
**Douek,** Haim *WhoRel 92*
**Douek,** Maurice 1948- *AmMWSc 92*
**Dougal,** Arwin A 1926- *AmMWSc 92*
**Dougal,** Malcolm Gordon 1938- *Who 92*
**Dougalis,** Vassilios 1949- *AmMWSc 92*
**Dougall,** Richard S 1937- *AmMWSc 92*
**Dougall,** Robert Neill 1913- *IntAu&W 91*
**Dougan,** Alexander Derek 1938- *Who 92*
**Dougan,** Arden Diane 1954- *AmMWSc 92*
**Dougan,** David John 1936- *Who 92*
**Dougan,** Jerome Wayne 1932- *WhoMW 92*
**Dougan,** Philip Jerome 1932- *WhoRel 92*
**Dougery,** John Robert 1940- *WhoFI 92*
**Dough,** Robert Lyle, Sr 1931- *AmMWSc 92*
**Doughan,** Thomas Bruce 1960- *WhoMW 92*
**Dougherty,** Bernard Glenn 1949- *WhoRel 92*
**Dougherty,** Blanford Barnard 1870-1957 *DcNCBi 2*
**Dougherty,** Celia Berniece 1935- *WhoWest 92*
**Dougherty,** Charles Michael 1944- *AmMWSc 92*
**Dougherty,** Charlotte Anne 1947- *WhoFI 92, WhoMW 92*
**Dougherty,** Dana Dean Lesley *WhoEnt 92*
**Dougherty,** Dauphin Disco 1869-1929 *DcNCBi 2*
**Dougherty,** David Francis 1956- *WhoMW 92*
**Dougherty,** Dennis 1865-1951 *RelLAm 91*
**Dougherty,** Dennis A 1952- *AmMWSc 92*
**Dougherty,** Edw J. 1937- *WhoEnt 92*
**Dougherty,** Edward Larry 1938- *WhoEnt 92*
**Dougherty,** Eugene P 1953- *AmMWSc 92*
**Dougherty,** Fred *DrAPF 91*
**Dougherty,** Harry L 1926- *AmMWSc 92*
**Dougherty,** Harry W *AmMWSc 92*
**Dougherty,** Ivan Noel 1907- *Who 92*
**Dougherty,** J Patrick 1948- *WhoAmP 91*
**Dougherty,** James B., Jr. 1955- *WhoAmL 92*
**Dougherty,** James Douglas 1936- *WhoFI 92*
**Dougherty,** James E. 1923- *ConAu 134*
**Dougherty,** James Joseph 1951- *WhoMW 92*
**Dougherty,** Jay *DrAPF 91*
**Dougherty,** John A 1943- *AmMWSc 92*
**Dougherty,** John Chrysostom, III 1915- *WhoAmL 92, WhoFI 92*
**Dougherty,** John Dennis, Jr. 1942- *WhoAmL 92*
**Dougherty,** John E 1922- *WhoAmP 91*
**Dougherty,** John James 1924- *WhoWest 92*
**Dougherty,** John Joseph 1907- *WhoRel 92*
**Dougherty,** John Joseph 1923- *AmMWSc 92*
**Dougherty,** John William 1925- *AmMWSc 92*
**Dougherty,** Joseph C 1934- *AmMWSc 92*
**Dougherty,** Margaret Jane 1956- *WhoFI 92*
**Dougherty,** Marion *IntMPA 92*
**Dougherty,** Mark Allen 1960- *WhoRel 92*
**Dougherty,** Michael Joseph 1949- *WhoWest 92*
**Dougherty,** Paul John 1953- *WhoEnt 92*
**Dougherty,** Raleigh Gordon 1928- *WhoWest 92*
**Dougherty,** Ralph C 1940- *AmMWSc 92*
**Dougherty,** Richard Evans, II 1959- *WhoWest 92*
**Dougherty,** Robert Charles 1929- *WhoWest 92*
**Dougherty,** Robert I. 1908- *WhoBlA 92*
**Dougherty,** Robert Malvin 1929- *AmMWSc 92*
**Dougherty,** Robert Watson 1904- *AmMWSc 92*
**Dougherty,** Ronald Jary 1936- *WhoWest 92*
**Dougherty,** Thomas John 1933- *AmMWSc 92*
**Dougherty,** William J 1934- *AmMWSc 92*
**Doughman,** Donald James 1933- *AmMWSc 92*
**Doughten,** Timothy Russell, Sr 1956- *WhoEnt 92*
**Doughtie,** Bonnie Lynn 1950- *WhoRel 92*
**Doughton,** Robert Lee 1863-1954 *DcNCBi 2*
**Doughton,** Rufus Alexander 1857-1945 *DcNCBi 2*
**Doughty,** A. Glenn 1942- *WhoRel 92*
**Doughty,** Charles Carter 1915- *AmMWSc 92*
**Doughty,** Charles Montagu *RfGEnL 91*
**Doughty,** Clyde Carl 1924- *AmMWSc 92*
**Doughty,** Francis W 1850-1917 *ScFEYrs*
**Doughty,** George Henry 1911- *Who 92*
**Doughty,** John Robert 1936- *WhoWest 92*
**Doughty,** Julian O 1933- *AmMWSc 92*
**Doughty,** Leslie John Trevalyn 1922- *WhoFI 92*
**Doughty,** Mark 1921- *AmMWSc 92*
**Doughty,** Michael Dean 1947- *WhoFI 92*
**Doughty,** Robin W. 1941- *WrDr 92*
**Doughty,** Warren Browe 1921- *WhoAmP 91*
**Doughty,** William 1925- *Who 92*
**Dougill,** John Wilson 1934- *Who 92*
**Douglas** *Who 92*
**Douglas,** Aaron 1899-1979 *FacFETw*
**Douglas,** Alexander Stuart 1921- *Who 92*
**Douglas,** Alice May 1865-1943 *AmPeW*
**Douglas,** Andrew 1932- *WhoAmL 92, WhoMW 92*
**Douglas,** Andrew Sholto 1953- *AmMWSc 92*
**Douglas,** Andy 1932- *WhoAmP 91*
**Douglas,** Arthur *WrDr 92*
**Douglas,** Arthur John Alexander 1920- *Who 92*
**Douglas,** Aubry Carter 1943- *WhoBlA 92*
**Douglas,** Barbara *WrDr 92*
**Douglas,** Barry 1960- *IntWW 91, Who 92*
**Douglas,** Ben Harold 1935- *AmMWSc 92*
**Douglas,** Betty C 1920- *WhoAmP 91*
**Douglas,** Bob W 1934- *WhoAmP 91*
**Douglas,** Bobby Eddie 1942- *WhoBlA 92*
**Douglas,** Bodie E 1924- *AmMWSc 92*
**Douglas,** Bruce L 1925- *AmMWSc 92*
**Douglas,** Bryce 1924- *AmMWSc 92*
**Douglas,** Buster 1960- *WhoBlA 92*
**Douglas,** Carroll Reece 1932- *AmMWSc 92*
**Douglas,** Charles Francis 1930- *AmMWSc 92*
**Douglas,** Charles Gwynne, III 1942- *WhoAmP 91*
**Douglas,** Charles Leigh 1930- *AmMWSc 92, WhoWest 92*
**Douglas,** Charles Primrose 1921- *IntWW 91, Who 92*
**Douglas,** Clarence James, Jr. 1924- *WhoFI 92*
**Douglas,** Clifford Eric 1958- *WhoAmL 92*
**Douglas,** Craig Carl 1954- *AmMWSc 92*
**Douglas,** David 1799-1834 *DcAmImH*
**Douglas,** David Lewis 1920- *AmMWSc 92*
**Douglas,** Debra Horner 1952- *WhoFI 92*
**Douglas,** Dexter Richard 1937- *AmMWSc 92*
**Douglas,** Donald 1911- *Who 92*
**Douglas,** Donald Willis, Jr. 1917- *IntWW 91*
**Douglas,** Donald Wills 1892-1981 *DcTwDes*
**Douglas,** Donald Wills, Jr 1917- *AmMWSc 92*
**Douglas,** Donald Wills, Sr 1892-1981 *FacFETw*
**Douglas,** Dorothy Ann 1951- *AmMWSc 92*
**Douglas,** Dwight Charles 1949- *WhoEnt 92*
**Douglas,** E. Sidney, III 1957- *WhoMW 92*
**Douglas,** Edna M. 1904- *WhoBlA 92*
**Douglas,** Edward Curtis 1940- *AmMWSc 92*
**Douglas,** Edward Sholto 1909- *Who 92*
**Douglas,** Elizabeth Asche 1930- *WhoBlA 92*
**Douglas,** Ellen *DrAPF 91*
**Douglas,** Ellen 1921- *ConNov 91*
**Douglas,** Florence M. 1933- *WhoBlA 92*
**Douglas,** Frederick William 1913- *WhoBlA 92*
**Douglas,** Gary 1945- *WhoWest 92*
**Douglas,** Gary Kent 1953- *WhoRel 92*
**Douglas,** Gavin 1474?-1522 *RfGEnL 91*
**Douglas,** Gavin Stuart 1932- *Who 92*
**Douglas,** George 1869-1902 *RfGEnL 91*
**Douglas,** George Halsey 1934- *WhoMW 92*
**Douglas,** George Warren 1938- *WhoAmP 91*
**Douglas,** Gordon 1907- *IntMPA 92*
**Douglas,** Gordon Watkins 1921- *AmMWSc 92*
**Douglas,** Gregory A. *DrAPF 91*
**Douglas,** H. Dwight 1943- *WhoAmL 92*
**Douglas,** H Eugene 1940- *WhoAmP 91*

**Douglas,** Harry E., III 1938- *WhoBlA 92*
**Douglas,** Helen Gahagan 1900-1980 *FacFETw, PorAmW [port]*
**Douglas,** Helen Mary 1900-1980 *HanAmWH*
**Douglas,** Henley L. 1929- *WhoBlA 92*
**Douglas,** Henry Russell 1925- *Who 92*
**Douglas,** Herbert P., Jr 1922- *BlkOlyM, WhoBlA 92*
**Douglas,** Hugh 1927- *AmMWSc 92*
**Douglas,** J M 1933- *AmMWSc 92*
**Douglas,** Jacqueline A. 1950- *WhoBlA 92*
**Douglas,** James 1837-1918 *BiInAmS*
**Douglas,** James 1914- *AmMWSc 92*
**Douglas,** James 1960- *WhoBlA 92*
**Douglas,** James Buster 1960- *IntWW 91*
**Douglas,** James Dixon 1922- *WrDr 92*
**Douglas,** James Holley 1951- *WhoAmP 91*
**Douglas,** James Matthew 1944- *WhoBlA 92*
**Douglas,** James Murray 1925- *Who 92*
**Douglas,** James Nathaniel 1935- *AmMWSc 92*
**Douglas,** James Sievers *AmMWSc 92*
**Douglas,** Janice Green 1944- *WhoBlA 92*
**Douglas,** Jocelyn Fielding 1927- *AmMWSc 92*
**Douglas,** Joe, Jr. 1928- *WhoBlA 92*
**Douglas,** John 1929- *WrDr 92*
**Douglas,** John Breed, III 1953- *WhoAmL 92*
**Douglas,** John Daniel 1945- *WhoBlA 92*
**Douglas,** John Edward 1926- *AmMWSc 92*
**Douglas,** John Edwin 1939- *WhoAmP 91*
**Douglas,** John Hoffmann 1920- *WhoFI 92*
**Douglas,** John W 1944- *WhoIns 92*
**Douglas,** Joseph Francis 1926- *AmMWSc 92, WhoBlA 92*
**Douglas,** Judith Navi 1962- *WhoFI 92*
**Douglas,** Keith 1920-1944 *FacFETw, RfGEnL 91*
**Douglas,** Kenneth 1920- *Who 92*
**Douglas,** Kenneth Jay 1922- *WhoFI 92, WhoMW 92*
**Douglas,** Kirk 1916- *FacFETw, IntWW 91*
**Douglas,** Kirk 1918- *IntMPA 92, WhoEnt 92, WrDr 92*
**Douglas,** Larry Joe 1937- *AmMWSc 92*
**Douglas,** Lee 1951- *WhoEnt 92*
**Douglas,** Lloyd C. 1877-1951 *BenetAL 91*
**Douglas,** Lloyd Cassel 1877-1951 *RelLAm 91*
**Douglas,** Lloyd Evans 1951- *AmMWSc 92*
**Douglas,** Louis H. 1907-1979 *ConAu 133*
**Douglas,** Lowell Arthur 1926- *AmMWSc 92*
**Douglas,** Mae Alice 1951- *WhoBlA 92*
**Douglas,** Mansfield, III 1930- *WhoBlA 92*
**Douglas,** Margaret Elizabeth 1934- *Who 92*
**Douglas,** Marion Joan 1940- *WhoFI 92, WhoWest 92*
**Douglas,** Marjorie Jamison 1926- *WhoEnt 92*
**Douglas,** Mary 1921- *Who 92*
**Douglas,** Mary Christine 1962- *WhoEnt 92*
**Douglas,** Matthew M 1949- *AmMWSc 92*
**Douglas,** Matthew Marion 1949- *WhoMW 92*
**Douglas,** Maurice *ScFEYrs*
**Douglas,** Melvyn 1901-1981 *ConAu 135, FacFETw*
**Douglas,** Michael *WrDr 92*
**Douglas,** Michael 1944- *IntMPA 92*
**Douglas,** Michael Anthony 1940- *IntWW 91*
**Douglas,** Michael Gilbert 1945- *AmMWSc 92*
**Douglas,** Michael Kirk 1944- *IntWW 91, WhoEnt 92*
**Douglas,** Michael Ray 1953- *WhoAmL 92*
**Douglas,** Mike *LesBEnT 92*
**Douglas,** Mike 1925- *IntMPA 92*
**Douglas,** N. John *WhoBlA 92*
**Douglas,** Neil Harrison 1932- *AmMWSc 92*
**Douglas,** Norman 1862-1946 *LiExTwC*
**Douglas,** Norman 1868-1952 *FacFETw, RfGEnL 91*
**Douglas,** Pamela Susan 1954- *AmMWSc 92*
**Douglas,** Paul Wolff 1926- *WhoFI 92*
**Douglas,** Peter Roderick 1950- *WhoAmL 92*
**Douglas,** R M *TwCSFW 91*
**Douglas,** Richard Giles 1932- *Who 92*
**Douglas,** Richard Wilson 1950- *WhoAmL 92*
**Douglas,** Robert 1813-1897 *BiInAmS*
**Douglas,** Robert 1899- *Who 92*
**Douglas,** Robert 1909- *WhoEnt 92*
**Douglas,** Robert Alden 1925- *AmMWSc 92*
**Douglas,** Robert G 1937- *AmMWSc 92*
**Douglas,** Robert Gordon, Jr 1934- *AmMWSc 92*
**Douglas,** Robert Hazard 1947- *AmMWSc 92*
**Douglas,** Robert James 1937- *AmMWSc 92*
**Douglas,** Robert Lawrence 1951- *WhoAmL 92*
**Douglas,** Robert Lee 1936- *WhoMW 92*
**Douglas,** Robert Martin 1849-1917 *DcNCBi 2*
**Douglas,** Roger Owen 1937- *IntWW 91, Who 92*
**Douglas,** Ronald Albert Neale 1922- *Who 92*
**Douglas,** Ronald George 1938- *AmMWSc 92*
**Douglas,** Ronald Walter 1910- *Who 92*
**Douglas,** Roy Rene 1938- *AmMWSc 92*
**Douglas,** Samuel Horace 1928- *WhoBlA 92*
**Douglas,** Sara Frances 1939- *WhoMW 92*
**Douglas,** Sheila 1924- *TwCPaSc*
**Douglas,** Sherman 1966- *WhoBlA 92*
**Douglas,** Sholto *Who 92*
**Douglas,** Sholto Johnstone 1871-1958 *TwCPaSc*
**Douglas,** Silas Hamilton 1816-1890 *BiInAmS*
**Douglas,** Stephen 1954- *WhoWest 92*
**Douglas,** Stephen A. 1813-1861 *BenetAL 91, RComAH*
**Douglas,** Stephen Arnold 1813-1861 *AmPolLe [port]*
**Douglas,** Steven Craig 1952- *WhoAmL 92*
**Douglas,** Steven Daniel 1939- *AmMWSc 92*
**Douglas,** Susan 1946- *WhoFI 92*
**Douglas,** T C 1904-1986 *FacFETw*
**Douglas,** Thomas Alexander 1926- *Who 92*
**Douglas,** Thorne *TwCWW 91*
**Douglas,** Tommy Charles 1946- *AmMWSc 92*
**Douglas,** Valerie *IntMPA 92*
**Douglas,** Vicki V 1937- *WhoAmP 91*
**Douglas,** Vincent Fredric 1949- *WhoMW 92*
**Douglas,** W.H. Russel 1952- *WhoWest 92*
**Douglas,** W J Murray 1927- *AmMWSc 92*
**Douglas,** Walter Edmond 1933- *WhoBlA 92*
**Douglas,** Walter Mark 1943- *WhoAmL 92*
**Douglas,** Willard H., Jr. 1932- *WhoBlA 92*
**Douglas,** William 1921- *Who 92*
**Douglas,** William Blakistone *ScFEYrs*
**Douglas,** William Ernest 1930- *WhoAmP 91, WhoFI 92*
**Douglas,** William Hugh 1938- *AmMWSc 92*
**Douglas,** William J 1941- *AmMWSc 92*
**Douglas,** William Kennedy 1922- *AmMWSc 92*
**Douglas,** William O. 1898-1980 *BenetAL 91, FacFETw, RComAH*
**Douglas,** William Orville 1898-1980 *AmPolLe*
**Douglas,** William Wilton 1922- *AmMWSc 92, IntWW 91, Who 92*
**Douglas And Clydesdale,** Marquess of 1978- *Who 92*
**Douglas-Chilton,** Cher *WhoHisp 92*
**Douglas-Hamilton** *Who 92*
**Douglas-Hamilton,** Diarmaid H 1940- *AmMWSc 92*
**Douglas-Hamilton,** James Alexander 1942- *Who 92, WrDr 92*
**Douglas-Home** *Who 92*
**Douglas-Home,** Alec *WrDr 92*
**Douglas-Home,** Alec 1903- *FacFETw*
**Douglas-Home,** David Alexander Cospatrick 1943- *Who 92*
**Douglas-Home,** William *Who 92*
**Douglas-Home,** William 1912- *IntWW 91*
**Douglas-Mann,** Bruce Leslie Home 1927- *Who 92*
**Douglas-Mann,** Keith John Sholto 1931- *Who 92*
**Douglas Miller,** Robert Alexander Gavin 1937- *Who 92*
**Douglas-Pennant** *Who 92*
**Douglas-Scott-Montagu** *Who 92*
**Douglas Williams,** Kordice Majella 1955- *WhoAmL 92*
**Douglas-Wilson,** Ian 1912- *Who 92*
**Douglas-Withers,** John Keppel Ingold 1919- *Who 92*
**Douglass,** Amanda Hart *ConAu 35NR*
**Douglass,** Andrew Ellicott 1819-1901 *BiInAmS*
**Douglass,** Andrew Ellicott 1867-1962 *FacFETw*
**Douglass,** Anna Murray 1813-1882 *NotBlAW 92 [port]*
**Douglass,** Arthur E. 1933- *WhoBlA 92*
**Douglass,** Billie *WrDr 92*
**Douglass,** Brooks 1963- *WhoAmP 91*
**Douglass,** Carl Dean 1925- *AmMWSc 92*
**Douglass,** Claudia Beth 1950- *AmMWSc 92*
**Douglass,** Clyde J 1925- *WhoAmP 91*
**Douglass,** D C *AmMWSc 92*
**Douglass,** David Holmes 1932- *AmMWSc 92*
**Douglass,** David Leslie 1931- *AmMWSc 92*
**Douglass,** Donald Robert 1934- *WhoWest 92*
**Douglass,** Ellsworth *ScFEYrs*
**Douglass,** Ellsworth and Pallander, Edwin *ScFEYrs*
**Douglass,** Enid Hart 1926- *WhoWest 92*
**Douglass,** Frank Russell 1933- *WhoAmL 92*
**Douglass,** Frederick 1817?-1895 *BlkLC [port], DcAmImH*
**Douglass,** Frederick 1818-1895 *BenetAL 91, RComAH*
**Douglass,** Gus R 1927- *WhoAmP 91*
**Douglass,** Herbert Edgar 1927- *WhoRel 92*
**Douglass,** Irwin Bruce 1904- *AmMWSc 92*
**Douglass,** James Edward 1928- *AmMWSc 92*
**Douglass,** James Edward 1930- *AmMWSc 92*
**Douglass,** James Wilson 1937- *AmPeW*
**Douglass,** Jane Dempsey 1933- *WhoRel 92*
**Douglass,** John H. 1933- *WhoBlA 92*
**Douglass,** John Jay 1922- *WhoAmL 92*
**Douglass,** John Jordan 1875-1940 *DcNCBi 2*
**Douglass,** John Michael 1939- *WhoWest 92*
**Douglass,** John W. 1942- *WhoBlA 92*
**Douglass,** John William 1942- *WhoAmP 91*
**Douglass,** Kenneth Harmon *AmMWSc 92*
**Douglass,** Lewis Lloyd 1930- *WhoBlA 92*
**Douglass,** Matthew McCartney 1926- *AmMWSc 92*
**Douglass,** Melvin Isadore 1948- *WhoBlA 92*
**Douglass,** Mike Reese 1955- *WhoBlA 92*
**Douglass,** Penny Moss 1956- *WhoEnt 92*
**Douglass,** Pritchard Calkins 1913- *AmMWSc 92*
**Douglass,** Raymond Charles 1923- *AmMWSc 92*
**Douglass,** Richard H. 1933- *WhoWest 92*
**Douglass,** Robert Duncan 1941- *WhoAmL 92*
**Douglass,** Robert Joseph, Jr. 1951- *WhoFI 92, WhoWest 92*
**Douglass,** Robert Lee 1928- *WhoAmP 91, WhoBlA 92*
**Douglass,** Robert Royal 1931- *WhoFI 92*
**Douglass,** Sarah Mapps 1806-1882 *NotBlAW 92*
**Douglass,** Terry Dean 1942- *AmMWSc 92*
**Douglass,** William 1691-1752 *BenetAL 91, BiInAmS*
**Douglass,** William Birch, III 1943- *WhoAmL 92*
**Douglass,** William Damon 1959- *WhoWest 92*
**Douglis,** Avron 1918- *AmMWSc 92*
**Doukas,** Harry Michael 1919- *AmMWSc 92*
**Doukhan,** Jacques Benjamin 1940- *WhoRel 92*
**Doulis,** Thomas *DrAPF 91*
**Doull,** John 1922- *AmMWSc 92*
**Doulton,** Alfred John Farre 1911- *Who 92*
**Doulton,** John Hubert Farre 1942- *Who 92*
**Douma,** Harry Hein 1933- *WhoMW 92*
**Douma,** Jacob H 1912- *AmMWSc 92*
**Doumakes,** Donald James 1955- *WhoAmP 91*
**Doumani,** George Alexander 1929- *AmMWSc 92*
**Doumar,** Robert George 1930- *WhoAmL 92*
**Doumas,** A C 1932- *AmMWSc 92*
**Doumas,** Basil T 1930- *AmMWSc 92*
**Doumas,** Basil Thomas 1930- *WhoMW 92*
**Doumas,** Gena Kathleen 1963- *WhoFI 92*
**Doumas,** Leonidas Paraskevas 1942- *WhoAmL 92*
**Doumaux,** Arthur Roy, Jr 1938- *AmMWSc 92*
**Doumenc,** Philippe 1934- *IntWW 91*
**Doumit,** Carl James 1945- *AmMWSc 92*
**Doumlele,** Ruth Hailey 1925- *WhoFI 92*
**Dounce,** Alexander Latham *AmMWSc 92*
**Doune,** Lord 1966- *Who 92*
**Dountas,** Mihalis 1932- *IntWW 91*
**Doupe,** Robert N. 1941- *WhoWest 92*
**Douple,** Evan Barr 1943- *AmMWSc 92*
**Doupnik,** Ben, Jr 1939- *AmMWSc 92*
**Dourado,** Autran 1926- *ConAu 34NR*
**Dourado,** Waldomiro Autran *ConAu 34NR*
**Dourif,** Brad 1950- *IntMPA 92*
**Dourney,** Martin W 1944- *WhoIns 92*
**Douro,** Marquess of 1945- *Who 92*
**Douros,** John Drenkle 1930- *AmMWSc 92*
**Dourova,** Alexandra *EncAmaz 91*
**Dours,** Jean 1913- *IntWW 91*
**Dousa,** Thomas Patrick 1937- *AmMWSc 92*
**Douse,** Steven Carl 1948- *WhoAmL 92*
**Douskey,** Franz *DrAPF 91*
**Douss,** Habib 1953- *WhoWest 92*
**Dout,** Anne Jacqueline 1955- *WhoFI 92*
**Douthat,** Daryl Allen 1942- *AmMWSc 92*
**Douthat,** James Fielding 1942- *WhoAmL 92*
**Douthit,** Harry Anderson, Jr 1935- *AmMWSc 92*
**Douthit,** William E. 1925- *WhoBlA 92*
**Douthwaite,** Patricia 1939- *TwCPaSc*
**Doutt,** Geraldine Moffatt 1927- *WhoMW 92*
**Doutt,** Jeffrey Thomas 1947- *WhoWest 92*
**Doutt,** Richard Leroy 1916- *AmMWSc 92*
**Doutt,** Sam Blair 1927- *WhoAmP 91*
**Douty,** Horace Dale 1932- *WhoRel 92*
**Douty,** Richard T 1930- *AmMWSc 92*
**Douty,** Robert Watson 1943- *WhoRel 92*
**Douvas,** Elaine *WhoEnt 92*
**Douvier,** Mary Ann 1932- *WhoAmP 91*
**Douville,** Arthur *WhoAmP 91*
**Douville,** Phillip Raoul 1936- *AmMWSc 92*
**Dova,** Pietro Andrea 1963- *WhoWest 92*
**DoVale,** Antonio Joseph, Jr. 1954- *WhoFI 92*
**Dovalina,** Fernando, Jr. 1942- *WhoHisp 92*
**Dove,** Arthur Allan 1933- *Who 92*
**Dove,** Arthur G 1880-1946 *FacFETw*
**Dove,** Derek Brian 1932- *AmMWSc 92*
**Dove,** Donald Augustine 1930- *WhoWest 92*
**Dove,** Evelyn Francyne 1954- *WhoBlA 92*
**Dove,** James Leroy 1960- *WhoWest 92*
**Dove,** Jeffrey Austin 1959- *WhoAmL 92*
**Dove,** John Edward 1930- *AmMWSc 92*
**Dove,** Lewis Dunbar 1934- *AmMWSc 92*
**Dove,** Pearlie C. *WhoBlA 92*
**Dove,** Ray Allen 1921- *AmMWSc 92*
**Dove,** Richard Allan 1958- *WhoAmL 92*
**Dove,** Rita *DrAPF 91*
**Dove,** Rita 1952- *BenetAL 91, ConPo 91, IntAu&W 91, NotBlAW 92, WrDr 92*
**Dove,** Rita Frances 1952- *WhoBlA 92*
**Dove,** William Francis 1933- *AmMWSc 92*
**Dove,** William Franklin 1936- *AmMWSc 92*
**Dovenmuehle,** Robert Henry 1924- *AmMWSc 92*
**Dover,** Suffragan Bishop of 1927- *Who 92*
**Dover,** Carl Bellman 1941- *AmMWSc 92*
**Dover,** Den 1938- *Who 92*
**Dover,** Jerry Dean 1939- *WhoWest 92*
**Dover,** K. J. 1920- *WrDr 92*
**Dover,** Kenneth James 1920- *IntAu&W 91, IntWW 91, Who 92*
**Dover,** William Edgar 1945- *WhoFI 92*
**Dover,** William J *WhoAmP 91*
**Dovermann,** Karl Heinz 1948- *AmMWSc 92*
**Doverspike,** Dennis 1954- *WhoMW 92*
**Doverspike,** Lynn D 1934- *AmMWSc 92*
**Doverspike,** Terry Richard 1951- *WhoAmL 92*
**Dovey,** Irma *DrAPF 91*
**Dovi,** Joseph Louis 1940- *WhoFI 92*
**Doviak,** Richard J 1933- *AmMWSc 92*
**Dovich,** Laurel May 1962- *WhoRel 92*
**Dovish,** Chuck 1954- *WhoEnt 92*
**Dovlatov,** Sergei 1941-1990 *LiExTwC*
**Dovlatyan,** Frunzik Vaginakovich 1927- *IntWW 91*
**Dovre,** Paul John 1935- *WhoMW 92*
**Dovring,** Folke 1916- *WhoFI 92*
**Dovring,** Karin Elsa Ingeborg 1919- *IntAu&W 91, WhoMW 92*
**Dovzhenko,** Aleksandr Petrovich 1894-1956 *SovUnBD*
**Dovzhenko,** Alexander 1894-1956 *IntDcF 2-2 [port]*
**Dovzhenko,** Alexander Petrovich 1894-1956 *FacFETw*
**Dow,** Arthur 1928- *WhoAmP 91*
**Dow,** Arthur 1948- *WhoFI 92, WhoMW 92*
**Dow,** Bruce MacGregor 1938- *AmMWSc 92*
**Dow,** Charles G *WhoAmP 91*
**Dow,** Christopher *Who 92*
**Dow,** Christopher 1916- *IntWW 91*
**Dow,** Daniel G 1930- *AmMWSc 92*
**Dow,** David O 1948- *WhoAmP 91*
**Dow,** Douglas Morrison 1935- *Who 92*
**Dow,** Frederick Warren 1917- *WhoWest 92*
**Dow,** Harold Peter Bourner 1921- *Who 92*
**Dow,** Herbert H 1866-1930 *FacFETw*
**Dow,** Herbert Hoyt 1943- *WhoEnt 92*
**Dow,** Irving Apgar, Jr. 1920- *WhoRel 92*
**Dow,** James Richard 1943- *WhoEnt 92*
**Dow,** Jean Louise 1955- *WhoFI 92, WhoMW 92*
**Dow,** Jody DeRoma 1935- *WhoAmP 91*
**Dow,** John Christopher 1916- *Who 92*
**Dow,** John Davis *AmMWSc 92*
**Dow,** John Goodchild 1905- *WhoAmP 91*
**Dow,** Katherine Rae 1957- *WhoWest 92*
**Dow,** Kevin Wayne 1950- *WhoAmL 92*
**Dow,** Lois Weyman 1942- *AmMWSc 92*

**Dow**, Mary Alexis 1949- *WhoFI 92, WhoWest 92*
**Dow**, Melvin Abbe 1928- *WhoAmL 92*
**Dow**, Norris F *AmMWSc 92*
**Dow**, Paul C, Jr 1927- *AmMWSc 92*
**Dow**, Philip *DrAPF 91*
**Dow**, Robert Lee 1958- *AmMWSc 92*
**Dow**, Robert Stone 1908- *AmMWSc 92, WhoWest 92*
**Dow**, Thomas Alva 1945- *AmMWSc 92*
**Dow**, Thomas Edward 1940- *WhoRel 92*
**Dow**, Tony Fares 1947- *WhoWest 92*
**Dow**, W G 1895- *AmMWSc 92*
**Dowaliby**, Margaret Susanne 1924- *AmMWSc 92*
**Dowben**, Peter Arnold 1955- *AmMWSc 92*
**Dowben**, Robert Morris 1927- *AmMWSc 92*
**Dowbenko**, Rostyslaw 1927- *AmMWSc 92*
**Dowd**, Andrew Joseph 1929- *WhoAmL 92*
**Dowd**, Clement 1832-1898 *DcNCBi 2*
**Dowd**, David D., Jr. 1929- *WhoAmL 92, WhoMW 92*
**Dowd**, Diane 1953- *WhoAmL 92, WhoWest 92*
**Dowd**, Frank, Jr 1939- *AmMWSc 92*
**Dowd**, Gary William 1953- *WhoEnt 92*
**Dowd**, James Edward 1899-1966 *DcNCBi 2*
**Dowd**, James F 1941- *WhoIns 92*
**Dowd**, James Patrick 1937- *WhoMW 92*
**Dowd**, John P 1938- *AmMWSc 92*
**Dowd**, Karl Edmund 1934- *WhoRel 92*
**Dowd**, Kevin Michael 1961- *WhoAmL 92*
**Dowd**, Laurence P. 1914-1980 *ConAu 133*
**Dowd**, Matthew Joseph 1943- *WhoAmL 92*
**Dowd**, Michael Edward 1934- *WhoFI 92*
**Dowd**, Ned 1950- *WhoEnt 92*
**Dowd**, Paul 1936- *AmMWSc 92*
**Dowd**, Sandra K 1950- *WhoAmP 91*
**Dowd**, Susan Ramseyer 1936- *AmMWSc 92*
**Dowd**, Timothy Charles 1953- *WhoAmL 92*
**Dowd**, Travis 1940- *WhoAmP 91*
**Dowd**, Wayne 1941- *WhoAmP 91*
**Dowd**, William 1922- *NewAmDM*
**Dowd**, William Carey, Jr. 1893-1949 *DcNCBi 2*
**Dowd**, William Francis 1943- *WhoAmP 91*
**Dowd**, William Timothy 1927- *WhoAmL 92*
**Dowda**, F William *AmMWSc 92*
**Dowdall**, John Michael 1944- *Who 92*
**Dowdalls**, Edward Joseph 1926- *Who 92*
**Dowdell**, Dennis 1919- *WhoBlA 92*
**Dowdell**, Dennis, Jr. 1945- *WhoBlA 92*
**Dowdell**, Kevin Crawford 1961- *WhoBlA 92*
**Dowdell**, Rodger B 1925- *AmMWSc 92*
**Dowden**, Anne Ophelia Todd 1907- *IntAu&W 91, WrDr 92*
**Dowden**, Craig Phillips 1947- *WhoMW 92*
**Dowden**, George *DrAPF 91*
**Dowden**, Richard George 1949- *Who 92*
**Dowden**, Thomas Clark 1935- *WhoEnt 92*
**Dowdeswell**, Wilfrid Hogarth 1914- *WrDr 92*
**Dowdeswell**, Windsor 1920- *Who 92*
**Dowding** *Who 92*
**Dowding**, Baron 1919- *Who 92*
**Dowding**, Henry Wallace *ScFEYrs*
**Dowding**, Michael Frederick d1991 *Who 92N*
**Dowding**, Peter M'Callum 1943- *Who 92*
**Dowdle**, James C. *LesBEnT 92*
**Dowdle**, Joseph C 1927- *AmMWSc 92*
**Dowdle**, Patrick Dennis 1948- *WhoAmL 92, WhoWest 92*
**Dowdle**, Walter R 1930- *AmMWSc 92*
**Dowds**, Richard E 1930- *AmMWSc 92*
**Dowdy**, C Wayne 1943- *WhoAmP 91*
**Dowdy**, Edward Joseph 1939- *AmMWSc 92*
**Dowdy**, Frances Rose 1944- *WhoWest 92*
**Dowdy**, Helen Marie 1930- *WhoRel 92*
**Dowdy**, James H. 1932- *WhoBlA 92*
**Dowdy**, John Vernard, Jr. 1942- *WhoAmL 92*
**Dowdy**, John Wesley 1912- *WhoRel 92*
**Dowdy**, John Wesley, Jr. 1935- *WhoMW 92, WhoRel 92*
**Dowdy**, Lewis C. 1917- *WhoBlA 92*
**Dowdy**, Robert H 1937- *AmMWSc 92*
**Dowdy**, William Louis 1937- *AmMWSc 92*
**Dowe**, Ralph M. 1942- *WhoBlA 92*
**Dowe**, Thomas Whitfield 1919- *AmMWSc 92*
**Dowell**, Anthony 1943- *FacFETw, Who 92*
**Dowell**, Anthony James 1943- *IntWW 91, WhoEnt 92*
**Dowell**, Armstrong Manly 1921- *AmMWSc 92*
**Dowell**, Clifton Enders 1932- *AmMWSc 92*
**Dowell**, Coleman 1925-1985 *BenetAL 91*
**Dowell**, Douglas C 1924- *AmMWSc 92*
**Dowell**, Earl Hugh 1937- *AmMWSc 92*
**Dowell**, Flonnie 1947- *AmMWSc 92*
**Dowell**, Ian Malcolm 1940- *Who 92*
**Dowell**, James Alfred, Jr. 1954- *WhoMW 92*
**Dowell**, James Dale 1932- *WhoAmL 92, WhoAmP 91*
**Dowell**, Jerry Tray 1938- *AmMWSc 92*
**Dowell**, John Derek 1935- *IntWW 91, Who 92*
**Dowell**, Michael Brendan 1942- *AmMWSc 92*
**Dowell**, Ollie Willette 1957- *WhoBlA 92*
**Dowell**, Patricia Linda 1948- *WhoEnt 92*
**Dowell**, Richard Walker 1931- *WhoMW 92*
**Dowell**, Robert James 1942- *WhoFI 92*
**Dowell**, Robert Vernon 1947- *AmMWSc 92*
**Dowell**, Russell Thomas 1941- *AmMWSc 92*
**Dowell**, Tim *WhoAmP 91*
**Dowell**, Virgil Eugene 1926- *AmMWSc 92*
**Dowell**, Vulus Raymond, Jr 1927- *AmMWSc 92*
**Dowell-Cerasoli**, Patricia R. 1957- *WhoBlA 92*
**Dower**, Catherine Anne 1924- *WhoEnt 92*
**Dower**, Gordon Ewbank 1923- *AmMWSc 92*
**Dower**, Natalie 1931- *TwCPaSc*
**Dower**, Penn *TwCWW 91*
**Dowery**, Mary *WhoBlA 92*
**Dowgiewicz**, Michael John 1952- *WhoMW 92*
**Dowhan**, William 1942- *AmMWSc 92*
**Dowhen**, Garrick Storm 1945- *WhoEnt 92*
**Dowiak**, George 1932- *WhoFI 92*
**Dowie**, Ian James 1938- *WhoFI 92*
**Dowie**, John Alexander 1847-1907 *RelLAm 91*
**Dowis**, Lenore 1934- *WhoAmL 92, WhoFI 92*
**Dowis**, W J 1908- *AmMWSc 92*
**Dowiyogo**, Bernard 1946- *IntWW 91*
**Dowker**, Ann *TwCPaSc*
**Dowkings**, Wendy Lanell 1964- *WhoBlA 92*
**Dowland**, John 1563-1626 *NewAmDM*
**Dowler**, Clyde Cecil 1933- *AmMWSc 92*
**Dowler**, James R. 1925- *TwCWW 91, WrDr 92*
**Dowler**, Randal Lee 1953- *WhoFI 92*
**Dowler**, William Minor 1932- *AmMWSc 92*
**Dowley**, Joel Edward 1952- *WhoAmL 92*
**Dowlin**, Charles Edwin 1933- *WhoWest 92*
**Dowlin**, Kenneth Everett 1941- *WhoWest 92*
**Dowling**, Basil 1910- *ConPo 91, WrDr 92*
**Dowling**, Basil Cairns 1910- *IntAu&W 91*
**Dowling**, Diane Mary 1935- *AmMWSc 92*
**Dowling**, Donald Cullinan, Jr. 1960- *WhoAmL 92*
**Dowling**, Edmund Augustine 1927- *AmMWSc 92*
**Dowling**, Edward Thomas 1938- *WhoFI 92*
**Dowling**, Ellen Catherine 1948- *WhoWest 92*
**Dowling**, Herndon Glenn 1921- *AmMWSc 92*
**Dowling**, James G., Jr. 1952- *WhoAmL 92*
**Dowling**, James Hamilton 1931- *IntWW 91*
**Dowling**, Jane 1925- *TwCPaSc*
**Dowling**, Jerome M 1931- *AmMWSc 92*
**Dowling**, John 1938- *AmMWSc 92*
**Dowling**, John Elliott 1935- *AmMWSc 92, IntWW 91*
**Dowling**, John J 1934- *AmMWSc 92*
**Dowling**, Joseph Francis 1933- *AmMWSc 92*
**Dowling**, Kenneth 1933- *Who 92*
**Dowling**, Marie Augustine 1924- *AmMWSc 92*
**Dowling**, Monroe Davis, Jr. 1934- *WhoBlA 92*
**Dowling**, Nadine Valery 1947- *WhoFI 92*
**Dowling**, Nancy Kabara 1946- *WhoAmL 92*
**Dowling**, Owen Douglas *Who 92*
**Dowling**, Patricia A 1942- *WhoAmP 91*
**Dowling**, Patrick Henry 1954- *WhoFI 92*
**Dowling**, Patrick Joseph 1939- *Who 92*
**Dowling**, Roderick Anthony 1940- *WhoFI 92*
**Dowling**, Ruby Heath 1898- *WhoEnt 92*
**Dowling**, Sylvia *WhoEnt 92*
**Dowling**, Terence Dennis 1946- *WhoEnt 92*
**Dowling**, Terry 1946- *TwCPaSc*
**Dowling**, Terry 1948- *TwCSFW 91*
**Dowling**, Thomas Mark 1957- *WhoMW 92*
**Dowling**, Timothy Paul 1955- *WhoAmL 92*
**Dowling**, Vincent 1929- *IntWW 91*
**Dowling**, Vincent John 1927- *WhoAmL 92*
**Down**, Alastair 1914- *Who 92*
**Down**, Alastair Frederick 1914- *IntWW 91*
**Down**, Antony Turnbull L. *Who 92*
**Down**, Barbara Langdon *Who 92*
**Down**, Lesley-Anne 1954- *IntMPA 92*
**Down**, Lesley-Anne 1955- *WhoEnt 92*
**Down**, William John Denbigh *Who 92*
**Down And Connor**, Bishop of 1931- *Who 92*
**Down And Dromore**, Bishop of 1934- *Who 92*
**Downard**, Bob Hanson 1946- *WhoEnt 92*
**Downe**, Viscount 1935- *Who 92*
**Downe**, Cheryl Lee 1958- *WhoWest 92*
**Downen**, Madeline Elizabeth 1930- *WhoMW 92*
**Downend**, Paul Eugene 1907- *WhoAmP 91*
**Downer**, Donald Newson 1944- *AmMWSc 92*
**Downer**, Hunt Blair, Jr 1946- *WhoAmP 91*
**Downer**, Jerol C. 1941- *WhoWest 92*
**Downer**, Luther Henry 1913- *WhoBlA 92*
**Downer**, Martin Craig 1931- *Who 92*
**Downer**, Nancy Wuerth 1943- *AmMWSc 92*
**Downer**, Robert Nelson 1939- *WhoAmL 92*
**Downer**, Roger George Hamill 1942- *AmMWSc 92*
**Downes**, Bryan 1939- *WrDr 92*
**Downes**, Bryan Trevor 1939- *WhoWest 92*
**Downes**, David A. 1927- *WrDr 92*
**Downes**, David Anthony 1927- *IntAu&W 91*
**Downes**, Dwight 1944- *WhoBlA 92*
**Downes**, Edward 1924- *Who 92*
**Downes**, Edward O. D. 1911- *NewAmDM*
**Downes**, Edward Olin Davenport 1911- *WhoEnt 92*
**Downes**, George Robert 1911- *Who 92*
**Downes**, George Stretton 1914- *Who 92*
**Downes**, Gregory 1939- *WhoFI 92*
**Downes**, John 1799-1882 *BiInAmS*
**Downes**, John Antony 1914- *AmMWSc 92*
**Downes**, John D 1919- *AmMWSc 92*
**Downes**, Kerry 1930- *IntAu&W 91, Who 92, WrDr 92*
**Downes**, M. P. *Who 92*
**Downes**, Olin 1886-1955 *NewAmDM*
**Downes**, Quentin *WrDr 92*
**Downes**, Ralph 1904- *IntWW 91, Who 92*
**Downes**, William A 1911- *AmMWSc 92*
**Downey**, Anne Elisabeth 1936- *Who 92*
**Downey**, Aurelia Richie 1917- *WhoBlA 92*
**Downey**, Bernard Joseph 1917- *AmMWSc 92*
**Downey**, Brian William 1960- *WhoAmL 92*
**Downey**, Charles Hart 1930- *WhoRel 92*
**Downey**, D'Ann Barbara 1940- *WhoWest 92*
**Downey**, Deoborah Ann 1958- *WhoFI 92, WhoMW 92*
**Downey**, Fairfax D 1893-1990 *SmATA 66*
**Downey**, Fairfax Davis 1893- *IntAu&W 91*
**Downey**, Gordon 1928- *IntWW 91, Who 92*
**Downey**, H Fred 1939- *AmMWSc 92*
**Downey**, James 1939- *IntWW 91*
**Downey**, James Aloysius, III 1946- *WhoAmL 92*
**Downey**, James Edgar 1950- *WhoWest 92*
**Downey**, James LeRoy 1950- *WhoRel 92*
**Downey**, James Merritt 1944- *AmMWSc 92*
**Downey**, John A 1930- *AmMWSc 92*
**Downey**, John Charles 1926- *AmMWSc 92*
**Downey**, John Chegwyn Thomas 1920- *Who 92*
**Downey**, John Harold 1956- *WhoFI 92*
**Downey**, John Kenneth 1948- *WhoRel 92*
**Downey**, John Redmond 1950- *WhoAmL 92*
**Downey**, John Wilham 1927- *WhoEnt 92*
**Downey**, Joseph Robert, Jr 1941- *AmMWSc 92*
**Downey**, Kathleen Mary *AmMWSc 92*
**Downey**, Michael Peter 1942- *WhoEnt 92*
**Downey**, Mortimer Leo, III 1936- *WhoAmP 91*
**Downey**, Norma Jean 1935- *WhoMW 92*
**Downey**, Richard Keith 1927- *AmMWSc 92*
**Downey**, Richard Lawrence 1948- *WhoAmL 92*
**Downey**, Richard Ralph 1934- *WhoAmL 92, WhoFI 92*
**Downey**, Robert, Jr. 1965- *IntMPA 92*
**Downey**, Ronald Dean 1950- *WhoRel 92*
**Downey**, Ronald J 1933- *AmMWSc 92*
**Downey**, Thomas J. 1949- *AlmAP 92 [port]*
**Downey**, Thomas Joseph 1949- *WhoAmP 91*
**Downey**, Timothy Richard 1935- *WhoFI 92*
**Downey**, William George 1912- *Who 92*
**Downhower**, Jerry F 1940- *AmMWSc 92*
**Downie**, Elizabeth Morris 1935- *WhoMW 92*
**Downie**, Freda 1929- *ConPo 91, WrDr 92*
**Downie**, Freda Christina 1929- *IntAu&W 91*
**Downie**, Harry G 1926- *AmMWSc 92*
**Downie**, John 1931- *AmMWSc 92*
**Downie**, John William 1945- *AmMWSc 92*
**Downie**, Leonard 1942- *IntAu&W 91*
**Downie**, Leonard, Jr. 1942- *IntWW 91, WrDr 92*
**Downie**, Mary Alice 1934- *WrDr 92*
**Downie**, Mary Alice Dawe 1934- *IntAu&W 91*
**Downie**, Penny *ConTFT 9*
**Downie**, R. S. 1933- *WrDr 92*
**Downie**, Robert Silcock 1933- *IntWW 91, Who 92*
**Downie**, Winsome Angela 1948- *WhoBlA 92*
**Downing**, Alvin Joseph 1916- *WhoBlA 92*
**Downing**, Anthony Leighton 1926- *Who 92*
**Downing**, Barry Howard 1938- *WhoRel 92*
**Downing**, Brian Thomas 1947- *WhoFI 92*
**Downing**, Carl Seldon 1935- *WhoAmL 92*
**Downing**, Catherine Frances 1958- *WhoAmL 92*
**Downing**, Christine Rosenblatt 1931- *WhoRel 92*
**Downing**, Cynthia Hurst 1942- *WhoMW 92*
**Downing**, Daniel Rex 1963- *WhoRel 92*
**Downing**, David Francis 1926- *Who 92*
**Downing**, David Royal 1939- *AmMWSc 92*
**Downing**, Delbert F 1931- *WhoAmP 91*
**Downing**, Donald Leonard 1931- *AmMWSc 92*
**Downing**, Donald Talbot 1929- *AmMWSc 92*
**Downing**, Forrest W *WhoIns 92*
**Downing**, Gary Albert 1958- *WhoFI 92*
**Downing**, George V, Jr 1923- *AmMWSc 92*
**Downing**, Henry Julian 1919- *Who 92*
**Downing**, Jack *BenetAL 91*
**Downing**, James Christie 1924- *WhoAmL 92*
**Downing**, John Scott 1940- *AmMWSc 92*
**Downing**, John William, Jr. 1936- *WhoBlA 92*
**Downing**, Kenton Benson 1940- *AmMWSc 92*
**Downing**, Lawrence DeWitt 1936- *WhoAmL 92*
**Downing**, Mancourt 1925- *AmMWSc 92*
**Downing**, Mary Brigetta 1938- *AmMWSc 92*
**Downing**, Michael Richard 1947- *AmMWSc 92*
**Downing**, Peter 1929- *TwCPaSc*
**Downing**, Robert Allan 1929- *WhoAmL 92*
**Downing**, Robert Franklin 1943- *WhoAmL 92*
**Downing**, Robert Gregory 1953- *AmMWSc 92*
**Downing**, Robin Wilson 1962- *WhoFI 92*
**Downing**, S Evans 1930- *AmMWSc 92*
**Downing**, Stephen 1950- *WhoBlA 92*
**Downing**, Stephen Ward 1943- *AmMWSc 92*
**Downing**, Vic *WhoAmP 91*
**Downing**, William 1680?-1739 *DcNCBi 2*
**Downing**, William Lawrence 1921- *AmMWSc 92*
**Downpatrick**, Lord 1988- *Who 92*
**Downs**, Bertram Wilson, Jr 1925- *AmMWSc 92*
**Downs**, Clark Evans 1946- *WhoAmL 92*
**Downs**, Crystal Eilene 1964- *WhoBlA 92*
**Downs**, Dale Dean 1934- *WhoMW 92*
**Downs**, Darrell Wayne 1962- *WhoAmL 92*
**Downs**, David Erskine 1955- *WhoEnt 92*
**Downs**, David Rutherford 1957- *WhoRel 92*
**Downs**, David S 1941- *AmMWSc 92*
**Downs**, David William 1954- *WhoRel 92*
**Downs**, Diarmuid 1922- *IntWW 91, Who 92*
**Downs**, Donald Alexander 1948- *IntAu&W 91*
**Downs**, Douglas Walker 1945- *WhoWest 92*
**Downs**, Frederick Jon 1939- *AmMWSc 92*
**Downs**, Gary Leslie 1959- *WhoWest 92*
**Downs**, George 1901-1983 *TwCPaSc*
**Downs**, George Samuel 1939- *AmMWSc 92*
**Downs**, George Wallingford, Mrs. *Who 92*
**Downs**, Harry 1932- *WhoAmL 92*
**Downs**, Hartley H., III 1949- *WhoFI 92*
**Downs**, Hugh *LesBEnT 92 [port]*
**Downs**, Hugh 1921- *IntMPA 92*
**Downs**, Hugh Malcolm 1921- *WhoEnt 92*
**Downs**, James Joseph 1928- *AmMWSc 92*
**Downs**, Jon Franklin 1938- *WhoEnt 92*
**Downs**, Katherine Watson 1931- *WhoAmL 92*
**Downs**, Kathleen Joan 1950- *WhoWest 92*
**Downs**, Kenneth T. d1991 *NewYTBS 91*
**Downs**, Lawrence Douglas 1938- *WhoFI 92*
**Downs**, Leslie Hall 1900- *Who 92*
**Downs**, Martin Luther 1910- *AmMWSc 92*
**Downs**, Michael 1953- *TwCPaSc*

**Downs,** Robert 1937- *WrDr 92*
**Downs,** Robert B. *ConAu 133*
**Downs,** Robert B. 1903- *WrDr 92*
**Downs,** Robert B. 1903-1991 *CurBio 91N*
**Downs,** Robert Bingham d1991 *NewYTBS 91*
**Downs,** Robert Bingham 1903- *IntAu&W 91*
**Downs,** Robert Bingham 1903-1991 *ConAu 133*
**Downs,** Robert C.S. *DrAPF 91*
**Downs,** Robert Conrad Smith 1937- *IntAu&W 91*
**Downs,** Robert Jack 1923- *AmMWSc 92*
**Downs,** Sturdie W. *WhoRel 92*
**Downs,** Theodore 1919- *AmMWSc 92*
**Downs,** Thomas D 1933- *AmMWSc 92*
**Downs,** Wilbur G. d1991 *NewYTBS 91*
**Downs,** Wilbur George 1913- *AmMWSc 92*
**Downs,** William Fredrick 1942- *AmMWSc 92, WhoWest 92*
**Downshire,** Marquess of 1929- *Who 92*
**Downside,** Abbot of *Who 92*
**Downward,** Peter Aldcroft 1924- *Who 92*
**Downward,** William 1912- *Who 92*
**Dows,** David Alan 1928- *AmMWSc 92*
**Dowse,** Harold Burgess 1945- *AmMWSc 92*
**Dowse,** Robert Edward *WrDr 92*
**Dowsett,** Charles James Frank 1924- *IntWW 91, Who 92*
**Dowsett,** Robert Chipman 1929- *WhoIns 92*
**Dowson,** Duncan 1928- *IntWW 91, Who 92*
**Dowson,** Ernest 1867-1900 *RfGEnL 91*
**Dowson,** Graham Randall 1923- *IntWW 91, Who 92*
**Dowson,** Philip 1924- *IntWW 91, Who 92*
**Dowst,** Somerby R. 1926-1990 *ConAu 133*
**Dowty,** Alan K. 1940- *WrDr 92*
**Dowty,** Alan Kent 1940- *WhoMW 92*
**Doxat,** John 1914- *IntAu&W 91*
**Doxey,** Ralph Hindman 1950- *WhoAmP 91*
**Doxtader,** Kenneth Guy 1938- *AmMWSc 92*
**Doyal,** Kerry Shawn 1961- *WhoRel 92*
**Doyel,** David Elmond 1946- *WhoWest 92*
**Doyen,** Ross O 1926- *WhoAmP 91*
**Doyle,** Alfred W. 1955- *WhoEnt 92*
**Doyle,** Allan Elwood 1929- *WhoFI 92*
**Doyle,** Anthony Peter 1953- *WhoAmL 92*
**Doyle,** Arthur Conan 1859-1930 *FacFETw [port], RfGEnL 91, ScFEYrs, TwCSFW 91*
**Doyle,** Arthur James 1923- *WhoFI 92, WhoMW 92*
**Doyle,** Austin Joseph, Jr. 1941- *WhoAmL 92*
**Doyle,** Bernard *Who 92*
**Doyle,** Brian 1935- *ConAu 135, SmATA 67 [port], WrDr 92*
**Doyle,** Brian Andre 1911- *IntWW 91, Who 92*
**Doyle,** Charles 1928- *ConPo 91, IntAu&W 91, WrDr 92*
**Doyle,** Charles Robert *WhoAmP 91*
**Doyle,** Constance Talcott Johnston 1945- *WhoMW 92*
**Doyle,** Daniel Dean 1938- *WhoAmL 92*
**Doyle,** Daniel G 1935- *WhoAmP 91*
**Doyle,** Darrell Joseph 1939- *AmMWSc 92*
**Doyle,** Daryl Joseph 1950- *AmMWSc 92*
**Doyle,** David *WhoAmP 91*
**Doyle,** David Allen 1959- *WhoAmL 92*
**Doyle,** David Wilson 1954- *WhoEnt 92*
**Doyle,** Donald Vincent 1925- *WhoAmP 91, WhoMW 92*
**Doyle,** Erie R. 1917- *WhoBlA 92*
**Doyle,** Eugenie F 1921- *AmMWSc 92*
**Doyle,** Fiona Mary 1956- *AmMWSc 92*
**Doyle,** Francis Xavier 1933- *WhoRel 92*
**Doyle,** Frank Lawrence 1926- *AmMWSc 92*
**Doyle,** Frederick Bernard 1940- *IntWW 91, Who 92*
**Doyle,** Frederick Joseph 1920- *AmMWSc 92*
**Doyle,** George Patrick, III 1956- *WhoMW 92*
**Doyle,** Gillian 1959- *WhoEnt 92*
**Doyle,** Gordon Phillip 1948- *WhoAmL 92*
**Doyle,** Harley Joseph 1942- *WhoWest 92*
**Doyle,** Helen Elizabeth 1936- *WhoAmP 91*
**Doyle,** Henry Eman 1910- *WhoBlA 92*
**Doyle,** James *DrAPF 91*
**Doyle,** James E 1945- *WhoAmP 91*
**Doyle,** James Edward 1945- *WhoAmL 92, WhoMW 92*
**Doyle,** James Joseph 1923- *WhoRel 92*
**Doyle,** James Leonard 1929- *WhoRel 92*
**Doyle,** James Thomas 1933- *WhoMW 92*
**Doyle,** Jane Frances 1950- *WhoAmP 91*
**Doyle,** Jean C. *Who 92*
**Doyle,** John *ConAu 36NR*
**Doyle,** John 1928- *TwCPaSc*
**Doyle,** John Paul 1942- *WhoAmP 91*
**Doyle,** John Peter 1942- *WhoIns 92*
**Doyle,** John Robert 1924- *AmMWSc 92*
**Doyle,** John Robert 1950- *WhoAmL 92*
**Doyle,** Jon 1954- *AmMWSc 92*
**Doyle,** Joseph Anthony 1920- *WhoAmL 92*
**Doyle,** Joseph Arthur 1920- *WhoMW 92*
**Doyle,** Joseph Theobald 1918- *AmMWSc 92*
**Doyle,** Joyce Ann 1937- *WhoAmP 91*
**Doyle,** Justin Emmett 1935- *WhoAmL 92*
**Doyle,** Kenneth Owen, Jr. 1943- *WhoMW 92*
**Doyle,** Kevin 1933- *IntMPA 92*
**Doyle,** Larry James 1943- *AmMWSc 92*
**Doyle,** Lawrence Edward 1909- *AmMWSc 92*
**Doyle,** Lawrence S 1943- *WhoIns 92*
**Doyle,** Lee Lee 1932- *AmMWSc 92*
**Doyle,** Lloyd Allen, III 1962- *WhoRel 92*
**Doyle,** Margaret Davis 1914- *AmMWSc 92*
**Doyle,** Mary Anne 1943- *WhoRel 92*
**Doyle,** Mary Dolores *WhoRel 92*
**Doyle,** Matthew Joseph 1956- *WhoMW 92*
**Doyle,** Maureen McLinden 1947- *WhoAmL 92*
**Doyle,** Michael 1899- *TwCPaSc*
**Doyle,** Michael Anthony 1937- *WhoAmL 92*
**Doyle,** Michael Anthony 1948- *WhoFI 92*
**Doyle,** Michael Colin 1958- *WhoMW 92*
**Doyle,** Michael James 1939- *WhoWest 92*
**Doyle,** Michael Matthew 1950- *WhoAmP 91*
**Doyle,** Michael P 1942- *AmMWSc 92*
**Doyle,** Michael Patrick 1949- *AmMWSc 92*
**Doyle,** Michelle Ann 1969- *WhoMW 92*
**Doyle,** Mike *WrDr 92*
**Doyle,** Miles Lawrence 1927- *AmMWSc 92*
**Doyle,** Paul A. 1925- *WrDr 92*
**Doyle,** Paul F. 1946- *WhoAmL 92*
**Doyle,** Peggy 1921- *WhoEnt 92*
**Doyle,** Peter 1938- *Who 92*
**Doyle,** Peter Thomas 1928- *WhoWest 92*
**Doyle,** Reginald 1929- *Who 92*
**Doyle,** Richard 1948- *IntAu&W 91, WrDr 92*
**Doyle,** Richard Francis 1930- *WhoMW 92*
**Doyle,** Richard Henry, IV 1949- *WhoAmL 92, WhoMW 92*
**Doyle,** Richard Robert 1937- *AmMWSc 92*
**Doyle,** Robert H 1942- *WhoAmP 91*
**Doyle,** Roger Whitney 1941- *AmMWSc 92*
**Doyle,** Terrence William 1942- *AmMWSc 92*
**Doyle,** Walter M 1937- *AmMWSc 92*
**Doyle,** Wilfred Emmett 1913- *WhoRel 92, WhoWest 92*
**Doyle,** William 1932- *IntWW 91*
**Doyle,** William 1942- *Who 92, WrDr 92*
**Doyle,** William David 1935- *AmMWSc 92*
**Doyle,** William Jay, II 1928- *WhoFI 92, WhoMW 92*
**Doyle,** William Lewis 1910- *AmMWSc 92*
**Doyle,** William Patrick 1932- *Who 92*
**Doyle,** William Stowell 1944- *WhoFI 92*
**Doyle,** William T 1929- *AmMWSc 92*
**Doyle,** William Thomas 1925- *AmMWSc 92*
**Doyle,** William Thompson 1926- *WhoAmP 91*
**Doyle-Feder,** Donald Perry 1918- *AmMWSc 92*
**Doyle-Kossick,** Patricia 1960- *WhoAmL 92*
**D'Oyly,** Nigel Hadley Miller 1914- *Who 92*
**Doyne,** Thomas Harry 1927- *AmMWSc 92*
**Doyon,** Gilles Joseph 1952- *AmMWSc 92*
**Doyon,** Leonard Roger 1923- *AmMWSc 92*
**Doyran,** Turhan 1920- *IntAu&W 91*
**Dozier,** Brent *DrAPF 91*
**Dozier,** Bruce Emmitt 1948- *WhoAmL 92*
**Dozier,** D. J. 1965- *WhoBlA 92*
**Dozier,** Daniel Preston 1944- *WhoAmP 91*
**Dozier,** Flora Grace 1937- *WhoWest 92*
**Dozier,** Glenn Joseph 1950- *WhoFI 92*
**Dozier,** James Crosby 1960- *WhoMW 92*
**Dozier,** Lewis Bryant 1947- *AmMWSc 92*
**Dozier,** Morris, Sr. 1921- *WhoBlA 92*
**Dozier,** Pat Kennedy 1921- *WhoAmP 91*
**Dozier,** Richard K. 1939- *WhoBlA 92*
**Dozier,** Rush Watkins, Jr 1950- *WhoAmP 91*
**Dozier,** Tillman 1936- *WhoBlA 92*
**Dozier,** Weldon Grady 1938- *WhoFI 92*
**Dozier,** William d1991 *LesBEnT 92, NewYTBS 91*
**Dozier,** Zoe *WrDr 92*
**Dozois,** Gardner 1947- *IntAu&W 91, TwCSFW 91, WrDr 92*
**Dozono,** Robert Ryoji 1941- *WhoWest 92*
**Dozsa,** Leslie 1924- *AmMWSc 92*
**Dr. A** *ConAu 36NR, IntAu&W 91X*
**Dr. John** 1941- *ConMus 7 [port]*
**Dr. Seuss** 1904- *FacFETw*
**Dr. Seuss** 1904-1991 *DcLB Y91N [port]*
**Dr Soft** *IntAu&W 91X*
**Draayer,** Jerry Paul 1942- *AmMWSc 92*
**Drabble,** Bernard J. 1925- *IntWW 91*
**Drabble,** Jane 1947- *Who 92*
**Drabble,** Margaret 1939- *CnDBLB 8 [port], ConAu 35NR, ConNov 91, FacFETw, IntAu&W 91, IntWW 91, RfGEnL 91, Who 92, WrDr 92*
**Drabek,** Charles Martin 1942- *AmMWSc 92*
**Drabek,** Jan 1935- *LiExTwC*
**Drabinowicz,** Theresa A R 1923- *WhoAmP 91*
**Drabinsky,** Garth 1948- *IntMPA 92*
**Drabiska,** Frank John 1950- *WhoRel 92*
**Drabkin,** David 1942- *WhoAmL 92*
**Drabkin,** Murray 1928- *WhoAmL 92*
**Drace-Francis,** Charles David Stephen 1943- *Who 92*
**Drach,** Ivan Fedorovych 1936- *SovUnBD*
**Drach,** Ivan Fyodorovich 1936- *IntWW 91*
**Drach,** John Charles 1939- *AmMWSc 92*
**Drachman,** Allan Warren 1937- *WhoAmL 92*
**Drachman,** Daniel Bruce 1932- *AmMWSc 92*
**Drachman,** David A 1932- *AmMWSc 92*
**Drachman,** Frank Emanuel, Jr. 1930- *WhoAmL 92*
**Drachman,** Richard Jonas 1930- *AmMWSc 92*
**Drachnik,** Catherine Meldyn 1924- *WhoWest 92*
**Drachsler,** Julius *DcAmImH*
**Dracht,** William H. 1937- *WhoMW 92*
**Drackett,** Phil 1922- *WrDr 92*
**Drackett,** Philip Arthur 1922- *IntAu&W 91*
**Dracontius** 450?-496? *EncEarC*
**Dracup,** John Albert 1934- *AmMWSc 92*
**Dracup,** Kathleen A 1942- *AmMWSc 92*
**Draeger,** Norman Arthur *AmMWSc 92*
**Draeger,** William Charles 1942- *AmMWSc 92*
**Draegert,** David Allison 1940- *WhoAmL 92*
**Dragan,** Joseph Constantin 1917- *IntWW 91*
**Drage,** Theodorus Swaine 1712?-1774 *DcNCBi 2*
**Drage,** Thomas Brochmann, Jr 1948- *WhoAmP 91*
**Dragisich,** Vera 1963- *WhoMW 92*
**Drago,** Eugene Joseph 1926- *WhoAmP 91*
**Drago,** Harry Sinclair 1888-1979 *TwCWW 91*
**Drago,** Russell Stephen 1928- *AmMWSc 92*
**Dragoin,** William Bailey 1939- *AmMWSc 92*
**Dragon,** Elizabeth Alice Oosterom 1948- *AmMWSc 92*
**Dragon,** William, Jr. 1942- *WhoWest 92*
**Dragonetti,** John Joseph 1931- *AmMWSc 92*
**Dragonwagon,** Crescent *DrAPF 91*
**Dragonwagon,** Crescent 1952- *ConAu 36NR, IntAu&W 91, SmATA 14AS [port]*
**Dragoo,** Alan Lewis 1938- *AmMWSc 92*
**Dragosin,** David Paul 1949- *WhoEnt 92*
**Dragosin,** Terry Adam 1951- *WhoFI 92*
**Dragoti,** Stan 1932- *IntMPA 92*
**Dragoumis,** Paul 1934- *WhoFI 92*
**Dragoun,** Frank J 1929- *AmMWSc 92*
**Dragovich,** Alexander 1924- *AmMWSc 92*
**Dragsdorf,** Russell Dean 1922- *AmMWSc 92*
**Dragseth,** Kenneth A. 1945- *WhoMW 92*
**Dragt,** Alexander James 1936- *AmMWSc 92*
**Dragun,** Henry L 1932- *AmMWSc 92*
**Dragun,** James *AmMWSc 92*
**Draheim,** Newt *WhoAmL 92*
**Drahmann,** Jean 1922- *WhoWest 92*
**Drahmann,** Theodore 1926- *WhoRel 92*
**Drahos,** David Joseph 1951- *AmMWSc 92*
**Drahovzal,** James Alan 1939- *AmMWSc 92*
**Drai,** Victor 1947- *IntMPA 92*
**Draime,** Douglas *DrAPF 91*
**Drain,** Alton Paul 1947- *WhoAmP 91*
**Drain,** Geoffrey Ayrton 1918- *Who 92*
**Drain,** Patricia Welch 1935- *WhoAmP 91*
**Draine,** Bruce T 1947- *AmMWSc 92*
**Draisen,** Marc D *WhoAmP 91*
**Drake,** Albert *DrAPF 91*
**Drake,** Albert 1935- *WrDr 92*
**Drake,** Albert Dee 1935- *IntAu&W 91*
**Drake,** Albert Estern 1927- *AmMWSc 92*
**Drake,** Alfred 1914- *FacFETw*
**Drake,** Alvin William 1935- *AmMWSc 92*
**Drake,** Antony Elliot d1990 *Who 92N*
**Drake,** Arthur Edwin 1918- *AmMWSc 92*
**Drake,** Arthur Eric 1910- *Who 92*
**Drake,** Avery Ala, Jr 1927- *AmMWSc 92*
**Drake,** Barbara *DrAPF 91*
**Drake,** Barbara 1876-1963 *BiDBrF 2*
**Drake,** Billy Blandin 1917- *AmMWSc 92*
**Drake,** Bonnie *WrDr 92*
**Drake,** Charles 1914- *IntMPA 92*
**Drake,** Charles D 1924- *IntAu&W 91, WrDr 92*
**Drake,** Charles George 1920- *AmMWSc 92*
**Drake,** Charles Hadley 1916- *AmMWSc 92*
**Drake,** Charles Lum 1924- *AmMWSc 92*
**Drake,** Charles Roy 1918- *AmMWSc 92*
**Drake,** Charles Whitney 1926- *AmMWSc 92*
**Drake,** Chester Lee 1946- *WhoRel 92*
**Drake,** Claudia Jean 1947- *WhoWest 92*
**Drake,** Daniel 1785-1852 *BenetAL 91, BiInAmS*
**Drake,** Daniel D. 1931- *WhoBlA 92*
**Drake,** Darrell Melvin 1935- *AmMWSc 92*
**Drake,** David A 1945- *TwCSFW 91, WrDr 92*
**Drake,** David Allyn 1937- *AmMWSc 92*
**Drake,** David H. B. 1947- *WhoEnt 92*
**Drake,** Deborah Ellen 1948- *WhoWest 92*
**Drake,** E Maylon 1920- *WhoWest 92*
**Drake,** Earl R. 1865-1916 *NewAmDM*
**Drake,** Edgar Nathaniel, II 1937- *AmMWSc 92*
**Drake,** Edward Curtis 1948- *WhoFI 92*
**Drake,** Edward Lawson 1930- *AmMWSc 92*
**Drake,** Elisabeth Mertz 1936- *AmMWSc 92*
**Drake,** Ellen Tan 1928- *AmMWSc 92*
**Drake,** Ellet Haller 1914- *WhoFI 92, WhoMW 92*
**Drake,** Eric *Who 92*
**Drake,** Eric 1910- *IntWW 91*
**Drake,** Ervin Maurice 1919- *WhoEnt 92*
**Drake,** Evelyn Downie 1940- *WhoWest 92*
**Drake,** Fabia 1904-1990 *AnObit 1990*
**Drake,** Francis 1543-1596 *HisDSpE*
**Drake,** Frank Donald 1930- *AmMWSc 92, FacFETw, IntWW 91, WhoWest 92*
**Drake,** Frederick Maurice 1923- *Who 92*
**Drake,** George Albert 1934- *WhoMW 92*
**Drake,** George Barr 1938- *WhoBlA 92*
**Drake,** George M, Jr 1932- *AmMWSc 92*
**Drake,** Gordon William Frederic 1943- *AmMWSc 92*
**Drake,** Grace *WhoAmP 91*
**Drake,** Harold Allen 1942- *WhoWest 92*
**Drake,** Herbert R 1923- *WhoAmP 91*
**Drake,** Hudson Billings 1935- *WhoFI 92*
**Drake,** Jack Thomas Arthur H. *Who 92*
**Drake,** James Perry 1797-1876 *DcNCBi 2*
**Drake,** Jean Elizabeth R. *Who 92*
**Drake,** Jessica 1956- *WhoEnt 92*
**Drake,** Joan *WrDr 92*
**Drake,** John Edmund Bernard d1991 *Who 92N*
**Drake,** John Edward 1936- *AmMWSc 92*
**Drake,** John Gair 1930- *Who 92*
**Drake,** John Gibbs St. Clair, Jr. 1911-1990 *WhoBlA 92N*
**Drake,** John W 1932- *AmMWSc 92*
**Drake,** Joseph Rodman 1795-1820 *BenetAL 91*
**Drake,** Judith D. *WhoEnt 92*
**Drake,** Justin R 1921- *AmMWSc 92*
**Drake,** Larry *WhoEnt 92*
**Drake,** Laura 1949- *WhoEnt 92*
**Drake,** Linda Kay 1957- *WhoMW 92*
**Drake,** Lon David 1939- *AmMWSc 92*
**Drake,** Lucius C., Jr. 1946- *WhoWest 92*
**Drake,** Maurice *Who 92*
**Drake,** Michael Cameron 1948- *AmMWSc 92*
**Drake,** Michael Julian 1946- *AmMWSc 92*
**Drake,** Michael L 1949- *AmMWSc 92*
**Drake,** Paulina 1942- *WhoEnt 92*
**Drake,** Pauline Lilie 1926- *WhoBlA 92*
**Drake,** Richard Francis 1927- *WhoAmP 91, WhoMW 92*
**Drake,** Richard Lee 1942- *WhoWest 92*
**Drake,** Richard Lee 1950- *AmMWSc 92*
**Drake,** Robert E 1943- *AmMWSc 92*
**Drake,** Robert Firth 1947- *AmMWSc 92*
**Drake,** Robert L 1926- *AmMWSc 92*
**Drake,** Robert M, Jr 1920- *AmMWSc 92*
**Drake,** Rodman Leland 1943- *WhoFI 92*
**Drake,** Shirley Jean 1927- *WhoAmP 91*
**Drake,** Stephen Ralph 1941- *AmMWSc 92*
**Drake,** Stillman 1910- *IntWW 91*
**Drake,** Sylvie 1930- *WhoEnt 92*
**Drake,** Thomas E *WhoAmP 91*
**Drake,** Thomas Gerard 1954- *WhoMW 92*
**Drake,** Timothy Scott 1952- *WhoFI 92*
**Drake,** W. Raymond 1913- *WrDr 92*
**Drake,** Walter Raymond 1913- *IntAu&W 91*
**Drake,** William Earle 1903- *WrDr 92*
**Drake,** William Everett 1939- *WhoAmL 92*
**Drake,** William Frank, Jr. 1932- *WhoFI 92*
**Drake-Brockman,** Thomas Charles 1919- *Who 92*
**Drakeford,** Jack 1937- *WhoBlA 92*
**Drakes,** Muriel B. 1935- *WhoBlA 92*
**Draklich,** Nick 1926- *IntMPA 92*

**Drakontides,** Anna Barbara 1933- *AmMWSc 92*
**Drakos,** Charles Peter 1945- *WhoFI 92*
**Dran,** Robert Joseph 1947- *WhoAmL 92*
**Drance,** S M 1925- *AmMWSc 92*
**Dranchuk,** Peter Michael 1928- *AmMWSc 92*
**Drane,** Charles Joseph, Jr 1927- *AmMWSc 92*
**Drane,** Gerald Vernon 1924- *WhoEnt 92*
**Drane,** John Wanzer 1933- *AmMWSc 92*
**Drane,** John William 1946- *WhoRel 92*
**Drane,** Robert Brent 1797?-1862 *DcNCBi 2*
**Drane,** Robert Brent 1851-1939 *DcNCBi 2*
**Dranetz,** Abraham Isaac 1922- *WhoFI 92*
**Drannan,** Walter Theodore 1922- *WhoMW 92*
**Dranoff,** Joshua S 1932- *AmMWSc 92*
**Dranoff,** Steven Mark 1943- *WhoAmL 92*
**Drapalik,** Donald Joseph 1934- *AmMWSc 92*
**Drape,** Mary Ann 1957- *WhoAmL 92*
**Drapeau,** Jean 1916- *IntWW 91*
**Drapeau,** William Lawrence 1929- *WhoAmP 91*
**Draper,** Alan Gregory 1926- *Who 92*
**Draper,** Albert Lee 1938- *WhoRel 92*
**Draper,** Alfred Ernest 1924- *IntAu&W 91, WrDr 92*
**Draper,** Allyn *ScFEYrs*
**Draper,** Arthur Lincoln 1923- *AmMWSc 92*
**Draper,** Carroll Isaac 1914- *AmMWSc 92*
**Draper,** Charles Stark 1901-1987 *FacFETw*
**Draper,** Daniel Clay 1920- *WhoAmL 92*
**Draper,** David Eugene 1949- *WhoRel 92*
**Draper,** Dorothy 1889-1969 *DcTwDes, FacFETw*
**Draper,** Edgar Daniel 1921- *WhoBlA 92*
**Draper,** Everett T., Jr. 1939- *WhoBlA 92*
**Draper,** Frances Murphy 1947- *WhoBlA 92*
**Draper,** Frederick Webster 1945- *WhoBlA 92*
**Draper,** George W *ScFEYrs*
**Draper,** Gerald Carter 1926- *Who 92*
**Draper,** Gerald Linden 1941- *WhoAmL 92, WhoMW 92*
**Draper,** Grenville 1950- *AmMWSc 92*
**Draper,** Hal 1914- *IntAu&W 91*
**Draper,** Harold Hugh 1924- *AmMWSc 92*
**Draper,** Hastings *IntAu&W 91X, WrDr 92*
**Draper,** Henry 1837-1882 *BiInAmS*
**Draper,** James Edward 1924- *AmMWSc 92*
**Draper,** James Thomas 1935- *WhoRel 92*
**Draper,** James Wilson 1926- *WhoAmL 92*
**Draper,** John Christopher 1835-1885 *BiInAmS*
**Draper,** John Daniel 1919- *AmMWSc 92*
**Draper,** John Haydn Paul 1916- *Who 92*
**Draper,** John Wiliam 1811-1882 *BiInAmS*
**Draper,** Kenneth 1944- *TwCPaSc*
**Draper,** Laura Blosser 1956- *WhoEnt 92*
**Draper,** Laurence Rene 1930- *AmMWSc 92*
**Draper,** Margaret Green 1727-1807 *HanAmWH*
**Draper,** Margaret Green 1730?-1807 *BlkwEAR*
**Draper,** Mary Anna Palmer 1839-1914 *BiInAmS*
**Draper,** Michael William 1928- *Who 92*
**Draper,** Norman Richard 1931- *AmMWSc 92*
**Draper,** Paul *Who 92*
**Draper,** Paul 1947- *TwCPaSc*
**Draper,** Peter Sydney 1935- *Who 92*
**Draper,** Polly *WhoEnt 92*
**Draper,** R. P. 1928- *WrDr 92*
**Draper,** Richard Noel 1937- *AmMWSc 92*
**Draper,** Richard William 1942- *AmMWSc 92*
**Draper,** Rockford Keith *AmMWSc 92*
**Draper,** Ronald Philip 1928- *IntAu&W 91, Who 92*
**Draper,** Roy Douglas 1933- *AmMWSc 92*
**Draper,** Ruth 1884-1956 *BenetAL 91*
**Draper,** Theodore 1912- *WrDr 92*
**Draper,** William Henry 1830-1901 *BiInAmS*
**Draper,** William Henry, III 1928- *IntWW 91, WhoAmP 91*
**Drasco,** Dennis J. 1948- *WhoAmL 92*
**Drasin,** David 1940- *AmMWSc 92*
**Drattell,** Eric Marc 1958- *WhoAmL 92*
**Dratz,** Edward Alexander 1940- *AmMWSc 92*
**Draughon,** Frances Ann 1952- *AmMWSc 92*
**Draughon,** Scott Wilson 1952- *WhoAmL 92, WhoFI 92*
**Drauglis,** Edmund 1933- *AmMWSc 92*
**Draus,** Frank John 1929- *AmMWSc 92*
**Dravecky,** Dave 1956- *News 92-1 [port]*
**Draves,** William A., IV 1949- *WhoMW 92*
**Dravins,** Dainis 1949- *IntWW 91*
**Drawbaugh,** Kevin Alan 1960- *WhoFI 92*
**Drawe,** D Lynn 1942- *AmMWSc 92*
**Drawicz,** Andrzej 1932- *IntWW 91*
**Drawyer,** June Michelle 1964- *WhoFI 92*
**Dray,** Mark S. 1943- *WhoAmL 92*
**Dray,** Sheldon 1920- *AmMWSc 92*
**Dray,** Tevian 1956- *WhoWest 92*
**Dray,** William Herbert 1921- *IntWW 91*
**Draycott,** Douglas Patrick 1918- *Who 92*
**Draycott,** Gerald Arthur 1911- *Who 92*
**Drayer,** Cynthia *WhoEnt 92*
**Drayer,** Dennis Edward *AmMWSc 92*
**Drayer,** Dennis Eugene 1928- *AmMWSc 92*
**Drayson,** Robert Quested 1919- *Who 92*
**Drayson,** Sydney Roland 1937- *AmMWSc 92*
**Drayton,** Henry S 1848-1923 *ScFEYrs*
**Drayton,** James Bradley 1946- *WhoFI 92*
**Drayton,** Mary Ann 1941- *WhoAmP 91*
**Drayton,** Michael 1563-1631 *RfGEnL 91*
**Drayton,** Otis Paul 1939- *BlkOlyM*
**Drayton,** William 1943- *WhoFI 92*
**Drazen,** Lori *IntMPA 92*
**Drazin,** Israel 1935- *WhoAmL 92*
**Drazin,** Michael Peter 1929- *AmMWSc 92*
**Drea,** Edward Joseph 1954- *WhoMW 92*
**Dreblow,** Darlene DeMarie 1952- *WhoMW 92*
**Drebsky,** Dennis Jay 1946- *WhoAmL 92*
**Drebus,** Richard William 1924- *WhoFI 92*
**Dreby,** Edwin Christian, III 1915- *AmMWSc 92*
**Drechsel,** Max Ulrich, Count von 1911-1944 *EncTR 91*
**Drechsel,** Paul David 1925- *AmMWSc 92*
**Drechsler,** Randall Richard 1945- *WhoWest 92*
**Drecktrah,** Harold Gene 1938- *AmMWSc 92*
**Dreeben,** Arthur B 1922- *AmMWSc 92*
**Drees,** David T 1933- *AmMWSc 92*
**Drees,** John Allen 1943- *AmMWSc 92*
**Drees,** Robert Gaither 1927- *WhoWest 92*
**Drees,** Willem 1886-1988 *EncTR 91, FacFETw*
**Drees,** Willem 1922- *IntWW 91*
**Dreesen,** Tom Eugene 1943- *WhoEnt 92*
**Dreesman,** Gordon Ronald 1935- *AmMWSc 92*
**Dreeszen,** Vincent Harold 1921- *AmMWSc 92*
**Dregalla,** Herbert Edward, Jr. 1947- *WhoMW 92*
**Dregne,** Harold Ernest 1916- *AmMWSc 92*
**Dreher,** Diane Elizabeth 1946- *WhoEnt 92*
**Dreher,** Lucille G. 1910- *WhoBlA 92*
**Dreher,** Mark William 1955- *WhoWest 92*
**Dreher,** Murphy Andrew, Jr 1930- *WhoAmP 91*
**Dreibelbis,** John Adam 1928- *AmMWSc 92*
**Dreibelbis,** John L. 1934- *WhoRel 92*
**Dreicer,** Harry 1927- *AmMWSc 92*
**Dreier,** David 1952- *AlmAP 92 [port], WhoAmP 91*
**Dreier,** David Timothy 1952- *WhoFI 92, WhoWest 92*
**Dreier,** Katherine Sophie 1877-1952 *HanAmWH*
**Dreier,** Ralf 1931- *IntWW 91*
**Dreier,** William Alan 1937- *WhoAmL 92*
**Dreier,** William Matthews, Jr 1937- *AmMWSc 92*
**Dreifke,** Gerald E 1918- *AmMWSc 92*
**Dreifus,** David 1952- *WhoAmL 92*
**Dreifus,** Leonard S 1924- *AmMWSc 92*
**Dreifuss,** Arthur *IntMPA 92*
**Dreifuss,** Arthur 1908- *WhoEnt 92*
**Dreifuss,** Fritz Emanuel 1926- *AmMWSc 92*
**Dreikorn,** Barry Allen 1939- *AmMWSc 92*
**Dreiling,** Charles Ernest 1941- *AmMWSc 92*
**Dreiling,** David A 1918- *AmMWSc 92*
**Dreiling,** Mark Jerome 1940- *AmMWSc 92*
**Dreimanis,** Aleksis 1914- *AmMWSc 92, IntWW 91*
**Dreisbach,** Albert Russel, Jr. 1934- *WhoRel 92*
**Dreisbach,** John Gustave 1939- *WhoFI 92, WhoWest 92*
**Dreisbach,** Joseph Herman 1949- *AmMWSc 92*
**Dreisbach,** Leroy E. 1940- *WhoFI 92*
**Dreisbach,** Robert Hastings 1916- *AmMWSc 92*
**Dreiser,** Theodore *SourALJ*
**Dreiser,** Theodore 1871-1945 *BenetAL 91, DcAmImH, FacFETw, RComAH*
**Dreiss,** Gerard Julius 1928- *AmMWSc 92*
**Dreith,** George H. 1952- *WhoMW 92*
**Dreitler,** Joseph Richard 1950- *WhoAmL 92*
**Dreizen,** Paul 1929- *AmMWSc 92*
**Dreizen,** Samuel 1918- *AmMWSc 92*
**Drelich,** Arthur 1920- *AmMWSc 92*
**Drell,** Sidney David 1926- *AmMWSc 92, IntWW 91, WhoWest 92*
**Dreman,** David Nasaniel 1936- *WhoFI 92*
**Dremin,** Leonard Lonnie Alexander 1953- *WhoWest 92*
**Dren,** Anthony Thomas 1936- *AmMWSc 92*
**Drengler,** Keith Allan 1953- *AmMWSc 92*
**Drengler,** William Allan John 1949- *WhoAmP 91*
**Drenick,** Ernst John *AmMWSc 92*
**Drenick,** Rudolf F 1914- *AmMWSc 92*
**Drennan,** Carol Frieden 1952- *WhoEnt 92*
**Drennan,** Donna Jane 1944- *WhoAmL 92*
**Drennan,** Dorothy Elizabeth Carter 1929- *WhoEnt 92*
**Drennan,** Harry Joseph 1933- *WhoRel 92*
**Drennan,** Joseph Peter 1956- *WhoAmL 92, WhoFI 92*
**Drennan,** Merrill William 1915- *WhoRel 92*
**Drennan,** Michael Eldon 1946- *WhoWest 92*
**Drennan,** Ollin Junior 1925- *AmMWSc 92*
**Drennan,** William Anthony 1960- *WhoAmL 92*
**Drennen,** Gordon 1947- *WhoBlA 92*
**Drennen,** Marcia Simonton 1915- *IntAu&W 91*
**Drennen,** William Miller 1914- *WhoAmL 92*
**Drennen,** William Miller, Jr. 1942- *WhoEnt 92*
**Drenth,** Pieter Johan Diederik 1935- *IntWW 91*
**Dreosti,** Ivor Eustace 1936- *AmMWSc 92*
**Dresang,** Craig 1962- *WhoMW 92*
**Dresbach,** David Philip 1947- *WhoMW 92*
**Dresbach,** Glenn 1889-1968 *BenetAL 91*
**Dresch,** Francis William 1913- *AmMWSc 92*
**Dresch,** Stephen Paul 1943- *WhoAmP 91*
**Drescher,** Dennis G *AmMWSc 92*
**Drescher,** Henrik 1955- *ConAu 135, SmATA 67 [port]*
**Drescher,** John Mummau 1928- *WhoRel 92*
**Drescher,** William Dana 1948- *WhoFI 92*
**Drescher,** William James 1918- *AmMWSc 92*
**Dreschfield,** Ralph Leonard Emmanuel 1911- *Who 92*
**Dreschhoff,** Gisela Auguste-Marie 1938- *AmMWSc 92*
**Dresden,** Carlton F 1931- *AmMWSc 92*
**Dresden,** Marc Henri 1938- *AmMWSc 92*
**Dresden,** Max 1918- *AmMWSc 92*
**Dresdner,** Richard David 1918- *AmMWSc 92*
**Drese,** Claus Helmut 1922- *IntWW 91*
**Dresh,** Lisa Marie 1953- *WhoWest 92*
**Dresher,** Paul Joseph 1951- *WhoEnt 92*
**Dreshfield,** Arthur C, Jr 1929- *AmMWSc 92*
**Dreshfield,** Robert Lewis 1933- *AmMWSc 92*
**Dreska,** Noel 1928- *AmMWSc 92*
**Dreskin,** Stephen Charles 1949- *WhoWest 92*
**Dresmal,** James Eugene *WhoIns 92*
**Dresner,** Bruce Michael 1948- *WhoFI 92*
**Dresner,** Byron 1927- *WhoAmL 92*
**Dresner,** Joseph 1927- *AmMWSc 92*
**Dresnick,** Ronald C. 1944- *WhoAmL 92*
**Dress,** William John 1918- *AmMWSc 92*
**Dressel,** Barry 1947- *WhoMW 92*
**Dressel,** Francis George 1904- *AmMWSc 92*
**Dressel,** Herman Otto 1926- *AmMWSc 92*
**Dressel,** Irene Emma Ringwald 1926- *WhoMW 92*
**Dressel,** Jon *DrAPF 91*
**Dressel,** Paul A. 1934- *WhoFI 92, WhoMW 92*
**Dressel,** Paul Leroy 1910- *AmMWSc 92*
**Dressel,** Ralph William 1922- *AmMWSc 92*
**Dressel,** Roy Robert 1923- *WhoFI 92*
**Dresselhaus,** Gene Frederick 1929- *AmMWSc 92*
**Dresselhaus,** Mildred S 1930- *AmMWSc 92*
**Dressell,** Larry Thomas 1944- *WhoAmL 92*
**Dresser,** Amos 1812-1904 *AmPeW*
**Dresser,** Christopher 1834-1904 *DcTwDes*
**Dresser,** Davis 1904-1977 *TwCWW 91*
**Dresser,** Horatio Willis 1866-1954 *RelLAm 91*
**Dresser,** Hugh W 1930- *AmMWSc 92*
**Dresser,** Jesse Dale 1906- *WhoWest 92*
**Dresser,** Miles Joel 1935- *AmMWSc 92*
**Dresser,** Paul 1857-1906 *BenetAL 91, NewAmDM*
**Dresser,** Phyllis Howe *WhoAmP 91*
**Dresser,** Sandy Grogan 1943- *WhoFI 92*
**Dressler,** Alan Michael 1948- *AmMWSc 92, WhoWest 92*
**Dressler,** Conrad 1856-1940 *TwCPaSc*
**Dressler,** Edward Thomas 1943- *AmMWSc 92*
**Dressler,** Hans 1926- *AmMWSc 92*
**Dressler,** Robert A. 1945- *WhoAmL 92*
**Dressler,** Robert Anthony 1945- *WhoAmP 91*
**Dressler,** Robert Eugene 1944- *AmMWSc 92*
**Dressler,** Robert Louis 1927- *AmMWSc 92*
**Dressler,** Susan Jean 1958- *WhoEnt 92*
**Dressler,** Undine Michaelle 1955- *WhoEnt 92*
**Dretchen,** Kenneth Lewis 1946- *AmMWSc 92*
**Dreumont,** Antonio Alcides 1939- *WhoHisp 92*
**Drevdahl,** Elmer R 1926- *AmMWSc 92*
**Drevenstedt,** Jean 1927- *WhoMW 92*
**Drever,** James 1910- *Who 92*
**Drever,** Richard Alston, Jr. 1936- *WhoWest 92*
**Drever,** Timothy 1935- *TwCPaSc*
**Dreves,** Robert G 1914- *AmMWSc 92*
**Drevlow,** Robert Reuben 1947- *WhoAmL 92*
**Drew,** Arthur 1912- *Who 92*
**Drew,** Bruce Arthur 1924- *AmMWSc 92*
**Drew,** Charles Milton 1921- *WhoWest 92*
**Drew,** Dan Dale 1926- *AmMWSc 92*
**Drew,** David A 1916- *AmMWSc 92*
**Drew,** Ernest Harold 1937- *WhoFI 92*
**Drew,** Frances L 1917- *AmMWSc 92*
**Drew,** Fraser 1913- *WrDr 92*
**Drew,** Fraser Bragg Robert 1913- *IntAu&W 91*
**Drew,** G John 1940- *WhoAmP 91*
**Drew,** George *DrAPF 91*
**Drew,** George A 1894-1973 *FacFETw*
**Drew,** George Charles 1911- *Who 92*
**Drew,** Gerald John 1939- *WhoIns 92*
**Drew,** Henry D 1941- *AmMWSc 92*
**Drew,** Horace Rainsford, Jr. 1918- *WhoAmL 92*
**Drew,** Howard Dennis 1939- *AmMWSc 92*
**Drew,** Jack Hunter 1925- *WhoAmP 91*
**Drew,** James 1929- *ConCom 92*
**Drew,** James 1930- *AmMWSc 92*
**Drew,** James Brown 1922- *WhoBlA 92*
**Drew,** James Mulcro 1929- *WhoEnt 92*
**Drew,** James V. 1930- *WhoWest 92*
**Drew,** Jane Beverly 1911- *IntWW 91, Who 92*
**Drew,** Joanna Marie 1929- *Who 92*
**Drew,** John 1719?-1819 *DcNCBi 2*
**Drew,** John Alexander 1907- *Who 92*
**Drew,** John H 1943- *AmMWSc 92*
**Drew,** John Sydney Neville 1936- *Who 92*
**Drew,** Judy Morine 1951- *WhoMW 92*
**Drew,** Larry Donnell 1958- *WhoBlA 92*
**Drew,** Lawrence James 1940- *AmMWSc 92*
**Drew,** Leland Overbey 1923- *AmMWSc 92*
**Drew,** Lucas 1935- *WhoEnt 92*
**Drew,** Nicholas *WrDr 92*
**Drew,** Pamela 1910-1989 *TwCPaSc*
**Drew,** Paul 1935- *WhoEnt 92*
**Drew,** Pete *WhoAmP 91*
**Drew,** Peter Robert Lionel 1927- *Who 92*
**Drew,** Philip 1943- *WrDr 92*
**Drew,** Philip Garfield 1932- *AmMWSc 92*
**Drew,** Randy 1953- *WhoEnt 92*
**Drew,** Robert d1991 *Who 92N*
**Drew,** Robert Taylor 1936- *AmMWSc 92*
**Drew,** Russell Cooper 1931- *AmMWSc 92, WhoFI 92*
**Drew,** Sannie *TwCPaSc*
**Drew,** Shirley Delores 1932- *WhoFI 92*
**Drew,** Stephen Richard 1949- *WhoBlA 92*
**Drew,** T John 1941- *AmMWSc 92*
**Drew,** Thelma Lucille *WhoBlA 92*
**Drew,** Thomas Shaw 1947- *WhoWest 92*
**Drew,** Timothy 1886-1929 *RelLAm 91*
**Drew,** Walter Harlow 1935- *WhoFI 92*
**Drew,** Wayland 1932- *TwCSFW 91*
**Drew,** Weldon 1935- *WhoBlA 92*
**Drew,** William 1770?-1827 *DcNCBi 2*
**Drew,** William Arthur 1929- *AmMWSc 92*
**Drew-Peeples,** Brenda 1947- *WhoBlA 92*
**Drewe,** Robert 1943- *ConNov 91, WrDr 92*
**Drewes,** Harald D 1927- *AmMWSc 92*
**Drewes,** Lester Richard 1943- *AmMWSc 92*
**Drewes,** Patricia Ann 1932- *AmMWSc 92*
**Drewes,** Robert Clifton 1942- *AmMWSc 92*
**Drewes,** Tom Charles 1941- *WhoFI 92*
**Drewitt,** Frank 1932- *Who 92*
**Drewry,** Cecelia Hodges *WhoBlA 92*
**Drewry,** David John 1947- *Who 92*
**Drewry,** Guy Carleton 1901-1991 *ConAu 135*
**Drewry,** Henry Nathaniel 1924- *WhoBlA 92*
**Drewry,** William Alton 1936- *AmMWSc 92*
**Drews,** Juergen 1933- *IntWW 91*
**Drews,** Mark William 1960- *WhoEnt 92*

**Drews**, Michael James 1945- *AmMWSc 92*
**Drews**, Richard 1953- *WhoEnt 92*
**Drexel**, Katharine 1858-1955 *FacFETw*
**Drexel**, Katharine Mary 1858-1955 *RelLAm 91*
**Drexler**, Anton 1884-1942 *BiDExR, EncTR 91 [port]*
**Drexler**, Arthur 1925-1987 *DcTwDes*
**Drexler**, Clyde 1962- *WhoBlA 92, WhoWest 92*
**Drexler**, Deborah Lynn 1957- *WhoAmL 92*
**Drexler**, Edward James 1938- *AmMWSc 92*
**Drexler**, Elias J. 1911- *IntMPA 92*
**Drexler**, Henry 1927- *AmMWSc 92*
**Drexler**, James Allen 1948- *WhoAmL 92*
**Drexler**, Joanne Lee 1944- *WhoFI 92*
**Drexler**, Kenneth 1941- *WhoAmL 92, WhoWest 92*
**Drexler**, Lawrence Samuel 1957- *WhoAmL 92*
**Drexler**, Mary Sanford 1954- *WhoFI 92, WhoMW 92*
**Drexler**, Michael David 1938- *WhoEnt 92, WhoFI 92*
**Drexler**, Millard S. 1944- *WhoWest 92*
**Drexler**, Nora Lee 1947- *WhoEnt 92*
**Drexler**, Paul 1947- *WhoWest 92*
**Drexler**, Richard Allan 1947- *WhoFI 92, WhoMW 92*
**Drexler**, Rosalyn *DrAPF 91*
**Drexler**, Rosalyn 1926- *IntAu&W 91, WrDr 92*
**Dreyer**, Carl T 1889-1968 *FacFETw*
**Dreyer**, Carl Theodor 1889-1968 *IntDcF 2-2*
**Dreyer**, Desmond 1910- *Who 92*
**Dreyer**, Douglas Charles 1940- *WhoFI 92*
**Dreyer**, Duane Arthur 1942- *AmMWSc 92*
**Dreyer**, Floye Katherine 1927- *WhoEnt 92*
**Dreyer**, Hans P *ScFEYrs*
**Dreyer**, John Edward 1929- *WhoAmL 92*
**Dreyer**, Kirt A 1939- *AmMWSc 92*
**Dreyer**, Robert Marx 1914- *AmMWSc 92*
**Dreyer**, William J 1928- *AmMWSc 92*
**Dreyfus**, Alfred Stanley 1921- *WhoRel 92*
**Dreyfus**, George 1928- *ConCom 92, IntWW 91*
**Dreyfus**, George Joseph 1920- *WhoEnt 92*
**Dreyfus**, Howard Marlow 1942- *WhoIns 92*
**Dreyfus**, John Gustave 1918- *Who 92*
**Dreyfus**, Lee Sherman 1926- *IntWW 91*
**Dreyfus**, Marc George 1926- *AmMWSc 92*
**Dreyfus**, Pierre 1907- *IntWW 91, Who 92*
**Dreyfus**, Pierre Marc 1923- *AmMWSc 92*
**Dreyfus**, Richard Baeck 1958- *WhoAmL 92*
**Dreyfus**, Russell Warren 1929- *AmMWSc 92*
**Dreyfus**, Stuart Ernest 1931- *AmMWSc 92*
**Dreyfuss**, Henry 1904-1972 *DcTwDes, FacFETw*
**Dreyfuss**, Jacques 1937- *AmMWSc 92*
**Dreyfuss**, Joel P. 1945- *WhoBlA 92*
**Dreyfuss**, Lorin *WhoEnt 92*
**Dreyfuss**, M Peter 1932- *AmMWSc 92*
**Dreyfuss**, Michael 1934- *WhoEnt 92*
**Dreyfuss**, Patricia 1932- *AmMWSc 92*
**Dreyfuss**, Richard 1947- *IntMPA 92*
**Dreyfuss**, Richard Stephan 1947- *IntWW 91, WhoEnt 92*
**Dreyfuss**, Robert George 1931- *AmMWSc 92*
**Dreyfuss**, Rochelle Cooper *WhoAmL 92*
**Drezdzon**, William Lawrence 1934- *WhoMW 92*
**Dreze**, Jean 1959- *ConAu 133*
**Dribin**, Daniel Maccabaeus 1913- *AmMWSc 92*
**Dribin**, Lori *AmMWSc 92*
**Drickamer**, Harry George 1908- *FacFETw*
**Drickamer**, Harry George 1918- *AmMWSc 92, IntWW 91*
**Drickamer**, Kurt 1952- *AmMWSc 92*
**Drickamer**, Lee Charles 1946- *AmMWSc 92, WhoMW 92*
**Dridan**, Julian Randal *Who 92N*
**Driedger**, Florence Gay 1933- *WhoRel 92*
**Driedzic**, William R 1948- *AmMWSc 92*
**Driegert**, Robert S 1942- *WhoAmP 91*
**Driehaus**, Robert J 1928- *WhoIns 92*
**Driehuys**, Leonardus Bastiaan 1932- *WhoEnt 92*
**Drielsma**, Claude Dunbar H. *Who 92*
**Drielsma**, Willem Frans Carel 1919- *WhoFI 92*
**Driemeyer**, Clark McAdams 1931- *WhoFI 92*
**Dries**, William Charles 1930- *AmMWSc 92*
**Driesbach**, David Fraiser 1922- *WhoMW 92*
**Driesch**, Albert John 1920- *AmMWSc 92*
**Driesch**, Hans Adolf Eduard 1867-1941 *FacFETw*
**Driesel**, Timothy Michaels 1951- *WhoWest 92*
**Driesens**, Robert James 1918- *AmMWSc 92*
**Driessel**, Kenneth Richard 1940- *WhoWest 92*
**Driessen**, Dan 1951- *WhoBlA 92*
**Driessen**, Henry, Jr. 1927- *WhoBlA 92*
**Drieu La Rochelle**, Pierre 1893-1945 *BiDExR*
**Drieu la Rochelle**, Pierre-Eugene 1893-1945 *GuFrLit 1*
**Driever**, Carl William 1938- *AmMWSc 92*
**Drifters**, The *NewAmDM*
**Driftmier**, James Lee 1951- *WhoFI 92*
**Driggers**, Frank Edgar 1919- *AmMWSc 92*
**Driggers**, Raymond Roland 1923- *WhoRel 92*
**Driggers**, Timothy Gerald 1947- *WhoAmP 91*
**Driggriss**, Daphne Bernice Sutherland *WhoBlA 92*
**Driggs**, Charles Mulford 1924- *WhoAmL 92*
**Driggs**, Don Wallace 1924- *WhoAmP 91*
**Driker**, Eugene 1937- *WhoAmL 92*
**Drill**, Lisa Marie 1959- *WhoAmL 92*
**Drill**, Victor Alexander 1925- *AmMWSc 92*
**Driml**, Richard Lee 1935- *WhoEnt 92*
**Drimmer**, Lillian Boehmer 1949- *WhoFI 92*
**Drimmer**, Melvin 1934- *WhoMW 92*
**Drinan**, Robert F. 1920- *IntWW 91*
**Drinan**, Robert Frederick 1920- *WhoAmL 92, WhoAmP 91*
**Drinane**, Suleika Cabrera 1943- *WhoHisp 92*
**Dring**, James 1905-1985 *TwCPaSc*
**Dring**, John d1991 *Who 92N*
**Dring**, Richard Paddison 1913- *Who 92*
**Dring**, Thomas 1758-1825 *BenetAL 91*
**Dring**, William d1990 *IntWW 91N, Who 92N*
**Dring**, William 1904-1990 *TwCPaSc*
**Drinkall**, John Kenneth 1922- *Who 92*
**Drinkard**, William Charles, Jr 1929- *AmMWSc 92*
**Drinkard**, William H *WhoAmP 91*
**Drinker**, Henry S. 1880-1965 *NewAmDM*
**Drinker**, Philip A 1932- *AmMWSc 92*
**Drinker**, Sophie Hutchinson 1888-1968 *NewAmDM*
**Drinko**, John Deaver 1921- *WhoAmL 92, WhoMW 92*
**Drinkrow**, John *Who 92, WrDr 92*
**Drinkwater**, Alpheus Walton 1875-1962 *DcNCBi 2*
**Drinkwater**, Herbert *WhoAmP 91*
**Drinkwater**, Herbert R. *WhoWest 92*
**Drinkwater**, John 1882-1937 *FacFETw, RfGEnL 91*
**Drinkwater**, John 1925- *Who 92*
**Drinkwater**, Penny 1929- *WrDr 92*
**Drinkwater**, Terry d1989 *LesBEnT 92*
**Drinkwater**, William Otho 1919- *AmMWSc 92*
**Drinkwine**, Edward Allen 1946- *WhoMW 92*
**Drinnan**, Alan John 1932- *AmMWSc 92*
**Driscoll**, Bernard F *AmMWSc 92*
**Driscoll**, Brigid *WhoRel 92*
**Driscoll**, Cecil Lillian 1915- *WhoRel 92*
**Driscoll**, Charles F 1950- *AmMWSc 92*
**Driscoll**, Charles Francis 1943- *WhoMW 92*
**Driscoll**, Daniel Henry 1947- *WhoAmL 92*
**Driscoll**, Dennis Michael 1934- *AmMWSc 92*
**Driscoll**, Donald Thomas 1931- *WhoRel 92*
**Driscoll**, Dorothy H 1924- *AmMWSc 92*
**Driscoll**, Edward Maurice 1936- *WhoAmP 91*
**Driscoll**, Egbert Gotzian 1929- *AmMWSc 92*
**Driscoll**, Eli *TwCWW 91*
**Driscoll**, Frances *DrAPF 91*
**Driscoll**, Geoffrey C 1953- *WhoAmP 91*
**Driscoll**, George C 1927- *AmMWSc 92*
**Driscoll**, Jacques Donnelly 1960- *WhoAmL 92, WhoMW 92*
**Driscoll**, James 1925- *Who 92*
**Driscoll**, James Philip 1943- *Who 92*
**Driscoll**, Jerry L 1944- *WhoAmP 91*
**Driscoll**, John Brian 1946- *WhoAmP 91*
**Driscoll**, John G 1933- *AmMWSc 92*
**Driscoll**, John Gerard 1933- *WhoRel 92*
**Driscoll**, John Patrick 1935- *WhoFI 92*
**Driscoll**, John R 1924- *WhoAmP 91*
**Driscoll**, John Stanford 1934- *AmMWSc 92*
**Driscoll**, Joseph Edward 1941- *WhoAmL 92*
**Driscoll**, Mary Harris *DrAPF 91*
**Driscoll**, Michael John 1934- *AmMWSc 92*
**Driscoll**, Peter 1942- *IntAu&W 91, WrDr 92*
**Driscoll**, Raymond L 1905- *AmMWSc 92*
**Driscoll**, Richard James 1928- *AmMWSc 92*
**Driscoll**, Richard Stark 1928- *AmMWSc 92*
**Driscoll**, Thomas John 1949- *WhoRel 92*
**Driscoll**, William *AmMWSc 92*
**Driscoll**, William J 1913- *WhoAmP 91*
**Driscoll**, William Mark 1953- *WhoEnt 92*
**Driska**, Steven P *AmMWSc 92*
**Driskell**, Claude Evans 1926- *WhoBlA 92*
**Driskell**, David C. 1931- *WhoBlA 92*
**Driskell**, Judy Anne 1943- *AmMWSc 92*
**Driskill**, James Lawrence 1920- *WhoRel 92*
**Driskill**, John R 1934- *WhoIns 92*
**Driskill**, Joseph Denver 1946- *WhoRel 92*
**Driskill**, Joseph L 1955- *WhoAmP 91*
**Driskill**, Kevin 1957- *WhoAmL 92*
**Driskill**, William David 1938- *AmMWSc 92*
**Drisko**, Barbara Lucille 1932- *WhoAmP 91*
**Drisko**, Richard Warren 1925- *AmMWSc 92*
**Driss**, Rachid 1917- *IntWW 91*
**Dristy**, Forrest E 1931- *AmMWSc 92*
**Dritschilo**, William 1946- *AmMWSc 92*
**Dritz**, Michael A. 1938- *WhoFI 92*
**Driver**, Antony 1920- *Who 92*
**Driver**, Bryan 1932- *Who 92*
**Driver**, C. J. 1939- *ConNov 91, WrDr 92*
**Driver**, C. Stephen 1936- *WhoFI 92*
**Driver**, Charles Henry 1921- *AmMWSc 92*
**Driver**, Charles Jonathan 1939- *IntAu&W 91, Who 92*
**Driver**, Christopher 1932- *WrDr 92*
**Driver**, Christopher Prout 1932- *IntAu&W 91, Who 92*
**Driver**, Elwood T. 1921- *WhoBlA 92*
**Driver**, Eric 1911- *Who 92*
**Driver**, Garth Edward 1923- *AmMWSc 92*
**Driver**, Joe Luther 1946- *WhoFI 92*
**Driver**, Johnie M. 1933- *WhoBlA 92*
**Driver**, Louie M., Jr. 1924- *WhoBlA 92*
**Driver**, Olga Lindholm *Who 92*
**Driver**, Paul William 1954- *IntAu&W 91*
**Driver**, Richard D 1948- *AmMWSc 92*
**Driver**, Richard John 1937- *WhoAmP 91*
**Driver**, Richard Sonny, Jr. 1926- *WhoBlA 92*
**Driver**, Rodney D 1932- *AmMWSc 92, WhoAmP 91*
**Driver**, Rogers W. 1921- *WhoBlA 92*
**Driver**, Tom Faw 1925- *WhoRel 92*
**Drizulis**, Aleksandrs 1920- *IntWW 91*
**Drlica**, Karl 1943- *AmMWSc 92*
**Drnevich**, Vincent Paul 1940- *AmMWSc 92, WhoMW 92*
**Drobeck**, Hans Peter 1923- *AmMWSc 92*
**Drobena**, Thomas John 1934- *WhoRel 92*
**Drobinski**, Roger J 1951- *WhoIns 92*
**Drobney**, Ronald DeLoss 1942- *AmMWSc 92*
**Drobnies**, Saul Isaac 1933- *AmMWSc 92*
**Drobnyk**, John Wendel 1935- *AmMWSc 92*
**Drobot**, Stefan 1913- *AmMWSc 92*
**Drobot**, Vladimir *AmMWSc 92*
**Droege**, Harrison David 1961- *WhoWest 92*
**Droege**, John Walter 1921- *AmMWSc 92*
**Droege**, Thomas Arthur 1931- *WhoRel 92*
**Droeger**, William H. d1991 *NewYTBS 91*
**Droel**, William Louis 1948- *WhoRel 92*
**Droessler**, Earl George 1920- *AmMWSc 92*
**Drogheda**, Earl of 1937- *Who 92*
**Drogin**, Eve Roshevsky 1946- *WhoRel 92*
**Drohojowska**, Hunter 1952- *WhoWest 92*
**Droit**, Michel 1923- *IntWW 91*
**Drolet**, Paul L 1928- *WhoAmP 91*
**Droll**, Henry Andrew 1926- *AmMWSc 92*
**Drollinger**, John, Jr. 1924- *WhoFI 92*
**Drolsom**, Paul Newell 1925- *AmMWSc 92*
**Dromer**, Jean 1929- *IntWW 91*
**Dromgold**, Luther D 1925- *AmMWSc 92*
**Dromgoole**, Edward 1751-1835 *DcNCBi 2*
**Dromgoole**, Jolyon 1926- *Who 92*
**Dromgoole**, Patrick 1930- *IntMPA 92*
**Dromgoole**, Patrick Shirley Brookes F 1930- *Who 92*
**Dromgoole**, Peter Pelham 1815- *DcNCBi 2*
**Dromi**, Jose Roberto 1945- *IntWW 91*
**Dromore**, Bishop of 1924- *Who 92*
**Dronen**, Norman Obert, Jr 1945- *AmMWSc 92*
**Dronenburg**, Ernest Justin, Jr 1943- *WhoAmP 91*
**Droney**, John F, Jr 1946- *WhoAmP 91*
**Dronfield**, Ronald 1924- *Who 92*
**Dronke**, Peter 1934- *IntWW 91, Who 92*
**Droogan**, Cornelius James 1948- *WhoAmL 92*
**Droogleever Fortuyn**, Jan 1906- *IntWW 91*
**Dropesky**, Bruce Joseph 1924- *AmMWSc 92*
**Dropkin**, Allen Hodes 1930- *WhoMW 92*
**Dropkin**, John Joseph 1910- *AmMWSc 92*
**Dropkin**, Victor Harry 1916- *AmMWSc 92*
**Dropko**, William G. 1938- *WhoRel 92*
**Dropp**, John Jerome 1940- *AmMWSc 92*
**Droppers**, Carl H 1918- *IntAu&W 91, WrDr 92*
**Droppert**, Vincent Marc 1951- *WhoWest 92*
**Droppo**, James Garnet, Jr 1943- *AmMWSc 92*
**Dror**, Michael 1940- *WhoMW 92*
**Drosdick**, John Girard 1943- *WhoWest 92*
**Drosdoff**, Matthew 1908- *AmMWSc 92*
**Drosos**, Argyris 1936- *WhoWest 92*
**Drossman**, Melvyn Miles 1937- *AmMWSc 92*
**Drossoyiannis**, Anthony 1922- *IntWW 91*
**Drost**, Cynthia Mae Van Veldhuizen 1961- *WhoAmP 91*
**Drost**, Patricia May 1947- *WhoAmL 92*
**Drost-Hansen**, Walter 1925- *AmMWSc 92*
**Droste**, Donald Casper *WhoAmL 92*
**Droste**, John Brown 1927- *AmMWSc 92*
**Drouilhet**, Paul R 1933- *AmMWSc 92*
**Drower**, Margaret Stefana 1911- *WrDr 92*
**Drown**, Eugene Ardent 1915- *WhoWest 92*
**Drown**, Merle *DrAPF 91*
**Drown**, Thomas Messinger 1842-1904 *BiInAmS*
**Drowne**, Solomon 1753-1834 *BiInAmS*
**Drowota**, Frank F., III 1938- *WhoAmL 92, WhoAmP 91*
**Droz**, Georges Andre Leopold 1931- *IntWW 91*
**Droz**, Henry 1926- *WhoEnt 92*
**Drozd**, Leon Frank, Jr. 1948- *WhoAmL 92, WhoWest 92*
**Drozd**, Mikhail Filippovich *IntWW 91*
**Drozda**, Joseph Michael 1943- *WhoFI 92, WhoMW 92*
**Drozda**, William 1948- *WhoAmP 91*
**Drozdeck**, Steven Richard 1951- *WhoFI 92*
**Drozdova**, Margarita Sergeyevna 1948- *IntWW 91*
**Drozdowicz**, Zbigniew Marian 1949- *AmMWSc 92*
**Drozdziel**, Marion John 1924- *WhoFI 92*
**Dru**, Joanne 1923- *IntMPA 92*
**Drube**, Joel Alan 1954- *WhoMW 92*
**Druck**, Mark *WhoEnt 92*
**Druck**, Michael Jon 1961- *WhoFI 92*
**Drucker**, A. Norman 1930- *WhoAmL 92*
**Drucker**, Arnold 1932- *AmMWSc 92*
**Drucker**, Barry Jules 1940- *WhoMW 92*
**Drucker**, Daniel Charles 1918- *AmMWSc 92, IntWW 91, WrDr 92*
**Drucker**, Daniel Stephen 1946- *WhoMW 92*
**Drucker**, E E 1924- *AmMWSc 92*
**Drucker**, H. M. 1942- *WrDr 92*
**Drucker**, Harris 1943- *AmMWSc 92*
**Drucker**, Harvey 1941- *AmMWSc 92*
**Drucker**, Henry Mathew 1942- *IntAu&W 91*
**Drucker**, Henry Matthew 1942- *Who 92*
**Drucker**, Jean Maurice 1941- *IntWW 91*
**Drucker**, John H. 1952- *WhoAmL 92*
**Drucker**, Judith R. 1934- *WhoEnt 92*
**Drucker**, Marsha 1937- *WhoMW 92*
**Drucker**, Mort 1929- *ConAu 133*
**Drucker**, Peter 1909- *Who 92, WrDr 92*
**Drucker**, Peter Ferdinand 1909- *IntWW 91, WhoWest 92*
**Drucker**, Rolf 1926- *WhoEnt 92*
**Drucker**, Sally Ann *DrAPF 91*
**Drucker**, Stanley 1929- *NewAmDM*
**Drucker**, William D 1929- *AmMWSc 92*
**Drucker**, William Richard 1922- *AmMWSc 92*
**Druckman**, Jacob 1928- *ConCom 92, NewAmDM*
**Druckman**, Jacob Raphael 1928- *WhoEnt 92*
**Druckrey**, Gerald Richard 1933- *WhoMW 92*
**Drudge**, J Harold 1922- *AmMWSc 92*
**Drudi**, John Louis 1935- *WhoMW 92*
**Druehl**, Louis D 1936- *AmMWSc 92*
**Druelinger**, Melvin L 1940- *AmMWSc 92*
**Drufenbrock**, Diane 1929- *AmMWSc 92*
**Drufenbrock**, Diane Joyce 1929- *WhoAmP 91, WhoMW 92*
**Druffel**, Larry Edward 1940- *AmMWSc 92*
**Drugan**, Cornelius Bernard 1946- *WhoMW 92*
**Drugan**, James Richard 1938- *AmMWSc 92*
**Druger**, Marvin 1934- *AmMWSc 92*
**Druger**, Stephen David 1942- *AmMWSc 92*
**Drugg**, Warren Sowle 1929- *AmMWSc 92*
**Drui**, Albert Burnell 1926- *AmMWSc 92*
**Drukaroff**, David Marc 1948- *WhoFI 92*
**Druker**, Henry Leo 1953- *WhoFI 92*
**Drukker**, William Richard 1946- *WhoWest 92*
**Druks**, Herbert 1937- *IntAu&W 91, WrDr 92*
**Drullinger**, Robert Eugene 1944- *AmMWSc 92*

**Drum,** Charles Monroe 1934- *AmMWSc 92*
**Drum,** I M 1913- *AmMWSc 92*
**Drum,** Ryan William 1939- *AmMWSc 92*
**Drum,** Scott Douglas 1949- *WhoMW 92*
**Drumheller,** Douglas Schaeffer 1942- *AmMWSc 92*
**Drumheller,** George Jesse 1933- *WhoWest 92*
**Drumheller,** Helen E 1931- *WhoAmP 91*
**Drumheller,** John Earl 1931- *AmMWSc 92, WhoWest 92*
**Drumheller,** Kirk 1925- *AmMWSc 92*
**Drumlanrig,** Viscount 1967- *Who 92*
**Drumm,** Bernhardt Charles, Jr. 1941- *WhoAmL 92*
**Drumm,** D B *TwCSFW 91*
**Drumm,** Manuel Felix 1922- *AmMWSc 92*
**Drumm,** Walter Gregory 1940- *Who 92*
**Drummer,** Donald Raymond 1941- *WhoFI 92, WhoWest 92*
**Drummeter,** Louis Franklin, Jr 1921- *AmMWSc 92*
**Drummond** *Who 92*
**Drummond,** Anthony John D. *Who 92*
**Drummond,** Boyce Alexander, III 1946- *AmMWSc 92*
**Drummond,** Carol Cramer 1933- *WhoEnt 92*
**Drummond,** Charles Henry, III 1944- *AmMWSc 92*
**Drummond,** David Classon 1928- *Who 92*
**Drummond,** David L., Sr. 1918- *WhoBlA 92*
**Drummond,** Emma *WrDr 92*
**Drummond,** Gerard Kasper 1937- *WhoFI 92, WhoWest 92*
**Drummond,** Hamilton 1857-1935 *ScFEYrs*
**Drummond,** Harold Dean 1916- *WhoWest 92*
**Drummond,** Ian M. 1933- *WrDr 92*
**Drummond,** Ivor *IntAu&W 91X, WrDr 92*
**Drummond,** John 1919- *WhoAmP 91*
**Drummond,** John Dobyns 1945- *WhoMW 92*
**Drummond,** John Richard Gray 1934- *Who 92*
**Drummond,** June 1923- *IntAu&W 91, WrDr 92*
**Drummond,** Kenneth Herbert 1922- *AmMWSc 92*
**Drummond,** Kevin *Who 92*
**Drummond,** Lewis A. *WhoRel 92*
**Drummond,** Malcolm 1880-1945 *TwCPaSc*
**Drummond,** Malcolm McAllister 1937- *WhoFI 92*
**Drummond,** Maldwin Andrew Cyril 1932- *Who 92*
**Drummond,** Margaret Crawford 1922- *AmMWSc 92*
**Drummond,** Michael 1960-1990 *FacFETw*
**Drummond,** Norman Walker 1952- *Who 92*
**Drummond,** Paula Grier 1950- *WhoAmL 92*
**Drummond,** Paulo Nacif 1966- *WhoFI 92*
**Drummond,** Richard Henry 1916- *WhoRel 92*
**Drummond,** Robert Kendig 1939- *WhoAmL 92*
**Drummond,** Roger Otto 1931- *AmMWSc 92*
**Drummond,** Terence Michael 1950- *WhoRel 92*
**Drummond,** Thomas Anthony Kevin 1943- *Who 92*
**Drummond,** Thornton B., Jr. 1927- *WhoBlA 92*
**Drummond,** Tucker 1948- *WhoAmL 92*
**Drummond,** V. H. 1911- *WrDr 92*
**Drummond,** Walter *ConAu 36NR*
**Drummond,** Willa H 1943- *AmMWSc 92*
**Drummond,** William 1585-1649 *RfGEnL 91*
**Drummond,** William 1620?-1677 *DcNCBi 2*
**Drummond,** William Eckel 1927- *AmMWSc 92*
**Drummond,** William Henry 1854-1907 *BenetAL 91*
**Drummond,** William Joe 1944- *WhoBlA 92, WhoWest 92*
**Drummond,** William Norman 1927- *Who 92*
**Drummond de Andrade,** Carlos 1902-1987 *FacFETw*
**Drummond Young,** James Edward 1950- *Who 92*
**Drumont,** Edouard Adolphe 1844-1917 *BiDExR*
**Drumwright,** Thomas Franklin, Jr 1928- *AmMWSc 92*
**Drungo,** Elbert, Jr. 1943- *WhoBlA 92*
**Druon,** Maurice Samuel Roger Charles 1918- *IntWW 91, Who 92*
**Drury,** Alfred 1856-1944 *TwCPaSc*
**Drury,** Allen 1918- *BenetAL 91, ConNov 91, FacFETw, WrDr 92*
**Drury,** Allen Stuart 1918- *IntAu&W 91, IntWW 91, Who 92*
**Drury,** Cathleen Joanne 1951- *WhoAmL 92*
**Drury,** Charles Mills d1991 *Who 92N*
**Drury,** Charles Mills 1912- *IntWW 91*
**Drury,** Colin Gordon 1941- *AmMWSc 92*
**Drury,** David J 1944- *WhoIns 92*
**Drury,** Dennis C. 1941- *WhoAmL 92*
**Drury,** Finvola d1991 *NewYTBS 91*
**Drury,** George *DrAPF 91*
**Drury,** James 1934- *IntMPA 92*
**Drury,** John *DrAPF 91*
**Drury,** John 1936- *ConAu 133*
**Drury,** John Henry 1936- *Who 92*
**Drury,** Liston Nathaniel 1924- *AmMWSc 92*
**Drury,** Malcolm John 1948- *AmMWSc 92*
**Drury,** Maxine Cole 1914- *WrDr 92*
**Drury,** Michael *Who 92*
**Drury,** Paul 1903-1987 *TwCPaSc*
**Drury,** Robert Norman 1947- *WhoEnt 92*
**Drury,** Stephen *WhoEnt 92*
**Drury,** Stephen Max 1948- *WhoRel 92*
**Drury,** Susie B 1927- *WhoAmP 91*
**Drury,** Thomas T. 1943- *WhoRel 92*
**Drury,** Victor William Michael 1926- *Who 92*
**Drury,** William Holland 1921- *AmMWSc 92*
**Druse-Manteuffel,** Mary Jeanne 1946- *AmMWSc 92*
**Drusedum,** John William, Jr. 1952- *WhoRel 92*
**Drushel,** Harry 1925- *AmMWSc 92*
**Drusin,** Lewis Martin 1939- *AmMWSc 92*
**Drutchas,** Gerrick Gilbert 1953- *WhoWest 92*
**Drutz,** David Jules 1938- *WhoFI 92*
**Druy,** Mark Arnold 1955- *AmMWSc 92*
**Druyan,** Mary Ellen 1938- *AmMWSc 92*
**Druz,** Walter S 1917- *AmMWSc 92*
**Druzhnikov,** Juri 1933- *LiExTwC*
**Drvota,** Mojmir 1923- *WhoEnt 92*
**Dry,** Marcus Baxter 1871-1946 *DcNCBi 2*
**Dry,** Michael Powell 1943- *WhoFI 92*
**Dry,** William, III 1720-1781 *DcNCBi 2*
**Dryce,** H. David 1930- *WhoFI 92*
**Dryden,** Charles Walter 1920- *WhoBlA 92*
**Dryden,** David Charles 1947- *WhoFI 92*
**Dryden,** Gale Emerson 1922- *WhoMW 92*
**Dryden,** Hugh L 1898-1965 *FacFETw*
**Dryden,** John *TwCWW 91*
**Dryden,** John 1631-1700 *CnDBLB 2 [port], RfGEnL 91*
**Dryden,** John 1943- *Who 92*
**Dryden,** John Clifford 1951- *WhoEnt 92*
**Dryden,** Pamela *WrDr 92*
**Dryden,** Phylis Campbell *DrAPF 91*
**Dryden,** Richard Lee 1945- *AmMWSc 92*
**Dryden,** Robert Eugene 1927- *WhoAmL 92, WhoWest 92*
**Drye,** Samuel T. *WhoRel 92*
**Dryer,** Clayton Christopher 1951- *WhoWest 92*
**Dryer,** Douglas Poole 1915- *IntWW 91*
**Dryer,** Ivan 1939- *WhoEnt 92*
**Dryer,** Murray 1925- *AmMWSc 92*
**Dryer,** Richard Edward 1930- *WhoRel 92*
**Dryfoos,** Nancy Proskauer 1918-1991 *NewYTBS 91*
**Dryfoos,** Robert J 1942- *WhoAmP 91*
**Dryhurst,** Glenn 1939- *AmMWSc 92*
**Dryland,** Gordon Boyce 1926- *IntAu&W 91*
**Drysdale,** Andrew 1935- *IntWW 91*
**Drysdale,** Don Michael 1947- *WhoAmL 92*
**Drysdale,** George Marsman 1954- *WhoWest 92*
**Drysdale,** James Wallace 1937- *AmMWSc 92*
**Drysdale,** Robert Swanston 1941- *WhoFI 92*
**Drysdale,** Thomas Henry 1942- *Who 92*
**Drysdale Wilson,** John Veitch 1929- *Who 92*
**Drzewiecki,** Tadeusz Maria 1943- *AmMWSc 92*
**D'Silva,** Themistocles Damasceno Joaquim 1932- *AmMWSc 92*
**D'Souza,** Anthony Frank 1929- *AmMWSc 92*
**D'Souza,** Eugene 1917- *IntWW 91*
**D'Souza,** Gerard Eugene 1956- *WhoFI 92*
**D'Souza,** Henry Sebastian *Who 92*
**Du Daozheng** 1923- *IntWW 91*
**Du Gong** *IntWW 91*
**Du Pengcheng** 1921- *IntWW 91*
**Du Ping** 1908- *IntWW 91*
**Du Runsheng** 1913- *IntWW 91*
**Du Yide** 1912- *IntWW 91*
**Du Yuzhou** 1942- *IntWW 91*
**Du,** David Hung-Chang 1951- *AmMWSc 92*
**Du,** Julie Tsai *AmMWSc 92*
**Du,** Li-Jen 1935- *AmMWSc 92*
**Dua,** Indardev 1907- *IntWW 91*
**Dua,** Prem Nath 1935- *AmMWSc 92*
**Dual,** J. Fred, Jr. 1942- *WhoBlA 92*
**Dual,** Joseph Frederick, Jr. 1942- *WhoFI 92*
**Dual,** Peter Alfred 1946- *WhoBlA 92*
**Duall,** John William 1928- *WhoFI 92*
**Duan Junyi** 1910- *IntWW 91*
**Duane,** David Bierlein 1934- *AmMWSc 92*
**Duane,** Diane *TwCSFW 91, WrDr 92*
**Duane,** James 1733-1797 *BlkwEAR*
**Duane,** John F 1953- *WhoAmP 91*
**Duane,** Thomas David 1917- *AmMWSc 92*
**Duane,** William Francis 1948- *WhoEnt 92*
**Duany,** Luis Alberto 1965- *WhoHisp 92*
**Duany,** Luis F, Jr 1919- *AmMWSc 92*
**Duarte,** Amalia Maria 1962- *WhoHisp 92*
**Duarte,** David *WhoHisp 92*
**Duarte,** Harold Jorge 1950- *WhoRel 92*
**Duarte,** Jose Napoleon 1925-1990 *AnObit 1990*
**Duarte,** Ramon Gonzalez 1948- *WhoWest 92*
**Duarte,** Roger Ariel 1942- *WhoFI 92*
**Duarte,** Y. E. 1948- *WhoHisp 92*
**Duarte Fuentes,** Jose Napoleon 1926-1990 *FacFETw*
**Duarte-Valverde,** Gloria A. 1950- *WhoHisp 92*
**Duax,** William Leo 1939- *AmMWSc 92*
**Dub,** Anthony V. 1949- *WhoFI 92*
**Dub,** Michael 1917- *AmMWSc 92*
**Duba,** Arlo Dean 1929- *WhoRel 92*
**Dubach,** Harold William 1920- *AmMWSc 92*
**Dubach,** Leland L 1923- *AmMWSc 92*
**Dubai,** Ruler of *IntWW 91*
**Du Bain,** Myron 1923- *IntWW 91*
**Duband,** Wayne *IntMPA 92*
**Dubanevich,** Keith Scott 1957- *WhoAmL 92*
**DuBar,** Jules R 1923- *AmMWSc 92*
**Dubas,** Lawrence Francis 1952- *AmMWSc 92*
**Dubasov,** F V 1845-1912 *FacFETw*
**DuBay,** Denis Thomas 1952- *AmMWSc 92*
**Dubay,** George Henry 1914- *AmMWSc 92*
**DuBay,** Keith Edward 1953- *WhoAmL 92*
**Dubaz,** Larry, Jr *WhoAmP 91*
**Dubbe,** Richard F 1929- *AmMWSc 92*
**Dubbelday,** Pieter Steven 1928- *AmMWSc 92*
**Dubbins,** Don Gene 1928- *WhoEnt 92*
**Dubbs,** Del Rose M 1928- *AmMWSc 92*
**Dubcek,** Alexander 1921- *FacFETw, IntWW 91*
**Dube,** Charles Lewis 1964- *WhoEnt 92*
**Dube,** David Gregory 1948- *AmMWSc 92*
**Dube,** Ellen C 1947- *WhoAmP 91*
**Dube,** Francois 1955- *AmMWSc 92*
**Dube,** Gregory P 1954- *AmMWSc 92*
**Dube,** Jackson E. *IntMPA 92*
**Dube,** James L. 1949- *WhoFI 92*
**Dube,** Lawrence Edward, Jr. 1948- *WhoAmL 92*
**Dube,** LeRoy S 1908- *WhoAmP 91*
**Dube,** Maurice Andrew *AmMWSc 92*
**Dube,** Roger Raymond 1949- *AmMWSc 92*
**Dube,** Thomas M. T. 1938- *WhoBlA 92*
**Dube-Kastner,** Cheryl Ann 1963- *WhoFI 92*
**Dubeck,** Leroy W 1939- *AmMWSc 92*
**Dubelyew,** Didi Susan *DrAPF 91*
**Dubenion,** Elbert 1933- *WhoBlA 92*
**Duberg,** John E 1917- *AmMWSc 92*
**Duberg,** John Edward 1917- *WhoFI 92*
**Duberman,** Marin Bauml 1930- *IntAu&W 91*
**Duberman,** Martin 1930- *WrDr 92*
**Duberstein,** Aaron D. d1991 *NewYTBS 91*
**Duberstein,** Helen *DrAPF 91*
**Duberstein,** Helen 1926- *WrDr 92*
**Duberstein,** Helen Laura 1926- *WhoEnt 92*
**Duberstein,** Kenneth Marc 1944- *WhoAmP 91*
**Duberstein,** Larry 1944- *ConAu 135*
**Dubery,** Fred 1926- *TwCPaSc*
**Dubes,** George Richard 1926- *AmMWSc 92*
**Dubes,** Richard C 1934- *AmMWSc 92*
**du Beth,** Donna Maria 1947- *WhoAmL 92*
**Dubetz,** Shirley Arlene 1927- *WhoAmL 92*
**Dubey,** Devendra P 1936- *AmMWSc 92*
**Dubey,** Jitender Prakash 1938- *AmMWSc 92*
**Dubey,** Rajendra Narain 1938- *AmMWSc 92*
**Dubey,** Satya D 1930- *AmMWSc 92*
**Dubey,** Stephen Arthur 1947- *WhoMW 92*
**Dubie,** Norman *DrAPF 91*
**Dubie,** Norman 1945- *BenetAL 91, ConPo 91, IntAu&W 91, WrDr 92*
**Dubie,** William 1953- *IntAu&W 91*
**Dubiel,** Mark Baldwin 1956- *WhoWest 92*
**Dubiel,** Russell F 1951- *AmMWSc 92*
**Dubilier,** Martin H. d1991 *NewYTBS 91 [port]*
**Dubin,** Alvin 1914- *AmMWSc 92*
**Dubin,** Charles S. *LesBEnT 92*
**Dubin,** Donald T 1932- *AmMWSc 92*
**Dubin,** Fred S 1914- *AmMWSc 92*
**Dubin,** Henry Charles 1943- *AmMWSc 92*
**Dubin,** James Michael 1946- *WhoFI 92*
**Dubin,** Joseph William 1948- *WhoFI 92*
**Dubin,** Mark William 1942- *AmMWSc 92*
**Dubin,** Maurice 1926- *AmMWSc 92*
**Dubin,** Michael 1943- *WhoFI 92*
**Dubin,** Morton Donald 1931- *WhoEnt 92*
**Dubin,** Norman H 1942- *AmMWSc 92*
**Dubin,** Paul L. 1941- *WhoMW 92*
**Dubin,** Paul Lee 1941- *AmMWSc 92*
**Dubin,** Steven E. 1949- *WhoEnt 92*
**Dubin,** Steven Hugh 1948- *WhoFI 92*
**Dubina,** Joel F *WhoAmP 91*
**Dubina,** Joel Fredrick 1947- *WhoAmL 92*
**Dubina,** Mary Regina 1922- *WhoRel 92*
**Dubinin,** Nikolay Petrovich 1907- *IntWW 91, SovUnBD*
**Dubinin,** Yuri Vladimirovich 1930- *IntWW 91*
**Dubinin,** Yuriy Vladimirovich 1930- *SovUnBD*
**Dubins,** Lester Eli 1920- *AmMWSc 92*
**Dubins,** Mortimer Ira 1919- *AmMWSc 92*
**Dubinski,** John Richard 1942- *WhoMW 92*
**Dubinsky,** Barry *AmMWSc 92*
**Dubinsky,** David 1892-1982 *FacFETw*
**Dubinsky,** Rostislav 1923- *ConAu 133*
**Dubisch,** Roy 1917- *AmMWSc 92*
**Dubisch,** Russell John 1945- *AmMWSc 92*
**Dubiski,** Stanislaw 1929- *AmMWSc 92*
**Dubitsky,** Ira L. 1941- *WhoAmL 92*
**Dubitzky,** Jonathan Benjamin 1951- *WhoAmL 92*
**Duble,** Harold G 1938- *WhoIns 92*
**Duble,** Richard Lee 1940- *AmMWSc 92*
**Dublin,** Archbishop of 1925- *Who 92*
**Dublin,** Archbishop of 1926- *Who 92*
**Dublin,** Auxiliary Bishop of *Who 92*
**Dublin,** Dean of *Who 92*
**Dublin,** Louis I. 1882-1969 *CurBio 91N*
**Dublin,** Thomas David 1912- *AmMWSc 92*
**Dubner,** Ronald 1934- *AmMWSc 92*
**Dubnick,** Bernard 1928- *AmMWSc 92*
**Dubnov,** Eugene 1949- *LiExTwC*
**Dubocovich,** Margarita L 1947- *AmMWSc 92*
**DuBoff,** Leonard David 1941- *WhoWest 92*
**Dubois,** Alton Clark 1944- *WhoMW 92*
**Dubois,** Andre T 1939- *AmMWSc 92*
**DuBois,** Arthur Brooks 1923- *AmMWSc 92*
**DuBois,** Asa Stephen 1929-1985 *WhoBlA 92N*
**DuBois,** Augustus Jay 1849-1915 *BiInAmS*
**DuBois,** Cora d1991 *NewYTBS 91 [port]*
**Dubois,** David Graham *DrAPF 91*
**Du Bois,** David Graham 1925- *WhoBlA 92*
**Du Bois,** Donald Frank 1932- *AmMWSc 92*
**Dubois,** Donald Ward 1923- *AmMWSc 92*
**Dubois,** Donna Marie 1946- *WhoFI 92*
**Dubois,** Duane R 1934- *WhoIns 92*
**DuBois,** Frank A., III 1947- *WhoWest 92*
**DuBois,** Frederick Williamson 1923- *AmMWSc 92*
**DuBois,** G. Macy 1929- *IntWW 91*
**DuBois,** Gary Lee 1953- *WhoWest 92*
**DuBois,** Grant Edwin 1946- *AmMWSc 92, WhoMW 92*
**Dubois,** Jacques-Emile 1920- *IntWW 91*
**DuBois,** James Clemens 1936- *WhoAmP 91*
**DuBois,** Jan E. 1931- *WhoAmL 92*
**Dubois,** Jean-Marie M 1944- *AmMWSc 92*
**DuBois,** John 1700?-1768 *DcNCBi 2*
**DuBois,** John 1921- *WhoAmP 91*
**DuBois,** John R 1934- *AmMWSc 92*
**Dubois,** Karen Marie 1956- *WhoWest 92*
**DuBois,** Leanne Perme 1956- *WhoAmL 92*
**DuBois,** Louis H. 1930- *WhoFI 92*
**Du Bois,** M *IntAu&W 91X, WrDr 92*
**DuBois,** Mark Benjamin 1955- *WhoMW 92*
**Du Bois,** Nelson S. D'Andrea, Jr. 1930- *WhoBlA 92*
**DuBois,** Peter Arnott 1947- *WhoFI 92*
**Du Bois,** Reynold Cooper 1940- *WhoFI 92*
**Dubois,** Robert Dean 1948- *AmMWSc 92*
**Du Bois,** Robert Lee 1924- *AmMWSc 92*
**Dubois,** Ronald Joseph 1942- *AmMWSc 92*
**Du Bois,** Shirley Graham 1904-1977 *NotBlAW 92*
**Dubois,** Theodore 1837-1924 *NewAmDM*
**DuBois,** Thomas David 1940- *AmMWSc 92*
**Dubois,** W.E.B. *DcAmImH*
**Du Bois,** W E B 1868-1963 *AfrAmW, BenetAL 91, BlkLC [port], ConAu 34NR, FacFETw [port], LiExTwC, RComAH*
**Du Bois,** William Edward Burghardt 1868-1963 *AmPeW*

**du Bois,** William Pene *SmATA 68*
**Du Bois,** William Pene 1916- *IntAu&W 91, WrDr 92*
**Dubon,** Charles F. 1945- *WhoHisp 92*
**Dubos,** Jean-Baptiste 1670-1742 *BlkwCEP*
**Dubos,** Rene Jules 1901-1982 *FacFETw*
**DuBose,** Charles Wilson 1949- *WhoAmL 92*
**DuBose,** Clarence R. 1943- *WhoBlA 92*
**Dubose,** Cullen Lanier 1935- *WhoBlA 92*
**DuBose,** Francis Marquis 1922- *WhoRel 92, WhoWest 92*
**DuBose,** Leo Edwin 1931- *AmMWSc 92*
**DuBose,** Maria Deborah 1952- *WhoHisp 92*
**DuBose,** Otelia 1949- *WhoBlA 92*
**DuBose,** Pierre Wilds, Jr. 1928- *WhoRel 92*
**Du Bose,** Robert Earl, Jr. 1927- *WhoBlA 92*
**Dubose,** Robert Trafton 1919- *AmMWSc 92*
**DuBose,** William Porcher 1836-1918 *RelLAm 91*
**du Boulay** *Who 92*
**Du Boulay,** Francis Robin Houssemayne 1920- *IntWW 91*
**Du Boulay,** Robin 1920- *Who 92*
**Dubovik,** G.J. *DrAPF 91*
**DuBow,** Michael Scott 1950- *AmMWSc 92*
**Dubowitz,** Victor 1931- *IntWW 91, Who 92*
**Dubowski,** Kurt M 1921- *AmMWSc 92*
**Dubowsky,** Steven 1942- *AmMWSc 92*
**Duboy,** Antonio 1963- *WhoHisp 92*
**Dubpernell,** George 1901- *AmMWSc 92*
**Dubravcic,** Milan Frane 1922- *AmMWSc 92*
**du Breuil,** Felix L 1921- *AmMWSc 92*
**DuBridge,** Lee A. 1901- *Who 92*
**DuBridge,** Lee Alvin 1901- *AmMWSc 92, IntWW 91*
**Dubro,** Alec 1944- *ConAu 133*
**DuBroff,** Donald Alan 1951- *WhoMW 92*
**Dubroff,** Lewis Michael 1947- *AmMWSc 92*
**DuBroff,** Richard Edward 1948- *AmMWSc 92, WhoMW 92*
**DuBroff,** William 1937- *AmMWSc 92*
**Dubrovay,** Jaeson 1955- *WhoFI 92, WhoWest 92*
**Dubrovin,** Aleksandr Ivanovich 1855-1918 *BiDExR*
**Dubrovin,** Kenneth P 1931- *AmMWSc 92*
**Dubrovin,** Vivian 1931- *SmATA 65*
**Dubrow,** Heather 1945- *IntAu&W 91*
**Dubrow,** Marsha Ann 1948- *WhoFI 92*
**DuBrul,** E Lloyd 1909- *AmMWSc 92*
**DuBrul,** Ernest 1943- *AmMWSc 92*
**Du Brul,** Liza Hirsch 1955- *WhoAmL 92*
**DuBrul,** Stephen McKenzie, Jr. 1929- *WhoFI 92*
**Dubs,** Alfred 1932- *Who 92*
**Dubs,** Arthur R. 1930- *IntMPA 92*
**Dubsky,** Mario 1939-1985 *TwCPaSc*
**Dubuc,** Paul U 1938- *AmMWSc 92*
**Dubuc,** Serge 1939- *AmMWSc 92*
**Dubuffet,** Jean 1901-1985 *FacFETw*
**Dubuque,** Kenneth Robert 1948- *WhoFI 92*
**Dubus,** Andre *DrAPF 91, IntAu&W 91*
**Dubus,** Andre 1936- *BenetAL 91, ConNov 91, WrDr 92*
**Dubus,** Andre, III *DrAPF 91*
**Duby,** Georges Michel Claude 1919- *IntWW 91*
**Duby,** Jean Jacques 1940- *IntWW 91*
**Duby,** John 1930- *AmMWSc 92*
**Duby,** Paul F 1933- *AmMWSc 92*
**Duby,** Robert T 1940- *AmMWSc 92*
**Du Camp,** Maxime 1822-1894 *GuFrLit 1*
**Du Cane,** John Peter 1921- *Who 92*
**du Cann,** Edward 1924- *Who 92*
**du Cann,** Edward Dillon Lott 1924- *IntWW 91*
**Du Cann,** Richard Dillon Lott 1929- *Who 92*
**Ducasse,** Roger *NewAmDM*
**Ducat-Amos,** Barbara Mary 1921- *Who 92*
**Ducatel,** Julius Timoleon 1796-1849 *BiInAmS*
**Ducceschi,** James Martin Michael 1936- *WhoFI 92*
**Ducci,** Roberto 1914- *IntWW 91, Who 92*
**Duce** *EncTR 91*
**Duce,** Ivy Oneita 1895- *RelLAm 91*
**Duce,** Robert Arthur 1935- *AmMWSc 92*
**Duce,** S. Alan 1961- *WhoRel 92*
**Duch,** David S 1943- *AmMWSc 92*
**Duch,** Thomas J 1956- *WhoAmP 91*
**Du Chaillu,** Paul B. 1835-1903 *BenetAL 91*
**DuChaillu,** Paul Belloni 1835-1903 *BiInAmS*
**Duchamp,** David James 1939- *AmMWSc 92*
**Duchamp,** Marcel 1887-1968 *FacFETw*
**Duchamp,** Thomas Eugene 1947- *AmMWSc 92*
**Duchamp-Villon,** Raymond 1876-1918 *FacFETw*
**DuCharme,** Donald Walter 1937- *AmMWSc 92*
**Ducharme,** Doris R *WhoAmP 91*
**DuCharme,** Ernest Peter 1916- *AmMWSc 92*
**duCharme,** Gillian Drusilla Brown 1938- *Who 92*
**Ducharme,** Jacques R 1928- *AmMWSc 92*
**Duchein,** Michel 1926- *ConAu 135*
**Duchek,** John Robert 1948- *AmMWSc 92*
**Duchemin,** Robert Anthony 1962- *WhoAmL 92*
**Duchene,** Louis-Francois 1927- *Who 92, WrDr 92*
**Duchessi,** Peter Joseph 1953- *WhoFI 92*
**Duchin,** Peter Oelrichs 1937- *WhoEnt 92*
**Duchnowski,** Edward Martin 1942- *WhoWest 92*
**Duchon,** Roseann Marie 1950- *WhoMW 92*
**Duchossois,** Richard Louis 1921- *WhoMW 92*
**Duchovic,** Ronald Joseph 1951- *WhoMW 92*
**Duci,** Frank Joseph 1922- *WhoAmP 91*
**Ducibella,** Tom 1947- *AmMWSc 92*
**Ducic,** Jovan 1871-1943 *LiExTwC*
**Ducie,** Earl of 1917- *Who 92*
**duCille,** Ann *DrAPF 91*
**Ducis,** Ilze 1947- *AmMWSc 92*
**Duck,** Bobby Neal 1939- *AmMWSc 92*
**Duck,** Hywel Ivor 1933- *Who 92*
**Duck,** Ian Morley 1933- *AmMWSc 92*
**Duck,** Ruth Carolyn 1947- *WhoRel 92*
**Duck,** Stephen 1705-1756 *RfGEnL 91*
**Duck,** William N, Jr 1920- *AmMWSc 92*
**Duckenfield,** Nathaniel 1746-1824 *DcNCBi 2*
**Duckenfield,** Thomas Adams 1935- *WhoAmL 92*
**Duckenfield,** William d1721? *DcNCBi 2*
**Ducker,** Herbert Charles 1900- *Who 92*
**Ducker,** Thomas Barbee 1937- *AmMWSc 92*
**Duckett,** Ann Lorraine 1951- *WhoAmL 92*
**Duckett,** Gregory Morris 1960- *WhoBlA 92*
**Duckett,** Hillery Keith, II 1952- *WhoAmL 92*
**Duckett,** Joan 1934- *WhoAmL 92*
**Duckett,** Kermit Earl 1936- *AmMWSc 92*
**Duckett,** Thomas Ross 1924- *WhoAmP 91*
**Duckles,** Sue Piper 1946- *AmMWSc 92, WhoWest 92*
**Duckmanton,** Talbot 1921- *Who 92*
**Duckmanton,** Talbot Sydney 1921- *IntWW 91*
**Duckstein,** Lucien 1932- *AmMWSc 92*
**Ducksworth,** Marilyn Jacoby *WhoBlA 92*
**Duckwall,** Edward Wiley 1866-1916 *BiInAmS*
**Duckwall,** Ralph 1925- *WhoAmP 91*
**Duckworth,** Brian Roy 1934- *Who 92*
**Duckworth,** Donald Reid 1945- *WhoMW 92*
**Duckworth,** Eric *Who 92*
**Duckworth,** Gerald 1871-1937 *DcLB 112 [port]*
**Duckworth,** Guy 1923- *WhoEnt 92*
**Duckworth,** Henry Edmison 1915- *AmMWSc 92*
**Duckworth,** Henry William 1943- *AmMWSc 92*
**Duckworth,** John Clifford 1916- *Who 92*
**Duckworth,** John Howard 1949- *WhoRel 92*
**Duckworth,** Kevin Jerome 1964- *WhoBlA 92*
**Duckworth,** Marvin E. 1942- *WhoAmL 92*
**Duckworth,** Richard Dyce 1918- *Who 92*
**Duckworth,** Robert H. *WhoFI 92, WhoWest 92*
**Duckworth,** Robert Vincent 1938- *WhoIns 92*
**Duckworth,** Roy 1929- *Who 92*
**Duckworth,** Ruth 1919- *TwCPaSc*
**Duckworth,** Sandra Lee 1936- *WhoAmP 91*
**Duckworth,** Walter Donald 1935- *AmMWSc 92*
**Duckworth,** Walter Eric 1925- *Who 92*
**Duckworth,** William C 1919- *AmMWSc 92*
**Duckworth,** William Clifford 1941- *AmMWSc 92*
**Duckworth,** Winston H 1918- *AmMWSc 92*
**Duclon,** Warren Eugene 1924- *WhoMW 92*
**Duclos,** Charles Pinot 1704-1772 *BlkwCEP*
**Duclos,** Steven J 1962- *AmMWSc 92*
**Duclow,** Geraldine 1946- *WhoEnt 92*
**Ducoff,** Howard S 1923- *AmMWSc 92*
**DuComb,** Robert James, Jr 1943- *WhoAmP 91*
**Ducommun,** Elie 1833-1906 *FacFETw, WhoNob 90*
**Ducornet,** Erica 1943- *ConAu 34NR*
**Ducornet,** Rikki *ConAu 34NR, DrAPF 91*
**Ducreux,** Louis Raymond 1911- *IntWW 91*
**Du Cros,** Claude Philip Arthur Mallet 1922- *Who 92*
**Ducsay,** Charles Andrew 1953- *AmMWSc 92*
**Duczek,** Lorne 1946- *AmMWSc 92*
**Duda,** Daryl Michael 1949- *WhoEnt 92*
**Duda,** Edwin 1928- *AmMWSc 92*
**Duda,** Eugene Edward 1940- *AmMWSc 92*
**Duda,** Francis X. 1942- *WhoMW 92*
**Duda,** J L 1936- *AmMWSc 92*
**Duda,** Karel 1926- *Who 92*
**Duda,** Richard Oswald 1936- *AmMWSc 92*
**Duda,** Zenon Michael 1955- *WhoMW 92*
**Dudar,** John Douglas 1940- *AmMWSc 92*
**Dudarova,** Veronika Borisovna 1916- *SovUnBD*
**Dudas,** Koloman 1934- *IntWW 91*
**Dudas,** Marvin Joseph 1943- *AmMWSc 92*
**Dudbridge,** Bryan James 1912- *Who 92*
**Dudbridge,** Glen 1938- *IntWW 91, Who 92*
**Dudbroke** *ScFEYrs*
**Dudchik,** Tom *WhoAmP 91*
**Duddey,** James E 1941- *AmMWSc 92*
**Duddles,** Charles Weller 1940- *WhoFI 92*
**Duddley,** Job *WhoRel 92*
**Dudeck,** Albert Eugene 1936- *AmMWSc 92*
**du Deffand,** Marquise 1697-1780 *FrenWW*
**Dudek,** F Edward 1947- *AmMWSc 92*
**Dudek,** Henry Thomas 1929- *WhoFI 92*
**Dudek,** Louis 1918- *BenetAL 91, ConAu 14AS [port], ConPo 91, IntAu&W 91, WrDr 92*
**Dudek,** R A 1926- *AmMWSc 92*
**Dudek,** Thomas Joseph 1934- *AmMWSc 92*
**Dudelheim,** Hans R. 1927- *IntMPA 92*
**Dudelsky,** Vladimir *NewAmDM*
**Dudelson,** Stanley E. 1924- *IntMPA 92*
**Duder,** Tessa 1940- *IntAu&W 91, WrDr 92*
**Duderstadt,** Edward C 1928- *AmMWSc 92*
**Duderstadt,** James 1942- *AmMWSc 92*
**Duderstadt,** James J. 1942- *IntWW 91*
**Duderstadt,** James Johnson 1942- *WhoMW 92*
**Dudewicz,** Edward John 1942- *AmMWSc 92*
**Dudgeon,** Antony Greville 1916- *Who 92*
**Dudgeon,** Dan Ed 1947- *AmMWSc 92*
**Dudgeon,** Robert Ellis 1820-1904 *ScFEYrs*
**Dudich,** John T. d1991 *NewYTBS 91*
**Dudick,** Michael Joseph 1917- *WhoRel 92*
**Dudikoff,** Michael *IntMPA 92*
**Dudine,** James Ray 1947- *WhoFI 92*
**Dudinskaya,** Nataliya Mikhaylovna 1912- *SovUnBD*
**Dudinskaya,** Natalya Mikhailovna 1912- *FacFETw, IntWW 91*
**Dudintsev,** Vladimir Dmitrievich 1918- *SovUnBD*
**Dudintsev,** Vladimir Dmitriyevich 1918- *FacFETw, IntWW 91*
**Dudkiewicz,** Alan Bernard *AmMWSc 92*
**Dudko,** Dmitriy Sergeevich 1922- *SovUnBD*
**Dudley,** Archdeacon of *Who 92*
**Dudley,** Baroness 1907- *Who 92*
**Dudley,** Bishop Suffragan of 1923- *Who 92*
**Dudley,** Earl of 1920- *Who 92*
**Dudley,** Albert LeRoy 1952- *WhoBlA 92*
**Dudley,** Alden Woodbury, Jr 1937- *AmMWSc 92*
**Dudley,** Calmeze Henike, Jr. 1947- *WhoBlA 92*
**Dudley,** Carl Safford 1932- *WhoRel 92*
**Dudley,** Charles Benjamin 1842-1909 *BiInAmS*
**Dudley,** Charles Edward 1927- *WhoBlA 92*
**Dudley,** Crayton T. 1928- *WhoBlA 92*
**Dudley,** Darle W 1917- *AmMWSc 92*
**Dudley,** Donald Larry 1936- *AmMWSc 92, WhoWest 92*
**Dudley,** Dudley W 1936- *WhoAmP 91*
**Dudley,** Durand Stowell 1926- *WhoMW 92*
**Dudley,** Edward Bishop 1789-1855 *DcNCBi 2*
**Dudley,** Edward R. 1911- *WhoBlA 92*
**Dudley,** Evelyn Kay 1935- *WhoAmP 91*
**Dudley,** Everett Haskell, Jr. 1930- *WhoAmL 92*
**Dudley,** Frank Mayo 1920- *AmMWSc 92*
**Dudley,** Fred R 1944- *WhoAmP 91*
**Dudley,** Gary A 1952- *AmMWSc 92*
**Dudley,** Geoffrey A. 1917- *WrDr 92*
**Dudley,** Geoffrey Arthur 1917- *IntAu&W 91*
**Dudley,** George William, Jr. 1931- *WhoFI 92*
**Dudley,** Godfrey D. 1944- *WhoBlA 92*
**Dudley,** Grenae' Denise 1952- *WhoMW 92*
**Dudley,** Guilford 1756-1833 *DcNCBi 2*
**Dudley,** Guilford, Jr 1917- *WhoAmP 91*
**Dudley,** Harry Joseph 1949- *WhoRel 92*
**Dudley,** Helen *IntAu&W 91X*
**Dudley,** Herman T. 1924- *WhoBlA 92*
**Dudley,** Horace Chester 1909- *AmMWSc 92*
**Dudley,** Hugh Arnold 1925- *IntWW 91*
**Dudley,** Hugh Arnold Freeman 1925- *Who 92*
**Dudley,** J Duane 1928- *AmMWSc 92*
**Dudley,** James Benson 1859-1925 *DcNCBi 2*
**Dudley,** James Gatewood 1955- *WhoFI 92*
**Dudley,** John Cleveland 1929- *WhoRel 92*
**Dudley,** John Minot 1926- *AmMWSc 92*
**Dudley,** John Wesley 1931- *AmMWSc 92, WhoMW 92*
**Dudley,** John Wesley, Jr. 1957- *WhoEnt 92*
**Dudley,** Juanita C. 1929- *WhoBlA 92*
**Dudley,** Kenneth Harrison 1937- *AmMWSc 92*
**Dudley,** Lonnie LeRoy 1948- *WhoWest 92*
**Dudley,** Merle Bland 1929- *WhoRel 92*
**Dudley,** Michael 1957- *AmMWSc 92*
**Dudley,** Norman Alfred 1916- *Who 92*
**Dudley,** Patricia 1929- *AmMWSc 92*
**Dudley,** Paul 1675-1751 *BiInAmS*
**Dudley,** Paul V. 1926- *WhoRel 92*
**Dudley,** Perry, Jr. 1928- *WhoFI 92*
**Dudley,** Peter Anthony 1938- *AmMWSc 92*
**Dudley,** Richard H 1931- *AmMWSc 92*
**Dudley,** Richard Mansfield 1938- *AmMWSc 92*
**Dudley,** Robert Hamilton 1933- *WhoAmP 91*
**Dudley,** Ronald Tyrone, Jr. 1962- *WhoAmL 92*
**Dudley,** Rose *Who 92*
**Dudley,** Susan D 1949- *AmMWSc 92*
**Dudley,** Thelma 1923- *WhoBlA 92*
**Dudley,** Theodore R 1936- *AmMWSc 92*
**Dudley,** Underwood 1937- *AmMWSc 92*
**Dudley,** William Henry 1811-1886 *BiInAmS*
**Dudley,** William Lofland 1859-1914 *BiInAmS*
**Dudley,** William Russel 1849-1911 *BiInAmS*
**Dudley,** William Stuart 1947- *Who 92*
**Dudley-Smith,** Carolyn J. 1946- *WhoBlA 92*
**Dudley-Smith,** Timothy 1926- *IntAu&W 91, Who 92, WrDr 92*
**Dudley-Washington,** Loise 1944- *WhoBlA 92*
**Dudley-Williams,** Alastair 1943- *Who 92*
**Dudman,** Richard Beebe 1918- *WhoEnt 92*
**Dudney,** Charles Sherman 1949- *AmMWSc 92*
**Dudney,** Nancy Johnston 1954- *AmMWSc 92*
**Dudock,** Bernard S 1939- *AmMWSc 92*
**Dudok,** Willem Marinus 1884-1974 *DcTwDes*
**Dudrick,** Stanley John 1935- *AmMWSc 92*
**Duduit,** James Michael 1954- *WhoRel 92*
**Dudukovic,** Milorad 1944- *AmMWSc 92*
**Dudum,** Ronald Akram 1956- *WhoWest 92*
**Dudycz,** Walter W 1950- *WhoAmP 91*
**Dudziak,** Donald John 1935- *AmMWSc 92*
**Dudziak,** Walter Francis 1923- *AmMWSc 92*
**Dudzik,** Ted Edward 1925- *WhoMW 92*
**Dudzinski,** Diane Marie 1946- *AmMWSc 92*
**Due,** Mary Jane Carter 1922- *WhoAmP 91*
**Due,** Ole 1931- *IntWW 91, Who 92*
**Dueck,** John 1941- *AmMWSc 92*
**Duecker,** Heyman Clarke 1929- *AmMWSc 92*
**Duecker,** Robert Sheldon 1926- *WhoMW 92, WhoRel 92*
**Duedall,** Iver Warren 1939- *AmMWSc 92*
**Duehmig,** Marjorie Ann 1960- *WhoMW 92*
**Dueitt,** George Malcolm 1955- *WhoRel 92*
**Duek,** Eduardo Enrique 1949- *AmMWSc 92, WhoHisp 92*
**Dueker,** David Kenneth 1944- *AmMWSc 92*
**Dueland,** Rudolf 1933- *AmMWSc 92*
**Duell,** Daniel Paul 1952- *WhoEnt 92*
**Duell,** Elizabeth Ann 1936- *AmMWSc 92*
**Duell,** Paul M 1924- *AmMWSc 92*
**Duell,** William *WhoEnt 92*
**Duellman,** William Edward 1930- *AmMWSc 92*
**Dueltgen,** Ronald Rex 1940- *AmMWSc 92*
**Duemeland,** George Skip 1941- *WhoFI 92*
**Duemer,** Joseph *DrAPF 91*
**Duemling,** Robert Werner 1929- *WhoAmP 91*
**Duenas,** Edward Ramirez 1936- *WhoAmP 91*
**Duenas,** Jose Ramirez 1930- *WhoAmP 91*
**Duenas,** Mario G. 1950- *WhoHisp 92*
**Duensing,** Carol Janet 1937- *WhoWest 92*
**Duer,** Shirley Powell *WhoAmP 91*
**Duerbeck,** Julian Joseph Francis 1949- *WhoRel 92*
**Duerdoth,** Philip Robert 1962- *TwCPaSc*

**Duerfeldt**, William F. 1947- *WhoMW 92*
**Duerinck**, Louis T. 1929- *WhoAmL 92, WhoFI 92, WhoMW 92*
**Duerksen**, George Louis 1934- *WhoEnt 92*
**Duerksen**, Gregory John 1957- *WhoFI 92*
**Duerr**, Alfred *WhoWest 92*
**Duerr**, Douglas Hanson 1963- *WhoAmL 92*
**Duerr**, Frederick G 1935- *AmMWSc 92*
**Duerr**, Hans-Peter Emil 1929- *IntWW 91*
**Duerr**, J Stephen 1943- *AmMWSc 92*
**Duerr**, Lehn 1949- *WhoFI 92*
**Duerr**, Robert Kenneth, Jr. 1954- *WhoEnt 92*
**Duerre**, John A 1930- *AmMWSc 92*
**Duerre**, John Arden 1930- *WhoMW 92*
**Duersch**, Ralph R 1926- *AmMWSc 92*
**Duerson**, Dave Russell 1960- *WhoBlA 92*
**Duerson**, David Russell 1960- *WhoMW 92*
**Duerson**, Richard A. 1950- *WhoEnt 92*
**Duerst**, Richard William 1940- *AmMWSc 92*
**Dues**, John Joseph 1948- *WhoFI 92*
**Duesberg**, Peter H 1936- *AmMWSc 92*
**Duesbery**, Michael Serge 1942- *AmMWSc 92*
**Duesenberg**, Richard William 1930- *WhoAmL 92, WhoFI 92*
**Duesenberg**, Robert H. 1930- *WhoAmL 92, WhoFI 92, WhoMW 92*
**Duesenberry**, James Stembel 1918- *IntWW 91*
**Dueser**, Raymond D 1945- *AmMWSc 92*
**Duesing**, Dale L. 1945- *WhoEnt 92*
**Duesterberg**, Theodor 1875-1950 *BiDExR, EncTR 91 [port]*
**Duesterhoeft**, William Charles, Jr 1921- *AmMWSc 92*
**Duet**, Rickey Joseph 1953- *WhoEnt 92*
**Duetsch**, John Edwin 1915- *WhoAmL 92*
**Duever**, Thomas Albert 1958- *AmMWSc 92*
**Duewer**, Elizabeth Ann 1937- *AmMWSc 92*
**Duewer**, Raymond George 1926- *AmMWSc 92*
**Duey**, Charles John, Sr. 1928- *WhoRel 92*
**Duez**, David Joseph 1947- *WhoAmL 92*
**Dufallo**, Richard 1933- *ConAu 133*
**Dufau**, Maria Luisa 1938- *AmMWSc 92*
**Dufault**, Mary Louise Selker 1937- *WhoAmL 92*
**Dufault**, Peter Kane *DrAPF 91*
**Dufault**, Peter Kane 1923- *WrDr 92*
**Dufault**, Wilfrid Joseph 1907- *WhoRel 92*
**Dufay**, Charles-Francois de Cisternai 1689-1739 *BlkwCEP*
**Dufay**, Guillaume 1400?-1474 *NewAmDM*
**Dufek**, George J 1903-1977 *FacFETw*
**Duff**, Angus MacLean 1939- *WhoWest 92*
**Duff**, Antony 1920- *IntWW 91, Who 92*
**Duff**, Brian Barnett 1930- *WhoAmL 92, WhoMW 92*
**Duff**, Cloyd Edgar 1915- *WhoEnt 92*
**Duff**, Dale Thomas 1930- *AmMWSc 92*
**Duff**, Fratis L 1910- *AmMWSc 92*
**Duff**, George Alexander 1931- *WhoFI 92*
**Duff**, George Francis Denton 1926- *AmMWSc 92, IntWW 91*
**Duff**, Graham 1947- *Who 92*
**Duff**, Ivan Francis 1915- *AmMWSc 92*
**Duff**, J E 1918- *AmMWSc 92*
**Duff**, James George 1938- *WhoFI 92, WhoWest 92*
**Duff**, James I 1931- *WhoIns 92*
**Duff**, James McConnell 1940- *AmMWSc 92*
**Duff**, James Michael 1954- *WhoEnt 92*
**Duff**, John Bernard 1931- *WhoAmP 91, WhoMW 92*
**Duff**, John Francis 1946- *WhoFI 92*
**Duff**, John Thomas 1903- *WhoBlA 92*
**Duff**, Leo 1954- *TwCPaSc*
**Duff**, Marc Charles 1961- *WhoAmP 91*
**Duff**, Patrick Craigmile 1922- *Who 92*
**Duff**, Patrick William d1991 *Who 92N*
**Duff**, Raymond Stanley 1923- *AmMWSc 92*
**Duff**, Robert Hodge 1929- *AmMWSc 92*
**Duff**, Ronald George 1936- *AmMWSc 92*
**Duff**, Russell Earl 1926- *AmMWSc 92*
**Duff**, Scott 1950- *WhoAmP 91*
**Duff**, Thomas Robert G. *Who 92*
**Duff**, William G 1936- *AmMWSc 92*
**Duff**, William Leroy, Jr. 1938- *WhoWest 92*
**Duff Gordon**, Andrew 1933- *Who 92*
**Duffalo**, Richard 1933- *NewAmDM*
**Duffee**, David Kevin 1959- *WhoAmL 92*
**Duffell**, Andrea Michelle 1958- *WhoMW 92*
**Duffell**, Peter Royson 1939- *Who 92*
**Dufferin And Clandeboye**, Baron 1916- *Who 92*
**Duffett**, Roger Hugh Edward 1936- *Who 92*
**Duffey**, David Scott 1963- *WhoMW 92*
**Duffey**, Dick 1917- *AmMWSc 92*
**Duffey**, Donald Creagh 1931- *AmMWSc 92*
**Duffey**, George Henry 1920- *AmMWSc 92*
**Duffey**, Joseph D 1932- *WhoAmP 91*
**Duffey**, Joseph Daniel 1932- *IntWW 91*
**Duffey**, Michael Eugene 1945- *AmMWSc 92*
**Duffey**, Paul Andrews 1920- *WhoRel 92*
**Duffey**, Paul S. 1939- *WhoWest 92*
**Duffey**, Paul Stephen 1939- *AmMWSc 92*
**Duffey**, Perry L. 1934- *WhoRel 92*
**Duffey**, Sean Stephen 1943- *AmMWSc 92*
**Duffey**, William Simon, Jr. 1952- *WhoAmL 92*
**Duffie**, John A 1925- *AmMWSc 92*
**Duffield**, Deborah Ann 1941- *AmMWSc 92*
**Duffield**, Gervase E. 1935- *WrDr 92*
**Duffield**, Jack Jay 1933- *AmMWSc 92*
**Duffield**, John Thomas 1823-1901 *BiInAmS*
**Duffield**, Robert McGregor 1935- *IntAu&W 91*
**Duffield**, Roger C 1937- *AmMWSc 92*
**Duffield**, Samuel Pearce 1833-1916 *BiInAmS*
**Duffield**, Wendell Arthur 1941- *AmMWSc 92*
**Duffield**, William Ward 1823-1907 *BiInAmS*
**Duffin**, John H 1919- *AmMWSc 92*
**Duffin**, Mark Reed 1953- *WhoAmP 91*
**Duffin**, Richard James 1909- *AmMWSc 92*
**Duffoo**, Frantz Michel 1954- *WhoBlA 92*
**Duffus**, Henry John 1925- *AmMWSc 92*
**Duffus**, Herbert 1908- *Who 92*
**Duffus**, James Edward 1929- *AmMWSc 92*
**Duffus**, R. L. 1888-1972 *BenetAL 91*
**Duffy**, Albert Edward Patrick 1920- *Who 92*
**Duffy**, Antonia Susan *Who 92*
**Duffy**, Barbara Jean 1938- *WhoWest 92*
**Duffy**, Bernard Karl 1948- *WhoWest 92*
**Duffy**, Brian J 1941- *WhoIns 92*
**Duffy**, Carol Ann 1955- *ConPo 91, IntAu&W 91, WrDr 92*
**Duffy**, Christopher James 1963- *WhoFI 92*
**Duffy**, Clarence John 1947- *AmMWSc 92*
**Duffy**, Dale William 1962- *WhoMW 92*
**Duffy**, Daniel 1929- *Who 92*
**Duffy**, Dennis Anthony 1940- *WhoMW 92*
**Duffy**, Dennis Paul 1957- *WhoAmL 92*
**Duffy**, E.A.J. 1916- *TwCPaSc*
**Duffy**, Edmund Charles 1942- *WhoAmL 92*
**Duffy**, Eugene Jones 1954- *WhoBlA 92*
**Duffy**, Frank Hopkins 1937- *AmMWSc 92*
**Duffy**, Gary John 1953- *WhoAmP 91*
**Duffy**, Gary Wayne 1950- *WhoAmL 92*
**Duffy**, Harry Arthur 1915- *WhoWest 92*
**Duffy**, Irene J. 1933- *WhoAmL 92*
**Duffy**, Jack Gilbert, Jr. 1956- *WhoAmL 92*
**Duffy**, Jacques Wayne 1922- *AmMWSc 92*
**Duffy**, James E. *LesBEnT 92*
**Duffy**, James E. 1926- *IntMPA 92*
**Duffy**, James Henry 1934- *WhoAmL 92*
**Duffy**, James Joseph 1917- *WhoMW 92*
**Duffy**, Jean Anne 1948- *WhoAmP 91*
**Duffy**, John Leonard 1947- *WhoAmL 92*
**Duffy**, Joseph *Who 92*
**Duffy**, Joseph Michael 1936- *Who 92*
**Duffy**, Joseph Patrick, III 1949- *WhoEnt 92*
**Duffy**, Julia 1951- *WhoEnt 92*
**Duffy**, Kent Haviland 1951- *WhoEnt 92*
**Duffy**, Kevin Thomas 1933- *WhoAmL 92*
**Duffy**, L. Dennis 1941- *WhoWest 92*
**Duffy**, Lawrence Kevin 1948- *AmMWSc 92, WhoWest 92*
**Duffy**, Marcia Tinkham 1936- *WhoAmP 91*
**Duffy**, Martin Edward 1940- *WhoFI 92*
**Duffy**, Martin Patrick 1942- *WhoAmL 92*
**Duffy**, Maureen 1933- *ConNov 91, ConPo 91, WrDr 92*
**Duffy**, Maureen Patricia 1933- *IntAu&W 91, Who 92*
**Duffy**, Michael John 1938- *IntWW 91*
**Duffy**, Nancy Keogh 1947- *WhoEnt 92*
**Duffy**, Nicole *WhoEnt 92*
**Duffy**, Norman Vincent, Jr 1938- *AmMWSc 92*
**Duffy**, Patrick *Who 92*
**Duffy**, Patrick 1949- *IntMPA 92, WhoEnt 92*
**Duffy**, Peter Clarke 1927- *Who 92*
**Duffy**, Philip 1923- *AmMWSc 92*
**Duffy**, Regina Maurice *AmMWSc 92*
**Duffy**, Robert A 1921- *AmMWSc 92*
**Duffy**, Robert E 1930- *AmMWSc 92*
**Duffy**, Roger F 1925- *WhoAmP 91*
**Duffy**, Stephen J *WhoAmP 91*
**Duffy**, Steven Kent 1962- *WhoFI 92*
**Duffy**, Terry 1948- *TwCPaSc*
**Duffy**, Thomas A *WhoAmP 91*
**Duffy**, Thomas Edward 1947- *WhoFI 92*
**Duffy**, V Michael *WhoAmP 91*
**Duffy**, W. Leslie 1939- *WhoAmL 92*
**Duffy**, Wayne Edward 1920- *WhoWest 92*
**Duffy**, William d1810 *DcNCBi 2*
**Duffy**, William Edward, Jr. 1931- *WhoMW 92*
**Duffy**, William Thomas 1962- *WhoFI 92*
**Duffy**, William Thomas, Jr 1930- *AmMWSc 92*
**Duflot**, Leo Scott 1919- *AmMWSc 92*
**Dufoe**, William Stewart 1950- *WhoAmL 92*
**Dufoix**, Georgina 1943- *IntWW 91*
**Dufour**, Alfred Paul 1933- *WhoMW 92*
**DuFour**, E James 1934- *WhoAmP 91*
**Dufour**, Jacques John 1939- *AmMWSc 92*
**Dufour**, Jean Jacques *DcAmImH*
**Dufour**, John James 1763?-1827 *BiInAmS*
**Dufour**, Reginald James 1948- *AmMWSc 92*
**DuFour**, Richard George 1943- *WhoMW 92*
**Dufourcq**, Norbert d1990 *IntWW 91N*
**Dufourt**, Hugues 1943- *ConCom 92*
**DuFrain**, Russell Jerome 1944- *AmMWSc 92*
**Dufrene**, Phoebe Lyles 1952- *WhoMW 92*
**DuFresne**, Albert Herman 1928- *AmMWSc 92*
**DuFresne**, Armand Frederick 1917- *WhoFI 92, WhoWest 92*
**Dufresne**, E. Donald 1934- *WhoAmL 92*
**Dufresne**, Hilaire Louis 1944- *WhoWest 92*
**Dufresne**, John *DrAPF 91*
**Dufresne**, Richard Frederick 1943- *AmMWSc 92*
**Dufresne**, Roger 1948- *WhoFI 92*
**Dufty**, James W 1940- *AmMWSc 92*
**Dufty**, Richard 1911- *Who 92*
**Dufy**, Raoul 1877-1953 *FacFETw*
**Duga**, Jules Joseph 1932- *AmMWSc 92*
**Dugaiczyk**, Achilles 1930- *AmMWSc 92*
**Dugal**, Charles James, Jr. 1929- *WhoMW 92*
**Dugal**, Hardev Singh 1937- *AmMWSc 92*
**Dugal**, Louis Paul 1911- *AmMWSc 92*
**Dugan**, Alan *DrAPF 91*
**Dugan**, Alan 1923- *BenetAL 91, ConPo 91, IntAu&W 91, WrDr 92*
**Dugan**, Charles Francis, II 1939- *WhoAmL 92, WhoMW 92*
**Dugan**, Charles Hammond 1931- *AmMWSc 92*
**Dugan**, Dennis 1946- *IntMPA 92*
**Dugan**, Eileen C 1945- *WhoAmP 91*
**Dugan**, Gary Edwin 1941- *AmMWSc 92*
**Dugan**, Gerard A 1945- *WhoIns 92*
**DuGan**, Gordon Frank 1966- *WhoFI 92*
**Dugan**, Herschel Cedric 1931- *WhoRel 92*
**Dugan**, Hugh Timothy 1959- *WhoFI 92*
**Dugan**, John Francis 1935- *WhoAmL 92*
**Dugan**, John Philip 1942- *AmMWSc 92*
**Dugan**, John Raymond, Jr. 1948- *WhoAmL 92*
**Dugan**, Kimiko Hatta 1924- *AmMWSc 92*
**Dugan**, LeRoy, Jr 1915- *AmMWSc 92*
**Dugan**, Mike *WhoAmP 91*
**Dugan**, Patrick R 1931- *AmMWSc 92*
**Dugan**, Robert Perry, Jr. 1932- *WhoRel 92*
**Dugan**, Ruth Puglisi 1947- *WhoAmP 91*
**Dugan**, Thomas Cannon 1958- *WhoEnt 92*
**Dugan**, Willis Edwin 1909- *WhoMW 92*
**Duganne**, Augustine Joseph Hickey 1823?-1884 *BenetAL 91*
**Dugard**, Arthur Claude 1904- *Who 92*
**Dugard**, George Alan 1932- *WhoWest 92*
**Dugas**, Henry C. 1917- *WhoBlA 92*
**Dugas**, Hermann 1942- *AmMWSc 92*
**Dugas**, Louis, Jr. 1928- *WhoAmL 92*
**Dugas**, Stephen Leonard 1950- *WhoAmL 92*
**Dugdale** *Who 92*
**Dugdale**, Grant Keith 1960- *WhoAmL 92*
**Dugdale**, John, Mrs. *Who 92*
**Dugdale**, John Robert Stratford 1923- *Who 92*
**Dugdale**, Kathryn Edith Helen 1923- *Who 92*
**Dugdale**, Marion 1928- *AmMWSc 92*
**Dugdale**, Norman 1921- *Who 92, WrDr 92*
**Dugdale**, Peter Robin 1928- *Who 92*
**Dugdale**, Richard Cooper 1928- *AmMWSc 92*
**Dugdale**, Thomas 1880-1952 *TwCPaSc*
**Dugdale**, William d1868 *DcLB 106*
**Dugdale**, William 1922- *Who 92*
**Dugersuren**, Mangalyn 1922- *IntWW 91*
**Duggal**, Shakti Prakash 1931- *AmMWSc 92*
**Duggan**, Bessie Lou 1931- *WhoAmP 91*
**Duggan**, Bryan Christopher 1949- *WhoEnt 92*
**Duggan**, Daniel Edward 1926- *AmMWSc 92*
**Duggan**, Dennis E 1930- *AmMWSc 92*
**Duggan**, Eileen 1894-1972 *RfGEnL 91*
**Duggan**, Ervin S *WhoAmP 91*
**Duggan**, Gordon Aldridge 1937- *Who 92*
**Duggan**, Helen Ann 1921- *AmMWSc 92*
**Duggan**, James Edgar 1961- *WhoAmL 92*
**Duggan**, James Franklyn 1956- *WhoFI 92*
**Duggan**, James H. 1935- *WhoFI 92*
**Duggan**, Jerome Lewis 1933- *AmMWSc 92*
**Duggan**, John Coote 1918- *Who 92*
**Duggan**, John Peter 1946- *WhoAmL 92*
**Duggan**, Joseph F 1928- *WhoAmP 91*
**Duggan**, Joseph John 1938- *WhoWest 92*
**Duggan**, Kevin 1944- *WhoFI 92*
**Duggan**, Lawrence James 1933- *WhoWest 92*
**Duggan**, Mary Kay 1938- *WhoEnt 92*
**Duggan**, Maurice 1922-1974 *RfGEnL 91*
**Duggan**, Michael J 1931- *AmMWSc 92*
**Duggan**, Patrick James 1933- *WhoAmL 92, WhoMW 92*
**Duggan**, Thomas Patrick 1946- *WhoFI 92*
**Duggar**, Benjamin Charles 1933- *AmMWSc 92*
**Duggar**, Benjamin Minge 1872-1956 *FacFETw*
**Dugger**, Edward, III 1949- *WhoBlA 92*
**Dugger**, Edwin Ellsworth 1940- *WhoEnt 92*
**Dugger**, John Edward 1836-1888 *DcNCBi 2*
**Dugger**, John Scott 1948- *IntWW 91*
**Dugger**, Myron W 1936- *WhoAmP 91*
**Dugger**, Shepherd Monroe 1854-1938 *DcNCBi 2*
**Dugger**, William Mayfield 1947- *WhoFI 92*
**Dugger**, Willie Mack, Jr 1919- *AmMWSc 92*
**Duggin**, Lorraine *DrAPF 91*
**Duggin**, Michael J 1937- *AmMWSc 92*
**Duggin**, Richard *DrAPF 91*
**Duggins**, William Edgar 1920- *AmMWSc 92*
**Dugle**, Janet Mary Rogge 1934- *AmMWSc 92*
**Duglin**, Robert Louis 1956- *WhoMW 92*
**Dugliss**, Charles H 1921- *AmMWSc 92*
**Dugmore**, Clifford William d1990 *Who 92N*
**Dugmore**, Kent Clyde 1939- *WhoAmL 92, WhoWest 92*
**Dugoff**, Howard 1936- *AmMWSc 92, WhoAmP 91*
**Dugolinsky**, Brent Kerns 1945- *AmMWSc 92*
**Dugow**, John Edward, Jr. 1945- *WhoWest 92*
**Dugre**, Robert 1949- *AmMWSc 92*
**Duguay**, Michel Albert 1939- *AmMWSc 92*
**Duguid**, Andrew Alexander 1944- *Who 92*
**Duguid**, James Otto 1940- *AmMWSc 92*
**Duguid**, James Paris 1919- *Who 92*
**Duguid**, John 1906-1961 *TwCPaSc*
**Duguid**, Sandra R. *DrAPF 91*
**Duguid**, William Paris 1927- *AmMWSc 92*
**du Guillet**, Pernette 1520?-1545 *FrenWW*
**Dugundji**, James 1919- *AmMWSc 92*
**Dugundji**, John 1925- *AmMWSc 92*
**Duhaime**, Ricky Edward 1953- *WhoEnt 92*
**Du Halde**, Jean-Baptiste 1674-1743 *BlkwCEP*
**Duhamel**, Denise *DrAPF 91*
**Duhamel**, Georges 1884-1966 *ConAu 35NR, GuFrLit 1*
**Duhamel**, Raymond C 1942- *AmMWSc 92*
**Duhart**, Harold B. 1938- *WhoBlA 92*
**Duhe**, John M, Jr 1933- *WhoAmP 91*
**Duhe**, John Malcolm, Jr. 1933- *WhoAmL 92*
**Duhe**, Theodore Louis 1946- *WhoAmP 91*
**Duhl**, David M 1953- *AmMWSc 92*
**Duhl**, David N 1939- *AmMWSc 92*
**Duhl**, Leonard 1926- *WhoWest 92*
**Duhl**, Leonard J 1926- *AmMWSc 92, WrDr 92*
**Duhl**, Stuart 1940- *WhoAmL 92*
**Duhl-Emswiler**, Barbara Ann 1952- *AmMWSc 92*
**Duhme**, Carol McCarthy 1917- *WhoMW 92*
**Duhnke**, Robert Emmet, Jr. 1935- *WhoWest 92*
**Duhring**, Eugen 1833-1921 *EncTR 91*
**Duhring**, John Lewis 1933- *AmMWSc 92*
**Duhrkopf**, Richard Edward 1949- *AmMWSc 92*
**Duich**, Joseph M 1928- *AmMWSc 92*
**Duigan**, John *IntMPA 92*
**Duignan**, Michael Thomas 1950- *AmMWSc 92*
**Duisenberg**, Willem Frederik 1935- *IntWW 91*
**Duisman**, Jack Arnold 1937- *AmMWSc 92*
**Dujardin**, Jean-Pierre L *AmMWSc 92*
**du Jardin**, Rosamond Neal 1902-1963 *BenetAL 91*
**Dujovne**, Carlos A 1937- *AmMWSc 92*
**Dukakis**, Katharine 1937?- *ConAu 135*
**Dukakis**, Kitty *ConAu 135*
**Dukakis**, Michael 1933- *FacFETw [port]*
**Dukakis**, Michael S 1933- *WhoAmP 91*
**Dukakis**, Michael Stanley 1933- *AmPolLe, IntWW 91, Who 92*

**Dukakis,** Olympia 1931- *CurBio 91 [port], IntMPA 92, WhoEnt 92*
**Dukas,** Paul 1865-1935 *FacFETw, NewAmDM*
**Dukas,** Philip Alexander 1954- *WhoMW 92*
**Dukatz,** Ervin L, Jr 1952- *AmMWSc 92*
**Duke** *Who 92*
**Duke,** A Don 1933- *WhoAmP 91*
**Duke,** Angier Biddle 1915- *IntWW 91, WhoAmP 91*
**Duke,** Benjamin Newton 1855-1929 *DcNCBi 2*
**Duke,** Bernard 1927- *WhoFI 92*
**Duke,** Bill *NewYTBS 91 [port]*
**Duke,** Bill 1943- *IntMPA 92*
**Duke,** Cecil Howard Armitage 1912- *Who 92*
**Duke,** Charles 1935- *FacFETw*
**Duke,** Charles 1942- *WhoAmP 91*
**Duke,** Charles Bryan 1938- *AmMWSc 92*
**Duke,** Charles Lewis 1940- *AmMWSc 92*
**Duke,** Claire Diane 1935- *WhoAmP 91*
**Duke,** David 1950- *WhoAmP 91*
**Duke,** David Allen 1935- *AmMWSc 92, WhoFI 92*
**Duke,** David Ernest 1950- *NewYTBS 91 [port]*
**Duke,** David Nelson 1950- *WhoRel 92*
**Duke,** Dennis Wayne 1948- *AmMWSc 92*
**Duke,** Donald 1929- *WrDr 92*
**Duke,** Douglas 1923- *AmMWSc 92*
**Duke,** Everette Loranza 1929- *AmMWSc 92*
**Duke,** Gary Earl 1937- *AmMWSc 92*
**Duke,** Gary Philip 1957- *WhoWest 92*
**Duke,** George 1946- *WhoEnt 92*
**Duke,** George M. 1946- *WhoBlA 92*
**Duke,** Gerald 1910- *Who 92*
**Duke,** J Dale 1938- *WhoIns 92*
**Duke,** James A 1929- *AmMWSc 92, ConAu 135*
**Duke,** James Buchanan 1856-1925 *DcNCBi 2, FacFETw*
**Duke,** James Oliver 1946- *WhoRel 92*
**Duke,** James Taylor 1933- *WhoWest 92*
**Duke,** Jerry Childress 1938- *WhoEnt 92*
**Duke,** Jim *ConAu 135*
**Duke,** Jodie Lee, Jr 1945- *AmMWSc 92*
**Duke,** John Christian, Jr 1951- *AmMWSc 92*
**Duke,** John Murray 1947- *AmMWSc 92*
**Duke,** John Walter 1937- *AmMWSc 92*
**Duke,** June Temple 1922- *AmMWSc 92*
**Duke,** Kenneth Lindsay 1912- *AmMWSc 92*
**Duke,** Laura J. *WhoRel 92*
**Duke,** Leslie Dowling, Sr. 1924- *WhoBlA 92*
**Duke,** Lucy 1955- *TwCPaSc*
**Duke,** Madelaine 1925- *IntAu&W 91, WrDr 92*
**Duke,** Merlin 1941- *WhoAmP 91*
**Duke,** Michael 1935- *AmMWSc 92*
**Duke,** Michael Geoffrey H. *Who 92*
**Duke,** Neville Frederick 1922- *Who 92*
**Duke,** Patty *LesBEnT 92*
**Duke,** Patty 1946- *IntMPA 92, WhoEnt 92*
**Duke,** Paul Robert 1929- *WhoAmL 92*
**Duke,** Richard Alter 1937- *AmMWSc 92*
**Duke,** Robert Dominick 1928- *WhoAmL 92, WhoFI 92*
**Duke,** Robin Chandler Tippett 1923- *WhoFI 92*
**Duke,** Roy Burt, Jr 1932- *AmMWSc 92*
**Duke,** Stanley Houston 1944- *AmMWSc 92*
**Duke,** Stephen Oscar 1944- *AmMWSc 92*
**Duke,** Steven Barry 1934- *WhoAmL 92*
**Duke,** Thomas Allen 1941- *WhoRel 92*
**Duke,** Vernon 1903-1969 *NewAmDM*
**Duke,** Victor Hal 1925- *AmMWSc 92*
**Duke,** Washington 1820-1905 *DcNCBi 2*
**Duke,** Will *IntAu&W 91X, WrDr 92*
**Duke,** William, Jr. 1720?-1793 *DcNCBi 2*
**Duke,** William Edward 1932- *WhoWest 92*
**Dukelow,** Donald Allen 1932- *AmMWSc 92*
**Dukelow,** W Richard 1936- *AmMWSc 92*
**Dukeminier,** Jesse 1925- *WhoAmL 92*
**Dukepoo,** Frank Charles 1943- *AmMWSc 92*
**Duker,** Nahum Johanan 1942- *AmMWSc 92*
**Dukert,** Betty Cole 1927- *WhoEnt 92*
**Dukert,** Joseph M. 1929- *WrDr 92*
**Dukert,** Joseph Michael 1929- *WhoAmP 91*
**Dukes of Dixieland** *NewAmDM*
**Dukes,** Alan M. 1945- *IntWW 91, Who 92*
**Dukes,** Constance T. *WhoBlA 92*
**Dukes,** David 1945- *IntMPA 92*
**Dukes,** Dorothy 1926- *WhoRel 92*
**Dukes,** Duane 1950- *WhoMW 92*
**Dukes,** Francis Xavier 1965- *WhoEnt 92*
**Dukes,** Gary Rinehart 1939- *AmMWSc 92*
**Dukes,** Gene W 1943- *WhoAmP 91*
**Dukes,** Hazel Nell 1932- *WhoAmP 91, WhoBlA 92*
**Dukes,** Jack Richard 1941- *WhoMW 92*
**Dukes,** Jerome Erwin 1938- *WhoBlA 92*
**Dukes,** Joan 1947- *WhoAmP 91*
**Dukes,** John Robert 1930- *WhoMW 92*
**Dukes,** Justin Paul 1941- *Who 92*
**Dukes,** Michael Dennis 1952- *AmMWSc 92*
**Dukes,** Ofield 1932- *WhoBlA 92*
**Dukes,** Paul 1934- *IntAu&W 91, WrDr 92*
**Dukes,** Peter Paul 1930- *AmMWSc 92*
**Dukes,** Philip Duskin 1931- *AmMWSc 92*
**Dukes,** Rebecca Weathers 1934- *WhoEnt 92*
**Dukes,** Ronald 1942- *WhoBlA 92*
**Dukes,** Walter L. 1933- *WhoBlA 92*
**Dukhonin,** Nikolai Nikolayevich 1876-1917 *FacFETw*
**Dukler,** A E 1925- *AmMWSc 92*
**Duklewski,** James Edmund 1949- *WhoFI 92*
**Dukore,** Bernard F. 1931- *WrDr 92*
**Dukore,** Bernard Frank 1931- *IntAu&W 91, WhoEnt 92*
**Dukore,** Margaret Mitchell *DrAPF 91*
**Dula,** Thomas C. 1844-1868 *DcNCBi 2*
**Dulac,** Edmund 1882-1953 *TwCPaSc*
**Dulac,** Germaine 1882-1942 *IntDcF 2-2 [port], ReelWom [port]*
**Dulaney,** Eugene Lambert 1919- *AmMWSc 92*
**Dulaney,** John Thornton 1937- *AmMWSc 92*
**Dulanto,** Juan Carlos 1958- *WhoHisp 92*
**Dulany,** Daniel, Jr 1722-1797 *BlkwEAR*
**Dulany,** Donelson Edwin, Jr. 1928- *WhoMW 92*
**Dulany,** Harris *DrAPF 91*
**DuLaux,** Russell Frederick 1918- *WhoAmL 92, WhoFI 92*
**Dulay,** Dion Joseph 1948- *WhoMW 92*
**Dulay,** Hardial Singh *WhoWest 92*
**Dulbecco,** Renato 1914- *AmMWSc 92, FacFETw, IntWW 91, Who 92, WhoNob 90, WhoWest 92*
**Dulchinos,** Peter 1935- *WhoAmL 92, WhoFI 92*
**Dulcich,** Thomas Vincent 1953- *WhoAmL 92*
**Duldulao,** Julie R 1947- *WhoAmP 91*
**Dulemba,** Arthur W. 1942- *WhoAmL 92*
**Duley,** Charlotte Dudley 1920- *WhoWest 92*
**Duley,** Donald Gordon 1936- *WhoWest 92*
**Dulgeroff,** Carl Richard 1929- *AmMWSc 92*
**Dulin,** Gene 1925- *WhoRel 92*
**Dulin,** Jacques M. *WhoFI 92*
**Dulin,** Patricia Ann 1952- *WhoWest 92*
**Dulin,** Robert O., Jr. 1941- *WhoBlA 92*
**Dulin,** Thomas N. 1949- *WhoAmL 92*
**Duling,** Brian R 1937- *AmMWSc 92*
**Dulis,** Edward J 1919- *AmMWSc 92*
**Dulk,** George A 1930- *AmMWSc 92*
**Dulka,** Joseph John 1951- *AmMWSc 92*
**Dull,** Gerald G 1930- *AmMWSc 92*
**Dull,** Robert J 1947- *WhoAmP 91*
**Dullaghan,** Matthew Peter 1957- *WhoAmL 92*
**Dullea,** Keir 1936- *IntMPA 92, WhoEnt 92*
**Duller,** Nelson M, Jr 1923- *AmMWSc 92*
**Dulles,** Allen 1893-1969 *EncTR 91 [port]*
**Dulles,** Allen Welsh 1893-1969 *AmPolLe, FacFETw*
**Dulles,** Avery 1918- *WhoRel 92, WrDr 92*
**Dulles,** John Foster 1888-1959 *AmPeW, AmPolLe [port], FacFETw [port], RComAH*
**Dullien,** Francis A L 1925- *AmMWSc 92*
**Dullien,** Robert Charles 1950- *WhoWest 92*
**Dullin,** Charles 1885-1949 *FacFETw*
**Dulloo,** Madum Murlidas 1949- *IntWW 91*
**Dully,** Joseph Henry 1940- *WhoWest 92*
**Dulmage,** Howard Taylor 1923- *AmMWSc 92*
**Dulmage,** William James 1919- *AmMWSc 92*
**Dulmes,** Steven Lee 1957- *WhoMW 92*
**Dulo,** Jane 1917- *WhoEnt 92*
**Dulock,** Victor A, Jr 1939- *AmMWSc 92*
**Dulude,** Gary Joseph 1966- *WhoWest 92*
**Dulude,** Richard 1933- *WhoFI 92*
**Dulverton,** Baron 1915- *Who 92*
**Duly,** Sidney John d1991 *Who 92N*
**Dumachev,** Anatoliy Panteleyevich 1932- *IntWW 91*
**DuMaine,** R. Pierre 1931- *WhoRel 92, WhoWest 92*
**Duman,** John Girard 1946- *AmMWSc 92*
**Dumaran,** Adele *DrAPF 91*
**Dumars,** Joe 1963- *WhoMW 92*
**Dumars,** Joe, III 1963- *WhoBlA 92*
**Du Marsais,** Cesar Chesneau 1676-1756 *BlkwCEP*
**Dumas,** Alexandre 1802-1870 *GuFrLit 1*
**Dumas,** Alexandre 1824-1895 *DramC 1 [port], GuFrLit 1*
**Dumas,** Charles Everett 1937- *BlkOlyM*
**Dumas,** Claudine *WrDr 92*
**Dumas,** D. Juaken 1957- *WhoRel 92*
**Dumas,** Darrell Olen 1960- *WhoRel 92*
**Dumas,** David W 1943- *WhoAmP 91*
**Dumas,** Floyd E. 1926- *WhoBlA 92*
**Dumas,** Gerald *DrAPF 91*
**Dumas,** Gerald John 1930- *WhoEnt 92*
**Dumas,** H Scott 1957- *AmMWSc 92*
**Dumas,** Herbert M, Jr 1927- *AmMWSc 92*
**Dumas,** Jean 1925- *AmMWSc 92*
**Dumas,** Jean-Louis Robert Frederic 1938- *IntWW 91*
**Dumas,** Karen Marie 1962- *WhoBlA 92*
**Dumas,** Lawrence 1908- *WhoAmL 92*
**Dumas,** Lawrence Bernard 1941- *AmMWSc 92*
**Dumas,** Louise Isabelle 1934- *WhoWest 92*
**Dumas,** Philip Conrad 1923- *AmMWSc 92*
**Dumas,** Pierre 1924- *IntWW 91*
**Dumas,** Rhetaugh Etheldra Graves 1928- *IntWW 91*
**Dumas,** Rhetaugh Graves *AmMWSc 92*
**Dumas,** Rhetaugh Graves 1928- *WhoBlA 92*
**Dumas,** Roland 1922- *IntWW 91, Who 92*
**Dumas-Dubourg,** Francoise Therese B. 1932- *IntWW 91*
**Du Maurier,** Daphne 1907- *IntAu&W 91*
**Du Maurier,** Daphne 1907-1989 *FacFETw [port], RfGEnL 91*
**du Maurier,** George 1834-1896 *RfGEnL 91, ScFEYrs*
**Du Maurier,** Gerald *FacFETw*
**Dumbadze,** Nina Yakovlevna 1919- *SovUnBD*
**Dumbadze,** Nodar Vladimirovich d1989 *IntWW 91N*
**Dumbaugh,** William Henry, Jr 1929- *AmMWSc 92*
**Dumbauld,** Edward 1905- *WhoAmL 92*
**Dumbell,** Keith Rodney 1922- *Who 92*
**Dumbri,** Austin C 1947- *AmMWSc 92*
**Dumbroff,** Erwin Bernard 1932- *AmMWSc 92*
**Dumbutshena,** Enoch 1920- *IntWW 91, Who 92*
**Dumenil,** Lloyd C 1920- *AmMWSc 92*
**Dumeny,** Marcel Jacque 1950- *WhoAmL 92*
**Dumfries,** Earl of 1958- *Who 92*
**Dumin,** David Joseph 1935- *AmMWSc 92*
**Dumini,** Amerigo 1896-1967 *BiDExR*
**Dumisai,** Kwame 1939- *WhoBlA 92*
**Dumit,** Thomas A. 1942- *WhoAmL 92*
**Dumitrescu,** Domnita *WhoWest 92*
**Dumke,** Barbara Ann 1946- *WhoRel 92*
**Dumke,** Mark Paul 1955- *WhoRel 92*
**Dumke,** Melvin Philip 1920- *WhoMW 92*
**Dumke,** Paul Rudolph *AmMWSc 92*
**Dumke,** Warren Lloyd 1928- *AmMWSc 92*
**Dumm,** Demetrius Robert 1923- *WhoRel 92*
**Dumm,** Mary Elizabeth 1916- *AmMWSc 92*
**Dummann,** Marlo Jean 1940- *WhoMW 92*
**Dummer,** Nancy Eileen 1951- *WhoFI 92*
**Dummett,** Ann 1930- *ConAu 135, Who 92*
**Dummett,** Clifton Orrin 1919- *AmMWSc 92, WhoBlA 92*
**Dummett,** George Anthony 1907- *Who 92*
**Dummett,** Jocelyn Angela 1956- *WhoBlA 92*
**Dummett,** M. A. E. 1925- *WrDr 92*
**Dummett,** Michael Anthony Eardley 1925- *IntWW 91, Who 92*
**Dumon,** Bernard Claude Jean-Pierre 1935- *IntWW 91*
**Dumonceaux,** Benedict Joseph 1956- *WhoMW 92*
**Dumont,** Allan E 1924- *AmMWSc 92*
**DuMont,** Allen B. d1965 *LesBEnT 92*
**DuMont,** Bruce *WhoEnt 92*
**Dumont,** Guy Albert 1951- *AmMWSc 92*
**Dumont,** James Nicholas 1935- *AmMWSc 92*
**Dumont,** Kent P 1941- *AmMWSc 92*
**Du Mont,** Nicolas 1954- *WhoHisp 92*
**Dumont,** Rene 1904- *IntWW 91*
**Dumont,** Robert E 1922- *WhoAmP 91*
**Dumont,** Wayne, Jr 1914- *WhoAmP 91*
**DuMontelle,** Paul Bertrand 1933- *AmMWSc 92*
**Dumouchel,** Paul 1911- *WhoRel 92*
**Dumouchel,** Robert Justin 1942- *WhoAmL 92*
**Dumoulin,** Charles Lucian 1956- *AmMWSc 92*
**Dumper,** Anthony Charles *Who 92*
**Dumpson,** James R. *WhoBlA 92*
**Dun,** Walter Angus 1857-1887 *BiInAmS*
**Dunaevsky,** Isaak Osipovich 1900-1955 *SovUnBD*
**Dunagan,** James Alan 1954- *WhoWest 92*
**Dunagan,** Sidney George 1943- *WhoAmL 92*
**Dunagan,** Tommy Tolson 1931- *AmMWSc 92*
**Dunagan,** Walter Benton 1937- *WhoAmL 92*
**Dunahay,** Terri Goodman 1954- *AmMWSc 92*
**Dunaif,** Alexandra Louise 1957- *WhoFI 92*
**Dunalley,** Baron 1912- *Who 92*
**Dunand,** Jean 1877-1942 *FacFETw*
**Dunant,** Jean Henri 1828-1910 *WhoNob 90*
**Dunant,** Yves 1912- *IntWW 91*
**Dunaskiss,** Mat J 1951- *WhoAmP 91*
**Dunavant,** Leonard Clyde 1919- *WhoAmP 91*
**Dunavant,** Richard Hannah 1952- *WhoAmP 91*
**Dunavin,** Leonard Sypret, Jr 1930- *AmMWSc 92*
**Dunaway,** David Bruce 1945- *WhoAmL 92*
**Dunaway,** David R. 1939- *WhoWest 92*
**Dunaway,** Donald Lucius 1937- *WhoFI 92*
**Dunaway,** Dorothy Faye 1941- *IntWW 91*
**Dunaway,** Ernest Ray 1930- *WhoWest 92*
**Dunaway,** Faye 1941- *IntMPA 92, WhoEnt 92*
**Dunaway,** George Alton, Jr 1941- *AmMWSc 92*
**Dunaway,** Johnny V. 1948- *WhoAmL 92*
**Dunaway,** Margaret Ann 1943- *WhoWest 92*
**Dunaway,** Marietta 1952- *AmMWSc 92*
**Dunaway,** Thomas Whitfield, III 1951- *WhoAmL 92*
**Dunaway,** Trudy Vincent 1951- *WhoWest 92*
**Dunaway-Mariano,** Debra *AmMWSc 92*
**Dunayer,** Marty Dennis 1953- *WhoEnt 92*
**Dunayevskaya,** Raya 1910-1987 *FacFETw*
**Dunayevsky,** Isaak 1900-1955 *FacFETw*
**Dunbar,** Alexander Arbuthnott 1929- *Who 92*
**Dunbar,** Andrea 1961- *IntAu&W 91, WrDr 92*
**Dunbar,** Anne Cynthia 1938- *WhoBlA 92*
**Dunbar,** Bonnie Sue 1948- *AmMWSc 92*
**Dunbar,** Brian Jay d1991 *NewYTBS 91*
**Dunbar,** Burdett Sheridan 1938- *AmMWSc 92*
**Dunbar,** Charles 1907- *Who 92*
**Dunbar,** Charles Edward, III 1926- *WhoAmP 91*
**Dunbar,** Charles F 1937- *WhoAmP 91*
**Dunbar,** David G. *WhoRel 92*
**Dunbar,** David H. *Who 92*
**Dunbar,** David Wesley 1952- *WhoFI 92*
**Dunbar,** Dennis Monroe 1945- *AmMWSc 92*
**Dunbar,** Evelyn 1906-1960 *TwCPaSc*
**Dunbar,** Harry B. 1925- *WhoBlA 92*
**Dunbar,** Holly Jean 1960- *WhoEnt 92*
**Dunbar,** Howard Stanford 1919- *AmMWSc 92*
**Dunbar,** J Scott 1921- *AmMWSc 92*
**Dunbar,** James V., Jr. 1937- *WhoAmL 92*
**Dunbar,** John Greenwell 1930- *Who 92*
**Dunbar,** Joseph C 1944- *AmMWSc 92, WhoBlA 92*
**Dunbar,** Joseph Edward 1924- *AmMWSc 92*
**Dunbar,** Lawrence Gregory, Sr. 1953- *WhoAmL 92*
**Dunbar,** Leslie W. 1921- *WrDr 92*
**Dunbar,** Marjorie Henderson 1932- *WhoBlA 92*
**Dunbar,** Mary Asmundson 1942- *WhoFI 92, WhoMW 92*
**Dunbar,** Maxwell 1914- *IntAu&W 91*
**Dunbar,** Maxwell John 1914- *AmMWSc 92, IntWW 91*
**Dunbar,** Michael Patrick 1949- *WhoWest 92*
**Dunbar,** Patricia Lynn 1953- *WhoWest 92*
**Dunbar,** Paul Hammond, III 1943- *WhoAmL 92*
**Dunbar,** Paul Laurence 1872-1906 *AfrAmW, BenetAL 91, BlkLC [port], FacFETw, ShSCr 8 [port]*
**Dunbar,** Philip Gordon 1955- *AmMWSc 92*
**Dunbar,** Phyllis Marguerite *AmMWSc 92*
**Dunbar,** Prescott Nelson 1942- *WhoFI 92*
**Dunbar,** Richard Alan 1940- *AmMWSc 92*
**Dunbar,** Richard Paul 1951- *WhoWest 92*
**Dunbar,** Robert Copeland 1943- *AmMWSc 92*
**Dunbar,** Robert E 1926- *ConAu 34NR*
**Dunbar,** Robert John 1948- *WhoFI 92*
**Dunbar,** Robert L. 1951- *WhoEnt 92*
**Dunbar,** Robert Standish, Jr 1921- *AmMWSc 92*
**Dunbar,** William 1460?-1513? *RfGEnL 91*
**Dunbar,** William 1749-1810 *BiInAmS*
**Dunbar,** William Charles 1942- *WhoAmP 91*
**Dunbar,** William Taylor, III 1939- *WhoEnt 92*
**Dunbar,** Wylene Wisby 1949- *WhoAmL 92*
**Dunbar-Nasmith,** David Arthur 1921- *Who 92*

**Dunbar-Nasmith**, James Duncan 1927- *Who 92*
**Dunbar-Nelson**, Alice 1875-1935 *NotBlAW 92 [port]*
**Dunbar of Durn**, Drummond Cospatrick N 1917- *Who 92*
**Dunbar of Hempriggs**, Maureen Daisy Helen 1906- *Who 92*
**Dunbar of Mochrum**, Jean Ivor 1918- *Who 92*
**Dunbar of Northfield**, Archibald 1927- *Who 92*
**Dunboyne**, Baron 1917- *Who 92*
**Dunboyne**, Lord 1917- *WrDr 92*
**Duncalf**, Deryck 1926- *AmMWSc 92*
**Duncalf**, Stephen 1951- *TwCPaSc*
**Duncan**, A. A. M. 1926- *WrDr 92*
**Duncan**, A. R. C. 1915- *WrDr 92*
**Duncan**, Acheson Johnston 1904- *AmMWSc 92*
**Duncan**, Agnes Lawrie Addie 1947- *Who 92*
**Duncan**, Alan Eugene 1951- *WhoFI 92*
**Duncan**, Alex *IntAu&W 91X, WrDr 92*
**Duncan**, Alice Geneva 1917- *WhoBlA 92*
**Duncan**, Andrew Malcolm 1960- *WhoWest 92*
**Duncan**, Anita F 1931- *WhoAmP 91*
**Duncan**, Ann Q *WhoAmP 91*
**Duncan**, Ansley McKinley 1932- *WhoFI 92, WhoWest 92*
**Duncan**, Anthony Douglas 1930- *IntAu&W 91, WrDr 92*
**Duncan**, Archibald Alexander McBeth 1926- *IntWW 91, Who 92*
**Duncan**, Archibald Sutherland 1914- *Who 92*
**Duncan**, Bettie 1933- *AmMWSc 92*
**Duncan**, Brian Arthur Cullum 1908- *Who 92*
**Duncan**, Bryan Lee 1942- *AmMWSc 92*
**Duncan**, Budd Lee 1936- *AmMWSc 92*
**Duncan**, Calvin L. 1925- *WhoBlA 92*
**Duncan**, Carl Neil 1945- *WhoAmL 92*
**Duncan**, Charles Clifford 1907- *AmMWSc 92*
**Duncan**, Charles Donald 1948- *AmMWSc 92*
**Duncan**, Charles Kenney 1911- *IntWW 91*
**Duncan**, Charles Lee 1939- *AmMWSc 92*
**Duncan**, Charles Tignor 1924- *WhoBlA 92*
**Duncan**, Christopher Brian *WhoEnt 92*
**Duncan**, Clyde Tangley 1936- *WhoRel 92*
**Duncan**, Daniel Lee 1956- *WhoAmL 92*
**Duncan**, Daniel Merritt 1938- *WhoFI 92*
**Duncan**, Dave 1933- *IntAu&W 91, TwCSFW 91*
**Duncan**, David 1913- *TwCSFW 91, WrDr 92*
**Duncan**, David Edward 1926- *WhoBlA 92*
**Duncan**, David Francis 1923- *Who 92*
**Duncan**, Deborah Lynne 1965- *WhoMW 92*
**Duncan**, Denis Macdonald 1920- *Who 92*
**Duncan**, Dennis Andrew 1929- *AmMWSc 92*
**Duncan**, Don Darryl 1939- *AmMWSc 92*
**Duncan**, Donald 1903- *AmMWSc 92*
**Duncan**, Donald Allen 1929- *WhoWest 92*
**Duncan**, Donald Gordon 1920- *AmMWSc 92*
**Duncan**, Donald Pendleton 1916- *AmMWSc 92, WhoMW 92*
**Duncan**, Donald Ross 1935- *WhoAmL 92*
**Duncan**, Doris Gottschalk 1944- *WhoWest 92*
**Duncan**, Douglas John Stewart 1945- *Who 92*
**Duncan**, Douglas Wallace 1934- *AmMWSc 92*
**Duncan**, Duke *TwCWW 91*
**Duncan**, Dwight Gerard 1951- *WhoAmL 92*
**Duncan**, Ed Eugene 1948- *WhoAmL 92*
**Duncan**, Erika *DrAPF 91*
**Duncan**, Ernest Louis, Jr. *WhoAmL 92*
**Duncan**, Frances Mary 1942- *IntAu&W 91*
**Duncan**, Freeman B 1946- *WhoAmP 91*
**Duncan**, Geneva 1935- *WhoBlA 92*
**Duncan**, Geoffrey Stuart 1938- *Who 92*
**Duncan**, George 1933- *Who 92*
**Duncan**, George Alexander 1902- *Who 92*
**Duncan**, George Comer 1941- *AmMWSc 92*
**Duncan**, George Douglas *Who 92*
**Duncan**, George H. 1931- *WhoEnt 92*
**Duncan**, George R. 1923- *WhoAmL 92*
**Duncan**, George Ronald 1923- *WhoIns 92*
**Duncan**, George Thomas 1942- *AmMWSc 92*
**Duncan**, Gordon Duke 1926- *AmMWSc 92*
**Duncan**, Gordon W 1932- *AmMWSc 92*
**Duncan**, Greg John 1948- *WhoFI 92*
**Duncan**, Harry Ernest 1936- *AmMWSc 92*
**Duncan**, I B R 1926- *AmMWSc 92*
**Duncan**, Irma W 1912- *AmMWSc 92*
**Duncan**, Irma Wagner 1912- *WhoWest 92*
**Duncan**, Isadora 1877-1927 *FacFETw [port], RComAH*
**Duncan**, Isadora 1878-1927 *BenetAL 91, HanAmWH*
**Duncan**, J Santford 1948- *WhoAmP 91*
**Duncan**, James 1927- *Who 92*
**Duncan**, James Alan 1945- *AmMWSc 92*
**Duncan**, James Anthony 1954- *WhoAmP 91*
**Duncan**, James Brian 1959- *WhoEnt 92*
**Duncan**, James Byron 1947- *AmMWSc 92*
**Duncan**, James H., Jr. 1947- *WhoEnt 92*
**Duncan**, James Knox 1928- *WhoAmP 91*
**Duncan**, James Lowell 1937- *AmMWSc 92*
**Duncan**, James M *AmMWSc 92*
**Duncan**, James Playford 1919- *AmMWSc 92, Who 92*
**Duncan**, James Reary 1951- *WhoMW 92, WhoRel 92*
**Duncan**, James Stuart d1986 *Who 92N*
**Duncan**, James Thayer 1932- *AmMWSc 92*
**Duncan**, James W 1926- *AmMWSc 92*
**Duncan**, James Ward 1963- *WhoEnt 92*
**Duncan**, James Wendell 1942- *WhoAmP 91*
**Duncan**, Jason Charlie 1929- *WhoAmP 91*
**Duncan**, Jean *TwCPaSc*
**Duncan**, Jimmie Walter 1925- *WhoAmP 91*
**Duncan**, Joan A. 1939- *WhoBlA 92*
**Duncan**, John 1866-1945 *TwCPaSc*
**Duncan**, John C. 1920- *WhoFI 92*
**Duncan**, John C., Jr. 1942- *WhoBlA 92*
**Duncan**, John Clarke 1967- *WhoMW 92*
**Duncan**, John Finch 1933- *Who 92*
**Duncan**, John J., Jr. 1947- *AlmAP 92 [port], WhoAmP 91*
**Duncan**, John L 1932- *AmMWSc 92*
**Duncan**, John Malvin 1934- *WhoRel 92*
**Duncan**, John Robert 1937- *AmMWSc 92*
**Duncan**, John Spenser Ritchie 1921- *IntWW 91, Who 92*
**Duncan**, John Wiley 1947- *WhoWest 92*
**Duncan**, Joseph 1920- *TwCPaSc*
**Duncan**, Joseph Wayman 1936- *WhoFI 92*
**Duncan**, Julia K. *ConAu 134, SmATA 65*
**Duncan**, Julia Nunnally *DrAPF 91*
**Duncan**, Kate Corbin 1942- *WhoWest 92*
**Duncan**, Katherine 1913- *AmMWSc 92*
**Duncan**, Kenneth Playfair 1924- *Who 92*
**Duncan**, Laura *Who 92*
**Duncan**, Lawrence Lee 1950- *WhoFI 92*
**Duncan**, Leonard Clinton 1936- *AmMWSc 92*
**Duncan**, Leroy Edward, Jr 1917- *AmMWSc 92*
**Duncan**, Lewis Mannan 1951- *AmMWSc 92*
**Duncan**, Lindsay *IntMPA 92*
**Duncan**, Lois 1934- *ConAu 36NR, IntAu&W 91, WrDr 92*
**Duncan**, Louis 1862-1916 *BiInAmS*
**Duncan**, Louis Davidson, Jr. 1932- *WhoBlA 92*
**Duncan**, Lynda J. *WhoBlA 92*
**Duncan**, Malachi, Jr. 1937- *WhoBlA 92*
**Duncan**, Malcolm McGregor 1922- *Who 92*
**Duncan**, Margaret Caroline 1930- *AmMWSc 92*
**Duncan**, Mariano 1963- *WhoHisp 92*
**Duncan**, Marion M, Jr 1927- *AmMWSc 92*
**Duncan**, Marvin E. 1939- *WhoBlA 92*
**Duncan**, Marvin R 1935- *WhoAmP 91*
**Duncan**, Melba Frances Hurd *WhoWest 92*
**Duncan**, Michael John Freeman d1991 *Who 92N*
**Duncan**, Michael Rayvonne 1949- *WhoRel 92*
**Duncan**, Michael Robert 1947- *AmMWSc 92*
**Duncan**, Nora Kathryn 1946- *WhoAmL 92*
**Duncan**, Norman 1871-1916 *BenetAL 91*
**Duncan**, Paul David 1947- *WhoRel 92*
**Duncan**, Richard Chrane 1946- *WhoRel 92*
**Duncan**, Richard Dale 1941- *AmMWSc 92*
**Duncan**, Richard H 1922- *AmMWSc 92*
**Duncan**, Robert 1919- *IntAu&W 91*
**Duncan**, Robert 1919-1988 *BenetAL 91, FacFETw*
**Duncan**, Robert Blackford 1920- *WhoAmP 91*
**Duncan**, Robert C 1923- *AmMWSc 92*
**Duncan**, Robert Case 1958- *WhoFI 92*
**Duncan**, Robert Gene 1932- *WhoAmL 92, WhoMW 92*
**Duncan**, Robert Kennedy 1868-1914 *BiInAmS*
**Duncan**, Robert L. 1927- *WrDr 92*
**Duncan**, Robert Leon, Jr 1951- *AmMWSc 92*
**Duncan**, Robert M. 1927- *WhoBlA 92*
**Duncan**, Robert Michael 1951- *WhoAmP 91, WhoFI 92*
**Duncan**, Robert Morton 1927- *WhoAmL 92*
**Duncan**, Robert Todd 1903- *WhoBlA 92*
**Duncan**, Robin Barclay 1956- *WhoBlA 92*
**Duncan**, Ronald 1914-1982 *RfGEnL 91*
**Duncan**, Ronny Rush 1946- *AmMWSc 92*
**Duncan**, Royal Robert 1952- *WhoMW 92*
**Duncan**, Ruby 1932- *WhoBlA 92*
**Duncan**, Samuel Edward, Jr. 1904-1968 *DcNCBi 2*
**Duncan**, Sandy *LesBEnT 92*
**Duncan**, Sandy 1946- *IntMPA 92, WhoEnt 92*
**Duncan**, Sara Jeannette 1861-1922 *BenetAL 91*
**Duncan**, Scott Richard 1954- *WhoEnt 92*
**Duncan**, Sean Bruce 1942- *Who 92*
**Duncan**, Stanley Frederick St. Clare 1927- *IntWW 91, Who 92*
**Duncan**, Stephan W. 1924- *WhoBlA 92*
**Duncan**, Stephen Mack 1941- *WhoAmL 92, WhoAmP 91*
**Duncan**, Stewart 1926- *AmMWSc 92*
**Duncan**, Terrence *WrDr 92*
**Duncan**, Thomas Osler 1948- *AmMWSc 92*
**Duncan**, Timothy Harold 1959- *WhoWest 92*
**Duncan**, Todd 1903- *NewAmDM*
**Duncan**, Verdell 1946- *WhoBlA 92*
**Duncan**, Verne Allen 1934- *WhoAmP 91, WhoWest 92*
**Duncan**, Wallace Lee 1956- *WhoAmL 92*
**Duncan**, Walter E 1910- *AmMWSc 92*
**Duncan**, Walter Marvin, Jr 1952- *AmMWSc 92*
**Duncan**, Wilbur Howard 1910- *AmMWSc 92*
**Duncan**, William 1717-1760 *BlkwCEP*
**Duncan**, William 1944- *WrDr 92*
**Duncan**, William Louis 1945- *WhoWest 92*
**Duncan**, William Millen 1939- *WhoFI 92*
**Duncan**, William Perry 1943- *AmMWSc 92*
**Duncan**, William Raymond 1949- *AmMWSc 92*
**Duncan-Jones**, Geri 1958- *WhoBlA 92*
**Duncan Millar**, Ian Alastair 1914- *Who 92*
**Duncan-Sandys**, Lord 1908-1987 *FacFETw*
**Duncanson**, Donald George 1928- *WhoMW 92*
**Duncanson**, Patricia A. 1944- *WhoBlA 92*
**Dunckhorst**, F T 1931- *AmMWSc 92*
**Duncklee**, Elizabeth Anne 1958- *WhoMW 92*
**Duncombe** *Who 92*
**DunCombe**, C. Beth 1948- *WhoBlA 92*
**Duncombe**, E 1916- *AmMWSc 92*
**Duncombe**, Philip Pauncefort- 1927- *Who 92*
**Duncombe**, Raynor Bailey 1942- *WhoAmL 92*
**Duncombe**, Raynor Lockwood 1917- *AmMWSc 92*
**Duncombe**, Roy 1925- *Who 92*
**Duncumb**, Peter 1931- *Who 92*
**Dundas** *Who 92*
**Dundas**, Hugh 1920- *Who 92*
**Dundas**, Hugh Spencer Lisle 1920- *IntWW 91*
**Dundas**, Philip Blair, Jr. 1948- *WhoAmL 92*
**Dundee**, Earl of 1949- *Who 92*
**Dundee**, Provost of *Who 92*
**Dundee**, Harold A 1924- *AmMWSc 92*
**Dunderdale**, Wilfred Albert d1990 *Who 92N*
**Dundonald**, Earl of 1961- *Who 92*
**Dundurs**, J 1922- *AmMWSc 92*
**Dundy**, Elaine 1927- *ConNov 91, WrDr 92*
**Dune**, Steve Charles 1931- *WhoAmL 92, WhoFI 92*
**Dune**, T L *WhoAmP 91*
**Dunedin**, Bishop of 1942- *Who 92*
**Duneer**, Arthur Gustav, Jr 1924- *AmMWSc 92*
**Dunegan**, James H 1940- *WhoAmP 91*
**Dunegan**, Stephen Dennis 1952- *WhoAmL 92*
**Dunell**, Basil Anderson 1923- *AmMWSc 92*
**Dunetz**, Lora *DrAPF 91*
**Dunetz**, Roger Martin 1963- *WhoAmL 92*
**Dunfee**, Thomas Wylie 1941- *WhoAmL 92*
**Dunfey**, Robert John 1928- *WhoAmP 91*
**Dunfey**, William L. d1991 *NewYTBS 91*
**Dunford**, Edsel D *AmMWSc 92*
**Dunford**, Hugh Brian 1927- *AmMWSc 92*
**Dunford**, James Marshall 1915- *AmMWSc 92*
**Dunford**, Max Patterson 1930- *AmMWSc 92, WhoWest 92*
**Dunford**, Raymond A 1914- *AmMWSc 92*
**Dunford**, Robert A. 1931- *WhoFI 92*
**Dunford**, Robert Walter 1946- *AmMWSc 92*
**Dung**, H C 1936- *AmMWSc 92*
**Dungan**, Kendrick Webb 1928- *AmMWSc 92*
**Dungan**, Malcolm Thon 1922- *WhoAmL 92*
**Dungan**, Shirley Ann 1932- *WhoRel 92*
**Dungan**, William Joseph, Jr. 1956- *WhoFI 92*
**Dungan**, William Thompson 1930- *AmMWSc 92*
**Dungee**, Margaret R. *WhoBlA 92*
**Dungey**, James Wynne 1923- *Who 92*
**Dungie**, Ruth Spigner *WhoBlA 92*
**Dunglass**, Lord *Who 92*
**Dunglison**, Robley 1798-1869 *BiInAmS*
**Dungworth**, Donald L 1931- *AmMWSc 92*
**Dungy**, Claibourne I. 1938- *WhoBlA 92*
**Dungy**, Madgetta Thornton *WhoBlA 92*
**Dunham**, Charles Burton 1938- *AmMWSc 92*
**Dunham**, Charles W 1922- *AmMWSc 92*
**Dunham**, Christine *WhoEnt 92*
**Dunham**, Christopher Cooper 1937- *WhoAmP 91*
**Dunham**, Clarence E. 1934- *WhoBlA 92*
**Dunham**, Corydon Bushnell 1927- *WhoFI 92*
**Dunham**, Dave 1941- *WhoAmP 91*
**Dunham**, David Waring 1942- *AmMWSc 92*
**Dunham**, Frank G, Jr 1930- *WhoIns 92*
**Dunham**, Frank Willard 1942- *WhoAmL 92*
**Dunham**, Glen Curtis 1956- *AmMWSc 92*
**Dunham**, James George 1950- *AmMWSc 92*
**Dunham**, Jewett 1924- *AmMWSc 92*
**Dunham**, John L. 1939- *WhoBlA 92*
**Dunham**, John Malcolm 1923- *AmMWSc 92*
**Dunham**, Katherine *IntWW 91, NewYTBS 91 [port]*
**Dunham**, Katherine 1909- *NotBlAW 92 [port]*
**Dunham**, Katherine 1910- *WhoBlA 92*
**Dunham**, Katherine 1912- *FacFETw*
**Dunham**, Kingsley 1910- *Who 92, WrDr 92*
**Dunham**, Kingsley C. 1910- *IntWW 91*
**Dunham**, Michael James 1966- *WhoFI 92*
**Dunham**, Philip Bigelow 1937- *AmMWSc 92*
**Dunham**, Robert 1932- *WhoBlA 92*
**Dunham**, Russell John 1965- *WhoRel 92*
**Dunham**, Stephen Sampson 1945- *WhoAmL 92*
**Dunham**, Valgene Loren 1940- *AmMWSc 92*
**Dunham**, William 1947- *ConAu 133*
**Dunham**, William Wade 1947- *AmMWSc 92, WhoMW 92*
**Dunham**, Wolcott Balestier 1900- *AmMWSc 92*
**Dunham**, Wolcott Balestier, Jr. 1943- *WhoAmL 92*
**Dunholter**, Dana Allen 1946- *WhoMW 92*
**Dunie**, Richard Behr 1949- *WhoFI 92*
**Dunifer**, Gerald Leroy 1941- *AmMWSc 92*
**Dunigan**, Dennis Wayne 1952- *WhoFI 92, WhoMW 92*
**Dunigan**, Edward P 1934- *AmMWSc 92*
**Dunigan**, Mayme O. 1921- *WhoBlA 92*
**Dunigan**, Paul Francis Xavier, Jr. 1948- *WhoWest 92*
**Dunikoski**, Leonard Karol, Jr 1945- *AmMWSc 92*
**Dunin**, Elsie Ivancich 1935- *WhoWest 92*
**Duning**, George 1908- *IntMPA 92*
**Dunio**, Donna Kay 1946- *WhoRel 92*
**Dunipace**, Donald William 1907- *AmMWSc 92*
**Dunipace**, Ian Douglas 1939- *WhoAmL 92, WhoWest 92*
**Dunipace**, Kenneth Robert 1929- *AmMWSc 92*
**Dunitz**, Jack David 1923- *IntWW 91, Who 92*
**Dunivent**, John Thomas 1928- *WhoMW 92*
**Duniway**, Abigail Jane Scott 1834-1915 *HanAmWH*
**Duniway**, John Mason 1942- *AmMWSc 92*
**Dunk**, George Montagu 1716-1771 *BlkwEAR*
**Dunkel**, Arthur 1932- *IntWW 91, Who 92*
**Dunkel**, Morris 1927- *AmMWSc 92*
**Dunkel**, Stuart *WhoEnt 92*
**Dunkel**, Virginia Catherine 1934- *AmMWSc 92*
**Dunkelberger**, Harry Edward, Jr. 1930- *WhoAmL 92*
**Dunkelberger**, Tobias Henry 1909- *AmMWSc 92*
**Dunkeld**, Bishop of 1941- *Who 92*
**Dunkelman**, Lawrence 1917- *AmMWSc 92*
**Dunker**, Alan Keith 1943- *AmMWSc 92*
**Dunker**, Melvin Frederick William 1913- *AmMWSc 92, WhoMW 92*
**Dunker**, Richard Bruce 1937- *WhoMW 92*
**Dunker**, Robert Ferdinand 1931- *WhoIns 92*
**Dunker**, Sandra Sue 1957- *WhoRel 92*
**Dunkerley**, Donald Austin 1936- *WhoRel 92*

**Dunkerley,** George William 1919- *Who 92*
**Dunkerly,** Inez Kathleen 1914- *WhoAmP 91*
**Dunkerson,** Dennis L 1947- *WhoIns 92*
**Dunkin,** Jonathan David 1963- *WhoRel 92*
**Dunkl,** Charles Francis 1941- *AmMWSc 92*
**Dunklau,** Rupert Louis 1927- *WhoMW 92*
**Dunkle,** Larry D 1943- *AmMWSc 92*
**Dunkle,** Randal Clinton 1956- *WhoAmL 92*
**Dunkle,** Sidney Warren *AmMWSc 92*
**Dunkle,** Stephen T 1951- *WhoAmP 91*
**Dunkley,** Carlyle Anthony 1939- *IntWW 91*
**Dunkley,** Christopher 1944- *IntAu&W 91, Who 92*
**Dunkley,** James Lewis 1908- *Who 92*
**Dunkley,** Sue 1942- *TwCPaSc*
**Dunkley,** Walter Lewis 1918- *AmMWSc 92*
**Dunklin,** Juni *DrAPF 91*
**Dunkly,** James Warren 1942- *WhoRel 92*
**Dunlap,** Bobby David 1938- *AmMWSc 92*
**Dunlap,** Brett Irving 1947- *AmMWSc 92*
**Dunlap,** Burnie Harold 1943- *WhoWest 92*
**Dunlap,** Carter Wesley 1914- *WhoAmP 91*
**Dunlap,** Catherine Mary 1927- *WhoRel 92*
**Dunlap,** Charles Edward 1908- *AmMWSc 92*
**Dunlap,** Charles Lee 1943- *WhoFI 92, WhoWest 92*
**Dunlap,** Clarence Rupert 1908- *Who 92*
**Dunlap,** Claud Evans, III 1946- *AmMWSc 92*
**Dunlap,** Connie Sue Zimmerman 1952- *WhoMW 92*
**Dunlap,** Dale Lee 1956- *WhoFI 92*
**Dunlap,** Daniel Girard 1948- *WhoFI 92*
**Dunlap,** David Graydon 1949- *WhoAmL 92*
**Dunlap,** David Houston 1947- *WhoMW 92*
**Dunlap,** David Morris 1953- *WhoEnt 92*
**Dunlap,** Donald Gene 1926- *AmMWSc 92*
**Dunlap,** Eileen Sepmeyer 1965- *WhoEnt 92*
**Dunlap,** Elden Dale 1921- *WhoRel 92*
**Dunlap,** Estelle Cecilia Diggs 1912- *WhoBlA 92*
**Dunlap,** F. Thomas, Jr. 1951- *WhoAmL 92*
**Dunlap,** Henry Francis 1916- *AmMWSc 92*
**Dunlap,** Jack Stuart 1930- *WhoWest 92*
**Dunlap,** James Lapham 1937- *WhoFI 92*
**Dunlap,** James R 1961- *WhoAmP 91*
**Dunlap,** James Riley, Sr. 1925- *WhoWest 92*
**Dunlap,** Jeffrey Lee 1955- *WhoMW 92, WhoRel 92*
**Dunlap,** John Frederick 1943- *WhoAmL 92*
**Dunlap,** Julian Lee 1932- *AmMWSc 92*
**Dunlap,** Lawrence H 1910- *AmMWSc 92*
**Dunlap,** Leslie W 1911- *IntAu&W 91, WrDr 92*
**Dunlap,** Pamela Sue 1946- *WhoFI 92*
**Dunlap,** Peter L. 1942- *WhoAmL 92*
**Dunlap,** Richard D. 1923- *IntMPA 92*
**Dunlap,** Richard Donovan 1923- *WhoEnt 92*
**Dunlap,** Richard M 1917- *AmMWSc 92*
**Dunlap,** Robert Bruce 1942- *AmMWSc 92*
**Dunlap,** Robert D 1922- *AmMWSc 92*
**Dunlap,** Robert Ellis 1942- *WhoEnt 92*
**Dunlap,** Robert Terren 1944- *WhoEnt 92*
**Dunlap,** Susan D. 1943- *WrDr 92*
**Dunlap,** William 1766-1839 *BenetAL 91*
**Dunlap,** William Crawford 1918- *AmMWSc 92*
**Dunlap,** William DeWayne, Jr. 1938- *WhoFI 92, WhoMW 92*
**Dunlap,** William Joe 1929- *AmMWSc 92*
**Dunlap,** William Phillip 1942- *WhoMW 92*
**Dunlap,** William Wayne 1933- *WhoWest 92*
**Dunlap King,** Virgie M. 1940- *WhoBlA 92*
**Dunlavey,** Dean Carl 1925- *WhoAmL 92*
**Dunlavy,** Howard Russell 1954- *WhoMW 92*
**Dunleath,** Baron 1933- *Who 92*
**Dunleavy,** James Patrick 1939- *WhoAmP 91*
**Dunleavy,** John M 1923- *AmMWSc 92*
**Dunleavy,** Mike *WhoWest 92*
**Dunleavy,** Patrick 1952- *WrDr 92*
**Dunleavy,** Philip 1915- *Who 92*
**Dunlevie,** Ernie G. 1917- *WhoWest 92*
**Dunlevy,** John Nevins 1958- *WhoFI 92*
**Dunlop,** Andrew Reed 1953- *WhoMW 92*
**Dunlop,** Colin Charles Harrison 1918- *Who 92*
**Dunlop,** D L 1925- *AmMWSc 92*
**Dunlop,** David Wallace 1942- *WhoFI 92*
**Dunlop,** Edward 1907- *Who 92*
**Dunlop,** Edward Clarence 1916- *AmMWSc 92*
**Dunlop,** Eileen 1938- *WrDr 92*
**Dunlop,** Ernest Edward 1907- *IntWW 91*
**Dunlop,** Frank 1927- *Who 92, WhoEnt 92*
**Dunlop,** Gordon *Who 92*
**Dunlop,** Ian 1925- *WrDr 92*
**Dunlop,** Ian Geoffrey David 1925- *Who 92*
**Dunlop,** John 1910- *Who 92*
**Dunlop,** John T. 1914- *IntWW 91, WrDr 92*
**Dunlop,** John Thomas 1914- *WhoAmP 91*
**Dunlop,** Laurence James 1939- *WhoRel 92, WhoWest 92*
**Dunlop,** Norman Gordon 1928- *Who 92*
**Dunlop,** R.O. 1894-1973 *TwCPaSc*
**Dunlop,** Richard 1921- *IntAu&W 91*
**Dunlop,** Richard B. *Who 92*
**Dunlop,** Stephen Richard 1944- *WhoMW 92*
**Dunlop,** Thomas 1912- *Who 92*
**Dunlop,** William 1914- *Who 92*
**Dunlop,** William Henry 1943- *AmMWSc 92*
**Dunlop,** William Robert 1916- *AmMWSc 92*
**Dunluce,** Viscount *Who 92*
**Dunluce,** Alexander 1935- *TwCPaSc*
**Dunluce,** Sarah 1941- *TwCPaSc*
**Dunmire,** Irvin Dale 1928- *WhoWest 92*
**Dunmire,** Ronald Warren 1937- *WhoFI 92, WhoMW 92*
**Dunmire-Hedenkamp,** Debra Kay 1958- *WhoMW 92*
**Dunmore** *BlkwEAR*
**Dunmore,** Earl of 1913- *Who 92*
**Dunmore,** Charlotte J. 1926- *WhoBlA 92*
**Dunmore,** John 1923- *IntAu&W 91, WrDr 92*
**Dunmore,** Lawrence A., Jr. 1923- *WhoBlA 92*
**Dunmore,** Spencer 1928- *IntAu&W 91*
**Dunmore,** Spencer S. 1928- *WrDr 92*
**Dunn,** Baroness 1940- *IntWW 91, Who 92*
**Dunn,** Adrian John 1943- *AmMWSc 92*
**Dunn,** Alan Michael 1953- *WhoAmL 92*
**Dunn,** Alfred 1937- *TwCPaSc*
**Dunn,** Andrew Fletcher 1922- *AmMWSc 92*
**Dunn,** Anne 1929- *TwCPaSc*
**Dunn,** Anne Roberts 1940- *AmMWSc 92*
**Dunn,** Arnold Samuel 1929- *AmMWSc 92*
**Dunn,** Arvin Gail 1930- *WhoRel 92*
**Dunn,** Ben Monroe 1945- *AmMWSc 92*
**Dunn,** Benjamin Allen 1941- *AmMWSc 92*
**Dunn,** Bruce 1948- *AmMWSc 92*
**Dunn,** Bruce Eric 1959- *WhoBlA 92*
**Dunn,** Bryant Winfield Culberson 1927- *WhoAmP 91*
**Dunn,** Cal 1915- *WhoEnt 92*
**Dunn,** Charles August, Jr. 1944- *WhoFI 92*
**Dunn,** Charles Nord 1936- *AmMWSc 92*
**Dunn,** Charles R. 1930- *WhoAmL 92*
**Dunn,** Charles Thomas 1930- *WhoFI 92*
**Dunn,** Charles W. 1915- *WrDr 92*
**Dunn,** Charles Wythe 1940- *WhoAmP 91*
**Dunn,** Christopher Allan 1951- *WhoAmL 92*
**Dunn,** Christopher David Reginald 1945- *AmMWSc 92*
**Dunn,** Christopher Paul 1954- *WhoMW 92*
**Dunn,** Clark A 1901- *AmMWSc 92*
**Dunn,** D W 1923- *AmMWSc 92*
**Dunn,** Daniel Craig 1961- *WhoEnt 92*
**Dunn,** Danny Leroy 1946- *AmMWSc 92*
**Dunn,** Darrel Eugene 1932- *AmMWSc 92*
**Dunn,** Daryl Raymond 1966- *WhoMW 92*
**Dunn,** David Baxter 1917- *AmMWSc 92*
**Dunn,** David Boyd 1955- *WhoMW 92*
**Dunn,** David Evan 1935- *AmMWSc 92*
**Dunn,** David J. 1930- *WhoWest 92*
**Dunn,** David John 1943- *WhoMW 92*
**Dunn,** David Lee 1948- *WhoRel 92*
**Dunn,** David N 1940- *WhoIns 92*
**Dunn,** Dean Alan 1954- *AmMWSc 92*
**Dunn,** Donald A 1925- *AmMWSc 92*
**Dunn,** Donald Jack 1945- *WhoAmL 92*
**Dunn,** Doris Marjory 1921- *WhoWest 92*
**Dunn,** Dorothy Fay *AmMWSc 92*
**Dunn,** Douglas 1942- *ConPo 91, WrDr 92*
**Dunn,** Douglas Eaglesham 1942- *IntAu&W 91, IntWW 91, Who 92*
**Dunn,** Duane Merle 1957- *WhoMW 92*
**Dunn,** Edgar M, Jr 1939- *WhoAmP 91*
**Dunn,** Edmond Joseph 1935- *WhoRel 92*
**Dunn,** Edward K., Jr. 1935- *WhoFI 92*
**Dunn,** Edward Paul, Jr. 1953- *WhoFI 92*
**Dunn,** Edwin Rydell 1942- *WhoAmL 92*
**Dunn,** Elizabeth Jucius 1951- *WhoAmL 92*
**Dunn,** Elwood 1906- *WhoRel 92*
**Dunn,** Eric 1927- *Who 92*
**Dunn,** Floyd 1924- *AmMWSc 92*
**Dunn,** Floyd Warren 1920- *AmMWSc 92*
**Dunn,** Francis Michael 1933- *WhoMW 92*
**Dunn,** Francis Vivian 1908- *Who 92*
**Dunn,** Frederick Lester 1928- *AmMWSc 92*
**Dunn,** Frederick Sherwood 1893-1962 *AmPeW*
**Dunn,** Gary Alan 1954- *WhoMW 92*
**Dunn,** George J. 1935- *WhoAmL 92*
**Dunn,** George Lawrence 1936- *AmMWSc 92*
**Dunn,** George William 1930- *WhoBlA 92*
**Dunn,** George Willoughby 1914- *Who 92*
**Dunn,** Glenn 1947- *WhoEnt 92*
**Dunn,** Gordon Harold 1932- *AmMWSc 92, WhoWest 92*
**Dunn,** H. Glenn Tolson 1944- *WhoAmL 92*
**Dunn,** Helene K. 1936- *WhoEnt 92*
**Dunn,** Henry George 1917- *AmMWSc 92*
**Dunn,** Holly 1957- *ConMus 7 [port]*
**Dunn,** Horton, Jr 1929- *AmMWSc 92, WhoFI 92, WhoMW 92*
**Dunn,** Howard Eugene 1938- *AmMWSc 92*
**Dunn,** Hugh Alexander 1923- *IntWW 91*
**Dunn,** Hugh Patrick 1916- *IntAu&W 91, WrDr 92*
**Dunn,** Irving John 1938- *AmMWSc 92*
**Dunn,** J Allan 1872-1941 *ScFEYrs*
**Dunn,** J Howard 1909- *AmMWSc 92*
**Dunn,** Jack Hibbard 1944- *WhoWest 92*
**Dunn,** Jacquelin 1942- *AmMWSc 92*
**Dunn,** James B *WhoAmP 91*
**Dunn,** James Bernard 1927- *WhoMW 92*
**Dunn,** James Earl 1955- *WhoAmP 91, WhoBlA 92*
**Dunn,** James Eldon 1936- *AmMWSc 92*
**Dunn,** James Milton 1932- *WhoRel 92*
**Dunn,** James R *WhoAmP 91*
**Dunn,** James Robert 1921- *AmMWSc 92, WhoFI 92*
**Dunn,** James Whitney 1943- *WhoAmP 91*
**Dunn,** Janet Elaine 1956- *WhoAmP 91*
**Dunn,** Jeffrey William 1947- *WhoMW 92*
**Dunn,** Jennifer Blackburn 1941- *WhoAmP 91*
**Dunn,** Jesse R., Jr. 1958- *WhoRel 92*
**Dunn,** John 1940- *WrDr 92*
**Dunn,** John Churchill 1934- *Who 92*
**Dunn,** John F 1936- *WhoAmP 91*
**Dunn,** John Francis 1936- *WhoAmL 92*
**Dunn,** John Frederick, Jr 1930- *AmMWSc 92*
**Dunn,** John Montfort 1940- *IntWW 91, Who 92*
**Dunn,** John Patrick James 1944- *AmMWSc 92*
**Dunn,** John Raymond, Jr. 1937- *WhoFI 92*
**Dunn,** John Robert 1930- *AmMWSc 92*
**Dunn,** John Ross d1783 *DcNCBi 2*
**Dunn,** John Thornton 1932- *AmMWSc 92*
**Dunn,** Jon D 1937- *AmMWSc 92*
**Dunn,** Jonathan C 1957- *AmMWSc 92*
**Dunn,** Joseph Charles *AmMWSc 92*
**Dunn,** Joseph McElroy 1926- *WhoFI 92, WhoWest 92*
**Dunn,** Kaye 1910- *WhoBlA 92*
**Dunn,** Keith Mervin 1959- *WhoAmL 92*
**Dunn,** Kenneth Arthur 1945- *AmMWSc 92*
**Dunn,** Lawrence L. *WhoRel 92*
**Dunn,** Lawrence William 1942- *WhoAmP 91*
**Dunn,** Lloyd W. d1991 *NewYTBS 91*
**Dunn,** Lloyd W. 1906-1991 *ConAu 134*
**Dunn,** Louise Brisbin d1902 *BiInAmS*
**Dunn,** Martin 1955- *Who 92*
**Dunn,** Martin J 1956- *WhoAmP 91*
**Dunn,** Marvin 1940- *WhoBlA 92*
**Dunn,** Marvin I 1927- *AmMWSc 92*
**Dunn,** Mary Catherine 1924- *AmMWSc 92*
**Dunn,** Mary Jarratt 1942- *WhoAmP 91*
**Dunn,** Matthew Joseph 1958- *WhoAmL 92*
**Dunn,** Melvin B 1936- *WhoIns 92*
**Dunn,** Michael David 1944- *WhoWest 92*
**Dunn,** Michael F 1939- *AmMWSc 92*
**Dunn,** Michael Hamilton 1944- *WhoEnt 92*
**Dunn,** Michael Joseph 1951- *WhoWest 92*
**Dunn,** Mignon 1931- *NewAmDM*
**Dunn,** Miriam D 1927- *WhoAmP 91*
**Dunn,** Morris Douglas 1944- *WhoAmL 92*
**Dunn,** Nell 1936- *ConNov 91, IntAu&W 91, WrDr 92*
**Dunn,** Patrice Marie 1956- *WhoEnt 92*
**Dunn,** Patricia Ann 1944- *WhoAmP 91*
**Dunn,** Patrick Hunter 1912- *Who 92*
**Dunn,** Paul James 1939- *WhoAmL 92*
**Dunn,** Peter 1946- *WhoIns 92*
**Dunn,** Peter Edward 1946- *AmMWSc 92*
**Dunn,** Peter Norman 1926- *WrDr 92*
**Dunn,** Phillip Clark 1953- *WhoRel 92*
**Dunn,** Poindexter 1834-1914 *DcNCBi 2*
**Dunn,** Ralph 1914- *WhoAmP 91*
**Dunn,** Randy Edwin 1954- *WhoAmL 92*
**Dunn,** Raymond Elmer, Jr. 1956- *WhoFI 92*
**Dunn,** Richard *LesBEnT 92*
**Dunn,** Richard Anthony 1963- *WhoFI 92*
**Dunn,** Richard B 1927- *AmMWSc 92*
**Dunn,** Richard Johann 1943- *Who 92*
**Dunn,** Richard Joseph 1924- *WhoFI 92*
**Dunn,** Richard Lee 1940- *AmMWSc 92*
**Dunn,** Richard Maxwell 1942- *WhoFI 92*
**Dunn,** Richard S. 1928- *ConAu 134*
**Dunn,** Richard Wayne 1957- *WhoRel 92*
**Dunn,** Rick Dwayne 1961- *WhoWest 92*
**Dunn,** Ricky Robert 1948- *WhoRel 92*
**Dunn,** Robert *DrAPF 91*
**Dunn,** Robert Bruce 1943- *AmMWSc 92*
**Dunn,** Robert G 1923- *WhoAmP 91*
**Dunn,** Robert Garvin 1917- *AmMWSc 92*
**Dunn,** Robert Howard 1948- *WhoMW 92*
**Dunn,** Robert James *AmMWSc 92*
**Dunn,** Robert John 1946- *Who 92*
**Dunn,** Robert John 1950- *WhoMW 92*
**Dunn,** Robert Sigler 1926- *WhoMW 92*
**Dunn,** Robin Horace Walford 1918- *Who 92*
**Dunn,** Ronald Holland 1937- *WhoFI 92*
**Dunn,** Ronald Leslie 1954- *WhoAmL 92*
**Dunn,** Ross *WhoBlA 92*
**Dunn,** S. Watson 1918- *WrDr 92*
**Dunn,** Samuel L 1940- *AmMWSc 92*
**Dunn,** Sandy Lee 1958- *WhoEnt 92*
**Dunn,** Stanley Austin 1921- *AmMWSc 92*
**Dunn,** Stephen *DrAPF 91*
**Dunn,** Stephen 1939- *ConPo 91, WrDr 92*
**Dunn,** Steven Allen 1948- *WhoWest 92*
**Dunn,** Stuart Thomas 1940- *WhoWest 92*
**Dunn,** Susan 1954- *WhoEnt 92*
**Dunn,** T. R. 1955- *WhoBlA 92*
**Dunn,** Ted Lawrence 1926- *WhoIns 92*
**Dunn,** Theresa Rose 1962- *WhoFI 92*
**Dunn,** Thomas 1925- *NewAmDM*
**Dunn,** Thomas Aquinas 1942- *WhoAmP 91, WhoMW 92*
**Dunn,** Thomas G *WhoAmP 91*
**Dunn,** Thomas Guy 1935- *AmMWSc 92*
**Dunn,** Thomas M 1929- *AmMWSc 92*
**Dunn,** Thomas Tinsley 1901- *WhoAmL 92*
**Dunn,** Virginia Rose 1940- *WhoFI 92*
**Dunn,** Vivian *Who 92*
**Dunn,** W Carleton 1932- *WhoIns 92*
**Dunn,** W. Michael 1940- *WhoAmL 92*
**Dunn,** W. Paul 1938- *WhoBlA 92*
**Dunn,** Wallace Burton 1940- *WhoAmL 92*
**Dunn,** Warren Howard 1934- *WhoFI 92*
**Dunn,** Wendell Earl, III 1945- *WhoFI 92*
**Dunn,** Wesley B 1951- *WhoAmP 91*
**Dunn,** William Arthur, Jr 1953- *AmMWSc 92*
**Dunn,** William Bradley 1939- *WhoAmL 92*
**Dunn,** William Francis N. *Who 92*
**Dunn,** William Howard 1942- *AmMWSc 92*
**Dunn,** William Hubert 1933- *Who 92*
**Dunn,** William Joseph 1941- *AmMWSc 92*
**Dunn,** William L. 1919- *WhoBlA 92*
**Dunn,** William L. 1936- *WhoFI 92*
**Dunn,** William Lawrie 1927- *AmMWSc 92*
**Dunn-Barker,** Lillian Joyce 1938- *WhoBlA 92*
**Dunn Madden,** Anne Marie 1945- *WhoRel 92*
**Dunn-Rankin,** Peter 1929- *WhoWest 92*
**Dunnachie,** James Francis 1930- *Who 92*
**Dunnam,** Francis Eugene, Jr 1931- *AmMWSc 92*
**Dunnam,** Spurgeon M., III 1943- *WhoRel 92*
**Dunnavant,** Anthony LeRoy 1954- *WhoRel 92*
**Dunnavant,** Ezra LeRoy 1924- *WhoRel 92*
**Dunnavant,** William Rexford 1931- *WhoMW 92*
**Dunnaville,** C. Christopher 1961- *WhoFI 92*
**Dunnaville,** Clarence M., Jr. 1933- *WhoBlA 92*
**Dunne,** Carol *DrAPF 91*
**Dunne,** Cindy Lou 1947- *WhoEnt 92*
**Dunne,** Dana Philip C. 1963- *WhoFI 92*
**Dunne,** Diane C. *WhoFI 92*
**Dunne,** Dominick *IntMPA 92*
**Dunne,** Dominick 1925?- *ConTFT 9, IntAu&W 91, WrDr 92*
**Dunne,** Finley Peter 1867-1936 *BenetAL 91, DcAmImH*
**Dunne,** Gerald Thomas 1919- *WhoAmL 92*
**Dunne,** Griffin 1955- *IntMPA 92*
**Dunne,** Irene 1898-1990 *AnObit 1990*
**Dunne,** Irene Marie 1898-1990 *FacFETw [port]*
**Dunne,** John Augustine 1871-1920 *BiInAmS*
**Dunne,** John Gregory *FacFETw*
**Dunne,** John Gregory 1932- *BenetAL 91, ConNov 91, WrDr 92*
**Dunne,** John Richard 1930- *WhoAmL 92, WhoAmP 91*
**Dunne,** John S. 1929- *WrDr 92*
**Dunne,** Joseph James 1926- *WhoRel 92*
**Dunne,** Michael W. 1955- *WhoEnt 92*
**Dunne,** Patrick d1988 *Who 92N*
**Dunne,** Philip 1908- *IntMPA 92, WhoEnt 92*
**Dunne,** Sean Anthony 1926- *WhoRel 92*
**Dunne,** Thomas 1943- *AmMWSc 92, WhoWest 92*
**Dunne,** Thomas Gregory 1930- *AmMWSc 92*
**Dunne,** Thomas Raymond 1933- *Who 92*
**Dunnebacke-Dixon,** Thelma Hudson 1925- *AmMWSc 92, WhoWest 92*
**Dunner,** David Louis 1940- *AmMWSc 92*

**Dunner,** Donald Robert 1931- *WhoAmL 92*
**Dunner,** Leslie B. 1956- *WhoBlA 92*
**Dunner,** Leslie Byron 1956- *WhoEnt 92*
**Dunnery,** John Anthony 1957- *WhoAmL 92*
**Dunnet,** George Mackenzie 1928- *Who 92*
**Dunnett,** Alastair M. 1908- *WrDr 92*
**Dunnett,** Alastair MacTavish 1908- *IntAu&W 91, IntWW 91, Who 92*
**Dunnett,** Charles William 1921- *AmMWSc 92*
**Dunnett,** Dennis George 1939- *WhoWest 92*
**Dunnett,** Denzil Inglis 1917- *Who 92*
**Dunnett,** Dorothy 1923- *ConNov 91, IntAu&W 91, WrDr 92*
**Dunnett,** Jack 1922- *Who 92*
**Dunnett,** James 1914- *Who 92*
**Dunnett,** Walter McGregor 1924- *WhoRel 92*
**Dunnette,** Marvin Dale 1926- *WhoMW 92*
**Dunnevant,** Emmett Douglas 1924- *WhoRel 92*
**Dunnewald,** David Alan 1960- *WhoFI 92*
**Dunnick,** June K *AmMWSc 92*
**Dunnigan,** Alice 1906-1983 *NotBlAW 92*
**Dunnigan,** Jacques 1935- *AmMWSc 92*
**Dunnigan,** Jerry 1941- *WhoBlA 92*
**Dunnigan,** Mary Ann 1915- *WhoWest 92*
**Dunnigan,** T. Kevin 1938- *WhoFI 92*
**Dunning,** Barbara Renkens *DrAPF 91*
**Dunning,** Carole Sue 1949- *WhoWest 92*
**Dunning,** Charles Hager 1953- *WhoEnt 92*
**Dunning,** Dorothy Covalt 1937- *AmMWSc 92*
**Dunning,** Ernest Leon 1920- *AmMWSc 92*
**Dunning,** Frank Barrymore 1945- *AmMWSc 92*
**Dunning,** Herbert Neal 1923- *AmMWSc 92*
**Dunning,** Hubert Ray 1926- *WhoRel 92*
**Dunning,** James M. d1991 *NewYTBS 91*
**Dunning,** James Morse 1904- *AmMWSc 92*
**Dunning,** Jeremy David 1951- *AmMWSc 92, WhoMW 92*
**Dunning,** John Ernest Patrick 1912- *Who 92*
**Dunning,** John H. 1927- *WrDr 92*
**Dunning,** John Harry 1927- *Who 92*
**Dunning,** John Ray 1907-1975 *FacFETw*
**Dunning,** John Ray, Jr 1937- *AmMWSc 92*
**Dunning,** John Walcott 1912- *AmMWSc 92*
**Dunning,** John Wallace 1939- *WhoRel 92*
**Dunning,** Joseph 1920- *Who 92*
**Dunning,** Kenneth Laverne 1914- *AmMWSc 92, WhoWest 92*
**Dunning,** Lawrence *DrAPF 91*
**Dunning,** Lawrence 1931- *IntAu&W 91*
**Dunning,** Lynn Eugene 1947- *WhoWest 92*
**Dunning,** Paris Chipman 1806-1884 *DcNCBi 2*
**Dunning,** Ranald G 1902- *AmMWSc 92*
**Dunning,** Richard Scarborough 1950- *Who 92*
**Dunning,** Robert L, Sr *WhoAmP 91*
**Dunning,** Roosevelt 1924- *WhoBlA 92*
**Dunning,** Simon 1939- *Who 92*
**Dunning,** Stephen *DrAPF 91*
**Dunning,** Thomas Harold, Jr 1943- *AmMWSc 92*
**Dunning,** Wilhelmina Frances 1904- *AmMWSc 92*
**Dunnington-Jefferson,** Mervyn 1943- *Who 92*
**Dunnock,** Mildred 1901-1991 *CurBio 91N, NewYTBS 91 [port]*
**Dunnuck,** Samuel R, III 1947- *WhoAmP 91*
**Dunny,** Stanley 1939- *AmMWSc 92*
**Dunoyer,** Philippe 1930- *WhoFI 92, WhoWest 92*
**Dunpark,** Lord d1991 *Who 92N*
**Dunphie,** Charles 1902- *Who 92*
**Dunphy,** Donal 1917- *AmMWSc 92*
**Dunphy,** James Francis 1930- *AmMWSc 92*
**Dunraven and Mount-Earl,** Earl of 1939- *Who 92*
**Dunrossil,** Viscount 1926- *IntWW 91, Who 92*
**Duns Scotus,** John 1266?-1308 *DcLB 115 [port]*
**Dunsany,** Baron 1906- *Who 92*
**Dunsany,** Lord 1878-1957 *RfGEnL 91, ScFEYrs, TwCSFW 91*
**Dunsany,** Edward John Drax Plunkett, Lord 1878-1957 *FacFETw*
**Dunshee,** Bryant R 1921- *AmMWSc 92*
**Dunsing,** Marilyn Magdalene 1926- *AmMWSc 92*
**Dunsire,** Peter Kenneth 1932- *WhoFI 92, WhoMW 92*
**Dunsirn,** Brian Lee 1958- *WhoFI 92*
**Dunsmore,** Elizabeth M 1913- *WhoAmP 91*
**Dunsmore,** George M 1942- *WhoAmP 91*
**Dunson,** Carrie Lee 1946- *WhoBlA 92*
**Dunson,** William Albert 1941- *AmMWSc 92*
**Dunst,** Laurence David 1941- *WhoFI 92*
**Dunstable,** John 1390?-1453 *NewAmDM*
**Dunstan,** Bernard 1920- *IntWW 91, TwCPaSc, Who 92*
**Dunstan,** Donald 1923- *Who 92*
**Dunstan,** Donald Allan 1926- *IntWW 91, Who 92*
**Dunstan,** Gordon Reginald 1917- *IntWW 91, Who 92*
**Dunstan,** Ivan 1930- *Who 92*
**Dunstan,** Larry Kenneth 1948- *WhoWest 92*
**Dunstan,** Robert Owen 1927- *WhoAmP 91*
**Dunstan,** William Morgan 1935- *AmMWSc 92*
**Dunster,** John 1922- *Who 92*
**Dunston,** Alfred G. 1915- *WhoBlA 92*
**Dunston,** Alfred Gilbert, Jr. 1915- *WhoRel 92*
**Dunston,** Leonard G. 1940- *WhoBlA 92*
**Dunston,** Shawon Donnell 1963- *WhoBlA 92*
**Dunston,** Victor 1926- *WhoBlA 92*
**Dunston,** Walter T. 1935- *WhoBlA 92*
**Dunstone,** Brian 1943- *TwCPaSc*
**Dunton,** Franklin Roy 1921- *WhoAmP 91*
**Dunton,** John 1659-1733 *BenetAL 91*
**Duntze,** Daniel 1926- *Who 92*
**Dunwich,** Bishop Suffragan of 1926- *Who 92*
**Dunwich,** Viscount 1961- *Who 92*
**Dunwoody,** Dana James 1959- *WhoAmL 92*
**Dunwoody,** Gwyneth 1930- *Who 92*
**Dunwoody,** John 1929- *Who 92*
**Dunwoody,** Sharon Lee 1947- *AmMWSc 92*
**Dunworth,** John Vernon 1917- *IntWW 91, Who 92*
**Duo Duo** 1951- *LiExTwC*
**Duparc,** Henri 1848-1933 *NewAmDM*
**Dupas,** Mark Kirby 1959- *WhoBlA 92*
**Duper,** Mark Super 1959- *WhoBlA 92*
**Duperon,** Donald Francis 1937- *AmMWSc 92*
**Duperron,** Bella 1926- *WhoAmP 91*
**du Perry,** Jean *ConAu 35NR*
**Dupin,** Clyde Clement 1933- *WhoRel 92*
**Duplantier,** Adrian Guy 1929- *WhoAmL 92*
**Du Plessis,** Barend Jacobus 1940- *IntWW 91, Who 92*
**Du Plessis,** Christian 1944- *IntWW 91*
**Du Plessis,** Daniel Jacob 1918- *IntWW 91, Who 92*
**Du Plessis,** David J. 1905-1987 *DcEcMov*
**Du Plessis,** David Johannes 1905-1987 *RelLAm 91*
**Duplessis,** Harry Y. 1915- *WhoBlA 92*
**du Plessis,** Nancy *DrAPF 91*
**Du Plessis,** Pieter Christiaan 1935- *IntWW 91*
**DuPlessis,** Rachel Blau *DrAPF 91*
**Duplessis,** Susan Dubay 1956- *WhoAmP 91*
**Duplissea,** William Patrick 1950- *WhoAmP 91*
**Du Ponceau,** Pierre Etienne 1760-1844 *BenetAL 91*
**Dupond,** Patrick *WhoEnt 92*
**Dupong,** Jean 1922- *IntWW 91*
**du Pont,** Alfred I 1864-1935 *RComAH*
**Dupont,** Andre Guy *AmMWSc 92*
**duPont,** Augustus Irenee 1951- *WhoAmL 92*
**Dupont,** Bo 1941- *AmMWSc 92*
**Dupont,** Claire Hammel 1933- *AmMWSc 92*
**DuPont,** Clifford W 1905-1978 *FacFETw*
**Dupont,** Colyer Lee 1957- *WhoEnt 92, WhoWest 92*
**Dupont,** E. A. 1891-1956 *IntDcF 2-2*
**Dupont,** Edward Charles, Jr 1950- *WhoAmP 91*
**DuPont,** Eleuthere Irenee 1771-1834 *BiInAmS*
**Du Pont,** Frances Marguerite 1944- *AmMWSc 92*
**DuPont,** Francis Gurney 1850-1905 *BiInAmS*
**DuPont,** Herbert Lancashire 1938- *AmMWSc 92*
**Dupont,** Jacqueline 1934- *AmMWSc 92*
**Dupont,** Jacques-Bernard 1922- *IntWW 91*
**DuPont,** James Benjamen 1953- *WhoAmP 91*
**Dupont,** John 1948- *WhoEnt 92*
**DuPont,** Michael Richard 1961- *WhoAmL 92*
**Dupont,** Monica 1948- *WhoEnt 92*
**Dupont,** Paul Emile 1941- *AmMWSc 92*
**Du Pont,** Pierre Samuel 1935- *WhoAmP 91*
**du Pont,** Pierre Samuel, IV 1935- *IntWW 91*
**Dupont,** Ralph Paul 1929- *WhoAmL 92*
**Dupont,** Richard G 1943- *WhoAmP 91*
**DuPont,** Robert L, Jr 1936- *AmMWSc 92*
**DuPont,** Robert Louis 1936- *WhoAmP 91*
**Dupont,** Todd F 1942- *AmMWSc 92*
**Dupont,** William Dudley 1946- *AmMWSc 92*
**Dupont de Nemours,** Pierre Samuel 1739-1817 *BlkwCEP*
**DuPont-Morales,** Maria A. Toni 1948- *WhoHisp 92*
**Duppa-Miller,** John Bryan Peter *Who 92*
**Dupplin,** Viscount 1962- *Who 92*
**Duppong,** Margie Ann Claus 1939- *WhoMW 92*
**Duprat,** Francois 1940-1978 *BiDExR*
**Dupre,** Catherine *IntAu&W 91*
**Du Pre,** Donald Bates 1942- *AmMWSc 92*
**Dupre,** Emilo Joseph 1945- *WhoAmP 91, WhoBlA 92*
**Dupre,** Heidi Hildegard 1942- *WhoWest 92*
**Du Pre,** Jacqueline 1945-1985 *NewAmDM*
**Du Pre,** Jacqueline 1945-1987 *FacFETw*
**DuPre,** John L. 1953- *WhoRel 92*
**Dupre,** John Lionel 1953- *WhoBlA 92*
**Dupre,** Louis *IntAu&W 91, WrDr 92*
**Dupre,** Marcel 1886-1971 *NewAmDM*
**Dupre,** Thomas L. 1933- *WhoRel 92*
**Dupree,** Andrea K 1939- *AmMWSc 92*
**Dupree,** Andrew Lane, Sr. 1956- *WhoEnt 92, WhoWest 92*
**DuPree,** Billy Joe 1950- *WhoBlA 92*
**DuPree,** Clifford H. R. 1950- *WhoAmL 92*
**Dupree,** Daniel Edward 1932- *AmMWSc 92*
**DuPree,** David 1946- *WhoBlA 92*
**Dupree,** David H. 1959- *WhoAmL 92, WhoBlA 92*
**DuPree,** Don Keck *DrAPF 91*
**Dupree,** Edward A. 1943- *WhoBlA 92*
**Dupree,** Harry K *AmMWSc 92*
**Dupree,** James William 1932- *WhoRel 92*
**Dupree,** Marcus 1964- *WhoBlA 92*
**Dupree,** Peter 1924- *Who 92*
**Dupree,** Sandra Kay 1956- *WhoBlA 92*
**DuPree,** Sherry Sherrod 1946- *WhoBlA 92*
**du Preez,** Ronald Alwyn Gerald 1951- *WhoRel 92*
**Duprey,** JoAnn 1945- *WhoAmP 91*
**Duprey,** Pierre 1922- *DcEcMov*
**Duprey,** Richard Lawrence 1962- *WhoAmP 91*
**Duprez,** Gilbert-Louis 1806-1896 *NewAmDM*
**DuPriest,** Douglas Millhollen 1951- *WhoAmL 92*
**Dupuch,** Etienne d1991 *Who 92N*
**Dupuis,** Adrian M. 1919- *WrDr 92*
**Du Puis,** George Bonello 1928- *IntWW 91*
**Dupuis,** Gilles 1943- *AmMWSc 92*
**Dupuis,** Josephine Mabel 1920- *WhoAmP 91*
**Dupuis,** Russell Dean 1947- *AmMWSc 92*
**Dupuis,** Sylvio Louis 1934- *WhoAmP 91*
**Dupuis,** Victor Edward 1960- *WhoFI 92*
**Dupuy,** Arnold C. 1962- *ConAu 135*
**DuPuy,** David Lorraine 1941- *AmMWSc 92*
**DuPuy,** Elbert Newton 1904- *WhoMW 92*
**Dupuy,** Eliza Ann 1814-1881 *BenetAL 91*
**Dupuy,** Harold Paul 1922- *AmMWSc 92*
**Dupuy,** Howard Moore, Jr. 1929- *WhoFI 92, WhoWest 92*
**Dupuy,** T N 1916- *IntAu&W 91, WrDr 92*
**Duque,** Henry McArthur 1931- *WhoWest 92*
**Duque,** Ricardo Ernesto 1944- *AmMWSc 92*
**Duquesne,** Jacques Henri Louis 1930- *IntWW 91*
**Duquesnoy,** Rene J 1938- *AmMWSc 92*
**Duquette,** Alfred L 1923- *AmMWSc 92*
**Duquette,** David J 1939- *AmMWSc 92*
**Duquette,** Diane Rhea 1951- *WhoWest 92*
**Duquette,** Donald Norman 1947- *WhoAmL 92*
**Duquette,** Donald Richard 1954- *WhoFI 92*
**Durac,** Jack *WrDr 92*
**Durack,** David Tulloch 1944- *AmMWSc 92*
**Durack,** Mary 1913- *IntAu&W 91, Who 92, WrDr 92*
**Duraczynski,** Donna Moore 1937- *WhoAmP 91*
**Durafour,** Michel Andre Francois 1920- *IntWW 91*
**Durai-Swamy,** Kandaswamy 1945- *AmMWSc 92*
**Duraiswamy,** Vijayalakshmi Diraviam *WhoAmL 92*
**Durall,** Dolis, Jr. 1943- *WhoBlA 92*
**Duran Duran** *NewAmDM*
**Duran,** Alfredo G. 1936- *WhoHisp 92*
**Duran,** Alfredo R. 1961- *WhoHisp 92*
**Duran,** Arthur Eligio 1937- *WhoHisp 92*
**Duran,** Benjamin S 1939- *AmMWSc 92, WhoHisp 92*
**Duran,** Beverly 1948- *WhoHisp 92*
**Duran,** Cathy L. 1946- *WhoHisp 92*
**Duran,** David 1950- *WhoHisp 92*
**Duran,** Dianna J. 1955- *WhoHisp 92*
**Duran,** Dick 1935- *WhoHisp 92*
**Duran,** Diego 1537-1588 *HisDSpE*
**Duran,** Elena 1948- *WhoHisp 92*
**Duran,** Jess 1953- *WhoHisp 92*
**Duran,** Julio C. 1937- *WhoHisp 92*
**Duran,** June Clark 1919- *WhoAmP 91*
**Duran,** Karin Jeanine 1948- *WhoHisp 92*
**Duran,** Lois Janine 1952- *WhoAmL 92*
**Duran,** Massimiliano *WhoHisp 92*
**Duran,** Michael Carl 1953- *WhoWest 92*
**Duran,** Michael S. 1958- *WhoHisp 92*
**Duran,** Natalie 1955- *WhoHisp 92*
**Duran,** Noel Ruben 1954- *WhoEnt 92*
**Duran,** Philip 1936- *WhoHisp 92*
**Duran,** Richard 1949- *WhoWest 92*
**Duran,** Richard Fierro *WhoHisp 92*
**Duran,** Roberto 1951- *IntWW 91, WhoHisp 92*
**Duran,** Ruben 1924- *AmMWSc 92*
**Duran,** Servet A 1920- *AmMWSc 92*
**Duran,** Tino *WhoHisp 92*
**Duran,** Victor Manuel 1947- *WhoHisp 92*
**Duran,** Walter Nunez 1942- *AmMWSc 92*
**Duran Salguero,** Carlos 1956- *WhoHisp 92*
**Durand,** Ann Marwood d1694? *DcNCBi 2*
**Durand,** Bernice Black 1942- *AmMWSc 92*
**Durand,** Charles *ThHEIm*
**Durand,** Dickon 1934- *Who 92*
**Durand,** Donald P 1929- *AmMWSc 92*
**Durand,** Edward Allen 1919- *AmMWSc 92*
**Durand,** Elias 1794-1873 *BiInAmS*
**Durand,** George 1632-1693? *DcNCBi 2*
**Durand,** Guy 1933- *WhoRel 92*
**Durand,** Hugo G 1930- *WhoAmP 91*
**Durand,** James Blanchard 1929- *AmMWSc 92*
**Durand,** Loyal 1931- *AmMWSc 92*
**Durand,** Marc L 1940- *AmMWSc 92*
**Durand,** Marie Auguste 1830-1909 *NewAmDM*
**Durand,** Ralph *ScFEYrs*
**Durand,** Ralph Anthony 1876-1945 *ScFEYrs*
**Durand,** Ralph Edward 1947- *AmMWSc 92*
**Durand,** Robert A *WhoAmP 91*
**Durand,** Shawn Phillip 1955- *WhoMW 92*
**Durand,** Victor Albert Charles *Who 92*
**Durand,** Whitney 1942- *WhoAmL 92*
**Durand,** William Frederick 1859-1958 *FacFETw*
**Durand,** Winsley, Jr. 1941- *WhoBlA 92*
**Durand-Rival,** Pierre J. H. 1930- *IntWW 91*
**Durand-Ruel,** Paul 1831-1922 *ThHEIm*
**Durang,** Christopher 1949- *WrDr 92*
**Durant,** Anita 1938- *WhoBlA 92*
**Durant,** Ann Marwood d1694? *DcNCBi 2*
**Durant,** Anthony *Who 92*
**Durant,** Ariel 1898-1981 *FacFETw*
**Durant,** Ariel K. 1898-1981 *BenetAL 91*
**Durant,** Celeste Millicent 1947- *WhoBlA 92*
**Durant,** Charles E. 1949- *WhoMW 92*
**Durant,** Charles Ferson 1805-1873 *BiInAmS*
**Durant,** David N 1925- *IntAu&W 91*
**Durant,** David Norton 1925- *WrDr 92*
**Durant,** George 1632-1693? *DcNCBi 2*
**Durant,** John 1662-1699? *DcNCBi 2*
**Durant,** John Alexander, III 1939- *AmMWSc 92*
**Durant,** John Ridgway 1930- *AmMWSc 92*
**Durant,** John Robert 1950- *Who 92*
**Durant,** Marc 1947- *WhoAmL 92*
**Durant,** Naomi C. 1938- *WhoBlA 92*
**Durant,** Robert Anthony 1928- *Who 92*
**DuRant,** Robert Marvin 1922- *WhoEnt 92*
**Durant,** Stanton Vincent 1942- *Who 92*
**Durant,** Thomas James, Jr. 1941- *WhoBlA 92*
**Durant,** Will 1885-1981 *BenetAL 91, FacFETw*
**Durant-Paige,** Beverly 1954- *WhoBlA 92*
**Durante,** Anthony Joseph 1943- *AmMWSc 92*
**Durante,** Jimmy d1980 *LesBEnT 92*
**Durante,** Jimmy 1893-1980 *FacFETw*
**Durante,** Vincent Anthony 1950- *AmMWSc 92*
**Durante,** Viviana Paola 1967- *IntWW 91*
**Duranti,** Francesca 1935- *ConAu 133*
**Duranty,** Louis Edmond 1833-1880 *ThHEIm*
**Duranty,** Walter 1884-1957 *BenetAL 91*
**Duras,** Claire de 1777-1828 *FrenWW*
**Duras,** Marguerite *IntAu&W 91, Who 92*
**Duras,** Marguerite 1914- *ConLC 68 [port], FacFETw, FrenWW, GuFrLit 1, IntDcF 2-2 [port], IntWW 91, NewYTBS 91 [port], ReelWom*
**Duras,** Victor Hugo 1880-1943 *AmPeW*
**Durasov,** Vladimir Aleksandrovich 1935- *IntWW 91*
**Durate,** Geneva M. 1949- *WhoHisp 92*
**Duray,** John R 1940- *AmMWSc 92*

**Durazo,** Guillermo, Jr. 1952- *WhoWest 92*
**Durazo,** Maria Elena *WhoHisp 92*
**Durazo,** Raymond 1942- *WhoHisp 92*
**Durban,** Pam *DrAPF 91*
**Durband,** Alan 1927- *IntAu&W 91, WrDr 92*
**Durbeck,** Robert C 1935- *AmMWSc 92*
**Durbetaki,** N. John 1955- *WhoWest 92*
**Durbetaki,** Pandeli 1928- *AmMWSc 92*
**Durbin,** Enoch Job 1922- *AmMWSc 92*
**Durbin,** Gregory 1950- *WhoEnt 92*
**Durbin,** James 1923- *Who 92*
**Durbin,** John Riley 1935- *AmMWSc 92*
**Durbin,** Leonel Damien 1935- *AmMWSc 92*
**Durbin,** Leslie 1913- *Who 92*
**Durbin,** Paul Thomas 1933- *AmMWSc 92*
**Durbin,** Richard Duane 1930- *AmMWSc 92*
**Durbin,** Richard J. 1944- *AlmAP 92 [port]*
**Durbin,** Richard Joseph 1944- *WhoAmP 91, WhoMW 92*
**Durbin,** Richard Louis, Jr. 1955- *WhoAmL 92*
**Durbin,** Ronald Priestley 1939- *AmMWSc 92*
**Durbin,** Rosamond 1952- *WhoMW 92*
**Durbin,** Timothy Terrell 1957- *WhoEnt 92*
**Durbney,** Clydrow John 1916- *WhoRel 92*
**Durborow,** Carol Ross *WhoEnt 92*
**Durbridge,** Francis 1912- *IntAu&W 91, Who 92, WrDr 92*
**Durcan,** Paul 1944- *ConAu 134, ConPo 91, IntAu&W 91, WrDr 92*
**Durcansky,** Ferdinand 1906-1974 *BiDExR*
**Durchslag,** Stephen P. 1940- *WhoAmL 92*
**Durda,** Daniel Joseph 1948- *WhoMW 92*
**Durdek,** Franne Alyce 1947- *WhoEnt 92*
**Durden,** Christopher John 1940- *AmMWSc 92*
**Durden,** David Alan 1943- *AmMWSc 92*
**Durden,** Earnel 1937- *WhoBlA 92*
**Durden,** John Apling, Jr 1928- *AmMWSc 92*
**Durden,** Robert F. 1925- *WrDr 92*
**Durden,** Robert Franklin 1925- *IntAu&W 91*
**Durden,** Robert J. 1947- *WhoAmL 92*
**Durden,** William L. *WhoAmL 92*
**Durdenevsky,** Vsevolod Nikolaevich 1889-1963 *SovUnBD*
**Durdey,** Edward 1954- *TwCPaSc*
**Durdik,** Jeannine Marie 1954- *WhoWest 92*
**Dure,** Leon S, III 1931- *AmMWSc 92*
**Durell,** Ann 1930- *SmATA 66*
**Duren,** Ann Marwood d1694? *DcNCBi 2*
**Duren,** Emma Thompson 1925- *WhoBlA 92*
**Duren,** George 1632-1693? *DcNCBi 2*
**Duren,** John 1662-1699? *DcNCBi 2*
**Duren,** John Wayne 1942- *WhoMW 92*
**Duren,** Leoatis 1936- *WhoRel 92*
**Duren,** Peter Larkin 1935- *AmMWSc 92, WhoMW 92*
**Durenberger,** Dave 1934- *AlmAP 92 [port]*
**Durenberger,** David F 1934- *WhoAmP 91*
**Durenberger,** David Ferdinand 1934- *IntWW 91, WhoMW 92*
**Duret,** Theodore 1838-1927 *ThHEIm [port]*
**Durette,** Philippe Lionel 1944- *AmMWSc 92*
**Durey,** Peter Burrell 1932- *IntWW 91*
**Durfee,** David Rising 1934- *WhoFI 92*
**Durfee,** Harold Allen 1920- *WhoRel 92*
**Durfee,** John B. *WhoRel 92*
**Durfee,** Raphael B 1918- *AmMWSc 92*
**Durfee,** Raymond M 1922- *WhoAmP 91*
**Durfee,** Robert Lewis 1936- *AmMWSc 92*
**Durfee,** Wayne King 1924- *AmMWSc 92*
**Durfee,** William Hetherington 1915- *AmMWSc 92*
**D'Urfey,** Thomas 1653-1723 *RfGEnL 91*
**Durflinger,** Elizabeth Ward 1913- *AmMWSc 92*
**Durflinger,** Jeffrey Duane 1961- *WhoWest 92*
**Durgan,** Andrew James 1922- *WhoBlA 92*
**Durgautti** *EncAmaz 91*
**Durgawati** *EncAmaz 91*
**Durgin,** Diane 1946- *WhoAmL 92, WhoFI 92*
**Durgin,** Don *LesBEnT 92*
**Durgin,** William W 1942- *AmMWSc 92*
**Durgin-Wiggins,** Maud Ann 1925- *WhoAmP 91*
**Durgnat,** Raymond 1932- *WrDr 92*
**Durgnat,** Raymond Eric 1932- *IntAu&W 91*
**Durgom-Powers,** Jane E. 1948- *WhoAmL 92*
**Durham,** Archdeacon of *Who 92*
**Durham,** Baron 1961- *Who 92*
**Durham,** Bishop of 1925- *Who 92*
**Durham,** Dean of *Who 92*
**Durham,** Earl of *Who 92*
**Durham,** Arthur Lee 1951- *WhoEnt 92*
**Durham,** Barbara 1942- *WhoAmL 92, WhoAmP 91, WhoWest 92*
**Durham,** Barbee William 1910- *WhoBlA 92*
**Durham,** Bennie Lewis 1958- *WhoRel 92*
**Durham,** Billy Gene, Jr. 1953- *WhoEnt 92*
**Durham,** Carey Winston 1897- *WhoBlA 92*
**Durham,** Carl Thomas 1892-1974 *DcNCBi 2*
**Durham,** Carroll 1937- *WhoEnt 92*
**Durham,** Christine 1945- *WhoAmP 91*
**Durham,** Christine Meaders 1945- *WhoAmL 92, WhoWest 92*
**Durham,** Clarence Orson, Jr 1920- *AmMWSc 92*
**Durham,** Columbus 1844-1895 *DcNCBi 2*
**Durham,** Eddie L., Sr. 1946- *WhoBlA 92*
**Durham,** Edward 1965- *WhoEnt 92*
**Durham,** Frank Edington 1935- *AmMWSc 92*
**Durham,** Franklin P 1921- *AmMWSc 92*
**Durham,** George Stone 1912- *AmMWSc 92*
**Durham,** Harry Blaine, III 1946- *WhoWest 92*
**Durham,** Harvey Ralph 1938- *AmMWSc 92*
**Durham,** James Ivey 1933- *AmMWSc 92*
**Durham,** James Michael, Sr. 1937- *WhoFI 92, WhoMW 92*
**Durham,** James Stafford 1956- *WhoRel 92*
**Durham,** James W. 1937- *WhoAmL 92, WhoFI 92*
**Durham,** John *TwCWW 91*
**Durham,** John Wyatt 1907- *AmMWSc 92*
**Durham,** Joseph Thomas 1923- *WhoBlA 92*
**Durham,** Kathrynann 1951- *WhoAmP 91*
**Durham,** Kenneth 1924- *IntWW 91, Who 92*
**Durham,** Kenneth Joe 1953- *WhoMW 92*
**Durham,** Leon 1957- *WhoBlA 92*
**Durham,** Leonard 1925- *AmMWSc 92*
**Durham,** Lois Jean 1931- *AmMWSc 92*
**Durham,** M. Freeman 1958- *WhoAmL 92*
**Durham,** Marilyn *DrAPF 91*
**Durham,** Marilyn 1930- *TwCWW 91, WrDr 92*
**Durham,** Michael Dean 1949- *AmMWSc 92*
**Durham,** Michael Jonathan 1951- *WhoFI 92*
**Durham,** Nicolene Angela 1947- *WhoRel 92*
**Durham,** Norman Nevill 1927- *AmMWSc 92*
**Durham,** Plato 1840-1875 *DcNCBi 2*
**Durham,** Richard Monroe 1954- *WhoAmL 92*
**Durham,** Robert Earl 1930- *WhoEnt 92*
**Durham,** Ross M 1930- *AmMWSc 92*
**Durham,** Sidney Down 1943- *WhoAmL 92*
**Durham,** Stephen K 1949- *AmMWSc 92*
**Durham,** Steven Jackson 1947- *WhoAmP 91*
**Durham,** Susan B 1939- *WhoAmP 91*
**Durham,** Terry 1936- *TwCPaSc*
**Durham,** Warren John 1925- *WhoEnt 92*
**Durham,** William Andrew 1956- *WhoAmL 92*
**Durham,** William Bryan 1947- *AmMWSc 92*
**Durham,** William Fay 1922- *AmMWSc 92*
**Durham,** William H. 1873-1912 *RelLAm 91*
**Durham,** William Harold *ScFEYrs*
**Durham,** William R. 1945- *WhoBlA 92*
**Durica,** Thomas Edward 1942- *AmMWSc 92*
**Durie,** Alexander 1915- *Who 92*
**Durie,** David Robert Campbell 1944- *Who 92*
**Durie,** Jack Frederick, Jr. 1944- *WhoAmL 92*
**Durieux,** Mademoiselle *EncAmaz 91*
**Durig,** James Robert 1935- *AmMWSc 92*
**Duringer,** Jacob Clyde 1956- *WhoWest 92*
**Durio,** Walter O'Neal 1938- *AmMWSc 92*
**Durisen,** Richard H 1946- *AmMWSc 92*
**Durkan,** James P 1934- *AmMWSc 92*
**Durkan,** Jenny Anne 1958- *WhoAmL 92*
**Durkan,** Joseph Daniel *WhoFI 92*
**Durkay,** John Joseph 1946- *WhoAmL 92*
**Durkee,** Jackson L 1922- *AmMWSc 92*
**Durkee,** LaVerne H 1927- *AmMWSc 92*
**Durkee,** Lenore T 1932- *AmMWSc 92*
**Durkee,** Sarah Bruce 1955- *WhoEnt 92*
**Durkee,** Silas 1798-1878 *BiInAmS*
**Durket,** Steven Lorne 1960- *WhoAmL 92*
**Durkheim,** Emile 1858-1917 *FacFETw*
**Durkin,** Debra Elizabeth 1952- *WhoEnt 92*
**Durkin,** Dominic J 1930- *AmMWSc 92*
**Durkin,** Helen Germaine *AmMWSc 92*
**Durkin,** Herbert 1922- *Who 92*
**Durkin,** Jerry Martin 1959- *WhoEnt 92*
**Durkin,** John A *WhoAmP 91*
**Durkin,** John Quinn 1947- *WhoAmL 92*
**Durkin,** Martin Anthony, Jr. 1957- *WhoAmL 92*
**Durkin,** Martin Patrick 1894-1955 *AmPolLe*
**Durkin,** Martin Timothy 1949- *WhoIns 92*
**Durkin,** Mary Lewis 1945- *WhoMW 92*
**Durkin,** Patrick Ralph 1946- *AmMWSc 92*
**Durkin,** Raymond Michael 1936- *WhoAmP 91*
**Durko,** George Paul, Jr. 1961- *WhoFI 92*
**Durko,** Zsolt 1934- *ConCom 92, IntWW 91*
**Durkot,** Michael John *AmMWSc 92*
**Durkovic,** Russell George 1940- *AmMWSc 92*
**Durland,** John R 1914- *AmMWSc 92*
**Durley,** Alexander 1912- *WhoBlA 92*
**Durley,** Richard Charles 1943- *AmMWSc 92*
**Durling,** Allen E 1934- *AmMWSc 92*
**Durling,** Robert Marlowe 1929- *WhoWest 92*
**Durman,** Kenneth Thomas 1920- *WhoRel 92*
**Durmann,** Glenn George 1947- *WhoAmL 92*
**Durn,** Raymond Joseph 1925- *WhoAmL 92*
**Durnbaugh,** Donald F. 1927- *WrDr 92*
**Durnbaugh,** Donald Floyd 1927- *WhoRel 92*
**Durney,** Carl H 1931- *AmMWSc 92*
**Durney,** Joseph James, Jr. 1955- *WhoAmL 92*
**Durney,** Michael Cavalier 1943- *WhoAmL 92*
**Durnford,** Robert F 1922- *AmMWSc 92*
**Durnick,** Thomas Jackson 1946- *AmMWSc 92*
**Durnil,** Gordon K 1936- *WhoAmP 91*
**Durnil,** Gordon Kay 1936- *WhoMW 92*
**Durnil,** John Michael 1961- *WhoMW 92*
**Durning,** Charles 1923- *WhoEnt 92*
**Durning,** Charles 1933- *IntMPA 92*
**Durning,** William Pershing 1918- *WhoWest 92*
**Durno,** John Dregge 1936- *WhoFI 92*
**Durnovo,** Peter Nikolayevich 1844-1915 *FacFETw*
**Duro,** Akin 1941- *WhoBlA 92*
**Durocher,** Daniel Leonard 1948- *WhoAmL 92*
**Du Rocher,** James Howard 1945- *WhoAmL 92*
**Durocher,** Leo 1905- *FacFETw*
**Durocher,** Leo 1905-1991 *NewYTBS 91 [port], News 92-2*
**Durocher,** Leo 1906-1991 *CurBio 91N*
**Durocher-Kaminski,** Bruno Bronislaw 1919- *IntAu&W 91*
**Durojaiye,** Prince 1931- *WhoBlA 92*
**Duron,** Armando 1954- *WhoHisp 92*
**Duron,** Eric Raymond 1960- *WhoWest 92*
**Duron,** Susan Budde 1947- *WhoWest 92*
**Duron,** Ysabel 1947- *WhoHisp 92*
**Duron,** Ziyad H. 1959- *WhoHisp 92*
**Duroni,** Charles Eugene 1933- *WhoAmL 92*
**DuRose,** Richard Arthur 1937- *WhoAmL 92*
**Duroselle,** Jean-Baptiste 1917- *IntWW 91*
**Duroy,** Edwin *WhoHisp 92*
**Durr,** Albert Matthew, Jr 1923- *AmMWSc 92*
**Durr,** Clifford J. d1975 *LesBEnT 92*
**Durr,** Friedrich 1933- *AmMWSc 92*
**Durr,** Heinz 1933- *IntWW 91*
**Durr,** Janis Joy 1947- *WhoEnt 92*
**Durr,** Kent Skelton 1941- *IntWW 91, Who 92*
**Durr,** Paul Rutledge 1959- *WhoAmL 92*
**Durr,** William K. 1924- *WrDr 92*
**Durrands,** Kenneth James 1929- *Who 92*
**Durrani,** Sajjad H 1928- *AmMWSc 92*
**Durrani,** Shakirullah 1928- *IntWW 91*
**Durrant,** Anthony Harrisson 1931- *Who 92*
**Durrant,** Barbara Susan 1949- *AmMWSc 92*
**Durrant,** Dean Oborn 1929- *WhoWest 92*
**Durrant,** James Thom d1990 *Who 92N*
**Durrant,** Jennifer 1942- *TwCPaSc*
**Durrant,** Jennifer Ann 1942- *IntWW 91*
**Durrant,** Roy Turner 1925- *TwCPaSc*
**Durrant,** William Henry Estridge 1901- *Who 92*
**Durrell,** Gerald 1925- *WrDr 92*
**Durrell,** Gerald Malcolm d1990 *IntWW 91N*
**Durrell,** Gerald Malcolm 1925- *IntAu&W 91, Who 92*
**Durrell,** Lawrence 1912-1990 *AnObit 1990, CnDBLB 7 [port], ConPo 91, CurBio 91N, FacFETw, LiExTwC, RfGEnL 91, TwCSFW 91*
**Durrell,** Lawrence George d1990 *Who 92N*
**Durrell,** Lawrence George 1912- *IntWW 91*
**Durrell,** William S 1931- *AmMWSc 92*
**Durrenberger,** Edward Paul 1943- *WhoMW 92*
**Durrenmatt,** Friedrich d1990 *IntWW 91N, Who 92N*
**Durrenmatt,** Friedrich 1921-1990 *AnObit 1990, CurBio 91N, FacFETw*
**Durrenmatt,** Peter Ulrich 1904- *IntWW 91*
**Durrer,** Richard Michael 1952- *WhoAmL 92*
**Durrett,** George Mann 1917- *WhoFI 92*
**Durrett,** James Frazer, Jr. 1931- *WhoAmL 92*
**Durrill,** Preston Lee 1936- *AmMWSc 92*
**Durrum,** Emmett Leigh 1916- *AmMWSc 92*
**Dursch,** Friedrich 1930- *AmMWSc 92*
**Dursi,** Elsie L. *WhoRel 92*
**Durso,** Donald Francis 1925- *AmMWSc 92*
**Durso,** John William 1938- *AmMWSc 92*
**D'Urso,** Joseph Paul 1943- *DcTwDes*
**Durst,** Alan 1883-1970 *TwCPaSc*
**Durst,** Eric *WhoEnt 92*
**Durst,** Gary Michael 1945- *WhoMW 92*
**Durst,** Harold Everett 1924- *AmMWSc 92*
**Durst,** Jack Rowland 1926- *AmMWSc 92*
**Durst,** James R. 1945- *WhoWest 92*
**Durst,** Lincoln Kearney 1924- *AmMWSc 92*
**Durst,** Michael Charles 1954- *WhoAmL 92*
**Durst,** Mose 1939- *WhoRel 92*
**Durst,** Paul 1921- *IntAu&W 91, TwCWW 91, WrDr 92*
**Durst,** Peggy M. 1952- *WhoMW 92*
**Durst,** Richard Allen 1937- *AmMWSc 92*
**Durst,** Richard Wayne 1945- *WhoEnt 92*
**Durst,** Tony 1938- *AmMWSc 92*
**Durston,** David E. 1925- *IntMPA 92*
**Durtsche,** Sheldon V. 1935- *WhoMW 92*
**Durufle,** Maurice 1902-1986 *NewAmDM*
**Durum,** Daryl Eugene 1940- *WhoIns 92*
**Durum,** Scott Kenneth 1947- *AmMWSc 92*
**Durvasula,** Srirama Sastri 1938- *WhoFI 92*
**Durward,** Graham 1956- *TwCPaSc*
**Durward,** Scott 1935- *Who 92*
**Durwood,** Richard M. 1929- *IntMPA 92*
**Durwood,** Stanley H. 1920- *IntMPA 92, WhoMW 92*
**Durworth,** John *ScFEYrs*
**Dury,** George H 1916- *AmMWSc 92*
**Dury,** Ian 1942- *ConTFT 9*
**Duryea,** Dan Kevin 1953- *WhoAmL 92*
**Duryea,** Lee Vaughn 1932- *WhoAmP 91*
**Duryea,** Perry Belmont, Jr 1921- *WhoAmP 91*
**Duryea,** William R 1938- *AmMWSc 92*
**Duryee,** David Anthony 1938- *WhoFI 92*
**Durzan,** Donald John 1936- *AmMWSc 92*
**Dusanic,** Donald G 1934- *AmMWSc 92*
**Dusanic,** Donald Gabriel 1934- *WhoMW 92*
**Dusansky,** Richard 1942- *WhoFI 92*
**Dusapin,** Pascal 1955- *ConCom 92*
**du Sautoy,** Peter Francis 1912- *Who 92*
**Duscha,** Lloyd A *AmMWSc 92*
**Duschinsky,** Robert 1900- *AmMWSc 92*
**Duse,** Eleanora 1859-1924 *FacFETw*
**Dusel-Bacon,** Cynthia 1946- *AmMWSc 92*
**Dusenberry,** William Earl 1943- *AmMWSc 92*
**Dusenbery,** David Brock 1942- *AmMWSc 92*
**Dusenbery,** Ruth Lillian 1944- *AmMWSc 92*
**Dusenbury,** David Allan 1940- *WhoWest 92*
**Dusenbury,** Joseph Hooker 1923- *AmMWSc 92*
**Dusenbury,** Ruth Cole 1929- *WhoAmP 91*
**Du Shane,** James William 1912- *AmMWSc 92*
**DuShane,** Phyllis Miller 1924- *WhoWest 92*
**Dushkin,** Samuel 1891-1976 *NewAmDM*
**Dusi,** Julian Luigi 1920- *AmMWSc 92*
**DuSimitiere,** Pierre Eugene 1736?-1784 *BiInAmS*
**Dusky,** Joan Agatha 1951- *AmMWSc 92*
**Dusl,** Frank 1918- *WhoAmP 91*
**Dusman,** Dianne Elaine 1953- *WhoAmL 92*
**Dusman,** Preston Henry 1927- *WhoRel 92*
**Du Souich,** Patrick 1944- *AmMWSc 92*
**Dussauce,** Hyppolite Etienne 1829-1869 *BiInAmS*
**Dussault,** Ann Mary 1946- *WhoAmP 91*
**Dussault,** Jean H 1941- *AmMWSc 92*
**Dussault,** Nancy 1936- *IntMPA 92*
**d'Usseau,** Arnaud 1916-1990 *AnObit 1990, ConTFT 9*
**Dusseau,** Jerry William 1941- *AmMWSc 92*
**d'Usseau,** Loring 1930- *WhoEnt 92*
**Dusseault,** C. Dean 1938- *WhoAmL 92*
**Dusseck,** Jacques 1936- *WhoEnt 92*
**Dussinger,** John Andrew 1935- *WhoMW 92*
**Dussman,** Judith Ann 1947- *WhoMW 92*
**Dust,** Philip Clarence 1936- *WhoMW 92*
**Dust,** Steven Joseph 1954- *WhoFI 92*

**Dustan,** Harriet Pearson 1920- *AmMWSc 92*
**Duster,** Alfreda M. 1904-1983 *NotBlAW 92*
**Duster,** Benjamin C. 1927- *WhoBlA 92*
**Duster,** Donald Leon 1932- *WhoBlA 92*
**Duster,** Troy 1936- *WhoBlA 92*
**Dustman,** John Henry 1940- *AmMWSc 92*
**Dusto,** Arthur Ronald 1929- *AmMWSc 92*
**Duston,** Hannah 1657?-1736? *EncAmaz 91*
**Duston,** Jennifer 1954- *WhoEnt 92*
**Duston,** Robert Lewis 1960- *WhoAmL 92*
**Duswalt,** Allen Ainsworth, Jr 1932- *AmMWSc 92*
**Duszynski,** Donald Walter 1943- *AmMWSc 92*
**Dutch,** Deborah Lizbeth 1959- *WhoEnt 92*
**Dutch,** Steven Ian 1947- *AmMWSc 92*
**Dutcher,** Clinton Harvey, Jr 1932- *AmMWSc 92*
**Dutcher,** Frank Albert 1909- *WhoRel 92*
**Dutcher,** James Dwight 1950- *AmMWSc 92*
**Dutcher,** Russell Richardson 1927- *AmMWSc 92*
**Dutcher,** Susan K. 1953- *WhoWest 92*
**Dutcher,** William 1846-1920 *BiInAmS*
**Dutcher Thornton,** Alice Marilyn 1934- *WhoEnt 92*
**DuTemple,** Octave J 1920- *AmMWSc 92*
**Dutfield,** Ray *IntMPA 92*
**Duthie,** Hamish 1938- *AmMWSc 92*
**Duthie,** Herbert Livingston 1929- *Who 92*
**Duthie,** Robert Buchan 1925- *Who 92*
**Duthie,** Robert Grieve 1928- *Who 92*
**Duthie,** Robert Wilson 1939- *WhoFI 92*
**Duthoy,** Raymond Julius 1929- *WhoRel 92*
**Dutile,** Fernand Neville 1940- *WhoAmL 92*
**Dutile,** Gordon 1941- *WhoRel 92*
**Dutille,** Harold Kenneth, Jr. 1952- *WhoRel 92*
**Dutilleux,** Henri 1916- *ConCom 92, IntWW 91, NewAmDM*
**Dutka,** Bernard J 1932- *AmMWSc 92*
**Dutka,** Jacques 1919- *AmMWSc 92*
**Dutkewych,** Jaroslav Ihor 1948- *WhoMW 92*
**Du Toit,** Alexander Logie 1878-1949 *FacFETw*
**Dutoit,** Charles 1936- *NewAmDM, WhoEnt 92*
**Dutoit,** Charles E. 1936- *IntWW 91*
**Dutra,** Frank Robert 1916- *AmMWSc 92*
**Dutra,** Gerard Anthony 1945- *AmMWSc 92*
**Dutra,** Ramiro Carvalho 1931- *AmMWSc 92*
**Dutremble,** Dennis L *WhoAmP 91*
**Dutremble,** Lucien A *WhoAmP 91*
**Dutreux,** Helene *EncAmaz 91*
**Dutro,** John Thomas, Jr 1923- *AmMWSc 92*
**Dutschke,** Rudi 1940-1979 *FacFETw*
**Dutson,** Thayne R 1942- *AmMWSc 92, WhoWest 92*
**Dutt,** Amitabh Kumar 1948- *WhoFI 92*
**Dutt,** Ashok Kumar 1931- *WhoMW 92*
**Dutt,** Gautam Shankar 1949- *AmMWSc 92*
**Dutt,** Gordon Richard 1929- *AmMWSc 92*
**Dutt,** Guru 1925-1964 *IntDcF 2-2 [port]*
**Dutt,** Nikil D *AmMWSc 92*
**Dutt,** Ray Horn 1913- *AmMWSc 92*
**Dutt,** Utpal 1929- *IntWW 91*
**Dutta,** Hiran M *AmMWSc 92*
**Dutta,** Kanak 1927- *WhoAmP 91*
**Dutta,** Mitra 1953- *AmMWSc 92*
**Dutta,** Pulak 1951- *AmMWSc 92*
**Dutta,** Purnendu 1937- *AmMWSc 92*
**Dutta,** Saradindu 1931- *AmMWSc 92*
**Dutta,** Shib Prasad 1935- *AmMWSc 92*
**Dutta,** Sisir Kamal 1928- *AmMWSc 92*
**Dutta,** Sunil 1937- *AmMWSc 92*
**Dutta-Roy,** Asim Kanti 1955- *AmMWSc 92*
**Duttaahmed,** A 1935- *AmMWSc 92*
**Duttenhaver,** Linda La Kretz 1955- *WhoWest 92*
**Duttera,** Brian Cleve 1963- *WhoMW 92*
**Dutton,** Allen Ayers 1922- *WhoFI 92*
**Dutton,** Arthur Morlan 1923- *AmMWSc 92*
**Dutton,** Charles 1951- *ConTFT 9*
**Dutton,** Charles Granville 1956- *WhoEnt 92*
**Dutton,** Clarence Benjamin 1917- *WhoAmL 92*
**Dutton,** Clarence Edward 1841-1912 *BiInAmS*
**Dutton,** Cynthia Baldwin 1929- *AmMWSc 92*
**Dutton,** Denis Chandraraj 1935- *WhoRel 92*
**Dutton,** Diana Cheryl 1944- *WhoAmL 92*
**Dutton,** Frederick Gary 1923- *WhoAmL 92*
**Dutton,** Gary Roger 1938- *AmMWSc 92*
**Dutton,** Geoffrey 1922- *ConNov 91, ConPo 91, RfGEnL 91, WrDr 92*
**Dutton,** Geoffrey Piers Henry 1922- *IntAu&W 91, IntWW 91*
**Dutton,** Guy G. S. *WhoWest 92*
**Dutton,** Guy Gordon Studdy 1923- *AmMWSc 92*
**Dutton,** Harold Vermont, Jr 1945- *WhoAmP 91*
**Dutton,** Herbert Jasper 1914- *AmMWSc 92*
**Dutton,** James Macfarlane 1922- *Who 92*
**Dutton,** John Altnow 1936- *AmMWSc 92*
**Dutton,** John C 1918- *AmMWSc 92*
**Dutton,** John Coatsworth, Jr. 1944- *WhoFI 92*
**Dutton,** John Edgar 1924- *WhoWest 92*
**Dutton,** Jonathan Craig 1951- *AmMWSc 92*
**Dutton,** Jonathan Joseph 1942- *AmMWSc 92*
**Dutton,** Judson Dunlap 1908- *WhoAmP 91*
**Dutton,** Nancy Hogan 1938- *WhoAmL 92*
**Dutton,** P Leslie *AmMWSc 92*
**Dutton,** Pauline Mae *WhoWest 92*
**Dutton,** Peter Leslie 1941- *Who 92*
**Dutton,** Reginald David Ley 1916- *Who 92*
**Dutton,** Richard W 1930- *AmMWSc 92*
**Dutton,** Robert Edward, Jr 1924- *AmMWSc 92*
**Dutton,** Robert W *AmMWSc 92*
**Dutton,** Roger 1941- *AmMWSc 92*
**Dutton,** Samuel Train 1849-1919 *AmPeW*
**Dutton,** W T 1852?-1914 *BiInAmS*
**Duttweiler,** Donald Lars 1944- *AmMWSc 92*
**Duttweiler,** Russell E 1938- *AmMWSc 92*
**Dutu,** Alexandru 1928- *IntWW 91*
**Duty,** Robert C 1931- *AmMWSc 92*
**Duty,** Robert R. 1945- *WhoFI 92*
**Dutz,** Werner 1928- *AmMWSc 92*
**Duva,** Donna Marie 1956- *WhoFI 92*
**Duva,** Lou *NewYTBS 91 [port]*
**D'Uva,** Robert Carmen 1920- *WhoFI 92*
**Duval,** Barry E *WhoAmP 91*
**Duval,** Charles Gaetan 1930- *Who 92*
**DuVal,** Clive L, II 1912- *WhoAmP 91*
**Duval,** Denise 1921- *NewAmDM*
**Duval,** Gaetan *Who 92*
**Duval,** Gaetan 1930- *IntWW 91*
**Duval,** Jeanne *IntAu&W 91X, WrDr 92*
**Duval,** John C. *BenetAL 91*
**Duval,** Katherine *WrDr 92*
**Duval,** Kathy J *WhoAmP 91*
**Duval,** Leon-Etienne 1903- *IntWW 91, WhoRel 92*
**Duval,** Leonard A 1921- *AmMWSc 92*
**Duval,** Leonard Anthony 1921- *WhoMW 92*
**Du Val,** Merlin Kearfott 1922- *AmMWSc 92*
**Duval,** Michael 1938- *WhoFI 92*
**Du Val,** Virginia *IntAu&W 91X*
**Duvalier,** Francois *DcAmImH*
**Duvalier,** Francois 1907-1971 *FacFETw [port]*
**Duvalier,** Jean-Claude *DcAmImH*
**Duvalier,** Jean-Claude 1951- *IntWW 91*
**Duvalier,** Simone 1913- *IntWW 91*
**Duvall,** Arndt John, III 1931- *AmMWSc 92*
**Duvall,** C Dale 1933- *WhoAmP 91*
**Duvall,** Charles Farmer 1935- *WhoRel 92*
**Duvall,** David Garland 1949- *WhoFI 92*
**Duvall,** Donald Knox 1925- *WhoAmL 92*
**Duvall,** Evelyn Millis 1906- *IntAu&W 91, WrDr 92*
**Duvall,** George Evered 1920- *AmMWSc 92*
**Duvall,** Harry Marean 1910- *AmMWSc 92*
**DuVall,** Jack 1946- *WhoFI 92*
**Duvall,** John Edward 1947- *WhoAmL 92*
**Duvall,** John Joseph 1936- *AmMWSc 92*
**Duvall,** Lawrence Del 1942- *WhoIns 92*
**Duvall,** Lawrence Delbert 1942- *WhoFI 92*
**Duvall,** Leslie 1924- *WhoAmP 91*
**Duvall,** Paul Frazier, Jr 1941- *AmMWSc 92*
**DuVall,** Raymonda *WhoRel 92*
**Duvall,** Richard Osgood 1942- *WhoAmL 92*
**Duvall,** Robert 1931- *IntMPA 92, WhoEnt 92*
**Duvall,** Ronald Nash 1924- *AmMWSc 92*
**Duvall,** Shelley *LesBEnT 92*
**Duvall,** Shelley 1949- *IntMPA 92, WhoEnt 92*
**Duvall,** Wilbur Irving 1915- *AmMWSc 92*
**Duvall-Itjen,** Phyllis 1951- *WhoFI 92*
**Duvalon,** Ramon *BlkOlyM*
**Duvar,** Ivan Ernest Hunter 1939- *WhoFI 92*
**DuVarney,** Raymond Charles 1940- *AmMWSc 92*
**DuVaul,** Virginia C. *WrDr 92*
**Duverger,** Maurice 1917- *IntWW 91*
**Duvernoy,** Roger *DrAPF 91*
**Duvick,** Donald Nelson 1924- *AmMWSc 92, WhoFI 92*
**Du Vigneaud,** Vincent 1901-1978 *WhoNob 90*
**Duvillard,** Henri 1910- *IntWW 91*
**Duvin,** Robert Phillip 1937- *WhoAmL 92*
**Du Vivier,** Edward Keyes 1919- *WhoMW 92*
**Duvivier,** Jean Fernand 1926- *AmMWSc 92*
**Duvivier,** Julien 1896-1967 *IntDcF 2-2 [port]*
**DuVivier,** Katharine Keyes 1953- *WhoAmL 92*
**Duvoisin,** Roger C 1927- *AmMWSc 92*
**Duwe,** Arthur Edward 1922- *AmMWSc 92*
**Duwell,** Ernest John 1929- *AmMWSc 92*
**Dux,** James Philip 1921- *AmMWSc 92*
**Duxbury,** Alyn Crandall 1932- *AmMWSc 92, WhoWest 92*
**Duxbury,** Barry 1934- *Who 92*
**Duxbury,** Dean David 1934- *AmMWSc 92*
**Duxbury,** Mitzi L *AmMWSc 92*
**Duxbury,** Philip Thomas 1928- *Who 92*
**Duxbury,** Robert N 1933- *WhoAmP 91*
**Duy,** Donald Lewis 1950- *WhoRel 92*
**Duyan,** Peter 1915- *AmMWSc 92*
**Duyckinck,** Evert Augustus 1816-1878 *BenetAL 91*
**Duyckinck,** George Long 1823-1863 *BenetAL 91*
**Duykers,** Ludwig Richard Benjamin 1929- *AmMWSc 92*
**Duysen,** Murray E 1936- *AmMWSc 92*
**Duysheyev,** Arstanbek 1932- *IntWW 91*
**Duzan,** Mary Elizabeth 1942- *WhoAmL 92*
**Duzan,** Stephen Andrew 1941- *WhoWest 92*
**Duzgunes,** Nejat *AmMWSc 92*
**Dveirin,** Jack L. 1958- *WhoAmL 92*
**Dvir-Djerassi,** Yaakov 1946- *WhoEnt 92*
**Dvonch,** William 1915- *AmMWSc 92*
**Dvoracek,** Marvin John 1932- *AmMWSc 92*
**Dvorak,** Ann Marie-Tompkins 1938- *AmMWSc 92*
**Dvorak,** Anton 1841-1904 *BenetAL 91*
**Dvorak,** Antonin 1841-1904 *NewAmDM*
**Dvorak,** Frank Allen 1942- *WhoAmL 92*
**Dvorak,** Frank Arthur 1939- *AmMWSc 92*
**Dvorak,** Harold Fisher 1937- *AmMWSc 92*
**Dvorak,** Jan 1944- *AmMWSc 92*
**Dvorak,** Jane Ann 1955- *WhoMW 92*
**Dvorak,** Marilyn Angeles 1927- *WhoRel 92*
**Dvorak,** Michael A 1948- *WhoAmP 91*
**Dvorak,** Ray P. 1931- *WhoWest 92*
**Dvorak,** Stanley Joseph 1935- *WhoFI 92*
**Dvorak,** Warren Lee 1931- *WhoAmP 91*
**Dvorchik,** Barry Howard 1944- *AmMWSc 92*
**Dvoretzky,** Edward 1930- *WrDr 92*
**Dvoretzky,** Isaac 1928- *AmMWSc 92*
**Dvorin,** Lawrence Adler 1961- *WhoAmL 92*
**Dvorkin,** Louis 1951- *WhoMW 92*
**Dvornik,** Dushan Michael 1923- *AmMWSc 92*
**Dvorsky,** Peter 1951- *IntWW 91*
**Dvorsky,** Robert E 1948- *WhoAmP 91*
**Dwan,** Allan 1885-1981 *FacFETw, IntDcF 2-2 [port]*
**Dwan,** Dennis Edwin 1958- *WhoEnt 92*
**Dwan,** Rebecca Wallace Hankins 1952- *WhoWest 92*
**Dwarakanath,** Manchagondanahalli H 1943- *AmMWSc 92*
**Dwass,** Meyer 1923- *AmMWSc 92*
**Dweck,** Sydney Stevan 1926- *WhoEnt 92*
**Dwek,** Cyril S. 1936- *WhoFI 92*
**Dwek,** Raymond Allen 1941- *Who 92*
**Dwelle,** Robert Bruce *AmMWSc 92*
**Dwenger,** Thomas Andrew 1945- *WhoMW 92*
**Dwiggins,** Alvin *WhoAmP 91*
**Dwiggins,** Claudius William, Jr 1933- *AmMWSc 92*
**Dwight,** John S. 1813-1893 *BenetAL 91*
**Dwight,** Katherine Hepsabeth 1918- *WhoWest 92*
**Dwight,** Olivia *DrAPF 91*
**Dwight,** Reginald Kenneth *Who 92*
**Dwight,** Reginald Kenneth 1947- *WhoEnt 92*
**Dwight,** Theodore 1764-1846 *BenetAL 91*
**Dwight,** Theodore, Jr. 1796-1866 *BenetAL 91*
**Dwight,** Thomas 1843-1911 *BiInAmS*
**Dwight,** Timothy 1752-1817 *BenetAL 91*
**Dwight,** Timothy 1828-1916 *BenetAL 91*
**Dwight,** William Buck 1833-1906 *BiInAmS*
**Dwight Orvis,** Marianne 1816-1901 *BenetAL 91*
**Dwinell,** Lane 1906- *WhoAmP 91*
**Dwinger,** Edwin Erich 1898-1981 *EncTR 91 [port]*
**Dwinger,** Philip 1914- *AmMWSc 92*
**Dwire,** Henry Randolph 1882-1944 *DcNCBi 2*
**Dwivedi,** Anil Mohan 1947- *AmMWSc 92*
**Dwivedi,** Chandradhar 1948- *AmMWSc 92*
**Dwivedi,** Radhey Shyam *AmMWSc 92*
**Dwivedy,** Ramesh C 1943- *AmMWSc 92*
**Dworak,** Donald N 1934- *WhoAmP 91*
**Dworak,** Joseph Edward 1954- *WhoAmL 92*
**Dworetzky,** Murray 1917- *AmMWSc 92*
**Dworjanyn,** Lee O 1934- *AmMWSc 92*
**Dwork,** David Peter 1951- *WhoAmL 92*
**Dworken,** Harvey J 1920- *AmMWSc 92*
**Dworkin,** Andrea 1946- *IntWW 91, WrDr 92*
**Dworkin,** Judith Marcia 1949- *AmMWSc 92*
**Dworkin,** Mark Bruce 1949- *AmMWSc 92*
**Dworkin,** Martin 1927- *AmMWSc 92, WhoMW 92*
**Dworkin,** Martin S. *DrAPF 91*
**Dworkin,** Michael Leonard 1947- *WhoAmL 92*
**Dworkin,** Paul David 1937- *Who 92*
**Dworkin,** Ronald 1931- *WrDr 92*
**Dworkin,** Ronald Myles 1931- *Who 92, WhoAmL 92*
**Dwornik,** Frances Pierson 1956- *WhoAmL 92*
**Dwornik,** Julian Jonathan 1938- *AmMWSc 92*
**Dworschack,** Robert George 1920- *AmMWSc 92*
**Dworschak,** Scott Justin 1960- *WhoAmP 91*
**Dworsky,** Steven Gene 1944- *WhoAmP 91*
**Dworzan,** Helene *DrAPF 91*
**Dworzecka,** Maria *AmMWSc 92*
**Dwyer,** Augusta 1956- *ConAu 133*
**Dwyer,** Bernard J. 1921- *AlmAP 92 [port], WhoAmP 91*
**Dwyer,** Claire Buckley 1930- *WhoAmP 91*
**Dwyer,** Cornelius J., Jr. 1943- *WhoAmL 92*
**Dwyer,** Darrell James 1946- *WhoFI 92*
**Dwyer,** David Aloysious 1917- *WhoMW 92*
**Dwyer,** Deanna *ConAu 36NR, WrDr 92*
**Dwyer,** Dennis D. 1943- *WhoFI 92, WhoMW 92*
**Dwyer,** Dennis Michael 1945- *AmMWSc 92*
**Dwyer,** Diane Marie 1958- *WhoAmL 92*
**Dwyer,** Don D 1934- *AmMWSc 92*
**Dwyer,** Francis Gerard 1931- *AmMWSc 92*
**Dwyer,** Frank *DrAPF 91*
**Dwyer,** Gary Colburn 1943- *WhoWest 92*
**Dwyer,** Gary Joseph 1958- *WhoAmL 92*
**Dwyer,** Gerald Paul, Jr. 1947- *WhoFI 92*
**Dwyer,** Harry, III 1945- *AmMWSc 92*
**Dwyer,** Herbert Edward 1940- *WhoRel 92*
**Dwyer,** James Gerard 1961- *WhoAmL 92*
**Dwyer,** James Michael 1931- *AmMWSc 92*
**Dwyer,** James Richard 1949- *WhoWest 92*
**Dwyer,** Jeffry R. 1946- *WhoAmL 92*
**Dwyer,** Johanna T 1938- *AmMWSc 92*
**Dwyer,** Johanna Todd 1938- *WhoFI 92*
**Dwyer,** John Duncan 1915- *AmMWSc 92*
**Dwyer,** John P. 1951- *WhoAmL 92*
**Dwyer,** K. R. *ConAu 36NR, WrDr 92*
**Dwyer,** Lawrence Arthur 1947- *AmMWSc 92*
**Dwyer,** Maureen Quinn 1947- *WhoIns 92*
**Dwyer,** Patricia R 1962- *WhoAmP 91*
**Dwyer,** Ralph Daniel, Jr. 1924- *WhoAmL 92*
**Dwyer,** Richard A. 1934- *ConAu 135*
**Dwyer,** Richard Bruce 1954- *WhoWest 92*
**Dwyer,** Robert Francis 1930- *AmMWSc 92*
**Dwyer,** Samuel J, III 1932- *AmMWSc 92*
**Dwyer,** Sean-Ashley 1966- *WhoWest 92*
**Dwyer,** Sean G 1945- *AmMWSc 92*
**Dwyer,** Terry M 1948- *AmMWSc 92*
**Dwyer,** Thomas A 1923- *AmMWSc 92*
**Dwyer,** Thomas Aloysius Walsh, III 1940- *AmMWSc 92*
**Dwyer,** William J 1934- *WhoAmP 91*
**Dwyer,** William L. 1929- *WhoAmL 92*
**Dwyer-Carpenter,** Aleta 1948- *WhoBlA 92*
**Dwyer-Dobbin,** Mary Alice 1942- *WhoEnt 92*
**Dwyer-Hallquist,** Patricia 1954- *AmMWSc 92*
**Dwyer-Joyce,** Alice 1913- *IntAu&W 91*
**Dwyre,** John Steven 1946- *WhoAmL 92*
**Dy,** Francisco Justiniano 1912- *IntWW 91*
**Dy,** Kian Seng 1940- *AmMWSc 92*
**Dyadkin,** Lev Joseph 1955- *WhoWest 92*
**Dyak,** Miriam *DrAPF 91*
**Dyakov,** Ivan Nikolayevich 1937- *IntWW 91*
**Dyal,** Desta Casey 1922- *WhoAmP 91*
**Dyal,** Palmer 1933- *AmMWSc 92*
**Dyalhis,** Nictzin 1879-1942 *ScFEYrs*
**Dyar,** James Ervin 1959- *WhoRel 92*
**Dyar,** James Joseph 1931- *AmMWSc 92*
**Dyas,** Patricia Ann 1952- *WhoBlA 92*
**Dyba,** Karel 1940- *IntWW 91*
**Dyball,** Christopher John 1951- *AmMWSc 92*
**Dybalski,** Jack Norbert 1924- *AmMWSc 92*

**Dybas,** Linda Kathryn 1942- *AmMWSc 92*
**Dybczak,** Z W 1924- *AmMWSc 92*
**Dybek,** Stuart *DrAPF 91*
**Dybek,** Stuart 1942- *IntAu&W 91*
**Dybel,** Michael Wayne 1946- *AmMWSc 92*
**Dybenko,** Nikolai Kirillovich 1928- *IntWW 91*
**Dybenko,** Paul Yefimovich 1889-1938 *FacFETw*
**Dybing,** Clifford Dean 1931- *AmMWSc 92*
**Dybka,** Darryl Joseph 1953- *WhoEnt 92*
**Dybkjaer,** Lone 1940- *IntWW 91*
**Dybowski,** Cecil Ray 1946- *AmMWSc 92*
**Dybvig,** Douglas Howard 1935- *AmMWSc 92*
**Dybvig,** Paul Henry 1955- *AmMWSc 92*
**Dyce,** Barbara J. *WhoBlA 92*
**Dyce,** Rolf Buchanan 1929- *AmMWSc 92*
**Dyche,** Leola Fern 1940- *WhoRel 92*
**Dyche,** Lewis Lindsay 1857-1915 *BiInAmS*
**Dychtwald,** Maddy Kent 1952- *WhoEnt 92*
**Dyck,** Andrew Roy 1947- *WhoWest 92*
**Dyck,** Gerald Wayne 1938- *AmMWSc 92*
**Dyck,** Harold Peter 1920- *WhoAmP 91*
**Dyck,** Peter Leonard 1929- *AmMWSc 92*
**Dyck,** Robert Gilkey 1930- *WhoAmP 91*
**Dyck,** Rudolph Henry 1931- *AmMWSc 92*
**Dyck,** Walter Peter 1935- *AmMWSc 92*
**Dyckes,** Douglas Franz 1942- *AmMWSc 92*
**Dyckman,** Daniel J. 1957- *WhoEnt 92*
**Dyckman,** Deborah Anne 1964- *WhoAmL 92*
**Dycus,** Susan Johnson 1953- *WhoAmL 92*
**Dyde,** John Horsfall 1905- *Who 92*
**Dye,** Alan Louis *WhoAmL 92*
**Dye,** Alan Page 1946- *WhoAmL 92*
**Dye,** Betty Lee 1921- *WhoAmP 91*
**Dye,** Bradford Johnson, Jr 1933- *WhoAmP 91*
**Dye,** Bru *DrAPF 91*
**Dye,** Carl Melvyn 1940- *WhoFI 92*
**Dye,** Charles Melvin 1933- *WhoFI 92*
**Dye,** Clinton Elworth, Jr. 1942- *WhoBlA 92*
**Dye,** David 1943- *WhoEnt 92*
**Dye,** David L 1925- *AmMWSc 92*
**Dye,** David Ray 1951- *WhoFI 92*
**Dye,** Dwight Latimer 1931- *WhoRel 92*
**Dye,** Erica Becher 1958- *WhoEnt 92*
**Dye,** Frank J 1942- *AmMWSc 92*
**Dye,** Henry Abel 1926- *AmMWSc 92*
**Dye,** Jack Bertie 1919- *Who 92*
**Dye,** James Eugene 1939- *AmMWSc 92*
**Dye,** James Louis 1927- *AmMWSc 92*
**Dye,** James W. 1934- *WhoMW 92*
**Dye,** Lewis William 1944- *WhoAmL 92*
**Dye,** Lowell Delano, Jr. 1955- *WhoMW 92*
**Dye,** Luther V. 1933- *WhoBlA 92*
**Dye,** Lyle 1930- *WhoEnt 92, WhoMW 92*
**Dye,** Myron L 1954- *WhoIns 92*
**Dye,** Patrick Fain, Jr. 1962- *WhoEnt 92*
**Dye,** Ralph Dean, Jr. 1931- *WhoAmL 92*
**Dye,** Robert Charles 1943- *WhoFI 92*
**Dye,** Robert F 1920- *AmMWSc 92*
**Dye,** Robert Harris 1918- *WhoFI 92*
**Dye,** Robert Lloyd 1952- *WhoFI 92*
**Dye,** Sherman 1915- *WhoAmL 92*
**Dye,** Thomas Alfred 1954- *WhoAmL 92*
**Dye,** William Ellsworth 1926- *WhoAmL 92*
**Dye,** William Thomson, Jr 1918- *AmMWSc 92*
**Dyen,** Isidore 1913- *WrDr 92*
**Dyer,** Alan Richard 1945- *AmMWSc 92*
**Dyer,** Alexander Patrick 1932- *WhoFI 92*
**Dyer,** Alice Mildred 1929- *WhoWest 92*
**Dyer,** Alistair George 1945- *WhoMW 92*
**Dyer,** Allan Edwin 1923- *AmMWSc 92*
**Dyer,** Carolyn Price 1931- *WhoWest 92*
**Dyer,** Charles 1928- *IntAu&W 91, Who 92, WrDr 92*
**Dyer,** Charles Arnold 1940- *WhoAmL 92*
**Dyer,** Charles Austen 1936- *AmMWSc 92, WhoBlA 92*
**Dyer,** Charles Chester 1946- *AmMWSc 92*
**Dyer,** Charles Robert 1951- *AmMWSc 92*
**Dyer,** David William 1910- *WhoAmL 92*
**Dyer,** Dennis Robert 1950- *WhoEnt 92*
**Dyer,** Denzel Leroy 1929- *AmMWSc 92*
**Dyer,** Donald Chester 1939- *AmMWSc 92*
**Dyer,** Edward James, Jr 1937- *WhoAmP 91*
**Dyer,** Elizabeth 1906- *AmMWSc 92*
**Dyer,** Frank Falkoner 1931- *AmMWSc 92*
**Dyer,** Frederick C. 1918- *WrDr 92*
**Dyer,** Frederick T 1941- *WhoAmP 91*
**Dyer,** Gary Don 1952- *WhoRel 92*
**Dyer,** Gregory Clark 1947- *WhoFI 92*
**Dyer,** Henry Peter Francis S. *Who 92*
**Dyer,** Howard *WhoAmP 91*
**Dyer,** Hubert Jerome 1914- *AmMWSc 92*
**Dyer,** Ira 1925- *AmMWSc 92*
**Dyer,** Ira Jack 1929- *WhoAmP 91*
**Dyer,** Isadore 1865-1920 *BiInAmS*
**Dyer,** James 1934- *WrDr 92*
**Dyer,** James Arthur 1932- *AmMWSc 92*
**Dyer,** James Frederick 1934- *IntAu&W 91*
**Dyer,** James Lee 1934- *AmMWSc 92*
**Dyer,** Joe, Jr. 1934- *WhoBlA 92*
**Dyer,** John 1699-1757 *RfGEnL 91*
**Dyer,** John 1935- *AmMWSc 92*
**Dyer,** John Kaye 1935- *AmMWSc 92*
**Dyer,** John M. 1920- *WrDr 92*
**Dyer,** John Norvell 1930- *AmMWSc 92*
**Dyer,** Judith Gretchen 1937- *AmMWSc 92*
**Dyer,** Kenneth Edwin 1949- *WhoFI 92*
**Dyer,** Lawrence D 1930- *AmMWSc 92*
**Dyer,** Lois Edith 1925- *Who 92*
**Dyer,** Mark 1928- *Who 92*
**Dyer,** Mary d1660 *HanAmWH*
**Dyer,** Melvin I 1932- *AmMWSc 92*
**Dyer,** Merton S 1930- *WhoAmP 91*
**Dyer,** Noel John 1913- *WhoAmL 92*
**Dyer,** Peggy Lynn 1946- *AmMWSc 92*
**Dyer,** Randolph H 1940- *AmMWSc 92*
**Dyer,** Raye Nell *WhoRel 92*
**Dyer,** Rolla McIntyre, Jr 1922- *AmMWSc 92*
**Dyer,** Simon 1939- *Who 92*
**Dyer,** T.A. *DrAPF 91*
**Dyer,** Thomas Michael 1945- *WhoAmL 92*
**Dyer,** Tim Alan 1958- *WhoWest 92*
**Dyer,** Walter Sullivan, III 1957- *WhoWest 92*
**Dyer,** Wayne W. 1940- *WrDr 92*
**Dyer,** William Allan, Jr. 1902- *WhoMW 92*
**Dyer,** William Gerald 1929- *AmMWSc 92*
**Dyer-Bennet,** John 1915- *AmMWSc 92*
**Dyer-Bennet,** Richard d1991 *NewYTBS 91 [port]*
**Dyer-Goode,** Pamela Theresa 1950- *WhoBlA 92*
**Dyer-Smith,** John Edward 1918- *Who 92*
**Dyess,** Edwin Earl 1949- *WhoWest 92*
**Dyess,** William J 1929- *WhoAmP 91*
**Dygard,** Thomas J. 1931- *Au&Arts 7 [port]*
**Dygert,** Harold Paul, Jr. 1919- *WhoWest 92*
**Dyk,** Timothy Belcher 1937- *WhoAmL 92, WhoEnt 92*
**Dykas,** James Donald 1940- *WhoFI 92*
**Dyke** *Who 92*
**Dyke,** Bennett *AmMWSc 92*
**Dyke,** Gregory 1947- *Who 92*
**Dyke,** Henry Van *DrAPF 91*
**Dyke,** Richard Warren 1922- *AmMWSc 92*
**Dyke,** Stephen Patrick 1964- *WhoFI 92*
**Dyke,** Thomas Robert 1944- *AmMWSc 92*
**Dykeman,** Wilma *WrDr 92*
**Dyken,** Mark Lewis 1928- *AmMWSc 92*
**Dyken,** Paul Richard 1934- *AmMWSc 92*
**Dykes,** Archie Reece 1931- *WhoFI 92*
**Dykes,** David Orlo 1953- *WhoRel 92*
**Dykes,** David Wilmer 1933- *Who 92*
**Dykes,** DeWitt S., Jr. 1938- *WhoBlA 92*
**Dykes,** DeWitt Sanford, Sr. 1903- *WhoBlA 92*
**Dykes,** Donna Stokes 1943- *WhoRel 92*
**Dykes,** Eva B. 1893-1986 *NotBlAW 92*
**Dykes,** Hugh John 1939- *Who 92*
**Dykes,** James E. *WhoWest 92*
**Dykes,** James McKendree, Jr. 1946- *WhoRel 92*
**Dykes,** James Tate 1948- *WhoRel 92*
**Dykes,** Marie Draper 1942- *WhoBlA 92*
**Dykes,** Osborne Jefferson, III 1944- *WhoAmL 92*
**Dykes,** Robert William 1943- *AmMWSc 92*
**Dykes,** Roland A. *WhoBlA 92*
**Dykes Bower,** S. E. 1903- *Who 92*
**Dykhouse,** David Jay 1936- *WhoAmL 92*
**Dykhouse,** David Wayne 1949- *WhoAmL 92*
**Dykhuizen,** Daniel Edward 1942- *AmMWSc 92*
**Dykla,** John J 1944- *AmMWSc 92*
**Dykman,** Joan Day 1959- *WhoEnt 92*
**Dykman,** Roscoe A 1920- *AmMWSc 92*
**Dyksterhuis,** Edsko Jerry 1908- *AmMWSc 92*
**Dykstra,** Clifford Elliot 1952- *AmMWSc 92, WhoMW 92*
**Dykstra,** Craig Richard 1947- *WhoRel 92*
**Dykstra,** David Allen 1938- *WhoMW 92*
**Dykstra,** David Charles 1941- *WhoWest 92*
**Dykstra,** Dewey Irwin, Jr 1947- *AmMWSc 92*
**Dykstra,** Jerald Paul 1946- *AmMWSc 92*
**Dykstra,** Lenny *NewYTBS 91 [port]*
**Dykstra,** Leona 1942- *WhoAmP 91*
**Dykstra,** Linda A 1944- *AmMWSc 92*
**Dykstra,** Mark Allan 1946- *AmMWSc 92*
**Dykstra,** Philip Rouse 1929- *WhoWest 92*
**Dykstra,** Richard Charles 1950- *WhoFI 92*
**Dykstra,** Richard L. 1942- *WhoMW 92*
**Dykstra,** Richard Lynn 1942- *AmMWSc 92*
**Dykstra,** Robert 1930- *WhoMW 92*
**Dykstra,** Stanley John 1924- *AmMWSc 92*
**Dykstra,** Thomas Karl 1935- *AmMWSc 92*
**Dykstra,** William Dwight 1927- *WhoFI 92*
**Dylan,** Bob 1941- *BenetAL 91, ConPo 91, CurBio 91 [port], FacFETw [port], IntAu&W 91, IntWW 91, NewAmDM, NewYTBS 91 [port], RComAH, WhoEnt 92, WrDr 92*
**Dylla,** Henry Frederick 1949- *AmMWSc 92*
**Dylla,** Larry Matthew 1942- *WhoFI 92*
**Dym,** Clive L 1942- *AmMWSc 92*
**Dym,** Elaine Marjorie 1925- *WhoAmP 91*
**Dymally,** Lynn V. 1958- *WhoBlA 92*
**Dymally,** Mervyn M. 1926- *AlmAP 92 [port], WhoAmP 91, WhoBlA 92*
**Dymally,** Mervyn Malcolm 1926- *WhoWest 92*
**Dyment,** John Cameron 1938- *AmMWSc 92*
**Dymerski,** Paul Peter 1947- *AmMWSc 92*
**Dymicky,** Michael 1920- *AmMWSc 92*
**Dymoke,** Anne *EncAmaz 91*
**Dymoke,** John Lindley Marmion 1926- *Who 92*
**Dymoke,** Juliet 1919- *IntAu&W 91, WrDr 92*
**Dymoke,** Lionel Dorian 1921- *Who 92*
**Dymond,** Charles Edward 1916- *Who 92*
**Dymshyts,** Venyamin Emmanuilovich 1910- *IntWW 91*
**Dymsza,** Henry A 1922- *AmMWSc 92*
**Dynamis,** Queen of Bosphorus d7? *EncAmaz 91*
**Dynan,** William Shelley 1954- *AmMWSc 92*
**Dyne,** Peter John 1926- *AmMWSc 92*
**Dynes,** J Robert 1922- *AmMWSc 92*
**Dynes,** Robert Carr 1942- *AmMWSc 92*
**Dynevor,** Baron 1935- *Who 92*
**Dynkin,** Eugene B 1924- *AmMWSc 92*
**Dyott,** Thomas Michael 1947- *AmMWSc 92*
**Dypski,** Cornell N 1931- *WhoAmP 91*
**Dyrberg,** Thomas Peter 1954- *AmMWSc 92*
**Dyregrov,** Michael 1931- *WhoMW 92*
**Dyremose,** Henning 1945- *IntWW 91*
**Dyrkacz,** W William 1919- *AmMWSc 92*
**Dyrness,** Christen Theodore 1933- *AmMWSc 92*
**Dyrness,** William A 1943- *ConAu 35NR, WrDr 92*
**Dyrness,** William Arthur 1943- *WhoRel 92*
**Dyroff,** David Ray 1940- *AmMWSc 92*
**Dyrstad,** Joanell M 1942- *WhoAmP 91, WhoMW 92*
**Dyrud,** Amos Oliver 1915- *WhoRel 92*
**Dyrud,** Jarl Edvard 1921- *AmMWSc 92*
**Dysart,** Countess of 1914- *Who 92*
**Dysart,** Benjamin Clay, III 1940- *AmMWSc 92, WhoFI 92*
**Dysart,** Paul Biff 1945- *WhoMW 92*
**Dysart,** Richard A. *WhoEnt 92*
**Dysart,** Richard A. 1929- *IntMPA 92*
**Dysart,** Richard James 1932- *AmMWSc 92*
**Dysart,** Robert Lewis 1956- *WhoAmL 92*
**Dysinger,** Paul William 1927- *AmMWSc 92*
**Dysken,** Maurice William 1942- *AmMWSc 92, WhoMW 92*
**Dyson,** A. E. 1928- *WrDr 92*
**Dyson,** Anthony Edward 1928- *IntAu&W 91*
**Dyson,** Anthony James 1953- *WhoEnt 92*
**Dyson,** Anthony Oakley 1935- *Who 92*
**Dyson,** Arthur Thomas 1940- *WhoWest 92*
**Dyson,** David Arnold 1951- *WhoFI 92*
**Dyson,** Derek C 1932- *AmMWSc 92*
**Dyson,** Frank Watson 1868-1939 *FacFETw*
**Dyson,** Freeman 1923- *FacFETw, IntAu&W 91, WrDr 92*
**Dyson,** Freeman John 1923- *AmMWSc 92, IntWW 91, Who 92*
**Dyson,** John Anthony 1943- *Who 92*
**Dyson,** John Douglas 1918- *AmMWSc 92*
**Dyson,** John Michael 1929- *Who 92*
**Dyson,** John Stuart 1943- *WhoAmP 91*
**Dyson,** Robert Duane 1939- *AmMWSc 92, WhoWest 92*
**Dyson,** Roger Franklin 1940- *Who 92*
**Dyson,** Ronnie 1950-1990 *WhoBlA 92N*
**Dyson,** Roy 1948- *WhoAmP 91*
**Dyson,** William Riley 1940- *WhoAmP 91, WhoBlA 92*
**Dyson-Hudson,** V Rada 1930- *AmMWSc 92*
**Dyvig,** Peter 1934- *Who 92*
**Dyville,** Jack 1945- *WhoEnt 92*
**Dywan,** Jeffery Joseph 1949- *WhoAmL 92*
**Dzasokhov,** Aleksandr Sergeevich 1934- *SovUnBD A*
**Dzerzhinsky,** Feliks Edmundovich 1877-1926 *SovUnBD*
**Dzerzhinsky,** Felix Edmundovich 1877-1926 *FacFETw*
**Dzerzhinsky,** Ivan 1909-1978 *NewAmDM*
**Dzerzhinsky,** Ivan Ivanovich 1909- *FacFETw*
**Dzerzhinsky,** Ivan Ivanovich 1909-1978 *SovUnBD*
**Dzhanibekov,** Vladimir 1942- *FacFETw*
**Dzhasokhov,** Aleksandr Sergeyevich 1934- *IntWW 91*
**Dzhelepov,** Venedikt Petrovich 1913- *IntWW 91*
**Dzhemilev,** Mustafa 1943- *IntWW 91, SovUnBD*
**Dzhigarkhanian,** Armen Borisovich 1935- *IntWW 91*
**Dziadek,** Fred 1934- *WhoFI 92*
**Dziadyk,** Bohdan 1948- *AmMWSc 92, WhoMW 92*
**Dziak,** Richard Frank 1952- *WhoFI 92*
**Dziak,** Rose Mary 1946- *AmMWSc 92*
**Dzialo,** Raymond John 1931- *WhoAmP 91*
**Dzidic,** Ismet 1939- *AmMWSc 92*
**Dzieciuch,** Matthew Andrew 1931- *AmMWSc 92*
**Dzielak,** David J 1954- *AmMWSc 92*
**Dzierzanowski,** Frank John 1929- *AmMWSc 92*
**Dziewanowski,** Kazimierz 1930- *IntWW 91*
**Dziewiecki,** Krzysztof 1955- *WhoEnt 92*
**Dziewonski,** Adam Marian 1936- *AmMWSc 92*
**Dzigan,** Efim L'vovich 1898-1984 *SovUnBD*
**Dzimianski,** John W 1924- *AmMWSc 92*
**Dziordz,** Walter Michael 1951- *WhoRel 92*
**Dziubla,** Robert W. 1952- *WhoAmL 92*
**Dziuk,** Harold Edmund 1930- *AmMWSc 92*
**Dziuk,** Philip J 1926- *AmMWSc 92*
**Dzodin,** Harvey Cary 1947- *WhoEnt 92*
**Dzombak,** William Charles 1921- *AmMWSc 92*
**Dzubas,** Friedel 1915- *FacFETw*
**Dzundza,** George 1945- *IntMPA 92*
**Dzurik,** John Gerard 1950- *WhoAmL 92*
**Dzurisin,** Daniel 1951- *AmMWSc 92*
**D'Zurko,** Arpad *WhoEnt 92*
**Dzyuba,** Ivan Mikhailovich 1931- *IntWW 91*
**Dzyubin,** Eduard Georg'evich *SovUnBD*

# E

**E**, Sheila *WhoHisp 92*
**E.M.** *DrAPF 91*
**E W** *ScFEYrs*
**Eaborn**, Colin 1923- *IntWW 91, Who 92, WrDr 92*
**Eachus**, Alan Campbell 1939- *AmMWSc 92*
**Eachus**, Joseph Jackson 1911- *AmMWSc 92*
**Eachus**, Paul 1944- *TwCPaSc*
**Eachus**, Raymond Stanley 1944- *AmMWSc 92*
**Eachus**, Spencer William 1944- *AmMWSc 92*
**Eade**, Dominique *WhoEnt 92*
**Eade**, Donald Wayne 1959- *WhoRel 92*
**Eade**, Kenneth Edgar 1926- *AmMWSc 92*
**Eaden**, Maurice Bryan 1923- *Who 92*
**Eades**, Charles Hubert, Jr 1916- *AmMWSc 92*
**Eades**, James B, Jr 1923- *AmMWSc 92*
**Eades**, James L 1921- *AmMWSc 92*
**Eades**, Joan *DrAPF 91*
**Eades**, John Alwyn 1939- *AmMWSc 92*
**Eades**, Kenneth Rae 1953- *WhoFI 92*
**Eades**, Robert Timothy 1957- *WhoAmL 92*
**Eades**, Vincent W. 1956- *WhoBlA 92*
**Eadie**, Alexander 1920- *Who 92*
**Eadie**, Arlton d1935 *ScFEYrs*
**Eadie**, David Alan 1944- *WhoRel 92*
**Eadie**, Douglas George Arnott 1931- *Who 92*
**Eadie**, Ellice 1912- *Who 92*
**Eadie**, George Robert 1923- *AmMWSc 92*
**Eadie**, Ian 1913-1973 *TwCPaSc*
**Eadie**, Robert 1877-1954 *TwCPaSc*
**Eadington**, William Richard 1946- *WhoFI 92*
**Eadon**, George Albert 1945- *AmMWSc 92*
**Eads**, B G 1940- *AmMWSc 92*
**Eads**, Darwin D d1906 *BiInAmS*
**Eads**, Ewin Alfred 1915- *AmMWSc 92*
**Eads**, George Curtis 1942- *WhoFI 92*
**Eads**, James Buchanan 1820-1887 *BiInAmS*
**Eads**, M Adela *WhoAmP 91*
**Eads**, Ora Wilbert 1914- *WhoRel 92*
**Eads**, Ronald Preston 1948- *WhoFI 92*
**Eady** *Who 92*
**Eady**, Cornelius Robert *DrAPF 91*
**Eady**, David 1943- *Who 92*
**Eady**, Harold J. *IntMPA 92*
**Eady**, Mary E. *WhoBlA 92*
**Eagan**, Claire V. 1950- *WhoAmL 92*
**Eagan**, Emma Louise 1928- *WhoBlA 92*
**Eagan**, George Daniel 1957- *WhoFI 92*
**Eagan**, James Joseph 1926- *WhoAmP 91*
**Eagan**, Robert John 1944- *AmMWSc 92*
**Eagan**, Sherman G. 1942- *WhoEnt 92*
**Eagan**, William Edward 1943- *WhoAmP 91*
**Eagan**, William Frank 1920- *WhoMW 92*
**Eagan**, William Leon 1928- *WhoAmL 92*
**Eagar**, Robert Gouldman, Jr 1947- *AmMWSc 92*
**Eagar**, Thomas W 1950- *AmMWSc 92*
**Eagen**, Charles Frederick 1946- *AmMWSc 92*
**Eagen**, Isaac Brent 1929- *WhoRel 92*
**Eagen**, L. John 1947- *WhoRel 92*
**Eagen**, Michael 1951- *WhoEnt 92*
**Eager**, George S, Jr 1915- *AmMWSc 92*
**Eager**, Richard Alvin 1945- *WhoEnt 92*
**Eager**, Richard Livingston 1917- *AmMWSc 92*
**Eager**, Robert W, Jr. 1944- *WhoIns 92*
**Eagers**, Derek 1924- *Who 92*
**Eagger**, Arthur Austin 1898- *Who 92*
**Eagland**, Martin 1942- *Who 92*
**Eagle**, Arnold Elliott 1941- *WhoBlA 92*
**Eagle**, Donald Frohlichstein 1933- *AmMWSc 92*
**Eagle**, Edward 1908- *AmMWSc 92*
**Eagle**, Harry 1905- *AmMWSc 92, IntWW 91*
**Eagle**, Jack 1926- *WhoEnt 92*
**Eagle**, Paul Andre 1939- *WhoMW 92*
**Eagle**, Raven Grey 1927- *WhoEnt 92*
**Eagle**, Sam 1912- *AmMWSc 92*
**Eagle**, Thomas G. 1961- *WhoAmL 92*
**Eagleburger**, Lawrence Sidney 1930- *IntWW 91, WhoAmP 91*
**Eagleman**, Joe R 1936- *AmMWSc 92*
**Eagles**, The *NewAmDM*
**Eagles**, Aloha Taylor 1916- *WhoAmP 91*
**Eagles**, Douglas Alan 1943- *AmMWSc 92*
**Eagles**, James 1918- *Who 92*
**Eaglesfield**, Francis *WrDr 92*
**Eagleson**, Gerald Wayne 1947- *AmMWSc 92*
**Eagleson**, Halson Vashon 1903- *AmMWSc 92, WhoBlA 92*
**Eagleson**, Peter Sturges 1928- *AmMWSc 92*
**Eagleton**, Aileen 1902- *TwCPaSc*
**Eagleton**, Clyde 1891-1958 *AmPeW*
**Eagleton**, Godfrey Paul 1935- *TwCPaSc*
**Eagleton**, Lee C 1923- *AmMWSc 92*
**Eagleton**, Robert Don 1937- *AmMWSc 92*
**Eagleton**, Terence 1943- *WrDr 92*
**Eagleton**, Terence Francis 1943- *IntAu&W 91, Who 92*
**Eagleton**, Thomas F 1929- *FacFETw, WhoAmP 91*
**Eagleton**, Thomas Francis 1929- *IntWW 91*
**Eaglin**, Fulton B. 1941- *WhoBlA 92*
**Eagling**, Wayne John *IntWW 91, Who 92*
**Eagon**, John Alonzo 1932- *AmMWSc 92*
**Eagon**, Patricia K *AmMWSc 92*
**Eagon**, Robert Garfield 1927- *AmMWSc 92*
**Eaken**, Bruce Webb, Jr. 1938- *WhoAmL 92*
**Eaker**, Charles Mayfield 1919- *AmMWSc 92*
**Eaker**, Charles William 1949- *AmMWSc 92*
**Eaker**, Ira 1922- *WhoEnt 92*
**Eaker**, Ira C 1896-1987 *FacFETw*
**Eaker**, Sherry Ellen 1949- *WhoEnt 92*
**Eakes**, Grady M *WhoAmP 91*
**Eakin**, Bertram E 1928- *AmMWSc 92*
**Eakin**, Charles Gillilan 1927- *WhoWest 92*
**Eakin**, Debbie Sue 1961- *WhoEnt 92*
**Eakin**, Garret Michael 1947- *WhoMW 92*
**Eakin**, Margaretta Morgan 1941- *WhoAmL 92*
**Eakin**, Richard Marshall 1910- *AmMWSc 92*
**Eakin**, Richard R 1938- *AmMWSc 92*
**Eakin**, Richard Timothy 1942- *AmMWSc 92*
**Eakin**, Thomas Capper 1933- *WhoFI 92, WhoMW 92*
**Eakin**, William Rowland 1958- *WhoRel 92*
**Eakin**, William Wayne 1949- *WhoAmL 92*
**Eakins**, Joel Kenneth 1930- *WhoRel 92, WhoWest 92*
**Eakins**, Kenneth E 1935- *AmMWSc 92*
**Eakins**, Patricia *DrAPF 91*
**Eakins**, Peter Russell 1927- *AmMWSc 92*
**Eakins**, Susan Hannah 1851-1938 *HanAmWH*
**Eakins**, Thomas 1844-1916 *RComAH*
**Eakins**, William Shannon 1951- *WhoAmL 92*
**Eaks**, Irving Leslie 1923- *AmMWSc 92*
**Eales**, John Geoffrey 1937- *AmMWSc 92*
**Eales**, Lennox 1918- *IntWW 91*
**Eales**, Victor Henry James 1922- *Who 92*
**Ealey**, Adolphus 1941- *WhoBlA 92*
**Ealey**, Juanita Yvonne 1938- *WhoWest 92*
**Ealey**, Mark E. 1926- *WhoBlA 92*
**Ealey**, Roland D 1914- *WhoAmP 91*
**Ealing**, Abbot of *Who 92*
**Ealy**, F. Ronald 1934- *WhoAmL 92*
**Ealy**, Jonathan Bruce 1960- *WhoAmL 92*
**Ealy**, Mary Newcomb 1948- *WhoBlA 92*
**Ealy**, Robert Phillip 1914- *AmMWSc 92*
**Eamer**, Richard Keith 1928- *WhoFI 92, WhoWest 92*
**Eames**, Arnold C 1930- *AmMWSc 92*
**Eames**, Charles 1907-1978 *DcTwDes, FacFETw*
**Eames**, Emma 1865-1952 *NewAmDM*
**Eames**, Eric James 1917- *Who 92*
**Eames**, John Byron 1941- *WhoAmL 92*
**Eames**, M C 1931- *AmMWSc 92*
**Eames**, Ray 1915-1988 *FacFETw*
**Eames**, Ray Kaiser 1915-1988 *DcTwDes*
**Eames**, Robert Henry Alexander *Who 92*
**Eames**, Robert Henry Alexander 1937- *IntWW 91, WhoRel 92*
**Eames**, Wilberforce 1855-1937 *BenetAL 91*
**Eames**, William 1929- *AmMWSc 92*
**Eames**, Wilmer B 1914- *AmMWSc 92*
**Eanes**, Antonio dos Santos Ramalho 1935- *IntWW 91*
**Eanes**, Edward David 1934- *AmMWSc 92*
**Eanes**, James Jeffrey 1956- *WhoAmP 91*
**Eanes**, Joseph Cabel, Jr 1935- *WhoIns 92*
**Eanes**, Raullo Mance 1966- *WhoMW 92*
**Eannace**, Ralph J, Jr *WhoAmP 91*
**Eardley**, Diane Douglas *AmMWSc 92*
**Eardley**, Joan 1921-1963 *TwCPaSc*
**Eardley**, Richard Roy 1928- *WhoAmP 91*
**Eardley-Wilmot**, John 1917- *Who 92*
**Eareckson**, William Milton, III 1922- *AmMWSc 92*
**Eargle**, George Marvin 1939- *AmMWSc 92*
**Eargle**, John Morgan 1931- *AmMWSc 92*
**Earhart**, Amelia 1897-1937 *HanAmWH, RComAH*
**Earhart**, Amelia 1898-1937? *FacFETw [port]*
**Earhart**, Charles Franklin, Jr 1941- *AmMWSc 92*
**Earhart**, H. Byron 1935- *WrDr 92*
**Earhart**, J Ronald 1941- *AmMWSc 92*
**Earhart**, Richard Wilmot 1940- *AmMWSc 92*
**Earhart**, Steven D. 1958- *WhoFI 92*
**Earing**, Mason Humphry 1921- *AmMWSc 92*
**Earl Mountbatten of Burma** *ConAu 133*
**Earl of Dunsmere**, Baron Horan of Antwerp 1950- *WhoRel 92*
**Earl**, Allan Edwin 1939- *AmMWSc 92*
**Earl**, Anthony S 1936- *WhoAmP 91*
**Earl**, Anthony Scully 1936- *WhoMW 92*
**Earl**, Archie William, Sr. 1946- *WhoBlA 92*
**Earl**, Boyd L 1927- *AmMWSc 92*
**Earl**, Boyd L 1944- *AmMWSc 92*
**Earl**, Charles Riley 1933- *AmMWSc 92*
**Earl**, Christopher Joseph 1925- *Who 92*
**Earl**, Daniel d1790 *DcNCBi 2*
**Earl**, David 1951- *ConCom 92*
**Earl**, Eric Stafford 1928- *Who 92*
**Earl**, Francis Lee 1924- *AmMWSc 92*
**Earl**, Harley J. 1893-1954 *DcTwDes, FacFETw*
**Earl**, James Arthur 1932- *AmMWSc 92*
**Earl**, John Richard 1934- *WhoIns 92*
**Earle**, Alice Morse 1853-1911 *BenetAL 91*
**Earle**, Alvin Mathews 1931- *AmMWSc 92*
**Earle**, Arthur Frederick 1921- *IntWW 91, Who 92*
**Earle**, Clifford John, Jr 1935- *AmMWSc 92*
**Earle**, David Prince, Jr 1910- *AmMWSc 92*
**Earle**, E. E. Maples 1900- *Who 92*
**Earle**, Elizabeth Deutsch 1937- *AmMWSc 92*
**Earle**, Eric Davis 1937- *AmMWSc 92*
**Earle**, Ernest Joseph *WhoAmP 91*
**Earle**, George *Who 92*
**Earle**, George Hughes 1925- *Who 92*
**Earle**, Hardman George *Who 92*
**Earle**, Henry 1935- *WhoAmL 92*
**Earle**, Ion 1916- *IntWW 91, Who 92*
**Earle**, Joel Vincent 1952- *Who 92*
**Earle**, John Baylis 1766-1836 *DcNCBi 2*
**Earle**, John Nicholas Francis 1926- *Who 92*
**Earle**, Julius Richard, Jr. 1954- *WhoWest 92*
**Earle**, Lewis Samuel 1933- *WhoAmP 91*
**Earle**, Maud d1943 *TwCPaSc*
**Earle**, Pliny 1809-1892 *BiInAmS*
**Earle**, Ralph, II 1928- *WhoAmP 91*
**Earle**, Ralph Hervey, Jr 1928- *AmMWSc 92*
**Earle**, Robert Barton 1958- *WhoWest 92*
**Earle**, Robert Ray 1937- *WhoAmL 92*
**Earle**, Sylvia *NewYTBS 91 [port]*
**Earle**, Sylvia Alice 1935- *WhoWest 92*
**Earle**, Victor Montagne, III 1933- *WhoAmL 92*
**Earle**, Warren *ScFEYrs*
**Earle**, William George 1940- *WhoAmL 92*
**Earles**, Rene Martin 1940- *WhoBlA 92*
**Earles**, Stanley William Edward 1929- *Who 92*
**Earley**, Anthony Francis, Jr. 1949- *WhoAmL 92*
**Earley**, Charity Edna 1918- *WhoBlA 92*
**Earley**, Charles Willard 1933- *AmMWSc 92*
**Earley**, Edward Joseph, Jr. 1952- *WhoEnt 92*
**Earley**, Jacqui *DrAPF 91*
**Earley**, Joseph Emmet 1932- *AmMWSc 92*
**Earley**, Laurence E 1931- *AmMWSc 92*
**Earley**, Mark L 1954- *WhoAmP 91*

**Earley**, Neal Christopher 1946- WhoRel 92
**Earley**, Robert 1960- WhoAmP 91
**Earley**, Stanley Armstead, Jr. 1919- WhoBlA 92
**Earley**, Tom 1911- IntAu&W 91, WrDr 92
**Earley**, Victor H. WhoEnt 92
**Earll**, Fred Nelson 1924- AmMWSc 92
**Earll**, Robert Edward 1853-1896 BiInAmS
**Earlougher**, Robert Charles, Jr 1941- AmMWSc 92
**Earls**, James Roe 1943- AmMWSc 92
**Earls**, Julian Manly 1942- WhoBlA 92
**Earls**, Paul 1934- WhoEnt 92
**Earls**, Zeren 1937- WhoEnt 92
**Early**, Alphonso James, III 1939- WhoFI 92
**Early**, Bert Hylton 1922- WhoAmL 92, WhoFI 92, WhoMW 92
**Early**, Deloreese Patricia 1931- WhoEnt 92
**Early**, Edward M 1935- WhoAmP 91
**Early**, Edward William 1934- WhoAmP 91
**Early**, Gerald 1952- ConAu 133, WhoBlA 92
**Early**, Jack Gavin, Jr. 1953- WhoFI 92
**Early**, James Counts 1947- WhoBlA 92
**Early**, James G 1937- AmMWSc 92
**Early**, James M 1922- AmMWSc 92
**Early**, James Michael 1922- WhoWest 92
**Early**, Jean Leslie Hartz 1945- WhoRel 92
**Early**, John Collins 1919- WhoAmL 92
**Early**, Joseph D. 1933- AlmAP 92 [port]
**Early**, Joseph Daniel 1933- WhoAmP 91
**Early**, Joseph E 1940- AmMWSc 92
**Early**, Judith K. 1954- WhoMW 92
**Early**, Kevin LeVoy 1951- WhoMW 92
**Early**, Patrick Joseph 1933- WhoFI 92, WhoMW 92
**Early**, Paul David 1963- WhoBlA 92
**Early**, Quinn Remar 1965- WhoBlA 92
**Early**, Rexford Carlisle 1934- WhoAmP 91
**Early**, Robert S. 1935- WhoBlA 92
**Early**, S. Allen, III 1946- WhoBlA 92
**Early**, Stephen Barry 1945- WhoAmL 92
**Early**, Sybil Theresa 1952- WhoBlA 92
**Early**, Tom TwCPaSc, TwCWW 91, WrDr 92
**Early**, Violet Theresa 1924- WhoBlA 92
**Early**, Willian Norman 1931- WhoAmL 92
**Earnest**, Andrew George 1949- AmMWSc 92
**Earnest**, John L 1944- WhoAmP 91
**Earnest**, Sue W 1907- AmMWSc 92
**Earnhart**, Milt 1918- WhoAmP 91
**Earnshaw**, Anthony 1924- TwCPaSc, WrDr 92
**Earnshaw**, John W 1939- AmMWSc 92
**Earnshaw**, Roy 1917- Who 92
**Earnshaw**, William C 1950- AmMWSc 92
**Earp**, Virgil TwCWW 91
**Earth**, Wind and Fire NewAmDM
**Earthrowl**, Eliab George 1878-1948 TwCPaSc
**Eartly**, David Paul 1942- AmMWSc 92
**Earwood**, J. Donald, Jr. 1963- WhoRel 92
**Earwood**, Joseph Alan 1956- WhoMW 92
**Easby**, Steve 1958- TwCPaSc
**Eash**, John T 1906- AmMWSc 92
**Easler**, Michael Anthony 1950- WhoBlA 92
**Easley**, Betty 1929- WhoAmP 91
**Easley**, Billy Harley 1925- WhoBlA 92
**Easley**, Brenda Vietta 1951- WhoBlA 92
**Easley**, David 1952- WhoFI 92
**Easley**, Eddie V. 1928- WhoBlA 92
**Easley**, George Washington 1933- WhoWest 92
**Easley**, Hugh WhoAmP 91
**Easley**, Jacqueline Ruth 1957- WhoBlA 92
**Easley**, Jimmy Parker 1939- WhoMW 92
**Easley**, Joanne L. 1952- WhoMW 92
**Easley**, Kenny 1959- WhoBlA 92
**Easley**, Kevin A 1960- WhoAmP 91
**Easley**, Loyce Anna 1918- WhoWest 92
**Easley**, Mack 1916- WhoAmP 91
**Easley**, Michael B. 1954- WhoFI 92
**Easley**, Paul Howard, Sr. 1930- WhoBlA 92
**Easley**, Robert Sheldon 1950- WhoMW 92
**Easley**, Stephen Phillip 1952- AmMWSc 92
**Easley**, Veo 1932- WhoAmP 91
**Easmon**, Charles Syrett Farrell 1946- Who 92
**Easmon**, R. Sarif WrDr 92
**Eason**, Eugene WhoAmP 91
**Eason**, Henry 1910- IntWW 91, Who 92
**Eason**, James L 1942- WhoAmP 91
**Eason**, John Verne 1926- WhoAmP 91
**Eason**, Paul Bauer 1953- WhoAmL 92
**Eason**, Peter Lawrence 1955- WhoWest 92
**Eason**, Robert Gaston 1924- AmMWSc 92
**Eason**, Robert Kinley 1908- Who 92
**Eason**, William Everette, Jr. 1943- WhoAmL 92
**Easson**, Richard 1948- TwCPaSc
**Easson**, William McAlpine 1931- AmMWSc 92
**East**, Alfred 1849-1913 TwCPaSc
**East**, Charles DrAPF 91
**East**, Charles Robert 1936- WhoIns 92
**East**, David Albert 1936- Who 92
**East**, Don G. 1935- WhoWest 92
**East**, Ernest Earl 1942- WhoAmL 92
**East**, Frank Howard 1937- WhoMW 92
**East**, Frederick Henry 1919- Who 92
**East**, Gerald Reginald Ricketts d1991 Who 92N
**East**, Ginny 1959- WhoEnt 92
**East**, Grahame Richard 1908- Who 92
**East**, James Lindsay 1936- AmMWSc 92
**East**, John 1937- WrDr 92
**East**, John Anthony 1930- Who 92
**East**, Kenneth Arthur 1921- Who 92
**East**, Larry Verne 1937- AmMWSc 92
**East**, Lewis Ronald 1899- Who 92
**East**, Michael WrDr 92
**East**, Morris IntAu&W 91X
**East**, Ronald Who 92
**East**, Ronald Joseph 1931- Who 92
**East**, Thomas 1535?-1608 NewAmDM
**East**, William Gordon 1902- Who 92, WrDr 92
**East Anglia**, Bishop of 1919- Who 92
**Eastaugh**, Kenneth 1929- IntAu&W 91, WrDr 92
**Eastburn**, James W. 1797-1819 BenetAL 91
**Eastburn**, Jeannette Rose 1916- WhoMW 92, WhoRel 92
**Eastburn**, Richard A. 1934- WhoFI 92, WhoMW 92
**Eastburn**, William Henry, III 1932- WhoAmL 92
**Eastchurch**, Thomas d1677? DcNCBi 2
**Eastcott**, Harry Hubert Grayson 1917- IntWW 91, Who 92
**Easter**, Donald Philips 1919- AmMWSc 92
**Easter**, Hezekiah H. 1921- WhoBlA 92
**Easter**, Hezekiah Herbert 1921- WhoAmP 91
**Easter**, James Hugh 1948- WhoAmP 91
**Easter**, John W 1946- WhoIns 92
**Easter**, Robert Arnold 1947- AmMWSc 92
**Easter**, Ruby L. 1918- WhoRel 92
**Easter**, Rufus Benjamin, Jr. 1928- WhoBlA 92
**Easter**, Stephen Sherman, Jr 1938- AmMWSc 92
**Easter**, Steven Wycliffe 1941- WhoFI 92
**Easter**, Wilfred Otis, Jr. 1941- WhoBlA 92
**Easter**, William Taylor 1931- AmMWSc 92
**Easterbrook**, Don J 1935- AmMWSc 92
**Easterbrook**, Eliot Knights 1927- AmMWSc 92
**Easterbrook**, Frank Hoover 1948- WhoAmL 92, WhoAmP 91
**Easterbrook**, Kenneth Brian 1935- AmMWSc 92
**Easterday**, Bernard Carlyle 1929- AmMWSc 92
**Easterday**, Harry Tyson 1922- AmMWSc 92
**Easterday**, Jack L 1928- AmMWSc 92
**Easterday**, James E. 1915- WhoRel 92
**Easterday**, Kenneth E 1933- AmMWSc 92
**Easterday**, Michael Joseph 1941- WhoFI 92
**Easterday**, Otho Dunreath 1924- AmMWSc 92
**Easterday**, Richard Lee 1938- AmMWSc 92
**Easterley**, Robert ScFEYrs
**Easterley**, Robert and Wilbraham, John ScFEYrs
**Easterlin**, John Howard 1962- WhoEnt 92
**Easterling**, Larry Byron 1942- WhoRel 92
**Easterling**, Patricia Elizabeth 1934- Who 92
**Easterling**, Rosanna Avonna 1957- WhoBlA 92
**Easterling**, Ruth M 1910- WhoAmP 91
**Easterling**, William Ewart, Jr 1930- AmMWSc 92
**Easterly**, Nathan William 1927- AmMWSc 92
**Easterly**, Tom 1940- WhoAmP 91
**Easterman**, Daniel WrDr 92
**Eastes**, Frank Elisha 1924- AmMWSc 92
**Eastham**, James Norman 1903- AmMWSc 92
**Eastham**, Jerome Fields 1924- AmMWSc 92
**Eastham**, Kenneth 1927- Who 92
**Eastham**, Michael 1920- Who 92
**Easthope**, Antony 1939- WrDr 92
**Eastick**, Philip Noel 1954- WhoEnt 92
**Eastin**, Delaine WhoAmP 91
**Eastin**, Emory Ford 1940- AmMWSc 92
**Eastin**, James Thomas 1938- WhoEnt 92
**Eastin**, Jane White 1915- WhoAmP 91
**Eastin**, Jerry Dean 1931- AmMWSc 92
**Eastin**, John A 1934- AmMWSc 92
**Eastin**, Keith E. 1940- WhoAmL 92
**Eastin**, Robert Eugene 1924- WhoAmP 91
**Eastin**, William Clarence, Jr 1940- AmMWSc 92
**Eastlake**, Charles Locke 1836-1900 DcTwDes
**Eastlake**, William DrAPF 91
**Eastlake**, William 1917- BenetAL 91, ConNov 91, TwCWW 91, WrDr 92
**Eastland**, David Meade 1922- AmMWSc 92
**Eastland**, George Warren, Jr 1939- AmMWSc 92
**Eastland**, James Hagan 1923- WhoRel 92
**Eastland**, James O 1904-1986 FacFETw
**Eastland**, Woods Eugene 1945- WhoFI 92
**Eastler**, Thomas Edward 1944- AmMWSc 92
**Eastlick**, Herbert Leonard 1908- AmMWSc 92
**Eastman**, Alan D 1946- AmMWSc 92
**Eastman**, Albert Theodore 1928- WhoRel 92
**Eastman**, Caroline Merriam 1946- AmMWSc 92
**Eastman**, Charles A. 1858-1939 BenetAL 91
**Eastman**, Charles Gamage 1816-1860 BenetAL 91
**Eastman**, Charles Rochester 1868-1918 BiInAmS
**Eastman**, Crystal 1881-1928 AmPeW, BiDBrF 2, PorAmW [port], RComAH
**Eastman**, Daniel Robert Peden 1933- AmMWSc 92
**Eastman**, David Willard 1939- AmMWSc 92
**Eastman**, Dean Eric 1940- AmMWSc 92, IntWW 91
**Eastman**, Derek Ian Tennent d1991 Who 92N
**Eastman**, Eleanor Corinna WhoBlA 92
**Eastman**, Ernest 1930- IntWW 91
**Eastman**, George 1854-1932 DcTwDes, FacFETw, RComAH
**Eastman**, George D. d1991 NewYTBS 91
**Eastman**, George H. 1949- WhoEnt 92
**Eastman**, Guy Warner 1881-1907 BiInAmS
**Eastman**, Harry Claude MacColl 1923- IntWW 91
**Eastman**, Hope Beth 1943- WhoAmL 92
**Eastman**, James Earl 1946- WhoEnt 92
**Eastman**, John Richard 1917- WhoFI 92
**Eastman**, John Robie 1836-1913 BiInAmS
**Eastman**, John W 1935- AmMWSc 92
**Eastman**, Joseph 1944- AmMWSc 92
**Eastman**, Lee V. d1991 NewYTBS 91
**Eastman**, Lester F 1928- AmMWSc 92
**Eastman**, Mary H. 1818-1880 BenetAL 91
**Eastman**, Max 1883-1969 BenetAL 91
**Eastman**, Max Forrester 1883-1969 AmPeW
**Eastman**, Michael Paul 1941- AmMWSc 92
**Eastman**, Philip Clifford 1932- AmMWSc 92
**Eastman**, R O ScFEYrs
**Eastman**, Richard Dare 1936- WhoWest 92
**Eastman**, Richard Hallenbeck 1918- AmMWSc 92
**Eastman**, Robert M 1918- AmMWSc 92
**Eastman**, Robert Merriam 1918- WhoMW 92
**Eastman**, Robert Todd 1953- WhoEnt 92
**Eastman**, Roger Herbert 1931- WhoWest 92
**Eastman**, Ronald D. 1941- WhoAmL 92
**Eastman**, Seth 1808-1875 BenetAL 91
**Eastman**, Susan Elizabeth 1948- WhoWest 92
**Eastment**, Thomas James 1950- WhoAmL 92
**Eastmond**, Elbert John 1915- AmMWSc 92
**Eastmond**, Joan Marcella 1940- WhoBlA 92
**Easton**, Albert Eddy 1938- WhoFI 92
**Easton**, David 1917- IntWW 91, WrDr 92
**Easton**, David John 1941- Who 92
**Easton**, David Williams 1944- WhoAmL 92
**Easton**, Dexter Morgan 1921- AmMWSc 92
**Easton**, Douglas P 1944- AmMWSc 92
**Easton**, Earnest Lee 1943- IntAu&W 91
**Easton**, Edward 1940- WhoEnt 92
**Easton**, Elizabeth Wynne 1956- ConAu 134
**Easton**, Elmer C 1909- AmMWSc 92
**Easton**, Florence 1882-1955 NewAmDM
**Easton**, Glenn Scott 1959- WhoRel 92
**Easton**, Ivan G 1916- AmMWSc 92
**Easton**, James 1908-1990 AnObit 1990
**Easton**, James 1931- Who 92
**Easton**, James Alfred d1990 Who 92N
**Easton**, John 1929- TwCPaSc
**Easton**, John Francis 1928- Who 92
**Easton**, John J, Jr 1943- WhoAmP 91
**Easton**, John Jay, Jr. 1943- WhoAmL 92
**Easton**, Loyd D. 1915- WrDr 92
**Easton**, Nelson Roy 1919- AmMWSc 92
**Easton**, Randall Craig 1955- WhoFI 92
**Easton**, Richard J 1938- AmMWSc 92
**Easton**, Richard James 1934- WhoBlA 92
**Easton**, Robert 1915- ConAu 14AS [port], TwCWW 91, WrDr 92
**Easton**, Robert 1922- Who 92
**Easton**, Robert 1930- WhoEnt 92
**Easton**, Robert Alexander 1948- Who 92
**Easton**, Robert Howard 1936- WhoMW 92
**Easton**, Robert Olney 1915- IntAu&W 91, WhoWest 92
**Easton**, Robert Walter 1941- AmMWSc 92
**Easton**, Roger David 1923- WhoWest 92
**Easton**, Roger L WhoAmP 91
**Easton**, Sheena 1959- WhoEnt 92
**Easton**, Stephen Douglas 1958- WhoAmL 92
**Easton**, William Heyden 1916- AmMWSc 92
**Easton**, William James Durant 1941- WhoWest 92
**Easton-O'Donnell**, Joey 1955- WhoEnt 92
**Eastwick**, James ScFEYrs
**Eastwood**, Abraham Bagot 1943- AmMWSc 92
**Eastwood**, Basil R 1936- AmMWSc 92
**Eastwood**, Basil Stephen Talbot 1944- Who 92
**Eastwood**, Clint 1930- FacFETw, IntMPA 92, IntWW 91, WhoEnt 92
**Eastwood**, Dana Alan 1947- WhoFI 92
**Eastwood**, DeLyle 1932- AmMWSc 92
**Eastwood**, Douglas William 1918- AmMWSc 92
**Eastwood**, Granville 1906- Who 92
**Eastwood**, Gregory Lindsay 1940- AmMWSc 92
**Eastwood**, John 1909- Who 92
**Eastwood**, John Stephen 1925- Who 92
**Eastwood**, Noel Anthony Michael 1932- Who 92
**Eastwood**, Raymond L 1940- AmMWSc 92
**Eastwood**, Ronald Alan 1961- WhoRel 92
**Eastwood**, Thomas Alexander 1920- AmMWSc 92
**Eastwood**, Walter 1867-1943 TwCPaSc
**Eastwood**, Wilfred 1923- Who 92
**Easty**, David Leohello 1933- Who 92
**Easty**, Dwight Buchanan 1934- AmMWSc 92
**Easum**, Donald B. 1923- IntWW 91
**Easwaran**, Eknath RelLAm 91
**Easydorchik**, Edwin 1949- TwCPaSc
**Eates**, Edward Caston 1916- Who 92
**Eather**, Kenneth William 1901- Who 92
**Eatherly**, John Hershel, III 1940- WhoRel 92
**Eatinger**, Robert Joseph, Jr. 1957- WhoAmL 92
**Eatman**, Brenda Alene 1957- WhoBlA 92
**Eatman**, Janice A. 1959- WhoBlA 92
**Eatock Taylor**, Rodney 1944- Who 92
**Eaton**, Alvah Augustus 1865-1908 BiInAmS
**Eaton**, Alvin Ralph 1920- AmMWSc 92
**Eaton**, Amos 1776-1842 BiInAmS
**Eaton**, Barbra L 1941- AmMWSc 92
**Eaton**, Brian Alexander 1916- Who 92
**Eaton**, Charles D. WhoHisp 92
**Eaton**, Charles Edward DrAPF 91
**Eaton**, Charles Edward 1915- IntAu&W 91
**Eaton**, Charles Edward 1916- ConPo 91, WrDr 92
**Eaton**, Clyde S 1907- WhoAmP 91
**Eaton**, Cyrus Stephen 1883-1979 FacFETw
**Eaton**, Daniel Adams 1956- WhoAmP 91
**Eaton**, Daniel Cady 1834-1895 BiInAmS
**Eaton**, Darwin G 1823?-1895 BiInAmS
**Eaton**, David 1949- WhoEnt 92
**Eaton**, David Fielder 1946- AmMWSc 92
**Eaton**, David Hilliard 1932- WhoBlA 92
**Eaton**, David J 1949- AmMWSc 92
**Eaton**, David Leo 1932- AmMWSc 92
**Eaton**, Derek Lionel Who 92
**Eaton**, Donald Rex 1932- AmMWSc 92
**Eaton**, Douglas Charles 1945- AmMWSc 92
**Eaton**, Edgar Philip, Jr. 1923- WhoFI 92
**Eaton**, Erin Marie 1961- WhoWest 92
**Eaton**, Evelyn Sybil Mary 1902- BenetAL 91
**Eaton**, Gareth Richard 1940- AmMWSc 92
**Eaton**, George 1942- IntWW 91
**Eaton**, George L. SmATA 65
**Eaton**, George T 1910- AmMWSc 92
**Eaton**, George Walter 1933- AmMWSc 92
**Eaton**, Glenn Alan 1917- WhoRel 92
**Eaton**, Gordon Gray 1941- AmMWSc 92
**Eaton**, Gordon Pryor 1929- AmMWSc 92
**Eaton**, Harvill Carlton 1948- AmMWSc 92
**Eaton**, Henry Felix 1925- WhoFI 92
**Eaton**, Henry Taft 1918- WhoWest 92
**Eaton**, J H 1933- AmMWSc 92
**Eaton**, James A. 1921- WhoBlA 92
**Eaton**, James Edward 1951- WhoRel 92

**Eaton**, James Nathaniel, Sr. 1930- WhoBlA 92
**Eaton**, James Thompson 1927- Who 92
**Eaton**, Jerome F 1941- AmMWSc 92
**Eaton**, Jerry Paul 1926- AmMWSc 92
**Eaton**, Joe Oscar 1920- WhoAmL 92
**Eaton**, Joel A 1948- AmMWSc 92
**Eaton**, John C. 1935- WhoEnt 92
**Eaton**, John Charles 1935- NewAmDM
**Eaton**, John Charles, Jr. 1954- WhoFI 92
**Eaton**, John Henry 1790-1856 DcNCBi 2
**Eaton**, John Herbert 1927- WrDr 92
**Eaton**, John Kelly 1954- AmMWSc 92
**Eaton**, John LeRoy 1939- AmMWSc 92
**Eaton**, John P 1926- IntAu&W 91
**Eaton**, John Rust 1772-1830 DcNCBi 2
**Eaton**, John Wallace 1941- AmMWSc 92
**Eaton**, Joli Fay 1951- WhoWest 92
**Eaton**, Joseph March 1901- WhoAmP 91
**Eaton**, Karl Francis 1925- WhoMW 92
**Eaton**, Kenneth 1934- Who 92
**Eaton**, Kim Diane 1956- WhoAmL 92
**Eaton**, L. Daniel 1940- WhoWest 92
**Eaton**, Larry Ralph 1944- WhoAmL 92
**Eaton**, Lela M. Z. 1946- WhoBlA 92
**Eaton**, Lewis Swift 1919- WhoFI 92
**Eaton**, Marilyn Sue 1955- WhoRel 92
**Eaton**, Merrill Thomas, Jr 1920- AmMWSc 92
**Eaton**, Michael William 1958- WhoAmL 92
**Eaton**, Minetta Gaylor 1912- WhoBlA 92
**Eaton**, Monroe Davis 1904- AmMWSc 92
**Eaton**, Morris Leroy 1939- AmMWSc 92
**Eaton**, Patricia Frances 1944- WhoBlA 92
**Eaton**, Paul Bernard 1917- AmMWSc 92
**Eaton**, Paul Wentland 1927- AmMWSc 92
**Eaton**, Peter 1914- Who 92
**Eaton**, Philip Eugene 1936- AmMWSc 92
**Eaton**, Richard Behrens 1914- WrDr 92
**Eaton**, Richard Selden 1943- WhoAmP 91
**Eaton**, Robert Charles 1946- AmMWSc 92
**Eaton**, Robert Edward Lee 1909- WhoFI 92
**Eaton**, Robert J. 1940- IntWW 91
**Eaton**, Robert James 1940- AmMWSc 92, WhoFI 92, WhoMW 92
**Eaton**, Roy F. 1930- WhoEnt 92
**Eaton**, Sandra Shaw 1946- AmMWSc 92
**Eaton**, Stephen Woodman 1918- AmMWSc 92
**Eaton**, Ted Frank 1942- WhoRel 92
**Eaton**, Thelma Lucile 1928- WhoBlA 92
**Eaton**, Theodore A 1950- WhoIns 92
**Eaton**, Thomas 1739?-1809 DcNCBi 2
**Eaton**, Thomas Clark 1952- WhoWest 92
**Eaton**, Thomas Eldon 1948- AmMWSc 92
**Eaton**, Timothy R. 1951- WhoEnt 92
**Eaton**, Trevor 1934- WrDr 92
**Eaton**, Tyrone 1943- WhoBlA 92
**Eaton**, Walter Prichard 1878-1957 BenetAL 91
**Eaton**, William, Jr. 1809-1881 DcNCBi 2
**Eaton**, William Allen 1938- AmMWSc 92
**Eaton**, William Clement 1898-1980 DcNCBi 2
**Eaton**, William Lee 1947- WhoAmL 92
**Eaton**, William Thomas 1938- AmMWSc 92
**Eatough**, Delbert J 1940- AmMWSc 92
**Eatough**, Norman L 1933- AmMWSc 92
**Eaves**, A. Reginald 1935- WhoBlA 92
**Eaves**, Allen Charles Edward 1941- AmMWSc 92
**Eaves**, Burchet Curtis 1938- AmMWSc 92
**Eaves**, David Magill 1933- AmMWSc 92
**Eaves**, George Newton 1935- AmMWSc 92
**Eaves**, Gerald R 1939- WhoAmP 91
**Eaves**, James Clifton 1912- AmMWSc 92
**Eaves**, James Edwin Ed 1953- WhoEnt 92
**Eaves**, John 1929- TwCPaSc
**Eaves**, Lucile 1869-1953 WomSoc
**Eaves**, Mary Marie 1939- WhoAmP 91
**Eaves**, Reuben Elco 1944- AmMWSc 92
**Eaves**, William Alfred 1962- WhoRel 92
**Eayrs**, John Thomas 1913- Who 92
**Ebach**, Earl A 1928- AmMWSc 92
**Ebacher**, Roger 1936- WhoRel 92
**Ebadi**, Manuchair 1935- AmMWSc 92
**Eban**, Abba 1915- IntWW 91, Who 92
**Ebanga**, Martin Ndongo BlkOlyM
**Ebashi**, Setsuro 1922- FacFETw
**Ebaugh**, David Paul 1930- WhoRel 92
**Ebaugh**, Frank Wright 1901- WhoFI 92
**Ebaugh**, Franklin G, Jr 1921- AmMWSc 92
**Ebaugh**, William L. 1930- WhoWest 92
**Ebb**, Fred 1936- WhoEnt 92
**Ebb**, Lawrence Forrest 1918- WhoAmL 92
**Ebbe**, Obi N. I. 1949- WhoBlA 92
**Ebbe**, Shirley Nadine AmMWSc 92
**Ebbers**, James Paul 1926- WhoRel 92
**Ebbert**, Arthur, Jr 1922- AmMWSc 92
**Ebbesen**, Lynn Royce 1948- AmMWSc 92
**Ebbesmeyer**, Curtis Charles 1943- AmMWSc 92
**Ebbesson**, Sven O E 1937- AmMWSc 92
**Ebbett**, Eve 1925- WrDr 92
**Ebbett**, Frances Eva 1925- IntAu&W 91
**Ebbin**, Allan J 1938- AmMWSc 92
**Ebbing**, Darrell Delmar 1933- AmMWSc 92
**Ebbisham**, Baron d1991 Who 92N
**Ebbitts**, Mark Hobart 1949- WhoMW 92
**Ebbs**, George Heberling, Jr. 1942- WhoFI 92
**Ebbs**, Jane Cotton 1912- AmMWSc 92
**Ebdon**, David William 1939- AmMWSc 92
**Ebdon**, Paul Robert 1950- WhoWest 92
**Ebeid**, Russell Joseph 1940- WhoFI 92, WhoMW 92
**Ebejer**, Francis 1925- IntAu&W 91
**Ebel**, David M WhoAmP 91
**Ebel**, David M. 1940- WhoAmL 92, WhoWest 92
**Ebel**, Marvin Emerson 1930- AmMWSc 92
**Ebel**, Richard E 1946- AmMWSc 92
**Ebel**, Suzanne IntAu&W 91, WrDr 92
**Ebel**, Thomas George 1941- WhoAmL 92
**Ebel**, Wilfred Louis 1930- WhoAmP 91
**Ebeling**, Alfred W 1931- AmMWSc 92
**Eben**, Petr 1929- ConCom 92, IntWW 91
**Ebener**, Brian Scott 1961- WhoAmL 92
**Eberhard**, Anatol 1938- AmMWSc 92
**Eberhard**, Eric Drake 1945- WhoAmL 92
**Eberhard**, Everett 1915- AmMWSc 92
**Eberhard**, Jeffrey Wayne 1950- AmMWSc 92
**Eberhard**, Philippe Henri 1929- AmMWSc 92
**Eberhard**, William Thomas 1952- WhoMW 92
**Eberhard**, Wynn Lowell 1944- AmMWSc 92
**Eberhardt**, Allen Craig 1950- AmMWSc 92
**Eberhardt**, Clifford 1947- WhoBlA 92
**Eberhardt**, Cornelius 1932- WhoEnt 92
**Eberhardt**, Daniel Hugo 1938- WhoAmL 92
**Eberhardt**, Isabelle 1877-1904 EncAmaz 91
**Eberhardt**, Johann Ludwig 1758-1839 DcNCBi 2
**Eberhardt**, Keith Randall 1947- AmMWSc 92
**Eberhardt**, Lester Lee 1923- AmMWSc 92
**Eberhardt**, Manfred Karl 1930- AmMWSc 92
**Eberhardt**, Nikolai 1930- AmMWSc 92
**Eberhardt**, William Henry 1920- AmMWSc 92
**Eberhart**, H D 1906- AmMWSc 92
**Eberhart**, James Gettins 1936- AmMWSc 92
**Eberhart**, Mignon 1899- BenetAL 91
**Eberhart**, Mignon G 1899- IntAu&W 91, WrDr 92
**Eberhart**, Nelle Richmond 1871-1944 BenetAL 91
**Eberhart**, Richard DrAPF 91
**Eberhart**, Richard 1904- BenetAL 91, ConPo 91, IntAu&W 91, IntWW 91, Who 92, WrDr 92
**Eberhart**, Robert Clyde 1937- AmMWSc 92
**Eberhart**, Robert J 1930- AmMWSc 92
**Eberhart**, Steve A 1931- AmMWSc 92, WhoWest 92
**Eberhart**, Steven Wesley 1952- WhoMW 92
**Eberius**, Klaus Otto 1940- WhoFI 92
**Eberl**, Irmfried 1910-1948 EncTR 91
**Eberle**, Don 1948- WhoAmP 91
**Eberle**, Edward J. 1955- WhoAmL 92
**Eberle**, Helen I 1932- AmMWSc 92
**Eberle**, James 1927- Who 92
**Eberle**, James Henry Fuller 1927- IntWW 91
**Eberle**, John 1787-1838 BiInAmS
**Eberle**, Jon William 1934- AmMWSc 92
**Eberle**, Leo Thomas 1948- WhoAmL 92
**Eberle**, Michael John 1954- WhoFI 92
**Eberle**, Peter Richard 1941- WhoRel 92, WhoWest 92
**Eberle**, Richard Michael 1942- WhoWest 92
**Eberle**, Robert Frank, Jr. 1946- WhoFI 92
**Eberle**, William Denman 1923- IntWW 91
**Eberlein**, George Donald 1920- AmMWSc 92
**Eberlein**, Patricia James 1925- AmMWSc 92
**Eberlein**, Patrick Barry 1944- AmMWSc 92
**Eberley**, Helen-Kay 1947- WhoEnt 92, WhoMW 92
**Eberly**, Donald Eugene 1953- WhoAmP 91
**Eberly**, Harry Landis 1924- WhoFI 92
**Eberly**, Joseph Henry 1935- AmMWSc 92
**Eberly**, Kathryn DrAPF 91
**Eberly**, William Robert 1926- AmMWSc 92
**Ebersohn**, Wessel 1940- IntAu&W 91, WrDr 92
**Ebersol**, Dick LesBEnT 92
**Ebersole**, Brian 1947- WhoAmP 91
**Ebersole**, Frederick Levi, Sr. 1939- WhoMW 92
**Ebersole**, George David 1936- WhoFI 92
**Ebersole**, J. Glenn, Jr. 1947- WhoFI 92
**Ebersole**, John Franklin 1946- AmMWSc 92
**Eberspacher**, Charles H 1947- WhoAmP 91
**Eberspacher**, E. C. 1949- WhoAmL 92
**Eberstein**, Arthur 1928- AmMWSc 92
**Ebert**, Alan 1935- IntAu&W 91, WrDr 92
**Ebert**, Andrew Gabriel 1936- AmMWSc 92
**Ebert**, Carol Anne 1945- WhoFI 92
**Ebert**, Charles H V 1924- AmMWSc 92
**Ebert**, Earl Ernest 1931- AmMWSc 92
**Ebert**, Friedrich 1871-1925 EncTR 91 [port]
**Ebert**, Gary Lee 1947- AmMWSc 92
**Ebert**, Gladys Eileen Meyer 1921- WhoMW 92
**Ebert**, James A. 1950- WhoEnt 92
**Ebert**, James D. 1921- WrDr 92
**Ebert**, James David 1921- AmMWSc 92, IntWW 91, WhoFI 92
**Ebert**, Jeff Scott 1962- WhoFI 92
**Ebert**, Lawrence Burton 1949- AmMWSc 92
**Ebert**, Lynn J 1920- AmMWSc 92
**Ebert**, Michael 1917- WhoAmL 92
**Ebert**, Norma J. 1931- WhoMW 92
**Ebert**, Patricia Dorothy 1949- AmMWSc 92
**Ebert**, Paul Allen 1932- AmMWSc 92, WhoMW 92
**Ebert**, Paul Joseph 1936- AmMWSc 92
**Ebert**, Peter 1918- IntWW 91, Who 92
**Ebert**, Philip E 1929- AmMWSc 92
**Ebert**, Regan Danielle 1954- WhoAmL 92
**Ebert**, Richard Vincent 1912- AmMWSc 92
**Ebert**, Robert H 1914- AmMWSc 92
**Ebert**, Robert Higgins 1914- IntWW 91
**Ebert**, Robert Leo 1961- WhoEnt 92
**Ebert**, Robert Raymond 1943- WhoFI 92
**Ebert**, Roger 1942- ConTFT 9, WrDr 92
**Ebert**, Roger Joseph 1942- WhoEnt 92, WhoMW 92
**Ebert**, Thomas A 1938- AmMWSc 92
**Ebert**, Wesley W 1926- AmMWSc 92
**Ebert**, William Robley 1928- AmMWSc 92
**Eberts**, Floyd S, Jr 1924- AmMWSc 92
**Eberts**, John David 1941- IntMPA 92, Who 92
**Eberts**, Ray Edward 1954- AmMWSc 92
**Eberts**, Robert Eugene 1931- AmMWSc 92
**Eberwein**, Barton Douglas 1951- WhoWest 92
**Eberwein**, Thomas Charles 1948- WhoAmL 92
**Ebetino**, Charles A., Jr. 1952- WhoFI 92
**Ebetino**, Frank Frederick 1927- AmMWSc 92
**Ebey**, Carl Finley 1940- WhoRel 92
**Ebie**, Teresa Hayes 1957- WhoWest 92
**Ebie**, William D. 1942- WhoWest 92
**Ebin**, David G 1942- AmMWSc 92
**Ebin**, Robert Felix 1940- WhoAmL 92
**Ebiner**, Robert Maurice 1927- WhoAmL 92
**Ebinger**, Warren Ralph 1927- WhoRel 92
**Ebitz**, David MacKinnon 1947- WhoWest 92
**Ebitz**, Elizabeth Kelly 1950- WhoAmL 92
**Eble**, John Nelson 1927- AmMWSc 92
**Eble**, Thomas Eugene 1923- AmMWSc 92
**Ebling**, William Lunder 1930- WhoRel 92
**Ebner**, Ford Francis 1934- AmMWSc 92
**Ebner**, Jerry Rudolph 1947- AmMWSc 92
**Ebner**, Kurt E 1931- AmMWSc 92
**Ebner**, Kurt Miller 1960- WhoFI 92
**Ebner**, Stanley Gadd 1933- AmMWSc 92
**Ebner**, Timothy John 1949- AmMWSc 92
**Ebo**, Antona 1924- WhoBlA 92
**Ebon**, Martin 1917- WrDr 92
**Ebrahim**, Currimbhoy 1935- Who 92
**Ebrahimi**, Fereshteh 1951- AmMWSc 92
**Ebrahimi**, Nader Dabir 1955- AmMWSc 92
**Ebrahimi**, Yaghoob Salamat 1945- WhoWest 92
**Ebrey**, Thomas G 1941- AmMWSc 92
**Ebright**, Peggy Linden Short 1928- WhoWest 92
**Ebright**, Timothy George 1954- WhoFI 92
**Ebrington**, Viscount 1951- Who 92
**Ebsen**, Buddy LesBEnT 92
**Ebsen**, Buddy 1908- IntMPA 92
**Ebsen**, Stephen Matthew 1962- WhoFI 92
**Ebsworth**, Ann Marian 1937- Who 92
**Ebsworth**, Evelyn Algernon Valentine 1933- Who 92
**Ebtehaj**, Abol Hassan 1899- IntWW 91
**Eburne**, Sidney 1918- IntWW 91, Who 92
**Ebury**, Baron 1934- Who 92
**Eby**, Al R 1935- WhoAmP 91
**Eby**, Charles J 1929- AmMWSc 92
**Eby**, Deborah Ruth 1956- WhoEnt 92
**Eby**, Denise 1917- AmMWSc 92
**Eby**, Edward Stuart, Sr 1934- AmMWSc 92
**Eby**, Frank Shilling 1924- AmMWSc 92
**Eby**, G Nelson 1944- AmMWSc 92
**Eby**, George W. 1914- IntMPA 92
**Eby**, Harold Hildenbrandt 1918- AmMWSc 92
**Eby**, John Edson 1933- AmMWSc 92
**Eby**, John Martin 1939- AmMWSc 92
**Eby**, John Oliver 1940- WhoRel 92
**Eby**, Lawrence Thornton 1916- AmMWSc 92
**Eby**, Robert Newcomer 1931- AmMWSc 92
**Eby**, Ronald Kraft 1929- AmMWSc 92
**Eby**, Solomon 1834-1931 RelLAm 91
**Eca De Queiros**, Antonio 1891-1968 BiDExR
**Ecanow**, Bernard 1923- AmMWSc 92
**Eccard**, Johannes 1553-1611 NewAmDM
**Eccard**, Walter Thomas 1946- WhoAmL 92
**Eccles** Who 92
**Eccles**, Viscount 1904- IntWW 91, Who 92
**Eccles**, Geoffrey 1925- Who 92
**Eccles**, Homer Gordon 1937- WhoAmP 91
**Eccles**, Hugh William Patrick 1946- Who 92
**Eccles**, Jack Fleming 1922- Who 92
**Eccles**, John 1903- WrDr 92
**Eccles**, John Carew 1903- FacFETw, IntWW 91, Who 92, WhoNob 90
**Eccles**, John Dawson 1931- Who 92
**Eccles**, Patrick Who 92
**Eccles**, Peter Wilson 1936- WhoBlA 92
**Eccles**, Samuel Franklin 1930- AmMWSc 92
**Eccles**, Spencer Fox 1934- WhoWest 92
**Eccles**, Ted IntMPA 92
**Eccles**, William J 1932- AmMWSc 92
**Eccles of Moulton**, Baroness 1933- Who 92
**Eccles-Williams**, Hilary a'Beckett 1917- Who 92
**Eccleshall**, Donald 1927- AmMWSc 92
**Eccleston**, Brendan 1960- WhoAmL 92
**Eccleston**, Harry 1923- TwCPaSc
**Eccleston**, Harry Norman 1923- Who 92
**Eccleston**, Lynn Ellen 1948- WhoAmL 92
**Ecclestone**, Jacob Andrew 1939- Who 92
**Ecevit**, Bulent 1925- FacFETw, IntWW 91
**Echandi**, Eddie 1926- AmMWSc 92
**Echandi Jimenez**, Mario 1915- IntWW 91
**Echavarren**, Roberto 1944- ConSpAP
**Echave Ibia**, Baltasar 1580?-1660 HisDSpE
**Echave Orio**, Baltasar 1548-1630 HisDSpE
**Echegaray Y Eizaguirre**, Jose 1832-1916 WhoNob 90
**Echegoyen**, Luis Alberto 1951- AmMWSc 92
**Echegoyen**, Luis Dernelio 1938- WhoHisp 92
**Echelberger**, Herbert Eugene 1938- AmMWSc 92
**Echelberger**, Wayne F, Jr 1934- AmMWSc 92
**Echenique**, Miguel 1923- WhoHisp 92
**Echeruo**, Michael 1937- ConPo 91, WrDr 92
**Echevarria**, Abraham 1942- WhoHisp 92
**Echevarria**, Angel M. WhoHisp 92
**Echevarria**, David Philip 1941- WhoHisp 92
**Echevarria**, Efrain Franco, Jr. 1949- WhoHisp 92
**Echevarria**, Margarita 1951- WhoHisp 92
**Echevarrieta**, John 1959- WhoHisp 92
**Echeverri-Carroll**, Elsie Lucia 1959- WhoHisp 92
**Echeverria**, Durand 1913- WrDr 92
**Echeverria**, Esteban 1805-1851 BenetAL 91
**Echeverria Alvarez**, Luis 1922- IntWW 91
**Echeveste**, John Anthony 1949- WhoHisp 92
**Echeveste**, Samuel P. WhoHisp 92
**Echikson**, William 1959- ConAu 134
**Echlin**, Norman David Fenton 1925- Who 92
**EchoHawk**, Larry 1948- WhoAmL 92, WhoAmP 91, WhoWest 92
**Echols**, Allan K. TwCWW 91
**Echols**, Alvin E. 1930- WhoBlA 92
**Echols**, Charles E 1924- AmMWSc 92
**Echols**, Clarence LeRoy, Jr. 1947- WhoBlA 92
**Echols**, David Lorimer 1937- WhoBlA 92
**Echols**, Dorothy Jung 1916- AmMWSc 92
**Echols**, Earl, Jr WhoAmP 91
**Echols**, Harrison 1933- AmMWSc 92
**Echols**, Ivor Tatum 1919- WhoBlA 92
**Echols**, James Albert 1950- WhoBlA 92
**Echols**, Joan 1932- AmMWSc 92
**Echols**, Joseph Todd, Jr 1936- AmMWSc 92
**Echols**, M. Eileen 1951- WhoAmL 92
**Echols**, Mary Ann 1950- WhoBlA 92
**Echols**, Paul L. 1943- WhoEnt 92
**Echols**, Sheila 1964- BlkOlyM

**Echols**, Tommy Gerald 1951- *WhoRel 92*
**Echtenkamp**, Mike G. 1934- *WhoFI 92*
**Echtenkamp**, Stephen Frederick 1951- *AmMWSc 92*
**Echternacht**, Arthur Charles 1939- *AmMWSc 92*
**Echtman**, Irwin Morton 1937- *WhoAmL 92*
**Eck**, Charles Paul 1956- *WhoMW 92*
**Eck**, David Lowell 1941- *AmMWSc 92*
**Eck**, David Wilson 1962- *WhoRel 92*
**Eck**, Dorothy 1924- *WhoAmP 91*
**Eck**, E C *WhoAmP 91*
**Eck**, George Gregory 1950- *WhoAmL 92*
**Eck**, Gerald Gilbert 1942- *AmMWSc 92*
**Eck**, Harold Victor 1924- *AmMWSc 92*
**Eck**, John Clifford 1909- *AmMWSc 92*
**Eck**, John Stark 1941- *AmMWSc 92*
**Eck**, Joseph Edward 1939- *WhoFI 92*
**Eck**, Michael John 1956- *WhoWest 92*
**Eck**, Paul 1931- *AmMWSc 92*
**Eck**, Robert Edwin 1938- *AmMWSc 92*
**Eck**, Robert Joseph 1939- *WhoAmL 92*
**Eck**, Thomas G 1929- *AmMWSc 92*
**Eckard**, Kathleen *AmMWSc 92*
**Eckard**, Ralph Edgar 1927- *WhoRel 92*
**Eckardt**, A. Roy 1918- *WrDr 92*
**Eckardt**, Alice Eliza Lyons 1923- *WhoRel 92*
**Eckardt**, Arthur Roy 1918- *IntAu&W 91, WhoRel 92*
**Eckardt**, Douglas Marsden 1954- *WhoMW 92, WhoRel 92*
**Eckardt**, Michael Jon 1943- *AmMWSc 92*
**Eckardt**, Robert E 1916- *AmMWSc 92*
**Eckart**, Dennis E. 1950- *AlmAP 92 [port]*
**Eckart**, Dennis Edward 1950- *WhoAmP 91, WhoMW 92*
**Eckart**, Dietrich 1868-1923 *BiDExR, EncTR 91 [port]*
**Eckart**, Mark Straud Franklin 1961- *WhoMW 92*
**Eckaus**, Richard Samuel 1926- *WhoFI 92*
**Eckberg**, Scott Brian 1955- *WhoMW 92*
**Eckblad**, Edith G. 1923- *WrDr 92*
**Eckblad**, James Wilbur 1941- *AmMWSc 92*
**Eckbo**, Garrett 1910- *IntAu&W 91, WrDr 92*
**Ecke**, Paul, Sr. d1991 *NewYTBS 91*
**Eckel**, Edwin Butt 1906- *AmMWSc 92*
**Eckel**, Frederick Monroe 1939- *AmMWSc 92*
**Eckel**, Malcolm David 1946- *WhoRel 92*
**Eckel**, Robert Edward 1918- *AmMWSc 92*
**Eckel**, Timothy J. 1961- *WhoEnt 92*
**Eckelbarger**, Kevin Jay 1944- *AmMWSc 92*
**Eckelberger**, Robert, Jr. 1917- *WhoAmL 92*
**Eckelman**, Carl A 1933- *AmMWSc 92*
**Eckelman**, Richard Joel 1951- *WhoWest 92*
**Eckelman**, Robert Harvey 1957- *WhoMW 92*
**Eckelmann**, Frank Donald 1929- *AmMWSc 92*
**Eckelmann**, Walter R 1929- *AmMWSc 92*
**Eckelmeyer**, Kenneth Hall 1943- *AmMWSc 92*
**Eckels**, Arthur R 1919- *AmMWSc 92*
**Eckels**, Jon *DrAPF 91*
**Eckels**, Kenneth Henry 1942- *AmMWSc 92*
**Eckels**, Robert Allen 1957- *WhoAmP 91*
**Eckenfelder**, William Wesley, Jr 1926- *AmMWSc 92*
**Eckenhoff**, James Benjamin 1943- *AmMWSc 92*
**Eckenhoff**, James Edward 1915- *AmMWSc 92*
**Eckenwalder**, James Emory 1949- *AmMWSc 92*
**Eckenwiler**, William Bruce 1945- *WhoRel 92*
**Ecker**, Allan Benjamin 1921- *WhoAmL 92, WhoEnt 92*
**Ecker**, Daniel B. 1953- *WhoFI 92*
**Ecker**, David John 1954- *AmMWSc 92*
**Ecker**, Deborah Pitluk 1954- *WhoAmL 92*
**Ecker**, Donald Ness *WhoFI 92, WhoWest 92*
**Ecker**, Edwin D 1934- *AmMWSc 92*
**Ecker**, Harry Allen 1935- *AmMWSc 92*
**Ecker**, Joseph George 1942- *AmMWSc 92*
**Ecker**, Peder Kaloides 1929- *WhoAmL 92, WhoAmP 91*
**Ecker**, Richard Eugene 1930- *AmMWSc 92*
**Ecker**, Robert Michael 1961- *WhoEnt 92*
**Eckerle**, Kenneth Lee 1936- *AmMWSc 92*
**Eckerlin**, Herbert Martin 1935- *AmMWSc 92*
**Eckerlin**, Ralph Peter 1938- *AmMWSc 92*
**Eckerman**, Jerome 1925- *AmMWSc 92*
**Eckerman**, Roy Emmanuel 1921- *WhoRel 92, WhoWest 92*
**Eckermann**, Gerald Carlton 1934- *WhoWest 92*
**Eckersley**, Alfred 1928- *AmMWSc 92*
**Eckersley**, Darrell 1939- *WhoWest 92*
**Eckersley**, Donald 1922- *Who 92*
**Eckersley**, Jay William 1949- *WhoMW 92*
**Eckersley**, Norman Chadwick 1924- *WhoWest 92*
**Eckersley**, Thomas 1914- *Who 92*
**Eckersley-Maslin**, David Michael 1929- *Who 92*
**Eckert**, Alfred Carl, Jr 1920- *AmMWSc 92*
**Eckert**, Barry S 1949- *AmMWSc 92*
**Eckert**, Bonnie Yedica 1951- *WhoMW 92*
**Eckert**, Charles 1914- *AmMWSc 92*
**Eckert**, Charles Alan 1938- *AmMWSc 92*
**Eckert**, Donald James 1949- *AmMWSc 92*
**Eckert**, Ernst R G 1904- *AmMWSc 92*
**Eckert**, George Arthur, Jr. 1927- *WhoEnt 92*
**Eckert**, George Frank 1924- *AmMWSc 92*
**Eckert**, Geraldine Gonzales 1948- *WhoWest 92*
**Eckert**, H. Charles 1929- *WhoRel 92*
**Eckert**, Hans Ulrich 1916- *AmMWSc 92*
**Eckert**, J Presper 1919- *AmMWSc 92*
**Eckert**, John M. *IntMPA 92*
**Eckert**, John S 1910- *AmMWSc 92*
**Eckert**, John Wallace 1939- *WhoEnt 92*
**Eckert**, Joseph Webster 1931- *AmMWSc 92*
**Eckert**, Juergen 1947- *AmMWSc 92*
**Eckert**, Laura E 1950- *WhoAmP 91*
**Eckert**, Lowell Edgar 1932- *WhoRel 92*
**Eckert**, Michael Joseph 1947- *WhoEnt 92, WhoFI 92*
**Eckert**, Ralph J 1929- *WhoIns 92*
**Eckert**, Richard E *WhoAmP 91*
**Eckert**, Richard Edgar, Jr 1929- *AmMWSc 92*
**Eckert**, Richard Raymond 1942- *AmMWSc 92*
**Eckert**, Roger E 1926- *AmMWSc 92*
**Eckert**, Roger Earl 1926- *WhoMW 92*
**Eckert**, Royal Winfred 1927- *WhoEnt 92*
**Eckert**, Winfield Scott 1936- *WhoMW 92*
**Eckes**, Alfred Edward, Jr 1942- *WhoAmP 91*
**Eckhard**, Jacob, Sr. 1757-1833 *NewAmDM*
**Eckhardt**, Craig Jon 1940- *AmMWSc 92*
**Eckhardt**, Donald Henry 1932- *AmMWSc 92*
**Eckhardt**, Eileen Theresa 1928- *AmMWSc 92*
**Eckhardt**, Gisela *AmMWSc 92*
**Eckhardt**, Michael Thomas 1957- *WhoWest 92*
**Eckhardt**, Richard Dale 1918- *AmMWSc 92*
**Eckhardt**, Robert Barry 1942- *AmMWSc 92*
**Eckhardt**, Roger Lee 1963- *WhoWest 92*
**Eckhardt**, Ronald A 1942- *AmMWSc 92*
**Eckhardt**, Sandor 1927- *IntWW 91*
**Eckhardt**, Shohreh B 1938- *AmMWSc 92*
**Eckhardt**, Tibor 1888-1972 *FacFETw*
**Eckhardt**, Wilfried Otto 1928- *AmMWSc 92*
**Eckhardt-Gramatte**, S.-C. 1902-1974 *NewAmDM*
**Eckhart**, Meister 1260?-1328? *DcLB 115*
**Eckhart**, James F 1923- *WhoAmP 91*
**Eckhart**, Joseph Chris 1935- *WhoMW 92*
**Eckhart**, Walter 1938- *AmMWSc 92*
**Eckhaus**, Jay Elliot 1944- *WhoAmL 92*
**Eckhause**, Morton 1935- *AmMWSc 92*
**Eckhoff**, Mary Ann *WhoRel 92*
**Eckhoff**, Norman Dean 1938- *AmMWSc 92*
**Eckhold**, Scott Reed 1953- *WhoAmL 92*
**Eckholt**, Lawrence Eugene 1945- *WhoMW 92*
**Eckhouse**, Richard Henry 1940- *AmMWSc 92*
**Eckl**, William Wray 1936- *WhoAmL 92*
**Eckland**, Jeff Howard 1957- *WhoAmL 92*
**Ecklebarger**, Kermit Allen 1935- *WhoRel 92*
**Eckler**, Albert Ross 1927- *AmMWSc 92, WhoFI 92*
**Eckler**, Paul Eugene 1946- *AmMWSc 92*
**Eckles**, Wesley Webster, Jr 1926- *AmMWSc 92*
**Eckley**, James Robert 1947- *WhoAmL 92*
**Ecklund**, Earl Frank, Jr 1945- *AmMWSc 92*
**Ecklund**, Paul Richard 1941- *AmMWSc 92*
**Ecklund**, Stanley Duane 1939- *AmMWSc 92*
**Eckman**, David Walter 1942- *WhoAmL 92*
**Eckman**, Frederick *DrAPF 91*
**Eckman**, Michael Kent 1942- *AmMWSc 92*
**Eckman**, Philip Keeley 1931- *WhoWest 92*
**Eckmann**, Inge-Lise 1950- *WhoWest 92*
**Eckner**, Friedrich August Otto 1926- *AmMWSc 92*
**Eckroat**, Larry Raymond 1941- *AmMWSc 92*
**Eckroth**, Charles Angelo 1934- *AmMWSc 92*
**Eckroth**, David Raymond 1939- *AmMWSc 92*
**Eckroth**, Tony *WhoAmP 91*
**Eckstein**, Arthur 1923- *WhoEnt 92*
**Eckstein**, Bernard Hans 1923- *AmMWSc 92*
**Eckstein**, Eugene Charles 1946- *AmMWSc 92*
**Eckstein**, Jerome 1925- *ConAu 36NR*
**Eckstein**, John Alan 1948- *WhoAmL 92*
**Eckstein**, John William 1923- *AmMWSc 92*
**Eckstein**, Jonathan *AmMWSc 92*
**Eckstein**, Michael Lehman 1954- *WhoEnt 92*
**Eckstein**, Peter Charles 1936- *WhoFI 92, WhoMW 92*
**Eckstein**, Richard Waldo 1911- *AmMWSc 92*
**Eckstein**, Yechiel 1951- *WhoRel 92*
**Eckstein**, Yoram 1938- *AmMWSc 92*
**Eckstine**, Billy 1914- *FacFETw, NewAmDM, WhoBlA 92, WhoEnt 92*
**Eckstrom**, Daniel W. 1947- *WhoHisp 92*
**Eckstrom**, Donald James *AmMWSc 92*
**Eckstrom**, Vance LeRoy 1931- *WhoRel 92*
**Eco**, Umberto 1932- *FacFETw, IntAu&W 91, IntWW 91*
**Ecobichon**, Donald John 1937- *AmMWSc 92*
**Economides**, Floyd A. 1928- *WhoWest 92*
**Economides**, Michael John 1949- *AmMWSc 92*
**Economides**, Nicholas Sophocles 1954- *WhoFI 92*
**Economos**, Geo 1919- *AmMWSc 92*
**Economou**, Demetre J 1958- *AmMWSc 92*
**Economou**, Eleftherios Nickolas 1940- *AmMWSc 92*
**Economou**, Elly Helen 1928- *WhoRel 92*
**Economou**, George *DrAPF 91*
**Economou**, George 1934- *ConPo 91, WrDr 92*
**Economou**, Steven George 1922- *AmMWSc 92*
**Economy**, George 1927- *AmMWSc 92*
**Economy**, James 1929- *AmMWSc 92*
**Ecton**, Virgil E. 1940- *WhoBlA 92*
**Eczacibasi**, Nejat F. 1913- *WhoEnt 92*
**Edamura**, Fred Y 1939- *AmMWSc 92*
**Edan**, Mark 1950- *WhoEnt 92*
**Edasery**, James P 1948- *AmMWSc 92*
**Edberg**, Donald L. 1956- *WhoWest 92*
**Edberg**, Rolf 1912- *IntWW 91*
**Edberg**, Stefan 1966- *IntWW 91*
**Edberg**, Stephen Charles 1945- *AmMWSc 92*
**Edberg**, Stephen J. 1952- *WhoWest 92*
**Edde**, Howard Jasper 1937- *AmMWSc 92*
**Edden**, Alan John d1991 *Who 92N*
**Eddery**, Patrick James John 1952- *Who 92*
**Eddey**, Howard Hadfield 1910- *Who 92*
**Eddie**, Russell J 1938- *WhoAmP 91*
**Eddinger**, Charles Robert 1939- *AmMWSc 92*
**Eddinger**, Ralph Tracy 1922- *AmMWSc 92*
**Eddings**, Cynthia *WhoBlA 92*
**Eddings**, David 1931- *ConAu 35NR, IntAu&W 91, TwCSFW 91*
**Eddings**, Michael Charles 1945- *WhoAmL 92*
**Eddington**, Arthur 1882-1944 *CurBio 91N*
**Eddington**, Arthur Stanley 1882-1944 *FacFETw*
**Eddington**, Carl Lee 1932- *AmMWSc 92*
**Eddington**, Herbert Hoover 1929- *WhoBlA 92*
**Eddington**, Paul 1927- *IntMPA 92, IntWW 91*
**Eddington**, Paul Clark- 1927- *Who 92*
**Eddington**, Thomas L. 1960- *WhoFI 92*
**Eddins**, Boyd L 1933- *WhoAmP 91*
**Eddins**, Dwight 1939- *WrDr 92*
**Eddison**, E R 1882-1945 *TwCSFW 91*
**Eddison**, Jonathan Bole 1952- *WhoAmL 92*
**Eddleman**, Bobby R 1937- *AmMWSc 92*
**Eddleman**, Clyde Davis 1902- *Who 92*
**Eddleman**, Elvia Etheridge, Jr 1922- *AmMWSc 92*
**Eddleman**, Floyd Eugene 1930- *WhoEnt 92*
**Eddleman**, G. David 1936- *WhoEnt 92*
**Eddleman**, Lee E 1937- *AmMWSc 92*
**Eddleman**, Peter 1762-1847 *DcNCBi 2*
**Eddleman**, William Roseman 1913- *WhoAmL 92*
**Eddleman**, William Thomas 1900- *WhoBlA 92*
**Eddlemon**, Gerald Kirk 1945- *AmMWSc 92*
**Eddlemon**, Paul Nelson, Jr. 1934- *WhoFI 92*
**Edds**, George Tyson 1913- *AmMWSc 92*
**Edds**, Kenneth Tiffany 1945- *AmMWSc 92*
**Edds**, Stephen Charles 1949- *WhoAmL 92*
**Eddy**, Alfred Alan 1926- *Who 92*
**Eddy**, Carlton Anthony 1942- *AmMWSc 92*
**Eddy**, Charles Alan 1948- *WhoMW 92*
**Eddy**, Clarence 1851-1937 *NewAmDM*
**Eddy**, David Lee 1956- *WhoAmL 92*
**Eddy**, David Maxon 1941- *AmMWSc 92*
**Eddy**, Dennis Eugene 1935- *AmMWSc 92*
**Eddy**, Duane O. 1942- *WhoMW 92*
**Eddy**, Edward A. 1938- *WhoBlA 92*
**Eddy**, Edward Mitchell 1940- *AmMWSc 92*
**Eddy**, Elizabeth *DrAPF 91*
**Eddy**, George Amos 1928- *AmMWSc 92*
**Eddy**, George Sherwood 1871-1963 *AmPeW*
**Eddy**, Glenn Steven 1961- *WhoAmL 92*
**Eddy**, Hubert Allen 1930- *AmMWSc 92*
**Eddy**, Imogen W d1904 *BiInAmS*
**Eddy**, Jerry Kenneth 1940- *AmMWSc 92*
**Eddy**, John Allen 1931- *AmMWSc 92*
**Eddy**, Lowell Perry 1920- *AmMWSc 92*
**Eddy**, Lynne J 1944- *AmMWSc 92*
**Eddy**, Marilyn Mecklenborg 1953- *WhoAmL 92*
**Eddy**, Mary Baker 1821-1910 *BenetAL 91, HanAmWH, RComAH*
**Eddy**, Mary Baker Glover 1821-1910 *RelLAm 91*
**Eddy**, Nelson 1901-1967 *NewAmDM*
**Eddy**, Nelson Wallace 1939- *AmMWSc 92*
**Eddy**, Robert Devereux 1914- *AmMWSc 92*
**Eddy**, Robert Phillip 1919- *WhoWest 92*
**Eddy**, Sherwood 1871-1963 *BenetAL 91*
**Eddy**, Shirley Kathryn 1922- *WhoAmP 91*
**Eddy**, Thomas A 1934- *AmMWSc 92*
**Eddy**, William Abner 1850-1909 *BiInAmS*
**Eddy**, William Bahret *WhoMW 92*
**Eddy**, William Frost 1944- *AmMWSc 92*
**Ede**, Alan Winthrop 1933- *AmMWSc 92*
**Ede**, Dennis 1931- *Who 92*
**Ede**, Jeffery Raymond 1918- *Who 92*
**Edeiken**, Jack 1923- *AmMWSc 92*
**Edel**, Abraham 1908- *WrDr 92*
**Edel**, Leon 1907- *BenetAL 91, IntAu&W 91, IntWW 91, Who 92, WhoWest 92, WrDr 92*
**Edel**, Matthew 1941-1990 *ConAu 133*
**Edel**, Matthew David 1941- *WhoFI 92*
**Edelberg**, Robert 1921- *AmMWSc 92*
**Edele**, Durand J. *IntMPA 92*
**Edelen**, Dominic Gardiner Bowling 1933- *AmMWSc 92*
**Edelen**, Mary Beaty 1944- *WhoAmP 91*
**Edelhauser**, Henry F 1937- *AmMWSc 92*
**Edelheit**, Abraham J. 1958- *ConAu 134*
**Edelheit**, Hershel 1926- *ConAu 134*
**Edelhuber**, Stephen William 1956- *WhoRel 92*
**Edelin**, Kenneth C. 1939- *WhoBlA 92*
**Edelin**, Ramona Hoage *WhoBlA 92*
**Edelin**, Ramona Hoage 1945- *NotBlAW 92 [port]*
**Edell**, Stephen Bristow 1932- *Who 92*
**Edelman**, Alan Irwin 1958- *WhoAmL 92*
**Edelman**, Alma Ann 1918- *WhoAmP 91*
**Edelman**, Alvin 1916- *WhoAmL 92*
**Edelman**, Bernard L 1946- *IntAu&W 91*
**Edelman**, Daniel Joseph 1920- *WhoFI 92, WhoMW 92*
**Edelman**, David Anthony 1938- *AmMWSc 92*
**Edelman**, Edmund Douglas 1930- *WhoAmP 91*
**Edelman**, Elaine *DrAPF 91*
**Edelman**, Fredric Mark 1958- *WhoFI 92*
**Edelman**, Gerald Maurice 1929- *AmMWSc 92, IntWW 91, Who 92, WhoNob 90*
**Edelman**, Gregg 1958- *ConTFT 9*
**Edelman**, Herbert 1933- *WhoEnt 92*
**Edelman**, Isidore Samuel 1920- *AmMWSc 92*
**Edelman**, Jay Barry 1951- *AmMWSc 92*
**Edelman**, Julian *AmMWSc 92*
**Edelman**, Kenneth Norman 1934- *WhoRel 92*
**Edelman**, Louis F. d1976 *LesBEnT 92*
**Edelman**, Marian Wright 1939- *NotBlAW 92 [port], WhoAmL 92, WhoBlA 92*
**Edelman**, Mark Howard 1950- *WhoEnt 92*
**Edelman**, Mark L 1943- *WhoAmP 91*
**Edelman**, Marvin 1939- *AmMWSc 92*
**Edelman**, Murray J. 1919- *WrDr 92*
**Edelman**, Norman H 1937- *AmMWSc 92*
**Edelman**, Paul David 1956- *WhoFI 92*
**Edelman**, Paul Sterling 1926- *WhoAmL 92*
**Edelman**, Raymond Howard 1956- *WhoAmL 92*
**Edelman**, Revell Judith 1941- *WhoFI 92*
**Edelman**, Robert 1936- *AmMWSc 92*
**Edelman**, Robert 1942- *AmMWSc 92*
**Edelman**, Walter E, Jr 1933- *AmMWSc 92*
**Edelmann**, Chester M, Jr 1930- *AmMWSc 92*

**Edelmann**, Johann Christian 1698-1767 *BlkwCEP*
**Edelmann**, Otto Karl 1917- *IntWW 91*
**Edelnant**, Jay Alan 1948- *WhoEnt 92*
**Edelsack**, Edgar Allen 1924- *AmMWSc 92*
**Edelson**, Allan L 1940- *AmMWSc 92*
**Edelson**, Burton Irving 1926- *AmMWSc 92*
**Edelson**, David 1927- *AmMWSc 92*
**Edelson**, Edward Harold 1947- *AmMWSc 92*
**Edelson**, Gilbert Seymour 1928- *WhoAmL 92*
**Edelson**, Ira J. 1946- *WhoFI 92, WhoMW 92*
**Edelson**, Jerome 1932- *AmMWSc 92*
**Edelson**, Julie Ilene 1957- *WhoAmL 92*
**Edelson**, Martin Charles 1943- *AmMWSc 92*
**Edelson**, Paul J 1943- *AmMWSc 92*
**Edelson**, Robert Ellis 1943- *AmMWSc 92*
**Edelson**, Sidney 1916- *AmMWSc 92*
**Edelstein**, Alan Shane 1936- *AmMWSc 92*
**Edelstein**, Alex S. 1920?- *ConAu 133*
**Edelstein**, Barry Allen 1945- *AmMWSc 92*
**Edelstein**, Charles Bruce 1959- *WhoMW 92*
**Edelstein**, David Northon 1910- *WhoAmL 92*
**Edelstein**, Edward 1952- *WhoAmL 92*
**Edelstein**, Gerald Fred 1939- *WhoEnt 92*
**Edelstein**, Harold 1938- *AmMWSc 92*
**Edelstein**, Jason Zelig 1930- *WhoRel 92*
**Edelstein**, Jerome Melvin 1924- *WhoWest 92*
**Edelstein**, Marcia Arlene 1957- *WhoEnt 92*
**Edelstein**, Raymond Lewis 1954- *WhoAmL 92*
**Edelstein**, Richard Malvin 1930- *AmMWSc 92*
**Edelstein**, Rose Marie 1935- *WhoWest 92*
**Edelstein**, Scott *DrAPF 91*
**Edelstein**, Stuart J 1941- *AmMWSc 92*
**Edelstein**, Terese 1950- *ConAu 135*
**Edelstein**, Teri J. 1951- *WhoMW 92*
**Edelstein**, Victor 1945- *IntWW 91*
**Edelstein**, Warren Stanley 1937- *AmMWSc 92*
**Edelstein**, William Alan *AmMWSc 92*
**Edelstone**, Daniel I 1946- *AmMWSc 92*
**Edem**, Benjamin G. 1952- *WhoWest 92*
**Eden** *Who 92*
**Eden**, Anthony 1897-1977 *FacFETw [port]*
**Eden**, Barbara 1934- *ConTFT 9, IntMPA 92*
**Eden**, Barbara Jean *WhoEnt 92*
**Eden**, Charles 1673-1722 *DcNCBi 2*
**Eden**, Conrad W. *Who 92*
**Eden**, James Gary 1950- *AmMWSc 92*
**Eden**, Jeffrey Scott 1960- *WhoAmL 92*
**Eden**, Lee Smythe 1937- *WhoEnt 92*
**Eden**, Leslie 1950- *WhoMW 92*
**Eden**, Murray 1920- *AmMWSc 92*
**Eden**, Nancy Lester 1949- *WhoFI 92*
**Eden**, Nathan E. 1944- *WhoAmL 92*
**Eden**, Raymond Ler 1925- *WhoFI 92*
**Eden**, Richard Carl 1939- *AmMWSc 92*
**Eden**, Richard John 1922- *Who 92*
**Eden**, Robert 1942- *WhoMW 92*
**Eden**, Robert Anthony 1897-1977 *EncTR 91 [port]*
**Eden**, Robert Elwood 1947- *WhoAmL 92*
**Eden**, Sidney 1936- *WhoEnt 92*
**Eden**, Susan Hendrickson 1939- *WhoEnt 92*
**Eden**, William Denis 1878-1949 *TwCPaSc*
**Eden Of Winton**, Baron 1925- *IntWW 91, Who 92*
**Edenberg**, Howard Joseph 1948- *AmMWSc 92*
**Edenfield**, Berry Avant 1934- *WhoAmL 92*
**Edenfield**, Thomas Keen, Jr. 1943- *WhoWest 92*
**Edenfield**, Virginia Anne 1949- *WhoAmL 92*
**Edens**, Arthur Hollis 1901-1968 *DcNCBi 2*
**Edens**, Frank Wesley 1946- *AmMWSc 92*
**Edens**, Gary Denton 1942- *WhoEnt 92, WhoWest 92*
**Edens**, Glenn Thomas 1952- *WhoWest 92*
**Edens**, Patrick Clinton 1947- *WhoWest 92*
**Edens**, Richard Woodward 1928- *WhoIns 92*
**Eder**, Bernard 1952- *Who 92*
**Eder**, Douglas Jules 1944- *AmMWSc 92*
**Eder**, Howard Abram 1917- *AmMWSc 92*
**Eder**, Richard Gray 1932- *WhoWest 92*
**Ederer**, Fred 1926- *AmMWSc 92*
**Ederer**, Ronald Frank 1943- *WhoAmL 92, WhoAmP 91*
**Ederle**, Gertrude 1906- *FacFETw*
**Edersheim**, Peggy 1964- *WhoFI 92*
**Edes**, Michael 1930- *Who 92*
**Edeskuty**, F J 1923- *AmMWSc 92*
**Edey**, Harold Cecil 1913- *Who 92*
**Edey**, Maitland A. 1910- *WrDr 92*
**Edgar**, Alan D 1935- *AmMWSc 92*
**Edgar**, Alvis, Jr. 1929- *WhoEnt 92, WhoWest 92*
**Edgar**, Archer Lindo 1938- *WhoFI 92*
**Edgar**, Arlan Lee 1926- *AmMWSc 92*
**Edgar**, Arthur d1913 *BiInAmS*
**Edgar**, David 1940- *IntWW 91*
**Edgar**, David 1948- *IntAu&W 91, WrDr 92*
**Edgar**, David Burman 1948- *Who 92*
**Edgar**, Gilbert Hammond, III 1947- *WhoFI 92*
**Edgar**, Harold Simmons Hull 1942- *WhoAmL 92*
**Edgar**, Jacqueline L. 1948- *WhoBlA 92*
**Edgar**, James 1946- *IntWW 91*
**Edgar**, James Macmillan, Jr. 1936- *WhoWest 92*
**Edgar**, Jim 1946- *AlmAP 92 [port], WhoAmP 91, WhoMW 92*
**Edgar**, Josephine *IntAu&W 91X, WrDr 92*
**Edgar**, Norman Terence 1933- *AmMWSc 92*
**Edgar**, Patrick Nisbett 1770?-1858? *DcNCBi 2*
**Edgar**, Robert Allan 1940- *WhoAmL 92*
**Edgar**, Robert Kent 1943- *AmMWSc 92*
**Edgar**, Robert Stuart 1930- *AmMWSc 92*
**Edgar**, Robert William 1943- *WhoAmP 91, WhoWest 92*
**Edgar**, Samuel Allen 1916- *AmMWSc 92*
**Edgar**, Thomas Flynn 1945- *AmMWSc 92*
**Edgar**, William 1938- *Who 92*
**Edgar**, William Henry 1942- *WhoFI 92*
**Edgcomb**, John H *AmMWSc 92*
**Edgcumbe** *Who 92*
**Edgcumbe**, Ursula 1900-1985 *TwCPaSc*
**Edge**, Arthur B, IV *WhoAmP 91*
**Edge**, Eldon 1926- *WhoAmP 91*
**Edge**, Findley Bartow 1916- *WhoRel 92*
**Edge**, Geoffrey 1943- *Who 92*
**Edge**, James Brannen, Jr. 1946- *WhoFI 92*
**Edge**, James Edward 1948- *WhoFI 92*
**Edge**, Julian Dexter, Jr. 1942- *WhoAmL 92*
**Edge**, Malcolm 1931- *Who 92*
**Edge**, Orlyn P 1939- *AmMWSc 92*
**Edge**, Raymond Cyril Alexander 1912- *Who 92*
**Edge**, Ronald 1929- *AmMWSc 92*
**Edge**, Stanley 1903-1990 *AnObit 1990*
**Edge**, Thomas Leslie 1935- *WhoRel 92*
**Edge**, William *Who 92*
**Edgecomb**, Daniel W 1840?-1915 *BiInAmS*
**Edgecombe**, Nydia R. 1951- *WhoHisp 92*
**Edgecumbe**, Craig Hamilton 1943- *WhoFI 92*
**Edgell**, Marshall Hall 1939- *AmMWSc 92*
**Edgell**, Robert L. d1991 *NewYTBS 91*
**Edgell**, Thomas John 1945- *WhoFI 92*
**Edgell**, Walter Francis 1916- *AmMWSc 92*
**Edgell**, Zee 1940- *ConAu 135*
**Edgell Hoff**, Isabel Julie 1959- *WhoMW 92*
**Edgemon**, Roy T., Jr. 1934- *WhoRel 92*
**Edgerley**, Dennis A 1948- *AmMWSc 92*
**Edgerley**, Edward, Jr 1931- *AmMWSc 92*
**Edgerly**, Charles George Morgan 1918- *AmMWSc 92*
**Edgerly**, William Skelton 1927- *WhoFI 92*
**Edgerson**, Reginald Maurice 1956- *WhoMW 92*
**Edgerton**, Art Joseph 1928- *WhoBlA 92*
**Edgerton**, Brenda Evans 1949- *WhoBlA 92, WhoFI 92*
**Edgerton**, Clyde 1944- *ConAu 134, WrDr 92*
**Edgerton**, H E 1903- *AmMWSc 92*
**Edgerton**, H Quincy, Jr 1950- *WhoAmP 91*
**Edgerton**, Harold 1903-1990 *AnObit 1990*
**Edgerton**, Harold Eugene 1903-1990 *FacFETw*
**Edgerton**, James Arthur 1869-1938 *RelLAm 91*
**Edgerton**, John Palmer 1917- *WhoAmP 91*
**Edgerton**, Louis James 1914- *AmMWSc 92*
**Edgerton**, Mary Alice 1920- *WhoEnt 92*
**Edgerton**, Milton Thomas, Jr 1921- *AmMWSc 92*
**Edgerton**, Richard 1911- *WhoFI 92*
**Edgerton**, Robert B. 1953- *WhoWest 92*
**Edgerton**, Robert Flint 1917- *AmMWSc 92*
**Edgerton**, Robert Howard 1933- *AmMWSc 92*
**Edgerton**, William Halsey 1935- *WhoEnt 92*
**Edgett**, Steven Dennis 1948- *WhoWest 92*
**Edgeworth**, Maria 1768-1849 *RfGEnL 91*
**Edgeworth**, Richard 1764-1796 *DcNCBi 2*
**Edgeworth Johnstone**, Robert *Who 92*
**Edghill**, John W. 1906- *WhoBlA 92*
**Edgington**, David Norman 1933- *AmMWSc 92*
**Edgington**, Eugene Sinclair 1924- *WrDr 92*
**Edgington**, Jeffrey Wayne 1958- *WhoRel 92*
**Edgington**, Thomas S 1932- *AmMWSc 92*
**Edginton**, John Arthur 1935- *WhoAmL 92*
**Edgley**, Michael Christopher 1943- *IntWW 91*
**Edgmand**, Michael Richard 1938- *WhoFI 92*
**Edgren**, Richard Arthur 1925- *AmMWSc 92*
**Edholm**, Rand Alan 1955- *WhoMW 92*
**Edidin**, Michael Aaron 1939- *AmMWSc 92*
**Edie**, John Monroe 1945- *WhoRel 92*
**Edie**, Thomas Ker 1916- *Who 92*
**Edie**, Wayne Paul 1942- *WhoRel 92*
**Ediger**, Nicholas Martin 1928- *WhoFI 92*
**Ediger**, Robert I 1937- *AmMWSc 92*
**Edil**, Tuncer Berat 1945- *AmMWSc 92, WhoMW 92*
**Edin**, Charles Thomas 1955- *WhoAmL 92*
**Edinburgh**, Bishop of 1933- *Who 92*
**Edinburgh**, Dean of *Who 92*
**Edinburgh**, Duke of 1921- *IntWW 91*
**Edinburgh**, Provost of *Who 92*
**Edinger**, Henry Milton 1943- *AmMWSc 92*
**Edinger**, Ronald Ward 1942- *WhoWest 92*
**Edinger**, Stanley Evan 1943- *AmMWSc 92*
**Edington**, Jeffrey William 1939- *AmMWSc 92*
**Edington**, Patricia Ann 1941- *WhoMW 92*
**Edington**, Patricia Gentry 1938- *WhoAmP 91*
**Edirisinghe**, Albert *WhoRel 92*
**Edis**, Richard John Smale 1943- *Who 92*
**Edison**, Allen Ray 1926- *AmMWSc 92*
**Edison**, Larry Alvin 1936- *AmMWSc 92*
**Edison**, Thomas A. 1847-1931 *BenetAL 91, RComAH*
**Edison**, Thomas Alva 1847-1931 *DcTwDes, FacFETw [port]*
**Edkins**, John 1931-1966 *TwCPaSc*
**Edlefsen**, Blaine Ellis 1930- *WhoMW 92*
**Edlen**, Bengt 1906- *FacFETw, IntWW 91*
**Edleson**, Michael Edward 1958- *WhoFI 92*
**Edley**, Bill 1948- *WhoAmP 91*
**Edley**, Christopher 1928- *ConBlB 2 [port]*
**Edley**, Christopher F., Jr. 1953- *WhoAmL 92, WhoBlA 92*
**Edley**, Christopher F., Sr. 1928- *WhoBlA 92*
**Edlich**, Richard French 1939- *AmMWSc 92*
**Edlin**, Frank E 1909- *AmMWSc 92*
**Edlin**, George Robert 1937- *AmMWSc 92*
**Edlin**, John Charles 1943- *AmMWSc 92*
**Edlin**, Morton Christy 1949- *WhoMW 92*
**Edling**, Jerald Woodrow 1950- *WhoEnt 92*
**Edlow**, Kenneth Lewis 1941- *WhoFI 92*
**Edlund**, Ian Keith 1942- *WhoEnt 92*
**Edlund**, Judith Leora 1945- *WhoWest 92*
**Edlund**, Lawrence Ronald 1942- *WhoFI 92*
**Edlund**, Mikael 1950- *ConCom 92*
**Edlund**, Milton Carl 1924- *AmMWSc 92*
**Edlund**, Philip Arthur 1941- *WhoWest 92*
**Edlund**, Richard 1940- *ConTFT 9*
**Edlund**, Richard J 1924- *WhoAmP 91*
**Edman**, David Arthur 1930- *WhoRel 92*
**Edman**, James R. 1936- *WhoMW 92*
**Edman**, James Richard 1936- *AmMWSc 92*
**Edman**, Janet Lee 1956- *WhoEnt 92*
**Edman**, Jeff Daniel 1952- *WhoEnt 92*
**Edman**, John David 1938- *AmMWSc 92*
**Edman**, John Richard 1927- *WhoFI 92, WhoMW 92*
**Edman**, Walter W 1913- *AmMWSc 92*
**Edmands**, J Rayner 1850?-1910 *BiInAmS*
**Edmenson**, Walter Alexander 1892- *Who 92*
**Edmerson**, John 1948- *WhoRel 92*
**Edmison**, Marvin Tipton 1912- *AmMWSc 92*
**Edmison**, Susan Kay 1953- *WhoRel 92*
**Edmisten**, Rufus Ligh 1941- *WhoAmP 91*
**Edmisten**, Stuart Allen 1960- *WhoRel 92*
**Edmiston**, Clyde 1937- *AmMWSc 92*
**Edmiston**, Guy S., Jr. *WhoRel 92*
**Edmiston**, Joseph Tasker 1948- *WhoWest 92*
**Edmiston**, Rebecca Anne 1953- *WhoRel 92*
**Edmond**, Alfred Adam, Jr. 1960- *WhoBlA 92*
**Edmond**, John Marmion 1943- *IntWW 91, Who 92*
**Edmond**, Lauris 1924- *ConPo 91, WrDr 92*
**Edmond**, Lauris Dorothy 1924- *IntAu&W 91*
**Edmond**, Mary 1929- *TwCPaSc*
**Edmond**, Murray 1949- *ConPo 91, WrDr 92*
**Edmond**, Paul Edward 1944- *WhoBlA 92*
**Edmonds**, Albert Joseph 1942- *WhoBlA 92*
**Edmonds**, Brian Oliver 1963- *WhoFI 92*
**Edmonds**, Campbell Ray 1930- *WhoBlA 92*
**Edmonds**, Carol R 1947- *WhoAmP 91*
**Edmonds**, Charles Henry 1919- *WhoWest 92*
**Edmonds**, Christian Peter 1952- *WhoAmL 92*
**Edmonds**, David Albert 1944- *Who 92*
**Edmonds**, Dean Stockett, Jr 1924- *AmMWSc 92*
**Edmonds**, Douglas James 1956- *WhoAmL 92*
**Edmonds**, Edith *TwCPaSc*
**Edmonds**, Elaine S 1946- *AmMWSc 92*
**Edmonds**, Frank Norman, Jr 1919- *AmMWSc 92*
**Edmonds**, Harvey Lee, Jr 1942- *AmMWSc 92*
**Edmonds**, Helen G. 1911- *NotBlAW 92 [port]*
**Edmonds**, Henry L. 1944- *WhoRel 92*
**Edmonds**, Ivy Gordon 1917- *WhoWest 92*
**Edmonds**, James D, Jr 1939- *AmMWSc 92*
**Edmonds**, James W 1943- *AmMWSc 92*
**Edmonds**, John Christopher 1921- *Who 92*
**Edmonds**, John Christopher Paul 1936- *Who 92*
**Edmonds**, John Walter 1944- *Who 92*
**Edmonds**, Josephine E. 1921- *WhoBlA 92*
**Edmonds**, Kenny *WhoBlA 92*
**Edmonds**, Mary P 1922- *AmMWSc 92*
**Edmonds**, Michael Darnell 1960- *WhoEnt 92*
**Edmonds**, Norman Douglas 1938- *WhoBlA 92*
**Edmonds**, Peter Derek 1929- *AmMWSc 92*
**Edmonds**, Richard H 1933- *AmMWSc 92*
**Edmonds**, Robert Humphrey Gordon 1920- *Who 92*
**Edmonds**, Robert L 1943- *AmMWSc 92*
**Edmonds**, Sarah 1841-1898 *EncAmaz 91*
**Edmonds**, Sheila May 1916- *Who 92*
**Edmonds**, Steven M. 1952- *WhoAmL 92*
**Edmonds**, Thomas Andrew 1938- *WhoAmL 92*
**Edmonds**, Thomas Leon 1932- *WhoAmL 92*
**Edmonds**, Thomas Nathaniel 1936- *WhoBlA 92*
**Edmonds**, Walter D. 1903- *BenetAL 91, WrDr 92*
**Edmonds**, Walter Dumaux 1903- *IntAu&W 91*
**Edmonds**, William Fleming 1923- *WhoFI 92*
**Edmonds**, Winston Godward 1912- *Who 92*
**Edmonds-Brown**, George 1939- *Who 92*
**Edmondson** *Who 92*
**Edmondson**, Andrew Joseph 1935- *AmMWSc 92*
**Edmondson**, Anthony Arnold 1920- *Who 92*
**Edmondson**, Betty Lavern 1924- *WhoAmP 91*
**Edmondson**, Brandon Lee 1959- *WhoFI 92*
**Edmondson**, Dale Edward 1942- *AmMWSc 92*
**Edmondson**, Ed 1919- *WhoAmP 91*
**Edmondson**, Frank K. 1912- *WhoMW 92*
**Edmondson**, Frank Kelley 1912- *AmMWSc 92*
**Edmondson**, Frank Kelley, Jr. 1936- *WhoAmL 92*
**Edmondson**, G. C. *WrDr 92*
**Edmondson**, G C 1922- *IntAu&W 91, TwCSFW 91*
**Edmondson**, Hugh Allen 1906- *AmMWSc 92*
**Edmondson**, J L *WhoAmP 91*
**Edmondson**, James Howard 1931- *WhoAmP 91*
**Edmondson**, James Larry 1947- *WhoAmL 92*
**Edmondson**, James W 1930- *WhoIns 92*
**Edmondson**, James William 1930- *WhoFI 92*
**Edmondson**, James Williams 1943- *WhoMW 92*
**Edmondson**, John Richard 1927- *WhoAmL 92, WhoFI 92*
**Edmondson**, Leonard Firby 1912- *Who 92*
**Edmondson**, Morris Stephen 1941- *AmMWSc 92*
**Edmondson**, Robert Edward 1872- *BiDExR*
**Edmondson**, Simon 1955- *TwCPaSc*
**Edmondson**, W Thomas 1916- *AmMWSc 92*
**Edmondson**, William R., Jr. 1926- *WhoBlA 92*
**Edmondston**, Catherine Ann Devereux 1823-1875 *DcNCBi 2*
**Edmonson**, Bernie L. 1918- *WhoBlA 92*
**Edmonson**, Don Elton 1925- *AmMWSc 92*
**Edmonson**, Munro S. 1924- *WrDr 92*
**Edmonstone**, Archibald 1934- *Who 92*
**Edmonton**, Archbishop of 1924- *Who 92*
**Edmonton**, Area Bishop of 1932- *Who 92*
**Edmonton**, Bishop of 1933- *Who 92*
**Edmund**, Alexander Gordon 1924- *AmMWSc 92*
**Edmund**, Rudolph William 1910- *AmMWSc 92*
**Edmund**, Sean *SmATA 68*
**Edmund-Davies** *Who 92*

**Edmund-Davies,** Baron 1906- *IntWW 91, Who 92*
**Edmundowicz,** John Michael 1938- *AmMWSc 92*
**Edmunds,** Douglas Andrew 1948- *WhoAmL 92*
**Edmunds,** Ferrell, Jr. 1965- *WhoBlA 92*
**Edmunds,** Jeffrey Garth 1953- *WhoAmL 92*
**Edmunds,** John Sanford 1943- *WhoAmL 92*
**Edmunds,** Joseph Edsel 1935- *IntWW 91*
**Edmunds,** Kenny *WhoEnt 92*
**Edmunds,** Leland Nicholas, Jr 1939- *AmMWSc 92*
**Edmunds,** Leon K 1929- *AmMWSc 92*
**Edmunds,** Louis Henry, Jr 1931- *AmMWSc 92*
**Edmunds,** Peter James 1961- *AmMWSc 92*
**Edmunds,** Walter Richard 1928- *WhoBlA 92*
**Edmundson,** Allen B 1932- *AmMWSc 92*
**Edmundson,** Bruce 1952- *IntAu&W 91*
**Edmundson,** Charles Wayne 1942- *WhoMW 92*
**Edmundson,** Harold Parkins 1921- *AmMWSc 92*
**Edmunson,** James 1951- *WhoAmP 91*
**Ednam,** Viscount 1947- *Who 92*
**Edney,** Norris Allen 1936- *AmMWSc 92*
**Edney,** Norris Allen, I 1936- *WhoBlA 92*
**Edney,** Steve 1917- *WhoBlA 92*
**Ednie,** Norman A 1920- *AmMWSc 92*
**Edoga,** Delia Virginia 1943- *WhoAmL 92*
**Edozien,** Joseph Chike 1925- *AmMWSc 92*
**Edric,** Robert 1956- *IntAu&W 91*
**Edrich,** Leslie Howard 1953- *WhoWest 92*
**Edrich,** W J 1916-1986 *FacFETw*
**Edris,** James Alan 1944- *WhoFI 92*
**Edris,** Paul Milburn 1909- *WhoRel 92*
**Edsall,** Deborah Christine 1942- *WhoMW 92*
**Edsall,** Howard Linn *DrAPF 91*
**Edsall,** Howard Linn 1904- *WhoFI 92*
**Edsall,** John Tileston 1902- *AmMWSc 92, FacFETw, IntWW 91*
**Edsberg,** John Christian *Who 92*
**Edsberg,** Robert Leslie 1922- *AmMWSc 92*
**Edse,** Rudolph 1913- *AmMWSc 92*
**Edsel,** Ernest Martin 1959- *WhoFI 92*
**Edson,** Andrew Stephen 1946- *WhoFI 92*
**Edson,** Arthur Woodbury d1905 *BiInAmS*
**Edson,** Bennett Montgomery 1946- *WhoFI 92*
**Edson,** Charles Grant 1916- *AmMWSc 92*
**Edson,** Charles Louis 1934- *WhoAmL 92*
**Edson,** Cyrus 1857-1903 *BiInAmS*
**Edson,** Edward Marshall 1947- *WhoAmL 92*
**Edson,** George C d1909 *BiInAmS*
**Edson,** Herbert Robbins 1931- *WhoFI 92*
**Edson,** J T 1928- *IntAu&W 91, TwCWW 91, WrDr 92*
**Edson,** James Edward, Jr 1942- *AmMWSc 92*
**Edson,** Milan C *ScFEYrs*
**Edson,** Norris Willis 1937- *WhoWest 92*
**Edson,** Russell *DrAPF 91*
**Edson,** Russell 1935- *ConPo 91, IntAu&W 91, WrDr 92*
**Edson,** Wayne E. 1947- *WhoMW 92*
**Edson,** William A 1912- *AmMWSc 92*
**Edson,** William Alden 1912- *WhoWest 92*
**Edstrom,** Elaine Marjorie 1931- *WhoEnt 92*
**Edstrom,** Eric Wayne 1950- *WhoFI 92*
**Edstrom,** Jan-Erik 1931- *IntWW 91*
**Edstrom,** John Olof 1926- *WhoFI 92*
**Edstrom,** Ronald Dwight 1936- *AmMWSc 92*
**Edvina,** Louise 1878-1948 *NewAmDM*
**Edwall,** Dennis Dean 1948- *AmMWSc 92*
**Edward VII** 1841-1910 *FacFETw [port]*
**Edward VIII,** Duke of Windsor 1894-1972 *FacFETw*
**Edward,** Prince 1964 *Who 92R*
**Edward,** David Alexander Ogilvy 1934- *IntWW 91, Who 92*
**Edward,** Deirdre Waldron 1923- *AmMWSc 92*
**Edward,** Gregory John 1956- *WhoEnt 92*
**Edward,** Harry Francis Vincent 1895-1973 *BlkOlyM*
**Edward,** John Thomas 1919- *AmMWSc 92*
**Edward,** Marcus 1957- *WhoFI 92*
**Edwardes** *Who 92*
**Edwardes,** May *TwCPaSc*
**Edwardes,** Michael 1930- *Who 92*
**Edwardes,** Michael Owen 1930- *IntWW 91*
**Edwards** *Who 92*
**Edwards,** A. Wilson 1908- *WhoBlA 92*
**Edwards,** Adrian L *AmMWSc 92*
**Edwards,** Al 1937- *WhoAmP 91*
**Edwards,** Al E. 1937- *WhoBlA 92*
**Edwards,** Alan Kent 1940- *AmMWSc 92*
**Edwards,** Alan M 1933- *AmMWSc 92*
**Edwards,** Albert Carlisle 1937- *WhoWest 92*
**Edwards,** Alberta Roon 1926- *WhoFI 92*
**Edwards,** Alejandra Cox 1954- *WhoFI 92*
**Edwards,** Alfred Kenneth 1926- *Who 92*
**Edwards,** Alfred L. 1920- *WhoBlA 92*
**Edwards,** Alison Edith 1952- *WhoWest 92*
**Edwards,** Allen Jack 1926- *WrDr 92*
**Edwards,** Alonzo Clay 1904-1968 *DcNCBi 2*
**Edwards,** Alva Eugene 1928- *WhoFI 92*
**Edwards,** Andrew John Cumming 1940- *Who 92*
**Edwards,** Anne 1927- *IntAu&W 91, WrDr 92*
**Edwards,** Anthony 1962- *IntMPA 92*
**Edwards,** Ardis Lavonne 1930- *WhoWest 92*
**Edwards,** Arthur Frank George 1920- *Who 92*
**Edwards,** Arthur James 1902- *WhoBlA 92*
**Edwards,** Arthur L 1933- *AmMWSc 92*
**Edwards,** Arthur Mead 1836-1914? *BiInAmS*
**Edwards,** Atticus Fitzgerald 1890- *WhoAmP 91*
**Edwards,** Audrey Marie 1947- *WhoBlA 92*
**Edwards,** Ben 1916- *ConTFT 9*
**Edwards,** Ben E 1935- *AmMWSc 92*
**Edwards,** Benjamin Harrison 1953- *WhoFI 92*
**Edwards,** Benjamin Thomas 1927- *WhoRel 92*
**Edwards,** Bessie Regina 1942- *WhoBlA 92*
**Edwards,** Betty *WhoRel 92*
**Edwards,** Betty 1926- *WrDr 92*
**Edwards,** Betty F 1915- *AmMWSc 92*
**Edwards,** Bingham David 1943- *WhoAmL 92, WhoAmP 91*
**Edwards,** Blake *LesBEnT 92*
**Edwards,** Blake 1922- *IntDcF 2-2 [port], IntMPA 92, IntWW 91, WhoEnt 92*
**Edwards,** Blake Alan 1959- *WhoFI 92*
**Edwards,** Blake Edison 1938- *WhoRel 92*
**Edwards,** Bob 1947- *WhoEnt 92*
**Edwards,** Brenda Kay 1946- *AmMWSc 92*
**Edwards,** Brian 1942- *Who 92*
**Edwards,** Brian F *AmMWSc 92*
**Edwards,** Brian Ronald 1944- *AmMWSc 92*
**Edwards,** Bruce George 1942- *WhoWest 92*
**Edwards,** Bruce Lee, Jr. 1952- *WhoRel 92*
**Edwards,** Bruce S 1949- *AmMWSc 92*
**Edwards,** Bryon Taggart 1937- *WhoFI 92*
**Edwards,** Byron N 1932- *AmMWSc 92*
**Edwards,** Carl Normand 1943- *WhoFI 92*
**Edwards,** Carleton Ephraim 1909- *WhoAmP 91*
**Edwards,** Carol Abe *AmMWSc 92*
**Edwards,** Cassie *DrAPF 91*
**Edwards,** Cecil Leroy 1906- *WhoWest 92*
**Edwards,** Cecile Hoover 1926- *AmMWSc 92, WhoBlA 92*
**Edwards,** Chancy Rudolph 1925- *WhoAmP 91*
**Edwards,** Charles 1925- *AmMWSc 92*
**Edwards,** Charles Archibald 1945- *WhoAmL 92*
**Edwards,** Charles Arthur 1940- *WhoMW 92*
**Edwards,** Charles Benton, Jr. 1944- *WhoEnt 92, WhoWest 92*
**Edwards,** Charles C 1923- *AmMWSc 92*
**Edwards,** Charles Cornell 1923- *WhoAmP 91, WhoWest 92*
**Edwards,** Charles Edward 1939- *WhoFI 92*
**Edwards,** Charles Elvin, Jr. 1953- *WhoEnt 92*
**Edwards,** Charles Harold 1913- *Who 92*
**Edwards,** Charles Henry, Jr 1937- *AmMWSc 92*
**Edwards,** Charles Marcus 1937- *Who 92*
**Edwards,** Charles Marvin 1925- *WhoAmP 91*
**Edwards,** Charles Mundy, III 1935- *WhoFI 92*
**Edwards,** Charles Richard 1931- *WhoWest 92*
**Edwards,** Charles Richard 1945- *AmMWSc 92, WhoMW 92*
**Edwards,** Charlotte 1907-1987 *ConAu 35NR*
**Edwards,** Chet 1951- *AlmAP 92 [port], WhoAmP 91*
**Edwards,** Christopher 1941- *Who 92*
**Edwards,** Christopher Andrew 1966- *AmMWSc 92*
**Edwards,** Clara 1887-1974 *NewAmDM*
**Edwards,** Claybon Jerome 1929- *WhoBlA 92*
**Edwards,** Clive *Who 92*
**Edwards,** Constance Carver 1949- *AmMWSc 92*
**Edwards,** Cyril 1902?- *TwCPaSc*
**Edwards,** Dale Ivan 1930- *AmMWSc 92*
**Edwards,** Daniel Paul 1940- *WhoAmL 92*
**Edwards,** Daniel Walden 1950- *WhoAmL 92, WhoWest 92*
**Edwards,** David 1929- *Who 92*
**Edwards,** David 1957- *WhoEnt 92*
**Edwards,** David C. 1948- *WhoBlA 92*
**Edwards,** David Elgan 1943- *Who 92*
**Edwards,** David Franklin 1928- *AmMWSc 92*
**Edwards,** David H., Jr. 1922- *WhoBlA 92*
**Edwards,** David J 1943- *AmMWSc 92*
**Edwards,** David Lawrence 1929- *Who 92*
**Edwards,** David Maurice Michael 1962- *WhoRel 92*
**Edwards,** David Michael 1940- *Who 92*
**Edwards,** David Olaf 1932- *AmMWSc 92, Who 92*
**Edwards,** David Owen 1930- *AmMWSc 92*
**Edwards,** Dawn Ann 1956- *WhoFI 92*
**Edwards,** Del Mount 1953- *WhoFI 92*
**Edwards,** Delores A. 1965- *WhoBlA 92*
**Edwards,** Dennis 1959- *WhoBlA 92*
**Edwards,** Dennis, Jr. 1922- *WhoBlA 92*
**Edwards,** Dennis L. 1941- *WhoBlA 92*
**Edwards,** Dennis S. *DrAPF 91*
**Edwards,** Derek 1931- *Who 92*
**Edwards,** Don 1915- *AlmAP 92 [port], WhoAmP 91, WhoWest 92*
**Edwards,** Donald 1904- *WrDr 92*
**Edwards,** Donald Isaac d1991 *Who 92N*
**Edwards,** Donald K 1932- *AmMWSc 92*
**Edwards,** Donald M 1938- *AmMWSc 92*
**Edwards,** Donald Matthew 1950- *WhoWest 92*
**Edwards,** Donald O. 1931- *WhoBlA 92*
**Edwards,** Donald Philip 1947- *WhoBlA 92*
**Edwards,** Doris Steck 1944- *WhoMW 92*
**Edwards,** Dorothy R 1911- *WhoAmP 91*
**Edwards,** Dorothy Wright 1914- *WhoBlA 92*
**Edwards,** Douglas d1990 *LesBEnT 92*
**Edwards,** Douglas 1917-1990 *AnObit 1990, CurBio 91N, FacFETw*
**Edwards,** Douglas Cameron 1925- *AmMWSc 92*
**Edwards,** Douglas John 1916- *Who 92*
**Edwards,** Doyle Ray 1938- *AmMWSc 92*
**Edwards,** Eddie 1954- *WhoBlA 92*
**Edwards,** Edith Martha 1945- *WhoAmL 92*
**Edwards,** Edna Jane 1934- *WhoEnt 92*
**Edwards,** Edward George 1914- *Who 92*
**Edwards,** Edwin W. *NewYTBS 91 [port]*
**Edwards,** Edwin W 1927- *WhoAmP 91*
**Edwards,** Edwin Washington 1927- *IntWW 91*
**Edwards,** Eleanor Cecile 1940- *WhoFI 92*
**Edwards,** Eleanor Mattiasich 1938- *WhoEnt 92*
**Edwards,** Elgan *Who 92*
**Edwards,** Elizabeth Alice 1937- *Who 92*
**Edwards,** Ella Raino 1938- *WhoBlA 92*
**Edwards,** Ellis 1947- *WhoAmP 91*
**Edwards,** Elton 1923- *WhoAmP 91*
**Edwards,** Eric Alan 1953- *WhoEnt 92*
**Edwards,** Ernest Preston 1919- *AmMWSc 92*
**Edwards,** Erwyd *Who 92*
**Edwards,** Esther Gordy *WhoBlA 92*
**Edwards,** Eugene H 1922- *AmMWSc 92*
**Edwards,** Eunice L. *WhoBlA 92*
**Edwards,** F E *IntAu&W 91X*
**Edwards,** Frederick Edward 1931- *Who 92*
**Edwards,** Frederick H 1915- *AmMWSc 92*
**Edwards,** Frederick Mason 1948- *WhoAmP 91*
**Edwards,** Gareath Owen 1947- *Who 92*
**Edwards,** Gareth Owen 1940- *Who 92*
**Edwards,** Gary Lee 1940- *WhoAmL 92*
**Edwards,** Gawain 1901-1987 *ScFEYrs*
**Edwards,** Gayle Dameron 1927- *AmMWSc 92*
**Edwards,** Gaylen Lee 1956- *AmMWSc 92*
**Edwards,** Geoff 1942- *TwCPaSc*
**Edwards,** Geoffrey Francis 1917- *Who 92*
**Edwards,** George 1908- *Who 92*
**Edwards,** George 1918- *AmMWSc 92*
**Edwards,** George 1943- *ConCom 92*
**Edwards,** George C 1948- *WhoAmP 91*
**Edwards,** George Clifton, Jr. 1914- *WhoMW 92*
**Edwards,** George R. 1938- *WhoBlA 92*
**Edwards,** George Robert 1908- *IntWW 91*
**Edwards,** George W., Jr. 1939- *WhoFI 92*
**Edwards,** Gerald Elmo 1942- *AmMWSc 92*
**Edwards,** Gilbert Franklin 1915- *WhoBlA 92*
**Edwards,** Ginny Lou 1954- *WhoMW 92*
**Edwards,** Glen Robert 1939- *AmMWSc 92*
**Edwards,** Glenn Jeffry 1949- *WhoMW 92*
**Edwards,** Gordon Stuart 1938- *AmMWSc 92*
**Edwards,** Grover Lewis, Sr. 1944- *WhoBlA 92*
**Edwards,** Gus 1879-1945 *BenetAL 91, NewAmDM*
**Edwards,** Guy Arthur 1950- *WhoAmP 91*
**Edwards,** H M 1921- *AmMWSc 92*
**Edwards,** Hank *TwCWW 91, WrDr 92*
**Edwards,** Hardy Malcolm, Jr 1929- *AmMWSc 92*
**Edwards,** Harold Henry 1932- *AmMWSc 92*
**Edwards,** Harold Herbert 1937- *AmMWSc 92, WhoMW 92*
**Edwards,** Harold M 1936- *AmMWSc 92*
**Edwards,** Harry 1942- *ConBlB 2 [port], WhoBlA 92, WhoWest 92*
**Edwards,** Harry LaFoy 1936- *WhoAmL 92, WhoFI 92*
**Edwards,** Harry Stillwell 1855-1938 *BenetAL 91*
**Edwards,** Harry T. 1940- *WhoAmL 92, WhoAmP 91, WhoBlA 92*
**Edwards,** Harry Wallace 1939- *AmMWSc 92*
**Edwards,** Harvey 1929- *WrDr 92*
**Edwards,** Harvey Lawrence 1929- *WhoEnt 92*
**Edwards,** Helen 1882- *TwCPaSc*
**Edwards,** Helen Thom 1936- *AmMWSc 92*
**Edwards,** Henry 1830-1891 *BiInAmS*
**Edwards,** Hilton 1903-1982 *FacFETw*
**Edwards,** Horace Burton 1925- *WhoBlA 92*
**Edwards,** Howard Milton, III 1955- *WhoRel 92*
**Edwards,** Hugh Mortimer 1942- *WhoFI 92*
**Edwards,** Huw William Edmund 1953- *Who 92*
**Edwards,** Ian Keith 1926- *WhoMW 92*
**Edwards,** India 1895-1990 *AnObit 1990*
**Edwards,** Iorwerth 1909- *WrDr 92*
**Edwards,** Iorwerth Eiddon Stephen 1909- *IntAu&W 91, IntWW 91, Who 92*
**Edwards,** Isaac d1775 *DcNCBi 2*
**Edwards,** Ivan Kenneth 1926- *WhoAmP 91*
**Edwards,** J Gordon 1919- *AmMWSc 92*
**Edwards,** J. Michele 1945- *WhoEnt 92*
**Edwards,** Jack 1928- *WhoAmP 91*
**Edwards,** Jack A. 1948- *WhoWest 92*
**Edwards,** Jack Trevor 1920- *Who 92*
**Edwards,** James Burrows 1927- *AmMWSc 92, IntWW 91, WhoAmP 91*
**Edwards,** James Dallas, III 1937- *WhoFI 92*
**Edwards,** James Edwin 1914- *WhoAmL 92, WhoFI 92*
**Edwards,** James Franklin 1955- *WhoBlA 92*
**Edwards,** James Griffith 1928- *Who 92*
**Edwards,** James H. 1927- *IntMPA 92*
**Edwards,** James Harrell 1926- *WhoAmP 91*
**Edwards,** James Malone 1931- *WhoAmL 92*
**Edwards,** James Mark 1956- *AmMWSc 92*
**Edwards,** James Richard 1951- *WhoAmL 92*
**Edwards,** James Robert 1945- *WhoRel 92*
**Edwards,** James Valentine 1925- *Who 92*
**Edwards,** James Wesley 1938- *AmMWSc 92*
**Edwards,** Jean Curtis 1929- *WhoAmP 91, WhoBlA 92*
**Edwards,** Jean Marie Grunklee 1952- *WhoFI 92*
**Edwards,** Jeffery 1945- *TwCPaSc*
**Edwards,** Jeremy John Cary 1937- *Who 92*
**Edwards,** Jerry Lee 1954- *WhoRel 92*
**Edwards,** Jesse Efrem 1911- *AmMWSc 92*
**Edwards,** Jimmie Garvin 1934- *AmMWSc 92*
**Edwards,** John 1938- *TwCPaSc*
**Edwards,** John Anthony 1935- *AmMWSc 92*
**Edwards,** John Auert 1930- *AmMWSc 92*
**Edwards,** John Basil 1909- *Who 92*
**Edwards,** John C 1913- *AmMWSc 92*
**Edwards,** John Charles 1925- *Who 92*
**Edwards,** John Clifford 1961- *WhoMW 92*
**Edwards,** John Clive 1916- *Who 92*
**Edwards,** John Coates 1934- *IntWW 91, Who 92*
**Edwards,** John Colin 1940- *TwCPaSc*
**Edwards,** John D 1925- *AmMWSc 92*
**Edwards,** John D. 1952- *TwCPaSc*
**Edwards,** John David 1958- *WhoMW 92*
**Edwards,** John Duncan 1953- *WhoAmL 92*
**Edwards,** John Henry 1930- *WhoWest 92*
**Edwards,** John Hilton 1928- *IntWW 91, Who 92*
**Edwards,** John L. 1930- *WhoBlA 92*
**Edwards,** John Lionel 1915- *Who 92*
**Edwards,** John Loyd, III 1948- *WhoBlA 92*
**Edwards,** John Michael 1925- *Who 92*
**Edwards,** John Oelhaf 1922- *AmMWSc 92*
**Edwards,** John Phillip 1927- *Who 92*
**Edwards,** John R 1937- *AmMWSc 92*
**Edwards,** John S 1931- *AmMWSc 92*
**Edwards,** John Saul 1943- *WhoAmL 92, WhoAmP 91*
**Edwards,** John W., Jr. 1933- *WhoBlA 92*
**Edwards,** John Wesley, Jr. 1933- *WhoWest 92*
**Edwards,** John Wilson 1942- *WhoBlA 92*
**Edwards,** Jonathan 1703-1758 *BenetAL 91, BlkwCEP, RComAH*
**Edwards,** Jonathan, Jr 1933- *AmMWSc 92*
**Edwards,** Jorge 1931- *LiExTwC*

**Edwards,** Joseph D, Jr 1924- *AmMWSc 92*
**Edwards,** Joseph Robert 1908- *Who 92*
**Edwards,** Joshua Leroy 1918- *AmMWSc 92*
**Edwards,** Juanelle Barbee 1923- *WhoAmP 91*
**Edwards,** Julia *SmATA 67*
**Edwards,** Julian Ward 1930- *WhoAmP 91*
**Edwards,** Julie Andrews *Who 92*
**Edwards,** June *IntAu&W 91X, WrDr 92*
**Edwards,** Kathryn Louise 1947- *AmMWSc 92*
**Edwards,** Kenneth *Who 92*
**Edwards,** Kenneth 1917- *WhoWest 92*
**Edwards,** Kenneth Anthony 1939- *WhoMW 92*
**Edwards,** Kenneth Bernard 1961- *WhoWest 92*
**Edwards,** Kenneth Earle 1926- *WhoMW 92*
**Edwards,** Kenneth J. 1947- *WhoBlA 92*
**Edwards,** Kenneth John Richard 1934- *IntWW 91, Who 92*
**Edwards,** Kenneth Ward 1933- *AmMWSc 92*
**Edwards,** Kenneth Westbrook 1934- *AmMWSc 92*
**Edwards,** Kevin 1965- *WhoBlA 92*
**Edwards,** Kevin James 1957- *WhoWest 92*
**Edwards,** Kirk Lewis 1950- *WhoWest 92*
**Edwards,** L. William 1946- *WhoWest 92*
**Edwards,** Laura Emily 1969- *WhoEnt 92*
**Edwards,** Lawrence Jay 1940- *AmMWSc 92*
**Edwards,** Leila 1937- *AmMWSc 92*
**Edwards,** Leila Scelonge 1935- *WhoMW 92*
**Edwards,** Leo Derek 1937- *WhoBlA 92*
**Edwards,** Leon Roger 1940- *AmMWSc 92*
**Edwards,** Leslie Erroll 1914- *AmMWSc 92*
**Edwards,** Lewis 1953- *WhoBlA 92*
**Edwards,** Lewis Hiram 1938- *AmMWSc 92*
**Edwards,** Lionel 1878-1966 *TwCPaSc*
**Edwards,** Llewellyn 1935- *Who 92*
**Edwards,** Lonnie *WhoBlA 92*
**Edwards,** Lonzy Fitzgerald, Sr. 1949- *WhoRel 92*
**Edwards,** Louis Laird, Jr 1936- *AmMWSc 92*
**Edwards,** Lucy Elaine 1952- *AmMWSc 92*
**Edwards,** Luther Howard 1954- *WhoBlA 92*
**Edwards,** Lydia Justice 1937- *WhoAmP 91, WhoWest 92*
**Edwards,** Malcolm John 1934- *Who 92*
**Edwards,** Marc Benjamin 1946- *AmMWSc 92*
**Edwards,** Marcus *Who 92*
**Edwards,** Margaret *DrAPF 91*
**Edwards,** Marie Babare *WhoWest 92*
**Edwards,** Martin Hassall 1927- *AmMWSc 92*
**Edwards,** Marvin E. 1943- *WhoBlA 92*
**Edwards,** Marvin H 1937- *WhoAmP 91*
**Edwards,** Mary Anne 1936- *WhoWest 92*
**Edwards,** Mary Matthews 1919- *WhoAmP 91*
**Edwards,** Mattie Smith 1931- *WhoBlA 92*
**Edwards,** Maurice 1922- *WhoEnt 92*
**Edwards,** McIver Williamson, Jr 1935- *AmMWSc 92*
**Edwards,** Merrill Arthur 1932- *AmMWSc 92*
**Edwards,** Michael *Who 92*
**Edwards,** Michael 1938- *IntAu&W 91, WrDr 92*
**Edwards,** Michael David 1955- *WhoWest 92*
**Edwards,** Michael Donald 1949- *WhoEnt 92*
**Edwards,** Mickey 1937- *AlmAP 92 [port]*
**Edwards,** Miles John 1929- *AmMWSc 92*
**Edwards,** Miles Stanley 1951- *WhoBlA 92, WhoMW 92*
**Edwards,** Monica 1912- *WrDr 92*
**Edwards,** Nancy *DrAPF 91*
**Edwards,** Nancy C 1936- *AmMWSc 92*
**Edwards,** Ninian Murry 1922- *WhoAmL 92*
**Edwards,** Norman *IntAu&W 91X, TwCSFW 91, WrDr 92*
**Edwards,** Norman L. *Who 92*
**Edwards,** Ogden Frazelle 1909- *AmMWSc 92*
**Edwards,** Oliver Edward 1920- *AmMWSc 92*
**Edwards,** Oscar Lee 1953- *WhoBlA 92*
**Edwards,** Oscar Wendell 1916- *AmMWSc 92*
**Edwards,** Otis Carl, Jr. 1928- *WhoRel 92*
**Edwards,** Ovie C 1929- *WhoAmP 91*
**Edwards,** Owen 1933- *Who 92*
**Edwards,** Page *DrAPF 91*
**Edwards,** Page, Jr. 1941- *WrDr 92*
**Edwards,** Page Lawrence, Jr 1941- *IntAu&W 91*
**Edwards,** Palmer Lowell 1923- *AmMWSc 92*
**Edwards,** Patricia Anne 1944- *Who 92*
**Edwards,** Patricia Burr 1918- *WhoWest 92*
**Edwards,** Paul Vernon 1954- *WhoWest 92*
**Edwards,** Peter D. 1959- *TwCPaSc*
**Edwards,** Peter Robert 1937- *Who 92*
**Edwards,** Philip 1923- *WrDr 92*
**Edwards,** Philip A 1907-1971 *BlkOlyM*
**Edwards,** Philip Walter 1923- *IntWW 91, Who 92*
**Edwards,** Phyllis Mae 1921- *WhoFI 92, WhoWest 92*
**Edwards,** Preston Joseph 1943- *WhoBlA 92*
**Edwards,** Quentin Tytler 1925- *Who 92*
**Edwards,** Ralph *LesBEnT 92*
**Edwards,** Ralph 1913- *IntMPA 92*
**Edwards,** Ralph 1934- *WhoAmL 92*
**Edwards,** Ralph M. 1933- *WhoWest 92*
**Edwards,** Raoul 1967- *WhoEnt 92*
**Edwards,** Ray Conway 1913- *WhoFI 92*
**Edwards,** Richard Alan 1934- *WhoRel 92*
**Edwards,** Richard Alan 1957- *WhoMW 92*
**Edwards,** Richard Ambrose 1922- *WhoAmL 92*
**Edwards,** Richard Archer 1908- *AmMWSc 92*
**Edwards,** Richard Augustus, III 1945- *WhoAmP 91*
**Edwards,** Richard Charles 1949- *WhoWest 92*
**Edwards,** Richard Glenn 1940- *AmMWSc 92*
**Edwards,** Richard Humphrey Tudor 1939- *Who 92*
**Edwards,** Richard Lawrence 1953- *WhoMW 92*
**Edwards,** Richard M 1920- *AmMWSc 92*
**Edwards,** Richard Milton 1951- *WhoFI 92*
**Edwards,** Rob 1963- *WhoEnt 92*
**Edwards,** Robert 1939- *WhoBlA 92*
**Edwards,** Robert Erskine 1904- *WhoBlA 92*
**Edwards,** Robert Geoffrey 1925- *IntWW 91, Who 92*
**Edwards,** Robert John 1925- *IntWW 91, Who 92*
**Edwards,** Robert Lee 1922- *AmMWSc 92*
**Edwards,** Robert Lomas 1920- *AmMWSc 92*
**Edwards,** Robert Nelson 1946- *WhoAmL 92*
**Edwards,** Robert Randle 1934- *WhoAmL 92*
**Edwards,** Robert Septimus Friar 1910- *Who 92*
**Edwards,** Robert V 1940- *AmMWSc 92*
**Edwards,** Robert Valentino 1940- *WhoBlA 92*
**Edwards,** Robin Anthony 1939- *Who 92*
**Edwards,** Roger Nicholas *IntWW 91*
**Edwards,** Roger Snowden 1904- *Who 92*
**Edwards,** Ron 1930- *IntAu&W 91*
**Edwards,** Ronald Alfred 1939- *WhoBlA 92*
**Edwards,** Ronald George 1930- *WrDr 92*
**Edwards,** Ronald Walter 1930- *Who 92*
**Edwards,** Ronald Wayne 1958- *WhoBlA 92*
**Edwards,** Rondle E. 1934- *WhoBlA 92*
**Edwards,** Ross 1943- *ConCom 92*
**Edwards,** Roy Lawrence 1922- *AmMWSc 92*
**Edwards,** Rupert L. 1929- *WhoBlA 92*
**Edwards,** Russell d1991 *NewYTBS 91*
**Edwards,** Ruth McCalla 1949- *WhoBlA 92*
**Edwards,** Ryan Hayes *WhoEnt 92*
**Edwards,** Sam 1928- *IntWW 91*
**Edwards,** Samuel Frederick 1928- *Who 92*
**Edwards,** Sandra Banyar 1940- *WhoMW 92*
**Edwards,** Sarah Emma *EncAmaz 91*
**Edwards,** Sebastian 1953- *WhoWest 92*
**Edwards,** Shirley Heard 1949- *WhoBlA 92*
**Edwards,** Sian *WhoEnt 92*
**Edwards,** Solomon 1932- *WhoBlA 92*
**Edwards,** Stephen Allen 1953- *WhoAmL 92*
**Edwards,** Steve 1930- *AmMWSc 92*
**Edwards,** Steven Alan 1956- *WhoAmL 92*
**Edwards,** Stewart Leslie 1914- *Who 92*
**Edwards,** Susan Roddy Shaw 1954- *WhoEnt 92*
**Edwards,** Suzan 1951- *AmMWSc 92*
**Edwards,** Sylvia 1947- *WhoBlA 92*
**Edwards,** Ted 1939- *IntAu&W 91*
**Edwards,** Teresa 1964- *BlkOlyM*
**Edwards,** Terry Winslow 1935- *AmMWSc 92*
**Edwards,** Theodore 1965- *WhoBlA 92*
**Edwards,** Theodore Thomas 1917- *WhoBlA 92*
**Edwards,** Theodore Unaldo 1934- *WhoBlA 92*
**Edwards,** Thomas Ashton 1960- *WhoFI 92*
**Edwards,** Thomas Claude 1943- *AmMWSc 92*
**Edwards,** Thomas Erwyd 1933- *Who 92*
**Edwards,** Thomas F 1927- *AmMWSc 92*
**Edwards,** Thomas Harvey 1924- *AmMWSc 92*
**Edwards,** Thomas Henry, Jr. 1918- *WhoFI 92*
**Edwards,** Thomas Oliver 1943- *WhoBlA 92*
**Edwards,** Thomas R. 1928- *WrDr 92*
**Edwards,** Thomas Stoneham, Jr. 1959- *WhoAmL 92*
**Edwards,** Timothy Ernest 1942- *WhoWest 92*
**Edwards,** Tom W, Jr 1929- *WhoAmP 91*
**Edwards,** Tony Mal 1950- *WhoAmL 92*
**Edwards,** Verba L. 1950- *WhoBlA 92*
**Edwards,** Vero C. W. *Who 92*
**Edwards,** Victor Henry 1940- *AmMWSc 92*
**Edwards,** Vinal N d1919 *BiInAmS*
**Edwards,** Vince 1928- *IntMPA 92*
**Edwards,** Virginia Davis 1927- *WhoEnt 92*
**Edwards,** Vivian J. 1915- *WhoBlA 92*
**Edwards,** W Cary, Jr 1944- *WhoAmP 91*
**Edwards,** W Farrell 1931- *AmMWSc 92*
**Edwards,** W Sterling 1920- *AmMWSc 92*
**Edwards,** Wallace Edward, Jr 1954- *WhoAmP 91*
**Edwards,** Ward Blowers 1885-1935 *DcNCBi 2*
**Edwards,** Weldon Nathaniel 1788-1873 *DcNCBi 2*
**Edwards,** Willard 1931- *AmMWSc 92*
**Edwards,** William 1938- *Who 92*
**Edwards,** William Brundige, III 1942- *AmMWSc 92*
**Edwards,** William Charles 1934- *AmMWSc 92, WhoAmP 91*
**Edwards,** William David 1925- *WhoMW 92*
**Edwards,** William Dean 1948- *AmMWSc 92*
**Edwards,** William Henry 1822-1909 *BiInAmS*
**Edwards,** William James 1915- *WhoEnt 92*
**Edwards,** William James 1939- *WhoFI 92*
**Edwards,** William Kermit 1953- *WhoFI 92*
**Edwards,** William Martin 1951- *WhoWest 92*
**Edwards,** William N 1929- *WhoIns 92*
**Edwards,** William Paul 1960- *WhoEnt 92*
**Edwards,** William Philip Neville 1904- *IntWW 91, Who 92*
**Edwards,** William Thomas, Jr. 1956- *WhoEnt 92*
**Edwards-Aschoff,** Patricia Joann 1940- *WhoBlA 92*
**Edwards-Beckett,** Joy Annette 1953- *WhoMW 92*
**Edwards-Jones,** Ian 1923- *Who 92*
**Edwards-Moss,** David John *Who 92*
**Edwards-Stuart,** Antony James Cobham 1946- *Who 92*
**Edwardson,** John Richard 1923- *AmMWSc 92*
**Edwars,** Philip Walter 1923- *IntAu&W 91*
**Edwin,** Edward M. 1917- *WhoFI 92*
**Edyvane,** John 1934- *AmMWSc 92*
**Eechambadi,** Naras Varadarajan 1956- *WhoFI 92*
**Eelbeck,** Montfort d1790 *DcNCBi 2*
**Eeles,** Henry 1910- *Who 92*
**Eells,** James 1926- *AmMWSc 92*
**Eells,** Pamela Lynn 1956- *WhoEnt 92*
**Eelsen,** Pierre Henri Maurice 1933- *IntWW 91*
**Eer Nisse,** Errol P 1940- *AmMWSc 92*
**Eesley,** Gary 1950- *AmMWSc 92*
**Efanov,** Vasiliy Profov'evich 1900-1978 *SovUnBD*
**Efaw,** Cary R. 1949- *WhoFI 92*
**Effer,** W R 1927- *AmMWSc 92*
**Effert,** Sven 1922- *IntWW 91*
**Effinger,** Cecil 1914- *NewAmDM*
**Effinger,** Charles Harvey Williams, Jr. 1935- *WhoFI 92*
**Effinger,** George Alec 1947- *IntAu&W 91, TwCSFW 91, WrDr 92*
**Effinger,** Virgil 1873-1955 *BiDExR*
**Effingham,** Earl of 1905- *Who 92*
**Effort,** Edmund D. 1949- *WhoBlA 92*
**Effren,** John Kenneth 1949- *WhoFI 92*
**Effron,** David Louis 1938- *WhoEnt 92*
**Effros,** Edward George 1935- *AmMWSc 92*
**Effros,** Richard Matthew 1935- *AmMWSc 92*
**Effros,** Rita B 1941- *AmMWSc 92*
**Effros,** Robert Carlton 1933- *WhoAmL 92*
**Effross,** Walter Alan 1963- *WhoAmL 92*
**Efholm,** Mogens 1910- *IntWW 91*
**Efi,** Taisi Tupuola Tufuga 1938- *IntWW 91*
**Efimov** *IntWW 91*
**Efird,** Ireneus Polycarp 1834-1902 *DcNCBi 2*
**Efird,** James Michael 1932- *WhoRel 92*
**Efird,** John Solomon Melanchthon 1857-1927 *DcNCBi 2*
**Efird,** Joseph Bivens 1883-1966 *DcNCBi 2*
**Efird,** Oscar Ogburn 1892-1974 *DcNCBi 2*
**Efland,** Simpson Lindsay 1913- *WhoFI 92*
**Efner,** Howard F 1944- *AmMWSc 92*
**Efroimson,** Vladimir Pavlovich 1908-1988 *SovUnBD*
**Efron,** Bradley 1938- *AmMWSc 92, WhoWest 92*
**Efron,** Herman Yale 1926- *AmMWSc 92*
**Efron,** Robert 1927- *AmMWSc 92*
**Efron,** Samuel 1915- *WhoAmL 92, WhoFI 92*
**Efros,** Susan *DrAPF 91*
**Efstathiou,** George Petros 1955- *Who 92*
**Efstathiou,** John Dimitrios 1949- *WhoFI 92*
**Efthimides,** Aris D. 1929- *WhoHisp 92*
**Efthymiou,** Constantine John 1930- *AmMWSc 92*
**Eftimiadi,** Helen 1946- *IntAu&W 91*
**Eftimoff,** Anita Kendall 1927- *WhoMW 92*
**Eftink,** Edward M. *WhoRel 92*
**Eftink,** Maurice R 1951- *AmMWSc 92*
**Egal,** Mohamed Ibrahim 1928- *IntWW 91*
**Egami,** Takeshi 1945- *AmMWSc 92*
**Egan,** Alece Blanche 1934- *WhoAmL 92*
**Egan,** Anne Hays 1950- *WhoRel 92*
**Egan,** B Zane 1937- *AmMWSc 92*
**Egan,** Candace Lee 1958- *WhoEnt 92*
**Egan,** Carol Ann 1938- *WhoEnt 92*
**Egan,** Charles Joseph, Jr. 1932- *WhoAmL 92*
**Egan,** Cheryl Cobb 1960- *WhoWest 92*
**Egan,** Daniel Francis 1915- *WhoRel 92*
**Egan,** Donald E., Jr. 1931- *WhoAmL 92*
**Egan,** Edmund Alfred 1941- *AmMWSc 92*
**Egan,** Edward M. 1932- *WhoRel 92*
**Egan,** Eileen Mary *WhoAmL 92*
**Egan,** Eileen Mary 1911- *AmPeW*
**Egan,** Ferol 1923- *IntAu&W 91, WrDr 92*
**Egan,** Francis P 1917- *AmMWSc 92*
**Egan,** Harvey Daniel 1937- *WhoRel 92*
**Egan,** Howard L 1938- *AmMWSc 92*
**Egan,** James Clayton 1956- *WhoAmL 92*
**Egan,** James John 1927- *AmMWSc 92*
**Egan,** James Joseph 1941- *AmMWSc 92*
**Egan,** Jerome P 1943- *WhoAmP 91*
**Egan,** John 1939- *Who 92*
**Egan,** John Frederick 1935- *AmMWSc 92*
**Egan,** John Joseph 1944- *WhoAmL 92*
**Egan,** John Leopold 1939- *IntWW 91*
**Egan,** John Lloyd, Jr. 1958- *WhoAmL 92*
**Egan,** John M. *WhoMW 92*
**Egan,** John Patrick, II 1944- *WhoRel 92*
**Egan,** John Tinnerman 1948- *WhoWest 92*
**Egan,** Joseph Richard 1954- *WhoAmL 92*
**Egan,** Keith James 1930- *WhoRel 92*
**Egan,** Kevin James 1950- *WhoAmL 92*
**Egan,** Laury Agnes 1950- *WhoEnt 92*
**Egan,** Lesley *IntAu&W 91X*
**Egan,** Marianne Louise 1942- *AmMWSc 92*
**Egan,** Michael James 1923- *WhoAmP 91*
**Egan,** Michael Joseph, Jr 1926- *WhoAmP 91*
**Egan,** Mike F. 1962- *WhoFI 92*
**Egan,** Phyllis Reitz 1936- *WhoRel 92*
**Egan,** Pierce 1772-1849 *RfGEnL 91*
**Egan,** Raymond D 1931- *AmMWSc 92*
**Egan,** Richard L 1917- *AmMWSc 92*
**Egan,** Richard Stephen 1941- *AmMWSc 92*
**Egan,** Robert Joseph 1931- *WhoAmP 91*
**Egan,** Robert L 1920- *AmMWSc 92*
**Egan,** Robert Marshall 1948- *WhoWest 92*
**Egan,** Robert Shaw 1945- *AmMWSc 92*
**Egan,** Robert Wheeler 1943- *AmMWSc 92*
**Egan,** Russell E 1907- *WhoAmP 91*
**Egan,** Sean Joseph 1957- *WhoFI 92*
**Egan,** Susan Chan 1946- *WhoFI 92*
**Egan,** Thomas J 1925- *AmMWSc 92*
**Egan,** Thomas J. 1944- *WhoFI 92*
**Egan,** Timothy S. 1961- *WhoEnt 92*
**Egan,** Walter George 1923- *AmMWSc 92*
**Egan,** William Michael 1944- *AmMWSc 92*
**Egar,** Joseph Michael 1930- *AmMWSc 92*
**Egar,** Margaret Wells 1934- *AmMWSc 92*
**Egar,** Thomas Arthur *WhoAmL 92*
**Egas Moniz,** Antonio Caetano Abreu Freire 1874-1955 *WhoNob 90*
**Egberg,** David Curtis 1942- *AmMWSc 92*
**Egbert,** H M *TwCSFW 91*
**Egbert,** H M 1879-1960 *ScFEYrs*
**Egbert,** Robert B 1916- *AmMWSc 92*
**Egbuna,** Obi 1938- *WrDr 92*
**Egbunike,** Innocent 1961- *BlkOlyM*
**Egdahl,** Richard H 1926- *AmMWSc 92, IntWW 91*
**Egdell,** John Duncan 1938- *Who 92*
**Ege,** Hans Alsnes 1924- *WhoFI 92*
**Ege,** Raimund K 1958- *AmMWSc 92*
**Ege,** Seyhan Nurettin 1931- *AmMWSc 92*
**Egeberg,** Roger O 1903- *AmMWSc 92*
**Egee** *EncAmaz 91*
**Egeland,** Byron Ricker 1938- *WhoMW 92*
**Egeland,** Leif 1903- *IntWW 91, Who 92*
**Egelhoff,** William Frederick, Jr 1949- *AmMWSc 92*
**Egelstaff,** Peter A 1925- *AmMWSc 92*
**Egelston,** William E. 1959- *WhoMW 92*
**Egendoerfer,** Eugene Robert 1931- *WhoRel 92*

**Egenes**, Karen Heine 1945- *WhoMW 92*
**Egenolf**, Robert F. 1946- *WhoAmL 92*
**Eger**, Denise Leese 1960- *WhoRel 92*
**Eger**, Edmond I, II *AmMWSc 92*
**Eger**, F Martin 1936- *AmMWSc 92*
**Eger**, John M. *LesBEnT 92*
**Eger**, Joseph 1925- *WhoEnt 92*
**Egermeier**, Elsie E 1890-1986 *SmATA 65*
**Egermeier**, R P 1927- *AmMWSc 92*
**Egerton** *Who 92*
**Egerton**, David Boswell 1914- *Who 92*
**Egerton**, George 1859-1945 *BiDBrF 2*
**Egerton**, John Alfred Roy 1918- *Who 92*
**Egerton**, Philip John Caledon G. *Who 92*
**Egerton**, Raymond Frank 1944- *AmMWSc 92*
**Egerton**, Seymour 1915- *Who 92*
**Egerton**, Stephen 1932- *Who 92*
**Egerton**, Stephen Loftus 1932- *IntWW 91*
**Egervari**, Tibor Janos 1938- *WhoEnt 92*
**Eggan**, Fred Russell 1906-1991 *IntWW 91, -91N, NewYTBS 91 [port]*
**Eggan**, Hugh Melford 1930- *WhoFI 92*
**Eggan**, Lawrence Carl 1935- *AmMWSc 92*
**Eggar**, David Augustus 1969- *WhoEnt 92*
**Eggar**, Lois Beth Jennings 1940- *WhoEnt 92*
**Eggar**, Samantha 1939- *IntMPA 92, WhoEnt 92*
**Eggar**, Timothy John Crommelin 1951- *Who 92*
**Egge**, Alfred Severin 1933- *AmMWSc 92*
**Eggen**, Donald T 1922- *AmMWSc 92*
**Eggen**, Douglas Ambrose 1925- *AmMWSc 92*
**Eggen**, Eric Carl 1946- *WhoAmP 91*
**Eggena**, Patrick 1938- *AmMWSc 92*
**Eggenberger**, Andrew Jon 1938- *AmMWSc 92*
**Egger**, Carl Thomas 1937- *AmMWSc 92, WhoMW 92*
**Egger**, Louis Magnus 1919- *WhoAmP 91*
**Egger**, M David 1936- *AmMWSc 92*
**Eggers**, A J, Jr 1922- *AmMWSc 92*
**Eggers**, David Frank, Jr 1922- *AmMWSc 92*
**Eggers**, Fred M 1946- *AmMWSc 92*
**Eggers**, George W Nordholtz, Jr 1929- *AmMWSc 92*
**Eggers**, Hans J 1927- *AmMWSc 92*
**Eggers**, James Wesley 1925- *WhoFI 92, WhoMW 92*
**Eggers**, Kathleen W. 1942- *WhoMW 92*
**Eggers**, Kurt 1905-1943 *EncTR 91*
**Eggers**, Larry Alan 1941- *WhoWest 92*
**Eggers**, Mark Lee 1956- *WhoMW 92*
**Eggers**, Paul Walter 1919- *WhoAmL 92, WhoFI 92*
**Eggers**, Richard Howell 1938- *WhoWest 92*
**Eggerstedt**, Otto 1886-1933 *EncTR 91*
**Eggert**, Arthur Arnold 1944- *AmMWSc 92*
**Eggert**, Debra Ann 1969- *WhoMW 92*
**Eggert**, Donald A 1934- *AmMWSc 92*
**Eggert**, Frank Michael 1945- *AmMWSc 92*
**Eggert**, Franklin Paul 1920- *AmMWSc 92*
**Eggert**, Robert Glenn 1927- *AmMWSc 92*
**Eggert**, Robert John, Sr. 1913- *WhoFI 92, WhoWest 92*
**Eggert**, Russell Raymond 1948- *WhoAmL 92, WhoMW 92*
**Eggertsen**, Ben Thomas 1953- *WhoAmL 92*
**Eggertsen**, Frank Thomas 1913- *WhoWest 92*
**Eggimann**, Wilhelm Hans 1929- *AmMWSc 92*
**Eggington**, William Robert Owen 1932- *Who 92*
**Egginton**, Anthony Joseph 1930- *Who 92*
**Egginton**, Frank 1908- *TwCPaSc*
**Egginton**, Wycliffe 1875-1951 *TwCPaSc*
**Eggler**, David Hewitt 1940- *AmMWSc 92*
**Eggleston**, Anthony Francis 1928- *Who 92*
**Eggleston**, Carl Ulysses 1950- *WhoAmP 91*
**Eggleston**, Charles Haggett 1941- *WhoFI 92*
**Eggleston**, Dennis Lee 1941- *WhoFI 92*
**Eggleston**, Edward 1837-1902 *BenetAL 91*
**Eggleston**, Forrest Cary 1920- *AmMWSc 92*
**Eggleston**, George Cary 1839-1911 *BenetAL 91*
**Eggleston**, Glen E 1923- *AmMWSc 92*
**Eggleston**, Harold Gordon 1921- *Who 92*
**Eggleston**, James Frederick 1927- *Who 92*
**Eggleston**, Jane R 1947- *AmMWSc 92*
**Eggleston**, John Marshall 1954- *AmMWSc 92*
**Eggleston**, Joseph C 1936- *AmMWSc 92*
**Eggleston**, Neverett, Jr. *WhoBlA 92*
**Eggleston**, Patricia Juanita 1941- *WhoMW 92*
**Eggleston**, Patrick Myron 1941- *AmMWSc 92*
**Eggleston**, Richard Moulton d1991 *Who 92N*
**Eggleston**, Samuel John 1926- *Who 92*
**Eggleton**, Anthony 1932- *Who 92*
**Eggleton**, Reginald Charles 1920- *AmMWSc 92*
**Eggum**, Arne 1936- *ConAu 134*
**Egiebor**, Sharon E. 1959- *WhoBlA 92*
**Egilsson**, Olafur 1936- *IntWW 91, Who 92*
**Eginton**, Warren William 1924- *WhoAmL 92*
**Egk**, Werner 1901-1983 *NewAmDM*
**Egk**, Werner 1901-1990 *FacFETw*
**Egle**, Davis Max 1939- *AmMWSc 92*
**Egle**, John Lee, Jr 1939- *AmMWSc 92*
**Eglee**, Charles Hamilton 1951- *WhoEnt 92*
**Egler**, Frank E. 1911- *WrDr 92*
**Egler**, Frank Edwin 1911- *AmMWSc 92*
**Egler**, Steven Lenhart 1949- *WhoMW 92*
**Egleston**, Fred R 1947- *WhoAmP 91*
**Egleston**, Thomas 1832-1900 *BiInAmS*
**Egleton**, Clive 1927- *WrDr 92*
**Egleton**, Clive Frederick William 1927- *IntAu&W 91*
**Egley**, Thomas Arthur 1945- *WhoWest 92*
**Egli**, Alphons 1924- *IntWW 91*
**Egli**, Dennis B 1942- *AmMWSc 92*
**Egli**, Peter 1933- *AmMWSc 92*
**Eglin**, Colin Wells 1925- *IntWW 91*
**Eglington**, Charles Richard John 1938- *Who 92*
**Eglinton**, Geoffrey 1927- *IntWW 91, Who 92*
**Eglinton and Winton**, Earl of 1939- *Who 92*
**Eglit**, Howard Charles 1942- *WhoAmL 92*
**Eglitis**, Irma 1907- *AmMWSc 92*
**Eglitis**, Martin Alexandris 1955- *AmMWSc 92*
**Egloff**, David Allen 1935- *AmMWSc 92*
**Egloff**, E. Ralph 1932- *WhoMW 92*
**Egloff**, Fred R 1934- *IntAu&W 91*
**Egloff**, John Lawrence 1953- *WhoAmL 92*
**Egloff**, Julius, III 1946- *AmMWSc 92*
**Egly**, Henry 1824-1890 *RelLAm 91*
**Egly**, Richard S 1914- *AmMWSc 92*
**Egmond**, Max van 1936- *NewAmDM*
**Egmont**, Earl of 1914- *Who 92*
**Egner**, Anthony John 1954- *WhoEnt 92*
**Egner**, Donald Otto 1928- *AmMWSc 92*
**Egnoski**, Tina *DrAPF 91*
**Egon**, Nicholas *TwCPaSc*
**Egorin**, Merril Jon *AmMWSc 92*
**Egremont**, Baron 1948- *Who 92*
**Egremont**, Max 1948- *ConAu 35NR*
**Egri**, Gladys 1930- *WhoHisp 92*
**Eguchi**, Kazuyuki 1952- *WhoFI 92*
**Eguchi**, Michael Steven 1947- *WhoEnt 92*
**Eguchi**, Teiji 1926- *IntWW 91*
**Eguchi**, Tomonaru 1920- *IntWW 91*
**Eguiara Eguren**, Juan Jose de 1696-1763 *HisDSpE*
**Eguren**, Jose Maria 1882-1942 *BenetAL 91*
**Egypt**, Ophelia Settle 1903-1984 *NotBlAW 92*
**Ehle**, Byron Leonard 1937- *AmMWSc 92*
**Ehle**, Fred Robert 1952- *AmMWSc 92*
**Ehle**, Jay Sutton 1950- *WhoAmL 92*
**Ehle**, John *DrAPF 91*
**Ehle**, John 1925- *WrDr 92*
**Ehle**, Robert Cannon 1939- *WhoWest 92*
**Ehler**, Arthur Wayne 1922- *AmMWSc 92*
**Ehler**, Kenneth Walter 1946- *AmMWSc 92*
**Ehler**, Lester Ervin 1946- *WhoWest 92*
**Ehler**, Richard Lee 1930- *WhoWest 92*
**Ehleringer**, James Russell 1949- *AmMWSc 92*
**Ehlermann**, Claus-Dieter 1931- *IntWW 91*
**Ehlers**, Alan Peter 1945- *WhoMW 92*
**Ehlers**, Deborah Layne 1950- *WhoEnt 92*
**Ehlers**, Eleanor May Collier 1920- *WhoWest 92*
**Ehlers**, Ernest George 1927- *AmMWSc 92*
**Ehlers**, Florence Raush 1925- *WhoEnt 92*
**Ehlers**, Francis Edward 1916- *AmMWSc 92*
**Ehlers**, James LeRoy 1950- *WhoMW 92*
**Ehlers**, Joseph Martin 1965- *WhoMW 92*
**Ehlers**, Kenneth Warren 1922- *AmMWSc 92*
**Ehlers**, Larry Lee 1953- *WhoFI 92*
**Ehlers**, Mario Ralf Werner 1959- *AmMWSc 92*
**Ehlers**, Richard M. 1951- *WhoMW 92*
**Ehlers**, Vern James 1934- *WhoAmP 91*
**Ehlers**, William Albert 1942- *WhoWest 92*
**Ehlert**, A. Benjamin 1937- *WhoFI 92*
**Ehlert**, Arnold Douglas 1909- *WhoRel 92*
**Ehlert**, Thomas Clarence 1931- *AmMWSc 92, WhoMW 92*
**Ehlig**, Perry Lawrence 1927- *AmMWSc 92*
**Ehlig-Economides**, Christine Anna 1949- *AmMWSc 92*
**Ehline**, David Alan 1938- *WhoRel 92*
**Ehlinger**, John Joseph, Jr. 1949- *WhoAmL 92*
**Ehlke**, Bruce Frederic 1942- *WhoAmL 92*
**Ehlmann**, Arthur J 1928- *AmMWSc 92*
**Ehlmann**, Steven E 1950- *WhoAmP 91*
**Ehmann**, Anthony Valentine 1935- *WhoAmL 92*
**Ehmann**, Edward Paul 1940- *AmMWSc 92*
**Ehmann**, Norman Robert 1924- *WhoWest 92*
**Ehmann**, Richard Stephen 1943- *WhoAmL 92*
**Ehmann**, Thomas Robert 1952- *WhoFI 92*
**Ehmann**, William Donald 1931- *AmMWSc 92*
**Ehmen**, Betty Hersey 1927- *WhoAmP 91*
**Ehmke**, Forrest D. 1951- *WhoMW 92*
**Ehmke**, Horst Paul August 1927- *IntWW 91*
**Ehmling**, Miles Allen 1955- *WhoAmL 92*
**Ehren**, Kenneth Walton 1939- *WhoMW 92*
**Ehrenberg**, Herbert 1926- *IntWW 91*
**Ehrenberg**, Margaret Ruth 1953- *IntAu&W 91*
**Ehrenberg**, Miriam 1930- *IntAu&W 91*
**Ehrenberger**, Vlastimil 1935- *IntWW 91*
**Ehrenburg**, Ilya 1891-1967 *LiExTwC*
**Ehrenburg**, Ilya Grigorovich 1891-1967 *FacFETw*
**Ehrenfeld**, David W 1938- *AmMWSc 92*
**Ehrenfeld**, Elvera 1942- *AmMWSc 92*
**Ehrenfeld**, John R 1931- *AmMWSc 92*
**Ehrenfeld**, Robert Louis 1921- *AmMWSc 92*
**Ehrenfeld**, Sylvain 1929- *AmMWSc 92*
**Ehrenhaft**, Johann L 1915- *AmMWSc 92*
**Ehrenpreis**, Leon 1930- *AmMWSc 92*
**Ehrenpreis**, Seymour 1927- *AmMWSc 92*
**Ehrenreich**, Henry 1928- *AmMWSc 92*
**Ehrenreich**, John Helmuth 1929- *AmMWSc 92*
**Ehrenreich**, Mark Shane 1954- *WhoFI 92*
**Ehrenreich**, Ron 1950- *WhoAmP 91*
**Ehrenreich**, Theodore 1913- *AmMWSc 92*
**Ehrenson**, Stanton Jay 1931- *AmMWSc 92*
**Ehrenstein**, David Augustus 1947- *WhoEnt 92*
**Ehrenstein**, Gerald 1931- *AmMWSc 92*
**Ehrenstorfer**, Sieglinde K M 1927- *AmMWSc 92*
**Ehrenthal**, Irving 1918- *AmMWSc 92*
**Ehrenwerth**, Charlene Reidbord 1949- *WhoAmL 92*
**Ehrenwerth**, David Harry 1947- *WhoAmL 92*
**Ehret**, Anne 1937- *AmMWSc 92*
**Ehret**, Christopher 1941- *IntAu&W 91, WrDr 92*
**Ehret**, Robert 1925- *IntWW 91*
**Ehrhardt**, Arthur 1896-1971 *BiDExR*
**Ehrhardt**, Hermann 1881-1971 *BiDExR, EncTR 91 [port]*
**Ehrhart**, Carl Yarkers 1918- *WhoRel 92*
**Ehrhart**, Earl *WhoAmP 91*
**Ehrhart**, Ina C 1941- *AmMWSc 92*
**Ehrhart**, Joseph Edward 1933- *WhoEnt 92*
**Ehrhart**, L Allen *AmMWSc 92*
**Ehrhart**, Llewellyn McDowell 1942- *AmMWSc 92*
**Ehrhart**, Steven E. *WhoWest 92*
**Ehrhart**, W.D. *DrAPF 91*
**Ehrhart**, W. D. 1948- *DcLB DS9 [port]*
**Ehrhart**, Wendell A 1934- *AmMWSc 92*
**Ehrhart**, William Daniel 1948- *IntAu&W 91*
**Ehrich**, F Frederick 1919- *AmMWSc 92*
**Ehrich**, Fredric F 1928- *AmMWSc 92*
**Ehrich**, Sandra K 1947- *WhoAmP 91*
**Ehricke**, Krafft A 1917-1984 *FacFETw*
**Ehrig**, Raymond John 1928- *AmMWSc 92*
**Ehringer**, Martha Lucy Miller 1940- *WhoWest 92*
**Ehringhaus**, John Christoph Blucher 1882-1949 *DcNCBi 2*
**Ehrke**, Mary Jane 1937- *AmMWSc 92*
**Ehrle**, Roy W 1928- *WhoIns 92*
**Ehrler**, Bremer *WhoAmP 91*
**Ehrlich**, Alexander Charles 1935- *AmMWSc 92*
**Ehrlich**, Alvin McIntyre 1950- *WhoAmL 92*
**Ehrlich**, Amy 1942- *SmATA 65 [port]*
**Ehrlich**, Anne Howland 1933- *AmMWSc 92*
**Ehrlich**, Bettina *WrDr 92*
**Ehrlich**, Clarence Eugene 1938- *WhoFI 92, WhoMW 92*
**Ehrlich**, Edna E. 1919- *WhoFI 92*
**Ehrlich**, Edward Norman 1928- *AmMWSc 92*
**Ehrlich**, Eugene 1922- *IntAu&W 91, WrDr 92*
**Ehrlich**, Georg 1897-1966 *TwCPaSc*
**Ehrlich**, George Edward 1928- *AmMWSc 92*
**Ehrlich**, Gert 1926- *AmMWSc 92*
**Ehrlich**, Gertrude 1923- *AmMWSc 92*
**Ehrlich**, Grant Conklin 1916- *WhoWest 92*
**Ehrlich**, Gretel *DrAPF 91, TwCWW 91*
**Ehrlich**, H Paul 1941- *AmMWSc 92*
**Ehrlich**, Henry Lutz 1925- *AmMWSc 92*
**Ehrlich**, Howard George 1924- *AmMWSc 92*
**Ehrlich**, I Robert 1926- *AmMWSc 92*
**Ehrlich**, Jack 1930- *TwCWW 91, WrDr 92*
**Ehrlich**, Jerome Harry 1937- *WhoAmL 92*
**Ehrlich**, Julian *AmMWSc 92*
**Ehrlich**, Kenneth Craig 1943- *AmMWSc 92*
**Ehrlich**, Kenneth James *WhoEnt 92*
**Ehrlich**, Kingston W. 1914- *WhoMW 92*
**Ehrlich**, Lawrence 1917- *WhoRel 92*
**Ehrlich**, Louis William 1927- *AmMWSc 92*
**Ehrlich**, Max 1909-1983 *TwCSFW 91*
**Ehrlich**, Mel 1938- *WhoFI 92*
**Ehrlich**, Melanie 1945- *AmMWSc 92*
**Ehrlich**, Melvin 1944- *WhoFI 92*
**Ehrlich**, Paul 1854-1915 *FacFETw [port], WhoNob 90*
**Ehrlich**, Paul 1923- *AmMWSc 92*
**Ehrlich**, Paul 1932- *IntAu&W 91, WrDr 92*
**Ehrlich**, Paul Ewing 1948- *AmMWSc 92*
**Ehrlich**, Paul Ralph 1932- *AmMWSc 92, IntWW 91, WhoWest 92*
**Ehrlich**, Raymond 1918- *WhoAmL 92, WhoAmP 91*
**Ehrlich**, Richard 1921- *AmMWSc 92*
**Ehrlich**, Richard 1924- *AmMWSc 92*
**Ehrlich**, Robert 1936- *AmMWSc 92*
**Ehrlich**, Robert 1938- *AmMWSc 92*
**Ehrlich**, Robert L, Jr 1957- *WhoAmP 91*
**Ehrlich**, Robert Stark 1940- *AmMWSc 92*
**Ehrlich**, Roseanne *IntMPA 92*
**Ehrlich**, Roy Melven 1928- *WhoAmP 91*
**Ehrlich**, S Paul, Jr 1932- *AmMWSc 92, IntWW 91*
**Ehrlich**, Sanford Howard 1931- *AmMWSc 92*
**Ehrlich**, Shirley A. 1951- *WhoAmL 92*
**Ehrlich**, Stanley L 1925- *AmMWSc 92*
**Ehrlich**, Thomas 1934- *IntWW 91*
**Ehrlich**, Walter 1915- *AmMWSc 92*
**Ehrlichman**, John *DrAPF 91*
**Ehrlichman**, John 1925- *IntAu&W 91, WrDr 92*
**Ehrlichman**, John Daniel 1925- *AmPolLe, IntWW 91*
**Ehrling**, Sixten 1918- *NewAmDM, WhoEnt 92*
**Ehrman**, Joachim Benedict 1929- *AmMWSc 92*
**Ehrman**, John 1920- *WrDr 92*
**Ehrman**, John Patrick William 1920- *IntWW 91, Who 92*
**Ehrman**, Lee 1935- *AmMWSc 92*
**Ehrman**, Leonard 1932- *AmMWSc 92*
**Ehrman**, Michael Alan 1953- *WhoWest 92*
**Ehrman**, Sally *DrAPF 91*
**Ehrman**, William Geoffrey 1950- *Who 92*
**Ehrmann**, Max 1872-1945 *ScFEYrs*
**Ehrmann**, Rita Mae 1928- *AmMWSc 92, WhoRel 92*
**Ehrmann**, Thomas William 1935- *WhoAmL 92*
**Ehrmantraut**, Harry Charles 1921- *AmMWSc 92*
**Ehrreich**, Albert LeRoy 1923- *AmMWSc 92*
**Ehrreich**, Stewart Joel 1936- *AmMWSc 92*
**Ehyophsta** *EncAmaz 91*
**Eian**, Gilbert Lee 1943- *AmMWSc 92, WhoMW 92*
**Eibeck**, Richard Elmer 1935- *AmMWSc 92*
**Eibel**, Deborah 1940- *IntAu&W 91*
**Eiben**, Galen J 1936- *AmMWSc 92*
**Eiben**, Michael R. 1943- *WhoMW 92*
**Eiben**, Robert Michael 1922- *AmMWSc 92*
**Eibert**, John, Jr 1918- *AmMWSc 92*
**Eibl-Eibesfeldt**, Irenaus 1928- *IntWW 91*
**Eibling**, James A 1917- *AmMWSc 92*
**Eich**, Robert 1923- *AmMWSc 92*
**Eich**, Stephen B. *WhoEnt 92*
**Eich**, Todd Gerard 1965- *WhoFI 92*
**Eich**, William 1938- *WhoAmL 92*
**Eichbaum**, Barlane Ronald 1926- *AmMWSc 92*
**Eichberg**, Jorg Wilhelm 1939- *AmMWSc 92*
**Eichberg**, Joseph 1935- *AmMWSc 92*
**Eichberger**, Joseph Michael 1947- *WhoMW 92*
**Eichberger**, Le Roy Carl 1927- *AmMWSc 92*
**Eichel**, Herman Joseph 1924- *AmMWSc 92*
**Eichelbaum**, Thomas 1931- *Who 92*
**Eichelberger**, Brenda 1939- *WhoBlA 92*
**Eichelberger**, Clark Mell 1896-1980 *AmPeW*
**Eichelberger**, Daniel Lee 1965- *WhoRel 92*
**Eichelberger**, Edward B 1934- *AmMWSc 92*
**Eichelberger**, Ethyl 1945-1990 *ConTFT 9*
**Eichelberger**, Frank, Jr. 1931- *WhoWest 92*
**Eichelberger**, John Charles 1948- *AmMWSc 92*
**Eichelberger**, John Henry, Jr 1958- *WhoAmP 91*

**Eichelberger**, Robert John 1921- AmMWSc 92
**Eichelberger**, Robert Leslie 1926- AmMWSc 92
**Eichelberger**, Ted David, II 1930- WhoWest 92
**Eichelberger**, W H 1921- AmMWSc 92
**Eichelberger**, William L. 1922- WhoBlA 92
**Eichelman**, Burr S, Jr 1943- AmMWSc 92
**Eichenbaum**, E. Charles 1907- WhoAmL 92
**Eichenbaum**, Luise 1952- IntAu&W 91
**Eichenbaum**, Martin Stewart 1954- WhoFI 92
**Eichenberg**, Fritz 1901-1990 ConAu 133
**Eichenberger**, Hans 1926- DcTwDes
**Eichenberger**, Hans P 1921- AmMWSc 92
**Eichenberger**, Jerry Alan 1947- WhoAmL 92
**Eichenberger**, Mark d1991? NewYTBS 91
**Eichenberger**, Rudolph John 1941- AmMWSc 92
**Eichenholz**, Alfred 1927- AmMWSc 92
**Eichenwald**, Heinz Felix 1926- AmMWSc 92
**Eicher**, Allison Boyd 1935- WhoEnt 92
**Eicher**, Don Lauren 1930- AmMWSc 92
**Eicher**, Eva Mae 1939- AmMWSc 92
**Eicher**, George J 1916- AmMWSc 92
**Eicher**, John Harold 1921- AmMWSc 92
**Eicher**, Lawrence D. 1938- IntWW 91
**Eicher**, Roma Jean 1942- WhoFI 92
**Eichholz**, Alexander 1926- AmMWSc 92
**Eichholz**, Geoffrey G 1920- AmMWSc 92
**Eichhorn**, Arthur David 1953- WhoEnt 92, WhoMW 92
**Eichhorn**, Barbara 1937- WhoMW 92
**Eichhorn**, Bradford Reese 1954- WhoMW 92
**Eichhorn**, Douglas DrAPF 91
**Eichhorn**, Gunther Louis 1927- AmMWSc 92
**Eichhorn**, Heinrich Karl 1927- AmMWSc 92
**Eichhorn**, J 1924- AmMWSc 92
**Eichhorn**, Lisa 1952- IntMPA 92
**Eichhorn**, Roger 1931- AmMWSc 92
**Eichinger**, Bruce Edward 1941- AmMWSc 92
**Eichinger**, Jack Waldo, Jr 1904- AmMWSc 92
**Eichinger**, Marilynne H. WhoWest 92
**Eichler**, Duane Curtis 1946- AmMWSc 92
**Eichler**, Franklin Roosevelt 1933- WhoFI 92
**Eichler**, Fritz 1911- DcTwDes
**Eichler**, Irena d1990 IntWW 91N
**Eichler**, Victor B 1941- AmMWSc 92
**Eichman**, Peter L 1925- AmMWSc 92
**Eichmann**, Adolf 1906-1962 BiDExR, EncTR 91 [port], FacFETw [port]
**Eichmann**, George 1936- AmMWSc 92
**Eichna**, Ludwig Waldemar 1908- AmMWSc 92
**Eichner**, Eduard 1905- AmMWSc 92
**Eichner**, Edward Randolph 1938- AmMWSc 92
**Eichner**, Hans 1921- WrDr 92
**Eichner**, Maura DrAPF 91
**Eichorst**, Gail Susan 1952- WhoMW 92
**Eichten**, Beatrice Mary 1943- WhoRel 92
**Eichten**, Estia Joseph 1946- AmMWSc 92
**Eichwald**, Ernest J 1913- AmMWSc 92
**Eichwald**, F. Ken 1954- WhoHisp 92
**Eick**, Gretchen Cassel 1942- WhoRel 92
**Eick**, Harry Arthur 1929- AmMWSc 92
**Eick**, James E 1937- WhoIns 92
**Eick**, Jurgen IntWW 91N
**Eick**, Norman John 1958- WhoEnt 92
**Eicke**, Theodor 1892-1943 EncTR 91 [port]
**Eickelberg**, W Warren B 1925- AmMWSc 92
**Eickhoff**, Margaret Kathryn 1939- WhoFI 92
**Eickhoff**, Theodore C 1931- AmMWSc 92
**Eickholt**, Theodore Henry 1932- AmMWSc 92
**Eicknof**, John R. 1956- WhoEnt 92
**Eickstaedt**, Lawrence Lee 1939- AmMWSc 92
**Eickstedt**, Egon, Freiherr von 1892-1965 EncTR 91
**Eickwort**, George Campbell 1940- AmMWSc 92
**Eid**, Mikel John 1930- WhoMW 92
**Eide**, Edward T. WhoRel 92
**Eide**, Robert Walter 1957- WhoMW 92
**Eidelberg**, Eduardo 1930- AmMWSc 92
**Eidell**, Ronald George 1944- WhoFI 92
**Eidelman**, Terry 1960- WhoMW 92
**Eidels**, Leon 1942- AmMWSc 92
**Eidem**, Bjarne Mork 1936- IntWW 91
**Eidem**, Orville Meidell 1931- WhoMW 92
**Eider**, Norman George 1930- AmMWSc 92
**Eidinger**, David 1931- AmMWSc 92
**Eidinoff**, Maxwell Leigh 1915- AmMWSc 92
**Eidman**, Richard August Louis 1936- AmMWSc 92
**Eidman**, Vernon Roy 1936- WhoMW 92
**Eidsmoe**, Daniel Clark 1962- WhoAmL 92
**Eidson**, Kindell Dee 1951- WhoFI 92
**Eidson**, Wanda Carroll 1922- WhoAmP 91
**Eidson**, William Whelan 1935- AmMWSc 92
**Eidt**, Douglas Conrad 1928- AmMWSc 92
**Eidt**, Robert C 1923- AmMWSc 92
**Eidus**, Janice DrAPF 91
**Eiduson**, Samuel 1918- AmMWSc 92
**Eidy**, Jean E WhoAmP 91
**Eielson**, Jorge Eduardo 1924- ConSpAP
**Eifert**, Donald A 1929- WhoIns 92
**Eiffel**, Alexandre Gustave 1832-1923 DcTwDes
**Eifler**, Carl Frederick 1906- WhoWest 92
**Eifler**, Gus Kearney, Jr 1908- AmMWSc 92
**Eifrig**, David Eric 1935- AmMWSc 92
**Eifrig**, Gail McGrew 1940- WhoRel 92
**Eige**, Lillian 1915- SmATA 65 [port]
**Eigel**, Christopher John WhoFI 92, WhoMW 92
**Eigel**, Edwin George, Jr 1932- AmMWSc 92
**Eigel**, Robert Louis 1937- WhoFI 92, WhoMW 92
**Eigen**, Edward 1923- AmMWSc 92
**Eigen**, Judith Ann 1938- WhoEnt 92
**Eigen**, Manfred 1927- FacFETw, IntWW 91, Who 92, WhoNob 90
**Eigenbrodt**, Harold John 1928- WhoRel 92
**Eigenfeld**, Roger Conrad 1940- WhoRel 92
**Eighme**, Lloyd Elwyn 1927- AmMWSc 92
**Eight**, The RComAH
**Eights**, James 1798-1882 BiInAmS
**Eigner**, Edwin Moss 1931- WhoWest 92
**Eigner**, Joseph 1933- AmMWSc 92
**Eigner**, Larry 1927- ConPo 91, IntAu&W 91, WrDr 92
**Eigner**, William Whitling 1959- WhoAmL 92
**Eigo**, J. DrAPF 91
**Eiguren**, Roy Lewis 1952- WhoAmL 92
**Eijkman**, Christiaan 1858-1930 FacFETw, WhoNob 90
**Eik-Nes**, Kristen Borger 1922- AmMWSc 92
**Eikel**, Robert 1906- WhoAmL 92
**Eikenbary**, Raymond Darrell 1929- AmMWSc 92
**Eikenberry**, Arthur Raymond 1920- WhoWest 92
**Eikenberry**, James Owen 1952- WhoRel 92
**Eikenberry**, Jill 1947- IntMPA 92, WhoEnt 92
**Eikenberry**, Jon Nathan 1942- AmMWSc 92
**Eikenberry**, Kenneth Otto 1932- WhoAmL 92, WhoAmP 91, WhoWest 92
**Eikerenkoetter**, Frederick J., II 1935- RelLAm 91, WhoBlA 92
**Eikerenkoetter**, Frederick Joseph, II 1935- WhoRel 92
**Eikrem**, Lynwood Olaf 1919- AmMWSc 92, WhoFI 92
**Eil**, Charles 1946- AmMWSc 92
**Eiland**, Gary Wayne 1951- WhoAmL 92
**Eiland**, Ray Maurice 1932- WhoBlA 92
**Eilbacher**, Lisa IntMPA 92
**Eilber**, Frederick Richard 1940- AmMWSc 92
**Eilberg**, Joshua 1921- WhoAmP 91
**Eilbott**, Don A 1950- WhoAmP 91
**Eilen**, Howard Scott 1954- WhoAmL 92
**Eilenberg**, Lawrence Ira 1947- WhoWest 92
**Eilenberg**, Samuel 1913- AmMWSc 92, IntWW 91
**Eiler**, David Richard 1933- WhoRel 92
**Eiler**, G Roger 1944- WhoIns 92
**Eiler**, Hugo 1935- AmMWSc 92
**Eiler**, James Olney 1961- WhoAmL 92
**Eiler**, John Joseph 1910- AmMWSc 92
**Eiler**, Larry Tracy 1939- WhoMW 92
**Eilerman**, Betty Jean 1942- WhoMW 92
**Eilerman**, Dale Joseph 1952- WhoMW 92
**Eilerman**, Theodore Lawrence 1942- WhoMW 92
**Eilers**, Carl G 1925- AmMWSc 92
**Eilers**, Frederic Anton 1839-1917 BiInAmS
**Eilers**, Frederick Irving 1938- AmMWSc 92
**Eilers**, Hazel Kraft 1910- WrDr 92
**Eilers**, Lawrence John 1927- AmMWSc 92
**Eilers**, Todd Alan 1964- WhoMW 92
**Eilert**, Arnold James 1962- WhoMW 92
**Eilert**, Ed WhoAmP 91
**Eilledge**, Elwyn Owen Morris 1935- Who 92
**Eilon**, Samuel 1923- Who 92, WrDr 92
**Eilts**, Hermann Frederick 1922- IntWW 91, WhoAmP 91
**Eimbeck**, William 1841-1909 BiInAmS
**Eime**, Lester Oscar 1922- AmMWSc 92
**Eimer**, Nathan Philip 1949- WhoAmL 92
**Eimerl**, David AmMWSc 92
**Eimert**, Herbert 1897-1972 NewAmDM
**Ein**, Daniel 1938- AmMWSc 92
**Einarson**, Baldvin Oliver 1934- WhoAmL 92
**Einarsson**, Alfred W 1915- AmMWSc 92
**Einarsson**, Sveinn 1934- IntAu&W 91
**Einaudi**, Franco 1937- AmMWSc 92
**Einaudi**, Giulio 1912- IntWW 91
**Einaudi**, Luigi R 1936- WhoAmP 91
**Einaudi**, Marco Tullio 1939- AmMWSc 92
**Einbond**, Bernard Lionel DrAPF 91
**Einbond**, Bernard Lionel 1937- WrDr 92
**Einem**, Gottfried von 1918- ConCom 92, IntWW 91, NewAmDM
**Einerson**, Jay Scott 1959- WhoMW 92
**Einerson**, Richard John 1935- WhoRel 92
**Einert**, Alfred Erwin 1939- AmMWSc 92
**Einertson**, Norris Leonard 1930- WhoRel 92
**Einhellig**, Frank Arnold 1938- AmMWSc 92
**Einhorn**, David Allen 1961- WhoAmL 92, WhoFI 92
**Einhorn**, Edward Martin 1936- WhoMW 92
**Einhorn**, Harold 1929- WhoAmL 92
**Einhorn**, Martin B 1942- AmMWSc 92, WhoWest 92
**Einhorn**, Michael Allan 1952- WhoFI 92
**Einhorn**, Philip A 1942- AmMWSc 92
**Einhorn**, Stephen Edward 1943- WhoFI 92, WhoMW 92
**Einhorn**, Wendy DrAPF 91
**Einiger**, Carol Blum 1949- WhoFI 92
**Einiger**, Roger W. 1947- WhoFI 92
**Einoder**, Camille Elizabeth 1937- WhoMW 92
**Einolf**, David Matthew 1960- WhoMW 92
**Einolf**, William Noel 1943- AmMWSc 92
**Einset**, Eystein 1925- AmMWSc 92
**Einset**, John William 1947- AmMWSc 92
**Einspahr**, Dean William 1923- AmMWSc 92
**Einspahr**, Howard Martin 1943- AmMWSc 92
**Einspruch**, Norman G 1932- AmMWSc 92
**Einstein**, Albert 1879-1955 AmPeW, BenetAL 91, ConAu 133, EncTR 91 [port], FacFETw [port], RComAH, WhoNob 90
**Einstein**, Carol Wind 1953- WhoAmL 92
**Einstein**, Clifford Jay 1939- WhoEnt 92
**Einstein**, Edwin Frank 1955- WhoAmL 92
**Einstein**, Elizabeth Roboz AmMWSc 92
**Einstein**, Frederick W B 1940- AmMWSc 92
**Einstein**, Stephen Jan 1945- WhoRel 92, WhoWest 92
**Einstein**, Theodore Lee 1947- AmMWSc 92
**Einthoven**, Willem 1860-1927 WhoNob 90
**Einwich**, Anna Maria 1917- AmMWSc 92
**Einzig**, Barbara DrAPF 91
**Einzig**, Barbara Ellen 1951- IntAu&W 91
**Einzig**, Stanley 1942- AmMWSc 92
**Einzig**, Susan 1922- TwCPaSc
**Einziger**, Robert E 1945- AmMWSc 92
**Eipper**, Betty Anne 1945- AmMWSc 92
**Eirich**, Frederick Roland 1905- AmMWSc 92
**Eirich**, Lynda Mary 1952- WhoMW 92
**Eirman**, Thomas Fredrick 1947- WhoEnt 92
**Eis**, Jacalyn DrAPF 91
**Eisa**, Hamdy Mahmoud 1938- AmMWSc 92
**Eisberg**, John Frederic 1938- WhoAmL 92
**Eisberg**, Robert Martin 1928- AmMWSc 92
**Eisch**, John Joseph 1930- AmMWSc 92
**Eisdorfer**, Carl 1930- AmMWSc 92
**Eise**, Kurt Frederick 1937- WhoFI 92
**Eisele**, Carolyn AmMWSc 92
**Eisele**, Charles Wesley 1906- AmMWSc 92
**Eisele**, Garnett Thomas 1923- WhoAmL 92
**Eisele**, Milton Douglas 1910- WhoWest 92
**Eisele**, Patricia O'Leary 1935- WhoFI 92
**Eisele**, Paul M. 1934- WhoEnt 92
**Eisele**, Robert H 1948- IntAu&W 91
**Eisele**, Robert Henry 1948- WhoEnt 92
**Eisele**, William David 1927- WhoFI 92
**Eiseley**, Loren 1907-1977 BenetAL 91
**Eiselstein**, Herbert Louis 1919- AmMWSc 92
**Eiseman**, A Quillen 1938- WhoAmP 91
**Eiseman**, Ben 1917- AmMWSc 92
**Eiseman**, Neal Martin 1955- WhoAmL 92
**Eisemann**, Kurt 1923- AmMWSc 92, WhoWest 92
**Eisen**, Carol G. ConAu 133
**Eisen**, David Spencer 1956- WhoEnt 92
**Eisen**, David Stuart 1956- WhoAmL 92
**Eisen**, Edwin Otto 1940- WhoFI 92
**Eisen**, Eric Anshel 1950- WhoAmL 92
**Eisen**, Eugene J 1938- AmMWSc 92
**Eisen**, Fred Henry 1929- AmMWSc 92
**Eisen**, Glenn Philip 1940- WhoFI 92
**Eisen**, Henry 1921- AmMWSc 92
**Eisen**, Herman N. 1918- IntWW 91
**Eisen**, Herman Nathaniel 1918- AmMWSc 92
**Eisen**, Rebecca Dianne 1949- WhoAmL 92
**Eisen**, Sydney 1929- ConAu 135
**Eisenach**, Robert L 1942- WhoAmP 91
**Eisenacher**, Craig E 1947- WhoIns 92
**Eisenbach**, Robert 1914- WhoEnt 92
**Eisenbarth**, Gary L 1947- WhoIns 92
**Eisenbarth**, George Stephen 1947- AmMWSc 92
**Eisenberg**, Adi 1935- AmMWSc 92
**Eisenberg**, Alan 1935- WhoEnt 92, WhoFI 92
**Eisenberg**, Albert Charles 1946- WhoAmP 91
**Eisenberg**, Barry Martin 1947- WhoFI 92
**Eisenberg**, Bennett 1942- AmMWSc 92
**Eisenberg**, Brenda Russell 1942- AmMWSc 92
**Eisenberg**, Carola AmMWSc 92
**Eisenberg**, David 1939- AmMWSc 92
**Eisenberg**, Deborah DrAPF 91
**Eisenberg**, Evan 1938- AmMWSc 92
**Eisenberg**, F. Marcella WhoEnt 92
**Eisenberg**, Frank, Jr 1920- AmMWSc 92
**Eisenberg**, Frederick Aaron 1931- WhoRel 92
**Eisenberg**, Howard Bruce 1946- WhoAmL 92
**Eisenberg**, James 1930- WhoMW 92
**Eisenberg**, Jeffrey S. 1958- WhoAmL 92
**Eisenberg**, John Frederick 1935- AmMWSc 92
**Eisenberg**, John Meyer 1946- AmMWSc 92
**Eisenberg**, Judah Moshe 1938- AmMWSc 92
**Eisenberg**, Larry 1919- TwCSFW 91, WrDr 92
**Eisenberg**, Lawrence 1919- AmMWSc 92
**Eisenberg**, Lawrence 1933- AmMWSc 92
**Eisenberg**, Lawrence D. 1943- WhoAmL 92
**Eisenberg**, Leon 1922- AmMWSc 92, IntWW 91
**Eisenberg**, M Michael 1931- AmMWSc 92
**Eisenberg**, Martin A 1940- AmMWSc 92
**Eisenberg**, Max 1941- AmMWSc 92
**Eisenberg**, Melvin A. 1934- WhoAmL 92
**Eisenberg**, Murray 1939- AmMWSc 92
**Eisenberg**, R. Neal 1936- WhoFI 92
**Eisenberg**, Randall Scot 1964- WhoWest 92
**Eisenberg**, Rebecca S. 1955- WhoAmL 92
**Eisenberg**, Richard 1943- AmMWSc 92
**Eisenberg**, Richard Martin 1942- AmMWSc 92
**Eisenberg**, Robert 1944- AmMWSc 92
**Eisenberg**, Robert C 1938- AmMWSc 92
**Eisenberg**, Robert Michael 1938- AmMWSc 92
**Eisenberg**, Robert Philip 1945- WhoMW 92
**Eisenberg**, Robert S 1942- AmMWSc 92
**Eisenberg**, Robin Ledgin 1951- WhoRel 92
**Eisenberg**, Ronald Lee AmMWSc 92
**Eisenberg**, Ruth F. DrAPF 91
**Eisenberg**, Scott Alan 1959- WhoFI 92
**Eisenberg**, Sheldon Merven 1942- AmMWSc 92
**Eisenberg**, Sidney Edwin 1913- AmMWSc 92
**Eisenberg**, Stewart 1950- WhoAmL 92
**Eisenberg**, Susan DrAPF 91
**Eisenberg**, Susan Nadler 1956- WhoAmL 92
**Eisenberg**, Sylvan 1913- AmMWSc 92
**Eisenberg**, Theodore 1947- WhoAmL 92
**Eisenberg**, Walter Leo 1920- WhoAmL 92, WhoFI 92
**Eisenberger**, Peter Michael 1941- AmMWSc 92
**Eisenbrand**, Gregory David 1957- WhoFI 92
**Eisenbrandt**, David Lee 1945- AmMWSc 92
**Eisenbrandt**, H. C. 1790-1861 NewAmDM
**Eisenbrandt**, Leslie Lee 1908- AmMWSc 92
**Eisenbraun**, Allan Alfred 1928- AmMWSc 92
**Eisenbraun**, Edmund Julius 1920- AmMWSc 92
**Eisenbraun**, Eric Charles 1955- WhoAmL 92
**Eisenbud**, David 1947- AmMWSc 92
**Eisenbud**, Leonard 1913- AmMWSc 92
**Eisenbud**, Merril 1915- AmMWSc 92
**Eisendrath**, Edwin 1958- WhoAmP 91
**Eisenfeld**, Arnold Joel 1936- AmMWSc 92
**Eisenfeld**, Jerome 1938- AmMWSc 92
**Eisenhardt**, Roy 1939- WhoWest 92

**Eisenhardt**, William Anthony, Jr 1942- *AmMWSc 92*
**Eisenhart**, Churchill 1913- *AmMWSc 92*
**Eisenhauer**, Charles Martin 1930- *AmMWSc 92*
**Eisenhauer**, Gregory John 1958- *WhoFI 92*
**Eisenhauer**, Hugh Ross 1927- *AmMWSc 92*
**Eisenhauer**, Wayne Harold 1949- *WhoAmL 92*
**Eisenhower**, Dwight D. 1890-1969 *BenetAL 91, EncTR 91 [port], FacFETw [port], RComAH*
**Eisenhower**, Dwight David 1890-1969 *AmPolLe [port]*
**Eisenhower**, John S. D. 1922- *WrDr 92*
**Eisenhower**, John Sheldon Doud 1922- *IntWW 91, WhoAmP 91*
**Eisenhower**, Milton S 1899-1985 *FacFETw*
**Eisenlohr**, W S, Jr 1907- *AmMWSc 92*
**Eisenman**, George 1929- *AmMWSc 92*
**Eisenman**, Leonard Max 1942- *AmMWSc 92*
**Eisenman**, Morris Reuben 1950- *WhoEnt 92*
**Eisenman**, Peter D. 1932- *WrDr 92*
**Eisenman**, Richard Leo 1928- *AmMWSc 92*
**Eisenman**, Selma Tamber d1991 *NewYTBS 91*
**Eisenmayer**, Ernst 1920- *TwCPaSc*
**Eisenreich**, Steven John 1947- *AmMWSc 92*
**Eisenson**, Jon 1907- *AmMWSc 92, IntAu&W 91, WrDr 92*
**Eisenstadt**, Arthur A 1918- *AmMWSc 92*
**Eisenstadt**, Bertram Joseph 1923- *AmMWSc 92*
**Eisenstadt**, Jerome Melvin 1926- *AmMWSc 92*
**Eisenstadt**, Maurice 1931- *AmMWSc 92*
**Eisenstadt**, Pauline Bauman 1938- *WhoAmP 91*
**Eisenstadt**, Raymond 1921- *AmMWSc 92*
**Eisenstadt**, Shmuel N. 1923- *IntWW 91*
**Eisenstadt**, Shmuel Noah *WrDr 92*
**Eisenstadt**, Shmuel Noah 1923- *IntAu&W 91*
**Eisenstaedt**, Alfred 1898- *FacFETw, IntWW 91*
**Eisenstaedt**, Robert Witlin 1953- *WhoEnt 92*
**Eisenstark**, Abraham 1919- *AmMWSc 92*
**Eisenstatt**, Phillip 1922- *AmMWSc 92*
**Eisenstein**, Barry I 1948- *AmMWSc 92*
**Eisenstein**, Barry Ira 1948- *WhoMW 92*
**Eisenstein**, Bob I 1939- *AmMWSc 92*
**Eisenstein**, Bruce A 1941- *AmMWSc 92*
**Eisenstein**, Edward Lewisohn 1955- *WhoMW 92*
**Eisenstein**, Julian 1921- *AmMWSc 92*
**Eisenstein**, Ken 1948- *WhoEnt 92*
**Eisenstein**, Laurence Jay 1960- *WhoAmL 92, WhoAmP 91*
**Eisenstein**, Michael 1950- *WhoAmL 92*
**Eisenstein**, Phyllis 1946- *ConAu 36NR, IntAu&W 91, TwCSFW 91, WrDr 92*
**Eisenstein**, Reuben 1929- *AmMWSc 92*
**Eisenstein**, Robert Alan 1942- *AmMWSc 92*
**Eisenstein**, Samuel A. *DrAPF 91*
**Eisenstein**, Sergei 1898-1948 *IntDcF 2-2 [port]*
**Eisenstein**, Sergei Mikhilovich 1898-1948 *FacFETw*
**Eisenstein**, Sergey Mikhaylovich 1898-1948 *SovUnBD*
**Eisenstein**, Toby K 1942- *AmMWSc 92*
**Eisenthal**, Stephen Earl 1940- *WhoEnt 92*
**Eisentraut**, Kent James 1938- *AmMWSc 92*
**Eisenzimmer**, Betty Wenner 1939- *WhoFI 92, WhoWest 92*
**Eiser**, Arthur L 1928- *AmMWSc 92*
**Eiserling**, Frederick A 1938- *AmMWSc 92*
**Eiserling**, Frederick Allen 1938- *WhoWest 92*
**Eisermann**, Eckehard Hermann 1943- *WhoMW 92*
**Eisinger**, Josef 1924- *AmMWSc 92*
**Eisinger**, Robert Peter 1929- *AmMWSc 92*
**Eisland**, June *WhoAmP 91*
**Eisler**, Ann Olmsted 1954- *WhoWest 92*
**Eisler**, Elfriede *EncTR 91*
**Eisler**, Gerhart 1897-1968 *EncTR 91*
**Eisler**, Hanns 1898-1962 *NewAmDM*
**Eisler**, Millard Marcus 1950- *WhoMW 92*
**Eisler**, Robert David 1952- *WhoWest 92*
**Eisler**, Ronald 1932- *AmMWSc 92*
**Eisley**, Joe G 1928- *AmMWSc 92*
**Eisman**, Roy Hendrick 1948- *WhoFI 92*
**Eismeier**, Elizabeth Anne Smith 1949- *WhoFI 92*
**Eisner**, Alan Mark 1943- *AmMWSc 92*
**Eisner**, Elliott Roy 1945- *WhoAmL 92*
**Eisner**, Elmer 1919- *AmMWSc 92*
**Eisner**, Gilbert Martin 1932- *AmMWSc 92*
**Eisner**, Gisela 1925- *IntAu&W 91, WrDr 92*
**Eisner**, Howard 1935- *AmMWSc 92*
**Eisner**, Janet Margaret 1940- *WhoRel 92*
**Eisner**, Leonard d1991 *NewYTBS 91*
**Eisner**, Mark Joseph 1938- *AmMWSc 92*
**Eisner**, Michael D. *LesBEnT 92*
**Eisner**, Michael D. 1942- *IntMPA 92*
**Eisner**, Michael Dammann 1942- *IntWW 91, WhoEnt 92, WhoFI 92, WhoWest 92*
**Eisner**, Neil Robert 1943- *WhoAmL 92*
**Eisner**, Philip Nathan 1934- *AmMWSc 92*
**Eisner**, Richard Alan 1934- *WhoFI 92*
**Eisner**, Robert 1922- *WhoFI 92, WhoMW 92, WrDr 92*
**Eisner**, Robert Linden 1927- *AmMWSc 92*
**Eisner**, Ronald Richard 1933- *WhoWest 92*
**Eisner**, Thomas 1929- *AmMWSc 92, IntWW 91*
**Eisner**, Thomas Sultan 1944- *WhoAmL 92*
**Eiss**, Abraham L 1934- *AmMWSc 92*
**Eiss**, Albert Frank 1910- *AmMWSc 92*
**Eiss**, Norman Smith, Jr 1931- *AmMWSc 92*
**Eissenberg**, David M 1929- *AmMWSc 92*
**Eissenberg**, Joel Carter 1955- *AmMWSc 92, WhoMW 92*
**Eissenstat**, Eric Spencer 1958- *WhoAmL 92*
**Eissler**, Robert L 1921- *AmMWSc 92*
**Eissmann**, Robert Fred 1924- *WhoFI 92*
**Eissner**, Robert M 1926- *AmMWSc 92*
**Eiszner**, James Richard 1927- *AmMWSc 92*
**Eiszner**, James Richard, Jr. 1953- *WhoAmL 92*
**Eitan**, Raphael 1929- *IntWW 91*
**Eiten**, George 1923- *AmMWSc 92*
**Eitenmiller**, Ronald Ray 1944- *AmMWSc 92*
**Eitner**, Lorenz E. A. 1919- *WrDr 92*
**Eitner**, Lorenz Edwin Alfred 1919- *WhoWest 92*
**Eitrheim**, Norman Duane 1929- *WhoMW 92, WhoRel 92*
**Eittreim**, Stephen L 1941- *AmMWSc 92*
**Eitzen**, Donald Gene 1942- *AmMWSc 92*
**Eitzen**, Linda Neun 1947- *WhoWest 92*
**Eitzman**, Donald V 1927- *AmMWSc 92*
**Eixenberger**, Charles Anthony 1951- *WhoWest 92*
**Eizenstat**, Stuart E. 1943- *WhoAmL 92*
**Eizenstat**, Stuart Elliot 1943- *WhoAmP 91*
**Ek**, Alan Ryan 1942- *AmMWSc 92*
**Ekandem**, Dominic Ignatius 1917- *IntWW 91, WhoRel 92*
**Ekangaki**, Nzo 1934- *IntWW 91*
**Ekberg**, Anita 1931- *IntMPA 92*
**Ekberg**, Carl E, Jr 1920- *AmMWSc 92*
**Ekberg**, Donald Roy 1928- *AmMWSc 92*
**Ekberg**, Kent Francis 1947- *WhoFI 92*
**Ekdahl**, Jon Nels 1942- *WhoAmL 92*
**Ekdale**, Allan Anton 1946- *AmMWSc 92*
**Eke**, Abudu Yesufu 1923- *IntWW 91*
**Eke**, Kenoye Kelvin 1956- *WhoBlA 92*
**Ekechi**, Felix K. 1934- *WhoBlA 92*
**Ekelberry**, Emogene 1934- *WhoAmP 91*
**Ekelof**, Per Olof 1903- *IntWW 91*
**Ekelund**, Vilhelm 1880-1949 *LiExTwC*
**Ekenes**, J Martin 1950- *AmMWSc 92*
**Eker**, Bjarne Reidar 1903- *IntWW 91*
**Ekerdt**, John Gilbert 1952- *AmMWSc 92*
**Ekern**, George Patrick 1931- *WhoAmL 92*
**Ekern**, Halvor O 1917- *WhoAmP 91*
**Ekern**, Paul Chester 1920- *AmMWSc 92*
**Ekern**, Ronald James 1938- *AmMWSc 92*
**Ekernas**, Sven Anders 1945- *WhoFI 92*
**Ekirch**, Arthur A., Jr. 1915- *WrDr 92*
**Ekis**, Imants 1943- *WhoFI 92*
**Ekizian**, Gregory H. 1963- *WhoFI 92*
**Ekk**, Nikolay Vladimirovich 1902-1976 *SovUnBD*
**Ekland**, Britt 1942- *IntMPA 92*
**Ekleberry**, Lee E. 1943- *WhoMW 92*
**Eklof**, Paul Christian 1942- *AmMWSc 92*
**Eklof**, Svea Christine 1951- *WhoEnt 92*
**Eklund**, Carl Andrew 1943- *WhoAmL 92*
**Eklund**, Claudia Rieth 1951- *WhoAmL 92*
**Eklund**, Curtis Einar 1931- *AmMWSc 92*
**Eklund**, Darrel Lee 1942- *AmMWSc 92*
**Eklund**, Gordon 1945- *IntAu&W 91, TwCSFW 91, WrDr 92*
**Eklund**, Karl E 1929- *AmMWSc 92*
**Eklund**, Melvin Wesley 1933- *AmMWSc 92*
**Eklund**, Sigvard 1911- *IntWW 91, Who 92*
**Ekman**, Carl Frederick W 1932- *AmMWSc 92*
**Ekman**, Frank 1917- *AmMWSc 92*
**Ekman**, Gershon 1954- *WhoAmL 92*
**Ekman**, Vagn Walfrid 1874-1954 *FacFETw*
**Eknoyan**, Garabed *AmMWSc 92*
**Eknoyan**, Ohannes 1944- *AmMWSc 92*
**Ekramoddoullah**, Abul Kalam M 1939- *AmMWSc 92*
**Ekren**, Christopher Wartenberg 1962- *WhoAmL 92*
**Ekrom**, Roy Herbert 1929- *WhoFI 92, WhoWest 92*
**Ekrut**, Jim 1951- *WhoRel 92*
**Ekstedt**, Richard Dean 1925- *AmMWSc 92*
**Eksteen**, Jacobus Adriaan 1942- *IntWW 91*
**Eksteins**, Modris 1943- *ConAu 34NR*
**Eksten**, Ronald Charles 1943- *WhoAmL 92*
**Ekster**, Aleksandra Aleksandrovna 1882-1949 *SovUnBD*
**Ekstrand**, Kenneth Eric 1942- *AmMWSc 92*
**Ekstroem**, Margareta 1930- *ConAu 135*
**Ekstrom**, Lincoln 1932- *AmMWSc 92*
**Ekstrom**, Margareta *ConAu 135*
**Ekstrom**, Martin Eugen 1887-1954 *BiDExR*
**Ekstrom**, Michael P 1939- *AmMWSc 92*
**Ekstrom**, Robert Carl 1917- *WhoEnt 92, WhoMW 92*
**Ekvall**, Bernt 1915- *WhoMW 92*
**Ekvall**, Shirley W 1934- *AmMWSc 92*
**Ekwensi**, C. O. D. *SmATA 66*
**Ekwensi**, Cyprian 1921- *BlkLC [port], ConNov 91, IntAu&W 91, IntWW 91, RfGEnL 91, SmATA 66, WrDr 92*
**Ekwueme**, Alex Ifeanyichukwu 1932- *IntWW 91*
**El-Aasser**, Mohamed S 1943- *AmMWSc 92*
**El-Abiad**, Ahmed H 1926- *AmMWSc 92*
**El-Amin**, Sa'ad 1940- *WhoBlA 92*
**El-Ashry**, Mohamed T 1940- *AmMWSc 92*
**El-Ashry**, Mohamed Taha 1940- *WhoAmP 91*
**El-Awady**, Abbas Abbas 1939- *AmMWSc 92*
**El-Bayoumi**, Mohamed Ashraf 1934- *AmMWSc 92*
**El-Baz**, Farouk 1938- *AmMWSc 92*
**El Dareer**, Salah *AmMWSc 92*
**El-Domeiri**, Ali A H 1935- *AmMWSc 92*
**El-Fishawy**, Saad Samuel 1924- *WhoFI 92*
**El-Genk**, Mohamed Shafik *WhoWest 92*
**El-Genk**, Mohamed Shafik 1947- *AmMWSc 92*
**El-Ghazaly**, Samir M 1959- *AmMWSc 92*
**El Guindy**, Mahmoud Ismail *AmMWSc 92*
**El-Hage**, Nabil Nazih 1958- *WhoFI 92*
**El Hassan**, Sayed Abdullah *Who 92*
**El-Hawary**, Mohamed El-Aref 1943- *AmMWSc 92*
**El-Ibiary**, Mohamed Yousif 1928- *AmMWSc 92*
**El-Kareh**, Auguste Badih 1932- *AmMWSc 92*
**El-Kati**, Mahhmoud 1936- *WhoBlA 92*
**El Khadem**, Hassan S 1923- *AmMWSc 92*
**El-Khatib**, Shukri M 1933- *AmMWSc 92*
**El-Masry**, Ezz Ismail *AmMWSc 92*
**El-Naggar**, Mohammed Ismail 1951- *AmMWSc 92*
**El-Negoumy**, Abdul Monem 1920- *AmMWSc 92*
**El-Ouali Mustapha Sayed** 1948?-1976 *HisDSpE*
**El Ramey**, Ralph 1926- *WhoAmP 91*
**El-Refai**, Mahmoud F *AmMWSc 92*
**El-Sadat**, Muhammed Anwar 1918-1981 *WhoNob 90*
**El-Saden**, Munir Ridha 1928- *AmMWSc 92*
**El Saffar**, Zuhair M 1934- *AmMWSc 92*
**El Sawi**, Amir 1921- *Who 92*
**El Sayed**, Hatem M. 1954- *WhoWest 92*
**El-Sayed**, Mostafa Amr 1933- *AmMWSc 92*
**El-Sharkawi**, Mohamed A 1948- *AmMWSc 92*
**El-Sherif**, Nabil 1938- *AmMWSc 92*
**El-Shiekh**, Aly H 1931- *AmMWSc 92*
**El-Shishini**, Ali Salem 1939- *WhoFI 92*
**El-Swaify**, Samir Aly 1937- *AmMWSc 92*
**El-Tawil**, Doris 1943- *WhoMW 92*
**El-The Moor**, Brother Joe *DrAPF 91*
**el-Toure**, Askia Muhammad Abu Bakr 1938- *WhoBlA 92*
**El-Wakil**, M 1921- *AmMWSc 92*
**El Wardani**, Sayed Aly 1927- *AmMWSc 92*
**Ela**, Erik 1957- *WhoEnt 92*
**Ela**, Patrick Hobson 1948- *WhoWest 92*
**Elachi**, Charles 1947- *AmMWSc 92*
**Elagin**, Ivan 1918-1987 *LiExTwC*
**Elaine**, Karen 1965- *WhoWest 92*
**Elakovich**, Stella Daisy 1945- *AmMWSc 92*
**Elam**, Andrew Gregory, II 1932- *WhoFI 92*
**Elam**, Caroline Mary 1945- *Who 92*
**Elam**, Dorothy R. 1904- *WhoBlA 92*
**Elam**, Elizabeth Ann 1951- *WhoAmL 92*
**Elam**, Harry Justin 1922- *WhoBlA 92*
**Elam**, Harry Penoy 1919- *WhoBlA 92*
**Elam**, Henry 1903- *Who 92*
**Elam**, Jack 1916- *IntMPA 92*
**Elam**, Jack Gordon 1921- *AmMWSc 92*
**Elam**, Lloyd C 1928- *AmMWSc 92, WhoBlA 92*
**Elam**, Nicholas 1939- *Who 92*
**Elam**, Pamela Lynn 1950- *WhoAmP 91*
**Elam**, William Warren 1929- *AmMWSc 92*
**Eland**, John 1872-1933 *TwCPaSc*
**Eland**, John Hugh David 1941- *AmMWSc 92*
**Elander**, Keliitane Robert 1959- *WhoRel 92*
**Elander**, Richard Paul 1932- *AmMWSc 92*
**Elashoff**, Janet Dixon 1942- *AmMWSc 92*
**Elath**, Eliahu d1990 *IntWW 91N*
**Elath**, Eliahu 1903-1990 *FacFETw*
**ElAttar**, Tawfik Mohammed Ali 1925- *AmMWSc 92*
**Elaw**, Zilpha 1790?- *NotBlAW 92*
**Elbadawi**, Ahmad *AmMWSc 92*
**Elbaum**, Charles 1926- *AmMWSc 92*
**Elbaum**, Jerome David 1939- *WhoAmL 92*
**Elbaum**, Marek 1941- *AmMWSc 92*
**Elbein**, Alan D 1933- *AmMWSc 92*
**Elbel**, Robert E 1925- *AmMWSc 92*
**Elberger**, Andrea June 1952- *AmMWSc 92*
**Elberger**, Ronald Edward 1945- *WhoAmL 92*
**Elbert**, George A. 1911- *ConAu 35NR*
**Elbert**, Jerome William 1942- *AmMWSc 92*
**Elbert**, Joanna *WhoFI 92*
**Elbert**, Joyce *WrDr 92*
**Elbert**, Sarah 1937- *ConAu 135*
**Elbert**, Virginie Fowler 1912- *ConAu 35NR*
**Elberty**, William Turner, Jr 1930- *AmMWSc 92*
**Elbin**, Paul Nowell 1905- *ConAu 35NR*
**Elbin Penchina**, Debbie 1951- *WhoEnt 92*
**Elble**, Rodger Jacob 1948- *AmMWSc 92*
**Elbling**, Irving Nelson 1920- *AmMWSc 92*
**Elbon**, Julia Lockridge 1941- *WhoAmP 91*
**Elcan**, Martha M. 1955- *WhoEnt 92*
**Elce**, John Shackleton 1938- *AmMWSc 92*
**Elchlepp**, Jane G 1921- *AmMWSc 92*
**Elcoat**, George Alastair 1922- *Who 92*
**Elcock**, Claudius Adolphus Rufus 1923- *WhoBlA 92*
**Elcock**, Howard 1942- *WrDr 92*
**Elcrat**, Alan Ross 1942- *AmMWSc 92*
**Eld**, Henry 1814-1850 *BiInAmS*
**Elde**, Robert Philip 1947- *AmMWSc 92*
**Eldefrawi**, Amira T 1937- *AmMWSc 92*
**Eldefrawi**, Mohyee E 1932- *AmMWSc 92*
**Eldem**, M. Necat 1928- *IntWW 91*
**Elden**, Douglas Lloyd 1947- *WhoAmL 92*
**Elden**, Gary Michael 1944- *WhoAmL 92*
**Elden**, Richard Edward 1923- *AmMWSc 92*
**Elder**, Alexander Stowell 1915- *AmMWSc 92*
**Elder**, Alfonso 1898-1974 *DcNCBi 2*
**Elder**, Almora Kennedy 1920- *WhoBlA 92*
**Elder**, Curtis Harold 1921- *AmMWSc 92, WhoWest 92*
**Elder**, David A 1942- *WhoAmP 91*
**Elder**, David Edward 1927- *WhoMW 92*
**Elder**, David Renwick 1920- *Who 92*
**Elder**, David W *WhoIns 92*
**Elder**, Eldon 1921- *WhoEnt 92*
**Elder**, Ellen Rozanne *WhoRel 92*
**Elder**, Ernie Dewey, Jr. 1955- *WhoRel 92*
**Elder**, Fred A 1929- *AmMWSc 92*
**Elder**, Fred F B 1947- *AmMWSc 92*
**Elder**, Fred Kingsley, Jr 1921- *AmMWSc 92*
**Elder**, Gary *DrAPF 91*
**Elder**, Geraldine H. 1937- *WhoBlA 92*
**Elder**, Gove Griffith 1937- *WhoRel 92*
**Elder**, H E 1924- *AmMWSc 92*
**Elder**, Harvey Lynn 1934- *AmMWSc 92*
**Elder**, Irma B. *WhoHisp 92*
**Elder**, James Carl 1947- *WhoAmL 92*
**Elder**, James Franklin, Jr 1949- *AmMWSc 92*
**Elder**, Jerry Matson 1960- *WhoRel 92*
**Elder**, Joan Elizabeth 1954- *WhoEnt 92*
**Elder**, Joe Allen 1941- *AmMWSc 92*
**Elder**, John 1933- *WrDr 92*
**Elder**, John 1947- *ConAu 133*
**Elder**, John Howard 1947- *WhoAmL 92*
**Elder**, John Philip 1931- *AmMWSc 92*
**Elder**, John Thompson, Jr 1927- *AmMWSc 92*
**Elder**, John William 1933- *AmMWSc 92*
**Elder**, John William, Jr. 1949- *WhoRel 92*
**Elder**, Karl *DrAPF 91*
**Elder**, Kelli Linn 1961- *WhoMW 92*
**Elder**, Lee 1934- *WhoBlA 92*
**Elder**, Lonne, III 1931- *BlkLC [port], WhoBlA 92, WrDr 92*
**Elder**, Mark 1947- *NewAmDM*
**Elder**, Mark Philip 1947- *IntWW 91, Who 92, WhoEnt 92*
**Elder**, Michael Aiken 1931- *IntAu&W 91, WrDr 92*
**Elder**, Murdoch George 1938- *Who 92*

**Elder,** Philip E. R. *WhoRel 92*
**Elder,** Rex Alfred 1917- *AmMWSc 92*
**Elder,** Richard Charles 1939- *AmMWSc 92*
**Elder,** Richard Daniel 1927- *WhoWest 92*
**Elder,** Robert Jay 1949- *WhoRel 92*
**Elder,** Robert Lee 1931- *AmMWSc 92*
**Elder,** Samuel Adams 1929- *AmMWSc 92*
**Elder,** Vincent Allen 1948- *AmMWSc 92*
**Elder,** William 1843-1903 *BiInAmS*
**Elder,** William Hanna 1913- *AmMWSc 92*
**Elder,** William John 1929- *WhoIns 92*
**Elderfield,** John 1943- *TwCPaSc*
**Elderfield,** Maurice 1926- *Who 92*
**Elderhorst,** William 1828-1861 *BiInAmS*
**Elderkin,** Charles Edwin 1930- *AmMWSc 92*
**Elderkin,** Dana Vance 1955- *WhoEnt 92*
**Elderkin,** Helaine Grace 1954- *WhoAmL 92*
**Elderkin,** Richard Howard 1945- *AmMWSc 92*
**Elders,** M. Joycelyn 1933- *WhoBlA 92*
**Elders,** Minnie Joycelyn 1933- *AmMWSc 92*
**Elders,** Wilfred Allan 1933- *AmMWSc 92*
**Eldershaw,** M Barnard 1897- *TwCSFW 91*
**Eldin,** Gerard 1927- *IntWW 91*
**Eldin,** Hamed Kamal 1924- *AmMWSc 92*
**Eldin,** Raymond *ConAu 133*
**Eldin-Taylor,** Kenneth Roy d1990 *Who 92N*
**Eldis,** George Thomas 1944- *AmMWSc 92*
**Eldjarn,** Kristjan 1916-1982 *FacFETw*
**Eldon,** Earl of 1937- *Who 92*
**Eldon,** Charles A 1926- *AmMWSc 92*
**Eldon,** Michael *WhoRel 92*
**Eldred,** Earl 1919- *AmMWSc 92*
**Eldred,** Gerald Marcus 1934- *WhoEnt 92*
**Eldred,** Kenneth M 1929- *AmMWSc 92*
**Eldred,** Nelson Richards 1921- *AmMWSc 92*
**Eldred,** Norman Orville 1916- *AmMWSc 92, WhoMW 92*
**Eldred,** William D 1950- *AmMWSc 92*
**Eldredge,** Ashton Goodliff, Jr. 1937- *WhoFI 92*
**Eldredge,** Charles Child, III 1944- *WhoMW 92*
**Eldredge,** Christopher Edward 1953- *WhoMW 92*
**Eldredge,** Donald Herbert 1921- *AmMWSc 92*
**Eldredge,** Edda Rogers 1915- *WhoWest 92*
**Eldredge,** Frank Aubrey, II 1940- *WhoWest 92*
**Eldredge,** H. Wentworth 1909-1991 *ConAu 133*
**Eldredge,** Jane MacDougal 1944- *WhoAmP 91*
**Eldredge,** Kelly Husbands 1921- *AmMWSc 92*
**Eldredge,** Lucius G 1938- *AmMWSc 92*
**Eldredge,** Niles 1943- *AmMWSc 92*
**Eldridge,** Bernard George 1934- *WhoWest 92*
**Eldridge,** Bruce Frederick 1933- *AmMWSc 92, WhoWest 92*
**Eldridge,** Charles A 1949- *AmMWSc 92*
**Eldridge,** Colin Clifford 1942- *IntAu&W 91, WrDr 92*
**Eldridge,** David Wyatt 1940- *AmMWSc 92*
**Eldridge,** Douglas Alan 1944- *WhoAmL 92*
**Eldridge,** Elleanor 1785-1865 *NotBlAW 92*
**Eldridge,** Eric William 1906- *Who 92*
**Eldridge,** Frederic L 1924- *AmMWSc 92*
**Eldridge,** George 1828?-1900 *BiInAmS*
**Eldridge,** George Homans 1854-1905 *BiInAmS*
**Eldridge,** Harold Percy 1923- *TwCPaSc*
**Eldridge,** James F 1946- *WhoIns 92*
**Eldridge,** James L., Jr. 1948- *WhoBlA 92*
**Eldridge,** John Barron 1919- *Who 92*
**Eldridge,** John C 1933- *WhoAmP 91*
**Eldridge,** John Charles 1942- *AmMWSc 92*
**Eldridge,** John Cole 1933- *WhoAmL 92*
**Eldridge,** John E. T. 1936- *WrDr 92*
**Eldridge,** John W 1921- *AmMWSc 92*
**Eldridge,** Klaus Emil 1938- *AmMWSc 92*
**Eldridge,** Marian 1936- *WrDr 92*
**Eldridge,** Maxwell Bruce 1942- *AmMWSc 92*
**Eldridge,** Mildred 1909- *TwCPaSc*
**Eldridge,** Richard Mark 1951- *WhoAmL 92*
**Eldridge,** Ronnie 1931- *WhoAmP 91*
**Eldridge,** Roswell 1934- *AmMWSc 92*
**Eldridge,** Roy 1911-1989 *FacFETw, NewAmDM*
**Eldridge,** Truman Kermit, Jr. 1944- *WhoAmL 92*
**Eldridge,** William Butler 1931- *WhoAmL 92*
**Eldumiati,** Ismail Ibrahim 1940- *AmMWSc 92*
**Eleanor of Aquitaine** 1122?-1204 *EncAmaz 91*
**Eleanor of Castile** 1240?-1290 *EncAmaz 91*
**Eleanor of Provence** 1220?-1293? *EncAmaz 91*
**Eleazer,** George Robert, Jr. 1956- *WhoBlA 92*
**Eleazer,** William Randolph 1932- *WhoAmL 92*
**Eleccion,** Marcelino 1936- *WhoWest 92*
**Electric Light Orchestra** *ConMus 7 [port]*
**Electric Light Orchestra,** The *NewAmDM*
**Elefante,** Tom *IntMPA 92*
**Elegant,** Robert 1928- *WrDr 92*
**Elegant,** Robert Sampson 1928- *IntAu&W 91*
**Elejarde,** Marlene 1950- *BlkOlyM*
**Elek,** Stephen Dyonis 1914- *Who 92*
**Elek,** Steven, III 1956- *WhoFI 92*
**Eleonora d'Arborea** 1347-1404 *EncAmaz 91*
**Eleonore of Toledo** *EncAmaz 91*
**Elespuru,** Rosalie K 1944- *AmMWSc 92*
**Elethea,** Abba *DrAPF 91*
**Eleuterio,** Herbert Sousa 1927- *AmMWSc 92*
**Eleuterio,** Marianne Kingsbury 1929- *AmMWSc 92*
**Eleuterius,** Lionel Numa 1936- *AmMWSc 92*
**Eleutherus** *EncEarC*
**Eleveld,** Robert Jay 1936- *WhoAmP 91*
**Elevitch,** M.D. *DrAPF 91*
**Elewonibi,** Mohammed Thomas David 1965- *WhoBlA 92*
**Eley,** Daniel Douglas 1914- *IntWW 91, Who 92*
**Eley,** Geoffrey d1990 *IntWW 91N*
**Eley,** James H 1940- *AmMWSc 92*
**Eley,** John Duane 1951- *WhoMW 92*
**Eley,** John L. *Who 92*
**Eley,** Richard Robert *AmMWSc 92*
**Elfand,** Martin 1937- *IntMPA 92*
**Elfant,** Robert F 1936- *AmMWSc 92*
**Elfbaum,** Stanley Goodman 1938- *AmMWSc 92*
**Elfenbein,** Gerald Jay 1945- *AmMWSc 92*
**Elfer,** David Francis 1941- *Who 92*
**Elfert,** Charles George, Jr. 1944- *WhoFI 92*
**Elfin,** Mel 1929- *WhoFI 92*
**Elfman,** Danny *WhoEnt 92*
**Elfman,** Danny 1953- *IntMPA 92*
**Elfman,** Danny 1954- *IntWW 91*
**Elfman,** Eric Michael 1954- *WhoAmL 92*
**Elfner,** Albert Henry, III 1944- *WhoFI 92*
**Elfner,** Eliot Sherburne 1941- *WhoMW 92*
**Elfner,** Lloyd F 1923- *AmMWSc 92*
**Elfner,** Lynn Edward 1944- *AmMWSc 92*
**Elfont,** Edna A *AmMWSc 92*
**Elford,** Howard Lee 1935- *AmMWSc 92*
**Elford,** Kevin Michael 1954- *WhoAmL 92*
**Elfring,** Robert Lowell 1921- *WhoIns 92*
**Elfstrom,** Gary Macdonald 1944- *AmMWSc 92*
**Elfving,** Donald Carl 1941- *AmMWSc 92*
**Elfyn,** Menna 1951- *IntAu&W 91*
**Elg,** Taina 1930- *IntMPA 92*
**Elgar,** Edward 1857-1934 *FacFETw [port], NewAmDM*
**Elgart,** Larry Joseph 1922- *WhoEnt 92*
**Elgavish,** Ada S 1946- *AmMWSc 92*
**Elgee,** Neil J 1926- *AmMWSc 92*
**Elgee,** Neil Johnson 1926- *IntWW 91*
**Elger,** William Robert, Jr. 1950- *WhoMW 92*
**Elgerd,** O I 1925- *AmMWSc 92*
**Elgert,** Klaus Dieter 1948- *AmMWSc 92*
**Elgert,** Louis George 1923- *WhoRel 92*
**Elgin,** Earl of 1924- *Who 92*
**Elgin,** Gita *WhoWest 92*
**Elgin,** James H, Jr 1942- *AmMWSc 92*
**Elgin,** Joseph C 1904- *AmMWSc 92*
**Elgin,** Robert Lawrence 1944- *AmMWSc 92*
**Elgin,** Sarah Carlisle Roberts 1945- *AmMWSc 92*
**Elgin,** Suzette Haden 1936- *TwCSFW 91, WrDr 92*
**Elhammer,** Ake P 1948- *AmMWSc 92*
**Elharrar,** Victor 1944- *AmMWSc 92*
**Elhilali,** Mostafa M 1937- *AmMWSc 92*
**Elia,** Victor John 1942- *AmMWSc 92*
**Eliade,** Mircea 1907-1986 *FacFETw, LiExTwC*
**Eliades,** Elias 1947- *IntWW 91*
**Eliades,** Theo I 1938- *AmMWSc 92*
**Eliahu,** Mordechai 1928- *WhoRel 92*
**Elias,** Abigail 1952- *WhoAmL 92*
**Elias,** Antonio L *AmMWSc 92*
**Elias,** Blas, Jr. 1936- *WhoHisp 92*
**Elias,** Brian 1948- *ConCom 92*
**Elias,** Gerard 1944- *Who 92*
**Elias,** Gracy 1958- *WhoMW 92*
**Elias,** Hal *IntMPA 92*
**Elias,** Hans Georg 1928- *AmMWSc 92*
**Elias,** Hendrick Josef 1902-1973 *BiDExR*
**Elias,** Homer 1955- *WhoBlA 92*
**Elias,** Houghton F. 1911- *WhoMW 92*
**Elias,** Jerry Carlos 1959- *WhoWest 92*
**Elias,** Karen *DrAPF 91*
**Elias,** Laurence 1946- *AmMWSc 92*
**Elias,** Lorne 1930- *AmMWSc 92*
**Elias,** Marisel 1956- *WhoHisp 92*
**Elias,** Norbert 1897-1990 *AnObit 1990*
**Elias,** Patrick 1947- *Who 92*
**Elias,** Peter 1923- *AmMWSc 92, IntWW 91*
**Elias,** Peter M 1941- *AmMWSc 92*
**Elias,** Robert William 1942- *AmMWSc 92*
**Elias,** Rosalind 1931- *NewAmDM*
**Elias,** Santiago 1948- *WhoHisp 92*
**Elias,** Sheila *WhoWest 92*
**Elias,** Taslim Olawale d1991 *NewYTBS 91, Who 92N*
**Elias,** Taslim Olawale 1914- *IntWW 91*
**Elias,** Thomas Ittan 1947- *AmMWSc 92*
**Elias,** Thomas S 1942- *AmMWSc 92, ConAu 35NR*
**Elias,** Thomas Sam 1942- *WhoWest 92*
**Elias,** Ziad Malek 1934- *WhoWest 92*
**Eliason,** Alan Lewis 1939- *WhoWest 92*
**Eliason,** Edward Best 1940- *WhoIns 92*
**Eliason,** Leslie Carol 1959- *WhoAmL 92*
**Eliason,** Morton A 1932- *AmMWSc 92*
**Eliason,** Phyllis Marie 1925- *WhoRel 92*
**Eliason,** Richard I *WhoAmP 91*
**Eliason,** Stanley B 1939- *AmMWSc 92*
**Eliassen,** Jon Eric 1947- *WhoWest 92*
**Eliassen,** Kjell 1929- *IntWW 91, Who 92*
**Eliassen,** Rolf 1911- *AmMWSc 92*
**Eliasson,** Anders 1947- *ConCom 92*
**Eliasson,** Jan 1940- *IntWW 91*
**Eliasson,** Sven Gustav 1928- *AmMWSc 92*
**Elibank,** Lord 1923- *Who 92*
**Elibank,** Master of 1964- *Who 92*
**Eliceiri,** George Louis 1939- *AmMWSc 92*
**Elich,** Joe 1918- *AmMWSc 92*
**Elicker,** Gordon Leonard 1940- *WhoAmL 92*
**Elicker,** Paul Hamilton 1923- *IntWW 91*
**Eliecer Neftali Reyes y Basoalto,** R 1904-1973 *WhoNob 90*
**Elieff,** Lewis Steven 1929- *WhoFI 92*
**Eliel,** Ernest L. 1921- *IntWW 91*
**Eliel,** Ernest Ludwig 1921- *AmMWSc 92*
**Elien,** Mona Marie 1932- *WhoWest 92*
**Eliezer,** Isaac *AmMWSc 92*
**Eliezer,** Naomi *AmMWSc 92*
**Eliezer,** Zwy 1933- *AmMWSc 92*
**Elikann,** Lawrence S. 1923- *WhoEnt 92*
**Elimelech,** Menachem 1955- *AmMWSc 92*
**Elin,** Ronald John 1939- *AmMWSc 92*
**Eling,** Thomas Edward 1941- *AmMWSc 92*
**Elings,** Virgil Bruce 1939- *AmMWSc 92*
**Elinson,** Henry David 1935- *WhoWest 92*
**Elinson,** Jack 1917- *AmMWSc 92, IntWW 91*
**Elinson,** Richard Paul *AmMWSc 92*
**Elio,** Francisco Xavier de 1767-1822 *HisDSpE*
**Elioff,** Irma Mercado 1956- *WhoHisp 92*
**Elioff,** Thomas 1933- *AmMWSc 92*
**Elion,** Gertrude B 1918- *FacFETw*
**Elion,** Gertrude Belle 1918- *AmMWSc 92, IntWW 91, Who 92, WhoNob 90*
**Elion,** Herbert A. 1923- *WhoFI 92, WhoWest 92*
**Eliot** *Who 92*
**Eliot,** Lord 1966- *Who 92*
**Eliot,** Charles W. 1834-1926 *BenetAL 91*
**Eliot,** Charles William 1834-1926 *AmPeW*
**Eliot,** Charles William John 1928- *IntWW 91*
**Eliot,** Dan *ConAu 36NR*
**Eliot,** Drew *WhoEnt 92*
**Eliot,** George 1819-1880 *CnDBLB 4 [port], RfGEnL 91*
**Eliot,** Jared 1685-1763 *BiInAmS*
**Eliot,** Jill Luise 1937- *WhoEnt 92*
**Eliot,** John 1604-1690 *BenetAL 91*
**Eliot,** John G. 1800-1881 *DcNCBi 2*
**Eliot,** Peter Charles 1910- *Who 92*
**Eliot,** Robert S 1929- *AmMWSc 92*
**Eliot,** T. S. 1888-1965 *BenetAL 91, FacFETw [port], LiExTwC, RfGEnL 91*
**Eliot,** Theodore Quentin 1954- *WhoAmL 92*
**Eliot,** Thomas H. d1991 *NewYTBS 91 [port]*
**Eliot,** Thomas H. 1907-1991 *ConAu 135*
**Eliot,** Thomas Hopkinson 1907- *WhoAmP 91*
**Eliot,** Thomas Stearns 1888-1965 *WhoNob 90*
**Eliott,** E C *IntAu&W 91X*
**Eliott of Stobs,** Charles 1937- *Who 92*
**Elisberg,** Bennett La Dolce 1925- *AmMWSc 92*
**Elisburg,** Donald E 1938- *WhoAmP 91*
**Elish,** Dan 1960- *SmATA 68 [port]*
**Elisha,** Ron 1951- *IntAu&W 91*
**Elishe Vardapet** d480? *EncEarC*
**Elissa** *EncAmaz 91*
**Elitzur,** Moshe 1944- *AmMWSc 92*
**Elizabeth** 1866-1941 *TwCLC 41 [port]*
**Elizabeth I** 1533-1603 *EncAmaz 91*
**Elizabeth II** 1926- *FacFETw [port], IntWW 91*
**Elizabeth Angela Marguerite** 1900- *IntWW 91*
**Elizabeth,** Queen 1900 *Who 92R*
**Elizabeth II,** Queen 1926 *Who 92R*
**Elizabeth,** Martha *DrAPF 91*
**Elizabeth,** von S *IntAu&W 91X*
**Elizalde,** Angel, Jr. 1953- *WhoHisp 92*
**Elizalde,** Felix 1931- *WhoHisp 92*
**Elizan,** Teresita S 1931- *AmMWSc 92*
**Elizondo,** Hector 1936- *IntMPA 92, WhoHisp 92*
**Elizondo,** Hector G. 1939- *WhoHisp 92*
**Elizondo,** Patricia Irene 1955- *WhoEnt 92, WhoHisp 92*
**Elizondo,** Paul *WhoHisp 92*
**Elizondo,** Paul 1935- *WhoAmP 91*
**Elizondo,** Rey Soto 1940- *WhoHisp 92*
**Elizondo,** Reynaldo S 1940- *AmMWSc 92*
**Elizondo,** Rita *WhoHisp 92*
**Elizondo,** Sergio D. *DrAPF 91*
**Elizondo,** Sergio D. 1930- *WhoHisp 92*
**Elizondo,** Sergio Danilo 1930- *WhoWest 92*
**Elizondo,** Tonatiuh 1953- *WhoHisp 92*
**Elizondo,** Virgil P. *WhoHisp 92*
**Elizur,** Joel 1952- *ConAu 135*
**Elk,** Seymour B 1932- *AmMWSc 92*
**Elkan,** Benno 1877-1960 *TwCPaSc*
**Elkan,** Gerald Hugh 1929- *AmMWSc 92*
**Elkan,** Walter 1923- *Who 92*
**Elkes,** Joel 1913- *AmMWSc 92, IntWW 91, Who 92*
**Elkholy,** Hussein A 1933- *AmMWSc 92*
**Elkin,** Alexander 1909- *IntWW 91, Who 92*
**Elkin,** Benjamin 1911- *WrDr 92*
**Elkin,** Lynne Osman 1946- *AmMWSc 92*
**Elkin,** Milton 1916- *AmMWSc 92*
**Elkin,** Robert Glenn 1953- *AmMWSc 92, WhoMW 92*
**Elkin,** Sonia Irene Linda 1932- *Who 92*
**Elkin,** Stanley *DrAPF 91, NewYTBS 91 [port]*
**Elkin,** Stanley 1925-1986 *FacFETw*
**Elkin,** Stanley 1930- *BenetAL 91, ConNov 91, IntAu&W 91, WrDr 92*
**Elkin,** Stanley Lawrence 1930- *IntWW 91*
**Elkin,** William Futter 1916- *AmMWSc 92*
**Elkind,** Jerome I 1929- *AmMWSc 92*
**Elkind,** Michael John 1922- *AmMWSc 92*
**Elkind,** Mortimer M 1922- *AmMWSc 92*
**Elkind,** Mortimer Murray 1922- *WhoWest 92*
**Elkind,** Sue Saniel *DrAPF 91*
**Elkington,** Geoffrey 1907- *Who 92*
**Elkington,** William C. *DrAPF 91*
**Elkins,** Aaron J 1935- *IntAu&W 91, WrDr 92*
**Elkins,** Angela Moncrief 1933- *WhoAmP 91*
**Elkins,** Connie Kay 1957- *WhoAmL 92*
**Elkins,** Donald Marcum 1940- *AmMWSc 92*
**Elkins,** Dov Peretz 1937- *IntAu&W 91, WhoMW 92, WhoRel 92, WrDr 92*
**Elkins,** Earleen Feldman 1933- *AmMWSc 92*
**Elkins,** Glen Ray 1933- *WhoWest 92*
**Elkins,** Hillard 1929- *IntMPA 92, WhoEnt 92*
**Elkins,** James Anderson, Jr. 1919- *WhoFI 92*
**Elkins,** James E *WhoAmP 91*
**Elkins,** James Paul 1924- *WhoMW 92*
**Elkins,** Jesse Roy 1955- *WhoRel 92*
**Elkins,** John Rush 1941- *AmMWSc 92*
**Elkins,** Judith Molinar 1935- *AmMWSc 92*
**Elkins,** Ken Joe 1937- *WhoEnt 92*
**Elkins,** Kenneth Earl 1945- *WhoRel 92*
**Elkins,** L E 1912- *AmMWSc 92*
**Elkins,** Lincoln F 1918- *AmMWSc 92*
**Elkins,** Lloyd Edwin, Sr. 1912- *WhoFI 92*
**Elkins,** Michael David 1966- *WhoBlA 92*
**Elkins,** Robert Hiatt 1918- *AmMWSc 92*
**Elkins,** Roland Lucien 1945- *WhoWest 92*
**Elkins,** Ronald C 1936- *AmMWSc 92*
**Elkins,** Russell Alexander 1948- *WhoRel 92*
**Elkins,** Saul 1907- *IntMPA 92*
**Elkins,** Steven Paul 1949- *WhoFI 92*
**Elkins,** Thomas Richard 1931- *WhoEnt 92*
**Elkins,** Virgil Lynn 1925- *WhoBlA 92*
**Elkins,** William L 1932- *AmMWSc 92*
**Elkinton,** J Russell 1910- *AmMWSc 92*
**Elkon,** Jon 1949- *ConAu 134*
**Elkus,** Lawrence M. 1954- *WhoAmL 92*
**Ell,** William M 1939- *AmMWSc 92*
**Ellacombe,** John Lawrence Wemyss 1920- *Who 92*
**Ellam,** Gunnar 1929- *WhoWest 92*
**Ellaraino** 1938- *WhoBlA 92*
**Ellard,** Henry 1961- *WhoBlA 92*
**Ellas,** John Wayne 1948- *WhoRel 92*
**Elledge,** Jim *DrAPF 91*
**Ellefsen,** Paul 1939- *AmMWSc 92*

**Ellefson**, Ralph Donald 1931- *AmMWSc 92*
**Ellefson**, Timothy Harold 1953- *WhoMW 92*
**Elleman**, Daniel Draudt 1931- *AmMWSc 92*
**Elleman**, Thomas Smith 1931- *AmMWSc 92*
**Ellemann-Jensen**, Uffe 1941- *IntWW 91*
**Ellen** *DrAPF 91*
**Ellen**, Eric Frank 1930- *Who 92*
**Ellen**, Patricia Mae Hayward *Who 92*
**Ellenberg**, Jonas Harold 1942- *AmMWSc 92*
**Ellenberg**, Susan Smith 1946- *AmMWSc 92*
**Ellenberger**, Herman Albert 1916- *AmMWSc 92*
**Ellenberger**, Matthew Scott 1963- *WhoAmL 92*
**Ellenbogen**, Leon 1927- *AmMWSc 92*
**Ellenborough**, Baron 1926- *Who 92*
**Ellenburg**, Janus Yentsch 1922- *AmMWSc 92*
**Ellens**, Jay Harold 1932- *WhoRel 92*
**Ellenshaw**, Peter 1913- *ConTFT 9*
**Ellenson**, Gordon Eugene 1950- *WhoWest 92*
**Ellenson**, James L 1946- *AmMWSc 92*
**Ellenwood**, Audrey Erlene 1951- *WhoMW 92*
**Ellenwood**, Henry Small 1790-1833 *DcNCBi 2*
**Eller**, Adolphus Hill 1861-1941 *DcNCBi 2*
**Eller**, Arthur L, Jr 1933- *AmMWSc 92*
**Eller**, Carl L. 1942- *WhoBlA 92*
**Eller**, Charles Howe 1904- *AmMWSc 92*
**Eller**, Frank O. 1938- *WhoFI 92*
**Eller**, James Edgar 1931- *WhoFI 92*
**Eller**, Leslie Robert 1949- *WhoAmL 92*
**Eller**, Phillip Gary 1947- *AmMWSc 92*
**Eller**, Raymon Ernest 1910- *WhoRel 92*
**Eller**, Vernard 1927- *WrDr 92*
**Ellerbe**, Clinton Todd 1964- *WhoRel 92*
**Ellerbeck**, Rosemary *WrDr 92*
**Ellerbeck**, Rosemary Anne L'Estrange *IntAu&W 91*
**Ellerbee**, Linda *LesBEnT 92 [port]*
**Ellerbrake**, Richard Paul 1933- *WhoRel 92*
**Ellerbrook**, Niel Cochran 1948- *WhoFI 92*
**Ellerby**, Scott Martin 1961- *WhoAmL 92*
**Ellerby**, William Mitchell 1946- *WhoAmP 91*
**Ellerby**, William Mitchell, Sr. 1946- *WhoBlA 92*
**Ellerd**, Robert A *WhoAmP 91*
**Ellerman**, John Robert 1946- *WhoFI 92*
**Ellers**, Erich Werner 1928- *AmMWSc 92*
**Ellers**, Joseph Clinton 1959- *WhoAmP 91*
**Ellersick**, Fred W 1933- *AmMWSc 92*
**Ellert**, Frederick J *AmMWSc 92*
**Ellert**, Martha Schwandt 1940- *AmMWSc 92, WhoMW 92*
**Ellerton**, Christopher Cecil 1952- *WhoFI 92*
**Ellerton**, Geoffrey James 1920- *Who 92*
**Ellertson**, R Lee 1936- *WhoAmP 91*
**Ellery Queen** *BenetAL 91*
**Ellery**, Dale Raphael 1939- *WhoMW 92*
**Ellery**, John Graem d1855 *BiInAmS*
**Elles** *Who 92*
**Elles**, Baroness 1921- *Who 92*
**Elles**, James Edmund Moncrieff 1949- *Who 92*
**Elles**, Neil Patrick Moncrieff 1919- *Who 92*
**Ellestad**, George A 1934- *AmMWSc 92*
**Ellestad**, Myrvin H 1921- *AmMWSc 92*
**Ellestad**, Reuben B 1900- *AmMWSc 92*
**Ellet**, Charles 1810-1862 *BiInAmS*
**Ellet**, William H 1806-1859 *BiInAmS*
**Ellett**, Clayton Wayne 1916- *AmMWSc 92*
**Ellett**, D Maxwell 1922- *AmMWSc 92*
**Ellett**, Edwin Willard 1925- *AmMWSc 92*
**Ellett**, Henry 1938- *WhoWest 92*
**Ellett**, John Spears, II 1923- *WhoAmL 92*
**Ellett**, William H 1929- *AmMWSc 92*
**Ellfeldt**, Howard James 1937- *WhoMW 92*
**Ellgaard**, Erik G 1939- *AmMWSc 92*
**Ellias**, Loretta Christine 1919- *AmMWSc 92*
**Ellickson**, Jean 1935- *WhoMW 92*
**Ellickson**, Robert Chester 1941- *WhoAmL 92*
**Ellicott**, Andrew 1754-1820 *BiInAmS*
**Ellicott**, John LeMoyne 1929- *WhoAmL 92*
**Ellicott**, Robert James 1927- *IntWW 91*
**Ellig**, Bruce Robert 1936- *WhoFI 92*
**Elligan**, Irvin, Jr. 1915- *WhoBlA 92*
**Elligett**, Raymond Thomas, Jr. 1953- *WhoAmL 92*
**Elliker**, Paul R 1911- *AmMWSc 92*
**Ellin**, Marvin 1923- *WhoAmL 92, WhoFI 92*
**Ellin**, Robert Isadore 1925- *AmMWSc 92*
**Elling**, David L 1952- *WhoAmP 91*
**Elling**, Laddie Joe 1917- *AmMWSc 92*
**Ellingboe**, Albert Harlan 1931- *AmMWSc 92*
**Ellingboe**, J K 1927- *AmMWSc 92*
**Ellingboe**, James 1937- *AmMWSc 92*
**Ellingboe**, John Keith 1950- *WhoAmL 92*
**Ellinger**, Carol Eloise 1931- *WhoAmP 91*
**Ellinger**, Dorthy Larraine 1947- *WhoMW 92*
**Ellinger**, John Henry 1919- *WrDr 92*
**Ellinger**, Mark Stephen 1949- *AmMWSc 92*
**Ellinger**, Royal 1951- *WhoMW 92*
**Ellinghaus**, William M. 1922- *IntWW 91*
**Ellinghausen**, Herman Charles, Jr 1926- *AmMWSc 92*
**Ellingsen**, Olav 1941- *WhoFI 92*
**Ellingson**, Bertrum Edwin 1921- *WhoAmP 91*
**Ellingson**, David P 1944- *WhoIns 92*
**Ellingson**, Dianne Gill 1945- *WhoWest 92*
**Ellingson**, Jack A *AmMWSc 92*
**Ellingson**, John S 1940- *AmMWSc 92*
**Ellingson**, Lynn Marie 1957- *WhoMW 92*
**Ellingson**, Reynold Wallace 1934- *WhoAmP 91*
**Ellingson**, Robert George 1945- *AmMWSc 92*
**Ellingson**, Robert James 1923- *AmMWSc 92*
**Ellingson**, Robert L *WhoAmP 91*
**Ellingson**, Rudolph Conrad 1911- *AmMWSc 92*
**Ellington**, Duke 1899-1974 *NewAmDM*
**Ellington**, Brenda Andrea 1960- *WhoBlA 92*
**Ellington**, Charles Ronald 1941- *WhoAmL 92*
**Ellington**, Douglas D. 1886-1960 *DcNCBi 2*
**Ellington**, Duke 1899-1974 *RComAH*
**Ellington**, Earl Franklin 1933- *AmMWSc 92*
**Ellington**, Edward Kennedy 1899-1974 *FacFETw [port]*
**Ellington**, James Jackson 1944- *AmMWSc 92*
**Ellington**, James Marion 1953- *WhoEnt 92*
**Ellington**, James Willard 1927- *WhoWest 92*
**Ellington**, Jim 1943- *WhoAmP 91*
**Ellington**, Joe J 1934- *AmMWSc 92*
**Ellington**, Joel William 1936- *WhoAmP 91*
**Ellington**, John Stephen 1950- *WhoWest 92*
**Ellington**, Kenneth Raynor 1888-1962 *DcNCBi 2*
**Ellington**, Mercedes *WhoBlA 92, WhoEnt 92*
**Ellington**, Mercer 1919- *NewAmDM*
**Ellington**, Mercer Kennedy 1919- *WhoEnt 92*
**Ellington**, Nathalie May 1939- *WhoFI 92*
**Ellington**, Noble 1942- *WhoAmP 91*
**Ellington**, Ronald Earle 1945- *WhoRel 92*
**Ellington**, William Ross 1949- *AmMWSc 92*
**Ellingwood**, Bruce Russell 1944- *AmMWSc 92*
**Ellingwood**, Herbert E 1931- *WhoAmP 91*
**Ellingworth**, Richard Henry 1926- *Who 92*
**Ellinwood**, Everett Hews, Jr 1934- *AmMWSc 92*
**Ellinwood**, Howard Lyman 1926- *AmMWSc 92*
**Ellinwood**, William Edward 1950- *AmMWSc 92*
**Ellion**, M Edmund 1923- *AmMWSc 92*
**Elliot** *Who 92*
**Elliot**, Alfred Johnston 1911- *AmMWSc 92*
**Elliot**, Alistair 1932- *ConPo 91, WrDr 92*
**Elliot**, Arthur McAuley 1928- *AmMWSc 92*
**Elliot**, Bruce *DrAPF 91*
**Elliot**, Daniel Giraud 1835-1915 *BiInAmS*
**Elliot**, David Hawksley 1936- *AmMWSc 92*
**Elliot**, Diane Alynn 1949- *WhoEnt 92*
**Elliot**, Douglas Gene 1941- *WhoFI 92*
**Elliot**, Gerald 1923- *Who 92*
**Elliot**, Harry 1920- *Who 92*
**Elliot**, James I 1938- *AmMWSc 92*
**Elliot**, James Ludlow 1943- *AmMWSc 92*
**Elliot**, Janet Lee 1955- *WhoMW 92*
**Elliot**, Jeffrey M. 1947- *WrDr 92*
**Elliot**, Joe Oliver 1923- *AmMWSc 92*
**Elliot**, Maud Howe d1948 *BenetAL 91*
**Elliot**, Ralph Gregory 1936- *WhoAmL 92*
**Elliot**, Ramey Robert 1949- *WhoEnt 92*
**Elliot**, Robert M. 1923- *WhoFI 92*
**Elliot**, Sarah Barnwell 1848-1928 *BenetAL 91*
**Elliot**, Willard Somers 1926- *WhoEnt 92*
**Elliot**, William Cater 1961- *WhoAmL 92*
**Elliot-Murray-Kynynmound** *Who 92*
**Elliot of Harwood**, Baroness 1903- *Who 92*
**Elliot-Smith**, Alan Guy 1904- *Who 92*
**Elliott** *Who 92*
**Elliott**, Lord 1922- *Who 92*
**Elliott**, A. Wright *WhoFI 92*
**Elliott**, Aaron Marshall 1844-1910 *DcNCBi 2*
**Elliott**, Alfred Marlyn 1905- *AmMWSc 92*
**Elliott**, Alice 1919- *AmMWSc 92*
**Elliott**, Anthony Daniel, III 1948- *WhoBlA 92*
**Elliott**, Anthony Michael Manton 1947- *Who 92*
**Elliott**, Archer Thomas, Jr. 1944- *WhoAmL 92*
**Elliott**, Arthur H 1848?-1918 *BiInAmS*
**Elliott**, Arthur James 1941- *WhoAmL 92*
**Elliott**, Arthur York 1936- *AmMWSc 92*
**Elliott**, Barbara Jean 1927- *WhoMW 92*
**Elliott**, Bernard Burton 1921- *AmMWSc 92*
**Elliott**, Betty F. *WhoMW 92*
**Elliott**, Bob *ConAu 134*
**Elliott**, Brady Gifford 1943- *WhoAmL 92*
**Elliott**, Brian Robinson 1910- *IntWW 91, WrDr 92*
**Elliott**, Bruce John 1927- *Who 92*
**Elliott**, Byron Kauffman 1899- *WhoAmL 92*
**Elliott**, Cathy 1956- *WhoBlA 92*
**Elliott**, Cecil Michael 1949- *AmMWSc 92*
**Elliott**, Charles Harold 1948- *AmMWSc 92*
**Elliott**, Charles Kennedy 1919- *Who 92*
**Elliott**, Charles Middleton 1939- *IntWW 91, Who 92*
**Elliott**, Charles Thomas 1939- *Who 92*
**Elliott**, Charles William 1953- *WhoAmL 92*
**Elliott**, Clive 1945- *Who 92*
**Elliott**, Craig 1947- *WhoAmP 91*
**Elliott**, D William 1925- *WhoIns 92*
**Elliott**, Daisy 1919- *NotBlAW 92*
**Elliott**, Dan Whitacre 1922- *AmMWSc 92*
**Elliott**, Dana Edgar 1923- *AmMWSc 92*
**Elliott**, Dana Ray 1945- *AmMWSc 92*
**Elliott**, Daniel Robert, Jr. 1939- *WhoAmL 92, WhoFI 92*
**Elliott**, Darrell Kenneth 1952- *WhoRel 92, WhoWest 92*
**Elliott**, Darrell Wayne 1955- *WhoRel 92*
**Elliott**, David Duncan 1930- *AmMWSc 92*
**Elliott**, David Joseph 1953- *WhoAmL 92*
**Elliott**, David LeRoy 1932- *AmMWSc 92*
**Elliott**, David Murray 1930- *Who 92*
**Elliott**, David Stuart 1949- *Who 92*
**Elliott**, Denholm 1922- *IntMPA 92*
**Elliott**, Denholm Mitchell 1922- *Who 92, WhoEnt 92*
**Elliott**, Denis Anthony 1946- *AmMWSc 92*
**Elliott**, Dennis Hall 1946- *WhoAmL 92*
**Elliott**, Derek Wesley 1958- *WhoBlA 92*
**Elliott**, Dick 1937- *WhoAmP 91*
**Elliott**, Don *ConAu 36NR*
**Elliott**, Donald B 1931- *WhoAmP 91*
**Elliott**, Douglas Charles 1952- *WhoWest 92*
**Elliott**, Douglas Floyd 1932- *AmMWSc 92*
**Elliott**, Ebenezer 1781-1849 *RfGEnL 91*
**Elliott**, Eddie Mayes 1938- *WhoMW 92*
**Elliott**, Edwin Donald, Jr. 1948- *WhoAmL 92*
**Elliott**, Erica Merriam 1948- *WhoWest 92*
**Elliott**, Eugene Willis 1916- *AmMWSc 92*
**Elliott**, Ewell H, Jr 1936- *WhoAmP 91*
**Elliott**, Ezekiel Brown 1823-1888 *BiInAmS*
**Elliott**, Floyd Matlock 1956- *WhoAmL 92*
**Elliott**, Francis Perry 1861-1924 *ScFEYrs*
**Elliott**, Frank Abercrombie 1910- *Who 92*
**Elliott**, Frank Alan 1937- *Who 92*
**Elliott**, Frank George 1913- *WhoBlA 92*
**Elliott**, Frank Wallace 1930- *WhoAmL 92*
**Elliott**, Gary Wayne 1949- *WhoMW 92*
**Elliott**, George 1932- *Who 92*
**Elliott**, George Algimon 1925- *AmMWSc 92*
**Elliott**, George Arthur 1945- *AmMWSc 92*
**Elliott**, George Byron 1928- *WhoFI 92*
**Elliott**, George Horton 1926- *WhoAmL 92*
**Elliott**, George P. 1918-1980 *BenetAL 91*
**Elliott**, Gilbert 1843-1895 *DcNCBi 2*
**Elliott**, Gordon Jefferson 1928- *WhoWest 92*
**Elliott**, H Margaret 1925- *AmMWSc 92*
**Elliott**, Harley *DrAPF 91*
**Elliott**, Harold Marshall 1943- *WhoWest 92*
**Elliott**, Harold William 1905- *Who 92*
**Elliott**, Harriet Wiseman 1884-1947 *DcNCBi 2*
**Elliott**, Howard Clyde 1924- *AmMWSc 92*
**Elliott**, Hugh Percival 1911- *Who 92*
**Elliott**, Humphrey Taylor 1933- *WhoAmP 91*
**Elliott**, Irvin Wesley 1925- *AmMWSc 92, WhoBlA 92*
**Elliott**, J. Russell *WhoBlA 92*
**Elliott**, James Alton 1904- *WhoAmP 91*
**Elliott**, James Arthur 1941- *AmMWSc 92*
**Elliott**, James Ballintine 1936- *WhoRel 92*
**Elliott**, James Brian 1962- *WhoEnt 92*
**Elliott**, James Carson 1845-1936 *DcNCBi 2*
**Elliott**, James Gary 1945- *AmMWSc 92*
**Elliott**, James H 1927- *AmMWSc 92*
**Elliott**, James Henry 1936- *WhoRel 92*
**Elliott**, James Philip 1929- *IntWW 91, Who 92*
**Elliott**, James Robert 1910- *WhoAmL 92*
**Elliott**, James Robert Francis 1961- *WhoMW 92*
**Elliott**, James Sewell 1922- *WhoAmP 91*
**Elliott**, James Ward 1954- *WhoAmL 92*
**Elliott**, James William, Jr. 1950- *WhoFI 92*
**Elliott**, Jane Elizabeth Inch 1911- *AmMWSc 92*
**Elliott**, Janice 1931- *ConNov 91, IntAu&W 91, WrDr 92*
**Elliott**, Jeanne Marie Koreltz 1943- *WhoWest 92*
**Elliott**, Jerry Chris 1943- *AmMWSc 92*
**Elliott**, Jim 1942- *WhoAmP 91*
**Elliott**, Joanne 1925- *AmMWSc 92*
**Elliott**, Joe *WhoAmP 91*
**Elliott**, John Dorman 1941- *Who 92*
**Elliott**, John Frank 1920- *AmMWSc 92*
**Elliott**, John Franklin 1915- *WhoRel 92*
**Elliott**, John G. *DcNCBi 2*
**Elliott**, John Gregory 1948- *WhoWest 92*
**Elliott**, John H. 1930- *IntAu&W 91*
**Elliott**, John Habersham 1913- *AmMWSc 92*
**Elliott**, John Hall 1935- *WhoRel 92*
**Elliott**, John Huxtable 1930- *IntWW 91, Who 92, WrDr 92*
**Elliott**, Joseph Robert 1923- *AmMWSc 92*
**Elliott**, Joy *WhoBlA 92*
**Elliott**, Lang 1949- *IntMPA 92*
**Elliott**, Larry Doc 1953- *WhoBlA 92*
**Elliott**, Larry Gene 1965- *WhoAmP 91*
**Elliott**, Larry Leroy 1955- *WhoAmP 91*
**Elliott**, Larry P 1938- *AmMWSc 92*
**Elliott**, Larry Paul 1931- *AmMWSc 92*
**Elliott**, Lawrence 1924- *IntAu&W 91*
**Elliott**, Lee Ann 1927- *WhoAmP 91*
**Elliott**, Lee Bruce 1951- *WhoMW 92*
**Elliott**, Lloyd Floren 1937- *AmMWSc 92*
**Elliott**, Lois Lawrence 1931- *AmMWSc 92, WhoMW 92*
**Elliott**, Lora Louise 1962- *WhoMW 92*
**Elliott**, Marianne 1948- *IntWW 91*
**Elliott**, Mark 1939- *Who 92*
**Elliott**, Meena Lulla 1963- *WhoAmL 92*
**Elliott**, Michael 1924- *IntWW 91, Who 92*
**Elliott**, Michael Alwyn 1936- *Who 92*
**Elliott**, Michael Norman 1932- *Who 92*
**Elliott**, Michael Robert 1964- *WhoEnt 92*
**Elliott**, Mildred Ellen 1927- *WhoAmP 91*
**Elliott**, Mitchell Lee 1958- *WhoFI 92*
**Elliott**, Norman 1903- *Who 92*
**Elliott**, Norman Randall 1903- *IntWW 91*
**Elliott**, Oliver Douglas 1925- *Who 92*
**Elliott**, Osborn 1924- *IntWW 91*
**Elliott**, Paul M 1922- *AmMWSc 92*
**Elliott**, Paul Russell 1933- *AmMWSc 92*
**Elliott**, Peter James 1963- *WhoMW 92*
**Elliott**, Philip Lovin, Sr. 1891-1961 *DcNCBi 2*
**Elliott**, R. Keith 1942- *WhoFI 92*
**Elliott**, Ralph H. 1925- *WhoRel 92*
**Elliott**, Randal 1922- *Who 92*
**Elliott**, Richard Amos 1937- *AmMWSc 92*
**Elliott**, Richard B. 1952- *IntMPA 92*
**Elliott**, Richard Gene 1948- *WhoFI 92*
**Elliott**, Richard Harold 1953- *WhoRel 92*
**Elliott**, Richard Howard 1933- *WhoAmL 92, WhoFI 92*
**Elliott**, Robert A 1924- *AmMWSc 92*
**Elliott**, Robert Anthony K. *Who 92*
**Elliott**, Robert B. 1923- *ConAu 134, WhoEnt 92*
**Elliott**, Robert Betzel 1926- *WhoMW 92*
**Elliott**, Robert Bruce 1956- *WhoFI 92*
**Elliott**, Robert Chadwick 1946- *WhoFI 92*
**Elliott**, Robert D. *Who 92*
**Elliott**, Robert Daryl 1935- *AmMWSc 92*
**Elliott**, Robert Earl 1949- *WhoMW 92*
**Elliott**, Robert F. 1938- *WhoEnt 92*
**Elliott**, Robert James 1940- *AmMWSc 92, WhoWest 92*
**Elliott**, Robert S 1921- *AmMWSc 92*
**Elliott**, Roger 1928- *IntWW 91, Who 92*
**Elliott**, Roger Harley 1931- *WhoAmP 91*
**Elliott**, Ronald 1918- *Who 92*
**Elliott**, Ronald Dean 1953- *WhoRel 92*
**Elliott**, Rosemary Waite 1934- *AmMWSc 92*
**Elliott**, Roy Fraser 1921- *WhoFI 92*
**Elliott**, Sam 1944- *IntMPA 92*
**Elliott**, Sean Michael 1968- *WhoBlA 92*
**Elliott**, Shelden Dougless, Jr 1931- *AmMWSc 92*
**Elliott**, Sheldon Ellwood 1925- *AmMWSc 92*
**Elliott**, Stephen 1771-1830 *BiInAmS*
**Elliott**, Steven Pell 1953- *WhoAmL 92*
**Elliott**, Stuart Bruce 1927- *AmMWSc 92*
**Elliott**, Stuart Jay 1952- *WhoFI 92*
**Elliott**, Sue 1941- *WhoRel 92*
**Elliott**, Sumner Locke 1917- *WrDr 92*

**Elliott,** Sumner Locke 1917-1991 *ConAu 134, NewYTBS 91 [port]*
**Elliott,** Susan Spoehrer 1937- *WhoMW 92*
**Elliott,** T Mark 1956- *WhoAmP 91*
**Elliott,** Theron Paul 1945- *WhoMW 92*
**Elliott,** Thomas Edward 1944- *WhoMW 92*
**Elliott,** Thomas Joseph 1941- *WhoWest 92*
**Elliott,** Thomas Renton 1877-1961 *FacFETw*
**Elliott,** Tyron Clifford 1942- *WhoAmP 91*
**Elliott,** Walter Archibald *Who 92*
**Elliott,** Ward Edward Yandell 1937- *WhoWest 92*
**Elliott,** Wayne Allen 1939- *WhoAmP 91*
**Elliott,** William David 1934- *WhoBlA 92*
**Elliott,** William Edward 1942- *WhoRel 92*
**Elliott,** William Gibson 1934- *WhoFI 92, WhoMW 92*
**Elliott,** William H 1918- *AmMWSc 92*
**Elliott,** William Hueckel 1918- *WhoMW 92*
**Elliott,** William I. *DrAPF 91*
**Elliott,** William J 1939- *AmMWSc 92*
**Elliott,** William John 1951- *AmMWSc 92, WhoMW 92*
**Elliott,** William Paul 1928- *AmMWSc 92*
**Elliott,** William Rowcliffe 1910- *Who 92, WrDr 92*
**Elliott of Morpeth,** Baron 1920- *Who 92*
**Elliott-Taylor,** Grace Mary 1908- *IntAu&W 91*
**Ellis** *Who 92*
**Ellis and White** *DcLB 106*
**Ellis,** Aaron Edmund 1954- *WhoWest 92*
**Ellis,** Albert 1913- *AmMWSc 92, WrDr 92*
**Ellis,** Albert Tromly 1917- *AmMWSc 92*
**Ellis,** Alec 1932- *WrDr 92*
**Ellis,** Alfred Wright 1943- *WhoAmL 92*
**Ellis,** Alice Thomas *IntAu&W 91, Who 92, WrDr 92*
**Ellis,** Alice Thomas 1932- *ConNov 91*
**Ellis,** Allan D. 1951- *WhoBlA 92*
**Ellis,** Alvin A, Jr 1936- *WhoAmP 91*
**Ellis,** Andrew Jackson, Jr. 1930- *WhoAmL 92*
**Ellis,** Andrew Steven 1952- *Who 92*
**Ellis,** Andy Widders 1951- *WhoEnt 92*
**Ellis,** Anne Elizabeth 1945- *WhoFI 92*
**Ellis,** Arthur John 1932- *Who 92*
**Ellis,** Arthur Robert Malcolm 1912- *Who 92*
**Ellis,** Arvilla d1889 *BiInAmS*
**Ellis,** Audrey *WrDr 92*
**Ellis,** Barnes Humphreys 1940- *WhoAmL 92*
**Ellis,** Benjamin F., Jr. 1939- *WhoBlA 92*
**Ellis,** Benjamin F., Jr. 1941- *WhoBlA 92*
**Ellis,** Bernice *WhoFI 92*
**Ellis,** Bobby James 1941- *WhoAmP 91*
**Ellis,** Boyd G 1932- *AmMWSc 92*
**Ellis,** Bret Easton 1964- *IntAu&W 91, WrDr 92*
**Ellis,** Bruce Boyd 1956- *WhoEnt 92*
**Ellis,** Bryan James 1934- *Who 92*
**Ellis,** C N 1952- *AmMWSc 92*
**Ellis,** Calvin H., III 1941- *WhoBlA 92*
**Ellis,** Carlton Case 1954- *WhoWest 92*
**Ellis,** Carol Jacqueline 1929- *Who 92*
**Ellis,** Carolyn Terry 1949- *WhoAmL 92*
**Ellis,** Charles Bernard 1941- *WhoFI 92*
**Ellis,** Charles John 1944- *WhoEnt 92*
**Ellis,** Charles W. 1944- *WhoEnt 92*
**Ellis,** Christine DuBoulay *WhoEnt 92*
**Ellis,** Clifford Roy 1941- *AmMWSc 92*
**Ellis,** Courtenay 1946- *WhoAmL 92*
**Ellis,** Craig *DrAPF 91*
**Ellis,** Dale 1960- *WhoBlA 92*
**Ellis,** Daniel B 1937- *AmMWSc 92*
**Ellis,** David Allen 1917- *AmMWSc 92*
**Ellis,** David Dale 1952- *WhoAmL 92*
**Ellis,** David Greenhill 1936- *AmMWSc 92*
**Ellis,** David M 1937- *AmMWSc 92*
**Ellis,** David Richard 1952- *WhoEnt 92*
**Ellis,** David Roy 1947- *WhoAmL 92*
**Ellis,** David Wertz 1936- *AmMWSc 92*
**Ellis,** Demetrius 1946- *AmMWSc 92*
**Ellis,** Derek V 1930- *AmMWSc 92*
**Ellis,** Don 1934-1978 *NewAmDM*
**Ellis,** Don Edwin 1908- *AmMWSc 92*
**Ellis,** Donald Edwin 1939- *AmMWSc 92*
**Ellis,** Donald Griffith 1940- *AmMWSc 92*
**Ellis,** Donald Lee 1950- *WhoAmL 92*
**Ellis,** Donald Llewellyn 1926- *WhoRel 92*
**Ellis,** Dorothy June 1926- *Who 92*
**Ellis,** Dorsey Daniel, Jr. 1938- *WhoAmL 92*
**Ellis,** Douglas, Jr. 1947- *WhoBlA 92*
**Ellis,** Duke Ellington 1933- *WhoBlA 92*
**Ellis,** Edgar Heb, Jr. 1935- *WhoRel 92*
**Ellis,** Edward Robb 1911- *IntAu&W 91, WrDr 92*
**Ellis,** Edward S. 1840-1916 *BenetAL 91, ScFEYrs*
**Ellis,** Edward V. 1924- *WhoBlA 92*
**Ellis,** Edward William 1918- *Who 92*
**Ellis,** Edwin M 1914- *AmMWSc 92*
**Ellis,** Effie O'Neal 1913- *AmMWSc 92, NotBlAW 92, WhoBlA 92*
**Ellis,** Eileen Mary 1933- *Who 92*
**Ellis,** Eldon Eugene 1922- *WhoWest 92*
**Ellis,** Elizabeth Carol *AmMWSc 92*
**Ellis,** Elizabeth G. *WhoBlA 92*
**Ellis,** Ella T. *WrDr 92*
**Ellis,** Ella Thorp *DrAPF 91*
**Ellis,** Ella Thorp 1928- *IntAu&W 91*
**Ellis,** Elliot F 1929- *AmMWSc 92*
**Ellis,** Elmer 1901- *IntWW 91*
**Ellis,** Elmo Israel 1918- *WhoEnt 92*
**Ellis,** Elward Dwayne 1948- *WhoBlA 92*
**Ellis,** Emory Nelson, Jr. 1929- *WhoAmL 92*
**Ellis,** Eric Hans 1935- *AmMWSc 92*
**Ellis,** Ernest W. 1940- *WhoBlA 92*
**Ellis,** Eugene Joseph 1919- *WhoWest 92*
**Ellis,** Eva Lillian 1920- *WhoWest 92*
**Ellis,** Evelyn 1894-1958 *NotBlAW 92*
**Ellis,** Everett Lincoln 1919- *AmMWSc 92*
**Ellis,** Frank C 1913- *WhoAmP 91*
**Ellis,** Frank Corley, Jr 1940- *WhoAmP 91*
**Ellis,** Frank Russell 1915- *AmMWSc 92*
**Ellis,** Franklin Henry, Jr 1920- *AmMWSc 92*
**Ellis,** Fred E 1926- *AmMWSc 92*
**Ellis,** Fred K 1939- *WhoIns 92*
**Ellis,** Fred Wilson 1914- *AmMWSc 92*
**Ellis,** Frederic L. 1915- *WhoBlA 92*
**Ellis,** Frederick Startridge 1830-1901 *DcLB 106 [port]*
**Ellis,** G A *ScFEYrs*
**Ellis,** Gene *DrAPF 91*
**Ellis,** George Edwin, Jr. 1921- *WhoFI 92, WhoWest 92*
**Ellis,** George Francis Rayner 1939- *IntWW 91*
**Ellis,** George Richard 1937- *WhoWest 92*
**Ellis,** George Thomas 1932- *WhoAmL 92*
**Ellis,** George Washington 1925- *WhoBlA 92*
**Ellis,** Gerry Lynn 1957- *WhoBlA 92*
**Ellis,** Gordon Elon 1950- *WhoRel 92*
**Ellis,** Gwynn Pennant *IntAu&W 91, WrDr 92*
**Ellis,** Harold 1926- *Who 92, WrDr 92*
**Ellis,** Harold Bernard 1917- *AmMWSc 92*
**Ellis,** Harold Eugene 1953- *WhoEnt 92*
**Ellis,** Harold Hal 1918- *AmMWSc 92*
**Ellis,** Harrell Victor 1923- *WhoAmP 91*
**Ellis,** Harry Bearse 1921- *WrDr 92*
**Ellis,** Harry Goodwin 1942- *WhoWest 92*
**Ellis,** Harvey 1852-1904 *DcTwDes*
**Ellis,** Havelock 1859-1939 *FacFETw, ScFEYrs*
**Ellis,** Henry 1721-1806 *BiInAmS*
**Ellis,** Henry Carlton 1927- *WhoWest 92*
**Ellis,** Herbert *Who 92*
**Ellis,** Herbert Wayne 1948- *WhoAmL 92*
**Ellis,** Homer Godsey 1933- *AmMWSc 92*
**Ellis,** Howard Woodrow 1914- *WhoRel 92*
**Ellis,** Humphry Francis 1907- *Who 92, WrDr 92*
**Ellis,** J S 1927- *AmMWSc 92*
**Ellis,** Jack Barry 1936- *AmMWSc 92*
**Ellis,** Jack Clare 1922- *WhoEnt 92*
**Ellis,** James D. 1943- *WhoAmL 92*
**Ellis,** James Leonard 1928- *WhoAmP 91*
**Ellis,** James Leonard 1947- *WhoEnt 92*
**Ellis,** James Reed 1921- *WhoAmL 92*
**Ellis,** James Watson 1927- *AmMWSc 92*
**Ellis,** Jane A *ScFEYrs*
**Ellis,** Janice Rider 1939- *WhoWest 92*
**Ellis,** Jason Arundel 1918- *AmMWSc 92*
**Ellis,** Jeffrey Raymond 1944- *AmMWSc 92*
**Ellis,** Jerry William 1937- *AmMWSc 92*
**Ellis,** Jim 1955- *WhoAmL 92*
**Ellis,** Job Bicknell 1829-1905 *BiInAmS*
**Ellis,** John *WhoAmP 91*
**Ellis,** John 1925- *Who 92*
**Ellis,** John 1930- *Who 92*
**Ellis,** John Carroll, Jr. 1948- *WhoFI 92*
**Ellis,** John Emmett 1943- *AmMWSc 92*
**Ellis,** John Fletcher 1937- *AmMWSc 92*
**Ellis,** John Francis 1922- *AmMWSc 92*
**Ellis,** John Hagood 1928- *WhoAmP 91*
**Ellis,** John Hubert 1931- *IntAu&W 91*
**Ellis,** John Martin 1936- *IntWW 91*
**Ellis,** John Munn, III *WhoFI 92*
**Ellis,** John Norman 1939- *Who 92*
**Ellis,** John Rogers 1916- *Who 92*
**Ellis,** John Romaine 1922- *Who 92*
**Ellis,** John Russell 1938- *Who 92*
**Ellis,** John Taylor 1920- *AmMWSc 92*
**Ellis,** John Tracy 1905- *IntWW 91, WhoRel 92*
**Ellis,** John W. 1928- *WhoWest 92*
**Ellis,** John Willis 1820-1861 *DcNCBi 2*
**Ellis,** Johnell A. 1945- *WhoBlA 92*
**Ellis,** Johnny *WhoAmP 91*
**Ellis,** Jonathan Richard 1946- *IntWW 91, Who 92*
**Ellis,** Joseph Louis 1916-1990 *WhoBlA 92N*
**Ellis,** Joseph Stanley 1907- *Who 92*
**Ellis,** Julie 1933- *WrDr 92*
**Ellis,** June *Who 92*
**Ellis,** Kate Ferguson *DrAPF 91*
**Ellis,** Keith 1927- *WrDr 92*
**Ellis,** Keith Osborne 1941- *AmMWSc 92*
**Ellis,** Kenneth Joseph 1944- *AmMWSc 92*
**Ellis,** Kerwin Ray 1959- *WhoBlA 92*
**Ellis,** Laurence Edward 1932- *Who 92*
**Ellis,** Leander Theodore, Jr. 1929- *WhoBlA 92*
**Ellis,** Lee 1924- *WhoWest 92*
**Ellis,** LeGrande Clark 1932- *AmMWSc 92*
**Ellis,** Leo H. 1925- *WhoWest 92*
**Ellis,** Leonard Culberth 1934- *AmMWSc 92*
**Ellis,** Leslie Lee, Jr 1925- *AmMWSc 92*
**Ellis,** Lionel 1903- *TwCPaSc*
**Ellis,** Lynda Betty 1945- *AmMWSc 92*
**Ellis,** Lynn W 1928- *AmMWSc 92*
**Ellis,** Malcolm Eugene 1929- *WhoRel 92*
**Ellis,** Marilyn Pope 1938- *WhoBlA 92*
**Ellis,** Mark 1945- *WrDr 92*
**Ellis,** Mark Ernest 1954- *WhoMW 92*
**Ellis,** Mark Karl 1945- *IntAu&W 91*
**Ellis,** Mark Randall 1956- *WhoAmL 92*
**Ellis,** Mary 1900- *Who 92*
**Ellis,** Maxwell 1906- *Who 92*
**Ellis,** Michael 1917- *WhoEnt 92*
**Ellis,** Michael Eugene 1946- *WhoMW 92*
**Ellis,** Michael G 1941- *WhoAmP 91*
**Ellis,** Michael G. 1962- *WhoBlA 92*
**Ellis,** Michael Paul 1946- *WhoAmP 91*
**Ellis,** Nan Jane 1956- *WhoEnt 92*
**Ellis,** Nanette C. 1943- *WhoMW 92*
**Ellis,** Neal *DrAPF 91*
**Ellis,** Noel 1917- *TwCPaSc*
**Ellis,** Norman David 1943- *Who 92*
**Ellis,** O. Herbert 1916- *WhoBlA 92*
**Ellis,** Osian Gwynn 1928- *IntWW 91, Who 92*
**Ellis,** P. J. 1911- *WhoBlA 92*
**Ellis,** Patricia Mench 1949- *AmMWSc 92*
**Ellis,** Patrick 1928- *WhoRel 92*
**Ellis,** Patrick D 1930- *WhoAmP 91*
**Ellis,** Paul B., III 1950- *WhoEnt 92*
**Ellis,** Paul John 1941- *AmMWSc 92*
**Ellis,** Perry 1940-1986 *DcTwDes*
**Ellis,** Perry Edwin 1940- *IntWW 91*
**Ellis,** Peter 1950- *TwCPaSc*
**Ellis,** Philip Paul 1923- *AmMWSc 92*
**Ellis,** Ray Wendel 1938- *WhoRel 92*
**Ellis,** Raymond Clinton, Jr. 1921- *WhoFI 92*
**Ellis,** Raymond Joseph 1923- *Who 92*
**Ellis,** Reginald John 1935- *IntWW 91, Who 92*
**Ellis,** Reid Duane 1962- *WhoRel 92*
**Ellis,** Rex *AmMWSc 92*
**Ellis,** Richard *DcNCBi 2*
**Ellis,** Richard 1960- *ConAu 135*
**Ellis,** Richard Akers 1928- *AmMWSc 92*
**Ellis,** Richard Bassett 1915- *AmMWSc 92*
**Ellis,** Richard John 1939- *AmMWSc 92*
**Ellis,** Richard Peter 1931- *Who 92*
**Ellis,** Richard Steven 1947- *AmMWSc 92*
**Ellis,** Robert Anderson, Jr 1927- *AmMWSc 92*
**Ellis,** Robert Bryan, Jr. 1957- *WhoAmL 92*
**Ellis,** Robert Griswold 1908- *WhoFI 92, WhoMW 92*
**Ellis,** Robert Harry 1928- *WhoEnt 92, WhoWest 92*
**Ellis,** Robert L 1938- *AmMWSc 92*
**Ellis,** Robert Lawson, Jr 1922- *WhoAmP 91*
**Ellis,** Robert Lee 1949- *WhoAmL 92*
**Ellis,** Robert Malcolm 1936- *AmMWSc 92*
**Ellis,** Robert Paul 1944- *WhoWest 92*
**Ellis,** Robert Thomas 1924- *Who 92*
**Ellis,** Robert William 1939- *AmMWSc 92*
**Ellis,** Robert William 1940- *AmMWSc 92*
**Ellis,** Robin Gareth 1935- *Who 92*
**Ellis,** Rodney 1954- *WhoBlA 92*
**Ellis,** Rodney G 1954- *WhoAmP 91*
**Ellis,** Roger Henry 1910- *Who 92*
**Ellis,** Roger Wykeham 1929- *Who 92*
**Ellis,** Romallis 1965- *BlkOlyM*
**Ellis,** Ronald 1925- *IntWW 91, Who 92*
**Ellis,** Ronald Lee 1939- *WhoMW 92*
**Ellis,** Rosemary 1919- *AmMWSc 92*
**Ellis,** Ross Courtland 1929- *AmMWSc 92*
**Ellis,** Roswell P 1934- *WhoIns 92*
**Ellis,** Royston 1941- *IntAu&W 91, WrDr 92*
**Ellis,** Samuel Benjamin 1904- *AmMWSc 92*
**Ellis,** Sarah 1952- *SmATA 68 [port]*
**Ellis,** Sophie Wenzel *ScFEYrs*
**Ellis,** Stanley 1923- *AmMWSc 92*
**Ellis,** Stephen Dean 1943- *AmMWSc 92*
**Ellis,** Sydney 1917- *AmMWSc 92*
**Ellis,** T Mullett 1850- *ScFEYrs*
**Ellis,** T. R. 1940- *WhoMW 92*
**Ellis,** Tellis B., III 1943- *WhoBlA 92*
**Ellis,** Terence Bruce 1958- *WhoRel 92*
**Ellis,** Terry *WhoAmP 91*
**Ellis,** Theodore Gunville 1829-1883 *BiInAmS*
**Ellis,** Thomas Jay 1959- *WhoAmL 92*
**Ellis,** Thomas Selby, III 1940- *WhoAmL 92*
**Ellis,** Thomas Stephen 1952- *AmMWSc 92*
**Ellis,** Tom *Who 92*
**Ellis,** Tom S., Jr. 1952- *WhoAmL 92*
**Ellis,** Tyrone 1946- *WhoAmP 91*
**Ellis,** Verlyn Alfred 1912- *WhoAmP 91*
**Ellis,** Verna Jeanne 1928- *WhoAmP 91*
**Ellis,** Vivian *Who 92*
**Ellis,** Vivian Elizabeth *WhoWest 92*
**Ellis,** Wade 1909- *AmMWSc 92*
**Ellis,** Wade 1909-1989 *WhoBlA 92N*
**Ellis,** Walter Leon 1941- *WhoRel 92*
**Ellis,** Walton P 1931- *AmMWSc 92*
**Ellis,** Wesley *ConAu 35NR*
**Ellis,** Wilfred Desmond d1990 *Who 92N*
**Ellis,** Willard Lee 1944- *WhoAmP 91*
**Ellis,** William Ben 1940- *WhoFI 92*
**Ellis,** William C 1931- *AmMWSc 92*
**Ellis,** William Franklin 1964- *WhoRel 92*
**Ellis,** William Grenville 1940- *WhoMW 92*
**Ellis,** William Hartshorne 1929- *WhoEnt 92*
**Ellis,** William Haynes 1931- *AmMWSc 92*
**Ellis,** William Herbert 1921- *Who 92*
**Ellis,** William Hobert 1928- *AmMWSc 92*
**Ellis,** William Homer, Jr. 1932- *WhoRel 92*
**Ellis,** William Reuben 1917- *WhoBlA 92*
**Ellis,** William Rufus 1940- *AmMWSc 92*
**Ellis,** Zachary L. *WhoBlA 92*
**Ellis-Menaghan,** John J *AmMWSc 92*
**Ellis-Rees,** Hugh Francis 1929- *Who 92*
**Ellis-Vant,** Karen McGee 1950- *WhoWest 92*
**Ellisen,** Stanley A. 1922- *ConAu 133*
**Ellison,** Alfred Harris 1923- *AmMWSc 92*
**Ellison,** Alton Lynn, Jr. 1950- *WhoAmL 92*
**Ellison,** Arthur James 1920- *Who 92*
**Ellison,** Bart T 1942- *AmMWSc 92*
**Ellison,** Craig William 1944- *WhoRel 92*
**Ellison,** Dale Leo 1963- *WhoMW 92*
**Ellison,** David Ernest 1921- *WhoWest 92*
**Ellison,** David Lee 1955- *WhoBlA 92*
**Ellison,** David Morris 1951- *WhoRel 92*
**Ellison,** Deborah Lynnette 1952- *WhoWest 92*
**Ellison,** Edwin Christopher 1950- *WhoMW 92*
**Ellison,** Frank Oscar 1926- *AmMWSc 92*
**Ellison,** Gayfree Barney 1943- *AmMWSc 92*
**Ellison,** Gerald Alexander 1910- *IntWW 91, Who 92*
**Ellison,** Gerald L. 1943- *WhoEnt 92*
**Ellison,** Harlan *DrAPF 91*
**Ellison,** Harlan 1934- *BenetAL 91, TwCSFW 91, WrDr 92*
**Ellison,** Harlan Jay 1934- *FacFETw, IntWW 91*
**Ellison,** Henry S. 1923- *WhoBlA 92*
**Ellison,** James Oliver 1929- *WhoAmL 92*
**Ellison,** Joan Audrey 1928- *WrDr 92*
**Ellison,** John *WhoRel 92*
**Ellison,** John Alexander *Who 92*
**Ellison,** John Harold 1916- *Who 92*
**Ellison,** John Vogelsanger 1919- *AmMWSc 92*
**Ellison,** Julian, Jr. 1942- *WhoFI 92*
**Ellison,** Lawrence J. 1944- *WhoWest 92*
**Ellison,** Lois Taylor 1923- *AmMWSc 92*
**Ellison,** Marlon L 1916- *AmMWSc 92*
**Ellison,** Nolen M. 1941- *WhoBlA 92*
**Ellison,** Orval S 1921- *WhoAmP 91*
**Ellison,** Pauline Allen *WhoBlA 92*
**Ellison,** Pervis 1967- *WhoBlA 92*
**Ellison,** Peter Kemp 1942- *WhoAmP 91*
**Ellison,** Ralph *DrAPF 91*
**Ellison,** Ralph 1914- *AfrAmW, BenetAL 91, BlkLC [port], ConNov 91, FacFETw, IntWW 91, RComAH, WrDr 92*
**Ellison,** Ralph Henry C. *Who 92*
**Ellison,** Ralph Waldo 1914- *WhoBlA 92*
**Ellison,** Richard Thomas, III 1951- *WhoWest 92*
**Ellison,** Robert A. 1915- *WhoBlA 92*
**Ellison,** Robert G 1916- *AmMWSc 92*
**Ellison,** Robert Hardy 1950- *AmMWSc 92*
**Ellison,** Robert L 1930- *AmMWSc 92*
**Ellison,** Rose Ruth 1923- *AmMWSc 92*
**Ellison,** Samuel Porter, Jr 1914- *AmMWSc 92*
**Ellison,** Solon Arthur 1922- *AmMWSc 92*
**Ellison,** Stewart 1832-1899 *DcNCBi 2*
**Ellison,** Theodore 1930- *AmMWSc 92*
**Ellison,** Victor Louis 1955- *WhoMW 92*
**Ellison,** Virginia Howell 1910- *IntAu&W 91, WrDr 92*
**Ellison,** Wanda Marie 1960- *WhoFI 92*
**Ellison,** William Theodore 1941- *AmMWSc 92*
**Elliston,** Deborah LaMonte 1962- *WhoEnt 92*
**Elliston,** John E 1944- *AmMWSc 92*
**Ellman,** Candace E. 1967- *WhoWest 92*
**Ellman,** George Leon 1923- *AmMWSc 92*
**Ellman,** Louise Joyce 1945- *Who 92*
**Ellman,** Roger Arnold 1952- *WhoEnt 92*
**Ellman-Brown,** Geoffrey 1910- *Who 92*

**Ellmann**, Douglas Stanley 1956- WhoAmL 92
**Ellmann**, Richard 1918-1987 FacFETw
**Ellmann**, Sheila Frenkel 1931- WhoFI 92, WhoMW 92
**Ellmann**, William Marshall 1921- WhoAmL 92
**Ellmaurer**, Dennis Jay 1949- WhoFI 92
**Ellner**, Paul Daniel 1925- AmMWSc 92
**Ellois**, Edward R., Jr. 1922- WhoBlA 92
**Ellor**, James W. 1951- WhoRel 92
**Ellrod**, Frederick Edward, III 1953- WhoAmL 92
**Ellroy**, James DcLB Y91 [port]
**Ellroy**, James 1948- WrDr 92
**Ells**, Charles Edward 1923- AmMWSc 92
**Ells**, Frederick Richard 1934- AmMWSc 92
**Ells**, James E 1931- AmMWSc 92
**Ells**, Victor Raymond 1914- AmMWSc 92
**Ellsaesser**, Hugh Walter 1920- WhoWest 92
**Ellsberg**, Daniel 1931- AmPeW
**Ellsberg**, Edward 1891-1983 CurBio 91N
**Ellsberg**, Robert Boyd 1955- WhoRel 92
**Ellsberry**, Elizabeth Prather 1923- WhoAmP 91
**Ellson**, Robert A 1934- AmMWSc 92
**Ellstrand**, Norman Carl 1952- AmMWSc 92, WhoWest 92
**Ellstrom-Calder**, Annette 1952- WhoMW 92
**Ellsworth**, Cynthia Ann 1950- WhoMW 92
**Ellsworth**, Jane Dewey d1991 NewYTBS 91
**Ellsworth**, Lincoln 1880-1951 FacFETw
**Ellsworth**, Louis Daniel 1917- AmMWSc 92
**Ellsworth**, Mary Litchfield AmMWSc 92
**Ellsworth**, Maurice Owens 1948- WhoAmL 92
**Ellsworth**, Oliver 1745-1807 AmPolLe
**Ellsworth**, Phoebe Clemencia 1944- WhoAmL 92
**Ellsworth**, Ralph E. 1907- IntWW 91, WrDr 92
**Ellsworth**, Ralph Eugene 1907- WhoWest 92
**Ellsworth**, Richard German 1950- WhoWest 92
**Ellsworth**, Robert 1926- Who 92
**Ellsworth**, Robert Fred 1926- WhoFI 92
**Ellsworth**, Robert King 1941- AmMWSc 92
**Ellsworth**, Steven Kay 1946- WhoFI 92
**Ellsworth**, William Wallace 1918- WhoAmP 91
**Ellul**, Jacques 1912- DcEcMov
**Ellwanger**, C Scott 1947- WhoIns 92
**Ellwanger**, J. David 1937- WhoAmL 92
**Ellwanger**, John Paul 1931- WhoRel 92
**Ellwein**, Leon Burnell 1942- AmMWSc 92
**Ellwood**, Aubrey 1897- Who 92
**Ellwood**, Brooks B AmMWSc 92
**Ellwood**, Charles A. 1873-1946 DcAmImH
**Ellwood**, Eric Louis 1922- AmMWSc 92
**Ellwood**, George 1875-1955 TwCPaSc
**Ellwood**, Paul M, Jr 1926- AmMWSc 92
**Ellwood**, Robert Scott, Jr. 1933- WhoRel 92
**Ellwood**, Scott 1936- WhoAmL 92
**Ellyin**, Fernand 1938- AmMWSc 92
**Ellzey**, Joanne Tontz 1937- AmMWSc 92
**Ellzey**, Marion Lawrence, Jr 1939- AmMWSc 92
**Ellzey**, Randal Edmond 1958- WhoFI 92
**Ellzey**, Samuel Edward, Jr 1931- AmMWSc 92
**Elmadjian**, Fred 1915- AmMWSc 92
**Elmaghraby**, Salah Eldin 1927- AmMWSc 92
**Elman**, Howard Lawrence 1938- WhoFI 92
**Elman**, Irving WhoEnt 92
**Elman**, Mischa 1891-1967 FacFETw, NewAmDM
**Elman**, Richard DrAPF 91
**Elman**, Richard 1934- IntAu&W 91
**Elman**, Stephen Edward 1949- WhoEnt 92
**Elman**, Ziggy 1914-1968 NewAmDM
**Elmandjra**, Mahdi 1933- IntWW 91
**Elmegreen**, Debra Meloy 1952- AmMWSc 92
**Elmendorf**, Charles Halsey, III 1913- AmMWSc 92
**Elmendorf**, Fritz M. 1954- WhoFI 92
**Elmer**, Jonathan 1745-1817 BiInAmS
**Elmer**, Otto Charles 1918- AmMWSc 92
**Elmer**, Thomas J 1948- WhoIns 92
**Elmer**, W Owen 1938- WhoAmP 91
**Elmer**, William Arthur 1938- AmMWSc 92
**Elmer**, William B 1901- AmMWSc 92
**Elmes**, Gregory Arthur 1950- AmMWSc 92
**Elmes**, Peter Cardwell 1921- Who 92
**Elmets**, Craig Allan 1949- WhoMW 92
**Elmets**, Douglas Gregory 1958- WhoFI 92, WhoWest 92
**Elmo**, Thomas Joseph 1963- WhoEnt 92
**El'Mohammed**, Ali Malik Bell 1944- WhoMW 92
**Elmore**, Carroll Dennis 1940- AmMWSc 92
**Elmore**, David 1945- AmMWSc 92
**Elmore**, Edward Whitehead 1938- WhoAmL 92
**Elmore**, Garland Craft 1946- WhoEnt 92
**Elmore**, Geraldine Catharine 1936- WhoWest 92
**Elmore**, Glenn Van Ness 1916- AmMWSc 92
**Elmore**, James B 1949- IntAu&W 91
**Elmore**, James Lewis 1948- AmMWSc 92
**Elmore**, John Jesse, Jr 1936- AmMWSc 92
**Elmore**, Joyce A. 1937- WhoBlA 92
**Elmore**, Kimberly Laurence 1956- AmMWSc 92
**Elmore**, Leonard Joseph 1952- WhoEnt 92
**Elmore**, Louie Franklin 1951- WhoAmL 92
**Elmore**, Matthew Bret 1951- WhoEnt 92
**Elmore**, Patricia DrAPF 91
**Elmore**, Stancliff Churchill 1921- WhoAmL 92
**Elmore**, Stanley McDowell 1933- AmMWSc 92
**Elmore**, Van Adney 1929- WhoAmL 92
**Elmquist**, Jack Douglas 1943- WhoAmL 92
**Elms**, Barry James 1949- WhoFI 92
**Elms**, Ben 1935- WhoEnt 92
**Elms**, David Tatum 1943- WhoRel 92
**Elms**, James Cornelius 1916- AmMWSc 92
**Elms**, James Cornelius, IV 1916- WhoFI 92
**Elms**, Richard Alden 1931- WhoWest 92
**Elmsley**, Alexander 1730-1797 DcNCBi 2
**Elmsley**, John 1762-1805 DcNCBi 2
**Elmslie**, Alexander Frederic Joseph 1905- Who 92
**Elmslie**, George Grant 1871-1952 DcTwDes
**Elmslie**, James Stewart 1930- AmMWSc 92
**Elmslie**, Kenward DrAPF 91
**Elmslie**, Kenward 1929- ConPo 91, WrDr 92
**Elmslie**, Kenward Gray 1929- IntAu&W 91
**Elmstrom**, Gary William 1939- AmMWSc 92
**Elmstrom**, George P. 1925- WhoWest 92
**Elniff**, Terrill Irwin 1941- WhoFI 92
**Elofson**, Richard Macleod 1919- AmMWSc 92
**Elon**, Amos 1926- WrDr 92
**Elon**, Florence DrAPF 91
**Elorduy**, Nancy Kathryn 1943- WhoFI 92
**Elovic**, Barbara DrAPF 91
**Elovitz**, Mark Harvey 1938- WhoAmL 92, WhoRel 92
**Elowe**, Louis N 1922- AmMWSc 92
**Elphick**, Robert Yule 1948- WhoFI 92
**Elphin**, Bishop of 1918- Who 92
**Elphinstone** Who 92
**Elphinstone**, Lord 1953- Who 92
**Elphinstone**, Master of 1980- Who 92
**Elphinstone**, Douglas Who 92
**Elphinstone**, Maurice Douglas 1909- Who 92
**Elphinstone of Glack**, John 1924- Who 92
**Elrick**, David Emerson 1931- AmMWSc 92
**Elrick**, George Seefurth 1921- IntAu&W 91
**Elrington**, Christopher Robin 1930- Who 92
**Elrod**, Alvon Creighton 1928- AmMWSc 92
**Elrod**, Bruce Clifford 1949- WhoEnt 92
**Elrod**, David Wayne 1952- AmMWSc 92
**Elrod**, Eugene Richard 1949- WhoAmL 92
**Elrod**, Harold G, Jr 1918- AmMWSc 92
**Elrod**, Jackolyn Kennett 1943- WhoMW 92
**Elrod**, Jerry David 1938- WhoRel 92
**Elrod**, Joseph Harrison 1941- AmMWSc 92
**Elrod**, Linda Diane Henry 1947- WhoAmL 92
**Elrod**, Lu 1935- WhoEnt 92
**Elrod**, Richard Bryan 1949- WhoAmL 92
**Elsaesser**, Robert James 1926- WhoFI 92
**Elsas**, Fritz 1890-1945 EncTR 91
**Elsas**, Louis Jacob, II 1937- AmMWSc 92
**Elsass**, Mike L. 1947- WhoMW 92
**Elsasser**, Glen Robert 1935- WhoEnt 92
**Elsasser**, Hans Friedrich 1929- IntWW 91
**Elsasser**, Walter M. d1991 NewYTBS 91
**Elsasser**, Walter M 1904- AmMWSc 92
**Elsasser**, Walter Maurice 1904- FacFETw
**Elsayed**, Elsayed Abdelrazik 1947- AmMWSc 92
**Elsayed**, Nabil M 1946- AmMWSc 92
**Elsbach**, Peter 1924- AmMWSc 92
**Elsberg**, John DrAPF 91
**Elsberg**, Louis 1836-1885 BiInAmS
**Elsbernd**, Helen 1938- AmMWSc 92
**Elsberry**, Eric Cerny 1960- WhoWest 92
**Elsberry**, Russell Leonard 1941- AmMWSc 92
**Elsberry**, Susan Davise 1953- WhoWest 92
**Elsden**, Sidney Reuben 1915- Who 92
**Else**, Carolyn Joan 1934- WhoWest 92
**Else**, James Prentiss 1920- WhoRel 92
**Else**, John 1911- Who 92
**Elsea**, Gene WhoAmP 91
**Elsea**, Steven William 1955- WhoWest 92
**Elsen**, Albert Edward 1927- IntAu&W 91, WrDr 92
**Elsen**, Sheldon Howard 1928- WhoAmL 92
**Elsenbaumer**, Ronald Lee 1951- AmMWSc 92
**Elsener**, Daniel J. WhoRel 92
**Elser**, Danny Ray 1953- WhoWest 92
**Elser**, Johann Georg 1903-1945 EncTR 91 [port]
**Elser**, John Robert 1912- WhoFI 92
**Elsesser**, Lionelle Hurley 1945- WhoMW 92
**Elsevier**, Ernest 1914- AmMWSc 92
**Elsevier**, Susan Maria 1945- AmMWSc 92
**Elsey**, David DrAPF 91
**Elsey**, George McKee 1918- WhoFI 92
**Elsey**, John C 1935- AmMWSc 92
**Elsey**, John H 1945- WhoIns 92
**Elsey**, Kent D 1941- AmMWSc 92
**Elsey**, Margaret Grace 1929- AmMWSc 92
**Elsherbeni**, Atef Zakaria 1954- AmMWSc 92
**Elshoff**, James David 1946- WhoAmL 92
**Elshoff**, James L 1944- AmMWSc 92
**Elshoff**, James Lester 1944- WhoMW 92
**Elshtain**, Jean Bethke 1941- IntAu&W 91
**Elsik**, William Clinton 1935- AmMWSc 92
**Elsila**, David August 1939- WhoMW 92
**Elslager**, Edward Faith 1924- AmMWSc 92
**Elslande**, Renaat van 1916- IntWW 91
**Elsman**, James Leonard, Jr. 1936- WhoAmL 92, WhoRel 92
**Elsmore**, Lloyd 1913- Who 92
**Elsner**, Henry Leopold 1857-1916 BiInAmS
**Elsner**, Norbert Bernard 1933- AmMWSc 92
**Elsner**, Robert 1920- AmMWSc 92
**ElSohly**, Mahmoud Ahmed 1945- AmMWSc 92
**Elsom**, Cecil Harry 1912- Who 92
**Elsom**, Clint Gary 1946- WhoWest 92
**Elsom**, John WrDr 92
**Elsom**, John Edward 1934- IntAu&W 91
**Elson**, Alex 1905- WhoAmL 92
**Elson**, Charles 1909- WhoEnt 92
**Elson**, Charles 1934- AmMWSc 92
**Elson**, Charles Myer 1959- WhoAmL 92
**Elson**, Charles O, III 1942- AmMWSc 92
**Elson**, Edward L. R. 1906- WrDr 92
**Elson**, Edward Lee Roy 1906- WhoRel 92
**Elson**, Elliot 1937- AmMWSc 92
**Elson**, Graham Peel 1949- Who 92
**Elson**, Hannah Friedman 1943- AmMWSc 92
**Elson**, Jesse 1910- AmMWSc 92
**Elson**, John Albert 1923- AmMWSc 92
**Elson**, John S. 1943- WhoAmL 92
**Elson**, JoLane Brothers 1937- WhoMW 92
**Elson**, Lee Stephen 1947- AmMWSc 92
**Elson**, R. N. WrDr 92
**Elson**, Robert ScFEYrs
**Elson**, Virginia DrAPF 91
**Elspas**, B 1925- AmMWSc 92
**Elstad**, George Stanley 1927- WhoRel 92
**Elstein**, David Keith 1944- Who 92
**Elster**, J. Robert 1938- WhoAmL 92
**Elstner**, Richard Chesney 1924- WhoWest 92
**Elstob**, Elizabeth 1683-1756 BlkwCEP
**Elstob**, Peter 1915- IntAu&W 91, Who 92, WrDr 92
**Elston**, Allan Vaughan 1887-1976 TwCWW 91
**Elston**, Arnold 1907-1971 NewAmDM
**Elston**, Charles William 1914- AmMWSc 92
**Elston**, Christopher David 1938- Who 92
**Elston**, Donald 1926- AmMWSc 92
**Elston**, Lester Charles 1929- WhoWest 92
**Elston**, Peter 1927- WhoIns 92
**Elston**, Stuart B 1946- AmMWSc 92
**Elston**, Wayne Ralph, Jr. 1948- WhoRel 92
**Elston**, William Steger 1940- WhoFI 92
**Elston**, Wolfgang Eugene 1928- AmMWSc 92
**Elswick**, Donald David 1966- WhoMW 92
**Elsworth**, Derek AmMWSc 92
**Elsy**, Mary IntAu&W 91, WrDr 92
**Elterich**, G Joachim 1930- AmMWSc 92
**Eltgroth**, Peter George 1940- AmMWSc 92
**Eltherington**, Lorne 1933- AmMWSc 92
**Elthon**, Donald L 1952- AmMWSc 92
**Elthon**, Thomas Eugene 1954- AmMWSc 92
**Eltimsahy**, Adel H 1936- AmMWSc 92
**Elting**, Everett E. 1936- WhoFI 92
**Elting**, John Winston 1943- WhoFI 92
**Eltinge**, Lamont 1926- AmMWSc 92
**Eltis**, Walter Alfred 1933- IntWW 91, Who 92
**Elton** Who 92
**Elton**, Baron 1930- IntWW 91, Who 92
**Elton**, Arnold 1920- Who 92
**Elton**, Ben IntAu&W 91
**Elton**, Benjamin Charles 1959- Who 92
**Elton**, Charles 1953- Who 92
**Elton**, Charles Sutherland d1991 Who 92N
**Elton**, Charles Sutherland 1900- FacFETw
**Elton**, Charles Sutherland 1900-1991 IntWW 91, -91N
**Elton**, Edward Francis 1935- AmMWSc 92
**Elton**, Geoffrey 1921- IntWW 91, Who 92
**Elton**, Geoffrey Rudolph 1921- IntAu&W 91, WrDr 92
**Elton**, George Alfred Hugh 1925- Who 92
**Elton**, Joe 1951- WhoAmP 91
**Elton**, John Who 92
**Elton**, John Goodenough 1905- Who 92
**Elton**, Lewis Richard Benjamin 1923- Who 92
**Elton**, Michael Anthony 1932- Who 92
**Elton**, Michael John 1933- WhoFI 92
**Elton**, Peter John 1924- Who 92
**Elton**, Raymond Carter AmMWSc 92
**Eltringham**, S. K. 1929- WrDr 92
**Eltz**, Robert Walter 1932- AmMWSc 92
**Eltz-Rubenach**, Paul, Baron von 1875-1943 EncTR 91 [port]
**Eltze**, Ervin Marvin 1938- AmMWSc 92
**Eltzroth**, Linda Elaine Scott 1949- WhoMW 92
**Eluard**, Paul 1895-1952 FacFETw, GuFrLit 1, TwCLC 41 [port]
**Elveback**, Lillian Rose 1915- AmMWSc 92
**Elveden**, Viscount 1969- Who 92
**Elvehjem**, Conrad Arnold 1901-1962 FacFETw
**Elverum**, Gerard William, Jr 1927- AmMWSc 92
**Elvig**, Merrywayne 1931- WhoMW 92
**Elvin**, Herbert Lionel 1905- IntWW 91, Who 92
**Elvin**, Violetta 1925- IntWW 91, Who 92
**Elvin-Lewis**, Memory P F 1933- AmMWSc 92
**Elving**, Bruce Fred 1935- WhoEnt 92
**Elving**, Philip Juliber 1913- AmMWSc 92
**Elvira** ConTFT 9
**Elvira** 1951- WhoEnt 92
**Elvira**, Pablo 1941- NewAmDM
**Elvira Delgado**, Narciso D. 1967- WhoHisp 92
**Elvove**, Carl X. 1919- WhoMW 92
**Elward-Berry**, Julianne 1946- AmMWSc 92
**Elway**, John Albert 1960- WhoWest 92
**Elwell**, Celia Candace 1954- WhoAmL 92
**Elwell**, David Leslie 1940- AmMWSc 92
**Elwell**, Frederick 1870-1958 TwCPaSc
**Elwell**, Herbert 1898-1974 NewAmDM
**Elwell**, William Earl 1958- WhoRel 92
**Elwert**, Charles DrAPF 91
**Elwes**, Cary 1962- IntMPA 92
**Elwes**, Jeremy Gervase Geoffrey Philip 1921- Who 92
**Elwes**, Jeremy Vernon 1937- Who 92
**Elwes**, Simon 1902- TwCPaSc
**Elwin**, Fountain 1736-1833 DcNCBi 2
**Elwin**, James William, Jr. 1950- WhoAmL 92, WhoMW 92
**Elwood**, Ann 1931- WrDr 92
**Elwood**, Brian 1933- Who 92
**Elwood**, Brian Clay 1958- WhoMW 92
**Elwood**, David Michael 1935- WhoAmL 92
**Elwood**, James Kenneth 1936- AmMWSc 92
**Elwood**, Jerry William 1940- AmMWSc 92
**Elwood**, John Clint 1930- AmMWSc 92
**Elwood**, Roger 1933- ScFEYrs
**Elwood**, Roger and Ghidalia, Vic ScFEYrs
**Elwood**, Walter M. WhoRel 92
**Elwood**, Wesley M 1922- WhoAmP 91
**Elwood**, William Edward 1943- WhoAmL 92
**Elwood**, William K 1928- AmMWSc 92
**Elwood**, William R. 1935- WhoEnt 92
**Elworthy** Who 92
**Elworthy**, Baron 1911- IntWW 91, Who 92
**Elworthy**, Peter 1935- Who 92
**Elworthy**, Timothy Charles 1938- Who 92
**Elwyn**, Alexander Joseph 1927- AmMWSc 92
**Elwyn**, David Hunter 1920- AmMWSc 92
**Elwyn**, John 1916- TwCPaSc
**Elwyn-Jones**, Lady 1904-1990 AnObit 1990
**Ely**, Archdeacon of Who 92
**Ely**, Bishop of 1939- Who 92
**Ely**, Dean of Who 92
**Ely**, Marquess of 1913- Who 92

**Ely**, Achsah Mount 1848-1904 *BiInAmS*
**Ely**, Berten E, III 1948- *AmMWSc 92*
**Ely**, Betty Jo 1947- *WhoWest 92*
**Ely**, Charles Adelbert 1933- *AmMWSc 92*
**Ely**, Daniel Lee 1945- *AmMWSc 92*
**Ely**, David *DrAPF 91*
**Ely**, David 1927- *ConNov 91, IntAu&W 91, WrDr 92*
**Ely**, Donald Gene 1937- *AmMWSc 92*
**Ely**, Donald Jean 1935- *WhoRel 92*
**Ely**, Frank Louis 1924- *WhoAmP 91*
**Ely**, Harold Edmund 1946- *WhoMW 92*
**Ely**, James Frank 1945- *AmMWSc 92*
**Ely**, James Wallace, Jr. 1938- *WhoAmL 92*
**Ely**, John Frederick 1930- *AmMWSc 92*
**Ely**, John Hart 1938- *WhoAmL 92*
**Ely**, John Slade 1860-1906 *BiInAmS*
**Ely**, John Thomas Anderson 1923- *AmMWSc 92*
**Ely**, Joseph Buell, II 1938- *WhoFI 92*
**Ely**, Kathryn R 1944- *AmMWSc 92*
**Ely**, Keith *Who 92*
**Ely**, Marica McCann 1907- *WhoWest 92*
**Ely**, Northcutt 1903- *WhoAmL 92*
**Ely**, Paul 1897-1975 *FacFETw*
**Ely**, Paul C., Jr. 1932- *WhoFI 92*
**Ely**, Philip Thomas 1936- *Who 92*
**Ely**, Ralph Lawrence, Jr 1917- *AmMWSc 92*
**Ely**, Raymond Lloyd 1919- *AmMWSc 92*
**Ely**, Richard Theodore 1854-1943 *DcAmImH*
**Ely**, Robert Eugene 1949- *WhoAmL 92*
**Ely**, Robert P, Jr 1930- *AmMWSc 92*
**Ely**, Scott *DrAPF 91*
**Ely**, Sydney Keith 1949- *Who 92*
**Ely**, Theodore Newel 1846-1916 *BiInAmS*
**Ely**, Thomas Harrison 1942- *AmMWSc 92*
**Ely**, Thomas Sharpless 1924- *AmMWSc 92*
**Elya**, John Adel 1928- *WhoRel 92*
**Elyan**, Victor 1909- *Who 92*
**Elyasiani**, Elyas 1949- *WhoFI 92*
**Elyn**, Mark 1932- *WhoEnt 92, WhoMW 92*
**Elyot**, Thomas 1490?-1546 *RfGEnL 91*
**Elystan-Morgan** *Who 92*
**Elystan-Morgan**, Baron 1932- *Who 92*
**Elytis**, Odysseus 1911- *FacFETw, IntAu&W 91, IntWW 91, Who 92, WhoNob 90*
**Elytis**, Odysseus 1912- *LiExTwC*
**Elzay**, Richard Paul 1931- *AmMWSc 92*
**Elzerman**, Alan William 1949- *AmMWSc 92*
**Elzerman**, James Hubert 1952- *WhoRel 92*
**Elzey**, James Alan 1964- *WhoWest 92*
**Elzinga**, D Jack 1939- *AmMWSc 92*
**Elzinga**, Marshall 1938- *AmMWSc 92*
**Elzinga**, Peter 1944- *WhoWest 92*
**Elzinga**, Richard John 1931- *AmMWSc 92*
**Elzy**, Amanda Belle *WhoBlA 92*
**Ema**, Yasuo 1945- *WhoEnt 92*
**Emami**, Bahman 1943- *AmMWSc 92*
**Eman**, J. H. A. *IntWW 91*
**Emanuel**, Aaron 1912- *Who 92*
**Emanuel**, Alexander Eigeles 1937- *AmMWSc 92*
**Emanuel**, Cleaver 1944- *WhoAmP 91*
**Emanuel**, David 1952- *Who 92*
**Emanuel**, Elizabeth Florence 1953- *IntWW 91, Who 92*
**Emanuel**, Frank 1865-1948 *TwCPaSc*
**Emanuel**, George 1931- *AmMWSc 92*
**Emanuel**, Herbert L 1930- *WhoIns 92*
**Emanuel**, Irvin 1926- *AmMWSc 92*
**Emanuel**, Jack Howard 1921- *AmMWSc 92*
**Emanuel**, James A. *DrAPF 91*
**Emanuel**, James A. 1921- *ConPo 91, WrDr 92*
**Emanuel**, James Andrew 1921- *WhoBlA 92*
**Emanuel**, Lynn *DrAPF 91*
**Emanuel**, Richard Wolff 1923- *Who 92*
**Emanuel**, Rodica L 1939- *AmMWSc 92*
**Emanuel**, William Joseph 1938- *WhoAmL 92*
**Emanuel**, William Robert 1949- *AmMWSc 92*
**Emanuele**, Luciano 1948- *WhoMW 92*
**Emanuelli**, Eduardo Rafael 1946- *WhoAmP 91*
**Emanuelson**, James Robert 1931- *WhoIns 92*
**Emas**, Sidney Wengrover 1947- *WhoMW 92*
**Embden**, Gustav George 1874-1933 *FacFETw*
**Emberley**, Ed 1931- *ConAu 36NR*
**Emberton**, Kenneth C 1948- *AmMWSc 92*
**Embey**, Philip *WrDr 92*
**Embleton**, Tom William 1918- *AmMWSc 92*
**Embleton**, Tony Frederick Wallace 1929- *AmMWSc 92*
**Embley**, David Wayne 1946- *AmMWSc 92*
**Embling**, John Francis 1909- *Who 92*
**Emboden**, William A, Jr. 1935- *ConAu 34NR*
**Emboden**, William Allen, Jr 1935- *AmMWSc 92*
**Embody**, Daniel Robert 1914- *AmMWSc 92*
**Embree**, Charles Gordon *AmMWSc 92*
**Embree**, Charles Monroe 1935- *WhoRel 92*
**Embree**, Earl Owen 1924- *AmMWSc 92*
**Embree**, Glenn Mitchell 1951- *WhoAmL 92*
**Embree**, Harland Dumond 1923- *AmMWSc 92*
**Embree**, James Arlington 1934- *WhoBlA 92*
**Embree**, James Willard, Jr 1948- *AmMWSc 92*
**Embree**, M L 1924- *AmMWSc 92*
**Embree**, Norris Dean 1911- *AmMWSc 92*
**Embree**, Robert William 1932- *AmMWSc 92*
**Embrey**, David Cray 1961- *WhoMW 92*
**Embrey**, Derek Morris 1928- *Who 92*
**Embrey**, Robert Edward 1942- *WhoIns 92*
**Embry**, Bertis L 1914- *AmMWSc 92*
**Embry**, Carlos Brogdon, Jr 1941- *WhoAmP 91*
**Embry**, Lawrence Bryan 1918- *AmMWSc 92*
**Embry**, Robert Campbell, Jr 1937- *WhoAmP 91*
**Embry**, Wanda Lou 1942- *WhoAmP 91*
**Embry**, Wayne, Sr. 1937- *WhoBlA 92*
**Embry**, Wayne Richard 1937- *WhoMW 92*
**Embry-Wardrop**, Mary Rodriguez 1933- *AmMWSc 92*
**Emburey**, John Ernest 1952- *IntWW 91*
**Embury**, Janon Frederick, Jr 1945- *AmMWSc 92*
**Embury**, John David 1939- *AmMWSc 92*
**Emch**, George Frederick 1925- *AmMWSc 92*
**Emch**, Gerard G 1936- *AmMWSc 92*
**Emde**, Katy Marie 1953- *WhoEnt 92*
**Emde**, Richard K. 1938- *WhoMW 92*
**Emecheta**, Buchi 1944- *BlkLC [port], ConNov 91, IntAu&W 91, LiExTwC, SmATA 66, Who 92, WrDr 92*
**Emeigh**, Donald A, Jr 1954- *WhoIns 92*
**Emeka**, Mauris L. P. 1941- *WhoBlA 92*
**Emele**, Jane Frances 1925- *AmMWSc 92*
**Emeleus**, Harry 1903- *IntWW 91*
**Emeleus**, Harry Julius 1903- *FacFETw, Who 92*
**Emelin**, Georgia 1969- *WhoEnt 92*
**Emeneau**, Murray Barnson 1904- *IntWW 91, WrDr 92*
**Emenegger**, Robert E. 1933- *WhoEnt 92*
**Emeny**, Brooks 1901-1980 *AmPeW*
**Emeric**, Damaso 1921- *WhoHisp 92*
**Emerich**, Donald Warren 1920- *AmMWSc 92*
**Emerick**, David William 1945- *WhoFI 92*
**Emerick**, Harold B 1913- *AmMWSc 92*
**Emerick**, Judson Johnson 1941- *WhoWest 92*
**Emerick**, Royce Jasper 1931- *AmMWSc 92*
**Emerick**, Sally Elaine 1947- *WhoMW 92*
**Emerman**, Joanne Tannis *AmMWSc 92*
**Emerson**, Lake and Palmer *NewAmDM*
**Emerson**, Alice B. *ConAu 134, SmATA 65, -67*
**Emerson**, Alton Calvin 1934- *WhoWest 92*
**Emerson**, Andi 1932- *WhoFI 92*
**Emerson**, Archie Paul 1945- *WhoRel 92*
**Emerson**, Barbara Marie 1946- *WhoRel 92*
**Emerson**, Bill 1938- *AlmAP 92 [port], WhoAmP 91*
**Emerson**, Billy 1846-1902 *NewAmDM*
**Emerson**, Cherry Kathleen 1940- *WhoWest 92*
**Emerson**, David 1900- *IntAu&W 91, WrDr 92*
**Emerson**, David Edwin 1932- *AmMWSc 92*
**Emerson**, David Winthrop 1928- *AmMWSc 92*
**Emerson**, Donald McGeachy, Jr. 1952- *WhoFI 92*
**Emerson**, Donald Orville 1931- *AmMWSc 92*
**Emerson**, Douglas 1974- *WhoEnt 92*
**Emerson**, Earl W. 1948- *WrDr 92*
**Emerson**, Edwin 1823-1908 *BiInAmS*
**Emerson**, Faye d1983 *LesBEnT 92*
**Emerson**, Frank Henry 1921- *AmMWSc 92*
**Emerson**, Frederick Beauregard, Jr 1935- *AmMWSc 92*
**Emerson**, Frederick Valentine 1871-1919 *BiInAmS*
**Emerson**, George Barrell 1797-1881 *BiInAmS*
**Emerson**, George H 1837-1864 *BiInAmS*
**Emerson**, Geraldine Mariellen 1925- *AmMWSc 92*
**Emerson**, Isaac Edward 1859-1931 *DcNCBi 2*
**Emerson**, James Harold 1957- *WhoEnt 92*
**Emerson**, James L 1938- *AmMWSc 92*
**Emerson**, James Lindley 1924- *WhoAmP 91*
**Emerson**, Jerome A *WhoAmP 91*
**Emerson**, John Bonnell 1954- *WhoAmP 91*
**Emerson**, John David 1946- *AmMWSc 92*
**Emerson**, John Wilford 1933- *AmMWSc 92*
**Emerson**, John Williams, II 1929- *WhoAmL 92*
**Emerson**, Junius M *WhoAmP 91*
**Emerson**, Kary Cadmus 1918- *AmMWSc 92*
**Emerson**, Kenneth 1931- *AmMWSc 92*
**Emerson**, Marion Preston 1918- *AmMWSc 92*
**Emerson**, Marvin Chester 1928- *WhoAmL 92*
**Emerson**, Merle T 1930- *AmMWSc 92*
**Emerson**, Michael Ronald 1940- *Who 92*
**Emerson**, Oliver John 1919- *WhoAmP 91*
**Emerson**, Peter Albert 1923- *Who 92*
**Emerson**, Peter H 1856-1936 *FacFETw*
**Emerson**, Ralph 1787-1863 *BiInAmS*
**Emerson**, Ralph Waldo 1803-1882 *AmPeW, BenetAL 91, RComAH*
**Emerson**, Robert 1878-1944 *TwCPaSc*
**Emerson**, Robert 1948- *WhoAmP 91*
**Emerson**, Robert Kennerly, Sr. 1922- *WhoAmL 92*
**Emerson**, Robert Wyatt 1957- *WhoAmL 92*
**Emerson**, Ronald *ConAu 36NR*
**Emerson**, Ru 1944- *IntAu&W 91, TwCSFW 91*
**Emerson**, Sandra Hawk 1943- *WhoAmP 91*
**Emerson**, Thomas Edward, Jr 1935- *AmMWSc 92, WhoWest 92*
**Emerson**, Thomas I. d1991 *NewYTBS 91*
**Emerson**, Thomas I. 1907- *WrDr 92*
**Emerson**, Thomas I. 1907-1991 *ConAu 134*
**Emerson**, Thomas James 1947- *AmMWSc 92*
**Emerson**, Warren Russell 1940- *WhoAmP 91*
**Emerson**, William 1938- *WhoMW 92*
**Emerson**, William Harry 1928- *WhoAmL 92*
**Emerson**, William Kary 1941- *WhoMW 92*
**Emerson**, William Keith 1925- *AmMWSc 92*
**Emerson**, William Stevenson 1913- *WhoFI 92*
**Emerson**, Willis George 1856-1918 *ScFEYrs*
**Emert**, Jack Isaac 1948- *AmMWSc 92*
**Emerton**, Audrey *Who 92*
**Emerton**, John Adney 1928- *IntWW 91, Who 92*
**Emerton**, Lawrence, Sr 1928- *WhoAmP 91*
**Emeruwa**, Leatrice Joy W. *DrAPF 91*
**Emery**, Alan Eglin Heathcote 1928- *IntWW 91, Who 92*
**Emery**, Alan Roy 1939- *AmMWSc 92, WhoMW 92*
**Emery**, Alden H, Jr 1925- *AmMWSc 92*
**Emery**, Ashley F 1934- *AmMWSc 92*
**Emery**, Austin H. 1931- *WhoRel 92*
**Emery**, Charles Edward 1838-1898 *BiInAmS*
**Emery**, David Farnham 1948- *WhoAmP 91*
**Emery**, Donald Allen 1928- *AmMWSc 92*
**Emery**, Donald F 1928- *AmMWSc 92*
**Emery**, Earl Eugene 1931- *WhoFI 92*
**Emery**, Edward Mortimer 1926- *AmMWSc 92*
**Emery**, Edwin 1914- *IntAu&W 91*
**Emery**, Eleanor Jean 1918- *Who 92*
**Emery**, Fred 1933- *Who 92*
**Emery**, George Edward 1920- *Who 92*
**Emery**, Glenn D. 1954- *ConAu 135*
**Emery**, Guy Trask 1931- *AmMWSc 92*
**Emery**, James Jackson 1954- *WhoFI 92*
**Emery**, James W *WhoAmP 91*
**Emery**, Janette 1964- *TwCPaSc*
**Emery**, Jill Houghton 1943- *WhoAmP 91*
**Emery**, Joan Dawson *Who 92*
**Emery**, John Cameron 1947- *IntAu&W 91*
**Emery**, Joyce Margaret *Who 92*
**Emery**, Keith Allen 1954- *AmMWSc 92*
**Emery**, Kendal Ray 1963- *WhoWest 92*
**Emery**, Kenneth 1914- *WrDr 92*
**Emery**, Kenneth O. 1914- *IntWW 91*
**Emery**, Kenneth Orris 1914- *AmMWSc 92*
**Emery**, Lina *Who 92*
**Emery**, Michael B. 1938- *WhoFI 92*
**Emery**, Oren Dale 1927- *WhoRel 92*
**Emery**, Peter 1926- *Who 92*
**Emery**, Philip Anthony 1934- *AmMWSc 92, WhoWest 92*
**Emery**, Richard Meyer 1939- *AmMWSc 92*
**Emery**, Robert Allan 1943- *WhoRel 92*
**Emery**, Robert Firestone 1927- *IntAu&W 91, WrDr 92*
**Emery**, Roy Saltsman 1928- *AmMWSc 92*
**Emery**, Sarah Elizabeth Van De Vort 1838-1895 *HanAmWH*
**Emery**, Thomas Fred 1931- *AmMWSc 92*
**Emery**, Victor John 1934- *AmMWSc 92*
**Emery**, W L 1915- *AmMWSc 92*
**Emery**, William Henry Perry 1924- *AmMWSc 92*
**Emery**, William Jackson 1946- *AmMWSc 92*
**Emery-Wallis**, Frederick Alfred John 1927- *Who 92*
**Emeson**, Eugene Edward 1934- *AmMWSc 92*
**Emett**, Rowland d1990 *Who 92N*
**Emett**, Rowland 1906-1990 *AnObit 1990, ConAu 133*
**Emick**, Dudley Joseph, Jr 1939- *WhoAmP 91*
**Emick**, William John 1931- *WhoFI 92*
**Emig**, Lois Irene Myers 1925- *WhoEnt 92*
**Emigh**, Charles Robert 1920- *AmMWSc 92*
**Emigh**, Elizabeth Evelyn 1924- *WhoWest 92*
**Emigh**, G Donald 1911- *AmMWSc 92*
**Emiliani**, Cesare 1922- *AmMWSc 92, FacFETw*
**Emiliani**, Vittorio 1935- *IntWW 91*
**Emilio** *IntWW 91*
**Emilio**, Frank Anthony 1935- *WhoAmP 91*
**Emily**, Joseph Todd 1968- *WhoEnt 92*
**Emin**, David 1941- *AmMWSc 92*
**Emin**, Gevork 1919- *IntWW 91*
**Eminescu**, Mihail 1850-1889 *NinCLC 33 [port]*
**Eminhizer**, Earl Eugene 1926- *WhoMW 92, WhoRel 92*
**Eminizer**, Donald Lee 1969- *WhoEnt 92*
**Emino**, Everett Raymond 1942- *AmMWSc 92*
**Eminov**, Ali M. 1941- *WhoMW 92*
**Emiroglu**, Metin 1943- *IntWW 91*
**Emison**, Sidney Tharp 1931- *WhoWest 92*
**Emken**, Edward Allen 1940- *AmMWSc 92*
**Emlemdi**, Hasan Bashir 1959- *AmMWSc 92*
**Emlen**, John Merritt 1938- *AmMWSc 92*
**Emlen**, John Thompson, Jr 1908- *AmMWSc 92*
**Emlen**, Robert P. 1946- *ConAu 135*
**Emlen**, Stephen Thompson 1940- *AmMWSc 92*
**Emlen**, Warren Metz 1932- *WhoFI 92*
**Emler**, Donald Gilbert 1939- *WhoRel 92*
**Emlet**, Harry Elsworth, Jr 1927- *AmMWSc 92*
**Emley**, Charles Lee 1927- *WhoAmP 91*
**Emley**, Christopher Fielding 1943- *WhoAmL 92*
**Emley**, William Earl 1948- *WhoAmP 91*
**Emling**, Bertin Leo 1905- *AmMWSc 92*
**Emlyn**, Viscount 1962- *Who 92*
**Emlyn Jones**, John Hubert 1915- *Who 92*
**Emma**, Countess of Norfolk *EncAmaz 91*
**Emma of Normandy** d1052 *EncAmaz 91*
**Emma**, Queen of France *EncAmaz 91*
**Emma**, Charles Joseph, Jr. 1956- *WhoAmL 92*
**Emmanouilides**, George Christos 1926- *AmMWSc 92*
**Emmanuel**, George 1925- *AmMWSc 92*
**Emmanuel**, Jorge Agustin 1954- *WhoWest 92*
**Emmanuel**, Lenny *DrAPF 91*
**Emmanuel**, Lenny 1932- *WhoMW 92*
**Emmanuel**, Michel George 1918- *WhoAmL 92*
**Emmanuel**, Tsegai 1940- *WhoBlA 92*
**Emmel**, Thomas C 1941- *AmMWSc 92*
**Emmel**, Victor Meyer 1913- *AmMWSc 92*
**Emmeluth**, Bruce Palmer 1940- *WhoFI 92, WhoWest 92*
**Emmens**, Clifford Walter 1913- *IntWW 91*
**Emmerich**, Andre 1924- *IntAu&W 91, WrDr 92*
**Emmerich**, Noah Nicholas 1965- *WhoEnt 92*
**Emmerich**, Toby 1963- *WhoEnt 92*
**Emmerich**, Werner Sigmund 1921- *AmMWSc 92*
**Emmerling**, David Alan 1948- *AmMWSc 92*
**Emmerling**, Edward J 1908- *AmMWSc 92*
**Emmerman**, Michael N 1945- *WhoFI 92*
**Emmers**, Raimond 1924- *AmMWSc 92*
**Emmerson**, John Lynn 1933- *AmMWSc 92*
**Emmerson**, Ralph 1913- *Who 92*
**Emmerson**, Simon 1950- *ConCom 92*
**Emmert**, Charles Michael 1954- *WhoRel 92*
**Emmert**, Gilbert A 1938- *AmMWSc 92*
**Emmert**, R E 1929- *AmMWSc 92*
**Emmet**, Dorothy Mary *WrDr 92*
**Emmet**, Dorothy Mary 1904- *IntWW 91, Who 92*

**Emmet,** John Patten 1796-1842 *BiInAmS*
**Emmet,** R D *ScFEYrs*
**Emmet,** Thomas Addis 1828-1919 *DcAmImH*
**Emmet,** Thomas Addis, Jr. 1930- *WhoWest 92*
**Emmet,** Timothy Goodsmith 1958- *WhoEnt 92*
**Emmett,** Bryan David 1941- *Who 92*
**Emmett,** Dan 1815-1904 *NewAmDM*
**Emmett,** Daniel Decatur 1815-1904 *BenetAL 91*
**Emmett,** Edward Anthony 1940- *AmMWSc 92*
**Emmett,** Edward Martin 1949- *WhoAmL 92, WhoAmP 91, WhoFI 92*
**Emmett,** Harold Leslie d1991 *Who 92N*
**Emmett,** James Robert 1940- *WhoAmL 92*
**Emmett,** John L 1939- *AmMWSc 92*
**Emmett,** Martin Frederick Cheere 1934- *IntWW 91*
**Emmett,** Michelle Ann 1953- *WhoMW 92*
**Emmett,** Robert 1921- *WhoEnt 92*
**Emmett,** Robert Addis, III 1943- *WhoAmL 92*
**Emmett,** Robert Andrew 1922- *WhoAmP 91*
**Emmett,** V.J., Jr. *DrAPF 91*
**Emmett,** Walter Charles 1925- *WhoFI 92*
**Emmett,** William W 1937- *AmMWSc 92*
**Emmett-Oglesby,** Michael Wayne 1947- *AmMWSc 92*
**Emmich,** Cliff 1936- *WhoEnt 92*
**Emmich,** Richard Alan 1957- *WhoFI 92*
**Emmick,** Thomas Lynn 1940- *AmMWSc 92*
**Emmit,** Dan 1815-1904 *NewAmDM*
**Emmons,** Alice M 1955- *WhoAmP 91*
**Emmons,** Cynthia Wagner *DrAPF 91*
**Emmons,** Dale Clifton 1952- *WhoAmP 91*
**Emmons,** Donald Ray 1965- *WhoBlA 92*
**Emmons,** Earl Russell, Jr. 1967- *WhoRel 92*
**Emmons,** Ebenezer 1799-1863 *BiInAmS, DcNCBi 2*
**Emmons,** Greg B. 1953- *WhoAmL 92*
**Emmons,** Hamilton 1930- *AmMWSc 92*
**Emmons,** Howard W 1912- *AmMWSc 92*
**Emmons,** Howard Wilson 1912- *IntWW 91*
**Emmons,** Joanne Clara 1934- *WhoAmP 91*
**Emmons,** Larrimore Browneller 1935- *AmMWSc 92*
**Emmons,** Linda N 1937- *WhoAmP 91*
**Emmons,** Lyman Randlett 1927- *AmMWSc 92*
**Emmons,** Phyllis M. 1946- *WhoMW 92*
**Emmons,** Rayford E. 1948- *WhoBlA 92*
**Emmons,** Richard Conrad 1898- *AmMWSc 92*
**Emmons,** Richard William 1931- *AmMWSc 92, WhoWest 92*
**Emmons,** Samuel Franklin 1841-1911 *BiInAmS*
**Emmons,** Scott W 1945- *AmMWSc 92*
**Emmons,** Sharon Kay 1953- *WhoMW 92*
**Emmons,** William David 1924- *AmMWSc 92*
**Emmott,** Lawrence Fielding 1952- *WhoWest 92*
**Emms,** David Acfield 1925- *Who 92*
**Emms,** John Frederick George d1990 *Who 92N*
**Emms,** Peter Fawcett 1935- *Who 92*
**Emond,** George T 1943- *AmMWSc 92*
**Emond,** Lionel Joseph 1932- *WhoFI 92*
**Emond,** Robert R J 1930- *WhoAmP 91*
**Emord,** Jonathan Walker 1961- *WhoAmL 92*
**Emory,** Emerson 1925- *WhoBlA 92*
**Emory,** Frederick Lincoln 1867-1919 *BiInAmS*
**Emory,** John Brooks, III 1942- *WhoFI 92*
**Emory,** John Druse 1938- *WhoFI 92*
**Emory,** Katharine B. 1960- *WhoEnt 92*
**Emory,** Linda B 1938- *WhoIns 92*
**Emory,** Samuel Thomas 1933- *WhoAmP 91*
**Emory,** William Hemsley 1811-1887 *BiInAmS*
**Emovon,** Emmanuel Uwumagbuhunmwun 1929- *IntWW 91*
**Empen,** Joseph A 1940- *AmMWSc 92*
**Emperaire,** Achille 1829-1910 *ThHEIm*
**Empey,** Gene F. 1923- *WhoWest 92*
**Empey,** Reginald Norman Morgan 1947- *Who 92*
**Empey,** Walton Newcombe Francis *Who 92*
**Empie,** Adam 1785-1860 *DcNCBi 2*
**Empie,** Paul C 1909-1979 *FacFETw*
**Emplit,** Raymond Henry 1948- *WhoFI 92*
**Empson,** Cindy *WhoAmP 91*
**Empson,** Derek 1918- *Who 92*
**Empson,** John Eugene 1960- *WhoEnt 92*
**Empson,** William 1906-1984 *FacFETw, LiExTwC, RfGEnL 91*
**Emr,** Scott David 1954- *AmMWSc 92*
**Emraghy,** Hoda Abdel-Kader 1945- *AmMWSc 92*
**Emrich,** Edmund Michael 1956- *WhoAmL 92*
**Emrich,** Grover Harry 1929- *AmMWSc 92*
**Emrich,** Lawrence James 1955- *AmMWSc 92*
**Emrich,** Raymond Jay 1917- *AmMWSc 92*
**Emrick,** Donald Day 1929- *AmMWSc 92, WhoMW 92*
**Emrick,** Edwin Roy 1929- *AmMWSc 92*
**Emrick,** Roy M 1932- *AmMWSc 92*
**Emrick,** Shannon Tee 1963- *WhoAmL 92*
**Emrit,** Ronald C. 1945- *WhoBlA 92*
**Emroch,** Walter H *WhoAmP 91*
**Emry,** Frederic Grant 1939- *WhoAmL 92*
**Emry,** Louis Knar 1911- *WhoAmP 91*
**Emry,** Robert John 1940- *AmMWSc 92*
**Emry,** Thomas Leyburn 1842-1910 *DcNCBi 2*
**Emshwiller,** Carol *DrAPF 91*
**Emshwiller,** Carol 1921- *TwCSFW 91, WrDr 92*
**Emshwiller,** Ed 1925-1990 *IntDcF 2-2*
**Emshwiller,** Maclellan 1927- *AmMWSc 92*
**Emsley,** James Alan Burns 1943- *AmMWSc 92*
**Emsley,** Michael Gordon 1930- *AmMWSc 92*
**Emslie** *Who 92*
**Emslie,** Baron 1919- *Who 92*
**Emslie,** Alfred George 1907- *AmMWSc 92*
**Emslie,** George Carlyle 1919- *IntWW 91*
**Emslie,** Nigel 1947- *Who 92*
**Emslie,** Ronald Douglas 1915- *Who 92*
**Emslie,** Ronald Frank 1932- *AmMWSc 92*
**Emson,** Harry Edmund 1927- *AmMWSc 92*
**Emson,** Reginald 1912- *Who 92*
**Emswiler,** Charles E., Jr. 1917- *WhoRel 92*
**Emswiler,** Tom Neufer 1941- *WhoRel 92*
**Emtage,** Peter Roesch 1935- *AmMWSc 92*
**Enahoro,** Anthony 1923- *IntWW 91*
**Enberg,** Denis Alan *WhoMW 92*
**Enberg,** Dick *LesBEnT 92*
**Enberg,** Henry Winfield 1940- *WhoAmL 92, WhoFI 92*
**Encina,** Juan del 1468-1529 *NewAmDM*
**Encinas,** Salvador, Jr. 1963- *WhoHisp 92*
**Encinias,** Art *WhoHisp 92*
**Enciso,** Jose Raul 1954- *WhoHisp 92*
**Encombe,** Viscount 1962- *Who 92*
**End,** John Michael 1946- *WhoAmL 92*
**End,** William Thomas 1947- *WhoFI 92*
**Endahl,** Gerald Leroy 1924- *AmMWSc 92*
**Endal,** Andrew Samson 1949- *AmMWSc 92*
**Endara,** Guillermo *IntWW 91*
**Endara,** Guillermo 1936- *CurBio 91 [port]*
**Ende,** Michael 1929- *ConAu 36NR*
**Ende,** Michael 1930?- *TwCSFW 91A*
**Ende,** Norman 1924- *AmMWSc 92*
**Endecott,** John 1589?-1665 *BenetAL 91*
**Endejan,** Judith Anne 1953- *WhoAmL 92*
**Endeley,** E. M. L. 1916- *IntWW 91*
**Endell,** Ernst M. August 1871-1925 *DcTwDes*
**Endeman,** Ronald Lee 1936- *WhoAmL 92*
**Endemann,** Carl T. *DrAPF 91*
**Endemann,** Samuel Theodore Hermann Carl 1842-1909 *BiInAmS*
**Ender,** Elma Teresa Salinas 1953- *WhoHisp 92*
**Ender,** Jack Lee 1951- *WhoRel 92*
**Ender,** Jon Terry 1942- *WhoFI 92, WhoMW 92*
**Ender,** Richard Louis 1945- *WhoWest 92*
**Enderby,** Charles Eldred 1934- *AmMWSc 92*
**Enderby,** John Edwin 1931- *Who 92*
**Enderby,** Kenneth Albert 1920- *Who 92*
**Enderby,** Keppel Earl 1926- *IntWW 91*
**Enderby,** Samuel 1907- *Who 92*
**Enderlin,** Lee 1951- *IntAu&W 91*
**Enders,** Alexandra 1946- *WhoWest 92*
**Enders,** Allen Coffin 1928- *AmMWSc 92*
**Enders,** George Crandell *AmMWSc 92*
**Enders,** George Leonhard, Jr 1945- *AmMWSc 92*
**Enders,** John Franklin 1897-1985 *FacFETw, WhoNob 90*
**Enders,** Murvin S. 1942- *WhoBlA 92*
**Enders,** Pat *DrAPF 91*
**Enders,** Robert *IntMPA 92*
**Enders,** Thomas O. 1931- *IntWW 91*
**Enders,** Thomas Ostrom 1931- *WhoAmP 91*
**Endersby,** Clive 1944- *ConAu 133*
**Endersby,** Clive Paul 1944- *IntAu&W 91*
**Enderson,** James H 1936- *AmMWSc 92*
**Enderton,** Herbert Bruce 1936- *AmMWSc 92*
**Enderud,** Wilbur Donald, Jr. 1945- *WhoWest 92*
**Endicott,** John 1589?-1665 *BenetAL 91*
**Endicott,** John F 1932- *AmMWSc 92*
**Endler,** John Arthur 1947- *AmMWSc 92*
**Endlich,** Leatrice Ann 1928- *WhoMW 92*
**Endo,** Burton Yoshiaki 1926- *AmMWSc 92*
**Endo,** Kaname 1915- *IntWW 91*
**Endo,** Robert Minoru 1925- *AmMWSc 92*
**Endo,** Shusaku Paul 1923- *IntWW 91*
**Endo,** Youichi 1949- *AmMWSc 92*
**Endow,** Sharyn Anne 1948- *AmMWSc 92*
**Endre,** Laszlo 1895-1946 *BiDExR*
**Endrenyi,** Janos 1927- *AmMWSc 92*
**Endrenyi,** Laszlo 1933- *AmMWSc 92*
**Endres,** Diane Elizabeth 1950- *WhoEnt 92*
**Endres,** John Carol 1946- *WhoRel 92*
**Endres,** Joseph George 1932- *AmMWSc 92*
**Endres,** Leland Sander 1936- *AmMWSc 92*
**Endres,** Paul Frank 1942- *AmMWSc 92*
**Endress,** Jay Wayne 1960- *WhoAmL 92*
**Endrezze,** Anita *DrAPF 91*
**Endris,** Glenn Edwin 1938- *WhoAmP 91*
**Endrizzi,** John Edwin 1923- *AmMWSc 92*
**Endrizzi,** Susan Marie 1947- *WhoEnt 92*
**Endsley,** Harry Barclay 1943- *WhoAmL 92*
**Endsley,** L E, Jr 1912- *AmMWSc 92*
**Endt,** Alvin Claude 1933- *WhoAmP 91*
**Endy,** Melvin Becker, Jr. 1938- *WhoRel 92*
**Endyke,** Debra Joan 1955- *WhoFI 92*
**Enea,** Vincenzo 1946- *AmMWSc 92*
**Eneguess,** Daniel Francis 1922- *WhoAmP 91*
**Enemark,** John Henry 1940- *AmMWSc 92*
**Enenstein,** Norman H 1923- *AmMWSc 92*
**Enersen,** Burnham 1905- *WhoAmL 92*
**Enesco,** Georges 1881-1955 *FacFETw*
**Enesco,** Hildegard Esper 1936- *AmMWSc 92*
**Enescu,** George 1881-1955 *NewAmDM*
**Eney,** Richard Harris 1937- *WhoFI 92*
**Enfield,** Viscount 1964- *Who 92*
**Enfield,** Carl George 1942- *AmMWSc 92*
**Enfield,** Donald Michael 1945- *WhoWest 92*
**Enfield,** Franklin D 1933- *AmMWSc 92*
**Eng,** Anne Chin 1950- *WhoFI 92*
**Eng,** Christopher Kamuela 1949- *WhoRel 92*
**Eng,** Genghmun 1951- *AmMWSc 92*
**Eng,** Lawrence F 1931- *AmMWSc 92*
**Eng,** Leslie 1941- *AmMWSc 92*
**Eng,** Robert H K 1948- *AmMWSc 92*
**Eng,** Steve *DrAPF 91*
**Eng,** Sverre T 1928- *AmMWSc 92*
**Eng-,** Tom *ConAu 133*
**Engberg,** Eric Jon 1941- *WhoEnt 92*
**Engblom,** Goran Magnus 1930- *IntWW 91*
**Engbrecht,** Michael Robert 1955- *WhoWest 92*
**Engbretson,** Gustav Alan 1943- *AmMWSc 92*
**Engbring,** Norman H 1925- *AmMWSc 92*
**Engdahl,** David Einar 1940- *WhoAmL 92*
**Engdahl,** Eric Robert 1937- *AmMWSc 92*
**Engdahl,** Lora Ann 1964- *WhoFI 92*
**Engdahl,** Per Claes Sven Edward 1909- *BiDExR*
**Engdahl,** Richard Bott 1914- *AmMWSc 92*
**Engdahl,** Sylvia 1933- *TwCSFW 91*
**Engdahl,** Sylvia L. 1933- *WrDr 92*
**Enge,** Harald Anton 1920- *AmMWSc 92*
**Engebrecht,** P.A. *DrAPF 91*
**Engebrecht,** Richard E. *WhoWest 92*
**Engebrecht,** Ronald Henry 1934- *AmMWSc 92*
**Engebretsen,** Alan C. *DrAPF 91*
**Engebretsen,** Arden Bernt *WhoFI 92*
**Engebretson,** Milton Benjamin 1920- *WhoRel 92*
**Engebrit,** Mari Jane 1938- *WhoEnt 92*
**Engebritson,** Scott J 1958- *WhoIns 92*
**Engebritson,** Scott Jay 1958- *WhoMW 92*
**Engel,** Adolph James 1929- *AmMWSc 92*
**Engel,** Albert Edward 1916- *IntWW 91*
**Engel,** Albert Edward John 1916- *AmMWSc 92*
**Engel,** Albert Joseph 1924- *WhoAmL 92, WhoMW 92*
**Engel,** Albert Joseph, III 1954- *WhoAmL 92*
**Engel,** Alfred J 1927- *AmMWSc 92*
**Engel,** Andrew G 1930- *AmMWSc 92*
**Engel,** Austin George, Jr 1928- *WhoAmP 91*
**Engel,** Bernard F. 1921- *WrDr 92*
**Engel,** Bernard Theodore 1928- *AmMWSc 92*
**Engel,** Brian K 1956- *WhoIns 92*
**Engel,** Carol Ann 1961- *WhoMW 92*
**Engel,** Charles F. 1937- *IntMPA 92*
**Engel,** Charles Robert 1922- *AmMWSc 92*
**Engel,** David Lewis 1947- *WhoAmL 92*
**Engel,** Eliot L. 1947- *AlmAP 92 [port], WhoAmP 91*
**Engel,** Eric 1925- *AmMWSc 92*
**Engel,** George Larry 1947- *WhoAmL 92*
**Engel,** George Libman 1913- *AmMWSc 92*
**Engel,** Gerald Lawrence 1942- *AmMWSc 92*
**Engel,** Howard 1931- *WrDr 92*
**Engel,** James Douglas 1947- *AmMWSc 92*
**Engel,** James Francis 1941- *AmMWSc 92*
**Engel,** Jan Marcin 1924- *AmMWSc 92*
**Engel,** Jerome, Jr 1938- *AmMWSc 92*
**Engel,** Joel S 1936- *AmMWSc 92*
**Engel,** Johannes K. 1927- *IntWW 91*
**Engel,** John Charles 1955- *WhoAmL 92*
**Engel,** John Francis 1942- *AmMWSc 92*
**Engel,** John Hal, Jr 1930- *AmMWSc 92*
**Engel,** John Jay 1941- *AmMWSc 92*
**Engel,** John Ronald 1936- *WhoRel 92*
**Engel,** Joseph H 1922- *AmMWSc 92*
**Engel,** Lawrence Bernard 1949- *WhoEnt 92*
**Engel,** Lawrence Edward 1943- *WhoIns 92*
**Engel,** Lawrence J 1929- *AmMWSc 92*
**Engel,** Lehman 1910-1982 *NewAmDM*
**Engel,** Linda Jeanne 1949- *WhoWest 92*
**Engel,** Lon 1959- *WhoAmL 92*
**Engel,** Mary 1912- *WhoEnt 92*
**Engel,** Matthew Lewis 1951- *IntAu&W 91*
**Engel,** Milton Baer 1916- *AmMWSc 92*
**Engel,** Monroe 1921- *WrDr 92*
**Engel,** Niels N 1904- *AmMWSc 92*
**Engel,** Owen Lawrence 1927- *WhoEnt 92*
**Engel,** Paul Sanford 1942- *AmMWSc 92*
**Engel,** Peter Andras 1935- *AmMWSc 92*
**Engel,** Ralph Manuel 1944- *WhoAmL 92*
**Engel,** Richard Gardner 1944- *WhoAmL 92*
**Engel,** Richard Lee 1936- *WhoAmL 92*
**Engel,** Robert David 1932- *AmMWSc 92*
**Engel,** Robert Gehrels 1932- *WhoFI 92*
**Engel,** Robert Ralph 1942- *AmMWSc 92*
**Engel,** Ronald Richard 1936- *WhoIns 92*
**Engel,** Ruben William 1912- *AmMWSc 92*
**Engel,** Rudolf 1904- *AmMWSc 92*
**Engel,** Stephen James 1952- *WhoMW 92*
**Engel,** Susan Shepard 1947- *WhoAmL 92*
**Engel,** Thomas Walter 1942- *AmMWSc 92*
**Engel,** Toby Ross 1942- *AmMWSc 92, WhoMW 92*
**Engel,** William King 1930- *AmMWSc 92*
**Engel,** William R 1930- *WhoIns 92*
**Engel-Arieli,** Susan Lee 1954- *WhoMW 92*
**Engeland,** William Charles *AmMWSc 92*
**Engelbach,** David 1946- *ConAu 133*
**Engelbach,** Florence 1872-1951 *TwCPaSc*
**Engelbart,** Douglas C 1925- *AmMWSc 92*
**Engelberg,** Joseph 1928- *AmMWSc 92*
**Engelberg,** Mort *IntMPA 92*
**Engelberger,** Joseph Frederick 1925- *AmMWSc 92*
**Engelbert,** Peter Jon Paul von 1962- *WhoAmL 92*
**Engelborghs,** Yves 1946- *AmMWSc 92*
**Engelbrecht,** David Michael 1954- *WhoRel 92*
**Engelbrecht,** R S 1926- *AmMWSc 92*
**Engelbrecht,** Robert Frank 1928- *WhoRel 92*
**Engelbrecht,** Robert Martin d1991 *NewYTBS 91*
**Engelbrecht,** Rudolf S 1928- *AmMWSc 92*
**Engelder,** Theodore Carl 1927- *AmMWSc 92*
**Engeleiter,** Susan Shannon 1952- *WhoFI 92*
**Engeler,** Gordon Frederick, Jr. 1931- *WhoAmL 92*
**Engeler,** William E 1928- *AmMWSc 92*
**Engel'gardt,** Vladimir Aleksandrovich 1894-1984 *SovUnBD*
**Engelhard,** Arthur William 1928- *AmMWSc 92*
**Engelhard,** Hans Arnold 1934- *IntWW 91*
**Engelhard,** Joseph Adolphus 1832-1879 *DcNCBi 2*
**Engelhard,** Robert J 1927- *AmMWSc 92*
**Engelhard,** Robert John 1927- *WhoAmP 91*
**Engelhard,** Victor H 1951- *AmMWSc 92*
**Engelhardt,** Albert George 1935- *AmMWSc 92, WhoWest 92*
**Engelhardt,** David M 1912- *AmMWSc 92*
**Engelhardt,** Dean Lee 1940- *AmMWSc 92*
**Engelhardt,** Donald Alfred 1921- *WhoEnt 92*
**Engelhardt,** Donald Wayne 1935- *AmMWSc 92*
**Engelhardt,** Edward Louis 1919- *AmMWSc 92*
**Engelhardt,** Helen *DrAPF 91*
**Engelhardt,** Hugo Tristram 1912- *AmMWSc 92*
**Engelhardt,** John Hugo 1946- *WhoAmL 92, WhoFI 92*
**Engelhardt,** Klaus 1932- *IntWW 91*
**Engelhardt,** M. Veronice 1912- *WrDr 92*
**Engelhardt,** Mark Robert 1961- *WhoFI 92*
**Engelhardt,** Martin Lewis 1955- *WhoFI 92*
**Engelhardt,** Thomas Alexander 1930- *ConAu 133*
**Engelhardt,** Tom *ConAu 133*
**Engelhardt,** Vaughn Arthur 1918- *AmMWSc 92*
**Engelhardt,** Vladimir Aleksandrovich 1894-1984 *SovUnBD*
**Engelhart,** Michael Steven 1953- *WhoFI 92*

**Engelhart**, Timothy Alan 1951- *WhoFI 92*
**Engelke**, Charles Edward 1930- *AmMWSc 92*
**Engelke**, John Leland 1930- *AmMWSc 92*
**Engelke**, Raymond Pierce 1938- *AmMWSc 92*
**Engelken**, Sheri J. 1956- *WhoAmL 92*
**Engelkes**, Donald J 1938- *WhoIns 92*
**Engelkes**, James Richard 1942- *WhoMW 92*
**Engelking**, Ellen Melinda 1942- *WhoFI 92, WhoMW 92*
**Engelking**, Paul Craig 1948- *AmMWSc 92, WhoWest 92*
**Engell**, Hans 1948- *IntWW 91*
**Engell**, James 1951- *ConAu 135*
**Engellant**, Kenneth Hans 1940- *WhoWest 92*
**Engelman**, Arthur 1930- *AmMWSc 92*
**Engelman**, Donald J. 1951- *WhoFI 92*
**Engelman**, Donald Max 1941- *AmMWSc 92*
**Engelmann**, Bernt J. 1921- *IntWW 91*
**Engelmann**, Franz 1928- *AmMWSc 92*
**Engelmann**, George 1809-1884 *BiInAmS*
**Engelmann**, George Julius 1847-1903 *BiInAmS*
**Engelmann**, Henry 1831-1899 *BiInAmS*
**Engelmann**, Manfred David 1930- *AmMWSc 92*
**Engelmann**, Reinhart Wolfgang H 1934- *AmMWSc 92*
**Engelmann**, Richard H 1923- *AmMWSc 92*
**Engels**, John *DrAPF 91*
**Engels**, John 1931- *ConPo 91, IntAu&W 91, WrDr 92*
**Engels**, Patricia Louise 1926- *WhoAmL 92*
**Engels**, Thomas Joseph 1958- *WhoMW 92*
**Engelsman**, Joan Chamberlain *WhoRel 92*
**Engelson**, Erik Turner 1959- *WhoFI 92, WhoWest 92*
**Engelson**, George Joseph 1921- *WhoEnt 92*
**Engelson**, Richard Jay 1936- *WhoMW 92*
**Engelstad**, Orvis P 1928- *AmMWSc 92*
**Engelstad**, Roxann Louise 1954- *AmMWSc 92*
**Engemann**, Joseph George 1928- *AmMWSc 92*
**Engen**, David Paul 1949- *WhoMW 92*
**Engen**, Donald Davenport 1924- *WhoAmP 91*
**Engen**, Glenn Forrest 1925- *AmMWSc 92*
**Engen**, Ivar A 1932- *AmMWSc 92*
**Engen**, Lee Emerson 1921- *WhoFI 92*
**Engen**, Rene Leopold Alexis 1918- *IntWW 91*
**Engen**, Richard Lee 1932- *AmMWSc 92*
**Enger**, Carl Christian 1929- *AmMWSc 92*
**Enger**, Merlin Duane 1937- *AmMWSc 92*
**Engerman**, Ronald Lester 1929- *AmMWSc 92*
**Engerman**, Stanley Lewis 1936- *WhoFI 92*
**Engerrand**, Kenneth G. 1952- *WhoAmL 92*
**Engert**, Martin 1938- *AmMWSc 92*
**Engeset**, Jetmund 1938- *Who 92*
**Enget**, June Y 1930- *WhoAmP 91*
**Enggaard**, Knud 1929- *IntWW 91*
**Engh**, Helmer A, Jr 1935- *AmMWSc 92*
**Engh**, M J 1933- *TwCSFW 91*
**Engheta**, Nader 1955- *AmMWSc 92*
**Engholm**, Bjorn 1939- *IntWW 91*
**Engholm**, Charles Rudy 1951- *WhoAmL 92*
**Engibous**, James Charles 1923- *AmMWSc 92*
**Engin**, Ali Erkan 1943- *AmMWSc 92*
**Engl**, Walter L. 1926- *IntWW 91*
**England**, Alan Coulter 1932- *AmMWSc 92*
**England**, Anthony W 1942- *AmMWSc 92*
**England**, Arthur Jay, Jr. 1932- *WhoAmL 92*
**England**, Barbara Lee 1943- *WhoRel 92*
**England**, Barry 1934- *WrDr 92*
**England**, Barry Grant 1940- *AmMWSc 92*
**England**, Bob Lyle 1946- *WhoRel 92*
**England**, David Charles 1922- *AmMWSc 92*
**England**, Elyse Haidak 1942- *WhoEnt 92*
**England**, Forrest William 1912- *WhoMW 92*
**England**, Frank Raymond Wilton 1911- *Who 92*
**England**, George Allan 1877-1936 *ScFEYrs, TwCSFW 91*
**England**, Gerald Ernest 1949- *WhoEnt 92*
**England**, Glyn 1921- *IntWW 91, Who 92*
**England**, James Donald 1937- *AmMWSc 92*
**England**, James Walton 1938- *AmMWSc 92*
**England**, John 1786-1842 *DcAmImH*
**England**, John Melvin 1932- *WhoAmL 92*
**England**, Joseph Walker 1940- *WhoFI 92*
**England**, Lynne Lipton 1949- *WhoAmL 92*
**England**, Norman *WrDr 92*
**England**, Richard Jay 1926- *AmMWSc 92*
**England**, Robert Eugene 1941- *WhoRel 92*
**England**, Robert Walter 1928- *WhoRel 92*
**England**, Rodney Wayne 1932- *WhoBlA 92*
**England**, Sandra J 1949- *AmMWSc 92*
**England**, Sharon E. 1939- *WhoWest 92*
**England**, Stephen James 1951- *WhoAmL 92*
**England**, Talmadge Ray 1929- *AmMWSc 92*
**England**, Walter Bernard 1942- *AmMWSc 92*
**Englande**, Andrew Joseph 1944- *AmMWSc 92*
**Englander**, Harold Robert 1923- *AmMWSc 92*
**Englander**, Lester 1911- *WhoEnt 92*
**Englander**, Morris K *IntMPA 92*
**Englander**, Roger *LesBEnT 92*
**Englander**, Roger Leslie 1926- *WhoEnt 92*
**Englander**, Sol Walter 1930- *AmMWSc 92*
**Englar**, John David 1947- *WhoAmL 92*
**Englard**, Sasha 1929- *AmMWSc 92*
**Engle**, Barbara L 1945- *WhoAmP 91*
**Engle**, Benjamin J. 1941- *WhoWest 92*
**Engle**, Betty Jean 1925- *WhoAmL 92*
**Engle**, Damon Lawson 1919- *AmMWSc 92*
**Engle**, David Elbert 1942- *WhoRel 92*
**Engle**, Donald Edward 1927- *WhoFI 92*
**Engle**, Ed, Jr. *DrAPF 91*
**Engle**, Eloise 1923- *WrDr 92*
**Engle**, Gail 1944- *WhoEnt 92*
**Engle**, George 1926- *Who 92*
**Engle**, Harrison 1940- *WhoEnt 92*
**Engle**, Howard Vernon, Jr. 1927- *WhoMW 92*
**Engle**, Irene May *AmMWSc 92*
**Engle**, James Bruce 1919- *WhoAmP 91*
**Engle**, James Wayne 1951- *WhoMW 92*
**Engle**, Jessie Ann 1918- *AmMWSc 92*
**Engle**, John D., Jr. *DrAPF 91*
**Engle**, John Franklin 1921- *AmMWSc 92*
**Engle**, Kenneth William 1937- *WhoWest 92*
**Engle**, Mary Allen English 1922- *AmMWSc 92*
**Engle**, Michael Jean *AmMWSc 92*
**Engle**, Paul *DrAPF 91*
**Engle**, Paul 1908- *ConPo 91, FacFETw, IntAu&W 91*
**Engle**, Paul 1908-1991 *BenetAL 91, ConAu 134, CurBio 91N, NewYTBS 91 [port]*
**Engle**, Paul Randal 1919- *AmMWSc 92*
**Engle**, Phillip Raymond 1940- *WhoWest 92*
**Engle**, Ralph Landis, Jr 1920- *AmMWSc 92*
**Engle**, Ray 1934- *WhoWest 92*
**Engle**, Richard Carlyle 1934- *WhoFI 92, WhoMW 92*
**Engle**, Robert Irwin 1945- *WhoWest 92*
**Engle**, Robert Rufus 1930- *AmMWSc 92*
**Engle**, Thelburn L. 1901- *WrDr 92*
**Engle**, Thelburn LaRoy 1901- *WhoMW 92*
**Engle**, Thomas William 1951- *AmMWSc 92*
**Engle**, William Bruce 1950- *WhoMW 92*
**Engle**, William Thomas, Jr. 1957- *WhoAmL 92*
**Engle-Paananen**, Eloise 1923- *IntAu&W 91*
**Englebach**, George 1941- *WhoAmP 91*
**Englefield**, Dermot John Tryal 1927- *Who 92*
**Englehardt**, Elaine Eliason 1953- *WhoWest 92*
**Englehart**, Bob *ConAu 133*
**Englehart**, Edwin Thomas, Jr 1921- *AmMWSc 92*
**Englehart**, Richard W 1938- *AmMWSc 92*
**Englehart**, Robert, Jr. 1945- *ConAu 133*
**Englehart**, Robert Michael 1943- *Who 92*
**Engleman**, Christian L *AmMWSc 92*
**Engleman**, Ephraim Philip 1911- *AmMWSc 92*
**Engleman**, Finis E. 1895-1978 *ConAu 134*
**Engleman**, Karl 1933- *AmMWSc 92*
**Engleman**, Rolf, Jr 1934- *AmMWSc 92*
**Engleman**, Victor Solomon 1940- *AmMWSc 92*
**Engler**, Arnold 1927- *AmMWSc 92*
**Engler**, Cady Roy 1947- *AmMWSc 92*
**Engler**, Colleen House 1952- *WhoAmP 91*
**Engler**, Edmund Arthur 1856-1918 *BiInAmS*
**Engler**, Edward Martin 1947- *AmMWSc 92*
**Engler**, Harold S 1923- *AmMWSc 92*
**Engler**, Heinrich Gustav Adolf 1844-1930 *FacFETw*
**Engler**, Henry Julius, Jr 1916- *WhoAmP 91*
**Engler**, J. Curtis 1947- *WhoFI 92*
**Engler**, John M. 1948- *AlmAP 92 [port], WhoAmP 91*
**Engler**, John Mathias 1948- *WhoMW 92*
**Engler**, Marguerite M. *WhoWest 92*
**Engler**, Mary B. *WhoWest 92*
**Engler**, Reto Arnold 1931- *AmMWSc 92*
**Engler**, Thomas Albert 1954- *WhoMW 92*
**Englert**, Dennis M. 1938- *WhoAmL 92*
**Englert**, Du Wayne Cleveland 1932- *AmMWSc 92*
**Englert**, Edwin, Jr 1926- *AmMWSc 92*
**Englert**, James O. 1952- *WhoMW 92, WhoRel 92*
**Englert**, Mary Elizabeth 1901- *AmMWSc 92*
**Englert**, Robert D 1920- *AmMWSc 92*
**Englert**, Roy Theodore 1922- *WhoAmL 92*
**Englert**, Roy Theodore, Jr. 1958- *WhoAmL 92*
**Engles**, David 1946- *WhoIns 92*
**Engles**, David Charles 1924- *WhoFI 92*
**Engles**, John L., Jr. 1937- *WhoFI 92*
**Englesbe**, Andrew Joseph 1950- *WhoIns 92*
**Englesberg**, Ellis 1921- *AmMWSc 92*
**Englesmith**, Tejas 1941- *WhoEnt 92*
**Engley**, Frank B, Jr 1919- *AmMWSc 92*
**English**, Alan Dale 1947- *AmMWSc 92*
**English**, Alan Taylor 1934- *AmMWSc 92*
**English**, Albert J. 1967- *WhoBlA 92*
**English**, Alex 1954- *WhoBlA 92*
**English**, Arthur William 1945- *AmMWSc 92*
**English**, Barbara 1933- *WrDr 92*
**English**, Barbara Jane 1955- *WhoAmL 92*
**English**, Beno Lee, Jr. 1937- *WhoFI 92, WhoWest 92*
**English**, Bill *WhoAmP 91*
**English**, Bill 1930- *WhoAmP 91*
**English**, Brenda H. *WrDr 92*
**English**, Bruce Vaughan 1921- *AmMWSc 92*
**English**, Charles Royal 1938- *WhoAmL 92*
**English**, Clarence R. 1915- *WhoBlA 92*
**English**, Clifford, Jr 1940- *WhoIns 92*
**English**, Cyril 1913- *Who 92*
**English**, Cyril 1923- *Who 92*
**English**, Darrel Starr 1936- *AmMWSc 92*
**English**, David 1931- *IntAu&W 91, IntWW 91, Who 92*
**English**, David Floyd 1948- *WhoAmL 92*
**English**, Deborah *WhoBlA 92*
**English**, Donald 1930- *Who 92*
**English**, Donald Marvin 1951- *WhoWest 92*
**English**, Elizabeth Ann 1962- *WhoEnt 92*
**English**, Ellen Darlene 1952- *WhoAmL 92, WhoEnt 92, WhoMW 92*
**English**, Floyd L 1934- *AmMWSc 92*
**English**, Floyd Leroy 1934- *WhoMW 92*
**English**, Gerald 1925- *Who 92*
**English**, Gerald Alan 1946- *AmMWSc 92*
**English**, Gerald Marion 1931- *WhoWest 92*
**English**, Glenn 1940- *AlmAP 92 [port], WhoAmP 91*
**English**, Grace 1891-1956 *TwCPaSc*
**English**, H. Elwood 1945- *WhoWest 92*
**English**, Henry L. 1942- *WhoBlA 92*
**English**, Isobel 1925- *ConNov 91, IntAu&W 91, WrDr 92*
**English**, Jackson Pollard 1915- *AmMWSc 92*
**English**, James David 1941- *WhoAmL 92*
**English**, James P. 1930- *WhoFI 92*
**English**, Jerry Bruce 1942- *WhoRel 92*
**English**, Jerry Fitzgerald 1934- *WhoAmP 91*
**English**, John Cammel 1934- *WhoMW 92, WhoRel 92*
**English**, John Douglas 1947- *WhoFI 92*
**English**, Joseph Louise *WhoRel 92*
**English**, Joseph T 1933- *AmMWSc 92*
**English**, Joseph Thomas 1933- *IntWW 91*
**English**, Karan 1939- *WhoAmP 91*
**English**, Kenneth 1947- *WhoBlA 92*
**English**, Lawrence William 1942- *WhoFI 92*
**English**, Leigh Howard 1955- *AmMWSc 92*
**English**, Leonard Stanley 1937- *AmMWSc 92*
**English**, Marion S. 1912- *WhoBlA 92*
**English**, Michael 1930- *Who 92*
**English**, Michael Charles 1959- *WhoEnt 92*
**English**, Molly Hyde 1954- *WhoFI 92*
**English**, Perry T., Jr. 1933- *WhoBlA 92*
**English**, Philip Sheridan 1956- *WhoAmP 91*
**English**, Richard *TwCSFW 91*
**English**, Richard A. 1936- *WhoBlA 92*
**English**, Robert E 1953- *AmMWSc 92*
**English**, Sally Ann 1946- *WhoFI 92*
**English**, Stanley 1908- *TwCPaSc*
**English**, Stephen Raymond 1946- *WhoAmL 92*
**English**, Terence 1932- *Who 92*
**English**, Terence Alexander Hawthorne 1932- *IntWW 91*
**English**, Terence Michael 1944- *Who 92*
**English**, Thomas Dunn 1819-1902 *BenetAL 91*
**English**, Thomas James 1942- *WhoFI 92, WhoMW 92*
**English**, Thomas Saunders 1928- *AmMWSc 92*
**English**, Vickie Anne 1959- *WhoRel 92*
**English**, Whittie 1917- *WhoBlA 92*
**English**, William Berkeley 1960- *WhoFI 92*
**English**, William E. 1934- *WhoBlA 92*
**English**, William Harley 1911- *AmMWSc 92*
**English**, William Joseph 1941- *AmMWSc 92*
**English**, William Kirk 1929- *AmMWSc 92*
**Englund**, Charles R 1936- *AmMWSc 92*
**Englund**, Einar 1916- *ConCom 92*
**Englund**, Gage Bush 1931- *WhoEnt 92*
**Englund**, George H. 1926- *IntMPA 92*
**Englund**, Gregory Joseph 1956- *WhoAmL 92*
**Englund**, John Arthur 1926- *AmMWSc 92*
**Englund**, John Caldwell 1952- *AmMWSc 92*
**Englund**, Ken 1914- *IntMPA 92*
**Englund**, Paul Theodore 1938- *AmMWSc 92*
**Englund**, Richard d1991 *NewYTBS 91 [port]*
**Englund**, Richard 1932?-1991 *News 91, -91-3*
**Englund**, Robert 1949- *IntMPA 92*
**Engman**, John *DrAPF 91*
**Engman**, Lewis August 1936- *IntWW 91, WhoAmL 92*
**Engo**, Paul Bamela 1931- *IntWW 91*
**Engolio**, Edward Nathaniel 1921- *WhoAmL 92*
**Engoron**, Edward David 1946- *WhoWest 92*
**Engram**, Beverly *WhoAmP 91*
**Engram**, Jonathan Mark 1957- *WhoAmL 92*
**Engs**, Robert Francis 1943- *WhoBlA 92*
**Engseth**, William 1933- *IntWW 91*
**Engster**, Henry Martin 1949- *AmMWSc 92*
**Engstrom**, Daniel Edward 1958- *WhoEnt 92*
**Engstrom**, Donald James 1948- *WhoWest 92*
**Engstrom**, Elizabeth *DrAPF 91*
**Engstrom**, Herbert Leonard 1941- *AmMWSc 92*
**Engstrom**, John Eric 1943- *WhoMW 92*
**Engstrom**, Lee Edward 1941- *AmMWSc 92*
**Engstrom**, Norman Ardell 1945- *AmMWSc 92*
**Engstrom**, Odd 1941- *IntWW 91*
**Engstrom**, Ralph Warren 1914- *AmMWSc 92*
**Engstrom**, Theodore Wilhelm 1916- *WhoRel 92*
**Engum**, Eric Stanley 1949- *WhoAmL 92*
**Engvall**, Eva Susanna 1940- *AmMWSc 92*
**Engvalson**, Kinley Irving 1956- *WhoAmL 92*
**Engvold**, Oddbjorn 1938- *IntWW 91*
**Enheduanna** *EncAmaz 91*
**Enhorning**, Constance Elisabet 1945- *WhoEnt 92*
**Enick**, Robert M 1958- *AmMWSc 92*
**Enis**, Thomas Joseph 1937- *WhoAmL 92*
**Enju** *EncAmaz 91*
**Enke**, Christie George 1933- *AmMWSc 92*
**Enke**, Glenn L 1909- *AmMWSc 92*
**Enkelmann**, Larry Karl 1951- *WhoMW 92*
**Enloe**, Jeff H, Jr 1914- *WhoAmP 91*
**Enloe**, Louis Henry 1933- *AmMWSc 92*
**Enlow**, Donald Hugh 1927- *AmMWSc 92*
**Enman**, Thomas *WhoEnt 92*
**Enna**, Salvatore Joseph 1944- *AmMWSc 92*
**Ennals** *Who 92*
**Ennals**, Baron 1922- *IntWW 91, Who 92*
**Ennals**, Kenneth Frederick John 1932- *Who 92*
**Ennals**, Martin d1991 *NewYTBS 91 [port]*
**Ennals**, Martin 1927- *Who 92*
**Enneking**, Eugene A 1940- *AmMWSc 92*
**Enneking**, Marjorie 1941- *AmMWSc 92*
**Enneking**, William Fisher 1926- *AmMWSc 92*
**Ennen**, Edith 1907- *IntWW 91*
**Ennenga**, Kirk Castle 1964- *WhoRel 92*
**Ennes**, James M, Jr. 1933- *ConAu 34NR*
**Ennever**, John Joseph 1920- *AmMWSc 92*
**Ennis**, Billie Michael 1959- *WhoEnt 92*
**Ennis**, Bruce C 1939- *WhoAmP 91*
**Ennis**, Bruce Clifford 1941- *WhoAmL 92*
**Ennis**, C. Brady 1954- *WhoWest 92*
**Ennis**, David H 1940- *WhoAmP 91*
**Ennis**, Dwayne Edwin 1940- *WhoFI 92*
**Ennis**, Edgar William, Jr. 1945- *WhoAmL 92*
**Ennis**, Ella Gray Wilson 1925- *AmMWSc 92*

**Ennis,** Francis A *AmMWSc 92*
**Ennis,** Herbert Leo 1932- *AmMWSc 92*
**Ennis,** Jacob d1890? *BiInAmS*
**Ennis,** James Guise 1947- *WhoAmL 92*
**Ennis,** Robert D *TwCSFW 91*
**Ennis,** Stephen Eugene 1933- *WhoRel 92*
**Ennis,** Thomas Michael 1931- *WhoFI 92, WhoWest 92*
**Enniskillen,** Earl of 1942- *Who 92*
**Ennismore,** Viscount 1964- *Who 92*
**Enniss,** Pinckney C. 1931- *WhoRel 92*
**Ennist,** David L 1957- *AmMWSc 92*
**Ennix,** Coyness Loyal, Jr. 1942- *WhoBlA 92*
**Ennodius** 473?-521 *EncEarC*
**Ennor,** Kenneth Stafford 1933- *AmMWSc 92*
**Enns,** Ernest Gerhard 1940- *AmMWSc 92*
**Enns,** John Hermann 1907- *AmMWSc 92*
**Enns,** Kevin Scott 1959- *WhoMW 92*
**Enns,** Mark K *AmMWSc 92*
**Enns,** Richard Harvey 1938- *AmMWSc 92*
**Enns,** Wilbur Ronald 1913- *AmMWSc 92*
**Eno,** Brian 1948- *NewAmDM, WhoEnt 92*
**Eno,** Charles Franklin 1920- *AmMWSc 92*
**Eno,** Larry E 1969- *WhoAmP 91*
**Eno,** Robert Bryan 1936- *WhoRel 92*
**Eno,** Zellma Anita 1919- *WhoRel 92*
**Enoch,** David William 1924- *WhoAmL 92*
**Enoch,** Hollace J. 1950- *WhoBlA 92*
**Enoch,** Jacob 1927- *AmMWSc 92*
**Enoch,** Jay Martin 1929- *AmMWSc 92*
**Enochs,** Edgar Earle 1932- *AmMWSc 92*
**Enos,** Joseph Clive, III 1942- *WhoEnt 92*
**Enos,** Paul 1934- *AmMWSc 92*
**Enos,** Paul R 1931- *WhoIns 92*
**Enos,** Ralph Gregory 1952- *WhoRel 92*
**Enos,** William 1955- *WhoAmP 91*
**Enouen,** William Albert 1928- *WhoFI 92*
**Enquist,** Irving Fritiof 1920- *AmMWSc 92*
**Enquist,** Lynn William 1945- *AmMWSc 92*
**Enrici,** Domenico 1909- *Who 92*
**Enrietto,** Joseph Francis 1931- *AmMWSc 92*
**Enright,** Cynthia Lee 1950- *WhoWest 92*
**Enright,** D. J. 1920- *ConPo 91, LiExTwC, WrDr 92*
**Enright,** Dennis Joseph 1920- *IntAu&W 91, IntWW 91, Who 92*
**Enright,** Derek Anthony 1935- *Who 92*
**Enright,** Edward Joseph 1947- *WhoRel 92*
**Enright,** James Thomas 1932- *AmMWSc 92*
**Enright,** Juanita 1911- *WhoHisp 92*
**Enright,** Michael Robert 1956- *WhoAmL 92*
**Enright,** Michael Stanley 1960- *WhoFI 92*
**Enright,** Stephanie Veselich 1929- *WhoFI 92, WhoWest 92*
**Enright,** William Benner 1925- *WhoAmL 92*
**Enright,** William Gerald 1935- *WhoRel 92*
**Enrile,** Juan Ponce *IntWW 91*
**Enrique Y Tarancon,** Vicente 1907- *IntWW 91, WhoRel 92*
**Enriques,** Terence Bill 1955- *WhoFI 92*
**Enriquez,** Diana 1963- *WhoRel 92*
**Enriquez,** Francisco Javier 1955- *WhoWest 92*
**Enriquez,** Jaime 1958- *WhoHisp 92*
**Enriquez,** Manuel 1926- *NewAmDM*
**Enriquez,** Oscar 1963- *WhoHisp 92*
**Enriquez de Ribera,** Payo 1612-1685 *HisDSpE*
**Enriquez-Dougherty,** Suzanne Provencio 1959- *WhoHisp 92*
**Enriquez-Salazar,** Manuel 1926- *NewAmDM*
**Enriquez Savignac,** Antonio 1931- *IntWW 91*
**Enroth,** Tess *DrAPF 91*
**Enroth-Cugell,** Christina 1919- *AmMWSc 92*
**Ens,** E Werner 1956- *AmMWSc 92*
**Ensenat,** Donald Burnham 1946- *WhoAmP 91*
**Ensenat,** Teresa 1960- *WhoEnt 92*
**Ensign,** David James 1950- *WhoAmL 92*
**Ensign,** Georgianne Carol 1940- *WhoEnt 92*
**Ensign,** Paul Roselle 1906- *AmMWSc 92*
**Ensign,** Richard Papworth 1919- *WhoWest 92*
**Ensign,** Ronald D 1922- *AmMWSc 92*
**Ensign,** Stewart Ellery 1925- *AmMWSc 92*
**Ensign,** Thomas Charles 1941- *AmMWSc 92*
**Ensinck,** John William 1931- *AmMWSc 92*
**Enslen,** David McKay 1925- *WhoAmL 92*
**Enslen,** Richard Alan 1931- *WhoAmL 92*
**Ensley,** George H 1927- *WhoIns 92*
**Ensley,** Georgeanna 1952- *WhoMW 92*
**Ensley,** Harry Eugene 1945- *AmMWSc 92*
**Ensley,** Rodney Gene 1934- *WhoIns 92*
**Enslin,** Morton S. 1897-1980 *ConAu 134*
**Enslin,** Theodore *DrAPF 91*
**Enslin,** Theodore 1925- *ConPo 91, WrDr 92*
**Enslow,** Mary Bernice 1957- *WhoRel 92*
**Ensminger,** Aldie *WhoAmP 91*
**Ensminger,** Dale 1923- *AmMWSc 92, WhoMW 92*
**Ensminger,** John C 1934- *WhoAmP 91*
**Ensminger,** Leonard Elroy 1912- *AmMWSc 92*
**Ensminger,** Mark Douglas 1955- *WhoWest 92*
**Ensom,** Donald 1926- *Who 92*
**Ensor,** David 1906- *IntAu&W 91*
**Ensor,** David 1924- *Who 92*
**Ensor,** David Samuel 1941- *AmMWSc 92*
**Ensor,** Gary Albert 1956- *WhoAmL 92*
**Ensor,** George Anthony 1936- *Who 92*
**Ensor,** Michael de Normann 1919- *Who 92*
**Ensor,** Phyllis Gail 1938- *AmMWSc 92*
**Ensor Walters,** P. H. B. *Who 92*
**Ensrud,** Earl Richard 1926- *WhoMW 92*
**Ensslin,** Norbert 1944- *AmMWSc 92*
**Enstine,** Raymond Wilton, Jr. 1946- *WhoFI 92*
**Enstrom,** James Eugene 1943- *AmMWSc 92, WhoWest 92*
**Enstrom,** Ronald Edward 1935- *AmMWSc 92*
**Ensworth,** Marvin D 1934- *WhoAmP 91*
**Entekhabi,** Dara 1961- *AmMWSc 92*
**Enters,** Angna 1907- *BenetAL 91*
**Enters,** David Thomas 1955- *WhoMW 92*
**Entin,** Jonathan Lowe 1947- *WhoAmL 92*
**Entin,** Martin A 1912- *AmMWSc 92*
**Entman,** Barbara Sue 1954- *WhoEnt 92*
**Entman,** Mark Lawrence 1938- *AmMWSc 92*
**Entov,** Revold M. 1931- *IntWW 91*
**Entratter,** Corinne 1937- *WhoEnt 92*
**Entrekin,** Charles *DrAPF 91*
**Entrekin,** Durward Neal 1926- *AmMWSc 92*
**Entremont,** Philippe 1934- *IntWW 91, NewAmDM, WhoEnt 92*
**Entriken,** Robert Kersey 1913- *WhoWest 92*
**Entriken,** Robert Kersey, Jr. 1941- *WhoMW 92*
**Entringer,** Robert Rufus 1938- *WhoAmP 91*
**Entringer,** Roger Charles 1931- *AmMWSc 92*
**Entsminger,** Raymond David 1951- *WhoMW 92*
**Entus,** Kerri Lee 1963- *WhoFI 92*
**Entwisle,** Eric Arthur 1900- *WrDr 92*
**Entwistle,** Andrew John 1959- *WhoAmL 92*
**Entwistle,** James Tobit 1944- *WhoIns 92*
**Entwistle,** John Nuttall Maxwell 1910- *Who 92*
**Entwistle,** Kenneth Mercer 1925- *Who 92*
**Entz,** Lewis H 1931- *WhoAmP 91*
**Entzminger,** John N 1936- *AmMWSc 92*
**Enukidze,** Guram Nikolayevich *IntWW 91*
**Envall,** Bjorn 1942- *DcTwDes*
**Enver Bey** 1881-1922 *FacFETw*
**Enwonu,** Benedict Chuka 1921- *IntWW 91*
**Eny,** Desire M 1915- *AmMWSc 92*
**Enya** 1962?- *ConMus 6 [port]*
**Enyart,** William L. 1949- *WhoAmL 92*
**Enyeart,** James L 1943- *IntAu&W 91, WrDr 92*
**Enz,** John Walter *AmMWSc 92*
**Enzenberger,** Hans Magnus 1929- *LiExTwC*
**Enzensberger,** Hans Magnus 1929- *IntWW 91*
**Enzer,** Norbert Beverley 1930- *AmMWSc 92*
**Enzi,** Michael B 1944- *WhoAmP 91*
**Enzinger,** Franz Michael 1923- *AmMWSc 92*
**Enzmann,** Robert D 1930- *AmMWSc 92*
**Eoff,** Kay M 1932- *AmMWSc 92*
**Eoff,** W S 1920- *WhoAmP 91*
**Eoff Grindstaff,** Thelma Louise 1925- *WhoAmP 91*
**Eoll,** John Gordon 1943- *AmMWSc 92*
**Eorsi,** Gyula 1922- *IntWW 91*
**Eotvos,** Peter *Who 92*
**Eotvos,** Peter 1944- *IntWW 91*
**Epand,** Richard Mayer 1937- *AmMWSc 92*
**Epcar,** Richard Michael 1955- *WhoWest 92*
**Epel,** David 1937- *AmMWSc 92*
**Epernay,** Mark *ConAu 34NR*
**Eperon,** Alastair David Peter 1949- *IntWW 91*
**Epes,** Travis F. 1936- *WhoAmL 92*
**Ephraem The Syrian** 306?-373 *EncEarC*
**Ephraim,** Charlesworth W. 1942- *WhoBlA 92*
**Ephraim,** Donald Morley 1932- *WhoEnt 92*
**Ephraim,** Lionel Arthur 1930- *WhoEnt 92*
**Ephram,** George 1934- *IntWW 91*
**Ephraums,** Roderick Jarvis 1927- *Who 92*
**Ephremides,** Anthony 1943- *AmMWSc 92*
**Ephron,** Delia 1944- *SmATA 65 [port], WrDr 92*
**Ephron,** Nora 1941- *IntWW 91, WhoEnt 92*
**Ephrussi,** Charles 1845-1905 *ThHEIm*
**Epifanio,** Charles Edward 1944- *AmMWSc 92*
**Epigonus** *EncEarC*
**Epinay,** Louise-Florence d'Esclavelles d' 1726-1783 *BlkwCEP*
**Epiphanes** *EncEarC*
**Epiphanius of Salamis** 315?-403 *EncEarC*
**Epler,** James L 1937- *AmMWSc 92*
**Epler,** Jerry L *WhoIns 92*
**Epley,** Marion Jay 1907- *WhoAmL 92*
**Epley,** Marion Jay, III 1937- *WhoAmL 92*
**Epley,** Richard Jess 1942- *AmMWSc 92*
**Epley-Shuck,** Barbara Jeanne 1936- *WhoRel 92*
**Epling,** Gary Arnold 1945- *AmMWSc 92*
**Eposito,** Theresa Harlow 1930- *WhoAmP 91*
**Epp,** Arthur Jacob 1939- *WhoFI 92*
**Epp,** Chirold Delain 1939- *AmMWSc 92*
**Epp,** Donald James 1939- *AmMWSc 92*
**Epp,** Edward Rudolph 1929- *AmMWSc 92*
**Epp,** Eldon Jay 1930- *WhoMW 92, WhoRel 92, WrDr 92*
**Epp,** Franz Xaver, Ritter von 1868-1946 *EncTR 91 [port]*
**Epp,** Franz Xavier, Ritter von 1868-1947 *BiDExR*
**Epp,** Jake 1939- *IntWW 91*
**Epp,** Leonard G 1944- *AmMWSc 92*
**Epp,** Margaret Agnes 1913- *IntAu&W 91, WrDr 92*
**Epp,** Mary Elizabeth 1941- *WhoFI 92, WhoMW 92*
**Epp,** Melvin David 1942- *AmMWSc 92*
**Eppenger,** John Arthur 1948- *WhoRel 92*
**Eppenstein,** Walter 1920- *AmMWSc 92*
**Epperley,** Linda Ann 1960- *WhoAmL 92*
**Epperly,** W Robert 1935- *AmMWSc 92*
**Eppers,** William C 1930- *AmMWSc 92*
**Epperson,** Barbara 1921- *WhoRel 92*
**Epperson,** David E. 1935- *WhoBlA 92*
**Epperson,** David Marcus 1962- *WhoAmL 92*
**Epperson,** Edward Roy 1932- *AmMWSc 92*
**Epperson,** Eleanor Louise 1916- *WhoWest 92*
**Epperson,** Eric Robert 1949- *WhoFI 92, WhoWest 92*
**Epperson,** Jay Barry, Jr. 1962- *WhoWest 92*
**Epperson,** Kraettli Quynton 1949- *WhoAmL 92*
**Epperson,** Ozell Marie 1931- *WhoMW 92*
**Epperson,** Vaughn Elmo 1917- *WhoFI 92, WhoWest 92*
**Epperson,** Wallace Wilkins, Jr. 1948- *WhoFI 92*
**Eppert,** James Frederic 1939- *WhoMW 92*
**Eppia** *EncAmaz 91*
**Eppink,** Jeffrey Francis 1955- *WhoWest 92*
**Eppink,** Richard Theodore 1931- *AmMWSc 92*
**Epple,** Anne Orth 1927- *WrDr 92*
**Epple,** Bob *WhoAmP 91*
**Epple,** Kat 1952- *WhoEnt 92*
**Eppler,** Jerry Mack 1939- *WhoFI 92, WhoWest 92*
**Eppler,** Richard A 1934- *AmMWSc 92*
**Eppley,** Richard Wayne 1931- *AmMWSc 92*
**Eppley,** Roland Raymond, Jr. 1932- *WhoFI 92*
**Eppolito,** Anthony Peter 1953- *WhoAmL 92*
**Epprecht,** Russell *DrAPF 91*
**Eppright,** Margaret 1913- *AmMWSc 92*
**Epps,** A. Glenn 1929- *WhoBlA 92*
**Epps,** Anna Cherrie 1930- *AmMWSc 92, WhoBlA 92*
**Epps,** C. Roy 1941- *WhoBlA 92*
**Epps,** Charles Harry, Jr. 1930- *WhoBlA 92*
**Epps,** Constance Arnettres 1950- *WhoBlA 92*
**Epps,** Dolzie C. B. 1907- *WhoBlA 92*
**Epps,** Edgar G. 1929- *WhoBlA 92*
**Epps,** Garrett *DrAPF 91*
**Epps,** George Allen, Jr. 1940- *WhoBlA 92*
**Epps,** Harland Warren 1936- *AmMWSc 92*
**Epps,** Jack, Jr. 1949- *ConAu 133*
**Epps,** James Haws, III 1936- *WhoAmL 92*
**Epps,** James Vernon 1928- *WhoIns 92*
**Epps,** Jon Albert 1942- *AmMWSc 92*
**Epps,** Lawrence Edward 1957- *WhoAmP 91*
**Epps,** Mary Ellen 1934- *WhoAmP 91*
**Epps,** Naomi Newby 1909- *WhoBlA 92*
**Epps,** Phillip Earl 1958- *WhoBlA 92*
**Epps,** Preston H. 1888-1982 *ConAu 133*
**Epps,** Roselyn Payne *WhoBlA 92*
**Epps,** William David 1951- *WhoRel 92*
**Epps,** William Monroe 1916- *AmMWSc 92*
**Eppstein,** Deborah Anne 1948- *AmMWSc 92*
**Epremian,** E 1921- *AmMWSc 92*
**Epstein,** Alan Bruce 1944- *WhoAmL 92*
**Epstein,** Alan Neil 1932- *AmMWSc 92*
**Epstein,** Alexander Maxim 1963- *WhoWest 92*
**Epstein,** Alvin 1925- *ConTFT 9*
**Epstein,** Anthony 1921- *Who 92*
**Epstein,** Arthur Joseph 1945- *AmMWSc 92, WhoMW 92*
**Epstein,** Arthur William 1923- *AmMWSc 92*
**Epstein,** Aubrey 1922- *AmMWSc 92*
**Epstein,** Barry D 1942- *AmMWSc 92*
**Epstein,** Bernard 1920- *AmMWSc 92*
**Epstein,** Beryl 1910- *ChILR 26 [port]*
**Epstein,** Charles Joseph 1933- *AmMWSc 92*
**Epstein,** Charlotte 1921- *IntAu&W 91, WrDr 92*
**Epstein,** Cynthia Fuchs 1933- *WrDr 92*
**Epstein,** Daniel Mark *DrAPF 91*
**Epstein,** David Gustav 1943- *WhoAmL 92*
**Epstein,** David L 1944- *AmMWSc 92*
**Epstein,** David Lee 1947- *WhoFI 92*
**Epstein,** David Mayer 1930- *WhoEnt 92*
**Epstein,** Donald Robert 1945- *WhoAmL 92*
**Epstein,** Edna Selan 1938- *WhoAmP 91, WhoMW 92*
**Epstein,** Edward Joseph 1920- *WhoFI 92*
**Epstein,** Edward Selig 1931- *AmMWSc 92*
**Epstein,** Edward Steven 1948- *WhoEnt 92*
**Epstein,** Elaine *DrAPF 91*
**Epstein,** Elissa 1933- *WhoAmP 91*
**Epstein,** Emanuel 1916- *AmMWSc 92, IntWW 91*
**Epstein,** Emanuel 1922- *AmMWSc 92*
**Epstein,** Ervin Harold 1909- *AmMWSc 92*
**Epstein,** Ervin Harold, Jr. 1941- *WhoWest 92*
**Epstein,** Frank Benjamin 1942- *WhoEnt 92*
**Epstein,** Franklin Harold 1924- *AmMWSc 92*
**Epstein,** Gabriel 1918- *IntWW 91*
**Epstein,** Gabriel Leo 1941- *AmMWSc 92*
**Epstein,** Gary Martin 1942- *AmMWSc 92*
**Epstein,** Gary Marvin 1946- *WhoAmL 92, WhoEnt 92*
**Epstein,** George 1926- *AmMWSc 92*
**Epstein,** George 1934- *AmMWSc 92*
**Epstein,** Gerald Lewis 1956- *AmMWSc 92*
**Epstein,** Harold 1923- *WhoFI 92*
**Epstein,** Harvey Irwin 1946- *AmMWSc 92*
**Epstein,** Henry 1927- *AmMWSc 92*
**Epstein,** Henry F 1944- *AmMWSc 92*
**Epstein,** Herman Theodore 1920- *AmMWSc 92*
**Epstein,** Howard I 1941- *AmMWSc 92*
**Epstein,** Ira Stephen 1941- *WhoAmL 92*
**Epstein,** Irving Robert 1945- *AmMWSc 92*
**Epstein,** Isadore 1919- *AmMWSc 92*
**Epstein,** Jack Burton 1935- *AmMWSc 92*
**Epstein,** Jacob 1880-1959 *FacFETw [port], TwCPaSc*
**Epstein,** James Arnold 1951- *WhoEnt 92*
**Epstein,** Jason 1928- *News 91*
**Epstein,** Jean 1897-1953 *IntDcF 2-2*
**Epstein,** Jennifer Ann 1954- *WhoAmP 91*
**Epstein,** Jerome Louis 1961- *WhoAmL 92*
**Epstein,** Jerome Michael 1943- *WhoRel 92*
**Epstein,** John Howard 1926- *AmMWSc 92*
**Epstein,** Joseph 1918- *AmMWSc 92*
**Epstein,** Joseph 1937- *WrDr 92*
**Epstein,** Joseph William 1938- *AmMWSc 92*
**Epstein,** Joshua 1940- *AmMWSc 92*
**Epstein,** Judith Ann 1942- *WhoAmL 92*
**Epstein,** Judith Sue *DrAPF 91*
**Epstein,** Julius J 1909- *FacFETw, IntMPA 92*
**Epstein,** Kenneth Richard 1948- *WhoEnt 92*
**Epstein,** L Ivan 1918- *AmMWSc 92*
**Epstein,** Lawrence Melvin 1923- *AmMWSc 92*
**Epstein,** Lee Joan 1958- *IntAu&W 91*
**Epstein,** Leo Francis 1913- *AmMWSc 92*
**Epstein,** Leon J 1917- *AmMWSc 92*
**Epstein,** Leslie *DrAPF 91*
**Epstein,** Leslie 1938- *WrDr 92*
**Epstein,** Lois Barth 1933- *AmMWSc 92*
**Epstein,** Marcelo 1944- *AmMWSc 92*
**Epstein,** Marjorie 1952- *WhoRel 92*
**Epstein,** Mark Sanford 1957- *WhoAmL 92*
**Epstein,** Marvin Phelps 1920- *AmMWSc 92*
**Epstein,** Mary A Farrell 1939- *AmMWSc 92*
**Epstein,** Max 1925- *AmMWSc 92*
**Epstein,** Mel 1910- *IntMPA 92*
**Epstein,** Melvin 1938- *WhoAmL 92*
**Epstein,** Michael Alan 1954- *WhoAmL 92*
**Epstein,** Michael Anthony 1921- *IntWW 91*

**Epstein,** Morton Batlan 1917- *AmMWSc 92*
**Epstein,** Murray 1937- *AmMWSc 92*
**Epstein,** Nathan Bernic 1924- *AmMWSc 92*
**Epstein,** Noel *DcAmImH*
**Epstein,** Norman 1923- *AmMWSc 92*
**Epstein,** Paul Mark 1946- *AmMWSc 92*
**Epstein,** Paul Stuart 1957- *WhoAmL 92*
**Epstein,** Philip G 1909-1952 *FacFETw*
**Epstein,** Robert B 1934- *AmMWSc 92*
**Epstein,** Robert Harry 1958- *WhoAmL 92*
**Epstein,** Robert Joseph 1941- *WhoEnt 92*
**Epstein,** Robert Marvin 1928- *AmMWSc 92*
**Epstein,** Roger Harris 1945- *WhoAmL 92*
**Epstein,** Sam 1909- *ChILR 26 [port]*
**Epstein,** Samuel 1919- *AmMWSc 92*
**Epstein,** Samuel D. 1946- *WhoFI 92*
**Epstein,** Samuel David 1946- *AmMWSc 92*
**Epstein,** Samuel Stanley 1926- *AmMWSc 92*
**Epstein,** Saul Theodore 1924- *AmMWSc 92*
**Epstein,** Selma 1927- *WhoEnt 92*
**Epstein,** Seymour *DrAPF 91*
**Epstein,** Seymour 1917- *IntAu&W 91, WrDr 92*
**Epstein,** Seymour 1921- *AmMWSc 92*
**Epstein,** Sidney 1923- *WhoFI 92, WhoMW 92*
**Epstein,** Stephen Edward 1935- *AmMWSc 92*
**Epstein,** Stephen Roger 1947- *WhoFI 92*
**Epstein,** Suzanne Louise *AmMWSc 92*
**Epstein,** Wallace Victor 1926- *AmMWSc 92*
**Epstein,** William 1912- *IntWW 91*
**Epstein,** William L 1925- *AmMWSc 92*
**Epstein,** William Warren 1931- *AmMWSc 92*
**Epstein,** Wolfgang 1931- *AmMWSc 92*
**Epstien,** Jay Alan 1951- *WhoAmL 92*
**Epting,** C. Christopher *WhoMW 92, WhoRel 92*
**Epting,** George Hagood 1949- *WhoEnt 92*
**Epting,** Marion *WhoBlA 92*
**Equale,** Paul *NewYTBS 91 [port]*
**Equi,** Elaine *DrAPF 91*
**Equiano,** Olaudah 1745?-1797? *BenetAL 91, BlkLC [port], LitC 16 [port]*
**Erard,** Sebastien 1752-1831 *NewAmDM*
**Erasmus,** Beth de Wet 1935- *AmMWSc 92*
**Erasmus,** Desiderius 1469?-1536 *LitC 16 [port]*
**Erath,** Louis W 1917- *AmMWSc 92*
**Erauso,** Catalina de 1592?-1650 *EncAmaz 91*
**Erazmus,** Walter Thomas 1947- *WhoFI 92*
**Erb,** Christian Stehman, Jr. 1931- *WhoAmL 92*
**Erb,** Clarence Leighton, Jr. 1917- *WhoRel 92*
**Erb,** David Henry 1957- *WhoFI 92*
**Erb,** Dennis J 1952- *AmMWSc 92*
**Erb,** Donald 1927- *ConCom 92, NewAmDM, WhoEnt 92*
**Erb,** Kenneth 1939- *AmMWSc 92*
**Erb,** Lillian Edgar 1922- *WhoAmP 91*
**Erb,** Michael Reif 1953- *WhoEnt 92*
**Erb,** Richard David 1941- *IntWW 91*
**Erb,** Richard Louis Lundin 1929- *WhoMW 92*
**Erb,** Robert Allan 1932- *AmMWSc 92*
**Erbach,** Christian 1570-1635 *NewAmDM*
**Erbacher,** John Kornel 1942- *AmMWSc 92*
**Erbacher,** Kathryn Anne 1947- *WhoWest 92*
**Erbakan,** Necmettin 1926- *IntWW 91*
**Erbar,** John Harold 1931- *AmMWSc 92*
**Erbe,** Bonnie Ginzburg 1954- *WhoAmL 92*
**Erbe,** Johannes Petrus 1927- *IntWW 91*
**Erbe,** Lawrence Wayne 1924- *AmMWSc 92*
**Erbe,** Pamela *DrAPF 91*
**Erbe,** Richard W 1939- *AmMWSc 92*
**Erbeck,** Robert Nelson 1948- *WhoEnt 92*
**Erben,** Heinrich Karl 1921- *IntWW 91*
**Erber,** Thomas 1930- *AmMWSc 92, WhoMW 92*
**Erbert,** Virgil 1924- *WhoFI 92*
**Erbes,** Paul Kenneth 1957- *WhoRel 92*
**Erbisch,** Frederic H 1937- *AmMWSc 92*
**Erbisch,** Frederic Harold 1937- *WhoMW 92*
**Erbsen,** Claude Ernest 1938- *WhoFI 92*
**Erbst,** Lawrence Arnold 1930- *WhoAmL 92*
**Erburu,** Robert F. 1930- *WhoWest 92*
**Erby,** William Arthur 1933- *AmMWSc 92*
**Ercilla y Zuniga,** Alonso 1533-1594 *HisDSpE*
**Erck,** Robert Alan 1954- *AmMWSc 92*
**Ercklentz,** Alexander Tonio 1936- *WhoFI 92*
**Erckmann,** Emile 1822-1899 *ScFEYrs*
**Erckmann,** Emile and Alexandre Chatrain *ScFEYrs*
**Erckmann-Chatrian** *ScFEYrs*
**Ercolano,** Dean Richard 1962- *WhoFI 92*
**Ercole,** Robert Michael 1954- *WhoAmL 92*
**Ercoli,** Ercole *ConAu 133*
**Ercoli,** Gail Sharon 1950- *WhoEnt 92*
**Erdahl,** Lowell O. 1931- *WhoMW 92, WhoRel 92*
**Erdal,** Bruce Robert 1939- *AmMWSc 92, WhoWest 92*
**Erdel,** Timothy Paul 1951- *WhoRel 92*
**Erdely,** Stephen Lajos 1921- *WhoEnt 92*
**Erdelyi,** Ivan Nicholas 1926- *AmMWSc 92*
**Erdelyi,** Miklos 1928- *IntWW 91*
**Erdem,** Kaya 1928- *IntWW 91*
**Erdley,** Harold F 1925- *AmMWSc 92*
**Erdman,** Anne Marie 1916- *AmMWSc 92*
**Erdman,** Arthur Guy 1945- *AmMWSc 92*
**Erdman,** Barbara 1936- *WhoEnt 92*
**Erdman,** Becky Lee 1954- *WhoMW 92*
**Erdman,** Dennis Robert *WhoEnt 92*
**Erdman,** Donald Robert 1931- *WhoFI 92*
**Erdman,** Edward Louis 1906- *Who 92*
**Erdman,** Howard E 1930- *AmMWSc 92*
**Erdman,** John Gordon 1919- *AmMWSc 92*
**Erdman,** John Wilson, Jr 1945- *AmMWSc 92*
**Erdman,** Joseph 1935- *WhoAmL 92*
**Erdman,** Kimball S 1937- *AmMWSc 92*
**Erdman,** Loula Grace d1976 *TwCWW 91*
**Erdman,** Nikolay Robertovich 1902-1970 *SovUnBD*
**Erdman,** Paul E. 1932- *WrDr 92*
**Erdman,** Richard 1925- *IntMPA 92*
**Erdman,** Timothy Robert 1944- *AmMWSc 92*
**Erdman,** William James, II 1921- *AmMWSc 92*
**Erdmann,** David E 1939- *AmMWSc 92*
**Erdmann,** Duane John 1946- *AmMWSc 92*
**Erdmann,** Joachim Christian 1928- *AmMWSc 92, WhoWest 92*
**Erdmann,** John Hugo 1964- *AmMWSc 92*
**Erdmann,** Karl Dietrich *IntWW 91N*
**Erdmann,** Lothar 1888-1939 *EncTR 91*
**Erdmann,** Marvin Elmer 1930- *WhoFI 92*
**Erdmann,** Robert Charles 1939- *AmMWSc 92*
**Erdmann,** Terry James 1943- *WhoEnt 92*
**Erdner,** Jon W. 1942- *WhoFI 92*
**Erdogan,** Fazil 1925- *AmMWSc 92*
**Erdos,** Andre 1941- *IntWW 91*
**Erdos,** Ervin George 1922- *AmMWSc 92*
**Erdos,** Gregory William 1945- *AmMWSc 92*
**Erdos,** Paul 1913- *IntWW 91*
**Erdreich,** Ben 1938- *AlmAP 92 [port], WhoAmP 91*
**Erdrich,** Karen Louise 1954- *IntWW 91*
**Erdrich,** Louise *NewYTBS 91 [port]*
**Erdrich,** Louise 1954- *BenetAL 91, ConNov 91, IntAu&W 91, TwCWW 91, WrDr 92*
**Erdtmann,** Bernd Dietrich 1939- *AmMWSc 92*
**Erdvig,** Lloyd Parker 1953- *WhoRel 92*
**Ereaut,** Frank 1919- *Who 92*
**Erecinska,** Maria 1939- *AmMWSc 92*
**Erede,** Alberto 1909- *NewAmDM*
**Eredia,** Elaine 1950- *WhoFI 92*
**Erediauwa,** Omo N'Oba N'Edo Uku-A 1923- *IntWW 91*
**Erem,** Simon Shimon 1922- *WhoWest 92*
**Eremin,** Oleg 1938- *Who 92*
**Erenburg,** Il'ya Grigor'evich 1891-1967 *SovUnBD*
**Erenburg,** Steven Alan 1937- *WhoFI 92*
**Ereng,** Paul 1968- *BlkOlyM [port]*
**Erenrich,** Eric Howard 1944- *AmMWSc 92*
**Erenrich,** Evelyn Schwartz 1946- *AmMWSc 92*
**Erens,** Patricia 1938- *WrDr 92*
**Erensel,** Brent Bonbright 1957- *WhoFI 92*
**Eret,** Donald 1931- *WhoAmP 91*
**Erevia,** Angela 1934- *WhoHisp 92*
**Erf,** Robert K 1931 *AmMWSc 92*
**Erfman,** David John 1953- *WhoAmP 91*
**Erford,** Esther *DrAPF 91*
**Erhan,** Semih M *AmMWSc 92*
**Erhard,** Ludwig 1897-1977 *FacFETw*
**Erhard,** Michael Paul 1948- *WhoAmL 92*
**Erhard,** Tom 1923- *IntAu&W 91, WrDr 92*
**Erhardt,** Paul William 1947- *AmMWSc 92*
**Erhardt,** Peter Franklin 1933- *AmMWSc 92*
**Erhardt,** Ron *WhoAmP 91*
**Erhart,** James Nelson 1953- *WhoAmL 92*
**Erhart,** Rainer R 1935- *AmMWSc 92*
**Eri,** Serei 1936- *Who 92*
**Eri,** Vincent 1936- *ConNov 91, WrDr 92*
**Eribes,** Richard A. *WhoHisp 92*
**Ericksen,** Charles Gunnard, Jr. 1952- *WhoMW 92*
**Ericksen,** Donald O. 1932- *WhoRel 92*
**Ericksen,** George Edward 1920- *AmMWSc 92*
**Ericksen,** Jerald LaVerne 1924- *AmMWSc 92*
**Ericksen,** Mary Frances 1925- *AmMWSc 92*
**Ericksen,** Michael Ross 1957- *WhoFI 92*
**Ericksen,** Richard Harold 1938- *AmMWSc 92*
**Ericksen,** Wilhelm Skjetstad 1912- *AmMWSc 92*
**Erickson,** Alan *WhoAmP 91*
**Erickson,** Alan Eric 1928- *AmMWSc 92*
**Erickson,** Andrew M 1939- *WhoIns 92*
**Erickson,** Anton Earl 1919- *AmMWSc 92*
**Erickson,** Arthur Charles 1924- *IntWW 91, WhoWest 92*
**Erickson,** Betsy *WhoEnt 92*
**Erickson,** Bruce Wayne 1942- *AmMWSc 92*
**Erickson,** Calvin Howard 1946- *WhoWest 92*
**Erickson,** Carlton Kuehl 1939- *AmMWSc 92*
**Erickson,** Carol Ann 1933- *WhoWest 92*
**Erickson,** Catherine *DrAPF 91*
**Erickson,** Charles Edward 1947- *WhoIns 92*
**Erickson,** Charles John 1931- *WhoWest 92*
**Erickson,** Charlotte J. 1923- *WrDr 92*
**Erickson,** Charlotte Joanne 1923- *Who 92*
**Erickson,** Christopher Andrew 1957- *WhoFI 92, WhoWest 92*
**Erickson,** Cyrus Conrad 1909- *AmMWSc 92*
**Erickson,** David Belnap 1951- *WhoAmL 92*
**Erickson,** David Bruce 1947- *WhoFI 92*
**Erickson,** David Edward 1931- *AmMWSc 92*
**Erickson,** David Hayes 1960- *WhoAmL 92*
**Erickson,** David James 1949- *WhoMW 92*
**Erickson,** David John 1964- *WhoWest 92*
**Erickson,** David Martin 1953- *WhoAmL 92*
**Erickson,** David R 1929- *AmMWSc 92*
**Erickson,** David Rae 1929- *WhoMW 92*
**Erickson,** Dennis Alseth 1954- *WhoAmP 91*
**Erickson,** Dennis Harold 1940- *WhoFI 92*
**Erickson,** Dennis John 1942- *AmMWSc 92*
**Erickson,** Diane Quinn 1959- *WhoAmL 92*
**Erickson,** Don 1937- *WhoAmP 91*
**Erickson,** Donna Mary Hacking 1940- *IntAu&W 91*
**Erickson,** Douglas Robert 1956- *WhoRel 92*
**Erickson,** Duane Gordon 1931- *AmMWSc 92*
**Erickson,** Duane Otto 1930- *AmMWSc 92*
**Erickson,** Edward Herbert 1944- *AmMWSc 92*
**Erickson,** Edwin Francis 1934- *AmMWSc 92*
**Erickson,** Edwin Sylvester, Jr 1928- *AmMWSc 92*
**Erickson,** Eric Douglas 1955- *WhoWest 92*
**Erickson,** Eric Herman, Jr 1940- *AmMWSc 92*
**Erickson,** Eugene E 1923- *AmMWSc 92*
**Erickson,** Frank William 1923- *WhoEnt 92*
**Erickson,** Gail 1934- *WhoAmL 92, WhoFI 92*
**Erickson,** Gene Lloyd 1951- *WhoWest 92*
**Erickson,** Gerald Meyer 1927- *WhoMW 92*
**Erickson,** Glen Walter 1934- *AmMWSc 92*
**Erickson,** Gregory Kevin 1953- *WhoIns 92*
**Erickson,** Harold Paul 1940- *AmMWSc 92*
**Erickson,** Howard Hugh 1936- *AmMWSc 92, WhoMW 92*
**Erickson,** Howard Ralph 1919- *AmMWSc 92*
**Erickson,** James C, III 1927- *AmMWSc 92*
**Erickson,** James Eldred 1949- *AmMWSc 92*
**Erickson,** James George 1929- *AmMWSc 92, WhoWest 92*
**Erickson,** James H. 1939- *WhoWest 92*
**Erickson,** James Huston 1931- *WhoRel 92*
**Erickson,** Jeanne Marie *AmMWSc 92*
**Erickson,** John 1923- *AmMWSc 92*
**Erickson,** John 1929- *Who 92*
**Erickson,** John David 1933- *WhoRel 92*
**Erickson,** John Gerhard 1917- *AmMWSc 92*
**Erickson,** John M 1918- *AmMWSc 92*
**Erickson,** John Mark 1943- *AmMWSc 92*
**Erickson,** John Robert 1939- *AmMWSc 92*
**Erickson,** John William 1925- *AmMWSc 92*
**Erickson,** Jon Jay 1941- *AmMWSc 92*
**Erickson,** Joseph Arthur 1957- *WhoMW 92*
**Erickson,** Karen Louise 1939- *AmMWSc 92*
**Erickson,** Kenneth Lynn 1946- *AmMWSc 92*
**Erickson,** Kenneth Neil 1940- *AmMWSc 92*
**Erickson,** Kent L *AmMWSc 92*
**Erickson,** Kim L. 1951- *WhoMW 92*
**Erickson,** Larry Eugene 1938- *AmMWSc 92*
**Erickson,** Laurence A 1953- *AmMWSc 92*
**Erickson,** Laurence Robert 1949- *WhoMW 92*
**Erickson,** LeRoy *WhoAmP 91*
**Erickson,** Louis Carl 1914- *AmMWSc 92*
**Erickson,** Luther E 1933- *AmMWSc 92*
**Erickson,** Lynden Edwin 1938- *AmMWSc 92*
**Erickson,** Michael Glenn 1955- *WhoFI 92*
**Erickson,** Michael Karl 1936- *WhoEnt 92*
**Erickson,** Millard John 1932- *WhoMW 92, WhoRel 92*
**Erickson,** Mitchell Drake 1950- *AmMWSc 92*
**Erickson,** Nils Anders 1951- *WhoEnt 92*
**Erickson,** Peter Brown 1945- *IntAu&W 91*
**Erickson,** Ralph Ernest 1928- *WhoAmL 92*
**Erickson,** Ralph Hull 1931- *WhoAmL 92*
**Erickson,** Ralph O 1914- *AmMWSc 92*
**Erickson,** Ralph Roger 1959- *WhoAmL 92*
**Erickson,** Randal Gary 1965- *WhoMW 92*
**Erickson,** Randall L 1939- *AmMWSc 92*
**Erickson,** Ray Charles 1918- *AmMWSc 92*
**Erickson,** Richard Ames 1923- *AmMWSc 92*
**Erickson,** Richard Beau 1952- *WhoFI 92, WhoWest 92*
**Erickson,** Richard Clark 1946- *WhoAmL 92*
**Erickson,** Richard John 1943- *IntWW 91*
**Erickson,** Richard Lee 1938- *WhoFI 92*
**Erickson,** Richard Norman 1949- *WhoRel 92*
**Erickson,** Richard Theodore 1932- *WhoFI 92*
**Erickson,** Robert 1917- *NewAmDM*
**Erickson,** Robert Allen 1940- *WhoWest 92*
**Erickson,** Robert Andrew 1940- *WhoWest 92*
**Erickson,** Robert Daniel 1943- *WhoFI 92*
**Erickson,** Robert Gregory 1944- *WhoWest 92*
**Erickson,** Robert L. 1929- *WhoAmL 92*
**Erickson,** Robert Lee *WhoRel 92*
**Erickson,** Robert Porter 1930- *AmMWSc 92*
**Erickson,** Robert Porter 1939- *AmMWSc 92*
**Erickson,** Robert Stanley 1944- *WhoAmL 92*
**Erickson,** Robert W 1929- *AmMWSc 92*
**Erickson,** Roland Axel 1913- *WhoFI 92*
**Erickson,** Rolf Herbert 1940- *WhoMW 92*
**Erickson,** Ronald E 1933- *AmMWSc 92*
**Erickson,** Roy Lydeen 1923- *WhoAmL 92, WhoFI 92*
**Erickson,** Scott Lee 1959- *WhoEnt 92*
**Erickson,** Stanley Arvid *AmMWSc 92*
**Erickson,** Stephen Emory 1945- *WhoFI 92*
**Erickson,** Stephen Michael 1950- *IntAu&W 91*
**Erickson,** Stephen Paul 1951- *WhoAmP 91*
**Erickson,** Steve 1950- *WrDr 92*
**Erickson,** Terrance Casper 1949- *WhoMW 92*
**Erickson,** Thomas J 1954- *WhoIns 92*
**Erickson,** Thomas Sherman *WhoAmL 92*
**Erickson,** Tricia K. 1952- *WhoEnt 92*
**Erickson,** Virginia Bemmels 1948- *WhoWest 92*
**Erickson,** Walter *WrDr 92*
**Erickson,** Walter Bruce 1938- *WhoFI 92*
**Erickson,** Wayne Douglas 1932- *AmMWSc 92*
**Erickson,** Wayne Francis 1946- *AmMWSc 92*
**Erickson,** Wendell O 1925- *WhoAmP 91*
**Erickson,** William Clarence 1930- *AmMWSc 92*
**Erickson,** William Eugene 1945- *WhoMW 92*
**Erickson,** William Harry 1916- *AmMWSc 92*
**Erickson,** William Hurt 1924- *WhoAmL 92, WhoAmP 91, WhoWest 92*
**Erickstad,** Ralph John 1922- *WhoAmL 92, WhoAmP 91, WhoMW 92*
**Ericson,** Alfred 1928- *AmMWSc 92*
**Ericson,** Avis J 1947- *AmMWSc 92*
**Ericson,** Bruce Alan 1952- *WhoAmL 92*
**Ericson,** Burton E. 1928- *WhoAmL 92*
**Ericson,** Carl Erland 1913- *WhoRel 92*
**Ericson,** Charles Hayden 1953- *WhoRel 92*
**Ericson,** David Paul 1949- *WhoWest 92*
**Ericson,** Grover Charles 1941- *AmMWSc 92*
**Ericson,** James Donald 1935- *WhoAmL 92, WhoMW 92*
**Ericson,** John 1926- *IntMPA 92*
**Ericson,** Leif *BenetAL 91*
**Ericson,** Richard Charles 1933- *WhoMW 92*

**Ericson**, Roger Delwin 1934- *WhoAmL 92, WhoFI 92*
**Ericson**, William Arnold 1934- *AmMWSc 92*
**Ericsson**, John 1803-1889 *BiInAmS*
**Ericsson**, Lowell Harold 1928- *AmMWSc 92*
**Ericsson**, Ronald James 1935- *AmMWSc 92*
**Eriks**, Klaas 1922- *AmMWSc 92*
**Eriksen**, Clyde Hedman 1933- *AmMWSc 92*
**Eriksen**, Dan Oluf 1925- *WhoEnt 92*
**Eriksen**, Gerald Bruce 1951- *WhoAmP 91*
**Eriksen**, John George 1918- *WhoMW 92*
**Eriksen**, Richard Eugene 1945- *WhoAmL 92*
**Eriksen**, Stuart P 1930- *AmMWSc 92*
**Eriksen**, Stuart Pierre 1930- *WhoWest 92*
**Erikson**, Erik H 1902- *FacFETw, WrDr 92*
**Erikson**, Erik Homburger 1902- *IntWW 91*
**Erikson**, George Emil 1920- *AmMWSc 92*
**Erikson**, Glenn Robert 1951- *WhoWest 92*
**Erikson**, J Alden 1926- *AmMWSc 92*
**Erikson**, J. Lance 1943- *WhoAmL 92*
**Erikson**, Jay Arthur 1922- *AmMWSc 92*
**Erikson**, Mary Jane 1930- *AmMWSc 92*
**Erikson**, Nancy Watson *DrAPF 91*
**Erikson**, Raymond Leo 1936- *AmMWSc 92*
**Eriksson**, Elof 1883-1965 *BiDExR*
**Eriksson**, Erik Alexander, Jr. 1953- *WhoAmL 92*
**Eriksson**, Goran Olof 1929- *IntWW 91*
**Eriksson**, James Ernest 1943- *WhoMW 92*
**Eriksson**, Karl-Erik Lennart 1932- *AmMWSc 92*
**Eriksson**, Kenneth Andrew 1946- *AmMWSc 92*
**Eriksson**, Larry John 1945- *AmMWSc 92*
**Eriksson**, LeAnn Marie Davis 1961- *WhoMW 92*
**Eriksson**, Per-Olof 1938- *IntWW 91*
**Eriksson**, Wendell H. *WhoMW 92*
**Erim**, Ahmet Martin 1952- *WhoAmL 92*
**Eringen**, Ahmed Cemal 1921- *AmMWSc 92*
**Eriquez**, Louis Anthony 1949- *AmMWSc 92*
**Erisman**, James A. 1940- *WhoAmL 92*
**Erith**, John 1904- *WrDr 92*
**Eriugena**, John Scottus 810?-877? *DcLB 115 [port]*
**Erk**, Frank Chris 1924- *AmMWSc 92*
**Erke**, Keith Howard 1938- *AmMWSc 92*
**Erkelenz**, Anton 1878-1945 *EncTR 91*
**Erkiletian**, Dickran Hagop 1913- *WhoMW 92*
**Erkiletian**, Dickran Hagop, Jr 1913- *AmMWSc 92*
**Erkin**, Feridun Cemal 1899- *Who 92*
**Erkmen**, Hayrettin 1915- *IntWW 91*
**Erlande-Brandenburg**, Alain 1937- *IntWW 91*
**Erlander**, Tage 1901-1985 *FacFETw*
**Erlandsen**, Stanley L 1941- *AmMWSc 92*
**Erlandson**, Arvid Leonard 1929- *AmMWSc 92*
**Erlandson**, Donna Mae 1940- *WhoFI 92*
**Erlandson**, Paul M 1920- *AmMWSc 92*
**Erlandson**, Robert F. 1943- *WhoMW 92*
**Erlanger**, Bernard Ferdinand 1923- *AmMWSc 92*
**Erlanger**, Joseph 1874-1965 *FacFETw, WhoNob 90*
**Erlanger**, Philippe 1903- *IntAu&W 91, IntWW 91*
**Erlanger**, Steven Jay 1952- *ConAu 133*
**Erlbach**, Erich 1933- *AmMWSc 92*
**Erlebacher**, Arlene Cernik 1946- *WhoAmL 92*
**Erleigh**, Viscount 1986- *Who 92*
**Erlenborn**, John Neal 1927- *WhoAmL 92*
**Erlenmeyer-Kimling**, L *AmMWSc 92*
**Erlich**, David C *AmMWSc 92*
**Erlich**, Hans *DcTwDes*
**Erlich**, Ronald Harvey 1945- *AmMWSc 92*
**Erlichman**, Jack *AmMWSc 92*
**Erlichson**, Herman 1931- *AmMWSc 92*
**Erlicht**, Lewis *LesBEnT 92*
**Erlicht**, Lewis H. *IntMPA 92*
**Erlicht**, Lewis Howard 1939- *WhoEnt 92*
**Erlick**, Everett Howard 1921- *WhoEnt 92*
**Erlij**, David 1938- *AmMWSc 92*
**Erling**, Jacque J 1925- *WhoAmP 91*
**Erman**, Don Coutre 1940- *AmMWSc 92*
**Erman**, James Edwin 1940- *AmMWSc 92*
**Erman**, John 1935- *IntMPA 92, WhoEnt 92*
**Erman**, Lee Daniel 1944- *AmMWSc 92*
**Erman**, William F 1931- *AmMWSc 92*
**Ermenc**, Eugene D 1919- *AmMWSc 92*
**Ermenc**, Joseph John 1912- *AmMWSc 92*
**Ermentrout**, George Bard 1954- *AmMWSc 92*
**Ermine**, Will *TwCWW 91*
**Ermler**, Fridrikh Markovich 1898-1967 *SovUnBD*
**Ermler**, Walter Carl 1946- *AmMWSc 92*
**Ermutlu**, Ilhan M 1927- *AmMWSc 92*
**Ern**, Ernest Henry 1933- *AmMWSc 92*
**Erne**, Earl of 1937- *Who 92*
**Ernemann**, Andre 1923- *IntWW 91*
**Ernenwein**, Leslie 1900?-1961 *TwCWW 91*
**Ernest**, Albert Devery, Jr. 1930- *WhoFI 92*
**Ernest**, David John 1929- *WhoEnt 92*
**Ernest**, J Terry 1935- *AmMWSc 92*
**Ernest**, John 1922- *TwCPaSc*
**Ernest**, John Arthur 1935- *AmMWSc 92*
**Ernest**, Jonathan Alexander 1961- *WhoAmL 92*
**Ernest**, Michael Jeffrey 1948- *AmMWSc 92*
**Ernesti**, Johann August 1707-1781 *BlkwCEP*
**Erni**, Hans 1909- *IntWW 91*
**Erni**, Henri 1822-1885 *BiInAmS*
**Erno**, Richard B. 1923- *WrDr 92*
**Ernsberger**, Fred Martin 1919- *AmMWSc 92*
**Ernst**, Carl Henry 1938- *AmMWSc 92*
**Ernst**, Daniel Pearson 1931- *WhoAmL 92, WhoMW 92*
**Ernst**, David John 1943- *AmMWSc 92*
**Ernst**, David N *AmMWSc 92*
**Ernst**, Ed William 1950- *WhoWest 92*
**Ernst**, Edward W 1924- *AmMWSc 92*
**Ernst**, Eldon Gilbert 1939- *WhoRel 92, WhoWest 92*
**Ernst**, Gene Frederick 1939- *WhoMW 92*
**Ernst**, George W 1939- *AmMWSc 92*
**Ernst**, John Louis 1932- *WhoEnt 92*
**Ernst**, Joseph Richard 1934- *WhoMW 92, WhoRel 92*
**Ernst**, K.S. *DrAPF 91*
**Ernst**, Karl 1904-1934 *EncTR 91 [port]*
**Ernst**, Linda Marie 1947- *WhoMW 92*
**Ernst**, Lisa 1956- *WhoFI 92*
**Ernst**, Marcia McCrory 1961- *WhoAmL 92*
**Ernst**, Mark Stuart 1949- *WhoFI 92*
**Ernst**, Martin L 1920- *AmMWSc 92*
**Ernst**, Matthew Lee 1963- *WhoFI 92*
**Ernst**, Max 1891-1976 *FacFETw [port]*
**Ernst**, Michael J 1966- *WhoAmP 91*
**Ernst**, Michael Joseph 1962- *WhoAmL 92*
**Ernst**, Norman Frank, Jr. 1942- *WhoFI 92, WhoIns 92*
**Ernst**, Paul 1866-1933 *EncTR 91 [port]*
**Ernst**, Paul 1900?- *ScFEYrs*
**Ernst**, Philip Anthony 1956- *WhoEnt 92*
**Ernst**, Ralph Ambrose 1938- *AmMWSc 92*
**Ernst**, Reginald H. 1928- *WhoBlA 92*
**Ernst**, Richard Dale 1951- *AmMWSc 92*
**Ernst**, Richard Edward 1942- *AmMWSc 92*
**Ernst**, Richard R *AmMWSc 92*
**Ernst**, Robert 1915- *WrDr 92*
**Ernst**, Robert Alexander 1948- *WhoFI 92*
**Ernst**, Roberta Dorothea 1944- *AmMWSc 92*
**Ernst**, Stephen Arnold 1940- *AmMWSc 92*
**Ernst**, Susan Gwenn 1946- *AmMWSc 92*
**Ernst**, Wallace Gary 1931- *AmMWSc 92*
**Ernst**, Walter 1901- *AmMWSc 92*
**Ernst**, William Robert 1943- *AmMWSc 92*
**Ernst**, Wolfgang E 1951- *AmMWSc 92*
**Ernst-Fonberg**, Marylou 1937- *AmMWSc 92*
**Ernster**, Jacquelyn 1939- *WhoRel 92*
**Ernsting**, John 1928- *Who 92*
**Ernstrom**, Carl Anthon 1922- *AmMWSc 92*
**Erod**, Ivan 1936- *ConCom 92*
**Erokan**, Dennis William 1950- *WhoWest 92*
**Eron**, Lewis John 1951- *WhoRel 92*
**Eror**, Nicholas George, Jr 1937- *AmMWSc 92*
**Eros**, Peter 1932- *WhoEnt 92, WhoWest 92*
**Eroschenko**, Victor Paul 1938- *AmMWSc 92*
**Erosh**, William Daniel 1956- *WhoFI 92*
**Erpelding**, Curtis Michael 1950- *WhoWest 92*
**Erpelding**, Kevin Luke 1968- *WhoMW 92*
**Erpenbeck**, Jerome John 1933- *AmMWSc 92*
**Erpino**, Michael James 1939- *AmMWSc 92*
**Erreca**, Charles M. *WhoHisp 92*
**Errecart**, Joyce Hier 1950- *WhoAmL 92*
**Errede**, Beverly Jean 1949- *AmMWSc 92*
**Errede**, Louis A 1923- *AmMWSc 92*
**Errede**, Steven Michael 1952- *AmMWSc 92*
**Errera**, Samuel J 1926- *AmMWSc 92*
**Errett**, Daryl Dale 1922- *AmMWSc 92*
**Errett**, Isaac 1820-1888 *AmPeW, RelLAm 91*
**Errichiello**, Susan Frances Julie 1960- *WhoMW 92*
**Errickson**, Marvin Orion 1943- *WhoAmL 92*
**Errington**, Geoffrey 1926- *Who 92*
**Errington**, Lancelot 1917- *Who 92*
**Errington**, Richard Percy 1904- *Who 92*
**Errington**, Stuart Grant 1929- *IntWW 91, Who 92*
**Erritt**, John 1931- *Who 92*
**Erroll**, Earl of 1948- *Who 92*
**Erroll Of Hale**, Baron 1914- *IntWW 91, Who 92*
**Erschik**, Richard William 1945- *WhoMW 92*
**Ersek**, Gregory Joseph Mark 1956- *WhoAmL 92, WhoFI 92*
**Ersgaard**, Ole Kristian 1948- *WhoFI 92*
**Ershad**, Hossain Mohammad 1930- *IntWW 91*
**Ershad**, Hussain Mohammed 1930- *FacFETw*
**Ershad**, Hussain Muhammad 1930- *Who 92*
**Ershoff**, Benjamin H 1914- *AmMWSc 92*
**Ersin**, Nurettin 1918- *IntWW 91*
**Erskin**, John *WhoAmP 91*
**Erskine** *Who 92*
**Erskine**, Lord 1949- *Who 92*
**Erskine**, Anthony J 1931- *AmMWSc 92*
**Erskine**, Charlene G. 1943- *WhoMW 92*
**Erskine**, Christopher Forbes 1927- *AmMWSc 92*
**Erskine**, David *Who 92*
**Erskine**, Donald B 1923- *AmMWSc 92*
**Erskine**, Douglas *ScFEYrs*
**Erskine**, Emma Payne 1853-1924 *DcNCBi 2*
**Erskine**, James Christian, Jr. 1937- *WhoMW 92*
**Erskine**, James Lorenzo 1942- *AmMWSc 92*
**Erskine**, John 1879-1951 *BenetAL 91, FacFETw*
**Erskine**, John Morse 1920- *WhoWest 92*
**Erskine**, John Robert 1931- *AmMWSc 92*
**Erskine**, Kenneth F. *WhoBlA 92*
**Erskine**, Margaret *WrDr 92*
**Erskine**, Ralph 1914- *IntWW 91, Who 92*
**Erskine**, Robert 1735-1780 *BiInAmS*
**Erskine**, Rosalind *IntAu&W 91X, WrDr 92*
**Erskine**, Thomas 1750-1823 *ScFEYrs*
**Erskine**, Thomas David 1912- *Who 92*
**Erskine**, Thomas Ralph 1933- *Who 92*
**Erskine**, Wilson Fiske 1911-1972? *ConAu 134*
**Erskine-Hill**, Alexander Roger 1949- *Who 92*
**Erskine-Hill**, Henry Howard 1936- *Who 92*
**Erskine-Hill**, Roger *Who 92*
**Erskine-Lindop**, Audrey Beatrice Noel *IntAu&W 91*
**Erskine-Murray** *Who 92*
**Erskine of Rerrick**, Baron 1926- *Who 92*
**Erslev**, Allan Jacob 1919- *AmMWSc 92*
**Erslev**, Eric Allan 1954- *AmMWSc 92*
**Ersoy**, Okan Kadri 1945- *AmMWSc 92, WhoMW 92*
**Ersoy**, Ugur 1932- *AmMWSc 92*
**Erspamer**, Jack Laverne 1918- *AmMWSc 92*
**Erstad**, Leon Robert 1947- *WhoAmL 92*
**Erstfeld**, Thomas Ewald 1951- *AmMWSc 92*
**Erte** 1892-1990 *AnObit 1990, FacFETw [port]*
**Ertegun**, Ahmet Munir 1923- *WhoEnt 92*
**Ertekin**, Turgay 1947- *AmMWSc 92*
**Ertel**, Allen Edward 1936- *WhoAmP 91*
**Ertel**, Gary Arthur 1954- *WhoMW 92*
**Ertel**, Grace Roscoe 1921- *IntAu&W 91*
**Ertel**, Norman H 1932- *AmMWSc 92*
**Ertel**, Robert James 1932- *AmMWSc 92*
**Ertelt**, Henry Robinson 1924- *AmMWSc 92*
**Ertesezek**, Olga d1989 *FacFETw*
**Erteza**, Ahmed 1924- *AmMWSc 92*
**Ertl**, Josef 1925- *IntWW 91*
**Ertl**, Robert Owen 1930- *WhoEnt 92*
**Ertler**, Joseph Dale 1948- *WhoMW 92*
**Ertman**, Earl Leslie 1932- *WhoMW 92*
**Ertz**, Edward 1862-1954 *TwCPaSc*
**Ertz**, Susan 1894-1985 *TwCWW 91*
**Erulkar**, Solomon David 1924- *AmMWSc 92*
**Ervanian**, Armen 1937- *WhoFI 92*
**Erve**, Peter Raymond 1926- *AmMWSc 92*
**Erven**, Bernard Lee 1938- *AmMWSc 92*
**Erven**, Ron D. 1946- *WhoMW 92*
**Ervin**, C Patrick 1943- *AmMWSc 92*
**Ervin**, Craig Lindsay 1961- *WhoRel 92*
**Ervin**, Deborah Green 1956- *WhoBlA 92*
**Ervin**, Eugene Day 1948- *WhoFI 92*
**Ervin**, Frank 1926- *AmMWSc 92*
**Ervin**, George, Jr. 1957- *WhoRel 92*
**Ervin**, Hazel Arnett 1948- *WhoBlA 92*
**Ervin**, Hollis Edward 1952- *AmMWSc 92*
**Ervin**, James Cree 1964- *WhoMW 92*
**Ervin**, John B. 1916- *WhoBlA 92*
**Ervin**, John Witherspoon 1823-1902 *DcNCBi 2*
**Ervin**, Joseph Wilson 1901-1945 *DcNCBi 2*
**Ervin**, Leroy, Jr. 1936- *WhoBlA 92*
**Ervin**, Patrick Franklin 1946- *WhoWest 92*
**Ervin**, Robert Marvin 1917- *WhoAmL 92*
**Ervin**, Sam 1896-1985 *FacFETw*
**Ervin**, Sam J, III 1926- *WhoAmP 91*
**Ervin**, Samuel James, III 1926- *WhoAmL 92*
**Ervin**, Samuel James, Jr. 1896-1985 *AmPolLe, DcNCBi 2*
**Ervin**, Tom J 1952- *WhoAmP 91*
**Ervin**, William Carson 1859-1943 *DcNCBi 2*
**Ervine**, St. John 1883-1971 *RfGEnL 91*
**Ervine**, St. John Greer 1883-1971 *FacFETw*
**Ervine-Andrews**, Harold Marcus 1911- *Who 92*
**Erving**, Claude Moore, Jr. 1952- *WhoWest 92*
**Erving**, Julius 1950- *FacFETw*
**Erving**, Julius Winfield 1950- *WhoBlA 92*
**Erway**, Lawrence Clifton, Jr 1938- *AmMWSc 92*
**Erwin**, Albert R 1931- *AmMWSc 92*
**Erwin**, Alexander 1750-1829? *DcNCBi 2*
**Erwin**, Chesley Para 1920- *AmMWSc 92*
**Erwin**, Chesley Para, Jr. 1953- *WhoAmL 92*
**Erwin**, Claude F., Sr. 1906- *WhoBlA 92*
**Erwin**, Clyde Atkinson 1897-1952 *DcNCBi 2*
**Erwin**, David B, Sr 1924- *AmMWSc 92*
**Erwin**, Dennis Keith 1953- *WhoAmP 91*
**Erwin**, Diane Jean 1946- *WhoAmP 91*
**Erwin**, Donald C 1920- *AmMWSc 92*
**Erwin**, Donald Carroll 1920- *WhoWest 92*
**Erwin**, Donald Earl 1935- *WhoFI 92*
**Erwin**, Douglas Homer 1954- *WhoFI 92*
**Erwin**, Edgar E 1920- *WhoAmP 91*
**Erwin**, Frederick Joseph 1925- *WhoEnt 92*
**Erwin**, Henry Eugene, Jr. 1949- *WhoRel 92*
**Erwin**, Inta D. 1951- *WhoEnt 92*
**Erwin**, James Otis 1922- *WhoBlA 92*
**Erwin**, James Robinson 1953- *WhoAmL 92*
**Erwin**, James V 1925- *AmMWSc 92*
**Erwin**, James Walter 1946- *WhoAmL 92*
**Erwin**, Jesse Harper 1864-1962 *DcNCBi 2*
**Erwin**, Joel D. 1956- *WhoMW 92*
**Erwin**, John Preston 1939- *WhoAmP 91*
**Erwin**, Judith Ann 1939- *WhoEnt 92*
**Erwin**, Lewis 1951- *AmMWSc 92*
**Erwin**, Nancy Morgan 1949- *WhoFI 92*
**Erwin**, Phyllis R 1929- *WhoAmP 91*
**Erwin**, Richard C. 1923- *WhoAmL 92, WhoBlA 92*
**Erwin**, Richard T. 1942- *WhoEnt 92*
**Erwin**, Robert Bartley 1936- *WhoMW 92*
**Erwin**, Robert Bruce 1928- *AmMWSc 92*
**Erwin**, Robert Earl 1943- *WhoAmP 91*
**Erwin**, Terry Hugh, Jr. 1963- *WhoRel 92*
**Erwin**, Timothy J *WhoAmP 91*
**Erwin**, Virgil Gene 1937- *AmMWSc 92*
**Erwin**, William Allen 1856-1932 *DcNCBi 2*
**Erwin**, William Walter 1925- *WhoAmP 91*
**Erzberger**, Matthias 1875-1921 *EncTR 91 [port]*
**Erzen**, Robert Francis 1937- *WhoFI 92*
**Erzinger**, Kim L 1952- *WhoAmP 91*
**Er'ziya**, Stepan Dmitrievich 1876-1959 *SovUnBD*
**Erzurumlu**, H Chik 1934- *AmMWSc 92*
**Erzurumlu**, H. Chik M. 1934- *WhoWest 92*
**Es-Said**, Omar Salim 1952- *WhoWest 92*
**Esahak**, George Michael 1958- *WhoAmL 92*
**Esaki**, Howard Yuji 1953- *WhoFI 92*
**Esaki**, Leo 1925- *AmMWSc 92, FacFETw, IntWW 91, Who 92, WhoNob 90*
**Esaki**, Masumi 1915- *IntWW 91*
**Esala**, Philip John 1949- *WhoRel 92*
**Esary**, Charles Ray 1953- *WhoRel 92*
**Esary**, James Daniel 1926- *AmMWSc 92*
**Esau**, Gilbert D 1919- *WhoAmP 91*
**Esau**, Katherine 1898- *AmMWSc 92*
**Esayian**, Gary Martin 1958- *WhoFI 92*
**Esbensen**, Barbara Juster *DrAPF 91*
**Esbensen**, Barbara Juster 1925- *ConAu 134*
**Esbenshade**, Kathryn Mitchell 1955- *WhoMW 92*
**Esber**, Henry Jemil 1938- *AmMWSc 92*
**Esbin**, Jerry 1931- *IntMPA 92*
**Esbjornson**, Robert Glendon 1918- *WhoRel 92*
**Escaja**, James Michael 1955- *WhoMW 92*
**Escaja**, Mark Paul 1955- *WhoFI 92*
**Escala**, Veronica *WhoHisp 92*
**Escalada**, Antonio Jose de 1753-1821 *HisDSpE*
**Escaladas**, Emilio, III 1948- *WhoHisp 92*
**Escalante**, Jaime 1930- *WhoHisp 92*
**Escalante**, Judson Robert 1930- *WhoFI 92*
**Escalante**, Roel 1937- *WhoHisp 92*
**Escalante Cooper**, Barbara 1967- *WhoHisp 92*
**Escalera**, Albert D. 1943- *WhoHisp 92*

**Escalet**, Edwin Michael 1952- WhoHisp 92
**Escalet**, Frank Diaz, Jr. 1930- WhoHisp 92
**Escamilla**, Gerardo M. 1958- WhoHisp 92
**Escamilla**, James R. 1959- WhoHisp 92
**Escamilla**, Linda Garcia 1952- WhoHisp 92
**Escamilla**, Manuel 1947- WhoHisp 92
**Escandell**, Noemi DrAPF 91
**Escandon**, Ralph 1928- WhoHisp 92
**Escarraz**, Donald Ray 1932- WhoFI 92, WhoMW 92
**Escarraz**, Enrique, III 1944- WhoAmL 92
**Esce**, Susan Nan 1961- WhoAmL 92
**Esch**, Fred Stephen 1951- WhoWest 92
**Esch**, Gerald Wisler 1936- AmMWSc 92
**Esch**, Harald Erich 1931- AmMWSc 92
**Esch**, Louis James 1932- AmMWSc 92
**Esch**, Michael Martin 1952- WhoMW 92
**Esch**, Robin E 1930- AmMWSc 92
**Eschbach**, Charles Scott 1946- AmMWSc 92
**Eschbach**, Jesse Ernest 1920- WhoAmL 92
**Eschbach**, Joseph W AmMWSc 92
**Escheikh**, Abdelhamid 1935- IntWW 91
**Eschen**, Marvin 1926- WhoAmL 92
**Eschenbach**, Arthur Edwin 1918- WhoWest 92
**Eschenbach**, Christoph 1940- IntWW 91, NewAmDM, Who 92, WhoEnt 92
**Eschenbacher**, Larry Watts 1965- WhoEnt 92
**Eschenberg**, Kathryn 1923- AmMWSc 92
**Eschenburg**, Emil Paul 1915- WhoWest 92
**Eschenburg**, Frederick William 1957- WhoRel 92
**Eschenfelder**, Andrew Herbert 1925- AmMWSc 92
**Eschenmoser**, Albert 1925- FacFETw, IntWW 91
**Eschenroeder**, Alan Quade 1933- AmMWSc 92
**Escher**, Doris Jane Wolf 1917- AmMWSc 92
**Escher**, Emanuel 1943- AmMWSc 92
**Escher**, Maurits C 1898-1972 FacFETw
**Escherich**, Georg 1870-1941 BiDExR
**Escherich**, Rudolf Johann 1923- IntWW 91
**Eschig**, Max 1872-1927 NewAmDM
**Eschle**, James Lee 1937- AmMWSc 92
**Eschman**, Donald Frazier 1923- AmMWSc 92
**Eschmann**, Jean 1896-1961 DcTwDes
**Eschmeyer**, Paul Henry 1916- AmMWSc 92
**Eschmeyer**, William Neil 1939- AmMWSc 92
**Eschner**, Arthur Richard 1925- AmMWSc 92
**Eschner**, Edward George 1913- AmMWSc 92
**Esco**, Fred, Jr. 1954- WhoBlA 92
**Escobar**, Anna Maria 1956- WhoHisp 92
**Escobar**, Christy Brad 1954- WhoAmL 92
**Escobar**, Javier I 1943- AmMWSc 92
**Escobar**, Javier I., Sr. 1943- WhoHisp 92
**Escobar**, Jesus Ernesto 1948- WhoHisp 92
**Escobar**, Juan Manuel 1950- WhoHisp 92
**Escobar**, Maria Luisa 1909- IntWW 91
**Escobar**, Mario R 1931- AmMWSc 92
**Escobar**, Roberto E. WhoHisp 92
**Escobar Cerda**, Luis 1927- IntWW 91
**Escobar-Haskins**, Lillian WhoHisp 92
**Escobedo**, Edmundo, Sr. 1932- WhoHisp 92
**Escobedo**, Lydia Martinez 1930- WhoHisp 92
**Escobedo**, Theresa WhoHisp 92
**Escolar Sobrino**, Hipolito 1919- IntWW 91
**Escontrias**, Manuel 1945- WhoHisp 92
**Escoriaza y Cardona**, Jose Euripides de 1828-1921 HisDSpE
**Escorza**, Monica Marie 1958- WhoHisp 92
**Escot**, Pozzi WhoEnt 92
**Escott**, Sundra Erma 1954- WhoBlA 92
**Escott Cox**, Brian Robert Who 92
**Escott-Russell**, Sundra Erma 1954- WhoAmP 91
**Escovar**, Fernando 1944- WhoHisp 92
**Escovar Salom**, Ramon 1926- IntWW 91
**Escovedo**, Pete M. 1935- WhoHisp 92
**Escover**, Thomas Frank 1947- WhoWest 92
**Escribano-Alberca**, Ignacio 1928- WhoRel 92
**Escritt**, Ewart d1990 Who 92N
**Escritt**, Frederick Knowles 1893- Who 92
**Escudero**, Ernesto 1953- WhoHisp 92
**Escudero**, Gilbert 1945- WhoHisp 92
**Escudero**, Robert WhoHisp 92
**Escue**, Richard Byrd, Jr 1919- AmMWSc 92
**Esdale**, G. P. R., Mrs. Who 92
**Esders**, Theodore Walter 1945- AmMWSc 92
**Esecson**, Robert M. 1950- WhoFI 92
**Esen**, Asim 1938- AmMWSc 92
**Esenin**, Sergei Alexandrovich 1895-1925 FacFETw
**Eser**, Gunter O. 1927- IntWW 91
**Eser**, Gunter Otto 1927- Who 92
**Esfahani**, Mojtaba 1939- AmMWSc 92
**Esfandiary**, F. M. LiExTwC
**Esfandiary**, Mary Sadigh 1929- WhoFI 92
**Esgate**, Thomas Wagner 1949- WhoAmP 91
**Esgdaille**, Elias 1953- WhoHisp 92
**Eshbach**, Clifton Donald 1955- WhoEnt 92
**Eshbach**, John Robert 1922- AmMWSc 92
**Eshbach**, Lloyd Arthur 1910- IntAu&W 91, TwCSFW 91, WrDr 92
**Eshbaugh**, William Hardy 1936- AmMWSc 92, WhoMW 92
**Eshe**, Aisha DrAPF 91
**Eshelman**, Enos Grant, Jr. 1943- WhoWest 92
**Eshelman**, John Leo, Jr 1927- WhoAmP 91
**Esher**, Viscount 1913- Who 92
**Esherick**, Joseph Wharton 1942- WhoWest 92
**Esherick**, Wharton 1887-1970 DcTwDes
**Eshetu**, Gwendelbert Lewis 1940- WhoMW 92
**Eshleman**, Clayton DrAPF 91
**Eshleman**, Clayton 1935- BenetAL 91, ConPo 91, WrDr 92
**Eshleman**, Daniel Sylvester 1937- WhoRel 92
**Eshleman**, Ronald L 1933- AmMWSc 92
**Eshleman**, Von R 1924- AmMWSc 92
**Eshoo**, Anna Georges 1942- WhoAmP 91
**Eshpai**, Andrei Yakovlevich 1925- IntWW 91
**Esiason**, Boomer 1961- News 91 [port]
**Eskandari**, Freydoon M. 1936- WhoMW 92
**Eskandarian**, Edward 1936- WhoFI 92
**Eskdaill**, Lord 1984- Who 92
**Eskelsen**, Todd Richard 1939- WhoAmL 92
**Eskelson**, Cleamond D 1927- AmMWSc 92
**Eskelund**, Kenneth H 1924- AmMWSc 92
**Eskenazi**, David 1929- WhoRel 92
**Eskenazi**, Gerard Andre 1931- IntWW 91
**Eskesen**, B. Hal DrAPF 91
**Eskesen**, Ruth E 1939- WhoAmP 91
**Eskew**, Cathleen Cheek 1953- WhoWest 92
**Eskew**, Cletis Theodore 1904- AmMWSc 92
**Eskew**, David Lewis 1950- AmMWSc 92
**Eskew**, Elbert Wendall 1925- WhoRel 92
**Eski**, John Robert 1932- WhoMW 92
**Eskin**, Barry Sanford 1943- WhoAmL 92
**Eskin**, Frada 1936- WrDr 92
**Eskin**, Jeffrey Laurence 1952- WhoAmL 92
**Eskin**, Neason Akiva Michael 1941- AmMWSc 92
**Eskind**, Jane Greenebaum 1933- WhoAmP 91
**Eskins**, Kenneth AmMWSc 92
**Eskoff**, Richard Joseph WhoWest 92
**Eskola**, Antti Aarre 1934- IntWW 91
**Eskow**, John DrAPF 91
**Eskra**, John Philip, Jr. 1964- WhoEnt 92
**Eskridge**, John Clarence 1943- WhoBlA 92
**Eskridge**, Virginia Cook 1943- WhoAmL 92
**Eskridge**, William Nichol, Jr. 1951- WhoAmL 92
**Eskuri**, Neil WhoEnt 92
**Esleck**, David Lee 1959- WhoEnt 92
**Esler**, Anthony DrAPF 91
**Esler**, Anthony James 1934- WrDr 92
**Esler**, Robert F. 1933- WhoFI 92
**Esler**, Tika Amelia 1949- WhoWest 92
**Eslick**, Dennis Lee 1952- WhoFI 92
**Eslick**, Donald Farrell 1934- WhoAmP 91
**Eslick**, Robert Freeman 1916- AmMWSc 92
**Eslien**, Howard Jerome 1941- WhoAmL 92
**Eslyn**, Wallace Eugene 1924- AmMWSc 92
**Esmail**, Mohamed Nabil 1942- AmMWSc 92
**Esmay**, Donald Levern 1917- AmMWSc 92
**Esmay**, Merle L 1920- AmMWSc 92
**Esmen**, Nurtan A 1940- AmMWSc 92
**Esmenard**, Francis 1936- IntWW 91
**Esmon**, Charles Thomas 1947- AmMWSc 92
**Esmond**, Carl WhoEnt 92
**Esmond**, Carl 1906- IntMPA 92
**Esmond**, Harriet IntAu&W 91X, WrDr 92
**Esmonde**, Thomas 1960- Who 92
**Esnault-Pelterie**, Robert 1881-1957 FacFETw
**Esogbue**, Augustine O 1940- AmMWSc 92, WhoBlA 92
**Espach**, Ralph H, Jr 1932- AmMWSc 92
**Espada**, Martin DrAPF 91, WhoHisp 92
**Espada**, Pedro, Jr. 1953- WhoHisp 92
**Espada y Landa**, Juan Jose Diaz de HisDSpE
**Espaillat**, Edwin R. 1934- WhoHisp 92
**Espaillat**, Rhina P. DrAPF 91
**Espaldon**, Ernesto Mercader 1926- WhoAmP 91, WhoWest 92
**Espana**, Carlos 1919- AmMWSc 92
**Espana**, Jose Maria 1761-1799 HisDSpE
**Espander**, William Robert 1947- WhoWest 92
**Esparza**, Debra Sue 1960- WhoFI 92
**Esparza**, Francisco Javier 1967- WhoRel 92
**Esparza**, Henry WhoHisp 92
**Esparza**, Jesus 1932- WhoHisp 92
**Esparza**, Lili V. 1937- WhoHisp 92
**Esparza**, Manuel, Jr. 1946- WhoHisp 92
**Esparza**, Moctesuma Diaz 1949- WhoAmP 91, WhoEnt 92, WhoHisp 92
**Esparza**, Phillip W. 1949- WhoHisp 92
**Esparza**, Ralph Robert 1947- WhoHisp 92
**Esparza**, Thomas, Jr. 1952- WhoHisp 92
**Espat**, Roberto E. WhoHisp 92
**Espe**, Roger Bradley 1944- WhoWest 92
**Espejo**, Francisco Javier de Santa Cruz HisDSpE
**Espeland**, Pamela 1951- WrDr 92
**Espelie**, Karl Edward 1946- AmMWSc 92
**Espelie**, Solveig 1940- AmMWSc 92
**Espenoza**, Cecelia M. 1958- WhoHisp 92
**Espenshade**, Edward Bowman, Jr 1910- AmMWSc 92
**Espenshade**, Keith Lynn 1962- WhoRel 92
**Espenson**, James Henry 1937- AmMWSc 92
**Esper**, William Joseph 1932- WhoEnt 92
**Esperian**, Kallen Rose 1961- WhoEnt 92
**Espersen**, George A 1906- AmMWSc 92
**Espey**, John DrAPF 91
**Espey**, John 1913- WrDr 92
**Espey**, Lawrence Lee 1935- AmMWSc 92
**Espey**, Lucille Maud 1951- WhoAmL 92
**Espich**, Jeffrey K WhoAmP 91
**Espie**, Frank 1917- Who 92
**Espin**, C. Elizabeth 1961- WhoAmL 92
**Espin**, Oliva Maria 1938- WhoHisp 92
**Espin**, Orlando Oscar 1947- WhoHisp 92
**Espinar**, Alonso de d1513 HisDSpE
**Espinasse**, Jacques Paul 1943- IntWW 91
**Espineira**, Andy, IV 1949- WhoWest 92
**Espino**, David Virgil 1956- WhoHisp 92
**Espino**, Federico 1939- WrDr 92
**Espino**, Federico Licsi, Jr 1939- IntAu&W 91
**Espino**, Fern R. WhoHisp 92
**Espino Ramirez**, Rosa Maria 1964- WhoHisp 92
**Espinosa**, Alma Olga 1942- WhoHisp 92
**Espinosa**, Augusto 1919- Who 92
**Espinosa**, Aurelio Macedonio, Jr. 1907- WhoHisp 92
**Espinosa**, Dula Joanne 1958- WhoHisp 92
**Espinosa**, Edmundo 1927- WhoHisp 92
**Espinosa**, Enrique AmMWSc 92
**Espinosa**, Fernando WhoHisp 92
**Espinosa**, Francisco C. WhoHisp 92
**Espinosa**, Gaspar 1484-1537 HisDSpE
**Espinosa**, Genevieve 1950- WhoHisp 92
**Espinosa**, Guillermo G. 1960- WhoHisp 92
**Espinosa**, Hector WhoHisp 92
**Espinosa**, Hector 1940- WhoWest 92
**Espinosa**, Isidro Felix de 1679-1755 HisDSpE
**Espinosa**, James 1938- WhoHisp 92
**Espinosa**, James Manuel 1942- AmMWSc 92
**Espinosa**, Jose Manuel, Jr. 1942- WhoHisp 92
**Espinosa**, Luisito WhoHisp 92
**Espinosa**, Paul 1950- WhoHisp 92
**Espinosa**, Paula Maria 1939- WhoWest 92
**Espinosa**, Reynaldo, Jr. 1945- WhoHisp 92
**Espinosa**, Ruben William WhoHisp 92
**Espinosa**, Rudy DrAPF 91
**Espinosa Medrano**, Juan 1640-1688 HisDSpE
**Espinosa y Almodovar**, Juan 1941- WhoHisp 92
**Espinoza**, Alvaro 1962- WhoHisp 92
**Espinoza**, Armida Marie WhoWest 92
**Espinoza**, Daniel Isadore 1951- WhoRel 92
**Espinoza**, Elena Emilia 1960- WhoHisp 92
**Espinoza**, Eloisa 1960- WhoHisp 92
**Espinoza**, Gerardo 1955- WhoHisp 92
**Espinoza**, Isidro 1958- WhoHisp 92
**Espinoza**, Laurie Edith 1943- WhoHisp 92
**Espinoza**, Luis R. 1943- WhoHisp 92
**Espinoza**, Luis Rolan AmMWSc 92
**Espinoza**, Manuel R. 1942- WhoHisp 92
**Espinoza**, Michael Dan WhoHisp 92
**Espinoza**, Noe 1954- WhoHisp 92
**Espinoza**, Orlando P. 1953- WhoHisp 92
**Espinoza**, Pete E., Jr. 1948- WhoHisp 92
**Espiru**, Salvador 1913-1985 LiExTwC
**Esplen**, John Graham 1932- Who 92
**Esplin**, Barbara AmMWSc 92
**Esplin**, Fredrick Charles 1947- WhoEnt 92, WhoWest 92
**Esplin**, Ian 1914- Who 92
**Esposito**, Albert C 1922- WhoAmP 91
**Esposito**, Anthony James 1943- FacFETw
**Esposito**, Bonnie Lou 1947- WhoFI 92, WhoMW 92
**Esposito**, Cheryl Lynne 1964- WhoAmL 92
**Esposito**, Dennis Harry 1947- WhoAmL 92
**Esposito**, F Paul 1944- AmMWSc 92
**Esposito**, Frank, Jr WhoAmP 91
**Esposito**, John Nicholas 1938- AmMWSc 92
**Esposito**, John Vincent 1946- WhoAmL 92
**Esposito**, Joseph Anthony 1941- WhoAmL 92
**Esposito**, Joseph L 1941- ConAu 35NR
**Esposito**, Joseph Louis 1941- WhoAmL 92
**Esposito**, Larry Wayne 1951- AmMWSc 92
**Esposito**, Michael Salvatore 1940- AmMWSc 92
**Esposito**, Nancy DrAPF 91
**Esposito**, Pasquale Bernard 1940- AmMWSc 92
**Esposito**, Paul Andrew 1944- WhoAmP 91
**Esposito**, Phil 1942- FacFETw
**Esposito**, Raffaele 1932- AmMWSc 92
**Esposito**, Ralph V. 1954- WhoFI 92
**Esposito**, Rochelle E 1941- AmMWSc 92
**Esposito**, Rose Marie 1956- WhoAmL 92
**Esposito**, Stephen Michael 1949- WhoWest 92
**Esposito**, Theresa H WhoAmP 91
**Esposito**, Vito Michael 1940- AmMWSc 92
**Espoy**, Henry Marti 1917- AmMWSc 92
**Espree**, Allen James 1941- WhoBlA 92
**Espree**, Elizabeth Grace 1954- WhoRel 92
**Espy**, Herbert Hastings 1931- AmMWSc 92, WhoRel 92
**Espy**, Isaac Pugh 1939- WhoAmL 92
**Espy**, James Pollard 1785-1860 BiInAmS
**Espy**, James William 1948- WhoFI 92
**Espy**, Michael WhoBlA 92
**Espy**, Mike 1953- AlmAP 92 [port], WhoAmP 91
**Esquea Guerrero**, Emmanuel T. 1944- IntWW 91
**Esquer**, Cecilia D 1942- WhoAmP 91
**Esquerra**, Manuel Romo 1943- WhoHisp 92
**Esquerre**, Jean Roland 1923- WhoBlA 92
**Esquevin**, Christian Raymond 1948- WhoWest 92
**Esquiroz**, Margarita 1945- WhoHisp 92
**Esquivel**, Agerico Liwag 1932- AmMWSc 92
**Esquivel**, Argelia Velez 1936- WhoBlA 92
**Esquivel**, Joe WhoHisp 92
**Esquivel**, Manuel 1940- IntWW 91, Who 92
**Esquivel**, Rita WhoHisp 92
**Esrey**, Elizabeth Gove Goodier 1964- WhoFI 92
**Esrey**, William Todd 1940- WhoFI 92
**Esrick**, Jerald Paul 1941- WhoAmL 92
**Esrig**, Melvin I 1930- AmMWSc 92
**Esry**, Carroll Dale 1933- WhoMW 92
**Ess**, Charles Melvin 1951- WhoMW 92
**Essa**, Lisa Beth 1955- WhoWest 92
**Essaafi**, M'Hamed 1930- IntWW 91, Who 92
**Essame**, Enid Mary Who 92
**Essary**, Loris DrAPF 91
**Essayan**, Michael 1927- Who 92
**Essberger**, Ruprecht 1923- IntWW 91
**Esse**, Robert Carlyle 1932- AmMWSc 92
**Esselen**, William B 1912- AmMWSc 92
**Esselman**, W H 1917- AmMWSc 92
**Essen**, Louis 1908- Who 92
**Essenberg**, Margaret Kottke 1943- AmMWSc 92
**Essenberg**, Richard Charles 1943- AmMWSc 92
**Essenburg**, F 1924- AmMWSc 92
**Essene**, Eric J 1939- AmMWSc 92
**Essenfeld**, Amy 1959- AmMWSc 92
**Essenfeld**, Barry 1936- IntMPA 92
**Essenwanger**, Oskar M 1920- AmMWSc 92
**Esser**, Alfred F 1940- AmMWSc 92
**Esser**, Aristide Henri 1930- AmMWSc 92
**Esser**, Carl Eric 1942- WhoAmL 92
**Esser**, Hermann 1900-1981 BiDExR, EncTR 91 [port]
**Esser**, Otto 1917- IntWW 91
**Esser**, Robin Charles 1935- IntAu&W 91, Who 92
**Esserman**, Charles Howard 1958- WhoFI 92
**Esserman**, Rachel 1955- WhoEnt 92
**Essert**, Gary 1938- IntMPA 92
**Essery**, David James 1938- Who 92
**Essery**, John M 1936- AmMWSc 92
**Esses**, Jeffrey Alan 1960- WhoAmL 92
**Essex**, Earl of 1920- Who 92

**Essex**, David 1947- *IntMPA 92, IntWW 91*
**Essex**, Francis 1929- *IntAu&W 91, Who 92*
**Essex**, Francis William 1916- *Who 92*
**Essex**, Harry J 1915- *IntAu&W 91, IntMPA 92, WhoEnt 92, WrDr 92*
**Essex**, Kenneth Franklin 1943- *WhoAmL 92*
**Essex**, Myron 1939- *AmMWSc 92*
**Essex**, Saran 1948- *TwCWW 91, WrDr 92*
**Essex**, Terry 1946- *WhoAmP 91*
**Essex-Cater**, Antony John 1923- *Who 92, WrDr 92*
**Essien**, Francine B 1943- *AmMWSc 92*
**Essien**, Victor Kwesi 1952- *WhoAmL 92*
**Essiet**, Evaleen Johnson 1933- *WhoBlA 92*
**Essig**, Alvin 1923- *AmMWSc 92*
**Essig**, Carl Fohl 1919- *AmMWSc 92*
**Essig**, Charles J 1827?-1901 *BiInAmS*
**Essig**, Frederick Burt 1947- *AmMWSc 92*
**Essig**, Gustave Alfred 1915- *AmMWSc 92*
**Essig**, Henry J 1926- *AmMWSc 92*
**Essig**, Henry Werner 1930- *AmMWSc 92*
**Essig**, Philippe Louis Charles Marie 1933- *Who 92*
**Essig**, Rodney Allen 1949- *WhoEnt 92*
**Essigmann**, John Martin 1947- *AmMWSc 92*
**Essigmann**, Martin W 1917- *AmMWSc 92*
**Essington**, Edward Herbert 1937- *AmMWSc 92*
**Essler**, Warren O 1924- *AmMWSc 92*
**Esslin**, Martin 1918- *IntAu&W 91, LiExTwC, WrDr 92*
**Esslin**, Martin Julius 1918- *Who 92*
**Esslinger**, Anna Mae Linthicum 1912- *WhoFI 92*
**Esslinger**, Hartmut 1945- *DcTwDes*
**Esslinger**, Jack Houston 1931- *AmMWSc 92*
**Esslinger**, Theodore Lee 1944- *AmMWSc 92*
**Esslinger**, William Glenn 1937- *AmMWSc 92*
**Essman**, Joseph Edward 1935- *AmMWSc 92*
**Essman**, Walter Bernard 1933- *AmMWSc 92*
**Essmyer**, Michael Martin 1949- *WhoAmL 92*
**Essner**, Edward Stanley 1927- *AmMWSc 92*
**Essonghe**, Jean-Baptiste 1927- *IntWW 91*
**Essono**, Samuel Nang *WhoRel 92*
**Essop**, Ahmed 1931- *ConNov 91, IntAu&W 91, WrDr 92*
**Essrig**, Harry 1912- *SmATA 66*
**Esswood**, Paul Lawrence Vincent 1942- *IntWW 91, Who 92*
**Essy**, Amara 1943- *IntWW 91*
**Estabrook**, Frank Behle 1922- *AmMWSc 92*
**Estabrook**, George Frederick 1942- *AmMWSc 92*
**Estabrook**, Kent Gordon 1943- *AmMWSc 92*
**Estabrook**, Ronald 1926- *AmMWSc 92*
**Estang**, Luc 1911- *IntWW 91*
**Estany**, Myriam E. 1946- *WhoHisp 92*
**Estavillo**, William 1946- *WhoWest 92*
**Esteb**, Adlai Albert 1901- *WhoRel 92*
**Esteban**, Ernesto Pedro 1951- *WhoHisp 92*
**Esteban**, Manuel A. 1940- *WhoHisp 92, WhoWest 92*
**Esteban**, Mariano 1944- *WhoHisp 92*
**Estee**, Charles Remington 1921- *AmMWSc 92*
**Estefan**, Gloria *News 91 [port]*
**Estefan**, Gloria 1958- *WhoHisp 92*
**Estela**, Efrain Antonio 1954- *WhoHisp 92*
**Estensen**, Richard D 1934- *AmMWSc 92*
**Estep**, Charles Blackburn 1923- *AmMWSc 92*
**Estep**, Gerald Doss 1951- *WhoRel 92*
**Estep**, Herschel Leonard 1929- *AmMWSc 92*
**Estep**, James Riley, Jr. 1963- *WhoRel 92*
**Estep**, John Hayes 1930- *WhoMW 92*
**Estep**, Preston Wayne 1939- *WhoFI 92*
**Estep**, Roger D. 1930- *WhoBlA 92*
**Estep**, Ronald Eugene 1951- *WhoEnt 92*
**Estergreen**, Steven Leslie 1958- *WhoWest 92*
**Estergreen**, Victor Line 1925- *AmMWSc 92*
**Esterhazy** *NewAmDM*
**Esterka**, Peter 1935- *WhoRel 92*
**Esterkin**, Thomas Lyle 1956- *WhoWest 92*
**Esterle**, Stan *WhoRel 92*
**Esterline**, Dan Allan 1942- *WhoRel 92*
**Esterling**, Donald M 1942- *AmMWSc 92*
**Esterly**, Nancy Burton 1935- *AmMWSc 92*
**Estermann**, Eva Frances 1932- *AmMWSc 92*
**Esters**, George Edward 1941- *WhoBlA 92*
**Esterson**, Gerald L 1927- *AmMWSc 92*
**Estervig**, David Nels 1952- *AmMWSc 92*
**Estervig**, Howard Raymond 1947- *WhoFI 92*
**Estes**, Carl Lewis, II 1936- *WhoAmL 92, WhoFI 92*
**Estes**, Carroll L 1938- *AmMWSc 92*
**Estes**, Charles Byron 1946- *WhoEnt 92*
**Estes**, Charles Nicholson, Jr. 1945- *WhoAmL 92*
**Estes**, Dennis Ray 1941- *AmMWSc 92*
**Estes**, Douglas Lee 1944- *WhoMW 92*
**Estes**, Edna E 1921- *AmMWSc 92*
**Estes**, Edward Harvey, Jr 1925- *AmMWSc 92*
**Estes**, Edward Richard 1925- *AmMWSc 92*
**Estes**, Elaine Rose Graham 1931- *WhoBlA 92*
**Estes**, Eleanor 1906-1988 *BenetAL 91*
**Estes**, Frances Lorraine 1915- *AmMWSc 92*
**Estes**, Harper 1956- *WhoAmL 92*
**Estes**, Jack Charles 1935- *WhoFI 92*
**Estes**, James Allen 1945- *AmMWSc 92*
**Estes**, James Russell 1937- *AmMWSc 92*
**Estes**, Jane Elizabeth 1964- *WhoWest 92*
**Estes**, John H 1916- *AmMWSc 92*
**Estes**, John M., Jr. 1928- *WhoBlA 92*
**Estes**, Jon Carleton 1944- *WhoFI 92*
**Estes**, Joseph Raymond 1945- *WhoEnt 92*
**Estes**, Luther Weldon 1954- *WhoRel 92*
**Estes**, Lynda Sherryl 1945- *WhoFI 92*
**Estes**, Mark Wayne 1955- *WhoWest 92*
**Estes**, Moreau Pinckney, IV 1917- *WhoFI 92*
**Estes**, Richard 1932- *AmMWSc 92*
**Estes**, Sidney Harrison 1932- *WhoBlA 92*
**Estes**, Simon 1938- *NewAmDM*
**Estes**, Simon Lamont 1938- *WhoBlA 92, WhoEnt 92*
**Estes**, Stephen C *WhoAmP 91*
**Estes**, Timothy King 1940- *AmMWSc 92*
**Estes**, William 1919- *WrDr 92*
**Estes**, William K. 1919- *IntWW 91*
**Estete**, Miguel de *HisDSpE*
**Esteve-Coll**, Elizabeth *IntWW 91*
**Esteve-Coll**, Elizabeth Anne Loosemore 1938- *Who 92*
**Esteves**, Sandra Maria *DrAPF 91*
**Esteves**, Sandra Maria 1948- *WhoHisp 92*
**Estevez**, Emilio 1962- *IntMPA 92, IntWW 91, WhoEnt 92, WhoHisp 92*
**Estevez**, Enrique Gonzalo 1948- *AmMWSc 92*
**Estevez**, George Thomas 1925- *WhoEnt 92*
**Estevez**, Juan A., Jr. 1949- *WhoHisp 92*
**Estevez**, L. Antonio 1950- *WhoHisp 92*
**Estevez**, Ramon 1940- *WhoEnt 92*
**Estevez**, Victor A., III 1938- *WhoHisp 92*
**Estey**, Audree Phipps 1910- *WhoEnt 92*
**Estey**, Kenneth Fuller 1906- *WhoRel 92*
**Estey**, Ralph Howard 1916- *AmMWSc 92*
**Estey**, Willard Zebedee 1919- *Who 92*
**Esther** *EncEarC*
**Estienne**, Mark Joseph 1960- *AmMWSc 92*
**Estier**, Claude 1925- *IntWW 91*
**Estilai**, Ali 1940- *AmMWSc 92*
**Estill**, Ann H. M. *WhoBlA 92*
**Estill**, John Staples, Jr. 1919- *WhoAmL 92*
**Estill**, Lester D. 1920- *WhoMW 92*
**Estill**, Robert Whitridge 1927- *WhoRel 92*
**Estill**, Scott Michael 1961- *WhoAmL 92*
**Estill**, Wesley Boyd 1924- *AmMWSc 92*
**Estin**, Ann Laquer 1956- *WhoAmL 92*
**Estin**, Arthur John 1927- *AmMWSc 92*
**Estin**, Robert William 1931- *AmMWSc 92*
**Estis**, Dennis Arnold 1947- *WhoAmP 91*
**Estivill-Lorenz**, Vincent 1925- *WhoHisp 92*
**Estle**, Thomas Leo 1931- *AmMWSc 92*
**Estleman**, Loren D 1952- *IntAu&W 91, TwCWW 91, WrDr 92*
**Estler**, Ron Carter 1949- *AmMWSc 92*
**Estock**, Michael Joseph 1947- *WhoFI 92*
**Estoril**, Jean *IntAu&W 91X, WrDr 92*
**Estrada**, Alfredo J. *WhoHisp 92*
**Estrada**, Anthony Jose 1957- *WhoHisp 92*
**Estrada**, Dan 1950- *WhoHisp 92*
**Estrada**, Erik 1949- *IntMPA 92, WhoHisp 92*
**Estrada**, Eudoro 1933- *WhoHisp 92*
**Estrada**, Gabriel M. 1933- *WhoHisp 92*
**Estrada**, Herbert 1903- *AmMWSc 92*
**Estrada**, Jim 1943- *WhoHisp 92*
**Estrada**, Jose Luis 1955- *WhoHisp 92*
**Estrada**, Jose Macario 1942- *WhoAmL 92*
**Estrada**, Leobardo 1945- *WhoHisp 92*
**Estrada**, Louisa Isabel 1933- *WhoAmP 91*
**Estrada**, Luz D. *WhoHisp 92*
**Estrada**, Marc Napoleon 1965- *WhoHisp 92*
**Estrada**, Norma Ruth 1926- *AmMWSc 92*
**Estrada**, Roberto 1938- *WhoHisp 92*
**Estrada**, Ruben Cervantes 1940- *WhoHisp 92*
**Estrada**, Silvio J. 1939- *WhoHisp 92*
**Estrada**, Theresa Frances 1960- *WhoHisp 92*
**Estrada Palma**, Tomas 1835-1907 *HisDSpE*
**Estragon**, Vladimir *ConAu 36NR*
**Estreicher**, Samuel 1948- *WhoAmL 92*
**Estrella**, Julia *WhoRel 92*
**Estrella**, Nicolas 1951- *WhoHisp 92*
**Estrich**, Susan Rachel 1952- *WhoAmL 92*
**Estridge**, Robin *WrDr 92*
**Estrin**, Allen *WhoEnt 92*
**Estrin**, Dario Ariel 1962- *WhoMW 92*
**Estrin**, Eric Charles 1953- *WhoEnt 92*
**Estrin**, Gerald 1921- *AmMWSc 92*
**Estrin**, Kari 1954- *WhoEnt 92*
**Estrin**, Mitchell Stewart 1956- *WhoEnt 92*
**Estrin**, Norman Frederick 1939- *AmMWSc 92*
**Estrin**, Thelma A 1924- *AmMWSc 92*
**Estroff**, Nadine *DrAPF 91*
**Estrup**, Faiza Fawaz 1933- *AmMWSc 92*
**Estrup**, Peder Jan Z 1931- *AmMWSc 92*
**Esty**, Daniel Cushing 1959- *WhoAmL 92*
**Esty**, Donald, Jr *WhoAmP 91*
**Esty**, William Cole 1838-1916 *BiInAmS*
**Eswein**, Bruce James, II 1951- *WhoFI 92*
**Eszterhas**, Joe *IntMPA 92, SourALJ*
**Eszterhaus**, Joe *WrDr 92*
**Etaix**, Pierre 1928- *IntWW 91*
**Etayo Miqueo**, Jose Javier 1926- *IntWW 91*
**Etchart**, Mark S 1923- *WhoAmP 91*
**Etchecopar**, Maximo 1912- *BiDExR*
**Etchegaray**, Roger 1922- *IntWW 91, WhoRel 92*
**Etchegaray Aubry**, Alberto 1946- *IntWW 91*
**Etchells**, Frederick 1886-1973 *TwCPaSc*
**Etchells**, Jessie 1892-1933 *TwCPaSc*
**Etchells**, Ruth 1931- *Who 92*
**Etchemendy**, Nancy Howell 1952- *IntAu&W 91*
**Etches**, Robert J 1948- *AmMWSc 92*
**Etcheverry**, Michel Adrien 1919- *IntWW 91*
**Etchison**, Cordell 1914- *WhoAmP 91*
**Eteki Mboumoua**, William-Aurelien 1933- *IntWW 91*
**Etemadi**, Nour Ahmad 1921- *IntWW 91*
**Eteson**, Donald Calvert 1927- *AmMWSc 92*
**Etessami**, Rambod 1960- *WhoWest 92*
**Etgen**, Garret Jay 1937- *AmMWSc 92*
**Etgen**, William M 1929- *AmMWSc 92*
**Etges**, Frank Joseph 1924- *AmMWSc 92, WhoMW 92*
**Ethelbert** d616 *EncEarC*
**Ethelsdatter**, Karen *DrAPF 91*
**Etheredge**, Edward Ezekiel 1939- *AmMWSc 92*
**Etheredge**, Ernest C. 1946- *WhoRel 92*
**Etheredge**, Forest D 1929- *WhoAmP 91*
**Etheredge**, Forest DeRoyce 1929- *WhoMW 92*
**Etheredge**, James W. 1941- *WhoBlA 92*
**Etheredge**, Randall Abraham Edmund 1959- *WhoEnt 92*
**Etheredge**, Zelma Verree 1935- *WhoFI 92*
**Etherege**, George 1636-1692 *RfGEnL 91*
**Etheria** *EncEarC*
**Etheridge**, Albert Louis 1940- *AmMWSc 92*
**Etheridge**, Bob *WhoAmP 91*
**Etheridge**, Bobby Ray 1941- *WhoAmP 91*
**Etheridge**, David Elliott 1918- *AmMWSc 92*
**Etheridge**, Henry Emerson 1819-1902 *DcNCBi 2*
**Etheridge**, Jack Paul 1927- *WhoAmL 92*
**Etheridge**, James E. 1921- *WhoRel 92*
**Etheridge**, Larry E 1959- *WhoAmP 91*
**Etheridge**, Melissa *WhoEnt 92*
**Etheridge**, Richard Emmett 1929- *AmMWSc 92*
**Etheridge**, Robert Bruce 1878-1964 *DcNCBi 2*
**Etherington**, Geoffrey, II 1928- *WhoFI 92*
**Etherington**, Harold 1900- *AmMWSc 92*
**Etherington-Smith**, Gordon 1914- *Who 92*
**Etherton**, Bud 1930- *AmMWSc 92*
**Etherton**, Terence Michael Elkan Barnet 1951- *Who 92*
**Etherton**, Terry D 1949- *AmMWSc 92*
**Ethington**, Robert Allen 1954- *WhoRel 92*
**Ethington**, Robert Loren 1932- *AmMWSc 92*
**Ethinton**, Raymond Lindsay 1929- *AmMWSc 92*
**Ethridge**, Bruce 1938- *WhoAmP 91*
**Ethridge**, Frank Gulde 1938- *AmMWSc 92, WhoWest 92*
**Ethridge**, Grant Columbus 1964- *WhoRel 92*
**Ethridge**, John E. *WhoBlA 92*
**Ethridge**, Noel Harold 1927- *AmMWSc 92*
**Ethridge**, Robert Wylie 1940- *WhoBlA 92*
**Ethridge**, Samuel B. 1923- *WhoBlA 92*
**Ethridge**, William Louis 1910- *WhoAmP 91*
**Etiang**, Paul Orono 1938- *IntWW 91, Who 92*
**Etiemble**, Rene 1909- *IntWW 91*
**Etienne**, Duane Joseph 1941- *WhoMW 92*
**Etienne-Martin** 1913- *IntWW 91*
**Etish**, Allen Abram 1949- *WhoAmL 92*
**Etkes**, Raphael 1930- *IntMPA 92*
**Etkin**, Asher 1943- *AmMWSc 92*
**Etkin**, Bernard 1918- *AmMWSc 92*
**Etkind**, Efim Grigorievich 1918- *IntWW 91*
**Etler**, Alvin 1913-1973 *NewAmDM*
**Etling**, John Charles 1935- *WhoFI 92, WhoIns 92*
**Etling**, Terry Douglas 1943- *WhoMW 92*
**Etlinger**, Amelia *DrAPF 91*
**Etlinger**, Joseph David 1946- *AmMWSc 92*
**Etnier**, David Allen 1938- *AmMWSc 92*
**Etnier**, Elizabeth d1991 *NewYTBS 91*
**Eto**, Takami 1925- *IntWW 91*
**Etoungou**, Simon Nko'o 1932- *IntWW 91*
**Etra**, Aaron 1941- *WhoAmL 92*
**Etra**, Jonathan 1952-1991 *ConAu 133*
**Etrog**, Sorel 1933- *IntWW 91*
**Ets**, Marie Hall *DcAmImH*
**Etsou-Nzabi-Bamungwabi**, Frederic 1930- *WhoRel 92*
**Ett**, Alan Paul 1952- *WhoEnt 92, WhoWest 92*
**Ettedgui**, Alain Michael 1963- *WhoWest 92*
**Ettel**, Victor Alexander 1937- *AmMWSc 92*
**Ettenberg**, M 1916- *AmMWSc 92*
**Ettenberg**, Michael 1943- *AmMWSc 92*
**Ettensohn**, Francis Robert 1947- *AmMWSc 92*
**Ettenson**, Melvin Walter 1933- *WhoFI 92*
**Etter**, Constance Lynne 1943- *WhoFI 92*
**Etter**, Dave *DrAPF 91*
**Etter**, Dave 1928- *WrDr 92*
**Etter**, David Scott 1969- *WhoRel 92*
**Etter**, Delores Maria 1947- *AmMWSc 92*
**Etter**, Douglas Albert 1960- *WhoRel 92*
**Etter**, James Walter 1943- *WhoEnt 92*
**Etter**, Margaret Cairns 1943- *AmMWSc 92*
**Etter**, Paul Courtney 1947- *AmMWSc 92*
**Etter**, Raymond Lewis, Jr 1931- *AmMWSc 92*
**Etter**, Robert Miller 1932- *AmMWSc 92*
**Etters**, Ronald Milton 1948- *WhoAmL 92*
**Ettighofer**, Paul Coelestin 1896-1975 *EncTR 91*
**Etting**, Ruth 1907-1978 *NewAmDM*
**Ettinger**, Cecil Ray 1922- *WhoRel 92*
**Ettinger**, Edwin D. 1921- *IntMPA 92*
**Ettinger**, Elzbieta *WrDr 92*
**Ettinger**, George Harold *AmMWSc 92*
**Ettinger**, Harry Joseph 1934- *AmMWSc 92*
**Ettinger**, Joseph Alan 1931- *WhoAmL 92, WhoMW 92*
**Ettinger**, Milton G 1930- *AmMWSc 92*
**Ettinger**, Murray J *AmMWSc 92*
**Ettinger**, Richard Charles 1947- *WhoMW 92*
**Ettinghoff**, Tracy H. 1953- *WhoAmL 92*
**Ettingoff**, Cindy Cole 1959- *WhoAmL 92*
**Ettl**, Harald 1947- *IntWW 91*
**Ettling**, Bruce Vincent 1930- *WhoWest 92*
**Ettlinger**, Gerard Herman 1935- *WhoRel 92*
**Ettlinger**, John A. 1924- *IntMPA 92*
**Ettlinger**, Michael Pauw 1959- *WhoFI 92*
**Ettlinger**, Robert Emil 1947- *WhoWest 92*
**Ettman**, Steven Lawrence 1964- *WhoEnt 92*
**Ettner**, Dann J. 1957- *WhoRel 92*
**Ettor**, Joseph *DcAmImH*
**Ettouney**, Osama Mohamed 1951- *WhoMW 92*
**Ettre**, Leslie Stephen 1922- *AmMWSc 92*
**Ettrick**, Marco Antonio 1945- *WhoFI 92*
**Ettwein**, John 1721-1802 *DcNCBi 2*
**Etzel**, Barbara Coleman 1926- *WhoMW 92*
**Etzel**, Howard Wesley 1922- *AmMWSc 92*
**Etzel**, James Edward 1929- *AmMWSc 92*
**Etzioni**, Amitai 1929- *IntAu&W 91, WrDr 92*
**Etzioni**, Amitai Werner 1929- *WhoFI 92*
**Etzler**, Dorr Homer 1915- *AmMWSc 92*
**Etzler**, Frank M 1952- *AmMWSc 92*
**Etzler**, Marilynn Edith 1940- *AmMWSc 92, WhoWest 92*
**Etzweiler**, George Arthur 1920- *AmMWSc 92*
**Etzwiler**, Donnell D 1927- *AmMWSc 92*
**Etzwiler**, Donnell Dencil 1927- *IntWW 91*
**Eu**, Byung Chan 1935- *AmMWSc 92*
**Eu**, March Fong *WhoAmP 91*
**Eu**, March Kong Fong 1922- *WhoWest 92*
**Euans**, Robert Earl 1941- *WhoMW 92*
**Euba**, Akin 1935- *ConCom 92*
**Euba**, Femi 1941- *WhoEnt 92*
**Eubank**, Harold Porter 1924- *AmMWSc 92*
**Eubank**, J. Thomas 1930- *WhoAmL 92*
**Eubank**, Philip Toby 1936- *AmMWSc 92*
**Eubank**, Randall Lester 1952- *AmMWSc 92*

**Eubank,** William Roderick 1919- *AmMWSc 92*
**Eubanks,** David L. *WhoRel 92*
**Eubanks,** Dayna C. 1957- *WhoBlA 92*
**Eubanks,** Elizabeth Ruberta *AmMWSc 92*
**Eubanks,** Eugene E. 1939- *WhoBlA 92*
**Eubanks,** Gary Leroy, Sr. 1933- *WhoAmL 92*
**Eubanks,** Isaac Dwaine 1938- *AmMWSc 92*
**Eubanks,** John Bunyan 1913- *WhoBlA 92*
**Eubanks,** L Stanley 1931- *AmMWSc 92*
**Eubanks,** Rachel Amelia *WhoBlA 92*
**Eubanks,** Robert A. 1926- *WhoBlA 92*
**Eubanks,** Robert Alonzo 1926- *AmMWSc 92*
**Eubanks,** Ronald W. 1946- *WhoAmL 92*
**Eubanks,** William Hunter 1921- *AmMWSc 92*
**Eubig,** Casimir 1940- *AmMWSc 92*
**Eucherius of Lyons** d449? *EncEarC*
**Eucken,** Rudolph Christoph 1846-1926 *WhoNob 90*
**Eucrateia** *EncAmaz 91*
**Eudaily,** Ralph S 1913- *WhoAmP 91*
**Eudaly,** Nathan Hoyt 1913- *WhoRel 92*
**Eudy,** William Wayne 1939- *AmMWSc 92*
**Euell,** Julian Thomas 1929- *WhoBlA 92*
**Eugel,** James Frederick 1934- *WhoRel 92*
**Eugen Francis of Savoy-Carignan** 1663-1736 *BlkwCEP*
**Eugen of Savoy** 1663-1736 *BlkwCEP*
**Eugene,** John 1940- *WhoAmL 92*
**Eugere,** Edward J. 1930- *WhoBlA 92*
**Eugere,** Edward Joseph 1930- *AmMWSc 92*
**Eugippius** d535? *EncEarC*
**Eugster,** A Konrad 1938- *AmMWSc 92*
**Eugster,** Jack Wilson 1945- *WhoFI 92, WhoMW 92*
**Eukel,** Warren W 1921- *AmMWSc 92*
**Eule,** Julian Nathan 1949- *WhoAmL 92*
**Eulenburg,** Ernst 1847-1926 *NewAmDM*
**Euler,** Kenneth L 1937- *AmMWSc 92*
**Euler,** Leonhardt 1707-1783 *BlkwCEP*
**Euler,** Russell Nelson 1950- *WhoMW 92*
**Euler,** Ulf von *FacFETw*
**Euler,** William Carl, Jr. 1960- *WhoFI 92*
**Euler-Chelpin,** Hans Karl August S von 1873-1964 *FacFETw, WhoNob 90*
**Eulo,** Ken 1939- *IntAu&W 91*
**Eulogius of Alexandria** d608 *EncEarC*
**Eunomius of Cyzicus** 325?-395? *EncEarC*
**Eure,** Dexter D., Sr. 1923- *WhoBlA 92*
**Eure,** Herman Edward 1947- *AmMWSc 92, WhoBlA 92*
**Eure,** James L. *WhoRel 92*
**Eure,** Jerry Holton, Sr. 1923- *WhoBlA 92*
**Eure,** Wesley *WhoEnt 92*
**Euresti,** Benjamin, Jr. 1949- *WhoHisp 92*
**Eurich,** Richard 1903- *TwCPaSc*
**Eurich,** Richard Ernst 1903- *IntWW 91, Who 92*
**Euringer,** Richard 1891-1953 *EncTR 91 [port]*
**Eury,** Lynn Wade 1937- *WhoFI 92*
**Eurydice** *EncAmaz 91*
**Eurydice of Egypt** *EncAmaz 91*
**Eurydice,** Queen of Macedonia *EncAmaz 91*
**Euryleonis** *EncAmaz 91*
**Eurypyle** *EncAmaz 91*
**Eurythmics** *ConMus 6 [port]*
**Eusden,** John Dykstra 1922- *WhoRel 92*
**Eusebius of Caesarea** 260?-339? *EncEarC*
**Eusebius of Nicomedia** d342 *EncEarC*
**Eusebius of Vercelli** d370? *EncEarC*
**Euskirchen,** George John 1941- *WhoFI 92, WhoMW 92*
**Eustace,** Dudley Graham 1936- *Who 92*
**Eustace,** Frank James 1934- *WhoIns 92*
**Eustace,** John Wesley 1936- *WhoMW 92*
**Eustace,** Joseph Lambert 1908- *IntWW 91*
**Eustace,** Lambert 1908- *Who 92*
**Eustache,** Paul *WhoRel 92*
**Eustaquio,** George Castro 1931- *WhoAmP 91*
**Eustathius of Antioch** *EncEarC*
**Eustice,** David Christopher 1952- *AmMWSc 92*
**Eustice,** Francis Joseph 1951- *WhoAmL 92*
**Eustice,** Russell Clifford 1919- *WhoFI 92*
**Eustis,** Helen 1916- *WrDr 92*
**Eustis,** Henry Lawrence 1819-1885 *BiInAmS*
**Eustis,** Richmond Minor 1945- *WhoAmL 92*
**Eustis,** Robert H 1920- *AmMWSc 92*
**Eustis,** William Henry 1921- *AmMWSc 92*
**Euston,** Earl of 1947- *Who 92*
**Eutherius of Tyana** *EncEarC*
**Eutropius** *EncEarC*
**Eutsler,** Mark Leslie 1958- *WhoMW 92*
**Eutsler,** Steve Dwight 1958- *WhoRel 92*
**Eutyches** *EncEarC*
**Evagrius of Pontus** 345-399 *EncEarC*
**Evagrius Scholasticus** 535?-600 *EncEarC*
**Evaige,** Wanda Jo 1935- *WhoBlA 92*
**Evain,** Elaine *DrAPF 91*
**Evaldson,** Rune L 1918- *AmMWSc 92*
**Evan,** Derek 1962- *WhoWest 92*
**Evan,** Paul *TwCWW 91*
**Evan-Cook,** John Edward 1902- *Who 92*
**Evanega,** George R 1936- *AmMWSc 92*
**Evanega,** George Ronald 1936- *WhoFI 92*
**Evangelista,** Alfredo Gonzales 1958- *WhoAmL 92*
**Evangelista,** Donato A. 1932- *WhoAmL 92, WhoFI 92*
**Evangelista,** Francisco Boki *WhoAmP 91*
**Evangelista,** Marylee *WhoFI 92*
**Evangelista,** Ramon Antonio 1952- *WhoRel 92*
**Evangelou,** Iason 1926- *IntAu&W 91*
**Evanger,** Jacqueline Ruth 1926- *WhoAmP 91*
**Evanier,** David *DrAPF 91*
**Evankovich,** George Joseph 1930- *WhoFI 92, WhoWest 92*
**Evanochko,** William Thomas 1951- *AmMWSc 92*
**Evanoff,** Douglas Darrell 1951- *WhoFI 92*
**Evanoff,** Vlad 1916- *WrDr 92*
**Evans** *Who 92*
**Evans and Novak** *FacFETw*
**Evans,** A. Briant 1909- *Who 92*
**Evans,** A C *WhoAmP 91*
**Evans,** A. Michael, Jr. 1948- *WhoEnt 92*
**Evans,** Abigail Rian 1937- *WhoRel 92*
**Evans,** Ada B. 1932- *WhoBlA 92*
**Evans,** Alan 1930- *IntAu&W 91, WrDr 92*
**Evans,** Alan G 1942- *AmMWSc 92*
**Evans,** Albert Edwin, Jr 1930- *AmMWSc 92*
**Evans,** Alexander John 1954- *WhoFI 92*
**Evans,** Alfred Spring 1917- *AmMWSc 92*
**Evans,** Alicia 1960- *WhoBlA 92*
**Evans,** Allen V 1939- *WhoAmP 91*
**Evans,** Allison Bickle 1910- *AmMWSc 92*
**Evans,** Alona Elizabeth 1917-1980 *AmPeW*
**Evans,** Alun *Who 92*
**Evans,** Alun S. *Who 92*
**Evans,** Amanda Louise Elliot 1958- *Who 92*
**Evans,** Amos James 1922- *WhoBlA 92*
**Evans,** Andrew C. *IntMPA 92*
**Evans,** Angela Marie 1956- *WhoRel 92*
**Evans,** Anthony *Who 92*
**Evans,** Anthony 1922- *Who 92*
**Evans,** Anthony 1934- *Who 92*
**Evans,** Anthony Glyn 1942- *AmMWSc 92*
**Evans,** Anthony John 1930- *Who 92*
**Evans,** Anthony Lawrence 1951- *WhoRel 92*
**Evans,** Anthony Thomas 1943- *Who 92*
**Evans,** Arthur L. 1931- *WhoBlA 92*
**Evans,** Arthur Mostyn 1925- *Who 92*
**Evans,** Arthur T 1919- *AmMWSc 92*
**Evans,** Audrey Elizabeth 1925- *AmMWSc 92*
**Evans,** Augusta J. 1835-1909 *BenetAL 91*
**Evans,** B J 1942- *AmMWSc 92*
**Evans,** Barry 1943- *IntMPA 92*
**Evans,** Ben Edward 1944- *AmMWSc 92*
**Evans,** Bergen *LesBEnT 92*
**Evans,** Bernard William 1934- *AmMWSc 92*
**Evans,** Beverly Ann 1944- *WhoAmP 91*
**Evans,** Bill *DrAPF 91*
**Evans,** Bill 1920- *WhoEnt 92*
**Evans,** Bill 1929-1980 *FacFETw, NewAmDM*
**Evans,** Bill 1940- *WhoEnt 92*
**Evans,** Bill L. *WhoEnt 92*
**Evans,** Billy J. 1942- *WhoBlA 92*
**Evans,** Bob Overton 1927- *AmMWSc 92*
**Evans,** Bradford *DrAPF 91*
**Evans,** Briant *Who 92*
**Evans,** Britt 1946- *WhoWest 92*
**Evans,** Bruce A. 1946- *ConAu 134*
**Evans,** Bruce Dwight 1934- *WhoAmL 92, WhoFI 92*
**Evans,** Bruce Haselton 1939- *WhoMW 92*
**Evans,** Bruce Read *Who 92*
**Evans,** Bryant Robert 1945- *WhoWest 92*
**Evans,** Burtis Robbins 1925- *WhoWest 92*
**Evans,** Burton Robert 1929- *AmMWSc 92*
**Evans,** Carole Yvonne Mims 1951- *WhoBlA 92*
**Evans,** Caswell Alves, Jr. 1943- *WhoBlA 92*
**Evans,** Charles *Who 92*
**Evans,** Charles 1890-1979 *FacFETw*
**Evans,** Charles Andrew, Jr 1942- *AmMWSc 92*
**Evans,** Charles E 1938- *WhoAmP 91*
**Evans,** Charles Hawes 1940- *AmMWSc 92*
**Evans,** Charles Napoleon Bonaparte 1812-1883 *DcNCBi 2*
**Evans,** Charles P 1930- *AmMWSc 92*
**Evans,** Charles Stephen 1948- *WhoRel 92*
**Evans,** Charles Wesley 1939- *WhoAmP 91*
**Evans,** Charlotte A. *WhoBlA 92*
**Evans,** Charlotte Thelma Weaver 1947- *WhoRel 92*
**Evans,** Cheryl Lynn 1950- *WhoBlA 92*
**Evans,** Christina Hambley *Who 92*
**Evans,** Christopher 1951- *TwCSFW 91*
**Evans,** Christopher Francis 1909- *Who 92*
**Evans,** Claudia T 1952- *AmMWSc 92*
**Evans,** Clay 1925- *WhoBlA 92*
**Evans,** Clive Ernest 1937- *Who 92*
**Evans,** Clyde Edsel 1927- *AmMWSc 92*
**Evans,** Colin Rodney 1935- *Who 92*
**Evans,** Cooper *WhoAmP 91*
**Evans,** Craig 1949- *WhoFI 92*
**Evans,** Crecy Ann 1915- *WhoBlA 92*
**Evans,** Cynthia Anne 1953- *WhoMW 92*
**Evans,** D. Bruce 1935- *WhoFI 92*
**Evans,** Daniel Budd 1952- *WhoAmL 92*
**Evans,** Daniel Donald 1920- *AmMWSc 92*
**Evans,** Daniel Jackson *WhoAmP 91*
**Evans,** Daniel Jackson 1925- *IntWW 91, WhoWest 92*
**Evans,** Daniel Scot 1953- *WhoAmP 91*
**Evans,** Daniel Warren 1956- *WhoAmL 92*
**Evans,** David 1929-1988 *TwCPaSc*
**Evans,** David 1935- *Who 92*
**Evans,** David 1937- *Who 92*
**Evans,** David A 1941- *AmMWSc 92*
**Evans,** David Alan Price 1927- *Who 92*
**Evans,** David Allan *DrAPF 91*
**Evans,** David Anthony 1939- *Who 92*
**Evans,** David Arnold 1938- *AmMWSc 92*
**Evans,** David Arthur 1939- *AmMWSc 92*
**Evans,** David Bush 1954- *WhoMW 92*
**Evans,** David C 1924- *AmMWSc 92, WhoWest 92*
**Evans,** David Eifion 1911- *Who 92*
**Evans,** David Ellis 1930- *Who 92, WrDr 92*
**Evans,** David George 1924- *Who 92*
**Evans,** David Henry 1949- *WhoMW 92*
**Evans,** David Howard 1944- *Who 92*
**Evans,** David Hudson 1940- *AmMWSc 92*
**Evans,** David Huhn, Jr. 1944- *WhoEnt 92*
**Evans,** David Hunden 1924- *AmMWSc 92*
**Evans,** David John 1935- *Who 92*
**Evans,** David L 1906- *AmMWSc 92*
**Evans,** David L 1946- *AmMWSc 92*
**Evans,** David Lane 1954- *AmMWSc 92*
**Evans,** David Lawrence 1939- *WhoBlA 92*
**Evans,** David Lloyd C. *Who 92*
**Evans,** David Lynn 1941- *WhoMW 92*
**Evans,** David Marshall 1937- *Who 92*
**Evans,** David Milne 1917- *Who 92*
**Evans,** David Philip 1908- *Who 92*
**Evans,** David R 1941- *AmMWSc 92*
**Evans,** David Richard John 1938- *Who 92*
**Evans,** David Roderick 1946- *Who 92*
**Evans,** David Stanley 1916- *AmMWSc 92, IntWW 91, WrDr 92*
**Evans,** David W 1933- *AmMWSc 92*
**Evans,** David Wesley 1954- *AmMWSc 92*
**Evans,** David Wyke 1934- *IntWW 91*
**Evans,** Dennis Frederick d1990 *IntWW 91N, Who 92N*
**Evans,** Dennis Hyde 1939- *AmMWSc 92*
**Evans,** Diana Powers 1928- *WhoAmP 91*
**Evans,** Diane G. 1959- *WhoFI 92*
**Evans,** Dik *ScFEYrs*
**Evans,** Don A. 1948- *WhoWest 92*
**Evans,** Donald 1884-1921 *BenetAL 91*
**Evans,** Donald B 1933- *AmMWSc 92*
**Evans,** Donald Eugene 1934- *WhoRel 92*
**Evans,** Donald Foster 1949- *WhoWest 92*
**Evans,** Donald John 1926- *WhoAmL 92*
**Evans,** Donald Lee 1943- *AmMWSc 92*
**Evans,** Donald LeRoy 1933- *WhoMW 92*
**Evans,** Donald Thomas 1938- *WhoEnt 92*
**Evans,** Donna Browder *WhoBlA 92*
**Evans,** Donna Janis 1944- *WhoFI 92*
**Evans,** Donovan Lee 1939- *AmMWSc 92*
**Evans,** Dorsey 1930- *WhoBlA 92*
**Evans,** Douglas Craig 1961- *WhoEnt 92*
**Evans,** Douglas Fennell 1937- *AmMWSc 92*
**Evans,** Douglas Hayward 1950- *WhoAmL 92*
**Evans,** Douglas Richard 1951- *WhoEnt 92*
**Evans,** Dwayne 1958- *BlkOlyM*
**Evans,** Dwight 1954- *WhoAmP 91, WhoBlA 92*
**Evans,** E. A. *IntWW 91*
**Evans,** E Chris 1928- *WhoAmP 91*
**Evans,** E Everett 1893-1958 *TwCSFW 91*
**Evans,** E Graham, Jr *AmMWSc 92*
**Evans,** Eben 1920- *Who 92*
**Evans,** Edgar E. 1908- *WhoBlA 92*
**Evans,** Edgar G 1884-1914 *BiInAmS*
**Evans,** Edward Butram 1894- *WhoBlA 92*
**Evans,** Edward Clark 1955- *WhoBlA 92*
**Evans,** Edward Lewis 1904- *Who 92*
**Evans,** Edward Stanley Price 1925- *Who 92*
**Evans,** Edward William 1932- *AmMWSc 92*
**Evans,** Edwin C. 1917- *IntWW 91*
**Evans,** Edwin Curtis 1917- *AmMWSc 92*
**Evans,** Edwin Victor 1914- *AmMWSc 92*
**Evans,** Eifion *Who 92*
**Evans,** Elbert Franklin 1947- *WhoMW 92*
**Evans,** Eleanor Juanita 1944- *WhoBlA 92*
**Evans,** Elizabeth *DrAPF 91*
**Evans,** Ellis *Who 92*
**Evans,** Emrys *Who 92*
**Evans,** Ena Winifred 1938- *Who 92*
**Evans,** Eric *Who 92*
**Evans,** Eric J. 1945- *WrDr 92*
**Evans,** Ernest Edward, Jr 1922- *AmMWSc 92*
**Evans,** Ernestine D. 1917- *WhoHisp 92*
**Evans,** Ernestine Duran 1917- *WhoAmP 91*
**Evans,** Ersel Arthur 1922- *AmMWSc 92*
**Evans,** Essi H 1950- *AmMWSc 92*
**Evans,** Eva L. 1935- *WhoBlA 92*
**Evans,** Evan *TwCWW 91*
**Evans,** Evan Cyfeiliog, III 1922- *AmMWSc 92*
**Evans,** Evan Franklin 1918- *AmMWSc 92*
**Evans,** F Dean 1955- *WhoAmP 91*
**Evans,** F Maurice 1930- *WhoAmP 91*
**Evans,** Fabyan Peter Leaf 1943- *Who 92*
**Evans,** Fay Jones 1909- *WhoAmP 91*
**Evans,** Foster 1915- *AmMWSc 92*
**Evans,** Frances *WrDr 92*
**Evans,** Francis Cope 1914- *AmMWSc 92*
**Evans,** Francis Eugene 1928- *AmMWSc 92*
**Evans,** Francis Gaynor 1907- *AmMWSc 92*
**Evans,** Francis Loring G. *Who 92*
**Evans,** Frank Bernard 1927- *ConAu 36NR*
**Evans,** Frank Edward 1923- *WhoAmP 91*
**Evans,** Franklin James, Jr 1921- *AmMWSc 92*
**Evans,** Frederick Anthony 1907- *Who 92*
**Evans,** Frederick Earl 1948- *AmMWSc 92*
**Evans,** Frederick Read 1913- *AmMWSc 92*
**Evans,** Frederick William 1808-1893 *AmPeW*
**Evans,** Gareth 1944- *Who 92*
**Evans,** Gareth John 1944- *IntWW 91*
**Evans,** Garth 1934- *TwCPaSc*
**Evans,** Gary John 1945- *WhoMW 92*
**Evans,** Gary Lee 1938- *WhoMW 92*
**Evans,** Gary R 1941- *AmMWSc 92*
**Evans,** Gary William 1940- *AmMWSc 92*
**Evans,** Gene 1924- *IntMPA 92*
**Evans,** Geoffrey 1935- *AmMWSc 92*
**Evans,** George *BenetAL 91, DrAPF 91*
**Evans,** George 1745?-1784? *DcNCBi 2*
**Evans,** George Edward 1932- *AmMWSc 92*
**Evans,** George Ewart 1909- *IntAu&W 91*
**Evans,** George James 1944- *Who 92*
**Evans,** George L., Jr. 1947- *WhoFI 92*
**Evans,** George Leonard 1931- *AmMWSc 92*
**Evans,** George R. 1920- *WhoEnt 92*
**Evans,** George Robert, Jr. 1931- *WhoFI 92*
**Evans,** Geraint 1922- *NewAmDM*
**Evans,** Geraint Llewellyn 1922- *IntWW 91, Who 92, WhoEnt 92*
**Evans,** Gerald Johnson 1945- *WhoRel 92*
**Evans,** Gerald William 1950- *AmMWSc 92*
**Evans,** Geraldine Ann 1939- *WhoMW 92*
**Evans,** Gil 1912-1988 *FacFETw, NewAmDM*
**Evans,** Gillian 1944- *IntAu&W 91*
**Evans,** Glenn Thomas 1946- *AmMWSc 92*
**Evans,** Godfrey *Who 92*
**Evans,** Gordon Emil 1932- *WhoAmP 91*
**Evans,** Gordon Heyd 1930- *WhoFI 92*
**Evans,** Gregory Bradshaw 1958- *WhoFI 92*
**Evans,** Gregory Herbert 1949- *AmMWSc 92*
**Evans,** Gregory James 1954- *WhoBlA 92*
**Evans,** Grose 1916- *IntAu&W 91, WrDr 92*
**Evans,** Gwendolyn *WhoBlA 92*
**Evans,** Gwynfor 1912- *IntWW 91, Who 92*
**Evans,** H Dean 1929- *WhoAmP 91*
**Evans,** H Gene 1941- *WhoAmP 91*
**Evans,** Harold 1928- *WrDr 92*
**Evans,** Harold Edward 1927- *WhoFI 92*
**Evans,** Harold J 1921- *AmMWSc 92, IntWW 91*
**Evans,** Harold Matthew 1928- *IntAu&W 91, IntWW 91, Who 92, WhoFI 92*
**Evans,** Harold Ray 1926- *WhoEnt 92*
**Evans,** Harrison Silas 1911- *AmMWSc 92*
**Evans,** Harry Kent 1935- *WhoEnt 92*
**Evans,** Haydn Barry 1936- *WhoRel 92*
**Evans,** Haydn T. *Who 92*
**Evans,** Hazel Atkinson 1931- *WhoAmP 91*
**Evans,** Helen Harrington 1924- *AmMWSc 92*
**Evans,** Henry 1760?-1810 *DcNCBi 2*
**Evans,** Henry 1934- *WhoAmP 91*
**Evans,** Henry John 1930- *Who 92*
**Evans,** Henry Mullen, Jr. 1936- *WhoRel 92*
**Evans,** Herbert B. 1919- *WhoBlA 92*
**Evans,** Herbert David 1944- *WhoRel 92*
**Evans,** Herbert John 1937- *AmMWSc 92*
**Evans,** Herschel 1909-1939 *NewAmDM*
**Evans,** Hilary 1929- *ScFEYrs*
**Evans,** Hiram John 1916- *AmMWSc 92*
**Evans,** Howard Edward 1922- *AmMWSc 92*
**Evans,** Howard Ensign 1919- *AmMWSc 92*

**Evans,** Howard Tasker, Jr 1919- *AmMWSc 92*
**Evans,** Hubert Carol 1921- *WhoAmP 91*
**Evans,** Hugh E 1934- *AmMWSc 92*
**Evans,** Hugh Lloyd 1941- *AmMWSc 92*
**Evans,** Huw Prideaux 1941- *Who 92*
**Evans,** Hywel Eifion 1910- *Who 92*
**Evans,** I O 1894-1977 *ScFEYrs*
**Evans,** Ian Philip 1948- *Who 92*
**Evans,** Irene M 1943- *AmMWSc 92*
**Evans,** Jack *WhoBlA 92*
**Evans,** Jack Barton 1948- *WhoFI 92*
**Evans,** James *TwCSFW 91*
**Evans,** James 1932- *Who 92*
**Evans,** James Allan S. 1931- *WrDr 92*
**Evans,** James Bowen 1930- *AmMWSc 92*
**Evans,** James Brainerd 1921- *AmMWSc 92*
**Evans,** James Carmichael 1900- *WhoBlA 92*
**Evans,** James Donald 1926- *Who 92*
**Evans,** James E. 1946- *WhoAmL 92*
**Evans,** James Ellis 1910- *Who 92*
**Evans,** James Eric Lloyd 1914- *AmMWSc 92*
**Evans,** James Forrest 1932- *WhoMW 92*
**Evans,** James Gilbert, Jr. 1924- *WhoAmL 92*
**Evans,** James H 1934- *WhoIns 92*
**Evans,** James H 1939- *WhoAmP 91*
**Evans,** James Harold 1939- *WhoAmL 92*
**Evans,** James Humphrey R. *Who 92*
**Evans,** James Ornette 1920- *AmMWSc 92*
**Evans,** James R 1931- *AmMWSc 92*
**Evans,** James Robert 1950- *WhoMW 92*
**Evans,** James Spurgeon 1931- *AmMWSc 92*
**Evans,** James Stuart 1941- *AmMWSc 92*
**Evans,** James Warren 1938- *AmMWSc 92*
**Evans,** James Weldon 1926- *WhoAmP 91*
**Evans,** James William 1908- *AmMWSc 92*
**Evans,** James William 1943- *AmMWSc 92, WhoWest 92*
**Evans,** Jan Roger 1942- *WhoAmL 92*
**Evans,** Jane 1944- *WhoFI 92*
**Evans,** Jane Franklin Bridges 1933- *WhoMW 92*
**Evans,** Janelle Jo 1927- *WhoAmP 91*
**Evans,** Janelle Johnson 1956- *WhoWest 92*
**Evans,** Janet Ann 1936- *WhoEnt 92*
**Evans,** Janice W 1937- *WhoAmP 91*
**Evans,** Jed Reeder 1929- *WhoWest 92*
**Evans,** Jeffrey Orvis 1953- *WhoFI 92, WhoMW 92*
**Evans,** Jennifer Jane 1947- *WhoEnt 92*
**Evans,** Jeremy David Agard 1936- *Who 92*
**Evans,** Jerry L 1931- *WhoAmP 91*
**Evans,** Jerry Lee 1931- *WhoWest 92*
**Evans,** Jesse 1937- *WhoAmP 91*
**Evans,** Joe B. 1929- *WhoBlA 92*
**Evans,** Joe Smith 1933- *AmMWSc 92*
**Evans,** Joel Raymond 1948- *WhoFI 92*
**Evans,** Johannes Sanao 1927- *WhoFI 92*
**Evans,** John *IntAu&W 91X, Who 92*
**Evans,** John 1812-1861 *BiInAmS*
**Evans,** John 1922- *WhoAmP 91*
**Evans,** John 1930- *Who 92*
**Evans,** John Alan Maurice 1936- *Who 92*
**Evans,** John Alfred Eaton 1933- *Who 92*
**Evans,** John Borden 1929- *WhoRel 92*
**Evans,** John C 1938- *AmMWSc 92*
**Evans,** John Charles, Jr 1944- *AmMWSc 92*
**Evans,** John David Gemmill 1942- *IntWW 91*
**Evans,** John Davies 1925- *Who 92*
**Evans,** John Derby 1944- *WhoFI 92*
**Evans,** John Edward 1925- *AmMWSc 92*
**Evans,** John Ellis 1914- *AmMWSc 92*
**Evans,** John Erik 1927- *WhoIns 92*
**Evans,** John F. *WhoRel 92*
**Evans,** John Fenton 1949- *AmMWSc 92*
**Evans,** John Field 1928- *Who 92*
**Evans,** John G. *Who 92*
**Evans,** John Isaac Glyn 1919- *Who 92*
**Evans,** John Joseph 1940- *WhoFI 92*
**Evans,** John Kerr Q. *Who 92*
**Evans,** John Marten Llewellyn 1909- *Who 92*
**Evans,** John Mascal 1915- *Who 92*
**Evans,** John Mervin 1949- *WhoAmL 92*
**Evans,** John Millard 1918- *WhoFI 92*
**Evans,** John N 1948- *AmMWSc 92*
**Evans,** John R 1929- *AmMWSc 92*
**Evans,** John R 1932- *WhoAmP 91*
**Evans,** John Robert 1929- *IntWW 91, Who 92*
**Evans,** John Roger W. *Who 92*
**Evans,** John Stanley 1943- *Who 92*
**Evans,** John Stanton 1921- *AmMWSc 92*
**Evans,** John Thomas 1948- *WhoAmL 92*
**Evans,** John Thornley 1938- *WhoAmL 92*
**Evans,** John V 1933- *AmMWSc 92*
**Evans,** John Victor 1925- *WhoAmP 91*
**Evans,** John W 1935- *AmMWSc 92*
**Evans,** John Wainwright, Jr 1909- *AmMWSc 92*
**Evans,** John Wynford 1934- *Who 92*
**Evans,** John Yorath Gwynne 1922- *Who 92*
**Evans,** Jonathan *IntAu&W 91X*
**Evans,** Joni 1942- *News 91 [port]*
**Evans,** Joseph Liston 1930- *AmMWSc 92*
**Evans,** Joseph Owen 1949- *WhoMW 92*
**Evans,** Julia 1913- *IntAu&W 91*
**Evans,** Junius Anthony 1911- *WhoWest 92*
**Evans,** Karen 1958- *WhoAmL 92*
**Evans,** Keith Ordway 1954- *WhoAmL 92*
**Evans,** Kelly R. 1953- *WhoAmL 92*
**Evans,** Kenneth, Jr 1941- *AmMWSc 92*
**Evans,** Kenneth Dawson 1915- *Who 92*
**Evans,** Kenneth Jack 1929- *AmMWSc 92*
**Evans,** Kenneth R. 1938- *ConAu 134*
**Evans,** Kent Steven 1946- *WhoMW 92*
**Evans,** Lance Saylor 1944- *AmMWSc 92*
**Evans,** Lane 1951- *AlmAP 92 [port], WhoAmP 91, WhoMW 92*
**Evans,** Larry Gerald 1943- *AmMWSc 92*
**Evans,** Larry Q 1948- *WhoAmP 91*
**Evans,** Lary Lewis 1939- *WhoFI 92*
**Evans,** Latimer Richard 1918- *AmMWSc 92*
**Evans,** Laurence James d1991 *Who 92N*
**Evans,** Laurie Edward 1933- *AmMWSc 92*
**Evans,** Lawrance Lee 1945- *WhoAmP 91*
**Evans,** Lawrence Alan 1958- *WhoEnt 92*
**Evans,** Lawrence B 1934- *AmMWSc 92*
**Evans,** Lawrence Eugene 1932- *AmMWSc 92*
**Evans,** Lawrence Jack, Jr. 1921- *WhoAmL 92, WhoWest 92*
**Evans,** Lawrence Timothy 1947- *WhoRel 92*
**Evans,** Lee 1933- *WhoEnt 92*
**Evans,** Lee 1947- *WhoBlA 92*
**Evans,** Lee E 1922- *AmMWSc 92*
**Evans,** Lee Edward 1947- *BlkOlyM*
**Evans,** Leon, Jr. 1953- *WhoBlA 92*
**Evans,** Leon Edward, Jr. 1942- *WhoBlA 92*
**Evans,** Leonard 1939- *AmMWSc 92, WhoMW 92*
**Evans,** LeRoy W. 1946- *WhoBlA 92*
**Evans,** Lewis 1700-1756 *BiInAmS*
**Evans,** Lillie R. 1913- *WhoBlA 92*
**Evans,** Linda *LesBEnT 92*
**Evans,** Linda 1942- *IntMPA 92, WhoEnt 92*
**Evans,** Lloyd Ranney 1932- *WhoEnt 92*
**Evans,** Lloyd Russell, Jr 1947- *WhoAmP 91*
**Evans,** Lloyd Thomas 1927- *IntWW 91, Who 92*
**Evans,** Loren Kenneth 1928- *WhoFI 92, WhoMW 92*
**Evans,** Lorenzo J. 1909- *WhoBlA 92*
**Evans,** Lynn Susan 1951- *WhoFI 92*
**Evans,** Malinda Murphey 1935- *WhoMW 92*
**Evans,** Margaret Ann 1947- *WhoMW 92*
**Evans,** Mari *DrAPF 91, WhoBlA 92, WrDr 92*
**Evans,** Mari 1923- *ConPo 91, NotBlAW 92*
**Evans,** Mark *WhoEnt 92*
**Evans,** Mark Armstrong 1940- *Who 92*
**Evans,** Mark L. 1942- *WhoAmL 92*
**Evans,** Mark Lewis 1956- *WhoAmL 92*
**Evans,** Marlene June 1933- *WhoRel 92*
**Evans,** Marlene Sandra 1946- *AmMWSc 92*
**Evans,** Martha *DrAPF 91*
**Evans,** Martin Frederic 1947- *WhoAmL 92*
**Evans,** Mary Adetta 1909- *WhoBlA 92*
**Evans,** Mary Jo 1935- *AmMWSc 92*
**Evans,** Matilda Arabella 1872-1935 *NotBlAW 92*
**Evans,** Matthew 1941- *IntWW 91, Who 92*
**Evans,** Maurice d1989 *LesBEnT 92*
**Evans,** Max 1924- *WrDr 92*
**Evans,** Max 1925- *IntAu&W 91, TwCWW 91*
**Evans,** Max Jay 1943- *WhoWest 92*
**Evans,** Melvin H. 1917-1984 *WhoBlA 92N*
**Evans,** Merlyn 1910-1973 *TwCPaSc*
**Evans,** Michael *Who 92*
**Evans,** Michael Allen 1943- *AmMWSc 92*
**Evans,** Michael B. 1946- *WhoAmL 92*
**Evans,** Michael Dean 1953- *WhoFI 92*
**Evans,** Michael Douglas 1959- *AmMWSc 92*
**Evans,** Michael Leigh 1941- *AmMWSc 92*
**Evans,** Michael Nordon 1915- *Who 92*
**Evans,** Michael Scott 1952- *WhoAmL 92*
**Evans,** Milton L. 1936- *WhoBlA 92*
**Evans,** Mostyn *Who 92*
**Evans,** Mostyn 1925- *IntWW 91*
**Evans,** Myra Lynn 1959- *WhoBlA 92*
**Evans,** Nancy *WhoAmP 91*
**Evans,** Nancy 1950- *ConAu 34NR, SmATA 65*
**Evans,** Nancy Jo 1947- *WhoMW 92*
**Evans,** Nancy Remage 1944- *AmMWSc 92*
**Evans,** Nathaniel 1742-1767 *BenetAL 91*
**Evans,** Neal John, II 1946- *AmMWSc 92*
**Evans,** Neil B 1947- *WhoAmP 91*
**Evans,** Neil Edward 1943- *WhoEnt 92*
**Evans,** Neil Kenneth 1936- *WhoAmL 92*
**Evans,** Newton Jasper, Jr 1940- *WhoAmP 91*
**Evans,** Nicholas 1907- *TwCPaSc*
**Evans,** Noel John 1933- *Who 92*
**Evans,** Norman A 1922- *AmMWSc 92*
**Evans,** Olen M. 1954- *WhoRel 92*
**Evans,** Oliver 1755-1819 *BiInAmS*
**Evans,** Orinda D. 1943- *WhoAmL 92*
**Evans,** Owen Carlyle 1920- *WhoWest 92*
**Evans,** Patricia E. 1946- *WhoBlA 92*
**Evans,** Patricia P. *WhoBlA 92*
**Evans,** Patrick Alexander Sidney 1943- *Who 92*
**Evans,** Paul M. 1954- *WhoWest 92*
**Evans,** Paul Vernon 1926- *WhoAmL 92*
**Evans,** Penney 1941- *WhoWest 92*
**Evans,** Peter 1781-1852 *DcNCBi 2*
**Evans,** Peter 1929- *Who 92*
**Evans,** Peter Angus 1929- *Who 92*
**Evans,** Peter Billow 1959- *WhoFI 92*
**Evans,** Phillip L. 1937- *WhoBlA 92*
**Evans,** Phyllis Mary Carlyon d1990 *Who 92N*
**Evans,** R. Daniel *DrAPF 91*
**Evans,** R Mont 1947- *WhoAmP 91*
**Evans,** R. Stanton 1961- *WhoMW 92*
**Evans,** Raeford G 1919- *AmMWSc 92*
**Evans,** Ralph Aiken 1924- *AmMWSc 92*
**Evans,** Ralph H, Jr 1929- *AmMWSc 92*
**Evans,** Ray 1915- *IntMPA 92*
**Evans,** Ray 1920- *TwCPaSc*
**Evans,** Raymond Arthur 1925- *AmMWSc 92*
**Evans,** Raymond Bernard 1915- *WhoEnt 92*
**Evans,** Raymond John Morda 1917- *Who 92*
**Evans,** Rees Thompson 1945- *WhoAmL 92*
**Evans,** Rhydwyn Harding 1900- *Who 92*
**Evans,** Rhys Sterling 1923- *WhoEnt 92*
**Evans,** Richard 1735?-1774? *DcNCBi 2*
**Evans,** Richard 1928- *Who 92*
**Evans,** Richard Alan 1934- *WhoAmP 91*
**Evans,** Richard Denman 1948- *WhoFI 92*
**Evans,** Richard John 1947- *IntWW 91*
**Evans,** Richard Lloyd 1935- *WhoWest 92*
**Evans,** Richard Mark 1928- *IntWW 91*
**Evans,** Richard N. 1924- *WhoAmL 92*
**Evans,** Richard Todd 1932- *AmMWSc 92*
**Evans,** Robert *AmMWSc 92*
**Evans,** Robert 1927- *IntWW 91, Who 92*
**Evans,** Robert 1930- *IntMPA 92*
**Evans,** Robert, Jr. 1932- *WhoFI 92*
**Evans,** Robert Charles 1918- *IntWW 91, Who 92*
**Evans,** Robert David 1945- *WhoAmL 92*
**Evans,** Robert Edward 1943- *WhoEnt 92*
**Evans,** Robert George, Jr. 1953- *WhoMW 92*
**Evans,** Robert J. 1930- *WhoEnt 92*
**Evans,** Robert John 1909- *AmMWSc 92, WhoWest 92*
**Evans,** Robert John 1928- *AmMWSc 92, WhoMW 92*
**Evans,** Robert John Weston 1943- *IntWW 91, Who 92*
**Evans,** Robert Lindsay, Sr. 1934- *WhoEnt 92*
**Evans,** Robert Morton 1917- *AmMWSc 92*
**Evans,** Robert Noel 1922- *Who 92*
**Evans,** Robert Owen 1919- *WrDr 92*
**Evans,** Robert Sheldon 1944- *WhoFI 92*
**Evans,** Robert Vincent 1958- *WhoWest 92*
**Evans,** Robert Warren 1927- *WhoBlA 92*
**Evans,** Roberta George 1938- *WhoAmL 92*
**Evans,** Robley D 1907- *AmMWSc 92*
**Evans,** Robley Dunglison 1907- *FacFETw*
**Evans,** Roderick *Who 92*
**Evans,** Rodney Earl 1939- *WhoFI 92*
**Evans,** Roger 1951- *WhoAmL 92*
**Evans,** Roger James *AmMWSc 92*
**Evans,** Roger Lynwood 1928- *AmMWSc 92, WhoMW 92*
**Evans,** Roger Malcolm 1935- *AmMWSc 92*
**Evans,** Roger W. *Who 92*
**Evans,** Ronald M *AmMWSc 92*
**Evans,** Ronald Wayne 1927- *WhoAmP 91*
**Evans,** Rowland, Jr 1921- *FacFETw, WhoAmP 91, WrDr 92*
**Evans,** Roxanne J. 1952- *WhoBlA 92*
**Evans,** Roy Lyon 1931- *Who 92*
**Evans,** Russell Wilmot 1922- *IntWW 91, Who 92*
**Evans,** Ruth Anne 1944- *WhoMW 92*
**Evans,** Ruthana Wilson 1932- *WhoBlA 92*
**Evans,** Samuel London 1902- *WhoBlA 92, WhoEnt 92*
**Evans,** Sara M. 1943- *WrDr 92*
**Evans,** Scott 1954- *WhoEnt 92*
**Evans,** Sherry Hartfield 1948- *WhoEnt 92*
**Evans,** Simon John 1937- *Who 92*
**Evans,** Slayton Alvin, Jr. 1943- *WhoBlA 92*
**Evans,** Spofford L. 1919- *WhoBlA 92*
**Evans,** Sticks 1923- *WhoBlA 92*
**Evans,** Stuart 1934- *IntAu&W 91*
**Evans,** Stuart Anthony 1951- *WhoWest 92*
**Evans,** Sylvia Ann 1951- *WhoMW 92*
**Evans,** T H 1906- *AmMWSc 92*
**Evans,** Tabor *ConAu 35NR, IntAu&W 91X, TwCWW 91, WrDr 92*
**Evans,** Taylor Herbert 1918- *AmMWSc 92*
**Evans,** Terence Thomas 1940- *WhoAmL 92, WhoMW 92*
**Evans,** Thelma Jean Mathis 1944- *WhoMW 92*
**Evans,** Therman E. 1944- *WhoBlA 92*
**Evans,** Thomas 1863-1907 *BiInAmS*
**Evans,** Thomas 1925- *WhoBlA 92*
**Evans,** Thomas Alun 1937- *Who 92*
**Evans,** Thomas Archie 1928- *WhoBlA 92*
**Evans,** Thomas Chives Newton 1947- *WhoFI 92*
**Evans,** Thomas Edgar, Jr. 1940- *WhoWest 92*
**Evans,** Thomas Edward 1939- *AmMWSc 92*
**Evans,** Thomas Eric 1928- *Who 92*
**Evans,** Thomas F 1924- *AmMWSc 92*
**Evans,** Thomas George 1934- *AmMWSc 92*
**Evans,** Thomas Godfrey 1920- *Who 92*
**Evans,** Thomas Henry 1907- *Who 92*
**Evans,** Thomas Michael 1930- *Who 92*
**Evans,** Thomas P 1921- *AmMWSc 92*
**Evans,** Thomas Walter 1923- *AmMWSc 92*
**Evans,** Thomas William 1930- *WhoAmL 92*
**Evans,** Timothy C 1943- *WhoAmP 91, WhoBlA 92*
**Evans,** Timothy Monroe 1945- *WhoWest 92*
**Evans,** Todd Edwin 1947- *AmMWSc 92*
**Evans,** Tommy Nicholas 1922- *AmMWSc 92*
**Evans,** Toni Lynn 1952- *WhoMW 92*
**Evans,** Trevor 1925- *AmMWSc 92*
**Evans,** Trevor 1927- *Who 92*
**Evans,** Trevor John 1947- *Who 92*
**Evans,** Van Holland 1924- *WhoRel 92*
**Evans,** Vernon D. 1950- *WhoBlA 92*
**Evans,** Victoria Regina 1963- *WhoHisp 92*
**Evans,** Vince Tobias 1955- *WhoBlA 92*
**Evans,** Vincent *Who 92*
**Evans,** Virginia John 1913- *AmMWSc 92*
**Evans,** W E 1938- *AmMWSc 92*
**Evans,** W. Ronald 1938- *WhoBlA 92*
**Evans,** Walker 1903-1975 *DcTwDes, FacFETw*
**Evans,** Warren Cleage 1948- *WhoBlA 92*
**Evans,** Warren D *WhoAmP 91*
**Evans,** Warren Felt 1817-1889 *RelLAm 91*
**Evans,** Warren William 1921- *AmMWSc 92*
**Evans,** Wayne Errol 1951- *AmMWSc 92*
**Evans,** Webb 1913- *WhoBlA 92*
**Evans,** Webster 1908-1982 *ConAu 133*
**Evans,** Wick *TwCWW 91*
**Evans,** William Andrew 1939- *Who 92*
**Evans,** William Buell 1918- *AmMWSc 92*
**Evans,** William C. 1899- *WhoBlA 92*
**Evans,** William Clayton 1944- *WhoBlA 92*
**Evans,** William David 1949- *Who 92*
**Evans,** William Davidson, Jr. 1943- *WhoAmL 92*
**Evans,** William E. 1931- *WhoBlA 92*
**Evans,** William Emrys 1924- *Who 92*
**Evans,** William George 1923- *AmMWSc 92*
**Evans,** William Halla 1950- *WhoRel 92*
**Evans,** William John 1947- *AmMWSc 92*
**Evans,** William John 1950- *WhoWest 92*
**Evans,** William L 1924- *AmMWSc 92*
**Evans,** William McKee 1923- *WrDr 92*
**Evans,** William Neal 1950- *WhoWest 92*
**Evans,** William Paul 1922- *AmMWSc 92*
**Evans,** William R *AmMWSc 92*
**Evans,** William Richard 1938- *WhoEnt 92*
**Evans,** William Thomas 1941- *WhoWest 92*
**Evans,** William Vincent 1915- *Who 92*
**Evans,** William Wallace 1923- *WhoAmL 92*
**Evans,** Winifred Doyle 1934- *AmMWSc 92*
**Evans,** Winston Kenneth 1928- *WhoFI 92*
**Evans,** Wynford *Who 92*
**Evans-Anfom,** Emmanuel 1919- *Who 92*
**Evans-Bevan,** Martyn Evan 1932- *Who 92*
**Evans Davies,** Gloria 1932- *IntAu&W 91*
**Evans-Dodd,** Theora Anita 1945- *WhoBlA 92*
**Evans-Freke** *Who 92*
**Evans-Le Blanc,** Candace Kay 1958- *WhoWest 92*
**Evans-Lombe,** Edward Christopher 1937- *Who 92*
**Evans-McNeill,** Elona Anita 1945- *WhoBlA 92*
**Evans of Claughton,** Baron 1928- *Who 92*
**Evans-Tranumn,** Shelia 1951- *WhoBlA 92*
**Evansen,** Virginia B. *WrDr 92*
**Evanson,** Barbara Gibbons 1944- *WhoAmP 91*

**Evanson,** Paul John 1941- *WhoFI 92*
**Evanson,** Robert Verne 1920- *AmMWSc 92*
**Evanswood,** Terrence Edward 1970- *WhoMW 92*
**Evanti,** Lillian 1890-1967 *NotBlAW 92*
**Evard,** Rene 1927- *AmMWSc 92*
**Evarts,** George William 1936- *WhoFI 92*
**Evarts,** Hal G. 1915-1989 *TwCWW 91*
**Evarts,** Hal G., Sr. 1887-1934 *TwCWW 91*
**Evarts,** Hal George 1887-1934 *BenetAL 91*
**Evarts,** Prescott, Jr. *DrAPF 91*
**Evarts,** Ritva Poukka 1932- *AmMWSc 92*
**Evarts,** William Maxwell 1818-1901 *AmPolLe*
**Evatt,** Bruce Lee 1939- *AmMWSc 92*
**Evatt,** Elizabeth Andreas 1933- *Who 92*
**Evatt,** Harmon Parker 1935- *WhoAmP 91*
**Evces,** Charles Richard 1938- *AmMWSc 92*
**Evdokim,** Archbishop 1869-1935 *RelLAm 91*
**Evdokimov,** Paul 1901-1970 *DcEcMov*
**Evdokimova,** Eva 1948- *WhoEnt 92*
**Eve** *EncEarC [port], Who 92*
**Eve,** Arthur O 1933- *WhoAmP 91, WhoBlA 92*
**Eve,** Christina M. 1917- *WhoBlA 92*
**Eve,** Trevor 1951- *ConTFT 9*
**Evege,** Walter L., Jr. 1943- *WhoBlA 92*
**Eveland,** Harmon Edwin 1924- *AmMWSc 92*
**Eveland,** Warren C 1904- *AmMWSc 92*
**Eveleigh,** Douglas Edward 1933- *AmMWSc 92*
**Eveleigh,** Edward Walter 1917- *Who 92*
**Eveleigh,** Eldon Spencer 1950- *AmMWSc 92*
**Eveleigh,** Geoffrey Charles 1912- *Who 92*
**Eveleigh,** Virgil W 1931- *AmMWSc 92*
**Eveleth,** George Stimson 1938- *WhoFI 92*
**Eveleth,** Peter Ames 1939- *WhoAmL 92*
**Eveling,** Stanley 1925- *IntAu&W 91, WrDr 92*
**Evelti,** Mary M 1920- *WhoAmP 91*
**Evelyn,** Gwyneth 1925- *WhoEnt 92*
**Evelyn,** John 1620-1706 *RfGEnL 91*
**Evelyn,** John Michael 1916- *IntAu&W 91*
**Evelyn,** Michael 1916- *Who 92*
**Even,** James A *WhoIns 92*
**Even,** William Roy, Jr 1952- *AmMWSc 92*
**Evenbeck,** Scott Edward 1946- *WhoMW 92*
**Evennett,** David Anthony 1949- *Who 92*
**Eveno,** Bertrand 1944- *IntWW 91*
**Evens,** F Monte 1932- *AmMWSc 92*
**Evens,** Leonard 1933- *AmMWSc 92*
**Evens,** Martha Walton 1935- *AmMWSc 92, WhoMW 92*
**Evens,** Ronald Gene 1939- *WhoMW 92*
**Evensen,** Alf John 1938- *WhoFI 92*
**Evensen,** Gregory Lance 1950- *WhoMW 92*
**Evensen,** James Millard 1931- *AmMWSc 92*
**Evensen,** Jens 1917- *IntWW 91*
**Evensen,** Kathleen Brown *AmMWSc 92*
**Evensen,** Thomas James 1933- *AmMWSc 92*
**Evenson,** Dennis David 1946- *WhoAmP 91*
**Evenson,** Donald Paul 1940- *AmMWSc 92*
**Evenson,** Edward B 1942- *AmMWSc 92*
**Evenson,** Kenneth Melvin 1932- *AmMWSc 92*
**Evenson,** Merle Armin 1934- *AmMWSc 92*
**Evenson,** Paul Arthur 1946- *AmMWSc 92*
**Evenson,** Robert Eugene 1934- *WhoFI 92*
**Evenson,** Russell Allen 1947- *WhoMW 92*
**Evenson,** S. Jeanne 1938- *WhoWest 92*
**Evenson,** William Edwin 1941- *AmMWSc 92*
**Evenstad,** Kenneth L. 1943- *WhoMW 92*
**Everaert,** Pierre Jean 1939- *WhoFI 92*
**Everard,** Christopher E. W. *Who 92*
**Everard,** Noel James 1923- *AmMWSc 92*
**Everard,** Richard 1683-1733 *DcNCBi 2*
**Everard,** Robin 1939- *Who 92*
**Everard,** Timothy John 1929- *Who 92*
**Everbach,** Otto George 1938- *WhoAmL 92, WhoFI 92*
**Everding,** August 1928- *IntWW 91*
**Everding,** Henry Edward, Jr. 1934- *WhoRel 92*
**Everding,** Robert George 1945- *WhoWest 92*
**Evered,** David Charles 1940- *IntWW 91, Who 92*
**Everest,** Allan S. 1913- *WrDr 92*
**Everest,** David Anthony 1926- *Who 92*
**Everest,** F Alton 1909- *AmMWSc 92*
**Everett,** Alexander Hill 1790-1847 *BenetAL 91*
**Everett,** Allen Edward 1933- *AmMWSc 92*
**Everett,** Ann Maxie 1959- *WhoEnt 92*
**Everett,** Ann Nevarez 1915- *WhoRel 92*
**Everett,** Ardell Gordon 1937- *AmMWSc 92*
**Everett,** Asa Brooks 1828-1875 *NewAmDM*
**Everett,** Bernard Jonathan 1943- *Who 92*
**Everett,** Bonnie Ellen 1951- *WhoAmL 92*
**Everett,** C. Curtis 1930- *WhoAmL 92*
**Everett,** Carl Nicholas 1926- *WhoFI 92*
**Everett,** Chad 1937- *IntMPA 92, WhoEnt 92*
**Everett,** Christopher Harris Doyle 1933- *Who 92*
**Everett,** Danny 1966- *BlkOlyM*
**Everett,** David Leon, II 1922-1990 *WhoBlA 92N*
**Everett,** Douglas Hugh 1916- *IntWW 91, Who 92, WrDr 92*
**Everett,** Edward 1794-1865 *AmPolLe [port], BenetAL 91*
**Everett,** Eileen *Who 92*
**Everett,** Elbert Kyle 1946- *WhoFI 92*
**Everett,** Glen Exner 1934- *AmMWSc 92*
**Everett,** Graham *DrAPF 91*
**Everett,** Guy M 1915- *AmMWSc 92*
**Everett,** Harry Day 1880?-1908 *BiInAmS*
**Everett,** Herbert Lyman 1922- *AmMWSc 92*
**Everett,** Hobart Ray, Jr. 1949- *WhoWest 92*
**Everett,** Howard Cheston 1909- *WhoWest 92*
**Everett,** J. Richard 1936- *WhoBlA 92*
**Everett,** James Joseph 1955- *WhoAmL 92*
**Everett,** James Legrand, III 1926- *AmMWSc 92*
**Everett,** James William 1951- *WhoRel 92*
**Everett,** James William, Jr. 1957- *WhoAmL 92, WhoFI 92*
**Everett,** Jeffrey Arthur 1964- *WhoFI 92*
**Everett,** Joann Marie *DrAPF 91*
**Everett,** John Wendell 1906- *AmMWSc 92*
**Everett,** Jonathan Jubal 1950- *WhoAmL 92*
**Everett,** K R 1934- *AmMWSc 92*
**Everett,** Karen J. 1926- *WhoMW 92*
**Everett,** Kay 1941- *WhoBlA 92*
**Everett,** Kenneth Gary 1942- *AmMWSc 92*
**Everett,** Lois Almen 1931- *WhoWest 92*
**Everett,** Lorne Gordon 1943- *AmMWSc 92*
**Everett,** Mark Allen 1928- *AmMWSc 92*
**Everett,** Mary Elizabeth 1929- *WhoFI 92*
**Everett,** Mike 1948- *WhoAmP 91*
**Everett,** Nell M. *WhoAmL 92*
**Everett,** Oliver William 1943- *Who 92*
**Everett,** Pamela Irene 1947- *WhoAmL 92, WhoFI 92, WhoWest 92*
**Everett,** Paul Marvin 1940- *AmMWSc 92*
**Everett,** Percival L. 1933- *WhoBlA 92*
**Everett,** Peter 1931- *IntAu&W 91*
**Everett,** Ralph B. 1951- *WhoBlA 92*
**Everett,** Ralph Bernard 1951- *WhoAmP 91*
**Everett,** Reuben Oscar 1879-1971 *DcNCBi 2*
**Everett,** Reynolds Melville, Jr. 1946- *WhoAmL 92*
**Everett,** Robert Andrew 1948- *WhoRel 92*
**Everett,** Robert R 1921- *AmMWSc 92*
**Everett,** Robert W, Jr 1921- *AmMWSc 92*
**Everett,** Robinson Oscar 1928- *WhoAmL 92*
**Everett,** Ronald Emerson 1937- *WhoMW 92*
**Everett,** Rupert 1959- *IntMPA 92*
**Everett,** Rupert 1960- *IntWW 91*
**Everett,** Sallie Baker 1888-1975 *DcNCBi 2*
**Everett,** Stephen Edward 1958- *WhoWest 92*
**Everett,** T. H. 1903?-1986 *ConAu 133*
**Everett,** Thomas Gregory 1964- *WhoBlA 92*
**Everett,** Thomas Henry Kemp 1932- *Who 92*
**Everett,** Tom *WhoEnt 92*
**Everett,** Wade 1941- *TwCWW 91*
**Everett,** Warren S 1910- *AmMWSc 92*
**Everett,** Wilbur Wayne 1932- *AmMWSc 92*
**Everett,** Woodrow W, III 1960- *AmMWSc 92*
**Everett,** Woodrow Wilson, Jr 1937- *AmMWSc 92*
**Everette,** Sharon Esther McLeod 1949- *WhoWest 92*
**Evergood,** Philip 1901-1973 *FacFETw*
**Everhard,** Martin Edward 1933- *AmMWSc 92*
**Everhart,** Benjamin Matlack 1818-1904 *BiInAmS*
**Everhart,** Denise *WhoAmP 91*
**Everhart,** Donald Lee 1932- *AmMWSc 92*
**Everhart,** Donald Lough 1917- *AmMWSc 92*
**Everhart,** Edgar 1920- *AmMWSc 92*
**Everhart,** Isaiah Fawkes 1840-1911 *BiInAmS*
**Everhart,** James G 1915- *AmMWSc 92*
**Everhart,** Katrina Luise 1961- *WhoMW 92*
**Everhart,** Leighton Phreaner, Jr 1942- *AmMWSc 92*
**Everhart,** Leon Eugene 1928- *WhoWest 92*
**Everhart,** Rex 1920- *WhoEnt 92*
**Everhart,** Robert Phillip 1936- *WhoEnt 92, WhoMW 92*
**Everhart,** Thomas E 1932- *AmMWSc 92*
**Everhart,** Thomas Eugene 1932- *WhoWest 92*
**Everidge,** Mary Jim 1930- *WhoAmP 91*
**Everill,** Richard Harold 1942- *WhoMW 92*
**Everill,** William Franklin 1926- *WhoAmL 92*
**Evering,** Frederick Christian, Jr 1936- *AmMWSc 92*
**Everingham,** Dale M. 1963- *WhoEnt 92*
**Everingham,** Douglas Nixon 1923- *IntWW 91*
**Everingham,** Harry Towner 1908- *WhoWest 92*
**Everitt,** Alan Milner 1926- *Who 92, WrDr 92*
**Everitt,** Anthony Michael 1940- *Who 92*
**Everitt,** C W Francis 1934- *AmMWSc 92*
**Everling,** Ulrich 1925- *IntWW 91*
**Everlove,** Nora Jean 1953- *WhoAmL 92*
**Everly Brothers** *NewAmDM*
**Everly,** Charles Ray 1944- *AmMWSc 92*
**Everly,** David Noble 1941- *WhoRel 92*
**Everly,** Don 1937- *NewAmDM*
**Everly,** Phil 1939- *NewAmDM*
**Everman,** Welch D. *DrAPF 91*
**Evermann,** James Frederick 1944- *AmMWSc 92*
**Evernden,** Margery 1916- *WrDr 92*
**Evers,** Carl Gustav 1934- *AmMWSc 92*
**Evers,** James Charles 1922- *WhoAmP 91, WhoBlA 92*
**Evers,** Larry 1946- *ConAu 135*
**Evers,** Medgar W 1926-1963 *FacFETw*
**Evers,** Myrlie *WhoBlA 92*
**Evers,** Robert C 1939- *AmMWSc 92*
**Evers,** Robert Clement 1939- *WhoMW 92*
**Evers,** William John 1932- *AmMWSc 92*
**Evers,** William L 1906- *AmMWSc 92*
**Everse,** Johannes 1931- *AmMWSc 92*
**Eversley,** David Edward Charles 1921- *Who 92*
**Eversmeyer,** Harold Edwin 1927- *AmMWSc 92*
**Eversole,** Kellye Anne 1958- *WhoAmP 91*
**Eversole,** Robert Matthew 1962- *WhoFI 92*
**Everson,** Alan Ray 1943- *AmMWSc 92*
**Everson,** Dale O 1930- *AmMWSc 92*
**Everson,** Diane Louise 1953- *WhoMW 92*
**Everson,** Everett Henry 1923- *AmMWSc 92*
**Everson,** Frederick 1910- *Who 92*
**Everson,** Howard E 1918- *AmMWSc 92*
**Everson,** John Andrew 1933- *Who 92*
**Everson,** Leonard Charles 1923- *WhoFI 92*
**Everson,** Ronald 1903- *WrDr 92*
**Everson,** Ronald Ward 1931- *AmMWSc 92*
**Everson,** Steven Lee 1950- *WhoAmL 92*
**Everson,** William *DrAPF 91*
**Everson,** William 1912- *BenetAL 91, ConPo 91, IntAu&W 91, WrDr 92*
**Everson,** William K. 1929- *IntMPA 92*
**Everstine,** Gordon Carl 1943- *AmMWSc 92*
**Eversz,** Robert McLeod 1954- *IntAu&W 91*
**Evert,** Chris 1954- *FacFETw [port]*
**Evert,** Chris Marie 1954- *IntWW 91*
**Evert,** Henry Earl 1915- *AmMWSc 92*
**Evert,** Militiades 1939- *IntWW 91*
**Evert,** Ray Franklin 1931- *AmMWSc 92*
**Everts,** Craig Hamilton 1939- *AmMWSc 92*
**Everts,** Edward Herman 1951- *WhoMW 92*
**Everts,** Margaret Jewett 1962- *WhoEnt 92*
**Everwine,** Peter 1930- *ConPo 91, WrDr 92*
**Every,** George 1909- *WrDr 92*
**Every,** Henry 1947- *Who 92*
**Eves,** David Charles Thomas 1942- *Who 92*
**Eves,** Jeffrey P. 1946- *WhoFI 92*
**Eves,** Reginald G. 1876-1941 *TwCPaSc*
**Eveslage,** Sylvester Lee 1923- *AmMWSc 92*
**Evett,** Arthur A 1925- *AmMWSc 92*
**Evett,** Jack B 1942- *AmMWSc 92*
**Evett,** Jay Fredrick 1931- *AmMWSc 92*
**Evett,** Malcolm 1942- *WhoWest 92*
**Evilia,** Ronald Frank 1943- *AmMWSc 92*
**Evin,** Andrew *WhoRel 92*
**Evin,** Claude 1949- *IntWW 91*
**Evinrude,** Frances Langford 1913- *WhoEnt 92*
**Evins,** David E. d1991 *NewYTBS 91 [port]*
**Evison,** Frank Foster 1922- *IntWW 91*
**Evitt,** William Robert 1923- *AmMWSc 92*
**Evjue,** William Theodore 1882-1970 *AmPeW*
**Evleth,** Earl Mansfield 1931- *AmMWSc 92*
**Evoe** *EncAmaz 91*
**Evola,** Giulio Cesare Andrea 1898-1974 *BiDExR*
**Evola,** Phillip A. 1949- *WhoEnt 92*
**Evora,** Paulino do Lovramento *WhoRel 92*
**Evoy,** William 1938- *AmMWSc 92*
**Evren,** Kenan 1917- *FacFETw*
**Evren,** Kenan 1918- *IntWW 91*
**Evron,** Ephraim 1920- *IntWW 91*
**Evtuhov,** Viktor 1935- *AmMWSc 92*
**Ewald,** Arno Wilfred 1918- *AmMWSc 92*
**Ewald,** Douglas R *WhoAmP 91*
**Ewald,** Fred Peterson, Jr 1932- *AmMWSc 92*
**Ewald,** Harold Kenneth, III 1947- *WhoWest 92*
**Ewald,** Rex Alan 1951- *WhoAmL 92*
**Ewald,** Robert Frederick 1924- *WhoFI 92, WhoIns 92, WhoMW 92*
**Ewald,** Sandra J *AmMWSc 92*
**Ewald,** Willaim Rudolph 1923- *WhoFI 92*
**Ewald,** William Philip 1922- *AmMWSc 92*
**Ewaldsen,** Hans Lorenz 1923- *IntWW 91*
**Ewan,** George T 1927- *AmMWSc 92*
**Ewan,** Joseph 1909- *AmMWSc 92*
**Ewan,** Richard Colin 1934- *AmMWSc 92*
**Ewan,** William Kenneth 1943- *WhoMW 92*
**Ewans,** Martin Kenneth 1928- *IntWW 91, Who 92*
**Ewart,** Ann 1957- *WhoAmL 92*
**Ewart,** David Shanks 1901-1965 *TwCPaSc*
**Ewart,** Douglas Randolph 1946- *WhoFI 92*
**Ewart,** Frank J. 1876-1947 *RelLAm 91*
**Ewart,** Gavin 1916- *ConPo 91, WrDr 92*
**Ewart,** Gavin Buchanan 1916- *IntAu&W 91, IntWW 91, Who 92*
**Ewart,** Hamilton Glover 1849-1918 *DcNCBi 2*
**Ewart,** Hugh Wallace, Jr 1939- *AmMWSc 92*
**Ewart,** Ivan 1919- *Who 92*
**Ewart,** Lani L. 1950- *WhoAmL 92*
**Ewart,** Mervyn H 1920- *AmMWSc 92*
**Ewart,** Phillip Smith 1938- *WhoMW 92*
**Ewart,** R Bradley 1932- *AmMWSc 92*
**Ewart,** Terry E 1934- *AmMWSc 92*
**Ewart-Biggs** *Who 92*
**Ewart-Biggs,** Baroness *Who 92*
**Ewazen,** Eric *WhoEnt 92*
**Ewbank,** Anthony 1925- *Who 92*
**Ewbank,** Inga-Stina 1932- *Who 92*
**Ewbank,** John Robert 1934- *WhoMW 92*
**Ewbank,** Michael Henry 1930- *Who 92*
**Ewbank,** Thomas 1792-1870 *BiInAmS*
**Ewbank,** Thomas Peters 1943- *WhoMW 92*
**Ewbank,** Walter Frederick 1918- *Who 92*
**Ewbank,** Wesley Bruce 1932- *AmMWSc 92*
**Ewell,** A. Ben, Jr. 1941- *WhoAmL 92, WhoWest 92*
**Ewell,** Barbara C 1947- *ConAu 35NR*
**Ewell,** Ervin Edgar 1867-1904 *BiInAmS*
**Ewell,** Henry Norwood 1918- *BlkOlyM*
**Ewell,** James John, Jr 1942- *AmMWSc 92*
**Ewell,** Raymond W. 1928- *WhoBlA 92*
**Ewell,** Tom 1909- *IntMPA 92*
**Ewen,** Alwyn Bradley 1932- *AmMWSc 92*
**Ewen,** Clark *WhoAmP 91*
**Ewen,** David Paul 1944- *WhoWest 92*
**Ewen,** Harold David 1933- *WhoEnt 92*
**Ewen,** Harold Irving 1922- *AmMWSc 92*
**Ewen,** Kenneth Andrew 1946- *WhoMW 92*
**Ewen,** Malcolm Dawes 1954- *WhoEnt 92*
**Ewen,** Paterson 1925- *IntWW 91*
**Ewen,** Peter 1903- *Who 92*
**Ewens,** John Qualtrough 1907- *Who 92*
**Ewer,** Tom Keightley 1911- *Who 92*
**Ewers,** Anne *WhoEnt 92*
**Ewers,** Hanns Heinz 1871-1943 *EncTR 91*
**Ewers,** James Benjamin, Jr. 1948- *WhoBlA 92*
**Ewers,** R. Darrell 1933- *WhoFI 92*
**Ewers,** Ralph O 1936- *AmMWSc 92*
**Ewers,** Roger Leonard 1935- *WhoRel 92*
**Ewert,** Adam 1927- *AmMWSc 92*
**Ewert,** Alan 1949- *WhoWest 92*
**Ewert,** Quentin Albert 1915- *WhoAmL 92*
**Ewig,** Carl Stephen 1945- *AmMWSc 92*
**Ewin,** David Ernest Thomas F. *Who 92*
**Ewing** *Who 92*
**Ewing,** Alastair *Who 92*
**Ewing,** Andrew Graham 1957- *AmMWSc 92*
**Ewing,** Barbara Lee 1945- *WhoBlA 92*
**Ewing,** Bayard d1991 *NewYTBS 91*
**Ewing,** Bayard 1916- *WhoAmP 91*
**Ewing,** Ben B 1924- *AmMWSc 92*
**Ewing,** Channing Lester 1927- *AmMWSc 92*
**Ewing,** Charles Patrick 1949- *WhoAmL 92*
**Ewing,** Clair Eugene 1915- *AmMWSc 92*
**Ewing,** David Charles 1942- *WhoMW 92*
**Ewing,** David Leon 1941- *AmMWSc 92*
**Ewing,** David Walkley 1923- *WrDr 92*
**Ewing,** David William 1957- *WhoMW 92*
**Ewing,** Dean Edgar 1932- *AmMWSc 92, WhoWest 92*
**Ewing,** Donald J, Jr 1931- *AmMWSc 92*
**Ewing,** Donna Marie 1936- *WhoMW 92*

**Ewing,** Edward Buchanan 1947- *WhoEnt 92*
**Ewing,** Edwin S, Jr 1924- *WhoIns 92*
**Ewing,** Elizabeth Cameron 1906- *IntAu&W 91, WrDr 92*
**Ewing,** Elmer Ellis 1931- *AmMWSc 92*
**Ewing,** Fayette Clay, Jr 1886?-1914 *BiInAmS*
**Ewing,** Galen Wood 1914- *AmMWSc 92*
**Ewing,** George Edward 1933- *AmMWSc 92*
**Ewing,** George McNaught 1907- *AmMWSc 92*
**Ewing,** Gerald Dean 1932- *AmMWSc 92*
**Ewing,** Gordon J 1931- *AmMWSc 92*
**Ewing,** Harry 1931- *Who 92*
**Ewing,** J Benjamin 1931- *WhoAmP 91*
**Ewing,** J J 1942- *AmMWSc 92*
**Ewing,** Jack David 1960- *WhoAmL 92*
**Ewing,** James Alfred 1855-1935 *FacFETw*
**Ewing,** John 1732-1802 *BiInAmS*
**Ewing,** John Alexander 1923- *AmMWSc 92*
**Ewing,** John Arthur 1912- *AmMWSc 92*
**Ewing,** John H 1918- *WhoAmP 91*
**Ewing,** John I 1924- *AmMWSc 92*
**Ewing,** John Kirby 1923- *WhoFI 92*
**Ewing,** John R. 1917- *WhoBlA 92*
**Ewing,** Joseph Neff, Jr. 1925- *WhoAmL 92*
**Ewing,** June Swift 1938- *AmMWSc 92*
**Ewing,** Ky Pepper, Jr. 1935- *WhoAmL 92*
**Ewing,** Larry Larue 1936- *AmMWSc 92*
**Ewing,** Mamie Hans 1939- *WhoBlA 92*
**Ewing,** Margaret Anne 1945- *Who 92*
**Ewing,** Maria 1950- *NewAmDM*
**Ewing,** Maria Louise *WhoEnt 92*
**Ewing,** Maria Louise 1950- *IntWW 91*
**Ewing,** Martin Sipple 1945- *AmMWSc 92*
**Ewing,** Mary Eileen 1926- *WhoMW 92*
**Ewing,** Patrick 1962- *BlkOlyM, CurBio 91 [port], WhoBlA 92*
**Ewing,** R A 1915- *AmMWSc 92*
**Ewing,** Randy L 1944- *WhoAmP 91*
**Ewing,** Raymond C 1936- *WhoAmP 91*
**Ewing,** Raymond Peyton 1925- *WhoFI 92, WhoMW 92*
**Ewing,** Richard Dwight 1930- *AmMWSc 92*
**Ewing,** Richard Edward 1946- *AmMWSc 92, WhoWest 92*
**Ewing,** Robert 1922- *WhoAmL 92, WhoFI 92*
**Ewing,** Robert Alastair 1909- *Who 92*
**Ewing,** Robert Clark 1957- *WhoAmL 92*
**Ewing,** Rodney Charles 1946- *AmMWSc 92*
**Ewing,** Ronald Ira 1935- *AmMWSc 92*
**Ewing,** Russ 1933- *WhoBlA 92*
**Ewing,** Russell Charles, II 1941- *WhoWest 92*
**Ewing,** Samuel Daniel, Jr. 1938- *WhoBlA 92*
**Ewing,** Sherman 1926- *WhoWest 92*
**Ewing,** Sidney Alton 1934- *AmMWSc 92*
**Ewing,** Solon Alexander 1930- *AmMWSc 92*
**Ewing,** Theodore Bode 1942- *WhoAmP 91*
**Ewing,** Thomas Edward 1954- *AmMWSc 92*
**Ewing,** Thomas W. 1935- *AlmAP 92 [port], WhoAmP 91, WhoMW 92*
**Ewing,** Wayne 1948- *WhoEnt 92*
**Ewing,** William Barton 1938- *WhoAmP 91*
**Ewing,** William Henszey 1939- *WhoAmL 92*
**Ewing,** William Hickman, Jr. 1942- *WhoAmL 92*
**Ewing,** William Howell 1914- *AmMWSc 92*
**Ewing,** William James 1936- *WhoBlA 92*
**Ewing,** William Maurice 1906- *FacFETw*
**Ewing,** Winifred Margaret 1929- *IntWW 91, Who 92*
**Ewins,** Arthur James 1882-1957 *FacFETw*
**Ewins,** David John 1942- *Who 92*
**Ewins,** Peter David 1943- *Who 92*
**Ewoldt,** Elda Mae 1934- *WhoAmP 91*
**Ewonus,** George Kimball 1949- *WhoMW 92*
**Ewusie,** Joseph Yanney 1927- *Who 92*
**Ewy,** Russell Lee 1958- *WhoMW 92*
**Exarhos,** Gregory James 1948- *AmMWSc 92*
**Excellent,** Matilda *IntAu&W 91X*
**Exe,** David Allen 1942- *WhoFI 92, WhoMW 92*
**Exetastes** *ConAu 134*
**Exeter,** Archdeacon of *Who 92*
**Exeter,** Bishop of 1929- *Who 92*
**Exeter,** Dean of *Who 92*
**Exeter,** Marquess of 1935- *Who 92*
**Exler,** Samuel *DrAPF 91*
**Exley,** Charles Errol, Jr. 1929- *IntWW 91, WhoFI 92, WhoMW 92*
**Exley,** Frederick *DrAPF 91*
**Exline,** Jerry Michael 1942- *WhoEnt 92*
**Exmouth,** Viscount 1940- *Who 92*
**Exner,** Virgil 1909-1973 *DcTwDes, FacFETw*
**Exon,** J. James 1921- *AlmAP 92 [port], IntWW 91, WhoAmP 91*
**Exon,** John James 1921- *WhoMW 92*
**Exton,** Clive 1930- *IntAu&W 91, Who 92, WrDr 92*
**Exton,** John Howard 1933- *AmMWSc 92*
**Exton,** Reginald John 1935- *AmMWSc 92*
**Exton,** Rodney Noel 1927- *Who 92*
**Exum,** Benjamin 1725?-1789 *DcNCBi 2*
**Exum,** James Gooden, Jr. 1935- *WhoAmL 92, WhoAmP 91*
**Exum,** Nathaniel *WhoAmP 91*
**Exum,** Thurman McCoy 1947- *WhoBlA 92*
**Eyadema,** Gnassingbe 1937- *IntWW 91*
**Eyberg,** Donald Theodore, Jr. 1944- *WhoMW 92*
**Eyck,** Frank 1921- *IntAu&W 91, WrDr 92*
**Eyckmans,** Luc A. F. 1930- *IntWW 91*
**Eyde,** Richard Husted 1928- *AmMWSc 92*
**Eyde,** Samuel 1866-1940 *FacFETw*
**Eydgahi,** Ali Mohammadzadeh 1957- *AmMWSc 92*
**Eye,** Robert V. *WhoAmL 92*
**Eyen,** Jerome *ConAu 134*
**Eyen,** Tom d1991 *NewYTBS 91*
**Eyen,** Tom 1941- *IntAu&W 91*
**Eyen,** Tom 1941-1991 *ConAu 134*
**Eyer,** Bruce Jarrett 1941- *WhoWest 92*
**Eyer,** Donald E. 1929- *WhoFI 92*
**Eyer,** James Arthur 1929- *AmMWSc 92*
**Eyer,** Jerome Arlan 1934- *AmMWSc 92*
**Eyer,** Lester Emery 1912- *AmMWSc 92*
**Eyerly,** George B 1917- *AmMWSc 92*
**Eyers,** Patrick Howard Caines 1933- *Who 92*
**Eyestone,** Willard Halsey 1918- *AmMWSc 92*
**Eyges,** Leonard James 1920- *AmMWSc 92*
**Eykhe,** Robert Indrikovich 1890-1940 *SovUnBD*
**Eykhenbaum,** Boris Mikhaylovich 1886-1959 *SovUnBD*
**Eykhoff,** Pieter 1929- *AmMWSc 92, IntWW 91*
**Eyler,** John Robert 1945- *AmMWSc 92*
**Eyman,** Darrell Paul 1937- *AmMWSc 92*
**Eyman,** Earl Duane 1925- *AmMWSc 92*
**Eyman,** Lyle Dean 1941- *AmMWSc 92*
**Eyman,** Richard Harrison 1930- *WhoFI 92*
**Eyman,** Roger Allen 1942- *WhoRel 92*
**Eyman,** Susanne Kohn 1956- *WhoMW 92*
**Eynon,** John Marles 1923- *Who 92*
**Eynon,** Robert 1941- *TwCWW 91, WrDr 92*
**Eynon,** Steven Scott 1961- *WhoRel 92*
**Eyraud,** Francis-Charles 1931- *IntWW 91*
**Eyre and Spottiswoode** *DcLB 106*
**Eyre,** Annette *WrDr 92*
**Eyre,** Brian Leonard 1933- *Who 92*
**Eyre,** Charles George 1925- *WhoRel 92*
**Eyre,** Dean Jack 1914- *Who 92*
**Eyre,** Graham 1931- *Who 92*
**Eyre,** Ivan 1935- *IntWW 91*
**Eyre,** James 1930- *Who 92*
**Eyre,** Peter 1936- *AmMWSc 92*
**Eyre,** Reginald 1924- *Who 92*
**Eyre,** Reginald John 1931- *WhoWest 92*
**Eyre,** Richard 1943- *IntWW 91*
**Eyre,** Richard Charles Hastings 1943- *Who 92*
**Eyre,** Richard Montague Stephens 1929- *Who 92*
**Eyre,** Ronald 1929- *IntAu&W 91, Who 92*
**Eyre,** S. Robert 1922- *WrDr 92*
**Eyre,** William H, Jr 1951- *WhoIns 92*
**Eyre,** William Hudson, Jr. 1951- *WhoWest 92*
**Eyre,** Wilson 1858-1944 *DcTwDes*
**Eyres,** Harry 1958- *WrDr 92*
**Eyres Monsell** *Who 92*
**Eyring,** Edward J 1934- *AmMWSc 92*
**Eyring,** Edward M 1931- *AmMWSc 92*
**Eyring,** Henry 1901-1981 *FacFETw*
**Eyring,** Henry Bennion 1933- *WhoRel 92, WhoWest 92*
**Eyring,** LeRoy 1919- *AmMWSc 92*
**Eysenck,** H. J. 1916- *WrDr 92*
**Eysenck,** Hans 1916- *IntAu&W 91*
**Eysenck,** Hans Jurgen 1916- *IntWW 91, Who 92*
**Eysenck,** Michael William 1944- *Who 92*
**Eyskens,** Gaston 1905-1988 *FacFETw*
**Eyskens,** Mark 1933- *IntWW 91*
**Eyster,** Eugene Henderson 1914- *AmMWSc 92*
**Eyster,** Henry Clyde 1910- *AmMWSc 92*
**Eyster,** Marshall Blackwell 1923- *AmMWSc 92*
**Eysymontt,** Jerzy 1937- *IntWW 91*
**Eytan,** Walter 1910- *IntWW 91*
**Eyton,** Anthony 1923- *TwCPaSc*
**Eyton,** Anthony John Plowden 1923- *IntWW 91, Who 92*
**Eyzaguirre,** Carlos 1923- *AmMWSc 92*
**Ezagui,** Alan Mark 1955- *WhoFI 92*
**Ezard,** Gary Carl 1963- *WhoEnt 92*
**Ezeilo,** James Okoye Chukuka 1930- *Who 92*
**Ezekiel** *EncEarC*
**Ezekiel,** Nissim 1924- *ConPo 91, IntAu&W 91, WrDr 92*
**Ezekowitz,** Michael David 1946- *AmMWSc 92*
**Ezell,** Annette Schram 1940- *WhoFI 92*
**Ezell,** Charlaine Louise 1950- *WhoMW 92*
**Ezell,** Eugene Mark 1941- *WhoAmP 91*
**Ezell,** Ronnie Lee 1944- *AmMWSc 92*
**Ezell,** Wayland Lee 1937- *AmMWSc 92*
**Ezell,** William Alexander 1924- *WhoBlA 92*
**Ezelle,** Curtis 1921- *WhoAmP 91*
**Ezersky,** William Martin 1951- *WhoAmL 92*
**Ezhuthachan,** Sudhakar Gopalan 1946- *WhoMW 92*
**Eziemefe,** Godslove Ajenavi 1955- *WhoBlA 92*
**Ezis,** Andre 1943- *WhoWest 92*
**Eznik** *EncEarC*
**Ezra** *EncEarC, Who 92*
**Ezra,** Baron 1919- *IntWW 91, Who 92*
**Ezra,** Arthur Abraham 1925- *AmMWSc 92*
**Ezra,** David A. 1947- *WhoAmL 92*
**Ezra,** Gregory Sion 1953- *AmMWSc 92*
**Ezrati,** Milton Joseph 1947- *WhoFI 92*
**Ezratty,** Harry Aaron 1933- *WhoAmL 92*
**Ezrin,** Calvin 1926- *AmMWSc 92*
**Ezrin,** Myer 1926- *AmMWSc 92*
**Ezzard,** Martha M 1938- *WhoAmP 91*
**Ezzat,** Hazem Ahmed 1942- *AmMWSc 92*
**Ezzell,** Ben Roach 1943- *WhoWest 92*
**Ezzell,** Robert Marvin *AmMWSc 92*

# F

**Faaborg,** John Raynor 1949- *AmMWSc 92*
**Faalevao,** Aviata Fano *WhoAmP 91*
**Faanes,** Ronald 1941- *AmMWSc 92*
**Fa'arman,** Alfred 1917- *AmMWSc 92*
**Faas,** Ekbert 1938- *WrDr 92*
**Faas,** Richard William 1931- *AmMWSc 92*
**Faatz,** Jeanne Ryan 1941- *WhoAmP 91*
**Fabares,** Shelley *WhoEnt 92*
**Fabares,** Shelley 1944- *IntMPA 92*
**Fabbi,** Brent Peter 1938- *AmMWSc 92*
**Fabbri,** Fabio 1933- *IntWW 91*
**Fabbri,** Inez 1831-1909 *NewAmDM*
**Fabel,** Thomas Lincoln 1946- *WhoAmL 92*
**Fabel,** Warren L 1933- *WhoIns 92*
**Fabela,** Augie K., Sr. *WhoHisp 92*
**Faber and Faber Limited** *DcLB 112*
**Faber and Gwyer Limited** *DcLB 112*
**Faber,** Albert John 1945- *AmMWSc 92*
**Faber,** Betty Lane 1944- *AmMWSc 92*
**Faber,** Carol Antoinette 1937- *WhoFI 92*
**Faber,** Donald S 1943- *AmMWSc 92*
**Faber,** George Donald 1921- *WhoEnt 92*
**Faber,** Georges 1926- *IntWW 91*
**Faber,** Heije 1907- *WhoRel 92*
**Faber,** James Edward 1951- *AmMWSc 92*
**Faber,** Jan Job 1934- *AmMWSc 92*
**Faber,** John 1918- *WrDr 92*
**Faber,** Julian Tufnell 1917- *Who 92*
**Faber,** Lee Edward 1942- *AmMWSc 92*
**Faber,** Lothar 1925- *NewAmDM*
**Faber,** Marcel D 1944- *AmMWSc 92*
**Faber,** Michael Leslie Ogilvie 1929- *Who 92*
**Faber,** Peter Lewis 1938- *WhoAmL 92*
**Faber,** Raymond Albert 1947- *WhoMW 92*
**Faber,** Richard 1924- *Who 92*
**Faber,** Richard Leon 1940- *AmMWSc 92*
**Faber,** Robert 1908- *WhoEnt 92*
**Faber,** Robertoh *DrAPF 91*
**Faber,** Roger Jack 1931- *AmMWSc 92*
**Faber,** Ronald Anthony 1933- *WhoEnt 92*
**Faber,** Sandra Moore 1944- *AmMWSc 92*
**Faber,** Shepard Mazor 1928- *AmMWSc 92*
**Faber,** Thomas Erle 1927- *Who 92*
**Faber,** Timothy T. 1964- *WhoRel 92*
**Faber,** Vance 1944- *AmMWSc 92*
**Fabes,** Eugene Barry 1937- *AmMWSc 92*
**Fabian** *EncEarC*
**Fabian,** Andrew Christopher 1948- *Who 92*
**Fabian,** Gary Lamar, Jr. 1966- *WhoRel 92*
**Fabian,** Jerome Francis 1943- *WhoFI 92*
**Fabian,** Lawrence E. 1944- *WhoAmL 92*
**Fabian,** Leonard Jay 1946- *WhoWest 92*
**Fabian,** Leonard William 1923- *AmMWSc 92*
**Fabian,** Mark 1956- *WhoEnt 92*
**Fabian,** Michael William 1931- *AmMWSc 92*
**Fabian,** Paul 1930- *Who 92*
**Fabian,** Raymond Fredrick 1921- *WhoRel 92*
**Fabian,** Robert John 1939- *AmMWSc 92*
**Fabiani,** Dante Carl 1917- *IntWW 91*
**Fabiani,** Simonetta *IntWW 91*
**Fabiano,** Roberta Mary 1952- *WhoEnt 92*
**Fabic,** Stanislav 1925- *AmMWSc 92*
**Fabietti,** Victor Armando 1920- *WhoFI 92*
**Fabila,** Jose Andres 1955- *WhoHisp 92*
**Fabilli,** Mary *DrAPF 91*
**Fabio,** Sarah Webster 1928-1979 *NotBlAW 92*
**Fabisch,** Judith P. 1938- *WhoMW 92*
**Fabish,** Thomas John 1938- *AmMWSc 92*
**Fabius,** Laurent 1946- *IntWW 91, Who 92*
**Fabray,** Nanette *WhoEnt 92*
**Fabray,** Nanette 1920- *IntMPA 92*
**Fabray,** Nanette 1922- *NewAmDM*
**Fabrazio,** Philip Terry *WhoEnt 92*
**Fabre,** Edwin G. 1945- *WhoBlA 92*
**Fabre,** Louis Fernand, Jr 1941- *AmMWSc 92*
**Fabre,** Niola Frachou 1951- *WhoWest 92*
**Fabre-Ramirez,** Miguel Juan 1950- *WhoAmP 91*
**Fabrega,** Jorge 1922- *IntWW 91*
**Fabrey,** James Douglas 1943- *AmMWSc 92*
**Fabri,** Zoltan 1917- *IntDcF 2-2, IntWW 91*
**Fabricand,** Burton Paul 1923- *AmMWSc 92*
**Fabricant,** Barbara Louise 1950- *AmMWSc 92*
**Fabricant,** Catherine G 1919- *AmMWSc 92*
**Fabricant,** Julius 1919- *AmMWSc 92*
**Fabrice** 1951- *WhoBlA 92*
**Fabricio,** Roberto C. 1946- *WhoHisp 92*
**Fabricius,** Dietrich M 1950- *AmMWSc 92*
**Fabricius,** Fritz 1919- *IntWW 91*
**Fabricius,** Valeda Clareen 1940- *WhoMW 92*
**Fabrikant,** Ilya I 1949- *AmMWSc 92*
**Fabrikant,** Irene Berger 1933- *AmMWSc 92*
**Fabrikant,** Valery Isaak 1940- *AmMWSc 92*
**Fabris,** Hubert 1926- *AmMWSc 92*
**Fabrizi,** Aldo 1905-1990 *AnObit 1990*
**Fabrizio,** Angelina Maria *AmMWSc 92*
**Fabrizio,** John Arthur, Jr 1923- *WhoAmP 91*
**Fabrizius,** Peter *WrDr 92*
**Fabro,** Sergio 1931- *AmMWSc 92*
**Fabry,** Andras 1937- *AmMWSc 92*
**Fabry,** Joseph B 1909- *IntAu&W 91, WrDr 92*
**Fabry,** Mary E Riepe 1942- *AmMWSc 92*
**Fabry,** Thomas Lester 1937- *AmMWSc 92*
**Fabrycky,** Wolter J 1932- *AmMWSc 92*
**Fabunmi,** James Ayinde 1950- *AmMWSc 92*
**Faccenda,** Philip John 1929- *WhoAmL 92*
**Facchiano,** Ferdinando 1927- *IntWW 91*
**Face,** Albert Ray 1919- *WhoAmP 91*
**Facemire,** Allen Stewart 1945- *WhoEnt 92*
**Facer,** Charles Richard 1949- *WhoEnt 92*
**Facer,** George Wesley 1937- *WhoMW 92*
**Facer,** Roger Lawrence Lowe 1933- *Who 92*
**Facey,** John Abbott 1926- *WhoIns 92*
**Fachet,** William F., Jr. 1943- *WhoFI 92*
**Facio,** Gonzalo J. 1918- *IntWW 91*
**Fack,** Robbert 1917- *Who 92*
**Fackelman,** Gustave Edward 1941- *AmMWSc 92*
**Fackenheim,** Emil L. 1916- *WrDr 92*
**Fackenthall,** Maryanne A. 1948- *WhoEnt 92*
**Fackler,** Benjamine Lloyd 1926- *WhoFI 92*
**Fackler,** Donald A., Jr. 1955- *WhoWest 92*
**Fackler,** Ernest Carl, III 1943- *WhoAmP 91*
**Fackler,** Glen Dale 1936- *WhoFI 92*
**Fackler,** Grant William 1965- *WhoMW 92*
**Fackler,** Martin L 1933- *AmMWSc 92*
**Fackler,** Martin Luther 1933- *WhoWest 92*
**Fackler,** Walter David 1921- *WhoMW 92*
**Fackler,** Walter Valentine, Jr 1920- *AmMWSc 92*
**Fackler,** William Marion 1938- *WhoFI 92*
**Fackre,** Gabriel Joseph 1926- *WhoRel 92*
**Fackrell,** Brian Patrick 1955- *WhoEnt 92*
**Facos,** James *DrAPF 91*
**Facos,** James Francis 1924- *IntAu&W 91*
**Factor,** Arnold 1936- *AmMWSc 92*
**Factor,** Davis, Sr. d1991 *NewYTBS 91*
**Factor,** Jan Robert 1950- *AmMWSc 92*
**Factor,** Max, III 1945- *WhoAmL 92, WhoWest 92*
**Factor,** Ralph Lance 1944- *WhoMW 92*
**Factor,** Stephen M 1942- *AmMWSc 92*
**Facundus of Hermiane** *EncEarC*
**Facusse,** Albert Shucry 1921- *WhoFI 92*
**Fadden,** Delmar McLean 1941- *WhoWest 92*
**Fadden,** Eileen Ann 1943- *WhoFI 92*
**Faddick,** Robert Raymond 1938- *AmMWSc 92*
**Fadeev,** Aleksandr Aleksandrovich 1901-1956 *SovUnBD*
**Fadeley,** Brett Duane 1953- *WhoFI 92*
**Fadeley,** Edward Norman 1929- *WhoAmL 92, WhoAmP 91, WhoWest 92*
**Fadeley,** Nancie Peacocke 1930- *WhoAmP 91*
**Fadell,** Albert George 1928- *AmMWSc 92*
**Fadell,** Edward Richard 1926- *AmMWSc 92*
**Fadem,** B. J. 1955- *WhoWest 92*
**Fadem,** Jerrold Alan 1926- *WhoAmL 92*
**Faden,** Howard *AmMWSc 92*
**Fader,** Daniel Nelson 1930- *WhoMW 92*
**Fader,** Henry Conrad 1946- *WhoAmL 92*
**Fader,** Walter John 1923- *AmMWSc 92*
**Fadeyechev,** Nikolay Borisovich 1933- *IntWW 91*
**Fadeyev,** Alexander Alexandrovich 1901-1956 *FacFETw*
**Fadeyev,** Ludvig Dmitriyevich 1934- *IntWW 91*
**Fadiman,** Clifton 1904- *IntAu&W 91, IntMPA 92, WrDr 92*
**Fadley,** Charles Sherwood 1941- *AmMWSc 92*
**Fadly,** Aly Mahmoud 1941- *AmMWSc 92*
**Fadner,** Thomas Alan 1929- *AmMWSc 92*
**Fadulu,** Sunday O. 1940- *WhoBlA 92*
**Fadum,** Ralph Eigil 1912- *AmMWSc 92*
**Faduma,** Orishatukeh 1855-1946 *DcNCBi 2*
**Faecke,** Peter 1940- *IntWW 91*
**Faehl,** William Russell 1954- *WhoFI 92*
**Faerstein,** Howard *DrAPF 91*
**Faesi,** Stephan 1948- *WhoEnt 92*
**Faessler,** Edwin Joseph 1944- *WhoMW 92*
**Faeth,** Gerard Michael 1936- *AmMWSc 92*
**Faeth,** Stanley Herman 1951- *AmMWSc 92*
**Fafenrodt,** Alexis Alexandrovitch 1937- *WhoAmL 92*
**Fafian,** Joseph, Jr 1939- *WhoIns 92*
**Faflick,** Carl E 1922- *AmMWSc 92*
**Fagal,** Harold Edward 1923- *WhoRel 92*
**Fagan,** Andrew Thomas 1953- *WhoFI 92*
**Fagan,** Brian Murray 1936- *IntAu&W 91, WrDr 92*
**Fagan,** Christopher Brendan 1937- *WhoAmL 92*
**Fagan,** Harold Leonard 1920- *WhoBlA 92*
**Fagan,** J R 1935- *AmMWSc 92*
**Fagan,** John Edward 1943- *AmMWSc 92*
**Fagan,** John Paul 1930- *WhoFI 92*
**Fagan,** Kate J. 1951- *WhoAmL 92*
**Fagan,** Kathy *DrAPF 91*
**Fagan,** Kathy 1958- *IntAu&W 91*
**Fagan,** Kevin Douglas 1956- *WhoEnt 92*
**Fagan,** Michael Joseph 1942- *WhoWest 92*
**Fagan,** Patrick Feltrim 1935- *Who 92*
**Fagan,** Paul V 1927- *AmMWSc 92*
**Fagan,** Peter Ledford 1951- *WhoAmL 92*
**Fagan,** Raymond 1914- *AmMWSc 92*
**Fagan,** Renny 1956- *WhoAmP 91*
**Fagan,** Thomas Perry 1932- *WhoMW 92*
**Fagan,** Timothy Charles 1947- *AmMWSc 92*
**Fagan,** Wayne Irwin 1943- *WhoAmL 92, WhoFI 92*
**Fagan,** William Lawrence 1927- *WhoWest 92*
**Fagan,** William Thomas 1945- *WhoAmL 92*
**Fagans,** Karl P. 1942- *WhoFI 92*
**Fagbayi,** Mutiu Olutoyin 1953- *WhoBlA 92*
**Fage,** John Donnelly 1921- *IntAu&W 91, Who 92, WrDr 92*
**Fagen,** Arthur Howard 1951- *WhoEnt 92*
**Fagen,** Laurie Napua 1953- *WhoEnt 92*
**Fagen,** Robert 1945- *AmMWSc 92*
**Fager,** Charles Eugene 1942- *WhoRel 92*
**Fager,** Everett Dean 1947- *WhoRel 92*
**Fager,** Vance E. 1956- *WhoWest 92*
**Fagerberg,** Dixon, Jr. 1909- *WhoWest 92*
**Fagerberg,** Roger Richard 1935- *WhoAmL 92, WhoFI 92, WhoMW 92*
**Fagerberg,** Wayne Robert 1944- *AmMWSc 92*
**Fagerburg,** David Richard 1942- *AmMWSc 92*
**Fagerholm,** Karl-August 1901-1984 *FacFETw*
**Fagerlind,** Marvin Carl 1951- *WhoMW 92*
**Fagerson,** Irving Seymour 1920- *AmMWSc 92*
**Fagerstrom,** Douglas Lee 1951- *WhoRel 92*
**Fagerstrom,** John Alfred 1930- *AmMWSc 92*
**Faget,** Maxime A 1921- *AmMWSc 92*
**Fagg,** Gary T. 1948- *WhoFI 92*
**Fagg,** Gary Thomas 1948- *WhoIns 92*
**Fagg,** George G *WhoAmP 91*
**Fagg,** George Gardner 1934- *WhoAmL 92, WhoMW 92*
**Fagg,** Harrison Grover 1931- *WhoAmP 91*
**Fagg,** Larry Ermel 1949- *WhoMW 92*
**Fagg,** Lawrence Wellburn 1923- *AmMWSc 92*
**Fagg,** Russell Charles 1960- *WhoAmP 91*
**Fagg,** Thomas Wood 1958- *WhoMW 92*
**Fagg,** William Buller 1914- *Who 92*
**Faggart,** Jonathan Efird 1958- *WhoRel 92*
**Fagge,** John William Frederick 1910- *Who 92*
**Faggs Starr,** Mae Heriwentha 1932- *BlkOlyM*

**Fagin**, Allen Ian 1949- *WhoAmL 92*
**Fagin**, Arnold David 1933- *WhoAmL 92*
**Fagin**, Claire M 1926- *AmMWSc 92*
**Fagin**, Claire Mintzer 1926- *IntWW 91*
**Fagin**, Darryl Hall 1942- *WhoBlA 92*
**Fagin**, David Kyle 1938- *WhoWest 92*
**Fagin**, Karin 1949- *AmMWSc 92*
**Fagin**, Katherine Diane *AmMWSc 92*
**Fagin**, Larry *DrAPF 91*
**Fagin**, Ronald 1945- *AmMWSc 92*
**Fagley**, Thomas Fisher 1913- *AmMWSc 92*
**Fagnant-Loughman**, Suzanne Claire 1960- *WhoEnt 92*
**Fagot**, John Albert, Jr. 1943- *WhoEnt 92*
**Fagot**, Wilfred Clark 1924- *AmMWSc 92*
**Faguet**, Guy B 1939- *AmMWSc 92*
**Fagundes**, Joseph H. 1955- *WhoAmL 92*
**Fagundes**, Joseph Marvin, III 1953- *WhoAmL 92*
**Fagundo**, Ana Maria 1938- *WhoWest 92*
**Fahd** 1923- *FacFETw*
**Fahd Ibn Abdul Aziz** 1923- *IntWW 91*
**Faherty**, Keith F 1931- *AmMWSc 92*
**Fahey**, Charles J 1933- *AmMWSc 92*
**Fahey**, Charles Joseph 1933- *WhoRel 92*
**Fahey**, Charles Joseph 1937- *WhoFI 92*
**Fahey**, Darryl Richard 1942- *AmMWSc 92*
**Fahey**, George Christopher, Jr 1949- *AmMWSc 92*
**Fahey**, James Edward 1953- *WhoFI 92*
**Fahey**, James J. d1991 *NewYTBS 91*
**Fahey**, James R 1951- *AmMWSc 92*
**Fahey**, Jane Elise 1954- *WhoAmL 92*
**Fahey**, John 1939- *NewAmDM*
**Fahey**, John Leonard 1944- *AmMWSc 92*
**Fahey**, John Leslie 1924- *AmMWSc 92*
**Fahey**, John Vincent 1948- *AmMWSc 92*
**Fahey**, Marcella Clifford 1934- *WhoAmP 91*
**Fahey**, Michael G 1943- *WhoAmP 91*
**Fahey**, Paul Farrell 1942- *AmMWSc 92*
**Fahey**, Richard Paul 1944- *WhoAmL 92*
**Fahey**, Robert C 1936- *AmMWSc 92*
**Fahey**, Walter John 1927- *AmMWSc 92*
**Fahidy**, Thomas Z 1934- *AmMWSc 92*
**Fahien**, Leonard A 1934- *AmMWSc 92*
**Fahien**, Ray W 1923- *AmMWSc 92*
**Fahim**, Mostafa Safwat 1931- *AmMWSc 92*
**Fahimi**, Hossein Dariush 1933- *AmMWSc 92*
**Fahl**, Charles Byron 1939- *AmMWSc 92*
**Fahl**, Roy Jackson, Jr 1925- *AmMWSc 92*
**Fahl**, William Edwin 1950- *AmMWSc 92*
**Fahlberg**, Constantin 1850-1910 *BiInAmS*
**Fahlberg**, Willson Joel 1918- *AmMWSc 92*
**Fahlen**, Theodore Stauffer 1941- *AmMWSc 92*
**Fahlman**, Gregory Gaylord 1944- *AmMWSc 92*
**Fahlquist**, Davis A 1926- *AmMWSc 92*
**Fahmy**, Abdel Aziz 1925- *AmMWSc 92*
**Fahmy**, Aly *AmMWSc 92*
**Fahmy**, Ismail 1922- *ConAu 133, IntWW 91*
**Fahmy**, Mohamed Ali 1920- *IntWW 91*
**Fahmy**, Mohamed Hamed 1940- *AmMWSc 92*
**Fahmy**, Moustafa Mahmoud 1929- *AmMWSc 92*
**Fahn**, Abraham 1916- *WrDr 92*
**Fahn**, Jay 1949- *WhoFI 92*
**Fahn**, Stanley 1933- *AmMWSc 92*
**Fahner**, Tyrone C. 1942- *WhoAmL 92*
**Fahnestock**, George Reeder 1914- *AmMWSc 92*
**Fahnestock**, Stephen Richard *AmMWSc 92*
**Fahning**, Melvyn Luverne 1936- *AmMWSc 92*
**Fahrbach**, Ruth C *WhoAmP 91*
**Fahrenbach**, Marvin Jay 1918- *AmMWSc 92*
**Fahrenbach**, Wolf Henrich 1932- *AmMWSc 92*
**Fahrenholtz**, Kenneth Earl 1934- *AmMWSc 92*
**Fahrenholtz**, Susan Roseno *AmMWSc 92*
**Fahrenkamp**, Bettye *WhoAmP 91*
**Fahrenkopf**, Frank J, Jr 1939- *WhoAmP 91*
**Fahrnbruch**, Dale E. 1924- *WhoAmL 92, WhoAmP 91, WhoMW 92*
**Fahrney**, Byron Weltie 1932- *WhoWest 92*
**Fahrney**, David Emory 1934- *AmMWSc 92*
**Fahselt**, Dianne 1941- *AmMWSc 92*
**Fahy**, Charles Laurence 1947- *WhoFI 92*
**Fahy**, Christopher *DrAPF 91*
**Fahy**, Joseph Thomas 1919- *WhoAmL 92*
**Fahy**, Terrence Gerard 1955- *WhoRel 92*
**Faich**, Gerald Alan 1942- *AmMWSc 92*
**Faiers**, Christopher Fordham 1948- *IntAu&W 91*
**Faiferman**, Isidore *AmMWSc 92*
**Faig**, Wolfgang 1939- *AmMWSc 92*
**Faigenbaum**, Bernard David 1958- *WhoAmL 92*
**Faignant**, John Paul 1953- *WhoAmL 92*
**Faiks**, Jan *WhoAmP 91*
**Faiks**, Jan Ogozalek 1945- *WhoWest 92*
**Fail**, Patricia A 1942- *AmMWSc 92*
**Failing**, William Latimer, Jr. 1940- *WhoEnt 92*
**Failinger**, Marie Anita 1952- *WhoAmL 92, WhoRel 92*
**Faill**, Rodger Tanner 1936- *AmMWSc 92*
**Failla**, Patricia McClement 1925- *AmMWSc 92*
**Faillace**, Louis A 1932- *AmMWSc 92*
**Faillace**, Michael Antonio 1957- *WhoAmL 92*
**Faillard**, Hans 1924- *IntWW 91*
**Failor**, Elwyn Elliott 1911- *WhoMW 92*
**Failor**, William Ned 1950- *WhoFI 92*
**Fails**, Madine Hester 1953- *WhoBlA 92*
**Fails**, Thomas Glenn 1928- *AmMWSc 92*
**Failyer**, George Henry 1849- *BiInAmS*
**Faiman**, Charles 1939- *AmMWSc 92*
**Faiman**, Michael 1935- *AmMWSc 92*
**Faiman**, Morris David 1932- *AmMWSc 92*
**Faiman**, Peter *IntMPA 92*
**Faiman**, Robert N 1923- *AmMWSc 92*
**Fain**, Gordon Lee 1946- *AmMWSc 92*
**Fain**, Haskell 1926- *WhoMW 92*
**Fain**, Jay Lindsey 1950- *WhoFI 92*
**Fain**, Joel Maurice 1953- *WhoAmL 92*
**Fain**, John Nicholas 1934- *AmMWSc 92*
**Fain**, John William 1953- *WhoRel 92*
**Fain**, Karen Kellogg 1940- *WhoWest 92*
**Fain**, Robert C 1936- *AmMWSc 92*
**Fain**, Sammy 1902-1989 *ConTFT 9*
**Fain**, Sammy 1902-1990 *NewAmDM*
**Fain**, Samuel Clark, Jr 1942- *AmMWSc 92*
**Fain**, Sandra Lynn Buchert 1961- *WhoEnt 92*
**Fain**, William Wharton 1927- *AmMWSc 92*
**Fainberg**, Anthony 1944- *AmMWSc 92*
**Fainberg**, Arnold Harold 1922- *AmMWSc 92*
**Fainberg**, Joseph 1930- *AmMWSc 92*
**Faingold**, Carl L 1943- *AmMWSc 92*
**Faini**, Maria Luisa Teresa *WhoEnt 92*
**Fainlight**, Ruth *DrAPF 91*
**Fainlight**, Ruth 1931- *ConPo 91, IntAu&W 91, WrDr 92*
**Fainstat**, Theodore 1929- *AmMWSc 92*
**Faint**, John Anthony Leonard 1942- *Who 92*
**Fair**, C. James 1951- *WhoMW 92*
**Fair**, Daryl S 1947- *AmMWSc 92*
**Fair**, Donald Robert Russell 1916- *Who 92*
**Fair**, Frank T. 1929- *WhoBlA 92*
**Fair**, Frank Thomas 1929- *WhoRel 92*
**Fair**, Harry David, Jr 1936- *AmMWSc 92*
**Fair**, Hudson Randolph 1953- *WhoMW 92*
**Fair**, James R 1920- *AmMWSc 92*
**Fair**, James R, Jr. 1920- *ConAu 34NR*
**Fair**, James Richard 1950- *WhoMW 92*
**Fair**, James Woodson 1927- *WhoRel 92*
**Fair**, Michael 1946- *WhoAmP 91*
**Fair**, Mike 1942- *WhoAmP 91*
**Fair**, Norman Arnold 1945- *WhoIns 92*
**Fair**, Patricia Anne 1952- *WhoAmP 91*
**Fair**, Rachel Ann 1965- *WhoFI 92*
**Fair**, Richard Barton 1942- *AmMWSc 92*
**Fair**, Ronald *DrAPF 91*
**Fair**, Ronald L. 1932- *WhoBlA 92*
**Fair**, Talmadge Willard 1939- *WhoBlA 92*
**Fairand**, Barry Philip 1934- *AmMWSc 92*
**Fairbairn**, Brooke *Who 92*
**Fairbairn**, David 1924- *Who 92*
**Fairbairn**, David Eric 1917- *Who 92*
**Fairbairn**, David Ritchie 1934- *Who 92*
**Fairbairn**, Douglas 1926- *WrDr 92*
**Fairbairn**, Douglas Foakes 1919- *Who 92*
**Fairbairn**, Harold Williams 1906- *AmMWSc 92*
**Fairbairn**, James Brooke 1930- *Who 92*
**Fairbairn**, John F, II 1922- *AmMWSc 92*
**Fairbairn**, John Sydney 1934- *IntWW 91, Who 92*
**Fairbairn**, Stephen Carl 1960- *WhoWest 92*
**Fairbairn of Fordell**, Nicholas 1933- *Who 92*
**Fairbairns**, Zoe 1948- *ConNov 91, TwCSFW 91, WrDr 92*
**Fairbairns**, Zoe Ann 1948- *IntAu&W 91*
**Fairbank**, Henry Alan 1918- *AmMWSc 92*
**Fairbank**, Holly Cannon 1953- *WhoEnt 92*
**Fairbank**, Janet Ayer 1879-1951 *BenetAL 91*
**Fairbank**, John K. 1907- *WrDr 92*
**Fairbank**, John K. 1907-1991 *ConAu 135, CurBio 91N, NewYTBS 91 [port]*
**Fairbank**, William Martin 1917- *AmMWSc 92*
**Fairbank**, William Martin 1917-1989 *FacFETw*
**Fairbank**, William Martin, Jr 1946- *AmMWSc 92*
**Fairbanks**, Charles Warren 1852-1918 *AmPolLe*
**Fairbanks**, Douglas 1883-1939 *FacFETw [port]*
**Fairbanks**, Douglas 1909- *Who 92*
**Fairbanks**, Douglas, Jr. *FacFETw*
**Fairbanks**, Douglas, Jr. 1909- *IntMPA 92*
**Fairbanks**, Douglas Elton, Jr 1909- *IntAu&W 91, IntWW 91, WhoEnt 92*
**Fairbanks**, Gilbert Wayne 1937- *AmMWSc 92*
**Fairbanks**, Grant 1940- *AmMWSc 92*
**Fairbanks**, Harold V 1915- *AmMWSc 92*
**Fairbanks**, Henry 1830-1918 *BiInAmS*
**Fairbanks**, Jerry 1904- *IntMPA 92*
**Fairbanks**, Laurence Dee 1926- *AmMWSc 92*
**Fairbanks**, Mary Kathleen 1948- *WhoWest 92*
**Fairbanks**, Richard M, III 1941- *WhoAmP 91*
**Fairbanks**, Richard Monroe 1912- *WhoEnt 92*
**Fairbanks**, Richard Monroe, III 1941- *WhoAmL 92*
**Fairbanks**, Robert Alvin 1944- *WhoAmL 92*
**Fairbanks**, Virgil 1930- *AmMWSc 92*
**Fairbanks**, William J 1931- *WhoIns 92*
**Fairbridge**, Rhodes Whitmore 1914- *AmMWSc 92*
**Fairbrothers**, David Earl 1925- *AmMWSc 92*
**Fairburn**, A.R.D. 1904-1957 *RfGEnL 91*
**Fairburn**, Eleanor 1928- *WrDr 92*
**Fairburn**, Eleanor M 1928- *IntAu&W 91*
**Fairchild**, Arvid Pershing 1925- *WhoWest 92*
**Fairchild**, Blair 1877-1933 *NewAmDM*
**Fairchild**, Bob 1943- *WhoAmP 91*
**Fairchild**, Clifford Eugene 1934- *AmMWSc 92*
**Fairchild**, David George 1939- *AmMWSc 92*
**Fairchild**, Edward Elwood, Jr 1949- *AmMWSc 92*
**Fairchild**, Edward H 1943- *AmMWSc 92*
**Fairchild**, Gary Lee 1943- *WhoAmL 92*
**Fairchild**, Graham Bell 1906- *AmMWSc 92*
**Fairchild**, Henry Brant, III 1945- *WhoMW 92*
**Fairchild**, Henry Pratt 1880-1956 *DcAmImH*
**Fairchild**, Homer Eaton 1921- *AmMWSc 92*
**Fairchild**, Jack 1928- *AmMWSc 92*
**Fairchild**, John Burr 1927- *WhoEnt 92, WhoFI 92*
**Fairchild**, Joseph Jerome 1949- *WhoAmP 91*
**Fairchild**, Joseph Virgil, Jr 1933- *AmMWSc 92, WhoFI 92*
**Fairchild**, Mahlon Lowell 1930- *AmMWSc 92*
**Fairchild**, Morgan 1950- *IntMPA 92, WhoEnt 92*
**Fairchild**, Philip Lee 1962- *WhoRel 92*
**Fairchild**, Ralph Grandison 1935- *AmMWSc 92*
**Fairchild**, Raymond Eugene 1923- *WhoFI 92*
**Fairchild**, Raymond Francis 1946- *WhoAmL 92*
**Fairchild**, Robert Wayne *AmMWSc 92*
**Fairchild**, Roger *WhoAmP 91*
**Fairchild**, Russell H 1947- *WhoAmP 91*
**Fairchild**, William 1918- *IntMPA 92*
**Fairchild**, William Warren 1938- *AmMWSc 92*
**Faircloth**, Larry V 1948- *WhoAmP 91*
**Faircloth**, Wayne Reynolds 1932- *AmMWSc 92*
**Faircloth**, William Turner 1829-1900 *DcNCBi 2*
**Fairclough**, Anthony John 1924- *IntWW 91, Who 92*
**Fairclough**, Ellen Louks 1905- *Who 92*
**Fairclough**, John 1930- *Who 92*
**Fairclough**, John Whitaker 1930- *IntWW 91*
**Fairclough**, Michael 1940- *TwCPaSc*
**Fairclough**, Wilfred 1907- *TwCPaSc, Who 92*
**Faire**, Zabrina *WrDr 92*
**Faires**, Barbara Trader 1943- *AmMWSc 92*
**Faires**, John Douglas 1941- *AmMWSc 92*
**Faires**, Olando Joe 1931- *WhoEnt 92*
**Faires**, Ross N. 1934- *WhoFI 92*
**Faires**, Wesley Lee 1932- *AmMWSc 92*
**Fairey**, Michael John 1933- *Who 92*
**Fairfax** *Who 92*
**Fairfax**, Beatrice *BenetAL 91*
**Fairfax**, James Oswald 1933- *Who 92*
**Fairfax**, John 1930- *IntAu&W 91, WrDr 92*
**Fairfax**, Marion 1875-1970 *ReelWom*
**Fairfax**, Robert *NewAmDM*
**Fairfax**, Roger Anthony 1951- *WhoBlA 92*
**Fairfax**, Sally Kirk 1944- *AmMWSc 92*
**Fairfax**, Vincent Charles 1909- *IntWW 91, Who 92*
**Fairfax-Lucy**, Edmund 1945- *Who 92*
**Fairfax of Cameron**, Lord 1956- *Who 92*
**Fairfield**, Darrell *IntAu&W 91X, WrDr 92*
**Fairfield**, John *DrAPF 91*
**Fairfield**, Richard Thomas 1937- *WhoMW 92*
**Fairfield**, Roy Phillip 1918- *WhoMW 92*
**Fairfield**, Sumner Lincoln 1803-1844 *BenetAL 91*
**Fairgrieve**, James H. 1944- *TwCPaSc*
**Fairgrieve**, Russell 1924- *Who 92*
**Fairhall**, Allen 1909- *Who 92*
**Fairhall**, Arthur William 1925- *AmMWSc 92*
**Fairhaven**, Baron 1936- *Who 92*
**Fairhurst**, C 1929- *AmMWSc 92*
**Fairhurst**, Jack Leslie 1905- *TwCPaSc*
**Fairleigh**, James Parkinson 1938- *WhoEnt 92*
**Fairleigh**, Marlane Paxson 1939- *WhoFI 92*
**Fairleigh**, Runa *WrDr 92*
**Fairley**, George 1920- *TwCPaSc*
**Fairley**, Henry Barrie Fleming 1927- *AmMWSc 92*
**Fairley**, James Lafayette, Jr 1920- *AmMWSc 92*
**Fairley**, James S. 1940- *WrDr 92*
**Fairley**, Richard L. 1933- *WhoBlA 92*
**Fairley**, William Merle 1928- *AmMWSc 92*
**Fairlie**, Alison 1917- *Who 92*
**Fairlie**, Henry 1924-1990 *AnObit 1990*
**Fairlie**, Hugh 1919- *Who 92*
**Fairlie-Cuninghame**, William Henry 1930- *Who 92*
**Fairman**, Frederick Walker 1935- *AmMWSc 92*
**Fairman**, Henry Clay *ScFEYrs*
**Fairman**, Jarrett Sylvester 1939- *WhoFI 92*
**Fairman**, Jimmy W. 1948- *WhoBlA 92*
**Fairman**, Joan Alexandra 1935- *WrDr 92*
**Fairman**, Joel Martin 1929- *WhoEnt 92*
**Fairman**, John Abbrey 1949- *WhoBlA 92*
**Fairman**, Paul W 1916-1977 *TwCSFW 91*
**Fairman**, Susanne Bank 1954- *WhoMW 92*
**Fairman**, William Duane 1929- *AmMWSc 92*
**Fairnie**, Ian James 1944- *WhoMW 92*
**Fairstein**, Linda 1948?- *News 91 [port], WhoAmL 92*
**Fairtlough**, Gerard Howard 1930- *Who 92*
**Fairweather**, Claude Cyril 1906- *Who 92*
**Fairweather**, Denys Vivian Ivor 1927- *Who 92*
**Fairweather**, Digby 1946- *IntAu&W 91*
**Fairweather**, Edwin Arthur 1916- *WhoWest 92*
**Fairweather**, Eric John 1942- *Who 92*
**Fairweather**, Frank Arthur 1928- *Who 92*
**Fairweather**, Graeme 1942- *AmMWSc 92*
**Fairweather**, Patrick Stanislaus 1936- *Who 92*
**Fairweather**, William Ross *AmMWSc 92*
**Fairweather-Tait**, Susan Jane 1949- *AmMWSc 92*
**Faisal** 1906-1975 *FacFETw*
**Faison**, Delores 1945- *WhoWest 92*
**Faison**, Derek E. 1948- *WhoBlA 92*
**Faison**, Frankie 1949- *WhoBlA 92*
**Faison**, Helen Smith 1924- *WhoBlA 92*
**Faison**, John Miller 1862-1915 *DcNCBi 2*
**Faison**, John W. 1908- *WhoBlA 92*
**Faison**, Lee Vell 1933- *WhoAmP 91*
**Faison**, Ollie William, Jr. 1947- *WhoAmL 92*
**Faison**, Samson Lane 1860-1940 *DcNCBi 2*
**Faison**, Sharon Gail 1955- *WhoBlA 92*
**Faison**, Thurman Lawrence 1938- *WhoBlA 92*
**Faissler**, William L 1938- *AmMWSc 92*
**Fait**, George A 1926- *WhoIns 92*
**Faith No More** *ConMus 7 [port]*
**Faith**, Adam 1940- *IntWW 91*
**Faith**, Carl Clifton 1927- *AmMWSc 92*
**Faith**, Percy 1908-1976 *NewAmDM*
**Faith**, Sheila 1928- *Who 92*
**Faithfull** *Who 92*
**Faithfull**, Baroness 1910- *Who 92*
**Faivre**, Jules Abel 1867-1945 *ThHEIm*
**Faivre d'Arcier**, Bernard 1944- *IntWW 91*
**Faivus**, Samuel N. 1950- *WhoAmL 92*
**Fajans**, Edgar W 1911- *AmMWSc 92*
**Fajans**, Jack 1922- *AmMWSc 92*
**Fajans**, Stefan Stanislaus 1918- *AmMWSc 92*
**Fajardo**, Frederick Joseph 1935- *WhoFI 92*
**Fajardo**, Jorge Elias 1942- *WhoHisp 92*
**Fajardo**, Juan Ramon, Jr. 1958- *WhoHisp 92*
**Fajardo**, Teresa Ana Guzman 1938- *WhoFI 92*
**Fajardo-Acosta**, Fidel 1960- *WhoHisp 92*
**Fajen**, John Herman 1929- *WhoRel 92*
**Fajer**, Abram Bencjan 1926- *AmMWSc 92*
**Fajer**, Jack 1936- *AmMWSc 92*

**Fajt,** Gregory C 1954- *WhoAmP 91*
**Fakhoury,** Rachid *IntWW 91*
**Fakhreddinov,** Rizautdin 1859-1936 *SovUnBD*
**Fakhrid-Deen,** Nashid Abdullah 1949- *WhoBlA 92*
**Fakley,** Dennis Charles 1924- *Who 92*
**Fakunding,** John Leonard 1945- *AmMWSc 92*
**Fakundiny,** Robert Harry 1940- *AmMWSc 92*
**Falagan-Girona,** Mildred 1950- *WhoHisp 92*
**Falana,** Lola 1943- *WhoBlA 92*
**Falb,** Peter L 1936- *AmMWSc 92*
**Falb,** Peter Lawrence 1936- *WhoFI 92*
**Falcao,** Armando Ribeiro 1920- *IntWW 91*
**Falcao,** Jose Freire 1925- *WhoRel 92*
**Falchuk,** Kenneth H 1940- *AmMWSc 92*
**Falci,** Kenneth Joseph *AmMWSc 92*
**Falck,** Colin 1934- *IntAu&W 91, WrDr 92*
**Falck,** Frank James 1925- *AmMWSc 92*
**Falco,** Charles Maurice 1948- *AmMWSc 92*
**Falco,** Edward *DrAPF 91*
**Falco,** Edward 1948- *ConAu 134*
**Falco,** James William 1942- *AmMWSc 92*
**Falco,** Louis 1942- *WhoEnt 92*
**Falco,** Maria Josephine 1932- *WhoMW 92*
**Falcon,** Angelo *WhoHisp 92*
**Falcon,** Carroll James 1941- *AmMWSc 92*
**Falcon,** David 1946- *Who 92*
**Falcon,** Dora 1936- *WhoHisp 92*
**Falcon,** Juan Manuel 1967- *WhoWest 92*
**Falcon,** Louis A 1932- *AmMWSc 92*
**Falcon,** Luis M. 1955- *WhoHisp 92*
**Falcon,** Mark 1940- *TwCWW 91, WrDr 92*
**Falcon,** Michael Gascoigne 1928- *Who 92*
**Falcon,** Norman Leslie 1904- *Who 92*
**Falcon,** Rafael 1947- *WhoHisp 92*
**Falcon,** Raymond Jesus, Jr. 1953- *WhoAmL 92, WhoFI 92*
**Falconbridge,** Brian 1950- *TwCPaSc*
**Falcone,** A B *AmMWSc 92*
**Falcone,** Alfonso Benjamin 1923- *WhoWest 92*
**Falcone,** Carmine 1946- *WhoFI 92, WhoWest 92*
**Falcone,** Charles Anthony 1942- *WhoFI 92*
**Falcone,** Domenick Joseph *AmMWSc 92*
**Falcone,** James Salvatore, Jr 1946- *AmMWSc 92*
**Falcone,** Louis A. 1955- *WhoAmL 92*
**Falcone,** Michael Frank 1948- *WhoEnt 92*
**Falcone,** Nola Maddox 1939- *WhoFI 92*
**Falcone,** Patricia Kuntz 1952- *AmMWSc 92*
**Falcone,** Philip Francis 1929- *WhoWest 92*
**Falcone,** Robert Edward 1950- *WhoMW 92*
**Falcone,** Sebastian Anthony 1927- *WhoRel 92*
**Falconer,** Alan David 1945- *WhoRel 92*
**Falconer,** Alexander 1940- *Who 92*
**Falconer,** Charles Leslie 1951- *Who 92*
**Falconer,** David Duncan 1940- *AmMWSc 92*
**Falconer,** Douglas 1914- *Who 92*
**Falconer,** Douglas Scott 1913- *IntWW 91, Who 92*
**Falconer,** Etta Zuber 1933- *AmMWSc 92*
**Falconer,** James *IntAu&W 91X*
**Falconer,** John Lucien 1946- *AmMWSc 92*
**Falconer,** Peter Serrell 1916- *Who 92*
**Falconer,** Thomas Hugh 1935- *AmMWSc 92*
**Falconer,** Warren Edgar 1936- *AmMWSc 92*
**Falconer,** William 1732-1769 *RfGEnL 91*
**Falconet,** Etienne Maurice 1716-1791 *BlkwCEP*
**Falcucci,** Franca 1926- *IntWW 91*
**Faldo,** Nicholas Alexander 1957- *Who 92*
**Faldo,** Nick *NewYTBS 91 [port]*
**Faldo,** Nick 1957- *IntWW 91*
**Falek,** Arthur 1924- *AmMWSc 92*
**Falen,** Becky 1963- *WhoEnt 92*
**Faleomavaega,** Eni F H *WhoAmP 91*
**Faleomavaega,** Eni F. H. 1943- *AlmAP 92, WhoWest 92*
**Faler,** Kenneth Turner 1931- *AmMWSc 92*
**Falero,** Frank 1937- *WhoWest 92*
**Fales,** Frank Weck 1914- *AmMWSc 92*
**Fales,** Haliburton, II 1919- *WhoAmL 92*
**Fales,** Henry Marshall 1927- *AmMWSc 92*
**Fales,** Steven Lewis 1947- *AmMWSc 92*
**Fales,** William Harold 1940- *AmMWSc 92*
**Falese,** Patricia Anne 1959- *WhoEnt 92*
**Faletau,** 'Inoke Fotu 1937- *IntWW 91, Who 92*
**Faletti,** Duane W 1934- *AmMWSc 92*
**Faletti,** Harold Everett 1952- *WhoAmL 92*
**Faletti,** Richard Joseph 1922- *WhoAmL 92*
**Faley,** Richard Scott 1947- *WhoAmL 92, WhoFI 92*
**Faley,** Robert Lawrence 1927- *WhoFI 92*
**Falgoust,** Dean Thomas 1958- *WhoAmL 92*
**Falgout,** William Donald 1941- *WhoRel 92*
**Falick,** Abraham Johnson 1920- *WhoWest 92*
**Falicov,** Leopoldo Maximo 1933- *AmMWSc 92, IntWW 91, WhoWest 92*
**Falin,** Valentin Mikhailovich 1926- *IntWW 91*
**Falin,** Valentin Mikhaylovich 1926- *SovUnBD*
**Falino,** Francis Joseph 1970- *WhoHisp 92*
**Falise,** Michel 1931- *IntWW 91*
**Falk,** Arnold Ross 1947- *WhoAmL 92*
**Falk,** Bruce Pembleton *WhoFI 92*
**Falk,** Candace 1947- *WrDr 92*
**Falk,** Catherine T 1939- *AmMWSc 92*
**Falk,** Charles David 1939- *AmMWSc 92*
**Falk,** Charles Eugene 1923- *AmMWSc 92*
**Falk,** Conrad Robert 1935- *WhoEnt 92*
**Falk,** Darrel Ross 1946- *AmMWSc 92*
**Falk,** Edward D 1925- *AmMWSc 92*
**Falk,** Elizabeth Moxley 1942- *WhoEnt 92*
**Falk,** Eugene D. 1953- *WhoEnt 92*
**Falk,** Gertrude 1925- *AmMWSc 92*
**Falk,** Harold 1933- *AmMWSc 92*
**Falk,** Harold Charles 1934- *AmMWSc 92*
**Falk,** Harvey Oscar 1932- *WhoRel 92*
**Falk,** Henry 1943- *AmMWSc 92*
**Falk,** James Harvey, Sr. 1938- *WhoAmL 92*
**Falk,** James Robert 1953- *WhoFI 92*
**Falk,** John Carl 1938- *AmMWSc 92*
**Falk,** John L 1927- *AmMWSc 92*
**Falk,** Julie Dawn 1961- *WhoMW 92*
**Falk,** Lawrence A, Jr 1938- *AmMWSc 92*
**Falk,** Lee *ConAu 133*
**Falk,** Leslie Alan 1915- *AmMWSc 92*
**Falk,** Lloyd L 1919- *AmMWSc 92*
**Falk,** Marcia *DrAPF 91*
**Falk,** Marshall Allen 1929- *AmMWSc 92, WhoMW 92*
**Falk,** Michael 1931- *AmMWSc 92*
**Falk,** Michael Philip 1953- *WhoMW 92*
**Falk,** Nancy Ellen Auer 1938- *WhoRel 92*
**Falk,** Peter *LesBEnT 92*
**Falk,** Peter 1927- *IntMPA 92, WhoEnt 92*
**Falk,** Randall M. 1921- *WhoRel 92*
**Falk,** Richard H 1938- *AmMWSc 92*
**Falk,** Robert Hardy 1948- *WhoAmL 92, WhoFI 92*
**Fal'k,** Robert Rafaylovich 1886-1958 *SovUnBD*
**Falk,** Roger 1910- *Who 92*
**Falk,** Roger Lee 1953- *WhoAmL 92*
**Falk,** Sam d1991 *NewYTBS 91*
**Falk,** Signi Lenea 1906- *WrDr 92*
**Falk,** Stanley Lawrence 1927- *WrDr 92*
**Falk,** Steven L. 1946- *WhoFI 92*
**Falk,** Sydney Westervelt, Jr. 1947- *WhoAmL 92*
**Falk,** Theodore J 1931- *AmMWSc 92*
**Falk,** Thomas 1926- *AmMWSc 92*
**Falk,** Werner David d1991 *NewYTBS 91*
**Falk,** Willie Robert 1937- *AmMWSc 92*
**Falk,** Ze'ev W. 1923- *WrDr 92*
**Falke,** Ernest Victor 1942- *AmMWSc 92*
**Falkehag,** S Ingemar 1930- *AmMWSc 92*
**Falkenbach,** George J 1927- *AmMWSc 92*
**Falkenberg,** Edward 1940- *WhoFI 92*
**Falkenberg,** Kort Adeler, III 1952- *WhoEnt 92*
**Falkenberg,** William Stevens 1927- *WhoWest 92*
**Falkenburg,** Jinx Lincoln 1919- *WhoEnt 92*
**Falkender,** Baroness 1932- *Who 92*
**Falkener,** Sarah DeRippe 1755-1819 *DcNCBi 2*
**Falkener,** William 1751-1819 *DcNCBi 2*
**Falkenhausen,** Alexander von 1878-1966 *EncTR 91 [port]*
**Falkenhorst,** Nikolaus von 1885-1968 *EncTR 91 [port]*
**Falkenstein,** Gary Lee 1937- *AmMWSc 92*
**Falkenstein,** Kathy Fay 1950- *AmMWSc 92*
**Falker,** John Richard 1940- *WhoMW 92*
**Falkie,** Thomas Victor 1934- *AmMWSc 92*
**Falkiewicz,** Michael Joseph 1942- *AmMWSc 92*
**Falkiner,** Edmond 1938- *Who 92*
**Falkingham,** John Norman 1917- *Who 92*
**Falkinham,** Joseph Oliver, III 1942- *AmMWSc 92*
**Falkirk,** Richard *IntAu&W 91X, WrDr 92*
**Falkland,** Master of 1963- *Who 92*
**Falkland,** Viscount 1935- *Who 92*
**Falkler,** William Alexander, Jr 1944- *AmMWSc 92*
**Falkner,** Bobbie E. *WhoBlA 92*
**Falkner,** Frank Tardrew 1918- *AmMWSc 92*
**Falkner,** James George 1952- *WhoWest 92*
**Falkner,** Keith 1900- *IntWW 91, Who 92*
**Falkner,** Robert Frank 1940- *WhoAmL 92*
**Falkner,** William C. 1825-1889 *BenetAL 91*
**Falkner,** William Carroll 1954- *WhoAmL 92*
**Falkow,** Stanley 1934- *AmMWSc 92*
**Falkowitz,** Daniel 1936- *WhoFI 92*
**Falkowski,** James Jerry 1953- *WhoMW 92*
**Falkowski,** Paul Gordon 1951- *AmMWSc 92*
**Falkus,** Hugh Edward Lance 1917- *IntAu&W 91, Who 92*
**Fall,** Albert 1861-1944 *FacFETw*
**Fall,** Albert Bacon 1861-1944 *AmPolLe*
**Fall,** Brian James Proetel 1937- *IntWW 91, Who 92*
**Fall,** Harry H 1920- *AmMWSc 92*
**Fall,** Ibrahima 1942- *IntWW 91*
**Fall,** Jane Murray 1950- *WhoFI 92*
**Fall,** Medoune 1919- *IntWW 91*
**Fall,** Michael William 1942- *AmMWSc 92*
**Fall,** R Ray 1943- *AmMWSc 92*
**Fall,** Timothy Lee 1960- *WhoAmL 92*
**Falla,** Enrique C. *WhoHisp 92*
**Falla,** Enrique Crabb 1939- *WhoFI 92*
**Falla,** Manuel de 1876-1946 *FacFETw, NewAmDM*
**Falla,** Paul Stephen 1913- *Who 92*
**Falla y Matheu,** Manuel de 1876-1946 *NewAmDM*
**Fallaci,** Oriana 1930- *IntAu&W 91, IntWW 91*
**Fallada,** Hans 1893-1947 *EncTR 91 [port]*
**Fallaw,** Michael John 1941- *WhoMW 92*
**Falldin,** Thorbjorn 1926- *IntWW 91*
**Fallding,** Margaret Hurlstone Hardy 1920- *AmMWSc 92*
**Falle,** Sam 1919- *Who 92*
**Falleder,** Arnold E. *DrAPF 91*
**Fallek,** Max Edward 1930- *WhoFI 92*
**Faller,** Alan Judson 1929- *AmMWSc 92*
**Faller,** James E 1934- *AmMWSc 92*
**Faller,** James George 1934- *AmMWSc 92*
**Faller,** John William 1942- *AmMWSc 92*
**Faller,** Lincoln Bruce 1943- *WhoMW 92*
**Faller,** Morton Alfred 1946- *WhoAmL 92*
**Faller,** Rhoda Dianne Grossberg 1946- *WhoAmL 92*
**Faller,** Susan Grogan 1950- *WhoAmL 92*
**Faller,** William Edward 1964- *WhoWest 92*
**Fallert,** Herbert C 1936- *WhoAmP 91*
**Falletta,** Charles Edward 1944- *AmMWSc 92*
**Falletta,** Jo Ann *WhoEnt 92A*
**Falletta,** John Matthew 1940- *AmMWSc 92*
**Fallick,** Gregg Vance 1959- *WhoAmL 92*
**Fallieros,** Stavros 1927- *AmMWSc 92*
**Falliers,** Constantine J 1924- *AmMWSc 92*
**Fallin,** James Holder 1945- *WhoAmP 91*
**Fallin,** Joseph Price, Jr 1947- *WhoAmP 91*
**Fallin,** Mary C 1954- *WhoAmP 91*
**Fallin,** Pat Finley 1941- *WhoAmP 91*
**Fallis,** Alexander Graham 1940- *AmMWSc 92*
**Fallis,** Laurence S. *DrAPF 91*
**Fallman,** Michael S. 1960- *WhoAmL 92*
**Fallon,** Ann Marie 1949- *AmMWSc 92*
**Fallon,** Brett David 1961- *WhoAmL 92*
**Fallon,** Christopher Chaffee, Jr. 1948- *WhoAmL 92*
**Fallon,** Eldon E. 1939- *WhoAmL 92*
**Fallon,** Frederick Walter *AmMWSc 92*
**Fallon,** George *IntAu&W 91X*
**Fallon,** Harold Joseph 1931- *AmMWSc 92*
**Fallon,** Hazel Rosemary *Who 92*
**Fallon,** Ivan Gregory 1944- *IntAu&W 91, Who 92*
**Fallon,** James Harry 1947- *AmMWSc 92*
**Fallon,** John Francis *AmMWSc 92*
**Fallon,** John Joseph 1923- *WhoAmL 92*
**Fallon,** John T 1946- *AmMWSc 92*
**Fallon,** Joseph Anthony 1941- *WhoAmP 91*
**Fallon,** Joseph Greenleaf 1911- *AmMWSc 92*
**Fallon,** Martin *IntAu&W 91X, Who 92, WrDr 92*
**Fallon,** Michael *DrAPF 91*
**Fallon,** Michael 1952- *Who 92*
**Fallon,** Michael David *AmMWSc 92*
**Fallon,** Michael P. 1941- *WhoHisp 92*
**Fallon,** Michael Patrick 1942- *WhoMW 92*
**Fallon,** Peter 1931- *Who 92*
**Fallon,** Peter 1951- *ConAu 133, ConPo 91*
**Fallon,** Richard H., Jr. 1952- *WhoAmL 92*
**Fallon,** Stephen Francis 1956- *WhoHisp 92, WhoIns 92*
**Fallon,** Thomas Anthony 1944- *WhoEnt 92*
**Fallon,** Tina K 1917- *WhoAmP 91*
**Fallon,** Tom *DrAPF 91*
**Fallon,** William Shield 1931- *WhoAmL 92*
**Falloon,** John H. *IntWW 91*
**Fallows,** Albert Bennett 1928- *Who 92*
**Fallows,** James Mackenzie 1949- *WrDr 92*
**Falls,** Arthur GrandPre 1901- *WhoMW 92*
**Falls,** C Frank 1934- *WhoAmP 91*
**Falls,** Edward Joseph 1920- *WhoAmL 92*
**Falls,** James Bruce 1923- *AmMWSc 92*
**Falls,** Kathleene Joyce 1949- *WhoMW 92*
**Falls,** Robert Arthur 1954- *WhoEnt 92, WhoMW 92*
**Falls,** William McKenzie 1948- *AmMWSc 92*
**Falls,** William Randolph, Sr 1929- *AmMWSc 92*
**Fallside,** Frank 1932- *Who 92*
**Falmar,** Leslie Karen 1961- *WhoHisp 92*
**Falmouth,** Viscount 1919- *Who 92*
**Faloon,** William Wassell 1920- *AmMWSc 92*
**Falquez-Certain,** Miguel Angel 1948- *WhoHisp 92*
**Falsetti,** Herman Leo 1934- *AmMWSc 92*
**Falsey,** John *LesBEnT 92*
**Falsgraf,** William Wendell 1933- *WhoAmL 92*
**Falstad,** David Bergfeld 1936- *WhoFI 92*
**Falstad,** William James 1934- *WhoAmP 91*
**Falstein,** Louis *DrAPF 91*
**Falter,** John Max 1930- *AmMWSc 92*
**Falthammar,** Carl-Gunne 1931- *IntWW 91*
**Faltin,** Bruce Charles 1947- *WhoWest 92*
**Faltings,** Gerd 1954- *AmMWSc 92*
**Faltynek,** Robert Allen 1948- *AmMWSc 92*
**Faludy,** George 1910- *LiExTwC*
**Falvey,** Caroline A. 1960- *WhoAmL 92*
**Falvey,** Patrick Joseph 1927- *WhoAmL 92*
**Falwell,** Jerry *LesBEnT 92*
**Falwell,** Jerry 1933- *FacFETw, RelLAm 91*
**Falwell,** Jerry L. 1933- *IntWW 91, WhoRel 92*
**Falwell,** Robert V 1948- *WhoAmP 91*
**Falzarano,** L Domenic 1940- *WhoAmP 91*
**Falzon,** Michael 1945- *IntWW 91*
**Falzone,** Nicholas 1945- *WhoAmL 92*
**Fama,** Donald Francis 1938- *AmMWSc 92*
**Fama,** Joseph Danford 1942- *WhoFI 92*
**Famadas,** Jose 1908- *WhoFI 92*
**Fambrough,** Douglas McIntosh 1941- *AmMWSc 92*
**Fambrough-Adamson,** Sheryl 1954- *WhoAmL 92*
**Famighetti,** Louise Orto 1930- *AmMWSc 92*
**Famiglietti,** Edward Virgil, Jr 1943- *AmMWSc 92*
**Famiglietti,** Nancy Zima 1956- *WhoFI 92*
**Family,** Fereydoon 1945- *AmMWSc 92*
**Famoye,** Kiya Felix 1956- *WhoMW 92*
**Famularo,** Kendall Ferris 1928- *AmMWSc 92*
**Fan,** Madam *EncAmaz 91*
**Fan Weitang** *IntWW 91*
**Fan Ziyu** 1914- *IntWW 91*
**Fan,** Chang-Yun 1918- *AmMWSc 92*
**Fan,** Chien 1930- *AmMWSc 92*
**Fan,** Dah-Nien 1937- *AmMWSc 92*
**Fan,** David P 1942- *AmMWSc 92*
**Fan,** Hsin Ya *AmMWSc 92*
**Fan,** Hsing Yun 1914- *AmMWSc 92*
**Fan,** Hsu Yun 1912- *AmMWSc 92*
**Fan,** Hung Y. 1947- *WhoWest 92*
**Fan,** John C C 1943- *AmMWSc 92*
**Fan,** Joyce Wang 1919- *AmMWSc 92*
**Fan,** Ky 1914- *AmMWSc 92*
**Fan,** Liang-Shih 1947- *AmMWSc 92*
**Fan,** Liang-Shing 1932- *WhoFI 92*
**Fan,** Liang-Tseng 1929- *AmMWSc 92*
**Fan,** Ningping 1954- *AmMWSc 92*
**Fan,** Pow-Foong 1933- *AmMWSc 92*
**Fan,** Stephen S 1934- *AmMWSc 92*
**Fanaka,** Jamaa 1942- *WhoBlA 92*
**Fanaro,** Barry Paul 1953- *WhoEnt 92*
**Fanaroff,** Avroy A 1938- *AmMWSc 92*
**Fanaroff,** Sheri Van Greenby 1955- *WhoAmL 92, WhoFI 92*
**Fancher,** Evelyn Pitts 1924- *WhoBlA 92*
**Fancher,** Llewellyn W 1917- *AmMWSc 92*
**Fancher,** Otis Earl 1916- *AmMWSc 92*
**Fancher,** Paul S 1932- *AmMWSc 92*
**Fancher,** Rick 1953- *WhoAmL 92*
**Fancher,** Robert T. 1954- *ConAu 135*
**Fanciulli,** Francesco 1853-1915 *NewAmDM*
**Fanconi,** Bruno Mario 1939- *AmMWSc 92*
**Fancutt,** Walter 1911- *WrDr 92*
**Fancy,** Patricia Barbara 1939- *WhoAmL 92*
**Fand,** Richard Meyer 1923- *AmMWSc 92*
**Fand,** Theodore Ira 1915- *AmMWSc 92*
**Fandel,** John *DrAPF 91*
**Fandel,** Michael Ralph 1955- *WhoWest 92*
**Fandrich,** Lamont H. 1951- *WhoWest 92*
**Fane** *Who 92*
**Fane,** Bron *IntAu&W 91X, TwCSFW 91, WrDr 92*
**Fane,** Harry Frank Brien 1915- *Who 92*
**Fane,** Julian 1927- *IntAu&W 91, WrDr 92*
**Fane Trefusis** *Who 92*
**Fanelli,** George Marion, Jr 1926- *AmMWSc 92*
**Fanestil,** Darrell Dean 1933- *AmMWSc 92*
**Faneuil,** Peter 1700-1743 *BenetAL 91*
**Fanfani,** Amintore 1908- *IntWW 91*

**Fang Lizhi** 1936- *ConAu 135, IntWW 91*
**Fang Lizhi** 1937- *FacFETw*
**Fang Qiang** 1911- *IntWW 91*
**Fang Weizhong** 1928- *IntWW 91*
**Fang Yi** 1916- *IntWW 91*
**Fang,** Cheng-Shen 1936- *AmMWSc 92*
**Fang,** Ching Seng 1938- *AmMWSc 92*
**Fang,** Fabian Tien-Hwa 1929- *AmMWSc 92*
**Fang,** Frank F 1930- *AmMWSc 92*
**Fang,** Jen-Ho 1929- *AmMWSc 92*
**Fang,** Joong J 1923- *AmMWSc 92*
**Fang,** L.Z. *ConAu 135*
**Fang,** Mary Ruth 1961- *WhoWest 92*
**Fang,** Sheng Chung 1916- *AmMWSc 92*
**Fang,** Victor Shengkuen 1929- *AmMWSc 92*
**Fangboner,** Raymond Franklin 1943- *AmMWSc 92*
**Fangel,** Jayne Grace 1959- *WhoMW 92*
**Fanger,** Bradford Otto 1956- *AmMWSc 92*
**Fanger,** Carleton G 1924- *AmMWSc 92*
**Fanger,** Michael Walter 1940- *AmMWSc 92*
**Fangio,** Juan Manuel 1911- *FacFETw, IntWW 91*
**Fangman,** Walton L 1939- *AmMWSc 92*
**Fangmeier,** Delmar Dean 1932- *AmMWSc 92, WhoWest 92*
**Fanguy,** Roy Charles 1929- *AmMWSc 92*
**Fanizza,** Joanne 1957- *WhoAmL 92*
**Fanjul,** Alfonso, Jr. *WhoHisp 92*
**Fanjul,** Andres *WhoHisp 92*
**Fanjul,** Jose *WhoHisp 92*
**Fankboner,** Peter Vaughn 1938- *AmMWSc 92*
**Fankhanel,** Edward H. 1958- *WhoHisp 92*
**Fankhauser,** Merrell Wayne 1943- *WhoEnt 92*
**Fann,** Huoo-Long 1931- *AmMWSc 92*
**Fanner,** Peter Duncan 1926- *Who 92*
**Fannin,** Bob M 1922- *AmMWSc 92*
**Fannin,** Carl Hendrix 1955- *WhoRel 92*
**Fannin,** Daniel Paul Clark 1942- *WhoWest 92*
**Fannin,** Paul Jones 1907- *WhoAmP 91*
**Fanning,** Clifford Wayne 1952- *WhoEnt 92*
**Fanning,** Dana Brian 1951- *WhoEnt 92*
**Fanning,** David *LesBEnT 92 [port]*
**Fanning,** David 1755-1825 *DcNCBi 2*
**Fanning,** Delvin Seymour 1931- *AmMWSc 92*
**Fanning,** Edmund 1737-1818 *DcNCBi 2*
**Fanning,** Eleanor 1949- *WhoAmL 92*
**Fanning,** Ellis Vinal, Jr 1935- *WhoAmP 91*
**Fanning,** George Richard 1936- *AmMWSc 92*
**Fanning,** Harold Dean 1952- *WhoRel 92*
**Fanning,** James Collier 1931- *AmMWSc 92*
**Fanning,** John Patton 1934- *WhoAmP 91*
**Fanning,** John Thomas 1837-1911 *BiInAmS*
**Fanning,** Kenneth James 1947- *WhoAmP 91*
**Fanning,** Kent Abram 1941- *AmMWSc 92*
**Fanning,** Nathaniel 1755-1805 *BenetAL 91*
**Fanning,** Peter Maurice 1955- *WhoEnt 92*
**Fanning,** Robert Arthur 1951- *WhoAmL 92*
**Fanning,** Ronald Heath 1935- *WhoMW 92*
**Fanning,** Thomas Andrew 1957- *WhoFI 92*
**Fanning,** Tolbert 1810-1874 *AmPeW*
**Fanning,** William 1728-1782 *DcNCBi 2*
**Fanny-Dell** 1939- *WhoWest 92*
**Fano,** Robert M 1917- *AmMWSc 92*
**Fano,** Ugo 1912- *AmMWSc 92, IntWW 91*
**Fanolio,** Richard Wayne 1935- *WhoEnt 92*
**Fanon,** Frantz 1925-1961 *BlkLC [port], LiExTwC*
**Fanon,** Frantz Omar 1925-1961 *FacFETw*
**Fanone,** Joseph Anthony 1949- *WhoAmL 92*
**Fanos,** John G 1926- *WhoAmP 91*
**Fanos,** William R. 1953- *WhoMW 92*
**Fanshawe,** George Drew d1991 *Who 92N*
**Fanshawe,** John Richardson, II 1906- *AmMWSc 92*
**Fanshawe,** Thomas Evelyn 1918- *Who 92*
**Fanshawe,** William Joseph 1926- *AmMWSc 92*
**Fanshawe of Richmond,** Baron 1927- *Who 92*
**Fansler,** Bradford S 1939- *AmMWSc 92*
**Fansler,** Kevin Spain 1938- *AmMWSc 92*
**Fansler,** Mary Adrienne 1947- *WhoWest 92*
**Fansler,** Todd David 1947- *WhoMW 92*
**Fanslow,** Alyce Muck 1935- *WhoMW 92*
**Fanslow,** Don J 1936- *AmMWSc 92*
**Fanslow,** Glenn E 1927- *AmMWSc 92*
**Fanslow,** Julia Earleen 1939- *WhoWest 92*
**Fant,** Clyde Edward, Jr. 1934- *WhoRel 92*
**Fant,** Ennis Maurice 1961- *WhoAmP 91*
**Fanta,** Donald Charles 1928- *WhoFI 92*
**Fanta,** George Frederick 1934- *AmMWSc 92*
**Fanta,** Paul Edward 1921- *AmMWSc 92*
**Fantasia,** Mary E 1919- *WhoAmP 91*
**Fantasia,** Nick *WhoAmP 91*
**Fante,** Ronald Louis 1936- *AmMWSc 92*
**Fanthorpe,** R Lionel 1935- *TwCSFW 91, WrDr 92*
**Fanthorpe,** Robert Lionel 1935- *IntAu&W 91*
**Fanthorpe,** U. A. 1929- *ConPo 91, WrDr 92*
**Fanthorpe,** Ursula Askham 1929- *IntAu&W 91*
**Fanticola,** Anthony Charles 1960- *WhoEnt 92*
**Fantin-Latour,** Ignace-Henri-Jean-T 1836-1904 *ThHEIm*
**Fantini,** Amedeo Alexander 1922- *AmMWSc 92*
**Fantino,** Lisa Maria *WhoEnt 92*
**Fantis,** Akis 1944- *IntWW 91*
**Fantl,** Susan *DrAPF 91*
**Fantoni,** Barry 1940- *TwCPaSc, WrDr 92*
**Fantoni,** Barry Ernest 1940- *Who 92*
**Fantozzi,** Tony 1933- *IntMPA 92*
**Fantry,** Catherine Huber 1948- *WhoAmP 91*
**Fantz,** Paul Richard 1941- *AmMWSc 92*
**Fanucci,** Allan Angelo 1953- *WhoAmL 92*
**Fanucci,** Jerome B 1924- *AmMWSc 92*
**Fanuele,** Michael Anthony 1938- *WhoFI 92*
**Fanuele,** Vincent James 1950- *WhoEnt 92*
**Faqir,** Fadia A. M. A. 1956- *LiExTwC*
**Farabaugh,** Gina Marie 1965- *WhoFI 92*
**Farabee,** Ray 1932- *WhoAmP 91*
**Farabi,** Al- 870?-950 *DcLB 115*
**Farace,** Joseph Francis 1941- *WhoEnt 92*
**Farach,** Horacio Andres 1955- *WhoAmL 92*
**Faraci,** Dominick Daniel 1938- *WhoAmL 92*
**Faraday,** Bruce 1919- *AmMWSc 92*
**Farag,** Ihab Hanna 1946- *AmMWSc 92*
**Farag,** Shawky Abdelmonem 1939- *WhoMW 92*
**Farage,** Donald J. *WhoAmL 92*
**Farago,** Joe 1948- *WhoEnt 92*
**Farago,** John 1917- *AmMWSc 92*
**Farah,** Empress of Iran *IntWW 91*
**Farah,** Abdulrahim Abby 1919- *IntWW 91*
**Farah,** Alfred Emil 1914- *AmMWSc 92*
**Farah,** Badie Naiem *AmMWSc 92*
**Farah,** Benjamin Frederick 1956- *WhoMW 92*
**Farah,** Fuad Salim 1929- *AmMWSc 92*
**Farah,** Greg Arthur 1965- *WhoFI 92*
**Farah,** Nuruddin 1945- *BlkLC [port], ConNov 91, IntAu&W 91, LiExTwC, WrDr 92*
**Farah,** Roger *WhoFI 92*
**Farah,** Tawfic Elias 1946- *WhoWest 92*
**Farah Dirir,** Saleh Hadji 1937- *IntWW 91*
**Faraj,** Bahjat Alfred *AmMWSc 92*
**Faraldi,** Lorna *WhoEnt 92*
**Faranda,** John Paul 1957- *WhoWest 92*
**Farao,** Lucia Victoria 1927- *WhoHisp 92*
**Faraone,** Juana 1940- *WhoHisp 92*
**Faraone,** Ted 1956- *WhoEnt 92*
**Faras,** Anthony James 1942- *AmMWSc 92*
**Farb,** Edith 1928- *AmMWSc 92*
**Farb,** Stanley Norman 1935- *WhoFI 92*
**Farb,** Thomas Forest 1956- *WhoFI 92*
**Farber,** Andrew R 1953- *AmMWSc 92*
**Farber,** Anne 1948- *WhoAmL 92*
**Farber,** Bart *IntMPA 92*
**Farber,** Bernard John 1948- *WhoAmL 92, WhoMW 92*
**Farber,** Donald Clifford 1923- *WhoAmL 92, WhoEnt 92*
**Farber,** Elliot 1932- *AmMWSc 92*
**Farber,** Elliott 1928- *AmMWSc 92*
**Farber,** Emmanuel 1918- *AmMWSc 92*
**Farber,** Erich A 1921- *AmMWSc 92*
**Farber,** Eugene M 1917- *AmMWSc 92*
**Farber,** Florence Eileen 1939- *AmMWSc 92*
**Farber,** Herman 1919- *AmMWSc 92*
**Farber,** Hugh Arthur 1933- *AmMWSc 92*
**Farber,** Isadore E. 1917- *WhoMW 92*
**Farber,** Jay Paul 1942- *AmMWSc 92*
**Farber,** John J. 1925- *WhoFI 92*
**Farber,** John Lewis *AmMWSc 92*
**Farber,** Jorge 1948- *AmMWSc 92*
**Farber,** Joseph 1924- *AmMWSc 92*
**Farber,** Marilyn Diane 1945- *AmMWSc 92*
**Farber,** Milton 1916- *AmMWSc 92*
**Farber,** Milton H. d1991 *NewYTBS 91 [port]*
**Farber,** Paul Alan 1938- *AmMWSc 92*
**Farber,** Paul Lawrence 1944- *WhoWest 92*
**Farber,** Phillip Andrew 1934- *AmMWSc 92*
**Farber,** Robert James 1946- *AmMWSc 92*
**Farber,** Rosann Alexander 1944- *AmMWSc 92*
**Farber,** Saul Joseph 1918- *AmMWSc 92*
**Farber,** Sergio Julio 1938- *AmMWSc 92*
**Farber,** Seth Jonathan 1962- *WhoAmL 92*
**Farber,** Seymour Morgan 1912- *AmMWSc 92*
**Farber,** Steven Glenn 1946- *WhoAmL 92*
**Farber,** Theodore Myles 1935- *AmMWSc 92*
**Farber,** Thomas *DrAPF 91*
**Farber,** William M. 1957- *WhoEnt 92*
**Farberman,** Harold 1929- *NewAmDM*
**Farberman,** Harold 1930- *WhoEnt 92*
**Farberman,** Harvey A 1939- *ConAu 35NR*
**Farbman,** Albert Irving 1934- *AmMWSc 92*
**Farbrother,** Barry John 1943- *WhoMW 92*
**Farbstein,** Leonard *WhoAmP 91*
**Farbstein,** Sol 1927- *WhoEnt 92*
**Farcasiu,** Dan 1937- *AmMWSc 92*
**Fardink,** Michael d1991 *NewYTBS 91*
**Fareed,** Ahmed Ali 1932- *WhoMW 92*
**Farel,** Paul Bertrand 1944- *AmMWSc 92*
**Farell,** Cesar Gustavo 1961- *WhoHisp 92*
**Farell Cubillas,** Arsenio 1921- *IntWW 91*
**Farely,** Alison *WrDr 92*
**Farentino,** Angela 1942- *WhoEnt 92*
**Farentino,** James 1938- *IntMPA 92, WhoEnt 92*
**Farese,** John Booth 1944- *WhoAmL 92*
**Farewell,** John P 1942- *AmMWSc 92*
**Farewell,** John Philip 1942- *WhoMW 92*
**Farewell,** Patricia *DrAPF 91*
**Farfan-Ramirez,** Lucrecia *WhoHisp 92*
**Fargas,** Laura *DrAPF 91*
**Fargason,** Eddie Wayne 1948- *WhoRel 92*
**Fargher,** Lawrence LeRoy 1932- *WhoAmP 91*
**Fargher,** Tim 1952- *TwCPaSc*
**Fargis,** George Aloysius 1854-1916 *BiInAmS*
**Fargo,** Donna 1945- *WhoEnt 92*
**Fargo,** Doone *IntAu&W 91X, TwCWW 91*
**Fargo,** Howard L 1928- *WhoAmP 91*
**Fargo,** James 1938- *IntMPA 92*
**Fargo,** John Jay 1950- *WhoAmL 92*
**Fargo,** Louis James 1938- *WhoEnt 92*
**Fargue,** Leon-Paul 1876-1947 *FacFETw*
**Farhadieh,** Rouyentan 1944- *AmMWSc 92*
**Farhang,** Ash Hashem 1934- *WhoFI 92*
**Farhat,** Debbie Daly 1954- *WhoAmP 91*
**Farhataziz,** Mr 1932- *AmMWSc 92*
**Farhi,** Diane C 1951- *AmMWSc 92*
**Farhi,** Edward 1952- *AmMWSc 92*
**Farhi,** Leon Elie 1923- *AmMWSc 92*
**Farhi,** Morris 1935- *LiExTwC*
**Faria,** Antonio F. 1948- *WhoHisp 92*
**Faria,** Gilberto 1942- *WhoHisp 92*
**Faria,** Joseph L 1947- *WhoAmP 91*
**Farias,** Edward J. *WhoHisp 92*
**Farias,** Fred, III 1957- *WhoHisp 92*
**Farias,** Jesse 1945- *WhoHisp 92*
**Farias,** Ramiro, Jr. 1949- *WhoHisp 92*
**Farias,** Victor 1940- *ConAu 135*
**Faricy,** Raymond White, Jr 1934- *WhoAmP 91*
**Faricy,** Robert L 1926- *ConAu 34NR, WrDr 92*
**Farid,** Nadir R 1944- *AmMWSc 92*
**Faries,** Dillard Wayne 1941- *AmMWSc 92*
**Faries,** McIntyre 1896- *WhoAmP 91*
**Farigoule,** Louis *ConAu 34NR*
**Farin,** Lisa Schulke 1958- *WhoWest 92*
**Farina,** Battista 1893-1966 *DcTwDes*
**Farina,** Joseph Peter 1931- *AmMWSc 92*
**Farina,** Julie Lynn 1950- *WhoAmL 92*
**Farina,** Lissette M. 1965- *WhoHisp 92*
**Farina,** Michael 1949- *WhoEnt 92*
**Farina,** Peter R 1946- *AmMWSc 92*
**Farina,** Richard 1936-1966 *BenetAL 91*
**Farina,** Robert Donald 1934- *AmMWSc 92*
**Farina,** Thomas Edward 1941- *AmMWSc 92*
**Farinacci,** Jorge A. 1924- *WhoHisp 92*
**Farinacci,** Roberto 1892-1945 *BiDExR*
**Farinella,** Salvatore *DrAPF 91*
**Farinelli** 1705-1782 *NewAmDM*
**Farinet,** Catherine Louise 1966- *WhoEnt 92*
**Faringdon,** Baron 1937- *Who 92*
**Faris,** Elmer L 1914- *WhoAmP 91*
**Faris,** Jane Theresa Cantwell 1931- *WhoAmP 91*
**Faris,** John Jay 1921- *AmMWSc 92*
**Faris,** Muhammed 1951- *FacFETw*
**Faris,** Mustapha 1933- *IntWW 91*
**Faris,** Sam Russell 1917- *AmMWSc 92*
**Faris,** William 1705?-1757? *DcNCBi 2*
**Faris,** William Guignard 1939- *AmMWSc 92*
**Faris-Stockem,** Debbie Anne 1955- *WhoWest 92*
**Farisani,** Tshenuwani Simon 1947- *ConAu 134*
**Farish,** Donald J. 1942- *WrDr 92*
**Farish,** Donald James 1942- *AmMWSc 92*
**Farish,** James Matthew 1946- *WhoFI 92*
**Farish,** Terry *DrAPF 91*
**Farison,** James Blair 1938- *AmMWSc 92, WhoMW 92*
**Fariss,** Bruce Lindsay 1934- *AmMWSc 92*
**Fariss,** Robert Hardy 1928- *AmMWSc 92*
**Farjeon,** Eleanor 1881-1965 *FacFETw*
**Farjeon,** Herbert 1887-1945 *FacFETw*
**Farkas,** Bertalan 1949- *FacFETw*
**Farkas,** Daniel Frederick 1933- *AmMWSc 92*
**Farkas,** Eugene 1926- *AmMWSc 92*
**Farkas,** Ferenc 1905- *IntWW 91, NewAmDM*
**Farkas,** Leslie Gabriel 1915- *AmMWSc 92*
**Farkas,** Philip 1914- *NewAmDM*
**Farkas,** Philip Francis 1914- *WhoEnt 92*
**Farkas,** Walter Robert 1933- *AmMWSc 92*
**Farkas-Himsley,** Hannah 1918- *AmMWSc 92*
**Farkass,** Imre 1919- *AmMWSc 92*
**Farland,** Eugene Hector 1918- *WhoWest 92*
**Farlee,** Rodney Dale 1952- *AmMWSc 92*
**Farleigh,** John 1900-1965 *TwCPaSc*
**Farley,** Andrew Newell 1934- *WhoAmL 92*
**Farley,** Barbara Suzanne 1949- *WhoAmL 92*
**Farley,** Belmont Greenlee 1920- *AmMWSc 92*
**Farley,** Blanche *DrAPF 91*
**Farley,** Bruce A 1943- *WhoAmP 91*
**Farley,** Carol 1936- *IntAu&W 91, WrDr 92*
**Farley,** Carole 1946- *IntWW 91, WhoEnt 92*
**Farley,** Charles Edward 1933- *WhoEnt 92*
**Farley,** Daniel W. 1955- *WhoAmL 92*
**Farley,** Donald B 1935- *WhoAmP 91*
**Farley,** Donald T, Jr 1933- *AmMWSc 92*
**Farley,** Donald William 1943- *WhoAmL 92*
**Farley,** Edward A. *IntWW 91*
**Farley,** Elton Dean 1937- *WhoFI 92*
**Farley,** Eugene Joseph 1950- *WhoFI 92*
**Farley,** Eugene Shedden, Jr 1927- *AmMWSc 92*
**Farley,** Frances *WhoAmP 91*
**Farley,** Francis James Macdonald 1920- *IntWW 91, Who 92*
**Farley,** Frank Donald 1928- *WhoMW 92*
**Farley,** George Edward 1929- *WhoAmP 91*
**Farley,** Gerald LaVerne 1931- *WhoMW 92*
**Farley,** Hale Ralph 1935- *WhoWest 92*
**Farley,** Harriet 1813-1907 *HanAmWH*
**Farley,** Harriet 1817-1907 *BenetAL 91*
**Farley,** Henry Edward 1930- *Who 92*
**Farley,** Hugh Thomas 1931- *WhoAmP 91*
**Farley,** James A 1888-1976 *FacFETw*
**Farley,** James Aloysius 1888-1976 *AmPolLe*
**Farley,** James Bernard 1930- *WhoFI 92*
**Farley,** James D 1938- *AmMWSc 92*
**Farley,** Jerry Michael *AmMWSc 92*
**Farley,** John 1936- *AmMWSc 92*
**Farley,** John Murphy 1842-1918 *RelLAm 91*
**Farley,** John William 1948- *AmMWSc 92*
**Farley,** Joseph McConnell 1927- *WhoFI 92*
**Farley,** Joseph Michael 1961- *IntAu&W 91*
**Farley,** Joseph P, Sr *WhoAmP 91*
**Farley,** Kathleen Murphy 1936- *WhoAmP 91*
**Farley,** Lloyd Edward 1915- *WhoMW 92*
**Farley,** Loida Leslie 1953- *WhoMW 92*
**Farley,** Margaret Ann 1935- *WhoRel 92*
**Farley,** Martyn Graham 1924- *Who 92*
**Farley,** Mary Nicholas 1913- *WhoRel 92*
**Farley,** Mary-Rose Christine *Who 92*
**Farley,** Peggy Ann 1947- *WhoFI 92*
**Farley,** Ralph Milne 1887-1963 *ScFEYrs, TwCSFW 91*
**Farley,** Reuben William 1940- *AmMWSc 92*
**Farley,** Rob *Who 92*
**Farley,** Robert Hugh 1950- *WhoMW 92*
**Farley,** Roger Dean *AmMWSc 92*
**Farley,** Terrence Michael 1930- *WhoFI 92*
**Farley,** Thomas Albert 1933- *AmMWSc 92*
**Farley,** Thomas T. 1934- *WhoAmL 92, WhoFI 92, WhoWest 92*
**Farley,** Timothy Joseph 1960- *WhoAmP 91*
**Farley,** Timothy Shawn 1956- *WhoEnt 92*
**Farley,** Wendy Lee 1958- *WhoRel 92*
**Farley,** William F. 1942- *WhoFI 92, WhoMW 92*
**Farley,** William Horace, Jr. 1950- *WhoBlA 92*
**Farley-Villalobos,** Robbie Jean 1953- *WhoEnt 92, WhoHisp 92*
**Farling,** Robert J. 1936- *WhoFI 92*
**Farlough,** H. Eugene, Jr. 1938- *WhoBlA 92*
**Farlow,** Stanley Jerome 1937- *AmMWSc 92*
**Farlow,** Tal 1921- *NewAmDM*
**Farlow,** Talmage Holt 1921- *IntWW 91*
**Farlow,** William Gilson 1844-1919 *BiInAmS*
**Farm,** Raymond John 1939- *AmMWSc 92*
**Farmakis,** George Leonard 1925- *WhoMW 92*
**Farman,** Allan George 1949- *AmMWSc 92*

**Farman,** Richard Donald 1935- *WhoFI 92, WhoWest 92*
**Farmanfarmaian,** Allahverdi 1929- *AmMWSc 92*
**Farmbrough,** David John *Who 92*
**Farmer,** Annette 1921- *WhoAmP 91*
**Farmer,** Anthony Lee 1960- *WhoMW 92*
**Farmer,** Art 1928- *NewAmDM*
**Farmer,** Barry Louis 1947- *AmMWSc 92*
**Farmer,** Bernard 1919- *TwCPaSc*
**Farmer,** Bertram Hughes 1916- *WrDr 92*
**Farmer,** Beverley 1941- *ConNov 91*
**Farmer,** Bruce *Who 92*
**Farmer,** Bruce Albert 1957- *WhoBlA 92*
**Farmer,** Bruce Jay 1927- *WhoFI 92*
**Farmer,** Bryce E 1951- *WhoIns 92*
**Farmer,** Chantal 1959- *AmMWSc 92*
**Farmer,** Clarence 1915- *WhoBlA 92*
**Farmer,** Crofton Bernard *AmMWSc 92*
**Farmer,** Dale F. 1959- *WhoFI 92*
**Farmer,** David Christopher 1945- *WhoAmL 92*
**Farmer,** David Ray 1940- *WhoAmL 92*
**Farmer,** Derek Maitland 1943- *WhoRel 92*
**Farmer,** Donald Arthur, Jr. 1944- *WhoAmL 92*
**Farmer,** Donald Jackson 1925- *AmMWSc 92*
**Farmer,** Douglas Jay 1960- *WhoAmL 92*
**Farmer,** Edward Campbell, Jr. 1918- *WhoAmL 92*
**Farmer,** Edward Desmond 1917- *Who 92*
**Farmer,** Edwin Bruce 1936- *Who 92*
**Farmer,** Elaine F 1937- *WhoAmP 91*
**Farmer,** Estella Louise 1942- *WhoMW 92*
**Farmer,** Fannie 1857-1915 *BenetAL 91*
**Farmer,** Forest J 1941- *ConBlB 1 [port], WhoBlA 92*
**Farmer,** Foy Elisabeth Johnson 1887-1971 *DcNCBi 2*
**Farmer,** Francesta Elizabeth 1949- *WhoBlA 92*
**Farmer,** Frank Reginald 1914- *IntWW 91, Who 92*
**Farmer,** George *Who 92*
**Farmer,** George Wallace 1929- *Who 92*
**Farmer,** Gerald 1945- *WhoFI 92*
**Farmer,** Guy 1912- *WhoAmL 92*
**Farmer,** Harold E. 1904-1990 *WhoBlA 92N*
**Farmer,** Helen Sweeney 1929- *WhoMW 92*
**Farmer,** Hilda Wooten 1950- *WhoBlA 92*
**Farmer,** Hugh Robert Macdonald 1907- *Who 92*
**Farmer,** Ian William 1935- *WhoWest 92*
**Farmer,** James 1920- *ConBlB 2 [port], WhoBlA 92*
**Farmer,** James Bernard 1928- *AmMWSc 92*
**Farmer,** James Lee 1938- *AmMWSc 92*
**Farmer,** James Leonard, Jr. 1920- *IntWW 91*
**Farmer,** James Prentice, Jr. 1951- *WhoAmL 92*
**Farmer,** Janene Elizabeth 1946- *WhoWest 92*
**Farmer,** Jeanette Ann 1964- *WhoEnt 92*
**Farmer,** Jeffrey E. *WhoRel 92*
**Farmer,** Jerome Richardson 1941- *WhoWest 92*
**Farmer,** John 1798-1859 *BiInAmS*
**Farmer,** John David 1939- *WhoWest 92*
**Farmer,** John James, III 1943- *AmMWSc 92*
**Farmer,** John M 1934- *WhoAmP 91*
**Farmer,** John Thomas 1952- *WhoAmL 92*
**Farmer,** John William 1947- *AmMWSc 92*
**Farmer,** Joseph Collin 1955- *WhoWest 92*
**Farmer,** Karen Batchelor 1951- *WhoBlA 92*
**Farmer,** Larry Bert 1936- *AmMWSc 92*
**Farmer,** Larry Clinton 1951- *WhoBlA 92*
**Farmer,** Lorelie Joy 1943- *WhoFI 92*
**Farmer,** Louis T. 1945- *WhoFI 92*
**Farmer,** Lovedin George 1908- *IntWW 91, Who 92*
**Farmer,** Malcolm, III 1939- *WhoAmL 92*
**Farmer,** Marjorie Nichols 1922- *WhoRel 92*
**Farmer,** Martin Eugene, Jr 1955- *WhoAmP 91*
**Farmer,** Mary Winifred 1939- *AmMWSc 92*
**Farmer,** Merle Louise 1906- *WhoAmP 91*
**Farmer,** Patrick Stewart 1942- *AmMWSc 92*
**Farmer,** Penelope 1939- *IntAu&W 91, WrDr 92*
**Farmer,** Peter 1936- *TwCPaSc*
**Farmer,** Peter John 1952- *Who 92*
**Farmer,** Philip Jose *DrAPF 91*
**Farmer,** Philip Jose 1918- *ConAu 35NR, TwCSFW 91, WrDr 92*
**Farmer,** Richard Gilbert 1931- *AmMWSc 92, IntWW 91*
**Farmer,** Robert Clarence 1941- *WhoBlA 92*
**Farmer,** Robert E, Jr 1930- *AmMWSc 92*
**Farmer,** Robert Frederick 1922- *Who 92*
**Farmer,** Robert L 1933- *WhoAmP 91*
**Farmer,** Robert William 1926- *WhoAmP 91*
**Farmer,** Rod *DrAPF 91*
**Farmer,** Roger Edward Alfred 1955- *WhoFI 92*
**Farmer,** Ryland Lee 1948- *WhoAmP 91*
**Farmer,** S. Brian 1962- *WhoAmL 92*
**Farmer,** Sarah Jane 1847-1916 *HanAmWH*
**Farmer,** Susan Lawson 1942- *WhoAmP 91, WhoEnt 92*
**Farmer,** Terry Gordon 1957- *WhoAmL 92*
**Farmer,** Thomas Laurence 1923- *WhoAmL 92, WhoAmP 91*
**Farmer,** Thomas Wohlsen 1914- *AmMWSc 92*
**Farmer,** Timothy David 1954- *WhoEnt 92*
**Farmer,** Tom M 1947- *WhoAmP 91*
**Farmer,** Walter Ashford 1927- *AmMWSc 92*
**Farmer,** Walter Joseph 1938- *AmMWSc 92*
**Farmer,** William Michael 1944- *AmMWSc 92*
**Farmer,** William R. 1921- *WrDr 92*
**Farmer,** William Robert 1952- *WhoEnt 92, WhoWest 92*
**Farmer,** William S, Jr 1922- *AmMWSc 92*
**Farmer,** Willie Sidney, Sr. 1930- *WhoBlA 92*
**Farmiloe,** Dorothy 1920- *WrDr 92*
**Farn,** Charles Luh-Sun 1934- *AmMWSc 92*
**Farnaby,** Giles 1565?-1640 *NewAmDM*
**Farnam,** Thomas Campbell 1945- *WhoAmL 92*
**Farnam,** Walter Edward 1941- *WhoIns 92*
**Farnan,** Joseph James, Jr. 1945- *WhoAmL 92*
**Farncombe,** Charles Frederick 1919- *Who 92*
**Farndale,** James *WrDr 92*
**Farndale,** Martin 1929- *Who 92*
**Farndale,** Martin Baker 1929- *IntWW 91*
**Farndale,** W. A. J. 1916- *WrDr 92*
**Farnell,** Albert Bennett 1917- *AmMWSc 92*
**Farnell,** Daniel Reese 1932- *AmMWSc 92*
**Farnell,** G W 1925- *AmMWSc 92*
**Farnell,** Graeme 1947- *Who 92*
**Farner,** Donald Sankey 1915- *AmMWSc 92*
**Farnes,** Patricia 1931- *AmMWSc 92*
**Farney,** Thomas Patrick 1948- *WhoMW 92*
**Farng,** Richard Kwang 1943- *AmMWSc 92*
**Farnham,** Baron 1931- *Who 92*
**Farnham,** Clayton Henson 1938- *WhoAmL 92*
**Farnham,** David James 1955- *WhoAmL 92*
**Farnham,** Eliza Wood Burham 1815-1864 *HanAmWH*
**Farnham,** John 1942- *TwCPaSc*
**Farnham,** Mary Glade Siemer 1924- *WhoWest 92*
**Farnham,** Paul Rex 1931- *AmMWSc 92*
**Farnham,** R H *ScFEYrs*
**Farnham,** Rouse Smith 1918- *AmMWSc 92*
**Farnham,** Sherman B 1912- *AmMWSc 92*
**Farnholtz,** Sharyn Ann 1945- *WhoRel 92*
**Farningham,** Alexander Ian 1923- *Who 92*
**Farnstrom,** Kim Lee 1956- *WhoMW 92*
**Farnsworth,** A. W. 1945- *WhoRel 92*
**Farnsworth,** Archie Verdell, Jr 1941- *AmMWSc 92*
**Farnsworth,** Carl Leon 1930- *AmMWSc 92*
**Farnsworth,** Donald Clyde 1940- *WhoRel 92*
**Farnsworth,** Edward Allan 1928- *WhoAmL 92*
**Farnsworth,** Harrison E 1896- *AmMWSc 92*
**Farnsworth,** Lee Winfield 1932- *WhoAmP 91*
**Farnsworth,** Marie 1896- *AmMWSc 92*
**Farnsworth,** Marjorie Whyte 1921- *AmMWSc 92*
**Farnsworth,** Norman R 1930- *AmMWSc 92*
**Farnsworth,** Patricia Nordstrom 1930- *AmMWSc 92*
**Farnsworth,** Paul Burton 1953- *AmMWSc 92*
**Farnsworth,** Philip Richeson 1941- *WhoAmL 92, WhoEnt 92*
**Farnsworth,** Philip Wesley 1947- *WhoRel 92*
**Farnsworth,** Philo T. d1971 *LesBEnT 92*
**Farnsworth,** Richard 1920- *IntMPA 92, WhoEnt 92*
**Farnsworth,** Richard Kent 1934- *AmMWSc 92*
**Farnsworth,** Robert *DrAPF 91*
**Farnsworth,** Roy Lothrop 1928- *AmMWSc 92*
**Farnsworth,** Susan *WhoAmP 91*
**Farnsworth,** T. Brooke 1945- *WhoAmL 92*
**Farnsworth,** Wells Eugene 1921- *AmMWSc 92, WhoMW 92*
**Farnum,** Bruce Wayne 1935- *AmMWSc 92*
**Farnum,** Donald G 1934- *AmMWSc 92*
**Farnum,** Eugene Howard 1942- *AmMWSc 92*
**Farnum,** Jonathan K 1939- *WhoAmP 91*
**Farnum,** Norman Allen 1955- *WhoEnt 92*
**Farnum,** Peter 1946- *AmMWSc 92*
**Farnum,** Sylvia A 1936- *AmMWSc 92*
**Farnum,** Wesley *WhoAmP 91*
**Farnworth,** Edward Robert 1947- *AmMWSc 92*
**Farnworth,** John David 1935- *Who 92*
**Farokhi,** Saeed 1952- *AmMWSc 92*
**Farole,** George P. 1955- *WhoFI 92*
**Faron,** Boleslaw 1937- *IntWW 91*
**Faron,** John Frank 1933- *WhoWest 92*
**Farona,** Michael F 1935- *AmMWSc 92*
**Farone,** William Anthony 1940- *AmMWSc 92*
**Farouk** 1920-1965 *FacFETw [port]*
**Farouk,** Bakhtier 1951- *AmMWSc 92*
**Farquhar,** Charles Don Petrie 1937- *Who 92*
**Farquhar,** David 1928- *ConCom 92*
**Farquhar,** Dion *DrAPF 91*
**Farquhar,** Gale Burton 1927- *AmMWSc 92*
**Farquhar,** George 1677?-1707 *RfGEnL 91*
**Farquhar,** Jane Colden *BiInAmS*
**Farquhar,** John William 1927- *AmMWSc 92, IntWW 91*
**Farquhar,** Karen Lee 1958- *WhoFI 92*
**Farquhar,** Marilyn Gist 1928- *AmMWSc 92*
**Farquhar,** Michael 1938- *Who 92*
**Farquhar,** Oswald Cornell 1921- *AmMWSc 92*
**Farquhar,** Peter Henry 1947- *AmMWSc 92*
**Farquhar,** Robert Michael 1954- *WhoAmL 92*
**Farquhar,** Robert Nichols 1936- *WhoAmL 92, WhoMW 92*
**Farquhar,** Robin Hugh 1938- *IntWW 91*
**Farquhar,** Ronald McCunn 1929- *AmMWSc 92*
**Farquharson,** Donald 1928- *Who 92*
**Farquharson,** James 1903- *Who 92*
**Farquharson,** Jonathan 1937- *Who 92*
**Farquharson,** Joseph 1846-1935 *TwCPaSc*
**Farquharson,** Paul Newman 1962- *WhoAmL 92*
**Farquharson,** Robert Alexander 1925- *Who 92*
**Farquharson,** Robert James 1824-1884 *BiInAmS*
**Farquharson,** Walter Henry 1936- *WhoRel 92*
**Farquharson of Invercauld,** Alwyne Arthur 1919- *Who 92*
**Farquharson of Whitehouse,** Colin Andrew 1923- *Who 92*
**Farr,** Alfred Derek 1930- *WrDr 92*
**Farr,** Andrew Grant *AmMWSc 92*
**Farr,** Charles Sims 1920- *WhoAmL 92*
**Farr,** David Frederick 1941- *AmMWSc 92*
**Farr,** Dennis Larry Ashwell 1929- *IntWW 91, Who 92*
**Farr,** Diana *IntAu&W 91, WrDr 92*
**Farr,** Donald Richard 1944- *WhoFI 92*
**Farr,** Felicia 1932- *IntMPA 92*
**Farr,** Gardner Neil 1932- *WhoAmL 92*
**Farr,** Herman *WhoBlA 92*
**Farr,** James David 1926- *WhoEnt 92*
**Farr,** Jamie 1934- *IntMPA 92, WhoEnt 92*
**Farr,** John 1922- *Who 92*
**Farr,** Kenneth E 1917- *AmMWSc 92*
**Farr,** Lee Edward 1907- *WhoWest 92*
**Farr,** Linus Gilbert 1951- *WhoAmL 92*
**Farr,** Llewellyn Goldstone 1928- *WhoBlA 92*
**Farr,** Louise Rose 1918- *WhoAmP 91*
**Farr,** Lynne Adams 1939- *AmMWSc 92*
**Farr,** Melvin 1944- *WhoBlA 92*
**Farr,** Melvin, Jr. 1966- *WhoBlA 92*
**Farr,** Norman Nelson 1928- *WhoFI 92*
**Farr,** Peter Gerald Desmond 1917- *Who 92*
**Farr,** Richard Studley 1922- *AmMWSc 92*
**Farr,** Robert *WhoAmP 91*
**Farr,** Sam 1941- *WhoAmP 91*
**Farr,** Tommy 1914-1986 *FacFETw*
**Farr,** Toney Lein 1960- *WhoAmP 91*
**Farr,** William Morris 1938- *AmMWSc 92, WhoAmP 91*
**Farr,** William S, Jr 1935- *WhoAmP 91*
**Farragher,** Clare M 1941- *WhoAmP 91*
**Farragher,** Sean T. *DrAPF 91*
**Farragut,** George Anthony Magin 1755-1817 *DcNCBi 2*
**Farrakhan,** Louis 1933- *ConBlB 2 [port], RelLAm 91, WhoBlA 92, WhoRel 92*
**Farral,** James Lee 1947- *WhoMW 92*
**Farran,** Roy Alexander 1921- *WrDr 92*
**Farrance,** Roger Arthur 1933- *Who 92*
**Farrand,** Clair Loring 1895-1981 *FacFETw*
**Farrand,** Julian Thomas 1935- *Who 92*
**Farrand,** Robert William 1934- *WhoAmP 91*
**Farrand,** Stephen Kendall 1945- *AmMWSc 92*
**Farrand,** William Richard 1931- *AmMWSc 92*
**Farrands,** John Law 1921- *Who 92*
**Farrant,** Elizabeth *DrAPF 91*
**Farrant,** Richard 1530?-1580 *NewAmDM*
**Farrant,** Trevor *IntAu&W 91*
**Farrar,** Aili R 1925- *WhoAmP 91*
**Farrar,** Bernard 1930- *Who 92*
**Farrar,** Constance Mosher 1925- *WhoFI 92*
**Farrar,** David Turner 1941- *AmMWSc 92*
**Farrar,** Donald B. 1935- *WhoEnt 92*
**Farrar,** Donald Keith 1938- *WhoFI 92*
**Farrar,** Elaine Willardson 1929- *WhoWest 92*
**Farrar,** Frank L. 1929- *IntWW 91, WhoAmP 91*
**Farrar,** George Elbert, Jr 1906- *AmMWSc 92*
**Farrar,** Geraldine 1882-1967 *FacFETw, NewAmDM*
**Farrar,** Grover Louis 1936- *AmMWSc 92*
**Farrar,** James Martin 1948- *AmMWSc 92*
**Farrar,** James Paul 1937- *WhoFI 92*
**Farrar,** John 1779-1853 *BiInAmS*
**Farrar,** John 1896-1974 *BenetAL 91*
**Farrar,** John 1927- *AmMWSc 92*
**Farrar,** John Dow 1959- *WhoMW 92*
**Farrar,** John J *AmMWSc 92*
**Farrar,** John Keith 1948- *AmMWSc 92*
**Farrar,** John Laird 1913- *AmMWSc 92*
**Farrar,** John Thruston 1920- *AmMWSc 92*
**Farrar,** Keith 1927- *WhoAmP 91*
**Farrar,** Marcia Gertrude 1941- *WhoFI 92*
**Farrar,** Mark Eldon 1950- *WhoAmL 92*
**Farrar,** Martha Ann 1943- *WhoRel 92*
**Farrar,** Pauline Elizabeth 1928- *WhoFI 92*
**Farrar,** R E 1917- *AmMWSc 92*
**Farrar,** Ralph Coleman 1930- *AmMWSc 92*
**Farrar,** Reginald Warren, Jr. 1922- *WhoAmL 92*
**Farrar,** Rex Gordon 1925- *Who 92*
**Farrar,** Robert Lynn, Jr 1921- *AmMWSc 92*
**Farrar,** Ronald T. 1935- *WrDr 92*
**Farrar,** Scott *WhoEnt 92*
**Farrar,** Sidney Bob 1928- *WhoEnt 92*
**Farrar,** Thomas C 1933- *AmMWSc 92*
**Farrar,** William Edmund 1933- *AmMWSc 92*
**Farrar,** William L 1950- *AmMWSc 92*
**Farrar,** William Wesley *AmMWSc 92*
**Farrar-Hockley,** Anthony Heritage 1924- *Who 92*
**Farrauto,** Robert Joseph 1941- *AmMWSc 92*
**Farrell,** Anthony 1945- *TwCPaSc*
**Farrell,** Arthur Denis d1990 *Who 92N*
**Farrell,** Austin James 1932- *WhoAmL 92*
**Farrell,** Barbara Lou 1935- *WhoWest 92*
**Farrell,** Ben *WrDr 92*
**Farrell,** Brian 1929- *ConAu 135*
**Farrell,** Bryan Henry 1923- *WhoWest 92*
**Farrell,** Charles 1900?-1990 *ConTFT 9*
**Farrell,** Charles 1901-1990 *AnObit 1990*
**Farrell,** Cheryl Layne 1955- *WhoBlA 92*
**Farrell,** Christine Marie 1949- *WhoAmL 92*
**Farrell,** Cliff 1899-1977 *TwCWW 91*
**Farrell,** David *IntAu&W 91X, WrDr 92*
**Farrell,** David Coakley 1933- *WhoFI 92, WhoMW 92*
**Farrell,** David E 1939- *AmMWSc 92, WhoRel 92*
**Farrell,** Edgar Henry 1924- *WhoFI 92*
**Farrell,** Edward Alan 1963- *WhoFI 92*
**Farrell,** Edward Joseph 1917- *AmMWSc 92*
**Farrell,** Eileen 1920- *IntWW 91, NewAmDM, WhoEnt 92*
**Farrell,** Eugene Patrick 1911- *AmMWSc 92*
**Farrell,** F Thomas 1929- *AmMWSc 92*
**Farrell,** Francine Annette 1948- *WhoWest 92*
**Farrell,** George Joseph, Jr 1930- *WhoAmP 91*
**Farrell,** Harold Maron, Jr 1940- *AmMWSc 92*
**Farrell,** Henry *IntMPA 92*
**Farrell,** Herman D, Jr *WhoAmP 91*
**Farrell,** Hobert Kenneth 1939- *WhoRel 92*
**Farrell,** J B 1923- *AmMWSc 92*
**Farrell,** J. G. 1935-1979 *ConAu 36NR, RfGEnL 91*
**Farrell,** J. Michael 1941- *WhoAmL 92*
**Farrell,** J. Michael 1953- *WhoAmL 92*
**Farrell,** James *Who 92*
**Farrell,** James Aloysius 1943- *Who 92*
**Farrell,** James Andrew 1957- *WhoAmL 92*
**Farrell,** James T. 1904-1975 *DcAmImH*
**Farrell,** James T. 1904-1979 *BenetAL 91, ConLC 66 [port], FacFETw*

**Farrell**, Jay Phillip AmMWSc 92
**Farrell**, Jeremiah Edward 1937- WhoMW 92
**Farrell**, Jim 1960- WhoAmP 91
**Farrell**, John A 1935- AmMWSc 92
**Farrell**, John Dennis 1951- WhoEnt 92
**Farrell**, John Stanislaus 1931- WhoFI 92
**Farrell**, John Timothy 1947- WhoMW 92
**Farrell**, Joseph Christopher 1935- WhoFI 92
**Farrell**, Kenneth Royden 1927- WhoWest 92
**Farrell**, Larry Charles 1941- WhoFI 92
**Farrell**, Larry Don 1942- AmMWSc 92
**Farrell**, Leighton Kirk 1930- WhoRel 92
**Farrell**, M. Catherine 1948- WhoAmL 92
**Farrell**, M. J. Who 92
**Farrell**, Margaret Alice 1932- AmMWSc 92
**Farrell**, Mark Macaulay WhoWest 92
**Farrell**, Michael 1940- TwCPaSc
**Farrell**, Michael Arthur 1933- Who 92
**Farrell**, Michael Brennan WhoAmL 92, WhoAmP 91
**Farrell**, Michael Flagg 1940- WhoEnt 92
**Farrell**, Michael Joseph 1938- WhoAmL 92
**Farrell**, Michael W WhoAmP 91
**Farrell**, Mike 1939- IntMPA 92, WhoEnt 92
**Farrell**, Monica Louise 1962- WhoMW 92
**Farrell**, Neal F. 1934- WhoAmL 92
**Farrell**, Odessa Wright 1908- WhoBlA 92
**Farrell**, Pamela Barnard 1943- IntAu&W 91
**Farrell**, Patrick Joseph 1951- WhoWest 92
**Farrell**, Paul Harry 1927- WhoAmL 92
**Farrell**, Perry 1960- News 92-2 [port]
**Farrell**, Phyllis Chase 1930- WhoAmP 91
**Farrell**, Richard Alfred 1939- AmMWSc 92
**Farrell**, Robert C 1936- WhoAmP 91, WhoBlA 92
**Farrell**, Robert Lawrence 1925- AmMWSc 92
**Farrell**, Robert Michael 1947- AmMWSc 92
**Farrell**, Robert Terence 1948- WhoAmP 91
**Farrell**, Roger Hamlin 1929- AmMWSc 92
**Farrell**, Samuel D. 1941- WhoBlA 92
**Farrell**, Suzanne WhoEnt 92
**Farrell**, Suzanne 1945- FacFETw
**Farrell**, Terence 1938- IntWW 91, Who 92
**Farrell**, Thomas Dinan 1948- WhoAmL 92
**Farrell**, Thomas Joseph 1926- WhoWest 92
**Farrell**, Timothy Robert Warwick 1943- Who 92
**Farrell**, William E 1948- WhoAmP 91
**Farrell**, William Edgar 1937- WhoFI 92, WhoWest 92
**Farrell-Donaldson**, Marie D. 1947- WhoBlA 92
**Farrell-Logan**, Vivian WhoEnt 92
**Farrelly**, Alexander 1923- WhoAmP 91
**Farrelly**, James Gerard 1939- AmMWSc 92
**Farrelly**, Peter John 1956- WhoEnt 92
**Farrelly**, Wallace Gregg 1948- WhoEnt 92
**Farren**, Ann Louise 1926- AmMWSc 92
**Farren**, Frank H, Jr WhoAmP 91
**Farren**, Mick 1943- TwCSFW 91, WrDr 92
**Farrenc**, Louise 1804-1875 NewAmDM
**Farrer**, Brian Ainsworth 1930- Who 92
**Farrer**, Charles Matthew 1929- Who 92
**Farrer**, David John 1943- Who 92
**Farrer**, John 1941- WhoEnt 92, WhoWest 92
**Farrer**, Julia 1950- TwCPaSc
**Farrer**, Katharine 1911- WrDr 92
**Farrer**, Margaret Irene 1914- Who 92
**Farrer**, Matthew Who 92
**Farrer**, Rosa Maria Zaldivar 1937- WhoHisp 92
**Farrer**, William Oliver 1926- Who 92
**Farrer-Brown**, Leslie 1904- IntWW 91, Who 92
**Farrere**, Claude 1876-1957 ScFEYrs
**Farrier**, Maurice Hugh 1926- AmMWSc 92
**Farrier**, Noel John 1937- AmMWSc 92
**Farrimond**, George Francis, Jr. 1932- WhoFI 92, WhoWest 92
**Farrimond**, Herbert Leonard 1924- Who 92
**Farrimond**, John 1913- IntAu&W 91
**Farringer**, Leland Dwight 1927- AmMWSc 92, WhoMW 92
**Farrington**, David Philip 1944- Who 92
**Farrington**, Dewey Lee 1956- WhoWest 92
**Farrington**, Donald Wayne 1946- WhoMW 92
**Farrington**, Gregory Charles 1946- AmMWSc 92
**Farrington**, Henry Francis Colden 1914- Who 92
**Farrington**, Ian S. 1947- WrDr 92
**Farrington**, Jerry S. 1934- WhoFI 92
**Farrington**, John P 1933- WhoIns 92
**Farrington**, John William 1944- AmMWSc 92
**Farrington**, Joseph Kirby 1948- AmMWSc 92
**Farrington**, Margot DrAPF 91
**Farrington**, Mark Nolan 1941- WhoEnt 92
**Farrington**, Paul Stephen 1919- AmMWSc 92
**Farrington**, Thomas Alex 1943- WhoBlA 92
**Farrington**, Thomas Allan 1941- AmMWSc 92
**Farrington**, William Benford 1921- AmMWSc 92, WhoFI 92
**Farrior**, J. Rex, Jr. 1927- WhoAmL 92, WhoFI 92
**Farris**, Ann 1937- WhoEnt 92
**Farris**, Christine DrAPF 91
**Farris**, David Allen 1928- AmMWSc 92, WhoWest 92
**Farris**, David Preston 1952- WhoWest 92
**Farris**, Donn Michael 1921- WhoRel 92
**Farris**, Edward Thompson 1925- WhoEnt 92
**Farris**, Forrest Leverne 1928- WhoRel 92
**Farris**, Frank Mitchell, Jr. 1915- WhoAmL 92
**Farris**, Jerome WhoAmP 91
**Farris**, Jerome 1930- WhoAmL 92, WhoBlA 92, WhoWest 92
**Farris**, John DrAPF 91
**Farris**, John Leo 1947- WhoFI 92
**Farris**, Joseph Harvey 1922- WhoAmP 91
**Farris**, Martin Theodore 1925- WhoFI 92
**Farris**, Michael Kerry 1956- WhoMW 92
**Farris**, Mitchel Eugene, Jr. 1946- WhoWest 92
**Farris**, Norma J 1931- WhoAmP 91
**Farris**, Paul Leonard 1919- WhoFI 92, WhoMW 92
**Farris**, Richard Austin 1943- AmMWSc 92
**Farris**, Robert E WhoAmP 91
**Farris**, Theodore N. 1953- WhoAmL 92
**Farris**, Thomas Chad 1954- WhoAmL 92
**Farris**, Thomas N. 1959- WhoMW 92
**Farris**, Vera King 1940- WhoBlA 92
**Farris**, William Clay 1948- WhoFI 92, WhoMW 92
**Farris**, William Harrison 1945- WhoAmL 92
**Farris**, William W WhoAmP 91
**Farrissey**, William Joseph, Jr 1931- AmMWSc 92
**Farrokh**, Reza 1943- WhoWest 92
**Farrow**, Bernard Edward 1936- WhoWest 92
**Farrow**, Christopher John 1937- Who 92
**Farrow**, David Marcus 1929- WhoEnt 92
**Farrow**, Harold Frank 1936- WhoBlA 92
**Farrow**, James S IntAu&W 91X, WrDr 92
**Farrow**, John H 1935- AmMWSc 92
**Farrow**, Leonilda Altman 1929- AmMWSc 92
**Farrow**, Margaret A 1934- WhoAmP 91
**Farrow**, Mark 1947- WhoAmP 91
**Farrow**, Mia NewYTBS 91 [port]
**Farrow**, Mia 1945- IntMPA 92, Who 92
**Farrow**, Mia Villiers 1945- IntWW 91, WhoEnt 92
**Farrow**, Robert Scott 1952- WhoFI 92
**Farrow**, Sallie A. 1942- WhoBlA 92
**Farrow**, Wendall Moore 1922- AmMWSc 92
**Farrow**, William McKnight, III 1955- WhoBlA 92
**Farrow**, Willie Lewis 1941- WhoBlA 92
**Farrug**, Eugene Joseph 1928- WhoAmL 92
**Farrug**, Eugene Joseph, Jr. 1961- WhoFI 92
**Farrukh**, Marwan Omar 1946- WhoFI 92
**Farrukh**, Usamah Omar 1944- AmMWSc 92
**Farry**, Michael Allen 1957- WhoAmL 92
**Farschman**, Marc Wayne 1955- WhoRel 92
**Farson**, Bruce ScFEYrs
**Farson**, Daniel 1927- WrDr 92
**Farson**, Daniel Negley 1927- IntAu&W 91, IntWW 91
**Farthing**, Barton Roby 1916- AmMWSc 92
**Farthing**, Bruce 1926- Who 92
**Farthing**, Penelope Sue 1945- WhoAmL 92
**Farthing**, Stephen 1950- TwCPaSc
**Faruki**, Charles Joseph 1949- WhoAmL 92
**Farulli**, Piero 1920- IntWW 91
**Faruqui**, Ahmad 1953- WhoFI 92
**Farvis**, William Ewart John 1911- Who 92
**Farvolden**, Robert Norman 1928- AmMWSc 92
**Farwell**, Arthur 1872-1952 NewAmDM
**Farwell**, Byron IntAu&W 91
**Farwell**, George Wells 1920- AmMWSc 92
**Farwell**, Hermon Waldo, Jr. 1918- WhoWest 92
**Farwell**, Robert William 1927- AmMWSc 92
**Farwell**, Sherry Owen 1944- AmMWSc 92
**Fary**, Mark WhoAmP 91
**Farzana Somru** EncAmaz 91
**Fas Alzamora**, Antonio J WhoAmP 91
**Fasanaro**, Charles Nicholas 1943- WhoRel 92
**Fasang**, Patrick Pad AmMWSc 92
**Fasano**, Ellen Claire 1957- WhoFI 92
**Fasano**, Kristine Marie 1951- WhoAmL 92
**Fasano**, Michael Benjamin 1958- WhoAmP 91
**Fasano**, Rhoda Kay 1945- WhoAmP 91
**Fasbender**, Lawrence William 1942- WhoAmP 91
**Fascell**, Dante B. 1917- AlmAP 92 [port], IntWW 91, WhoAmP 91
**Fasch**, Johann Friedrich 1688-1758 NewAmDM
**Fasching**, Darrell J. WhoRel 92
**Fasching**, James Le Roy 1942- AmMWSc 92
**Fasciani**, John Guy 1955- WhoFI 92
**Fasco**, Michael John AmMWSc 92
**Fase**, Martin M. G. 1937- IntWW 91
**Fasel**, Ida DrAPF 91
**Fasel**, Ida 1909- IntAu&W 91
**Fasella**, Paolo Maria 1930- Who 92
**Fash**, Michael William 1940- WhoEnt 92
**Fashbaugh**, Howard Dilts, Jr. 1922- WhoAmL 92, WhoFI 92
**Fashena**, Gladys Jeannette 1910- AmMWSc 92
**Fashing**, Edward Michael 1936- WhoMW 92
**Fashing**, Norman James 1943- AmMWSc 92
**Fasi**, Frank Francis 1920- WhoAmP 91, WhoWest 92
**Fasi**, Joseph Mario, II 1954- WhoAmL 92
**Fasi**, Mohammed El 1908- IntWW 91
**Fask**, Alan S 1945- AmMWSc 92
**Fasman**, Barry Alan 1946- WhoEnt 92
**Fasman**, Gerald David 1925- AmMWSc 92
**Fasman**, Zachary Dean 1948- WhoAmL 92
**Faso**, John J 1952- WhoAmP 91
**Faso**, Laurie Joseph 1946- WhoEnt 92
**Faso**, Steven Michael 1961- WhoMW 92
**Fasola**, Alfred Francis 1919- AmMWSc 92
**Fass**, Arnold Lionel 1922- AmMWSc 92
**Fass**, Barbara 1940- WhoAmP 91
**Fass**, Charles Raymond 1926- WhoEnt 92
**Fass**, David N AmMWSc 92
**Fass**, M. Monroe 1901- IntMPA 92
**Fass**, Paula Shirley 1947- WhoWest 92
**Fass**, Peter Michael 1937- WhoAmL 92
**Fass**, Richard A 1943- AmMWSc 92
**Fass**, Stephen M 1938- AmMWSc 92
**Fassbaender**, Brigitte 1939- IntWW 91, WhoEnt 92
**Fassbander**, Brigitte 1939- NewAmDM
**Fassbinder**, Rainer W 1946-1982 FacFETw
**Fassbinder**, Rainer Werner 1946-1982 IntDcF 2-2 [port]
**Fassel**, Velmer Arthur 1919- AmMWSc 92, WhoWest 92
**Fassett**, David Walter 1908- AmMWSc 92
**Fassett**, James Ernest 1933- AmMWSc 92
**Fassett**, John David 1951- AmMWSc 92
**Fassett**, Kaffe 1937- Who 92
**Fassio**, Danny Lee 1947- WhoAmL 92
**Fassio**, Virgil 1927- WhoFI 92, WhoWest 92
**Fassler**, Charles 1946- WhoAmL 92
**Fassler**, Crystal G. 1942- WhoMW 92
**Fassler**, Joseph K. 1942- WhoWest 92
**Fassnacht**, John Hartwell 1933- AmMWSc 92
**Fasso**, James Anthony 1959- WhoEnt 92
**Fassoulis**, Satiris Galahad 1922- WhoFI 92
**Fast**, Alvin Lewis 1923- WhoEnt 92
**Fast**, Arlo Wade 1940- AmMWSc 92
**Fast**, C R 1921- AmMWSc 92
**Fast**, Dale Eugene 1945- AmMWSc 92
**Fast**, Eric Carson 1949- WhoFI 92
**Fast**, Henryk 1925- AmMWSc 92
**Fast**, Howard 1914- BenetAL 91, ConNov 91, CurBio 91 [port], FacFETw, IntWW 91, TwCSFW 91, TwCWW 91, WrDr 92
**Fast**, Howard Melvin 1914- WhoEnt 92
**Fast**, Jonathan 1948- ConAu 34NR, IntAu&W 91, TwCSFW 91, WrDr 92
**Fast**, Marion Everett 1932- WhoRel 92
**Fast**, Nathaniel Anthony 1916- WhoEnt 92
**Fast**, Patricia E 1943- AmMWSc 92
**Fast**, Robert Erwin 1932- WhoAmP 91
**Fast**, Ronald Walter 1934- AmMWSc 92
**Fast**, Thomas Normand 1922- AmMWSc 92
**Fastenberg**, David 1951- WhoFI 92
**Faster**, Walter William 1933- WhoFI 92
**Fasthuber-Grande**, Traudy 1950- WhoFI 92
**Fastidius** EncEarC
**Fatayi-Williams**, Atanda 1918- IntWW 91, Who 92
**Fatchen**, Max 1920- WrDr 92
**Fatchen**, Maxwell Edgar 1920- IntAu&W 91
**Fatchett**, Derek John 1945- Who 92
**Fate**, Martin Eugene, Jr. 1933- WhoFI 92
**Fateh**, A. F. M. Abul 1926- IntWW 91
**Fateh**, Abul Fazal Muhammad Abul 1926- Who 92
**Fateley**, William Gene 1929- AmMWSc 92, WhoMW 92
**Fateman**, Richard J 1946- AmMWSc 92, WhoWest 92
**Fatemi**, Emad Aldin-Mohammad 1960- WhoMW 92
**Fatemi**, Shireen 1958- WhoWest 92
**Fates**, Gil LesBEnT 92
**Fates**, Joseph Gilbert 1914- WhoEnt 92
**Fateyev**, Anatoliy Mikhailovich 1931- IntWW 91
**Fath**, George R 1938- AmMWSc 92
**Fath**, Jacques 1912-1954 DcTwDes
**Fath**, Joseph 1925- AmMWSc 92
**Fathauer**, Theodore Frederick 1946- WhoWest 92
**Fathman**, C Garrison 1942- AmMWSc 92
**Fatiadi**, Alexander Johann 1923- AmMWSc 92
**Fatima** EncAmaz 91
**Fatio**, Louise 1904- WrDr 92
**Fatisha** DrAPF 91
**Fatland**, James R. WhoWest 92
**Fator**, Gertrude Yvonne 1935- WhoWest 92
**Fatora**, Joachim Robert 1928- WhoRel 92
**Fatouros**, Arghyrios A. 1932- WrDr 92
**Fatt**, Irving 1920- AmMWSc 92
**Fatt**, Paul IntWW 91, Who 92
**Fatt**, William Robert 1951- WhoFI 92
**Fattah**, Chaka 1956- WhoAmP 91, WhoBlA 92
**Fattah**, Falaka 1931- WhoBlA 92
**Fattal**, Dia Allah El- 1927- IntWW 91
**Fattes**, Edwin Roy 1942- WhoFI 92
**Fattic**, LoNita Susan 1955- WhoMW 92
**Fattig**, John J 1924- WhoIns 92
**Fattig**, W Donald 1936- AmMWSc 92
**Fattorini**, Hector Osvaldo 1938- AmMWSc 92, WhoWest 92
**Fatzinger**, Carl Warren 1938- AmMWSc 92
**Faubion**, Billy Don 1942- AmMWSc 92
**Faubion**, Daniel Joseph 1963- WhoMW 92
**Faubion**, Jerry Tolbert 1917- WhoFI 92
**Faubl**, Hermann 1942- AmMWSc 92
**Faubus**, Orval 1910-1980 FacFETw
**Faucera**, Allen Anthony 1949- WhoEnt 92
**Faucett**, Barbara J. WhoBlA 92
**Faucett**, Robert E 1926- AmMWSc 92
**Faucett**, T R 1920- AmMWSc 92
**Faucett**, William Munroe 1916- AmMWSc 92
**Fauchald**, Kristian 1935- AmMWSc 92
**Faucher**, Albert 1915- IntWW 91
**Faucher**, Real DrAPF 91
**Faucheux**, Ronald Anthony 1950- WhoAmP 91
**Fauci**, Anthony S 1940- AmMWSc 92
**Faucon**, Bernard 1950- IntWW 91
**Faudman**, David Allen 1959- WhoFI 92, WhoWest 92
**Faudree**, Ralph Jasper, Jr 1939- AmMWSc 92
**Faught**, Harold Franklin 1924- WhoFI 92
**Faught**, John Brian 1942- AmMWSc 92
**Faul**, Denis O'Beirne 1932- IntWW 91
**Faulcon**, Clarence Augustus, II 1928- WhoBlA 92
**Faulconer**, Bruce Laland 1951- WhoEnt 92
**Faulconer**, Kay Anne 1945- WhoWest 92
**Faulconer**, Robert Jamieson 1923- AmMWSc 92
**Faulders**, C. Thomas, III 1949- WhoFI 92
**Faulders**, Charles R 1927- AmMWSc 92
**Faulding**, Charles 1916- WhoBlA 92
**Faulding**, Juliette J. 1952- WhoBlA 92
**Faulds**, Andrew Matthew William 1923- Who 92
**Faulhaber**, Charles Bailey 1941- WhoWest 92
**Faulhaber**, L Michael 1937- WhoIns 92
**Faulhaber**, Michael 1869-1952 EncTR 91 [port]
**Faulise**, Anthony Samuel 1964- WhoWest 92
**Fauliso**, Joseph J 1916- WhoAmP 91
**Faulk**, Anne O'Dell 1956- WhoFI 92
**Faulk**, Dennis D. 1936- WhoMW 92
**Faulk**, Dennis Derwin 1936- AmMWSc 92
**Faulk**, Dwight WhoAmP 91
**Faulk**, Estelle A. WhoBlA 92
**Faulk**, John Henry LesBEnT 92
**Faulk**, John Henry 1913-1990 AnObit 1990, FacFETw
**Faulk**, Joseph Erastus 1945- WhoAmL 92
**Faulk**, Michael Anthony 1953- WhoAmL 92

**Faulk**, Odie B 1933- *IntAu&W 91, WrDr 92*
**Faulk**, Richard Oran 1951- *WhoAmL 92*
**Faulkenberry**, Gerald David 1937- *AmMWSc 92*
**Faulkin**, Leslie J, Jr 1930- *AmMWSc 92*
**Faulkner**, Amanda 1953- *TwCPaSc*
**Faulkner**, Charles Herman 1937- *WrDr 92*
**Faulkner**, D John 1942- *AmMWSc 92*
**Faulkner**, David Ewart Riley 1934- *Who 92*
**Faulkner**, Dennis *Who 92*
**Faulkner**, Dexter Harold 1937- *WhoWest 92*
**Faulkner**, Douglas 1929- *Who 92*
**Faulkner**, Edwin J 1911- *WhoIns 92*
**Faulkner**, Edwin Jerome 1911- *WhoMW 92*
**Faulkner**, Eric 1914- *Who 92*
**Faulkner**, Eric Odin 1914- *IntWW 91*
**Faulkner**, Frank David 1915- *AmMWSc 92, WhoWest 92*
**Faulkner**, Gary Doyle 1944- *AmMWSc 92*
**Faulkner**, Gavin John *AmMWSc 92*
**Faulkner**, Geanie *WhoBlA 92*
**Faulkner**, Harry George Basil 1931- *IntWW 91*
**Faulkner**, Howard J. 1945- *ConAu 135*
**Faulkner**, Hugh 1916- *Who 92*
**Faulkner**, Hugh Charles 1912- *Who 92*
**Faulkner**, J. Hugh 1933- *IntWW 91*
**Faulkner**, James Dennis 1926- *Who 92*
**Faulkner**, James Earl 1928- *AmMWSc 92*
**Faulkner**, James Reed 1950- *WhoMW 92*
**Faulkner**, James Vincent, Jr. 1944- *WhoAmL 92*
**Faulkner**, Jerry A 1936- *WhoIns 92*
**Faulkner**, John 1937- *AmMWSc 92*
**Faulkner**, John A 1923- *AmMWSc 92*
**Faulkner**, John Edward 1920- *AmMWSc 92*
**Faulkner**, John Richard Hayward 1941- *Who 92*
**Faulkner**, John Samuel 1932- *AmMWSc 92*
**Faulkner**, Juanita Smith 1935- *WhoFI 92*
**Faulkner**, Kenneth Keith 1926- *AmMWSc 92*
**Faulkner**, Larry Ray 1944- *AmMWSc 92, WhoMW 92*
**Faulkner**, Leonard Anthony *Who 92*
**Faulkner**, Lloyd 1926- *AmMWSc 92*
**Faulkner**, Lynn L 1941- *AmMWSc 92*
**Faulkner**, Marquetta Larneita 1953- *WhoBlA 92*
**Faulkner**, Maurice Ervin 1912- *WhoEnt 92, WhoWest 92*
**Faulkner**, Patricia 1946- *TwCPaSc*
**Faulkner**, Patricia Anne 1944- *WhoAmP 91*
**Faulkner**, Percy d1990 *Who 92N*
**Faulkner**, Peter 1929- *AmMWSc 92*
**Faulkner**, Richard Oliver 1946- *Who 92*
**Faulkner**, Russell Conklin, Jr 1920- *AmMWSc 92*
**Faulkner**, Scot MacDonald 1953- *WhoAmP 91*
**Faulkner**, Sewell Ford 1924- *WhoWest 92*
**Faulkner**, Thomas Richard 1947- *AmMWSc 92*
**Faulkner**, Trevor 1929- *TwCPaSc*
**Faulkner**, Walter Thomas 1928- *WhoAmL 92*
**Faulkner**, Willard Riley 1915- *AmMWSc 92*
**Faulkner**, William 1897-1962 *Au&Arts 7 [port], BenetAL 91, ConLC 68 [port], FacFETw [port], RComAH*
**Faulkner**, William Cuthbert 1897-1962 *WhoNob 90*
**Faulkner of Downpatrick**, Lady 1925- *Who 92*
**Faulknor**, Cliff 1913- *IntAu&W 91, WrDr 92*
**Faulks**, Peter Ronald 1917- *Who 92*
**Faulks**, Sebastian Charles 1953- *Who 92*
**Faull**, Ellen *WhoEnt 92*
**Faulstich**, Albert Joseph 1910- *WhoFI 92*
**Faulstich**, James R. 1933- *WhoFI 92*
**Faulstich**, Janet Kay 1942- *WhoAmP 91*
**Faunce**, Charles M 1867?-1899 *BiInAmS*
**Faunce**, Sherman P. 1938- *WhoAmL 92*
**Fauntleroy**, John Douglass, Sr. 1920-1989 *WhoBlA 92N*
**Fauntroy**, Walter E 1933- *WhoAmP 91, WhoBlA 92*
**Faupel**, David William 1944- *WhoRel 92*
**Faupel**, Joseph H 1916- *AmMWSc 92*
**Fauquier**, Francis 1704?-1768 *BlkwEAR*
**Faur**, Jose 1934- *WhoRel 92*
**Faure**, Edgar 1908-1988 *FacFETw*
**Faure**, Gabriel 1845-1924 *NewAmDM*
**Faure**, Gabriel Urbain 1845-1924 *FacFETw*
**Faure**, Gunter 1934- *AmMWSc 92*
**Faure**, Jean-Baptiste 1830-1914 *ThHEIm*
**Faure**, John Edward 1956- *WhoAmP 91*
**Faure**, Maurice Henri 1922- *IntWW 91*
**Faure**, Roland 1926- *IntWW 91*
**Fauri**, Eric Joseph 1942- *WhoAmL 92*
**Fauroux**, Roger 1926- *IntWW 91*
**Fausak**, William Arthur 1938- *WhoMW 92*
**Fausch**, David Arthur 1935- *WhoFI 92*
**Fausch**, Homer David 1919- *AmMWSc 92*
**Fauser**, Louis 1910- *WhoIns 92*
**Fauset**, Crystal Dreda Bird 1893-1965 *NotBlAW 92*
**Fauset**, Jessie 1882-1961 *ModAWWr*
**Fauset**, Jessie Redmon 1882-1961 *BlkLC [port], HanAmWH, NotBlAW 92 [port]*
**Fauset**, Jessie Redmon 1884?-1961 *BenetAL 91*
**Fausett**, Donald Wright 1940- *AmMWSc 92*
**Fausett**, Laurene van Camp 1943- *AmMWSc 92*
**Fausey**, Norman Ray 1938- *AmMWSc 92*
**Fausset**, Shelley 1920- *TwCPaSc*
**Faust**, Charles Harry, Jr 1943- *AmMWSc 92*
**Faust**, Charles L 1906- *AmMWSc 92*
**Faust**, Charles R *AmMWSc 92*
**Faust**, Claude Marie 1917- *AmMWSc 92*
**Faust**, Frederick 1892-1944 *BenetAL 91*
**Faust**, George Huddleston 1915- *WhoAmL 92*
**Faust**, George Tobias 1908- *AmMWSc 92*
**Faust**, Irvin *DrAPF 91*
**Faust**, Irvin 1924- *BenetAL 91, ConNov 91, WrDr 92*
**Faust**, Irving M *AmMWSc 92*
**Faust**, John Philip 1924- *AmMWSc 92*
**Faust**, John Roosevelt, Jr. 1932- *WhoAmL 92*
**Faust**, John William, Jr 1922- *AmMWSc 92*
**Faust**, Maria Anna *AmMWSc 92*
**Faust**, Mark Joseph 1966- *WhoMW 92*
**Faust**, Miklos 1927- *AmMWSc 92*
**Faust**, Naomi F. *DrAPF 91*
**Faust**, Naomi Flowe *WhoBlA 92*
**Faust**, Norma Jean 1948- *WhoMW 92*
**Faust**, Richard Ahlvers 1921- *AmMWSc 92*
**Faust**, Richard Edward 1927- *AmMWSc 92*
**Faust**, Robert Gilbert 1932- *AmMWSc 92*
**Faust**, Samuel Denton 1929- *AmMWSc 92*
**Faust**, Walter Luck 1934- *AmMWSc 92*
**Faust**, William Paul 1929- *WhoAmP 91*
**Faust**, William R 1918- *AmMWSc 92*
**Faustinus** *EncEarC*
**Fausto**, Nelson 1936- *AmMWSc 92*
**Fausto**, Nicholas Matthew 1957- *WhoAmL 92*
**Fausto-Gil**, Fidel 1955- *WhoHisp 92*
**Fausto-Sterling**, Anne 1944- *AmMWSc 92*
**Faustus of Byzantium** *EncEarC*
**Faustus of Riez** d490? *EncEarC*
**Faut**, Owen Donald 1936- *AmMWSc 92*
**Fauteck**, Paul Karsten 1935- *WhoMW 92*
**Fauth**, David Jonathan 1951- *AmMWSc 92*
**Fauth**, Mae Irene 1913- *AmMWSc 92*
**Fautin**, Daphne Gail 1946- *AmMWSc 92*
**Fautsko**, Timothy Frank 1945- *WhoWest 92*
**Fauvelle**, Michael Henry 1920- *Who 92*
**Fauver**, Scribner L 1931- *WhoAmP 91*
**Fauver**, Vernon A 1928- *AmMWSc 92*
**Fauvet**, Jacques 1914- *IntWW 91*
**Fava**, Francis R 1860?-1896 *BiInAmS*
**Fava**, Ronald Stephen 1949- *WhoAmL 92*
**Favale**, Anthony John 1935- *AmMWSc 92*
**Favalora**, John Clement 1935- *WhoRel 92*
**Favaro**, Dennis Ray 1961- *WhoAmL 92*
**Favazza**, Armando Riccardo 1941- *AmMWSc 92, WhoFI 92*
**Favell**, Anthony Rowland 1939- *Who 92*
**Favier**, Jean 1932- *IntWW 91*
**Favila**, Rodolfo Gomez 1951- *WhoHisp 92*
**Favill**, Henry Baird 1860-1916 *BiInAmS*
**Faville**, Curtis *DrAPF 91*
**Favorite**, Felix 1925- *AmMWSc 92*
**Favorite**, John R 1916- *AmMWSc 92*
**Favors**, Jerry Lewis 1953- *WhoMW 92*
**Favors**, Kathryne Taylor 1924- *WhoBlA 92*
**Favorsky**, Vladimir Andreevich 1886-1964 *SovUnBD*
**Favour**, Cutting Broad 1913- *AmMWSc 92*
**Favre**, Alexandre Jean Auguste 1911- *IntWW 91*
**Favre**, Henri Albert 1926- *AmMWSc 92*
**Favreau**, Irene B 1950- *WhoAmP 91*
**Favret**, A G 1925- *AmMWSc 92*
**Favrholdt**, David Cornaby 1931- *IntWW 91*
**Favro**, Lawrence Dale 1932- *AmMWSc 92*
**Favrot**, Henri Mortimer, Jr. 1930- *WhoFI 92*
**Favrot**, Leo Mortimer, III 1941- *WhoAmL 92*
**Faw**, Barbara Ann 1936- *WhoBlA 92*
**Faw**, Duane Leslie 1920- *WhoRel 92*
**Faw**, Richard E 1936- *AmMWSc 92*
**Faw**, Wade Farris 1942- *AmMWSc 92*
**Fawaz**, George 1913- *AmMWSc 92*
**Fawbush**, Andrew Jackson 1946- *WhoAmL 92*
**Fawbush**, Wayne H 1944- *WhoAmP 91*
**Fawcett**, Catherine *IntAu&W 91X*
**Fawcett**, Charles Winton 1946- *WhoAmL 92*
**Fawcett**, Colin 1923- *Who 92*
**Fawcett**, Colvin Peter 1935- *AmMWSc 92*
**Fawcett**, David Blakley, Jr. 1927- *WhoAmL 92*
**Fawcett**, Don Wayne 1917- *AmMWSc 92, IntWW 91, WhoWest 92*
**Fawcett**, E Douglas 1866-1960 *ScFEYrs*
**Fawcett**, Edgar 1847-1904 *BenetAL 91, ScFEYrs*
**Fawcett**, Eric 1927- *AmMWSc 92*
**Fawcett**, Farrah *LesBEnT 92*
**Fawcett**, Farrah 1947- *IntMPA 92*
**Fawcett**, Farrah Leni 1947- *WhoEnt 92*
**Fawcett**, Howard Hoy 1916- *WhoFI 92*
**Fawcett**, James Davidson *AmMWSc 92*
**Fawcett**, James Davidson 1933- *WhoMW 92*
**Fawcett**, James Edmund Sandford d1991 *Who 92N*
**Fawcett**, James Edmund Sandford 1913- *IntWW 91*
**Fawcett**, James Jeffrey 1936- *AmMWSc 92*
**Fawcett**, John Harold 1929- *Who 92*
**Fawcett**, Kay-Tee *Who 92*
**Fawcett**, Mark Stanley 1932- *AmMWSc 92*
**Fawcett**, Nancy Drudge 1936- *WhoAmP 91*
**Fawcett**, Newton Creig *AmMWSc 92*
**Fawcett**, Raymond 1934- *TwCPaSc*
**Fawcett**, Richard Steven 1948- *AmMWSc 92*
**Fawcett**, Rosemary 1947- *TwCPaSc*
**Fawcett**, Sherwood Luther 1919- *AmMWSc 92*
**Fawcett**, Stancine Brenna *WhoFI 92, WhoWest 92*
**Fawcett**, Susan C. *DrAPF 91*
**Fawcett**, Timothy Goss 1953- *AmMWSc 92, WhoMW 92*
**Fawcett**, William Frederick 1937- *WhoEnt 92*
**Fawcus**, Graham Ben 1937- *Who 92*
**Fawcus**, Peter 1915- *Who 92*
**Fawcus**, Simon James David 1938- *Who 92*
**Fawdry**, Marguerite 1912- *ConAu 135*
**Fawell**, Beverly 1930- *WhoAmP 91*
**Fawell**, Harris W. 1929- *AlmAP 92 [port], WhoAmP 91, WhoMW 92*
**Fawer**, Michael Seth 1936- *WhoAmL 92*
**Fawkes**, Beth G. *DrAPF 91*
**Fawkes**, Randol 1924- *Who 92*
**Fawkes**, Richard Brian 1944- *IntAu&W 91*
**Fawkes**, Wally 1924- *Who 92*
**Fawley**, John Philip 1945- *AmMWSc 92*
**Fawsett**, Evelyn *TwCPaSc*
**Fawsett**, Patricia Combs 1943- *WhoAmL 92*
**Fawson**, Jay 1929- *WhoAmP 91*
**Fawver**, J Jay 1940- *WhoAmP 91*
**Fawwaz**, Rashid 1935- *AmMWSc 92*
**Fawzi**, Mahmoud 1900-1981 *FacFETw*
**Fax**, Elton C. 1909- *WhoBlA 92*
**Faxon**, Charles Edward 1846-1918 *BiInAmS*
**Faxon**, Jack 1936- *WhoAmP 91*
**Faxon**, Thomas Baker 1924- *WhoAmL 92*
**Faxon**, Walter 1848-1920 *BiInAmS*
**Fay brothers** *FacFETw*
**Fay**, Abbott Eastman 1926- *WhoWest 92*
**Fay**, Alice D Awtrey 1926- *AmMWSc 92*
**Fay**, Allen 1934- *WrDr 92*
**Fay**, Amy 1844-1928 *NewAmDM*
**Fay**, Donald B *WhoAmP 91*
**Fay**, Douglas Brian 1957- *WhoEnt 92*
**Fay**, Edgar Stewart 1908- *Who 92*
**Fay**, Francis Hollis 1927- *AmMWSc 92*
**Fay**, Frank J 1870-1931 *FacFETw*
**Fay**, Fredric S *AmMWSc 92*
**Fay**, Homer 1928- *AmMWSc 92*
**Fay**, Humphrey Michael 1949- *Who 92*
**Fay**, James A 1923- *AmMWSc 92*
**Fay**, John David d1991 *Who 92N*
**Fay**, John Edward, II 1934- *AmMWSc 92*
**Fay**, John J, Jr 1927- *WhoAmP 91*
**Fay**, John Thomas 1936- *WhoMW 92*
**Fay**, Julie *DrAPF 91*
**Fay**, Julie Diane 1950- *WhoAmL 92*
**Fay**, Marcus J 1921- *AmMWSc 92*
**Fay**, Maureen A. *WhoRel 92*
**Fay**, Michael *Who 92*
**Fay**, Patrick J. 1916- *IntMPA 92*
**Fay**, Peter Carlyle 1958- *WhoMW 92*
**Fay**, Peter P. 1945- *WhoMW 92*
**Fay**, Peter T *WhoAmP 91*
**Fay**, Peter Thorp 1929- *WhoAmL 92*
**Fay**, Philip S 1921- *AmMWSc 92*
**Fay**, Regan Joseph 1948- *WhoAmL 92*
**Fay**, Richard James 1935- *WhoWest 92*
**Fay**, Richard Rozzell 1944- *AmMWSc 92, WhoMW 92*
**Fay**, Robert Clinton 1936- *AmMWSc 92*
**Fay**, Robert W 1940- *WhoAmP 91*
**Fay**, Ruthann Christina 1968- *WhoEnt 92*
**Fay**, Stanley *ConAu 133*
**Fay**, Temple Harold 1960- *AmMWSc 92*
**Fay**, Theodore 1807-1898 *BenetAL 91*
**Fay**, Thomas Frederic 1940- *WhoAmL 92, WhoAmP 91*
**Fay**, Toni G. 1947- *WhoBlA 92*
**Fay**, Warren Henry 1929- *AmMWSc 92*
**Fay**, William George 1872-1947 *FacFETw*
**Fay**, William Michael *WhoAmL 92*
**Fayard**, Calvin C, Jr 1943- *WhoAmP 91*
**Fayat**, Henri 1908- *IntWW 91*
**Faye**, Jean Pierre 1925- *IntWW 91*
**Fayed**, Mohamed 1933- *IntWW 91*
**Fayer**, Michael David 1947- *AmMWSc 92*
**Fayer**, Ronald 1939- *AmMWSc 92*
**Fayers**, Norman Owen 1945- *Who 92*
**Fayez**, Mohamad al-Ali al- 1937- *IntWW 91*
**Fayko**, Aleksey Mikhaylovich 1893-1978 *SovUnBD*
**Fayle**, Harlan Downing 1907- *AmMWSc 92*
**Faymon**, Karl A 1927- *AmMWSc 92*
**Fayntsimmer**, Aleksandr Mikhaylovich 1906-1982 *SovUnBD*
**Fayon**, A M 1920- *AmMWSc 92*
**Fayorsey**, Clarence Bawa 1922- *WhoFI 92*
**Fayos**, Juan Vallvey 1929- *AmMWSc 92*
**Fayrer**, John 1944- *Who 92*
**Fayrfax**, Robert 1464-1521 *NewAmDM*
**Fayter**, Richard George, Jr 1937- *AmMWSc 92*
**Fazan**, Adrienne d1965 *ReelWom*
**Fazande**, Hilliard C., II 1943- *WhoBlA 92*
**Fazekas**, Arpad Gyula 1936- *AmMWSc 92*
**Fazio**, Anthony Lee 1937- *WhoFI 92, WhoMW 92*
**Fazio**, Giovanni Gene 1933- *AmMWSc 92*
**Fazio**, Paul 1939- *AmMWSc 92*
**Fazio**, Peter Victor, Jr. 1940- *WhoAmL 92, WhoFI 92, WhoMW 92*
**Fazio**, Ronald C 1944- *WhoIns 92*
**Fazio**, Steve 1916- *AmMWSc 92*
**Fazio**, Vic 1942- *AlmAP 92 [port], WhoWest 92*
**Fazio**, Victor H 1942- *WhoAmP 91*
**Fazzari**, Steven Mark 1955- *WhoFI 92, WhoMW 92*
**Fazzini**, Georgia Carol 1946- *WhoWest 92*
**Fazzini**, Mark Allen 1952- *WhoMW 92*
**Fazzino**, Alex J 1923- *WhoAmP 91*
**Fea**, William Wallace 1907- *Who 92*
**Feachem**, Richard George Andrew 1947- *Who 92*
**Fead**, John William Norman 1923- *AmMWSc 92*
**Feagans**, William Marion 1927- *AmMWSc 92*
**Feagin**, Eugene Lloyd 1950- *WhoRel 92*
**Feagin**, Frank J 1914- *AmMWSc 92*
**Feagin**, Frederick F 1931- *AmMWSc 92*
**Feagin**, Roy C 1914- *AmMWSc 92*
**Feagin**, Terry 1945- *AmMWSc 92*
**Feagles**, Gerald Franklin 1934- *WhoMW 92*
**Feagles**, Robert West 1920- *WhoFI 92*
**Feagley**, Michael Rowe 1945- *WhoAmL 92*
**Feairheller**, Stephen Henry 1933- *AmMWSc 92*
**Feairheller**, William Russell, Jr 1931- *AmMWSc 92*
**Feakes**, Frank 1923- *AmMWSc 92*
**Fealk**, Martin N. 1941- *WhoAmL 92*
**Fear**, J Van Dyck 1925- *AmMWSc 92*
**Fearer**, William Potter, III 1959- *WhoAmL 92*
**Fearheiley**, Nancy P. 1952- *WhoEnt 92*
**Fearing**, John T. 1916- *WhoBlA 92*
**Fearing**, Kenneth 1902-1961 *BenetAL 91, FacFETw*
**Fearing**, Olin S 1928- *AmMWSc 92*
**Fearing**, Ralph Burton 1918- *AmMWSc 92*
**Fearl**, Clifford *WhoEnt 92*
**Fearn**, Dean Henry 1943- *WhoWest 92*
**Fearn**, James Ernest 1920- *AmMWSc 92*
**Fearn**, John Martin 1916- *Who 92*
**Fearn**, John Russell 1908-1960 *TwCSFW 91, TwCWW 91*
**Fearn**, Richard L 1937- *AmMWSc 92*
**Fearn**, Robin 1934- *Who 92*
**Fearn**, Ronald Cyril 1931- *Who 92*
**Fearn-Banks**, Kathleen 1941- *WhoBlA 92*
**Fearnley**, Lawrence 1932- *AmMWSc 92*
**Fearnot**, Neal Edward 1953- *AmMWSc 92*
**Fearnsides**, John Joseph *AmMWSc 92*
**Fearon**, Douglas T 1942- *AmMWSc 92*
**Fearon**, Frederick William Gordon 1938- *AmMWSc 92*
**Fearon**, James George 1960- *WhoAmL 92*
**Fearon**, Lee Charles 1938- *WhoWest 92*
**Fearon**, Peter 1942- *WrDr 92*
**Fearons**, George Hadsall 1927- *WhoIns 92*

**Fearrington,** Willa Anne 1949- WhoAmL 92
**Fears,** Emery Lewis, Jr. 1925- WhoBlA 92
**Fears,** William Earl 1920- WhoAmP 91
**Feasley,** Charles Frederick 1915- AmMWSc 92
**Feast,** Michael William 1926- IntWW 91
**Feaster,** Carl Vance 1921- AmMWSc 92
**Feaster,** Gene R 1918- AmMWSc 92
**Feaster,** John Pipkin 1920- AmMWSc 92
**Feaster,** LaVerne Williams 1926- WhoBlA 92
**Feaster,** Robert DrAPF 91
**Feates,** Francis Stanley 1932- Who 92
**Feather,** David Hoover 1943- AmMWSc 92
**Feather,** John Pliny 1947- Who 92
**Feather,** Lawrence Steven 1955- WhoWest 92
**Feather,** Leonard 1914- WrDr 92
**Feather,** Merlin Chester 1929- WhoRel 92
**Feather,** Milton S 1936- AmMWSc 92
**Feather,** Yan Kel 1920- TwCPaSc
**Featherly,** Henry Frederick 1930- WhoAmL 92
**Featherly,** Walter Thomas, III 1955- WhoAmL 92
**Featherman,** Bernard 1929- WhoFI 92
**Feathers,** William D 1927- AmMWSc 92
**Featherston,** Bill 1927- TwCPaSc
**Featherston,** Frank Hunter 1929- AmMWSc 92
**Featherstonaugh,** Henry Gordon 1917- WhoMW 92
**Featherstone,** Bruce Alan 1953- WhoAmL 92
**Featherstone,** Hugh Robert 1926- Who 92
**Featherstone,** John Douglas Bernard 1944- AmMWSc 92
**Featherstonhaugh,** George William 1780-1866 BiInAmS
**Featherstonhaugh,** James Duane 1944- WhoAmL 92
**Feaver,** Douglas David 1921- WhoWest 92
**Feaver,** Douglas Russell 1914- Who 92
**Feaver,** William 1942- WrDr 92
**Feaver,** William Andrew 1942- Who 92
**Feay,** Darrell Charles 1927- AmMWSc 92
**Feay,** Wiliam T 1803?-1879 BiInAmS
**Feazel,** Charles Elmo, Jr 1921- AmMWSc 92
**Feazel,** Charles Tibbals 1945- AmMWSc 92
**Feazell,** Thomas Lee 1937- WhoAmL 92
**Febel,** Joel William 1938- WhoMW 92
**Febres Cordero Rivadeneira,** Leon IntWW 91
**Fecan,** Ivan LesBEnT 92
**Fech,** Dennis Gerard 1950- WhoMW 92
**Fech,** Edward Bruce 1933- WhoMW 92, WhoRel 92
**Fechenbach,** Hermann 1897- TwCPaSc
**Fecher,** Conrad Christopher 1946- WhoFI 92
**Fecher,** Constance WrDr 92
**Fecher,** Vincent John 1924- WhoRel 92
**Fechheimer,** Marcus 1952- AmMWSc 92
**Fechheimer,** Nathan S 1925- AmMWSc 92
**Fechner,** Gilbert Henry 1922- AmMWSc 92
**Fechtel,** Vince, Jr 1936- WhoAmP 91
**Fechtel,** Vincent J. 1936- WhoAmL 92
**Fechter,** Alan Edward 1934- AmMWSc 92, WhoFI 92
**Fechter,** Laurence David AmMWSc 92
**Fechter,** Robert Bernard 1940- AmMWSc 92, WhoMW 92
**Feczko,** Albert G., Jr. 1939- WhoAmL 92
**Fedak,** George 1940- AmMWSc 92
**Fedalen,** Richard J 1939- WhoIns 92
**Fedarb,** Daphne 1912- TwCPaSc
**Fedarb,** Ernest 1905- TwCPaSc
**Fedde,** Elizabeth 1850-1921 RelLAm 91
**Fedde,** Marion Roger 1935- AmMWSc 92
**Fedden,** Mary 1915- TwCPaSc
**Fedden,** Romilly 1875-1939 TwCPaSc
**Fedder,** Norman Joseph 1934- IntAu&W 91, WhoEnt 92, WrDr 92
**Fedder,** Steven Lee 1950- AmMWSc 92
**Feddern,** Henry A 1938- AmMWSc 92
**Fedders,** John Michael 1941- WhoAmL 92
**Fedders,** Peter Alan 1939- AmMWSc 92
**Fedderson,** Don LesBEnT 92
**Fedderson,** Yvonne Lime 1935- WhoWest 92
**Feddoes,** Sadie C. WhoBlA 92
**Fede,** Andrew Thomas 1956- WhoAmL 92
**Fedele,** Ivan 1953- ConCom 92
**Fedele,** Philip A 1939- WhoAmP 91
**Fedele,** Stephen 1931- WhoMW 92
**Feder,** Arthur A. 1927- WhoAmL 92
**Feder,** Bernard 1924- WrDr 92
**Feder,** David O 1924- AmMWSc 92
**Feder,** Edward M 1940- WhoIns 92
**Feder,** Gottfried 1883-1941 BiDExR, EncTR 91 [port]
**Feder,** Harvey Herman 1940- AmMWSc 92
**Feder,** Howard Mitchell 1922- AmMWSc 92
**Feder,** Joseph 1932- AmMWSc 92
**Feder,** Ralph 1922- AmMWSc 92
**Feder,** Raymond L 1920- AmMWSc 92
**Feder,** Robert 1930- WhoAmL 92
**Feder,** Robert 1956- WhoEnt 92
**Feder,** Saul E. 1943- WhoAmL 92, WhoFI 92
**Feder,** Steve Charles 1958- WhoFI 92
**Feder,** William Adolph 1920- AmMWSc 92
**Federbush,** Paul Gerard 1934- AmMWSc 92
**Federer,** C Anthony 1939- AmMWSc 92
**Federer,** Herbert 1920- AmMWSc 92
**Federer,** Walter Theodore 1915- AmMWSc 92
**Federici,** Brian Anthony 1943- AmMWSc 92
**Federici,** Dennis Carl 1950- WhoFI 92
**Federici,** William R WhoAmP 91
**Federico,** Andrew John 1950- WhoFI 92
**Federico,** Gene 1918- DcTwDes, WhoEnt 92
**Federico,** Gloria Cabralez 1953- WhoHisp 92
**Federico,** Hugo A. 1947- WhoHisp 92
**Federico,** James Joseph, Jr 1946- WhoAmP 91
**Federico,** Joe, Jr. 1935- WhoHisp 92
**Federico,** Olga Maria 1923- AmMWSc 92
**Federighi,** Enrico Thomas 1927- AmMWSc 92
**Federighi,** Francis D 1931- AmMWSc 92
**Federle,** Katherine Hunt 1958- WhoAmL 92
**Federle,** Thomas Walter 1952- AmMWSc 92
**Federman,** Daniel D 1928- AmMWSc 92
**Federman,** Micheline 1939- AmMWSc 92
**Federman,** Raymond DrAPF 91
**Federman,** Raymond 1928- BenetAL 91, ConNov 91, IntAu&W 91, WrDr 92
**Federmann,** Bernard Robert 1956- WhoRel 92
**Federmann,** Franklin Howard 1939- WhoFI 92
**Federmann,** Nikolaus 1501-1546 HisDSpE
**Federowicz,** Alexander John 1935- AmMWSc 92
**Federspiel,** Charles Foster 1929- AmMWSc 92
**Federspiel,** Thomas Holger 1935- IntWW 91
**Federzoni,** Luigi 1878-1967 BiDExR, EncTR 91
**Fedewa,** Lawrence John 1937- WhoFI 92
**Fedida,** Sam 1918- Who 92
**Fedin,** Konstantin Aleksandrovich 1892-1977 SovUnBD
**Fedin,** Konstantin Alexandrovich 1892-1977 FacFETw
**Fedinec,** Alexander 1926- AmMWSc 92
**Fedirko,** Pavel Stefanovich 1932- IntWW 91
**Fedor,** Edward John 1924- AmMWSc 92
**Fedor,** Leo Richard 1934- AmMWSc 92
**Fedorchak,** Timothy Hill 1958- WhoFI 92
**Fedorchuk,** Vitaliy Vasil'evich 1918- SovUnBD
**Fedorenko,** Nikolay Prokofiyevich 1917- IntWW 91
**Fedorenko,** Nikolay Trofimovich 1912- IntWW 91
**Fedorko,** Charles Andrew, Jr. 1947- WhoWest 92
**Fedoroff,** Nina V 1942- AmMWSc 92
**Fedoroff,** Sergey 1925- AmMWSc 92
**Fedorov,** Svyatoslav Nikolaevich 1927- IntWW 91, SovUnBD
**Fedorov,** Viktor Stepanovich 1912- IntWW 91
**Fedorovsky,** Fedor Fedorovich 1883-1955 SovUnBD
**Fedors,** John, Jr. 1953- WhoAmL 92
**Fedors,** Robert Francis 1934- AmMWSc 92
**Fedoruk,** Sylvia O. 1927- WhoWest 92
**Fedoryka,** Damian Paul 1940- WhoFI 92
**Fedoseev,** Petr Nikolaevich 1908- SovUnBD
**Fedoseev,** Vladimir Ivanovich 1932- SovUnBD
**Fedoseyev,** Pyotr Nikolayevich 1908- IntWW 91
**Fedoseyev,** Vladimir Ivanovich 1932- IntWW 91
**Fedosov,** Yevgeny Aleksandrovich 1929- IntWW 91
**Fedotov,** Sergey Aleksandrovich 1931- IntWW 91
**Fedrick,** Geoffrey Courtis 1937- Who 92
**Fedrick,** James Love 1930- AmMWSc 92
**Feduccia,** John Alan 1943- AmMWSc 92
**Fee,** James Arthur 1939- AmMWSc 92
**Fee,** Thomas J 1931- WhoAmP 91
**Feehan,** John Joseph 1953- WhoAmL 92
**Feeks,** J. Michael 1942- WhoFI 92
**Feeley,** Gregory 1955- ConAu 135
**Feeley,** Henry Joseph, Jr. 1940- WhoFI 92, WhoMW 92
**Feeley,** John Cornelius 1933- AmMWSc 92
**Feeley,** Kathleen 1929- WhoRel 92
**Feeley,** Malcolm M. 1942- WhoAmL 92
**Feeley,** Sharon Denise 1949- WhoMW 92
**Feeley,** Theresa Gouvin 1947- WhoAmP 91
**Feelings,** Muriel Grey 1938- WhoBlA 92
**Feelings,** Thomas 1933- WhoBlA 92
**Feely,** Anne Marie 1953- WhoWest 92
**Feely,** Frank Joseph, Jr 1918- AmMWSc 92
**Feely,** Herbert William 1928- AmMWSc 92
**Feely,** Michael Lamon 1963- WhoRel 92
**Feely,** Richard Alan 1947- AmMWSc 92
**Feely,** Wayne E 1931- AmMWSc 92
**Feeman,** George Franklin 1930- AmMWSc 92, WhoMW 92
**Feeman,** James Frederic 1922- AmMWSc 92
**Feemster,** John Arthur 1939- WhoBlA 92
**Feeney,** Dennis Michael 1953- WhoAmL 92
**Feeney,** Don Joseph, Jr. 1948- WhoMW 92
**Feeney,** Floyd Fulton 1933- WhoAmL 92
**Feeney,** Gloria Comulada 1925- AmMWSc 92
**Feeney,** Patricia Sharon 1948- WhoFI 92
**Feeney,** Richard Michael, II 1954- WhoAmL 92
**Feeney,** Robert Earl 1913- AmMWSc 92
**Feeney,** Robert K 1938- AmMWSc 92
**Feeney,** Tom 1958- WhoAmP 91
**Feeney-Burns,** Mary Lynette 1931- AmMWSc 92
**Feenker,** Cherie Diane 1950- WhoAmL 92
**Feenstra,** Ernest Star 1917- AmMWSc 92
**Feeny,** Max Howard 1928- Who 92
**Feeny,** Paul Patrick 1940- AmMWSc 92
**Feeny,** Thomas DrAPF 91
**Feerick,** John David 1936- WhoAmL 92
**Feero,** William E 1938- AmMWSc 92
**Feerst,** Irwin 1927- AmMWSc 92
**Fees,** James Richard 1931- WhoFI 92
**Fees,** John T. 1967- WhoWest 92
**Fees,** Nancy Fardelius 1950- WhoWest 92
**Feese,** Bennie Taylor 1937- AmMWSc 92
**Feeser,** Larry James 1937- AmMWSc 92
**Feezel,** Jerry David 1938- WhoMW 92
**Feezor-Stewart,** Barbara Yvonne 1950- WhoWest 92
**Fefer,** Itsik 1900-1952 FacFETw
**Feferman,** Solomon 1928- AmMWSc 92
**Feffer,** Paul Evan 1921- WhoFI 92
**Fefferman,** Charles Louis 1949- AmMWSc 92
**Fegan,** Kevin 1962- WhoMW 92
**Fegelein,** Hermann 1906-1945 EncTR 91 [port]
**Feger,** Claudius 1948- AmMWSc 92
**Feggans,** Edward L. 1919- WhoBlA 92
**Feggins,** James C. WhoRel 92
**Feggins,** Virginia L 1940- WhoAmP 91
**Feghali,** Georges Maurice 1953- WhoMW 92
**Fegley,** Kenneth A 1923- AmMWSc 92
**Feheney,** John Matthew 1932- WhoRel 92
**Feher,** Elsa 1932- AmMWSc 92
**Feher,** Frank J 1958- AmMWSc 92
**Feher,** George 1924- AmMWSc 92, IntWW 91
**Feher,** Joseph John 1949- AmMWSc 92
**Fehette,** H Van Derck 1916- AmMWSc 92
**Fehl,** Philipp P. 1920- WrDr 92
**Fehler,** Michael C 1951- AmMWSc 92
**Fehlner,** Francis Paul 1934- AmMWSc 92
**Fehlner,** Thomas Patrick 1937- AmMWSc 92
**Fehn,** Jeffrey Martin 1963- WhoFI 92
**Fehnel,** Edward Adam 1922- AmMWSc 92
**Fehon,** Jack Harold 1926- AmMWSc 92
**Fehr,** Basil Henry Frank 1912- Who 92
**Fehr,** J. Will 1926- WhoWest 92
**Fehr,** Larry Michael 1952- WhoWest 92
**Fehr,** Lee A. 1961- WhoEnt 92
**Fehr,** Robert O 1911- AmMWSc 92
**Fehr,** Rudi 1911- IntMPA 92
**Fehr,** Walter R 1939- AmMWSc 92
**Fehrenbach,** Charles Max 1914- IntWW 91
**Fehrenbach,** Konstantin 1852-1926 EncTR 91 [port]
**Fehrenbach,** Mark David 1962- WhoEnt 92
**Fehrenbach,** T. R. 1925- WrDr 92
**Fehrenbacher,** Don Edward 1920- WrDr 92
**Fehrer,** Steven Craig 1951- WhoWest 92
**Fehribach,** Ronald Steven 1949- WhoMW 92, WhoWest 92
**Fehring,** Lawrence Joseph 1958- WhoAmL 92
**Fehrman,** Carl 1915- ConAu 133
**Fei Xiaotong** 1910- IntWW 91
**Fei,** Cheng-Wu 1914- TwCPaSc
**Feibel,** Frederick Arthur 1942- WhoFI 92
**Feibel,** Robert Marks 1943- WhoMW 92
**Feibelman,** Peter Julian 1942- AmMWSc 92
**Feibelman,** Walter A 1925- AmMWSc 92
**Feibes,** Walter 1928- AmMWSc 92
**Feibleman,** James Kern, Mrs. 1929- WhoEnt 92
**Feibleman,** Peter S. 1930- BenetAL 91
**Feibusch,** Hans 1898- TwCPaSc, Who 92
**Feichter,** Patton L 1945- WhoAmP 91
**Feichtinger,** Mark Rudolph 1948- WhoAmL 92
**Feichtner,** John David 1930- AmMWSc 92, WhoWest 92
**Feick,** John Mitchell 1951- WhoAmL 92
**Feiden,** Bart Joseph 1937- WhoFI 92
**Feiden,** Larraine Vogel 1962- WhoAmL 92
**Feider,** Paul 1951- ConAu 35NR
**Feier,** Claudette D. 1933- WhoFI 92
**Feier,** Robert Ruven 1933- WhoWest 92
**Feiertag,** Thomas Harold 1935- AmMWSc 92
**Feifel,** Herman 1915- AmMWSc 92
**Feiffer,** Jules 1929- FacFETw [port], IntAu&W 91, IntWW 91, WhoEnt 92, WrDr 92
**Feig,** Gerald 1932- AmMWSc 92
**Feig,** Larry Allen 1952- AmMWSc 92
**Feig,** Marsha Anne 1946- WhoFI 92
**Feig,** Stephen Arthur 1937- WhoWest 92
**Feigal,** David William, Jr 1949- AmMWSc 92
**Feigal,** Ellen G 1954- AmMWSc 92
**Feige,** Edgar Louis 1937- WhoFI 92
**Feige,** Norman G 1931- AmMWSc 92
**Feigelson,** Eric Dennis 1953- AmMWSc 92
**Feigelson,** Muriel 1926- AmMWSc 92
**Feigelson,** Philip 1925- AmMWSc 92
**Feigelson,** Robert Saul 1935- AmMWSc 92
**Feigen,** Brenda S. 1944- WhoEnt 92
**Feigen,** Larry Philip 1942- AmMWSc 92
**Feigenbaum,** Abraham Samuel 1929- AmMWSc 92
**Feigenbaum,** Armand Vallin 1920- WhoFI 92
**Feigenbaum,** Bob 1948- WhoAmP 91
**Feigenbaum,** Brian Alexander 1954- WhoEnt 92
**Feigenbaum,** Edward A 1936- AmMWSc 92, ConAu 134
**Feigenbaum,** Edward Albert 1936- WhoWest 92
**Feigenbaum,** Edward D. 1958- WhoAmL 92
**Feigenbaum,** Harvey 1933- AmMWSc 92
**Feigenbaum,** Jay Lawrence 1952- WhoAmP 91
**Feigenbaum,** Judah Marvin 1950- WhoFI 92
**Feigenbaum,** Mitchell Jay 1944- AmMWSc 92
**Feigenson,** Gerald William 1946- AmMWSc 92
**Feigerle,** Charles Stephen 1950- AmMWSc 92
**Feighan,** Edward F. 1947- AlmAP 92 [port]
**Feighan,** Edward Farrell 1947- WhoAmP 91, WhoMW 92
**Feighan,** Maria Josita 1932- AmMWSc 92
**Feighner,** Scott Dennis 1951- AmMWSc 92
**Feight,** Cheryl LeAnn 1949- WhoEnt 92
**Feigin,** Barbara Sommer 1937- WhoFI 92
**Feigin,** Irwin Harris 1915- AmMWSc 92
**Feigin,** Ralph David 1938- AmMWSc 92
**Feigl,** Dorothy M 1938- AmMWSc 92
**Feigl,** Eric O 1933- AmMWSc 92
**Feigl,** Frank Joseph 1936- AmMWSc 92
**Feigl,** Fred 1884-1965 TwCPaSc
**Feigl,** Polly Catherine 1935- AmMWSc 92
**Feign,** David 1923- AmMWSc 92
**Feigner,** Vera EncAmaz 91
**Feigon,** Lee 1945- WrDr 92
**Feijoo y Montenegro,** Benito Jeronimo 1676-1764 BlkwCEP
**Feikema,** Feike TwCWW 91, WrDr 92
**Feikens,** John 1917- WhoAmL 92, WhoMW 92
**Feikens,** Robert Houwing 1955- WhoAmL 92
**Feiker,** George E, Jr 1918- AmMWSc 92
**Feil,** Edward Rosewater 1924- WhoEnt 92
**Feil,** Frank J., Jr. 1926- WhoAmL 92
**Feil,** Linda Mae 1948- WhoWest 92
**Feil,** Paul Arnold 1922- WhoAmP 91
**Feild,** Kay Carol 1938- WhoAmP 91
**Feild,** Maurice 1905-1988 TwCPaSc
**Feilden,** Bernard 1919- Who 92
**Feilden,** Bernard Melchior 1919- IntWW 91
**Feilden,** Geoffrey Bertram Robert 1917- IntWW 91, Who 92
**Feilden,** Henry 1916- Who 92
**Feilding** Who 92
**Feilding,** Viscount 1970- Who 92
**Feiler,** Jane Abeshouse 1936- WhoFI 92
**Feiler,** Paul 1918- TwCPaSc
**Feiler,** William A, Jr 1940- AmMWSc 92

**Feiler,** William S. 1946- *WhoAmL 92*
**Feiman,** Ronald Mark 1951- *WhoEnt 92*
**Fein,** Burton Ira 1940- *AmMWSc 92*
**Fein,** Cheri *DrAPF 91*
**Fein,** Ethan 1948- *WhoEnt 92*
**Fein,** Harvey L 1936- *AmMWSc 92*
**Fein,** Herbert 1922- *WhoFI 92*
**Fein,** Irving Ashley 1911- *WhoEnt 92*
**Fein,** Jack M 1940- *AmMWSc 92*
**Fein,** Jay Sheldon 1937- *AmMWSc 92*
**Fein,** Marvin Michael 1923- *AmMWSc 92*
**Fein,** Melanie Lippincott 1949- *WhoAmL 92*
**Fein,** R S 1923- *AmMWSc 92*
**Fein,** Rashi 1926- *AmMWSc 92, IntWW 91*
**Fein,** Richard J. 1929- *WrDr 92*
**Fein,** Roger Gary 1940- *WhoAmL 92, WhoMW 92*
**Fein,** Ronald Lawrence 1943- *WhoAmL 92*
**Fein,** Stephen Joel 1946- *WhoAmL 92*
**Fein,** Steven 1958- *WhoFI 92*
**Fein,** Thomas Paul 1946- *WhoMW 92*
**Fein,** William 1933- *WhoWest 92*
**Feinberg,** Barry N *AmMWSc 92*
**Feinberg,** Barry Vincent 1938- *IntAu&W 91*
**Feinberg,** Benjamin Allen 1944- *AmMWSc 92*
**Feinberg,** David B. 1956- *ConAu 135*
**Feinberg,** Evgueniy Lvovich 1912- *IntWW 91*
**Feinberg,** Gerald 1933- *AmMWSc 92, WrDr 92*
**Feinberg,** Gregg Michael 1958- *WhoAmL 92*
**Feinberg,** Harold 1922- *AmMWSc 92*
**Feinberg,** Joy Marilyn *WhoAmL 92*
**Feinberg,** Lee F 1947- *WhoAmP 91*
**Feinberg,** Leonard 1914- *IntAu&W 91, WrDr 92*
**Feinberg,** Martin Robert 1942- *AmMWSc 92*
**Feinberg,** Matthew Harris 1942- *WhoAmL 92*
**Feinberg,** Milton *IntMPA 92*
**Feinberg,** Norman Maurice 1934- *WhoFI 92*
**Feinberg,** Paul Stuart 1942- *WhoAmL 92*
**Feinberg,** Robert Edward 1935- *WhoEnt 92*
**Feinberg,** Robert Ira 1956- *WhoAmL 92*
**Feinberg,** Robert Jacob 1931- *AmMWSc 92*
**Feinberg,** Robert S. 1934- *WhoFI 92*
**Feinberg,** Robert Samuel 1940- *AmMWSc 92*
**Feinberg,** Rosa Castro 1939- *WhoHisp 92*
**Feinberg,** Stewart Carl 1947- *AmMWSc 92*
**Feinberg,** Wilfred *WhoAmP 91*
**Feinberg,** Wilfred 1920- *WhoAmL 92*
**Feinblatt,** Joel David *AmMWSc 92*
**Feinbloom,** Richard I. 1935- *ConAu 135*
**Feinblum,** David Alan 1940- *AmMWSc 92*
**Feindel,** William Howard 1918- *AmMWSc 92*
**Feinendegen,** Ludwig E. 1927- *IntWW 91*
**Feiner,** Alexander 1928- *AmMWSc 92*
**Feiner,** Harry Alan 1953- *WhoEnt 92*
**Feinglas,** Mitchel Alan 1948- *WhoFI 92*
**Feingold,** Adolph 1920- *AmMWSc 92*
**Feingold,** Alex Jay 1950- *AmMWSc 92*
**Feingold,** Alfred 1941- *AmMWSc 92*
**Feingold,** Arnold Moses 1920- *AmMWSc 92*
**Feingold,** Ben F 1900- *AmMWSc 92*
**Feingold,** David Sidney 1922- *AmMWSc 92*
**Feingold,** Earl 1924- *AmMWSc 92*
**Feingold,** Eugene 1931- *WrDr 92*
**Feingold,** Janice Carol Moore 1949- *WhoFI 92*
**Feingold,** Russell D 1953- *WhoAmP 91*
**Feingold,** S. Norman *WrDr 92*
**Feingold,** Stephen Wise 1956- *WhoAmL 92*
**Feinhandler,** Edward Sanford 1948- *WhoWest 92*
**Feininger,** Tomas 1935- *AmMWSc 92*
**Feinland,** Raymond 1928- *AmMWSc 92*
**Feinleib,** Julius 1936- *AmMWSc 92*
**Feinleib,** Manning 1935- *AmMWSc 92*
**Feinleib,** Mary Ella 1938- *AmMWSc 92*
**Feinleib,** Morris 1924- *AmMWSc 92*
**Feinman,** Alvin *DrAPF 91*
**Feinman,** J 1928- *AmMWSc 92*
**Feinman,** Mark 1955- *WhoAmL 92*
**Feinman,** Max L 1905- *AmMWSc 92*
**Feinman,** Richard David 1940- *AmMWSc 92*
**Feinman,** Steven Allyn 1961- *WhoAmL 92*
**Feinman,** Susan 1930- *AmMWSc 92*
**Feinn,** Barbara Ann 1925- *WhoFI 92*
**Feinsinger,** Peter 1948- *AmMWSc 92*
**Feinsod,** Paul Martin 1955- *WhoAmL 92*
**Feinstein,** Alan 1941- *IntMPA 92*
**Feinstein,** Alan Laurence 1941- *WhoEnt 92*
**Feinstein,** Alan Shawn 1931- *WhoFI 92*
**Feinstein,** Alejandro 1929- *AmMWSc 92*
**Feinstein,** Allen Irwin 1940- *AmMWSc 92*
**Feinstein,** Allen Lewis 1929- *WhoAmL 92*
**Feinstein,** Alvan Richard 1925- *AmMWSc 92, IntWW 91*
**Feinstein,** Charles David 1946- *AmMWSc 92*
**Feinstein,** Charles Hilliard 1932- *IntWW 91, Who 92*
**Feinstein,** David 1946- *ConAu 135, WhoWest 92*
**Feinstein,** Dianne 1933- *IntWW 91, WhoWest 92*
**Feinstein,** Dianne Goldman 1933- *WhoAmP 91*
**Feinstein,** Elaine 1930- *ConNov 91, ConPo 91, IntAu&W 91, WrDr 92*
**Feinstein,** Fred Ira 1945- *WhoAmL 92*
**Feinstein,** Hyman Israel 1911- *AmMWSc 92*
**Feinstein,** Irwin K 1914- *AmMWSc 92*
**Feinstein,** Jeffrey E. 1957- *WhoAmL 92*
**Feinstein,** John 1956- *ConAu 133, WrDr 92*
**Feinstein,** Joseph 1925- *AmMWSc 92*
**Feinstein,** Louis 1912- *AmMWSc 92*
**Feinstein,** Marguerite d1991 *NewYTBS 91*
**Feinstein,** Marion Finke 1925- *WhoEnt 92*
**Feinstein,** Mark Robert 1955- *WhoEnt 92*
**Feinstein,** Martin 1921- *WhoEnt 92*
**Feinstein,** Maurice B 1929- *AmMWSc 92*
**Feinstein,** Michael 1956- *ConMus 6 [port]*
**Feinstein,** Michael Jay 1956- *WhoEnt 92*
**Feinstein,** Miles Roger 1941- *WhoAmL 92*
**Feinstein,** Morley Todd 1954- *WhoRel 92*
**Feinstein,** Myron Elliot 1943- *AmMWSc 92*
**Feinstein,** Otto 1930- *WhoAmP 91*
**Feinstein,** Paul Louis 1955- *WhoAmL 92*
**Feinstein,** Robert Norman 1915- *AmMWSc 92*
**Feinstein,** Roni 1954- *ConAu 134*
**Feinstein,** S. Michael 1948- *WhoFI 92*
**Feinstein,** Sheldon Israel 1950- *AmMWSc 92*
**Feinstein,** William Lewis 1957- *WhoAmL 92*
**Feinstone,** Stephen Mark 1944- *AmMWSc 92*
**Feintuch,** Philip 1937- *WhoAmL 92*
**Feiock,** Frank Donald 1936- *AmMWSc 92*
**Feiock,** John Paul 1944- *WhoFI 92*
**Feir,** Dorothy Jean 1929- *AmMWSc 92*
**Feir,** Marvin Leonard 1940- *WhoWest 92*
**Feirstein,** Bruce Jon 1953- *WhoEnt 92*
**Feirstein,** Frederick *DrAPF 91*
**Feis,** Herbert 1893-1972 *AmPeW*
**Feisal I** 1885-1933 *FacFETw*
**Feisal II** 1935-1958 *FacFETw*
**Feisel,** Lyle Dean 1935- *AmMWSc 92*
**Feiss,** Hugh Bernard 1939- *WhoRel 92*
**Feiss,** Paul Geoffrey 1943- *AmMWSc 92*
**Feissner,** Karl George 1931- *WhoAmL 92*
**Feist,** Alvin John 1955- *WhoFI 92*
**Feist,** Dale Daniel 1938- *AmMWSc 92*
**Feist,** F. Lee 1943- *WhoFI 92*
**Feist,** Gene 1930- *WhoEnt 92*
**Feist,** Nancy Lynn 1965- *WhoMW 92*
**Feist,** Raymond E *TwCSFW 91*
**Feist,** William Charles 1934- *AmMWSc 92*
**Feist,** Wolfgang Martin 1927- *AmMWSc 92*
**Feit,** Carl 1945- *AmMWSc 92*
**Feit,** Christian 1921- *IntWW 91*
**Feit,** David 1937- *AmMWSc 92*
**Feit,** Eugene David 1935- *AmMWSc 92*
**Feit,** Glenn M. 1929- *WhoAmL 92*
**Feit,** Ira 1940- *AmMWSc 92*
**Feit,** Irving N 1942- *AmMWSc 92*
**Feit,** Julius 1919- *AmMWSc 92*
**Feit,** Michael 1928- *WhoMW 92*
**Feit,** Michael Dennis 1942- *AmMWSc 92, WhoWest 92*
**Feit,** Sidnie Marilyn 1935- *AmMWSc 92*
**Feit,** Walter 1930- *AmMWSc 92*
**Feitelson,** Jerald Stuart 1953- *WhoWest 92*
**Feitelson,** Robert Joel 1935- *WhoAmL 92*
**Feith,** Douglas Jay 1953- *WhoAmL 92*
**Feith,** Kathy Lynn 1956- *WhoFI 92*
**Feitler,** David 1952- *AmMWSc 92*
**Feito,** Jose 1929- *WhoFI 92*
**Feitshans,** Buzz *IntMPA 92*
**Feitshans,** Fred Rollin 1937- *WhoEnt 92*
**Feitshans,** Matthew Grant 1969- *WhoEnt 92*
**Feivou,** Jack 1965- *WhoEnt 92*
**Feiwel,** George Richard 1929- *WhoFI 92*
**Feiwell,** Murray Jay 1937- *WhoAmL 92*
**Fejer,** Stephen Oscar 1916- *AmMWSc 92*
**Fejeran,** Moses Tydingco *WhoAmP 91*
**Fejos,** Paul 1897-1963 *IntDcF 2-2*
**Fekaris,** Dino George 1945- *WhoWest 92*
**Fekete,** Antal E 1932- *AmMWSc 92*
**Fekete,** George Otto *WhoAmL 92*
**Fekete,** Janos 1918- *IntWW 91*
**Fekety,** F Robert, Jr 1929- *AmMWSc 92*
**Fekkes,** Jan, III 1954- *WhoRel 92*
**Fela** 1938- *ConBlB 1 [port]*
**Feland,** Gary 1939- *WhoAmP 91*
**Felando,** Gerald Nicholas 1934- *WhoAmP 91*
**Felbeck,** David K 1926- *AmMWSc 92*
**Felbeck,** George Theodore, Jr 1924- *AmMWSc 92*
**Felber,** Anselma *DcAmImH*
**Felber,** Franklin Stanton 1950- *AmMWSc 92*
**Felber,** Rene 1933- *IntWW 91*
**Felberbaum,** Carol Ann 1939- *WhoMW 92*
**Felcey,** Trevor 1945- *TwCPaSc*
**Felch,** Charles H, Sr 1926- *WhoAmP 91*
**Felch,** Patricia Anne 1947- *WhoAmL 92, WhoEnt 92*
**Felch,** William C *AmMWSc 92*
**Felch,** William Campbell 1920- *IntWW 91*
**Felcher,** Gian Piero 1936- *AmMWSc 92*
**Felciano,** Richard 1930- *ConCom 92, NewAmDM, WhoEnt 92*
**Feld,** Alan David 1936- *WhoAmL 92*
**Feld,** Bernard Taub 1919- *AmMWSc 92*
**Feld,** Connie Burton 1951- *WhoMW 92*
**Feld,** Edward 1943- *WhoRel 92*
**Feld,** Eliot 1942- *FacFETw, WhoEnt 92*
**Feld,** Franklin Fred 1923- *WhoAmL 92*
**Feld,** Fritz 1900- *IntMPA 92, WhoEnt 92*
**Feld,** Jindrich 1925- *ConCom 92*
**Feld,** Joseph 1919- *WhoFI 92*
**Feld,** Karen Irma 1947- *IntAu&W 91*
**Feld,** Leonard Bernard 1950- *WhoAmL 92*
**Feld,** Michael S 1940- *AmMWSc 92*
**Feld,** Myron Xane 1915- *WhoWest 92*
**Feld,** Ross *DrAPF 91*
**Feld,** Steven Alan 1955- *WhoEnt 92*
**Feld,** Steven Eric 1954- *WhoAmL 92*
**Feld,** Werner J 1910- *IntAu&W 91, WrDr 92*
**Feld,** William Adam 1944- *AmMWSc 92*
**Feldacker,** Bruce S. 1940- *WhoAmL 92*
**Feldaverd,** Nicholas Edward, III 1949- *WhoWest 92*
**Feldbaek,** Ole 1936- *IntWW 91*
**Feldberg,** Meyer 1942- *WhoFI 92*
**Feldberg,** Ross Sheldon 1943- *AmMWSc 92*
**Feldberg,** Stephen William 1937- *AmMWSc 92*
**Feldberg,** Sumner Lee 1924- *WhoFI 92*
**Feldberg,** Wilhelm Siegmund 1900- *IntWW 91, Who 92*
**Feldbin,** Abraham Isaac 1916- *WhoRel 92*
**Feldblum,** Philip F. 1906- *WhoAmL 92*
**Feldbrill,** Victor 1924- *NewAmDM, WhoEnt 92*
**Feldbusch,** Michael F. 1951- *WhoMW 92*
**Feldbush,** Robert Harold 1933- *WhoEnt 92*
**Feldbush,** Thomas Lee 1939- *AmMWSc 92*
**Feldenkreis,** George 1935- *WhoHisp 92*
**Felder,** Brian Otis 1967- *WhoWest 92*
**Felder,** Cain Hope 1943- *WhoBlA 92*
**Felder,** Darryl Lambert 1947- *AmMWSc 92*
**Felder,** Harvey 1955- *WhoBlA 92*
**Felder,** John Gressette 1944- *WhoAmP 91*
**Felder,** Loretta Kay 1956- *WhoBlA 92*
**Felder,** Michael Lee 1959- *WhoRel 92*
**Felder,** Myrna 1941- *WhoAmL 92*
**Felder,** Raoul Lionel 1934- *WhoAmL 92, WhoFI 92*
**Felder,** Richard Mark 1939- *AmMWSc 92*
**Felder,** Thomas E. *WhoBlA 92*
**Felder,** Tyree Preston, II 1927- *WhoBlA 92*
**Felder,** William 1943- *AmMWSc 92*
**Felder,** Willie W 1927- *WhoAmP 91*
**Felder-Hoehne,** Felicia Harris *WhoBlA 92*
**Felderman,** Eric *DrAPF 91*
**Feldhamer,** George Alan 1947- *AmMWSc 92*
**Feldhaus,** Richard Joseph 1929- *AmMWSc 92*
**Feldhaus,** Stephen Martin 1945- *WhoAmL 92*
**Feldhausen,** John Michael 1939- *WhoWest 92*
**Feldherr,** Carl M 1934- *AmMWSc 92*
**Feldhusen,** Hazel J. 1928- *WhoMW 92*
**Feldkamp,** John Calvin 1939- *WhoAmL 92*
**Feldkirchner,** Barbara JoAnn 1936- *WhoEnt 92*
**Feldlaufer,** Mark Francis 1948- *AmMWSc 92*
**Feldmaier,** Douglas Alan 1954- *WhoMW 92*
**Feldman,** Alan *DrAPF 91*
**Feldman,** Alan Sidney 1927- *AmMWSc 92*
**Feldman,** Albert 1936- *AmMWSc 92*
**Feldman,** Alfred Philip 1923- *AmMWSc 92*
**Feldman,** Allan Maurice 1943- *WhoFI 92*
**Feldman,** Allan Roy 1945- *WhoFI 92*
**Feldman,** Andrew 1943- *WhoAmL 92*
**Feldman,** Annette 1913-198-? *ConAu 34NR*
**Feldman,** Annette Young 1916- *WhoWest 92*
**Feldman,** Arthur 1931- *AmMWSc 92*
**Feldman,** B Robert 1934- *AmMWSc 92*
**Feldman,** Barry Joel 1944- *AmMWSc 92*
**Feldman,** Barry Stewart 1940- *WhoIns 92*
**Feldman,** Basil 1926- *Who 92*
**Feldman,** Bernard Joseph 1946- *AmMWSc 92*
**Feldman,** Bruce Michael 1943- *WhoAmL 92*
**Feldman,** Charles 1924- *AmMWSc 92*
**Feldman,** Charles Franklin 1945- *WhoAmL 92*
**Feldman,** Charles Lawrence 1935- *AmMWSc 92*
**Feldman,** Chester *WhoEnt 92*
**Feldman,** Chester 1920- *AmMWSc 92, WhoMW 92*
**Feldman,** Corey 1971- *IntMPA 92*
**Feldman,** Daniel Lee 1949- *WhoAmP 91*
**Feldman,** Daniel S 1926- *AmMWSc 92*
**Feldman,** Dave W. 1960- *WhoEnt 92*
**Feldman,** David 1921- *AmMWSc 92*
**Feldman,** David 1927- *AmMWSc 92*
**Feldman,** David Hall 1956- *WhoFI 92*
**Feldman,** Dick 1925- *WhoEnt 92*
**Feldman,** Donald William 1931- *AmMWSc 92*
**Feldman,** Dorel 1924- *AmMWSc 92*
**Feldman,** Dot Welber *WhoMW 92*
**Feldman,** Edgar A 1937- *AmMWSc 92*
**Feldman,** Edward S. 1929- *IntMPA 92*
**Feldman,** Edwin B 1925- *AmMWSc 92*
**Feldman,** Elaine Bossak 1926- *AmMWSc 92*
**Feldman,** Elliot Jay 1947- *WhoAmL 92*
**Feldman,** Ernesto V. *IntWW 91*
**Feldman,** Franklin 1927- *WhoAmL 92, WhoEnt 92*
**Feldman,** Fred 1942- *AmMWSc 92*
**Feldman,** Fredric J 1940- *AmMWSc 92*
**Feldman,** Fredric Joel 1940- *WhoWest 92*
**Feldman,** Gary Jay 1942- *AmMWSc 92*
**Feldman,** Gary Mitchell 1957- *WhoAmL 92*
**Feldman,** Gerald D 1937- *IntAu&W 91, WrDr 92*
**Feldman,** Gordon 1928- *AmMWSc 92*
**Feldman,** Harold Raymond 1918- *WhoFI 92*
**Feldman,** Harris Joseph 1942- *WhoMW 92*
**Feldman,** Henry Robert 1932- *AmMWSc 92*
**Feldman,** Irving *DrAPF 91*
**Feldman,** Irving 1928- *ConPo 91, WrDr 92*
**Feldman,** Irwin Miles 1939- *WhoAmL 92*
**Feldman,** Isaac 1918- *AmMWSc 92*
**Feldman,** Jack, Rabbi *DrAPF 91*
**Feldman,** Jack Glenn 1952- *WhoAmL 92*
**Feldman,** Jack L 1948- *AmMWSc 92*
**Feldman,** Jacob 1928- *AmMWSc 92*
**Feldman,** Jacob J *AmMWSc 92*
**Feldman,** James Michael 1933- *AmMWSc 92*
**Feldman,** Jay N. 1936- *WhoFI 92*
**Feldman,** Jeffrey C 1953- *WhoAmP 91*
**Feldman,** Jeffrey Marc 1949- *WhoAmL 92*
**Feldman,** Jerome A 1938- *AmMWSc 92*
**Feldman,** Jerome Myron 1935- *IntWW 91*
**Feldman,** Jerry F 1942- *AmMWSc 92*
**Feldman,** Jonathan *WhoEnt 92*
**Feldman,** Jose M 1927- *AmMWSc 92*
**Feldman,** Joseph Aaron 1925- *AmMWSc 92*
**Feldman,** Joseph David 1916- *AmMWSc 92*
**Feldman,** Joseph Gerald 1940- *AmMWSc 92*
**Feldman,** Joseph Louis 1938- *AmMWSc 92*
**Feldman,** Julian 1915- *AmMWSc 92, WhoMW 92*
**Feldman,** Kenneth Scott 1956- *AmMWSc 92*
**Feldman,** Kevin Dennis 1956- *WhoMW 92*
**Feldman,** Larry Howard 1942- *AmMWSc 92*
**Feldman,** Lawrence 1922- *AmMWSc 92*
**Feldman,** Lawrence A 1938- *AmMWSc 92*
**Feldman,** Leonard 1923- *AmMWSc 92*
**Feldman,** Leonard Cecil 1939- *AmMWSc 92*
**Feldman,** Leonid Ariel 1953- *WhoRel 92*
**Feldman,** Louis A 1941- *AmMWSc 92*
**Feldman,** Louis Arnold 1941- *WhoWest 92*
**Feldman,** Marcus William 1942- *AmMWSc 92*
**Feldman,** Martin 1935- *AmMWSc 92*
**Feldman,** Martin L. C. 1934- *WhoAmL 92, WhoAmP 91*
**Feldman,** Martin Leonard 1937- *AmMWSc 92*
**Feldman,** Martin Louis 1941- *AmMWSc 92*
**Feldman,** Martin Robert 1938- *AmMWSc 92*
**Feldman,** Marvin Herschel 1945- *WhoFI 92*
**Feldman,** Matthew 1919- *WhoAmP 91*

**Feldman,** Michael 1926- *IntWW 91*
**Feldman,** Michael Brent 1956- *WhoAmP 91*
**Feldman,** Milton Alexander 1931- *WhoAmL 92*
**Feldman,** Milton H 1918- *AmMWSc 92*
**Feldman,** Mitchell Robert 1956- *WhoEnt 92*
**Feldman,** Morton 1926-1987 *NewAmDM*
**Feldman,** Myer 1917- *IntWW 91, WhoEnt 92*
**Feldman,** Nathaniel E 1925- *AmMWSc 92*
**Feldman,** Nicholas 1924- *AmMWSc 92*
**Feldman,** Paul Arnold 1940- *AmMWSc 92*
**Feldman,** Paul Donald 1939- *AmMWSc 92*
**Feldman,** Peter Michael 1941- *WhoFI 92*
**Feldman,** Phil 1922- *IntMPA 92*
**Feldman,** Richard *WhoEnt 92*
**Feldman,** Richard Jay 1952- *WhoAmP 91*
**Feldman,** Richard Martin 1944- *AmMWSc 92*
**Feldman,** Robert H L 1943- *AmMWSc 92*
**Feldman,** Roberta Kirsch 1952- *WhoAmL 92*
**Feldman,** Roger David 1943- *WhoAmL 92*
**Feldman,** Ruth *DrAPF 91*
**Feldman,** Ruth 1911- *IntAu&W 91*
**Feldman,** Samuel M 1933- *AmMWSc 92*
**Feldman,** Shel 1936- *WhoMW 92*
**Feldman,** Simone Yellen d1991 *NewYTBS 91 [port]*
**Feldman,** Stanley G *WhoAmP 91*
**Feldman,** Stanley George 1933- *WhoAmL 92, WhoWest 92*
**Feldman,** Steven Lewis 1962- *WhoFI 92*
**Feldman,** Stuart 1941- *AmMWSc 92*
**Feldman,** Susan Beth 1949- *WhoEnt 92*
**Feldman,** Susan C 1943- *AmMWSc 92*
**Feldman,** Thomas Myron 1950- *WhoEnt 92*
**Feldman,** Uri 1935- *AmMWSc 92*
**Feldman,** Victor Fred 1935- *WhoMW 92*
**Feldman,** William 1917- *AmMWSc 92*
**Feldman,** William A 1945- *AmMWSc 92*
**Feldman,** William Charles 1940- *AmMWSc 92*
**Feldman,** William T. 1953- *WhoEnt 92*
**Feldman,** Yael S. 1941- *WhoRel 92*
**Feldmann,** Annette *DrAPF 91*
**Feldmann,** Edward George 1930- *AmMWSc 92*
**Feldmann,** Louis George 1909- *WhoAmL 92*
**Feldmann,** Rodney Mansfield 1939- *AmMWSc 92*
**Feldmann,** Roger Scott 1961- *WhoFI 92, WhoWest 92*
**Feldmeier,** Joseph Robert 1916- *AmMWSc 92*
**Feldmeir,** Diane L. 1956- *WhoFI 92*
**Feldmesser,** Julius 1918- *AmMWSc 92*
**Feldmeth,** Carl Robert 1942- *AmMWSc 92*
**Feldon,** Barbara 1941- *IntMPA 92*
**Feldshuh,** Tovah 1953- *IntMPA 92*
**Feldshuh,** Tovah S. 1952- *WhoEnt 92*
**Feldsott,** Edward 1956- *WhoEnt 92*
**Feldstein,** Alan 1933- *AmMWSc 92*
**Feldstein,** Charles Robert 1922- *WhoMW 92*
**Feldstein,** Donald 1931- *WhoRel 92*
**Feldstein,** Martin Stuart 1939- *IntWW 91, Who 92, WhoFI 92*
**Feldstein,** Nathan 1937- *AmMWSc 92*
**Feldstein Soto,** Luis A. 1960- *WhoHisp 92*
**Feldt,** Allan Gunnar 1932- *WhoMW 92*
**Feldt,** David Allan 1957- *WhoMW 92*
**Feldt,** John Harrell 1940- *WhoAmL 92*
**Feldt,** Kjell-Olof 1931- *IntWW 91*
**Feldt,** Leonard Samuel 1925- *AmMWSc 92*
**Feldt,** Ralph Leo 1941- *WhoMW 92*
**Feleciano,** Paul, Jr. *WhoHisp 92*
**Feleciano,** Paul, Jr 1942- *WhoAmP 91*
**Felgenhauer,** H.R. *DrAPF 91*
**Felger,** Maurice Monroe 1908- *AmMWSc 92*
**Felger,** Ralph William 1919- *WhoMW 92*
**Felgner,** Philip Louis 1950- *AmMWSc 92*
**Felice,** Cynthia 1942- *IntAu&W 91, TwCSFW 91, WrDr 92*
**Felice,** Fortunato Bartolomeo di 1723-1789 *BlkwCEP*
**Felice,** John *WhoEnt 92*
**Felice,** Nicholas R 1927- *WhoAmP 91*
**Felice,** Roger Alex 1948- *WhoAmL 92*
**Felicetta,** Vincent Frank 1919- *AmMWSc 92*
**Felici,** Angelo 1919- *IntWW 91, WhoRel 92*
**Feliciana,** Jerrye Brown 1951- *WhoBlA 92*
**Feliciano,** Ellen Sanders 1947- *WhoFI 92*
**Feliciano,** Jose 1945- *WhoEnt 92, WhoHisp 92*
**Feliciano,** Jose C. 1950- *WhoHisp 92*
**Feliciano,** Jose Celso 1950- *WhoAmL 92*
**Feliciano,** Jose R. 1956- *WhoHisp 92*
**Feliciano,** Juan G. 1951- *WhoHisp 92*
**Feliciotti,** Enio 1926- *AmMWSc 92*
**Felicita,** James Thomas 1947- *WhoFI 92, WhoWest 92*
**Felicitas** *EncEarC*
**Felien,** Alice Mildred 1913- *WhoAmP 91*
**Felig,** Philip 1936- *AmMWSc 92*
**Felinski,** William Walter 1953- *WhoFI 92*
**Felipe,** Leon 1884-1968 *DcLB 108 [port]*
**Feliu,** David Noel 1957- *WhoAmL 92*
**Felix I** *EncEarC*
**Felix II** *EncEarC*
**Felix III** *EncEarC*
**Felix IV** *EncEarC*
**Felix of Nola** *EncEarC*
**Felix Tan'-dem** 1845-1924 *WhoNob 90*
**Felix,** Arthur, Jr. 1945- *WhoHisp 92*
**Felix,** Arthur M 1938- *AmMWSc 92*
**Felix,** Daniel Mendiola 1950- *WhoHisp 92*
**Felix,** Dudley E. *WhoBlA 92*
**Felix,** Fred *WhoHisp 92*
**Felix,** Jack Otto 1945- *WhoEnt 92*
**Felix,** Jeanette S 1944- *AmMWSc 92*
**Felix,** Jennings Patrick 1921- *WhoAmL 92*
**Felix,** Junior Francisco 1967- *WhoHisp 92*
**Felix,** Kelvin Edward 1933- *WhoRel 92*
**Felix,** Raul 1938- *WhoHisp 92*
**Felix,** Ray d1991 *NewYTBS 91*
**Felix,** Raymond Anthony 1946- *AmMWSc 92*
**Felix,** Richard James 1944- *WhoFI 92, WhoWest 92*
**Felix,** Robert Hanna 1904- *AmMWSc 92*
**Felix,** Ted Mark 1947- *WhoFI 92*
**Felixson,** Scott Lee 1966- *WhoEnt 92*
**Felker,** David R. 1957- *WhoFI 92*
**Felker,** Donald William *WhoMW 92*
**Felker,** Harry *WhoAmP 91*
**Felker,** Jean Howard 1919- *AmMWSc 92*
**Felker,** Joseph B. 1926- *WhoBlA 92*
**Felker,** William H. 1953- *WhoEnt 92*
**Fell,** Anthony 1914- *Who 92*
**Fell,** Barry 1917- *WrDr 92*
**Fell,** Bert Hoadley, Jr. 1957- *WhoMW 92*
**Fell,** Colin 1930- *AmMWSc 92*
**Fell,** David 1943- *Who 92*
**Fell,** David Lee 1946- *WhoMW 92*
**Fell,** George Brady 1916- *AmMWSc 92*
**Fell,** Howard Barraclough 1917- *AmMWSc 92*
**Fell,** James Michael Gardner 1923- *AmMWSc 92*
**Fell,** John Louis 1927- *WhoEnt 92*
**Fell,** Michael 1939- *TwCPaSc*
**Fell,** Norman 1924- *IntMPA 92*
**Fell,** Paul Erven 1937- *AmMWSc 92*
**Fell,** Richard Taylor 1948- *Who 92*
**Fell,** Robert 1921- *IntWW 91, Who 92*
**Fell,** Ronald Dean 1949- *AmMWSc 92*
**Fell,** Sheila 1931-1979 *TwCPaSc*
**Fella Przybylowski,** Michelle 1958- *WhoEnt 92*
**Fellechner,** Frederick Gustave, III 1948- *WhoEnt 92*
**Feller,** Benjamin E. 1947- *WhoFI 92*
**Feller,** Charles W. 1934- *WhoMW 92*
**Feller,** Dannis R 1941- *AmMWSc 92*
**Feller,** David E. 1916- *WhoAmL 92*
**Feller,** Fred d1991 *NewYTBS 91*
**Feller,** Lee Arthur 1950- *WhoEnt 92*
**Feller,** Lloyd Harris 1942- *WhoAmL 92*
**Feller,** Ralph Paul 1934- *AmMWSc 92*
**Feller,** Robert Jarman 1945- *AmMWSc 92*
**Feller,** Robert Livingston 1919- *AmMWSc 92*
**Feller,** Robert S., Sr. *WhoFI 92, WhoWest 92*
**Feller,** Robert William Andrew 1918- *WhoEnt 92*
**Feller,** William 1925- *AmMWSc 92*
**Fellerman,** Linden Jan 1956- *WhoFI 92*
**Fellers,** David Anthony 1935- *AmMWSc 92*
**Fellers,** Francis Xavier 1922- *AmMWSc 92*
**Fellers,** James Davison 1913- *WhoAmL 92*
**Fellers,** James Davison, Jr. 1948- *WhoMW 92*
**Fellers,** Rhonda Gay 1955- *WhoAmL 92, WhoFI 92*
**Fellers,** Rufus Gustavus 1920- *AmMWSc 92*
**Felley,** Donald Louis 1921- *AmMWSc 92*
**Fellgett,** Peter Berners 1922- *IntWW 91, Who 92*
**Fellgiebel,** Fritz Erich 1886-1944 *EncTR 91*
**Fellhauer,** David E. 1939- *WhoRel 92*
**Fellhauer,** James Dale 1949- *WhoEnt 92*
**Fellin,** Octavia Antoinette 1913- *WhoWest 92*
**Felling,** Darrell Edward *WhoAmP 91*
**Felling,** Donna M *WhoAmP 91*
**Felling,** William E 1924- *AmMWSc 92*
**Fellinger,** L L 1915- *AmMWSc 92*
**Fellinger,** Robert C 1922- *AmMWSc 92*
**Fellingham,** David Andrew 1937- *WhoFI 92*
**Fellini,** Federico 1920- *FacFETw, IntDcF 2-2 [port], IntMPA 92, IntWW 91, Who 92*
**Fellman,** Arnold Charles 1943- *WhoMW 92*
**Fellman,** Daniel R. 1943- *IntMPA 92*
**Fellman,** Gerry Louis 1932- *WhoAmL 92*
**Fellman,** John Keegan 1952- *WhoWest 92*
**Fellman,** Nat D. 1910- *IntMPA 92*
**Fellman,** Richard Mayer 1935- *WhoAmP 91*
**Fellman,** Steven John 1938- *WhoAmL 92*
**Fellmann,** Robert Paul 1924- *AmMWSc 92*
**Fellner,** Baruch Abraham 1944- *WhoAmL 92*
**Fellner,** Fritz 1922- *IntWW 91*
**Fellner,** Michael Joseph 1949- *WhoMW 92*
**Fellner,** Peter John 1943- *Who 92*
**Fellner,** Susan K 1936- *AmMWSc 92*
**Fellner,** William Henry 1942- *AmMWSc 92*
**Fellowes** *Who 92*
**Fellowes,** Edmund H. 1870-1951 *NewAmDM*
**Fellowes,** Peter *DrAPF 91*
**Fellowes,** Robert 1941- *Who 92*
**Fellows,** Catherine *WrDr 92*
**Fellows,** Derek Edward 1927- *Who 92*
**Fellows,** Edith Marilyn 1923- *WhoEnt 92*
**Fellows,** Edward Frank 1930- *Who 92*
**Fellows,** George Wesley 1945- *WhoIns 92*
**Fellows,** Henry David, Jr. 1954- *WhoAmL 92*
**Fellows,** Jeffrey Keith 1940- *Who 92*
**Fellows,** John A 1906- *AmMWSc 92*
**Fellows,** John Staurt 1952- *WhoFI 92*
**Fellows,** John Walter 1938 *Who 92*
**Fellows,** Larry Dean 1934- *AmMWSc 92, WhoWest 92*
**Fellows,** Malcolm Stuart 1924- *IntAu&W 91*
**Fellows,** Robert Ellis, Jr 1933- *AmMWSc 92*
**Fellows,** Ward Jay 1913- *WhoRel 92*
**Fellrath,** Richard Frederic 1940- *WhoAmL 92*
**Fells,** Ian 1932- *Who 92*
**Fells,** Robert Marshall 1950- *WhoAmL 92*
**Felman,** James Evan 1962- *WhoAmL 92*
**Felman,** Yehudi M 1938- *AmMWSc 92*
**Felmlee,** William John 1930- *AmMWSc 92*
**Felmley,** Jerry John 1933- *WhoWest 92*
**Felos,** George James 1952- *WhoAmL 92*
**Felper,** David Michael 1954- *WhoAmL 92*
**Felrice,** Barry 1945- *WhoAmP 91*
**Fels,** Charles Wentworth Baker 1943- *WhoAmL 92*
**Fels,** James Alexander 1944- *WhoAmL 92*
**Fels,** Joseph 1853-1914 *DcNCBi 2*
**Fels,** Nicholas Wolff 1943- *WhoAmL 92*
**Fels,** Stephen Brook 1940- *AmMWSc 92*
**Felsen,** Leopold Benno 1924- *AmMWSc 92*
**Felsenfeld,** Carl 1927- *WhoAmL 92*
**Felsenfeld,** Gary 1929- *AmMWSc 92*
**Felsenstein,** Joseph 1942- *AmMWSc 92*
**Felsenthal,** Gerald 1941- *AmMWSc 92*
**Felsenthal,** Steven Altus 1949- *WhoAmL 92, WhoMW 92*
**Felsher,** Murray 1936- *AmMWSc 92*
**Felson,** Ethan Joseph 1965- *WhoRel 92*
**Felstein,** Ivor 1933- *WrDr 92*
**Felstiner,** William Lorell Franklin 1929- *WhoAmL 92, WhoMW 92*
**Felt,** James Patterson 1950- *WhoWest 92*
**Felt,** James Wright 1926- *WhoWest 92*
**Felt,** Rowland Earl 1936- *AmMWSc 92*
**Feltch,** Brent A 1931- *WhoAmP 91*
**Felten,** David L 1948- *AmMWSc 92*
**Felten,** James Edgar 1934- *AmMWSc 92*
**Felten,** John James 1937- *AmMWSc 92*
**Feltenstein,** Mary Belle 1947- *WhoAmL 92*
**Felter,** Jeffrey Bishop 1957- *WhoEnt 92*
**Felter,** John Kenneth 1950- *WhoFI 92*
**Felter,** Paul 1947- *WhoWest 92*
**Feltey,** Kathryn Margaret 1954- *WhoMW 92*
**Feltham,** Kerry Bonnycastle 1944- *WhoEnt 92*
**Feltham,** Lewellyn Allister Woodrow 1926- *AmMWSc 92*
**Feltham,** Robert Dean 1932- *AmMWSc 92*
**Felthouse,** Jack Calvin 1925- *WhoAmL 92*
**Felthouse,** Timothy R 1951- *AmMWSc 92*
**Felthouse,** Timothy Roy 1951- *WhoMW 92*
**Feltman,** Nancy J. *WhoWest 92*
**Feltman,** Reuben 1907- *AmMWSc 92*
**Feltner,** Kurt C 1931- *AmMWSc 92*
**Feltner-Kapornyai,** Daniel Kalman 1936- *WhoRel 92*
**Feltner-Kapornyai,** G. Raye 1945- *WhoRel 92*
**Felton,** Ann Shirey 1941- *WhoBlA 92*
**Felton,** B. *DrAPF 91*
**Felton,** Catherine 1916- *WhoRel 92*
**Felton,** Charles B 1936- *WhoAmP 91*
**Felton,** Deborah Jean 1949- *WhoMW 92*
**Felton,** Dorothy Wood 1929- *WhoAmP 91*
**Felton,** Guy Page, III 1937- *WhoFI 92*
**Felton,** James A. 1919- *WhoBlA 92*
**Felton,** James A. 1945- *WhoBlA 92*
**Felton,** James Edward, Jr. 1932- *WhoBlA 92*
**Felton,** James Steven 1945- *AmMWSc 92*
**Felton,** Jean Spencer 1911- *AmMWSc 92*
**Felton,** Jule Wimberly, Jr. 1932- *WhoAmL 92*
**Felton,** Kenneth E 1920- *AmMWSc 92*
**Felton,** Lewis P 1938- *AmMWSc 92*
**Felton,** Norman *LesBEnT 92*
**Felton,** Norman Francis 1913- *WhoEnt 92*
**Felton,** Otis Leverna 1946- *WhoBlA 92*
**Felton,** Rebecca Ann Latimer 1835-1930 *AmPeW*
**Felton,** Robert Stayton 1928- *WhoIns 92*
**Felton,** Ronald H 1938- *AmMWSc 92*
**Felton,** Samuel Page 1919- *AmMWSc 92, WhoWest 92*
**Felton,** Staley Lee 1920- *AmMWSc 92*
**Felton,** William Raymond 1956- *WhoAmL 92*
**Felton,** Zora Belle 1930- *WhoBlA 92*
**Felts,** Diana J. *DrAPF 91*
**Felts,** James Martin *AmMWSc 92*
**Felts,** John Harvey 1924- *AmMWSc 92*
**Felts,** John Pate 1951- *WhoFI 92*
**Felts,** Wayne Moore 1912- *AmMWSc 92*
**Felts,** William Joseph Lawrence 1924- *AmMWSc 92*
**Felts,** William Robert 1923- *AmMWSc 92*
**Felts,** William Robert, Jr. 1923- *IntWW 91*
**Feltsman,** Vladimir 1952- *FacFETw*
**Feltus,** James, Jr. 1921- *WhoBlA 92*
**Felty,** Evan J 1932- *AmMWSc 92*
**Felty,** Kriss Delbert 1954- *WhoAmL 92*
**Felty,** Wayne Lee 1943- *AmMWSc 92*
**Feltz,** Donald Everett 1933- *AmMWSc 92*
**Feltzin,** Joseph 1921- *AmMWSc 92*
**Felver,** Charles Stanley 1916- *WrDr 92*
**Felzenberg,** Leonard Jerome 1933- *WhoAmP 91*
**Felzer,** Jordan Wayne 1958- *WhoAmL 92*
**Feman,** Stephen Sosin 1940- *AmMWSc 92*
**Femenia,** Jose 1942- *AmMWSc 92*
**Femino,** Jim 1952- *WhoEnt 92*
**Femling,** Jean *DrAPF 91*
**Femminella,** Charles J., Jr. 1938- *WhoFI 92*
**Fenady,** Andrew J. 1928- *IntMPA 92*
**Fenburr,** Herbert L 1913- *AmMWSc 92*
**Fenby,** Eric 1906- *WrDr 92*
**Fenby,** Eric William 1906- *IntWW 91, Who 92*
**Fenchak,** Richard *WhoRel 92*
**Fenchel,** Tom Michael 1940- *IntWW 91*
**Fencl,** Vladimir *AmMWSc 92*
**Fendall,** Neville Rex Edwards 1917- *IntWW 91, Who 92*
**Fendall,** Roger K 1935- *AmMWSc 92*
**Fendel,** Daniel 1946- *AmMWSc 92*
**Fendelman,** Burton M 1937- *WhoAmL 92*
**Fender,** Brian Edward Frederick 1934- *IntWW 91, Who 92*
**Fender,** Clarence Leo *NewAmDM*
**Fender,** Clarence Leo d1991 *NewYTBS 91 [port]*
**Fender,** Derek Henry 1918- *AmMWSc 92*
**Fender,** Freddy 1936- *NewAmDM*
**Fender,** Freddy 1937- *WhoEnt 92, WhoHisp 92*
**Fender,** Leo 1909-1991 *News 92-1*
**Fender,** P G H 1892-1985 *FacFETw*
**Fenderson,** Bruce Andrew 1952- *AmMWSc 92*
**Fendick,** Thomas J. 1959- *WhoAmL 92*
**Fendler,** Augustus 1813-1883 *BiInAmS*
**Fendler,** Eleanor Johnson 1939- *AmMWSc 92*
**Fendler,** Janos Hugo 1937- *AmMWSc 92*
**Fendler,** Oscar 1909- *WhoAmL 92, WhoAmP 91*
**Fendler,** Paul Bernard 1962- *WhoMW 92*
**Fendley,** Ted Wyatt 1939- *AmMWSc 92*
**Fendrich,** Roger Paul 1943- *WhoAmL 92*
**Fenech,** Henri J 1925- *AmMWSc 92*
**Fenech,** Joseph Charles 1950- *WhoAmL 92*
**Fenech-Adami,** Edward 1934- *IntWW 91, Who 92*
**Fenelon,** Francois DeSalignac DeLaMothe 1651-1715 *BlkwCEP*
**Feneon,** Felix 1861-1944 *ThHEIm*
**Fenerty,** Laurie Donald 1936- *WhoRel 92*
**Feng Depei** 1906- *IntWW 91*
**Feng Duan** 1923- *IntWW 91*
**Feng He** 1931- *IntWW 91*
**Feng Jinsong** 1934- *IntWW 91*
**Feng Jinwen** 1924- *IntWW 91*
**Feng Jixin** *IntWW 91*
**Feng Kang** 1920- *IntWW 91*
**Feng Lanrui** 1920- *IntWW 91*
**Feng Wenbin** 1911- *IntWW 91*
**Feng Zhi** 1905- *LiExTwC*
**Feng,** Albert Shih-Hung *AmMWSc 92*
**Feng,** Anita N. *DrAPF 91*
**Feng,** Chuan C D 1922- *AmMWSc 92*

**Feng,** Da-Fei *AmMWSc 92*
**Feng,** Da Hsuan *AmMWSc 92*
**Feng,** Joseph Shao-Ying *AmMWSc 92*
**Feng,** Joseph Shao-Ying 1948- *WhoWest 92*
**Feng,** Lingzhi 1940- *IntAu&W 91*
**Feng,** Paul Yen-Hsiung 1926- *AmMWSc 92*
**Feng,** Rong 1962- *AmMWSc 92*
**Feng,** Sung Yen 1929- *AmMWSc 92*
**Feng,** Theo-dric 1953- *WhoEnt 92*
**Feng,** Tse-yun 1928- *AmMWSc 92*
**Feng,** Youlan d1990 *IntWW 91N*
**Fenger,** Joan Cruff 1927- *WhoAmP 91*
**Fenger Moller,** Grethe 1941- *IntWW 91*
**Fengler,** John Peter 1928- *WhoEnt 92*
**Fenhagen,** James Corner 1929- *WhoRel 92*
**Fenhalls,** Richard Dorian 1943- *Who 92*
**Fenichel,** Gerald M 1935- *AmMWSc 92*
**Fenichel,** Henry 1938- *AmMWSc 92, WhoMW 92*
**Fenichel,** Jay Steven 1954- *WhoEnt 92*
**Fenichel,** Norman Stewart 1924- *WhoFI 92*
**Fenichel,** Richard Lee 1925- *AmMWSc 92*
**Feniger,** Jerome Roland, Jr. 1927- *WhoEnt 92*
**Feniger,** Siegmund *WrDr 92*
**Fenimore,** David Clarke 1930- *AmMWSc 92*
**Fenimore,** Jeffrey Scott 1963- *WhoMW 92*
**Fenlason,** Edward James 1937- *WhoRel 92*
**Fenlon,** Jack 1940- *WhoAmP 91*
**Fenn,** Charles 1907- *IntAu&W 91, WrDr 92*
**Fenn,** Dan Huntington, Jr 1923- *WhoAmP 91*
**Fenn,** Douglas Roydon 1957- *WhoEnt 92*
**Fenn,** H N 1907- *AmMWSc 92*
**Fenn,** Ingemund 1907- *IntWW 91*
**Fenn,** John Bennett 1917- *AmMWSc 92*
**Fenn,** Nicholas 1936- *Who 92*
**Fenn,** Nicholas M. 1936- *IntWW 91*
**Fenn,** Ormon William, Jr. 1927- *WhoFI 92*
**Fenn,** Robert William, III 1941- *AmMWSc 92*
**Fenna,** Roger Edward 1947- *AmMWSc 92*
**Fennario,** David *WrDr 92*
**Fennario,** David 1947- *IntAu&W 91*
**Fennebresque,** Kim Samuel 1950- *WhoFI 92*
**Fennel,** Ron *WhoAmP 91*
**Fennel,** William Edward 1923- *AmMWSc 92*
**Fennell,** Christine Elizabeth 1948- *WhoWest 92*
**Fennell,** Christopher Connor 1961- *WhoAmL 92*
**Fennell,** Desmond 1933- *Who 92*
**Fennell,** Diane Marie 1944- *WhoFI 92, WhoWest 92*
**Fennell,** Frederick 1914- *NewAmDM*
**Fennell,** Hazel 1936- *TwCPaSc*
**Fennell,** John Allison 1928- *WhoRel 92*
**Fennell,** John Lister Illingworth 1918- *IntAu&W 91, Who 92, WrDr 92*
**Fennell,** Peter Edward 1954- *WhoIns 92*
**Fennell,** Robert E 1942- *AmMWSc 92*
**Fennell,** Thomas E. 1950- *WhoAmL 92*
**Fennell,** Thomas F., II d1991 *NewYTBS 91*
**Fennelly,** Brian 1937- *NewAmDM*
**Fennelly,** Brian Leo 1937- *WhoEnt 92*
**Fennelly,** Jane Corey 1942- *WhoAmL 92*
**Fennelly,** Paul Francis 1945- *AmMWSc 92*
**Fennelly,** Tony 1945- *IntAu&W 91*
**Fennelly,** Vincent M. *LesBEnT 92*
**Fennelly,** Vincent M. 1920- *IntMPA 92*
**Fennema,** Owen Richard 1929- *AmMWSc 92*
**Fenneman,** George 1919- *IntMPA 92*
**Fenneman,** George Watt 1919- *WhoEnt 92*
**Fenner,** Carol 1929- *IntAu&W 91, WrDr 92*
**Fenner,** Derrick Steven 1967- *WhoBlA 92*
**Fenner,** Donald Dean 1929- *WhoRel 92*
**Fenner,** Frank John 1914- *IntWW 91, Who 92, WrDr 92*
**Fenner,** Gary Eugene 1954- *WhoRel 92*
**Fenner,** Heinrich 1924- *AmMWSc 92*
**Fenner,** James R *IntAu&W 91X, WrDr 92*
**Fenner,** Peggy 1922- *Who 92*
**Fenner,** Peter 1937- *AmMWSc 92*
**Fenner,** Rachel 1939- *TwCPaSc*
**Fenner,** Renee Lynette 1954- *WhoEnt 92*
**Fenner,** Richard d1766? *DcNCBi 2*
**Fenner,** Richard 1758-1828 *DcNCBi 2*
**Fenner,** Robert 1755?-1816 *DcNCBi 2*
**Fenner,** Roger T. 1943- *WrDr 92*
**Fenner,** Wayne Robert 1939- *AmMWSc 92*
**Fenner-Crisp,** Penelope Ann 1939- *AmMWSc 92*
**Fennessey,** Paul V 1942- *AmMWSc 92*
**Fennessy,** Edward 1912- *Who 92*
**Fennessy,** John James 1933- *AmMWSc 92, WhoMW 92*
**Fennessy,** Marsha Beach Stewart 1952- *WhoEnt 92*
**Fennewald,** Michael Andrew 1951- *AmMWSc 92*
**Fenney,** Nicholas William 1906- *AmMWSc 92*
**Fenney,** Roger Johnson 1916- *Who 92*
**Fenning,** Lisa Hill 1952- *WhoAmL 92, WhoWest 92*
**Fenno,** James Robert 1943- *WhoMW 92*
**Fenno,** Nathan R. 1958- *WhoAmL 92*
**Fenoglio,** Cecilia M 1943- *AmMWSc 92*
**Fenoglio,** Richard Andrew 1941- *AmMWSc 92*
**Fenollosa,** Ernest F. 1853-1908 *BenetAL 91*
**Fenrich,** Richard Karl 1962- *AmMWSc 92*
**Fenrick,** Harold William 1935- *AmMWSc 92*
**Fenrick,** Maureen Helen 1946- *AmMWSc 92*
**Fenselau,** Allan Herman 1937- *AmMWSc 92*
**Fenselau,** Catherine Clarke 1939- *AmMWSc 92*
**Fenske,** Alfred 1934- *WhoMW 92*
**Fenske,** George R *AmMWSc 92*
**Fenske,** Jerald Allan 1960- *WhoRel 92*
**Fenske,** Paul Roderick 1925- *AmMWSc 92*
**Fensom,** David Strathern 1916- *AmMWSc 92*
**Fenster,** Aaron 1947- *AmMWSc 92*
**Fenster,** Frederic Michael 1943- *WhoFI 92*
**Fenster,** Herbert Lawrence 1935- *WhoAmL 92*
**Fenster,** Robert David 1946- *WhoAmL 92*
**Fenster,** Saul K 1933- *AmMWSc 92*
**Fenstermacher,** Charles Alvin 1928- *AmMWSc 92, WhoWest 92*
**Fenstermacher,** Joseph Don 1934- *AmMWSc 92*
**Fenstermacher,** Robert Lane 1941- *AmMWSc 92*
**Fenstermaker,** Perry Molan 1926- *WhoWest 92*
**Fenstermaker,** Roger William 1942- *AmMWSc 92*
**Fenstermaker,** Vesle *DrAPF 91*
**Fensterstock,** Blair Courtney 1950- *WhoIns 92*
**Fensterwald,** Bernard, Jr. 1921-1991 *NewYTBS 91*
**Fentem,** Peter Harold 1933- *Who 92*
**Fenter,** Felix West 1926- *AmMWSc 92*
**Fenter,** Randy Lynn 1953- *WhoRel 92*
**Fenters,** James Dean 1936- *AmMWSc 92, WhoMW 92*
**Fentiman,** Allison Foulds, Jr 1937- *AmMWSc 92*
**Fenton,** Alexander 1929- *IntWW 91, Who 92*
**Fenton,** Bruce Stuart 1946- *WhoFI 92*
**Fenton,** Charles E. *WhoAmL 92*
**Fenton,** D. X. 1932- *WrDr 92*
**Fenton,** David George 1932- *AmMWSc 92*
**Fenton,** Donald Mason 1929- *AmMWSc 92, WhoWest 92*
**Fenton,** Edward 1917- *ConAu 34NR, IntAu&W 91, WrDr 92*
**Fenton,** Edward Warren 1937- *AmMWSc 92*
**Fenton,** Elaine Poliakoff 1948- *WhoAmL 92*
**Fenton,** George *ConTFT 9*
**Fenton,** Harold Arthur 1909- *Who 92*
**Fenton,** Howard Nathan, III 1950- *WhoMW 92*
**Fenton,** Isabelle B 1922- *WhoAmP 91*
**Fenton,** James 1949- *ConPo 91, WrDr 92*
**Fenton,** James J 1925- *WhoAmP 91*
**Fenton,** James Martin 1949- *IntAu&W 91, Who 92*
**Fenton,** John Charles 1921- *Who 92, WrDr 92*
**Fenton,** John William, II 1939- *AmMWSc 92*
**Fenton,** Julia *ConAu 135*
**Fenton,** Kathryn Marie 1953- *WhoAmL 92*
**Fenton,** M Brock 1943- *AmMWSc 92*
**Fenton,** Marilyn Ruth 1942- *AmMWSc 92*
**Fenton,** Mark *IntAu&W 91X*
**Fenton,** Mary Jo 1928- *WhoAmP 91*
**Fenton,** Matthew John 1954- *AmMWSc 92*
**Fenton,** Priscilla Jane 1947- *WhoWest 92*
**Fenton,** Robert E 1933- *AmMWSc 92*
**Fenton,** Robert George 1931- *AmMWSc 92*
**Fenton,** Robert L. 1929- *ConAu 135*
**Fenton,** Robert S. 1949- *WhoAmL 92*
**Fenton,** Stuart William 1922- *AmMWSc 92*
**Fenton,** Thomas Conner 1954- *WhoAmL 92*
**Fenton,** Thomas E 1933- *AmMWSc 92*
**Fenton,** Thomas Eugene 1933- *WhoMW 92*
**Fenton,** Wayne Alexander 1945- *AmMWSc 92*
**Fentress,** John Carroll 1939- *AmMWSc 92*
**Fentress,** Robert H. 1921- *WhoBlA 92*
**Fentress,** Shirley B. 1937- *WhoBlA 92*
**Fenves,** Steven J 1931- *AmMWSc 92*
**Fenwick,** Catherine 1955- *TwCPaSc*
**Fenwick,** Charles Ghequiere 1880-1973 *AmPeW*
**Fenwick,** Elizabeth 1920- *WrDr 92*
**Fenwick,** Gary Lindel 1943- *WhoWest 92*
**Fenwick,** Harry 1922- *AmMWSc 92*
**Fenwick,** Ian 1941- *IntAu&W 91, WrDr 92*
**Fenwick,** James Clarke 1940- *AmMWSc 92*
**Fenwick,** Jeffery Robert 1930- *Who 92*
**Fenwick,** John James 1932- *Who 92*
**Fenwick,** Millicent 1910- *IntWW 91*
**Fenwick,** Millicent Hammond 1910- *WhoAmP 91*
**Fenwick,** Robert B 1936- *AmMWSc 92*
**Fenyes,** Joseph Gabriel Egon 1925- *AmMWSc 92*
**Fenyves,** Ervin J 1924- *AmMWSc 92*
**Fenyves,** Lorand 1918- *NewAmDM*
**Fenyves,** Marta *DrAPF 91*
**Fenzl,** Terry Earle 1945- *WhoAmL 92*
**Feola,** Jose Maria 1926- *AmMWSc 92*
**Feola,** Mario *AmMWSc 92*
**Fer,** Ahmet Ferit *WhoMW 92*
**Feraca,** Jean *DrAPF 91*
**Feraday,** Melville Albert 1929- *AmMWSc 92*
**Feramisco,** James Robert 1952- *AmMWSc 92*
**Feran,** Russell G. 1948- *WhoFI 92*
**Ferbel,** Thomas 1937- *AmMWSc 92*
**Ferber,** Al *DrAPF 91*
**Ferber,** Edna 1885-1968 *FacFETw [port], HanAmWH, TwCWW 91*
**Ferber,** Edna 1887-1968 *BenetAL 91*
**Ferber,** Herbert 1906-1991 *CurBio 91N, NewYTBS 91*
**Ferber,** Kelvin Halket 1910- *AmMWSc 92*
**Ferber,** Mel *LesBEnT 92*
**Ferber,** Norman Alan 1948- *WhoWest 92*
**Ferber,** Robert R 1935- *AmMWSc 92*
**Ferber,** Robert Rudolf 1935- *WhoWest 92*
**Ferchau,** Hugo Alfred 1929- *AmMWSc 92*
**Ferchaud,** John B 1912- *AmMWSc 92*
**Ferden,** Bruce 1949- *WhoEnt 92*
**Ferder,** John Edward 1961- *WhoEnt 92*
**Ferderber-Hersonski,** Boris Constantin 1943- *WhoFI 92*
**Ferdig,** Sue Harford 1940- *WhoWest 92*
**Ferdinand I** 1861-1948 *FacFETw*
**Ferdinand VI** 1712-1759 *HisDSpE*
**Ferdinand VII** 1783-1833 *HisDSpE*
**Ferdinand of Aragon** 1452-1516 *HisDSpE*
**Ferdinand,** Keith C. 1950- *WhoBlA 92*
**Ferdinand,** Larry 1947- *WhoAmP 91*
**Ferdinandi,** Eckhardt Stevan *AmMWSc 92*
**Ferdinandov,** Boris Alekseevich 1889-1959 *SovUnBD*
**Ferdman,** Alejandro Jose 1962- *WhoHisp 92*
**Ferdon,** Edwin Nelson, Jr. 1913- *WhoWest 92*
**Ferdon,** Julie 1950- *WhoAmP 91*
**FerDon,** Lee Monroe 1942- *WhoRel 92*
**Ferdowsi,** Abdollah 1951- *WhoMW 92*
**Ferdun,** Gareth Stanley 1937- *WhoWest 92*
**Fereaud-Farber,** Zulima V. 1944- *WhoHisp 92*
**Ferebee,** Claude T., Sr. 1901- *WhoBlA 92*
**Ferebee,** Dennis Dozier 1815-1884 *DcNCBi 2*
**Ferebee,** Dorothy Boulding 1890-1980 *NotBlAW 92*
**Ferebee,** John Spencer, Jr. 1947- *WhoFI 92*
**Ferebee,** Percy Bell 1891-1970 *DcNCBi 2*
**Feren,** David *DrAPF 91*
**Ferenbach,** Carl, III 1942- *WhoFI 92*
**Ference,** Helen Marie 1946- *WhoWest 92*
**Ference,** Michael, Jr 1911- *AmMWSc 92*
**Ferencsik,** Janos 1907-1984 *FacFETw, NewAmDM*
**Ferencz,** Charlotte 1921- *AmMWSc 92*
**Ferencz,** Nicholas 1937- *AmMWSc 92*
**Ferencz,** Robert Arnold 1946- *WhoAmL 92*
**Ferenczi,** Ronald James 1950- *WhoFI 92, WhoMW 92*
**Ferenczy,** Oto 1921- *IntWW 91*
**Ferens,** Thomas 1903- *Who 92*
**Ferensztajn,** Bogumil 1934- *IntWW 91*
**Ferentz,** Melvin 1928- *AmMWSc 92*
**Ferer,** Kenneth Michael 1937- *AmMWSc 92*
**Ferere,** Gerard Alphonse 1930- *WhoBlA 92*
**Fergani,** Yacine 1946- *IntWW 91*
**Fergerson,** Mable 1955- *BlkOlyM*
**Fergerson,** Miriam N. 1941- *WhoBlA 92*
**Fergin,** Richard Kenneth 1933- *AmMWSc 92*
**Fergus,** Gary Scott 1954- *WhoWest 92*
**Fergus,** James d1989 *Who 92N*
**Fergus,** John 1741-1802 *DcNCBi 2*
**Fergus,** Patricia Marguerita 1918- *WhoMW 92*
**Fergus,** Scott C *WhoAmP 91*
**Ferguson,** Adam 1723-1816 *BlkwCEP*
**Ferguson,** Adlai Cleveland, Jr. 1919- *WhoMW 92*
**Ferguson,** Alastair Victor 1955- *AmMWSc 92*
**Ferguson,** Albert Barnett 1919- *AmMWSc 92*
**Ferguson,** Albert Hayden 1928- *AmMWSc 92*
**Ferguson,** Alexander Cunningham *AmMWSc 92*
**Ferguson,** Allen Richmond 1919- *WhoFI 92*
**Ferguson,** Andrew L. *WhoBlA 92*
**Ferguson,** Anita Perez *WhoHisp 92*
**Ferguson,** Benny Winfield 1944- *WhoRel 92*
**Ferguson,** Bradford Lee 1947- *WhoAmL 92*
**Ferguson,** Bruce Alan 1956- *WhoFI 92*
**Ferguson,** Bruce W. 1954- *WhoAmL 92*
**Ferguson,** C Alan 1940- *WhoIns 92*
**Ferguson,** C. David *IntWW 91*
**Ferguson,** C. E. 1928-1972 *ConAu 134*
**Ferguson,** Catherine 1779?-1854 *NotBlAW 92*
**Ferguson,** Cecil 1931- *WhoBlA 92*
**Ferguson,** Charles W 1927- *WhoAmP 91*
**Ferguson,** Colin C 1921- *AmMWSc 92*
**Ferguson,** Dale Curtis 1948- *AmMWSc 92*
**Ferguson,** Dale E 1922- *WhoAmP 91*
**Ferguson,** Dale Vernon 1943- *AmMWSc 92*
**Ferguson,** Dallas Eugene 1945- *WhoAmL 92*
**Ferguson,** David B 1926- *AmMWSc 92*
**Ferguson,** David James 1947- *WhoFI 92, WhoWest 92*
**Ferguson,** David John 1939- *AmMWSc 92*
**Ferguson,** David L. 1947- *WhoRel 92*
**Ferguson,** David Lawrence 1949- *AmMWSc 92*
**Ferguson,** Dennis J *WhoAmP 91*
**Ferguson,** Dennis Lorne 1950- *WhoHisp 92*
**Ferguson,** Derek Talmar 1965- *WhoBlA 92*
**Ferguson,** Donald John 1916- *AmMWSc 92*
**Ferguson,** Donald Leon 1930- *AmMWSc 92*
**Ferguson,** Douglas Edward 1940- *WhoFI 92*
**Ferguson,** Earl J 1925- *AmMWSc 92*
**Ferguson,** Earl Wilson 1943- *AmMWSc 92*
**Ferguson,** Edward A., Jr. 1942- *WhoBlA 92*
**Ferguson,** Edward C, III 1926- *AmMWSc 92*
**Ferguson,** Elliott LaRoy, II 1965- *WhoBlA 92*
**Ferguson,** Ernest Alexander 1917- *Who 92*
**Ferguson,** Eugene Gaylord 1914- *WhoEnt 92*
**Ferguson,** Everett 1933- *WrDr 92*
**Ferguson,** Fred Ernest, Jr. 1935- *WhoAmL 92*
**Ferguson,** Frederick Palmer 1916- *AmMWSc 92*
**Ferguson,** G. Alan 1947- *WhoAmL 92*
**Ferguson,** Garland Sevier, Jr. 1878-1963 *DcNCBi 2*
**Ferguson,** Gary Gene 1940- *AmMWSc 92*
**Ferguson,** Gary Gilbert 1941- *AmMWSc 92*
**Ferguson,** Gary Jack 1943- *WhoIns 92*
**Ferguson,** George A. 1923- *WhoBlA 92*
**Ferguson,** George Alonzo 1923- *AmMWSc 92*
**Ferguson,** George E 1906- *AmMWSc 92*
**Ferguson,** George Ray 1915- *AmMWSc 92*
**Ferguson,** George Robert, Jr 1933- *WhoAmP 91*
**Ferguson,** George W *WhoIns 92*
**Ferguson,** Gerald Paul 1951- *WhoAmL 92*
**Ferguson,** Gil 1923- *WhoAmP 91*
**Ferguson,** Glenn Walker 1929- *IntWW 91*
**Ferguson,** Harley Bascum 1875-1968 *DcNCBi 2*
**Ferguson,** Harley Robert 1936- *WhoFI 92*
**Ferguson,** Harold Allen, Jr. 1960- *WhoMW 92*
**Ferguson,** Harry 1914- *AmMWSc 92*
**Ferguson,** Harry Ian Symons 1920- *AmMWSc 92*
**Ferguson,** Helaman Rolfe Pratt 1940- *AmMWSc 92*
**Ferguson,** Herman White 1916- *AmMWSc 92*
**Ferguson,** Holly Anne 1953- *WhoEnt 92*
**Ferguson,** Howard 1908- *ConCom 92*
**Ferguson,** Hugh Carson 1921- *AmMWSc 92*
**Ferguson,** Idell *WhoBlA 92*
**Ferguson,** Isaac Clyde 1943- *WhoRel 92*
**Ferguson,** Jacqueline Ann 1950- *WhoWest 92*
**Ferguson,** James 1710-1776 *BlkwCEP*
**Ferguson,** James 1797-1867 *BiInAmS*
**Ferguson,** James Brown Provan 1935- *Who 92*

**Ferguson,** James E 1946- WhoAmP 91
**Ferguson,** James Edward 1871-1944 FacFETw
**Ferguson,** James Elliot, II 1942- WhoAmL 92
**Ferguson,** James Homer 1936- AmMWSc 92
**Ferguson,** James Joseph, Jr 1926- AmMWSc 92
**Ferguson,** James Kenneth Wallace 1907- AmMWSc 92
**Ferguson,** James L. 1926- IntWW 91
**Ferguson,** James L 1947- AmMWSc 92
**Ferguson,** James Malcolm 1931- AmMWSc 92
**Ferguson,** James Mecham 1941- AmMWSc 92
**Ferguson,** James Peter 1937- WhoFI 92
**Ferguson,** James Phillip 1958- WhoAmP 91
**Ferguson,** James Warner 1950- WhoEnt 92
**Ferguson,** Jay A. 1947- WhoEnt 92
**Ferguson,** Jay Preston 1946- WhoEnt 92
**Ferguson,** Jeffrey William 1948- WhoMW 92
**Ferguson,** John Alexander 1927- Who 92
**Ferguson,** John Allen 1941- WhoEnt 92
**Ferguson,** John Allen 1945- AmMWSc 92
**Ferguson,** John Barclay 1947- AmMWSc 92
**Ferguson,** John Carruthers 1937- AmMWSc 92
**Ferguson,** John Charles, Jr 1938- WhoAmP 91
**Ferguson,** John Fredrick 1932- WhoWest 92
**Ferguson,** John Howard 1902- AmMWSc 92
**Ferguson,** John McIntyre 1915- Who 92
**Ferguson,** Johnnie Nathaniel 1943- WhoBlA 92
**Ferguson,** Joseph DrAPF 91
**Ferguson,** Joseph Gantt 1921- AmMWSc 92
**Ferguson,** Joseph Luther, Jr 1941- AmMWSc 92
**Ferguson,** Karen Anne 1942- AmMWSc 92
**Ferguson,** Kaye Irene 1939- WhoMW 92
**Ferguson,** Keith Tyrone 1959- WhoBlA 92
**Ferguson,** Ken 1937- TwCPaSc
**Ferguson,** Kenneth Alan 1953- WhoRel 92
**Ferguson,** Laing 1935- AmMWSc 92
**Ferguson,** Larry R 1937- WhoAmP 91
**Ferguson,** Lawrence J 1946- WhoAmP 91
**Ferguson,** Le Baron O 1939- AmMWSc 92
**Ferguson,** Leonard Price 1951- WhoFI 92
**Ferguson,** Leslie Lee, Jr. 1940- WhoWest 92
**Ferguson,** Lewis Hamilton, III 1944- WhoAmL 92
**Ferguson,** Lloyd Elbert 1942- WhoWest 92
**Ferguson,** Lloyd N. 1918- WhoBlA 92
**Ferguson,** Lloyd Noel 1918- AmMWSc 92
**Ferguson,** M. Dwight 1933- WhoRel 92
**Ferguson,** Malcolm James 1960- WhoFI 92
**Ferguson,** Malcolm Stuart 1908- AmMWSc 92
**Ferguson,** Marion Lee 1923- AmMWSc 92
**Ferguson,** Mary Hobson 1927- AmMWSc 92
**Ferguson,** Maynard 1928- ConMus 7 [port], FacFETw, NewAmDM, WhoEnt 92
**Ferguson,** Michael Charles 1943- WhoAmL 92
**Ferguson,** Michael John 1941- AmMWSc 92
**Ferguson,** Michael William 1947- AmMWSc 92
**Ferguson,** Milton WhoRel 92
**Ferguson,** Milton Carr, Jr. 1931- WhoAmL 92
**Ferguson,** Miriam A 1875-1961 FacFETw
**Ferguson,** Neil Edward J. Who 92
**Ferguson,** Noel Moore 1907- AmMWSc 92
**Ferguson,** Norman Wayne 1933- WhoRel 92
**Ferguson,** Pamela A 1943- AmMWSc 92
**Ferguson,** Pamela Anderson 1943- WhoMW 92
**Ferguson,** Paul 1943- IntWW 91
**Ferguson,** Peter 1933- WrDr 92
**Ferguson,** Ralph 1955- WhoBlA 92
**Ferguson,** Raymond Craig 1922- AmMWSc 92
**Ferguson,** Renee 1949- WhoBlA 92
**Ferguson,** Richard 1935- Who 92
**Ferguson,** Richard Oliver 1962- WhoFI 92
**Ferguson,** Robert DcNCBi 2
**Ferguson,** Robert 1948- ConAu 135
**Ferguson,** Robert A. WhoAmL 92
**Ferguson,** Robert Bury 1920- AmMWSc 92
**Ferguson,** Robert Carmel 1938- WhoRel 92
**Ferguson,** Robert Ernest 1937- WhoAmP 91
**Ferguson,** Robert Lee, Sr. 1932- WhoBlA 92
**Ferguson,** Robert Lynn 1932- AmMWSc 92
**Ferguson,** Robert Nicholas 1944- AmMWSc 92
**Ferguson,** Robert R., III WhoFI 92
**Ferguson,** Roger K 1937- AmMWSc 92
**Ferguson,** Ronald 1939- ConAu 134
**Ferguson,** Ronald E 1942- WhoIns 92
**Ferguson,** Ronald James 1939- AmMWSc 92
**Ferguson,** Ronald M AmMWSc 92
**Ferguson,** Rosetta 1920- WhoBlA 92
**Ferguson,** Roy A WhoAmP 91
**Ferguson,** Ruth H 1895- WhoAmP 91
**Ferguson,** Samuel 1810-1886 NinCLC 33 [port], RfGEnL 91
**Ferguson,** Sarah 1959- ConAu 135, SmATA 66 [port]
**Ferguson,** Sharon Hermine 1953- WhoMW 92
**Ferguson,** Shellie Alvin 1943- WhoBlA 92
**Ferguson,** Sherlon Lee 1949- WhoBlA 92
**Ferguson,** Sherman E. 1944- WhoBlA 92
**Ferguson,** Shirley Martha 1923- AmMWSc 92
**Ferguson,** St. Julian 1935- WhoBlA 92
**Ferguson,** Stephen Mason 1939- AmMWSc 92
**Ferguson,** Susan Katharine Stover 1944- WhoMW 92
**Ferguson,** Tee 1950- WhoAmP 91
**Ferguson,** Thomas 1921- AmMWSc 92
**Ferguson,** Thomas Edward 1928- WhoAmP 91
**Ferguson,** Thomas Lee 1942- AmMWSc 92
**Ferguson,** Thomas S 1929- AmMWSc 92
**Ferguson,** Tim Wayne 1955- WhoFI 92
**Ferguson,** Ward P 1931- WhoAmP 91
**Ferguson,** Warren John 1920- WhoAmL 92, WhoWest 92
**Ferguson,** Whitworth, III 1954- WhoAmL 92
**Ferguson,** Wilfred 1917- WhoAmP 91
**Ferguson,** Wilkie Demeritte, Jr. 1939- WhoBlA 92
**Ferguson,** William DrAPF 91
**Ferguson,** William Allen 1917- AmMWSc 92
**Ferguson,** William Charles 1930- WhoFI 92
**Ferguson,** William Davidson, Jr. 1961- WhoMW 92
**Ferguson,** William Duncan 1953- WhoMW 92
**Ferguson,** William E 1921- AmMWSc 92
**Ferguson,** William Everett 1933- WhoRel 92
**Ferguson,** William Sidney 1927- AmMWSc 92
**Ferguson,** William Warren 1940- WhoAmL 92
**Ferguson Davie,** Antony 1952- Who 92
**Ferguson-Miller,** Shelagh Mary 1942- AmMWSc 92
**Ferguson-Smith,** Malcolm Andrew 1931- IntWW 91, Who 92
**Fergusson,** Adam 1932- Who 92
**Fergusson,** Ewen Alastair John 1932- IntWW 91, Who 92
**Fergusson,** Harvey 1890-1971 BenetAL 91, TwCWW 91
**Fergusson,** J.D. 1874-1961 TwCPaSc
**Fergusson,** James David d1991 Who 92N
**Fergusson,** James H. H. C. Who 92
**Fergusson,** Robert 1750-1774 DcLB 109 [port], RfGEnL 91
**Fergusson,** Robert George 1911- WhoWest 92
**Fergusson,** William Blake 1924- AmMWSc 92
**Fergusson of Kilkerran,** Charles 1931- Who 92
**Feria,** Abraham H. 1946- WhoHisp 92
**Feria,** Floridano 1937- WhoHisp 92
**Fericano,** Paul DrAPF 91
**Ferin,** Juraj AmMWSc 92
**Feringa,** Earl Robert 1932- AmMWSc 92
**Ferington,** Thomas Edwin 1926- AmMWSc 92
**Ferino,** Christopher Kenneth 1961- WhoFI 92, WhoMW 92
**Ferkingstad,** Susanne M. 1955- WhoMW 92
**Ferko,** Andrew Paul 1942- AmMWSc 92
**Ferl,** Robert Joseph 1954- AmMWSc 92
**Ferlan,** Arthur 1922- WhoAmP 91
**Ferland,** E. James 1942- WhoFI 92
**Ferland,** Gary Joseph 1951- AmMWSc 92
**Ferlinghetti,** Lawrence DrAPF 91
**Ferlinghetti,** Lawrence 1919- BenetAL 91, ConPo 91, CurBio 91 [port], FacFETw, IntAu&W 91
**Ferlinghetti,** Lawrence 1920- IntWW 91, WrDr 92
**Ferlinz,** Jack 1942- WhoMW 92
**Ferlita,** Ernest 1927- WrDr 92
**Ferlita,** Ernest Charles 1927- IntAu&W 91
**Ferlo,** Joseph Anthony 1959- WhoEnt 92
**Ferm,** Anders 1938- IntWW 91
**Ferm,** Deane William 1927- WhoRel 92
**Ferm,** John Charles 1925- AmMWSc 92
**Ferm,** Lois Roughan 1918- WhoRel 92
**Ferm,** Richard L 1924- AmMWSc 92
**Ferm,** Robert Livingston 1931- WhoRel 92
**Ferm,** Vergil Harkness 1924- AmMWSc 92
**Ferman,** Irving 1919- WhoAmL 92, WhoFI 92
**Ferman,** James Alan 1930- Who 92
**Fermi,** Enrico 1901-1954 FacFETw [port], WhoNob 90
**Fermi,** Giulio 1936- AmMWSc 92
**Fermin,** Cesar Danilo AmMWSc 92
**Fermin,** Felix Jose 1963- WhoHisp 92
**Fermor,** Patrick Michael Leigh 1915- Who 92
**Fermor-Hesketh** Who 92
**Fermoso Garcia,** Julio 1948- IntWW 91
**Fermoy,** Baron 1967- Who 92
**Fermoy,** Dowager Lady 1908- Who 92
**Fern,** Fanny BenetAL 91
**Fern,** Raymond Joseph 1940- WhoMW 92
**Fernald,** Arthur Thomas 1917- AmMWSc 92
**Fernald,** Chester Bailey 1869-1938 BenetAL 91
**Fernald,** Russell Dawson 1941- AmMWSc 92
**Fernan,** Mary Brigid 1958- WhoAmL 92
**Fernandes,** Angelo Who 92
**Fernandes,** Angelo Innocent 1913- IntWW 91
**Fernandes,** Daniel James 1948- AmMWSc 92
**Fernandes,** Gabriel 1936- AmMWSc 92
**Fernandes,** Gaspar 1570?-1629 NewAmDM
**Fernandes,** George 1930- IntWW 91
**Fernandes,** John Henry 1924- AmMWSc 92
**Fernandes,** Lehua 1949- WhoHisp 92
**Fernandes,** Pedro Infante 1957- WhoHisp 92
**Fernandes,** Prabhavathi Bhat 1949- AmMWSc 92
**Fernandes,** Simon 1538?-1600? DcNCBi 2
**Fernandes Salling,** Lehua 1949- WhoAmP 91
**Fernandez,** Abel A. 1952- WhoHisp 92
**Fernandez,** Adolfo, Jr 1951- WhoAmP 91, WhoHisp 92
**Fernandez,** Albert Bades WhoHisp 92
**Fernandez,** Alberto Antonio 1925- AmMWSc 92
**Fernandez,** Alberto Miguel 1958- WhoHisp 92
**Fernandez,** Alex 1969- WhoHisp 92
**Fernandez,** Alfonso 1951- WhoHisp 92
**Fernandez,** Alfred P. 1934- WhoHisp 92
**Fernandez,** Alfredo Jose 1957- WhoMW 92
**Fernandez,** Alvaro Alfonso 1938- WhoHisp 92
**Fernandez,** Andres Jose 1940- WhoHisp 92
**Fernandez,** Angel d1991 NewYTBS 91, WhoHisp 92N
**Fernandez,** Anthony Soter WhoRel 92
**Fernandez,** Aymara 1960- WhoHisp 92
**Fernandez,** Ben Joseph 1958- WhoEnt 92
**Fernandez,** Benedict Joseph, III 1936- WhoHisp 92
**Fernandez,** Benito R. WhoHisp 92
**Fernandez,** Carlos Jesus 1951- WhoHisp 92
**Fernandez,** Carlos M. 1953- WhoHisp 92
**Fernandez,** Carol 1949- WhoHisp 92
**Fernandez,** Carole Fragoza 1941- WhoHisp 92
**Fernandez,** Castor A. WhoHisp 92
**Fernandez,** Celestino 1949- WhoHisp 92
**Fernandez,** Charles M. WhoHisp 92
**Fernandez,** Chico WhoHisp 92
**Fernandez,** Daniel DrAPF 91
**Fernandez,** Dennis Sunga 1961- WhoAmL 92
**Fernandez,** Dolores M. 1944- WhoHisp 92
**Fernandez,** Dominique 1929- IntWW 91
**Fernandez,** Doria Goodrich 1958- WhoHisp 92
**Fernandez,** Eduardo B. 1936- WhoHisp 92
**Fernandez,** Emilio 1904-1986 FacFETw, IntDcF 2-2
**Fernandez,** Enrique WhoHisp 92
**Fernandez,** Erasto WhoHisp 92
**Fernandez,** Eugenia 1957- WhoHisp 92
**Fernandez,** Eustasio, Jr. 1919- WhoHisp 92
**Fernandez,** Ferdinand F WhoAmP 91
**Fernandez,** Ferdinand Francis 1937- WhoAmL 92, WhoHisp 92
**Fernandez,** Fernando Lawrence 1938- WhoHisp 92
**Fernandez,** Fidel Juan 1959- WhoHisp 92
**Fernandez,** Frances WhoHisp 92
**Fernandez,** Francisco WhoHisp 92
**Fernandez,** Frank WhoHisp 92
**Fernandez,** Geraldine Sandra 1938- WhoMW 92
**Fernandez,** Gigi 1964- WhoHisp 92
**Fernandez,** Gilbert, Jr. 1938- WhoHisp 92
**Fernandez,** Gilbert G. 1936- WhoHisp 92
**Fernandez,** Guillermo G. WhoHisp 92
**Fernandez,** Gustavo Antonio 1944- WhoHisp 92
**Fernandez,** Hector R C 1937- AmMWSc 92, WhoHisp 92
**Fernandez,** Henry Anthony 1949- WhoHisp 92
**Fernandez,** Hugo Lathrop 1940- AmMWSc 92
**Fernandez,** Iris Virginia 1955- WhoHisp 92
**Fernandez,** J. M. WhoHisp 92
**Fernandez,** Jack Eugene 1930- AmMWSc 92
**Fernandez,** Jack Eugene, Sr. 1930- WhoHisp 92
**Fernandez,** John 1935- WhoHisp 92
**Fernandez,** John Anthony 1940- WhoHisp 92
**Fernandez,** John D. 1947- WhoHisp 92
**Fernandez,** John Peter 1941- WhoBlA 92
**Fernandez,** Jorge Antonio 1944- WhoHisp 92
**Fernandez,** Jose WhoEnt 92, WhoHisp 92
**Fernandez,** Jose Martin AmMWSc 92
**Fernandez,** Jose Ramon, Jr. 1944- WhoHisp 92
**Fernandez,** Jose Walfredo 1955- WhoAmL 92
**Fernandez,** Joseph 1935- News 91 [port], -91-3 [port]
**Fernandez,** Joseph A. 1935- WhoHisp 92
**Fernandez,** Juan Carlos WhoHisp 92
**Fernandez,** Julian, Jr. WhoHisp 92
**Fernandez,** Leticia 1956- WhoHisp 92
**Fernandez,** Lillian 1954- WhoHisp 92
**Fernandez,** Liz 1959- WhoHisp 92
**Fernandez,** Lloyd WhoHisp 92
**Fernandez,** Louis, Jr. WhoHisp 92
**Fernandez,** Louis Agnelo 1944- AmMWSc 92
**Fernandez,** Louis Anthony 1939- AmMWSc 92, WhoHisp 92
**Fernandez,** Louise Ann 1953- WhoHisp 92
**Fernandez,** Luis F. 1951- WhoHisp 92
**Fernandez,** Luis Felipe 1958- WhoHisp 92
**Fernandez,** Lynne Ann 1957- WhoBlA 92
**Fernandez,** M. H. WhoHisp 92
**Fernandez,** Manny 1952- WhoFI 92
**Fernandez,** Manuel B. 1925- WhoHisp 92
**Fernandez,** Manuel G. WhoHisp 92
**Fernandez,** Manuel Jose 1946- WhoHisp 92
**Fernandez,** Manuel Joseph 1939- WhoHisp 92
**Fernandez,** Maria Isabel 1953- WhoHisp 92
**Fernandez,** Mark Antonio 1960- WhoHisp 92
**Fernandez,** Marlene WhoHisp 92
**Fernandez,** Mary Joe 1971- WhoHisp 92
**Fernandez,** Miguel HisDSpE
**Fernandez,** Miguel Angel 1939- WhoFI 92
**Fernandez,** Mildred WhoHisp 92
**Fernandez,** Nelda T. 1948- WhoRel 92
**Fernandez,** Nelson WhoHisp 92
**Fernandez,** Nestor A., Sr. WhoHisp 92
**Fernandez,** Nino J. WhoHisp 92
**Fernandez,** Nohema del Carmen 1944- WhoEnt 92, WhoHisp 92
**Fernandez,** Osvaldo J. 1959- WhoFI 92
**Fernandez,** Rafael Edward 1952- WhoAmL 92
**Fernandez,** Rafael Ludovino 1948- WhoHisp 92
**Fernandez,** Ramiro A. 1951- WhoHisp 92
**Fernandez,** Ramon 1958- WhoHisp 92
**Fernandez,** Ramon S. 1934- WhoHisp 92
**Fernandez,** Raul A. 1945- WhoHisp 92
**Fernandez,** Rene 1961- WhoMW 92
**Fernandez,** Ricardo 1940- WhoHisp 92
**Fernandez,** Ricardo, III 1970- WhoHisp 92
**Fernandez,** Ricardo Jesus 1953- WhoHisp 92
**Fernandez,** Richard R. WhoRel 92
**Fernandez,** Robert I. 1956- WhoHisp 92
**Fernandez,** Roberto G. 1951- WhoHisp 92
**Fernandez,** Rodney E. WhoHisp 92
**Fernandez,** Rodolfo 1940- WhoHisp 92
**Fernandez,** Roger Rodriguez 1934- WhoHisp 92
**Fernandez,** Ruben D. 1949- WhoHisp 92
**Fernandez,** Ruben Mark 1954- WhoHisp 92
**Fernandez,** Rudy WhoHisp 92
**Fernandez,** Rudy M., Jr. 1948- WhoHisp 92
**Fernandez,** Sally Garza 1958- WhoHisp 92
**Fernandez,** Theresa M. WhoHisp 92
**Fernandez,** Thomas L. 1930- WhoHisp 92
**Fernandez,** Tomas I. 1925- WhoHisp 92
**Fernandez,** Tony 1962- WhoBlA 92, WhoHisp 92

**Fernandez,** Valentin, Jr. 1953- *WhoHisp 92*
**Fernandez,** Wilfredo 1961- *WhoHisp 92*
**Fernandez,** Zandra Luz 1954- *WhoHisp 92*
**Fernandez,** Zenaida 1954- *WhoHisp 92*
**Fernandez Arteaga,** Jose 1933- *WhoRel 92*
**Fernandez-Baca,** David Fernando 1959- *WhoHisp 92*
**Fernandez-Baca,** Jaime A. 1954- *WhoHisp 92*
**Fernandez-Baca,** Jaime Alberto 1954- *AmMWSc 92*
**Fernandez-Chardiet,** Miguel *WhoHisp 92*
**Fernandez-Cruz,** Eduardo P 1946- *AmMWSc 92*
**Fernandez Cuesta Y Merelo,** Raimundo 1896- *BiDExR*
**Fernandez de Enciso,** Martin 1470-1528 *HisDSpE*
**Fernandez de Heredia y Valdez,** Juan A 1478-1557 *HisDSpE*
**Fernandez de Lizardi,** Jose Joaquin 1776-1827 *BenetAL 91, HisDSpE*
**Fernandez de Oviedo y Valdes,** Gonzalo *HisDSpE*
**Fernandez de Piedrahita,** Lucas 1624-1688 *HisDSpE*
**Fernandez de Recalde,** Juan d1615 *HisDSpE*
**Fernandez-Esteva,** Frank 1931- *WhoHisp 92*
**Fernandez-Franco,** Sonia M. 1938- *WhoHisp 92*
**Fernandez-Gonzalez,** Justo 1952- *WhoAmL 92*
**Fernandez Haar,** Ana Maria 1951- *WhoHisp 92*
**Fernandez-Iznaola,** Ricardo Jaime 1949- *WhoEnt 92*
**Fernandez-Jimenez,** Juan 1946- *WhoHisp 92*
**Fernandez-Madrid,** Felix 1927- *AmMWSc 92, WhoHisp 92*
**Fernandez Maldonado Solari,** Jorge 1922- *IntWW 91*
**Fernandez-Morera,** Dario *WhoHisp 92*
**Fernandez-Muro,** Jose Antonio 1920- *IntWW 91*
**Fernandez Olmos,** Margarite 1949- *WhoHisp 92*
**Fernandez Ordonez,** Francisco 1930- *IntWW 91*
**Fernandez Pacheco,** Ismael *WhoAmP 91, WhoHisp 92*
**Fernandez-Palmer,** Lydia *WhoHisp 92*
**Fernandez-Pol,** Jose Alberto 1943- *AmMWSc 92*
**Fernandez-Repollet,** Emma D 1951- *AmMWSc 92*
**Fernandez Retamar,** Roberto 1930- *ConSpAP, IntWW 91*
**Fernandez Sanz,** Matilde 1950- *IntWW 91*
**Fernandez-Torriente,** Gaston F. 1924- *WhoHisp 92*
**Fernandez-Torrijos,** Vivian 1966- *WhoHisp 92*
**Fernandez-Vazquez,** Antonio A. 1949- *WhoHisp 92*
**Fernandez-Velazquez,** Juan R. 1936- *WhoHisp 92*
**Fernandez y Cossio,** Hector Rafael 1937- *AmMWSc 92*
**Fernandez-Zayas,** Marcelo R. 1938- *WhoHisp 92*
**Fernando,** Constantine Herbert 1929- *AmMWSc 92*
**Fernando,** Harindra Joseph 1955- *AmMWSc 92*
**Fernando,** Joseph Anicetus Patrick 1959- *WhoFI 92, WhoMW 92*
**Fernando,** Nicholas Marcus *Who 92*
**Fernando,** Nicholas Marcus 1932- *IntWW 91*
**Fernando,** Quintus 1926- *AmMWSc 92*
**Fernando,** Rohan Luigi 1952- *AmMWSc 92*
**Fernando,** Simon 1538?-1600? *DcNCBi 2*
**Fernando,** Sumith D. Peter 1952- *WhoRel 92*
**Fernando,** Thusew Samuel 1906- *IntWW 91*
**Fernbach,** Donald Joseph 1925- *AmMWSc 92*
**Fernbach,** John R. 1920- *WhoAmL 92*
**Fernbach,** Sidney 1917- *AmMWSc 92, WhoWest 92*
**Ferncase,** Richard Kendrick 1954- *WhoEnt 92*
**Fernee,** Kenneth 1926- *TwCPaSc*
**Fernelius,** Nils Conard 1934- *AmMWSc 92*
**Ferner,** John William *AmMWSc 92*
**Ferneyhough,** Brian 1943- *ConCom 92, NewAmDM*
**Ferneyhough,** Brian John Peter 1943- *IntWW 91, Who 92*
**Ferng,** Douglas Ming-Haw 1945- *WhoMW 92*
**Ferngren,** Gary Burt 1942- *WhoWest 92*
**Fernholz,** Eunice Charlotte 1927- *WhoAmP 91*
**Fernholz,** Martin Anthony 1952- *WhoFI 92, WhoMW 92*
**Fernicola,** Gregory Anthony 1957- *WhoAmL 92*
**Fernie,** Bruce Frank 1948- *AmMWSc 92*
**Fernie,** Eric Campbell 1939- *Who 92*
**Fernie,** John Donald 1933- *AmMWSc 92*
**Fernig,** Felicite *EncAmaz 91*
**Fernig,** Theophile *EncAmaz 91*
**Ferniot,** Jean 1918- *IntWW 91*
**Fernow,** Richard Clinton 1947- *AmMWSc 92*
**Ferns,** Henry Stanley 1913- *Who 92*
**Ferns,** W. Paterson *LesBEnT 92*
**Fernsler,** John Paul 1940- *WhoAmL 92*
**Fernstrom,** John Dickson 1947- *AmMWSc 92*
**Fernstrum,** David Ross 1950- *WhoAmL 92*
**Fernyhough,** Bernard 1932- *Who 92*
**Fernyhough,** Ernest 1908- *Who 92*
**Feroe,** John Albert 1946- *AmMWSc 92*
**Ferone,** Robert 1936- *AmMWSc 92*
**Feroz,** Ehsan Habib 1952- *WhoMW 92*
**Feroze,** Rustam Moolan 1920- *Who 92*
**Ferra,** Lorraine *DrAPF 91*
**Ferra,** Max 1937- *WhoEnt 92, WhoHisp 92*
**Ferrabosco,** Alfonso 1543-1588 *NewAmDM*
**Ferrabosco,** Alfonso 1578-1628 *NewAmDM*
**Ferraby,** Paul 1951- *TwCPaSc*
**Ferradas,** Renaldo 1932- *WhoHisp 92*
**Ferraez,** Martha Elizabeth 1937- *WhoRel 92*
**Ferragamo,** Salvatore 1898-1960 *DcTwDes*
**Ferragut,** Rene *WhoHisp 92*
**Ferraioli,** Armando 1949- *WhoFI 92*
**Ferraiolo,** Angela 1958- *WhoEnt 92*
**Ferrall,** Raymond 1906- *Who 92*
**Ferrall,** Victor Eugene, Jr. 1936- *WhoMW 92*
**Ferrand,** Frederick Owen 1959- *WhoAmL 92*
**Ferrand,** Stephen Lee 1787-1830 *DcNCBi 2*
**Ferrand,** William Pugh, Sr. 1789-1874 *DcNCBi 2*
**Ferrandis,** Bruno 1960- *WhoEnt 92*
**Ferrans,** Victor Joaquin 1937- *AmMWSc 92*
**Ferrante,** Michael John 1930- *AmMWSc 92*
**Ferrante,** W R 1928- *AmMWSc 92*
**Ferranti,** Sebastian Basil Joseph Z de *Who 92*
**Ferrantino,** Michael Joseph 1958- *WhoFI 92*
**Ferrar,** Harold 1935- *WrDr 92*
**Ferrar,** Joseph C 1939- *AmMWSc 92*
**Ferrara,** Anthony Joseph 1947- *WhoAmL 92*
**Ferrara,** Arthur Vincent 1930- *WhoFI 92*
**Ferrara,** Bartolomeo Peter 1931- *WhoEnt 92*
**Ferrara,** Dominick John, III 1939- *WhoEnt 92*
**Ferrara,** Franco 1911-1985 *NewAmDM*
**Ferrara,** Louis W 1923- *AmMWSc 92*
**Ferrara,** Peter J. *WhoAmL 92*
**Ferrara,** Peter J 1955- *WhoAmP 91*
**Ferrara,** Salvatore Stephen 1931- *WhoAmL 92*
**Ferrara,** Thomas Ciro 1947- *AmMWSc 92*
**Ferrara,** William Leonard 1930- *WhoFI 92*
**Ferrarelli,** Rina *DrAPF 91*
**Ferrari,** Andrew 1839?-1915 *BiInAmS*
**Ferrari,** David G 1944- *WhoAmP 91*
**Ferrari,** Domenic J *WhoAmP 91*
**Ferrari,** Domenico 1940- *AmMWSc 92, WhoWest 92*
**Ferrari,** Donna Mae 1931- *WhoFI 92*
**Ferrari,** Douglas Paul 1956- *WhoEnt 92*
**Ferrari,** Enzo 1898-1988 *FacFETw*
**Ferrari,** Harry M 1932- *AmMWSc 92*
**Ferrari,** Juan 1950- *WhoFI 92*
**Ferrari,** Lawrence A 1937- *AmMWSc 92*
**Ferrari,** Leonard 1943- *AmMWSc 92*
**Ferrari,** Luc 1929- *ConCom 92, NewAmDM*
**Ferrari,** Mary *DrAPF 91*
**Ferrari,** Melissa Rico 1955- *WhoAmL 92*
**Ferrari,** Michael David 1945- *WhoMW 92*
**Ferrari,** Michael Richard, Jr. 1940- *WhoMW 92*
**Ferrari,** R.L. 1930- *ConAu 135*
**Ferrari,** Richard Alan 1932- *AmMWSc 92*
**Ferrari,** Richard Francis 1944- *WhoAmP 91*
**Ferrari,** Richard H. 1956- *WhoFI 92*
**Ferrari,** Robert Joseph 1936- *WhoFI 92*
**Ferrario,** Carlos Maria *AmMWSc 92*
**Ferrario,** Joseph A. 1926- *WhoRel 92, WhoWest 92*
**Ferraris,** Fred *DrAPF 91*
**Ferraris,** John Patrick 1947- *AmMWSc 92*
**Ferraro,** Anthony Michael, Sr 1935- *WhoAmP 91*
**Ferraro,** Arnaldo A 1936- *WhoAmP 91*
**Ferraro,** Bernadette A 1952- *IntAu&W 91*
**Ferraro,** Betty M 1925- *WhoAmP 91*
**Ferraro,** Charles Domenic 1913- *WhoMW 92*
**Ferraro,** Charles Frank 1924- *AmMWSc 92*
**Ferraro,** Charles Michael 1955- *WhoIns 92*
**Ferraro,** Douglas P *AmMWSc 92*
**Ferraro,** Geraldine 1935- *FacFETw [port], HanAmWH, RComAH*
**Ferraro,** Geraldine A. *NewYTBS 91 [port]*
**Ferraro,** Geraldine A 1935- *WhoAmP 91*
**Ferraro,** Geraldine Anne 1935- *AmPolLe, IntWW 91*
**Ferraro,** John *WhoHisp 92*
**Ferraro,** John Anthony 1946- *AmMWSc 92*
**Ferraro,** John J 1931- *AmMWSc 92*
**Ferraro,** John Ralph 1918- *AmMWSc 92, WhoMW 92*
**Ferraro,** Kenneth Frank 1954- *WhoMW 92*
**Ferraro,** Michael Francis 1952- *WhoFI 92*
**Ferraro,** Richard Edward 1924- *WhoAmP 91*
**Ferraro,** Robert Donald 1954- *WhoFI 92*
**Ferrars,** E. X. *WrDr 92*
**Ferrars,** Elizabeth 1907- *IntAu&W 91, WrDr 92*
**Ferras,** Christian 1933-1982 *NewAmDM*
**Ferrat,** Jacques Jean *TwCSFW 91*
**Ferraudi,** Guillermo Jorge 1942- *AmMWSc 92*
**Ferrazza,** Carl J. 1920- *IntMPA 92*
**Ferrazzetta,** Settimio Arturo *WhoRel 92*
**Ferrazzi,** Ferruccio 1891- *IntWW 91*
**Ferre,** Antonio Luis 1934- *WhoFI 92, WhoHisp 92*
**Ferre,** Antonio R. *WhoHisp 92*
**Ferre,** Frederick 1933- *IntAu&W 91, WrDr 92*
**Ferre,** Gianfranco 1944- *CurBio 91 [port], IntWW 91*
**Ferre,** Helen Aguirre 1957- *WhoHisp 92*
**Ferre,** Luis A 1904- *WhoAmP 91, WhoHisp 92*
**Ferre,** Maurice Antonio 1935- *WhoHisp 92*
**Ferre,** Nels Fredrik Solomon 1908-1971 *RelLAm 91*
**Ferre,** Rosario 1942- *ConSpAP, SpAmWW, WhoHisp 92*
**Ferrebee,** Donna Elaine 1958- *WhoMW 92*
**Ferrebee,** Thomas G. 1937- *WhoBlA 92*
**Ferree,** Carolyn Ruth 1944- *AmMWSc 92*
**Ferree,** David C 1943- *AmMWSc 92*
**Ferree,** John Newton, Jr. 1946- *WhoWest 92*
**Ferree,** Thurman Nealon 1931- *WhoMW 92*
**Ferree,** Thurman Thomas *WhoAmP 91*
**Ferreira,** Daniel Alves 1944- *WhoMW 92*
**Ferreira,** Francis Joseph, Jr 1938- *WhoAmP 91*
**Ferreira,** Gail Veronica 1952- *WhoFI 92*
**Ferreira,** Jesse T 1917- *WhoAmP 91*
**Ferreira,** Jo Ann Jeanette Chanoux 1943- *WhoFI 92*
**Ferreira,** Jose, Jr. 1956- *WhoFI 92*
**Ferreira,** Judith Anne 1940- *WhoWest 92*
**Ferreira,** Laurence E 1928- *AmMWSc 92*
**Ferreira,** Thomas Henry 1959- *WhoFI 92*
**Ferreira-Worth,** Deirdre Charlyn 1958- *WhoWest 92*
**Ferreiro,** Claudio Eduardo 1939- *WhoHisp 92*
**Ferrel,** Cipriano *WhoHisp 92*
**Ferrel,** William 1817-1891 *BiInAmS*
**Ferrell,** Blaine Richard 1951- *AmMWSc 92*
**Ferrell,** Calvin L 1949- *AmMWSc 92*
**Ferrell,** Conchata 1943- *IntMPA 92*
**Ferrell,** Conchata Galen 1943- *WhoEnt 92*
**Ferrell,** D Thomas, Jr 1922- *AmMWSc 92*
**Ferrell,** Daniel Lee 1949- *WhoWest 92*
**Ferrell,** Edward F 1914- *AmMWSc 92*
**Ferrell,** Howard H 1929- *AmMWSc 92*
**Ferrell,** James K 1923- *AmMWSc 92*
**Ferrell,** James Robert 1949- *WhoFI 92*
**Ferrell,** Jeffrey Clark 1946- *WhoFI 92*
**Ferrell,** Joe C 1947- *WhoAmP 91*
**Ferrell,** John Atkinson 1880-1965 *DcNCBi 2*
**Ferrell,** John Frederick 1942- *WhoFI 92*
**Ferrell,** Milton Morgan, Jr. 1951- *WhoAmL 92*
**Ferrell,** Nancy Warren 1932- *WhoWest 92*
**Ferrell,** Ray Edward, Jr 1941- *AmMWSc 92*
**Ferrell,** Richard Allan 1926- *AmMWSc 92*
**Ferrell,** Robert Edward 1943- *AmMWSc 92*
**Ferrell,** Rosie E. 1915- *WhoBlA 92*
**Ferrell,** William James 1940- *AmMWSc 92*
**Ferrell,** William Kreiter 1919- *AmMWSc 92*
**Ferrell,** William Russell 1932- *AmMWSc 92*
**Ferrell Edmondson,** Barbara Ann 1947- *BlkOlyM*
**Ferren,** John Maxwell 1937- *WhoAmL 92, WhoAmP 91*
**Ferren,** Larry Gene 1948- *AmMWSc 92*
**Ferren,** Richard Anthony 1931- *AmMWSc 92*
**Ferrendelli,** James Anthony 1936- *AmMWSc 92*
**Ferrer,** Betzaida 1943- *WhoHisp 92*
**Ferrer,** Fernando 1950- *WhoHisp 92*
**Ferrer,** Gloria Esther 1952- *WhoHisp 92*
**Ferrer,** Jennifer Klatsky 1956- *WhoMW 92*
**Ferrer,** John David 1944- *WhoHisp 92*
**Ferrer,** Jorge F *AmMWSc 92*
**Ferrer,** Jose 1912- *IntMPA 92, IntWW 91*
**Ferrer,** Jose 1912-1992 *WhoHisp 92N*
**Ferrer,** Jose Vicente 1912- *Who 92, WhoEnt 92*
**Ferrer,** Mel 1917- *IntMPA 92*
**Ferrer,** Miguel *ConTFT 9, WhoHisp 92*
**Ferrer,** Miguel 1954- *IntMPA 92*
**Ferrer,** Rafael Douglas Paul 1957- *WhoAmL 92*
**Ferrer,** Rafael George 1930- *WhoAmL 92*
**Ferrer La Hera,** Juan *BlkOlyM*
**Ferrera,** Robert James 1937- *WhoMW 92*
**Ferreri,** Marco 1928- *IntAu&W 91, IntDcF 2-2*
**Ferreri,** Vito Richard 1949- *WhoAmL 92*
**Ferrero,** Guillermo E. 1954- *WhoHisp 92*
**Ferrero,** Louis Peter 1942- *WhoMW 92*
**Ferrers,** Earl 1929- *Who 92*
**Ferrers,** Maude *EncAmaz 91*
**Ferretti,** Aldo 1929- *AmMWSc 92*
**Ferretti,** James Alfred 1939- *AmMWSc 92*
**Ferretti,** Joseph Jerome 1937- *AmMWSc 92*
**Ferretti Di Val D'Era,** Lando 1895-1977 *BiDExR*
**Ferrey,** Jeffrey Baker 1943- *WhoWest 92*
**Ferrey,** Marie Esperanza 1964- *WhoHisp 92*
**Ferreyra,** Guillermo S. 1953- *WhoHisp 92*
**Ferri,** Alessandra Maria 1963- *WhoEnt 92*
**Ferri,** Baldassare 1610-1680 *NewAmDM*
**Ferri,** Guy d1991 *NewYTBS 91*
**Ferri,** Roger C. d1991 *NewYTBS 91*
**Ferrians,** Oscar John, Jr 1928- *AmMWSc 92*
**Ferrie,** Alexander Martin 1923- *Who 92*
**Ferriell,** Jeffrey Thomas 1953- *WhoAmL 92*
**Ferriell,** Peter Paul 1955- *WhoMW 92*
**Ferrier,** Baron 1900- *Who 92*
**Ferrier,** Barbara May 1932- *AmMWSc 92*
**Ferrier,** Gregory R 1943- *AmMWSc 92*
**Ferrier,** Jack Moreland 1943- *AmMWSc 92*
**Ferrier,** Johan Henri Eliza 1910- *IntWW 91*
**Ferrier,** Kathleen 1912-1953 *FacFETw, NewAmDM*
**Ferrier,** Leslie Kenneth 1941- *AmMWSc 92*
**Ferrier,** Lucy *ConAu 35NR*
**Ferrier,** Robert Patton 1934- *Who 92*
**Ferrier,** Susan 1782-1854 *RfGEnL 91*
**Ferriero,** Diana 1959- *WhoAmL 92*
**Ferrigno,** Peter D 1927- *AmMWSc 92*
**Ferrigno,** Robert *ConLC 65 [port]*
**Ferrigno,** Thomas Howard 1925- *AmMWSc 92*
**Ferril,** Thomas Hornsby 1896-1988 *BenetAL 91*
**Ferrill,** Alan Michael 1955- *WhoAmL 92*
**Ferrill,** John Wesley 1947- *WhoMW 92*
**Ferrillo,** John *WhoEnt 92*
**Ferrin,** Mark Allen 1950- *WhoAmL 92*
**Ferrini,** Burt 1942 *WhoEnt 92*
**Ferrini,** James Thomas 1938- *WhoAmL 92*
**Ferrini,** Vincent *DrAPF 91*
**Ferris** *Who 92*
**Ferris,** Ann M 1945- *AmMWSc 92*
**Ferris,** Benjamin Greeley, Jr 1919- *AmMWSc 92*
**Ferris,** Bernard Joe 1922- *AmMWSc 92*
**Ferris,** Charles D. *LesBEnT 92*
**Ferris,** Charles Daniel 1933- *WhoAmP 91*
**Ferris,** Clifford D 1935- *AmMWSc 92*
**Ferris,** Clinton S, Jr 1933- *AmMWSc 92*
**Ferris,** Deam Hunter 1912- *AmMWSc 92*
**Ferris,** Evelyn Scott *WhoWest 92*
**Ferris,** Francis 1932- *Who 92*
**Ferris,** Frederick L 1946- *AmMWSc 92*
**Ferris,** Horace Garfield 1913- *AmMWSc 92*
**Ferris,** J David 1937- *WhoIns 92*
**Ferris,** James Peter 1932- *AmMWSc 92*
**Ferris,** John Mason *AmMWSc 92, WhoMW 92*
**Ferris,** Joseph Edward 1929- *WhoMW 92*

**Ferris**, Mark Leslie 1947- WhoFI 92
**Ferris**, Nancy Ann 1955- WhoAmL 92
**Ferris**, Paul 1929- IntAu&W 91, WrDr 92
**Ferris**, Paul Frederick 1929- Who 92
**Ferris**, Philip 1930- AmMWSc 92
**Ferris**, Raphael Ellis 1953- WhoAmL 92
**Ferris**, Robert Monsour 1938- AmMWSc 92
**Ferris**, Ronald Curry Who 92
**Ferris**, Ronald Curry 1945- WhoRel 92, WhoWest 92
**Ferris**, Steven Howard 1943- AmMWSc 92
**Ferris**, Sydney 1902- TwCPaSc
**Ferris**, Thomas Francis 1930- AmMWSc 92
**Ferris**, Timothy 1944- WrDr 92
**Ferris**, Timothy Allan 1947- WhoFI 92
**Ferris**, Tony 1928- WhoAmL 92
**Ferris**, Virginia Rogers AmMWSc 92, WhoMW 92
**Ferris**, Wayne Robert AmMWSc 92
**Ferris**, William L 1941- WhoIns 92
**Ferris**, William Michael 1948- WhoAmL 92
**Ferris-Prabhu**, Albert Victor Michael AmMWSc 92
**Ferriss**, Abbott Lamoyne 1915- WrDr 92
**Ferriss**, Donald P 1924- AmMWSc 92
**Ferriss**, Gregory Stark 1924- AmMWSc 92
**Ferriss**, Lucy 1954- IntAu&W 91
**Ferritor**, Daniel Edward 1939- ConAu 35NR
**Ferro**, Anthony J. WhoHisp 92
**Ferro**, Benedict WhoHisp 92
**Ferro**, David Newton 1946- AmMWSc 92
**Ferro**, John Joseph 1961- WhoFI 92
**Ferro**, Jorge 1948- WhoHisp 92
**Ferro**, Ramon 1941- WhoHisp 92
**Ferro**, Simon WhoHisp 92
**Ferro**, Simon 1953- WhoAmP 91
**Ferro**, Thomas Louis 1947- WhoEnt 92
**Ferroli**, John Anthony 1958- WhoAmL 92
**Ferron**, Jean H 1948- AmMWSc 92
**Ferron**, John R 1926- AmMWSc 92
**Ferrone**, Frank Anthony 1947- AmMWSc 92
**Ferrone**, Soldano 1940- AmMWSc 92
**Ferrucci**, Sheila Corrigan 1953- WhoAmL 92
**Ferry**, Alexander 1931- Who 92
**Ferry**, Andrew P 1929- AmMWSc 92
**Ferry**, Arthur George, Jr. 1938- WhoRel 92
**Ferry**, David DrAPF 91
**Ferry**, David 1957- TwCPaSc
**Ferry**, David K 1940- AmMWSc 92
**Ferry**, Donald J WhoAmP 91
**Ferry**, James A 1937- AmMWSc 92
**Ferry**, John Allen 1962- WhoMW 92
**Ferry**, John Christopher 1949- WhoAmL 92
**Ferry**, John Douglass 1912- AmMWSc 92, IntWW 91, WrDr 92
**Ferry**, John Farwell 1877-1910 BiInAmS
**Ferry**, John Mott 1949- AmMWSc 92
**Ferry**, John Yeoman 1953- WhoAmP 91
**Ferry**, Joseph Dean 1954- WhoAmL 92
**Ferry**, Mary MacConnell 1943- WhoAmL 92
**Ferry**, Michael James 1957- WhoMW 92
**Ferry**, Miles Yeoman 1932- WhoAmP 91
**Ferry**, Richard Michael 1937- WhoFI 92
**Fersht**, Alan Roy 1943- IntWW 91, Who 92
**Fershtman**, Julie Ilene 1961- WhoAmL 92, WhoMW 92
**Fersman**, Aleksandr Yevgen'evich 1883-1945 SovUnBD
**Ferst**, Jeanne Rolfe 1918- WhoAmP 91
**Ferstandig**, Louis Lloyd 1924- AmMWSc 92
**Fertig**, Ralph David Hays 1930- WhoAmP 91
**Fertig**, Stanford Newton 1919- AmMWSc 92
**Fertig**, Ted Brian O'Day 1937- WhoWest 92
**Fertis**, Demeter G 1926- AmMWSc 92
**Fertitta**, Robert S. 1940- WhoAmL 92
**Fertl**, Walter Hans 1940- AmMWSc 92
**Fertziger**, Allen Philip 1941- AmMWSc 92
**Ferwerda**, Vernon LeRoy 1918- WhoRel 92
**Fery**, John Bruce 1930- IntWW 91, WhoFI 92, WhoWest 92
**Fery**, Richard Lee 1943- AmMWSc 92
**Fery-Bognar**, Marie von EncAmaz 91
**Ferzacca**, William 1927- WhoMW 92
**Ferziger**, Joel H 1937- AmMWSc 92
**Fesenmair**, Helene 1937- TwCPaSc
**Fesh**, Robert M 1937- WhoAmP 91
**Fesh**, Stephen James, Jr 1943- WhoAmP 91
**Feshbach**, Herman 1917- AmMWSc 92, IntWW 91
**Fesjian**, Sezar 1943- AmMWSc 92
**Fesko**, Timothy WhoAmP 91
**Feskoe**, Gaffney Jon 1949- WhoFI 92
**Fesmire**, Charles Wayne 1932- WhoRel 92
**Fesmire**, Walker Eugene 1929- WhoMW 92
**Fesperman**, John T. 1925- WrDr 92
**Fesperman**, John Thomas, Jr 1925- IntAu&W 91
**Fessenden**, Anne Lathrop DrAPF 91
**Fessenden**, Peter 1937- AmMWSc 92
**Fessenden**, Ralph James 1932- AmMWSc 92
**Fessenden**, Reginald Aubrey 1866-1932 DcNCBi 2, FacFETw
**Fessenden**, Richard Warren 1934- AmMWSc 92
**Fessenden**, Thomas Green 1771-1837 BenetAL 91
**Fessenden-MacDonald**, June Marion 1937- AmMWSc 92
**Fessey**, Mereth Cecil 1917- Who 92
**Fessler**, John Hans 1928- AmMWSc 92
**Fessler**, Liselotte I AmMWSc 92
**Fessler**, Raymond R AmMWSc 92
**Fessler**, Richard Donald 1943- WhoAmP 91
**Festa**, Costanzo 1480?-1545 NewAmDM
**Festa**, Roger Reginald 1950- AmMWSc 92, WhoMW 92
**Festa**, William J. 1959- WhoFI 92
**Feste**, Charles Allen 1928- WhoAmL 92
**Fester**, Dale A 1932- AmMWSc 92
**Fester**, Keith Edward 1942- AmMWSc 92
**Festetics**, Sandor 1882-1956 BiDExR
**Festoff**, Barry William 1940- WhoMW 92
**Fetch**, Alan Michael 1953- WhoEnt 92, WhoMW 92
**Fetcher**, E S 1909- AmMWSc 92
**Fetchin**, John Allan 1942- WhoMW 92
**Fetchit**, Stepin 1902-1985 FacFETw
**Fetcho**, Joseph Robert 1957- AmMWSc 92
**Feth**, Frederick Charles 1938- WhoWest 92
**Feth**, George C 1931- AmMWSc 92
**Feth**, Joseph S. 1945- WhoMW 92
**Fetherolf**, Fred Arthur 1944- WhoRel 92
**Fetherolf**, Joyce Wilson 1952- WhoWest 92
**Fetherston-Dilke**, Charles Beaumont 1921- Who 92
**Fetherston-Dilke**, Mary Stella 1918- Who 92
**Fetkovich**, John Gabriel 1931- AmMWSc 92
**Fetler**, Andrew DrAPF 91
**Fetler**, Dan Gregor 1952- WhoEnt 92
**Fetler**, Paul 1920- WhoEnt 92
**Fetner**, Robert Henry 1922- AmMWSc 92
**Fetridge**, Bonnie-Jean Clark 1915- WhoMW 92
**Fetridge**, Clark Worthington 1946- WhoAmP 91, WhoFI 92, WhoMW 92
**Fetridge**, William Harrison 1906- WhoAmP 91
**Fetscher**, Charles Arthur 1912- AmMWSc 92
**Fetscher**, Iring 1922- IntWW 91
**Fetsko**, Jacqueline Marie 1926- AmMWSc 92
**Fett**, John D 1933- AmMWSc 92
**Fett**, Robert Walter 1928- WhoWest 92
**Fett**, William Frederick 1952- AmMWSc 92
**Fetter**, Alexander Lees 1937- AmMWSc 92
**Fetter**, Bernard Frank 1921- AmMWSc 92
**Fetter**, Charles Willard, Jr 1942- AmMWSc 92, WhoMW 92
**Fetter**, Frank Whitson 1899-1991 ConAu 135
**Fetter**, Kathryn A. 1950- WhoMW 92
**Fetter**, Manuel 1809-1889 DcNCBi 2
**Fetter**, Theodore Henry 1906- WhoEnt 92
**Fetter**, William Allan 1928- AmMWSc 92
**Fetterhoff**, Carl Elmer 1938- WhoRel 92
**Fetterly**, Lynn Lawrence 1947- WhoFI 92
**Fetterman**, Carole L. 1953- WhoEnt 92
**Fetterman**, Harold Ralph 1941- AmMWSc 92
**Fetterman**, James C. 1947- WhoAmL 92
**Fetterolf**, Carlos de la Mesa, Jr 1926- AmMWSc 92
**Fetterolf**, Charles Frederick 1928- IntWW 91, WhoFI 92
**Fetters**, James Williams 1944- WhoMW 92
**Fetters**, Karl L 1909- AmMWSc 92
**Fetters**, Lewis 1936- AmMWSc 92
**Fetters**, Paul R. WhoRel 92
**Fetters**, Samuel Max 1928- WhoAmL 92
**Fettes**, Edward Mackay 1918- AmMWSc 92
**Fetting**, Otto 1871-1933 RelLAm 91
**Fetting**, Rainer 1949- WorArt 1980
**Fettinger**, George Edgar 1929- WhoAmP 91
**Fettiplace**, Robert 1946- Who 92
**Fettweis**, Alfred Leo Maria 1926- AmMWSc 92, IntWW 91
**Fettweis**, Gunter Bernhard Leo 1924- IntWW 91
**Fetty**, Maurice Allen 1936- WhoRel 92
**Fetyatter**, Gary L. 1949- WhoMW 92
**Fetzer**, Brian Charles 1950- WhoAmL 92
**Fetzer**, Herman 1899-1935 ScFEYrs
**Fetzer**, Homer D 1932- AmMWSc 92
**Fetzer**, John d1991 NewYTBS 91
**Fetzer**, John Charles 1953- AmMWSc 92
**Fetzer**, John E. d1991 LesBEnT 92
**Fetzer**, John E. 1901- IntMPA 92
**Fetzer**, Leland 1930- ScFEYrs
**Fetzer**, Mark Stephen 1950- WhoAmL 92
**Fetzer**, Michael Stephan 1953- WhoMW 92
**Feucht**, Donald Lee 1933- AmMWSc 92
**Feucht**, James Roger 1933- AmMWSc 92
**Feuchtenberger**, Pat Waltman 1933- WhoEnt 92
**Feuchtenberger**, William Pence 1930- WhoAmP 91
**Feuchtwang**, Thomas Emanuel 1930- AmMWSc 92
**Feuchtwanger**, Lewis 1805-1876 BiInAmS
**Feuchtwanger**, Lion 1884-1958 EncTR 91 [port], FacFETw, LiExTwC
**Feudale**, Barry Francis 1946- WhoAmL 92
**Feuer**, Cy 1911- WhoEnt 92
**Feuer**, George 1921- AmMWSc 92
**Feuer**, Henry 1912- AmMWSc 92
**Feuer**, Joseph N 1940- WhoAmP 91
**Feuer**, Mark David 1953- AmMWSc 92
**Feuer**, Paula Berger 1922- AmMWSc 92
**Feuer**, Richard Dennis 1940- AmMWSc 92
**Feuer**, Robert Adley 1941- WhoAmL 92
**Feuer**, Robert Charles 1936- AmMWSc 92
**Feuer**, Steven Z. 1959- WhoAmL 92
**Feuer**, William Wallace 1925- WhoAmL 92
**Feuerberg**, Mark Stanley 1942- WhoFI 92
**Feuerherd**, Victor Edmond 1925- WhoFI 92
**Feuerlicht**, Roberta Strauss 1931-1991 ConAu 135, NewYTBS 91
**Feuermann**, Claudio A. WhoHisp 92
**Feuermann**, Emanuel 1902-1942 NewAmDM
**Feuerstein**, Alan Ricky 1950- WhoAmL 92
**Feuerstein**, Donald Martin 1937- WhoAmL 92
**Feuerstein**, Georg W. 1947- WrDr 92
**Feuerstein**, Heinrich 1877-1942 EncTR 91
**Feuerstein**, Herbert 1927- WhoFI 92
**Feuerstein**, Irwin 1939- AmMWSc 92
**Feuerstein**, Marcy Berry 1950- WhoWest 92
**Feuerstein**, Martin 1924- WhoAmP 91
**Feuerstein**, Sandra Jeanne 1946- WhoAmL 92
**Feuerstein**, Seymour 1931- AmMWSc 92
**Feuerwerker**, Albert 1927- WrDr 92
**Feuillade**, Louis 1873-1925 IntDcF 2-2
**Feuillere**, Edwige Who 92
**Feuillere**, Edwige 1910- IntWW 91
**Feulner**, Edwin John, Jr 1941- WhoAmP 91, WhoFI 92
**Feury**, Richard John 1950- WhoEnt 92
**Feustel**, Edward Alvin 1940- AmMWSc 92
**Feversham**, Baron 1945- Who 92
**Fevin**, Antoine de 1474?-1512? NewAmDM
**Fevold**, Harry Richard 1935- AmMWSc 92
**Fevurly**, Keith Robert 1951- WhoAmL 92
**Few**, Adelaide Gonzalez 1937- WhoAmL 92
**Few**, Arthur Allen 1939- AmMWSc 92
**Few**, Elsie 1909-1980 TwCPaSc
**Few**, James 1746-1771 DcNCBi 2
**Few**, Kimberly Denise 1967- WhoFI 92
**Few**, Terry Lee 1948- WhoBlA 92
**Few**, William, Jr. 1748-1828 DcNCBi 2
**Few**, William Preston 1867-1940 DcNCBi 2
**Fewel**, Harriett 1943- WhoAmL 92
**Fewell**, Charles Kenneth, Jr. 1943- WhoAmL 92
**Fewell**, Danna Nolan 1958- WhoRel 92
**Fewell**, Jeannie Louise 1948- WhoFI 92
**Fewell**, Kenneth Robert 1948- WhoIns 92
**Fewell**, Richard 1937- WhoBlA 92
**Fewer**, Darrell R 1923- AmMWSc 92
**Fewkes**, Robert Charles Joseph 1935- AmMWSc 92
**Fex**, Jorgen 1924- AmMWSc 92
**Fey**, Curt F 1932- AmMWSc 92
**Fey**, Emil 1886-1938 BiDExR
**Fey**, George 1944- AmMWSc 92
**Fey**, George Ting-Kuo 1940- AmMWSc 92
**Fey**, Robert Michael 1942- WhoWest 92
**Fey**, Thomas H 1954- WhoAmP 91
**Feydeau**, Georges 1862-1921 FacFETw, GuFrLit 1
**Feyder**, Jacques 1885-1948 IntDcF 2-2
**Feyder**, Jean 1947- IntWW 91
**Feye**, Lyle John 1953- WhoFI 92
**Feyerabend**, Paul K. 1924- WrDr 92
**Feyerherm**, Arlin Martin 1925- AmMWSc 92
**Feyide**, Meshach Otokiti 1926- IntWW 91
**Feynman**, Joan 1927- AmMWSc 92
**Feynman**, Richard Phillips 1918-1988 FacFETw, WhoNob 90
**Feyns**, Liviu Valentin 1938- AmMWSc 92
**Feyock**, Stefan 1942- AmMWSc 92
**Feyzioglu**, Turhan 1922- IntWW 91
**Fezandie**, Clement 1865- ScFEYrs
**Fezer**, Karl Dietrich 1930- AmMWSc 92
**Ffitch**, George Norman 1929- Who 92
**ffolkes**, Robert 1943- Who 92
**Fforde**, John Standish 1921- IntWW 91, Who 92
**Ffowcs Williams**, John Eirwyn 1935- Who 92
**Ffrangcon-Davies**, Gwen 1891- Who 92
**ffrench** Who 92
**ffrench**, Baron 1956- Who 92
**Ffrench-Beytagh**, Gonville Aubie d1991 Who 92N
**Ffrench-Davis**, Ricardo 1936- IntWW 91
**ffytche**, Timothy John 1936- Who 92
**Fiacc**, Padraic 1924- IntAu&W 91, WrDr 92
**Fiacco**, Benny Richard 1954- WhoEnt 92
**Fiad**, Roberto Eduardo 1958- WhoHisp 92
**Fiala**, Alan Dale 1942- AmMWSc 92
**Fiala**, David Marcus 1946- WhoAmL 92, WhoFI 92, WhoMW 92
**Fiala**, Emerich Silvio 1938- AmMWSc 92
**Fiala**, Ernst 1928- IntWW 91
**Fialer**, Philip A 1938- AmMWSc 92
**Fialer**, Philip Anthony 1938- WhoWest 92
**Fialka**, Ladislav 1931-1991 IntWW 91, -91N
**Fialkoff**, Jay R. 1951- WhoAmL 92
**Fialkow**, Aaron David 1911- AmMWSc 92
**Fialkow**, Philip Jack 1934- AmMWSc 92, WhoWest 92
**Fialkow**, Steven 1943- WhoFI 92
**Fialkowski**, Barbara DrAPF 91
**Fialky**, Gary Lewis 1942- WhoAmL 92
**Fialla**, Frank R. DcTwDes
**Fiammenghi**, Gioia 1929- SmATA 66 [port]
**Fibich**, Felix 1917- WhoEnt 92
**Fibiger**, Johannes Andreas Grib 1867-1928 WhoNob 90
**Fibiger**, John Andrew 1932- WhoFI 92
**Fibonacci**, Leonardo d1250? DcTwDes
**Ficano**, Robert Anthony 1952- WhoAmP 91
**Ficenec**, John Robert 1938- AmMWSc 92
**Ficeto**, Michael Joseph 1951- WhoEnt 92
**Fich**, Sylvan 1910- AmMWSc 92
**Ficher**, Miguel 1922- AmMWSc 92
**Fichera**, Lewis Carmen 1949- WhoAmL 92
**Fichte**, Johann Gottlieb 1762-1814 BlkwCEP
**Fichtel**, Carl Edwin 1933- AmMWSc 92
**Fichtenau**, Heinrich 1912- IntWW 91
**Fichter**, George 1922- IntAu&W 91
**Fichter**, George S. 1922- WrDr 92
**Fichter**, Joseph H. 1908- WhoRel 92
**Fick**, Gary Warren 1943- AmMWSc 92
**Fick**, Herbert John 1937- AmMWSc 92
**Ficke**, Arthur Davison 1883-1945 BenetAL 91
**Fickel**, Robert Bruce 1946- WhoAmL 92
**Ficken**, Millicent Sigler 1933- AmMWSc 92
**Ficken**, Robert W 1932- AmMWSc 92
**Ficker**, Robin WhoAmP 91
**Fickert**, Kurt J. 1920- WrDr 92
**Fickert**, Kurt Jon 1920- IntAu&W 91
**Fickess**, Douglas Ricardo 1931- AmMWSc 92
**Fickett**, Bob H 1924- WhoAmP 91
**Fickett**, Frederick Roland 1937- AmMWSc 92
**Fickett**, Lewis Perley, Jr 1926- WhoAmP 91
**Fickett**, Wildon 1927- AmMWSc 92
**Fickey**, Timothy Lynn 1963- WhoRel 92
**Fickies**, Robert H 1944- AmMWSc 92
**Fickinger**, Wayne Joseph 1926- WhoFI 92, WhoMW 92
**Fickinger**, William Joseph 1934- AmMWSc 92
**Fickle**, William Dick 1943- WhoMW 92
**Fickling**, Benjamin William 1909- Who 92
**Fickling**, William Arthur, Jr. 1932- WhoFI 92
**Ficks**, Robert Leslie, Jr. 1919- WhoFI 92
**Ficquette**, Sharon Elaine 1956- WhoAmL 92
**Ficsor**, Gyula 1936- AmMWSc 92
**Ficzeri**, Paul Daniel 1946- WhoRel 92
**Fiddes**, James Raffan 1919- Who 92
**Fiddick**, Paul William 1949- WhoEnt 92
**Fiddick**, Peter Ronald 1938- Who 92
**Fiddler**, Walter 1936- AmMWSc 92
**Fidel**, Joseph A 1923- WhoAmP 91, WhoHisp 92
**Fidel**, Noel Alan 1945- WhoAmL 92
**Fidelle**, Thomas Patrick 1939- AmMWSc 92
**Fidellow**, Edward Andre, Jr. 1946- WhoRel 92
**Fidelman**, Jack 1935- WhoFI 92
**Fidis**, Coventine 1947- WhoHisp 92
**Fidjestol**, Bjarne 1937- IntWW 91

**Fidlar**, Marion M 1909- *AmMWSc 92*
**Fidler**, Carol Ann 1942- *WhoMW 92*
**Fidler**, Isaiah J 1936- *AmMWSc 92*
**Fidler**, Jan 1927- *Who 92*
**Fidler**, John M 1947- *AmMWSc 92*
**Fidler**, Walther Balderson 1923- *WhoAmL 92*
**Fidler-Simpson**, John Cody *Who 92*
**Fidone**, Salvatore Joseph 1939- *AmMWSc 92*
**Fidrych**, Stanley Francis, Jr. 1950- *WhoFI 92*
**Fiebach**, H. Robert 1939- *WhoAmL 92*
**Fiebelman**, Kenneth Franklin 1941- *WhoAmP 91*
**Fiebert**, Gary Bruce 1947- *WhoFI 92*
**Fiebig**, Gregory Vernon 1957- *WhoRel 92*
**Fiebiger**, Daniel Joseph 1951- *WhoEnt 92*
**Fiebiger**, Stephen Charles 1958- *WhoAmL 92*
**Fiebrink**, Mark Edward 1951- *WhoIns 92*
**Fiedel**, Barry Allen *AmMWSc 92*
**Fiedelman**, Howard W 1916- *AmMWSc 92*
**Fiedelman**, Howard William 1916- *WhoMW 92*
**Fiedler**, Arthur 1894-1979 *ConMus 6 [port], NewAmDM*
**Fiedler**, Bobbi 1937- *WhoAmP 91*
**Fiedler**, Edward Henry, Jr. 1932- *WhoAmL 92*
**Fiedler**, Fred E 1922- *IntAu&W 91, WrDr 92*
**Fiedler**, George J *AmMWSc 92*
**Fiedler**, H C 1924- *AmMWSc 92*
**Fiedler**, Harold Joseph 1924- *AmMWSc 92*
**Fiedler**, J. Bernard 1949- *WhoFI 92*
**Fiedler**, Jean *DrAPF 91*
**Fiedler**, John *IntMPA 92*
**Fiedler**, John Amberg 1941- *WhoWest 92*
**Fiedler**, Leslie A. *DrAPF 91*
**Fiedler**, Leslie A. 1917- *BenetAL 91, ConNov 91, IntAu&W 91, IntWW 91, WrDr 92*
**Fiedler**, Leslie Aaron 1917- *WhoEnt 92*
**Fiedler**, Marc 1955- *WhoAmL 92*
**Fiedler**, Paul Charles 1953- *AmMWSc 92*
**Fiedler**, Sally A. *DrAPF 91*
**Fiedler**, Virginia Carol *AmMWSc 92*
**Fiedler-Nagy**, Christa 1943- *AmMWSc 92*
**Fief**, Madame de *EncAmaz 91*
**Fiegener**, Craig Allen 1971- *WhoWest 92*
**Fiel**, Robyn Ilene 1961- *WhoFI 92*
**Field**, A J 1924- *AmMWSc 92*
**Field**, Ada Martitia 1887-1972 *DcNCBi 2*
**Field**, Alexander James 1949- *WhoFI 92*
**Field**, Andrea Bear 1949- *WhoAmL 92*
**Field**, Anne 1926- *Who 92*
**Field**, Arnold 1917- *Who 92*
**Field**, Arthur Kirk 1938- *AmMWSc 92*
**Field**, Arthur Norman 1935- *WhoAmL 92*
**Field**, Barry John Anthony 1946- *Who 92*
**Field**, Byron Dustin 1918- *AmMWSc 92, WhoMW 92*
**Field**, Charles *TwCWW 91*
**Field**, Charles W. 1934- *WhoWest 92*
**Field**, Christopher Bower 1953- *AmMWSc 92*
**Field**, Corey 1956- *WhoEnt 92*
**Field**, Curtis Lincoln 1949- *WhoRel 92*
**Field**, Cyrus West 1933- *AmMWSc 92*
**Field**, D. M. *WrDr 92*
**Field**, David 1944- *ConAu 133*
**Field**, David Anthony *AmMWSc 92*
**Field**, David Charles 1953- *WhoAmL 92*
**Field**, David Dudley 1805-1894 *AmPeW*
**Field**, David Ellis 1953- *WhoAmL 92*
**Field**, David M. *IntMPA 92*
**Field**, Edward *DrAPF 91*
**Field**, Edward 1924- *ConPo 91, IntAu&W 91, WrDr 92*
**Field**, Edward John 1936- *Who 92*
**Field**, Edward Joseph 1958- *WhoRel 92*
**Field**, Ellen *WhoAmP 91*
**Field**, Eugene 1850-1895 *BenetAL 91*
**Field**, Frances *WhoAmP 91*
**Field**, Frank 1942- *Who 92, WrDr 92*
**Field**, Frank Chester *TwCWW 91*
**Field**, Frank Henry 1922- *AmMWSc 92*
**Field**, Frederick Gorham, Jr 1932- *WhoAmP 91*
**Field**, Geoffrey William 1941- *Who 92*
**Field**, George Brooks 1929- *AmMWSc 92*
**Field**, George Francis 1934- *AmMWSc 92*
**Field**, George Robert 1919- *AmMWSc 92*
**Field**, Hartry 1946- *IntWW 91*
**Field**, Helen 1951- *IntWW 91*
**Field**, Henry Frederick 1941- *WhoAmL 92*
**Field**, Herbert Cyre 1930- *AmMWSc 92*
**Field**, Hermann Haviland 1910- *AmMWSc 92, ConAu 135*
**Field**, Howard Lawrence 1928- *AmMWSc 92*
**Field**, Hugh Meyer 1944- *WhoAmL 92*
**Field**, Ian Trevor 1933- *Who 92*
**Field**, Jack Everett 1927- *AmMWSc 92*
**Field**, James Bernard 1926- *AmMWSc 92*
**Field**, Jay Ernest 1947- *AmMWSc 92*
**Field**, Jeffrey Frederic 1954- *WhoWest 92*
**Field**, Jill Margaret 1934- *Who 92*
**Field**, Joanna *IntAu&W 91X, WrDr 92*
**Field**, John d1991 *NewYTBS 91, Who 92N*
**Field**, John 1782-1837 *NewAmDM*
**Field**, Joseph M. 1810-1856 *BenetAL 91*
**Field**, Jules B. 1919- *WhoEnt 92*
**Field**, Julie Kunce 1959- *WhoAmL 92*
**Field**, Karen Ann 1936- *WhoMW 92*
**Field**, Katharine G 1951- *AmMWSc 92*
**Field**, Kent A. 1952- *WhoRel 92*
**Field**, Kurt William 1944- *AmMWSc 92*
**Field**, Lamar 1922- *AmMWSc 92*
**Field**, Leslie 1926- *WhoMW 92*
**Field**, Lester 1918- *AmMWSc 92*
**Field**, Lynda Katherine 1962- *WhoEnt 92*
**Field**, M. Patricia 1958- *WhoAmL 92*
**Field**, Malcolm David 1937- *Who 92*
**Field**, Mark G. 1923- *WrDr 92*
**Field**, Marlo *ScFEYrs*
**Field**, Marshall 1834-1906 *RComAH*
**Field**, Marshall 1941- *WhoFI 92, WhoMW 92*
**Field**, Marshall, III 1893-1956 *FacFETw [port]*
**Field**, Marshall Hayward 1930- *Who 92*
**Field**, Martha Amanda 1943- *WhoAmL 92*
**Field**, Martin 1773-1833 *BiInAmS*
**Field**, Marvin Frederick 1926- *AmMWSc 92*
**Field**, Michael *TwCLC 43 [port]*
**Field**, Michael 1914- *AmMWSc 92*
**Field**, Michael 1933- *AmMWSc 92*
**Field**, Michael Ehrenhart 1945- *AmMWSc 92*
**Field**, Michael Jay 1943- *WhoMW 92*
**Field**, Michael Walter 1948- *IntWW 91, Who 92*
**Field**, Nathan 1587-1619? *RfGEnL 91*
**Field**, Nathan David 1925- *AmMWSc 92*
**Field**, Noel Macdonald, Jr. 1934- *WhoAmL 92*
**Field**, Norman 1917- *TwCPaSc*
**Field**, Norman J 1922- *AmMWSc 92*
**Field**, Paul Eugene 1934- *AmMWSc 92*
**Field**, Paul L. 1925- *WhoFI 92*
**Field**, Peter *TwCWW 91*
**Field**, Peter 1926- *WhoAmP 91*
**Field**, Rachel 1894-1942 *BenetAL 91*
**Field**, Randi Sue 1956- *WhoAmL 92*
**Field**, Ray A 1933- *AmMWSc 92*
**Field**, Richard Alan 1947- *Who 92*
**Field**, Richard Clark 1940- *WhoAmL 92*
**Field**, Richard D 1944- *AmMWSc 92*
**Field**, Richard Jeffrey 1941- *AmMWSc 92, WhoWest 92*
**Field**, Robert Edward 1945- *WhoAmL 92, WhoFI 92, WhoMW 92*
**Field**, Robert Steven 1949- *WhoMW 92*
**Field**, Robert Warren 1944- *AmMWSc 92*
**Field**, Ronald James 1946- *AmMWSc 92*
**Field**, Ruth Bisen 1927- *AmMWSc 92*
**Field**, Sally *LesBEnT 92*
**Field**, Sally 1946- *IntMPA 92, WhoEnt 92*
**Field**, Sampson R. d1991 *NewYTBS 91*
**Field**, Sandra Gusciora 1958- *WhoAmL 92*
**Field**, Shirley Anne 1938- *IntMPA 92*
**Field**, Stanley *DrAPF 91*
**Field**, Ted *IntMPA 92, WhoEnt 92, WhoWest 92*
**Field**, Thomas George, Jr. 1942- *WhoAmL 92*
**Field**, William Bruce 1941- *WhoAmP 91*
**Field**, William James 1909- *Who 92*
**Field**, Wright *ScFEYrs*
**Field-Fisher**, Thomas Gilbert 1915- *Who 92*
**Field-Hyde**, Margaret 1905- *NewAmDM*
**Fielde**, Adele Marion 1839-1916 *BiInAmS*
**Fielden**, C. Franklin, III 1946- *WhoWest 92*
**Fielden**, Frank 1915- *Who 92*
**Fielder**, Barbara Lee 1942- *WhoWest 92*
**Fielder**, Cecil 1963- *WhoMW 92*
**Fielder**, Cecil Grant 1963- *WhoBlA 92*
**Fielder**, Charles William 1957- *WhoMW 92*
**Fielder**, D C 1917- *AmMWSc 92*
**Fielder**, Douglas Stratton 1940- *AmMWSc 92*
**Fielder**, Fred Charles 1933- *WhoBlA 92*
**Fielder**, Leslie A 1917- *FacFETw*
**Fielder**, Mildred 1913- *IntAu&W 91, WrDr 92*
**Fielder**, Rita Liggins 1944- *WhoMW 92*
**Fieldhouse** *Who 92*
**Fieldhouse**, Baron 1928- *IntWW 91, Who 92*
**Fieldhouse**, Brian 1933- *Who 92*
**Fieldhouse**, David K. 1925- *WrDr 92*
**Fieldhouse**, David Kenneth 1925- *Who 92*
**Fieldhouse**, David Kenneth 1927- *IntWW 91*
**Fieldhouse**, Donald John 1925- *AmMWSc 92*
**Fieldhouse**, Harold d1991 *Who 92N*
**Fieldhouse**, John W 1941- *AmMWSc 92*
**Fieldhouse**, Richard Arnold d1990 *Who 92N*
**Fieldhouse**, W.L. *TwCWW 91*
**Fieldhouse**, William *TwCWW 91*
**Fielding**, A.W. *ConAu 135*
**Fielding**, A W 1918- *IntAu&W 91, WrDr 92*
**Fielding**, Brian 1933-1987 *TwCPaSc*
**Fielding**, Christopher J 1942- *AmMWSc 92*
**Fielding**, Colin 1926- *Who 92*
**Fielding**, David Robert 1948- *WhoFI 92*
**Fielding**, Donald Howerton 1938- *WhoRel 92*
**Fielding**, Elizabeth May 1917- *WhoAmP 91*
**Fielding**, Fenella Marion 1934- *Who 92*
**Fielding**, Frank Stanley d1990 *Who 92N*
**Fielding**, Fred F 1939- *WhoAmP 91*
**Fielding**, Fred Fisher 1939- *WhoAmL 92*
**Fielding**, Harold Preston 1930- *WhoWest 92*
**Fielding**, Henry 1707-1754 *BlkwCEP, CnDBLB 2 [port], RfGEnL 91*
**Fielding**, Herbert U 1923- *WhoAmP 91*
**Fielding**, Herbert Ulysses 1923- *WhoBlA 92*
**Fielding**, Howard 1861-1929 *ScFEYrs*
**Fielding**, Leslie 1932- *IntWW 91, Who 92*
**Fielding**, Raymond 1931- *WrDr 92*
**Fielding**, Raymond Edwin 1931- *IntAu&W 91, WhoEnt 92*
**Fielding**, Richard Walter 1933- *Who 92*
**Fielding**, Ronald Herbert 1949- *WhoFI 92*
**Fielding**, Sarah 1710-1768 *BlkwCEP, RfGEnL 91*
**Fielding**, Stuart 1939- *AmMWSc 92*
**Fielding**, William J. 1886-1973 *ConAu 134*
**Fielding**, Xan *ConAu 135, IntAu&W 91X, WrDr 92*
**Fielding-Russell**, George Samuel 1939- *AmMWSc 92*
**Fieldler**, Cecil 1963- *ConBlB 2 [port]*
**Fieldman**, Gale 1941- *WhoAmL 92*
**Fieldman**, Wayne Lyle 1944- *WhoMW 92*
**Fields**, A. Leo 1947- *WhoBlA 92*
**Fields**, Alan *IntMPA 92*
**Fields**, Alfred E 1937- *AmMWSc 92*
**Fields**, Alva Dotson 1929- *WhoBlA 92*
**Fields**, Annie Adams 1834-1915 *BenetAL 91*
**Fields**, Arlonda M. 1963- *WhoBlA 92*
**Fields**, Barry Lee 1953- *WhoMW 92*
**Fields**, Bernard N 1938- *AmMWSc 92*
**Fields**, C Virginia 1946- *WhoAmP 91*
**Fields**, Clark Leroy 1937- *AmMWSc 92*
**Fields**, Cleo *WhoBlA 92*
**Fields**, Cleo 1962- *WhoAmP 91*
**Fields**, Curtis Grey 1933- *WhoFI 92, WhoMW 92*
**Fields**, Curtland Eugene 1951- *WhoFI 92*
**Fields**, Darrel Rex 1925- *WhoWest 92*
**Fields**, David C 1937- *WhoAmP 91*
**Fields**, David Edward 1944- *AmMWSc 92*
**Fields**, David Jon 1959- *WhoRel 92*
**Fields**, Davis S, Jr 1929- *AmMWSc 92*
**Fields**, Dennis Franklin, Sr. 1947- *WhoRel 92*
**Fields**, Dennis H 1945- *WhoAmP 91*
**Fields**, Dexter L. 1944- *WhoBlA 92*
**Fields**, Donald Brian 1950- *WhoAmL 92*
**Fields**, Donald Lee 1932- *AmMWSc 92*
**Fields**, Dorothy 1904-1974 *FacFETw*
**Fields**, Duggie 1945- *TwCPaSc*
**Fields**, Duncan Stanley 1956- *WhoAmL 92*
**Fields**, Earl Grayson 1935- *WhoBlA 92*
**Fields**, Edward E. 1918- *WhoBlA 92*
**Fields**, Ellis Kirby 1917- *AmMWSc 92*
**Fields**, Ewaugh Finney *WhoBlA 92*
**Fields**, Frank *TwCWW 91*
**Fields**, Freddie 1923- *IntMPA 92*
**Fields**, Gerald S 1929- *AmMWSc 92*
**Fields**, Gracie 1898-1979 *FacFETw*
**Fields**, Hanoch Michael 1961- *WhoRel 92*
**Fields**, Henry Michael 1946- *WhoAmL 92*
**Fields**, Howard Lincoln 1939- *AmMWSc 92*
**Fields**, Hugh G 1930- *WhoAmP 91*
**Fields**, Inez C. *WhoBlA 92*
**Fields**, Jack M., Jr. 1952- *AlmAP 92 [port], WhoAmP 91*
**Fields**, James Edward, Jr. 1963- *WhoRel 92*
**Fields**, James Perry 1932- *AmMWSc 92*
**Fields**, James T. 1817-1881 *BenetAL 91*
**Fields**, Jason Roy 1970- *WhoEnt 92*
**Fields**, Jennie *DrAPF 91*
**Fields**, Jerry L 1936- *AmMWSc 92*
**Fields**, Julia *DrAPF 91*
**Fields**, Kay Louise 1941- *AmMWSc 92*
**Fields**, Kenneth 1962- *WhoBlA 92*
**Fields**, Kim 1969- *WhoBlA 92*
**Fields**, Lewis Maurice 1867-1941 *BenetAL 91*
**Fields**, M. Joan 1934- *WhoBlA 92*
**Fields**, Marion Lee 1926- *AmMWSc 92*
**Fields**, Marjory Diana 1942- *WhoAmL 92*
**Fields**, Mary *EncAmaz 91*
**Fields**, Mary 1832?-1914 *NotBlAW 92*
**Fields**, Nathaniel 1949- *WhoBlA 92*
**Fields**, Paul Robert 1919- *AmMWSc 92*
**Fields**, Peppy 1907- *WhoEnt 92*
**Fields**, R Wayne 1941- *AmMWSc 92, WhoWest 92*
**Fields**, Reuben Elbert 1916- *AmMWSc 92*
**Fields**, Richard A. 1950- *WhoBlA 92*
**Fields**, Richard Joel 1947- *AmMWSc 92*
**Fields**, Rick *DrAPF 91*
**Fields**, Robbie Shannon 1952- *WhoEnt 92*
**Fields**, Robert William 1920- *AmMWSc 92*
**Fields**, Robin F. 1955- *WhoAmL 92*
**Fields**, Samuel Bennie 1925- *WhoBlA 92*
**Fields**, Samuel Preston, Jr. 1918- *WhoRel 92*
**Fields**, Savoynne Morgan 1950- *WhoBlA 92*
**Fields**, Scott 1956- *ConAu 134*
**Fields**, Stanley 1930- *WhoBlA 92*
**Fields**, Stuart Howard 1943- *WhoFI 92*
**Fields**, Terence 1937- *Who 92*
**Fields**, Theodore 1922- *AmMWSc 92, WhoMW 92*
**Fields**, Thomas Eric 1948- *WhoAmP 91*
**Fields**, Thomas Gibson 1920- *WhoEnt 92*
**Fields**, Thomas Henry 1930- *AmMWSc 92*
**Fields**, Thomas Lynn 1925- *AmMWSc 92*
**Fields**, Verna 1918-1982 *ReelWom*
**Fields**, Victor Hugo 1907- *WhoBlA 92*
**Fields**, W C 1879-1946 *FacFETw*
**Fields**, Wayne *WrDr 92*
**Fields**, Wayne 1942- *ConAu 134*
**Fields**, William Gordon 1912- *AmMWSc 92*
**Fields**, William I., Jr. 1944- *WhoBlA 92*
**Fields**, William Straus 1913- *AmMWSc 92*
**Fields**, Wilmer Clemont 1922- *WhoRel 92*
**Fieldsend**, John Charles Rowell 1921- *IntWW 91, Who 92*
**Fieldsteel**, Jan Ellen 1960- *WhoAmL 92*
**Fieleke**, Norman Siegfried 1932- *WhoFI 92*
**Fienberg**, Stephen Elliott 1942- *AmMWSc 92*
**Fienen**, Daniel Henry 1952- *WhoRel 92*
**Fienen**, David Norman 1946- *WhoMW 92*
**Fiennes** *Who 92*
**Fiennes**, Maurice 1907- *Who 92*
**Fiennes**, Oliver W Twisleton-Wykeham- 1926- *Who 92*
**Fiennes**, Ranulph 1944- *WrDr 92*
**Fiennes**, Ranulph Twisleton-Wykeham 1944- *IntAu&W 91, IntWW 91, Who 92*
**Fiennes-Clinton** *Who 92*
**Fienup**, James R 1948- *AmMWSc 92*
**Fienup**, James Ray 1948- *WhoMW 92*
**Fierberg**, Steven Edward 1954- *WhoEnt 92*
**Fierce**, Hughlyn F. *WhoBlA 92*
**Fierce**, Milfred C. 1937- *WhoBlA 92*
**Fierer**, Joshua A 1937- *AmMWSc 92*
**Fiering**, Myron B 1934- *AmMWSc 92*
**Fierlinger**, Paul 1936- *WhoEnt 92*
**Fierman**, Paula A. *WhoEnt 92*
**Fiero**, George William, Jr 1936- *AmMWSc 92*
**Fiero**, Patricia G *WhoAmP 91*
**Fierro**, Alex 1927- *WhoHisp 92*
**Fierro**, Enrique 1941- *ConSpAP*
**Fierro**, Eugene John 1941- *WhoAmL 92*
**Fierros**, Juan Enrique 1951- *WhoHisp 92*
**Fierros**, Mario 1926- *WhoHisp 92*
**Fiers**, Alan Dale, Jr. 1939- *NewYTBS 91 [port]*
**Fierstein**, Harvey *IntWW 91*
**Fierstein**, Harvey 1954- *BenetAL 91, IntMPA 92, WrDr 92*
**Fierstein**, Harvey Forbes 1954- *WhoEnt 92*
**Fierstine**, Harry Lee 1932- *AmMWSc 92*
**Fiesinger**, Donald William 1943- *AmMWSc 92*
**Fiesler**, Emile *AmMWSc 92*
**Fiess**, Harold Alvin 1917- *AmMWSc 92*
**Fiete**, Richard Wayne 1938- *WhoRel 92*
**Fietsam**, Robert Charles 1927- *WhoFI 92, WhoMW 92*
**Fietz**, William Adolf 1931- *AmMWSc 92*
**Fieve**, Ronald Robert 1930- *AmMWSc 92*
**Fife**, Duke of 1929- *Who 92*
**Fife**, Barbara J *WhoAmP 91*
**Fife**, David Joel 1950- *WhoRel 92*
**Fife**, David Lee 1936- *WhoRel 92*
**Fife**, Dennis Jensen 1945- *WhoWest 92*
**Fife**, Elaine Harner 1950- *WhoAmL 92*
**Fife**, G. Patric 1946- *WhoRel 92*
**Fife**, Joan Blanche Tucker 1961- *WhoAmL 92*
**Fife**, John Douglas, Jr. 1955- *WhoFI 92*
**Fife**, Lorin Merrill, III 1953- *WhoWest 92*
**Fife**, Paul Chase 1930- *AmMWSc 92*
**Fife**, Thomas Harley 1931- *AmMWSc 92*
**Fife**, William Franklin 1921- *WhoFI 92*
**Fife**, William Paul 1917- *AmMWSc 92*
**Fife**, Wilmer Krafft 1933- *AmMWSc 92, WhoMW 92*
**Fifer**, Ken *DrAPF 91*
**Fifer**, Robert Alan 1943- *AmMWSc 92*
**Fifield**, Esther L *WhoAmP 91*

**Fifield**, Richard Delmage 1946- WhoRel 92
**Fifkova**, Eva 1932- AmMWSc 92
**Fifner**, Douglas Karl 1953- WhoAmL 92
**Fifoot**, Erik Richard Sidney 1925- Who 92
**Fifoot**, Paul Ronald Ninnes 1928- Who 92
**Figa**, Candace Cole 1951- WhoAmL 92
**Figa**, Phillip Sam 1951- WhoAmL 92
**Figaro**, Mark O. 1921- WhoBlA 92
**Figart**, Deborah M. 1959- WhoMW 92
**Figart**, Thomas Orlando 1925- WhoRel 92
**Figdor**, Sanford Kermit 1926- AmMWSc 92
**Figes**, Eva 1932- ConNov 91, IntAu&W 91, LiExTwC, WrDr 92
**Figg**, Leonard 1923- Who 92
**Figg**, Mary 1934- WhoAmP 91
**Figg**, Robert McCormick, Jr. 1901- WhoAmL 92
**Figg**, William Carl, Jr. 1949- WhoWest 92
**Figge**, Charlene Elizabeth 1948- WhoRel 92
**Figge**, David C 1925- AmMWSc 92
**Figge**, F. J., II WhoFI 92
**Figgess**, John 1909- Who 92
**Figgie**, Harry E., Jr. 1923- WhoMW 92
**Figgins**, Letha Arlene 1916- WhoMW 92
**Figgis**, Anthony St John Howard 1940- Who 92
**Figgis**, Arthur Lenox 1918- Who 92
**Figgis**, Brian Norman 1930- IntWW 91
**Figgures**, Frank 1910-1990 AnObit 1990
**Figgures**, Frank Edward d1990 Who 92N
**Figley**, Melvin Morgan 1920- AmMWSc 92
**Figlioli**, Jerry V. 1957- WhoFI 92
**Figliozzi**, John Philip 1946- WhoFI 92, WhoMW 92
**Figman**, Elliot DrAPF 91
**Fignar**, Eugene Michael 1946- WhoAmL 92
**Fignar**, Rosemary Casey 1945- WhoFI 92
**Figucia**, Joseph Charles, Jr. 1957- WhoEnt 92
**Figueira**, Joseph Franklin 1943- AmMWSc 92
**Figueiredo**, Elisio de 1940- IntWW 91
**Figueiredo**, Hubert Fernandes 1958- WhoWest 92
**Figueiredo**, Joao Baptista de 1918- IntWW 91
**Figuera**, Angela 1902-1984 DcLB 108 [port]
**Figueras**, John 1924- AmMWSc 92
**Figueras**, Patricia Ann McVeigh 1933- AmMWSc 92
**Figueredo**, Candelaria EncAmaz 91
**Figueredo**, Danilo H. 1951- WhoHisp 92
**Figueredo**, Luis Rene 1959- WhoAmL 92
**Figueres**, Jose 1906-1990 AnObit 1990
**Figueres Ferrer**, Jose d1990 IntWW 91N
**Figueres Ferrer**, Jose 1906-1990 FacFETw
**Figueroa**, Adolfo 1941- IntWW 91
**Figueroa**, Alfredo WhoHisp 92
**Figueroa**, Angela WhoHisp 92
**Figueroa**, Angelo 1957- WhoHisp 92
**Figueroa**, Antonio WhoHisp 92
**Figueroa**, Benito, Jr. 1947- WhoHisp 92
**Figueroa**, Daphne Elizabeth 1960- WhoHisp 92
**Figueroa**, Darryl Lynette 1959- WhoHisp 92
**Figueroa**, Edna WhoHisp 92
**Figueroa**, Enrique Esquivel 1951- WhoHisp 92
**Figueroa**, Howard George 1930- WhoFI 92
**Figueroa**, J. Fernando 1957- WhoHisp 92
**Figueroa**, John 1920- WrDr 92
**Figueroa**, John 1949- WhoHisp 92
**Figueroa**, John J 1920- ConPo 91
**Figueroa**, Jose-Angel DrAPF 91
**Figueroa**, Juan A. 1953- WhoHisp 92
**Figueroa**, Juan Alberto 1953- WhoAmP 91
**Figueroa**, Julian 1943- WhoHisp 92
**Figueroa**, Liz 1951- WhoHisp 92
**Figueroa**, Luis 1951- WhoFI 92
**Figueroa**, Luis Guillermo 1954- WhoAmL 92
**Figueroa**, Manuel 1959- WhoHisp 92
**Figueroa**, Mario WhoHisp 92
**Figueroa**, Michael Otto 1943- WhoWest 92
**Figueroa**, Nicholas 1933- WhoHisp 92
**Figueroa**, Octavio Alfonso 1949- WhoHisp 92
**Figueroa**, Octavio D., Jr. 1942- WhoHisp 92
**Figueroa**, Raul 1946- WhoHisp 92
**Figueroa**, Raymond 1947- WhoAmP 91, WhoHisp 92
**Figueroa**, Roberto WhoHisp 92
**Figueroa**, Samuel I. 1955- WhoHisp 92
**Figueroa**, Sandra 1946- WhoHisp 92
**Figueroa**, Sandra L. WhoHisp 92
**Figueroa**, William Gutierrez 1921- AmMWSc 92
**Figueroa Chapel**, Ramon DrAPF 91
**Figueroa-Orozco**, Victor WhoHisp 92
**Figueroa-Sarriera**, Heidi Judith 1958- WhoHisp 92
**Figuerola Camue**, Enrique 1938- BlkOlyM
**Figueur**, Theresa 1774-1839 EncAmaz 91
**Figuieras**, John Steven 1953- WhoMW 92
**Figura**, Roger Stanley 1945- WhoFI 92
**Figures**, Colin 1925- Who 92
**Figures**, Michael 1947- WhoBlA 92
**Figures**, Michael A 1947- WhoAmP 91
**Figures**, Thomas H. 1944- WhoBlA 92
**Figurski**, David Henry 1947- AmMWSc 92
**Figurski**, Gerald Anthony 1945- WhoAmL 92
**Figwer**, J Jacek 1928- AmMWSc 92
**Fihn**, Jeffrey Glaser 1949- WhoAmL 92
**Fiil**, Niels Peter 1941- IntWW 91
**Fijalkowski**, Stanislaw 1922- IntWW 91
**Fijolek**, Richard Marion 1958- WhoAmL 92
**Fike**, Barry Don 1955- WhoRel 92
**Fike**, Edward Lake 1920- WhoWest 92
**Fike**, Harold Lester 1926- AmMWSc 92
**Fike**, William Thomas, Jr 1928- AmMWSc 92
**Fike**, Winston 1921- AmMWSc 92
**Fikentscher**, Wolfgang 1928- IntWW 91
**Fikre-Selassie**, Wogderess IntWW 91
**Filachione**, Edward Mario 1909- AmMWSc 92
**Filadelfi-Keszi**, Mary Ann Stephanie 1952- AmMWSc 92
**Filak**, David Francis 1952- WhoMW 92
**Filali**, Abdellatif 1928- IntWW 91
**Filandro**, Anthony Salvatore 1930- AmMWSc 92
**Filangieri**, Gaetano 1752-1788 BlkwCEP
**Filano**, Albert E 1925- AmMWSc 92
**Filante**, William Jules 1929- WhoAmP 91
**Filardi**, Constantine Basil 1930- WhoAmL 92
**Filardo**, Leonor IntWW 91
**Filaret** IntWW 91
**Filas**, Robert William 1947- AmMWSc 92
**Filastrius of Brescia** d397? EncEarC
**Filatchev**, Oleg Pavlovich 1937- SovUnBD
**Filatov**, Aleksandr Pavlovich 1922- IntWW 91
**Filatov**, Sergey Mironovich 1925- SovUnBD
**Filatova**, Ludmila Pavlovna 1935- IntWW 91
**Filbert**, Augustus Myers 1933- AmMWSc 92
**Filbert**, Gary Preston 1929- WhoMW 92
**Filbey**, Allen Howard 1927- AmMWSc 92
**Filbin**, James 1932- IntAu&W 91
**Filbin**, Thomas DrAPF 91
**Filbinger**, Hans Karl 1913- IntWW 91
**Filby**, P. William 1911- WrDr 92
**Filby**, Royston Herbert 1934- AmMWSc 92
**Filby**, William Charles Leonard 1933- Who 92
**Filcek**, Rodney Raymond 1953- WhoMW 92
**Filchock**, Ethel WhoMW 92
**Fildes**, Luke 1843-1927 TwCPaSc
**File**, Joseph 1923- AmMWSc 92
**Filene**, Edward Albert 1860-1937 FacFETw
**Filener**, Millard Lee 1946- WhoFI 92
**Filer**, Crist Nicholas 1949- AmMWSc 92
**Filer**, Denis Edwin 1932- Who 92
**Filer**, Kelvin Dean 1955- WhoBlA 92
**Filer**, Lloyd Jackson, Jr 1919- AmMWSc 92
**Filer**, Randall Keith 1952- WhoFI 92
**Filer**, Theodore H, Jr 1928- AmMWSc 92
**Filerman**, Michael LesBEnT 92
**Filerman**, Michael Herman 1938- WhoEnt 92
**Files**, Gordon Louis 1912- WhoWest 92
**Files**, Mark Willard 1941- WhoFI 92
**Files**, Richard Lloyd 1941- WhoFI 92
**Filevich**, Basil WhoRel 92, WhoWest 92
**Filgo**, Holland Cleveland, Jr 1926- AmMWSc 92
**Filhiol**, Georgia Blanchard 1934- WhoRel 92
**Filiatrault**, Edward John, Jr. 1938- WhoFI 92
**Filiault**, Joss Richard 1956- WhoAmL 92
**Filice**, Francis P 1922- AmMWSc 92
**Filing**, Nicholas A 1947- WhoIns 92
**Filiol**, Jean Paul Robert 1909- BiDExR
**Filip**, Joseph Stuart 1947- WhoAmP 91
**Filipacchi**, Daniel 1928- IntWW 91
**Filipchenko**, Yury Aleksandrovich 1882-1930 SovUnBD
**Filipek**, Stephan John 1959- WhoAmL 92
**Filipescu**, Nicolae 1935- AmMWSc 92
**Filipo**, Liufau WhoAmP 91
**Filipov**, Grisha 1919- IntWW 91
**Filipovich**, Alexandra H AmMWSc 92
**Filipp**, Mark Richard 1955- WhoAmL 92
**Filippenko**, Alexei Vladimir 1958- AmMWSc 92
**Filippenko**, Vladimir I 1930- AmMWSc 92
**Filippine**, Edward Louis 1930- WhoAmL 92
**Filippone**, Ella Finger 1935- WhoFI 92
**Filippou**, Filip C 1955- AmMWSc 92
**Filipps**, Frank Peter 1947- WhoFI 92, WhoIns 92
**Filippuzzi**, Richard Alan 1959- WhoWest 92
**Filipski**, Alan James 1946- WhoWest 92
**Filisko**, Frank Edward 1942- AmMWSc 92
**Filisola**, Vicente HisDSpE
**Filkin**, Elizabeth 1940- Who 92
**Filkins**, James P 1936- AmMWSc 92
**Filkke**, Arnold M 1919- AmMWSc 92
**Fill**, Gerald A Andrew 1938- WhoAmP 91
**Fillebrown**, Thomas 1836-1908 BiInAmS
**Filler**, Lewis 1928- AmMWSc 92
**Filler**, Robert 1923- AmMWSc 92, WhoMW 92
**Filler**, Ronald Howard 1948- WhoAmL 92
**Filler**, Susan Melanie 1947- WhoEnt 92
**Fillers**, R. P. 1955- WhoEnt 92
**Fillerup**, Melvin McDonald 1924- WhoWest 92
**Fillet**, Mitchell Harris 1948- WhoFI 92
**Fillet**, Robert E. 1921- WhoWest 92
**Filleul**, Peter Amy 1929- Who 92
**Filley**, Bette Elaine 1933- WhoWest 92
**Filley**, Denise Kay 1964- WhoMW 92
**Filley**, Giles Franklin 1915- AmMWSc 92
**Filliben**, James John 1943- AmMWSc 92
**Fillicaro**, Barbara Jean WhoMW 92
**Filling**, Richard Rice 1932- WhoAmP 91
**Fillingham**, Patricia DrAPF 91
**Fillion**, Paul R 1920- WhoAmP 91
**Fillios**, Louis Charles 1923- AmMWSc 92
**Fillioud**, Georges 1929- IntWW 91
**Fillipi**, Gordon Michael 1940- AmMWSc 92
**Fillippone**, Walter R 1921- AmMWSc 92
**Fillius**, Walker 1937- AmMWSc 92
**Fillmer**, Leslie Donald 1949- WhoEnt 92
**Fillmore**, Charles Sherlock 1854-1948 RelLAm 91
**Fillmore**, Henry 1881-1956 NewAmDM
**Fillmore**, Millard 1800-1874 AmPolLe [port], BenetAL 91, RComAH
**Fillmore**, Myrtle 1845-1931 RelLAm 91
**Fillmore**, Peter Arthur 1936- AmMWSc 92
**Fillmore**, Scott James 1960- WhoMW 92
**Fillmore**, William L. WhoWest 92
**Fillo**, Joseph Francis 1953- WhoFI 92
**Filmer**, David Lee 1932- AmMWSc 92
**Filmon**, Gary Albert 1942- WhoMW 92
**Filner**, Barbara 1941- AmMWSc 92
**Filner**, Philip 1939- AmMWSc 92
**Filon**, Sidney Philip Lawrence 1905- Who 92
**Filonov**, Pavel Nikolaevich 1883-1941 SovUnBD
**Filosa**, Gary 1931- WrDr 92
**Filosa**, Gary Fairmont Randolph V., II 1931- WhoEnt 92, WhoFI 92, WhoWest 92
**Filosa**, Renato IntWW 91
**Filseth**, Stephen V 1936- AmMWSc 92
**Fil'shin**, Gennadiy Innokent'evich 1931- SovUnBD
**Filshin**, Gennadiy Innokentovich 1931- IntWW 91
**Filson**, Brent DrAPF 91
**Filson**, Don P 1931- AmMWSc 92
**Filson**, John 1747?-1788 BenetAL 91
**Filson**, Malcolm Harold 1907- AmMWSc 92
**Filson**, Marguerite B. 1935- WhoAmL 92
**Filteau**, Gabriel 1918- AmMWSc 92
**Filter**, Eunice M. 1940- WhoFI 92
**Filtzer**, Donald 1948- IntAu&W 91
**Fimbres**, Gabrielle M. 1963- WhoHisp 92
**Fimbres**, Martha M. 1948- WhoHisp 92
**Fimian**, Walter Joseph, Jr 1926- AmMWSc 92
**Fina**, Louis R 1918- AmMWSc 92
**Finaish**, Mohamed 1936- IntWW 91
**Finale**, Frank Louis DrAPF 91
**Finale**, Frank Louis 1942- IntAu&W 91
**Finan**, Ellen Cranston 1951- WhoWest 92
**Finan**, Richard H 1934- WhoAmP 91
**Finan**, W Timothy 1950- WhoAmP 91
**Finando**, Steven J 1948- AmMWSc 92
**Finau**, Patelisio Punou-Ki-Hihifo WhoRel 92
**Finazzo**, Christopher Steven 1954- WhoAmL 92
**Finberg**, James Michael 1958- WhoAmL 92
**Finberg**, Laurence 1923- AmMWSc 92
**Finberg**, Robert William 1950- AmMWSc 92
**Fincastle**, Viscount 1946- Who 92
**Finch**, Anne RfGEnL 91
**Finch**, Anne 1661-1720 BlkwCEP
**Finch**, Annie DrAPF 91
**Finch**, C R 1928- AmMWSc 92
**Finch**, Caleb Ellicott 1939- AmMWSc 92, WhoWest 92
**Finch**, Christopher 1939- WrDr 92
**Finch**, Clement Alfred 1915- AmMWSc 92
**Finch**, Deborah Marie 1954- WhoWest 92
**Finch**, Edward Francis 1947- WhoMW 92
**Finch**, Edward Ridley, Jr. 1919- WhoAmL 92
**Finch**, Flora 1947- WhoWest 92
**Finch**, Floyd Raymond, Jr WhoAmP 91
**Finch**, Floyd Raymond, Jr. 1953- WhoAmL 92
**Finch**, Francis Miles 1827-1907 BenetAL 91
**Finch**, Gaylord Kirkwood 1923- AmMWSc 92
**Finch**, George Augustus 1884-1957 AmPeW
**Finch**, George Ingle 1888-1970 FacFETw
**Finch**, George Nelson 1926- WhoFI 92
**Finch**, Gregory Martin 1951- WhoBlA 92
**Finch**, Harold Bertram, Jr. 1927- WhoFI 92, WhoMW 92
**Finch**, Harry C 1917- AmMWSc 92
**Finch**, Jack Norman 1923- AmMWSc 92
**Finch**, James Earl 1958- WhoMW 92
**Finch**, James Larry 1953- WhoEnt 92
**Finch**, Janet M. 1950- WhoBlA 92
**Finch**, John Vernor 1917- AmMWSc 92
**Finch**, Jon 1942- IntMPA 92
**Finch**, Jon Nicholas 1943- IntWW 91
**Finch**, Josiah John 1814-1850 DcNCBi 2
**Finch**, Kenneth Allen 1959- WhoRel 92
**Finch**, Matthew IntAu&W 91X, WrDr 92
**Finch**, Merton IntAu&W 91X, WrDr 92
**Finch**, Michael Paul 1946- WhoAmL 92
**Finch**, Michael Steven 1952- WhoAmL 92
**Finch**, Pearl Lamm 1927- WhoAmP 91
**Finch**, Peter 1947- IntAu&W 91, WrDr 92
**Finch**, Raymond Lawrence 1940- WhoBlA 92
**Finch**, Robert 1900- ConPo 91, IntAu&W 91, WrDr 92
**Finch**, Robert Allen 1941- AmMWSc 92
**Finch**, Robert D 1938- AmMWSc 92
**Finch**, Robert Hutchison 1925- WhoAmP 91
**Finch**, Rogers B 1920- AmMWSc 92
**Finch**, Ronald Corydon 1934- WhoAmL 92
**Finch**, Ruth L. 1950- WhoAmL 92
**Finch**, Samuel Prestley, III 1942- WhoWest 92
**Finch**, Sheila 1935- IntAu&W 91
**Finch**, Stephen Clark 1929- Who 92
**Finch**, Stephen Joseph 1945- AmMWSc 92
**Finch**, Stuart Cecil 1921- AmMWSc 92
**Finch**, Stuart McIntyre 1919- AmMWSc 92
**Finch**, Thomas Austin, Sr. 1890-1943 DcNCBi 2
**Finch**, Thomas Jefferson 1861-1929 DcNCBi 2
**Finch**, Thomas Lassfolk 1926- AmMWSc 92
**Finch**, Thomas Wesley 1946- AmMWSc 92, WhoWest 92
**Finch**, Walter Goss Gilchrist 1918- WhoFI 92
**Finch**, Warren Irvin 1924- AmMWSc 92, WhoWest 92
**Finch**, William G. H. d1990 IntWW 91N
**Finch**, William H. 1924- WhoBlA 92
**Finch Hatton** Who 92
**Finch-Knightley** Who 92
**Fincham**, John Robert Stanley 1926- IntWW 91, Who 92
**Finchell**, A. Richard 1927- WhoFI 92
**Fincher**, Beatrice Gonzalez 1941- WhoHisp 92
**Fincher**, Bobby Lee 1934- AmMWSc 92
**Fincher**, Edward Lester 1921- AmMWSc 92
**Fincher**, George Truman 1939- AmMWSc 92
**Fincher**, John Albert 1911- AmMWSc 92
**Fincher**, Julian H 1935- AmMWSc 92
**Fincher**, W W, Jr WhoAmP 91
**Finck**, Douglas Parsons 1951- WhoEnt 92
**Finck**, Heinrich 1445-1527 NewAmDM
**Finck**, Kevin William 1954- WhoAmL 92
**Fincke**, Gary DrAPF 91
**Fincke**, Margaret Louise 1900- AmMWSc 92
**Fincke**, Waring Roberts 1945- WhoAmL 92
**Finckenstein**, Stefan, Graf Finck von 1961- IntWW 91
**Finckh**, Ludwig 1876-1964 EncTR 91
**Finckley**, Thomas d1695? DcNCBi 2
**Finco**, Arthur A 1932- AmMWSc 92
**Finco**, Delmar R 1936- AmMWSc 92
**Finder**, Alan Eliot 1952- WhoFI 92
**Finder**, Theodore Roosevelt 1914- WhoAmL 92
**Finder-Stone**, Patricia Ann 1929- WhoMW 92
**Findlay**, Alastair Donald Fraser 1944- Who 92
**Findlay**, Alice M. WhoRel 92
**Findlay**, David W. 1946- WhoWest 92
**Findlay**, Donald Russell 1951- Who 92
**Findlay**, Glen Marshall 1940- WhoMW 92

**Findlay,** Ian Herbert Fyfe 1918- *IntWW 91, Who 92*
**Findlay,** James Stewart 1934- *WhoRel 92*
**Findlay,** John A 1936- *AmMWSc 92*
**Findlay,** John W A 1945- *AmMWSc 92*
**Findlay,** John Wilson 1915- *AmMWSc 92*
**Findlay,** Raymond D 1938- *AmMWSc 92*
**Findlay,** Roberta 1952- *WhoEnt 92*
**Findlay,** Timothy 1930- *BenetAL 91*
**Findler,** Nicholas Victor 1930- *AmMWSc 92*
**Findley,** Don Aaron 1926- *WhoFI 92*
**Findley,** F A 1918- *WhoAmP 91*
**Findley,** Hazel Winifred Rockwell 1911- *WhoAmP 91*
**Findley,** James E. 1923- *WhoWest 92*
**Findley,** James Smith 1926- *AmMWSc 92*
**Findley,** Kristin Wallace 1942- *WhoAmP 91*
**Findley,** Lawrence Arne 1947- *WhoMW 92*
**Findley,** Marshall E 1927- *AmMWSc 92*
**Findley,** Mary Baker 1943- *WhoEnt 92*
**Findley,** Mary Lou McBroom 1945- *WhoMW 92*
**Findley,** Paul 1921- *WhoAmP 91*
**Findley,** Stephen Charles 1949- *WhoAmL 92*
**Findley,** Timothy 1930- *ConNov 91, WrDr 92*
**Findley,** Timothy Irving Frederick 1930- *IntAu&W 91*
**Findley,** William N 1914- *AmMWSc 92*
**Findley,** William Ray, Jr 1920- *AmMWSc 92*
**Findley,** William Robert 1935- *AmMWSc 92*
**Findling,** John Ellis 1941- *WhoMW 92*
**Fine,** Adrian 1945- *AmMWSc 92*
**Fine,** Albert Samuel 1923- *AmMWSc 92*
**Fine,** Anne 1947- *ChlLR 25 [port], IntAu&W 91, WrDr 92*
**Fine,** Arthur Kenneth 1937- *WhoAmL 92*
**Fine,** Barry Kenneth 1938- *WhoFI 92*
**Fine,** Ben Sion 1928- *AmMWSc 92*
**Fine,** Benjamin 1948- *AmMWSc 92*
**Fine,** Bob 1949- *WhoFI 92*
**Fine,** Burton *WhoEnt 92*
**Fine,** David H 1942- *AmMWSc 92*
**Fine,** David Jeffrey 1950- *WhoFI 92*
**Fine,** Deborah Jane 1942- *WhoEnt 92*
**Fine,** Donald I. 1922- *IntWW 91*
**Fine,** Donald Lee 1943- *AmMWSc 92*
**Fine,** Douglas P 1943- *AmMWSc 92*
**Fine,** Dwight Albert 1933- *AmMWSc 92*
**Fine,** Edward Haskell *WhoAmL 92*
**Fine,** Eric Douglas 1966- *WhoFI 92*
**Fine,** Franklin Marshall 1947- *WhoWest 92*
**Fine,** Gregory Monroe 1957- *WhoRel 92*
**Fine,** Howard Alan 1941- *WhoFI 92*
**Fine,** Howard Floyd 1950- *WhoAmL 92*
**Fine,** Irving 1914-1962 *NewAmDM*
**Fine,** James Allen 1934- *WhoFI 92*
**Fine,** Jo-David 1950- *AmMWSc 92*
**Fine,** John Van Antwerp 1939- *IntAu&W 91*
**Fine,** Joseph Loyd, Jr 1937- *WhoAmP 91*
**Fine,** Kenneth Richard 1956- *WhoFI 92*
**Fine,** Lawrence Oliver 1917- *AmMWSc 92*
**Fine,** Leonard W 1935- *AmMWSc 92*
**Fine,** Marlene Rosen *DrAPF 91*
**Fine,** Michael 1953- *WhoMW 92*
**Fine,** Michael Lawrence 1946- *AmMWSc 92*
**Fine,** Morris Eugene 1918- *AmMWSc 92*
**Fine,** Morris M 1914- *AmMWSc 92*
**Fine,** Neal Harvey 1944- *WhoAmL 92*
**Fine,** Paul Leonard 1962- *WhoFI 92*
**Fine,** Ralph 1928- *WhoFI 92*
**Fine,** Ralph Adam 1941- *WhoAmL 92*
**Fine,** Rana Arnold 1944- *AmMWSc 92*
**Fine,** Richard Eliot 1942- *AmMWSc 92*
**Fine,** Richard Isaac 1940- *WhoAmL 92, WhoFI 92, WhoWest 92*
**Fine,** Roberta Sue 1957- *WhoAmL 92*
**Fine,** Samuel 1925- *AmMWSc 92*
**Fine,** Sidney 1920- *WhoMW 92, WrDr 92*
**Fine,** Terrence Leon 1939- *AmMWSc 92*
**Fine,** Verna 1920- *WhoEnt 92*
**Fine,** Vivian 1913- *ConCom 92, NewAmDM, WhoEnt 92*
**Fine,** William Irwin 1928- *WhoMW 92*
**Finebaum,** Murray L. 1942- *WhoFI 92*
**Fineberg,** Charles 1921- *AmMWSc 92*
**Fineberg,** Harvey V 1945- *AmMWSc 92*
**Fineberg,** Herbert 1915- *AmMWSc 92*
**Fineberg,** Naomi Schwartz 1940- *WhoMW 92*
**Fineberg,** Richard Arnold 1922- *AmMWSc 92*
**Fineberg,** Robert Alan 1948- *WhoAmL 92*
**Finefield,** Suzanne Seibel 1950- *WhoRel 92*
**Fineg,** Jerry 1928- *AmMWSc 92*
**Finegan,** Jack 1908- *IntAu&W 91, WrDr 92*
**Finegan,** Patrick T'ung 1959- *WhoAmL 92*
**Finegold,** Leonard X 1935- *AmMWSc 92*
**Finegold,** Milton J 1935- *AmMWSc 92*
**Finegold,** Ronald 1942- *WhoFI 92*
**Finegold,** Sydney Martin 1921- *AmMWSc 92*
**Finelli,** Anthony Francis 1922- *AmMWSc 92*
**Finello,** Daniel J, Jr 1951- *WhoAmP 91*
**Fineman,** Daniel David 1949- *WhoWest 92*
**Fineman,** Howard 1948- *ConAu 133*
**Fineman,** Howard David 1948- *WhoEnt 92*
**Fineman,** Irving 1893- *BenetAL 91*
**Fineman,** Karen 1963- *WhoEnt 92*
**Fineman,** Manuel Nathan 1920- *AmMWSc 92*
**Fineman,** Martin Lee 1957- *WhoAmL 92*
**Fineman,** Morton A 1919- *AmMWSc 92*
**Fineman,** S. David 1945- *WhoAmL 92*
**Finer,** Elliot Geoffrey 1944- *Who 92*
**Finer,** Jeffry Keith 1955- *WhoAmL 92*
**Finer,** Michael Scott 1964- *WhoFI 92*
**Finer,** Samuel 1915- *IntAu&W 91, WrDr 92*
**Finer,** Samuel Edward 1915- *Who 92*
**Finerman,** A 1925- *AmMWSc 92*
**Finerman,** Scott Curtis 1960- *WhoMW 92*
**Finerty,** John Charles 1914- *AmMWSc 92*
**Fineshriber,** William H., Jr. 1909- *IntMPA 92, WhoEnt 92*
**Finesilver,** Jay Mark 1955- *WhoAmL 92, WhoFI 92*
**Finesilver,** Sherman Glenn 1927- *WhoAmL 92, WhoWest 92*
**Finestein,** Israel 1921- *Who 92*
**Finestone,** Albert Justin 1921- *AmMWSc 92*
**Finestone,** Laurie Ann 1949- *TwCPaSc*
**Finet,** Scott 1958- *WhoAmL 92*
**Finetta,** Regis 1934- *IntWW 91*
**Finfrock,** Bruce Daniel 1950- *WhoRel 92*
**Fingar,** Walter Wiggs 1934- *AmMWSc 92*
**Finger,** Anne *DrAPF 91*
**Finger,** Bernard L. 1927- *WhoFI 92*
**Finger,** Charles J 1861-1941 *ScFEYrs*
**Finger,** Charles J. 1869-1941 *BenetAL 91*
**Finger,** Irving 1924- *AmMWSc 92*
**Finger,** James Walter, II 1951- *WhoMW 92*
**Finger,** Jerry Elliott 1932- *WhoFI 92*
**Finger,** John Holden 1913- *WhoAmL 92, WhoFI 92, WhoWest 92*
**Finger,** Kenneth F 1929- *AmMWSc 92*
**Finger,** Larry W 1940- *AmMWSc 92*
**Finger,** Louis Judah 1920- *WhoAmL 92*
**Finger,** Seymour 1915- *WrDr 92*
**Finger,** Sidney Michael 1837-1896 *DcNCBi 2*
**Finger,** Terry Richard 1948- *AmMWSc 92*
**Finger,** Thomas Emanuel 1949- *AmMWSc 92*
**Finger,** William Whitney 1961- *WhoMW 92*
**Fingerhut,** Eric D *WhoAmP 91*
**Fingerhut,** John Hyman 1910- *Who 92*
**Fingerman,** Milton 1928- *AmMWSc 92*
**Fingerman,** Sue Whitsell 1932- *AmMWSc 92*
**Fingl,** Edward 1923- *AmMWSc 92*
**Fingland,** Stanley 1919- *Who 92*
**Fingleton,** David Melvin 1941- *Who 92*
**Fingret,** Peter 1934- *Who 92*
**Finholt,** Albert Edward 1918- *AmMWSc 92*
**Finholt,** James E 1933- *AmMWSc 92*
**Fini,** Leonor 1908- *FacFETw*
**Fini,** Leonor 1918- *IntWW 91*
**Finigan,** Vincent P., Jr. 1946- *WhoAmL 92*
**Finin,** Timothy Wilking 1949- *AmMWSc 92*
**Finitzo-Hieber,** Terese 1947- *AmMWSc 92*
**Finizio,** Michael 1938- *AmMWSc 92*
**Fink,** Aaron Herman 1916- *WhoFI 92*
**Fink,** Anthony Lawrence 1943- *AmMWSc 92*
**Fink,** Arlington M 1932- *AmMWSc 92*
**Fink,** Austin Ira 1920- *AmMWSc 92*
**Fink,** Bernard Raymond 1914- *AmMWSc 92*
**Fink,** Carole 1940- *ConAu 135, WrDr 92*
**Fink,** Charles Augustin 1929- *WhoFI 92*
**Fink,** Charles Lloyd 1944- *AmMWSc 92*
**Fink,** Chester Walter 1928- *AmMWSc 92*
**Fink,** Colin Ethelbert 1910- *AmMWSc 92*
**Fink,** Daniel J 1926- *AmMWSc 92*
**Fink,** David Howard 1952- *WhoMW 92*
**Fink,** David Jordan 1943- *AmMWSc 92*
**Fink,** David Warren 1944- *AmMWSc 92*
**Fink,** Don Roger 1931- *AmMWSc 92*
**Fink,** Donald G 1911- *AmMWSc 92*
**Fink,** Dwayne Harold 1932- *AmMWSc 92*
**Fink,** Earl Barton 1919- *WhoAmP 91*
**Fink,** Edward Murray 1934- *WhoAmL 92*
**Fink,** Edward Robert 1929- *WhoAmL 92*
**Fink,** George 1936- *Who 92*
**Fink,** George Erwin 1949- *WhoFI 92*
**Fink,** Gerald R. 1940- *IntWW 91*
**Fink,** Gerald Ralph 1940- *AmMWSc 92*
**Fink,** Gordon Ian 1953- *WhoAmL 92*
**Fink,** Gregory Burnell 1928- *AmMWSc 92*
**Fink,** Harold Kenneth 1916- *WhoWest 92*
**Fink,** Herman Joseph 1930- *AmMWSc 92*
**Fink,** James Brewster 1943- *AmMWSc 92, WhoWest 92*
**Fink,** James Paul 1940- *AmMWSc 92*
**Fink,** Jeffrey Neil 1963- *WhoAmL 92*
**Fink,** Jerold Albert 1941- *WhoAmL 92*
**Fink,** Jerrold Evan 1946- *WhoAmL 92*
**Fink,** Joanne Krupey 1945- *AmMWSc 92*
**Fink,** John Bergeman 1945- *WhoMW 92*
**Fink,** Jonathan Harry 1951- *AmMWSc 92*
**Fink,** Jordan Norman 1934- *AmMWSc 92*
**Fink,** Joseph Allen 1942- *WhoAmL 92*
**Fink,** Joyce McGrew 1942- *WhoRel 92*
**Fink,** Kathryn Ferguson 1917- *AmMWSc 92*
**Fink,** Kenn C. 1951- *WhoEnt 92*
**Fink,** Kenneth Howard 1914- *AmMWSc 92*
**Fink,** Kenneth Lee 1939- *WhoMW 92*
**Fink,** Kerry Leif 1961- *WhoFI 92*
**Fink,** Leon 1948- *ConAu 135*
**Fink,** Lester Harold 1925- *AmMWSc 92*
**Fink,** Linda Susan 1958- *AmMWSc 92*
**Fink,** Louis Maier 1942- *AmMWSc 92*
**Fink,** Loyd Kenneth, Jr 1936- *AmMWSc 92*
**Fink,** Lyman R 1912- *AmMWSc 92*
**Fink,** Manfred 1937- *AmMWSc 92*
**Fink,** Martin Ronald 1931- *AmMWSc 92*
**Fink,** Mary Alexander 1919- *AmMWSc 92*
**Fink,** Max 1923- *AmMWSc 92*
**Fink,** Merton 1921- *IntAu&W 91, WrDr 92*
**Fink,** Michael Armand 1939- *WhoEnt 92*
**Fink,** Mike 1770?-1823? *BenetAL 91*
**Fink,** Norman Stiles 1926- *WhoAmL 92*
**Fink,** Peter 1948- *TwCPaSc*
**Fink,** Philip H. 1935- *WhoRel 92*
**Fink,** Rachel Deborah 1956- *AmMWSc 92*
**Fink,** Richard David 1936- *AmMWSc 92*
**Fink,** Richard Walter 1928- *AmMWSc 92*
**Fink,** Robert A. *DrAPF 91*
**Fink,** Robert David 1942- *AmMWSc 92*
**Fink,** Robert M 1915- *AmMWSc 92*
**Fink,** Robert Morgan 1915- *WhoWest 92*
**Fink,** Robert Steven 1943- *WhoAmL 92*
**Fink,** Rodney James 1934- *AmMWSc 92, WhoMW 92*
**Fink,** Scott Alan 1953- *WhoAmL 92*
**Fink,** Stewart Charles 1956- *WhoAmL 92*
**Fink,** Stuart Howard 1948- *WhoWest 92*
**Fink,** Thomas A 1934- *WhoAmP 91*
**Fink,** Thomas Andrew 1954- *WhoFI 92*
**Fink,** Thomas Edward 1940- *WhoMW 92*
**Fink,** Thomas Robert 1943- *AmMWSc 92*
**Fink,** Tom *WhoWest 92*
**Fink,** Tom 1928- *WhoAmP 91*
**Fink,** William Henry 1941- *AmMWSc 92*
**Fink,** William Lee 1946- *AmMWSc 92*
**Finkbeiner,** Herman Lawrence 1931- *AmMWSc 92*
**Finkbeiner,** John A 1917- *AmMWSc 92*
**Finkbeiner,** Otto Karl 1923- *WhoRel 92*
**Finke,** Guenther Bruno 1930- *AmMWSc 92*
**Finke,** James Harold 1944- *AmMWSc 92*
**Finke,** Reinald Guy 1928- *AmMWSc 92*
**Finke,** Richard Gerald 1950- *AmMWSc 92*
**Finke,** Robert Forge 1941- *WhoAmL 92*
**Finkel,** Asher Joseph 1915- *AmMWSc 92*
**Finkel,** Bernard 1926- *WhoMW 92*
**Finkel,** Bob *LesBEnT 92*
**Finkel,** Donald *DrAPF 91*
**Finkel,** Donald 1929- *ConPo 91, IntAu&W 91, WrDr 92*
**Finkel,** Gerald Michael 1941- *WhoAmL 92*
**Finkel,** Herman J 1918- *AmMWSc 92*
**Finkel,** Leonard 1931- *AmMWSc 92*
**Finkel,** Madelon Lubin 1949- *AmMWSc 92*
**Finkel,** Raphael Ari 1951- *AmMWSc 92*
**Finkelday,** John Paul 1943- *WhoFI 92*
**Finkelday,** Karen Lynn 1944- *WhoFI 92*
**Finkelhoffe,** Fred L. *BenetAL 91*
**Finkelman,** Fred Douglass 1947- *AmMWSc 92*
**Finkelman,** Ken *IntMPA 92*
**Finkelman,** Robert Barry 1943- *AmMWSc 92*
**Finkelman Cox,** Penney 1951- *WhoEnt 92*
**Finkelmeier,** Philip Renner 1914- *WhoMW 92*
**Finkelstein,** Abraham Bernard 1923- *AmMWSc 92*
**Finkelstein,** Allen Lewis 1943- *WhoAmL 92*
**Finkelstein,** Caroline *DrAPF 91*
**Finkelstein,** David 1911- *AmMWSc 92*
**Finkelstein,** David 1929- *AmMWSc 92*
**Finkelstein,** David 1956- *WhoAmP 91*
**Finkelstein,** David B 1945- *AmMWSc 92*
**Finkelstein,** Edward Sydney 1925- *WhoFI 92*
**Finkelstein,** Jack, Jr. 1952- *WhoFI 92*
**Finkelstein,** Jacob 1910- *AmMWSc 92*
**Finkelstein,** Jacob Noah 1949- *AmMWSc 92*
**Finkelstein,** James Arthur 1952- *WhoWest 92*
**Finkelstein,** James David 1933- *AmMWSc 92*
**Finkelstein,** Jay Jon 1959- *WhoAmL 92*
**Finkelstein,** Jay Laurence 1938- *AmMWSc 92*
**Finkelstein,** Jerome 1941- *AmMWSc 92*
**Finkelstein,** Jesse Adam 1955- *WhoAmL 92, WhoFI 92*
**Finkelstein,** Lois Rosalyn 1951- *WhoAmL 92*
**Finkelstein,** Louis 1895-1991 *NewYTBS 91 [port]*
**Finkelstein,** Ludwik 1929- *Who 92*
**Finkelstein,** Manuel 1928- *AmMWSc 92*
**Finkelstein,** Mark Jon 1947- *WhoFI 92*
**Finkelstein,** Miriam *DrAPF 91*
**Finkelstein,** Mozes *WhoRel 92*
**Finkelstein,** Norman M. *DrAPF 91*
**Finkelstein,** Paul 1922- *AmMWSc 92*
**Finkelstein,** Richard Alan 1930- *AmMWSc 92, WhoMW 92*
**Finkelstein,** Robert 1942- *AmMWSc 92*
**Finkelstein,** Robert Jay 1916- *AmMWSc 92*
**Finkelstein,** Seth 1956- *WhoFI 92*
**Finkelstein,** Stanley Michael 1941- *AmMWSc 92*
**Finkenbinder,** Paul Edwin 1921- *WhoRel 92*
**Finkes,** Barbara Faith 1956- *WhoRel 92*
**Finkl,** Charles William, II 1941- *AmMWSc 92*
**Finkle,** Bernard Joseph 1921- *AmMWSc 92*
**Finklea,** Harry Osborn 1949- *AmMWSc 92*
**Finklea,** John F 1933- *AmMWSc 92*
**Finklea,** Robert Weir, III 1944- *WhoFI 92*
**Finklea,** Tula Ellice 1923- *WhoEnt 92*
**Finkler,** Paul 1936- *AmMWSc 92*
**Finkner,** Morris Dale 1921- *AmMWSc 92*
**Finkner,** Ralph Eugene 1925- *AmMWSc 92*
**Finks,** Robert Melvin 1927- *AmMWSc 92*
**Finlay,** Alexander William 1921- *Who 92*
**Finlay,** Barton Brett 1959- *AmMWSc 92*
**Finlay,** Charles Hector 1910- *Who 92*
**Finlay,** David 1963- *Who 92*
**Finlay,** Frank 1926- *IntMPA 92, IntWW 91, Who 92*
**Finlay,** Ian *Who 92*
**Finlay,** Ian 1906- *WrDr 92*
**Finlay,** Ian Hamilton 1925- *ConPo 91, IntAu&W 91, TwCPaSc, WrDr 92*
**Finlay,** Joseph Bryan 1943- *AmMWSc 92*
**Finlay,** Joseph Burton 1921- *AmMWSc 92*
**Finlay,** Mary Fleming 1944- *AmMWSc 92*
**Finlay,** Peter Stevenson 1924- *AmMWSc 92*
**Finlay,** Robert Derek 1932- *WhoFI 92*
**Finlay,** Roger W 1935- *AmMWSc 92*
**Finlay,** Terence Edward *Who 92, WhoRel 92*
**Finlay,** Thomas Aloysius 1922- *IntWW 91, Who 92*
**Finlay,** Thomas Hiram 1938- *AmMWSc 92*
**Finlay,** Walter L 1923- *AmMWSc 92*
**Finlay,** William *IntAu&W 91X, WrDr 92*
**Finlay,** William Ian 1906- *Who 92*
**Finlay-Maxwell,** David Campbell 1923- *Who 92*
**Finlayson,** Birdwell 1932- *AmMWSc 92*
**Finlayson,** Bruce Alan 1939- *AmMWSc 92*
**Finlayson,** George 1943- *Who 92*
**Finlayson,** George Ferguson 1924- *Who 92*
**Finlayson,** Henry C 1930- *AmMWSc 92*
**Finlayson,** James Bruce 1937- *AmMWSc 92*
**Finlayson,** Jock Kinghorn 1921- *IntWW 91*
**Finlayson,** John Sylvester 1933- *AmMWSc 92*
**Finlayson,** Richard S 1934- *WhoAmP 91*
**Finlayson,** Robert Douglas 1909- *WhoEnt 92*
**Finlayson,** Robert G. *Who 92*
**Finlayson,** Roderick 1904- *ConNov 91, RfGEnL 91, WrDr 92*
**Finlayson,** William E. 1924- *WhoBlA 92*
**Finlayson-Pitts,** Barbara Jean 1948- *WhoWest 92*
**Finletter,** Thomas Knight 1893-1980 *AmPeW*
**Finley,** Allen Brown 1929- *WhoRel 92*
**Finley,** Arlington Levart 1948- *AmMWSc 92*
**Finley,** Arthur Marion 1918- *AmMWSc 92*
**Finley,** Betty M. 1941- *WhoBlA 92*
**Finley,** Daniel Mark 1957- *WhoMW 92*
**Finley,** David 1890-1977 *FacFETw*
**Finley,** David Emanuel 1935- *AmMWSc 92*
**Finley,** David Raymond 1952- *WhoMW 92*

**Finley,** D'Linell, Sr. 1948- *WhoBlA 92*
**Finley,** Doyle Cifford 1936- *WhoRel 92*
**Finley,** George Alvin, III 1938- *WhoFI 92*
**Finley,** Glenna 1925- *WrDr 92*
**Finley,** Jack Dwight 1927- *WhoFI 92*
**Finley,** James Bradley 1781-1856 *DcNCBi 2*
**Finley,** James Daniel 1941- *WhoWest 92*
**Finley,** James Daniel, III 1941- *AmMWSc 92*
**Finley,** James Edward 1933- *WhoRel 92*
**Finley,** James H. 1947- *WhoMW 92*
**Finley,** James William 1967- *WhoWest 92*
**Finley,** Jeanne *DrAPF 91*
**Finley,** Joanne Elizabeth 1922- *AmMWSc 92*
**Finley,** John *BenetAL 91*
**Finley,** John Charles 1950- *WhoMW 92*
**Finley,** John Jordan 1946- *WhoAmL 92*
**Finley,** John Miller 1953- *WhoRel 92*
**Finley,** John P 1945- *AmMWSc 92*
**Finley,** John Westcott 1942- *AmMWSc 92*
**Finley,** Joseph Howard 1931- *AmMWSc 92*
**Finley,** Joseph Michael 1952- *WhoAmL 92*
**Finley,** Julie Michele 1941- *WhoAmL 92*
**Finley,** Kathleen S. 1949- *WhoWest 92*
**Finley,** Kay Thomas 1934- *AmMWSc 92*
**Finley,** Leon 1907- *WhoAmL 92*
**Finley,** Lewis Merren 1929- *WhoFI 92*
**Finley,** Martha Farquharson 1828-1909 *BenetAL 91*
**Finley,** Michael *DrAPF 91*
**Finley,** Michael Craig 1950- *IntAu&W 91*
**Finley,** Michael John 1932- *Who 92*
**Finley,** Morris 1939- *WhoBlA 92*
**Finley,** Peter 1919- *Who 92*
**Finley,** Philip Bruce 1930- *WhoMW 92*
**Finley,** Robert Byron, Jr 1917- *AmMWSc 92*
**Finley,** Robert Corpening 1905-1976 *DcNCBi 2*
**Finley,** Robert James 1947- *AmMWSc 92*
**Finley,** Robert Van Eaton 1922- *WhoRel 92*
**Finley,** Sara Crews 1930- *AmMWSc 92*
**Finley,** Skip 1948- *WhoBlA 92, WhoEnt 92*
**Finley,** Wayne House 1927- *AmMWSc 92*
**Finley,** William Lloyd 1926- *WhoFI 92*
**Finley,** William Thompson, Jr. 1936- *WhoAmL 92*
**Finlinson,** Fred W 1942- *WhoAmP 91*
**Finlon,** Francis P 1924- *AmMWSc 92*
**Finn,** Arthur Leonard 1934- *AmMWSc 92*
**Finn,** Bruce Leon 1956- *WhoEnt 92*
**Finn,** Chester Evans, Jr. 1944- *NewYTBS 91 [port]*
**Finn,** D L 1924- *AmMWSc 92*
**Finn,** Daniel Rush 1947- *WhoFI 92, WhoMW 92, WhoRel 92*
**Finn,** David 1921- *WhoFI 92*
**Finn,** David Anthony 1954- *WhoMW 92*
**Finn,** Doug *DrAPF 91*
**Finn,** Edward J 1930- *AmMWSc 92*
**Finn,** Elizabeth 1933- *TwCPaSc*
**Finn,** Frances M 1937- *AmMWSc 92*
**Finn,** Harold M 1922- *AmMWSc 92*
**Finn,** Harold R 1948- *WhoAmP 91*
**Finn,** James Crampton, Jr 1924- *AmMWSc 92*
**Finn,** James Walter 1946- *AmMWSc 92*
**Finn,** Janet Lorraine 1942- *WhoMW 92*
**Finn,** Joan Lockwood *WhoFI 92*
**Finn,** John Martin 1919- *AmMWSc 92*
**Finn,** John McMaster 1947- *AmMWSc 92*
**Finn,** John R 1923- *WhoAmP 91*
**Finn,** John Stephen 1951- *WhoAmL 92*
**Finn,** John Thomas 1948- *AmMWSc 92*
**Finn,** John William 1942- *WhoBlA 92*
**Finn,** Judith Ann Fiedler 1940- *WhoRel 92*
**Finn,** Lila Everett 1909- *WhoEnt 92*
**Finn,** Mary Murphy 1939- *WhoEnt 92*
**Finn,** Mike *DrAPF 91*
**Finn,** Patricia Ann *AmMWSc 92*
**Finn,** Patricia Gloria 1949- *WhoAmL 92*
**Finn,** Peter 1954- *WhoFI 92*
**Finn,** R K 1920- *AmMWSc 92*
**Finn,** R. L. 1922- *WrDr 92*
**Finn,** Ralph Leslie 1912- *IntAu&W 91*
**Finn,** Robert *AmMWSc 92*
**Finn,** Robert 1930- *WhoEnt 92*
**Finn,** Robert Green 1941- *WhoBlA 92*
**Finn,** Ronald Dennet 1944- *AmMWSc 92*
**Finn,** Sara Shiels *WhoWest 92*
**Finn,** Stephen Martin 1949- *WhoEnt 92*
**Finn,** Thomas James 1940- *WhoFI 92*
**Finn,** Thomas Macy 1927- *WhoRel 92*
**Finn,** Timothy John 1950- *WhoAmL 92*
**Finn,** Vincent 1930- *IntWW 91*
**Finn,** William Daniel Liam 1933- *AmMWSc 92*
**Finnan,** John O'Neill 1953- *WhoFI 92*
**Finnane,** Daniel F. *WhoWest 92*
**Finnbogadottir,** Vigdis 1930- *IntWW 91*
**Finnegan,** Cyril Vincent 1922- *AmMWSc 92*
**Finnegan,** Frances 1941- *WrDr 92*
**Finnegan,** James *DrAPF 91*
**Finnegan,** James John, Jr. 1948- *WhoMW 92*
**Finnegan,** John Francis 1957- *WhoAmL 92*
**Finnegan,** John J 1938- *WhoAmP 91*
**Finnegan,** Lawrence J 1930- *WhoIns 92*
**Finnegan,** Mary Jeremy 1907- *ConAu 135*
**Finnegan,** Michael 1941- *AmMWSc 92*
**Finnegan,** Michael J. 1941- *WhoMW 92*
**Finnegan,** Richard Allen 1932- *AmMWSc 92*
**Finnegan,** Richard G. 1931- *WhoWest 92*
**Finnegan,** Terrence Edward 1956- *WhoMW 92*
**Finnegan,** Thomas Joseph 1900- *WhoAmL 92, WhoMW 92*
**Finnegan,** Thomas Joseph, Jr. 1935- *WhoAmL 92, WhoFI 92*
**Finnegan,** Walter Daniel 1923- *AmMWSc 92*
**Finnegan,** Walter James 1944- *WhoAmL 92*
**Finnegan,** William Robinson 1928- *WhoEnt 92*
**Finnegan-Pinchuk** *LesBEnT 92*
**Finnell,** Charles Adkins 1943- *WhoAmP 91*
**Finnell,** Dallas Grant 1931- *WhoFI 92*
**Finnell,** Matthew James 1955- *WhoAmL 92*
**Finnell,** Robert Kirtley, III 1949- *WhoAmP 91*
**Finnemore,** Douglas K 1934- *AmMWSc 92*
**Finnemore,** John 1937- *WhoWest 92*
**Finnemore,** Joseph 1860-1939 *TwCPaSc*
**Finner-Williams,** Paris Michele 1951- *WhoMW 92*
**Finneran,** Emmett John 1944- *WhoIns 92*
**Finneran,** Ethan Vincent 1952- *WhoAmL 92*
**Finneran,** Richard J 1943- *IntAu&W 91, WrDr 92*
**Finneran,** Susan Rogers 1947- *WhoAmL 92*
**Finneran,** Thomas M 1950- *WhoAmP 91*
**Finnerty,** Danny James 1956- *WhoFI 92*
**Finnerty,** Frank Ambrose, Jr 1923- *AmMWSc 92*
**Finnerty,** James Lawrence 1927- *AmMWSc 92*
**Finnerty,** John Dudley 1949- *WhoFI 92*
**Finnerty,** Joseph Edward 1945- *WhoFI 92*
**Finnerty,** Tony Robert 1954- *WhoFI 92*
**Finnerty,** William Robert 1929- *AmMWSc 92*
**Finnerud,** Kenneth Percival 1933- *WhoFI 92*
**Finney,** Albert *Who 92*
**Finney,** Albert 1936- *FacFETw, IntMPA 92, IntWW 91, WhoEnt 92*
**Finney,** Bartlett John 1939- *WhoMW 92*
**Finney,** David John 1917- *IntWW 91, Who 92*
**Finney,** Ernest A., Jr. 1931- *WhoBlA 92*
**Finney,** Ernest Adolphus, Jr. 1931- *WhoAmL 92, WhoAmP 91*
**Finney,** Ernest J. *ConAu 134*
**Finney,** Essex Eugene, Jr 1937- *AmMWSc 92, WhoBlA 92*
**Finney,** Frederick Marshall 1941- *WhoMW 92*
**Finney,** Jack *ConAu 133*
**Finney,** Jack 1911- *IntAu&W 91, TwCSFW 91, WrDr 92*
**Finney,** James 1920- *Who 92*
**Finney,** James Nathaniel 1938- *WhoAmL 92*
**Finney,** Jarlath John 1930- *Who 92*
**Finney,** Jervis Spencer 1931- *WhoAmL 92*
**Finney,** Jim *DrAPF 91*
**Finney,** Joan 1925- *AlmAP 92 [port], WhoAmP 91*
**Finney,** Joan Marie McInroy 1925- *IntWW 91, WhoMW 92*
**Finney,** John Edgar, III 1943- *WhoFI 92, WhoWest 92*
**Finney,** John H. 1938- *WhoBlA 92*
**Finney,** John Thornley 1932- *Who 92*
**Finney,** Joseph Claude Jeans 1927- *WhoAmL 92*
**Finney,** Joseph J 1927- *AmMWSc 92*
**Finney,** Karl Frederick 1911- *AmMWSc 92*
**Finney,** Leon D., Jr. 1938- *WhoBlA 92*
**Finney,** Madge *WhoAmP 91*
**Finney,** Mark *IntAu&W 91X*
**Finney,** Michael Anthony 1956- *WhoBlA 92*
**Finney,** Paul Dustin, Jr 1952- *WhoAmP 91*
**Finney,** Robert G. 1935- *WhoEnt 92*
**Finney,** Ross Lee 1906- *ConCom 92, NewAmDM, WhoEnt 92*
**Finney,** Ross Lee, III 1933- *AmMWSc 92*
**Finney,** Roy Pelham 1924- *AmMWSc 92*
**Finney,** Shan 1944- *SmATA 65*
**Finney,** Stanley Charles 1947- *AmMWSc 92*
**Finney,** Walter Braden 1921- *ConAu 133*
**Finney,** Willard Rhoades 1926- *WhoAmP 91*
**Finnian** d549? *EncEarC*
**Finnican,** Mark H 1957- *WhoIns 92*
**Finnicum,** Betty Jo 1930- *WhoAmP 91*
**Finnie,** Clarence Herbert 1930- *WhoWest 92*
**Finnie,** Doris G. 1919- *WhoWest 92*
**Finnie,** I 1928- *AmMWSc 92*
**Finnie,** Linda Agnes 1952- *IntWW 91*
**Finnie,** Phillip Powell 1933- *WhoWest 92*
**Finnie,** Rogers L., Sr. 1945- *WhoBlA 92*
**Finnigan,** Dennis Michael 1928- *WhoWest 92*
**Finnigan,** J W 1924- *AmMWSc 92*
**Finnigan,** Joan 1925- *ConPo 91, IntAu&W 91, WrDr 92*
**Finnigan,** Joseph Townsend 1944- *WhoFI 92, WhoMW 92*
**Finnis,** John Mitchell 1940- *IntWW 91, Who 92*
**Finnissy,** Michael 1946- *ConCom 92*
**Finniston,** Montague d1991 *IntWW 91N, Who 92N*
**Fino,** Marie Georgette Keck 1923- *WhoFI 92*
**Finogenov,** Pavel Vasilyevich 1919- *IntWW 91*
**Fins,** Francisco M. 1961- *WhoHisp 92*
**Fins,** Lauren 1945- *AmMWSc 92*
**Finsberg,** Geoffrey 1926- *Who 92*
**Finsen,** Niels Ryberg 1860-1904 *FacFETw, WhoNob 90*
**Finseth,** Dennis Henry 1945- *AmMWSc 92*
**Finstad,** Carl Derald 1929- *WhoMW 92*
**Finstad,** Donald Lee 1945- *WhoAmP 91*
**Finstein,** Melvin S 1931- *AmMWSc 92*
**Finster,** Mieczyslaw 1924- *AmMWSc 92*
**Finston,** Harmon Leo 1922- *AmMWSc 92*
**Finston,** Roland A 1937- *AmMWSc 92*
**Fintrie,** Lord 1973- *Who 92*
**Finucan,** John Thomas 1930- *WhoRel 92*
**Finucane,** Ronald C. *ConAu 135*
**Finzel,** Rodney Brian 1951- *AmMWSc 92*
**Finzi,** Aldo 1891-1944 *BiDExR*
**Finzi,** Gerald 1901- *FacFETw*
**Finzi,** Gerald 1901-1956 *NewAmDM*
**Fiol,** Maria Angeles 1933- *WhoHisp 92*
**Fiolet,** Herman Antonius 1920- *IntWW 91*
**Fiondella,** Robert William 1942- *WhoFI 92*
**Fioravanti,** Nancy Eleanor 1935- *WhoFI 92*
**Fiore,** Anthony William 1920- *AmMWSc 92*
**Fiore,** Carl 1928- *AmMWSc 92*
**Fiore,** James Louis, Jr. 1935- *WhoFI 92*
**Fiore,** James Patrick 1953- *WhoRel 92*
**Fiore,** Jordan Hugh Faust 1954- *WhoAmL 92, WhoAmP 91*
**Fiore,** Joseph Vincent 1920- *AmMWSc 92*
**Fiore,** Nicholas F 1939- *AmMWSc 92*
**Fiore,** Nicholas Joseph 1953- *WhoAmL 92*
**Fiorella,** Edward Anthony, Jr. 1959- *WhoAmL 92*
**Fiorella,** Kenneth Scott 1953- *WhoAmL 92*
**Fiorelli,** Joseph Stephen 1950- *WhoWest 92*
**Fiorelli,** Paul E. 1956- *WhoMW 92*
**Fiorentini,** James John 1947- *WhoAmL 92*
**Fiorentino,** Carmine 1932- *WhoAmL 92*
**Fiorentino,** Imero *LesBEnT 92*
**Fiorentino,** Imero Ovidio 1928- *WhoEnt 92*
**Fiorentino,** Thomas Martin 1959- *WhoAmL 92*
**Fiorenza,** Francis P. 1941- *WhoRel 92*
**Fiorenza,** Joseph A. 1931- *WhoRel 92*
**Fiorenzano,** Frank John 1949- *WhoAmP 91*
**Fiori,** Bart J 1930- *AmMWSc 92*
**Fiorica,** Vincent 1931- *WhoMW 92*
**Fiorindo,** Robert Philip 1935- *AmMWSc 92*
**Fiorino,** Angelo John 1943- *WhoMW 92*
**Fiorino,** John Wayne 1946- *WhoWest 92*
**Fiorito,** Edward Gerald 1936- *WhoAmL 92*
**Fiorito,** Ralph Bruno 1941- *AmMWSc 92*
**Fiorucci,** Cesare 1941- *WhoFI 92*
**Fiorucci,** Elio 1935- *DcTwDes*
**Fiquet,** Hortense 1850-1918 *ThHElm [port]*
**Firari,** Harvey 1921- *WhoEnt 92*
**Firbank,** Ronald 1886-1926 *FacFETw, RfGEnL 91*
**Firby,** James R 1933- *AmMWSc 92*
**Firchow,** Peter 1937- *WrDr 92*
**Firchow,** Peter Edgerly 1937- *WhoMW 92*
**Firdman,** Henry Eric 1936- *AmMWSc 92*
**Fire,** Edward L 1936- *WhoAmP 91*
**Fire,** John 1895-1976 *RelLAm 91*
**Fire,** Philip 1925- *AmMWSc 92*
**Firebaugh,** Morris W 1937- *AmMWSc 92*
**Firehammer,** Richard Armin, Jr. 1957- *WhoAmL 92*
**Fireman,** Edward Leonard 1922- *AmMWSc 92*
**Fireman,** Karen Schreiber 1959- *WhoFI 92*
**Fireman,** Paul 1944- *WhoFI 92*
**Fireman,** Philip 1932- *AmMWSc 92*
**Firer,** Susan *DrAPF 91*
**Fireside,** Harvey F. 1929- *WrDr 92*
**Firestone,** Alexander 1940- *AmMWSc 92*
**Firestone,** Debra Kay 1958- *WhoMW 92*
**Firestone,** Eddie W. 1920- *WhoEnt 92*
**Firestone,** Frederick Norton 1931- *WhoWest 92*
**Firestone,** Ira Joel 1941- *WhoMW 92*
**Firestone,** Keith Norman 1954- *WhoAmL 92*
**Firestone,** Raymond A 1931- *AmMWSc 92*
**Firestone,** Rena Loderhose 1952- *WhoFI 92*
**Firestone,** Reuven 1952- *WhoRel 92*
**Firestone,** Richard Francis 1926- *AmMWSc 92*
**Firestone,** Ross Francis 1932- *AmMWSc 92*
**Firestone,** William L 1921- *AmMWSc 92*
**Firetog,** Theodore Warren 1950- *WhoAmL 92*
**Firey,** Joseph Carl 1918- *AmMWSc 92*
**Firey,** Walter Irving 1916- *WrDr 92*
**Firey,** William James 1923- *AmMWSc 92*
**Firk,** Frank William Kenneth 1930- *AmMWSc 92*
**Firkins,** John Frederick 1935- *AmMWSc 92*
**Firkins,** John Lionel 1942- *AmMWSc 92*
**Firkins,** Peter Charles 1926- *WrDr 92*
**Firkusny,** Rudolf 1912- *IntWW 91, NewAmDM, WhoEnt 92*
**Firle,** Tomas E 1926- *AmMWSc 92*
**Firlit,** Casimir Francis 1939- *AmMWSc 92*
**Firmage,** D Allan 1918- *AmMWSc 92*
**Firmage,** Edwin Brown *WhoAmL 92*
**Firman,** Steve C. 1953- *WhoMW 92*
**Firmat,** Francisco F. *WhoHisp 92*
**Firment,** Lawrence Edward 1950- *AmMWSc 92*
**Firmicus Maternus** d350? *EncEarC*
**Firmilian** d268 *EncEarC*
**Firminger,** Harlan Irwin 1918- *AmMWSc 92*
**Firmston-Williams,** Peter 1918- *Who 92*
**Firmstone,** David 1943- *TwCPaSc*
**Firmstone,** Frank 1846-1917 *BiInAmS*
**Firnberg,** David 1930- *Who 92*
**Firnberg,** Hertha 1909- *IntWW 91*
**Firnkas,** Sepp 1925- *AmMWSc 92*
**Firor,** Hugh Valentine 1929- *WhoMW 92*
**Firor,** John 1927- *WrDr 92*
**Firor,** John William 1927- *AmMWSc 92*
**Firriolo,** Domenic 1933- *AmMWSc 92*
**Firschein,** Hilliard E 1927- *AmMWSc 92*
**Firsching,** Ferdinand Henry 1923- *AmMWSc 92*
**Firshein,** William 1930- *AmMWSc 92*
**Firsova,** Elena 1950- *ConCom 92*
**First,** Harry 1945- *WhoAmL 92*
**First,** Melvin William 1914- *AmMWSc 92*
**First,** Neal L 1930- *AmMWSc 92*
**First,** Wesley 1920- *WhoFI 92*
**Firstenberg,** Jean 1936- *WhoEnt 92*
**Firstenberg,** Samuel 1950- *WhoEnt 92*
**Firstenberger,** B G 1917- *AmMWSc 92*
**Firstenberger,** Lester William 1962- *WhoAmL 92*
**Firstman,** Eric Jacob 1957- *WhoAmL 92*
**Firstman,** Sidney I 1931- *AmMWSc 92*
**Firth,** Andrew Trevor 1922- *Who 92*
**Firth,** Arthur Percival 1928- *IntAu&W 91*
**Firth,** Brian William 1926- *WhoWest 92*
**Firth,** Charles Edward Anson 1902- *Who 92*
**Firth,** Colin 1930- *Who 92*
**Firth,** Colin 1960- *ConTFT 9, IntMPA 92*
**Firth,** Derek 1939- *WhoWest 92*
**Firth,** Edward Michael Tyndall 1903- *Who 92*
**Firth,** Everett Joseph 1930- *WhoEnt 92*
**Firth,** Joan Margaret 1935- *Who 92*
**Firth,** Peter 1953- *IntMPA 92, IntWW 91*
**Firth,** Peter James *Who 92*
**Firth,** Raymond 1901- *Who 92, WrDr 92*
**Firth,** Raymond William 1901- *IntWW 91*
**Firth,** Ronnie Lynn 1954- *WhoMW 92*
**Firth,** Tazeena Mary 1935- *Who 92*
**Firth,** William Charles, Jr 1934- *AmMWSc 92*
**Fisanick,** Georgia Jeanne 1950- *AmMWSc 92*
**Fiscal,** Paula Calderon Castillo 1950- *WhoWest 92*
**Fiscarel,** Barbara *WhoFI 92*
**Fisch,** Adrian Brian 1948- *WhoMW 92*
**Fisch,** Charles 1921- *AmMWSc 92*
**Fisch,** Forest Norland 1918- *AmMWSc 92*
**Fisch,** Harold 1923- *WrDr 92*
**Fisch,** Herbert A 1923- *AmMWSc 92*
**Fisch,** Oscar 1934- *AmMWSc 92*
**Fisch,** Robert O 1925- *AmMWSc 92*
**Fisch,** Ronald 1951- *AmMWSc 92*
**Fisch,** Sanford Michael 1955- *WhoWest 92*
**Fisch-Thomsen,** Niels 1939- *IntWW 91*
**Fischbach,** Charles Peter 1939- *WhoAmL 92, WhoFI 92*

Fischbach, David Bibb 1926- AmMWSc 92
Fischbach, Deloris R 1923- WhoAmP 91
Fischbach, Ephraim 1942- AmMWSc 92
Fischbach, Fritz Albert 1937- AmMWSc 92
Fischbach, Gerald David 1938- AmMWSc 92
Fischbach, Henry 1914- AmMWSc 92
Fischbach, Joseph W 1917- AmMWSc 92
Fischback, Bryant C 1926- AmMWSc 92
Fischbarg, Jorge 1935- AmMWSc 92, WhoHisp 92
Fischbeck, Helmut J 1928- AmMWSc 92
Fischel, Daniel R. 1950- WhoAmL 92
Fischel, David 1936- AmMWSc 92
Fischel, Edward Elliot 1920- AmMWSc 92
Fischel, Shelley Duckstein 1950- WhoEnt 92
Fischell, David R 1953- AmMWSc 92
Fischell, Robert E 1929- AmMWSc 92
Fischell, Tim Alexander 1956- AmMWSc 92
Fischer, A Alan 1928- AmMWSc 92
Fischer, Aaron Jack 1947- WhoMW 92
Fischer, Alan Dean 1947- WhoRel 92
Fischer, Albert G 1928- AmMWSc 92
Fischer, Albert Karl 1931- AmMWSc 92, WhoMW 92
Fischer, Alfred George 1920- AmMWSc 92
Fischer, Alvin Eugene, Jr. 1942- WhoFI 92
Fischer, Annie 1914- IntWW 91, Who 92
Fischer, Barry Steven 1961- WhoAmL 92
Fischer, Brent S. C. 1964- WhoEnt 92
Fischer, Bruce R 1949- WhoIns 92
Fischer, Bruno 1908- IntAu&W 91, WrDr 92
Fischer, C Rutherford 1934- AmMWSc 92
Fischer, Carey Michael 1950- WhoAmL 92
Fischer, Carl 1849-1923 NewAmDM
Fischer, Carl 1924- WhoEnt 92
Fischer, Charlotte Froese 1929- AmMWSc 92
Fischer, Colette Barbara 1947- WhoWest 92
Fischer, D. Clare 1928- WhoEnt 92
Fischer, David Arnold 1943- WhoAmL 92
Fischer, David C 1948- WhoAmP 91
Fischer, David John 1928- AmMWSc 92
Fischer, David Jon 1952- WhoAmL 92
Fischer, Deborah Elene 1958- WhoRel 92
Fischer, Diana Bradbury 1934- AmMWSc 92
Fischer, Edmond H 1920- AmMWSc 92, IntWW 91
Fischer, Edmond Henri 1920- WhoWest 92
Fischer, Edward 1914- IntAu&W 91
Fischer, Edward A. 1914- WrDr 92
Fischer, Edward G 1916- AmMWSc 92
Fischer, Edwin 1886-1960 NewAmDM
Fischer, Emil Herman 1852-1919 WhoNob 90
Fischer, Emil Hermann 1852-1919 FacFETw
Fischer, Eric Robert 1945- WhoAmL 92
Fischer, Erik 1920- IntWW 91
Fischer, Ernst Otto 1918- FacFETw, IntWW 91, Who 92, WhoNob 90
Fischer, Eugen 1874-1967 EncTR 91
Fischer, Eugene Charles 1940- AmMWSc 92
Fischer, Ferdinand Joseph 1940- AmMWSc 92
Fischer, Floyd Brand 1916- WhoAmP 91
Fischer, Frederick William 1939- WhoAmL 92
Fischer, George A 1939- AmMWSc 92
Fischer, George J 1925- AmMWSc 92
Fischer, George K 1923- AmMWSc 92
Fischer, Gerhard Emil 1928- AmMWSc 92
Fischer, Glenn Albert 1922- AmMWSc 92
Fischer, Grace Mae 1927- AmMWSc 92
Fischer, Hans 1881-1945 FacFETw, WhoNob 90
Fischer, Harry William 1921- AmMWSc 92
Fischer, Henry Fred 1938- WhoAmP 91
Fischer, Howard B 1959- WhoIns 92
Fischer, Imre A 1935- AmMWSc 92
Fischer, Irene Kaminka 1907- AmMWSc 92
Fischer, Irwin 1903-1977 NewAmDM
Fischer, Irwin 1927- AmMWSc 92
Fischer, Ivan 1951- IntWW 91, WhoEnt 92
Fischer, James Adrian 1916- WhoRel 92
Fischer, James Edward 1946- WhoMW 92
Fischer, James Joseph 1936- AmMWSc 92
Fischer, James Roland 1945- AmMWSc 92
Fischer, Janet Jordan 1923- AmMWSc 92
Fischer, Jay Martin 1950- WhoFI 92
Fischer, Johann Christian 1733-1800 NewAmDM
Fischer, John D. WhoRel 92
Fischer, John Edward 1939- AmMWSc 92
Fischer, John Hans 1928- WhoRel 92
Fischer, Joseph Alfred 1931- WhoFI 92
Fischer, June S 1931- WhoAmP 91
Fischer, Karen Alta 1952- WhoEnt 92
Fischer, Karen Ann 1947- WhoWest 92
Fischer, Karl Ingmar Roman 1922- IntWW 91
Fischer, Kenneth Christian 1944- WhoEnt 92
Fischer, Lawrence J 1937- AmMWSc 92
Fischer, Leewellyn C 1937- AmMWSc 92
Fischer, Louis Wayne 1952- WhoEnt 92
Fischer, Ludwig 1745-1825 NewAmDM
Fischer, Lynn Helen 1943- IntAu&W 91
Fischer, Lynn Suzanne 1951- WhoWest 92
Fischer, Marilyn Carol 1936- WhoRel 92
Fischer, Mark Alan 1950- WhoAmL 92, WhoEnt 92
Fischer, Mark Benjamin 1949- AmMWSc 92
Fischer, Mark Frederick 1951- WhoRel 92
Fischer, Marsha Leigh 1955- WhoFI 92
Fischer, Martin A 1937- WhoIns 92
Fischer, Mary Allison 1951- WhoMW 92
Fischer, Michael 1947- AmMWSc 92
Fischer, Michael John 1948- WhoWest 92
Fischer, Neil Jeffrey 1955- WhoWest 92
Fischer, Nikolaus Hartmut 1936- AmMWSc 92
Fischer, Nora Barry 1951- WhoAmL 92
Fischer, Norman, Jr. 1924- WhoEnt 92
Fischer, Oskar 1923- IntWW 91
Fischer, Patrick Carl 1935- AmMWSc 92
Fischer, Paul 1936- WhoAmP 91
Fischer, Paul Hamilton AmMWSc 92
Fischer, Paul Henning 1919- IntWW 91
Fischer, R B 1920- AmMWSc 92
Fischer, Ralph Frederick 1924- WhoRel 92
Fischer, Richard Bernard 1919- AmMWSc 92
Fischer, Richard Lawrence 1936- WhoAmL 92, WhoFI 92
Fischer, Richard Martin, Jr 1947- AmMWSc 92
Fischer, Robert B 1917- AmMWSc 92
Fischer, Robert Blanchard 1920- AmMWSc 92
Fischer, Robert George 1920- AmMWSc 92
Fischer, Robert H. 1918- WrDr 92
Fischer, Robert James 1943- FacFETw, IntWW 91
Fischer, Robert Leigh 1926- AmMWSc 92
Fischer, Robert Warren 1935- WhoEnt 92
Fischer, Roger Raymond 1941- WhoAmP 91
Fischer, Roland Lee 1924- AmMWSc 92
Fischer, Ronald Francis 1955- WhoAmL 92
Fischer, Ronald Howard 1942- AmMWSc 92
Fischer, Russell Jon 1960- AmMWSc 92
Fischer, Ruth 1895-1961 EncTR 91
Fischer, Stanley 1943- IntWW 91, WhoFI 92
Fischer, Stanley Henry 1943- WhoAmL 92
Fischer, Stephen Gary 1947- WhoAmL 92
Fischer, Stephen Heiberg 1943- WhoFI 92
Fischer, Steve 1951- WhoAmL 92
Fischer, Susan Marie 1947- AmMWSc 92
Fischer, Theodore Vernon 1939- AmMWSc 92
Fischer, Thomas Covell 1938- WhoAmL 92
Fischer, Traugott Erwin 1932- AmMWSc 92
Fischer, Vic WhoAmP 91
Fischer, William Donald 1928- WhoMW 92
Fischer, William Henry 1921- AmMWSc 92
Fischer, William Raymond 1926- WhoAmP 91
Fischer, William S. 1935- WhoBlA 92
Fischer, William Samuel 1935- WhoEnt 92
Fischer, Zoe Ann 1939- WhoFI 92, WhoWest 92
Fischer-Appelt, Peter 1932- IntWW 91
Fischer-Dieskau, Dietrich 1925- FacFETw, IntWW 91, NewAmDM, Who 92, WhoEnt 92
Fischer-Jorgensen, Eli 1911- IntWW 91
Fischer von Erlach, Johann Bernhard 1656?-1723 BlkwCEP
Fischhoff, David Allen 1952- AmMWSc 92
Fischinger, Peter John 1937- AmMWSc 92
Fischl, Charles Frederick 1950- WhoWest 92
Fischl, Eric 1948- IntWW 91, WorArt 1980 [port]
Fischler, Drake Anthony 1923- AmMWSc 92
Fischler, Franz 1946- IntWW 91
Fischler, Martin A 1932- AmMWSc 92
Fischler, Marvin Glenn 1957- WhoAmL 92
Fischler, Shirley SmATA 66
Fischler, Stan SmATA 66 [port]
Fischlschweiger, Werner 1932- AmMWSc 92
Fischman, Donald A 1936- AmMWSc 92
Fischman, Harlow Kenneth 1932- AmMWSc 92
Fischman, Leonard Lipman 1919- WhoFI 92
Fischman, Marian Weinbaum 1939- AmMWSc 92
Fischman, Myrna Leah WhoFI 92
Fischman, Stuart L 1935- AmMWSc 92
Fischmar, Richard Mayer 1938- WhoFI 92, WhoMW 92
Fischoff, Gary Charles 1954- WhoAmL 92
Fischoff, George Allan 1938- WhoEnt 92
Fischoff, Richard IntMPA 92
Fischthal, Glenn Jay 1948- WhoEnt 92
Fiscus, Alvin G 1930- AmMWSc 92
Fiscus, Edwin Lawson 1942- AmMWSc 92
Fiscus, Jack, III 1967- WhoRel 92
Fiser, Paul S 1938- AmMWSc 92
Fiset, Paul 1922- AmMWSc 92
Fish, A. Joe 1942- WhoAmL 92
Fish, Anthony d1991 Who 92N
Fish, Barbara 1920- AmMWSc 92
Fish, Charles Robert, Jr. 1954- WhoWest 92
Fish, Cheryl DrAPF 91
Fish, David Earl 1936- WhoFI 92
Fish, Donald C 1937- AmMWSc 92
Fish, Donald Winston 1930- WhoAmL 92
Fish, Eleanor N 1952- AmMWSc 92
Fish, F H, Jr 1923- AmMWSc 92
Fish, Ferol F, Jr 1930- AmMWSc 92
Fish, Francis 1924- Who 92
Fish, Frank Eliot 1953- AmMWSc 92
Fish, Gordon E 1951- AmMWSc 92
Fish, Hamilton 1808-1893 AmPolLe
Fish, Hamilton 1888-1991 CurBio 91N, NewYTBS 91 [port], News 91, -91-3
Fish, Hamilton, Jr. 1926- AlmAP 92 [port], WhoAmP 91
Fish, Hugh 1923- Who 92
Fish, Irving 1938- AmMWSc 92
Fish, James E 1945- AmMWSc 92
Fish, James Henry 1947- WhoWest 92
Fish, Jefferson 1942- AmMWSc 92
Fish, Jerry Richard 1949- WhoAmL 92
Fish, John 1920- Who 92
Fish, John Frederick 1925- WhoRel 92
Fish, John G 1938- AmMWSc 92
Fish, Jonathan Severance 1944- WhoFI 92
Fish, Jonathon Kevin 1955- WhoEnt 92, WhoWest 92
Fish, Joseph Leroy 1943- AmMWSc 92
Fish, Leslie 1956- IntAu&W 91
Fish, Marleen 1934- WhoAmP 91
Fish, Mary Ann Tinklepaugh 1930- WhoAmP 91
Fish, Mary Martha 1930- WhoFI 92
Fish, Ody J 1925- WhoAmP 91
Fish, Paul Waring 1933- WhoAmL 92, WhoFI 92
Fish, Peter Graham 1937- WhoAmL 92
Fish, Richard Wayne 1934- AmMWSc 92
Fish, Robert A. WhoFI 92
Fish, Ruby Mae Bertram 1918- WhoWest 92
Fish, Sewall Lawrence DcNCBi 2
Fish, Stanley 1938- IntAu&W 91
Fish, Stanley E. 1938- WrDr 92
Fish, Stanley Eugene 1938- WhoAmL 92
Fish, Stewart Allison 1925- AmMWSc 92
Fish, Thomas Edward, Jr. 1951- WhoRel 92
Fish, Wayne William 1941- AmMWSc 92
Fish, William 1956- AmMWSc 92
Fish, William Arthur 1921- AmMWSc 92
Fishacre, Richard 1205?-1248 DcLB 115
Fishbach, Philip David 1941- WhoFI 92
Fishback, Price Vanmeter 1955- WhoFI 92
Fishback, William Thompson 1922- AmMWSc 92, WhoMW 92
Fishbein, Eileen Greif 1936- AmMWSc 92
Fishbein, Irwin Harvey 1931- WhoRel 92
Fishbein, Martin 1936- WhoMW 92
Fishbein, Peter Melvin 1934- WhoAmL 92
Fishbein, William AmMWSc 92
Fishbein, William Nichols 1933- AmMWSc 92
Fishbone ConMus 7 [port]
Fishbone, Leslie Gary 1946- AmMWSc 92
Fishburn, Angela Mary 1933- WrDr 92
Fishburn, Dudley 1946- Who 92
Fishburn, Kay Maurine 1939- WhoFI 92, WhoMW 92
Fishburne, Edward Stokes, III 1936- AmMWSc 92
Fishburne, Larry 1963- IntMPA 92
Fishburne, Laurence John, III 1961- WhoBlA 92
Fishburne, Raymond Paul 1918- WhoAmL 92
Fishe, Gerald Raymond Aylmer 1926- WhoFI 92
Fishel, Andrew S WhoAmP 91
Fishel, Charles Vinton 1938- WhoFI 92
Fishel, David Burton 1948- WhoFI 92
Fishel, Derry Lee 1929- AmMWSc 92
Fishel, Douglas Ray 1954- WhoRel 92
Fishel, James Dean 1953- WhoMW 92
Fishel, James Joseph 1959- WhoAmL 92
Fishel, John B 1914- AmMWSc 92
Fishel, Paul Richard, Jr. 1957- WhoMW 92
Fishel, Stanley Irvyng 1914- WhoEnt 92
Fishelman, Bruce C. 1949- WhoAmL 92
Fisher Who 92
Fisher, Baron 1921- Who 92
Fisher, A. James 1950- WhoMW 92
Fisher, Ada 1924- NotBlAW 92
Fisher, Ada L. 1924- WhoBlA 92
Fisher, Adam D. DrAPF 91
Fisher, Aileen 1906- IntAu&W 91, WrDr 92
Fisher, Al IntMPA 92
Fisher, Alan W. 1939- WrDr 92
Fisher, Albert Lee 1920- WhoMW 92
Fisher, Alexander Metcalf 1794-1822 BilnAmS
Fisher, Allan Campbell 1943- WhoFI 92
Fisher, Allan Everett 1943- WhoRel 92
Fisher, Allen 1944- ConPo 91, WrDr 92
Fisher, Alma Z. 1945- WhoBlA 92
Fisher, Andrew Eugene 1961- WhoEnt 92
Fisher, Andrew Somes 1948- WhoEnt 92
Fisher, Ann Elizabeth 1953- WhoAmL 92
Fisher, Ann Houston 1946- WhoRel 92
Fisher, Anne Who 92
Fisher, Anne B. 1957- ConAu 135
Fisher, Art LesBEnT 92
Fisher, Arthur Douglas 1952- AmMWSc 92
Fisher, Arthur J. Who 92
Fisher, Avery 1906- NewAmDM
Fisher, Barry Alan 1943- WhoAmL 92, WhoWest 92
Fisher, Bart Steven 1943- WhoAmL 92
Fisher, Ben 1924- AmMWSc 92
Fisher, Bennett Greg 1956- WhoEnt 92
Fisher, Bennett Lawson 1942- WhoFI 92
Fisher, Bernard 1918- AmMWSc 92
Fisher, Bertram Dore 1928- WhoAmL 92
Fisher, Bonnell H. 1933- WhoRel 92
Fisher, Brady Alan 1952- WhoAmL 92
Fisher, Brenda B. WhoMW 92
Fisher, Bruce Barry 1951- WhoEnt 92
Fisher, Bruce David 1949- WhoWest 92
Fisher, C Page, Jr 1921- AmMWSc 92
Fisher, Carl A. 1945- WhoRel 92, WhoWest 92
Fisher, Carl Anthony 1945- WhoBlA 92
Fisher, Carrie 1956- ConAu 135, CurBio 91 [port], IntMPA 92, News 91 [port], WrDr 92
Fisher, Carrie Frances 1956- WhoEnt 92
Fisher, Champe Andrews 1928- WhoAmL 92
Fisher, Charles 1789-1849 DcNCBi 2
Fisher, Charles Frederick 1816-1861 DcNCBi 2
Fisher, Charles Harold 1906- AmMWSc 92
Fisher, Charles Osborne, Jr 1943- WhoAmP 91
Fisher, Charles Thomas, III 1929- WhoFI 92, WhoMW 92
Fisher, Clark Alan 1933- AmMWSc 92
Fisher, Clarkson Sherman 1921- WhoAmL 92
Fisher, Clarkson Sherman, Jr. 1952- WhoAmL 92
Fisher, Clay BenetAL 91, ConAu 135, IntAu&W 91X, TwCWW 91, WrDr 92
Fisher, Cletus G 1922- AmMWSc 92
Fisher, Craig Becker 1932- WhoEnt 92
Fisher, D. Joseph 1937- WhoMW 92
Fisher, D Michael 1944- WhoAmP 91
Fisher, Dale John 1925- AmMWSc 92
Fisher, Darrell R 1951- AmMWSc 92
Fisher, David 1946- WrDr 92
Fisher, David Andrew 1948- WhoEnt 92, WhoFI 92
Fisher, David Andrew 1958- WhoBlA 92
Fisher, David Clarence 1960- WhoWest 92
Fisher, David E 1932- AmMWSc 92, WrDr 92
Fisher, David Jay 1959- WhoAmL 92
Fisher, David L. DrAPF 91
Fisher, David Scot 1961- WhoAmL 92
Fisher, Deborah May 1968- WhoRel 92
Fisher, Delbert A 1928- AmMWSc 92
Fisher, Delbert Arthur 1928- WhoWest 92
Fisher, Dennis Roy 1941- WhoFI 92
Fisher, Desmond 1920- Who 92
Fisher, Don Lowell 1941- AmMWSc 92
Fisher, Donald 1931- Who 92
Fisher, Donald B 1935- AmMWSc 92
Fisher, Donald D 1929- AmMWSc 92
Fisher, Donald G. 1928- WhoWest 92
Fisher, Donald Wiener 1923- WhoAmL 92
Fisher, Donald William 1922- AmMWSc 92
Fisher, Donne Francis 1938- WhoEnt 92, WhoFI 92
Fisher, Doris G. 1907- Who 92
Fisher, Dorothy Canfield 1879-1958 BenetAL 91, FacFETw
Fisher, Dudley Henry 1922- Who 92
Fisher, E. Carleton 1934- WhoBlA 92

**Fisher,** E Eugene 1922- *AmMWSc 92*
**Fisher,** Earl Monty 1938- *WhoWest 92*
**Fisher,** Eddie *LesBEnT 92*
**Fisher,** Eddie 1928- *IntMPA 92*
**Fisher,** Edith Maureen 1944- *WhoBlA 92*
**Fisher,** Edward 1913- *AmMWSc 92*
**Fisher,** Edward Allen 1950- *AmMWSc 92*
**Fisher,** Edward Carrington 1809-1890 *DcNCBi 2*
**Fisher,** Edward G. 1932- *WhoBlA 92*
**Fisher,** Edward George K. *Who 92*
**Fisher,** Edward Richard 1938- *AmMWSc 92*
**Fisher,** Edward S 1921- *AmMWSc 92*
**Fisher,** Edward Stanley 1921- *WhoMW 92*
**Fisher,** Edwin Ralph 1923- *AmMWSc 92*
**Fisher,** Elisabeth Neill 1944- *Who 92*
**Fisher,** Ellsworth Henry 1911- *AmMWSc 92*
**Fisher,** Elwood 1926- *AmMWSc 92*
**Fisher,** Eric O'Neill 1954- *WhoFI 92*
**Fisher,** Erman Caldwell 1923- *WhoMW 92*
**Fisher,** Everett 1920- *WhoAmL 92*
**Fisher,** Farley 1938- *AmMWSc 92*
**Fisher,** Frances Christine *DcNCBi 2*
**Fisher,** Francis George Robson 1921- *Who 92*
**Fisher,** Francis John Fulton 1926- *AmMWSc 92*
**Fisher,** Frank M, Jr 1931- *AmMWSc 92*
**Fisher,** Franklin A 1929- *AmMWSc 92*
**Fisher,** Franklin E 1933- *AmMWSc 92*
**Fisher,** Franklin M. 1934- *WrDr 92*
**Fisher,** Franklin Marvin 1934- *WhoFI 92*
**Fisher,** Fred 1875-1942 *NewAmDM*
**Fisher,** Frederick Hendrick 1926- *AmMWSc 92, WhoWest 92*
**Fisher,** Frederick Stephen 1937- *AmMWSc 92*
**Fisher,** Fredy *Who 92*
**Fisher,** Gail *WhoBlA 92*
**Fisher,** Gail Feimster 1928- *AmMWSc 92*
**Fisher,** Galen Bruce 1945- *AmMWSc 92*
**Fisher,** Gary Alan 1955- *WhoEnt 92*
**Fisher,** Gene Jordan 1931- *AmMWSc 92*
**Fisher,** Geoffrey Francis 1887-1972 *DcEcMov, FacFETw*
**Fisher,** George A, Jr 1912- *AmMWSc 92*
**Fisher,** George Carver 1939- *WhoBlA 92*
**Fisher,** George Egbert 1863-1920 *BiInAmS*
**Fisher,** George Harold, Jr 1943- *AmMWSc 92*
**Fisher,** George Mark 1949- *WhoRel 92*
**Fisher,** George Myles Cordell 1940- *WhoFI 92*
**Fisher,** George Park 1827-1909 *EncEarC, RelLAm 91*
**Fisher,** George Phillip 1938- *AmMWSc 92*
**Fisher,** George Read 1903- *Who 92*
**Fisher,** George Robert 1928- *AmMWSc 92*
**Fisher,** George Wescott 1937- *AmMWSc 92*
**Fisher,** George William *DrAPF 91*
**Fisher,** Gerald F 1943- *WhoIns 92*
**Fisher,** Gerald Lionel 1946- *AmMWSc 92*
**Fisher,** Gerald Saul 1931- *WhoAmL 92*
**Fisher,** Glenn Duane 1947- *WhoMW 92*
**Fisher,** Gordon McCrea 1925- *AmMWSc 92*
**Fisher,** Gordon P 1922- *AmMWSc 92*
**Fisher,** Greg *WhoAmP 91*
**Fisher,** Gregory James 1950- *WhoFI 92*
**Fisher,** Hans 1928- *AmMWSc 92*
**Fisher,** Harold L 1910- *WhoAmP 91*
**Fisher,** Harold Leonard 1910- *WhoAmL 92*
**Fisher,** Harold M 1940- *AmMWSc 92*
**Fisher,** Harold Stephen 1950- *WhoMW 92*
**Fisher,** Harold Wallace 1904- *AmMWSc 92, Who 92*
**Fisher,** Harold Wilbur 1928- *AmMWSc 92*
**Fisher,** Harrison *DrAPF 91*
**Fisher,** Harvey Franklin 1923- *AmMWSc 92*
**Fisher,** Henry 1918- *Who 92*
**Fisher,** Henry Arthur Pears 1918- *IntWW 91*
**Fisher,** Henry Lee 1874-1947 *RelLAm 91*
**Fisher,** Irving Norton 1867-1947 *AmPeW*
**Fisher,** Irving Sanborn 1920- *AmMWSc 92*
**Fisher,** Jack 1952- *WhoEnt 92*
**Fisher,** Jack Bernard 1943- *AmMWSc 92*
**Fisher,** James Atherton 1909- *Who 92*
**Fisher,** James Delbert 1942- *AmMWSc 92*
**Fisher,** James Harold 1919- *AmMWSc 92, WhoMW 92*
**Fisher,** James Lee 1944- *WhoAmL 92*
**Fisher,** James Neil 1917- *Who 92*
**Fisher,** James R 1955- *WhoIns 92*
**Fisher,** James Raymond 1951- *WhoAmL 92*
**Fisher,** James Robert 1946- *WhoWest 92*
**Fisher,** James Russell 1940- *AmMWSc 92*
**Fisher,** James Thomas 1946- *AmMWSc 92*
**Fisher,** James W 1925- *AmMWSc 92*
**Fisher,** James W., Jr. 1942- *WhoFI 92*
**Fisher,** Jimmie Lou 1941- *WhoAmP 91*
**Fisher,** Jimmy Don 1947- *WhoEnt 92*
**Fisher,** Joel 1947- *IntWW 91*
**Fisher,** Joel Marshall 1935- *WhoAmP 91*
**Fisher,** John 1892-1983 *FacFETw*
**Fisher,** John 1938- *TwCPaSc*
**Fisher,** John Andre 1931- *WhoMW 92*
**Fisher,** John Arbuthnot 1841-1920 *FacFETw*
**Fisher,** John Berton 1951- *AmMWSc 92*
**Fisher,** John C *WhoAmP 91*
**Fisher,** John Crocker 1919- *AmMWSc 92*
**Fisher,** John E 1929- *WhoIns 92*
**Fisher,** John E. 1930- *WhoMW 92*
**Fisher,** John Edwin 1929- *WhoFI 92, WhoMW 92*
**Fisher,** John Edwin 1941- *WhoAmL 92*
**Fisher,** John F 1937- *AmMWSc 92*
**Fisher,** John Francis 1933- *WhoIns 92*
**Fisher,** John Harrison 1949- *WhoEnt 92*
**Fisher,** John Herbert 1921- *AmMWSc 92*
**Fisher,** John Morris 1922- *WhoFI 92*
**Fisher,** John Mortimer 1915- *Who 92*
**Fisher,** John Philip 1927- *WhoFI 92*
**Fisher,** John Sergio 1934- *WhoWest 92*
**Fisher,** John Welton, II 1942- *WhoAmL 92*
**Fisher,** John William 1931- *AmMWSc 92*
**Fisher,** Jon Herbert 1947- *WhoFI 92*
**Fisher,** Joseph 1933- *WhoBlA 92*
**Fisher,** Joseph Lyman 1914- *WhoAmP 91*
**Fisher,** Joseph Stewart 1933- *WhoWest 92*
**Fisher,** Judith Danelle 1951- *WhoBlA 92*
**Fisher,** Jules Edward 1937- *WhoEnt 92*
**Fisher,** June Marion 1933- *AmMWSc 92*
**Fisher,** Kathleen MacPhee 1955- *WhoWest 92*
**Fisher,** Kathleen Mary Flynn 1938- *AmMWSc 92*
**Fisher,** Kenneth D 1932- *AmMWSc 92*
**Fisher,** Kenneth K *WhoAmP 91*
**Fisher,** Kenneth Robert Stanley 1942- *AmMWSc 92*
**Fisher,** Kenneth Walter 1931- *AmMWSc 92*
**Fisher,** Kevin Bruce 1959- *WhoAmL 92*
**Fisher,** Knute Adrian 1941- *AmMWSc 92*
**Fisher,** Lawrence N. *WhoAmL 92*
**Fisher,** Lee I. *WhoAmL 92, WhoMW 92*
**Fisher,** Lee I 1951- *WhoAmP 91*
**Fisher,** Leon Harold 1918- *AmMWSc 92*
**Fisher,** Leonard 1924- *WhoAmL 92*
**Fisher,** Leonard Everett 1924- *IntAu&W 91, WrDr 92*
**Fisher,** Leonard M 1944- *WhoIns 92*
**Fisher,** Leonard Thomas 1947- *WhoFI 92*
**Fisher,** Leonard V 1929- *AmMWSc 92*
**Fisher,** Leslie John 1940- *AmMWSc 92*
**Fisher,** Lester Emil 1921- *WhoMW 92*
**Fisher,** Lillian S. 1921- *WhoAmL 92*
**Fisher,** Linda 1943- *ConTFT 9, WhoEnt 92*
**Fisher,** Linda E 1947- *AmMWSc 92*
**Fisher,** Linda Elaine 1947- *WhoMW 92*
**Fisher,** Lloyd B. 1942- *WhoBlA 92*
**Fisher,** Lloyd D 1939- *AmMWSc 92*
**Fisher,** Lou *DrAPF 91*
**Fisher,** Louis 1934- *WrDr 92*
**Fisher,** Lucy 1949- *IntMPA 92*
**Fisher,** Lucy J. 1949- *WhoEnt 92*
**Fisher,** Lyman McArthur 1923- *AmMWSc 92*
**Fisher,** M.F.K. *DrAPF 91*
**Fisher,** M F K 1908- *FacFETw*
**Fisher,** Marc James 1948- *WhoMW 92*
**Fisher,** Marc Louis 1958- *WhoFI 92*
**Fisher,** Margery Lilian Edith 1913- *IntAu&W 91, Who 92*
**Fisher,** Maria d1991 *NewYTBS 91*
**Fisher,** Mark 1841-1923 *TwCPaSc*
**Fisher,** Mark 1944- *Who 92*
**Fisher,** Mark Miles 1899-1970 *RelLAm 91*
**Fisher,** Martin Joseph 1944- *AmMWSc 92*
**Fisher,** Marvin 1927- *WrDr 92*
**Fisher,** Marvin Mark 1927- *WhoWest 92*
**Fisher,** Mary Maurine 1929- *WhoFI 92*
**Fisher,** Mattie Cook 1921- *WhoBlA 92*
**Fisher,** Maurice 1924- *Who 92*
**Fisher,** Max Henry 1922- *IntWW 91, Who 92*
**Fisher,** Merwyn T 1937- *WhoAmP 91*
**Fisher,** Michael 1918- *Who 92*
**Fisher,** Michael Bruce 1945- *WhoFI 92*
**Fisher,** Michael Ellis 1931- *AmMWSc 92, IntWW 91, Who 92*
**Fisher,** Michael Lee 1957- *WhoMW 92*
**Fisher,** Milton Leonard 1922- *WhoAmL 92*
**Fisher,** Montgomery Ross 1921- *WhoWest 92*
**Fisher,** Morton Poe, Jr. 1936- *WhoAmL 92*
**Fisher,** Myron R. 1935- *WhoAmL 92*
**Fisher,** Myrta 1917- *TwCPaSc*
**Fisher,** Nancy 1941- *WhoEnt 92*
**Fisher,** Nancy Collins 1950- *WhoEnt 92*
**Fisher,** Nancy Kathleen *Who 92*
**Fisher,** Neal Floyd 1936- *WhoRel 92*
**Fisher,** Newman 1928- *AmMWSc 92*
**Fisher,** Nicholas Seth 1949- *AmMWSc 92*
**Fisher,** Nigel 1913- *IntAu&W 91, Who 92, WrDr 92*
**Fisher,** Nola Jan 1953- *WhoAmL 92*
**Fisher,** O. H., Mrs. *Who 92*
**Fisher,** Orval George 1952- *WhoRel 92*
**Fisher,** Patricia 1921- *Who 92*
**Fisher,** Paul Andrew 1952- *AmMWSc 92*
**Fisher,** Paul Douglas 1954- *AmMWSc 92*
**Fisher,** Pearl Davidowitz 1920- *AmMWSc 92*
**Fisher,** Perry Wright *AmMWSc 92*
**Fisher,** Peter L. 1963- *WhoEnt 92*
**Fisher,** Philip Arthur 1907- *WhoWest 92*
**Fisher,** Philip Chapin 1926- *AmMWSc 92*
**Fisher,** Philip Clyde 1938- *WhoMW 92*
**Fisher,** Philip Condon 1930- *WhoWest 92*
**Fisher,** Philip M 1878-1932 *ScFEYrs*
**Fisher,** Phyllis Anne 1913- *Who 92*
**Fisher,** Ralph Talcott, Jr. 1920- *WrDr 92*
**Fisher,** Ray W 1921- *AmMWSc 92*
**Fisher,** Reed Edward 1932- *AmMWSc 92*
**Fisher,** Reuben 1923- *WhoEnt 92*
**Fisher,** Richard Alan 1950- *WhoEnt 92*
**Fisher,** Richard Allen 1947- *WhoRel 92*
**Fisher,** Richard B. 1936- *WhoFI 92*
**Fisher,** Richard Colomb 1923- *Who 92*
**Fisher,** Richard Forrest 1941- *AmMWSc 92*
**Fisher,** Richard Gary 1952- *AmMWSc 92*
**Fisher,** Richard L. *WhoRel 92*
**Fisher,** Richard L 1947- *WhoAmP 91*
**Fisher,** Richard Laymon 1934- *WhoBlA 92*
**Fisher,** Richard Paul 1948- *AmMWSc 92*
**Fisher,** Richard R 1941- *AmMWSc 92*
**Fisher,** Richard Virgil 1928- *AmMWSc 92*
**Fisher,** Robert *WhoAmP 91*
**Fisher,** Robert Alan 1943- *AmMWSc 92*
**Fisher,** Robert Amos, Jr 1934- *AmMWSc 92*
**Fisher,** Robert Bruce 1937- *WhoRel 92*
**Fisher,** Robert C. 1950- *WhoWest 92*
**Fisher,** Robert D *WhoIns 92*
**Fisher,** Robert Earl 1939- *AmMWSc 92*
**Fisher,** Robert Elwood 1931- *WhoRel 92*
**Fisher,** Robert F. 1936- *WhoBlA 92*
**Fisher,** Robert George 1917- *AmMWSc 92*
**Fisher,** Robert I. 1939- *WhoAmL 92*
**Fisher,** Robert L *AmMWSc 92*
**Fisher,** Robert Lloyd 1925- *AmMWSc 92*
**Fisher,** Robert Louis 1944- *WhoAmL 92*
**Fisher,** Robert Scott 1960- *WhoAmL 92*
**Fisher,** Robert Stephen 1939- *AmMWSc 92*
**Fisher,** Robert Walter 1948- *WhoAmL 92*
**Fisher,** Robert Warren 1952- *WhoMW 92*
**Fisher,** Robin Scott 1952- *AmMWSc 92*
**Fisher,** Roger 1919- *TwCPaSc*
**Fisher,** Roger 1922- *WrDr 92*
**Fisher,** Roger Anthony 1936- *Who 92*
**Fisher,** Roger Dummer 1922- *WhoAmL 92*
**Fisher,** Ronald C. 1950- *WhoFI 92*
**Fisher,** Ronald Richard 1941- *AmMWSc 92*
**Fisher,** Rosalind Anita 1956- *WhoMW 92*
**Fisher,** Rosalind Lum 1946- *WhoFI 92*
**Fisher,** Rowland 1885-1969 *TwCPaSc*
**Fisher,** Roy 1930- *ConPo 91, IntAu&W 91, WrDr 92*
**Fisher,** Rubin Ivan 1948- *WhoBlA 92*
**Fisher,** Rudolph 1897-1934 *BlkLC [port]*
**Fisher,** Russell S 1949- *WhoIns 92*
**Fisher,** Ruth *WhoAmP 91*
**Fisher,** Sallie Ann 1923- *AmMWSc 92*
**Fisher,** Sally *DrAPF 91*
**Fisher,** Samuel Melton 1860-1939 *TwCPaSc*
**Fisher,** Samuel Sturm 1938- *AmMWSc 92*
**Fisher,** Sandra 1947- *TwCPaSc*
**Fisher,** Saul Harrison 1913- *AmMWSc 92*
**Fisher,** Seymour 1922- *AmMWSc 92*
**Fisher,** Seymour 1925- *AmMWSc 92*
**Fisher,** Shelley Marie 1942- *WhoBlA 92*
**Fisher,** Shirley Ida A. 1935- *WhoWest 92*
**Fisher,** Stanley Morton 1928- *WhoFI 92*
**Fisher,** Stanley Parkins 1919- *AmMWSc 92*
**Fisher,** Stephen D 1941- *AmMWSc 92*
**Fisher,** Steven Kay 1942- *AmMWSc 92*
**Fisher,** Stuart Gordon 1943- *AmMWSc 92*
**Fisher,** Sylvia Gwendoline Victoria *Who 92*
**Fisher,** T Richard 1921- *AmMWSc 92*
**Fisher,** Ted V 1941- *WhoAmP 91*
**Fisher,** Terence 1904-1980 *IntDcF 2-2 [port]*
**Fisher,** Theodore William 1921- *AmMWSc 92*
**Fisher,** Thomas Edward 1926- *WhoAmL 92*
**Fisher,** Thomas George 1931- *WhoAmL 92*
**Fisher,** Thomas Gilbert F. *Who 92*
**Fisher,** Thomas Graham 1940- *WhoAmL 92, WhoMW 92*
**Fisher,** Thomas Henry 1938- *AmMWSc 92*
**Fisher,** Thornton Roberts 1937- *AmMWSc 92*
**Fisher,** Tom Lyons 1942- *AmMWSc 92*
**Fisher,** Vance Addicks 1935- *WhoAmL 92*
**Fisher,** Vardis 1895-1968 *BenetAL 91, TwCWW 91*
**Fisher,** Vincent J 1930- *AmMWSc 92*
**Fisher,** Wade *IntAu&W 91X, TwCWW 91*
**Fisher,** Waldo Reynolds 1930- *AmMWSc 92*
**Fisher,** Walter 1916- *WhoBlA 92*
**Fisher,** Walter Taylor d1991 *NewYTBS 91*
**Fisher,** Warner Douglass 1923- *AmMWSc 92*
**Fisher,** Wayne 1937- *WhoAmL 92*
**Fisher,** Wendy Astley-Bell 1944- *WhoFI 92*
**Fisher,** Weston Joseph *WhoWest 92*
**Fisher,** William Francis 1941- *AmMWSc 92*
**Fisher,** William Gary 1947- *AmMWSc 92*
**Fisher,** William Henry 1912- *WhoWest 92*
**Fisher,** William Lawrence 1932- *AmMWSc 92*
**Fisher,** William Redwood 1808-1842 *BiInAmS*
**Fisher,** Zack Buchanan 1941- *WhoAmP 91*
**Fisher of Rednal,** Baroness 1919- *Who 92*
**Fisherman,** Mark Frederic 1950- *WhoAmL 92*
**Fishkin,** Arthur Frederic 1930- *AmMWSc 92*
**Fishkin,** James S. *WhoAmL 92*
**Fishkin,** Leslie Jay 1954- *WhoFI 92*
**Fishlin,** Lewis Harvey 1943- *WhoAmL 92*
**Fishlock,** David Jocelyn 1932- *Who 92, WrDr 92*
**Fishlock,** Trevor 1941- *IntAu&W 91, Who 92*
**Fishman,** Alfred Paul 1918- *AmMWSc 92*
**Fishman,** Alvin 1927- *WhoAmP 91*
**Fishman,** Bernard Philip 1950- *WhoRel 92*
**Fishman,** Charles *DrAPF 91*
**Fishman,** Charles 1942- *IntAu&W 91*
**Fishman,** David H 1939- *AmMWSc 92*
**Fishman,** David Hirsch 1939- *WhoAmL 92*
**Fishman,** Edward Marc 1946- *WhoAmL 92*
**Fishman,** Elliot Keith 1953- *AmMWSc 92*
**Fishman,** Frank J, Jr 1931- *AmMWSc 92*
**Fishman,** Fred Norman 1925- *WhoAmL 92*
**Fishman,** George Samuel 1937- *AmMWSc 92*
**Fishman,** Gerald Jay 1943- *AmMWSc 92*
**Fishman,** Harvey Morton 1937- *AmMWSc 92*
**Fishman,** Irving Yale 1920- *AmMWSc 92*
**Fishman,** Jack 1930- *AmMWSc 92*
**Fishman,** Jacob Robert 1930- *WhoFI 92*
**Fishman,** James Bart 1954- *WhoAmL 92*
**Fishman,** Jerry Haskel 1923- *AmMWSc 92*
**Fishman,** Joshua A 1926- *ConAu 34NR*
**Fishman,** Kenneth Jay 1950- *WhoAmL 92*
**Fishman,** Lewis Warren 1951- *WhoAmL 92*
**Fishman,** Libby G. 1940- *WhoAmL 92*
**Fishman,** Lillian 1915- *WhoWest 92*
**Fishman,** Mark Brian 1951- *WhoFI 92*
**Fishman,** Marshall Lewis 1937- *AmMWSc 92*
**Fishman,** Marvin 1928- *AmMWSc 92*
**Fishman,** Marvin Joseph 1932- *AmMWSc 92*
**Fishman,** Morris 1939- *AmMWSc 92*
**Fishman,** Myer M 1918- *AmMWSc 92*
**Fishman,** Norman 1924- *AmMWSc 92*
**Fishman,** Peter Harvey 1939- *AmMWSc 92*
**Fishman,** Philip M 1943- *AmMWSc 92*
**Fishman,** Richard Glenn 1952- *WhoAmL 92*
**Fishman,** Robert Allen 1924- *AmMWSc 92*
**Fishman,** Robert Sumner 1932- *AmMWSc 92*
**Fishman,** S. James 1943- *WhoAmL 92*
**Fishman,** Sherold 1925- *AmMWSc 92*
**Fishman,** Steven Gerald 1942- *AmMWSc 92*
**Fishman,** William Harold 1914- *AmMWSc 92, WhoWest 92*
**Fishman,** William S. d1991 *NewYTBS 91 [port]*
**Fishwick,** Avril 1924- *Who 92*
**Fishwick,** Clifford 1923- *TwCPaSc*
**Fisiak,** Jacek 1936- *IntWW 91*
**Fisk,** Carlton Ernest 1947- *WhoMW 92*
**Fisk,** Charles Brenton 1925-1983 *NewAmDM*
**Fisk,** David John 1947- *Who 92*
**Fisk,** Edward Ray 1924- *WhoWest 92*
**Fisk,** Frank Wilbur 1914- *AmMWSc 92*
**Fisk,** George Ayrs 1941- *AmMWSc 92*
**Fisk,** Ian Terrasatti 1968- *WhoFI 92*
**Fisk,** Jack *IntMPA 92*
**Fisk,** James B 1910-1981 *FacFETw*
**Fisk,** Lanny Herbert 1944- *AmMWSc 92*

**Fisk,** Linda Lorean 1944- *WhoWest 92*
**Fisk,** Merlin Edgar 1921- *WhoAmL 92*
**Fisk,** Nicholas 1923- *IntAu&W 91, TwCSFW 91, WrDr 92*
**Fisk,** Pauline 1948- *SmATA 66 [port]*
**Fisk,** Robert F, Jr 1949- *WhoAmP 91*
**Fisk,** Robert Spencer 1939- *AmMWSc 92*
**Fiske,** Arland Orin 1927- *WhoRel 92*
**Fiske,** Dudley Astley d1991 *Who 92N*
**Fiske,** John 1842-1901 *BenetAL 91, BiInAmS*
**Fiske,** Milan Derbyshire 1914- *AmMWSc 92*
**Fiske,** Nathan 1733-1799 *BenetAL 91*
**Fiske,** Richard 1962- *WhoEnt 92*
**Fiske,** Richard Allen 1933- *WhoEnt 92*
**Fiske,** Richard Sewell 1932- *AmMWSc 92*
**Fiske,** Robert B. d1991 *NewYTBS 91 [port]*
**Fiske,** Robert Bishop, Jr. 1930- *WhoAmL 92*
**Fiske,** Sharon *WrDr 92*
**Fiske,** Tarleton *IntAu&W 91X*
**Fiskell,** John Garth Austin 1917- *AmMWSc 92*
**Fisko,** James J. *WhoRel 92*
**Fisler,** George Frederick 1931- *AmMWSc 92*
**Fison,** David Charles 1908- *IntAu&W 91, WrDr 92*
**Fison,** Guy 1917- *Who 92*
**Fiss,** Owen M. 1938- *WhoAmL 92, WrDr 92*
**Fisser,** Herbert George 1926- *AmMWSc 92*
**Fistoulari,** Anatole 1907- *IntWW 91, Who 92*
**Fiszbach,** Tadeusz 1935- *IntWW 91*
**Fitch,** Alanah 1953- *AmMWSc 92*
**Fitch,** Asa 1809-1879 *BiInAmS*
**Fitch,** Bonnie Lynn 1953- *WhoEnt 92*
**Fitch,** Clarence E. 1929- *WhoBlA 92*
**Fitch,** Clyde 1865-1909 *BenetAL 91, FacFETw*
**Fitch,** Coy Dean 1934- *AmMWSc 92*
**Fitch,** David Paul 1950- *WhoFI 92*
**Fitch,** Donald Everett 1928- *WhoWest 92*
**Fitch,** Douglas Bernard Stocker 1927- *Who 92*
**Fitch,** Douglas Hodges 1959- *WhoAmL 92*
**Fitch,** Ernest Chester, Jr 1924- *AmMWSc 92*
**Fitch,** Frank Wesley 1929- *AmMWSc 92*
**Fitch,** George 1877-1915 *BenetAL 91*
**Fitch,** Gregory Scott 1962- *WhoRel 92*
**Fitch,** Harrison Arnold 1943- *WhoBlA 92*
**Fitch,** Henry Sheldon 1909- *AmMWSc 92*
**Fitch,** Howard Mercer 1909- *WhoAmL 92*
**Fitch,** Jack *WhoWest 92*
**Fitch,** John Henry 1944- *AmMWSc 92*
**Fitch,** John William, III 1938- *AmMWSc 92*
**Fitch,** Jonathan Stuart 1950- *WhoAmP 91*
**Fitch,** Kenneth Leonard 1929- *AmMWSc 92*
**Fitch,** Marcus Felix Brudenell 1908- *Who 92*
**Fitch,** Mark Keith 1957- *WhoAmL 92*
**Fitch,** Martha Jean 1960- *WhoRel 92*
**Fitch,** Mary Killeen 1949- *WhoFI 92*
**Fitch,** Milton F, Jr *WhoAmP 91, WhoBlA 92*
**Fitch,** Raymond William 1931- *WhoAmL 92*
**Fitch,** Richard 1929- *Who 92*
**Fitch,** Robert McLellan 1928- *AmMWSc 92, WhoFI 92*
**Fitch,** Rodney Arthur 1938- *Who 92*
**Fitch,** Steven Joseph 1930- *AmMWSc 92*
**Fitch,** Val Logsdon 1923- *AmMWSc 92, FacFETw, IntWW 91, WhoNob 90*
**Fitch,** W Chester 1916- *AmMWSc 92*
**Fitch,** Walter M 1929- *AmMWSc 92*
**Fitch,** Walter Stewart 1926- *AmMWSc 92*
**Fitch,** William Edwards 1867-1949 *DcNCBi 2*
**Fitchen,** Douglas Beach 1936- *AmMWSc 92*
**Fitchen,** Franklin Charles 1928- *AmMWSc 92*
**Fitchett,** Dorothy Marie 1946- *WhoRel 92*
**Fitchett,** Gilmer Trower 1920- *AmMWSc 92*
**Fitchew,** Geoffrey Edward 1939- *IntWW 91, Who 92*
**Fitchue,** M. Anthony 1943- *WhoBlA 92*
**Fite,** Lloyd Emery 1930- *AmMWSc 92*
**Fite,** Wade Lanford 1925- *AmMWSc 92*
**Fitelson,** H. William 1905- *IntMPA 92*
**Fiterman,** Charles 1933- *IntWW 91*
**Fites,** Donald Vester 1934- *WhoFI 92, WhoMW 92*
**Fitgerald,** F Scott 1896-1940 *FacFETw [port]*
**Fitgerald,** Robert Stuart 1910-1985 *FacFETw*
**Fithian,** Floyd J 1928- *WhoAmP 91*
**Fithian,** Robert Arthur 1927- *WhoAmP 91*
**Fitial,** Benigno R 1945- *WhoAmP 91*
**Fitilis,** Art Constantine *WhoFI 92*
**Fitouri,** Mohamed 1925- *IntWW 91*
**Fitoussi,** Jean-Paul Samuel 1908- *IntWW 91*
**Fitt** *Who 92*
**Fitt,** Baron 1925- *IntWW 91*
**Fitt,** Baron 1926- *Who 92*
**Fitt,** Michael George *WhoIns 92*
**Fitt,** Peter Stanley 1931- *AmMWSc 92*
**Fitt,** Robert Louis 1905- *Who 92*
**Fitt,** William K *AmMWSc 92*
**Fittall,** Betty Daphne C. *Who 92*
**Fitter,** Richard 1913- *WrDr 92*
**Fitter,** Richard Sidney Richmond 1913- *IntAu&W 91, Who 92*
**Fitterer,** G R 1901- *AmMWSc 92*
**Fitterer,** John Angus 1922- *WhoRel 92*
**Fitteron,** John Joseph 1941- *WhoFI 92*
**Fitting-Gifford,** Marjorie Ann Premo 1933- *AmMWSc 92*
**Fittipaldi,** Emerson 1946- *IntWW 91*
**Fittipaldi,** Santiago Antonio 1960- *WhoHisp 92*
**Fitton,** James 1889-1982 *TwCPaSc*
**Fitts,** C. Austin 1950- *WhoFI 92*
**Fitts,** Charles Thomas 1932- *AmMWSc 92*
**Fitts,** Donald Dennis 1932- *AmMWSc 92*
**Fitts,** Dudley 1903-1968 *BenetAL 91*
**Fitts,** James Walter 1913- *AmMWSc 92*
**Fitts,** Kenneth L. 1945- *WhoEnt 92*
**Fitts,** Leroy 1944- *WhoBlA 92*
**Fitts,** Martin Russell 1954- *WhoFI 92*
**Fitts,** R. Lewis 1930- *WhoRel 92*
**Fitts,** Richard Earl 1931- *AmMWSc 92*
**Fittz,** Senga Nengudi 1943- *WhoBlA 92*
**Fitz,** Harold Carlton, Jr 1926- *AmMWSc 92*
**Fitz,** Henry 1808-1863 *BiInAmS*
**Fitz,** James Francis 1946- *WhoRel 92*
**Fitz,** Raymond L. 1941- *WhoRel 92*
**Fitz,** Reginald Herber 1843-1913 *BiInAmS*
**Fitzalan-Howard** *Who 92*
**FitzAlan-Howard,** Bennett-Thomas Henry R. 1955- *WhoFI 92*
**Fitzalan-Howard,** Michael 1916- *Who 92*
**Fitzball,** Edward 1793-1873 *RfGEnL 91*
**Fitzclarence** *Who 92*
**Fitzer,** Gary Dean 1957- *WhoWest 92*
**Fitzer,** Herbert Clyde 1910- *Who 92*
**Fitzer,** Jack 1926- *AmMWSc 92*
**Fitzerald,** John Warner 1924- *WhoAmL 92*
**FitzGeorge-Balfour,** Victor 1913- *Who 92*
**Fitzgeorge-Parker,** Tim 1920- *WrDr 92*
**Fitzgerald** *Who 92*
**Fitzgerald,** Anthony Michael 1944- *WhoAmL 92*
**Fitzgerald,** Barbara *IntAu&W 91X*
**Fitzgerald,** Barry 1888-1961 *FacFETw*
**Fitzgerald,** Brian Lee 1961- *WhoMW 92*
**Fitzgerald,** Bridget Mary 1964- *WhoEnt 92*
**Fitzgerald,** Captain Hugh *ConAu 133*
**Fitzgerald,** Carl *AmMWSc 92*
**Fitzgerald,** Carrie Eugenia 1929- *WhoBlA 92*
**Fitzgerald,** Charles Patrick 1902- *IntWW 91, Who 92, WrDr 92*
**Fitzgerald,** Charlotte Diane 1949- *WhoBlA 92*
**Fitzgerald,** Daniel Patrick 1916- *Who 92*
**FitzGerald,** David J P 1956- *AmMWSc 92*
**Fitzgerald,** David John 1955- *WhoEnt 92*
**Fitz-Gerald,** Desmond John Villiers 1937- *Who 92*
**Fitzgerald,** Donald Ray 1923- *AmMWSc 92*
**Fitzgerald,** Duane Glenn 1931- *AmMWSc 92*
**Fitzgerald,** Edith Jackson 1932- *WhoFI 92*
**Fitzgerald,** Edmund B. 1926- *IntWW 91*
**Fitzgerald,** Edmund Bacon 1926- *WhoFI 92*
**FitzGerald,** Edward 1809-1883 *RfGEnL 91*
**Fitzgerald,** Edward Aloysius 1942- *AmMWSc 92*
**Fitzgerald,** Edward Thomas d1988 *Who 92N*
**Fitzgerald,** Edwin Roger 1923- *AmMWSc 92*
**Fitzgerald,** Ella 1918- *FacFETw [port], IntWW 91, NewAmDM, NotBlAW 92 [port], RComAH, WhoBlA 92, WhoEnt 92*
**Fitzgerald,** Ernest Abner 1925- *WhoRel 92, WrDr 92*
**Fitzgerald,** F. Scott 1896-1940 *BenetAL 91, LiExTwC, RComAH, ScFEYrs*
**Fitzgerald,** Frances 1940- *BenetAL 91, IntWW 91, WrDr 92*
**Fitzgerald,** Frank 1929- *Who 92*
**Fitzgerald,** Frank Moore 1955- *WhoAmP 91*
**FitzGerald,** Frederick 1825-1866 *DcNCBi 2*
**Fitzgerald,** Garret 1926- *IntWW 91, Who 92, WrDr 92*
**FitzGerald,** George 1917- *Who 92*
**Fitzgerald,** George Patrick 1922- *AmMWSc 92*
**Fitzgerald,** Gerald Edward 1941- *Who 92*
**Fitzgerald,** Gerald Loftus 1907- *Who 92*
**Fitzgerald,** Gerald Roland 1930- *AmMWSc 92*
**Fitzgerald,** Geraldine 1914- *IntMPA 92*
**Fitzgerald,** Gerard John 1949- *AmMWSc 92*
**Fitzgerald,** Glenna Gibbs *AmMWSc 92*
**Fitz Gerald,** Gregory *DrAPF 91*
**Fitzgerald,** Herbert H. 1928- *WhoBlA 92*
**Fitzgerald,** Howard David 1938- *WhoBlA 92*
**Fitzgerald,** J Edmund 1923- *AmMWSc 92*
**Fitzgerald,** James Alfred, Jr. 1956- *WhoMW 92*
**Fitzgerald,** James Allen 1941- *AmMWSc 92*
**Fitzgerald,** James Edward 1931- *AmMWSc 92*
**Fitzgerald,** James Francis 1926- *WhoEnt 92*
**Fitzgerald,** James Michael *WhoAmP 91*
**Fitzgerald,** James Michael 1929- *WhoMW 92*
**Fitzgerald,** James Patrick 1946- *WhoAmL 92*
**Fitzgerald,** James W 1942- *AmMWSc 92*
**Fitzgerald,** Janet Anne 1935- *WhoRel 92*
**FitzGerald,** Jerry 1936- *WhoWest 92*
**Fitzgerald,** Jerry Dale 1959- *WhoEnt 92*
**Fitzgerald,** Jerry Mack 1937- *AmMWSc 92*
**FitzGerald,** John Bernard, III 1956- *WhoAmL 92*
**Fitzgerald,** John Charles, Jr. 1941- *WhoFI 92*
**Fitzgerald,** John Desmond 1928- *AmMWSc 92*
**FitzGerald,** John Edward, III 1945- *WhoAmL 92*
**Fitzgerald,** John Moonan 1923- *WhoAmL 92*
**Fitzgerald,** John Patrick 1936- *WhoEnt 92*
**Fitzgerald,** John Thomas, Jr. 1948- *WhoRel 92*
**Fitzgerald,** John Warner 1924- *WhoAmP 91*
**FitzGerald,** Joseph Arthur 1925- *AmMWSc 92*
**Fitzgerald,** Joseph C. 1922- *WhoWest 92*
**Fitzgerald,** Joseph Michael, Jr. 1943- *WhoAmL 92*
**Fitzgerald,** Julia 1943- *IntAu&W 91*
**Fitzgerald,** Kenneth Wayne 1945- *WhoWest 92*
**FitzGerald,** Kevin Michael 1956- *WhoAmL 92*
**Fitzgerald,** Kevin W 1950- *WhoAmP 91*
**Fitzgerald,** Laurence Rockwell 1916- *AmMWSc 92*
**Fitzgerald,** Laurie Ann 1950- *WhoFI 92*
**Fitzgerald,** Lawrence Terrell 1938- *AmMWSc 92*
**Fitzgerald,** Marie Anton 1922- *AmMWSc 92*
**Fitzgerald,** Maureen Elizabeth 1920- *IntAu&W 91*
**Fitzgerald,** Maurice E 1932- *AmMWSc 92*
**FitzGerald,** Maurice Pim Valter 1939- *AmMWSc 92*
**Fitzgerald,** Michael Anthony 1944- *WhoFI 92*
**FitzGerald,** Michael Frederick Clive 1936- *Who 92*
**Fitzgerald,** Michael L 1951- *WhoAmP 91*
**Fitzgerald,** Michael Lee 1951- *WhoMW 92*
**Fitzgerald,** Oscar Penn 1829-1911 *DcNCBi 2*
**Fitzgerald,** Patrick Henry 1943- *AmMWSc 92*
**Fitzgerald,** Patrick James 1913- *AmMWSc 92*
**Fitzgerald,** Patrick John 1928- *Who 92*
**Fitzgerald,** Patrick Thomas 1944- *WhoEnt 92*
**Fitzgerald,** Patrick William 1953- *WhoAmL 92*
**Fitzgerald,** Patrishya Anne 1952- *WhoEnt 92*
**Fitzgerald,** Paul A 1937- *WhoIns 92*
**Fitzgerald,** Paul Jackson 1924- *AmMWSc 92*
**Fitzgerald,** Paul Joseph 1953- *WhoMW 92*
**Fitzgerald,** Paul Ray 1920- *AmMWSc 92*
**Fitzgerald,** Paula Marie Dean 1949- *AmMWSc 92*
**Fitzgerald,** Penelope 1916- *ConNov 91, WrDr 92*
**Fitzgerald,** Penelope Mary 1916- *IntAu&W 91, IntWW 91, Who 92*
**Fitzgerald,** Peter Hanley 1929- *IntWW 91*
**FitzGerald,** Richard Joseph, Jr. 1930- *WhoAmL 92*
**Fitzgerald,** Richard Patrick 1950- *WhoWest 92*
**Fitzgerald,** Robert D 1902- *IntAu&W 91*
**FitzGerald,** Robert D. 1902-1987 *RfGEnL 91*
**Fitzgerald,** Robert George 1840-1919 *DcNCBi 2*
**Fitzgerald,** Robert Hannon, Jr 1942- *AmMWSc 92*
**Fitzgerald,** Robert James 1918- *AmMWSc 92*
**Fitzgerald,** Robert Lynn 1939- *WhoWest 92*
**Fitzgerald,** Robert S. 1910- *BenetAL 91*
**Fitzgerald,** Robert Schaefer 1931- *AmMWSc 92*
**Fitzgerald,** Robert William 1931- *AmMWSc 92*
**Fitz-Gerald,** Roger Miller 1935- *WhoAmL 92*
**Fitzgerald,** Roosevelt 1941- *WhoBlA 92*
**Fitzgerald,** Roy Lee 1911- *WhoBlA 92*
**Fitzgerald,** Sallyanne Huffaker 1944- *WhoMW 92*
**FitzGerald,** Stephen Arthur 1938- *IntWW 91*
**Fitzgerald,** Thomas Francis Kelly 1959- *WhoEnt 92*
**Fitzgerald,** Thomas James 1938- *AmMWSc 92*
**Fitzgerald,** Thomas James 1943- *AmMWSc 92*
**FitzGerald,** Thomas Joe 1941- *WhoMW 92*
**Fitzgerald,** Thomas Michael 1936- *AmMWSc 92*
**Fitzgerald,** Tikhon 1932- *WhoRel 92*
**Fitzgerald,** Tikhon Lee R. H. 1932- *WhoWest 92*
**Fitzgerald,** Vincent James 1950- *WhoWest 92*
**Fitzgerald,** Walter David 1941- *WhoFI 92*
**Fitzgerald,** Walter George 1936- *WhoFI 92*
**Fitzgerald,** William B. *WhoBlA 92*
**Fitzgerald,** William Brendan 1936- *WhoAmL 92, WhoWest 92*
**Fitzgerald,** William Francis *AmMWSc 92*
**Fitzgerald,** William Francis 1908- *WhoFI 92*
**Fitzgerald,** William Knight d1991 *Who 92N*
**Fitzgerald,** William Thomas 1926- *WhoFI 92, WhoMW 92*
**Fitzgerald,** Zelda 1899-1948 *BenetAL 91*
**Fitzgerald,** Zelda 1900-1948 *HanAmWH*
**Fitzgerald-Brown,** Benita 1961- *BlkOlyM*
**Fitzgerald-Lombard,** Charles 1941- *Who 92*
**FitzGibbon,** Constantine 1919-1983 *TwCSFW 91*
**FitzGibbon,** Joanne Eileen Theodora W 1916- *IntAu&W 91*
**FitzGibbon,** Louis Theobald Dillon 1925- *Who 92*
**FitzGibbon,** Theodora 1916- *WrDr 92*
**Fitzgibbon,** William Edward, III 1945- *AmMWSc 92*
**Fitzgibbons,** J D 1922- *AmMWSc 92*
**Fitzhardinge,** Joan Margaret 1912- *ConAu 36NR*
**FitzHarris,** Viscount 1946- *Who 92*
**Fitzharris,** Joseph Charles 1946- *WhoMW 92*
**Fitzharris,** Timothy Patrick 1944- *AmMWSc 92*
**Fitzherbert** *Who 92*
**FitzHerbert,** Giles Eden 1935- *Who 92*
**FitzHerbert,** Richard 1963- *Who 92*
**Fitzherbert-Brockholes,** Michael John 1920- *Who 92*
**Fitzhugh,** Calvin Craig 1950- *WhoAmL 92*
**Fitzhugh,** David Michael 1946- *WhoAmL 92*
**Fitzhugh,** Henry Allen 1939- *AmMWSc 92*
**Fitzhugh,** Howard Naylor 1909- *WhoBlA 92*
**Fitzhugh,** Kathryn Corrothers 1950- *WhoBlA 92*
**Fitzhugh,** Louise 1928-1974 *ConAu 34NR*
**Fitzhugh,** Oscar Garth 1901- *AmMWSc 92*
**Fitzhugh,** Patrick Armand 1965- *WhoFI 92*
**Fitzhugh,** Percy Keese 1876-1950 *ConAu 133, SmATA 65*
**FitzHugh,** Richard 1922- *AmMWSc 92*
**Fitzhugh-Bell,** Kathleen *AmMWSc 92*
**Fitz-James,** Philip Chester 1920- *AmMWSc 92*
**Fitzjohn,** David 1963- *TwCPaSc*
**Fitzloff,** John Frederick 1940- *AmMWSc 92*
**Fitz-Maurice** *Who 92*
**Fitzmaurice,** Desmond FitzJohn 1893- *Who 92*
**Fitzmaurice,** George 1877-1963 *FacFETw, RfGEnL 91*
**Fitzmaurice,** Leona Claire 1945- *WhoWest 92*
**Fitzmaurice,** Nessan 1959- *AmMWSc 92*
**Fitzmyer,** Joseph Augustine 1920- *WhoRel 92*
**Fitzner,** Richard Earl 1946- *AmMWSc 92*
**Fitzpane,** Mary 1928- *TwCPaSc*
**FitzPatrick,** Alan Joseph 1937- *WhoRel 92*

**Fitzpatrick,** Albert E. 1928- *WhoBlA 92*
**Fitzpatrick,** Ben, Jr 1932- *AmMWSc 92*
**Fitzpatrick,** Charles R 1938- *WhoIns 92*
**Fitzpatrick,** Christine Morris 1920- *WhoMW 92*
**FitzPatrick,** David Beatty 1920- *Who 92*
**Fitzpatrick,** Dennis John 1948- *WhoAmL 92*
**Fitzpatrick,** Derrick Milas 1959- *WhoRel 92*
**Fitzpatrick,** Desmond 1912- *IntWW 91, Who 92*
**Fitzpatrick,** Don William 1940- *WhoMW 92*
**Fitzpatrick,** Duross 1934- *WhoAmL 92*
**Fitzpatrick,** Edward B. *WhoBlA 92*
**Fitzpatrick,** Edwin Bernard 1930- *WhoMW 92*
**Fitzpatrick,** Ellen 1957- *WhoFI 92*
**Fitzpatrick,** Ernest Hugh *ScFEYrs*
**Fitzpatrick,** Francis Anthony 1947- *AmMWSc 92*
**FitzPatrick,** Francis James 1916- *WhoAmL 92, WhoFI 92*
**Fitzpatrick,** Gary Owen 1943- *AmMWSc 92*
**Fitzpatrick,** George 1946- *AmMWSc 92*
**Fitzpatrick,** Harold Francis 1947- *WhoAmL 92, WhoFI 92*
**Fitzpatrick,** Hugh Michael 1920- *AmMWSc 92*
**Fitzpatrick,** J F, Jr 1932- *AmMWSc 92*
**Fitzpatrick,** James Bernard 1930- *Who 92*
**Fitzpatrick,** James Franklin 1933- *WhoAmL 92*
**Fitzpatrick,** Jimmie Doile 1938- *AmMWSc 92*
**Fitzpatrick,** Joe Allen 1959- *WhoRel 92*
**Fitzpatrick,** John 1929- *Who 92*
**Fitzpatrick,** John Hitchcock 1923- *WhoAmP 91*
**Fitzpatrick,** John J. 1918- *WhoRel 92*
**Fitzpatrick,** John J 1943- *WhoAmP 91*
**Fitzpatrick,** John K., Jr. 1962- *WhoFI 92*
**Fitzpatrick,** John Leo 1922- *WhoAmP 91*
**Fitzpatrick,** John Malcolm 1924- *WhoFI 92*
**Fitzpatrick,** John Ronald 1923- *Who 92*
**Fitzpatrick,** John Weaver 1951- *AmMWSc 92*
**Fitzpatrick,** Joseph A 1944- *AmMWSc 92*
**Fitzpatrick,** Joseph Mark 1925- *WhoAmL 92*
**Fitzpatrick,** Joseph T *WhoAmP 91*
**Fitzpatrick,** Jude *WhoRel 92*
**Fitzpatrick,** Julia C. *WhoBlA 92*
**FitzPatrick,** Kevin *DrAPF 91*
**Fitzpatrick,** Lloyd Charles 1937- *AmMWSc 92*
**Fitzpatrick,** Mary Anne Theresa 1949- *WhoMW 92*
**Fitzpatrick,** Max Ray 1934- *WhoMW 92*
**Fitzpatrick,** Michael John 1948- *WhoFI 92*
**Fitzpatrick,** Michael Thomas 1967- *WhoMW 92*
**Fitzpatrick,** Patrick Michael 1946- *AmMWSc 92*
**Fitzpatrick,** Philip Matthew 1915- *AmMWSc 92*
**Fitzpatrick,** Robert Charles 1926- *AmMWSc 92*
**Fitzpatrick,** Rosalyn M 1911- *WhoAmP 91*
**Fitzpatrick,** Ruth McDonough 1933- *WhoRel 92*
**Fitzpatrick,** Sean Kevin 1941- *WhoFI 92*
**Fitzpatrick,** Terence John 1948- *WhoMW 92*
**Fitzpatrick,** Thomas Bernard 1919- *AmMWSc 92*
**Fitzpatrick,** Thomas David 1947- *WhoEnt 92*
**Fitzpatrick,** Whitfield Westfeldt 1942- *WhoAmL 92*
**Fitzpatrick,** William *WhoMW 92*
**Fitzpatrick,** William 1949- *WhoEnt 92*
**Fitzpatrick,** William J. 1889- *WhoBlA 92*
**Fitzporter,** John L *ScFEYrs*
**FitzRalph,** Matthew *ConAu 34NR*
**FitzRoy** *Who 92*
**FitzRoy,** Charles d1989 *Who 92N*
**Fitzroy,** Nancy Deloye 1927- *AmMWSc 92*
**FitzRoy Newdegate** *Who 92*
**Fitzsimmons,** Barry Patrick 1961- *WhoEnt 92*
**Fitzsimmons,** Delbert Wayne 1932- *AmMWSc 92*
**Fitzsimmons,** Frank E 1908-1981 *FacFETw*
**Fitzsimmons,** Joseph John 1934- *WhoMW 92*
**Fitzsimmons,** Lisa Lynn 1964- *WhoWest 92*
**Fitzsimmons,** Lowell Cotton 1931- *WhoWest 92*
**Fitzsimmons,** Richard Stewart 1950- *WhoAmP 91*
**Fitzsimmons,** Robert Hameil 1940- *WhoFI 92*
**Fitzsimmons,** Robert Patrick 1952- *WhoAmP 91*
**Fitzsimmons,** Thomas *DrAPF 91*
**Fitzsimmons,** Thomas 1926- *IntAu&W 91*
**Fitzsimmons,** Timothy 1952- *WhoFI 92*
**Fitzsimmons,** William Kennedy 1909- *Who 92*
**Fitzsimon,** James Joseph 1932- *WhoEnt 92*
**Fitzsimonds,** Roger Leon 1938- *WhoFI 92, WhoMW 92*
**Fitzsimons,** Anthony *Who 92*
**Fitzsimons,** George K. 1928- *WhoRel 92*
**Fitzsimons,** James Thomas 1928- *Who 92*
**FitzSimons,** Maureen *WhoEnt 92*
**Fitzsimons,** P. Anthony 1946- *Who 92*
**Fitzsimons,** Patrick S. 1930- *WhoWest 92*
**FitzSimons,** Sharon Russell 1945- *WhoFI 92*
**Fitzsimons,** Thomas Patrick 1953- *WhoMW 92*
**Fitzwalter,** Baron 1914- *Who 92*
**Fitzwater,** Donald 1930- *AmMWSc 92*
**Fitzwater,** Margaret Gwen 1955- *WhoRel 92*
**Fitzwater,** Marlin 1942- *IntWW 91*
**Fitzwater,** Martha Amanda 1961- *WhoAmL 92*
**Fitzwater,** Max Marlin 1942- *WhoAmP 91*
**Fitzwater,** Robert N 1924- *AmMWSc 92*
**Fitzwater,** Sidney Allen 1953- *WhoAmL 92*
**Fiumara,** Nicholas J 1912- *AmMWSc 92*
**Five Pennies,** The *NewAmDM*
**Five,** Billy *ConAu 135*
**Five,** Kaci Kullmann 1951- *IntWW 91*
**Fivecoat,** Martha Hodge 1944- *WhoMW 92*
**Fivel,** Daniel I 1932- *AmMWSc 92*
**Fives-Taylor,** Paula Marie 1933- *AmMWSc 92*
**Fivizzani,** Albert John, Jr 1946- *AmMWSc 92*
**Fivozinsky,** Sherman Paul 1938- *AmMWSc 92*
**Fix,** Alfred Harold 1930- *WhoFI 92*
**Fix,** Brian David 1944- *WhoAmL 92*
**Fix,** Delbert Dale 1926- *AmMWSc 92*
**Fix,** George Arthur 1925- *WhoAmP 91*
**Fix,** George Joseph 1939- *AmMWSc 92*
**Fix,** Helen Herrink 1922- *WhoAmP 91*
**Fix,** James D 1931- *AmMWSc 92*
**Fix,** John Dekle 1941- *AmMWSc 92*
**Fix,** John Neilson 1937- *WhoMW 92*
**Fix,** Kathleen A 1960- *AmMWSc 92*
**Fix,** Richard Conrad 1930- *AmMWSc 92*
**Fix,** Ronald Edward 1941- *AmMWSc 92*
**Fix,** Wilbur James 1927- *WhoFI 92, WhoWest 92*
**Fixel,** Lawrence *DrAPF 91*
**Fixell,** Lester G. 1919- *WhoFI 92*
**Fixman,** Marshall 1930- *AmMWSc 92, IntWW 91*
**Fizdale,** Robert 1920- *NewAmDM*
**Fizer,** William J. *WhoRel 92*
**Fjarlie,** Earl J 1932- *AmMWSc 92*
**Fjeld,** Phyllis *WhoRel 92*
**Fjeld,** Robert Alan 1947- *AmMWSc 92*
**Fjeld,** Roger Willard 1933- *WhoMW 92, WhoRel 92*
**Fjelde,** Rolf 1926- *IntAu&W 91, WrDr 92*
**Fjeldgaard,** Kjeld 1946- *WhoFI 92*
**Fjellman,** Anel Gilbert 1917- *WhoRel 92*
**Fjelstad,** Eric Jon 1962- *WhoAmL 92*
**Fjelstad,** Paul 1954- *WhoAmL 92*
**Fjordbotten,** Alf Lee 1952- *WhoRel 92*
**Fjordbotten,** Edwin LeRoy 1938- *WhoWest 92*
**Fjoslien,** Dave 1936- *WhoAmP 91*
**Flaagan,** Odell D 1938- *WhoAmP 91*
**Flaanders,** Ernest William 1935- *WhoRel 92*
**Flaccus** *BenetAL 91*
**Flaccus,** Edward 1921- *AmMWSc 92*
**Flach,** Frederic Francis 1927- *AmMWSc 92*
**Flach,** Klaus Werner 1927- *AmMWSc 92*
**Flach,** Werner 1935- *WhoFI 92*
**Flachsbart,** Peter George 1944- *AmMWSc 92, WhoWest 92*
**Flachskam,** Robert Louis, Jr 1946- *AmMWSc 92*
**Flack,** Bertram Anthony 1924- *Who 92*
**Flack,** Charles Haynes 1927- *WhoMW 92*
**Flack,** Harley Eugene 1943- *WhoBlA 92*
**Flack,** J E 1929- *AmMWSc 92*
**Flack,** John T *WhoAmP 91*
**Flack,** Roberta 1939- *WhoBlA 92, WhoEnt 92*
**Flack,** Ronald Dumont, Jr 1947- *AmMWSc 92*
**Flack,** Warren Wade 1956- *WhoWest 92*
**Flacke,** Joan Wareham 1931- *AmMWSc 92*
**Flacke,** Werner Ernst 1924- *AmMWSc 92*
**Flaco,** El *DrAPF 91*
**Fladeland,** Betty 1919- *IntAu&W 91, WrDr 92*
**Flading,** John Joseph 1960- *WhoFI 92*
**Fladung,** Jerome F *WhoAmP 91*
**Fladung,** Richard Denis 1953- *WhoAmL 92*
**Flaesgarten,** Grace Ludmila 1932- *WhoMW 92*
**Flagan,** Richard Charles 1947- *AmMWSc 92*
**Flagello,** Ezio 1931- *NewAmDM*
**Flagello,** Ezio Domenico 1932- *WhoEnt 92*
**Flagello,** Nicolas 1928- *NewAmDM*
**Flagg,** David 1937- *WhoAmP 91*
**Flagg,** Douglas Bryan 1962- *WhoWest 92*
**Flagg,** E. Alma W. 1918- *WhoBlA 92*
**Flagg,** Francis 1898-1946 *ScFEYrs*
**Flagg,** J. Thomas 1917- *WhoBlA 92*
**Flagg,** James Montgomery 1877-1960 *BenetAL 91*
**Flagg,** John Ferard 1914- *AmMWSc 92*
**Flagg,** John William Hawkins 1929- *Who 92*
**Flagg,** Joseph H. 1914-1990 *WhoBlA 92N*
**Flagg,** Michael James 1958- *WhoMW 92*
**Flagg,** Neal P. 1959- *WhoAmL 92*
**Flagg,** Norman Lee 1932- *WhoWest 92*
**Flagg,** Raymond Osbourn 1933- *AmMWSc 92*
**Flagg,** Ronald Simon 1953- *WhoAmL 92*
**Flagg,** Thomas Wilson 1805-1884 *BiInAmS*
**Flaggs,** George, Jr 1953- *WhoAmP 91*
**Flagle,** Charles D 1919- *AmMWSc 92*
**Flagler,** Terrence 1964- *WhoBlA 92*
**Flagler,** William Lawrence 1922- *WhoWest 92*
**Flagstad,** Kirsten 1895-1962 *FacFETw, NewAmDM*
**Flaherty,** Brian J 1965- *WhoAmP 91*
**Flaherty,** Charles Frances, Jr 1938- *WhoAmP 91*
**Flaherty,** Daniel Leo 1929- *WhoRel 92*
**Flaherty,** David T *WhoAmP 91*
**Flaherty,** David Thomas, Jr. 1953- *WhoAmL 92, WhoFI 92*
**Flaherty,** Doug *DrAPF 91*
**Flaherty,** Francis Joseph 1935- *AmMWSc 92*
**Flaherty,** Francis X 1947- *WhoAmP 91*
**Flaherty,** Franklin Trimby, Jr 1934- *AmMWSc 92*
**Flaherty,** Gerald Stanley 1938- *WhoFI 92*
**Flaherty,** Gloria *WhoEnt 92*
**Flaherty,** John Edmund 1948- *WhoAmL 92*
**Flaherty,** John Joseph 1932- *WhoFI 92*
**Flaherty,** John P *WhoAmP 91*
**Flaherty,** John P., Jr. 1931- *WhoAmL 92*
**Flaherty,** John Thomas 1941- *AmMWSc 92*
**Flaherty,** Joseph *LesBEnT 92*
**Flaherty,** Joseph E 1943- *AmMWSc 92*
**Flaherty,** Kenneth Mathew 1964- *WhoMW 92*
**Flaherty,** Larry Paul 1943- *WhoWest 92*
**Flaherty,** Michael Francis 1936- *WhoAmP 91*
**Flaherty,** Nancy H *WhoAmP 91*
**Flaherty,** Patrick Francis 1950- *WhoAmL 92*
**Flaherty,** Peter F 1925- *WhoAmP 91*
**Flaherty,** Richard Alan 1952- *WhoFI 92*
**Flaherty,** Robert 1884-1951 *FacFETw, IntDcF 2-2*
**Flaherty,** Robert Coleman 1917- *WhoRel 92*
**Flaherty,** Robert Edward 1948- *WhoAmP 91*
**Flaherty,** Robert J. 1884-1951 *BenetAL 91*
**Flaherty,** Ronald David 1952- *WhoFI 92*
**Flaherty,** Susan L.Q. 1955- *WhoAmL 92*
**Flaherty,** Virginia Chatfield 1921- *WhoAmP 91*
**Flahibe,** Mary Elizabeth 1948- *AmMWSc 92*
**Flahiff,** George Bernard 1905- *RelLAm 91, WhoRel 92*
**Flaim,** Francis Richard 1913- *AmMWSc 92*
**Flaim,** Kathryn Erskine 1949- *AmMWSc 92*
**Flaim,** Stephen Frederick 1948- *AmMWSc 92, WhoWest 92*
**Flaim,** Thomas Alfred 1946- *AmMWSc 92*
**Flake,** Floyd H. 1945- *AlmAP 92 [port], WhoAmP 91, WhoBlA 92*
**Flake,** Nancy 1917-1968 *DcNCBi 2*
**Flake,** Nancy Aline 1956- *WhoBlA 92*
**Flakes,** Dennis *WhoRel 92*
**Flakes,** Larry Joseph 1947- *WhoBlA 92*
**Flaks,** Joel George 1927- *AmMWSc 92*
**Flaks,** Stephen 1941- *IntMPA 92*
**Flam,** Eric 1935- *AmMWSc 92*
**Flam,** Jack *DrAPF 91*
**Flamand,** Paul Henri 1909- *IntWW 91*
**Flambeau,** Blossom *ConAu 135*
**Flamer,** John H., Jr. 1938- *WhoBlA 92*
**Flamm,** Bryce Conway 1927- *WhoAmP 91*
**Flamm,** Daniel Lawrence 1943- *AmMWSc 92, WhoWest 92*
**Flamm,** Donald 1899- *WhoFI 92*
**Flamm,** Leonard Nathan 1943- *WhoAmL 92*
**Flammang,** Susann 1950- *IntAu&W 91, WhoRel 92*
**Flammarion,** Camille 1842-1925 *ScFEYrs*
**Flammarion,** Charles-Henri 1946- *IntWW 91*
**Flammer,** George Herbert 1947- *WhoAmL 92*
**Flammer,** Gordon H 1926- *AmMWSc 92*
**Flamson,** Richard J., III d1991 *NewYTBS 91*
**Flamson,** Richard J., III 1929- *IntWW 91*
**Flanagan,** Barry 1941- *IntWW 91, TwCPaSc, Who 92, WorArt 1980*
**Flanagan,** Bernard Joseph 1908- *WhoRel 92*
**Flanagan,** Carroll Edward 1911- *AmMWSc 92*
**Flanagan,** Christie Stephen 1938- *WhoAmL 92*
**Flanagan,** Edward Gaskill 1875-1942 *DcNCBi 2*
**Flanagan,** Edward Joseph 1886-1948 *FacFETw [port], RelLAm 91*
**Flanagan,** Edward Joseph 1931- *WhoMW 92*
**Flanagan,** Edward William 1950- *WhoEnt 92*
**Flanagan,** Fionnula Manon 1941- *WhoEnt 92*
**Flanagan,** Harry Paul 1933- *WhoMW 92*
**Flanagan,** James Henry, Jr. 1934- *WhoAmL 92*
**Flanagan,** James Joseph, III 1950- *WhoFI 92*
**Flanagan,** James L 1925- *AmMWSc 92*
**Flanagan,** James Loton 1925- *IntWW 91*
**Flanagan,** James Philip 1954- *WhoAmP 91*
**Flanagan,** John 1829-1902 *DcNCBi 2*
**Flanagan,** John Anthony 1942- *WhoAmL 92*
**Flanagan,** John J 1961- *WhoAmP 91*
**Flanagan,** Joseph Patrick 1938- *WhoFI 92, WhoMW 92*
**Flanagan,** Joseph Patrick, Jr. 1924- *WhoAmL 92*
**Flanagan,** Joye Boggs 1927- *WhoAmP 91*
**Flanagan,** Judith Ann 1950- *WhoFI 92*
**Flanagan,** Judy Claire 1958- *WhoAmL 92*
**Flanagan,** Kevin West 1958- *WhoRel 92*
**Flanagan,** Larry 1953- *WhoEnt 92*
**Flanagan,** Mark Donnell 1962- *WhoAmL 92*
**Flanagan,** Michael Joseph 1946- *Who 92*
**Flanagan,** Michael Leonard 1935- *WhoAmL 92*
**Flanagan,** Mike 1950- *ConAu 133*
**Flanagan,** Natalie Smith 1913- *WhoAmP 91*
**Flanagan,** Patrick Anthony 1938- *WhoAmP 91*
**Flanagan,** Patrick Joseph 1940- *IntAu&W 91*
**Flanagan,** Peter J 1930- *WhoIns 92*
**Flanagan,** Peter Rutledge 1945- *AmMWSc 92*
**Flanagan,** Richard *DrAPF 91*
**Flanagan,** Robert *DrAPF 91*
**Flanagan,** Robert B., Sr. 1929- *WhoBlA 92*
**Flanagan,** Robert Joseph 1924- *AmMWSc 92*
**Flanagan,** Robert Joseph 1941- *WhoFI 92*
**Flanagan,** Robert Lawrence 1945- *WhoAmP 91*
**Flanagan,** Stephen Paul 1950- *WhoEnt 92*
**Flanagan,** Stephen Roger 1956- *WhoFI 92*
**Flanagan,** Steven Douglas 1948- *AmMWSc 92*
**Flanagan,** T. Earl, Jr. 1937- *WhoBlA 92*
**Flanagan,** T.P. 1929- *TwCPaSc*
**Flanagan,** Ted Benjamin 1929- *AmMWSc 92*
**Flanagan,** Theodore Ross 1920- *AmMWSc 92*
**Flanagan,** Thomas 1923- *BenetAL 91, ConNov 91, WrDr 92*
**Flanagan,** Thomas Donald 1935- *AmMWSc 92*
**Flanagan,** Thomas Leo 1916- *AmMWSc 92*
**Flanagan,** Thomas Patrick *WhoMW 92*
**Flanagan,** Thomas Raymond 1951- *AmMWSc 92*
**Flanagan,** Wayne 1955- *WhoFI 92*
**Flanagan,** William 1923-1969 *NewAmDM*
**Flanagan,** William F 1927- *AmMWSc 92*
**Flanagan,** William Lee 1939- *WhoRel 92*
**Flanagan-Simpson,** Katherine *DrAPF 91*
**Flanagin,** Neil 1930- *WhoAmL 92*
**Flanagin,** Patrick Henry 1948- *WhoAmP 91*
**Flanary,** Gareth Dean 1961- *WhoRel 92*
**Flanary,** James Lee 1955- *WhoAmL 92*
**Flanders,** Allen F. 1945- *WhoWest 92*
**Flanders,** Clifford Auten 1911- *AmMWSc 92*
**Flanders,** David A 1939- *WhoAmP 91*

Flanders, Dennis 1915- TwCPaSc, Who 92
Flanders, Donald Hargis 1924- WhoFI 92
Flanders, Dwight Prescott 1909- WhoFI 92, WhoMW 92
Flanders, Edward Paul 1934- WhoEnt 92
Flanders, George James 1960- WhoWest 92
Flanders, Harley 1925- AmMWSc 92
Flanders, Harry E 1912- WhoAmP 91
Flanders, Henry Jackson, Jr. 1921- WhoRel 92
Flanders, Jane DrAPF 91
Flanders, John W, Sr 1927- WhoAmP 91
Flanders, Kathleen Corey 1956- AmMWSc 92
Flanders, Peggy DrAPF 91
Flanders, Raymond Alan 1929- WhoMW 92
Flanders, Robert Vern 1947- AmMWSc 92
Flanders, Scott Nelson 1956- WhoFI 92
Flanders, Wayne C. 1949- WhoRel 92
Flandrau, Charles Macomb 1871-1938 BenetAL 91
Flandro, Gary A 1934- AmMWSc 92
Flandro, Millie L 1954- WhoAmP 91
Flanery, David 1828-1900 BiInAmS
Flanick, Jill Ellin 1958- WhoFI 92
Flanigan, Donna Marie Herring 1957- WhoWest 92
Flanigan, James 1936- ConAu 134
Flanigan, Norbert James 1918- AmMWSc 92
Flanigan, Richard D 1941- WhoAmP 91
Flanigan, Robert Daniel, Jr. 1949- WhoFI 92
Flanigan, Rosemary 1926- WhoMW 92
Flanigan, Stevenson 1926- AmMWSc 92
Flanigan, Teresa Marie 1959- WhoAmL 92
Flanigan, Virgil James 1938- AmMWSc 92
Flanigan, William Francis, Jr 1939- AmMWSc 92
Flanigan, William J 1930- AmMWSc 92
Flanigen, Edith Marie 1929- AmMWSc 92
Flank, William H 1932- AmMWSc 92
Flannagan, Eric Goodyear 1892-1970 DcNCBi 2
Flannagan, John Fullan 1940- AmMWSc 92
Flannagan, Roy Catesby, Jr. 1938- WhoMW 92
Flannelly, Kevin J. 1949- WhoWest 92
Flannelly, Laura T. 1952- WhoWest 92
Flannelly, William G 1931- AmMWSc 92
Flanner, Janet 1892-1978 BenetAL 91, FacFETw, LiExTwC
Flannery, Arthur Daniel 1944- WhoEnt 92
Flannery, Brian Paul 1948- AmMWSc 92
Flannery, Christopher Patrick 1956- WhoAmL 92
Flannery, Ellen Joanne 1951- WhoAmL 92
Flannery, Harry Audley 1947- WhoAmL 92
Flannery, John B, Jr 1941- AmMWSc 92
Flannery, John Francis 1928- WhoAmL 92
Flannery, John Philip, II 1946- WhoAmL 92
Flannery, Joseph Patrick 1932- IntWW 91, WhoFI 92
Flannery, Kate EncAmaz 91
Flannery, Martin Henry 1918- Who 92
Flannery, Martin Raymond 1941- AmMWSc 92
Flannery, Rebecca R. 1952- WhoEnt 92
Flannigan, J. J. 1968- WhoBlA 92
Flansburgh, Earl Robert 1931- WhoFI 92
Flanter, Jill Selevan 1960- WhoEnt 92
Flasar, F Michael 1946- AmMWSc 92
Flasch, Bert 1930- WhoEnt 92
Flaschen, Evan Daniel 1957- WhoAmL 92
Flaschen, Steward Samuel 1926- WhoFI 92
Flaschka, Hermenegild Arved 1915- AmMWSc 92
Flashman, Stuart Milton 1948- AmMWSc 92
Flashner, Michael 1942- AmMWSc 92
Flaskamp, Ruth Ehmen Staack 1927- WhoMW 92
Flaspohler, David 1939- AmMWSc 92
Flaster, Lawrence Michael 1951- WhoAmL 92
Flaster, Richard Joel 1943- WhoAmL 92
Flatau, Carole Joan 1935- WhoEnt 92
Flateau, John 1950- WhoBlA 92
Flateau-Gooding, Adele Marie 1951- WhoFI 92
Flaten, Betty Arlene 1938- WhoAmP 91
Flaten, Robert A 1934- WhoAmP 91
Flath, Robert Arthur 1933- AmMWSc 92
Flather Who 92
Flather, Baroness Who 92
Flather, Gary Denis Who 92
Flathman, Richard Earl 1934- IntWW 91
Flatley, Derek Comedy 1920- Who 92
Flatley, Lawrence Edward 1950- WhoAmL 92
Flato, Jud B 1940- AmMWSc 92, WhoFI 92
Flato, William Roeder, Jr. 1945- WhoFI 92
Flatt and Scruggs NewAmDM
Flatt, Adrian Ede 1921- AmMWSc 92
Flatt, Carter J 1943- WhoIns 92
Flatt, Daniel Lewis 1960- WhoAmL 92
Flatt, Elmer E WhoAmP 91
Flatt, Ernest LesBEnT 92
Flatt, Ernest Orville 1918- WhoEnt 92
Flatt, Jean-Pierre 1933- AmMWSc 92
Flatt, Lester 1914-1979 NewAmDM
Flatt, Michael Oliver 1938- WhoWest 92
Flatt, William Perry 1931- AmMWSc 92
Flatte, Stanley Martin 1940- AmMWSc 92
Flattely, Alistair 1922- TwCPaSc
Flatter, Joseph Otto 1894- TwCPaSc
Flattery, David Kevin 1960- AmMWSc 92
Flattery, Paul Charles 1935- WhoMW 92
Flattery, Thomas L. 1922- IntMPA 92
Flattery, Thomas Long 1922- WhoAmL 92
Flatto, Leopold 1929- AmMWSc 92
Flatts, Barbara Ann 1951- WhoBlA 92
Flaubert, Gustave 1821-1880 GuFrLit 1
Flaugh, Michael Edward 1941- AmMWSc 92
Flaugher, Jeanine Karen Sue WhoMW 92
Flaum, Joel M WhoAmP 91
Flaum, Joel Martin 1936- WhoAmL 92, WhoMW 92
Flaum, Marshall Allen WhoEnt 92
Flaum, Sander Allen 1937- WhoFI 92
Flaumenhaft, Eugene AmMWSc 92
Flautt, Thomas Joseph, Jr 1932- AmMWSc 92
Flavell, Geoffrey 1913- Who 92
Flavell, Richard Anthony 1945- AmMWSc 92, IntWW 91, Who 92
Flavell, Richard Bailey 1943- Who 92
Flavelle, David 1921- Who 92
Flavian d449 EncEarC
Flavin, Dan 1933- IntWW 91
Flavin, Glennon P. 1916- WhoRel 92
Flavin, Martin 1883-1967 BenetAL 91
Flavin, Martin 1920- AmMWSc 92
Flavin, Michael Austin 1932- AmMWSc 92
Flawn, Peter Tyrrell 1926- AmMWSc 92
Flax, Alexander H 1921- AmMWSc 92
Flax, Barbara Ann 1961- WhoAmL 92
Flax, Lawrence 1934- AmMWSc 92
Flax, Martin Howard 1928- AmMWSc 92
Flax, Stephen Wayne 1946- AmMWSc 92
Flaxen, David William 1941- Who 92
Flaxer, David 1935- WhoAmL 92
Flaxman, David 1939- WhoAmL 92
Flaxman, John 1755-1826 BlkwCEP
Flaxman, John P. 1934- IntMPA 92
Flaxman, Rosalind 1907- WhoEnt 92
Flay, Brian Richard 1947- AmMWSc 92
Flayhart, Robert Keyser 1959- WhoRel 92
Fleagle, John G 1948- AmMWSc 92
Fleagle, Patrick Elvin 1951- WhoAmP 91
Fleagle, Robert Guthrie 1918- AmMWSc 92
Fleary, George McQuinn 1922- WhoBlA 92
Flecha, Roberto, Jr. 1958- WhoHisp 92
Flechsig, Alfred J, Jr AmMWSc 92
Flechtheim, Ossip K. 1909- IntWW 91
Flechtner, Harry Marshal 1951- WhoAmL 92
Flechtner, Thomas Welch 1943- AmMWSc 92
Fleck, Arthur C 1936- AmMWSc 92
Fleck, Charles J., Jr. 1940- WhoAmL 92
Fleck, George Morrison 1934- AmMWSc 92
Fleck, Gerald Robert 1947- WhoEnt 92
Fleck, Gordon Pierce 1931- WhoFI 92
Fleck, Joseph Amadeus, Jr 1928- AmMWSc 92
Fleck, Lisa DrAPF 91
Fleck, Marlys WhoAmP 91
Fleck, Paul Duncan 1934- WhoWest 92
Fleck, Richard F. DrAPF 91
Fleck, Richard Francis 1937- WhoWest 92
Fleck, Stephen 1912- AmMWSc 92
Fleck, William G 1940- AmMWSc 92
Fleck, Zachary Thomas 1961- WhoMW 92
Fleckenstein, Albrecht 1917- AmMWSc 92
Fleckenstein, Gunther 1925- IntWW 91
Fleckenstein, John Thomas 1942- WhoMW 92
Fleckenstein, William Dale 1934- WhoMW 92
Flecker, James Elroy 1884-1915 RfGEnL 91, ScFEYrs, TwCLC 43 [port]
Flecker, James William 1939- Who 92
Fleckman, Philip Howard 1946- WhoWest 92
Fleddermann, Richard G 1922- AmMWSc 92
Fleder, Robert Charles 1948- WhoAmL 92
Fleeger, John Wayne 1949- AmMWSc 92
Fleeker, James R 1937- AmMWSc 92
Fleeman, Daniel James 1954- WhoMW 92
Fleeman, Mary Grace 1947- WhoAmL 92
Fleener, Robert Francis 1951- WhoRel 92
Fleenor, Edgar, Jr. 1933- WhoMW 92
Fleenor, Marvin Bension 1939- AmMWSc 92
Fleer, David 1953- WhoRel 92
Fleer, Keith George 1943- WhoAmL 92, WhoEnt 92
Fleeson, William 1915- AmMWSc 92
Fleet, Kenneth George 1929- IntAu&W 91, Who 92
Fleet, Stephen George 1936- Who 92
Fleetwood Mac FacFETw, NewAmDM
Fleetwood, Charles Wesley 1904- AmMWSc 92
Fleetwood, Frances 1902- IntAu&W 91
Fleetwood, George Sherman 1953- WhoMW 92
Fleetwood, Mary Annis 1931- WhoFI 92
Fleetwood, Mick 1947- WhoEnt 92
Fleetwood, Mildred Kaiser 1945- AmMWSc 92
Fleetwood, Susan Maureen 1944- Who 92
Fleetwood, Thirvin Dow 1922- WhoAmP 91
Fleetwood-Walker, Bernard 1893-1963 TwCPaSc
Fleezanis, Jorja Kay 1952- WhoEnt 92
Flegal, Arthur Russell, Jr 1946- AmMWSc 92, WhoWest 92
Flegal, Cal J 1936- AmMWSc 92
Flegal, Robert Melvin 1941- AmMWSc 92
Flegenheimer, Diana Vaughn 1945- WhoWest 92
Flegenheimer, Harold H 1924- AmMWSc 92
Fleharty, Eugene 1934- AmMWSc 92
Fleharty, Rosemary Ann 1951- WhoFI 92
Fleig, Albert J, Jr 1937- AmMWSc 92
Fleisch, Jerome Herbert 1941- AmMWSc 92
Fleischaker, Marc L. 1945- WhoAmL 92
Fleischaker, Ted 1950- WhoEnt 92
Fleischauer, Paul Dell 1942- AmMWSc 92
Fleischer, Alfred J WhoAmP 91
Fleischer, Allan A 1931- AmMWSc 92
Fleischer, Arthur, Jr. 1933- WhoAmL 92
Fleischer, Arthur C 1952- AmMWSc 92
Fleischer, Becca Catherine 1930- AmMWSc 92
Fleischer, Carl August 1936- WhoFI 92
Fleischer, Charles 1950- ConTFT 9
Fleischer, Daniel WhoRel 92
Fleischer, Everly B 1936- AmMWSc 92
Fleischer, Ezra 1928- IntWW 91
Fleischer, Gerald A 1933- AmMWSc 92
Fleischer, Henry 1923- AmMWSc 92
Fleischer, Henry 1938- WhoAmL 92
Fleischer, Herbert Oswald 1913- AmMWSc 92
Fleischer, Hugh William 1938- WhoAmP 91
Fleischer, Isidore 1927- AmMWSc 92
Fleischer, Joseph Linden 1943- WhoFI 92
Fleischer, Max 1883-1972 FacFETw
Fleischer, Michael 1908- AmMWSc 92
Fleischer, Peter 1941- AmMWSc 92
Fleischer, Richard O. WhoEnt 92
Fleischer, Richard O. 1916- IntMPA 92, IntWW 91
Fleischer, Robert Louis 1930- AmMWSc 92
Fleischer, Sidney 1930- AmMWSc 92
Fleischer, Thomas B 1929- AmMWSc 92
Fleischer, Walter Hersch 1940- WhoAmL 92
Fleischhauer, Carl-August 1930- IntWW 91
Fleischli, George Robert 1940- WhoAmL 92
Fleischmajer, Raul WhoHisp 92
Fleischmajer, Raul 1924- AmMWSc 92
Fleischman, Alan R 1946- AmMWSc 92
Fleischman, Albert Sid 1920- IntAu&W 91
Fleischman, Darrell Eugene 1934- AmMWSc 92
Fleischman, Edward H 1932- WhoAmP 91
Fleischman, Edward Hirsh 1932- WhoAmL 92, WhoFI 92
Fleischman, Harry 1914- WrDr 92
Fleischman, Herman Israel 1950- WhoAmL 92
Fleischman, James Paul 1956- WhoFI 92
Fleischman, Julian B 1933- AmMWSc 92
Fleischman, Marvin 1937- AmMWSc 92
Fleischman, Paul 1952- WrDr 92
Fleischman, Paul Taylor 1952- IntAu&W 91
Fleischman, Robert Werder 1937- AmMWSc 92
Fleischman, Sid 1920- WrDr 92
Fleischman, Sol Joseph 1910- WhoEnt 92
Fleischman, Stephen LesBEnT 92
Fleischman, Stephen 1954- WhoMW 92
Fleischman, Ted DrAPF 91
Fleischmann, Charles Werner 1936- AmMWSc 92
Fleischmann, Ernest Martin 1924- WhoEnt 92, WhoWest 92
Fleischmann, Hans Hermann 1933- AmMWSc 92
Fleischmann, Martin 1927- IntWW 91, Who 92
Fleischmann, Paul 1946- WhoRel 92
Fleischmann, Rudolf 1903- IntWW 91
Fleischmann, William Robert, Jr 1944- AmMWSc 92
Fleischmann-Fellowes, Dagmar 1958- WhoAmL 92
Fleisher, Bernice DrAPF 91
Fleisher, Edwin A. 1877-1959 NewAmDM
Fleisher, Frederic E 1933- IntAu&W 91
Fleisher, Gary Mitchell 1941- WhoFI 92
Fleisher, Harold 1921- AmMWSc 92
Fleisher, Jerrilyn 1952- WhoFI 92
Fleisher, Leon 1928- NewAmDM
Fleisher, Marcy Beth 1964- WhoEnt 92
Fleisher, Martin 1935- AmMWSc 92
Fleisher, Penrod Jay 1937- AmMWSc 92
Fleisher, Risselle Rosenthal 1934- WhoAmP 91
Fleisher, Steven M. 1945- WhoAmL 92
Fleisher, Thomas A 1946- AmMWSc 92
Fleishman, Alan Michael 1939- WhoWest 92
Fleishman, Alfred 1905- WhoMW 92
Fleishman, Avrom 1933- IntAu&W 91, WrDr 92
Fleishman, Bernard Abraham 1925- AmMWSc 92
Fleishman, Joel Lawrence 1934- WhoAmL 92
Fleishman, Lazar 1944- ConAu 133
Fleishman, Seymour 1918- ConAu 133, SmATA 66
Fleishmann, Arthur 1896-1990 TwCPaSc
Fleisig, Ross 1921- AmMWSc 92
Fleiss, Joseph L 1937- AmMWSc 92
Fleissner, Robert F. 1932- WhoMW 92
Fleit, Howard B 1952- AmMWSc 92
Flemal, Ronald Charles 1942- AmMWSc 92
Fleming, Bishop 1906-1990 AnObit 1990
Fleming, A M 1868- ScFEYrs
Fleming, Alan Wayne 1939- AmMWSc 92
Fleming, Alexander 1881-1955 FacFETw [port], WhoNob 90
Fleming, Alice 1928- IntAu&W 91, WrDr 92
Fleming, Alicia DeLaMothe WhoBlA 92
Fleming, Amalia 1909-1986 FacFETw
Fleming, Andrew Macdonald 1963- WhoEnt 92
Fleming, Anthony Caldwell 1939- WhoFI 92
Fleming, Arthur Sherwood 1905- RelLAm 91
Fleming, Arthur Wallace 1935- WhoBlA 92
Fleming, Attie Anderson 1921- AmMWSc 92
Fleming, Berry IntAu&W 91
Fleming, Bruce E. 1921- WhoBlA 92
Fleming, Bruce Ingram 1941- AmMWSc 92
Fleming, Caroline WrDr 92
Fleming, Carolyn 1946- WhoBlA 92
Fleming, Carolyn Elizabeth 1946- WhoRel 92
Fleming, Charles Walter 1928- WhoBlA 92
Fleming, Dalton Dick, III 1953- WhoEnt 92
Fleming, Daniel E 1940- WhoAmP 91
Fleming, David 1937- Who 92
Fleming, David L. 1934- WhoRel 92
Fleming, Deborah DrAPF 91
Fleming, Donald Joseph 1935- WhoAmL 92
Fleming, Donovan Ernest 1932- AmMWSc 92
Fleming, Douglas Riley 1922- WhoFI 92
Fleming, Edward Homer, Jr 1925- AmMWSc 92
Fleming, Edward J. 1920- WhoRel 92
Fleming, Ellis T. 1933- WhoBlA 92
Fleming, Faye 1943- WhoAmP 91
Fleming, G. James 1904- WhoBlA 92
Fleming, George 1938- WhoBlA 92
Fleming, Gerald DrAPF 91
Fleming, Gordon N 1936- AmMWSc 92
Fleming, Graham Richard 1949- AmMWSc 92
Fleming, Grahame Ritchie 1949- Who 92
Fleming, Gus WhoEnt 92A
Fleming, Henry Pridgen 1932- AmMWSc 92
Fleming, Ian 1906- TwCPaSc, Who 92
Fleming, Ian 1908-1964 CnDBLB 7 [port], FacFETw [port], RfGEnL 91
Fleming, J Gordon WhoIns 92
Fleming, James Charles 1938- AmMWSc 92
Fleming, James Emmitt 1947- AmMWSc 92
Fleming, James George 1929- WhoAmL 92
Fleming, James Joseph 1917- AmMWSc 92
Fleming, James Preston 1944- WhoAmP 91

**Fleming,** James Richard 1944- *WhoAmL 92*
**Fleming,** James Stuart 1936- *AmMWSc 92*
**Fleming,** James T *WhoAmP 91*
**Fleming,** Janet Blair 1944- *IntMPA 92*
**Fleming,** Jerry Aldin 1948- *WhoRel 92*
**Fleming,** Joel Fredric 1931- *WhoMW 92*
**Fleming,** John 1904- *Who 92*
**Fleming,** John 1919- *Who 92*
**Fleming,** John Bryden 1918- *Who 92*
**Fleming,** John Emory 1944- *WhoBlA 92*
**Fleming,** John F 1934- *AmMWSc 92*
**Fleming,** John Grant 1914- *WhoAmP 91*
**Fleming,** John Gunther 1919- *WhoAmL 92*
**Fleming,** John Howland 1957- *WhoMW 92*
**Fleming,** John Marley 1930- *Who 92*
**Fleming,** Jonathan Wight 1934- *WhoAmP 91*
**Fleming,** Joseph Clifton, Jr. 1942- *WhoAmL 92*
**Fleming,** Joseph Z. 1941- *WhoAmL 92*
**Fleming,** Juanita W *AmMWSc 92, WhoBlA 92*
**Fleming,** June H. 1938- *WhoBlA 92*
**Fleming,** Kay 1958- *WhoEnt 92*
**Fleming,** Laura Memhard 1957- *WhoFI 92*
**Fleming,** Laurence William Howie 1929- *IntAu&W 91, WrDr 92*
**Fleming,** Lawrence Thomas 1913- *AmMWSc 92*
**Fleming,** Lethia C. 1876-1963 *NotBlAW 92*
**Fleming,** Lisa L. 1961- *WhoAmL 92*
**Fleming,** Louis K. 1925- *WhoEnt 92*
**Fleming,** Mack Gerald 1932- *WhoAmL 92*
**Fleming,** Margaret Lindsey 1955- *WhoAmL 92*
**Fleming,** Martin Kharis 1956- *WhoAmP 91*
**Fleming,** Melvin J. 1926- *WhoBlA 92*
**Fleming,** Michael Paul 1948- *AmMWSc 92*
**Fleming,** Michael Paul 1963- *WhoAmL 92*
**Fleming,** Michael Thomas 1962- *WhoFI 92*
**Fleming,** Miles 1919-1978 *ConAu 134*
**Fleming,** Patricia Stubbs 1937- *WhoBlA 92*
**Fleming,** Patrick John 1947- *AmMWSc 92*
**Fleming,** Paul Daniel, III 1943- *AmMWSc 92*
**Fleming,** Peggy Gale 1948- *FacFETw*
**Fleming,** Peter B 1941- *AmMWSc 92*
**Fleming,** Phyllis Jane 1924- *AmMWSc 92*
**Fleming,** Quince D., Sr. 1915- *WhoBlA 92*
**Fleming,** Raylton Arthur 1925- *Who 92*
**Fleming,** Raymond Richard 1945- *WhoBlA 92*
**Fleming,** Reid *ConAu 135*
**Fleming,** Renee L. 1959- *WhoEnt 92*
**Fleming,** Rhonda *IntMPA 92, WhoEnt 92*
**Fleming,** Rhonda Kye 1951- *WhoEnt 92*
**Fleming,** Richard Allan 1929- *AmMWSc 92*
**Fleming,** Richard Cornwell 1932- *AmMWSc 92*
**Fleming,** Richard J 1938- *AmMWSc 92*
**Fleming,** Richard Scott 1947- *WhoWest 92*
**Fleming,** Richard Seaman 1939- *AmMWSc 92*
**Fleming,** Robben W. *LesBEnT 92*
**Fleming,** Robben Wright 1916- *IntWW 91*
**Fleming,** Robert 1921-1976 *NewAmDM*
**Fleming,** Robert 1932- *Who 92*
**Fleming,** Robert McLemore 1946- *AmMWSc 92*
**Fleming,** Robert Willerton 1919- *AmMWSc 92*
**Fleming,** Robert William 1936- *AmMWSc 92*
**Fleming,** Roger Lee 1957- *WhoMW 92*
**Fleming,** Rose Ann 1932- *WhoRel 92*
**Fleming,** Samuel Crozier, Jr. 1940- *WhoFI 92*
**Fleming,** Scott 1923- *IntWW 91*
**Fleming,** Sharon Elayne 1949- *AmMWSc 92*
**Fleming,** Stanley Louis 1933- *WhoBlA 92*
**Fleming,** Steven Robert 1951- *WhoRel 92*
**Fleming,** Stuart *ConAu 36NR*
**Fleming,** Susan Alice 1949- *WhoRel 92*
**Fleming,** Suzanne M 1927- *AmMWSc 92*
**Fleming,** Sydney Winn 1924- *AmMWSc 92*
**Fleming,** Theodore Harris 1942- *AmMWSc 92*
**Fleming,** Thomas 1927- *WrDr 92*
**Fleming,** Thomas James 1953- *WhoAmL 92*
**Fleming,** Thomas Jeffery 1955- *WhoFI 92*
**Fleming,** Thomas Michael 1951- *WhoMW 92*
**Fleming,** Thomas Smith, Jr. 1948- *WhoWest 92*
**Fleming,** Timothy Woodbridge 1944- *WhoEnt 92*
**Fleming,** Vern 1961- *BlkOlyM, WhoBlA 92*
**Fleming,** Vernon Cornelious 1952- *WhoBlA 92*
**Fleming,** Victor 1883-1949 *IntDcF 2-2 [port]*
**Fleming,** Walter 1919- *AmMWSc 92*
**Fleming,** Warren R 1922- *AmMWSc 92*
**Fleming,** Weldon Gary, Jr. 1944- *WhoBlA 92*
**Fleming,** Wendell Helms 1928- *AmMWSc 92*
**Fleming,** William 1909- *WrDr 92*
**Fleming,** William Calvin 1936- *WhoAmP 91*
**Fleming,** William Herbert 1925- *AmMWSc 92*
**Fleming,** William Launcelot Scott d1990 *IntWW 91N*
**Fleming,** William Leroy 1905- *AmMWSc 92*
**Fleming,** William Neal 1960- *WhoAmL 92*
**Fleming,** William Robert 1960- *WhoRel 92*
**Fleming,** William Sloan 1937- *WhoFI 92*
**Fleming,** William Wright 1932- *AmMWSc 92*
**Fleming,** Williamina Paton Stevens 1857-1911 *BiInAmS, FacFETw*
**Fleminger,** Abraham 1925- *AmMWSc 92*
**Flemings,** Merton Corson 1929- *AmMWSc 92*
**Flemington,** Roger 1932- *Who 92*
**Flemington,** William Frederick d1991 *Who 92N*
**Flemish knight,** The *EncAmaz 91*
**Flemister,** Launcelot Johnson 1913- *AmMWSc 92*
**Flemister,** Sarah C 1913- *AmMWSc 92*
**Flemm,** Eugene William 1944- *WhoEnt 92*
**Flemma,** John Ernest 1923- *WhoAmL 92*
**Flemming,** Arthur Sherwood 1905- *IntWW 91, WhoAmP 91*
**Flemming,** Charles Stephen 1948- *WhoBlA 92*
**Flemming,** Harry S 1940- *WhoAmP 91*
**Flemming,** Howard Joseph 1943- *WhoWest 92*
**Flemming,** John Stanton 1941- *IntWW 91, Who 92*
**Flemming,** Joseph Hale 1941- *WhoFI 92*
**Flemming,** Leonard 1880-1946 *ScFEYrs*
**Flemming,** Lillian Brock 1949- *WhoBlA 92*
**Flemming,** Ronald Raymond 1944- *WhoWest 92*
**Flemming,** Stanley Lalit Kumar 1953- *WhoWest 92*
**Flemmons,** Jerry 1936- *IntAu&W 91*
**Flemmons,** Kenneth Alan 1956- *WhoEnt 92*
**Flemyng,** Robert 1912- *IntMPA 92*
**Flender,** Harold 1924-1975 *ConAu 135*
**Flender,** Rodman 1962- *WhoEnt 92*
**Flenniken,** Cecil Stephenson 1925- *WhoFI 92*
**Flenniken,** John Michael 1951- *WhoMW 92*
**Flerov,** Georgi 1913- *FacFETw*
**Flerov,** Georgiy Nikolayevich 1913-1990 *IntWW 91, -91N*
**Flesch,** Carl 1873-1944 *NewAmDM*
**Flesch,** David C 1944- *AmMWSc 92*
**Flesch,** Michael Charles 1940- *Who 92*
**Flescher,** Irwin 1926- *WrDr 92*
**Fleshel,** Marcia Fran 1946- *WhoAmL 92*
**Flesher,** Dale Lee 1945- *IntAu&W 91*
**Flesher,** Hubert Louis 1933- *WhoRel 92*
**Flesher,** James Wendell 1925- *AmMWSc 92*
**Fleshler,** Bertram 1928- *AmMWSc 92*
**Fleshman,** James Wilson, Jr *AmMWSc 92*
**Flessa,** Karl Walter 1946- *AmMWSc 92*
**Flessner,** Bruce William 1953- *WhoMW 92*
**Fletchall,** Oscar Hale 1920- *AmMWSc 92*
**Fletcher** *Who 92*
**Fletcher,** Aaron Nathaniel 1925- *AmMWSc 92*
**Fletcher,** Adam *IntAu&W 91X*
**Fletcher,** Alan 1907- *Who 92*
**Fletcher,** Alan G 1925- *AmMWSc 92*
**Fletcher,** Alan Gerard 1931- *Who 92*
**Fletcher,** Alan Mackay *WhoEnt 92*
**Fletcher,** Alan Philip 1914- *Who 92*
**Fletcher,** Ann *DrAPF 91*
**Fletcher,** Ann Elizabeth Mary *Who 92*
**Fletcher,** Anthony L. 1935- *WhoAmL 92*
**Fletcher,** Anthony Phillips 1919- *AmMWSc 92*
**Fletcher,** Archibald Ian 1924- *Who 92*
**Fletcher,** Archibald Peter 1930- *Who 92*
**Fletcher,** Arthur Allen 1924- *WhoAmP 91, WhoBlA 92*
**Fletcher,** Augustus James Voisey 1928- *Who 92*
**Fletcher,** Barbara Miller 1956- *WhoRel 92*
**Fletcher,** Barry Davis 1935- *AmMWSc 92*
**Fletcher,** Betty B *WhoAmP 91*
**Fletcher,** Betty B. 1923- *WhoAmL 92, WhoWest 92*
**Fletcher,** Carlos Alfredo Torres 1959- *WhoEnt 92*
**Fletcher,** Cathy Ann 1949- *WhoFI 92*
**Fletcher,** Charles Montague 1911- *Who 92*
**Fletcher,** Clarence Shelby 1914- *WhoAmL 92*
**Fletcher,** Clifton Maurice 1935- *WhoAmP 91*
**Fletcher,** Colin 1922- *IntAu&W 91, WrDr 92*
**Fletcher,** Craig Steven 1967- *WhoWest 92*
**Fletcher,** David 1940- *IntAu&W 91*
**Fletcher,** David Ross 1959- *WhoRel 92*
**Fletcher,** David Todd 1958- *WhoEnt 92*
**Fletcher,** Dean Charles 1921- *AmMWSc 92*
**Fletcher,** Dirk *TwCWW 91*
**Fletcher,** Donald James 1951- *AmMWSc 92*
**Fletcher,** Donald Warren 1929- *AmMWSc 92*
**Fletcher,** Douglas Kim 1952- *WhoRel 92*
**Fletcher,** Edward A 1924- *AmMWSc 92*
**Fletcher,** Edward Abraham 1924- *WhoMW 92*
**Fletcher,** Edward Royce 1937- *AmMWSc 92*
**Fletcher,** Frank William 1937- *AmMWSc 92*
**Fletcher,** Garth L 1936- *AmMWSc 92*
**Fletcher,** Geoffrey Bernard Abbott 1903- *Who 92*
**Fletcher,** Geoffrey Scowcroft *Who 92*
**Fletcher,** George P. 1939- *WhoAmL 92*
**Fletcher,** Giles 1546-1611 *RfGEnL 91*
**Fletcher,** Giles 1585?-1623 *RfGEnL 91*
**Fletcher,** Gordon Alan 1942- *IntAu&W 91*
**Fletcher,** Harry Edward 1942- *WhoRel 92*
**Fletcher,** Harry Huntington 1907- *AmMWSc 92*
**Fletcher,** Harvey 1884-1981 *FacFETw*
**Fletcher,** Harvey Junior 1923- *AmMWSc 92*
**Fletcher,** Homer Lee 1928- *WhoWest 92*
**Fletcher,** Horace 1849-1919 *BiInAmS*
**Fletcher,** Horace Grant 1913- *WhoEnt 92*
**Fletcher,** Howard R. 1924- *WhoBlA 92*
**Fletcher,** Hugh Alasdair 1947- *IntWW 91*
**Fletcher,** Inglis 1879-1969 *DcNCBi 2*
**Fletcher,** J S 1863-1935 *ScFEYrs*
**Fletcher,** James 1919- *FacFETw*
**Fletcher,** James Allen 1947- *WhoEnt 92, WhoWest 92*
**Fletcher,** James Andrew 1945- *WhoBlA 92*
**Fletcher,** James C. 1919-1991 *NewYTBS 91 [port]*
**Fletcher,** James C., Jr. 1934- *WhoBlA 92*
**Fletcher,** James Chipman 1919- *AmMWSc 92, IntWW 91, WhoAmP 91*
**Fletcher,** James Erving 1935- *AmMWSc 92, WhoEnt 92*
**Fletcher,** James Muir Cameron 1914- *Who 92*
**Fletcher,** James Thomas d1990 *Who 92N*
**Fletcher,** James W 1943- *AmMWSc 92*
**Fletcher,** John 1579-1625 *RfGEnL 91*
**Fletcher,** John Antony 1918- *Who 92*
**Fletcher,** John Caldwell 1931- *WhoRel 92*
**Fletcher,** John Edward 1937- *AmMWSc 92*
**Fletcher,** John Edwin 1941- *Who 92*
**Fletcher,** John George 1934- *AmMWSc 92*
**Fletcher,** John Gould 1886-1950 *BenetAL 91, FacFETw*
**Fletcher,** John Lynn 1925- *AmMWSc 92*
**Fletcher,** John Samuel 1938- *AmMWSc 92*
**Fletcher,** John Sheidley 1953- *WhoAmL 92*
**Fletcher,** John Walter James 1937- *IntAu&W 91, WrDr 92*
**Fletcher,** Joseph 1905-1991 *ConAu 135*
**Fletcher,** Joseph F. d1991 *NewYTBS 91 [port]*
**Fletcher,** Judith Ann 1943- *WhoWest 92*
**Fletcher,** Kenneth 1954- *WhoRel 92*
**Fletcher,** Kenneth Steele, III 1941- *AmMWSc 92*
**Fletcher,** Kim 1927- *WhoFI 92, WhoWest 92*
**Fletcher,** Leland Vernon 1946- *WhoWest 92*
**Fletcher,** Leroy S 1936- *AmMWSc 92*
**Fletcher,** Leslie 1906- *Who 92*
**Fletcher,** Leslie 1922- *Who 92*
**Fletcher,** Lewis John 1943- *WhoAmL 92*
**Fletcher,** Louisa Adaline 1919- *WhoBlA 92*
**Fletcher,** Louise 1934- *IntMPA 92*
**Fletcher,** Louise 1936- *WhoEnt 92*
**Fletcher,** Lowell W 1920- *AmMWSc 92*
**Fletcher,** Lucille 1912- *WrDr 92*
**Fletcher,** Marilyn Lowen *DrAPF 91*
**Fletcher,** Marjorie *DrAPF 91*
**Fletcher,** Marjorie Helen 1932- *Who 92*
**Fletcher,** Martin J 1932- *AmMWSc 92*
**Fletcher,** Mary Ann 1937- *AmMWSc 92*
**Fletcher,** Neil 1944- *Who 92*
**Fletcher,** Neil Russel 1933- *AmMWSc 92*
**Fletcher,** Neville Horner 1930- *IntWW 91*
**Fletcher,** Norman *WhoAmL 92, WhoAmP 91*
**Fletcher,** Oscar Jasper, Jr 1938- *AmMWSc 92*
**Fletcher,** Paul Chipman 1926- *AmMWSc 92*
**Fletcher,** Paul Litton, Jr 1941- *AmMWSc 92*
**Fletcher,** Paul Louie 1930- *WhoFI 92*
**Fletcher,** Paul Thomas 1912- *Who 92*
**Fletcher,** Paul Wayne 1951- *AmMWSc 92*
**Fletcher,** Peter 1939- *AmMWSc 92*
**Fletcher,** Peter C 1935- *AmMWSc 92*
**Fletcher,** Peter Carteret 1916- *Who 92*
**Fletcher,** Philip B. *WhoMW 92*
**Fletcher,** Philip John 1946- *Who 92*
**Fletcher,** Phineas 1582?-1650 *RfGEnL 91*
**Fletcher,** Randol Beryle 1957- *WhoAmP 91*
**Fletcher,** Ray C *WhoAmP 91*
**Fletcher,** Raymond d1991 *Who 92N*
**Fletcher,** Richard Alexander 1944- *WrDr 92*
**Fletcher,** Riley Eugene 1912- *WhoAmL 92*
**Fletcher,** Robert 1823-1912 *BiInAmS*
**Fletcher,** Robert Chipman 1921- *AmMWSc 92*
**Fletcher,** Robert E. 1938- *WhoBlA 92*
**Fletcher,** Robert Hillman 1940- *AmMWSc 92*
**Fletcher,** Robin Anthony 1922- *Who 92*
**Fletcher,** Ronald 1921- *WrDr 92*
**Fletcher,** Ronald Austin 1931- *AmMWSc 92*
**Fletcher,** Ronald D 1933- *AmMWSc 92*
**Fletcher,** Ronald Stanley 1937- *Who 92*
**Fletcher,** Roy Jackson 1935 *AmMWSc 92*
**Fletcher,** Stephen Edwin 1927- *WhoRel 92*
**Fletcher,** Stewart G 1918- *AmMWSc 92*
**Fletcher,** Suzanne W 1940- *AmMWSc 92*
**Fletcher,** Thomas Francis 1937- *AmMWSc 92*
**Fletcher,** Thomas Harvey 1955- *AmMWSc 92*
**Fletcher,** Thomas Lloyd 1917- *AmMWSc 92*
**Fletcher,** Thomas William 1924- *WhoAmP 91*
**Fletcher,** Tyrone P. 1939- *WhoBlA 92*
**Fletcher,** Virginia Carol 1944- *WhoAmP 91*
**Fletcher,** W Fred 1928- *WhoAmP 91*
**Fletcher,** William A. 1945- *WhoAmL 92*
**Fletcher,** William Adrin 1948- *WhoRel 92*
**Fletcher,** William Ellis 1936- *AmMWSc 92*
**Fletcher,** William H *AmMWSc 92*
**Fletcher,** William Henry 1916- *AmMWSc 92*
**Fletcher,** William L *AmMWSc 92*
**Fletcher,** William Mahar 1924- *WhoRel 92*
**Fletcher,** William Sigourney 1927- *AmMWSc 92*
**Fletcher,** William Thomas 1934- *AmMWSc 92*
**Fletcher,** Winona Lee 1926- *WhoBlA 92*
**Fletcher-Cooke,** Charles 1914- *Who 92*
**Fletcher-Vane** *Who 92*
**Flett,** Ethel Snelson 1912- *IntAu&W 91*
**Flett,** Nancy Jo W 1936- *WhoAmP 91*
**Fletterick,** Robert John 1943- *AmMWSc 92*
**Flettner,** Marianne 1933- *WhoWest 92*
**Fleurant,** Gerdes 1939- *WhoBlA 92*
**Fleuriet,** Kenneth R 1968- *WhoAmP 91*
**Fleury,** Ellen Joanne 1955- *WhoEnt 92*
**Fleury,** Lorraine M 1936- *WhoAmP 91*
**Fleury,** Paul A 1939- *AmMWSc 92*
**Flew,** Antony 1923- *WrDr 92*
**Flew,** Antony Garrard Newton 1923- *Who 92*
**Flewellen,** Icabod 1916- *WhoBlA 92*
**Flex,** Walter 1887-1917 *EncTR 91 [port]*
**Flexer,** David 1909- *IntMPA 92*
**Flexman,** Edmund A, Jr 1940- *AmMWSc 92*
**Flexner,** Anne Crawford 1874-1955 *BenetAL 91*
**Flexner,** James Thomas 1908- *IntAu&W 91, IntWW 91, WrDr 92*
**Flexner,** John M 1926- *AmMWSc 92*
**Flexner,** Louis Barkhouse 1902- *AmMWSc 92*
**Flexner,** Simon 1863-1946 *FacFETw*
**Flexner,** Stuart B. 1928- *WrDr 92*
**Flexner,** Stuart Berg 1928- *IntAu&W 91*
**Flexner,** Stuart Berg 1928-1990 *ConAu 133*
**Flexner,** William Alan 1942- *WhoMW 92*
**Flexon,** Floyd David 1948- *WhoMW 92*
**Flexser,** Leo Aaron 1910- *AmMWSc 92*
**Flick,** Carl 1926- *AmMWSc 92*
**Flick,** Cathy 1949- *AmMWSc 92*
**Flick,** Charles Philip 1952- *WhoAmL 92*
**Flick,** Friedrich 1883-1972 *EncTR 91 [port]*
**Flick,** George Joseph, Jr 1940- *AmMWSc 92*
**Flick,** John A 1917- *AmMWSc 92*
**Flick,** Mark Emmet 1954- *WhoEnt 92*

**Flick,** Parke Kinsey 1946- *AmMWSc 92, WhoMW 92*
**Flick,** Paul Townsend 1961- *WhoAmL 92*
**Flick,** Robert J 1944- *WhoAmP 91*
**Flick,** Thomas Michael 1954- *WhoMW 92*
**Flick,** William Fredrick 1940- *WhoWest 92*
**Flicker,** Herbert 1930- *AmMWSc 92*
**Flicker,** Theodore J. *LesBEnT 92*
**Flicker,** Yuval Zvi 1955- *AmMWSc 92*
**Flickinger,** Charles John 1938- *AmMWSc 92*
**Flickinger,** Charles M. 1953- *WhoAmL 92*
**Flickinger,** George Latimore, Jr 1933- *AmMWSc 92*
**Flickinger,** Harry Harner 1936- *WhoAmL 92*
**Flickinger,** Joe Arden 1949- *WhoWest 92*
**Flickinger,** Reed Adams 1924- *AmMWSc 92*
**Flickinger,** Stephen Albert 1942- *AmMWSc 92*
**Flieder,** John Joseph 1936- *WhoFI 92*
**Fliedner,** Leonard John, Jr 1937- *AmMWSc 92*
**Fliegel,** Frederick Martin 1956- *AmMWSc 92*
**Fliegel,** Henry Frederick 1936- *AmMWSc 92*
**Fliegelman,** Avra Leah *WhoEnt 92*
**Flier,** Michael Stephen 1941- *IntAu&W 91, WrDr 92*
**Flier,** Yakov Vladimirovich 1912-1977 *SovUnBD*
**Fliere,** Yakov Vladimirovich 1912-1977 *SovUnBD*
**Fliess,** Peter Joachim 1915- *WrDr 92*
**Fligg,** James Edward 1936- *WhoMW 92*
**Fligg,** Loren L 1940- *WhoIns 92*
**Flight,** Claude 1881-1955 *TwCPaSc*
**Fligman,** Raymond Brian 1961- *WhoMW 92*
**Fligstein,** Neil 1951- *ConAu 135*
**Flimm,** Jurgen 1941- *IntWW 91*
**Flindall,** Jacqueline 1932- *Who 92*
**Flinders,** Jerran T 1937- *AmMWSc 92*
**Flinders,** Neil J. 1934- *WrDr 92*
**Flindt,** Flemming 1936- *WhoEnt 92*
**Flindt,** Flemming Ole 1936- *IntWW 91*
**Flink,** Edmund Berney 1914- *AmMWSc 92*
**Flink,** Edward B. 1951- *WhoAmL 92*
**Flink,** Richard Allen 1935- *WhoAmL 92*
**Flinkstrom,** Henry Allan 1933- *WhoFI 92*
**Flinn,** Charles Gallagher 1938- *WhoAmL 92*
**Flinn,** David Lynnfield 1943- *WhoFI 92*
**Flinn,** Edward Ambrose 1931- *AmMWSc 92*
**Flinn,** Eugene C. *DrAPF 91*
**Flinn,** James Edwin 1934- *AmMWSc 92*
**Flinn,** Jane Margaret 1938- *AmMWSc 92*
**Flinn,** John C. 1917- *IntMPA 92*
**Flinn,** Michael de Vlaming 1941- *WhoFI 92*
**Flinn,** Michael Joseph 1958- *WhoFI 92*
**Flinn,** Monroe Lawrence 1917- *WhoAmP 91*
**Flinn,** Patricia Ellen *DrAPF 91*
**Flinn,** Paul Anthony 1926- *AmMWSc 92*
**Flinn,** Richard A 1916- *AmMWSc 92*
**Flinn,** Roberta Jeanne 1947- *WhoWest 92*
**Flinn,** Thomas Hance 1922- *WhoFI 92*
**Flinn,** Thomas Michael 1961- *WhoAmL 92*
**Flinner,** Jack L 1931- *AmMWSc 92*
**Flint,** Anthony Patrick Fielding 1943- *Who 92*
**Flint,** Austin 1812-1886 *BiInAmS*
**Flint,** Austin, Jr 1836-1915 *BiInAmS*
**Flint,** Betty Margaret 1920- *WrDr 92*
**Flint,** Daniel Waldo Boone 1926- *WhoAmL 92*
**Flint,** David 1919- *Who 92*
**Flint,** Delos Edward 1918- *AmMWSc 92*
**Flint,** Delos Edward, Jr. 1956- *WhoAmL 92*
**Flint,** Elizabeth Parker 1951- *AmMWSc 92*
**Flint,** Franklin Ford 1925- *AmMWSc 92*
**Flint,** Gordon B 1919- *WhoAmP 91*
**Flint,** Harrison Leigh 1929- *AmMWSc 92*
**Flint,** Hollis Mitchell 1938- *AmMWSc 92*
**Flint,** Homer Eon 1892-1924 *ScFEYrs, TwCSFW 91*
**Flint,** James Milton 1838-1919 *BiInAmS*
**Flint,** Jean-Jacques 1943- *AmMWSc 92*
**Flint,** John Edgar 1930- *IntAu&W 91, WrDr 92*
**Flint,** Lou Jean 1934- *WhoWest 92*
**Flint,** Michael Frederick 1932- *Who 92*
**Flint,** Norman Keith 1921- *AmMWSc 92*
**Flint,** Oliver Simeon, Jr 1931- *AmMWSc 92*
**Flint,** Patricia Robins 1946- *WhoWest 92*
**Flint,** Rachael H. *Who 92*
**Flint,** Robert Purves 1883-1947 *TwCPaSc*
**Flint,** Roland *DrAPF 91*
**Flint,** Sarah Jane *AmMWSc 92*
**Flint,** Timothy 1780-1840 *BenetAL 91*
**Flint,** William Russell 1880-1969 *TwCPaSc*
**Flippen,** Frances Morton *WhoBlA 92*
**Flippen,** Greg 1950- *WhoBlA 92*
**Flippen,** James Howard, Jr. 1929- *WhoAmL 92*
**Flippen,** Richard Bernard 1930- *AmMWSc 92*
**Flippen-Anderson,** Judith Lee 1941- *AmMWSc 92*
**Flippin,** Gilmer Franklin 1947- *WhoAmL 92*
**Flippin,** Kay Stewart 1906- *NotBlAW 92*
**Flippin,** Keith Alan 1961- *WhoRel 92*
**Flippin,** Tancrede Wayman 1961- *WhoRel 92*
**Flippin,** William Edward 1952- *WhoRel 92*
**Flippo,** John William 1948- *WhoAmL 92*
**Flippo,** Ronnie G 1937- *WhoAmP 91*
**Flipse,** John E 1921- *AmMWSc 92*
**Flipse,** Martin Eugene 1919- *AmMWSc 92*
**Flipse,** Robert Joseph 1923- *AmMWSc 92*
**Fliri,** Franz 1918- *IntWW 91*
**Flischel,** Susan Frances 1959- *WhoFI 92*
**Fliss,** Edward Roger 1953- *WhoMW 92*
**Fliss,** Raphael M. 1930- *WhoRel 92*
**Fliszar,** Sandor 1927- *AmMWSc 92*
**Flitcraft,** R K, II 1920- *AmMWSc 92*
**Flitcraft,** Richard Kirby, II 1920- *WhoFI 92*
**Flitner,** Andreas 1922- *IntWW 91*
**Flitter,** David 1913- *AmMWSc 92*
**Flittner,** Glenn Arden 1928- *AmMWSc 92*
**Floberg,** John Forrest 1915- *WhoAmL 92*
**Flocchini,** Richard James 1939- *WhoWest 92*
**Floch,** Morton Hugh 1934- *WhoFI 92*
**Flock,** Donald Louis 1930- *AmMWSc 92*
**Flock,** Gail Curry 1917- *WhoWest 92*
**Flock,** Henry H. 1935- *WhoFI 92*
**Flock,** Jeffrey Charles 1958- *WhoMW 92*
**Flock,** John William 1947- *AmMWSc 92*
**Flock,** Warren L 1920- *AmMWSc 92*
**Flocken,** John W 1939- *AmMWSc 92*
**Floden,** Gillis Scott 1950- *WhoWest 92*
**Flodin,** N W 1915- *AmMWSc 92*
**Floding,** Matthew Duane 1955- *WhoRel 92*
**Flohn,** Hermann 1912- *IntWW 91*
**Flokstra,** Gerard John, III 1956- *WhoRel 92*
**Flokstra,** John Hilbert 1925- *AmMWSc 92*
**Flom,** Donald Gordon 1924- *AmMWSc 92*
**Flom,** Edward Leonard 1929- *WhoFI 92*
**Flom,** Gerald Trossen 1930- *WhoAmL 92*
**Flom,** Joseph Harold 1923- *WhoAmL 92, WhoFI 92*
**Flom,** Merton Clyde 1926- *AmMWSc 92*
**Flono,** Fannie 1952- *WhoBlA 92*
**Flood,** Brian Robert 1948- *AmMWSc 92*
**Flood,** Charles Bracelen 1929- *IntAu&W 91, WrDr 92*
**Flood,** Christopher 1936- *TwCWW 91*
**Flood,** Clifford Arrington, Jr 1939- *AmMWSc 92*
**Flood,** Daniel J 1903- *WhoAmP 91*
**Flood,** David Andrew 1955- *Who 92*
**Flood,** Dorothy Garnett 1951- *AmMWSc 92*
**Flood,** E. Thadeus 1932-1977 *ConAu 133*
**Flood,** James Joseph, Jr. 1931- *WhoAmL 92*
**Flood,** James Tyrrell 1934- *WhoEnt 92, WhoWest 92*
**Flood,** Joan Moore 1941- *WhoAmL 92*
**Flood,** Joe *WhoAmP 91*
**Flood,** John Daniel 1958- *WhoFI 92*
**Flood,** John Edward 1925- *Who 92*
**Flood,** John H *WhoAmP 91*
**Flood,** John Joseph 1951- *WhoAmL 92*
**Flood,** John Martin 1939- *Who 92*
**Flood,** Kevin Patrick 1939- *WhoAmL 92*
**Flood,** Michael Donovan 1949- *Who 92*
**Flood,** Norman 1935- *ConAu 134*
**Flood,** Patrick *WhoRel 92*
**Flood,** Patrick 1960-1990 *NewYTBS 91 [port]*
**Flood,** Peter Frederick 1940- *AmMWSc 92*
**Flood,** Randolph Gene 1950- *WhoAmP 91*
**Flood,** Shearlene Davis 1938- *WhoBlA 92*
**Flood,** Thomas Charles 1945- *AmMWSc 92*
**Flood,** Walter A 1927- *AmMWSc 92*
**Floody,** C Wallace 1918-1989 *FacFETw*
**Flook,** Maria *DrAPF 91*
**Flook,** William Mowat, Jr 1921- *AmMWSc 92*
**Flor,** Claus Peter 1953- *WhoEnt 92*
**Flor,** Loy Lorenz 1919- *WhoWest 92*
**Flora June** 1925- *WhoEnt 92*
**Flora,** Edward B 1929- *AmMWSc 92*
**Flora,** George Claude 1923- *AmMWSc 92*
**Flora,** Jairus Dale, Jr 1944- *AmMWSc 92*
**Flora,** James 1914- *WrDr 92*
**Flora,** James Royer 1914- *IntAu&W 91*
**Flora,** Joseph M. 1934- *WrDr 92*
**Flora,** Joseph Martin 1934- *IntAu&W 91*
**Flora,** Kent Allen 1944- *WhoMW 92*
**Flora,** Lewis Franklin 1947- *AmMWSc 92*
**Flora,** Maria Joan 1949- *WhoAmL 92*
**Flora,** Philip Craig 1950- *WhoEnt 92*
**Flora,** Robert Henry 1944- *AmMWSc 92*
**Flora,** Robert Montgomery 1938- *AmMWSc 92*
**Flora,** Roger E 1939- *AmMWSc 92*
**Florakis,** Charilaos Ioannoy 1914- *IntWW 91*
**Floran,** Robert John 1947- *AmMWSc 92*
**Florance,** Edwin R 1942- *AmMWSc 92*
**Florant,** Gregory Lester 1951- *AmMWSc 92*
**Florea,** Harold R 1914- *AmMWSc 92*
**Florea,** John 1916- *IntMPA 92*
**Florea,** John Ted 1916- *WhoEnt 92*
**Floreen,** Stephen 1932- *AmMWSc 92*
**Florek,** Kenneth F. 1960- *WhoAmL 92*
**Floren,** Lee 1910- *IntAu&W 91, TwCWW 91*
**Florence,** Alexander Taylor 1940- *Who 92*
**Florence,** Craig Buck 1962- *WhoAmL 92*
**Florence,** Jerry DeWayne 1948- *WhoFI 92*
**Florence,** Johnny C. 1930- *WhoBlA 92*
**Florence,** Joseph Howard 1932- *WhoWest 92*
**Florence,** Kenneth James 1943- *WhoAmL 92, WhoWest 92*
**Florence,** Lella Faye Secor 1887-1966 *AmPeW*
**Florence,** Mary Sargent 1857-1954 *TwCPaSc*
**Florence,** Robert Edwin 1963- *WhoFI 92*
**Florence,** Ronald 1942- *IntAu&W 91*
**Florence,** Verena Magdalena 1946- *WhoWest 92*
**Florence,** Virginia Proctor Powell 1897- *WhoBlA 92*
**Florensky,** Paul Alexandrovich 1892- *FacFETw*
**Florentin,** Rudolfo Aranda *AmMWSc 92*
**Florentino,** Vincent 1948- *WhoIns 92*
**Florentz,** Jean-Louis 1947- *IntWW 91*
**Flores,** Alberto Sierra 1956- *WhoHisp 92*
**Flores,** Alex 1959- *WhoHisp 92*
**Flores,** Alfonso J. 1949- *WhoHisp 92*
**Flores,** Alfred, Jr. 1958- *WhoHisp 92*
**Flores,** Alma 1960- *WhoHisp 92*
**Flores,** Andrew F. 1940- *WhoWest 92*
**Flores,** Antonio R. 1947- *WhoHisp 92*
**Flores,** Apolonio 1940- *WhoHisp 92*
**Flores,** Armando, Jr. 1945- *WhoHisp 92*
**Flores,** Armida S. 1945- *WhoHisp 92*
**Flores,** Aurelio 1931- *WhoWest 92*
**Flores,** Aurora 1954- *WhoHisp 92*
**Flores,** Benny E. *WhoHisp 92*
**Flores,** Bernie 1934- *WhoHisp 92*
**Flores,** Candida 1951- *WhoHisp 92*
**Flores,** Connie 1944- *WhoHisp 92*
**Flores,** Daniel *WhoHisp 92*
**Flores,** David 1951- *WhoHisp 92*
**Flores,** Dionicio *WhoHisp 92*
**Flores,** Don *WhoHisp 92*
**Flores,** Eddie, Jr. 1946- *WhoWest 92*
**Flores,** Eduardo 1957- *WhoHisp 92*
**Flores,** Eileen *WhoHisp 92*
**Flores,** Eliezer 1959- *WhoHisp 92*
**Flores,** Elizabeth Lopez 1940- *WhoHisp 92*
**Flores,** Elmo Rivera, Jr. 1943- *WhoHisp 92*
**Flores,** Enrique Antonio 1943- *WhoHisp 92*
**Flores,** Ernie *WhoHisp 92*
**Flores,** Francisco Jose 1934- *WhoHisp 92*
**Flores,** Frank *WhoHisp 92*
**Flores,** Frank Fausto 1930- *WhoEnt 92, WhoFI 92*
**Flores,** Gerry *WhoHisp 92*
**Flores,** Heidi Lee 1963- *WhoWest 92*
**Flores,** Henry, II 1944- *WhoHisp 92*
**Flores,** Hernan R., Jr. 1961- *WhoHisp 92*
**Flores,** Ismael 1958- *WhoHisp 92*
**Flores,** Ivan 1923- *AmMWSc 92, WhoHisp 92, WrDr 92*
**Flores,** J. O. 1954- *WhoHisp 92*
**Flores,** Jess *WhoHisp 92*
**Flores,** Joe *WhoHisp 92*
**Flores,** Joe, Jr. 1951- *WhoHisp 92*
**Flores,** John 1952- *WhoHisp 92*
**Flores,** John Ruben 1956- *WhoAmL 92*
**Flores,** Jose Ramon 1967- *WhoHisp 92*
**Flores,** Joseph Alfred 1934- *WhoHisp 92*
**Flores,** Joseph R. 1935- *WhoBlA 92*
**Flores,** Juan Jose 1801-1864 *HisDSpE*
**Flores,** Juan Manuel 1951- *WhoHisp 92*
**Flores,** Laura Jane 1951- *WhoHisp 92*
**Flores,** Lauro H. 1950- *WhoHisp 92*
**Flores,** Leonard Lopez, Jr. 1937- *WhoHisp 92*
**Flores,** Manuel, Jr. 1923- *WhoHisp 92*
**Flores,** Manuel R. *WhoHisp 92*
**Flores,** Maria Carolina *WhoHisp 92*
**Flores,** Maria Teresa 1962- *WhoHisp 92*
**Flores,** Matthew Gilbert 1962- *WhoHisp 92*
**Flores,** Mayra 1968- *WhoHisp 92*
**Flores,** Norma Louise 1958- *WhoHisp 92*
**Flores,** Orlando 1946- *WhoHisp 92*
**Flores,** Pablo H. 1933- *WhoHisp 92*
**Flores,** Patricio Fernandez 1929- *WhoHisp 92*
**Flores,** Patrick F. 1929- *WhoRel 92*
**Flores,** Philip Joseph 1949- *WhoAmP 91*
**Flores,** Raymond Jose 1929- *WhoHisp 92*
**Flores,** Rene James, Sr. 1943- *WhoWest 92*
**Flores,** Roberto J. 1935- *WhoHisp 92*
**Flores,** Romeo M 1939- *AmMWSc 92, WhoWest 92*
**Flores,** Rosa Alba 1958- *WhoWest 92*
**Flores,** Rosemary 1959- *WhoHisp 92*
**Flores,** Ruben, Jr. 1954- *WhoHisp 92*
**Flores,** Rudy B. 1947- *WhoHisp 92*
**Flores,** Samson Sol 1922- *AmMWSc 92*
**Flores,** Silvia S. *WhoHisp 92*
**Flores,** Stephen William 1952- *WhoEnt 92*
**Flores,** Suzanne 1931- *WhoFI 92*
**Flores,** Thomas R. 1937- *WhoWest 92*
**Flores,** Thomas Richard 1940- *WhoWest 92*
**Flores,** Tom 1937- *WhoHisp 92*
**Flores,** Wayne R. 1957- *WhoHisp 92*
**Flores de Apodaca,** Roberto 1951- *WhoHisp 92*
**Flores-Hughes,** Grace 1946- *WhoHisp 92*
**Flores Napolitano,** Graciela *WhoHisp 92*
**Flores Torres,** Jorge 1929- *IntWW 91*
**Flores-Velasquez,** Elizabeth Ann 1957- *WhoHisp 92*
**Floresca,** Felipe *WhoHisp 92*
**Florescu,** William Ilie, Jr. 1955- *WhoMW 92*
**Florestano,** Dana Joseph 1945- *WhoFI 92, WhoMW 92*
**Floreth,** Frederick Dennis 1956- *WhoAmL 92*
**Florey,** Charles du Ve 1934- *Who 92*
**Florey,** Howard Walter 1898-1968 *WhoNob 90*
**Florey,** Klaus 1919- *AmMWSc 92*
**Florey,** Robert 1900-1979 *IntDcF 2-2 [port]*
**Florez,** Edward T. 1949- *WhoHisp 92*
**Florez,** Ernestine Armendariz 1939- *WhoAmP 91*
**Florez,** John *WhoHisp 92*
**Florez,** Rey *WhoAmP 91*
**Florian,** Frank Lee 1933- *WhoFI 92*
**Florian,** Friedrich Karl 1894- *EncTR 91*
**Florian,** Friedrich Karl 1894-1975 *BiDExR*
**Florian,** Marianna Bolognesi *WhoMW 92*
**Florian,** Mario 1937- *WhoHisp 92*
**Florian,** Robert Bruce 1930- *WhoRel 92*
**Florie,** Terry Lynn 1956- *WhoWest 92*
**Florig,** Henry Keith 1954- *AmMWSc 92*
**Florin,** Roland Eric 1915- *AmMWSc 92*
**Florin,** Wil Hermann 1955- *WhoAmL 92*
**Florine** *EncAmaz 91*
**Florini,** James Ralph 1931- *AmMWSc 92*
**Florinus** *EncEarC*
**Florio,** Andrea Nicola 1927- *WhoEnt 92*
**Florio,** Caryl 1843-1920 *NewAmDM*
**Florio,** Dominic Anthony 1946- *WhoFI 92*
**Florio,** Ermanno 1954- *WhoEnt 92*
**Florio,** James J. 1937- *News 91 [port]*
**Florio,** James Joseph 1937- *WhoAmP 91*
**Florio,** Jim 1937- *AlmAP 92 [port]*
**Florio,** Pasquale J, Jr 1936- *AmMWSc 92*
**Florit,** Eugenio 1903- *BenetAL 91, WhoHisp 92*
**Florjancic,** Frederick Joseph, Jr. 1947- *WhoMW 92*
**Florman,** Alfred Leonard 1912- *AmMWSc 92*
**Florman,** Edwin F 1904- *AmMWSc 92*
**Florman,** Monte 1926- *AmMWSc 92*
**Florman,** Samuel C 1925- *AmMWSc 92*
**Flornoy,** Louis 1846-1904 *ThHEIm*
**Florovsky,** Georges Vasilievich 1893-1979 *DcEcMov*
**Florschuetz,** Leon W 1935- *AmMWSc 92*
**Florschutz,** Darko 1945- *WhoMW 92*
**Florsheim,** Charles 1949- *WhoAmL 92*
**Florsheim,** Stewart *DrAPF 91*
**Florsheim,** Warner Hanns 1922- *AmMWSc 92*
**Flory,** Eldon Ray 1948- *WhoMW 92*
**Flory,** Jeffrey Allen 1963- *WhoMW 92*
**Flory,** Leslie E 1907- *AmMWSc 92*
**Flory,** Paul John 1910-1985 *WhoNob 90*
**Flory,** Robert Mikesell 1912- *WhoFI 92*
**Flory,** Sheldon *DrAPF 91*
**Flory,** Thomas Reherd 1946- *AmMWSc 92*
**Flosdorf,** Jim *DrAPF 91*
**Floss,** Frederick George 1957- *WhoFI 92*
**Floss,** Gary D. 1941- *WhoMW 92*
**Floss,** Heinz G 1934- *AmMWSc 92*
**Flotow,** Friedrich 1812-1883 *NewAmDM*
**Flotron,** Francis E, Jr 1954- *WhoAmP 91*
**Flott,** Leslie William 1934- *WhoMW 92*
**Flott,** Robert Leslie 1963- *WhoEnt 92*
**Flottman,** Dorothy Higginbottom 1924- *WhoAmP 91*
**Floud,** Jean Esther 1915- *Who 92*
**Floud,** Roderick Castle 1942- *Who 92*
**Flouret,** George R 1935- *AmMWSc 92*
**Flournoy,** Dayl Jean 1944- *AmMWSc 92*

**Flournoy,** Houston Irvine 1929- *WhoWest 92*
**Flournoy,** Philip James 1955- *WhoRel 92*
**Flournoy,** Robert Lane 1941- *WhoAmP 91*
**Flournoy,** Robert Wilson 1936- *AmMWSc 92*
**Flournoy,** Selwyn Lester, Jr 1941- *WhoIns 92*
**Flournoy,** Valerie Rose 1952- *WhoBlA 92*
**Floutz,** William Vaughn 1935- *AmMWSc 92, WhoMW 92*
**Flowe,** Benjamin Hugh, Jr. 1956- *WhoAmL 92*
**Flowe,** Carol Connor 1950- *WhoAmL 92*
**Flower** *Who 92*
**Flower,** Amanda Cameron 1863-1940 *RelLAm 91*
**Flower,** Antony John Frank 1951- *Who 92*
**Flower,** B O 1858-1918 *DcAmImH*
**Flower,** Desmond John Newman 1907- *IntAu&W 91, Who 92*
**Flower,** Edward James William 1923- *Who 92*
**Flower,** Jake *WrDr 92*
**Flower,** Joann 1935- *WhoAmP 91*
**Flower,** John Arnold 1921- *WhoMW 92*
**Flower,** John Matthew 1929- *WrDr 92*
**Flower,** Joseph James Roswell 1888-1970 *RelLAm 91*
**Flower,** Joseph Reynolds 1913- *WhoRel 92*
**Flower,** Michael Llowarch Warburton 1935- *Who 92*
**Flower,** Phillip John 1948- *AmMWSc 92*
**Flower,** Robert Walter 1941- *AmMWSc 92*
**Flower,** Rousseau Hayner 1913- *AmMWSc 92*
**Flower,** Terrence Frederick 1941- *AmMWSc 92*
**Flower,** Walter Chew, III 1939- *WhoFI 92*
**Flowerday,** Albert Dale 1927- *AmMWSc 92*
**Flowerdew,** Phyllis *IntAu&W 91, WrDr 92*
**Flowers** *Who 92*
**Flowers,** Baron 1924- *IntWW 91, Who 92*
**Flowers,** Allan Dale 1946- *AmMWSc 92*
**Flowers,** Charles E *WhoAmP 91*
**Flowers,** Charles E, Jr 1920- *AmMWSc 92*
**Flowers,** Daniel F 1920- *AmMWSc 92*
**Flowers,** Daniel Gregory 1959- *WhoMW 92*
**Flowers,** Glen Dale 1940- *WhoRel 92*
**Flowers,** Gregory *WhoEnt 92*
**Flowers,** Harold L 1917- *AmMWSc 92*
**Flowers,** Joe D 1943- *AmMWSc 92*
**Flowers,** John 1935- *WhoAmL 92*
**Flowers,** John Wilson 1910- *AmMWSc 92*
**Flowers,** Loma Kaye 1944- *WhoBlA 92*
**Flowers,** Mary E *WhoAmP 91*
**Flowers,** Michael Lynn 1952- *WhoAmL 92*
**Flowers,** Nancy Carolyn 1928- *AmMWSc 92*
**Flowers,** Nancy Jo 1945- *WhoAmP 91*
**Flowers,** Ralph L. 1936- *WhoBlA 92*
**Flowers,** Ralph Wills 1948- *AmMWSc 92*
**Flowers,** Robert Lee 1870-1951 *DcNCBi 2*
**Flowers,** Ronald Bruce 1935- *WhoRel 92*
**Flowers,** Runette 1945- *WhoBlA 92*
**Flowers,** Russell Sherwood, Jr 1951- *AmMWSc 92*
**Flowers,** Sally A. 1954- *WhoBlA 92*
**Flowers,** Sonny 1946- *WhoBlA 92*
**Flowers,** Steve 1951- *WhoAmP 91*
**Flowers,** W. Harold, Sr. 1913-1990 *WhoBlA 92N*
**Flowers,** William Harold, Jr. 1946- *WhoBlA 92*
**Flowers,** William Howard, Jr. 1913- *WhoFI 92*
**Flowers,** William Knox, Jr. 1916- *WhoBlA 92*
**Flowers,** William Washington 1874-1941 *DcNCBi 2*
**Floy,** Charles R 1934- *WhoIns 92*
**Floyd** 1901-1934 *FacFETw*
**Floyd,** Alton David 1941- *AmMWSc 92, WhoMW 92*
**Floyd,** Angela Sue 1964- *WhoFI 92*
**Floyd,** Angeleita Stevens 1952- *WhoEnt 92*
**Floyd,** Billie J 1929- *WhoAmP 91*
**Floyd,** Carey E, Jr *AmMWSc 92*
**Floyd,** Carlisle 1926- *NewAmDM, WhoEnt 92*
**Floyd,** Charles Allen 1960- *WhoFI 92*
**Floyd,** Christina 1949- *TwCPaSc*
**Floyd,** Craig William 1956- *WhoAmP 91, WhoFI 92*
**Floyd,** Dean Allen 1951- *WhoBlA 92*
**Floyd,** Dolphin Ward 1807-1836 *DcNCBi 2*
**Floyd,** Edwin Earl 1924- *AmMWSc 92*
**Floyd,** Eldra Moore, Jr 1920- *WhoAmP 91*
**Floyd,** Elson Sylvester 1956- *WhoWest 92*
**Floyd,** Eric A. 1960- *WhoBlA 92*
**Floyd,** Ervin Richard 1934- *WhoAmP 91*
**Floyd,** Gary Leon 1940- *AmMWSc 92*
**Floyd,** Giles 1932- *Who 92*
**Floyd,** Glenn Eldon 1937- *WhoAmP 91*
**Floyd,** J F R 1915- *AmMWSc 92*
**Floyd,** Jack *WhoAmP 91*
**Floyd,** Jack William 1934- *WhoAmL 92*
**Floyd,** James Kemper 1933- *WhoWest 92*
**Floyd,** James M *WhoAmP 91*
**Floyd,** James T. *WhoBlA 92*
**Floyd,** James Timothy 1951- *WhoRel 92*
**Floyd,** Jeremiah 1932- *WhoBlA 92*
**Floyd,** John Anthony 1923- *Who 92*
**Floyd,** John Claiborne, Jr 1927- *AmMWSc 92, WhoMW 92*
**Floyd,** John Lincoln 1954- *WhoWest 92*
**Floyd,** John Taylor 1942- *WhoFI 92*
**Floyd,** Johnny W 1938- *WhoAmP 91*
**Floyd,** Joseph Calvin 1941- *AmMWSc 92*
**Floyd,** Kenneth Eugene 1955- *WhoRel 92*
**Floyd,** Lin Axamethy 1953- *WhoAmL 92*
**Floyd,** Madge Black 1935- *WhoRel 92*
**Floyd,** Mark S. 1958- *WhoBlA 92*
**Floyd,** Marquette L. 1928- *WhoBlA 92*
**Floyd,** Mary Joan 1949- *WhoFI 92*
**Floyd,** Michael Dennis 1953- *WhoAmL 92*
**Floyd,** Otis L., Jr. *WhoBlA 92*
**Floyd,** Richard E 1931- *WhoAmP 91*
**Floyd,** Robert A 1940- *AmMWSc 92*
**Floyd,** Robert W 1936- *AmMWSc 92*
**Floyd,** Roderick 1904- *TwCPaSc*
**Floyd,** Samuel A., Jr. 1937- *WhoBlA 92*
**Floyd,** Steve William 1950- *WhoEnt 92*
**Floyd,** Vernon Clinton 1927- *WhoBlA 92*
**Floyd,** Vircher B. 1928- *WhoBlA 92*
**Floyd,** William Beckwith 1930- *AmMWSc 92*
**Floyd,** Willis Waldo 1903- *AmMWSc 92*
**Floyd,** Winston Cordell 1948- *WhoBlA 92*
**Floyd Anderson,** Dionne Camille 1965- *WhoBlA 92*
**Floyd Ewin,** David Ernest Thomas 1911- *Who 92*
**Floyd-Teniya,** Kathleen 1953- *WhoFI 92*
**Floyer,** Michael Antony 1920- *Who 92*
**Flubacher,** Joseph Francis 1914- *WhoFI 92*
**Fluck,** Eugene Richards 1934- *AmMWSc 92*
**Fluck,** Michele Marguerite 1940- *AmMWSc 92*
**Fluck,** Richard Allen 1945- *AmMWSc 92*
**Fluck,** Richard Conard 1938- *AmMWSc 92*
**Flueck,** John A 1933- *AmMWSc 92*
**Fluegel,** Elizabeth Leigh 1959- *WhoEnt 92*
**Fluellen,** Joel 1908-1990 *ConTFT 9*
**Fluellen,** Joel M. 1908-1990 *WhoBlA 92N*
**Fluent,** Craig Michael 1952- *IntAu&W 91*
**Flug,** James Franklin 1939- *WhoAmL 92*
**Flugaur,** Rick Anthony 1961- *WhoAmL 92*
**Flugger,** Penelope Ann 1942- *WhoFI 92*
**Fluharty,** Arvan Lawrence 1934- *AmMWSc 92*
**Fluharty,** Charles William 1947- *WhoMW 92*
**Fluharty,** David Lincoln 1946- *AmMWSc 92*
**Fluharty,** Jesse Ernest 1916- *WhoWest 92*
**Fluke,** Donald John 1923- *AmMWSc 92*
**Fluke,** John Maurice, Jr. 1942- *WhoWest 92*
**Fluke,** Lyla Schram *WhoWest 92*
**Fluke,** William Albert 1942- *WhoMW 92*
**Fluker,** Philip A. 1920- *WhoBlA 92*
**Flum,** Ralph Allen 1954- *WhoIns 92*
**Flum,** Robert S, Sr 1925- *AmMWSc 92*
**Flumerfelt,** Raymond W 1939- *AmMWSc 92*
**Fluno,** Jere David 1941- *WhoFI 92*
**Flurett,** Garfield William 1928- *WhoAmP 91*
**Flurry,** Robert Luther, Jr 1933- *AmMWSc 92*
**Flury,** Alvin Godfrey 1920- *AmMWSc 92*
**Flusche,** Annamarie 1944- *WhoEnt 92*
**Flusser,** Peter R 1930- *AmMWSc 92*
**Flute,** Peter Thomas 1928- *Who 92*
**Fly,** Claude Lee 1905- *AmMWSc 92*
**Fly,** Frank Morriss 1945- *WhoAmP 91*
**Fly,** James Lawrence d1966 *LesBEnT 92*
**Fly,** James Lawrence, Jr. 1928- *WhoFI 92*
**Flye,** M. Wayne 1942- *WhoMW 92*
**Flyg,** Nils Svante 1891-1943 *BiDExR*
**Flyger,** Vagn Folkmann 1922- *AmMWSc 92*
**Flying Officer X** *ConAu 34NR*
**Flynn,** Alvin Nash 1946- *WhoAmL 92*
**Flynn,** Anita A 1916- *WhoAmP 91*
**Flynn,** Ann Dolores 1912- *WhoAmP 91*
**Flynn,** Annette Theresa 1953- *WhoFI 92*
**Flynn,** Barbara *ConTFT 9*
**Flynn,** Beverly Collora *WhoMW 92*
**Flynn,** Carol 1933- *WhoAmP 91*
**Flynn,** Charles Milton, Jr. 1940- *WhoWest 92*
**Flynn,** Colin Peter 1935- *AmMWSc 92*
**Flynn,** Daniel Joseph 1959- *WhoFI 92*
**Flynn,** David *DrAPF 91*
**Flynn,** Edward J 1920- *WhoAmP 91*
**Flynn,** Edward Joseph 1942- *AmMWSc 92*
**Flynn,** Edward Robert 1934- *AmMWSc 92*
**Flynn,** Elizabeth Anne 1951- *WhoFI 92, WhoWest 92*
**Flynn,** Elizabeth Gurley 1890-1964 *DcAmImH, HanAmWH, RComAH*
**Flynn,** Errol 1909-1959 *FacFETw [port]*
**Flynn,** Eugene John 1949- *WhoAmL 92*
**Flynn,** F. Patrick 1949- *WhoFI 92*
**Flynn,** Francis J 1916- *WhoAmP 91*
**Flynn,** Frank 1906- *WrDr 92*
**Flynn,** Frederick Valentine 1924- *Who 92*
**Flynn,** Gary Alan 1950- *AmMWSc 92*
**Flynn,** Gary Clark 1954- *WhoAmL 92*
**Flynn,** George *DrAPF 91, TwCWW 91*
**Flynn,** George P 1936- *AmMWSc 92*
**Flynn,** George William 1937- *WhoMW 92*
**Flynn,** George William 1938- *AmMWSc 92*
**Flynn,** Harry Joseph 1933- *WhoRel 92*
**Flynn,** Jackson *TwCWW 91, WrDr 92*
**Flynn,** James Arthur, III 1940- *WhoFI 92*
**Flynn,** James Bernard 1924- *WhoRel 92*
**Flynn,** James P *WhoAmP 91*
**Flynn,** James Patrick 1924- *AmMWSc 92*
**Flynn,** James Robert 1934- *WrDr 92*
**Flynn,** James T *WhoAmP 91*
**Flynn,** Jeffrey Paul 1959- *WhoAmL 92*
**Flynn,** John *IntMPA 92*
**Flynn,** John Allen 1945- *WhoAmL 92*
**Flynn,** John Gerrard 1937- *IntWW 91, Who 92*
**Flynn,** John J *WhoAmP 91*
**Flynn,** John Joseph 1955- *AmMWSc 92*
**Flynn,** John Joseph, Jr 1931- *AmMWSc 92*
**Flynn,** John M 1929- *AmMWSc 92*
**Flynn,** John Thomas 1948- *AmMWSc 92*
**Flynn,** Joseph Henry 1922- *AmMWSc 92*
**Flynn,** Karen Jean 1950- *WhoFI 92*
**Flynn,** Kevin Francis 1927- *AmMWSc 92*
**Flynn,** Kirtland, Jr. 1922- *WhoFI 92*
**Flynn,** Leslie Bruce 1918- *WrDr 92*
**Flynn,** Margaret A 1915- *AmMWSc 92*
**Flynn,** Matthew 1947- *WhoAmP 91*
**Flynn,** Michael A. 1957- *WhoWest 92*
**Flynn,** Michael Francis 1935- *WhoRel 92*
**Flynn,** Michael J 1932- *WhoAmP 91*
**Flynn,** Michael J 1934- *AmMWSc 92*
**Flynn,** Michael James 1920- *WhoFI 92*
**Flynn,** Michael Matthew 1935- *WhoFI 92*
**Flynn,** Nancy *DrAPF 91*
**Flynn,** Padraig 1939- *IntWW 91*
**Flynn,** Patrick 1929- *AmMWSc 92*
**Flynn,** Paul Arthur 1946- *WhoMW 92*
**Flynn,** Paul D 1926- *AmMWSc 92*
**Flynn,** Paul Phillip 1935- *Who 92*
**Flynn,** Pauline T. 1942- *WhoMW 92*
**Flynn,** Peter Anthony 1942- *WhoAmL 92, WhoMW 92*
**Flynn,** Peter Earl 1961- *WhoFI 92*
**Flynn,** Philip Patrick 1950- *WhoFI 92*
**Flynn,** Ralph Melvin, Jr. 1944- *WhoWest 92*
**Flynn,** Raymond L 1939- *WhoAmP 91*
**Flynn,** Richard *DrAPF 91*
**Flynn,** Richard James 1928- *WhoAmL 92, WhoFI 92*
**Flynn,** Robert *DrAPF 91*
**Flynn,** Robert 1932- *IntAu&W 91, TwCWW 91, WrDr 92*
**Flynn,** Robert Emmett 1933- *WhoMW 92*
**Flynn,** Robert James 1923- *AmMWSc 92*
**Flynn,** Robert W 1934- *AmMWSc 92*
**Flynn,** Ronald Thomas 1947- *AmMWSc 92*
**Flynn,** Sharon Ann 1955- *WhoFI 92*
**Flynn,** T F 1927- *AmMWSc 92*
**Flynn,** T.T. 1902- *TwCWW 91*
**Flynn,** Thomas *Who 92*
**Flynn,** Thomas Charles 1950- *WhoFI 92*
**Flynn,** Thomas Geoffrey 1937- *AmMWSc 92*
**Flynn,** Thomas Joseph 1936- *WhoAmL 92, WhoFI 92*
**Flynn,** Thomas Lee 1946- *WhoAmL 92*
**Flynn,** Thomas M 1933- *AmMWSc 92*
**Flynn,** Thomas William 1955- *WhoEnt 92*
**Flynn,** Timothy John 1962- *WhoAmP 91*
**Flynn,** William Edward 1938- *WhoAmP 91*
**Flynn,** William J 1932- *WhoIns 92*
**Flynn,** William J, Jr 1933- *WhoAmP 91*
**Flynn,** William Joseph 1926- *WhoFI 92, WhoIns 92*
**Flynn,** William Joseph, Jr 1949- *WhoAmP 91*
**Flynn,** William Thomas 1947- *WhoIns 92*
**Flynn,** Wilson Paul 1926- *WhoAmP 91*
**Flynn Peterson,** Kathleen A. 1954- *WhoAmL 92*
**Flynt,** Candace *DrAPF 91*
**Flynt,** Clifton William 1953- *WhoMW 92*
**Flynt,** Crisp B 1949- *WhoAmP 91*
**Flynt,** John J, Jr 1914- *WhoAmP 91*
**Flynt,** Josiah *BenetAL 91*
**Flys,** Carlos Ricardo 1963- *WhoHisp 92*
**Flythe,** Starkey, Jr. *DrAPF 91*
**FM-20 30** *WrDr 92*
**Fo,** Dario 1926- *FacFETw, Who 92*
**Fo,** Dario 1954- *IntWW 91*
**Foa,** Conrad Mario 1941- *WhoFI 92*
**Foa,** J V 1909- *AmMWSc 92*
**Foa,** Piero Pio 1911- *AmMWSc 92, WhoMW 92*
**Foakes,** Reginald Anthony 1923- *Who 92*
**Foale,** Colin Henry 1930- *Who 92*
**Foale,** Marion Ann 1939- *IntWW 91*
**Foard,** Donald Edward 1929- *AmMWSc 92*
**Foard,** Frederick Carter 1945- *WhoBlA 92, WhoFI 92*
**Foard,** Frederick Theophilus, Jr. 1889-1966 *DcNCBi 2*
**Foard,** John Frederick 1827-1909 *DcNCBi 2*
**Foard,** John Hanby 1901-1977 *DcNCBi 2*
**Foard,** Osborne Giles 1820-1882 *DcNCBi 2*
**Foat,** Linda 1951- *WhoEnt 92*
**Fobare,** William Floyd 1954- *AmMWSc 92*
**Fobes,** John Edwin 1918- *IntWW 91*
**Fobes,** Melcher Prince 1911- *AmMWSc 92*
**Foccart,** Jacques 1913- *IntWW 91*
**Focella,** Antonino 1924- *AmMWSc 92*
**Foch,** Ferdinand 1851-1929 *FacFETw*
**Foch,** Nina 1924- *IntMPA 92, WhoEnt 92, WhoWest 92*
**Focht,** Dennis Douglass 1941- *AmMWSc 92*
**Focht,** John Arnold, Jr 1923- *AmMWSc 92, WhoFI 92*
**Focht,** Theodore Harold 1934- *WhoAmL 92*
**Fock,** Jeno 1916- *IntWW 91*
**Focke,** Alfred Bosworth 1906- *AmMWSc 92*
**Focke,** Arthur E 1904- *AmMWSc 92*
**Focke,** Heinrich 1890-1979 *FacFETw*
**Focke,** Katharina 1922- *IntWW 91*
**Focke,** Paul Everard Justus 1937- *Who 92*
**Fockler,** Herbert Hill 1922- *WhoFI 92*
**Fodden,** John Henry 1918- *AmMWSc 92*
**Foden,** Arthur d1990 *Who 92N*
**Foden,** Harry Gartside, Jr. 1924- *WhoFI 92*
**Foden-Pattinson,** Peter Lawrence 1925- *Who 92*
**Foderaro,** Anthony Harolde 1926- *AmMWSc 92*
**Fodiman,** Aaron Rosen 1937- *WhoFI 92*
**Fodor,** Eugene d1991 *NewYTBS 91 [port]*
**Fodor,** Eugene 1905-1991 *ConAu 133*
**Fodor,** Eugene 1906?-1991 *News 91, -91-3*
**Fodor,** Eugene Nicholas 1950- *WhoEnt 92*
**Fodor,** Gabor 1915- *AmMWSc 92*
**Fodor,** George E 1932- *AmMWSc 92*
**Fodor,** Gerald Michael 1947- *WhoFI 92*
**Fodor,** Janice Hoyer 1937- *WhoMW 92*
**Fodor,** Lawrence Martin 1937- *AmMWSc 92*
**Fodrea,** Carolyn Wrobel 1943- *WhoMW 92*
**Fody,** Edward Paul 1947- *WhoMW 92*
**Foecke,** Harold Anthony 1926- *AmMWSc 92*
**Foege,** William Herbert 1936- *AmMWSc 92*
**Foegh,** Marie Ladefoged 1942- *AmMWSc 92*
**Foehl,** Edward Albert 1942- *WhoFI 92*
**Foehr,** Edward Gotthard 1917- *AmMWSc 92*
**Foehrkolb,** Susan Mary 1948- *WhoMW 92*
**Foell,** John David 1931- *WhoFI 92*
**Foelsche,** Horst Wilhelm Julius 1937- *AmMWSc 92*
**Foerch,** Bruce Frederick 1949- *WhoWest 92*
**Foernzler,** Ernest Carl 1935- *AmMWSc 92*
**Foerst,** John George, Jr. 1927- *WhoFI 92*
**Foerster,** Edward L, Sr 1919- *AmMWSc 92*
**Foerster,** George Stephen 1929- *AmMWSc 92*
**Foerster,** Mark Richard 1955- *WhoAmL 92*
**Foerster,** Norman 1887-1972 *BenetAL 91*
**Foerster,** Richard *DrAPF 91*
**Foerster,** Robert F 1883-1941 *DcAmImH*
**Foex,** Pierre 1935- *Who 92*
**Foflygen,** Ronald Wayne 1944- *WhoWest 92*
**Fofonoff,** Nicholas Paul 1929- *AmMWSc 92*
**Foft,** John William 1928- *AmMWSc 92*
**Fogal,** Daniel Steven 1951- *WhoMW 92*
**Fogam,** Margaret Hanorah *WhoBlA 92*
**Fogarassy,** Helen *DrAPF 91*
**Fogartie,** James Eugene 1924- *WhoRel 92*
**Fogarty,** Charles Joseph 1955- *WhoAmP 91*
**Fogarty,** Christopher Winthrop 1921- *Who 92*
**Fogarty,** Daniel P 1924- *WhoAmP 91*
**Fogarty,** Gerald Philip 1939- *WhoRel 92*
**Fogarty,** Jack V. *IntMPA 92*
**Fogarty,** John Charde 1934- *AmMWSc 92*
**Fogarty,** John Patrick Cody 1958- *WhoAmL 92*
**Fogarty,** Joseph R. *LesBEnT 92*
**Fogarty,** Michael Patrick 1916- *Who 92, WrDr 92*
**Fogarty,** Raymond W 1957- *WhoAmP 91*

**Fogarty**, Robert Stephen 1938- *WhoMW 92*
**Fogarty**, William Joseph 1932- *AmMWSc 92*
**Fogden**, Michael Ernest George 1936- *Who 92*
**Fogderud**, Patricia Ann 1938- *WhoRel 92*
**Fogel**, Aaron *DrAPF 91*
**Fogel**, Adelaide Forst 1915- *WhoFI 92*
**Fogel**, Alan Dale 1945- *WhoWest 92*
**Fogel**, Barry Steven 1952- *WhoFI 92*
**Fogel**, Bernard J 1936- *AmMWSc 92*
**Fogel**, Charles M 1913- *AmMWSc 92*
**Fogel**, Daniel Mark *DrAPF 91*
**Fogel**, David Alan 1942- *WhoAmP 91*
**Fogel**, Edward 1943- *WhoRel 92*
**Fogel**, Irving Martin 1929- *WhoFI 92*
**Fogel**, Jeremy Don 1949- *WhoAmL 92*
**Fogel**, Jerry 1936- *WhoMW 92*
**Fogel**, Joan Cathy 1943- *WhoAmL 92*
**Fogel**, Norman 1924- *AmMWSc 92*
**Fogel**, Paul David 1949- *WhoAmL 92*
**Fogel**, Richard 1932- *WhoAmL 92*
**Fogel**, Robert Dale 1947- *AmMWSc 92*
**Fogel**, Robert W. 1926- *Who 92*
**Fogel**, Robert William 1926- *IntWW 91, WrDr 92*
**Fogel**, Seymour 1919- *AmMWSc 92*
**Fogel**, Sheldon Leslie 1942- *WhoFI 92*
**Fogel'**, Vladimir Petrovich 1902-1929 *SovUnBD*
**Fogel**, Wayne A., II 1941- *WhoFI 92*
**Fogelberg**, Daniel Grayling 1951- *WhoEnt 92*
**Fogelberg**, Jay Carl 1945- *WhoAmL 92*
**Fogelberg**, Paul Alan 1951- *WhoMW 92*
**Fogelholm**, Markus 1946- *IntWW 91*
**Fogelman**, Evan Marr 1960- *WhoEnt 92*
**Fogelnest**, Robert 1946- *WhoAmL 92*
**Fogelson**, Andrew 1942- *IntMPA 92*
**Fogelson**, David Eugene 1926- *AmMWSc 92*
**Fogelson**, James H. d1991 *NewYTBS 91 [port]*
**Fogelsonger**, Ned Raymond 1947- *WhoFI 92*
**Fogerty**, Arthur Joseph 1938- *WhoFI 92*
**Fogerty**, James Edward 1945- *WhoMW 92*
**Fogg**, Alan 1921- *Who 92*
**Fogg**, Blaine Viles 1940- *WhoAmL 92*
**Fogg**, Cyril Percival 1914- *Who 92*
**Fogg**, Donald Ernest 1922- *AmMWSc 92*
**Fogg**, Edward T 1927- *AmMWSc 92*
**Fogg**, Ernest Leslie 1920- *WhoRel 92*
**Fogg**, Gordon Elliott 1919- *IntWW 91, Who 92, WrDr 92*
**Fogg**, James 1937- *WhoMW 92*
**Fogg**, Linda Jean 1955- *WhoEnt 92*
**Fogg**, Peter John 1931- *AmMWSc 92*
**Fogg**, Ralph Everett, Jr. 1932- *WhoRel 92*
**Fogg**, Ray B. 1964- *WhoEnt 92*
**Fogg**, Rebecca Snider 1949- *WhoWest 92*
**Foggie**, Charles H. 1912- *WhoBlA 92*
**Foggie**, Charles Herbert 1912- *WhoRel 92*
**Foggon**, George 1913- *Who 92*
**Foggs**, Edward J. *WhoMW 92, WhoRel 92*
**Foggs**, Edward L. 1934- *WhoBlA 92*
**Foggs**, Joyce D. 1930- *WhoBlA 92*
**Foggy Mountain Boys** *NewAmDM*
**Fogh-Andersen**, Poul 1913- *IntWW 91*
**Fogiel**, Adolf W *AmMWSc 92*
**Fogle**, Ellen L. 1951- *WhoEnt 92*
**Fogle**, Harold Warman 1918- *AmMWSc 92*
**Fogle**, James 1936- *ConAu 134*
**Fogleman**, Alfred 1937- *WhoRel 92*
**Fogleman**, Guy 1924- *WhoAmP 91*
**Fogleman**, John Albert 1911- *WhoAmP 91*
**Fogleman**, Ralph William 1926- *AmMWSc 92*
**Fogleman**, Wavell Wainwright 1942- *AmMWSc 92*
**Fogler**, Hugh Scott 1939- *AmMWSc 92*
**Foglesong**, Mark Allen 1949- *AmMWSc 92*
**Foglia**, Thomas Anthony 1940- *AmMWSc 92*
**Foglietta**, Thomas M. 1928- *AlmAP 92 [port], WhoAmP 91*
**Foglio**, Mario Eusebio 1931- *AmMWSc 92*
**Foglio**, Susana 1924- *AmMWSc 92*
**Fogt**, Thomas M. 1945- *WhoMW 92*
**Fogus**, Kathleen Marie 1963- *WhoMW 92*
**Fogwell**, Joseph Wray 1915- *AmMWSc 92*
**Fohl**, Timothy 1934- *AmMWSc 92*
**Fohlen**, George Marcel 1919- *AmMWSc 92*
**Fohlmeister**, Jurgen Fritz 1941- *AmMWSc 92*
**Fohn**, Gerald Anthony 1945- *WhoAmL 92*
**Foighel**, Isi 1927- *IntWW 91*
**Foigny**, Gabriel De 1640-1692 *ScFEYrs*
**Foil**, Robert Rodney 1934- *AmMWSc 92*
**Foiles**, Carl Luther 1935- *AmMWSc 92*
**Foiles**, James Larry 1950- *WhoMW 92*
**Foiles**, Stephen Martin 1956- *AmMWSc 92*
**Fois**, Andrew 1958- *WhoAmL 92*
**Foise**, Jonathan Walter 1958- *WhoMW 92*
**Foister**, Robert Thomas 1949- *AmMWSc 92*
**Foisy**, Hector B 1936- *AmMWSc 92*
**Foit**, Franklin Frederick, Jr 1942- *AmMWSc 92*
**Fojtik**, Jan 1928- *IntWW 91*
**Fok**, Agnes Kwan 1940- *AmMWSc 92*
**Fok**, Samuel S M 1926- *AmMWSc 92*
**Fok**, Samuel Shiu-Ming 1926- *WhoWest 92*
**Fok**, Siu Yuen 1937- *AmMWSc 92*
**Fok**, Thomas Dso Yun 1921- *AmMWSc 92, WhoFI 92, WhoMW 92*
**Fok**, Yu-Si 1932- *AmMWSc 92*
**Fokes**, William B, II *WhoIns 92*
**Fokin**, Mikhail Mikhaylovich 1880-1942 *SovUnBD*
**Fokin**, Yurii Yevgenyevich 1936- *IntWW 91*
**Fokine**, Irine 1922- *WhoEnt 92*
**Fokine**, Michael 1880-1942 *FacFETw*
**Fokine**, Michel 1880-1942 *SovUnBD*
**Fokker**, Anton Hermann Gerard 1890-1939 *FacFETw*
**Folan**, Lorcan Michael 1960- *AmMWSc 92*
**Foland**, Kenneth Austin 1945- *AmMWSc 92*
**Foland**, Neal Eugene 1929- *AmMWSc 92*
**Foland**, William Douglas 1926- *AmMWSc 92*
**Folberg**, Harold Jay 1941- *WhoAmL 92*
**Folberth**, William Mitchell, III 1944- *WhoFI 92*
**Folch-Pi**, Diana Maria 1951- *WhoAmL 92*
**Folden**, Robert William 1945- *WhoEnt 92*
**Foldes**, Andor 1913- *IntWW 91, NewAmDM, Who 92*
**Foldes**, Francis Ferenc 1910- *AmMWSc 92*
**Foldes**, Lawrence David 1959- *WhoEnt 92*
**Foldes**, Lucien Paul 1930- *Who 92*
**Foldessy**, Edward Patrick 1941- *IntAu&W 91*
**Foldi**, Andrew Harry 1926- *WhoEnt 92*
**Foldi**, Andrew Peter 1931- *AmMWSc 92*
**Folds**, James Donald 1940- *AmMWSc 92*
**Foldvary**, Elmer 1935- *AmMWSc 92*
**Foldy**, Leslie Lawrance 1919- *AmMWSc 92*
**Folen**, Vincent James 1924- *AmMWSc 92*
**Foley** *Who 92*
**Foley**, Baron 1923- *Who 92*
**Foley**, Brian Charles 1910- *Who 92*
**Foley**, Brian T. 1959- *WhoAmL 92*
**Foley**, Daniel Edmund 1926- *WhoFI 92, WhoWest 92*
**Foley**, Daniel Patrick 1920- *WhoMW 92*
**Foley**, Daniel Ronald 1941- *WhoAmL 92*
**Foley**, Daniel Thomas 1957- *WhoAmL 92*
**Foley**, David E. 1930- *WhoRel 92*
**Foley**, Dean Carroll 1925- *AmMWSc 92*
**Foley**, Dennis Joseph 1945- *AmMWSc 92*
**Foley**, Dennis Michael 1960- *WhoAmL 92*
**Foley**, Duane H *AmMWSc 92*
**Foley**, Duncan Karl 1942- *WhoFI 92*
**Foley**, Edward Leo 1930- *AmMWSc 92*
**Foley**, Edward W 1937- *WhoIns 92*
**Foley**, Eileen 1918- *WhoAmP 91*
**Foley**, Eugene Arthur 1953- *WhoFI 92*
**Foley**, Francis Joseph, III 1941- *WhoAmL 92*
**Foley**, George Edward 1912- *AmMWSc 92*
**Foley**, H Thomas 1933- *AmMWSc 92*
**Foley**, Helen A 1953- *WhoAmP 91*
**Foley**, Henry Charles 1956- *AmMWSc 92*
**Foley**, Henry Michael 1917- *AmMWSc 92*
**Foley**, Hugh Smith 1939- *Who 92*
**Foley**, Jack *DrAPF 91*
**Foley**, James David 1942- *AmMWSc 92*
**Foley**, James E 1950- *AmMWSc 92*
**Foley**, James F, Jr 1942- *WhoIns 92*
**Foley**, James Patrick 1953- *WhoAmP 91*
**Foley**, Johanna Mary 1945- *IntAu&W 91, Who 92*
**Foley**, John F 1931- *AmMWSc 92*
**Foley**, John Francis 1928- *WhoAmL 92*
**Foley**, John Patrick 1935- *WhoRel 92*
**Foley**, John Paul 1939- *Who 92*
**Foley**, Joseph Michael 1916- *AmMWSc 92*
**Foley**, Kathleen M 1944- *AmMWSc 92*
**Foley**, Kenneth John 1936- *AmMWSc 92*
**Foley**, Kevin 1950- *WhoIns 92*
**Foley**, Larry Don 1954- *WhoEnt 92*
**Foley**, Leo Thomas 1928- *WhoAmP 91*
**Foley**, Lewis Michael 1938- *WhoFI 92*
**Foley**, Lila A. 1925- *WhoHisp 92*
**Foley**, Louise Munro 1933- *IntAu&W 91, WrDr 92*
**Foley**, Lucille C 1936- *WhoAmP 91*
**Foley**, Mark 1954- *WhoAmP 91*
**Foley**, Martha 1897?-1977 *BenetAL 91*
**Foley**, Maurice 1925- *IntWW 91, Who 92*
**Foley**, Michael Glen 1945- *AmMWSc 92*
**Foley**, Noel *Who 92*
**Foley**, Patrick Joseph 1930- *WhoAmL 92, WhoFI 92, WhoIns 92*
**Foley**, Patrick Joseph 1934- *WhoAmP 91*
**Foley**, Paul Allen 1934- *WhoAmL 92*
**Foley**, Peter Michael 1947- *WhoAmL 92*
**Foley**, Red 1910-1968 *NewAmDM*
**Foley**, Richard, Jr 1949- *WhoAmP 91*
**Foley**, Robert Douglas 1954- *WhoEnt 92*
**Foley**, Robert H. 1930- *WhoFI 92*
**Foley**, Robert John 1958- *WhoAmL 92*
**Foley**, Robert L., Sr. *WhoRel 92*
**Foley**, Robert Matthew 1943- *WhoAmL 92*
**Foley**, Robert Thomas 1918- *AmMWSc 92*
**Foley**, Ronald E, Jr *WhoIns 92*
**Foley**, Ronald F 1950- *WhoAmP 91*
**Foley**, Ronald Graham Gregory 1923- *Who 92*
**Foley**, Thomas John 1954- *WhoAmL 92*
**Foley**, Thomas John Noel 1914- *Who 92*
**Foley**, Thomas Lester 1956- *WhoRel 92*
**Foley**, Thomas Preston, Jr 1937- *AmMWSc 92*
**Foley**, Thomas S. 1929- *AlmAP 92 [port]*
**Foley**, Thomas Stephen 1929- *AmPolLe, IntWW 91, Who 92, WhoAmP 91, WhoWest 92*
**Foley**, Walter P 1936- *WhoIns 92*
**Foley**, William Arthur *AmMWSc 92*
**Foley**, William Edward, Jr. 1952- *WhoRel 92*
**Foley**, William Leonard 1941- *WhoRel 92*
**Foley**, William M 1929- *AmMWSc 92*
**Foley**, William Thomas 1911- *AmMWSc 92*
**Foley-Berkeley** *Who 92*
**Folger**, Alonzo Dillard 1888-1941 *DcNCBi 2*
**Folger**, David W 1931- *AmMWSc 92*
**Folger**, Henry Clay 1857-1930 *BenetAL 91*
**Folger**, John Hamlin 1880-1963 *DcNCBi 2*
**Folger**, Lee Merritt 1934- *WhoFI 92*
**Folger**, Peter 1617?-1690? *BenetAL 91*
**Folger**, Walter 1765-1849 *BiInAmS*
**Folinas**, Helen 1927- *AmMWSc 92*
**Folingsby**, Kenneth *ScFEYrs*
**Folinsbee**, Robert Edward 1917- *AmMWSc 92*
**Folio**, Fred *ScFEYrs*
**Foljambe** *Who 92*
**Folk**, Earl Donald 1939- *AmMWSc 92*
**Folk**, Frank Stewart 1932- *WhoBlA 92*
**Folk**, George Edgar, Jr 1914- *AmMWSc 92*
**Folk**, George Nathaniel 1831-1896 *DcNCBi 2*
**Folk**, John Edward 1925- *AmMWSc 92*
**Folk**, Robert Louis 1925- *AmMWSc 92*
**Folk**, Robert Thomas 1927- *AmMWSc 92*
**Folk**, Russell Harter 1947- *WhoFI 92*
**Folk**, Stewart H 1915- *AmMWSc 92*
**Folk**, Theodore Lamson 1940- *AmMWSc 92*
**Folk**, William Robert 1944- *AmMWSc 92*
**Folke**, Will *IntAu&W 91X*
**Folkenflik**, Max 1948- *WhoAmL 92*
**Folker**, Alfred August 1946- *WhoEnt 92*
**Folkers**, Karl 1906- *IntWW 91*
**Folkers**, Karl August 1906- *AmMWSc 92*
**Folkers**, Winston Edward 1935- *WhoMW 92*
**Folkert**, Jay Ernest 1916- *AmMWSc 92*
**Folkerts**, George William 1938- *AmMWSc 92*
**Folkerts**, Thomas Mason 1926- *AmMWSc 92, WhoMW 92*
**Folkes**, Peter L. 1923- *TwCPaSc*
**Folkestone**, Viscount 1955- *Who 92*
**Folkinga**, Celia Gould 1957- *WhoAmP 91*
**Folkman**, Moses Judah 1933- *AmMWSc 92*
**Folks**, Francis Neil 1939- *WhoWest 92*
**Folks**, Homer 1867-1963 *DcAmImH*
**Folks**, Homer Clifton 1923- *AmMWSc 92*
**Folks**, John Leroy 1929- *AmMWSc 92*
**Folks**, John M 1948- *WhoAmP 91*
**Folks**, L. Scott 1955- *WhoEnt 92*
**Folks**, Leslie Scott 1955- *WhoBlA 92*
**Folland**, Gerald Budge 1947- *AmMWSc 92*
**Folland**, Nathan Orlando 1937- *AmMWSc 92*
**Follari**, Gregorio 1940-1991 *NewYTBS 91*
**Follesdal**, Dagfinn 1932- *IntWW 91*
**Follett**, Brian Keith 1939- *Who 92*
**Follett**, James 1939- *ConAu 134*
**Follett**, Ken 1949- *IntAu&W 91, IntWW 91, WrDr 92*
**Follett**, Robert J R 1928- *WhoAmP 91*
**Follett**, Robert John Richard 1928- *WhoMW 92*
**Follett**, Roy Hunter 1935- *AmMWSc 92, WhoWest 92*
**Follett**, Wilbur Irving 1901- *AmMWSc 92*
**Follette**, Patricia 1929- *TwCPaSc*
**Folley**, Clyde H. 1927- *WhoFI 92*
**Follick**, Edwin Duane 1935- *WhoAmL 92, WhoFI 92, WhoWest 92*
**Follin**, Michael Roger 1951- *WhoMW 92*
**Follingstad**, Henry George 1922- *AmMWSc 92*
**Follis**, Elaine Russell 1944- *WhoRel 92*
**Follis**, John Victorine 1923- *WhoEnt 92*
**Follmer**, John Scott 1951- *WhoEnt 92*
**Follo**, Carl R 1944- *WhoIns 92*
**Follot**, Paul 1877-1941 *DcTwDes*
**Follows**, Alan Greaves 1921- *AmMWSc 92*
**Follstad**, Merle Norman 1931- *AmMWSc 92*
**Follstaedt**, David Martin 1947- *AmMWSc 92*
**Follweiler**, Douglas MacArthur 1942- *AmMWSc 92*
**Follweiler**, Joanne Schaaf 1942- *AmMWSc 92*
**Folmar**, Emory M 1930- *WhoAmP 91*
**Folmar**, Joel Michael 1936- *WhoAmP 91*
**Folse**, Dean Sydney 1921- *AmMWSc 92*
**Folse**, Raymond Francis, Jr 1940- *AmMWSc 92*
**Folsey**, George, Jr. 1939- *IntMPA 92*
**Folso**, Michael James 1948- *WhoEnt 92*
**Folsom**, Charles Follen 1842-1907 *BiInAmS*
**Folsom**, Frank M. d1970 *LesBEnT 92*
**Folsom**, Franklin Brewster 1907- *IntAu&W 91, WrDr 92*
**Folsom**, Henry R 1913- *WhoAmP 91*
**Folsom**, Henry Richard 1913- *WhoFI 92*
**Folsom**, James E 1908-1987 *FacFETw*
**Folsom**, James Elisha, Jr 1949- *WhoAmP 91*
**Folsom**, Richard G 1907- *AmMWSc 92*
**Folsom**, Sallie Stark 1930- *WhoAmP 91*
**Folsom**, Theodore Robert 1908- *AmMWSc 92*
**Folsom**, Victor Clarence 1909- *WhoAmL 92*
**Folsome**, Clair Edwin 1935- *AmMWSc 92*
**Folster**, David 1937- *ConAu 134*
**Folta**, Samuel Nathan 1965- *WhoRel 92*
**Foltinek**, Herbert 1930- *IntWW 91*
**Folts**, David Jacob 1958- *WhoMW 92*
**Folts**, Dwight David 1947- *AmMWSc 92*
**Folts**, John D 1938- *AmMWSc 92*
**Folts**, Sylvia Maxine 1932- *WhoMW 92*
**Foltz**, Craig Billig 1952- *AmMWSc 92*
**Foltz**, Donald Joseph 1933- *WhoWest 92*
**Foltz**, Donald Richard 1926- *AmMWSc 92*
**Foltz**, Eldon Leroy 1919- *AmMWSc 92*
**Foltz**, George Edward 1924- *AmMWSc 92*
**Foltz**, Michael Craig 1957- *WhoAmL 92*
**Foltz**, Nevin D 1940- *AmMWSc 92*
**Foltz**, Rodger L 1934- *AmMWSc 92*
**Foltz**, Roger Ernest 1950- *WhoEnt 92*
**Foltz**, Thomas Roberts, Jr 1920- *AmMWSc 92*
**Foltz-Gray**, Dorothy *DrAPF 91*
**Folweiler**, Robert Cooper 1933- *AmMWSc 92*
**Folwell**, Dale Robbins 1958- *WhoFI 92*
**Folwell**, William Hopkins 1924- *WhoRel 92*
**Folz**, Carol Ann 1951- *WhoFI 92, WhoMW 92*
**Folz**, Sylvester D 1941- *AmMWSc 92*
**Fomichenko**, Konstantin Yefimovich 1927- *IntWW 91*
**Fomin** *ConAu 134*
**Fomin**, Ivan Aleksandrovich 1872-1936 *SovUnBD*
**Fomon**, Samuel Joseph 1923- *AmMWSc 92, WhoMW 92*
**Fomufod**, Antoine Kofi 1940- *WhoBlA 92*
**Fonaroff**, Leonard Schuyler 1928- *AmMWSc 92*
**Fonarow**, Jerry 1935- *WhoEnt 92*
**Fonash**, Stephan J 1941- *AmMWSc 92*
**Foncha**, John Ngu 1916- *IntWW 91*
**Fonck**, Eugene J 1954- *AmMWSc 92*
**Fonck**, Raymond John 1951- *AmMWSc 92*
**Fonda**, Bridget 1964- *IntMPA 92*
**Fonda**, Donald Albert, Jr. 1938- *WhoRel 92*
**Fonda**, Henry 1905-1983 *FacFETw [port]*
**Fonda**, Jane 1937- *FacFETw [port], HanAmWH, IntMPA 92, IntWW 91, WhoEnt 92, WrDr 92*
**Fonda**, Margaret Lee 1942- *AmMWSc 92*
**Fonda**, Peter 1939- *IntMPA 92*
**Fonda**, Peter 1940- *WhoEnt 92*
**Fonda**, Richard Weston 1940- *AmMWSc 92*
**Fondacaro**, Joseph D 1943- *AmMWSc 92*
**Fondahl**, John W 1924- *AmMWSc 92*
**Fondren**, Doris Gray 1930- *WhoAmL 92*
**Fondren**, Kervin 1963- *IntAu&W 91*
**Fondren**, Larry E 1947- *WhoIns 92*
**Fondy**, Joseph J. 1959- *WhoEnt 92*
**Fondy**, Thomas Paul 1937- *AmMWSc 92*
**Foner**, Eric 1943- *WrDr 92*
**Foner**, Henry Joseph 1919- *WhoAmP 91*
**Foner**, Philip S. 1910- *WrDr 92*
**Foner**, Samuel Newton 1920- *AmMWSc 92*
**Foner**, Simon 1925- *AmMWSc 92*
**Fones**, William H D 1917- *WhoAmP 91*
**Fones**, William Hardin Davis 1917- *WhoAmL 92*
**Fonfara**, John W *WhoAmP 91*
**Fong**, Billy Jaw 1955- *WhoRel 92*
**Fong**, Bruce William 1952- *WhoRel 92*
**Fong**, Carl S. 1959- *WhoWest 92*
**Fong**, Ching-Yao 1935- *AmMWSc 92*
**Fong**, Francis K 1938- *AmMWSc 92*

**Fong,** Franklin 1947- AmMWSc 92
**Fong,** Godwin Wing-Kin 1950- AmMWSc 92
**Fong,** Harold Michael 1938- WhoAmL 92, WhoWest 92
**Fong,** Harry H S 1935- AmMWSc 92
**Fong,** Hiram 1907- IntWW 91
**Fong,** Hiram L. 1906- WhoFI 92, WhoWest 92
**Fong,** Hiram Leong 1906- WhoAmP 91
**Fong,** Jack Sun-Chik 1941- AmMWSc 92
**Fong,** James T 1927- AmMWSc 92
**Fong,** Jeffery Tse-Wei 1934- AmMWSc 92
**Fong,** John Richard 1950- WhoWest 92
**Fong,** Jones W 1936- AmMWSc 92
**Fong,** Julita Angela 1933- WhoWest 92
**Fong,** Kei-Lai Lau 1950- AmMWSc 92
**Fong,** Kenneth Tom 1961- WhoAmL 92
**Fong,** Kevin M. 1955- WhoAmL 92
**Fong,** Marc Alan 1949- WhoAmL 92
**Fong,** Peter 1924- AmMWSc 92
**Fong,** Peter C. K. 1955- WhoAmL 92
**Fong,** Shao-Ling AmMWSc 92
**Fong,** Wenda WhoEnt 92
**Fong,** Wilfred Wai Fai 1959- WhoRel 92
**Fonger,** William Hamilton 1925- AmMWSc 92
**Fonjallaz,** Arthur Robert Gaston 1875-1944 BiDExR
**Fonkalsrud,** Eric W 1932- AmMWSc 92
**Fonken,** David W 1931- AmMWSc 92
**Fonken,** Gerhard Joseph 1928- AmMWSc 92
**Fonken,** Gunther Siegfried 1926- AmMWSc 92
**Fonner,** David Kent 1957- WhoAmL 92
**Fonnesbeck,** Paul Vance 1931- AmMWSc 92
**Fono,** Andrew 1923- AmMWSc 92
**Fonong,** Tekum 1952- AmMWSc 92
**Fonrose,** Harold Anthony 1925- WhoBlA 92
**Fons,** August Marion, III 1951- WhoWest 92
**Fonseca,** Aloysius 1915- WrDr 92
**Fonseca,** Aloysius Joseph IntAu&W 91
**Fonseca,** Anthony Gutierre 1940- AmMWSc 92
**Fonseca,** Horacio Ricardo 1940- WhoHisp 92
**Fonseca,** James Francis 1923- WhoHisp 92
**Fonseca,** Juan de Rodriguez 1451-1524 HisDSpE
**Fonseca,** Juan E. 1919- WhoHisp 92
**Fonseca,** Orlando R WhoAmP 91, WhoHisp 92
**Fonseca,** Santiago V. 1936- WhoHisp 92
**Font,** Robert G 1940- AmMWSc 92
**Font,** William Francis 1944- AmMWSc 92
**Fontaine,** Andre 1921- IntWW 91
**Fontaine,** Andre Lucien Georges 1921- Who 92
**Fontaine,** Arthur Robert 1929- AmMWSc 92
**Fontaine,** Charles Philip, III 1960- WhoAmL 92
**Fontaine,** Denis Louis 1940- WhoFI 92
**Fontaine,** Gilles Joseph 1948- AmMWSc 92
**Fontaine,** Joan 1917- IntMPA 92
**Fontaine,** John C. WhoAmL 92
**Fontaine,** Julia Clare 1920- AmMWSc 92
**Fontaine,** Marc F 1926- AmMWSc 92
**Fontaine,** Mary Elizabeth 1947- WhoRel 92
**Fontaine,** Maurice Alfred 1904- IntWW 91
**Fontaine,** Peter 1691-1757? DcNCBi 2
**Fontaine,** T. Lamar 1956- WhoWest 92
**Fontaine,** Thomas Davis 1916- AmMWSc 92
**Fontaine,** Valerie Anne 1955- WhoAmL 92
**Fontaine,** William Morris 1835-1913 BiInAmS
**Fontana,** Anthony Jerome, Jr 1950- WhoAmP 91
**Fontana,** Daniel John 1949- WhoFI 92
**Fontana,** Ernest Leonard 1941- WhoMW 92
**Fontana,** Mario H 1933- AmMWSc 92
**Fontana,** Peter R 1935- AmMWSc 92
**Fontana,** Robert E 1915- AmMWSc 92
**Fontana,** Thomas Michael 1951- WhoEnt 92
**Fontana,** Vincent J 1923- AmMWSc 92
**Fontana,** Vincent Robert 1939- WhoAmL 92
**Fontanella,** John Joseph 1945- AmMWSc 92
**Fontanelle,** Bernard De Bovier De ScFEYrs B
**Fontanet,** Alvaro L. 1940- WhoHisp 92
**Fontanez,** Angel Gabriel 1960- WhoHisp 92
**Fontanez,** Dale W. 1967- WhoHisp 92
**Fontanne,** Lynn FacFETw
**Fontayne,** K. Nicole WhoBlA 92
**Fontenay,** Charles L 1917- TwCSFW 91, WrDr 92
**Fontendot,** Elvin Clemence 1952- WhoAmP 91
**Fontenelle,** Bernard le Bovier de 1657-1757 BlkwCEP
**Fontenelle,** Lydia Julia 1938- AmMWSc 92
**Fonteno,** Myrtle C. 1927-1980 WhoBlA 92N
**Fontenot,** Herman 1963- WhoBlA 92
**Fontenot,** Joseph Paul 1927- AmMWSc 92
**Fontenot,** Ken DrAPF 91
**Fontenot,** Louis K. 1918- WhoBlA 92
**Fontenot,** Martin Mayance, Jr 1944- AmMWSc 92
**Fontenot,** Mary Alice 1910- WrDr 92
**Fontenot,** Wonda Lee 1948- WhoRel 92
**Fontenot-Jamerson,** Berlinda 1947- WhoBlA 92
**Fontenoy,** Jean 1899-1945 BiDExR
**Fontes,** Brian F. 1950- WhoHisp 92
**Fontes,** Evandro Martine 1961- WhoEnt 92
**Fontes,** Wayne 1939- WhoMW 92
**Fonteyn,** Margot ConAu 133
**Fonteyn,** Margot 1919-1991 CurBio 91N, FacFETw [port], NewYTBS 91 [port], News 91, -91-3
**Fonteyn,** Paul John 1946- AmMWSc 92
**Fonteyn de Arias,** Margot 1919-1991 ConAu 133
**Fontheim,** Claude G.B. 1955- WhoAmL 92, WhoFI 92
**Fontheim,** Ernest Gunter 1922- AmMWSc 92
**Fontijn,** Arthur 1928- AmMWSc 92
**Fontyn,** Jacqueline 1930- ConCom 92
**Fonvielle,** William Harold 1943- WhoBlA 92
**Fonville,** Danny D. WhoBlA 92
**Fonville,** Dee DrAPF 91
**Fonvizen,** Artur Vladimirovich 1882-1973 SovUnBD
**Fooden,** Jack 1927- AmMWSc 92
**Fookes,** Janet 1936- Who 92
**Foon,** Dennis 1951- WrDr 92
**Foon,** Dennis Todd 1951- IntAu&W 91
**Foor,** W Eugene 1936- AmMWSc 92
**Foorman,** James Louis 1948- WhoAmL 92
**Foos,** K. Michael 1943- WhoMW 92
**Foos,** Kenneth Michael 1943- AmMWSc 92
**Foos,** Raymond Anthony 1928- AmMWSc 92
**Foos,** Robert Young 1922- AmMWSc 92
**Foose,** Richard Martin 1915- AmMWSc 92
**Foose,** Thomas John 1945- AmMWSc 92
**Foot** Who 92
**Foot,** Baron 1909- Who 92
**Foot,** Adeline EncAmaz 91
**Foot,** David Lovell 1939- Who 92
**Foot,** Geoffrey 1915- Who 92
**Foot,** Michael 1913- FacFETw, Who 92, WrDr 92
**Foot,** Michael Colin 1935- Who 92
**Foot,** Michael David Kenneth Willoughby 1946- Who 92
**Foot,** Michael Mackintosh 1913- IntAu&W 91, IntWW 91
**Foot,** Michael Richard Daniell 1919- IntAu&W 91, Who 92, WrDr 92
**Foot,** Paul Mackintosh 1937- IntAu&W 91, Who 92
**Foot,** Philippa Ruth 1920- IntWW 91, Who 92
**Foot,** Victorine 1920- TwCPaSc
**Foote,** Albert E 1846-1895 BiInAmS
**Foote,** Arthur 1853-1937 NewAmDM
**Foote,** Avon Edward 1937- WhoEnt 92
**Foote,** Benjamin Archer 1928- AmMWSc 92
**Foote,** Bobbie Leon 1940- AmMWSc 92
**Foote,** Carlton Dan 1935- AmMWSc 92
**Foote,** Christopher S 1935- AmMWSc 92
**Foote,** David Ward, Jr. 1958- WhoMW 92
**Foote,** Edward Thaddeus, II 1937- WhoAmL 92
**Foote,** Eli 1747-1792 DcNCBi 2
**Foote,** Emmerline 1955- WhoAmL 92
**Foote,** Florence Martindale 1911- AmMWSc 92
**Foote,** Freeman 1908- AmMWSc 92
**Foote,** Garvin Brant 1942- AmMWSc 92
**Foote,** Geoffrey 1950- WrDr 92
**Foote,** Henry Robert Bowreman 1904- Who 92
**Foote,** Herbert N, Sr 1934- WhoAmP 91
**Foote,** Horton 1916- ConAu 34NR, IntAu&W 91, IntMPA 92, WhoEnt 92, WrDr 92
**Foote,** James Herbert 1929- AmMWSc 92
**Foote,** Janet Lorraine 1943- WhoEnt 92
**Foote,** Jeffrey Paul 1949- WhoAmL 92
**Foote,** Joe Reeder 1919- AmMWSc 92
**Foote,** Joe Stephen 1949- WhoAmP 91
**Foote,** Joel Lindsley 1928- AmMWSc 92
**Foote,** John Taintor 1881-1950 BenetAL 91
**Foote,** Kenneth Gerald 1935- AmMWSc 92
**Foote,** Kenneth Taylor 1954- WhoEnt 92
**Foote,** Leonard Hobson Buchanon 1898- WhoBlA 92
**Foote,** Margie Ellen 1929- WhoAmP 91
**Foote,** Martha Louisa 1957- WhoAmL 92
**Foote,** Mary Hallock 1847-1918 HanAmWH
**Foote,** Mary Hallock 1847-1938 BenetAL 91
**Foote,** Mary Hallock 1876-1938 TwCWW 91
**Foote,** Murray Wilbur 1916- AmMWSc 92
**Foote,** Paul Sheldon 1946- WhoFI 92, WhoWest 92
**Foote,** Percy Wright 1879-1961 DcNCBi 2
**Foote,** Peter Godfrey 1924- Who 92
**Foote,** Ray Palmer, Jr. 1933- WhoFI 92
**Foote,** Raymond Eugene 1922- WhoEnt 92
**Foote,** Richard Herbert 1918- AmMWSc 92
**Foote,** Richard Martin 1950- AmMWSc 92
**Foote,** Robert Hutchinson 1922- AmMWSc 92
**Foote,** Robert S 1922- AmMWSc 92
**Foote,** Samuel 1721?-1777 RfGEnL 91
**Foote,** Shelby DrAPF 91
**Foote,** Shelby 1916- BenetAL 91, ConNov 91, CurBio 91 [port], News 91 [port], WrDr 92
**Foote,** Shelby Dade 1916- IntAu&W 91
**Foote,** Sherrill Lynne 1940- WhoMW 92
**Foote,** Vernon Stuart, Jr 1924- AmMWSc 92
**Foote,** W. David 1940- WhoFI 92
**Foote,** Warren Christopher 1927- AmMWSc 92
**Foote,** Wilford Darrell 1931- AmMWSc 92
**Foote,** William Henry 1794-1869 DcNCBi 2
**Foote,** Wilson Hoover 1920- AmMWSc 92
**Foote,** Yvonne 1949- WhoBlA 92
**Foote-Smith,** Elizabeth DrAPF 91
**Footman,** Charles Worthington Fowden 1905- Who 92
**Footman,** Gordon Elliott 1927- WhoWest 92
**Footman,** Robert 1916- IntAu&W 91
**Foots,** James 1916- IntWW 91, Who 92
**Foottit,** Anthony Charles 1935- Who 92
**Fopeano,** John Vincent, Jr 1928- AmMWSc 92
**Fopeano,** Stephan Mark 1963- WhoEnt 92
**Fopp,** Michael Anton 1947- Who 92
**Forain,** Jean-Louis 1852-1931 ThHEIm
**Foraker,** David Alan 1956- WhoWest 92
**Foraker-Thompson,** Jane 1937- WhoAmL 92
**Foral,** Ralph Francis 1934- AmMWSc 92
**Foran,** David John 1937- WhoMW 92
**Foran,** James Michael 1942- AmMWSc 92
**Foran,** John Francis 1930- WhoAmP 91
**Foran,** Kenneth Lawrence 1941- WhoAmP 91
**Forbat,** John Egon 1928- WhoFI 92
**Forbath,** William E. 1952- WhoAmL 92
**Forbes** Who 92
**Forbes,** Lord 1918- Who 92
**Forbes,** Master of 1946- Who 92
**Forbes,** Alastair 1908- Who 92
**Forbes,** Albert Ronald 1931- AmMWSc 92
**Forbes,** Aleck TwCWW 91
**Forbes,** Alexander 1882- ScFEYrs
**Forbes,** Alexander James 1923- IntWW 91
**Forbes,** Alexandra Elizabeth 1958- WhoEnt 92
**Forbes,** Alfred A., III 1940- WhoWest 92
**Forbes,** Alfred Dean 1941- WhoRel 92
**Forbes,** Alfred Dixon 1953- WhoEnt 92
**Forbes,** Allan Louis 1928- AmMWSc 92
**Forbes,** Anthony David Arnold William 1938- Who 92
**Forbes,** Arthur Lee, III 1928- WhoAmL 92
**Forbes,** Barbara WhoEnt 92
**Forbes,** Bruce Jordan 1953- WhoRel 92
**Forbes,** Bryan 1926- IntAu&W 91, IntMPA 92, IntWW 91, Who 92, WrDr 92
**Forbes,** Calvin DrAPF 91
**Forbes,** Calvin 1945- WhoBlA 92
**Forbes,** Charles 1844-1917 BiInAmS
**Forbes,** Charles Edward 1944- AmMWSc 92
**Forbes,** Christopher 1950- WhoFI 92
**Forbes,** Colin IntAu&W 91, WrDr 92
**Forbes,** Colin 1928- Who 92
**Forbes,** Daniel IntAu&W 91X, WrDr 92
**Forbes,** Daniel Merrill 1954- WhoRel 92
**Forbes,** David 1945- IntMPA 92
**Forbes,** David Craig 1938- WhoEnt 92
**Forbes,** David Richard 1944- WhoIns 92
**Forbes,** DeLoris Stanton 1923- IntAu&W 91
**Forbes,** Donald James 1921- Who 92
**Forbes,** Donna Jean 1942- AmMWSc 92
**Forbes,** Edward Coyle 1915- WhoFI 92
**Forbes,** Elliot 1917- NewAmDM, WhoEnt 92
**Forbes,** Esther 1891-1967 BenetAL 91, FacFETw
**Forbes,** Francis Blackwell 1840?-1908 BiInAmS
**Forbes,** Franklin Sim 1936- WhoAmL 92
**Forbes,** Fred William 1936- WhoFI 92
**Forbes,** George L. 1931- WhoBlA 92
**Forbes,** Gilbert Burnett 1915- AmMWSc 92
**Forbes,** Graham John Thomson 1951- Who 92
**Forbes,** Hamish 1916- Who 92
**Forbes,** Ian 1914- Who 92
**Forbes,** Ian 1920- AmMWSc 92
**Forbes,** J Randy 1952- WhoAmP 91
**Forbes,** Jack Edwin 1928- AmMWSc 92
**Forbes,** James 1910- AmMWSc 92
**Forbes,** James 1923- IntWW 91, Who 92
**Forbes,** James 1952- BlkOlyM
**Forbes,** James Franklin 1941- AmMWSc 92
**Forbes,** Jerry Wayne 1941- AmMWSc 92
**Forbes,** John 1950- ConPo 91, WrDr 92
**Forbes,** John Edward 1925- WhoFI 92
**Forbes,** John Morrison 1925- Who 92
**Forbes,** John Stuart 1936- Who 92
**Forbes,** Judith L 1942- AmMWSc 92
**Forbes,** Kathryn 1909-1966 BenetAL 91
**Forbes,** Kenneth Albert Faucher 1922- WhoWest 92
**Forbes,** Kevin Francis 1955- WhoFI 92
**Forbes,** Leonard 1940- WhoWest 92
**Forbes,** Malcolm 1919-1990 AnObit 1990
**Forbes,** Malcolm Holloway 1933- AmMWSc 92
**Forbes,** Malcolm Stevenson 1919- IntAu&W 91
**Forbes,** Malcolm Stevenson 1919-1990 FacFETw [port]
**Forbes,** Malcolm Stevenson, Jr 1947- WhoAmP 91, WhoFI 92
**Forbes,** Martin 1920- AmMWSc 92
**Forbes,** Michael Shepard 1945- AmMWSc 92
**Forbes,** Milton L 1930- AmMWSc 92
**Forbes,** Morton Gerald 1938- WhoAmL 92
**Forbes,** Muriel Rose d1991 Who 92N
**Forbes,** Nanette Who 92
**Forbes,** Oliver Clifford 1927- AmMWSc 92
**Forbes,** Paul Donald 1936- AmMWSc 92
**Forbes,** Richard Brainard 1921- AmMWSc 92
**Forbes,** Richard Bryan 1936- AmMWSc 92
**Forbes,** Richard Mather 1916- AmMWSc 92
**Forbes,** Ronald 1947- TwCPaSc
**Forbes,** Rose Dabney Malcolm 1875?-1947 AmPeW
**Forbes,** Stanhope Alexander 1857-1947 TwCPaSc
**Forbes,** Stanton IntAu&W 91X
**Forbes,** Stanton 1923- WrDr 92
**Forbes,** Stephen W 1942- WhoIns 92
**Forbes,** Terry Gene 1946- AmMWSc 92
**Forbes,** Thayne John 1938- Who 92
**Forbes,** Thomas Rogers 1911- AmMWSc 92
**Forbes,** Vivian 1891-1937 TwCPaSc
**Forbes,** Warren C 1939- AmMWSc 92
**Forbes,** William d1751? DcNCBi 2
**Forbes,** William Frederick 1924- AmMWSc 92
**Forbes,** William Frederick Eustace 1932- Who 92
**Forbes,** William Smith 1831-1905 BiInAmS
**Forbes,** William Stuart- 1935- Who 92
**Forbes-Leith of Fyvie,** Andrew 1929- Who 92
**Forbes of Craigievar,** Ewan d1991 Who 92N
**Forbes of Craigievar,** Ewan 1912- Who 92
**Forbes of Pitsligo,** Charles E Stuart- d1985 Who 92N
**Forbes-Sempill** Who 92
**Forbis,** Bryan Lester 1957- WhoMW 92
**Forbis,** Clinton Sherman, Jr. 1944- WhoAmL 92
**Forbis,** James Edwin 1931- WhoAmP 91
**Forbis,** Jeff E. 1950- WhoFI 92
**Forbis,** John W 1939- WhoAmP 91
**Forbis,** Orie Lester, Jr 1922- AmMWSc 92
**Forbrich,** Carl A, Jr 1939- AmMWSc 92
**Forbus,** Ina B. WrDr 92
**Forbus,** Wiley Davis 1894-1976 DcNCBi 2
**Forbush,** Bliss, III 1945- AmMWSc 92
**Forbush,** Scott E 1904-1984 FacFETw
**Force,** Carlton Gregory 1926- AmMWSc 92
**Force,** Don Clement 1928- AmMWSc 92
**Force,** Manning Ferguson 1824-1899 BiInAmS
**Force,** Peter 1790-1868 BenetAL 91
**Force,** Ronald Clarence 1917- WhoMW 92
**Forche,** Carolyn DrAPF 91
**Forche,** Carolyn 1950- ConPo 91, WrDr 92
**Forche,** Jennifer Roth 1960- WhoMW 92
**Forchelli,** Jeffrey David 1947- WhoAmL 92
**Forchhammer,** Jes 1934- IntWW 91

**Forchheimer**, Frederick 1853-1913 *BiInAmS*
**Forchheimer**, Otto Louis 1926- *AmMWSc 92*
**Forchielli**, Americo Lewis 1922- *AmMWSc 92*
**Forcier**, George Arthur 1938- *AmMWSc 92*
**Forcier**, Gerald Raymond 1928- *WhoAmP 91*
**Forcier**, Lawrence Kenneth 1943- *AmMWSc 92*
**Forcinio**, Hallie Eunice 1952- *WhoMW 92*
**Forcione**, Alban Keith 1938- *WrDr 92*
**Ford**, Adam 1940- *Who 92*
**Ford**, Aileen W. 1934- *WhoBlA 92*
**Ford**, Albert Lewis, Jr 1946- *AmMWSc 92*
**Ford**, Albert S. 1929- *WhoBlA 92*
**Ford**, Alec George 1926- *WrDr 92*
**Ford**, Alonzo Anthony 1953- *WhoRel 92*
**Ford**, Andrew 1943- *Who 92*
**Ford**, Anita 1948- *TwCPaSc*
**Ford**, Anthony *Who 92*
**Ford**, Antoinette 1941- *WhoBlA 92*
**Ford**, Antony 1944- *Who 92*
**Ford**, Arnold Josiah 1890?-1935? *RelLAm 91*
**Ford**, Arthur Augustus 1897-1971 *RelLAm 91*
**Ford**, Arthur B 1932- *AmMWSc 92*
**Ford**, Ausbra 1935- *WhoBlA 92*
**Ford**, Austin Francis, Jr. 1941- *WhoWest 92*
**Ford**, Barbara *ConAu 134*
**Ford**, Benjamin Thomas 1925- *Who 92*
**Ford**, Bert H 1918- *WhoAmP 91*
**Ford**, Betty Bloomer 1918- *WhoWest 92*
**Ford**, Boris 1917- *IntAu&W 91, Who 92, WrDr 92*
**Ford**, Bowles C. 1911- *WhoBlA 92*
**Ford**, Brian J 1939- *ConAu 34NR*
**Ford**, Brian John 1939- *IntAu&W 91, WrDr 92*
**Ford**, Brinsley *Who 92*
**Ford**, Bryan B. 1958- *WhoAmL 92*
**Ford**, C Quentin 1923- *AmMWSc 92*
**Ford**, Carolyn 1953- *WhoAmP 91*
**Ford**, Cecil Atha 1941- *WhoAmL 92*
**Ford**, Charles 1936- *WhoBlA 92*
**Ford**, Charles Edmund 1912- *Who 92*
**Ford**, Charles Henri *DrAPF 91*
**Ford**, Charles Henri 1913- *ConPo 91, WrDr 92*
**Ford**, Charles Reed 1931- *WhoAmP 91*
**Ford**, Charles T. 1907- *WhoBlA 92*
**Ford**, Christopher Dale 1961- *WhoRel 92*
**Ford**, Clark Fugier 1953- *AmMWSc 92*
**Ford**, Claudette Franklin 1942- *WhoBlA 92*
**Ford**, Clinita Arnsby 1928- *AmMWSc 92*
**Ford**, Clinton Banker 1913- *AmMWSc 92*
**Ford**, Colin John 1934- *Who 92*
**Ford**, Corey 1902-1969 *BenetAL 91*
**Ford**, Corydon La 1813-1894 *BiInAmS*
**Ford**, Dan 1952- *WhoBlA 92*
**Ford**, Daniel 1931- *WrDr 92*
**Ford**, Daniel Morgan 1942- *AmMWSc 92*
**Ford**, Danny R 1952- *WhoAmP 91*
**Ford**, David *WrDr 92*
**Ford**, David 1935- *Who 92*
**Ford**, David A 1935- *AmMWSc 92*
**Ford**, David Clayton 1949- *WhoAmL 92, WhoAmP 91*
**Ford**, David Fairbanks 1962- *WhoEnt 92*
**Ford**, David Frank 1948- *Who 92*
**Ford**, David K. 1948- *WhoWest 92*
**Ford**, David Leon, Jr. 1944- *WhoBlA 92*
**Ford**, David Lynn 1959- *WhoRel 92*
**Ford**, David Robert 1935- *IntWW 91*
**Ford**, Dawn W. 1955- *WhoEnt 92*
**Ford**, Deborah Lee 1945- *WhoBlA 92*
**Ford**, Denys Kensington 1923- *AmMWSc 92*
**Ford**, Donald A. 1928- *WhoBlA 92*
**Ford**, Donald Hoskins 1930- *AmMWSc 92*
**Ford**, Donis W. *DrAPF 91*
**Ford**, Donna Irene 1959- *WhoMW 92*
**Ford**, Donna Lou 1937- *WhoRel 92*
**Ford**, Douglas 1914- *WrDr 92*
**Ford**, Douglas Albert 1917- *Who 92*
**Ford**, Douglas Waldo 1941- *WhoMW 92*
**Ford**, Douglas William C. *Who 92*
**Ford**, Dwain *AmMWSc 92*
**Ford**, Edsel Bryant 1893-1943 *FacFETw*
**Ford**, Edward 1910- *Who 92*
**Ford**, Edward 1930- *WhoAmP 91*
**Ford**, Eileen Otte 1922- *WhoEnt 92*
**Ford**, Elaine *DrAPF 91*
**Ford**, Elbur *IntAu&W 91X, Who 92, WrDr 92*
**Ford**, Ellen Hodson 1913- *WhoEnt 92, WhoMW 92*
**Ford**, Emory A 1940- *AmMWSc 92*
**Ford**, Evern D. 1952- *WhoBlA 92*
**Ford**, Faith *WhoEnt 92*
**Ford**, Floyd Mallory 1921- *AmMWSc 92*
**Ford**, Ford B 1922- *WhoAmP 91*
**Ford**, Ford Maddox 1873-1939 *FacFETw*
**Ford**, Ford Madox 1873-1939 *CnDBLB 6 [port], LiExTwC, RfGEnL 91*
**Ford**, Fred, Jr. 1930- *WhoBlA 92*
**Ford**, Frederick Jay 1960- *WhoRel 92*
**Ford**, Frederick Ross 1936- *WhoFI 92, WhoMW 92*
**Ford**, Frederick W. *LesBEnT 92*
**Ford**, Freeman Arms 1941- *WhoWest 92*
**Ford**, Gary Henry 1952- *WhoMW 92*
**Ford**, Gary Holloway 1945- *WhoMW 92*
**Ford**, Gary L. 1944- *WhoBlA 92*
**Ford**, Geoffrey 1923- *Who 92*
**Ford**, George Burt 1923- *WhoAmL 92*
**Ford**, George Dudley 1940- *AmMWSc 92*
**Ford**, George H 1914- *IntAu&W 91, WrDr 92*
**Ford**, George Henry 1912- *TwCPaSc*
**Ford**, George Johnson 1916- *Who 92*
**Ford**, George Peter 1949- *AmMWSc 92*
**Ford**, George Pratt 1919- *AmMWSc 92*
**Ford**, George Washington, III 1924- *WhoBlA 92*
**Ford**, George Willard 1927- *AmMWSc 92*
**Ford**, Gerald 1913- *FacFETw [port], RComAH*
**Ford**, Gerald R. 1913- *BenetAL 91, WhoAmP 91*
**Ford**, Gerald Rudolph 1913- *Who 92*
**Ford**, Gerald Rudolph, Jr. 1913- *AmPolLe [port], IntWW 91, WhoWest 92*
**Ford**, Gerald Wayne 1948- *WhoRel 92*
**Ford**, Geraldine Bledsoe *WhoBlA 92*
**Ford**, Gertrude *DrAPF 91*
**Ford**, Gilbert Clayton 1923- *AmMWSc 92*
**Ford**, Gillian Rachel 1934- *Who 92*
**Ford**, Glenn 1916- *IntMPA 92, WhoEnt 92*
**Ford**, Glyn *Who 92*
**Ford**, Gordon Buell, Jr 1937- *IntAu&W 91, WhoFI 92, WhoMW 92, WrDr 92*
**Ford**, Graham B. d1991 *NewYTBS 91*
**Ford**, Gregory Clay 1955- *WhoFI 92*
**Ford**, Gregory John 1961- *WhoAmL 92*
**Ford**, Hamilton Gates d1991 *NewYTBS 91*
**Ford**, Harold E. 1945- *AlmAP 92 [port]*
**Ford**, Harold Eugene 1945- *WhoAmP 91, WhoBlA 92*
**Ford**, Harold Frank 1915- *Who 92*
**Ford**, Harold Warner 1915- *WhoWest 92*
**Ford**, Harrison 1942- *IntMPA 92, IntWW 91, WhoEnt 92*
**Ford**, Harrison B. 1928- *WhoWest 92*
**Ford**, Henry *DcAmImH*
**Ford**, Henry 1863-1947 *DcTwDes, FacFETw [port], RComAH*
**Ford**, Henry, II 1917- *FacFETw*
**Ford**, Herbert 1927- *WrDr 92*
**Ford**, Herbert Paul 1927- *IntAu&W 91*
**Ford**, Hilary *WrDr 92*
**Ford**, Hilda Eileen 1924- *WhoBlA 92*
**Ford**, Holland Cole 1940- *AmMWSc 92*
**Ford**, Hugh 1913- *IntWW 91, Who 92*
**Ford**, J. Doug 1943- *WhoWest 92*
**Ford**, James 1927- *AmMWSc 92*
**Ford**, James Allan 1920- *IntAu&W 91, Who 92, WrDr 92*
**Ford**, James Arthur 1934- *AmMWSc 92*
**Ford**, James Carlton 1937- *WhoWest 92*
**Ford**, James David 1931- *WhoRel 92*
**Ford**, James Glyn 1950- *Who 92*
**Ford**, James L C, Jr 1933- *AmMWSc 92*
**Ford**, James Stephen 1943- *WhoFI 92*
**Ford**, James W. *WhoBlA 92*
**Ford**, James W. 1922- *WhoBlA 92*
**Ford**, Jane 1944- *TwCPaSc*
**Ford**, Jean *WhoAmP 91*
**Ford**, Jean Elizabeth 1923- *WhoMW 92*
**Ford**, Jesse Hill 1928- *BenetAL 91, ConNov 91, IntAu&W 91, WrDr 92*
**Ford**, Joan Elizabeth *DrAPF 91*
**Ford**, Joe M *WhoAmP 91*
**Ford**, Joe T 1937- *WhoAmP 91*
**Ford**, Joe Thomas 1937- *WhoFI 92, WhoMW 92*
**Ford**, John 1586?- *CnDBLB 1*
**Ford**, John 1586?-1639? *RfGEnL 91*
**Ford**, John 1895-1973 *BenetAL 91, FacFETw, IntDcF 2-2 [port]*
**Ford**, John Albert, Jr 1931- *AmMWSc 92*
**Ford**, John Anthony 1938- *Who 92*
**Ford**, John Archibald 1922- *IntWW 91, Who 92*
**Ford**, John Charles 1942- *WhoEnt 92, WhoFI 92*
**Ford**, John M *TwCSFW 91*
**Ford**, John Newton 1942- *WhoAmP 91, WhoBlA 92*
**Ford**, John Peter 1912- *Who 92*
**Ford**, John Philip 1930- *AmMWSc 92*
**Ford**, John Stephen 1957- *WhoFI 92*
**Ford**, John T., Jr. 1953- *WhoEnt 92, WhoWest 92*
**Ford**, Johnny L. 1942- *WhoBlA 92*
**Ford**, Johnny L, Sr 1942- *WhoAmP 91*
**Ford**, Johny Joe 1944- *AmMWSc 92*
**Ford**, Joseph 1914- *WhoAmL 92*
**Ford**, Joseph 1927- *AmMWSc 92*
**Ford**, Joseph Dillon 1952- *WhoEnt 92*
**Ford**, Joseph Francis 1912- *Who 92*
**Ford**, Judith Ann 1935- *WhoFI 92*
**Ford**, Judith Donna 1935- *WhoBlA 92*
**Ford**, Kathleen *DrAPF 91*
**Ford**, Kay Louise 1944- *WhoMW 92*
**Ford**, Keith John 1944- *WhoAmP 91*
**Ford**, Kenneth 1908- *WhoWest 92*
**Ford**, Kenneth A. 1949- *WhoBlA 92*
**Ford**, Kenneth William 1926- *AmMWSc 92*
**Ford**, Kirk *TwCWW 91, WrDr 92*
**Ford**, L. H. *WhoRel 92*
**Ford**, Laura 1961- *TwCPaSc*
**Ford**, Lawrence Howard 1948- *AmMWSc 92*
**Ford**, Lee Ellen 1917- *WhoAmL 92, WhoMW 92, WrDr 92*
**Ford**, Leslie *AmMWSc 92*
**Ford**, Lester Randolph, Jr 1927- *AmMWSc 92*
**Ford**, Lewis *TwCWW 91*
**Ford**, Lewis Stanley 1933- *WhoRel 92*
**Ford**, Lincoln Edmond 1938- *AmMWSc 92*
**Ford**, Loretta C 1920- *AmMWSc 92*
**Ford**, Louis H 1935- *WhoAmP 91*
**Ford**, Lucy Karen 1954- *WhoWest 92*
**Ford**, Luther L. 1931- *WhoBlA 92*
**Ford**, Lynette Rae 1945- *WhoAmP 91*
**Ford**, Marcella Woods *WhoBlA 92*
**Ford**, Marion George, Jr. 1937- *WhoBlA 92*
**Ford**, Mark Patrick 1956- *WhoMW 92*
**Ford**, Mark Timothy 1956- *WhoEnt 92*
**Ford**, Mark William 1966- *WhoMW 92*
**Ford**, Marlene Lynch 1954- *WhoAmP 91*
**Ford**, Mary Alice 1935- *WhoAmP 91*
**Ford**, Michael Edward 1948- *AmMWSc 92*
**Ford**, Michael P. 1953- *WhoMW 92*
**Ford**, Michael Q. 1949- *WhoWest 92*
**Ford**, Miller Clell, Jr 1929- *AmMWSc 92*
**Ford**, Nancy Howard 1942- *WhoBlA 92*
**Ford**, Nancy Louise 1935- *WhoEnt 92*
**Ford**, Nancy M *WhoAmP 91*
**Ford**, Neville Finch 1934- *AmMWSc 92*
**Ford**, Norman Cornell, Jr 1932- *AmMWSc 92*
**Ford**, Norman Lee 1934- *AmMWSc 92*
**Ford**, Patrick 1837-1913 *DcAmImH*
**Ford**, Patrick Kelley 1949- *WhoEnt 92*
**Ford**, Patrick Lang 1927- *AmMWSc 92*
**Ford**, Paul Leicester 1865-1902 *BenetAL 91*
**Ford**, Peter *Who 92*
**Ford**, Peter 1930- *Who 92*
**Ford**, Peter 1936- *IntAu&W 91*
**Ford**, Peter 1937- *TwCPaSc*
**Ford**, Peter Campbell 1941- *AmMWSc 92*
**Ford**, Peter George Tipping 1931- *Who 92*
**Ford**, Philip Jackson, Jr 1956- *BlkOlyM*
**Ford**, Pronty L. 1921- *WhoBlA 92*
**Ford**, R. A. D. 1915- *ConPo 91, WrDr 92*
**Ford**, Ralph Eugene 1963- *WhoEnt 92*
**Ford**, Raymond Eustace 1898- *Who 92*
**Ford**, Richard *DrAPF 91*
**Ford**, Richard 1944- *BenetAL 91, ConNov 91, IntWW 91, WrDr 92*
**Ford**, Richard Brinsley 1908- *Who 92*
**Ford**, Richard D. 1935- *WhoBlA 92*
**Ford**, Richard Earl 1933- *AmMWSc 92*
**Ford**, Richard Edmond 1927- *WhoAmL 92*
**Ford**, Richard Fiske 1934- *AmMWSc 92*
**Ford**, Richard Westaway 1930- *AmMWSc 92*
**Ford**, Robert 1923- *Who 92*
**Ford**, Robert 1948- *WhoBlA 92*
**Ford**, Robert Alan 1950- *WhoEnt 92*
**Ford**, Robert Arthur Douglass 1915- *IntWW 91*
**Ford**, Robert Benjamin, Jr. 1935- *WhoBlA 92*
**Ford**, Robert Blackman 1924- *WhoBlA 92*
**Ford**, Robert David 1956- *WhoAmL 92*
**Ford**, Robert Sedgwick 1916- *AmMWSc 92*
**Ford**, Robert Stanley 1929- *Who 92*
**Ford**, Robert Webster 1923- *Who 92*
**Ford**, Roger Julian, Sr. 1934- *WhoRel 92*
**Ford**, Roy Arthur 1925- *Who 92*
**Ford**, Ruth *WhoEnt 92*
**Ford**, Sarah Ann 1951- *WhoBlA 92*
**Ford**, Sarah Litsey 1901- *IntAu&W 91*
**Ford**, Seabury Hurd 1902- *WhoAmL 92*
**Ford**, Sewell 1868-1946 *BenetAL 91*
**Ford**, Stephen Paul 1948- *AmMWSc 92*
**Ford**, Susan Heim 1943- *AmMWSc 92*
**Ford**, Tennessee Ernie d1991 *LesBEnT 92*
**Ford**, Tennessee Ernie 1919- *IntMPA 92*
**Ford**, Tennessee Ernie 1919-1991 *NewYTBS 91 [port], News 92-2*
**Ford**, Terry Everett 1956- *WhoFI 92*
**Ford**, Thomas 1580?-1648 *NewAmDM*
**Ford**, Thomas Aven 1917- *AmMWSc 92*
**Ford**, Thomas Jeffers 1930- *WhoFI 92*
**Ford**, Thomas Matthews 1931- *AmMWSc 92*
**Ford**, Thomas Patrick, Jr. 1944- *WhoAmL 92*
**Ford**, Timothy Alan 1951- *WhoAmP 91*
**Ford**, Tony 1925- *IntMPA 92*
**Ford**, Vernon N. 1945- *WhoBlA 92*
**Ford**, Victoria 1946- *WhoWest 92*
**Ford**, Virginia 1914- *WhoBlA 92*
**Ford**, Wallace *TwCWW 91*
**Ford**, Wallace L., II 1950- *WhoBlA 92*
**Ford**, Wallace Roy 1937- *WhoRel 92*
**Ford**, Warren Thomas 1942- *AmMWSc 92*
**Ford**, Wayne 1931- *AmMWSc 92*
**Ford**, Wayne Keith 1953- *AmMWSc 92*
**Ford**, Webster *ConAu 133*
**Ford**, Wendell H. 1924- *AlmAP 92 [port], WhoAmP 91*
**Ford**, Wendell Hampton 1924- *IntWW 91*
**Ford**, Wilbur Leonard, Jr 1937- *WhoAmP 91*
**Ford**, Wilfred Franklin 1920- *Who 92*
**Ford**, William *DrAPF 91*
**Ford**, William Clay 1925- *IntWW 91, WhoMW 92*
**Ford**, William D. 1927- *AlmAP 92 [port]*
**Ford**, William David 1927- *WhoAmP 91, WhoMW 92*
**Ford**, William Ellsworth 1950- *AmMWSc 92*
**Ford**, William F. 1936- *WhoWest 92*
**Ford**, William Francis 1925- *WhoFI 92*
**Ford**, William Frank 1934- *AmMWSc 92*
**Ford**, William Kent, Jr 1931- *AmMWSc 92*
**Ford**, William L., Jr. 1941- *WhoBlA 92*
**Ford**, William Patric 1955- *WhoRel 92*
**Ford**, William R. 1933- *WhoBlA 92*
**Ford-Choyke**, Phyllis *DrAPF 91*
**Ford Davies**, Oliver *ConTFT 9*
**Ford-Hutchinson**, Anthony W 1947- *AmMWSc 92*
**Ford-Robertson**, Francis Calder 1901- *Who 92*
**Ford-Robertson**, Julian 1935- *IntAu&W 91*
**Forde**, Christopher Theophilus 1907- *WhoBlA 92*
**Forde**, Fraser Philip, Jr. 1943- *WhoBlA 92*
**Forde**, George Stephen, Jr. 1934- *WhoAmL 92*
**Forde**, Harold McDonald 1916- *Who 92*
**Forde**, Henry deBoulay 1933- *IntWW 91*
**Forde**, James Albert 1927- *WhoBlA 92*
**Forde-Johnston**, James 1927- *WrDr 92*
**Fordemwalt**, James Newton 1932- *AmMWSc 92, WhoWest 92*
**Forder**, Anthony 1925- *WrDr 92*
**Forder**, Charles Robert 1907- *Who 92, WrDr 92*
**Forder**, Kenneth John 1925- *Who 92*
**Fordham**, Christopher Columbus, III 1926- *AmMWSc 92*
**Fordham**, James Lynn 1924- *AmMWSc 92*
**Fordham**, John Jeremy 1933- *Who 92*
**Fordham**, Joseph Raymond 1937- *AmMWSc 92*
**Fordham**, Laurence Sherman 1929- *WhoAmL 92*
**Fordham**, Monroe 1939- *WhoBlA 92*
**Fordham**, Paul T 1917- *WhoAmP 91*
**Fordham**, William David 1939- *AmMWSc 92*
**Fordham**, Willmon Albert 1926- *WhoRel 92*
**Fordice**, Daniel Kirkwood, Jr. 1934- *WhoFI 92*
**Fordice**, Kirk 1934- *NewYTBS 91*
**Fordon**, Wilfred Aaron 1927- *AmMWSc 92*
**Fordyce**, David Buchanan 1924- *AmMWSc 92*
**Fordyce**, Edward Winfield, Jr. 1941- *WhoAmL 92*
**Fordyce**, James Stuart 1931- *AmMWSc 92*
**Fordyce**, Wayne Edgar *AmMWSc 92*
**Foreback**, Craig Carl 1946- *WhoMW 92*
**Foree**, Edward G 1941- *AmMWSc 92*
**Foree**, Jack Clifford 1935- *WhoBlA 92*
**Foregger**, Nikolay Mikhaylovich 1892-1939 *SovUnBD*
**Foregger**, Thomas H 1946- *AmMWSc 92*
**Forehand**, Jennie Meador 1935- *WhoAmP 91*
**Forehand**, Robert Jackson 1951- *WhoRel 92*
**Forehand**, Vernon Thomas, Jr 1947- *WhoAmP 91*
**Forehand**, Winfred Brian 1945- *WhoAmP 91*
**Foreht**, Stephen R. 1959- *WhoEnt 92*
**Forell**, George Wolfgang 1919- *WhoRel 92*
**Forella**, June B 1927- *WhoAmP 91*
**Forelle**, Helen 1936- *IntAu&W 91*
**Forelli**, Frank John 1932- *AmMWSc 92*
**Foreman**, Bruce Milburn, Jr 1932- *AmMWSc 92*
**Foreman**, Calvin 1910- *AmMWSc 92*
**Foreman**, Carl 1914-1984 *FacFETw*
**Foreman**, Charles Frederick 1920- *AmMWSc 92*

**Foreman,** Charles William 1923- *AmMWSc 92*
**Foreman,** Christopher H. 1925- *WhoBlA 92*
**Foreman,** Darhl Lois 1924- *AmMWSc 92*
**Foreman,** Dennis Walden, Jr 1929- *AmMWSc 92*
**Foreman,** Diana 1949- *WhoRel 92*
**Foreman,** Doyle 1933- *WhoBlA 92*
**Foreman,** Edward Rawson 1939- *WhoAmL 92*
**Foreman,** Edwin Francis 1931- *WhoFI 92*
**Foreman,** Fred 1948- *WhoAmL 92, WhoMW 92*
**Foreman,** George 1949- *BlkOlyM, ConBlB 1 [port], FacFETw, NewYTBS 91 [port]*
**Foreman,** George Edward 1949- *WhoBlA 92*
**Foreman,** Harold W 1938- *WhoAmP 91*
**Foreman,** Harry 1915- *AmMWSc 92, WhoMW 92*
**Foreman,** James Louis 1927- *WhoAmL 92, WhoMW 92*
**Foreman,** Jeff 1951- *WhoAmP 91*
**Foreman,** Joe Cornelius, Jr. 1943- *WhoBlA 92*
**Foreman,** John *IntMPA 92*
**Foreman,** John Charles 1951- *WhoFI 92*
**Foreman,** John Daniel 1940- *WhoFI 92*
**Foreman,** John E K 1922- *AmMWSc 92*
**Foreman,** John Frederick 1947- *WhoAmL 92*
**Foreman,** Joyce B. 1948- *WhoBlA 92*
**Foreman,** Kenneth M 1925- *AmMWSc 92*
**Foreman,** Kim Hyun-Deok 1951- *WhoWest 92*
**Foreman,** L.L. 1901- *TwCWW 91*
**Foreman,** Laura *WhoEnt 92*
**Foreman,** Lee *TwCWW 91*
**Foreman,** Lee David 1946- *WhoAmL 92*
**Foreman,** Leland Don 1943- *WhoRel 92*
**Foreman,** Lucille Elizabeth 1923- *WhoBlA 92*
**Foreman,** Margaret 1951- *TwCPaSc*
**Foreman,** Matthew D 1957- *AmMWSc 92*
**Foreman,** Michael 1938- *IntAu&W 91, Who 92, WrDr 92*
**Foreman,** Michael Loren 1944- *WhoAmL 92*
**Foreman,** Michael Marcellus 1941- *WhoAmP 91*
**Foreman,** Milton Edward, Jr. 1932- *WhoMW 92*
**Foreman,** Paul *DrAPF 91*
**Foreman,** Percy 1902-1988 *FacFETw*
**Foreman,** Philip 1923- *Who 92*
**Foreman,** Richard 1937- *WhoEnt 92, WrDr 92*
**Foreman,** Robert Dale 1946- *AmMWSc 92*
**Foreman,** Robert Walter 1923- *AmMWSc 92*
**Foreman,** Ronald Eugene 1938- *AmMWSc 92*
**Foreman,** Ronald Louis 1937- *AmMWSc 92*
**Foreman,** S. Beatrice 1917- *WhoBlA 92*
**Foreman,** Terry Hancock 1943- *WhoRel 92*
**Foreman,** William 1939- *TwCPaSc*
**Foreman,** William Edwin 1929- *AmMWSc 92*
**Foremaster,** Errol J 1954- *WhoEnt 92*
**Forenti,** John Henry 1946- *WhoWest 92*
**Forenza,** Salvatore 1946- *AmMWSc 92*
**Forer,** Anne *DrAPF 91*
**Forer,** Arthur H 1935- *AmMWSc 92*
**Forer,** Morris Leon 1912- *WhoAmL 92*
**Forero,** Enrique 1942- *AmMWSc 92*
**Forero De Saade,** Maria Teresa 1939- *IntWW 91*
**Forese,** James John 1935- *WhoFI 92*
**Foresman,** James Buckey 1935- *WhoMW 92*
**Foresman,** Kerry Ryan 1948- *AmMWSc 92*
**Forest,** Antonia *WrDr 92*
**Forest,** Charlene Lynn 1947- *AmMWSc 92*
**Forest,** Edward 1933- *AmMWSc 92*
**Forest,** Eva Brown 1941- *WhoWest 92*
**Forest,** Frank John 1947- *WhoEnt 92*
**Forest,** Herman Silva 1921- *AmMWSc 92*
**Forest,** James Hendrickson 1941- *AmPeW*
**Forest,** Philip Earle 1931- *WhoFI 92*
**Forestell,** James Terence 1925- *WhoRel 92*
**Forester** *Who 92*
**Forester,** Baron 1938- *Who 92*
**Forester,** C S 1899-1966 *FacFETw, RfGEnL 91*
**Forester,** Donald Charles 1943- *AmMWSc 92*
**Forester,** Donald Wayne 1937- *AmMWSc 92*
**Forester,** Frank *BenetAL 91*
**Forester,** Karl S. 1940- *WhoAmL 92*
**Forester,** Larry Wayne 1951- *WhoRel 92*
**Forester,** Ralph H 1928- *AmMWSc 92*
**Forester,** Richard Monroe 1947- *AmMWSc 92*
**Foresti,** Roy J, Jr 1925- *AmMWSc 92*
**Forestier,** Danielle 1943- *WhoWest 92*
**Forestier-Walker,** Michael 1949- *Who 92*
**Forestieri,** Americo F 1929- *AmMWSc 92*
**Foret,** James A 1921- *AmMWSc 92*
**Foret,** John Emil 1937- *AmMWSc 92*
**Foret,** Mickey Phillip 1945- *WhoFI 92*
**Forey,** Martin Rudolph 1817-1881 *DcNCBi 2*
**Forfar,** John Oldroyd 1916- *Who 92*
**Forgac,** John Michael 1949- *AmMWSc 92*
**Forgacs,** Gabor 1949- *AmMWSc 92*
**Forgacs,** Joseph 1917- *AmMWSc 92*
**Forgacs,** Otto Lionel 1931- *AmMWSc 92*
**Forgan,** Elizabeth Anne Lucy 1944- *Who 92*
**Forgash,** Andrew John 1923- *AmMWSc 92*
**Forge,** Andrew 1923- *TwCPaSc*
**Forge,** Andrew Murray 1923- *Who 92*
**Forge,** Helen Cecilia 1923- *WhoMW 92*
**Forge,** Thomas Roger 1963- *WhoMW 92*
**Forgeng,** W D 1909- *AmMWSc 92*
**Forgeot,** Jean 1915- *IntWW 91*
**Forger,** Alexander Darrow 1923- *WhoAmL 92*
**Forges Davanzati,** Roberto 1880-1936 *BiDExR*
**Forget,** Bernard G 1939- *AmMWSc 92*
**Forgey,** Tom 1939- *WhoAmP 91*
**Forghani,** Bagher 1936- *WhoWest 92*
**Forghani-Abkenari,** Bagher 1936- *AmMWSc 92*
**Forgione,** Louis J 1930- *WhoIns 92*
**Forgotson,** Florence Frances 1908- *WhoAmL 92*
**Forgotson,** James Morris, Jr 1930- *AmMWSc 92*
**Forgues,** Jorge Raul 1955- *WhoFI 92*
**Forgus,** Ronald Henry 1928- *WhoMW 92*
**Forgy,** Charles Lanny 1949- *AmMWSc 92*
**Forgy,** Lawrence *WhoAmP 91*
**Forgy,** Lawrence E., Jr. 1939- *WhoAmL 92*
**Forist,** Arlington Ardeane 1922- *AmMWSc 92*
**Fork,** David Charles 1929- *AmMWSc 92*
**Fork,** Richard Lynn 1935- *AmMWSc 92*
**Forker,** David 1937- *WhoIns 92*
**Forker,** E Lee 1930- *AmMWSc 92*
**Forkert,** Clifford Arthur 1916- *WhoWest 92*
**Forkey,** David Medrick 1940- *AmMWSc 92*
**Forkin,** Thomas S. 1937- *WhoAmL 92*
**Forland,** Marvin 1933- *AmMWSc 92*
**Forlani,** Arnaldo 1925- *IntWW 91*
**Forlano,** Frederick Peter 1947- *WhoAmL 92*
**Forlines,** Franklin Leroy 1926- *WhoRel 92*
**Forlini,** Frank John, Jr. 1941- *WhoMW 92*
**Formal,** Samuel Bernard 1923- *AmMWSc 92*
**Forman,** Beth Rosalyne 1949- *WhoMW 92*
**Forman,** Bryan Torrey 1962- *WhoAmL 92*
**Forman,** Charles William 1916- *WhoRel 92, WrDr 92*
**Forman,** David Avrum 1942- *WhoAmL 92*
**Forman,** David S 1942- *AmMWSc 92*
**Forman,** David Sholem 1942- *WhoAmL 92*
**Forman,** Debra L 1957- *AmMWSc 92*
**Forman,** Denis 1917- *IntMPA 92, Who 92*
**Forman,** Donald T 1932- *AmMWSc 92*
**Forman,** Earl Julian 1929- *AmMWSc 92*
**Forman,** Francis Nigel 1943- *Who 92*
**Forman,** G Lawrence 1942- *AmMWSc 92*
**Forman,** George Lawrence 1942- *WhoMW 92*
**Forman,** George W 1919- *AmMWSc 92*
**Forman,** Graham Neil 1930- *Who 92*
**Forman,** Guy 1906- *AmMWSc 92*
**Forman,** H. Chandlee d1991 *NewYTBS 91*
**Forman,** Henry Jay 1947- *WhoWest 92*
**Forman,** Howard C 1946- *WhoAmP 91*
**Forman,** Howard I 1917- *WhoAmP 91*
**Forman,** J Charles 1931- *AmMWSc 92*
**Forman,** James 1939- *AmMWSc 92*
**Forman,** James Ross, III 1947- *WhoAmL 92*
**Forman,** Jeanne Leach 1916- *WhoEnt 92*
**Forman,** Jerome A. *IntMPA 92*
**Forman,** Joan *IntAu&W 91, WrDr 92*
**Forman,** John Denis *Who 92*
**Forman,** John Denis 1917- *IntWW 91*
**Forman,** Joshua 1777-1848 *DcNCBi 2*
**Forman,** Linda Helaine 1943- *WhoMW 92*
**Forman,** Mark Leonard 1949- *WhoEnt 92*
**Forman,** McLain J 1928- *AmMWSc 92*
**Forman,** Michael Bertram 1921- *Who 92*
**Forman,** Michele R 1950- *AmMWSc 92*
**Forman,** Milos 1932- *FacFETw, IntDcF 2-2, IntMPA 92, IntWW 91, Who 92, WhoEnt 92*
**Forman,** Miriam Ausman 1939- *AmMWSc 92*
**Forman,** Nessa Ruth 1943- *WhoEnt 92*
**Forman,** Nigel *Who 92*
**Forman,** Paul 1937- *AmMWSc 92*
**Forman,** Paula *WhoFI 92*
**Forman,** Peter Vandyne 1958- *WhoAmP 91*
**Forman,** Ralph 1921- *AmMWSc 92*
**Forman,** Richard Allan 1939- *AmMWSc 92*
**Forman,** Richard T T 1935- *AmMWSc 92*
**Forman,** Richard Thomas 1935- *WhoFI 92, WhoWest 92*
**Forman,** Roy 1931- *Who 92*
**Forman,** Sheila Hedda 1960- *WhoAmL 92*
**Forman,** Tom 1936- *WhoEnt 92*
**Forman,** Weldon Warren 1927- *WhoRel 92*
**Forman,** William 1914- *AmMWSc 92*
**Forman,** William Harper, Jr. 1936- *WhoAmL 92*
**Formanek,** Edward William 1942- *AmMWSc 92*
**Formanek,** Luella Helen 1924- *WhoMW 92*
**Formanek,** R J 1922- *AmMWSc 92*
**Formanowicz,** Daniel Robert, Jr 1954- *AmMWSc 92*
**Formartine,** Viscount 1983- *Who 92*
**Formby,** Bent Clark 1940- *WhoWest 92*
**Formby,** Jim Earn 1920- *WhoAmP 91*
**Formby,** John Paul 1940- *WhoFI 92*
**Formby,** Myles Landseer 1901- *Who 92*
**Formeister,** Richard B 1946- *AmMWSc 92*
**Formeller,** Daniel Richard 1949- *WhoAmL 92*
**Formento,** Daniel 1954- *WhoEnt 92*
**Former Resident of the Hub,** A *ScFEYrs*
**Formey,** Jean-Henri-Samuel 1711-1797 *BlkwCEP*
**Formhals,** Danny Lee 1966- *WhoRel 92*
**Formica,** Gianni 1922- *IntWW 91*
**Formica,** Joseph Victor 1929- *AmMWSc 92*
**Formica,** Salvatore 1927- *IntWW 91*
**Formichelli,** Anthony 1949- *WhoEnt 92*
**Formigoni,** Roberto 1947- *IntWW 91*
**Formston,** Clifford 1907- *Who 92*
**Formwalt,** William Alexander 1951- *WhoWest 92*
**Fornace,** Albert J, Jr 1949- *AmMWSc 92*
**Fornaciari,** Gilbert Martin 1946- *WhoMW 92*
**Fornaess,** John Erik 1946- *AmMWSc 92*
**Fornara,** Charles William 1935- *WrDr 92*
**Fornasetti,** Piero 1913-1988 *DcTwDes*
**Fornatto,** Elio Joseph 1928- *WhoMW 92*
**Fornay,** Alfred R., Jr. *WhoBlA 92*
**Fornberg,** Bengt 1946- *AmMWSc 92*
**Fornefeld,** Eugene Joseph 1920- *AmMWSc 92*
**Forner,** Elmira *WhoAmP 91*
**Fornes,** Maria Irene 1930- *LiExTwC, WhoHisp 92, WrDr 92*
**Fornes,** Raymond Earl 1943- *AmMWSc 92*
**Forney,** Albert J 1915- *AmMWSc 92*
**Forney,** Bill E 1921- *AmMWSc 92*
**Forney,** Daniel Munroe 1784-1847 *DcNCBi 2*
**Forney,** G David, Jr 1940- *AmMWSc 92*
**Forney,** J F *WhoAmP 91*
**Forney,** John Horace 1829-1902 *DcNCBi 2*
**Forney,** Larry J 1944- *AmMWSc 92*
**Forney,** Mary Jane 1949- *WhoBlA 92*
**Forney,** Peter 1756-1834 *DcNCBi 2*
**Forney,** R C 1927- *AmMWSc 92*
**Forney,** Robert Burns 1916- *AmMWSc 92*
**Forney,** Robert Clyde 1927- *WhoFI 92*
**Forney,** William Henry 1823-1894 *DcNCBi 2*
**Fornoff,** Frank, Jr. 1914- *WhoFI 92*
**Fornshell,** Dave Lee 1937- *WhoMW 92*
**Foroulis,** Z Andrew 1926- *AmMWSc 92*
**Forquer,** Sandra Lynne 1943- *AmMWSc 92*
**Forray,** Marvin Julian 1922- *AmMWSc 92*
**Forren,** Johnnie Ray 1954- *WhoWest 92*
**Forrer,** Max P 1925- *AmMWSc 92*
**Forres,** Baron 1946- *Who 92*
**Forrest,** Allen *TwCWW 91*
**Forrest,** Alvane M. 1916- *WhoBlA 92*
**Forrest,** Andrew Patrick 1923- *Who 92*
**Forrest,** Arthur *LesBEnT 92*
**Forrest,** Aston *ScFEYrs*
**Forrest,** Bruce James 1950- *AmMWSc 92*
**Forrest,** David *WrDr 92*
**Forrest,** Edgar H 1916- *WhoAmP 91*
**Forrest,** Edgar Hull 1916- *WhoRel 92*
**Forrest,** Edwin 1806-1872 *BenetAL 91*
**Forrest,** Frederic *WhoEnt 92*
**Forrest,** Frederic 1936- *IntMPA 92*
**Forrest,** Geoffrey 1909- *Who 92*
**Forrest,** Geoffrey Cornish 1898- *Who 92*
**Forrest,** Herbert Emerson 1923- *WhoAmL 92, WhoFI 92*
**Forrest,** Hugh Sommerville 1924- *AmMWSc 92*
**Forrest,** Irene Stephanie 1908- *AmMWSc 92*
**Forrest,** James 1905- *Who 92*
**Forrest,** James Alexander 1905- *IntWW 91*
**Forrest,** James Benjamin 1935- *AmMWSc 92*
**Forrest,** John Charles 1936- *AmMWSc 92*
**Forrest,** John Richard 1943- *Who 92*
**Forrest,** John Samuel 1907- *IntWW 91, Who 92*
**Forrest,** Joseph Michael 1946- *WhoMW 92*
**Forrest,** Katherine V. 1939- *WrDr 92*
**Forrest,** Kenton Harvey 1944- *WhoWest 92*
**Forrest,** Leon 1937- *ConNov 91, IntAu&W 91, WrDr 92*
**Forrest,** Leon Richard 1937- *WhoBlA 92*
**Forrest,** Lou 1943- *WhoEnt 92*
**Forrest,** Melba June 1931- *WhoMW 92*
**Forrest,** Norman John 1898- *TwCPaSc*
**Forrest,** Patrick *Who 92*
**Forrest,** Richard 1932- *WrDr 92*
**Forrest,** Richard Michael 1954- *WhoAmL 92*
**Forrest,** Richard Stockton 1932- *IntAu&W 91*
**Forrest,** Robert Neagle 1925- *AmMWSc 92*
**Forrest,** Ronald 1923- *Who 92*
**Forrest,** Ronnie Reed 1951- *WhoRel 92*
**Forrest,** Sidney 1918- *WhoEnt 92*
**Forrest,** Steve 1925- *IntMPA 92*
**Forrest,** Suzanne Sims 1926- *WhoWest 92*
**Forrest,** Thomas *BenetAL 91*
**Forrest,** Thomas Douglas 1933- *AmMWSc 92*
**Forrest,** William George Grieve 1925- *Who 92, WrDr 92*
**Forrest,** William Ivon Norman 1914- *Who 92*
**Forrest-Carter,** Audrey Faye 1956- *WhoBlA 92*
**Forrestal,** James V 1892-1949 *FacFETw*
**Forrestal,** James Vincent 1892-1949 *AmPolLe*
**Forrester,** Alan McKay 1940- *WhoMW 92*
**Forrester,** Alvin Theodore 1918- *AmMWSc 92*
**Forrester,** David Michael 1944- *Who 92*
**Forrester,** Donald Jason 1937- *AmMWSc 92*
**Forrester,** Duncan Baillie 1933- *Who 92*
**Forrester,** Eugene Priest 1926- *WhoFI 92*
**Forrester,** Gary 1946- *WhoAmP 91*
**Forrester,** Giles Charles Fielding 1939- *Who 92*
**Forrester,** Helen *IntAu&W 91X, WrDr 92*
**Forrester,** Helen 1919- *IntAu&W 91*
**Forrester,** Ian Stewart 1945- *Who 92*
**Forrester,** J. Owen 1939- *WhoAmL 92*
**Forrester,** James *WhoAmP 91*
**Forrester,** Jay W 1918- *AmMWSc 92*
**Forrester,** Jay Wright 1918- *WhoFI 92*
**Forrester,** Joe D. 1946- *WhoWest 92*
**Forrester,** John Paul 1953- *WhoAmL 92*
**Forrester,** John Stuart 1924- *Who 92*
**Forrester,** Maureen 1930- *FacFETw, NewAmDM*
**Forrester,** Michael 1917- *Who 92*
**Forrester,** Michael Lee 1959- *WhoAmL 92*
**Forrester,** Peter Garnett 1917- *Who 92*
**Forrester,** Rex 1928- *WrDr 92*
**Forrester,** Robin 1937- *TwCPaSc*
**Forrester,** Rosemary Wellington 1953- *WhoMW 92*
**Forrester,** Sherri Rhoda 1936- *AmMWSc 92*
**Forrester,** Warren David 1925- *AmMWSc 92*
**Forrester,** William Donald 1931- *WhoFI 92*
**Forrester,** William Ray 1911- *WrDr 92*
**Forrester-Paton,** Douglas Shaw 1921- *Who 92*
**Forrette,** John Elmer 1922- *AmMWSc 92*
**Forrey,** Arden W 1932- *AmMWSc 92*
**Forro,** Frederick, Jr 1924- *AmMWSc 92*
**Forrow,** Brian Derek 1927- *WhoAmL 92, WhoFI 92*
**Fors,** Elton W 1934- *AmMWSc 92*
**Forsbach,** Jack Alan 1932- *WhoAmL 92, WhoEnt 92, WhoFI 92, WhoWest 92*
**Forsberg,** Carl Earl 1920- *WhoEnt 92*
**Forsberg,** Cecil Wallace 1942- *AmMWSc 92*
**Forsberg,** Charles Alton 1944- *WhoWest 92*
**Forsberg,** Dennis Patrick 1942- *WhoMW 92*
**Forsberg,** Franklin S *WhoAmP 91*
**Forsberg,** Gerald 1912- *Who 92, WrDr 92*
**Forsberg,** Jim d1991 *NewYTBS 91*
**Forsberg,** John Herbert 1942- *AmMWSc 92*
**Forsberg,** Kevin 1934- *AmMWSc 92*
**Forsberg,** Kevin John 1934- *WhoWest 92*
**Forsberg,** Mark *WhoRel 92*
**Forsberg,** Robert Arnold 1930- *AmMWSc 92*
**Forsberg,** Terry George 1940- *WhoEnt 92*
**Forsblad,** Ingemar Bjorn 1927- *AmMWSc 92*
**Forscher,** Bernard Kronman 1927- *AmMWSc 92*
**Forscher,** Frederick 1918- *AmMWSc 92*

**Forsdyke,** Donald Roy 1938- *AmMWSc 92*
**Forsee,** William Anthony 1948- *WhoMW 92*
**Forsen,** Harold K 1932- *AmMWSc 92*
**Forsen,** K. Sture 1932- *IntWW 91*
**Forseth,** Roger Daniels 1927- *WhoMW 92*
**Forseth,** Scott Lawrence 1962- *WhoAmL 92*
**Forsey,** Eugene A. d1991 *NewYTBS 91*
**Forsh,** Ol'ga Dmitrievna 1873-1961 *SovUnBD*
**Forsham,** Peter Hugh 1915- *AmMWSc 92*
**Forshaw,** Peter 1936- *Who 92*
**Forshay-Lunsford,** Cin 1965- *IntAu&W 91*
**Forshey,** Caleb Goldsmith 1812-1881 *BiInAmS*
**Forshey,** Chester Gene 1925- *AmMWSc 92*
**Forshey,** J. Patrick 1959- *WhoWest 92*
**Forsiak,** Walter William 1935- *WhoEnt 92, WhoWest 92*
**Forslund,** David Wallace 1944- *AmMWSc 92*
**Forslund,** Thomas Odell 1951- *WhoWest 92*
**Forsman,** Alpheus Edwin 1941- *WhoAmL 92*
**Forsman,** Avis Clapper 1931- *WhoAmL 92*
**Forsman,** Chuck 1944- *WhoWest 92*
**Forsman,** Earl N 1936- *AmMWSc 92*
**Forsman,** M E 1912- *AmMWSc 92*
**Forsman,** William C 1929- *AmMWSc 92*
**Forssander,** Paul Richard 1944- *WhoFI 92, WhoWest 92*
**Forssen,** Eric Anton 1951- *AmMWSc 92*
**Forssmann,** Werner Theodor Otto 1904-1979 *FacFETw, WhoNob 90*
**Forsstrom,** Per Gustaf 1950- *WhoEnt 92*
**Forst,** Edmund Charles, Jr. 1961- *WhoMW 92*
**Forst,** John Kelly 1960- *WhoMW 92*
**Forst,** Judith Doris 1943- *WhoEnt 92*
**Forst,** Marion Francis 1910- *WhoRel 92*
**Forst,** Wendell 1926- *AmMWSc 92*
**Forst,** Willi 1903-1980 *EncTR 91 [port]*
**Forstadt,** Joseph Lawrence 1940- *WhoAmL 92*
**Forstall,** Kweku Dwayne 1960- *WhoBlA 92*
**Forstall,** Terrence Christopher 1945- *WhoAmL 92*
**Forstall,** Walton, Jr 1909- *AmMWSc 92*
**Forstater,** Mark 1943- *IntMPA 92*
**Forstchen,** William R *TwCSFW 91, WrDr 92*
**Forste,** Norman Lee 1935- *WhoFI 92, WhoWest 92*
**Forster,** Albert 1902-1948 *EncTR 91 [port]*
**Forster,** Albert 1902-1954? *BiDExR*
**Forster,** Andrew *TwCPaSc*
**Forster,** Anthony 1785-1820 *DcNCBi 2*
**Forster,** Archibald 1928- *Who 92*
**Forster,** Bruce Alexander 1948- *WhoFI 92*
**Forster,** Cecil R. 1911- *WhoBlA 92*
**Forster,** Cecil R., Jr. 1943- *WhoBlA 92*
**Forster,** Charles Ian Kennerley 1911- *Who 92*
**Forster,** Clifford 1913- *WhoAmL 92*
**Forster,** Cornelius Philip 1919- *WhoRel 92*
**Forster,** D Lynn 1946- *AmMWSc 92*
**Forster,** Denis 1941- *AmMWSc 92*
**Forster,** Dianna Ruth 1937- *WhoAmP 91*
**Forster,** Donald 1920- *Who 92*
**Forster,** Donald Murray 1929- *Who 92*
**Forster,** E. M. 1879-1970 *CnDBLB 6 [port], FacFETw, RfGEnL 91, ScFEYrs*
**Forster,** Eric Brown 1917- *Who 92*
**Forster,** Eric Otto 1918- *AmMWSc 92*
**Forster,** Francis Michael 1912- *AmMWSc 92*
**Forster,** Fred Kurt 1944- *AmMWSc 92*
**Forster,** Friedrich 1895-1958 *EncTR 91*
**Forster,** Garey James 1950- *WhoAmP 91*
**Forster,** Garth Andrew 1955- *WhoRel 92*
**Forster,** Harriet Herta *AmMWSc 92*
**Forster,** Homer W. 1944- *WhoFI 92*
**Forster,** Hubert Vincent *AmMWSc 92*
**Forster,** James Francis 1956- *WhoAmL 92*
**Forster,** Julian 1918- *AmMWSc 92*
**Forster,** Kurt 1915- *AmMWSc 92*
**Forster,** Leonard Wilson 1913- *Who 92*
**Forster,** Leslie Stewart 1924- *AmMWSc 92*
**Forster,** Margaret 1938- *ConAu 133, ConNov 91, IntAu&W 91, IntWW 91, Who 92, WrDr 92*
**Forster,** Michael Jay 1923- *AmMWSc 92*
**Forster,** Neil Milward 1927- *Who 92*
**Forster,** Noel 1932- *TwCPaSc*
**Forster,** Norvela 1931- *Who 92*
**Forster,** Oliver 1925- *Who 92*
**Forster,** Oliver Grantham 1925- *IntWW 91*
**Forster,** Peter Hans 1942- *WhoMW 92*
**Forster,** Raymond Robert 1922- *IntWW 91*
**Forster,** Robert 1941- *IntMPA 92*
**Forster,** Robert E, II 1919- *AmMWSc 92*
**Forster,** Roy Philip 1911- *AmMWSc 92*
**Forster,** Susan Joan 1962- *WhoFI 92*
**Forster,** Warren Schumann 1914- *AmMWSc 92*
**Forster,** William 1921- *Who 92*
**Forster,** William Owen 1927- *AmMWSc 92*
**Forsthoefel,** Paulinus Frederick 1915- *AmMWSc 92*
**Forsthoff,** Ernst 1902-1974 *EncTR 91*
**Forstman,** Henry Jackson 1929- *WhoRel 92*
**Forstner,** Janet Ferguson 1937- *AmMWSc 92*
**Forstrom,** June Rochelle 1932- *WhoWest 92*
**Forsyne,** Ida 1883- *NotBlAW 92*
**Forsyte,** Charles *Who 92*
**Forsyth,** Ben Ralph 1934- *AmMWSc 92, WhoFI 92, WhoWest 92*
**Forsyth,** Benjamin 1760?-1814 *DcNCBi 2*
**Forsyth,** Bill 1947- *IntDcF 2-2 [port], IntMPA 92, IntWW 91, Who 92*
**Forsyth,** Bruce *Who 92*
**Forsyth,** Dale Marvin 1945- *AmMWSc 92*
**Forsyth,** Douglas John 1946- *AmMWSc 92*
**Forsyth,** Elliott Christopher 1924- *IntWW 91*
**Forsyth,** Eric Boyland 1932- *AmMWSc 92*
**Forsyth,** Frank Russell 1922- *AmMWSc 92*
**Forsyth,** Frederick *IntWW 91*
**Forsyth,** Frederick 1938- *ConNov 91, IntAu&W 91, WrDr 92*
**Forsyth,** George H, Jr. d1991 *NewYTBS 91*
**Forsyth,** George H., Jr. 1901-1991 *ConAu 133*
**Forsyth,** Ilene Haering 1928- *WhoMW 92*
**Forsyth,** J S 1916- *AmMWSc 92*
**Forsyth,** James 1913- *WrDr 92*
**Forsyth,** James Lorin 1942- *WhoWest 92*
**Forsyth,** James M 1942- *AmMWSc 92*
**Forsyth,** Jane Louise 1921- *AmMWSc 92*
**Forsyth,** Jennifer Mary 1924- *Who 92*
**Forsyth,** Jessie 1847-1937 *HanAmWH*
**Forsyth,** John 1780-1841 *AmPolLe*
**Forsyth,** John Wiley 1913- *AmMWSc 92*
**Forsyth,** Karen 1953- *TwCPaSc*
**Forsyth,** Kerry Seneca 1954- *WhoWest 92*
**Forsyth,** Michael 1951- *ConAu 133*
**Forsyth,** Michael Bruce 1954- *Who 92*
**Forsyth,** Paul Francis 1928- *AmMWSc 92*
**Forsyth,** Peter Allan 1922- *AmMWSc 92*
**Forsyth,** Raymond Arthur 1928- *WhoWest 92*
**Forsyth,** Thomas Henry 1942- *AmMWSc 92*
**Forsyth,** William Douglass 1909- *Who 92*
**Forsyth-Johnson,** Bruce Joseph 1928- *Who 92*
**Forsyth of That Ilk,** Alistair Charles W. 1929- *Who 92*
**Forsythe,** Alan Barry 1940- *AmMWSc 92, WhoFI 92, WhoWest 92*
**Forsythe,** Charles Wayne 1949- *WhoRel 92*
**Forsythe,** Clifford 1929- *Who 92*
**Forsythe,** Dennis Martin 1942- *AmMWSc 92*
**Forsythe,** Douglass 1913- *WhoAmP 91*
**Forsythe,** Eric 1947- *WhoEnt 92*
**Forsythe,** Henderson 1917- *WhoEnt 92*
**Forsythe,** Howard Yost, Jr 1931- *AmMWSc 92*
**Forsythe,** James Roy 1920- *Who 92*
**Forsythe,** Janet W. 1957- *WhoAmL 92*
**Forsythe,** John 1918- *IntMPA 92, WhoEnt 92*
**Forsythe,** John Edward 1937- *WhoAmP 91*
**Forsythe,** Malcolm 1936- *Who 92*
**Forsythe,** Mary MacCornack 1920- *WhoAmP 91*
**Forsythe,** Paddy *Who 92*
**Forsythe,** Patricia Hays *WhoMW 92*
**Forsythe,** Randall D 1952- *AmMWSc 92*
**Forsythe,** Richard Hamilton *AmMWSc 92*
**Forsythe,** Robert Elliott 1949- *WhoFI 92, WhoMW 92*
**Forsythe,** Roger d1991 *NewYTBS 91*
**Forsythe,** William *IntMPA 92*
**Fort,** Charles *DrAPF 91*
**Fort,** Charles 1874-1932 *BenetAL 91, ScFEYrs*
**Fort,** Charles Hoy *ScFEYrs B*
**Fort,** Edward B. *WhoBlA 92*
**Fort,** Gerald Marshall 1919- *WhoMW 92*
**Fort,** James Tomlinson 1928- *WhoAmL 92*
**Fort,** Jane 1938- *WhoBlA 92*
**Fort,** Jean 1915- *Who 92*
**Fort,** John Franklin, III 1941- *WhoFI 92*
**Fort,** Lee Earthmon 1950- *WhoWest 92*
**Fort,** Lyman Rankin 1922- *WhoAmL 92*
**Fort,** Maeve Geraldine 1940- *Who 92*
**Fort,** Paul 1872-1960 *GuFrLit 1*
**Fort,** Raymond Cornelius, Jr 1938- *AmMWSc 92*
**Fort,** Robert Bradley 1948- *WhoRel 92*
**Fort,** Timothy Lyman 1958- *WhoMW 92*
**Fort,** Tomlinson, Jr 1932- *AmMWSc 92*
**Fort,** Wilkinson Davis 1926- *WhoAmP 91*
**Fort,** William H. 1915- *WhoBlA 92*
**Fort-Brescia,** Bernardo *WhoHisp 92*
**Fortado,** Michael George 1943- *WhoAmL 92*
**Fortas,** Abe 1910-1982 *FacFETw [port]*
**Forte** *Who 92*
**Forte,** Baron 1908- *IntWW 91, Who 92*
**Forte,** Chet *LesBEnT 92*
**Forte,** Dan 1953- *WhoEnt 92*
**Forte,** David Francis 1941- *WhoAmL 92*
**Forte,** Fabian 1943- *IntMPA 92*
**Forte,** Fabian Anthony 1943- *WhoEnt 92*
**Forte,** James Peter 1936- *WhoEnt 92*
**Forte,** John Gaetano 1934- *AmMWSc 92*
**Forte,** Johnie, Jr. 1936- *WhoBlA 92*
**Forte,** Joseph Michael 1954- *WhoAmL 92*
**Forte,** Joseph Peter 1944- *WhoMW 92*
**Forte,** Leonard Ralph 1941- *AmMWSc 92*
**Forte,** Michael B 1952- *WhoAmP 91*
**Forte,** Minnie T. 1916- *WhoBlA 92*
**Forte,** Rocco 1945- *IntWW 91, Who 92*
**Forte,** Wayne Francis 1950- *WhoEnt 92*
**Forte,** Wesley E 1933- *WhoIns 92*
**Forte,** Wesley Elbert 1933- *WhoAmL 92, WhoFI 92*
**Forten,** Charlotte 1837-1914 *PorAmW [port]*
**Forten,** Charlotte L. 1837?-1914 *BlkLC [port]*
**Forten,** Margaretta 1808-1875 *NotBlAW 92*
**Forten Grimke,** Charlotte L. 1837-1914 *NotBlAW 92 [port]*
**Fortenbach,** Ray Thomas 1927- *WhoAmL 92*
**Fortenbaugh,** Samuel Byrod, III 1933- *WhoAmL 92, WhoFI 92*
**Fortenberry,** Louis W *WhoAmP 91*
**Fortenberry,** Rick 1946- *WhoAmP 91*
**Fortes,** George 1944- *AmMWSc 92*
**Fortescue** *Who 92*
**Fortescue,** Earl 1922- *Who 92*
**Fortescue,** Adrian 1941- *Who 92*
**Fortescue,** Trevor Victor Norman 1916- *Who 92*
**Fortescue-Brickdale,** Eleanor 1872-1945 *TwCPaSc*
**Forteviot,** Baron 1906- *Who 92*
**Forth,** Eric 1944- *Who 92*
**Forth,** Kevin Bernard 1949- *WhoFI 92, WhoWest 92*
**Forth,** Mark Timothy 1959- *WhoFI 92*
**Fortier,** Jean-Marie *Who 92*
**Fortier,** Jean-Marie 1920- *IntWW 91, WhoRel 92*
**Fortier,** L. Yves 1935- *IntWW 91*
**Fortier,** Quincy Ernest 1912- *WhoWest 92*
**Fortier,** Theodore T. 1926- *WhoBlA 92*
**Fortin,** Andre Francis 1951- *AmMWSc 92*
**Fortin,** Joseph Thomas 1954- *WhoMW 92*
**Fortin-Brochu,** Debra Ann 1960- *WhoEnt 92*
**Fortinberry,** Toxey Thomas 1908- *WhoAmP 91*
**Fortini,** Victor Scott 1962- *WhoFI 92*
**Fortis,** Louis G 1947- *WhoAmP 91*
**Fortman,** John Joseph 1939- *AmMWSc 92*
**Fortman,** Marvin 1930- *WhoAmL 92*
**Fortna,** Lixi 1913- *WhoAmP 91*
**Fortner,** Brand I 1955- *AmMWSc 92*
**Fortner,** George William 1938- *AmMWSc 92*
**Fortner,** Hueston Gilmore 1959- *WhoAmL 92, WhoEnt 92*
**Fortner,** Joseph Gerald 1921- *AmMWSc 92*
**Fortner,** Rosanne White 1945- *AmMWSc 92*
**Fortner,** Wendell Lee 1935- *AmMWSc 92*
**Fortner,** Wolfgang 1907-1987 *NewAmDM*
**Fortney,** Doyle Wright 1933- *WhoRel 92*
**Fortney,** Judith A 1938- *AmMWSc 92*
**Fortney,** Lloyd Ray 1936- *AmMWSc 92*
**Fortney,** Steven *DrAPF 91*
**Fortnum,** Donald Holly 1932- *AmMWSc 92*
**Fortsen,** Mary d1664? *DcNCBi 2*
**Fortson,** Edward Norval 1936- *AmMWSc 92*
**Fortson,** Eleanor Ann 1904- *WhoAmP 91*
**Fortson,** Elnora Agnes 1943- *WhoBlA 92*
**Fortson,** Henry David, Jr. 1946- *WhoBlA 92*
**Fortson,** Mary d1664? *DcNCBi 2*
**Fortuin,** Thomas Mark 1946- *WhoAmL 92*
**Fortuna,** Edward Michael, Jr 1951- *AmMWSc 92*
**Fortuna,** William Frank 1948- *WhoMW 92*
**Fortunato,** Buddy 1946- *WhoAmP 91*
**Fortunato,** Peter *DrAPF 91*
**Fortune,** Alvin V. 1935- *WhoBlA 92*
**Fortune,** Bill 1948- *WhoEnt 92*
**Fortune,** Gwendoline Y. *WhoBlA 92*
**Fortune,** H Terry 1941- *AmMWSc 92*
**Fortune,** James Michael 1947- *WhoWest 92*
**Fortune,** Joanne C. 1941- *WhoAmL 92*
**Fortune,** Joanne Elizabeth 1945- *AmMWSc 92*
**Fortune,** Lowell 1941- *WhoAmL 92*
**Fortune,** Marie M. *WhoRel 92*
**Fortune,** Michael Joseph 1922- *WhoRel 92*
**Fortune,** Richard Cordova 1938- *WhoHisp 92*
**Fortune,** Roger Gerard 1963- *WhoEnt 92*
**Fortune,** Roma Coxey 1879-1942 *DcNCBi 2*
**Fortune,** T Thomas 1856-1928 *RComAH*
**Fortune,** Terence John 1946- *WhoAmL 92*
**Fortuno,** Luis G. 1960- *WhoHisp 92*
**Fortuno,** Victor M. 1952- *WhoAmL 92*
**Fortuny,** Lucia 1937- *WhoWest 92*
**Fortuny,** Mariano 1871-1949 *DcTwDes*
**Forty,** Arthur John 1928- *Who 92*
**Forty,** Francis John d1990 *Who 92N*
**Forty,** George 1927- *ConAu 34NR*
**Forward,** David Ross 1934- *WhoAmP 91*
**Forward,** Richard Blair, Jr 1943- *AmMWSc 92*
**Forward,** Robert L 1932- *AmMWSc 92, TwCSFW 91, WrDr 92*
**Forward,** Robert Lull 1932- *IntAu&W 91*
**Forwell,** George Dick 1928- *Who 92*
**Forwood,** Dudley 1912- *Who 92*
**Forwood,** Nicholas James 1948- *Who 92*
**Forys,** Leonard J 1941- *AmMWSc 92*
**Forziati,** Alphonse Frank 1911- *AmMWSc 92*
**Fosback,** Norman George 1947- *WhoFI 92*
**Fosbender,** William Ross, Jr. 1940- *WhoMW 92*
**Fosberg,** Maynard Axel 1919- *AmMWSc 92*
**Fosberg,** Theodore M 1934- *AmMWSc 92*
**Foscante,** Raymond Eugene 1942- *AmMWSc 92*
**Foschini,** Gerard Joseph 1940- *AmMWSc 92*
**Foschino,** Paul 1952- *WhoFI 92*
**Fosco,** Angelo *WhoFI 92*
**Foscolos,** Anthony E 1930- *AmMWSc 92*
**Foscolos,** Nicoloas *WhoRel 92*
**Foscue,** David Edward 1944- *WhoAmL 92*
**Fosdick,** Charles Austin 1842-1915 *BenetAL 91*
**Fosdick,** Harry Emerson 1878-1969 *AmPeW, BenetAL 91, RelLAm 91*
**Fosdick,** Lloyd D 1928- *AmMWSc 92*
**Fosdick,** Nellie d1917 *BiInAmS*
**Fosdick,** Raymond Blaine 1883-1972 *AmPeW*
**Fosdick,** Roger L 1936- *AmMWSc 92*
**Fosgate,** David M, Sr *WhoAmP 91*
**Foshee,** E Crum, Jr 1937- *WhoAmP 91*
**Foshee,** Howard Bryce 1925- *WhoRel 92*
**Foshee,** Hubert Lynn 1941- *WhoRel 92*
**Fosheim,** Douglas G *WhoAmP 91*
**Fosheim,** Douglas G. 1953- *WhoMW 92*
**Fosheim,** Jon R 1923- *WhoAmP 91*
**Fosher,** Donald Hobart 1935- *WhoFI 92, WhoMW 92*
**Fosket,** Donald Elston 1936- *AmMWSc 92*
**Foskett,** Daphne 1911- *IntAu&W 91, WrDr 92*
**Foskett,** David Robert 1949- *Who 92*
**Foskett,** Douglas John 1918- *Who 92, WrDr 92*
**Foskit,** Barry M. 1938- *WhoMW 92*
**Fosmire,** Fred Randall 1926- *WhoFI 92*
**Fosnacht,** Donald Ralph 1950- *AmMWSc 92*
**Fosness,** Irene Waugh 1906- *WhoAmP 91*
**Fosnough,** Larry Wayne 1957- *WhoRel 92*
**Foss,** Alan Stuart 1929- *AmMWSc 92*
**Foss,** Charles R. 1945- *WhoMW 92*
**Foss,** Donald C 1938- *AmMWSc 92*
**Foss,** Frederic A 1922- *WhoAmP 91*
**Foss,** Frederick William, Jr 1933- *AmMWSc 92*
**Foss,** Harlan d1991 *NewYTBS 91*
**Foss,** Harlan Funston 1918- *WhoRel 92*
**Foss,** John E 1932- *AmMWSc 92*
**Foss,** John F 1938- *AmMWSc 92*
**Foss,** John G 1930- *AmMWSc 92*
**Foss,** Judith C *WhoAmP 91*
**Foss,** Kathleen 1925- *Who 92*
**Foss,** Lukas 1922- *ConCom 92, IntWW 91, NewAmDM, WhoEnt 92*
**Foss,** Martha Ann 1933- *WhoFI 92*
**Foss,** Martyn 1918- *AmMWSc 92*
**Foss,** Mary Kay Ann 1944- *WhoWest 92*
**Foss,** Patricia H *WhoAmP 91*
**Foss,** Peter Herbert 1959- *WhoMW 92*
**Foss,** Phillip *DrAPF 91*
**Foss,** Ralph Scot 1945- *WhoFI 92*
**Foss,** Richard John 1944- *WhoRel 92*
**Foss,** Robert Paul 1937- *AmMWSc 92*
**Foss,** Sam Walter 1858-1911 *BenetAL 91*
**Fossan,** David B 1934- *AmMWSc 92*
**Fosse,** Bob 1927-1987 *FacFETw, IntDcF 2-2*
**Fosse,** Lucretia Ann 1962- *WhoEnt 92*
**Fossel,** Eric Thor 1941- *AmMWSc 92*
**Fossenkemper,** Marius Emig 1902- *WhoEnt 92, WhoMW 92*

**Fosset**, Andre 1918- *IntWW 91*
**Fossey**, Brigitte 1947- *IntMPA 92*
**Fossey**, Dian 1932-1985 *ConAu 34NR, FacFETw*
**Fossick**, Michael 1947- *TwCPaSc*
**Fossier**, Robert 1927- *IntWW 91*
**Fossland**, Joeann Jones 1948- *WhoWest 92*
**Fossland**, Robert Gerard 1918- *AmMWSc 92*
**Fosslien**, Egil 1935- *AmMWSc 92*
**Fossum**, Guilford O 1918- *AmMWSc 92*
**Fossum**, Jarl Egil 1946- *WhoRel 92*
**Fossum**, Jerry G 1943- *AmMWSc 92*
**Fossum**, Robert H 1923- *IntAu&W 91, WrDr 92*
**Fossum**, Robert Merle 1938- *AmMWSc 92, WhoMW 92*
**Fossum**, Steve P 1941- *AmMWSc 92*
**Fossum**, Timothy V 1942- *AmMWSc 92*
**Fost**, Dennis L 1944- *AmMWSc 92*
**Foster** *Who 92*
**Foster**, A. Mickey 1956- *WhoFI 92*
**Foster**, Abby Kelley 1811-1887 *HanAmWH*
**Foster**, Alan Dean 1946- *IntAu&W 91, TwCSFW 91, WhoWest 92, WrDr 92*
**Foster**, Albert Earl 1931- *AmMWSc 92*
**Foster**, Alfred Carville, Jr 1932- *WhoAmP 91*
**Foster**, Alfred Field 1915- *AmMWSc 92*
**Foster**, Allan 1926- *Who 92*
**Foster**, Alvin Garfield 1934- *WhoBlA 92*
**Foster**, Andrew D. 1919-1987 *WhoBlA 92N*
**Foster**, Andrew Lee, Jr. 1946- *WhoRel 92*
**Foster**, Andrew William 1944- *Who 92*
**Foster**, Arthur Key, Jr. 1933- *WhoAmL 92*
**Foster**, Arthur R 1924- *AmMWSc 92*
**Foster**, Ashley 1922- *WhoWest 92*
**Foster**, Barbara Anne 1955- *WhoEnt 92*
**Foster**, Ben 1926- *WhoAmP 91*
**Foster**, Billy Glen 1932- *AmMWSc 92*
**Foster**, Brendan 1948- *IntWW 91, Who 92*
**Foster**, Brian Lee 1938- *WhoWest 92*
**Foster**, Bruce Parks 1925- *AmMWSc 92*
**Foster**, Carl Oscar, Jr. 1926- *WhoBlA 92*
**Foster**, Cary D 1951- *WhoAmP 91*
**Foster**, Catherine Rierson 1935- *WhoFI 92*
**Foster**, Caxton Croxford 1929- *AmMWSc 92*
**Foster**, Charles 1830-1882 *DcNCBi 2*
**Foster**, Charles Allen 1931- *WhoIns 92*
**Foster**, Charles Allen 1941- *WhoAmL 92*
**Foster**, Charles Crawford 1941- *WhoAmL 92*
**Foster**, Charles David Owen 1938- *AmMWSc 92*
**Foster**, Charles Henry Wheelwright 1927- *AmMWSc 92*
**Foster**, Charles Howard 1947- *AmMWSc 92*
**Foster**, Charles I. 1898-197-? *ConAu 134*
**Foster**, Charles Matthews, II 1929- *WhoRel 92*
**Foster**, Charles Raiford, III 1953- *WhoFI 92*
**Foster**, Charles Stephen 1942- *AmMWSc 92*
**Foster**, Charles Thomas, Jr 1949- *AmMWSc 92*
**Foster**, Christine 1943- *IntMPA 92*
**Foster**, Christopher 1930- *Who 92*
**Foster**, Christopher David 1930- *IntWW 91*
**Foster**, Christopher Norman 1946- *Who 92*
**Foster**, Clyde 1931- *WhoBlA 92*
**Foster**, Colin *TwCPaSc*
**Foster**, Craig Alan 1951- *WhoWest 92*
**Foster**, Daniel George 1958- *WhoRel 92*
**Foster**, Daniel W 1930- *AmMWSc 92*
**Foster**, David 1929- *IntMPA 92*
**Foster**, David 1944- *ConNov 91*
**Foster**, David Bernard 1914- *AmMWSc 92*
**Foster**, David George 1957- *WhoWest 92*
**Foster**, David H. *LesBEnT 92*
**Foster**, David Lee 1933- *WhoAmL 92*
**Foster**, David Manning 1944- *IntAu&W 91, WrDr 92*
**Foster**, David Mark 1932- *WhoRel 92*
**Foster**, David Ramsey 1920- *WhoFI 92*
**Foster**, David Scott 1938- *WhoAmL 92*
**Foster**, David Skaats 1852-1920 *ScFEYrs*
**Foster**, David William 1940- *WrDr 92*
**Foster**, David William 1961- *WhoRel 92*
**Foster**, Deborah Jean 1952- *WhoEnt 92*
**Foster**, Deborah Valrie 1955- *WhoBlA 92*
**Foster**, Debra Courtney 1953- *WhoRel 92*
**Foster**, Delores Jackson 1938- *WhoBlA 92*
**Foster**, Dennis 1931- *Who 92*
**Foster**, Dennis James 1952- *WhoEnt 92*
**Foster**, Derek 1937- *Who 92*
**Foster**, Diana Harris 1644?- *DcNCBi 2*
**Foster**, Don 1948- *IntAu&W 91*
**Foster**, Donald Herbert 1934- *WhoMW 92*
**Foster**, Donald Myers 1938- *AmMWSc 92*
**Foster**, Donnie Ted 1948- *WhoAmP 91*
**Foster**, Douglas Layne 1944- *AmMWSc 92*
**Foster**, Douglas Leroy 1931- *WhoBlA 92*
**Foster**, Dudley Edwards, Jr. 1935- *WhoEnt 92, WhoWest 92*
**Foster**, Duncan Graham, Jr 1929- *AmMWSc 92*
**Foster**, E C 1939- *WhoAmP 91, WhoBlA 92*
**Foster**, E Gordon 1919- *AmMWSc 92*
**Foster**, Edson L. 1927- *WhoFI 92*
**Foster**, Edward, Sr. 1945- *WhoBlA 92*
**Foster**, Edward Halsey 1942- *IntAu&W 91, WrDr 92*
**Foster**, Edward Staniford, Jr 1913- *AmMWSc 92*
**Foster**, Edwin Michael 1917- *AmMWSc 92*
**Foster**, Edwin Powell 1942- *AmMWSc 92*
**Foster**, Elizabeth Read 1912- *WrDr 92*
**Foster**, Ellis L 1923- *AmMWSc 92*
**Foster**, Eric H. 1943- *WhoFI 92*
**Foster**, Eugene A 1927- *AmMWSc 92*
**Foster**, Eugene L 1922- *AmMWSc 92*
**Foster**, Evan *TwCWW 91*
**Foster**, Frances 1924- *WhoEnt 92*
**Foster**, Frances Helen 1924- *WhoBlA 92*
**Foster**, Frances Smith 1944- *ConAu 135, WhoBlA 92*
**Foster**, Francis d1735? *DcNCBi 2*
**Foster**, Frank 1920- *TwCPaSc*
**Foster**, Frank B., III 1928- *WhoBlA 92*
**Foster**, Frank Pierce 1841-1911 *BiInAmS*
**Foster**, Gary Dean 1944- *WhoRel 92*
**Foster**, George *WrDr 92*
**Foster**, George A, Jr 1938- *AmMWSc 92*
**Foster**, George Arthur 1948- *WhoBlA 92*
**Foster**, George Arthur C. *Who 92*
**Foster**, George Burman 1858-1918 *RelLAm 91*
**Foster**, George C 1893- *ScFEYrs*
**Foster**, George Rainey 1943- *AmMWSc 92*
**Foster**, George William, Jr. 1919- *WhoAmL 92*
**Foster**, Giraud Vernam 1928- *AmMWSc 92*
**Foster**, Gladys M. 1927- *WhoBlA 92*
**Foster**, Gloria *WhoBlA 92*
**Foster**, Greg 1958- *BlkOlyM*
**Foster**, Greg 1959- *WhoBlA 92*
**Foster**, Hannah Webster *BenetAL 91*
**Foster**, Harold Douglas 1943- *AmMWSc 92*
**Foster**, Harold Edward 1939- *WhoFI 92*
**Foster**, Harold Marvin 1928- *AmMWSc 92*
**Foster**, Harry *TwCWW 91*
**Foster**, Helen Laura 1919- *AmMWSc 92*
**Foster**, Henry D 1912- *AmMWSc 92*
**Foster**, Henry Louis 1925- *AmMWSc 92, WhoFI 92*
**Foster**, Henry Wendell 1933- *AmMWSc 92, WhoBlA 92*
**Foster**, Horatio Alvah 1858-1913 *BiInAmS*
**Foster**, Ian Hampden 1946- *Who 92*
**Foster**, Iris *IntAu&W 91X, WrDr 92*
**Foster**, Irving Gordon 1912- *AmMWSc 92*
**Foster**, J Earl 1929- *AmMWSc 92*
**Foster**, James Franklin *WhoMW 92*
**Foster**, James H. 1931- *WhoBlA 92*
**Foster**, James H 1955- *WhoIns 92*
**Foster**, James Hadlei 1938- *WhoBlA 92*
**Foster**, James Henderson 1946- *AmMWSc 92*
**Foster**, James Henry 1930- *AmMWSc 92*
**Foster**, James Henry 1933- *WhoFI 92*
**Foster**, James L. 1943- *WhoBlA 92*
**Foster**, James Leroy 1944- *WhoAmP 91*
**Foster**, James Norton, Jr. 1954- *WhoAmL 92*
**Foster**, James Reuben 1930- *WhoFI 92*
**Foster**, Janet L. 1955- *WhoEnt 92*
**Foster**, Janice Martin 1946- *WhoBlA 92*
**Foster**, Jeanne *DrAPF 91, TwCWW 91*
**Foster**, Jo Graham 1915- *WhoAmP 91*
**Foster**, Joan Mary 1923- *Who 92*
**Foster**, Joanna Katharine 1939- *Who 92*
**Foster**, Jodie 1962- *IntMPA 92, IntWW 91, NewYTBS 91 [port], WhoEnt 92*
**Foster**, Joe B. 1934- *WhoFI 92*
**Foster**, John 1814?-1897 *BiInAmS*
**Foster**, John 1927- *Who 92*
**Foster**, John 1951- *TwCPaSc*
**Foster**, John Bentley, Jr. 1951- *WhoRel 92*
**Foster**, John Clayton 1935- *WhoAmP 91*
**Foster**, John Edward 1940- *AmMWSc 92*
**Foster**, John Hoskins 1921- *AmMWSc 92*
**Foster**, John McGaw 1928- *AmMWSc 92*
**Foster**, John McNeely 1949- *WhoFI 92*
**Foster**, John Peter 1919- *Who 92*
**Foster**, John Robert 1916- *Who 92*
**Foster**, John Robert 1940- *WhoAmL 92*
**Foster**, John Robert 1947- *AmMWSc 92*
**Foster**, John Stuart 1958- *WhoWest 92*
**Foster**, John Stuart, Jr 1922- *AmMWSc 92*
**Foster**, John Watson 1836-1917 *AmPeW, AmPolLe*
**Foster**, John Webster 1923- *AmMWSc 92*
**Foster**, John Wells 1815-1873 *BiInAmS*
**Foster**, John William 1921- *Who 92*
**Foster**, John Witherspoon 1948- *WhoFI 92*
**Foster**, Jonathan Rowe 1947- *Who 92*
**Foster**, Joseph E. 1954- *WhoAmL 92*
**Foster**, Joyce Geraldine 1951- *AmMWSc 92*
**Foster**, Julia 1944- *IntMPA 92*
**Foster**, Julie Irene 1955- *WhoAmL 92*
**Foster**, Katherine D 1924- *WhoAmP 91*
**Foster**, Kathryn Briggs 1943- *WhoAmP 91*
**Foster**, Ken Wood 1950- *AmMWSc 92*
**Foster**, Kenneth William 1944- *AmMWSc 92*
**Foster**, Kennith Earl 1945- *AmMWSc 92*
**Foster**, Kent Ellsworth 1943- *AmMWSc 92*
**Foster**, Kim Alan 1956- *WhoWest 92*
**Foster**, LaDoris J. 1933- *WhoBlA 92*
**Foster**, Lawrence 1941- *IntWW 91, NewAmDM, Who 92, WhoEnt 92*
**Foster**, Leila Merrell 1929- *WhoRel 92*
**Foster**, Leslie D. *DrAPF 91*
**Foster**, Leslie Donley 1930- *WhoMW 92*
**Foster**, Leslie Sheila 1941- *WhoWest 92*
**Foster**, Lester Anderson, Jr. 1929- *WhoFI 92*
**Foster**, Linda Nemec *DrAPF 91*
**Foster**, Linda Nemec 1950- *IntAu&W 91*
**Foster**, Lloyd A. 1940- *WhoMW 92*
**Foster**, Lloyd Bennett 1911- *WhoAmL 92*
**Foster**, Lloyd L. 1930- *WhoBlA 92*
**Foster**, Lorraine L 1938- *AmMWSc 92*
**Foster**, Luther H. 1913- *WhoBlA 92*
**Foster**, Lynn 1952- *WhoAmL 92*
**Foster**, M A 1939- *TwCSFW 91, WrDr 92*
**Foster**, M Glenys *AmMWSc 92*
**Foster**, Malcolm Burton 1931- *WrDr 92*
**Foster**, Margaret C 1935- *AmMWSc 92*
**Foster**, Maria Elena 1956- *WhoHisp 92*
**Foster**, Mark Edward 1948- *WhoFI 92*
**Foster**, Mark Stephen 1948- *WhoAmL 92*
**Foster**, Marta 1941- *WhoHisp 92*
**Foster**, Martin Conroy 1953- *WhoAmL 92*
**Foster**, Mary Christine 1943- *WhoEnt 92*
**Foster**, Mary Frazer 1914- *WhoWest 92*
**Foster**, Mary Melville 1890-1968 *TwCPaSc*
**Foster**, Maurice David *IntMPA 92*
**Foster**, Meg 1948- *IntMPA 92*
**Foster**, Melissa 1953- *WhoEnt 92*
**Foster**, Melvin Edward Tim 1938- *WhoWest 92*
**Foster**, Melvon Lamphere, III 1957- *WhoMW 92*
**Foster**, Merrill W 1939- *AmMWSc 92*
**Foster**, Merrill White 1939- *WhoMW 92*
**Foster**, Michael Edward 1949- *WhoMW 92*
**Foster**, Michael Ralph 1943- *AmMWSc 92*
**Foster**, Michael Simmler 1942- *AmMWSc 92*
**Foster**, Michael William 1940- *WhoWest 92*
**Foster**, Mike 1955- *WhoAmP 91*
**Foster**, Mildred Thomas 1927- *WhoBlA 92*
**Foster**, Murphy James, Jr 1930- *WhoAmP 91*
**Foster**, Neal Robert 1937- *AmMWSc 92*
**Foster**, Neil William 1945- *AmMWSc 92*
**Foster**, Norman *DcTwDes, LesBEnT 92*
**Foster**, Norman 1935- *Who 92*
**Foster**, Norman Charles 1947- *AmMWSc 92*
**Foster**, Norman George 1919- *AmMWSc 92*
**Foster**, Norman Holland 1934- *AmMWSc 92*
**Foster**, Norman Leslie 1909- *Who 92*
**Foster**, Norman Robert 1935- *IntWW 91*
**Foster**, Paul 1931- *IntAu&W 91, WhoEnt 92, WrDr 92*
**Foster**, Pearl D. 1922- *WhoBlA 92*
**Foster**, Perry Alanson, Jr 1925- *AmMWSc 92*
**Foster**, Peter *Who 92*
**Foster**, Peter Beaufoy 1921- *Who 92*
**Foster**, Peter Martin 1924- *Who 92*
**Foster**, Philip A *WhoAmP 91*
**Foster**, Philip Carey 1947- *WhoAmP 91*
**Foster**, Pops 1892?-1969 *NewAmDM*
**Foster**, Portia L. 1953- *WhoBlA 92*
**Foster**, Randolph Sinks 1820-1903 *RelLAm 91*
**Foster**, Raunell H. 1938- *WhoBlA 92*
**Foster**, Raymond Orrville 1921- *AmMWSc 92*
**Foster**, Richard *WhoAmP 91*
**Foster**, Richard 1622?- *DcNCBi 2*
**Foster**, Richard 1945- *TwCPaSc*
**Foster**, Richard Anthony 1941- *Who 92*
**Foster**, Richard B 1916- *AmMWSc 92*
**Foster**, Richard J 1942- *ConAu 34NR*
**Foster**, Richard James 1942- *WhoRel 92*
**Foster**, Richard Layne 1955- *WhoWest 92*
**Foster**, Richard N 1941- *AmMWSc 92*
**Foster**, Richard Vincent 1935- *WhoEnt 92*
**Foster**, Robert 1913- *Who 92*
**Foster**, Robert Allen 1955- *WhoFI 92*
**Foster**, Robert Davis 1929- *WhoBlA 92*
**Foster**, Robert Earl, III 1948- *WhoWest 92*
**Foster**, Robert Edward, II 1920- *AmMWSc 92*
**Foster**, Robert Estill 1939- *WhoEnt 92*
**Foster**, Robert Fitzroy 1949- *Who 92*
**Foster**, Robert H 1920- *AmMWSc 92*
**Foster**, Robert Joe 1924- *AmMWSc 92*
**Foster**, Robert John 1929- *AmMWSc 92*
**Foster**, Robert Lawson 1925- *WhoRel 92*
**Foster**, Robert Leon 1939- *WhoBlA 92*
**Foster**, Robert Sidney 1913- *IntWW 91*
**Foster**, Robert W 1920- *WhoAmP 91*
**Foster**, Robin Bradford 1945- *AmMWSc 92*
**Foster**, Rockwood Hoar 1923- *WhoAmP 91*
**Foster**, Rodney Patrick 1951- *WhoRel 92*
**Foster**, Roger Sherman, Jr 1936- *AmMWSc 92*
**Foster**, Rosebud Lightbourn 1934- *WhoBlA 92*
**Foster**, Roy *Who 92*
**Foster**, Roy Allen 1960- *WhoBlA 92*
**Foster**, Ruth Mary 1927- *WhoWest 92*
**Foster**, Ruth Sullivan 1929- *WhoAmP 91*
**Foster**, Samuel R 1932- *WhoAmP 91*
**Foster**, Shannon Raine 1961- *WhoAmL 92*
**Foster**, Simon *IntAu&W 91X, WrDr 92*
**Foster**, Stephen 1826-1864 *BenetAL 91*
**Foster**, Stephen Collins 1826-1864 *NewAmDM*
**Foster**, Stephen John 1953-1978 *TwCPaSc*
**Foster**, Stephen Symonds 1809-1881 *AmPeW*
**Foster**, Steven 1957- *ConAu 135*
**Foster**, Steven Wayne 1949- *WhoRel 92*
**Foster**, Stillman Allen, Jr. 1939- *WhoRel 92*
**Foster**, Susan J *AmMWSc 92*
**Foster**, Terry Joe 1948- *WhoAmL 92*
**Foster**, Terry Lynn 1943- *AmMWSc 92*
**Foster**, Theodore Dean 1929- *AmMWSc 92*
**Foster**, Thomas Ashcroft 1934- *Who 92*
**Foster**, Thomas P 1939- *WhoIns 92*
**Foster**, Thomas Scott 1947- *AmMWSc 92*
**Foster**, Tim 1951- *TwCPaSc*
**Foster**, Tim 1957- *WhoAmP 91*
**Foster**, Tonita Minge 1944- *WhoAmL 92*
**Foster**, Tony 1932- *WhoEnt 92*
**Foster**, V. Alyce 1909- *WhoBlA 92*
**Foster**, Vicky Ann 1952- *WhoFI 92*
**Foster**, Virginia 1914- *AmMWSc 92*
**Foster**, Vivienne 1936- *TwCPaSc*
**Foster**, W. Bert 1869-1929 *TwCWW 91*
**Foster**, W F 1916- *WhoAmP 91*
**Foster**, Walter Edward 1924- *AmMWSc 92*
**Foster**, Walter Herbert, Jr. 1919- *WhoFI 92*
**Foster**, Walter Tad *WhoMW 92*
**Foster**, Wanell Baize 1928- *WhoWest 92*
**Foster**, Wendell 1929- *WhoAmP 91*
**Foster**, Wilfred John Daniel 1937- *AmMWSc 92*
**Foster**, William B 1931- *WhoIns 92*
**Foster**, William Burnham 1930- *AmMWSc 92*
**Foster**, William J 1959- *AmMWSc 92*
**Foster**, William James, III 1953- *WhoWest 92*
**Foster**, William K. 1933- *WhoBlA 92*
**Foster**, William Patrick 1919- *WhoBlA 92*
**Foster**, William Silas, Jr. 1939- *WhoRel 92*
**Foster**, William Walter 1922- *WhoAmP 91*
**Foster**, Willis Roy 1928- *AmMWSc 92*
**Foster**, Winthrop D 1880?-1918 *BiInAmS*
**Foster-Brown**, Roy Stephenson 1904- *Who 92*
**Foster-Sutton**, Stafford William Powell 1898- *IntWW 91, Who 92*
**Fostervoll**, Alv Jakob 1932- *IntWW 91*
**Fota**, Constantin *IntWW 91*
**Fota**, Frank George 1921- *WhoMW 92*
**Foth**, Henry Donald 1923- *AmMWSc 92*
**Foth**, Richard B. *WhoRel 92*
**Fotherby**, Lesley 1946- *TwCPaSc*
**Fothergill**, Anthony 1732?-1813 *BiInAmS*
**Fothergill**, Brian 1921- *IntAu&W 91*
**Fothergill**, Dorothy Joan 1923- *Who 92*
**Fothergill**, Richard Humphrey Maclean 1937- *Who 92*
**Foti**, Margaret A *AmMWSc 92*
**Foti**, Steven M 1958- *WhoAmP 91*
**Fotino**, Marilena *AmMWSc 92*
**Fotino**, Mircea 1927- *AmMWSc 92*
**Fotsch**, Dan Robert 1947- *WhoWest 92*
**Fottrell**, Patrick 1933- *IntWW 91*
**Fou Ts'ong** 1934- *IntWW 91, Who 92*
**Fou**, Cheng-Ming 1936- *AmMWSc 92*
**Fouad**, Abdel Aziz 1928- *AmMWSc 92*
**Foucault**, Alan Arthur 1953- *WhoWest 92*
**Foucault**, Michel 1926-1984 *ConAu 34NR, ConLC 69 [port], FacFETw, GuFrLit 1*
**Fouchard**, Joseph James 1928- *WhoAmP 91*
**Fouche**, Jacobus Johannes 1898-1980 *FacFETw*
**Foucher**, W D 1936- *AmMWSc 92*
**Foudin**, Arnold S *AmMWSc 92*
**Fougere**, Jean 1914- *IntAu&W 91*

**Fougere,** Paul Francis 1932- *AmMWSc 92*
**Fougeron,** Myron George 1932- *AmMWSc 92*
**Fougerousse,** Philip 1945- *WhoAmL 92*
**Fought,** Sheryl Kristine 1949- *WhoFI 92*
**Fouhy,** Ed *LesBEnT 92*
**Foulds,** Elfrida Vipont 1902- *IntAu&W 91, WrDr 92*
**Foulds,** John Douglas *AmMWSc 92*
**Foulds,** Jon 1932- *Who 92*
**Foulger,** Keith 1925- *Who 92*
**Foulis,** David James 1930- *AmMWSc 92*
**Foulis,** Iain 1937- *Who 92*
**Foulk,** Clinton Ross 1930- *AmMWSc 92*
**Foulk,** Grover C 1926- *WhoAmP 91*
**Foulk,** Jack 1941- *WhoAmP 91*
**Foulke,** Bruce Randall 1951- *WhoEnt 92*
**Foulke,** Edwin G, Jr *WhoAmP 91*
**Foulke,** Edwin Gerhart, Jr. 1952- *WhoAmL 92*
**Foulkes,** Ernest Charles 1924- *AmMWSc 92*
**Foulkes,** George 1942- *Who 92*
**Foulkes,** Nigel 1919- *Who 92*
**Foulkes,** Nigel Gordon 1919- *IntWW 91*
**Foulkes,** Peter 1936- *WrDr 92*
**Foulkes,** Robert Hugh 1918- *AmMWSc 92*
**Foulkrod,** Marc Jonathan 1955- *WhoWest 92*
**Foulks,** Carl Alvin 1947- *WhoBlA 92*
**Foulks,** James Grigsby 1916- *AmMWSc 92*
**Foulks,** Marva Jean Shipman 1952- *WhoMW 92*
**Foulks Foster,** Ivadale Marie 1922- *WhoBlA 92*
**Foulser,** David A 1933- *AmMWSc 92*
**Foulston,** Nola Tedesco 1940- *WhoAmL 92*
**Founds,** Henry William 1942- *AmMWSc 92*
**Fountain,** Alan 1946- *Who 92*
**Fountain,** Anthony Gerald 1963- *WhoRel 92*
**Fountain,** Cherryl 1950- *TwCPaSc*
**Fountain,** Edwin Byrd 1930- *WhoRel 92*
**Fountain,** Ernest Kristoffer Jones 1956- *WhoFI 92*
**Fountain,** Freeman Percival 1921- *WhoWest 92*
**Fountain,** Henry Francis, Jr. 1924- *WhoFI 92*
**Fountain,** John, Jr. 1960- *WhoWest 92*
**Fountain,** John Crothers 1947- *AmMWSc 92*
**Fountain,** John William 1944- *AmMWSc 92*
**Fountain,** L H 1913- *WhoAmP 91*
**Fountain,** Leonard Du Bois 1929- *AmMWSc 92*
**Fountain,** Lewis Spencer 1917- *AmMWSc 92*
**Fountain,** Linda Kathleen 1954- *WhoFI 92*
**Fountain,** Pete 1930- *ConMus 7 [port], NewAmDM*
**Fountain,** Peter Dewey, Jr. 1930- *WhoEnt 92*
**Fountain,** Richard Tillman 1885-1945 *DcNCBi 2*
**Fountain,** Ronald Glenn 1939- *WhoFI 92*
**Fountain,** Venoal M., Sr. *WhoBlA 92*
**Fountain,** William Stanley 1920- *WhoBlA 92*
**Fountos,** William Joseph, III 1956- *WhoMW 92*
**Fouquet,** Georges 1862-1957 *DcTwDes*
**Fouquet,** Julie 1958- *AmMWSc 92*
**Fouquette,** Martin John, Jr 1930- *AmMWSc 92*
**Four Brothers** *NewAmDM*
**Four Horseman** *NewAmDM*
**Four Tops,** The *NewAmDM*
**Fourastie,** Jean d1990 *IntWW 91N*
**Fourcade,** Jean-Pierre 1929- *IntWW 91, Who 92*
**Fourcaud,** Louis de 1853-1914 *ThHEIm*
**Fourcroy,** Antoine Francois, comte de 1755-1809 *BlkwCEP*
**Fourer,** Robert 1950- *AmMWSc 92*
**Fourest,** Henry-Pierre 1911- *IntWW 91*
**Fourie,** Bernardus Gerhardus 1916- *IntWW 91*
**Fourier,** Charles 1772-1837 *BenetAL 91*
**Fourier,** Francois Charles Marie 1772-1837 *ScFEYrs B*
**Fournelle,** Raymond Albert 1941- *AmMWSc 92*
**Fournelle,** Thomas Albert 1946- *AmMWSc 92, WhoMW 92*
**Fournet,** Jean 1913- *NewAmDM*
**Fourney,** M E 1936- *AmMWSc 92*
**Fournie,** John William 1952- *AmMWSc 92*
**Fournie,** Raymond Richard 1951- *WhoAmL 92, WhoEnt 92*
**Fournier,** Bernard 1938- *Who 92*
**Fournier,** Cheryl J. 1960- *WhoRel 92*
**Fournier,** Collette V. 1952- *WhoBlA 92*
**Fournier,** Donald Frederick 1934- *WhoWest 92*
**Fournier,** Jacques 1929- *IntWW 91*
**Fournier,** Jean 1914- *Who 92*
**Fournier,** John J F 1942- *AmMWSc 92*
**Fournier,** Maurille Joseph, Jr 1940- *AmMWSc 92*
**Fournier,** Michel 1954- *AmMWSc 92*
**Fournier,** Pierre 1906-1986 *NewAmDM*
**Fournier,** Pierre 1906-1986 *FacFETw*
**Fournier,** R E Keith 1949- *AmMWSc 92*
**Fournier,** Robert Orville 1932- *AmMWSc 92*
**Fournier,** Serge Raymond-Jean 1931- *WhoEnt 92*
**Fournier,** Walter Frank 1912- *WhoWest 92*
**Fournier-Acuna,** Fernando 1916- *IntWW 91*
**Fourquet,** Michel Martin Leon 1914- *IntWW 91*
**Fourrier,** Clay Joseph 1950- *WhoEnt 92*
**Fourtner,** Charles Russell 1944- *AmMWSc 92*
**Fourtouni,** Eleni *DrAPF 91*
**Fousekis,** James Thomas 1938- *WhoAmL 92*
**Foushee,** Geraldine George 1947- *WhoBlA 92*
**Foushee,** Sandra *DrAPF 91*
**Fouss,** James L 1936- *AmMWSc 92*
**Fouss,** Robert Eugene, II 1964- *WhoEnt 92*
**Foust,** Julius Isaac 1865-1946 *DcNCBi 2*
**Foust,** Paul McClain 1929- *WhoAmP 91*
**Foust,** Richard Duane, Jr. 1945- *WhoWest 92*
**Foust,** Robert S 1941- *WhoAmP 91*
**Foust,** Rosanne Skibo 1964- *WhoWest 92*
**Foutch,** Gary Lynn 1954- *AmMWSc 92*
**Foutch,** Harley Wayne 1944- *AmMWSc 92*
**Foutch,** Michael James 1951- *WhoEnt 92*
**Fouts,** James Ralph 1929- *AmMWSc 92*
**Fouts,** Kenneth Allen, Jr. 1941- *WhoEnt 92*
**Fouty,** Marvin Francis 1936- *WhoMW 92*
**Foutz,** Devin Jon 1970- *WhoEnt 92*
**Foutz,** Samuel Theodore 1945- *WhoBlA 92*
**Fouyas,** Methodios 1925- *Who 92*
**Fow,** Louis Fairchild 1939- *WhoMW 92*
**Fowble,** William Franklin 1938- *WhoFI 92*
**Fowden,** Leslie 1925- *IntWW 91, Who 92*
**Fowell,** Andrew John 1936- *AmMWSc 92*
**Fowells,** Joseph Dunthorne Briggs 1916- *Who 92*
**Fowke,** David 1950- *Who 92*
**Fowke,** Edith Margaret 1913- *IntAu&W 91, WrDr 92*
**Fowke,** H Shirley 1914- *IntAu&W 91*
**Fowke,** Lawrence Carroll 1941- *AmMWSc 92*
**Fowke,** Philip Francis 1950- *IntWW 91*
**Fowkes,** Frederick Mayhew 1915- *AmMWSc 92*
**Fowlds,** Derek 1937- *ConTFT 9*
**Fowle,** Daniel Gould 1831-1891 *DcNCBi 2*
**Fowle,** Eleanor Cranston *WhoAmP 91*
**Fowle,** Frank Fuller 1908- *WhoAmL 92*
**Fowler,** Abe Neal 1939- *WhoAmP 91*
**Fowler,** Alan B 1928- *AmMWSc 92*
**Fowler,** Alastair 1930- *IntAu&W 91, WrDr 92*
**Fowler,** Alastair David Shaw 1930- *Who 92*
**Fowler,** Alfred 1868-1940 *FacFETw*
**Fowler,** Anne Blankenburg 1948- *WhoAmL 92*
**Fowler,** Arnold K 1936- *AmMWSc 92*
**Fowler,** Audree Vernee 1933- *AmMWSc 92*
**Fowler,** Austine Brown 1936- *WhoFI 92*
**Fowler,** Beryl *Who 92*
**Fowler,** Betty Janmae 1925- *WhoEnt 92*
**Fowler,** Bonny Long 1964- *WhoMW 92*
**Fowler,** Bruce Andrew 1945- *AmMWSc 92*
**Fowler,** Bruce Wayne 1948- *AmMWSc 92*
**Fowler,** Caleb L. *WhoMW 92*
**Fowler,** Calvin 1940- *BlkOlyM*
**Fowler,** Charles A 1920- *AmMWSc 92*
**Fowler,** Charles Arman, Jr 1912- *AmMWSc 92*
**Fowler,** Charles Benjamin 1962- *WhoEnt 92*
**Fowler,** Charles Lewis 1877-1974 *DcNCBi 2*
**Fowler,** Christopher B. *Who 92*
**Fowler,** Christopher George 1959- *WhoFI 92*
**Fowler,** Clarence Maxwell 1918- *AmMWSc 92*
**Fowler,** Clyde Bernard 1924- *WhoAmP 91*
**Fowler,** Conrad Murphree 1918- *WhoAmP 91*
**Fowler,** Daniel Lee 1954- *WhoAmL 92*
**Fowler,** David Covington 1921- *WhoRel 92*
**Fowler,** Dennis Houston 1924- *Who 92*
**Fowler,** Derek 1929- *Who 92*
**Fowler,** Don D 1936- *IntAu&W 91, WrDr 92*
**Fowler,** Don Dee 1936- *WhoWest 92*
**Fowler,** Don Wall 1944- *WhoAmL 92*
**Fowler,** Dona J. 1928- *WhoWest 92*
**Fowler,** Dona Jane 1928- *AmMWSc 92*
**Fowler,** Donald Lionel 1935- *WhoAmP 91*
**Fowler,** Donald Paige 1932- *AmMWSc 92*
**Fowler,** Donald Raymond 1926- *WhoAmL 92*
**Fowler,** Earle Cabell 1921- *AmMWSc 92*
**Fowler,** Edward Herbert 1936- *AmMWSc 92*
**Fowler,** Edward Michael 1929- *IntWW 91, Who 92*
**Fowler,** Edwin Earl 1955- *WhoWest 92*
**Fowler,** Elbert Wentzell 1915- *WhoAmP 91*
**Fowler,** Elizabeth 1943- *AmMWSc 92*
**Fowler,** Emil Eugene 1923- *AmMWSc 92*
**Fowler,** Eric Beaumont 1914- *AmMWSc 92*
**Fowler,** Frank Cavan 1918- *AmMWSc 92*
**Fowler,** Frank Wilson 1941- *AmMWSc 92*
**Fowler,** Gene 1890-1960 *BenetAL 91*
**Fowler,** Gene 1931- *ConPo 91, WrDr 92*
**Fowler,** George *ScFEYrs*
**Fowler,** George J., III 1950- *WhoHisp 92*
**Fowler,** George Selton, Jr. 1920- *WhoMW 92*
**Fowler,** Gerald Allan 1934- *AmMWSc 92*
**Fowler,** Gerald Teasdale 1935- *Who 92*
**Fowler,** Giles Merrill 1934- *WhoMW 92*
**Fowler,** Gregory L 1934- *AmMWSc 92*
**Fowler,** H M, Sr *WhoAmP 91*
**Fowler,** H Seymour 1919- *AmMWSc 92*
**Fowler,** Hammond 1901- *WhoAmP 91*
**Fowler,** Harold Douglas 1927- *WhoRel 92*
**Fowler,** Harry 1926- *IntMPA 92*
**Fowler,** Henry Hamill 1908- *IntWW 91, Who 92, WhoAmP 91*
**Fowler,** Howland Auchincloss 1930- *AmMWSc 92*
**Fowler,** Hugh Charles 1926- *WhoAmP 91*
**Fowler,** Ian 1932- *Who 92*
**Fowler,** James A 1923- *AmMWSc 92*
**Fowler,** James Daniel, Jr. 1944- *WhoBlA 92*
**Fowler,** James Edward 1931- *WhoAmL 92, WhoFI 92*
**Fowler,** James Lowell 1935- *AmMWSc 92*
**Fowler,** James M. 1939- *WhoWest 92*
**Fowler,** James Wiley, III 1940- *WhoRel 92*
**Fowler,** Jay Bradford *DrAPF 91*
**Fowler,** Jennifer 1939- *ConCom 92*
**Fowler,** Jerry M 1940- *WhoAmP 91*
**Fowler,** Joanna S 1942- *AmMWSc 92*
**Fowler,** John Alvis 1921- *AmMWSc 92*
**Fowler,** John D. 1931- *WhoBlA 92*
**Fowler,** John Dale, Jr. 1957- *WhoFI 92*
**Fowler,** John Edgar 1865-1930 *DcNCBi 2*
**Fowler,** John Francis 1925- *Who 92*
**Fowler,** John J *WhoAmP 91*
**Fowler,** John Milton 1945- *WhoAmL 92*
**Fowler,** John Rayford 1943- *AmMWSc 92*
**Fowler,** Jon Frederick 1943- *WhoWest 92*
**Fowler,** Karen Joy 1950- *TwCSFW 91*
**Fowler,** Kenneth A. 1900-1987 *TwCWW 91*
**Fowler,** Kenneth Abrams 1900- *IntAu&W 91*
**Fowler,** Lee Allan 1961- *WhoRel 92*
**Fowler,** Leon, Jr. 1943- *WhoBlA 92*
**Fowler,** Leslie R 1924- *WhoAmP 91*
**Fowler,** Linda Marilyn 1936- *WhoAmP 91*
**Fowler,** Lorenzo Niles 1811-1896 *BiInAmS*
**Fowler,** Lydia Folger 1822-1879 *BiInAmS*
**Fowler,** Malcolm McFarland 1943- *AmMWSc 92*
**Fowler,** Marian Elizabeth 1929- *IntAu&W 91*
**Fowler,** Mark S. *LesBEnT 92*
**Fowler,** Michael *Who 92*
**Fowler,** Michael 1938- *AmMWSc 92*
**Fowler,** Murray Elwood 1928- *AmMWSc 92*
**Fowler,** Nancy Crowley 1922- *WhoWest 92*
**Fowler,** Nathaniel Eugene 1922- *WhoWest 92*
**Fowler,** Noble Owen 1919- *AmMWSc 92*
**Fowler,** Norma Lee 1952- *AmMWSc 92*
**Fowler,** Norman *IntWW 91, Who 92*
**Fowler,** Orson Squire 1809-1887 *BiInAmS*
**Fowler,** Patricia Cervantes Romero 1944- *WhoHisp 92*
**Fowler,** Peter Howard 1923- *IntWW 91, Who 92*
**Fowler,** Peter James 1936- *Who 92*
**Fowler,** Peter Jon 1936- *Who 92*
**Fowler,** Peter Niles 1951- *WhoAmL 92*
**Fowler,** Peter Norman 1938- *IntWW 91, Who 92*
**Fowler,** Queen Dunlap *WhoBlA 92*
**Fowler,** Richard A. 1948- *ConAu 36NR*
**Fowler,** Richard Gildart 1916- *AmMWSc 92*
**Fowler,** Richard Michael 1954- *WhoEnt 92*
**Fowler,** Richard Nicholas 1946- *Who 92*
**Fowler,** Robert *WhoAmP 91*
**Fowler,** Robert Asa 1928- *Who 92*
**Fowler,** Robert M. 1950- *WhoRel 92*
**Fowler,** Robert McSwain 1906- *AmMWSc 92*
**Fowler,** Rollen Charles 1962- *WhoWest 92*
**Fowler,** Ronald Frederick 1910- *Who 92*
**Fowler,** Ross Miller 1959- *WhoFI 92*
**Fowler,** Samuel Frank, Jr. 1928- *WhoAmL 92*
**Fowler,** Scott Wellington 1941- *AmMWSc 92*
**Fowler,** Stanley D 1942- *AmMWSc 92*
**Fowler,** Stephen C *AmMWSc 92*
**Fowler,** Stephen Eugene 1940- *WhoMW 92*
**Fowler,** Stephen Mark 1959- *WhoAmL 92*
**Fowler,** Susan Robinson 1946- *WhoEnt 92*
**Fowler,** Sydney *TwCSFW 91*
**Fowler,** Thaddeus Postelle, Jr. *WhoBlA 92*
**Fowler,** Thomas Geoffrey 1924- *WhoWest 92*
**Fowler,** Thomas Kenneth 1931- *AmMWSc 92*
**Fowler,** Timothy John 1938- *AmMWSc 92*
**Fowler,** Tom *WhoAmP 91*
**Fowler,** Tony Ray 1961- *WhoRel 92*
**Fowler,** Vivian Delores 1946- *WhoFI 92*
**Fowler,** W Wyche, Jr 1940- *WhoAmP 91*
**Fowler,** Wallace T 1938- *AmMWSc 92*
**Fowler,** Walton Berry 1946- *WhoFI 92*
**Fowler,** William Alfred 1911- *AmMWSc 92, FacFETw, IntWW 91, Who 92, WhoNob 90, WhoWest 92*
**Fowler,** William Dix 1940- *WhoFI 92*
**Fowler,** William E., Jr. 1921- *WhoBlA 92*
**Fowler,** William Mayo, Jr 1926- *AmMWSc 92*
**Fowler,** William Michael 1953- *WhoEnt 92*
**Fowler,** William Raymond 1944- *WhoEnt 92*
**Fowler,** William Stewart 1924- *IntAu&W 91*
**Fowler,** William Wyche, Jr. 1940- *IntWW 91*
**Fowler,** Wyche, Jr. 1940- *AlmAP 92 [port]*
**Fowler,** Wyman Beall, Jr 1937- *AmMWSc 92*
**Fowler Howitt,** William *Who 92*
**Fowles,** George Richard 1928- *AmMWSc 92*
**Fowles,** Grant Robert 1919- *AmMWSc 92*
**Fowles,** John 1926- *CnDBLB 8 [port], ConNov 91, FacFETw, IntAu&W 91, IntWW 91, RfGEnL 91, Who 92, WrDr 92*
**Fowles,** Patrick Ernest 1938- *AmMWSc 92*
**Fowley,** Douglas 1911- *IntMPA 92*
**Fowlis,** William Webster 1937- *AmMWSc 92*
**Fowlkes,** Dane Winstead 1960- *WhoRel 92*
**Fowlkes,** Doretha P. 1944- *WhoBlA 92*
**Fowlkes,** Joe *WhoAmP 91*
**Fowlkes,** Nancy P. *WhoBlA 92*
**Fowlkes,** Nelson J. 1934- *WhoBlA 92*
**Fowls,** Elida White Merrick 1929- *WhoMW 92*
**Fox Sisters** *RelLAm 91*
**Fox,** A Gardner 1912- *AmMWSc 92*
**Fox,** Adrian Samuel 1936- *AmMWSc 92*
**Fox,** Aileen 1907- *IntAu&W 91, WrDr 92*
**Fox,** Alan 1920- *WrDr 92*
**Fox,** Alan Martin 1938- *Who 92*
**Fox,** Anne Chisholm 1941- *WhoAmP 91*
**Fox,** Anthony *IntAu&W 91X, WrDr 92*
**Fox,** Anthony John 1946- *Who 92*
**Fox,** Arthur Charles 1926- *AmMWSc 92*
**Fox,** Barbara Saxton 1957- *AmMWSc 92*
**Fox,** Barry Jay 1956- *WhoWest 92*
**Fox,** Bennett L 1938- *AmMWSc 92*
**Fox,** Bernard Lawrence 1940- *AmMWSc 92*
**Fox,** Bernard Michael 1942- *WhoFI 92*
**Fox,** Betty 1935- *WhoFI 92*
**Fox,** Betty Lee 1948- *WhoMW 92*
**Fox,** Bradley Alan 1963- *AmMWSc 92*
**Fox,** Brian Michael 1944- *Who 92*
**Fox,** Byron Neal 1948- *WhoAmL 92*
**Fox,** C Fred 1937- *AmMWSc 92*
**Fox,** C. P. 1913- *WrDr 92*
**Fox,** Carl Alan 1950- *AmMWSc 92*
**Fox,** Carol 1926-1981 *NewAmDM*
**Fox,** Catherine d1892 *RelLAm 91*
**Fox,** Charles Ira 1940- *WhoEnt 92*
**Fox,** Charles L d1898 *BiInAmS*
**Fox,** Charles Martin 1953- *WhoAmL 92*
**Fox,** Charles Philip 1913- *IntAu&W 91*
**Fox,** Chester 1934- *WhoEnt 92*
**Fox,** Chester David 1931- *AmMWSc 92*
**Fox,** Christine 1922- *TwCPaSc*
**Fox,** Christine R 1947- *WhoAmP 91*
**Fox,** Connie *DrAPF 91, WrDr 92*
**Fox,** Dale Bennett 1939- *AmMWSc 92*
**Fox,** Daniel Michael 1938- *WhoFI 92*
**Fox,** Daniel Wayne 1923- *AmMWSc 92*
**Fox,** Danny Gene 1940- *AmMWSc 92*
**Fox,** David 1920- *AmMWSc 92*
**Fox,** David Eliot 1960- *WhoEnt 92*
**Fox,** David Martin 1948- *WhoEnt 92*
**Fox,** David Wayne 1931- *WhoFI 92, WhoMW 92*
**Fox,** David William 1928- *AmMWSc 92*
**Fox,** David William 1959- *WhoAmL 92*
**Fox,** Dean Frederick 1944- *WhoFI 92*

**Fox,** Derrick Sean 1964- *WhoWest 92*
**Fox,** Donald A 1948- *AmMWSc 92*
**Fox,** Donald Lee 1943- *AmMWSc 92*
**Fox,** Donald Melville 1942- *WhoIns 92*
**Fox,** Donald William 1922- *WhoAmP 91*
**Fox,** Douglas Allan 1927- *WhoRel 92*
**Fox,** Douglas Eugene 1956- *WhoFI 92*
**Fox,** Douglas Gary 1941- *AmMWSc 92*
**Fox,** Douglas Lee 1951- *WhoAmL 92*
**Fox,** Edgar Leroy 1934- *WhoRel 92*
**Fox,** Edward 1937- *IntMPA 92, IntWW 91, Who 92*
**Fox,** Edward A 1920- *AmMWSc 92*
**Fox,** Edward A. 1936- *WhoFI 92*
**Fox,** Edward A 1950- *AmMWSc 92*
**Fox,** Edward Hanton 1945- *WhoAmL 92*
**Fox,** Edward L. 1938-1983 *ConAu 134*
**Fox,** Eleanor Josephine 1953- *WhoFI 92*
**Fox,** Eleanor Mae Cohen 1936- *WhoAmL 92*
**Fox,** Elizabeth *DrAPF 91*
**Fox,** Emmet 1886-1951 *RelLAm 91*
**Fox,** Erika 1936- *ConCom 92*
**Fox,** Eugene N 1927- *AmMWSc 92*
**Fox,** Everett V. 1915- *WhoBlA 92*
**Fox,** Frances Farnsworth 1928- *WhoAmP 91*
**Fox,** Francis Henry 1923- *AmMWSc 92*
**Fox,** Frederick d1991 *NewYTBS 91*
**Fox,** Frederick Alfred 1931- *WhoEnt 92*
**Fox,** Frederick Glenn 1918- *AmMWSc 92*
**Fox,** G. Richard 1942- *WhoAmL 92, WhoMW 92*
**Fox,** G Sidney 1928- *AmMWSc 92*
**Fox,** Gardner F 1911- *TwCSFW 91*
**Fox,** Geoffrey *DrAPF 91*
**Fox,** Geoffrey Charles 1944- *AmMWSc 92*
**Fox,** George A *AmMWSc 92*
**Fox,** George Edward 1945- *AmMWSc 92*
**Fox,** Gerald 1923- *AmMWSc 92*
**Fox,** Gerard F *AmMWSc 92*
**Fox,** Gloria L *WhoAmP 91*
**Fox,** Hamilton Phillips, III 1945- *WhoAmL 92*
**Fox,** Hanna *DrAPF 91*
**Fox,** Harold 1943- *WhoFI 92*
**Fox,** Harold Munro 1889-1967 *FacFETw*
**Fox,** Harry Judd, Jr. 1951- *WhoAmL 92*
**Fox,** Hazel Mary 1928- *Who 92*
**Fox,** Hazel Metz 1921- *AmMWSc 92*
**Fox,** Henry Murray 1912- *IntWW 91, Who 92*
**Fox,** Herbert Leon 1930- *AmMWSc 92*
**Fox,** Howard Tall, Jr. 1920- *WhoMW 92*
**Fox,** Hugh *DrAPF 91*
**Fox,** Hugh 1932- *WrDr 92*
**Fox,** Irving 1912- *AmMWSc 92*
**Fox,** Irving Harvey 1943- *AmMWSc 92*
**Fox,** Irwin *LesBEnT 92*
**Fox,** J Bradley *WhoAmP 91*
**Fox,** J Eugene 1934- *AmMWSc 92*
**Fox,** Jack 1940- *WhoWest 92*
**Fox,** Jack Jay 1916- *AmMWSc 92*
**Fox,** Jack Lawrence 1941- *AmMWSc 92*
**Fox,** James 1939- *IntMPA 92, IntWW 91, Who 92*
**Fox,** James 1941- *WhoEnt 92*
**Fox,** James Carroll 1928- *WhoAmL 92*
**Fox,** James David 1943- *AmMWSc 92*
**Fox,** James Erwin 1945- *WhoAmL 92*
**Fox,** James Gahan 1943- *AmMWSc 92*
**Fox,** James Hoppes 1948- *WhoAmL 92*
**Fox,** James M. *DrAPF 91*
**Fox,** James Michael 1953- *WhoEnt 92*
**Fox,** James N. 1942- *WhoFI 92*
**Fox,** James Richard 1943- *WhoFI 92*
**Fox,** James Robert 1950- *WhoAmL 92*
**Fox,** Jay B, Jr 1927- *AmMWSc 92*
**Fox,** Jean 1941- *WhoEnt 92*
**Fox,** Jean A. 1947- *WhoMW 92*
**Fox,** Jeanne Jones 1929- *WhoBlA 92*
**Fox,** Jeannine Elise 1946- *WhoFI 92*
**Fox,** Jeff *WhoAmP 91*
**Fox,** Jeffrey James 1956- *WhoAmP 91*
**Fox,** Jimi 1946- *WhoEnt 92*
**Fox,** Joan Elizabeth Bothwell 1947- *AmMWSc 92*
**Fox,** Joel S 1939- *AmMWSc 92*
**Fox,** John *DrAPF 91, Who 92*
**Fox,** John 1907-1984 *FacFETw*
**Fox,** John, Jr. 1863-1919 *BenetAL 91*
**Fox,** John Arthur 1924- *AmMWSc 92*
**Fox,** John David 1929- *AmMWSc 92*
**Fox,** John Frederick 1945- *AmMWSc 92*
**Fox,** John Lindsay 1958- *WhoFI 92*
**Fox,** John Marcus 1927- *Who 92*
**Fox,** John Wayne 1947- *WhoAmP 91*
**Fox,** Jon D 1947- *WhoAmP 91*
**Fox,** Jonathan T. 1960- *WhoEnt 92*
**Fox,** Joseph Leland 1938- *WhoWest 92*
**Fox,** Joseph M, III 1922- *AmMWSc 92*
**Fox,** Joseph Marlin 1915- *WhoFI 92*
**Fox,** Joseph S 1947- *AmMWSc 92*
**Fox,** Joseph William *WhoIns 92*
**Fox,** Karl A. 1917- *WrDr 92*
**Fox,** Karl August 1917- *WhoFI 92, WhoMW 92*
**Fox,** Karl Richard 1942- *AmMWSc 92*
**Fox,** Kathy Pinkstaff 1942- *WhoAmL 92*
**Fox,** Kaye Edward 1932- *AmMWSc 92*
**Fox,** Kenneth 1935- *AmMWSc 92, WhoAmL 92*
**Fox,** Kenneth Ian 1943- *AmMWSc 92*
**Fox,** Kenneth Lambert 1927- *Who 92*
**Fox,** Kevin A 1939- *AmMWSc 92*
**Fox,** Kevin Christopher 1963- *WhoMW 92*
**Fox,** Langton Douglas 1917- *Who 92*
**Fox,** Laurel R 1946- *AmMWSc 92*
**Fox,** Leah 1814?-1890 *RelLAm 91*
**Fox,** Len 1905- *WrDr 92*
**Fox,** Leon 1951- *WhoAmL 92*
**Fox,** Leslie 1918- *Who 92*
**Fox,** Levi 1914- *IntAu&W 91, WrDr 92*
**Fox,** Logan Jordan 1922- *WhoRel 92*
**Fox,** Lucia *DrAPF 91*
**Fox,** M. W. 1937- *WrDr 92*
**Fox,** Marci Jane 1951- *WhoAmL 92*
**Fox,** Marcus *Who 92*
**Fox,** Margaret d1893 *RelLAm 91*
**Fox,** Mark Richard 1953- *WhoAmL 92*
**Fox,** Martin 1929- *AmMWSc 92*
**Fox,** Martin Dale 1946- *AmMWSc 92*
**Fox,** Marvin 1922- *WhoRel 92*
**Fox,** Mary *ScFEYrs, TwCPaSc*
**Fox,** Mary, and Richard Whateley *ScFEYrs*
**Fox,** Mary Catherine 1956- *WhoAmP 91*
**Fox,** Mary Eleanor 1919- *AmMWSc 92*
**Fox,** Mary Frances 1940- *AmMWSc 92*
**Fox,** Marye Anne 1947- *AmMWSc 92*
**Fox,** Matthew d1964 *LesBEnT 92*
**Fox,** Matthew 1940- *News 92-2 [port]*
**Fox,** Matthew Steven 1946- *WhoFI 92*
**Fox,** Matthew Timothy 1940- *RelLAm 91*
**Fox,** Mattie Rae Spivey 1923- *AmMWSc 92*
**Fox,** Maurice Sanford 1924- *AmMWSc 92, IntWW 91*
**Fox,** Mem 1946- *IntAu&W 91*
**Fox,** Merrill C 1947- *WhoAmP 91*
**Fox,** Merritt B. 1946- *WhoAmL 92*
**Fox,** Michael Allen 1948- *WhoAmP 91*
**Fox,** Michael Henry 1946- *AmMWSc 92*
**Fox,** Michael J. 1961- *IntMPA 92, IntWW 91, WhoEnt 92*
**Fox,** Michael James 1944- *WhoAmL 92*
**Fox,** Michael Jean 1941- *AmMWSc 92*
**Fox,** Michael John 1921- *Who 92*
**Fox,** Michael Leonard 1825-1888 *DcNCBi 2*
**Fox,** Michael Scott 1963- *WhoAmL 92*
**Fox,** Michael Vass 1940- *WhoRel 92*
**Fox,** Michael Wilson 1937- *AmMWSc 92*
**Fox,** Milton E 1926- *WhoAmP 91*
**Fox,** Mona Alexis *WrDr 92*
**Fox,** Murray *Who 92*
**Fox,** Neil Stewart 1945- *AmMWSc 92*
**Fox,** Norman A. 1911-1960 *TwCWW 91*
**Fox,** Oscar Chapman 1830-1902 *BiInAmS*
**Fox,** Owen Forrest 1944- *AmMWSc 92, WhoMW 92*
**Fox,** Patricia Sain 1954- *WhoMW 92*
**Fox,** Patrick Bernard 1948- *WhoRel 92*
**Fox,** Paul 1925- *Who 92*
**Fox,** Paul Jeffrey 1941- *AmMWSc 92*
**Fox,** Paul Leonard 1925- *IntWW 91*
**Fox,** Paula *DrAPF 91*
**Fox,** Paula 1923- *ConAu 36NR, IntAu&W 91, WrDr 92*
**Fox,** Peter George 1940- *WhoEnt 92*
**Fox,** Peter Kendrew 1949- *IntWW 91*
**Fox,** Phyllis 1923- *AmMWSc 92*
**Fox,** Phyllis Gordon 1931- *WhoWest 92*
**Fox,** Ralph Edward 1929- *WhoRel 92*
**Fox,** Raymond Charles 1930- *WhoEnt 92*
**Fox,** Rebecca J. *WhoAmL 92*
**Fox,** Renee Claire 1928- *IntWW 91*
**Fox,** Richard *IntMPA 92*
**Fox,** Richard A. 1929- *IntMPA 92*
**Fox,** Richard Carr 1933- *AmMWSc 92*
**Fox,** Richard Henry 1938- *AmMWSc 92*
**Fox,** Richard K., Jr. 1925- *WhoBlA 92*
**Fox,** Richard Romaine 1934- *AmMWSc 92*
**Fox,** Richard Shirley 1943- *AmMWSc 92*
**Fox,** Robert 1938- *Who 92, WrDr 92*
**Fox,** Robert August 1937- *WhoFI 92, WhoWest 92*
**Fox,** Robert Bernard 1922- *AmMWSc 92*
**Fox,** Robert Dean 1936- *AmMWSc 92*
**Fox,** Robert Joseph 1953- *WhoFI 92*
**Fox,** Robert Kriegbaum 1907- *AmMWSc 92*
**Fox,** Robert Lee 1923- *AmMWSc 92*
**Fox,** Robert R. *DrAPF 91*
**Fox,** Robert William 1934- *AmMWSc 92*
**Fox,** Roberta 1943- *WhoAmP 91*
**Fox,** Roberta Fulton 1943- *WhoAmL 92*
**Fox,** Robin 1934- *ConAu 135*
**Fox,** Robin James L. *Who 92*
**Fox,** Ronald Ernest 1936- *WhoMW 92*
**Fox,** Ronald Forrest 1943- *AmMWSc 92*
**Fox,** Ronald Lee 1952- *WhoWest 92*
**Fox,** Roy 1920- *Who 92*
**Fox,** Russell Elwell 1916- *AmMWSc 92*
**Fox,** Ruth W. *Who 92*
**Fox,** Sally G 1951- *WhoAmP 91*
**Fox,** Sally Ingersoll 1925- *AmMWSc 92*
**Fox,** Sally Vreseis 1955- *WhoWest 92*
**Fox,** Samuel 1908- *WrDr 92*
**Fox,** Samuel J. 1919- *WhoRel 92*
**Fox,** Samuel Mickle, III 1923- *AmMWSc 92*
**Fox,** Selena 1949- *RelLAm 91*
**Fox,** Selena Marie 1949- *WhoRel 92*
**Fox,** Sidney Walter 1912- *AmMWSc 92, FacFETw*
**Fox,** Stanley Forrest 1946- *AmMWSc 92*
**Fox,** Stephen Cress 1948- *WhoEnt 92*
**Fox,** Stephen R. 1945- *WrDr 92*
**Fox,** Stephen Sorin 1933- *AmMWSc 92*
**Fox,** Steven Alan 1953- *WhoMW 92*
**Fox,** Steven Richard 1959- *WhoAmL 92*
**Fox,** Stuart Ira 1945- *WhoWest 92*
**Fox,** Sunny Jessica 1946- *WhoWest 92*
**Fox,** Susan *DrAPF 91*
**Fox,** Susan Rogan 1946- *WhoAmL 92*
**Fox,** Ted 1954- *WrDr 92*
**Fox,** Terry 1958-1981 *FacFETw*
**Fox,** Terry Curtis 1948- *WhoEnt 92*
**Fox,** Theodore B. 1912-1988 *WhoBlA 92N*
**Fox,** Theodore J. *WrDr 92*
**Fox,** Thomas Allen 1926- *AmMWSc 92*
**Fox,** Thomas David 1950- *AmMWSc 92*
**Fox,** Thomas E., Jr. 1963- *WhoBlA 92*
**Fox,** Thomas George 1942- *WhoWest 92*
**Fox,** Thomas Oren 1945- *AmMWSc 92*
**Fox,** Thomas Walton 1923- *AmMWSc 92*
**Fox,** Timothy Patrick 1958- *WhoEnt 92*
**Fox,** Uffa 1898-1972 *DcTwDes, FacFETw*
**Fox,** Vernon 1916- *ConAu 35NR*
**Fox,** Virgil 1912-1980 *NewAmDM*
**Fox,** Virginia Gaines 1939- *WhoEnt 92*
**Fox,** Wallace 1920- *Who 92*
**Fox,** William 1914- *AmMWSc 92*
**Fox,** William 1928- *Who 92*
**Fox,** William B 1928- *AmMWSc 92*
**Fox,** William Cassidy 1926- *AmMWSc 92*
**Fox,** William F., Jr. 1942- *IntWW 91*
**Fox,** William K. 1917- *WhoBlA 92*
**Fox,** William L. *DrAPF 91*
**Fox,** William Lloyd, Jr. 1953- *WhoRel 92*
**Fox,** William R 1936- *AmMWSc 92*
**Fox,** William Templeton 1932- *AmMWSc 92*
**Fox,** William Thornton Rickert 1912-1988 *AmPeW*
**Fox,** William Walter, Jr 1945- *AmMWSc 92*
**Fox,** Winifred Marjorie *Who 92*
**Fox-Andrews,** James Roland Blake 1922- *Who 92*
**Fox Bassett,** Nigel 1929- *Who 92*
**Fox-Genovese,** Elizabeth 1941- *WrDr 92*
**Fox-Pitt,** Douglas 1864-1922 *TwCPaSc*
**Fox-Strangways** *Who 92*
**Foxall,** Colin 1947- *Who 92*
**Foxall,** Martha Jean 1931- *WhoBlA 92*
**Foxall,** Raymond 1916- *IntAu&W 91, WrDr 92*
**Foxell,** Clive Arthur Peirson 1930- *Who 92*
**Foxell,** Nigel 1931- *WrDr 92*
**Foxen,** Gene Louis 1936- *WhoFI 92*
**Foxhall,** George Frederic 1939- *AmMWSc 92*
**Foxhoven,** Jerry Ray 1952- *WhoAmL 92*
**Foxhoven,** Michael John 1949- *WhoFI 92, WhoWest 92*
**Foxlee,** James Brazier 1921- *Who 92*
**Foxley,** Alejandro 1939- *IntWW 91*
**Foxley,** William Noall 1949- *WhoWest 92*
**Foxley-Norris,** Christopher 1917- *Who 92*
**Foxley Rioseco,** Alejandro 1940- *IntWW 91*
**Foxman,** Bruce Mayer 1942- *AmMWSc 92*
**Foxman,** Stephen Mark 1946- *WhoAmL 92*
**Foxon,** David Fairweather 1923- *Who 92*
**Foxon,** Harold Peter 1919- *Who 92*
**Foxton,** Edwin Frederick 1914- *Who 92*
**Foxwell,** Ivan 1914- *IntMPA 92*
**Foxwell,** Julia Elena 1944- *WhoHisp 92*
**Foxworth,** Eugene D, Jr 1927- *WhoAmP 91*
**Foxworth,** John Edwin, Jr. 1932- *WhoMW 92*
**Foxworth,** Robert 1941- *IntMPA 92*
**Foxworthy,** Bruce L 1925- *AmMWSc 92*
**Foxworthy,** James E 1930- *AmMWSc 92*
**Foxx,** Daniel LeRoy, Jr. 1939- *WhoWest 92*
**Foxx,** Dave 1950- *WhoEnt 92*
**Foxx,** Jack *WrDr 92*
**Foxx,** Jimmie 1907-1967 *FacFETw*
**Foxx,** Redd d1991 *LesBEnT 92, NewYTBS 91 [port]*
**Foxx,** Redd 1922- *IntMPA 92, WhoBlA 92*
**Foxx,** Redd 1922-1991 *ConAu 135, ConBlB 2 [port], News 92-2*
**Foxx,** Richard Michael 1944- *AmMWSc 92*
**Foy,** Benny Earl 1948- *WhoMW 92*
**Foy,** C Allan 1944- *AmMWSc 92*
**Foy,** Charles Daley 1923- *AmMWSc 92*
**Foy,** Chester Larrimore 1928- *AmMWSc 92*
**Foy,** Herbert Miles, III 1945- *WhoAmL 92*
**Foy,** Hjordis M 1926- *AmMWSc 92*
**Foy,** James 1772-1823 *DcNCBi 2*
**Foy,** Robert Bastian 1928- *AmMWSc 92*
**Foy,** Ruth Ann 1942- *WhoWest 92*
**Foy,** Thomas Patrick 1951- *WhoAmP 91*
**Foy,** Thomas Paul 1914- *WhoAmP 91*
**Foy,** Wade H 1925- *AmMWSc 92*
**Foy,** Walter Lawrence 1921- *AmMWSc 92*
**Foye,** Laurance V, Jr 1925- *AmMWSc 92*
**Foye,** Patrick Joseph 1957- *WhoAmL 92*
**Foye,** Thomas Harold 1930- *WhoAmL 92*
**Foye,** William Owen 1923- *AmMWSc 92*
**Foye-Eberhardt,** Ladye Antoinette 1943- *WhoBlA 92, WhoMW 92*
**Foyer,** Jean 1921- *IntWW 91*
**Foyle,** Christina Agnes Lilian *Who 92*
**Foyle,** Christina Agnes Lilian 1911- *IntWW 91*
**Foyle,** Dolores Hartley 1928- *WhoAmP 91*
**Foyo,** George William 1946- *WhoHisp 92*
**Foyt,** A J 1935- *FacFETw*
**Foyt,** Arthur George, Jr 1937- *AmMWSc 92*
**Fozard,** James Leonard 1930- *AmMWSc 92*
**Fozard,** John William 1928- *IntWW 91, Who 92*
**Fozzard,** George Broward 1939- *AmMWSc 92*
**Fozzard,** Harry A 1931- *AmMWSc 92*
**Fra Elbertus** *BenetAL 91*
**Fraad,** Lewis M 1907- *AmMWSc 92*
**Fraas,** Arthur P 1915- *AmMWSc 92*
**Fracanzani,** Carlo 1935- *IntWW 91*
**Fracassi,** Michael A. 1957- *WhoAmL 92*
**Fracchia,** Pearl Garza 1950- *WhoHisp 92*
**Fracci,** Carla 1936- *FacFETw, WhoEnt 92*
**Frack,** Joseph E 1948- *WhoIns 92*
**Fradan,** Cyril 1928- *TwCPaSc*
**Frade,** Peter Daniel 1946- *AmMWSc 92*
**Fradin,** Frank Yale 1941- *AmMWSc 92*
**Fradkin,** Cheng-Mei Wang 1928- *AmMWSc 92*
**Fradkin,** David Milton 1931- *AmMWSc 92, WhoMW 92*
**Fradkin,** Judith Elaine 1949- *AmMWSc 92*
**Fradkin,** Mindy Sue 1955- *WhoEnt 92*
**Fraedrich,** Karl Emil 1939- *WhoFI 92*
**Fraenkel,** Dan Gabriel 1937- *AmMWSc 92*
**Fraenkel,** George Kessler 1921- *AmMWSc 92*
**Fraenkel,** Gideon 1932- *AmMWSc 92*
**Fraenkel,** Jack R. 1932- *WrDr 92*
**Fraenkel,** Peter Maurice 1915- *Who 92*
**Fraenkel,** Stephen Joseph 1917- *AmMWSc 92, WhoMW 92*
**Fraenkel-Conrat,** Heinz 1910- *IntWW 91*
**Fraenkel-Conrat,** Heinz L 1910- *FacFETw*
**Fraenkel-Conrat,** Heinz Ludwig 1910- *AmMWSc 92*
**Fraenkel-Conrat,** Jane E 1915- *AmMWSc 92*
**Fraga,** Juan R. 1924- *WhoHisp 92*
**Fraga,** Lupe *WhoHisp 92*
**Fraga,** Robert Joseph 1939- *WhoMW 92*
**Fraga,** Rosa *WhoHisp 92*
**Fraga,** Serafin 1931- *AmMWSc 92*
**Fraga Iribarne,** Manuel 1922- *IntWW 91, Who 92*
**Fragale,** Ron 1950- *WhoAmP 91*
**Fragaszy,** Richard J 1950- *AmMWSc 92*
**Frager,** Malcolm 1935- *NewAmDM*
**Frager,** Malcolm 1935-1991 *CurBio 91N, NewYTBS 91 [port]*
**Frago-Zito,** Ivy Marie 1956- *WhoFI 92*
**Fragola,** Anthony *DrAPF 91*
**Fragola,** Anthony 1943- *IntAu&W 91*
**Fragonard,** Jean Honore 1732-1806 *BlkwCEP*
**Fragos,** Berrien *DrAPF 91*
**Fraguela,** Javier *WhoHisp 92*
**Fraguela,** Rafael Jose 1955- *WhoHisp 92*
**Fraher,** David J. *DrAPF 91*
**Frahm,** Charles Peter 1938- *AmMWSc 92*
**Frahm,** Donald R 1932- *WhoIns 92*
**Frahm,** Herbert Ernst Karl 1913- *WhoNob 90*
**Frahm,** Marilyn Grace 1934- *WhoMW 92*
**Frahm,** Richard R 1939- *AmMWSc 92*
**Frahm,** Robert George, II 1951- *WhoFI 92*
**Frahm,** Sheila 1945- *WhoAmP 91, WhoMW 92*
**Frahmann,** Dennis George 1953- *WhoWest 92*
**Fraiberg,** Lawrence P. *LesBEnT 92 [port]*
**Fraiberg,** Lawrence Phillip 1921- *WhoEnt 92*
**Fraiche,** Donna DiMartino 1951- *WhoAmL 92*
**Fraiden,** Norman Arthur 1943- *WhoAmL 92*
**Fraidin,** Stephen 1939- *WhoAmL 92*
**Fraikor,** Frederick John 1937- *AmMWSc 92*
**Fraikorn,** Beth Ilene 1960- *WhoEnt 92*
**Fraile,** Medardo 1925- *IntAu&W 91*
**Frailey,** Dennis J 1944- *AmMWSc 92*
**Fraim,** John Herbert 1926- *WhoEnt 92*
**Frair,** Karen Lee 1945- *AmMWSc 92*
**Frair,** Wayne 1926- *AmMWSc 92*

**Fraise,** Eugene 1932- *WhoAmP 91*
**Fraiser,** John J, Jr *WhoAmP 91*
**Fraitag,** Leonard Alan 1961- *WhoWest 92*
**Frajola,** Walter Joseph 1916- *AmMWSc 92*
**Fraker,** Anna Clyde 1935- *AmMWSc 92*
**Fraker,** Barth Lyle 1967- *WhoRel 92*
**Fraker,** Bill *ConTFT 9*
**Fraker,** John Richard 1934- *AmMWSc 92*
**Fraker,** Mark Arnott 1944- *WhoWest 92*
**Fraker,** Pamela Jean 1944- *AmMWSc 92*
**Fraker,** William *ConTFT 9*
**Fraker,** William A. 1923- *ConTFT 9, IntMPA 92*
**Frakes,** Elizabeth 1922- *AmMWSc 92*
**Frakes,** George Edward 1932- *WhoWest 92, WrDr 92*
**Frakes,** Lawrence Austin 1933- *AmMWSc 92*
**Frakes,** Phillip E 1929- *WhoIns 92*
**Frakes,** Rodney Vance 1930- *AmMWSc 92*
**Fraknoi,** Andrew 1948- *WhoWest 92*
**Fraknoi,** Andrew Gabriel 1948- *AmMWSc 92*
**Fraleigh,** John Walter 1945- *WhoMW 92*
**Fraleigh,** Peter Charles 1942- *AmMWSc 92*
**Fraley,** Carl D. 1928- *WhoFI 92*
**Fraley,** Elwin E 1934- *AmMWSc 92*
**Fraley,** Jo Ann Budd 1938- *WhoAmL 92*
**Fraley,** Mark Thomas 1952- *WhoAmL 92*
**Fraley,** Robert Thomas 1953- *AmMWSc 92*
**Fraley,** Russell Scott 1957- *WhoAmL 92*
**Fraley,** Ruth Ann 1942- *WhoAmL 92*
**Fralick,** Richard Allston 1937- *AmMWSc 92*
**Fralicx,** Ronald Ray 1950- *WhoAmL 92*
**Fram,** Harvey 1918- *AmMWSc 92*
**Frame,** Alistair 1929- *Who 92*
**Frame,** Alistair Gilchrist 1929- *IntWW 91*
**Frame,** Clarence George 1918- *WhoFI 92, WhoWest 92*
**Frame,** Cynthia Solt *DrAPF 91*
**Frame,** David James 1941- *WhoRel 92*
**Frame,** David William 1934- *Who 92*
**Frame,** Donald M. 1911-1991 *ConAu 133*
**Frame,** Donald Murdoch d1991 *NewYTBS 91 [port]*
**Frame,** Donald Murdoch 1911- *IntAu&W 91, WrDr 92*
**Frame,** Frank Riddell 1930- *IntWW 91, Who 92*
**Frame,** Harlan D 1933- *AmMWSc 92*
**Frame,** James Sutherland 1907- *AmMWSc 92, WhoMW 92*
**Frame,** Janet *ConAu 36NR*
**Frame,** Janet 1924- *ConLC 66 [port], ConNov 91, FacFETw, IntAu&W 91, IntWW 91, RfGEnL 91, WrDr 92*
**Frame,** John Timothy 1930- *Who 92, WhoRel 92*
**Frame,** John W 1916- *AmMWSc 92*
**Frame,** Paul S *AmMWSc 92*
**Frame,** Raymond C. 1946- *WhoFI 92*
**Frame,** Robert Roy 1939- *AmMWSc 92*
**Frame,** Robert Thomas 1948- *WhoMW 92*
**Frame,** Ronald 1953- *ConNov 91, WrDr 92*
**Frame,** Ted Ronald 1929- *WhoWest 92*
**Frame,** William Verner 1938- *WhoFI 92*
**Framer,** Walt *LesBEnT 92*
**Framke,** Donna M. 1963- *WhoMW 92*
**Framme,** Lawrence Henry, III 1949- *WhoAmL 92, WhoAmP 91*
**Frampton,** Elon Wilson 1924- *AmMWSc 92*
**Frampton,** George 1860-1928 *TwCPaSc*
**Frampton,** George Thomas 1917- *WhoAmL 92*
**Frampton,** Hollis 1936-1984 *IntDcF 2-2*
**Frampton,** Meredith 1894-1982 *TwCPaSc*
**Frampton,** Paul Howard 1943- *AmMWSc 92*
**Frampton,** Peter 1950- *FacFETw, NewAmDM, WhoEnt 92*
**Fran,** Paul E. d1991 *NewYTBS 91*
**Frana,** Jerry Louis 1949- *WhoMW 92*
**Franca,** Celia 1921- *WhoEnt 92*
**Franca,** Jose-Augusto 1922- *IntWW 91*
**Francais,** Jean 1920- *IntWW 91*
**Francaix,** Jean 1912- *ConCom 92, NewAmDM*
**Francavilla,** Thomas L 1939- *AmMWSc 92*
**France,** Anatole 1844-1922 *FacFETw*
**France,** Anatole 1844-1924 *GuFrLit 1, ScFEYrs, WhoNob 90*
**France,** Arnold William 1911- *Who 92*
**France,** Belinda Takach 1964- *WhoFI 92*
**France,** Christopher 1934- *Who 92*
**France,** Erwin A. 1938- *WhoBlA 92*
**France,** Frederick Doug, Jr. 1953- *WhoBlA 92*
**France,** James Thomas 1956- *WhoFI 92*
**France,** Joseph David 1953- *WhoFI 92*
**France,** Peter 1935- *Who 92*
**France,** Peter William 1938- *AmMWSc 92*
**France,** Richard Thomas 1938- *Who 92*
**France,** Tab *DrAPF 91*
**France,** Thomas Douglas 1937- *WhoMW 92*
**France,** Valerie Edith 1935- *Who 92*
**France,** W DeWayne, Jr 1940- *AmMWSc 92*
**France,** Walter DeWayne, Jr. 1940- *WhoMW 92*
**Frances Mary Jacqueline of La Tour** 1600-1645 *EncAmaz 91*
**Frances,** Andrew Robert 1950- *WhoEnt 92*
**Frances,** Saul 1910- *AmMWSc 92*
**Frances,** Susan Frances 1948- *WhoFI 92*
**Francesca,** Alba 1950- *WhoEnt 92*
**Francescatti,** Zino d1991 *NewYTBS 91 [port]*
**Francescatti,** Zino 1902- *IntWW 91, NewAmDM*
**Francescatti,** Zino 1905-1991 *CurBio 91N*
**Franceschetti,** Donald Ralph 1947- *AmMWSc 92*
**Franceschi,** Ernest Joseph, Jr. 1957- *WhoAmL 92, WhoWest 92*
**Franceschina,** John Charles 1947- *WhoEnt 92*
**Franceschini,** Guy Arthur 1918- *AmMWSc 92*
**Franceschini,** Remo 1928- *AmMWSc 92*
**Francesconi,** Ralph P 1939- *AmMWSc 92*
**Francfort,** Alfred John, Jr. 1939- *WhoFI 92*
**Franch,** Richard Thomas 1942- *WhoAmL 92*
**Franch,** Robert H 1927- *AmMWSc 92*
**Franchi,** JonCarlo *WhoEnt 92*
**Franchi,** Jorge 1965- *WhoHisp 92*
**Franchi,** Rafael L. 1927- *WhoHisp 92*
**Franchini,** Gene Edward 1935- *WhoAmL 92, WhoAmP 91, WhoWest 92*
**Franchini,** Roxanne 1951- *WhoFI 92*
**Franchon,** Lisa *IntAu&W 91X*
**Franchot,** Peter 1947- *WhoAmP 91*
**Francia,** Jose Gaspar Rodriguez de 1766-1840 *HisDSpE*
**Franciosa,** Anthony 1928- *IntMPA 92, WhoEnt 92*
**Franciosa,** Joseph Anthony 1936- *AmMWSc 92*
**Francis,** Alun 1943- *WhoEnt 92*
**Francis,** Amadeo I.D. 1931- *WhoFI 92*
**Francis,** Anne 1932- *IntMPA 92*
**Francis,** Anthony Huston 1942- *AmMWSc 92*
**Francis,** Arlene *LesBEnT 92*
**Francis,** Arlene 1908- *IntMPA 92*
**Francis,** Arokiasamy Joseph 1941- *AmMWSc 92*
**Francis,** Bettina Magnus 1943- *AmMWSc 92*
**Francis,** C. D. E. *WrDr 92*
**Francis,** Charles *SmATA 66*
**Francis,** Charles K 1939- *AmMWSc 92*
**Francis,** Charles S. L. 1943- *WhoBlA 92*
**Francis,** Cheryl Margaret 1949- *WhoBlA 92*
**Francis,** Chester Wayne 1936- *AmMWSc 92*
**Francis,** Clare 1946- *ConAu 34NR, IntAu&W 91, WrDr 92*
**Francis,** Clare Mary 1946- *Who 92*
**Francis,** Clinton William 1951- *WhoAmL 92*
**Francis,** Connie 1938- *IntMPA 92*
**Francis,** David Albert *WhoBlA 92*
**Francis,** David R. 1933- *ConAu 133*
**Francis,** David Rowland 1850-1927 *FacFETw*
**Francis,** David W 1936- *AmMWSc 92*
**Francis,** David Wesson 1918- *AmMWSc 92*
**Francis,** Delma J. 1953- *WhoBlA 92*
**Francis,** Dennis P 1943- *WhoIns 92*
**Francis,** Dick *IntWW 91*
**Francis,** Dick 1920- *CnDBLB 8 [port], ConNov 91, FacFETw, Who 92, WrDr 92*
**Francis,** Donald Pinkston 1942- *AmMWSc 92*
**Francis,** Dorothy Brenner 1926- *IntAu&W 91, WrDr 92*
**Francis,** Drew M. 1957- *WhoEnt 92*
**Francis,** E. Aracelis 1939- *WhoBlA 92*
**Francis,** Edith V. *WhoBlA 92*
**Francis,** Edward Howel 1924- *Who 92*
**Francis,** Edward Reginald 1929- *Who 92*
**Francis,** Erle William 1909- *WhoAmL 92*
**Francis,** Eugene 1917- *WhoEnt 92*
**Francis,** Eugene A 1927- *AmMWSc 92*
**Francis,** Evan Eugene, Jr. 1942- *WhoRel 92*
**Francis,** Faith Ellen 1929- *AmMWSc 92*
**Francis,** Freddie 1917- *IntMPA 92, WhoEnt 92*
**Francis,** Frederick John 1921- *AmMWSc 92*
**Francis,** Gary Stuart 1943- *AmMWSc 92*
**Francis,** George Konrad 1939- *AmMWSc 92*
**Francis,** Gerald Peter 1936- *AmMWSc 92*
**Francis,** Gilbert H. 1930- *WhoBlA 92*
**Francis,** Gwyn Jones 1930- *Who 92*
**Francis,** H.E. *DrAPF 91*
**Francis,** H. E., Jr. 1924- *WrDr 92*
**Francis,** Henry Minton 1922- *WhoBlA 92*
**Francis,** Herbert Edward, Jr 1924- *IntAu&W 91*
**Francis,** Horace William 1926- *Who 92*
**Francis,** Howard Thomas 1917- *AmMWSc 92*
**Francis,** Ivor Stuart 1938- *AmMWSc 92*
**Francis,** James 1968- *WhoBlA 92*
**Francis,** James Ashby 1948- *WhoMW 92*
**Francis,** James Bicheno 1815-1892 *BiInAmS*
**Francis,** James L. 1943- *WhoBlA 92*
**Francis,** John Elbert 1937- *AmMWSc 92*
**Francis,** John Elsworth 1932- *AmMWSc 92*
**Francis,** John L. 1928- *WhoRel 92*
**Francis,** John Michael 1939- *Who 92*
**Francis,** John William 1966- *WhoFI 92*
**Francis,** Jon Hoyer 1940- *WhoEnt 92*
**Francis,** Joseph A. 1923- *WhoBlA 92, WhoRel 92*
**Francis,** Julie Anne 1961- *WhoWest 92*
**Francis,** Kevin 1949- *IntMPA 92*
**Francis,** Laurie 1918- *Who 92*
**Francis,** Leroy Andrew 1910- *WhoMW 92*
**Francis,** Livingston S. 1929- *WhoBlA 92*
**Francis,** Lois Dahlin 1945- *WhoWest 92*
**Francis,** Lyman L 1920- *AmMWSc 92*
**Francis,** Marion David 1923- *AmMWSc 92*
**Francis,** Mary 1921- *WhoRel 92*
**Francis,** Mary Frances Van Dyke 1925- *WhoFI 92*
**Francis,** Merrill Richard 1932- *WhoAmL 92*
**Francis,** Michael 1922- *TwCPaSc*
**Francis,** Michael Kpakala *WhoRel 92*
**Francis,** Mike 1938- *TwCPaSc*
**Francis,** Mike McD *AmMWSc 92*
**Francis,** Norman *Who 92*
**Francis,** Norman 1922- *AmMWSc 92*
**Francis,** Norman C. *WhoBlA 92*
**Francis,** Owen 1912- *Who 92*
**Francis,** Patricia Anne Shaud 1961- *WhoAmL 92*
**Francis,** Patricia Rose 1948- *WhoMW 92, WhoRel 92*
**Francis,** Patrick John 1964- *WhoBlA 92*
**Francis,** Peter David 1934- *WhoAmP 91, WhoWest 92*
**Francis,** Peter Schuyler 1927- *AmMWSc 92*
**Francis,** Philip *IntAu&W 91X*
**Francis,** Philip Hamilton 1938- *AmMWSc 92*
**Francis,** Ray Llewellyn 1921- *AmMWSc 92, WhoMW 92*
**Francis,** Ray William, Jr. 1927- *WhoBlA 92*
**Francis,** Richard 1945- *IntAu&W 91, WrDr 92*
**Francis,** Richard Arden 1938- *WhoAmL 92*
**Francis,** Richard L. 1919- *WhoBlA 92*
**Francis,** Richard L 1933- *AmMWSc 92*
**Francis,** Richard Lane 1938- *AmMWSc 92*
**Francis,** Richard Mark 1947- *Who 92*
**Francis,** Richard Norman 1949- *WhoWest 92*
**Francis,** Richard Stanley *Who 92*
**Francis,** Richard Stanley 1920- *IntAu&W 91, IntWW 91*
**Francis,** Richard Trevor Langford 1934- *IntWW 91, Who 92*
**Francis,** Robert 1901- *IntAu&W 91*
**Francis,** Robert 1901-1987 *BenetAL 91*
**Francis,** Robert Colgate 1942- *AmMWSc 92*
**Francis,** Robert Dorl 1920- *AmMWSc 92*
**Francis,** Ronald Bernard 1964- *WhoBlA 92*
**Francis,** Sam 1923- *IntWW 91*
**Francis,** Samuel Hopkins 1943- *AmMWSc 92*
**Francis,** Sharron H 1944- *AmMWSc 92*
**Francis,** Shirley Ann 1934- *WhoAmP 91*
**Francis,** Spencer Lee 1943- *WhoFI 92*
**Francis,** Stanley Arthur 1919- *AmMWSc 92*
**Francis,** Thomas, Jr 1900-1969 *FacFETw*
**Francis,** Thomas Edward 1933- *WhoAmP 91*
**Francis,** Timothy Duane 1956- *WhoWest 92*
**Francis,** William *Who 92*
**Francis,** William Charles 1937- *WhoMW 92*
**Francis,** William Connett 1922- *AmMWSc 92*
**Francis,** William Howard 1941- *WhoAmL 92*
**Francis,** William Lancelot 1906- *Who 92*
**Francis,** William Norman 1921- *Who 92*
**Francis,** William Porter 1940- *AmMWSc 92*
**Francis,** Yvette Fay *WhoBlA 92*
**Francisci Di Baschi,** Marco 1920- *IntWW 91*
**Francisco,** Anthony M. 1960- *WhoBlA 92*
**Francisco,** James L. 1937- *WhoMW 92*
**Francisco,** James Lee 1937- *WhoAmP 91*
**Francisco,** Jerry Thomas 1932- *AmMWSc 92*
**Francisco,** Joseph Salvadore, Jr 1955- *AmMWSc 92, WhoBlA 92*
**Francisco,** Juan, Jr. 1952- *WhoHisp 92*
**Francisco,** Julia M 1947- *WhoAmP 91*
**Francisco,** Kenneth Dale 1941- *WhoAmP 91*
**Francisco,** Marcia Madora 1958- *WhoBlA 92*
**Francisco,** Patricia Weaver *DrAPF 91*
**Francisco,** Peter 1760?-1831 *DcNCBi 2*
**Francisco,** Virginia Royster 1942- *WhoEnt 92*
**Francisco,** Wayne Markland 1943- *WhoFI 92, WhoWest 92*
**Francisco,** William H. 1947- *WhoFI 92*
**Franciscovich,** George 1954- *WhoEnt 92*
**Franciscus,** James d1991 *LesBEnT 92, NewYTBS 91 [port]*
**Franciscus,** James 1934-1991 *News 92-1*
**Franck,** Ardath Amond 1925- *WhoMW 92*
**Franck,** Cesar 1822-1890 *NewAmDM*
**Franck,** Frederick 1909- *IntAu&W 91, WrDr 92*
**Franck,** Harry A. 1881-1962 *BenetAL 91*
**Franck,** James 1882-1964 *FacFETw, WhoNob 90*
**Franck,** John Martin 1680?-1745 *DcNCBi 2*
**Franck,** Jorge L. 1959- *WhoEnt 92*
**Franck,** Kay 1911- *DcTwDes*
**Franck,** Michael 1932- *WhoAmL 92, WhoFI 92*
**Franck,** Richard W 1936- *AmMWSc 92*
**Franck,** Thomas Martin 1931- *IntAu&W 91, WhoAmL 92, WrDr 92*
**Franck,** Wallace Edmundt 1933- *AmMWSc 92*
**Francka,** Catherine Cantwell 1937- *WhoAmP 91*
**Francke,** August Hermann 1663-1727 *BlkwCEP*
**Francke,** Oscar F 1950- *AmMWSc 92*
**Francke,** Uta 1942- *AmMWSc 92*
**Franckenstein,** Joseph von, Baroness *Who 92*
**Franckiewicz,** Victor John, Jr 1954- *WhoAmP 91*
**Francklin,** Philip 1913- *Who 92*
**Francko,** David Alex 1952- *AmMWSc 92, WhoMW 92*
**Franco** 1939-1989 *FacFETw*
**Franco,** Adolfo Mariano 1922- *WhoHisp 92*
**Franco,** Angel 1951- *WhoHisp 92*
**Franco,** Armando 1935- *WhoFI 92, WhoHisp 92*
**Franco,** Barbara Alice 1945- *WhoMW 92*
**Franco,** Carole Ann 1948- *WhoEnt 92*
**Franco,** Charles, Sr. *WhoHisp 92*
**Franco,** David Michael 1948- *WhoRel 92*
**Franco,** Francisco 1892-1975 *EncTR 91 [port], FacFETw [port]*
**Franco,** Frank 1945- *WhoWest 92*
**Franco,** Gloria Lopez *WhoHisp 92*
**Franco,** Harry *BenetAL 91*
**Franco,** Hernan R. 1942- *WhoHisp 92*
**Franco,** John Albert 1942- *WhoAmL 92*
**Franco,** John Vincent 1947- *WhoMW 92*
**Franco,** Jorge 1929- *WhoWest 92*
**Franco,** Jose, Jr. 1966- *WhoHisp 92*
**Franco,** Juan Roberto 1937- *WhoHisp 92*
**Franco,** Julio 1961- *WhoHisp 92*
**Franco,** Julio Cesar 1961- *WhoBlA 92*
**Franco,** Madeleine 1949- *WhoWest 92*
**Franco,** Nicholas Benjamin 1938- *AmMWSc 92*
**Franco,** Paul Roy 1947- *WhoHisp 92*
**Franco,** Philip Joseph 1922- *WhoFI 92*
**Franco,** Ralph Abraham 1921- *WhoAmL 92*
**Franco,** Ramon Luis 1963- *WhoHisp 92*
**Franco,** Richard Anthony 1941- *WhoFI 92*
**Franco,** Robert J., II 1957- *WhoAmL 92*
**Franco,** Ruben 1947- *WhoHisp 92*
**Franco,** Rudolph Lopez 1929- *WhoHisp 92*
**Franco,** Thomas S *WhoIns 92*
**Franco,** Victor 1937- *AmMWSc 92*
**Franco,** Victor Manuel 1949- *WhoHisp 92*
**Franco Bahamonde,** Francisco 1893-1975 *HisDSpE*
**Franco-Saenz,** Roberto 1937- *AmMWSc 92*
**Franco Y Bahamonde,** Francisco 1892-1975 *BiDExR*
**Francoeur,** Robert Thomas 1931- *AmMWSc 92, WrDr 92*
**Francois,** Emmanuel Saturnin 1938- *WhoBlA 92*
**Francois,** Gary Ray 1937- *WhoMW 92*

**Francois,** Georges Charles Clement G 1910-1969 *WhoNob 90*
**Francois,** Josephus Alphonsus Marie 1901- *BiDExR*
**Francois,** Richard K. 1947- *WhoWest 92*
**Francois,** Terry A. 1921- *WhoBlA 92*
**Francois,** Theodore Victor 1938- *WhoBlA 92*
**Francois-Poncet,** Andre 1887-1978 *EncTR 91 [port]*
**Francois-Poncet,** Jean Andre 1928- *IntWW 91, Who 92*
**Francomano,** George 1933- *WhoIns 92*
**Francome,** John 1952- *IntAu&W 91, Who 92*
**Francq,** Edward Nathaniel Lloyd 1934- *AmMWSc 92*
**Francuch,** Paul Charles 1950- *WhoMW 92*
**Francy,** David Bruce 1932- *AmMWSc 92*
**Franda,** Robert Josef 1966- *WhoMW 92*
**Frandina,** Anthony Frank 1937- *WhoFI 92*
**Frandsen,** Henry 1933- *AmMWSc 92*
**Frandsen,** John Christian 1933- *AmMWSc 92*
**Frandsen,** Lloyd 1948- *WhoAmP 91*
**Frandson,** Rowen Dale 1920- *AmMWSc 92*
**Franey,** Philip David 1948- *WhoFI 92*
**Franey,** Ros 1946- *WrDr 92*
**Franger,** Lynn Marie 1959- *WhoMW 92*
**Frangione,** Blas *AmMWSc 92*
**Frangiosa,** Lawrence Michael 1961- *WhoAmL 92*
**Frangipane,** Francis A. 1946- *WhoRel 92*
**Frangopol,** Dan Mircea 1946- *AmMWSc 92*
**Frangopoulos,** Zissimos A. 1944- *WhoFI 92*
**Frangos,** James George 1934- *WhoAmL 92*
**Frangsmyr,** Tore 1938- *IntWW 91*
**Franjieh,** Suleiman 1910- *IntWW 91*
**Franju,** Georges 1912-1987 *IntDcF 2-2*
**Frank,** Alan Donald 1917- *Who 92*
**Frank,** Alan M 1944- *AmMWSc 92*
**Frank,** Albert Bernard 1939- *AmMWSc 92*
**Frank,** Alfred Swift, Jr 1924- *WhoAmP 91*
**Frank,** Allan Lee 1964- *WhoFI 92*
**Frank,** Andre Gunder 1929- *WrDr 92*
**Frank,** Andrew *Who 92*
**Frank,** Andrew Julian 1925- *AmMWSc 92*
**Frank,** Anne 1929-1945 *ConAu 133, EncTR 91 [port], FacFETw*
**Frank,** Anthony M. 1931- *CurBio 91 [port], News 92-1 [port]*
**Frank,** Arlen W 1928- *AmMWSc 92*
**Frank,** Arne 1925- *AmMWSc 92*
**Frank,** Arnie 1929- *WhoEnt 92*
**Frank,** Arthur J. 1946- *WhoAmL 92*
**Frank,** Arthur Jesse 1945- *AmMWSc 92*
**Frank,** Barney 1940- *AlmAP 92 [port], WhoAmP 91*
**Frank,** Barry *LesBEnT 92*
**Frank,** Barry 1941- *AmMWSc 92*
**Frank,** Barry H. 1938- *WhoAmL 92*
**Frank,** Bernard 1913- *WhoAmL 92*
**Frank,** Bruce Hill 1938- *AmMWSc 92, WhoMW 92*
**Frank,** Bruce Howard 1937- *WhoFI 92*
**Frank,** Bruno 1887-1945 *LiExTwC*
**Frank,** Caroline Kachura 1943- *WhoFI 92*
**Frank,** Carolyn 1952- *AmMWSc 92*
**Frank,** Charles *Who 92*
**Frank,** Charles 1911- *IntWW 91*
**Frank,** Charles Edward 1914- *AmMWSc 92*
**Frank,** Charles Marvin 1932- *WhoEnt 92*
**Frank,** Charles R. 1937- *WrDr 92*
**Frank,** Claude 1925- *NewAmDM, WhoEnt 92*
**Frank,** Claudia Pat 1936- *WhoAmP 91*
**Frank,** David Lewis 1943- *AmMWSc 92*
**Frank,** David Stanley 1944- *AmMWSc 92*
**Frank,** Don J 1937- *WhoAmP 91*
**Frank,** Don Michael 1943- *WhoFI 92*
**Frank,** Donald Herbert 1931- *WhoRel 92, WhoWest 92*
**Frank,** Donald Joseph 1926- *AmMWSc 92*
**Frank,** Donald Louis 1955- *WhoRel 92*
**Frank,** Douglas 1916- *Who 92*
**Frank,** Edmond 1945- *IntMPA 92*
**Frank,** Elizabeth 1945- *IntAu&W 91*
**Frank,** Eugene Maxwell 1907- *WhoRel 92*
**Frank,** Floyd William 1922- *AmMWSc 92*
**Frank,** Forrest Jay 1937- *AmMWSc 92*
**Frank,** Frederick 1932- *WhoFI 92*
**Frank,** Frederick Charles 1911- *Who 92*
**Frank,** George Barry 1929- *AmMWSc 92*
**Frank,** Gerald Wendel 1923- *WhoAmP 91*
**Frank,** Glenn William 1928- *AmMWSc 92*
**Frank,** H Lee 1941- *AmMWSc 92*
**Frank,** Hans 1900-1946 *BiDExR, EncTR 91 [port]*
**Frank,** Harriet, Jr. *ReelWom*
**Frank,** Helmut J. *WrDr 92*
**Frank,** Henry Sorg 1902- *AmMWSc 92*
**Frank,** Hilda Rhea Kaplan 1939- *WhoEnt 92*
**Frank,** Hilmer Aaron 1923- *AmMWSc 92*
**Frank,** Howard 1941- *AmMWSc 92*
**Frank,** Ilya Mikaylovich 1908-1990 *WhoNob 90*
**Frank,** Ilya Mikhailovich d1990 *IntWW 91N*
**Frank,** J. Louis 1936- *WhoFI 92*
**Frank,** Jacob 1936- *WhoAmL 92*
**Frank,** Jacqueline 1953- *WhoEnt 92*
**Frank,** James Albert 1952- *WhoEnt 92*
**Frank,** James Richard 1951- *AmMWSc 92*
**Frank,** Jay Allan 1943- *WhoAmL 92*
**Frank,** Jean A. 1942- *WhoWest 92*
**Frank,** Jean Ann 1929- *AmMWSc 92*
**Frank,** Jean-Michel 1895-1981 *DcTwDes*
**Frank,** Jeffrey *DrAPF 91*
**Frank,** Joan Patricia 1925- *AmMWSc 92*
**Frank,** Joel Lawrence 1961- *WhoAmL 92*
**Frank,** John Bernard, Jr. 1947- *WhoWest 92*
**Frank,** John Bernkopf 1956- *WhoAmL 92*
**Frank,** John Howard 1942- *AmMWSc 92*
**Frank,** John L 1935- *AmMWSc 92*
**Frank,** John LeRoy 1952- *WhoAmL 92*
**Frank,** John Nicholas 1953- *WhoMW 92*
**Frank,** John Paul 1917- *WhoAmL 92*
**Frank,** John V. 1936- *WhoFI 92, WhoMW 92*
**Frank,** Josef 1885-1967 *DcTwDes*
**Frank,** Joseph 1918- *WrDr 92*
**Frank,** Joseph Nathaniel 1918- *IntAu&W 91*
**Frank,** Joy Sopis *AmMWSc 92*
**Frank,** Karl Hermann 1898-1946 *BiDExR, EncTR 91 [port]*
**Frank,** Kozi 1930- *AmMWSc 92*
**Frank,** Laurence Michael 1943- *WhoEnt 92*
**Frank,** Lawrence 1915- *AmMWSc 92*
**Frank,** Leo *FacFETw*
**Frank,** Leonard Harold 1930- *AmMWSc 92*
**Frank,** Lily *WhoRel 92*
**Frank,** Lloyd 1925- *WhoAmL 92*
**Frank,** Lorraine Weiss 1923- *WhoAmP 91*
**Frank,** Louis Albert 1938- *AmMWSc 92*
**Frank,** Martin 1947- *AmMWSc 92*
**Frank,** Martin J 1928- *AmMWSc 92*
**Frank,** Mary 1933- *WorArt 1980 [port]*
**Frank,** Maurice Jerome 1942- *AmMWSc 92*
**Frank,** Max 1927- *AmMWSc 92*
**Frank,** Michael Ian 1960- *WhoEnt 92*
**Frank,** Michael Jay 1945- *WhoFI 92*
**Frank,** Michael M 1937- *AmMWSc 92*
**Frank,** Michael Robert 1949- *WhoEnt 92*
**Frank,** Milton 1919- *WhoAmP 91*
**Frank,** Nancy G 1943- *WhoAmP 91*
**Frank,** Neil LaVerne 1931- *AmMWSc 92*
**Frank,** Oscar 1932- *AmMWSc 92*
**Frank,** Pat 1907-1964 *TwCSFW 91*
**Frank,** Patricia Anne 1929- *WhoAmP 91*
**Frank,** Patricia Luciana 1956- *WhoEnt 92*
**Frank,** Paul 1918- *IntWW 91*
**Frank,** Paul A., III 1955- *WhoEnt 92*
**Frank,** Paul Justin 1967- *WhoEnt 92*
**Frank,** Peter *DrAPF 91*
**Frank,** Peter Bruce 1943- *WhoWest 92*
**Frank,** Peter Christensen 1943- *WhoEnt 92*
**Frank,** Peter Wolfgang 1923- *AmMWSc 92*
**Frank,** Philip Marquis 1924- *WhoRel 92*
**Frank,** Rebecca Brumfield 1961- *WhoFI 92*
**Frank,** Reuven *LesBEnT 92*
**Frank,** Rich *LesBEnT 92 [port]*
**Frank,** Richard A 1936- *WhoAmP 91*
**Frank,** Richard Allin 1961- *WhoAmL 92*
**Frank,** Richard Harvey 1942- *WhoEnt 92, WhoWest 92*
**Frank,** Richard Horton, Jr. 1928- *WhoEnt 92*
**Frank,** Richard L. 1931- *WhoBlA 92*
**Frank,** Richard Stephen 1940- *AmMWSc 92*
**Frank,** Robert Allen 1932- *WhoFI 92*
**Frank,** Robert Andrew 1964- *Who 92*
**Frank,** Robert Carl 1927- *AmMWSc 92*
**Frank,** Robert G., Jr. 1943- *ConAu 134*
**Frank,** Robert Joseph 1939- *WhoWest 92*
**Frank,** Robert Loeffler 1914- *AmMWSc 92*
**Frank,** Robert Louis 1958- *WhoAmL 92*
**Frank,** Robert M. 1946- *WhoMW 92*
**Frank,** Robert McKinley, Jr 1932- *AmMWSc 92*
**Frank,** Robert Morris 1920- *AmMWSc 92*
**Frank,** Robert Neil 1939- *AmMWSc 92*
**Frank,** Roland Walter 1956- *WhoFI 92*
**Frank,** Ronald Edward 1933- *WhoFI 92*
**Frank,** Ronald W. 1947- *WhoFI 92*
**Frank,** Ruby Merinda 1920- *WhoFI 92*
**Frank,** Sally Belinkoff 1959- *WhoAmL 92*
**Frank,** Samuel B 1909- *AmMWSc 92*
**Frank,** Sanders Thalheimer 1938- *WhoWest 92*
**Frank,** Sandy *LesBEnT 92*
**Frank,** Sheldon *DrAPF 91*
**Frank,** Sidney Raymond 1919- *AmMWSc 92*
**Frank,** Simon 1921- *AmMWSc 92*
**Frank,** Stanley 1926- *AmMWSc 92*
**Frank,** Stanley Donald 1932- *WhoFI 92*
**Frank,** Stephen Edward 1941- *WhoFI 92*
**Frank,** Stephen Ira 1942- *WhoMW 92*
**Frank,** Stephen Richard 1942- *WhoAmL 92, WhoWest 92*
**Frank,** Steve *WhoAmP 91*
**Frank,** Steven Jay 1961- *WhoAmL 92*
**Frank,** Steven Neil 1947- *AmMWSc 92*
**Frank,** Sylvan Gerald 1939- *AmMWSc 92*
**Frank,** Thaisa *DrAPF 91*
**Frank,** Theodore David 1941- *WhoAmL 92*
**Frank,** Thomas Paul 1956- *AmMWSc 92*
**Frank,** Thomas Stolley 1931- *AmMWSc 92*
**Frank,** Victor Samuel 1919- *AmMWSc 92*
**Frank,** Waldo 1889-1967 *BenetAL 91*
**Frank,** Walter 1905-1945 *EncTR 91*
**Frank,** William Benson 1928- *AmMWSc 92*
**Frank,** William Charles 1940- *AmMWSc 92, WhoMW 92*
**Frank,** William Fielding 1944- *WhoFI 92*
**Frank,** William H. 1943- *WhoFI 92*
**Frank,** William Harris 1948- *WhoAmL 92*
**Frank,** William Nelson 1953- *WhoFI 92*
**Frank,** William Pendleton 1941- *WhoFI 92*
**Frank,** William Richard 1947- *WhoAmL 92*
**Frank,** Wilson James 1923- *AmMWSc 92*
**Frankart,** William A 1943- *AmMWSc 92*
**Franke,** Ann Harriet 1952- *WhoAmL 92*
**Franke,** Arnold Gene 1932- *WhoFI 92*
**Franke,** Charles H 1933- *AmMWSc 92*
**Franke,** Christopher *DrAPF 91*
**Franke,** Donald Edward 1937- *AmMWSc 92*
**Franke,** Egon 1913- *IntWW 91*
**Franke,** Ernest A 1939- *AmMWSc 92*
**Franke,** Ernst Karl 1911- *AmMWSc 92*
**Franke,** Frederick Rahde 1918- *AmMWSc 92*
**Franke,** Gene Louis 1951- *AmMWSc 92*
**Franke,** Herbert 1914- *IntWW 91*
**Franke,** Herbert W 1927- *TwCSFW 91A*
**Franke,** John Charles 1937- *WhoMW 92*
**Franke,** John Erwin 1946- *AmMWSc 92*
**Franke,** John J, Jr 1930- *WhoAmP 91*
**Franke,** Lee E. *DrAPF 91*
**Franke,** Linda Frederick 1947- *WhoAmL 92*
**Franke,** Michael Wolfgang 1948- *WhoMW 92*
**Franke,** Milton Eugene 1931- *AmMWSc 92, WhoMW 92*
**Franke,** Richard Homer 1937- *WhoWest 92*
**Franke,** Richard James 1931- *WhoFI 92*
**Franke,** Robert G 1933- *AmMWSc 92*
**Frankel,** Alona 1937- *ConAu 135, SmATA 66 [port]*
**Frankel,** Arthur 1928- *WhoEnt 92*
**Frankel,** Arthur Irving 1918- *AmMWSc 92*
**Frankel,** Benjamin Harrison 1930- *WhoAmL 92*
**Frankel,** C. David 1953- *WhoEnt 92*
**Frankel,** Daniel 1903- *IntMPA 92*
**Frankel,** Edward Irwin 1941- *WhoWest 92*
**Frankel,** Edwin N 1928- *AmMWSc 92*
**Frankel,** Ellen 1938- *IntAu&W 91*
**Frankel,** Ellen 1951- *ConAu 135*
**Frankel,** Ephraim A. 1942- *WhoMW 92*
**Frankel,** Evan M. d1991 *NewYTBS 91 [port]*
**Frankel,** Fred Harold 1924- *AmMWSc 92*
**Frankel,** Fred Robert 1934- *AmMWSc 92*
**Frankel,** Gene 1923- *WhoEnt 92*
**Frankel,** Gerhart 1901-1965 *TwCPaSc*
**Frankel,** Harry Meyer 1927- *AmMWSc 92*
**Frankel,** Herbert *Who 92*
**Frankel,** Herbert 1914- *AmMWSc 92*
**Frankel,** Jack William 1925- *AmMWSc 92*
**Frankel,** James Burton 1924- *WhoAmL 92*
**Frankel,** Joseph 1935- *AmMWSc 92*
**Frankel,** Julie 1947- *ConAu 36NR*
**Frankel,** Julius 1935- *AmMWSc 92*
**Frankel,** Kenneth 1941- *ConTFT 9*
**Frankel,** Kenneth Reid 1942- *WhoEnt 92*
**Frankel,** Larry 1928- *AmMWSc 92*
**Frankel,** Lawrence 1941- *AmMWSc 92*
**Frankel,** Leonard Jay 1941- *WhoAmL 92*
**Frankel,** Lois J 1948- *WhoAmP 91*
**Frankel,** Martin Richard 1943- *AmMWSc 92, WhoFI 92*
**Frankel,** Marvin E. 1920- *WhoAmL 92*
**Frankel,** Max 1930- *IntAu&W 91, IntWW 91*
**Frankel,** Michael Henry 1939- *WhoAmL 92, WhoFI 92*
**Frankel,** Michael Jay 1947- *AmMWSc 92*
**Frankel,** Michael S. 1946- *WhoWest 92*
**Frankel,** Otto 1900- *Who 92*
**Frankel,** Otto Herzberg 1900- *IntWW 91*
**Frankel,** Paul David *WhoAmL 92*
**Frankel,** Paul Herzberg 1903- *Who 92*
**Frankel,** Phyllis Sarah 1936- *WhoAmP 91*
**Frankel,** Richard Barry 1939- *AmMWSc 92*
**Frankel,** Robert F 1943- *WhoAmP 91*
**Frankel,** Russell Morris 1947- *WhoFI 92*
**Frankel,** Sally Herbert 1903- *IntWW 91, Who 92*
**Frankel,** Sandor 1943- *WrDr 92*
**Frankel,** Sherman 1922- *AmMWSc 92*
**Frankel,** Sidney 1910- *AmMWSc 92*
**Frankel,** Stanley Arthur 1918- *WhoFI 92*
**Frankel,** Theodore Thomas 1929- *AmMWSc 92*
**Frankel,** Victor H 1925- *AmMWSc 92*
**Frankel,** William 1917- *Who 92*
**Frankel,** William George 1954- *WhoEnt 92*
**Franken,** Hendrik 1936- *IntWW 91*
**Franken,** Peter Alden 1928- *AmMWSc 92*
**Franken,** Rose 1895-1988 *BenetAL 91*
**Franken,** Stephen Robert 1932- *WhoEnt 92*
**Frankenberg,** Dirk 1937- *AmMWSc 92*
**Frankenberg,** Julian Myron 1938- *AmMWSc 92*
**Frankenberg,** Naomi *WhoRel 92*
**Frankenburg,** Peter Edgar 1926- *AmMWSc 92*
**Frankenburg,** Richard James 1929- *WhoAmP 91*
**Frankenfeld,** John William 1932- *AmMWSc 92*
**Frankenhaeuser,** Marianne 1925- *IntWW 91*
**Frankenheim,** Samuel 1932- *WhoAmL 92, WhoEnt 92, WhoFI 92*
**Frankenheimer,** John *LesBEnT 92*
**Frankenheimer,** John 1930- *FacFETw, IntDcF 2-2, IntMPA 92*
**Frankenheimer,** John Michael 1930- *IntWW 91, WhoEnt 92*
**Frankenstein,** John 1940- *WhoFI 92*
**Frankenstein,** William Abe 1941- *WhoFI 92*
**Frankenthal,** Robert Peter 1930- *AmMWSc 92*
**Frankenthaler,** Helen 1928- *FacFETw, IntWW 91*
**Franker,** Stephen Grant 1949- *WhoMW 92*
**Frankevich,** Yevgeniy Leonidovich 1930- *IntWW 91*
**Frankfater,** Allen 1941- *AmMWSc 92*
**Frankfather,** William 1944- *WhoEnt 92*
**Frankfort,** Rona S. 1947- *WhoMW 92*
**Frankforter,** Weldon D 1920- *AmMWSc 92*
**Frankfurt,** Stephen Owen 1931- *IntWW 91*
**Frankfurter,** David 1909-1982 *EncTR 91 [port]*
**Frankfurter,** Felix 1882-1965 *AmPolLe, FacFETw [port], RComAH*
**Frankham,** Harold Edward 1911- *Who 92*
**Frankhauser,** Sandra Jane 1963- *WhoMW 92*
**Frankhouser,** Floyd Richard 1944- *WrDr 92*
**Frankhouser,** Homer Sheldon, Jr. 1927- *WhoFI 92*
**Frankhouser,** William Lester 1924- *WhoFI 92*
**Frankie,** Gordon William 1940- *AmMWSc 92*
**Frankino,** Steven P. 1936- *WhoAmL 92*
**Frankish,** Brian Edward 1943- *WhoEnt 92, WhoWest 92*
**Frankish,** H *ScFEYrs*
**Frankl,** Daniel Richard 1922- *AmMWSc 92*
**Frankl,** Paul T. 1887-1958 *DcTwDes*
**Frankl,** Peter 1935- *IntWW 91, Who 92*
**Frankl,** Razelle 1932- *ConAu 133*
**Frankl,** William S 1928- *AmMWSc 92*
**Frankland** *Who 92*
**Frankland,** Anthony Noble 1922- *Who 92*
**Frankland,** Noble *Who 92*
**Frankland,** Noble 1922- *IntAu&W 91, WrDr 92*
**Frankland,** Trevor 1931- *TwCPaSc*
**Frankle,** Edward Alan 1946- *WhoAmL 92*
**Frankle,** Reva Treelisky *AmMWSc 92*
**Frankle,** William Ernest 1944- *AmMWSc 92*
**Franklin,** Alan Douglas 1922- *AmMWSc 92*
**Franklin,** Albert Andrew Ernst 1914- *Who 92*
**Franklin,** Alexander John 1921- *IntAu&W 91, WrDr 92*
**Franklin,** Allan David 1938- *AmMWSc 92*
**Franklin,** Allen D. 1945- *WhoBlA 92*
**Franklin,** Alton David 1940- *WhoEnt 92*
**Franklin,** Ann 1696-1763 *BenetAL 91*
**Franklin,** Aretha 1942- *IntWW 91, NewAmDM, NotBlAW 92 [port], WhoBlA 92*
**Franklin,** Barbara H. *NewYTBS 91*
**Franklin,** Ben 1918- *TwCPaSc*
**Franklin,** Benjamin 1706-1790 *AmPolLe [port], BenetAL 91, BiInAmS,*

*BlkwCEP, BlkwEAR [port], NewAmDM, RComAH*
**Franklin,** Benjamin 1812-1878 *AmPeW*
**Franklin,** Benjamin 1925- *WhoAmL 92*
**Franklin,** Benjamin 1934- *WhoBlA 92*
**Franklin,** Benjamin Barnum 1944- *WhoMW 92*
**Franklin,** Benjamin Edward 1922- *WhoBlA 92*
**Franklin,** Benjamin Nolan 1946- *WhoAmP 91*
**Franklin,** Bernard W. *WhoBlA 92, WhoRel 92*
**Franklin,** Beryl Cletis 1923- *AmMWSc 92*
**Franklin,** Blake Timothy 1942- *WhoAmL 92*
**Franklin,** Bonnie 1944- *IntMPA 92*
**Franklin,** Bruce Walter 1936- *WhoAmL 92, WhoMW 92*
**Franklin,** Byron Paul 1958- *WhoBlA 92*
**Franklin,** Carl C 1922- *WhoAmP 91*
**Franklin,** Carol Bertha 1947- *WhoRel 92*
**Franklin,** Carol Lee 1952- *WhoFI 92*
**Franklin,** Charlotte White *NotBlAW 92*
**Franklin,** Chester Arthur, Jr. 1934- *WhoWest 92*
**Franklin,** Clarence Frederick 1945- *WhoBlA 92*
**Franklin,** Clyde 1929-1979 *WhoBlA 92N*
**Franklin,** Costella M. 1932- *WhoBlA 92*
**Franklin,** Curtis U., Jr. 1929- *WhoBlA 92*
**Franklin,** David Lee 1943- *WhoFI 92*
**Franklin,** David M. 1943- *WhoBlA 92*
**Franklin,** Dolores Mercedes *WhoBlA 92*
**Franklin,** Donald Bruce 1942- *WhoMW 92*
**Franklin,** Edgar 1879- *ScFEYrs*
**Franklin,** Eric 1910- *Who 92*
**Franklin,** Eugene T., Jr. 1945- *WhoBlA 92*
**Franklin,** Eve 1954- *WhoAmP 91*
**Franklin,** Floyd 1929- *WhoBlA 92*
**Franklin,** Frances Stark 1930- *WhoEnt 92*
**Franklin,** Fred Aldrich 1932- *AmMWSc 92*
**Franklin,** Frederick Russell 1929- *WhoAmL 92, WhoMW 92*
**Franklin,** Gail Elizabeth 1952- *WhoEnt 92*
**Franklin,** Gayle Jessup 1957- *WhoBlA 92*
**Franklin,** Gene F 1927- *AmMWSc 92*
**Franklin,** George Henry 1923- *Who 92*
**Franklin,** George Joseph 1920- *AmMWSc 92*
**Franklin,** Gordon Herbert 1933- *Who 92*
**Franklin,** Grant L. 1918- *WhoBlA 92*
**Franklin,** H Bruce 1934- *ScFEYrs*
**Franklin,** Harold A. *WhoBlA 92*
**Franklin,** Harry 1906- *IntAu&W 91*
**Franklin,** Herbert Lehman, Jr 1940- *WhoAmP 91*
**Franklin,** Herman 1935- *WhoBlA 92*
**Franklin,** J.E. *DrAPF 91*
**Franklin,** J. E. 1937- *NotBlAW 92, WhoBlA 92*
**Franklin,** James 1697-1735 *BenetAL 91*
**Franklin,** James Curry 1933- *AmMWSc 92*
**Franklin,** James McWillie 1942- *AmMWSc 92*
**Franklin,** James Russell 1944- *WhoAmP 91*
**Franklin,** Jerrold 1930- *AmMWSc 92*
**Franklin,** Jerry Forest 1936- *AmMWSc 92*
**Franklin,** Jesse 1760-1823 *DcNCBi 2*
**Franklin,** Jimmie Lewis 1939- *IntAu&W 91*
**Franklin,** Joe *LesBEnT 92*
**Franklin,** Joe 1926- *ConAu 134*
**Franklin,** Joel Nicholas 1930- *AmMWSc 92*
**Franklin,** John *Who 92*
**Franklin,** John H. 1915- *WrDr 92*
**Franklin,** John Hope 1915- *FacFETw, IntAu&W 91, IntWW 91, WhoBlA 92*
**Franklin,** John Patrick *WhoWest 92*
**Franklin,** Kenneth Linn 1923- *AmMWSc 92*
**Franklin,** Larry Daniel 1942- *WhoFI 92*
**Franklin,** Leonard 1914- *WhoAmL 92*
**Franklin,** Linda Campbell 1941- *WrDr 92*
**Franklin,** Linda Lawrence 1950- *WhoEnt 92*
**Franklin,** Luther Edward 1929- *AmMWSc 92*
**Franklin,** Marc Adam 1932- *WhoAmL 92*
**Franklin,** Margaret Lavona Barnum 1905- *WhoMW 92*
**Franklin,** Marion McCoy 1938- *WhoRel 92*
**Franklin,** Mark A 1940- *AmMWSc 92*
**Franklin,** Marshall 1929- *WhoWest 92*
**Franklin,** Martha Lois 1956- *WhoBlA 92*
**Franklin,** Martha Minerva 1870-1968 *NotBlAW 92*
**Franklin,** Marvin Michael 1952- *WhoFI 92*
**Franklin,** Mervyn 1932- *AmMWSc 92*
**Franklin,** Meshack 1772-1839 *DcNCBi 2*
**Franklin,** Michael 1927- *Who 92*
**Franklin,** Michael 1952- *WhoFI 92*
**Franklin,** Michael Harold 1923- *IntMPA 92*
**Franklin,** Michael R 1944- *AmMWSc 92*
**Franklin,** Miles 1879-1954 *FacFETw, LiExTwC, RfGEnL 91*
**Franklin,** Milton B., Jr. 1950- *WhoBlA 92*
**Franklin,** Naomi C 1929- *AmMWSc 92*
**Franklin,** Nick 1943- *WhoAmP 91*
**Franklin,** Oliver St. Clair, Jr. 1945- *WhoBlA 92*
**Franklin,** Pamela 1950- *IntMPA 92*
**Franklin,** Percy 1926- *WhoBlA 92*
**Franklin,** Ralph E 1934- *AmMWSc 92*
**Franklin,** Raoul Norman 1935- *IntWW 91, Who 92*
**Franklin,** Raymond W. 1946- *WhoEnt 92*
**Franklin,** Renty Benjamin 1945- *AmMWSc 92, WhoBlA 92*
**Franklin,** Richard 1934- *WhoAmP 91*
**Franklin,** Richard 1948- *IntMPA 92*
**Franklin,** Richard Arnold 1956- *WhoWest 92*
**Franklin,** Richard B. 1948- *WhoEnt 92*
**Franklin,** Richard Crawford 1915- *AmMWSc 92*
**Franklin,** Richard Harrington d1991 *Who 92N*
**Franklin,** Richard Langdon 1925- *WrDr 92*
**Franklin,** Richard Mark 1947- *WhoAmL 92*
**Franklin,** Richard Morris 1930- *AmMWSc 92*
**Franklin,** Robert A. *IntMPA 92*
**Franklin,** Robert Drury 1935- *WhoFI 92*
**Franklin,** Robert Louis 1935- *AmMWSc 92*
**Franklin,** Robert M. 1954- *ConAu 135*
**Franklin,** Robert Michael 1954- *WhoBlA 92*
**Franklin,** Robert Ray 1928- *AmMWSc 92*
**Franklin,** Robert Vernon, Jr. 1926- *WhoBlA 92*
**Franklin,** Ronald *AmMWSc 92*
**Franklin,** Ronald Lee 1939- *WhoRel 92*
**Franklin,** Ronald Monroe 1953- *WhoRel 92*
**Franklin,** Roosevelt 1933- *WhoRel 92*
**Franklin,** Rosa *WhoAmP 91*
**Franklin,** Rosalind 1920-1958 *FacFETw*
**Franklin,** Rudolph Michael *AmMWSc 92*
**Franklin,** Rudolph Thomas 1928- *AmMWSc 92*
**Franklin,** Ruth 1948- *TwCPaSc*
**Franklin,** Samuel Gregg 1946- *AmMWSc 92*
**Franklin,** Samuel Harvey 1928- *WrDr 92*
**Franklin,** Scott Harrison 1954- *WhoWest 92*
**Franklin,** Shirley Clarke 1945- *WhoBlA 92*
**Franklin,** Shirley Marie 1930- *WhoMW 92*
**Franklin,** Stanley Phillip 1931- *AmMWSc 92*
**Franklin,** Stephen David 1941- *WhoRel 92*
**Franklin,** Steve Anthony 1951- *WhoFI 92*
**Franklin,** Sylvan L. 1934- *WhoFI 92*
**Franklin,** Thomas Chester 1923- *AmMWSc 92*
**Franklin,** Thomas Doyal, Jr 1941- *AmMWSc 92*
**Franklin,** Thomas E. 1947- *WhoBlA 92*
**Franklin,** Ursula Martius 1921- *AmMWSc 92*
**Franklin,** Walt *DrAPF 91*
**Franklin,** Warren *WhoEnt 92*
**Franklin,** Warwick Orlando 1938- *IntWW 91*
**Franklin,** Wayne L. 1955- *WhoBlA 92*
**Franklin,** Wilbur A 1942- *AmMWSc 92*
**Franklin,** Wilbur Alan 1942- *WhoWest 92*
**Franklin,** William 1730?-1813 *BenetAL 91*
**Franklin,** William Alfred 1916- *Who 92*
**Franklin,** William B. 1948- *WhoBlA 92*
**Franklin,** William Edwin 1930- *WhoRel 92*
**Franklin,** William Elwood 1931- *AmMWSc 92*
**Franklin,** William Jay 1945- *WhoAmL 92*
**Franklin,** William John 1927- *Who 92*
**Franklin,** William Lloyd 1941- *AmMWSc 92*
**Franklin,** William P. 1953- *WhoFI 92, WhoMW 92*
**Franklin,** William Webster 1941- *WhoAmP 91*
**Franklyn,** Audrey Pozen 1930- *WhoEnt 92*
**Franklyn,** Lesley 1938- *TwCPaSc*
**Franko,** Bernard Vincent 1922- *AmMWSc 92*
**Franko,** Joseph R. 1946- *WhoWest 92*
**Franko,** Robert Matthew 1947- *WhoWest 92*
**Franko-Filipasic,** Borivoj Richard Simon 1922- *AmMWSc 92*
**Frankoski,** Stanley P 1944- *AmMWSc 92*
**Frankovich,** M.J. 1910- *IntMPA 92*
**Frankovich,** Mike J. 1910- *WhoEnt 92*
**Frankovich,** Mike John, Jr. 1942- *WhoEnt 92*
**Franks** *Who 92*
**Franks,** Baron 1905- *IntWW 91, Who 92*
**Franks,** Allen P 1936- *AmMWSc 92*
**Franks,** Arthur Temple 1920- *Who 92*
**Franks,** C Ronald *WhoAmP 91*
**Franks,** Cecil Simon 1935- *Who 92*
**Franks,** David A 1929- *AmMWSc 92*
**Franks,** Desmond Gerald Fergus 1928- *Who 92*
**Franks,** Dick *Who 92*
**Franks,** Dobbs 1933- *WhoEnt 92A*
**Franks,** Donald *WhoRel 92*
**Franks,** Edwin Clark 1937- *AmMWSc 92*
**Franks,** Everlee Gordon 1931- *WhoBlA 92*
**Franks,** Gary 1954?- *ConBlB 2 [port]*
**Franks,** Gary A. 1953- *AlmAP 92 [port], WhoBlA 92*
**Franks,** Gary Alvin 1953- *WhoAmP 91*
**Franks,** Helen 1934- *ConAu 133*
**Franks,** Herbert Hoover 1934- *WhoAmL 92, WhoMW 92*
**Franks,** Herschel Pickens 1930- *WhoAmL 92*
**Franks,** Jack Darrow 1963- *WhoAmL 92*
**Franks,** Janice 1950- *WhoAmL 92*
**Franks,** John Anthony, Jr 1935- *AmMWSc 92*
**Franks,** John Gerald 1905- *Who 92*
**Franks,** John Julian 1929- *AmMWSc 92*
**Franks,** Jon Michael 1941- *WhoAmL 92*
**Franks,** Julius, Jr. 1922- *WhoBlA 92*
**Franks,** Larry Allen 1934- *AmMWSc 92*
**Franks,** Lewis Embree 1931- *AmMWSc 92*
**Franks,** Martin Davis 1950- *WhoAmP 91*
**Franks,** Michael Lee 1954- *WhoAmP 91*
**Franks,** Neal Edward 1936- *AmMWSc 92*
**Franks,** Richard Lee 1941- *AmMWSc 92*
**Franks,** Robert D 1951- *WhoAmP 91*
**Franks,** Stephen G 1950- *WhoIns 92*
**Franks,** Stephen Guest 1946- *AmMWSc 92*
**Franks,** Trent 1957- *WhoAmP 91*
**Franks,** Vaudry Lee 1921- *WhoAmP 91*
**Franks,** William Brown 1948- *WhoFI 92*
**Frankum,** Ronald Bruce 1935- *WhoAmP 91*
**Frann,** Mary *WhoEnt 92*
**Frano,** Andrew Joseph 1953- *WhoAmL 92*
**Franqui,** Carlos 1921- *LiExTwC*
**Frans,** Robert Earl 1927- *AmMWSc 92*
**Franse,** Renard 1948- *AmMWSc 92*
**Franson,** Carl Irvin 1934- *WhoWest 92*
**Franson,** Marc Paul 1955- *WhoAmL 92*
**Franson,** Raymond Lee 1959- *AmMWSc 92*
**Franson,** Richard Carl 1943- *AmMWSc 92*
**Frant,** Martin S 1926- *AmMWSc 92*
**Franta,** William Alfred 1913- *AmMWSc 92*
**Franta,** William Roy 1942- *AmMWSc 92*
**Franti,** Charles Elmer 1933- *AmMWSc 92*
**Frantsi,** Christopher 1942- *AmMWSc 92*
**Frantsve,** Dennis John 1938- *WhoEnt 92*
**Frantti,** Gordon Earl 1928- *AmMWSc 92*
**Frantz,** Andrew Gibson 1930- *AmMWSc 92*
**Frantz,** Beryl May 1943- *AmMWSc 92*
**Frantz,** Daniel Raymond 1943- *AmMWSc 92*
**Frantz,** Dean Leslie 1919- *WhoMW 92*
**Frantz,** Douglas 1949- *IntAu&W 91*
**Frantz,** Gregory Clayton 1947- *AmMWSc 92*
**Frantz,** Ivan DeRay, Jr 1916- *AmMWSc 92*
**Frantz,** Jack Thomas 1939- *WhoFI 92*
**Frantz,** Jeffrey Lloyd 1960- *WhoMW 92*
**Frantz,** Joe B 1917- *IntAu&W 91, WrDr 92*
**Frantz,** Joseph Foster 1933- *AmMWSc 92*
**Frantz,** Julia McBride 1924- *WhoEnt 92*
**Frantz,** Justus *IntWW 91*
**Frantz,** Leroy, Jr 1927- *WhoAmP 91*
**Frantz,** Marc 1951- *WhoMW 92*
**Frantz,** Martin 1952- *WhoAmP 91*
**Frantz,** Michael D. 1955- *WhoMW 92*
**Frantz,** Paul Lewis 1955- *WhoAmL 92*
**Frantz,** Robert Lewis 1925- *WhoAmL 92*
**Frantz,** Robert Wesley 1950- *WhoAmL 92*
**Frantz,** Stephen Richard 1958- *WhoMW 92*
**Frantz,** Theodore Claude 1922- *WhoWest 92*
**Frantz,** Wendelin R 1929- *AmMWSc 92*
**Frantz,** William Lawrence 1927- *AmMWSc 92*
**Frantzen,** Allen J. 1947- *WrDr 92*
**Frantzis,** Theodosios George 1941- *WhoFI 92*
**Frantzve,** Jerri Lyn 1942- *WhoFI 92*
**Franz Ferdinand** 1863-1914 *FacFETw*
**Franz Joseph II** 1906- *FacFETw*
**Franz,** Anselm 1900- *AmMWSc 92*
**Franz,** Arthur 1920- *IntMPA 92*
**Franz,** Caroline Jones 1947- *WhoEnt 92*
**Franz,** Craig Joseph 1953- *AmMWSc 92*
**Franz,** Curtis Allen 1940- *AmMWSc 92*
**Franz,** Daniel Thomas 1949- *WhoFI 92, WhoMW 92*
**Franz,** David Alan 1942- *AmMWSc 92*
**Franz,** Delton Willis 1932- *WhoRel 92*
**Franz,** Donald Eugene, Jr. 1944- *WhoFI 92*
**Franz,** Donald Norbert 1932- *AmMWSc 92*
**Franz,** Edgar Arthur 1919- *AmMWSc 92*
**Franz,** Edmund C 1920- *AmMWSc 92*
**Franz,** Frank Andrew 1937- *AmMWSc 92*
**Franz,** Frederick William 1893- *WhoRel 92*
**Franz,** Gunter Norbert 1935- *AmMWSc 92*
**Franz,** Herbert 1908- *IntWW 91*
**Franz,** James Alan 1948- *AmMWSc 92*
**Franz,** John Edward 1929- *AmMWSc 92*
**Franz,** John Matthias 1927- *AmMWSc 92*
**Franz,** Judy R 1938- *AmMWSc 92*
**Franz,** Keith S 1954- *WhoAmP 91*
**Franz,** Kevin Gerhard 1953- *Who 92*
**Franz,** Kurt Hubert 1904- *EncTR 91*
**Franz,** Laurence Werner 1939- *WhoFI 92*
**Franz,** Louis Joseph 1931- *WhoRel 92*
**Franz,** Lydia Millicent Truc 1924- *WhoFI 92*
**Franz,** Norman Charles 1925- *AmMWSc 92*
**Franz,** Otto Gustav 1931- *AmMWSc 92*
**Franz,** Robert 1815-1892 *NewAmDM*
**Franz,** William Scott 1957- *WhoWest 92*
**Franz,** Wolfgang Wilhelm 1934- *WhoFI 92*
**Franzak,** Edmund George 1930- *AmMWSc 92*
**Franzblau,** Carl 1934- *AmMWSc 92*
**Franzen,** Charles Rice 1957- *WhoRel 92*
**Franzen,** Dorothea Susanna 1912- *AmMWSc 92*
**Franzen,** Hugo Friedrich 1934- *AmMWSc 92*
**Franzen,** James 1934- *AmMWSc 92*
**Franzen,** Jonathan *DrAPF 91*
**Franzen,** Kay Louise 1950- *AmMWSc 92*
**Franzen,** Lavern Gerhard 1926- *WhoRel 92*
**Franzen,** Ulrich J. 1921- *IntWW 91*
**Franzen,** Wolfgang 1922- *AmMWSc 92*
**Franzetta,** Benedict C. 1921- *WhoRel 92*
**Franzi,** Richard Anthony 1958- *WhoWest 92*
**Franzia,** Joseph Stephen 1942- *WhoWest 92*
**Franzin,** William Gilbert 1946- *AmMWSc 92*
**Franzke,** Richard Albert 1935- *WhoAmL 92*
**Franzkowski,** Rainer 1935- *WhoFI 92*
**Franzl,** Robert E 1921- *AmMWSc 92*
**Franzmeier,** Alvin Henry 1933- *WhoRel 92*
**Franzmeier,** Donald Paul 1935- *AmMWSc 92, WhoMW 92*
**Franzoi,** Stephen Louis 1953- *WhoMW 92*
**Franzon,** Paul Damian 1961- *AmMWSc 92*
**Franzoni,** Charles M 1932- *WhoAmP 91*
**Franzosa,** Edward Sykes 1945- *AmMWSc 92*
**Franzusoff,** Alex Jacob 1954- *WhoWest 92*
**Frappia,** Linda Ann 1946- *WhoWest 92*
**Frappier,** Armand 1904- *AmMWSc 92, IntWW 91*
**Frappier,** Cara Munshaw 1942- *WhoMW 92*
**Frarey,** Murray James 1917- *AmMWSc 92*
**Frary,** Hobart Dickinson 1887-1920 *BiInAmS*
**Frary,** Richard Spencer 1924- *WhoWest 92*
**Frasca,** Jeremiah Niblo 1936- *WhoFI 92*
**Frascella,** Daniel W 1934- *AmMWSc 92*
**Frasch,** Brian Bernard 1956- *WhoAmL 92*
**Frasch,** Carl Edward 1943- *AmMWSc 92*
**Frasch,** Herman 1851-1914 *BiInAmS*
**Frasche,** Dean F 1906- *AmMWSc 92*
**Frascino,** Edward *ConAu 35NR*
**Frasco,** David Lee 1931- *AmMWSc 92*
**Frascotti,** John Anthony 1960- *WhoEnt 92*
**Fraser** *Who 92*
**Fraser,** Baron 1945- *IntWW 91*
**Fraser,** Alan Richard 1944- *AmMWSc 92*
**Fraser,** Alasdair MacLeod 1946- *Who 92*
**Fraser,** Albert Donald 1949- *AmMWSc 92*
**Fraser,** Alex Stewart 1923- *AmMWSc 92*
**Fraser,** Alexander 1940- *TwCPaSc*
**Fraser,** Alexander Macdonald 1921- *Who 92*
**Fraser,** Alistair Bisson 1939- *AmMWSc 92*
**Fraser,** Alvardo M. 1922- *WhoBlA 92*
**Fraser,** Angus 1928- *Who 92*
**Fraser,** Angus Simon James 1945- *Who 92*
**Fraser,** Ann Davina Elizabeth 1954- *AmMWSc 92*
**Fraser,** Anthea *WrDr 92*
**Fraser,** Anthea Mary *IntAu&W 91*
**Fraser,** Anthony Walkinshaw 1934- *Who 92*
**Fraser,** Antonia 1932- *IntAu&W 91, IntWW 91, Who 92, WrDr 92*
**Fraser,** Basil 1920- *Who 92*
**Fraser,** Blair Allen 1948- *AmMWSc 92*
**Fraser,** Brian John 1947- *WhoRel 92*
**Fraser,** Bruce 1910- *Who 92*
**Fraser,** Campbell *IntWW 91, Who 92*
**Fraser,** Charles 1928- *Who 92*

**Fraser**, Clarence Malcolm 1926- *AmMWSc 92*
**Fraser**, Claud Lovat 1890-1921 *TwCPaSc*
**Fraser**, Colin Angus Ewen 1918- *Who 92*
**Fraser**, Conon 1930- *WrDr 92*
**Fraser**, Cynthia *TwCPaSc*
**Fraser**, D Ian 1931- *WhoIns 92*
**Fraser**, David 1920- *Who 92*
**Fraser**, David Allison 1922- *AmMWSc 92*
**Fraser**, David Charles 1942- *WhoFI 92*
**Fraser**, David William 1944- *AmMWSc 92*
**Fraser**, Dean 1916- *AmMWSc 92*
**Fraser**, Donald 1921- *AmMWSc 92*
**Fraser**, Donald Alexander Stuart 1925- *AmMWSc 92*
**Fraser**, Donald Blake 1910- *Who 92*
**Fraser**, Donald Boyd 1930- *AmMWSc 92*
**Fraser**, Donald C 1941- *AmMWSc 92*
**Fraser**, Donald Hamilton 1929- *TwCPaSc, Who 92*
**Fraser**, Donald MacKay 1924- *WhoAmP 91, WhoMW 92*
**Fraser**, Donald Ross 1927- *WhoAmP 91*
**Fraser**, Dorothy 1926- *Who 92*
**Fraser**, Douglas 1910- *WrDr 92*
**Fraser**, Douglas Andrew 1916- *IntWW 91*
**Fraser**, Douglas Fyfe 1941- *AmMWSc 92*
**Fraser**, Douglas Were d1988 *Who 92N*
**Fraser**, Earl Donald 1912- *WhoWest 92*
**Fraser**, Earl W., Jr. 1947- *WhoBlA 92*
**Fraser**, Edward *Who 92*
**Fraser**, Eric 1902-1983 *TwCPaSc*
**Fraser**, Everett MacKay 1921- *WhoAmL 92*
**Fraser**, Frank Clarke 1920- *AmMWSc 92*
**Fraser**, George C. 1945- *WhoBlA 92*
**Fraser**, George MacDonald 1925- *IntAu&W 91, Who 92, WrDr 92*
**Fraser**, Gerald Timothy 1957- *AmMWSc 92*
**Fraser**, Gordon Simon 1946- *AmMWSc 92*
**Fraser**, Grant Adam 1943- *AmMWSc 92*
**Fraser**, Harry 1937- *WrDr 92*
**Fraser**, Harvey R 1916- *AmMWSc 92*
**Fraser**, Henry Paterson 1907- *Who 92*
**Fraser**, Hugh Vincent 1908- *Who 92*
**Fraser**, Ian 1901- *Who 92*
**Fraser**, Ian 1933- *TwCPaSc, WhoEnt 92*
**Fraser**, Ian Edward 1920- *Who 92*
**Fraser**, Ian James 1923- *Who 92*
**Fraser**, Ian McLennan 1927- *AmMWSc 92*
**Fraser**, Ian Watson 1907- *Who 92, WrDr 92*
**Fraser**, J T 1923- *AmMWSc 92*
**Fraser**, James *WrDr 92*
**Fraser**, James 1924- *Who 92*
**Fraser**, James Campbell 1923- *IntWW 91, Who 92*
**Fraser**, James Earle 1876-1953 *FacFETw*
**Fraser**, James Edward 1931- *Who 92*
**Fraser**, James Mattison 1925- *AmMWSc 92*
**Fraser**, James Millan 1925- *AmMWSc 92*
**Fraser**, James Owen Arthur 1937- *Who 92*
**Fraser**, Jane *IntAu&W 91X, WrDr 92*
**Fraser**, Jean Ethel 1923- *WhoBlA 92*
**Fraser**, Jill 1952- *WhoEnt 92*
**Fraser**, John Allen 1931- *IntWW 91, Who 92*
**Fraser**, John Denis 1934- *Who 92*
**Fraser**, John Foster 1930- *WhoFI 92*
**Fraser**, John Gillies 1914- *WhoRel 92*
**Fraser**, John Malcolm 1930- *Who 92*
**Fraser**, John Stewart 1931- *Who 92*
**Fraser**, John Stiles 1921- *AmMWSc 92*
**Fraser**, John Wayne 1944- *WhoFI 92*
**Fraser**, Jon 1955- *WhoEnt 92*
**Fraser**, Julie Ann 1959- *WhoMW 92*
**Fraser**, Karen *WhoAmP 91*
**Fraser**, Kathleen *DrAPF 91*
**Fraser**, Kathleen 1937- *ConPo 91, WrDr 92*
**Fraser**, Kenneth John Alexander 1929- *Who 92*
**Fraser**, Kenneth William, Jr. 1937- *WhoFI 92*
**Fraser**, Lemuel Anderson 1918- *AmMWSc 92*
**Fraser**, Leo W 1926- *WhoAmP 91*
**Fraser**, Leon Allison 1921- *WhoBlA 92*
**Fraser**, Malcolm *Who 92*
**Fraser**, Malcolm 1930- *FacFETw, IntWW 91*
**Fraser**, Malcolm Henry 1939- *WhoEnt 92*
**Fraser**, Margaret Shirley *AmMWSc 92*
**Fraser**, Margot 1936- *ConAu 135*
**Fraser**, Mark Robert 1953- *WhoWest 92*
**Fraser**, Michael Neely 1960- *WhoFI 92*
**Fraser**, Michael Raymond 1960- *WhoRel 92*
**Fraser**, Morris 1941- *IntAu&W 91, WrDr 92*
**Fraser**, Nigel William 1947- *AmMWSc 92*
**Fraser**, Norah Anne *WhoEnt 92*
**Fraser**, Paterson *Who 92*
**Fraser**, Peter Arthur 1928- *AmMWSc 92*
**Fraser**, Peter Marshall 1918- *IntWW 91, Who 92*
**Fraser**, Randall Orin 1949- *WhoEnt 92*
**Fraser**, Renee White 1952- *WhoWest 92*
**Fraser**, Rhonda Beverly 1960- *WhoBlA 92*
**Fraser**, Robert 1947- *ConAu 134*
**Fraser**, Robert Donald Bruce 1924- *IntWW 91*
**Fraser**, Robert Gordon 1921- *AmMWSc 92*
**Fraser**, Robert Rowntree 1931- *AmMWSc 92*
**Fraser**, Robert Stewart 1922- *AmMWSc 92*
**Fraser**, Robert Stuart 1923- *AmMWSc 92*
**Fraser**, Rodger Alvin 1944- *WhoBlA 92*
**Fraser**, Ronald Chester 1919- *AmMWSc 92*
**Fraser**, Ronald Petrie 1917- *Who 92*
**Fraser**, Russell A. 1927- *WrDr 92*
**Fraser**, Simon 1950- *TwCPaSc*
**Fraser**, Simon William Hetherington 1951- *Who 92*
**Fraser**, Stanley Charles 1951- *WhoMW 92*
**Fraser**, Sylvia Lois 1935- *IntAu&W 91*
**Fraser**, Thomas Cameron 1949- *WhoEnt 92*
**Fraser**, Thomas Hunter 1948- *AmMWSc 92*
**Fraser**, Thomas Jefferson 1932- *WhoAmP 91*
**Fraser**, Thomas Robert 1962- *WhoWest 92*
**Fraser**, Thomas Russell 1908- *Who 92*
**Fraser**, Troy L 1949- *WhoAmP 91*
**Fraser**, Veronica Mary 1933- *Who 92*
**Fraser**, W. Hamish 1941- *WrDr 92*
**Fraser**, William d1990 *IntWW 91N*
**Fraser**, William Hamish 1941- *IntAu&W 91*
**Fraser**, William James 1921- *Who 92*
**Fraser**, William Kerr 1929- *IntWW 91, Who 92*
**Fraser**, William Lawrence 1929- *WhoFI 92*
**Fraser McLuskey**, James *Who 92*
**Fraser of Carmyllie**, Baron 1945- *Who 92*
**Fraser Of Kilmorack**, Baron 1915- *IntWW 91, Who 92*
**Fraser-Reid**, Bertram Oliver 1934- *AmMWSc 92*
**Fraser-Smith**, Antony Charles 1938- *AmMWSc 92*
**Fraser-Tytler**, Christian Helen 1897- *Who 92*
**Frasher**, Wallace G, Jr 1920- *AmMWSc 92*
**Frashier**, Loyd Dola 1916- *AmMWSc 92*
**Frasier**, Gary W. 1937- *WhoWest 92*
**Frasier**, Gary Wayne 1937- *AmMWSc 92*
**Frasier**, George E. 1942- *WhoAmL 92, WhoWest 92*
**Frasier**, Jim 1940- *WhoAmP 91*
**Frasier**, Leroy B. 1910- *WhoBlA 92*
**Frasier**, Mary Mack 1938- *WhoBlA 92*
**Frasier**, Ralph Kennedy 1938- *WhoAmL 92, WhoBlA 92, WhoFI 92*
**Frasier**, S Douglas 1932- *AmMWSc 92*
**Frassetto**, Floriana Domina 1950- *WhoEnt 92*
**Frassinelli**, Guido Joseph 1927- *WhoWest 92*
**Frasure**, Evan *WhoAmP 91*
**Frasure**, Kenneth William 1955- *WhoEnt 92*
**Frasyniuk**, Wladyslaw 1954- *IntWW 91*
**Fratantoni**, Joseph Charles 1938- *AmMWSc 92*
**Fratcher**, William Franklin 1913- *WhoAmL 92, WhoMW 92, WrDr 92*
**Frater**, Alexander 1937- *WrDr 92*
**Frater**, Maurice Alan 1939- *WhoAmL 92*
**Frater**, Robert William Mayo 1928- *AmMWSc 92*
**Frates**, Gregory Frank 1960- *WhoWest 92*
**Frati**, William 1931- *AmMWSc 92*
**Fratianni**, Michele Ugo 1941- *WhoMW 92*
**Fratiello**, Anthony 1936- *AmMWSc 92*
**Fratini**, Georgina Carolin 1931- *IntWW 91*
**Frattali**, Rose E 1931- *WhoIns 92*
**Frattali**, Victor Paul 1938- *AmMWSc 92*
**Fratti**, Mario 1927- *IntAu&W 91, WhoEnt 92, WrDr 92*
**Frattini**, Gianfranco 1926- *DcTwDes*
**Frattini**, Paul L 1958- *AmMWSc 92*
**Fratus**, Jeffrey Richard 1963- *WhoMW 92*
**Fratzke**, Charles Edward 1927- *WhoIns 92*
**Fratzke**, Michael Julius 1950- *WhoMW 92*
**Frauchiger**, Fritz Arnold 1941- *WhoWest 92*
**Frauenfeld**, Alfred Eduard 1898-1977 *BiDExR, EncTR 91 [port]*
**Frauenfelder**, Hans 1922- *AmMWSc 92*
**Frauenglas**, Robert A. *DrAPF 91*
**Frauenglass**, Elliott 1934- *AmMWSc 92*
**Frauenthal**, James Clay 1944- *AmMWSc 92*
**Fraughan**, Charles 1929- *TwCPaSc*
**Fraumeni**, Joseph F, Jr 1933- *AmMWSc 92*
**Fraunfelder**, Frederick Theodor 1934- *AmMWSc 92*
**Fraunfelder**, Frederick Theodore 1934- *WhoWest 92*
**Fraunfelter**, George H 1927- *AmMWSc 92*
**Frausto**, Marco Antonio 1950- *WhoHisp 92*
**Frautschi**, Steven Clark 1933- *AmMWSc 92, WhoWest 92*
**Frautschi**, Timothy Clark 1937- *WhoAmL 92*
**Frautschy**, Jeffery Dean 1919- *AmMWSc 92*
**Frawley**, Anthony Denis 1949- *AmMWSc 92*
**Frawley**, Daniel S 1943- *WhoAmP 91*
**Frawley**, James 1937- *IntMPA 92*
**Frawley**, John Paul 1927- *AmMWSc 92*
**Frawley**, Mark David 1959- *WhoEnt 92*
**Frawley**, Nile Nelson 1950- *AmMWSc 92*
**Frawley**, Robert Donald 1947- *WhoFI 92*
**Frawley**, Thomas Francis 1919- *AmMWSc 92*
**Frawley**, William James 1937- *AmMWSc 92*
**Fray**, Peter Richard 1946- *WhoFI 92, WhoMW 92*
**Fray**, Robert Dutton 1939- *AmMWSc 92*
**Frayer**, Warren Edward 1939- *AmMWSc 92*
**Frayling**, Christopher John 1946- *Who 92*
**Frayling**, Nicholas Arthur 1944- *Who 92*
**Frayn**, Michael 1933- *ConNov 91, IntAu&W 91, IntWW 91, TwCSFW 91, Who 92, WrDr 92*
**Frayne**, Anne Marie 1954- *WhoAmL 92*
**Frayne**, David Patrick 1965- *WhoWest 92*
**Frayser**, Katherine Regina 1926- *AmMWSc 92*
**Fraysse**, Jean-Pierre 1930- *IntWW 91*
**Frazao**, Sergio Armando 1917- *IntWW 91*
**Fraze**, Candida *DrAPF 91*
**Fraze**, Candida 1945- *IntAu&W 91*
**Frazee**, Jane 1936- *WhoEnt 92*
**Frazee**, Jerry D 1929- *AmMWSc 92*
**Frazee**, John Powell, Jr. 1944- *WhoFI 92*
**Frazee**, Mary Ann 1934- *WhoAmP 91*
**Frazee**, Robert C 1928- *WhoAmP 91*
**Frazee**, Ronald Leroy 1946- *WhoAmL 92*
**Frazee**, Rowland C. 1921- *IntWW 91*
**Frazee**, Steve 1909- *IntAu&W 91, TwCWW 91, WrDr 92*
**Frazer**, Alan 1943- *AmMWSc 92*
**Frazer**, Andrew *IntAu&W 91X*
**Frazer**, Benjamin Chalmers 1922- *AmMWSc 92*
**Frazer**, Bryan Douglas 1942- *AmMWSc 92*
**Frazer**, Cloyce Clemon 1919- *WhoWest 92*
**Frazer**, Eva Louise 1957- *WhoBlA 92*
**Frazer**, Ira 1954- *WhoAmL 92*
**Frazer**, J Ronald 1923- *AmMWSc 92*
**Frazer**, Jack Winfield 1924- *AmMWSc 92*
**Frazer**, John Fries 1812-1872 *BiInAmS*
**Frazer**, John P 1914- *AmMWSc 92*
**Frazer**, Joseph Atchison 1961- *WhoFI 92*
**Frazer**, L Neil 1948- *AmMWSc 92*
**Frazer**, Malcolm John 1931- *Who 92*
**Frazer**, Marshall Everett 1944- *AmMWSc 92*
**Frazer**, Persifor 1844-1909 *BiInAmS*
**Frazer**, Susane Irene *WhoMW 92*
**Frazer**, Thomas Lee 1945- *WhoFI 92*
**Frazer**, W Donald 1937- *AmMWSc 92*
**Frazer**, Wendy 1943- *WhoMW 92*
**Frazer**, William Henry 1873-1953 *DcNCBi 2*
**Frazer**, William Johnson, Jr. 1924- *WhoFI 92*
**Frazer**, William Miller 1864-1961 *TwCPaSc*
**Frazer**, William Robert 1933- *AmMWSc 92*
**Frazier**, A. D., Jr. 1944- *WhoFI 92*
**Frazier**, A Joel 1938- *AmMWSc 92*
**Frazier**, Adolphus Cornelious *WhoAmP 91, WhoBlA 92*
**Frazier**, Allie Robert 1933- *WhoAmL 92*
**Frazier**, Arthur *IntAu&W 91X, WrDr 92*
**Frazier**, Audrey Lee 1927- *WhoBlA 92*
**Frazier**, Benjamin West 1841-1905 *BiInAmS*
**Frazier**, Charles Douglas 1939- *WhoBlA 92*
**Frazier**, Claude Clinton, III 1948- *AmMWSc 92, WhoMW 92*
**Frazier**, Clifford B. *WhoBlA 92*
**Frazier**, Dan E., Sr. 1949- *WhoBlA 92*
**Frazier**, Dennis Allen 1955- *WhoAmP 91*
**Frazier**, Donald Tha 1935- *AmMWSc 92*
**Frazier**, Douglas Byron 1957- *WhoFI 92*
**Frazier**, Edward Clarence 1953- *WhoEnt 92*
**Frazier**, Edward Nelson 1939- *AmMWSc 92*
**Frazier**, Edward O Neil 1946- *WhoAmP 91*
**Frazier**, Eufaula Smith 1924- *WhoBlA 92*
**Frazier**, Francis Marie 1932- *WhoAmP 91*
**Frazier**, George Clark, Jr 1930- *AmMWSc 92*
**Frazier**, Gregory Craig 1950- *WhoRel 92*
**Frazier**, Henry B, III 1934- *WhoAmP 91*
**Frazier**, Herman Ronald 1954- *BlkOlyM, WhoBlA 92*
**Frazier**, Hillman Terome 1950- *WhoAmP 91*
**Frazier**, Howard Stanley 1926- *AmMWSc 92*
**Frazier**, Ian 1951- *WrDr 92*
**Frazier**, James Lewis 1943- *AmMWSc 92*
**Frazier**, James Russell 1962- *WhoRel 92*
**Frazier**, Jimmy Leon 1939- *WhoBlA 92*
**Frazier**, Joe 1944- *FacFETw, WhoBlA 92*
**Frazier**, John *WhoAmP 91*
**Frazier**, John Melvin 1944- *AmMWSc 92*
**Frazier**, John Phillip 1939- *WhoFI 92*
**Frazier**, Joseph 1944- *BlkOlyM*
**Frazier**, Joseph Norris 1925- *WhoBlA 92*
**Frazier**, Julie A. 1962- *WhoBlA 92*
**Frazier**, Kimberlee Gonterman 1953- *WhoMW 92*
**Frazier**, Larry Gene 1931- *WhoMW 92*
**Frazier**, Lawrence Alan 1936- *WhoIns 92*
**Frazier**, Lee Rene 1946- *WhoBlA 92*
**Frazier**, Leon 1932- *WhoBlA 92*
**Frazier**, Leslie Antonio 1959- *WhoBlA 92*
**Frazier**, Levi, Jr. 1951- *WhoBlA 92*
**Frazier**, Lincoln B 1905- *WhoAmP 91*
**Frazier**, Loy William, Jr 1938- *AmMWSc 92*
**Frazier**, Mark Christopher 1952- *WhoFI 92*
**Frazier**, Michael Wallace 1956- *WhoMW 92*
**Frazier**, Patrick Louis, Jr. 1949- *WhoRel 92*
**Frazier**, Peggy Kaluz 1943- *WhoAmP 91*
**Frazier**, Ramona Yancey 1941- *WhoBlA 92*
**Frazier**, Randal Terry 1958- *WhoMW 92*
**Frazier**, Ranta A. 1915- *WhoBlA 92*
**Frazier**, Ray Jerrell 1943- *WhoBlA 92*
**Frazier**, Regina Jollivette 1943- *WhoBlA 92*
**Frazier**, Reginald Lee 1934- *WhoBlA 92*
**Frazier**, Richard Glenn 1931- *WhoRel 92*
**Frazier**, Richard H 1900- *AmMWSc 92*
**Frazier**, Rick C. 1936- *WhoBlA 92*
**Frazier**, Robert Carl 1932- *AmMWSc 92*
**Frazier**, Royce Eldon 1952- *WhoRel 92*
**Frazier**, S. N. *WhoRel 92*
**Frazier**, Sheila E. 1948- *IntMPA 92*
**Frazier**, Stephen Earl 1939- *AmMWSc 92*
**Frazier**, Thomas Vernon 1921- *AmMWSc 92*
**Frazier**, Todd Mearl 1925- *AmMWSc 92*
**Frazier**, Tom John 1948- *WhoEnt 92*
**Frazier**, Walt 1945- *WhoBlA 92*
**Frazier**, Walter Ronald 1939- *WhoFI 92*
**Frazier**, William Allen 1908- *AmMWSc 92*
**Frazier**, William Edward, Jr. 1922- *WhoFI 92*
**Frazier**, William Francis, Jr. 1957- *WhoAmL 92*
**Frazier**, William James 1942- *WhoBlA 92*
**Frazier**, William Tucker 1928- *WhoMW 92*
**Frazier**, Wynetta Artricia 1942- *WhoBlA 92, WhoMW 92*
**Frazza**, Everett Joseph 1924- *AmMWSc 92*
**Frazza**, George S. 1934- *WhoAmL 92, WhoFI 92*
**Frazza**, Robert Thomas 1962- *WhoEnt 92*
**Frea**, James Irving 1937- *AmMWSc 92*
**Freadman**, Marvin Alan 1949- *AmMWSc 92*
**Freaney**, Vincent 1945- *WhoIns 92*
**Frear**, Donald Stuart 1929- *AmMWSc 92*
**Frears**, Stephen 1941- *IntDcF 2-2 [port], IntMPA 92*
**Frears**, Stephen Arthur 1941- *IntWW 91, Who 92*
**Freas**, Alan D 1910- *AmMWSc 92*
**Freas**, Charles Anthony 1952- *WhoAmL 92*
**Freas**, William 1946- *AmMWSc 92*
**Freauf**, Elizabeth S 1936- *WhoAmP 91*
**Freberg**, C Roger 1916- *AmMWSc 92*
**Freberg**, Stanley 1926- *WhoEnt 92*
**Freborg**, Layton *WhoAmP 91*
**Freburger**, William Joseph 1940- *IntAu&W 91*
**Freccia**, Massimo 1906- *IntWW 91*
**Frech**, Harry Edward, III 1946- *WhoFI 92*
**Frech**, Roger 1941- *AmMWSc 92*
**Freche**, John C 1923- *AmMWSc 92*
**Frechet**, Jean M J 1944- *AmMWSc 92*
**Frechette**, Alfred Leo 1909- *AmMWSc 92*
**Frechette**, Louis 1839-1908 *BenetAL 91*
**Frechette**, Myles Robert Rene 1936- *WhoAmP 91*
**Frechette**, Roland A 1927- *WhoAmP 91*
**Freck**, Peter G 1934- *AmMWSc 92*
**Freckmann**, Robert W 1939- *AmMWSc 92*
**Freda**, Aldo 1921- *WhoAmP 91*
**Fredd**, Chester Arthur *WhoBlA 92*
**Frede**, Michael 1940- *Who 92*
**Frede**, Richard *DrAPF 91*
**Fredeen**, Howard T 1921- *AmMWSc 92*

**Fredegonde of Neustria** 545-597 *EncAmaz 91*
**Freden,** Stanley Charles 1927- *AmMWSc 92*
**Fredenburg,** Robert Love 1921- *AmMWSc 92*
**Frederic,** Harold 1856-1898 *BenetAL 91*
**Frederic,** Mike *IntAu&W 91X*
**Frederici,** C. Carleton 1938- *WhoAmL 92*
**Frederick II** 1712-1786 *BlkwCEP, NewAmDM*
**Frederick the Great** 1712-1786 *BlkwCEP*
**Frederick WilliamI** 1688-1740 *BlkwCEP*
**Frederick,** Beebe Ray, Jr 1938- *WhoAmP 91*
**Frederick,** Charles Boscawen 1919- *Who 92*
**Frederick,** Cyndie Louise 1961- *WhoFI 92*
**Frederick,** Daniel 1925- *AmMWSc 92*
**Frederick,** David Charles 1951- *WhoFI 92*
**Frederick,** David Eugene 1931- *AmMWSc 92*
**Frederick,** David John 1957- *WhoEnt 92*
**Frederick,** Dean Kimball 1934- *AmMWSc 92*
**Frederick,** Edward C 1930- *AmMWSc 92*
**Frederick,** Edward Charles 1930- *WhoMW 92*
**Frederick,** Gary Donnell 1947- *WhoWest 92*
**Frederick,** George Francis 1937- *WhoFI 92*
**Frederick,** George Leonard 1930- *AmMWSc 92*
**Frederick,** Gersami Karen *DrAPF 91*
**Frederick,** J George 1882- *ScFEYrs*
**Frederick,** James R 1946- *AmMWSc 92*
**Frederick,** Jane Runkel 1952- *WhoMW 92*
**Frederick,** Jeanne M *AmMWSc 92*
**Frederick,** Jerrell Lee 1930- *WhoEnt 92*
**Frederick,** John *TwCWW 91*
**Frederick,** John Edgar 1940- *AmMWSc 92*
**Frederick,** K.C. *DrAPF 91*
**Frederick,** Kenneth Jacob 1913- *AmMWSc 92*
**Frederick,** Lafayette 1923- *AmMWSc 92*
**Frederick,** Larry 1957- *WhoRel 92*
**Frederick,** Lloyd Randall 1921- *AmMWSc 92*
**Frederick,** Marcel Sal 1926- *WhoAmP 91*
**Frederick,** Mark Allen 1951- *WhoEnt 92*
**Frederick,** Mary Ellen 1931- *WhoWest 92*
**Frederick,** Melvin Lyle 1929- *WhoAmP 91*
**Frederick,** Paul Anthony 1925- *WhoFI 92, WhoMW 92*
**Frederick,** Pauline *LesBEnT 92*
**Frederick,** Pauline 1906-1990 *AnObit 1990*
**Frederick,** Pauline 1918-1990 *FacFETw*
**Frederick,** Randy *WhoAmP 91*
**Frederick,** Raymond H 1923- *AmMWSc 92*
**Frederick,** Richard 1954- *WhoAmP 91*
**Frederick,** Robert Rice 1926- *IntWW 91*
**Frederick,** Samuel Adams 1946- *WhoAmL 92*
**Frederick,** Sue Ellen 1946- *AmMWSc 92*
**Frederick,** Thomas James 1956- *WhoAmL 92*
**Frederick,** Virginia Fiester 1916- *WhoAmP 91*
**Frederick,** Willard Drawn, Jr 1934- *WhoAmP 91*
**Frederick,** William George DeMott 1936- *AmMWSc 92*
**Fredericks,** Barry Irwin 1936- *WhoAmL 92*
**Fredericks,** Christopher M 1944- *AmMWSc 92*
**Fredericks,** Claude 1923- *WhoEnt 92*
**Fredericks,** Daniel Carl 1950- *WhoRel 92*
**Fredericks,** Francis 1935- *WhoAmP 91*
**Fredericks,** Frank, Dr. *WrDr 92*
**Fredericks,** Henry St. Clair 1942- *WhoEnt 92*
**Fredericks,** Isiah 1930- *WhoAmP 91*
**Fredericks,** Leroy Owen 1924- *WhoBlA 92*
**Fredericks,** Marshall Maynard 1908- *WhoMW 92*
**Fredericks,** Robert Joseph 1934- *AmMWSc 92*
**Fredericks,** Ward Arthur 1939- *WhoFI 92, WhoWest 92*
**Fredericks,** Wesley Charles, Jr. 1948- *WhoAmL 92, WhoFI 92*
**Fredericks,** William John 1924- *AmMWSc 92*
**Fredericksen,** James Monroe 1919- *AmMWSc 92*
**Fredericksen,** Tommy L 1946- *AmMWSc 92*
**Frederickson,** Arman Frederick 1918- *AmMWSc 92*
**Frederickson,** David J 1944- *WhoAmP 91*
**Frederickson,** Dennis R 1939- *WhoAmP 91*
**Frederickson,** Dennis Russel 1939- *WhoMW 92*
**Frederickson,** Evan Lloyd 1922- *AmMWSc 92*
**Frederickson,** Greg N 1947- *AmMWSc 92*
**Frederickson,** H. Gray, Jr. 1937- *IntMPA 92*
**Frederickson,** Harry Gray, Jr. 1937- *WhoEnt 92*
**Frederickson,** Lyle L 1905- *WhoAmP 91*
**Frederickson,** Richard Gordon 1944- *AmMWSc 92*
**Fredericton,** Bishop of 1932- *Who 92*
**Frederik,** Hendrik *WhoRel 92*
**Frederika** 1917-1981 *FacFETw*
**Frederikse,** Hans Pieter Roetert 1920- *AmMWSc 92*
**Frederiksen,** Dixie Ward 1942- *AmMWSc 92*
**Frederiksen,** Richard Allan 1933- *AmMWSc 92*
**Frederikson,** Edna *DrAPF 91*
**Frederking,** Traugott Heinrich Karl 1926- *WhoWest 92*
**Fredette,** William Joseph 1966- *WhoEnt 92*
**Fredga,** Arne 1902- *IntWW 91*
**Frediani,** Harold Arthur 1911- *AmMWSc 92*
**Fredin,** Leif G R 1945- *AmMWSc 92*
**Fredin,** Reynold A 1923- *AmMWSc 92*
**Fredkin,** Donald Roy 1935- *AmMWSc 92*
**Fredlund,** Ray 1925- *WhoAmP 91*
**Fredman,** Michael Lawrence 1947- *AmMWSc 92*
**Fredman,** Samuel George 1924- *WhoAmP 91*
**Fredman,** Stephen *DrAPF 91*
**Fredmann,** Martin 1943- *WhoEnt 92*
**Fredner,** Rolf Morten 1913- *WhoFI 92*
**Fredrich,** Augustine Joseph 1939- *AmMWSc 92*
**Fredrick,** Earl E., Jr. 1929- *WhoBlA 92*
**Fredrick,** Jerome Frederick 1926- *AmMWSc 92*
**Fredrick,** Laurence William 1927- *AmMWSc 92*
**Fredrick,** Marilyn Theriot 1950- *WhoWest 92*
**Fredrick,** Michael Todd 1957- *WhoMW 92*
**Fredricks,** Edgar John 1942- *WhoAmP 91*
**Fredricks,** Richard 1933- *WhoEnt 92*
**Fredricks,** Terry L. 1957- *WhoAmL 92*
**Fredricks,** Walter William 1935- *AmMWSc 92*
**Fredrickson,** Arnold G 1932- *AmMWSc 92*
**Fredrickson,** Bryan Timothy 1956- *WhoAmL 92*
**Fredrickson,** Donald Sharp 1924- *AmMWSc 92, IntWW 91, WhoAmP 91*
**Fredrickson,** Hope Linette 1955- *WhoAmL 92*
**Fredrickson,** John E 1919- *AmMWSc 92*
**Fredrickson,** John Murray 1931- *AmMWSc 92*
**Fredrickson,** Lawrence Thomas 1928- *WhoEnt 92*
**Fredrickson,** Leigh H 1939- *AmMWSc 92*
**Fredrickson,** Lola Jean 1945- *WhoMW 92*
**Fredrickson,** Lowry Clifford 1932- *WhoMW 92*
**Fredrickson,** Richard William 1919- *AmMWSc 92*
**Fredrickson,** Sharon Wong 1956- *WhoMW 92*
**Fredrickson,** Vance O 1928- *WhoIns 92*
**Fredrik,** Burry 1925- *WhoEnt 92*
**Fredriksson,** Kurt A 1926- *AmMWSc 92*
**Free** *ConAu 35NR*
**Free,** Alfred Henry 1913- *AmMWSc 92*
**Free,** Charles Alfred 1936- *AmMWSc 92*
**Free,** Helen M 1923- *AmMWSc 92*
**Free,** John Ulric 1941- *AmMWSc 92*
**Free,** Joseph Carl 1935- *AmMWSc 92*
**Free,** Kenneth A. 1936- *WhoBlA 92*
**Free,** Marvin Davis, Jr. 1947- *WhoMW 92*
**Free,** Michael John 1937- *AmMWSc 92*
**Free,** Ray D 1910- *WhoAmP 91*
**Free,** Stephen J 1948- *AmMWSc 92*
**Free,** World B. 1953- *WhoBlA 92*
**Freeberg,** Debra Lynn 1955- *WhoEnt 92*
**Freeberg,** Fred E 1937- *AmMWSc 92*
**Freeberg,** John Arthur 1932- *AmMWSc 92*
**Freebody,** Wilfred Leslie d1991 *Who 92N*
**Freeborn,** Edmund Tiers, III 1952- *WhoRel 92*
**Freeborn,** Richard 1926- *WrDr 92*
**Freeborn,** Richard Harry 1926- *IntAu&W 91*
**Freed,** Alan 1922-1965 *NewAmDM*
**Freed,** Alvyn Mark 1913- *WhoWest 92*
**Freed,** Ann Sybl 1945- *WhoEnt 92*
**Freed,** Arthur Nelson 1952- *AmMWSc 92*
**Freed,** Arvy Glenn 1863-1931 *RelLAm 91*
**Freed,** Barry *ConAu 35NR*
**Freed,** Bennett George 1957- *WhoWest 92*
**Freed,** Bert 1919- *WhoEnt 92*
**Freed,** Carl Robert 1956- *WhoEnt 92*
**Freed,** Charles 1926- *AmMWSc 92*
**Freed,** Daniel Josef 1927- *WhoAmL 92*
**Freed,** DeBow 1925- *WhoMW 92*
**Freed,** Elaine Eilers 1934- *WhoAmP 91, WhoWest 92*
**Freed,** Eric Robert 1950- *WhoWest 92*
**Freed,** Fred d1974 *LesBEnT 92*
**Freed,** Hirsh 1910- *WhoAmL 92*
**Freed,** Howard A 1926- *WhoAmP 91*
**Freed,** Isadore 1900-1960 *NewAmDM*
**Freed,** Jack H 1938- *AmMWSc 92*
**Freed,** James Melvin 1939- *AmMWSc 92*
**Freed,** Jerome James 1928- *AmMWSc 92*
**Freed,** John Howard 1943- *AmMWSc 92*
**Freed,** Jonathan Michael 1954- *WhoEnt 92*
**Freed,** Karl F 1942- *AmMWSc 92*
**Freed,** Karl Frederick 1942- *WhoMW 92*
**Freed,** Kenneth Alan 1957- *WhoAmL 92*
**Freed,** Leonard Alan 1947- *AmMWSc 92*
**Freed,** Lynn *DrAPF 91*
**Freed,** Lynn Ruth 1945- *WrDr 92*
**Freed,** Marcia 1948- *WhoWest 92*
**Freed,** Mayer Goodman 1945- *WhoAmL 92*
**Freed,** Meier Ezra 1925- *AmMWSc 92*
**Freed,** Merrill Alan 1929- *WhoAmL 92*
**Freed,** Michael Abraham 1953- *AmMWSc 92*
**Freed,** Murray Monroe 1924- *AmMWSc 92*
**Freed,** Norman 1936- *AmMWSc 92*
**Freed,** Paul Ernest 1918- *WhoRel 92*
**Freed,** Ray *DrAPF 91*
**Freed,** Richard 1928- *WhoEnt 92*
**Freed,** Robert Lloyd 1950- *AmMWSc 92*
**Freed,** Simon 1899- *AmMWSc 92*
**Freed,** Virgil Haven 1919- *AmMWSc 92*
**Freed,** Walter *WhoAmP 91*
**Freedberg,** Abraham Stone 1908- *AmMWSc 92*
**Freedberg,** David Adrian 1948- *Who 92*
**Freedberg,** Irwin Mark 1931- *AmMWSc 92*
**Freedberg,** Sydney Joseph 1914- *IntAu&W 91, IntWW 91, WrDr 92*
**Freedenberg,** Paul 1943- *WhoAmP 91*
**Freedgood,** Morton 1912- *IntAu&W 91*
**Freedland,** Michael 1934- *WrDr 92*
**Freedland,** Michael Rodney 1934- *IntAu&W 91*
**Freedland,** Richard A 1931- *AmMWSc 92*
**Freedman,** Aaron David 1922- *AmMWSc 92*
**Freedman,** Albert Z. *WhoEnt 92*
**Freedman,** Alfred Mordecai 1917- *AmMWSc 92*
**Freedman,** Allen Roy 1940- *AmMWSc 92*
**Freedman,** Amelia 1940- *Who 92*
**Freedman,** Andrew 1951- *AmMWSc 92*
**Freedman,** Anita 1927- *WhoAmP 91*
**Freedman,** Anthony Stephen 1945- *WhoAmP 91*
**Freedman,** Arthur Jacob 1924- *AmMWSc 92*
**Freedman,** Barnett 1901-1958 *TwCPaSc*
**Freedman,** Bart Joseph 1955- *WhoAmL 92*
**Freedman,** Beatrice Claudia 1904- *TwCPaSc*
**Freedman,** Bernard Benjamin 1939- *WhoAmL 92*
**Freedman,** Carla 1944- *WhoRel 92*
**Freedman,** Charles 1925- *Who 92*
**Freedman,** Daniel X 1921- *AmMWSc 92, WhoWest 92*
**Freedman,** Daniel Z 1939- *AmMWSc 92*
**Freedman,** David A 1938- *AmMWSc 92*
**Freedman,** David Asa 1918- *AmMWSc 92*
**Freedman,** David Noel 1922- *WhoRel 92*
**Freedman,** Dawn Angela 1942- *Who 92*
**Freedman,** Eli 1927- *AmMWSc 92*
**Freedman,** Eric 1949- *IntAu&W 91*
**Freedman,** Eugene M. 1932- *WhoFI 92*
**Freedman,** Forrest Scott 1961- *WhoAmL 92*
**Freedman,** Frank Harlan 1924- *WhoAmL 92*
**Freedman,** George 1921- *AmMWSc 92*
**Freedman,** Gerald M. 1943- *WhoAmL 92*
**Freedman,** Harold Hersh 1924- *AmMWSc 92*
**Freedman,** Harriet 1949- *TwCPaSc*
**Freedman,** Harry 1922- *NewAmDM, WhoEnt 92*
**Freedman,** Helen Rosengren 1952- *IntAu&W 91*
**Freedman,** Henry Hillel 1919- *AmMWSc 92*
**Freedman,** Herbert Irving 1940- *AmMWSc 92*
**Freedman,** Howard Martin 1953- *WhoFI 92*
**Freedman,** Howard Samuel 1941- *WhoFI 92*
**Freedman,** James Joseph 1958- *WhoAmL 92*
**Freedman,** Jay Weil 1942- *WhoAmL 92*
**Freedman,** Jeffrey Carl 1945- *AmMWSc 92*
**Freedman,** Jeffrey Charles 1944- *WhoAmL 92*
**Freedman,** Jerome 1916- *AmMWSc 92*
**Freedman,** Jerrold *IntMPA 92*
**Freedman,** Joel 1948- *WhoIns 92*
**Freedman,** Jon Bruce 1959- *WhoAmL 92*
**Freedman,** Joyce Beth 1945- *WhoMW 92*
**Freedman,** Judith 1939- *WhoAmP 91*
**Freedman,** Jules 1933- *AmMWSc 92*
**Freedman,** Kenneth David 1947- *WhoAmL 92*
**Freedman,** Laurence Joel 1962- *WhoAmL 92*
**Freedman,** Lawrence David 1948- *Who 92*
**Freedman,** Lawrence Zelic 1919- *AmMWSc 92, WhoMW 92*
**Freedman,** Leon David 1921- *AmMWSc 92*
**Freedman,** Lewis *LesBEnT 92*
**Freedman,** Lewis Simon 1936- *AmMWSc 92*
**Freedman,** Louis 1917- *Who 92*
**Freedman,** M David 1938- *AmMWSc 92*
**Freedman,** Marshall Kevin 1962- *WhoFI 92*
**Freedman,** Marvin I 1939- *AmMWSc 92*
**Freedman,** Maryann Saccomando 1934- *WhoAmL 92*
**Freedman,** Melvin H. 1920- *WhoEnt 92*
**Freedman,** Melvin Harris 1939- *AmMWSc 92*
**Freedman,** Mervin Burton 1920- *WrDr 92*
**Freedman,** Michael Hartley 1951- *AmMWSc 92, WhoWest 92*
**Freedman,** Michael Lewis 1942- *AmMWSc 92*
**Freedman,** Monroe Henry 1928- *WhoAmL 92*
**Freedman,** Nancy 1920- *WrDr 92*
**Freedman,** Philip 1926- *AmMWSc 92*
**Freedman,** Richard 1932-1991 *ConAu 134*
**Freedman,** Robert *DrAPF 91*
**Freedman,** Robert Brandeis 1943- *WhoAmL 92*
**Freedman,** Robert Russell 1947- *AmMWSc 92, WhoMW 92*
**Freedman,** Robert Wagner 1915- *AmMWSc 92*
**Freedman,** Ronald 1917- *IntWW 91, WrDr 92*
**Freedman,** Samuel 1908- *Who 92*
**Freedman,** Samuel Orkin 1928- *AmMWSc 92*
**Freedman,** Samuel Sumner 1927- *WhoAmL 92, WhoAmP 91*
**Freedman,** Sandra Warshaw 1943- *WhoAmP 91*
**Freedman,** Stanley Arnold 1922- *WhoAmL 92*
**Freedman,** Steven I 1935- *AmMWSc 92*
**Freedman,** Steven Leslie 1935- *AmMWSc 92*
**Freedman,** Stuart Jay 1944- *AmMWSc 92*
**Freedman,** Stuart Joel 1939- *WhoAmL 92*
**Freedman,** Theodore Levy 1947- *WhoAmL 92*
**Freedman,** Walter G. 1938- *WhoMW 92*
**Freedman,** Winifred Deborah 1957- *WhoEnt 92*
**Freedom,** Nancy 1932- *WhoWest 92*
**Freedy,** Amos 1938- *AmMWSc 92*
**Freeh,** Louis J. 1950- *WhoAmL 92*
**Freehling,** Allen Isaac 1932- *WhoRel 92, WhoWest 92*
**Freehling,** Daniel Joseph 1950- *WhoAmL 92*
**Freehling,** Harold George, Jr. 1947- *WhoMW 92*
**Freehling,** William W. 1935- *WrDr 92*
**Freel,** Phillip Leroy, Jr. 1968- *WhoMW 92*
**Freeland,** Charles 1940- *WhoAmL 92*
**Freeland,** Charles Johnston, III 1940- *WhoRel 92*
**Freeland,** Darryl Creighton 1939- *WhoWest 92*
**Freeland,** Flora Ellen 1930- *WhoEnt 92*
**Freeland,** Frances Webb 1944- *WhoFI 92*
**Freeland,** George Lockwood 1931- *AmMWSc 92*
**Freeland,** Herbert Thomas 1953- *WhoRel 92*
**Freeland,** James M. Jackson 1927- *WhoAmL 92*
**Freeland,** John Redvers 1927- *Who 92*
**Freeland,** Mark Sydnes 1943- *WhoFI 92*
**Freeland,** Mary Graham *Who 92*
**Freeland,** Max 1920- *AmMWSc 92*
**Freeland,** Michael Willis 1941- *WhoAmL 92*
**Freeland,** Robert Frederick 1919- *WhoWest 92*
**Freeland,** Robert Lenward, Jr. 1939- *WhoBlA 92*
**Freeland,** Russell L. 1929- *WhoBlA 92*
**Freeland,** Thomas Breen 1936- *WhoWest 92*
**Freeland,** W. Michael 1949- *WhoMW 92*
**Freeland,** William Thomas 1944- *WhoFI 92*
**Freeland-Graves,** Jeanne H 1948- *AmMWSc 92*
**Freeling,** Michael 1945- *AmMWSc 92*
**Freeling,** Nicholas 1927- *IntAu&W 91*

**Freeling,** Nicolas 1927- *ConNov 91, Who 92, WrDr 92*
**Freels,** Larry Ellis 1941- *WhoRel 92*
**Freels,** Willard Dudley 1924- *WhoAmP 91*
**Freeman,** Al, Jr. 1934- *IntMPA 92*
**Freeman,** Alan R 1937- *AmMWSc 92*
**Freeman,** Albert Cornelius, Jr. *WhoBlA 92*
**Freeman,** Albert Eugene 1931- *AmMWSc 92*
**Freeman,** Anne Hobson *DrAPF 91*
**Freeman,** Anne Hobson 1934- *IntAu&W 91*
**Freeman,** Antoinette Rosefeldt 1937- *WhoAmL 92*
**Freeman,** Arnold I 1937- *AmMWSc 92*
**Freeman,** Arthur 1925- *AmMWSc 92*
**Freeman,** Arthur James 1927- *WhoRel 92*
**Freeman,** Arthur Jay 1930- *AmMWSc 92*
**Freeman,** Arthur Scott 1955- *AmMWSc 92*
**Freeman,** Barbara 1937- *TwCPaSc*
**Freeman,** Barbara C. 1906- *WrDr 92*
**Freeman,** Beth Labson 1953- *WhoAmP 91*
**Freeman,** Bill 1938- *WrDr 92*
**Freeman,** Bob A 1926- *AmMWSc 92*
**Freeman,** Brian A. 1940- *WhoAmL 92*
**Freeman,** Bruce Alan 1952- *AmMWSc 92*
**Freeman,** Bruce L, Jr 1949- *AmMWSc 92*
**Freeman,** Bud 1906-1991 *NewAmDM*
**Freeman,** C 1933- *WhoAmP 91*
**Freeman,** Carolyn Ruth 1950- *AmMWSc 92*
**Freeman,** Catherine 1931- *Who 92*
**Freeman,** Charles E. 1915- *WhoBlA 92*
**Freeman,** Charles Edward, Jr 1941- *AmMWSc 92*
**Freeman,** Charles Eldridge 1933- *WhoBlA 92*
**Freeman,** Charles Townsend 1943- *WhoFI 92*
**Freeman,** Charles W, Jr 1943- *WhoAmP 91*
**Freeman,** Charles Wellman, Jr. 1943- *IntWW 91*
**Freeman,** Clifford Echols, Jr. 1959- *WhoFI 92*
**Freeman,** Colette 1937- *AmMWSc 92*
**Freeman,** Corinne 1926- *WhoAmP 91*
**Freeman,** Corwin Stuart, Jr. 1947- *WhoMW 92*
**Freeman,** Darlene Marie 1951- *WhoHisp 92*
**Freeman,** David 1927- *WhoWest 92*
**Freeman,** David 1945- *WrDr 92*
**Freeman,** David Calvin, Sr. 1942- *WhoBlA 92*
**Freeman,** David Charles 1952- *Who 92*
**Freeman,** David Franklin, Jr. 1959- *WhoAmL 92*
**Freeman,** David Haines 1931- *AmMWSc 92*
**Freeman,** David John 1928- *Who 92*
**Freeman,** David John 1948- *WhoAmL 92*
**Freeman,** David Lynn 1924- *WhoAmL 92*
**Freeman,** David Ralph 1934- *WhoAmL 92*
**Freeman,** David Scott 1961- *WhoAmL 92*
**Freeman,** Davis *ConAu 134*
**Freeman,** Devery *DrAPF 91*
**Freeman,** Dewayne *WhoAmP 91*
**Freeman,** Dick *WhoWest 92*
**Freeman,** Donald Wilford 1929- *WhoFI 92*
**Freeman,** Douglas Southall 1886-1953 *BenetAL 91*
**Freeman,** Dwight Carl 1951- *AmMWSc 92*
**Freeman,** Ed 1942- *WhoEnt 92*
**Freeman,** Edgar James 1917- *Who 92*
**Freeman,** Edmund B. 1795-1868 *DcNCBi 2*
**Freeman,** Edward Anderson 1914- *WhoBlA 92*
**Freeman,** Edward C. *WhoBlA 92*
**Freeman,** Edward C 1906- *WhoAmP 91*
**Freeman,** Edward Gordon 1926- *WhoFI 92*
**Freeman,** Eldridge Thomas, Jr. 1926- *WhoMW 92*
**Freeman,** Elizabeth d1792 *BlkwEAR*
**Freeman,** Elizabeth 1744?-1829 *NotBlAW 92*
**Freeman,** Ernest Allan 1932- *Who 92*
**Freeman,** Ernest Michael 1937- *Who 92*
**Freeman,** Ernest Robert 1933- *AmMWSc 92*
**Freeman,** Evelyn 1940- *WhoBlA 92*
**Freeman,** Everett d1991 *LesBEnT 92, NewYTBS 91*
**Freeman,** Fillmore 1936- *AmMWSc 92*
**Freeman,** Forster 1927- *WhoRel 92*
**Freeman,** Frankie M. 1916- *WhoBlA 92*
**Freeman,** Fred W 1924- *AmMWSc 92*
**Freeman,** Gaylord A. d1991 *NewYTBS 91 [port]*
**Freeman,** George Clemon, Jr. 1929- *WhoAmL 92*
**Freeman,** George R 1918- *AmMWSc 92*
**Freeman,** George Ross, Jr. 1945- *WhoRel 92*
**Freeman,** George Vincent 1911- *Who 92*
**Freeman,** George Washington 1789-1858 *DcNCBi 2*
**Freeman,** Gill Sherryl 1949- *WhoAmL 92*
**Freeman,** Gillian 1929- *ConNov 91, IntAu&W 91, WrDr 92*
**Freeman,** Glynna W. 1945- *WhoAmL 92*
**Freeman,** Gordon Russel 1930- *AmMWSc 92*
**Freeman,** Gregory Bruce 1956- *WhoBlA 92*
**Freeman,** Gustave 1909- *AmMWSc 92*
**Freeman,** Habern *WhoAmP 91*
**Freeman,** Harold Adolph 1909- *AmMWSc 92*
**Freeman,** Harold P. 1933- *WhoBlA 92*
**Freeman,** Harold Stanley 1951- *AmMWSc 92*
**Freeman,** Harold Wayne 1929- *WhoMW 92*
**Freeman,** Harold Webber 1899- *Who 92*
**Freeman,** Harry Cleveland 1925- *AmMWSc 92*
**Freeman,** Harry Lawrence 1869-1954 *NewAmDM*
**Freeman,** Harry Louis 1932- *WhoFI 92*
**Freeman,** Herbert 1925- *AmMWSc 92*
**Freeman,** Herbert Edmund 1947- *WhoMW 92*
**Freeman,** Herbert James 1941- *WhoWest 92*
**Freeman,** Horatio Putnam 1924- *AmMWSc 92*
**Freeman,** Houghton 1921- *WhoIns 92*
**Freeman,** Hugh J *AmMWSc 92*
**Freeman,** Hugh Lionel 1929- *Who 92*
**Freeman,** Ifan Charles Harold d1990 *Who 92N*
**Freeman,** Isadore 1912- *WhoEnt 92*
**Freeman,** James *Who 92*
**Freeman,** James A. 1950- *WhoRel 92*
**Freeman,** James Atticus, III 1947- *WhoAmL 92*
**Freeman,** James Darcy d1991 *Who 92N*
**Freeman,** James Darcy 1907- *WhoRel 92*
**Freeman,** James Darcy 1907-1991 *IntWW 91, -91N*
**Freeman,** James David 1958- *WhoFI 92*
**Freeman,** James Harrison 1922- *AmMWSc 92*
**Freeman,** James J 1940- *AmMWSc 92*
**Freeman,** James Jasper 1907-1990 *WhoBlA 92N*
**Freeman,** James Robin *Who 92*
**Freeman,** James William 1946- *WhoAmP 91*
**Freeman,** Jeff 1960- *WhoAmP 91*
**Freeman,** Jeffrey VanDuyne 1934- *AmMWSc 92*
**Freeman,** Jennifer 1956- *WhoAmL 92*
**Freeman,** Jere Evans 1936- *AmMWSc 92*
**Freeman,** Jeremiah Patrick 1929- *AmMWSc 92*
**Freeman,** Jo 1945- *WrDr 92*
**Freeman,** Joe Bailey 1937- *WhoFI 92*
**Freeman,** Joel 1922- *IntMPA 92, WhoEnt 92*
**Freeman,** Joel Arthur 1954- *WhoRel 92*
**Freeman,** John *Who 92*
**Freeman,** John 1915- *IntAu&W 91, IntWW 91*
**Freeman,** John 1958- *TwCPaSc*
**Freeman,** John A 1938- *AmMWSc 92*
**Freeman,** John A 1948- *AmMWSc 92*
**Freeman,** John Alderman 1917- *AmMWSc 92*
**Freeman,** John Allen 1912- *Who 92*
**Freeman,** John Anthony 1937- *Who 92*
**Freeman,** John Clinton, Jr 1920- *AmMWSc 92*
**Freeman,** John Daniel 1941- *AmMWSc 92*
**Freeman,** John J 1941- *AmMWSc 92*
**Freeman,** John Jerome 1933- *AmMWSc 92*
**Freeman,** John Mark 1933- *AmMWSc 92*
**Freeman,** John Paul 1937- *AmMWSc 92*
**Freeman,** John Richardson 1927- *AmMWSc 92*
**Freeman,** John Wright, Jr 1935- *AmMWSc 92*
**Freeman,** Joseph 1897-1965 *BenetAL 91*
**Freeman,** Joseph Michael 1947- *WhoRel 92*
**Freeman,** Joseph Theodore 1908- *AmMWSc 92*
**Freeman,** Joseph William 1914- *Who 92*
**Freeman,** Josh 1949- *WhoEnt 92*
**Freeman,** Joyce 1927- *WhoAmP 91*
**Freeman,** Judson, Jr. 1943- *WhoAmL 92*
**Freeman,** Julia Berg 1940- *AmMWSc 92*
**Freeman,** Karen Marie 1960- *WhoBlA 92*
**Freeman,** Karl Boruch 1934- *AmMWSc 92*
**Freeman,** Kenneth Alfrey 1912- *AmMWSc 92*
**Freeman,** Kenneth Donald 1912- *WhoBlA 92*
**Freeman,** Kerlin, Jr. 1930- *WhoBlA 92*
**Freeman,** Kevin Lane 1957- *WhoEnt 92*
**Freeman,** Lawrence 1906-1991 *NewYTBS 91 [port]*
**Freeman,** Lelabelle Christine 1923- *WhoBlA 92*
**Freeman,** Leon David 1920- *AmMWSc 92*
**Freeman,** Leon Howard, Jr. 1949- *WhoAmL 92*
**Freeman,** Leonard d1973 *LesBEnT 92*
**Freeman,** Louis Barton 1935- *AmMWSc 92*
**Freeman,** Louis S. 1940- *WhoFI 92*
**Freeman,** Lucy 1916- *WrDr 92*
**Freeman,** Marc Edward 1944- *AmMWSc 92*
**Freeman,** Marianne *WhoAmP 91*
**Freeman,** Marie Joyce 1934- *Who 92*
**Freeman,** Mark William 1949- *WhoEnt 92*
**Freeman,** Martin 1944- *WhoWest 92*
**Freeman,** Mary E. Wilkins 1852-1930 *BenetAL 91, ModAWWr*
**Freeman,** Mary Eleanor Wilkins 1852-1930 *HanAmWH*
**Freeman,** Mary Lamb *DrAPF 91*
**Freeman,** Mary Louise 1941- *WhoAmP 91*
**Freeman,** Max James 1934- *AmMWSc 92*
**Freeman,** Maynard Lloyd 1950- *AmMWSc 92*
**Freeman,** McKinley Howard, Sr. 1920- *WhoBlA 92*
**Freeman,** Michael 1936- *TwCPaSc*
**Freeman,** Michael Alexander Reykers 1931- *IntWW 91, Who 92*
**Freeman,** Michael E. 1937- *WhoAmL 92*
**Freeman,** Michael John 1951- *WhoAmP 91*
**Freeman,** Michael O 1948- *WhoAmP 91*
**Freeman,** Milton Malcolm Roland 1934- *AmMWSc 92*
**Freeman,** Milton Victor 1911- *WhoAmL 92, WhoFI 92*
**Freeman,** Morgan 1937- *ConBlB 2 [port], CurBio 91 [port], IntMPA 92, WhoBlA 92, WhoEnt 92*
**Freeman,** Muriel Messinger 1920- *WhoEnt 92*
**Freeman,** Myron L 1930- *AmMWSc 92*
**Freeman,** Nancy Cecile 1944- *WhoBlA 92*
**Freeman,** Nancy Jean 1948- *WhoEnt 92*
**Freeman,** Nancy Leigh 1960- *WhoWest 92*
**Freeman,** Neil 1948- *WhoFI 92, WhoWest 92*
**Freeman,** Neil Julian 1939- *AmMWSc 92*
**Freeman,** Nelson R. 1924- *WhoBlA 92*
**Freeman,** Norman E., Sr. 1950- *WhoBlA 92*
**Freeman,** Orville Lothrop 1918- *IntWW 91, WhoAmP 91*
**Freeman,** Palmer 1944- *WhoAmL 92*
**Freeman,** Palmer, Jr 1944- *WhoAmP 91*
**Freeman,** Patricia Elizabeth 1924- *WhoWest 92*
**Freeman,** Paul 1916- *Who 92*
**Freeman,** Paul 1936- *NewAmDM*
**Freeman,** Paul D. 1936- *WhoBlA 92*
**Freeman,** Paul Douglas 1939- *WhoEnt 92*
**Freeman,** Paul Douglas 1946- *WhoMW 92*
**Freeman,** Paul Illife *Who 92*
**Freeman,** Peter Kent 1931- *AmMWSc 92*
**Freeman,** Peter Sunderlin 1944- *WhoFI 92*
**Freeman,** Preston Garrison 1933- *WhoBlA 92*
**Freeman,** R. B. 1915-1986 *ConAu 133*
**Freeman,** Ralf *DcNCBi 2*
**Freeman,** Ralph 1911- *IntWW 91, Who 92*
**Freeman,** Ralph 1945- *TwCPaSc*
**Freeman,** Ralph David 1939- *AmMWSc 92*
**Freeman,** Raymond 1932- *AmMWSc 92, IntWW 91, Who 92*
**Freeman,** Reino Samuel 1919- *AmMWSc 92*
**Freeman,** Richard B 1931- *AmMWSc 92*
**Freeman,** Richard C. 1926- *WhoAmL 92*
**Freeman,** Richard Carl 1929- *AmMWSc 92*
**Freeman,** Richard Dean 1928- *WhoFI 92*
**Freeman,** Richard Dwaine 1945- *WhoRel 92*
**Freeman,** Richard Francis 1934- *WhoFI 92*
**Freeman,** Richard Gavin 1910- *Who 92*
**Freeman,** Richard Merrell 1921- *WhoAmP 91*
**Freeman,** Richard Reiling 1944- *AmMWSc 92*
**Freeman,** Richard Weldon 1931- *WhoAmL 92*
**Freeman,** Robert *AmMWSc 92*
**Freeman,** Robert Arnold 1927- *WhoMW 92*
**Freeman,** Robert Clarence 1927- *AmMWSc 92*
**Freeman,** Robert David 1930- *AmMWSc 92*
**Freeman,** Robert DeCorps 1921- *WhoAmP 91*
**Freeman,** Robert Glen 1927- *AmMWSc 92*
**Freeman,** Robert L 1934- *WhoAmP 91*
**Freeman,** Robert Lee *WhoBlA 92*
**Freeman,** Robert Louis 1956- *WhoAmP 91*
**Freeman,** Robert Mallory 1941- *WhoFI 92*
**Freeman,** Robert Mark 1961- *WhoRel 92*
**Freeman,** Robert Schofield 1935- *WhoEnt 92*
**Freeman,** Robert Turner, Jr. 1918- *WhoBlA 92*
**Freeman,** Roger A. d1991 *NewYTBS 91*
**Freeman,** Roger A. 1904- *WrDr 92*
**Freeman,** Roger Dante 1933- *AmMWSc 92*
**Freeman,** Roger Norman 1942- *Who 92*
**Freeman,** Ronald J. 1947- *WhoBlA 92*
**Freeman,** Ronald J., II 1947- *BlkOlyM*
**Freeman,** Ruby E. 1921- *WhoBlA 92*
**Freeman,** Ruges R. 1917- *WhoBlA 92*
**Freeman,** Russell Adams 1932- *WhoAmL 92, WhoFI 92*
**Freeman,** Sarah 1940- *ConAu 133, SmATA 66*
**Freeman,** Shirley Ann 1930- *WhoAmP 91*
**Freeman,** Sidney Lee 1927- *WhoRel 92*
**Freeman,** Simon 1952- *ConAu 133*
**Freeman,** Theodore H., Jr. 1950- *WhoBlA 92*
**Freeman,** Thomas *WrDr 92*
**Freeman,** Thomas d1821 *BiInAmS*
**Freeman,** Thomas Edward 1930- *AmMWSc 92*
**Freeman,** Thomas F. 1920- *WhoBlA 92*
**Freeman,** Thomas G 1937- *WhoAmP 91*
**Freeman,** Thomas J 1932- *AmMWSc 92*
**Freeman,** Thomas J A 1841-1907 *BiInAmS*
**Freeman,** Thomas Patrick 1938- *AmMWSc 92*
**Freeman,** Thomas Walter 1908- *IntAu&W 91*
**Freeman,** Todd Ira 1953- *WhoAmL 92*
**Freeman,** Tom M. 1952- *WhoAmL 92*
**Freeman,** Tony *ConAu 134*
**Freeman,** Travis 1925- *WhoAmP 91*
**Freeman,** Tyler Ira 1934- *WhoMW 92*
**Freeman,** Val LeRoy 1926- *WhoWest 92*
**Freeman,** Varel Daniel, Jr. 1949- *WhoFI 92*
**Freeman,** Verne Crawford 1900- *AmMWSc 92*
**Freeman,** Vivian L 1927- *WhoAmP 91*
**Freeman,** Wade Austin 1940- *AmMWSc 92*
**Freeman,** Walter Eugene 1928- *WhoBlA 92*
**Freeman,** Walter Jackson, III 1927- *AmMWSc 92*
**Freeman,** William M 1926- *WhoAmP 91, WhoBlA 92*
**Freeman,** William T. *DrAPF 91*
**Freeman,** William Taft, Jr. 1937- *WhoRel 92, WhoWest 92*
**Freeman Allen,** Geoffrey 1922- *WrDr 92*
**Freeman-Grenville** *Who 92*
**Freeman-Grenville,** Greville Stewart P 1918- *IntAu&W 91, WrDr 92*
**Freeman-Lindsay,** Diane *WhoBlA 92*
**Freeman-Pollard,** Jhivaun Rose 1963- *WhoWest 92*
**Freemantle,** Brian 1936- *WrDr 92*
**Freemantle,** Brian Harry 1936- *IntAu&W 91*
**Freemantle,** Chloe 1950- *TwCPaSc*
**Freemen,** Barbara Constance 1906- *IntAu&W 91*
**Freemon,** Frank Reed 1938- *AmMWSc 92*
**Freemont,** James McKinley 1942- *WhoBlA 92*
**Freer,** Charles Edward Jesse 1901- *Who 92*
**Freer,** Eleanor Everest 1864-1942 *NewAmDM*
**Freer,** Lyle Leroy 1925- *WhoAmP 91*
**Freer,** Mavis 1927- *TwCPaSc*
**Freer,** Paul Caspar 1862-1912 *BiInAmS*
**Freer,** Richard John 1942- *AmMWSc 92*
**Freer,** Robert 1923- *Who 92*
**Freer,** Robert Elliott, Jr. 1941- *WhoAmL 92*
**Freer,** Stephan T 1933- *AmMWSc 92*
**Freericks,** Mary *DrAPF 91*
**Freerks,** Marshall Cornelius 1912- *AmMWSc 92*
**Freerksen,** Deborah Lynne 1956- *AmMWSc 92*
**Freerksen,** Enno 1910- *IntWW 91*
**Freerksen,** Gregory Nathan 1951- *WhoAmL 92*
**Freerksen,** Robert Wayne 1952- *AmMWSc 92*
**Frees,** David M., III 1960- *WhoAmL 92*
**Freese,** Ernst 1925- *AmMWSc 92*
**Freese,** Frank E 1940- *WhoIns 92*
**Freese,** George E, Jr 1920- *WhoAmP 91*
**Freese,** John Philip 1947- *WhoAmL 92*
**Freese,** Katherine 1957- *AmMWSc 92*
**Freese,** Kenneth Brooks 1949- *AmMWSc 92*
**Freese,** Mathias B. *DrAPF 91*
**Freese,** Ralph 1943- *WhoWest 92*
**Freese,** Ralph 1946- *AmMWSc 92*
**Freese,** Raymond William 1934- *AmMWSc 92*
**Freese,** Richard 1937- *WhoAmP 91*
**Freese,** Robert Gerard 1929- *WhoFI 92*
**Freese,** Sigrid Halvorson 1939- *WhoAmP 91*
**Freese,** Stephen J 1960- *WhoAmP 91*
**Freese,** Uwe Ernst 1925- *AmMWSc 92*

**Freese**, William P, II 1934- *AmMWSc 92*
**Freeson**, Reginald 1926- *Who 92*
**Freeston**, W Denney, Jr 1936- *AmMWSc 92*
**Freeth**, Denzil Kingson 1924- *Who 92*
**Freeth**, Gordon 1914- *IntWW 91, Who 92*
**Freeth**, H. Andrew 1912- *TwCPaSc*
**Freeth**, Peter 1938- *TwCPaSc*
**Freeth**, Peter Stewart 1938- *Who 92*
**Freethey**, Geoffrey Ward 1945- *AmMWSc 92*
**Freeze**, James Gordon 1957- *WhoEnt 92*
**Freeze**, Richard 1948- *WhoEnt 92*
**Freeze**, Roy Allan 1939- *AmMWSc 92*
**Freger**, Craig Jeffrey 1958- *WhoAmL 92*
**Fregia**, Darrell Leon 1949- *WhoBlA 92*
**Fregia**, Paul Douglas 1958- *WhoMW 92*
**Fregly**, Melvin James 1925- *AmMWSc 92*
**Fregolle**, David Edward 1954- *WhoAmL 92*
**Fregoso**, Thomas G. 1958- *WhoHisp 92*
**Frehm**, Walter 1915- *WhoEnt 92*
**Frehn**, John 1936- *AmMWSc 92*
**Frei**, Emil, III 1924- *AmMWSc 92*
**Frei**, Ephraim Heinrich 1912- *IntWW 91*
**Frei**, Jaroslav Vaclav 1929- *AmMWSc 92*
**Frei**, John Karen, Sister *AmMWSc 92*
**Frei Montalva**, Eduardo 1911-1982 *FacFETw*
**Freiberg**, Brenda Randall 1938- *WhoFI 92*
**Freiberg**, Lowell Carl 1939- *WhoFI 92*
**Freiberg**, Samuel Robert 1924- *AmMWSc 92*
**Freiberger**, Walter Frederick 1924- *AmMWSc 92, WhoFI 92*
**Freibert**, Pat 1936- *WhoAmP 91*
**Freibott**, George August 1954- *WhoWest 92*
**Freiburg**, Richard Eighme 1923- *AmMWSc 92*
**Freiday**, Dean 1915- *WhoRel 92*
**Freidberg**, Sidney 1914- *WhoAmL 92*
**Freidin**, John 1941- *WhoAmP 91*
**Freidin**, Seymour d1991 *NewYTBS 91*
**Freidin**, Seymour K. 1917-1991 *ConAu 134*
**Freidinger**, Roger Merlin 1947- *AmMWSc 92*
**Freidline**, Charles Eugene 1937- *AmMWSc 92*
**Freier**, Esther Fay 1925- *AmMWSc 92*
**Freier**, George David 1915- *AmMWSc 92*
**Freier**, Herbert Edward 1921- *AmMWSc 92, WhoMW 92*
**Freier**, Jerome Bernard 1916- *AmMWSc 92*
**Freier**, Phyllis S 1921- *AmMWSc 92*
**Freier**, Susan Marcie 1953- *WhoEnt 92*
**Freier**, Tom *WhoAmP 91*
**Freiert**, William Kendall 1941- *WhoMW 92*
**Freiheit**, Ronald Ray 1956- *WhoEnt 92*
**Freiherr von Kleydorff**, Ludwig Otto A. 1926- *WhoFI 92*
**Freile**, Juan Rodriguez *HisDSpE*
**Freilich**, Gerald 1926- *AmMWSc 92*
**Freilich**, Jeff 1948- *WhoEnt 92, WhoWest 92*
**Freilich**, Joshua 1951- *WhoWest 92*
**Freilicher**, Jane 1924- *WorArt 1980 [port]*
**Freilicher**, Melvyn *DrAPF 91*
**Freilicher**, Melvyn 1946- *IntAu&W 91*
**Freilicher**, Morton 1931- *WhoAmL 92*
**Freiling**, Edward Clawson 1922- *AmMWSc 92*
**Freiling**, Michael Joseph 1950- *AmMWSc 92*
**Freiman**, Charles 1932- *AmMWSc 92*
**Freiman**, David Galland 1911- *AmMWSc 92*
**Freiman**, Howard Arthur 1956- *WhoFI 92*
**Freiman**, Paul E. 1932- *WhoWest 92*
**Freiman**, Stephen Weil 1942- *AmMWSc 92*
**Freimanis**, Atis K 1925- *AmMWSc 92*
**Freimanis**, Atis Kristaps 1925- *WhoMW 92*
**Freimann**, John Raymond 1926- *WhoEnt 92*
**Freimark**, Jeffrey Philip 1955- *WhoFI 92*
**Freimark**, Linda H. 1955- *WhoAmL 92*
**Freimer**, Earl Howard 1926- *AmMWSc 92, WhoMW 92*
**Freimer**, Marshall Leonard 1932- *AmMWSc 92*
**Freimuth**, Henry Charles 1912- *AmMWSc 92*
**Freimuth**, Joseph Michael 1944- *WhoAmL 92*
**Freimuth**, Kenneth Charles 1941- *WhoWest 92*
**Freind**, John 1675-1728 *BlkwCEP*
**Freind**, Stephen F 1944- *WhoAmP 91*
**Freinkel**, Norbert 1926- *AmMWSc 92*
**Freinkel**, Ruth Kimmelstiel 1926- *AmMWSc 92*
**Freire**, Ernesto I 1949- *AmMWSc 92*
**Freire**, Paulo Reglus Neves 1921- *DcEcMov*
**Freire Falcao**, Jose 1925- *WhoRel 92*
**Freire Serrano**, Ramon 1787-1851 *HisDSpE*
**Freireich**, Emil J 1927- *AmMWSc 92*
**Freis**, Edward David 1912- *AmMWSc 92*
**Freis**, Robert P 1931- *AmMWSc 92*
**Freise**, Earl J 1935- *AmMWSc 92*
**Freisen**, Gil *WhoBlA 92*
**Freiser**, Henry 1920- *AmMWSc 92*
**Freiser**, Lawrence M. 1942- *WhoAmL 92*
**Freiser**, Marvin Joseph 1926- *AmMWSc 92*
**Freisheim**, James Harold 1937- *AmMWSc 92*
**Freisinger**, Randall R. *DrAPF 91*
**Freisler**, Roland 1893-1945 *EncTR 91 [port]*
**Freitag**, David Franklin, II 1945- *WhoMW 92*
**Freitag**, Dean R 1926- *AmMWSc 92*
**Freitag**, Edward George 1946- *WhoFI 92*
**Freitag**, Frederick Gerald 1952- *WhoMW 92*
**Freitag**, Harlow 1936- *AmMWSc 92*
**Freitag**, James Milton 1953- *WhoEnt 92*
**Freitag**, Julia Louise 1927- *AmMWSc 92*
**Freitag**, Michael 1961- *WhoWest 92*
**Freitag**, Peter Roy 1943- *WhoWest 92*
**Freitag**, Robert Frederick 1920- *AmMWSc 92*
**Freitag**, Steven John 1951- *WhoMW 92*
**Freitas**, Antoinette Juni 1944- *WhoFI 92*
**Freitas**, Beatrice Botty 1938- *WhoEnt 92*
**Freitas**, John Eugene 1945- *WhoMW 92*
**Freitas**, Robert Archibald, Jr. 1952- *WhoWest 92*
**Freitas**, Stephen Joseph 1958- *WhoWest 92*
**Freitas Do Amaral**, Diogo *IntWW 91*
**Freivalds**, Laila 1942- *IntWW 91*
**Freiwald**, Eric William 1927- *WhoEnt 92*
**Freiwald**, Ronald Charles 1943- *AmMWSc 92*
**Freizer**, Louis A. 1931- *WhoEnt 92, WhoFI 92*
**Frejacques**, Claude 1924- *IntWW 91*
**Freke**, John 1688-1756 *BlkwCEP*
**Freleng**, Friz 1906- *IntMPA 92, WhoEnt 92*
**Frelich**, Phyllis 1944- *WhoEnt 92*
**Frelinger**, Andrew L 1953- *AmMWSc 92*
**Frelinger**, Jeffrey 1948- *AmMWSc 92*
**Frelinghuysen**, Frederick Theodore 1817-1885 *AmPolLe*
**Frelinghuysen**, Joseph S. 1912- *ConAu 134*
**Frelinghuysen**, Rodney 1946- *WhoAmP 91*
**Frelow**, Robert Dean 1932- *WhoBlA 92*
**Frelow**, Robert Lee, Jr. 1966- *WhoBlA 92*
**Fremantle** *Who 92*
**Fremantle**, Anne 1910- *IntAu&W 91*
**Fremantle**, John Tapling 1927- *Who 92*
**Fremaux**, Louis Joseph Felix 1921- *IntWW 91, Who 92*
**Fremgen**, James Morgan 1933- *WrDr 92*
**Fremlin**, Celia 1914- *IntAu&W 91, WrDr 92*
**Fremling**, Calvin R 1929- *AmMWSc 92*
**Fremling**, Warren Charles 1947- *WhoEnt 92*
**Fremming**, Benjamin DeWitt 1924- *AmMWSc 92*
**Fremont**, Jessie Benton d1902 *BenetAL 91*
**Fremont**, John C. 1813-1890 *BenetAL 91*
**Fremont**, John Charles 1813-1890 *AmPolLe*
**Fremont**, Sewall Lawrence 1816-1886 *DcNCBi 2*
**Fremont-Smith**, Marion R. 1926- *WhoAmL 92*
**Fremount**, Henry Neil 1933- *AmMWSc 92*
**Fremouw**, Edward Joseph 1934- *AmMWSc 92*
**Fremstad**, Olive 1871-1951 *NewAmDM*
**Frenay**, Henri 1905-1988 *FacFETw*
**French** *Who 92*
**French**, Mrs. *NewAmDM*
**French**, Alan Raymond 1946- *AmMWSc 92*
**French**, Alexander Murdoch 1920- *AmMWSc 92*
**French**, Alfred 1916- *IntAu&W 91, IntWW 91, WrDr 92*
**French**, Alfred Dexter 1943- *AmMWSc 92*
**French**, Alice 1850-1934 *BenetAL 91*
**French**, Allen Lee 1939- *AmMWSc 92*
**French**, Annie 1872-1965 *TwCPaSc*
**French**, Anthony Philip 1920- *Who 92*
**French**, Becky Russell 1953- *WhoAmL 92*
**French**, Bevan Meredith 1937- *AmMWSc 92*
**French**, Brian *TwCPaSc*
**French**, Bruce Hartung 1915- *WhoAmL 92*
**French**, Carroll Davies 1928- *WhoAmL 92*
**French**, Catherine 1946- *WhoEnt 92*
**French**, Cecil Charles John 1926- *Who 92*
**French**, Charles Stacy 1907- *AmMWSc 92, IntWW 91*
**French**, Christopher James Saunders 1925- *Who 92*
**French**, Clarence Levi, Jr. 1925- *WhoFI 92, WhoWest 92*
**French**, David *DrAPF 91*
**French**, David 1939- *IntAu&W 91, WrDr 92*
**French**, David 1947- *Who 92*
**French**, David Milton 1914- *AmMWSc 92*
**French**, David N 1936- *AmMWSc 92*
**French**, David W 1921- *AmMWSc 92*
**French**, Dick 1946- *TwCPaSc*
**French**, Douglas Charles 1944- *Who 92*
**French**, E. LaVon *WhoAmL 92*
**French**, Edward P 1924- *AmMWSc 92*
**French**, Ernest W 1929- *AmMWSc 92*
**French**, Fiona 1944- *IntAu&W 91, WrDr 92*
**French**, Frances Elizabeth 1947- *WhoEnt 92*
**French**, Francis William 1927- *AmMWSc 92*
**French**, Frank Elwood, Jr 1935- *AmMWSc 92*
**French**, Frank Louis 1952- *WhoEnt 92*
**French**, George Wesley 1928- *WhoBlA 92*
**French**, Georgine Louise 1934- *WhoWest 92*
**French**, Gerald 1927- *TwCPaSc*
**French**, Gordon Nichols 1919- *AmMWSc 92*
**French**, Hadley Mack 1952- *WhoMW 92*
**French**, Harold Stanley 1921- *WhoFI 92*
**French**, Harold Wendell 1930- *WhoRel 92*
**French**, Henry Pierson, Jr. 1934- *WhoFI 92*
**French**, Henry William 1910- *Who 92*
**French**, Howard W. 1957- *WhoBlA 92*
**French**, J Barry 1931- *AmMWSc 92*
**French**, James C 1930- *AmMWSc 92*
**French**, James Edwin 1942- *AmMWSc 92*
**French**, James J. 1926- *WhoBlA 92*
**French**, Jeptha Victor 1936- *AmMWSc 92*
**French**, Joan *DrAPF 91*
**French**, John, III 1932- *WhoAmL 92, WhoFI 92*
**French**, John Denton 1852-1925 *FacFETw*
**French**, John Donald 1923- *AmMWSc 92*
**French**, John Douglas 1911- *AmMWSc 92*
**French**, John Dwyer 1933- *WhoAmL 92*
**French**, John Robert 1818-1890 *DcNCBi 2*
**French**, Joseph H 1928- *AmMWSc 92*
**French**, Joseph Henry 1928- *WhoBlA 92*
**French**, Judson Cull 1922- *AmMWSc 92*
**French**, Kenneth Edward 1929- *AmMWSc 92*
**French**, Larry J 1940- *AmMWSc 92*
**French**, Layne Bryan 1950- *WhoAmL 92*
**French**, Leslie Richard 1904- *Who 92*
**French**, Linda Jean 1947- *WhoAmL 92*
**French**, Lisa 1953- *WhoIns 92*
**French**, Lyle Albert 1915- *AmMWSc 92*
**French**, Marilyn 1929- *BenetAL 91, ConNov 91, IntWW 91, WrDr 92*
**French**, MaryAnn 1952- *WhoBlA 92*
**French**, Neville Arthur Irwin 1920- *Who 92*
**French**, Nicole Renee 1966- *WhoMW 92*
**French**, Paul *ConAu 36NR, IntAu&W 91X, TwCSFW 91*
**French**, Philip 1933- *IntAu&W 91, WrDr 92*
**French**, Philip Franks 1932- *WhoFI 92, WhoMW 92*
**French**, Philip Neville 1933- *Who 92*
**French**, Phyllis Olivia 1953- *WhoEnt 92*
**French**, Ray 1927- *WhoAmP 91*
**French**, Raymond 1920- *WhoFI 92*
**French**, Richard Collins 1922- *AmMWSc 92*
**French**, Richard Edwin 1926- *WhoWest 92*
**French**, Richard Frederic 1915- *WhoEnt 92*
**French**, Robert Dexter 1939- *AmMWSc 92*
**French**, Robert Leonard 1933- *AmMWSc 92*
**French**, Robert P 1919- *WhoAmP 91, WhoBlA 92*
**French**, Samuel d1898 *DcLB 106 [port]*
**French**, Simon 1957- *WrDr 92*
**French**, Stephen Warren 1934- *WhoWest 92*
**French**, Susan F. 1943- *WhoAmL 92*
**French**, Victor *LesBEnT 92*
**French**, Walter Russell, Jr 1923- *AmMWSc 92*
**French**, Warren B, Jr 1923- *WhoAmP 91*
**French**, Warren G. 1922- *WrDr 92*
**French**, Warren Graham 1922- *IntAu&W 91*
**French**, Wilbur Lile 1929- *AmMWSc 92*
**French**, William Edwin 1936- *AmMWSc 92*
**French**, William George 1943- *AmMWSc 92*
**French**, William Harold 1926- *IntAu&W 91*
**French**, William Stanley 1940- *AmMWSc 92*
**Frend**, William 1916- *WrDr 92*
**Frend**, William Hugh Clifford 1916- *IntWW 91, Who 92*
**Freneau**, Philip 1752-1832 *BenetAL 91, BlkwEAR*
**Frenger**, Paul F 1946- *AmMWSc 92*
**Freni**, Mirella 1935- *IntWW 91, NewAmDM*
**Frenke**, Eugene 1907- *IntMPA 92*
**Frenkel**, Albert W 1919- *AmMWSc 92*
**Frenkel**, Douglas N. 1947- *WhoAmL 92*
**Frenkel**, Eugene Phillip 1929- *AmMWSc 92*
**Frenkel**, Gerald Daniel 1944- *AmMWSc 92*
**Frenkel**, Jacob *NewYTBS 91 [port]*
**Frenkel**, Jacob Karl 1921- *AmMWSc 92*
**Frenkel**, Krystyna 1941- *AmMWSc 92*
**Frenkel**, Marvin Allen 1926- *WhoFI 92, WhoMW 92*
**Frenkel**, Michael 1936- *WhoAmL 92*
**Frenkel**, Nama Rachel 1951- *WhoEnt 92*
**Frenkel**, Niza B 1947- *AmMWSc 92*
**Frenkel**, Rene A 1932- *AmMWSc 92*
**Frenkel-Brunswik**, Else 1908-1958 *WomPsyc*
**Frenkiel**, Richard H *AmMWSc 92*
**Frenklach**, Michael Y 1947- *AmMWSc 92*
**Frenock**, Larry 1956- *WhoEnt 92*
**Frensdorff**, H Karl 1922- *AmMWSc 92*
**Frensley**, A C *WhoAmP 91*
**Frensley**, William Robert *AmMWSc 92*
**Frenssen**, Gustav 1863-1945 *EncTR 91*
**Frenster**, John H 1928- *AmMWSc 92*
**Frenster**, John Henry 1928- *WhoWest 92*
**Frentz**, David Edwin 1947- *WhoEnt 92*
**Frenzel**, Charles Alfon 1940- *WhoWest 92*
**Frenzel**, Hugh N 1918- *AmMWSc 92*
**Frenzel**, Louis Daniel, Jr 1920- *AmMWSc 92*
**Frenzel**, Lydia Ann Melcher 1944- *AmMWSc 92*
**Frenzel**, Otto N., III 1930- *WhoFI 92, WhoMW 92*
**Frenzel**, William Eldridge 1928- *WhoAmP 91*
**Frenzen**, Christopher Lee 1954- *AmMWSc 92*
**Frenzen**, Paul 1924- *AmMWSc 92*
**Frenzer**, Peter F 1934- *WhoIns 92*
**Frenzer**, Peter Frederick 1934- *WhoFI 92*
**Frere**, James Arnold 1920- *Who 92*
**Frere**, Jean 1919- *IntWW 91*
**Frere**, John Hookham 1769-1846 *RfGEnL 91*
**Frere**, Maurice Herbert 1932- *AmMWSc 92*
**Frere**, Richard Tobias 1938- *Who 92*
**Frere**, S. S. 1916- *WrDr 92*
**Frere**, Sheppard Sunderland 1916- *IntWW 91, Who 92*
**Frere-Smith**, Matthew 1923- *TwCPaSc*
**Freret**, Nicolas 1688-1749 *BlkwCEP*
**Freret**, Rene Joseph 1944- *WhoRel 92*
**Frerichs**, Donald L 1931- *WhoAmP 91*
**Frerichs**, Ernest Sunley 1925- *WhoRel 92*
**Frerichs**, Kent Elmer 1946- *WhoAmP 91*
**Frerichs**, William Charles Anthony 1829-1905 *DcNCBi 2*
**Frerichs**, William Edward 1939- *AmMWSc 92*
**Frerking**, Kenneth Lee 1932- *WhoRel 92*
**Frerking**, Margaret Ann 1950- *AmMWSc 92*
**Frerman**, Frank Edward 1942- *AmMWSc 92*
**Freron**, Elie-Catherine 1718-1776 *BlkwCEP*
**Fresco**, Jacques Robert 1928- *AmMWSc 92*
**Fresco**, James Martin 1926- *AmMWSc 92*
**Fresco**, Robert M. 1928- *IntMPA 92*
**Frescobaldi**, Girolamo 1583-1643 *NewAmDM*
**Fresconi**, Therese Marie 1961- *WhoRel 92*
**Frescura**, Bert Louis 1936- *AmMWSc 92*
**Frese**, Edward Scheer, Jr. 1944- *WhoFI 92*
**Frese**, Frederick Joseph, III 1940- *WhoMW 92*
**Fresh**, Edith McCullough 1942- *WhoBlA 92*
**Fresh**, James Henry 1922- *WhoRel 92*
**Fresh**, James W 1926- *AmMWSc 92*
**Freshour**, Peter James 1948- *WhoRel 92*
**Freshwater**, David 1950- *WhoFI 92*
**Freshwater**, Donald Cole 1924- *Who 92*
**Fresia**, Elmo James 1931- *AmMWSc 92*
**Freskos**, John Nicholas 1958- *WhoMW 92*
**Fresno**, Leonides 1927- *WhoHisp 92*
**Fresno Larrain**, Juan Francisco 1914- *IntWW 91, WhoRel 92*
**Fresquez**, Catalina Lourdes 1937- *AmMWSc 92*
**Fresquez**, Edward J. *WhoHisp 92*
**Fresquez**, Ernest C. 1955- *WhoHisp 92*
**Fresquez**, Ralph E. 1934- *WhoHisp 92*
**Fresquez**, Sonny *WhoHisp 92*
**Freston**, James W 1936- *AmMWSc 92*
**Freston**, Tom *LesBEnT 92 [port]*

**Freter**, Kurt Rudolf 1929- *AmMWSc 92*
**Freter**, Mark Allen 1947- *WhoWest 92*
**Freter**, Rolf Gustav 1926- *AmMWSc 92*
**Fretheim**, Terence Erling 1936- *WhoRel 92*
**Fretter**, William Bache 1916- *AmMWSc 92*
**Fretwell**, Carl Quention, II 1951- *WhoBlA 92*
**Fretwell**, Craig Bailey 1954- *WhoWest 92*
**Fretwell**, Elizabeth *Who 92*
**Fretwell**, Estil Van 1952- *WhoAmP 91*
**Fretwell**, George Herbert d1991 *Who 92N*
**Fretwell**, John 1930- *Who 92*
**Fretwell**, John Emsley 1930- *IntWW 91*
**Fretwell**, Lyman Jefferson, Jr 1934- *AmMWSc 92*
**Fretwell**, Nancy Houx 1944- *WhoAmP 91*
**Fretz**, David Eldon 1963- *WhoAmL 92*
**Fretz**, Donald Robert 1922- *WhoAmL 92*
**Fretz**, Patricia Lynn 1950- *WhoMW 92*
**Fretz**, Thomas Alvin 1942- *AmMWSc 92*
**Freuchen-Gale**, Dagmar d1991 *NewYTBS 91*
**Freud**, Anna 1895-1982 *ConAu 34NR, FacFETw, WomPsyc*
**Freud**, Clement 1924- *Who 92, WrDr 92*
**Freud**, John Sigmund 1956- *WhoAmL 92*
**Freud**, Lucian 1922- *IntWW 91, TwCPaSc, Who 92*
**Freud**, Paul J 1938- *AmMWSc 92*
**Freud**, Sigmund 1856-1939 *ConAu 133, EncTR 91 [port], FacFETw, LiExTwC*
**Freud**, Sophie 1924- *ConAu 134*
**Freudberg**, Seth D 1959- *WhoIns 92*
**Freudenberg**, Edgar 1927- *WhoFI 92*
**Freudenberger**, C. Dean 1930- *ConAu 135*
**Freudenberger**, Herman 1922- *WrDr 92*
**Freudenberger**, Theobald 1904- *WhoRel 92*
**Freudenstein**, Ferdinand 1926- *AmMWSc 92*
**Freudenthal**, Hugo David 1930- *AmMWSc 92*
**Freudenthal**, Peter 1934- *AmMWSc 92*
**Freudenthal**, Ralph Ira 1940- *AmMWSc 92*
**Freudenthal**, Steven F 1949- *WhoAmP 91*
**Freudmann**, Axel I 1946- *WhoIns 92*
**Freund**, Doris Isabelle 1920- *WhoAmP 91*
**Freund**, Fred A. 1928- *WhoAmL 92*
**Freund**, Gerhard 1926- *AmMWSc 92*
**Freund**, Harry 1917- *AmMWSc 92*
**Freund**, Howard John 1946- *AmMWSc 92*
**Freund**, Jack 1917- *AmMWSc 92*
**Freund**, James Coleman 1934- *WhoAmL 92*
**Freund**, John Ernst 1921- *AmMWSc 92*
**Freund**, Kenneth Robert 1950- *WhoWest 92*
**Freund**, Lambert Ben 1942- *AmMWSc 92*
**Freund**, Matthew J 1928- *AmMWSc 92*
**Freund**, Mitchell David 1953- *WhoEnt 92*
**Freund**, Paul Abraham 1908- *WhoAmL 92*
**Freund**, Peter George Oliver 1936- *AmMWSc 92*
**Freund**, Peter Richard 1935- *AmMWSc 92*
**Freund**, Philip 1909- *WrDr 92*
**Freund**, Richard A 1924- *AmMWSc 92*
**Freund**, Robert M 1953- *AmMWSc 92*
**Freund**, Robert Stanley 1939- *AmMWSc 92*
**Freund**, Roland Wilhelm 1955- *AmMWSc 92*
**Freund**, Rudolf Jakob 1927- *AmMWSc 92*
**Freund**, Samuel J. 1949- *WhoAmL 92*
**Freund**, Susan Marguerite 1945- *WhoAmL 92*
**Freund**, Thomas Steven 1944- *AmMWSc 92*
**Freund**, William Curt 1926- *WhoFI 92*
**Freund**, York Paul 1947- *WhoFI 92*
**Freund-Rosenthal**, Miriam Kottler 1906- *IntWW 91*
**Freundlich**, Martin 1930- *AmMWSc 92*
**Freundlich**, Martin M 1905- *AmMWSc 92*
**Frevel**, Ludo Karl 1910- *AmMWSc 92, WhoMW 92*
**Frevert**, James Wilmot 1922- *WhoFI 92*
**Frevert**, Richard Anton 1956- *WhoEnt 92*
**Frevert**, Richard Keller 1914- *AmMWSc 92*
**Frew**, Donald Hudson, III 1960- *RelLAm 91*
**Frew**, Patricia A 1953- *WhoAmP 91*
**Frewer**, Glyn 1931- *WrDr 92*
**Frewer**, Glyn Mervyn Louis 1931- *IntAu&W 91*
**Frewer**, Louis Benson 1906- *IntAu&W 91*
**Frewer**, Matt 1958- *IntMPA 92*
**Frey**, Andrew Lewis 1938- *WhoAmL 92*
**Frey**, Bertram Christopher 1947- *WhoAmL 92, WhoMW 92*
**Frey**, Bruce Edward 1945- *AmMWSc 92*
**Frey**, Carl *AmMWSc 92*
**Frey**, Charles Frederick 1929- *AmMWSc 92*
**Frey**, Chris M 1923- *AmMWSc 92*
**Frey**, Dale Franklin 1932- *WhoFI 92*
**Frey**, David Allen 1935- *AmMWSc 92*
**Frey**, David Grover 1915- *AmMWSc 92*
**Frey**, Dennis Frederick 1941- *AmMWSc 92*
**Frey**, Donald N 1923- *AmMWSc 92*
**Frey**, Douglas D 1955- *AmMWSc 92*
**Frey**, Elmer Jacob 1918- *AmMWSc 92*
**Frey**, Frank William 1947- *WhoAmL 92*
**Frey**, Frederick August 1938- *AmMWSc 92*
**Frey**, Frederick James 1950- *WhoIns 92*
**Frey**, Frederick Wolff, Jr 1930- *AmMWSc 92*
**Frey**, Gerard Louis 1914- *WhoRel 92*
**Frey**, Gerhard Michael 1933- *BiDExR*
**Frey**, Glenn 1948- *WhoEnt 92*
**Frey**, Harley Harrison, Jr. 1920- *WhoMW 92*
**Frey**, Henry Charles 1948- *WhoAmL 92*
**Frey**, Henry Richard 1932- *AmMWSc 92*
**Frey**, Herman S. 1920- *WhoFI 92*
**Frey**, James R 1932- *AmMWSc 92*
**Frey**, Jeffrey 1939- *AmMWSc 92*
**Frey**, John Erhart 1930- *AmMWSc 92*
**Frey**, Kenneth John 1923- *AmMWSc 92*
**Frey**, Kenneth O *WhoAmP 91*
**Frey**, Louis, Jr. 1934- *WhoAmL 92*
**Frey**, Martin Alan 1939- *WhoAmL 92*
**Frey**, Mary Anne Bassett 1934- *AmMWSc 92*
**Frey**, Maurice G 1913- *AmMWSc 92*
**Frey**, Merwin Lester 1932- *AmMWSc 92*
**Frey**, Nancy 1946- *WhoFI 92*
**Frey**, Nicholas F. 1949- *WhoAmL 92*
**Frey**, Nicholas Martin 1948- *AmMWSc 92*
**Frey**, Perry Allen 1935- *AmMWSc 92*
**Frey**, Philip Gregory 1960- *WhoAmL 92*
**Frey**, Philip Sigmund 1941- *WhoAmL 92*
**Frey**, Robert G *WhoAmP 91*
**Frey**, Sheldon Ellsworth 1921- *AmMWSc 92*
**Frey**, Stuart Macklin 1925- *WhoFI 92*
**Frey**, Susan Hamilton 1944- *WhoAmL 92*
**Frey**, Terrence G 1948- *AmMWSc 92*
**Frey**, Thomas G 1943- *AmMWSc 92*
**Frey**, Timothy John 1955- *WhoEnt 92*
**Frey**, Todd Matthew 1962- *WhoRel 92*
**Frey**, Virginia Ann 1942- *WhoRel 92*
**Frey**, William Adrian 1951- *AmMWSc 92*
**Frey**, William Carl 1923- *AmMWSc 92*
**Frey**, William Carl 1930- *WhoRel 92, WhoWest 92*
**Frey**, William Francis 1933- *AmMWSc 92*
**Frey**, William Howard, II 1947- *AmMWSc 92*
**Freyberg** *Who 92*
**Freyberg**, Baron 1923- *Who 92*
**Freyberg**, Paul 1923- *ConAu 135*
**Freyberger**, Wilfred L 1928- *AmMWSc 92*
**Freyburger**, Walter Alfred 1920- *AmMWSc 92*
**Freyd**, Peter John 1936- *AmMWSc 92*
**Freyd**, William Pattinson 1933- *WhoFI 92*
**Freydberg**, Margaret Howe *DrAPF 91*
**Freydis** *EncAmaz 91*
**Freyer**, Ellen Jacobs 1940- *WhoEnt 92*
**Freyer**, Gustav John 1931- *AmMWSc 92*
**Freyer**, Hans 1887-1969 *EncTR 91*
**Freyermuth**, Harlan Benjamin 1917- *AmMWSc 92*
**Freygang**, Walter Henry, Jr 1924- *AmMWSc 92*
**Freymann**, John Gordon 1922- *AmMWSc 92*
**Freymann**, Moye Wicks 1925- *AmMWSc 92*
**Freymond**, Jacques 1911- *IntWW 91*
**Freymuth**, Peter 1936- *AmMWSc 92, WhoWest 92*
**Freyndlikh**, Alisa Brunovna 1934- *IntWW 91*
**Freyre**, Ernesto, Jr. 1942- *WhoHisp 92*
**Freyre**, Raoul Manuel 1931- *AmMWSc 92*
**Freyss**, David 1933- *WhoEnt 92*
**Freyssinet**, Eugene 1879-1962 *DcTwDes, FacFETw*
**Freytag**, Lucy 1941- *WhoAmP 91*
**Freytag**, Paul Harold 1934- *AmMWSc 92*
**Freytag**, Richard Arthur 1933- *WhoFI 92*
**Freytag**, Sharon Nelson 1943- *WhoAmL 92*
**Freytag**, Svend O *AmMWSc 92*
**Frezon**, Sherwood Earl 1921- *AmMWSc 92*
**Frezza**, Bernard, Jr 1952- *WhoAmP 91*
**Fri**, Robert Wheeler 1935- *WhoAmP 91*
**Friar**, Billy W 1931- *AmMWSc 92*
**Friar**, Daniel Boone 1800-1858 *DcNCBi 2*
**Friar**, James Lewis 1940- *AmMWSc 92*
**Friar**, Robert Edsel 1933- *AmMWSc 92*
**Friars**, Gerald W 1929- *AmMWSc 92*
**Frias**, Christina R. 1938- *WhoHisp 92*
**Frias**, Linda *WhoHisp 92*
**Frias**, Louis A. *WhoHisp 92*
**Frias**, Louis Jaime 1946- *WhoHisp 92*
**Friauf**, Robert J 1926- *AmMWSc 92*
**Friauf**, Robert James 1926- *WhoMW 92*
**Friaz**, Guadalupe Mendez 1953- *WhoHisp 92*
**Fribance**, George Walter 1950- *WhoWest 92*
**Friberg**, Arnold 1913- *WhoWest 92*
**Friberg**, Emil Edwards 1935- *AmMWSc 92*
**Friberg**, James Frederick 1943- *AmMWSc 92*
**Friberg**, Karl Arthur 1945- *WhoFI 92*
**Friberg**, LaVerne Marvin 1949- *AmMWSc 92*
**Friberg**, Ronald Leroy 1944- *WhoRel 92*
**Friberg**, Stig E 1930- *AmMWSc 92*
**Fribourg**, Henry August 1929- *AmMWSc 92*
**Fribourg**, Michel *WhoFI 92*
**Fribourgh**, James H 1926- *AmMWSc 92*
**Fric**, Martin 1902-1968 *IntDcF 2-2*
**Fricano**, John Charles 1930- *WhoAmL 92*
**Fricano**, Tom Salvatore 1930- *WhoWest 92*
**Frick**, Arthur Charles 1923- *WhoMW 92*
**Frick**, Bob Scott 1940- *WhoEnt 92*
**Frick**, C. H. *WrDr 92*
**Frick**, Charles Mayser 1938- *WhoFI 92*
**Frick**, Ford C 1894-1978 *FacFETw*
**Frick**, Frank Smith 1938- *WhoRel 92*
**Frick**, Gottlob 1906- *IntWW 91, NewAmDM*
**Frick**, Henry Clay 1849-1919 *RComAH*
**Frick**, Ivan Eugene 1928- *WhoRel 92*
**Frick**, James William 1924- *WhoMW 92*
**Frick**, John Bartolet 1950- *WhoFI 92*
**Frick**, John P 1944- *AmMWSc 92*
**Frick**, John William 1951- *WhoMW 92*
**Frick**, Kerry Diana 1958- *WhoWest 92*
**Frick**, Murray Allan, Jr. 1954- *WhoRel 92*
**Frick**, Neil Huntington 1933- *AmMWSc 92*
**Frick**, Oscar L 1923- *AmMWSc 92*
**Frick**, Pieter A 1942- *AmMWSc 92*
**Frick**, Robert Hathaway 1924- *WhoAmL 92, WhoFI 92*
**Frick**, Wilhelm 1877-1946 *BiDExR, EncTR 91 [port]*
**Fricke**, Arthur Lee 1934- *AmMWSc 92*
**Fricke**, Edwin Francis 1910- *AmMWSc 92*
**Fricke**, Gerd 1946- *AmMWSc 92*
**Fricke**, Gordon Hugh 1937- *AmMWSc 92*
**Fricke**, Howard R 1936- *WhoIns 92*
**Fricke**, Kenneth Arthur 1918- *WhoAmL 92*
**Fricke**, Manfred 1936- *IntWW 91*
**Fricke**, Martin Paul 1937- *AmMWSc 92, WhoWest 92*
**Fricke**, Thomas Scott 1959- *WhoFI 92*
**Fricke**, William G, Jr 1926- *AmMWSc 92*
**Fricken**, Raymond Lee 1937- *AmMWSc 92*
**Fricker**, Anthony Nigel 1937- *Who 92*
**Fricker**, Joachim Carl 1927- *Who 92*
**Fricker**, Mary 1940- *ConAu 134*
**Fricker**, Peter Racine 1920- *NewAmDM*
**Fricker**, Peter Racine 1920-1990 *ConCom 92*
**Frickey**, Paul Henry 1931- *AmMWSc 92*
**Fricklas**, Anita Alper 1937- *WhoRel 92*
**Fricklas**, Michael David 1960- *WhoAmL 92, WhoFI 92*
**Fricks**, Ernest Eugene 1948- *WhoFI 92*
**Fricks**, Richard *DrAPF 91*
**Fricon**, Terri Madeline 1943- *WhoEnt 92*
**Fricsay**, Ferenc 1914-1963 *NewAmDM*
**Friday**, Elbert W, Jr 1939- *AmMWSc 92*
**Friday**, Fritz Carleton 1933- *WhoMW 92*
**Friday**, Herschel Hugar 1922- *WhoAmL 92*
**Friday**, Nancy *WrDr 92*
**Friday**, William Clyde 1920- *IntWW 91*
**Friderichs**, Hans 1931- *IntWW 91*
**Fridh**, Ake Josefsson 1918- *IntWW 91*
**Fridh**, Gertrude 1921- *IntWW 91*
**Fridholm**, George H. 1921- *WhoFI 92*
**Fridholm**, Roger Theodore 1941- *WhoFI 92, WhoMW 92*
**Fridinger**, Tomas Lee 1940- *AmMWSc 92*
**Fridland**, Arnold *AmMWSc 92*
**Fridlender**, Georgy Mikhailovich 1915- *IntWW 91*
**Fridley**, Robert B 1934- *AmMWSc 92*
**Fridley**, Saundra Lynn 1948- *WhoWest 92*
**Fridlund**, Paul Russell 1920- *AmMWSc 92*
**Fridman**, Josef Josel 1945- *WhoFI 92*
**Fridovich**, Irwin 1929- *AmMWSc 92, IntWW 91*
**Fridovich-Keil**, Judith Lisa 1961- *AmMWSc 92*
**Fridson**, Martin Steven 1952- *WhoFI 92*
**Fridy**, John Albert 1937- *AmMWSc 92*
**Friebel**, David Lee 1939- *WhoMW 92*
**Friebele**, Edward Joseph 1946- *AmMWSc 92*
**Friebert**, Robert *WhoAmP 91*
**Friebert**, Stuart *DrAPF 91*
**Fried**, Alfred 1864-1921 *FacFETw*
**Fried**, Alfred Hermann 1864-1921 *WhoNob 90*
**Fried**, Bernard 1933- *AmMWSc 92*
**Fried**, Burton David 1925- *AmMWSc 92*
**Fried**, Burton Theodore 1940- *WhoAmL 92, WhoFI 92*
**Fried**, Charles 1935- *IntWW 91, WhoAmL 92*
**Fried**, Charles A. 1945- *WhoFI 92*
**Fried**, David L 1933- *AmMWSc 92*
**Fried**, Donald David 1936- *WhoAmL 92*
**Fried**, Elaine June 1943- *WhoWest 92*
**Fried**, Elliot *DrAPF 91*
**Fried**, Emanuel *DrAPF 91*
**Fried**, Erich 1921- *IntAu&W 91, LiExTwC*
**Fried**, Erwin 1922- *AmMWSc 92*
**Fried**, Ferdinand 1898-1967 *EncTR 91*
**Fried**, George H 1926- *AmMWSc 92*
**Fried**, Herbert Daniel 1928- *WhoFI 92*
**Fried**, Herbert Martin 1929- *AmMWSc 92*
**Fried**, Howard Mark *AmMWSc 92*
**Fried**, Jeffrey Michael 1953- *WhoFI 92*
**Fried**, Jerrold 1937- *AmMWSc 92*
**Fried**, Jim *WhoAmP 91*
**Fried**, Joel Ethan 1954- *WhoEnt 92, WhoMW 92*
**Fried**, Joel R. 1946- *WhoMW 92*
**Fried**, Joel Robert 1946- *AmMWSc 92*
**Fried**, John 1929- *AmMWSc 92*
**Fried**, John H 1924- *AmMWSc 92*
**Fried**, John H. 1929- *WhoFI 92*
**Fried**, Josef 1914- *AmMWSc 92, IntWW 91*
**Fried**, Lewis Fredrick 1943- *WhoMW 92*
**Fried**, Louis Lester 1930- *WhoWest 92*
**Fried**, Martin L. 1934- *WhoAmL 92*
**Fried**, Maurice 1920- *AmMWSc 92*
**Fried**, Max 1910- *IntMPA 92*
**Fried**, Melvin 1924- *AmMWSc 92*
**Fried**, Paula Arden 1957- *WhoMW 92*
**Fried**, Philip *DrAPF 91*
**Fried**, Victor A *AmMWSc 92*
**Fried**, Vojtech 1921- *AmMWSc 92*
**Fried**, Walter 1935- *AmMWSc 92*
**Fried**, Walter Rudolf 1923- *AmMWSc 92*
**Fried**, William C. 1938- *WhoAmL 92*
**Friedan**, Betty 1921- *BenetAL 91, FacFETw [port], HanAmWH, IntWW 91, PorAmW [port], RComAH, WhoAmP 91, WhoEnt 92, WrDr 92*
**Friedberg**, A. Alan 1932- *IntMPA 92*
**Friedberg**, Alan Charles 1945- *WhoAmL 92*
**Friedberg**, Barry Sewell 1941- *WhoFI 92*
**Friedberg**, Carl E *AmMWSc 92*
**Friedberg**, Errol Clive 1937- *AmMWSc 92*
**Friedberg**, Felix 1921- *AmMWSc 92*
**Friedberg**, Gertrude 1908-1989 *TwCSFW 91*
**Friedberg**, Leon 1947- *WhoAmL 92*
**Friedberg**, Lionel 1944- *WhoEnt 92*
**Friedberg**, Martha Asher *DrAPF 91*
**Friedberg**, Maurice 1929- *IntAu&W 91, WrDr 92*
**Friedberg**, Michael 1939- *AmMWSc 92*
**Friedberg**, Richard Michael 1935- *AmMWSc 92*
**Friedberg**, Simeon Adlow 1925- *AmMWSc 92*
**Friedberg**, Stephen Howard 1940- *AmMWSc 92*
**Friedberg**, Stephen M. 1935- *WhoFI 92*
**Friedberg**, Thomas Harold 1939- *WhoIns 92*
**Friedberg**, Wallace 1927- *AmMWSc 92*
**Friedberger**, John Peter William 1937- *Who 92*
**Friedburg**, Louis Henry 1846- *BiInAmS*
**Friede**, Reinhard L 1926- *AmMWSc 92*
**Friedeburg**, Hans Georg von 1895-1945 *EncTR 91 [port]*
**Friedel**, Arthur W 1937- *AmMWSc 92*
**Friedel**, Jacques 1921- *IntWW 91*
**Friedel**, Wolfgang F 1946- *WhoIns 92*
**Friedell**, Ellen Silberstein 1948- *WhoAmL 92*
**Friedell**, Gilbert H 1927- *AmMWSc 92*
**Friedell**, Hymer Louis 1911- *AmMWSc 92*
**Friedell**, John C 1929- *AmMWSc 92*
**Friedeman**, Gerald R *WhoAmP 91*
**Friedemann**, Zygmunt Jerzy 1922- *WhoAmP 91*
**Frieden**, Bernard J 1930- *IntAu&W 91, WrDr 92*
**Frieden**, Bernard Roy 1936- *AmMWSc 92*
**Frieden**, Carl 1928- *AmMWSc 92*
**Frieden**, Earl 1921- *AmMWSc 92*
**Friedenberg**, Gary Howard 1940- *WhoAmL 92*
**Friedenberg**, Joan Ellen 1951- *WhoMW 92*
**Friedenberg**, Richard M 1926- *AmMWSc 92*
**Friedensohn**, Elias d1991 *NewYTBS 91*
**Friedenstein**, Hanna *AmMWSc 92*
**Friedenthal**, Jack H. 1931- *WhoAmL 92*
**Frieder**, Gideon 1937- *AmMWSc 92*
**Frieder**, Sol Lehrman 1919- *WhoEnt 92*
**Friederich**, Diane Marie 1962- *WhoRel 92*
**Friederich**, Mary Anna 1931- *WhoWest 92*
**Friederichs**, Norman Paul 1936- *WhoAmL 92, WhoFI 92, WhoMW 92*
**Friederici**, Hartmann H R 1927- *AmMWSc 92*
**Friedersdorf**, Max Lee 1929- *WhoAmP 91*
**Friedewald**, William Thomas 1939- *AmMWSc 92*

**Friedfertig,** Richard Bruce 1952- *WhoAmL 92*
**Friedgen,** Christina Julia 1943- *WhoEnt 92*
**Friedheim,** Jerry Warden 1934- *WhoAmP 91, WhoFI 92*
**Friedheim,** Michael 1943- *WhoFI 92*
**Friedhofer,** James Earl 1962- *WhoAmL 92*
**Friedhoff,** Arnold Jerome 1923- *AmMWSc 92*
**Friedkin,** John 1926- *IntMPA 92*
**Friedkin,** Morris Enton 1918- *AmMWSc 92*
**Friedkin,** William 1939- *IntDcF 2-2 [port], IntMPA 92, IntWW 91, WhoEnt 92*
**Friedl,** Francis Peter 1917- *WhoRel 92*
**Friedl,** Frank Edward 1931- *AmMWSc 92*
**Friedl,** Rick 1947- *WhoWest 92*
**Friedlaender,** Fritz J 1925- *AmMWSc 92*
**Friedlaender,** Fritz Josef 1925- *WhoMW 92*
**Friedlaender,** Jonathan Scott 1940- *AmMWSc 92*
**Friedland,** Beatrice L 1914- *AmMWSc 92*
**Friedland,** Bernard 1930- *AmMWSc 92*
**Friedland,** Claire Edith 1929- *WhoMW 92*
**Friedland,** Daniel 1916- *AmMWSc 92*
**Friedland,** Fritz 1910- *AmMWSc 92*
**Friedland,** Jack Arthur 1940- *WhoWest 92*
**Friedland,** Jerry Herbert 1937- *WhoAmL 92*
**Friedland,** Joan Martha 1936- *AmMWSc 92*
**Friedland,** Joanne Benazzi 1953- *WhoAmL 92*
**Friedland,** John E 1937- *WhoAmP 91*
**Friedland,** Louis N. 1913- *WhoEnt 92*
**Friedland,** Melvyn 1932- *AmMWSc 92*
**Friedland,** Philip Jay 1946- *WhoFI 92*
**Friedland,** Seth Douglas 1951- *WhoAmL 92*
**Friedland,** Seymour 1928- *WhoFI 92*
**Friedland,** Stephen Sholom 1921- *AmMWSc 92*
**Friedland,** Waldo Charles 1923- *AmMWSc 92*
**Friedland,** William H. 1923- *WrDr 92*
**Friedlander,** Alan L 1936- *AmMWSc 92*
**Friedlander,** Albert H. 1927- *WrDr 92*
**Friedlander,** Arthur Henry 1942- *WhoWest 92*
**Friedlander,** Carl B 1949- *AmMWSc 92*
**Friedlander,** Carl I. d1991 *NewYTBS 91*
**Friedlander,** Charles Douglas 1928- *WhoWest 92*
**Friedlander,** Edward Robert 1952- *WhoRel 92*
**Friedlander,** Eric Mark 1944- *AmMWSc 92*
**Friedlander,** Frederick Gerard 1917- *IntWW 91, Who 92*
**Friedlander,** Gary Scott 1959- *WhoAmL 92*
**Friedlander,** Gerhart 1916- *AmMWSc 92*
**Friedlander,** Henry Z *AmMWSc 92*
**Friedlander,** Herbert Norman 1922- *AmMWSc 92*
**Friedlander,** Ira Ray 1953- *AmMWSc 92*
**Friedlander,** James Stuart 1942- *WhoAmL 92*
**Friedlander,** John Benjamin 1941- *AmMWSc 92*
**Friedlander,** Lee 1934- *ModArCr 2*
**Friedlander,** Martin *AmMWSc 92*
**Friedlander,** Michael J 1950- *AmMWSc 92*
**Friedlander,** Michael Wulf 1928- *AmMWSc 92*
**Friedlander,** Miriam 1914- *WhoAmP 91*
**Friedlander,** Miriam Alice 1947- *WhoMW 92*
**Friedlander,** Patricia Ann 1944- *WhoMW 92*
**Friedlander,** Sheldon K 1927- *AmMWSc 92*
**Friedlander,** Susan Jean 1946- *AmMWSc 92*
**Friedlander,** Tzvi Hersh 1946- *WhoRel 92*
**Friedlander,** Walter Jay 1919- *AmMWSc 92*
**Friedlander,** William Sheffield 1930- *AmMWSc 92*
**Friedler,** Robert M 1936- *AmMWSc 92*
**Friedlob,** Raymond Louis 1945- *WhoAmL 92*
**Friedly,** John C 1938- *AmMWSc 92*
**Friedman,** Abraham S 1921- *AmMWSc 92*
**Friedman,** Alan *DrAPF 91*
**Friedman,** Alan Charles 1947- *WhoMW 92*
**Friedman,** Alan E 1945- *AmMWSc 92*
**Friedman,** Alan Herbert 1937- *AmMWSc 92*
**Friedman,** Alan Howard 1928- *IntAu&W 91*
**Friedman,** Alan Victor 1938- *WhoAmL 92*
**Friedman,** Alan Warren 1939- *WrDr 92*
**Friedman,** Alexander Herbert 1925- *AmMWSc 92*
**Friedman,** Alfred Leo 1917- *WhoRel 92*
**Friedman,** Alvin Edward 1919- *WhoFI 92*
**Friedman,** Amy 1952- *ConAu 133*
**Friedman,** Arnold Carl 1951- *AmMWSc 92*
**Friedman,** Arnold J. *IntMPA 92*
**Friedman,** Arnold M. *WhoAmL 92*
**Friedman,** Arthur Daniel 1940- *AmMWSc 92, WhoFI 92*
**Friedman,** Avner 1932- *AmMWSc 92*
**Friedman,** B.H. *DrAPF 91*
**Friedman,** B. H. 1926- *WrDr 92*
**Friedman,** Barbara Bernstein 1946- *WhoFI 92*
**Friedman,** Barry 1938- *WhoWest 92*
**Friedman,** Barry 1954- *WhoAmL 92*
**Friedman,** Barry Ira 1962- *WhoAmL 92*
**Friedman,** Ben I 1926- *AmMWSc 92*
**Friedman,** Bernard 1940- *TwCPaSc*
**Friedman,** Bernard Alvin 1943- *WhoAmL 92, WhoMW 92*
**Friedman,** Bernard Samuel 1907- *AmMWSc 92*
**Friedman,** Berwyn Leonard 1930- *WhoFI 92*
**Friedman,** Bradley David 1955- *WhoEnt 92*
**Friedman,** Bruce 1936- *WhoFI 92*
**Friedman,** Bruce A. 1935- *WhoWest 92*
**Friedman,** Bruce Jay *DrAPF 91*
**Friedman,** Bruce Jay 1930- *BenetAL 91, ConNov 91, IntAu&W 91, WrDr 92*
**Friedman,** Carol *WhoEnt 92*
**Friedman,** Charles Nathaniel 1946- *AmMWSc 92*
**Friedman,** Charles William 1928- *WhoEnt 92*
**Friedman,** Clifford Hall 1959- *WhoFI 92*
**Friedman,** Constance Livingstone 1920- *AmMWSc 92*
**Friedman,** Cynthia 1933- *WhoAmP 91*
**Friedman,** Dana Beth 1964- *WhoWest 92*
**Friedman,** Daniel Lester 1936- *AmMWSc 92*
**Friedman,** Daniel Mortimer 1916- *WhoAmL 92*
**Friedman,** David F. 1923- *ConAu 134, IntMPA 92*
**Friedman,** David Peter 1944- *Who 92*
**Friedman,** Debbie *DrAPF 91*
**Friedman,** Dennis Carl 1948- *WhoFI 92*
**Friedman,** Don Gene 1925- *AmMWSc 92*
**Friedman,** Dorothy *DrAPF 91*
**Friedman,** Ed *DrAPF 91*
**Friedman,** Edward Alan 1935- *AmMWSc 92, WhoFI 92*
**Friedman,** Edward David *WhoAmL 92*
**Friedman,** Edward David 1912- *WhoAmP 91*
**Friedman,** Edward Marc 1949- *WhoRel 92*
**Friedman,** Edwin Fritz 1950- *WhoEnt 92*
**Friedman,** Eileen Anne *AmMWSc 92*
**Friedman,** Eitan *AmMWSc 92*
**Friedman,** Eli A 1933- *AmMWSc 92*
**Friedman,** Elias *WrDr 92*
**Friedman,** Elizabeth S 1894-1980 *FacFETw*
**Friedman,** Emanuel A 1926- *AmMWSc 92*
**Friedman,** Emil Martin 1948- *AmMWSc 92, WhoMW 92*
**Friedman,** Ephraim 1930- *AmMWSc 92*
**Friedman,** Erick 1939- *WhoEnt 92*
**Friedman,** Ernest Harvey 1931- *WhoMW 92*
**Friedman,** Eugene Stuart 1941- *WhoAmL 92*
**Friedman,** Ferne Sandra 1952- *WhoEnt 92*
**Friedman,** Frank L 1942- *AmMWSc 92*
**Friedman,** Fred Jay 1951- *AmMWSc 92*
**Friedman,** Fred K 1952- *AmMWSc 92*
**Friedman,** Gary David 1934- *AmMWSc 92*
**Friedman,** George 1934- *WhoAmP 91*
**Friedman,** George Henry 1954- *WhoAmL 92, WhoFI 92*
**Friedman,** George J 1928- *AmMWSc 92*
**Friedman,** Gerald Alan 1952- *WhoMW 92*
**Friedman,** Gerald Manfred 1921- *AmMWSc 92*
**Friedman,** Ginger *WhoEnt 92*
**Friedman,** Harold Bertrand 1904- *AmMWSc 92*
**Friedman,** Harold Leo 1923- *AmMWSc 92*
**Friedman,** Harvey Martin 1948- *AmMWSc 92, WhoMW 92*
**Friedman,** Harvey Paul 1935- *AmMWSc 92*
**Friedman,** Helen Lowenthal 1924- *AmMWSc 92*
**Friedman,** Herbert 1916- *AmMWSc 92, FacFETw, WrDr 92*
**Friedman,** Herbert A. 1918- *WhoRel 92*
**Friedman,** Herbert Alter 1937- *AmMWSc 92*
**Friedman,** Herman 1931- *AmMWSc 92*
**Friedman,** Howard Martin 1941- *WhoAmL 92, WhoMW 92*
**Friedman,** Howard Martin 1948- *WhoFI 92*
**Friedman,** Howard Stephen 1948- *AmMWSc 92*
**Friedman,** Irving 1920- *AmMWSc 92*
**Friedman,** Irwin 1929- *AmMWSc 92*
**Friedman,** Jack P 1939- *AmMWSc 92*
**Friedman,** Jacob Horace 1916- *WrDr 92*
**Friedman,** James Moss 1941- *WhoAmL 92*
**Friedman,** James Winstein 1936- *WhoFI 92*
**Friedman,** Jerome Isaac 1930- *AmMWSc 92, WhoNob 90*
**Friedman,** Jessica Ruth 1959- *WhoAmL 92*
**Friedman,** Jim 1955- *WhoEnt 92*
**Friedman,** Joel Mitchel 1947- *AmMWSc 92*
**Friedman,** Joel Stephen 1937- *WhoFI 92*
**Friedman,** John *WrDr 92*
**Friedman,** John Maxwell, Jr. 1944- *WhoAmL 92*
**Friedman,** John Robert 1941- *WhoAmL 92*
**Friedman,** John Steven 1949- *WhoRel 92*
**Friedman,** Jon George 1951- *WhoAmL 92*
**Friedman,** Joseph *IntMPA 92*
**Friedman,** Joseph 1955- *WhoFI 92*
**Friedman,** Joshua M 1941- *IntAu&W 91*
**Friedman,** Joyce Barbara 1928- *AmMWSc 92*
**Friedman,** Jules Daniel 1928- *AmMWSc 92, WhoWest 92*
**Friedman,** Julian Richard 1936- *WhoAmL 92*
**Friedman,** Julius Jay 1926- *AmMWSc 92*
**Friedman,** Ken *DrAPF 91*
**Friedman,** Kenneth Harris 1944- *WhoFI 92*
**Friedman,** Kenneth Joseph 1943- *AmMWSc 92*
**Friedman,** Kenneth Todd *WhoWest 92*
**Friedman,** Kinky *WrDr 92*
**Friedman,** Lawrence *AmMWSc 92*
**Friedman,** Lawrence A. 1951- *WhoAmL 92*
**Friedman,** Lawrence Boyd 1939- *AmMWSc 92*
**Friedman,** Lawrence David 1932- *AmMWSc 92*
**Friedman,** Lawrence M. 1930- *WhoAmL 92, WrDr 92*
**Friedman,** Lawrence Milton 1945- *WhoIns 92*
**Friedman,** Leonard 1929- *AmMWSc 92*
**Friedman,** Lewis 1922- *AmMWSc 92*
**Friedman,** Lillian Siegel 1906- *WhoAmL 92*
**Friedman,** Lionel Robert 1933- *AmMWSc 92*
**Friedman,** Lisa Lane 1963- *WhoAmL 92*
**Friedman,** Lonnie Rae 1947- *WhoWest 92*
**Friedman,** Luba 1949- *WhoMW 92*
**Friedman,** M H *AmMWSc 92*
**Friedman,** Maralyn *DrAPF 91*
**Friedman,** Marc Mitchell *AmMWSc 92*
**Friedman,** Marcia *WhoRel 92*
**Friedman,** Mark David 1953- *WhoRel 92*
**Friedman,** Mark Menachem 1953- *WhoAmL 92*
**Friedman,** Martin 1925- *WhoMW 92*
**Friedman,** Marvin Harold 1923- *AmMWSc 92*
**Friedman,** Mary Brooks 1947- *WhoAmL 92*
**Friedman,** Matthew Joel 1940- *AmMWSc 92*
**Friedman,** Maurice Harold 1903-1991 *NewYTBS 91*
**Friedman,** Maurice Stanley 1921- *WhoRel 92*
**Friedman,** Melvin 1930- *AmMWSc 92*
**Friedman,** Melvin J. 1928- *WrDr 92*
**Friedman,** Mendel 1933- *AmMWSc 92*
**Friedman,** Michael 1949- *WhoAmP 91*
**Friedman,** Michael A 1943- *AmMWSc 92*
**Friedman,** Michael E 1937- *AmMWSc 92*
**Friedman,** Michael Elliot 1951- *WhoAmL 92*
**Friedman,** Michael Howard 1944- *WhoWest 92*
**Friedman,** Michael Phillip 1951- *WhoAmL 92*
**Friedman,** Michael Steven 1953- *WhoAmL 92*
**Friedman,** Milton 1912- *FacFETw, IntAu&W 91, IntWW 91, Who 92, WhoFI 92, WhoNob 90, WhoWest 92, WrDr 92*
**Friedman,** Mischa Elliot 1922- *AmMWSc 92*
**Friedman,** Mitchell 1944- *AmMWSc 92*
**Friedman,** Morton 1928- *AmMWSc 92*
**Friedman,** Morton Harold 1935- *AmMWSc 92*
**Friedman,** Morton Henry 1938- *AmMWSc 92*
**Friedman,** Murray 1926- *WhoAmP 91*
**Friedman,** Myrna Elaine 1949- *WhoAmL 92*
**Friedman,** Naftali Robert 1962- *WhoFI 92*
**Friedman,** Nancy Bengis *DrAPF 91*
**Friedman,** Nathan Baruch 1911- *AmMWSc 92*
**Friedman,** Neil Alan 1953- *WhoEnt 92*
**Friedman,** Neil Stuart 1934- *WhoFI 92*
**Friedman,** Nicholas R. 1946- *WhoAmL 92*
**Friedman,** Norman *DrAPF 91*
**Friedman,** Norman 1925- *WrDr 92*
**Friedman,** Orrie Max 1915- *AmMWSc 92*
**Friedman,** Paul *DrAPF 91, LesBEnT 92*
**Friedman,** Paul 1931- *AmMWSc 92*
**Friedman,** Paul 1937- *WrDr 92*
**Friedman,** Paul Alan 1937- *WhoMW 92*
**Friedman,** Paul D 1953- *WhoAmP 91*
**Friedman,** Paul J 1937- *AmMWSc 92*
**Friedman,** Paul Lawrence 1944- *WhoAmL 92*
**Friedman,** Penny 1951- *WhoFI 92, WhoMW 92*
**Friedman,** Philip 1944- *WhoEnt 92*
**Friedman,** Raymond 1922- *AmMWSc 92*
**Friedman,** Reuben Isidore 1946- *WhoAmL 92*
**Friedman,** Richard *DrAPF 91*
**Friedman,** Richard D. 1951- *WhoAmL 92*
**Friedman,** Richard Elliott 1946- *WhoRel 92*
**Friedman,** Richard M 1930- *AmMWSc 92*
**Friedman,** Robert 1947- *WhoEnt 92*
**Friedman,** Robert Bernard 1938- *AmMWSc 92*
**Friedman,** Robert D. 1950- *WhoAmL 92*
**Friedman,** Robert David 1935- *AmMWSc 92*
**Friedman,** Robert Harold 1924- *AmMWSc 92*
**Friedman,** Robert James 1956- *WhoEnt 92*
**Friedman,** Robert L. 1930- *IntMPA 92*
**Friedman,** Robert Laurence 1943- *WhoAmL 92*
**Friedman,** Robert Lee 1930- *WhoEnt 92*
**Friedman,** Robert Michael 1950- *WhoAmL 92, WhoFI 92*
**Friedman,** Robert Morris 1932- *AmMWSc 92*
**Friedman,** Robert Paul 1952- *WhoAmL 92*
**Friedman,** Ronald Marvin 1930- *AmMWSc 92*
**Friedman,** Ronald Samuel 1962- *WhoMW 92*
**Friedman,** Rosemary 1929- *IntAu&W 91, WrDr 92*
**Friedman,** Roy *DrAPF 91*
**Friedman,** Ruth T 1936- *AmMWSc 92*
**Friedman,** S.L. *DrAPF 91*
**Friedman,** Samuel Arthur 1927- *AmMWSc 92*
**Friedman,** Samuel Selig 1935- *WhoAmL 92*
**Friedman,** Sanford *DrAPF 91*
**Friedman,** Selwyn Marvin 1929- *AmMWSc 92*
**Friedman,** Seymour K 1928- *AmMWSc 92*
**Friedman,** Seymour Mark 1917- *IntMPA 92*
**Friedman,** Sheila Natasha Simrod *DrAPF 91*
**Friedman,** Sheldon Edward 1936- *WhoFI 92*
**Friedman,** Shelly Arnold 1949- *WhoWest 92*
**Friedman,** Sholem 1949- *WhoAmL 92*
**Friedman,** Sidney 1926- *AmMWSc 92*
**Friedman,** Sigmund W. 1938- *WhoEnt 92*
**Friedman,** Simon 1945- *WhoAmL 92*
**Friedman,** Solomon Philip 1931- *WhoAmL 92*
**Friedman,** Sonya *DrAPF 91*
**Friedman,** Stanley 1922- *WhoWest 92*
**Friedman,** Stanley 1925- *AmMWSc 92*
**Friedman,** Stephen 1937- *IntMPA 92, WhoEnt 92*
**Friedman,** Stephen Burt 1931- *AmMWSc 92*
**Friedman,** Stephen James 1938- *WhoAmL 92*
**Friedman,** Steve *LesBEnT 92 [port]*
**Friedman,** Steven Eric 1954- *WhoEnt 92*
**Friedman,** Steven J. 1960- *WhoAmL 92*
**Friedman,** Stuart Alan 1944- *WhoAmL 92*
**Friedman,** Sue Tyler 1925- *WhoFI 92*
**Friedman,** Susan Stanford 1943- *WhoMW 92*
**Friedman,** Sydney Murray 1916- *AmMWSc 92*
**Friedman,** Terry B 1949- *WhoAmP 91*
**Friedman,** Thea Marla *AmMWSc 92*
**Friedman,** Thomas Baer 1944- *AmMWSc 92*
**Friedman,** Thomas L. 1953- *WrDr 92*
**Friedman,** Townsend B, Jr 1940- *WhoAmP 91*
**Friedman,** Victor Stanley 1933- *WhoAmL 92*
**Friedman,** Viktor 1938- *WhoEnt 92*
**Friedman,** Wilbur Harvey 1907- *WhoAmL 92*
**Friedman,** Will Joel 1950- *WhoWest 92*
**Friedman,** William *FacFETw*
**Friedman,** William Albert 1938- *AmMWSc 92*

**Friedman**, William Foster 1936- *AmMWSc 92*
**Friedman**, Yochanan 1945- *AmMWSc 92*
**Friedmann**, Alexander Alexandrovich 1888-1925 *FacFETw*
**Friedmann**, E Imre 1921- *AmMWSc 92*
**Friedmann**, Gerhart B 1929- *AmMWSc 92*
**Friedmann**, Herbert Claus 1927- *AmMWSc 92*
**Friedmann**, Jacques Henri 1932- *IntWW 91, Who 92*
**Friedmann**, Paul 1933- *AmMWSc 92*
**Friedmann**, Peretz Peter 1938- *AmMWSc 92, WhoWest 92*
**Friedmann**, Thelma Mae 1939- *WhoRel 92*
**Friedmann**, Theodore 1935- *AmMWSc 92*
**Friedmann**, Thomas *DrAPF 91*
**Friedmann**, Yohanan 1936- *WrDr 92*
**Friedmeyer**, Martha Sue 1937- *WhoWest 92*
**Friedner**, Lewis R 1956- *WhoAmP 91*
**Friedrich**, Anthony Paul, Jr. 1947- *WhoMW 92*
**Friedrich**, Benjamin C 1929- *AmMWSc 92*
**Friedrich**, Bruce H 1936- *AmMWSc 92*
**Friedrich**, Christen Louise 1963- *WhoRel 92*
**Friedrich**, Craig William 1946- *WhoAmL 92*
**Friedrich**, Donald Martin 1944- *AmMWSc 92*
**Friedrich**, Dwight P 1913- *WhoAmP 91*
**Friedrich**, Edwin Carl 1936- *AmMWSc 92*
**Friedrich**, Henry Walter August 1928- *WhoRel 92*
**Friedrich**, James Wayne 1952- *AmMWSc 92*
**Friedrich**, Louis Elbert 1941- *AmMWSc 92*
**Friedrich**, Otto Martin, Jr 1939- *AmMWSc 92*
**Friedrich**, Paul *DrAPF 91*
**Friedrich**, Paul 1927- *WrDr 92*
**Friedrich**, Robert Edmund, Jr. 1948- *WhoRel 92*
**Friedrich**, Rose Marie 1941- *WhoMW 92*
**Friedrich**, Stephen Miro 1932- *WhoFI 92*
**Friedrichs**, Niels Georg 1929- *WhoFI 92, WhoMW 92*
**Friedstat**, Charles David 1946- *WhoMW 92*
**Friel**, Arthur O 1885-1959 *ScFEYrs*
**Friel**, Bernard Preston 1930- *WhoAmL 92, WhoMW 92*
**Friel**, Brian *NewYTBS 91 [port]*
**Friel**, Brian 1929- *FacFETw, IntAu&W 91, IntWW 91, RfGEnL 91, Who 92, WhoEnt 92, WrDr 92*
**Friel**, Daniel Denwood 1920- *AmMWSc 92*
**Friel**, Leroy Lawrence 1938- *AmMWSc 92*
**Friels**, Colin *IntMPA 92*
**Frieman**, Edward Allan 1926- *AmMWSc 92, WhoWest 92*
**Friemel**, Jerome L 1932- *WhoAmP 91*
**Friend**, Amy Susan 1958- *WhoAmP 91*
**Friend**, Archibald Gordon 1912- *Who 92*
**Friend**, Barbara *DrAPF 91*
**Friend**, Bernard Ernest 1924- *Who 92*
**Friend**, Bruce Bidwell 1957- *WhoEnt 92*
**Friend**, Charlotte 1921-1987 *FacFETw*
**Friend**, Cynthia Marie 1955- *AmMWSc 92*
**Friend**, Daniel S 1933- *AmMWSc 92*
**Friend**, David Robert 1956- *WhoWest 92*
**Friend**, Helen Margaret 1931- *WhoMW 92*
**Friend**, James Philip 1929- *AmMWSc 92*
**Friend**, Jed 1958- *WhoWest 92*
**Friend**, Johnny Dale 1956- *WhoRel 92*
**Friend**, Jonathon D *AmMWSc 92*
**Friend**, Judith H 1941- *AmMWSc 92*
**Friend**, Kelsey E 1922- *WhoAmP 91*
**Friend**, Lionel 1945- *IntWW 91, Who 92*
**Friend**, Milton 1935- *AmMWSc 92*
**Friend**, Oscar 1897-1963 *TwCWW 91*
**Friend**, Patric Lee 1938- *AmMWSc 92*
**Friend**, Phyllis 1922- *Who 92*
**Friend**, Robert *DrAPF 91*
**Friend**, Robert 1913- *WrDr 92*
**Friend**, Robert Dale 1955- *WhoRel 92*
**Friend**, Robert Nathan 1930- *WhoMW 92*
**Friend**, William Benedict 1931- *WhoRel 92*
**Friend**, William George 1928- *AmMWSc 92*
**Friendly**, Andrew S. H. 1951- *WhoEnt 92*
**Friendly**, David T. 1956- *WhoEnt 92*
**Friendly**, Ed *LesBEnT 92*
**Friendly**, Ed 1922- *WhoEnt 92*
**Friendly**, Edwin S., III 1957- *WhoEnt 92*
**Friendly**, Fred W. *LesBEnT 92 [port]*
**Friendly**, Fred W. 1915- *IntMPA 92, IntWW 91, WrDr 92*
**Friendly**, Lynda E. *WhoFI 92*
**Frier**, Bruce W. 1943- *WhoAmL 92*
**Friermood**, Elisabeth H. 1903- *WrDr 92*
**Friermood**, Elisabeth Hamilton 1903- *IntAu&W 91*
**Frierson**, Charles Davis, III 1932- *WhoAmP 91*
**Frierson**, James Gordon 1940- *WhoAmL 92*
**Frierson**, Meade 1940- *WhoAmL 92*
**Frierson**, William Joe 1907- *AmMWSc 92*
**Fries**, Adelaide Lisetta 1871-1949 *DcNCBi 2*
**Fries**, Arthur Lawrence 1937- *WhoFI 92*
**Fries**, Cara Rosendale 1942- *AmMWSc 92*
**Fries**, Charles W. *LesBEnT 92*
**Fries**, Charles W. 1928- *IntMPA 92*
**Fries**, David Samuel 1945- *AmMWSc 92*
**Fries**, Donald E 1943- *WhoIns 92*
**Fries**, Francis Henry 1855-1931 *DcNCBi 2*
**Fries**, Francis Levin 1812-1863 *DcNCBi 2*
**Fries**, Henry Elias 1857-1949 *DcNCBi 2*
**Fries**, Jakob Friedrich 1773-1843 *EncTR 91*
**Fries**, James Andrew 1943- *AmMWSc 92*
**Fries**, John William 1846-1927 *DcNCBi 2*
**Fries**, Joseph Howard 1952- *WhoEnt 92*
**Fries**, Kenny *DrAPF 91*
**Fries**, Philip J., Jr. 1958- *WhoAmL 92*
**Fries**, Ralph Jay 1930- *AmMWSc 92*
**Fries**, Sharon Lavonne 1959- *WhoBlA 92*
**Friese**, Christopher Ryan 1975- *WhoEnt 92*
**Friese**, George Ralph 1936- *WhoAmL 92, WhoFI 92*
**Friese**, Robert Charles 1943- *WhoWest 92*
**Friesecke**, Raymond Francis 1937- *WhoFI 92, WhoWest 92*
**Friesel**, Dennis Lane 1942- *AmMWSc 92*
**Friesel**, Evyatar 1930- *ConAu 135*
**Friesem**, Albert Asher 1936- *AmMWSc 92*
**Friesen**, Benjamin S 1928- *AmMWSc 92*
**Friesen**, Donald Kent 1941- *AmMWSc 92*
**Friesen**, Earl Wayne 1927- *AmMWSc 92*
**Friesen**, Ernest Clare, Jr. 1928- *WhoAmL 92*
**Friesen**, Henry George 1934- *AmMWSc 92*
**Friesen**, James Donald 1935- *AmMWSc 92*
**Friesen**, Mahlon G. 1949- *WhoRel 92*
**Friesen**, Rhinehart F 1914- *AmMWSc 92*
**Friesen**, Richard Aldon 1928- *WhoEnt 92*
**Friesen**, Richard David 1947- *WhoEnt 92*
**Friesen**, Rick *WhoEnt 92*
**Friesen**, Ronald Lee 1939- *WhoMW 92*
**Friesen**, Stanley Richard 1918- *AmMWSc 92*
**Friesen**, Wolfgang Otto 1942- *AmMWSc 92*
**Frieser**, Rudolf Gruenspan 1920- *AmMWSc 92*
**Friesinger**, Gottlieb Christian 1929- *AmMWSc 92*
**Friesner**, Esther M 1951- *TwCSFW 91*
**Friess**, Seymour Louis 1922- *AmMWSc 92*
**Frietze**, Jose Victor 1943- *WhoHisp 92*
**Frieze**, Harold Delbert 1943- *WhoAmL 92*
**Frigerio**, Charles Straith 1957- *WhoAmL 92*
**Frigerio**, Ismael 1955- *WhoHisp 92*
**Frigerio**, Ronald Joseph 1940- *WhoAmP 91*
**Friggieri**, Oliver 1947- *IntAu&W 91*
**Frigo**, James Peter Paul 1942- *WhoFI 92*
**Frigon**, Chris Darwin 1949- *WhoEnt 92*
**Frigon**, Henry Frederick 1934- *WhoFI 92*
**Frigon**, Judith Ann 1945- *WhoWest 92*
**Frigyesi**, Tamas L 1927- *AmMWSc 92*
**Friihauf**, Edward Joe 1936- *AmMWSc 92*
**Friis**, Erik J. 1913- *WrDr 92*
**Friis**, Henning Kristian 1911- *IntWW 91*
**Friis-Baastad**, Babbis Ellinor 1921-1970 *ConAu 134*
**Frilot**, Bert Clark 1939- *WhoEnt 92*
**Friman**, Alice *DrAPF 91*
**Friman**, Paul Lawrence 1959- *WhoEnt 92*
**Friml**, Rudolf 1879-1972 *NewAmDM*
**Frimmer**, Rick Leslie 1951- *WhoAmL 92*
**Frimoth**, Bud 1926- *WhoEnt 92, WhoRel 92*
**Frimpong-Ansah**, Jonathan Herbert 1930- *IntWW 91*
**Frimpter**, George W 1928- *AmMWSc 92*
**Frimpter**, Michael Howard 1934- *AmMWSc 92*
**Frindall**, Bill *ConAu 135*
**Frindall**, William Howard 1939- *ConAu 135, IntAu&W 91*
**Frindt**, Robert Frederick 1939- *AmMWSc 92*
**Frings**, Christopher Stanton 1940- *AmMWSc 92*
**Frings**, Ketti 1915-1981 *BenetAL 91*
**Frings**, Manfred Servatius 1925- *WhoMW 92*
**Frink**, Charles Richard 1931- *AmMWSc 92*
**Frink**, Donald W 1933- *AmMWSc 92*
**Frink**, Elisabeth 1930- *IntWW 91, Who 92*
**Frink**, Elizabeth 1930- *TwCPaSc*
**Frink**, Frederick T 1920- *WhoAmP 91*
**Frink**, George Malancthan Dame 1931- *WhoRel 92*
**Frink**, Jno. Spencer 1930- *WhoIns 92*
**Frink**, John Spencer 1930- *WhoBlA 92*
**Frink**, Ronald Murice 1959- *WhoBlA 92*
**Frink**, Samuel H. 1944- *WhoBlA 92*
**Frink Reed**, Caroliese Ingrid 1949- *WhoBlA 92*
**Frinta**, Mojmir S 1922- *IntAu&W 91*
**Friou**, George Jacob 1919- *AmMWSc 92*
**Friou**, Stuart Norwood 1966- *WhoFI 92*
**Fripp**, Alfred Thomas 1899- *Who 92*
**Fripp**, Archibald Linley 1939- *AmMWSc 92*
**Fripp**, Paul 1890-1945 *TwCPaSc*
**Frisa**, Daniel 1955- *WhoAmP 91*
**Frisancho**, A Roberto 1939- *AmMWSc 92*
**Frisbee**, Don Calvin 1923- *WhoFI 92, WhoWest 92*
**Frisbee**, Lee *DrAPF 91*
**Frisbie**, Charles 1939- *WhoAmL 92*
**Frisbie**, Curtis Lynn, Jr. 1943- *WhoAmL 92*
**Frisbie**, James Daniel 1949- *WhoRel 92*
**Frisbie**, Raymond Edward 1945- *AmMWSc 92*
**Frisbie**, William Floyd, Jr. 1960- *WhoEnt 92*
**Frisby**, Audrey Mary *Who 92*
**Frisby**, Herbert Russell, Jr. 1950- *WhoAmL 92*
**Frisby**, James Curtis 1930- *AmMWSc 92*
**Frisby**, Robert W 1920- *WhoAmP 91*
**Frisby**, Roger Harry Kilbourne 1921- *Who 92*
**Frisby**, Terence 1932- *Who 92, WrDr 92*
**Frisch**, Alfred Shelby 1935- *AmMWSc 92*
**Frisch**, Celia *WhoEnt 92*
**Frisch**, Fred I. 1935- *WhoFI 92*
**Frisch**, Harry David 1954- *WhoAmL 92*
**Frisch**, Harry Lloyd 1928- *AmMWSc 92*
**Frisch**, Henry Jonathan 1944- *AmMWSc 92*
**Frisch**, I T 1937- *AmMWSc 92*
**Frisch**, Jack Eugene 1929- *WhoEnt 92*
**Frisch**, Joseph 1921- *AmMWSc 92*
**Frisch**, Kurt Charles 1918- *AmMWSc 92*
**Frisch**, Max 1911-1991 *ConAu 134, CurBio 91N, FacFETw, NewYTBS 91*
**Frisch**, Max Rudolf 1911- *IntAu&W 91*
**Frisch**, Max Rudolf 1911-1991 *IntWW 91, -91N*
**Frisch**, P Douglas 1945- *AmMWSc 92*
**Frisch**, Ragnar Kittil Anton 1895-1973 *WhoNob 90*
**Frisch**, Randy Steven 1962- *WhoEnt 92*
**Frisch**, Rose Epstein 1918- *AmMWSc 92*
**Frischenmeyer**, Michael Leo 1951- *WhoFI 92*
**Frischenschlager**, Friedhelm 1943- *IntWW 91*
**Frischer**, Henri 1934- *AmMWSc 92*
**Frischkorn**, David Ephraim Keasbey, Jr. 1951- *WhoFI 92*
**Frischman**, Dan 1959- *WhoEnt 92*
**Frischmann**, Donald W 1921- *WhoIns 92*
**Frischmann**, Wilem William *Who 92*
**Frischmeyer**, Linda Elizabeth 1955- *WhoAmL 92*
**Frischmeyer**, Michael Joseph 1953- *WhoFI 92*
**Frischmuth**, Robert Alfred 1940- *WhoEnt 92, WhoFI 92*
**Frischmuth**, Robert Wellington 1940- *AmMWSc 92*
**Frisco**, Kenneth Lawrence 1948- *WhoFI 92*
**Frisco**, L J 1923- *AmMWSc 92*
**Frisell**, Wilhelm Richard 1920- *AmMWSc 92*
**Frisell-Schroder**, Sonja Bettie 1937- *WhoEnt 92*
**Frishberg**, Carol 1947- *AmMWSc 92*
**Frishe**, Jim 1946- *WhoAmP 91*
**Frishkoff**, Patricia Ann 1944- *WhoWest 92*
**Frishkoff**, Paul *WhoWest 92*
**Frishkopf**, Lawrence Samuel 1930- *AmMWSc 92*
**Frishman**, Austin Michael 1940- *AmMWSc 92*
**Frishman**, Daniel 1919- *AmMWSc 92*
**Frishman**, Eileen Steinberg 1946- *WhoWest 92*
**Frishman**, Fred 1923- *AmMWSc 92*
**Frishman**, Laura J 1947- *AmMWSc 92*
**Frishman**, William Howard 1946- *AmMWSc 92*
**Frisillo**, Albert Lawrence 1943- *AmMWSc 92*
**Frisinger**, H Howard, II 1933- *AmMWSc 92*
**Frisinger**, Haakan H. J. 1928- *IntWW 91*
**Frisk**, George Vladimir 1946- *AmMWSc 92*
**Frisk**, Jack Eugene 1942- *WhoFI 92*
**Frisken**, William Ross 1933- *AmMWSc 92*
**Frisman**, Roger Lawrence 1952- *WhoMW 92*
**Frison**, Lee A. 1941- *WhoBlA 92*
**Frissel**, Harry Frederick 1920- *AmMWSc 92*
**Frist**, Thomas Fearn 1910- *WhoFI 92*
**Frist**, Thomas Fearn, Jr. 1938- *WhoFI 92*
**Fristedt**, Bert 1937- *AmMWSc 92*
**Fristrom**, Dianne 1940- *AmMWSc 92*
**Fristrom**, James W 1936- *AmMWSc 92*
**Fristrom**, Robert Maurice 1922- *AmMWSc 92*
**Friswold**, Fred Ravndahl 1937- *WhoFI 92*
**Fritch**, Le Ann 1937- *WhoAmP 91*
**Fritch**, Wayne Alan 1962- *WhoRel 92*
**Fritcher**, Earl Edwin 1923- *WhoWest 92*
**Fritchle**, Frank Paul 1922- *AmMWSc 92*
**Fritchman**, Harry Kier, II 1923- *AmMWSc 92*
**Frith**, Anthony Ian Donald 1929- *Who 92*
**Frith**, Arthur J d1913 *BiInAmS*
**Frith**, David Edward John 1937- *IntAu&W 91, Who 92*
**Frith**, Donald Alfred 1918- *Who 92*
**Frith**, Edward Leslie 1919- *Who 92*
**Frith**, Henry 1840- *ScFEYrs*
**Frith**, Jack *TwCPaSc*
**Frith**, Mary 1584?-1659 *EncAmaz 91*
**Frith**, Michael William 1951- *WhoWest 92*
**Fritsch**, Albert J. 1933- *WrDr 92*
**Fritsch**, Albert Joseph 1933- *IntAu&W 91*
**Fritsch**, Arnold Rudolph 1932- *AmMWSc 92*
**Fritsch**, Billy Dale, Jr. 1956- *WhoFI 92*
**Fritsch**, Carl Walter 1928- *AmMWSc 92*
**Fritsch**, Charles A 1936- *AmMWSc 92*
**Fritsch**, Edward Francis 1950- *AmMWSc 92*
**Fritsch**, Elizabeth 1940- *Who 92*
**Fritsch**, Klaus 1941- *AmMWSc 92*
**Fritsch**, Robert Lawrence 1943- *WhoWest 92*
**Fritsch**, Theodor 1852-1933 *BiDExR, EncTR 91 [port]*
**Fritsch**, Thomas Joseph 1947- *WhoFI 92*
**Fritsch**, Werner, Baron von 1880-1939 *EncTR 91 [port]*
**Fritsche**, Claudia 1952- *IntWW 91*
**Fritsche**, David Emil, Sr. 1939- *WhoRel 92*
**Fritsche**, Herbert Ahart, Jr 1941- *AmMWSc 92*
**Fritsche**, Richard T 1936- *AmMWSc 92*
**Fritschel**, Ted C 1932- *WhoAmP 91*
**Fritschen**, Leo J 1930- *AmMWSc 92*
**Fritschen**, Robert David 1935- *AmMWSc 92*
**Fritschy**, J Melvin 1921- *AmMWSc 92*
**Fritter**, Randy Joe 1955- *WhoAmP 91*
**Fritton**, Daniel Dale 1942- *AmMWSc 92*
**Fritton**, Karl Andrew 1955- *WhoAmL 92*
**Fritts**, Edward O. *WhoEnt 92A*
**Fritts**, Guy Anthony 1943- *WhoFI 92*
**Fritts**, Harold Clark 1928- *AmMWSc 92*
**Fritts**, Harry Washington, Jr 1921- *AmMWSc 92*
**Fritts**, Robert Washburn 1924- *AmMWSc 92*
**Fritts**, Steven Hugh 1948- *AmMWSc 92*
**Fritts**, Tom Duff 1926- *WhoRel 92*
**Fritts-Williams**, Mary Louise Monica 1940- *AmMWSc 92*
**Fritz**, Donald Wayne 1933- *WhoEnt 92, WhoMW 92*
**Fritz**, George H 1919- *WhoAmP 91*
**Fritz**, George John 1927- *AmMWSc 92*
**Fritz**, George Richard, Jr 1932- *AmMWSc 92*
**Fritz**, Georgia T 1933- *AmMWSc 92*
**Fritz**, Gilbert Geiger 1942- *AmMWSc 92*
**Fritz**, Harry 1937- *WhoAmP 91*
**Fritz**, Herbert Ira 1935- *AmMWSc 92*
**Fritz**, Irving Bamdas 1927- *AmMWSc 92*
**Fritz**, James B. 1927- *WhoBlA 92*
**Fritz**, James John 1920- *AmMWSc 92*
**Fritz**, James Sherwood 1924- *AmMWSc 92*
**Fritz**, James William 1952- *WhoAmL 92*
**Fritz**, Jean 1915- *IntAu&W 91, WrDr 92*
**Fritz**, John 1822-1913 *BiInAmS*
**Fritz**, Joseph N 1931- *AmMWSc 92*
**Fritz**, K E 1918- *AmMWSc 92*
**Fritz**, Katherine Elizabeth 1918- *AmMWSc 92*
**Fritz**, Kenneth M. 1938- *WhoEnt 92*
**Fritz**, Lawrence William 1937- *AmMWSc 92*
**Fritz**, Madeleine Alberta *AmMWSc 92*
**Fritz**, Marc Anthony 1951- *AmMWSc 92*
**Fritz**, Mary G 1938- *WhoAmP 91*
**Fritz**, Mary Theresa 1940- *WhoRel 92*
**Fritz**, Michael E 1938- *AmMWSc 92*
**Fritz**, Michael Henry 1940- *WhoMW 92*
**Fritz**, Michael John 1950- *WhoAmL 92*
**Fritz**, Moses Kelly 1904- *WhoBlA 92*
**Fritz**, Paul John 1929- *AmMWSc 92*
**Fritz**, Peter 1937- *AmMWSc 92*
**Fritz**, Richard Blair 1936- *AmMWSc 92*
**Fritz**, Robert B 1937- *AmMWSc 92*
**Fritz**, Robert J 1923- *AmMWSc 92*
**Fritz**, Robert S. 1936- *WhoWest 92*
**Fritz**, Ronald Mathew 1956- *WhoMW 92*
**Fritz**, Roy Fredolin 1915- *AmMWSc 92*
**Fritz**, Russell Joseph 1958- *WhoEnt 92*
**Fritz**, Ruth Ann 1931- *WhoAmP 91*
**Fritz**, Samuel 1650- *HisDSpE*
**Fritz**, Sigmund 1914- *AmMWSc 92*

**Fritz**, Terrence Lee 1943- WhoFI 92
**Fritz**, Thomas Edward 1933- AmMWSc 92
**Fritz**, Thomas Vincent 1934- WhoFI 92
**Fritz**, Walter Helmut 1929- IntAu&W 91, IntWW 91
**Fritz**, William Harold 1928- AmMWSc 92
**Fritz**, William J 1953- AmMWSc 92
**Fritz**, William Richard, Sr. 1920- WhoRel 92
**Fritzberg**, Bruce Edward 1945- WhoEnt 92
**Fritze**, Curtis W 1922- AmMWSc 92
**Fritze**, James Napier 1925- WhoFI 92
**Fritzell**, Erik Kenneth 1946- AmMWSc 92
**Fritzell**, Peter A. 1940- ConAu 133
**Fritzhand**, Marek 1913- IntWW 91
**Fritzius**, John Earl 1949- WhoFI 92
**Fritzlen**, Glenn A 1919- AmMWSc 92
**Fritzler**, Gerald John 1953- WhoWest 92
**Fritzsche**, Alfred Keith 1943- AmMWSc 92
**Fritzsche**, David J. 1940- WhoWest 92
**Fritzsche**, Hans 1900-1953 EncTR 91 [port]
**Fritzsche**, Hellmut 1927- AmMWSc 92, WhoMW 92
**Friz**, Carl T 1927- AmMWSc 92
**Frizell**, Joseph Palmer 1832-1910 BiInAmS
**Frizzel**, Terry WhoWest 92
**Frizzel**, Terry 1927- WhoAmP 91
**Frizzell**, Gregory Kent 1956- WhoAmL 92
**Frizzell**, Kerri L. 1961- WhoWest 92
**Frizzell**, Lefty 1928- NewAmDM
**Frizzell**, Leon Albert 1947- AmMWSc 92
**Frizzell**, Martha McDanolds 1902- WhoAmP 91
**Frizzell**, Thomas William 1953- WhoWest 92
**Frizzelle**, Nolan 1921- WhoAmP 91
**Frizzera**, Glauco 1939- AmMWSc 92
**Frobe**, Roger Paul 1937- WhoRel 92
**Frobel**, Ronald Kenneth 1946- WhoWest 92
**Froberger**, Johann Jakob 1616-1667 NewAmDM
**Frobish**, Lowell T 1940- AmMWSc 92
**Frodey**, Ray Charles 1923- AmMWSc 92
**Frodsham**, Anthony Freer 1919- Who 92
**Frodsham**, John David 1930- IntWW 91
**Frodsham**, Stanley 1882-1969 RelLAm 91
**Frodyma**, Michael Mitchell 1920- AmMWSc 92
**Froe**, Dreyfus Walter 1914- WhoBlA 92
**Froe**, Otis David 1912- WhoBlA 92
**Froeb**, Donald Forrest 1930- WhoAmL 92
**Froebel**, Friedrich 1782-1852 DcTwDes
**Froeber**, Richard Reinhold 1929- WhoEnt 92
**Froede**, Harry Curt 1934- AmMWSc 92
**Froehle**, Charles WhoRel 92
**Froehlich**, Anne Liese 1923- WhoAmP 91
**Froehlich**, Fritz Edgar 1925- AmMWSc 92
**Froehlich**, Harold Vernon 1932- WhoAmP 91
**Froehlich**, Jeffrey Paul 1943- AmMWSc 92
**Froehlich**, Joseph Daniel 1958- WhoMW 92
**Froehlich**, Karlfried 1930- WhoRel 92
**Froehlich**, Laurence Alan 1951- WhoAmL 92
**Froehlich**, Luz 1928- AmMWSc 92
**Froehlig**, Celia B. 1953- WhoEnt 92
**Froelich**, Albert Joseph 1929- AmMWSc 92
**Froelich**, Carl August 1875-1953 EncTR 91 [port]
**Froelich**, Ernest 1912- AmMWSc 92
**Froelich**, Frederick Karl 1946- WhoFI 92
**Froelich**, Gary L. 1943- WhoAmL 92
**Froelich**, Jeffrey Earl 1946- WhoAmL 92
**Froelich**, Kevin Mark 1955- WhoRel 92
**Froelich**, Philip Nissen 1946- AmMWSc 92
**Froelich**, Robert Earl 1929- AmMWSc 92
**Froelich**, Susan G. 1951- WhoMW 92
**Froelke**, David Ray 1948- WhoFI 92
**Froelker**, Jim 1949- WhoAmP 91
**Froemke**, Jon 1941- AmMWSc 92
**Froemsdorf**, Donald Hope 1934- AmMWSc 92
**Froerer**, Fredrick, III 1944- WhoAmL 92
**Froes**, Francis Herbert 1940- AmMWSc 92
**Froese**, Alison Barbara 1945- AmMWSc 92
**Froese**, Arnold 1934- AmMWSc 92
**Froese**, Gerd 1926- AmMWSc 92
**Froessl**, Horst Waldemar 1929- WhoFI 92
**Froewiss**, Kenneth Clark 1945- WhoFI 92
**Frogel**, Jay Albert 1944- AmMWSc 92
**Froggatt**, Leslie 1920- IntWW 91, Who 92
**Froggatt**, Peter 1928- Who 92
**Frogge**, William Thomas 1951- WhoFI 92
**Frohlich**, Albrecht 1916- IntWW 91, Who 92
**Frohlich**, Ali Can 1958- WhoWest 92
**Frohlich**, Edward David 1931- AmMWSc 92
**Frohlich**, Gerhard J 1929- AmMWSc 92
**Frohlich**, Herbert d1991 IntWW 91N, Who 92N
**Frohlich**, Jiri J 1942- AmMWSc 92
**Frohlich**, Kenneth 1945- WhoIns 92
**Frohlich**, Kenneth R. 1945- WhoFI 92
**Frohlichstein**, Alan 1953- WhoMW 92
**Frohlichstein**, David Lee 1956- WhoMW 92
**Frohliger**, John Owen 1930- AmMWSc 92
**Frohm**, Robert George 1942- WhoFI 92
**Frohman**, Charles 1860-1915 BenetAL 91
**Frohman**, Charles Edward 1921- AmMWSc 92
**Frohman**, Daniel 1851-1940 BenetAL 91
**Frohman**, Lawrence Asher 1935- AmMWSc 92
**Frohman**, Roland H. 1928- WhoBlA 92
**Frohmberg**, Richard P 1920- AmMWSc 92
**Frohne**, Richard F. 1954- WhoMW 92
**Frohne**, Vincent Sauter 1936- WhoEnt 92
**Frohnen**, Richard Gene 1930- WhoWest 92
**Frohnhoefer**, Francis William 1939- WhoFI 92
**Frohnhofen**, Herbert 1955- WhoRel 92
**Frohnmayer**, David Braden 1940- WhoAmL 92, WhoAmP 91, WhoWest 92
**Frohnmayer**, John Edward 1942- NewYTBS 91 [port], WhoEnt 92
**Frohnsdorff**, Geoffrey James Carl 1928- AmMWSc 92
**Frohock**, John d1772 DcNCBi 2
**Frohrib**, Darrell A 1930- AmMWSc 92
**Frohsin**, Henry I. 1943- WhoAmL 92
**Froikin**, Murray Arthur 1952- WhoEnt 92
**Froiland**, Sven Gordon 1922- AmMWSc 92
**Froiland**, Thomas Gordon 1943- AmMWSc 92
**Frojmovic**, Maurice Mony 1943- AmMWSc 92
**Frolander**, Herbert Farley 1922- AmMWSc 92
**Frolik**, Charles Alan 1945- AmMWSc 92
**Frolik**, Elvin Frank 1909- AmMWSc 92
**Frolik**, Lawrence Anton 1944- WhoAmL 92
**Frolov**, Ivan Timofeevich 1929- SovUnBD
**Frolov**, Ivan Timofeyevich 1929- IntWW 91
**Frolov**, Konstantin Vasilevich 1932- IntWW 91, SovUnBD
**From**, Alvin 1943- WhoAmP 91
**From**, Arthur Harvey Leigh 1936- AmMWSc 92
**From**, Charles A, Jr 1915- AmMWSc 92
**From**, Harry WhoEnt 92
**Fromageot**, Henri Pierre-Marcel 1937- AmMWSc 92
**Froman**, Bradley Ray 1957- WhoEnt 92
**Froman**, Darol Kenneth 1906- AmMWSc 92
**Froman**, Sandra Sue 1949- WhoAmL 92
**Froman**, Seymour 1920- AmMWSc 92
**Fromberg**, Malcolm Hubert 1935- WhoAmL 92
**Fromberg**, Paul David 1960- WhoRel 92
**Frome**, Michael 1920- WrDr 92
**Froment**, Frank Livingston 1909- WhoFI 92
**Froment-Meurice**, Henri 1923- IntWW 91
**Fromentin**, Eugene 1820-1876 GuFrLit 1
**Fromhold**, Albert Thomas, Jr 1935- AmMWSc 92
**Fromkin**, Victoria A 1923- AmMWSc 92
**Fromknecht**, Mary 1940- WhoRel 92
**Fromm**, David 1939- AmMWSc 92
**Fromm**, Eli 1939- AmMWSc 92
**Fromm**, Erich 1900-1980 BenetAL 91, FacFETw [port]
**Fromm**, Erwin Frederick 1933- WhoFI 92
**Fromm**, Friedrich 1888-1945 EncTR 91 [port]
**Fromm**, Gerhard Hermann 1931- AmMWSc 92
**Fromm**, Hans 1939- AmMWSc 92
**Fromm**, Hans Walther Herbert 1919- IntWW 91
**Fromm**, Herbert Jerome 1929- AmMWSc 92
**Fromm**, Jeffery Bernard 1947- WhoAmL 92
**Fromm**, Joseph L. 1930- WhoFI 92
**Fromm**, Paul 1907-1987 NewAmDM
**Fromm**, Paul Oliver 1923- AmMWSc 92
**Fromm**, Sandra Jeanette 1944- WhoAmL 92
**Fromme**, Friedrich Karl 1930- IntWW 91
**Frommer**, Gabriel Paul 1936- AmMWSc 92
**Frommer**, Harvey 1937- IntAu&W 91
**Frommer**, Henry 1943- WhoFI 92
**Frommer**, Jack 1918- AmMWSc 92
**Frommer**, Peter Leslie 1932- AmMWSc 92
**Frommhold**, Lothar Werner 1930- AmMWSc 92
**Fromovitz**, Stan 1936- AmMWSc 92
**Fromowitz**, Frank B AmMWSc 92
**Fromstein**, Mitchell S. 1928- IntWW 91
**Fronczak**, Robert Eugene 1952- WhoFI 92
**Fronczek**, Frank Rolf 1948- AmMWSc 92
**Frondel**, Clifford 1907- AmMWSc 92
**Frondizi**, Arturo 1908- IntWW 91
**Fronek**, Arnost 1923- AmMWSc 92
**Fronek**, Donald Karel 1937- AmMWSc 92
**Fronek**, Kitty 1925- AmMWSc 92
**Froning**, Glenn Wesley 1930- AmMWSc 92, WhoMW 92
**Fronke**, Alan Robert 1955- WhoEnt 92
**Front**, Marshall Bernard 1937- WhoFI 92
**Frontenac**, Louis de Baude, Comte de 1620-1698 BenetAL 91
**Frontiere**, Dominic 1931- IntMPA 92
**Frontiere**, Georgia WhoWest 92
**Frontis**, Stephen 1792-1867 DcNCBi 2
**Frood**, Alan Campbell 1926- Who 92
**Frood**, Hester 1882-1971 TwCPaSc
**Froom**, Georgia Amelia 1944- WhoEnt 92
**Frooydarlund**, Jan-Anker 1911- IntAu&W 91
**Frosch**, Craig Edmond 1960- WhoAmL 92
**Frosch**, Robert Alan 1928- AmMWSc 92, WhoFI 92
**Frosch**, William Arthur 1932- AmMWSc 92
**Froseth**, John Allen 1942- AmMWSc 92
**Frosh**, Brian E 1946- WhoAmP 91
**Frossard**, Andre 1915- IntWW 91
**Frossard**, Charles 1922- Who 92
**Frost**, A. B. 1851-1928 BenetAL 91
**Frost**, A. Corwin 1934- WhoFI 92
**Frost**, Abraham Edward Hardy 1918- Who 92
**Frost**, Albert D 1922- AmMWSc 92
**Frost**, Albert Edward 1914- Who 92
**Frost**, Alison Ann 1962- WhoEnt 92
**Frost**, Anthony 1951- TwCPaSc
**Frost**, Arthur Atwater 1909- AmMWSc 92
**Frost**, Barrie James 1939- AmMWSc 92
**Frost**, Barry Warren 1947- WhoAmL 92
**Frost**, Bobby Jean 1932- WhoEnt 92
**Frost**, Brian George 1935- WhoRel 92
**Frost**, Brian R T 1926- AmMWSc 92
**Frost**, Brian Standish 1958- WhoAmL 92
**Frost**, Bruce Wesley 1941- AmMWSc 92
**Frost**, Carleton Pennington 1830?-1896 BiInAmS
**Frost**, Carol DrAPF 91
**Frost**, Celestine DrAPF 91
**Frost**, Charles Christopher 1806-1880 BiInAmS
**Frost**, David LesBEnT 92 [port]
**Frost**, David 1925- AmMWSc 92
**Frost**, David 1939- Who 92, WrDr 92
**Frost**, David Cregreen 1929- AmMWSc 92
**Frost**, David Paradine 1939- IntAu&W 91, IntWW 91
**Frost**, E A M 1938- AmMWSc 92
**Frost**, Elton Taylor 1957- WhoRel 92
**Frost**, Frances 1905-1959 BenetAL 91
**Frost**, Frederick TwCWW 91
**Frost**, Frederick G., Jr. d1991 NewYTBS 91
**Frost**, Gavin 1930- RelLAm 91
**Frost**, George 1935- Who 92
**Frost**, H Bonnell 1923- AmMWSc 92
**Frost**, Hardy Lee 1935- WhoFI 92
**Frost**, Harold Maurice, III 1942- AmMWSc 92
**Frost**, Herbert Hamilton 1917- AmMWSc 92
**Frost**, Hugh A. 1926- WhoBlA 92
**Frost**, Jackie Gene 1937- AmMWSc 92
**Frost**, James Marion 1848-1916 RelLAm 91
**Frost**, James Raymond 1953- WhoFI 92
**Frost**, Jeffrey Michael Torbet 1938- Who 92
**Frost**, Jerry William 1940- WhoRel 92
**Frost**, John Dutton 1912- Who 92
**Frost**, John Elliott 1924- WhoFI 92
**Frost**, John Kingsbury 1922- AmMWSc 92
**Frost**, Jonas Martin 1942- WhoAmP 91
**Frost**, Kenneth Almeron, Jr 1944- AmMWSc 92
**Frost**, Kid WhoHisp 92
**Frost**, L S 1922- AmMWSc 92
**Frost**, Lawrence William 1920- AmMWSc 92
**Frost**, Linda Smith 1956- IntMPA 92
**Frost**, Mark WhoEnt 92
**Frost**, Mark Edward 1948- WhoEnt 92
**Frost**, Martin 1942- AlmAP 92 [port]
**Frost**, Norma W 1927- WhoAmP 91
**Frost**, Olivia Pleasants WhoBlA 92
**Frost**, Peter Kip 1936- IntAu&W 91
**Frost**, Phyllis Irene 1917- Who 92
**Frost**, Richard DrAPF 91
**Frost**, Robert 1874-1963 BenetAL 91, FacFETw [port], RComAH
**Frost**, Robert 1939- WhoFI 92
**Frost**, Robert Edwin 1932- AmMWSc 92
**Frost**, Robert Hartwig 1917- AmMWSc 92
**Frost**, Robert T 1924- AmMWSc 92
**Frost**, Ryker TwCWW 91, WrDr 92
**Frost**, S D 1930- WhoAmP 91
**Frost**, S. Newell 1935- WhoWest 92
**Frost**, Stanley Brice 1913- WrDr 92
**Frost**, Sydney Who 92
**Frost**, Terence 1915- Who 92
**Frost**, Terrence Parker 1921- AmMWSc 92
**Frost**, Terry 1915- TwCPaSc
**Frost**, Thomas Clayborne 1927- WhoFI 92
**Frost**, Thomas Pearson 1933- IntWW 91, Who 92
**Frost**, Thomas Sydney 1916- Who 92
**Frost**, W. Gregory 1949- WhoFI 92
**Frost**, Walter 1935- AmMWSc 92
**Frost**, William Henry 1930- WhoBlA 92
**Frost**, Wilson WhoAmP 91, WhoBlA 92
**Frost**, Winston Lyle 1958- WhoAmL 92
**Frost**, Yvonne 1931- RelLAm 91
**Frost-Mason**, Sally Kay 1950- AmMWSc 92
**Frothingham**, Octavius Brooks 1822-1895 RelLAm 91
**Frothingham**, Thomas Eliot 1926- AmMWSc 92
**Froud**, Ethel E 1880?-1941 BiDBrF 2
**Froud**, Jonathan 1958- TwCPaSc
**Frounfelker**, Robert E 1925- AmMWSc 92
**Frowein**, Jochen Abraham 1934- IntWW 91
**Frowen**, Stephen Francis 1923- IntAu&W 91, WhoFI 92
**Froy**, Herald IntAu&W 91X
**Froy**, Martin 1926- TwCPaSc, Who 92
**Froyd**, James Donald 1939- AmMWSc 92
**Froyen**, Sverre 1951- AmMWSc 92
**Frucht**, Richard Charles 1951- WhoMW 92
**Fruchtenbaum**, Arnold Genekovich 1943- WhoRel 92
**Fruchter**, Benjamin 1914- WrDr 92
**Fruchter**, Jonathan S 1945- AmMWSc 92
**Fruchter**, Jonathan Sewell 1945- WhoWest 92
**Fruchthendler**, Fred Barry 1951- WhoWest 92
**Fruchtman**, Milton A. IntMPA 92, LesBEnT 92
**Fruchtman**, Milton Allen WhoEnt 92
**Fruechtenicht**, Hans Heinrich 1943- WhoEnt 92
**Fruechtenicht**, Thomas Eric 1940- WhoAmP 91
**Frueckert**, Rolf Herbert 1945- WhoFI 92
**Frueh**, Alfred Joseph, Jr 1919- AmMWSc 92
**Frueh**, Curt David 1959- WhoRel 92
**Fruehan**, Richard J 1942- AmMWSc 92
**Fruehling**, Rosemary T 1933- ConAu 35NR
**Frug**, Gerald E. 1939- WhoAmL 92
**Frugoli**, Amadeo 1932- IntWW 91
**Frugoni**, Orazio 1921- NewAmDM
**Fruh**, Eugen 1914- IntWW 91
**Fruhauf**, Hans 1904- IntWW 91
**Fruhbeck De Burgos**, Rafael 1933- IntWW 91, NewAmDM
**Fruhman**, George Joshua 1924- AmMWSc 92
**Fruin**, Mark Edward 1956- WhoWest 92
**Fruin**, Roger Joseph 1915- WhoAmL 92
**Fruit**, Sandra Kay Shelton 1952- WhoMW 92
**Fruitman**, Frederick Howard 1950- WhoFI 92
**Fruitt**, Ronald L. 1937- WhoMW 92
**Frum**, Carlos M. 1945- WhoHisp 92
**Frumerman**, Robert 1924- AmMWSc 92
**Frumkes**, Herbert M. 1926- WhoFI 92
**Frumkes**, Lewis Burke DrAPF 91
**Frumkes**, Lewis Burke 1939- ConAu 36NR
**Frumkes**, Thomas Eugene 1941- AmMWSc 92
**Frumkin**, Allan 1926- IntWW 91
**Frumkin**, Boris DcAmImH
**Frumkin**, Gene DrAPF 91
**Frumkin**, Gene 1928- IntAu&W 91, WhoWest 92, WrDr 92
**Frump**, John Adams 1921- AmMWSc 92
**Frungillo**, Nicholas Anthony, Jr. 1960- WhoFI 92
**Frunze**, Mikhail Vasilevich 1885-1925 FacFETw, SovUnBD
**Frush**, James Carroll, Jr. 1930- WhoWest 92
**Frushour**, Bruce George 1947- AmMWSc 92
**Fruth**, Beryl Rose 1952- WhoMW 92
**Fruth**, Terence Melling 1938- WhoAmL 92
**Fruthaler**, George James, Jr 1925- AmMWSc 92
**Frutiger**, Robert Lester 1946- AmMWSc 92
**Fruton**, Joseph S 1912- ConAu 34NR, WrDr 92
**Fruton**, Joseph Stewart 1912- AmMWSc 92, IntWW 91
**Fry**, Albert Joseph 1937- AmMWSc 92
**Fry**, Anne Evans 1939- AmMWSc 92, WhoMW 92
**Fry**, Anthony 1927- TwCPaSc
**Fry**, Arthur James 1921- AmMWSc 92
**Fry**, Beverly Jane WhoEnt 92

**Fry**, Charles George 1936- WhoMW 92, WhoRel 92
**Fry**, Christopher 1907- ConPo 91, FacFETw, IntAu&W 91, IntWW 91, RfGEnL 91, SmATA 66 [port], Who 92, WrDr 92
**Fry**, Cleota Gage 1910- AmMWSc 92
**Fry**, Craig R 1952- WhoAmP 91
**Fry**, Cynthia Anne 1953- WhoAmL 92
**Fry**, Darrell 1963- WhoBlA 92
**Fry**, David Allen 1959- WhoMW 92
**Fry**, David Lloyd George 1918- AmMWSc 92
**Fry**, David Stow 1949- WhoAmL 92
**Fry**, Donald C WhoAmP 91
**Fry**, Donald Lewis 1924- AmMWSc 92
**Fry**, Donald Michael 1943- WhoWest 92
**Fry**, Donald William 1910- IntWW 91, Who 92
**Fry**, Edward B. 1925- WrDr 92
**Fry**, Edward Donald, II 1956- WhoAmP 91
**Fry**, Edward Irad 1924- AmMWSc 92
**Fry**, Edward Strauss 1940- AmMWSc 92
**Fry**, Eldon Ervin 1946- WhoRel 92
**Fry**, Elizabeth 1780-1845 BlkwCEP
**Fry**, Francis J 1920- AmMWSc 92
**Fry**, Franklin Clark 1900-1968 DcEcMov, RelLAm 91
**Fry**, Frederick Ernest Joseph 1908- AmMWSc 92
**Fry**, Harold Philip 1941- WhoMW 92
**Fry**, Harry Wellman 1932- WhoFI 92
**Fry**, Ian Kelsey 1923- Who 92
**Fry**, Jack L 1930- AmMWSc 92
**Fry**, James Lawrence 1957- WhoWest 92
**Fry**, James Leslie 1941- AmMWSc 92, WhoMW 92
**Fry**, James N 1952- AmMWSc 92
**Fry**, James Palmer 1939- AmMWSc 92
**Fry**, James Wilson 1939- WhoMW 92
**Fry**, John 1922- Who 92
**Fry**, John Craig 1926- AmMWSc 92
**Fry**, John Sedgwick 1929- AmMWSc 92
**Fry**, Jonathan Michael 1937- IntWW 91
**Fry**, Joshua 1700?-1754 BiInAmS
**Fry**, Joyce Elaine 1943- WhoRel 92
**Fry**, K Edward 1943- WhoAmP 91
**Fry**, Laura Anne 1857-1943 HanAmWH
**Fry**, LeRoy F 1918- WhoAmP 91
**Fry**, Leslie McGee 1913- WhoAmP 91
**Fry**, Lewis George 1860-1933 TwCPaSc
**Fry**, Linda Sue 1961- WhoFI 92, WhoWest 92
**Fry**, Louis Edwin, Jr. 1928- WhoBlA 92
**Fry**, Louis Rummel 1928- AmMWSc 92
**Fry**, Lowell Lawrence 1956- WhoRel 92
**Fry**, Malcolm Craig 1928- WhoRel 92
**Fry**, Margaret 1931- Who 92
**Fry**, Marion Golda 1932- IntWW 91
**Fry**, Maxwell 1899- DcTwDes
**Fry**, Maxwell 1899-1987 FacFETw
**Fry**, Michael Lynn 1951- WhoRel 92
**Fry**, Morton Harrison, II 1946- WhoAmL 92
**Fry**, Peggy Crooke 1928- AmMWSc 92
**Fry**, Peter Derek 1931- Who 92
**Fry**, Peter George Robin Plantagenet S. Who 92
**Fry**, Richard Henry 1900- Who 92
**Fry**, Richard Jeremy Michael 1925- AmMWSc 92
**Fry**, Roger 1866-1934 FacFETw, TwCPaSc
**Fry**, Roger Eliot 1866-1934 DcTwDes
**Fry**, Ronald Ernest 1925- Who 92
**Fry**, Rosalie K. 1911- WrDr 92
**Fry**, Rosalie Kingsmill 1911- IntAu&W 91
**Fry**, Roy Henry 1931- WhoMW 92
**Fry**, Sam, Jr. d1991 NewYTBS 91
**Fry**, Simon 1944- TwCPaSc
**Fry**, Simon 1947- WhoBlA 92
**Fry**, Stephen John 1957- Who 92
**Fry**, Thomas R 1923- AmMWSc 92
**Fry**, Thomas Richard 1948- WhoFI 92
**Fry**, Wayne Lyle 1922- AmMWSc 92
**Fry**, William Earl 1944- AmMWSc 92
**Fry**, William Edward 1954- WhoRel 92
**Fry**, William Finley, Jr. 1924- WrDr 92
**Fry**, William Frederick 1921- AmMWSc 92
**Fry**, William Gordon 1909- Who 92
**Fry**, William Henry 1813-1864 NewAmDM
**Fry**, William James 1928- AmMWSc 92
**Fry**, William Norman H. Who 92
**Fryar**, Irving Dale 1962- WhoBlA 92
**Fryatt**, John E. WhoAmL 92
**Fryback**, William Max 1921- WhoAmP 91
**Fryberg**, Abraham 1901- Who 92
**Fryberger**, David 1931- AmMWSc 92
**Fryczkowski**, Andrzej Witold 1939- WhoMW 92
**Frydenberg**, Erling 1953- WhoWest 92
**Frydendall**, Merrill J 1934- AmMWSc 92
**Frydland**, Rachmiel 1919-1985 RelLAm 91
**Frydman**, Paul 1906- WhoMW 92
**Frye**, Alva L 1922- AmMWSc 92
**Frye**, C G 1918- AmMWSc 92
**Frye**, Cecil Leonard 1928- AmMWSc 92
**Frye**, Charles Alton 1936- WhoAmP 91
**Frye**, Charles Anthony 1946- WhoBlA 92
**Frye**, Charles Isaac 1935- AmMWSc 92
**Frye**, Clayton Wesley, Jr. 1930- WhoFI 92
**Frye**, David Scott 1955- WhoIns 92
**Frye**, Ellen DrAPF 91
**Frye**, Gerald Dalton 1950- AmMWSc 92
**Frye**, Glenn McKinley, Jr 1926- AmMWSc 92
**Frye**, Helen Jackson 1930- WhoAmL 92
**Frye**, Henry E. 1932- WhoAmL 92, WhoAmP 91, WhoBlA 92
**Frye**, Herman Northrop d1991 IntWW 91N
**Frye**, Herschel Gordon 1920- AmMWSc 92
**Frye**, James Sayler 1945- AmMWSc 92
**Frye**, Jennings Bryan, Jr 1918- AmMWSc 92
**Frye**, John H, Jr 1908- AmMWSc 92
**Frye**, Judith Eleen Minor WhoFI 92, WhoWest 92
**Frye**, Keith 1935- AmMWSc 92
**Frye**, Michael John Ernest 1945- Who 92
**Frye**, Nadine Grace WhoBlA 92
**Frye**, Northrop 1912-1991 BenetAL 91, ConAu 133, CurBio 91N, FacFETw, NewYTBS 91 [port], News 91, -91-3
**Frye**, Reginald Stanley 1936- WhoBlA 92
**Frye**, Richard Arthur 1948- WhoAmL 92
**Frye**, Richard Nelson 1920- IntWW 91, WrDr 92
**Frye**, Robert Bruce 1949- AmMWSc 92
**Frye**, Robert Edward 1936- WhoBlA 92
**Frye**, Roland 1921- WrDr 92
**Frye**, Roland Mushat 1921- IntAu&W 91, WhoRel 92
**Frye**, Roland Mushat, Jr. 1950- WhoAmL 92
**Frye**, Russell Scott 1953- WhoAmL 92
**Frye**, Timothy Wayne 1956- WhoMW 92
**Frye**, Walter NewAmDM
**Frye**, Wilbur Wayne 1933- AmMWSc 92
**Frye**, William IntMPA 92
**Frye**, William Emerson 1917- AmMWSc 92
**Frye**, William Sinclair 1924- WhoBlA 92
**Fryefield**, Peter Jay 1949- WhoAmL 92
**Fryer**, Appleton 1927- WhoFI 92
**Fryer**, Charles W 1928- AmMWSc 92
**Fryer**, David Richard 1936- Who 92
**Fryer**, E. Reeseman d1991 NewYTBS 91
**Fryer**, Elsie Beth 1925- AmMWSc 92
**Fryer**, Geoffrey 1927- IntWW 91, Who 92
**Fryer**, Gladys Constance 1923- WhoWest 92
**Fryer**, Holly Claire 1908- AmMWSc 92
**Fryer**, John Louis 1929- AmMWSc 92
**Fryer**, Jonathan 1950- IntAu&W 91, WrDr 92
**Fryer**, Jonathan Paul 1955- WhoAmL 92
**Fryer**, Judith Dorothy 1950- WhoAmL 92
**Fryer**, Lester K WhoAmP 91
**Fryer**, Malcolm 1937- TwCPaSc
**Fryer**, Minot Packer 1925- AmMWSc 92
**Fryer**, Patrick J. 1956- WhoWest 92
**Fryer**, Robert Sherwood 1920- WhoEnt 92
**Fryer**, Rodney Ian 1930- AmMWSc 92
**Fryer**, Wilfred George 1900- Who 92
**Frykenberg**, Robert E. 1930- WrDr 92
**Frykenberg**, Robert Eric 1930- WhoMW 92
**Fryklund**, Verne Charles, Jr 1920- AmMWSc 92
**Fryling**, Robert Howard 1921- AmMWSc 92
**Frym**, Gloria DrAPF 91
**Fryman**, Louis William 1935- WhoAmL 92
**Fryman**, Virgil Thomas, Jr. 1940- WhoAmL 92
**Frymer**, Murry 1934- WhoWest 92
**Frymire**, Richard L 1931- WhoAmP 91
**Fryrear**, Donald W 1936- AmMWSc 92
**Fryson**, Sim E. WhoBlA 92
**Frystak**, Ronald Wayne 1941- AmMWSc 92
**Fryt**, Michael David 1955- WhoAmL 92
**Fryt**, Monte Stanislaus 1949- WhoFI 92
**Fryxell**, Fritiof Melvin 1900- AmMWSc 92
**Fryxell**, Greta Albrecht 1926- AmMWSc 92
**Fryxell**, Paul Arnold 1927- AmMWSc 92
**Fryxell**, Robert Edward 1923- AmMWSc 92
**Fryxell**, Ronald C 1938- AmMWSc 92
**Ftaclas**, Christ AmMWSc 92
**Fthenakis**, Emanuel John 1928- AmMWSc 92, WhoFI 92
**Fu Chongbi** 1916- IntWW 91
**Fu Hao** 1916- IntWW 91
**Fu Kuiqing** IntWW 91
**Fu Qifeng** 1941- IntWW 91
**Fu Quanyou** 1930- IntWW 91
**Fu Tianchou** d1990 IntWW 91N
**Fu Tianlin** 1946- IntWW 91
**Fu Tieshan** 1932- IntWW 91
**Fu Zhuanzuo** 1914- IntWW 91
**Fu**, Cheng-Tze 1949- AmMWSc 92
**Fu**, Hui-Hsing 1947- AmMWSc 92
**Fu**, Jerry Hui Ming 1932- AmMWSc 92
**Fu**, Kuan-Chen 1933- AmMWSc 92
**Fu**, Lee Lueng 1950- AmMWSc 92
**Fu**, Li-Sheng William AmMWSc 92
**Fu**, Lorraine Shao-Yen 1939- AmMWSc 92
**Fu**, Peter Pi-Cheng 1941- AmMWSc 92
**Fu**, Shou-Cheng Joseph 1924- AmMWSc 92
**Fu**, Shu Man 1942- AmMWSc 92
**Fu**, Wallace Yamtak 1943- AmMWSc 92
**Fu**, Wei-ning 1925- AmMWSc 92
**Fu**, Xiang 1962- WhoWest 92
**Fu**, Yuan C 1930- AmMWSc 92
**Fu**, Yun-Lung 1942- AmMWSc 92
**Fua**, Giorgio 1919- IntWW 91
**Fuad I** 1868-1936 FacFETw
**Fuad**, Kutlu Tekin 1926- Who 92
**Fuavai**, Te'o WhoAmP 91
**Fubini**, Eugene G 1913- AmMWSc 92
**Fubini**, Eugene Ghiron 1913- WhoFI 92
**Fuccella**, Carl J. 1927- WhoFI 92
**Fucci**, Donald James 1941- AmMWSc 92
**Fucci**, Joseph Leonard 1950- WhoFI 92
**Fucci**, Michael J. 1956- WhoAmL 92
**Fuchel**, Jennifer Ruth 1964- WhoEnt 92
**Fuchigami**, Leslie H 1942- AmMWSc 92
**Fuchs**, Alan D. 1936- WhoRel 92
**Fuchs**, Albert Frederick 1938- AmMWSc 92
**Fuchs**, Anke 1937- IntWW 91
**Fuchs**, Anna-Riitta AmMWSc 92
**Fuchs**, Daniel DrAPF 91
**Fuchs**, Daniel 1909- BenetAL 91, ConNov 91, WrDr 92
**Fuchs**, Elaine V 1950- AmMWSc 92
**Fuchs**, Elinor 1933- WhoEnt 92
**Fuchs**, Ewald Franz 1939- AmMWSc 92
**Fuchs**, Frank Joseph 1954- WhoEnt 92
**Fuchs**, Franklin 1931- AmMWSc 92
**Fuchs**, Fritz Friedrich 1918- AmMWSc 92
**Fuchs**, H O 1907- AmMWSc 92
**Fuchs**, Henry 1948- AmMWSc 92
**Fuchs**, Jack Frederick 1952- WhoAmL 92
**Fuchs**, Jacob 1923- AmMWSc 92
**Fuchs**, James Allen 1943- AmMWSc 92
**Fuchs**, James Claiborne Allred 1938- AmMWSc 92
**Fuchs**, Jay R 1955- WhoIns 92
**Fuchs**, Jerome Herbert 1922- WhoFI 92
**Fuchs**, Joseph WhoEnt 92
**Fuchs**, Joseph 1900- NewAmDM
**Fuchs**, Joseph Herman 1917- WhoAmP 91
**Fuchs**, Josephine S WhoAmP 91
**Fuchs**, Julius Jakob 1927- AmMWSc 92
**Fuchs**, Klaus 1911-1988 FacFETw
**Fuchs**, Laszlo 1924- AmMWSc 92
**Fuchs**, Leo L. 1929- IntMPA 92
**Fuchs**, Lillian WhoEnt 92
**Fuchs**, Lillian 1903- NewAmDM
**Fuchs**, Lucy 1935- WrDr 92
**Fuchs**, Michael LesBEnT 92
**Fuchs**, Michael 1946- IntMPA 92
**Fuchs**, Michael Alvin 1949- WhoMW 92
**Fuchs**, Michael J. 1946- WhoEnt 92
**Fuchs**, Morton S 1932- AmMWSc 92
**Fuchs**, Norman H 1938- AmMWSc 92
**Fuchs**, Olivia Anne Morris 1949- WhoAmL 92
**Fuchs**, Owen George 1951- WhoFI 92
**Fuchs**, Peter Cornelius 1936- WhoWest 92
**Fuchs**, Richard 1926- AmMWSc 92
**Fuchs**, Richard E 1936- AmMWSc 92
**Fuchs**, Robert F. 1924- WhoAmL 92
**Fuchs**, Robert L 1929- AmMWSc 92
**Fuchs**, Roland John 1933- AmMWSc 92
**Fuchs**, Ronald 1932- AmMWSc 92
**Fuchs**, Stephen Lewis 1946- WhoRel 92
**Fuchs**, Thomas 1942- WhoEnt 92
**Fuchs**, Victor Robert 1924- AmMWSc 92, IntWW 91, WhoFI 92
**Fuchs**, Vivian 1908- Who 92, WrDr 92
**Fuchs**, Vivian Ernest IntAu&W 91
**Fuchs**, Vivian Ernest 1908- IntWW 91
**Fuchs**, Vivien Ernest 1908- FacFETw
**Fuchs**, Vladimir 1935- AmMWSc 92
**Fuchs**, W Kent 1954- AmMWSc 92
**Fuchs**, Walter 1932- AmMWSc 92
**Fuchs**, William D. 1947- WhoFI 92
**Fuchs**, Wolfgang Heinrich 1915- AmMWSc 92
**Fuchsman**, Charles H 1917- AmMWSc 92
**Fuchsman**, William Harvey 1941- AmMWSc 92
**Fucik**, Donald Edward 1955- WhoAmL 92
**Fucik**, Edward Montford 1914- AmMWSc 92
**Fucik**, John Edward 1928- AmMWSc 92
**Fuda**, Michael George 1938- AmMWSc 92
**Fudali**, Robert F 1933- AmMWSc 92
**Fudenberg**, H Hugh 1928- AmMWSc 92
**Fudge**, Ann Marie WhoBlA 92
**Fudge**, Danny Hugh 1962- WhoRel 92
**Fudge**, Joe Allen 1939- WhoAmP 91
**Fudge**, Roy Smith 1920- WhoRel 92
**Fudger**, Arthur Wolfe 1933- WhoAmL 92
**Fudro**, Stanley J 1918- WhoAmP 91
**Fuegi**, John 1936- WrDr 92
**Fuehrer**, Mark Edwin DrAPF 91
**Fuelberg**, Henry Ernest 1948- AmMWSc 92
**Fuellhart**, David Clark 1938- WhoEnt 92
**Fuelling**, Clinton Paul 1937- AmMWSc 92
**Fuenfhausen**, Kenneth Lee 1958- WhoRel 92
**Fuenning**, Samuel Isaiah 1916- AmMWSc 92
**Fuente**, Claudio Jesus 1950- WhoEnt 92
**Fuentealba**, Victor William 1922- WhoEnt 92
**Fuentes**, Carlos 1928- BenetAL 91, DcLB 113 [port], FacFETw, IntAu&W 91, IntWW 91, LiExTwC, Who 92, WhoHisp 92
**Fuentes**, Carlos De IntDcF 2-2
**Fuentes**, Daisy 1966- WhoHisp 92
**Fuentes**, Elia Ivonne WhoHisp 92
**Fuentes**, Ernesto WhoHisp 92
**Fuentes**, Ernesto Venegas 1947- WhoHisp 92
**Fuentes**, Fernando Luis 1952- WhoHisp 92
**Fuentes**, Humberto WhoHisp 92
**Fuentes**, John WhoHisp 92
**Fuentes**, Leopoldo C. 1949- WhoHisp 92
**Fuentes**, Manuel 1955- WhoHisp 92
**Fuentes**, Martha Ayers 1923- WhoEnt 92
**Fuentes**, Pete Acosta 1952- WhoHisp 92
**Fuentes**, R. Alan 1949- WhoHisp 92
**Fuentes**, Ricardo, Jr 1948- AmMWSc 92
**Fuentes**, Tina Guerrero 1949- WhoHisp 92
**Fuentes-Chao**, Rene WhoHisp 92
**Fuentes y Guzman**, Francisco Antonio de 1643-1700 HisDSpE
**Fuentez**, Lucio 1944- WhoHisp 92
**Fuerbringer**, Alfred Ottomar 1903- WhoRel 92
**Fuerniss**, Gloria Villasana 1949- WhoHisp 92
**Fuerniss**, Stephen Joseph 1945- AmMWSc 92
**Fuerst**, Adolph 1925- AmMWSc 92
**Fuerst**, Carlton Dwight 1955- AmMWSc 92
**Fuerst**, Paul Anthony 1948- AmMWSc 92
**Fuerst**, Robert 1921- AmMWSc 92
**Fuerstenau**, D W 1928- AmMWSc 92
**Fuerstenau**, M C 1933- AmMWSc 92
**Fuertes**, Estevan Antonio 1838-1903 BiInAmS
**Fuertes**, Gloria 1918- DcLB 108 [port]
**Fuertes**, Raul A. 1940- WhoHisp 92
**Fuess**, Billings Sibley, Jr. 1928- WhoEnt 92
**Fuess**, Frederick William, III 1927- AmMWSc 92
**Fuess**, Harold George 1910- WhoRel 92
**Fuest**, Robert 1927- IntMPA 92
**Fugal**, Jared Widdison 1963- WhoWest 92
**Fugard**, Athol 1932- FacFETw, IntWW 91, RfGEnL 91, Who 92, WrDr 92
**Fugard**, Athol Harold 1932- IntAu&W 91
**Fugard**, Michael Teape 1933- Who 92
**Fugate**, Donald James 1953- WhoRel 92
**Fugate**, Edward 1956- WhoRel 92
**Fugate**, Ivan Dee 1928- WhoFI 92
**Fugate**, Joseph B 1933- AmMWSc 92
**Fugate**, Judith WhoEnt 92
**Fugate**, Kearby Joe 1934- AmMWSc 92
**Fugate**, Wilbur Lindsay 1913- WhoAmL 92
**Fugelso**, Leif Erik 1935- AmMWSc 92
**Fuget**, Charles Robert 1929- AmMWSc 92, WhoBlA 92
**Fuget**, Henry Eugene 1925- WhoBlA 92
**Fugger**, Joseph 1921- AmMWSc 92
**Fugiel**, Frank Paul 1950- WhoFI 92
**Fugina**, Peter X WhoAmP 91
**Fugitt**, Billy Wayne 1935- WhoMW 92
**Fuglede**, Bent 1925- IntWW 91
**Fuglei-Lazebnik**, Kate Marie 1955- WhoEnt 92
**Fugler**, Jon Edward 1956- WhoRel 92
**Fugler**, Michael Roy 1949- WhoAmL 92
**Fugo**, Nicholas William 1913- AmMWSc 92
**Fuhlbrigge**, Peter Martin 1957- WhoMW 92
**Fuhlhage**, Donald Wayne 1931- AmMWSc 92
**Fuhlrodt**, Norman Theodore 1910- WhoFI 92
**Fuhr**, Ann Barton Mosher 1941- WhoRel 92
**Fuhr**, Grant 1962- ConBlB 1 [port]
**Fuhr**, Irvin 1913- AmMWSc 92
**Fuhr**, Jeffrey Robert 1946- AmMWSc 92
**Fuhr**, Joseph Ernest 1936- AmMWSc 92
**Fuhr**, Samuel E. 1918- WhoBlA 92
**Fuhrer**, Arthur K. 1926- WhoEnt 92
**Fuhriman**, D K 1918- AmMWSc 92
**Fuhrken**, Gebhard 1930- AmMWSc 92
**Fuhrken**, Marie Rose 1960- WhoFI 92
**Fuhrman**, Albert William 1921- AmMWSc 92
**Fuhrman**, Bruce Livermore 1936- WhoWest 92

**Fuhrman**, Charles Michael 1952- *WhoRel 92*
**Fuhrman**, Frederick Alexander 1915- *AmMWSc 92*
**Fuhrman**, Harold Henry 1923- *WhoAmL 92*
**Fuhrman**, Jed Alan 1956- *AmMWSc 92, WhoWest 92*
**Fuhrman**, Linn 1944- *WhoAmP 91*
**Fuhrman**, Robert Alexander 1925- *AmMWSc 92, IntWW 91, WhoFI 92, WhoWest 92*
**Fuhrman**, Steve *WhoAmP 91*
**Fuhrman**, Wayne James 1944- *WhoMW 92*
**Fuhrmann**, Barbara Clara 1949- *WhoRel 92*
**Fuhrmann**, Charles J., II 1945- *WhoFI 92*
**Fuhrmann**, Horst 1926- *IntWW 91*
**Fuhs**, Allen E 1927- *AmMWSc 92*
**Fuhs**, Henry G 1941- *WhoAmP 91*
**Fuhs**, Wendy L. 1950- *WhoMW 92*
**Fuiava**, Mike *WhoAmP 91*
**Fuiks**, L.J. 1954- *WhoFI 92*
**Fuimaono**, A U 1923- *WhoAmP 91*
**Fuimaono**, Lutu Tenari 1930- *WhoAmP 91*
**Fuiten**, Joseph Benjamin 1949- *WhoRel 92*
**Fuji**, Hiroshi 1930- *AmMWSc 92*
**Fujii**, Jack K 1940- *AmMWSc 92*
**Fujii**, Jack Koji 1940- *WhoWest 92*
**Fujii**, Kiyo 1921- *WhoWest 92*
**Fujii**, Richard M. 1932- *WhoWest 92*
**Fujikawa**, Eva Eiko 1958- *WhoFI 92, WhoWest 92*
**Fujikawa**, Gyo 1908- *ChlLR 25 [port]*
**Fujikawa**, Norma Sutton 1928- *AmMWSc 92*
**Fujimori**, Alberto Kenyo 1939- *IntWW 91*
**Fujimori**, Masamichi 1921- *IntWW 91*
**Fujimori**, Tetsuo 1919- *IntWW 91*
**Fujimoto**, Atsuko Ono 1935- *AmMWSc 92*
**Fujimoto**, George Iwao 1920- *AmMWSc 92*
**Fujimoto**, Gordon Takeo 1952- *AmMWSc 92*
**Fujimoto**, James G 1957- *AmMWSc 92*
**Fujimoto**, James Masao 1928- *AmMWSc 92*
**Fujimoto**, Minoru 1926- *AmMWSc 92*
**Fujimoto**, Shigeyoshi 1936- *AmMWSc 92*
**Fujimoto**, Takao 1931- *IntWW 91*
**Fujimoto**, Wilfred Y 1940- *AmMWSc 92*
**Fujimura**, Osamu 1927- *AmMWSc 92*
**Fujimura**, Robert 1933- *AmMWSc 92*
**Fujinami**, Robert S 1949- *AmMWSc 92*
**Fujinami**, Takao 1932- *IntWW 91*
**Fujino**, Hirotake 1933- *IntWW 91*
**Fujinoye** *EncAmaz 91*
**Fujioka**, Masao 1924- *IntWW 91*
**Fujioka**, Roger Sadao 1938- *AmMWSc 92*
**Fujisaki**, Akira 1917- *IntWW 91*
**Fujita**, Dawn Masayo 1967- *WhoWest 92*
**Fujita**, Donald J 1943- *AmMWSc 92*
**Fujita**, Shigeji 1929- *AmMWSc 92*
**Fujita**, Tetsuya T 1920- *AmMWSc 92*
**Fujita**, Yoshio 1908- *IntWW 91*
**Fujitani**, Martin Tomio 1968- *WhoWest 92*
**Fujiwara**, Elizabeth Jubin 1945- *WhoAmL 92*
**Fujiwara**, Hamao 1947- *WhoEnt 92*
**Fujiwara**, Hideo 1946- *AmMWSc 92*
**Fujiwara**, Keigi 1944- *AmMWSc 92*
**Fujiyama**, Naraichi 1915- *Who 92*
**Fujiyoshi**, Tsuguhide 1913- *IntWW 91*
**Fuka**, Louis Richard 1937- *AmMWSc 92*
**Fukai**, Junichiro 1938- *AmMWSc 92*
**Fukaya**, Takashi *IntWW 91*
**Fuks**, Ladislav 1923- *IntAu&W 91*
**Fukubayashi**, Harold Haruhisa 1936- *WhoMW 92*
**Fukuda**, Haruko 1946- *WrDr 92*
**Fukuda**, Margaret Mary 1948- *WhoAmL 92*
**Fukuda**, Minoru 1945- *AmMWSc 92*
**Fukuda**, Takeo 1905- *IntWW 91*
**Fukuhara**, Francis M 1925- *AmMWSc 92*
**Fukuhara**, Henry 1913- *WhoWest 92*
**Fukui**, H 1927- *AmMWSc 92*
**Fukui**, Hatsuaki 1927- *WhoFI 92*
**Fukui**, Kenichi 1918- *IntWW 91, Who 92, WhoNob 90*
**Fukuji**, Brian Courtney 1962- *WhoEnt 92*
**Fukumoto**, Benjamin I. 1938- *WhoWest 92*
**Fukumoto**, Bert Ken 1955- *WhoAmL 92*
**Fukumoto**, Brian Michael 1967- *WhoWest 92*
**Fukumoto**, Leslie Satsuki 1955- *WhoAmL 92*
**Fukunaga**, Carol A 1947- *WhoAmP 91*
**Fukunaga**, Keinosuke 1930- *AmMWSc 92*
**Fukunaga**, Tadamichi 1931- *AmMWSc 92*
**Fukushima**, Barbara Naomi 1948- *WhoFI 92, WhoWest 92*
**Fukushima**, David Kenzo 1917- *AmMWSc 92*
**Fukushima**, Eiichi 1936- *AmMWSc 92*
**Fukushima**, Joji 1927- *IntWW 91*
**Fukushima**, Toshiyuki 1921- *AmMWSc 92*
**Fukuta**, Norihiko 1931- *AmMWSc 92*
**Fukutake**, Tadashi 1917- *WrDr 92*
**Fukuto**, Tetsuo Roy 1923- *AmMWSc 92*
**Fukuyama**, Kimie 1927- *AmMWSc 92*
**Fukuyama**, Thomas T 1927- *AmMWSc 92*
**Fukuyama**, Tohru 1948- *AmMWSc 92*
**Fulbright**, Dennis Wayne 1952- *AmMWSc 92*
**Fulbright**, Harry Wilks 1918- *AmMWSc 92*
**Fulbright**, J William 1905- *FacFETw, Who 92, WrDr 92*
**Fulbright**, James William 1905- *AmPolLe, WhoAmP 91*
**Fulbright**, John William 1952- *WhoWest 92*
**Fulbright**, Junus Cymore 1942- *WhoRel 92*
**Fulbright**, Maquestia J. 1955- *WhoFI 92*
**Fulbright**, Timothy Edward 1953- *AmMWSc 92*
**Fulbright**, William 1905- *IntWW 91*
**Fulcher**, Carolyn Jean 1956- *WhoFI 92*
**Fulcher**, Derick Harold 1917- *Who 92*
**Fulcher**, William Ernest 1931- *AmMWSc 92*
**Fulci**, Francesco Paolo 1931- *IntWW 91*
**Fulco**, Armand J 1932- *AmMWSc 92*
**Fulco**, Frank 1908- *WhoAmP 91*
**Fulco**, Jose Roque 1927- *AmMWSc 92*
**Fulcomer**, James Joseph 1943- *WhoAmP 91*
**Fuld**, Bracha d1946 *EncAmaz 91*
**Fulda**, Myron Oscar 1930- *AmMWSc 92*
**Fulde**, Roland Charles 1926- *AmMWSc 92*
**Fulde**, Walter John 1935- *WhoWest 92*
**Fuleihan**, Anis 1900-1970 *NewAmDM*
**Fuleki**, Tibor 1931- *AmMWSc 92*
**Fulenwider**, John 1756?-1826 *DcNCBi 2*
**Fulfer**, John Keith 1959- *WhoRel 92*
**Fulford**, David 1925- *WhoEnt 92*
**Fulford**, James Arthur 1937- *WhoFI 92*
**Fulford**, Margaret Hannah 1904- *AmMWSc 92*
**Fulford**, Robert John 1923- *Who 92*
**Fulford**, William James 1949- *WhoAmP 91*
**Fulgentius of Ruspe** 467?-533 *EncEarC*
**Fulgenzi**, Benjamin 1925- *WhoFI 92, WhoMW 92*
**Fulger**, Charles V 1932- *AmMWSc 92*
**Fulgham**, Roietta Goodwin 1948- *WhoBlA 92*
**Fulghum**, Brice Elwin 1919- *WhoFI 92*
**Fulghum**, Robert *WrDr 92*
**Fulghum**, Robert 1937- *IntAu&W 91*
**Fulghum**, Robert Schmidt 1929- *AmMWSc 92*
**Fulginiti**, Vincent Anthony 1931- *AmMWSc 92*
**Fulham**, Bishop Suffragan of 1931- *Who 92*
**Fulk**, H. Roger 1956- *WhoMW 92*
**Fulk**, Judith Ann 1949- *WhoMW 92*
**Fulk**, Kenneth S. 1953- *WhoMW 92*
**Fulk**, Lance Monroe 1964- *WhoMW 92*
**Fulkerson**, James 1945- *ConCom 92*
**Fulkerson**, John Frederick 1922- *AmMWSc 92*
**Fulkerson**, William 1935- *AmMWSc 92*
**Fulkes**, Jean Aston *WhoMW 92*
**Fulks**, Paula Jean 1954- *WhoAmL 92*
**Fulks**, Watson 1919- *AmMWSc 92*
**Full**, Jerome Kendrick 1926- *WhoFI 92*
**Full**, Robert Witmer 1949- *WhoAmL 92*
**Fullagar**, Paul David 1938- *AmMWSc 92*
**Fullam**, Harold Thomas 1927- *AmMWSc 92*
**Fullam**, John Cronin 1951- *WhoEnt 92*
**Fullard**, George 1923-1974 *TwCPaSc*
**Fullen**, Floyd Russell 1938- *WhoAmP 91*
**Fullen**, Harry James 1952- *WhoMW 92*
**Fuller**, Albert *WhoEnt 92*
**Fuller**, Albert Clinton 1920- *WhoAmP 91*
**Fuller**, Alice W *ScFEYrs*
**Fuller**, Almyra Oveta 1955- *WhoBlA 92*
**Fuller**, Alvarado M 1851- *ScFEYrs*
**Fuller**, Andrew S 1828-1896 *BiInAmS*
**Fuller**, Arthur Orpen 1926- *IntWW 91*
**Fuller**, Barbara Fink Brockway 1936- *AmMWSc 92*
**Fuller**, Bartholomew 1829-1882 *DcNCBi 2*
**Fuller**, Benjamin Franklin, Jr 1922- *AmMWSc 92*
**Fuller**, Beverly Jean 1927- *WhoEnt 92*
**Fuller**, Blair *DrAPF 91*
**Fuller**, Blind Boy *DcNCBi 2*
**Fuller**, Blind Boy 1909?-1941 *NewAmDM*
**Fuller**, Brian Leslie 1936- *Who 92*
**Fuller**, Buckminster 1895-1983 *DcTwDes*
**Fuller**, Cecil Gary 1943- *WhoEnt 92*
**Fuller**, Charles 1939- *BenetAL 91, BlkLC [port], DramC 1 [port], WhoBlA 92, WhoEnt 92, WrDr 92*
**Fuller**, Charles Edward 1887-1968 *RelLAm 91*
**Fuller**, Christopher Robert 1953- *AmMWSc 92*
**Fuller**, Craig L 1951- *WhoAmP 91*
**Fuller**, Curtis D. 1934- *WhoBlA 92*
**Fuller**, David Otis, Jr. 1939- *WhoAmL 92*
**Fuller**, Derek Joseph Haggard 1917- *AmMWSc 92, WhoMW 92*
**Fuller**, Dewey C. 1934- *WhoBlA 92*
**Fuller**, Diana Clare 1953- *WhoAmL 92*
**Fuller**, Don Edgar 1928- *WhoAmP 91*
**Fuller**, Donald Edward *WhoMW 92*
**Fuller**, Doris Jean 1945- *WhoBlA 92*
**Fuller**, Dudley D 1913- *AmMWSc 92*
**Fuller**, E Bert 1898- *WhoAmP 91*
**Fuller**, Edmund 1914- *WrDr 92*
**Fuller**, Edwin Wiley 1847-1876 *DcNCBi 2*
**Fuller**, Ellen Oneil *AmMWSc 92*
**Fuller**, Eugene George 1938- *AmMWSc 92*
**Fuller**, Everett G 1920- *AmMWSc 92*
**Fuller**, Everett J 1929- *AmMWSc 92*
**Fuller**, Forst Donald 1916- *AmMWSc 92*
**Fuller**, Francis Brock 1927- *AmMWSc 92*
**Fuller**, Fred H. d1991 *NewYTBS 91*
**Fuller**, Frederick T *ScFEYrs*
**Fuller**, G. M. 1920- *WhoAmL 92*
**Fuller**, Gail Elaine 1953- *WhoAmL 92*
**Fuller**, Gary Albert 1941- *WhoWest 92*
**Fuller**, Geoffrey Herbert 1927- *Who 92*
**Fuller**, George C. *WhoRel 92*
**Fuller**, Gerald Arthur 1939- *AmMWSc 92*
**Fuller**, Gerald M 1935- *AmMWSc 92*
**Fuller**, Glenn 1929- *AmMWSc 92*
**Fuller**, Gloria Ann 1952- *WhoBlA 92*
**Fuller**, Harold David 1937- *WhoBlA 92*
**Fuller**, Harold Q 1907- *AmMWSc 92*
**Fuller**, Harold Wayne 1925- *AmMWSc 92*
**Fuller**, Harry Laurance 1938- *WhoFI 92, WhoMW 92*
**Fuller**, Haynes R 1928- *WhoAmP 91*
**Fuller**, Henry B. 1857-1929 *BenetAL 91*
**Fuller**, Henry Lester 1916- *AmMWSc 92*
**Fuller**, Herbert Harold 1946- *WhoEnt 92*
**Fuller**, Homer Taylor 1838-1908 *BiInAmS*
**Fuller**, Horace Bartlet, Jr. 1935- *WhoRel 92*
**Fuller**, Ivan Walter 1963- *WhoEnt 92*
**Fuller**, Jack Lewis 1945- *WhoBlA 92*
**Fuller**, Jack William 1946- *WhoFI 92*
**Fuller**, Jackson Franklin 1920- *AmMWSc 92*
**Fuller**, James J. 1946- *WhoBlA 92*
**Fuller**, James Osborn 1912- *AmMWSc 92, WhoMW 92*
**Fuller**, Jean Overton 1915- *WrDr 92*
**Fuller**, Jean Violet Overton 1915- *IntAu&W 91*
**Fuller**, Jesse 1896-1976 *NewAmDM*
**Fuller**, John 1916- *IntAu&W 91, WrDr 92*
**Fuller**, John 1917- *Who 92*
**Fuller**, John 1937- *ConPo 91, WrDr 92*
**Fuller**, John Edward 1943- *WhoMW 92*
**Fuller**, John Frederick Charles 1878-1966 *BiDExR*
**Fuller**, John G. 1913-1990 *ConAu 133, SmATA 65 [port]*
**Fuller**, John L 1937- *IntAu&W 91*
**Fuller**, John Leopold 1937- *Who 92*
**Fuller**, John W. 1940- *WhoFI 92*
**Fuller**, John William Fleetwood 1936- *Who 92*
**Fuller**, Kenneth C *WhoAmP 91*
**Fuller**, Kent Ralph 1938- *AmMWSc 92*
**Fuller**, Lee Dennison 1910- *WhoMW 92*
**Fuller**, Leonard Eugene 1919- *AmMWSc 92*
**Fuller**, Leonard John 1891-1973 *TwCPaSc*
**Fuller**, Loie 1862-1928 *FacFETw*
**Fuller**, Loula Moore 1950- *WhoAmL 92*
**Fuller**, Lynn Fenton 1947- *AmMWSc 92*
**Fuller**, Margaret 1810-1850 *BenetAL 91, HanAmWH, PorAmW [port], RComAH*
**Fuller**, Marian Jane 1940- *AmMWSc 92*
**Fuller**, Mark Adin, Jr. 1933- *WhoFI 92*
**Fuller**, Mark K. 1960- *WhoMW 92*
**Fuller**, Mark Roy 1946- *AmMWSc 92*
**Fuller**, Martin 1943- *TwCPaSc*
**Fuller**, Martin Emil 1930- *AmMWSc 92*
**Fuller**, Maurice DeLano, Jr. 1930- *WhoAmL 92*
**Fuller**, Melville Weston 1833-1910 *AmPolLe*
**Fuller**, Melvin Stuart 1931- *AmMWSc 92*
**Fuller**, Meta Warrick 1877-1968 *NotBlAW 92 [port]*
**Fuller**, Michael D 1934- *AmMWSc 92*
**Fuller**, Michael John 1932- *Who 92*
**Fuller**, Mike Douglas 1957- *WhoAmL 92*
**Fuller**, Milton E 1926- *AmMWSc 92*
**Fuller**, Mozelle James 1909- *WhoRel 92*
**Fuller**, Norvell Ricardo 1953- *WhoBlA 92*
**Fuller**, Perry Lucian 1922- *WhoMW 92*
**Fuller**, Peter 1947-1990 *AnObit 1990*
**Fuller**, Peter McAfee 1943- *AmMWSc 92*
**Fuller**, R Buckminster 1895-1983 *FacFETw*
**Fuller**, Ray W 1935- *AmMWSc 92*
**Fuller**, Reginald Horace 1915- *WhoRel 92, WrDr 92*
**Fuller**, Richard H 1928- *AmMWSc 92*
**Fuller**, Richard Kenneth 1935- *AmMWSc 92*
**Fuller**, Richard M 1933- *AmMWSc 92*
**Fuller**, Rickey Wayne 1955- *WhoRel 92*
**Fuller**, Robert Allen 1953- *WhoWest 92*
**Fuller**, Robert Charles 1952- *WhoRel 92*
**Fuller**, Robert Earl 1938- *WhoRel 92, WhoWest 92*
**Fuller**, Robert Edwin 1949- *WhoWest 92*
**Fuller**, Robert Gohl 1935- *AmMWSc 92*
**Fuller**, Robert Kenneth 1942- *WhoWest 92*
**Fuller**, Robert Leander 1943- *WhoAmL 92, WhoFI 92*
**Fuller**, Robert Russell 1947- *WhoMW 92*
**Fuller**, Robert Thomas 1824?- *DcNCBi 2*
**Fuller**, Ron 1948- *WhoAmP 91*
**Fuller**, Roy 1912- *ConNov 91, ConPo 91, FacFETw, RfGEnL 91, WrDr 92*
**Fuller**, Roy 1912-1991 *ConAu 135*
**Fuller**, Roy Broadbent 1912- *IntAu&W 91, IntWW 91, Who 92*
**Fuller**, Roy Joseph 1939- *AmMWSc 92*
**Fuller**, Rufus Clinton 1925- *AmMWSc 92*
**Fuller**, Ruth Louvenia 1937- *WhoWest 92*
**Fuller**, Samuel 1911- *IntAu&W 91, IntDcF 2-2 [port]*
**Fuller**, Samuel 1912- *IntMPA 92*
**Fuller**, Samuel Ashby 1924- *WhoAmL 92*
**Fuller**, Samuel Henry 1946- *AmMWSc 92*
**Fuller**, Simon William John 1943- *Who 92*
**Fuller**, Stephen William 1945- *AmMWSc 92*
**Fuller**, Terry Ray 1953- *WhoAmL 92*
**Fuller**, Thomas Blount 1857-1927 *DcNCBi 2*
**Fuller**, Thomas Charles 1832-1901 *DcNCBi 2*
**Fuller**, Thomas Charles 1918- *AmMWSc 92*
**Fuller**, Thomas Oscar 1867-1942 *DcNCBi 2, RelLAm 91*
**Fuller**, Thomas S. 1934- *WhoBlA 92*
**Fuller**, Violet 1920- *TwCPaSc*
**Fuller**, Wallace Hamilton 1915- *AmMWSc 92*
**Fuller**, Wanda 1938- *WhoAmP 91*
**Fuller**, Wayne Arthur 1931- *AmMWSc 92*
**Fuller**, Wayne Maurice 1946- *WhoFI 92*
**Fuller**, Wayne P 1932- *WhoAmP 91*
**Fuller**, Wendy Webb 1952- *AmMWSc 92*
**Fuller**, William Albert 1924- *AmMWSc 92*
**Fuller**, William P *WhoAmP 91*
**Fuller**, William Richard 1920- *AmMWSc 92*
**Fuller**, William Roger 1949- *WhoWest 92*
**Fuller**, Williamson Whitehead 1858-1934 *DcNCBi 2*
**Fuller-Acland-Hood**, William *Who 92*
**Fullerton**, Alexander 1924- *WrDr 92*
**Fullerton**, Alexander Fergus 1924- *IntAu&W 91*
**Fullerton**, Charles Michael 1932- *AmMWSc 92, WhoWest 92*
**Fullerton**, Charlotte Louise 1967- *WhoEnt 92*
**Fullerton**, David Stanley 1941- *AmMWSc 92*
**Fullerton**, Dwight Story 1943- *AmMWSc 92*
**Fullerton**, Gail 1927- *WrDr 92*
**Fullerton**, Gail Jackson 1927- *WhoWest 92*
**Fullerton**, H P 1912- *AmMWSc 92*
**Fullerton**, Larry Wayne 1950- *AmMWSc 92*
**Fullerton**, Lawrence Rae 1952- *WhoAmL 92*
**Fullerton**, Mark Davis 1950- *WhoAmL 92*
**Fullerton**, Peter George Patrick Downing 1930- *Who 92*
**Fullerton**, R. Donald 1931- *IntWW 91, WhoFI 92*
**Fullerton**, Ralph O 1931- *AmMWSc 92*
**Fullerton**, Thomas Mankin, Jr. 1959- *WhoFI 92*
**Fullerton**, William Hugh 1939- *IntWW 91, Who 92*
**Fullhart**, Lawrence, Jr 1920- *AmMWSc 92*
**Fullhart**, Robert Lee 1931- *WhoFI 92*
**Fullilove**, Paul A., Sr. 1916- *WhoBlA 92*
**Fulling**, Stephen Albert 1945- *AmMWSc 92*
**Fullman**, R L 1922- *AmMWSc 92*
**Fullmer**, Charles Walter 1932- *WhoRel 92*
**Fullmer**, George Clinton 1922- *AmMWSc 92*
**Fullmer**, Harold Milton 1918- *AmMWSc 92*
**Fullmer**, June Zimmerman 1920- *AmMWSc 92*
**Fullmer**, Lee Wayne 1931- *WhoRel 92*
**Fullmer**, Ronald K *WhoAmP 91*
**Fullmer**, Steven Mark 1956- *WhoFI 92, WhoWest 92*
**Fullmer**, Timothy Shawn 1963- *WhoWest 92*
**Fullwood**, Brent Lanard 1963- *WhoBlA 92*
**Fullwood**, Harlow, Jr. 1941- *WhoBlA 92*
**Fullwood**, Ralph Roy 1928- *AmMWSc 92*
**Fulmer**, Charles V 1920- *AmMWSc 92*
**Fulmer**, Elton 1864-1916 *BiInAmS*

**Fulmer**, Glenn Elton 1928- *AmMWSc 92*
**Fulmer**, Hugh Scott 1928- *AmMWSc 92*
**Fulmer**, Joseph G. 1950- *WhoEnt 92*
**Fulmer**, Michael Clifford 1954- *WhoFI 92, WhoMW 92*
**Fulmer**, R. Britt 1954- *WhoMW 92*
**Fulmer**, Richard W 1930- *AmMWSc 92*
**Fulmer**, Ronald Calhoun 1945- *WhoAmP 91*
**Fulmer**, Scott Gordon 1950- *WhoFI 92*
**Fulmer**, Vincent Anthony 1927- *WhoFI 92*
**Fulmor**, William 1913- *AmMWSc 92*
**Fulop**, Milford 1927- *AmMWSc 92*
**Fulop**, Robert Ernest 1926- *WhoMW 92, WhoRel 92*
**Fulop-Miller**, Rene 1891-1963 *LiExTwC*
**Fulop-Muller**, Rene 1891-1963 *LiExTwC*
**Fulp**, James Alan 1951- *WhoFI 92*
**Fulp**, Ronald Owen 1936- *AmMWSc 92*
**Fulthorpe**, Henry Joseph 1916- *Who 92*
**Fulton**, Alice *DrAPF 91*
**Fulton**, Alice 1952- *ConPo 91*
**Fulton**, Burt J. 1925- *WhoAmL 92*
**Fulton**, Chandler Montgomery 1934- *AmMWSc 92*
**Fulton**, Darrell Nelson 1946- *WhoFI 92, WhoMW 92*
**Fulton**, David Bryant 1863?-1941 *DcNCBi 2*
**Fulton**, David Campbell 1956- *WhoFI 92*
**Fulton**, Davie 1916- *Who 92*
**Fulton**, Donald Lee 1935- *WhoBlA 92*
**Fulton**, Dorothy Margaret Young 1926- *WhoMW 92*
**Fulton**, George P 1914- *AmMWSc 92*
**Fulton**, Hamilton d1834 *DcNCBi 2*
**Fulton**, Hamish 1946- *TwCPaSc*
**Fulton**, Henry W., Jr. 1934- *WhoAmL 92*
**Fulton**, J C 1923- *AmMWSc 92*
**Fulton**, James 1930- *DcTwDes*
**Fulton**, James W 1928- *AmMWSc 92*
**Fulton**, James Wayte, Jr. 1911- *WhoRel 92*
**Fulton**, James William 1921- *WhoMW 92*
**Fulton**, Joe Kirk, Jr. 1957- *WhoFI 92*
**Fulton**, John David 1937- *AmMWSc 92*
**Fulton**, John Francis 1933- *Who 92*
**Fulton**, Joseph Patton 1917- *AmMWSc 92*
**Fulton**, Len *DrAPF 91*
**Fulton**, Lorin Watkins 1963- *WhoEnt 92*
**Fulton**, Norman Robert 1935- *WhoFI 92, WhoWest 92*
**Fulton**, Paul 1934- *WhoFI 92*
**Fulton**, Paul F 1916- *AmMWSc 92*
**Fulton**, Richard Alsina 1926- *WhoAmL 92*
**Fulton**, Richard Delbert 1945- *WhoWest 92*
**Fulton**, Richard Harmon 1927- *WhoAmP 91*
**Fulton**, Robert 1765-1815 *BiInAmS, RComAH*
**Fulton**, Robert Andrew 1944- *Who 92*
**Fulton**, Robert Brank 1911- *WhoAmP 91*
**Fulton**, Robert Burwell 1849-1919 *BiInAmS*
**Fulton**, Robert D 1929- *WhoAmP 91*
**Fulton**, Robert E 1931- *AmMWSc 92*
**Fulton**, Robert Henry 1926- *WhoBlA 92*
**Fulton**, Robert John 1937- *AmMWSc 92*
**Fulton**, Robert Lester 1926- *WhoMW 92*
**Fulton**, Robert Lester 1935- *AmMWSc 92*
**Fulton**, Robert Paul 1958- *WhoRel 92*
**Fulton**, Robert Watt 1914- *AmMWSc 92*
**Fulton**, Robert Wesley 1942- *AmMWSc 92*
**Fulton**, Robin 1937- *ConPo 91, IntAu&W 91, WrDr 92*
**Fulton**, Sandy Michael 1943- *WhoFI 92*
**Fulton**, Thomas 1927- *AmMWSc 92*
**Fulton**, Thomas Benjamin 1918- *WhoRel 92*
**Fulton**, Tony E 1951- *WhoAmP 91*
**Fulton**, Winston Cordell 1943- *AmMWSc 92*
**Fulton-Bereal**, Arlene R. 1946- *WhoFI 92*
**Fults**, Daniel Webster, III 1953- *WhoWest 92*
**Fultyn**, Robert Victor 1933- *AmMWSc 92*
**Fultz**, Brent T 1955- *AmMWSc 92*
**Fultz**, Dave 1921- *AmMWSc 92*
**Fultz**, Philip Nathaniel 1943- *WhoWest 92*
**Fultz**, R Paul 1923- *AmMWSc 92*
**Fultz**, Robert Edward 1941- *WhoAmL 92*
**Fulvia** d40BC *EncAmaz 91*
**Fulwood**, Sam, III 1956- *WhoBlA 92*
**Fumagalli**, John David 1961- *WhoMW 92*
**Fumagalli**, Orazio 1921- *WhoMW 92*
**Fumento**, Rocco *DrAPF 91*
**Fumento**, Rocco 1923- *WrDr 92*
**Fumo**, Vincent J 1943- *WhoAmP 91*
**Funahashi**, Akira 1928- *WhoMW 92*
**Funahashi**, Masao 1913- *IntWW 91*
**Funck**, Dennis Light 1926- *AmMWSc 92*
**Funck**, Larry Lehman 1942- *AmMWSc 92*
**Funcke**, Liselotte 1918- *IntWW 91*
**Funder**, Friedrich 1872-1959 *EncTR 91*
**Funderburg**, I. Owen 1924- *WhoBlA 92*
**Funderburgh**, James Louis 1945- *AmMWSc 92*
**Funderburk**, Charles Edward 1961- *WhoRel 92*
**Funderburk**, David 1944- *WhoAmP 91*
**Funderburk**, David Clarkson 1945- *WhoWest 92*
**Funderburk**, Kenneth LeRoy 1936- *WhoAmP 91*
**Funderburk**, Larry Bryce 1939- *WhoAmL 92*
**Funderburk**, Raymond 1944- *WhoAmL 92*
**Funderburk**, William Watson 1931- *WhoBlA 92*
**Fundoianu**, Barbu 1898- *LiExTwC*
**Funes**, Gregorio 1749-1829 *HisDSpE*
**Funes Villalpando**, Ambrosio de *HisDSpE*
**Fung**, Adrian K 1936- *AmMWSc 92*
**Fung**, Daniel Yee Chak 1942- *AmMWSc 92*
**Fung**, Henry C, Jr 1939- *AmMWSc 92*
**Fung**, Ho-Leung 1943- *AmMWSc 92*
**Fung**, Honpong 1920- *AmMWSc 92*
**Fung**, K Y 1948- *AmMWSc 92*
**Fung**, Kenneth Ping-Fan 1911- *Who 92*
**Fung**, Leslie Wo-Mei 1946- *AmMWSc 92*
**Fung**, Shun Chong 1943- *AmMWSc 92*
**Fung**, Steven 1951- *AmMWSc 92*
**Fung**, Sui-an 1922- *AmMWSc 92*
**Fung**, Yuan-Cheng B 1919- *AmMWSc 92*
**Funge**, Robert *DrAPF 91*
**Funger**, Hans 1891-1945 *EncTR 91*
**Funk**, Albert Peter 1919- *WhoAmL 92*
**Funk**, Cyril Reed, Jr 1928- *AmMWSc 92*
**Funk**, David Albert 1927- *WhoAmL 92, WhoMW 92*
**Funk**, David Charles 1947- *WhoEnt 92*
**Funk**, David Crozier 1922- *AmMWSc 92*
**Funk**, David Truman 1929- *AmMWSc 92*
**Funk**, Emerson Gornflow, Jr 1931- *AmMWSc 92*
**Funk**, Glenn Albert 1942- *AmMWSc 92*
**Funk**, James Ellis 1932- *AmMWSc 92*
**Funk**, James William, Jr. 1947- *WhoMW 92*
**Funk**, John Fretz 1835-1930 *AmPeW, RelLAm 91*
**Funk**, John Leon 1909- *AmMWSc 92*
**Funk**, Joyce Anne 1952- *WhoRel 92*
**Funk**, Milton Albert 1918- *WhoWest 92*
**Funk**, Richard Cullen 1934- *AmMWSc 92*
**Funk**, Robert Francis 1930- *WhoEnt 92*
**Funk**, S. Jeff 1959- *WhoAmL 92*
**Funk**, Sherman Maxwell 1925- *WhoAmP 91*
**Funk**, Terri Florin 1961- *WhoFI 92*
**Funk**, Virgil Clarence 1937- *WhoRel 92*
**Funk**, Walther 1890-1960 *EncTR 91 [port]*
**Funk**, Walther Emanuel 1890-1960 *BiDExR*
**Funk**, William Henry 1933- *AmMWSc 92*
**Funka**, Thomas Howard 1946- *WhoRel 92*
**Funkadelic** *NewAmDM*
**Funke**, David Eric 1961- *WhoAmL 92*
**Funke**, Gosta Werner 1906- *IntWW 91*
**Funke**, Phillip T 1932- *AmMWSc 92*
**Funkenbusch**, Walter W 1918- *AmMWSc 92*
**Funkhouser**, David Edward 1941- *WhoAmL 92*
**Funkhouser**, Edward Allen 1945- *AmMWSc 92*
**Funkhouser**, Erica *DrAPF 91*
**Funkhouser**, Erica 1949- *ConAu 135*
**Funkhouser**, Jane D 1939- *AmMWSc 92*
**Funkhouser**, Jeffrey Gregg 1961- *WhoMW 92*
**Funkhouser**, John Tower 1928- *AmMWSc 92*
**Funkhouser**, Morton Littell, Jr. 1943- *WhoRel 92*
**Funkhouser**, Richard 1917- *WhoAmP 91*
**Funkhouser**, Richard Daniel Brunk 1935- *WhoMW 92*
**Funkhouser**, Tzena Lynn 1958- *WhoEnt 92*
**Funn**, Carlton A., Sr. 1932- *WhoBlA 92*
**Funn**, Courtney Harris 1941- *WhoBlA 92*
**Funsten**, Herbert Oliver, III 1962- *AmMWSc 92*
**Funston**, Frederick 1865-1917 *FacFETw*
**Funston**, G. Keith 1910- *Who 92*
**Funt**, Allen 1914- *ConTFT 9, IntMPA 92*
**Funt**, B Lionel 1924- *AmMWSc 92*
**Funt**, Nancy Bodner 1949- *WhoFI 92*
**Funteas**, Roula Ellyse 1966- *WhoEnt 92*
**Fuoco**, Philip Stephen 1946- *WhoAmL 92*
**Fuoss**, Raymond Matthew 1905- *AmMWSc 92*
**Fuqua**, Don 1933- *WhoAmP 91*
**Fuqua**, Harry Matthew 1959- *WhoAmL 92*
**Fuqua**, John Brooks 1918- *WhoFI 92*
**Fuqua**, Mary Elizabeth 1922- *AmMWSc 92*
**Fuqua**, Robert Verne 1928- *WhoRel 92*
**Fuqua**, Thomas Edward 1942- *WhoAmP 91*
**Fuquay**, James Jenkins 1924- *AmMWSc 92*
**Fuquay**, John Wade 1933- *AmMWSc 92*
**Fur**, Lajos 1938- *IntWW 91*
**Furan**, Rodney Luke Leroy 1927- *WhoWest 92*
**Furay**, Catherine J. 1952- *WhoAmL 92*
**Furbay**, Walter M. 1920- *WhoFI 92*
**Furber**, Robert 1921- *Who 92*
**Furbish**, Francis Scott 1940- *AmMWSc 92*
**Furby**, Neal Washburn 1912- *AmMWSc 92*
**Furby**, Tommy Eugene 1953- *WhoAmL 92*
**Furches**, David Moffatt 1832-1908 *DcNCBi 2*
**Furchgott**, Robert Francis 1916- *AmMWSc 92*
**Furcinitti**, Paul Stephen 1949- *AmMWSc 92*
**Furco**, Joseph John 1951- *WhoMW 92*
**Furcolo**, Foster 1917- *WhoAmP 91*
**Furcon**, John Edward 1942- *WhoMW 92*
**Furdyna**, Jacek K 1933- *AmMWSc 92*
**Furer**, Arthur Carl Othmar 1920- *IntWW 91*
**Furer-Haimendorf**, Christoph von 1909- *Who 92*
**Furesz**, John 1927- *AmMWSc 92*
**Furet**, Francois 1927- *IntWW 91*
**Furey**, Dorothy 1940- *WhoHisp 92*
**Furey**, James Joseph 1938- *WhoFI 92*
**Furey**, John J. 1949- *WhoAmL 92*
**Furey**, Patrick Dennis 1954- *WhoAmL 92, WhoWest 92*
**Furey**, Robert Joseph 1956- *WhoMW 92*
**Furey**, Robert Lawrence 1941- *AmMWSc 92*
**Furey**, Sherman Francis, Jr. 1919- *WhoAmL 92*
**Furfari**, Frank A 1915- *AmMWSc 92*
**Furfine**, Charles Stuart 1936- *AmMWSc 92*
**Furgason**, Robert Roy 1935- *AmMWSc 92*
**Furgiuele**, Angelo Ralph 1929- *AmMWSc 92*
**Furgler**, Kurt 1924- *IntWW 91*
**Furhiman**, Robert Lee 1940- *WhoWest 92*
**Furie**, Bruce 1944- *AmMWSc 92*
**Furie**, Sidney J 1933- *IntMPA 92*
**Furimsky**, Stephen, Jr. 1924- *WhoWest 92*
**Furkin**, David Scott 1957- *WhoAmL 92*
**Furlan**, Valentin 1942- *AmMWSc 92*
**Furlanetto**, Richard W 1945- *AmMWSc 92*
**Furlaud**, Richard Mortimer 1923- *WhoFI 92*
**Furlong**, Charles Richard 1950- *WhoFI 92*
**Furlong**, Edward V., Jr. 1937- *WhoFI 92*
**Furlong**, Henry T 1928- *WhoIns 92*
**Furlong**, Ira E 1931- *AmMWSc 92*
**Furlong**, Monica 1930- *Who 92*
**Furlong**, Nicholas 1929- *IntAu&W 91*
**Furlong**, Norman Burr, Jr 1931- *AmMWSc 92*
**Furlong**, Patrick David 1948- *WhoMW 92*
**Furlong**, Richard W 1929- *AmMWSc 92*
**Furlong**, Robert B 1934- *AmMWSc 92*
**Furlong**, Robert Joseph 1954- *WhoEnt 92*
**Furlong**, Robert Stafford 1904- *Who 92*
**Furlong**, Ronald *Who 92*
**Furlonger**, Robert William 1921- *Who 92*
**Furlow**, Mack Vernon, Jr. 1931- *WhoMW 92*
**Furlow**, Mary Beverley 1933- *WhoWest 92*
**Furlow**, Rita *WhoAmP 91*
**Furman**, Anthony Michael 1934- *WhoFI 92*
**Furman**, David Stephen 1945- *WhoWest 92*
**Furman**, Deane Philip 1915- *AmMWSc 92*
**Furman**, Evelyn Edith 1913- *WhoEnt 92*
**Furman**, Howard 1938- *WhoAmL 92*
**Furman**, James B. 1937- *WhoBlA 92*
**Furman**, James Merle 1932- *WhoMW 92*
**Furman**, Laura *DrAPF 91*
**Furman**, Marc 1953- *WhoAmL 92*
**Furman**, Rexford D. 1943- *WhoRel 92*
**Furman**, Robert Howard 1918- *AmMWSc 92*
**Furman**, Robert McKnight 1846-1904 *DcNCBi 2*
**Furman**, Roy Lance 1939- *WhoFI 92*
**Furman**, Seymour 1931- *AmMWSc 92*
**Furman**, Stan 1932- *WhoAmP 91*
**Furman**, Walter Laurie 1913- *WhoRel 92*
**Furmanov**, Dimitri Andreyevich 1891-1926 *FacFETw*
**Furmanov**, Dmitriy Andreevich 1891-1926 *SovUnBD*
**Furmanski**, Philip 1946- *AmMWSc 92*
**Furmston**, Bentley Edwin 1931- *Who 92*
**Furmston**, Michael Philip 1933- *Who 92*
**Furnas**, David William 1931- *AmMWSc 92*
**Furnell**, Raymond 1935- *Who 92*
**Furner**, Derek Jack 1921- *Who 92*
**Furner**, Raymond Lynn 1943- *AmMWSc 92*
**Furness** *Who 92*
**Furness**, Viscount 1929- *Who 92*
**Furness**, Alan Edwin 1937- *Who 92*
**Furness**, Betty *LesBEnT 92*
**Furness**, Betty 1916- *IntMPA 92, WhoEnt 92*
**Furness**, Frank 1839-1912 *DcTwDes*
**Furness**, Horace Howard 1833-1912 *BenetAL 91*
**Furness**, Horace Howard, Jr. 1865-1930 *BenetAL 91*
**Furness**, Peter John 1956- *WhoAmL 92*
**Furness**, Rex L 1923- *WhoAmP 91*
**Furness**, Robin *Who 92*
**Furness**, Simon John 1936- *Who 92*
**Furness**, Stephen 1933- *Who 92*
**Furney**, Linda Jeanne 1947- *WhoAmP 91, WhoMW 92*
**Furnier**, Vincent 1948- *WhoEnt 92*
**Furnish**, Dorothy Jean 1921- *WhoRel 92*
**Furnish**, Raymond Douglas 1949- *WhoWest 92*
**Furnish**, Victor Paul 1931- *WhoRel 92, WrDr 92*
**Furnish**, Zelma M 1927- *WhoAmP 91*
**Furniss**, Delma 1934- *WhoAmP 91*
**Furniss**, Peter 1919- *Who 92*
**Furniss**, Susan West 1924- *WhoAmP 91*
**Furnival**, George Mason 1925- *AmMWSc 92*
**Furnival**, George Mitchell 1908- *WhoWest 92*
**Furnival**, John 1933- *TwCPaSc*
**Furnival Jones**, Martin 1912- *Who 92*
**Furnivall**, Barony 1933- *Who 92*
**Furnweger**, Karen 1951- *WhoMW 92*
**Furois**, Michael Carl 1960- *WhoFI 92, WhoMW 92*
**Furphy**, Joseph 1843-1912 *RfGEnL 91*
**Furr**, Aaron Keith 1932- *AmMWSc 92*
**Furr**, Ann Longwell 1945- *WhoAmL 92*
**Furr**, Carter Branham Snow 1932- *WhoAmL 92*
**Furr**, Gary Allison 1954- *WhoRel 92*
**Furr**, Quint Eugene 1921- *WhoFI 92*
**Furr**, Richard Michael 1942- *WhoFI 92*
**Furr**, Robert Bivens, Jr. 1957- *WhoAmL 92*
**Furrer**, James Douglas 1952- *WhoEnt 92*
**Furrer**, John D 1920- *AmMWSc 92*
**Furrer**, John Rudolf 1927- *WhoFI 92*
**Furrer**, Lawrence Austin 1934- *WhoMW 92*
**Furrh**, Lemuel Christopher 1921- *WhoAmP 91*
**Furrow**, Gregory Paul 1960- *WhoMW 92*
**Furrow**, Stanley Donald 1934- *AmMWSc 92*
**Furry**, Benjamin K 1923- *AmMWSc 92*
**Furry**, Ronald B 1931- *AmMWSc 92*
**Fursa**, Edmond Carl 1947- *WhoFI 92*
**Fursdon**, Francis William Edward 1925- *Who 92*
**Furse**, Clare Taylor 1931- *AmMWSc 92*
**Furse**, Paul 1904- *TwCPaSc*
**Furshpan**, Edwin Jean 1928- *AmMWSc 92*
**Furst**, Alan 1941- *ConAu 34NR*
**Furst**, Anton d1991 *NewYTBS 91*
**Furst**, Arthur 1914- *AmMWSc 92*
**Furst**, Austin O. *IntMPA 92*
**Furst**, Henry d1967 *LiExTwC*
**Furst**, Henry Fairchild 1951- *WhoAmL 92*
**Furst**, Janos Kalman 1935- *IntWW 91*
**Furst**, John Douglas 1959- *WhoFI 92*
**Furst**, Lilian R. 1931- *WrDr 92*
**Furst**, Merrick Lee 1955- *AmMWSc 92*
**Furst**, Milton 1921- *AmMWSc 92*
**Furst**, Patricia Ann *WhoIns 92*
**Furst**, Stephen Andrew *Who 92*
**Furst**, Ulrich Richard 1913- *AmMWSc 92*
**Furste**, Wesley Leonard, II 1915- *WhoMW 92*
**Furstenberg**, Hillel *AmMWSc 92*
**Furstman**, Shirley Elsie Daddow 1930- *WhoFI 92*
**Furtado**, Dolores 1938- *AmMWSc 92, WhoMW 92*
**Furtado**, Robert Audley 1912- *Who 92*
**Furtado**, Stephen Eugene 1942- *WhoEnt 92*
**Furtado**, Victor Cunha 1937- *AmMWSc 92*
**Furtak**, Thomas Elton 1949- *AmMWSc 92*
**Furter**, W F 1931- *AmMWSc 92*
**Furth**, David George 1945- *AmMWSc 92*
**Furth**, Eugene David 1929- *AmMWSc 92*
**Furth**, Frederick Paul 1934- *WhoAmP 91*
**Furth**, George 1932- *WhoEnt 92, WrDr 92*
**Furth**, Harold Paul 1930- *AmMWSc 92, IntWW 91*
**Furth**, John J 1929- *AmMWSc 92*
**Furth**, Warren Wolfgang 1928- *IntWW 91*
**Furthmayr**, Heinz 1941- *AmMWSc 92*
**Furtick**, Russell Harry 1958- *WhoFI 92*
**Furtney**, Diane *DrAPF 91*
**Furton**, George C *WhoAmP 91*
**Furtseva**, Yekaterina Alekseevna 1910-1974 *SovUnBD*
**Furtwangler**, Virginia *DrAPF 91*
**Furtwangler**, Virginia Ann 1932- *IntAu&W 91*
**Furtwangler**, Wilhelm 1886-1954 *EncTR 91 [port], FacFETw, NewAmDM*
**Furubotn**, Eirik Grundtvig 1923- *WhoFI 92*
**Furugard**, Birger 1887-1961 *BiDExR*

**Furuhata,** Taketo 1930- *WhoFI 92*
**Furui,** Yoshimi *IntWW 91*
**Furukawa,** David Hiroshi 1938- *AmMWSc 92*
**Furukawa,** George Tadaharu 1921- *AmMWSc 92*
**Furukawa,** Shiro Bruce 1953- *WhoFI 92*
**Furukawa,** Toshiharu 1948- *AmMWSc 92*
**Furumoto,** Augustine S 1927- *AmMWSc 92*
**Furumoto,** Horace Wataru 1931- *AmMWSc 92*
**Furumoto,** Warren Akira 1934- *AmMWSc 92*
**Furusawa,** Eiichi 1928- *AmMWSc 92*
**Furuta,** Tokuji 1925- *AmMWSc 92*
**Furutan,** Ali-Akbar 1905- *WhoRel 92*
**Furuto,** Donald K 1948- *AmMWSc 92*
**Furuya,** Toru 1909- *IntWW 91*
**Fusaro,** Bernard A 1924- *AmMWSc 92*
**Fusaro,** Craig Allen 1948- *AmMWSc 92*
**Fusaro,** Ramon Michael 1927- *AmMWSc 92*
**Fusaro,** Robert Francis Xavier 1941- *WhoAmL 92*
**Fuscaldo,** Anthony Alfred 1939- *AmMWSc 92*
**Fuscaldo,** Kathryn Elizabeth 1931- *AmMWSc 92*
**Fusco,** Andrew G. 1948- *WhoAmL 92*
**Fusco,** Angelo 1953- *WhoAmP 91*
**Fusco,** Anthony Salvatore 1954- *WhoFI 92*
**Fusco,** Carmen Louise *AmMWSc 92*
**Fusco,** David Michael 1959- *WhoAmL 92*
**Fusco,** Gabriel Carmine 1936- *AmMWSc 92*
**Fusco,** Jay William 1949- *WhoAmL 92*
**Fusco,** Louis Michael 1949- *WhoAmP 91*
**Fusco,** Madeline M 1924- *AmMWSc 92*
**Fusco,** Robert Angelo 1941- *AmMWSc 92*
**Fusco,** Sal M. 1932- *WhoWest 92*
**Fusco,** Victor 1949- *WhoAmL 92*
**Fuse,** Bobby LeAndrew, Jr. 1952- *WhoBlA 92*
**Fusek,** Serena *DrAPF 91*
**Fuseler,** John William 1943- *AmMWSc 92*
**Fuselier,** Louis Alfred 1932- *WhoAmL 92*
**Fushtey,** Stephen George 1924- *AmMWSc 92*
**Fusi,** Juan Pablo 1945- *IntWW 91*
**Fusillier,** Richard 1923- *WhoEnt 92*
**Fusillo,** Lisa Ann 1951- *WhoEnt 92*
**Fusner,** Neal Henry 1958- *WhoMW 92*
**Fuson,** Anne Beaty 1928- *WhoAmP 91*
**Fuson,** Ben W. 1911- *WrDr 92*
**Fuson,** Benjamin Willis 1911- *IntAu&W 91*
**Fuson,** Douglas Finley 1944- *WhoAmL 92*
**Fuson,** Ernest Wayne 1947- *AmMWSc 92*
**Fuson,** Nelson 1913- *AmMWSc 92*
**Fuson,** Rickey Lee 1954- *WhoRel 92*
**Fuson,** Robert L 1932- *AmMWSc 92*
**Fuson,** Roger Baker 1916- *AmMWSc 92*
**Fuss,** John M. 1930- *WhoFI 92*
**Fusscas,** J Peter *WhoAmP 91*
**Fussell,** Aaron E *WhoAmP 91*
**Fussell,** Catharine Pugh 1919- *AmMWSc 92*
**Fussell,** Michael 1927-1974 *TwCPaSc*
**Fussell,** Paul 1924- *ConAu 35NR, IntAu&W 91, IntWW 91, WrDr 92*
**Fussell,** Ronald Moi 1956- *WhoFI 92*
**Fussichen,** Kenneth 1950- *WhoMW 92*
**Fussner,** Frank Smith 1920- *WrDr 92*
**Fuste,** Jose Antonio 1943- *WhoAmL 92*
**Fuster,** Jaime B. 1941- *AlmAP 92 [port], WhoAmP 91, WhoHisp 92*
**Fuster,** Joaquin Maria 1930- *AmMWSc 92*
**Fuston,** James Lynn 1959- *WhoEnt 92*
**Futabatei Shimei** 1864-1909 *TwCLC 44*
**Futch,** Archer Hamner 1925- *AmMWSc 92, WhoWest 92*
**Futch,** David Gardner 1932- *AmMWSc 92*
**Futch,** Edward 1911- *WhoBlA 92*
**Futcher,** Anthony Graham 1941- *AmMWSc 92*
**Futcher,** Palmer Howard 1910- *AmMWSc 92*
**Futey,** Bohdan A. 1939- *WhoAmL 92*
**Futia,** Leo R 1919- *WhoIns 92*
**Futoran,** Herbert S 1942- *WhoIns 92*
**Futral,** James Robert 1944- *WhoRel 92*
**Futral,** Larry Lee 1942- *WhoRel 92*
**Futrell,** Ashley Brown, Jr 1956- *WhoAmP 91*
**Futrell,** J William 1941- *AmMWSc 92*
**Futrell,** Jean H 1933- *AmMWSc 92*
**Futrell,** Mary Feltner 1924- *AmMWSc 92*
**Futrell,** Mary Hatwood 1940- *NotBlAW 92 [port], WhoBlA 92*
**Futrell,** Robert Frank 1917- *WhoFI 92*
**Futrell,** Stephan Ray 1956- *WhoAmL 92*
**Futrell,** William Benjamin, III 1942- *WhoEnt 92*
**utrelle,** Jacques 1875-1912 *ScFEYrs*
**utrelle,** Robert Peel 1937- *AmMWSc 92*
**utterer,** Karen Lehner 1953- *WhoEnt 92*
**utuyma,** Douglas Joel 1942- *AmMWSc 92*
**Fux,** Johann Joseph 1660-1741 *NewAmDM*
**Fuxa,** James Roderick 1949- *AmMWSc 92*
**Fuzak,** John Francis 1948- *WhoAmL 92*
**Fuzek,** John Frank 1921- *AmMWSc 92*
**Fuzesi,** Stephen, Jr. 1948- *WhoAmL 92*
**Fyans,** Thomas *WhoRel 92*
**Fye,** Deryk 1947- *TwCPaSc*
**Fye,** Robert Eaton 1924- *AmMWSc 92*
**Fye,** Rodney Wayne 1928- *WhoWest 92*
**Fyfe,** H B 1918- *TwCSFW 91*
**Fyfe,** I Millar 1925- *AmMWSc 92*
**Fyfe,** James Arthur 1941- *AmMWSc 92*
**Fyfe,** Maria 1938- *Who 92*
**Fyfe,** Richard Ross 1941- *AmMWSc 92*
**Fyfe,** Robert Joseph 1956- *WhoMW 92*
**Fyfe,** William Arthur 1916- *WhoAmP 91*
**Fyfe,** William Sefton 1927- *AmMWSc 92, IntWW 91, Who 92*
**Fyffe,** Barry Keith 1936- *WhoEnt 92*
**Fyffe,** Darrel Wayne 1941- *WhoMW 92*
**Fyffe,** David Eugene 1925- *AmMWSc 92*
**Fyfield,** Frances *ConAu 135*
**Fyhrie,** David Paul 1955- *AmMWSc 92*
**Fyjis-Walker,** Richard Alwyne 1927- *Who 92*
**Fykes,** Leroy Matthews, Jr. 1945- *WhoBlA 92*
**Fyler,** Carl John 1921- *WhoMW 92*
**Fyles,** Franklin 1847-1911 *BenetAL 91*
**Fyles,** John Gladstone 1923- *AmMWSc 92*
**Fymat,** Alain L 1938- *AmMWSc 92*
**Fyne,** Neal *ScFEYrs*
**Fysh,** Robert Michael 1940- *Who 92*
**Fysh,** Wilmot Hudson 1895-1974 *ConAu 134*
**Fyson,** J. G. 1904- *WrDr 92*
**Fyson,** Jenny Grace 1904- *IntAu&W 91*
**Fystrom,** Dell O 1937- *AmMWSc 92*
**Fytelson,** Milton 1917- *AmMWSc 92*

# G

**G H P** 1844-1930 *ScFEYrs*
**Gaafar,** Sayed Mohammed 1924- *AmMWSc 92*
**Gaal,** Ilse Lisl Novak 1924- *AmMWSc 92*
**Gaal,** Istvan 1933- *IntDcF 2-2*
**Gaal,** James Geza 1960- *WhoMW 92*
**Gaal,** Jeffrey Andrew 1956- *WhoFI 92*
**Gaal,** John 1952- *WhoAmL 92*
**Gaal,** Robert A P 1929- *AmMWSc 92*
**Gaal,** Steven Alexander 1924- *AmMWSc 92*
**Gaalova,** Barbara Kanzler 1953- *WhoFI 92*
**Gaalswyk,** Arie 1918- *AmMWSc 92*
**Gaan,** Margaret 1914- *IntAu&W 91, SmATA 65 [port], WrDr 92*
**Gaar,** Kermit Albert, Jr 1934- *AmMWSc 92*
**Gaar,** Marilyn A. Wiegraffe 1946- *WhoMW 92*
**Gaar,** Norman Edward 1929- *WhoAmL 92, WhoMW 92*
**Gaard,** Thomas J 1939- *WhoIns 92*
**Gaarder,** Newell Thomas 1939- *AmMWSc 92*
**Gaarenstroom,** Stephen William 1950- *AmMWSc 92, WhoMW 92*
**Gabain,** Ethel 1883-1950 *TwCPaSc*
**Gabaldon,** Benjamin Alfonso 1926- *WhoHisp 92*
**Gabaldon,** Julia K. 1947- *WhoHisp 92*
**Gabaldon,** Tony *WhoAmP 91*
**Gabaldon,** Tony 1930- *WhoHisp 92*
**Gaballah,** Saeed S *AmMWSc 92*
**Gabathuler,** Erwin 1933- *Who 92*
**Gabay,** Diane Martin 1954- *WhoWest 92*
**Gabay,** Donald D 1935- *WhoIns 92*
**Gabay,** Jonathan Glenn 1956- *AmMWSc 92*
**Gabay,** Sabit 1922- *AmMWSc 92*
**Gabb,** Harry 1909- *Who 92*
**Gabb,** Timothy Paul 1958- *AmMWSc 92*
**Gabb,** William More 1839-1878 *BiInAmS*
**Gabbai,** Moni E 1943- *WhoIns 92*
**Gabbard,** Douglas, II 1952- *WhoAmL 92*
**Gabbard,** Fletcher 1930- *AmMWSc 92*
**Gabbard,** G.N. *DrAPF 91*
**Gabbard,** Gregory Alan 1949- *WhoAmL 92*
**Gabbard,** Ralph *WhoEnt 92*
**Gabbard,** Thomas Eugene 1955- *WhoEnt 92*
**Gabbe,** John Daniel 1929- *AmMWSc 92*
**Gabbert,** Daniel Franklin 1952- *WhoEnt 92*
**Gabbert,** Janice Jean 1940- *WhoMW 92*
**Gabbert,** Paul George 1935- *AmMWSc 92*
**Gabbert,** William Lee 1915- *WhoRel 92*
**Gabbiani,** Giulio 1937- *AmMWSc 92*
**Gabbin,** Alexander Lee 1945- *WhoBlA 92*
**Gabbin,** Joanne Veal 1946- *WhoBlA 92*
**Gabel,** Albert A 1930- *AmMWSc 92*
**Gabel,** Dorothy Lillian 1936- *WhoMW 92*
**Gabel,** Edward Alexander 1947- *WhoIns 92*
**Gabel,** Frederick D 1912- *WhoIns 92*
**Gabel,** Frederick Daniel, Jr 1938- *WhoIns 92*
**Gabel,** Gary Joseph 1949- *WhoMW 92*
**Gabel,** George DeSaussure, Jr. 1940- *WhoAmL 92, WhoFI 92*
**Gabel,** James Gray, III 1935- *WhoMW 92*
**Gabel,** James Russel 1918- *AmMWSc 92*
**Gabel,** Johannes Karl 1952- *WhoAmL 92*
**Gabel,** Joseph C *AmMWSc 92*
**Gabel,** Richard Allen 1946- *AmMWSc 92*
**Gabelman,** Irving J 1918- *AmMWSc 92*
**Gabelman,** Irving Jacob 1918- *WhoFI 92*
**Gabelman,** John Warren 1921- *WhoWest 92*
**Gabelman,** Warren Henry 1921- *AmMWSc 92*
**Gabelnick,** Henry Lewis 1940- *AmMWSc 92*
**Gaber,** Bruce Paul 1941- *AmMWSc 92*
**Gaber,** Frank Charles, III 1958- *WhoWest 92*
**Gaber,** George Joseph 1916- *WhoEnt 92*
**Gaber,** Jason Lee 1957- *WhoRel 92*
**Gaberino,** John Anthony, Jr. 1941- *WhoAmL 92*
**Gaberman,** Harry 1913- *WhoAmL 92, WhoFI 92*
**Gaberman,** Judith *DrAPF 91*
**Gaberman,** Richard Miles 1938- *WhoAmL 92*
**Gaberson,** Howard Axel 1931- *WhoWest 92*
**Gabert,** Alex W. *WhoHisp 92*
**Gabert,** Michael Allen 1948- *WhoMW 92*
**Gabet,** Stephen J *WhoAmP 91*
**Gabiera,** Fernando 1941- *LiExTwC*
**Gabinet,** Leon 1927- *WhoAmL 92*
**Gabinski,** Theris M 1938- *WhoAmP 91*
**Gabis,** Damien Anthony 1942- *AmMWSc 92*
**Gable,** Christopher *IntWW 91*
**Gable,** Clark 1901-1960 *FacFETw [port]*
**Gable,** David Lee 1943- *WhoRel 92*
**Gable,** Frederick W. 1947- *WhoEnt 92*
**Gable,** G. Ellis 1905- *WhoAmL 92*
**Gable,** George Daniel 1863-1911 *BiInAmS*
**Gable,** James Jackson, Jr 1918- *AmMWSc 92*
**Gable,** Karen Elaine 1939- *WhoMW 92*
**Gable,** Michael F 1945- *AmMWSc 92*
**Gable,** Nancy Eileen 1955- *WhoRel 92*
**Gable,** Ralph William 1929- *AmMWSc 92*
**Gable,** Richard Warren 1938- *WhoAmL 92*
**Gable,** Robert Elledy 1934- *WhoAmP 91, WhoFI 92*
**Gablentz,** Otto von der 1930- *IntWW 91*
**Gabler,** Robert Clair 1933- *WhoWest 92*
**Gabler,** Robert Earl 1927- *AmMWSc 92*
**Gabler,** Russell Allan 1922- *WhoRel 92*
**Gabler,** Walter Louis 1931- *AmMWSc 92*
**Gabler-Hover,** Janet A. 1953- *ConAu 135*
**Gablik,** Suzi 1934- *WrDr 92*
**Gabliks,** Janis 1924- *AmMWSc 92*
**Gabo,** Naum 1890-1977 *FacFETw, ModArCr 2 [port], SovUnBD*
**Gaboimilla** *EncAmaz 91*
**Gabor,** Al *DrAPF 91*
**Gabor,** Andrew John 1935- *AmMWSc 92*
**Gabor,** Carol Ann Evelyn 1946- *WhoMW 92*
**Gabor,** Dennis 1900-1979 *FacFETw, WhoNob 90*
**Gabor,** Frank 1918- *WhoFI 92, WhoIns 92*
**Gabor,** Jeffrey Alan 1942- *WhoFI 92*
**Gabor,** John Dewain 1932- *AmMWSc 92*
**Gabor,** Thomas 1925- *AmMWSc 92*
**Gabor,** Zsa Zsa 1917- *WhoEnt 92*
**Gabor,** Zsa Zsa 1918- *IntMPA 92*
**Gabour,** Jim 1947- *WhoEnt 92*
**Gabourel,** John Dustan 1928- *AmMWSc 92*
**Gaboury,** Glen Arthur 1957- *WhoRel 92*
**Gabovitch,** Steven Alan 1953- *WhoAmL 92*
**Gabovitch,** William 1922- *WhoAmL 92*
**Gabovitch,** William Neal 1962- *WhoAmL 92*
**Gabre-Sellassie,** Zewde 1926- *IntWW 91*
**Gabria,** Joanne Bakaitis 1945- *WhoFI 92*
**Gabrick,** Robert William 1940- *WhoMW 92*
**Gabridge,** Michael Gregory 1943- *AmMWSc 92*
**Gabriel,** Barbra L 1953- *AmMWSc 92*
**Gabriel,** Benjamin Moses 1931- *WhoBlA 92*
**Gabriel,** Cedric John 1935- *AmMWSc 92*
**Gabriel,** Daniel *DrAPF 91*
**Gabriel,** Dennis R. 1950- *WhoHisp 92*
**Gabriel,** Eberhard John 1942- *WhoAmL 92, WhoMW 92*
**Gabriel,** Edward George 1946- *AmMWSc 92*
**Gabriel,** Edwin Z 1913- *AmMWSc 92*
**Gabriel,** Eileen M 1951- *WhoIns 92*
**Gabriel,** Ethel Mary 1921- *WhoEnt 92, WhoFI 92*
**Gabriel,** Eugene Richard 1949- *WhoEnt 92*
**Gabriel,** Garabet J 1935- *AmMWSc 92*
**Gabriel,** Henry 1914- *AmMWSc 92*
**Gabriel,** Israel El 1944- *WhoWest 92*
**Gabriel,** Jacques-Ange 1698-1782 *BlkwCEP*
**Gabriel,** John R 1931- *AmMWSc 92*
**Gabriel,** Juri 1940- *WrDr 92*
**Gabriel,** Juri Evald 1940- *IntAu&W 91*
**Gabriel,** Karl Leonard 1929- *AmMWSc 92*
**Gabriel,** Larry E 1946- *WhoAmP 91*
**Gabriel,** Lester H 1928- *AmMWSc 92*
**Gabriel,** Michal 1960- *IntWW 91*
**Gabriel,** Mordecai Lionel 1918- *AmMWSc 92*
**Gabriel,** Oscar V 1946- *AmMWSc 92*
**Gabriel,** Peter 1950- *IntWW 91, WhoEnt 92*
**Gabriel,** R Othmar 1925- *AmMWSc 92*
**Gabriel,** Rennie 1948- *WhoWest 92*
**Gabriel,** Richard Francis 1920- *AmMWSc 92*
**Gabriel,** Richard Lance 1962- *WhoAmL 92*
**Gabriel,** William Francis 1925- *AmMWSc 92*
**Gabriele,** Orlando Frederick 1927- *AmMWSc 92*
**Gabriele,** Thomas L 1940- *AmMWSc 92*
**Gabrieli,** Andrea 1510?-1586 *NewAmDM*
**Gabrieli,** Giovanni 1555?-1612 *NewAmDM*
**Gabrielian,** Armen 1940- *WhoFI 92*
**Gabrielides,** Andreas 1949- *IntWW 91*
**Gabrielli,** Adolfo Ricardo Pablo 1911- *IntWW 91*
**Gabrielli,** Thomas Robert 1947- *WhoEnt 92*
**Gabrielse,** Hubert 1926- *AmMWSc 92*
**Gabrielsen,** Ann Emily 1925- *AmMWSc 92*
**Gabrielsen,** Bernard L 1934- *AmMWSc 92*
**Gabrielsen,** Bjarne 1941- *AmMWSc 92*
**Gabrielsen,** Trygve O 1930- *AmMWSc 92*
**Gabrielson,** Dave *WhoAmP 91*
**Gabrielson,** Richard Lewis 1931- *AmMWSc 92*
**Gabrielson,** Shirley Gail 1934- *WhoWest 92*
**Gabrilovich,** Ossip 1878-1936 *NewAmDM*
**Gabrilovich,** Yevgeny Osipovich 1899- *SovUnBD*
**Gabrilowitsch,** Ossip 1878-1936 *FacFETw*
**Gabrusewycz-Garcia,** Natalia 1934- *AmMWSc 92*
**Gabrynowicz,** Joanne Irene 1949- *WhoMW 92*
**Gaburo,** Kenneth 1926- *NewAmDM*
**Gabuzda,** Thomas George 1930- *AmMWSc 92*
**Gaby,** William Lawrence 1917- *AmMWSc 92*
**Gac,** Edward John 1944- *WhoAmL 92*
**Gac,** Frank David 1951- *WhoWest 92*
**Gacano,** Carl B. 1954- *WhoWest 92*
**Gach,** Gary G. *DrAPF 91*
**Gachet,** Paul 1818-1909 *ThHEIm*
**Gachette,** Louise Foston 1911- *WhoBlA 92*
**Gacic,** Radisa 1938- *IntWW 91*
**Gackle,** William Frederick 1927- *WhoAmP 91*
**Gacs,** Peter 1947- *AmMWSc 92*
**Gad,** Lance Stewart 1945- *WhoFI 92*
**Gad,** Urban 1879-1947 *IntDcF 2-2*
**Gad-el-Hak,** Mohamed 1945- *AmMWSc 92*
**Gadalla,** Mahmoud Saad 1932- *WhoWest 92*
**Gadamer,** Ernst Oscar 1924- *AmMWSc 92*
**Gadamer,** Hans-Georg 1900- *IntWW 91*
**Gadberry,** Howard M 1922- *AmMWSc 92*
**Gadbois,** Richard A., Jr. 1932- *WhoAmL 92, WhoWest 92*
**Gadd,** John 1925- *Who 92*
**Gadd,** Staffan 1934- *Who 92*
**Gadd,** Steve 1945- *NewAmDM*
**Gadda Conti,** Piero 1902- *IntWW 91*
**Gaddafi,** Mu'ammar Muhammad al- 1942- *IntWW 91*
**Gaddafi,** Wanis *IntWW 91*
**Gaddam,** Encik Kasitah bin 1947- *IntWW 91*
**Gaddes,** Gordon 1936- *Who 92*
**Gaddes,** Richard 1942- *WhoEnt 92, WhoMW 92*
**Gaddie,** Ellen Downing 1961- *WhoWest 92*
**Gaddis,** Monica Louise 1955- *AmMWSc 92*
**Gaddis,** Vincent Hayes 1913- *WrDr 92*
**Gaddis,** William *DrAPF 91*
**Gaddis,** William 1922- *BenetAL 91, ConNov 91, FacFETw, IntAu&W 91, IntWW 91, WrDr 92*
**Gaddis-Rose,** Marilyn 1930- *WrDr 92*
**Gaddum-Rosse,** Penelope 1941- *AmMWSc 92*
**Gaddy,** Beatrice 1933- *WhoBlA 92*
**Gaddy,** Carolyn C 1910- *WhoAmP 91*
**Gaddy,** Charles Winfred 1880-1941 *DcNCBi 2*
**Gaddy,** James Leoma 1932- *AmMWSc 92*
**Gaddy,** M Gordon 1936- *WhoIns 92*
**Gaddy,** Oscar 1932- *AmMWSc 92*
**Gade,** Daniel W 1936- *AmMWSc 92*
**Gade,** Edward Herman Henry, III 1936- *AmMWSc 92*
**Gade,** Henry *TwCSFW 91*
**Gade,** Niels 1817-1890 *NewAmDM*

**Gade**, Sandra Ann 1937- *AmMWSc 92*
**Gadebusch**, Hans Henning 1924- *AmMWSc 92*
**Gadek**, Frank Joseph 1941- *AmMWSc 92*
**Gaden**, Barbara Joan 1954- *WhoAmL 92*
**Gaden**, Elmer L, Jr 1923- *AmMWSc 92*
**Gadgil**, Vithal Narhar 1928- *IntWW 91*
**Gadler**, Hakan Eric 1956- *WhoFI 92*
**Gadney**, Reg 1941- *WrDr 92*
**Gadol**, Nancy *AmMWSc 92*
**Gadol**, Peter 1964- *ConAu 134*
**Gadola**, Paul V. 1929- *WhoAmL 92, WhoMW 92*
**Gadomski**, Robert Eugene 1947- *WhoFI 92*
**Gadon**, Steven Franklin 1931- *WhoAmL 92*
**Gadsby**, Dwight Maxon 1932- *AmMWSc 92*
**Gadsby**, Neville 1914- *Who 92*
**Gadsden**, Christopher 1724-1805 *BlkwEAR*
**Gadsden**, Christopher Henry 1946- *WhoAmL 92*
**Gadsden**, Eugene Hinson 1912- *WhoBlA 92*
**Gadsden**, James 1788-1858 *AmPolLe*
**Gadsden**, James 1949- *WhoAmL 92*
**Gadsden**, Marie D. 1919- *NotBlAW 92*
**Gadsden**, Nathaniel J., Jr. 1950- *WhoBlA 92*
**Gadsden**, Peter 1929- *Who 92*
**Gadsden**, Peter Drury Haggerston 1929- *IntWW 91*
**Gadsden**, Richard Hamilton, Sr 1925- *AmMWSc 92*
**Gadson**, Rosetta E. 1938- *WhoBlA 92*
**Gadwood**, Robert Charles 1952- *AmMWSc 92*
**Gadye**, Clifford Scott 1955- *WhoAmL 92*
**Gadzhiev**, Rauf Soltan ogly 1922- *IntWW 91*
**Gadzuk**, John William 1941- *AmMWSc 92*
**Gaebelein**, Arno C. 1861-1945 *RelLAm 91*
**Gaebelein**, Paul Whitefield, Jr. 1919- *WhoWest 92*
**Gaebler**, Rainer 1938- *IntWW 91*
**Gaebler**, Richard H 1930- *WhoIns 92*
**Gaebler**, Robert Adams 1932- *WhoMW 92*
**Gaede**, Anton Henry, Jr. 1939- *WhoAmL 92*
**Gaedke**, Rudolph Meggs 1938- *AmMWSc 92*
**Gaehtgens**, Thomas Wolfgang 1940- *IntWW 91*
**Gaekle**, Robert E. 1949- *WhoMW 92*
**Gaeng**, Gerard Joseph 1953- *WhoAmL 92*
**Gaensler**, Edward Arnold 1921- *AmMWSc 92*
**Gaenzl**, Kurt 1946- *ConAu 134*
**Gaer**, Marvin Charles 1935- *AmMWSc 92*
**Gaertner**, Donell J. 1932- *WhoMW 92*
**Gaertner**, Frank Herbert 1938- *AmMWSc 92*
**Gaertner**, Gary M. *WhoAmL 92*
**Gaertner**, Joel P. 1964- *WhoRel 92*
**Gaertner**, Ken *DrAPF 91*
**Gaertner**, Richard F 1933- *AmMWSc 92*
**Gaertner**, Van Russell 1924- *AmMWSc 92*
**Gaertner**, Wolfgang Wilhelm 1929- *AmMWSc 92*
**Gaerttner**, Martin R 1944- *AmMWSc 92*
**Gaess**, Roger *DrAPF 91*
**Gaeta**, Gerald 1955- *WhoHisp 92*
**Gaetani**, Jan de *NewAmDM*
**Gaetano**, Cortesi 1912- *IntWW 91*
**Gaetanos**, Christ 1953- *WhoAmL 92*
**Gaete Rojas**, Sergio 1939- *IntWW 91*
**Gaeth**, M Ben 1921- *WhoAmP 91*
**Gaewsky**, David 1960- *WhoRel 92*
**Gafarian**, Antranig Vaughn 1924- *AmMWSc 92*
**Gaff**, Brian Michael 1962- *WhoFI 92*
**Gaffar**, Abdul 1939- *AmMWSc 92*
**Gaffey**, Cornelius Thomas 1928- *AmMWSc 92*
**Gaffey**, Michael James 1945- *AmMWSc 92*
**Gaffey**, William Robert 1924- *AmMWSc 92*
**Gaffield**, William 1935- *AmMWSc 92*
**Gaffigan**, Michael A. 1936- *WhoFI 92*
**Gaffke**, Howard William 1918- *WhoAmP 91*
**Gaffney** *Who 92*
**Gaffney**, Barbara Lundy 1944- *AmMWSc 92*
**Gaffney**, Edwin Vincent *AmMWSc 92*
**Gaffney**, Elizabeth *DrAPF 91*
**Gaffney**, F J 1912- *AmMWSc 92*
**Gaffney**, Floyd 1930- *WhoBlA 92*
**Gaffney**, Gary Steven 1952- *WhoAmL 92*
**Gaffney**, James 1931- *WhoRel 92*
**Gaffney**, James Anthony 1928- *Who 92*
**Gaffney**, James Anthony 1929- *WhoEnt 92*
**Gaffney**, Jeffrey Steven 1949- *AmMWSc 92*
**Gaffney**, John Francis 1939- *WhoWest 92*
**Gaffney**, John W. 1930- *WhoBlA 92*
**Gaffney**, Lauren *NewYTBS 91 [port]*
**Gaffney**, Mark William 1951- *WhoAmL 92*
**Gaffney**, Martin d1991 *NewYTBS 91 [port]*
**Gaffney**, Mary Louise *WhoBlA 92*
**Gaffney**, Michael William 1953- *WhoEnt 92*
**Gaffney**, Patrick M 1951- *AmMWSc 92*
**Gaffney**, Paul Cotter 1917- *AmMWSc 92*
**Gaffney**, Paul G, II 1946- *AmMWSc 92*
**Gaffney**, Peter Edward 1931- *AmMWSc 92*
**Gaffney**, Robert 1931- *IntMPA 92*
**Gaffney**, Robert J 1944- *WhoAmP 91*
**Gaffney**, Thomas Daniel 1933- *WhoBlA 92*
**Gaffney**, Thomas Edward 1930- *AmMWSc 92*
**Gaffney**, Thomas Francis 1945- *WhoMW 92*
**Gafford**, Charlotte *DrAPF 91*
**Gafford**, Lanelle Guyton 1930- *AmMWSc 92*
**Gafford**, William R 1924- *AmMWSc 92*
**Gaffurius**, Franchinus 1451-1522 *NewAmDM*
**Gafke**, Roger Adams 1939- *WhoMW 92*
**Gafny**, Arnon 1932- *IntWW 91*
**Gag**, Wanda 1893-1946 *BenetAL 91*
**Gagain**, Edward Francis, Jr. 1947- *WhoFI 92*
**Gagar**, Eleuterio Castro 1935- *WhoWest 92*
**Gagarin**, Yuri 1934-1968 *FacFETw [port]*
**Gagarin**, Yuriy Alekseevich 1934-1968 *SovUnBD*
**Gagarov**, Dmitriy Nikolaevich 1938- *SovUnBD*
**Gagarov**, Dmitriy Nikolayevich 1938- *IntWW 91*
**Gage** *Who 92*
**Gage**, Viscount 1932- *Who 92*
**Gage**, Andrew Arthur 1922- *AmMWSc 92*
**Gage**, Berkeley 1904- *Who 92*
**Gage**, Beverly Anne 1934- *WhoAmP 91*
**Gage**, Carl Webster 1955- *WhoAmP 91*
**Gage**, Charles Quincey 1946- *WhoAmL 92*
**Gage**, Clarke Lyman 1921- *AmMWSc 92*
**Gage**, Delwyn 1930- *WhoAmP 91*
**Gage**, Donald S 1930- *AmMWSc 92*
**Gage**, Edward 1925- *TwCPaSc*
**Gage**, Edwin C., III 1940- *WhoFI 92*
**Gage**, Elliot Howes 1923- *WhoMW 92*
**Gage**, Frances Dana 1808-1884 *BenetAL 91*
**Gage**, Fred Kelton 1925- *WhoAmL 92*
**Gage**, Frederick Worthington 1912- *AmMWSc 92, WhoMW 92*
**Gage**, Gaston Hemphill 1930- *WhoAmL 92*
**Gage**, George Henry 1924- *WhoFI 92*
**Gage**, Harlow W. 1911- *IntWW 91*
**Gage**, Hilda R. 1939- *WhoAmL 92*
**Gage**, Hy *ScFEYrs A*
**Gage**, Jack James 1931- *WhoMW 92*
**Gage**, John 1937- *WhoEnt 92*
**Gage**, John Sloatman 1948- *WhoMW 92*
**Gage**, Joy P. 1930- *ConAu 35NR*
**Gage**, Kenneth Seaver 1942- *AmMWSc 92*
**Gage**, L Patrick 1942- *AmMWSc 92*
**Gage**, Leland Scott 1952- *WhoRel 92*
**Gage**, Martin 1934- *WhoEnt 92*
**Gage**, Mary 1940- *WhoEnt 92*
**Gage**, Matilda Joslyn 1826-1898 *HanAmWH*
**Gage**, Michael Henry 1945- *WhoMW 92*
**Gage**, Michael Lester 1955- *WhoRel 92*
**Gage**, Nathaniel Lees 1917- *IntWW 91*
**Gage**, Nicholas 1939- *IntAu&W 91*
**Gage**, Peter William 1937- *IntWW 91*
**Gage**, Robert 1921- *DcTwDes*
**Gage**, Robert Clifford 1941- *WhoRel 92*
**Gage**, Robert Jeffrey 1951- *WhoAmL 92*
**Gage**, Ronald H. *WhoFI 92*
**Gage**, Ruth Elva 1940- *WhoAmP 91*
**Gage**, S. R. 1945- *ConAu 134*
**Gage**, Susanna Phelps 1857-1915 *BiInAmS*
**Gage**, Thomas *HisDSpE*
**Gage**, Thomas 1596?-1656 *BenetAL 91*
**Gage**, Thomas 1720?-1787 *BlkwEAR*
**Gage**, Thomas Underwood 1960- *WhoAmP 91*
**Gage**, Tommy Wilton 1935- *AmMWSc 92*
**Gage**, William James 1932- *WhoEnt 92*
**Gage**, William Marcus 1938- *Who 92*
**Gage**, Wilson *WrDr 92*
**Gagen**, J. Wilfrid *WhoEnt 92*
**Gagen**, James Edwin 1935- *AmMWSc 92*
**Gagen**, Marilyn Jean 1949- *WhoFI 92*
**Gager**, Forrest Lee, Jr 1922- *AmMWSc 92*
**Gager**, William Ballantine 1928- *AmMWSc 92*
**Gagge**, Adolf Pharo 1908- *AmMWSc 92*
**Gaggioli**, Richard A 1934- *AmMWSc 92*
**Gagliano**, Frank 1931- *IntAu&W 91, WrDr 92*
**Gagliano**, Frank Joseph 1931- *WhoEnt 92*
**Gagliano**, Gerard Anthony 1954- *WhoWest 92*
**Gagliano**, Marco da 1582-1643 *NewAmDM*
**Gagliano**, Nicholas Charles 1927- *AmMWSc 92*
**Gagliano**, S Thomas 1931- *WhoAmP 91*
**Gagliano**, Sherwood Moneer 1935- *AmMWSc 92*
**Gagliardi**, Elaine Hightower 1960- *WhoAmL 92*
**Gagliardi**, George N 1930- *AmMWSc 92*
**Gagliardi**, L John 1935- *AmMWSc 92*
**Gagliardi**, Pat 1950- *WhoAmP 91*
**Gagliardi**, Raymond Alfred 1922- *WhoMW 92*
**Gagliardi**, Robert M 1934- *AmMWSc 92*
**Gagliardi**, Ugo Oscar 1931- *AmMWSc 92*
**Gagliardo**, John G. 1933- *WrDr 92*
**Gaglio**, Samuel Steven 1949- *WhoMW 92*
**Gaglione**, Robert J. 1958- *WhoAmL 92*
**Gagna**, Claude Eugene 1956- *AmMWSc 92*
**Gagne**, Armand Joseph, Jr. 1936- *WhoFI 92*
**Gagne**, Gregory Allan 1948- *WhoEnt 92*
**Gagne**, Jean-Marie 1932- *AmMWSc 92*
**Gagne**, Paul Ernest 1946- *WhoFI 92*
**Gagne**, Raymond J 1935- *AmMWSc 92*
**Gagne**, Robert Raymond 1948- *AmMWSc 92*
**Gagne**, Verne Clarence 1926- *WhoEnt 92*
**Gagne**, Walter Paul 1944- *WhoRel 92*
**Gagne**, William Roderick 1955- *WhoAmL 92*
**Gagnebin**, Albert P. 1909- *IntWW 91*
**Gagnebin**, Albert Paul 1909- *AmMWSc 92*
**Gagnier**, J-J 1885-1949 *NewAmDM*
**Gagnon**, Camilien Joseph Xavier 1929- *AmMWSc 92*
**Gagnon**, Claude 1950- *AmMWSc 92*
**Gagnon**, Donald Joseph 1939- *WhoWest 92*
**Gagnon**, Edith Morrison 1909- *WhoEnt 92*
**Gagnon**, Edouard 1918- *IntWW 91, WhoRel 92*
**Gagnon**, Ernest 1834-1915 *NewAmDM*
**Gagnon**, Eugene Gerald 1936- *AmMWSc 92*
**Gagnon**, Eugene L 1943- *WhoAmP 91*
**Gagnon**, Gabrielle Virginia 1913- *WhoAmP 91*
**Gagnon**, Jean-Marie 1933- *IntWW 91*
**Gagnon**, Lee Albert 1937- *WhoFI 92*
**Gagnon**, Leo Paul 1929- *AmMWSc 92*
**Gagnon**, Marcel 1928- *AmMWSc 92*
**Gagnon**, Real 1924- *AmMWSc 92*
**Gagnon**, Stewart Walter 1949- *WhoAmL 92*
**Gagnon**, Wayne Joseph 1949- *WhoWest 92*
**Gago**, Jenny *WhoHisp 92*
**Gagola**, Stephen Michael, Jr 1947- *AmMWSc 92*
**Gahan**, Kathleen Mason 1940- *WhoWest 92*
**Gaherty**, Geoffrey George 1941- *AmMWSc 92*
**Gahl**, William A 1950- *AmMWSc 92*
**Gahler**, Arnold Robert 1919- *AmMWSc 92*
**Gai**, Madge E 1944- *WhoAmP 91*
**Gaia**, Pam *WhoAmP 91*
**Gaiber**, Lawrence Jay 1960- *WhoFI 92, WhoWest 92*
**Gaiber**, Maxine Diane 1949- *WhoWest 92*
**Gaidinliu**, Rani *EncAmaz 91*
**Gaidis**, James Michael 1940- *AmMWSc 92*
**Gaidis**, Michael Christopher 1967- *AmMWSc 92*
**Gaidos**, James A 1936- *AmMWSc 92*
**Gaiever**, Ivar 1929- *FacFETw*
**Gaik**, Geraldine Catherine 1942- *AmMWSc 92*
**Gail**, Barbara *WrDr 92*
**Gail**, Maxwell Trowbridge, Jr. 1943- *WhoEnt 92*
**Gail**, Otto 1896-1956 *TwCSFW 91A*
**Gail**, Otto Willi 1896-1956 *ScFEYrs*
**Gail**, Scanlon 1949- *WhoEnt 92*
**Gailani**, Salman 1926- *AmMWSc 92*
**Gailar**, Norman Milton 1918- *AmMWSc 92*
**Gailar**, Owen H 1925- *AmMWSc 92*
**Gailey**, Charles Franklin, Jr. 1926- *WhoFI 92*
**Gailey**, Franklin Bryan 1918- *AmMWSc 92*
**Gailey**, Kenneth Durwood 1947- *AmMWSc 92*
**Gaillard**, Bernard 1944- *WhoBlA 92*
**Gaillard**, Eugene 1862-1933 *DcTwDes*
**Gaillard**, George Siday, III 1941- *WhoFI 92*
**Gaillard**, Larry Dexter 1940- *WhoIns 92*
**Gaillard**, Marie-Anne *ThHEIm*
**Gaillard**, Mary Katharine 1939- *AmMWSc 92, WhoWest 92*
**Gaillard**, Ralph C., Sr. 1943- *WhoBlA 92*
**Gaillard**, Slim d1991 *NewYTBS 91*
**Gaillard**, Stephen *ScFEYrs*
**Gailys**, John M. 1941- *WhoWest 92*
**Gaiman**, Neil 1960- *ConAu 133*
**Gain**, Ronald Ellsworth 1940- *AmMWSc 92*
**Gaine**, Hugh 1727-1807 *BenetAL 91*
**Gainen**, Susan Rose 1950- *WhoAmL 92*
**Gainer**, Andrew A. 1919- *WhoBlA 92*
**Gainer**, Carl E *WhoAmP 91*
**Gainer**, Frank Edward 1938- *AmMWSc 92, WhoBlA 92*
**Gainer**, Glen Bertram, Jr 1927- *WhoAmP 91*
**Gainer**, Harold 1935- *AmMWSc 92*
**Gainer**, John F. 1954- *WhoBlA 92*
**Gainer**, John Lloyd 1938- *AmMWSc 92*
**Gainer**, Joseph Henry 1924- *AmMWSc 92*
**Gainer**, Michael Kizinski 1933- *AmMWSc 92*
**Gainer**, Robert Timothy 1957- *WhoEnt 92*
**Gainer**, Ronald Lee 1934- *WhoAmL 92*
**Gainer**, Ruby Jackson *WhoBlA 92*
**Gaines**, Adriane Theresa 1947- *WhoBlA 92, WhoEnt 92*
**Gaines**, Alan McCulloch 1938- *AmMWSc 92*
**Gaines**, Albert L 1920- *AmMWSc 92*
**Gaines**, Ava Candace 1963- *WhoBlA 92*
**Gaines**, Bennett Gilbert 1947- *WhoAmL 92*
**Gaines**, Charles Kelsey 1854-1944 *ScFEYrs*
**Gaines**, Clarence E., Sr. 1923- *WhoBlA 92*
**Gaines**, Clarence L. 1914- *WhoBlA 92*
**Gaines**, Corey Yasuto 1965- *WhoBlA 92*
**Gaines**, Cristina E. 1946- *WhoHisp 92*
**Gaines**, Deborah Kay 1946- *WhoAmL 92*
**Gaines**, Donald Frank 1936- *AmMWSc 92*
**Gaines**, Dora Belle 1927-1990 *WhoBlA 92N*
**Gaines**, Edward Everett 1937- *AmMWSc 92*
**Gaines**, Edward M 1913- *AmMWSc 92*
**Gaines**, Edythe J. 1922- *WhoBlA 92*
**Gaines**, Ernest 1933- *BlkLC [port]*
**Gaines**, Ernest J. *DrAPF 91*
**Gaines**, Ernest J 1933- *AfrAmW, BenetAL 91, ConNov 91, WhoBlA 92, WrDr 92*
**Gaines**, Francis Pendleton 1892-1963 *DcNCBi 2*
**Gaines**, Frank D 1934- *WhoAmP 91*
**Gaines**, Fred Neil 1959- *WhoAmL 92*
**Gaines**, Frederick *DrAPF 91*
**Gaines**, George Loweree, Jr 1930- *AmMWSc 92*
**Gaines**, Gordon Bradford 1923- *AmMWSc 92*
**Gaines**, Gregory 1950- *AmMWSc 92*
**Gaines**, H Michael 1945- *WhoIns 92*
**Gaines**, Haydon Decatur 1943- *WhoWest 92*
**Gaines**, Herschel Davis 1942- *WhoBlA 92*
**Gaines**, Howard Clarke 1909- *WhoAmL 92*
**Gaines**, Irene McCoy 1892-1964 *NotBlAW 92*
**Gaines**, Irving David 1923- *WhoAmL 92*
**Gaines**, J H 1931- *AmMWSc 92*
**Gaines**, Jack Raymond 1927- *AmMWSc 92*
**Gaines**, James Abner 1927- *AmMWSc 92*
**Gaines**, James Donald 1936- *WhoMW 92*
**Gaines**, James R 1935- *AmMWSc 92*
**Gaines**, Jaunell Wallace 1942- *WhoBlA 92*
**Gaines**, John Adrian 1955- *WhoWest 92*
**Gaines**, John Andrew 1942- *WhoFI 92*
**Gaines**, Leslie Doran 1912- *WhoBlA 92*
**Gaines**, Manyles B., Jr. 1938- *WhoBlA 92*
**Gaines**, Mark L *WhoAmP 91*
**Gaines**, Mary E. *WhoBlA 92*
**Gaines**, Michael Stephen 1943- *AmMWSc 92*
**Gaines**, Natalie Mallie *WhoMW 92*
**Gaines**, Oscar Cornell 1954- *WhoBlA 92*
**Gaines**, Paul Laurence, Sr. 1932- *WhoBlA 92*
**Gaines**, Peter Mathew 1951- *WhoAmL 92*
**Gaines**, Philip Walter 1960- *WhoAmL 92*
**Gaines**, Ray D. 1932- *WhoBlA 92*
**Gaines**, Richard David 1944- *WhoAmL 92*
**Gaines**, Richard Kendall 1947- *WhoBlA 92*
**Gaines**, Robert D 1933- *AmMWSc 92*
**Gaines**, Robert Darryl 1951- *WhoMW 92*
**Gaines**, Robert E 1923- *WhoAmP 91*
**Gaines**, Robert Earl 1941- *AmMWSc 92*
**Gaines**, Robert Martin 1931- *WhoAmL 92*
**Gaines**, Samuel Stone 1938- *WhoBlA 92*
**Gaines**, Sedalia Mitchell 1917- *WhoBlA 92*
**Gaines**, Sylvester, Jr. 1921- *WhoBlA 92*
**Gaines**, Thurston Lenwood, Jr. 1922- *WhoBlA 92*
**Gaines**, Tinsley Powell 1939- *AmMWSc 92*
**Gaines**, Tyler Belt 1924- *WhoAmL 92, WhoMW 92*
**Gaines**, Victor Pryor 1939- *WhoBlA 92*
**Gaines**, Weaver Henderson, Jr. 1943- *WhoAmL 92*

**Gaines**, Wesley John 1840-1912 *RelLAm 91*
**Gaines**, William Chester 1933- *WhoMW 92*
**Gaines**, William Maxwell 1922- *WhoEnt 92, WhoFI 92*
**Gaines**, Willys Ann 1938- *WhoEnt 92*
**Gainey**, Leonard Dennis, II 1927- *WhoBlA 92*
**Gainey**, Louis Franklin, Jr 1947- *AmMWSc 92*
**Gainey**, Robert Michael 1953- *WhoMW 92*
**Gainford**, Baron 1921- *Who 92*
**Gainham**, Rachel 1922- *Who 92*
**Gainham**, Sarah *IntAu&W 91X*
**Gainham**, Sarah 1922- *WrDr 92*
**Gains**, Lawrence Howard 1948- *AmMWSc 92*
**Gainsborough**, Earl of 1923- *Who 92*
**Gainsborough**, George Fotheringham 1915- *Who 92*
**Gainsborough**, Michael 1938- *Who 92*
**Gainsborough**, Thomas 1727?-1788 *BlkwCEP*
**Gainsbourg**, Serge 1928-1991 *IntWW 91, -91N, NewYTBS 91*
**Gainsford**, Ian Derek 1930- *Who 92*
**Gaintner**, John Richard 1936- *AmMWSc 92*
**Gair**, George Frederick 1926- *Who 92*
**Gair**, Jacob Eugene 1922- *AmMWSc 92*
**Gairy**, Eric Matthew 1922- *IntWW 91, Who 92*
**Gaiser**, Gerd 1908-1976 *EncTR 91*
**Gaiser**, Jody 1939- *WhoMW 92*
**Gaiseric** d477 *EncEarC*
**Gaisford**, John Scott 1934- *Who 92*
**Gaisford**, Paul 1941- *TwCPaSc*
**Gaisinovich**, Abba Yevseevich 1906-1989 *SovUnBD*
**Gaisser**, Thomas Korff 1940- *AmMWSc 92*
**Gait**, Robert Irwin 1938- *AmMWSc 92*
**Gaitan**, Antonio C., Jr. 1933- *WhoHisp 92*
**Gaitan**, Fernando J., Jr. 1948- *WhoBlA 92*
**Gaitan**, Jose E. 1951- *WhoAmL 92*
**Gaitan**, Ramon 1934- *WhoHisp 92*
**Gaitan Duran**, Jorge 1924-1962 *ConSpAP*
**Gaither**, Alonzo Smith 1903- *WhoBlA 92*
**Gaither**, Basil d1803 *DcNCBi 2*
**Gaither**, Bill 1936- *RelLAm 91*
**Gaither**, Burgess Sidney 1807-1892 *DcNCBi 2*
**Gaither**, Cornelius E. 1928- *WhoBlA 92*
**Gaither**, Dorothy B. 1941- *WhoBlA 92*
**Gaither**, Edmund B. 1944- *WhoBlA 92*
**Gaither**, Ephraim Lash 1850-1943 *DcNCBi 2*
**Gaither**, Gloria 1942- *RelLAm 91*
**Gaither**, James C. 1937- *WhoAmL 92*
**Gaither**, James Louis 1931- *WhoRel 92*
**Gaither**, James W., Jr. 1954- *WhoBlA 92*
**Gaither**, John F. 1949- *WhoMW 92*
**Gaither**, John F., Jr. *WhoAmL 92*
**Gaither**, John Francis 1918- *WhoFI 92*
**Gaither**, Lewis Joe 1948- *WhoRel 92*
**Gaither**, Magalene Dulin 1928- *WhoBlA 92*
**Gaither**, Nathan 1788-1862 *DcNCBi 2*
**Gaither**, R. Trent 1957- *WhoAmL 92*
**Gaither**, Richard A. 1939- *WhoBlA 92*
**Gaither**, Robert Barker 1929- *AmMWSc 92*
**Gaither**, Thomas W. 1938- *WhoBlA 92*
**Gaither**, Thomas Walter 1938- *AmMWSc 92*
**Gaither**, William Samuel 1932- *AmMWSc 92*
**Gaitskell**, Hugh 1906-1963 *FacFETw [port]*
**Gaitskill**, Mary 1954- *ConLC 69 [port]*
**Gaitz**, Charles M 1922- *AmMWSc 92*
**Gaius** *EncEarC*
**Gaius**, Saimon 1920- *Who 92*
**Gaj**, Ljudevit *DcAmImH*
**Gajan**, Raymond Joseph 1920- *AmMWSc 92*
**Gajardo**, Joel *WhoHisp 92*
**Gajda**, Radola 1892-1948 *BiDExR*
**Gajdusek**, D. Carleton 1923- *WrDr 92*
**Gajdusek**, Daniel Carleton 1923- *AmMWSc 92, IntWW 91, Who 92, WhoNob 90*
**Gaje Ghale** 1922- *Who 92*
**Gajec**, John Joseph 1918- *WhoEnt 92, WhoMW 92*
**Gajec**, Lucile Cruz *WhoHisp 92*
**Gajendar**, Nandigam 1940- *AmMWSc 92*
**Gajewski**, Fred John 1912- *AmMWSc 92*
**Gajewski**, Joseph J 1939- *AmMWSc 92*
**Gajewski**, Ryszard 1930- *AmMWSc 92*
**Gajewski**, W M 1923- *AmMWSc 92*
**Gajewski**, Waclaw 1911- *IntWW 91*
**Gajewski**, Wieslaw Peter 1946- *WhoMW 92*
**Gajjar**, Jagdish T 1940- *AmMWSc 92*
**Gajus**, Gregory Lyle 1973- *WhoEnt 92*
**Gakenheimer**, Walter Christian 1916- *AmMWSc 92*
**Gal**, Andrew Eugene 1918- *AmMWSc 92*
**Gal**, George 1921- *AmMWSc 92*
**Gal**, Joseph *AmMWSc 92*
**Gal**, Kenneth Maurice 1954- *WhoFI 92*
**Gal**, Richard John 1957- *WhoFI 92*
**Gal**, Susannah 1958- *AmMWSc 92*
**Gal-Or**, Esther 1951- *WhoFI 92*
**Gala**, Richard R 1935- *AmMWSc 92*
**Galaburda**, Albert Mark 1948- *AmMWSc 92*
**Galadari**, Abdel-Wahab 1938- *IntWW 91*
**Galainena**, Mariano Luis 1922- *WhoHisp 92*
**Galaj**, Dyzma 1915- *IntWW 91*
**Galambos**, Janos 1940- *AmMWSc 92*
**Galambos**, John Thomas 1921- *AmMWSc 92*
**Galambos**, Robert 1914- *AmMWSc 92*
**Galambos**, Theodore V 1929- *AmMWSc 92*
**Galamian**, Ivan 1903-1981 *NewAmDM*
**Galamison**, Milton A. 1923-1988 *WhoBlA 92N*
**Galan**, Juan Arturo, Jr. 1944- *WhoHisp 92*
**Galan**, Louis 1928- *AmMWSc 92, WhoMW 92*
**Galan**, Nely 1964- *WhoHisp 92*
**Galan Alvarez**, Victor J. 1933- *WhoHisp 92*
**Galane**, Irma Adele Bereston 1921- *WhoFI 92*
**Galane**, Irma B 1921- *AmMWSc 92*
**Galane**, Morton Robert 1926- *WhoAmL 92, WhoWest 92*
**Galanis**, George J *WhoAmP 91*
**Galanis**, John William 1937- *WhoAmL 92*
**Galanis**, Nicolas 1939- *AmMWSc 92*
**Galanos**, James 1924- *IntWW 91*
**Galant**, Herbert Lewis 1928- *WhoAmL 92*
**Galante**, Jane Hohfeld 1924- *WhoEnt 92*
**Galante**, M. Christina 1942- *IntMPA 92*
**Galante**, Pierre 1909- *WrDr 92*
**Galanter**, Marc Selig 1931- *WhoAmL 92, WhoMW 92*
**Galanter**, Robert Allen 1945- *WhoAmL 92*
**Galanti**, Paul Edward 1939- *WhoFI 92*
**Galantucci**, Robert Louis 1945- *WhoAmL 92*
**Galanty**, Mark Allan 1958- *WhoEnt 92*
**Galardi**, Dino Gale 1957- *WhoAmL 92*
**Galardy**, Richard Edward *AmMWSc 92*
**Galarraga**, Andres Jose 1961- *WhoHisp 92*
**Galarza**, Ernesto *DcAmImH*
**Galarza**, Ernesto 1905-1984 *RComAH*
**Galarza**, Gabino E. 1941- *WhoHisp 92*
**Galas**, David John 1944- *AmMWSc 92*
**Galassi**, Jonathan *DrAPF 91*
**Galasso**, Francis Salvatore 1931- *AmMWSc 92*
**Galasso**, George John 1932- *AmMWSc 92*
**Galasso**, John Michael 1944- *WhoAmL 92*
**Galasso**, Joseph F., Jr. 1940- *WhoEnt 92*
**Galat**, Eugene R. *WhoRel 92*
**Galati**, Frank Joseph 1943- *WhoEnt 92, WhoMW 92*
**Galati**, Gregg 1961- *WhoEnt 92*
**Galati**, Michael Anthony 1930- *WhoIns 92*
**Galati**, Michael Bernard 1931- *WhoRel 92*
**Galatianos**, Gus Athanassios 1947- *WhoFI 92*
**Galatz**, Henry Francis 1947- *WhoAmL 92*
**Galatz**, Neil Gilbert 1933- *WhoAmL 92*
**Galaway**, Ronald Alvin 1943- *AmMWSc 92*
**Galaxan**, Sol *TwCSFW 91*
**Galayda**, John Nicolas 1948- *AmMWSc 92*
**Galazka**, Helen Gordon MacRobert 1915- *WhoRel 92*
**Galbi**, Elmer W. 1934- *WhoAmL 92*
**Galbiati**, Enzo Emilio 1897- *BiDExR*
**Galbiati**, Louis J 1925- *AmMWSc 92*
**Galbis**, Ignacio R. M. *WhoHisp 92*
**Galbis**, Ignacio Ricardo Maria 1931- *WhoWest 92*
**Galbis**, Ricardo 1936- *WhoHisp 92*
**Galbraith** *Who 92*
**Galbraith**, Barry Ward 1941- *WhoMW 92*
**Galbraith**, Bruce W. 1940- *WhoEnt 92*
**Galbraith**, Donald Barrett 1937- *AmMWSc 92*
**Galbraith**, Evan Griffith 1928- *WhoAmP 91*
**Galbraith**, Gary Gene 1934- *WhoWest 92*
**Galbraith**, Harry Wilson 1918- *AmMWSc 92*
**Galbraith**, J. Kenneth 1908- *IntWW 91*
**Galbraith**, James Hunter 1925- *Who 92*
**Galbraith**, James Nelson, Jr 1936- *AmMWSc 92*
**Galbraith**, James Ronald 1936- *WhoFI 92*
**Galbraith**, Jean 1906- *WrDr 92*
**Galbraith**, John Allen 1923- *WhoAmP 91*
**Galbraith**, John Drummond, Jr. 1919- *WhoMW 92*
**Galbraith**, John Kenneth 1908- *BenetAL 91, ConAu 34NR, FacFETw [port], Who 92, WhoAmP 91, WrDr 92*
**Galbraith**, John Robert 1935- *WhoFI 92*
**Galbraith**, John Robert 1938- *WhoWest 92*
**Galbraith**, John William 1921- *WhoFI 92*
**Galbraith**, Marie W *WhoAmP 91*
**Galbraith**, Neil 1911- *Who 92*
**Galbraith**, Nicol Spence 1927- *IntWW 91*
**Galbraith**, Peter Woodard 1950- *WhoAmP 91*
**Galbraith**, Robert Michael 1947- *AmMWSc 92*
**Galbraith**, Ruth Legg 1923- *AmMWSc 92*
**Galbraith**, Samuel Laird 1945- *Who 92*
**Galbraith**, William 1945- *AmMWSc 92*
**Galbraith**, William Campbell 1935- *Who 92*
**Galbreath**, Anthony Dale 1954- *WhoBlA 92*
**Galbreath**, Edwin Carter 1913- *AmMWSc 92*
**Galbreath**, Jacquelyn Rodgers 1958- *WhoWest 92*
**Galbreath**, Theodore Ralph 1953- *WhoMW 92*
**Galbut**, Martin Richard 1946- *WhoAmL 92*
**Galdes**, Alphonse 1952- *AmMWSc 92*
**Galdone**, Paul 1907?-1986 *SmATA 66 [port]*
**Galdston**, Morton 1912- *AmMWSc 92*
**Gale**, Andy Mark 1947- *WhoEnt 92*
**Gale**, Bob *ConAu 133*
**Gale**, Bob 1951- *IntMPA 92*
**Gale**, Charles 1926- *AmMWSc 92*
**Gale**, Charles C, Jr 1926- *AmMWSc 92*
**Gale**, Christopher 1679?-1735 *DcNCBi 2*
**Gale**, Connie Ruth 1946- *WhoAmL 92*
**Gale**, Daniel Bailey 1933- *WhoWest 92*
**Gale**, David 1921- *AmMWSc 92*
**Gale**, Douglas Shannon, II 1942- *AmMWSc 92*
**Gale**, Edmund d1738 *DcNCBi 2*
**Gale**, Ernest Frederick 1914- *IntWW 91, Who 92*
**Gale**, Fay *Who 92*
**Gale**, Forest McClure, Jr. 1940- *WhoRel 92*
**Gale**, Fournier Joseph, III 1944- *WhoAmL 92*
**Gale**, George *IntMPA 92*
**Gale**, George Alexander 1906- *Who 92*
**Gale**, George Osborne 1931- *AmMWSc 92*
**Gale**, George Stafford d1990 *Who 92N*
**Gale**, George Stafford 1927- *IntAu&W 91*
**Gale**, Glen Roy 1929- *AmMWSc 92*
**Gale**, Gwendoline Fay 1932- *IntWW 91, Who 92*
**Gale**, Harold Walter 1939- *AmMWSc 92*
**Gale**, Henry H *AmMWSc 92*
**Gale**, James Lyman 1934- *AmMWSc 92*
**Gale**, John 1929- *Who 92*
**Gale**, John Albert 1956- *WhoEnt 92*
**Gale**, Laird Housel 1935- *AmMWSc 92*
**Gale**, Leonard Dunnell 1800-1883 *BiInAmS*
**Gale**, Malcolm Ruthven d1990 *Who 92N*
**Gale**, Maradel Krummel 1939- *WhoWest 92*
**Gale**, Mary Ellen 1940- *WhoAmL 92*
**Gale**, Michael 1932- *Who 92*
**Gale**, Michael R 1952- *WhoAmP 91*
**Gale**, Michael Robert 1951- *ConAu 133, WhoEnt 92*
**Gale**, Michael Sadler 1919- *Who 92*
**Gale**, Nord Loran 1938- *AmMWSc 92*
**Gale**, Paula Jane 1946- *AmMWSc 92*
**Gale**, Richard 1896-1982 *FacFETw*
**Gale**, Robert Peter 1945- *AmMWSc 92, WhoWest 92*
**Gale**, Roger James 1943- *Who 92*
**Gale**, Stephen Bruce 1940- *AmMWSc 92*
**Gale**, Vi *DrAPF 91*
**Gale**, William Arthur 1939- *AmMWSc 92*
**Gale**, Zona *DrAPF 91*
**Gale**, Zona 1874-1938 *AmPeW, BenetAL 91, ScFEYrs*
**Galea**, Louis 1947- *IntWW 91*
**Galeana**, Frank H. 1929- *WhoHisp 92*
**Galeano**, Cesar 1926- *AmMWSc 92*
**Galeano**, Eduardo 1904- *LiExTwC*
**Galeano**, Hermenegildo 1762-1814 *HisDSpE*
**Galeano**, Sergio F 1934- *AmMWSc 92*
**Galeazzi**, Francesco 1758-1819 *NewAmDM*
**Galecke**, Robert Michael 1942- *WhoFI 92*
**Galecki**, Gregory Michael 1961- *WhoFI 92*
**Galeener**, Frank Lee 1936- *AmMWSc 92, WhoWest 92*
**Galef**, Andrew Geoffrey 1932- *WhoWest 92*
**Galef**, Steven Allen 1940- *WhoAmL 92*
**Galehouse**, Jon Scott 1939- *AmMWSc 92*
**Galehouse**, Lawrence David 1946- *WhoAmL 92*
**Galella**, Ron 1931- *IntAu&W 91*
**Galen**, Clemens August, Count von 1878-1946 *EncTR 91 [port]*
**Galenson**, Walter 1914- *WrDr 92*
**Galeotti**, Steven 1952- *WhoFI 92*
**Galer**, Donna Lynn 1949- *WhoIns 92*
**Galer**, Mary Jane 1924- *WhoAmP 91*
**Galerius** 250?-311 *EncEarC*
**Gales**, Edwin Alan 1921- *WhoFI 92*
**Gales**, James 1922- *WhoBlA 92*
**Gales**, Joseph 1761-1841 *DcNCBi 2*
**Gales**, Joseph, Jr. 1786-1860 *DcNCBi 2*
**Gales**, Kathleen Emily 1927- *Who 92*
**Gales**, Robert Robinson 1941- *WhoAmL 92*
**Gales**, Robert Sydney 1914- *AmMWSc 92*
**Gales**, Samuel Joel 1930- *WhoWest 92*
**Gales**, Seaton 1828-1878 *DcNCBi 2*
**Gales**, Weston Raleigh 1802-1848 *DcNCBi 2*
**Gales**, Winifred Marshall 1761-1839 *DcNCBi 2*
**Galetto**, William George 1939- *AmMWSc 92*
**Galey**, John Apt 1928- *AmMWSc 92*
**Galey**, William Raleigh 1943- *AmMWSc 92*
**Galeyev**, Albert Abubakirovich 1940- *IntWW 91*
**Galgano**, Thomas Michael 1949- *WhoAmL 92*
**Galganski**, Terry James 1954- *WhoAmL 92*
**Galian**, Laurence Joseph Anthony Michael 1954- *WhoEnt 92*
**Galiani**, Ferdinand 1728-1787 *BlkwCEP*
**Galiardo**, John William 1933- *WhoAmL 92*
**Galiazzo**, Connie C *WhoAmP 91*
**Galib-Frangie**, Jussef M 1938- *WhoAmP 91*
**Galiber**, Joseph L. 1924- *WhoBlA 92*
**Galiber**, Joseph Lionel 1924- *WhoAmP 91*
**Galibois**, Andre 1938- *AmMWSc 92*
**Galich**, Aleksandr Arkadievich 1919-1977 *SovUnBD*
**Galich**, Alexander 1919-1977 *LiExTwC*
**Galician**, Mary-Lou 1946- *IntAu&W 91, WhoEnt 92*
**Galie**, Catherine Ann 1947- *WhoEnt 92*
**Galie**, Louis Michael 1945- *WhoFI 92*
**Galifianakis**, Nick 1928- *WhoAmP 91*
**Galil**, Fahmy 1925- *AmMWSc 92*
**Galil**, Khadry Ahmed 1942- *AmMWSc 92*
**Galilei**, Vincenzo 1520?-1591 *NewAmDM*
**Galili**, Israel 1911-1986 *FacFETw*
**Galimi**, Dominick Joseph 1945- *WhoFI 92*
**Galimir**, Felix 1910- *WhoEnt 92*
**Galimore**, Michael Oliver 1947- *WhoFI 92*
**Galin**, Aleksandr 1942- *IntWW 91*
**Galin**, David 1936- *AmMWSc 92*
**Galin**, Miles A 1932- *AmMWSc 92*
**Galindez**, Emilio 1943- *WhoHisp 92*
**Galindo**, Anibal H 1929- *AmMWSc 92*
**Galindo**, Blas 1910- *ConCom 92*
**Galindo**, Cezar 1954- *WhoHisp 92*
**Galindo**, Eileen 1966- *WhoHisp 92*
**Galindo**, Felipe 1957- *WhoHisp 92*
**Galindo**, Israel 1954- *WhoRel 92*
**Galindo**, Kelly Elaine 1963- *WhoEnt 92*
**Galindo**, P. 1929- *WhoHisp 92*
**Galindo**, Rafael *WhoHisp 92*
**Galindo**, Ramon Gracia 1921- *WhoHisp 92*
**Galindo**, Xiomara Inez 1961- *WhoHisp 92*
**Galindo Dimas**, Blas 1910- *ConCom 92*
**Galindo-Elvira**, Carlos 1967- *WhoHisp 92*
**Galine**, Donald Leslie 1945- *WhoAmL 92*
**Galinsky**, Alvin M 1931- *AmMWSc 92*
**Galinsky**, Irving 1921- *AmMWSc 92*
**Galinsky**, Karl 1942- *WrDr 92*
**Galinsky**, Marsha Dee 1958- *WhoAmL 92*
**Galinsky**, Raymond Ethan 1948- *AmMWSc 92*
**Galioto**, Salvatore *DrAPF 91*
**Galioto**, Salvatore 1925- *IntAu&W 91*
**Galipeau**, Steven Arthur 1948- *WhoWest 92*
**Galitski**, Thomas B. 1943- *WhoFI 92*
**Galitz**, Donald S 1935- *AmMWSc 92*
**Galitz**, Robert Frederick 1931- *WhoMW 92, WhoRel 92*
**Galivan**, John H 1939- *AmMWSc 92*
**Galjaard**, Hans 1935- *IntWW 91*
**Galkin**, Dmitri Prokhovovich 1926- *IntWW 91*
**Galkowski**, Catherine Helen 1957- *WhoMW 92*
**Galkowski**, Theodore Thaddeus 1921- *AmMWSc 92*
**Gall**, A. Philip 1952- *WhoEnt 92*
**Gall**, Carl Evert 1931- *AmMWSc 92*
**Gall**, David Anthony 1941- *WhoMW 92*
**Gall**, Donald Alan 1934- *AmMWSc 92, WhoWest 92*
**Gall**, Donald Arthur 1936- *WhoRel 92*
**Gall**, Elizabeth Benson 1944- *WhoMW 92*
**Gall**, Eugene Harvey 1946- *WhoRel 92*
**Gall**, Graham A E 1936- *AmMWSc 92*

**Gall**, Henderson Alexander 1927- *IntAu&W 91, Who 92*
**Gall**, James William 1942- *AmMWSc 92*
**Gall**, Joseph Grafton 1928- *AmMWSc 92, IntWW 91*
**Gall**, Lawrence Howard 1917- *WhoAmL 92*
**Gall**, Lenore Rosalie 1943- *WhoBlA 92*
**Gall**, Martin 1944- *AmMWSc 92*
**Gall**, Robert Stephen 1958- *WhoRel 92*
**Gall**, Sally M. *DrAPF 91*
**Gall**, Sally Moore 1941- *IntAu&W 91*
**Gall**, Sandy *Who 92*
**Gall**, Walter George 1929- *AmMWSc 92*
**Gall**, William Einar 1942- *AmMWSc 92*
**Galla Placidia** 392?-450 *EncEarC*
**Gallacher** *Who 92*
**Gallacher**, Baron 1920- *Who 92*
**Gallacher**, Bernard 1949- *Who 92*
**Gallacher**, John 1931- *Who 92*
**Gallacher**, Tom 1934- *WrDr 92*
**Gallager**, Gale *ConAu 35NR*
**Gallager**, Mike John 1945- *WhoBlA 92*
**Gallager**, Robert G 1931- *AmMWSc 92*
**Gallagher**, Abisola Helen 1950- *WhoBlA 92*
**Gallagher**, Alan C 1936- *AmMWSc 92*
**Gallagher**, Anne Porter 1950- *WhoFI 92*
**Gallagher**, Annette 1924- *WhoRel 92*
**Gallagher**, Blanche Marie 1922- *WhoMW 92*
**Gallagher**, Brad K 1944- *WhoIns 92*
**Gallagher**, Brent S 1939- *AmMWSc 92*
**Gallagher**, Brian A 1957- *WhoAmP 91*
**Gallagher**, Brian Boru 1934- *AmMWSc 92*
**Gallagher**, Buell Gordon 1904-1978 *ConAu 133*
**Gallagher**, Charles Clifton 1937- *AmMWSc 92*
**Gallagher**, David Alden 1949- *AmMWSc 92*
**Gallagher**, Dennis Hugh 1936- *WhoEnt 92*
**Gallagher**, Dennis Joseph 1939- *WhoAmP 91*
**Gallagher**, Dennis Vincent 1952- *WhoEnt 92*
**Gallagher**, Francis George Kenna 1917- *IntWW 91, Who 92*
**Gallagher**, Francis Heath 1905- *Who 92*
**Gallagher**, George Arthur 1923- *AmMWSc 92*
**Gallagher**, Idella Jane Smith 1917- *WhoMW 92*
**Gallagher**, J Jack, Jr *WhoAmP 91*
**Gallagher**, Jack Burt 1947- *WhoEnt 92*
**Gallagher**, James A 1926- *AmMWSc 92*
**Gallagher**, James Aloysius 1926- *WhoMW 92*
**Gallagher**, James J 1922- *AmMWSc 92*
**Gallagher**, James J A 1927- *WhoAmP 91*
**Gallagher**, James Michael 1946- *WhoFI 92*
**Gallagher**, James Roswell 1903- *IntAu&W 91, WrDr 92*
**Gallagher**, Jane Chispa 1950- *AmMWSc 92*
**Gallagher**, Joel Peter 1942- *AmMWSc 92*
**Gallagher**, John 1919-1980 *ConAu 133*
**Gallagher**, John Andrew 1955- *WhoEnt 92*
**Gallagher**, John Clarence 1934- *WhoRel 92*
**Gallagher**, John Joseph, Jr 1940- *AmMWSc 92*
**Gallagher**, John Leslie 1935- *AmMWSc 92*
**Gallagher**, John M, Jr 1927- *AmMWSc 92*
**Gallagher**, John Michael *WhoFI 92*
**Gallagher**, John Patrick 1924- *WhoRel 92*
**Gallagher**, John Robert, Jr. 1941- *WhoMW 92*
**Gallagher**, John Sill 1947- *AmMWSc 92*
**Gallagher**, Kenna *Who 92*
**Gallagher**, Kent Grey 1933- *WhoEnt 92, WhoMW 92*
**Gallagher**, Kevin M 1932- *WhoIns 92*
**Gallagher**, Kim 1964- *BlkOlyM*
**Gallagher**, Leo Aloysius 1923- *WhoFI 92*
**Gallagher**, Lori 1950- *WhoEnt 92*
**Gallagher**, Maire Teresa 1933- *Who 92*
**Gallagher**, Margie Lee *AmMWSc 92*
**Gallagher**, Mark Steven 1956- *WhoFI 92*
**Gallagher**, Mark Thomas 1956- *WhoAmL 92*
**Gallagher**, Mary Kevin 1926- *WhoRel 92*
**Gallagher**, Michael 1934- *Who 92*
**Gallagher**, Michael Patrick 1958- *WhoEnt 92*
**Gallagher**, Michael Terrance 1943- *AmMWSc 92*
**Gallagher**, Monica *Who 92*
**Gallagher**, Neal Charles 1949- *AmMWSc 92*
**Gallagher**, Neil Ignatius 1926- *AmMWSc 92*
**Gallagher**, Patricia *WrDr 92*
**Gallagher**, Patrick Francis Xavier 1952- *WhoMW 92*
**Gallagher**, Patrick Joseph 1921- *Who 92*
**Gallagher**, Patrick Kent 1931- *AmMWSc 92, WhoMW 92*
**Gallagher**, Patrick Ximenes 1935- *AmMWSc 92*
**Gallagher**, Peter 1955- *ConTFT 9, IntMPA 92*
**Gallagher**, Peter Freeman 1957- *WhoFI 92*
**Gallagher**, Phil C 1926- *WhoIns 92*
**Gallagher**, Richard Hugo 1927- *AmMWSc 92*
**Gallagher**, Richard S. 1942- *WhoAmL 92*
**Gallagher**, Robert Melvin 1950- *WhoFI 92*
**Gallagher**, Sean Joseph 1963- *WhoAmL 92*
**Gallagher**, Terence Joseph 1934- *WhoAmL 92*
**Gallagher**, Tess *DrAPF 91, WrDr 92*
**Gallagher**, Tess 1932- *ConPo 91*
**Gallagher**, Thomas Allen 1942- *WhoAmL 92*
**Gallagher**, Thomas Francis 1944- *AmMWSc 92*
**Gallagher**, Thomas George 1941- *WhoRel 92*
**Gallagher**, Thomas J 1949- *WhoIns 92*
**Gallagher**, Thomas Joseph 1949- *WhoFI 92*
**Gallagher**, Tom 1944- *WhoAmP 91, WhoFI 92*
**Gallagher**, William Davis 1808-1894 *BenetAL 91*
**Gallagher**, William J 1931- *AmMWSc 92*
**Gallaher**, Art, Jr 1925- *IntAu&W 91, WrDr 92*
**Gallaher**, Charles Morris 1944- *WhoWest 92*
**Gallaher**, Cynthia *DrAPF 91*
**Gallaher**, Daniel David 1952- *AmMWSc 92*
**Gallaher**, James Alexander 1957- *WhoAmP 91*
**Gallaher**, Lawrence Joseph 1925- *AmMWSc 92*
**Gallaher**, William Richard 1944- *AmMWSc 92*
**Gallais**, Fernand Georges 1908- *IntWW 91*
**Galland**, Adolf 1912- *EncTR 91 [port]*
**Gallander**, James Francis 1937- *AmMWSc 92*
**Gallant Fox** 1927-1954 *FacFETw*
**Gallant**, Donald 1929- *AmMWSc 92*
**Gallant**, Esther May 1943- *AmMWSc 92*
**Gallant**, James *DrAPF 91*
**Gallant**, Jonathan A 1937- *AmMWSc 92*
**Gallant**, Mavis *DrAPF 91*
**Gallant**, Mavis 1922- *BenetAL 91, ConNov 91, FacFETw, LiExTwC, RfGEnL 91, WrDr 92*
**Gallant**, Noelle *WrDr 92*
**Gallant**, Roy A. 1924- *SmATA 68 [port]*
**Gallant**, Roy Arthur 1924- *IntAu&W 91, WrDr 92*
**Gallant**, Timothy Lee 1952- *WhoWest 92*
**Gallanty**, Alan Todd 1959- *WhoAmL 92*
**Gallar**, John Joseph 1936- *WhoWest 92*
**Gallardo**, David Felipe 1958- *WhoHisp 92*
**Gallardo**, Dora Castillo 1947- *WhoHisp 92*
**Gallardo**, Guadalupe 1962- *WhoHisp 92*
**Gallardo**, Joseph Inez 1951- *WhoHisp 92*
**Gallardo**, Ramon A. 1937- *WhoHisp 92*
**Gallardo**, Sara 1931-1988 *SpAmWW*
**Gallardo**, Silvana Sandra *WhoHisp 92*
**Gallardo-Carpentier**, Adriana 1930- *AmMWSc 92*
**Gallardo Garcia**, Rafael 1927- *WhoRel 92*
**Gallary**, Peter Hayden 1945- *WhoFI 92*
**Gallati**, Walter William 1927- *AmMWSc 92*
**Gallatin**, Albert *DcAmImH*
**Gallatin**, Albert 1761-1849 *AmPolLe, BenetAL 91*
**Gallaway**, Bob Mitchel 1916- *AmMWSc 92*
**Gallaway**, Guy Austin 1938- *WhoAmP 91*
**Gallaway**, James d1798 *DcNCBi 2*
**Gallaway**, John Marion 1835-1909 *DcNCBi 2*
**Gallaway**, John Mark 1925- *WhoAmP 91*
**Galle**, Emile 1846-1904 *DcTwDes*
**Galle**, Kurt R 1925- *AmMWSc 92*
**Gallea**, Anthony Michael 1949- *WhoFI 92*
**Gallea**, Christina 1942- *WhoEnt 92*
**Gallegly**, Elton 1944- *AlmAP 92 [port], WhoAmP 91*
**Gallegly**, Elton William 1944- *WhoWest 92*
**Gallegly**, Mannon Elihu 1923- *AmMWSc 92*
**Gallegly**, Wayne Edwin 1943- *WhoAmP 91*
**Gallego**, Augustine *WhoHisp 92*
**Gallego**, Daniel Tapia 1935- *WhoHisp 92*
**Gallego**, Guillermo 1957- *WhoHisp 92*
**Gallego**, Mike 1960- *WhoHisp 92*
**Gallego**, Pete *WhoHisp 92*
**Gallego**, Pete 1961- *WhoAmP 91*
**Gallegos**, Abigail Marquez 1952- *WhoHisp 92*
**Gallegos**, Alphonse 1931- *WhoRel 92, WhoWest 92*
**Gallegos**, Andrew Lalo 1940- *WhoHisp 92*
**Gallegos**, Arnold Jose 1938- *WhoHisp 92*
**Gallegos**, Carlos *WhoHisp 92*
**Gallegos**, Carlos A. 1940- *WhoHisp 92*
**Gallegos**, Emilio Juan 1932- *AmMWSc 92*
**Gallegos**, Esteban Guillermo 1956- *WhoEnt 92, WhoHisp 92*
**Gallegos**, Eugene 1935- *WhoAmP 91*
**Gallegos**, Jake Eugene 1935- *WhoHisp 92*
**Gallegos**, John Paul 1935- *WhoHisp 92*
**Gallegos**, Jose Ramon 1948- *WhoEnt 92*
**Gallegos**, Larry A., Sr. 1944- *WhoHisp 92*
**Gallegos**, Larry Duayne 1951- *WhoAmL 92*
**Gallegos**, Laura Matilde 1924- *WhoHisp 92*
**Gallegos**, Leonardo Eufemio 1940- *WhoHisp 92*
**Gallegos**, Louis E. 1943- *WhoHisp 92*
**Gallegos**, Luis Eloy-Alfonso 1936- *WhoHisp 92*
**Gallegos**, Lupe Leticia 1957- *WhoHisp 92*
**Gallegos**, Mario, Jr *WhoAmP 91*
**Gallegos**, Mario V., Jr. *WhoHisp 92*
**Gallegos**, Mark S. 1955- *WhoHisp 92*
**Gallegos**, Mark Steven 1955- *WhoAmL 92*
**Gallegos**, Martin 1956- *WhoHisp 92*
**Gallegos**, Mary Ellen 1949- *WhoHisp 92*
**Gallegos**, Michael Sharon 1952- *WhoHisp 92*
**Gallegos**, Michel Rose 1944- *WhoRel 92*
**Gallegos**, Pete 1940- *WhoHisp 92*
**Gallegos**, Raymond Robert 1935- *WhoHisp 92*
**Gallegos**, Robert A. 1956- *WhoHisp 92*
**Gallegos**, Robert C. 1940- *WhoHisp 92*
**Gallegos**, Romulo 1884-1969 *BenetAL 91, FacFETw*
**Gallegos**, Rudolph T. 1944- *WhoHisp 92*
**Gallegos**, Sandra Luz 1951- *WhoHisp 92*
**Gallegos**, Steve D. *WhoHisp 92*
**Gallegos**, Thomas Gilbert 1946- *WhoHisp 92*
**Gallegos**, Tony E. 1924- *WhoHisp 92*
**Gallegos**, Vincent *WhoAmP 91, WhoHisp 92*
**Galleher**, Stephen Cary 1942- *WhoEnt 92*
**Gallela**, Francis Anthony 1943- *WhoFI 92*
**Gallelli**, Joseph F 1936- *AmMWSc 92*
**Gallen**, James J 1928- *WhoAmP 91*
**Gallen**, Joel A. 1957- *WhoEnt 92*
**Gallen**, William J 1924- *AmMWSc 92*
**Gallenberg**, Loretta A 1957- *AmMWSc 92*
**Galleno**, Humberto 1943- *WhoFI 92*
**Gallenstein**, Edward Francis 1922- *WhoMW 92*
**Gallent**, John Bryant 1902- *AmMWSc 92*
**Galler**, Bernard Aaron 1928- *AmMWSc 92, WhoMW 92*
**Galler**, Janina Regina *AmMWSc 92*
**Galler**, Sidney Roland 1922- *AmMWSc 92*
**Galler**, William Sylvan 1929- *AmMWSc 92*
**Galles**, Duane LeRoy Charles Mealman 1948- *WhoMW 92*
**Galletta**, Gene John 1929- *AmMWSc 92*
**Galletta**, Joseph Leo 1935- *WhoWest 92*
**Galletta**, Nunzio 1927- *WhoFI 92*
**Galletti**, Pierre Marie 1927- *AmMWSc 92*
**Galley**, Robert 1921- *IntWW 91*
**Galley**, Robert Albert Ernest 1909- *Who 92*
**Galley**, Roy 1947- *Who 92*
**Galleymore**, Frances 1946- *WrDr 92*
**Gallez**, Bernard 1938- *AmMWSc 92*
**Galli**, Caterina 1723?-1804 *NewAmDM*
**Galli**, Darrell Joseph 1948- *WhoWest 92*
**Galli**, John Ronald 1936- *AmMWSc 92*
**Galli-Curci**, Amelita 1882-1963 *NewAmDM*
**Galli-Marie**, Celestine 1840-1905 *NewAmDM*
**Gallian**, Joseph A 1942- *AmMWSc 92*
**Gallian**, Leslie Jane 1964- *WhoRel 92*
**Gallian**, Russell Joseph 1948- *WhoAmL 92*
**Galliano**, Alina 1950- *WhoHisp 92*
**Gallico**, Paul 1897-1976 *BenetAL 91, FacFETw*
**Gallie**, Thomas Muir 1925- *AmMWSc 92*
**Gallie**, Walter Bryce 1912- *Who 92*
**Gallienne**, Paul Malcolm 1955- *WhoEnt 92*
**Gallienus** 218?-268 *EncEarC*
**Galliers-Pratt**, Anthony Malcolm 1926- *Who 92*
**Galliford**, David George 1925- *Who 92*
**Galligan**, Frank Daniel 1938- *WhoMW 92*
**Galligan**, James M 1931- *AmMWSc 92*
**Galligan**, John D 1932- *AmMWSc 92*
**Galligan**, Sara Ann 1949- *WhoAmL 92*
**Galligan**, Zach 1964- *IntMPA 92*
**Galligan**, Zachary Wolfe 1964- *WhoEnt 92*
**Galliher**, Keith Edwin, Jr. 1947- *WhoFI 92*
**Gallik**, Janice Susan *WhoWest 92*
**Galliker**, Franz 1926- *IntWW 91*
**Gallimard**, Claude 1914-1991 *IntWW 91, -91N, NewYTBS 91*
**Gallin**, John I 1943- *AmMWSc 92*
**Gallina**, Charles Onofrio 1943- *WhoMW 92*
**Gallinaro**, Nicholas Francis 1930- *WhoFI 92*
**Galliner**, Edith 1914- *TwCPaSc*
**Galliner**, Peter 1920- *IntWW 91, Who 92*
**Gallini**, John B 1934- *AmMWSc 92*
**Gallinot**, Ruth Maxine 1925- *WhoMW 92*
**Gallipeau**, Richard William 1928- *WhoAmP 91*
**Gallistel**, Charles Ransom 1941- *AmMWSc 92*
**Gallivan**, James Bernard 1938- *AmMWSc 92*
**Gallivan**, John William 1915- *WhoWest 92*
**Gallizioli**, Steve 1924- *AmMWSc 92*
**Gallo**, Anthony Edward, Jr 1931- *AmMWSc 92*
**Gallo**, August Anthony 1951- *AmMWSc 92*
**Gallo**, Charles Francis 1935- *AmMWSc 92*
**Gallo**, Dean A. 1935- *AlmAP 92 [port], WhoAmP 91*
**Gallo**, Duane Gordon 1926- *AmMWSc 92*
**Gallo**, Eduardo Felix 1945- *WhoMW 92*
**Gallo**, Ernest 1909- *WhoWest 92*
**Gallo**, Frank J 1921- *AmMWSc 92*
**Gallo**, Joseph Charles 1950- *WhoEnt 92*
**Gallo**, Joseph Edward 1917- *WhoWest 92*
**Gallo**, Julio 1910- *WhoWest 92*
**Gallo**, Lillian *LesBEnT 92*
**Gallo**, Linda Lou 1937- *AmMWSc 92*
**Gallo**, Louis *DrAPF 91*
**Gallo**, Robert 1937- *IntWW 91, News 91 [port]*
**Gallo**, Robert C 1937- *AmMWSc 92*
**Gallo**, Robert Vincent 1941- *AmMWSc 92*
**Gallo**, Thomas A *WhoAmP 91*
**Gallo**, Vincent John 1943- *WhoFI 92*
**Gallo-Fox**, Lesley Ann 1957- *WhoEnt 92*
**Gallo-Torres**, Hugo E *AmMWSc 92*
**Gallob**, Joel Aurom 1951- *WhoWest 92*
**Gallogly**, James Lawrence 1952- *WhoAmL 92*
**Gallois**, Louis 1944- *IntWW 91*
**Gallon**, Dennis P. *WhoBlA 92*
**Gallon**, Ray 1947- *WhoEnt 92*
**Gallone**, Carmine 1886-1973 *IntDcF 2-2 [port]*
**Gallop**, Paul Myron 1927- *AmMWSc 92*
**Gallopo**, Andrew Robert 1940- *AmMWSc 92*
**Gallopoulos**, Gregory Stratis 1959- *WhoAmL 92*
**Gallot**, Richard Joseph 1936- *WhoBlA 92*
**Gallow**, Amanda 1960- *WhoEnt 92*
**Galloway**, Bishop of 1926- *Who 92*
**Galloway**, Earl of 1928- *Who 92*
**Galloway**, Abraham H. d1870 *DcNCBi 2*
**Galloway**, Allan Douglas 1920- *Who 92, WrDr 92*
**Galloway**, Dale Frederick 1923- *WhoMW 92*
**Galloway**, Daniel Lee 1958- *WhoMW 92*
**Galloway**, David Alexander 1943- *WhoFI 92*
**Galloway**, Donald *WhoAmP 91*
**Galloway**, Ernestine Royal 1928- *WhoRel 92*
**Galloway**, Ethan Charles 1930- *AmMWSc 92*
**Galloway**, Frank Coffey, III 1962- *WhoAmL 92*
**Galloway**, Frank Coffey, Jr. 1938- *WhoAmL 92*
**Galloway**, George 1954- *Who 92*
**Galloway**, Gordon Lynn 1936- *AmMWSc 92*
**Galloway**, Grace Crowden d1782 *BlkwEAR*
**Galloway**, Gregory Bruce 1959- *WhoEnt 92*
**Galloway**, Harvey S, Jr 1934- *WhoIns 92*
**Galloway**, Harvey Scott, Jr. 1934- *WhoFI 92*
**Galloway**, James Neville 1944- *AmMWSc 92*
**Galloway**, Janice 1956- *WrDr 92*
**Galloway**, Joseph 1731?-1803 *BlkwEAR*
**Galloway**, Kenneth Franklin 1941- *AmMWSc 92, WhoWest 92*
**Galloway**, Kenneth Gardiner 1917- *Who 92*
**Galloway**, Lee 1945- *WhoEnt 92*
**Galloway**, Lillian Carroll 1934- *WhoEnt 92*
**Galloway**, Margaret Elinor 1927- *WhoMW 92*
**Galloway**, Pamela Eilene 1952- *WhoWest 92*
**Galloway**, Priscilla 1930- *SmATA 66 [port]*
**Galloway**, Raymond Alfred 1928- *AmMWSc 92*
**Galloway**, Raymond Forrest 1941- *WhoAmL 92*
**Galloway**, Richard H. 1940- *WhoAmL 92*
**Galloway**, Robert Edward 1931- *WhoMW 92*
**Galloway**, Robert Gene 1949- *WhoRel 92*

**Galloway,** Shirley A 1934- *WhoAmP 91*
**Galloway,** Tom Taylor 1957- *WhoEnt 92*
**Galloway,** William 1877-1952 *FacFETw*
**Galloway,** William Don 1939- *AmMWSc 92*
**Galloway,** William Edmond 1944- *AmMWSc 92*
**Galloway,** William Joyce 1924- *AmMWSc 92*
**Gallu,** Samuel G. d1991 *NewYTBS 91*
**Gallucci,** Robert Russell 1950- *AmMWSc 92*
**Galluccio,** Douglas Francis 1965- *WhoEnt 92*
**Gallun,** Raymond Z 1911- *TwCSFW 91, WrDr 92*
**Gallun,** Raymond Zinke 1911- *IntAu&W 91*
**Gallun,** Robert Louis 1924- *AmMWSc 92*
**Gallup,** Bonnie Lee 1948- *WhoWest 92*
**Gallup,** David Norris 1940- *WhoWest 92*
**Gallup,** Dick *DrAPF 91*
**Gallup,** Donald Noel 1931- *AmMWSc 92*
**Gallup,** George H 1901-1984 *FacFETw*
**Gallup,** Lee *WhoEnt 92*
**Gallus** *NewAmDM*
**Gallus Mag** *EncAmaz 91*
**Gallwey,** Philip Frankland P. *Who 92*
**Gallwey,** Sydney H. 1921- *WhoBlA 92*
**Gallwey,** W. Timothy 1938- *WrDr 92*
**Galm,** John Arnold 1934- *WhoWest 92*
**Galm,** Robert Woods 1942- *WhoAmP 91*
**Galmarino,** Alberto Raul 1928- *AmMWSc 92*
**Galmot,** Yves 1931- *IntWW 91*
**Galnick,** Mitchell Neil 1953- *WhoAmL 92*
**Galonsky,** Aaron Irving 1929- *AmMWSc 92*
**Galosy,** Richard Allen 1946- *AmMWSc 92*
**Galouye,** Daniel F 1911?-1976 *TwCSFW 91*
**Galouye,** Daniel Francis 1920-1976 *ConAu 134*
**Galper,** Jonas Bernard *AmMWSc 92*
**Galperin,** Irving 1926- *AmMWSc 92*
**Galperin,** Si Hirsch, Jr 1931- *WhoAmP 91*
**Galpern** *Who 92*
**Galpern,** Baron 1903- *Who 92*
**Galpin,** Brian John Francis 1921- *Who 92*
**Galpin,** Donald R 1933- *AmMWSc 92*
**Galpin,** Francis W. 1858-1945 *NewAmDM*
**Galpin,** Rodney D. 1932- *IntWW 91*
**Galpin,** Rodney Desmond 1932- *Who 92*
**Galsky,** Alan Gary 1942- *AmMWSc 92*
**Galstad,** Robin Rose Mlada 1963- *WhoMW 92*
**Galstaun,** Lionel Samuel 1913- *AmMWSc 92*
**Galster,** Richard W 1930- *AmMWSc 92*
**Galster,** William Allen 1932- *AmMWSc 92, WhoWest 92*
**Galston,** Arthur William 1920- *AmMWSc 92*
**Galston,** Clarence E 1909- *WhoIns 92*
**Galsworthy,** Anthony Charles 1944- *Who 92*
**Galsworthy,** Arthur Michael 1944- *Who 92*
**Galsworthy,** John 1867-1933 *CnDBLB 5 [port], FacFETw, RfGEnL 91, WhoNob 90*
**Galsworthy,** John 1919- *IntWW 91, Who 92*
**Galsworthy,** Michael *Who 92*
**Galsworthy,** Peter Robert 1939- *AmMWSc 92*
**Galsworthy,** Sara B 1938- *AmMWSc 92*
**Galt,** Charles Parker, Jr 1942- *AmMWSc 92*
**Galt,** Jack E 1923- *WhoAmP 91*
**Galt,** John 1779-1839 *BenetAL 91, RfGEnL 91*
**Galt,** John 1925- *AmMWSc 92*
**Galt,** John Kirtland 1920- *AmMWSc 92, WhoWest 92*
**Galt,** John William 1940- *WhoEnt 92*
**Galt,** Robert Thomas 1953- *WhoRel 92*
**Galter,** Paul Elbert 1930- *WhoAmL 92*
**Galterio,** Louis 1951- *WhoFI 92*
**Galtieri,** Leopoldo Fortunato 1926- *FacFETw, IntWW 91*
**Galton,** Peter Malcolm 1942- *AmMWSc 92*
**Galton,** Raymond Percy 1930- *IntAu&W 91, Who 92*
**Galton,** Valerie Anne 1934- *AmMWSc 92*
**Galtung,** Johan 1930- *IntWW 91*
**Galuppi,** Baldassare 1706-1785 *BlkwCEP, NewAmDM*
**Galush,** William John 1942- *WhoMW 92*
**Galusha,** Joseph G, Jr 1945- *AmMWSc 92*
**Galuszka,** Mary Helene 1945- *WhoMW 92, WhoRel 92*
**Galvan,** Anthony, III 1946- *WhoWest 92*
**Galvan,** Eddie 1927- *WhoHisp 92*
**Galvan,** Jose Manuel 1952- *WhoHisp 92*
**Galvan,** Juan Manuel 1952- *WhoHisp 92*
**Galvan,** Manuel P. 1949- *WhoHisp 92*
**Galvan,** Manuel Paul 1949- *WhoMW 92*
**Galvan,** Mary Grace 1958- *WhoHisp 92*
**Galvan,** Mary Theresa 1957- *WhoMW 92*
**Galvan,** Noemi Ethel 1939- *WhoHisp 92*
**Galvan,** Robert J. 1921- *WhoHisp 92*
**Galvan,** Roberto A. *DrAPF 91*
**Galvano,** Mauro *WhoHisp 92*
**Galvao Filho,** Orlando 1940- *IntWW 91*
**Galveas,** Ernane 1922- *IntWW 91*
**Galvez,** Arnaldo E. 1940- *WhoHisp 92*
**Galvez,** Jorge F. 1940- *WhoHisp 92*
**Galvez,** Jose de 1720-1787 *HisDSpE*
**Galvez,** Manuel 1882-1962 *BenetAL 91, BiDExR*
**Galvin,** Aaron A 1932- *AmMWSc 92*
**Galvin,** Bernard Vincent Joseph 1933- *Who 92*
**Galvin,** Brendan *DrAPF 91*
**Galvin,** Brendan 1938- *ConPo 91, WrDr 92*
**Galvin,** Cyril Jerome, Jr 1935- *AmMWSc 92*
**Galvin,** Emma Corinne 1909- *WhoBlA 92*
**Galvin,** Fred 1936- *AmMWSc 92*
**Galvin,** Jene Maurice 1943- *WhoAmP 91*
**Galvin,** John Rogers 1929- *IntWW 91, Who 92*
**Galvin,** Madeline Sheila 1948- *WhoAmL 92, WhoFI 92*
**Galvin,** Martin *DrAPF 91*
**Galvin,** Mary Eleanor 1926- *WhoRel 92*
**Galvin,** Michael *WhoAmP 91*
**Galvin,** Patrick 1927- *ConPo 91, WrDr 92*
**Galvin,** Patrick G 1926- *WhoAmP 91*
**Galvin,** Robert J. 1938- *WhoAmL 92*
**Galvin,** Robert W 1922- *AmMWSc 92, IntWW 91*
**Galvin,** Thomas Joseph 1934- *AmMWSc 92*
**Galvin,** William C *WhoAmP 91*
**Galvin,** William F *WhoAmP 91*
**Galvin-Harrison,** Christopher 1956- *TwCPaSc*
**Galway,** Viscount 1922- *Who 92*
**Galway,** James 1939- *IntWW 91, NewAmDM, Who 92, WhoEnt 92*
**Galway,** Robert Conington *IntAu&W 91X*
**Galway And Kilmacduagh,** Bishop of 1927- *Who 92*
**Galwey,** Geoffrey 1912- *WrDr 92*
**Galyean,** John Gilmer 1952- *WhoEnt 92*
**Galyean,** Michael Lee 1951- *AmMWSc 92*
**Galysh,** Robert Alan 1954- *WhoMW 92*
**Gam,** Paul Jonathan 1959- *WhoMW 92*
**Gamache,** Joey *WhoHisp 92*
**Gamache,** Kathleen Anne 1956- *WhoAmL 92*
**Gamache,** Richard Donald 1935- *WhoFI 92*
**Gamache,** Valerie Anne *WhoFI 92*
**Gamades,** Alexandra 1930- *WhoRel 92*
**Gamage,** Herbert Lee 1935- *WhoMW 92*
**Gamaleya,** Nikolay Fedorovich 1859-1949 *SovUnBD*
**Gamar,** Reginald William 1936- *WhoEnt 92*
**Gamarra,** Agustin 1785-1841 *HisDSpE*
**Gamarro,** Pedro J 1955- *BlkOlyM*
**Gamary,** Bonnie Lee 1962- *WhoMW 92*
**Gamassi,** Mohamed Abdul Ghani al- 1921- *IntWW 91*
**Gamba,** John Jerome 1944- *WhoFI 92*
**Gamba,** Pedro Sarmiento de *HisDSpE*
**Gamba,** Piero 1936- *NewAmDM*
**Gamba-Stonehouse,** Virginia 1954- *ConAu 134*
**Gambal,** David 1931- *AmMWSc 92, WhoMW 92*
**Gambale,** Ganine 1961- *WhoAmL 92*
**Gambara** *EncAmaz 91*
**Gambardella,** William V 1960- *WhoAmP 91*
**Gambari,** Ibrahim Agboola 1944- *IntWW 91*
**Gambaro,** Ernest Umberto 1938- *WhoWest 92*
**Gambaro,** Griselda 1928- *SpAmWW*
**Gambee,** Robert Rankin 1942- *WhoFI 92*
**Gambel,** Michael Lawrence 1943- *WhoMW 92*
**Gambel,** William 1823-1849 *BiInAmS*
**Gambert,** Steven Ross 1949- *AmMWSc 92*
**Gambescia,** Joseph Marion 1919- *AmMWSc 92*
**Gambetta,** Jack 1949- *WhoFI 92*
**Gambhirwala,** Devang Chandravadan 1964- *WhoFI 92*
**Gambier,** Dominique 1947- *IntWW 91*
**Gambill,** Bruce Warren 1930- *WhoAmP 91*
**Gambill,** Calvin 1924- *WhoAmP 91*
**Gambill,** Christopher Brett 1957- *WhoAmL 92*
**Gambill,** John Douglas *AmMWSc 92*
**Gambill,** Robert Arnold 1927- *AmMWSc 92*
**Gambill,** Sue *DrAPF 91*
**Gambill,** Terry A. 1942- *WhoMW 92*
**Gambill,** Walter Ray 1922- *WhoAmL 92*
**Gambino,** Diane R *IntAu&W 91*
**Gambino,** Jerome James 1925- *WhoWest 92*
**Gambino,** Richard Joseph 1935- *AmMWSc 92*
**Gambino,** S Raymond 1926- *AmMWSc 92*
**Gambino,** Thomas Dominic 1942- *WhoEnt 92*
**Gamble,** Andrew Michael 1947- *IntAu&W 91, WrDr 92*
**Gamble,** David 1966- *Who 92*
**Gamble,** Dean Franklin 1920- *AmMWSc 92*
**Gamble,** Dennis Bruce, I 1956- *WhoRel 92*
**Gamble,** Douglas Irvin 1953- *WhoMW 92*
**Gamble,** Ed 1943- *ConAu 133*
**Gamble,** Edward Hill 1943- *WhoEnt 92*
**Gamble,** Eva M. 1952- *WhoBlA 92*
**Gamble,** Francis Trevor 1928- *AmMWSc 92*
**Gamble,** Fred Ridley, Jr 1941- *AmMWSc 92*
**Gamble,** James Lawder, Jr 1921- *AmMWSc 92*
**Gamble,** Janet Helen 1917- *WhoBlA 92*
**Gamble,** John Reeves, Jr 1922- *WhoAmP 91*
**Gamble,** John Robert 1921- *AmMWSc 92*
**Gamble,** Joseph Graham, Jr. 1926- *WhoAmL 92*
**Gamble,** Kenneth 1943- *WhoBlA 92*
**Gamble,** Kenneth L. 1941- *WhoBlA 92*
**Gamble,** Kevin Douglas 1965- *WhoBlA 92*
**Gamble,** Lee St. Clair 1954- *WhoWest 92*
**Gamble,** Oscar Charles 1949- *WhoBlA 92*
**Gamble,** Richard Craig 1955- *WhoMW 92, WhoRel 92*
**Gamble,** Richard John 1948- *WhoEnt 92*
**Gamble,** Robert Lewis 1947- *WhoBlA 92*
**Gamble,** Robert Oscar 1935- *AmMWSc 92*
**Gamble,** Ron 1933- *WhoAmP 91*
**Gamble,** Theodore Robert, Jr. 1953- *WhoFI 92*
**Gamble,** Thomas Dean 1947- *AmMWSc 92*
**Gamble,** Tracy Joseph 1954- *WhoEnt 92*
**Gamble,** Wilbert 1932- *AmMWSc 92, WhoBlA 92*
**Gamble,** William F. 1950- *WhoBlA 92*
**Gamble,** William Leo 1936- *AmMWSc 92*
**Gamblian,** Stan Harrison 1952- *WhoMW 92*
**Gamblin,** Marty Nolan 1944- *WhoEnt 92*
**Gambling,** William Alexander 1926- *IntWW 91, Who 92*
**Gamboa,** Alejandro 1948- *WhoHisp 92*
**Gamboa,** Anthony H. 1942- *WhoHisp 92*
**Gamboa,** Darlene 1948- *WhoHisp 92*
**Gamboa,** Erasmo 1941- *WhoHisp 92*
**Gamboa,** George Charles 1923- *WhoWest 92*
**Gamboa,** George John 1946- *AmMWSc 92*
**Gamboa,** Harry, Jr. 1951- *WhoHisp 92*
**Gamboa,** John C. 1941- *WhoHisp 92*
**Gamboa,** Reymundo *DrAPF 91*
**Gamboa,** Theodore David 1951- *WhoHisp 92*
**Gambon,** Michael 1940- *IntMPA 92*
**Gambon,** Michael John 1940- *IntWW 91, Who 92*
**Gamborg,** Oluf Lind 1924- *AmMWSc 92*
**Gambrell,** Carroll B, Jr 1924- *AmMWSc 92*
**Gambrell,** David Henry 1929- *IntWW 91, WhoAmL 92, WhoAmP 91*
**Gambrell,** Lydia Jahn 1904- *AmMWSc 92*
**Gambrell,** Samuel C, Jr 1935- *AmMWSc 92*
**Gambrell,** Sarah Belk 1918- *WhoFI 92*
**Gambrill,** Eileen 1934- *ConAu 34NR*
**Gambro,** Michael S. 1954- *WhoAmL 92, WhoWest 92*
**Gambs,** Carl M. 1943- *WhoFI 92, WhoMW 92*
**Gambs,** Gerard Charles 1918- *AmMWSc 92*
**Gambs,** Roger Duane *AmMWSc 92*
**Game,** John Charles 1946- *AmMWSc 92*
**Gamedze,** A. B. 1921- *IntWW 91*
**Gamelin,** Maurice-Gustave 1872-1958 *EncTR 91 [port]*
**Gamelin,** Theodore W 1939- *AmMWSc 92*
**Gamer,** Nancy Crews 1937- *WhoWest 92*
**Gamero Del Castillo,** Pedro 1910-1984 *BiDExR*
**Gameros,** L. Ignacio 1939- *WhoHisp 92*
**Games,** Abram 1914- *Who 92*
**Games,** Keith Max 1928- *WhoMW 92*
**Gamet,** Donald Max 1916- *WhoFI 92*
**Gamez,** Antonio 1955- *WhoHisp 92*
**Gamez,** Kathy Joe 1956- *WhoHisp 92*
**Gamez,** Robert 1968- *WhoHisp 92*
**Gaminara,** Albert William 1913- *Who 92*
**Gamkrelidze,** Thomas V. 1929- *IntWW 91*
**Gamm,** Gordon Julius 1939- *WhoAmL 92*
**Gamm,** Stanford Ralph 1917- *WhoWest 92*
**Gammage,** Henry Burcher 1947- *WhoEnt 92*
**Gammage,** Richard Bertram 1937- *AmMWSc 92*
**Gammage,** Robert Alton 1938- *WhoAmP 91*
**Gammal,** Albert Abraham, Jr 1928- *WhoAmP 91*
**Gammal,** Elias Bichara 1930- *AmMWSc 92*
**Gammel,** George Michael 1952- *AmMWSc 92*
**Gammel,** John Ledel 1924- *AmMWSc 92*
**Gammelgaard,** Lars P. 1945- *IntWW 91*
**Gammell,** Gloria Ruffner 1948- *WhoWest 92*
**Gammell,** James Gilbert Sydney 1920- *Who 92*
**Gammell,** John Frederick 1921- *Who 92*
**Gammell,** Paul M 1939- *AmMWSc 92*
**Gammell,** Stephen 1943- *ConAu 135*
**Gammell,** Wayne William 1940- *WhoMW 92*
**Gammell-Byas,** Denyce 1946- *WhoMW 92*
**Gammie,** Gordon Edward 1922- *Who 92*
**Gammill,** Darryl Curtis 1950- *WhoFI 92, WhoWest 92*
**Gammill,** John Stewart 1923- *WhoIns 92*
**Gammill,** Lee M, Jr 1934- *WhoIns 92*
**Gammill,** Lee Morgan, Jr. 1934- *WhoFI 92*
**Gammill,** Ronald Bruce 1948- *AmMWSc 92*
**Gammon,** E Ann 1933- *WhoAmP 91*
**Gammon,** James *IntMPA 92*
**Gammon,** James Alan 1934- *WhoAmL 92, WhoEnt 92*
**Gammon,** James Edwin, Sr. 1944- *WhoRel 92*
**Gammon,** James Robert 1930- *AmMWSc 92, WhoMW 92*
**Gammon,** Janice Carlene 1946- *WhoAmP 91*
**Gammon,** Malcolm Ernest, Sr. 1947- *WhoFI 92*
**Gammon,** Mattie Jean 1924- *WhoFI 92, WhoWest 92*
**Gammon,** Nathan, Jr 1914- *AmMWSc 92*
**Gammon,** Ray Eugene 1933- *WhoAmL 92*
**Gammon,** Reg 1894- *TwCPaSc*
**Gammon,** Reginald Adolphus 1921- *WhoBlA 92, WhoMW 92*
**Gammon,** Richard Anthony 1937- *AmMWSc 92*
**Gammon,** Richard Harriss 1943- *AmMWSc 92*
**Gammon,** Robert Winston 1940- *AmMWSc 92*
**Gammon,** Walter Ray 1942- *AmMWSc 92*
**Gammon,** William Clarence 1955- *WhoRel 92*
**Gammons,** Peter 1945- *WhoEnt 92*
**Gammons,** Peter T., Jr. 1936- *WhoIns 92*
**Gamo,** Hideya 1924- *AmMWSc 92*
**Gamon,** Hugh Wynell 1921- *Who 92*
**Gamoran,** Abraham Carmi 1926- *WhoFI 92*
**Gamoran,** Emanuel 1895-1962 *DcAmImH*
**Gamota,** George 1939- *AmMWSc 92*
**Gamow,** George 1904-1968 *FacFETw*
**Gamow,** Rustem Igor 1935- *AmMWSc 92*
**Gamroth,** Arthur Paul 1930- *WhoFI 92*
**Gams,** Sylvia S 1943- *WhoAmP 91*
**Gamsakhurdia,** Zviad Konstantinovich 1939- *IntWW 91, SovUnBD*
**Gamsey,** David Lee 1957- *WhoFI 92*
**Gamsky,** Neal Richard 1931- *WhoMW 92*
**Gamso,** Jeffrey Michael 1949- *WhoAmL 92*
**Gamson,** Bernard W 1917- *AmMWSc 92*
**Gamson,** Leland Pablo *DrAPF 91*
**Gamson,** William A. 1934- *WrDr 92*
**Gamst,** Frederick Charles 1936- *WrDr 92*
**Gamwell,** Franklin I. *WhoRel 92*
**Gamzatov,** Rasul Gamzatovich 1923- *IntWW 91*
**Gamzu,** Elkan R 1943- *AmMWSc 92*
**Gan Zhijian** *IntWW 91*
**Gan Ziyu** 1929- *IntWW 91*
**Gan,** Jose Cajilig 1933- *AmMWSc 92*
**Ganao,** David-Charles 1928- *IntWW 91*
**Ganapathy,** Ramachandran 1939- *AmMWSc 92*
**Ganapathy,** Seetha N 1932- *AmMWSc 92*
**Ganapol,** Barry Douglas 1944- *AmMWSc 92*
**Ganas,** Perry S 1937- *AmMWSc 92*
**Ganatra,** Jayant K. 1939- *WhoMW 92*
**Ganaway,** James Rives 1927- *AmMWSc 92*
**Ganbaatar,** Adyagiin 1959- *IntWW 91*
**Ganbold,** Davaadorjiin 1957- *IntWW 91*
**Gancarz,** Alexander John 1948- *AmMWSc 92*
**Gance,** Abel 1889-1981 *FacFETw, IntDcF 2-2 [port]*
**Gancer,** Donald Charles 1933- *WhoAmL 92*
**Ganchiff,** Robert Lee 1935- *WhoMW 92*
**Ganchoff,** John Christopher 1933- *AmMWSc 92*
**Ganchrow,** Donald 1940- *AmMWSc 92*
**Gancy,** Alan Brian 1932- *AmMWSc 92*
**Gandar,** Leslie Walter 1919- *Who 92*
**Gandara,** Daniel 1948- *WhoHisp 92*
**Gandara,** Jose Raul 1957- *WhoHisp 92*

**Gandara-Schwartz**, Rebecca Christine 1964- *WhoEnt 92*
**Gandee**, John Stephen 1909- *Who 92*
**Gandee**, Robert Lester 1947- *WhoMW 92*
**Gandelman**, Nona 1946- *WhoEnt 92*
**Gandelman**, Ronald Jay 1944- *AmMWSc 92*
**Gander**, Forrest *DrAPF 91*
**Gander**, Frederick W 1921- *AmMWSc 92*
**Gander**, George William 1930- *AmMWSc 92*
**Gander**, John E 1925- *AmMWSc 92*
**Gander**, Robert Johns 1918- *AmMWSc 92*
**Gander**, Stephen James 1950- *WhoEnt 92*
**Ganders**, Fred Russell 1945- *AmMWSc 92*
**Gandevia**, Bryan Harle 1925- *WrDr 92*
**Gandhi**, Harendra Sakarlal 1941- *AmMWSc 92*
**Gandhi**, Indira 1917-1984 *FacFETw [port]*
**Gandhi**, Maneka Anand 1956- *IntWW 91*
**Gandhi**, Manmohan Purushottam 1901- *Who 92*
**Gandhi**, Mohandas K 1869-1948 *FacFETw [port]*
**Gandhi**, Mukesh Vashumal 1956- *WhoMW 92*
**Gandhi**, Om P 1934- *AmMWSc 92*
**Gandhi**, Om Parkash 1934- *WhoWest 92*
**Gandhi**, Prem Parkash 1936- *WhoFI 92*
**Gandhi**, Rajiv d1991 *Who 92N*
**Gandhi**, Rajiv 1944- *IntWW 91*
**Gandhi**, Rajiv 1944-1991 *CurBio 91N, NewYTBS 91, News 91*
**Gandhi**, Rajiv 1945-1991 *FacFETw*
**Gandhi**, Sonia *NewYTBS 91 [port]*
**Gandia**, Aldo Ray 1958- *WhoHisp 92*
**Gandler**, Joseph Rubin 1949- *AmMWSc 92*
**Gandley**, Kenneth Royce *WrDr 92*
**Gandley**, Kenneth Royce 1920- *IntAu&W 91*
**Gandois**, Jean Guy Alphonse 1930- *IntWW 91*
**Gandolfi**, A Jay 1946- *AmMWSc 92*
**Gandolfo**, Joseph John 1959- *WhoAmL 92*
**Gandolfo**, Lucian John 1954- *WhoRel 92*
**Gandour**, Richard David 1945- *AmMWSc 92*
**Gandurski**, Ronald Edward 1941- *WhoMW 92*
**Gandy**, Christopher Thomas 1917- *Who 92*
**Gandy**, David Stewart 1932- *Who 92*
**Gandy**, Dean Murray 1927- *WhoAmL 92*
**Gandy**, H. Conway 1934- *WhoAmL 92*
**Gandy**, Michael Charles 1945- *WhoAmL 92*
**Gandy**, Roland A., Jr. 1924- *WhoBlA 92*
**Gandy**, Ronald Herbert 1917- *Who 92*
**Gane**, Barrie Charles 1935- *Who 92*
**Gane**, Michael 1927- *Who 92*
**Ganeff**, John Joseph 1942- *WhoRel 92*
**Ganelin Trio** *NewAmDM*
**Ganelin**, Vyacheslav 1944- *IntWW 91*
**Ganelius**, Tord Hjalmar 1925- *IntWW 91*
**Ganellin**, Charon Robin 1934- *IntWW 91, Who 92*
**Ganem**, Bruce 1948- *AmMWSc 92*
**Ganem**, John 1960- *WhoWest 92*
**Ganesan**, Adayapalam T 1932- *AmMWSc 92*
**Ganesan**, Ann K 1933- *AmMWSc 92*
**Ganesan**, Devaki 1940- *AmMWSc 92*
**Ganesan**, Nanda Kumar 1952- *WhoWest 92*
**Ganesh**, Orekonde 1941- *WhoMW 92*
**Ganet**, Abner S 1925- *WhoAmP 91*
**Ganey**, George Till, Jr. 1927- *WhoAmL 92*
**Ganey**, James Hobson 1944- *WhoBlA 92*
**Ganfield**, David Judd 1941- *AmMWSc 92*
**Gang**, Stephen R. 1951- *WhoEnt 92*
**Gangarosa**, Eugene J 1926- *AmMWSc 92*
**Gangarosa**, Louis Paul, Sr 1929- *AmMWSc 92*
**Gange**, Richard William 1945- *AmMWSc 92*
**Gangel**, Kenneth Otto 1935- *WhoRel 92*
**Gangemi**, Francis A 1929- *AmMWSc 92*
**Gangemi**, Francis Anthony 1929- *WhoMW 92*
**Gangemi**, Kenneth *DrAPF 91*
**Gangemi**, Kenneth 1937- *ConNov 91*
**Gangi**, Anthony Frank 1929- *AmMWSc 92*
**Gangi**, Rayna Marie 1950- *WhoFI 92*
**Gangjee**, Aleem 1948- *AmMWSc 92*
**Gangle**, Sandra Smith 1943- *WhoAmL 92*
**Gangloff**, Pierre 1941- *AmMWSc 92*
**Gangloff**, Richard Paul 1948- *AmMWSc 92*
**Gangnat**, Maurice 1856-1924 *ThHEIm*
**Gangstad**, Edward Otis 1917- *AmMWSc 92*
**Gangstad**, John Erik 1948- *WhoAmL 92*
**Gangulee**, Amitava 1941- *AmMWSc 92*
**Ganguli**, Mukul Chandra 1938- *AmMWSc 92*
**Ganguly**, Ashit K 1934- *AmMWSc 92*
**Ganguly**, Bishwa Nath 1942- *AmMWSc 92*
**Ganguly**, Jibamitra 1938- *AmMWSc 92*
**Ganguly**, Pankaj 1939- *AmMWSc 92*
**Ganguly**, Rama *AmMWSc 92*
**Ganguly**, Suman 1942- *AmMWSc 92*
**Gangwal**, Santosh Kumar 1947- *AmMWSc 92*
**Gangwer**, Thomas E 1946- *AmMWSc 92*
**Gangwere**, Heather Hendry 1964- *WhoWest 92*
**Gangwere**, Robert Lloyd 1952- *WhoAmL 92*
**Gangwere**, Stanley Kenneth 1925- *AmMWSc 92*
**Gangwisch**, Kathy A. *WhoEnt 92*
**Gani**, Joseph Mark 1924- *IntWW 91*
**Gani**, Shafiqul 1946- *IntWW 91*
**Ganick**, John Gershon 1939- *WhoAmL 92*
**Ganilau**, Penaia Kanatabatu 1918- *IntWW 91, Who 92*
**Ganion**, Larry Robert 1941- *WhoMW 92*
**Ganis**, Frank Michael Gangarosa 1924- *AmMWSc 92*
**Ganis**, Sidney M. 1940- *IntMPA 92*
**Ganis**, Stephen Lane 1951- *WhoAmL 92*
**Ganister**, Ruth Eileen 1950- *WhoAmL 92*
**Ganley**, Beatrice *DrAPF 91*
**Ganley**, Helen 1940- *TwCPaSc*
**Ganley**, James Joseph 1946- *WhoEnt 92*
**Ganley**, James Powell 1937- *AmMWSc 92*
**Ganley**, Oswald Harold 1929- *AmMWSc 92*
**Ganley**, W Paul 1934- *AmMWSc 92*
**Gann**, Donald L 1940- *WhoAmP 91*
**Gann**, Donald Stuart 1932- *AmMWSc 92*
**Gann**, Ernest K. 1910- *BenetAL 91, WrDr 92*
**Gann**, Ernest Kellogg d1991 *NewYTBS 91 [port]*
**Gann**, Ernest Kellogg 1910- *WhoEnt 92*
**Gann**, Glenn Alan 1955- *WhoRel 92*
**Gann**, Gregory Charles 1950- *WhoFI 92*
**Gann**, Lewis Henry 1924- *IntAu&W 91, WrDr 92*
**Gann**, Pamela Brooks 1948- *WhoAmL 92*
**Gann**, Paul 1912-1989 *FacFETw*
**Gann**, Richard George 1944- *AmMWSc 92*
**Gann**, Walter *TwCWW 91*
**Gann**, William D 1878- *ScFEYrs*
**Gannatal**, Joseph Paul 1955- *WhoWest 92*
**Gannaway**, Charles Everett 1962- *WhoEnt 92*
**Gannaway**, Nancy Harrison 1929- *WhoBlA 92*
**Gannes**, Abraham P. 1911- *WhoRel 92*
**Gannett**, Ann Cole 1916- *WhoAmP 91*
**Gannett**, Benjamin Hamlen 1942- *WhoFI 92*
**Gannett**, Damon L. 1947- *WhoAmL 92*
**Gannett**, Deborah Sampson 1760-1827 *BlkwEAR*
**Gannett**, Diana Ruth 1947- *WhoEnt 92*
**Gannett**, Henry 1846-1914 *BiInAmS*
**Gannett**, R. G. *WhoRel 92*
**Gannett**, Robert T 1917- *WhoAmP 91*
**Gannett**, Ruth Stiles 1923- *WrDr 92*
**Gannon**, Alice H 1954- *WhoIns 92*
**Gannon**, Christopher J. I. 1962- *WhoAmL 92*
**Gannon**, Frances Virginia 1929- *WhoWest 92*
**Gannon**, J. Truett 1930- *WhoRel 92*
**Gannon**, Jane Ann 1963- *WhoFI 92*
**Gannon**, John 1950- *WhoAmP 91*
**Gannon**, John Sexton 1927- *WhoAmL 92*
**Gannon**, Leo J 1950- *WhoAmP 91*
**Gannon**, Mark Stephen 1950- *WhoAmL 92*
**Gannon**, Mary Carol *AmMWSc 92*
**Gannon**, Paul J *WhoAmP 91*
**Gannon**, Richard Galen 1950- *WhoAmP 91*
**Gannon**, Robert P. *WhoWest 92*
**Gannon**, Thomas P 1943- *WhoAmP 91*
**Gano**, James Edward 1941- *AmMWSc 92*
**Gano**, John 1727-1804 *DcNCBi 2*
**Gano**, Richard W 1956- *AmMWSc 92*
**Gano**, Robert Daniel 1922- *AmMWSc 92*
**Ganong**, William Francis 1924- *AmMWSc 92*
**Ganopole**, Deidre Susan 1950- *WhoAmL 92*
**Ganote**, Charles Edgar 1937- *AmMWSc 92*
**Ganpat** 1886-1951 *ScFEYrs*
**Gans**, Bruce M. 1951- *WhoMW 92*
**Gans**, Bruce Michael *DrAPF 91*
**Gans**, Carl 1923- *AmMWSc 92*
**Gans**, David 1907- *AmMWSc 92*
**Gans**, Dennis Joseph 1949- *WhoFI 92*
**Gans**, Eric L. 1941- *WrDr 92*
**Gans**, Eric Lawrence 1941- *WhoWest 92*
**Gans**, Erna Irene *WhoMW 92*
**Gans**, Eugene Howard 1929- *AmMWSc 92*
**Gans**, Herbert J. 1927- *WrDr 92*
**Gans**, Joachim *DcNCBi 2*
**Gans**, Joseph Herbert 1922- *AmMWSc 92*
**Gans**, Manfred 1922- *AmMWSc 92*
**Gans**, Paul Jonathan 1933- *AmMWSc 92*
**Gans**, Roger Frederick 1941- *AmMWSc 92*
**Gans**, Samuel Myer 1925- *WhoFI 92*
**Gansauer**, Bruce W. 1949- *WhoMW 92*
**Gansberg**, Judith M. 1947- *WhoEnt 92*
**Ganschow**, Clifford Laurence 1935- *WhoMW 92*
**Ganschow**, Roger Elmer 1937- *AmMWSc 92*
**Ganshof Van Der Meersch**, Walter 1900- *IntWW 91*
**Gansler**, Jacques Singleton 1934- *ConAu 135*
**Gansz**, David C.D. *DrAPF 91*
**Gant**, Catherine Adamski 1936- *WhoAmL 92*
**Gant**, Donald Ross 1928- *WhoFI 92*
**Gant**, Fred Allan 1936- *AmMWSc 92*
**Gant**, Horace Zed 1914- *WhoAmL 92*
**Gant**, John William, Jr. 1955- *WhoAmL 92*
**Gant**, Jonathan *IntAu&W 91X, TwCWW 91*
**Gant**, Joseph Erwin 1912- *WhoWest 92*
**Gant**, Joseph Erwin, Jr 1912- *WhoAmP 91*
**Gant**, Kathy Savage 1947- *AmMWSc 92*
**Gant**, Norman Ferrell, Jr 1939- *AmMWSc 92*
**Gant**, Phillip M., III 1949- *WhoBlA 92*
**Gant**, Raymond Leroy 1961- *WhoBlA 92*
**Gant**, Richard *IntAu&W 91X, WrDr 92*
**Gant**, Ronald Edwin 1965- *WhoBlA 92*
**Gant**, Wanda Adele 1949- *WhoBlA 92*
**Gant**, William M 1939- *WhoAmP 91*
**Ganten**, Detlev 1941- *AmMWSc 92*
**Gantenbein**, Rex Earl 1950- *WhoWest 92*
**Ganter**, Bernard J. 1928- *WhoRel 92*
**Ganter**, Daniel Dean 1935- *WhoEnt 92*
**Ganter**, Gladys Marie 1908- *WhoMW 92*
**Ganter**, Susan Lynn 1964- *WhoWest 92*
**Ganther**, Howard Edward 1937- *AmMWSc 92*
**Ganthony**, Richard *ScFEYrs*
**Ganti**, Venkat Rao 1928- *AmMWSc 92*
**Gantin**, Bernardin 1922- *IntWW 91, WhoRel 92*
**Gantley**, Patrick Eugene 1944- *WhoFI 92*
**Gantman**, Geraldine Ann 1945- *WhoFI 92*
**Gantner**, Carrillo Baillieu 1944- *IntWW 91*
**Gantner**, George E, Jr 1927- *AmMWSc 92*
**Gantner**, Neilma *WrDr 92*
**Gantt**, David F 1941- *WhoAmP 91*
**Gantt**, Elisabeth 1934- *AmMWSc 92*
**Gantt**, Gloria 1945- *WhoBlA 92*
**Gantt**, Harvey *WhoAmP 91*
**Gantt**, Harvey 1943- *ConBlB 1 [port]*
**Gantt**, Harvey Bernard 1943- *WhoBlA 92*
**Gantt**, James Richard 1933- *WhoRel 92*
**Gantt**, Michael David 1951- *WhoRel 92*
**Gantt**, Ralph Raymond 1936- *AmMWSc 92*
**Gantt**, Rebecca Esler 1909- *WhoRel 92*
**Gantt**, Walter N. 1921- *WhoBlA 92*
**Gantz**, Bruce Jay 1946- *WhoMW 92*
**Gantz**, Frank Carlton 1960- *WhoRel 92*
**Gantz**, John G., Jr. 1948- *WhoFI 92, WhoIns 92*
**Gantz**, Nancy Rollins 1949- *WhoWest 92*
**Gantz**, Ralph Lee 1932- *AmMWSc 92*
**Gantz**, Wilbur H., III 1937- *IntWW 91*
**Gantz**, Wilbur Henry, III 1937- *WhoFI 92, WhoMW 92*
**Gantzel**, Peter Kellogg 1934- *AmMWSc 92*
**Gantzer**, John Carroll 1947- *WhoWest 92*
**Gantzer**, Mary Lou 1950- *AmMWSc 92*
**Ganus**, Clifton Loyd, III 1945- *WhoEnt 92*
**Ganz**, Aaron 1924- *AmMWSc 92*
**Ganz**, Albert Frederick 1872-1917 *BiInAmS*
**Ganz**, Bruno 1941- *IntMPA 92*
**Ganz**, Charles Robert 1942- *AmMWSc 92*
**Ganz**, David L. 1951- *WhoAmL 92, WhoFI 92*
**Ganz**, Felix 1959- *WhoFI 92*
**Ganz**, Lowell 1948- *WhoEnt 92*
**Ganz**, Mark B. 1960- *WhoAmL 92*
**Ganz**, Paul Michael 1956- *WhoMW 92*
**Ganz**, Peter Felix 1920- *Who 92*
**Ganz**, Rudolph 1877-1972 *NewAmDM*
**Ganz**, Tony *ConTFT 9, IntMPA 92*
**Ganza**, Kresimir Peter 1948- *AmMWSc 92*
**Ganzerla**, John Thomas 1955- *WhoEnt 92*
**Ganzi**, Victor Frederick 1947- *WhoAmL 92*
**Ganzl**, Kurt *ConAu 134*
**Ganzler**, Cathy E. 1961- *WhoEnt 92*
**Ganzoni** *Who 92*
**Ganzuri**, Kamal Al- 1933- *IntWW 91*
**Gao Dezhan** 1932- *IntWW 91*
**Gao Fenglian** 1964- *IntWW 91*
**Gao Houliang** 1915- *IntWW 91*
**Gao Jianzhong** *IntWW 91*
**Gao Jingde** 1922- *IntWW 91*
**Gao Shangquan** 1929- *IntWW 91*
**Gao Yang** *IntWW 91*
**Gao Yangwen** 1917- *IntWW 91*
**Gao Ying** 1929- *IntWW 91*
**Gao Zhanxiang** 1935- *IntWW 91*
**Gao**, Chun Xin 1956- *WhoMW 92*
**Gao**, Jiali 1962- *AmMWSc 92*
**Gao**, Kuixiong 1937- *AmMWSc 92*
**Gaon**, Solomon 1912- *Who 92*
**Gaona**, Tomas M. 1922- *WhoHisp 92*
**Gapon**, Georgi Apollonovich 1870-1906 *FacFETw*
**Gaponenko**, Taras Gur'evich 1906- *SovUnBD*
**Gaponov-Grekhov**, Andrey Viktorovich 1926- *IntWW 91*
**Gaposchkin**, Peter John Arthur 1940- *AmMWSc 92, WhoWest 92*
**Gapp**, David Alger 1945- *AmMWSc 92*
**Gapp**, Karen Anne 1941- *WhoRel 92*
**Gappa**, Judith M. *WhoMW 92*
**Gaprindashvili**, Nona Terent'evna 1941- *SovUnBD*
**Gapurov**, Mukhamednazar 1922- *IntWW 91*
**Gara**, Aaron Delano 1935- *AmMWSc 92*
**Gara**, Otto Gabriel *WhoAmL 92*
**Gara**, Robert I 1931- *AmMWSc 92*
**Garabedian**, Michael Douglas 1967- *WhoFI 92*
**Garabedian**, Paul R. 1927- *IntWW 91*
**Garabedian**, Paul Roesel 1927- *AmMWSc 92*
**Garabito**, Juan de Santiago y Leon *HisDSpE*
**Garafalo**, Sebastian Joseph 1932- *WhoAmP 91*
**Garafola**, Lynn 1946- *ConAu 135*
**Garagiola**, Joe *LesBEnT 92*
**Garahan**, Peter Thomas 1946- *WhoFI 92*
**Garaikoetxea Urriza**, Carlos 1939- *IntWW 91*
**Garajalde**, Fernando Alberto 1953- *WhoFI 92*
**Garamendi**, John 1945- *NewYTBS 91 [port]*
**Garamendi**, John R 1945- *WhoAmP 91*
**Garand**, Christopher Pierre 1947- *WhoIns 92*
**Garand**, Ronald Stephen 1956- *WhoMW 92*
**Garang**, John 1943- *IntWW 91*
**Garango**, Tiemoko Marc 1927- *IntWW 91*
**Garant**, Eric Matthew 1957- *WhoEnt 92*
**Garant**, Serge 1929-1986 *NewAmDM*
**Garas**, Klara 1919- *IntWW 91*
**Garascia**, Richard Joseph 1917- *AmMWSc 92*
**Garat**, Gerald Miguel 1935- *WhoWest 92*
**Garaudy**, Roger Jean Charles 1913- *IntWW 91*
**Garavaglia**, Abdon Lewis 1915- *WhoRel 92*
**Garavaglia**, John Charles 1951- *WhoAmL 92*
**Garavel**, Paul James 1958- *WhoAmP 91*
**Garavelli**, John Stephen 1947- *AmMWSc 92*
**Garaway**, Michael *TwCPaSc*
**Garay**, Andrew Steven 1926- *AmMWSc 92*
**Garay**, Antonio Francisco 1947- *WhoHisp 92*
**Garay**, Gustav John 1933- *AmMWSc 92*
**Garay**, Jose Manuel 1965- *WhoHisp 92*
**Garay**, Juan de 1528-1584 *HisDSpE*
**Garay**, Leslie Andrew 1924- *AmMWSc 92*
**Garay**, Val Christian 1942- *WhoHisp 92*
**Garayalde**, Allen *WhoHisp 92*
**Garayua**, Mary Isa 1945- *WhoHisp 92*
**Garb**, Andrew Steven 1942- *WhoAmL 92*
**Garb**, Solomon 1920- *IntAu&W 91*
**Garba**, Joseph Nanven 1943- *IntWW 91*
**Garbaccio**, Donald Howard 1930- *AmMWSc 92*
**Garbacz**, Gerald George 1936- *WhoFI 92*
**Garbacz**, Robert J 1933- *AmMWSc 92*
**Garbacz**, Ron Rand 1938- *WhoFI 92*
**Garbaczewski**, Daniel Frank 1950- *WhoMW 92*
**Garbarini**, Edgar Joseph 1910- *AmMWSc 92*
**Garbarini**, Victor C 1926- *AmMWSc 92*
**Garbarino**, Robert Paul 1929- *WhoAmL 92*
**Garbark**, Melvin D. 1930- *WhoMW 92*
**Garbe**, Louis Richard 1876-1957 *TwCPaSc*
**Garber**, Alan J 1943- *AmMWSc 92*
**Garber**, Alan Michael 1955- *WhoFI 92*
**Garber**, Anne Theresa 1946- *WhoEnt 92*
**Garber**, Charles A 1941- *AmMWSc 92*
**Garber**, Cynthia Ann 1956- *WhoRel 92*
**Garber**, Dale Jay 1951- *WhoFI 92*
**Garber**, Daniel Elliot 1949- *WhoMW 92*
**Garber**, David H 1918- *AmMWSc 92*
**Garber**, David J. 1949- *WhoMW 92*
**Garber**, Davis 1829?-1896 *BiInAmS*
**Garber**, Donald I 1936- *AmMWSc 92*
**Garber**, Edward David 1918- *AmMWSc 92*
**Garber**, Eugene K. *DrAPF 91*
**Garber**, Floyd Wayne 1941- *AmMWSc 92*
**Garber**, H Newton 1930- *AmMWSc 92*
**Garber**, Harold Jerome 1913- *AmMWSc 92*
**Garber**, Harry Douglas 1928- *WhoFI 92*
**Garber**, Helen Kolikow 1954- *WhoEnt 92*
**Garber**, James Noble, II 1933- *WhoAmL 92*
**Garber**, Janice Winter 1950- *WhoWest 92*

**Garber,** Jerold Allan 1942- *WhoEnt 92*
**Garber,** John Douglas 1920- *AmMWSc 92*
**Garber,** Lawrence L 1942- *AmMWSc 92*
**Garber,** Lawrence Lee 1942- *WhoMW 92*
**Garber,** Meyer 1928- *AmMWSc 92*
**Garber,** Milton 1925- *WhoAmL 92*
**Garber,** Morris Joseph 1912- *AmMWSc 92*
**Garber,** Murray S 1934- *AmMWSc 92*
**Garber,** Paul L. 1942- *WhoRel 92*
**Garber,** Paul Neff 1899-1972 *DcNCBi 2*
**Garber,** Reuben Lee 1929- *WhoRel 92*
**Garber,** Richard Hammerle 1921- *AmMWSc 92*
**Garber,** Richard Lincoln 1950- *AmMWSc 92*
**Garber,** Robert Alan 1931- *WhoAmL 92*
**Garber,** Robert William 1943- *AmMWSc 92*
**Garber,** Samuel Baugh 1934- *WhoAmL 92, WhoFI 92, WhoMW 92*
**Garber,** Sheldon 1920- *WhoMW 92*
**Garber,** Stanley S. 1953- *WhoEnt 92*
**Garber,** Victor 1949- *ConTFT 9*
**Garber,** William Macy 1922- *WhoEnt 92*
**Garber,** Zev 1941- *WhoRel 92, WhoWest 92*
**Garberding,** Larry Gilbert 1938- *WhoMW 92*
**Garbers,** Christoph Friedrich 1929- *IntWW 91*
**Garbers,** David Lorn 1944- *AmMWSc 92*
**Garbett,** Bryson *WhoAmP 91*
**Garbey,** Barbaro 1957- *WhoBlA 92*
**Garbey,** Rolando 1947- *BlkOlyM*
**Garbis,** Andrew Nicholas 1936- *WhoFI 92*
**Garbis,** Marvin Joseph 1936- *WhoAmL 92*
**Garbo,** Greta 1905-1990 *AnObit 1990, ConTFT 9, FacFETw [port], RComAH*
**Garbona,** Edgar *WhoHisp 92*
**Garbose,** Doris Rhoda 1924- *WhoAmP 91*
**Garbrecht,** Louis 1949- *WhoAmL 92*
**Garbrecht,** William Lee 1923- *AmMWSc 92*
**Garbuny,** Max 1912- *AmMWSc 92*
**Garbus,** Martin 1934- *ConAu 133*
**Garbutt,** Eugene James 1925- *WhoMW 92*
**Garbutt,** John Thomas 1929- *AmMWSc 92*
**Garbutt,** Richard *WhoEnt 92*
**Garces,** Francisco 1934- *IntWW 91*
**Garces,** Francisco Tomas 1738-1781 *HisDSpE*
**Garces,** Francisco Tomas Hermenegildo 1738-1781 *BenetAL 91*
**Garces,** Julian 1447-1542 *HisDSpE*
**Garces,** Rich 1971- *WhoHisp 92*
**Garchik,** Leah 1945- *ConAu 133*
**Garcia,** A C *WhoAmP 91*
**Garcia,** Adalberto Carlos 1954- *WhoHisp 92*
**Garcia,** Adalberto Moreno 1943- *WhoHisp 92*
**Garcia,** Adolfo Ramon 1948- *WhoAmL 92*
**Garcia,** Adriana 1941- *WhoHisp 92*
**Garcia,** Adrienne Lucia Regina 1947- *WhoEnt 92*
**Garcia,** Albert B 1944- *AmMWSc 92, WhoHisp 92*
**Garcia,** Albert Joseph 1951- *WhoFI 92*
**Garcia,** Alberto *WhoHisp 92*
**Garcia,** Alberto 1930- *WhoHisp 92*
**Garcia,** Alberto, Jr. 1930- *WhoHisp 92*
**Garcia,** Alberto A. 1945- *WhoHisp 92*
**Garcia,** Alberto Ureta 1926- *WhoHisp 92*
**Garcia,** Alfonso E., Sr. 1933- *WhoHisp 92*
**Garcia,** Alfred R. *WhoHisp 92*
**Garcia,** Alfred Robert 1957- *WhoWest 92*
**Garcia,** Alfredo *WhoHisp 92*
**Garcia,** Alfredo Mariano 1927- *AmMWSc 92*
**Garcia,** Alicia Rangel 1964- *WhoHisp 92*
**Garcia,** Alma *WhoHisp 92*
**Garcia,** Amando S., Sr. 1934- *WhoHisp 92*
**Garcia,** Andres 1948- *WhoHisp 92*
**Garcia,** Andrew E., Sr. *WhoHisp 92*
**Garcia,** Andy 1956- *IntMPA 92, WhoHisp 92*
**Garcia,** Anthony Edward 1951- *WhoHisp 92*
**Garcia,** Antonio E. 1901- *WhoHisp 92*
**Garcia,** Antonio E. 1924- *WhoHisp 92*
**Garcia,** Antonio Jose 1959- *WhoHisp 92*
**Garcia,** Antonio M. 1946- *WhoHisp 92*
**Garcia,** Arcenio A, Sr 1947- *WhoAmP 91*
**Garcia,** Arcenio Arturo, Sr. 1947- *WhoHisp 92*
**Garcia,** Ariel Antonio 1953- *WhoHisp 92*
**Garcia,** Armando *WhoHisp 92*
**Garcia,** Armando 1931- *WhoHisp 92*
**Garcia,** Armando 1951- *WhoHisp 92*
**Garcia,** Arnulfo 1946- *WhoHisp 92*
**Garcia,** Arnulfo, Jr. 1948- *WhoHisp 92*
**Garcia,** Arthur 1924- *Who 92*
**Garcia,** Bernardo Alejandro 1941- *WhoHisp 92*
**Garcia,** Bernardo Ramon 1956- *WhoHisp 92*
**Garcia,** Blanche 1946- *WhoHisp 92*
**Garcia,** Carlos *WhoHisp 92*
**Garcia,** Carlos 1967- *WhoHisp 92*
**Garcia,** Carlos A. 1935- *WhoHisp 92*
**Garcia,** Carlos E. *WhoHisp 92*
**Garcia,** Carlos E 1936- *AmMWSc 92*
**Garcia,** Carlos Emilio 1942- *WhoHisp 92*
**Garcia,** Carlos Ernesto 1936- *WhoHisp 92*
**Garcia,** Carlos Fernando 1953- *WhoHisp 92*
**Garcia,** Carmen M. *WhoHisp 92*
**Garcia,** Carol Henderson 1956- *WhoAmL 92*
**Garcia,** Casimiro Gilbert 1930- *WhoWest 92*
**Garcia,** Castelar Medardo 1942- *WhoAmL 92*
**Garcia,** Catalina Esperanza 1944- *WhoHisp 92*
**Garcia,** Catherine Arlita 1951- *WhoWest 92*
**Garcia,** Celso-Ramon 1921- *AmMWSc 92, WhoHisp 92*
**Garcia,** Cesar *WhoHisp 92*
**Garcia,** Clara L. 1948- *WhoHisp 92*
**Garcia,** Conrad, Jr. *WhoHisp 92*
**Garcia,** Cordelia Villarreal 1951- *WhoHisp 92*
**Garcia,** Crisostomo Bautista 1948- *WhoFI 92*
**Garcia,** Crispin, Jr. 1945- *WhoHisp 92*
**Garcia,** Cristina 1958- *WhoHisp 92*
**Garcia,** Damaso Domingo 1957- *WhoHisp 92*
**Garcia,** Daniel 1947- *WhoHisp 92*
**Garcia,** Daniel, Jr. 1944- *WhoHisp 92*
**Garcia,** Daniel Albert 1946- *WhoHisp 92*
**Garcia,** Daniel Margarito 1963- *WhoMW 92*
**Garcia,** David *WhoHisp 92*
**Garcia,** David H. 1949- *WhoHisp 92*
**Garcia,** David J. *WhoHisp 92*
**Garcia,** David Joseph 1946- *WhoHisp 92*
**Garcia,** David M. 1956- *WhoHisp 92*
**Garcia,** David Richard 1953- *WhoHisp 92*
**Garcia,** Dawn E. 1959- *WhoHisp 92*
**Garcia,** Delano J *WhoAmP 91, WhoHisp 92*
**Garcia,** Dennis *WhoHisp 92*
**Garcia,** Dennis R. 1954- *WhoHisp 92*
**Garcia,** Diego 1471- *HisDSpE*
**Garcia,** Domingo 1940- *WhoHisp 92*
**Garcia,** Domingo A. 1958- *WhoHisp 92*
**Garcia,** Edith V 1931- *WhoAmP 91*
**Garcia,** Eduardo 1964- *WhoHisp 92*
**Garcia,** Edward 1958- *WhoHisp 92*
**Garcia,** Edward Coronado 1946- *WhoHisp 92*
**Garcia,** Edward J. 1928- *WhoAmL 92, WhoHisp 92, WhoWest 92*
**Garcia,** Edwina 1944- *WhoAmP 91, WhoHisp 92*
**Garcia,** Efraim S. 1931- *WhoHisp 92*
**Garcia,** Eleuterio M. 1943- *WhoHisp 92*
**Garcia,** Elias *WhoHisp 92*
**Garcia,** Eligio, Jr. 1939- *WhoHisp 92*
**Garcia,** Elizabeth Mildred 1956- *WhoHisp 92*
**Garcia,** Elsa Laura 1954- *WhoHisp 92*
**Garcia,** Elvira Elena 1938- *WhoHisp 92*
**Garcia,** Enildo Albert 1932- *WhoHisp 92*
**Garcia,** Enrique A. 1947- *WhoHisp 92*
**Garcia,** Ernest Eugene 1946- *WhoAmP 91, WhoHisp 92*
**Garcia,** Esther 1945- *WhoHisp 92*
**Garcia,** Eugene N 1925- *AmMWSc 92*
**Garcia,** Eugene Nicholas 1925- *WhoHisp 92*
**Garcia,** Eva 1950- *WhoHisp 92*
**Garcia,** Evelyn 1952- *WhoHisp 92*
**Garcia,** Evelyn Jasso 1948- *WhoHisp 92*
**Garcia,** Everardo *WhoHisp 92*
**Garcia,** F. Chris 1940- *WhoHisp 92*
**Garcia,** Felix M. *WhoHisp 92*
**Garcia,** Fernando *WhoHisp 92*
**Garcia,** Fernando 1946- *WhoFI 92*
**Garcia,** Fernando Salcedo 1960- *WhoFI 92*
**Garcia,** Frances 1941- *WhoHisp 92*
**Garcia,** Frances Josephine 1938- *WhoHisp 92*
**Garcia,** Francisco Cesareo, III 1946- *WhoHisp 92*
**Garcia,** Francisco Jose 1920- *WhoHisp 92*
**Garcia,** Frank C. 1924- *WhoHisp 92*
**Garcia,** George A. 1945- *WhoRel 92*
**Garcia,** Gilbert 1945- *WhoHisp 92*
**Garcia,** Gregorio Martin 1932- *WhoFI 92*
**Garcia,** Gustavo *WhoHisp 92*
**Garcia,** Guy D. 1955- *WhoHisp 92*
**Garcia,** H. F. 1925- *WhoHisp 92*
**Garcia,** Hector *WhoHisp 92*
**Garcia,** Hector D 1946- *AmMWSc 92*
**Garcia,** Hector Gomez 1931- *WhoHisp 92*
**Garcia,** Hector Perez 1914- *WhoHisp 92*
**Garcia,** Hector Santos 1957- *WhoHisp 92*
**Garcia,** Henry F. 1943- *WhoHisp 92*
**Garcia,** Herlinda 1944- *WhoHisp 92*
**Garcia,** Herman S. 1950- *WhoHisp 92*
**Garcia,** Hipolito Frank 1925- *WhoAmL 92*
**Garcia,** Ignacio Razon 1953- *WhoAmL 92*
**Garcia,** Iris Ana 1954- *WhoHisp 92*
**Garcia,** Isidro *WhoHisp 92*
**Garcia,** Israel 1937- *WhoHisp 92*
**Garcia,** Iva *WhoHisp 92*
**Garcia,** Jane C. *WhoHisp 92*
**Garcia,** Jane C 1948- *WhoAmP 91*
**Garcia,** Jasper 1939- *WhoAmP 91*
**Garcia,** Javier N. 1948- *WhoHisp 92*
**Garcia,** Jerry 1942- *FacFETw, WhoEnt 92, WhoHisp 92*
**Garcia,** Jess *WhoHisp 92*
**Garcia,** Jesus 1941- *WhoHisp 92*
**Garcia,** Jesus Enrique 1946- *WhoHisp 92*
**Garcia,** Jesus G. *WhoHisp 92*
**Garcia,** Jesus G 1956- *WhoAmP 91*
**Garcia,** Joaquin 1940- *WhoHisp 92*
**Garcia,** Joe Baldemar 1942- *WhoHisp 92*
**Garcia,** Joe G., Jr. 1946- *WhoHisp 92*
**Garcia,** Joe Manuel, Jr. 1952- *WhoHisp 92*
**Garcia,** John 1917- *AmMWSc 92, WhoHisp 92*
**Garcia,** John Anthony 1955- *WhoHisp 92*
**Garcia,** John F. 1964- *WhoHisp 92*
**Garcia,** John Martin 1949- *WhoHisp 92*
**Garcia,** Jorge Jesus 1955- *WhoHisp 92*
**Garcia,** Jorge Logan 1950- *WhoHisp 92*
**Garcia,** Jose *WhoHisp 92*
**Garcia,** Jose Bautista 1966- *WhoHisp 92*
**Garcia,** Jose D., Jr. 1936- *WhoHisp 92*
**Garcia,** Jose De Jesus 1943- *WhoMW 92*
**Garcia,** Jose Dolores, Jr 1936- *AmMWSc 92*
**Garcia,** Jose F. 1928- *WhoHisp 92*
**Garcia,** Jose-Guadalupe Villarreal 1947- *WhoHisp 92*
**Garcia,** Jose Guillermo 1959- *WhoHisp 92*
**Garcia,** Jose Joel 1946- *WhoHisp 92*
**Garcia,** Jose Luix 1949- *WhoMW 92*
**Garcia,** Jose Mauricio Nunes 1767-1830 *NewAmDM*
**Garcia,** Jose Zebedeo 1945- *WhoAmP 91, WhoHisp 92, WhoWest 92*
**Garcia,** Josefina M. 1906- *WhoHisp 92*
**Garcia,** Josefina Margarita 1906- *WhoEnt 92*
**Garcia,** Joseph 1962- *WhoHisp 92*
**Garcia,** Joseph, Jr. 1941- *WhoHisp 92*
**Garcia,** Joseph E. 1950- *WhoHisp 92*
**Garcia,** Joseph Guadalupe 1931- *WhoHisp 92*
**Garcia,** Josie Alaniz 1946- *WhoHisp 92*
**Garcia,** Juan Andres 1967- *WhoHisp 92*
**Garcia,** Juan C. 1944- *WhoHisp 92*
**Garcia,** Juan Carlos 1961- *WhoHisp 92*
**Garcia,** Juan Castanon 1949- *WhoHisp 92*
**Garcia,** Juan F. 1950- *WhoHisp 92*
**Garcia,** Juan G. 1933- *WhoHisp 92*
**Garcia,** Juan Manuel 1953- *WhoHisp 92*
**Garcia,** Juan Ramon 1947- *WhoHisp 92*
**Garcia,** Juanita *WhoHisp 92*
**Garcia,** Juanita Garcia 1934- *WhoHisp 92*
**Garcia,** Julian Steve 1960- *WhoWest 92*
**Garcia,** Juliet Villarreal 1949- *WhoHisp 92*
**Garcia,** Julio H. *WhoHisp 92*
**Garcia,** Julio H 1933- *AmMWSc 92*
**Garcia,** Julio Ralph, Sr. 1932- *WhoHisp 92*
**Garcia,** Kelly 1964- *WhoMW 92*
**Garcia,** Kerry J. 1952- *WhoHisp 92*
**Garcia,** Kwame N. 1946- *WhoBlA 92*
**Garcia,** Laura Diana 1961- *WhoHisp 92*
**Garcia,** Lauro *WhoHisp 92*
**Garcia,** Lauro, III *WhoHisp 92*
**Garcia,** Lawrence Dean 1936- *WhoHisp 92*
**Garcia,** Lawrence R. 1951- *WhoHisp 92*
**Garcia,** Leo A. *WhoHisp 92*
**Garcia,** Leon M. N. *WhoHisp 92*
**Garcia,** Lino, Jr. 1934- *WhoHisp 92*
**Garcia,** Lionel Gonzalo 1935- *WhoHisp 92*
**Garcia,** Lloyd Bert 1957- *WhoWest 92*
**Garcia,** Louie Joe 1954- *WhoHisp 92*
**Garcia,** Louis *WhoHisp 92*
**Garcia,** Louis Lawrence 1947- *WhoMW 92*
**Garcia,** Louis R. 1931- *WhoIns 92*
**Garcia,** Luis Alonzo 1954- *WhoHisp 92*
**Garcia,** Luis Cesareo 1949- *WhoAmL 92*
**Garcia,** Luis M. *WhoHisp 92*
**Garcia,** Luis R 1949- *WhoHisp 92*
**Garcia,** Luis Rene, Jr. 1945- *WhoHisp 92*
**Garcia,** Lydia Maria 1936- *WhoHisp 92*
**Garcia,** Magdalena *WhoHisp 92*
**Garcia,** Manuel 1775-1832 *NewAmDM*
**Garcia,** Manuel 1805-1906 *NewAmDM*
**Garcia,** Manuel, Jr. *WhoHisp 92*
**Garcia,** Manuel Blas 1942- *WhoHisp 92*
**Garcia,** Manuel Domingo 1952- *WhoAmL 92*
**Garcia,** Manuel J. *WhoHisp 92*
**Garcia,** Manuel Mariano 1938- *AmMWSc 92*
**Garcia,** Marcelo Horacio 1959- *AmMWSc 92*
**Garcia,** Margaret A. 1950- *WhoHisp 92*
**Garcia,** Margaret Louise 1963- *WhoHisp 92*
**Garcia,** Maria 1955- *WhoHisp 92*
**Garcia,** Maria S. T. *WhoHisp 92*
**Garcia,** Mariano 1918- *AmMWSc 92*
**Garcia,** Mario, Jr. 1959- *WhoHisp 92*
**Garcia,** Mario Leopoldo 1940- *AmMWSc 92*
**Garcia,** Mario T. 1944- *WhoHisp 92*
**Garcia,** Marlene Linares 1956- *WhoHisp 92*
**Garcia,** Marta Irma 1946- *WhoWest 92*
**Garcia,** Mary Ann 1937- *WhoHisp 92*
**Garcia,** Mary Dolores 1949- *WhoHisp 92*
**Garcia,** Mary Inez 1931- *WhoAmP 91*
**Garcia,** Mary Jane 1936- *WhoHisp 92*
**Garcia,** Mary Jane M 1936- *WhoAmP 91*
**Garcia,** Marz John 1937- *WhoAmP 91*
**Garcia,** Melva Ybarra 1950- *WhoHisp 92*
**Garcia,** Meredith Mason *AmMWSc 92*
**Garcia,** Michael *WhoHisp 92*
**Garcia,** Michael John 1948- *WhoHisp 92*
**Garcia,** Michael Omar 1948- *AmMWSc 92*
**Garcia,** Michael Orlando 1957- *WhoFI 92*
**Garcia,** Michael T. *WhoHisp 92*
**Garcia,** Miguel A., Jr. 1952- *WhoHisp 92*
**Garcia,** Miguel Angel 1938- *WhoHisp 92*
**Garcia,** Mildred 1952- *WhoHisp 92*
**Garcia,** Nasario 1936- *ConAu 134*
**Garcia,** Neftali G. 1943- *WhoHisp 92*
**Garcia,** Nicolas Bruce 1961- *WhoHisp 92*
**Garcia,** Nora *WhoHisp 92*
**Garcia,** Norma G. 1950- *WhoHisp 92*
**Garcia,** Ofelia *WhoHisp 92*
**Garcia,** Olga Chaidez 1957- *WhoHisp 92*
**Garcia,** Olivia 1953- *WhoHisp 92*
**Garcia,** Orlando 1952- *WhoHisp 92*
**Garcia,** Orlando L 1952- *WhoAmP 91*
**Garcia,** Oscar Manuel 1950- *WhoHisp 92*
**Garcia,** Oscar Nicolas 1936- *AmMWSc 92, WhoHisp 92*
**Garcia,** Otto Luis 1947- *WhoHisp 92*
**Garcia,** Pauline J. 1948- *WhoHisp 92*
**Garcia,** Pedro Vasquez 1937- *WhoHisp 92*
**Garcia,** Peter 1930- *WhoHisp 92*
**Garcia,** Peter Angel 1960- *WhoHisp 92*
**Garcia,** Peter C. *WhoHisp 92*
**Garcia,** Pilar A 1926- *AmMWSc 92*
**Garcia,** Rafael I. *WhoHisp 92*
**Garcia,** Ralph, Jr. 1943- *WhoHisp 92*
**Garcia,** Raquel Elena 1946- *WhoHisp 92*
**Garcia,** Raul 1935- *AmMWSc 92*
**Garcia,** Raul A. 1949- *WhoHisp 92*
**Garcia,** Raul C. 1946- *WhoHisp 92*
**Garcia,** Raul P., Jr. 1947- *WhoHisp 92*
**Garcia,** Ray 1960- *WhoHisp 92*
**Garcia,** Raymond 1963- *WhoEnt 92*
**Garcia,** Raymond E. 1941- *WhoHisp 92*
**Garcia,** Rene 1939- *WhoHisp 92*
**Garcia,** Rene Luis 1945- *WhoHisp 92*
**Garcia,** Ricardo Alberto 1946- *WhoHisp 92*
**Garcia,** Ricardo H. *WhoHisp 92*
**Garcia,** Ricardo J. 1947- *WhoHisp 92*
**Garcia,** Ricardo Romano 1938- *WhoHisp 92*
**Garcia,** Rich *WhoHisp 92*
**Garcia,** Richard *WhoHisp 92*
**Garcia,** Richard 1930- *AmMWSc 92*
**Garcia,** Richard Amado 1941- *WhoHisp 92*
**Garcia,** Rita Zamora 1937- *WhoHisp 92*
**Garcia,** Robert 1933- *WhoAmP 91*
**Garcia,** Robert Allen 1952- *WhoHisp 92*
**Garcia,** Robert Eugene 1934- *WhoMW 92*
**Garcia,** Robert George 1956- *WhoHisp 92*
**Garcia,** Robert L. 1948- *WhoHisp 92*
**Garcia,** Robert N 1937- *WhoAmP 91*
**Garcia,** Robert S. *WhoHisp 92*
**Garcia,** Robert Stanley 1958- *WhoHisp 92*
**Garcia,** Roberto *WhoHisp 92*
**Garcia,** Rod *WhoHisp 92*
**Garcia,** Rodolfo, Jr 1963- *WhoAmP 91, WhoHisp 92*
**Garcia,** Roland, Jr. 1958- *WhoHisp 92*
**Garcia,** Roland B. *WhoHisp 92*
**Garcia,** Rose *WhoHisp 92*
**Garcia,** Ruben *WhoHisp 92*
**Garcia,** Rudolph 1951- *WhoAmL 92*
**Garcia,** Rupert 1941- *WhoHisp 92*
**Garcia,** Salvador 1948- *WhoMW 92*
**Garcia,** Sam *WhoHisp 92*
**Garcia,** Sam 1957- *WhoHisp 92*
**Garcia,** Santos 1947- *WhoHisp 92*
**Garcia,** Sheila *WhoHisp 92*
**Garcia,** Sid 1959- *WhoHisp 92*
**Garcia,** Silas T *WhoAmP 91*
**Garcia,** Stephen Trinidad 1944- *WhoHisp 92*
**Garcia,** Susana 1956- *WhoHisp 92*
**Garcia,** Sylvia R. 1950- *WhoHisp 92*
**Garcia,** Teofilo 1942- *WhoHisp 92*
**Garcia,** Terry Donato 1953- *WhoAmL 92*
**Garcia,** Thomas Alfred 1951- *WhoWest 92*
**Garcia,** Victor *BlkOlyM*
**Garcia,** Wanda *WhoHisp 92*
**Garcia,** William Burres 1940- *WhoBlA 92*
**Garcia,** William T. 1958- *WhoAmL 92*
**Garcia,** Yvonne 1949- *WhoHisp 92*
**Garcia,** Yvonne 1956- *WhoHisp 92*
**Garcia Anoveros,** Jaime 1932- *IntWW 91*
**Garcia-Araiza,** Leonardo R. 1947- *WhoHisp 92*
**Garcia-Ayvens,** Francisco *WhoHisp 92*
**Garcia-Barcena,** Yanira E. 1950- *WhoHisp 92*
**Garcia-Barrera,** Gloria 1952- *WhoHisp 92*

**Garcia-Bengochea,** Francisco 1917- *AmMWSc 92*
**Garcia Berlanga,** Luis 1921- *IntDcF 2-2*
**Garcia-Borras,** Thomas 1926- *WhoWest 92*
**Garcia-Botero,** Alfonso 1960- *WhoFI 92*
**Garcia-Bunuel,** Luis 1931- *WhoWest 92*
**Garcia-Cartagena,** Esther 1945- *WhoHisp 92*
**Garcia-Castro,** Ivette 1937- *AmMWSc 92*
**Garcia-Cisneros,** Florencio 1924- *WhoHisp 92*
**Garcia-Clyne,** Sonia 1957- *WhoHisp 92*
**Garcia-Colin,** Leopoldo Scherer 1930- *AmMWSc 92*
**Garcia De Jalon,** Alejandro Bedox 1925- *WhoHisp 92*
**Garcia de Oteyza,** Juan 1962- *WhoHisp 92*
**Garcia de Polavieja,** Camilo 1838-1914 *HisDSpE*
**Garcia-Diaz,** Alberto 1945- *WhoHisp 92*
**Garcia Diez,** Juan Antonio 1940- *IntWW 91*
**Garcia Fuste,** Tomas *WhoHisp 92*
**Garcia-Godoy,** Franklin 1952- *WhoHisp 92*
**Garcia-Gomez,** Jorge 1937- *WhoHisp 92*
**Garcia Gonzalez,** Rafael 1926- *WhoRel 92*
**Garcia Goyena,** Rafael 1766-1823 *HisDSpE*
**Garcia-Granados,** Sergio Eduardo 1942- *WhoFI 92*
**Garcia Iniguez,** Calixto 1839-1898 *HisDSpE*
**Garcia Jofre de Loaysa,** Juan *HisDSpE*
**Garcia-Kone,** Anna Y. 1953- *WhoHisp 92*
**Garcia Lanza,** Jose Manuel d1828 *HisDSpE*
**Garcia Lopez,** Estela 1966- *WhoHisp 92*
**Garcia Lorca,** Federico 1898-1936 *DcLB 108 [port], DramC 2 [port], FacFETw, PoeCrit 3 [port]*
**Garcia-Manzanedo,** Hector 1926- *WhoHisp 92*
**Garcia Marquez,** Gabriel *Who 92*
**Garcia Marquez,** Gabriel 1928- *BenetAL 91, ConLC 68 [port], DcLB 113 [port], FacFETw [port], IntWW 91, LiExTwC, ShScr 8 [port]*
**Garcia Marquez,** Gabriel Jose 1928- *WhoNob 90*
**Garcia-Marquez,** Vicente 1953- *ConAu 134*
**Garcia Millan,** Angel 1953- *WhoHisp 92*
**Garcia-Munoz,** Moises 1922- *AmMWSc 92*
**Garcia-Nakata,** Lorraine 1950- *WhoHisp 92*
**Garcia Nieto,** Jose 1914- *IntWW 91*
**Garcia-Nunez,** Fernando 1944- *WhoHisp 92*
**Garcia-Oliva,** Manolo 1938- *WhoHisp 92*
**Garcia Oller,** Jose Luis 1923- *WhoHisp 92*
**Garcia-Palmieri,** Mario R 1927- *AmMWSc 92*
**Garcia-Palmieri,** Mario Ruben 1927- *WhoHisp 92*
**Garcia-Parra,** Jaime 1931- *Who 92*
**Garcia Pelaez,** Raul 1922- *IntWW 91*
**Garcia-Pena,** Roberto 1910- *IntAu&W 91, IntWW 91*
**Garcia Perez,** Alan 1949- *IntWW 91*
**Garcia Pinto,** Magdalena 1943- *WhoHisp 92*
**Garcia-Prats,** Joseph A. 1944- *WhoHisp 92*
**Garcia Pumacahua,** Mateo 1755?-1815 *HisDSpE*
**Garcia Ramirez,** Sergio 1938- *IntWW 91*
**Garcia Ramos,** Juan 1915- *AmMWSc 92*
**Garcia-Rangel,** Sara Marina 1939- *WhoHisp 92*
**Garcia-Rill,** Edgar E 1948- *AmMWSc 92*
**Garcia-Rios,** Jose M. 1957- *WhoHisp 92*
**Garcia Robles,** Alfonso d1991 *Who 92N*
**Garcia Robles,** Alfonso 1911- *IntWW 91, WhoNob 90*
**Garcia Robles,** Alfonso 1911-1991 *NewYTBS 91*
**Garcia-Rodriguez,** Sergio 1961- *WhoHisp 92*
**Garcia-Rosaly,** Leticia 1949- *WhoHisp 92*
**Garcia-Sainz,** J Adolfo 1952- *AmMWSc 92*
**Garcia-Santesmases,** Jose Miguel 1952- *AmMWSc 92*
**Garcia-Santiago,** Ramon *WhoAmP 91, WhoHisp 92*
**Garcia-Serrano,** Maria Victoria 1959- *WhoHisp 92*
**Garcia Vargas,** Julian 1946- *IntWW 91*
**Garcia-Verdugo,** Luisa 1960- *WhoHisp 92*
**Garcia Yebra,** Valentin 1917- *IntWW 91*
**Garcilaso de la Vega** 1539-1616 *BenetAL 91, HisDSpE*
**Gard,** Beverly 1940- *WhoAmP 91*
**Gard,** David Lynn *AmMWSc 92*
**Gard,** David Richard 1953- *AmMWSc 92, WhoMW 92*
**Gard,** Don Irvin 1926- *AmMWSc 92*
**Gard,** Gary Lee 1937- *AmMWSc 92*
**Gard,** Janice *IntAu&W 91X, SmATA 68, WrDr 92*
**Gard,** Janice Koles 1954- *AmMWSc 92*
**Gard,** John 1963- *WhoAmP 91*
**Gard,** Joyce 1911- *WrDr 92*
**Gard,** O W 1921- *AmMWSc 92*
**Gard,** Orin Peneton 1909- *WhoRel 92*
**Gard,** Richard 1928- *AmMWSc 92*
**Gard,** Richard Abbott 1914- *WhoRel 92*
**Gard,** Steven Jay 1949- *WhoAmL 92*
**Garda,** Donna J. 1961- *WhoEnt 92*
**Gardam,** David Hill 1922- *Who 92*
**Gardam,** Jane 1928- *WrDr 92*
**Gardam,** Jane Mary *Who 92*
**Gardam,** Jane Mary 1928- *IntAu&W 91*
**Garde,** Betty 1905-1989 *ConTFT 9*
**Garde,** Billie Pirner 1953- *WhoAmL 92*
**Garde,** John Charles 1961- *WhoAmL 92*
**Gardea,** Aili Tapio 1964- *WhoHisp 92*
**Gardebring,** Sandra S. *WhoAmL 92, WhoAmP 91, WhoMW 92*
**Gardella,** Hazel L 1915- *WhoAmP 91*
**Gardella,** Joseph Augustus, Jr 1955- *AmMWSc 92*
**Gardella,** Libero Anthony 1935- *AmMWSc 92*
**Gardelli,** Lamberto 1915- *IntWW 91, NewAmDM*
**Gardeman,** Geneva E *WhoAmP 91*
**Garden,** Alexander 1730-1791 *BiInAmS*
**Garden,** Bruce *IntAu&W 91X, WrDr 92*
**Garden,** Edward 1930- *WrDr 92*
**Garden,** Mary 1874-1967 *FacFETw, NewAmDM*
**Garden,** Nancy 1938- *IntAu&W 91, WrDr 92*
**Garden,** Timothy 1944- *Who 92*
**Garden,** William Fraser 1856-1921 *TwCPaSc*
**Gardener,** Helen Hamilton 1853-1925 *RelLAm 91*
**Gardenhire,** Gary Wayne 1945- *WhoAmP 91*
**Gardenia,** Vincent 1921- *WhoEnt 92*
**Gardenia,** Vincent 1922- *IntMPA 92*
**Gardenier,** John Stark 1937- *AmMWSc 92*
**Gardenier,** Turkan Kumbaraci 1941- *AmMWSc 92*
**Gardent,** Paul 1921- *IntWW 91*
**Garder,** Arthur 1925- *AmMWSc 92*
**Gardham,** Marcus Maxwell d1991 *Who 92N*
**Gardier,** Robert Woodward 1927- *AmMWSc 92*
**Gardin,** Julius M 1949- *AmMWSc 92*
**Gardin,** Lori Ann 1967- *WhoEnt 92*
**Gardin,** Vladimir Rostislavovich 1877-1965 *SovUnBD*
**Gardiner,** Lord 1900-1990 *AnObit 1990*
**Gardiner,** Alex T. 1954- *WhoMW 92*
**Gardiner,** Brian 1932- *TwCPaSc*
**Gardiner,** Christopher *BenetAL 91*
**Gardiner,** Clive 1891-1960 *TwCPaSc*
**Gardiner,** Donald Andrew 1922- *AmMWSc 92*
**Gardiner,** Donald K 1939- *WhoIns 92*
**Gardiner,** Donald Kent 1939- *WhoFI 92*
**Gardiner,** Dorothy 1894-1979 *TwCWW 91*
**Gardiner,** Duncan *Who 92*
**Gardiner,** E. Nicholas P. 1939- *WhoFI 92*
**Gardiner,** Edgar *ScFEYrs*
**Gardiner,** Edward Gardiner 1854-1907 *BiInAmS*
**Gardiner,** Frederic 1858-1917 *BiInAmS*
**Gardiner,** George 1935- *Who 92*
**Gardiner,** George L. 1933- *WhoBlA 92*
**Gardiner,** Gerald 1902- *TwCPaSc*
**Gardiner,** Gerald Austin 1900-1990 *FacFETw*
**Gardiner,** Harry Walter 1938- *WhoMW 92*
**Gardiner,** Helen 1901- *Who 92*
**Gardiner,** James Terry 1842-1912 *BiInAmS*
**Gardiner,** Jeremy 1957- *TwCPaSc*
**Gardiner,** John 1862?-1900 *BiInAmS*
**Gardiner,** John Alden 1938- *AmMWSc 92*
**Gardiner,** John Brooke 1929- *AmMWSc 92*
**Gardiner,** John Duncan 1937- *Who 92*
**Gardiner,** John Eliot 1943- *CurBio 91 [port], IntWW 91, NewAmDM, Who 92*
**Gardiner,** John Ralph 1946- *Who 92*
**Gardiner,** Kenneth William 1917- *AmMWSc 92*
**Gardiner,** Lester Raymond, Jr. 1931- *WhoAmL 92*
**Gardiner,** Lion Frederick 1938- *AmMWSc 92*
**Gardiner,** Lora Jean *DrAPF 91*
**Gardiner,** Muriel 1901-1985 *FacFETw*
**Gardiner,** Patrick 1922- *WrDr 92*
**Gardiner,** Patrick Lancaster 1922- *IntAu&W 91, Who 92*
**Gardiner,** Peter Alexander Jack 1935- *WhoFI 92*
**Gardiner,** Peter Dod Robin 1927- *Who 92*
**Gardiner,** Peter R. 1949- *IntMPA 92*
**Gardiner,** Robert 1914- *Who 92*
**Gardiner,** Robert 1929- *WhoEnt 92*
**Gardiner,** Robert Kweku Atta 1914- *IntWW 91*
**Gardiner,** Victor Alec 1929- *Who 92*
**Gardiner,** William Cecil, Jr 1933- *AmMWSc 92*
**Gardiner-Scott,** William 1906- *Who 92*
**Gardini,** Raul 1933- *IntWW 91, Who 92*
**Gardinier,** Suzanne *DrAPF 91*
**Gardino,** Vincent Anthony 1953- *WhoFI 92*
**Gardis,** Gilda J. 1944- *WhoWest 92*
**Gardlund,** Zachariah Gust 1937- *AmMWSc 92*
**Gardner** *Who 92*
**Gardner,** A. Barclay 1930- *WhoWest 92*
**Gardner,** Alan Joel 1945- *WhoAmL 92*
**Gardner,** Alvin Frederick 1920- *AmMWSc 92*
**Gardner,** Andrew Leroy 1919- *AmMWSc 92*
**Gardner,** Ann 1937- *WhoAmP 91*
**Gardner,** Antony John 1927- *Who 92*
**Gardner,** Arthur *IntMPA 92*
**Gardner,** Arthur Wendel 1924- *AmMWSc 92*
**Gardner,** Autrey Thaddeus, Jr. 1939- *WhoWest 92*
**Gardner,** Ava 1922-1990 *AnObit 1990, ConTFT 9, FacFETw*
**Gardner,** Barbara *WhoAmP 91*
**Gardner,** Bernard 1931- *AmMWSc 92*
**Gardner,** Bettye J *WhoBlA 92*
**Gardner,** Booth 1936- *WhoAmP 91, WhoWest 92*
**Gardner,** Bradford Arthur 1949- *WhoFI 92*
**Gardner,** Brenda Sue 1952- *WhoMW 92*
**Gardner,** Brian 1931- *WrDr 92*
**Gardner,** Brian Collis 1959- *WhoAmL 92*
**Gardner,** Brian E. 1952- *WhoAmL 92*
**Gardner,** Bruce D 1951- *WhoIns 92*
**Gardner,** Bruce Herbert 1948- *WhoWest 92*
**Gardner,** Bryant Rogers 1930- *AmMWSc 92*
**Gardner,** Carroll F 1934- *WhoAmP 91*
**Gardner,** Caryn Sue 1960- *WhoAmL 92*
**Gardner,** Cedric Boyer 1946- *WhoBlA 92*
**Gardner,** Charles Olda 1919- *AmMWSc 92*
**Gardner,** Charles Olda, Jr 1949- *AmMWSc 92*
**Gardner,** Charlotte A 1931- *WhoAmP 91*
**Gardner,** Chester Stone 1947- *AmMWSc 92*
**Gardner,** Clifford S 1924- *AmMWSc 92*
**Gardner,** Clyde Edward 1931- *WhoFI 92, WhoMW 92*
**Gardner,** Craig Shaw 1949- *TwCSFW 91*
**Gardner,** Dan Nobles 1942- *WhoRel 92*
**Gardner,** Daniel 1945- *AmMWSc 92*
**Gardner,** Daniel Pereira d1853 *BiInAmS*
**Gardner,** David Arnold 1939- *AmMWSc 92, WhoFI 92*
**Gardner,** David Godfrey 1936- *AmMWSc 92*
**Gardner,** David John 1953- *WhoEnt 92, WhoFI 92*
**Gardner,** David Milton 1928- *AmMWSc 92*
**Gardner,** David Morgan 1936- *WhoMW 92*
**Gardner,** David Pierpont 1933- *IntWW 91, Who 92, WhoWest 92*
**Gardner,** David R 1942- *AmMWSc 92*
**Gardner,** Dee Ray 1925- *WhoEnt 92*
**Gardner,** Diana *TwCPaSc*
**Gardner,** Don R. 1935- *WhoAmL 92*
**Gardner,** Donald Eugene 1931- *AmMWSc 92*
**Gardner,** Donald Glenn 1931- *AmMWSc 92*
**Gardner,** Donald Murray 1928- *AmMWSc 92*
**Gardner,** Douglas Bruce B. *Who 92*
**Gardner,** Douglas Frank 1943- *Who 92*
**Gardner,** E. Marie 1930- *WhoWest 92*
**Gardner,** Earl William, Jr 1928- *AmMWSc 92*
**Gardner,** Edward 1912- *Who 92*
**Gardner,** Edward, Jr 1925- *AmMWSc 92*
**Gardner,** Edward Clinton 1920- *WhoRel 92, WrDr 92*
**Gardner,** Edward Eugene 1923- *AmMWSc 92*
**Gardner,** Edward G. 1925- *WhoBlA 92*
**Gardner,** Eldon John 1909- *AmMWSc 92*
**Gardner,** Eliot Lawrence 1940- *AmMWSc 92*
**Gardner,** Elmer Claude 1925- *WhoFI 92*
**Gardner,** Eric 1949- *WhoEnt 92*
**Gardner,** Erle Stanley 1889-1970 *BenetAL 91, FacFETw, ScFEYrs*
**Gardner,** Esther Polinsky 1941- *AmMWSc 92*
**Gardner,** Evelyn Amel 1943- *WhoWest 92*
**Gardner,** Fay Webb 1885-1969 *DcNCBi 2*
**Gardner,** Floyd M 1929- *AmMWSc 92*
**Gardner,** Frank S 1916- *AmMWSc 92*
**Gardner,** Frank W. 1923- *WhoBlA 92*
**Gardner,** Franklin Pierce 1924- *AmMWSc 92*
**Gardner,** Fred Marvin 1922- *AmMWSc 92*
**Gardner,** Frederick Albert 1927- *AmMWSc 92*
**Gardner,** Gary David 1949- *WhoEnt 92*
**Gardner,** Gary Edward 1952- *WhoMW 92*
**Gardner,** George F. 1924- *WhoEnt 92*
**Gardner,** Gerald Brousseau 1884-1964 *RelLAm 91*
**Gardner,** Gerald Henry Fraser 1926- *AmMWSc 92*
**Gardner,** Harold Wayne 1935- *AmMWSc 92*
**Gardner,** Henry L. 1944- *WhoBlA 92*
**Gardner,** Herb 1934- *WrDr 92*
**Gardner,** Herbert 1921- *Who 92*
**Gardner,** Homer Jay 1942- *WhoWest 92*
**Gardner,** Howard *IntAu&W 91*
**Gardner,** Howard Garry 1943- *WhoMW 92*
**Gardner,** Howard Shafer 1908- *AmMWSc 92*
**Gardner,** Hoyt Devane 1923- *WhoAmP 91*
**Gardner,** Ian 1944- *TwCPaSc*
**Gardner,** Isabella 1915-1981 *BenetAL 91*
**Gardner,** J. Stephen 1944- *WhoAmL 92*
**Gardner,** Jackie Randolph 1930- *WhoBlA 92*
**Gardner,** James 1907- *Who 92*
**Gardner,** James Barrington 1934- *WhoFI 92*
**Gardner,** James Carson 1933- *WhoAmP 91*
**Gardner,** James Jesse 1932- *Who 92*
**Gardner,** James Piers 1954- *Who 92*
**Gardner,** James Richard 1944- *WhoFI 92*
**Gardner,** James Vincent 1940- *AmMWSc 92*
**Gardner,** Jeffery Fay *AmMWSc 92*
**Gardner,** Jeremy *WrDr 92*
**Gardner,** Jerome 1932- *TwCWW 91, WrDr 92*
**Gardner,** Jerry David 1941- *AmMWSc 92*
**Gardner,** Jerry Louis, Jr. 1932- *WhoAmL 92*
**Gardner,** Jewelle Baker 1925- *WhoFI 92*
**Gardner,** Jim 1946- *WhoAmP 91*
**Gardner,** Joan Elizabeth 1926- *WhoEnt 92*
**Gardner,** John 1917- *ConCom 92*
**Gardner,** John 1926- *IntAu&W 91, WrDr 92*
**Gardner,** John 1933-1982 *BenetAL 91, FacFETw*
**Gardner,** John Arvy, Jr 1939- *AmMWSc 92*
**Gardner,** John Frederick 1958- *WhoAmL 92*
**Gardner,** John Hale 1922- *AmMWSc 92*
**Gardner,** John Linton 1917- *Who 92*
**Gardner,** John Lowell 1923- *WhoFI 92*
**Gardner,** John Pickens, Jr 1952- *WhoAmP 91*
**Gardner,** John R 1937- *WhoIns 92*
**Gardner,** John Reed, II 1925- *WhoIns 92*
**Gardner,** John William 1912- *IntWW 91, Who 92, WhoAmP 91*
**Gardner,** Joseph Arthur Frederick 1919- *AmMWSc 92*
**Gardner,** Joseph Eugene 1946- *WhoAmP 91*
**Gardner,** Joseph Henry 1935- *WhoMW 92*
**Gardner,** Kathleen D. 1947- *WhoAmL 92*
**Gardner,** Kay Louise 1941- *WhoEnt 92*
**Gardner,** Keith A. St. H. 1929- *BlkOlyM*
**Gardner,** Kenneth Burslam 1924- *IntWW 91, Who 92*
**Gardner,** Kenneth Drake, Jr 1929- *AmMWSc 92*
**Gardner,** LaMaurice Holbrook 1936- *WhoBlA 92*
**Gardner,** Larry Allan 1929- *WhoRel 92*
**Gardner,** Laureen Marie 1957- *WhoFI 92*
**Gardner,** Leonard Burton, II 1927- *WhoWest 92*
**Gardner,** Leonard Foster 1921- *WhoAmP 91*
**Gardner,** Lewis *DrAPF 91*
**Gardner,** Liz 1932- *WhoEnt 92*
**Gardner,** Lytt Irvine 1917- *AmMWSc 92*
**Gardner,** Marjorie Hyer 1923- *AmMWSc 92*
**Gardner,** Marsha Lou Stull 1942- *WhoWest 92*
**Gardner,** Meghan Stengel 1968- *WhoEnt 92*
**Gardner,** Miriam *WrDr 92*
**Gardner,** Monroe Evans 1895-1975 *DcNCBi 2*
**Gardner,** Murray Briggs 1929- *AmMWSc 92*
**Gardner,** Nancy Hazard 1949- *WhoFI 92*
**Gardner,** Nellie E *ScFEYrs*
**Gardner,** Nord Arling 1923- *WhoWest 92*
**Gardner,** Norman Keith Ayliffe 1925- *Who 92*

**Gardner**, Oliver Maxwell 1882-1947 *DcNCBi 2*
**Gardner**, Paul E *WhoIns 92*
**Gardner**, Paul F 1930- *WhoAmP 91*
**Gardner**, Paul Jay 1929- *AmMWSc 92*
**Gardner**, Pete D 1927- *AmMWSc 92*
**Gardner**, Philip *WhoEnt 92*
**Gardner**, Phillip John 1941- *AmMWSc 92*
**Gardner**, Phyllis Ann 1937- *WhoAmP 91*
**Gardner**, Piers *Who 92*
**Gardner**, R. H. 1918- *WhoEnt 92*
**Gardner**, Ralph Bennett 1919- *Who 92*
**Gardner**, Ralph D. 1923- *WrDr 92*
**Gardner**, Randy 1958- *WhoAmP 91*
**Gardner**, Randy Cecil 1952- *WhoRel 92*
**Gardner**, Randy Clyburn 1952- *WhoEnt 92*
**Gardner**, Ray Dean, Jr. 1954- *WhoAmL 92*
**Gardner**, Reed McArthur 1937- *AmMWSc 92*
**Gardner**, Richard A. 1931- *ConAu 34NR, WrDr 92*
**Gardner**, Richard A 1941- *AmMWSc 92*
**Gardner**, Richard Bruce 1940- *WhoRel 92*
**Gardner**, Richard Hartwell 1934- *WhoFI 92*
**Gardner**, Richard Kevin 1961- *WhoFI 92*
**Gardner**, Richard Lavenham 1943- *IntWW 91, Who 92*
**Gardner**, Richard Lynn 1934- *AmMWSc 92*
**Gardner**, Richard Newton 1927- *IntWW 91, WhoAmL 92, WhoAmP 91*
**Gardner**, Robert B 1939- *AmMWSc 92*
**Gardner**, Robert Dickson Robertson 1924- *Who 92*
**Gardner**, Robert Granville 1924- *WhoRel 92*
**Gardner**, Robert Harkins 1947- *WhoEnt 92*
**Gardner**, Robert Harry 1913- *WhoMW 92*
**Gardner**, Robert Heys 1960- *WhoAmL 92*
**Gardner**, Robert Meade 1927- *WhoMW 92*
**Gardner**, Robert Wayne 1928- *AmMWSc 92*
**Gardner**, Robin P 1934- *AmMWSc 92*
**Gardner**, Rose Marie 1926- *WhoEnt 92*
**Gardner**, Russell, Jr 1938- *AmMWSc 92*
**Gardner**, Russell Menese 1920- *WhoAmL 92*
**Gardner**, Samuel C. 1931- *WhoBlA 92*
**Gardner**, Sandra *DrAPF 91*
**Gardner**, Sara A 1938- *AmMWSc 92*
**Gardner**, Sherwin 1928- *AmMWSc 92*
**Gardner**, Shirley Mae 1932- *WhoFI 92*
**Gardner**, Stephen *DrAPF 91*
**Gardner**, Steve *WhoAmP 91*
**Gardner**, Steven 1959- *WhoAmL 92*
**Gardner**, Sue Shaffer 1931- *WhoAmL 92*
**Gardner**, Sylvia Alice 1947- *AmMWSc 92*
**Gardner**, Thomas Michael 1952- *WhoWest 92*
**Gardner**, Thomas William 1949- *AmMWSc 92*
**Gardner**, Todd Whitney 1955- *WhoAmL 92*
**Gardner**, Trudi York 1947- *WhoFI 92*
**Gardner**, Valerie S. 1951- *WhoFI 92*
**Gardner**, Victor F. *WhoRel 92*
**Gardner**, W. Booth 1936- *IntWW 91*
**Gardner**, Walter Everett 1940- *WhoAmP 91*
**Gardner**, Walter Hale 1917- *AmMWSc 92, WhoWest 92*
**Gardner**, Wanda Joyce 1950- *WhoEnt 92*
**Gardner**, Warren E., Jr. 1922- *WhoBlA 92*
**Gardner**, Warren Joseph, Jr. 1951- *WhoFI 92*
**Gardner**, Wayland Downing 1928- *WhoMW 92*
**Gardner**, Wayne Scott 1920- *AmMWSc 92*
**Gardner**, Wayne Stanley 1941- *AmMWSc 92*
**Gardner**, Weston Deuain 1917- *AmMWSc 92*
**Gardner**, Wilford Robert 1925- *AmMWSc 92, IntWW 91*
**Gardner**, Willard Hale 1925- *WhoAmP 91*
**Gardner**, William Albert, Jr 1939- *AmMWSc 92*
**Gardner**, William Booth 1936- *AlmAP 92 [port]*
**Gardner**, William Howlett 1902- *AmMWSc 92*
**Gardner**, William Lee 1940- *AmMWSc 92*
**Gardner**, William Leonard 1942- *WhoAmL 92*
**Gardner**, William Maving 1914- *Who 92*
**Gardner**, William Michael 1948- *WhoAmP 91*
**Gardner**, Winston W, Jr 1938- *WhoAmP 91*
**Gardner**, Woodford Lloyd, Jr. 1945- *WhoAmL 92*
**Gardner-Chavis**, Ralph Alexander 1922- *AmMWSc 92*
**Gardner-Medwin**, Robert Joseph 1907- *Who 92*
**Gardner of Parkes**, Baroness 1927- *Who 92*
**Gardner-Thorpe**, Ronald 1917- *Who 92*
**Gardocki**, Joseph F 1926- *AmMWSc 92*
**Gardom**, Garde Basil 1924- *Who 92*
**Gardon**, John Leslie 1928- *AmMWSc 92*
**Gardonier**, Al 1940- *WhoFI 92*
**Gardons**, S. S. *ConAu 36NR, IntAu&W 91X, WrDr 92*
**Garduno**, Juan Jose Jesus 1922- *WhoFI 92*
**Gardyn**, George Edwards 1928- *WhoHisp 92*
**Gareau**, Joseph H 1947- *WhoIns 92*
**Garebian**, Keith 1943- *IntAu&W 91*
**Garel-Jones**, Tristan 1941- *Who 92*
**Garelick**, David Arthur 1937- *AmMWSc 92*
**Garelick**, Mordecai Lusby 1957- *WhoAmL 92*
**Garelick**, Richard Jay 1954- *WhoMW 92*
**Garen**, Alan 1926- *AmMWSc 92*
**Garetovski**, Nikolay 1926- *IntWW 91*
**Garetz**, Bruce Allen 1949- *AmMWSc 92*
**Garey**, Carroll Laverne 1917- *AmMWSc 92*
**Garey**, Charles Thomson 1947- *WhoEnt 92*
**Garey**, Donald Lee 1931- *WhoFI 92, WhoWest 92*
**Garey**, Kerry Anne 1957- *WhoWest 92*
**Garey**, Michael Randolph 1945- *AmMWSc 92*
**Garey**, Terry A. *DrAPF 91*
**Garey**, Walter Francis 1926- *AmMWSc 92*
**Garff**, Robert H *WhoAmP 91*
**Garfield**, Alan J *AmMWSc 92*
**Garfield**, Allen 1939- *IntMPA 92*
**Garfield**, Bernard Howard 1924- *WhoEnt 92*
**Garfield**, Brad Lewis 1957- *WhoEnt 92*
**Garfield**, Brian 1939- *TwCWW 91, WrDr 92*
**Garfield**, Brian Wynne 1939- *WhoEnt 92*
**Garfield**, Ernest 1932- *WhoAmP 91*
**Garfield**, Eugene 1925- *AmMWSc 92*
**Garfield**, Genie May 1921- *WhoWest 92*
**Garfield**, Howard Michael 1942- *WhoAmL 92, WhoWest 92*
**Garfield**, James A. 1831-1881 *BenetAL 91, RComAH*
**Garfield**, James Abram 1831-1881 *AmPolLe [port]*
**Garfield**, Johanna *DrAPF 91*
**Garfield**, Leon 1921- *Au&Arts 8 [port], IntAu&W 91, Who 92, WrDr 92*
**Garfield**, Leslie Jerome 1932- *WhoFI 92*
**Garfield**, Nancy Ellen 1954- *WhoMW 92*
**Garfield**, Robert Edward 1939- *AmMWSc 92*
**Garfield**, Sanford Allen 1943- *AmMWSc 92*
**Garfin**, David Edward 1940- *AmMWSc 92*
**Garfin**, Louis 1917- *AmMWSc 92*
**Garfinkel**, Arthur Frederick 1934- *AmMWSc 92*
**Garfinkel**, Barry Herbert 1928- *WhoAmL 92*
**Garfinkel**, Boris 1904- *AmMWSc 92*
**Garfinkel**, David 1930- *AmMWSc 92*
**Garfinkel**, David Abot 1955- *WhoFI 92*
**Garfinkel**, Harmon Mark 1933- *AmMWSc 92*
**Garfinkel**, Lawrence 1922- *AmMWSc 92*
**Garfinkel**, Michelle Robin 1961- *WhoFI 92*
**Garfinkel**, Neil B. 1964- *WhoAmL 92*
**Garfinkel**, Patricia *DrAPF 91*
**Garfinkel**, Patricia Gail 1938- *IntAu&W 91*
**Garfinkel**, Paul Earl 1946- *AmMWSc 92*
**Garfinkle**, Barry David 1946- *AmMWSc 92*
**Garfinkle**, Craig Stuart 1964- *WhoEnt 92*
**Garfinkle**, Louis 1928- *IntMPA 92*
**Garfinkle**, Louis Alan 1928- *WhoEnt 92*
**Garfit**, William 1944- *TwCPaSc*
**Garfitt**, Alan 1920- *Who 92*
**Garfitt**, Roger 1944- *ConPo 91, IntAu&W 91, WrDr 92*
**Garforth**, Francis William 1917- *WrDr 92*
**Garfunkel**, Art 1941- *IntWW 91, NewAmDM, WhoEnt 92*
**Garfunkel**, Art 1942- *IntMPA 92*
**Garfunkel**, Myron Paul 1923- *AmMWSc 92*
**Garg**, Arun *AmMWSc 92*
**Garg**, Arun 1947- *WhoMW 92*
**Garg**, Arun K 1946- *AmMWSc 92*
**Garg**, Bhagwan D 1940- *AmMWSc 92*
**Garg**, Devendra 1948- *WhoFI 92*
**Garg**, Devendra Prakash 1934- *AmMWSc 92*
**Garg**, Diwakar 1952- *AmMWSc 92*
**Garg**, Hari G 1931- *AmMWSc 92*
**Garg**, Jagadish Behari 1929- *AmMWSc 92*
**Garg**, Krishna Murari 1932- *AmMWSc 92*
**Garg**, Lal Chand 1933- *AmMWSc 92*
**Garg**, Umesh 1953- *AmMWSc 92*
**Gargallo**, Pablo 1881-1934 *FacFETw*
**Gargan**, Thomas Joseph 1952- *WhoWest 92*
**Gargano**, Charles A *WhoAmP 91*
**Gargano**, Francine Ann 1957- *WhoAmL 92*
**Gargaro**, Anthony 1942- *AmMWSc 92*
**Gargaro**, Christopher A. 1958- *WhoMW 92*
**Garges**, Susan 1953- *AmMWSc 92*
**Gargiulo**, Andrea Weiner 1946- *WhoAmL 92*
**Gargus**, James L 1922- *AmMWSc 92*
**Garibaldi**, Angelo 1815-1892 *DcNCBi 2*
**Garibaldi**, Antoine Michael 1950- *WhoBlA 92*
**Garibaldi**, John Attilio 1916- *AmMWSc 92*
**Garibaldi**, Marie L 1934- *WhoAmP 91*
**Garibaldi**, Marie Louise 1934- *WhoAmL 92*
**Garibaldi**, Peter P 1931- *WhoAmP 91*
**Gariepy**, Claude 1954- *AmMWSc 92*
**Gariepy**, Fred B. 1958- *WhoWest 92*
**Gariepy**, Ronald F 1940- *AmMWSc 92*
**Garik**, Vladimir L 1913- *AmMWSc 92*
**Garin**, David L 1939- *AmMWSc 92*
**Garin**, Erast Pavlovich 1902-1980 *SovUnBD*
**Garin**, Marita *DrAPF 91*
**Garin**, Mary S. Painter d1991 *NewYTBS 91*
**Garing**, John Seymour 1930- *AmMWSc 92*
**Garing**, William Henry 1910- *Who 92*
**Garinger**, Elmer Henry 1891-1982 *DcNCBi 2*
**Garinger**, Louis Daniel *WhoRel 92*
**Garino**, John Robert 1930- *WhoMW 92*
**Garino**, Terry Joseph 1960- *WhoWest 92*
**Garis**, Howard R. 1873-1962 *BenetAL 91, ScFEYrs*
**Garisto**, John Albert 1951- *WhoRel 92*
**Garitano**, Rita *DrAPF 91*
**Garito**, Anthony Frank *AmMWSc 92*
**Garl**, Michael Joseph 1949- *WhoEnt 92*
**Garland**, Abe J. 1913- *WhoAmL 92*
**Garland**, Akhil D. 1964- *WhoEnt 92*
**Garland**, Basil 1920- *Who 92*
**Garland**, Bennett *TwCWW 91, WrDr 92*
**Garland**, Beverly 1930- *IntMPA 92*
**Garland**, Carl Wesley 1929- *AmMWSc 92*
**Garland**, Cedric Frank 1946- *AmMWSc 92*
**Garland**, Charles E 1926- *AmMWSc 92*
**Garland**, David Ellsworth 1947- *WhoRel 92*
**Garland**, David Wayne 1948- *WhoAmL 92*
**Garland**, Donita L 1940- *AmMWSc 92*
**Garland**, Douglas Milton 1947- *WhoRel 92*
**Garland**, Douglas Walter 1942- *WhoRel 92*
**Garland**, Ed 1885-1980 *NewAmDM*
**Garland**, Evelyn Claire 1952- *WhoAmL 92*
**Garland**, Floyd Richard 1938- *WhoRel 92*
**Garland**, Frances Vaughan 1924- *WhoAmP 91*
**Garland**, Frederick Peter 1912- *Who 92*
**Garland**, Garfield Garrett 1945- *WhoWest 92*
**Garland**, Gary David 1964- *WhoFI 92*
**Garland**, Geoff 1926- *WhoEnt 92*
**Garland**, George *WrDr 92*
**Garland**, George 1904-1985 *TwCWW 91*
**Garland**, George David 1926- *IntWW 91*
**Garland**, Gregory *WhoRel 92*
**Garland**, Hamlin 1860-1940 *BenetAL 91, FacFETw, TwCWW 91*
**Garland**, Hazel Barbara 1913- *WhoBlA 92*
**Garland**, Hereford 1905- *AmMWSc 92*
**Garland**, Howard 1937- *AmMWSc 92*
**Garland**, James Boyce 1920- *WhoAmL 92*
**Garland**, James C 1942- *AmMWSc 92*
**Garland**, James H. 1931- *WhoRel 92*
**Garland**, James W 1933- *AmMWSc 92*
**Garland**, John Kenneth 1935- *AmMWSc 92*
**Garland**, Joseph A *WhoAmP 91*
**Garland**, Judy d1969 *LesBEnT 92*
**Garland**, Judy 1922-1969 *ConMus 6 [port], FacFETw [port], NewAmDM*
**Garland**, Madge 1898-1990 *AnObit 1990*
**Garland**, Margaret 1900-1977 *TwCPaSc*
**Garland**, Marie Tarvin 1943- *WhoAmP 91*
**Garland**, Michael McKee 1939- *AmMWSc 92*
**Garland**, Nicholas Withycombe 1935- *Who 92*
**Garland**, Patrick 1935- *IntWW 91*
**Garland**, Patrick Ewart 1935- *Who 92*
**Garland**, Patrick Neville 1929- *Who 92*
**Garland**, Paul Griffith 1930- *WhoAmL 92*
**Garland**, Peter *Who 92*
**Garland**, Peter Bryan 1934- *Who 92*
**Garland**, Phyllis T. 1935- *NotBlAW 92, WhoBlA 92*
**Garland**, Ray Lucian 1934- *WhoAmP 91*
**Garland**, Richard Roger 1958- *WhoAmL 92*
**Garland**, Robert Bruce 1932- *AmMWSc 92*
**Garland**, Robert Lee 1932- *WhoWest 92*
**Garland**, Sara Gay 1946- *WhoAmP 91*
**Garland**, Sylvia Dillof 1919- *WhoAmL 92*
**Garland**, Thomas Jack 1934- *WhoAmP 91*
**Garland**, Victor 1934- *IntWW 91, Who 92*
**Garland**, William 1923-1984 *FacFETw*
**Garland**, William Arthur 1945- *AmMWSc 92*
**Garland**, William Calvin, Jr. 1951- *WhoRel 92*
**Garland**, William James 1948- *AmMWSc 92*
**Garland**, Winston Kinnard 1964- *WhoBlA 92*
**Garlathy**, Frank Bryan 1946- *WhoRel 92*
**Garlett**, Marti Watson 1945- *WhoMW 92*
**Garlich**, Jimmy Dale 1936- *AmMWSc 92*
**Garlick**, George Donald 1934- *AmMWSc 92*
**Garlick**, George Frederick John 1919- *Who 92*
**Garlick**, Helen Patricia 1958- *IntAu&W 91*
**Garlick**, James Graham 1936- *WhoAmP 91*
**Garlick**, John 1921- *Who 92*
**Garlick**, Kenneth John 1916- *Who 92*
**Garlick**, Michael 1944- *WhoAmL 92*
**Garlick**, Raymond 1926- *ConPo 91, WrDr 92*
**Garlick**, Robert L 1949- *AmMWSc 92*
**Garlick**, Theodatus 1805-1884 *BiInAmS*
**Garlid**, Keith David 1934- *AmMWSc 92*
**Garlid**, Kermit L 1929- *AmMWSc 92*
**Garlin**, Douglas James 1957- *WhoFI 92*
**Garling**, David John Haldane 1937- *Who 92*
**Garlinski**, Jozef 1913- *IntAu&W 91, WrDr 92*
**Garlo**, Olgierd Casimir 1919- *WhoMW 92*
**Garlock**, Steven Jay 1949- *WhoMW 92*
**Garlough**, William Glenn 1924- *WhoFI 92, WhoWest 92*
**Garmaise**, David Lyon 1923- *AmMWSc 92*
**Garmaise**, Freda 1928- *ConAu 134*
**Garman**, Brian Lee 1945- *AmMWSc 92*
**Garman**, David K 1957- *WhoAmP 91*
**Garman**, Harry St. Clair 1945- *WhoAmL 92*
**Garman**, John Andrew 1921- *AmMWSc 92*
**Garman**, Mary Minnette 1932- *WhoAmP 91*
**Garman**, Merle Edward, Jr. 1942- *WhoMW 92*
**Garman**, Robert Harvey 1941- *AmMWSc 92*
**Garman**, Teresa A 1937- *WhoAmP 91*
**Garmany**, Catharine Doremus 1946- *AmMWSc 92*
**Garmatis**, Iakovos *WhoRel 92*
**Garmendia**, Francisco 1924- *WhoRel 92*
**Garmer**, William Robert 1946- *WhoAmL 92*
**Garmey**, Ronald 1937- *WhoAmP 91*
**Garmezy**, R H 1923- *AmMWSc 92*
**Garmire**, Elsa Meints 1939- *AmMWSc 92*
**Garmire**, Gordon Paul 1937- *AmMWSc 92*
**Garmon**, Lucille Burnett 1936- *AmMWSc 92*
**Garmon**, Ronald Gene 1934- *AmMWSc 92*
**Garmoyle**, Viscount 1965- *Who 92*
**Garn**, Edwin Jacob 1932- *AlmAP 92 [port], IntWW 91, WhoAmP 91, WhoWest 92*
**Garn**, Jake 1932- *FacFETw*
**Garn**, Kevin S 1955- *WhoAmP 91*
**Garn**, Paul Donald 1920- *AmMWSc 92*
**Garn**, Stanley Marion 1922- *AmMWSc 92, IntWW 91*
**Garnar**, Thomas E, Jr 1922- *AmMWSc 92*
**Garnaut**, Ross Gregory 1946- *IntWW 91*
**Garne**, Gaston *ScFEYrs*
**Garneau**, Francois-Xavier 1809-1866 *BenetAL 91*
**Garneau**, Francois Xavier 1936- *AmMWSc 92*
**Garneau**, Marc 1949- *FacFETw*
**Garner**, Alan 1934- *IntAu&W 91, Who 92, WrDr 92*
**Garner**, Albert Y 1925- *AmMWSc 92*
**Garner**, Andrew 1945- *AmMWSc 92*
**Garner**, Anthony 1927- *Who 92*
**Garner**, Bob 1960- *WhoEnt 92*
**Garner**, Bryan Andrew 1958- *WhoAmL 92*
**Garner**, Carlene Ann 1945- *WhoWest 92*
**Garner**, Charles 1931- *WhoBlA 92*
**Garner**, Cyril Wilbur Luther 1940- *AmMWSc 92*
**Garner**, Daniel Dee 1947- *AmMWSc 92*
**Garner**, Donald Eugene 1935- *WhoFI 92*
**Garner**, Duane LeRoy 1936- *AmMWSc 92*
**Garner**, Edward, Jr. 1942- *WhoBlA 92*
**Garner**, Edwin Leon, Jr. 1959- *WhoRel 92*
**Garner**, Erroll 1923-1977 *NewAmDM*
**Garner**, Frederic Francis 1910- *Who 92*
**Garner**, Frederick Leonard 1920- *Who 92*

**Garner**, George Bernard 1927- *AmMWSc 92*
**Garner**, Grayce Scott 1922- *WhoBlA 92*
**Garner**, Harold E 1935- *AmMWSc 92*
**Garner**, Harry Hyman 1910-1973 *ConAu 134*
**Garner**, Harry Richard 1935- *AmMWSc 92*
**Garner**, Harvey L 1926- *AmMWSc 92*
**Garner**, Helen 1942- *ConNov 91, IntAu&W 91, WrDr 92*
**Garner**, Herschel Whitaker 1936- *AmMWSc 92*
**Garner**, Hessle Filmore 1926- *AmMWSc 92*
**Garner**, Hugh 1913-1979 *BenetAL 91*
**Garner**, Jac Buford 1954- *WhoMW 92*
**Garner**, Jackie Bass 1934- *AmMWSc 92*
**Garner**, James *LesBEnT 92*
**Garner**, James 1928- *ConTFT 9, IntMPA 92, IntWW 91, WhoEnt 92*
**Garner**, James G 1938- *AmMWSc 92*
**Garner**, James Parent 1923- *WhoAmL 92*
**Garner**, James Wilford 1871-1938 *AmPeW*
**Garner**, Jasper Henry Barkdoll 1921- *AmMWSc 92*
**Garner**, Jim D 1963- *WhoAmP 91*
**Garner**, Joe 1942- *WhoMW 92*
**Garner**, John Charles 1949- *WhoWest 92*
**Garner**, John Donald 1931- *Who 92*
**Garner**, John Nance 1868-1967 *AmPolLe, FacFETw*
**Garner**, John W. 1924- *WhoBlA 92*
**Garner**, Joseph Dee 1951- *WhoEnt 92*
**Garner**, Judy Ann 1944- *WhoWest 92*
**Garner**, June B. 1923- *WhoBlA 92*
**Garner**, Kent Howard 1945- *WhoRel 92*
**Garner**, La Forrest Dean 1933- *WhoBlA 92*
**Garner**, LaForrest D 1933- *AmMWSc 92*
**Garner**, Linda Nanella 1946- *WhoFI 92*
**Garner**, Lon L. 1927- *WhoBlA 92*
**Garner**, Lynn E 1941- *AmMWSc 92*
**Garner**, Marie G 1924- *WhoAmP 91*
**Garner**, Mary E. *WhoBlA 92*
**Garner**, Mary Martin *WhoAmL 92*
**Garner**, Maurice Richard 1915- *Who 92*
**Garner**, Melvin C. 1941- *WhoBlA 92*
**Garner**, Meridon Vestal 1928- *AmMWSc 92*
**Garner**, Michael Scott 1939- *Who 92*
**Garner**, Mildred Maxine 1919- *WhoRel 92*
**Garner**, Nathan Warren 1944- *WhoBlA 92*
**Garner**, Phil 1949- *WhoMW 92*
**Garner**, Reuben John 1921- *AmMWSc 92*
**Garner**, Richard Warren 1948- *WhoIns 92*
**Garner**, Robert Edward Lee 1946- *WhoAmL 92*
**Garner**, Robert F. 1920- *WhoRel 92*
**Garner**, Robert Henry 1933- *AmMWSc 92*
**Garner**, Robert L *ScFEYrs B*
**Garner**, Steven Brett 1961- *WhoMW 92*
**Garner**, Thomas L. 1930- *WhoBlA 92*
**Garner**, Timothy L. 1957- *WhoMW 92*
**Garner**, Val Z 1932- *WhoAmP 91*
**Garner**, Velvia M. 1941- *WhoBlA 92*
**Garner**, Wayne *WhoAmP 91*
**Garner**, Wendell 1921- *WrDr 92*
**Garner**, Wendell Richard 1921- *IntWW 91*
**Garner**, William *IntAu&W 91*
**Garner**, William 1920- *WrDr 92*
**Garner**, William Darrell 1933- *WhoFI 92*
**Garner**, William Vivian Nigel 1944- *IntAu&W 91*
**Garnes**, Eugene Ellsworth 1955- *WhoEnt 92*
**Garnes**, Glenn Keith 1961- *WhoAmL 92*
**Garnes**, William A. 1924- *WhoBlA 92*
**Garnet**, Hyman R 1920- *AmMWSc 92*
**Garnet**, Sarah 1831-1911 *NotBlAW 92 [port]*
**Garnett**, Angelica 1918- *TwCPaSc*
**Garnett**, Bernard E. 1940- *WhoBlA 92*
**Garnett**, David *TwCSFW 91*
**Garnett**, David 1892-1981 *RfGEnL 91*
**Garnett**, Edward F., Jr. 1947- *WhoFI 92*
**Garnett**, Edward John, Jr. 1954- *WhoAmL 92*
**Garnett**, Eve C R *IntAu&W 91, WrDr 92*
**Garnett**, Eve C. R. 1900-1991 *ConAu 134*
**Garnett**, Jess 1924- *WhoAmP 91*
**Garnett**, John *Who 92*
**Garnett**, John 1748?-1820 *BiInAmS*
**Garnett**, Kevin Mitchell 1950- *Who 92*
**Garnett**, Marion Winston 1919- *WhoAmL 92, WhoBlA 92*
**Garnett**, Mayn Clew 1866- *ScFEYrs*
**Garnett**, Richard 1923- *IntAu&W 91, WrDr 92*
**Garnett**, Richard Lewis 1952- *WhoWest 92*
**Garnett**, Richard Wingfield, Jr 1915- *AmMWSc 92*
**Garnett**, Ronald Leon 1945- *WhoBlA 92*
**Garnett**, Stanley Iredale, II 1943- *WhoAmL 92*
**Garnett**, Tay *LesBEnT 92*
**Garnett**, Tay 1894-1977 *IntDcF 2-2 [port]*
**Garnett**, Thomas Ronald 1915- *Who 92*
**Garnett**, Wendall d1991 *NewYTBS 91*
**Garnett**, William John 1921- *Who 92*
**Garnett-Orme**, Ion d1991 *Who 92N*
**Garnette**, Booker Thomas 1930- *WhoBlA 92*
**Garnham**, John Charles 1959- *WhoFI 92*
**Garnham**, Percy Cyril Claude 1901- *IntWW 91, Who 92, WrDr 92*
**Garnichaud**, Brian Doston 1941- *WhoMW 92*
**Garnier**, John 1934- *Who 92*
**Garnock**, Viscount 1990- *Who 92*
**Garnons Williams**, Basil Hugh 1906- *Who 92*
**Garnsey**, David Arthur 1909- *Who 92*
**Garnsey**, Stephen Michael 1937- *AmMWSc 92*
**Garnsey**, Walter Wood, Jr. 1945- *WhoAmL 92*
**Garnsworthy**, Lewis Samuel 1922- *IntWW 91*
**Garodnick**, Joseph 1945- *AmMWSc 92*
**Garofalo**, Robert Louis 1944- *WhoEnt 92*
**Garofalo**, Terri Jane Comerford 1963- *WhoEnt 92*
**Garofalo**, Vincent James 1939- *WhoMW 92*
**Garofola**, Anthony Charles 1954- *WhoMW 92*
**Garofolo**, John Joseph, Jr. 1957- *WhoWest 92*
**Garoian**, George 1927- *AmMWSc 92*
**Garon**, Claude Francis 1942- *AmMWSc 92, WhoWest 92*
**Garon**, Olivier 1928- *AmMWSc 92*
**Garon**, Olivier Marie 1946- *WhoEnt 92*
**Garone**, John Edward *AmMWSc 92*
**Garonzik**, Sara E. 1951- *WhoEnt 92*
**Garou**, Louis P. *ConAu 134, SmATA 67*
**Garoufalis**, Angelo George 1929- *WhoFI 92*
**Garoufalis**, Maria Elaine 1957- *WhoMW 92*
**Garouste**, Gerard 1946- *WorArt 1980*
**Garoutte**, Bill Charles 1921- *AmMWSc 92*
**Garr**, Carl Robert 1927- *WhoFI 92*
**Garr**, Louis J., Jr. 1939- *WhoAmL 92, WhoFI 92*
**Garr**, Ronald Warren 1944- *WhoRel 92*
**Garr**, Teri 1949- *IntMPA 92*
**Garr**, Teri 1952- *WhoEnt 92*
**Garr**, Thomas Merrill 1954- *WhoMW 92*
**Garrabrandt**, John Neafie, Jr. 1917- *WhoRel 92*
**Garrahy**, J Joseph 1930- *WhoAmP 91*
**Garrambone**, Leonard James 1947- *WhoEnt 92*
**Garramone**, Raymond *WhoAmP 91*
**Garran**, Peter d1991 *Who 92N*
**Garrard**, Charles 1952- *TwCPaSc*
**Garrard**, Christopher S 1945- *AmMWSc 92*
**Garrard**, Lancelot Austin 1904- *Who 92, WrDr 92*
**Garrard**, Lewis, II 1829-1887 *BenetAL 91*
**Garrard**, Norma Lee 1945- *WhoEnt 92*
**Garrard**, Peter John 1929- *TwCPaSc*
**Garrard**, Richard 1937- *Who 92*
**Garrard**, Rose 1946- *IntWW 91, TwCPaSc*
**Garrard**, Sterling Davis 1919- *AmMWSc 92*
**Garrard**, Verl Grady 1923- *AmMWSc 92*
**Garrard**, William Irwin 1932- *WhoAmL 92*
**Garrard**, William Lash, Jr 1940- *AmMWSc 92*
**Garrard**, William T 1942- *AmMWSc 92*
**Garratty**, George 1935- *AmMWSc 92*
**Garraty**, John A. 1920- *ConAu 36NR*
**Garraway**, Michael Oliver 1934- *AmMWSc 92, WhoBlA 92*
**Garreau**, Louis-Armand 1817-1865 *BenetAL 91*
**Garrelick**, Joel Marc 1941- *AmMWSc 92*
**Garrell**, Martin Henry 1939- *AmMWSc 92*
**Garrels**, Dennis Earl 1942- *WhoRel 92*
**Garrels**, Helen Ann 1940- *WhoFI 92*
**Garrels**, James I 1948- *AmMWSc 92*
**Garrels**, John Carlyle 1914- *Who 92*
**Garrels**, Robert M. *IntWW 91N*
**Garrels**, Robert Minard 1916- *AmMWSc 92*
**Garrelts**, Jewell Milan 1903- *AmMWSc 92*
**Garren**, Henry Wilburn 1925- *AmMWSc 92*
**Garren**, Kenneth Albert 1951- *WhoEnt 92*
**Garren**, Ralph, Jr 1921- *AmMWSc 92*
**Garrenton**, Linwood Wilson 1941- *WhoRel 92*
**Garretson**, Ann Black 1955- *WhoAmL 92*
**Garretson**, Craig Martin 1924- *AmMWSc 92*
**Garretson**, Harold H 1911- *AmMWSc 92*
**Garretson**, James Edmund 1828-1895 *BiInAmS*
**Garretson**, O.L. 1912- *WhoWest 92*
**Garretson**, Robert Mark 1951- *WhoWest 92*
**Garretson**, Steven Michael 1950- *WhoWest 92*
**Garrett**, Albert Charles 1915- *TwCPaSc*
**Garrett**, Alfred Benjamin 1906- *AmMWSc 92*
**Garrett**, Aline M. 1944- *WhoBlA 92*
**Garrett**, Andrew 1823-1887 *BiInAmS*
**Garrett**, Anthony David 1928- *Who 92*
**Garrett**, Barry B 1935- *AmMWSc 92*
**Garrett**, Benjamin Caywood 1949- *AmMWSc 92*
**Garrett**, Betty 1919- *IntMPA 92*
**Garrett**, Betty Lou 1930- *WhoMW 92*
**Garrett**, Bowman Staples 1922- *AmMWSc 92*
**Garrett**, Cain, Jr. 1942- *WhoBlA 92*
**Garrett**, Carleton Theodore *AmMWSc 92*
**Garrett**, Carol Ann 1956- *WhoMW 92*
**Garrett**, Charles C. *TwCWW 91*
**Garrett**, Charles Geoffrey Blythe 1925- *AmMWSc 92*
**Garrett**, Charles Hope 1953- *WhoRel 92*
**Garrett**, Charles Thomasson 1954- *WhoEnt 92*
**Garrett**, Charles Walter 1873- *ScFEYrs*
**Garrett**, Charlotte *DrAPF 91*
**Garrett**, Cheryl Ann 1946- *WhoBlA 92*
**Garrett**, David 1951- *WhoRel 92*
**Garrett**, David L 1944- *AmMWSc 92*
**Garrett**, David M. 1941- *WhoAmL 92*
**Garrett**, Deborra Elizabeth 1951- *WhoAmL 92*
**Garrett**, Donald E 1923- *AmMWSc 92*
**Garrett**, Duejean Clements 1942- *WhoFI 92*
**Garrett**, E. Wyman 1933- *WhoBlA 92*
**Garrett**, Edgar Ray 1921- *AmMWSc 92*
**Garrett**, Edward Robert 1920- *AmMWSc 92*
**Garrett**, Emanuel 1951- *WhoEnt 92*
**Garrett**, Ephraim Spencer, III 1937- *AmMWSc 92*
**garrett**, evvy *DrAPF 91*
**Garrett**, Florence Rome 1912- *WrDr 92*
**Garrett**, George *DrAPF 91*
**Garrett**, George 1929- *BenetAL 91, ConNov 91, ConPo 91, IntAu&W 91, WrDr 92*
**Garrett**, Godfrey John 1937- *Who 92*
**Garrett**, Gordon *TwCSFW 91*
**Garrett**, Guy Thomas, Jr. 1932- *WhoBlA 92*
**Garrett**, H. Lawrence 1939- *IntWW 91*
**Garrett**, H Lawrence, III 1939- *WhoAmP 91*
**Garrett**, Helen Marie *WhoAmP 91*
**Garrett**, Henry Berry 1948- *AmMWSc 92*
**Garrett**, Henry Edmund Melvill Lennox 1924- *Who 92*
**Garrett**, J Marshall 1932- *AmMWSc 92*
**Garrett**, J Richard 1945- *WhoIns 92*
**Garrett**, James F. d1991 *NewYTBS 91*
**Garrett**, James Leo, Jr. 1925- *WhoRel 92*
**Garrett**, James M 1941- *AmMWSc 92*
**Garrett**, James Richard 1917- *AmMWSc 92*
**Garrett**, Jay Spencer 1947- *WhoAmL 92*
**Garrett**, Jerry Dale 1940- *AmMWSc 92*
**Garrett**, John 1920- *DcEcMov*
**Garrett**, John Laurence 1931- *Who 92*
**Garrett**, John Patrick 1954- *WhoMW 92*
**Garrett**, Joseph Patrick 1955- *WhoFI 92*
**Garrett**, Joy Irene 1946- *WhoEnt 92*
**Garrett**, Joyce F. 1931- *WhoBlA 92*
**Garrett**, Kelly Suzanne 1969- *WhoWest 92*
**Garrett**, Kenneth James 1953- *WhoWest 92*
**Garrett**, L W, Jr 1925- *AmMWSc 92*
**Garrett**, Lawrence G, Jr. 1942- *IntMPA 92*
**Garrett**, Leroy 1913- *WhoBlA 92*
**Garrett**, Leslie *DrAPF 91*
**Garrett**, Louis Henry 1960- *WhoBlA 92*
**Garrett**, Madeline Elizabeth *WhoFI 92*
**Garrett**, Margo 1949- *WhoEnt 92*
**Garrett**, Mark Whitney 1951- *WhoAmL 92*
**Garrett**, Maxie 1931- *WhoAmP 91*
**Garrett**, Melvin Alboy 1936- *WhoBlA 92*
**Garrett**, Michael Benjamin 1941- *AmMWSc 92*
**Garrett**, N. Dumas 1960- *WhoFI 92*
**Garrett**, Naomi M. 1906- *WhoBlA 92*
**Garrett**, Nathan Taylor 1931- *WhoBlA 92*
**Garrett**, Pat 1951- *WhoEnt 92*
**Garrett**, Paul 1863-1940 *DcNCBi 2*
**Garrett**, Paul C. 1946- *WhoBlA 92*
**Garrett**, Paul Conrad 1946- *WhoAmL 92*
**Garrett**, Paul Daniel 1961- *AmMWSc 92*
**Garrett**, Peter Wayne 1933- *AmMWSc 92*
**Garrett**, Randall 1927-1988 *TwCSFW 91*
**Garrett**, Raymond 1900- *Who 92*
**Garrett**, Reginald Hooker 1939- *AmMWSc 92*
**Garrett**, Richard 1920- *IntAu&W 91, WrDr 92*
**Garrett**, Richard Anthony 1918- *Who 92*
**Garrett**, Richard E 1933- *AmMWSc 92*
**Garrett**, Richard Edward 1922- *AmMWSc 92*
**Garrett**, Robert Austin 1919- *AmMWSc 92*
**Garrett**, Robert Dean 1933- *WhoFI 92, WhoMW 92*
**Garrett**, Robert Ogden 1933- *AmMWSc 92*
**Garrett**, Robert Roth 1921- *AmMWSc 92*
**Garrett**, Robert Sheldon 1926- *WhoAmL 92*
**Garrett**, Robert Stephens 1937- *WhoWest 92*
**Garrett**, Roger W. 1949- *WhoEnt 92*
**Garrett**, Romeo Benjamin 1910- *WhoBlA 92*
**Garrett**, Ronnie Lee 1944- *WhoRel 92, WhoWest 92*
**Garrett**, Ruby Grant 1941- *WhoBlA 92, WhoEnt 92*
**Garrett**, Ruby Joyce Burriss 1946- *AmMWSc 92, WhoAmL 92*
**Garrett**, Sandy 1943- *WhoAmP 91*
**Garrett**, Scott *WhoAmP 91*
**Garrett**, Stacy F., III 1944- *WhoAmL 92*
**Garrett**, Steven Lurie 1949- *AmMWSc 92*
**Garrett**, Terence 1929- *Who 92*
**Garrett**, Thaddeus, Jr. 1948- *WhoBlA 92*
**Garrett**, Theodore Louis 1943- *WhoAmL 92*
**Garrett**, Thomas Boyd 1941- *AmMWSc 92*
**Garrett**, Thomas John 1927- *Who 92*
**Garrett**, Thomas Leroy, Jr. 1953- *WhoFI 92*
**Garrett**, Thomas Miles 1830-1864 *DcNCBi 2*
**Garrett**, Tim 1951- *WhoAmP 91*
**Garrett**, Tom 1954- *WhoAmP 91*
**Garrett**, Virginia Bonner 1922- *WhoAmP 91*
**Garrett**, William Edward 1920- *Who 92*
**Garrett**, William Floyd, Jr. 1947- *WhoWest 92*
**Garrett**, William Norbert 1926- *AmMWSc 92*
**Garrett**, William Ray 1937- *AmMWSc 92*
**Garrett**, William Walton 1926- *WhoAmL 92*
**Garrett Harshaw**, Karla 1955- *WhoBlA 92*
**Garretto**, Leonard Anthony, Jr. 1925- *WhoFI 92*
**Garrettson**, Lorne Keith 1934- *AmMWSc 92*
**Garrick**, B John 1930- *AmMWSc 92*
**Garrick**, David 1717-1779 *BlkwCEP [port], RfGEnL 91*
**Garrick**, Isadore Edward 1910- *AmMWSc 92*
**Garrick**, Jan Dianne 1952- *WhoAmL 92*
**Garrick**, Laura Morris 1945- *AmMWSc 92*
**Garrick**, Michael D 1938- *AmMWSc 92*
**Garrick**, Rita Anne *AmMWSc 92*
**Garrick**, Ronald 1940- *Who 92*
**Garrick**, Thomas S. 1966- *WhoBlA 92*
**Garrido**, Jorge L. *WhoHisp 92*
**Garrido**, Jose A., Jr. 1953- *WhoHisp 92*
**Garriga**, Julio 1955- *WhoHisp 92*
**Garrigan**, Richard Thomas 1938- *WhoFI 92*
**Garrigan**, William Henry, III 1954- *WhoMW 92*
**Garrigle**, William Aloysius 1941- *WhoAmL 92*
**Garrigo**, Jose R. 1936- *WhoHisp 92*
**Garrigue**, Jean 1914-1972 *BenetAL 91*
**Garrigues**, Gayle Lynne 1955- *WhoWest 92*
**Garrigues**, Henry Jacques 1831-1913 *BiInAmS*
**Garrigus**, Charles Byford 1914- *WhoWest 92*
**Garrigus**, Upson Stanley 1917- *AmMWSc 92*
**Garrioch**, Henry 1916- *Who 92*
**Garriott**, Edward Bennett 1853-1910 *BiInAmS*
**Garriott**, James Clark 1938- *AmMWSc 92*
**Garriott**, Michael Lee 1951- *AmMWSc 92, WhoMW 92*
**Garripoli**, Mary 1956- *WhoEnt 92*
**Garris**, Curtis Wayne 1952- *WhoEnt 92*
**Garris**, Robert Eugene 1930- *WhoRel 92*
**Garrison**, Allen K 1931- *AmMWSc 92*
**Garrison**, Althea 1940- *WhoFI 92*
**Garrison**, Arthur Wayne 1934- *AmMWSc 92*
**Garrison**, Barbara Jane 1949- *AmMWSc 92*
**Garrison**, Betty Bernhardt 1932- *AmMWSc 92, WhoWest 92*
**Garrison**, Charles Eugene 1943- *WhoMW 92*
**Garrison**, David *DrAPF 91*
**Garrison**, David Louis 1941- *WhoAmL 92*
**Garrison**, Dee 1934- *WrDr 92*
**Garrison**, Esther F. 1922- *WhoBlA 92*
**Garrison**, Gary 1934- *WhoFI 92*
**Garrison**, Greg *LesBEnT 92*
**Garrison**, Hazel Jeanne 1928- *AmMWSc 92*
**Garrison**, James C 1943- *AmMWSc 92*
**Garrison**, James Edwin 1949- *WhoFI 92*

**Garrison**, Jewell K. 1946- *WhoBlA 92*
**Garrison**, Jimmy 1934-1976 *NewAmDM*
**Garrison**, John Carson 1935- *AmMWSc 92, WhoFI 92*
**Garrison**, John Dresser 1922- *AmMWSc 92*
**Garrison**, Joseph *DrAPF 91*
**Garrison**, Larry Richard 1951- *WhoMW 92*
**Garrison**, Lester Boyd 1948- *WhoWest 92*
**Garrison**, Lewis K. 1932- *WhoAmL 92*
**Garrison**, Lisa *DrAPF 91*
**Garrison**, Lloyd K. d1991 *NewYTBS 91 [port]*
**Garrison**, Lloyd K. 1897-1991 *CurBio 91N*
**Garrison**, Norman Eugene 1943- *AmMWSc 92*
**Garrison**, Omar V 1913- *IntAu&W 91, WrDr 92*
**Garrison**, Paul Cornell 1935- *WhoMW 92*
**Garrison**, Peggy *DrAPF 91*
**Garrison**, Pitser Hardeman 1912- *WhoAmL 92*
**Garrison**, Robert E., Jr. 1923- *WhoBlA 92*
**Garrison**, Robert Edward 1932- *AmMWSc 92*
**Garrison**, Robert Frederick 1936- *AmMWSc 92*
**Garrison**, Robert Gene 1925- *AmMWSc 92*
**Garrison**, Robert J 1944- *AmMWSc 92*
**Garrison**, Sidney Clarence 1887-1945 *DcNCBi 2*
**Garrison**, Stephen Allan 1940- *WhoFI 92*
**Garrison**, Thomas Edmond 1922- *WhoAmP 91*
**Garrison**, Thomas Edwin 1949- *WhoMW 92*
**Garrison**, U. Edwin 1928- *WhoWest 92*
**Garrison**, Walter R. 1926- *WhoFI 92*
**Garrison**, Warren Manford 1915- *AmMWSc 92*
**Garrison**, Wendell Phillips 1840-1907 *ScFEYrs*
**Garrison**, William Emmett, Jr 1933- *AmMWSc 92*
**Garrison**, William Lloyd 1805-1879 *AmPeW, BenetAL 91, RComAH*
**Garrison**, William Lloyd 1939- *WhoMW 92*
**Garrison**, William Lloyd, Jr. 1838-1909 *AmPeW*
**Garrison**, Zina 1963- *BlkOlyM, ConBlB 2 [port], IntWW 91*
**Garrison**, Zina Lynna 1963- *WhoBlA 92*
**Garrison-Corbin**, Patricia Ann 1947- *WhoBlA 92*
**Garrity**, Dennis Gerard 1953- *WhoAmL 92*
**Garrity**, John Joseph *WhoAmP 91*
**Garrity**, Juan David 1961- *WhoHisp 92*
**Garrity**, Michael K 1942- *AmMWSc 92*
**Garrity**, Monique P. 1941- *WhoBlA 92*
**Garrity**, Paul Gerard 1923- *WhoFI 92*
**Garrity**, Robert T 1949- *WhoAmP 91*
**Garrity**, Thomas F 1943- *AmMWSc 92*
**Garrity**, Thomas John 1949- *WhoFI 92*
**Garro**, Anthony Joseph 1942- *AmMWSc 92*
**Garro**, Barbara 1943- *WhoFI 92*
**Garro**, Elena 1920- *SpAmWW*
**Garro**, Samuel Joseph, Jr. 1954- *WhoAmL 92*
**Garrod**, Claude 1932- *AmMWSc 92*
**Garrod**, John Robert 1952- *WhoEnt 92*
**Garrod**, Martin 1935- *Who 92*
**Garrone**, Gabriel Marie 1901- *IntWW 91, WhoRel 92*
**Garrop**, Barbara Ann 1941- *WhoWest 92*
**Garrott**, Homer L. 1914- *WhoBlA 92*
**Garrott**, Idamae 1916- *WhoAmP 91*
**Garrott**, Isham Warren 1816-1863 *DcNCBi 2*
**Garrott**, Jay Gregory 1948- *WhoMW 92*
**Garrou**, Philip Ernest 1949 *AmMWSc 92*
**Garrow**, David J 1953- *IntAu&W 91, WrDr 92*
**Garrow**, Robert Joseph 1929- *AmMWSc 92*
**Garroway**, Allen N 1943- *AmMWSc 92*
**Garroway**, Dave d1982 *LesBEnT 92*
**Garruto**, John Anthony 1952- *WhoFI 92, WhoWest 92*
**Garruto**, Michelle Bartok 1961- *WhoWest 92*
**Garruto**, Ralph Michael 1943- *AmMWSc 92*
**Garry**, Benjamin Thomas 1960- *WhoAmL 92*
**Garry**, Charles R. 1909-1991 *NewYTBS 91 [port]*
**Garry**, Frederick W 1921- *AmMWSc 92*
**Garry**, John Thomas, II 1923- *WhoAmL 92*
**Garry**, Philip J 1933- *AmMWSc 92*
**Garry**, Robert Campbell 1900- *Who 92*
**Garry**, Stacey Lynne 1952- *WhoWest 92*
**Garsek**, Edward Harold 1946- *WhoRel 92*
**Garsia**, Adriano Mario 1928- *AmMWSc 92*
**Garside**, Brian K 1940- *AmMWSc 92*
**Garside**, Edward Thomas 1930- *AmMWSc 92*
**Garside**, Jack Clifford 1924- *IntAu&W 91*
**Garside**, Jane 1936- *Who 92*
**Garside**, Larry Joe 1943- *AmMWSc 92, WhoWest 92*
**Garside**, Marlene Elizabeth 1933- *WhoFI 92*
**Garside**, Oswald 1879-1942 *TwCPaSc*
**Garside**, Roger Ramsay 1938- *Who 92*
**Garside**, Steven L. 1957- *WhoWest 92*
**Garske**, David Herman 1937- *AmMWSc 92*
**Garske**, Jay Toring 1936- *WhoWest 92*
**Garson**, George 1930- *TwCPaSc*
**Garson**, Greer 1908- *IntMPA 92, Who 92, WhoEnt 92*
**Garson**, Robin William 1921- *Who 92*
**Garst**, David Nelson 1959- *WhoAmL 92*
**Garst**, John Eric 1946- *AmMWSc 92*
**Garst**, John Fredric 1932- *AmMWSc 92*
**Garst**, Richard Sylvester 1936- *WhoAmP 91*
**Garstang**, Michael 1930- *AmMWSc 92*
**Garstang**, Roy Henry 1925- *AmMWSc 92, WhoWest 92*
**Garstang**, Walter Lucian 1908- *Who 92*
**Garstens**, Martin Aaron 1911- *AmMWSc 92*
**Garstin**, Alethea 1894- *TwCPaSc*
**Garstin**, Crosbie 1887-1930 *ScFEYrs*
**Garstin**, Norman 1847-1926 *TwCPaSc*
**Gart**, Herbert Steven 1937- *WhoEnt 92*
**Gart**, John Jacob 1931- *AmMWSc 92*
**Garte**, Seymour Jay 1947- *AmMWSc 92*
**Garten**, Charles Thomas, Jr 1948- *AmMWSc 92*
**Gartenberg**, Dov Moshe 1954- *WhoRel 92*
**Gartenberg**, Seymour Lee 1931- *WhoEnt 92, WhoFI 92*
**Gartenhaus**, Solomon 1929- *AmMWSc 92*
**Garth**, Bryant Geoffrey 1949- *WhoAmL 92*
**Garth**, Eleanor 1940- *WhoEnt 92*
**Garth**, John Campbell 1934- *AmMWSc 92*
**Garth**, John Shrader 1909- *AmMWSc 92*
**Garth**, Leonard I. 1921- *WhoAmL 92*
**Garth**, Richard Edwin 1926- *AmMWSc 92*
**Garth**, Samuel 1661-1719 *RfGEnL 91*
**Garthe**, William A 1936- *AmMWSc 92*
**Garther**, John G 1951- *AmMWSc 92*
**Garthoff**, Raymond L. 1929- *WrDr 92*
**Garthoff**, Raymond Leonard 1929- *WhoAmP 91*
**Garthwaite**, Susan Marie 1950- *AmMWSc 92*
**Garthwaite**, William 1906- *Who 92*
**Gartlan**, Joseph V, Jr 1925- *WhoAmP 91*
**Gartland**, John C 1940- *WhoAmP 91*
**Gartland**, Jude T. 1944- *WhoFI 92*
**Gartland**, William Joseph 1941- *AmMWSc 92*
**Gartler**, Stanley Michael 1923- *AmMWSc 92, WhoWest 92*
**Gartley**, Markham Ligon 1944- *WhoAmP 91*
**Gartlir**, Kenneth T. 1950- *WhoAmL 92*
**Gartner**, Alan 1935- *ConAu 34NR*
**Gartner**, Chloe Maria 1916- *IntAu&W 91, WrDr 92*
**Gartner**, Daniel Lee 1945- *WhoMW 92*
**Gartner**, Edward A 1928- *AmMWSc 92*
**Gartner**, Harold Henry, III 1948- *WhoAmL 92, WhoWest 92*
**Gartner**, Kenneth Lawrence 1952- *WhoAmL 92*
**Gartner**, Lawrence Mitchel 1933- *AmMWSc 92, WhoMW 92*
**Gartner**, Leslie Paul 1943- *AmMWSc 92*
**Gartner**, Michael G. *LesBEnT 92 [port]*
**Gartner**, Michael G. 1938- *IntMPA 92*
**Gartner**, Michael Gay 1938- *WhoFI 92, WhoMW 92*
**Gartner**, Murray 1922- *WhoAmL 92*
**Gartner**, Nathan Hart 1939- *AmMWSc 92*
**Gartner**, Stefan, Jr 1937- *AmMWSc 92*
**Gartner**, T Kent *AmMWSc 92*
**Gartner**, W. Joseph 1928- *WhoFI 92*
**Gartner**, William Joseph 1942- *WhoWest 92*
**Garton**, David Wendell 1953- *AmMWSc 92*
**Garton**, Gena Marie 1958- *WhoRel 92*
**Garton**, George Alan 1922- *IntWW 91, Who 92*
**Garton**, Janet 1944- *ConAu 36NR*
**Garton**, John Henry 1941- *Who 92*
**Garton**, John Leslie 1916- *Who 92*
**Garton**, Robert Dean 1933- *WhoAmP 91, WhoMW 92*
**Garton**, Roland Lee 1953- *WhoFI 92*
**Garton**, Ronald Ray 1935- *AmMWSc 92*
**Garton**, Roy Lewis 1953- *WhoEnt 92, WhoWest 92*
**Garton**, William Reginald Stephen 1912- *IntWW 91, Who 92*
**Garton Ash**, Timothy *WrDr 92*
**Gartrell**, Charles Frederick 1951- *AmMWSc 92*
**Gartrell**, Joseph Lee 1961- *WhoWest 92*
**Gartrell**, Luther R. 1940- *WhoBlA 92*
**Gartshore**, Ian Stanley 1935- *AmMWSc 92*
**Gartside**, Peter Stuart 1937- *AmMWSc 92*
**Gartside**, Robert N 1918- *AmMWSc 92*
**Garty**, Kenneth Thomas 1916- *AmMWSc 92*
**Garty**, Robert Townsend 1957- *WhoFI 92*
**Gartz**, Linda Louise 1949- *WhoEnt 92*
**Garvagh**, Baron 1920- *Who 92*
**Garvan**, Stephen Bond 1952- *WhoEnt 92*
**Garve**, Andrew 1908- *WrDr 92*
**Garven**, Floyd Charles 1922- *AmMWSc 92*
**Garver**, Connie J. 1962- *WhoWest 92*
**Garver**, David Chester 1944- *WhoRel 92*
**Garver**, David L 1939- *AmMWSc 92*
**Garver**, Frederick Albert 1936- *AmMWSc 92*
**Garver**, Frederick Merrill 1945- *WhoFI 92, WhoMW 92*
**Garver**, James R. 1955- *WhoMW 92*
**Garver**, Oliver Bailey, Jr. 1925- *WhoRel 92, WhoWest 92*
**Garver**, Raymond James 1939- *WhoWest 92*
**Garver**, Robert S. 1942- *WhoFI 92*
**Garver**, Robert Vernon 1932- *AmMWSc 92*
**Garver**, William Sherman, IV 1962- *WhoWest 92*
**Garverick**, Charles Michael 1936- *WhoRel 92*
**Garvey**, Doris Burmester 1936- *WhoWest 92*
**Garvey**, Ellen Gruber *DrAPF 91*
**Garvey**, Gerald Thomas 1935- *AmMWSc 92*
**Garvey**, James Anthony 1923- *WhoAmL 92*
**Garvey**, James F 1957- *AmMWSc 92*
**Garvey**, James Sutherland 1922- *WhoAmP 91*
**Garvey**, Jane Roberts 1919- *WhoAmL 92*
**Garvey**, John Burwell 1952- *WhoAmL 92*
**Garvey**, John Charles 1921- *WhoEnt 92*
**Garvey**, John Hugh 1948- *WhoAmL 92*
**Garvey**, John Leo 1927- *WhoAmL 92*
**Garvey**, Justine Spring 1922- *AmMWSc 92*
**Garvey**, Kenneth Thomas 1946- *WhoAmL 92*
**Garvey**, Marcus 1887-1940 *BlkLC [port], ConBlB 1 [port], DcAmImH, FacFETw [port], RComAH, TwCLC 41 [port]*
**Garvey**, Mona C. 1934- *ConAu 34NR*
**Garvey**, Patrick d1810 *DcNCBi 2*
**Garvey**, R Michael 1947- *AmMWSc 92*
**Garvey**, Richard Anthony 1950- *WhoAmL 92*
**Garvey**, Rita *WhoAmP 91*
**Garvey**, Ronald Herbert d1991 *Who 92N*
**Garvey**, Roy George 1941- *AmMWSc 92*
**Garvey**, Steve 1948- *ConAu 133*
**Garvey**, Terence Brian 1952- *WhoAmL 92*
**Garvey**, Thomas 1936- *Who 92*
**Garvey**, Thomas Joseph 1931- *WhoRel 92*
**Garvick**, Kenneth Ryan 1945- *WhoEnt 92*
**Garvin**, Abbott Julian *AmMWSc 92*
**Garvin**, Charles David 1929- *WhoMW 92*
**Garvin**, Clarence Alexander, Jr. 1921- *WhoFI 92*
**Garvin**, Clifton C., Jr. 1921- *IntWW 91*
**Garvin**, Clifton Canter, Jr. 1921- *Who 92*
**Garvin**, David 1923- *AmMWSc 92*
**Garvin**, Donald Frank 1932- *AmMWSc 92*
**Garvin**, Harold Whitman 1924- *WhoAmP 91*
**Garvin**, James Brian 1956- *AmMWSc 92*
**Garvin**, Jeffrey Lawrence 1957- *AmMWSc 92*
**Garvin**, Jonathan 1932- *WhoBlA 92*
**Garvin**, Mildred Barry 1929- *WhoAmP 91, WhoBlA 92*
**Garvin**, Paul Joseph, Jr 1928- *AmMWSc 92*
**Garvin**, Paul Lawrence 1939- *AmMWSc 92*
**Garvin**, Todd Jeffrey 1954- *WhoWest 92*
**Garvine**, Richard William 1940- *AmMWSc 92*
**Garwin**, Charles A 1944- *AmMWSc 92*
**Garwin**, Edward Lee 1933- *AmMWSc 92*
**Garwin**, Richard L. 1928- *IntWW 91*
**Garwin**, Richard Lawrence 1928- *AmMWSc 92*
**Garwood**, Douglas Leon 1944- *AmMWSc 92*
**Garwood**, Ellen Clayton *WhoAmP 91*
**Garwood**, Julia Marie 1951- *WhoAmL 92*
**Garwood**, Maurice F 1907- *AmMWSc 92*
**Garwood**, Roland William, Jr 1945- *AmMWSc 92*
**Garwood**, Tirzah 1908-1951 *TwCPaSc*
**Garwood**, Victor Paul 1917- *AmMWSc 92*
**Garwood**, Will *WhoAmP 91*
**Garwood**, William Everett 1919- *AmMWSc 92*
**Garwood**, William Lockhart 1931- *WhoAmL 92*
**Gary**, Alonzo G., Jr. 1928- *WhoBlA 92*
**Gary**, Cheryl Lynn 1955- *WhoWest 92*
**Gary**, Emily Gregory Gilliam 1867-1962 *DcNCBi 2*
**Gary**, James Frederick 1920- *WhoFI 92*
**Gary**, James H 1921- *AmMWSc 92*
**Gary**, James William 1947- *WhoMW 92*
**Gary**, John Godfrey, Jr 1943- *WhoAmP 91*
**Gary**, Judson Emmet, III 1954- *WhoRel 92*
**Gary**, Julia Thomas 1929- *WhoRel 92*
**Gary**, Lawrence Edward 1939- *WhoBlA 92*
**Gary**, Lesley *Who 92*
**Gary**, Lorraine 1937- *IntMPA 92*
**Gary**, Melvin L. 1938- *WhoBlA 92*
**Gary**, Nancy E *AmMWSc 92*
**Gary**, Norman Erwin 1933- *AmMWSc 92*
**Gary**, Richard David 1949- *WhoAmL 92*
**Gary**, Robert 1928- *AmMWSc 92*
**Gary**, Robert W 1938- *WhoIns 92*
**Gary**, Roger Vanstrom 1946- *WhoAmP 91*
**Gary**, Roland Thacher 1916- *AmMWSc 92*
**Gary**, Stephen Peter 1939- *AmMWSc 92*
**Garza**, Adolph Aranda 1959- *WhoEnt 92*
**Garza**, Angie 1948- *WhoHisp 92*
**Garza**, Anita Hernandez 1936- *WhoHisp 92*
**Garza**, Antonio O., Jr. *WhoHisp 92*
**Garza**, Augustine *WhoHisp 92*
**Garza**, Betty V. *WhoHisp 92*
**Garza**, Carlos *WhoHisp 92*
**Garza**, Carlos, Jr. 1944- *WhoHisp 92*
**Garza**, Carmen Lomas *WhoHisp 92*
**Garza**, Cipriano *WhoHisp 92*
**Garza**, Cutberto 1947- *AmMWSc 92, WhoHisp 92*
**Garza**, Cyndy 1956- *WhoHisp 92*
**Garza**, Daniel *DrAPF 91*
**Garza**, Edmund T. 1943- *WhoHisp 92*
**Garza**, Edward 1947- *WhoHisp 92*
**Garza**, Emilio M. 1947- *WhoAmL 92, WhoAmP 91, WhoHisp 92*
**Garza**, Enola 1953- *WhoHisp 92*
**Garza**, Federico, Jr. 1958- *WhoHisp 92*
**Garza**, Fidencio Gustavo, Jr. 1932- *WhoHisp 92*
**Garza**, Francisco Xavier 1952- *WhoHisp 92*
**Garza**, G. Jaime *WhoHisp 92*
**Garza**, Geoffrey Rene 1964- *WhoHisp 92*
**Garza**, Jaime R. 1954- *WhoHisp 92*
**Garza**, Jaime Rene 1941- *WhoHisp 92*
**Garza**, Javier *WhoHisp 92*
**Garza**, Javier Joaquin 1955- *WhoHisp 92*
**Garza**, Jose G. 1932- *WhoHisp 92*
**Garza**, Jose Leyva 1942- *WhoHisp 92*
**Garza**, Juan *WhoHisp 92*
**Garza**, Juanita Elizondo 1939- *WhoHisp 92*
**Garza**, Lalo *WhoHisp 92*
**Garza**, Lloyd *WhoHisp 92*
**Garza**, M. Antoinette 1939- *WhoHisp 92*
**Garza**, Marco *WhoHisp 92*
**Garza**, Margarito *WhoHisp 92*
**Garza**, Margarito P. *WhoHisp 92*
**Garza**, Maria C. 1959- *WhoHisp 92*
**Garza**, Maria Luisa *WhoHisp 92*
**Garza**, Martin Edward 1965- *WhoHisp 92*
**Garza**, Mary *WhoHisp 92*
**Garza**, Michael Diaz 1949- *WhoFI 92*
**Garza**, Oliver P. 1941- *WhoHisp 92*
**Garza**, Rachel Delores 1952- *WhoHisp 92*
**Garza**, Raymond Robles 1931- *WhoHisp 92*
**Garza**, Raynaldo T. 1957- *WhoHisp 92*
**Garza**, Reynaldo G. 1915- *WhoHisp 92*
**Garza**, Richard Robert 1947- *WhoHisp 92*
**Garza**, Rick Earnest 1952- *WhoHisp 92*
**Garza**, Robert *WhoHisp 92*
**Garza**, Roberto 1942- *WhoHisp 92*
**Garza**, Roberto Jesus 1934- *WhoHisp 92*
**Garza**, Roberto Montes 1951- *WhoHisp 92*
**Garza**, Rogelio Cantu 1946- *WhoHisp 92*
**Garza**, Rosalinda Perez 1948- *WhoRel 92*
**Garza**, Roy 1951- *WhoHisp 92*
**Garza**, Ruben Cesar, Sr. 1935- *WhoHisp 92*
**Garza**, Salvador, Jr. 1955- *WhoHisp 92*
**Garza**, San Juanita 1955- *WhoHisp 92*
**Garza**, Thomas A. 1962- *WhoHisp 92*
**Garza**, Thomas F. 1965- *WhoHisp 92*
**Garza**, Thomas Jesus 1958- *WhoHisp 92*
**Garza**, Trini *WhoHisp 92*
**Garza**, Vicki 1932- *WhoAmP 91*
**Garza**, William Alfred 1950- *WhoHisp 92*
**Garza**, Ygnacio *WhoHisp 92*
**Garza**, Ygnacio 1953- *WhoAmP 91*
**Garza**, Yolanda 1955- *WhoHisp 92*
**Garza-Adame**, Maria Dolores 1946- *WhoHisp 92*
**Garza-Gongora**, Sara R. *WhoHisp 92*
**Garza Schmilewski**, Diva *WhoHisp 92*
**Garzarelli**, Elaine Marie 1951- *WhoFI 92*
**Garzia**, John 1700?-1744 *DcNCBi 2*
**Garzoli**, Silvia *WhoHisp 92*

**Garzon**, Max 1953- AmMWSc 92
**Garzon**, Ruben Dario 1937- AmMWSc 92
**Garzone**, George WhoEnt 92
**Gasaway**, Laura Nell 1945- WhoAmL 92
**Gasbarre**, Louis Charles 1948- AmMWSc 92
**Gasbarro**, Pasco, Jr. 1944- WhoAmL 92
**Gasca**, Pedro de la 1485-1567 HisDSpE
**Gascar**, Pierre 1916- IntWW 91
**Gasch**, Pauline Diana Who 92
**Gasche**, Rodolphe 1938- ConAu 135
**Gaschen**, Francis Allan 1950- WhoAmP 91
**Gascho**, Gary John 1941- AmMWSc 92
**Gascoigne**, Bamber 1935- IntAu&W 91, Who 92, WrDr 92
**Gascoigne**, George 1539?-1577 RfGEnL 91
**Gascoigne**, George Edward 1896-1971 TwCPaSc
**Gascoigne**, John 1951- ConAu 133
**Gascoigne**, Nicholas Robert John 1958- AmMWSc 92
**Gascoigne**, Stanley 1914- Who 92
**Gascon**, Jean 1920-1988 FacFETw
**Gascoyne**, David 1916- ConPo 91, RfGEnL 91, WrDr 92
**Gascoyne**, David Emery 1916- IntAu&W 91
**Gasdorf**, Edgar Carl 1931- AmMWSc 92
**Gasek**, Stanley P. 1917- WhoRel 92
**Gash**, Jonathan 1933- IntAu&W 91, WrDr 92
**Gash**, Kenneth Blaine 1933- AmMWSc 92
**Gash**, Lauren Beth 1960- WhoMW 92
**Gash**, Norman 1912- IntWW 91, Who 92, WrDr 92
**Gash**, Virgil Walter 1919- AmMWSc 92
**Gasic**, Gabriel J 1912- AmMWSc 92
**Gasich**, Welko E 1922- AmMWSc 92
**Gasich**, Welko Elton 1922- WhoFI 92
**Gasidlo**, Joseph Michael 1935- AmMWSc 92
**Gasiorkiewicz**, Eugene Anthony 1950- WhoAmL 92
**Gasiorkiewicz**, Eugene Constantine 1920- AmMWSc 92
**Gasiorowicz**, Stephen G 1928- AmMWSc 92
**Gasis**, Andrew 1909- IntWW 91
**Gask**, Daphne Irvine Prideaux 1920- Who 92
**Gaskell**, Colin Simister 1937- Who 92
**Gaskell**, David R 1940- AmMWSc 92
**Gaskell**, Elizabeth 1810-1865 CnDBLB 4 [port], RfGEnL 91
**Gaskell**, George Percival 1868-1934 TwCPaSc
**Gaskell**, Ivan George Alexander de Wend 1955- IntAu&W 91
**Gaskell**, Jane 1941- IntAu&W 91, TwCSFW 91, WrDr 92
**Gaskell**, Peter 1917- AmMWSc 92
**Gaskell**, Philip 1926- Who 92, WrDr 92
**Gaskell**, Richard 1936- Who 92
**Gaskell**, Robert Eugene 1912- AmMWSc 92
**Gaskell**, Robert Weyand 1945- AmMWSc 92
**Gaskill**, Herbert Leo 1923- WhoWest 92
**Gaskill**, Herbert Stockton 1909- AmMWSc 92
**Gaskill**, Irving E 1922- AmMWSc 92
**Gaskill**, Jack Donald 1935- AmMWSc 92
**Gaskill**, Robert Clarence, Sr. 1931- WhoBlA 92
**Gaskill**, William 1930- IntWW 91, Who 92
**Gaskin**, Catherine 1929- Who 92, WrDr 92
**Gaskin**, Catherine Marjella 1929- IntAu&W 91
**Gaskin**, David Edward 1939- AmMWSc 92
**Gaskin**, Felicia 1943- AmMWSc 92
**Gaskin**, Frances Christian 1936- WhoBlA 92
**Gaskin**, Jack Michael 1943- AmMWSc 92
**Gaskin**, Jeanine 1945- WhoBlA 92
**Gaskin**, Juanita 1946- WhoEnt 92
**Gaskin**, Leonard O. 1920- WhoBlA 92
**Gaskin**, Leroy 1924- WhoBlA 92
**Gaskin**, Maxwell 1921- Who 92
**Gaskins**, Eura DuVal, Jr. 1941- WhoAmL 92
**Gaskins**, H Rex 1958- AmMWSc 92
**Gaskins**, Louise Elizabeth 1930- WhoBlA 92
**Gaskins**, Murray Hendricks 1927- AmMWSc 92
**Gasmer**, Alan M. 1959- WhoEnt 92
**Gaspar**, Anna Louise 1935- WhoWest 92
**Gaspar**, Gary J 1949- WhoIns 92
**Gaspar**, Max Raymond 1915- AmMWSc 92
**Gaspar**, Peter Paul 1935- AmMWSc 92
**Gaspar**, Rogelio G. 1965- WhoWest 92
**Gaspard**, Kathryn Jane AmMWSc 92
**Gaspard**, Marcus Stuart 1948- WhoAmP 91
**Gaspard**, Patrice T. 1954- WhoBlA 92
**Gaspard**, Perry A. 1949- WhoRel 92
**Gaspard**, Ray ConTFT 9
**Gaspard**, Raymond L. 1949- ConTFT 9
**Gaspari**, Remo 1921- IntWW 91
**Gasparini**, Francesco 1668-1727 NewAmDM
**Gasparini**, Francis Marino 1941- AmMWSc 92
**Gasparovic**, Richard Francis 1941- AmMWSc 92
**Gasparrini**, Claudia AmMWSc 92
**Gasparyan**, Goar Mikaelovna 1924- SovUnBD
**Gaspe**, Philippe Aubert de 1786-1871 BenetAL 91
**Gasper**, Gary John 1958- WhoAmL 92
**Gasper**, George, Jr 1939- AmMWSc 92
**Gasper**, Joseph J. 1942- WhoMW 92
**Gasper**, Louis 1911- WhoWest 92
**Gasper**, Mark 1956- WhoEnt 92
**Gasper**, Ruth Eileen 1934- WhoFI 92, WhoMW 92
**Gasperoni**, Emil, Sr. 1926- WhoFI 92
**Gasque**, Harrison 1958- WhoEnt 92
**Gasquet**, Joachim 1873-1921 ThHEIm
**Gass**, Clinton Burke 1920- AmMWSc 92
**Gass**, Frederick Stuart 1943- AmMWSc 92
**Gass**, George Hiram 1924- AmMWSc 92
**Gass**, Ian 1926- WrDr 92
**Gass**, Ian Graham 1926- IntWW 91, Who 92
**Gass**, James Ronald 1924- Who 92
**Gass**, Raymond William 1937- WhoAmL 92
**Gass**, Richard Brian 1967- WhoRel 92
**Gass**, Saul Irving 1926- AmMWSc 92
**Gass**, Sylvester Francis 1911- WhoRel 92
**Gass**, Timothy Jon 1955- WhoAmL 92
**Gass**, William 1924- WrDr 92
**Gass**, William H. DrAPF 91
**Gass**, William H. 1924- BenetAL 91, ConNov 91, FacFETw
**Gassaway**, James D 1932- AmMWSc 92
**Gassaway**, Michael 1950- WhoAmL 92
**Gassel**, Philip Michael 1947- WhoAmL 92
**Gassen**, Joseph Albert 1926- WhoAmL 92
**Gassend**, Pierre 1592-1655 BlkwCEP
**Gassendi** 1592-1655 BlkwCEP
**Gassensmith**, Norbert John 1932- WhoEnt 92
**Gasser**, Charles Scott 1955- AmMWSc 92
**Gasser**, David Lloyd 1943- AmMWSc 92
**Gasser**, Heinz 1932- AmMWSc 92
**Gasser**, Herbert Spencer 1888-1963 FacFETw, WhoNob 90
**Gasser**, Raymond Frank 1935- AmMWSc 92
**Gasser**, William 1923- AmMWSc 92
**Gassie**, Edward William 1925- AmMWSc 92
**Gassier**, Pierre 1915- ConAu 34NR
**Gassman**, Alan Scott 1959- WhoAmL 92
**Gassman**, Lewis 1910- Who 92
**Gassman**, Merrill Loren 1943- AmMWSc 92
**Gassman**, Paul G 1935- AmMWSc 92
**Gassman**, Paul George 1935- WhoMW 92
**Gassman**, Victor Alan 1935- WhoFI 92
**Gassman**, Vittorio 1922- IntMPA 92, IntWW 91
**Gassmann**, Florian Leopold 1729-1774 NewAmDM
**Gassmann**, Gunther 1931- IntWW 91
**Gassmann**, Henry 1927- WhoAmP 91
**Gassner**, John W. 1903-1967 BenetAL 91
**Gasson**, Barry 1935- Who 92
**Gasson**, John Gustav Haycraft 1931- Who 92
**Gast**, Aaron Edward 1927- WhoRel 92
**Gast**, Bruce Jeffrey 1961- WhoEnt 92
**Gast**, Dwight V 1951- IntAu&W 91
**Gast**, Harry T, Jr 1920- WhoAmP 91
**Gast**, James Avery 1929- AmMWSc 92
**Gast**, Jay Arnold 1956- WhoFI 92
**Gast**, Lyle Everett 1919- AmMWSc 92
**Gast**, Nancy Lou 1941- WhoWest 92
**Gast**, Robert Gale 1931- AmMWSc 92
**Gast**, Robert Henry, Jr. 1946- WhoWest 92
**Gastaut**, Henri Jean 1915- IntWW 91
**Gasteiger**, Tina Lyn 1970- WhoEnt 92
**Gaster**, Gordon Devon 1934- WhoFI 92
**Gastev**, Alexei Kapitonovich 1882-1939 FacFETw
**Gastevich**, Vladimir 1933- WhoAmL 92
**Gastil**, R Gordon 1928- AmMWSc 92
**Gastineau**, Clifford Felix 1920- AmMWSc 92
**Gastineau**, John Edward 1957- WhoMW 92
**Gastineau**, Michael Keith 1957- WhoIns 92
**Gastion**, Hillary, Sr. 1946- WhoRel 92
**Gastl**, George Clifford 1938- AmMWSc 92
**Gastoldi**, Giovanni Giacomo 1550?-1622 NewAmDM
**Gaston**, Alexander 1735?-1781 DcNCBi 2
**Gaston**, Arnett W. 1938- WhoBlA 92
**Gaston**, Arthur G., Sr. 1892- WhoBlA 92
**Gaston**, Bill WrDr 92
**Gaston**, Cito 1944- WhoBlA 92
**Gaston**, Dennis Dudley 1951- WhoEnt 92
**Gaston**, Edwin Willmer, Jr. 1925- WrDr 92
**Gaston**, H A ScFEYrs
**Gaston**, Henry Victor 1943- WhoAmP 91
**Gaston**, Hugh Philip 1910- WhoFI 92, WhoMW 92
**Gaston**, Judith Ann 1950- WhoMW 92
**Gaston**, Linda Saulsby 1947- WhoBlA 92
**Gaston**, Lyle Kenneth 1930- AmMWSc 92
**Gaston**, Mack Charles 1940- WhoBlA 92
**Gaston**, Marilyn Hughes 1939- WhoBlA 92
**Gaston**, Minnie L. 1909- WhoBlA 92
**Gaston**, Patrick David 1951- WhoAmL 92
**Gaston**, Paul Kenneth 1934- WhoAmL 92
**Gaston**, Robert E 1939- WhoAmP 91
**Gaston**, William James 1927- WrDr 92
**Gaston**, William Joseph 1778-1844 DcNCBi 2
**Gaston**, William W. 1926- IntWW 91
**Gastony**, Gerald Joseph 1940- AmMWSc 92
**Gastwirth**, Bart Wayne AmMWSc 92
**Gastwirth**, Joseph L 1938- AmMWSc 92
**Gastwirth**, Stuart Lawrence 1939- WhoAmL 92
**Gaswick**, Dennis C 1942- AmMWSc 92
**Gat**, Joel R. 1926- IntWW 91
**Gat**, Nahum 1947- AmMWSc 92
**Gat**, Uri 1936- AmMWSc 92
**Gatch**, Milton McCormick 1932- IntAu&W 91
**Gatch**, Milton McCormick, Jr. 1932- WhoRel 92, WrDr 92
**Gate**, Simon 1883-1945 DcTwDes
**Gatehouse**, Graham Gould 1935- Who 92
**Gatehouse**, Robert Alexander 1924- Who 92
**Gately**, Alexander Patrick 1949- WhoFI 92
**Gately**, Christopher Dewar 1952- WhoEnt 92
**Gately**, David F WhoAmP 91
**Gately**, Mark Donohue 1952- WhoAmL 92
**Gately**, Maurice Kent 1946- AmMWSc 92
**Gatenby**, Anthony Arthur 1951- AmMWSc 92
**Gatenby**, Greg 1950- ConPo 91, WrDr 92
**Gates**, Albert ConAu 133
**Gates**, Allen H, Jr 1929- AmMWSc 92
**Gates**, Arthur Roland, II 1941- WhoFI 92
**Gates**, Audrey Castine 1937- WhoBlA 92
**Gates**, Beatrix DrAPF 91
**Gates**, Bill NewYTBS 91 [port]
**Gates**, Bob 1951- WhoAmP 91
**Gates**, Bruce C 1940- AmMWSc 92
**Gates**, Caroyln 1935- WhoAmP 91
**Gates**, Charles Cassius 1921- WhoFI 92, WhoWest 92
**Gates**, Charles Edgar 1926- AmMWSc 92
**Gates**, Charles Matthew 1964- WhoFI 92
**Gates**, Clifford E., Jr. 1946- WhoBlA 92
**Gates**, Clifton W. 1923- WhoBlA 92
**Gates**, Crawford Marion 1921- WhoEnt 92
**Gates**, D W 1921- AmMWSc 92
**Gates**, Daryl Francis 1926- WhoWest 92
**Gates**, David G 1931- AmMWSc 92
**Gates**, David Murray 1921- AmMWSc 92
**Gates**, Donald Robert 1949- WhoFI 92
**Gates**, Doris 1901- IntAu&W 91
**Gates**, Earl Raymond 1931- WhoMW 92
**Gates**, Eleanor 1875-1951 BenetAL 91
**Gates**, Eleanor 1957- TwCPaSc
**Gates**, Gary Lynn 1950- WhoRel 92
**Gates**, George O 1905- AmMWSc 92
**Gates**, Gerald Otis 1939- AmMWSc 92
**Gates**, Glodean Kent Kerkmann 1934- WhoEnt 92
**Gates**, Halbert Frederick 1919- AmMWSc 92
**Gates**, Henry Louis 1950- WrDr 92
**Gates**, Henry Louis, Jr. ConLC 65 [port]
**Gates**, Henry Louis, Jr 1950- IntAu&W 91, WhoBlA 92
**Gates**, Henry Stillman 1929- AmMWSc 92
**Gates**, Horatio 1727?-1806 BenetAL 91, BlkwEAR
**Gates**, Hugh H WhoAmP 91
**Gates**, Jacquelyn Knight 1951- WhoBlA 92
**Gates**, James Edward 1943- AmMWSc 92
**Gates**, James Lloyd, Jr. 1957- WhoAmL 92
**Gates**, Jimmie Earl 1956- WhoBlA 92
**Gates**, Jodie WhoEnt 92
**Gates**, John E 1927- AmMWSc 92
**Gates**, John Edward 1924- WhoMW 92
**Gates**, Joseph Spencer 1935- AmMWSc 92
**Gates**, Keith L WhoAmP 91
**Gates**, Larry 1915- WhoEnt 92
**Gates**, Leslie Dean, Jr 1922- AmMWSc 92
**Gates**, Lewis E. 1860-1924 BenetAL 91
**Gates**, M. Mike WhoIns 92
**Gates**, Marshall De Motte, Jr. 1915- IntWW 91
**Gates**, Marshall DeMotte, Jr 1915- AmMWSc 92
**Gates**, Martina Marie 1957- WhoMW 92
**Gates**, Mary D. 1926- WhoMW 92
**Gates**, Michael Andrew 1946- AmMWSc 92
**Gates**, Milo Sedgwick 1923- WhoFI 92
**Gates**, Moine R 1940- WhoAmP 91
**Gates**, Nina Jane 1947- WhoBlA 92
**Gates**, Norman T. 1914- WrDr 92
**Gates**, Olcott 1919- AmMWSc 92
**Gates**, Otis A., III 1935- WhoBlA 92
**Gates**, Paul Edward 1945- WhoBlA 92
**Gates**, Paul W. 1901- WrDr 92
**Gates**, Philomene 1918- ConAu 134
**Gates**, Philomene Asher 1918- WhoAmL 92
**Gates**, Raymond Dee 1925- AmMWSc 92
**Gates**, Rebecca Twilley 1932- WhoAmP 91
**Gates**, Reginald Eugene 1947- WhoEnt 92
**Gates**, Richard Daniel 1942- WhoMW 92
**Gates**, Robert E 1920- WhoAmP 91
**Gates**, Robert Franklin, Jr. 1944- WhoEnt 92
**Gates**, Robert Leroy 1917- AmMWSc 92
**Gates**, Robert M. 1943- News 92-2 [port], WhoAmP 91
**Gates**, Robert Maynard 1918- AmMWSc 92, WhoMW 92
**Gates**, Robert Michael 1943- NewYTBS 91 [port]
**Gates**, Robert Pfarr 1942- WhoAmL 92
**Gates**, Ronald Cecil 1923- Who 92
**Gates**, Ronald Eugene 1941- AmMWSc 92
**Gates**, Samuel Kent 1938- WhoAmL 92
**Gates**, Susa Amelia Young 1856-1933 RelLAm 91
**Gates**, Sylvester J, Jr 1950- AmMWSc 92
**Gates**, Theodore Allan, Jr. 1933- WhoWest 92
**Gates**, Thomas Michael 1943- WhoBlA 92
**Gates**, Todd Michael 1943- WhoMW 92
**Gates**, William Allman, III 1949- WhoAmL 92
**Gates**, William H. 1925- WhoAmL 92
**Gates**, William H. 1955- CurBio 91 [port]
**Gates**, William Henry 1955- WhoWest 92
**Gates**, William Lawrence 1928- AmMWSc 92
**Gates**, William S. 1944- WhoIns 92
**Gates**, William Thomas George d1990 Who 92N
**Gatewood**, Algie C. 1951- WhoBlA 92
**Gatewood**, Arthur Smith 1945- WhoRel 92
**Gatewood**, Buford Echols 1913- AmMWSc 92
**Gatewood**, Dean Charles 1925- AmMWSc 92
**Gatewood**, George David 1940- AmMWSc 92
**Gatewood**, James C WhoAmP 91
**Gatewood**, Judith Anne 1944- WhoFI 92
**Gatewood**, Lael Cranmer 1938- AmMWSc 92
**Gatewood**, Lucian B. 1945- WhoBlA 92
**Gatewood**, Rita Patricia 1946- WhoMW 92
**Gatewood**, Tela Lynne WhoAmL 92
**Gatewood**, Wallace Lavell 1946- WhoBlA 92
**Gath**, Carl H 1912- AmMWSc 92
**Gathe**, Joseph C. 1929- WhoBlA 92
**Gathercoal**, Allan M. 1953- WhoRel 92
**Gathercole**, John Robert 1937- Who 92
**Gathercole**, Roy 1945- TwCPaSc
**Gathers**, George Roger 1936- AmMWSc 92, WhoWest 92
**Gathers**, James 1930- BlkOlyM
**Gatherum**, Gordon Elwood 1923- AmMWSc 92
**Gathings**, William Edward AmMWSc 92
**Gathorne-Hardy** Who 92
**Gathorne-Hardy**, Jonathan 1933- IntAu&W 91, WrDr 92
**Gathright**, Howard T. 1935- WhoAmL 92
**Gati**, John 1927- WhoEnt 92
**Gati**, William Eugene WhoFI 92
**Gatipon**, Glenn Blaise 1940- AmMWSc 92
**Gatland**, Ian Robert 1936- AmMWSc 92
**Gatland**, Kenneth William 1924- WrDr 92
**Gatley**, Ian 1950- AmMWSc 92
**Gatley**, William Stuart 1932- AmMWSc 92
**Gatley**, William Stuart, Sr. 1932- WhoWest 92
**Gatlin**, Alfred Moore 1790- DcNCBi 2
**Gatlin**, Daniel G. 1957- WhoWest 92
**Gatlin**, Delbert Monroe, III 1958- AmMWSc 92
**Gatlin**, Elissa L. 1948- WhoBlA 92
**Gatlin**, Fred 1948- WhoAmP 91
**Gatlin**, Larry Wayne 1948- WhoEnt 92
**Gatlin**, Lila L AmMWSc 92
**Gatlin**, Michael Gerard 1956- WhoAmL 92
**Gatlin**, Richard Caswell 1809-1896 DcNCBi 2
**Gatling**, James Henry 1816-1879 DcNCBi 2
**Gatling**, Richard Gerald, Sr. 1944- WhoRel 92
**Gatling**, Richard Jordan 1818-1903 DcNCBi 2
**Gatling**, Robert Riddick AmMWSc 92

**Gatos,** H C 1921- *AmMWSc 92*
**Gatos,** Stephanie *WrDr 92*
**Gatrall,** Jeffrey 1948- *WhoEnt 92*
**Gatrousis,** Christopher 1928- *AmMWSc 92, WhoWest 92*
**Gatschet,** Albert Samuel 1832-1907 *BiInAmS*
**Gatsik,** Stephen 1949- *WhoWest 92*
**Gatski,** Ron Bernard 1935- *WhoAmP 91*
**Gatski,** Thomas Bernard 1948- *AmMWSc 92*
**Gatson,** Wilina Ione 1925- *WhoBlA 92*
**Gatt,** Lawrence 1941- *IntWW 91*
**Gattaz,** Yvon 1925- *IntWW 91*
**Gattegno,** Christophe Jacques 1962- *WhoMW 92*
**Gattegno,** Jean 1935- *IntWW 91*
**Gatten,** Robert Edward, Jr 1944- *AmMWSc 92*
**Gatten,** Tom *DrAPF 91*
**Gatterdam,** Paul Esch 1929- *AmMWSc 92*
**Gattey,** Charles Neilson 1921- *IntAu&W 91, WrDr 92*
**Gatti,** Anthony Roger 1935- *AmMWSc 92*
**Gatti,** Daniel Jon 1946- *WhoWest 92*
**Gatti-Casazza,** Giulio 1869-1940 *NewAmDM*
**Gatting,** Michael William 1957- *IntWW 91*
**Gattinger,** Augustin 1825-1903 *BiInAmS*
**Gattinger,** Richard Larry 1937- *AmMWSc 92*
**Gattis,** Samuel Mallett 1863-1931 *DcNCBi 2*
**Gattis,** William Anthony 1959- *WhoRel 92*
**Gattison,** Kenneth Clay 1964- *WhoBlA 92*
**Gatto,** Alfonso 1909-1976 *DcLB 114 [port]*
**Gatto,** Janice 1960- *WhoAmL 92*
**Gatto,** Joseph Daniel 1956- *WhoFI 92*
**Gatto,** Louis Albert 1950- *AmMWSc 92*
**Gatton,** Becky Kingsbury 1960- *WhoMW 92*
**Gatton,** Steven Lee 1954- *WhoMW 92*
**Gattone,** Vincent H, II 1951- *AmMWSc 92*
**Gattone,** Vincent Henry, II 1951- *WhoMW 92*
**Gattozzi,** Marianna Storto 1949- *WhoMW 92*
**Gatts,** Thomas F 1933- *AmMWSc 92*
**Gattsek,** William Allan 1957- *WhoEnt 92*
**Gattuso,** James Leslie 1957- *WhoAmL 92*
**Gatty,** Trevor Thomas 1930- *Who 92*
**Gatu,** John 1925- *DcEcMov*
**Gatward,** James *IntMPA 92, LesBEnT 92*
**Gatward,** James 1938- *Who 92*
**Gatz,** Arthur John, Jr 1947- *AmMWSc 92*
**Gatz,** Carole R 1933- *AmMWSc 92*
**Gatz,** Henning 1951- *WhoWest 92*
**Gatz,** Randall Neal 1943- *AmMWSc 92*
**Gatza,** James 1933- *WhoIns 92*
**Gatzak,** John Peter 1949- *WhoEnt 92*
**Gatzke,** Hans W 1915- *IntAu&W 91*
**Gatzy,** John T, Jr 1936- *AmMWSc 92*
**Gau,** John Glen Mackay 1940- *Who 92*
**Gau,** John N 1945- *AmMWSc 92*
**Gaubatz,** Lynn Marie 1956- *WhoEnt 92*
**Gaubert,** Ronald Joseph 1946- *WhoFI 92*
**Gaucher,** Ellen Jean 1941- *WhoMW 92*
**Gaucher,** George Maurice 1938- *AmMWSc 92*
**Gauci,** Victor J. 1931- *IntWW 91*
**Gauck,** Carl Richard 1942- *WhoRel 92*
**Gaud,** William S 1943- *AmMWSc 92*
**Gaudentius of Brescia** *EncEarC*
**Gaudet,** Frances Joseph 1861-1934 *NotBlAW 92*
**Gaudette,** Henri Eugene 1932- *AmMWSc 92*
**Gaudette,** Leo Eward 1925- *AmMWSc 92*
**Gaudi i Cornet,** Antonio 1852-1926 *DcTwDes, FacFETw*
**Gaudian,** David John 1960- *WhoFI 92*
**Gaudibert,** Louis-Joachim 1812-1878 *ThHEIm*
**Gaudier-Brzeska,** Henri 1891-1915 *FacFETw, TwCPaSc*
**Gaudin,** Anthony J 1938- *AmMWSc 92*
**Gaudin,** Edward Clark 1931- *WhoAmP 91*
**Gaudino,** Mario 1918- *AmMWSc 92*
**Gaudio,** Arthur Ralph, Sr. 1942- *WhoAmL 92*
**Gaudio,** Frank Salvatore 1957- *WhoAmL 92*
**Gaudio,** John James 1945- *WhoMW 92*
**Gaudio,** Robert Joseph John *WhoMW 92*
**Gaudioso,** Stephen Lawrence 1945- *AmMWSc 92*
**Gaudry,** Roger 1913- *AmMWSc 92, IntWW 91, Who 92*
**Gaudy,** Anthony F, Jr 1925- *AmMWSc 92*
**Gauer,** Donald L 1932- *WhoIns 92*
**Gauer,** Edward H. d1991 *NewYTBS 91*
**Gauff,** Joseph F., Jr. 1939- *WhoBlA 92*
**Gaufin,** Arden Rupert 1911- *AmMWSc 92*
**Gaugain,** Paul-Octave 1850-1904 *ThHEIm*
**Gauger,** David Kenyon 1958- *WhoMW 92*
**Gauger,** Martin 1905-1941 *EncTR 91*
**Gauger,** Randy Jay 1947- *WhoRel 92*
**Gauger,** Wendell Lee 1927- *AmMWSc 92*
**Gaughan,** John Anthony 1947- *WhoAmP 91*
**Gaughan,** Norbert F. 1921- *WhoRel 92*
**Gaughan,** Renata Rysnik *AmMWSc 92*
**Gaughan,** Roger Grant 1951- *AmMWSc 92*
**Gaughran,** George Richard Lawrence 1919- *AmMWSc 92*
**Gaugl,** John F 1937- *AmMWSc 92*
**Gaugler,** Robert Walter 1940- *AmMWSc 92*
**Gauguin,** Paul 1848-1903 *ThHEIm*
**Gauhar,** Aruna 1940- *AmMWSc 92*
**Gauk,** Aleksandr Vasil'evich 1893-1963 *SovUnBD*
**Gaukler,** George 1936- *WhoAmP 91*
**Gaul,** Dewie Joseph 1928- *WhoAmL 92*
**Gaul,** George Brubaker 1916- *WhoFI 92*
**Gaul,** Malinda Ann 1958- *WhoAmL 92*
**Gaul,** Richard Joseph 1929- *AmMWSc 92*
**Gauld,** David 1866-1936 *TwCPaSc*
**Gauld,** William Wallace 1919- *Who 92*
**Gaulden,** Mary Esther 1921- *AmMWSc 92*
**Gaulden,** Ray 1914- *TwCWW 91*
**Gauldie,** Enid Elizabeth 1928- *IntAu&W 91, WrDr 92*
**Gauldie,** Jack *AmMWSc 92*
**Gaulin,** Jean 1942- *Who 92*
**Gaulke,** Mary Florence 1923- *WhoWest 92*
**Gaull,** Gerald E 1930- *AmMWSc 92*
**Gaull,** Gerald Edward 1930- *WhoMW 92*
**Gaulle,** Charles de 1890-1970 *EncTR 91 [port]*
**Gault,** Annabel 1952- *TwCPaSc*
**Gault,** Charles Alexander 1908- *Who 92*
**Gault,** David Hamilton 1928- *Who 92*
**Gault,** Donald E 1923- *AmMWSc 92*
**Gault,** Francis Beers 1875-1946 *DcNCBi 2*
**Gault,** Frederick Paul 1933- *AmMWSc 92*
**Gault,** George 1916- *TwCPaSc*
**Gault,** John Stanley 1942- *WhoMW 92*
**Gault,** Kate 1954- *TwCPaSc*
**Gault,** Marian Holness 1934- *WhoBlA 92*
**Gault,** N L, Jr 1920- *AmMWSc 92, WhoMW 92*
**Gault,** Nancy Pate 1957- *WhoFI 92*
**Gault,** Stanley Carleton 1926- *WhoFI 92, WhoMW 92*
**Gault,** Terrell Wilson 1951- *WhoWest 92*
**Gault,** William Campbell 1910- *IntAu&W 91, WrDr 92*
**Gault,** Willie 1960- *News 91 [port]*
**Gault,** Willie James 1960- *WhoBlA 92*
**Gaulter,** Derek Vivian 1924- *Who 92*
**Gaultier,** Jean-Paul 1952- *IntWW 91*
**Gaultier de La Ferriere,** Jacques Marie G 1923- *IntWW 91*
**Gaultney,** John Orton 1915- *WhoFI 92*
**Gaultois,** Dallas Rose 1940- *WhoEnt 92*
**Gaum,** Carl H 1922- *AmMWSc 92*
**Gaumer,** Albert Edwin Hellick 1926- *AmMWSc 92*
**Gaumer,** Herman Richard 1941- *AmMWSc 92*
**Gaumnitz,** Erwin Alfred 1907- *AmMWSc 92*
**Gaumond,** Charles Frank 1950- *AmMWSc 92*
**Gaunaurd,** Guillermo C 1940- *AmMWSc 92*
**Gaunt,** Abbot Stott 1936- *AmMWSc 92*
**Gaunt,** Graham *WrDr 92*
**Gaunt,** James Joseph 1934- *WhoRel 92*
**Gaunt,** Janet Lois 1947- *WhoAmL 92*
**Gaunt,** John Thixton 1936- *AmMWSc 92*
**Gaunt,** Paul 1932- *AmMWSc 92*
**Gaunt,** Robert 1907- *AmMWSc 92*
**Gaunt,** Stanley Newkirk 1915- *AmMWSc 92*
**Gaunt,** William 1900-1980 *TwCPaSc*
**Gaunt Suddards,** Henry *Who 92*
**Gauntier,** Gene 1891-1966 *ReelWom [port]*
**Gauntlett,** David Allan 1954- *WhoAmL 92*
**Gauntt,** William Amor 1926- *AmMWSc 92*
**Gaunya,** William Stephen 1920- *AmMWSc 92*
**Gaupp,** Andrew Christopher 1954- *WhoEnt 92*
**Gauri,** Kharaiti Lal 1933- *AmMWSc 92*
**Gaus,** Arthur Edward 1924- *AmMWSc 92*
**Gaus,** Gunter 1929- *IntWW 91*
**Gaus,** Paul Louis 1949- *AmMWSc 92*
**Gausden,** Ronald 1921- *Who 92*
**Gause,** Donald C 1934- *AmMWSc 92*
**Gause,** Evelyn Pauline 1946- *AmMWSc 92*
**Gause,** Georgiy Frantsevich 1910-1988 *SovUnBD*
**Gause,** Lucien Coatsworth 1836-1880 *DcNCBi 2*
**Gause,** Norma Neal 1920- *WhoRel 92*
**Gauss,** Christian 1878-1951 *BenetAL 91*
**Gaustad,** Edwin Scott 1923- *WhoRel 92*
**Gaustad,** John Eldon 1938- *AmMWSc 92*
**Gauster,** Wilhelm Belrupt 1940- *AmMWSc 92*
**Gauster,** Wilhelm Friedrich 1901- *AmMWSc 92*
**Gaut,** Janice Rae 1952- *WhoMW 92*
**Gaut,** Zane Noel 1929- *AmMWSc 92*
**Gautam,** Surhid P. 1956- *WhoFI 92*
**Gautheret,** Roger 1910- *IntWW 91*
**Gauthier,** Didier 1954- *AmMWSc 92*
**Gauthier,** Fernand Marcel 1923- *AmMWSc 92*
**Gauthier,** George James 1940- *AmMWSc 92*
**Gauthier,** Geraldine Florence 1931- *AmMWSc 92*
**Gauthier,** Joseph Delphis 1909- *WhoRel 92*
**Gauthier,** Mary Elizabeth 1917- *WhoMW 92*
**Gauthier,** Roland Joseph 1915- *WhoRel 92*
**Gauthier,** Victor Joseph 1941- *WhoWest 92*
**Gauthier,** Wendell Haynes 1943- *WhoAmL 92*
**Gauthreaux,** Sidney Anthony 1940- *AmMWSc 92*
**Gautier,** Dick 1937- *WhoEnt 92*
**Gautier,** Eduardo Emilio 1927- *WhoHisp 92*
**Gautier,** Judith 1845-1917 *FrenWW*
**Gautier,** Theophile 1811-1872 *GuFrLit 1, ThHEIm*
**Gautier,** Thomas Nicholas Boudet 1764-1848 *DcNCBi 2*
**Gautier-Smith,** Peter Claudius 1929- *Who 92*
**Gautieri,** Ronald Francis 1933- *AmMWSc 92*
**Gautreau,** Ronald 1940- *AmMWSc 92*
**Gautreaux,** Marcelian Francis 1930- *AmMWSc 92*
**Gautreaux,** Timothy Martin *DrAPF 91*
**Gautrey,** Peter 1918- *Who 92*
**Gautsch,** James Willard 1941- *AmMWSc 92*
**Gautschi,** Walter 1927- *AmMWSc 92, WhoMW 92*
**Gauvain,** Timothy John Lund 1942- *Who 92*
**Gauvey,** David Howard 1938- *WhoFI 92*
**Gauvin,** J N Laurie 1929- *AmMWSc 92*
**Gauvin,** Michel 1919- *IntWW 91*
**Gauvin,** William H 1913- *AmMWSc 92*
**Gauvin,** William Henry 1913- *IntWW 91*
**Gauvreau,** Emile 1891-1956 *BenetAL 91*
**Gauvreau,** N Paul 1948- *WhoAmP 91*
**Gauze,** Georgiy Frantsevich 1910-1988 *SovUnBD*
**Gava,** Antonio 1930- *IntWW 91*
**Gavac,** Donna B 1926- *IntAu&W 91*
**Gavac,** Donna Broderick 1926- *WhoWest 92*
**Gavalas,** Alexander Beary 1945- *WhoEnt 92*
**Gavalas,** George R 1936- *AmMWSc 92*
**Gavaldon,** Edward Adolph 1945- *WhoHisp 92*
**Gavan,** James Anderson 1916- *AmMWSc 92, WhoMW 92*
**Gavande,** Sampat A *AmMWSc 92*
**Gavasci,** Anna Teresa 1924- *AmMWSc 92*
**Gavaskar,** Sunil 1949- *IntWW 91*
**Gavaskar,** Sunil Manohar 1949- *FacFETw, Who 92*
**Gavazzeni,** Gianandrea 1919- *IntWW 91*
**Gaveau,** Joseph 1824-1903 *NewAmDM*
**Gavenda,** John David 1933- *AmMWSc 92*
**Gaver,** Chasen *DrAPF 91*
**Gaver,** Donald Paul 1926- *AmMWSc 92*
**Gaver,** Mary Virginia 1906- *ConAu 34NR*
**Gaver,** Robert Calvin 1938- *AmMWSc 92*
**Gavey,** James Edward 1942- *WhoFI 92*
**Gavian,** Peter Wood 1932- *WhoFI 92*
**Gavin,** Carney Edward 1939- *WhoRel 92*
**Gavin,** Catherine *IntAu&W 91*
**Gavin,** Catherine 1907- *WrDr 92*
**Gavin,** Charles 1944- *TwCPaSc*
**Gavin,** David Francis 1939- *AmMWSc 92*
**Gavin,** Delane Michael 1935- *WhoEnt 92*
**Gavin,** Donald Arthur 1931- *AmMWSc 92*
**Gavin,** Donald Glenn 1942- *WhoAmL 92*
**Gavin,** Elizabeth 1938- *WhoAmP 91*
**Gavin,** Gerard Brennan 1923- *AmMWSc 92*
**Gavin,** James 1907-1990 *AnObit 1990*
**Gavin,** James Maurice 1907-1990 *FacFETw*
**Gavin,** James Merricks Lewis 1911- *Who 92*
**Gavin,** James Raphael, III 1945- *WhoBlA 92*
**Gavin,** John 1932- *IntMPA 92, IntWW 91*
**Gavin,** John Anthony 1932- *WhoEnt 92*
**Gavin,** John Anthony Golenor 1932- *WhoHisp 92*
**Gavin,** John J 1920- *WhoAmP 91*
**Gavin,** John Joseph 1922- *AmMWSc 92*
**Gavin,** Joseph Gleason, Jr 1920- *AmMWSc 92*
**Gavin,** Kelley Louise 1962- *WhoAmL 92*
**Gavin,** L. Katherine *WhoBlA 92*
**Gavin,** Lloyd Alvin 1943- *AmMWSc 92, WhoWest 92*
**Gavin,** Louis Brooks 1907- *WhoAmL 92*
**Gavin,** Robert M, Jr 1940- *AmMWSc 92*
**Gavin,** T. Edward 1922- *WhoFI 92*
**Gavin,** Thomas *DrAPF 91*
**Gavin,** Thomas Joseph 1953- *WhoFI 92*
**Gavin,** Walter Harris 1947- *WhoEnt 92*
**Gavin-Singer,** Betty Ann 1954- *WhoEnt 92*
**Gavina,** Dino 1932- *DcTwDes*
**Gavina,** Pedro L. *WhoHisp 92*
**Gavini,** Muralidhara B 1947- *AmMWSc 92*
**Gaviria,** Cesar *IntWW 91*
**Gaviria Trujillo,** Cesar *NewYTBS 91 [port]*
**Gavis,** Jerome 1928- *AmMWSc 92*
**Gavish,** Yeshayahu 1925- *IntWW 91*
**Gavito,** Olga Leticia 1951- *WhoHisp 92*
**Gavlin,** Gilbert 1920- *AmMWSc 92*
**Gavlock,** Eugene Harlan 1925- *WhoFI 92*
**Gavora,** Jan Samuel 1933- *AmMWSc 92*
**Gavras,** Constantin 1933- *WhoEnt 92*
**Gavrilov,** Andrei 1955- *IntWW 91*
**Gavrity,** John D 1940- *WhoIns 92*
**Gavron,** Robert 1930- *Who 92*
**Gavronsky,** Serge *DrAPF 91*
**Gavronsky,** Serge 1932- *IntAu&W 91, WrDr 92*
**Gavurin,** Lillian *AmMWSc 92*
**Gaw,** C Vernon 1942- *AmMWSc 92*
**Gaw,** David George 1951- *WhoFI 92*
**Gawain Poet** *RfGEnL 91*
**Gawalt,** Gerard Wilfred 1943- *WhoAmL 92*
**Gawarecki,** Stephen Jerome 1929- *AmMWSc 92*
**Gawer,** Albert Henry 1935- *AmMWSc 92*
**Gawienowski,** Anthony Michael 1924- *AmMWSc 92*
**Gawley,** Irwin H, Jr 1927- *AmMWSc 92*
**Gawley,** Robert Edgar 1948- *AmMWSc 92*
**Gawron,** Oscar 1914- *AmMWSc 92*
**Gawsworth,** John *ConAu 34NR*
**Gawthrop,** Robert S., III 1942- *WhoAmL 92*
**Gay,** Alice Felts 1949- *WhoFI 92*
**Gay,** Amelia *WrDr 92*
**Gay,** Ben Allen 1946- *WhoFI 92*
**Gay,** Ben Douglas 1942- *AmMWSc 92*
**Gay,** Benjamin 1916- *WhoBlA 92*
**Gay,** Bernard 1921- *TwCPaSc*
**Gay,** Birdie Spivey 1918- *WhoBlA 92*
**Gay,** Bonnie Lewis 1942- *WhoAmL 92*
**Gay,** Bruce Wallace, Jr 1940- *AmMWSc 92*
**Gay,** Carl Lloyd 1950- *WhoAmL 92*
**Gay,** Carol Virginia Lovejoy 1940- *AmMWSc 92*
**Gay,** Charles Francis 1946- *AmMWSc 92*
**Gay,** Craig Matthew 1955- *WhoRel 92*
**Gay,** Don Douglas 1944- *AmMWSc 92*
**Gay,** E. Phelps 1952- *WhoAmL 92*
**Gay,** Eddie C. 1940- *WhoBlA 92*
**Gay,** Emil Laurence 1923- *WhoAmL 92, WhoFI 92*
**Gay,** Francis Vernon 1930- *WhoAmL 92*
**Gay,** Frank P 1925- *AmMWSc 92*
**Gay,** Geoffrey Charles Lytton 1914- *IntWW 91, Who 92*
**Gay,** George Arthur 1916- *WhoRel 92*
**Gay,** George Wilsmore 1913- *Who 92*
**Gay,** Helen 1918- *AmMWSc 92*
**Gay,** Helen Parker 1920- *WhoBlA 92*
**Gay,** Jackson Gilbert 1932- *AmMWSc 92*
**Gay,** James 1744-1819 *DcNCBi 2*
**Gay,** James Edward 1949- *WhoWest 92*
**Gay,** James F. 1942- *WhoBlA 92*
**Gay,** Joan Dabkowski 1940- *WhoAmP 91*
**Gay,** John 1685-1732 *BlkwCEP, NewAmDM, RfGEnL 91*
**Gay,** John 1924- *ConTFT 9, IntMPA 92*
**Gay,** Joyce Domingue 1930- *WhoEnt 92*
**Gay,** Kathlyn R. 1930- *WrDr 92*
**Gay,** Kathlyn Ruth 1930- *IntAu&W 91*
**Gay,** Lloyd Wesley 1933- *AmMWSc 92*
**Gay,** Marie-Louise 1952- *ConAu 135, SmATA 68 [port]*
**Gay,** Marilyn Fanelli Martin 1925- *IntAu&W 91, WhoEnt 92*
**Gay,** Martin 1803-1850 *BiInAmS*
**Gay,** Michael Howard 1943- *AmMWSc 92*
**Gay,** Milton F., Jr. 1942- *WhoBlA 92*
**Gay,** Naomi C 1907- *IntAu&W 91*
**Gay,** Peter 1923- *IntAu&W 91, IntWW 91, WrDr 92*
**Gay,** Philip Thomas 1949- *WhoWest 92*
**Gay,** Renate Erika 1949- *AmMWSc 92*
**Gay,** Richard Leslie 1950- *AmMWSc 92, WhoWest 92*
**Gay,** Robert Laird 1940- *WhoWest 92*
**Gay,** Robert Stephen 1947- *WhoFI 92*
**Gay,** Steffen 1948- *AmMWSc 92*
**Gay,** Theodis *WhoAmP 91*
**Gay,** Thomas John 1940- *AmMWSc 92*
**Gay,** Tom David 1947- *WhoEnt 92*
**Gay,** William 1955- *WhoBlA 92*
**Gay,** William Ingalls 1926- *AmMWSc 92*
**Gayan,** Anil Kumarsingh 1948- *IntWW 91*
**Gayarre,** Charles Etienne Arthur 1805-1895 *BenetAL 91*
**Gaydon,** Alfred Gordon 1911- *IntWW 91, Who 92, WrDr 92*

**Gaydos**, Joseph M. 1926- *AlmAP 92 [port]*
**Gaydos**, Joseph Matthew 1926- *WhoAmP 91*
**Gaydos**, Michael Edward, IV 1956- *WhoFI 92*
**Gaye**, Amadou Karim 1913- *IntWW 91*
**Gaye**, Marvin 1939-1984 *ConBlB 2 [port], FacFETw, NewAmDM*
**Gayed**, Sobhy Kamel 1924- *AmMWSc 92*
**Gayer**, Karl Herman 1913- *AmMWSc 92*
**Gayhart**, Keith Alan 1954- *WhoEnt 92*
**Gayl**, Wilhelm, Baron von 1879-1945 *EncTR 91*
**Gayle**, Addison, Jr. d1991 *NewYTBS 91*
**Gayle**, Addison, Jr. 1932- *WhoBlA 92*
**Gayle**, Addison, Jr. 1932-1991 *ConAu 135*
**Gayle**, Crystal *WhoEnt 92*
**Gayle**, Emma *IntAu&W 91X, WrDr 92*
**Gayle**, Gibson, Jr. 1926- *WhoAmL 92*
**Gayle**, Helene Doris 1955- *WhoBlA 92*
**Gayle**, Irving Charles 1920- *WhoBlA 92*
**Gayle**, Lucille Jordan 1920- *WhoBlA 92*
**Gayle**, Peter *IntMPA 92*
**Gayle-Thompson**, Delores J. 1938- *WhoBlA 92*
**Gayler**, Charles 1820-1892 *BenetAL 91*
**Gayles**, Anne Richardson 1923- *WhoBlA 92*
**Gayles**, Franklin Johnson *WhoBlA 92*
**Gayles**, Joseph Nathan, Jr 1937- *AmMWSc 92*
**Gayles**, Joseph Nathan Webster, Jr. 1937- *WhoBlA 92*
**Gayles**, Lindsey, Jr. 1953- *WhoBlA 92*
**Gayley**, James 1855-1920 *BiInAmS*
**Gaylin**, Willard 1925- *AmMWSc 92, WrDr 92*
**Gaylinn**, Marlene Sonya 1933- *WhoEnt 92*
**Gaylor**, Adolph Darnell 1950- *WhoBlA 92*
**Gaylor**, Anne Nicol 1926- *RelLAm 91*
**Gaylor**, David William 1930- *AmMWSc 92*
**Gaylor**, James Leroy 1934- *AmMWSc 92*
**Gaylor**, Michael James 1947- *AmMWSc 92*
**Gaylor**, Robert Gene 1939- *WhoMW 92*
**Gaylord**, Albert Stanley 1942- *WhoWest 92*
**Gaylord**, Brian Stuart 1944- *WhoFI 92*
**Gaylord**, Eber William 1922- *AmMWSc 92*
**Gaylord**, Edward Lewis 1919- *WhoEnt 92*
**Gaylord**, Ellihue, Sr. 1922- *WhoBlA 92*
**Gaylord**, James Earl 1940- *WhoAmL 92*
**Gaylord**, Karen Whitacre 1951- *WhoFI 92*
**Gaylord**, Mary Fletcher 1915- *WhoAmP 91*
**Gaylord**, Norman Grant 1923- *AmMWSc 92*
**Gaylord**, Richard J 1947- *AmMWSc 92*
**Gaylord**, S. Murray 1942- *WhoFI 92*
**Gaylord**, Thomas Keith 1943- *AmMWSc 92*
**Gaylord**, Willis 1792-1844 *BiInAmS*
**Gaymon**, Nicholas Edward 1928- *WhoBlA 92*
**Gayner**, Glen B, Jr 1927- *WhoAmP 91*
**Gaynes**, Albert H. d1991 *NewYTBS 91*
**Gaynor**, Alan Sims 1928- *WhoAmL 92*
**Gaynor**, Dean Scott 1964- *WhoWest 92*
**Gaynor**, Florence S. 1920- *WhoBlA 92*
**Gaynor**, Harry J. *ConAu 134*
**Gaynor**, John James 1953- *AmMWSc 92*
**Gaynor**, Joseph 1925- *AmMWSc 92, WhoWest 92*
**Gaynor**, Kevin Allen 1948- *WhoAmL 92*
**Gaynor**, Mitzi 1931- *IntMPA 92*
**Gaynor**, Ronald Kevin 1952- *WhoWest 92*
**Gaynor**, Samuel Dennison 1933- *WhoMW 92*
**Gaynor**, Vere Egerton 1947- *WhoMW 92*
**Gayoom**, Maumoon Abdul 1937- *FacFETw, IntWW 91*
**Gayoso**, Antonio 1939- *WhoHisp 92*
**Gayre of Gayre and Nigg**, Robert *Who 92*
**Gayre Of Gayre And Nigg**, Robert 1907- *WrDr 92*
**Gayton**, Bertram *ScFEYrs*
**Gayton**, Gary D. 1933- *WhoBlA 92*
**Gayton**, Joseph W. *WhoHisp 92*
**Gayton**, Nelson 1963- *WhoHisp 92*
**Gayton**, Ronald B. 1938- *WhoHisp 92*
**Gazaway**, James Austin 1955- *WhoRel 92*
**Gazaway**, Larry Galen 1965- *WhoMW 92*
**Gazda**, I W 1941- *AmMWSc 92*
**Gazdanov**, Gaito 1903-1971 *LiExTwC*
**Gazdar**, Adi F 1937- *AmMWSc 92*
**Gazdar**, Gerald James Michael 1950- *Who 92*
**Gaze**, R. Michael 1927- *WrDr 92*
**Gaze**, Raymond Michael 1927- *IntWW 91, Who 92*
**Gazenko**, Oleg Georgievich 1918- *IntWW 91*
**Gazin**, Charles Lewis 1904- *AmMWSc 92*
**Gazis**, Denos Constantinos 1930- *AmMWSc 92*
**Gazit**, Shlomo 1926- *IntWW 91*
**Gazley**, Carl, Jr 1922- *AmMWSc 92*
**Gazo**, Stephen P. 1955- *WhoFI 92*
**Gazouleas**, Panagiotis J. 1927- *WhoRel 92*
**Gaztambide**, Mario F. 1945- *WhoHisp 92*
**Gaztambide**, Mario Francisco, Jr 1945- *WhoAmP 91*
**Gaztambide**, Peter *WhoHisp 92*
**Gazunis**, Katherine-Teressa 1954- *WhoWest 92*
**Gazzaniga**, Giuseppe 1743-1818 *NewAmDM*
**Gazzaniga**, Michael Saunders 1939- *AmMWSc 92*
**Gazzar**, Abdel Hadi el 1925- *IntWW 91*
**Gazzara**, Ben 1930- *IntMPA 92, WhoEnt 92*
**Gazzard**, Roy James Albert 1923- *Who 92*
**Gazzelloni**, Severino 1919- *NewAmDM*
**Gazzo**, Michael Vincente 1923- *WhoEnt 92*
**Gazzola**, Robert Allen 1938- *WhoAmL 92*
**Gazzoli**, John Joseph, Jr. 1947- *WhoAmL 92*
**Gbeho**, James Victor 1935- *IntWW 91*
**Gbewonyo**, Sylvestre Kwadzo 1942- *WhoFI 92*
**Gbezera-Bria**, Michel 1946- *IntWW 91*
**Gdlyan**, Tel'man Khorenovich 1940- *SovUnBD*
**Gdlyan**, Trelman Khorenovich 1940- *IntWW 91*
**Gdowski**, Diana 1951- *WhoWest 92*
**Gdowski**, Walter J 1946- *WhoIns 92*
**Ge Gan-ru** 1954- *ConCom 92*
**Ge Tingsui** 1913- *IntWW 91*
**Ge Wujue** 1937- *IntWW 91*
**Ge**, Weikun 1942- *AmMWSc 92*
**Ge**, Wujue 1937- *IntAu&W 91*
**Ge**, Zhong 1963- *WhoWest 92*
**Geach**, Christine 1930- *IntAu&W 91, WrDr 92*
**Geach**, George Alwyn 1913- *AmMWSc 92*
**Geach**, Gertrude Elizabeth Margaret *Who 92*
**Geach**, Peter Thomas 1916- *Who 92*
**Geacintov**, Nicholas 1935- *AmMWSc 92*
**Geadelmann**, Jon Lee 1944- *AmMWSc 92*
**Geake**, Raymond Robert 1936- *WhoAmP 91*
**Gealer**, Roy L 1932- *AmMWSc 92*
**Gealt**, Adelheid 1946- *ConAu 36NR*
**Gealt**, Michael Alan 1948- *AmMWSc 92*
**Gealy**, Elizabeth Lee 1923- *AmMWSc 92*
**Gealy**, John Robert 1930- *AmMWSc 92*
**Gealy**, William James 1925- *AmMWSc 92*
**Gean**, Donald H *WhoAmP 91*
**Geanangel**, Russell Alan 1941- *AmMWSc 92*
**Geaney**, John Joseph 1937- *WhoRel 92*
**Geankoplis**, Christie J 1921- *AmMWSc 92*
**Gear**, Adrian R L 1939- *AmMWSc 92*
**Gear**, Charles William 1935- *AmMWSc 92*
**Gear**, James Richard 1935- *AmMWSc 92*
**Gear**, Michael Frederick 1934- *Who 92*
**Gear**, Sara Moreau 1941- *WhoAmP 91*
**Gear**, William 1915- *TwCPaSc, Who 92*
**Gearen**, John J. 1943- *WhoAmL 92*
**Gearhart**, Jane Annette Simpson 1918- *WhoWest 92*
**Gearhart**, John Wesley, III 1950- *WhoEnt 92*
**Gearhart**, Marilyn Kaye 1950- *WhoMW 92*
**Gearhart**, Patricia Johanna *AmMWSc 92*
**Gearhart**, Ray Leroy 1946- *WhoEnt 92*
**Gearhart**, Roger A 1935- *AmMWSc 92*
**Gearheart**, Bill R. 1928- *WrDr 92*
**Gearien**, James Edward 1919- *AmMWSc 92*
**Gearing**, Juanita Newman 1945- *AmMWSc 92*
**Gearing-Thomas**, G *IntAu&W 91X*
**Gearring**, Joel Kenneth 1936- *WhoBlA 92*
**Gearty**, Edward Joseph 1923- *WhoAmP 91*
**Gearty**, Timothy Fredrik 1955- *WhoAmL 92*
**Geary**, Anthony 1947- *IntMPA 92*
**Geary**, Barbara Ann 1935- *WhoEnt 92*
**Geary**, Clarence Butler 1912- *WhoBlA 92*
**Geary**, David A. 1943- *WhoRel 92*
**Geary**, David Leslie 1947- *WhoFI 92*
**Geary**, James Michael 1956- *WhoFI 92*
**Geary**, John Charles 1945- *AmMWSc 92*
**Geary**, Kevin 1952- *TwCPaSc*
**Geary**, Leo Charles 1942- *AmMWSc 92*
**Geary**, Mike 1932- *TwCPaSc*
**Geary**, Norcross D 1947- *AmMWSc 92*
**Geary**, Patricia 1951- *ConAu 134*
**Geary**, Paul C. 1954- *WhoEnt 92*
**Geary-O'Brien**, Kimberly Anne 1964- *WhoWest 92*
**Geballe**, Gordon Theodore 1947- *AmMWSc 92*
**Geballe**, Ronald 1918- *AmMWSc 92*
**Geballe**, Theodore Henry 1920- *AmMWSc 92*
**Geballe**, Thomas Ronald 1944- *AmMWSc 92*
**Gebauer**, Kurt Manfred 1951- *WhoEnt 92*
**Gebauer**, Peter Anthony 1943- *AmMWSc 92, WhoMW 92*
**Gebauer**, Phyllis *DrAPF 91*
**Gebauer**, Victor Earl 1938- *WhoMW 92, WhoRel 92*
**Gebben**, Alan Irwin 1931- *AmMWSc 92*
**Gebber**, Gerard L 1939- *AmMWSc 92*
**Gebbie**, Katharine Blodgett 1932- *AmMWSc 92*
**Gebel-Williams**, Gunther 1934- *WhoEnt 92*
**Gebelein**, Charles G 1929- *AmMWSc 92*
**Gebelein**, Richard Stephen 1946- *WhoAmP 91*
**Gebelt**, Robert Eugene 1937- *AmMWSc 92*
**Geber**, William Frederick 1923- *AmMWSc 92*
**Gebert**, Herman John 1949- *WhoRel 92*
**Gebhard**, Roger Lee 1945- *AmMWSc 92*
**Gebhardt**, Bryan Matthew *AmMWSc 92*
**Gebhardt**, Fred 1925- *IntMPA 92*
**Gebhardt**, Joseph Davis 1946- *WhoAmP 91*
**Gebhardt**, Joseph John 1923- *AmMWSc 92*
**Gebhart**, Benjamin 1923- *AmMWSc 92*
**Gebhart**, Joseph Gilbert 1953- *WhoAmL 92*
**Gebhart**, Michael James 1956- *WhoMW 92*
**Gebler**, Carlo 1954- *ConAu 133*
**Gebler**, Ernest 1915- *IntAu&W 91, WrDr 92*
**Gebuhr**, Otto 1877-1954 *EncTR 91 [port]*
**Gecau**, Kimani J. 1947- *WhoBlA 92*
**Gecel**, Claudine 1957- *WhoFI 92*
**Geck**, Duane Michael 1959- *WhoAmL 92*
**Geckle**, William Jude 1955- *AmMWSc 92*
**Gecowets**, Gregory Alton Stephens 1963- *WhoWest 92*
**Geczik**, Ronald Joseph 1933- *AmMWSc 92*
**Gedalecia**, David 1942- *WhoMW 92*
**Gedalge**, Andre 1856-1926 *NewAmDM*
**Gedda**, Nicolai 1925- *IntWW 91, NewAmDM*
**Geddes** *Who 92*
**Geddes**, Baron 1937- *Who 92*
**Geddes**, Alexander MacIntosh 1934- *Who 92*
**Geddes**, Ann 1943- *WhoEnt 92*
**Geddes**, Anthony Reay 1912- *Who 92*
**Geddes**, Barbara Sheryl 1944- *WhoWest 92*
**Geddes**, Charles Lynn 1928- *WhoWest 92*
**Geddes**, David Darwin 1922- *AmMWSc 92*
**Geddes**, Diana Elizabeth Campbell 1947- *IntAu&W 91*
**Geddes**, Fionna 1949- *TwCPaSc*
**Geddes**, Ford Irvine 1913- *IntWW 91, Who 92*
**Geddes**, Gary 1940- *ConPo 91, IntAu&W 91, WrDr 92*
**Geddes**, Gary Lee 1950- *WhoWest 92*
**Geddes**, George 1809-1883 *BiInAmS*
**Geddes**, John Joseph 1940- *AmMWSc 92, WhoMW 92*
**Geddes**, John Maxwell 1941- *ConCom 92*
**Geddes**, Keith Oliver 1947- *AmMWSc 92*
**Geddes**, LaNelle Evelyn 1935- *AmMWSc 92*
**Geddes**, Leslie Alexander 1921- *AmMWSc 92*
**Geddes**, Lorna *WhoEnt 92*
**Geddes**, Margaret 1914- *TwCPaSc*
**Geddes**, Michael Dawson 1944- *Who 92*
**Geddes**, Norman Bel 1893-1958 *BenetAL 91*
**Geddes**, Paul *IntAu&W 91*
**Geddes**, Reay *Who 92*
**Geddes**, Robert C 1927- *WhoAmP 91*
**Geddes**, Robert Dale 1938- *WhoFI 92*
**Geddes**, Sylvia Myers 1935- *WhoAmL 92*
**Geddes**, Virgil 1897- *BenetAL 91*
**Geddes**, Wilburt Hale 1926- *AmMWSc 92*
**Geddes**, William George Nicholson 1913- *Who 92*
**Geddie**, John Jay 1937- *WhoAmP 91*
**Geddie**, Thomas Edwin 1930- *WhoFI 92*
**Geddie**, William Fredrick 1955- *WhoEnt 92*
**Geddis**, Timothy Patrick 1966- *WhoMW 92*
**Geddy**, John 1748-1799 *DcNCBi 2*
**Gede**, Thomas Frederick 1948- *WhoAmL 92, WhoAmP 91*
**Gedeon**, Geza S 1914- *AmMWSc 92*
**Gedgaudas**, Eugene 1924- *WhoMW 92*
**Gedicks**, Albert Joseph 1948- *WhoMW 92*
**Gedling**, Donnie 1939- *WhoAmP 91*
**Gedling**, Raymond 1917- *Who 92*
**Gedney**, Larry Daniel 1938- *AmMWSc 92*
**Geduldig**, Donald 1932- *AmMWSc 92*
**Gedzhev**, Nedyo *WhoRel 92*
**Gee**, Adrian Philip 1952- *AmMWSc 92*
**Gee**, Al 1942- *WhoBlA 92*
**Gee**, Allen 1924- *AmMWSc 92*
**Gee**, Anthony Hall 1948- *Who 92*
**Gee**, Charles William 1936- *AmMWSc 92*
**Gee**, Charlotte *IntMPA 92*
**Gee**, Chuck Yim 1933- *WhoFI 92*
**Gee**, Dan Mar 1951- *WhoFI 92*
**Gee**, David Charles Laycock 1947- *Who 92*
**Gee**, David Easton 1923- *AmMWSc 92*
**Gee**, Earl Justin 1953- *WhoAmP 91*
**Gee**, Edwin Austin 1920- *AmMWSc 92, IntWW 91*
**Gee**, Elwood Gordon 1944- *WhoMW 92*
**Gee**, Gayle Catherine 1934- *WhoAmP 91*
**Gee**, Geoffrey 1910- *IntWW 91, Who 92*
**Gee**, J Bernard L 1927- *AmMWSc 92*
**Gee**, James David 1934- *WhoRel 92*
**Gee**, John Henry 1936- *AmMWSc 92*
**Gee**, Juliet Leslie 1954- *WhoAmL 92*
**Gee**, Louis Stark 1922- *WhoFI 92*
**Gee**, Lynn LaMarr 1912- *AmMWSc 92*
**Gee**, Maggie 1948- *ConNov 91, WrDr 92*
**Gee**, Matthew Lane 1959- *WhoAmL 92*
**Gee**, Maurice 1931- *ConNov 91, WrDr 92*
**Gee**, Maurice Gough 1931- *IntAu&W 91*
**Gee**, Norman 1952- *AmMWSc 92*
**Gee**, Richard 1942- *Who 92*
**Gee**, Robert LeRoy 1926- *WhoMW 92*
**Gee**, Robert William 1936- *AmMWSc 92*
**Gee**, Sherman 1937- *AmMWSc 92*
**Gee**, Shirley 1932- *IntAu&W 91, WrDr 92*
**Gee**, Shirley Jane 1963- *WhoWest 92*
**Gee**, Terry W 1940- *WhoAmP 91*
**Gee**, Thomas Gibbs *WhoAmP 91*
**Gee**, Thomas Gibbs 1925- *WhoAmL 92*
**Gee**, Timothy Hugh 1936- *Who 92*
**Gee**, Walter 1927- *WhoAmP 91*
**Gee**, William 1931- *AmMWSc 92*
**Gee**, William Rowland, Jr. 1940- *WhoBlA 92*
**Geelan**, Peter Brian Kenneth 1929- *WhoWest 92*
**Geelhoed**, Glenn William 1942- *AmMWSc 92*
**Geelkerken**, Cornelis van 1901-1976 *BiDExR*
**Geelong**, Bishop of *Who 92*
**Geels**, Edwin James 1940- *AmMWSc 92*
**Geen**, Glen Howard 1933- *AmMWSc 92*
**Geen**, Russell Glenn 1932- *WhoMW 92*
**Geen**, Sherri Lynn 1964- *WhoMW 92*
**Geene**, Paul Frederick 1956- *WhoMW 92*
**Geens**, Andre 1941- *IntWW 91*
**Geens**, Gaston 1931- *IntWW 91*
**Geentiens**, Gaston Petrus, Jr. 1935- *WhoFI 92*
**Geer**, Ann *WhoRel 92*
**Geer**, Billy W 1935- *AmMWSc 92*
**Geer**, Henry Daniel 1922- *WhoEnt 92*
**Geer**, Ira W 1935- *AmMWSc 92*
**Geer**, Jack Charles 1927- *AmMWSc 92*
**Geer**, James Francis 1940- *AmMWSc 92*
**Geer**, Mary Lou 1947- *WhoRel 92*
**Geer**, Richard P 1938- *AmMWSc 92*
**Geer**, Ronald L 1926- *AmMWSc 92*
**Geer**, Thomas Lee 1951- *WhoAmL 92, WhoFI 92*
**Geerdes**, Harold Paul 1916- *WhoEnt 92*
**Geering**, Emil John 1924- *AmMWSc 92*
**Geering**, Ian Walter 1947- *Who 92*
**Geering**, R. G. 1918- *ConAu 133, WrDr 92*
**Geers**, Thomas L 1939- *AmMWSc 92*
**Geertz**, Armin Wilbert 1948- *WhoRel 92*
**Geertz**, Clifford 1926- *ConAu 36NR, IntWW 91, WrDr 92*
**Geertz**, Clifford James 1926- *IntAu&W 91*
**Geeseman**, Gordon E 1921- *AmMWSc 92*
**Geeseman**, Robert George 1944- *WhoAmL 92*
**Geeslin**, Roger Harold 1931- *AmMWSc 92*
**Geeson**, Judy 1948- *IntMPA 92*
**Geeting**, Joyce Ann 1944- *WhoEnt 92*
**Geffen**, Abraham 1916- *AmMWSc 92*
**Geffen**, Betty Ada 1911- *WhoEnt 92*
**Geffen**, David 1943- *IntMPA 92, WhoEnt 92*
**Geffen**, M. David 1938- *WhoRel 92*
**Geffen**, T M 1922- *AmMWSc 92*
**Geffen**, Terence John 1921- *Who 92*
**Geffroy**, Gustave 1855-1926 *ThHEIm*
**Gefsky**, Harold Leon 1917- *WhoEnt 92*
**Gefter**, Malcolm Lawrence 1942- *AmMWSc 92*
**Gefter**, William Irvin 1915- *AmMWSc 92*
**Gegel**, Harold L 1933- *AmMWSc 92*
**Gegenheimer**, Peter Albert 1950- *AmMWSc 92*
**Gegesi Kiss**, Pal 1900- *IntWW 91*
**Geggus**, David Patrick 1949- *IntAu&W 91*
**Geghman**, Yahya Hamoud 1934- *IntWW 91*
**Geh**, Hans-Peter 1934- *IntWW 91*
**Geha**, Alexander Salim 1936- *AmMWSc 92*
**Geha**, Joseph 1944- *ConAu 134*
**Geha**, Joseph Albert 1944- *WhoEnt 92*
**Geha**, Raif S 1945- *AmMWSc 92*
**Gehan**, Edmund A 1929- *AmMWSc 92*
**Gehlbach**, Frederick Renner 1935- *AmMWSc 92*
**Gehlen**, Arnold 1904-1976 *EncTR 91*
**Gehlen**, Reinhard 1902-1979 *EncTR 91 [port]*
**Gehlhaar**, Rolf 1943- *ConCom 92*
**Gehlhoff**, Walter 1922- *IntWW 91*

**Gehlmann**, John Brown 1950- *WhoMW 92*
**Gehlmann**, Timothy Shawn 1960- *WhoFI 92*
**Gehlsen**, Kurt Ronald 1956- *WhoWest 92*
**Gehm**, Charlene *WhoEnt 92*
**Gehm**, David Eugene 1952- *WhoMW 92*
**Gehman**, Bruce Lawrence 1937- *AmMWSc 92*
**Gehman**, Larry K. 1943- *WhoAmL 92*
**Gehman**, Terry Lee 1947- *WhoEnt 92*
**Geho**, Walter Blair 1939- *AmMWSc 92*
**Gehr**, Thomas Yeats, Jr. 1953- *WhoMW 92*
**Gehrels**, Jurgen Carlos 1935- *Who 92*
**Gehrels**, Tom 1925- *AmMWSc 92*
**Gehrenbeck**, Richard Keith 1934- *AmMWSc 92*
**Gehres**, Eleanor Mount 1932- *WhoWest 92*
**Gehres**, James 1932- *WhoAmL 92, WhoWest 92*
**Gehres**, Ruth 1933- *WhoRel 92*
**Gehres**, Walter Arnold 1920- *WhoAmP 91*
**Gehri**, Dennis Clark 1937- *AmMWSc 92*
**Gehrig**, James Joseph 1921- *WhoAmP 91*
**Gehrig**, John D 1924- *AmMWSc 92*
**Gehrig**, Lou 1903-1941 *FacFETw [port]*
**Gehrig**, Michael Ford 1947- *WhoAmL 92*
**Gehrig**, Robert Frank 1928- *AmMWSc 92*
**Gehring**, David Austin 1930- *WhoFI 92*
**Gehring**, Frederick William 1925- *AmMWSc 92*
**Gehring**, George Joseph, Jr. 1931- *WhoWest 92*
**Gehring**, George Michael 1958- *WhoWest 92*
**Gehring**, Harvey Thomas 1911- *AmMWSc 92*
**Gehring**, James Joseph 1946- *WhoFI 92*
**Gehring**, John Gunter 1952- *WhoAmL 92*
**Gehring**, Matthew James 1964- *WhoFI 92*
**Gehring**, Perry James 1936- *AmMWSc 92*
**Gehring**, Robert Joseph 1954- *WhoAmL 92*
**Gehring**, Ronald Kent 1941- *WhoAmL 92*
**Gehring**, Stephen Evan 1942- *WhoAmL 92*
**Gehring**, Walter Jakob 1939- *IntWW 91*
**Gehris**, Clarence Winfred 1917- *AmMWSc 92*
**Gehrke**, Charles William 1917- *AmMWSc 92*
**Gehrke**, Henry 1936- *AmMWSc 92*
**Gehrke**, Robert James 1940- *AmMWSc 92, WhoWest 92*
**Gehrke**, Susan Irene 1961- *WhoMW 92*
**Gehrke**, Timothy Robert 1960- *WhoMW 92*
**Gehrke**, Willard H 1920- *AmMWSc 92*
**Gehrmann**, Adolph 1868-1920 *BiInAmS*
**Gehrmann**, An Rose 1945- *WhoEnt 92*
**Gehrmann**, John Edward 1941- *AmMWSc 92*
**Gehrs**, Carl William 1941- *AmMWSc 92*
**Gehrs**, Jason Paul 1955- *WhoMW 92*
**Gehrt**, Floyd Eugene 1929- *WhoAmL 92*
**Gehry**, Frank O. 1929- *DcTwDes*
**Gehry**, Frank Owen 1929- *IntWW 91, WhoWest 92*
**Gehrz**, Robert Douglas 1944- *AmMWSc 92*
**Geibel**, Grace Ann 1937- *WhoRel 92*
**Geibel**, Jon Frederick 1950- *AmMWSc 92*
**Geidel**, Gwendelyn 1953- *AmMWSc 92*
**Geidner**, Charles Frederick 1948- *WhoAmL 92*
**Geiduschek**, E. Peter 1928- *IntWW 91*
**Geiduschek**, Ernest Peter 1928- *AmMWSc 92*
**Geier**, James Aylward Develin 1925- *WhoFI 92, WhoMW 92*
**Geier**, Joan Austin *DrAPF 91*
**Geier**, Marcus 1959- *WhoWest 92*
**Geiersbach**, Ronald Paul 1952- *WhoAmL 92*
**Geigel**, Kenneth Francis 1938- *WhoHisp 92*
**Geiger**, Alexander 1950- *WhoAmL 92*
**Geiger**, Benjamin 1947- *AmMWSc 92*
**Geiger**, C. Edward *WhoRel 92*
**Geiger**, David Kenneth 1956- *AmMWSc 92*
**Geiger**, David Nathaniel 1933- *WhoBlA 92*
**Geiger**, David Scott 1928- *WhoMW 92*
**Geiger**, Donald R 1933- *AmMWSc 92*
**Geiger**, Donald Raymond 1933- *WhoMW 92*
**Geiger**, Edwin Otto 1939- *AmMWSc 92*
**Geiger**, Gene E 1928- *AmMWSc 92*
**Geiger**, Glenn Charles 1952- *WhoAmL 92*
**Geiger**, Gordon Harold 1937- *AmMWSc 92*
**Geiger**, H Jack 1925- *AmMWSc 92*
**Geiger**, Hans Wilhelm 1882-1945 *FacFETw*
**Geiger**, Helmut 1928- *IntWW 91*
**Geiger**, Howard W. d1991 *NewYTBS 91*
**Geiger**, James Norman 1932- *WhoAmL 92*
**Geiger**, James Stephen 1929- *AmMWSc 92*
**Geiger**, John Grigsby 1960- *IntAu&W 91*
**Geiger**, Jon Ross 1943- *AmMWSc 92*
**Geiger**, Karla Mary 1964- *WhoMW 92*
**Geiger**, Klaus Wilhelm 1921- *AmMWSc 92*
**Geiger**, Loren Dennis 1946- *WhoEnt 92*
**Geiger**, Mark Watson 1949- *WhoFI 92*
**Geiger**, Michael James 1952- *WhoFI 92*
**Geiger**, Paul Frank 1932- *AmMWSc 92*
**Geiger**, Paul Jerome 1930- *AmMWSc 92*
**Geiger**, Randall L 1949- *AmMWSc 92*
**Geiger**, Richard Lawrence 1917- *WhoFI 92*
**Geiger**, Rupprecht 1908- *IntWW 91*
**Geiger**, William Ebling, Jr 1944- *AmMWSc 92*
**Geiges**, K S 1908- *AmMWSc 92*
**Geihs**, Frederick Siegfried 1935- *WhoAmL 92, WhoFI 92*
**Geil**, Phillip H 1930- *AmMWSc 92*
**Geil**, Wilma Jean 1939- *WhoEnt 92*
**Geilker**, Charles Don 1933- *AmMWSc 92*
**Geils Band**, The J. *NewAmDM*
**Geils**, Jerome *NewAmDM*
**Geiman**, J. Robert 1931- *WhoAmL 92, WhoMW 92*
**Geimer**, James Philip 1936- *WhoFI 92*
**Geimer**, Roger Anthony 1932- *WhoMW 92*
**Geinisman**, Yuri 1931- *AmMWSc 92*
**Geis**, Aelred Dean 1929- *AmMWSc 92*
**Geis**, Gerald E 1933- *WhoAmP 91*
**Geis**, Jerome Arthur 1946- *WhoAmL 92*
**Geis**, Norman Winer 1925- *WhoAmL 92*
**Geisbuhler**, Timothy Paul 1954- *AmMWSc 92*
**Geise**, Harry Fremont 1920- *WhoFI 92*
**Geise**, Marie Clabeaux 1941- *AmMWSc 92*
**Geisel**, Ernesto 1907- *IntWW 91*
**Geisel**, Henry Jules 1947- *WhoAmL 92*
**Geisel**, Martin Simon 1941- *WhoFI 92*
**Geisel**, Robert Carl 1920- *WhoAmP 91*
**Geisel**, Theodor d1991 *LesBEnT 92*
**Geisel**, Theodor 1904-1991 *News 92-2*
**Geisel**, Theodor Seuss *BenetAL 91*
**Geisel**, Theodor Seuss 1904-1991 *ConAu 135, CurBio 91N, DcLB Y91N [port], NewYTBS 91 [port], SmATA 67*
**Geiselman**, Paula J 1944- *AmMWSc 92*
**Geisendorfer**, James Vernon 1929- *WhoMW 92, WhoRel 92*
**Geiser**, James 1949- *WhoFI 92*
**Geiser**, Theodore William 1925- *WhoAmL 92*
**Geisert**, Arthur 1941- *WrDr 92*
**Geisert**, Gregory Wayne 1948- *WhoFI 92*
**Geisert**, Wayne Frederick 1921- *WhoFI 92*
**Geishecker**, John Andrew, Jr. 1937- *WhoFI 92*
**Geisheimer**, Fred 1926- *WhoFI 92*
**Geisler**, C D 1933- *AmMWSc 92*
**Geisler**, Dick G. 1928- *WhoWest 92*
**Geisler**, Fred Harden 1947- *AmMWSc 92*
**Geisler**, Grace 1912- *AmMWSc 92*
**Geisler**, Hans Emanuel 1935- *WhoMW 92*
**Geisler**, Harlynne 1950- *WhoEnt 92*
**Geisler**, Herbert George, Jr. 1949- *WhoEnt 92*
**Geisler**, Jerry Hubert 1934- *WhoAmP 91*
**Geisler**, John 1962- *WhoEnt 92*
**Geisler**, John Edmund 1934- *AmMWSc 92*
**Geisler**, Nathan David 1946- *WhoFI 92*
**Geisler**, Norman 1932- *WrDr 92*
**Geisler**, Thomas Milton, Jr. 1943- *WhoAmL 92*
**Geisman**, Raymond August, Sr 1921- *AmMWSc 92*
**Geismar**, Ludwig Leo 1921- *IntAu&W 91, WrDr 92*
**Geismar**, Maxwell 1909-1979 *BenetAL 91*
**Geismar**, Richard Lee 1927- *WhoEnt 92*
**Geismar**, Thomas 1931- *DcTwDes*
**Geismar**, Thomas H. 1931- *WhoEnt 92*
**Geismer**, Alan Stearn, Jr. 1948- *WhoAmL 92*
**Geison**, Ronald Leon *AmMWSc 92*
**Geiss**, David Richard 1953- *WhoMW 92*
**Geiss**, Gunther R 1938- *AmMWSc 92*
**Geiss**, Janice Marie 1950- *WhoAmL 92*
**Geiss**, Johannes 1926- *IntWW 91*
**Geiss**, Roy Howard 1937- *AmMWSc 92*
**Geissbuhler**, Stephan 1942- *WhoEnt 92*
**Geisser**, Seymour 1929- *AmMWSc 92*
**Geissert**, Katy 1926- *WhoAmP 91, WhoWest 92*
**Geissinger**, Hans Dieter 1930- *AmMWSc 92*
**Geissinger**, Ladnor Dale 1938- *AmMWSc 92*
**Geissler**, Ernst D 1915- *AmMWSc 92*
**Geissler**, Heiner 1930- *IntWW 91*
**Geissler**, Ludwig A *ScFEYrs*
**Geissler**, Paul Robert 1932- *AmMWSc 92*
**Geissler**, Suzanne Burr 1950- *WhoRel 92*
**Geissman**, John William 1952- *AmMWSc 92*
**Geissman**, Mary Joan 1939- *WhoAmP 91*
**Geist**, Ernest Edward 1938- *WhoRel 92*
**Geist**, Gretel 1941- *WhoEnt 92*
**Geist**, Harold 1916- *IntAu&W 91, WrDr 92*
**Geist**, J C 1915- *AmMWSc 92*
**Geist**, Jacob M 1921- *AmMWSc 92*
**Geist**, Jerry Douglas 1934- *WhoWest 92*
**Geist**, Karin Ruth Tammeus Mcphail 1938- *WhoWest 92*
**Geist**, Richard A 1944- *WhoAmP 91*
**Geist**, Ronald Peter 1964- *WhoEnt 92*
**Geist**, Valerius 1938- *AmMWSc 92*
**Geisterfer-Lowrance**, Anja A T *AmMWSc 92*
**Geistfeld**, Loren V. 1945- *WhoMW 92*
**Geistfeld**, Ronald Elwood 1933- *WhoMW 92*
**Geistweidt**, Gerald 1948- *WhoAmP 91*
**Geithner**, Paul Herman, Jr. 1930- *WhoFI 92*
**Geitz**, Michael M. 1952- *WhoAmL 92*
**Geitz**, R C 1919- *AmMWSc 92*
**Gejdenson**, Sam 1948- *WhoAmP 91*
**Gejdenson**, Samuel 1948- *AlmAP 92 [port]*
**Gekas**, George W. 1930- *AlmAP 92 [port]*
**Gekas**, George William 1930- *WhoAmP 91*
**Gekker**, Chris *WhoEnt 92*
**Gelaga-King**, George 1932- *IntWW 91*
**Gelardin**, Jacques P. *WhoFI 92*
**Gelasius I** *EncEarC*
**Gelasius of Caesarea** d395 *EncEarC*
**Gelasius of Cyzicus** *EncEarC*
**Gelatt**, Charles Daniel, Jr 1947- *AmMWSc 92*
**Gelb**, Alan 1950- *IntAu&W 91*
**Gelb**, Arthur 1937- *AmMWSc 92*
**Gelb**, Bruce S *WhoAmP 91*
**Gelb**, Fritzi Gina 1949- *WhoAmL 92*
**Gelb**, George Edward 1946- *WhoAmL 92*
**Gelb**, Johanna Lynn 1963- *WhoAmL 92*
**Gelb**, Joseph Donald 1923- *WhoAmL 92, WhoFI 92*
**Gelb**, Judith Anne 1935- *WhoAmL 92*
**Gelb**, Judith C. 1937- *WhoFI 92*
**Gelb**, Leonard Louis 1918- *AmMWSc 92*
**Gelb**, Leslie Howard 1937- *WhoAmP 91*
**Gelb**, Richard Lee 1924- *WhoFI 92*
**Gelband**, Alan Bruce 1944- *WhoFI 92*
**Gelband**, Henry 1936- *AmMWSc 92*
**Gelband**, Stephen Laurence 1931- *WhoAmL 92*
**Gelbard**, Alan Stewart 1934- *AmMWSc 92*
**Gelbard**, Fernando 1940- *IntWW 91*
**Gelbard**, Robert S *WhoAmP 91*
**Gelbart**, Abe 1911- *AmMWSc 92*
**Gelbart**, Larry *LesBEnT 92*
**Gelbart**, Larry 1925- *IntMPA 92, WhoEnt 92, WrDr 92*
**Gelbart**, Larry 1928- *IntAu&W 91, IntWW 91*
**Gelbart**, Stephen Samuel 1946- *AmMWSc 92*
**Gelbart**, William M 1946- *AmMWSc 92*
**Gelbaum**, Bernard Russell 1922- *AmMWSc 92*
**Gelber**, Don Jeffrey 1940- *WhoAmL 92, WhoWest 92*
**Gelber**, Jack 1932- *BenetAL 91, WhoEnt 92, WrDr 92*
**Gelber**, Louise Carp *WhoAmL 92*
**Gelber**, Louise Carp 1921- *WhoAmP 91*
**Gelber**, Richard David 1947- *AmMWSc 92*
**Gelber**, Robert Cary 1951- *WhoAmL 92*
**Gelberd**, Sewell Frederick 1945- *WhoMW 92*
**Gelberg**, Alan 1928- *AmMWSc 92*
**Gelberman**, Joseph H. 1912- *RelLAm 91*
**Gelbke**, Claus-Konrad 1947- *AmMWSc 92*
**Gelboin**, Harry Victor 1929- *AmMWSc 92*
**Gelbutis**, Tracy Joyce 1963- *WhoEnt 92*
**Gelbwachs**, Jerry A *AmMWSc 92*
**Geldenhuys**, Hendrik Albertus 1925- *IntWW 91*
**Gelder**, James R *WhoIns 92*
**Gelder**, John William 1933- *WhoAmL 92*
**Gelder**, Michael Graham 1929- *Who 92*
**Gelderloos**, Orin Glenn 1939- *AmMWSc 92*
**Gelderman**, Carol 1935- *WrDr 92*
**Geldmacher**, Joan Elizabeth 1931- *WhoRel 92*
**Geldmacher**, R C 1917- *AmMWSc 92*
**Geldof**, Bob 1954- *IntWW 91, Who 92, WhoEnt 92*
**Geldreich**, Edwin E 1922- *AmMWSc 92*
**Gelehrter**, George Ludwig 1948- *WhoMW 92*
**Gelehrter**, Thomas David 1936- *AmMWSc 92, WhoMW 92*
**Gelenberg**, Alan Jay 1944- *WhoWest 92*
**Gelerinter**, Edward 1936- *AmMWSc 92, WhoMW 92*
**Gelernter**, Herbert Leo 1929- *AmMWSc 92*
**Gelert**, William Joseph 1951- *WhoIns 92*
**Geleta**, Greg *DrAPF 91*
**Geleta**, James Edward 1953- *WhoFI 92*
**Gelfan**, Gregory *IntMPA 92*
**Gelfand**, Alan Enoch 1945- *AmMWSc 92*
**Gelfand**, David H 1944- *AmMWSc 92*
**Gelfand**, Erwin William 1941- *AmMWSc 92*
**Gelfand**, Henry Morris 1920- *AmMWSc 92*
**Gelfand**, Israil Moiseyevich 1913- *IntWW 91*
**Gelfand**, Ivan 1927- *WhoFI 92, WhoMW 92*
**Gelfand**, Jack Jacob 1944- *AmMWSc 92*
**Gelfand**, Jennifer *WhoEnt 92*
**Gelfand**, Marshall M. 1927- *WhoWest 92*
**Gelfand**, Neal 1944- *WhoFI 92*
**Gelfand**, Norman Mathew 1939- *AmMWSc 92*
**Gelfant**, Seymour 1922- *AmMWSc 92*
**Gelfond**, Gordon 1936- *WhoAmL 92*
**Gelfond**, Rhoda *DrAPF 91*
**Gelhaus**, Robert Joseph 1941- *WhoAmL 92*
**Gelhorn**, Martha *DrAPF 91*
**Geliebter**, Allan 1947- *AmMWSc 92*
**Gelin**, Daniel Yves 1921- *IntWW 91*
**Gelin**, Franklin Charles 1945- *WhoWest 92*
**Gelinas**, David L 1951- *WhoAmP 91*
**Gelinas**, Douglas Alfred 1940- *AmMWSc 92*
**Gelinas**, Gratien 1909- *IntAu&W 91, IntWW 91*
**Gelinas**, Robert Joseph 1937- *AmMWSc 92*
**Gelineau**, Louis Edward 1928- *WhoRel 92*
**Gell**, Carl Leddin 1943- *WhoAmL 92*
**Gell**, Frank *ConAu 35NR*
**Gell**, John J. 1948- *WhoFI 92*
**Gell**, Maurice L 1937- *AmMWSc 92*
**Gell**, Philip George Houthem 1914- *Who 92*
**Gell-Mann**, Murray 1929- *AmMWSc 92, FacFETw, IntWW 91, Who 92, WhoNob 90, WhoWest 92, WrDr 92*
**Gellai**, Miklos 1930- *AmMWSc 92*
**Gellard**, Jacques 1931- *WhoRel 92*
**Geller**, Andrew Michael 1924- *WhoFI 92*
**Geller**, Arthur Michael 1941- *AmMWSc 92*
**Geller**, Brian L. 1948- *IntMPA 92*
**Geller**, Bruce *LesBEnT 92*
**Geller**, David Melville 1930- *AmMWSc 92*
**Geller**, Edward 1928- *AmMWSc 92*
**Geller**, Eric P. *WhoAmL 92*
**Geller**, Harold Arthur 1954- *WhoFI 92*
**Geller**, Harvey 1921- *AmMWSc 92*
**Geller**, Henry *LesBEnT 92*
**Geller**, Herbert M 1945- *AmMWSc 92*
**Geller**, Irving 1925- *AmMWSc 92*
**Geller**, Jerome William 1914- *WhoEnt 92*
**Geller**, Kenneth N 1930- *AmMWSc 92*
**Geller**, Kenneth Steven 1947- *WhoAmL 92*
**Geller**, Lisa Michelle 1965- *WhoEnt 92*
**Geller**, Margaret Joan 1947- *AmMWSc 92*
**Geller**, Marvin Alan 1943- *AmMWSc 92*
**Geller**, Milton 1922- *AmMWSc 92*
**Geller**, Mitchell Jed 1953- *WhoAmL 92*
**Geller**, Myer 1926- *AmMWSc 92*
**Geller**, Nancy L 1944- *AmMWSc 92*
**Geller**, Norman Harvey 1934- *WhoEnt 92*
**Geller**, Robert James 1937- *WhoFI 92*
**Geller**, Robert James 1952- *AmMWSc 92*
**Geller**, Ronald G 1943- *AmMWSc 92*
**Geller**, Ruth *DrAPF 91*
**Geller**, Seymour 1921- *AmMWSc 92*
**Geller**, Stephen Arthur 1939- *AmMWSc 92, WhoWest 92*
**Geller**, Steven Anthony 1958- *WhoAmP 91*
**Geller**, Stuart M. 1942- *WhoRel 92*
**Geller**, Susan Carol 1948- *AmMWSc 92*
**Gellermann**, William Prescott 1929- *WhoFI 92*
**Gellerstedt**, Marie Ada 1926- *WhoFI 92, WhoMW 92*
**Gellert**, Christian Furchtegott 1715-1769 *BlkwCEP*
**Gellert**, Martin Frank 1929- *AmMWSc 92*
**Gellert**, Michael Erwin 1931- *WhoFI 92*
**Gellert**, Natalya Vladimirovna 1953- *IntWW 91*
**Gellert**, Ronald J 1935- *AmMWSc 92*
**Gelles**, David Stephen 1945- *AmMWSc 92*
**Gelles**, Isadore Leo 1925- *AmMWSc 92*
**Gelles**, S H 1930- *AmMWSc 92*
**Gellhorn**, Alfred 1913- *AmMWSc 92*
**Gellhorn**, Ernest Albert Eugene 1935- *WhoAmL 92*
**Gellhorn**, Jaquelin Ann Silker 1935- *WhoWest 92*
**Gellhorn**, Martha *IntWW 91*
**Gellhorn**, Martha 1906- *BenetAL 91*
**Gellhorn**, Martha 1908- *ConNov 91, IntAu&W 91, WrDr 92*
**Gellhorn**, Peter 1912- *Who 92*
**Gellineau**, Victor Marcel, Jr. 1942- *WhoBlA 92*
**Gellis**, Barrie *DrAPF 91*
**Gellis**, Barrie Fabian 1950- *WhoEnt 92*

**Gellis,** Roberta 1927- *WrDr 92*
**Gellis,** Roberta Leah 1927- *IntAu&W 91*
**Gellis,** Sydney Saul 1914- *AmMWSc 92*
**Gellman,** Charles 1916- *AmMWSc 92*
**Gellman,** Gloria Gae Seeburger Schick 1947- *WhoFI 92, WhoWest 92*
**Gellman,** Isaiah 1928- *AmMWSc 92*
**Gellman,** Rachel Lee 1950- *WhoEnt 92*
**Gellner,** Ernest 1925- *WrDr 92*
**Gellner,** Ernest Andre 1925- *IntWW 91, Who 92*
**Gelman,** Aleksandr Isaakovich 1933- *IntWW 91*
**Gelman,** Andrew Richard 1946- *WhoAmL 92*
**Gelman,** Donald 1938- *AmMWSc 92*
**Gelman,** Harry 1935- *AmMWSc 92*
**Gelman,** I. Lawrence 1946- *WhoAmL 92*
**Gelman,** Juan 1930- *ConSpAP*
**Gelman,** Larry 1930- *WhoEnt 92*
**Gelman,** Liebe Kazan *DrAPF 91*
**Gelman,** Polina *EncAmaz 91*
**Gelman,** Sandor M. 1938- *WhoAmL 92*
**Gelman,** Scott Alan 1955- *WhoEnt 92*
**Gelman,** Simon 1936- *AmMWSc 92*
**Gelmann,** Edward P 1950- *AmMWSc 92*
**Gelmetti,** Gianluigi 1945- *WhoEnt 92*
**Gelmis,** Joseph Stephan 1935- *WhoEnt 92*
**Gelnett,** Ronald Howard 1933- *WhoWest 92*
**Gelnovatch,** V *AmMWSc 92*
**Gelopulos,** Demosthenes Peter 1938- *AmMWSc 92*
**Gelotte,** Bob Gunnar 1950- *WhoEnt 92*
**Gelovani,** Mikhail Georgievich 1893-1956 *SovUnBD*
**Gelperin,** Alan 1941- *AmMWSc 92*
**Gelpi,** Albert 1931- *IntAu&W 91, WrDr 92*
**Gelpi,** Michael Anthony 1940- *WhoMW 92*
**Gelpi,** William R. 1937- *WhoHisp 92*
**Gels,** Patty Artrip 1951- *WhoMW 92*
**Gelsi,** Frederick A *WhoAmP 91*
**Gelsomino,** Gerald Joseph 1952- *WhoWest 92*
**Gelston,** Louis Merwin 1879-1905 *BiInAmS*
**Gelston,** Mortimer Ackley 1920- *WhoAmP 91*
**Gelt,** Howard B *WhoAmP 91*
**Gelt,** Louis Eleazar 1908- *WhoAmL 92*
**Geltman,** Elizabeth A. Glass 1962- *WhoAmL 92*
**Geltman,** Sydney 1927- *AmMWSc 92*
**Gel'tser,** Yekaterina Vasil'evna 1876-1962 *SovUnBD*
**Geltzer,** Robert Lawrence 1945- *WhoAmL 92*
**Geluso,** Kenneth Nicholas 1945- *AmMWSc 92*
**Gelven,** Michael Paul 1946- *WhoFI 92*
**Gelzer,** Justus 1929- *AmMWSc 92*
**Gelzer,** Michael 1916- *IntWW 91*
**Gem,** Richard David Harvey 1945- *Who 92*
**Geman,** Staurt Alan 1949- *AmMWSc 92*
**Gemayel,** Amin 1942- *IntWW 91*
**Gemayel,** Boutros 1932- *WhoRel 92*
**Gembala,** Joseph John 1957- *WhoRel 92*
**Gemballa,** Eric Eckhard 1943- *WhoEnt 92*
**Gembicki,** Stanley Arthur 1941- *AmMWSc 92*
**Gemeinhardt,** Walter Frederick 1923- *WhoAmL 92*
**Gemeinhart,** Thomas James 1932- *WhoRel 92*
**Gemignani,** Michael C 1938- *AmMWSc 92*
**Geminder,** Robert 1935- *AmMWSc 92*
**Geminiani,** Francesco 1687-1762 *NewAmDM*
**Gemma,** Anthony Nicholas 1951- *WhoAmL 92*
**Gemma,** John P 1939- *WhoIns 92*
**Gemma,** Peter B, Jr 1950- *WhoAmP 91*
**Gemmell,** David A 1948- *TwCSFW 91*
**Gemmell,** Gordon D 1921- *AmMWSc 92*
**Gemmell,** Kathleen *DrAPF 91*
**Gemmell,** Robert S 1933- *AmMWSc 92*
**Gemmer,** Robert Valentine 1946- *AmMWSc 92, WhoMW 92*
**Gemperline,** Margaret Mary Cetera 1953- *AmMWSc 92*
**Gemperline,** Paul Joseph *AmMWSc 92*
**Gempp,** Walter 1878-1939 *EncTR 91*
**Gemrich,** Alfred John 1936- *WhoAmL 92*
**Gems,** Pam 1925- *WrDr 92*
**Gemsa,** Diethard 1937- *AmMWSc 92*
**Gemski,** Peter 1936- *AmMWSc 92*
**Gen,** Martin 1926- *WhoFI 92*
**Genabith,** Richard Carl 1946- *WhoAmL 92, WhoFI 92*
**Genader,** Ann Marie 1932- *WhoRel 92*
**Genaidy,** Ashraf Mohamed 1957- *AmMWSc 92, WhoMW 92*
**Genaro,** Donald Michael 1932- *WhoFI 92*
**Genaro,** Joseph M. 1930- *WhoHisp 92*
**Genato,** Vincent Michael 1946- *WhoEnt 92*
**Genauer,** Emily *WrDr 92*
**Genberg,** Ira 1947- *WhoAmL 92*
**Gencarelli,** Jane B 1929- *WhoAmP 91*
**Genco,** Joseph Michael 1939- *AmMWSc 92*
**Genco,** Robert J 1938- *AmMWSc 92*
**Gencsoy,** Hasan Tahsin 1924- *AmMWSc 92*
**Genda,** Minoru 1904-1989 *FacFETw*
**Gendece,** Brian *IntMPA 92*
**Gendel,** Eugene B. 1948- *WhoFI 92, WhoWest 92*
**Gendel,** Steven Michael *AmMWSc 92*
**Gendernalik,** Sue Aydelott *AmMWSc 92*
**Genders,** Roger Alban Marson 1919- *Who 92*
**Gendler,** Sandra J 1944- *AmMWSc 92*
**Gendreau,** Richard James 1946- *WhoMW 92*
**Gendreau-Massaloux,** Michele 1944- *IntWW 91*
**Gendron,** Joseph Saul 1938- *WhoAmP 91*
**Gendron,** Maurice 1920- *NewAmDM*
**Gendron,** Maurice 1920-1990 *AnObit 1990*
**Gendron,** Odore Joseph 1921- *WhoRel 92*
**Geneaux,** Nancy Lynne 1942- *AmMWSc 92*
**Genechten,** Robert van 1895-1945 *BiDExR*
**Genecin,** Abraham 1918- *AmMWSc 92*
**Geneen,** Harold Sydney 1910- *IntWW 91*
**Genega,** Paul *DrAPF 91*
**Genel,** Myron 1936- *AmMWSc 92*
**Genensky,** Samuel Milton 1927- *AmMWSc 92*
**Gener,** Jose M. *WhoHisp 92*
**General,** John Arthur 1943- *WhoFI 92*
**Generes,** Tasker 1942- *WhoHisp 92*
**Generoso,** Walderico Malinawan 1941- *AmMWSc 92*
**Generous,** Eric Yves Jacques 1960- *WhoFI 92*
**Genes,** Andrew Nicholas 1932- *AmMWSc 92*
**Genesis** *NewAmDM*
**Genest,** Fernand A 1923- *WhoAmP 91*
**Genest,** Jacques 1919- *AmMWSc 92, IntWW 91*
**Genest,** Jean-Baptiste 1927- *WhoRel 92*
**Genet,** Jean 1910-1986 *FacFETw, GuFrLit 1*
**Genet,** Rene P H 1920- *AmMWSc 92*
**Genetelli,** Emil J 1937- *AmMWSc 92*
**Genetti,** William Ernest 1942- *AmMWSc 92*
**Genevieve,** Saint 423-501 *EncAmaz 91*
**Geng Biao** 1909- *IntWW 91*
**Geng,** Shu 1942- *AmMWSc 92*
**Geng,** Steven Michael 1961- *WhoMW 92*
**Geng,** Thomas William 1958- *WhoAmP 91*
**Genge,** Kenneth Lyle *Who 92, WhoRel 92, WhoWest 92*
**Genge,** Mark 1927- *Who 92*
**Genge,** Milton Henry, Jr. 1950- *WhoMW 92*
**Genge,** William Harrison 1923- *WhoFI 92*
**Gengenbach,** Burle Gene 1944- *AmMWSc 92*
**Gengor,** Virginia Anderson 1927- *WhoFI 92, WhoWest 92*
**Gengozian,** Nazareth 1929- *AmMWSc 92*
**Geniesse,** Robert John 1929- *WhoAmL 92*
**Genillard,** Robert Louis 1929- *IntWW 91*
**Genin,** Dennis Joseph 1938- *AmMWSc 92*
**Genin,** Joseph 1934- *AmMWSc 92*
**Genini,** Ronald Walter 1946- *WhoWest 92*
**Geniusz,** Ronald Robert 1946- *WhoMW 92*
**Genkin,** Barry Howard 1949- *WhoAmL 92*
**Genlis,** Comtesse de 1746-1830 *FrenWW*
**Genlis,** Stephanie Felicite, comtesse de 1746-1830 *BlkwCEP*
**Genn,** Gilbert J 1952- *WhoAmP 91*
**Genn,** Mordecai Halevi 1946- *WhoRel 92*
**Gennadios,** Bishop 1924- *WhoRel 92*
**Gennadios,** Bishop of Paphos 1910-1986 *FacFETw*
**Gennadius** *EncEarC*
**Gennadius I of Constantinople** d471 *EncEarC*
**Gennari,** F John 1937- *AmMWSc 92*
**Gennaro,** Alfonso Robert 1925- *AmMWSc 92*
**Gennaro,** Antonio L. 1934- *WhoWest 92*
**Gennaro,** Antonio Louis 1934- *AmMWSc 92*
**Gennaro,** Joseph Francis 1924- *AmMWSc 92*
**Gennaro,** Joseph J 1919- *AmMWSc 92*
**Gennaro,** Robert Nash 1940- *AmMWSc 92*
**Gennep,** Arnold van 1873-1957 *FacFETw*
**Gennes,** Pierre G. de 1932- *IntWW 91*
**Gennis,** Robert Bennett 1944- *AmMWSc 92*
**Genone,** Hudor 1843-1915 *ScFEYrs*
**Genoud,** Ernest G 1880?-1918 *BiInAmS*
**Genova,** Diane Melisano 1948- *WhoFI 92*
**Genova,** James John 1946- *AmMWSc 92*
**Genova,** Joseph Steven 1952- *WhoAmL 92*
**Genova,** Peter J 1944- *WhoAmP 91*
**Genoves,** Juan 1930- *IntWW 91*
**Genovese,** Alfred *WhoEnt 92*
**Genovese,** Denny *WhoEnt 92*
**Genovese,** Edgar Nicholas 1942- *WhoWest 92*
**Genovese,** Francis Charles 1921- *WhoFI 92*
**Genovese,** Kitty d1964 *FacFETw*
**Genovese,** Thomas Leonardo 1936- *WhoAmL 92, WhoFI 92*
**Genovese,** Vito 1897-1969 *FacFETw*
**Genovesi,** Anthony J *WhoAmP 91*
**Genovesi,** Vincent Joseph 1938- *WhoRel 92*
**Genoways,** Hugh Howard 1940- *AmMWSc 92, WhoMW 92*
**Genrich,** Willard Adolph 1915- *WhoAmL 92*
**Gens,** Peter D. 1940- *WhoAmL 92*
**Gens,** Ralph S 1924- *AmMWSc 92*
**Gens,** Richard Howard 1929- *WhoAmL 92*
**Gensamer,** Maxwell 1902- *AmMWSc 92*
**Genscher,** Hans-Dietrich 1927- *IntWW 91, Who 92*
**Gensel,** Patricia Gabbey 1944- *AmMWSc 92*
**Gensert,** Richard Michael 1922- *WhoFI 92*
**Genshaw,** Marvin Alden 1939- *AmMWSc 92, WhoMW 92*
**Gensler,** Kinereth *DrAPF 91*
**Gensler,** Kinereth Dushkin 1922- *IntAu&W 91*
**Gensous,** Pierre 1925- *IntWW 91*
**Gent,** Alan Neville 1927- *AmMWSc 92*
**Gent,** David 1935- *Who 92*
**Gent,** Martin Paul Neville 1950- *AmMWSc 92*
**Gent,** Michael 1934- *AmMWSc 92*
**Genter,** John Robert 1957- *WhoFI 92*
**Gentes,** Julie L. 1947- *WhoFI 92*
**Genth,** Anthony Rees 1945- *WhoHisp 92*
**Genth,** Frederick Augustus, Jr 1855-1910 *BiInAmS*
**Genth,** Frederick Augustus, Sr 1820-1893 *BiInAmS*
**Gentile,** Anthony 1920- *WhoFI 92*
**Gentile,** Anthony L 1930- *AmMWSc 92*
**Gentile,** Arthur Christopher 1926- *AmMWSc 92*
**Gentile,** David Louis 1945- *WhoMW 92*
**Gentile,** Dominick E 1932- *AmMWSc 92*
**Gentile,** Francesco Carlo d1990 *IntWW 91N*
**Gentile,** George G 1921- *WhoAmP 91*
**Gentile,** Giovanni 1875-1944 *BiDExR, FacFETw*
**Gentile,** Jack Vito 1950- *WhoFI 92*
**Gentile,** James Michael 1946- *AmMWSc 92*
**Gentile,** John Robert 1956- *WhoFI 92*
**Gentile,** Louis Joseph 1917- *WhoAmP 91*
**Gentile,** Mark Joseph 1956- *WhoAmL 92*
**Gentile,** Peter A 1952- *WhoIns 92*
**Gentile,** Peter M. 1965- *WhoEnt 92*
**Gentile,** Philip 1923- *AmMWSc 92*
**Gentile,** Ralph G 1914- *AmMWSc 92*
**Gentile,** Richard J 1929- *AmMWSc 92*
**Gentile,** Thomas Joseph 1953- *AmMWSc 92*
**Gentili-Lynn,** Elizabeth V. 1950- *WhoFI 92*
**Gentle,** James Eddie 1943- *AmMWSc 92*
**Gentle,** Kenneth W 1940- *AmMWSc 92*
**Gentle,** Mary 1956- *TwCSFW 91, WrDr 92*
**Gentle,** Mary Rosalyn 1956- *IntAu&W 91*
**Gentle,** Nicola 1951- *TwCPaSc*
**Gentleman Johnny** *BenetAL 91*
**Gentleman,** David 1930- *TwCPaSc, Who 92, WrDr 92*
**Gentleman,** Jane Forer 1940- *AmMWSc 92*
**Gentleman,** William Morven 1942- *AmMWSc 92*
**Gentlewoman,** A *IntAu&W 91X*
**Gentner,** Claudia Alene 1953- *WhoFI 92*
**Gentner,** Donald Richard 1940- *WhoWest 92*
**Gentner,** Donald S. 1949- *WhoMW 92*
**Gentner,** Norman Elwood 1943- *AmMWSc 92*
**Gentner,** Paul LeFoe 1944- *WhoFI 92*
**Gentner,** Robert F 1938- *AmMWSc 92*
**Gentrup,** Clarice 1937- *WhoRel 92*
**Gentry,** Albert Newman, III 1956- *WhoBlA 92*
**Gentry,** Alvin *WhoBlA 92*
**Gentry,** Alwyn Howard 1945- *AmMWSc 92*
**Gentry,** Ann Denise 1948- *WhoEnt 92*
**Gentry,** Atron A. *WhoBlA 92*
**Gentry,** Charles Ezell 1921- *WhoAmP 91*
**Gentry,** Charles Lewis, Jr. 1954- *WhoMW 92*
**Gentry,** Claude Edwin 1930- *AmMWSc 92*
**Gentry,** Curt 1931- *WrDr 92*
**Gentry,** Deborah Brown 1954- *WhoAmL 92*
**Gentry,** Dennis Louis 1959- *WhoBlA 92*
**Gentry,** Don Kenneth 1939- *WhoMW 92*
**Gentry,** Donald William 1943- *AmMWSc 92*
**Gentry,** Gavin Miller 1930- *WhoAmL 92*
**Gentry,** Glenn Aden 1931- *AmMWSc 92*
**Gentry,** Ivey Clenton 1919- *AmMWSc 92*
**Gentry,** James O'Conor 1926- *WhoIns 92*
**Gentry,** James William 1926- *WhoWest 92*
**Gentry,** Jane *DrAPF 91*
**Gentry,** John Tilmon 1921- *AmMWSc 92*
**Gentry,** Joyce Ann 1942- *WhoEnt 92*
**Gentry,** Karl Ray 1938- *AmMWSc 92*
**Gentry,** LaMar Duane 1946- *WhoBlA 92*
**Gentry,** Larry E 1949- *WhoAmP 91*
**Gentry,** Marshall Bruce 1953- *WhoMW 92*
**Gentry,** Martha Imogen 1926- *WhoWest 92*
**Gentry,** Meredith Poindexter 1809-1866 *DcNCBi 2*
**Gentry,** Michael Jay 1959- *WhoMW 92*
**Gentry,** Michael Lee 1942- *WhoWest 92*
**Gentry,** Michael Ray 1951- *WhoRel 92*
**Gentry,** Nolden I. 1937- *WhoBlA 92*
**Gentry,** Richard Hayden 1933- *WhoAmP 91*
**Gentry,** Robert Bryan 1936- *IntAu&W 91*
**Gentry,** Robert Cecil 1916- *AmMWSc 92*
**Gentry,** Robert Francis 1921- *AmMWSc 92*
**Gentry,** Robert Vance 1933- *AmMWSc 92*
**Gentry,** Roger Lee 1938- *AmMWSc 92*
**Gentry,** Samuel James 1952- *WhoRel 92*
**Gentry,** Steven Gordon 1952- *WhoAmL 92*
**Gentry,** Thomas George 1843-1905 *BiInAmS*
**Gentry,** Thomas Lee 1960- *WhoAmP 91*
**Gentry,** Willard Max, Jr 1923- *AmMWSc 92*
**Gentry,** William George 1899- *Who 92*
**Gentry,** William Norton 1908- *WhoFI 92*
**Gentry,** William Ronald 1942- *AmMWSc 92*
**Gentsch,** Madison Brent 1958- *WhoFI 92*
**Genty,** Richard Daniel 1926- *WhoAmL 92*
**Gentz,** Gerald Thomas 1949- *WhoAmP 91*
**Gentzler,** Robert E 1943- *AmMWSc 92*
**Genuario,** Robert L *WhoAmP 91*
**Genus,** Karl *LesBEnT 92*
**Genuth,** Saul M 1931- *AmMWSc 92*
**Genys,** John B 1923- *AmMWSc 92*
**Genzen,** Gary Carl 1944- *WhoRel 92*
**Genzer,** Jerome Daniel 1925- *AmMWSc 92*
**Genzer,** Stephen Bruce 1952- *WhoAmL 92*
**Genzler,** Christopher John 1960- *WhoMW 92*
**Genzmer,** Harald 1909- *IntWW 91*
**Geo-Karis,** Adeline Jay 1918- *WhoAmP 91*
**Geoffreys,** Stephen 1959- *IntMPA 92*
**Geoffrin,** Marie Therese 1699-1777 *BlkwCEP*
**Geoffroy,** Etienne Francois 1672-1731 *BlkwCEP*
**Geoffroy,** Gregory Lynn 1946- *AmMWSc 92*
**Geoffroy Saint-Hilaire,** Etienne 1772-1844 *BlkwCEP*
**Geoga,** Douglas Gerard 1955- *WhoAmL 92*
**Geoghegan,** Patricia 1947- *WhoAmL 92*
**Geoghegan,** Ross 1943- *AmMWSc 92*
**Geoghegan,** Thomas Edward *AmMWSc 92*
**Geoghegan,** William David 1943- *AmMWSc 92*
**Geoghegan,** William Davidson 1922- *WhoRel 92*
**Geok-Lin Lim,** Shirley 1955?- *LiExTwC*
**Geokas,** Michael C 1924- *AmMWSc 92*
**Geokezas,** Meletios 1936- *AmMWSc 92*
**Geolot,** Alan Charles 1954- *WhoAmL 92*
**Geoppinger,** James Carl 1940- *WhoMW 92*
**Geores,** Ronald Joseph 1939- *WhoEnt 92*
**Georgadze,** Mikhail Porfir'evich 1912-1982 *SovUnBD*
**Georgakakos,** Konstantine P 1954- *AmMWSc 92*
**Georgakas,** Dan *DrAPF 91*
**Georgakis,** Christos *AmMWSc 92*
**Georgakis,** Constantine 1937- *AmMWSc 92*
**Georgala,** Douglas Lindley 1934- *Who 92*
**Georgalis,** Nicholas Christos 1947- *WhoMW 92*
**Georganas,** Nicolas D 1943- *AmMWSc 92*
**Georgantones** 1940- *WhoEnt 92*
**George** *Who 92*
**George** 1943- *WorArt 1980 [port]*
**George I** 1660-1727 *BlkwCEP*
**George II** 1683-1760 *BlkwCEP*
**George III** 1738-1820 *BlkwCEP, BlkwEAR [port]*
**George V** 1865-1936 *FacFETw*
**George VI** d1952 *FacFETw [port]*
**George VI** 1895-1952 *EncTR 91 [port]*
**George of Laodicea** *EncEarC*
**George of Pisidia** *EncEarC*
**George,** St. *EncEarC*
**George,** A R 1938- *AmMWSc 92*

**George**, Adrian 1944- TwCPaSc
**George**, Albert El Deeb 1936- AmMWSc 92
**George**, Alexander Andrew 1938- WhoAmL 92
**George**, Alfred Raymond 1912- Who 92
**George**, Allen 1935- WhoBlA 92
**George**, Anne Denise 1941- AmMWSc 92
**George**, Anthony Sanderson 1928- Who 92
**George**, Arthur 1915- Who 92
**George**, Boyd Winston 1925- AmMWSc 92
**George**, Bruce Douglas 1957- WhoMW 92
**George**, Bruce Thomas 1942- Who 92
**George**, Camille 1927- WhoAmP 91
**George**, Carl Joseph Winder 1930- AmMWSc 92
**George**, Carrie Leigh 1915- WhoBlA 92, WhoRel 92
**George**, Charles Redgenal 1938- AmMWSc 92
**George**, Claude C. 1922- WhoBlA 92
**George**, Claude S., Jr. 1920- WrDr 92
**George**, Clifford Eugene 1942- AmMWSc 92
**George**, Collins Crusor 1909-1980 ConAu 133
**George**, Danny 1953- WhoAmP 91
**George**, David Alan 1942- WhoFI 92
**George**, David Bruce 1944- WhoMW 92
**George**, Dick Leon 1936- AmMWSc 92
**George**, Donald Wayne 1921- AmMWSc 92
**George**, Donald William 1926- IntWW 91, Who 92
**George**, Earl 1924- WhoEnt 92
**George**, Earl Duncan 1911- WhoEnt 92
**George**, Edward WhoBlA 92
**George**, Edward Alan John 1938- Who 92
**George**, Edward Thomas 1925- AmMWSc 92
**George**, Eliot WrDr 92
**George**, Elizabeth IntAu&W 91
**George**, Elizabeth 1949- WrDr 92
**George**, Elmer, Jr 1928- AmMWSc 92
**George**, Elmer Joseph 1944- WhoAmP 91
**George**, Emery DrAPF 91
**George**, Emery E. 1933- ConAu 36NR
**George**, Emily WrDr 92
**George**, Ernest Thornton, III 1950- WhoFI 92
**George**, Fredrick William 1946- AmMWSc 92
**George**, Gary R 1954- WhoAmP 91
**George**, Gary Raymond 1954- WhoBlA 92, WhoMW 92
**George**, George Louis 1907- IntMPA 92
**George**, George W. 1920- IntMPA 92
**George**, George Warren 1920- WhoEnt 92
**George**, Gerald Eugene 1935- WhoWest 92
**George**, Graham Elias 1912- WhoEnt 92
**George**, Griffith Owen 1902- Who 92
**George**, Harry Allan 1948- WhoFI 92
**George**, Harvey 1935- AmMWSc 92
**George**, Heinrich 1893-1946 EncTR 91 [port]
**George**, Henry ScFEYrs B
**George**, Henry 1839-1897 BenetAL 91, RComAH
**George**, Henry Ridyard 1921- Who 92
**George**, Hermon, Jr. 1945- WhoBlA 92
**George**, Hywel 1924- Who 92
**George**, Ian Gordon Combe Who 92
**George**, James Alfred 1950- WhoRel 92
**George**, James E 1938- AmMWSc 92
**George**, James Edward 1943- WhoFI 92
**George**, James Francis 1929- AmMWSc 92
**George**, James Henry Bryn 1929- AmMWSc 92
**George**, James Raymond 1945- WhoFI 92
**George**, James Z 1922- AmMWSc 92
**George**, Jean Craighead 1919- Au&Arts 8 [port], IntAu&W 91, SmATA 68 [port], WrDr 92
**George**, Jimmy 1940- WhoEnt 92
**George**, John, Jr 1946- WhoAmP 91
**George**, John Angelos 1934- AmMWSc 92
**George**, John Caleekal 1921- AmMWSc 92
**George**, John Harold 1935- AmMWSc 92
**George**, John Lothar 1916- AmMWSc 92
**George**, John Martin, Jr. 1947- WhoAmL 92
**George**, John Ronald 1940- AmMWSc 92
**George**, Johnny 1953- WhoMW 92
**George**, Jonathan IntAu&W 91X, WrDr 92
**George**, Joseph A 1936- WhoAmP 91
**George**, Joyce Jackson 1936- WhoAmL 92
**George**, Kalankamary Pily 1933- AmMWSc 92
**George**, Kathleen E. DrAPF 91
**George**, Kathleen Elizabeth 1943- WhoEnt 92
**George**, Kenneth Desmond 1937- Who 92
**George**, Kenneth Dudley 1916- AmMWSc 92
**George**, Kenneth Montague 1930- IntWW 91
**George**, Larry Wayne 1954- WhoAmL 92
**George**, Laura W. WhoBlA 92
**George**, Llewellyn Norman Havard 1925- Who 92
**George**, Lloyd D. 1930- WhoAmL 92
**George**, Lloyd R 1926- WhoAmP 91
**George**, Louis 1935- IntMPA 92
**George**, Lynda Day 1946- WhoEnt 92
**George**, M Colleen 1938- AmMWSc 92
**George**, Marcus 1760?-1810 DcNCBi 2
**George**, Mary 1916- WhoAmP 91
**George**, Mary Alice 1938- WhoHisp 92
**George**, Melvin Douglas 1936- AmMWSc 92, WhoMW 92
**George**, Michael James 1941- AmMWSc 92
**George**, Michael Todd 1953- WhoEnt 92
**George**, Milon Fred 1944- AmMWSc 92
**George**, Nicholas 1937- AmMWSc 92
**George**, Nicholas 1962- WhoFI 92
**George**, Orlando J, Jr 1945- WhoAmP 91
**George**, Patricia Margaret 1948- AmMWSc 92
**George**, Patrick 1923- TwCPaSc
**George**, Patrick Herbert 1923- Who 92
**George**, Patrick Joseph 1951- WhoEnt 92
**George**, Paula Louise 1952- WhoWest 92
**George**, Peter 1924-1966 TwCSFW 91
**George**, Peter John 1919- Who 92
**George**, Peter Kurt 1942- AmMWSc 92
**George**, Peter T. 1929- WhoWest 92
**George**, Phil DrAPF 91
**George**, Philip 1920- AmMWSc 92
**George**, Philip Donald 1921- AmMWSc 92
**George**, Phyllis LesBEnT 92
**George**, Phyllis 1949- WhoEnt 92
**George**, Randolph Oswald WhoRel 92
**George**, Raymond Who 92
**George**, Raymond S 1936- AmMWSc 92
**George**, Robert 1923- AmMWSc 92
**George**, Robert Curtis 1939- WhoFI 92
**George**, Robert Eugene 1929- AmMWSc 92
**George**, Robert Glen 1939- WhoMW 92
**George**, Robert Hyland 1929- WhoAmP 91
**George**, Robert Peter 1955- WhoAmL 92
**George**, Robert Porter 1937- AmMWSc 92
**George**, Ronald Baylis 1932- AmMWSc 92
**George**, Ronald Edison 1937- AmMWSc 92
**George**, Ronald Glen 1941- WhoWest 92
**George**, Roy Kenneth 1934- WhoRel 92
**George**, Sally DrAPF 91
**George**, Sandra Lynn 1957- WhoEnt 92
**George**, Sarah B 1956- AmMWSc 92
**George**, Simon 1931- AmMWSc 92
**George**, Stefan 1868-1933 EncTR 91 [port], FacFETw
**George**, Stephen Anthony 1943- AmMWSc 92
**George**, Stephen L 1943- AmMWSc 92
**George**, Susan 1950- IntMPA 92, IntWW 91
**George**, Susanae 1953- WhoWest 92
**George**, T Adrian 1942- AmMWSc 92
**George**, Tate Claude 1968- WhoBlA 92
**George**, Ted Mason 1922- AmMWSc 92
**George**, Theodore Roosevelt, Jr. 1934- WhoBlA 92
**George**, Thom Ritter 1942- WhoEnt 92
**George**, Thomas D 1940- AmMWSc 92
**George**, Thomas Frederick 1947- AmMWSc 92
**George**, Timothy Gordon 1958- AmMWSc 92
**George**, Timothy John Burr 1937- Who 92
**George**, Vance WhoEnt 92, WhoWest 92
**George**, W. H. Krome 1918- IntWW 91
**George**, W. Peyton 1936- WhoAmL 92
**George**, Walter 1929- WhoAmP 91
**George**, Wilfred Raymond 1928- WhoFI 92
**George**, William 1925- AmMWSc 92
**George**, William David 1943- Who 92
**George**, William Douglas, Jr. 1932- WhoFI 92
**George**, William F. 1939 WhoRel 92
**George**, William Jacob 1938- AmMWSc 92
**George**, William Kenneth, Jr 1945- AmMWSc 92
**George**, William Leo, Jr 1938- AmMWSc 92
**George**, Zelma Watson 1903- NotBlAW 92 [port], WhoBlA 92
**George-Brown**, Lord 1914-1985 FacFETw
**George-Nascimento**, Carlos 1945- AmMWSc 92
**George-Weinstein**, Mindy 1953- AmMWSc 92
**Georgel**, Pierre 1943- IntWW 91
**Georgenson**, Philip Michael 1949- WhoMW 92
**Georgeoglou**, Nitsa-Athina 1922- IntAu&W 91
**Georges**, Georges Martin ConAu 35NR
**Georges**, John A. 1931- WhoFI 92
**Georges**, Peter John 1940- WhoAmL 92
**Georges**, Philip Telford 1923- IntWW 91
**Georges**, Telford 1923- Who 92
**Georgesco**, Victor 1948- WhoFI 92
**Georgescu**, Peter Andrew 1939- WhoFI 92
**Georgeson**, Byron Paul 1932- WhoMW 92
**Georgeson**, Scott F. 1956- WhoMW 92
**Georghiou**, George Paul 1925- AmMWSc 92
**Georghiou**, Michael 1932- WhoFI 92
**Georghiou**, Paris Elias 1946- AmMWSc 92
**Georghiou**, Solon 1939- AmMWSc 92
**Georgi**, Daniel Taylan 1948- AmMWSc 92
**Georgi**, Howard 1947- AmMWSc 92
**Georgi**, Jay R 1928- AmMWSc 92
**Georgia Minstrels** NewAmDM
**Georgiade**, Nicholas George 1918- AmMWSc 92
**Georgiades**, Gabriel George 1956- WhoWest 92
**Georgiadis**, John G 1959- AmMWSc 92
**Georgian**, Vlasios 1919- AmMWSc 92
**Georgiana**, John Thomas 1942- WhoMW 92
**Georgiana**, Joseph Samuel 1933- WhoAmL 92
**Georgiev**, Vassil St 1936- AmMWSc 92
**Georgine**, Robert A WhoIns 92
**Georgiou**, George 1959- AmMWSc 92
**Georgitsis**, Nicolas Mike 1934- WhoFI 92
**Georgius**, John R. 1944- WhoFI 92
**Georgopapadakou**, Nafsika Eleni 1950- AmMWSc 92
**Georgopoulos**, Apostolos P AmMWSc 92
**Georgopoulos**, Constantine Panos 1942- AmMWSc 92
**Georgopulos**, Peter Demetrios 1944- AmMWSc 92
**Gepford**, William George 1927- WhoRel 92
**Gephardt**, Donald Louis 1937- WhoEnt 92
**Gephardt**, Richard A. 1941- AlmAP 92 [port]
**Gephardt**, Richard Andrew 1941- IntWW 91, WhoAmP 91, WhoMW 92
**Gephart**, Landis Stephen 1917- AmMWSc 92
**Gepner**, Ivan Alan 1945- AmMWSc 92
**Geppaart**, Chris P. A. 1931- IntWW 91
**Geppert**, Gerard Allen 1932- AmMWSc 92
**Geppert**, John Gustave 1956- WhoAmL 92
**Geppert**, Walter 1939- IntWW 91
**Ger**, Shaw-Shyong 1959- WhoWest 92
**Gerace**, Larry R 1951- AmMWSc 92
**Gerace**, Michael Joseph 1944- AmMWSc 92
**Gerace**, Paul Louis 1934- AmMWSc 92
**Geraci**, Joseph E 1916- AmMWSc 92
**Geraci**, Mari 1961- WhoEnt 92
**Geraghty**, J. Richard 1953- WhoWest 92
**Geraghty**, James Joseph 1920- AmMWSc 92
**Geraghty**, Jeanne WhoAmP 91
**Geraghty**, Michael A 1930- AmMWSc 92
**Geraghty**, Thomas F. 1944- WhoAmL 92
**Gerald**, Arthur Thomas, Jr. 1947- WhoBlA 92
**Gerald**, Gilberto Ruben 1950- WhoBlA 92
**Gerald**, Helen IntMPA 92
**Gerald**, James A. 1937- WhoEnt 92
**Gerald**, John Bart DrAPF 91
**Gerald**, Matthew D. 1957- WhoFI 92
**Gerald**, Melvin Douglas, Sr. 1942- WhoBlA 92
**Gerald**, Michael Charles 1939- AmMWSc 92
**Gerald**, Park S 1921- AmMWSc 92
**Gerald**, William 1918- WhoBlA 92
**Geraldson**, Carroll Morton 1918- AmMWSc 92
**Geraldson**, Raymond I. 1911- WhoAmL 92
**Geraldson**, Raymond I., Jr. 1940- WhoAmL 92
**Gerali**, Steven Peter 1956- WhoRel 92
**Gerami**, Shahin 1950- WhoMW 92
**Geran**, Joseph, Jr. 1945- WhoBlA 92
**Gerard** Who 92
**Gerard**, Baron 1918- Who 92
**Gerard**, Alexander 1728-1795 BlkwCEP
**Gerard**, Cleveland Joseph 1924- AmMWSc 92
**Gerard**, Gary Floyd 1944- AmMWSc 92
**Gerard**, Geoffrey Who 92
**Gerard**, Gil 1943- IntMPA 92
**Gerard**, Jean B S 1938- WhoAmP 91
**Gerard**, Jean Broward Shevlin 1938- IntWW 91
**Gerard**, Jeffrey McKeighan 1960- WhoWest 92
**Gerard**, Jesse Thomas 1941- AmMWSc 92
**Gerard**, Jim DrAPF 91
**Gerard**, Joseph Eugene 1944- WhoRel 92
**Gerard**, Jules Bernard 1929- WhoAmL 92
**Gerard**, Lillian IntMPA 92
**Gerard**, Philip DrAPF 91
**Gerard**, Philip R. 1913- IntMPA 92
**Gerard**, Ronald 1925- Who 92
**Gerard**, Stephen Stanley 1936- WhoAmL 92
**Gerard**, Susan WhoAmP 91
**Gerard**, Valrie Ann 1948- AmMWSc 92
**Gerard**, William Geoffrey 1907- Who 92
**Gerard**, William John 1935- WhoAmL 92
**Gerard-Pearse**, John Roger Southey 1924- Who 92
**Gerardi**, Bob WhoEnt 92
**Gerardi**, Michael Frank 1965- WhoMW 92
**Gerardi**, Ralph 1941- WhoWest 92
**Gerardo**, James Bernard 1936- AmMWSc 92
**Gerardo**, Nori 1956- WhoFI 92
**Gerarge**, Anthony Thomas 1933- WhoWest 92
**Geras**, Adele 1944- WrDr 92
**Geras**, Adele Daphne 1944- IntAu&W 91
**Geras**, Norman 1943- WrDr 92
**Geras**, Norman Myron 1943- IntAu&W 91
**Geraschenko**, Victor 1937- IntWW 91
**Gerasimov**, Aleksandr Mikhaylovich 1881-1963 SovUnBD
**Gerasimov**, Anatoliy Nikolayevich 1931- IntWW 91
**Gerasimov**, Gennadi Ivanovich 1930- IntWW 91
**Gerasimov**, Gennadiy Ivanovich 1930- SovUnBD
**Gerasimov**, Ivan Aleksandrovich 1921- IntWW 91
**Gerasimov**, Sergei 1906-1985 IntDcF 2-2
**Gerasimov**, Sergey Apollinar'evich 1906-1985 SovUnBD
**Gerasimov**, Sergey Vasil'evich 1885-1964 SovUnBD
**Gerasimowicz**, Walter Vladimir 1952- AmMWSc 92
**Gerassi**, John 1931- WrDr 92
**Geratz**, Joachim Dieter 1929- AmMWSc 92
**Gerba**, Charles Peter 1945- AmMWSc 92, WhoWest 92
**Gerbasi**, Vicente 1913- ConSpAP
**Gerber**, Abraham 1925- WhoFI 92
**Gerber**, Albert B. 1913- WhoAmL 92
**Gerber**, Barry Eldon 1942- WhoWest 92
**Gerber**, Bernard Robert 1935- AmMWSc 92
**Gerber**, Charles Waas 1961- WhoFI 92
**Gerber**, Dan DrAPF 91
**Gerber**, David IntMPA 92, LesBEnT 92
**Gerber**, Donald Albert 1932- AmMWSc 92
**Gerber**, Donald Jeff 1960- WhoFI 92
**Gerber**, Donald Wayne 1963- WhoFI 92
**Gerber**, Douglas E. 1933- WrDr 92
**Gerber**, Eduard A 1907- AmMWSc 92
**Gerber**, Edward F. 1932- WhoAmL 92
**Gerber**, Elizabeth Daniel 1940- WhoAmP 91
**Gerber**, Eugene J. 1931- WhoRel 92
**Gerber**, George Hilton 1942- AmMWSc 92
**Gerber**, H Joseph 1924- AmMWSc 92
**Gerber**, Howard 1957- WhoAmL 92
**Gerber**, Israel Joshua 1918- WhoRel 92
**Gerber**, Jay Dean AmMWSc 92
**Gerber**, Joel 1940- WhoAmL 92
**Gerber**, John C. 1908- WrDr 92
**Gerber**, John Francis 1930- AmMWSc 92
**Gerber**, John George AmMWSc 92
**Gerber**, Leon E 1941- AmMWSc 92
**Gerber**, Linda M 1953- AmMWSc 92
**Gerber**, Merrill Joan DrAPF 91
**Gerber**, Merrill Joan 1938- WrDr 92
**Gerber**, Michael A 1939- AmMWSc 92
**Gerber**, Michael H. 1944- IntMPA 92
**Gerber**, Naomi Lynn Hurwitz AmMWSc 92
**Gerber**, Robert Evan 1947- WhoAmL 92
**Gerber**, Roger Alan 1939- WhoAmL 92
**Gerber**, Rudolph Joseph 1938- WhoAmL 92
**Gerber**, Samuel Michael 1920- AmMWSc 92
**Gerber**, Steven 1953- WhoAmL 92
**Gerber**, Thomas Allen 1947- WhoAmL 92
**Gerber**, Warren Charles, Jr. 1955- WhoFI 92
**Gerber**, William 1908- WrDr 92
**Gerberding**, Greta Elaine 1960- WhoAmL 92
**Gerberding**, John Habighorst 1922- WhoRel 92
**Gerberding**, Miles Carston 1930- WhoFI 92
**Gerberding**, William Passavant 1929- WhoWest 92
**Gerberg**, Eugene Jordan 1919- AmMWSc 92
**Gerberg**, Judith Levine 1940- WhoFI 92
**Gerberge** EncAmaz 91
**Gerberich**, John Barnes 1916- AmMWSc 92
**Gerberich**, William Warren 1935- AmMWSc 92
**Gerberick**, M. Ekola DrAPF 91
**Gerberry**, Ronald Vincent 1953- WhoAmP 91
**Gerbi**, Susan Alexandra 1944- AmMWSc 92
**Gerbie**, Albert B 1927- AmMWSc 92
**Gerbner**, George 1919- IntWW 91

**Gerbracht**, Robert Thomas 1924- *WhoWest 92*
**Gerde**, Carlyle Noyes 1946- *WhoAmL 92*
**Gerdeen**, James C 1937- *AmMWSc 92*
**Gerdeen**, Joel Wallace 1948- *WhoMW 92*
**Gerdener**, John Gerhard 1949- *WhoMW 92*
**Gerdener**, Theo J. A. 1916- *IntWW 91*
**Gerdes**, Carl Edward, Jr. 1960- *WhoAmL 92*
**Gerdes**, Charles Frederick 1945- *AmMWSc 92*
**Gerdes**, David A 1942- *WhoAmP 91*
**Gerdes**, Henry Carsten 1940- *WhoWest 92*
**Gerdes**, Jerrell Foster 1948- *WhoMW 92*
**Gerdes**, Karl Frederick 1949- *WhoWest 92*
**Gerdes**, Kenneth Lee 1943- *WhoEnt 92*
**Gerdes**, Neil Wayne 1943- *WhoMW 92, WhoRel 92*
**Gerdes**, Ralph Donald 1951- *WhoMW 92*
**Gerdil**, Giacinto Sigismondi 1718-1802 *BlkwCEP*
**Gerding**, Benjamin Franklin, III 1916- *WhoFI 92*
**Gerding**, Dale Nicholas 1940- *AmMWSc 92, WhoMW 92*
**Gerding**, Donna Ethel 1922- *WhoAmP 91*
**Gerding**, Thomas G 1930- *AmMWSc 92*
**Gerdovich**, Carl John 1956- *WhoMW 92*
**Gerdt**, Yelizaveta Pavlovna 1891-1975 *SovUnBD*
**Gerdts**, Charles William, III 1953- *WhoAmL 92*
**Gerdts**, Donald Duane 1932- *WhoEnt 92*
**Gerdy**, James Robert 1943- *AmMWSc 92*
**Gere**, Charles 1869-1957 *TwCPaSc*
**Gere**, James Monroe 1925- *AmMWSc 92*
**Gere**, John Arthur Giles 1921- *Who 92*
**Gere**, Margaret 1878-1965 *TwCPaSc*
**Gere**, Richard 1949- *IntMPA 92, IntWW 91, Who 92, WhoEnt 92*
**Gereben**, Istvan B 1933- *AmMWSc 92*
**Gereboff**, Joel David 1950- *WhoRel 92*
**Gerecht**, J Fred 1915- *AmMWSc 92*
**Gereighty**, Andrea S. *DrAPF 91*
**Gereke**, Gunther 1893-1970 *EncTR 91*
**Geremek**, Bronislaw 1932- *IntWW 91*
**Geren**, Collis Ross 1945- *AmMWSc 92*
**Geren**, Gerald S. 1939- *WhoAmL 92, WhoFI 92*
**Geren**, Pete *WhoAmP 91*
**Geren**, Pete 1952- *AlmAP 92 [port]*
**Gerena**, Victor M 1935- *WhoAmP 91*
**Gerencser**, George A *AmMWSc 92*
**Gerencser**, Mary Ann 1927- *AmMWSc 92*
**Gerencser**, Vincent Frederic 1927- *AmMWSc 92*
**Gerentz**, Sven 1921- *IntWW 91*
**Gerety**, Peter Leo 1912- *WhoRel 92*
**Gerety**, Robert John 1939- *AmMWSc 92*
**Gerety**, T. Michael 1942- *IntMPA 92*
**Gerety**, Tom 1946- *WhoAmL 92*
**Gerevich**, Aladar 1910- *IntWW 91*
**Gerez**, Victor 1934- *AmMWSc 92*
**Gerfen**, Charles Otto 1920- *AmMWSc 92*
**Gergacz**, John William 1950- *WhoAmL 92*
**Gergely**, John 1919- *AmMWSc 92*
**Gergely**, Peter 1936- *AmMWSc 92*
**Gergen**, Mark P. 1956- *WhoAmL 92*
**Gerges**, Abraham G 1934- *WhoAmP 91*
**Gergiannakis**, Anthony Emmanuel 1935- *WhoRel 92*
**Gergiev**, Valery 1953- *IntWW 91*
**Gergis**, Samir D *AmMWSc 92*
**Gerhard**, Derek James 1927- *Who 92*
**Gerhard**, Earl R 1922- *AmMWSc 92*
**Gerhard**, Glen Carl 1935- *AmMWSc 92*
**Gerhard**, Harry E., Jr. 1925- *WhoFI 92*
**Gerhard**, John Bruce 1948- *WhoMW 92*
**Gerhard**, Lee C 1937- *AmMWSc 92*
**Gerhard**, Roberto 1896-1970 *NewAmDM*
**Gerhard**, Walter Ulrich *AmMWSc 92*
**Gerhardi**, William 1895-1977 *ScFEYrs*
**Gerhardie**, William 1895-1977 *RfGEnL 91*
**Gerhardsen**, Tove Strand 1946- *IntWW 91*
**Gerhardt**, Clarence William 1940- *WhoAmL 92*
**Gerhardt**, Dan W *WhoAmP 91*
**Gerhardt**, Don John 1943- *AmMWSc 92*
**Gerhardt**, George William 1915- *AmMWSc 92*
**Gerhardt**, Glenn Rodney 1923- *WhoFI 92*
**Gerhardt**, H Carl, Jr 1945- *AmMWSc 92*
**Gerhardt**, Jon Stuart 1943- *AmMWSc 92*
**Gerhardt**, Klaus Otto 1935- *AmMWSc 92*
**Gerhardt**, Lester A 1940- *AmMWSc 92*
**Gerhardt**, Mark S 1946- *AmMWSc 92*
**Gerhardt**, Paul Donald 1917- *AmMWSc 92*
**Gerhardt**, Philipp 1921- *AmMWSc 92*
**Gerhardt**, Reid Richard 1941- *AmMWSc 92*
**Gerhart**, Emanuel Vogel 1817-1904 *RelLAm 91*
**Gerhart**, Frederick John 1946- *WhoAmL 92*
**Gerhart**, James Basil 1928- *AmMWSc 92*
**Gerhart**, John C 1936- *AmMWSc 92*
**Gerhart**, Mary J. 1935- *WhoRel 92*
**Gerhart**, Peter Milton 1945- *WhoAmL 92*
**Gerhart**, Steven George 1948- *WhoAmL 92*
**Gerhold**, George A 1937- *AmMWSc 92*
**Gerhold**, Henry Dietrich 1931- *AmMWSc 92*
**Gerich**, John Edward *AmMWSc 92*
**Gericke**, Otto Luke 1907- *AmMWSc 92*
**Gericke**, Otto Reinhard 1921- *AmMWSc 92*
**Gericke**, Paul William 1924- *WhoEnt 92, WhoRel 92*
**Gericke**, Wilhelm 1845-1925 *NewAmDM*
**Gerig**, Donald D. *WhoRel 92*
**Gerig**, Jeffrey Lee 1962- *WhoRel 92*
**Gerig**, John Thomas 1938- *AmMWSc 92*
**Gerig**, Thomas Michael 1942- *AmMWSc 92*
**Gerig**, Wesley Lee 1930- *WhoRel 92*
**Gerik**, James Stephen 1956- *AmMWSc 92*
**Gerike**, Paul William 1956- *WhoEnt 92*
**Gerima**, Haile *IntDcF 2-2*
**Gerin**, John Louis 1937- *AmMWSc 92*
**Gering**, Linda Ann 1953- *WhoFI 92*
**Gering**, Robert Lee 1920- *AmMWSc 92*
**Geringer**, James E 1944- *WhoAmP 91*
**Geringer**, Susan Diane 1954- *WhoWest 92*
**Geringer**, William C., Sr. 1954- *WhoMW 92*
**Gerischer**, Heinz 1919- *IntWW 91*
**Gerjuoy**, Edward 1918- *AmMWSc 92*
**Gerke**, Harold Edward 1912- *WhoAmP 91*
**Gerke**, John Royal 1927- *AmMWSc 92*
**Gerke**, Scott Charles 1965- *WhoMW 92*
**Gerken**, George Manz 1933- *AmMWSc 92*
**Gerken**, John Raymond, Jr 1926- *WhoAmP 91*
**Gerken**, Robert William Frank 1932- *Who 92*
**Gerken**, Walter Bland 1922- *WhoWest 92*
**Gerkin**, Charles Vincent 1922- *WhoRel 92*
**Gerking**, Shelby Delos 1918- *AmMWSc 92*
**Gerl**, James *WhoAmP 91*
**Gerl**, James 1952- *WhoAmL 92*
**Gerlach**, A A 1920- *AmMWSc 92*
**Gerlach**, Don R. 1932- *WhoMW 92, WrDr 92*
**Gerlach**, Eberhard 1934- *AmMWSc 92*
**Gerlach**, Edward Rudolph 1931- *AmMWSc 92*
**Gerlach**, Franklin Theodore 1935- *WhoAmL 92*
**Gerlach**, G. Donald 1933- *WhoAmL 92*
**Gerlach**, Helmut Georg von 1866-1935 *EncTR 91 [port]*
**Gerlach**, Howard G, Jr 1940- *AmMWSc 92*
**Gerlach**, James William 1955- *WhoAmP 91*
**Gerlach**, John *DrAPF 91*
**Gerlach**, John Louis *AmMWSc 92*
**Gerlach**, John Norman 1947- *AmMWSc 92*
**Gerlach**, Larry R. 1941- *ConAu 133*
**Gerlach**, Manfred 1928- *IntWW 91*
**Gerlach**, Robert Louis 1940- *AmMWSc 92*
**Gerlach**, Scott B 1948- *WhoIns 92*
**Gerlach**, Terrence Melvin *AmMWSc 92*
**Gerle**, Ladislav 1936- *IntWW 91*
**Gerlich**, Fritz 1883-1934 *EncTR 91 [port]*
**Gerling**, Hans 1915- *IntWW 91*
**Gerling**, William Curtis 1937- *WhoAmP 91*
**Gerlits**, Francis Joseph 1931- *WhoAmL 92*
**Gerlitz**, Curtis Neal 1944- *WhoMW 92*
**Gerlitz**, Dennis Eugene 1937- *WhoIns 92*
**Gerloff**, Gerald Carl 1920- *AmMWSc 92*
**Gerloff**, M. 1922- *WhoMW 92*
**Gerlt**, John Alan 1947- *AmMWSc 92*
**Germain**, Albert E. 1934- *WhoAmL 92, WhoFI 92*
**Germain**, George 1716-1785 *BlkwEAR*
**Germain**, Gerald 1942- *WhoFI 92*
**Germain**, Hubert 1920- *IntWW 91*
**Germain**, Paul 1920- *IntWW 91*
**Germain**, Ronald N 1948- *AmMWSc 92*
**Germain**, Stuart Lloyd 1941- *WhoEnt 92*
**Germaine**, Diane N. 1944- *WhoEnt 92*
**German**, His Holiness 1899- *IntWW 91*
**German**, Aleksey Borisovich 1938- *SovUnBD*
**German**, Aleksey Georgievich 1938- *IntWW 91*
**German**, Ann Louise *WhoBlA 92*
**German**, Bessie Jones 1945- *WhoRel 92*
**German**, Don Everett 1959- *WhoRel 92*
**German**, Dwight Charles 1944- *AmMWSc 92*
**German**, Edward Cecil 1921- *WhoAmL 92*
**German**, James Lafayette, III 1926- *AmMWSc 92*
**German**, James Randolph 1948- *WhoFI 92*
**German**, Jeffrey Neal 1957- *WhoAmL 92*
**German**, Jill S. 1964- *WhoMW 92*
**German**, Norman *DrAPF 91*
**German**, Victor Frederick *AmMWSc 92*
**German**, William 1919- *WhoWest 92*
**Germane**, Charlotte Suzanne 1954- *WhoAmL 92*
**Germane**, Geoffrey James 1950- *AmMWSc 92*
**Germani**, Fernando 1906- *IntWW 91*
**Germann**, Albert Frederick Ottomar, II 1929- *AmMWSc 92*
**Germann**, Richard P 1918- *AmMWSc 92*
**Germann**, Richard Paul 1918- *WhoFI 92, WhoMW 92*
**Germano**, Arthur Charles 1951- *WhoFI 92*
**Germanos** 1872-1951 *DcEcMov*
**Germanotta**, Jeffrey Steven 1958- *WhoMW 92*
**Germanus of Auxerre** 375?-437? *EncEarC*
**Germanus of Constantinople** 634?-733? *EncEarC*
**Germany**, Albert 1942- *WhoBlA 92*
**Germany**, Archie Herman 1917- *AmMWSc 92*
**Germany**, Sylvia Marie Armstrong 1950- *WhoBlA 92*
**Germer**, Adolph 1881-1966 *DcAmImH*
**Germer**, Richard Eliason 1946- *WhoWest 92*
**Germeshausen**, Kenneth J 1907- *AmMWSc 92*
**Germi**, Pietro 1914-1974 *IntDcF 2-2 [port]*
**Germinario**, Ralph Joseph 1943- *AmMWSc 92*
**Germino**, Felix Joseph 1930- *AmMWSc 92*
**Germond**, Jack 1928- *WrDr 92*
**Germovnik**, Francis 1915- *WhoRel 92*
**Germroth**, Ted Calvin 1952- *AmMWSc 92*
**Gernant**, Robert Everett 1941- *AmMWSc 92*
**Gerner**, Eugene Willard 1947- *AmMWSc 92, WhoWest 92*
**Gerner**, Ken *DrAPF 91*
**Gernert**, Herbert Everett, Jr. 1925- *WhoFI 92*
**Gernes**, Julius E. 1939- *WhoMW 92*
**Gernes**, Sonia *DrAPF 91*
**Gernhardt**, Karen Kay 1949- *WhoMW 92*
**Gernreich**, Rudi 1922-1985 *DcTwDes*
**Gerns**, Fred Rudolph 1925- *AmMWSc 92*
**Gernsback**, Hugo 1884-1967 *BenetAL 91, TwCSFW 91*
**Gernsback**, Hugo 1887-1964 *ScFEYrs*
**Gernsheim**, Helmut 1913- *WrDr 92*
**Gernsheim**, Helmut Erich Robert 1913- *IntWW 91, Who 92*
**Gerntholz**, Gereld F 1936- *WhoAmP 91*
**Gero**, Alexander 1907- *AmMWSc 92*
**Gero**, James Farrington 1945- *WhoFI 92*
**Geroch**, Robert Paul 1942- *AmMWSc 92*
**Gerola**, Humberto Cayetano 1943- *AmMWSc 92*
**Gerolimatos**, Barbara 1950- *AmMWSc 92*
**Gerome**, Jean-Leon 1824-1904 *ThHEIm*
**Geron**, George Henry 1944- *WhoAmP 91*
**Gerone**, Peter John 1928- *AmMWSc 92*
**Geronimo** 1829?-1909 *BenetAL 91, RComAH, RelLAm 91*
**Gerosa**, Peter Norman 1928- *Who 92*
**Gerould**, Gordon Hall 1877-1953 *BenetAL 91*
**Gerould**, Katherine Fuller 1879-1944 *BenetAL 91*
**Gerow**, Clare William 1927- *AmMWSc 92*
**Gerow**, Edwin Mahaffey 1931- *WhoRel 92*
**Gerow**, James A 1911- *WhoAmP 91*
**Gerow**, Margit Wallace 1935- *WhoAmL 92*
**Gerow**, Stephen Albyn 1942- *WhoFI 92*
**Gerowin**, Mina *WhoFI 92*
**Gerpheide**, John H 1925- *AmMWSc 92*
**Gerpheide**, John Henry 1925- *WhoWest 92*
**Gerra**, Martin Jerome, Jr. 1927- *WhoFI 92*
**Gerra**, Rosa A. *WhoHisp 92*
**Gerrald**, Kathy 1944- *WhoAmP 91*
**Gerrard**, A.J. *ConAu 135*
**Gerrard**, Alfred Horace 1899- *Who 92*
**Gerrard**, Basil Harding 1919- *Who 92*
**Gerrard**, Charles 1750?-1797 *DcNCBi 2*
**Gerrard**, Charles Robert 1892-1964 *TwCPaSc*
**Gerrard**, David Keith Robin 1939- *Who 92*
**Gerrard**, John 1944- *ConAu 135*
**Gerrard**, John Henry 1920- *Who 92*
**Gerrard**, John Watson 1916- *AmMWSc 92*
**Gerrard**, Jonathan M 1947- *AmMWSc 92*
**Gerrard**, Keith 1935- *WhoAmL 92*
**Gerrard**, Peter Noel 1930- *Who 92*
**Gerrard**, Ronald Tilbrook 1918- *Who 92*
**Gerrard**, Theresa Lee *AmMWSc 92*
**Gerrard**, Thomas Aquinas 1933- *AmMWSc 92*
**Gerrard-Wright**, Richard Eustace John 1930- *Who 92*
**Gerrare**, Wirt 1862- *ScFEYrs*
**Gerrath**, Joseph Fredrick 1936- *AmMWSc 92*
**Gerraughty**, Robert Joseph 1928- *AmMWSc 92, WhoMW 92*
**Gerring**, Irving 1909- *AmMWSc 92*
**Gerringer-Busenbark**, Elizabeth J. 1934- *WhoFI 92, WhoWest 92*
**Gerrish**, Brian Albert 1931- *IntAu&W 91, WhoMW 92, WhoRel 92, WrDr 92*
**Gerrish**, Frederic Henry 1845-1920 *BiInAmS*
**Gerrish**, Hollis G. 1907- *WhoFI 92*
**Gerrish**, James Ramsay 1956- *AmMWSc 92*
**Gerrish**, Martin Frederic 1926- *WhoEnt 92*
**Gerritsen**, Alexander Nicolaas 1913- *AmMWSc 92*
**Gerritsen**, Franciscus 1923- *AmMWSc 92*
**Gerritsen**, George Contant 1926- *AmMWSc 92*
**Gerritsen**, Hendrik Jurjen 1927- *AmMWSc 92*
**Gerritsen**, Jeroen 1951- *AmMWSc 92*
**Gerritsen**, Mary Ellen 1953- *AmMWSc 92*
**Gerrity**, Robert M. *WhoMW 92*
**Gerrity**, Ross Gordon 1945- *AmMWSc 92*
**Gerrodette**, Timothy 1946- *AmMWSc 92*
**Gerrold**, David 1944- *IntAu&W 91, SmATA 66, TwCSFW 91, WrDr 92*
**Gerry**, Edward T 1938- *AmMWSc 92*
**Gerry**, Elbridge 1744-1814 *AmPolLe, BlkwEAR*
**Gerry**, Elbridge Thomas 1908- *WhoFI 92*
**Gerry**, Elbridge Thomas, Jr. 1933- *WhoFI 92*
**Gerry**, John Francis 1925- *WhoAmL 92*
**Gerry**, Joseph John 1928- *WhoRel 92*
**Gerry**, Martin Hughes, IV 1943- *WhoAmP 91*
**Gerry**, Michael Charles Lewis 1939- *AmMWSc 92*
**Gerry**, Richard Woodman 1914- *AmMWSc 92*
**Gers**, Harvey 1947- *WhoFI 92, WhoMW 92*
**Gersami** *DrAPF 91*
**Gersbacher**, Willard Marion 1906- *AmMWSc 92*
**Gersch**, Charles Emanuel 1930- *WhoEnt 92*
**Gersch**, Charles Frant 1942- *WhoAmL 92*
**Gersch**, Harold Arthur 1922- *AmMWSc 92*
**Gersch**, Will 1929- *AmMWSc 92*
**Gerschbacher**, Corine Marie 1961- *WhoFI 92*
**Gerschefski**, Edwin 1909- *WhoEnt 92*
**Gerschenson**, Lazaro E 1936- *AmMWSc 92*
**Gersh**, Eileen Sutton 1913- *AmMWSc 92*
**Gersh**, Michael Elliot 1943- *AmMWSc 92*
**Gershator**, David *DrAPF 91*
**Gershator**, Phillis *DrAPF 91*
**Gershbein**, Leon Lee 1917- *AmMWSc 92, WhoMW 92*
**Gershberg**, Herbert 1917- *AmMWSc 92*
**Gershel**, Seth David 1957- *WhoEnt 92*
**Gershenfeld**, Mitchell Eric 1957- *WhoEnt 92*
**Gershengorn**, Marvin Carl 1946- *AmMWSc 92*
**Gershenowitz**, Harry 1926- *AmMWSc 92*
**Gershenson**, Hillel Halkin 1935- *AmMWSc 92*
**Gershenson**, Sergey Mikhaylovich 1906- *SovUnBD*
**Gershenzon**, M 1928- *AmMWSc 92*
**Gershenzon**, Sergey Mikhaylovich 1906- *SovUnBD*
**Gershevitch**, Ilya 1914- *IntWW 91, Who 92*
**Gershgoren**, Sid *DrAPF 91*
**Gershinowitz**, Harold 1910- *AmMWSc 92*
**Gershman**, Lewis C 1938- *AmMWSc 92*
**Gershman**, Louis Leo 1920- *AmMWSc 92*
**Gershman**, Melvin 1927- *AmMWSc 92*
**Gershman**, Stephen Allen 1950- *WhoAmL 92*
**Gershoff**, Stanley Norton *AmMWSc 92*
**Gershon**, Anne A 1938- *AmMWSc 92*
**Gershon**, Elizabeth Lewis 1955- *WhoFI 92*
**Gershon**, Elliot Sheldon 1940- *AmMWSc 92*
**Gershon**, Fredric Benjamin 1939- *WhoEnt 92*
**Gershon**, Gary Nichols 1946- *WhoAmL 92, WhoFI 92, WhoMW 92*
**Gershon**, Herman 1921- *AmMWSc 92*
**Gershon**, Howard Jeffrey 1948- *WhoFI 92*
**Gershon**, Karen 1923- *IntAu&W 91, WrDr 92*
**Gershon**, Michael David 1938- *AmMWSc 92*
**Gershon**, Norm 1947- *WhoAmP 91*
**Gershon**, Samuel 1927- *AmMWSc 92*
**Gershon**, Sol D 1910- *AmMWSc 92*
**Gershon**, William I. 1934- *WhoMW 92*
**Gershowitz**, Henry 1924- *AmMWSc 92*
**Gershun**, Theodore Leonard 1924- *AmMWSc 92*
**Gershuny**, Donald Nevin 1944- *WhoFI 92*
**Gershwin**, George 1898-1937 *BenetAL 91, FacFETw [port], NewAmDM, RComAH*
**Gershwin**, Ira 1896-1983 *BenetAL 91, FacFETw [port]*
**Gershwin**, Jerry 1926- *WhoEnt 92, WhoWest 92*

**Gersie**, Michael H 1948- *WhoIns 92*
**Gersin**, Robert P. 1929-1989 *DcTwDes*
**Gerske**, Janet Fay 1950- *WhoAmL 92*
**Gerson**, Carol Roberts 1948- *WhoMW 92*
**Gerson**, Corinne *DrAPF 91*
**Gerson**, David 1953- *WhoAmP 91*
**Gerson**, Elliot F 1952- *WhoIns 92*
**Gerson**, Gary Stanford 1945- *WhoMW 92, WhoRel 92*
**Gerson**, Jerome Howard 1928- *WhoAmL 92*
**Gerson**, John Henry Cary 1945- *Who 92*
**Gerson**, Levi ben 1288-1344 *DcLB 115*
**Gerson**, Lowell Walter 1942- *AmMWSc 92*
**Gerson**, Mark 1921- *IntWW 91*
**Gerson**, Mauricio 1953- *WhoHisp 92*
**Gerson**, Ralph Joseph 1949- *WhoAmL 92*
**Gerson**, Robert 1923- *AmMWSc 92*
**Gerson**, Stuart Michael 1944- *WhoAmL 92*
**Gersonides** 1288-1344 *DcLB 115*
**Gersovitz**, Mark 1949- *WhoMW 92*
**Gersper**, Paul Logan 1936- *AmMWSc 92*
**Gerst**, Cornelius Gary 1939- *WhoMW 92*
**Gerst**, Irving 1912- *AmMWSc 92*
**Gerst**, Jeffery William 1944- *AmMWSc 92*
**Gerst**, Paul Howard 1927- *AmMWSc 92*
**Gerstacker**, Friedrich 1816-1872 *BenetAL 91*
**Gerstein**, Allen Harvey 1937- *WhoAmL 92*
**Gerstein**, Bernard Clemence 1932- *AmMWSc 92*
**Gerstein**, David Brown 1936- *WhoFI 92*
**Gerstein**, George Leonard 1933- *AmMWSc 92*
**Gerstein**, Kenneth Stephen 1951- *WhoAmL 92*
**Gerstein**, Kurt 1905-1945 *EncTR 91 [port]*
**Gerstein**, Larry J 1940- *AmMWSc 92*
**Gerstein**, Melvin 1922- *AmMWSc 92*
**Gerstein**, Mordicai 1935- *ConAu 36NR*
**Gerstel**, Dan Ulrich 1914- *AmMWSc 92*
**Gerstell**, A. Frederick 1938- *WhoFI 92, WhoWest 92*
**Gersten**, Jerome William 1917- *AmMWSc 92*
**Gersten**, Joel Irwin 1942- *AmMWSc 92*
**Gersten**, Joseph Morris 1947- *WhoAmP 91*
**Gersten**, Stephen M 1940- *AmMWSc 92*
**Gerstenberg**, Frank Eric 1941- *Who 92*
**Gerstenberg**, Richard Charles 1909- *Who 92*
**Gerstenberger**, Donna 1929- *WrDr 92*
**Gerstenfeld**, Gerald F. 1931- *WhoAmL 92*
**Gerstenhaber**, Murray 1927- *AmMWSc 92*
**Gerstenhaber**, Ronald Alan 1947- *WhoAmP 91*
**Gerstenmaier**, Eugen 1906-1986 *EncTR 91 [port]*
**Gerstenmaier**, Eugen Karl Albrecht 1906-1986 *FacFETw*
**Gerster**, Robert Arnold 1920- *AmMWSc 92*
**Gerster**, Robert Gibson 1945- *WhoEnt 92*
**Gersting**, John Marshall, Jr 1940- *AmMWSc 92*
**Gersting**, Judith Lee 1940- *AmMWSc 92*
**Gerstl**, Bruno *AmMWSc 92*
**Gerstl**, Siegfried Adolf Wilhelm 1939- *AmMWSc 92*
**Gerstle**, Francis Peter, Jr 1942- *AmMWSc 92*
**Gerstle**, Kurt H 1923- *AmMWSc 92*
**Gerstle**, Kurt Herman 1923- *WhoWest 92*
**Gerstler**, Amy *DrAPF 91*
**Gerstman**, Henry 1938- *WhoFI 92*
**Gerstman**, Hubert Louis 1934- *AmMWSc 92*
**Gerstman**, Sharon Stern 1952- *WhoAmL 92*
**Gerstner**, Louis V. 1942- *CurBio 91 [port]*
**Gerstner**, Louis Vincent, Jr. 1942- *IntWW 91, WhoFI 92*
**Gerstner**, Richard Thomas 1939- *WhoFI 92*
**Gerstner**, Robert W 1934 *AmMWSc 92*
**Gerstner**, Robert William 1934- *WhoMW 92*
**Gerstorff**, Jeffrey Dale 1960- *WhoMW 92*
**Gersz**, Steven R. 1957- *WhoAmL 92*
**Gerteis**, Robert Louis 1936- *AmMWSc 92*
**Gerteisen**, Thomas Jacob 1943- *AmMWSc 92*
**Gerth**, Donald R. 1928- *IntWW 91*
**Gerth**, Donald Rogers 1928- *WhoWest 92*
**Gerth**, Frank E, III 1945- *AmMWSc 92*
**Gertis**, Neill Allan 1943- *WhoFI 92*
**Gertjejansen**, Roland O 1936- *AmMWSc 92*
**Gertjejansen**, Roland Orlen 1936- *WhoMW 92*
**Gertler**, Mark 1891-1939 *TwCPaSc*
**Gertler**, Menard M 1919- *AmMWSc 92*
**Gertler**, Meyer H. 1945- *WhoAmL 92*
**Gertner**, David A. 1961- *WhoFI 92*
**Gertner**, Michael Harvey 1941- *WhoAmL 92, WhoMW 92*
**Gertner**, Sheldon Bernard 1927- *AmMWSc 92*
**Gertsacov**, Adam Greenblatt 1964- *WhoFI 92*
**Gertych**, Zbigniew 1922- *IntWW 91, Who 92*
**Gertz**, Elmer 1906- *WhoMW 92*
**Gertz**, Gedaliah 1929- *WhoMW 92, WhoRel 92*
**Gertz**, Irving 1915- *IntMPA 92*
**Gertz**, Jami 1965- *IntMPA 92*
**Gertz**, Neal Morrison 1919- *WhoMW 92*
**Gertz**, Samuel David 1947- *AmMWSc 92*
**Gertz**, Steven Michael 1943- *AmMWSc 92*
**Gerughty**, Ronald Mills 1932- *AmMWSc 92*
**Gervais**, C. H. 1946- *ConPo 91, WrDr 92*
**Gervais**, Darwin 1921- *WhoFI 92*
**Gervais**, Floyd 1931- *WhoAmP 91*
**Gervais**, Francine 1951- *AmMWSc 92*
**Gervais**, Judith Ann 1957- *WhoFI 92*
**Gervais**, Marcel Andre 1931- *WhoRel 92*
**Gervais**, Paul 1915- *AmMWSc 92*
**Gervais**, Paul Nelson 1947- *WhoFI 92*
**Gervais**, Steven 1955- *WhoWest 92*
**Gervat**, Thomas Vincent 1946- *WhoEnt 92*
**Gervay**, Joseph Edmund 1931- *AmMWSc 92*
**Gervex**, Henri 1852-1929 *ThHElm*
**Gervin**, Derrick Eugene 1963- *WhoBlA 92*
**Gervin**, George 1952- *WhoBlA 92*
**Gervis Meyrick** *Who 92*
**Gerwe**, Raymond Daniel 1904- *AmMWSc 92*
**Gerwick**, Ben Clifford, III 1953- *AmMWSc 92*
**Gerwick**, Ben Clifford, Jr 1919- *AmMWSc 92, IntWW 91, WhoFI 92*
**Gerwick-Brodeur**, Madeline Carol 1951- *WhoWest 92*
**Gerwin**, Brenda Isen 1939- *AmMWSc 92*
**Gerwin**, Donald 1937- *IntAu&W 91*
**Gerwin**, Leslie Ellen 1950- *WhoAmL 92*
**Gerwin**, Richard A 1934- *AmMWSc 92*
**Gery**, Igal *AmMWSc 92*
**Gery**, John *DrAPF 91*
**Gery**, Marie Vogl *DrAPF 91*
**Gery**, Michael E *WhoAmP 91*
**Gery**, Robert Lucian W. *Who 92*
**Geryol**, Andrew John 1942- *WhoFI 92*
**Gerzog**, Lawrence David 1956- *WhoAmL 92*
**Gesang Doje** 1936- *IntWW 91*
**Gesch**, Roy 1920- *WrDr 92*
**Geschke**, Charles Matthew 1939- *AmMWSc 92*
**Geschwind**, Stanley 1921- *AmMWSc 92*
**Geschwind**, Stuart Mark 1947- *WhoAmL 92*
**Geseck**, Rosemary Barbara 1956- *WhoEnt 92*
**Gesell**, Arnold L 1880-1961 *FacFETw*
**Gesell**, Gerhard Alden 1910- *WhoAmL 92*
**Gesell**, Thomas Frederick 1940- *AmMWSc 92*
**Geselowitz**, David B 1930- *AmMWSc 92*
**Geshay**, Jeffrey John 1952- *WhoRel 92*
**Geshell**, Richard Steven 1943- *WhoAmL 92, WhoWest 92*
**Geshner**, Robert Andrew 1928- *AmMWSc 92*
**Gesinski**, Raymond Marion 1932- *AmMWSc 92*
**Geske**, Alvin Jay 1942- *WhoAmL 92*
**Geske**, Janine Patricia 1949- *WhoAmL 92*
**Geskin**, Ernest S 1935- *AmMWSc 92*
**Gesler**, Alan Edward 1945- *WhoAmL 92*
**Gesmer**, Ellen Frances 1950- *WhoAmL 92*
**Gesner**, Bayard Rustin 1950- *WhoFI 92*
**Gesner**, Bruce D 1938- *AmMWSc 92*
**Gesner**, Carol 1922- *WrDr 92*
**Gess**, Albin Horst 1942- *WhoAmL 92*
**Gess**, Denise 1952- *ConAu 135*
**Gessaman**, James A 1939- *AmMWSc 92*
**Gessaman**, Margaret Palmer 1934- *AmMWSc 92*
**Gesse**, Tabb Steven 1969- *WhoMW 92*
**Gessel**, Ira Martin 1951- *AmMWSc 92*
**Gessel**, Stanley Paul 1916- *AmMWSc 92*
**Gessell**, John Maurice 1920- *WhoRel 92*
**Gessen**, Boris Mikhaylovich 1883-1938 *SovUnBD*
**Gesser**, Hyman Davidson 1929- *AmMWSc 92*
**Gessert**, Autumn Roberta 1958- *WhoWest 92*
**Gessert**, Carl F 1923- *AmMWSc 92*
**Gessert**, Walter Louis 1919- *AmMWSc 92*
**Gessler**, Albert Murray 1918- *AmMWSc 92*
**Gessler**, Johannes 1936- *AmMWSc 92*
**Gessler**, Otto 1875-1955 *EncTR 91 [port]*
**Gessner**, Adolf Wilhelm 1928- *AmMWSc 92*
**Gessner**, Charles Herman 1938- *WhoFI 92*
**Gessner**, Frederick B 1937- *AmMWSc 92*
**Gessner**, Ira Harold 1931- *AmMWSc 92*
**Gessner**, Lynne 1919- *WrDr 92*
**Gessner**, Matthew A. 1967- *WhoMW 92*
**Gessner**, Peter K 1931- *AmMWSc 92*
**Gessner**, Richard *DrAPF 91*
**Gessner**, Robert V 1948- *AmMWSc 92*
**Gessner**, Salomon 1730-1788 *BlkwCEP*
**Gessner**, Teresa 1933- *AmMWSc 92*
**Gessow**, Alfred 1922- *AmMWSc 92*
**Gest**, Howard 1921- *AmMWSc 92*
**Gest**, Howard David 1952- *WhoAmL 92*
**Gestefeld**, Ursula Newell 1845-1921 *RelLAm 91*
**Gesteland**, Raymond Frederick 1938- *AmMWSc 92*
**Gesteland**, Robert Charles 1930- *AmMWSc 92*
**Gestetner**, David 1937- *Who 92*
**Gestetner**, Jonathan 1940- *Who 92*
**Geston**, Mark *DrAPF 91*
**Geston**, Mark S 1946- *TwCSFW 91, WrDr 92*
**Gestrin**, Kristian 1929- *IntWW 91*
**Gesualdo**, Carlo 1560?-1613 *NewAmDM*
**Gesund**, Hans 1928- *AmMWSc 92*
**Getchell**, Earle Duncan 1916- *WhoAmP 91*
**Getchell**, Thomas V 1939- *AmMWSc 92*
**Getchell**, Thomas Vincent *AmMWSc 92*
**Getches**, David Harding 1942- *WhoAmL 92*
**Gethers**, Peter *DrAPF 91*
**Gethin**, Richard 1949- *Who 92*
**Gething**, Richard Templeton 1911- *Who 92*
**Gethmann**, Richard Charles 1941- *AmMWSc 92*
**Gethner**, Jon Steven 1946- *AmMWSc 92*
**Getis**, Joel Brian 1966- *WhoFI 92*
**Getler**, Helen 1925- *WhoAmP 91*
**Getman**, Willard Etheridge 1949- *WhoAmL 92*
**Getnick**, Michael Elliot 1944- *WhoAmL 92*
**Getnick**, Neil Victor 1953- *WhoAmL 92*
**Getoor**, Ronald Kay 1929- *AmMWSc 92*
**Getreu**, Ian Edwin 1943- *WhoWest 92*
**Getreu**, Sanford 1930- *WhoWest 92*
**Getsi**, Joseph Marie 1953- *WhoEnt 92*
**Getsi**, Lucia C. *DrAPF 91*
**Getsinger**, William J 1924- *AmMWSc 92*
**Gettel**, James Joseph 1959- *WhoAmL 92*
**Gettier**, Glenn Howard, Jr. 1942- *WhoFI 92*
**Getting**, Carol Jean 1938- *WhoRel 92*
**Getting**, Ivan Alexander 1912- *AmMWSc 92*
**Getting**, Peter Alexander 1944- *AmMWSc 92*
**Gettings**, Don E 1923- *WhoAmP 91*
**Gettins**, Peter 1953- *AmMWSc 92*
**Gettleman**, Jeffrey Warren 1946- *WhoWest 92*
**Gettler**, Joseph Daniel 1916- *AmMWSc 92*
**Gettner**, Alan Frederick 1941- *WhoAmL 92*
**Gettner**, Marvin 1934- *AmMWSc 92*
**Getto**, Ernest John 1944- *WhoAmL 92*
**Getto**, Virgil M 1924- *WhoAmP 91*
**Getty**, Bill 1926- *WhoEnt 92*
**Getty**, Donald 1933- *IntWW 91*
**Getty**, Donald Ross 1933- *Who 92, WhoWest 92*
**Getty**, Estelle 1923- *IntMPA 92, WhoEnt 92*
**Getty**, Gerald Winkler 1913- *WhoAmL 92*
**Getty**, J. Ronald 1929- *IntMPA 92*
**Getty**, Jean Paul 1892-1976 *RComAH*
**Getty**, Robert J 1922- *AmMWSc 92*
**Getty**, Ward Douglas 1933- *AmMWSc 92*
**Getz**, Bert Atwater 1937- *WhoFI 92*
**Getz**, Don 1920- *IntMPA 92*
**Getz**, George Fulmer, Jr. 1908- *WhoFI 92, WhoWest 92*
**Getz**, Godfrey S 1930- *AmMWSc 92*
**Getz**, James Edward 1950- *WhoMW 92*
**Getz**, John *IntMPA 92*
**Getz**, Lowell Lee 1931- *AmMWSc 92*
**Getz**, Lowell Vernon 1932- *WhoFI 92*
**Getz**, Michael John 1944- *AmMWSc 92*
**Getz**, Stan 1927- *IntWW 91*
**Getz**, Stan 1927-1991 *CurBio 91N, FacFETw, NewAmDM, NewYTBS 91 [port], News 91*
**Getzels**, Jacob Warren 1912- *IntWW 91*
**Getzen**, Forrest William 1928- *AmMWSc 92*
**Getzen**, Rufus Thomas 1944- *AmMWSc 92*
**Getzendaner**, Milton Edmond 1918- *AmMWSc 92*
**Getzendanner**, Susan 1939- *WhoAmL 92, WhoMW 92*
**Getzin**, Louis William 1933- *AmMWSc 92*
**Getzin**, Paula Mayer 1941- *AmMWSc 92*
**Getzoff**, William Morey 1947- *WhoAmL 92*
**Getzwiller**, Polly 1924- *WhoAmP 91*
**Geu**, Thomas Earl 1957- *WhoAmL 92*
**Geuder**, Frederick William 1954- *WhoMW 92*
**Geumei**, Aida M *AmMWSc 92*
**Geurts**, Marie Anne H L 1947- *AmMWSc 92*
**Geuss**, Gary George 1958- *WhoAmL 92*
**Geuther**, Robert Otto 1909- *WhoMW 92*
**Gevantman**, Lewis Herman 1921- *AmMWSc 92*
**Gevarter**, William Bradley 1927- *AmMWSc 92*
**Gevecker**, Vernon A C 1909- *AmMWSc 92*
**Geveden**, Charles R 1940- *WhoAmP 91*
**Gevers**, Marcia Bonita 1946- *WhoAmL 92*
**Gevertz**, John Neil 1956- *WhoAmL 92*
**Gevinson**, Alan Cary 1953- *WhoEnt 92*
**Gewanter**, Herman Louis 1927- *AmMWSc 92*
**Gewartowski**, J W 1930- *AmMWSc 92*
**Gewertz**, Bruce Labe 1949- *AmMWSc 92*
**Gewertz**, Kenneth A *WhoAmP 91*
**Gewirtz**, Allan 1931- *AmMWSc 92*
**Gewirtz**, David A 1948- *AmMWSc 92*
**Gewirtz**, Leonard Benjamin 1918- *WhoRel 92*
**Gewirtz**, Paul D. 1947- *WhoAmL 92*
**Gewurz**, Henry 1936- *AmMWSc 92*
**Gex**, Walter Joseph, III 1939- *WhoAmL 92*
**Geyer**, Barbara Ann 1940- *WhoAmP 91*
**Geyer**, Edward B., Jr. 1929- *WhoBlA 92*
**Geyer**, Georgie Anne 1935- *IntAu&W 91, WrDr 92*
**Geyer**, James David 1943- *WhoAmL 92*
**Geyer**, John Charles 1906- *AmMWSc 92*
**Geyer**, Kenneth Albert 1927- *WhoEnt 92*
**Geyer**, Mark Allen 1944- *AmMWSc 92*
**Geyer**, Richard Adam 1914- *AmMWSc 92*
**Geyer**, Robert Pershing 1918- *AmMWSc 92*
**Geyer**, Sidna Priest 1943- *WhoMW 92*
**Geyer**, Stanley J 1949- *AmMWSc 92*
**Geyer**, Thomas H. 1952- *WhoAmL 92*
**Geyer**, William Richard 1948- *WhoAmL 92*
**Geyling**, F Th 1926- *AmMWSc 92*
**Geyman**, John P. 1931- *WrDr 92*
**Geyman**, John Payne 1931- *AmMWSc 92*
**Gezon**, Horace Martin 1914- *AmMWSc 92*
**Gezurian**, Dorothy Ellen 1956- *WhoFI 92*
**Gfeller**, Eduard 1937- *AmMWSc 92*
**Ghafar Baba**, Abdul 1925- *IntWW 91*
**Ghafari**, Yousif Butrus 1952- *WhoMW 92*
**Ghaffar**, Abdul 1942- *AmMWSc 92*
**Ghaffari**, Abolghassem 1909- *IntWW 91*
**Ghaffari**, Ebrahim Abe 1945- *WhoRel 92*
**Ghai**, Dharam P. 1936- *ConAu 34NR*
**Ghai**, Geetha R 1946- *AmMWSc 92*
**Ghai**, Om Prakash 1919- *IntWW 91*
**Ghaidan**, Saadoun 1930- *IntWW 91*
**Ghale**, Subedar Gaje *Who 92*
**Ghalem**, Nadia 1941- *IntAu&W 91*
**Ghali**, Boutros Boutros 1922- *NewYTBS 91*
**Ghali**, Moheb Amin 1939- *WhoWest 92*
**Ghalib**, Sharif 1942- *WhoFI 92*
**Ghaly**, Tharwat Shahata 1939- *AmMWSc 92*
**Ghanaba** 1923- *NewAmDM*
**Ghanayem**, Burhan I 1952- *AmMWSc 92*
**Ghandakly**, Adel Ahmad 1945- *AmMWSc 92*
**Ghandehari**, Mohammad Hossein 1943- *AmMWSc 92*
**Ghandhi**, Sorab Khushro 1928- *AmMWSc 92*
**Ghanem**, Mohamed Hafez 1925- *IntWW 91*
**Ghani**, Ashraf Muhammad 1931- *WhoFI 92*
**Gharekhan**, Chinmaya Rajaninath 1937- *IntWW 91*
**Gharrett**, Anthony John 1945- *AmMWSc 92*
**Ghasimi**, Mohammad Reza 1947- *IntWW 91*
**Ghassemi**, Masood 1940- *AmMWSc 92*
**Ghatak**, Ritwik 1925-1976 *IntDcF 2-2*
**Ghate**, Suhas Ramkrishna 1946- *AmMWSc 92*
**Ghausi**, Mohammed Shuaib 1930- *AmMWSc 92*
**Ghazala**, Mohamed Abdel Halim Abu- *IntWW 91*
**Ghazali**, Al- 1058-1111 *DcLB 115*
**Ghazanfar**, Shaikh Mohammed 1937- *WhoFI 92, WhoWest 92*
**Ghazarian**, Jacob G 1937- *AmMWSc 92*
**Ghazi**, Juliane Kay 1955- *WhoAmL 92*
**Ghaznavi**, John Jahangir 1935- *WhoFI 92*
**Ghebrehiwet**, Berhane 1946- *AmMWSc 92*
**Ghecas**, Anthony George 1961- *WhoAmP 91*
**Gheddo**, Piero 1929- *WhoRel 92*
**Ghee**, Doug *WhoAmP 91*
**Gheen**, James *DcNCBi 2*
**Gheith**, Mohamed A 1925- *AmMWSc 92*
**Ghelerode**, Michel de 1898-1962 *FacFETw*
**Ghen**, David C 1939- *AmMWSc 92*
**Ghent**, Arthur W 1927- *AmMWSc 92*
**Ghent**, Arthur Warren 1927- *WhoMW 92*
**Ghent**, Bob 1925- *WhoEnt 92*
**Ghent**, Edward Dale 1937- *AmMWSc 92*
**Ghent**, Emmanuel 1925- *NewAmDM*
**Ghent**, Henri Hermann 1926- *WhoBlA 92*

**Ghent**, Kenneth Smith 1911- *AmMWSc 92*
**Ghent**, William Robert 1922- *AmMWSc 92*
**Gheorghe**, Stefan *IntWW 91*
**Gheorghiu**, Ion 1929- *IntWW 91*
**Gheorghiu**, Mihail Mihnea 1919- *IntWW 91*
**Gheorghiu**, Paul 1916- *AmMWSc 92*
**Gheorghiu-Dej**, Gheorghe 1901-1965 *FacFETw*
**Gherab**, Mohamed Habib 1926- *IntWW 91*
**Gheraieb**, Abdelkrim 1935- *Who 92*
**Gherardi**, Gherardo Joseph 1921- *AmMWSc 92*
**Gherardi**, James Louis 1951- *WhoMW 92*
**Ghering**, Mary Virgil 1910- *AmMWSc 92*
**Ghering**, Walter L 1930- *AmMWSc 92*
**Gherlein**, Gerald Lee 1938- *WhoAmL 92, WhoFI 92*
**Gherlone**, Mildred Streeter 1925- *WhoAmP 91*
**Gherman**, Beverly 1934- *SmATA 68 [port]*
**Gherna**, Robert Larry 1937- *AmMWSc 92*
**Ghersi**, Michele Giuseppe Vittorio 1968- *WhoEnt 92*
**Gherson**, Adolph Randolph Albert 1928- *IntWW 91*
**Ghertner**, Edward L. 1957- *WhoEnt 92*
**Gherty**, John E. 1944- *WhoMW 92*
**Ghesquiere**, Virginie *EncAmaz 91*
**Ghetia**, Gail *DrAPF 91*
**Ghetti**, Bernardino Francesco 1941- *WhoMW 92*
**Ghezal**, Ahmed 1930- *IntWW 91*
**Ghezzi**, Bert 1941- *ConAu 133*
**Ghezzo**, Mario 1937- *AmMWSc 92*
**Ghia**, Giancinto 1887-1944 *DcTwDes, FacFETw*
**Ghia**, Kirti N *AmMWSc 92*
**Ghiara**, Paolo 1958- *AmMWSc 92*
**Ghiardi**, James Domenic 1918- *WhoAmL 92*
**Ghiardi**, John Felix Linus 1918- *WhoFI 92*
**Ghiaurov**, Nicolai 1929- *IntWW 91, NewAmDM*
**Ghicas**, Dimitrios Christos 1952- *WhoFI 92*
**Ghidoni**, John Joseph 1931- *AmMWSc 92*
**Ghiglia**, Oscar Alberto 1938- *WhoEnt 92*
**Ghigna**, Charles *DrAPF 91*
**Ghigo**, Frank Dunnington 1945- *AmMWSc 92*
**Ghika**, Nicolas 1906- *IntWW 91*
**Ghilardi**, Melinda Christina 1958- *WhoAmL 92*
**Ghiorso**, Albert 1915- *AmMWSc 92*
**Ghiorso**, Mark Stefan 1954- *AmMWSc 92*
**Ghiraldini**, Joan 1951- *WhoFI 92*
**Ghirardelli**, Robert George 1930- *AmMWSc 92*
**Ghiron**, Camillo A 1932- *AmMWSc 92*
**Ghiselin**, Brewster *DrAPF 91*
**Ghiselin**, Brewster 1903- *ConPo 91, IntAu&W 91, WrDr 92*
**Ghiselin**, Michael Tenant 1939- *AmMWSc 92*
**Ghista**, Dhanjoo Noshir 1940- *AmMWSc 92*
**Ghitalla**, Armando 1925- *NewAmDM*
**Ghitterman**, Allan Sydney 1924- *WhoAmL 92*
**Ghiuselev**, Nicola 1936- *IntWW 91*
**Ghiz**, Joseph Atallah 1945- *IntWW 91, Who 92*
**Ghizikis**, Phaidon 1917- *IntWW 91*
**Ghnassia**, Maurice 1920- *ConAu 34NR*
**Ghnem**, Edward *WhoAmP 91*
**Ghobashy**, Omar Zaki 1924- *WhoAmL 92*
**Gholson**, General James, Jr. 1944- *WhoBlA 92*
**Gholson**, Larry Estie 1949- *AmMWSc 92*
**Gholson**, Robert Karl 1930- *AmMWSc 92*
**Gholston**, Betty J. 1942- *WhoBlA 92*
**Ghoneim**, Mohamed Mansour 1934- *AmMWSc 92*
**Ghoneim**, Youssef Ahmed *AmMWSc 92*
**Ghoraski**, Gholam Reza 1948- *WhoFI 92*
**Ghorbal**, Ashraf *IntWW 91*
**Ghosananda**, Maha 1924- *RelLAm 91*
**Ghose**, Hirendra M *AmMWSc 92*
**Ghose**, John Elliot *WhoRel 92*
**Ghose**, Manmohan 1869-1924 *RfGEnL 91*
**Ghose**, Rabindra Nath 1925- *AmMWSc 92, WhoFI 92*
**Ghose**, Subrata *AmMWSc 92*
**Ghose**, Tarunendu 1928- *AmMWSc 92*
**Ghose**, Zulfikar *DrAPF 91*
**Ghose**, Zulfikar 1935- *ConNov 91, ConPo 91, IntAu&W 91, LiExTwC, WrDr 92*
**Ghosh**, Ajit Kumar 1919- *IntAu&W 91*
**Ghosh**, Amal Kumar 1926- *AmMWSc 92*
**Ghosh**, Amal Kumar 1931- *AmMWSc 92*
**Ghosh**, Amitav 1956- *IntAu&W 91, WrDr 92*
**Ghosh**, Amitava 1957- *AmMWSc 92*
**Ghosh**, Anil Chandra 1936- *AmMWSc 92*
**Ghosh**, Arati 1936- *AmMWSc 92*
**Ghosh**, Arun Kumar 1930- *WhoFI 92, WrDr 92*
**Ghosh**, Arup Kumar 1950- *AmMWSc 92*
**Ghosh**, Asoke Kumar 1938- *AmMWSc 92*
**Ghosh**, Bhaskar Kumar 1936- *AmMWSc 92*
**Ghosh**, Bijan K 1935- *AmMWSc 92*
**Ghosh**, Chitta Ranjan 1936- *AmMWSc 92*
**Ghosh**, Christopher Paul 1961- *WhoAmP 91*
**Ghosh**, Dipak K 1947- *AmMWSc 92*
**Ghosh**, Gautam 1950- *IntWW 91*
**Ghosh**, Hara Prasad 1937- *AmMWSc 92*
**Ghosh**, Mriganka M 1935- *AmMWSc 92*
**Ghosh**, Nimai Kumar 1937- *AmMWSc 92*
**Ghosh**, Rashbehari 1937- *IntAu&W 91*
**Ghosh**, Sakti P 1935- *AmMWSc 92*
**Ghosh**, Sambhunath 1935- *AmMWSc 92*
**Ghosh**, Sanjib Kumar 1925- *AmMWSc 92*
**Ghosh**, Satyendra Kumar 1945- *AmMWSc 92*
**Ghosh**, Subir 1950- *AmMWSc 92*
**Ghosh**, Swapan Kumar 1942- *AmMWSc 92*
**Ghosh**, Vinita Johri 1949- *AmMWSc 92*
**Ghoshal**, Nani Gopal 1934- *AmMWSc 92, WhoMW 92*
**Ghoshtagore**, Rathindra Nath 1937- *AmMWSc 92*
**Ghougassian**, Joseph 1944- *WhoAmP 91*
**Ghowsi**, Kiumars 1960- *AmMWSc 92*
**Ghozali**, Sid Ahmed 1937- *IntWW 91*
**Ghozati**, Seyed-Ali 1944- *AmMWSc 92*
**Ghrib**, Mohamed 1943- *IntWW 91*
**Ghuman**, Gian Singh 1929- *AmMWSc 92*
**Ghurburrun**, Beergoonath 1928- *IntWW 91*
**Ghurburrun**, Rabindrah 1929- *Who 92*
**Ghurye**, Sudhish G 1924- *AmMWSc 92*
**Ghusayni**, Badih Najib 1954- *WhoMW 92*
**Ghylin**, Clair 1929- *WhoFI 92*
**Gia-Russo**, Anthony Paul 1910- *WhoRel 92*
**Giacalone**, Frank T. 1951- *WhoFI 92*
**Giacalone**, Joseph Anthony 1938- *WhoFI 92*
**Giacchetti**, Athos 1921- *AmMWSc 92*
**Giacco**, Alexander Fortunatus *AmMWSc 92*
**Giacco**, Alexander Fortunatus 1919- *IntWW 91*
**Giacconi**, Riccardo 1931- *AmMWSc 92, IntWW 91*
**Giachello**, Aida L. Maisonet 1945- *WhoHisp 92*
**Giacobbe**, Paul A. 1949- *WhoIns 92*
**Giacobbe**, Thomas Joseph 1941- *AmMWSc 92*
**Giacobini**, Ezio *AmMWSc 92*
**Giacoletto**, L J 1916- *AmMWSc 92*
**Giacomazzi**, Frank Paul 1931- *WhoFI 92*
**Giacomelli**, Filiberto 1928- *AmMWSc 92*
**Giacomelli**, Giorgio 1930- *IntWW 91*
**Giacometti**, Alberto 1901-1966 *FacFETw*
**Giacometti**, Diego 1902-1985 *FacFETw*
**Giacometti**, Luigi 1926- *AmMWSc 92*
**Giacometti**, Marcel Alain 1951- *WhoFI 92*
**Giacometto**, Leo A 1962- *WhoAmP 91*
**Giaever**, Ivar 1929- *AmMWSc 92, IntWW 91, Who 92, WhoNob 90*
**Giaimo**, Robert N 1919- *WhoAmP 91*
**Giaimo**, Robert Nicholas 1919- *WhoAmL 92*
**Gialamas**, George Thomas 1938- *WhoMW 92*
**Gialamas**, Stefanos Panagiotis 1955- *WhoMW 92*
**Gialanella**, Philip Thomas 1930- *WhoWest 92*
**Giallanza**, Charles Philip 1950- *WhoAmL 92*
**Giallorenzi**, Thomas Gaetano 1943- *AmMWSc 92*
**Giam**, Choo-Seng 1931- *AmMWSc 92*
**Giamati**, Charles C, Jr 1927- *AmMWSc 92*
**Giamatti**, A Bart 1938-1989 *FacFETw*
**Giambattista**, Michele Donato 1934- *WhoWest 92*
**Giambone**, Anthony Francis 1964- *WhoWest 92*
**Giambra**, Joel A 1957- *WhoAmP 91*
**Giambrone**, Joseph James 1950- *AmMWSc 92*
**Giambrone**, Timothy Paul 1957- *WhoFI 92*
**Giamei**, Anthony Francis 1940- *AmMWSc 92*
**Giammara**, Berverly L Turner Sites 1938- *AmMWSc 92*
**Giammatteo**, Hollis *DrAPF 91*
**Giammona**, Charles P, Jr 1948- *AmMWSc 92*
**Giammona**, Samuel T 1930- *AmMWSc 92*
**Giampapa**, Guy Henry 1927- *WhoEnt 92*
**Giampapa**, Mark Steven 1954- *AmMWSc 92*
**Giampietro**, Wayne Bruce 1942- *WhoAmL 92*
**Gianakaris**, Constantine John 1934- *IntAu&W 91, WhoEnt 92, WrDr 92*
**Gianaris**, Bill 1965- *WhoAmL 92*
**Gianaris**, Nicholas Vasil 1929- *WhoFI 92*
**Giancana**, Sam 1908-1975 *FacFETw*
**Giancola**, Mary Rose 1952- *WhoMW 92*
**Gianelly**, Anthony Alfred 1936- *AmMWSc 92*
**Gianetto**, Robert 1927- *AmMWSc 92*
**Gianfranceschi**, Jean Holden 1955- *WhoAmL 92*
**Gianinno**, Susan McManama 1948- *WhoFI 92*
**Gianino**, John Joseph 1935- *WhoFI 92*
**Gianino**, Peter Dominic 1932- *AmMWSc 92*
**Gianitsos**, Anestis Nicholas 1961- *WhoMW 92*
**Giannakopoulos**, Panagiotis Konstantine 1949- *WhoRel 92*
**Giannelis**, Emmanuel P 1957- *AmMWSc 92*
**Giannetti**, Louis Daniel 1937- *WhoEnt 92*
**Giannetti**, Ronald A 1946- *AmMWSc 92*
**Giannettino**, John Mark 1959- *WhoEnt 92*
**Gianni**, Angelo R., Jr. 1946- *WhoMW 92*
**Giannini**, A James 1947- *AmMWSc 92*
**Giannini**, A P 1870-1949 *FacFETw*
**Giannini**, Cynthia *WhoEnt 92*
**Giannini**, Dante Henry, Jr. 1952- *WhoFI 92*
**Giannini**, David *DrAPF 91*
**Giannini**, Dusolina 1900-1986 *NewAmDM*
**Giannini**, Enzo 1946- *SmATA 68 [port]*
**Giannini**, Gabriel Maria 1905- *AmMWSc 92*
**Giannini**, Giancarlo 1942- *IntMPA 92*
**Giannini**, Margaret Joan 1921- *AmMWSc 92*
**Giannini**, Matthew Carlo 1950- *WhoMW 92*
**Giannini**, Vittorio 1903-1966 *NewAmDM*
**Giannone**, Pietro 1676-1748 *BlkwCEP*
**Giannopoulos**, Joanne *WhoMW 92*
**Giannotti**, Edward, Jr. 1948- *WhoFI 92*
**Giannotti**, Ralph Alfred 1942- *AmMWSc 92*
**Giannovario**, Joseph Anthony 1948- *AmMWSc 92*
**Gianola**, Umberto Ferdinando 1927- *AmMWSc 92*
**Gianoli**, Paul *DrAPF 91*
**Gianopulos**, George A. 1940- *WhoRel 92*
**Gianopulos**, John William 1931- *WhoMW 92*
**Gianoulakis**, John Louis 1938- *WhoAmL 92*
**Giants**, Thomas W 1940- *AmMWSc 92*
**Gianturco**, Delio E. 1940- *WhoFI 92*
**Gianturco**, Elizabeth Jordan 1941- *WhoAmL 92*
**Gianturco**, Maurizio 1928- *AmMWSc 92*
**Gianturco**, Maurizio Antonio 1928- *WhoFI 92*
**Gianturco**, Paola 1939- *WhoFI 92*
**Gianviti**, Francois Paul Frederic 1938- *IntWW 91*
**Giap**, Vo Nguyen *FacFETw, IntWW 91*
**Giapitsoglou**, Antoni 1960- *WhoEnt 92*
**Giaquinta**, Ben 1922- *WhoAmP 91*
**Giaquinta**, Robert T 1947- *AmMWSc 92*
**Giardelli**, Arthur 1911- *TwCPaSc*
**Giardina**, Denise *DrAPF 91*
**Giardina**, Richard Cono 1944- *WhoWest 92*
**Giardini**, Armando Alfonzo 1925- *AmMWSc 92*
**Giarini**, Orio 1936- *WhoFI 92*
**Giarola**, Attilio Jose 1930- *AmMWSc 92*
**Giaroli**, John Nello 1928- *AmMWSc 92*
**Giarrusso**, Frederick Frank 1936- *AmMWSc 92*
**Giarrusso**, Michael Thomas 1955- *WhoAmP 91*
**Giauque**, Gerald Stone 1941- *WhoWest 92*
**Giauque**, William Francis 1895-1982 *WhoNob 90*
**Gibala**, Ronald 1938- *AmMWSc 92, WhoMW 92*
**Gibaldi**, Milo 1938- *AmMWSc 92*
**Gibans**, James David 1930- *WhoFI 92*
**Gibas**, Allen Henry 1945- *WhoAmL 92*
**Gibb**, Andrew 1927- *Who 92*
**Gibb**, Andrew Thomas Fotheringham 1947- *Who 92*
**Gibb**, Arthur 1908- *WhoAmP 91*
**Gibb**, Barry 1946- *WhoEnt 92*
**Gibb**, Francis Ross 1927- *IntWW 91, Who 92*
**Gibb**, Ian Pashley 1926- *Who 92*
**Gibb**, James Woolley 1933- *AmMWSc 92*
**Gibb**, Lee *IntAu&W 91X*
**Gibb**, Maurice 1949- *WhoEnt 92*
**Gibb**, Phelan 1870-1948 *TwCPaSc*
**Gibb**, Richard A 1936- *AmMWSc 92*
**Gibb**, Robert *DrAPF 91*
**Gibb**, Robin 1949- *WhoEnt 92*
**Gibb**, Sara Lee 1937- *WhoEnt 92*
**Gibb**, Thomas Robinson Pirie 1916- *AmMWSc 92*
**Gibb**, Walter Frame 1919- *Who 92*
**Gibb**, William Eric 1911- *Who 92*
**Gibbard**, Bruce 1942- *AmMWSc 92*
**Gibbard**, H Frank 1940- *AmMWSc 92*
**Gibbens**, Barnaby John 1935- *Who 92*
**Gibbens**, John Monnett 1927- *WhoMW 92*
**Gibbens**, Robert Parker 1928- *AmMWSc 92*
**Gibbens**, Thomas Earl 1947- *WhoMW 92*
**Gibberd**, Kathleen 1897- *WrDr 92*
**Gibbes**, Emily V. 1915- *WhoBlA 92, WhoRel 92*
**Gibbes**, Lewis Reeve 1810-1894 *BiInAmS*
**Gibbes**, Robert Wilson 1809-1866 *BiInAmS*
**Gibbes**, William Holman 1930- *WhoAmL 92*
**Gibbings**, Peter 1929- *Who 92*
**Gibbings**, Robert 1889-1958 *TwCPaSc*
**Gibbins**, Betty Jane 1923- *AmMWSc 92*
**Gibbins**, Elizabeth Mary 1911- *Who 92*
**Gibbins**, Gordon A 1948- *WhoIns 92*
**Gibbins**, Ronald Charles *Who 92*
**Gibbins**, Sidney Gore 1926- *AmMWSc 92*
**Gibble**, Stephen Robert 1956- *WhoAmP 91*
**Gibble**, Walter Paul 1916- *WhoWest 92*
**Gibbon**, Edward 1737-1794 *BlkwCEP, EncEarC, RfGEnL 91*
**Gibbon**, John 1827-1896 *DcNCBi 2*
**Gibbon**, John 1917- *Who 92*
**Gibbon**, Lewis Grassic 1901-1935 *RfGEnL 91*
**Gibbon**, Michael 1930- *Who 92*
**Gibbon**, Norman Charles 1929- *AmMWSc 92*
**Gibbon**, Ralph Hailer 1916- *WhoAmL 92*
**Gibbon**, William Monk 1896- *IntAu&W 91*
**Gibbons**, Ashton Frank Eleazer 1935- *AmMWSc 92*
**Gibbons**, Barbara Hollingworth 1932- *AmMWSc 92*
**Gibbons**, Celia Victoria Townsend 1911- *WhoFI 92*
**Gibbons**, Christopher 1615-1676 *NewAmDM*
**Gibbons**, Daniel Bay 1957- *WhoAmL 92*
**Gibbons**, David *Who 92*
**Gibbons**, David Louis 1946- *AmMWSc 92*
**Gibbons**, Donald Frank 1926- *AmMWSc 92*
**Gibbons**, Edward John d1990 *Who 92N*
**Gibbons**, Elizabeth B. 1931- *WhoRel 92*
**Gibbons**, Faye 1938- *SmATA 65*
**Gibbons**, Floyd 1886-1939 *ScFEYrs*
**Gibbons**, Gene 1951- *WhoEnt 92*
**Gibbons**, Gregory Dennis 1953- *WhoRel 92*
**Gibbons**, H. Thomas 1947- *WhoAmL 92*
**Gibbons**, Ian Read 1931- *AmMWSc 92, IntWW 91, Who 92*
**Gibbons**, J Whitfield 1939- *AmMWSc 92, ConAu 35NR*
**Gibbons**, James 1834-1921 *BenetAL 91, DcNCBi 2, RelLAm 91*
**Gibbons**, James 1924- *IntWW 91*
**Gibbons**, James 1944- *WhoAmP 91*
**Gibbons**, James Anthony 1957- *WhoAmL 92*
**Gibbons**, James Arthur 1944- *WhoAmL 92, WhoWest 92*
**Gibbons**, James F 1931- *AmMWSc 92*
**Gibbons**, James Joseph 1946- *AmMWSc 92*
**Gibbons**, Jean Dickinson 1938- *AmMWSc 92*
**Gibbons**, Joel Clarke 1942- *WhoFI 92*
**Gibbons**, John *WhoEnt 92*
**Gibbons**, John 1949- *TwCPaSc*
**Gibbons**, John 1956- *WhoBlA 92*
**Gibbons**, John David *IntWW 91*
**Gibbons**, John David 1927- *Who 92*
**Gibbons**, John Ernest 1940- *Who 92*
**Gibbons**, John Howard 1929- *AmMWSc 92*
**Gibbons**, John Joseph 1924- *WhoAmL 92*
**Gibbons**, Joseph F 1948- *WhoAmP 91*
**Gibbons**, Joseph H 1934- *AmMWSc 92*
**Gibbons**, Julia Smith 1950- *WhoAmL 92*
**Gibbons**, Keith Alan 1957- *WhoRel 92*
**Gibbons**, Kenneth Harry 1931- *Who 92*
**Gibbons**, Kenneth Thomas 1926- *WhoAmL 92*
**Gibbons**, Larry Eugene 1943- *WhoRel 92*
**Gibbons**, Larry V 1932- *AmMWSc 92*
**Gibbons**, Loren Kenneth 1938- *AmMWSc 92*
**Gibbons**, Louis Charles 1914- *AmMWSc 92*
**Gibbons**, Maribeth Vivian 1952- *WhoWest 92*
**Gibbons**, Maritza 1962- *WhoFI 92*
**Gibbons**, Mark Hanley 1952- *WhoAmP 91*
**Gibbons**, Mathew Gerald 1919- *AmMWSc 92*

**Gibbons**, Michael Francis, Jr 1941- AmMWSc 92
**Gibbons**, Orlando 1583-1625 NewAmDM
**Gibbons**, Patrick C 1943- AmMWSc 92
**Gibbons**, Reginald DrAPF 91
**Gibbons**, Robert J 1945- WhoIns 92
**Gibbons**, Robert John 1944- WhoAmL 92
**Gibbons**, Robert Joseph 1945- WhoFI 92
**Gibbons**, Robert Philip 1933- WhoFI 92
**Gibbons**, Ronald J 1932- AmMWSc 92
**Gibbons**, Sam M. 1920- AlmAP 92 [port], WhoAmP 91
**Gibbons**, Stella Dorothea 1902- IntAu&W 91
**Gibbons**, Steven Van 1955- WhoAmL 92
**Gibbons**, Walter E. 1952- WhoBlA 92
**Gibbons**, Whit ConAu 35NR
**Gibbons**, William Edward Doran 1948- Who 92
**Gibbons**, William John 1947- WhoAmL 92
**Gibbons**, William Peters 1812-1897 BiInAmS
**Gibbs** Who 92
**Gibbs**, Alan Gregory 1939- AmMWSc 92
**Gibbs**, Alma G. 1914- WhoBlA 92
**Gibbs**, Alonzo 1915- WrDr 92
**Gibbs**, Alonzo Lawrence 1915- IntAu&W 91
**Gibbs**, Ann 1940- AmMWSc 92
**Gibbs**, Anthony Matthews 1933- IntWW 91, WrDr 92
**Gibbs**, Arnold James 1923- WhoAmL 92
**Gibbs**, Barbara DrAPF 91
**Gibbs**, Betty Lenore 1943- WhoFI 92
**Gibbs**, C. Earl 1935- WhoRel 92
**Gibbs**, C. Jeanean DrAPF 91
**Gibbs**, Charles Howard 1940- AmMWSc 92
**Gibbs**, Charles Kenneth 1953- WhoRel 92
**Gibbs**, Charles Melvin 1921- Who 92
**Gibbs**, Clarence Joseph, Jr 1924- AmMWSc 92
**Gibbs**, Daniel 1943- AmMWSc 92
**Gibbs**, David 1944- IntMPA 92
**Gibbs**, David Lee 1948- AmMWSc 92
**Gibbs**, David Neil 1958- WhoFI 92
**Gibbs**, Dennis C 1952- WhoIns 92
**Gibbs**, Doon Laurence 1954- AmMWSc 92
**Gibbs**, Edwin C. 1949- WhoWest 92
**Gibbs**, Elizabeth Villa 1935- WhoAmP 91
**Gibbs**, Eustace Hubert Beilby 1929- Who 92
**Gibbs**, Evelyn 1905- TwCPaSc
**Gibbs**, Finley P 1940- AmMWSc 92
**Gibbs**, Frederic Andrews 1903- AmMWSc 92
**Gibbs**, Geoff 1960- WhoEnt 92
**Gibbs**, George 1776-1833 BiInAmS
**Gibbs**, George 1815-1873 BiInAmS
**Gibbs**, Gerald Ernest 1896- Who 92
**Gibbs**, Gerald V 1929- AmMWSc 92
**Gibbs**, Gordon Everett 1911- AmMWSc 92
**Gibbs**, Harold Cuthbert 1928- AmMWSc 92
**Gibbs**, Harry 1917- IntWW 91, Who 92
**Gibbs**, Hugh Harper 1930- AmMWSc 92
**Gibbs**, Humphrey 1902-1990 AnObit 1990
**Gibbs**, Humphrey Vicary d1990 IntWW 91N, Who 92N
**Gibbs**, Humphrey Vicary 1902-1990 FacFETw
**Gibbs**, Hyatt McDonald 1938- AmMWSc 92
**Gibbs**, James Alanson 1935- WhoFI 92
**Gibbs**, James Albert 1917- AmMWSc 92
**Gibbs**, James Gendron, Jr 1938- AmMWSc 92
**Gibbs**, Janet Ann Bentley 1939- WhoRel 92
**Gibbs**, Janne Roberta 1949- WhoWest 92
**Gibbs**, Jewelle Taylor 1933- WhoBlA 92
**Gibbs**, John DcNCBi 2
**Gibbs**, John 1917- Who 92
**Gibbs**, John Dorance 1951- WhoMW 92
**Gibbs**, John Gamble 1930- WhoRel 92
**Gibbs**, John Patrick 1948- WhoFI 92
**Gibbs**, Jonathan 1953- TwCPaSc
**Gibbs**, Jonathan C. 1827-1874 RelLAm 91
**Gibbs**, Josiah Willard 1839-1903 BenetAL 91, BiInAmS
**Gibbs**, June Nesbitt 1922- WhoAmP 91
**Gibbs**, Karen Patricia 1952- WhoBlA 92
**Gibbs**, L James 1947- WhoAmP 91
**Gibbs**, Lancelot Richard 1934- IntWW 91
**Gibbs**, Lippman Martin 1938- WhoAmL 92
**Gibbs**, Marla WhoBlA 92
**Gibbs**, Marla 1931- IntMPA 92, WhoEnt 92
**Gibbs**, Martin 1922- AmMWSc 92
**Gibbs**, Martin St John Valentine 1917- Who 92
**Gibbs**, Marvin E 1934- AmMWSc 92
**Gibbs**, Michael John 1962- WhoFI 92
**Gibbs**, Mike 1937- NewAmDM
**Gibbs**, Molly 1912- Who 92
**Gibbs**, Morris M d1908 BiInAmS
**Gibbs**, Norman 1910-1990 AnObit 1990
**Gibbs**, Norman Edgar 1941- AmMWSc 92
**Gibbs**, Oswald Moxley 1927- IntWW 91, Who 92
**Gibbs**, Patt A. 1942- WhoAmL 92
**Gibbs**, Peter 1924- AmMWSc 92
**Gibbs**, R Darnley 1904- AmMWSc 92, IntWW 91, WrDr 92
**Gibbs**, Red 1947- WhoWest 92
**Gibbs**, Richard John 1943- Who 92
**Gibbs**, Richard John Hedley 1941- Who 92
**Gibbs**, Richard Lynn 1939- AmMWSc 92
**Gibbs**, Robert John 1926- AmMWSc 92
**Gibbs**, Roger Geoffrey 1934- Who 92
**Gibbs**, Roland 1921- Who 92
**Gibbs**, Roland Christopher 1921- IntWW 91
**Gibbs**, Ronald John 1933- AmMWSc 92
**Gibbs**, Rosalyn Davenport 1936- WhoAmL 92
**Gibbs**, Samuel Julian 1932- AmMWSc 92
**Gibbs**, Sandra E. 1942- WhoBlA 92
**Gibbs**, Sarah Preble 1930- AmMWSc 92
**Gibbs**, Stephen 1920- IntWW 91, Who 92
**Gibbs**, Stephen Thomas 1942- WhoMW 92
**Gibbs**, Terry 1924- NewAmDM
**Gibbs**, Terry Ralph 1937- AmMWSc 92
**Gibbs**, Thomas W 1932- AmMWSc 92
**Gibbs**, Timothy 1923- TwCPaSc
**Gibbs**, Timothy Durant 1938- IntWW 91
**Gibbs**, Tony 1953- WhoRel 92
**Gibbs**, Vernon D. G. 1951- WhoBlA 92
**Gibbs**, Warmoth T. 1892- WhoBlA 92
**Gibbs**, William Eugene 1930- AmMWSc 92
**Gibbs**, William Francis 1886-1967 DcTwDes, FacFETw
**Gibbs**, William Royal 1934- AmMWSc 92
**Gibbs**, Wolcott 1822-1908 BiInAmS
**Gibbs**, Wolcott 1902-1958 BenetAL 91
**Gibbs-Albanesius**, Janet DrAPF 91
**Gibeault**, Patricia M. 1953- WhoAmL 92
**Gibeault**, Victor Andrew 1941- AmMWSc 92
**Gibeon**, Leonard 1945- WhoFI 92
**Giberson**, Francis Eugene 1947- WhoAmL 92
**Gibert**, Peter 1942- WhoHisp 92
**Gibes**, Patricia A. 1937- WhoRel 92
**Gibian**, Gary Lee 1949- AmMWSc 92
**Gibian**, Morton J 1939- AmMWSc 92
**Gibian**, Thomas George 1922- AmMWSc 92
**Gibilaro**, Jason 1962- TwCPaSc
**Gibilisco**, Joseph 1924- AmMWSc 92
**Gibinski**, Kornel 1915- IntWW 91
**Giblett**, Eloise R. 1921- IntWW 91
**Giblett**, Eloise Rosalie 1921- AmMWSc 92
**Giblett**, Phylis Lee Walz 1945- WhoWest 92
**Gibley**, Charles W, Jr 1934- AmMWSc 92
**Giblin**, Denis Richard 1927- AmMWSc 92
**Giblin**, Frank Joseph 1942- AmMWSc 92
**Giblin**, Louis 1944- WhoMW 92
**Giblin**, Patrick David 1932- WhoFI 92
**Giblin-Davis**, Robin Michael 1955- AmMWSc 92
**Gibney**, Frank Bray 1924- WhoWest 92
**Gibney**, Lawrence John 1932- WhoIns 92
**Gibofsky**, Allan 1949- AmMWSc 92, WhoAmL 92, WhoFI 92
**Gibor**, Ahron 1925- AmMWSc 92
**Gibori**, Geula 1945- AmMWSc 92
**Gibraltar In Europe**, Auxiliary Bishop of Who 92
**Gibraltar In Europe**, Bishop of 1925- Who 92
**Gibraltar In Europe**, Suffragan Bishop of 1936- Who 92
**Gibran**, Kahlil DcAmImH
**Gibran**, Kahlil 1883-1931 FacFETw, LiExTwC
**Gibs**, John DcNCBi 2
**Gibson** Who 92
**Gibson**, Baron 1916- IntWW 91, Who 92
**Gibson**, Albert 1918- WhoBlA 92
**Gibson**, Alexander 1926- NewAmDM, Who 92
**Gibson**, Alexander Cameron 1926- ConAu 134
**Gibson**, Alexander Drummond 1926- IntWW 91
**Gibson**, Althea 1927- HanAmWH, NotBlAW 92 [port], WhoBlA 92
**Gibson**, Anne 1940- Who 92
**Gibson**, Anthony Lorenza 1942- WhoRel 92
**Gibson**, Antonio Marice 1962- WhoBlA 92
**Gibson**, Arthur Charles 1947- WhoWest 92
**Gibson**, Atholl Allen Vear 1940- AmMWSc 92
**Gibson**, Audrey Jane 1924- AmMWSc 92
**Gibson**, Benjamin F. 1931- WhoAmL 92, WhoBlA 92
**Gibson**, Benjamin Franklin, V 1938- AmMWSc 92
**Gibson**, Betty M. 1938- WhoBlA 92
**Gibson**, Bob 1935- FacFETw [port]
**Gibson**, Bob Dean 1931- WhoRel 92
**Gibson**, Bruce 1953- WhoAmP 91
**Gibson**, Bynum WhoAmP 91
**Gibson**, Camille Mary 1937- WhoAmP 91
**Gibson**, Carl H 1934- AmMWSc 92
**Gibson**, Carlton Wayne 1934- WhoAmP 91
**Gibson**, Catherine Antionette 1954- WhoWest 92
**Gibson**, Charles Dana 1867-1944 BenetAL 91
**Gibson**, Charles E 1916- IntAu&W 91, WrDr 92
**Gibson**, Charles Richard 1956- WhoMW 92, WhoRel 92
**Gibson**, Christopher 1921- Who 92
**Gibson**, Colvin Lee 1918- AmMWSc 92
**Gibson**, Count Dillon, Jr 1921- AmMWSc 92
**Gibson**, David 1922- Who 92
**Gibson**, David 1939- Who 92
**Gibson**, David F 1942- AmMWSc 92
**Gibson**, David Frederic 1942- WhoWest 92
**Gibson**, David Mark 1923- AmMWSc 92
**Gibson**, David Michael 1945- AmMWSc 92
**Gibson**, David Paul 1946- WhoRel 92
**Gibson**, David Thomas 1938- AmMWSc 92
**Gibson**, Dennis James 1952- WhoWest 92
**Gibson**, Dennis Leslie, Jr. 1935- WhoMW 92
**Gibson**, Derek 1945- IntMPA 92, WhoWest 92
**Gibson**, Dewey Elvin 1933- WhoRel 92
**Gibson**, Don Bishop, Jr. 1948- WhoEnt 92
**Gibson**, Donald B. 1933- WhoBlA 92
**Gibson**, Donald Bancroft 1928- WhoAmP 91
**Gibson**, Donald Cameron Ernest Forbes 1916- Who 92
**Gibson**, Donald Evelyn Edward 1908- Who 92
**Gibson**, Dorothy Hinds 1933- AmMWSc 92
**Gibson**, Earl Doyle 1923- AmMWSc 92
**Gibson**, Edward F 1937- AmMWSc 92
**Gibson**, Edward George 1936- AmMWSc 92
**Gibson**, Edward Lee 1933- WhoRel 92
**Gibson**, Edward Lewis 1932- WhoBlA 92
**Gibson**, Eleanor Jack 1910- IntWW 91, WomPsyc
**Gibson**, Elisabeth Jane 1937- WhoWest 92
**Gibson**, Elizabeth Harris WhoMW 92
**Gibson**, Elvis Edward 1937- WhoBlA 92
**Gibson**, Emmalene 1944- WhoRel 92
**Gibson**, Ernest Gerard 1961- WhoBlA 92
**Gibson**, Ernest Robinson 1920- WhoBlA 92
**Gibson**, Ernest W, III 1927- WhoAmP 91
**Gibson**, Ernest Willard, III 1927- WhoAmL 92
**Gibson**, Eva 1939- ConAu 35NR
**Gibson**, Everett Kay, Jr 1940- AmMWSc 92
**Gibson**, F. Michie 1950- WhoAmL 92
**Gibson**, Flash 1944- AmMWSc 92
**Gibson**, Floyd Robert 1910- WhoAmL 92, WhoMW 92
**Gibson**, Frank Byron 1945- WhoAmL 92
**Gibson**, Frank William Ernest 1923- IntWW 91, Who 92
**Gibson**, Gary Eugene 1945- AmMWSc 92
**Gibson**, Gayril 1958- WhoRel 92
**Gibson**, George 1909- AmMWSc 92
**Gibson**, George 1931- AmMWSc 92
**Gibson**, George Edward 1909- WhoMW 92
**Gibson**, George L ScFEYrs
**Gibson**, George R 1905- AmMWSc 92
**Gibson**, Gerald W 1937- AmMWSc 92
**Gibson**, Gordon 1926- AmMWSc 92
**Gibson**, Grace Evelyn Loving DrAPF 91
**Gibson**, Greg 1953- BlkOlyM
**Gibson**, Gregory A. 1948- WhoBlA 92
**Gibson**, Gregory James 1958- WhoMW 92
**Gibson**, Guadalupe 1917- WhoHisp 92
**Gibson**, Harold F 1921- AmMWSc 92
**Gibson**, Harold J 1909- AmMWSc 92
**Gibson**, Harold Leslie George 1917- Who 92
**Gibson**, Harris, Jr. 1936- WhoBlA 92
**Gibson**, Harry Clark IntAu&W 91X
**Gibson**, Harry Gene 1938- WhoMW 92
**Gibson**, Harry H. C. 1913- WhoBlA 92, WhoIns 92
**Gibson**, Harry William 1941- AmMWSc 92
**Gibson**, Helen 1894-1977 ReelWom
**Gibson**, Helena Christine 1937- WhoFI 92
**Gibson**, Henry 1935- IntMPA 92
**Gibson**, Henry Clay, Jr 1922- AmMWSc 92
**Gibson**, Hugh Simons 1883-1954 AmPeW
**Gibson**, Ian 1939- WrDr 92
**Gibson**, J Murray 1954- AmMWSc 92
**Gibson**, Jack 1920- WhoAmP 91
**Gibson**, James 1928- AmMWSc 92
**Gibson**, James 1948- TwCPaSc
**Gibson**, James A 1867?-1917 BiInAmS
**Gibson**, James Clark 1950- WhoRel 92
**Gibson**, James Darrell 1934- AmMWSc 92
**Gibson**, James Donald 1912- AmMWSc 92
**Gibson**, James Edwin 1941- AmMWSc 92
**Gibson**, James H 1930- AmMWSc 92
**Gibson**, James Isaac 1925- WhoAmP 91
**Gibson**, James John 1923- AmMWSc 92
**Gibson**, James O. 1934- WhoBlA 92
**Gibson**, Jay 1950- WhoAmP 91
**Gibson**, Jean 1935- TwCPaSc
**Gibson**, John A. WhoBlA 92
**Gibson**, John E 1926- AmMWSc 92
**Gibson**, John Francis 1966- WhoMW 92
**Gibson**, John Frank 1959- WhoRel 92
**Gibson**, John Hoadley 1906- WhoMW 92
**Gibson**, John Knight 1957- AmMWSc 92
**Gibson**, John M. 1899-19--? ConAu 134
**Gibson**, John Michael 1940- AmMWSc 92
**Gibson**, John Peter 1929- Who 92
**Gibson**, John Phillips 1930- AmMWSc 92
**Gibson**, John R WhoAmP 91
**Gibson**, John Robert 1925- WhoAmL 92, WhoMW 92
**Gibson**, John S WhoIns 92
**Gibson**, John Sibbald 1923- Who 92
**Gibson**, John Thomas 1948- WhoBlA 92
**Gibson**, John Vernon Morice 1937- WhoAmP 91
**Gibson**, John Walter 1922- Who 92
**Gibson**, John Wheat 1946- WhoAmL 92
**Gibson**, Johnnie M. M. 1949- WhoBlA 92
**Gibson**, Joseph 1916- Who 92
**Gibson**, Joseph David 1928- Who 92
**Gibson**, Joseph Lee 1940- WhoAmL 92
**Gibson**, Joseph W, Jr 1922- AmMWSc 92
**Gibson**, Joseph Woodward 1917- AmMWSc 92
**Gibson**, Josephine IntAu&W 91X, WrDr 92
**Gibson**, Joyce Correy 1948- AmMWSc 92
**Gibson**, Kathleen Rita 1942- AmMWSc 92
**Gibson**, Keith Patrick 1953- WhoAmL 92
**Gibson**, Kenneth Allen 1932- WhoBlA 92
**Gibson**, Kenneth David 1926- AmMWSc 92
**Gibson**, Kenneth O, Sr WhoAmP 91
**Gibson**, Kenneth Richard, III 1943- WhoMW 92
**Gibson**, L. Anthony 1939- WhoAmL 92
**Gibson**, Lee B 1926- AmMWSc 92
**Gibson**, Leonard Young 1911- Who 92
**Gibson**, Leslie Donovan 1910-1969 TwCPaSc
**Gibson**, Lloyd 1945- TwCPaSc
**Gibson**, Lois K 1929- WhoAmP 91
**Gibson**, Lois Naomi 1933- WhoRel 92
**Gibson**, Luther Ralph 1933- AmMWSc 92
**Gibson**, Margaret DrAPF 91
**Gibson**, Mary Jane 1933- WhoAmP 91
**Gibson**, Mary Morton 1939- AmMWSc 92
**Gibson**, Matthew Lee 1957- WhoRel 92
**Gibson**, Maurice 1960- WhoBlA 92
**Gibson**, Mel 1956- IntMPA 92, IntWW 91, WhoEnt 92
**Gibson**, Melvin Roy 1920- AmMWSc 92, WhoWest 92
**Gibson**, Michael Alfred 1944- WhoEnt 92
**Gibson**, Michael Bradford 1929- Who 92
**Gibson**, Michael Jay 1956- WhoMW 92
**Gibson**, Michael John 1939- Who 92
**Gibson**, Michael Ray 1954- WhoRel 92
**Gibson**, Miles 1947- IntAu&W 91, WrDr 92
**Gibson**, Morgan DrAPF 91
**Gibson**, Muscoe Minor, II 1923- WhoFI 92
**Gibson**, N. S. WhoRel 92
**Gibson**, P.J. DrAPF 91
**Gibson**, Patricia Ann 1942- WhoMW 92
**Gibson**, Paul, Jr. 1927- WhoBlA 92
**Gibson**, Paul Alexander 1941- Who 92
**Gibson**, Paul Raymond 1924- WhoWest 92
**Gibson**, Peter 1934- IntWW 91
**Gibson**, Peter Cecil 1913- Who 92
**Gibson**, Peter Leslie 1934- Who 92
**Gibson**, Peter Murray 1939- AmMWSc 92
**Gibson**, Pryor A 1957- WhoAmP 91
**Gibson**, Quentin 1913- WrDr 92
**Gibson**, Quentin Howieson 1918- AmMWSc 92, IntWW 91, Who 92
**Gibson**, Ralph 1922- Who 92
**Gibson**, Ralph Milton 1923- WhoBlA 92
**Gibson**, Raymond Edward 1946- AmMWSc 92
**Gibson**, Raymond Eugene 1924- WhoRel 92
**Gibson**, Reginald Walker 1927- WhoAmL 92, WhoBlA 92
**Gibson**, Rex 1931- IntAu&W 91, IntWW 91
**Gibson**, Richard C 1919- AmMWSc 92
**Gibson**, Richard Ingram 1948- WhoWest 92
**Gibson**, Robert 1927- WrDr 92
**Gibson**, Robert 1935- WhoBlA 92
**Gibson**, Robert Alfred 1932- WhoAmP 91
**Gibson**, Robert Dennis 1942- IntWW 91, Who 92

**Gibson**, Robert Donald Davidson 1927- *Who 92*
**Gibson**, Robert Harry 1938- *AmMWSc 92*
**Gibson**, Robert Law, Jr. 1936- *WhoAmL 92*
**Gibson**, Robert Wilder 1917- *AmMWSc 92*
**Gibson**, Rosalind Susan 1940- *AmMWSc 92*
**Gibson**, Roy 1924- *IntWW 91, Who 92*
**Gibson**, Royce Wesley 1964- *WhoFI 92*
**Gibson**, Sam Thompson 1916- *AmMWSc 92*
**Gibson**, Sarah L. 1927- *WhoBlA 92*
**Gibson**, Scott Douglas 1956- *WhoAmL 92*
**Gibson**, Scott Wilbert 1948- *WhoMW 92*
**Gibson**, Stephen Lee 1942- *WhoAmL 92*
**Gibson**, Stephen M. *DrAPF 91*
**Gibson**, Stephen Miller 1952- *WhoFI 92*
**Gibson**, Steven A. 1952- *WhoEnt 92*
**Gibson**, Terence Allen 1937- *Who 92*
**Gibson**, Thelma Jean 1934- *WhoAmP 91*
**Gibson**, Thomas 1915- *Who 92*
**Gibson**, Thomas Alvin, Jr 1919- *AmMWSc 92*
**Gibson**, Thomas Chometon 1921- *AmMWSc 92*
**Gibson**, Thomas George 1934- *AmMWSc 92*
**Gibson**, Thomas Joseph 1935- *WhoAmL 92, WhoFI 92*
**Gibson**, Thomas Richard 1951- *AmMWSc 92*
**Gibson**, Thomas William 1935- *AmMWSc 92*
**Gibson**, Treva Kay 1938 *WhoWest 92*
**Gibson**, Truman K., Jr. 1912- *WhoBlA 92*
**Gibson**, Verna Kaye 1942- *WhoFI 92*
**Gibson**, Walter 1897-1985 *FacFETw*
**Gibson**, Walter Maxwell 1930- *AmMWSc 92*
**Gibson**, Walter Samuel 1932- *IntAu&W 91, WrDr 92*
**Gibson**, Warren Arnold 1941- *WhoBlA 92*
**Gibson**, Warren Wolcott 1927- *WhoAmL 92*
**Gibson**, Wendy Joan 1953- *WhoAmL 92*
**Gibson**, Wilford Henry 1924- *Who 92*
**Gibson**, William 1914- *BenetAL 91, IntAu&W 91, SmATA 66 [port], WrDr 92*
**Gibson**, William 1948- *ConAu 133, IntAu&W 91, TwCSFW 91, WrDr 92*
**Gibson**, William Alfred 1866-1931 *TwCPaSc*
**Gibson**, William Allen 1955- *WhoWest 92*
**Gibson**, William Andrew *AmMWSc 92*
**Gibson**, William C *WhoAmP 91*
**Gibson**, William David 1925- *Who 92*
**Gibson**, William Edward 1921- *WhoRel 92*
**Gibson**, William Edward 1944- *WhoMW 92*
**Gibson**, William Hamilton 1850-1896 *BiInAmS*
**Gibson**, William Howard, Jr. 1941- *WhoBlA 92*
**Gibson**, William Lee 1949- *WhoFI 92*
**Gibson**, William Loane 1944- *AmMWSc 92*
**Gibson**, William M. 1934- *WhoBlA 92*
**Gibson**, William Michael 1956- *WhoAmL 92*
**Gibson**, William Ray 1962- *WhoEnt 92*
**Gibson**, William Raymond 1923- *AmMWSc 92*
**Gibson**, William S 1933- *WhoIns 92*
**Gibson**, William Wallace 1928- *AmMWSc 92*
**Gibson**, William Willard, Jr. 1932- *WhoAmL 92*
**Gibson-Barboza**, Mario 1918- *IntWW 91, Who 92*
**Gibson-Craig-Carmichael**, David Peter W 1946- *Who 92*
**Gibson-Watt**, Baron 1918- *Who 92*
**Gick**, Philip David 1913- *Who 92*
**Giclas**, Henry Lee 1910- *AmMWSc 92*
**Giclas**, Patricia C *AmMWSc 92*
**Giczi**, Gregory Joseph 1948- *WhoEnt 92*
**Gidal**, George 1934- *AmMWSc 92*
**Gidari**, Anthony Salvatore 1943- *AmMWSc 92*
**Gidaspov**, Boris Veniaminovich 1933- *IntWW 91, SovUnBD*
**Gidda**, Jaswant Singh 1946- *AmMWSc 92*
**Gidden**, Barry Owen Barton 1915- *Who 92*
**Giddens**, Anthony 1938- *Who 92*
**Giddens**, Charles Edwin 1944- *WhoEnt 92*
**Giddens**, Don P 1940- *AmMWSc 92*
**Giddens**, Joel Edwin 1917- *AmMWSc 92*
**Giddens**, Paul Joseph 1944- *WhoMW 92*
**Giddens**, William Ellis, Jr 1937- *AmMWSc 92*
**Giddings**, Clifford Frederick 1936- *WhoFI 92*
**Giddings**, Franklin Henry 1855-1931 *AmPeW*
**Giddings**, George Gosselin 1937- *AmMWSc 92*
**Giddings**, John Calvin 1930- *AmMWSc 92, WrDr 92*
**Giddings**, Joshua Reed 1795-1864 *AmPolLe*
**Giddings**, Michael 1920- *Who 92*
**Giddings**, Paula 1947- *NotBlAW 92*
**Giddings**, Paula Jane 1947- *WhoBlA 92*
**Giddings**, Raymond W, Sr 1922- *WhoAmP 91*
**Giddings**, Sydney Arthur 1929- *AmMWSc 92*
**Giddings**, Thomas H, Jr *AmMWSc 92*
**Giddings**, William Paul 1933- *AmMWSc 92*
**Gide**, Andre 1869-1951 *FacFETw, GuFrLit 1*
**Gide**, Andre Paul Guillaume 1869-1951 *WhoNob 90*
**Gidel**, Robert Hugh 1951- *WhoFI 92*
**Gideon**, Kenneth W 1946- *WhoAmP 91*
**Gideon**, Kenneth Wayne 1946- *WhoFI 92*
**Gideon**, Lee Burton 1938- *WhoEnt 92*
**Gideon**, Miriam 1906- *NewAmDM, WhoEnt 92*
**Gideon**, Richard Walter 1928- *WhoFI 92*
**Gideon-Hawke**, Pamela Lawrence 1945- *WhoWest 92*
**Gidez**, Lewis Irwin 1927- *AmMWSc 92*
**Gidley**, J L 1924- *AmMWSc 92*
**Gidley**, William Jeremiah 1926- *WhoFI 92*
**Gidney**, Calvin L. 1930- *WhoBlA 92*
**Giduz**, Roland 1925- *WhoEnt 92*
**Gidwani**, Ram N 1936- *AmMWSc 92*
**Gidwitz**, Betsy R. 1940- *WhoRel 92*
**Gidwitz**, Gerald 1906- *WhoFI 92, WhoMW 92*
**Gidwitz**, John David 1941- *WhoEnt 92*
**Gidwitz**, Joseph Leon 1905- *WhoFI 92*
**Gidwitz**, Ronald J. 1945- *WhoMW 92*
**Giebisch**, Gerhard Hans 1927- *AmMWSc 92*
**Giebner**, Cara Rae 1940- *WhoMW 92*
**Gieck**, Jack Edgar 1923- *WhoEnt 92*
**Giedion**, Sigfried 1894-1968 *DcTwDes, FacFETw*
**Giedt**, W H 1920- *AmMWSc 92*
**Giedt**, Walvin Roland 1905- *WhoWest 92*
**Gieg**, Carol Suzanne 1957- *WhoWest 92*
**Giegel**, Joseph Lester 1938- *AmMWSc 92*
**Gieger**, Loren Glenn 1937- *WhoRel 92*
**Giegerich**, Thomas William 1955- *WhoAmL 92*
**Giele**, Janet Z. 1934- *ConAu 36NR*
**Gielen**, Michael 1927- *ConCom 92*
**Gielen**, Michael Andreas 1927- *IntWW 91*
**Gielgud**, John *NewYTBS 91 [port]*
**Gielgud**, John 1904- *FacFETw, IntMPA 92, IntWW 91, Who 92, WhoEnt 92, WrDr 92*
**Gielgud**, Maina 1945- *Who 92, WhoEnt 92*
**Gielisse**, Peter Jacob Maria 1934- *AmMWSc 92*
**Gielissen**, A. James 1928- *WhoWest 92*
**Gielow**, Richard William 1943- *WhoRel 92*
**Giem**, Ross Nye, Jr. 1923- *WhoWest 92*
**Gienow**, Herbert Hans Walter 1926- *IntWW 91*
**Gier**, Audra May Calhoon 1940- *WhoMW 92*
**Gier**, Karan Hancock 1947- *WhoWest 92*
**Gier**, Nicholas Francis 1944- *WhoRel 92*
**Gierasch**, Lila Mary 1948- *AmMWSc 92*
**Gierasch**, Peter Jay 1940- *AmMWSc 92*
**Gierbolini-Ortiz**, Gilberto 1926- *WhoAmL 92*
**Giere**, Frederic Arthur 1923- *AmMWSc 92*
**Gierek**, Edward 1913- *FacFETw, IntWW 91*
**Gierer**, Paul L *AmMWSc 92*
**Gierer**, Vincent A., Jr. 1947- *WhoFI 92*
**Gierhart**, Roger Lee 1931- *WhoAmL 92*
**Giering**, John Edgar 1929- *AmMWSc 92*
**Giering**, Richard Herbert 1929- *WhoFI 92, WhoMW 92*
**Giering**, Warren Percival 1941- *AmMWSc 92*
**Gierke**, Craig Sherman 1950- *WhoAmP 91*
**Gierke**, Herman Fredrick, III 1943- *WhoAmL 92, WhoAmP 91, WhoMW 92*
**Gierke**, Timothy Dee 1946- *AmMWSc 92*
**Gierowski**, Stefan 1925- *IntWW 91*
**Giersch**, Herbert 1921- *IntWW 91*
**Gierster**, Hans 1925- *IntWW 91*
**Giertz**, J. Fred 1943- *WhoFI 92, WhoMW 92*
**Giertz**, Robert William 1925- *WhoFI 92, WhoMW 92*
**Gierut**, Casimir Frank 1919- *WhoRel 92*
**Gies**, Martha *DrAPF 91*
**Gies**, Ronald Bruce 1965- *WhoFI 92*
**Giesa**, Michael William 1943- *WhoWest 92*
**Giesbert**, Franz-Olivier 1949- *IntWW 91*
**Giesbrecht**, Herbert Jacob 1925- *WhoRel 92*
**Giesbrecht**, John 1922- *AmMWSc 92*
**Giesbrecht**, Lawrence *WhoRel 92*
**Giesbrecht**, Martin Gerhard 1933- *WhoFI 92*
**Gieschen**, Charles Arthur 1958- *WhoRel 92*
**Gieschen**, Donald Werner 1924- *WhoWest 92*
**Giese**, Arthur Charles 1904- *AmMWSc 92*
**Giese**, Cary William 1942- *WhoWest 92*
**Giese**, Clayton 1931- *AmMWSc 92*
**Giese**, David E 1942- *WhoAmP 91*
**Giese**, David Lyle 1933- *AmMWSc 92*
**Giese**, Edgar William 1941- *WhoAmP 91*
**Giese**, Elizabeth Ann 1943- *WhoAmP 91*
**Giese**, Gerald Paul 1956- *WhoFI 92*
**Giese**, Graham Sherwood 1931- *AmMWSc 92*
**Giese**, Heiner 1944- *WhoAmL 92*
**Giese**, John H 1915- *AmMWSc 92*
**Giese**, Robert Frederick 1943- *AmMWSc 92*
**Giese**, Robert James 1950- *WhoRel 92*
**Giese**, Robert Paul 1936- *AmMWSc 92*
**Giese**, Roger Wallace 1943- *AmMWSc 92*
**Giese**, Ronald Lawrence 1934- *AmMWSc 92*
**Giese**, Rossman Frederick, Jr 1936- *AmMWSc 92*
**Giese**, Vincent 1923- *WhoRel 92*
**Giese**, Warren Kenneth 1924- *WhoAmP 91*
**Giesecke**, Adolph H 1932- *AmMWSc 92*
**Gieseke**, James Arnold 1936- *AmMWSc 92*
**Gieseking**, John Eldon 1905- *AmMWSc 92*
**Gieseking**, Walter 1895-1956 *FacFETw, NewAmDM*
**Giesel**, James Theodore 1941- *AmMWSc 92*
**Giesela**, Countess of Eltz *EncAmaz 91*
**Gieseler**, Daniel J., Jr. 1938- *WhoIns 92*
**Gieselman**, Kenneth E 1920- *WhoAmP 91*
**Gieselman**, Robert Dale 1932- *WhoMW 92*
**Giesen**, Arthur Rossa, Jr 1932- *WhoAmP 91*
**Giesen**, Francis Henry 1932- *WhoMW 92*
**Giesen**, Herman Mills 1928- *WhoFI 92*
**Gieser**, Charles Kenneth 1939- *WhoRel 92*
**Giesey**, Harry George 1933- *WhoIns 92*
**Giesler**, Gregg Carl 1944- *AmMWSc 92*
**Giesler**, John Hanford 1931- *WhoRel 92*
**Giesmann**, Donald John 1949- *WhoMW 92, WhoRel 92*
**Giess**, Edward August 1929- *AmMWSc 92*
**Giessen**, Bill C 1932- *AmMWSc 92*
**Giessinger**, Peter W 1920- *WhoAmP 91*
**Giesy**, J U 1877-1947 *TwCSFW 91*
**Giesy**, J U 1877-1948 *ScFEYrs*
**Giesy**, J U and Smith, Junius B *ScFEYrs*
**Giesy**, John Paul, Jr 1948- *AmMWSc 92, WhoMW 92*
**Giesy**, Robert 1922- *AmMWSc 92*
**Gietzen**, Dorothy Winter *AmMWSc 92*
**Giever**, John Bertram 1919- *AmMWSc 92*
**Gieysztor**, Aleksander 1916- *IntWW 91*
**Giffard** *Who 92*
**Giffard**, Adam Edward 1934- *Who 92*
**Giffard**, Sydney 1926- *Who 92*
**Giffen**, John A. 1938- *IntWW 91, WhoFI 92*
**Giffen**, Lawrence Everett, Sr. 1923- *WhoMW 92*
**Giffen**, Martin Brener 1919- *AmMWSc 92*
**Giffen**, Robert H 1922- *AmMWSc 92*
**Giffen**, William Martin, Jr 1933- *AmMWSc 92*
**Giffin**, Emily Buchholtz 1947- *AmMWSc 92*
**Giffin**, Gordon Davies 1949- *WhoAmP 91*
**Giffin**, Kenneth Neal 1944- *WhoAmP 91, WhoFI 92*
**Giffin**, Kenneth S. 1943- *WhoWest 92*
**Giffin**, Mary Elizabeth 1919- *WhoRel 92*
**Giffin**, Reggie Craig 1942- *WhoAmL 92, WhoMW 92*
**Giffin**, Walter C 1936- *AmMWSc 92*
**Giffin**, Walter Charles 1936- *WhoWest 92*
**Gifford** *Who 92*
**Gifford**, Baron 1940- *Who 92*
**Gifford**, Anita Sheree 1964- *WhoAmL 92*
**Gifford**, Arthur Roy 1937- *WhoWest 92*
**Gifford**, Barry *DrAPF 91*
**Gifford**, Barry 1946- *WrDr 92*
**Gifford**, Barry Colby 1946- *IntAu&W 91*
**Gifford**, Bernard R. 1943- *WhoBlA 92*
**Gifford**, Cameron Edward 1931- *AmMWSc 92*
**Gifford**, Carol Lynn 1942- *WhoAmP 91*
**Gifford**, Charles Henry 1913- *IntWW 91*
**Gifford**, Charles Kilvert 1942- *WhoFI 92*
**Gifford**, Chuck *WhoAmP 91*
**Gifford**, David Stevens 1924- *AmMWSc 92*
**Gifford**, Denis 1927- *IntAu&W 91, WrDr 92*
**Gifford**, Donald Arthur 1945- *WhoAmL 92*
**Gifford**, Donald George 1952- *WhoAmL 92*
**Gifford**, Edward Stewart, Jr. 1907- *WrDr 92*
**Gifford**, Ernest Milton 1920- *AmMWSc 92*
**Gifford**, Frank *LesBEnT 92*
**Gifford**, Franklin Andrew, Jr 1922- *AmMWSc 92*
**Gifford**, George Edwin 1924- *AmMWSc 92*
**Gifford**, Gerald F 1939- *AmMWSc 92*
**Gifford**, Gloria 1951- *WhoEnt 92*
**Gifford**, Harold 1906- *AmMWSc 92*
**Gifford**, Helen 1935- *ConCom 92, NewAmDM*
**Gifford**, Henry 1913- *Who 92*
**Gifford**, James Fergus 1940- *AmMWSc 92*
**Gifford**, Jerri Jacklyn 1946- *WhoWest 92*
**Gifford**, John A 1947- *AmMWSc 92*
**Gifford**, John Irving 1930- *WhoMW 92*
**Gifford**, Kathie Lee 1953- *News 92-2 [port]*
**Gifford**, Matt *TwCWW 91*
**Gifford**, Michael Brian 1936- *IntWW 91, Who 92*
**Gifford**, Michael Richard 1959- *WhoRel 92*
**Gifford**, Nelson Sage 1930- *WhoFI 92*
**Gifford**, Ray Wallace, Jr 1923- *AmMWSc 92*
**Gifford**, Sara Elizabeth 1952- *WhoMW 92*
**Gifford**, Thomas 1937- *WrDr 92*
**Gifford**, Timothy Penny 1947- *WhoEnt 92*
**Gifford**, William *DrAPF 91*
**Gifford**, William C. 1941- *WhoAmL 92*
**Gifford**, William Leo 1930- *WhoAmP 91*
**Gifford**, Zerbanoo 1950- *IntAu&W 91*
**Gifter**, Mordecai *WhoMW 92*
**Giftos**, P. Michael 1947- *WhoAmL 92*
**Gigee**, Brian Keith 1954- *WhoRel 92*
**Giger**, Adolf J 1927- *AmMWSc 92*
**Gigerenzer**, Gerd 1947- *ConAu 135*
**Giggal**, Kenneth 1927- *IntAu&W 91*
**Giggall**, George Kenneth 1914- *Who 92*
**Gigger**, Helen C. 1944- *WhoBlA 92*
**Gigger**, Nathaniel Jay 1944- *WhoBlA 92*
**Gigli**, Beniamino 1890-1957 *FacFETw, NewAmDM*
**Gigli**, Irma 1931- *AmMWSc 92*
**Giglio**, Anthony *WhoAmP 91*
**Giglio**, Frank 1933- *WhoAmP 91*
**Giglio**, Frank Peter, Jr. 1960- *WhoEnt 92*
**Giglio**, Paula Alice Moss 1946- *WhoAmL 92*
**Giglio**, Richard John 1937- *AmMWSc 92*
**Giglio**, Steven Rene 1952- *WhoAmL 92*
**Gigliotti**, Donna 1954- *IntMPA 92*
**Gigliotti**, Frank J 1942- *WhoAmP 91*
**Gigliotti**, Helen Jean 1936- *AmMWSc 92*
**Gignac**, Judith Ann 1939- *WhoAmP 91*
**Giguere**, Joseph Charles 1939- *AmMWSc 92*
**Giguere**, Michael Joseph 1947- *WhoAmL 92*
**Giguere**, Roland 1929- *BenetAL 91*
**Gihon**, Albert Leary 1833-1901 *BiInAmS*
**Gijon y Robles**, Rafael 1925- *WhoHisp 92*
**Gikas**, Paul William 1928- *AmMWSc 92*
**Gil**, Andres Valerio 1954- *WhoAmL 92*
**Gil**, Carlos B. 1937- *WhoHisp 92*
**Gil**, David Georg 1924- *IntAu&W 91, WrDr 92*
**Gil**, Federico Guillermo 1915- *WrDr 92*
**Gil**, Francis Rene 1961- *WhoHisp 92*
**Gil**, Gustavo 1950- *WhoHisp 92*
**Gil**, Joan 1940- *AmMWSc 92*
**Gil**, Lourdes 1951- *WhoHisp 92*
**Gil**, Luis A. 1950- *WhoHisp 92*
**Gil**, Mieczyslaw 1944- *IntWW 91*
**Gil**, Salvador 1950- *AmMWSc 92*
**Gil de Biedma**, Jaime 1929-1990 *DcLB 108 [port]*
**Gil de Lamadrid**, Jesus 1926- *AmMWSc 92*
**Gil de Montes**, Roberto 1950- *WhoHisp 92*
**Gil-Robles**, Jose Maria 1899-1980 *FacFETw*
**Gilani**, Shamshad H 1937- *AmMWSc 92*
**Gilardi**, Edward Francis 1936- *AmMWSc 92*
**Gilardi**, Richard D. 1936- *WhoAmL 92*
**Gilardi**, Richard Dean 1940- *AmMWSc 92*
**Gilashvili**, Pavel Georgievich 1918- *IntWW 91*
**Gilb**, Corinne Lathrop 1925- *WhoMW 92*
**Gilb**, Dagoberto *DrAPF 91*
**Gilb**, Dagoberto 1950- *WhoHisp 92*
**Gilbarg**, David 1918- *AmMWSc 92*
**Gilbart**, Andrew James 1950- *Who 92*
**Gilbart-Denham**, Seymour Vivian 1939- *Who 92*
**Gilberd**, Bruce Carlyle *Who 92*
**Gilberg**, Kenneth Roy 1951- *WhoAmL 92*
**Gilbert** *Who 92*
**Gilbert** 1942- *WorArt 1980 [port]*
**Gilbert** 1943- *TwCPaSc*
**Gilbert and George** *TwCPaSc, WorArt 1980 [port]*
**Gilbert**, A. C. *DcTwDes*
**Gilbert**, Alan 1944- *WrDr 92*
**Gilbert**, Alan Jay 1951- *WhoAmL 92*
**Gilbert**, Albert C. 1924- *WhoBlA 92*
**Gilbert**, Alfred 1854-1934 *TwCPaSc*

**Gilbert**, Allan Henry 1929- *AmMWSc 92*
**Gilbert**, Alton Lee 1942- *AmMWSc 92*
**Gilbert**, Amy M. 1895-1980 *ConAu 133*
**Gilbert**, Anna 1916- *IntAu&W 91, WrDr 92*
**Gilbert**, Anthony 1934- *ConCom 92*
**Gilbert**, Arthur C *WhoAmP 91*
**Gilbert**, Arthur Charles 1926- *AmMWSc 92*
**Gilbert**, Arthur Donald 1916- *AmMWSc 92*
**Gilbert**, Arthur Joseph 1915- *WhoRel 92*
**Gilbert**, Arthur N. 1920- *IntMPA 92*
**Gilbert**, Barrie 1937- *AmMWSc 92*
**Gilbert**, Barry Jay 1943- *AmMWSc 92*
**Gilbert**, Barry Kent 1944- *AmMWSc 92*
**Gilbert**, Benjamin Davis 1835-1907 *BiInAmS*
**Gilbert**, Benjamin Franklin 1918- *WrDr 92*
**Gilbert**, Bentley Brinkerhoff 1924- *IntAu&W 91, WrDr 92*
**Gilbert**, Bil 1927- *ConAu 134*
**Gilbert**, Blaine Louis 1940- *WhoAmL 92*
**Gilbert**, Bob 1939- *WhoAmP 91*
**Gilbert**, Brian E 1942- *AmMWSc 92*
**Gilbert**, Bruce 1947- *ConTFT 9, IntMPA 92*
**Gilbert**, Carter Rowell 1930- *AmMWSc 92*
**Gilbert**, Cass 1859-1934 *DcTwDes, FacFETw*
**Gilbert**, Celia *DrAPF 91*
**Gilbert**, Charles Breed, III 1922- *WhoAmP 91*
**Gilbert**, Charles E., III 1949- *WhoAmL 92*
**Gilbert**, Charles Merwin 1910- *AmMWSc 92*
**Gilbert**, Christopher *DrAPF 91*
**Gilbert**, Christopher 1949- *WhoBlA 92*
**Gilbert**, Clark William *WhoIns 92*
**Gilbert**, Clyde Coulter *WhoAmP 91*
**Gilbert**, Creighton Eddy 1924- *WrDr 92*
**Gilbert**, Daniel Lee 1925- *AmMWSc 92*
**Gilbert**, Dave 1930- *WhoEnt 92*
**Gilbert**, David Erwin 1939- *AmMWSc 92*
**Gilbert**, David Lee 1956- *WhoRel 92*
**Gilbert**, Denise Marie 1957- *WhoFI 92*
**Gilbert**, Dewayne Everett 1924- *AmMWSc 92*
**Gilbert**, Don Dale 1934- *AmMWSc 92*
**Gilbert**, Donald 1900-1961 *TwCPaSc*
**Gilbert**, Donald Keith 1955- *WhoRel 92*
**Gilbert**, Dorothy *DrAPF 91*
**Gilbert**, Douglas L 1925- *AmMWSc 92, IntAu&W 91*
**Gilbert**, E. Beth 1949- *WhoEnt 92*
**Gilbert**, E O 1930- *AmMWSc 92*
**Gilbert**, Ed 1943- *WhoAmP 91*
**Gilbert**, Edgar Nelson 1923- *AmMWSc 92*
**Gilbert**, Edward E 1925- *AmMWSc 92*
**Gilbert**, Edward Peter 1956- *WhoAmL 92*
**Gilbert**, Eldridge H. E. 1912- *WhoBlA 92*
**Gilbert**, Elmer G 1930- *AmMWSc 92*
**Gilbert**, Ethel Schaefer 1939- *AmMWSc 92*
**Gilbert**, Eugene Charles 1942- *AmMWSc 92*
**Gilbert**, Felix 1905-1991 *IntWW 91, -91N, NewYTBS 91 [port]*
**Gilbert**, Francis Evalo 1916- *AmMWSc 92*
**Gilbert**, Frank 1934- *WhoAmP 91*
**Gilbert**, Frank Albert 1900- *AmMWSc 92*
**Gilbert**, Franklin Andrew, Sr 1919- *AmMWSc 92*
**Gilbert**, Fred 1941- *AmMWSc 92*
**Gilbert**, Fred D., Jr. 1947- *WhoBlA 92*
**Gilbert**, Fred Ivan, Jr 1920- *AmMWSc 92*
**Gilbert**, Frederick Carnes 1867-1946 *RelLAm 91*
**Gilbert**, Frederick Emerson, Jr 1941- *AmMWSc 92*
**Gilbert**, Frederick Franklin 1941- *AmMWSc 92*
**Gilbert**, Frederick Spofford, Jr. 1939- *WhoFI 92*
**Gilbert**, Gareth E 1921- *AmMWSc 92*
**Gilbert**, Geoffrey Alan 1917- *IntWW 91, Who 92*
**Gilbert**, George Carlton, Sr. 1947- *WhoRel 92*
**Gilbert**, George Lewis 1933- *AmMWSc 92*
**Gilbert**, George Thomas 1954- *WhoEnt 92*
**Gilbert**, Glenn G. 1936- *WrDr 92*
**Gilbert**, Glyn Charles Anglim 1920- *Who 92*
**Gilbert**, Grove Karl 1843-1918 *BiInAmS*
**Gilbert**, Harold Frederick 1916- *WhoFI 92, WhoMW 92*
**Gilbert**, Harriet S 1930- *AmMWSc 92*
**Gilbert**, Harriett 1948- *WrDr 92*
**Gilbert**, Harriett Sarah 1948- *IntAu&W 91*
**Gilbert**, Heather Campbell 1944- *WhoWest 92*
**Gilbert**, Helen Odell 1922- *WhoWest 92*
**Gilbert**, Henry F. 1868-1928 *NewAmDM*
**Gilbert**, Herbert Alan 1931- *WhoAmP 91*
**Gilbert**, Herman Cromwell 1923- *WhoBlA 92*
**Gilbert**, Howard Alden 1935- *WhoMW 92*
**Gilbert**, Howard David 1944- *WhoMW 92*
**Gilbert**, Hugh Campbell 1926- *Who 92*
**Gilbert**, Humphrey 1539?-1583 *BenetAL 91*
**Gilbert**, Ian Grant 1925- *Who 92*
**Gilbert**, Ilsa *DrAPF 91*
**Gilbert**, Ilsa 1933- *IntAu&W 91*
**Gilbert**, J. Freeman 1931- *IntWW 91*
**Gilbert**, Jack *DrAPF 91*
**Gilbert**, Jack 1925- *IntAu&W 91*
**Gilbert**, Jack Pittard 1925- *AmMWSc 92*
**Gilbert**, Jacqueline Ann 1954- *WhoFI 92*
**Gilbert**, James Alan Longmore 1918- *AmMWSc 92*
**Gilbert**, James Cayce 1925- *WhoRel 92*
**Gilbert**, James Freeman 1931- *AmMWSc 92*
**Gilbert**, James Robert 1946- *AmMWSc 92*
**Gilbert**, Jean P. 1928- *WhoBlA 92*
**Gilbert**, Jerome B *AmMWSc 92*
**Gilbert**, Jimmie D 1934- *AmMWSc 92*
**Gilbert**, Joel Sterling 1935- *AmMWSc 92*
**Gilbert**, John Andrew 1948- *AmMWSc 92*
**Gilbert**, John Barry 1937- *AmMWSc 92*
**Gilbert**, John Cannon 1908- *Who 92*
**Gilbert**, John Carl 1939- *AmMWSc 92*
**Gilbert**, John Jouett 1937- *AmMWSc 92*
**Gilbert**, John Laurence 1950- *WhoAmL 92*
**Gilbert**, John Nunneley, Jr. *WhoIns 92*
**Gilbert**, John Orman 1907- *Who 92*
**Gilbert**, John Raphael 1926- *IntAu&W 91, WrDr 92*
**Gilbert**, John William 1927- *Who 92*
**Gilbert**, Joseph 1931- *Who 92*
**Gilbert**, Judith Arlene 1946- *WhoAmL 92*
**Gilbert**, Judith May 1934- *WhoRel 92*
**Gilbert**, Katherine Everett 1886-1952 *DcNCBi 2*
**Gilbert**, Kenneth 1931- *NewAmDM*
**Gilbert**, Kenneth Albert 1931- *IntWW 91, WhoEnt 92*
**Gilbert**, Larry Alan 1945- *WhoRel 92*
**Gilbert**, Lawrence Irwin 1929- *AmMWSc 92*
**Gilbert**, Lewis 1920- *ConTFT 9, IntMPA 92, IntWW 91*
**Gilbert**, Lorna A. 1943- *WhoAmL 92*
**Gilbert**, Margaret Lois 1928- *AmMWSc 92*
**Gilbert**, Margot R 1949- *WhoAmP 91*
**Gilbert**, Marie *DrAPF 91*
**Gilbert**, Mark Joseph 1959- *WhoAmL 92*
**Gilbert**, Martin 1936- *CurBio 91 [port], IntAu&W 91, IntWW 91, Who 92, WrDr 92*
**Gilbert**, Mary *WrDr 92*
**Gilbert**, Melissa 1964- *WhoEnt 92*
**Gilbert**, Michael *NewYTBS 91 [port]*
**Gilbert**, Michael 1912- *ConAu 15AS [port], IntAu&W 91, WrDr 92*
**Gilbert**, Michael Dale 1951- *WhoRel 92, WhoWest 92*
**Gilbert**, Michael Francis 1912- *Who 92*
**Gilbert**, Michael William 1954- *WhoEnt 92*
**Gilbert**, Murray Charles 1936- *AmMWSc 92*
**Gilbert**, Myron B 1921- *AmMWSc 92*
**Gilbert**, Pamela Jayne 1946- *WhoWest 92*
**Gilbert**, Patrick Nigel Geoffrey 1934- *Who 92, WhoRel 92*
**Gilbert**, Paul T 1876- *ScFEYrs*
**Gilbert**, Paul Wilner 1916- *AmMWSc 92*
**Gilbert**, Perry Webster 1912- *AmMWSc 92*
**Gilbert**, Phillip Evans 1962- *WhoFI 92*
**Gilbert**, R J 1923- *AmMWSc 92*
**Gilbert**, Rachel Shaw *WhoAmP 91, WhoWest 92*
**Gilbert**, Ralph James 1929- *WhoAmL 92*
**Gilbert**, Ray Wilson, Jr. 1951- *WhoFI 92*
**Gilbert**, Richard 1957- *TwCPaSc*
**Gilbert**, Richard Carl 1927- *AmMWSc 92*
**Gilbert**, Richard Dean 1920- *AmMWSc 92*
**Gilbert**, Richard E 1933- *AmMWSc 92*
**Gilbert**, Richard Gene 1935- *AmMWSc 92*
**Gilbert**, Richard Joel 1948- *WhoAmL 92*
**Gilbert**, Richard Lannear 1921- *WhoBlA 92*
**Gilbert**, Richard Lapham, Jr 1916- *AmMWSc 92*
**Gilbert**, Robert 1924- *AmMWSc 92*
**Gilbert**, Robert Andrew 1942- *IntAu&W 91*
**Gilbert**, Robert L 1931- *AmMWSc 92*
**Gilbert**, Robert Patrick 1952- *WhoEnt 92*
**Gilbert**, Robert Pertsch 1932- *AmMWSc 92*
**Gilbert**, Robert Pettibone 1917- *AmMWSc 92*
**Gilbert**, Robert Wolfe 1920- *WhoWest 92*
**Gilbert**, Roger Whitney 1932- *WhoIns 92*
**Gilbert**, Ronald Rhea 1942- *WhoAmL 92*
**Gilbert**, Ross Joseph 1953- *WhoFI 92, WhoMW 92*
**Gilbert**, Ruth 1917- *WrDr 92*
**Gilbert**, Sandra M. *DrAPF 91*
**Gilbert**, Sandra M. 1936- *BenetAL 91, WrDr 92*
**Gilbert**, Scott F 1949- *AmMWSc 92*
**Gilbert**, Seymour George 1914- *AmMWSc 92*
**Gilbert**, Sharon May 1948- *WhoRel 92*
**Gilbert**, Stanley Leon 1940- *WhoAmL 92*
**Gilbert**, Stephen 1910- *IntWW 91*
**Gilbert**, Stephen Alan 1939- *WhoFI 92, WhoIns 92*
**Gilbert**, Stephen L. 1943- *WhoWest 92*
**Gilbert**, Stephen Marc 1941- *AmMWSc 92*
**Gilbert**, Steven Edward 1943- *WhoWest 92*
**Gilbert**, Steven Jeffrey 1947- *WhoEnt 92*
**Gilbert**, Stuart William 1926- *Who 92*
**Gilbert**, Susan Ann 1950- *WhoWest 92*
**Gilbert**, Susan Cosby 1964- *WhoRel 92*
**Gilbert**, Susan Pond *AmMWSc 92*
**Gilbert**, Theodore William, Jr 1929- *AmMWSc 92*
**Gilbert**, Thomas Angus 1948- *WhoWest 92*
**Gilbert**, Thomas Edward 1952- *WhoMW 92*
**Gilbert**, Thomas Lewis 1922- *AmMWSc 92*
**Gilbert**, Thomas Rexford 1946- *AmMWSc 92*
**Gilbert**, Vincent Newton 1955- *WhoMW 92*
**Gilbert**, Virginia *DrAPF 91*
**Gilbert**, W D 1910- *AmMWSc 92*
**Gilbert**, W.S. 1836-1911 *RfGEnL 91*
**Gilbert**, Walter 1932- *AmMWSc 92, IntWW 91, Who 92, WhoNob 90*
**Gilbert**, Walter Wilson 1922- *AmMWSc 92*
**Gilbert**, William 1735-1790 *DcNCBi 2*
**Gilbert**, William Best 1921- *AmMWSc 92*
**Gilbert**, William Henry, III 1939- *AmMWSc 92*
**Gilbert**, William Irwin 1915- *AmMWSc 92*
**Gilbert**, William James 1916- *AmMWSc 92*
**Gilbert**, William S. 1836-1911 *NewAmDM*
**Gilbert**, William Spencer 1927- *AmMWSc 92*
**Gilbert-Barness**, Enid F 1927- *AmMWSc 92*
**Gilbert-Brinkman**, Melissa 1964- *IntMPA 92*
**Gilbertsen**, Ralph Wayne 1954- *WhoMW 92*
**Gilbertsen**, Richard B *AmMWSc 92*
**Gilbertsen**, Victor Adolph 1924- *AmMWSc 92*
**Gilbertson**, Donald Edmund 1934- *AmMWSc 92*
**Gilbertson**, Eric Raymond 1945- *WhoMW 92*
**Gilbertson**, Geoffrey d1991 *Who 92N*
**Gilbertson**, John R 1929- *AmMWSc 92*
**Gilbertson**, Michael 1945- *AmMWSc 92*
**Gilbertson**, Oswald Irving 1927- *WhoFI 92, WhoWest 92*
**Gilbertson**, Peter Allan 1953- *WhoFI 92*
**Gilbertson**, Robert Lee 1925- *AmMWSc 92*
**Gilbertson**, Sherry Marie 1959- *WhoAmL 92*
**Gilbertson**, Steven Edward 1951- *WhoMW 92*
**Gilbertson**, Terry Joel 1939- *AmMWSc 92*
**Gilbey** *Who 92*
**Gilbey**, Derek 1913- *Who 92*
**Gilbo**, Anna-Carolyn Stirewalt *DrAPF 91*
**Gilboa**, Yehoshua A. 1918-1981 *ConAu 35NR*
**Gilbody**, Wendolyn Marie 1945- *WhoWest 92*
**Gilboe**, Daniel Pierre 1934- *AmMWSc 92*
**Gilboe**, David Dougherty 1929- *AmMWSc 92*
**Gilboy**, Michael Russell 1950- *WhoFI 92*
**Gilbreath**, Freida Carol 1949- *WhoFI 92*
**Gilbreath**, Jerry Michael 1948- *WhoAmP 91*
**Gilbreath**, Sidney Gordon, III 1931- *AmMWSc 92*
**Gilbreath**, William Pollock 1936- *AmMWSc 92*
**Gilbrech**, Donald Albert 1927- *AmMWSc 92*
**Gilbreth**, Lillian Evelyn 1878-1972 *HanAmWH*
**Gilbreth**, Lillian Moller 1878-1972 *WomPsyc*
**Gilbreth**, Robert M 1920- *WhoAmP 91*
**Gilbride**, William Donald 1924- *WhoAmL 92*
**Gilby**, Stephen Warner 1939- *AmMWSc 92*
**Gilchrest**, Thornton Charles 1931- *WhoMW 92*
**Gilchrest**, Wayne T. 1946- *AlmAP 92 [port], WhoAmP 91*
**Gilchriest**, Lorenzo 1938- *WhoBlA 92*
**Gilchrist**, Andrew 1910- *Who 92*
**Gilchrist**, Andrew Graham 1910- *IntWW 91*
**Gilchrist**, Andrew Rae 1899- *Who 92*
**Gilchrist**, Archibald 1929- *Who 92*
**Gilchrist**, Bruce 1930- *AmMWSc 92*
**Gilchrist**, Carlton Chester 1935- *WhoBlA 92*
**Gilchrist**, Charles W 1936- *WhoAmP 91*
**Gilchrist**, Charles Waters 1936- *WhoRel 92*
**Gilchrist**, Elizabeth *DrAPF 91*
**Gilchrist**, Ellen *DrAPF 91*
**Gilchrist**, Ellen 1935- *BenetAL 91, ConNov 91, WrDr 92*
**Gilchrist**, Essie Ford 1950- *WhoWest 92*
**Gilchrist**, Jack Philip 1961- *WhoAmL 92*
**Gilchrist**, Jay 1952- *WhoRel 92*
**Gilchrist**, John *WrDr 92*
**Gilchrist**, Kelvin Keith 1951- *WhoMW 92*
**Gilchrist**, Peter Spence 1861-1947 *DcNCBi 2*
**Gilchrist**, Philip Thomson 1865-1956 *TwCPaSc*
**Gilchrist**, Rae *Who 92*
**Gilchrist**, Ralph E 1926- *AmMWSc 92*
**Gilchrist**, Richard Irwin 1946- *WhoWest 92*
**Gilchrist**, Robertson 1926- *WhoBlA 92*
**Gilchrist**, Thomas 1735?-1789 *DcNCBi 2*
**Gilchrist**, William Risque, Jr. 1944- *WhoFI 92*
**Gilcreast**, Conway, Sr. 1924- *WhoBlA 92*
**Gilcrest**, Roger Allen 1955- *WhoAmL 92*
**Gildas** *EncEarC*
**Gilde**, Hans-Georg 1933- *AmMWSc 92, WhoMW 92*
**Gildea**, Brian Michael 1939- *WhoAmL 92*
**Gildehaus**, Thomas Arthur 1940- *WhoFI 92, WhoMW 92*
**Gilden**, Carol Valerie 1956- *WhoAmL 92*
**Gilden**, Donald Harvey 1937- *AmMWSc 92*
**Gilden**, Glen Garth 1926- *WhoRel 92*
**Gilden**, K. B. *ConAu 134*
**Gilden**, Katya Alpert d1991 *NewYTBS 91*
**Gilden**, Katya Alpert 1919?-1991 *ConAu 134*
**Gilden**, Raymond Victor 1935- *AmMWSc 92*
**Gilden**, Richard Henry 1946- *WhoAmL 92*
**Gildenberg**, Philip Leon 1935- *AmMWSc 92*
**Gildenhorn**, Hyman L 1921- *AmMWSc 92*
**Gildenhorn**, Joseph B 1929- *WhoAmP 91*
**Gildenhorn**, Stanton J 1942- *WhoAmP 91*
**Gilder**, Richard Watson 1844-1909 *BenetAL 91*
**Gilder**, Robert Charles 1923- *Who 92*
**Gildersleeve**, Basil L. 1831-1924 *BenetAL 91*
**Gildersleeve**, Benjamin 1907- *AmMWSc 92*
**Gildersleeve**, Larry Benjamin 1949- *WhoFI 92*
**Gildersleeve**, Nathaniel 1871-1919 *BiInAmS*
**Gildersleeve**, Richard E 1914- *AmMWSc 92*
**Gildersleeve**, Thomas 1927- *IntAu&W 91*
**Gildersleeve**, Virginia Crocheron 1877-1965 *AmPeW*
**Gildner**, Gary *DrAPF 91*
**Gildner**, Gary 1938- *ConPo 91, WrDr 92*
**Gildner**, Gregory Lawrence 1956- *WhoFI 92*
**Gildred**, Theodore E 1935- *WhoAmP 91*
**Gildred**, Theodore Edmonds 1935- *IntWW 91*
**Gildseth**, Wayne 1935- *AmMWSc 92*
**Gildston**, Phyllis *WhoEnt 92*
**Gile**, David Russell 1959- *WhoMW 92*
**Gile**, Leland Henry 1920- *AmMWSc 92*
**Gilels**, Emil 1916-1985 *FacFETw, NewAmDM*
**Gilel's**, Emil' Grigor'evich 1916-1985 *SovUnBD*
**Giler**, David *IntMPA 92*
**Giles** *Who 92*
**Giles Corey** *BenetAL 91*
**Giles of Rome** 1243?-1316 *DcLB 115*
**Giles**, Abraham L *WhoAmP 91*
**Giles**, Allen 1924- *WhoEnt 92*
**Giles**, Althea B. 1926- *WhoBlA 92*
**Giles**, Anne Diener 1948- *WhoEnt 92*
**Giles**, Carl Ronald 1916- *Who 92*
**Giles**, Charles Winston 1942- *WhoBlA 92*
**Giles**, Clarence Alfred 1946- *WhoFI 92*
**Giles**, Conrad Leslie 1934- *WhoMW 92*
**Giles**, Eugene 1933- *AmMWSc 92*
**Giles**, Everett L 1917- *WhoAmP 91*
**Giles**, Frank 1919- *ConAu 133*
**Giles**, Frank Thomas Robertson 1919- *IntAu&W 91, Who 92*
**Giles**, Geoffrey Reginald 1936- *Who 92*
**Giles**, Gerald Lynn 1943- *WhoWest 92*
**Giles**, Graham 1942- *TwCPaSc*
**Giles**, Gregory Ross 1962- *WhoAmL 92*
**Giles**, Henrietta 1962- *WhoBlA 92*
**Giles**, Homer Wayne 1919- *WhoFI 92, WhoMW 92*
**Giles**, Jack 1945- *TwCWW 91, WrDr 92*
**Giles**, James T. *WhoBlA 92*
**Giles**, James T. 1943- *WhoAmL 92*
**Giles**, Jesse Albion, III 1931- *AmMWSc 92*

**Giles**, Jimmie, Jr. 1954- *WhoBlA 92*
**Giles**, Jimmie Drexal 1939- *WhoEnt 92*
**Giles**, Joe L. 1943- *WhoBlA 92*
**Giles**, John 1921- *WrDr 92*
**Giles**, John Crutchlow 1934- *AmMWSc 92*
**Giles**, Judith Margaret 1939- *WhoRel 92*
**Giles**, Kris *IntAu&W 91X*
**Giles**, Maggi 1938- *TwCPaSc*
**Giles**, Mark Allen 1965- *WhoFI 92*
**Giles**, Michael Arthur 1943- *AmMWSc 92*
**Giles**, Michael Kent 1945- *AmMWSc 92*
**Giles**, Molly *DrAPF 91*
**Giles**, Morgan Charles M. *Who 92*
**Giles**, Nancy 1960- *WhoBlA 92*
**Giles**, Norman Henry 1915- *AmMWSc 92*
**Giles**, Pauline *Who 92*
**Giles**, Percy 1952- *WhoAmP 91*
**Giles**, Peter Cobb 1929- *AmMWSc 92*
**Giles**, Ralph E 1941- *AmMWSc 92*
**Giles**, Ray A 1923- *WhoAmP 91*
**Giles**, Robert Frederick 1918- *Who 92*
**Giles**, Robert H, Jr 1933- *AmMWSc 92*
**Giles**, Robert Hartmann 1933- *WhoMW 92*
**Giles**, Robin 1926- *AmMWSc 92*
**Giles**, Robin Arthur 1936- *AmMWSc 92*
**Giles**, Roy Curtis 1932- *Who 92*
**Giles**, Sondra Leah 1940- *WhoAmL 92*
**Giles**, Thomas Davis 1938- *AmMWSc 92*
**Giles**, Tony 1925- *TwCPaSc*
**Giles**, Waldron H. 1932- *WhoBlA 92*
**Giles**, Warren 1896-1979 *FacFETw*
**Giles**, William Jefferson, III 1936- *WhoAmL 92*
**Giles**, William R. 1925- *WhoBlA 92*
**Giles**, Willie Anthony, Jr. 1941- *WhoBlA 92*
**Giles-Gee**, Helen Foster 1950- *WhoBlA 92*
**Giletti**, Bruno John 1929- *AmMWSc 92*
**Gilfeather**, Frank L 1942- *AmMWSc 92*
**Gilfert**, James C 1927- *AmMWSc 92*
**Gilfillan**, Alasdair Mitchell 1956- *AmMWSc 92*
**Gilfillan**, Merrill *DrAPF 91*
**Gilfillan**, Robert Frederick 1923- *AmMWSc 92*
**Gilfix**, Edward Leon 1923- *AmMWSc 92*
**Gilford**, Jack 1907-1990 *AnObit 1990, FacFETw*
**Gilford**, Leon 1917- *AmMWSc 92*
**Gilford**, Rotea J. 1927- *WhoBlA 92*
**Gilford**, Steven Ross 1952- *WhoAmL 92*
**Gilfrich**, John Valentine 1927- *AmMWSc 92*
**Gilg**, Joseph George 1926- *WhoWest 92*
**Gilgan**, Michael Wilson 1938- *AmMWSc 92*
**Gilger**, Paul Douglass 1954- *WhoWest 92*
**Gilgore**, Sheldon Gerald 1932- *WhoMW 92*
**Gilgun**, John F. *DrAPF 91*
**Gilgun**, John Joseph 1937- *WhoAmP 91*
**Gilham**, Peter Thomas 1930- *AmMWSc 92*
**Gilhespy**, Tom 1944- *TwCPaSc*
**Gili**, Katherine 1948- *TwCPaSc*
**Giliberti**, Barbara Claire 1954- *WhoAmL 92*
**Gilij**, Felipe Salvador 1721-1789 *HisDSpE*
**Gililland**, Michael Lane 1946- *WhoMW 92*
**Gilinsky**, Victor 1934- *AmMWSc 92, WhoAmP 91*
**Gilinson**, Philip J, Jr 1914- *AmMWSc 92*
**Giliomee**, Hermann Buhr 1938- *IntWW 91*
**Gilje**, John 1939- *AmMWSc 92*
**Gilkerson**, William Richard 1926- *AmMWSc 92*
**Gilkes**, Arthur Gwyer 1915- *WhoAmL 92, WhoMW 92*
**Gilkes**, Cheryl Townsend 1947- *WhoBlA 92*
**Gilkeson**, M Mack 1922- *AmMWSc 92*
**Gilkeson**, Raymond Allen 1921- *AmMWSc 92*
**Gilkeson**, Robert Fairbairn 1917- *AmMWSc 92*
**Gilkey**, Gordon Waverly 1912- *WhoWest 92*
**Gilkey**, J. L. *WhoRel 92*
**Gilkey**, John Clark *AmMWSc 92*
**Gilkey**, Langdon Brown 1919- *WhoRel 92*
**Gilkey**, Peter Belden 1946- *AmMWSc 92*
**Gilkey**, Russell 1920- *AmMWSc 92*
**Gilkey**, William C. 1932- *WhoBlA 92*
**Gilkie**, Robert James 1935- *WhoAmP 91*
**Gilkison**, Alan Fleming d1990 *Who 92N*
**Gill** 1840-1885 *ThHElm*
**Gill**, Anthony Keith 1930- *IntWW 91, Who 92*
**Gill**, Ardian 1929- *WhoIns 92*
**Gill**, Arthur Eric Rowton 1882-1940 *DcTwDes, FacFETw*
**Gill**, Ayesha Elenin 1933- *AmMWSc 92*
**Gill**, B. M. *WrDr 92*
**Gill**, Barbara A *WhoAmP 91*
**Gill**, Bartholomew *WrDr 92*
**Gill**, Betty 1921- *WhoAmP 91*
**Gill**, Bikram Singh *AmMWSc 92*
**Gill**, Brendan *DrAPF 91*
**Gill**, Brendan 1914- *ConNov 91, IntWW 91, WrDr 92*
**Gill**, Brian 1942- *Who 92*
**Gill**, C Burroughs 1921- *AmMWSc 92*
**Gill**, Christopher John Fred 1936- *Who 92*
**Gill**, Clifford Cressey 1921- *AmMWSc 92*
**Gill**, Colin Unwin 1892-1940 *TwCPaSc*
**Gill**, Cyril James 1904- *Who 92*
**Gill**, David 1928- *Who 92*
**Gill**, David 1934- *ConPo 91, IntAu&W 91, WrDr 92*
**Gill**, David Gordon 1947- *WhoWest 92*
**Gill**, David Lloyd 1949- *WhoAmL 92*
**Gill**, David Meeker 1934- *WhoAmL 92*
**Gill**, David Michael 1940- *AmMWSc 92*
**Gill**, David Walter 1946- *WhoRel 92*
**Gill**, Dhanwant Singh 1941- *AmMWSc 92*
**Gill**, Douglas Edward 1944- *AmMWSc 92*
**Gill**, E. Ann 1951- *WhoAmL 92*
**Gill**, Edwin Maurice 1899-1978 *DcNCBi 2*
**Gill**, Elbert T, Jr *WhoAmP 91*
**Gill**, Eric 1882-1940 *TwCPaSc*
**Gill**, Frank Bennington 1941- *AmMWSc 92*
**Gill**, Gail Louise 1955- *WhoMW 92*
**Gill**, George Malcolm 1934- *Who 92*
**Gill**, George Wilhelm 1941- *AmMWSc 92, WhoWest 92*
**Gill**, Gerald Robert 1948- *WhoBlA 92*
**Gill**, Gillian *ConAu 134*
**Gill**, Gillian C. 1942- *ConAu 134*
**Gill**, Gordon Nelson 1937- *AmMWSc 92*
**Gill**, Gregory William 1962- *WhoAmL 92*
**Gill**, Gurcharan S 1935- *AmMWSc 92*
**Gill**, Harmohindar Singh 1933- *AmMWSc 92*
**Gill**, Harold Edward 1957- *WhoAmL 92*
**Gill**, Harold Hatfield 1921- *AmMWSc 92*
**Gill**, Harry 1922- *Who 92*
**Gill**, Harry Douglas 1861?-1918 *BiInAmS*
**Gill**, Ian Gordon 1919- *Who 92*
**Gill**, Jack 1930- *Who 92*
**Gill**, James Edward 1931- *AmMWSc 92*
**Gill**, James Kenneth 1920- *Who 92*
**Gill**, Jeffrey Harold 1955- *WhoRel 92*
**Gill**, Jerry H. 1933- *WrDr 92*
**Gill**, Jerry Henry 1933- *IntAu&W 91*
**Gill**, John J. 1932- *WhoAmL 92*
**Gill**, John J. 1959- *WhoFI 92*
**Gill**, John Leslie 1935- *AmMWSc 92, WhoMW 92*
**Gill**, John Paul, Jr 1937- *AmMWSc 92*
**Gill**, John Russell, Jr 1929- *AmMWSc 92*
**Gill**, John Welch, Jr. 1942- *WhoAmL 92*
**Gill**, Keith Hubert 1929- *WhoAmL 92*
**Gill**, Kendall Cedric 1968- *WhoBlA 92*
**Gill**, Kenneth 1927- *Who 92*
**Gill**, Kenneth Duane 1946- *WhoRel 92*
**Gill**, Kenneth Edward 1932- *Who 92*
**Gill**, Leonard William George 1918- *Who 92*
**Gill**, Louis John 1940- *WhoAmP 91*
**Gill**, Lyle Bennett 1916- *WhoMW 92*
**Gill**, Macdonald 1884-1947 *TwCPaSc*
**Gill**, Madge 1882-1961 *TwCPaSc*
**Gill**, Malcolm *Who 92*
**Gill**, Margaret Gaskins 1940- *WhoAmL 92*
**Gill**, Margaret S *WhoAmP 91*
**Gill**, Mary S 1921- *IntAu&W 91*
**Gill**, Merton 1914- *AmMWSc 92*
**Gill**, Michael *LesBEnT 92*
**Gill**, Milton Randall 1950- *WhoRel 92*
**Gill**, Myrna Lakshmi 1943- *WrDr 92*
**Gill**, Patrick David 1944- *WhoAmL 92*
**Gill**, Patrick F 1955- *WhoAmP 91*
**Gill**, Patrick William 1952- *WhoEnt 92*
**Gill**, Peter 1939- *Who 92, WrDr 92*
**Gill**, Piara Singh 1940- *AmMWSc 92*
**Gill**, Randall Allen 1958- *WhoAmL 92*
**Gill**, Rebecca LaLosh 1944- *WhoWest 92*
**Gill**, Richard Lawrence 1946- *WhoAmL 92*
**Gill**, Richard Thomas 1927- *WhoEnt 92*
**Gill**, Robert Anthony 1928- *AmMWSc 92*
**Gill**, Robert Lewis 1912- *WhoBlA 92*
**Gill**, Robert T. 1946- *WhoAmL 92*
**Gill**, Robert Wager 1940- *AmMWSc 92*
**Gill**, Robert William 1929- *IntAu&W 91*
**Gill**, Robin Denys 1927- *Who 92*
**Gill**, Ronald Crispin 1916- *WrDr 92*
**Gill**, Ronald Lee 1949- *AmMWSc 92*
**Gill**, Rosa Underwood 1944- *WhoBlA 92*
**Gill**, Samuel A. 1932- *WhoBlA 92*
**Gill**, Stanley Jensen 1929- *AmMWSc 92*
**Gill**, Stanley Sanderson 1923- *Who 92*
**Gill**, Stephen Joel 1947- *WhoMW 92*
**Gill**, Stephen Paschall 1938- *AmMWSc 92*
**Gill**, Theodore Nicholas 1837-1914 *BiInAmS*
**Gill**, Thomas James, III 1932- *AmMWSc 92*
**Gill**, Thomas M 1941- *WhoIns 92*
**Gill**, Thomas Stratton 1941- *WhoAmL 92*
**Gill**, Troy D. 1937- *WhoBlA 92*
**Gill**, Vince 1957- *ConMus 7 [port]*
**Gill**, Walter Harris 1937- *WhoMW 92*
**Gill**, Wanda Eileen 1945- *WhoEnt 92*
**Gill**, Wilfred George 1912- *WhoFI 92*
**Gill**, William D 1935- *AmMWSc 92*
**Gill**, William Joseph 1944- *AmMWSc 92*
**Gill**, William N 1928- *AmMWSc 92*
**Gill**, William Robert 1920- *AmMWSc 92*
**Gillam**, Basil Early 1913- *AmMWSc 92*
**Gillam**, Denys Edgar d1991 *Who 92N*
**Gillam**, Harry Lee, Jr. 1954- *WhoAmL 92*
**Gillam**, Isaac Thomas, IV 1932- *WhoBlA 92*
**Gillam**, John B, III 1946- *WhoAmP 91*
**Gillam**, Marshall Robert 1942- *WhoRel 92*
**Gillam**, Max Lee 1926- *WhoAmL 92*
**Gillam**, Patrick John 1933- *IntWW 91, Who 92, WhoFI 92*
**Gillam**, Stanley George 1915- *Who 92*
**Gillan**, Maria Mazziotti *DrAPF 91*
**Gillan**, Maria Mazziotti 1940- *WhoEnt 92*
**Gilland**, Gina Ruth 1955- *WhoRel 92*
**Gillanders**, Lewis Alexander 1925- *Who 92*
**Gillard**, Baiba Kurins 1946- *AmMWSc 92*
**Gillard**, Francis George 1908- *IntWW 91, Who 92*
**Gillard**, Stuart Thomas 1946- *WhoEnt 92*
**Gillary**, Howard L 1940- *AmMWSc 92*
**Gillaspy**, James Edward 1917- *AmMWSc 92*
**Gillaspy**, Richard *LesBEnT 92*
**Gillaspy**, Richard M. 1927- *IntMPA 92*
**Gillchrest**, Robert Raymond 1946- *WhoRel 92*
**Gille**, John Charles 1934- *AmMWSc 92*
**Gillece**, James Patrick, Jr. 1944- *WhoAmL 92*
**Gilleland**, Ken Orrin 1952- *WhoEnt 92*
**Gilleland**, Martha Jane 1940- *AmMWSc 92*
**Gillels**, Elizaveta 1919- *IntWW 91*
**Gillen**, James Robert 1937- *WhoAmL 92*
**Gillen**, Keith Thomas 1942- *AmMWSc 92*
**Gillen**, Kenneth Todd 1942- *AmMWSc 92*
**Gillen**, William Albert 1914- *WhoAmL 92*
**Gillenwater**, Jay Young 1933- *AmMWSc 92*
**Giller**, E B 1918- *AmMWSc 92*
**Giller**, Edward Bonfoy 1918- *WhoWest 92*
**Giller**, Molly 1942- *WhoRel 92*
**Giller**, Norman Myer 1918- *WhoFI 92*
**Gillerman**, Gerald 1924- *WhoAmL 92*
**Gillers**, Stephen 1943- *WhoAmL 92*
**Gilles**, Daniel 1917- *IntWW 91*
**Gilles**, Dennis Cyril 1925- *Who 92*
**Gilles**, Floyd Harry 1930- *AmMWSc 92*
**Gilles**, Herbert Michael Joseph 1921- *Who 92*
**Gilles**, Kenneth Albert 1922- *AmMWSc 92*
**Gilles**, Paul Wilson 1921- *AmMWSc 92*
**Gillespie**, Alastair William 1922- *IntWW 91*
**Gillespie**, Arthur Samuel, Jr 1931- *AmMWSc 92*
**Gillespie**, Asa Isekiar 1928- *WhoRel 92*
**Gillespie**, Avon E. 1938- *WhoBlA 92*
**Gillespie**, Bonita 1951- *WhoBlA 92*
**Gillespie**, Carolyn Mary 1948- *WhoEnt 92*
**Gillespie**, Charles A, Jr 1935- *WhoAmP 91*
**Gillespie**, Charles Anthony, Jr. 1935- *IntWW 91*
**Gillespie**, Claude Milton 1932- *AmMWSc 92*
**Gillespie**, Colleen Patricia 1958- *WhoAmL 92*
**Gillespie**, Cynthia K. 1941- *ConAu 133*
**Gillespie**, Daniel Thomas 1938- *AmMWSc 92*
**Gillespie**, Dizzy 1917- *ConBlB 1 [port], ConMus 6 [port], NewAmDM, WhoBlA 92, WhoEnt 92*
**Gillespie**, Elizabeth 1936- *AmMWSc 92*
**Gillespie**, Eugene 1922- *WhoAmP 91*
**Gillespie**, G Richard 1926- *AmMWSc 92*
**Gillespie**, Gardest 1943- *WhoAmP 91*
**Gillespie**, Gary Don 1943- *WhoMW 92*
**Gillespie**, George H 1945- *AmMWSc 92*
**Gillespie**, George Joseph, III 1930- *WhoAmL 92*
**Gillespie**, George Yancey 1943- *AmMWSc 92*
**Gillespie**, Gerald 1933- *WrDr 92*
**Gillespie**, Gerald Leroy 1949- *WhoMW 92*
**Gillespie**, Henry d1991 *LesBEnT 92*
**Gillespie**, Houston Oliver, Jr. 1941- *WhoEnt 92*
**Gillespie**, Iain E. 1931- *IntWW 91*
**Gillespie**, Iain Erskine 1931- *Who 92*
**Gillespie**, J. Martin 1949- *WhoFI 92, WhoMW 92*
**Gillespie**, James 1747-1805 *DcNCBi 2*
**Gillespie**, James Davis 1955- *WhoAmL 92*
**Gillespie**, James Howard 1917- *AmMWSc 92*
**Gillespie**, James Laurence 1946- *WhoMW 92*
**Gillespie**, Jane Lee 1957- *WhoAmP 91*
**Gillespie**, Jerry *WhoAmP 91*
**Gillespie**, Jerry Ray 1937- *AmMWSc 92*
**Gillespie**, Jesse Samuel, Jr 1921- *AmMWSc 92*
**Gillespie**, Joe Daniel 1947- *WhoFI 92*
**Gillespie**, John 1936- *AmMWSc 92*
**Gillespie**, John Birks 1917- *FacFETw [port], IntWW 91*
**Gillespie**, John Fagan 1936- *WhoFI 92*
**Gillespie**, John Spence 1926- *Who 92*
**Gillespie**, Judith *WhoRel 92*
**Gillespie**, L. Kay 1940- *WhoWest 92*
**Gillespie**, LaRoux King 1942- *AmMWSc 92*
**Gillespie**, Marcia A. 1944- *WhoBlA 92*
**Gillespie**, Marcia Ann 1944- *ConAu 134*
**Gillespie**, Marilyn Iola 1940- *WhoAmP 91*
**Gillespie**, Michael 1929- *TwCPaSc*
**Gillespie**, Netta *DrAPF 91*
**Gillespie**, O Stanley 1916- *WhoAmP 91*
**Gillespie**, Rena Harrell 1949- *WhoBlA 92*
**Gillespie**, Rhondda 1941- *IntWW 91*
**Gillespie**, Robert B. *WrDr 92*
**Gillespie**, Robert B 1917- *IntAu&W 91*
**Gillespie**, Robert Howard 1916- *AmMWSc 92*
**Gillespie**, Robert Paul 1947- *WhoMW 92*
**Gillespie**, Robert Wayne 1944- *WhoMW 92*
**Gillespie**, Ronald James 1924- *AmMWSc 92, IntWW 91, Who 92*
**Gillespie**, Rowan 1953- *TwCPaSc*
**Gillespie**, Terry James 1941- *AmMWSc 92*
**Gillespie**, Thomas David 1939- *AmMWSc 92*
**Gillespie**, Thomas William 1928- *WhoRel 92*
**Gillespie**, Todd Allen 1962- *WhoMW 92*
**Gillespie**, Tom P., Jr. *WhoBlA 92*
**Gillespie**, Walter Lee 1930- *AmMWSc 92*
**Gillespie**, William G. 1931- *WhoBlA 92*
**Gillespie**, William Harry 1931- *AmMWSc 92*
**Gillespie**, William Hewitt 1905- *Who 92*
**Gillespy**, Clark Sutton 1961- *WhoAmL 92*
**Gillett**, Charlie 1942- *IntAu&W 91, WrDr 92*
**Gillett**, David Keith 1945- *Who 92*
**Gillett**, Fran 1928- *WhoAmP 91*
**Gillett**, Frederick Huntington 1851-1935 *AmPolLe*
**Gillett**, George Nield, Jr. 1938- *WhoEnt 92, WhoWest 92*
**Gillett**, Jack James 1943- *WhoEnt 92*
**Gillett**, Lawrence B 1931- *AmMWSc 92*
**Gillett**, Margaret 1930- *IntAu&W 91, WrDr 92*
**Gillett**, Robin 1925- *Who 92*
**Gillett**, Robin Danvers Penrose 1925- *IntWW 91*
**Gillett**, Tedford A 1935- *AmMWSc 92*
**Gillett**, Victor William, Jr. 1932- *WhoFI 92*
**Gillett**, William Coe 1964- *WhoEnt 92*
**Gillette** *IntAu&W 91X*
**Gillette**, Anita 1938- *WhoEnt 92*
**Gillette**, Bob *WrDr 92*
**Gillette**, David Duane 1946- *AmMWSc 92*
**Gillette**, Dean 1925- *AmMWSc 92*
**Gillette**, Edward LeRoy 1932- *AmMWSc 92*
**Gillette**, Eric Allison 1935- *WhoWest 92*
**Gillette**, Ethel 1923- *IntAu&W 91*
**Gillette**, Frankie Jacobs 1925- *WhoBlA 92*
**Gillette**, George Frederick 1925- *WhoRel 92*
**Gillette**, Harriet Ellen 1914- *WhoMW 92*
**Gillette**, James Robert 1928- *AmMWSc 92*
**Gillette**, Jay Michael 1939- *WhoEnt 92*
**Gillette**, John Albert 1958- *WhoFI 92*
**Gillette**, Kevin Keith 1961- *AmMWSc 92*
**Gillette**, Kevin Mark 1955- *WhoAmP 91*
**Gillette**, Lyra Stephanie 1930- *WhoBlA 92*
**Gillette**, Martha Ulbrick 1945- *AmMWSc 92*
**Gillette**, Mary Kathleen 1961- *WhoAmL 92*
**Gillette**, Minnie 1929- *WhoAmP 91*
**Gillette**, Norman John 1911- *AmMWSc 92*
**Gillette**, Paul Crawford 1942- *AmMWSc 92*
**Gillette**, Philip Roger 1917- *AmMWSc 92*
**Gillette**, Rhanor 1943- *AmMWSc 92*
**Gillette**, Richard F 1934- *AmMWSc 92*
**Gillette**, Robert West 1934- *WhoAmP 91*
**Gillette**, Ronald William *AmMWSc 92*
**Gillette**, Ruth 1904- *WhoEnt 92*
**Gillette**, W. Michael 1941- *WhoAmL 92, WhoAmP 91, WhoWest 92*
**Gillette**, William 1855-1937 *BenetAL 91*
**Gilley**, Mickey 1937?- *ConMus 7 [port]*
**Gilley**, Mickey Leroy 1936- *WhoEnt 92*
**Gilley**, Sheridan 1945- *ConAu 133*
**Gilley**, Smith E *WhoAmP 91*
**Gilley**, Wayne 1915- *WhoAmP 91*
**Gillford**, Lord 1960- *Who 92*
**Gillham**, Grant David 1957- *WhoWest 92*
**Gillham**, John K 1930- *AmMWSc 92*
**Gillham**, Nicholas Wright 1932- *AmMWSc 92*
**Gillham**, Robert Winston 1940- *AmMWSc 92*
**Gilliam**, Arleen Fain 1949- *WhoBlA 92*
**Gilliam**, Armon Louis 1964- *WhoBlA 92*
**Gilliam**, Bates McCluer 1918- *WhoAmP 91*
**Gilliam**, Carroll Lewis 1929- *WhoAmL 92*

**Gilliam,** Charles Homer 1952- *AmMWSc 92*
**Gilliam,** Charles Stanley 1924- *WhoWest 92*
**Gilliam,** Daniel Charles 1959- *WhoEnt 92*
**Gilliam,** Dorothy Butler *WhoBlA 92*
**Gilliam,** Du-Bois Layfelt 1951- *WhoBlA 92*
**Gilliam,** E G *ScFEYrs*
**Gilliam,** Earl B. 1931- *WhoBlA 92*
**Gilliam,** Earl Ben 1931- *WhoAmL 92*
**Gilliam,** Frank Delano *WhoBlA 92*
**Gilliam,** George Harrison 1942- *WhoAmP 91*
**Gilliam,** Herman Arthur, Jr. 1943- *WhoBlA 92*
**Gilliam,** Jackson Earle 1920- *WhoRel 92*
**Gilliam,** James H., Jr. 1945- *WhoAmL 92, WhoBlA 92*
**Gilliam,** James H., Sr. 1920- *WhoBlA 92*
**Gilliam,** James M 1942- *AmMWSc 92*
**Gilliam,** James Wendell 1938- *AmMWSc 92*
**Gilliam,** Jean Marie 1923- *WhoAmP 91*
**Gilliam,** John Eugene, Jr. 1954- *WhoFI 92*
**Gilliam,** John Rally 1945- *WhoBlA 92*
**Gilliam,** Marvin L. 1941- *WhoBlA 92*
**Gilliam,** Mary 1928- *WhoWest 92*
**Gilliam,** Otis Randolph 1924- *AmMWSc 92*
**Gilliam,** Reginald Earl 1944- *WhoAmP 91*
**Gilliam,** Reginald Earl, Jr. 1944- *WhoBlA 92*
**Gilliam,** Robert M., Sr. 1926- *WhoBlA 92*
**Gilliam,** Roosevelt Sandy, Jr. 1932- *WhoBlA 92*
**Gilliam,** Sam, Jr. 1933- *WhoBlA 92*
**Gilliam,** Sharon *WhoBlA 92*
**Gilliam,** Steven Philip, Sr. 1949- *WhoAmL 92*
**Gilliam,** Terry 1940- *ConAu 35NR, IntDcF 2-2 [port], IntMPA 92, Who 92*
**Gilliam,** Terry Vance 1940- *IntWW 91, WhoEnt 92*
**Gilliam,** Vincent Carver 1944- *WhoRel 92*
**Gilliams,** Tyrone 1941- *WhoBlA 92*
**Gillian,** Jerry *ConAu 35NR*
**Gilliard,** Joseph Wadus 1914- *WhoBlA 92*
**Gilliat,** Leslie 1917- *IntMPA 92*
**Gilliat,** Martin 1913- *Who 92*
**Gilliat,** Sidney *IntDcF 2-2*
**Gilliatt,** Neal 1917- *WhoFI 92*
**Gilliatt,** Penelope *DrAPF 91, IntAu&W 91, IntWW 91, WrDr 92*
**Gilliatt,** Penelope 1932- *ConNov 91, FacFETw*
**Gilliatt,** Penelope Ann Douglass Conner 1932- *Who 92*
**Gilliatt,** Roger William d1991 *Who 92N*
**Gillibrand,** Sydney 1934- *Who 92*
**Gillice,** Sondra Jupin *WhoFI 92*
**Gillich,** William John 1935- *AmMWSc 92*
**Gillick,** Ernest George 1874-1951 *TwCPaSc*
**Gillick,** John 1916- *Who 92*
**Gillick,** Mary d1965 *TwCPaSc*
**Gillie,** Ann 1906- *TwCPaSc*
**Gillie,** Christopher 1914- *IntAu&W 91, WrDr 92*
**Gillies,** Alastair J 1924- *AmMWSc 92*
**Gillies,** Charles Wesley 1946- *AmMWSc 92*
**Gillies,** George Thomas 1952- *AmMWSc 92*
**Gillies,** Gordon 1916- *Who 92*
**Gillies,** John Arthur 1947- *WhoWest 92*
**Gillies,** Patricia Ann 1929- *WhoWest 92*
**Gillies,** Valerie 1948- *ConPo 91, WrDr 92*
**Gillies,** William 1898-1973 *TwCPaSc*
**Gilligan,** Diana Mary *AmMWSc 92*
**Gilligan,** Edmund 1899-1973 *BenetAL 91*
**Gilligan,** Francis Atwood 1939- *WhoAmL 92*
**Gilligan,** John Philip, III 1930- *WhoEnt 92*
**Gilligan,** Lawrence G 1948- *AmMWSc 92*
**Gilligan,** Mary Ann 1956- *WhoAmL 92*
**Gilligan,** Robert F 1942- *WhoAmP 91*
**Gilligan,** Robert G *WhoAmP 91*
**Gilligan,** William Lee 1924- *WhoAmP 91*
**Gillikin,** Jesse Edward, Jr 1952- *AmMWSc 92*
**Gillikin,** Richard Charles 1952- *WhoMW 92*
**Gillikin,** Virginia 1952- *WhoAmL 92*
**Gillilan,** James Horace 1932- *AmMWSc 92*
**Gillilan,** Lois Adell 1911- *AmMWSc 92*
**Gillilan,** Strickland 1869-1954 *BenetAL 91*
**Gilliland,** Alexis A 1931- *IntAu&W 91, TwCSFW 91, WrDr 92*
**Gilliland,** Bobby Eugene 1936- *AmMWSc 92*
**Gilliland,** David *Who 92*
**Gilliland,** David Jervois Thetford 1932- *Who 92*
**Gilliland,** Dennis Crippen 1938- *AmMWSc 92*
**Gilliland,** Eric Raymond 1962- *WhoEnt 92*
**Gilliland,** Floyd Ray, Jr 1939- *AmMWSc 92*
**Gilliland,** Hap 1918- *WhoWest 92*
**Gilliland,** Harold Eugene 1937- *AmMWSc 92*
**Gilliland,** James Andrew David 1937- *Who 92*
**Gilliland,** James Norman 1950- *WhoWest 92*
**Gilliland,** Jennifer *Who 92*
**Gilliland,** Joe E 1927- *AmMWSc 92*
**Gilliland,** John Campbell, II 1945- *WhoAmL 92*
**Gilliland,** John L, Jr 1910- *AmMWSc 92*
**Gilliland,** Lance Galen 1967- *WhoFI 92*
**Gilliland,** Mary *DrAPF 91*
**Gilliland,** Neil Edgar 1943- *WhoRel 92*
**Gilliland,** Richard *WhoEnt 92*
**Gilliland,** Robert McMurtry 1921- *AmMWSc 92*
**Gilliland,** Ronald Lynn 1952- *AmMWSc 92*
**Gilliland,** Stanley Eugene 1940- *AmMWSc 92*
**Gilliland,** William Nathan 1919- *AmMWSc 92*
**Gillin,** Donald T. 1914- *IntMPA 92*
**Gillin,** James 1925- *AmMWSc 92*
**Gillin,** Kathryn Lorraine 1945- *WhoWest 92*
**Gillin,** Malvin James, Jr. 1946- *WhoAmL 92*
**Gillin,** Philip Howard 1937- *WhoWest 92*
**Gilling,** Lancelot Cyril Gilbert 1920- *Who 92*
**Gillingham,** Bryan Reginald 1944- *WhoEnt 92*
**Gillingham,** David Ronald 1947- *WhoMW 92*
**Gillingham,** James Clark 1944- *AmMWSc 92*
**Gillingham,** James Morris 1924- *AmMWSc 92*
**Gillingham,** John 1916- *Who 92*
**Gillingham,** Michael John 1933- *Who 92*
**Gillingham,** Peter Llewellyn 1914- *Who 92*
**Gillingham,** Robert J 1923- *AmMWSc 92*
**Gillingham,** Tim 1958- *TwCPaSc*
**Gillings,** Gary Dean 1955- *WhoMW 92*
**Gilliom,** Morris Eugene 1932- *WhoMW 92*
**Gilliom,** Richard D 1934- *AmMWSc 92*
**Gillis,** Ann 1927- *IntMPA 92*
**Gillis,** Bernard Benjamin *Who 92*
**Gillis,** Bernard Thomas 1931- *AmMWSc 92, WhoMW 92*
**Gillis,** Beth Marie 1945- *WhoRel 92*
**Gillis,** Carl L, Jr 1917- *WhoAmP 91*
**Gillis,** Charles Norman 1933- *AmMWSc 92*
**Gillis,** Christine Diest-Lorgion *WhoFI 92*
**Gillis,** Christopher *WhoEnt 92*
**Gillis,** Don 1912-1978 *NewAmDM*
**Gillis,** Donald Paul 1941- *WhoEnt 92*
**Gillis,** Hugh Andrew 1935- *AmMWSc 92*
**Gillis,** Hugh Marion, Sr 1918- *WhoAmP 91*
**Gillis,** James E, Jr 1920- *AmMWSc 92*
**Gillis,** James J. 1927- *WhoEnt 92*
**Gillis,** James Thompson 1956- *AmMWSc 92*
**Gillis,** John Ericsen 1943- *AmMWSc 92*
**Gillis,** John H., Jr. 1951- *WhoAmL 92*
**Gillis,** John William 1937- *WhoWest 92*
**Gillis,** Kathy 1960- *WhoEnt 92*
**Gillis,** Lee Elwood *WhoAmP 91*
**Gillis,** Margaret Rose 1953- *WhoEnt 92*
**Gillis,** Marina N 1934- *AmMWSc 92*
**Gillis,** Marvin Bob 1920- *WhoFI 92*
**Gillis,** Murlin Fern 1935- *AmMWSc 92*
**Gillis,** Nelson Scott 1953- *WhoFI 92*
**Gillis,** Paul Leonard 1953- *WhoWest 92*
**Gillis,** Peter Paul 1930- *AmMWSc 92*
**Gillis,** Richard A 1938- *AmMWSc 92*
**Gillis,** Shirley J. Barfield 1943- *WhoBlA 92*
**Gillis,** Theresa McKinzy 1945- *WhoBlA 92*
**Gillis,** William Freeman 1948- *WhoBlA 92*
**Gillispie,** Gregory David 1949- *AmMWSc 92*
**Gillispie,** Harold Leon 1933- *WhoMW 92*
**Gillispie,** Lucy Anthony 1928- *WhoAmP 91*
**Gillispie,** William Henry 1927- *WhoBlA 92*
**Gilliss,** Edward Johnson 1955- *WhoAmL 92*
**Gilliss,** James Melville 1811-1865 *BiInAmS*
**Gilliss,** Walter 1855-1925 *BenetAL 91*
**Gillman,** Bernard Arthur 1927- *Who 92*
**Gillman,** David 1938- *AmMWSc 92*
**Gillman,** Florence Morgan 1947- *WhoRel 92*
**Gillman,** Henry 1833-1915 *BiInAmS*
**Gillman,** Hyman David 1941- *AmMWSc 92*
**Gillman,** John Leo 1948- *WhoRel 92*
**Gillman,** Leonard 1917- *AmMWSc 92*
**Gillman,** Richard *DrAPF 91*
**Gillman,** Richard 1931- *WhoWest 92*
**Gillman,** Tricia 1951- *TwCPaSc*
**Gillmar,** Stanley Frank 1935- *WhoAmL 92, WhoFI 92, WhoWest 92*
**Gillmor,** John Edward 1937- *WhoAmL 92*
**Gillmor,** Paul E. 1939- *AlmAP 92 [port], WhoMW 92*
**Gillmor,** Paul Eugene 1939- *WhoAmP 91*
**Gillmor,** R N 1906- *AmMWSc 92*
**Gillmore,** Alan David 1905- *Who 92*
**Gillmore,** Alver James, III 1947- *WhoAmP 91*
**Gillmore,** David 1934- *Who 92*
**Gillmore,** David Howe 1934- *IntWW 91*
**Gillmore,** Donald W 1919- *AmMWSc 92*
**Gillmore,** Inez Haynes 1873-1970 *ScFEYrs*
**Gillock,** Edgar Hardin 1928- *WhoAmP 91*
**Gillock,** Gerald Seth 1950- *WhoRel 92*
**Gillock,** Jon *WhoEnt 92*
**Gillom,** Jennifer 1964- *BlkOlyM*
**Gillon,** Adam 1921- *IntAu&W 91, WrDr 92*
**Gillon,** Katie Troncale 1949- *WhoEnt 92*
**Gillon,** Luc-Pierre-A. 1920- *IntWW 91*
**Gillon,** Raanan Evelyn Zvi 1941- *Who 92*
**Gillooly,** Edna Rae 1932- *WhoEnt 92*
**Gillooly,** George Rice 1930- *AmMWSc 92*
**Gilloteaux,** Jacques Jean-Marie A 1944- *AmMWSc 92*
**Gillott,** Donald H 1931- *AmMWSc 92*
**Gillow,** Edward William 1939- *AmMWSc 92*
**Gillum,** Amanda McKee 1947- *AmMWSc 92*
**Gillum,** Perry Eugene 1933- *WhoRel 92*
**Gillum,** Ronald Lee 1938- *AmMWSc 92*
**Gillum,** Ronald M. 1939- *WhoBlA 92*
**Gilman,** Albert F, III 1931- *AmMWSc 92*
**Gilman,** Alfred G 1941- *AmMWSc 92*
**Gilman,** Arthur 1837-1909 *BenetAL 91*
**Gilman,** Benjamin A. 1922- *AlmAP 92 [port], WhoAmP 91*
**Gilman,** Caroline Howard 1794-1888 *BenetAL 91*
**Gilman,** Charles 1946- *WhoFI 92*
**Gilman,** Charles Alan 1949- *WhoAmL 92*
**Gilman,** Charlotte Anna Perkins 1860-1935 *HanAmWH*
**Gilman,** Charlotte Perkins 1860-1935 *BenetAL 91, ModAWWr, PorAmW [port], RComAH, ScFEYrs, TwCSFW 91, WomSoc*
**Gilman,** Daniel Coit 1831-1908 *BenetAL 91*
**Gilman,** David Alan 1933- *WhoMW 92*
**Gilman,** Donald Lawrence 1931- *AmMWSc 92*
**Gilman,** Dorothy 1923- *IntAu&W 91, WrDr 92*
**Gilman,** Dugan *DrAPF 91*
**Gilman,** Frederick Joseph 1940- *AmMWSc 92*
**Gilman,** George G 1936- *IntAu&W 91, TwCWW 91, WrDr 92*
**Gilman,** George L *WhoAmP 91*
**Gilman,** Harold 1876-1919 *TwCPaSc*
**Gilman,** Irvin Edward 1926- *WhoEnt 92*
**Gilman,** Jane P 1945- *AmMWSc 92*
**Gilman,** John Joseph 1925- *AmMWSc 92*
**Gilman,** John Richard, Jr 1925- *AmMWSc 92*
**Gilman,** Kenneth David 1951- *WhoEnt 92*
**Gilman,** Lauren Cundiff 1914- *AmMWSc 92*
**Gilman,** Martin Robert 1937- *AmMWSc 92*
**Gilman,** Nicholas 1938- *WhoAmL 92*
**Gilman,** Norman Washburn 1938- *AmMWSc 92*
**Gilman,** Paul Brewster, Jr 1929- *AmMWSc 92*
**Gilman,** Peter A 1941- *AmMWSc 92*
**Gilman,** Richard 1925- *IntAu&W 91, WhoEnt 92, WrDr 92*
**Gilman,** Richard Atwood 1935- *AmMWSc 92*
**Gilman,** Robert Cham *TwCSFW 91, WrDr 92*
**Gilman,** Robert Edward 1932- *AmMWSc 92*
**Gilman,** Robert Hugh 1942- *AmMWSc 92*
**Gilman,** Ronald Keith 1942- *WhoMW 92*
**Gilman,** Ronald Lee 1942- *WhoAmL 92*
**Gilman,** S John Frances 1930- *AmMWSc 92*
**Gilman,** Sheldon Glenn 1943- *WhoAmL 92*
**Gilman,** Sid 1932- *AmMWSc 92*
**Gilman,** Steven Christopher 1952- *AmMWSc 92*
**Gilmartin,** Amy Jean 1932- *AmMWSc 92*
**Gilmartin,** Hugh 1923- *Who 92*
**Gilmartin,** John A. 1942- *WhoFI 92*
**Gilmartin,** Karen Baust 1961- *WhoAmL 92*
**Gilmartin,** Malvern 1926- *AmMWSc 92*
**Gilmartin,** Platt Jay 1952- *WhoWest 92*
**Gilmartin,** Thomas Joseph 1940- *AmMWSc 92*
**Gilmer,** Charles Thomas 1933- *WhoAmP 91*
**Gilmer,** David Seeley 1937- *AmMWSc 92*
**Gilmer,** Donald H 1945- *WhoAmP 91*
**Gilmer,** Elizabeth Meriwether 1870-1951 *BenetAL 91*
**Gilmer,** George Hudson 1937- *AmMWSc 92*
**Gilmer,** Jeremy Francis 1818-1883 *DcNCBi 2*
**Gilmer,** John Adams 1805-1868 *DcNCBi 2*
**Gilmer,** Penny Jane 1943- *AmMWSc 92*
**Gilmer,** Robert 1938- *AmMWSc 92*
**Gilmer,** Robert D. 1858-1924 *DcNCBi 2*
**Gilmer,** Robert McCullough 1920- *AmMWSc 92*
**Gilmer,** Robert William, III 1946- *WhoFI 92*
**Gilmer,** Steven Lee 1949- *WhoEnt 92*
**Gilmer,** Thomas Edward, Jr 1925- *AmMWSc 92*
**Gilmer,** Wendell Jerome 1950- *WhoEnt 92*
**Gilmer,** William Franklin 1901-1954 *DcNCBi 2*
**Gilmere,** Julie Ann 1958- *WhoAmL 92*
**Gilmont,** Ernest Rich 1929- *AmMWSc 92*
**Gilmont,** Roger 1916- *AmMWSc 92*
**Gilmor,** Robert 1774-1848 *BiInAmS*
**Gilmore,** Al Tony 1946- *WhoBlA 92*
**Gilmore,** Alvan Ray 1921- *AmMWSc 92*
**Gilmore,** Anthony *TwCSFW 91*
**Gilmore,** Art 1912- *WhoEnt 92*
**Gilmore,** Arthur W 1920- *AmMWSc 92*
**Gilmore,** Artis 1948- *WhoBlA 92*
**Gilmore,** Brian Terence 1937- *Who 92*
**Gilmore,** Carol Jacqueline *Who 92*
**Gilmore,** Carter 1926- *WhoAmP 91*
**Gilmore,** Carter C. 1926- *WhoBlA 92*
**Gilmore,** Catherine Rye 1947- *WhoEnt 92*
**Gilmore,** Charles Arthur 1919- *WhoBlA 92*
**Gilmore,** Charles Edmund 1948- *WhoRel 92*
**Gilmore,** Christopher John 1961- *WhoWest 92*
**Gilmore,** Clarence Percy 1926- *IntAu&W 91*
**Gilmore,** David D. 1943- *ConAu 133*
**Gilmore,** Don E 1928- *WhoAmP 91*
**Gilmore,** Don William 1959- *WhoWest 92*
**Gilmore,** Dulcie Corkill 1951- *WhoEnt 92*
**Gilmore,** Earl C 1930- *AmMWSc 92*
**Gilmore,** Earl Howard 1923- *AmMWSc 92*
**Gilmore,** Edwin 1931- *WhoBlA 92*
**Gilmore,** Forrest Richard 1922- *AmMWSc 92*
**Gilmore,** Gary R 1950- *WhoAmP 91*
**Gilmore,** Gloria Louise 1954- *WhoRel 92*
**Gilmore,** Grant William 1961- *WhoEnt 92*
**Gilmore,** Harold James 1961- *WhoEnt 92*
**Gilmore,** Helen Carol *WhoMW 92*
**Gilmore,** Horace Weldon 1918- *WhoAmL 92, WhoMW 92*
**Gilmore,** James Eugene 1927- *AmMWSc 92*
**Gilmore,** James Stanley, Jr 1926- *WhoAmP 91, WhoEnt 92*
**Gilmore,** James Stuart, III 1949- *WhoAmP 91*
**Gilmore,** John *DrAPF 91*
**Gilmore,** John 1951- *ConAu 133*
**Gilmore,** John T 1931- *AmMWSc 92*
**Gilmore,** John T. 1935- *WhoBlA 92*
**Gilmore,** Joseph Patrick 1928- *AmMWSc 92*
**Gilmore,** June Ellen 1927- *WhoMW 92*
**Gilmore,** Kathi 1944- *WhoAmP 91*
**Gilmore,** Lloyd Marshall 1925- *WhoFI 92*
**Gilmore,** Mark, Jr 1939- *WhoAmP 91*
**Gilmore,** Marshall *WhoRel 92*
**Gilmore,** Marshall 1931- *WhoBlA 92*
**Gilmore,** Mary 1865-1962 *RfGEnL 91*
**Gilmore,** Mary Jean Cameron 1865-1962 *FacFETw*
**Gilmore,** Maurice Eugene 1938- *AmMWSc 92*
**Gilmore,** Mikal George 1951- *WhoWest 92*
**Gilmore,** Patrick S. 1829-1892 *NewAmDM*
**Gilmore,** Paul Carl 1925- *AmMWSc 92*
**Gilmore,** Richard G. 1927- *WhoBlA 92*
**Gilmore,** Richard Harvey 1942- *WhoEnt 92*
**Gilmore,** Robert Beattie 1913- *AmMWSc 92*
**Gilmore,** Robert G. *WhoAmL 92*
**Gilmore,** Robert McKinley, Sr. 1952- *WhoBlA 92*
**Gilmore,** Robert Snee 1938- *AmMWSc 92*
**Gilmore,** Robert Witter 1933- *WhoMW 92*
**Gilmore,** Rosalind Edith Jean 1937- *Who 92*
**Gilmore,** Shirley Ann 1935- *AmMWSc 92*
**Gilmore,** Stuart Irby 1930- *AmMWSc 92*
**Gilmore,** Susan Astrid Lytle 1942- *WhoWest 92*
**Gilmore,** Thomas Meyer 1942- *AmMWSc 92, WhoFI 92*
**Gilmore,** Thomas Odell, Sr 1936- *WhoAmP 91*

**Gilmore**, Timothy Jonathan 1949- WhoFI 92, WhoWest 92
**Gilmore**, Walter Murchison 1869-1946 DcNCBi 2
**Gilmore**, William Franklin 1935- AmMWSc 92
**Gilmore**, William Harold 1932- WhoMW 92
**Gilmore**, William Rhodes, II 1946- WhoAmP 91
**Gilmore**, William S. 1934- IntMPA 92
**Gilmour**, Alan Breck 1928- Who 92
**Gilmour**, Alexander Clement 1931- Who 92
**Gilmour**, Allan 1916- Who 92
**Gilmour**, Allan Dana 1934- WhoFI 92, WhoMW 92
**Gilmour**, Campbell Morrison 1916- AmMWSc 92
**Gilmour**, Ernest Henry 1936- AmMWSc 92
**Gilmour**, Hugh Stewart Allen 1926- AmMWSc 92
**Gilmour**, Ian 1926- IntWW 91, Who 92
**Gilmour**, Jeff L 1947- WhoAmP 91
**Gilmour**, John 1912- Who 92
**Gilmour**, Marion Nyholm H 1928- AmMWSc 92
**Gilmour**, Mavis Gwendolyn 1926- IntWW 91
**Gilmour**, Nigel Benjamin Douglas 1947- Who 92
**Gilmour**, Thomas Henry Johnstone 1936- AmMWSc 92
**Gilmour-Stallsworth**, Lisa K 1959- AmMWSc 92
**Giloth-David**, King R. 1940- WhoBlA 92
**Gilow**, Helmuth Martin 1933- AmMWSc 92
**Gilpatric**, Guy 1896-1950 BenetAL 91
**Gilpatrick**, Janet Louise 1944- WhoAmP 91
**Gilpin**, Alan 1924- WrDr 92
**Gilpin**, Clemmie Edward 1942- WhoBlA 92
**Gilpin**, Michael James 1941- AmMWSc 92
**Gilpin**, Roger Keith 1947- AmMWSc 92
**Gilpin**, W. Clark WhoRel 92
**Gilpin**, William 1724-1804 BlkwCEP
**Gilpin**, William 1813?-1894 BenetAL 91
**Gilray**, James ConAu 133
**Gilreath**, Coot, Jr. 1937- WhoBlA 92
**Gilreath**, James Preston 1947- AmMWSc 92
**Gilroy**, Beryl 1924- ConAu 135
**Gilroy**, Beryl Agatha IntAu&W 91
**Gilroy**, Frank 1925- IntMPA 92
**Gilroy**, Frank D. DrAPF 91
**Gilroy**, Frank D. 1925- BenetAL 91, IntAu&W 91, WrDr 92
**Gilroy**, Frank Daniel 1925- WhoEnt 92
**Gilroy**, James Joseph 1926- AmMWSc 92
**Gilroy**, John 1925- AmMWSc 92
**Gilroy**, Mark Kevin 1958- WhoRel 92
**Gilroy**, Norman T 1896-1977 FacFETw
**Gilroy**, Tracy Anne Hunsaker 1959- WhoMW 92
**Gilroy Bevan**, David Who 92
**Gilruth**, Robert R 1913- AmMWSc 92
**Gilruth**, Robert Rowe 1913- FacFETw, IntWW 91
**Gilsdorf**, Thomas Ernest 1958- WhoMW 92
**Gilsenan**, Michael Dermot Cole 1940- Who 92
**Gilson**, Arnold Leslie 1931- WhoFI 92
**Gilson**, Earl Arthur 1923- WhoAmP 91
**Gilson**, Estelle DrAPF 91
**Gilson**, James Russell 1951- WhoAmL 92
**Gilson**, Jerome 1931- WhoAmL 92
**Gilson**, Nanette Clinch 1951- WhoAmL 92
**Gilson**, Nigel Langley 1922- Who 92
**Gilson**, Ronald Jay 1946- WhoAmL 92
**Gilson**, W E, Jr 1936- WhoIns 92
**Gilson**, Warren Edwin, Jr. 1936- WhoFI 92
**Gilstein**, Jacob Burrill 1923- AmMWSc 92
**Gilstrap**, Franklin Ephriam 1944- AmMWSc 92
**Gilstrap**, James Jeffrey 1947- WhoFI 92
**Gilstrap**, Robert Edward, Jr. 1961- WhoRel 92
**Giltinan**, David Anthony 1936- AmMWSc 92
**Giltner**, Otis Beryl 1931- WhoFI 92
**Gilton**, Donna L. 1950- WhoBlA 92
**Gilula**, Louis Arnold 1942- AmMWSc 92
**Gilula**, Norton Bernard 1944- AmMWSc 92
**Gilvarg**, Charles 1925- AmMWSc 92
**Gilvarry**, John James 1917- AmMWSc 92
**Gilvary**, James Joseph 1929- WhoAmL 92
**Gilven**, Hezekiah 1927- WhoBlA 92
**Gilway**, Barry John 1945- WhoIns 92
**Gim**, Joy WhoEnt 92
**Gimarc**, Benjamin M 1934- AmMWSc 92
**Gimbel**, Franklyn M. 1936- WhoMW 92
**Gimbel**, J. William, Jr. 1908- WhoMW 92
**Gimbel**, John 1922- WrDr 92
**Gimbel**, Louis S, III 1929- WhoAmP 91
**Gimbel**, Norman WhoEnt 92
**Gimbel**, Roger 1925- IntMPA 92
**Gimble**, Jeffrey M 1955- AmMWSc 92
**Gimbrone**, Michael Anthony, Jr 1943- AmMWSc 92
**Gimelli**, Salvatore Paul 1919- AmMWSc 92
**Gimenez**, Carlos 1954- WhoHisp 92
**Gimenez**, Jose Raul 1955- WhoHisp 92
**Gimenez Caballero**, Ernesto 1899- BiDExR
**Gimenez-Porrata**, Alfonso 1937- WhoHisp 92
**Gimeno**, Emil 1921- WhoHisp 92
**Gimferrer**, Pere 1945- IntWW 91
**Gimingham**, Charles Henry 1923- Who 92
**Gimlett**, James I 1929- AmMWSc 92
**Gimmarro**, Steven Paul 1959- WhoMW 92
**Gimmestad**, Michael Jon 1943- WhoWest 92
**Gimple**, Glenn Edward 1940- AmMWSc 92
**Gimson**, Ernest 1864-1919 DcTwDes
**Gimson**, George Stanley 1915- Who 92
**Gin**, Jackson 1934- WhoMW 92
**Gin**, Jerry Ben 1943- AmMWSc 92
**Gin**, W 1928- AmMWSc 92
**Ginader**, Barbara Malia 1956- WhoFI 92
**Ginalski**, Mark 1960- WhoWest 92
**Ginastera**, Alberto 1916-1983 FacFETw, NewAmDM
**Ginden**, Kathryn WhoEnt 92
**Ginder**, Gordon Dean 1949- WhoMW 92
**Ginder**, Peter Craig 1946- WhoAmL 92
**Gindes**, Philip Haddington WhoWest 92
**Gindin**, James 1926- WrDr 92
**Gindin**, James Jack 1926- IntAu&W 91
**Gindin**, William Howard 1931- WhoAmL 92
**Gindler**, James Edward 1925- AmMWSc 92
**Gindsberg**, Joseph 1920- AmMWSc 92
**Gine-Masdeu**, Evarist 1944- AmMWSc 92
**Ginell**, Robert 1912- AmMWSc 92
**Ginell**, William Seaman 1923- AmMWSc 92
**Giner**, Jose Domingo 1928- AmMWSc 92
**Giner-Sorolla**, Alfredo 1919- AmMWSc 92
**Gineris**, Marc A. 1959- WhoFI 92
**Gines**, Ralph Junior 1933- WhoAmP 91
**Ginesi**, Edna 1902- TwCPaSc
**Ginevan**, Michael Edward 1946- AmMWSc 92
**Ginex**, Louis Joseph 1937- WhoWest 92
**Ging**, Rosalie J 1921- AmMWSc 92
**Gingell**, John 1925- Who 92
**Gingell**, John 1935- TwCPaSc
**Gingell**, Laurie William Albert 1925- Who 92
**Gingell**, Ralph 1945- AmMWSc 92
**Gingell**, Robert Arthur 1923- WhoAmL 92
**Ginger**, Ann F. 1925- WrDr 92
**Ginger**, Laura Ann 1954- WhoAmL 92
**Ginger**, Leonard George 1918- AmMWSc 92
**Ginger**, Phyllis Ethel 1907- Who 92
**Gingerich**, Dennis Daniel 1953- WhoRel 92
**Gingerich**, Florine Rose 1951- WhoAmL 92
**Gingerich**, Karl Andreas 1927- AmMWSc 92
**Gingerich**, Owen 1930- AmMWSc 92
**Gingerich**, Philip Derstine 1946- AmMWSc 92, WhoMW 92
**Gingerich**, Willard DrAPF 91
**Gingery**, Roy Evans 1942- AmMWSc 92
**Gingher**, Marianne DrAPF 91
**Gingle**, Alan Raymond 1949- AmMWSc 92
**Gingold**, Dan IntMPA 92
**Gingold**, Daniel Tan 1928- WhoEnt 92
**Gingold**, Dennis Marc 1949- WhoAmL 92, WhoFI 92
**Gingold**, Harlan Bruce 1946- WhoAmL 92
**Gingold**, Josef 1909- ConMus 6 [port], NewAmDM
**Gingold**, Kurt 1929- AmMWSc 92
**Gingras**, Armando Rosario 1941- WhoWest 92
**Gingras**, Bernard Arthur 1927- AmMWSc 92
**Gingras**, Frank Edwin 1919- WhoRel 92
**Gingras**, John Richard 1949- WhoAmL 92
**Gingrass**, Ruedi Peter 1932- AmMWSc 92
**Gingrich**, Arnold 1903-1976 BenetAL 91
**Gingrich**, C. David 1951- WhoFI 92
**Gingrich**, John Nelson 1947- WhoEnt 92
**Gingrich**, Newell Shiffer 1906- AmMWSc 92
**Gingrich**, Newt 1943- AlmAP 92 [port], IntWW 91, News 91 [port], WhoAmP 91
**Gini**, Maria Luigia 1946- AmMWSc 92
**Ginis**, Asterios Michael 1945- AmMWSc 92
**Ginley**, Marcia Sue 1952- WhoAmL 92
**Ginley**, Thomas J. 1938- WhoMW 92
**Ginn**, Alfred Stephen 1932- WhoRel 92
**Ginn**, David 1951- WhoAmP 91
**Ginn**, Edwin 1838-1914 AmPeW
**Ginn**, H Earl 1931- AmMWSc 92
**Ginn**, H. Rand 1942- WhoWest 92
**Ginn**, Jeffery Byron 1961- WhoRel 92
**Ginn**, John Charles 1937- WhoFI 92
**Ginn**, M. Stanly 1911- WhoFI 92
**Ginn**, Robert Ford 1931- AmMWSc 92
**Ginn**, Ronald Bryan 1934- WhoAmP 91
**Ginn**, Sam L. 1937- WhoWest 92
**Ginn**, Thomas Clifford 1946- AmMWSc 92
**Ginna**, Robert Emmett, Jr. 1925- IntMPA 92
**Ginnard**, Charles Raymond 1947- AmMWSc 92
**Ginner**, Charles 1878-1952 TwCPaSc
**Ginnetti**, John P 1945- WhoIns 92
**Ginning**, P R 1923- AmMWSc 92
**Ginnings**, Gerald Keith 1928- AmMWSc 92
**Ginns**, James Herbert 1938- AmMWSc 92
**Ginocchio**, Joseph Natale 1936- AmMWSc 92
**Ginorio**, Angela Beatriz 1947- WhoHisp 92
**Ginos**, George Edwin 1929- WhoAmL 92
**Ginos**, James Zissis 1923- AmMWSc 92
**Ginsberg**, Allen DrAPF 91
**Ginsberg**, Allen 1926- AmPeW, BenetAL 91, ConLC 69 [port], ConPo 91, FacFETw [port], IntAu&W 91, IntWW 91, PoeCrit 4 [port], RComAH, WhoEnt 92, WrDr 92
**Ginsberg**, Alvin Paul 1932- AmMWSc 92
**Ginsberg**, Barry Howard 1945- AmMWSc 92
**Ginsberg**, David Morton 1951- WhoEnt 92
**Ginsberg**, Donald Maurice 1933- AmMWSc 92
**Ginsberg**, Edward S 1938- AmMWSc 92
**Ginsberg**, Emily Suzanne 1935- WhoFI 92
**Ginsberg**, Ernest 1931- WhoAmL 92, WhoFI 92
**Ginsberg**, Harold Samuel 1917- AmMWSc 92
**Ginsberg**, Hersh Meier 1928- WhoRel 92
**Ginsberg**, Jeffrey Scott 1962- WhoEnt 92
**Ginsberg**, Jerry Hal 1944- AmMWSc 92
**Ginsberg**, Jonathan I 1941- AmMWSc 92
**Ginsberg**, Lewis Robbins 1932- WhoAmL 92
**Ginsberg**, Louis 1896-1976 BenetAL 91
**Ginsberg**, Mark Howard 1945- AmMWSc 92
**Ginsberg**, Melvin R. 1942- WhoAmL 92
**Ginsberg**, Michael 1943- TwCPaSc
**Ginsberg**, Murry B 1928- AmMWSc 92
**Ginsberg**, Myron 1943- WhoMW 92
**Ginsberg**, Myron David 1939- AmMWSc 92
**Ginsberg**, Ronald Erwin 1946- WhoAmP 91
**Ginsberg**, Sidney 1920- IntMPA 92
**Ginsberg**, Theodore 1933- AmMWSc 92
**Ginsberg**, Theodore 1941- AmMWSc 92
**Ginsberg**, William Roy 1930- WhoAmL 92
**Ginsberg-Fellner**, Fredda Vita 1937- AmMWSc 92
**Ginsburg**, Ann 1932- AmMWSc 92
**Ginsburg**, Arthur Jay 1941- WhoAmL 92
**Ginsburg**, Benson Earl 1918- AmMWSc 92
**Ginsburg**, Carl DrAPF 91
**Ginsburg**, Charles David 1912- WhoAmL 92, WhoFI 92
**Ginsburg**, Charles P 1920- AmMWSc 92
**Ginsburg**, David 1920- AmMWSc 92
**Ginsburg**, David 1921- Who 92
**Ginsburg**, Douglas H WhoAmP 91
**Ginsburg**, Douglas Howard 1946- WhoAmL 92
**Ginsburg**, Edward M. 1932- WhoAmL 92
**Ginsburg**, Ellin Louis WhoFI 92
**Ginsburg**, Faye D. 1952- ConAu 133
**Ginsburg**, Helen WhoFI 92
**Ginsburg**, Herbert 1928- AmMWSc 92
**Ginsburg**, Jack Martin 1928- AmMWSc 92
**Ginsburg**, Kenneth Alan 1954- WhoMW 92
**Ginsburg**, Lawrence David 1947- WhoAmL 92
**Ginsburg**, Lewis S. 1914- IntMPA 92
**Ginsburg**, Martin David 1932- WhoAmL 92
**Ginsburg**, Merrill Stuart 1935- AmMWSc 92
**Ginsburg**, Mirra IntAu&W 91
**Ginsburg**, Nathan 1910- AmMWSc 92
**Ginsburg**, Robert Nathan 1925- AmMWSc 92
**Ginsburg**, Ruth Bader 1933- WhoAmL 92, WhoAmP 91
**Ginsburg**, Seymour 1927- AmMWSc 92, WhoWest 92
**Ginsburg**, Victor 1930- AmMWSc 92
**Ginsburg-Wolf**, Frances Ruth 1953- WhoRel 92
**Ginsburgh**, Irwin 1926- AmMWSc 92
**Ginsburgh**, Robert Howard 1956- WhoAmL 92
**Ginsburgs**, George 1932- WrDr 92
**Ginsbury**, Norman 1902- IntAu&W 91, Who 92
**Ginski**, John Martin 1926- AmMWSc 92
**Ginsky**, Marvin H. 1930- WhoAmL 92, WhoFI 92
**Ginsparg**, Paul H AmMWSc 92
**Ginsparg**, Sylvia Levine 1931- WhoMW 92
**Gintautas**, Jonas 1938- AmMWSc 92
**Ginter**, Marshall L 1935- AmMWSc 92
**Ginter**, Melissa Ann WhoMW 92
**Ginther**, Joan R. 1947- WhoWest 92
**Ginther**, Robert J 1917- AmMWSc 92
**Ginther**, Vance Curtis 1946- WhoRel 92, WhoWest 92
**Gintis**, Herbert Malena 1940- WhoFI 92
**Ginyard**, Martin Cecil 1952- WhoFI 92
**Ginzberg**, Eli 1911- AmMWSc 92, IntAu&W 91, IntWW 91, WrDr 92
**Ginzburg**, Abram Moiseevich 1878-193-? SovUnBD
**Ginzburg**, Aleksandr Il'ich 1936- SovUnBD
**Ginzburg**, Aleksandr Ilyich 1936- IntWW 91
**Ginzburg**, Alexander 1936- FacFETw
**Ginzburg**, Carlo NewYTBS 91 [port]
**Ginzburg**, Lev R 1945- AmMWSc 92
**Ginzburg**, Lidia Yakovlevna 1902- IntWW 91
**Ginzburg**, Moisey Yakovlevich 1892-1946 SovUnBD
**Ginzburg**, Natalia d1991 NewYTBS 91 [port]
**Ginzburg**, Natalia 1916- FacFETw, IntWW 91
**Ginzburg**, Natalia 1916-1991 ConAu 135, CurBio 91N
**Ginzburg**, Shimon DcAmImH
**Ginzburg**, Vitaly Lazarevich 1916- IntWW 91
**Ginzburg**, Yevgeniya Semenovna 1904-1977 SovUnBD
**Ginzel**, Karl-Heinz 1921- AmMWSc 92
**Ginzton**, Edward Leonard 1915- AmMWSc 92, IntWW 91, WhoWest 92
**Gioannini**, Theresa Lee 1949- AmMWSc 92
**Giobbi**, Monica Joan 1953- WhoWest 92
**Giocomo**, Gary WhoEnt 92
**Gioffre**, Bruno Joseph 1934- WhoAmL 92
**Gioffre Baird**, Lisa Ann 1961- WhoAmL 92
**Gioggia**, Robert Stephen 1943- AmMWSc 92
**Gioia**, Angelo Joseph 1951- WhoMW 92
**Gioia**, Anthony Alfred 1934- AmMWSc 92
**Gioia**, Dana DrAPF 91
**Gioia**, Ted 1957- IntAu&W 91
**Gioiella**, Russell Michael 1954- WhoAmL 92
**Gioiello**, John Leslie 1955- WhoAmL 92
**Gioioso**, Joseph Vincent 1939- WhoMW 92
**Giolitti**, Antonio 1915- IntWW 91, Who 92
**Giolitti**, Giovanni 1842-1928 FacFETw
**Giolli**, Roland A 1934- AmMWSc 92
**Giometti**, Carol Smith 1950- AmMWSc 92
**Giometti**, Gulio Mario 1960- WhoMW 92
**Gion**, Edmund 1929- AmMWSc 92
**Gionfriddo**, James Gregory 1954- WhoFI 92
**Gionfriddo**, Paul 1953- WhoAmP 91
**Giono**, Jean 1895-1970 ConAu 35NR, GuFrLit 1
**Giordano**, Amodio 1962- WhoEnt 92
**Giordano**, Anthony B 1915- AmMWSc 92
**Giordano**, Arthur Anthony 1941- AmMWSc 92
**Giordano**, August Thomas 1923- WhoEnt 92
**Giordano**, Clara 1924- WhoAmP 91
**Giordano**, Ernest 1926- WhoFI 92
**Giordano**, Gary S 1950- WhoAmP 91
**Giordano**, Gerard Raymond 1946- WhoWest 92
**Giordano**, John Read 1937- WhoEnt 92
**Giordano**, Joseph, Jr 1946- WhoAmP 91
**Giordano**, Joseph, Jr. 1953- WhoFI 92
**Giordano**, Larry F 1945- WhoAmP 91
**Giordano**, Lawrence Francis 1953- WhoAmL 92
**Giordano**, Michele 1930- IntWW 91, WhoRel 92
**Giordano**, Nicholas Anthony 1943- WhoFI 92
**Giordano**, Nicholas J 1951- AmMWSc 92
**Giordano**, Paul Gregory 1956- WhoWest 92
**Giordano**, Paul M 1936- AmMWSc 92
**Giordano**, Richard Vincent 1934- IntWW 91, Who 92, WhoFI 92
**Giordano**, Thomas Henry 1950- AmMWSc 92

**Giordano**, Tony 1939- WhoEnt 92
**Giordano**, Tony 1960- AmMWSc 92
**Giordano**, Umberto 1867-1948 NewAmDM
**Giordmaine**, Joseph Anthony 1933- AmMWSc 92
**Giorgi**, Angelo Louis 1917- AmMWSc 92
**Giorgi**, E J 1921- WhoAmP 91
**Giorgi**, Elsie A AmMWSc 92
**Giorgi**, Janis V 1947- AmMWSc 92
**Giorgio**, Anthony Joseph 1930- AmMWSc 92
**Giorgio**, Marosa di 1932- ConSpAP
**Giorgio**, Paul Joseph 1950- WhoAmP 91
**Giori**, Claudio 1938- AmMWSc 92, WhoAmL 92
**Giorno**, John DrAPF 91
**Giosan**, Nicolae d1990 IntWW 91N
**Gioseffi**, Daniela DrAPF 91
**Giotes**, Artie George 1941- WhoAmL 92
**Giotti**, Virgilio 1885-1957 DcLB 114 [port]
**Giovacchini**, Peter L 1922- AmMWSc 92
**Giovacchini**, Rubert Peter 1928- AmMWSc 92
**Giovando**, John W. 1943- WhoEnt 92
**Giovanella**, Beppino C 1932- AmMWSc 92
**Giovanelli**, Riccardo 1946- AmMWSc 92
**Giovanielli**, Damon V 1943- AmMWSc 92
**Giovanni**, Nikki DrAPF 91
**Giovanni**, Nikki 1943- BenetAL 91, BlkLC [port], ConPo 91, FacFETw, NotBlAW 92 [port], WhoBlA 92, WrDr 92
**Giovanni**, Paul 1940-1990 ConTFT 9
**Giovanniello**, Joseph, Jr. 1958- WhoAmL 92
**Giovanniello**, Margaret Montgomery Torr 1927- WhoAmL 92
**Giovannitti**, Arturo 1884-1959 BenetAL 91
**Giovannitti**, Arturo Massimo 1884-1959 DcAmImH
**Giovannitti**, Len DrAPF 91
**Giovannoni**, Stephen Joseph 1951- WhoWest 92
**Giovine**, Giulio 1947- WhoFI 92
**Giovinetto**, Mario Bartolome 1933- AmMWSc 92
**Gipp**, Chuck 1947- WhoAmP 91
**Gippin**, Morris 1908- AmMWSc 92
**Gippius**, Zinaida LiExTwC
**Gippius**, Zinaida Nikolayevna 1867-1945 FacFETw
**Gipps**, Ruth 1921- NewAmDM
**Gipps**, Ruth Dorothy Louisa 1921- WhoEnt 92
**Gippsland**, Bishop of 1929- Who 92
**Gips**, Donald Henry 1960- WhoFI 92
**Gipson**, Arthur A. 1935- WhoBlA 92
**Gipson**, Bernard Franklin, Sr. 1921- WhoBlA 92
**Gipson**, Donna Hays 1959- WhoMW 92
**Gipson**, Francis E. 1923- WhoBlA 92
**Gipson**, Fred 1908-1973 TwCWW 91
**Gipson**, Ilene Kay 1944- AmMWSc 92
**Gipson**, James William 1945- WhoRel 92
**Gipson**, Lovelace Preston, II 1942- WhoBlA 92
**Gipson**, Mack, Jr 1931- AmMWSc 92, WhoBlA 92
**Gipson**, Philip 1943- AmMWSc 92
**Gipson**, Reve WhoBlA 92
**Gipson**, Robert Malone 1939- AmMWSc 92
**Gipstein**, Milton Fivenson 1951- WhoAmL 92, WhoWest 92
**Gipstein**, Robert Malcolm 1936- WhoWest 92
**Gipstein**, Todd Alan 1952- WhoEnt 92
**Giral**, Angela 1935- WhoHisp 92
**Giraldi**, Wanda Williamson 1943- WhoAmL 92
**Giraldo**, Alvaro A 1945- AmMWSc 92
**Giraldo**, Rene WhoHisp 92
**Giramonti**, Piero Danilo 1964- WhoEnt 92
**Girard**, Alexander 1907- DcTwDes
**Girard**, Ann Olson 1959- WhoAmL 92
**Girard**, Charles Frederic 1822-1895 BiInAmS
**Girard**, Deborah Ann 1954- WhoEnt 92
**Girard**, Dennis Michael 1939- AmMWSc 92
**Girard**, Francis Henry 1935- AmMWSc 92
**Girard**, G Tanner 1952- AmMWSc 92, WhoMW 92
**Girard**, James Emery 1945- AmMWSc 92
**Girard**, James Louis 1953- WhoAmP 91
**Girard**, James P. DrAPF 91
**Girard**, Kenneth Francis 1924- AmMWSc 92
**Girard**, Leonard Arthur 1942- WhoAmL 92, WhoFI 92
**Girard**, Nettabell 1938- WhoAmL 92
**Girard**, Rene Noel 1923- IntWW 91
**Girard**, Stephen 1750-1831 DcAmImH
**Girard De Charbonnieres**, Guy de 1907- IntWW 91
**Girard-diCarlo**, Constance Bricker 1947- WhoFI 92
**Girardeau**, Arnett E 1929- WhoAmP 91
**Girardeau**, Marvin Denham, Jr 1930- AmMWSc 92
**Girardi**, Anthony Joseph 1926- AmMWSc 92
**Girardi**, Laurence Leonard 1953- WhoEnt 92
**Girardin**, David Walter 1951- WhoWest 92
**Girardin**, Delphine Gay De 1804-1855 FrenWW
**Girardin**, Holly Hurtt 1940- WhoMW 92
**Girardin**, Rene-Louis, marquis de 1735-1808 BlkwCEP
**Girardot**, Annie 1931- IntMPA 92
**Girardot**, Annie Suzanne 1931- IntWW 91
**Girardot**, Jean Marie Denis 1944- AmMWSc 92
**Girardot**, Norman John 1943- WhoRel 92
**Girardot**, Peter Raymond 1922- AmMWSc 92
**Giraud**, Andre Louis Yves 1925- IntWW 91
**Giraud**, Henri-Honore 1879-1949 EncTR 91, FacFETw [port]
**Giraud**, Jacob P, Jr 1811?-1870 BiInAmS
**Giraud**, Michel 1929- IntWW 91
**Giraudet**, Pierre 1919- IntWW 91
**Giraudi**, Carlo 1926- AmMWSc 92
**Giraudi**, Patrick 1961- WhoEnt 92
**Giraudier**, Antonio A., Jr. 1926- WhoHisp 92
**Giraudo**, John Peter 1953- WhoAmL 92
**Giraudoux**, Jean 1882-1944 FacFETw, GuFrLit 1
**Girault**, Lawrence Joseph 1915- WhoWest 92
**Giray**, I. Safa 1931- IntWW 91
**Gird**, Steven Richard 1943- AmMWSc 92
**Girden**, Eugene Lawrence 1930- WhoAmL 92
**Girdwood**, Ronald Haxton 1917- IntWW 91, Who 92
**Gire**, Sharon L 1944- WhoAmP 91
**Girello**, Paul Vincent 1951- WhoEnt 92
**Girenko**, Andrey Nikolaevich 1936- SovUnBD
**Girenko**, Andrey Nikolayevich 1936- IntWW 91
**Girer**, Irvin 1920- WhoMW 92
**Girerd**, Rene Jean 1920- AmMWSc 92
**Girgenti**, John Alexander 1947- WhoAmP 91
**Giri**, Jagannath 1933- AmMWSc 92
**Giri**, Lallan AmMWSc 92
**Giri**, Narayan C 1928- AmMWSc 92
**Giri**, Shri N 1934- AmMWSc 92
**Giri**, Tulsi 1926- IntWW 91
**Giri**, V V 1894-1980 FacFETw
**Girifalco**, Louis A 1928- AmMWSc 92
**Girijavallabhan**, Viyyoor Moopil 1942- AmMWSc 92
**Girion**, Barbara 1937- SmATA 14AS [port]
**Girit**, Ibrahim Cem 1951- AmMWSc 92
**Giritlian**, James Sarkis 1948- WhoEnt 92
**Girling**, John 1926- WrDr 92
**Girling**, John Lawrence Scott 1926- IntAu&W 91
**Girling**, Peter Howard d1991 Who 92N
**Girling**, Sheila TwCPaSc
**Girod**, Frank Paul 1908- WhoWest 92
**Girod**, Jean-Philippe WhoEnt 92
**Girodias**, Maurice 1919-1990 AnObit 1990
**Girolami**, Lisa S. 1960- WhoEnt 92
**Girolami**, Paul 1926- IntWW 91, Who 92
**Girolami**, Roland Louis 1924- AmMWSc 92
**Giron**, Jose Alberto 1948- WhoHisp 92
**Giron**, Juan Rene WhoRel 92
**Giron**, Robert LeRoy 1952- WhoHisp 92
**Giron De Velasco**, Jose Antonio 1911- BiDExR
**Girone**, Maria Elena 1939- WhoHisp 92
**Girotti**, Albert William 1937- AmMWSc 92
**Girou**, Michael L 1947- AmMWSc 92
**Girouard**, Fernand E 1938- AmMWSc 92
**Girouard**, Mark 1931- Who 92, WrDr 92
**Girouard**, Peggy Jo Fulcher 1933- WhoEnt 92
**Girouard**, Ronald Maurice 1936- AmMWSc 92
**Giroud**, Francoise 1916- IntWW 91
**Giroux**, Andre 1916- FacFETw
**Giroux**, E. X. WrDr 92
**Giroux**, Guy 1926- AmMWSc 92
**Giroux**, Joye 1930- IntAu&W 91
**Giroux**, Roger M. 1945- WhoMW 92
**Giroux**, Vincent A 1921- AmMWSc 92
**Giroux**, Yves M 1935- AmMWSc 92
**Girovich**, Mark Jacob 1934- WhoFI 92
**Girri**, Alberto 1919- ConSpAP
**Girsch**, Stephen John 1946- AmMWSc 92
**Girse**, Robert Donald 1948- AmMWSc 92
**Girth**, Marjorie Louisa 1939- WhoAmL 92
**Girton**, Lance 1942- WhoWest 92
**Girty**, Simon TwCWW 91
**Girty**, Simon 1741-1818 BenetAL 91
**Girtz**, Joseph Michael 1896- WhoRel 92
**Girvigian**, Raymond 1926- WhoWest 92
**Girvin**, Eb Carl 1917- AmMWSc 92
**Girvin**, Gary Edward 1951- WhoAmP 91
**Girvin**, John Patterson 1934- AmMWSc 92
**Girvin**, Richard Allen 1926- WhoEnt 92, WhoFI 92
**Girvin**, Steven M 1950- AmMWSc 92
**Girzone**, Joseph F. 1930- WrDr 92
**Gisbert**, Nelson 1946- WhoHisp 92
**Gisborough**, Baron 1927- Who 92
**Giscard D'Estaing**, Francois 1926- IntWW 91
**Giscard d'Estaing**, Valery 1926- FacFETw [port], IntWW 91, Who 92
**Gisch**, Daryl John 1955- WhoMW 92
**Giscombe**, C.S. DrAPF 91
**Gisel**, Pierre 1947- WhoRel 92
**Gisevius**, Hans Bernd 1904-1974 EncTR 91 [port]
**Gish**, Annabeth IntMPA 92
**Gish**, Duane Tolbert 1921- AmMWSc 92
**Gish**, Edward Rutledge 1908- WhoMW 92
**Gish**, Glenwood Littleton 1931- WhoFI 92
**Gish**, Lawrence Lee 1930- WhoAmP 91
**Gish**, Lillian WhoEnt 92
**Gish**, Lillian 1896?- FacFETw, IntMPA 92, ReelWom
**Gish**, Lillian Diana 1899- IntWW 91, Who 92
**Gish**, Robert F. 1940- ConAu 133
**Gish**, Robert Franklin 1940- WhoMW 92
**Gish**, Rodney Wayne 1946- WhoRel 92
**Gislason**, Eric Arni 1940- AmMWSc 92
**Gislason**, Gylfi Th. 1917- IntWW 91
**Gislason**, I Lee 1943- AmMWSc 92
**Gisler**, Galen Ross 1950- AmMWSc 92
**Gismondi**, Emma DcTwDes
**Gismondi**, Ernesto DcTwDes
**Gisolfi**, Carl Vincent 1942- AmMWSc 92, WhoMW 92
**Gisriel**, Michael 1951- WhoAmP 91
**Gissen**, Aaron J 1917- AmMWSc 92
**Gissendanner**, John M. 1939- WhoBlA 92
**Gissing**, George 1857-1903 RfGEnL 91
**Gissler**, Sig 1935- ConAu 134
**Gissler**, Sigvard Gunnar, Jr. 1935- WhoMW 92
**Gist**, Carole 1970?- ConBlB 1 [port]
**Gist**, Christopher 1706?-1759 BenetAL 91
**Gist**, Eloice ReelWom
**Gist**, Herman C WhoAmP 91
**Gist**, Howard Battle, Jr. 1919- WhoAmL 92
**Gist**, Jessie M. Gilbert 1925- WhoBlA 92
**Gist**, Karen Wingfield 1950- WhoBlA 92
**Gist**, Lewis Alexander, Jr 1921- AmMWSc 92, WhoBlA 92
**Giszczak**, Thaddeus 1916- AmMWSc 92
**Gitaitis**, Ronald David 1950- AmMWSc 92
**Gitalov**, Aleksandr Vasilyevich 1915- IntWW 91
**Gitch**, David William 1939- WhoWest 92
**Gitchel**, Wallace Dent 1941- WhoAmL 92
**Gite**, Lloyd Anthony 1951- WhoBlA 92
**Giteck**, Janice 1946- ConCom 92
**Gitelman**, Hillel J 1932- AmMWSc 92
**Githens**, John Horace, Jr 1922- AmMWSc 92
**Githii**, Ethel Waddell WhoBlA 92
**Gitin**, David DrAPF 91
**Gitin**, Maria DrAPF 91
**Gitin**, Seymour 1936- WhoRel 92
**Gitlin**, Chris 1933- WhoAmP 91
**Gitlin**, Harris Martlin 1914- AmMWSc 92
**Gitlin**, Irving d1967 LesBEnT 92
**Gitlin**, Todd DrAPF 91
**Gitlin**, Todd 1943- WhoWest 92
**Gitlin**, Todd A. 1943- WrDr 92
**Gitlitz**, Melvin H 1940- AmMWSc 92
**Gitlitz**, Stuart Hal 1951- WhoAmL 92
**Gitlow**, Allan Michael 1943- WhoMW 92
**Gitney**, James John 1955- WhoFI 92
**Gitnick**, Gary L 1939- AmMWSc 92
**Gitnick**, Gary Lee 1939- WhoWest 92
**Gitomer**, Steven Joel 1942- WhoWest 92
**Gitt**, Robert Roper 1941- WhoEnt 92
**Gittelman**, Bernard 1932- AmMWSc 92
**Gittelman**, Donald Henry 1929- AmMWSc 92
**Gittelman**, Phillip Bruce 1938- WhoEnt 92
**Gittelsohn**, Roland B. 1910- WrDr 92
**Gittelsohn**, Roland Bertram 1910- WhoRel 92
**Gittelson**, Abraham Jacob 1928- WhoRel 92
**Gittens**, James Philip 1952- WhoBlA 92
**Gittens**, Robert Preston 1952- WhoAmL 92
**Gittens**, Sheila Sledge 1948- WhoEnt 92
**Gitter**, Max 1943- WhoAmL 92
**Gitter**, Robert Jeffrey 1950- WhoFI 92, WhoMW 92
**Gittes**, Frederick M. 1947- WhoAmL 92
**Gittes**, Ruben Foster 1934- AmMWSc 92
**Gittings**, Harold John 1947- Who 92
**Gittings**, Robert 1911- ConPo 91, IntAu&W 91, Who 92, WrDr 92
**Gittings**, Steven Vernley 1955- WhoFI 92
**Gittins**, Arthur Richard 1926- AmMWSc 92
**Gittins**, John 1932- AmMWSc 92
**Gittleman**, Arthur P 1941- AmMWSc 92
**Gittleman**, Arthur Paul 1941- WhoWest 92
**Gittleman**, Jonathan I 1926- AmMWSc 92
**Gittleman**, Morris 1912- WhoFI 92
**Gittlen**, Barry M. 1943- WhoRel 92
**Gittler**, Franz Ludwig 1924- AmMWSc 92
**Gittler**, Joseph B. 1912- WrDr 92
**Gittler**, Sydney d1991 NewYTBS 91 [port]
**Gittleson**, Stephen Mark 1938- AmMWSc 92
**Gittlin**, Arthur Sam 1914- WhoFI 92
**Gittus**, Gary Alan 1960- WhoAmL 92
**Gittus**, John Henry 1930- Who 92
**Gitzendanner**, L G 1919- AmMWSc 92
**Giudici**, Franco William 1928- WhoRel 92
**Giuffra**, Robert Joseph 1930- WhoAmL 92
**Giuffrai**, Gerald Leroy 1935- WhoEnt 92
**Giuffre**, Jimmy WhoEnt 92
**Giuffre**, Jimmy 1921- NewAmDM
**Giuffrida**, Barbara Ann 1952- WhoFI 92
**Giuffrida**, Elio 1919- IntWW 91
**Giuffrida**, Robert Eugene 1928- AmMWSc 92
**Giuffrida**, Thomas Salvatore 1949- AmMWSc 92
**Giugiaro**, Giorgio 1938- DcTwDes
**Giulianelli**, James Louis 1940- AmMWSc 92
**Giuliani**, Alex 1927- WhoAmP 91
**Giuliani**, Peter 1907- WhoAmP 91
**Giuliani**, Rudolph 1944- WhoAmP 91
**Giuliano**, Neil Gerard 1956- WhoWest 92
**Giuliano**, Robert Michael 1954- AmMWSc 92
**Giuliano**, Vincent E 1929- AmMWSc 92
**Giulianti**, Mara Selena 1944- WhoAmP 91
**Giulietti**, Giuseppe 1879-1953 BiDExR
**Giulietti**, James D WhoAmP 91
**Giulini**, Carlo Maria 1914- FacFETw, IntWW 91, NewAmDM, Who 92
**Giunchigliani**, Chris WhoAmP 91
**Giunta**, Anthony John 1928- WhoAmP 91
**Giunta**, Francesco 1887-1971 BiDExR
**Giunta**, Joseph 1951- WhoEnt 92, WhoMW 92
**Giunta**, Raymond 1960- WhoRel 92
**Giuranna**, Bruno 1933- IntWW 91
**Giurescu**, Dinu C. 1927- IntWW 91
**Giuriati**, Giovanni Battista 1876-1970 BiDExR
**Giurlando**, Lorraine Mary 1966- WhoFI 92
**Gius**, John Armes 1908- AmMWSc 92
**Giussani**, Pablo d1991 NewYTBS 91
**Giusti**, William Roger 1947- WhoAmL 92
**Giusto**, Thomas Michael 1953- WhoEnt 92
**Givan**, Boyd Eugene WhoFI 92
**Givan**, Lori Rey 1960- WhoMW 92
**Givan**, Richard M 1921- WhoAmP 91
**Givan**, Richard Martin 1921- WhoAmL 92, WhoMW 92
**Givant**, Philip Joachim 1935- WhoFI 92, WhoWest 92
**Givas**, Thomas Peter 1957- WhoAmL 92
**Givaudan**, Ben Trested, III 1936- WhoEnt 92
**Givelber**, Daniel James 1940- WhoAmL 92
**Given**, Edward Ferguson 1919- Who 92
**Given**, Peter Hervey 1918- AmMWSc 92
**Given**, Phyllis WhoAmP 91
**Given**, Robert R 1932- AmMWSc 92
**Givenchy**, Hubert de 1927- IntWW 91
**Givenchy**, Hubert Taffin de 1927- DcTwDes, FacFETw
**Givens**, Arthur A, Jr 1936- WhoAmP 91
**Givens**, Clementina M. 1921- WhoBlA 92
**Givens**, David W. 1932- WhoFI 92, WhoMW 92
**Givens**, Donovahn Heston 1930- WhoBlA 92
**Givens**, E. Terrian 1930- WhoBlA 92
**Givens**, Edwin Neil 1935- AmMWSc 92
**Givens**, Ernest P. 1964- WhoBlA 92
**Givens**, Henry, Jr. WhoBlA 92
**Givens**, Jack Rodman 1928- WhoAmL 92
**Givens**, James Robert 1930- AmMWSc 92
**Givens**, James Wallace, Jr. 1910- WhoWest 92
**Givens**, Jeanne WhoAmP 91
**Givens**, Joshua Edmond 1953- WhoBlA 92
**Givens**, Ken 1947- WhoAmP 91
**Givens**, Lawrence 1938- WhoBlA 92
**Givens**, Leonard David 1943- WhoBlA 92
**Givens**, Maurice 1945- WhoMW 92
**Givens**, Paul Edward 1934- AmMWSc 92
**Givens**, Richard Ayres 1932- WhoAmL 92
**Givens**, Richard Spencer 1940- AmMWSc 92
**Givens**, Robin WhoEnt 92
**Givens**, Robin 1965- WhoBlA 92
**Givens**, Ron D 1952- WhoAmP 91
**Givens**, Roy E 1929- WhoAmP 91
**Givens**, Samuel Virtue 1946- AmMWSc 92
**Givens**, Stann William 1950- WhoAmL 92
**Givens**, Terry Stuart 1945- WhoAmL 92
**Givens**, William Geary 1932- AmMWSc 92

**Givens,** William L. 1940- *WhoWest 92*
**Givens,** Willie Alan 1938- *Who 92*
**Givens,** Wyatt Wendell 1932- *AmMWSc 92*
**Givhan,** Mercer A., Jr. 1943- *WhoBlA 92*
**Givhan,** Robin Deneen 1964- *WhoBlA 92*
**Givhan,** Thomas Bartram 1926- *WhoAmL 92*
**Givi,** Peyman 1958- *AmMWSc 92*
**Givins,** Abe, Jr. 1951- *WhoBlA 92*
**Givler,** Robert L 1931- *AmMWSc 92*
**Givone,** Donald Daniel 1936- *AmMWSc 92*
**Givot,** Steven Ira 1950- *WhoMW 92*
**Giza,** Chester Anthony 1930- *AmMWSc 92*
**Giza,** Yueh-Hua Chen 1929- *AmMWSc 92*
**Gizis,** Evangelos John 1934- *AmMWSc 92*
**Gizouli,** Dafallah *IntWW 91*
**Gizzi,** Michael *DrAPF 91*
**Gjaerevoll,** Olav 1916- *IntWW 91*
**Gjedde,** Albert 1946- *AmMWSc 92*
**Gjellerup,** Karl 1857-1919 *FacFETw*
**Gjellerup,** Karl Adolph 1857-1919 *WhoNob 90*
**Gjelsness,** Barent *DrAPF 91*
**Gjerde,** Bjartmar 1931- *IntWW 91*
**Gjerde,** Kristina Maria 1957- *WhoAmL 92*
**Gjere,** Linda Janssen 1950- *WhoRel 92*
**Gjerness,** Omar Norman 1922- *WhoRel 92*
**Gjerstad,** Diane A 1957- *WhoAmP 91*
**Gjertsen,** Astrid 1928- *IntWW 91*
**Gjessing,** Helen Witton 1927- *AmMWSc 92*
**Gjostein,** Norman A 1931- *AmMWSc 92*
**Gjovig,** Bruce Quentin 1951- *WhoMW 92*
**Glabe,** Charles G 1952- *AmMWSc 92*
**Glabe,** Elmer Frederick 1911- *WhoMW 92*
**Glaberson,** William I 1944- *AmMWSc 92*
**Glabman,** Sheldon 1932- *AmMWSc 92*
**Glacel,** Barbara Pate 1948- *WhoFI 92*
**Glackens,** William 1870-1938 *FacFETw*
**Glackin,** William Charles 1917- *WhoEnt 92*
**Glacking,** Marjorie Joyce Straub 1936- *WhoMW 92*
**Glad,** Dain Sturgis 1932- *WhoWest 92*
**Glad,** Edward Newman 1919- *WhoAmL 92*
**Glad,** John 1941- *ConAu 133*
**Glad,** Suzanne Lockley 1929- *WhoWest 92*
**Gladd,** Neil Laurence 1955- *WhoEnt 92*
**Gladden,** Brenda Winckler 1943- *WhoBlA 92*
**Gladden,** Bruce 1951- *AmMWSc 92*
**Gladden,** Dean Robert 1953- *WhoEnt 92, WhoMW 92*
**Gladden,** James Walter, Jr. 1940- *WhoAmL 92*
**Gladden,** Joseph Rhea, Jr. 1942- *WhoAmL 92*
**Gladden,** Major P. 1935- *WhoBlA 92*
**Gladden,** Thomas Christopher 1948- *WhoEnt 92*
**Gladden,** Washington 1836-1918 *RelLAm 91*
**Gladding,** Gary Earle 1944- *AmMWSc 92*
**Gladding,** Walter St.George 1936- *WhoFI 92*
**Glade,** Richard William 1928- *AmMWSc 92*
**Gladeck,** Joseph M, Jr 1950- *WhoAmP 91*
**Gladfelter,** Wayne Lewis 1953- *AmMWSc 92*
**Gladfelter,** Wilbert Eugene 1928- *AmMWSc 92*
**Gladilin,** Anatoliy Tikhonovich 1935- *IntWW 91, SovUnBD*
**Glading,** Jan *DrAPF 91*
**Gladkin,** Peter 1947- *WhoFI 92*
**Gladkov,** Fedor Vasil'evich 1883-1958 *SovUnBD*
**Gladky,** Ivan Ivanovich 1930- *IntWW 91*
**Gladman,** Charles Herman 1917- *AmMWSc 92*
**Gladner,** Marc Stefan 1952- *WhoWest 92*
**Gladney,** Henry M 1938- *AmMWSc 92*
**Gladney,** Marcellious 1949- *WhoBlA 92*
**Gladrow,** Elroy Merle 1915- *AmMWSc 92*
**Gladson,** Guy Allen, Jr. 1928- *WhoAmL 92*
**Gladstein,** Robert David 1943- *WhoEnt 92*
**Gladstone,** Arthur M 1921- *IntAu&W 91, WrDr 92*
**Gladstone,** David Arthur Steuart 1935- *IntWW 91, Who 92*
**Gladstone,** Eve *ConAu 34NR*
**Gladstone,** Harold Maurice 1932- *AmMWSc 92*
**Gladstone,** Kenneth Alan 1948- *WhoEnt 92*
**Gladstone,** Maggie *WrDr 92*
**Gladstone,** Matthew Theodore 1919- *AmMWSc 92*
**Gladstone,** William 1925- *IntWW 91, Who 92*
**Gladstone,** William Louis 1931- *WhoFI 92*
**Gladstone,** William Turnbull 1931- *AmMWSc 92*
**Gladue,** Brian Anthony 1950- *AmMWSc 92*
**Gladush,** Ivan Dmitrievich *IntWW 91*
**Gladwell,** Beatrice Howard 1914- *WhoAmP 91*
**Gladwell,** Graham M L 1934- *AmMWSc 92*
**Gladwell,** Ian 1944- *AmMWSc 92*
**Gladwell,** Rodney 1928- *TwCPaSc*
**Gladwin,** Derek Oliver 1930- *Who 92*
**Gladwin,** John Warren 1942- *Who 92*
**Gladwin,** William Joseph, Jr. 1946- *WhoAmL 92*
**Gladwyn,** Baron 1900- *IntWW 91, Who 92*
**Gladwyn,** Lord 1900- *WrDr 92*
**Gladysz,** John A 1952- *AmMWSc 92*
**Gladysz,** John Andrew 1952- *WhoWest 92*
**Glaenzer,** Richard H 1933- *AmMWSc 92*
**Glaeser,** Hans Hellmut 1934- *AmMWSc 92*
**Glaeser,** Robert M 1937- *AmMWSc 92*
**Glaeser,** William A 1923- *AmMWSc 92*
**Glagov,** Seymour 1925- *AmMWSc 92*
**Glahe,** Fred R. 1934- *WrDr 92*
**Glahn,** Harry Robert 1928- *AmMWSc 92*
**Glaid,** Andrew Joseph, III 1923- *AmMWSc 92*
**Glaister,** Lesley 1956- *ConAu 134*
**Glaisyer,** Hugh 1930- *Who 92*
**Glamann,** Kristof 1923- *IntWW 91, Who 92*
**Glamis,** Lord 1986- *Who 92*
**Glamis,** Walter *TwCSFW 91*
**Glamkowski,** Edward Joseph 1936- *AmMWSc 92*
**Glamorgan,** Earl of 1989- *Who 92*
**Glance,** Harvey 1957- *BlkOlyM*
**Glancey,** Burnett Michael 1930- *AmMWSc 92*
**Glancy,** Alfred Robinson, III 1938- *WhoFI 92, WhoMW 92*
**Glancy,** David L 1934- *AmMWSc 92*
**Glancy,** Diane *DrAPF 91*
**Glancy,** Dorothy Jean 1944- *WhoAmL 92*
**Glancz,** Ronald Robert 1943- *WhoAmL 92*
**Gland,** John Louis 1947- *AmMWSc 92*
**Glanden,** William Donald 1951- *WhoEnt 92*
**Glander,** Charles Franklin 1933- *WhoAmL 92*
**Glandine,** Viscount 1967- *Who 92*
**Glandt,** Eduardo Daniel 1945- *AmMWSc 92*
**Glang,** Gabriele *DrAPF 91*
**Glanstein,** Eleanor Elovich 1944- *WhoAmL 92*
**Glanstein,** Joel Charles 1940- *WhoAmL 92*
**Glanstein,** Ralph 1933- *WhoAmL 92*
**Glanton,** John Lee 1952- *WhoMW 92*
**Glanton,** Luther Thomas, Jr. 1913-1991 *WhoBlA 92N*
**Glanton,** Lydia Jackson 1909- *WhoBlA 92*
**Glanton,** Richard H. 1946- *WhoAmL 92*
**Glanton,** Richard Howard 1946- *WhoAmP 91*
**Glanton,** Sadye Lyerson 1900- *WhoBlA 92*
**Glantz,** David M. 1942- *ConAu 135*
**Glantz,** Gina Stritzler 1943- *WhoAmP 91*
**Glantz,** Raymon M 1941- *AmMWSc 92*
**Glantz,** Stanton Arnold 1946- *AmMWSc 92*
**Glantz,** Wendy Newman 1956- *WhoAmL 92*
**Glanusk,** Baron 1917- *Who 92*
**Glanville,** Alec William 1921- *Who 92*
**Glanville,** Brian 1931- *ConNov 91, WrDr 92*
**Glanville,** Brian Lester *IntAu&W 91*
**Glanville,** Brian Lester 1931- *Who 92*
**Glanville,** Cecil E. 1925- *WhoBlA 92*
**Glanville,** Dorian Anthony 1946- *WhoWest 92*
**Glanville,** James Oliver 1941- *AmMWSc 92*
**Glanville,** John Hart 1954- *WhoFI 92*
**Glanville Brown,** William *Who 92*
**Glanville-Hicks,** Peggy 1912- *NewAmDM*
**Glanville-Hicks,** Peggy 1912-1990 *AnObit 1990*
**Glanville-Jones,** Thomas *Who 92*
**Glanz,** Filson H 1934- *AmMWSc 92*
**Glanz,** Karen 1953- *ConAu 135*
**Glanz,** Peter K 1941- *AmMWSc 92*
**Glanz,** William Edward 1949- *AmMWSc 92*
**Glanzer,** David William 1943- *WhoAmL 92*
**Glanzer,** Mona Naomi 1931- *WhoAmL 92*
**Glanzman,** Steven Blaise 1955- *WhoFI 92*
**Glanzrock,** Stephen Andrew 1948- *WhoEnt 92*
**Glaphyra** *EncAmaz 91*
**Glapinski,** Adam 1950- *IntWW 91*
**Glapthorne,** Henry 1610?-1643? *RfGEnL 91*
**Glar,** Martha *EncAmaz 91*
**Glareanus,** Henricus 1488-1563 *NewAmDM*
**Glaros,** George Raymond 1941- *AmMWSc 92*
**Glarum,** Sivert Herth 1933- *AmMWSc 92*
**Glasberg,** Paula Drillman 1939- *WhoFI 92*
**Glasbergen,** Willem 1923- *IntWW 91*
**Glasby,** Ian 1931- *Who 92*
**Glasco,** Anita L. 1942- *WhoBlA 92*
**Glasco,** Kimberly *WhoEnt 92*
**Glascock,** Homer Hopson, II 1929- *AmMWSc 92*
**Glascock,** Michael Dean 1949- *AmMWSc 92*
**Glasel,** Jay Arthur 1934- *AmMWSc 92*
**Glaser,** Alvin 1932- *WhoFI 92*
**Glaser,** Arthur Henry 1947- *WhoAmL 92*
**Glaser,** Charles Barry *AmMWSc 92*
**Glaser,** Charles Vernon 1936- *WhoEnt 92*
**Glaser,** Christopher Roy 1950- *WhoRel 92*
**Glaser,** Comstock *WrDr 92*
**Glaser,** David Hugo 1956- *WhoFI 92*
**Glaser,** David Martin 1957- *WhoAmL 92*
**Glaser,** Donald Arthur 1926- *AmMWSc 92, IntWW 91, Who 92, WhoNob 90, WhoWest 92*
**Glaser,** Donald H. 1941- *WhoAmL 92, WhoWest 92*
**Glaser,** Douglas Edward 1951- *WhoFI 92*
**Glaser,** Edmund M 1927- *AmMWSc 92*
**Glaser,** Edward L 1929- *AmMWSc 92*
**Glaser,** Elton *DrAPF 91*
**Glaser,** Elton Albert, II 1945- *WhoMW 92*
**Glaser,** Frederic M 1935- *AmMWSc 92*
**Glaser,** Frederick Bernard 1935- *AmMWSc 92*
**Glaser,** Gareth Evan 1952- *WhoAmL 92*
**Glaser,** Gilbert Herbert 1920- *AmMWSc 92*
**Glaser,** Harold 1924- *AmMWSc 92*
**Glaser,** Herman 1923- *AmMWSc 92*
**Glaser,** Isabel Joshlin *DrAPF 91*
**Glaser,** Janet H 1944- *AmMWSc 92*
**Glaser,** Joseph Bernard 1925- *WhoRel 92*
**Glaser,** Keith Brian 1960- *AmMWSc 92*
**Glaser,** Kenneth B., Jr. 1926- *WhoAmL 92*
**Glaser,** Kurt 1914- *WrDr 92*
**Glaser,** Kurt 1915- *AmMWSc 92*
**Glaser,** Leslie 1937- *AmMWSc 92*
**Glaser,** Luis 1932- *AmMWSc 92*
**Glaser,** Michael 1945- *AmMWSc 92, WhoMW 92*
**Glaser,** Michael S. *DrAPF 91*
**Glaser,** Milton 1929- *DcTwDes, FacFETw, WhoEnt 92*
**Glaser,** Milton Arthur 1912- *AmMWSc 92*
**Glaser,** Myron B 1927- *AmMWSc 92*
**Glaser,** Nancy Ellen 1945- *WhoWest 92*
**Glaser,** Norman Dale 1921- *WhoAmP 91*
**Glaser,** Paul Michael 1943- *IntMPA 92, WhoEnt 92*
**Glaser,** Peter E 1923- *AmMWSc 92*
**Glaser,** Robert 1921- *AmMWSc 92, IntWW 91*
**Glaser,** Robert Edward 1935- *WhoAmL 92*
**Glaser,** Robert Harvey, Sr. 1935- *WhoRel 92*
**Glaser,** Robert J 1942- *AmMWSc 92*
**Glaser,** Robert Joy 1918- *AmMWSc 92, IntWW 91*
**Glaser,** Robert L. *LesBEnT 92*
**Glaser,** Robert Leonard 1929- *WhoEnt 92*
**Glaser,** Roger Michael 1944- *AmMWSc 92*
**Glaser,** Ronald 1939- *AmMWSc 92*
**Glaser,** Sidney 1912- *IntMPA 92*
**Glaser,** Steven Jay 1957- *WhoAmL 92*
**Glaser,** Susan Jo Rosenblum 1948- *WhoWest 92*
**Glaser,** Thomas John 1957- *WhoFI 92*
**Glaser,** Walter 1929- *IntAu&W 91*
**Glaser,** Warren 1928- *AmMWSc 92*
**Glaser,** William 1940- *WhoAmP 91*
**Glaser,** William Arnold 1925- *WrDr 92*
**Glaser de Lugo,** Frank *AmMWSc 92*
**Glasford,** Glenn M 1918- *AmMWSc 92*
**Glasgo,** Mark Albert 1964- *WhoMW 92*
**Glasgow,** Archbishop of *Who 92*
**Glasgow,** Auxiliary Bishop of *Who 92*
**Glasgow,** Earl of 1939- *Who 92*
**Glasgow,** Provost of *Who 92*
**Glasgow,** Dale William 1925- *AmMWSc 92*
**Glasgow,** David Gerald 1936- *AmMWSc 92*
**Glasgow,** David Leroy 1942- *WhoEnt 92*
**Glasgow,** Douglas G. *WhoBlA 92*
**Glasgow,** Edwin 1874-1955 *TwCPaSc*
**Glasgow,** Edwin John 1945- *Who 92*
**Glasgow,** Ellen 1873-1945 *ModAWWr*
**Glasgow,** Ellen 1874-1945 *BenetAL 91*
**Glasgow,** James 1735?-1819 *DcNCBi 2*
**Glasgow,** James Alan 1945- *WhoAmL 92*
**Glasgow,** John Charles 1932- *AmMWSc 92*
**Glasgow,** Louis Charles 1943- *AmMWSc 92*
**Glasgow,** Lowell Alan 1932- *AmMWSc 92*
**Glasgow,** Norman Milton 1922- *WhoAmL 92*
**Glasgow,** Robert Joe 1942- *WhoAmP 91*
**Glasgow,** Thomas William, Jr. 1947- *WhoFI 92*
**Glasgow,** Vicki Louise 1947- *WhoMW 92*
**Glasgow,** Willene Graythen 1939- *WhoFI 92*
**Glasgow,** William Jacob 1946- *WhoAmL 92, WhoFI 92*
**Glasgow And Galloway,** Bishop of 1932- *Who 92*
**Glasgow And Galloway,** Dean of *Who 92*
**Glashausser,** Charles Michael 1939- *AmMWSc 92*
**Glashow,** Sheldon Lee 1932- *AmMWSc 92, IntWW 91, Who 92, WhoNob 90*
**Glaskin,** G M 1923- *IntAu&W 91, WrDr 92*
**Glasky,** Alvin Jerald 1933- *AmMWSc 92*
**Glasner,** Ann K. *DrAPF 91*
**Glasner,** Daniel Mayer 1940- *WhoFI 92*
**Glasner,** Moses 1942- *AmMWSc 92*
**Glasoe,** Paul Kirkwold 1913- *AmMWSc 92*
**Glaspell,** Susan 1876-1948 *ModAWWr, TwCWW 91*
**Glaspell,** Susan 1882-1948 *BenetAL 91*
**Glaspey,** John Warren 1944- *AmMWSc 92*
**Glaspie,** April C *WhoAmP 91*
**Glaspie,** April Catherine 1942- *NewYTBS 91*
**Glaspie,** Donald Lee 1922- *AmMWSc 92*
**Glaspie,** Peyton Scott 1946- *AmMWSc 92*
**Glasrud,** Bruce Alden 1940- *WhoWest 92*
**Glasrud,** Clarence A. 1911- *WrDr 92*
**Glass,** Alastair Malcolm 1940- *AmMWSc 92*
**Glass,** Alexander Jacob 1933- *AmMWSc 92*
**Glass,** Andrew *ConAu 134*
**Glass,** Andrew Martin William 1944- *WhoMW 92*
**Glass,** Anthony Trevor 1940- *Who 92*
**Glass,** Arthur Warren 1921- *AmMWSc 92*
**Glass,** Benjamin d1991 *NewYTBS 91*
**Glass,** Benjamin 1911- *WhoAmL 92*
**Glass,** Beth Ann 1957- *WhoFI 92*
**Glass,** Billy Price 1940- *AmMWSc 92*
**Glass,** Bryan Pettigrew 1919- *AmMWSc 92*
**Glass,** Daniel S. *WhoEnt 92*
**Glass,** David Bankes 1947- *AmMWSc 92*
**Glass,** David Carter 1930- *AmMWSc 92*
**Glass,** David D. 1935- *WhoFI 92*
**Glass,** Edward Brown 1913- *Who 92*
**Glass,** Edward Hadley 1917- *AmMWSc 92*
**Glass,** Edward Nathan *AmMWSc 92*
**Glass,** Fred Stephen 1940- *WhoAmL 92*
**Glass,** Geoffrey Theodore 1954- *WhoAmL 92*
**Glass,** George 1936- *AmMWSc 92*
**Glass,** George B Jerzy 1903- *AmMWSc 92*
**Glass,** Gerald Damon 1967- *WhoBlA 92*
**Glass,** Graham Percy 1938- *AmMWSc 92*
**Glass,** H. Bentley 1906- *IntWW 91*
**Glass,** Herbert 1934- *WhoEnt 92*
**Glass,** Herbert David 1915- *AmMWSc 92*
**Glass,** Hiram Bentley 1906- *AmMWSc 92*
**Glass,** Howard George 1909- *AmMWSc 92*
**Glass,** Hugh d1833? *BenetAL 91*
**Glass,** I I 1918- *AmMWSc 92*
**Glass,** James 1928- *WhoBlA 92*
**Glass,** James Clifford 1937- *AmMWSc 92*
**Glass,** James William 1946- *WhoEnt 92*
**Glass,** Jesse, Jr. *DrAPF 91*
**Glass,** John Richard 1917- *AmMWSc 92*
**Glass,** Jonathan Thaddeus 1957- *WhoRel 92*
**Glass,** Jonathan Wilson 1957- *WhoRel 92*
**Glass,** Joseph E. 1940- *WhoAmL 92*
**Glass,** Laurel Ellen 1923- *AmMWSc 92*
**Glass,** Leo 1936- *WhoAmL 92*
**Glass,** Linda Mae 1952- *WhoEnt 92*
**Glass,** Malcolm *DrAPF 91*
**Glass,** Mark 1947- *WhoAmL 92*
**Glass,** Michael Stuart, II 1963- *WhoFI 92*
**Glass,** Molly 1925- *IntAu&W 91*
**Glass,** Montague *DcAmImH*
**Glass,** Montague 1877-1934 *BenetAL 91*
**Glass,** Murray 1924- *WhoEnt 92*
**Glass,** Nathaniel E 1949- *AmMWSc 92*
**Glass,** Philip 1937- *ConCom 92, FacFETw, IntWW 91, NewAmDM, News 91 [port], WhoEnt 92*
**Glass,** Richard Lawrence 1931- *WhoMW 92*
**Glass,** Richard Lee 1932- *WhoRel 92*
**Glass,** Richard Steven 1943- *AmMWSc 92*
**Glass,** Richard Thomas 1941- *AmMWSc 92*
**Glass,** Robert 1940- *WhoAmL 92*
**Glass,** Robert David 1922- *WhoAmP 91*
**Glass,** Robert Davis 1922- *WhoAmL 92, WhoBlA 92*
**Glass,** Robert Louis 1923- *AmMWSc 92*
**Glass,** Roger I M 1946- *AmMWSc 92*
**Glass,** Ronald 1945- *WhoBlA 92*
**Glass,** Ronald Lee 1946- *WhoFI 92*
**Glass,** Ruth 1912-1990 *AnObit 1990*
**Glass,** Stephen Joseph 1917- *WhoWest 92*

**Glass**, Thomas 1945- WhoAmP 91
**Glass**, Todd Irwin 1961- WhoMW 92
**Glass**, Virginia M. 1927- WhoBlA 92
**Glass**, Werner 1927- AmMWSc 92
**Glass**, William A 1931- AmMWSc 92
**Glass**, William Lawrence 1955- WhoFI 92
**Glass**, William Mervyn 1885-1965 TwCPaSc
**Glassbrenner**, Charles J 1928- AmMWSc 92
**Glassco**, John 1909-1981 BenetAL 91
**Glasscock**, Amnesia ConAu 35NR
**Glasscock**, Anne WrDr 92
**Glasscock**, James Samuel 1931- WhoAmP 91
**Glasscock**, John Lewis 1928- Who 92
**Glasscock**, Kent WhoAmP 91
**Glasscock**, Weldon Alexander 1963- WhoFI 92, WhoWest 92
**Glasse**, John Howell 1922- WhoRel 92
**Glasse**, Thomas Henry 1898- Who 92
**Glasser**, Alan Herbert 1943- AmMWSc 92
**Glasser**, Arthur Charles 1921- AmMWSc 92
**Glasser**, Eugene Robert 1925- WhoRel 92
**Glasser**, Ira Saul 1938- WhoAmL 92
**Glasser**, Israel Leo 1924- WhoAmL 92
**Glasser**, Jay Howard 1935- AmMWSc 92
**Glasser**, John Weakley 1944- AmMWSc 92
**Glasser**, Julian 1912- AmMWSc 92
**Glasser**, Leo George 1916- AmMWSc 92
**Glasser**, M Lawrence 1933- AmMWSc 92
**Glasser**, Perry DrAPF 91
**Glasser**, Richard Lee 1927- AmMWSc 92
**Glasser**, Robert Gene 1929- AmMWSc 92
**Glasser**, Stanley Richard 1926- AmMWSc 92
**Glasser**, Stephen Avodeau 1944- WhoAmL 92
**Glasser**, Thomas Daniel 1946- WhoAmL 92
**Glasser**, Wolfgang Gerhard 1941- AmMWSc 92
**Glassett**, Tim Scott 1956- WhoWest 92
**Glassgold**, Alfred Emanuel 1929- AmMWSc 92
**Glassgow**, M Edward 1934- WhoAmP 91
**Glassgow**, Willis Allen 1934- WhoFI 92
**Glassheim**, Eliot Alan 1938- WhoAmP 91
**Glassick**, Charles Etzweiler 1931- AmMWSc 92
**Glassley**, William Edward 1947- AmMWSc 92
**Glassman**, Abraham 1933- WhoAmP 91
**Glassman**, Armand Barry 1938- AmMWSc 92
**Glassman**, Caroline D WhoAmP 91
**Glassman**, Caroline Duby 1922- WhoAmL 92
**Glassman**, Edward 1929- AmMWSc 92
**Glassman**, Gerald Seymour 1932- WhoFI 92
**Glassman**, Harold Nelson 1912- AmMWSc 92
**Glassman**, Howard Theodore 1934- WhoAmL 92
**Glassman**, Irvin 1923- AmMWSc 92
**Glassman**, Jerome Martin 1919- AmMWSc 92
**Glassman**, Paulette Marie WhoEnt 92
**Glassman**, Richard Alan 1949- WhoAmL 92
**Glassman**, Ronald M. 1937- ConAu 134
**Glassman**, Seth 1946- WhoEnt 92
**Glassman**, Sidney Frederick 1919- AmMWSc 92
**Glassman**, Stuart Lewis 1929- WhoEnt 92
**Glassmeyer**, Steven Kyle 1950- WhoEnt 92
**Glassmoyer**, Thomas Parvin 1915- WhoAmL 92
**Glassner**, Barry 1952- ConAu 135
**Glassner**, Martin Ira 1932- ConAu 34NR
**Glassock**, Richard James AmMWSc 92
**Glasson**, Linda 1947- WhoFI 92
**Glasson**, William Henry 1874-1946 DcNCBi 2
**Glasspole**, Florizel 1909- Who 92
**Glasspole**, Florizel Augustus 1909- IntWW 91
**Glasstone**, Samuel 1897- AmMWSc 92
**Glaston**, W.B. TwCWW 91
**Glastris**, William Vlasios, Jr. 1960- WhoMW 92
**Glater**, Irving William 1927- WhoFI 92
**Glatfelter**, Noah Miller 1837-1911 BiInAmS
**Glatstein**, Eli J 1938- AmMWSc 92
**Glatstein**, Jacob 1896-1971 LiExTwC
**Glatzer**, Louis 1940- AmMWSc 92
**Glatzer**, Robert Anthony 1932- WhoFI 92, WhoWest 92
**Glauber**, Roy Jay 1925- AmMWSc 92
**Glauber**, Stephen LesBEnT 92
**Glauberman**, George Isaac 1941- AmMWSc 92
**Glauberman**, Melvin L. 1927- WhoAmL 92
**Glaubiger**, Merel Pomeranz 1943- WhoAmL 92
**Glaubinger**, Lawrence David 1925- WhoFI 92
**Glaubman**, Michael Juda 1924- AmMWSc 92
**Glauch**, Alden Glenwood 1919- WhoMW 92
**Glaude**, Stephen A. 1954- WhoBlA 92
**Glaudemans**, Cornelis P 1932- AmMWSc 92
**Glauert**, Audrey Marion 1925- Who 92
**Glauert**, Howard Perry 1952- AmMWSc 92
**Glauner**, Alfred William 1936- WhoAmL 92
**Glaunsinger**, William Stanley 1945- AmMWSc 92
**Glauser**, Elinor Mikelberg 1931- AmMWSc 92
**Glauser**, Frederick Louis 1937- AmMWSc 92
**Glauser**, Stanley Charles 1931- AmMWSc 92
**Glauz**, Robert Doran 1927- AmMWSc 92
**Glauz**, William Donald 1933- AmMWSc 92
**Glaves-Smith**, Frank William 1919- Who 92
**Glaviano**, Vincent Valentino 1920- AmMWSc 92
**Glavich**, Thomas Anthony 1950- WhoWest 92
**Glavin**, A. Rita Chandellier 1937- WhoAmL 92
**Glavin**, Anthony DrAPF 91
**Glavin**, Gary Bertrun 1949- AmMWSc 92
**Glavin**, James Henry, III 1931- WhoAmL 92, WhoAmP 91
**Glavin**, William F. 1932- IntWW 91
**Glavin**, William Francis 1932- Who 92
**Glawe**, Lloyd Neil 1932- AmMWSc 92
**Glaze**, Andrew DrAPF 91
**Glaze**, Andrew 1920- IntAu&W 91
**Glaze**, Andrew Louis 1920- WrDr 92
**Glaze**, Bob 1927- WhoAmP 91
**Glaze**, Eleanor DrAPF 91
**Glaze**, Michael John Carlisle 1935- Who 92
**Glaze**, Richard Edward 1930- WhoAmL 92
**Glaze**, Robert P 1933- AmMWSc 92
**Glaze**, Tom 1938- WhoAmL 92, WhoAmP 91
**Glaze**, William H 1934- AmMWSc 92
**Glazebrook**, Carla Rae 1958- WhoWest 92
**Glazebrook**, Mark 1936- Who 92
**Glazebrook**, Philip 1937- WrDr 92
**Glazebrook**, Philip Kirkland 1937- IntAu&W 91
**Glazener**, Edward Walker 1922- AmMWSc 92
**Glazer**, Alexander Namiot 1935- AmMWSc 92
**Glazer**, Andrew Norman Shafron 1955- WhoAmL 92
**Glazer**, Avram A. 1960- WhoAmL 92
**Glazer**, Barry 1936- WhoEnt 92
**Glazer**, Barry David 1948- WhoAmL 92
**Glazer**, Donald Jack 1942- WhoFI 92
**Glazer**, Donald Wayne 1944- WhoAmL 92
**Glazer**, Edward Louis 1946- WhoAmL 92
**Glazer**, Esther WhoEnt 92
**Glazer**, Guilford 1921- WhoFI 92
**Glazer**, Jack Henry 1928- WhoAmL 92
**Glazer**, Mark Jonathan 1949- WhoFI 92
**Glazer**, Michael H. 1948- WhoAmL 92
**Glazer**, Michael Joseph 1955- WhoAmL 92
**Glazer**, Miriyam Myra 1945- WhoWest 92
**Glazer**, Nathan 1923- IntWW 91, WrDr 92
**Glazer**, Rachelle Hoffman 1958- WhoAmL 92
**Glazer**, Rea Helene 1944- WhoWest 92
**Glazer**, Robert Arnold 1954- WhoFI 92
**Glazer**, Robert Irwin 1942- AmMWSc 92
**Glazer**, Scott F. 1962- WhoMW 92
**Glazer**, Steven Donald 1948- WhoAmL 92
**Glazer**, Steven Mark 1951- WhoAmL 92
**Glazer**, Tom 1914- WhoEnt 92
**Glazer**, Walter Philip, Jr. 1958- WhoFI 92
**Glazer**, William IntMPA 92
**Glazier**, Gregory Kent 1951- WhoEnt 92
**Glazier**, Loss Pequeno WhoHisp 92
**Glazier**, Lyle DrAPF 91
**Glazier**, Robert Henry 1926- AmMWSc 92
**Glazier**, Sidney 1918- IntMPA 92
**Glazko**, Anthony Joachim 1914- AmMWSc 92
**Glazman**, Yuli M 1911- AmMWSc 92
**Glazner**, Raymond Charles WhoMW 92
**Glazunov**, Alexander 1865-1936 NewAmDM
**Glazunov**, Alexander Konstantinovich 1865-1936 FacFETw
**Glazunov**, Ilya 1930- IntWW 91
**Glazunov**, Il'ya Sergeevich 1930- SovUnBD
**Gleasner**, Diana 1936- IntAu&W 91
**Gleason**, Alan Harold 1917- WhoMW 92
**Gleason**, Alfred M. 1930- WhoWest 92
**Gleason**, Alice Bryant 1940- WhoFI 92
**Gleason**, Andrew Mattei 1921- AmMWSc 92, IntWW 91
**Gleason**, Charles Thomas 1950- WhoAmL 92, WhoMW 92
**Gleason**, Clarence Henry 1922- AmMWSc 92
**Gleason**, Darlene Harriette 1933- WhoMW 92
**Gleason**, David WhoAmP 91
**Gleason**, David Russell 1958- WhoAmL 92
**Gleason**, Douglas Renwick 1956- WhoWest 92
**Gleason**, Edward Hinsdale, Jr 1927- AmMWSc 92
**Gleason**, Eliza 1909- NotBlAW 92, WhoBlA 92
**Gleason**, Francis Gilbert, Jr. 1959- WhoAmL 92
**Gleason**, Fred Gene 1933- WhoRel 92
**Gleason**, Frederick Grant 1848-1903 NewAmDM
**Gleason**, Gale R, Jr 1927- AmMWSc 92
**Gleason**, Geoffrey Irving 1923- AmMWSc 92
**Gleason**, Gerald Michael 1929- WhoMW 92
**Gleason**, Gerald Wayne 1911- WhoAmL 92, WhoMW 92
**Gleason**, Harold Anthony 1945- WhoFI 92
**Gleason**, Jackie d1987 LesBEnT 92 [port]
**Gleason**, Jackie 1916-1987 FacFETw
**Gleason**, James Gordon 1915- AmMWSc 92
**Gleason**, James Mullaney 1948- WhoAmL 92
**Gleason**, Jean Wilbur 1943- WhoAmL 92
**Gleason**, Joanna 1950- WhoEnt 92
**Gleason**, Joel Page, Sr. 1943- WhoFI 92
**Gleason**, John F. 1950- WhoAmL 92
**Gleason**, John Francis 1928- WhoEnt 92
**Gleason**, John James 1941- WhoEnt 92
**Gleason**, John Patrick, Jr. 1941- WhoFI 92
**Gleason**, Judith DrAPF 91
**Gleason**, Larry 1938- IntMPA 92
**Gleason**, Larry Neil 1939- AmMWSc 92
**Gleason**, Linda K. 1956- WhoMW 92
**Gleason**, Mabel Mallens 1957- WhoEnt 92
**Gleason**, Maurice Francis 1909- WhoBlA 92
**Gleason**, Neil P WhoAmP 91
**Gleason**, Philip Wayne 1943- WhoAmP 91
**Gleason**, Ray Edward 1931- AmMWSc 92
**Gleason**, Robert A, Sr 1909- WhoAmP 91
**Gleason**, Robert Davis 1935- WhoAmP 91
**Gleason**, Robert Willard 1932- AmMWSc 92
**Gleason**, Thomas Daues 1936- WhoFI 92, WhoMW 92
**Gleason**, Thomas E. 1946- WhoMW 92
**Gleason**, Thomas James 1941- AmMWSc 92
**Gleason**, William Ewing 1941- WhoMW 92
**Gleason**, William F., Jr. WhoAmL 92
**Gleason**, William James, III 1960- WhoMW 92
**Gleaton**, Harriet Elizabeth 1937- AmMWSc 92
**Gleave**, John T. 1917- WrDr 92
**Gleaves**, Earl William 1930- AmMWSc 92
**Gleaves**, John Thompson 1946- AmMWSc 92
**Glebe**, Brian Douglas 1948- AmMWSc 92
**Glebocki**, Robert 1940- IntWW 91
**Gleckman**, Philip Landon 1961- AmMWSc 92
**Gleckner**, Robert F 1925- IntAu&W 91, WrDr 92
**Gledhill**, Anthony John 1938- Who 92
**Gledhill**, Barton L 1936- AmMWSc 92
**Gledhill**, Barton LeVan 1936- WhoWest 92
**Gledhill**, David Anthony 1934- IntWW 91, Who 92
**Gledhill**, David Edward 1941- WhoFI 92
**Gledhill**, Robert Hamor 1931- AmMWSc 92
**Gledhill**, Ronald James 1914- AmMWSc 92
**Gledhill**, William Emerson 1941- AmMWSc 92
**Glee**, George, Jr. 1938- WhoBlA 92
**Gleed**, William H 1933- WhoIns 92
**Glees**, Anthony 1948- ConAu 134
**Gleeson**, Anthony Murray 1938- Who 92
**Gleeson**, Austin M 1938- AmMWSc 92
**Gleeson**, James Newman 1940- AmMWSc 92
**Gleeson**, James William 1920- Who 92
**Gleeson**, Jeremy Michael 1953- WhoWest 92
**Gleeson**, Paul Francis 1941- WhoAmL 92
**Gleeson**, Richard Alan 1947- AmMWSc 92
**Gleeson**, Thomas Alexander 1920- AmMWSc 92
**Gleeson**, Thomas F. WhoRel 92
**Gleghorn**, G J 1927- AmMWSc 92
**Gleghorn**, George Jay 1927- WhoWest 92
**Gleich**, Carol S 1935- AmMWSc 92
**Gleich**, Gerald J 1931- AmMWSc 92
**Gleich**, Walter A. 1924- IntWW 91
**Gleicher**, Gerald Jay 1939- AmMWSc 92
**Gleichert**, Gregg Charles 1948- WhoMW 92
**Gleichman**, John Alan 1944- WhoMW 92
**Gleichman**, Pamela Walton 1944- WhoAmP 91
**Gleichman**, Peter Alan 1953- WhoAmL 92
**Gleick**, James IntAu&W 91
**Gleig**, Charles 1862- ScFEYrs
**Gleijeses**, Mario 1955- WhoFI 92
**Gleim**, Clyde Edgar 1913- AmMWSc 92
**Gleim**, Elmer Quentin 1917- WhoRel 92
**Gleim**, Paul Stanley 1923- AmMWSc 92
**Gleim**, Robert David 1946- AmMWSc 92
**Gleiser**, Chester Alexander AmMWSc 92
**Gleiss**, Henry Weston 1928- WhoAmL 92, WhoMW 92
**Gleissner**, Gene Heiden 1928- AmMWSc 92
**Gleissner**, Heinrich 1927- IntWW 91, Who 92
**Gleit**, Chester Eugene 1933- AmMWSc 92
**Gleit**, Milton Ralph 1937- WhoAmL 92
**Gleiter**, Melvin Earl 1926- AmMWSc 92
**Glekel**, Jeffrey Ives 1947- WhoAmL 92
**Glembotski**, Christopher Charles 1952- AmMWSc 92
**Glemp**, Jozef 1929- IntWW 91, WhoRel 92
**Glemser**, Oskar Max 1911- IntWW 91
**Glen**, Alexander 1912- Who 92
**Glen**, Alexander Richard 1912- IntWW 91
**Glen**, Archibald 1909- Who 92
**Glen**, Duncan 1933- ConPo 91, WrDr 92
**Glen**, Duncan Munro 1933- IntAu&W 91
**Glen**, Emilie DrAPF 91
**Glen**, Frank Grenfell 1933- WrDr 92
**Glen**, John 1932- IntMPA 92
**Glen**, Robert 1905- AmMWSc 92
**Glen Haig**, Mary Alison 1918- Who 92
**Glenamara**, Baron 1912- IntWW 91, Who 92
**Glenapp**, Viscount 1943- Who 92
**Glenarthur**, Baron 1944- Who 92
**Glenconner**, Baron 1926- Who 92
**Glencross**, David 1936- Who 92
**Glende**, Eric A, Jr 1938- AmMWSc 92
**Glendening**, Norman Willard 1913- AmMWSc 92
**Glendenning**, Don TwCWW 91
**Glendenning**, George William 1931- WhoIns 92
**Glendenning**, Norman Keith 1931- AmMWSc 92
**Glendevon**, Baron 1912- Who 92
**Glendining**, Alan 1924- Who 92
**Glendinning**, James Garland 1919- Who 92
**Glendinning**, Victoria 1937- IntAu&W 91, IntWW 91, Who 92
**Glendon**, George ScFEYrs
**Glendon**, Mary Ann 1938- WhoAmL 92
**Glendower**, Rose WrDr 92
**Glendyne**, Baron 1926- Who 92
**Glenesk**, Gail Belle 1955- WhoMW 92
**Glenister**, Brian Frederick 1928- AmMWSc 92, WhoMW 92
**Glenister**, Paul Robson 1918- AmMWSc 92
**Glenister**, Tony William 1923- Who 92
**Glenn**, Alan Holton 1950- AmMWSc 92
**Glenn**, Alfred Hill 1921- AmMWSc 92
**Glenn**, Annette Williams 1963- WhoWest 92
**Glenn**, Archibald IntWW 91, Who 92
**Glenn**, Barbara Peterson AmMWSc 92
**Glenn**, Belinda 1963- WhoWest 92
**Glenn**, Bertis Lamon 1922- AmMWSc 92
**Glenn**, Cecil E. 1938- WhoBlA 92
**Glenn**, Charles Edward 1944- WhoRel 92
**Glenn**, Charles Kenneth 1934- WhoRel 92
**Glenn**, Charles Owen 1938- IntMPA 92
**Glenn**, Clayton Ray 1957- WhoMW 92
**Glenn**, Cleta Mae 1921- WhoAmL 92
**Glenn**, David Wright 1943- WhoFI 92
**Glenn**, Dennis Eugene 1948- WhoBlA 92
**Glenn**, Don Allen 1936- WhoRel 92
**Glenn**, Donald Taylor, Jr. 1948- WhoFI 92
**Glenn**, Edward C., Jr. 1922- WhoBlA 92
**Glenn**, Edwin Forbis 1857-1926 DcNCBi 2
**Glenn**, Furman Eugene 1944- AmMWSc 92
**Glenn**, Gene W 1928- WhoAmP 91
**Glenn**, George R 1923- AmMWSc 92
**Glenn**, Gerald Marvin 1942- WhoFI 92
**Glenn**, Grant Matthew 1951- WhoAmL 92
**Glenn**, Guy Charles 1930- WhoWest 92
**Glenn**, James TwCWW 91
**Glenn**, James D., Jr. 1934- WhoWest 92
**Glenn**, James Francis 1928- AmMWSc 92
**Glenn**, Jane Siobhan 1956- WhoAmL 92
**Glenn**, Joe Davis, Jr. 1921- WhoFI 92
**Glenn**, John, Jr 1921- FacFETw [port]

**Glenn**, John H., Jr. 1921- AlmAP 92 [port], Who 92
**Glenn**, John Herschel, Jr. 1921- IntWW 91, WhoAmP 91, WhoMW 92
**Glenn**, Joseph Leonard 1925- AmMWSc 92
**Glenn**, Joseph Robert Archibald 1911- IntWW 91, Who 92
**Glenn**, Karen DrAPF 91
**Glenn**, Kevin Challon 1954- AmMWSc 92
**Glenn**, Lane Adam 1967- WhoEnt 92
**Glenn**, Laura WhoEnt 92
**Glenn**, Lewis Alan 1936- AmMWSc 92
**Glenn**, Loyd Lee 1952- AmMWSc 92
**Glenn**, Marion Edward, Jr. 1941- WhoAmL 92
**Glenn**, Michael Leo 1956- WhoRel 92
**Glenn**, Patricia Campbell 1942- WhoBlA 92
**Glenn**, Patricia Lee 1954- WhoFI 92
**Glenn**, Ramona Martin 1931- WhoAmP 91
**Glenn**, Richard A 1925- AmMWSc 92
**Glenn**, Robert Brodnax 1854-1920 DcNCBi 2
**Glenn**, Robin Day 1947- WhoAmL 92
**Glenn**, Rollin Copper 1927- AmMWSc 92
**Glenn**, Ronald Fedric 1943- WhoAmP 91
**Glenn**, Roy Johnson 1920- WhoFI 92
**Glenn**, Scott 1942- IntMPA 92, WhoEnt 92
**Glenn**, Steven Claude 1947- WhoFI 92
**Glenn**, Thomas M 1940- AmMWSc 92
**Glenn**, Tyree 1912-1974 NewAmDM
**Glenn**, Valerie Rose 1954- WhoWest 92
**Glenn**, William 1840-1907 BiInAmS
**Glenn**, William Grant 1916- AmMWSc 92
**Glenn**, William Henry, Jr 1937- AmMWSc 92
**Glenn**, William Wallace Lumpkin 1914- AmMWSc 92
**Glenn**, Wynola 1932- WhoBlA 92
**Glenn-Lewin**, David Carl 1943- AmMWSc 92
**Glennan**, T Keith 1905- AmMWSc 92, FacFETw, IntWW 91
**Glenne**, Bard 1935- AmMWSc 92
**Glennen**, Robert Eugene, Jr. 1933- WhoMW 92
**Glenner**, E J 1926- AmMWSc 92
**Glenner**, George Geiger 1927- AmMWSc 92, WhoWest 92
**Glenner**, Richard Allen 1934- WhoMW 92
**Glenner**, Steve Charles 1966- WhoEnt 92
**Glenney**, Daniel Martin 1962- WhoFI 92
**Glennie**, Angus James Scott 1950- Who 92
**Glennie**, Evelyn Elizabeth Ann 1965- Who 92
**Glennon**, James M. 1942- IntMPA 92
**Glennon**, James Michael 1942- WhoEnt 92
**Glennon**, John Joseph 1862-1946 RelLAm 91
**Glennon**, John Robert 1957- WhoFI 92
**Glennon**, Joseph Anthony 1931- AmMWSc 92
**Glennon**, Patrick Joseph 1963- WhoWest 92
**Glennon**, Theresa 1958- WhoAmL 92
**Glenny**, Robert Joseph Ervine 1923- Who 92
**Glentoran**, Baron 1912- Who 92
**Glentworth**, Viscount 1963- Who 92
**Gleser**, Leon Jay 1939- AmMWSc 92
**Glesing**, Charles Richard, Jr. 1955- WhoAmL 92
**Gleske**, Leonhard 1921- IntWW 91
**Gless**, Elmer E 1928- AmMWSc 92
**Gless**, George E 1917- AmMWSc 92
**Gless**, Sharon WhoEnt 92
**Gless**, Sharon 1943- IntMPA 92
**Glessner**, Alfred Joseph 1943- AmMWSc 92
**Glessner**, Gary David 1960- WhoRel 92
**Glessner**, Harry David 1960- WhoEnt 92
**Glessner**, Thomas Allen 1952- WhoAmL 92
**Glester**, John William 1946- Who 92
**Gletsos**, Constantine 1934- AmMWSc 92
**Glew**, David Neville 1928- AmMWSc 92
**Glewwe**, Carl W 1927- AmMWSc 92
**Gleyre**, Charles 1808-1874 ThHEIm
**Gleysteen**, John Jacob 1941- AmMWSc 92
**Gleyzal**, Andre 1908- AmMWSc 92
**Glezen**, William Paul 1931- AmMWSc 92
**Gliauda**, Jurgis 1906- IntAu&W 91, WrDr 92
**Glick**, Andrew Justus 1948- WhoEnt 92
**Glick**, Arnold J 1931- AmMWSc 92
**Glick**, Bernard Robert 1945- AmMWSc 92
**Glick**, Bruce 1927- AmMWSc 92
**Glick**, Carl 1890-1971 BenetAL 91
**Glick**, Charles Frey 1917- AmMWSc 92
**Glick**, David 1908- AmMWSc 92
**Glick**, David M 1936- AmMWSc 92
**Glick**, Deborah J WhoAmP 91
**Glick**, Deborah Kelly 1953- WhoFI 92
**Glick**, Edward Bernard 1929- IntAu&W 91, WrDr 92
**Glick**, Forrest Irving 1934- AmMWSc 92
**Glick**, Garland Wayne 1921- WhoRel 92
**Glick**, Gerald 1934- AmMWSc 92
**Glick**, Harold Alan AmMWSc 92
**Glick**, Hyman J. 1904- IntMPA 92
**Glick**, Ian Bernard 1948- Who 92
**Glick**, J Leslie 1940- AmMWSc 92
**Glick**, Jane Mills 1943- AmMWSc 92
**Glick**, John H 1943- AmMWSc 92
**Glick**, John Henry, Jr 1924- AmMWSc 92
**Glick**, Karen Andrea 1962- WhoAmL 92
**Glick**, Mary 1951- WhoFI 92
**Glick**, Mary Catherine AmMWSc 92
**Glick**, Milton Don 1937- AmMWSc 92, WhoMW 92
**Glick**, Phyllis IntMPA 92
**Glick**, Reuven 1951- WhoFI 92
**Glick**, Richard Edwin 1927- AmMWSc 92
**Glick**, Robert L 1934- AmMWSc 92
**Glick**, Samuel Shipley 1900- AmMWSc 92
**Glick**, Stanley Dennis 1944- AmMWSc 92
**Glick**, Steven Marc 1947- WhoWest 92
**Glick**, Thomas F 1939- ConAu 34NR
**Glickfeld**, Carole L. DrAPF 91
**Glickman**, Dan 1944- AlmAP 92 [port]
**Glickman**, Daniel Robert 1944- WhoAmP 91, WhoMW 92
**Glickman**, Harry 1924- WhoWest 92
**Glickman**, Jeffrey Bruce 1948- WhoWest 92
**Glickman**, Lawrence Theodore 1942- AmMWSc 92
**Glickman**, Louis 1933- WhoFI 92
**Glickman**, Marlene 1936- WhoFI 92
**Glickman**, Norman J. 1942- ConAu 135
**Glickman**, Richard WhoFI 92
**Glickman**, Ronald C 1956- WhoAmP 91
**Glickman**, Samuel Arthur 1918- AmMWSc 92
**Glickman**, Sylvia Roberta 1932- WhoEnt 92
**Glickman**, Walter A 1938- AmMWSc 92
**Glicksberg**, Charles Irving 1900- IntAu&W 91, WrDr 92
**Glicksman**, Arvin Sigmund 1924- AmMWSc 92
**Glicksman**, Gail Gaisin 1956- WhoRel 92
**Glicksman**, Martin E 1937- AmMWSc 92
**Glicksman**, Maurice 1928- AmMWSc 92
**Glickson**, Andrew Asher 1949- WhoAmP 91
**Glickstein**, Joseph 1917- AmMWSc 92
**Glickstein**, Mitchell 1931- AmMWSc 92
**Glickstein**, Stanley S 1933- AmMWSc 92
**Glickstein**, Steven Howard 1960- WhoFI 92
**Glidden**, Frederick D. BenetAL 91
**Glidden**, Frederick Dilley TwCWW 91
**Glidden**, Jonathan TwCWW 91
**Glidden**, Richard Mills 1924- AmMWSc 92
**Glidden**, Robert Burr 1936- WhoEnt 92
**Glidden**, Ronald C 1939- WhoIns 92
**Glidewell**, Iain 1924- IntWW 91, Who 92
**Glieberman**, Cary Hirsch 1943- WhoEnt 92
**Glieberman**, Herbert Allen 1930- WhoMW 92
**Gliedman**, Marvin L 1929- AmMWSc 92
**Gliege**, John Gerhardt 1948- WhoAmL 92
**Glier**, Reyngol'd Moritsevich 1875-1956 SovUnBD
**Gliere**, Reinhold 1875-1956 NewAmDM
**Gliere**, Reinhold Moritzovich 1875-1956 FacFETw
**Gliere**, Reyngol'd Moritsevich 1875-1956 SovUnBD
**Gliewe**, Unada G. 1927- WrDr 92
**Gligor-Habian**, Lisa Danielle 1964- WhoRel 92
**Gligorov**, Kiro 1917- IntWW 91
**Gliha**, John Lee 1953- WhoMW 92
**Glimcher**, Melvin Jacob 1925- AmMWSc 92
**Glime**, Janice Mildred 1941- AmMWSc 92, WhoMW 92
**Glime**, Raymond George 1931- WhoAmL 92
**Glimm**, Adele DrAPF 91
**Glimm**, James Gilbert 1934- AmMWSc 92
**Glimmerveen**, Joop 1928- BiDExR
**Glin**, Knight of Who 92
**Glinka**, Mikhail Ivanovich 1804-1857 NewAmDM
**Glinski**, Barbara Michalina 1953- WhoMW 92
**Glinski**, Richard M. 1929- WhoRel 92
**Glinski**, Ronald P 1941- AmMWSc 92
**Glinsmann**, Walter H AmMWSc 92
**Glisdorf**, Mary Jo B. 1957- WhoAmL 92
**Glissant**, Edouard 1928- ConLC 68 [port]
**Glisson**, Allen Wilburn, Jr 1951- AmMWSc 92
**Glisson**, Floyd Wright 1947- WhoFI 92
**Glisson**, Jackie 1954- WhoAmP 91
**Glisson**, Jerry Lee 1923- WhoRel 92
**Glisson**, Silas Nease 1941- AmMWSc 92
**Glist**, Paul 1953- WhoAmL 92
**Glista**, Jonathan Eugene 1964- WhoRel 92
**Glistrup**, Mogens 1926- IntWW 91
**Glitman**, Karen Micquela 1963- WhoAmP 91
**Glitman**, Maynard W WhoAmP 91
**Glitman**, Maynard Wayne 1933- IntWW 91
**Glitz**, Dohn George 1936- AmMWSc 92
**Glitzenstein**, Eric Robert 1957- WhoAmL 92
**Glizer**, Yudif' Samoilovna 1904-1968 SovUnBD
**Gloag**, John 1896-1981 DcTwDes, TwCSFW 91
**Gloag**, Julian 1930- ConNov 91, IntAu&W 91, WrDr 92
**Gloak**, Graeme Frank 1921- Who 92
**Globe**, Samuel 1916- AmMWSc 92
**Globensky**, Yvon Raoul 1937- AmMWSc 92
**Glober**, George Edward, Jr. 1944- WhoAmL 92
**Globke**, Hans 1889-1973 EncTR 91 [port]
**Globocnik**, Odilo 1904-1945 BiDExR, EncTR 91 [port]
**Globokar**, Vinko 1934- ConCom 92, NewAmDM
**Globoke**, Joseph Raymond 1955- WhoMW 92
**Globus**, Albert 1931- AmMWSc 92
**Globus**, Yoram IntMPA 92, WhoEnt 92
**Globus**, Yoram 1943- IntWW 91
**Glock**, Marvin David 1912- WrDr 92
**Glock**, Robert Dean 1936- AmMWSc 92
**Glock**, Waldo Sumner 1897- AmMWSc 92
**Glock**, William 1908- Who 92
**Glock**, William Frederick 1908- IntWW 91
**Glocker**, Edwin Merriam 1910- AmMWSc 92
**Glocklin**, Vera Charlotte 1926- AmMWSc 92
**Glockner**, Peter G 1929- AmMWSc 92
**Glod**, Edward Francis 1942- AmMWSc 92
**Glod**, Marie Annette 1962- WhoAmL 92
**Glode**, Leonard Michael 1947- AmMWSc 92
**Glodis**, William J, Jr 1934- WhoAmP 91
**Gloeckler**, George 1937- AmMWSc 92
**Gloeden**, Elisabeth Charlotte 1903-1944 EncTR 91
**Gloege**, George Herman 1904- AmMWSc 92
**Gloeggler**, Tony DrAPF 91
**Gloer**, William Hulitt 1950- WhoRel 92
**Gloersen**, Per 1927- AmMWSc 92
**Gloge**, Detlef Christoph 1936- AmMWSc 92
**Glogovsky**, Robert L 1936- AmMWSc 92
**Glogovsky**, Robert Louis 1936- WhoMW 92
**Glogowski**, Patricia Carol 1942- WhoFI 92
**Glomb**, Diana WhoAmP 91
**Glomb**, Walter L 1925- AmMWSc 92
**Glommen**, Harvey Hamilton 1928- WhoMW 92
**Glomset**, John A 1928- AmMWSc 92
**Glomski**, Chester Anthony 1928- AmMWSc 92
**Glonek**, Thomas 1941- AmMWSc 92
**Gloor**, Christopher Barta 1949- WhoFI 92
**Gloor**, Pierre 1923- AmMWSc 92
**Gloor**, Robert Louis 1940- WhoAmP 91
**Gloor**, Walter Ervin 1907- AmMWSc 92
**Gloor**, Walter Thomas, Jr 1924- AmMWSc 92
**Glooschenko**, Walter Arthur 1938- AmMWSc 92
**Glore**, John Frederick 1955- WhoEnt 92
**Glorig**, Aram 1906- AmMWSc 92
**Glorioso**, Carl Anthony 1970- WhoEnt 92
**Glorioso**, Joseph Charles, III 1945- AmMWSc 92
**Glorioso**, Robert M 1940- AmMWSc 92
**Glorsky**, Maxine Julie 1940- WhoEnt 92
**Glosband**, Daniel Martin 1944- WhoAmL 92
**Gloshen**, Donna Rae 1938- WhoMW 92
**Gloss**, Steven Paul 1944- AmMWSc 92
**Glossbrenner**, Ernestine Viola 1932- WhoAmP 91
**Glosser**, Robert 1937- AmMWSc 92
**Glosser**, Ronald Dean 1933- WhoFI 92
**Glossop**, Peter 1928- IntWW 91, Who 92
**Glossop**, Reginald ScFEYrs
**Glosten**, Lawrence R AmMWSc 92
**Gloster**, Elizabeth 1949- Who 92
**Gloster**, Hugh Morris 1911- WhoBlA 92
**Gloster**, Jesse E. 1915- WhoBlA 92
**Gloster**, John 1922- Who 92
**Gloster**, John Gaines 1928- WhoBlA 92
**Gloster**, Thomas Benn 1763-1819 DcNCBi 2
**Glosup**, Lorene 1911- WhoEnt 92
**Gloth**, Richard Edward 1941- AmMWSc 92
**Glotta**, Ronald Delon 1941- WhoAmL 92
**Glotzer**, Albert 1908- ConAu 133
**Glotzer**, Cary Ian 1961- WhoEnt 92
**Glotzer**, David DrAPF 91
**Gloucester**, Archdeacon of Who 92
**Gloucester**, Bishop of Who 92
**Gloucester**, Dean of Who 92
**Gloucester**, The Duke of 1944- IntWW 91, Who 92R
**Glouner**, Richard C. 1931- WhoEnt 92
**Glovach**, Linda R 1947- IntAu&W 91
**Glover**, Agnes W. 1925- WhoBlA 92
**Glover**, Alan Harney 1949- WhoAmP 91
**Glover**, Albert Downing 1907- WhoMW 92
**Glover**, Allen Donald 1938- AmMWSc 92
**Glover**, Anthony Richard Haysom 1934- Who 92
**Glover**, Archibald F. 1902- WhoBlA 92
**Glover**, Arthur Lewis, Jr. 1912- WhoBlA 92
**Glover**, Arthur McDaniel, Jr. 1941- WhoAmL 92
**Glover**, Benjamin Howell 1916- AmMWSc 92
**Glover**, Bernard E. 1933- WhoBlA 92
**Glover**, Billy Joe 1938- WhoAmP 91
**Glover**, Bobby L 1936- WhoAmP 91
**Glover**, Bruce Hellion 1932- WhoEnt 92
**Glover**, Chester Artis 1954- WhoBlA 92
**Glover**, Claiborne V C, III 1947- AmMWSc 92
**Glover**, Clarence Ernest, Jr. 1956- WhoBlA 92
**Glover**, Crispin 1964- IntMPA 92
**Glover**, Crispin Hellion 1964- WhoEnt 92
**Glover**, Danny 1947- IntMPA 92, WhoBlA 92, WhoEnt 92
**Glover**, Danny 1948- ConBlB 1 [port]
**Glover**, David Val 1932- AmMWSc 92
**Glover**, Deborah Dianne 1963- WhoAmL 92
**Glover**, Delone Bradford 1924- WhoAmP 91
**Glover**, Denis 1912-1980 RfGEnL 91
**Glover**, Denise M. 1952- WhoBlA 92
**Glover**, Diana M. 1948- WhoBlA 92
**Glover**, Donald H 1918- WhoAmP 91
**Glover**, Elsa Margaret 1939- AmMWSc 92
**Glover**, Eric 1935- Who 92
**Glover**, Eula E. 1907- WhoBlA 92
**Glover**, Francis Nicholas 1925- AmMWSc 92
**Glover**, Fred William 1937- AmMWSc 92
**Glover**, George Irvin 1940- AmMWSc 92
**Glover**, Gilbert Louis 1921- WhoAmP 91
**Glover**, Gleason 1934- WhoBlA 92
**Glover**, Gregory Leonard 1966- WhoRel 92
**Glover**, Jacqueline Renee 1951- WhoWest 92
**Glover**, James 1929- IntWW 91, Who 92
**Glover**, James Franklin 1957- WhoEnt 92
**Glover**, Jane Alison 1949- IntWW 91, Who 92, WhoEnt 92
**Glover**, Janet Reaveley 1912- WrDr 92
**Glover**, Jeffrey Allan 1963- WhoFI 92
**Glover**, Jerry Wayne 1949- WhoFI 92
**Glover**, Jimmy Ray 1945- WhoAmP 91
**Glover**, John 1944- IntMPA 92
**Glover**, John L 1943- WhoAmP 91
**Glover**, John Neville 1913- Who 92
**Glover**, Jon 1943- ConAu 133
**Glover**, Judith 1943- IntAu&W 91, WrDr 92
**Glover**, Keith 1946- Who 92
**Glover**, Kenneth Elijah 1952- WhoBlA 92
**Glover**, Kenneth Frank 1920- Who 92
**Glover**, Kenneth Merle 1928- AmMWSc 92
**Glover**, Larry Hodges 1954- WhoRel 92
**Glover**, Leon Conrad, Jr 1935- AmMWSc 92
**Glover**, Linda F. 1951- WhoBlA 92
**Glover**, Lynn, III 1928- AmMWSc 92
**Glover**, Maggie Wallace 1948- WhoAmP 91
**Glover**, Michael James Kevin 1940- IntWW 91
**Glover**, Myles Howard 1928- Who 92
**Glover**, Paul W 1947- WhoIns 92
**Glover**, Peter James 1913- Who 92
**Glover**, R. Edward 1943- WhoFI 92
**Glover**, Robert E 1896- AmMWSc 92
**Glover**, Robert Finlay 1917- Who 92
**Glover**, Robert G. 1931- WhoBlA 92
**Glover**, Roland Leigh 1911- AmMWSc 92
**Glover**, Rolfe Eldridge, III 1924- AmMWSc 92
**Glover**, Roy Andrew 1941- AmMWSc 92
**Glover**, Ruth Champion 1926- WhoAmP 91
**Glover**, Sandra Jean 1939- AmMWSc 92
**Glover**, Sarah L. 1954- WhoBlA 92
**Glover**, Shirley 1951- WhoEnt 92
**Glover**, Stephen Charles Morton 1952- Who 92
**Glover**, Townend 1813-1883 BiInAmS
**Glover**, Trevor David 1940- Who 92
**Glover**, Victor 1932- Who 92
**Glover**, Victor Norman 1948- WhoBlA 92
**Glover**, William d1712 DcNCBi 2
**Glover**, William Harper 1911- WhoEnt 92
**Glover**, William James 1924- Who 92
**Glovsky**, M Michael 1936- AmMWSc 92

**Glovsky**, Susan G. L. 1955- *WhoAmL 92*
**Glovsky**, William Moses 1921- *WhoAmL 92*
**Glowa**, John Robert 1946- *AmMWSc 92*
**Glowacki**, Janusz 1938- *LiExTwC*
**Glowacki**, Julie 1944- *AmMWSc 92*
**Glowacki**, Matthew John 1954- *WhoMW 92*
**Glower**, Donald D 1926- *AmMWSc 92*
**Glower**, Jacob Sean 1962- *WhoFI 92*
**Glowienka**, Emerine Frances 1920- *WhoWest 92*
**Glowienka**, John Clement 1948- *AmMWSc 92*
**Glowik-Johnson**, Linda Ann 1951- *WhoEnt 92*
**Gloyd**, Lawrence Eugene 1932- *WhoFI 92*
**Gloyer**, Stewart Edward 1942- *AmMWSc 92*
**Gloyer**, Stewart Wayne 1910- *AmMWSc 92*
**Gloyna**, Earnest F 1921- *AmMWSc 92*
**Glubb**, John Bagot 1897-1986 *FacFETw*
**Glubok**, Shirley 1933- *SmATA 68 [port]*
**Gluck** 1895-1976 *TwCPaSc*
**Gluck**, Alma 1884-1938 *NewAmDM*
**Gluck**, Christoph Willibald 1714-1787 *BlkwCEP, NewAmDM*
**Gluck**, Dale Richard 1952- *WhoWest 92*
**Gluck**, Felix 1923-1981 *TwCPaSc*
**Gluck**, Hazel Frank 1933- *WhoAmP 91*
**Gluck**, Josiah Nicholas 1959- *WhoEnt 92*
**Gluck**, Louis 1924- *AmMWSc 92*
**Gluck**, Louise *DrAPF 91*
**Gluck**, Louise 1943- *BenetAL 91, ConPo 91, IntAu&W 91, WrDr 92*
**Gluck**, Richard Alan 1958- *WhoFI 92*
**Gluck**, Ronald Monroe 1937- *AmMWSc 92*
**Gluck**, Tereze *DrAPF 91*
**Gluckman**, Bernard Louis 1909- *WhoEnt 92*
**Glucks**, Richard 1889-1945 *EncTR 91*
**Glucksman**, Ernest D. *LesBEnT 92*
**Gluckstein**, Fritz Paul 1927- *AmMWSc 92*
**Gluckstein**, Martin E 1928- *AmMWSc 92*
**Gluckstern**, Robert Leonard 1924- *AmMWSc 92*
**Glue**, George Thomas 1917- *Who 92*
**Glueck**, Ann Laura 1924- *WhoAmP 91*
**Glueck**, Bernard Charles 1914- *AmMWSc 92*
**Glueck**, Eleanor Touroff 1898-1972 *FacFETw*
**Glueck**, Helen Iglauer 1907- *AmMWSc 92*
**Glueck**, Sheldon *FacFETw*
**Glueckman**, Alan Jay 1944- *WhoEnt 92*
**Glukhov**, Arkadiy Mikhailovich 1925- *IntWW 91*
**Gluntz**, Martin L 1931- *AmMWSc 92*
**Glusband**, Steven Joseph 1947- *WhoAmL 92*
**Glushchenko**, Ivan Yevdokimovich 1907-1987 *SovUnBD*
**Glushenko**, Yevgeniya Konstatinovna 1952- *IntWW 91*
**Glushien**, Arthur Samuel 1911- *AmMWSc 92, WhoWest 92*
**Glushko**, Valentin Pavlovich 1908-1988 *SovUnBD*
**Glushko**, Valentin Petrovich 1906-1989 *FacFETw*
**Glushko**, Victor 1946- *AmMWSc 92*
**Glusker**, Jenny Pickworth 1931- *AmMWSc 92*
**Gluskin**, Robert Wayne 1946- *WhoMW 92*
**Gluskoter**, Harold Jay 1935- *AmMWSc 92*
**Glusman**, Murray 1914- *AmMWSc 92*
**Glut**, Don F 1944- *IntAu&W 91, WrDr 92*
**Glut**, Donald F. 1944- *WhoEnt 92*
**Gluth**, Diane Marie 1961- *WhoRel 92*
**Gluyas**, Constance 1920- *IntAu&W 91, WrDr 92*
**Gluyas**, Richard Edwin 1921- *AmMWSc 92*
**Gluys**, Charles Byron 1928- *WhoFI 92*
**Glyde**, Henry Russell 1937- *AmMWSc 92*
**Glymph**, Eakin Milton 1915- *AmMWSc 92*
**Glyn** *Who 92*
**Glyn**, Alan 1918- *Who 92*
**Glyn**, Anthony 1922- *IntAu&W 91, Who 92, WrDr 92*
**Glyn**, Elinor 1864-1943 *ReelWom*
**Glyn**, Hilary B. 1916- *Who 92*
**Glyn**, Richard 1943- *Who 92*
**Glyn Jones**, Kenneth 1915- *IntAu&W 91*
**Glynn**, Alan Anthony 1923- *Who 92*
**Glynn**, Carlin 1940- *IntMPA 92, WhoEnt 92*
**Glynn**, Gary Allen 1946- *WhoFI 92*
**Glynn**, Ian Michael 1928- *IntWW 91, Who 92*
**Glynn**, James A. 1941- *WhoWest 92*
**Glynn**, James Vincent 1938- *WhoIns 92*
**Glynn**, John Joseph, Jr 1941- *WhoAmP 91*
**Glynn**, Peter W 1933- *AmMWSc 92*
**Glynn**, William Allen 1935- *AmMWSc 92*
**Glynn**, William C. 1944- *WhoWest 92*
**Gmeiner**, Herman 1919-1986 *FacFETw*
**Gmelch**, George 1944- *WrDr 92*
**Gmelch**, Sharon 1947- *WrDr 92*
**Gnade**, Bruce E 1955- *AmMWSc 92*
**Gnaedinger**, John P 1926- *AmMWSc 92*
**Gnaedinger**, Richard H 1930- *AmMWSc 92*
**Gnam**, Adrian 1940- *WhoEnt 92, WhoWest 92*
**Gnanadesikan**, Ramanathan 1932- *AmMWSc 92*
**Gnanam**, A. 1932- *IntWW 91*
**Gnanapragasasam**, Jabez Jebasir *WhoRel 92*
**Gnarowski**, Michael 1934- *WrDr 92*
**Gnat**, Thomas J. *WhoRel 92*
**Gnatt**, Poul Rudolph 1923- *IntWW 91*
**Gnau**, John Russell, Jr 1930- *WhoAmP 91*
**Gnecco**, Louis T. 1945- *WhoHisp 92*
**Gnehm**, Max Willi 1943- *WhoWest 92*
**Gneiser**, Douglas Todd 1961- *WhoWest 92*
**Gnerlich**, Rod Lawrence 1948- *WhoMW 92*
**Gnessin**, Michael Febianovich 1883-1957 *FacFETw*
**Gneuss**, Helmut Walter Georg 1927- *IntWW 91*
**Gnichtel**, William Van Orden 1934- *WhoAmL 92*
**Gniewek**, Raymond 1931- *WhoEnt 92*
**Gniffke**, Terry Lee 1952- *WhoWest 92*
**Gnodtke**, Carl F 1936- *WhoAmP 91*
**Gnuse**, Robert Karl 1947- *WhoRel 92*
**Go**, Mateo Lian Poa 1918- *AmMWSc 92*
**Go**, Robert A. 1955- *WhoMW 92*
**Go**, Vay Liang 1938- *AmMWSc 92*
**Goad**, Clyde Clarenton 1946- *AmMWSc 92*
**Goad**, Colin 1914- *Who 92*
**Goad**, Judy Ann 1946- *WhoAmP 91*
**Goad**, Nolen E 1941- *WhoAmP 91*
**Goad**, Walter Benson, Jr 1925- *AmMWSc 92*
**Goadby**, Hector Kenneth d1990 *Who 92N*
**Goaley**, Donald Joseph 1935- *WhoIns 92*
**Goans**, Judy Winegar 1949- *WhoAmL 92*
**Goans**, Ronald Earl 1946- *AmMWSc 92*
**Goates**, Donald Ray 1943- *WhoRel 92*
**Goates**, James Rex 1920- *AmMWSc 92*
**Goates**, Steven Rex 1951- *AmMWSc 92*
**Goay**, Michael Song-Chye 1964- *WhoWest 92*
**Goaz**, Paul William 1922- *AmMWSc 92*
**Gobar**, Alfred Julian 1932- *WhoFI 92, WhoWest 92*
**Gobar**, Sally Randall 1933- *WhoWest 92*
**Gobat**, Albert 1843-1914 *FacFETw*
**Gobat**, Charles Albert 1843-1914 *WhoNob 90*
**Gobbell**, Ronald Vance 1948- *WhoFI 92*
**Gobbi**, Tito 1913-1984 *FacFETw, NewAmDM*
**Gobbo**, James 1931- *Who 92*
**Gobby**, Thomas John 1939- *WhoMW 92*
**Gobel**, Frederick L 1935- *AmMWSc 92*
**Gobel**, George d1991 *LesBEnT 92, NewYTBS 91 [port]*
**Gobel**, George 1920-1991 *CurBio 91N, News 91*
**Gobel**, Harriet 1922- *WhoMW 92*
**Gobel**, Stephen 1938- *AmMWSc 92*
**Gober**, Mark Sterling 1964- *WhoEnt 92*
**Gobetti**, Daniela 1952- *WhoMW 92*
**Gobeyn**, Bruce Barrett 1944- *WhoFI 92, WhoMW 92*
**Gobillard**, Yves 1838-1893 *ThHEIm*
**Gobineau**, Arthur de 1816-1882 *EncTR 91 [port]*
**Gobineau**, Joseph-Arthur, Comte de 1816-1882 *GuFrLit 1*
**Goble**, Alfred Theodore 1909- *AmMWSc 92*
**Goble**, Anthony 1943- *TwCPaSc*
**Goble**, David Franklin 1940- *AmMWSc 92*
**Goble**, Edward Earl 1938- *WhoAmP 91*
**Goble**, Frans Cleon 1913- *AmMWSc 92*
**Goble**, George G 1929- *AmMWSc 92*
**Goble**, Gerald Leroy, Jr 1953- *WhoAmP 91*
**Goble**, John Frederick 1925- *Who 92*
**Goble**, Robert Joseph 1960- *WhoFI 92*
**Goble**, Thomas Lee 1935- *WhoRel 92*
**Goblirsch**, Richard Paul 1930- *AmMWSc 92*
**Gobran**, Ramsis 1932- *AmMWSc 92*
**Goburdhun**, Jagdishwar 1946- *IntWW 91*
**Gochenaur**, Sally Elizabeth 1932- *AmMWSc 92*
**Gochenour**, Douglas Allen 1962- *WhoRel 92*
**Gochenour**, William Sylva 1916- *AmMWSc 92*
**Gochman**, Mark Adam 1960- *WhoEnt 92*
**Gochman**, Nathan 1933- *AmMWSc 92*
**Gochnauer**, Thomas Alexander 1919- *AmMWSc 92*
**Gock**, Terry Sai-Wah 1951- *WhoWest 92*
**Gockel**, John Raymond 1947- *WhoFI 92*
**Gockley**, David 1943- *WhoEnt 92*
**Gockley**, David Woodrow 1918- *WhoRel 92*
**Godager**, Jane Ann 1943- *WhoWest 92*
**Godar**, Edith Marie 1921- *AmMWSc 92*
**Godar**, Thomas Paul 1955- *WhoAmL 92*
**Godard**, Benjamin 1849-1895 *NewAmDM*
**Godard**, Donald Wesley 1947- *WhoWest 92*
**Godard**, Hugh P 1914- *AmMWSc 92*
**Godard**, Jean-Luc 1930- *FacFETw, IntDcF 2-2 [port], IntMPA 92, IntWW 91, WhoEnt 92*
**Godbe**, William Samuel 1833-1902 *RelLAm 91*
**Godbee**, H W 1928- *AmMWSc 92*
**Godbee**, John F 1926- *WhoAmP 91*
**Godbee**, Richard Greene, II 1951- *AmMWSc 92*
**Godbee**, Thomasina D. 1946- *WhoBlA 92*
**Godber**, Geoffrey Chapham 1912- *Who 92*
**Godber**, George 1908- *Who 92*
**Godber**, John 1956- *IntAu&W 91, WrDr 92*
**Godbey**, Allen Howard 1864-1948 *DcNCBi 2*
**Godbey**, John Kirby 1921- *AmMWSc 92*
**Godbey**, William Givens 1919- *AmMWSc 92*
**Godbold**, Donald Horace 1928- *WhoBlA 92*
**Godbold**, E. Stanly, Jr. 1942- *WrDr 92*
**Godbold**, Francis Stanley 1943- *WhoFI 92*
**Godbold**, Gene Hamilton 1936- *WhoAmL 92*
**Godbold**, Geoff 1935- *IntMPA 92*
**Godbold**, Jake M *WhoAmP 91*
**Godbold**, John Cooper 1920- *WhoAmL 92*
**Godbold**, N Terry 1948- *WhoIns 92*
**Godbold**, Wilford Darrington, Jr. 1938- *WhoAmL 92, WhoFI 92*
**Godbole**, Sadashiva Shankar 1939- *AmMWSc 92*
**Godchaux**, Walter, III 1939- *AmMWSc 92*
**Goddard**, Allison F 1936- *WhoAmP 91*
**Goddard**, Ann Felicity 1936- *Who 92*
**Goddard**, Burton Leslie 1910- *WhoRel 92*
**Goddard**, Charles K 1937- *AmMWSc 92*
**Goddard**, Charles William 1880-1951 *BenetAL 91*
**Goddard**, Daniel C 1950- *WhoIns 92*
**Goddard**, David Benjamin 1947- *WhoMW 92*
**Goddard**, David Rodney 1927- *Who 92*
**Goddard**, Dean Allen 1942- *WhoRel 92*
**Goddard**, Duane Philip 1952- *WhoAmP 91*
**Goddard**, Dwight 1861-1939 *RelLAm 91*
**Goddard**, Earl G 1917- *AmMWSc 92*
**Goddard**, Eric Norman 1897- *Who 92*
**Goddard**, Gene Oliver 1949- *WhoFI 92*
**Goddard**, Harold Keith 1936- *Who 92*
**Goddard**, Hazel Bryan 1912- *WhoRel 92*
**Goddard**, Hazel Idella Firth 1911- *IntAu&W 91*
**Goddard**, Henry H 1866- *DcAmImH*
**Goddard**, Joe Dean 1936- *AmMWSc 92*
**Goddard**, John Burgess 1943- *Who 92*
**Goddard**, John Burnham 1942- *AmMWSc 92*
**Goddard**, John Wesley 1941- *WhoEnt 92*
**Goddard**, Leonard 1925- *IntWW 91*
**Goddard**, Mary Katherine 1738-1816 *BlkwEAR*
**Goddard**, Murray Cowdery 1924- *AmMWSc 92*
**Goddard**, Paul Beck 1811-1866 *BiInAmS*
**Goddard**, Paul Douglas, Jr 1944- *WhoAmP 91*
**Goddard**, Paulette 1905?-1990 *AnObit 1990*
**Goddard**, Paulette 1911?-1990 *ConTFT 9, FacFETw*
**Goddard**, Peter 1945- *Who 92*
**Goddard**, Pliny Earle 1869-1928 *BenetAL 91*
**Goddard**, Ray Everett 1922- *AmMWSc 92*
**Goddard**, Richard Patrick 1952- *WhoAmL 92*
**Goddard**, Robert 1954- *ConAu 134*
**Goddard**, Robert H 1882-1945 *FacFETw [port]*
**Goddard**, Rosalind Kent 1944- *WhoBlA 92*
**Goddard**, Ross Millard, Jr. 1927- *WhoAmL 92*
**Goddard**, Roy 1939- *Who 92*
**Goddard**, Ruth 1923- *WhoAmP 91*
**Goddard**, Samuel Pearson 1919- *IntWW 91*
**Goddard**, Samuel Pearson, Jr 1919- *WhoAmP 91*
**Goddard**, Sandra Kay 1947- *WhoMW 92*
**Goddard**, Stephen 1937- *AmMWSc 92*
**Goddard**, Stuart Leslie 1954- *WhoEnt 92*
**Goddard**, Terrence Patrick 1944- *AmMWSc 92*
**Goddard**, Terry *WhoWest 92*
**Goddard**, Terry 1947- *WhoAmP 91*
**Goddard**, William Andrew, III 1937- *AmMWSc 92, WhoWest 92*
**Goddard-Callender**, Beverley 1956- *BlkOlyM*
**Godden**, Charles Henry 1922- *Who 92*
**Godden**, Geoffrey Arthur 1929- *WrDr 92*
**Godden**, Malcolm Reginald 1945- *Who 92*
**Godden**, Mark *WhoEnt 92*
**Godden**, Max Leon 1923- *Who 92*
**Godden**, Rumer 1907- *ConAu 36NR, ConNov 91, FacFETw, IntAu&W 91, IntWW 91, Who 92, WrDr 92*
**Godden**, Tony Richard Hillier 1927- *Who 92*
**Goddin**, C S 1914- *AmMWSc 92*
**Goddu**, Robert Fenno 1925- *AmMWSc 92*
**Godeaux**, Jean 1922- *IntWW 91*
**Godec**, Ciril J 1937- *AmMWSc 92*
**Godel**, Kurt 1906-1978 *FacFETw*
**Godenne**, Ghislaine D 1924- *AmMWSc 92*
**Goder**, Harold Arthur 1924- *AmMWSc 92*
**Goderich**, Mario P. *WhoHisp 92*
**Godet**, Maurice R. 1930- *IntWW 91*
**Godey**, John *IntAu&W 91X*
**Godey**, Louis A. 1804-1878 *BenetAL 91*
**Godfrey**, A. A. *WhoRel 92*
**Godfrey**, Albert Blanton 1941- *WhoFI 92*
**Godfrey**, Andrew Elliott 1940- *AmMWSc 92*
**Godfrey**, Angela 1939- *TwCPaSc*
**Godfrey**, Arthur d1983 *LesBEnT 92*
**Godfrey**, Brendan Berry 1945- *AmMWSc 92*
**Godfrey**, Brett Marshall 1959- *WhoAmL 92*
**Godfrey**, Charles *WrDr 92*
**Godfrey**, Charles S 1918- *AmMWSc 92*
**Godfrey**, Cullen Michael 1945- *WhoAmL 92*
**Godfrey**, Darrell Daniel 1958- *WhoRel 92*
**Godfrey**, Dave 1938- *ConNov 91, WrDr 92*
**Godfrey**, David Robert 1961- *WhoEnt 92*
**Godfrey**, Donald Albert 1944- *AmMWSc 92, WhoMW 92*
**Godfrey**, Emile Sylvester, Jr. 1950- *WhoBlA 92*
**Godfrey**, Francis d1675 *DcNCBi 2*
**Godfrey**, Gary Lunt 1946- *AmMWSc 92*
**Godfrey**, George Lawrence 1943- *AmMWSc 92*
**Godfrey**, Gerald Michael 1933- *Who 92*
**Godfrey**, H P 1941- *AmMWSc 92*
**Godfrey**, Harold William *Who 92, WhoRel 92*
**Godfrey**, Hollis 1874-1936 *ScFEYrs*
**Godfrey**, Howard Anthony 1946- *Who 92*
**Godfrey**, James Edward 1950- *WhoAmP 91*
**Godfrey**, James Michael 1955- *WhoRel 92*
**Godfrey**, John *DrAPF 91*
**Godfrey**, John Carl 1929- *AmMWSc 92*
**Godfrey**, John Joseph 1941- *AmMWSc 92*
**Godfrey**, John M 1945- *IntAu&W 91*
**Godfrey**, Keith d1976 *LesBEnT 92*
**Godfrey**, Louise Sarah 1950- *Who 92*
**Godfrey**, Malcolm Paul Weston 1926- *Who 92*
**Godfrey**, Martyn N 1949- *IntAu&W 91*
**Godfrey**, Norman Eric 1927- *Who 92*
**Godfrey**, Paul Bard 1927- *WhoAmL 92*
**Godfrey**, Paul Jeffrey 1940- *AmMWSc 92*
**Godfrey**, Paul Russell 1914- *AmMWSc 92*
**Godfrey**, Paul Victor 1939- *WhoEnt 92*
**Godfrey**, Peter 1924- *Who 92*
**Godfrey**, R H *TwCSFW 91*
**Godfrey**, Richard Cartier 1954- *WhoAmL 92*
**Godfrey**, Richard George 1927- *WhoWest 92*
**Godfrey**, Robert Allen 1944- *AmMWSc 92*
**Godfrey**, Robert D 1948- *WhoAmP 91*
**Godfrey**, Robert R. 1947- *WhoFI 92*
**Godfrey**, Susan Sturgis 1944- *AmMWSc 92*
**Godfrey**, Thomas 1704-1749 *BiInAmS*
**Godfrey**, Thomas 1736-1763 *BenetAL 91*
**Godfrey**, Thomas, Jr. 1736-1763 *DcNCBi 2*
**Godfrey**, Thomas Francis 1944- *WhoAmL 92*
**Godfrey**, Thomas Nigel King 1927- *AmMWSc 92*
**Godfrey**, W Lynn 1939- *AmMWSc 92*
**Godfrey**, Wesley *WhoBlA 92*
**Godfrey**, William *Who 92*
**Godfrey**, William Ashley 1938- *WhoMW 92*
**Godfrey**, William Earl 1910- *AmMWSc 92*
**Godfrey**, William R. 1948- *WhoBlA 92*
**Godhwani**, Arjun 1941- *AmMWSc 92*
**Godick**, Neil Barnett 1942- *WhoFI 92*
**Godiksen**, Carol Lorenzen 1952- *WhoMW 92*
**Godin**, Claude 1926- *AmMWSc 92*
**Godin**, Wilfred Lucien 1937- *WhoAmP 91*
**Godine**, David R. 1944- *IntWW 91*
**Godine**, John Elliott 1947- *AmMWSc 92*
**Godiner**, Donald Leonard 1933- *WhoAmL 92*
**Godinez**, Hector G. *WhoHisp 92*
**Godinez**, Maria Elena 1950- *WhoHisp 92*

**Godinez Flores**, Ramon 1936- *WhoRel 92*
**Goding**, James Watson 1946- *AmMWSc 92*
**Godino**, Charles F 1934- *AmMWSc 92*
**Godke**, Robert Alan 1944- *AmMWSc 92*
**Godkin**, Celia 1948- *ConAu 133, SmATA 66*
**Godkin**, E. L. 1831-1902 *BenetAL 91*
**Godkin**, Roy Lynn 1946- *WhoFI 92*
**Godley** *Who 92*
**Godley**, Gene Edwin 1939- *WhoAmP 91*
**Godley**, Georgina 1955- *IntWW 91*
**Godley**, W. A. H. 1926- *WrDr 92*
**Godley**, Willie Cecil 1922- *AmMWSc 92*
**Godley**, Wynne Alexander Hugh 1926- *Who 92*
**Godman**, Arthur 1916- *IntAu&W 91, WrDr 92*
**Godman**, Gabriel C 1921- *AmMWSc 92*
**Godman**, John Davidson 1794-1830 *BiInAmS*
**Godman**, Norman Anthony 1938- *Who 92*
**Godman Irvine**, Bryant *Who 92*
**Godnick**, Gilbert G 1927- *WhoAmP 91*
**Godofsky**, Stanley 1928- *WhoAmL 92*
**Godollei**, Rachel 1952- *WhoMW 92*
**Godolphin**, Sidney 1610?-1643? *RfGEnL 91*
**Godolphin**, William 1941- *AmMWSc 92*
**Godowsky**, Leopold 1870-1938 *NewAmDM*
**Godoy**, Gustavo G. *WhoHisp 92*
**Godoy**, Manuel de 1767-1851 *HisDSpE*
**Godoy**, Virginia Flores *WhoHisp 92*
**Godoy Alcayaga**, Lucila 1889-1957 *WhoNob 90*
**Godoy Perez**, Ramona *WhoHisp 92*
**Godrej**, Adi Burjor 1942- *IntWW 91*
**Godrick**, Joseph Adam 1942- *AmMWSc 92*
**Godsay**, Madhu 1932- *AmMWSc 92*
**Godschalk**, David Robinson 1931- *AmMWSc 92*
**Godsell**, Stanley Harry 1920- *Who 92*
**Godsey**, C. Wayne 1946- *WhoEnt 92, WhoWest 92*
**Godsey**, John Drew 1922- *IntAu&W 91, WhoRel 92, WrDr 92*
**Godsey**, Kyle Lee 1963- *WhoRel 92*
**Godshalk**, Gordon Lamar 1948- *AmMWSc 92*
**Godshall**, Fredric Allen 1934- *AmMWSc 92*
**Godshall**, Robert W 1933- *WhoAmP 91*
**Godsil**, Richard William 1953- *WhoRel 92*
**Godsoe**, Peter Cowperthwaite 1938- *WhoFI 92*
**Godson**, Godfrey Nigel 1936- *AmMWSc 92*
**Godson**, Warren Lehman 1920- *AmMWSc 92*
**Godston**, Peter Phillips 1961- *WhoWest 92*
**Godt**, Henry Charles, Jr 1925- *AmMWSc 92*
**Godt**, Robert Eugene 1942- *AmMWSc 92*
**Godunov**, Aleksandr 1949- *IntWW 91, SovUnBD*
**Godunov**, Alexander 1949- *IntMPA 92*
**Godunov**, Alexander Boris 1949- *WhoEnt 92*
**Godwin**, Anne 1897- *Who 92*
**Godwin**, Archibald Campbell 1831-1864 *DcNCBi 2*
**Godwin**, Bruce Roger 1957- *WhoEnt 92*
**Godwin**, David Ottis, Jr. 1954- *WhoAmL 92*
**Godwin**, Donald Everett 1947- *WhoAmL 92*
**Godwin**, Fay S. 1931- *IntWW 91*
**Godwin**, Francis 1562-1633 *ScFEYrs*
**Godwin**, Gail *DrAPF 91*
**Godwin**, Gail 1937- *BenetAL 91, ConLC 69 [port], ConNov 91, WrDr 92*
**Godwin**, Hannibal Lafayette 1873-1929 *DcNCBi 2*
**Godwin**, Howard Gibson 1902-1976 *DcNCBi 2*
**Godwin**, I. Lamond 1942- *WhoBlA 92*
**Godwin**, James Basil, Jr 1924- *AmMWSc 92*
**Godwin**, Janice Rivero 1953- *WhoRel 92*
**Godwin**, John 1922- *WrDr 92*
**Godwin**, John 1928- *IntAu&W 91*
**Godwin**, John Thomas 1917- *AmMWSc 92*
**Godwin**, Keith 1916- *TwCPaSc*
**Godwin**, Kimberly Ann 1960- *WhoAmL 92*
**Godwin**, King David 1951- *WhoEnt 92*
**Godwin**, Larry W 1948- *WhoAmP 91*
**Godwin**, Mary Wollstonecraft *RfGEnL 91*
**Godwin**, Mills Edwin, Jr 1914- *WhoAmP 91*
**Godwin**, Parke 1816-1904 *BenetAL 91*
**Godwin**, Paul Milton 1942- *WhoEnt 92*
**Godwin**, Peter Christopher 1957- *IntAu&W 91*
**Godwin**, R. Wayne 1941- *WhoFI 92*
**Godwin**, Ralph Lee, Jr. 1954- *WhoFI 92*
**Godwin**, Robert Anthony 1938- *WhoAmL 92*
**Godwin**, Robert O 1935- *AmMWSc 92*
**Godwin**, Robert Paul 1937- *AmMWSc 92*
**Godwin**, Robert William 1951- *WhoMW 92*
**Godwin**, Tom 1915- *TwCSFW 91*
**Godwin**, William 1756-1836 *BlkwCEP, CnDBLB 3 [port], RfGEnL 91, ScFEYrs*
**Godwin**, William Henry 1923- *Who 92*
**Godwin-Austen**, Pamela 1952- *WhoEnt 92*
**Godycki**, Ludwig Edward 1921- *AmMWSc 92*
**Godzeski**, Carl William 1926- *AmMWSc 92*
**Goe**, Gerald Lee 1942- *AmMWSc 92*
**Goeas**, Edward A, III 1952- *WhoAmP 91*
**Goebbels**, Joseph 1887-1945 *CurBio 91N*
**Goebbels**, Joseph 1897-1945 *EncTR 91 [port], FacFETw [port]*
**Goebbels**, Paul Joseph 1897-1945 *BiDExR*
**Goebel**, Carl Jerome 1929- *AmMWSc 92*
**Goebel**, Charles Gale 1917- *AmMWSc 92*
**Goebel**, Charles James 1930- *AmMWSc 92*
**Goebel**, Chilton Godfrey, Jr. 1944- *WhoFI 92*
**Goebel**, Christopher Jay 1966- *WhoMW 92*
**Goebel**, David Kenneth 1961- *WhoMW 92*
**Goebel**, Edward William, Jr. 1938- *WhoAmL 92*
**Goebel**, Edwin DeWayne 1923- *AmMWSc 92*
**Goebel**, Jack Bruce 1932- *AmMWSc 92*
**Goebel**, Maristella 1915- *AmMWSc 92*
**Goebel**, Richard Alan 1944- *WhoMW 92*
**Goebel**, Ronald William 1947- *AmMWSc 92*
**Goebel**, Ulf *DrAPF 91*
**Goebel**, Walther F. 1899- *IntWW 91*
**Goebel**, Walther Frederick 1899- *AmMWSc 92*
**Goebel**, William Horn 1941- *WhoAmL 92*
**Goebert**, Robert J. 1941- *WhoFI 92*
**Goeckeritz**, Felix Leo *ScFEYrs*
**Goeckner**, Norbert Anthony 1930- *AmMWSc 92*
**Goedde**, Alan George 1948- *WhoFI 92*
**Goedde**, William Richard 1930- *WhoIns 92*
**Goeddel**, David V 1951- *AmMWSc 92*
**Goede**, C. Wayne 1938- *WhoMW 92*
**Goedecke**, David Stewart 1929- *WhoEnt 92*
**Goedecke**, George Harold 1933- *WhoWest 92*
**Goedeker**, Edward Joseph 1937- *WhoFI 92*
**Goeden**, Richard Dean 1935- *AmMWSc 92*
**Goedicke**, Jean 1908- *WhoWest 92*
**Goedicke**, Patricia *DrAPF 91*
**Goedicke**, Patricia 1931- *ConPo 91, IntAu&W 91, WrDr 92*
**Goedicke**, Victor Alfred 1912- *AmMWSc 92*
**Goedken**, Virgil Linus 1940- *AmMWSc 92*
**Goefft**, L. Michael 1952- *WhoWest 92*
**Goeglein**, Gloria *WhoAmP 91*
**Goeglein**, Richard John 1934- *WhoWest 92*
**Goehler**, Brigitte Hanna 1926- *AmMWSc 92*
**Goehr**, Alexander 1932- *ConCom 92, IntWW 91, NewAmDM, Who 92*
**Goehring**, Charles B. 1952- *WhoFI 92*
**Goehring**, Edward Lee 1929- *WhoFI 92*
**Goehring**, John Brown 1935- *AmMWSc 92*
**Goehring**, William Earl 1952- *WhoAmL 92*
**Goei**, Bernard Thwan-Poo 1938- *WhoWest 92*
**Goeke**, Dale E 1950- *WhoAmP 91*
**Goeke**, George Leonard 1942- *AmMWSc 92*
**Goeke**, Leo Francis *WhoEnt 92*
**Goeken**, Nancy Ellen *AmMWSc 92*
**Goel**, Amrit Lal 1938- *AmMWSc 92*
**Goel**, Kailash C 1937- *AmMWSc 92*
**Goel**, Narendra Swarup 1941- *AmMWSc 92*
**Goel**, Om Prakash 1943- *AmMWSc 92*
**Goel**, Prem Kumar 1943- *AmMWSc 92*
**Goel**, Ram Parkash 1942- *AmMWSc 92*
**Goela**, Jitendra Singh 1951- *AmMWSc 92*
**Goelkel**, Gary Morgan 1953- *WhoFI 92*
**Goell**, James E 1939- *AmMWSc 92*
**Goeltz**, Richard Karl 1942- *WhoFI 92*
**Goelz**, John Matthew 1957- *WhoMW 92*
**Goelz**, Robert Dean 1951- *WhoAmL 92*
**Goelzer**, Daniel Lee 1947- *WhoAmL 92, WhoFI 92*
**Goelzer**, Kathryn Ann 1964- *WhoWest 92*
**Goen**, Clarence C., Jr. 1924-1990 *ConAu 133*
**Goenka**, Harsh Vardhan 1957- *IntWW 91*
**Goepel**, Charles Albert 1953- *AmMWSc 92*
**Goepp**, Robert August 1930- *AmMWSc 92*
**Goerch**, Carl 1891-1974 *DcNCBi 2*
**Goerdeler**, Carl Friedrich 1884-1945 *EncTR 91 [port]*
**Goergen**, Donald Joseph 1943- *WhoRel 92*
**Goergen**, Michael James 1952- *WhoAmL 92*
**Goering**, Bradley Paul 1967- *WhoMW 92*
**Goering**, Carroll Eugene 1934- *AmMWSc 92*
**Goering**, Gordon E. 1937- *WhoAmL 92*
**Goering**, Harlan Lowell 1921- *AmMWSc 92*
**Goering**, Helga *ConAu 35NR*
**Goering**, Hermann 1893-1946 *FacFETw [port]*
**Goering**, John James 1934- *AmMWSc 92*
**Goering**, Kenneth Justin 1913- *AmMWSc 92*
**Goering**, Leonard Lowell 1938- *WhoRel 92, WhoWest 92*
**Goering**, Wiston Keith 1928- *WhoWest 92*
**Goeringer**, Gerald Conrad 1933- *AmMWSc 92*
**Goeritz**, Mathias 1915-1990 *FacFETw*
**Goerke**, Jon 1929- *AmMWSc 92*
**Goerner**, Joseph Kofahl 1925- *AmMWSc 92*
**Goertemiller**, Clarence C, Jr 1928- *AmMWSc 92*
**Goertz**, Christoph Klaus 1944- *AmMWSc 92*
**Goertz**, Grayce Edith 1919- *AmMWSc 92*
**Goertz**, John William 1929- *AmMWSc 92*
**Goertzel**, Gerald 1919- *AmMWSc 92*
**Goerz**, David Jonathan, Jr 1934- *AmMWSc 92*
**Goes**, Albrecht 1908- *IntWW 91*
**Goes**, Robert Kenneth 1963- *WhoMW 92*
**Goeske**, Janet L 1911- *WhoAmP 91*
**Goessmann**, Charles Anthony 1827-1910 *BiInAmS*
**Goetchius**, Eugene Van Ness 1921- *WhoRel 92*
**Goetel**, Ferdynand 1890-1960 *LiExTwC*
**Goethals**, Angela *NewYTBS 91 [port]*
**Goethals**, George Washington 1858-1928 *FacFETw*
**Goethe**, Johann Wolfgang von 1749-1832 *BlkwCEP, NinCLC 34 [port]*
**Goethert**, B H 1907- *AmMWSc 92*
**Goetinck**, Paul Firmin 1933- *AmMWSc 92*
**Goetsch**, Dennis Donald 1924- *AmMWSc 92*
**Goetsch**, Gerald D 1923- *AmMWSc 92*
**Goetsch**, John Hubert 1933- *WhoFI 92*
**Goetsch**, Robert George 1933- *WhoAmP 91*
**Goetschel**, Charles Thomas 1935- *AmMWSc 92*
**Goettel**, Gerard Louis 1928- *WhoAmL 92*
**Goettelman**, Scott Victor 1963- *WhoAmL 92*
**Goettemoeller**, William Anthony 1937- *WhoMW 92*
**Goetting**, Bradley *WhoAmP 91*
**Goettler**, Lloyd Arnold 1939- *AmMWSc 92*
**Goettlich Riemann**, Wilhelmina Maria Anna 1934- *AmMWSc 92*
**Goettling-Krause**, Gisela Erika Waltraud 1926- *WhoEnt 92, WhoMW 92*
**Goettsch**, Robert 1927- *AmMWSc 92*
**Goetz**, Abraham 1926- *AmMWSc 92*
**Goetz**, Alexander Franklin Hermann 1938- *AmMWSc 92*
**Goetz**, Augustus *BenetAL 91*
**Goetz**, Charles Albert 1908- *AmMWSc 92*
**Goetz**, Charles Frederick 1956- *WhoFI 92*
**Goetz**, Charles J. 1939- *WhoAmL 92*
**Goetz**, David Michael 1950- *WhoEnt 92*
**Goetz**, Elizabeth Morey 1927- *WhoMW 92*
**Goetz**, Frederick Charles *AmMWSc 92*
**Goetz**, Frederick William, Jr 1950- *AmMWSc 92*
**Goetz**, George Arthur 1921- *WhoMW 92*
**Goetz**, George Washington 1856-1897 *BiInAmS*
**Goetz**, Harold 1932- *AmMWSc 92*
**Goetz**, Kenneth Lee 1932- *AmMWSc 92*
**Goetz**, Marisa 1956- *WhoAmL 92*
**Goetz**, Masa Aiba 1928- *WhoWest 92*
**Goetz**, Maurice Harold 1924- *WhoAmL 92*
**Goetz**, Raymond 1922- *WhoAmL 92*
**Goetz**, Richard W 1936- *AmMWSc 92*
**Goetz**, Roger Melvin 1940- *WhoRel 92*
**Goetz**, Rudolph W 1942- *AmMWSc 92*
**Goetz**, Ruth *BenetAL 91*
**Goetz**, William Charles 1954- *WhoAmL 92*
**Goetz**, William G 1944- *WhoAmP 91*
**Goetz**, William H 1914- *AmMWSc 92*
**Goetze**, Mary 1943- *WhoMW 92*
**Goetzel**, Claus G 1913- *AmMWSc 92*
**Goetzinger**, Cornelius Peter 1911- *AmMWSc 92*
**Goetzke**, Gary Albert 1956- *WhoMW 92*
**Goetzke**, Gloria Louise *WhoWest 92*
**Goetzke**, Ronald Richard 1933- *WhoIns 92*
**Goeudevert**, Daniel 1942- *IntWW 91*
**Goez**, J. L. 1939- *WhoHisp 92*
**Goff** *Who 92*
**Goff**, Byron Heazelton, Jr. 1940- *WhoAmL 92*
**Goff**, Charles W 1941- *AmMWSc 92*
**Goff**, Christopher Godfrey 1945- *AmMWSc 92*
**Goff**, Colleen Mullen 1948- *WhoAmL 92*
**Goff**, Donald L 1947- *WhoAmP 91*
**Goff**, Donald Leslie 1947- *WhoMW 92*
**Goff**, Doris Mildred 1920- *WhoEnt 92*
**Goff**, Emmet Stull 1852-1902 *BiInAmS*
**Goff**, Gerald K 1925- *AmMWSc 92*
**Goff**, Harold Milton 1947- *AmMWSc 92*
**Goff**, James Franklin 1928- *AmMWSc 92*
**Goff**, Jerry Eason, II 1969- *WhoEnt 92*
**Goff**, Jesse Paul 1955- *AmMWSc 92*
**Goff**, Jim *WhoRel 92*
**Goff**, John Samuel 1931- *WhoWest 92*
**Goff**, Kenneth Odell 1953- *WhoRel 92*
**Goff**, Kenneth W 1928- *AmMWSc 92*
**Goff**, Lynda June 1949- *AmMWSc 92*
**Goff**, Martyn 1923- *IntAu&W 91, Who 92, WrDr 92*
**Goff**, Norvel 1949- *WhoAmP 91*
**Goff**, Philip Bruce 1953- *IntWW 91*
**Goff**, Regina Mary 1917- *WhoBlA 92*
**Goff**, Robert 1955- *Who 92*
**Goff**, Robert Edward 1952- *WhoFI 92*
**Goff**, Robert William, Jr. 1946- *WhoAmL 92*
**Goff**, Stephen Payne 1951- *AmMWSc 92*
**Goff**, Wilhelmina Delores 1940- *WhoBlA 92*
**Goff**, Wilmer Scott 1923- *WhoMW 92*
**Goff Of Chieveley**, Baron 1926- *IntWW 91, Who 92*
**Goffe**, Art *WhoAmP 91*
**Goffe**, Arthur d1737? *DcNCBi 2*
**Goffe**, William 1605?-1679? *BenetAL 91*
**Goffinet**, Edward P, Jr 1930- *AmMWSc 92*
**Goffman**, Erving 1922-1982 *FacFETw*
**Goffman**, Martin 1940- *AmMWSc 92*
**Goffredo**, Daniel Louis 1923- *WhoFI 92*
**Gofman**, John William 1918- *AmMWSc 92*
**Goforth**, Charles Preston 1950- *WhoWest 92*
**Goforth**, Charles Wayne 1931- *WhoAmP 91*
**Goforth**, Deretha Rainey 1944- *AmMWSc 92*
**Goforth**, Ellen *IntAu&W 91X, WrDr 92*
**Goforth**, Kenneth H., Jr. 1947- *WhoRel 92*
**Goforth**, Nathan Dan 1951- *WhoWest 92*
**Goforth**, Thomas Tucker 1937- *AmMWSc 92*
**Goforth**, William Clements 1937- *WhoAmL 92*
**Goga**, Octavian 1881-1938 *BiDExR, EncTR 91 [port]*
**Gogan**, James Wilson 1938- *WhoFI 92*
**Gogan**, Niall Joseph 1941- *AmMWSc 92*
**Gogarten**, Friedrich 1887-1967 *EncTR 91, FacFETw*
**Gogarty**, Oliver St. John 1878-1957 *LiExTwC, RfGEnL 91*
**Gogarty**, W B 1930- *AmMWSc 92*
**Gogarty**, William Barney 1930- *WhoWest 92*
**Gogel**, Germaine E 1952- *AmMWSc 92*
**Goger**, Pauline Rohm 1913- *AmMWSc 92*
**Gogerty**, John Harry 1933- *AmMWSc 92*
**Goggans**, James F 1920- *AmMWSc 92*
**Goggin**, Dan 1943- *IntAu&W 91*
**Goggin**, Joseph Robert 1926- *WhoFI 92*
**Goggin**, Robert Allan 1931- *WhoWest 92*
**Goggins**, Horace 1929- *WhoBlA 92*
**Goggins**, Jean A 1947- *AmMWSc 92*
**Goggins**, John Francis 1933- *AmMWSc 92*
**Goggins**, Juanita Willmon 1934- *WhoAmP 91*
**Gogh**, Theo van 1857-1891 *ThHEIm [port]*
**Gogh**, Vincent van 1853-1890 *ThHEIm*
**Gogin**, Charles 1845-1931 *TwCPaSc*
**Gogisgi** *DrAPF 91*
**Goglia**, Charles A., Jr. 1931- *WhoAmL 92*
**Goglia**, Gennaro Louis 1921- *AmMWSc 92*
**Goglia**, M J 1916- *AmMWSc 92*
**Gogliettino**, John Carmine 1952- *WhoFI 92*
**Gogo**, Gregory 1943- *WhoAmL 92*
**Gogoberidze**, Lana Levanovna 1928- *IntWW 91*
**Gogol**, John Michael 1938- *WhoWest 92*
**Gogol**, Nikolai 1809-1852 *DramC 1 [port], NinCLC 31 [port]*
**Gogolewski**, Raymond Paul 1941- *AmMWSc 92*
**Gogolin**, Marilyn Tompkins 1946- *WhoWest 92*
**Gogos**, Costas G 1938- *AmMWSc 92*
**Goguen**, Emile J *WhoAmP 91*
**Goguen**, Joseph A, Jr 1941- *AmMWSc 92*
**Goguen**, Joseph Amadee 1941- *Who 92*
**Goh Chok Tong** 1941- *IntWW 91, Who 92*
**Goh Keng Swee** 1918- *IntWW 91*

**Goh**, Edward Hua Seng 1942- AmMWSc 92
**Goheen**, Austin Clement 1917- AmMWSc 92
**Goheen**, David Wade 1920- AmMWSc 92, WhoWest 92
**Goheen**, Harry Earl 1915- AmMWSc 92
**Goheen**, Lola Coleman 1948- AmMWSc 92
**Goheen**, Robert 1919- WrDr 92
**Goheen**, Robert F 1919- WhoAmP 91
**Goheen**, Robert Francis 1919- IntWW 91, Who 92
**Goheen**, Steven Charles 1951- AmMWSc 92
**Gohel**, Jayvantsinhji 1915- Who 92
**Gohil**, Pratapsinh 1950- WhoMW 92
**Gohil**, Punit 1957- WhoWest 92
**Gohlke**, Florence Margaret 1914- WhoAmP 91
**Gohmert**, Louis Buller, Jr. 1953- WhoAmL 92
**Gohn**, A. Janelle 1955- WhoMW 92
**Gohr**, Frank August 1922- AmMWSc 92
**Goico**, Pedro Geronimo 1808-1890 HisDSpE
**Goicoechea**, Jose Antonio 1735-1814 HisDSpE
**Goicouria**, Pedro A. WhoHisp 92
**Goicuria Cabrera**, Domingo 1804-1870 HisDSpE
**Goihman-Yahr**, Mauricio 1938- AmMWSc 92
**Goimarac**, Peter Paul 1964- WhoFI 92
**Goin**, Carey R. 1960- WhoEnt 92
**Goines**, Donald 1937?-1974 BlkLC [port]
**Goines**, Leonard 1934- WhoBlA 92, WhoEnt 92
**Going**, John 1936- ConTFT 9, WhoEnt 92
**Going**, Robert Neil 1951- WhoAmP 91
**Goings**, Everett Vernon 1945- WhoFI 92
**Goins**, Frances Floriano 1950- WhoAmL 92
**Goins**, James Allen 1930- WhoRel 92
**Goins**, Mary G. 1929- WhoBlA 92
**Goins**, N. Walter WhoBlA 92
**Goins**, Neal Rodney 1952- AmMWSc 92
**Goins**, Rosemarie 1940- WhoRel 92
**Goins**, Truman 1920- AmMWSc 92
**Goins**, William C, Jr AmMWSc 92
**Goiporia**, Maneck Nadirshaw 1932- IntWW 91
**Goishi**, Wataru 1928- AmMWSc 92
**Goitein**, Michael 1939- AmMWSc 92
**Goizueta**, Roberto 1931- IntWW 91
**Goizueta**, Roberto C. 1931- WhoHisp 92
**Goizueta**, Roberto Crispulo 1931- WhoFI 92
**Goizueta**, Roberto Segundo 1954- WhoHisp 92
**Gojmerac**, Walter Louis 1925- AmMWSc 92
**Gojmerac-Leiner**, Georgia DrAPF 91
**Gojny**, Frank 1952- AmMWSc 92
**Goka**, Richard Shunji 1947- WhoWest 92
**Gokcen**, Nev A 1921- AmMWSc 92
**Gokee**, Donald LeRoy 1933- WhoRel 92
**Gokel**, George William 1946- AmMWSc 92
**Goken**, Garold Lee 1937- AmMWSc 92
**Gokey**, Franklin Charles 1916- WhoIns 92
**Gokhale**, Datta Vasudeo 1944- WhoEnt 92
**Gokhale**, Dattaprabhakar V 1936- AmMWSc 92
**Goksel**, Mehmet Adnan 1924- AmMWSc 92
**Goktepe**, Omer Faruk 1939- AmMWSc 92
**Gokul** 1944- WhoEnt 92
**Gol**, Jean 1942- IntWW 91
**Golab**, Tomasz 1922- AmMWSc 92
**Golan**, Martin DrAPF 91
**Golan**, Menahem 1929- IntMPA 92, IntWW 91, WhoEnt 92
**Golan**, Stephen Leonard 1951- WhoAmL 92
**Goland**, Allen Nathan 1930- AmMWSc 92
**Goland**, Martin 1919- AmMWSc 92
**Golanski**, Alani 1954- WhoAmL 92
**Golant**, William 1937- WrDr 92
**Golarz-De Bourne**, Maria Nelly 1934- AmMWSc 92
**Golashesky**, Chrysa Zofia 1957- WhoFI 92
**Golasinski**, Michael Joseph 1943- WhoFI 92
**Golaski**, Walter Michael 1913- WhoFI 92
**Golay**, Marcel Jules Edouard 1902- AmMWSc 92
**Golay**, Michael W AmMWSc 92
**Golbar**, Ashton Afshin 1963- WhoFI 92
**Golbey**, Robert 1922- AmMWSc 92
**Golbus**, Mitchell S 1939- AmMWSc 92
**Golchan**, Frederic IntMPA 92
**Golchan**, Frederic Alfred 1953- WhoEnt 92
**Golchert**, Norbert William 1935- AmMWSc 92
**Golcuklu**, Ahmet Feyyaz 1926- IntWW 91
**Gold**, Alan Stephen 1944- WhoAmL 92
**Gold**, Albert 1935- AmMWSc 92
**Gold**, Allen 1918- AmMWSc 92
**Gold**, Allen Morton 1930- AmMWSc 92
**Gold**, Alvin Hirsh 1932- AmMWSc 92
**Gold**, Andrew Vick 1934- AmMWSc 92
**Gold**, Armand Joel 1926- AmMWSc 92
**Gold**, Arnold Henry 1932- WhoAmL 92
**Gold**, Arthur 1917- NewAmDM, Who 92
**Gold**, Barry Ira 1946- AmMWSc 92
**Gold**, Barry Irwin 1946- AmMWSc 92
**Gold**, Bernard 1923- AmMWSc 92
**Gold**, Daisy Hendley 1893-1975 DcNCBi 2
**Gold**, Daniel Howard 1929- AmMWSc 92
**Gold**, Daniel P 1954- AmMWSc 92
**Gold**, David Percy 1933- AmMWSc 92
**Gold**, Don 1931- WhoMW 92
**Gold**, Edward DrAPF 91
**Gold**, Edward 1941- AmMWSc 92
**Gold**, Eli 1920- AmMWSc 92
**Gold**, Elijah Herman 1936- AmMWSc 92
**Gold**, Emanuel R 1935- WhoAmP 91
**Gold**, Erica Louise 1959- WhoEnt 92
**Gold**, Ernest 1921- IntMPA 92, WhoEnt 92
**Gold**, George Myron 1935- WhoAmL 92
**Gold**, Gerald 1927- AmMWSc 92
**Gold**, Gerald 1945- WhoMW 92
**Gold**, Gordon Stanford 1946- WhoAmL 92
**Gold**, H L 1914- FacFETw, TwCSFW 91, WrDr 92
**Gold**, Harold Arthur 1929- WhoAmL 92
**Gold**, Harold Eugene 1928- AmMWSc 92
**Gold**, Harris 1936- AmMWSc 92
**Gold**, Harvey Joseph 1932- AmMWSc 92
**Gold**, Harvey Saul 1952- AmMWSc 92
**Gold**, Herbert DrAPF 91
**Gold**, Herbert 1924- BenetAL 91, ConNov 91, FacFETw, WrDr 92
**Gold**, Herbert Frank 1939- WhoFI 92
**Gold**, Herman DrAPF 91
**Gold**, Hyman 1914- WhoEnt 92
**Gold**, I. Randall 1951- WhoAmL 92
**Gold**, Irwin Neal 1957- WhoFI 92
**Gold**, Ivan DrAPF 91
**Gold**, Jack 1930- IntWW 91, Who 92, WhoEnt 92
**Gold**, James Sommers 1951- WhoFI 92
**Gold**, Jay D. 1942- WhoFI 92
**Gold**, Jay Joseph 1923- AmMWSc 92
**Gold**, Jeff WhoEnt 92
**Gold**, Jeffrey Mark 1945- WhoFI 92
**Gold**, John 1925- Who 92
**Gold**, John Rush 1946- AmMWSc 92
**Gold**, Joseph 1912- IntWW 91, Who 92
**Gold**, Judith Hammerling 1941- AmMWSc 92
**Gold**, Kenneth Arthur 1954- WhoFI 92
**Gold**, Kenneth Harris 1942- WhoMW 92
**Gold**, Laurence Stephen 1936- WhoAmL 92
**Gold**, Leonard Singer 1934- WhoRel 92
**Gold**, Lewis Peter 1935- AmMWSc 92
**Gold**, Lorne W 1928- AmMWSc 92
**Gold**, Mark Stephen 1949- AmMWSc 92
**Gold**, Martin 1932- AmMWSc 92
**Gold**, Martin I 1928- AmMWSc 92
**Gold**, Marvin B 1933- AmMWSc 92
**Gold**, Marvin H 1915- AmMWSc 92
**Gold**, Marvin H 1936- AmMWSc 92
**Gold**, Melissa d1991 NewYTBS 91
**Gold**, Melvin 1909- IntMPA 92
**Gold**, Melvin Louis 1909- WhoEnt 92
**Gold**, Michael DcAmImH
**Gold**, Michael 1894-1967 BenetAL 91
**Gold**, Michael Howard 1941- AmMWSc 92
**Gold**, Michael Nathan 1952- WhoWest 92
**Gold**, Morton 1933- WhoEnt 92
**Gold**, Neil D. 1948- WhoAmL 92
**Gold**, Norman Irving 1921- AmMWSc 92
**Gold**, Paul Ernest 1945- AmMWSc 92
**Gold**, Phil 1936- AmMWSc 92, IntWW 91
**Gold**, Philip William 1944- AmMWSc 92
**Gold**, Phillip 1937- WhoAmL 92
**Gold**, Pleasant Daniel 1833-1920 DcNCBi 2
**Gold**, Raymond 1927- AmMWSc 92
**Gold**, Richard Horace 1935- AmMWSc 92
**Gold**, Richard Michael 1937- AmMWSc 92
**Gold**, Richard N. 1945- WhoFI 92
**Gold**, Richard Robert 1930- AmMWSc 92
**Gold**, Robert 1942- AmMWSc 92
**Gold**, Roger Eugene 1944- AmMWSc 92
**Gold**, Ronald Marc 1953- WhoEnt 92
**Gold**, Sherry Pearl 1935- WhoEnt 92
**Gold**, Shirley Jeanne 1925- WhoAmP 91, WhoWest 92
**Gold**, Simeon 1949- WhoAmL 92
**Gold**, Stanley P. 1942- WhoFI 92
**Gold**, Stephen B. 1946- WhoAmL 92
**Gold**, Stephen Charles 1915- Who 92
**Gold**, Steve 1944- WhoEnt 92
**Gold**, Steven Harvey 1946- AmMWSc 92
**Gold**, Steven Michael 1953- WhoAmL 92
**Gold**, Steven William 1963- WhoAmL 92
**Gold**, Stuart Alan 1953- WhoAmL 92
**Gold**, Stuart Walter 1949- WhoAmL 92
**Gold**, Sydell Perlmutter 1941- AmMWSc 92
**Gold**, Sylviane 1948- WhoEnt 92
**Gold**, Theodore Sedgwick 1818-1906 BiInAmS
**Gold**, Thomas 1920- AmMWSc 92, IntWW 91, Who 92
**Gold**, Vera Johnson 1951- WhoFI 92
**Gold**, Warren Maxwell 1934- AmMWSc 92
**Gold**, Wendy Lee 1955- WhoEnt 92
**Gold**, William 1923- AmMWSc 92
**Gold**, William Buchanan, Jr. 1914- WhoAmL 92
**Goldak**, Paul Joseph 1946- WhoMW 92
**Goldan**, Paul David 1933- AmMWSc 92
**Goldanskii**, Vitalii Iosifovich 1923- IntWW 91
**Goldaper**, Gabriele Gay 1937- WhoWest 92
**Goldbarth**, Albert DrAPF 91
**Goldbarth**, Albert 1948- BenetAL 91, ConPo 91, WrDr 92
**Goldbeck**, George P 1925- WhoIns 92
**Goldberg**, A Jon 1947- AmMWSc 92
**Goldberg**, Aaron 1917- AmMWSc 92
**Goldberg**, Aaron Joseph 1943- AmMWSc 92
**Goldberg**, Abraham 1923- IntWW 91, Who 92
**Goldberg**, Alan Herbert 1931- AmMWSc 92, WhoMW 92
**Goldberg**, Alan Joel 1943- WhoAmL 92
**Goldberg**, Alan Marvin 1939- AmMWSc 92
**Goldberg**, Alan Samuel 1953- WhoRel 92
**Goldberg**, Alfred 1923- AmMWSc 92
**Goldberg**, Alfred L 1942- AmMWSc 92
**Goldberg**, Allan Roy 1941- AmMWSc 92
**Goldberg**, Andrew Franklin 1960- WhoFI 92
**Goldberg**, Andrew Paul 1945- AmMWSc 92
**Goldberg**, Arthur 1908-1990 AnObit 1990, RComAH
**Goldberg**, Arthur Abba 1940- WhoFI 92
**Goldberg**, Arthur H 1935- AmMWSc 92
**Goldberg**, Arthur H. 1942- WhoFI 92
**Goldberg**, Arthur J 1908-1990 FacFETw [port]
**Goldberg**, Arthur Joseph 1908-1990 AmPolLe
**Goldberg**, Arthur M. d1991 NewYTBS 91
**Goldberg**, Aubrey 1940- WhoAmL 92
**Goldberg**, Avram Jacob 1930- WhoFI 92
**Goldberg**, Barbara DrAPF 91
**Goldberg**, Benjamin 1915- AmMWSc 92
**Goldberg**, Bernard 1932- IntMPA 92
**Goldberg**, Bertram J. 1942- WhoRel 92
**Goldberg**, Bertrand 1913- IntWW 91
**Goldberg**, Billy B 1915- WhoAmP 91
**Goldberg**, Bruce David WhoFI 92
**Goldberg**, Bruce Edward 1948- WhoWest 92
**Goldberg**, Burton David 1927- AmMWSc 92
**Goldberg**, Charles Ned 1941- WhoAmL 92
**Goldberg**, Colman 1924- AmMWSc 92
**Goldberg**, Conrad Stewart 1943- AmMWSc 92
**Goldberg**, Danny 1950- WhoEnt 92
**Goldberg**, David WhoRel 92
**Goldberg**, David 1934- WhoAmL 92
**Goldberg**, David Arthur 1954- WhoAmL 92
**Goldberg**, David Ben 1956- WhoEnt 92
**Goldberg**, David C 1921- AmMWSc 92
**Goldberg**, David Elliott 1932- AmMWSc 92
**Goldberg**, David Gerard 1947- Who 92
**Goldberg**, David Myer 1933- AmMWSc 92
**Goldberg**, Dick 1947- WhoEnt 92
**Goldberg**, Don Harvey 1941- WhoRel 92
**Goldberg**, Edward 1940- WhoFI 92
**Goldberg**, Edward B 1935- AmMWSc 92
**Goldberg**, Edward D 1921- AmMWSc 92
**Goldberg**, Edward David 1921- IntWW 91
**Goldberg**, Edward Morris 1931- WhoWest 92
**Goldberg**, Edwin A 1916- AmMWSc 92
**Goldberg**, Elaine Catherine 1944- WhoMW 92
**Goldberg**, Erwin 1930- AmMWSc 92
**Goldberg**, Estelle Maxine 1934- AmMWSc 92
**Goldberg**, Eugene 1927- AmMWSc 92
**Goldberg**, Eugene P 1928- AmMWSc 92
**Goldberg**, Fred 1921- IntMPA 92
**Goldberg**, Fred Sellmann 1941- WhoFI 92, WhoWest 92
**Goldberg**, Fred T., Jr. WhoAmL 92
**Goldberg**, Gail Lovell 1947- WhoAmL 92
**Goldberg**, Gary David LesBEnT 92
**Goldberg**, Gary David 1944- WhoEnt 92
**Goldberg**, Gary Syd 1948- WhoAmP 91
**Goldberg**, Gerald Jay DrAPF 91
**Goldberg**, Gershon Morton 1924- AmMWSc 92
**Goldberg**, Harry 1918- AmMWSc 92
**Goldberg**, Harvey 1940- WhoFI 92
**Goldberg**, Henry L. d1991 NewYTBS 91 [port]
**Goldberg**, Herbert Sam 1926- AmMWSc 92
**Goldberg**, Herman R 1915- WhoAmP 91
**Goldberg**, Hillel 1946- IntAu&W 91, WhoRel 92
**Goldberg**, Howard Alan 1948- WhoEnt 92
**Goldberg**, Howard S 1936- AmMWSc 92
**Goldberg**, Hyman 1939- AmMWSc 92
**Goldberg**, Ira Barry 1943- AmMWSc 92
**Goldberg**, Irvin H 1926- AmMWSc 92
**Goldberg**, Irving David 1921- AmMWSc 92
**Goldberg**, Irving Loeb 1906- WhoAmL 92
**Goldberg**, Ivan Baer 1939- WhoFI 92
**Goldberg**, Ivan D 1934- AmMWSc 92
**Goldberg**, Jacob 1926- AmMWSc 92
**Goldberg**, Janet E. 1951- WhoAmL 92
**Goldberg**, Jay Aaron 1949- WhoEnt 92
**Goldberg**, Jay M 1935- AmMWSc 92
**Goldberg**, Jerold Martin 1938- WhoEnt 92
**Goldberg**, Jerry David 1964- WhoWest 92
**Goldberg**, Jerry M. 1940- WhoEnt 92
**Goldberg**, Jolande Elisabeth 1931- WhoAmL 92
**Goldberg**, Jonathan Jacob 1947- Who 92
**Goldberg**, Joseph 1923- AmMWSc 92
**Goldberg**, Joseph Louis 1909- AmMWSc 92
**Goldberg**, Joshua Norman 1925- AmMWSc 92
**Goldberg**, Joshua Rabb 1957- WhoFI 92
**Goldberg**, Judith Ilana 1962- WhoAmL 92
**Goldberg**, Judy Hiller 1933- WhoWest 92
**Goldberg**, Kenneth Philip 1945- AmMWSc 92
**Goldberg**, Lawrence Spencer 1940- AmMWSc 92
**Goldberg**, Lee Dresden 1937- AmMWSc 92
**Goldberg**, Lee Winicki 1932- WhoFI 92, WhoWest 92
**Goldberg**, Leon Isadore 1926- AmMWSc 92
**Goldberg**, Leonard 1934- IntMPA 92, WhoEnt 92, WhoFI 92
**Goldberg**, Leonard H 1945- AmMWSc 92
**Goldberg**, Leslie Ellen 1964- WhoAmL 92
**Goldberg**, Lester DrAPF 91
**Goldberg**, Lester 1924- IntAu&W 91
**Goldberg**, Louis 1908- WrDr 92
**Goldberg**, Louis J 1936- AmMWSc 92
**Goldberg**, M. Roy 1962- WhoAmL 92
**Goldberg**, Marc Evan 1957- WhoFI 92
**Goldberg**, Mark Arthur 1934- AmMWSc 92, WhoWest 92
**Goldberg**, Mark Barry 1946- WhoWest 92
**Goldberg**, Martin 1930- AmMWSc 92
**Goldberg**, Martin A 1929- AmMWSc 92
**Goldberg**, Marvin 1939- AmMWSc 92
**Goldberg**, Matthew Sohn 1955- WhoFI 92
**Goldberg**, Melvin Arthur 1923- WhoEnt 92
**Goldberg**, Melvin Leonard 1932- AmMWSc 92
**Goldberg**, Merrill B 1943- AmMWSc 92
**Goldberg**, Michael Ellis 1941- AmMWSc 92
**Goldberg**, Michael Ian 1944- AmMWSc 92
**Goldberg**, Morris 1928- WhoWest 92
**Goldberg**, Morris M. d1991 NewYTBS 91
**Goldberg**, Morton Edward 1932- AmMWSc 92
**Goldberg**, Morton Falk 1937- AmMWSc 92
**Goldberg**, Moses Haym 1940- WhoEnt 92
**Goldberg**, Myra DrAPF 91
**Goldberg**, Neil A. 1947- WhoAmL 92
**Goldberg**, Nelson D 1931- AmMWSc 92
**Goldberg**, Norman 1921- AmMWSc 92
**Goldberg**, Norman Albert 1918- WhoEnt 92, WhoMW 92
**Goldberg**, Norman L. 1906-1982 ConAu 133
**Goldberg**, Pamela Winer 1955- WhoFI 92
**Goldberg**, Paul 1932- WhoFI 92
**Goldberg**, Paul 1959- ConAu 135
**Goldberg**, Paula Bursztyn 1938- AmMWSc 92
**Goldberg**, R J 1950- AmMWSc 92
**Goldberg**, Richard Aran 1936- AmMWSc 92
**Goldberg**, Richard Robert 1941- WhoAmL 92
**Goldberg**, Richard Robinson 1931- AmMWSc 92
**Goldberg**, Robert D 1951- WhoAmP 91
**Goldberg**, Robert Jack 1914- AmMWSc 92
**Goldberg**, Robert M. 1941- WhoAmL 92
**Goldberg**, Robert Nathan 1943- AmMWSc 92
**Goldberg**, Rube 1883-1970 FacFETw
**Goldberg**, Sabine Ruth 1958- AmMWSc 92
**Goldberg**, Samuel 1925- AmMWSc 92
**Goldberg**, Samuel 1928- WhoFI 92
**Goldberg**, Samuel I 1923- AmMWSc 92
**Goldberg**, Samuel Louis 1926- IntWW 91, WrDr 92
**Goldberg**, Sandra Gail 1940- WhoAmP 91

**Goldberg**, Seth A. 1953- *WhoAmL 92*
**Goldberg**, Seymour 1927- *AmMWSc 92*
**Goldberg**, Seymour 1928- *AmMWSc 92*
**Goldberg**, Sherman I. *WhoAmL 92*
**Goldberg**, Sidney 1931- *WhoFI 92*
**Goldberg**, Simon *TwCPaSc*
**Goldberg**, Stanley 1934- *AmMWSc 92*
**Goldberg**, Stanley Irwin 1930- *AmMWSc 92*
**Goldberg**, Stanley Irwin 1934- *WhoFI 92*
**Goldberg**, Stephen 1942- *AmMWSc 92*
**Goldberg**, Stephen B. 1932- *WhoAmL 92*
**Goldberg**, Stephen Robert 1941- *AmMWSc 92*
**Goldberg**, Stephen Zalmund 1947- *AmMWSc 92*
**Goldberg**, Steven F 1950- *WhoIns 92*
**Goldberg**, Steven R 1941- *AmMWSc 92*
**Goldberg**, Stuart 1956- *WhoFI 92*
**Goldberg**, Susan Solomon 1944- *WhoMW 92*
**Goldberg**, Szymon 1909- *NewAmDM*
**Goldberg**, Victor Joel 1933- *WhoFI 92*
**Goldberg**, Victor Paul 1941- *WhoAmL 92*
**Goldberg**, Vladislav V 1936- *AmMWSc 92*
**Goldberg**, Walter M 1946- *AmMWSc 92*
**Goldberg**, Whoopi *WhoBlA 92*
**Goldberg**, Whoopi 1949- *IntMPA 92*
**Goldberg**, Whoopi 1950- *NotBlAW 92*
**Goldberg**, Whoopi 1955- *WhoEnt 92*
**Goldberger**, Amy 1957- *AmMWSc 92*
**Goldberger**, Arthur Stanley 1930- *WhoFI 92*
**Goldberger**, David Alan 1941- *WhoAmL 92*
**Goldberger**, George Stefan 1947- *WhoFI 92*
**Goldberger**, Marvin Leonard 1922- *AmMWSc 92, IntWW 91, Who 92*
**Goldberger**, Michael Eric 1935- *AmMWSc 92*
**Goldberger**, Robert Frank 1933- *AmMWSc 92*
**Goldberger**, W M 1928- *AmMWSc 92*
**Goldblatt**, Barry Lance 1945- *WhoFI 92*
**Goldblatt**, David Ira 1937- *WhoAmL 92*
**Goldblatt**, Hal Michael 1952- *WhoEnt 92, WhoWest 92*
**Goldblatt**, Irwin Leonard 1940- *AmMWSc 92*
**Goldblatt**, Mark Lawrence 1948- *WhoEnt 92*
**Goldblatt**, Peter 1943- *AmMWSc 92*
**Goldblatt**, Peter Jerome *AmMWSc 92*
**Goldblatt**, Simon *Who 92*
**Goldblith**, Samuel Abraham 1919- *AmMWSc 92*
**Goldbloom**, David Ellis 1933- *AmMWSc 92*
**Goldbloom**, Richard B 1924- *AmMWSc 92*
**Goldblum**, Jeff 1952- *IntMPA 92, IntWW 91, WhoEnt 92*
**Goldblum**, Martin T. 1940- *WhoAmL 92*
**Goldbrunner**, Josef *WhoRel 92*
**Goldburg**, Arnold 1927- *AmMWSc 92*
**Goldburg**, Walter Isaac 1927- *AmMWSc 92*
**Goldby**, Frank 1903- *Who 92*
**Golde**, David William 1940- *AmMWSc 92*
**Golde**, Hellmut 1930- *AmMWSc 92*
**Goldemberg**, Isaac *DrAPF 91*
**Goldemberg**, Isaac 1945- *WhoHisp 92*
**Goldemberg**, Robert Lewis 1925- *AmMWSc 92*
**Golden**, Abner 1918- *AmMWSc 92*
**Golden**, Abraham J. 1918- *WhoAmL 92, WhoEnt 92*
**Golden**, Alfred 1908- *AmMWSc 92*
**Golden**, Alva Morgan 1920- *AmMWSc 92*
**Golden**, Archie Sidney 1931- *AmMWSc 92*
**Golden**, Arthur F. 1946- *WhoAmL 92*
**Golden**, Arthur Ivanhoe 1926- *WhoBlA 92*
**Golden**, Balfour Henry 1922- *WhoFI 92*
**Golden**, Ben Roy 1937- *AmMWSc 92*
**Golden**, Bill d1959 *LesBEnT 92*
**Golden**, Bruce Paul 1943- *WhoAmL 92*
**Golden**, Carole Ann 1942- *AmMWSc 92*
**Golden**, Christopher Anthony 1937- *WhoAmL 92*
**Golden**, Daniel Lewis 1913- *WhoAmL 92*
**Golden**, David E 1932- *AmMWSc 92*
**Golden**, David Mark 1935- *AmMWSc 92*
**Golden**, Donald Leon 1940- *WhoBlA 92*
**Golden**, Edward Scott 1955- *WhoAmL 92*
**Golden**, Elliott 1926- *WhoAmL 92*
**Golden**, Evelyn Davis 1951- *WhoBlA 92*
**Golden**, Francis St Clair 1936- *Who 92*
**Golden**, Fred Stephan 1945- *WhoFI 92*
**Golden**, Gail Kadison *DrAPF 91*
**Golden**, Gerald Samuel 1935- *WhoRel 92*
**Golden**, Gerald Seymour 1933- *AmMWSc 92*
**Golden**, Grace 1904- *TwCPaSc*
**Golden**, Grace Lydia 1904- *Who 92*
**Golden**, Gregg Hannan Stewart 1953- *WhoAmL 92*
**Golden**, Harry 1902-1981 *BenetAL 91*
**Golden**, Harry Lewis 1902-1981 *DcNCBi 2*
**Golden**, Herbert L. *IntMPA 92*
**Golden**, Jacqueline Audry 1935- *WhoAmP 91*
**Golden**, Jerome B 1917- *IntMPA 92*
**Golden**, John 1874-1955 *BenetAL 91*
**Golden**, John Dennis 1954- *WhoAmL 92*
**Golden**, John Joseph, Jr. 1943- *WhoFI 92*
**Golden**, John O 1937- *AmMWSc 92*
**Golden**, John Terence 1932- *AmMWSc 92*
**Golden**, Jonathan Lohr 1954- *WhoRel 92*
**Golden**, Joyce Cheryl 1955- *WhoMW 92*
**Golden**, Julius 1929- *WhoWest 92*
**Golden**, Kelly Paul 1943- *AmMWSc 92*
**Golden**, Kenneth Ivan 1932- *AmMWSc 92*
**Golden**, Laron E 1920- *AmMWSc 92*
**Golden**, Louie 1940- *WhoBlA 92*
**Golden**, Louis Joseph 1952- *WhoFI 92*
**Golden**, Marita 1950- *WhoBlA 92*
**Golden**, Mark 1948- *ConAu 135*
**Golden**, Marvin Darnell 1955- *WhoBlA 92*
**Golden**, Michael *WhoAmL 92, WhoAmP 91*
**Golden**, Michael 1942- *WhoWest 92*
**Golden**, Michael Edward 1944- *WhoFI 92*
**Golden**, Michael Joseph 1862-1918 *BiInAmS*
**Golden**, Michael R. 1950- *WhoEnt 92*
**Golden**, Michael Stanley 1942- *AmMWSc 92*
**Golden**, Mike *DrAPF 91*
**Golden**, Pat d1991 *NewYTBS 91*
**Golden**, Patricia Pagie Woodson 1951- *WhoEnt 92*
**Golden**, Paul A 1918- *WhoAmP 91*
**Golden**, Paul Lloyd 1939- *WhoRel 92*
**Golden**, Phillip Harry 1958- *WhoFI 92*
**Golden**, Rima *DrAPF 91*
**Golden**, Robert Bennett 1948- *WhoMW 92*
**Golden**, Robert Charles 1946- *WhoFI 92*
**Golden**, Robert Irving 1947- *WhoRel 92*
**Golden**, Robert K 1925- *AmMWSc 92*
**Golden**, Robert Nelson 1940- *WhoAmL 92*
**Golden**, Ronald Allen 1944- *WhoBlA 92*
**Golden**, Samuel Lewis 1921- *WhoBlA 92*
**Golden**, Sidney 1917- *AmMWSc 92*
**Golden**, Tim Robert 1954- *WhoAmP 91*
**Golden**, William 1911-1959 *DcTwDes*
**Golden**, William B *WhoAmP 91*
**Golden**, Willie L. 1952- *WhoBlA 92*
**Golden**, Wilson 1948- *WhoAmL 92*
**Golden**, Woodrow Wilson, Jr 1948- *WhoAmP 91*
**Goldenbaum**, George Charles 1936- *AmMWSc 92*
**Goldenbaum**, Paul Ernest 1943- *AmMWSc 92*
**Goldenberg**, Andrew Avi 1945- *AmMWSc 92*
**Goldenberg**, Barbara Lou 1952- *AmMWSc 92*
**Goldenberg**, Barton Joshua 1955- *WhoFI 92*
**Goldenberg**, David Jay 1955- *WhoMW 92*
**Goldenberg**, David Milton 1938- *AmMWSc 92*
**Goldenberg**, George 1929- *WhoFI 92*
**Goldenberg**, Gerald J 1933- *AmMWSc 92*
**Goldenberg**, Harris Seymour 1942- *WhoMW 92*
**Goldenberg**, Judith Elena 1953- *WhoAmL 92*
**Goldenberg**, Martin Irwin 1933- *AmMWSc 92*
**Goldenberg**, Marvin M 1935- *AmMWSc 92*
**Goldenberg**, Naomi *WhoRel 92*
**Goldenberg**, Neal 1935- *AmMWSc 92*
**Goldenberg**, Ronald Edwin 1931- *WhoMW 92*
**Goldenberg**, Stephen Fred 1946- *WhoAmL 92*
**Goldenberg**, Susan 1944- *ConAu 134*
**Goldenhersh**, Robert Stanley 1922- *WhoAmL 92, WhoMW 92*
**Goldensohn**, Barry *DrAPF 91*
**Goldensohn**, Eli Samuel 1915- *AmMWSc 92*
**Goldensohn**, Lorrie *DrAPF 91*
**Goldenson**, Jerome 1912- *AmMWSc 92*
**Goldenson**, Leonard H. *LesBEnT 92 [port]*
**Goldenson**, Leonard H. 1905- *IntMPA 92*
**Goldenson**, Leonard Harry 1905- *WhoEnt 92*
**Goldenson**, Robert M. 1908- *WrDr 92*
**Goldenthal**, Edwin Ira 1930- *AmMWSc 92*
**Goldenthal**, Jolene Bleich *WhoEnt 92*
**Goldenthal**, Robert Howard 1948- *WhoMW 92*
**Golder**, Morris Ellis 1913- *RelLAm 91, WhoRel 92*
**Golder**, Richard Harry 1922- *AmMWSc 92*
**Golder**, Thomas Keith 1942- *AmMWSc 92*
**Golderman**, Cynthia R. *DrAPF 91*
**Goldey**, James Mearns 1926- *AmMWSc 92*
**Goldfarb**, Bernard Sanford 1917- *WhoAmL 92, WhoFI 92, WhoMW 92*
**Goldfarb**, David 1917- *WhoAmP 91*
**Goldfarb**, David Barnett 1954- *WhoFI 92*
**Goldfarb**, David S 1956- *AmMWSc 92*
**Goldfarb**, Donald 1941- *AmMWSc 92*
**Goldfarb**, Eric Daniel 1964- *WhoMW 92*
**Goldfarb**, Howard Gerald 1941- *IntMPA 92*
**Goldfarb**, I. Jay 1933- *WhoFI 92, WhoWest 92*
**Goldfarb**, Irene Dale 1929- *WhoFI 92*
**Goldfarb**, Johanna 1950- *WhoMW 92*
**Goldfarb**, Joseph 1943- *AmMWSc 92*
**Goldfarb**, Mitchell 1953- *WhoEnt 92*
**Goldfarb**, Muriel Bernice 1920- *WhoFI 92*
**Goldfarb**, Nathan 1913- *AmMWSc 92*
**Goldfarb**, Peter 1941- *WhoEnt 92*
**Goldfarb**, Reuven *DrAPF 91*
**Goldfarb**, Robert Lawrence 1951- *WhoFI 92*
**Goldfarb**, Ronald 1933- *WrDr 92*
**Goldfarb**, Ronald B *AmMWSc 92*
**Goldfarb**, Ronald Lawrence 1933- *WhoAmL 92*
**Goldfarb**, Roy David 1947- *AmMWSc 92*
**Goldfarb**, Russell M. 1934- *WrDr 92*
**Goldfarb**, Sidney *DrAPF 91*
**Goldfarb**, Stanley 1931- *AmMWSc 92*
**Goldfarb**, Theodore D 1935- *AmMWSc 92*
**Goldfeder**, Anna 1897- *AmMWSc 92*
**Goldfein**, Alan *DrAPF 91*
**Goldfeld**, Dorian 1947- *AmMWSc 92*
**Goldfeld**, Stephen Michael 1940- *WhoFI 92*
**Goldfield**, Edwin David 1918- *AmMWSc 92*
**Goldfien**, Alan 1923- *AmMWSc 92*
**Goldfine**, Howard 1932- *AmMWSc 92*
**Goldfine**, Ira D 1943- *AmMWSc 92*
**Goldfine**, Lewis John *AmMWSc 92*
**Goldfinger**, Andrew David 1945- *AmMWSc 92*
**Goldfinger**, Erno 1902- *DcTwDes*
**Goldfischer**, Sidney L 1926- *AmMWSc 92*
**Goldfrank**, Max 1911- *AmMWSc 92*
**Goldfried**, Marvin R 1936- *AmMWSc 92*
**Goldhaber**, Alfred Scharff 1940- *AmMWSc 92*
**Goldhaber**, Gerson 1924- *AmMWSc 92*
**Goldhaber**, Gertrude Scharff 1911- *AmMWSc 92, IntWW 91*
**Goldhaber**, Jacob Kopel 1924- *AmMWSc 92*
**Goldhaber**, Maurice 1911- *AmMWSc 92, IntWW 91*
**Goldhaber**, Paul 1924- *AmMWSc 92*
**Goldham**, Bob d1991 *NewYTBS 91*
**Goldhammer**, Paul 1929- *AmMWSc 92*
**Goldheim**, Samuel Lewis 1910- *AmMWSc 92*
**Goldhirsh**, Julius 1935- *AmMWSc 92*
**Goldhoff**, Kenneth Louis 1961- *WhoFI 92*
**Goldhor**, Susan 1939- *AmMWSc 92*
**Goldich**, Robert Michael 1953- *WhoAmL 92*
**Goldich**, Samuel Stephen 1909- *AmMWSc 92*
**Goldie**, Archibald Richardson 1925- *WhoRel 92*
**Goldie**, Grace Wyndham 1905?-1986 *FacFETw*
**Goldie**, James Hugh 1937- *AmMWSc 92*
**Goldie**, Mark 1926- *AmMWSc 92*
**Goldie**, Peter Lawrence 1946- *Who 92*
**Goldie**, Ray Robert 1920- *WhoAmL 92, WhoWest 92*
**Goldie**, Ron Robert 1951- *WhoAmL 92*
**Goldin**, Abraham Samuel 1917- *AmMWSc 92*
**Goldin**, Augusta 1906- *WrDr 92*
**Goldin**, Bernard *IntMPA 92*
**Goldin**, Daniel 1960- *WhoEnt 92*
**Goldin**, Edwin 1938- *AmMWSc 92*
**Goldin**, Gerald Alan 1943- *AmMWSc 92*
**Goldin**, Judah 1914- *WhoRel 92*
**Goldin**, Kathleen McKinney 1943- *ConAu 133*
**Goldin**, Larry Marc 1955- *WhoAmL 92*
**Goldin**, Marc Stuart 1962- *WhoAmL 92*
**Goldin**, Martin Bruce 1938- *WhoMW 92*
**Goldin**, Milton 1917- *AmMWSc 92*
**Goldin**, Nikolay Vasiliyevich 1910- *IntWW 91*
**Goldin**, Stanley Michael 1948- *AmMWSc 92*
**Goldin**, Stephen *DrAPF 91*
**Goldin**, Stephen 1947- *IntAu&W 91, TwCSFW 91, WrDr 92*
**Golding**, Alfred Siemon 1924- *WhoMW 92*
**Golding**, Brage 1920- *AmMWSc 92*
**Golding**, Brage, Jr 1942- *AmMWSc 92*
**Golding**, Bruce 1947- *IntWW 91*
**Golding**, Cecilie Monica 1902- *Who 92*
**Golding**, Cornelius E 1947- *WhoIns 92*
**Golding**, David 1915- *IntMPA 92*
**Golding**, Douglas Lawrence 1931- *AmMWSc 92*
**Golding**, George Earl 1925- *WhoWest 92*
**Golding**, Hana 1949- *AmMWSc 92*
**Golding**, John 1929- *TwCPaSc, Who 92*
**Golding**, John 1931- *Who 92*
**Golding**, John Anthony 1920- *Who 92*
**Golding**, John Simon Rawson 1921- *Who 92*
**Golding**, John Thomas 1957- *WhoAmL 92*
**Golding**, Leonard S 1935- *AmMWSc 92*
**Golding**, Llinos 1933- *Who 92*
**Golding**, Lois Hamblett 1921- *WhoWest 92*
**Golding**, Martin Philip 1930- *WhoAmL 92*
**Golding**, Monica *Who 92*
**Golding**, Paul Alfred 1943- *WhoEnt 92*
**Golding**, Peter 1947- *IntAu&W 91, WrDr 92*
**Golding**, Raymund Marshall 1935- *Who 92, WrDr 92*
**Golding**, Terence Edward 1932- *Who 92*
**Golding**, William 1911- *CnDBLB 7 [port], ConNov 91, IntAu&W 91, IntWW 91, RfGEnL 91, TwCSFW 91, Who 92, WrDr 92*
**Golding**, William Gerald 1911- *FacFETw, WhoNob 90*
**Goldingay**, John 1942- *Who 92*
**Goldings**, Herbert Jeremy 1929- *AmMWSc 92*
**Goldish**, Dorothy May 1934- *AmMWSc 92*
**Goldish**, Elihu 1928- *AmMWSc 92*
**Goldkette**, Jean 1899-1962 *NewAmDM*
**Goldklang**, Lori M. *WhoEnt 92*
**Goldknopf**, Ira Leonard 1946- *AmMWSc 92*
**Goldleaf**, Steven 1953- *IntAu&W 91*
**Goldmacher**, Victor S 1952- *AmMWSc 92*
**Goldman**, Aaron Sampson 1932- *AmMWSc 92*
**Goldman**, Albert 1927- *WrDr 92*
**Goldman**, Alex J 1917- *SmATA 65, WhoRel 92*
**Goldman**, Allan Larry 1943- *AmMWSc 92*
**Goldman**, Allen Marshall 1937- *AmMWSc 92*
**Goldman**, Allen S 1929- *AmMWSc 92*
**Goldman**, Andrew Charles 1947- *WhoEnt 92*
**Goldman**, Anne Ipsen 1935- *AmMWSc 92*
**Goldman**, Antony John 1940- *Who 92*
**Goldman**, Armond Samuel 1930- *AmMWSc 92*
**Goldman**, Arnold 1936- *IntAu&W 91, WrDr 92*
**Goldman**, Arthur Joseph 1934- *AmMWSc 92*
**Goldman**, Barbara Deren 1949- *WhoEnt 92*
**Goldman**, Benjamin Edward 1940- *WhoAmL 92*
**Goldman**, Bernard 1926- *WhoFI 92*
**Goldman**, Berthold 1913- *IntWW 91*
**Goldman**, Bo 1932- *IntMPA 92*
**Goldman**, Bobbie *DrAPF 91*
**Goldman**, Brad Michael 1954- *WhoFI 92*
**Goldman**, Bruce Dale 1940- *AmMWSc 92*
**Goldman**, Carl Lonny 1953- *WhoEnt 92*
**Goldman**, Charles Norton 1932- *WhoAmL 92, WhoFI 92*
**Goldman**, Charles R. 1930- *WrDr 92*
**Goldman**, Charles Remington 1930- *AmMWSc 92*
**Goldman**, Clint *WhoEnt 92*
**Goldman**, Daniel Ware 1952- *AmMWSc 92*
**Goldman**, David 1952- *AmMWSc 92*
**Goldman**, David Eliot 1910- *AmMWSc 92*
**Goldman**, David Tobias 1933- *AmMWSc 92*
**Goldman**, Dexter Stanley 1925- *AmMWSc 92*
**Goldman**, Donald A. 1947- *WhoAmL 92*
**Goldman**, E.S. *DrAPF 91*
**Goldman**, Edmund 1906- *IntMPA 92*
**Goldman**, Edward Aron 1941- *WhoRel 92*
**Goldman**, Edward M. *DrAPF 91*
**Goldman**, Edwin Franko 1878-1956 *NewAmDM*
**Goldman**, Emanuel 1945- *AmMWSc 92*
**Goldman**, Emma 1869-1940 *AmPeW, BenetAL 91, DcAmImH, FacFETw [port], HanAmWH, LiExTwC, RComAH*
**Goldman**, Ernest Harold 1922- *AmMWSc 92*
**Goldman**, Gary Craig 1951- *WhoAmL 92*
**Goldman**, Gerald 1934- *WhoAmP 91*
**Goldman**, Hal 1919- *WhoEnt 92*
**Goldman**, Harold 1927- *AmMWSc 92*
**Goldman**, Harvey 1932- *AmMWSc 92*
**Goldman**, Heath Marshall 1964- *WhoEnt 92*
**Goldman**, Henry Howard 1936- *WhoFI 92*
**Goldman**, Henry M 1911- *AmMWSc 92*
**Goldman**, Israel David 1936- *AmMWSc 92*
**Goldman**, Jack 1937- *WhoAmP 91*
**Goldman**, Jack Leslie 1935- *AmMWSc 92*
**Goldman**, Jacob E 1921- *AmMWSc 92*
**Goldman**, James 1927- *IntAu&W 91, WhoEnt 92, WrDr 92*
**Goldman**, James Allan 1935- *AmMWSc 92*
**Goldman**, James Eliot 1946- *AmMWSc 92*
**Goldman**, Jamie Lee 1957- *WhoFI 92*
**Goldman**, Jane *IntMPA 92*
**Goldman**, Jay 1930- *AmMWSc 92*

**Goldman**, Jerry Stephen 1951- *WhoAmL 92, WhoEnt 92*
**Goldman**, Joel Harvey 1943- *AmMWSc 92*
**Goldman**, Joel J. 1940- *WhoAmL 92*
**Goldman**, John Abner 1940- *AmMWSc 92*
**Goldman**, Joseph L 1932- *AmMWSc 92*
**Goldman**, Joseph Richard 1943- *WhoMW 92*
**Goldman**, Judy *DrAPF 91*
**Goldman**, Kenneth M 1922- *AmMWSc 92*
**Goldman**, Lawrence 1936- *AmMWSc 92*
**Goldman**, Leonard Manuel 1925- *AmMWSc 92*
**Goldman**, Lloyd *DrAPF 91*
**Goldman**, Louis 1928- *WhoMW 92*
**Goldman**, Malcolm 1929- *AmMWSc 92*
**Goldman**, Manuel 1932- *AmMWSc 92*
**Goldman**, Marc *WhoEnt 92*
**Goldman**, Marshall I. 1930- *WrDr 92*
**Goldman**, Marshall Irwin 1930- *WhoFI 92*
**Goldman**, Martin Mayer 1910- *WhoAmL 92*
**Goldman**, Marvin 1928- *AmMWSc 92*
**Goldman**, Max 1920- *AmMWSc 92*
**Goldman**, Mia Ashforth 1954- *WhoEnt 92*
**Goldman**, Michael *DrAPF 91*
**Goldman**, Michael F. 1939- *IntMPA 92*
**Goldman**, Michael Frederic 1939- *WhoEnt 92*
**Goldman**, Moises Julian 1949- *WhoMW 92*
**Goldman**, Nahum 1894-1982 *FacFETw*
**Goldman**, Nancy Joan Kramer 1953- *WhoEnt 92*
**Goldman**, Nathan Carliner 1950- *WhoAmL 92*
**Goldman**, Neal *WhoFI 92*
**Goldman**, Norman L 1933- *AmMWSc 92*
**Goldman**, Oscar 1925- *AmMWSc 92*
**Goldman**, Patricia Ann 1942- *WhoAmP 91*
**Goldman**, Paul *NewYTBS 91 [port], WhoAmP 91*
**Goldman**, Paul H J 1950- *IntAu&W 91*
**Goldman**, Peter 1929- *AmMWSc 92*
**Goldman**, Rachel Bok 1937- *WhoMW 92*
**Goldman**, Ralph 1919- *AmMWSc 92*
**Goldman**, Ralph Frederick 1928- *AmMWSc 92*
**Goldman**, Richard Franko 1910-1980 *NewAmDM*
**Goldman**, Richard Stewart 1948- *WhoAmL 92*
**Goldman**, Robert Barnett 1927- *AmMWSc 92*
**Goldman**, Robert Craig 1942- *WhoMW 92*
**Goldman**, Robert David 1939- *AmMWSc 92*
**Goldman**, Robert Huron 1918- *WhoAmL 92, WhoFI 92*
**Goldman**, Ronald 1933- *AmMWSc 92*
**Goldman**, Roy Lawrence 1954- *WhoAmL 92*
**Goldman**, S Robert 1937- *AmMWSc 92*
**Goldman**, Samuel 1912- *IntWW 91, Who 92*
**Goldman**, Shepard *IntMPA 92*
**Goldman**, Simon 1913- *WhoEnt 92, WhoFI 92*
**Goldman**, Solomon 1893-1953 *RelLAm 91*
**Goldman**, Stanford 1907- *AmMWSc 92*
**Goldman**, Stephen Allen 1946- *AmMWSc 92*
**Goldman**, Stephen Dana 1960- *WhoAmL 92*
**Goldman**, Stephen L 1942- *AmMWSc 92*
**Goldman**, Stephen Shepard 1941- *AmMWSc 92*
**Goldman**, Steven *AmMWSc 92*
**Goldman**, Steven Jason 1947- *WhoAmL 92, WhoFI 92*
**Goldman**, Stuart A. 1948- *WhoEnt 92*
**Goldman**, Terrence Jack 1947- *AmMWSc 92*
**Goldman**, Theodore Daniel 1946- *AmMWSc 92*
**Goldman**, Thomas William, Jr. 1944- *WhoRel 92*
**Goldman**, Virginia Veronica 1919- *WhoAmP 91*
**Goldman**, Vladimir J *AmMWSc 92*
**Goldman**, William 1931- *ConNov 91, IntMPA 92, IntWW 91, WrDr 92*
**Goldman**, William 1932- *IntAu&W 91*
**Goldman**, Yale E *AmMWSc 92*
**Goldman-Rakic**, Patricia S *AmMWSc 92*
**Goldmann**, Kurt 1921- *AmMWSc 92*
**Goldmark**, Carl Peter 1906-1977 *FacFETw*
**Goldmark**, Josephine 1867-1950 *DcAmImH*
**Goldmark**, Karl 1830-1915 *NewAmDM*
**Goldmark**, Peter C. d1977 *LesBEnT 92*
**Goldmark**, Rubin 1872-1936 *NewAmDM*
**Goldner**, Adreas M 1934- *AmMWSc 92*
**Goldner**, Anna F. 1939- *WhoRel 92*
**Goldner**, Bonnie 1956- *WhoEnt 92*
**Goldner**, Harriet J. 1949- *WhoMW 92*
**Goldner**, Herman 1928- *AmMWSc 92*
**Goldner**, Jesse Alan 1948- *WhoAmL 92*
**Goldner**, Joseph Leonard 1918- *AmMWSc 92*
**Goldner**, Ronald B 1935- *AmMWSc 92*
**Goldoni**, Carlo 1707-1793 *BlkwCEP*
**Goldovsky**, Boris 1908- *NewAmDM, WhoEnt 92*
**Goldowsky**, Barbara *DrAPF 91*
**Goldreich**, Gloria *DrAPF 91*
**Goldreich**, Peter 1939- *AmMWSc 92, IntWW 91*
**Goldrein**, Iain Saville 1952- *IntAu&W 91*
**Goldrein**, Neville Clive *Who 92*
**Goldress**, Jerry E. *WhoFI 92*
**Goldrich**, Stanley Gilbert 1937- *AmMWSc 92*
**Goldring**, John Bernard 1944- *Who 92*
**Goldring**, Lionel Solomon 1922- *AmMWSc 92*
**Goldring**, Mary Sheila *Who 92*
**Goldring**, Norman Max 1937- *WhoFI 92, WhoMW 92*
**Goldring**, Patrick 1921- *WrDr 92*
**Goldring**, Roberta M 1929- *AmMWSc 92*
**Goldring**, Sidney 1923- *AmMWSc 92*
**Golds**, Anthony Arthur 1919- *IntWW 91, Who 92*
**Goldsack**, Alan Raymond 1947- *Who 92*
**Goldsack**, Douglas Eugene 1939- *AmMWSc 92*
**Goldsack**, John Redman 1932- *Who 92*
**Goldsamt**, Bonnie Blume 1946- *WhoAmL 92*
**Goldsand**, Robert d1991 *NewYTBS 91*
**Goldsberry**, Richard Eugene 1956- *WhoFI 92*
**Goldsberry**, Ronald Eugene 1942- *WhoBlA 92*
**Goldsborough**, John Paul 1934- *AmMWSc 92*
**Goldsby**, Arthur Raymond 1904- *AmMWSc 92*
**Goldsby**, Richard Allen 1934- *AmMWSc 92*
**Goldsby**, W. Dean, Sr. *WhoBlA 92*
**Goldscheider**, Calvin 1941- *WhoRel 92*
**Goldschmid**, Harvey Jerome 1940- *WhoAmL 92*
**Goldschmid**, Mary Tait Seibert 1947- *WhoFI 92*
**Goldschmid**, Otto 1910- *AmMWSc 92*
**Goldschmidt**, Bernard Morton 1936- *AmMWSc 92*
**Goldschmidt**, Berthold 1903- *IntWW 91*
**Goldschmidt**, Bertrand 1912- *IntWW 91*
**Goldschmidt**, Eric Nathan 1927- *AmMWSc 92*
**Goldschmidt**, Millicent 1926- *AmMWSc 92*
**Goldschmidt**, Neil Edward 1940- *IntWW 91, WhoAmP 91, WhoWest 92*
**Goldschmidt**, Peter Graham 1945- *AmMWSc 92*
**Goldschmidt**, Raul Max 1941- *AmMWSc 92*
**Goldschmidt**, Victor W 1936- *AmMWSc 92, WhoHisp 92*
**Goldschmidt**, Yaaqov 1927- *WrDr 92*
**Goldschmidt**, Yadin Yehuda 1949- *AmMWSc 92*
**Goldschneider**, Irving 1937- *AmMWSc 92*
**Goldsholl**, Morton 1911- *DcTwDes*
**Goldsmith**, Alexander Kinglake 1938- *Who 92*
**Goldsmith**, Amy Bochner 1960- *WhoAmL 92*
**Goldsmith**, Ann *DrAPF 91*
**Goldsmith**, Arnold Louis 1928- *WhoMW 92*
**Goldsmith**, Arthur 1926- *WrDr 92*
**Goldsmith**, Barbara *DrAPF 91*
**Goldsmith**, Barbara 1931- *WrDr 92*
**Goldsmith**, Barry Richard 1949- *WhoAmL 92*
**Goldsmith**, Bram 1923- *WhoFI 92*
**Goldsmith**, Charles Harry 1939- *AmMWSc 92*
**Goldsmith**, Christopher C. 1947- *WhoMW 92*
**Goldsmith**, Christopher William 1964- *WhoEnt 92*
**Goldsmith**, Dale Preston Joel 1916- *AmMWSc 92*
**Goldsmith**, David Jonathan 1931- *AmMWSc 92*
**Goldsmith**, Donald Alan 1943- *WhoAmL 92*
**Goldsmith**, Donald Leon 1937- *AmMWSc 92*
**Goldsmith**, Donald William 1943- *WhoAmL 92*
**Goldsmith**, Edward 1923- *AmMWSc 92*
**Goldsmith**, Edward Rene David 1928- *IntAu&W 91, Who 92*
**Goldsmith**, Eli David 1907- *AmMWSc 92*
**Goldsmith**, Ethel Frank 1919- *WhoMW 92*
**Goldsmith**, Frederica *DrAPF 91*
**Goldsmith**, George Jason 1923- *AmMWSc 92*
**Goldsmith**, Harry L 1928- *AmMWSc 92*
**Goldsmith**, Harry Sawyer 1929- *AmMWSc 92*
**Goldsmith**, Harvey 1946- *IntWW 91*
**Goldsmith**, Henry Arnold 1910- *AmMWSc 92*
**Goldsmith**, Howard *DrAPF 91*
**Goldsmith**, Jack Richard 1958- *WhoWest 92*
**Goldsmith**, James 1933- *Who 92*
**Goldsmith**, James Michael 1933- *IntWW 91*
**Goldsmith**, Jeanette Erlbaum *DrAPF 91*
**Goldsmith**, Jerry 1929- *IntMPA 92, WhoEnt 92*
**Goldsmith**, Jewett 1919- *AmMWSc 92*
**Goldsmith**, Joel Sol 1892-1964 *RelLAm 91*
**Goldsmith**, John Rothchild 1922- *AmMWSc 92*
**Goldsmith**, John Stuart 1924- *Who 92*
**Goldsmith**, Julian Royce 1918- *AmMWSc 92*
**Goldsmith**, Karen Lee 1946- *WhoAmL 92*
**Goldsmith**, Kathleen Mawhinney 1957- *WhoFI 92*
**Goldsmith**, Larry D. 1952- *WhoEnt 92*
**Goldsmith**, Laura Tobi 1950- *AmMWSc 92*
**Goldsmith**, Lowell Alan 1938- *AmMWSc 92*
**Goldsmith**, Lynn Natalie 1948- *WhoEnt 92*
**Goldsmith**, Marshall J. 1940- *WhoAmL 92*
**Goldsmith**, Martin M. 1913- *IntMPA 92*
**Goldsmith**, Marvin 1931- *WhoAmL 92*
**Goldsmith**, Mary Helen Martin 1933- *AmMWSc 92*
**Goldsmith**, Melissa Kay 1958- *WhoEnt 92*
**Goldsmith**, Merrill E 1946- *AmMWSc 92*
**Goldsmith**, Merwin 1937- *WhoEnt 92*
**Goldsmith**, Michael Allen 1946- *AmMWSc 92*
**Goldsmith**, Michael David 1962- *WhoRel 92*
**Goldsmith**, Oliver 1728?-1774 *BlkwCEP*
**Goldsmith**, Oliver 1730?-1774 *CnDBLB 2 [port], DcLB 109 [port], RfGEnL 91*
**Goldsmith**, Paul Felix 1948- *AmMWSc 92*
**Goldsmith**, Paul Kenneth 1942- *AmMWSc 92*
**Goldsmith**, Peter Henry 1950- *Who 92*
**Goldsmith**, Philip 1930- *Who 92*
**Goldsmith**, Ralph Samuel 1931- *AmMWSc 92*
**Goldsmith**, Raymond Stuart 1950- *WhoEnt 92*
**Goldsmith**, Richard 1918- *AmMWSc 92*
**Goldsmith**, Richard E. 1933- *WhoAmL 92*
**Goldsmith**, Robert Frederick Kinglake 1907- *Who 92*
**Goldsmith**, Robert Holloway 1930- *WhoWest 92*
**Goldsmith**, Ruth 1924- *WhoAmP 91*
**Goldsmith**, Silvianna *WhoEnt 92*
**Goldsmith**, Stanley Alan 1956- *WhoAmL 92*
**Goldsmith**, Stephen 1946- *WhoAmL 92, WhoMW 92*
**Goldsmith**, Timothy Henshaw 1932- *AmMWSc 92*
**Goldsmith**, Walter Kenneth 1938- *Who 92*
**Goldsmith**, Werner 1924- *AmMWSc 92*
**Goldsmith**, William 1931- *TwCPaSc*
**Goldsmith**, Willis Jay 1947- *WhoAmL 92*
**Goldson**, Alfred Lloyd 1946- *WhoBlA 92*
**Goldspiel**, Arnold Nelson 1949- *WhoFI 92*
**Goldspiel**, Solomon 1913- *AmMWSc 92*
**Goldspiel**, Steven Ira 1946- *WhoFI 92*
**Goldstein**, Abraham M B 1914- *AmMWSc 92*
**Goldstein**, Abraham S. 1925- *IntWW 91, WhoAmL 92, WrDr 92*
**Goldstein**, Albert 1928- *AmMWSc 92*
**Goldstein**, Albert 1938- *AmMWSc 92, WhoMW 92*
**Goldstein**, Alfred 1926- *Who 92*
**Goldstein**, Alfred George 1932- *WhoFI 92, WhoMW 92*
**Goldstein**, Allan Avrum 1951- *WhoEnt 92*
**Goldstein**, Allan L 1937- *AmMWSc 92*
**Goldstein**, Allen A 1925- *AmMWSc 92*
**Goldstein**, Ann L *AmMWSc 92*
**Goldstein**, Arthur Murray 1922- *AmMWSc 92*
**Goldstein**, August, Jr 1920- *AmMWSc 92*
**Goldstein**, Avram 1919- *AmMWSc 92, IntWW 91*
**Goldstein**, Barry Bruce 1947- *WhoWest 92*
**Goldstein**, Bernard 1935- *AmMWSc 92*
**Goldstein**, Bernard David 1939- *AmMWSc 92*
**Goldstein**, Bernard Herbert 1907- *WhoAmL 92*
**Goldstein**, Bruce William 1946- *WhoEnt 92*
**Goldstein**, Burton Jack 1930- *AmMWSc 92*
**Goldstein**, Byron Bernard 1939- *AmMWSc 92*
**Goldstein**, Charles Arthur 1936- *WhoAmL 92*
**Goldstein**, Charles Irwin 1940- *AmMWSc 92*
**Goldstein**, Charles M 1929- *AmMWSc 92*
**Goldstein**, Charles Meyer 1921- *WhoWest 92*
**Goldstein**, Daniel Frank 1948- *WhoAmL 92*
**Goldstein**, David 1929- *AmMWSc 92*
**Goldstein**, David Joel 1947- *AmMWSc 92*
**Goldstein**, David Louis 1957- *AmMWSc 92*
**Goldstein**, David Stanley 1948- *AmMWSc 92*
**Goldstein**, Dora Benedict 1922- *AmMWSc 92*
**Goldstein**, E Bruce 1941- *AmMWSc 92*
**Goldstein**, Edward 1923- *AmMWSc 92*
**Goldstein**, Elisheva 1947- *AmMWSc 92*
**Goldstein**, Elizabeth 1955- *WhoIns 92*
**Goldstein**, Elliot 1934- *AmMWSc 92*
**Goldstein**, Elliott Stuart 1942- *AmMWSc 92*
**Goldstein**, Fern 1935- *WhoMW 92*
**Goldstein**, Frank Robert 1943- *WhoAmL 92*
**Goldstein**, Franz 1922- *AmMWSc 92*
**Goldstein**, Fred Bernard 1924- *AmMWSc 92*
**Goldstein**, Frederick J 1942- *AmMWSc 92*
**Goldstein**, Gary S. 1954- *WhoFI 92*
**Goldstein**, Gerald 1922- *AmMWSc 92*
**Goldstein**, Gerald 1930- *AmMWSc 92*
**Goldstein**, Gideon 1937- *AmMWSc 92*
**Goldstein**, Gilbert 1914- *AmMWSc 92*
**Goldstein**, Glenn Alan 1954- *WhoAmL 92*
**Goldstein**, Gloria 1931- *WhoAmL 92*
**Goldstein**, Gordon D 1917- *AmMWSc 92*
**Goldstein**, Harold William 1931- *AmMWSc 92*
**Goldstein**, Harris Sidney 1934- *AmMWSc 92*
**Goldstein**, Harvey 1939- *WrDr 92*
**Goldstein**, Herbert 1922- *AmMWSc 92*
**Goldstein**, Herbert Jay 1923- *AmMWSc 92*
**Goldstein**, Herman Bernard 1917- *AmMWSc 92*
**Goldstein**, Howard Bernard 1943- *WhoFI 92*
**Goldstein**, Howard Sheldon 1952- *WhoAmL 92*
**Goldstein**, Howard Warren 1949- *WhoAmL 92*
**Goldstein**, Inge F 1930- *AmMWSc 92*
**Goldstein**, Irving Solomon 1921- *AmMWSc 92*
**Goldstein**, Jack 1930- *AmMWSc 92*
**Goldstein**, Jack Charles 1942- *WhoAmL 92*
**Goldstein**, Jack Stanley 1925- *AmMWSc 92*
**Goldstein**, Jacob Herman 1915- *AmMWSc 92*
**Goldstein**, Jeffrey Jay 1957- *AmMWSc 92*
**Goldstein**, Jeffrey L. 1950- *WhoEnt 92*
**Goldstein**, Jeffrey Marc 1947- *AmMWSc 92*
**Goldstein**, Jeremy S. 1962- *WhoFI 92*
**Goldstein**, Jerome 1931- *WrDr 92*
**Goldstein**, Jerome Arthur 1941- *AmMWSc 92*
**Goldstein**, Jerome Charles 1935- *AmMWSc 92*
**Goldstein**, Joan 1932- *ConAu 35NR*
**Goldstein**, Joan Delano *Who 92*
**Goldstein**, John Cecil 1944- *AmMWSc 92*
**Goldstein**, Jonathan Amos 1929- *WhoMW 92, WrDr 92*
**Goldstein**, Jorge Alberto 1949- *AmMWSc 92, WhoAmL 92*
**Goldstein**, Joseph 1923- *WhoAmL 92, WrDr 92*
**Goldstein**, Joseph I 1939- *AmMWSc 92*
**Goldstein**, Joseph Leonard 1940- *AmMWSc 92, IntWW 91, Who 92, WhoNob 90*
**Goldstein**, Joyce Allene 1941- *AmMWSc 92*
**Goldstein**, Julius L 1935- *AmMWSc 92*
**Goldstein**, Kenneth B. 1949- *WhoAmL 92*
**Goldstein**, Kenneth F 1944- *WhoIns 92*
**Goldstein**, Kenneth Mark 1946- *WhoMW 92*
**Goldstein**, Kenneth Spike 1969- *WhoEnt 92*
**Goldstein**, Larry Joel 1944- *AmMWSc 92*
**Goldstein**, Laurence *DrAPF 91*
**Goldstein**, Laurence Alan 1943- *WhoMW 92*
**Goldstein**, Lawrence Gerald 1936- *WhoFI 92*
**Goldstein**, Lawrence Howard 1952- *AmMWSc 92*
**Goldstein**, Lawrence S B 1956- *AmMWSc 92*
**Goldstein**, Lee 1954- *WhoEnt 92*
**Goldstein**, Leon 1933- *AmMWSc 92*
**Goldstein**, Leonide 1914- *AmMWSc 92*

**Goldstein,** Lester 1924- *AmMWSc 92*
**Goldstein,** Lewis Charles 1917- *AmMWSc 92*
**Goldstein,** Lionel Alvin 1932- *WhoFI 92*
**Goldstein,** Lisa 1953- *TwCSFW 91*
**Goldstein,** Louis 1904- *AmMWSc 92*
**Goldstein,** Louis Arnold 1907- *AmMWSc 92*
**Goldstein,** Louis L 1913- *WhoAmP 91*
**Goldstein,** Louis Philip 1960- *WhoFI 92*
**Goldstein,** Lynn Adrian 1948- *WhoAmL 92*
**Goldstein,** Manfred 1927- *WhoFI 92*
**Goldstein,** Marcia Landweber 1952- *WhoAmL 92*
**Goldstein,** Marcus Solomon 1906- *AmMWSc 92*
**Goldstein,** Margaret Ann 1939- *AmMWSc 92*
**Goldstein,** Marion *DrAPF 91*
**Goldstein,** Mark David 1947- *WhoFI 92*
**Goldstein,** Mark Kane 1938- *AmMWSc 92*
**Goldstein,** Mark L. 1958- *WhoRel 92*
**Goldstein,** Martin 1919- *AmMWSc 92*
**Goldstein,** Martin Edward 1934- *WhoAmL 92*
**Goldstein,** Marvin E 1938- *AmMWSc 92*
**Goldstein,** Marvin Mark 1944- *WhoAmL 92*
**Goldstein,** Marvin Sherwood 1934- *AmMWSc 92*
**Goldstein,** Max 1920- *AmMWSc 92*
**Goldstein,** Maxine Shapiro 1926- *WhoAmP 91*
**Goldstein,** Melvin E 1936- *AmMWSc 92*
**Goldstein,** Melvin Joseph 1933- *AmMWSc 92*
**Goldstein,** Melvyn L 1943- *AmMWSc 92*
**Goldstein,** Menek 1924- *AmMWSc 92*
**Goldstein,** Michael *WhoFI 92*
**Goldstein,** Michael 1928- *WhoFI 92*
**Goldstein,** Michael 1939- *Who 92*
**Goldstein,** Michael Gerald 1946- *WhoAmL 92*
**Goldstein,** Milton 1926- *IntMPA 92*
**Goldstein,** Milton Norman 1925- *AmMWSc 92*
**Goldstein,** Mindy Sue *AmMWSc 92*
**Goldstein,** Moise Herbert, Jr 1926- *AmMWSc 92*
**Goldstein,** Morton Norman 1936- *WhoAmL 92*
**Goldstein,** Murray 1925- *AmMWSc 92*
**Goldstein,** Myron 1935- *AmMWSc 92*
**Goldstein,** N. Linda 1953- *WhoAmL 92*
**Goldstein,** Nancy Beth 1957- *WhoEnt 92*
**Goldstein,** Neil Warren 1950- *WhoEnt 92*
**Goldstein,** Norma Ornstein 1921- *AmMWSc 92*
**Goldstein,** Norman 1934- *WhoWest 92*
**Goldstein,** Norman N *AmMWSc 92*
**Goldstein,** Norman Philip 1921- *AmMWSc 92*
**Goldstein,** Norman Phillip 1940- *AmMWSc 92*
**Goldstein,** Paul 1943- *WhoAmL 92*
**Goldstein,** Paul Henry 1936- *WhoMW 92*
**Goldstein,** Paul Irwin 1926- *WhoAmL 92*
**Goldstein,** Peter Dobkin 1953- *WhoAmL 92*
**Goldstein,** Philip 1930- *AmMWSc 92*
**Goldstein,** R J 1928- *AmMWSc 92*
**Goldstein,** Raymond 1931- *AmMWSc 92*
**Goldstein,** Richard 1939- *AmMWSc 92*
**Goldstein,** Richard Bruce 1946- *WhoFI 92*
**Goldstein,** Richard David 1957- *WhoAmL 92*
**Goldstein,** Richard M. 1952- *WhoAmL 92*
**Goldstein,** Richard Neal 1943- *AmMWSc 92*
**Goldstein,** Robert 1912- *AmMWSc 92*
**Goldstein,** Robert 1924- *AmMWSc 92*
**Goldstein,** Robert Arnold 1941- *AmMWSc 92*
**Goldstein,** Robert David 1947- *WhoAmL 92*
**Goldstein,** Robert Lawrence 1931- *AmMWSc 92*
**Goldstein,** Robert Lee 1951- *WhoFI 92*
**Goldstein,** Robin 1952- *ConAu 133*
**Goldstein,** Robin Sheryl 1953- *AmMWSc 92*
**Goldstein,** Rosalie 1937- *WhoEnt 92*
**Goldstein,** Rubin 1933- *AmMWSc 92*
**Goldstein,** Samuel Joseph 1925- *AmMWSc 92*
**Goldstein,** Samuel R. 1918- *WhoFI 92*
**Goldstein,** Sandu M 1936- *AmMWSc 92*
**Goldstein,** Selma 1949- *AmMWSc 92*
**Goldstein,** Seth Richard 1939- *AmMWSc 92*
**Goldstein,** Sheldon 1947- *AmMWSc 92*
**Goldstein,** Sheldon Mark 1943- *WhoAmL 92*
**Goldstein,** Sidney 1927- *WhoFI 92, WrDr 92*
**Goldstein,** Sidney 1930- *AmMWSc 92*
**Goldstein,** Sidney 1932- *AmMWSc 92*
**Goldstein,** Simon Alfred 1935- *Who 92*
**Goldstein,** Solomon 1929- *AmMWSc 92*
**Goldstein,** Stanley P 1923- *AmMWSc 92*
**Goldstein,** Stanley P. 1934- *WhoFI 92*
**Goldstein,** Steven David 1951- *WhoFI 92*
**Goldstein,** Steven Edward 1948- *WhoWest 92*
**Goldstein,** Steven Jay 1951- *WhoFI 92*
**Goldstein,** Stuart Frederick 1939- *AmMWSc 92*
**Goldstein,** Stuart Wolf 1931- *WhoAmL 92, WhoWest 92*
**Goldstein,** Sylvia Beatrice 1919- *WhoEnt 92, WhoFI 92*
**Goldstein,** Theodore Philip 1928- *AmMWSc 92*
**Goldstein,** Thomas 1944- *WhoAmL 92*
**Goldstein,** Walter Elliott 1940- *AmMWSc 92*
**Goldstein,** William M. 1942- *WhoEnt 92, WhoWest 92*
**Goldstein-Jackson,** Kevin 1946- *WrDr 92*
**Goldstein-Jackson,** Kevin Grierson 1946- *Who 92*
**Goldstick,** Thomas Karl 1934- *AmMWSc 92*
**Goldstine,** Herman Heine 1913- *AmMWSc 92, IntWW 91*
**Goldston,** Barbara M. Harral 1937- *WhoFI 92, WhoWest 92*
**Goldston,** Harold M 1930- *WhoIns 92*
**Goldston,** Linda Leebov 1942- *WhoAmL 92*
**Goldston,** Michael Eugene 1954- *WhoFI 92*
**Goldston,** Nathaniel R., III 1938- *WhoBlA 92*
**Goldston,** Ralph Peter 1929- *WhoBlA 92*
**Goldston,** Stephen Eugene 1931- *WhoMW 92*
**Goldston,** William D, Jr *WhoAmP 91*
**Goldstone,** Alfred D *AmMWSc 92*
**Goldstone,** David Israel 1908- *Who 92*
**Goldstone,** David Joseph 1929- *Who 92*
**Goldstone,** Hilary F 1947- *WhoAmP 91*
**Goldstone,** James 1931- *ConTFT 9, IntMPA 92, WhoEnt 92*
**Goldstone,** Jeffrey 1933- *AmMWSc 92, IntWW 91, Who 92*
**Goldstone,** Jerry 1940- *WhoWest 92*
**Goldstone,** Mark Lewis 1959- *WhoAmL 92*
**Goldstone,** Peter Walter 1926- *Who 92*
**Goldstone,** Philip David 1950- *AmMWSc 92*
**Goldstone,** Richard 1912- *IntMPA 92*
**Goldstone,** Robert 1952- *WhoIns 92*
**Goldstone,** Steven F. 1946- *WhoAmL 92*
**Goldstrand,** Dennis Joseph 1952- *WhoWest 92*
**Goldstucker,** Eduard 1913- *IntWW 91*
**Goldstucker,** Mark Edwin 1955- *WhoAmL 92*
**Goldsworth,** Andy 1956- *TwCPaSc*
**Goldsworthy,** Graeme 1934- *ConAu 35NR*
**Goldsworthy,** J. L. 1962- *WhoEnt 92*
**Goldsworthy,** Peter 1951- *ConPo 91, WrDr 92*
**Goldsworthy,** Robert Flood, Jr 1943- *WhoAmP 91*
**Goldsworthy,** Stanley 1926- *Who 92*
**Goldszmit,** Henryk *SmATA 65*
**Goldszmit,** Henryk 1878-1942 *ConAu 133*
**Goldthorpe,** Brian Lees 1933- *Who 92*
**Goldthorpe,** John Harry 1935- *IntWW 91, Who 92*
**Goldthwait,** David Atwater 1921- *AmMWSc 92, WhoMW 92*
**Goldthwait,** R G 1919- *AmMWSc 92*
**Goldthwait,** Richard Parker 1911- *AmMWSc 92*
**Goldthwaite,** Duncan 1927- *AmMWSc 92*
**Goldware,** David 1916- *WhoWest 92*
**Goldwasser,** Edwin Leo 1919- *AmMWSc 92, WhoMW 92*
**Goldwasser,** Eugene 1922- *AmMWSc 92*
**Goldwasser,** Samuel M *AmMWSc 92*
**Goldwasser,** Thomas 1939- *ConAu 135*
**Goldwater,** Barry 1909- *FacFETw [port]*
**Goldwater,** Barry, Jr 1938- *WhoAmP 91*
**Goldwater,** Barry M. 1909- *Who 92, WrDr 92*
**Goldwater,** Barry Morris 1909- *AmPolLe, IntWW 91, WhoAmP 91, WhoWest 92*
**Goldwater,** Leonard John 1903- *AmMWSc 92*
**Goldwater,** Marilyn 1927- *WhoAmP 91*
**Goldwater,** William Henry 1921- *AmMWSc 92*
**Goldwein,** Manfred Isaac 1924- *AmMWSc 92*
**Goldwhite,** Harold 1931- *AmMWSc 92*
**Goldwin,** Robert 1922- *WrDr 92*
**Goldwin,** Robert A 1922- *WhoAmP 91*
**Goldwitz,** Susan *DrAPF 91*
**Goldworm,** Robert d1991 *NewYTBS 91*
**Goldwyn,** Ralph Norman 1925- *WhoFI 92*
**Goldwyn,** Roger M 1936- *AmMWSc 92*
**Goldwyn,** Samuel 1882-1974 *BenetAL 91, FacFETw*
**Goldwyn,** Samuel, Jr. 1926- *IntMPA 92*
**Goldwyn,** Samuel John, Jr. 1926- *WhoEnt 92*
**Goldy,** Daniel Louis 1915- *WhoAmP 91*
**Goldyne,** Marc E 1944- *AmMWSc 92*
**Gole,** James Leslie 1945- *AmMWSc 92*
**Golebiowski,** Stefan 1900- *IntAu&W 91*
**Goleman,** Denzil Lyle 1924- *AmMWSc 92*
**Golemba,** Frank John 1943- *AmMWSc 92*
**Golemon,** Ronald Kinnan 1938- *WhoAmL 92*
**Golenberg,** Sanford Leonard 1945- *WhoMW 92*
**Goler,** Donald Stuart 1937- *WhoAmL 92*
**Goler,** William Harvey 1846-1939 *DcNCBi 2*
**Goles,** Gordon George 1934- *AmMWSc 92*
**Golestaneh,** Ahmad Ali 1920- *AmMWSc 92*
**Golet,** Francis Charles 1945- *AmMWSc 92*
**Goleyzovsky,** Kas'yan Yaroslavovich 1892-1970 *SovUnBD*
**Golgi,** Camillo 1843-1926 *WhoNob 90*
**Golias,** Helen Lihvar 1920- *WhoMW 92*
**Golibart,** Robert Washington, Jr. 1955- *WhoEnt 92*
**Goliber,** Edward William 1920- *AmMWSc 92*
**Golibersuch,** David Clarence 1942- *AmMWSc 92*
**Golicz,** Lawrence John 1944- *WhoFI 92*
**Goliday,** Willie V. 1956- *WhoBlA 92*
**Goliger,** Nancy *IntMPA 92*
**Goligher,** John Cedric 1912- *Who 92*
**Golightly,** Lena Mills *WhoBlA 92, WhoEnt 92*
**Gollghtly,** Robert Arnette 1946- *WhoFI 92*
**Golightly,** Rodney Dean 1962- *WhoMW 92, WhoRel 92*
**Golin,** Stuart 1938- *AmMWSc 92*
**Golinkin,** Herbert Sheldon 1940- *AmMWSc 92*
**Golino,** Carlo L. d1991 *NewYTBS 91*
**Golino,** Valeria 1966- *IntMPA 92*
**Golis,** Paul Robert 1954- *WhoAmL 92*
**Golishev,** Efim 1897-1970 *NewAmDM*
**Golitz,** Loren Eugene 1941- *WhoWest 92*
**Golka,** Friedemann Walter 1942- *WhoRel 92*
**Golkin,** Jeffrey 1957- *WhoAmL 92*
**Goll,** Darrel Eugene 1936- *AmMWSc 92*
**Goll,** Gerald Eugene 1931- *WhoWest 92*
**Goll,** James E 1927- *WhoAmP 91*
**Goll,** Peter 1947- *WhoAmP 91*
**Goll,** Robert John 1926- *AmMWSc 92*
**Goll,** Sherrie Markin 1946- *WhoAmP 91*
**Goll,** Yvan 1891-1950 *LiExTwC*
**Gollahalli,** Subramanyam Ramappa 1942- *AmMWSc 92*
**Gollaher,** Michael Monroe 1953- *WhoAmP 91*
**Gollamudi,** Ramachander 1934- *AmMWSc 92*
**Gollan,** Frank 1909-1988 *FacFETw*
**Gollancz,** Livia Ruth 1920- *Who 92*
**Gollancz,** Victor 1893-1967 *DcLB 112 [port], FacFETw*
**Golledge,** Reginald George 1937- *WhoWest 92*
**Gollehon-Smith,** Deborah Ann 1961- *WhoWest 92*
**Goller,** Edwin John 1940- *AmMWSc 92*
**Golley,** Frank Benjamin 1930- *AmMWSc 92*
**Gollhofer,** Richard Arnold 1955- *WhoAmL 92*
**Gollin,** Alfred M. 1926- *Who 92*
**Gollin,** Susanne Merle *AmMWSc 92*
**Gollmar,** Dorothy May 1927- *AmMWSc 92*
**Gollner,** Theodor 1929- *IntWW 91*
**Gollnick,** Philip D 1934- *AmMWSc 92*
**Gollob,** Fred 1927- *AmMWSc 92*
**Gollob,** Lawrence *AmMWSc 92*
**Gollomb,** Joseph 1881-1950 *BenetAL 91*
**Gollon,** Peter J *AmMWSc 92*
**Gollott,** Thomas Arlin 1935- *WhoAmP 91*
**Gollub,** Jerry Paul 1944- *AmMWSc 92*
**Gollub,** Seymour 1925- *AmMWSc 92*
**Golniewicz,** Francis Xavier, Jr. 1920- *WhoAmL 92*
**Golod,** William Hersh 1933- *AmMWSc 92*
**Golodner,** Adam Marc 1959- *WhoWest 92*
**Golomb,** Frederick M 1924- *AmMWSc 92*
**Golomb,** Harvey Morris 1943- *AmMWSc 92*
**Golomb,** Michael 1909- *AmMWSc 92, WhoMW 92*
**Golomb,** Solomon Wolf 1932- *AmMWSc 92*
**Golombek,** Harry 1911- *Who 92*
**Golomski,** William Arthur *AmMWSc 92*
**Golomstock,** Igor 1929- *ConAu 134*
**Goloskie,** Raymond 1930- *AmMWSc 92*
**Golosov,** Il'ya Aleksandrovich 1883-1945 *SovUnBD*
**Golosov,** Panteleimon Aleksandrovich 1882-1945 *SovUnBD*
**Golovanov,** Nikolay Semenovich 1891-1953 *SovUnBD*
**Golovchenko,** Ivan Kharitonovich *IntWW 91*
**Golovin,** Michael N 1923- *AmMWSc 92*
**Golovnya,** Anatoliy Dmitrievich 1900-1982 *SovUnBD*
**Golowich,** Eugene 1939- *AmMWSc 92*
**Golphin,** Vincent F. A. 1952- *WhoBlA 92*
**Gols,** A. George 1928- *WhoFI 92*
**Golschmann,** Vladimir 1893-1972 *NewAmDM*
**Golson,** Benny 1929- *NewAmDM*
**Golsong,** Heribert 1927- *IntWW 91*
**Golt,** Sidney 1910- *Who 92*
**Golton,** William Charles 1936- *AmMWSc 92*
**Gol'tsman,** Abram Zinov'evich 1894-1933 *SovUnBD*
**Goltz,** H A 1924- *WhoAmP 91*
**Goltz,** Robert W 1923- *AmMWSc 92*
**Goltz,** Robert William 1923- *WhoWest 92*
**Goltzer,** Albert *WhoEnt 92*
**Goltzer,** Harold *WhoEnt 92*
**Goltzman,** David 1944- *AmMWSc 92*
**Golub,** Abraham 1921- *AmMWSc 92*
**Golub,** Barry Eric 1957- *WhoIns 92*
**Golub,** Edward S 1934- *AmMWSc 92*
**Golub,** Efim I 1934- *AmMWSc 92*
**Golub,** Ellis Eckstein 1942- *AmMWSc 92*
**Golub,** Gene H 1932- *AmMWSc 92*
**Golub,** Gene Howard 1932- *WhoWest 92*
**Golub,** Glen M. 1955- *WhoEnt 92*
**Golub,** Harvey 1939- *WhoFI 92, WhoIns 92, WhoMW 92*
**Golub,** Howard Victor 1945- *WhoAmL 92*
**Golub,** Leon 1922- *WorArt 1980 [port]*
**Golub,** Lewis 1931- *WhoFI 92*
**Golub,** Lorne Malcolm 1941- *AmMWSc 92*
**Golub,** Morton Allan 1925- *AmMWSc 92*
**Golub,** Peter Richard 1952- *WhoEnt 92*
**Golub,** Samuel J 1915- *AmMWSc 92*
**Golub,** Sharon Bramson 1937- *AmMWSc 92*
**Golub,** Sidney Harris 1943- *AmMWSc 92*
**Golub,** Thomas A *WhoIns 92*
**Golub,** William Weldon 1914- *WhoAmL 92*
**Goluba,** Raymond William 1939- *AmMWSc 92*
**Golubic,** Stephan 1934- *AmMWSc 92*
**Golubic,** Theodore Roy 1928- *WhoWest 92*
**Golubitsky,** Martin Aaron 1945- *AmMWSc 92*
**Golubjatnikov,** Rjurik 1931- *AmMWSc 92*
**Golubkina,** Anna Semenova 1864-1927 *SovUnBD*
**Golubnichny,** Vladimir Ivanovich 1936- *SovUnBD*
**Golubovic,** Aleksandar 1920- *AmMWSc 92*
**Golubow,** Julius 1929- *AmMWSc 92*
**Golubski,** Joseph Frank 1953- *WhoMW 92*
**Golueke,** Clarence George 1911- *AmMWSc 92*
**Golumbic,** Calvin 1912- *AmMWSc 92*
**Golumbic,** Martin Charles 1948- *AmMWSc 92*
**Golumbic,** Norma 1916- *AmMWSc 92*
**Golusin,** Millard R. 1947- *WhoMW 92*
**Golway,** Peter L *AmMWSc 92*
**Golz,** James F 1947- *WhoIns 92*
**Golz,** Ronald Alfred 1934- *WhoFI 92*
**Goma,** Louis Sylvain 1941- *IntWW 91*
**Gomara,** Francisco Lopez de *HisDSpE*
**Gomard,** Bernhard 1926- *IntWW 91*
**Gomatos,** Peter John 1929- *AmMWSc 92*
**Gomba,** John Edward 1952- *WhoFI 92*
**Gombar,** Charles T 1952- *AmMWSc 92*
**Gomberg,** Edith S. Lisansky 1920- *WhoMW 92*
**Gomberg,** Henry J 1918- *AmMWSc 92*
**Gomberg,** Joan Susan 1957- *AmMWSc 92*
**Gomberg,** Louis Roos 1907- *WhoWest 92*
**Gomberg,** Maury Leslie 1946- *WhoEnt 92*
**Gomberg,** Sydelle *WhoEnt 92*
**Gombert,** Nicolas 1495?-1560? *NewAmDM*
**Gombojav,** Damdingiyn 1919- *IntWW 91*
**Gombos,** Andrew Michael, Jr 1948- *AmMWSc 92*
**Gombos,** Gyula 1886-1936 *BiDExR*
**Gombos von Jakfa,** Gyula 1886-1936 *EncTR 91 [port]*
**Gombosuren,** Tserenpiliin 1943- *IntWW 91*
**Gombrich,** Ernst 1909- *IntWW 91, Who 92, WrDr 92*
**Gombrich,** Richard Francis 1937- *Who 92*
**Gombrowicz,** Witold 1904-1969 *LiExTwC*
**Gomer,** Richard Hans 1956- *AmMWSc 92*
**Gomer,** Robert 1924- *AmMWSc 92, IntWW 91*
**Gomersall,** Stephen John 1948- *Who 92*
**Gomery,** Douglas *IntAu&W 91*
**Gomery,** Douglas 1945- *WhoEnt 92*
**Gomes,** Edward Clayton, Jr. 1933- *WhoMW 92*
**Gomes,** Francisco da Costa 1914- *IntWW 91*

**Gomes**, Lydia B. 1954- *WhoWest 92*
**Gomes**, Norman Vincent 1914- *WhoFI 92*
**Gomes**, Peter John 1942- *WhoBlA 92, WhoRel 92*
**Gomes**, Wayne Reginald 1938- *AmMWSc 92*
**Gomez**, Adelina Marquez 1930- *WhoHisp 92*
**Gomez**, Adelina S. *WhoHisp 92*
**Gomez**, Al Ralph 1957- *WhoEnt 92*
**Gomez**, Alain Michel 1938- *IntWW 91*
**Gomez**, Alfred *WhoHisp 92*
**Gomez**, Alfredo C. 1939- *WhoHisp 92*
**Gomez**, Andy Santiago 1954- *WhoHisp 92*
**Gomez**, Antonio A. 1945- *WhoHisp 92*
**Gomez**, Armelio Juan 1947- *WhoHisp 92*
**Gomez**, Arturo 1951- *AmMWSc 92*
**Gomez**, Aurelia F. 1937- *WhoHisp 92*
**Gomez**, Basil Anthony, Jr. 1936- *WhoHisp 92*
**Gomez**, Ben *WhoHisp 92*
**Gomez**, Carlos R. 1937- *WhoHisp 92*
**Gomez**, Carmen 1957- *WhoHisp 92*
**Gomez**, Charles Lawrence 1934- *WhoHisp 92*
**Gomez**, Cynthia Ann 1958- *WhoHisp 92*
**Gomez**, Daniel J. 1926- *WhoBlA 92*
**Gomez**, David Frederick 1940- *WhoAmL 92, WhoWest 92*
**Gomez**, Dennis Craig 1948- *WhoBlA 92*
**Gomez**, Drexel *WhoRel 92*
**Gomez**, Eduardo 1930- *WhoHisp 92*
**Gomez**, Edward Casimiro 1938- *WhoHisp 92*
**Gomez**, Elias Galvan 1934- *WhoHisp 92*
**Gomez**, Elsa 1938- *WhoHisp 92*
**Gomez**, Ernesto Alvarado 1946- *WhoHisp 92*
**Gomez**, Faustino 1935- *WhoHisp 92*
**Gomez**, Fausto B. 1954- *WhoHisp 92*
**Gomez**, Francis D. 1941- *WhoHisp 92*
**Gomez**, Francis Dean 1941- *WhoFI 92*
**Gomez**, George *WhoHisp 92*
**Gomez**, George 1958- *WhoAmP 91*
**Gomez**, Guillermo G. 1933- *WhoHisp 92*
**Gomez**, Ildefonso Luis 1928- *AmMWSc 92*
**Gomez**, Isabel 1941- *WhoHisp 92*
**Gomez**, Jaime Armando *WhoHisp 92*
**Gomez**, Jesus Albert 1954- *WhoHisp 92*
**Gomez**, Jewelle *DrAPF 91*
**Gomez**, Jill *IntWW 91, Who 92*
**Gomez**, Jodie Dawn Bean 1953- *WhoMW 92*
**Gomez**, John R., Sr. 1923- *WhoHisp 92*
**Gomez**, Jorge Luis 1964- *WhoHisp 92*
**Gomez**, Jose 1959- *BlkOlyM*
**Gomez**, Jose Felix 1949- *WhoHisp 92*
**Gomez**, Jose Miguel 1858-1921 *HisDSpE*
**Gomez**, Jose Pantaleon, III 1956- *WhoHisp 92*
**Gomez**, Juan 1854-1933 *HisDSpE*
**Gomez**, Juan Vicente 1857-1935 *FacFETw*
**Gomez**, Kevin Lawrence Johnson 1950- *WhoBlA 92*
**Gomez**, Lawrence J. 1946- *WhoHisp 92*
**Gomez**, Lawrence T. 1940- *WhoHisp 92*
**Gomez**, Leo 1967- *WhoHisp 92*
**Gomez**, Leonel, Jr. 1965- *WhoHisp 92*
**Gomez**, LeRoy Marcial 1934- *WhoHisp 92*
**Gomez**, Louis Salazar 1939- *WhoWest 92*
**Gomez**, Luis David 1955- *WhoFI 92*
**Gomez**, Luis Oscar 1943- *WhoHisp 92, WhoRel 92*
**Gomez**, Manuel *WhoHisp 92*
**Gomez**, Manuel Octavio 1934-1988 *IntDcF 2-2*
**Gomez**, Margaret Juarez 1944- *WhoHisp 92*
**Gomez**, Margarita 1940- *WhoHisp 92*
**Gomez**, Maria Rosario 1941- *WhoHisp 92*
**Gomez**, Mario J. 1956- *WhoHisp 92*
**Gomez**, Mark 1959- *WhoRel 92*
**Gomez**, Martin J. 1951- *WhoHisp 92*
**Gomez**, Mary Louise 1950- *WhoHisp 92*
**Gomez**, Michael 1942- *WhoHisp 92*
**Gomez**, Michael Joseph 1964- *WhoFI 92*
**Gomez**, Mike 1951- *WhoHisp 92*
**Gomez**, Orlando A. *WhoHisp 92*
**Gomez**, Oscar C. 1946- *WhoHisp 92*
**Gomez**, Paul 1957- *WhoHisp 92*
**Gomez**, Pedro Judas 1962- *WhoHisp 92*
**Gomez**, Pete *WhoHisp 92*
**Gomez**, Raul 1948- *WhoHisp 92*
**Gomez**, Reynaldo A. 1949- *WhoHisp 92*
**Gomez**, Ricardo Eduardo 1938- *WhoHisp 92*
**Gomez**, Ricardo G. 1955- *WhoWest 92*
**Gomez**, Richard A., Sr. 1954- *WhoHisp 92*
**Gomez**, Robert Pastor, II 1948- *WhoHisp 92*
**Gomez**, Rod J. *WhoHisp 92*
**Gomez**, Roland Herman, Jr. 1938- *WhoAmL 92*
**Gomez**, Ronald J 1934- *WhoAmP 91*
**Gomez**, Rudolph *WhoHisp 92*
**Gomez**, Rudolph Vasquez 1944- *WhoHisp 92*
**Gomez**, Ruth 1938- *WhoHisp 92*
**Gomez**, Salvador *WhoHisp 92*
**Gomez**, Sara 1943-1974 *IntDcF 2-2 [port]*
**Gomez**, Sharon Jeanneene 1954- *WhoHisp 92*
**Gomez**, Stephen Jesus 1957- *WhoHisp 92*
**Gomez**, Tom Philip 1954- *WhoHisp 92*
**Gomez**, Tony *WhoHisp 92*
**Gomez**, Victor J. 1941- *WhoHisp 92*
**Gomez**, Walter Vasquez 1916- *WhoRel 92*
**Gomez-Acebo**, Luis d1991 *NewYTBS 91*
**Gomez-Baisden**, Gladys Esther 1943- *WhoHisp 92*
**Gomez Berges**, Victor 1940- *IntWW 91*
**Gomez-Bethke**, Irene Marie 1935- *WhoHisp 92*
**Gomez-Calderon**, Javier 1948- *WhoHisp 92*
**Gomez-Cambronero**, Julian 1959- *AmMWSc 92*
**Gomez de Avellaneda**, Gertrudis 1814-1873 *HisDSpE, SpAmWW*
**Gomez Gil**, Alfredo 1936- *WhoHisp 92*
**Gomez-Martinez**, Jose Luis 1943- *WhoHisp 92*
**Gomez Palacio**, Enrique 1947- *WhoHisp 92*
**Gomez-Quinones**, Juan *DrAPF 91*
**Gomez-Quinones**, Juan 1940- *WhoHisp 92*
**Gomez-Quintero**, Ela R. *WhoHisp 92*
**Gomez-Quiroz**, Juan 1939- *WhoHisp 92*
**Gomez-Rodriguez**, Manuel 1940- *AmMWSc 92, WhoHisp 92*
**Gomez Rosa**, Alexis 1950- *WhoHisp 92*
**Gomez-Tumpkins-Preston**, Cheryl Annette 1954- *WhoHisp 92*
**Gomez-Vega**, Ibis del Carmen 1952- *WhoHisp 92*
**Gomez y Baez**, Maximo 1836-1905 *HisDSpE*
**Gomezplata**, Albert 1930- *AmMWSc 92, WhoHisp 92*
**Gomillion**, Charles Goode 1900- *WhoBlA 92*
**Gomm**, Richard Culling C. *Who 92*
**Gomme**, Robert Anthony 1930- *Who 92*
**Gommel**, William Raymond 1924- *AmMWSc 92*
**Gomoll**, Allen W 1933- *AmMWSc 92*
**Gomory**, Ralph E 1929- *AmMWSc 92*
**Gomory**, Ralph Edward 1929- *IntWW 91, WhoFI 92*
**Gompa**, Raghu Ramaiah 1960- *WhoMW 92*
**Gompers**, Joseph Alan 1924- *WhoAmL 92*
**Gompers**, Samuel 1850-1924 *BenetAL 91, FacFETw [port], RComAH*
**Gompertz**, Jeremy 1937- *Who 92*
**Gompertz**, Michael L 1912- *AmMWSc 92*
**Gomringer**, Eugen 1925- *IntWW 91*
**Gomsi**, Donald Edwin 1954- *WhoWest 92*
**Gomulka**, Wladyslaw 1905-1982 *FacFETw*
**Gona**, Amos G 1933- *AmMWSc 92*
**Gona**, Ophelia Delaine *AmMWSc 92*
**Gona**, Ophelia Delaine 1936- *WhoBlA 92*
**Gonano**, Aulo Ivo 1952- *WhoAmP 91*
**Gonano**, John Roland 1939- *AmMWSc 92*
**Gonas**, John Samuel, Jr. 1939- *WhoAmL 92*
**Goncalves**, Fatima *WhoHisp 92*
**Goncalves**, Nancy Henriques 1952- *WhoEnt 92*
**Goncalves**, Vasco dos Santos 1921- *IntWW 91*
**Goncalves Dias**, Antonio 1823-1864 *BenetAL 91*
**Gonce-Cartwright**, Noreen Callihan 1937- *WhoFI 92*
**Goncerzewicz**, Maria Irena 1917- *IntWW 91*
**Gonchar**, Aleksandr Terent'evich 1918- *SovUnBD*
**Gonchar**, Oles' 1918- *IntWW 91*
**Goncharov**, Andrey Dmitrievich 1903-1979 *SovUnBD*
**Goncharov**, Leongard Vasilevich 1929- *IntWW 91*
**Gonchigdorj**, Radnaasumbeliin 1954- *IntWW 91*
**Goncourt**, Edmond 1822-1896 *FacFETw, ThHEIm*
**Goncourt**, Edmond de 1822-1896 *GuFrLit 1*
**Goncourt**, Jules de 1830-1870 *GuFrLit 1, ThHEIm*
**Goncz**, Arpad 1922- *IntWW 91*
**Gonda**, Jan 1905- *IntWW 91*
**Gonda**, Matthew Allen 1949- *AmMWSc 92*
**Gondek**, Diana Stasia 1948- *WhoAmL 92*
**Gondek**, Therese Marie 1950- *WhoMW 92*
**Gondelman**, Jay Leon 1948- *WhoEnt 92*
**Gonder**, Eric Charles 1950- *AmMWSc 92*
**Gondos**, Bernard 1935- *AmMWSc 92*
**Goneau**, Sherry Anne 1967- *WhoRel 92*
**Gonen**, Shmuel d1991 *NewYTBS 91*
**Gong Benyan** 1927- *IntWW 91*
**Gong Pusheng** 1913- *IntWW 91*
**Gong**, Christopher Gregory *WhoWest 92*
**Gong**, Henry, Jr. 1947- *WhoWest 92*
**Gong**, Mamie Poggio 1951- *WhoWest 92*
**Gong**, William C 1948- *AmMWSc 92*
**Gonga**, Dawilli 1946- *WhoBlA 92*
**Gonges**, Olympe de d1792 *EncAmaz 91*
**Goni**, Michael Frank 1953- *WhoFI 92*
**Goni**, Paul 1929- *WhoHisp 92*
**Gonick**, Catherine *DrAPF 91*
**Gonick**, Ely 1925- *AmMWSc 92*
**Gonick**, Harvey C 1930- *AmMWSc 92*
**Gonlubol**, Ahmet Sakip 1958- *WhoAmL 92*
**Gonnella**, Patricia Anne 1949- *AmMWSc 92*
**Gonnering**, Russell Stephen 1949- *WhoMW 92*
**Gonnerman**, Daniel Lu 1959- *WhoRel 92*
**Gonor**, Jefferson John 1932- *AmMWSc 92*
**Gonor**, Robert F 1949- *WhoIns 92*
**Gonos**, Robert Anthony 1951- *WhoAmL 92*
**Gonsalves**, Dennis 1943- *AmMWSc 92*
**Gonsalves**, June Miles 1939- *WhoBlA 92*
**Gonsalves**, Lenine M 1927- *AmMWSc 92*
**Gonsalves**, Neil Ignatius 1938- *AmMWSc 92*
**Gonsalves**, Paul 1920-1974 *NewAmDM*
**Gonsalves-Middleton**, Edith Ann 1957- *WhoAmL 92*
**Gonsalvez**, David Joseph Antony 1956- *WhoFI 92*
**Gonser**, Bruce Winfred 1899- *AmMWSc 92*
**Gonser**, Stephen George 1945- *WhoEnt 92*
**Gonshor**, Harry 1928- *AmMWSc 92*
**Gonso**, James Rodney 1955- *WhoFI 92*
**Gonson**, S. Donald 1936- *WhoAmL 92*
**Gonthier**, Giovinella *IntWW 91*
**Gontier**, Jean Roger 1927- *AmMWSc 92*
**Gontrum**, Peter Baer 1932- *WhoWest 92*
**Gonya**, Donald Alan 1934- *WhoAmL 92*
**Gonye**, Laszlo K. 1922- *WhoIns 92*
**Gonyea**, William Joseph 1942- *AmMWSc 92*
**Gonzales**, A. Nick 1946- *WhoHisp 92*
**Gonzales**, Alex D. 1927- *WhoHisp 92*
**Gonzales**, Alexis 1931- *WhoEnt 92, WhoHisp 92*
**Gonzales**, Alfred *WhoHisp 92*
**Gonzales**, Ambrose Elliot 1857-1926 *BenetAL 91*
**Gonzales**, Aurora H. 1932- *WhoHisp 92*
**Gonzales**, Betty J. *WhoHisp 92*
**Gonzales**, Bridget Anneliese 1960- *WhoHisp 92*
**Gonzales**, Cesar A. 1952- *WhoHisp 92*
**Gonzales**, Ciriaco *WhoHisp 92*
**Gonzales**, Ciriaco Q 1933- *AmMWSc 92*
**Gonzales**, David Fidel 1943- *WhoHisp 92*
**Gonzales**, Diana Espana 1947- *WhoHisp 92*
**Gonzales**, Dorothy 1943- *WhoHisp 92*
**Gonzales**, Eduardo 1954- *WhoHisp 92*
**Gonzales**, Edward 1947- *WhoHisp 92*
**Gonzales**, Eloisa Aragon 1952- *WhoHisp 92*
**Gonzales**, Elwood John 1927- *AmMWSc 92*
**Gonzales**, Eva 1849-1883 *ThHEIm [port]*
**Gonzales**, Federico 1921- *AmMWSc 92*
**Gonzales**, Francisco 1947- *WhoHisp 92*
**Gonzales**, Isabel *WhoHisp 92*
**Gonzales**, Jake, Jr. 1928- *WhoHisp 92*
**Gonzales**, Joe *WhoHisp 92*
**Gonzales**, Joe 1949- *WhoHisp 92*
**Gonzales**, Joe Anthony 1957- *WhoHisp 92*
**Gonzales**, John *WhoAmP 91*
**Gonzales**, Jose *WhoHisp 92*
**Gonzales**, Juan L., Jr. 1945- *WhoHisp 92*
**Gonzales**, Leo *WhoHisp 92*
**Gonzales**, Lily L. *WhoHisp 92*
**Gonzales**, Liz 1957- *WhoHisp 92*
**Gonzales**, Marcia Joan 1953- *WhoAmL 92, WhoHisp 92*
**Gonzales**, Marjorie Elaine 1927- *WhoEnt 92*
**Gonzales**, Michael David 1951- *WhoHisp 92*
**Gonzales**, Nancy Alderete 1948- *WhoAmP 91*
**Gonzales**, Nita *WhoHisp 92*
**Gonzales**, Pablo 1949- *WhoHisp 92*
**Gonzales**, Pancho 1928- *WhoHisp 92*
**Gonzales**, Patti Ann 1956- *WhoMW 92*
**Gonzales**, Pedro Antonio 1930- *WhoHisp 92*
**Gonzales**, Rafael Alfred 1951- *WhoWest 92*
**Gonzales**, Rafael Chipeco 1933- *WhoAmL 92, WhoWest 92*
**Gonzales**, Rebecca 1946- *WhoHisp 92*
**Gonzales**, Rebecca Ann 1966- *WhoHisp 92*
**Gonzales**, Rene 1961- *WhoHisp 92*
**Gonzales**, Richard Alonzo 1928- *WhoHisp 92*
**Gonzales**, Richard Joseph 1950- *WhoAmL 92, WhoWest 92*
**Gonzales**, Richard L. 1938- *WhoHisp 92*
**Gonzales**, Richard Robert 1945- *WhoWest 92*
**Gonzales**, Richard S. 1954- *WhoHisp 92*
**Gonzales**, Rick 1959- *WhoHisp 92*
**Gonzales**, Robert E 1936- *WhoAmP 91*
**Gonzales**, Roberta Marie *WhoHisp 92*
**Gonzales**, Ron *WhoAmP 91*
**Gonzales**, Ron 1951- *WhoHisp 92*
**Gonzales**, Serge 1936- *AmMWSc 92*
**Gonzales**, Severiano H. 1942- *WhoHisp 92*
**Gonzales**, Stanley James 1929- *WhoHisp 92*
**Gonzales**, Stephanie 1950- *WhoAmP 91, WhoHisp 92, WhoWest 92*
**Gonzales**, Stephen Elliott 1955- *WhoAmP 91*
**Gonzales**, Thomas 1940- *WhoHisp 92*
**Gonzales**, Thomas A. *WhoHisp 92*
**Gonzales**, Tomasa Calixta 1948- *WhoHisp 92*
**Gonzales Alvarez**, Juvencio 1917- *WhoRel 92*
**Gonzales Martin**, Marcelo 1918- *WhoRel 92*
**Gonzales Posada**, Luis 1945- *IntWW 91*
**Gonzales Rogers**, Donna Jean 1959- *WhoHisp 92*
**Gonzales-Thornell**, Consuelo *WhoHisp 92*
**Gonzalez**, A. C. *WhoHisp 92*
**Gonzalez**, Aida Argentina 1940- *WhoHisp 92*
**Gonzalez**, Al *WhoAmP 91*
**Gonzalez**, Alan Francis 1951- *WhoAmL 92*
**Gonzalez**, Alberto 1947- *WhoHisp 92*
**Gonzalez**, Alejandro 1960- *WhoHisp 92*
**Gonzalez**, Alex Ramon 1932- *WhoHisp 92*
**Gonzalez**, Alexander 1945- *WhoHisp 92*
**Gonzalez**, Alexander G. 1952- *WhoHisp 92*
**Gonzalez**, Alfonso 1944- *WhoHisp 92*
**Gonzalez**, Alfonso, Jr. 1938- *WhoHisp 92*
**Gonzalez**, Alfredo *WhoHisp 92*
**Gonzalez**, Andrew Manuel 1927- *WhoHisp 92*
**Gonzalez**, Angel 1925- *DcLB 108 [port]*
**Gonzalez**, Angela 1947- *WhoHisp 92*
**Gonzalez**, Angelo 1943- *WhoHisp 92*
**Gonzalez**, Annabella Quintanilla 1941- *WhoEnt 92, WhoHisp 92*
**Gonzalez**, Antonio Erman 1935- *IntWW 91*
**Gonzalez**, Arleen Caballero 1957- *WhoHisp 92*
**Gonzalez**, Armando L. *WhoHisp 92*
**Gonzalez**, Arnie *WhoHisp 92*
**Gonzalez**, Atanacio Barrera 1941- *WhoMW 92*
**Gonzalez**, Atanacio Barrera, III 1941- *WhoHisp 92*
**Gonzalez**, Avelino Juan 1951- *WhoHisp 92*
**Gonzalez**, Bernardo Antonio 1950- *WhoHisp 92*
**Gonzalez**, Bradley Joseph 1954- *WhoEnt 92*
**Gonzalez**, Bryan B. *WhoHisp 92*
**Gonzalez**, Caleb 1929- *WhoHisp 92*
**Gonzalez**, Cambell 1918- *WhoBlA 92*
**Gonzalez**, Carlos *WhoHisp 92*
**Gonzalez**, Carlos Alberto 1958- *WhoHisp 92*
**Gonzalez**, Carlos F. *WhoHisp 92*
**Gonzalez**, Carlos Juan 1945- *WhoHisp 92*
**Gonzalez**, Carlos Manuel 1946- *WhoHisp 92*
**Gonzalez**, Celedonio 1923- *WhoHisp 92*
**Gonzalez**, Cesar Augusto 1931- *WhoHisp 92, WhoWest 92*
**Gonzalez**, Charles A. 1945- *WhoHisp 92*
**Gonzalez**, Conrado A. 1945- *WhoHisp 92*
**Gonzalez**, Constantino Jose 1956- *WhoHisp 92*
**Gonzalez**, Crispin, Jr. 1936- *WhoHisp 92*
**Gonzalez**, Cristina 1951- *WhoHisp 92*
**Gonzalez**, Dale V. *WhoHisp 92*
**Gonzalez**, Daniel J. 1946- *WhoHisp 92*
**Gonzalez**, Dario R. 1953- *WhoHisp 92*
**Gonzalez**, David John 1951- *WhoHisp 92*
**Gonzalez**, David Lawrence 1957- *WhoHisp 92*
**Gonzalez**, David R. 1944- *WhoHisp 92*
**Gonzalez**, Deena J. 1952- *WhoHisp 92*
**Gonzalez**, Diana 1946- *WhoHisp 92*
**Gonzalez**, Diane Kathryn 1947- *WhoMW 92*
**Gonzalez**, Edgar 1924- *AmMWSc 92, WhoHisp 92*
**Gonzalez**, Edgar R. 1957- *WhoHisp 92*
**Gonzalez**, Eduardo *WhoHisp 92*
**Gonzalez**, Edward, Jr. 1931- *WhoHisp 92*
**Gonzalez**, Efrain, Jr 1948- *WhoAmP 91, WhoHisp 92*
**Gonzalez**, Elena Isabel 1965- *WhoHisp 92*
**Gonzalez**, Elma 1942- *AmMWSc 92, WhoHisp 92*
**Gonzalez**, Elmo *WhoHisp 92*
**Gonzalez**, Emiliano 1955- *IntAu&W 91*
**Gonzalez**, Enrico Raul 1967- *WhoWest 92*
**Gonzalez**, Enrique Luis 1955- *WhoHisp 92*
**Gonzalez**, Ernest Paul 1937- *WhoHisp 92*
**Gonzalez**, Ernesto 1930- *WhoEnt 92*
**Gonzalez**, Eugene Robert *WhoHisp 92*

**Gonzalez**, Eulogio Raphael 1948- *AmMWSc 92*
**Gonzalez**, Felipe Marquez 1942- *FacFETw*
**Gonzalez**, Fernando L. 1954- *WhoHisp 92*
**Gonzalez**, Francisco Javier 1958- *WhoFI 92*
**Gonzalez**, Francisco Manuel 1933- *AmMWSc 92*
**Gonzalez**, Francisco Ramon 1944- *WhoAmP 91*
**Gonzalez**, Frank, Jr. 1948- *WhoHisp 92, WhoMW 92*
**Gonzalez**, Frank J 1953- *AmMWSc 92*
**Gonzalez**, Frank Woodward 1951- *WhoHisp 92*
**Gonzalez**, Fredrick J. 1949- *WhoHisp 92*
**Gonzalez**, Genaro 1930- *WhoHisp 92*
**Gonzalez**, Genaro 1949- *WhoHisp 92*
**Gonzalez**, Genaro, Jr. 1957- *WhoHisp 92*
**Gonzalez**, Georgina S. *WhoHisp 92*
**Gonzalez**, Gerardo M. 1950- *WhoHisp 92*
**Gonzalez**, Gisela A. 1949- *WhoHisp 92*
**Gonzalez**, Gladys 1955- *AmMWSc 92*
**Gonzalez**, Gladys M. 1955- *WhoHisp 92*
**Gonzalez**, Gualberto G. 1953- *WhoHisp 92*
**Gonzalez**, Guillermo 1944- *AmMWSc 92*
**Gonzalez**, Guillermo 1949- *WhoHisp 92*
**Gonzalez**, Hector Gerardo 1962- *WhoHisp 92*
**Gonzalez**, Hector Hugo 1937- *WhoHisp 92*
**Gonzalez**, Hector Xavier, Jr. 1956- *WhoHisp 92*
**Gonzalez**, Henry B. 1916- *AlmAP 92 [port]*
**Gonzalez**, Henry Barbosa 1916- *WhoAmP 91, WhoFI 92, WhoHisp 92*
**Gonzalez**, Henry E., Jr. 1950- *WhoHisp 92*
**Gonzalez**, Henry John 1958- *WhoWest 92*
**Gonzalez**, Hernan 1949- *WhoAmL 92*
**Gonzalez**, Humberto *WhoHisp 92*
**Gonzalez**, Jaime A 1933- *WhoAmP 91, WhoHisp 92*
**Gonzalez**, James V. *WhoHisp 92*
**Gonzalez**, Jim 1948- *WhoHisp 92*
**Gonzalez**, Jim 1950- *WhoHisp 92*
**Gonzalez**, Joaquin 1948- *WhoHisp 92*
**Gonzalez**, Joaquin F. 1938- *WhoAmL 92*
**Gonzalez**, Joe Manuel 1950- *WhoFI 92*
**Gonzalez**, Joe Paul 1957- *WhoHisp 92*
**Gonzalez**, John E. *WhoHisp 92*
**Gonzalez**, John Lloyd 1943- *WhoHisp 92*
**Gonzalez**, Jorge A. 1952- *WhoHisp 92*
**Gonzalez**, Jorge Augusto 1932- *WhoHisp 92*
**Gonzalez**, Jorge E. 1957- *WhoHisp 92*
**Gonzalez**, Jorge Gerardo 1961- *WhoFI 92*
**Gonzalez**, Jorge R. *DrAPF 91*
**Gonzalez**, Jose 1959- *WhoHisp 92*
**Gonzalez**, Jose Alejandro, Jr. 1931- *WhoAmL 92, WhoHisp 92*
**Gonzalez**, Jose Emilio *DrAPF 91*
**Gonzalez**, Jose Gamaliel 1933- *WhoHisp 92*
**Gonzalez**, Jose Luis 1936- *WhoHisp 92*
**Gonzalez**, Jose Luis 1939- *WhoHisp 92*
**Gonzalez**, Jose Luis 1966- *WhoHisp 92*
**Gonzalez**, Jose Manuel, I 1964- *WhoHisp 92*
**Gonzalez**, Jose R. 1930- *WhoHisp 92*
**Gonzalez**, Joseph Frank 1941- *WhoHisp 92*
**Gonzalez**, Juan 1969- *WhoHisp 92*
**Gonzalez**, Juan-Antonio 1950- *WhoHisp 92*
**Gonzalez**, Juan J. 1949- *WhoHisp 92*
**Gonzalez**, Juan Manuel, Sr. 1948- *WhoHisp 92*
**Gonzalez**, Julio 1876-1942 *FacFETw*
**Gonzalez**, Justo L. 1937- *WhoHisp 92, WrDr 92*
**Gonzalez**, Karen 1963- *WhoEnt 92*
**Gonzalez**, Kenneth 1953- *WhoHisp 92*
**Gonzalez**, Kimberly Regina 1964- *WhoWest 92*
**Gonzalez**, Lauren Yvonne 1952- *WhoHisp 92*
**Gonzalez**, Lee *WhoHisp 92*
**Gonzalez**, Lohr H. 1930- *WhoHisp 92*
**Gonzalez**, Louie *WhoHisp 92*
**Gonzalez**, Louis Max 1948- *WhoRel 92*
**Gonzalez**, Lucas E. 1940- *WhoHisp 92*
**Gonzalez**, Lucia C. 1936- *WhoHisp 92*
**Gonzalez**, Luis A. *WhoHisp 92*
**Gonzalez**, Luis Alberto *WhoHisp 92*
**Gonzalez**, Luis Augusto 1950- *WhoHisp 92*
**Gonzalez**, Luis Emilio 1967- *WhoHisp 92*
**Gonzalez**, Luis Guillermo 1932- *WhoEnt 92*
**Gonzalez**, Luis Jorge 1936- *WhoHisp 92, WhoWest 92*
**Gonzalez**, Luis Jose 1942- *WhoHisp 92*
**Gonzalez**, Luis L 1928- *AmMWSc 92, WhoHisp 92*
**Gonzalez**, Macario Amador 1944- *WhoHisp 92*
**Gonzalez**, Manuel 1944- *WhoEnt 92*
**Gonzalez**, Manuel E. *WhoHisp 92*
**Gonzalez**, Manuel F. 1930- *WhoHisp 92*
**Gonzalez**, Manuel George, IV 1954- *WhoHisp 92*
**Gonzalez**, Margaret *WhoHisp 92*
**Gonzalez**, Margarita 1954- *WhoHisp 92*
**Gonzalez**, Mario J 1941- *AmMWSc 92*
**Gonzalez**, Mario J., Jr. 1941- *WhoHisp 92*
**Gonzalez**, Mario M. *WhoHisp 92*
**Gonzalez**, Martha Alicia 1952- *WhoHisp 92*
**Gonzalez**, Martin 1929- *WhoHisp 92*
**Gonzalez**, Martin 1944- *WhoHisp 92*
**Gonzalez**, Martin Michael 1955- *WhoHisp 92*
**Gonzalez**, Mary Lou 1955- *WhoHisp 92*
**Gonzalez**, Mary Lou C. 1954- *WhoHisp 92*
**Gonzalez**, Mauricio Martinez 1945- *WhoHisp 92*
**Gonzalez**, Michael J. 1962- *WhoHisp 92*
**Gonzalez**, Miguel *WhoHisp 92*
**Gonzalez**, Miriam Santiago 1953- *WhoHisp 92*
**Gonzalez**, Mirta A. 1941- *WhoHisp 92*
**Gonzalez**, Mirza L. 1938- *WhoHisp 92*
**Gonzalez**, Mirza Laura 1938- *WhoMW 92*
**Gonzalez**, N.V.M. *DrAPF 91*
**Gonzalez**, Nicasio, III 1946- *WhoHisp 92*
**Gonzalez**, Nivia 1946- *WhoHisp 92*
**Gonzalez**, Norberto Carlos 1937- *AmMWSc 92*
**Gonzalez**, Norma Leticia 1962- *WhoHisp 92*
**Gonzalez**, Ondina Ester 1958- *WhoHisp 92*
**Gonzalez**, Orsini 1949- *WhoHisp 92*
**Gonzalez**, Patricia 1958- *WhoHisp 92, WorArt 1980 [port]*
**Gonzalez**, Paul *WhoHisp 92*
**Gonzalez**, Paula 1932- *AmMWSc 92, WhoHisp 92*
**Gonzalez**, Pedro, Jr. 1945- *WhoHisp 92*
**Gonzalez**, Rafael C 1942- *AmMWSc 92, WhoHisp 92*
**Gonzalez**, Rafael Jesus *DrAPF 91*
**Gonzalez**, Rafael Jesus 1935- *WhoHisp 92*
**Gonzalez**, Ralph Edward 1961- *WhoHisp 92*
**Gonzalez**, Ralph P. 1955- *WhoHisp 92*
**Gonzalez**, Ramiro 1954- *WhoHisp 92*
**Gonzalez**, Ramon Rafael, Jr 1940- *AmMWSc 92, WhoHisp 92*
**Gonzalez**, Raul A *WhoAmP 91*
**Gonzalez**, Raul A 1933- *AmMWSc 92*
**Gonzalez**, Raul A. 1940- *WhoAmL 92, WhoHisp 92*
**Gonzalez**, Raymond Emmanuel 1924- *WhoAmP 91, WhoHisp 92*
**Gonzalez**, Raymond L. 1939- *WhoHisp 92*
**Gonzalez**, Refugio A. 1947- *WhoHisp 92*
**Gonzalez**, Refugio Amador 1947- *WhoWest 92*
**Gonzalez**, Rene D. 1957- *WhoHisp 92*
**Gonzalez**, Rene Jose 1937- *WhoEnt 92*
**Gonzalez**, Ricardo A. 1946- *WhoHisp 92*
**Gonzalez**, Richard 1953- *WhoHisp 92*
**Gonzalez**, Richard Alonzo 1928- *FacFETw*
**Gonzalez**, Richard Charles 1929- *WhoHisp 92*
**Gonzalez**, Richard D. 1932- *WhoHisp 92*
**Gonzalez**, Richard Donald 1932- *AmMWSc 92*
**Gonzalez**, Richard Rafael 1942- *AmMWSc 92, WhoHisp 92*
**Gonzalez**, Rick 1961- *WhoHisp 92*
**Gonzalez**, Robert Anthony 1945- *AmMWSc 92*
**Gonzalez**, Robert J. *WhoHisp 92*
**Gonzalez**, Robert Lee 1939- *WhoHisp 92*
**Gonzalez**, Roberto 1951- *WhoHisp 92*
**Gonzalez**, Roberto-Juan 1953- *WhoHisp 92*
**Gonzalez**, Roberto Octavio 1950- *WhoHisp 92*
**Gonzalez**, Rodolfo 1926- *WhoHisp 92*
**Gonzalez**, Rolando Noel 1947- *WhoHisp 92, WhoRel 92*
**Gonzalez**, Romualdo 1947- *WhoHisp 92*
**Gonzalez**, Ronald Louis 1946- *WhoHisp 92*
**Gonzalez**, Rose T. 1934- *WhoHisp 92*
**Gonzalez**, Roseann Duenas 1948- *WhoHisp 92*
**Gonzalez**, Ruben *WhoEnt 92*
**Gonzalez**, Ruben 1947- *WhoHisp 92*
**Gonzalez**, Rudy Gustavo 1955- *WhoHisp 92*
**Gonzalez**, Sabina Nieto 1950- *WhoHisp 92*
**Gonzalez**, Salvador 1954- *WhoHisp 92*
**Gonzalez**, Sandra Lynn 1955- *WhoHisp 92*
**Gonzalez**, Sigifredo, Jr 1956- *WhoAmP 91*
**Gonzalez**, Silvia Laura 1959- *WhoAmL 92*
**Gonzalez**, Socorro Quinones 1954- *WhoHisp 92*
**Gonzalez**, Steve John 1958- *WhoHisp 92*
**Gonzalez**, Teofilo F. 1948- *WhoHisp 92*
**Gonzalez**, Thomasa 1954- *WhoHisp 92*
**Gonzalez**, Velda *WhoHisp 92*
**Gonzalez**, Victoria Elena 1931- *WhoHisp 92*
**Gonzalez**, Vidal, Jr. 1950- *WhoFI 92, WhoHisp 92*
**Gonzalez**, Vincent F., III 1947- *WhoHisp 92*
**Gonzalez**, Wilfredo J. 1943- *WhoHisp 92*
**Gonzalez**, Xavier 1898- *WhoHisp 92*
**Gonzalez**, Yolanda Martinez 1958- *WhoHisp 92*
**Gonzalez-Alexopoulos** 1945- *WhoRel 92*
**Gonzalez-Angulo**, Amador 1933- *AmMWSc 92*
**Gonzalez-Argueso**, Luis R. 1942- *WhoHisp 92*
**Gonzalez-Avellanet**, Ileana 1959- *WhoHisp 92*
**Gonzalez Balcarce**, Antonio 1774-1819 *HisDSpE*
**Gonzalez Balcarce**, Diego 1784-1816 *HisDSpE*
**Gonzalez Balcarce**, Juan Ramon 1773-1836 *HisDSpE*
**Gonzalez Balcarce**, Marcos 1777-1832 *HisDSpE*
**Gonzalez-Calvo**, Judith Teresa 1953- *WhoHisp 92*
**Gonzalez Casanova**, Pablo 1922- *IntWW 91*
**Gonzalez-Chavez**, Ernesto 1941- *WhoHisp 92*
**Gonzalez-Crussi**, Francisco 1936- *WhoHisp 92*
**Gonzalez-Crussi**, Frank 1936- *IntAu&W 91*
**Gonzalez Cruz**, Hector *WhoAmP 91, WhoHisp 92*
**Gonzalez-Cruz**, Luis F. 1943- *WhoHisp 92*
**Gonzalez Davila**, Gil *HisDSpE*
**Gonzalez De Alvarez**, Genoveva 1926- *AmMWSc 92*
**Gonzalez Del Valle**, Jorge *IntWW 91*
**Gonzalez-del-Valle**, Luis Tomas 1946- *WhoWest 92*
**Gonzalez de Modestti**, Velda *WhoAmP 91*
**Gonzalez de Pesante**, Anarda 1950- *WhoHisp 92*
**Gonzalez de Santa Cruz**, Roque 1576-1628 *HisDSpE*
**Gonzalez-Dominguez**, Olympia B. *WhoHisp 92*
**Gonzalez-Durruthy**, Diana Maria 1957- *WhoHisp 92*
**Gonzalez-Echevarria**, Roberto 1943- *LiExTwC, WhoHisp 92*
**Gonzalez-Echeverria**, Roberto 1943- *WrDr 92*
**Gonzalez-Fernandez**, Jose Maria 1922- *AmMWSc 92*
**Gonzalez-Gerth**, Miguel *DrAPF 91*
**Gonzalez-Gonzalez**, Pedro 1925- *IntMPA 92*
**Gonzalez-Harvilan**, Aida 1940- *WhoHisp 92*
**Gonzalez-Levy**, Sandra B. 1950- *WhoHisp 92*
**Gonzalez-Lima**, Francisco 1955- *AmMWSc 92, WhoHisp 92*
**Gonzalez Marquez**, Felipe 1942- *IntWW 91, Who 92*
**Gonzalez Martin**, Marcelo 1918- *IntWW 91*
**Gonzalez-Martinez**, Ernesto 1938- *WhoHisp 92*
**Gonzalez-Martinez**, Merbil 1941- *WhoHisp 92*
**Gonzalez-Novo**, Enrique 1927- *WhoHisp 92*
**Gonzalez Oyola**, Ana Hilda 1948- *WhoHisp 92*
**Gonzalez Pantaleon**, Rafael 1937- *IntWW 91*
**Gonzalez-Pita**, J. Alberto 1954- *WhoAmL 92*
**Gonzalez-Quevedo**, Arnhilda 1947- *WhoAmP 91, WhoHisp 92*
**Gonzalez-Ramos**, Gladys M. 1954- *WhoHisp 92*
**Gonzalez-Sanfeliu**, Angel Juan 1961- *WhoFI 92*
**Gonzalez-Santin**, Edwin *WhoHisp 92*
**Gonzalez-T.**, Cesar A. *DrAPF 91*
**Gonzalez-Vales**, Luis Ernesto 1930- *WhoHisp 92*
**Gonzalez-Velasco**, Enrique Alberto 1940- *WhoHisp 92*
**Gonzalez Vicen**, Luis 1910- *BiDExR*
**Gonzalez Von Marees**, Jorge 1900-1962 *BiDExR*
**Gonzalez Zumarraga**, Antonio Jose 1925- *WhoRel 92*
**Gonzaque**, Ozie Bell 1925- *WhoBlA 92*
**Gonze**, Peter Charles 1949- *WhoFI 92*
**Goo**, Donald Wah Yung 1934- *WhoWest 92*
**Goo**, Edward Kwock Wai 1956- *AmMWSc 92*
**Gooch**, Anthony Cushing 1937- *WhoAmL 92*
**Gooch**, Brad *DrAPF 91*
**Gooch**, Brison D. 1925- *WrDr 92*
**Gooch**, Gary Duane 1936- *WhoRel 92*
**Gooch**, Graham Alan 1953- *IntWW 91*
**Gooch**, James Blanton 1947- *WhoRel 92*
**Gooch**, John 1945- *IntAu&W 91, Who 92*
**Gooch**, Lawrence Boyd 1942- *WhoFI 92*
**Gooch**, Peter *Who 92*
**Gooch**, Richard John Sherlock 1930- *Who 92*
**Gooch**, Robert Douglas d1989 *Who 92N*
**Gooch**, Robert Francis 1918- *WhoAmL 92*
**Gooch**, Stanley 1932- *WrDr 92*
**Gooch**, Stanley Alfred 1932- *IntAu&W 91*
**Gooch**, Steve 1945- *IntAu&W 91, WrDr 92*
**Gooch**, Trevor Sherlock 1915- *Who 92*
**Gooch**, Valerie Lynn 1957- *WhoRel 92*
**Gooch**, Van Douglas 1945- *AmMWSc 92*
**Gooch**, William Kevin 1954- *WhoFI 92*
**Goochee**, Herman Francis 1921- *AmMWSc 92*
**Good**, A L 1921- *AmMWSc 92*
**Good**, Adolphus Clemens 1856-1894 *BiInAmS*
**Good**, Anne Haines 1931- *AmMWSc 92*
**Good**, Anthony Bruton Meyrick 1933- *IntWW 91*
**Good**, Betsey Sprei *WhoEnt 92*
**Good**, Carl M, III 1944- *AmMWSc 92*
**Good**, Carter V. 1897- *WrDr 92*
**Good**, Charles E. 1922- *IntMPA 92*
**Good**, David Franklin 1943- *WhoMW 92*
**Good**, Don L 1921- *AmMWSc 92*
**Good**, Donal Bernard Waters 1907- *Who 92*
**Good**, Douglas Jay 1947- *WhoAmL 92*
**Good**, Edwin Marshall 1928- *WhoRel 92*
**Good**, Edwin Mitchell 1927- *WhoAmP 91*
**Good**, Ernest Eugene 1913- *AmMWSc 92*
**Good**, Gladysmae Cissna 1922- *WhoMW 92*
**Good**, Glenn Edward 1954- *WhoMW 92*
**Good**, Harold Marquis 1920- *AmMWSc 92*
**Good**, Irving John 1916- *AmMWSc 92*
**Good**, Janet Lois 1938- *WhoWest 92*
**Good**, Janet R *WhoAmP 91*
**Good**, Janis Caroline 1958- *WhoAmL 92*
**Good**, John Henry 1965- *WhoWest 92*
**Good**, John K. *Who 92*
**Good**, Joseph 1920- *WhoAmL 92*
**Good**, Joseph Cole, Jr. 1945- *WhoAmL 92*
**Good**, Kenneth 1942- *ConAu 134*
**Good**, Kenneth J. 1945- *WhoMW 92*
**Good**, Mary Lowe 1931- *AmMWSc 92, WhoFI 92*
**Good**, Myron Lindsay 1923- *AmMWSc 92*
**Good**, Norma Frauendorf 1939- *AmMWSc 92*
**Good**, Norman Everett 1917- *AmMWSc 92*
**Good**, Ralph E. d1991 *NewYTBS 91*
**Good**, Ralph Edward 1937- *AmMWSc 92*
**Good**, Reginald J. 1948- *WhoFI 92*
**Good**, Richard Albert 1917- *AmMWSc 92*
**Good**, Robert Alan 1922- *AmMWSc 92*
**Good**, Robert Campbell 1926- *AmMWSc 92*
**Good**, Robert Gaylen 1953- *WhoMW 92*
**Good**, Robert Howard 1931- *AmMWSc 92*
**Good**, Robert J *WhoAmP 91*
**Good**, Robert James 1920- *AmMWSc 92*
**Good**, Roland Hamilton, Jr 1923- *AmMWSc 92*
**Good**, Ronald D'Oyley 1896- *Who 92*
**Good**, Roy Sheldon 1924- *WhoFI 92*
**Good**, Ruth *DrAPF 91*
**Good**, Sheldon Fred 1933- *WhoMW 92*
**Good**, Steven Loren 1956- *WhoAmL 92*
**Good**, Susan M 1949- *WhoAmP 91*
**Good**, Thomas Arnold 1925- *WhoWest 92*
**Good**, Timothy Jay 1947- *WhoMW 92*
**Good**, Wilfred Manly 1913- *AmMWSc 92*
**Good**, Willa W. 1915- *WhoBlA 92*
**Good**, William Allen 1949- *WhoMW 92*
**Good**, William Breneman 1920- *AmMWSc 92*
**Good**, William E 1916- *AmMWSc 92*
**Good-Brown**, Sue Ann 1960- *WhoWest 92*
**Goodacre**, Kenneth 1910- *Who 92*
**Goodacre**, Robert Leslie 1947- *AmMWSc 92*
**Goodale**, Cecil Paul 1918- *Who 92*
**Goodale**, Fairfield 1923- *AmMWSc 92*
**Goodale**, James Campbell 1933- *WhoAmL 92, WhoEnt 92*
**Goodall**, Anthony Charles 1916- *Who 92*
**Goodall**, Arthur David 1931- *Who 92*
**Goodall**, David 1931- *IntWW 91*
**Goodall**, David William 1914- *Who 92*
**Goodall**, Frances Louise 1915- *WhoWest 92*
**Goodall**, Hurley 1927- *WhoAmP 91*
**Goodall**, Hurley Charles, Sr. 1927- *WhoBlA 92*
**Goodall**, Jackson Wallace, Jr. 1938- *WhoFI 92, WhoWest 92*
**Goodall**, Jane 1934- *CurBio 91 [port], FacFETw, News 91 [port], WrDr 92*
**Goodall**, John S 1908- *ChlLR 25 [port], SmATA 66 [port]*
**Goodall**, Leon Steele 1925- *WhoIns 92*
**Goodall**, Maurice John 1928- *Who 92*
**Goodall**, Norman 1896-1985 *DcEcMov*
**Goodall**, Peter 1920- *Who 92*

**Goodall,** Reginald 1901-1990 NewAmDM
**Goodall,** Reginald 1905-1990 AnObit 1990
**Goodall,** Valorie 1936- WhoEnt 92
**Goodart,** Elizabeth Mae 1944- WhoRel 92
**Goodarzi,** Fariborz 1940- AmMWSc 92
**Goodbody,** Terry George 1944- WhoWest 92
**Goodby,** Donald Rhodes 1926- WhoIns 92
**Goodby,** James Eugene 1929- WhoAmP 91
**Goodby,** Jeffrey WhoWest 92
**Goodchild,** David Hicks 1926- Who 92
**Goodchild,** David Lionel Napier 1935- Who 92
**Goodchild,** Max 1952- TwCPaSc
**Goodchild,** Peter Robert Edward 1939- Who 92
**Goodchild,** Robert Marshall 1933- WhoFI 92
**Goodchild,** Ronald Cedric Osbourne 1910- Who 92
**Goodchild,** Sidney 1903- Who 92
**Goodden,** Robert Yorke 1909- Who 92
**Goodding,** John Alan 1922- AmMWSc 92
**Goode,** Andrea Horrocks 1957- WhoWest 92
**Goode,** Anthony William 1944- IntWW 91
**Goode,** Calvin C 1927- WhoAmP 91, WhoBlA 92
**Goode,** Cary 1947- Who 92
**Goode,** Chris K. 1963- WhoBlA 92
**Goode,** George Brown 1851-1896 BiInAmS
**Goode,** George Ray 1930- WhoBlA 92
**Goode,** Harry C, Jr 1938- WhoAmP 91
**Goode,** Harry Donald 1912- AmMWSc 92
**Goode,** Helen Harper ScFEYrs
**Goode,** James Edward 1943- WhoBlA 92
**Goode,** John Wolford 1939- AmMWSc 92
**Goode,** Julia Pratt 1929- AmMWSc 92
**Goode,** Lemuel 1921- AmMWSc 92
**Goode,** Malvin R. 1908- WhoBlA 92
**Goode,** Margaret Ann 1924- WhoMW 92
**Goode,** Melvyn Dennis 1940- AmMWSc 92
**Goode,** Mervyn 1948- TwCPaSc
**Goode,** Monroe Jack 1928- AmMWSc 92
**Goode,** P Wayne 1937- WhoAmP 91
**Goode,** Philip Ranson 1943- AmMWSc 92
**Goode,** Richard 1916- WrDr 92
**Goode,** Richard 1943- NewAmDM
**Goode,** Richard Stephen 1943- WhoEnt 92
**Goode,** Richard Urquhart 1858-1903 BiInAmS
**Goode,** Robert J 1932- AmMWSc 92
**Goode,** Robert P 1936- AmMWSc 92
**Goode,** Royston Miles 1933- Who 92
**Goode,** Scott Roy 1948- AmMWSc 92
**Goode,** Steven 1951- WhoAmL 92
**Goode,** Victor M. 1947- WhoBlA 92
**Goode,** Virgil Hamlin, Jr 1946- WhoAmP 91
**Goode,** W Wilson WhoAmP 91
**Goode,** W. Wilson 1938- WhoBlA 92
**Goode,** Wayne 1937- WhoMW 92
**Goode,** Wendell Lynn 1952- WhoFI 92
**Goode,** William Henry 1814-1897 BiInAmS
**Goodearl,** Kenneth Ralph 1945- AmMWSc 92
**Goodell,** Charles Leroy 1854-1937 RelLAm 91
**Goodell,** Fred Lonyo 1915- WhoMW 92
**Goodell,** Horace Grant 1925- AmMWSc 92
**Goodell,** John Dewitte 1909- WhoMW 92
**Goodell,** Larry DrAPF 91
**Goodell,** Rae Simpson 1944- AmMWSc 92
**Gooden,** Arthur Henry TwCWW 91
**Gooden,** Arthur Henry 1879- ScFEYrs
**Gooden,** Cherry Ross 1942- WhoBlA 92
**Gooden,** Dwight NewYTBS 91 [port]
**Gooden,** Dwight Eugene 1964- WhoBlA 92
**Gooden,** Pamela Joyce 1954- WhoAmL 92
**Gooden,** Reginald Heber 1910- WhoRel 92
**Gooden,** Samuel Ellsworth 1916- WhoBlA 92
**Gooden,** Stephen 1892-1955 TwCPaSc
**Gooden,** Winston Earl WhoBlA 92
**Goodenough,** Andrew Lewis 1955- WhoFI 92
**Goodenough,** Anthony Michael 1941- Who 92
**Goodenough,** Cecilia Phyllis 1905- Who 92
**Goodenough,** Daniel Adino 1944- AmMWSc 92
**Goodenough,** David George 1942- AmMWSc 92
**Goodenough,** David John 1944- AmMWSc 92
**Goodenough,** Eugene Ross 1946- AmMWSc 92
**Goodenough,** Florence Laura 1886-1959 WomPsyc
**Goodenough,** Frederick Roger 1927- Who 92
**Goodenough,** J.B. DrAPF 91
**Goodenough,** John Bannister 1922- AmMWSc 92, Who 92
**Goodenough,** Judith Elizabeth 1948- AmMWSc 92
**Goodenough,** Keith 1956- WhoAmP 91
**Goodenough,** Richard 1925- Who 92
**Goodenough,** Ursula Wiltshire 1943- AmMWSc 92
**Goodenough,** Ward Hunt 1919- IntWW 91, WrDr 92
**Goodenow,** Karen Kolbe 1938- WhoMW 92
**Goodenow,** Rita M R 1943- WhoAmP 91
**Gooder,** Harry 1928- AmMWSc 92
**Gooders,** John 1937- IntAu&W 91, WrDr 92
**Goodes,** Melvin Russell 1935- IntWW 91, WhoFI 92
**Goodeve,** Allan McCoy 1923- AmMWSc 92
**Goodey,** Ila Marie 1948- WhoWest 92
**Goodey,** Paul Ronald 1946- AmMWSc 92
**Goodfellow,** Brent H 1940- WhoAmP 91
**Goodfellow,** Edward 1828-1899 BiInAmS
**Goodfellow,** Mark Aubrey 1931- Who 92
**Goodfellow,** Reginald 1894-1985 TwCPaSc
**Goodfellow,** Robin Irene 1945- WhoMW 92
**Goodfellow,** Rosalind Erica 1927- Who 92
**Goodfellow,** Susan Stucklen 1943- WhoEnt 92
**Goodfield,** June 1927- IntAu&W 91, WrDr 92
**Goodfriend,** Herbert Jay 1926- WhoAmL 92
**Goodfriend,** Lawrence AmMWSc 92
**Goodfriend,** Lewis S 1923- AmMWSc 92
**Goodfriend,** Paul Louis 1930- AmMWSc 92
**Goodfriend,** Robert Edward 1941- WhoAmL 92
**Goodfriend,** Theodore L 1931- AmMWSc 92
**Goodgal,** Sol Howard 1921- AmMWSc 92
**Goodgame,** Gordon Clifton 1934- WhoRel 92
**Goodgame,** Thomas H 1921- AmMWSc 92
**Goodge,** William Russell 1928- AmMWSc 92
**Goodgold,** Joseph 1920- AmMWSc 92
**Goodhart,** Lady 1939- Who 92
**Goodhart,** Charles Albert Eric 1936- Who 92
**Goodhart,** Nicholas 1919- Who 92
**Goodhart,** Philip 1925- Who 92
**Goodhart,** Robert 1948- Who 92
**Goodhart,** Robert Stanley 1909- AmMWSc 92
**Goodhart,** William 1933- Who 92
**Goodhartz,** Gerald 1938- WhoAmL 92
**Goodheart,** Barbara Jean 1934- WhoFI 92
**Goodheart,** Clarence F 1916- AmMWSc 92
**Goodheart,** Clyde Raymond 1931- AmMWSc 92
**Goodheart,** Eugene 1931- IntAu&W 91, WrDr 92
**Goodheart,** Karen 1958- WhoFI 92
**Goodheart,** Lawrence B. 1944- ConAu 135
**Goodhew,** Harry Who 92
**Goodhew,** Howard Ralph, Jr. 1923- WhoMW 92
**Goodhew,** Richard Henry 1931- Who 92
**Goodhew,** Victor 1919- Who 92
**Goodhue,** Bertram Grosvenor 1869-1924 DcTwDes, FacFETw
**Goodhue,** Charles Thomas 1932- AmMWSc 92
**Goodhue,** Mary B WhoAmP 91
**Goodhue,** Steven James 1954- WhoAmL 92
**Goodill,** William Earl 1961- WhoFI 92
**Goodin,** Joe Ray 1934- AmMWSc 92
**Goodin,** Stephen Anthony 1959- WhoEnt 92
**Gooding,** Anthony James Joseph S. Who 92
**Gooding,** Gretchen Ann Wagner 1935- AmMWSc 92
**Gooding,** Guy V, Jr 1931- AmMWSc 92
**Gooding,** James Leslie 1950- AmMWSc 92
**Gooding,** Judson 1926- WrDr 92
**Gooding,** Keith Horace 1913- Who 92
**Gooding,** Linda R 1945- AmMWSc 92
**Gooding,** Robert C 1918- AmMWSc 92
**Gooding,** Ronald Harry 1936- AmMWSc 92
**Goodings,** Allen 1925- Who 92, WhoRel 92
**Goodings,** David Ambery 1935- AmMWSc 92
**Goodings,** John Martin 1937- AmMWSc 92
**Goodisman,** Jerry 1939- AmMWSc 92
**Goodison,** Alan 1926- Who 92
**Goodison,** Lorna 1947- ConPo 91, WrDr 92
**Goodison,** Nicholas 1934- Who 92
**Goodison,** Nicholas Proctor 1934- IntWW 91
**Goodison,** Robin Reynolds 1912- Who 92
**Goodjohn,** Albert J 1928- AmMWSc 92
**Goodkin,** Jerome 1929- AmMWSc 92
**Goodkin,** Lewis Michael 1935- WhoFI 92
**Goodkind,** Conrad George 1944- WhoAmL 92
**Goodkind,** John M 1934- AmMWSc 92
**Goodkind,** Morton Jay 1928- AmMWSc 92
**Goodkind,** Richard Jerry 1937- AmMWSc 92
**Goodkind,** Thomas Stone 1953- WhoEnt 92
**Goodlad,** Alastair Robertson 1943- Who 92
**Goodlad,** John I. 1920- IntWW 91, WrDr 92
**Goodland,** John S. 1931- WhoAmL 92
**Goodland,** Judith Mary 1938- Who 92
**Goodland,** Robert James A 1945- AmMWSc 92
**Goodlatte,** Robert William 1952- WhoAmL 92, WhoAmP 91
**Goodlett,** Berry Christopher 1931- WhoAmP 91
**Goodlett,** Carlton B 1914- WhoAmP 91, WhoBlA 92
**Goodlin,** Gary Russell 1953- WhoRel 92
**Goodling,** Bill 1927- AlmAP 92 [port]
**Goodling,** Joshua Loren 1966- WhoRel 92
**Goodling,** William Franklin 1927- WhoAmP 91
**Goodloe,** Celestine Wilson 1954- WhoBlA 92
**Goodloe,** Daniel Reaves 1814-1902 DcNCBi 2
**Goodloe,** James William, Jr. 1942- WhoAmL 92
**Goodloe,** Paul Miller, II 1911- AmMWSc 92
**Goodluck,** James Robert 1954- WhoAmL 92
**Goodman** Who 92
**Goodman,** Baron 1913- IntWW 91, Who 92
**Goodman,** A M 1930- AmMWSc 92
**Goodman,** Abraham H 1910- AmMWSc 92
**Goodman,** Adolph Winkler 1915- AmMWSc 92
**Goodman,** Adrienne Joy 1948- WhoAmP 91
**Goodman,** Alan Lawrence 1938- AmMWSc 92
**Goodman,** Alan Leonard 1941- AmMWSc 92
**Goodman,** Albert 1927- AmMWSc 92
**Goodman,** Alfred 1920- WhoEnt 92
**Goodman,** Alfred Nelson 1945- WhoAmL 92
**Goodman,** Alix Meier 1953- WhoWest 92
**Goodman,** Arthur H 1935- WhoAmP 91
**Goodman,** Barbara 1932- Who 92
**Goodman,** Barbara Eason 1949- AmMWSc 92
**Goodman,** Beatrice May 1933- WhoWest 92
**Goodman,** Benny 1909-1986 FacFETw [port], NewAmDM, RComAH
**Goodman,** Bernard 1923- AmMWSc 92, WhoMW 92
**Goodman,** Beverly Alice 1951- WhoWest 92
**Goodman,** Billy Lee 1930- AmMWSc 92
**Goodman,** Carol 1945- WhoAmL 92
**Goodman,** Charles David 1928- AmMWSc 92, WhoMW 92
**Goodman,** Charles Schaffner, Jr. 1949- WhoFI 92
**Goodman,** Charles Thomas 1954- WhoAmP 91
**Goodman,** Charlotte Margolis 1934- ConAu 134
**Goodman,** Corey Scott 1951- AmMWSc 92
**Goodman,** Craig Guy 1950- WhoAmL 92
**Goodman,** Craig Stephen 1957- WhoEnt 92
**Goodman,** David Who 92
**Goodman,** David Barry Poliakoff 1942- AmMWSc 92
**Goodman,** David Joel 1939- AmMWSc 92
**Goodman,** David Wayne 1945- AmMWSc 92
**Goodman,** David Z. IntMPA 92
**Goodman,** DeWitt S. d1991 NewYTBS 91 [port]
**Goodman,** DeWitt Stetten 1930- AmMWSc 92
**Goodman,** Donald 1933- AmMWSc 92
**Goodman,** Donald Charles 1927- AmMWSc 92
**Goodman,** Donald Joseph 1922- WhoMW 92
**Goodman,** Donald Patrick 1930- WhoAmL 92
**Goodman,** Edward William 1948- WhoAmL 92
**Goodman,** Eli I 1929- AmMWSc 92
**Goodman,** Elizabeth Ann 1950- WhoAmL 92
**Goodman,** Ellen 1941- WrDr 92
**Goodman,** Elliot R. 1923- WrDr 92
**Goodman,** Elliott Irvin 1934- WhoAmL 92
**Goodman,** Erik David 1944- WhoMW 92
**Goodman,** Erika WhoEnt 92
**Goodman,** Eugene Marvin 1937- AmMWSc 92
**Goodman,** Evan Besey 1940- WhoMW 92
**Goodman,** Frank I. 1932- WhoAmL 92
**Goodman,** Frank R 1943- AmMWSc 92
**Goodman,** Fred 1928- AmMWSc 92
**Goodman,** Gary Alan 1947- WhoMW 92
**Goodman,** Gene IntMPA 92
**Goodman,** Geoffrey Alan 1951- WhoWest 92
**Goodman,** Geoffrey George 1921- Who 92
**Goodman,** George D. 1940- WhoBlA 92
**Goodman,** Gerald Joseph 1942- AmMWSc 92
**Goodman,** Gordon Louis 1933- AmMWSc 92
**Goodman,** Gwendolyn Ann 1955- WhoWest 92
**Goodman,** Harold Orbeck 1924- AmMWSc 92
**Goodman,** Henry J. 1932- WhoMW 92
**Goodman,** Henry Maurice 1934- AmMWSc 92
**Goodman,** Howard Who 92
**Goodman,** Howard Charles 1920- AmMWSc 92
**Goodman,** Howard Michael 1938- AmMWSc 92
**Goodman,** Hubert Thorman 1933- WhoMW 92
**Goodman,** Irving 1917- AmMWSc 92
**Goodman,** Ivy DrAPF 91
**Goodman,** Jacob Eli 1933- AmMWSc 92
**Goodman,** James Anthony 1936- WhoAmP 91
**Goodman,** James Arthur, Sr. 1933- WhoBlA 92
**Goodman,** James R 1933- AmMWSc 92
**Goodman,** Jay Irwin 1943- AmMWSc 92
**Goodman,** Jerome 1926- AmMWSc 92
**Goodman,** Joan Elizabeth 1950- IntAu&W 91
**Goodman,** Joan Wright 1925- AmMWSc 92
**Goodman,** Joel Mitchell 1948- AmMWSc 92
**Goodman,** Joel Warren 1933- AmMWSc 92
**Goodman,** John NewYTBS 91 [port], WhoEnt 92
**Goodman,** John 1952- ConTFT 9, IntMPA 92
**Goodman,** John David 1932- Who 92
**Goodman,** John Francis Bradshaw 1940- Who 92
**Goodman,** Jonathan 1933- IntAu&W 91, WrDr 92
**Goodman,** Joseph Magnus 1918- WhoEnt 92
**Goodman,** Joseph Wilfred 1936- AmMWSc 92, WhoWest 92
**Goodman,** Jules Eckert 1876-1962 BenetAL 91
**Goodman,** Julian LesBEnT 92
**Goodman,** Julian 1922- IntMPA 92, IntWW 91
**Goodman,** Julius 1935- AmMWSc 92
**Goodman,** Kenneth James 1961- WhoFI 92
**Goodman,** L E 1920- AmMWSc 92
**Goodman,** Lawrence Judd 1935- WhoEnt 92
**Goodman,** Lee Hugh 1953- WhoAmL 92
**Goodman,** Lenn Evan 1944- WhoWest 92
**Goodman,** Leon 1920- AmMWSc 92
**Goodman,** Leon Judias 1930- AmMWSc 92
**Goodman,** Leonard Seymour 1921- AmMWSc 92
**Goodman,** Lionel 1927- AmMWSc 92
**Goodman,** Louis E 1913- AmMWSc 92
**Goodman,** Louis Sanford 1906- AmMWSc 92
**Goodman,** Louis Wolf 1942- WrDr 92
**Goodman,** Madeleine Joyce 1945- WhoWest 92
**Goodman,** Madelene Joyce 1945- AmMWSc 92
**Goodman,** Major M 1938- AmMWSc 92
**Goodman,** Mark 1939- IntAu&W 91
**Goodman,** Mark N. 1952- WhoAmL 92, WhoWest 92
**Goodman,** Mark William 1960- AmMWSc 92
**Goodman,** Mary A. 1934- WhoWest 92
**Goodman,** Mason Ross 1948- WhoMW 92
**Goodman,** Max A. 1924- WhoAmL 92
**Goodman,** Melinda DrAPF 91
**Goodman,** Michael Bradley 1930- Who 92
**Goodman,** Michael Frederick 1951- WhoFI 92
**Goodman,** Michael G. 1946- WhoWest 92
**Goodman,** Michael Gordon 1946- AmMWSc 92
**Goodman,** Michael Jack 1931- Who 92
**Goodman,** Michelle Lynn 1960- WhoMW 92
**Goodman,** Mitchell DrAPF 91
**Goodman,** Morris 1925- AmMWSc 92

**Goodman,** Morse Lamb 1917- *Who 92*
**Goodman,** Mort 1910- *IntMPA 92*
**Goodman,** Murray 1928- *AmMWSc 92*
**Goodman,** Myron F 1939- *AmMWSc 92*
**Goodman,** Nan Louise 1964- *WhoRel 92*
**Goodman,** Nelson 1906- *IntAu&W 91, IntWW 91, WrDr 92*
**Goodman,** Nelson 1932- *AmMWSc 92*
**Goodman,** Nicholas Alfred 1953- *WhoAmL 92*
**Goodman,** Nicolas Daniels 1940- *AmMWSc 92*
**Goodman,** Norman L 1931- *AmMWSc 92*
**Goodman,** Norton Victor 1936- *WhoAmL 92*
**Goodman,** Paul 1911-1972 *BenetAL 91, ConAu 34NR, FacFETw*
**Goodman,** Paul Fredrick 1952- *WhoRel 92*
**Goodman,** Perry 1932- *Who 92*
**Goodman,** Philip 1925- *AmMWSc 92*
**Goodman,** Raymond John 1916- *IntWW 91, WhoFI 92*
**Goodman,** Richard E 1935- *AmMWSc 92*
**Goodman,** Richard E 1938- *AmMWSc 92*
**Goodman,** Richard Edwin 1935- *WhoEnt 92*
**Goodman,** Richard Henry *AmMWSc 92*
**Goodman,** Richard Lanahan 1946- *WhoAmL 92*
**Goodman,** Richard S 1934- *AmMWSc 92*
**Goodman,** Rick Edward 1948- *WhoRel 92*
**Goodman,** Robert Cedric 1956- *WhoAmL 92*
**Goodman,** Robert Howard 1928- *Who 92*
**Goodman,** Robert M 1920- *AmMWSc 92*
**Goodman,** Robert Merwin 1945- *AmMWSc 92*
**Goodman,** Robert Mitchell 1953- *WhoEnt 92*
**Goodman,** Robert Norman 1921- *AmMWSc 92*
**Goodman,** Robert O., Jr. 1956- *WhoBlA 92*
**Goodman,** Roe William 1938- *AmMWSc 92*
**Goodman,** Roger B. 1919- *WrDr 92*
**Goodman,** Ronald Keith 1929- *AmMWSc 92*
**Goodman,** Roy M 1930- *WhoAmP 91*
**Goodman,** Russell Brian 1945- *WhoWest 92*
**Goodman,** Ruth Weber 1939- *WhoEnt 92*
**Goodman,** Sam Richard 1930- *WhoFI 92, WhoWest 92*
**Goodman,** Sarah Anne 1945- *AmMWSc 92*
**Goodman,** Seymour 1933- *AmMWSc 92*
**Goodman,** Sherri Wasserman 1959- *WhoAmL 92*
**Goodman,** Shirley d1991 *NewYTBS 91 [port]*
**Goodman,** Stacey Jennifer 1964- *WhoEnt 92*
**Goodman,** Stephen H. 1944- *WhoFI 92*
**Goodman,** Stephen Kent 1949- *WhoWest 92*
**Goodman,** Steven Richard 1949- *AmMWSc 92*
**Goodman,** Stuart Lauren 1938- *WhoAmL 92*
**Goodman,** Sue Ellen 1946- *AmMWSc 92*
**Goodman,** Terence James 1950- *WhoWest 92*
**Goodman,** Theodore R 1925- *AmMWSc 92*
**Goodman,** Theodore R. 1927- *WhoFI 92*
**Goodman,** Thomas Henry 1961- *WhoRel 92*
**Goodman,** Toby Ray 1948- *WhoAmP 91*
**Goodman,** Victor Herke 1918- *AmMWSc 92*
**Goodman,** Victor Wayne 1943- *AmMWSc 92*
**Goodman,** Victoria *TwCPaSc*
**Goodman,** Walter 1927- *WhoEnt 92*
**Goodman,** William, III 1931- *WhoFI 92*
**Goodman,** William Beehler 1923- *WhoEnt 92*
**Goodman,** William Lee 1946- *WhoWest 92*
**Goodman,** William R, III 1952- *WhoAmP 91*
**Goodman,** William Richard 1930- *WhoFI 92*
**Goodman,** William Seay 1940- *WhoAmL 92*
**Goodman,** William Wolf 1917- *WhoAmP 91*
**Goodman,** Yitzchak Meir 1933- *WhoRel 92*
**Goodman-Malamuth,** Leo, II 1924- *WhoMW 92*
**Goodner,** Charles Joseph 1929- *AmMWSc 92*
**Goodner,** Dwight Benjamin 1913- *AmMWSc 92*
**Goodner,** Homer Wade 1929- *WhoFI 92*
**Goodner,** John Green *WhoAmP 91*
**Goodney,** David Edgar 1949- *AmMWSc 92*
**Goodnight,** Patricia Ann 1947- *WhoAmP 91*
**Goodno,** Barry John 1947- *AmMWSc 92*
**Goodno,** Kevin P 1963- *WhoAmP 91*
**Goodnow,** Jacqueline Jarrett 1924- *WomPsyc*
**Goodnow,** James Dorn 1941- *WhoMW 92*
**Goodover,** Pat M 1916- *WhoAmP 91*
**Goodpaster,** Andrew Jackson 1915- *IntWW 91, Who 92*
**Goodpasture,** Benjamin Cordell 1895-1977 *RelLAm 91*
**Goodpasture,** H. McKennie 1929- *ConAu 134*
**Goodpasture,** Jessie Carrol 1952- *AmMWSc 92*
**Goodrich,** Alan Owens 1958- *WhoAmL 92*
**Goodrich,** Arthur 1878-1941 *BenetAL 91*
**Goodrich,** Cecilie Ann 1941- *AmMWSc 92*
**Goodrich,** Chauncey Enoch 1801-1864? *BiInAmS*
**Goodrich,** Chris 1956- *ConAu 134*
**Goodrich,** Craig Robert 1949- *WhoWest 92*
**Goodrich,** David 1941- *Who 92*
**Goodrich,** Dorthee *WhoAmP 91*
**Goodrich,** Frances 1891-1984 *ReelWom [port]*
**Goodrich,** Frances Louisa 1856-1944 *DcNCBi 2*
**Goodrich,** Frank Bott 1826-1894 *BenetAL 91*
**Goodrich,** Glenn A 1925- *WhoAmP 91*
**Goodrich,** Harold Thomas 1931- *WhoBlA 92*
**Goodrich,** Ira Michael 1957- *WhoAmL 92*
**Goodrich,** James F *WhoAmP 91*
**Goodrich,** Joseph 1795-1852 *BiInAmS*
**Goodrich,** Judson Earl 1922- *AmMWSc 92*
**Goodrich,** Julian R 1943- *WhoAmP 91*
**Goodrich,** Leigh Earl 1948- *WhoMW 92*
**Goodrich,** Marcus 1897- *BenetAL 91*
**Goodrich,** Marcus Aurelius d1991 *NewYTBS 91*
**Goodrich,** Maurice Keith 1935- *WhoFI 92*
**Goodrich,** Max 1905- *AmMWSc 92*
**Goodrich,** Michael Alan 1933- *AmMWSc 92*
**Goodrich,** Philip Harold Ernest *Who 92*
**Goodrich,** Richard Douglas 1936- *AmMWSc 92*
**Goodrich,** Robert Emmett 1940- *IntMPA 92*
**Goodrich,** Robert Kent 1941- *AmMWSc 92*
**Goodrich,** Roy Gordon 1938- *AmMWSc 92*
**Goodrich,** Samuel G 1793-1860 *ScFEYrs*
**Goodrich,** Samuel Griswold 1793-1860 *BenetAL 91*
**Goodrich,** Thelma E. 1933- *WhoBlA 92*
**Goodrich,** Thomas Michael 1945- *WhoAmL 92*
**Goodrich,** Wallace 1871-1952 *NewAmDM*
**Goodrick,** Harry Joseph, Sr. 1928- *WhoAmL 92*
**Goodrick,** Mick *WhoEnt 92*
**Goodrick,** Richard Edward 1941- *AmMWSc 92, WhoWest 92*
**Goodridge,** Alan G 1937- *AmMWSc 92*
**Goodridge,** Noel Herbert Alan 1930- *Who 92*
**Goodridge,** Tracy Rochelle 1965- *WhoAmP 91*
**Goodrum,** Rebecca 1951- *WhoMW 92*
**Goodrum,** Wayne Louis 1934- *WhoAmL 92*
**Goodsell,** David Scott, Jr. 1961- *WhoWest 92*
**Goodsitt,** Robert Donald 1933- *WhoWest 92*
**Goodsman,** James Melville 1947- *Who 92*
**Goodsmith,** Kenneth Scott 1956- *WhoAmL 92*
**Goodson,** Alan Leslie 1933- *AmMWSc 92*
**Goodson,** Annie Jean *WhoBlA 92*
**Goodson,** Carl Edward 1917- *WhoRel 92*
**Goodson,** Ernest Jerome 1953- *WhoBlA 92*
**Goodson,** Frances Elizabeth *WhoBlA 92*
**Goodson,** Guy Neil 1951- *WhoAmL 92*
**Goodson,** Jack David 1930- *WhoRel 92*
**Goodson,** James Abner, Jr. 1921- *WhoBlA 92*
**Goodson,** James Brown, Jr 1915- *AmMWSc 92*
**Goodson,** Leroy Beverly 1933- *WhoBlA 92*
**Goodson,** Louie Aubrey, Jr 1922- *AmMWSc 92*
**Goodson,** Mark 1915- *WhoEnt 92, WhoWest 92*
**Goodson,** Mark 1918- *IntMPA 92*
**Goodson,** Mark 1925- *Who 92*
**Goodson,** Martin L., Jr. 1943- *WhoBlA 92*
**Goodson,** Michael John 1937- *Who 92*
**Goodson,** Patricia Randolph 1954- *WhoEnt 92*
**Goodson,** Raymond Eugene 1935- *AmMWSc 92, WhoFI 92*
**Goodson,** Richard Carle, Jr. 1945- *WhoFI 92*
**Goodson,** Walter Kenneth 1912- *WhoRel 92*
**Goodson,** William Wilson, Jr. 1951- *WhoEnt 92*
**Goodson Campen,** Cathy Anne 1963- *WhoAmL 92*
**Goodson-Todman** *LesBEnT 92*
**Goodson-Wickes,** Charles 1945- *Who 92*
**Goodspeed,** Edgar Johnson 1871-1962 *BenetAL 91, RelLAm 91*
**Goodspeed,** Frederick Maynard 1914- *AmMWSc 92*
**Goodspeed,** Robert Marshall 1938- *AmMWSc 92*
**Goodspeed,** Scott Winans 1954- *WhoFI 92*
**Goodstein,** David Louis 1939- *AmMWSc 92*
**Goodstein,** Madeline P 1920- *AmMWSc 92*
**Goodstein,** Richard Edward 1953- *WhoEnt 92*
**Goodstein,** Robert 1926- *AmMWSc 92*
**Goodstein,** Sanders Abraham 1918- *WhoMW 92*
**Goodstone,** Edward H 1934- *WhoIns 92*
**Goodtimes,** Art *DrAPF 91*
**Goodwill,** Robert 1936- *AmMWSc 92*
**Goodwilling,** Philip Louis 1935- *WhoMW 92*
**Goodwin,** Albert 1906- *Who 92*
**Goodwin,** Alfred Theodore 1923- *WhoAmL 92, WhoAmP 91, WhoWest 92*
**Goodwin,** Arthur 1922- *TwCPaSc*
**Goodwin,** Arthur VanKleek 1940- *AmMWSc 92*
**Goodwin,** B. E. *WhoRel 92*
**Goodwin,** Barry Kent 1960- *WhoMW 92*
**Goodwin,** Bennie Eugene, II 1933- *WhoRel 92*
**Goodwin,** Bill 1942- *IntAu&W 91, WhoAmP 91*
**Goodwin,** Bradford Scott 1954- *WhoFI 92*
**Goodwin,** Bruce K 1931- *AmMWSc 92*
**Goodwin,** Charles Arthur 1947- *AmMWSc 92*
**Goodwin,** Dale Eugene 1955- *WhoWest 92*
**Goodwin,** Della McGraw 1931- *WhoBlA 92*
**Goodwin,** Dennis Michael 1950- *WhoBlA 92*
**Goodwin,** Donald G *WhoIns 92*
**Goodwin,** Donald William 1931- *WhoMW 92*
**Goodwin,** Dorothy C 1914- *WhoAmP 91*
**Goodwin,** E. Marvin 1936- *WhoBlA 92*
**Goodwin,** Earl 1911- *WhoAmP 91*
**Goodwin,** Edwin Spencer *Who 92*
**Goodwin,** Eric Thomson 1913- *Who 92*
**Goodwin,** Evelyn Louise 1949- *WhoBlA 92*
**Goodwin,** Everett Carlton 1944- *WhoRel 92*
**Goodwin,** Felix L. 1919- *WhoBlA 92*
**Goodwin,** Francis E 1927- *AmMWSc 92*
**Goodwin,** Frank Erik 1954- *AmMWSc 92*
**Goodwin,** Frederick King 1936- *AmMWSc 92*
**Goodwin,** Gene M 1941- *AmMWSc 92*
**Goodwin,** Geoffrey 1916- *WrDr 92*
**Goodwin,** Geoffrey Lawrence 1916- *Who 92*
**Goodwin,** George Edward 1924- *WhoAmP 91*
**Goodwin,** Gerald FuQuay *WhoEnt 92*
**Goodwin,** Hal *SmATA 65*
**Goodwin,** Harold L 1914-1990 *SmATA 65*
**Goodwin,** Hugh Wesley 1921- *WhoBlA 92*
**Goodwin,** James Crawford 1926- *AmMWSc 92*
**Goodwin,** James Gordon, Jr 1945- *AmMWSc 92*
**Goodwin,** James Osby 1939- *WhoBlA 92*
**Goodwin,** James Simeon 1945- *AmMWSc 92*
**Goodwin,** Jean McClung 1946- *WhoMW 92*
**Goodwin,** Jesse Francis 1929- *AmMWSc 92, WhoBlA 92*
**Goodwin,** Jill 1939- *WhoEnt 92*
**Goodwin,** Joe William 1928- *WhoAmP 91*
**Goodwin,** John Forrest 1918- *IntWW 91, Who 92*
**Goodwin,** John Robert 1929- *WhoAmL 92, WhoWest 92*
**Goodwin,** John Robert 1952- *WhoFI 92, WhoMW 92*
**Goodwin,** John Thomas, Jr 1914- *AmMWSc 92*
**Goodwin,** Joseph Robert 1942- *WhoAmP 91*
**Goodwin,** Julie D. *WhoAmL 92*
**Goodwin,** Kathleen Watson 1940- *WhoAmP 91*
**Goodwin,** Kelly Oliver Perry 1911- *WhoBlA 92*
**Goodwin,** Kenneth 1920- *AmMWSc 92*
**Goodwin,** Larry 1945- *WhoAmP 91*
**Goodwin,** Leonard George 1915- *IntWW 91, Who 92*
**Goodwin,** Lester Kepner 1928- *AmMWSc 92*
**Goodwin,** Martin David 1964- *WhoBlA 92*
**Goodwin,** Maryellen 1965- *WhoAmP 91*
**Goodwin,** Matthew 1929- *Who 92*
**Goodwin,** Maud Wilder 1856-1935 *BenetAL 91*
**Goodwin,** Melvin Harris, Jr 1917- *AmMWSc 92*
**Goodwin,** Mercedier Cassandra de Freitas *WhoBlA 92*
**Goodwin,** Noel *Who 92*
**Goodwin,** Norma J. 1937- *WhoBlA 92*
**Goodwin,** Norman J 1913- *WhoAmP 91, WhoMW 92*
**Goodwin,** Paul Beale 1938- *WhoMW 92*
**Goodwin,** Paul Newcomb 1926- *AmMWSc 92*
**Goodwin,** Peter Austin 1929- *Who 92*
**Goodwin,** Peter Warren 1936- *AmMWSc 92*
**Goodwin,** Rex Dean 1909- *WhoRel 92*
**Goodwin,** Richard 1934- *IntMPA 92*
**Goodwin,** Richard G. 1935- *WhoFI 92*
**Goodwin,** Richard Hale 1910- *AmMWSc 92*
**Goodwin,** Richard Murphey 1913- *Who 92*
**Goodwin,** Robert Archer, Jr 1914- *AmMWSc 92*
**Goodwin,** Robert Daniel, Jr 1950- *WhoAmP 91*
**Goodwin,** Robert Earl 1926- *AmMWSc 92*
**Goodwin,** Robert Kerr 1948- *WhoBlA 92*
**Goodwin,** Robert T., Sr. 1915- *WhoBlA 92*
**Goodwin,** Ronald 1925- *IntMPA 92*
**Goodwin,** Ronald Alfred 1925- *WhoEnt 92*
**Goodwin,** Ronald Hayse 1933- *AmMWSc 92*
**Goodwin,** Rosanne 1954- *WhoWest 92*
**Goodwin,** Samuel Dennis 1951- *WhoRel 92*
**Goodwin,** Sidney S 1906- *AmMWSc 92*
**Goodwin,** Stephen *DrAPF 91*
**Goodwin,** Suzanne *IntAu&W 91X, WrDr 92*
**Goodwin,** Terry Lee 1949- *WhoMW 92*
**Goodwin,** Thomas Elton 1947- *AmMWSc 92*
**Goodwin,** Thomas LaRoi 1961- *WhoRel 92*
**Goodwin,** Tommy Lee 1936- *AmMWSc 92*
**Goodwin,** Trevor Noel 1927- *Who 92*
**Goodwin,** Trevor W. 1916- *WrDr 92*
**Goodwin,** Trevor Walworth 1916- *IntWW 91, Who 92*
**Goodwin,** Vaughn Allen 1968- *WhoBlA 92*
**Goodwin,** Vickie Lee 1948- *WhoAmP 91*
**Goodwin,** Warren Herbert 1925- *WhoAmP 91*
**Goodwin,** William Jennings 1925- *AmMWSc 92*
**Goodwin,** William Olin 1945- *WhoFI 92*
**Goodwin,** William Pierce, Jr. 1949- *WhoBlA 92*
**Goodwine,** James K, Jr 1930- *AmMWSc 92, WhoWest 92*
**Goodwine,** John William 1940- *WhoMW 92*
**Goodwyn,** Jack Ray 1934- *AmMWSc 92*
**Goodwyn,** Larry Don 1958- *WhoAmL 92*
**Goody,** John R. 1919- *WrDr 92*
**Goody,** John Rankine 1919- *Who 92*
**Goody,** Launcelot John 1908- *Who 92*
**Goody,** Richard 1921- *AmMWSc 92*
**Goody,** Sam 1904-1991 *NewYTBS 91 [port], News 92-1*
**Goodyear,** Charles 1800-1860 *BiInAmS*
**Goodyear,** Edward Stephen, Jr. 1954- *WhoFI 92*
**Goodyear,** Nelson 1811-1857 *BiInAmS*
**Goodyear,** Watson Andrews 1838-1891 *BiInAmS*
**Goodyear,** Wayne David 1951- *WhoFI 92*
**Goodyear,** William Frederick, Jr 1929- *AmMWSc 92*
**Goodyer,** Allan Victor 1918- *AmMWSc 92*
**Goodzeit,** Carl Leonard 1928- *AmMWSc 92*
**Googe,** Barnabe 1540-1594 *RfGEnL 91*
**Googin,** John M 1922- *AmMWSc 92*
**Googins,** Louise Paulson 1941- *WhoFI 92*
**Googins,** Robert R 1937- *WhoIns 92*
**Gookin,** Daniel 1612-1687 *BenetAL 91*
**Gookin,** R. Burt 1914- *IntWW 91*
**Gookin,** Thomas Allen Jaudon 1951- *WhoFI 92, WhoWest 92*
**Gookin,** William Scudder 1914- *WhoWest 92*
**Goold** *Who 92*
**Goold,** Baron 1934- *Who 92*
**Goold,** Florence Wilson 1912- *WhoMW 92*
**Goold,** George 1923- *Who 92*
**Goold,** J William 1953- *WhoAmP 91*
**Goold,** Oliver 1923- *WhoFI 92*
**Goold-Adams,** Richard John Moreton 1916- *Who 92*
**Goolden,** Barbara d1990 *Who 92N*
**Goolden,** Barbara 1900- *IntAu&W 91*
**Gooley,** Charles E. 1953- *WhoBlA 92*
**Goolrick,** Robert Mason 1934- *WhoAmL 92*

**Goolsbee,** Charles Thomas 1935- *WhoAmL 92*
**Goolsby,** Tony 1933- *WhoAmP 91*
**Goon,** David James Wong 1942- *AmMWSc 92*
**Gooneratne,** Malini Yasmine 1935- *IntAu&W 91*
**Gooneratne,** Tilak Eranga 1919- *IntWW 91, Who 92*
**Goonetilleke,** Albert 1936- *IntWW 91*
**Goonewardene,** Hilary Felix 1925- *AmMWSc 92, WhoMW 92*
**Goor,** Charles G 1912- *AmMWSc 92*
**Goor,** Ronald Stephen 1940- *AmMWSc 92*
**Goorey,** Nancy Reynolds *AmMWSc 92*
**Goormaghtigh,** John Victor 1919- *IntWW 91*
**Goorvitch,** David 1941- *AmMWSc 92*
**Goos,** Bernd *IntWW 91*
**Goos,** Roger Delmon 1924- *AmMWSc 92*
**Goosby,** Zuretti L. 1922- *WhoBlA 92*
**Goosman,** David R 1941- *AmMWSc 92*
**Goosman,** Eleanor McKee 1917- *WhoMW 92*
**Goossen,** Duane A 1955- *WhoAmP 91*
**Goossen,** Jacob Frederic 1927- *WhoEnt 92*
**Goossens,** Eugene 1893-1962 *NewAmDM*
**Goossens,** John Charles 1928- *AmMWSc 92*
**Goossens,** Leon 1897-1988 *FacFETw, NewAmDM*
**Goostree,** Robert Edward 1923- *WhoAmL 92*
**Goote,** Thor 1899-1940 *EncTR 91*
**Gootenberg,** Joseph Eric 1949- *AmMWSc 92*
**Gootman,** Norman Lerner 1933- *AmMWSc 92*
**Gootman,** Phyllis Myrna Adler 1938- *AmMWSc 92*
**Gootnick,** Margery Fischbein 1927- *WhoAmL 92*
**Goott,** Alan Franklin 1947- *WhoAmL 92*
**Gopal,** Raj 1942- *AmMWSc 92*
**Gopal,** Sara 1965- *WhoFI 92*
**Gopal,** Sarvepalli 1923- *IntWW 91, Who 92, WrDr 92*
**Gopal-Chowdhury,** Paul 1949- *TwCPaSc*
**Gopalakrishna,** K V 1944- *AmMWSc 92*
**Gopalakrishnan,** Kakkala 1942- *AmMWSc 92*
**Gopalan,** Coluthur 1918- *IntWW 91, Who 92*
**Gopikanth,** M L 1954- *AmMWSc 92*
**Goplen,** Bernard Peter 1930- *AmMWSc 92*
**Goplerud,** Clifford P 1924- *AmMWSc 92*
**Gopman,** Howard Z. 1940- *WhoAmL 92*
**Gopon,** Gene George 1944- *WhoFI 92, WhoIns 92*
**Goppel,** Alfons 1905- *IntWW 91*
**Gora,** Edwin Karl 1911- *AmMWSc 92*
**Gora,** Thaddeus F, Jr 1941- *AmMWSc 92*
**Gora,** William Alan 1946- *WhoEnt 92*
**Goradia,** Chandra P 1939- *AmMWSc 92*
**Gorai,** Dinesh Chandra *Who 92*
**Gorai,** Dinesh Chandra 1934- *IntWW 91*
**Goran,** Michael I 1961- *AmMWSc 92*
**Goran,** Morris 1916- *AmMWSc 92, WrDr 92*
**Goran,** Robert Charles 1917- *AmMWSc 92*
**Gorans,** Gerald Elmer 1922- *WhoFI 92, WhoWest 92*
**Goranson,** Edwin Alexander 1904- *AmMWSc 92*
**Goranson,** H T 1947- *AmMWSc 92*
**Goransson,** Bengt 1932- *IntWW 91*
**Gorard,** Anthony John 1927- *Who 92*
**Goray,** Narayan Ganesh 1907- *IntWW 91, Who 92*
**Gorbach,** Sherwood Leslie 1934- *AmMWSc 92*
**Gorbachev,** Mikhail 1931- *FacFETw [port]*
**Gorbachev,** Mikhail S. *NewYTBS 91 [port]*
**Gorbachev,** Mikhail Sergeevich 1931- *SovUnBD*
**Gorbachev,** Mikhail Sergeyevich 1931- *IntWW 91, Who 92, WhoNob 90*
**Gorbachev,** Raisa Maksimovna 1934- *IntWW 91*
**Gorbacheva,** Raisa Maksimovna 1932- *SovUnBD*
**Gorbanevskaya,** Natal'ya Yevgen'evna 1936- *SovUnBD*
**Gorbatkin,** Steven M 1960- *AmMWSc 92*
**Gorbatsevich,** Serge N 1922- *AmMWSc 92*
**Gorbaty,** Martin Leo 1942- *AmMWSc 92*
**Gorbet,** Daniel Wayne 1942- *AmMWSc 92*
**Gorbett,** David S. 1946- *WhoMW 92*
**Gorbman,** Aubrey 1914- *AmMWSc 92*
**Gorbovsky,** Gleb Yakovlevich 1931- *SovUnBD*
**Gorbsky,** Gary James 1955- *AmMWSc 92*
**Gorbunoff,** Marina J 1927- *AmMWSc 92*
**Gorbunov,** Anatoliy Valer'yanovich 1942- *SovUnBD*
**Gorbunovs,** Anatoliis 1942- *SovUnBD*
**Gorbunovs,** Anatoliys 1942- *IntWW 91*
**Gorcey,** Elizabeth Ann 1965- *WhoEnt 92*
**Gorchakov,** Nikolay Mikhaylovich 1899-1958 *SovUnBD*
**Gorchakov,** Pyotr Andreyevich 1917- *IntWW 91*
**Gorcheff,** Nick A. 1958- *WhoMW 92*
**Gorchov,** David Louis 1958- *AmMWSc 92*
**Gorczynski,** Dale Michael 1950- *WhoAmP 91*
**Gorczynski,** Reginald Meiczyslaw 1947- *AmMWSc 92*
**Gordan,** Andrew Leb 1923- *WhoMW 92*
**Gordan,** Gilbert Saul 1916- *AmMWSc 92*
**Gordan,** Judith Allison 1956- *WhoEnt 92, WhoWest 92*
**Gordan-Feller,** Carla Janine 1936- *WhoRel 92*
**Gordee,** Robert Stouffer 1932- *AmMWSc 92*
**Gorden,** Berner J 1939- *AmMWSc 92*
**Gorden,** Fred A. 1940- *WhoBlA 92*
**Gorden,** Gerald Niccola 1950- *WhoFI 92*
**Gorden,** Gregrey Wayne 1954- *WhoEnt 92*
**Gorden,** Jeffrey Michael 1955- *WhoFI 92*
**Gorden,** Phillip 1934- *AmMWSc 92*
**Gorden,** Robert Wayne 1932- *AmMWSc 92*
**Gorder,** William E *WhoAmP 91*
**Gordes,** Joel N 1946- *WhoAmP 91*
**Gordesky,** Morton 1929- *WhoAmL 92*
**Gordetsky,** Gordon Richard 1944- *WhoFI 92*
**Gordey,** Michel 1913- *IntAu&W 91, IntWW 91*
**Gordeyev,** Vyacheslav Mikhailovich 1948- *IntWW 91*
**Gordh,** George Rudolph, Jr 1944- *AmMWSc 92*
**Gordh,** Gordon 1945- *AmMWSc 92*
**Gordich,** Lawrence Alan 1957- *WhoAmL 92*
**Gordienko,** Aleksey Fyodorovich 1917- *IntWW 91*
**Gordimer,** Nadine 1923- *ConNov 91, DcLB Y91 [port], FacFETw, IntAu&W 91, IntWW 91, NewYTBS 91 [port], RfGEnL 91, Who 92, WrDr 92*
**Gordin,** Jacob 1853-1909 *BenetAL 91*
**Gordin,** Richard Davis 1928- *WhoMW 92*
**Gordine,** Dora 1906- *TwCPaSc, Who 92*
**Gordis,** Enoch 1931- *AmMWSc 92*
**Gordis,** Kent Kryloff 1961- *WhoEnt 92*
**Gordis,** Leon 1934- *AmMWSc 92*
**Gordis,** Robert 1908- *IntWW 91, WhoRel 92, WrDr 92*
**Gordley,** James Russell 1946- *WhoAmL 92*
**Gordon** *Who 92*
**Gordon,** Aaron Z. 1929- *WhoBlA 92*
**Gordon,** Adelbert M., Jr. 1928- *WhoRel 92*
**Gordon,** Adoniram Judson 1836-1895 *RelLAm 91*
**Gordon,** Adrienne Sue *AmMWSc 92*
**Gordon,** Alan Craig 1954- *WhoEnt 92*
**Gordon,** Albert McCague 1934- *AmMWSc 92*
**Gordon,** Albert Raye 1939- *AmMWSc 92*
**Gordon,** Albert Saul 1910- *AmMWSc 92*
**Gordon,** Alex 1922- *IntMPA 92*
**Gordon,** Alexander Esme 1910- *Who 92*
**Gordon,** Alexander H., II 1944- *WhoBlA 92*
**Gordon,** Alexander John 1917- *Who 92*
**Gordon,** Allan M. 1933- *WhoBlA 92*
**Gordon,** Allen 1948- *WhoAmP 91*
**Gordon,** Alvin S 1914- *AmMWSc 92*
**Gordon,** Andrew C. L. D. *Who 92*
**Gordon,** Annette Waters 1937- *AmMWSc 92*
**Gordon,** Archibald Ronald 1927- *Who 92*
**Gordon,** Arnold J 1937- *AmMWSc 92*
**Gordon,** Arnold L 1940- *AmMWSc 92*
**Gordon,** Arnold Mark 1937- *WhoAmL 92*
**Gordon,** Arnold Saul 1941- *WhoEnt 92*
**Gordon,** Aubrey Abraham 1925- *Who 92*
**Gordon,** Barbara C 1935- *WhoAmP 91*
**Gordon,** Baron Jack 1953- *WhoFI 92*
**Gordon,** Barry 1934- *WrDr 92*
**Gordon,** Barry Joel 1945- *WhoFI 92*
**Gordon,** Barry Maxwell 1930- *AmMWSc 92*
**Gordon,** Barry Monroe 1947- *AmMWSc 92*
**Gordon,** Bart 1949- *AlmAP 92 [port]*
**Gordon,** Barton Jennings 1949- *WhoAmP 91*
**Gordon,** Benjamin Edward 1916- *AmMWSc 92*
**Gordon,** Benjamin J, Jr 1932- *WhoAmP 91*
**Gordon,** Bernard 1918- *WhoEnt 92*
**Gordon,** Bernard 1922- *WhoMW 92*
**Gordon,** Bernard Ludwig 1931- *AmMWSc 92*
**Gordon,** Bernard M 1927- *AmMWSc 92*
**Gordon,** Bert I. *IntMPA 92*
**Gordon,** Bertha Comer 1916- *WhoBlA 92*
**Gordon,** Bill *TwCWW 91*
**Gordon,** Bonnie *DrAPF 91*
**Gordon,** Boyd 1926- *Who 92*
**Gordon,** Bradley Howell 1954- *WhoMW 92*
**Gordon,** Brian William 1926- *Who 92*
**Gordon,** Bridgette 1967- *BlkOlyM*
**Gordon,** Bruce 1929- *IntMPA 92*
**Gordon,** Bruce S. 1946- *WhoBlA 92*
**Gordon,** Burton K. 1945- *WhoFI 92*
**Gordon,** Burton LeRoy 1920- *AmMWSc 92*
**Gordon,** Carl Jackson, Jr 1944- *WhoAmP 91*
**Gordon,** Caroline 1895-1981 *BenetAL 91, ConAu 36NR*
**Gordon,** Carolyn Sue 1950- *AmMWSc 92*
**Gordon,** Charles *IntMPA 92*
**Gordon,** Charles 1918- *Who 92*
**Gordon,** Charles D. 1934- *WhoBlA 92*
**Gordon,** Charles Edward 1941- *WhoRel 92*
**Gordon,** Charles Eugene 1938- *WhoBlA 92*
**Gordon,** Charles F. *DrAPF 91*
**Gordon,** Charles Franklin 1921- *WhoBlA 92*
**Gordon,** Charles Robert 1935- *WhoAmP 91*
**Gordon,** Charles William 1860-1937 *BenetAL 91, RelLAm 91*
**Gordon,** Chester Duncan 1920- *AmMWSc 92*
**Gordon,** Chester Murray 1918- *AmMWSc 92*
**Gordon,** Christopher John 1953- *AmMWSc 92*
**Gordon,** Claire Catherine 1954- *AmMWSc 92*
**Gordon,** Claude Eugene 1916- *WhoEnt 92, WhoWest 92*
**Gordon,** Clifford Wesley *WhoBlA 92*
**Gordon,** Clyde Howard 1933- *WhoWest 92*
**Gordon,** Coco *DrAPF 91*
**Gordon,** Constance Mary Brand 1956- *WhoEnt 92*
**Gordon,** Corey Lee 1956- *WhoAmL 92*
**Gordon,** Cosmo Gerald 1945- *Who 92*
**Gordon,** Courtney Parks 1939- *AmMWSc 92*
**Gordon,** Craig Jeffrey 1953- *WhoMW 92*
**Gordon,** Cyrus H. 1908- *Who 92*
**Gordon,** Cyrus Herzl 1908- *WrDr 92*
**Gordon,** Dana 1958- *WhoAmL 92*
**Gordon,** Dane Rex 1925- *WhoRel 92*
**Gordon,** Daniel Bowman 1950- *WhoEnt 92*
**Gordon,** Daniel Israel 1920- *AmMWSc 92*
**Gordon,** Daniel R. 1951- *WhoAmL 92*
**Gordon,** Darrell R. 1926- *WhoBlA 92*
**Gordon,** David *TwCSFW 91*
**Gordon,** David 1916- *WhoMW 92*
**Gordon,** David Buddy 1918- *AmMWSc 92*
**Gordon,** David Eliot 1949- *WhoAmL 92*
**Gordon,** David Jamieson 1947- *WhoEnt 92*
**Gordon,** David Sorrell 1941- *Who 92*
**Gordon,** David Stewart *AmMWSc 92*
**Gordon,** David Zevi 1943- *WhoAmL 92*
**Gordon,** Deborah *WrDr 92*
**Gordon,** Deborah Leigh 1950- *WhoAmL 92*
**Gordon,** Dennis T 1941- *AmMWSc 92*
**Gordon,** Derek E. 1954- *WhoBlA 92*
**Gordon,** Desmond Spencer 1911- *Who 92*
**Gordon,** Dexter 1922-1990 *FacFETw*
**Gordon,** Dexter 1923-1990 *AnObit 1990, NewAmDM*
**Gordon,** Dexter Keith 1923-1990 *WhoBlA 92N*
**Gordon,** Diana *IntAu&W 91X, WrDr 92*
**Gordon,** Don 1926- *WhoEnt 92*
**Gordon,** Donald *IntAu&W 91X, WrDr 92*
**Gordon,** Donald 1929- *WrDr 92*
**Gordon,** Donald 1930- *IntWW 91*
**Gordon,** Donald 1939- *AmMWSc 92*
**Gordon,** Donald C. 1911- *WrDr 92*
**Gordon,** Donald Howard 1954- *WhoWest 92*
**Gordon,** Donald Jay 1941- *WhoMW 92*
**Gordon,** Donald Ramsay 1929- *IntAu&W 91*
**Gordon,** Donald Theile 1935- *AmMWSc 92*
**Gordon,** Donna Grace 1934- *WhoWest 92*
**Gordon,** Donovan 1934- *AmMWSc 92*
**Gordon,** Douglas *Who 92*
**Gordon,** Douglas Littleton 1924- *AmMWSc 92*
**Gordon,** Edgar George 1924- *WhoAmL 92*
**Gordon,** Edmund W. 1921- *WhoBlA 92*
**Gordon,** Edward Earl 1949- *WhoMW 92*
**Gordon,** Edward Lansing, Jr 1906-1971 *BlkOlyM*
**Gordon,** Edwin Jason 1952- *WhoBlA 92*
**Gordon,** Elaine Y 1931- *WhoAmP 91*
**Gordon,** Ellen Rubin *WhoMW 92*
**Gordon,** Ellis Davis 1913- *AmMWSc 92*
**Gordon,** Eric *Who 92*
**Gordon,** Eric Bruce 1961- *WhoEnt 92*
**Gordon,** Eric Michael 1946- *AmMWSc 92*
**Gordon,** Ernest 1916- *WhoRel 92, WrDr 92*
**Gordon,** Esme *Who 92*
**Gordon,** Esme 1910- *TwCPaSc*
**Gordon,** Ethel E. 1915- *WrDr 92*
**Gordon,** Ethel M. 1911- *WhoBlA 92*
**Gordon,** Eugene Andrew 1917- *WhoAmL 92*
**Gordon,** Eugene Irving 1930- *AmMWSc 92*
**Gordon,** Evan L. 1941- *WhoAmL 92*
**Gordon,** Fannetta Nelson 1919- *WhoBlA 92*
**Gordon,** Florence S *AmMWSc 92*
**Gordon,** Forrest Lyle 1926- *WhoRel 92*
**Gordon,** Francis 1928- *WhoAmP 91*
**Gordon,** Frank X *WhoAmP 91*
**Gordon,** Frank X., Jr. 1929- *WhoAmL 92, WhoWest 92*
**Gordon,** Fred *DrAPF 91*
**Gordon,** Gale 1906- *ConTFT 9, IntMPA 92*
**Gordon,** Gary Donald 1928- *AmMWSc 92*
**Gordon,** Gary Frederick 1947- *WhoMW 92*
**Gordon,** Geoffrey Arthur 1948- *AmMWSc 92*
**Gordon,** George Angier 1853-1929 *RelLAm 91*
**Gordon,** George E, III *WhoAmP 91*
**Gordon,** George Eric 1905- *Who 92*
**Gordon,** George N. 1926- *WrDr 92*
**Gordon,** George Selbie 1919- *AmMWSc 92*
**Gordon,** Gerald *Who 92*
**Gordon,** Gerald Arthur 1934- *AmMWSc 92*
**Gordon,** Gerald Bernard 1934- *AmMWSc 92*
**Gordon,** Gerald Henry 1929- *Who 92*
**Gordon,** Gerald M 1931- *AmMWSc 92*
**Gordon,** Gerald Timothy *DrAPF 91*
**Gordon,** Gilbert 1933- *AmMWSc 92*
**Gordon,** Giles 1940- *ConNov 91, WrDr 92*
**Gordon,** Giles Alexander Esme 1940- *IntAu&W 91, Who 92*
**Gordon,** Glen Everett 1935- *AmMWSc 92*
**Gordon,** Glenn Stuart 1961- *WhoAmL 92*
**Gordon,** Gordon 1906- *WrDr 92*
**Gordon,** Hal *SmATA 65*
**Gordon,** Hannah Cambell Grant 1941- *Who 92*
**Gordon,** Hannah Elizabeth 1920- *WhoAmP 91*
**Gordon,** Harold Thomas 1918- *AmMWSc 92*
**Gordon,** Harrison J. 1950- *WhoAmL 92*
**Gordon,** Harry H 1938- *WhoIns 92*
**Gordon,** Harry Haskin 1906- *AmMWSc 92*
**Gordon,** Harry William 1924- *AmMWSc 92*
**Gordon,** Hayden S 1910- *AmMWSc 92*
**Gordon,** Helen A. 1923- *WhoBlA 92*
**Gordon,** Helen Alice 1944- *WhoMW 92*
**Gordon,** Helen Heightsman 1932- *WhoWest 92*
**Gordon,** Helmut Albert 1908- *AmMWSc 92*
**Gordon,** Herbert David 1938- *WhoFI 92*
**Gordon,** Hilda May 1874-1972 *TwCPaSc*
**Gordon,** Howard Allan 1943- *AmMWSc 92*
**Gordon,** Howard Lyon 1930- *WhoFI 92*
**Gordon,** Howard R 1940- *AmMWSc 92*
**Gordon,** Hugh 1930- *AmMWSc 92*
**Gordon,** Hymie 1926- *AmMWSc 92*
**Gordon,** Ian Alistair 1908- *IntAu&W 91, Who 92, WrDr 92*
**Gordon,** Irvin H 1912- *WhoAmP 91*
**Gordon,** Irving 1914- *AmMWSc 92*
**Gordon,** Irving 1922- *AmMWSc 92*
**Gordon,** Irving Martin 1926- *WhoMW 92*
**Gordon,** Isabel S & Sorkin, Sophie *ScFEYrs*
**Gordon,** Isidor 1913- *IntWW 91*
**Gordon,** J. E. *WhoRel 92*
**Gordon,** Jack 1929- *IntMPA 92*
**Gordon,** Jack D 1922- *WhoAmP 91*
**Gordon,** Jaimy *DrAPF 91*
**Gordon,** James Byron 1822-1864 *DcNCBi 2*
**Gordon,** James Houston 1946- *WhoAmP 91*
**Gordon,** James Lee 1932- *WhoMW 92, WhoRel 92*
**Gordon,** James Patrick 1950- *WhoMW 92*
**Gordon,** James Power 1928- *AmMWSc 92*
**Gordon,** James S. 1941- *WhoAmL 92*
**Gordon,** James Samuel 1941- *AmMWSc 92*
**Gordon,** James Stuart 1936- *Who 92*
**Gordon,** James Wylie 1934- *AmMWSc 92*
**Gordon,** Janine M. 1946- *WhoFI 92*
**Gordon,** Jay Fisher 1926- *WhoAmL 92*
**Gordon,** Jeanne Brown *WhoAmP 91*
**Gordon,** Jeffrey I *AmMWSc 92*
**Gordon,** Jeffrey Miles 1949- *AmMWSc 92*
**Gordon,** Jeffrey Neil 1949- *WhoAmL 92*
**Gordon,** Joan 1923- *AmMWSc 92*
**Gordon,** Joan May 1946- *WhoMW 92*
**Gordon,** Joel Ethan 1930- *AmMWSc 92*
**Gordon,** John 1925- *WrDr 92*
**Gordon,** John Bowie 1921- *Who 92*
**Gordon,** John C 1939- *AmMWSc 92*

**Gordon,** John E. *WhoAmL 92*
**Gordon,** John Edward 1931- *AmMWSc 92*
**Gordon,** John Fraser 1916- *IntAu&W 91, WrDr 92*
**Gordon,** John Gunn Drummond 1909- *Who 92*
**Gordon,** John Keith 1940- *Who 92*
**Gordon,** John Lynn 1933- *WhoWest 92*
**Gordon,** John P 1928- *AmMWSc 92*
**Gordon,** John S 1931- *AmMWSc 92*
**Gordon,** John William 1925- *IntAu&W 91*
**Gordon,** Jon W 1949- *AmMWSc 92*
**Gordon,** Joseph Cooper 1959- *WhoAmP 91*
**Gordon,** Joseph G., II 1945- *WhoBlA 92*
**Gordon,** Joseph Grover, II 1945- *AmMWSc 92*
**Gordon,** Joseph K. *WhoAmL 92*
**Gordon,** Joseph R 1924- *AmMWSc 92*
**Gordon,** Judith 1943- *WhoFI 92*
**Gordon,** Julius 1932- *AmMWSc 92*
**Gordon,** Katharine 1916- *WrDr 92*
**Gordon,** Katherine 1954- *AmMWSc 92*
**Gordon,** Keith *IntAu&W 91X*
**Gordon,** Keith 1906- *Who 92*
**Gordon,** Keith 1961- *IntMPA 92*
**Gordon,** Kenneth Richard 1945- *AmMWSc 92*
**Gordon,** Kirpal *DrAPF 91*
**Gordon,** Kurtiss Jay 1940- *AmMWSc 92*
**Gordon,** Lancaster 1962- *WhoBlA 92*
**Gordon,** Lance Kenneth 1947- *AmMWSc 92*
**Gordon,** Larry David 1938- *WhoMW 92*
**Gordon,** Lawrence 1936- *IntMPA 92*
**Gordon,** Leland J. 1897-1982 *ConAu 133*
**Gordon,** Leland James 1927- *WhoAmL 92*
**Gordon,** Leonard Herman David 1928- *WhoMW 92*
**Gordon,** Levan 1933- *WhoBlA 92*
**Gordon,** Lew *IntAu&W 91X, TwCWW 91, WrDr 92*
**Gordon,** Lewis Alexander 1937- *WhoMW 92*
**Gordon,** Lincoln 1913- *IntWW 91*
**Gordon,** Lionel Eldred Peter S. *Who 92*
**Gordon,** Lois Barbara 1947- *WhoAmL 92*
**Gordon,** Lois G. 1938- *WrDr 92*
**Gordon,** Lois Jackson 1932- *WhoBlA 92*
**Gordon,** Lonny Joseph 1942- *WhoEnt 92*
**Gordon,** Louis 1946- *AmMWSc 92*
**Gordon,** Louis Irwin 1928- *AmMWSc 92*
**Gordon,** Lyle J 1926- *AmMWSc 92*
**Gordon,** MacDonnell *DrAPF 91*
**Gordon,** Malcolm Stephen 1933- *AmMWSc 92*
**Gordon,** Malcolm Wofsy 1917- *AmMWSc 92*
**Gordon,** Manuel Joe 1922- *AmMWSc 92*
**Gordon,** Margaret Shaughnessy 1910- *WhoWest 92*
**Gordon,** Margret King 1927- *WhoAmP 91*
**Gordon,** Marilyn 1940- *WhoWest 92*
**Gordon,** Marjorie *WhoEnt 92*
**Gordon,** Mark 1926- *WhoEnt 92*
**Gordon,** Mark A 1937- *AmMWSc 92*
**Gordon,** Mark Stephen 1942- *AmMWSc 92*
**Gordon,** Marvin Jay 1946- *WhoWest 92*
**Gordon,** Mary *BenetAL 91, DrAPF 91*
**Gordon,** Mary 1949- *ConNov 91, IntAu&W 91, WrDr 92*
**Gordon,** Mary McDougall 1929- *WhoWest 92*
**Gordon,** Maurice Kirby, II 1944- *WhoAmL 92*
**Gordon,** Max 1903-1989 *FacFETw*
**Gordon,** Max 1931-1990 *AnObit 1990*
**Gordon,** Maxie S., Sr. 1910- *WhoBlA 92*
**Gordon,** Maxwell 1921- *AmMWSc 92*
**Gordon,** Mel 1943- *TwCPaSc*
**Gordon,** Melinda Sue 1957- *WhoEnt 92*
**Gordon,** Michael 1909- *IntMPA 92, WhoEnt 92, WhoWest 92*
**Gordon,** Michael Andrew *AmMWSc 92*
**Gordon,** Michael Gerald Francis 1941- *WhoRel 92*
**Gordon,** Michael Mackin 1950- *WhoAmL 92*
**Gordon,** Michael Robert 1939- *WhoWest 92*
**Gordon,** Michael Robert 1947- *WhoAmP 91*
**Gordon,** Mildred 1923- *Who 92*
**Gordon,** Mildred Kobrin *AmMWSc 92*
**Gordon,** Millard F 1921- *AmMWSc 92*
**Gordon,** Milton 1929- *AmMWSc 92*
**Gordon,** Milton A. 1935- *WhoBlA 92*
**Gordon,** Milton Andrew 1935- *AmMWSc 92*
**Gordon,** Milton Paul 1930- *AmMWSc 92*
**Gordon,** Mitchell Ira 1957- *WhoFI 92*
**Gordon,** Morris Aaron 1920- *AmMWSc 92*
**Gordon,** Morton Lawrence 1924- *WhoRel 92*
**Gordon,** Morton Maurice 1924- *AmMWSc 92*
**Gordon,** Myra 1939- *AmMWSc 92*
**Gordon,** Nadia *Who 92*
**Gordon,** Nathan 1917- *AmMWSc 92*
**Gordon,** Nathan Lee 1915- *WhoEnt 92*
**Gordon,** Nicholas 1928- *WhoEnt 92*
**Gordon,** Nora Antonia 1866-1901 *NotBlAW 92*
**Gordon,** P 1918- *AmMWSc 92*
**Gordon,** Pamela Joan 1936- *Who 92*
**Gordon,** Patrick Duff 1719-1773 *DcNCBi 2*
**Gordon,** Patrick W. *Who 92*
**Gordon,** Paul *DrAPF 91*
**Gordon,** Paul David 1941- *WhoFI 92*
**Gordon,** Paul Perry 1927- *WhoAmP 91*
**Gordon,** Paul Stewart 1963- *WhoMW 92*
**Gordon,** Paula Rossbacher 1953- *WhoEnt 92*
**Gordon,** Peter *Who 92*
**Gordon,** Peter Macie 1919- *Who 92*
**Gordon,** Philip N 1919- *AmMWSc 92*
**Gordon,** Philip Ray 1955- *AmMWSc 92*
**Gordon,** Portia Beverly 1952- *AmMWSc 92*
**Gordon,** R 1917- *AmMWSc 92*
**Gordon,** Randall Joe 1941- *WhoMW 92*
**Gordon,** Rex *IntAu&W 91X, WrDr 92*
**Gordon,** Rex 1917- *TwCSFW 91*
**Gordon,** Richard 1921- *Who 92, WrDr 92*
**Gordon,** Richard 1925- *IntMPA 92*
**Gordon,** Richard 1943- *AmMWSc 92*
**Gordon,** Richard F., Jr. 1929- *IntWW 91*
**Gordon,** Richard Lee 1935- *AmMWSc 92*
**Gordon,** Richard M. Erik 1949- *WhoFI 92*
**Gordon,** Richard Seymour 1925- *AmMWSc 92*
**Gordon,** Rob 1965- *WhoEnt 92*
**Gordon,** Robert Boyd 1929- *AmMWSc 92*
**Gordon,** Robert Bruce 1948- *WhoEnt 92*
**Gordon,** Robert Cameron 1941- *WhoEnt 92*
**Gordon,** Robert Charles Frost 1920- *WhoAmP 91*
**Gordon,** Robert Dixon 1936- *AmMWSc 92*
**Gordon,** Robert Douglas 1936- *Who 92*
**Gordon,** Robert Edward 1925- *AmMWSc 92*
**Gordon,** Robert Edward 1938- *WhoWest 92*
**Gordon,** Robert Eugene 1932- *WhoAmL 92, WhoEnt 92*
**Gordon,** Robert Fitzgerald 1928- *WhoBlA 92*
**Gordon,** Robert Gary 1946- *WhoFI 92*
**Gordon,** Robert H 1852?-1910 *BiInAmS*
**Gordon,** Robert James 1932- *Who 92*
**Gordon,** Robert James 1940- *WhoFI 92, WhoMW 92*
**Gordon,** Robert Jay 1944- *AmMWSc 92*
**Gordon,** Robert Julian 1923- *AmMWSc 92*
**Gordon,** Robert L. 1941- *WhoBlA 92*
**Gordon,** Robert W. 1941- *WhoAmL 92*
**Gordon,** Robert Wilson 1915- *Who 92*
**Gordon,** Roberta Gail *WhoEnt 92*
**Gordon,** Roger Hall 1949- *WhoMW 92*
**Gordon,** Roger L. *WhoWest 92*
**Gordon,** Ronald *Who 92*
**Gordon,** Ronald E 1949- *AmMWSc 92*
**Gordon,** Ronald Eugene 1946- *WhoBlA 92*
**Gordon,** Ronald John 1954- *WhoHisp 92*
**Gordon,** Ronald Stanton 1937- *AmMWSc 92*
**Gordon,** Ronald William 1942- *WhoMW 92*
**Gordon,** Roy Gerald 1940- *AmMWSc 92*
**Gordon,** Rusty 1942- *WhoEnt 92*
**Gordon,** Ruth 1896-1985 *FacFETw, ReelWom*
**Gordon,** Ruth Evelyn *AmMWSc 92*
**Gordon,** Ruth Vida 1926- *AmMWSc 92, WhoWest 92*
**Gordon,** Ryan Russell 1965- *WhoRel 92*
**Gordon,** Samuel M. 1898- *WhoWest 92*
**Gordon,** Samuel Morris 1898- *AmMWSc 92*
**Gordon,** Samuel Neal 1950- *WhoMW 92, WhoRel 92*
**Gordon,** Samuel Robert 1943- *AmMWSc 92*
**Gordon,** Saul 1925- *AmMWSc 92*
**Gordon,** Scott 1949- *WhoEnt 92*
**Gordon,** Serena 1963- *ConTFT 9*
**Gordon,** Seymour Arthur 1936- *WhoAmL 92*
**Gordon,** Sheffield 1916- *AmMWSc 92*
**Gordon,** Sheldon P 1942- *AmMWSc 92*
**Gordon,** Sheldon Robert 1949- *AmMWSc 92*
**Gordon,** Siamon 1938- *Who 92*
**Gordon,** Sidney 1917- *Who 92*
**Gordon,** Stanley H 1925- *AmMWSc 92*
**Gordon,** Stephen L 1944- *AmMWSc 92*
**Gordon,** Stephen Louis 1956- *WhoAmL 92*
**Gordon,** Steven Eric 1960- *WhoEnt 92, WhoWest 92*
**Gordon,** Steven Joe 1956- *WhoFI 92*
**Gordon,** Steven Michael 1949- *WhoAmL 92*
**Gordon,** Stewart *TwCWW 91, WrDr 92*
**Gordon,** Stuart 1947- *TwCSFW 91, WhoEnt 92, WrDr 92*
**Gordon,** Stuart James 1930- *WhoAmL 92*
**Gordon,** Sydney Jeter 1946- *WhoWest 92*
**Gordon,** Sydney Michael 1939- *AmMWSc 92*
**Gordon,** Tavia 1917- *AmMWSc 92*
**Gordon,** Terry Douglas 1954- *WhoAmL 92*
**Gordon,** Thomas 1918- *WrDr 92*
**Gordon,** Thomas 1967- *WhoBlA 92*
**Gordon,** Vera Kate *Who 92*
**Gordon,** Victor Reese 1950- *WhoRel 92*
**Gordon,** Vivian V. 1934- *WhoBlA 92*
**Gordon,** Walter 1906-1987 *FacFETw*
**Gordon,** Walter Carl, Jr. 1927- *WhoBlA 92*
**Gordon,** Walter Lear, III 1942- *WhoBlA 92*
**Gordon,** Wayne Alan 1946- *AmMWSc 92*
**Gordon,** Wayne Lecky 1952- *AmMWSc 92*
**Gordon,** William 1728-1807 *BlkwEAR*
**Gordon,** William A. 1950- *ConAu 135*
**Gordon,** William Bernard 1935- *AmMWSc 92*
**Gordon,** William Bingham 1950- *WhoWest 92*
**Gordon,** William Brice 1941- *WhoFI 92*
**Gordon,** William E 1918- *AmMWSc 92*
**Gordon,** William Edwin 1918- *IntWW 91*
**Gordon,** William Edwin 1919- *AmMWSc 92*
**Gordon,** William George 1931- *WhoAmP 91*
**Gordon,** William Howat Leslie 1914- *Who 92*
**Gordon,** William John 1939- *AmMWSc 92*
**Gordon,** William Livingston 1927- *AmMWSc 92*
**Gordon,** William Ransome 1943- *AmMWSc 92*
**Gordon,** Winfield James 1926- *WhoBlA 92*
**Gordon-Brown,** Alexander Douglas 1927- *Who 92*
**Gordon-Cumming,** Alexander Roualeyn 1924- *Who 92*
**Gordon Cumming,** William Gordon 1928- *Who 92*
**Gordon Davies,** John *Who 92*
**Gordon de Figols,** Priscilla Ann 1938- *WhoEnt 92*
**Gordon-Duff,** Thomas Robert 1911- *Who 92*
**Gordon-Finlayson,** Robert 1916- *Who 92*
**Gordon Jones,** Edward 1914- *Who 92*
**Gordon-Lennox** *Who 92*
**Gordon Lennox,** Lord 1931- *IntWW 91*
**Gordon Lennox,** Bernard Charles 1932- *Who 92*
**Gordon Lennox,** Nicholas Charles 1931- *Who 92*
**Gordon-Shelby,** Lurdys Marie 1963- *WhoBlA 92*
**Gordon-Smith,** David Gerard 1925- *Who 92*
**Gordon-Smith,** Ralph 1905- *IntWW 91, Who 92*
**Gordone,** Charles 1925- *BenetAL 91, WhoBlA 92, WrDr 92*
**Gordone,** Charles 1927- *WhoEnt 92*
**Gordons,** The *WrDr 92*
**Gordus,** Adon Alden 1932- *AmMWSc 92*
**Gordy,** Berry 1929- *IntMPA 92, WhoEnt 92*
**Gordy,** Berry, Jr. 1929- *ConBlB 1 [port], ConMus 6 [port], WhoBlA 92*
**Gordy,** Desiree D'Laura 1956- *WhoBlA 92*
**Gordy,** Edwin 1925- *AmMWSc 92*
**Gordy,** John Pancoast 1851-1908 *BiInAmS*
**Gordy,** Stephen Ellison 1920- *WhoAmP 91*
**Gordy,** Thomas D 1915- *AmMWSc 92*
**Gordziel,** Steven A 1946- *AmMWSc 92*
**Gore** *Who 92*
**Gore,** Al 1948- *NewYTBS 91 [port]*
**Gore,** Albert, Jr. 1948- *AlmAP 92 [port], IntWW 91, WhoAmP 91*
**Gore,** Blinzy L. 1921- *WhoBlA 92*
**Gore,** Bryan Frank 1938- *AmMWSc 92, WhoWest 92*
**Gore,** Catherine 1799-1861 *RfGEnL 91*
**Gore,** David Curtiss 1964- *WhoFI 92*
**Gore,** David Eugene 1935- *WhoFI 92*
**Gore,** David L. 1937- *WhoBlA 92*
**Gore,** David Lee 1937- *WhoMW 92*
**Gore,** David Ormsby *FacFETw*
**Gore,** Donald Ray 1936- *WhoMW 92*
**Gore,** Dorothy J 1926- *AmMWSc 92*
**Gore,** Ernest Stanley 1942- *AmMWSc 92*
**Gore,** Francis St John 1921- *Who 92*
**Gore,** Frederick 1913- *TwCPaSc*
**Gore,** Frederick John Pym 1913- *IntWW 91, Who 92*
**Gore,** Ira 1913- *AmMWSc 92*
**Gore,** John Squires 1957- *WhoMW 92*
**Gore,** Joseph A. *WhoBlA 92*
**Gore,** Joshua Walker 1852-1908 *DcNCBi 2*
**Gore,** Louise 1925- *WhoAmP 91*
**Gore,** Madhav 1921- *IntWW 91*
**Gore,** Marion Tanner 1937- *WhoMW 92*
**Gore,** Martin Wayne 1955- *WhoRel 92*
**Gore,** Michael 1951- *IntMPA 92*
**Gore,** Michael Edward John 1935- *Who 92*
**Gore,** Natalie Elizabeth 1962- *WhoWest 92*
**Gore,** Pamela J W 1955- *AmMWSc 92*
**Gore,** Paul Annesley 1921- *Who 92*
**Gore,** Richard 1954- *Who 92*
**Gore,** Robert Cummins 1907- *AmMWSc 92*
**Gore,** Samuel Thomas 1933- *WhoAmP 91*
**Gore,** Spencer 1878-1914 *TwCPaSc*
**Gore,** St John *Who 92*
**Gore,** Timothy Clearence 1956- *WhoRel 92*
**Gore,** Wilbert Lee 1912- *AmMWSc 92*
**Gore,** William Earl 1946- *AmMWSc 92*
**Gore,** Willis C 1926- *AmMWSc 92*
**Gore-Booth,** Angus 1920- *Who 92*
**Gore-Booth,** David Alwyn 1943- *Who 92*
**Gore-Langton** *Who 92*
**Gorecki,** Henryk 1933- *ConCom 92*
**Gorecki,** Henryk Mikolaj 1933- *IntWW 91*
**Goree,** James Gleason 1935- *AmMWSc 92*
**Goree,** Janie Glymph 1921- *WhoBlA 92*
**Gorelczenko,** Mark Allan 1950- *WhoEnt 92*
**Gorelic,** Lester Sylvan 1940- *AmMWSc 92*
**Gorelick,** Jerry Lee 1946- *AmMWSc 92*
**Gorelick,** Kenneth J 1952- *AmMWSc 92, WhoWest 92*
**Gorelik,** Mordecai 1899-1990 *ConTFT 9*
**Gorell,** Baron 1927- *Who 92*
**Gorell,** Thomas Andrew 1940- *AmMWSc 92*
**Goremykin,** Ivan Longinovich 1839-1917 *FacFETw*
**Goren,** Alan Charles 1946- *AmMWSc 92*
**Goren,** Bruce Neal 1956- *WhoEnt 92*
**Goren,** Charles H. 1901-1991 *ConAu 134, CurBio 91N, NewYTBS 91 [port], News 91*
**Goren,** Howard Joseph 1941- *AmMWSc 92*
**Goren,** Judith *DrAPF 91*
**Goren,** Mayer Bear 1921- *AmMWSc 92*
**Goren,** Roberta C. 1943-1983 *ConAu 135*
**Goren,** Shlomo 1917- *IntWW 91*
**Goren,** Simon L 1936- *AmMWSc 92*
**Gorena,** Sam Luis 1958- *WhoHisp 92*
**Gorenberg,** Robin 1960- *WhoAmL 92*
**Gorenstein,** Charles 1950- *WhoAmL 92*
**Gorenstein,** Daniel *AmMWSc 92*
**Gorenstein,** David George 1945- *AmMWSc 92*
**Gorenstein,** Edward 1936- *WhoFI 92*
**Gorenstein,** Marc Victor 1950- *AmMWSc 92*
**Gorenstein,** Paul 1934- *AmMWSc 92*
**Gorenstein,** Shirley Slotkin 1928- *AmMWSc 92*
**Gores,** Christopher Merrel 1943- *WhoAmL 92*
**Gores,** Gregory J 1955- *AmMWSc 92*
**Gores,** Joe 1931- *IntAu&W 91, WrDr 92*
**Gores,** Joseph Nicholas 1931- *WhoEnt 92*
**Gores,** Landis d1991 *NewYTBS 91*
**Goresky,** Carl A 1932- *AmMWSc 92*
**Goretta,** Claude 1929- *IntDcF 2-2, IntWW 91*
**Goretta,** Louis Alexander 1922- *AmMWSc 92*
**Gorev,** Nikolay Nikolayevich 1900- *IntWW 91*
**Gorewitz,** Rubin Leon 1924- *WhoFI 92*
**Gorey,** Brent Steven 1951- *WhoAmL 92*
**Gorey,** Edward 1925- *BenetAL 91, WrDr 92*
**Gorfien,** Harold 1924- *AmMWSc 92*
**Gorfien,** Stephen Frank 1958- *AmMWSc 92*
**Gorgans,** Mark Thomas 1957- *WhoRel 92*
**Gorgas,** William Crawford 1854-1920 *BiInAmS, FacFETw*
**Gorges,** Ferdinando 1566?-1647 *BenetAL 91*
**Gorges,** Heinz A 1913- *AmMWSc 92*
**Gorges,** Heinz August 1913- *WhoFI 92*
**Gorgey,** Gabor 1929- *IntAu&W 91*
**Gorgone,** John 1941- *AmMWSc 92*
**Gorham,** Bradford 1935- *WhoAmP 91*
**Gorham,** Daniel John 1929- *WhoRel 92*
**Gorham,** David L. 1932- *WhoFI 92*
**Gorham,** Elaine Deborah 1945- *AmMWSc 92*
**Gorham,** Eville 1925- *AmMWSc 92*
**Gorham,** James 1745-1804 *DcNCBi 2*
**Gorham,** John 1783-1829 *BiInAmS*
**Gorham,** John Francis 1921- *AmMWSc 92*
**Gorham,** John Richard 1922- *AmMWSc 92*
**Gorham,** John Richard 1931- *AmMWSc 92*
**Gorham,** Michael *IntAu&W 91X, WrDr 92*
**Gorham,** Paul Raymond 1918- *AmMWSc 92*
**Gorham,** R C *AmMWSc 92*
**Gorham,** Sarah *DrAPF 91*
**Gorham,** Thelma Thurston 1913- *WhoBlA 92*
**Gorham,** William Franklin 1926- *AmMWSc 92*
**Gori,** Antonio Francesco 1691-1757 *BlkwCEP*

**Gori**, Gio Batta 1931- AmMWSc 92
**Goria**, Giovanni 1943- IntWW 91
**Goribar**, Nicolas Javier de d1736 HisDSpE
**Gorin**, George 1925- AmMWSc 92
**Gorin**, Philip Albert James 1931- AmMWSc 92
**Gorin**, Ralph Edgar 1948- WhoWest 92
**Gorin**, Steven Barry 1962- WhoAmL 92
**Goring**, David Arthur Ingham 1920- AmMWSc 92
**Goring**, Emmy 1893-1973 EncTR 91 [port]
**Goring**, Geoffrey E 1920- AmMWSc 92
**Goring**, Hermann 1893-1946 EncTR 91 [port]
**Goring**, Hermann Wilhelm 1893-1946 BiDExR
**Goring**, Karin 1888-1931 EncTR 91
**Goring**, Marius 1912- IntMPA 92, IntWW 91, Who 92
**Goring**, Peter Allan Elliott 1943- WhoFI 92
**Goring**, William 1933- Who 92
**Goring**, William S. 1943- WhoBlA 92
**Gorini**, Catherine Ann 1949- WhoMW 92
**Gorinovich**, Gorald Nikolayevich 1929- IntWW 91
**Gorinson**, Stanley M. 1945- WhoAmL 92
**Gorkin**, Jess 1913-1985 FacFETw
**Gor'ky**, Maksim 1868-1936 SovUnBD
**Gorky**, Maxim 1868-1936 FacFETw [port], LiExTwC
**Gorla**, Rama S R AmMWSc 92
**Gorland**, Scott Lance 1949- WhoAmL 92
**Gorland**, Sol H 1941- AmMWSc 92
**Gorley Putt**, Samuel Who 92
**Gorlick**, Dennis 1944- AmMWSc 92
**Gorlick**, Laurence Karl 1951- WhoWest 92
**Gorlin**, Cathy Ellen 1953- WhoAmL 92
**Gorlin**, Richard 1926- AmMWSc 92
**Gorlin**, Robert James 1923- AmMWSc 92
**Gormalley**, Joan Patricia 1938- WhoAmP 91
**Gorman**, Alexander M. 1814-1865 DcNCBi 2
**Gorman**, Arthur Daniel 1946- AmMWSc 92
**Gorman**, Barbara Rose 1945- WhoWest 92
**Gorman**, Benjamin Frank 1931- WhoFI 92
**Gorman**, Bertha Gaffney 1940- WhoBlA 92
**Gorman**, Christopher 1955- WhoEnt 92
**Gorman**, Clem 1942- IntAu&W 91, WrDr 92
**Gorman**, Cliff WhoEnt 92
**Gorman**, Colum A 1936- AmMWSc 92
**Gorman**, Cornelia M 1951- AmMWSc 92
**Gorman**, Deborah Ewing 1946- WhoRel 92
**Gorman**, Ed 1941- TwCWW 91, WrDr 92
**Gorman**, Eugene Francis 1926- AmMWSc 92
**Gorman**, Francis J WhoAmP 91
**Gorman**, Gary Eugene 1944- WhoRel 92
**Gorman**, George Charles 1941- AmMWSc 92
**Gorman**, George E 1921- WhoAmP 91
**Gorman**, Gerald Otis 1937- WhoWest 92
**Gorman**, Gerald Warner 1933- WhoAmL 92, WhoMW 92
**Gorman**, Gertrude Alberta WhoBlA 92
**Gorman**, Ginny WrDr 92
**Gorman**, Herbert S. 1893-1954 BenetAL 91
**Gorman**, John Edward 1942- WhoFI 92
**Gorman**, John Joseph 1950- WhoEnt 92
**Gorman**, John Peter 1927- Who 92
**Gorman**, John R. WhoRel 92
**Gorman**, John Reginald 1923- Who 92
**Gorman**, John Richard 1913- AmMWSc 92
**Gorman**, Joseph Gregory, Jr. 1939- WhoAmL 92
**Gorman**, Joseph Thomas, Jr. 1957- WhoAmL 92
**Gorman**, Joseph Tolle 1937- IntWW 91, WhoFI 92, WhoMW 92
**Gorman**, Joseph Tolle, Jr. 1961- WhoFI 92
**Gorman**, Karen Machmer 1955- WhoMW 92
**Gorman**, Kenneth J 1932- WhoIns 92
**Gorman**, Kevin Charles 1951- WhoAmP 91
**Gorman**, Lawrence James 1948- WhoFI 92
**Gorman**, Leo Joseph 1929- WhoRel 92
**Gorman**, Marcie Sothern 1949- WhoFI 92
**Gorman**, Mark Scott WhoAmP 91
**Gorman**, Marvin 1928- AmMWSc 92
**Gorman**, Mary E. DcNCBi 2
**Gorman**, Maureen J. 1955- WhoAmL 92
**Gorman**, Melville 1910- AmMWSc 92
**Gorman**, Michael 1938- TwCPaSc
**Gorman**, Michael Joseph 1954- WhoRel 92
**Gorman**, Michael S. 1957- WhoEnt 92
**Gorman**, Michael Stephen 1951- WhoWest 92
**Gorman**, Ned WhoEnt 92
**Gorman**, Richard 1946- TwCPaSc
**Gorman**, Richard E 1950- WhoAmP 91
**Gorman**, Robert A. 1937- WhoAmL 92
**Gorman**, Robert Roland 1944- AmMWSc 92
**Gorman**, Stephen Thomas 1924- WhoAmP 91
**Gorman**, Teresa Ellen 1931- Who 92
**Gorman**, William Alan 1925- AmMWSc 92
**Gorman**, William Moore 1923- IntWW 91, Who 92
**Gormanston**, Viscount 1939- Who 92
**Gorme**, Eydie WhoEnt 92
**Gormezano**, Keith Stephen 1955- WhoFI 92, WhoWest 92
**Gormican**, Annette 1924- AmMWSc 92
**Gormley** Who 92
**Gormley**, Baron 1917- IntWW 91, Who 92
**Gormley**, Antony 1950- IntWW 91, TwCPaSc
**Gormley**, Dennis James 1939- WhoMW 92
**Gormley**, Franics Xavier, Jr. 1953- WhoWest 92
**Gormley**, Michael Francis 1939- AmMWSc 92
**Gormley**, William L 1946- WhoAmP 91
**Gormley**, William Thomas 1915- AmMWSc 92
**Gormly**, Allan Graham 1937- Who 92
**Gormly**, Barbara Diesner 1943- WhoFI 92
**Gormly**, William Mowry 1941- WhoFI 92, WhoWest 92
**Gormus**, Bobby Joe 1941- AmMWSc 92
**Gorn**, Saul 1912- AmMWSc 92
**Gornall**, Allan Godfrey 1914- AmMWSc 92
**Gorney**, Jay 1896-1990 AnObit 1990
**Gorney**, Karen Lynn WhoEnt 92
**Gorney**, Roderic 1924- AmMWSc 92
**Gorniak**, Gerard Charles 1949- AmMWSc 92
**Gorniak**, Michael John 1953- WhoEnt 92
**Gornick**, Alan Lewis 1908- WhoAmL 92
**Gornick**, Fred 1929- AmMWSc 92
**Gornick**, Vivian 1935- WrDr 92
**Gornish**, Gerald 1937- WhoAmL 92
**Gornto**, Albert Brooks, Jr. 1929- WhoFI 92
**Gornto**, Richard Francis 1946- WhoFI 92
**Gorodetsky**, Sergei Mitrofanovich 1884-1967 FacFETw
**Gorodetzky**, Charles W 1937- AmMWSc 92
**Gorody**, Anthony Wagner 1949- AmMWSc 92
**Goroff**, Diana K AmMWSc 92
**Gorog**, Istvan 1938- AmMWSc 92
**Gorog**, Laszlo 1903- IntMPA 92
**Gorog**, William Christopher WhoEnt 92
**Gorostiza**, Luis Roberto 1957- WhoHisp 92
**Gorovsky**, Martin A 1941- AmMWSc 92
**Gorozdos**, Richard E 1928- AmMWSc 92
**Gorr**, Ivan William WhoFI 92, WhoMW 92
**Gorr**, Jon Carl 1958- WhoEnt 92
**Gorr**, Rita 1926- NewAmDM
**Gorrafa**, Adly Abdel-Moniem 1935- AmMWSc 92
**Gorrell**, David Anthony 1943- WhoMW 92
**Gorrell**, Frank Cheatham 1927- WhoAmP 91
**Gorrell**, Joseph Hendren 1868-1942 DcNCBi 2
**Gorrell**, Lorraine WhoEnt 92
**Gorrell**, Ralph 1803-1875 DcNCBi 2
**Gorrell**, Robert 1914- WrDr 92
**Gorrell**, Robert Pinkney 1955- WhoEnt 92
**Gorrell**, Thomas Earl 1950- AmMWSc 92
**Gorriaran**, Michael 1960- WhoWest 92
**Gorrill**, William R 1921- AmMWSc 92
**Gorrin**, Eugene 1956- WhoAmL 92
**Gorrin-Peralta**, Jose Juan 1942- WhoHisp 92
**Gorringe**, Christopher John 1945- Who 92
**Gorringe**, Sandi Lee 1952- WhoWest 92
**Gorrissen**, Jacques WhoEnt 92
**Gorriti**, Juana Manuela 1818-1892 SpAmWW
**Gorrod**, John William 1931- Who 92
**Gorry**, G Anthony AmMWSc 92
**Gorse**, Joseph 1945- AmMWSc 92
**Gorse**, Robert August, Jr 1942- AmMWSc 92
**Gorshin**, Frank 1934- WhoEnt 92
**Gorshkov**, Leonid Aleksandrovich 1930- IntWW 91
**Gorshkov**, Sergei G 1910-1988 FacFETw
**Gorshkov**, Sergey Georgievich 1910-1988 SovUnBD
**Gorsic**, Joseph 1924- AmMWSc 92
**Gorsica**, Henry Jan 1907- AmMWSc 92
**Gorske**, Robert Herman 1932- WhoAmL 92
**Gorski**, Andrzej 1946- AmMWSc 92
**Gorski**, Dennis T WhoAmP 91
**Gorski**, Hedwig Irene DrAPF 91
**Gorski**, Jack 1931- AmMWSc 92
**Gorski**, Jeffrey Paul 1947- AmMWSc 92
**Gorski**, Leon John 1938- AmMWSc 92
**Gorski**, Robert Alexander 1922- AmMWSc 92
**Gorski**, Roger Anthony 1935- AmMWSc 92
**Gorski**, Walter Joseph 1943- WhoAmL 92
**Gorski**, William Edward 1950- WhoRel 92
**Gorski-Simon**, Kathleen M. 1958- WhoMW 92
**Gorsky**, Aleksandr Alekseevich 1871-1924 SovUnBD
**Gorsline**, Donn Sherrin 1926- AmMWSc 92
**Gorsline**, Robert Ainslee, Jr. 1942- WhoFI 92
**Gorsline**, Russell Elvin 1943- WhoEnt 92
**Gorson**, Robert O 1923- AmMWSc 92
**Gorst**, Harold E 1868-1950 ScFEYrs
**Gorst**, John Michael 1928- Who 92
**Gorsuch**, Richard Lee 1937- WhoRel 92
**Gort**, Viscount 1916- Who 92
**Gort**, Michael 1923- WhoFI 92
**Gort**, Sam TwCWW 91
**Gortatowski**, Melvin Jerome 1925- AmMWSc 92
**Gorthy**, Willis Charles 1934- AmMWSc 92
**Gortler**, Leon Bernard 1935- AmMWSc 92
**Gortner**, Marjoe 1944- IntMPA 92
**Gortner**, Robert Vanderbilt 1930- WhoMW 92
**Gortner**, Ross Aiken, Jr 1912- AmMWSc 92
**Gortner**, Susan Reichert 1932- AmMWSc 92
**Gortner**, Willis Alway 1913- AmMWSc 92
**Gorton**, Clarence Lynn 1911- WhoEnt 92
**Gorton**, Cynthia Ruth 1951- WhoWest 92
**Gorton**, John 1911- Who 92
**Gorton**, John Greg 1947- WhoWest 92
**Gorton**, John Grey 1911- IntWW 91
**Gorton**, Lesley Ann 1939- TwCPaSc
**Gorton**, Richard C. 1939- WhoFI 92
**Gorton**, Robert Lester 1931- AmMWSc 92
**Gorton**, Samuel 1592?-1677 BenetAL 91
**Gorton**, Slade 1928- AlmAP 92 [port], IntWW 91, WhoAmP 91, WhoWest 92
**Gorton**, Thomas Arthur 1910- WhoEnt 92
**Gortsema**, Frank Peter 1933- AmMWSc 92
**Gortvai**, Rosalinde Who 92
**Gorup**, Gregory James 1948- WhoFI 92
**Gorveatte**, Kenneth Layton 1935- WhoRel 92
**Gorz**, Herman Jacob 1920- AmMWSc 92
**Gorzelski**, Roman 1934- IntAu&W 91
**Gorzynski**, Eugene Arthur 1919- AmMWSc 92
**Gorzynski**, Janusz Gregory 1940- AmMWSc 92
**Gorzynski**, Timothy James 1950- AmMWSc 92
**Gosar**, Antone John 1930- WhoAmP 91
**Gosch**, Delores Marlene 1946- WhoMW 92
**Goschen** Who 92
**Goschen**, Viscount 1965- Who 92
**Goschen**, Edward 1913- Who 92
**Gosciewski**, Robert Louis 1957- WhoFI 92
**Gosdeck**, Thomas Joseph 1951- WhoAmL 92
**Gose**, Earl E 1934- AmMWSc 92
**Gose**, Elliott Bickley 1926- WhoWest 92
**Gose**, Richard Vernie 1927- WhoAmL 92, WhoFI 92, WhoWest 92
**Gosfield**, Edward, Jr 1918- AmMWSc 92
**Gosford**, Earl of 1942- Who 92
**Gosh**, Bobby 1936- WhoEnt 92
**Goshaw**, Alfred Thomas 1937- AmMWSc 92
**Goshen-Gottstein**, Moshe d1991 NewYTBS 91
**Goshgarian**, Robert Nelson 1956- WhoAmL 92
**Goshi**, Keiichi 1927- WhoWest 92
**Gosho**, Heinosuke 1902-1981 IntDcF 2-2
**Gosink**, Joan P 1941- AmMWSc 92
**Goskirk**, Ian 1932- Who 92
**Goskirk**, William Ian Macdonald 1932- IntWW 91
**Goslee**, Leonard Thomas 1932- WhoBlA 92
**Gosliga**, Martha DeGraaf 1954- WhoFI 92
**Goslin**, Roy Nelson 1904- AmMWSc 92
**Gosline**, John M 1943- AmMWSc 92
**Gosline**, Norman Abbot 1935- WhoFI 92
**Gosling**, Allan Gladstone 1933- Who 92
**Gosling**, Donald 1929- Who 92
**Gosling**, J. C. B. 1930- WrDr 92
**Gosling**, John Thomas 1938- AmMWSc 92
**Gosling**, Justin Cyril Bertrand 1930- IntWW 91, Who 92
**Gosling**, Paula 1939- WrDr 92
**Gosling**, Paula Louise 1939- IntAu&W 91
**Gosling**, Richard Bennett 1914- Who 92
**Goslow**, George E, Jr 1939- AmMWSc 92
**Gosman**, Albert Louis 1923- AmMWSc 92, WhoMW 92
**Gosman**, Robert F 1927- WhoAmP 91
**Gosnell**, Aubrey Brewer 1929- AmMWSc 92
**Gosnell**, Beverly Jones WhoAmP 91
**Gosnell**, Ricky Dale 1958- WhoRel 92
**Gosnell**, Thomas Hale 1920- WhoAmP 91
**Goss**, Carol 1947- WhoEnt 92
**Goss**, Charles Rapp, Jr 1937- AmMWSc 92
**Goss**, Clayton 1946- WhoBlA 92
**Goss**, Daniel Frederick 1932- WhoFI 92
**Goss**, David 1937- AmMWSc 92
**Goss**, David A 1948- AmMWSc 92
**Goss**, Frank, Jr. 1952- WhoBlA 92
**Goss**, Galen Lewis 1949- WhoFI 92
**Goss**, Gary Jack 1946- AmMWSc 92
**Goss**, George Robert 1952- AmMWSc 92
**Goss**, Glenn Richard 1932- WhoRel 92
**Goss**, James Arthur 1924- AmMWSc 92
**Goss**, Jay Bryan 1955- WhoAmL 92
**Goss**, Jerome Eldon 1935- WhoWest 92
**Goss**, Joel Francis 1955- WhoEnt 92
**Goss**, John Bradford 1956- WhoAmL 92
**Goss**, John Douglas 1942- AmMWSc 92
**Goss**, John R 1923- AmMWSc 92
**Goss**, Leonard George 1947- WhoFI 92, WhoMW 92, WhoRel 92
**Goss**, Linda WhoBlA 92
**Goss**, Louis George 1951- WhoMW 92
**Goss**, Nathaniel S 1826-1891 BiInAmS
**Goss**, Oscar Eugene 1926- WhoAmP 91
**Goss**, Porter J 1938- WhoAmP 91
**Goss**, Porter Johnston 1938- AlmAP 92 [port]
**Goss**, Richard John 1928- IntWW 91
**Goss**, Richard Johnson 1925- AmMWSc 92
**Goss**, Richard Oliver 1929- Who 92
**Goss**, Robert Charles 1929- AmMWSc 92
**Goss**, Robert Nichols 1921- AmMWSc 92
**Goss**, Robert Pike, Jr. 1943- WhoFI 92, WhoWest 92
**Goss**, Theresa Carter 1932- WhoBlA 92
**Goss**, Thomas Ashworth 1912- Who 92
**Goss**, Wilbur Hummon 1911- AmMWSc 92
**Goss**, William Epp 1941- WhoBlA 92
**Goss**, William Paul 1938- AmMWSc 92
**Goss-Seeger**, Debra A. 1958- WhoBlA 92
**Gossai**, Hemchand 1954- WhoRel 92
**Gossain**, Ved Vyas 1941- AmMWSc 92
**Gossan**, Brian Wesley 1954- WhoMW 92, WhoRel 92
**Gossard**, Arthur Charles 1935- AmMWSc 92
**Gossard**, Earl Everett 1923- AmMWSc 92, WhoWest 92
**Gosschalk**, Joseph Bernard 1936- Who 92
**Gosse**, Edmund 1849-1928 RfGEnL 91
**Gosse**, Sylvia 1881-1965 TwCPaSc
**Gossec**, Francois-Joseph 1734-1829 NewAmDM
**Gossel**, Thomas Alvin 1941- AmMWSc 92
**Gosselin**, Arthur Joseph AmMWSc 92
**Gosselin**, Edward A. 1943- WhoWest 92
**Gosselin**, Edward Alberic 1943- AmMWSc 92
**Gosselin**, Frances M 1930- WhoAmP 91
**Gosselin**, Gerald O 1931- WhoAmP 91
**Gosselin**, John William 1934- WhoAmL 92
**Gosselin**, Kenneth Stuart 1932- WhoRel 92
**Gosselin**, Peter G. 1951- ConAu 133
**Gosselin**, Richard A WhoAmP 91
**Gosselin**, Richard Pettengill 1921- AmMWSc 92
**Gosselin**, Robert Edmond 1919- AmMWSc 92
**Gosselin**, Timothy Richard 1955- WhoAmL 92
**Gosselink**, Eugene Paul 1937- AmMWSc 92
**Gosselink**, James G 1931- AmMWSc 92
**Gossels**, Claus Peter Rolf 1930- WhoAmL 92
**Gosser**, Lawrence Wayne 1938- AmMWSc 92
**Gosset**, Louis, Jr. 1936- IntMPA 92
**Gossett**, Barbara Jean 1956- WhoMW 92
**Gossett**, Billy Joe 1935- AmMWSc 92
**Gossett**, Charles Robert 1929- AmMWSc 92
**Gossett**, Dorsey McPeake 1931- AmMWSc 92
**Gossett**, Earl Fowler, Jr. 1933- WhoRel 92
**Gossett**, Hattie DrAPF 91
**Gossett**, James D 1924- WhoAmP 91
**Gossett**, James Michael 1950- AmMWSc 92
**Gossett**, Jon Kevin 1955- WhoEnt 92
**Gossett**, Kathryn Myers WhoMW 92
**Gossett**, Leigh Ann 1966- WhoFI 92
**Gossett**, Louis, Jr. 1936- WhoBlA 92, WhoEnt 92
**Gossett**, Oscar Milton 1925- WhoFI 92
**Gossett**, Philip 1941- WhoEnt 92, WhoMW 92
**Gossett**, Richard Glenn 1945- WhoMW 92
**Gossett**, Robert Francis, Jr. 1943- WhoFI 92
**Gossett**, Suzanne 1941- WhoMW 92
**Gossfeld**, Glenn Walter 1958- WhoMW 92
**Gosslee**, David Gilbert 1922- AmMWSc 92

**Gossling**, Jennifer 1934- AmMWSc 92
**Gossman**, Francis Joseph 1930- WhoRel 92
**Gossmann**, Hans Joachim 1955- AmMWSc 92
**Gostev**, Boris Ivanovich 1927- IntWW 91
**Gostin**, Jennifer DrAPF 91
**Gostin**, Larry 1949- Who 92
**Gostkowski**, Theodore P 1931- WhoIns 92
**Goswami**, Amit 1936- AmMWSc 92
**Goswami**, Bhuvenesh C 1937- AmMWSc 92
**Goswell**, Brian 1935- Who 92
**Goswitz**, Francis Andrew 1931- AmMWSc 92
**Goswitz**, Helen Vodopick 1931- AmMWSc 92
**Gosz**, James Roman 1940- AmMWSc 92
**Gotanda**, Philip Kan WhoEnt 92
**Gotbaum**, Joshua 1951- WhoFI 92
**Gotch**, Mike WhoAmP 91
**Gotch**, Tarquin 1952- WhoEnt 92
**Gotch**, Thomas Cooper 1854-1931 TwCPaSc
**Gotcher**, Jack Everett 1949- AmMWSc 92
**Gotcher**, James Ronald 1947- WhoAmL 92
**Gotelli**, David M 1943- AmMWSc 92
**Gotesky**, Rubin 1906- WhoMW 92
**Gotfryd**, Alexander d1991 NewYTBS 91
**Gotfryd**, Bernard 1924- ConAu 133
**Goth**, Andres 1914- AmMWSc 92
**Goth**, John W 1927- AmMWSc 92
**Goth**, John William 1927- WhoWest 92
**Goth**, Robert W 1927- AmMWSc 92
**Gothard**, Barbara Wheatley 1937- WhoBlA 92
**Gothard**, Donald L. 1934- WhoBlA 92
**Gothelf**, Bernard 1928- AmMWSc 92
**Gothoni**, Rene Reinhold 1950- WhoRel 92
**Gotimer**, Harry Albert 1947- WhoAmL 92
**Gotkin**, Michael Stanley 1942- WhoFI 92
**Gotlib**, Henryk 1890-1966 TwCPaSc
**Gotlieb**, Allan Ezra 1928- IntWW 91
**Gotlieb**, Avrum I 1946- AmMWSc 92
**Gotlieb**, C C 1921- AmMWSc 92
**Gotlieb**, Irwin I. 1949- WhoEnt 92
**Gotlieb**, Lawrence Barry 1948- WhoAmL 92
**Gotlieb**, Phyllis 1926- IntAu&W 91, TwCSFW 91, WrDr 92
**Goto**, Kimio 1926- WhoFI 92
**Goto**, Masao 1913- IntWW 91
**Goto**, Yasuo 1923- IntWW 91
**Gotoda**, Masaharu 1914- IntWW 91
**Gotoff**, Samuel P 1933- AmMWSc 92
**Gotolski**, William H 1926- AmMWSc 92
**Gots**, Joseph Simon 1917- AmMWSc 92
**Gotsch**, Peter Micah 1964- WhoMW 92
**Gotschalk**, Felix C 1929- TwCSFW 91, WrDr 92
**Gotschlich**, Emil C 1935- AmMWSc 92
**Gotsdiner**, Murray Bennett 1953- WhoMW 92
**Gotshall**, Daniel Warren 1929- AmMWSc 92
**Gotshall**, Jan Doyle 1942- WhoFI 92
**Gotshall**, Mark Edward 1960- WhoMW 92
**Gotshall**, Robert William 1945- AmMWSc 92
**Gotsopoulos**, Barbara Lynn 1948- WhoFI 92
**Gott**, Euyen 1915- AmMWSc 92
**Gott**, George DrAPF 91
**Gott**, Harold Dean 1953- WhoRel 92
**Gott**, J Richard, III 1947- AmMWSc 92
**Gott**, Karel 1939- IntWW 91
**Gott**, Preston Frazier 1919- AmMWSc 92
**Gott**, Richard 1938- WrDr 92
**Gott**, Robert Dean 1946- WhoAmP 91
**Gott**, Vincent Lynn 1927- AmMWSc 92
**Gotte**, Klaus 1932- IntWW 91
**Gotterer**, Gerald S 1933- AmMWSc 92
**Gotterer**, Malcolm Harold 1924- AmMWSc 92
**Gottesfeld**, Zehava AmMWSc 92
**Gottesman**, Elihu 1919- AmMWSc 92
**Gottesman**, Meyer 1935- WhoEnt 92
**Gottesman**, Michael 1946- AmMWSc 92
**Gottesman**, Roy Tully 1928- AmMWSc 92
**Gottesman**, Scott 1957- WhoIns 92
**Gottesman**, Stephen T 1939- AmMWSc 92
**Gottesman**, Stuart IntMPA 92
**Gottfried**, Bradley M 1950- AmMWSc 92
**Gottfried**, Byron S 1934- AmMWSc 92
**Gottfried**, Eugene Leslie 1929- AmMWSc 92, WhoWest 92
**Gottfried**, Kurt 1929- AmMWSc 92
**Gottfried**, Mark Ellis 1953- WhoFI 92
**Gottfried**, Paul 1927- AmMWSc 92
**Gottfried**, Richard Norman 1947- WhoAmP 91
**Gottfried**, Robert Lewis 1950- WhoEnt 92
**Gottheil**, Edward 1924- AmMWSc 92
**Gottheil**, William Samuel 1859-1920 BilnAmS
**Gottheimer**, George M., Jr. 1933- WhoIns 92
**Gotthelf**, Beth 1958- WhoAmL 92
**Gottlander**, Robert Jan Lars 1956- WhoMW 92
**Gottlieb**, A Arthur AmMWSc 92
**Gottlieb**, Abraham Mitchell 1909- AmMWSc 92
**Gottlieb**, Alan Merril 1947- WhoWest 92
**Gottlieb**, Allan 1945- AmMWSc 92
**Gottlieb**, Alma 1954- IntAu&W 91
**Gottlieb**, Amy DrAPF 91
**Gottlieb**, Annie 1946- ConAu 135
**Gottlieb**, Arlan J 1933- AmMWSc 92
**Gottlieb**, Barry Nelson 1944- WhoFI 92
**Gottlieb**, Bernard 1913- Who 92
**Gottlieb**, Carl 1938- IntMPA 92
**Gottlieb**, Charles F 1944- AmMWSc 92
**Gottlieb**, Daniel Henry 1937- AmMWSc 92, WhoMW 92
**Gottlieb**, Daniel Seth 1954- WhoAmL 92
**Gottlieb**, Darcy DrAPF 91
**Gottlieb**, David Neil 1947- WhoEnt 92
**Gottlieb**, Elaine DrAPF 91
**Gottlieb**, Elizabeth Geyer 1951- WhoEnt 92
**Gottlieb**, Frank P. 1945- WhoEnt 92
**Gottlieb**, Frederick Jay 1935- AmMWSc 92
**Gottlieb**, Gerald Lane 1941- AmMWSc 92
**Gottlieb**, Gidon Alain Guy 1932- WhoAmL 92
**Gottlieb**, Gilbert 1929- AmMWSc 92
**Gottlieb**, Irvin M 1921- AmMWSc 92
**Gottlieb**, James R 1947- WhoAmP 91
**Gottlieb**, Jane Ellen 1954- WhoEnt 92
**Gottlieb**, Janet 1954- WhoAmL 92
**Gottlieb**, Karen Ann 1951- AmMWSc 92
**Gottlieb**, Leon Herbert 1927- WhoWest 92
**Gottlieb**, Leonard Solomon 1927- AmMWSc 92
**Gottlieb**, Lester M. 1932- WhoFI 92
**Gottlieb**, Marise Suss 1938- AmMWSc 92
**Gottlieb**, Melvin Burt 1917- AmMWSc 92
**Gottlieb**, Melvin Harvey 1929- AmMWSc 92
**Gottlieb**, Michael Stuart 1947- AmMWSc 92
**Gottlieb**, Milton 1933- AmMWSc 92
**Gottlieb**, Morton Edgar 1921- WhoEnt 92
**Gottlieb**, Otto Richard 1920- AmMWSc 92
**Gottlieb**, Paul 1935- IntWW 91
**Gottlieb**, Paul David 1943- AmMWSc 92
**Gottlieb**, Paul E. 1936- WhoEnt 92
**Gottlieb**, Paul Mitchel 1954- WhoAmL 92
**Gottlieb**, Paula Gribetz 1957- WhoRel 92
**Gottlieb**, Peter 1935- AmMWSc 92
**Gottlieb**, Robert Adams 1931- IntWW 91, Who 92
**Gottlieb**, Sanford 1926- WhoAmP 91
**Gottlieb**, Scott C. 1952- WhoAmL 92
**Gottlieb**, Sheldon F 1932- AmMWSc 92
**Gottlieb**, Steven Arthur 1952- AmMWSc 92, WhoMW 92
**Gottling**, James Goe 1932- AmMWSc 92
**Gottmann**, Jean 1915- Who 92
**Gottmann**, Jean-Iona 1915- IntWW 91
**Gotto**, Antonio Marion, Jr 1935- AmMWSc 92
**Gottovi**, Karen Elizabeth 1941- WhoAmP 91
**Gottron**, Francis Robert, III 1953- WhoMW 92
**Gottry**, Steven Roger 1946- WhoEnt 92
**Gottschalg**, Melvin G 1921- WhoAmP 91
**Gottschalk**, Alexander 1932- AmMWSc 92
**Gottschalk**, Alfred 1930- WhoMW 92, WhoRel 92
**Gottschalk**, Arthur William 1952- WhoEnt 92
**Gottschalk**, Bernard 1935- AmMWSc 92
**Gottschalk**, Carl William 1922- AmMWSc 92, IntWW 91
**Gottschalk**, Donald Eugene 1934- WhoMW 92
**Gottschalk**, Frank Klaus 1932- WhoFI 92
**Gottschalk**, Gerhard 1935- IntWW 91
**Gottschalk**, Joachim 1904-1941 EncTR 91 [port]
**Gottschalk**, John Simison 1912- AmMWSc 92
**Gottschalk**, Laura Riding ConAu 135, WrDr 92
**Gottschalk**, Leonard 1924- WhoEnt 92
**Gottschalk**, Louis August 1916- AmMWSc 92
**Gottschalk**, Louis Moreau 1829-1869 NewAmDM
**Gottschalk**, Mark Jon 1952- WhoEnt 92
**Gottschalk**, Mary Therese 1931- WhoRel 92
**Gottschalk**, Max Jules 1909- WhoWest 92
**Gottschalk**, Nathan 1915- WhoEnt 92
**Gottschalk**, Patrick Owen 1953- WhoAmL 92
**Gottschalk**, Robert Neal 1928- AmMWSc 92
**Gottschalk**, Stephen Elmer 1947- WhoAmL 92
**Gottschalk**, Thomas A. 1942- WhoAmL 92
**Gottschall**, Edward M. 1915- ConAu 133
**Gottschall**, Robert James 1935- AmMWSc 92
**Gottschall**, W Carl 1938- AmMWSc 92
**Gottschang**, Jack Louis 1923- AmMWSc 92
**Gottsched**, Johann Christoph 1700-1766 BlkwCEP
**Gottschlich**, Chad F 1929- AmMWSc 92
**Gottscho**, Alfred M 1919- AmMWSc 92
**Gottscho**, Richard Alan 1952- AmMWSc 92
**Gottsegen**, Robert 1919- AmMWSc 92
**Gottshall**, Franklin H. 1902- WrDr 92
**Gottstein**, Barnard Jacob 1925- WhoFI 92, WhoWest 92
**Gottstein**, Barney J WhoAmP 91
**Gottstein**, William J 1929- AmMWSc 92
**Gottwald**, Floyd Dewey, Jr. 1922- WhoFI 92
**Gottwald**, George J. 1914- WhoRel 92
**Gottwald**, Jimmy Thorne 1938- AmMWSc 92
**Gottwald**, Klement 1896-1953 FacFETw [port]
**Gottwald**, Richard Landolin 1941- WhoMW 92
**Gottwald**, Timothy R 1953- AmMWSc 92
**Gotwald**, William Harrison, Jr 1939- AmMWSc 92
**Gotz**, Alexander 1928- IntWW 91
**Gotz**, Ignacio L. 1933- WrDr 92
**Gotze**, Heinz 1912- IntWW 91
**Goubau**, Georg 1906-1980 FacFETw
**Goubau**, Wolfgang M 1944- AmMWSc 92
**Goubran**, Emile Zola 1942- WhoWest 92
**Goud**, Paul A 1937- AmMWSc 92
**Goudarzi**, Gus 1918- AmMWSc 92
**Goudev**, Vladimir Victorovich 1940- IntWW 91
**Goudey**, Maurice Russel 1907- WhoEnt 92
**Goudge**, Eileen 1950- IntAu&W 91
**Goudie**, Andrew Shaw 1945- Who 92
**Goudie**, James Who 92
**Goudie**, John Carrick 1919- Who 92
**Goudie**, Thomas James 1942- Who 92
**Goudie**, William Henry 1916- Who 92
**Goudimel**, Claude 1515?-1572 NewAmDM
**Goudinoff**, Peter WhoAmP 91
**Goudsmit**, Esther Marianne 1933- AmMWSc 92
**Goudsmit**, Samuel A 1902-1978 FacFETw
**Goudy**, Andrew James 1943- WhoBlA 92
**Goudy**, Eugene 1961- WhoFI 92
**Goudy**, Frederic W. 1865-1947 DcTwDes, FacFETw
**Goudy**, Frederic William 1865-1947 BenetAL 91
**Goudy**, James Joseph Ralph 1952- WhoMW 92
**Goudy**, Josephine Gray 1925- WhoMW 92
**Goudy**, Willis John 1942- WhoMW 92
**Gouge**, Edward Max 1947- AmMWSc 92
**Gouge**, Susan Cornelia Jones 1924- AmMWSc 92
**Gougelman**, Paul Reina 1951- WhoAmL 92
**Gougeon**, Len 1947- ConAu 135
**Gouges**, Olympe de 1748-1793 BlkwCEP
**Gough** Who 92
**Gough**, Viscount 1941- Who 92
**Gough**, Barry Morton 1938- IntWW 91
**Gough**, Brandon Who 92
**Gough**, Cecil Ernest Freeman 1911- Who 92
**Gough**, Charles Brandon 1937- Who 92
**Gough**, David Arthur 1946- AmMWSc 92
**Gough**, Denis Ian 1922- AmMWSc 92
**Gough**, Francis Jacob 1928- AmMWSc 92
**Gough**, Frank Dixon, II 1959- WhoRel 92
**Gough**, Harrison Gould 1921- WhoWest 92
**Gough**, Hugh Rowlands 1905- IntWW 91, Who 92
**Gough**, John 1910- Who 92
**Gough**, John Francis 1934- WhoAmL 92
**Gough**, Larry Phillips 1944- AmMWSc 92
**Gough**, Lillian 1918- AmMWSc 92
**Gough**, Michael 1917- IntMPA 92, IntWW 91
**Gough**, Michael 1939- AmMWSc 92
**Gough**, Michael John 1939- WhoIns 92
**Gough**, Oran Dean 1937- WhoEnt 92
**Gough**, Paul 1958- TwCPaSc
**Gough**, Robert Edward 1949- AmMWSc 92
**Gough**, Robert George 1939- AmMWSc 92
**Gough**, Sidney Roger 1938- AmMWSc 92
**Gough**, Stephen Bradford 1950- AmMWSc 92
**Gough**, Walter C. 1943- WhoBlA 92
**Gough**, William Cabot 1930- WhoWest 92
**Gough**, William John 1945- WhoEnt 92
**Gough-Calthorpe** Who 92
**Gougis**, Lorna Gail 1948- WhoBlA 92
**Gouhier**, Henri Gaston 1898- IntWW 91
**Gouin**, Francis R 1938- AmMWSc 92
**Gouin**, Warner Peter 1954- WhoMW 92
**Gouk**, Alan 1939- TwCPaSc
**Gouke**, Cecil Granville 1928- WhoFI 92, WhoMW 92
**Goukouni Oueddei** IntWW 91
**Goulah**, Dorothy Maria WhoEnt 92
**Goulard**, Bernard 1933- AmMWSc 92
**Goulart**, Ron 1933- TwCSFW 91, WrDr 92
**Goulazian**, Peter Robert 1940- WhoEnt 92, WhoFI 92
**Goulbourne**, Donald Samuel, Jr. 1950- WhoBlA 92
**Gould**, A Lawrence 1941- AmMWSc 92
**Gould**, Adair Brasted 1916- AmMWSc 92
**Gould**, Alan I. 1940- WhoAmL 92
**Gould**, Anne Bramlee 1928- AmMWSc 92
**Gould**, Arthur 1924- WhoEnt 92
**Gould**, Augustus Addison 1805-1866 BilnAmS
**Gould**, Barbara Bodichon Ayrton 1886-1950 BiDBrF 2
**Gould**, Benjamin Apthorp, Jr 1824-1896 BilnAmS
**Gould**, Bette WhoRel 92
**Gould**, Bryan Charles 1939- IntWW 91, Who 92
**Gould**, Cecil 1918- WrDr 92
**Gould**, Cecil Hilton Monk 1918- Who 92
**Gould**, Celia R 1957- WhoAmP 91
**Gould**, Charles F 1932- WhoAmP 91
**Gould**, Charles Jay 1912- AmMWSc 92
**Gould**, Chester 1900-1985 Au&Arts 7 [port], FacFETw
**Gould**, Christopher M 1951- AmMWSc 92
**Gould**, Christopher Robert 1944- AmMWSc 92
**Gould**, Clio LaVerne 1919- WhoWest 92
**Gould**, David 1940- WhoAmL 92
**Gould**, David Foster, III 1952- WhoAmL 92
**Gould**, David Huntington 1921- AmMWSc 92
**Gould**, Debra Frances 1952- WhoEnt 92
**Gould**, Diana WhoEnt 92
**Gould**, Donald 1919- Who 92
**Gould**, Donald Everett 1932- WhoFI 92
**Gould**, Donald Paul 1958- WhoWest 92
**Gould**, Douglas Jay 1923- AmMWSc 92
**Gould**, Edward John Humphrey 1943- Who 92
**Gould**, Edward Ward 1957- WhoAmL 92
**Gould**, Edwin 1933- AmMWSc 92
**Gould**, Edwin Sheldon 1926- AmMWSc 92
**Gould**, Elliott 1938- IntMPA 92, IntWW 91, WhoEnt 92
**Gould**, Ernest Morton, Jr 1918- AmMWSc 92
**Gould**, G G 1913- AmMWSc 92
**Gould**, Gary Howard 1938- WhoAmP 91
**Gould**, George D. 1927- WhoFI 92
**Gould**, George Edwin 1905- AmMWSc 92
**Gould**, Geraldine Suzanne 1943- WhoHisp 92
**Gould**, Geri Jimenez 1943- WhoHisp 92
**Gould**, Glenn 1932-1982 FacFETw, NewAmDM
**Gould**, Glenn Hunting 1949- WhoFI 92
**Gould**, Harold 1923- IntMPA 92, WhoEnt 92
**Gould**, Harry Edward, Jr. 1938- WhoFI 92
**Gould**, Harry J, III 1947- AmMWSc 92
**Gould**, Harvey A 1938- AmMWSc 92
**Gould**, Harvey Allen 1945- AmMWSc 92
**Gould**, Henry Wadsworth 1928- AmMWSc 92
**Gould**, Herbert J. 1927- WhoWest 92
**Gould**, Howard M. 1962- WhoWest 92
**Gould**, Howard Ross 1921- AmMWSc 92
**Gould**, Jack LesBEnT 92
**Gould**, Jack Richard 1922- AmMWSc 92
**Gould**, James A. 1922- WrDr 92
**Gould**, James L 1945- AmMWSc 92, WrDr 92
**Gould**, James P AmMWSc 92
**Gould**, James Spencer 1922- WhoFI 92
**Gould**, Jay 1836-1892 RComAH
**Gould**, Jay Sheldon 1947- WhoFI 92
**Gould**, John 1908- BenetAL 91
**Gould**, John Charles 1915- Who 92
**Gould**, John Michael 1949- AmMWSc 92
**Gould**, John Philip, Jr. 1939- WhoFI 92
**Gould**, Joseph 1915- IntMPA 92
**Gould**, Joyce Brenda 1932- Who 92
**Gould**, K Lance 1938- AmMWSc 92
**Gould**, Kenneth 1967- BlkOlyM
**Gould**, Kenneth Alan 1949- AmMWSc 92
**Gould**, Kenneth B. 1955- WhoAmL 92
**Gould**, Kenneth G 1943- AmMWSc 92
**Gould**, Lawrence A 1930- AmMWSc 92
**Gould**, Leonard A 1927- AmMWSc 92
**Gould**, Lewis Henry 1950- WhoEnt 92
**Gould**, Lewis Jerome 1932- WhoAmL 92
**Gould**, Lois DrAPF 91, WrDr 92
**Gould**, Margery Lemlech 1965- WhoWest 92
**Gould**, Mark WhoEnt 92
**Gould**, Mark D 1946- AmMWSc 92
**Gould**, Martha B. 1931- WhoWest 92
**Gould**, Marty Leon 1949- WhoRel 92
**Gould**, Maxine Lubow 1942- WhoFI 92, WhoWest 92

**Gould**, Michael Nathan 1947- *AmMWSc 92*
**Gould**, Morton 1913- *ConCom 92, IntWW 91, NewAmDM, WhoEnt 92*
**Gould**, Patricia 1924- *Who 92*
**Gould**, Peter 1932- *WrDr 92*
**Gould**, Phillip 1940- *AmMWSc 92*
**Gould**, Phillip L 1937- *AmMWSc 92*
**Gould**, R Budd 1937- *WhoAmP 91*
**Gould**, R. Martin 1941- *WhoFI 92*
**Gould**, Richard A *WhoAmP 91*
**Gould**, Robert George 1947- *AmMWSc 92*
**Gould**, Robert Henderson 1919- *AmMWSc 92*
**Gould**, Robert James 1954- *AmMWSc 92*
**Gould**, Robert Joseph 1935- *AmMWSc 92*
**Gould**, Robert K 1929- *AmMWSc 92*
**Gould**, Robert Kinkade 1940- *AmMWSc 92*
**Gould**, Robert L. 1938- *WhoFI 92*
**Gould**, Robert R *WhoAmP 91*
**Gould**, Robert Simonton 1826-1904 *DcNCBi 2*
**Gould**, Robert William 1934- *AmMWSc 92*
**Gould**, Roberta *DrAPF 91*
**Gould**, Roy W 1927- *AmMWSc 92*
**Gould**, Sam 1942- *WhoMW 92*
**Gould**, Stephen Jay 1941- *AmMWSc 92, FacFETw, IntWW 91, WrDr 92*
**Gould**, Steven James 1946- *AmMWSc 92*
**Gould**, Syd S. 1912- *WhoFI 92*
**Gould**, Terry Allen 1942- *WhoAmL 92*
**Gould**, Thomas William 1914- *Who 92*
**Gould**, Walter Leonard 1923- *AmMWSc 92*
**Gould**, Walter Phillip 1925- *AmMWSc 92*
**Gould**, Wilbur Alphonso 1920- *AmMWSc 92*
**Gould**, William Allen 1941- *AmMWSc 92*
**Gould**, William Benjamin, IV 1936- *WhoAmL 92, WhoBlA 92*
**Gould**, William Blair 1924- *WhoRel 92*
**Gould**, William Douglas 1944- *AmMWSc 92*
**Gould**, William E 1934- *AmMWSc 92*
**Gould**, William F 1934- *WhoIns 92*
**Gould**, William Max 1939- *WhoMW 92*
**Gould**, William Richard 1919- *AmMWSc 92*
**Gould**, William Robert, III 1931- *AmMWSc 92*
**Gould-Somero**, Meredith 1940- *AmMWSc 92*
**Goulden**, Clyde Edward 1936- *AmMWSc 92*
**Goulden**, John 1941- *Who 92*
**Goulden**, Joseph C 1934- *IntAu&W 91, WrDr 92*
**Goulden**, Peter Derrick 1930- *AmMWSc 92*
**Goulder**, Diane Kessler 1950- *WhoAmL 92*
**Goulder**, Gerald Polster 1953- *WhoFI 92*
**Gouldey**, Bruce K. 1952- *WhoFI 92*
**Gouldey**, Glenn Charles 1952- *WhoFI 92, WhoMW 92*
**Goulding**, Charles Edwin, Jr 1916- *AmMWSc 92*
**Goulding**, Edmund 1891-1959 *IntDcF 2-2 [port]*
**Goulding**, Francis Robert 1810-1881 *BenetAL 91*
**Goulding**, Irvine 1910- *Who 92*
**Goulding**, Lingard *Who 92*
**Goulding**, Marrack Irvine 1936- *IntWW 91, Who 92*
**Goulding**, Miriam Bower 1942- *WhoAmL 92*
**Goulding**, Nora 1944- *WhoEnt 92*
**Goulding**, Paul Edmund 1934- *WhoAmP 91*
**Goulding**, Ray 1922-1990 *AnObit 1990, ConAu 36NR*
**Goulding**, Robert Lee, Jr 1920- *AmMWSc 92*
**Goulding**, William Lingard 1940- *Who 92*
**Gouldthorpe**, Kenneth Alfred Percival 1928- *WhoWest 92*
**Gouled Aptidon**, Hassan 1916- *IntWW 91*
**Goulet**, Harvey E, Jr 1941- *WhoAmP 91*
**Goulet**, Jacques 1946- *AmMWSc 92*
**Goulet**, John *DrAPF 91*
**Goulet**, Maurice 1932- *WhoAmP 91*
**Goulet**, Robert 1933- *IntMPA 92*
**Goulet**, Robert Gerard 1933- *WhoEnt 92*
**Goulet**, William Dawson 1941- *WhoWest 92*
**Goulian**, Dicran 1927- *AmMWSc 92*
**Goulian**, Mehran 1929- *AmMWSc 92, IntWW 91, WhoWest 92*
**Goulianos**, Konstantin 1935- *AmMWSc 92*
**Goulli**, Slaheddine El 1919- *IntWW 91*
**Goulson**, Hilton Thomas 1930- *AmMWSc 92*
**Goulty**, Alan Fletcher 1947- *Who 92*
**Gounaris**, Anne Demetra 1924- *AmMWSc 92*
**Gounelle De Pontanel**, Hugues 1903- *IntWW 91*
**Gounis**, Peter Edgar 1944- *WhoRel 92*
**Gounley**, Dennis Joseph 1950- *WhoAmL 92*
**Gounod**, Charles 1818-1893 *NewAmDM*
**Goupil**, Adolphe 1806-1893 *ThHEIm*
**Gour**, Betty 1914- *WhoEnt 92, WhoMW 92*
**Gourad Hamadou**, Barkad *IntWW 91*
**Gouraige**, Ghislain, Jr. 1959- *WhoFI 92*
**Gourary**, Barry Sholom 1923- *AmMWSc 92*
**Gouras**, Peter 1930- *AmMWSc 92*
**Gouraud**, Marie-Michel d1991 *NewYTBS 91*
**Gourdeau**, Raymond H 1936- *WhoAmP 91*
**Gourdie**, Tom 1913- *WrDr 92*
**Gourdin**, David Irvin, Jr. 1949- *WhoWest 92*
**Gourdin**, Edward Orval 1897-1966 *BlkOlyM*
**Gourdine**, Delcie Southall *DrAPF 91*
**Gourdine**, Meredith C 1929- *BlkOlyM*
**Gourdine**, Meredith Charles 1929- *AmMWSc 92*
**Gourdine**, Simon Peter 1940- *WhoBlA 92*
**Gourdon**, Alain 1928- *IntWW 91*
**Gourishankar**, V 1929- *AmMWSc 92*
**Gourisse**, Daniel 1939- *IntWW 91*
**Gourlay**, Basil Ian 1920- *Who 92*
**Gourlay**, David 1922- *WrDr 92*
**Gourlay**, Ian *Who 92*
**Gourlay**, Janet *Who 92*
**Gourlay**, Simon 1934- *Who 92*
**Gourley**, Desmond Robert Hugh 1922- *AmMWSc 92*
**Gourley**, Eugene Vincent 1940- *AmMWSc 92*
**Gourley**, James Leland 1919- *WhoFI 92*
**Gourley**, James Walter, III 1941- *WhoFI 92*
**Gourley**, Lloyd Eugene, Jr 1923- *AmMWSc 92*
**Gourley**, Paul Lee 1952- *AmMWSc 92*
**Gourmont**, Remy de 1858-1915 *GuFrLit 1*
**Gournay**, Marie Le Jars de 1565-1645 *FrenWW*
**Goursaud**, Anne Renee Mauricette D. *WhoWest 92*
**Gourse**, Jerome Allen 1929- *AmMWSc 92*
**Gourse**, Richard Lawrence 1949- *AmMWSc 92*
**Gourvitz**, Elliot Howard 1945- *WhoAmL 92*
**Gourzis**, James Theophile 1928- *AmMWSc 92*
**Gouse**, S William, Jr 1931- *AmMWSc 92, WhoAmP 91*
**Goust**, Jean Michel 1941- *AmMWSc 92*
**Goustin**, Anton Scott 1953- *AmMWSc 92*
**Goutard**, Noel 1931- *IntWW 91*
**Gouterman**, Martin 1931- *AmMWSc 92*
**Goutman**, Lois Clair 1923- *WhoEnt 92*
**Goutmann**, Michel Marcel 1939- *AmMWSc 92*
**Gouttiere**, John P. 1949- *WhoAmL 92*
**Gouvin**, Eric Joseph 1961- *WhoAmL 92*
**Gouw**, T H 1933- *AmMWSc 92*
**Gouwens**, David J. 1948- *WhoRel 92*
**Gouyon**, Paul 1910- *IntWW 91, WhoRel 92*
**Gouyou Beauchamps**, Xavier 1937- *IntWW 91*
**Govan**, Daniel Chevilette 1829-1911 *DcNCBi 2*
**Govan**, Duncan Eben 1923- *AmMWSc 92*
**Govan**, Lawrence 1919- *Who 92*
**Govan**, Ronald M. 1931- *WhoBlA 92*
**Govan**, Sandra Yvonne 1948- *WhoBlA 92*
**Gove**, Anna Maria 1867-1948 *DcNCBi 2*
**Gove**, Harry Edmund 1922- *AmMWSc 92*
**Gove**, Norwood Babcock 1932- *AmMWSc 92*
**Goveia**, Stephen Arthur 1951- *WhoFI 92*
**Gover**, Alan Shore 1948- *WhoAmL 92*
**Gover**, David Howe 1940- *WhoMW 92*
**Gover**, James E 1940- *AmMWSc 92*
**Gover**, James Edwin 1940- *WhoFI 92*
**Gover**, Robert 1929- *BenetAL 91, ConNov 91, IntAu&W 91, WrDr 92*
**Gover**, Timothy Daniel 1938- *WhoFI 92*
**Governale**, Constance Ann 1947- *WhoFI 92*
**Governale**, Frank Michael 1958- *WhoEnt 92*
**Governo**, David Michael 1956- *WhoAmL 92*
**Govett**, Gerald James 1932- *AmMWSc 92*
**Govett**, William John Romaine 1937- *Who 92*
**Govi**, O. *WrDr 92*
**Govier**, G W 1917- *AmMWSc 92*
**Govier**, Gordon 1946- *TwCPaSc*
**Govier**, Gordon Oliver 1951- *WhoEnt 92*
**Govier**, William Charles 1936- *AmMWSc 92*
**Govier**, William Miller 1915- *AmMWSc 92*
**Govil**, Narendra Kumar 1940- *AmMWSc 92*
**Govil**, Sanjay 1962- *AmMWSc 92*
**Govin**, Charles Thomas, Jr 1946- *AmMWSc 92*
**Govind**, Choonilal Keshav 1938- *AmMWSc 92*
**Govinda**, Anagarika 1898-1985 *RelLAm 91*
**Govindarajulu**, Zakkula 1933- *AmMWSc 92*
**Govindjee**, M 1933- *AmMWSc 92*
**Govoni**, Corrado 1884-1965 *DcLB 114 [port]*
**Govoni**, Stephen James 1949- *WhoFI 92*
**Govorov**, Leonid Aleksandrovich 1897-1955 *SovUnBD*
**Govorov**, Vladimir Leonidovich 1924- *IntWW 91, SovUnBD*
**Gow**, Ian 1937-1990 *AnObit 1990*
**Gow**, Jack Frank 1920- *WhoFI 92*
**Gow**, James Ellis 1877-1914 *BiInAmS*
**Gow**, James Michael 1924- *Who 92*
**Gow**, Jane 1944- *Who 92*
**Gow**, John Stobie 1933- *Who 92*
**Gow**, K V 1919- *AmMWSc 92*
**Gow**, Leonard Maxwell H. *Who 92*
**Gow**, Linda Yvonne Cherwin 1948- *WhoFI 92*
**Gow**, Michael *Who 92*
**Gow**, Michael 1924- *IntWW 91*
**Gow**, Neil 1932- *Who 92*
**Gow**, Ronald 1897- *WrDr 92*
**Gow**, Wendy *Who 92*
**Gow**, William Alexander 1920- *AmMWSc 92*
**Gow**, William Connell 1909- *Who 92*
**Gowan**, Joseph Patrick, Jr. 1939- *WhoFI 92*
**Gowans**, Alan 1923- *WrDr 92*
**Gowans**, Charles Shields 1923- *AmMWSc 92*
**Gowans**, Gregory *Who 92*
**Gowans**, James 1924- *Who 92*
**Gowans**, James L 1924- *AmMWSc 92*
**Gowans**, James Learmonth 1924- *IntWW 91*
**Gowans**, James Palmer 1930- *Who 92*
**Gowans**, Urban Gregory 1904- *Who 92*
**Gowar**, Norman William 1940- *Who 92*
**Goward**, Richard French, Jr. 1955- *WhoWest 92*
**Goward**, Russell 1935- *WhoAmP 91*
**Goward**, Russell A. 1935- *WhoBlA 92*
**Gowda**, Deve Javare 1918- *Who 92*
**Gowda**, Narasimhan Ramaiah 1949- *WhoFI 92, WhoMW 92*
**Gowda**, Netkal M Made 1947- *AmMWSc 92*
**Gowdey**, Charles Willis 1920- *AmMWSc 92*
**Gowdy**, Curt *LesBEnT 92*
**Gowdy**, Curt 1919- *IntMPA 92*
**Gowdy**, David Clive 1946- *Who 92*
**Gowdy**, Franklin Brockway 1945- *WhoAmL 92*
**Gowdy**, John Norman 1945- *AmMWSc 92*
**Gowdy**, Kenneth King 1932- *AmMWSc 92*
**Gowdy**, Robert C 1943- *WhoIns 92*
**Gowdy**, Robert Henry 1941- *AmMWSc 92*
**Gowdy**, Spenser O 1941- *AmMWSc 92*
**Gowe**, Robb Shelton 1921- *AmMWSc 92*
**Gowell**, Gilbert M 1845?-1908 *BiInAmS*
**Gowen**, Doris Dean 1928- *WhoMW 92*
**Gowen**, George W. 1929- *WhoAmL 92*
**Gowen**, James A. 1928-1981 *ConAu 134*
**Gowen**, Richard J 1935- *AmMWSc 92*
**Gowen**, Richard Joseph 1935- *WhoMW 92*
**Gowenlock**, Brian Glover 1926- *Who 92*
**Gowens**, Walter, II 1954- *WhoFI 92*
**Gower** *Who 92*
**Gower**, David Ivon 1957- *IntWW 91*
**Gower**, Godfrey Philip 1899- *Who 92*
**Gower**, Iris 1939- *WrDr 92*
**Gower**, Jim *Who 92*
**Gower**, John 1330?-1408 *RfGEnL 91*
**Gower**, John Clark 1941- *WhoAmP 91*
**Gower**, John Hugh 1925- *Who 92*
**Gower**, Laurence Cecil Bartlett 1913- *Who 92*
**Gower**, Thomas Charles 1926- *WhoAmP 91*
**Gower Isaac**, Anthony John *Who 92*
**Gowers**, Mont Alva 1915- *WhoWest 92*
**Gowgiel**, Joseph Michael 1926- *AmMWSc 92*
**Gowing**, Lawrence 1918- *IntAu&W 91, TwCPaSc, WrDr 92*
**Gowing**, Lawrence 1918-1991 *ConAu 133, NewYTBS 91 [port]*
**Gowing**, Lawrence Burnett d1991 *Who 92N*
**Gowing**, Margaret Mary 1921- *IntWW 91, Who 92, WrDr 92*
**Gowing**, Noel Frank Collett 1917- *Who 92*
**Gowland**, M.L. *DrAPF 91*
**Gowland**, William d1991 *Who 92N*
**Gowlland**, Mark 1943- *Who 92*
**Gowon**, Yakuba 1934- *FacFETw*
**Gowon**, Yakubu 1934- *IntWW 91, Who 92*
**Gowrie**, Earl of 1939- *Who 92*
**Gowrie**, The Earl of 1939- *IntWW 91*
**Goy**, David John Lister 1949- *Who 92*
**Goy**, Robert William 1924- *AmMWSc 92*
**Goya y Lucientes**, Francisco Jose de 1746-1828 *BlkwCEP*
**Goyal**, Megh R 1949- *AmMWSc 92*
**Goyal**, Raj K *AmMWSc 92*
**Goyal**, Suresh 1960- *AmMWSc 92*
**Goyan**, Jere Edwin 1930- *AmMWSc 92*
**Goyco**, Rafael *WhoHisp 92*
**Goyco-Graziani**, Ana Nisi *WhoAmP 91*
**Goyder**, Daniel George 1938- *Who 92*
**Goyder**, George Armin 1908- *Who 92, WrDr 92*
**Goyen**, William 1915-1983 *BenetAL 91*
**Goyenche**, Jose Manuel 1775-1846 *HisDSpE*
**Goyeneche y Barreda**, Pedro Mariano 1772-1844 *HisDSpE*
**Goyer**, Jean-Pierre 1932- *IntWW 91*
**Goyer**, Robert Andrew 1927- *AmMWSc 92*
**Goyer**, Robert G 1938- *AmMWSc 92*
**Goyer**, Virginia L. 1942- *WhoFI 92*
**Goyert**, Sanna Mather *AmMWSc 92*
**Goyette**, Geoffrey Robert 1948- *WhoMW 92*
**Goyings**, Lloyd Samuel 1933- *AmMWSc 92*
**Goytisolo**, Agustin de 1924- *WhoHisp 92*
**Goytisolo**, Juan 1931- *LiExTwC*
**Goz**, Barry 1937- *AmMWSc 92*
**Goz**, Harry G. 1932- *WhoEnt 92*
**Gozon**, Jozsef Stephan 1933- *WhoMW 92*
**Gozonsky**, Edwin S. 1930- *WhoFI 92*
**Gozzano**, Guido 1883-1916 *DcLB 114 [port]*
**Gozzo**, James J 1943- *AmMWSc 92*
**Graae**, Johan E A 1909- *AmMWSc 92*
**Graaff**, de Villiers, Sir 1913- *IntWW 91, Who 92*
**Grab**, Eugene Granville, Jr 1914- *AmMWSc 92*
**Graba**, Jayson L *WhoAmP 91*
**Grabar**, Andre d1990 *IntWW 91N*
**Grabar'**, Igor' Emmanuilovich 1871-1960 *SovUnBD*
**Grabar'**, Vladimir Emmanuilovich 1865-1956 *SovUnBD*
**Grabarek**, William Christian 1939- *WhoAmL 92*
**Grabarz**, Donald Francis 1941- *WhoWest 92*
**Grabarz**, Joseph S, Jr 1956- *WhoAmP 91*
**Grabeel**, Nancy G 1957- *WhoAmP 91*
**Grabek**, James Robert 1945- *WhoMW 92*
**Grabel**, Arvin 1935- *AmMWSc 92*
**Grabelle**, Toby 1940- *WhoAmL 92*
**Grabemann**, Karl W. 1929- *WhoAmL 92*
**Graben**, Henry Willingham 1934- *AmMWSc 92*
**Grabenstetter**, James Emmett 1946- *AmMWSc 92*
**Graber**, Ben 1948- *WhoAmP 91*
**Graber**, Charles David 1917- *AmMWSc 92*
**Graber**, Doris Appel 1923- *WhoFI 92*
**Graber**, Eric Scarth 1940- *WhoFI 92*
**Graber**, George 1940- *AmMWSc 92*
**Graber**, Harlan Duane 1935- *AmMWSc 92*
**Graber**, Harris David 1939- *WhoFI 92*
**Graber**, Howard Melvin 1931- *WhoRel 92*
**Graber**, Leland D 1924- *AmMWSc 92*
**Graber**, Martin Lyle 1952- *WhoMW 92*
**Graber**, Pierre 1908- *IntWW 91*
**Graber**, Richard Rex 1924- *AmMWSc 92*
**Graber**, Richard William 1956- *WhoAmL 92*
**Graber**, Robert Philip 1918- *AmMWSc 92*
**Graber**, Steven Wayne 1950- *WhoAmL 92*
**Graber**, Susan P. 1949- *WhoAmL 92, WhoAmP 91*
**Graber**, T M 1917- *AmMWSc 92*
**Graber**, Vincent James 1931- *WhoAmP 91*
**Graber**, Virgil Edward 1911- *IntAu&W 91*
**Graber-Pastrone**, Sylvia Lujean 1952- *WhoAmL 92*
**Grabham**, Anthony 1930- *Who 92*
**Grabia**, Stanley 1947- *WhoAmL 92*
**Grabiel**, Charles Edward 1927- *AmMWSc 92*
**Grabiel**, Julio 1946- *WhoHisp 92*
**Grabill**, Jim *DrAPF 91*
**Grabill**, Paul E. *DrAPF 91*
**Grabin**, Vasiliy Gavrilovich 1900-1980 *SovUnBD*
**Grabiner**, Anthony Stephen 1945- *Who 92*
**Grabiner**, Judith Victor 1938- *AmMWSc 92*
**Grabiner**, Sandy 1939- *AmMWSc 92, WhoWest 92*
**Grable**, Albert E 1939- *AmMWSc 92*
**Grable**, Betty 1916-1973 *FacFETw*
**Grable**, Reginald Harold 1917- *WhoMW 92*
**Grabman**, Richard *DrAPF 91*

**Grabo**, Anders P 1950- *WhoIns 92*
**Grabois**, Neil 1935- *AmMWSc 92*
**Grabosky**, Terri Jo 1949- *WhoMW 92*
**Grabow**, Jack David 1929- *WhoMW 92*
**Grabow**, John Charles 1956- *WhoAmL 92*
**Grabow**, Raymond John 1932- *WhoAmL 92*
**Grabowski**, Casimer Thaddeus 1927- *AmMWSc 92*
**Grabowski**, Edward Joseph John 1940- *AmMWSc 92*
**Grabowski**, Joseph J 1956- *AmMWSc 92*
**Grabowski**, Kenneth S 1952- *AmMWSc 92*
**Grabowski**, Roger J. 1947- *WhoFI 92*
**Grabowski**, Sandra Reynolds 1943- *AmMWSc 92*
**Grabowski**, Thomas J 1950- *AmMWSc 92*
**Grabowski**, Walter John 1949- *AmMWSc 92*
**Grabowski**, Zbigniew 1930- *IntWW 91*
**Grabowski**, Zbigniew Wojciech 1931- *AmMWSc 92, WhoMW 92*
**Grabscheid**, William Henry 1931- *WhoFI 92*
**Grabska**, Stanislawa Halina 1922- *WhoRel 92*
**Gracchus** *BlkwCEP*
**Grace**, Princess of Monaco 1928-1982 *FacFETw [port]*
**Grace**, Augusto F *WhoAmP 91*
**Grace**, Brian Guiles 1942- *WhoAmL 92*
**Grace**, Corinne Bissette 1929- *WhoFI 92, WhoWest 92*
**Grace**, Donald J 1926- *AmMWSc 92*
**Grace**, Edward Everett 1927- *AmMWSc 92*
**Grace**, George *DrAPF 91*
**Grace**, H. David 1936- *WhoFI 92*
**Grace**, Harold P 1919- *AmMWSc 92*
**Grace**, Horace R. 1943- *WhoBlA 92*
**Grace**, J. Peter 1913- *IntWW 91, WhoFI 92*
**Grace**, Jason Roy 1936- *WhoFI 92*
**Grace**, John Michael 1953- *WhoEnt 92*
**Grace**, John Ross 1943- *AmMWSc 92*
**Grace**, John Thomas 1934- *WhoAmL 92*
**Grace**, John William 1921- *WhoWest 92*
**Grace**, Marcellus 1947- *AmMWSc 92, WhoBlA 92*
**Grace**, Marcia Bell 1937- *WhoFI 92*
**Grace**, Nancy Terrell 1944- *WhoRel 92*
**Grace**, Norman David 1936- *AmMWSc 92*
**Grace**, O Donn 1936- *AmMWSc 92*
**Grace**, Oliver Davies 1914- *AmMWSc 92*
**Grace**, Patricia 1937- *ConNov 91, WrDr 92*
**Grace**, Peter J 1913- *IntAu&W 91*
**Grace**, Richard E 1930- *AmMWSc 92*
**Grace**, Richard Edward 1930- *WhoMW 92*
**Grace**, Robert Archibald 1938- *AmMWSc 92*
**Grace**, Sue *WhoAmP 91*
**Grace**, Sweet Daddy 1881-1960 *RelLAm 91*
**Grace**, Thom P 1955- *AmMWSc 92*
**Grace**, Thomas Lee 1955- *WhoFI 92*
**Grace**, Thomas Michael 1938- *AmMWSc 92*
**Grace**, Thomas Paul 1946- *WhoAmL 92*
**Grace**, Thomas Peter 1955- *WhoMW 92*
**Grace**, Thomas Terry 1927- *WhoFI 92*
**Gracey**, Howard 1935- *Who 92*
**Gracey**, John Halliday 1925- *Who 92*
**Gracia**, Glenda *WhoEnt 92*
**Gracia**, Homero G. 1951- *WhoHisp 92*
**Gracia**, John Matthew 1965- *WhoHisp 92*
**Gracia**, Jorge J. E. 1942- *WhoHisp 92*
**Gracia**, Luis 1926- *WhoHisp 92*
**Gracia**, Norma Elida 1940- *WhoHisp 92*
**Gracia-Machuca**, Rafael G. 1948- *WhoHisp 92*
**Gracia-Pena**, Idilio 1940- *WhoHisp 92*
**Gracias**, Maurice 1923- *WhoFI 92*
**Gracida**, Joaquin Chaussee *WhoHisp 92*
**Gracida**, Rene Henry 1923- *WhoHisp 92, WhoRel 92*
**Gracie**, G 1930- *AmMWSc 92*
**Gracq**, Julien 1910- *GuFrLit 1, IntWW 91*
**Gracy**, David B., II 1941- *WrDr 92*
**Gracy**, Robert Wayne 1941- *AmMWSc 92*
**Grad**, Arthur 1918- *AmMWSc 92*
**Grad**, Bernard Raymond 1920- *AmMWSc 92*
**Grad**, Eli 1928- *WhoRel 92*
**Grad**, Frank Paul 1924- *WhoAmL 92*
**Grad**, John Joseph 1938- *WhoFI 92*
**Grad**, Neil Elliott Marshall 1954- *WhoAmL 92*
**Graddick**, Charles Allen 1944- *WhoAmP 91*
**Graddy**, Elizabeth Ann 1950- *WhoFI 92*
**Graddy**, Sam 1964- *BlkOlyM*
**Grade** *Who 92*
**Grade**, Baron 1906- *IntWW 91, Who 92*
**Grade**, Chaim 1910-1982 *LiExTwC*
**Grade**, Lew *LesBEnT 92*
**Grade**, Lew 1906- *FacFETw, IntMPA 92, WhoEnt 92*
**Grade**, Lorna Jean 1954- *WhoMW 92*
**Grade**, Michael *LesBEnT 92*
**Grade**, Michael 1943- *IntMPA 92*
**Grade**, Michael Ian 1943- *IntWW 91, Who 92*
**Gradeless**, Donald Eugene 1949- *WhoMW 92*
**Gradie**, Jonathan Carey 1951- *AmMWSc 92*
**Gradin**, Anita 1933- *IntWW 91*
**Gradinger**, Ed *LesBEnT 92*
**Gradisar**, Nicholas Anthony 1949- *WhoAmL 92*
**Gradison**, Heather Jane 1952- *WhoAmP 91, WhoFI 92*
**Gradison**, Willis D. 1928- *AlmAP 92 [port]*
**Gradison**, Willis David, Jr 1928- *WhoAmP 91, WhoMW 92*
**Gradle**, Henry 1855-1911 *BiInAmS*
**Grado**, John Angelo 1953- *WhoFI 92*
**Gradstein**, Felix Marcel 1941- *AmMWSc 92*
**Gradus**, Ben 1918- *WhoEnt 92*
**Gradwohl**, David Mayer 1934- *WhoMW 92*
**Grady**, Benjamin Franklin 1831-1914 *DcNCBi 2*
**Grady**, Brenda Jayne 1953- *WhoFI 92*
**Grady**, Cecil Paul Leslie, Jr 1938- *AmMWSc 92*
**Grady**, David F. 1938- *WhoFI 92*
**Grady**, David J 1941- *WhoIns 92*
**Grady**, Duane Elmer 1957- *WhoRel 92*
**Grady**, Edward J 1933- *WhoAmP 91*
**Grady**, Elizabeth Moloney *WhoAmP 91*
**Grady**, Gregory 1945- *WhoAmL 92*
**Grady**, Harold James 1920- *AmMWSc 92*
**Grady**, Harold Roy 1922- *AmMWSc 92*
**Grady**, Henry Alexander 1871-1958 *DcNCBi 2*
**Grady**, Henry W. 1850-1889 *BenetAL 91*
**Grady**, Jack *DrAPF 91*
**Grady**, James Thomas 1949- *WhoEnt 92*
**Grady**, John F. 1929- *WhoAmL 92*
**Grady**, John Joseph 1951- *WhoAmP 91*
**Grady**, Joseph Edward 1927- *AmMWSc 92*
**Grady**, Joseph Patrick 1958- *WhoMW 92*
**Grady**, Lee Timothy 1937- *AmMWSc 92*
**Grady**, M. G. *WhoRel 92*
**Grady**, Mark F. 1948- *WhoAmL 92*
**Grady**, Mary Forte 1921- *WhoBlA 92*
**Grady**, Maureen Frances 1960- *WhoAmL 92*
**Grady**, Paul Davis 1890-1970 *DcNCBi 2*
**Grady**, Perry Linwood 1940- *AmMWSc 92*
**Grady**, Peter *WrDr 92*
**Grady**, Robert *WhoAmP 91*
**Grady**, Terence 1924- *Who 92*
**Grady**, Thomas J. 1914- *WhoRel 92*
**Grady**, Thomas Michael 1952- *WhoAmL 92*
**Grady**, Walter E. *WhoBlA 92*
**Grady**, William Earl 1953- *WhoMW 92*
**Grady**, Zedekiah L. 1931- *WhoBlA 92*
**Graebe**, Annette Mulvany 1943- *WhoMW 92*
**Graebe**, Herman 1901-1986 *FacFETw*
**Graebel**, Benjamin David 1955- *WhoFI 92*
**Graebel**, William P 1932- *AmMWSc 92*
**Graeber**, Charlotte Towner *ConAu 134*
**Graeber**, Clyde D 1933- *WhoAmP 91*
**Graeber**, Edward John 1934- *AmMWSc 92*
**Graeber**, Max Charler 1928- *WhoAmP 91*
**Graebert**, Eric W 1924- *AmMWSc 92*
**Graebner**, August Lawrence 1849-1904 *RelLAm 91*
**Graebner**, Jim Grubb 1950- *WhoEnt 92*
**Graebner**, Norman Arthur 1915- *WrDr 92*
**Graedel**, Thomas Eldon 1938- *AmMWSc 92*
**Graedener**, Hermann 1878-1956 *EncTR 91*
**Graef**, Luther William 1931- *WhoMW 92*
**Graef**, Philip Edwin 1923- *AmMWSc 92*
**Graef**, Roger 1936- *WrDr 92*
**Graef**, Roger Arthur 1936- *IntAu&W 91, Who 92*
**Graef**, Walter L 1938- *AmMWSc 92*
**Graefe**, Thomas Martyn 1948- *WhoEnt 92*
**Graeff**, David Wayne 1946- *WhoFI 92*
**Graeff**, Leslie Dale 1945- *WhoWest 92*
**Graeme**, Alexander 1943- *IntAu&W 91*
**Graeme**, Ian Rollo 1913- *Who 92*
**Graeme**, Roderic *IntAu&W 91X, WrDr 92*
**Graener**, Paul 1872-1944 *EncTR 91 [port]*
**Graese**, Judith Ann 1940- *WhoEnt 92*
**Graesser**, Alastair Stewart Durward 1915- *Who 92*
**Graessley**, William W 1933- *AmMWSc 92*
**Graetz**, Donald Alvin 1942- *AmMWSc 92*
**Graetz**, Michael J. 1944- *WhoAmL 92*
**Graetzer**, Hans Gunther 1930- *AmMWSc 92*
**Graetzer**, Reinhard 1933- *AmMWSc 92*
**Graf**, Andrew Louis 1956- *WhoMW 92*
**Graf**, Arnold 1870-1898 *BiInAmS*
**Graf**, Bayard Mayhew 1926- *WhoAmL 92*
**Graf**, Billy 1945- *IntMPA 92*
**Graf**, Donald Lee 1925- *AmMWSc 92*
**Graf**, E R 1931- *AmMWSc 92*
**Graf**, Edward Louis, Jr. 1938- *WhoFI 92*
**Graf**, Erlend Haakon 1939- *AmMWSc 92*
**Graf**, Ervin Donald 1930- *WhoWest 92*
**Graf**, Gary Lynn 1952- *WhoWest 92*
**Graf**, George *AmMWSc 92*
**Graf**, Hans 1931- *IntWW 91*
**Graf**, Hans Peter 1952- *AmMWSc 92*
**Graf**, Isabel Kathryn 1959- *WhoFI 92*
**Graf**, Jess *DrAPF 91*
**Graf**, Joseph Charles 1928- *WhoFI 92*
**Graf**, Lloyd Herbert 1919- *AmMWSc 92*
**Graf**, Melvin William 1955- *WhoMW 92*
**Graf**, Oskar Maria 1894-1967 *EncTR 91, LiExTwC*
**Graf**, Peter Emil 1930- *AmMWSc 92*
**Graf**, Richard Byron, Jr. 1939- *WhoRel 92*
**Graf**, Robert Arlan 1933- *WhoFI 92*
**Graf**, Steffi *NewYTBS 91 [port]*
**Graf**, Steffi 1969- *FacFETw, IntWW 91*
**Graf**, Thomas J 1948- *WhoIns 92*
**Graf**, William L 1947- *AmMWSc 92*
**Graf**, William N. 1912- *IntMPA 92*
**Graf Palffy von Erdoed**, Alexander Franz 1924- *WhoWest 92*
**Grafe**, Warren Blair 1954- *WhoWest 92*
**Graff**, Darrell Jay 1936- *AmMWSc 92*
**Graff**, Douglas Eric 1953- *WhoAmL 92*
**Graff**, Erik 1951- *WhoAmP 91*
**Graff**, F.T., Jr. 1939- *WhoAmL 92*
**Graff**, George Stephen 1917- *AmMWSc 92*
**Graff**, Gustav *AmMWSc 92*
**Graff**, Henry Franklin 1921- *IntAu&W 91, WrDr 92*
**Graff**, Ilene *ConTFT 9*
**Graff**, Johann Michael 1714-1782 *DcNCBi 2*
**Graff**, Karen E. 1948- *WhoWest 92*
**Graff**, Morris Morse 1910- *AmMWSc 92*
**Graff**, N. Walter 1939- *WhoAmL 92*
**Graff**, Randy 1955- *ConTFT 9*
**Graff**, Richard B. *IntMPA 92*
**Graff**, Robert A 1933- *AmMWSc 92*
**Graff**, Robert Alan 1953- *WhoMW 92*
**Graff**, Roger David 1955- *WhoFI 92*
**Graff**, Samuel M 1945- *AmMWSc 92*
**Graff**, Sigmund 1898-1979 *EncTR 91*
**Graff**, Stephen Ney 1934- *WhoMW 92*
**Graff**, Thomas D 1926- *AmMWSc 92*
**Graff**, William 1923- *AmMWSc 92*
**Graff**, William H. 1955- *WhoEnt 92*
**Graff**, William J, Jr 1923- *AmMWSc 92*
**Graffam**, Ward Irving 1940- *WhoAmL 92*
**Graffe**, John Coleman, Jr. 1955- *WhoAmL 92*
**Graffenried**, Christoph, baron von 1661-1743 *DcNCBi 2*
**Graffeo**, Anthony Philip 1947- *AmMWSc 92*
**Graffeo**, John Jude 1956- *WhoEnt 92*
**Graffigny**, Francoise d'Issembourg d'A de 1695-1758 *BlkwCEP*
**Graffigny**, Francoise d'Issembourg de 1695-1758 *FrenWW*
**Graffin**, Guillaume *WhoEnt 92*
**Graffis**, Don Warren 1928- *AmMWSc 92*
**Graffius**, James Herbert 1928- *AmMWSc 92*
**Graffman**, Gary 1928- *IntWW 91, NewAmDM, WhoEnt 92*
**Grafius**, Edward John 1948- *AmMWSc 92*
**Grafstein**, Bernice 1929- *AmMWSc 92*
**Grafstein**, Daniel 1927- *AmMWSc 92*
**Grafton**, Duchess of *Who 92*
**Grafton**, Duke of 1919- *Who 92*
**Grafton**, David 1930- *IntAu&W 91*
**Grafton**, Martin John 1919- *Who 92*
**Grafton**, Peter Witheridge 1916- *Who 92*
**Grafton**, Robert Bruce 1935- *AmMWSc 92*
**Grafton**, Sue 1940- *IntAu&W 91, WrDr 92*
**Grafton**, Thurman Stanford 1923- *AmMWSc 92*
**Grafton NSW**, Bishop of 1932- *Who 92*
**Grage**, Glenn Gordon 1956- *WhoRel 92*
**Grage**, Theodor B 1927- *AmMWSc 92*
**Gragg**, Billy Hardin 1928- *WhoAmP 91*
**Gragg**, Donald E 1939- *WhoAmP 91*
**Gragg**, Douglas Lloyd 1957- *WhoRel 92*
**Gragg**, Karl Lawrence 1946- *WhoAmL 92*
**Gragg**, Rod 1950- *ConAu 134*
**Gragg**, William Bryant, Jr 1936- *AmMWSc 92*
**Graglia**, Lino Anthony 1930- *WhoAmL 92*
**Graham** *Who 92*
**Graham**, Brother *WrDr 92*
**Graham**, Marquis of 1935- *Who 92*
**Graham**, A Richard 1934- *AmMWSc 92, WhoMW 92*
**Graham**, A Ronald 1917- *AmMWSc 92*
**Graham**, Ada 1931- *IntAu&W 91, WrDr 92*
**Graham**, Alan Keith 1934- *AmMWSc 92*
**Graham**, Alan Richard 1950- *WhoMW 92*
**Graham**, Alastair 1906- *Who 92*
**Graham**, Alastair Carew 1932- *Who 92*
**Graham**, Albertha L. *WhoBlA 92*
**Graham**, Alexander 1844-1934 *DcNCBi 2*
**Graham**, Alexander 1938- *Who 92*
**Graham**, Alexander Hawkins 1890-1977 *DcNCBi 2*
**Graham**, Alexander John 1930- *WrDr 92*
**Graham**, Alexander Michael 1938- *IntWW 91*
**Graham**, Alistair *Who 92*
**Graham**, Alma Eleanor 1936- *WhoRel 92*
**Graham**, Alvin Hartfort 1950- *WhoWest 92*
**Graham**, Andrew Alexander Kenny *Who 92*
**Graham**, Andrew Winston Mawdsley 1942- *Who 92*
**Graham**, Angus 1919-1991 *ConAu 134*
**Graham**, Angus Charles d1991 *Who 92N*
**Graham**, Angus Charles 1919- *IntWW 91*
**Graham**, Angus Frederick 1916- *AmMWSc 92*
**Graham**, Anna M 1932- *WhoAmP 91*
**Graham**, Anne *WhoAmP 91*
**Graham**, Anne Silvia 1934- *Who 92*
**Graham**, Antony Richard Malise 1928- *Who 92*
**Graham**, Arnold Harold 1917- *WhoAmL 92*
**Graham**, Arthur H 1933- *AmMWSc 92*
**Graham**, Arthur Renfree 1919- *AmMWSc 92*
**Graham**, Augustus Washington 1849-1936 *DcNCBi 2*
**Graham**, Beardsley 1914- *AmMWSc 92, WhoWest 92*
**Graham**, Benjamin Franklin 1920- *AmMWSc 92*
**Graham**, Bernadette Elizabeth 1960- *WhoMW 92*
**Graham**, Bettie Jean 1941- *AmMWSc 92*
**Graham**, Betty June 1917- *WhoAmP 91*
**Graham**, Bill d1991 *NewYTBS 91 [port]*
**Graham**, Bill 1931-1991 *News 92-2*
**Graham**, Billy *IntWW 91, Who 92*
**Graham**, Billy 1918- *FacFETw, News 92-1 [port], RComAH, RelLAm 91, WhoRel 92, WrDr 92*
**Graham**, Bob 1936- *AlmAP 92 [port]*
**Graham**, Bob 1942- *WrDr 92*
**Graham**, Bonnie J. 1943- *WhoWest 92*
**Graham**, Brian 1945- *TwCPaSc*
**Graham**, Bruce Allan 1938- *AmMWSc 92*
**Graham**, Bruce Douglas 1915- *AmMWSc 92*
**Graham**, Bruce Edward 1953- *WhoEnt 92*
**Graham**, Bruce Warner 1952- *WhoEnt 92*
**Graham**, C Ann 1940- *WhoAmP 91*
**Graham**, C Benjamin 1931- *AmMWSc 92*
**Graham**, Carlotta *ConAu 35NR*
**Graham**, Carol Ethlyn 1941- *WhoFI 92*
**Graham**, Caroline 1931- *WrDr 92*
**Graham**, Catherine Macaulay *BlkwCEP*
**Graham**, Catherine S. 1920- *WhoBlA 92*
**Graham**, Charles 1919- *Who 92*
**Graham**, Charles 1937- *AmMWSc 92, WhoMW 92*
**Graham**, Charles Benjamin, Jr. 1954- *WhoAmL 92*
**Graham**, Charles D, Jr 1929- *AmMWSc 92*
**Graham**, Charles DeVaughn 1939- *WhoEnt 92*
**Graham**, Charles Edward 1919- *AmMWSc 92*
**Graham**, Charles Edward 1932- *WhoWest 92*
**Graham**, Charles John 1929- *WhoMW 92*
**Graham**, Charles Lee 1931- *AmMWSc 92*
**Graham**, Charles Raymond, Jr 1940- *AmMWSc 92*
**Graham**, Charles S *IntAu&W 91X, WrDr 92*
**Graham**, Chestie Marie 1917- *WhoBlA 92*
**Graham**, Chris Dean 1960- *WhoRel 92*
**Graham**, Christopher Forbes 1940- *IntWW 91, Who 92*
**Graham**, Clifford 1937- *Who 92*
**Graham**, Clyde Benjamin, Jr. 1931- *WhoWest 92*
**Graham**, Colin *WhoEnt 92*
**Graham**, Colin 1931- *Who 92*
**Graham**, Colin C 1942- *AmMWSc 92*
**Graham**, Cynthia *WhoEnt 92*
**Graham**, Cynthia J. 1953- *WhoMW 92*
**Graham**, D Robert 1936- *WhoAmP 91*
**Graham**, Dale Elliott 1944- *AmMWSc 92*
**Graham**, Dan Duane 1953- *WhoRel 92*
**Graham**, Daniel Robert 1936- *IntWW 91*
**Graham**, David *Who 92*
**Graham**, David 1926- *TwCPaSc*
**Graham**, David Alec d1991 *Who 92N*
**Graham**, David Antony 1953- *WhoAmL 92*
**Graham**, David Bolden 1927- *WhoFI 92*
**Graham**, David Hoyt 1954- *WhoEnt 92*
**Graham**, David Lee 1939- *AmMWSc 92*
**Graham**, David M. *DrAPF 91*
**Graham**, David Tredway 1917- *AmMWSc 92*
**Graham**, Dee McDonald 1927- *AmMWSc 92*
**Graham**, Delores Metcalf 1929- *WhoBlA 92*
**Graham**, Denis David 1941- *WhoWest 92*
**Graham**, Desmond 1940- *WrDr 92*
**Graham**, Don 1947- *ConAu 133*

**Graham,** Donald C W 1932- *AmMWSc 92*
**Graham,** Donald Edward 1945- *IntAu&W 91, IntWW 91*
**Graham,** Donald Houston, Jr. 1914- *WhoWest 92*
**Graham,** Donald James 1932- *WhoMW 92*
**Graham,** Douglas *Who 92*
**Graham,** Douglas Arthur Montrose 1942- *IntWW 91*
**Graham,** Douglas Garrick, Jr. 1952- *WhoFI 92*
**Graham,** Douglas John 1934- *WhoWest 92*
**Graham,** Douglas Leslie d1991 *Who 92N*
**Graham,** Doyle Gene 1942- *AmMWSc 92*
**Graham,** Duncan 1942- *WhoFI 92*
**Graham,** Duncan Gilmour 1936- *Who 92*
**Graham,** Dunstan 1922- *AmMWSc 92*
**Graham,** Edmund F 1924- *AmMWSc 92*
**Graham,** Edward Henry 1935- *WhoAmL 92*
**Graham,** Edward Kidder 1876-1918 *DcNCBi 2*
**Graham,** Edward Kidder, Jr. 1911-1976 *DcNCBi 2*
**Graham,** Edward Underwood 1943- *AmMWSc 92*
**Graham,** Euan Douglas 1924- *Who 92*
**Graham,** Frances Keesler 1918- *AmMWSc 92*
**Graham,** Frank, Jr 1925- *IntAu&W 91, WrDr 92*
**Graham,** Frank Lawson 1942- *AmMWSc 92*
**Graham,** Frank Porter 1886-1972 *DcNCBi 2*
**Graham,** Fred *LesBEnT 92*
**Graham,** Frederick Mitchell 1921- *WhoBlA 92*
**Graham,** Gene 1932- *WhoAmP 91*
**Graham,** George 1882-1949 *TwCPaSc*
**Graham,** George Alfred Cecil 1939- *AmMWSc 92*
**Graham,** George Boughen 1920- *Who 92*
**Graham,** George G 1923- *AmMWSc 92*
**Graham,** George G 1931- *WhoAmP 91*
**Graham,** George Rex 1813-1894 *BenetAL 91*
**Graham,** George Ronald Gibson 1939- *Who 92*
**Graham,** George Washington, Jr. 1949- *WhoBlA 92*
**Graham,** Gordon *Who 92*
**Graham,** Gordon 1920- *Who 92*
**Graham,** Gwethalyn 1913-1965 *BenetAL 91*
**Graham,** Hardy Moore 1912- *WhoAmL 92*
**Graham,** Harold L 1930- *AmMWSc 92*
**Graham,** Harold Nathaniel 1921- *AmMWSc 92*
**Graham,** Harold Steven 1950- *WhoAmL 92*
**Graham,** Harry *TwCWW 91*
**Graham,** Harry Edward 1940- *WhoMW 92*
**Graham,** Harry Morgan 1929- *AmMWSc 92*
**Graham,** Helen W. *WhoBlA 92*
**Graham,** Henry 1930- *ConPo 91, IntAu&W 91, TwCPaSc, WrDr 92*
**Graham,** Henry Collins 1934- *AmMWSc 92*
**Graham,** Howard Lee, Sr. 1942- *WhoFI 92*
**Graham,** Hugh 1936- *WrDr 92*
**Graham,** Hugh Davis 1936- *IntAu&W 91*
**Graham,** Ian James Alastair 1923- *Who 92*
**Graham,** Irvin 1909- *WhoEnt 92*
**Graham,** Jack Bennett 1913- *AmMWSc 92*
**Graham,** Jack Raymond 1925- *AmMWSc 92*
**Graham,** Jack W. 1925- *WhoMW 92*
**Graham,** James *IntAu&W 91X, WrDr 92*
**Graham,** James 1793-1851 *DcNCBi 2*
**Graham,** James 1960- *WhoAmP 91*
**Graham,** James A 1921- *WhoAmP 91*
**Graham,** James Bellingham 1940- *Who 92*
**Graham,** James Bernard 1923- *WhoAmP 91*
**Graham,** James C., Jr. 1945- *WhoBlA 92*
**Graham,** James Carl 1941- *AmMWSc 92*
**Graham,** James Duncan 1799-1865 *BiInAmS*
**Graham,** James Herbert 1921- *WhoWest 92*
**Graham,** James Jay 1957- *WhoFI 92*
**Graham,** James L 1939- *WhoAmP 91*
**Graham,** James Lowery 1932- *Who 92*
**Graham,** James Thompson 1929- *Who 92*
**Graham,** James W 1932- *AmMWSc 92*
**Graham,** Jean Charters 1914- *WhoAmP 91*
**Graham,** Jesse Japnet, II 1950- *WhoAmL 92*
**Graham,** Jewel *WhoRel 92*
**Graham,** Jo-Ann Clara *WhoBlA 92*
**Graham,** John d1991 *NewYTBS 91 [port]*
**Graham,** John 1847-1921 *DcNCBi 2*
**Graham,** John 1908-1991 *CurBio 91N*
**Graham,** John 1918- *Who 92*
**Graham,** John 1926- *Who 92, WrDr 92*
**Graham,** John 1933- *AmMWSc 92*
**Graham,** John 1940- *AmMWSc 92*
**Graham,** John A 1911- *WhoAmP 91*
**Graham,** John Alan 1949- *WhoEnt 92*
**Graham,** John Alexander Noble 1926- *IntWW 91*
**Graham,** John Alistair 1942- *Who 92*
**Graham,** John Borden 1918- *AmMWSc 92*
**Graham,** John Dalby 1937- *WhoFI 92*
**Graham,** John David Carew 1923- *Who 92*
**Graham,** John Elwood 1933- *AmMWSc 92*
**Graham,** John H. 1915- *WhoBlA 92*
**Graham,** John J. 1913- *WhoRel 92*
**Graham,** John Moodie 1938- *Who 92*
**Graham,** John Patrick 1906- *Who 92*
**Graham,** John R 1945- *WhoIns 92*
**Graham,** John Strathie 1950- *Who 92*
**Graham,** John W *AmMWSc 92*
**Graham,** John Washington 1838-1928 *DcNCBi 2*
**Graham,** Jorie *DrAPF 91*
**Graham,** Jorie 1951- *BenetAL 91, ConPo 91, WrDr 92*
**Graham,** Joseph 1759-1836 *DcNCBi 2*
**Graham,** Joseph H 1933- *AmMWSc 92*
**Graham,** Joseph Harry 1921- *AmMWSc 92*
**Graham,** Jul Eliot 1953- *WhoAmL 92, WhoFI 92*
**Graham,** Katharine 1917- *WhoFI 92*
**Graham,** Katharine M. *LesBEnT 92*
**Graham,** Katharine Meyer 1917- *IntWW 91*
**Graham,** Kathleen 1947- *WhoWest 92*
**Graham,** Kathleen Mary *Who 92*
**Graham,** Kenneth 1922- *Who 92*
**Graham,** Kenneth Judson 1947- *AmMWSc 92*
**Graham,** Kenneth L. 1915- *WhoEnt 92*
**Graham,** Kirsten R. 1946- *WhoWest 92*
**Graham,** Larry, Jr. 1946- *WhoBlA 92*
**Graham,** Laura S.E. 1964- *WhoEnt 92*
**Graham,** Lawrence E 1936- *WhoIns 92*
**Graham,** Lawrence Lee 1935- *WhoEnt 92*
**Graham,** Le Roy Cullen 1926- *AmMWSc 92*
**Graham,** Lenore Templeton 1955- *WhoAmL 92*
**Graham,** LeRoy Maxwell, Jr. 1954- *WhoBlA 92*
**Graham,** Linda Kay Edwards 1946- *AmMWSc 92*
**Graham,** Linda Marie 1947- *WhoWest 92*
**Graham,** Lisa *WhoAmP 91*
**Graham,** Lois Charlotte 1917- *WhoWest 92*
**Graham,** Lois Laverne 1933- *WhoWest 92*
**Graham,** Lola Amanda 1896- *WhoWest 92*
**Graham,** Loren R 1933- *AmMWSc 92*
**Graham,** Louis Atkins 1925- *AmMWSc 92*
**Graham,** Louise McClary 1903-1986 *WhoBlA 92N*
**Graham,** Lowell E 1937- *WhoAmP 91*
**Graham,** Malcolm 1923- *AmMWSc 92*
**Graham,** Malcolm Gray Douglas 1930- *Who 92*
**Graham,** Margaret Helen *AmMWSc 92*
**Graham,** Mariah 1946- *WhoBlA 92*
**Graham,** Marilyn A 1935- *WhoAmP 91*
**Graham,** Martha d1991 *Who 92N*
**Graham,** Martha 1894- *HanAmWH*
**Graham,** Martha 1894-1991 *ConAu 134, CurBio 91N, FacFETw, IntWW 91, -91N, NewYTBS 91 [port], News 91, RComAH*
**Graham,** Martin 1929- *Who 92*
**Graham,** Martin H 1926- *AmMWSc 92*
**Graham,** Mary Bertha 1934- *WhoHisp 92*
**Graham,** Mary Owen 1872-1957 *DcNCBi 2*
**Graham,** Matt Patrick 1950- *WhoRel 92*
**Graham,** Matthew *DrAPF 91*
**Graham,** Michael Angelo 1921- *WhoBlA 92*
**Graham,** Michael Edward 1959- *WhoWest 92*
**Graham,** Michael John 1940- *AmMWSc 92*
**Graham,** Milton H. 1919- *WhoWest 92*
**Graham,** Nason Sherwood 1958- *WhoAmP 91*
**Graham,** Nicholas 1960?- *News 91 [port]*
**Graham,** Norman 1913- *Who 92*
**Graham,** Odell 1931- *WhoBlA 92*
**Graham,** Olivia Elaine 1946- *WhoRel 92*
**Graham,** P Anderson d1925 *ScFEYrs*
**Graham,** Pamela Smith 1944- *WhoFI 92, WhoWest 92*
**Graham,** Pamela Wold 1955- *WhoWest 92*
**Graham,** Parker Lee, II 1957- *WhoMW 92*
**Graham,** Patricia 1949- *WhoBlA 92*
**Graham,** Patricia Albjerg 1935- *IntWW 91*
**Graham,** Patricia Lynn 1959- *WhoMW 92*
**Graham,** Patrick *Who 92*
**Graham,** Paul Whitener Link 1939- *AmMWSc 92*
**Graham,** Peter 1922- *Who 92*
**Graham,** Peter 1934- *Who 92*
**Graham,** Peter Alfred 1922- *IntWW 91*
**Graham,** Peter Walter 1937- *Who 92*
**Graham,** Philip *DrAPF 91*
**Graham,** Philip Jeremy 1932- *Who 92*
**Graham,** Precious Jewel 1925- *WhoBlA 92, WhoMW 92*
**Graham,** Priscilla Mann 1915- *WhoWest 92*
**Graham,** R.B. Cunninghame 1852-1936 *RfGEnL 91*
**Graham,** Ralph Stuart 1950- *Who 92*
**Graham,** Ralph Wolfe d1988 *Who 92N*
**Graham,** Ray Logan 1934- *AmMWSc 92*
**Graham,** Raymond 1935- *AmMWSc 92*
**Graham,** Richard 1934- *ConAu 34NR*
**Graham,** Richard 1941- *WhoFI 92*
**Graham,** Richard A. 1936- *WhoBlA 92*
**Graham,** Richard Charles Burwell 1926- *AmMWSc 92*
**Graham,** Richard Newell 1947- *WhoFI 92*
**Graham,** Richard S 1942- *WhoAmP 91*
**Graham,** Rigby 1931- *TwCPaSc*
**Graham,** Robert *TwCSFW 91, WrDr 92*
**Graham,** Robert 1906- *AmMWSc 92*
**Graham,** Robert 1943- *AmMWSc 92*
**Graham,** Robert Albert 1931- *AmMWSc 92*
**Graham,** Robert Clare, III 1955- *WhoAmL 92*
**Graham,** Robert D. 1954- *WhoEnt 92*
**Graham,** Robert Davidson 1842-1905 *DcNCBi 2*
**Graham,** Robert Grant 1931- *WhoFI 92*
**Graham,** Robert Leslie 1926- *AmMWSc 92*
**Graham,** Robert Lockhart 1921- *AmMWSc 92*
**Graham,** Robert M 1948- *AmMWSc 92*
**Graham,** Robert Martin 1930- *Who 92*
**Graham,** Robert Montrose 1929- *AmMWSc 92*
**Graham,** Robert Orlando 1853-1911 *BiInAmS*
**Graham,** Robert Reavis 1925- *AmMWSc 92*
**Graham,** Robert Vincent 1921- *WhoAmP 91*
**Graham,** Robert William 1922- *AmMWSc 92, WhoMW 92*
**Graham,** Robin Bruce 1941- *WhoWest 92*
**Graham,** Roger John *WhoWest 92*
**Graham,** Roger Kenneth 1929- *AmMWSc 92*
**Graham,** Roger Neill 1941- *AmMWSc 92*
**Graham,** Ron 1948- *ConAu 133*
**Graham,** Ron Joseph 1964- *WhoMW 92*
**Graham,** Ronald A 1924- *AmMWSc 92*
**Graham,** Ronald Cairns 1931- *Who 92*
**Graham,** Ronald F. 1951- *WhoAmL 92*
**Graham,** Ronald Lewis 1935- *AmMWSc 92*
**Graham,** Ronald Powell 1915- *AmMWSc 92*
**Graham,** Ronald William 1918- *WhoRel 92*
**Graham,** Samuel Horatio 1912- *Who 92*
**Graham,** Saundra M 1941- *WhoAmP 91, WhoBlA 92*
**Graham,** Seldon Bain, Jr. 1926- *WhoAmL 92*
**Graham,** Sheila 1908?-1988 *FacFETw*
**Graham,** Shirley Ann 1935- *AmMWSc 92*
**Graham,** Stanley Paul 1952- *WhoWest 92*
**Graham,** Stephan Alan 1950- *AmMWSc 92, WhoWest 92*
**Graham,** Stephen Arthur 1954- *WhoEnt 92*
**Graham,** Stephen Douglas Andrews 1955- *WhoFI 92*
**Graham,** Stephen Michael 1951- *WhoAmL 92, WhoWest 92*
**Graham,** Stewart David 1934- *Who 92*
**Graham,** Stuart Twentyman 1921- *Who 92*
**Graham,** Susan Lois 1942- *AmMWSc 92*
**Graham,** Taylor *DrAPF 91*
**Graham,** Tecumseh Xavier 1925- *WhoBlA 92*
**Graham,** Terry Edward 1940- *AmMWSc 92*
**Graham,** Theodore N. 1930- *WhoBlA 92*
**Graham,** Thomas 1944- *Who 92*
**Graham,** Thomas Christopher 1946- *WhoAmP 91*
**Graham,** Thomas Wallace 1953- *WhoWest 92*
**Graham,** Tom *ConAu 133*
**Graham,** Tom 1888-1951 *ScFEYrs*
**Graham,** Tom Maness 1937- *AmMWSc 92*
**Graham,** Toni *DrAPF 91*
**Graham,** Toni 1945- *WhoWest 92*
**Graham,** Tony M. 1949- *WhoAmL 92*
**Graham,** Vanessa *IntAu&W 91X*
**Graham,** Vernon R. *WhoRel 92*
**Graham,** Victor Ernest 1920- *IntAu&W 91, WrDr 92*
**Graham,** W Donald 1919- *AmMWSc 92*
**Graham,** W. Fred 1930- *WrDr 92*
**Graham,** W.S. 1918-1986 *RfGEnL 91*
**Graham,** Walter A 1936- *WhoAmP 91*
**Graham,** Walter Gerald Cloete 1906- *Who 92*
**Graham,** Walter Waverly, III 1933- *AmMWSc 92*
**Graham,** Wilfred Jackson 1925- *Who 92*
**Graham,** William Albert 1943- *WhoRel 92*
**Graham,** William Alexander 1804-1875 *DcNCBi 2*
**Graham,** William Alexander 1873-1943 *DcNCBi 2*
**Graham,** William Alexander, Jr. 1839-1923 *DcNCBi 2*
**Graham,** William Arthur Grover 1930- *AmMWSc 92*
**Graham,** William B. 1911- *IntWW 91, WhoFI 92, WhoMW 92*
**Graham,** William Doyce, Jr 1939- *AmMWSc 92*
**Graham,** William Edgar, Jr. 1929- *WhoAmL 92, WhoFI 92*
**Graham,** William F. 1918- *DcEcMov, IntAu&W 91*
**Graham,** William Franklin 1918- *IntWW 91, Who 92, WhoRel 92*
**Graham,** William Fred 1930- *WhoRel 92*
**Graham,** William Gordon 1920- *Who 92*
**Graham,** William Hardin 1932- *WhoAmP 91*
**Graham,** William Howard 1926- *WhoEnt 92*
**Graham,** William Joseph 1932- *AmMWSc 92*
**Graham,** William Muir 1929- *AmMWSc 92*
**Graham,** William R 1937- *WhoAmP 91*
**Graham,** William Rendall 1938- *AmMWSc 92*
**Graham,** William Richard Montgomery 1944- *AmMWSc 92*
**Graham,** William Robert 1938- *WhoEnt 92*
**Graham,** William Thomas 1933- *WhoFI 92*
**Graham,** Winston *WrDr 92*
**Graham,** Winston 1910- *ConNov 91*
**Graham,** Winston Mawdsley *IntAu&W 91, Who 92*
**Graham,** Winthrop 1965- *BlkOlyM*
**Graham-Bryce,** Ian James 1937- *Who 92*
**Graham-Bryce,** Isabel 1902- *Who 92*
**Graham-Campbell,** David John 1912- *Who 92*
**Graham-Dixon,** Anthony Philip 1929- *IntWW 91, Who 92*
**Graham-Gazaway,** Courtenay *DrAPF 91*
**Graham Hall,** Jean *Who 92*
**Graham-Harrison,** Francis Laurence T 1914- *Who 92*
**Graham-Harrison,** Robert Montagu 1943- *Who 92*
**Graham-Hurd,** Melissa Ann 1956- *WhoAmL 92*
**Graham-Moon,** Peter Wilfred Giles *Who 92*
**Graham of Edmonton,** Baron 1925- *Who 92*
**Graham-Smith,** Francis *Who 92*
**Graham-Toler** *Who 92*
**Graham-Yooll,** Andrew 1944- *LiExTwC*
**Graham-Yooll,** Andrew Michael 1944- *IntAu&W 91*
**Grahame,** Kenneth 1859-1932 *RfGEnL 91*
**Grahame,** Orville Francis Booth 1904- *WhoAmL 92*
**Grahame-Smith,** David Grahame 1933- *Who 92*
**Grahamstown,** Bishop of 1938- *Who 92*
**Grahl-Madsen,** Atle 1922- *IntWW 91*
**Grahmann,** Charles V. 1931- *WhoRel 92*
**Grahn,** Ann Wagoner 1932- *WhoMW 92*
**Grahn,** Barbara Joan 1949- *WhoAmL 92*
**Grahn,** Douglas 1923- *AmMWSc 92*
**Grahn,** Edgar Howard 1919- *AmMWSc 92*
**Grahn,** Judy *DrAPF 91*
**Grahn,** Ulf 1942- *ConCom 92*
**Grahn,** Ulf Ake Wilhelm 1942- *WhoEnt 92*
**Graiff,** Leonard B 1933- *AmMWSc 92*
**Graikoski,** John T 1924- *AmMWSc 92*
**Grainger,** Cedric Anthony 1944- *AmMWSc 92*
**Grainger,** Charles Edward 1937- *WhoAmP 91*
**Grainger,** David William 1927- *WhoMW 92*
**Grainger,** Esther *TwCPaSc*
**Grainger,** James 1721?-1766 *RfGEnL 91*
**Grainger,** James 1956- *TwCPaSc*
**Grainger,** John Cameron 1950- *WhoEnt 92*
**Grainger,** John Joseph 1934- *AmMWSc 92*
**Grainger,** John Noel Rowland 1925- *IntWW 91*
**Grainger,** Leslie 1917- *Who 92*
**Grainger,** Percy 1882-1961 *NewAmDM*
**Grainger,** Percy 1892-1961 *FacFETw*
**Grainger,** Robert Ball 1923- *AmMWSc 92*
**Grainger,** Robert Michael 1948- *AmMWSc 92*
**Grainger,** Rowan 1936- *TwCPaSc*
**Grainger,** Scott 1947- *WhoWest 92*
**Grainger,** Thomas Hutcheson, Jr 1913- *AmMWSc 92*
**Grainville,** Patrick 1947- *IntWW 91*

**Grajek**, Michael Arthur 1944- *WhoMW 92*
**Grala**, Jane Marie *WhoFI 92*
**Grale**, Debora Ann 1959- *WhoMW 92*
**Gralla**, Edward Joseph 1932- *AmMWSc 92*
**Gralla**, Jay Douglas 1948- *AmMWSc 92*
**Gralnick**, Beth 1942- *WhoAmP 91*
**Gralnick**, Jeff *LesBEnT 92*
**Gralnick**, Samuel Louis 1944- *AmMWSc 92*
**Gram**, Joseph 1955- *WhoEnt 92*
**Gram**, Laurence Carter, Jr 1932- *WhoAmP 91*
**Gram**, Theodore Edward 1934- *AmMWSc 92*
**Grambling**, Jeffrey A 1953- *AmMWSc 92*
**Grambsch**, Clyde R 1917- *WhoAmP 91*
**Gramer**, Gary Edward *WhoMW 92*
**Gramer**, Rod Eugene 1953- *WhoWest 92*
**Gramera**, Robert Eugene 1936- *AmMWSc 92*
**Grames**, Conan Paul 1946- *WhoAmL 92*
**Gramiak**, Raymond 1924- *AmMWSc 92*
**Gramick**, Jeannine 1942- *AmMWSc 92*
**Graminski**, Edmond Leonard 1929- *AmMWSc 92*
**Gramlich**, B D 1938- *WhoIns 92*
**Gramlich**, James Vandle 1939- *AmMWSc 92*
**Gramling**, Lea Gene 1908- *AmMWSc 92*
**Gramm**, Donald 1927-1983 *NewAmDM*
**Gramm**, Phil 1942- *AlmAP 92 [port], WhoAmP 91*
**Gramm**, Warren Stanley 1920- *WhoWest 92*
**Gramm**, Wendy Lee *WhoFI 92*
**Gramm**, William Philip 1942- *IntWW 91*
**Grammater**, Rudolf Dimitri 1910- *WhoWest 92*
**Grammer**, Kelsey *WhoEnt 92*
**Grammer**, Michael B. 1961- *WhoRel 92*
**Gramov**, Marat Vladimirovich 1927- *IntWW 91*
**Grampp**, William D. 1914- *WrDr 92*
**Grampp**, William Dyer 1914- *WhoFI 92, WhoMW 92*
**Grampsas**, Tony 1936- *WhoAmP 91*
**Grams**, Anne P 1947- *AmMWSc 92*
**Grams**, Betty Jane 1926- *WhoRel 92*
**Grams**, Gary Wallace 1942- *AmMWSc 92*
**Grams**, Gerald William 1938- *AmMWSc 92*
**Grams**, Theodore Carl William 1918- *WhoWest 92*
**Grams**, William Edmund 1943- *WhoIns 92*
**Gramsci**, Antonio 1891-1937 *FacFETw*
**Gramza**, Anthony Francis 1936- *AmMWSc 92, WhoMW 92*
**Gran**, Gale I *WhoIns 92*
**Gran**, Richard J 1940- *AmMWSc 92*
**Granado**, Donald Casimir 1915- *Who 92*
**Granados**, Carmen 1965- *WhoHisp 92*
**Granados**, Enrique 1867-1916 *NewAmDM*
**Granados**, Frank L. *WhoHisp 92*
**Granados**, Jose *WhoHisp 92*
**Granados**, Mimi I. 1946- *WhoHisp 92*
**Granados**, Paul *IntAu&W 91X, WrDr 92*
**Granados y Campina**, Enrique 1867-1916 *NewAmDM*
**Granai**, Edwin Carpenter 1931- *WhoAmP 91*
**Granard**, Earl of 1915- *Who 92*
**Granat**, Richard Stuart 1940- *WhoAmL 92*
**Granat**, Robert *DrAPF 91*
**Granata**, Linda M. 1951- *WhoAmL 92*
**Granatek**, Alphonse Peter 1920- *AmMWSc 92*
**Granath**, Herbert A. *LesBEnT 92 [port]*
**Granath**, James Wilton 1949- *AmMWSc 92*
**Granato**, Andrew Vincent 1926- *AmMWSc 92*
**Granato**, Carol *DrAPF 91*
**Granatstein**, Victor Lawrence 1935- *AmMWSc 92*
**Granberg**, Aleksandr Grigorevich 1936- *IntWW 91*
**Granberg**, Charles Boyd 1921- *AmMWSc 92*
**Granberg**, Kurt M 1953- *WhoAmP 91*
**Granberry**, Darbie Merwin 1943- *AmMWSc 92*
**Granberry**, James Madison, Jr. 1914- *WhoBlA 92*
**Granborg**, Bertil Svante Mikael 1923- *AmMWSc 92*
**Granby**, Marquis of 1959- *Who 92*
**Granby**, Milton *ConAu 35NR*
**Granchelli**, Felix Edward 1923- *AmMWSc 92*
**Granchi**, Michael Patrick 1946- *AmMWSc 92*
**Grand Funk Railroad** *NewAmDM*
**Grand**, James Joseph 1931- *WhoMW 92*
**Grand**, Richard Joseph 1937- *AmMWSc 92*
**Grand**, Sarah 1854-1943 *BiDBrF 2*
**Grand**, Stanley 1927- *AmMWSc 92*
**Grand**, Theodore I 1938- *AmMWSc 92*
**Granda**, Allen Manuel 1929- *AmMWSc 92*
**Granda**, Carlos 1961- *WhoHisp 92*
**Grandage**, Arnold Herbert Edward 1918- *AmMWSc 92*
**Grandbois**, Alain 1900-1975 *BenetAL 91*
**Grande**, B. Lynda 1957- *WhoAmL 92*
**Grande**, Frank *WhoHisp 92*
**Grande**, John Joseph, Jr. 1942- *WhoFI 92*
**Grandel**, Eugene Robert 1933- *AmMWSc 92*
**Grandhi**, Raja Ratnam 1938- *AmMWSc 92*
**Grandi**, Alessandro 1580?-1630 *NewAmDM*
**Grandi**, Dino 1895-1988 *BiDExR, FacFETw*
**Grandi**, Steven Aldridge 1950- *AmMWSc 92*
**Grandi di Mordano**, Dino 1895-1988 *EncTR 91*
**Grandin**, Temple 1947- *WhoMW 92*
**Grandinetti**, Michael Lawrence 1960- *WhoFI 92*
**Grandis**, Leslie Allan 1944- *WhoAmL 92*
**Grandison**, Earl Michael 1950- *WhoBlA 92*
**Grandjany**, Marcel 1891-1975 *NewAmDM*
**Grandjean**, Carter Jules 1941- *AmMWSc 92*
**Grandma Moses** 1860-1961 *FacFETw*
**Grandmaison**, J Joseph 1943- *WhoAmP 91*
**Grandolfo**, Marian Carmela 1943- *AmMWSc 92*
**Grandower**, Elissa *IntAu&W 91X, WrDr 92*
**Grandstrand**, David Paul 1955- *WhoFI 92, WhoMW 92*
**Grandstrand**, Karen Louise 1955- *WhoAmL 92*
**Grandtner**, Miroslav Marian 1928- *AmMWSc 92*
**Grandy**, Charles Creed 1928- *AmMWSc 92*
**Grandy**, Fred 1948- *AlmAP 92 [port], WhoAmP 91, WhoMW 92*
**Grandy**, John 1913- *IntWW 91, Who 92*
**Grandy**, Nita Mary 1915- *WhoWest 92*
**Grandy**, Walter Thomas, Jr 1933- *AmMWSc 92*
**Grane**, Leif 1928- *IntWW 91*
**Graneau**, Peter 1921- *AmMWSc 92*
**Granelli**, Luigi 1929- *IntWW 91*
**Granet**, Bert 1910- *IntMPA 92, WhoEnt 92*
**Granet**, Irving 1924- *AmMWSc 92*
**Graneto**, Philip Anthony 1942- *WhoEnt 92*
**Graney**, Daniel O 1936- *AmMWSc 92*
**Graney**, Michael Proctor 1943- *WhoAmL 92*
**Granfield**, Patrick Richard 1930- *WhoRel 92*
**Granfil**, Toma 1913- *IntWW 91*
**Grange**, Harold 1903-1991 *FacFETw, NewYTBS 91 [port]*
**Grange**, Kenneth Henry 1929- *Who 92*
**Grange**, Larry William 1937- *WhoWest 92*
**Grange**, Peter *IntAu&W 91X, WrDr 92*
**Grange**, Raymond A 1910- *AmMWSc 92*
**Grange**, Red 1903-1991 *News 91, -91-3*
**Grange**, Russell Dean 1921- *WhoAmP 91*
**Grange**, William Marshall 1947- *WhoEnt 92*
**Granger**, Bill 1941- *IntAu&W 91, WrDr 92*
**Granger**, Bruce Ingham 1920- *WrDr 92*
**Granger**, Carl V 1928- *AmMWSc 92*
**Granger**, Carl Victor 1928- *WhoBlA 92*
**Granger**, Charles Franklin 1959- *WhoRel 92*
**Granger**, D Niel *AmMWSc 92*
**Granger**, David William 1951- *WhoWest 92*
**Granger**, Donald Lee 1943- *AmMWSc 92*
**Granger**, Edwina C. *WhoBlA 92*
**Granger**, Eleanor 1938- *WhoRel 92*
**Granger**, Farley 1925- *IntMPA 92*
**Granger**, Gale A 1937- *AmMWSc 92*
**Granger**, Harvey, Jr. 1928- *WhoFI 92*
**Granger**, Herbert Curry 1923- *WhoAmP 91*
**Granger**, Joey Paul *AmMWSc 92*
**Granger**, John Van Nuys 1918- *AmMWSc 92*
**Granger**, Kay 1943- *WhoAmP 91*
**Granger**, Lisa A. 1962- *WhoAmL 92*
**Granger**, Michael 1924- *TwCPaSc*
**Granger**, Philip Richard 1943- *WhoMW 92, WhoRel 92*
**Granger**, Robert A, II 1928- *AmMWSc 92*
**Granger**, Robert Mark 1953- *WhoAmL 92*
**Granger**, Rodney J. 1935- *WhoFI 92*
**Granger**, Shelton B. 1921- *WhoBlA 92*
**Granger**, Stewart 1913- *IntMPA 92, IntWW 91, Who 92*
**Granger-Taylor**, Nicolas 1963- *TwCPaSc*
**Granich**, Irving *BenetAL 91*
**Granick**, David 1926- *WrDr 92*
**Granick**, Steve 1953- *AmMWSc 92*
**Granier De Lilliac**, Rene 1919- *IntWW 91*
**Granieri**, Vincent James 1957- *WhoMW 92*
**Granik**, Theodore d1970 *LesBEnT 92*
**Granillo**, Frank *WhoHisp 92*
**Granin**, Daniel Aleksandrovich 1918- *IntWW 91*
**Granin**, Daniil Aleksandrovich 1919- *SovUnBD*
**Granirer**, Edmond 1935- *AmMWSc 92*
**Granit**, Ragnar Arthur d1991 *Who 92N*
**Granit**, Ragnar Arthur 1900- *IntWW 91, WhoNob 90*
**Granite**, Tony *WrDr 92*
**Granito**, Charles Edward 1937- *AmMWSc 92*
**Granito**, Frank H., Jr. 1931- *WhoAmL 92*
**Granlund**, Barbara *WhoAmP 91*
**Granlund**, Thomas Arthur 1951- *WhoWest 92*
**Grann**, Phyllis 1937- *IntWW 91*
**Grannan**, William Stephen 1929- *WhoMW 92*
**Granneman**, Vernon Henry 1953- *WhoAmL 92*
**Grannemann**, Glenn Niel 1944- *AmMWSc 92*
**Grannemann**, W W 1923- *AmMWSc 92*
**Granner**, Daryl Kitley 1936- *AmMWSc 92*
**Grannes**, A Janice 1937- *WhoAmP 91*
**Grannis**, Alexander Banks 1942- *WhoAmP 91*
**Grannis**, Paul Dutton 1938- *AmMWSc 92*
**Grano**, Olavi Johannes 1925- *IntWW 91*
**Grano**, Vicki Cornell 1955- *WhoFI 92*
**Granof**, Eugene B. 1936- *WhoAmL 92*
**Granoff**, Allan 1923- *AmMWSc 92*
**Granoff**, Alvin Roy 1948- *WhoAmP 91*
**Granoff**, Barry 1938- *AmMWSc 92*
**Granoff**, Barry 1940- *AmMWSc 92*
**Granoff**, Dan Martin 1944- *AmMWSc 92*
**Granoff**, Gail Patricia 1952- *WhoAmL 92*
**Granoff**, Gary Charles 1948- *WhoAmL 92, WhoFI 92*
**Granosky**, Eileen Margaret 1939- *WhoWest 92*
**Granovsky**, Aleksandr Andreevich 1860-1927 *SovUnBD*
**Granowitz**, Marian S 1914- *WhoAmP 91*
**Granquist**, Theodore Vernon 1935- *WhoRel 92*
**Granroth**, Ronald Alvin 1944- *WhoFI 92*
**Granston**, David Wilfred 1939- *WhoFI 92*
**Granstrom**, Marvin L 1920- *AmMWSc 92*
**Grant** *Who 92*
**Grant**, Alan Leslie 1962- *AmMWSc 92*
**Grant**, Alberta 1946- *WhoFI 92*
**Grant**, Alec Alan 1932- *Who 92*
**Grant**, Alexander 1925- *Who 92*
**Grant**, Alexander Marshall 1928- *WhoEnt 92*
**Grant**, Alicia Brown 1945- *WhoFI 92*
**Grant**, Alistair *Who 92*
**Grant**, Alistair 1925- *TwCPaSc*
**Grant**, Allan Kerr 1924- *IntWW 91*
**Grant**, Allan Wallace 1911- *Who 92*
**Grant**, Amy 1961?- *ConMus 7 [port]*
**Grant**, Andrew Francis Joseph 1911- *Who 92*
**Grant**, Andrew Young 1946- *Who 92*
**Grant**, Anna Augusta Fredrina *WhoBlA 92*
**Grant**, Anne McVicar 1755- *DcAmImH*
**Grant**, Anne McVickar 1755-1838 *BenetAL 91*
**Grant**, Anthony *IntAu&W 91X, WrDr 92*
**Grant**, Anthony 1925- *Who 92*
**Grant**, Art 1927- *WhoWest 92*
**Grant**, Arthur E 1923- *AmMWSc 92*
**Grant**, Arthur H. 1930- *WhoBlA 92*
**Grant**, B. Donald *LesBEnT 92*
**Grant**, B. Richard 1937- *WhoEnt 92*
**Grant**, Barbara Dianne *AmMWSc 92*
**Grant**, Ben Z 1939- *WhoAmP 91*
**Grant**, Bernard Alexander Montgomery 1944- *Who 92*
**Grant**, Bethany 1939- *WhoEnt 92*
**Grant**, Bill 1943- *WhoAmP 91*
**Grant**, Bob 1926- *WhoAmP 91*
**Grant**, Brad Warner 1960- *WhoMW 92, WhoRel 92*
**Grant**, Brian *Who 92*
**Grant**, Bruce 1925- *WrDr 92*
**Grant**, Bruce Alexander 1925- *IntAu&W 91, IntWW 91*
**Grant**, Bruce S 1942- *AmMWSc 92*
**Grant**, Burton Fred 1938- *WhoAmL 92*
**Grant**, C. B. S. *WrDr 92*
**Grant**, C.D. *DrAPF 91*
**Grant**, Carl N. 1939- *WhoEnt 92*
**Grant**, Carl Richard, Jr. 1951- *WhoWest 92*
**Grant**, Cary 1904-1986 *FacFETw*
**Grant**, Cecil Greene 1922- *WhoAmP 91*
**Grant**, Cedric Hilburn 1936- *IntWW 91*
**Grant**, Cedric Steven 1952- *WhoBlA 92*
**Grant**, Charles L 1942- *IntAu&W 91, TwCSFW 91, WrDr 92*
**Grant**, Charles Truman 1946- *WhoBlA 92, WhoMW 92*
**Grant**, Cheryl 1944- *WhoWest 92*
**Grant**, Cheryl Dayne 1944- *WhoBlA 92*
**Grant**, Clarence Lewis 1930- *AmMWSc 92*
**Grant**, Claude DeWitt 1944- *WhoBlA 92*
**Grant**, Clifford 1929- *Who 92*
**Grant**, Conrad Joseph 1956- *AmMWSc 92*
**Grant**, Cynthia Ann 1958- *AmMWSc 92*
**Grant**, Cynthia D. *DrAPF 91*
**Grant**, Dale Walter 1923- *AmMWSc 92*
**Grant**, David *WrDr 92*
**Grant**, David Evans 1924- *AmMWSc 92*
**Grant**, David Graham 1937- *AmMWSc 92*
**Grant**, David James 1922- *Who 92*
**Grant**, David James William 1937- *AmMWSc 92, WhoMW 92*
**Grant**, David Marshall 1955- *IntMPA 92*
**Grant**, David Miller *AmMWSc 92*
**Grant**, David Morris 1931- *AmMWSc 92, WhoWest 92*
**Grant**, Debora Felita 1956- *WhoBlA 92*
**Grant**, Dell Omega 1951- *WhoBlA 92*
**Grant**, Derek Aldwin 1915- *Who 92*
**Grant**, Donald Blane 1921- *Who 92*
**Grant**, Donald David 1924- *Who 92*
**Grant**, Donald Lloyd 1938- *AmMWSc 92*
**Grant**, Donald R 1932- *AmMWSc 92*
**Grant**, Doris Leona 1915- *WhoMW 92*
**Grant**, Douglas Hope 1934- *AmMWSc 92*
**Grant**, Douglas Marr Kelso 1917- *Who 92*
**Grant**, Douglas Roderick 1939- *AmMWSc 92*
**Grant**, Douglass Lloyd 1946- *AmMWSc 92*
**Grant**, Duncan 1885-1975 *TwCPaSc*
**Grant**, Duncan 1885-1978 *DcTwDes, FacFETw*
**Grant**, Duncan Alistair 1925- *Who 92*
**Grant**, Edward 1915- *Who 92*
**Grant**, Edward R 1947- *AmMWSc 92*
**Grant**, Edward Robert 1947- *WhoMW 92*
**Grant**, Edwin Randolph 1943- *WhoFI 92*
**Grant**, Ellen Catherine Gardner 1934- *IntAu&W 91*
**Grant**, Eneas Henry George 1901- *Who 92*
**Grant**, Ernest Walter 1918- *AmMWSc 92*
**Grant**, Eugene F 1917- *AmMWSc 92*
**Grant**, Eugene Lodewick 1897- *AmMWSc 92*
**Grant**, Ferris Nelson d1991 *Who 92N*
**Grant**, Fiona M. 1948- *TwCPaSc*
**Grant**, Frederic Delano, Jr. 1954- *WhoAmL 92*
**Grant**, Frederick Anthony 1949- *WhoFI 92*
**Grant**, Frederick Cyril 1925- *AmMWSc 92*
**Grant**, Frederick William 1834-1902 *RelLAm 91*
**Grant**, Gary 1965- *WhoBlA 92*
**Grant**, Gary C 1937- *WhoAmP 91*
**Grant**, Gary Rudolph 1943- *WhoBlA 92*
**Grant**, Gary S 1934- *WhoAmP 91*
**Grant**, George 1897-1982 *FacFETw*
**Grant**, George 1918-1988 *FacFETw*
**Grant**, George 1924- *Who 92*
**Grant**, George C 1929- *AmMWSc 92*
**Grant**, George C. 1939- *WhoBlA 92*
**Grant**, George Monro 1835-1902 *BenetAL 91*
**Grant**, Gregory Alan 1949- *AmMWSc 92, WhoMW 92*
**Grant**, Gregory Alan 1966- *WhoBlA 92*
**Grant**, Hallidie 1959- *WhoFI 92*
**Grant**, Harvey 1965- *WhoBlA 92*
**Grant**, Heber Jeddy 1856-1945 *RelLAm 91*
**Grant**, Herbert Lewis 1928- *WhoWest 92*
**Grant**, Hiram Louis 1843-1922 *DcNCBi 2*
**Grant**, Homer Hamilton, Jr. 1908- *WhoWest 92*
**Grant**, Horace Junior 1965- *WhoBlA 92*
**Grant**, Howard P. 1925- *WhoBlA 92*
**Grant**, Hubert Brian 1917- *Who 92*
**Grant**, Hugh *IntMPA 92*
**Grant**, Ian David 1943- *Who 92*
**Grant**, Ian Hallam L. *Who 92*
**Grant**, Ian Macdonald 1904- *TwCPaSc*
**Grant**, Ian Nicholas 1948- *Who 92*
**Grant**, Ian S 1940- *AmMWSc 92*
**Grant**, Jacquelyn 1948- *WhoBlA 92*
**Grant**, James 1932- *WhoBlA 92*
**Grant**, James, III 1812-1891 *DcNCBi 2*
**Grant**, James Alexander 1931- *Who 92*
**Grant**, James Alexander 1935- *AmMWSc 92*
**Grant**, James Ardern 1885-1973 *TwCPaSc*
**Grant**, James J, Jr 1935- *AmMWSc 92*
**Grant**, James Pineo 1922- *IntWW 91, Who 92*
**Grant**, James Russell 1924- *IntAu&W 91, WrDr 92*
**Grant**, James Shaw 1910- *Who 92*
**Grant**, James William Angus 1955- *AmMWSc 92*
**Grant**, John 1908- *Who 92*
**Grant**, John Alexander, Jr. 1923- *WhoFI 92*
**Grant**, John Andrew, Jr 1941- *AmMWSc 92*
**Grant**, John Anthony *Who 92*
**Grant**, John Audley 1943- *WhoAmP 91*
**Grant**, John Carrington 1937- *WhoWest 92*
**Grant**, John Donald 1926- *Who 92*
**Grant**, John Douglas 1932- *Who 92*
**Grant**, John Gaston 1858-1923 *DcNCBi 2*

Grant, John H., Sr. 1927- WhoBlA 92
Grant, John James 1914- Who 92
Grant, John Leonard 1960- WhoMW 92
Grant, John T 1920- WhoAmP 91
Grant, John Thomas 1920- WhoAmL 92, WhoMW 92
Grant, John Wallace 1946- AmMWSc 92
Grant, John Webster 1919- WrDr 92
Grant, Joseph J. 1951- WhoFI 92
Grant, Joseph N. 1925- WhoBlA 92
Grant, Julius 1901- IntAu&W 91
Grant, Keith 1930- TwCPaSc
Grant, Keith Frederick 1930- IntWW 91
Grant, Keith Wallace 1934- Who 92
Grant, Kingsley B. 1931- WhoBlA 92
Grant, Landon TwCWW 91
Grant, Lawrence 1938- WhoIns 92
Grant, Lee ReelWom
Grant, Lee 1931- IntMPA 92, WhoEnt 92
Grant, Leland F 1913- AmMWSc 92
Grant, Leonard J. 1933- WhoWest 92
Grant, Louis Russell, Jr 1928- AmMWSc 92
Grant, Louis Z. 1907- WhoAmL 92
Grant, M. Duncan 1950- WhoAmL 92
Grant, Madison 1865-1937 DcAmImH
Grant, Malcolm Etheridge 1944- Who 92
Grant, Marcia DrAPF 91
Grant, Mark TwCSFW 91
Grant, Martin 1956- AmMWSc 92
Grant, Mary 1947- WhoMW 92
Grant, Matthew Alistair 1937- Who 92
Grant, Maxwell FacFETw, IntAu&W 91X
Grant, McNair 1925- WhoBlA 92
Grant, Merrill LesBEnT 92
Grant, Merwin Darwin 1944- WhoAmL 92, WhoWest 92
Grant, Micah 1964- WhoEnt 92
Grant, Michael 1914- IntAu&W 91, Who 92, WrDr 92
Grant, Michael Clarence 1942- AmMWSc 92
Grant, Michael P 1936- AmMWSc 92
Grant, Michael Peter 1936- WhoFI 92
Grant, Michael Philip 1945- WhoAmP 91
Grant, Nathaniel 1943- WhoBlA 92
Grant, Neil 1938- ConAu 34NR, WrDr 92
Grant, Neil David Mountfield 1938- IntAu&W 91
Grant, Neil George 1937- AmMWSc 92
Grant, Nicholas Who 92
Grant, Nicholas J 1915- AmMWSc 92
Grant, Nigel 1932- WrDr 92
Grant, Norman Howard 1927- AmMWSc 92
Grant, Patrick Alexander 1945- WhoAmL 92, WhoAmP 91
Grant, Patrick Michael 1944- AmMWSc 92
Grant, Paul Bernard 1931- WhoFI 92, WhoMW 92
Grant, Paul Michael 1935- AmMWSc 92
Grant, Paula DiMeo 1943- WhoAmL 92
Grant, Percy Stickney 1860-1927 BenetAL 91
Grant, Peter James 1929- IntWW 91, Who 92
Grant, Peter John 1926- Who 92
Grant, Peter Malcolm 1933- AmMWSc 92
Grant, Peter Raymond 1936- AmMWSc 92, IntWW 91, Who 92
Grant, Peter Stanley 1952- WhoFI 92
Grant, Philip 1924- AmMWSc 92
Grant, Philip R, Jr AmMWSc 92
Grant, Philip Robert, Jr. 1930- WhoFI 92
Grant, R, O'Reilly, J B, J S of Dale ScFEYrs
Grant, Raymond Thomas 1957- WhoEnt 92
Grant, Rhoda 1902- AmMWSc 92, WhoMW 92
Grant, Richard WrDr 92
Grant, Richard E. 1957- IntMPA 92
Grant, Richard Earl 1935- WhoWest 92
Grant, Richard Evans 1927- AmMWSc 92
Grant, Richard J 1918- AmMWSc 92
Grant, Richard Lee 1955- WhoFI 92
Grant, Robert 1852-1940 BenetAL 91, ScFEYrs
Grant, Robert Allen 1905- WhoAmL 92, WhoMW 92
Grant, Robert C. 1943- WhoBlA 92
Grant, Robert George 1947- WhoMW 92
Grant, Robert Nathan 1930- WhoAmL 92
Grant, Roderick 1941- IntAu&W 91, WrDr 92
Grant, Roderick M, Jr 1935- AmMWSc 92
Grant, Rodney A 1960?- News 92-1 [port]
Grant, Ron E. WhoEnt 92
Grant, Ronald 1910- AmMWSc 92
Grant, Ronald W 1937- AmMWSc 92
Grant, Sheldon Kerry 1939- AmMWSc 92
Grant, Stanley Cameron 1931- AmMWSc 92
Grant, Stephen Allen 1938- WhoAmL 92
Grant, Stewart Walter Leslie 1948- WhoEnt 92
Grant, Susan 1954- WhoEnt 92
Grant, Susan Irene 1953- WhoAmL 92
Grant, Thomas James 1957- WhoEnt 92
Grant, Timothy Jerome 1965- WhoBlA 92
Grant, Ulysses S. 1822-1885 BenetAL 91, RComAH
Grant, Ulysses Simpson 1822-1885 AmPolLe [port]
Grant, Verne 1917- AmMWSc 92, WrDr 92
Grant, Verne E. 1917- IntWW 91
Grant, Walter Lawrence 1922- IntWW 91
Grant, Walter Leroy 1936- WhoFI 92
Grant, Walter Matthews 1945- WhoAmL 92, WhoFI 92
Grant, Walter Morton 1915- AmMWSc 92
Grant, Warren Herbert 1933- AmMWSc 92
Grant, Willard H 1923- AmMWSc 92
Grant, William A WhoAmP 91
Grant, William B 1942- AmMWSc 92
Grant, William Chase, Jr 1924- AmMWSc 92
Grant, William Downing 1917- WhoIns 92
Grant, William Frederick 1924- AmMWSc 92
Grant, William Packer, Jr. 1942- WhoFI 92
Grant, William T 1876-1972 FacFETw
Grant, William W. 1934- WhoBlA 92
Grant, William West, III 1932- WhoFI 92, WhoWest 92
Grant, Wilmer, Jr. 1940- WhoBlA 92
Grant, Wyn 1947- ConAu 35NR
Grant, Zilpah P. 1794-1874 HanAmWH
Grant-Adamson, Lesley 1942- WrDr 92
Grant-Ferris Who 92
Grant-Ferris, Piers Henry Michael 1933- WhoRel 92
Grant of Dalvey, Patrick Alexander B 1953- Who 92
Grant of Monymusk, Archibald 1954- Who 92
Grant-Suttie, Philip Who 92
Grantchester, Baron 1921- Who 92
Granter, Sharon Savoy 1940- WhoMW 92
Grantham, Bishop Suffragan of 1942- Who 92
Grantham, Guy 1900- Who 92
Grantham, Jared James 1936- AmMWSc 92
Grantham, Jasper Edward 1922- WhoFI 92
Grantham, Joseph Michael, Jr. 1947- WhoFI 92
Grantham, Leroy Francis 1929- AmMWSc 92
Grantham, Preston Hubert 1930- AmMWSc 92
Grantham, Roy Aubrey 1926- Who 92
Grantley, Baron 1923- Who 92
Grantley, Robert Clark 1948- WhoBlA 92
Grantmyre, Edward Bartlett 1931- AmMWSc 92
Grantom, Mark S. 1954- WhoAmL 92
Grants, Valdis 1942- WhoFI 92, WhoMW 92
Grantz, Arthur 1927- AmMWSc 92
Grantz, David Arthur 1951- AmMWSc 92
Granville Who 92
Granville, Earl 1918- Who 92
Granville, Austyn W ScFEYrs
Granville, Patty 1945- WhoEnt 92
Granville, William, Jr. 1940- WhoBlA 92
Granville-Barker, Harley RfGEnL 91
Granville-Barker, Harley 1877-1946 FacFETw
Granville of Eye, Baron 1899- Who 92
Granville Slack, George Who 92
Granz, Norman 1918- NewAmDM
Granzow, Kenneth Donald 1933- AmMWSc 92
Graper, Edward Bowen 1947- AmMWSc 92
Grapes, David Gene, II 1951- WhoEnt 92
Grapes, Jack DrAPF 91
Graphix, Michael J. 1957- WhoWest 92
Grappelli, Stephane 1908- IntWW 91, NewAmDM, Who 92
Grasdalen, Gary 1945- AmMWSc 92
Grasgreen, Martin 1925- IntMPA 92
Grasham, William Wesley 1930- WhoRel 92
Grass, Albert M 1910- AmMWSc 92
Grass, Alexander 1927- WhoFI 92
Grass, Gunter 1927- FacFETw [port], IntWW 91, LiExTwC
Grass, Gunter Wilhelm 1927- Who 92
Grass, Martin Lehrman 1954- WhoFI 92
Grass, William Ellis, Jr. 1943- WhoMW 92
Grassano, Thomas David 1961- WhoRel 92
Grassberger, Roland 1905- IntWW 91
Grasse, Peter Brunner 1956- AmMWSc 92, WhoFI 92
Grasse-Rouville, Francois-Joseph-Paul de 1722-1788 BlkwEAR
Grasselli, Eugene Ramiro 1810-1882 BiInAmS
Grasselli, Jeanette Gecsy 1928- AmMWSc 92
Grasselli, Robert Karl 1930- AmMWSc 92
Grasselly, Gilbert WhoRel 92
Grasser, Bruce Howard 1941- AmMWSc 92
Grassetti, Davide Riccardo 1920- AmMWSc 92
Grasshoff, Alex IntMPA 92, WhoEnt 92
Grasshoff, Jurgen Michael 1936- AmMWSc 92
Grassi, Anthony Prentice 1944- WhoFI 92
Grassi, Ellen Elizabeth 1949- WhoFI 92
Grassi, James Edward 1943- WhoWest 92
Grassi, Joseph F. 1949- WhoAmL 92
Grassi, Raymond Charles 1918- AmMWSc 92
Grassi, Vincent G 1956- AmMWSc 92
Grassia, Thomas Charles 1946- WhoAmL 92
Grassie, Charles Wesley, Jr 1952- WhoAmP 91
Grassino, Alejandro E AmMWSc 92
Grassl, Steven Miller 1952- AmMWSc 92
Grassle, John Frederick 1939- AmMWSc 92
Grassle, Judith Payne 1936- AmMWSc 92
Grassle, Karen WhoEnt 92
Grassley, Charles E. 1933- AlmAP 92 [port], IntWW 91, WhoAmP 91
Grassley, Charles Ernest 1933- WhoMW 92
Grassman, Paul Douglas 1945- WhoMW 92
Grassman, Raymond Fred 1939- WhoMW 92
Grassmick, Robert Alan 1936- AmMWSc 92
Grasso, Anthony Robert 1951- WhoRel 92
Grasso, Bobby 1938- WhoEnt 92, WhoWest 92
Grasso, Christopher Anthony 1950- WhoMW 92
Grasso, Donald Paul 1954- WhoMW 92
Grasso, Ella T 1919-1981 FacFETw
Grasso, Gerardo 1953- WhoFI 92
Grasso, Joseph Anthony 1935- AmMWSc 92
Grasso, Louis Joseph 1949- WhoEnt 92
Grasso, Mary Ann 1952- IntMPA 92, WhoEnt 92, WhoWest 92
Grasso, Richard A. WhoFI 92
Grasty, Robert Alvin 1925- WhoFI 92
Grasz, Lynne Anne Morian 1943- WhoEnt 92
Gratacap, Louis Pope 1851-1917 BiInAmS, ScFEYrs
Gratch, Serge 1921- AmMWSc 92
Grate, Isaac, Jr. 1952- WhoBlA 92
Grateful Dead, The FacFETw, NewAmDM
Grathwohl, Susan Maria DrAPF 91
Gratian 359-383 EncEarC
Gratian, J Warren 1918- AmMWSc 92
Gratias, Arthur Louis 1920- WhoAmP 91
Gratovich, Eugene Alexis 1941- WhoEnt 92
Grattan, C. Hartley 1902-1980 BenetAL 91
Grattan, Donald Henry 1926- Who 92
Grattan, James Alex 1948- AmMWSc 92
Grattan, Jerome Francis 1912- AmMWSc 92
Grattan-Bellew, Henry Charles 1933- Who 92
Grattan-Cooper, Sidney 1911- Who 92
Gratton, Enrico 1946- AmMWSc 92
Gratton, Jean 1924- WhoRel 92
Gratton, Patrick John Francis 1933- WhoFI 92
Gratus, Jack 1935- IntAu&W 91, WrDr 92
Gratwick, John 1918- Who 92
Gratwick, Stephen 1924- Who 92
Gratz, Leopold 1929- IntWW 91
Gratz, Norman G 1925- AmMWSc 92
Gratz, Rebecca 1781-1869 DcAmImH
Gratz, Ronald Karl 1946- AmMWSc 92
Gratz, Roy Fred 1942- AmMWSc 92
Gratzek, John B 1931- AmMWSc 92
Gratzer, George 1936- AmMWSc 92
Gratzios, Agamemnon 1922- IntWW 91
Gratzner, Howard G 1934- AmMWSc 92
Grau, Albert A 1918- AmMWSc 92
Grau, Charles Richard 1920- AmMWSc 92
Grau, Craig Robert 1946- AmMWSc 92
Grau, Edward Gordon 1946- AmMWSc 92
Grau, Fred V 1902- AmMWSc 92
Grau, James W. WhoEnt 92
Grau, Juan WhoHisp 92
Grau, Marcy Beinish 1950- WhoFI 92
Grau, Paul Andrew 1951- WhoAmL 92
Grau, Robert George 1943- WhoEnt 92
Grau, Shirley Ann DrAPF 91
Grau, Shirley Ann 1929- BenetAL 91, WhoEnt 92, WrDr 92
Grau, Shirley Ann 1930- ConNov 91, IntAu&W 91
Grau, Thomas Paul 1960- WhoMW 92
Graubard, John Joseph 1944- WhoAmL 92
Graubard, Mark 1904- WrDr 92
Graubard, Mark Aaron 1904- AmMWSc 92
Graubart, Jeffrey Lowell 1940- WhoAmL 92, WhoEnt 92
Graue, Dennis Jerome 1939- AmMWSc 92
Graue, Louis Charles 1923- AmMWSc 92
Grauer, Albert D 1942- AmMWSc 92
Grauer, Amelie L 1899- AmMWSc 92
Grauer, Donald John 1946- WhoRel 92
Grauer, Douglas Dale 1956- WhoMW 92
Grauer, Millard Joel 1927- WhoFI 92
Grauer, Rhoda Sheila 1944- WhoEnt 92
Grauert, Johannes 1930- IntWW 91
Graul, Christopher Welling 1950- WhoAmL 92
Graul, Leland Eden 1949- WhoFI 92
Graul, Walter Dale 1944- AmMWSc 92
Graulty, Robert Thomas 1928- AmMWSc 92
Grauman, Joseph Uri 1941- AmMWSc 92
Graumann, Hugo Oswalt 1913- AmMWSc 92
Graun, Carl Heinrich 1704-1759 NewAmDM
Graupe, Daniel 1934- AmMWSc 92
Grausam, Jeffrey Leonard 1943- WhoAmL 92
Grava, Janis 1920- AmMWSc 92
Gravani, Robert Bernard 1945- AmMWSc 92
Gravanis, Michael Basil 1929- AmMWSc 92
Gravatt, Claude Carrington, Jr 1939- AmMWSc 92
Grave, Gilman Drew 1941- AmMWSc 92
Grave, Walter Wyatt 1901- IntWW 91, Who 92
Graveel, John Gerard 1953- AmMWSc 92
Gravel, Camille F, Jr 1915- WhoAmP 91
Gravel, Denis Fernand 1935- AmMWSc 92
Gravel, Mike 1930- IntWW 91, WhoAmP 91
Graveline, Daniel Anthony 1941- WhoEnt 92
Graveline, Edward Paul 1947- WhoRel 92
Gravell, Maneth 1932- AmMWSc 92
Gravelle, Jane Gibson 1947- WhoFI 92
Gravelle, Karen 1942- ConAu 135
Gravely, Melvin J. 1940- WhoBlA 92
Gravely, Sally Margaret 1947- AmMWSc 92
Gravely, Samuel L., Jr. 1922- WhoBlA 92
Gravely, William Bernard 1939- WhoRel 92
Graven, Stanley N 1932- AmMWSc 92
Gravenberg, Eric Von 1950- WhoBlA 92
Gravenstein, Joachim Stefan 1925- AmMWSc 92
Graver, Elizabeth 1964- ConAu 135
Graver, Jack Edward 1935- AmMWSc 92
Graver, Lawrence Stanley 1931- IntAu&W 91, WrDr 92
Graver, Richard Byrd 1932- AmMWSc 92
Graver, Steven Francis 1951- WhoFI 92
Graver, William Robert 1947- AmMWSc 92
Gravereaux, David Claude 1966- WhoEnt 92
Gravers, Renate 1944- WhoFI 92
Graves Who 92
Graves, Baron 1911- Who 92
Graves, Albert Richard 1927- WhoMW 92
Graves, Alice 1942- WhoAmP 91
Graves, Allen Willis 1915- WhoRel 92
Graves, Anna Melissa 1875-1964 AmPeW
Graves, Anne Carol Finger 1933- AmMWSc 92
Graves, Austin T. d1991 NewYTBS 91
Graves, Bari Cordia 1947- WhoEnt 92
Graves, Brian Kenneth 1962- WhoMW 92
Graves, Bruce Bannister 1928- AmMWSc 92
Graves, C L 1856-1944 ScFEYrs
Graves, C L & Lucas, E V ScFEYrs
Graves, Calvin 1804-1877 DcNCBi 2
Graves, Carl N AmMWSc 92
Graves, Carol Kenney 1937- WhoFI 92, WhoMW 92
Graves, Carole A. 1938- WhoBlA 92
Graves, Charles E 1931- WhoAmP 91
Graves, Charles Norman 1930- AmMWSc 92, WhoMW 92
Graves, Clifford W. 1939- WhoBlA 92
Graves, Clifford Wayne 1939- WhoFI 92
Graves, Clinton Hannibal, Jr 1927- AmMWSc 92
Graves, Curtis M. 1938- WhoBlA 92
Graves, David E 1950- AmMWSc 92
Graves, David J 1941- AmMWSc 92
Graves, David William 1958- WhoRel 92
Graves, Denyce Antoinette 1964- WhoEnt 92
Graves, Donald C 1942- AmMWSc 92
Graves, Donald J 1933- AmMWSc 92
Graves, Earl G. 1935- ConBlB 1 [port], WhoBlA 92
Graves, Earl Gilbert 1935- WhoFI 92
Graves, Ernest 1880-1953 DcNCBi 2
Graves, Ernest Eugene 1947- WhoRel 92

Graves, Francis Porter, Jr 1923- WhoAmP 91
Graves, Frederick ScFEYrs
Graves, Gerald William 1924- WhoAmP 91
Graves, Glen Atkins 1927- AmMWSc 92
Graves, Glenn William 1929- AmMWSc 92
Graves, Hannon B 1943- AmMWSc 92
Graves, Harold E 1909- AmMWSc 92
Graves, Harry Hammond 1956- WhoMW 92
Graves, Harvey W, Jr 1927- AmMWSc 92
Graves, Helen Mataya 1925- WhoMW 92
Graves, Henry Lee 1813-1881 DcNCBi 2
Graves, Herbert Cornelius 1869-1919 BiInAmS
Graves, Irene Amelia 1906- WhoBlA 92
Graves, Jackie 1926- WhoBlA 92
Graves, James Robinson 1820-1893 RelLAm 91
Graves, Jerrod Franklin 1930- WhoBlA 92
Graves, Jerry Brook 1935- AmMWSc 92
Graves, Jesse Dickens 1819-1884 DcNCBi 2
Graves, John 1920- TwCWW 91, WrDr 92
Graves, John Clifford 1963- WhoBlA 92
Graves, John Harvey 1929- WhoMW 92
Graves, Ka Kathleen R. 1938- WhoWest 92
Graves, Kimberly Anne 1970- WhoRel 92
Graves, Kirk Andrew 1964- WhoEnt 92
Graves, Leon C 1951- WhoAmP 91
Graves, Leroy D 1912- AmMWSc 92
Graves, Leslie Theresa 1956- WhoBlA 92
Graves, Lester Baldwin 1958- WhoRel 92
Graves, Lewis Spottswood 1943- WhoRel 92
Graves, Lorraine Elizabeth 1957- WhoEnt 92
Graves, Louis 1883-1965 DcNCBi 2
Graves, Matthew Carl 1956- WhoFI 92
Graves, Maureen Ann 1946- WhoMW 92
Graves, Melanie Wallbillich 1963- WhoFI 92
Graves, Michael 1934- DcTwDes, FacFETw
Graves, Michael Phillip 1943- WhoEnt 92
Graves, Milford Robert 1941- NewAmDM
Graves, Morris 1910- FacFETw
Graves, Nancy 1940- WorArt 1980 [port]
Graves, Patrick Lee 1945- WhoAmL 92
Graves, Peter 1911- IntMPA 92
Graves, Peter 1926- IntMPA 92, WhoEnt 92
Graves, Ralph Henry 1817-1876 DcNCBi 2
Graves, Ralph Henry, III 1878-1939 DcNCBi 2
Graves, Ray Reynolds 1946- WhoAmL 92, WhoBlA 92
Graves, Raymond Lee 1928- WhoBlA 92
Graves, Richard 1715-1804 RfGEnL 91
Graves, Richard Perceval 1945- IntAu&W 91
Graves, Robert 1895-1985 CnDBLB 6 [port], ConAu 36NR, FacFETw, LiExTwC, RfGEnL 91
Graves, Robert Charles 1930- AmMWSc 92
Graves, Robert Earl 1938- AmMWSc 92
Graves, Robert Edward 1929- WhoWest 92
Graves, Robert Gage 1942- AmMWSc 92
Graves, Robert John 1945- AmMWSc 92
Graves, Robert Joseph 1952- AmMWSc 92
Graves, Robert Lawrence 1926- AmMWSc 92
Graves, Roderick Lawrence 1959- WhoBlA 92
Graves, Roy Neil DrAPF 91
Graves, Roy William, Jr 1915- AmMWSc 92
Graves, Rupert 1963- IntMPA 92
Graves, Scott Stoll 1952- AmMWSc 92
Graves, Sherman Teen 1905- WhoBlA 92
Graves, Shirley Patrick 1932- WhoWest 92
Graves, Sid Foster, Jr. 1946- WhoEnt 92
Graves, Spencer Bryce 1944- WhoFI 92
Graves, Thomas Browning 1932- WhoFI 92
Graves, Thomas Henry 1947- WhoRel 92
Graves, Toby Robert 1946- AmMWSc 92
Graves, Valerie WrDr 92
Graves, Valerie Jo 1950- WhoBlA 92
Graves, Vashti Sylvia 1967- WhoMW 92
Graves, Victoria 1941- AmMWSc 92
Graves, Wallace DrAPF 91
Graves, Wayne H 1925- AmMWSc 92
Graves, William 1937- WhoAmP 91
Graves, William Earl 1941- AmMWSc 92
Graves, William Ewing 1930- AmMWSc 92
Graves, William Howard 1940- AmMWSc 92
Graves, William Preston 1953- WhoAmP 91, WhoMW 92
Graves, Willie I. 1951- WhoRel 92
Gravesande, William Jacob 's 1688-1742 BlkwCEP
Graveson, Ronald Harry d1991 Who 92N
Gravett, Howard L 1911- AmMWSc 92
Gravett, Linda Sue 1950- WhoMW 92
Gravier, Charles 1719-1787 BlkwEAR
Graving, Richard John 1929- WhoAmL 92
Gravitt, Grant Harris 1934- WhoEnt 92
Gravitz, Sidney I 1932- AmMWSc 92
Grawe, Carol Ann 1938- WhoRel 92
Gray Who 92
Gray, Lord 1931- Who 92
Gray, Master of 1964- Who 92
Gray, A G, Jr ScFEYrs
Gray, A H, Jr 1936- AmMWSc 92
Gray, Alan 1926- AmMWSc 92
Gray, Alasdair 1934- ConNov 91, IntAu&W 91, WrDr 92
Gray, Alexander Stuart 1905- Who 92
Gray, Alfred 1939- AmMWSc 92
Gray, Alfred M. 1928- IntWW 91
Gray, Alfred Orren 1914- WrDr 92
Gray, Alice Ann 1947- WhoMW 92
Gray, Alice Wirth DrAPF 91
Gray, Allan, Jr 1930- AmMWSc 92
Gray, Allan P 1922- AmMWSc 92
Gray, Allen 1920- WhoEnt 92
Gray, Allen G 1915- AmMWSc 92
Gray, Andrew, III 1945- WhoFI 92
Gray, Andrew Aitken 1912- Who 92
Gray, Andrew Jackson 1924- WhoBlA 92
Gray, Andrew P 1916- AmMWSc 92
Gray, Angela IntAu&W 91X, WrDr 92
Gray, Ann Maynard 1945- WhoEnt 92
Gray, Anthony Who 92
Gray, Anthony James 1936- Who 92
Gray, Archibald Duncan, Jr. 1938- WhoAmL 92
Gray, Arthur L. 1918- WhoBlA 92
Gray, Asa 1810-1888 BenetAL 91, BiInAmS
Gray, Barbara E WhoAmP 91
Gray, Barbara Jean 1926- WhoAmP 91
Gray, Billy 1934- WhoAmP 91
Gray, Bowman 1874-1935 DcNCBi 2
Gray, Bowman, Jr. 1907-1969 DcNCBi 2
Gray, Brayton 1940- AmMWSc 92, WhoMW 92
Gray, Brian Mark 1939- WhoAmL 92
Gray, Bruce WhoRel 92
Gray, Bruce William 1937- AmMWSc 92
Gray, C Boyden WhoAmP 91
Gray, C. Vernon 1939- WhoBlA 92
Gray, Carl Thomas 1943- WhoMW 92
Gray, Carol Coleman 1946- WhoBlA 92
Gray, Caroline WrDr 92
Gray, Charles A 1938- AmMWSc 92
Gray, Charles Antony St John 1942- Who 92
Gray, Charles Augustus 1928- WhoFI 92
Gray, Charles Buffum 1934- WhoEnt 92
Gray, Charles Henry 1919-1986 WhoBlA 92N
Gray, Charles Horace 1911- Who 92
Gray, Charles Ireland 1929- Who 92
Gray, Charles Jackson 1947- WhoFI 92
Gray, Charlie William 1934- WhoEnt 92
Gray, Christine 1922- WhoBlA 92
Gray, Clarence Cornelius, III 1917- WhoBlA 92
Gray, Clarke Thomas 1919- AmMWSc 92
Gray, Clayton 1918- WrDr 92
Gray, Clifford Lawrence 1943- WhoEnt 92
Gray, Cliffton Herschel, Jr 1925- AmMWSc 92
Gray, Coleen 1922- IntMPA 92, WhoEnt 92
Gray, Constance Helen 1926- AmMWSc 92
Gray, D Anthony 1950- AmMWSc 92
Gray, Daniel Farnum 1963- WhoRel 92
Gray, David 1914- Who 92
Gray, David Bertsch 1944- AmMWSc 92
Gray, David Franklin 1917- WhoRel 92
Gray, David Julian 1953- WhoEnt 92
Gray, David Lee, Sr. 1931- WhoRel 92
Gray, David Robert 1945- AmMWSc 92
Gray, Denis Everett 1926- Who 92
Gray, Denis John Pereira 1935- Who 92
Gray, Dennis John 1953- AmMWSc 92
Gray, Derek Geoffrey 1941- AmMWSc 92
Gray, Diane 1941- WhoEnt 92
Gray, Don Norman 1931- AmMWSc 92
Gray, Donald Clifford 1930- Who 92
Gray, Donald Harford 1936- AmMWSc 92
Gray, Donald James 1908- AmMWSc 92
Gray, Donald Melvin 1938- AmMWSc 92
Gray, Donald Peter 1937- WhoRel 92
Gray, Dorothy Peyton 1943- WhoBlA 92
Gray, Dorothy Randall DrAPF 91
Gray, Douglas 1930- IntAu&W 91, Who 92, WrDr 92
Gray, Douglas Carmon 1938- AmMWSc 92
Gray, Douglas Stanning 1890-1959 TwCPaSc
Gray, Dulcie Who 92
Gray, Dulcie 1919- IntMPA 92
Gray, Dulcie 1920- WrDr 92
Gray, Dulcie Winifred 1920- IntAu&W 91
Gray, Duncan Montgomery, Jr. 1926- WhoRel 92
Gray, E Arthur 1925- WhoAmP 91
Gray, E. George 1924- IntWW 91
Gray, Earl E 1929- AmMWSc 92
Gray, Earl Ermont, Jr. 1952- WhoRel 92
Gray, Earl Haddon 1929- WhoBlA 92
Gray, Earnest 1957- WhoBlA 92
Gray, Edman Lowell 1939- WhoMW 92
Gray, Edward George 1924- Who 92
Gray, Edward Ray 1938- AmMWSc 92
Gray, Edward Samuel 1949- WhoEnt 92
Gray, Edward Theodore, Jr 1950- AmMWSc 92
Gray, Edward Wesley, Jr. 1946- WhoBlA 92
Gray, Edwin R 1931- AmMWSc 92
Gray, Eileen 1878-1976 DcTwDes
Gray, Elisha 1835-1901 BiInAmS
Gray, Elizabeth Janet WrDr 92
Gray, Ellen 1878-1976 FacFETw
Gray, Elmer 1934- AmMWSc 92
Gray, Elmon Taylor 1925- WhoAmP 91
Gray, Eoin Wedderburn 1942- AmMWSc 92
Gray, Ernest David 1930- AmMWSc 92
Gray, Ernest Paul 1926- AmMWSc 92
Gray, Ezio Maria 1885-1969 BiDExR
Gray, F Gail 1943- AmMWSc 92
Gray, Faith Harriet 1940- AmMWSc 92
Gray, Fenton 1916- AmMWSc 92
Gray, Francine du Plessix DrAPF 91
Gray, Francine du Plessix 1930- FacFETw, IntAu&W 91, WrDr 92
Gray, Francis Anthony 1917- Who 92
Gray, Francis Campbell 1940- WhoRel 92
Gray, Frank Davis, Jr 1916- AmMWSc 92
Gray, Franklin Emeric 1961- WhoFI 92
Gray, Fred David WhoBlA 92
Gray, Fred Ernest 1911- WhoAmP 91
Gray, Fred J 1942- WhoIns 92
Gray, Frederick Thomas, Jr 1951- WhoAmP 91
Gray, Frederick William 1918- AmMWSc 92
Gray, Frieda Gersh 1917- AmMWSc 92
Gray, Gary D 1936- AmMWSc 92
Gray, Gary Lee 1956- WhoFI 92
Gray, Gary M 1933- AmMWSc 92
Gray, Gary Ronald 1942- AmMWSc 92
Gray, Geoffrey Leicester 1905- Who 92
Gray, George A 1921- AmMWSc 92
Gray, George Alexander 1851-1912 DcNCBi 2
Gray, George Andrew David 1941- WhoFI 92
Gray, George Henry 1950- WhoAmL 92
Gray, George McBurney 1941- WhoRel 92
Gray, George Thomas Alexander 1949- Who 92
Gray, George W., III 1945- WhoBlA 92
Gray, George Wayne 1940- WhoFI 92
Gray, George William 1926- IntWW 91, Who 92
Gray, Georgia Neese WhoMW 92
Gray, Gilbert 1928- Who 92
Gray, Glenith Charlene 1948- WhoAmP 91
Gray, Gordon 1905- IntMPA 92
Gray, Gordon 1909-1982 DcNCBi 2
Gray, Gordon Cecil 1927- WhoFI 92
Gray, Gordon Joseph 1910- IntWW 91, Who 92, WhoRel 92
Gray, Gordon Thomas Seccombe 1911- Who 92
Gray, Grace Warner 1924- AmMWSc 92
Gray, Gregory Edward 1954- AmMWSc 92, WhoWest 92
Gray, H J 1924- AmMWSc 92
Gray, Hanna Holborn 1930- Who 92, WhoMW 92
Gray, Harold 1894-1968 BenetAL 91
Gray, Harold James 1907- Who 92, WrDr 92
Gray, Harry B 1935- AmMWSc 92
Gray, Harry Barkus 1935- IntWW 91
Gray, Harry Edward 1943- AmMWSc 92
Gray, Harry J. 1919- IntWW 91
Gray, Helen Theresa Gott 1942- WhoRel 92
Gray, Henry David 1908- WhoRel 92
Gray, Henry Hamilton 1922- AmMWSc 92
Gray, Herbert E. 1931- IntWW 91
Gray, Herbert Harold, III 1953- WhoAmL 92
Gray, Horace Benton, Jr 1941- AmMWSc 92
Gray, Howard William 1960- WhoWest 92
Gray, Hugh 1916- Who 92
Gray, Ian 1944- AmMWSc 92
Gray, Ina Turner 1926- WhoMW 92
Gray, Irving 1920- AmMWSc 92
Gray, J. Charles 1932- WhoAmL 92
Gray, J R 1938- WhoAmP 91
Gray, J. Stephen 1947- WhoAmL 92
Gray, Jack 1927- WrDr 92
Gray, James 1899-1984 BenetAL 91
Gray, James Alexander 1889-1952 DcNCBi 2
Gray, James Austin, II 1946- WhoBlA 92
Gray, James Clarke 1902- AmMWSc 92
Gray, James E. WhoBlA 92
Gray, James Edward 1932- AmMWSc 92
Gray, James Howard 1943- WhoBlA 92
Gray, James Larry 1932- WhoFI 92
Gray, James Martin 1851-1935 RelLAm 91
Gray, James P AmMWSc 92
Gray, James Patrick 1958- WhoMW 92
Gray, James R. 1953- WhoRel 92
Gray, James S AmMWSc 92
Gray, James S. 1943- WhoAmL 92
Gray, James Samuel 1936- WhoWest 92
Gray, James William 1945- WhoEnt 92
Gray, Jan Charles 1947- WhoAmL 92, WhoFI 92, WhoWest 92
Gray, Jane 1931- AmMWSc 92
Gray, Jeanne 1917- WhoEnt 92, WhoWest 92
Gray, Jerry 1961- WhoBlA 92
Gray, Jo Anne Hastings 1921- WhoAmP 91
Gray, Joan Maurisse WhoAmP 91
Gray, Joanne Maria 1958- WhoAmL 92
Gray, Joanne S. 1943- WhoBlA 92
Gray, Joe William 1946- AmMWSc 92
Gray, Joel Edward 1943- AmMWSc 92
Gray, John Who 92
Gray, John 1866-1934 RfGEnL 91
Gray, John 1913- Who 92
Gray, John 1918- Who 92
Gray, John 1942- TwCPaSc
Gray, John 1946- WrDr 92
Gray, John, II 1956- WhoAmP 91
Gray, John Archibald Browne 1918- IntWW 91
Gray, John Augustus, III 1924- AmMWSc 92
Gray, John B., Jr. 1951- WhoIns 92
Gray, John Calhoon 1955- WhoAmL 92
Gray, John Charles 1943- WhoAmL 92
Gray, John David 1928- WhoAmP 91
Gray, John Delton 1919- WhoFI 92
Gray, John Edward 1949- AmMWSc 92
Gray, John Magnus 1915- Who 92
Gray, John Malcolm 1940- AmMWSc 92
Gray, John Martin Fisher 1963- WhoAmL 92
Gray, John Michael Dudgeon 1913- Who 92
Gray, John Richard 1929- Who 92
Gray, John Stephens 1910- AmMWSc 92
Gray, John Walker 1931- AmMWSc 92
Gray, John Walton David 1936- Who 92
Gray, Johnnie Lee 1953- WhoBlA 92
Gray, Joseph Who 92
Gray, Joseph 1890-1963 TwCPaSc
Gray, Joseph B 1915- AmMWSc 92
Gray, Joseph William 1938- WhoBlA 92
Gray, Julius Alexander 1833-1891 DcNCBi 2
Gray, Karen G. WhoBlA 92
Gray, Karla M. WhoAmL 92, WhoWest 92
Gray, Karla M 1947- WhoAmP 91
Gray, Keith A., Jr. 1947- WhoBlA 92
Gray, Ken 1943- TwCPaSc
Gray, Kenneth Edward 1944- WhoAmL 92
Gray, Kenneth Eugene 1930- AmMWSc 92
Gray, Kenneth Fairbanks 1954- WhoAmL 92
Gray, Kenneth J 1924- WhoAmP 91
Gray, Kenneth Stewart 1945- AmMWSc 92
Gray, Kenneth W 1944- AmMWSc 92
Gray, Kenneth Walter 1939- Who 92
Gray, Kenneth Wayne 1944- WhoFI 92
Gray, Landon Carter 1850-1900 BiInAmS
Gray, Larry Allen 1943- WhoEnt 92
Gray, Laruth H. WhoBlA 92
Gray, Lawrence Firman 1949- AmMWSc 92
Gray, Leo Milton, Jr. 1946- WhoBlA 92
Gray, Leon 1951- WhoBlA 92
Gray, Leon Lorlan 1940- WhoMW 92
Gray, Leonard W 1942- WhoAmP 91
Gray, Lewis Richard 1936- AmMWSc 92
Gray, Linda WhoEnt 92
Gray, Linda 1940- IntMPA 92
Gray, Linda Esther 1948- Who 92
Gray, Linda Lou 1951- WhoAmL 92
Gray, Linsley Shepard, Jr 1929- AmMWSc 92
Gray, Louis Patrick 1916- IntWW 91
Gray, Louise Maxine 1938- WhoMW 92
Gray, Lynn Rene 1968- WhoEnt 92
Gray, Lyons 1942- WhoAmP 91
Gray, Maceo 1940- WhoBlA 92
Gray, Marcus J 1936- WhoAmP 91, WhoBlA 92
Gray, Margaret Ann 1950- WhoMW 92
Gray, Margaret Caroline 1913- Who 92
Gray, Marie Elise 1914- WhoWest 92
Gray, Mark William 1916- WhoAmL 92
Gray, Marvin W. 1944- WhoBlA 92
Gray, Mary Jane 1924- AmMWSc 92
Gray, Mary Wheat 1939- AmMWSc 92

**Gray,** Mattie Evans 1935- *WhoBlA 92*
**Gray,** Mayo L. *DrAPF 91*
**Gray,** Michael Stuart 1932- *Who 92*
**Gray,** Michael William 1943- *AmMWSc 92*
**Gray,** Michelle Eileen 1960- *WhoFI 92*
**Gray,** Milner Connorton 1899- *Who 92*
**Gray,** Milton Hefter 1910- *WhoAmL 92*
**Gray,** Monique Sylvaine *Who 92*
**Gray,** Moses W. 1937- *WhoBlA 92*
**Gray,** Myrtle Edwards 1914- *WhoBlA 92*
**Gray,** Nancy M 1954- *AmMWSc 92*
**Gray,** Naomi T. 1924- *WhoBlA 92*
**Gray,** Nicolete 1911- *WrDr 92*
**Gray,** Oscar Shalom 1926- *WhoAmL 92*
**Gray,** Pat *DrAPF 91*
**Gray,** Patricia Joyce 1951- *WhoWest 92*
**Gray,** Patrick James Murphy 1945- *WhoEnt 92*
**Gray,** Patrick Worth *DrAPF 91*
**Gray,** Paul 1930- *AmMWSc 92*
**Gray,** Paul Edward 1932- *AmMWSc 92, IntWW 91, Who 92*
**Gray,** Paul Eugene 1938- *AmMWSc 92*
**Gray,** Paul R *AmMWSc 92*
**Gray,** Paul Richard Charles 1948- *Who 92*
**Gray,** Paul Russell 1942- *WhoWest 92*
**Gray,** Paulette S 1943- *AmMWSc 92*
**Gray,** Pearl Spears 1945- *WhoBlA 92*
**Gray,** Peter 1926- *IntWW 91, Who 92*
**Gray,** Peter Francis 1937- *Who 92*
**Gray,** Peter Norman 1940- *AmMWSc 92*
**Gray,** Peter Vance 1928- *AmMWSc 92*
**Gray,** Philip Howard 1926- *WhoWest 92*
**Gray,** Rachel G *WhoAmP 91*
**Gray,** Ralph D. 1933- *WhoMW 92*
**Gray,** Ralph Donald, Jr 1938- *AmMWSc 92*
**Gray,** Ralph J 1923- *AmMWSc 92*
**Gray,** Raymond Francis 1926- *AmMWSc 92*
**Gray,** Raymond Leroy, Sr. 1915- *WhoBlA 92*
**Gray,** Reed Alden 1921- *AmMWSc 92*
**Gray,** Reginald 1932- *TwCPaSc*
**Gray,** Reginald John 1916- *Who 92*
**Gray,** Richard 1929- *IntAu&W 91, WrDr 92*
**Gray,** Richard Arden 1935- *WhoWest 92*
**Gray,** Richard Butler 1922- *IntAu&W 91, WrDr 92*
**Gray,** Richard Edwin, III 1950- *WhoAmL 92*
**Gray,** Richard Jules 1927- *WhoWest 92*
**Gray,** Richard Moss 1924- *WhoWest 92*
**Gray,** Robert 1928- *Who 92*
**Gray,** Robert 1942- *ConAu 134*
**Gray,** Robert 1945- *ConPo 91, WrDr 92*
**Gray,** Robert Alan 1955- *WhoEnt 92*
**Gray,** Robert Dean 1941- *WhoBlA 92*
**Gray,** Robert Dee 1941- *AmMWSc 92*
**Gray,** Robert Donald 1924- *WhoWest 92*
**Gray,** Robert H 1940- *AmMWSc 92*
**Gray,** Robert Howard 1937- *AmMWSc 92*
**Gray,** Robert J 1918- *AmMWSc 92*
**Gray,** Robert Keith 1923- *IntWW 91, WhoFI 92*
**Gray,** Robert Michael Ker *Who 92*
**Gray,** Robert Molten 1943- *AmMWSc 92, WhoWest 92*
**Gray,** Robert R. 1910- *WhoBlA 92*
**Gray,** Robert Winston 1938- *WhoFI 92*
**Gray,** Robin 1924- *Who 92*
**Gray,** Robin 1940- *Who 92*
**Gray,** Robin 1944- *Who 92*
**Gray,** Robin B 1925- *AmMWSc 92*
**Gray,** Robin Trevor 1940- *IntWW 91*
**Gray,** Roger Ibbotson 1921- *Who 92*
**Gray,** Roland, III 1943- *WhoAmL 92*
**Gray,** Ronald 1868-1951 *TwCPaSc*
**Gray,** Ronald Frederick 1944- *WhoWest 92*
**Gray,** Ronald Loren 1964- *WhoAmL 92*
**Gray,** Ruben L. 1938- *WhoBlA 92*
**Gray,** Russell *WrDr 92*
**Gray,** Russell Houston 1918- *AmMWSc 92*
**Gray,** Samuel Hutchison 1948- *AmMWSc 92*
**Gray,** Sarah Delcenia 1934- *AmMWSc 92*
**Gray,** Simon 1936- *RfGEnL 91, WrDr 92*
**Gray,** Simon James Holliday 1936- *FacFETw, IntWW 91, Who 92*
**Gray,** Simon John Halliday 1936- *IntAu&W 91*
**Gray,** Spalding 1941- *IntAu&W 91, IntMPA 92, WrDr 92*
**Gray,** Spaulding 1941- *WhoEnt 92*
**Gray,** Stephen d1736 *BlkwCEP*
**Gray,** Stephen Thomas 1950- *WhoMW 92*
**Gray,** Stephen Wood 1915- *AmMWSc 92*
**Gray,** Sterling Perkins, Jr. 1943- *WhoBlA 92*
**Gray,** Susan Simons 1950- *WhoWest 92*
**Gray,** Sylvia Mary d1991 *Who 92N*
**Gray,** Ted Fay 1942- *WhoRel 92*
**Gray,** Theodore Flint, Jr 1939- *AmMWSc 92*
**Gray,** Theodore Milton 1927- *WhoAmP 91*
**Gray,** Thomas 1716-1771 *BlkwCEP, CnDBLB 2 [port], DcLB 109 [port], RfGEnL 91*
**Gray,** Thomas 1850-1908 *BiInAmS*
**Gray,** Thomas Cecil 1913- *Who 92*
**Gray,** Thomas James 1917- *AmMWSc 92*
**Gray,** Thomas K. *IntMPA 92*
**Gray,** Thomas Knox *WhoEnt 92*
**Gray,** Thomas Merrill 1929- *AmMWSc 92*
**Gray,** Timothy Kenney 1939- *AmMWSc 92*
**Gray,** Tom J 1937- *AmMWSc 92*
**Gray,** Tony 1922- *IntAu&W 91, WrDr 92*
**Gray,** Truman S 1906- *AmMWSc 92*
**Gray,** Valerie Hamilton 1959- *WhoBlA 92*
**Gray,** Wallace Gale 1927- *WhoMW 92, WhoRel 92*
**Gray,** Walter C 1919- *AmMWSc 92*
**Gray,** Walter Franklin 1929- *WhoAmL 92*
**Gray,** Walter J *WhoAmP 91*
**Gray,** Walter Steven 1938- *AmMWSc 92*
**Gray,** Wardell 1921-1955 *NewAmDM*
**Gray,** Whitmore 1932- *WhoAmL 92*
**Gray,** Wilfred Douglas 1937- *WhoBlA 92*
**Gray,** William 1928- *Who 92*
**Gray,** William 1955- *Who 92*
**Gray,** William A. 1939- *WhoMW 92*
**Gray,** William Addison 1960- *WhoFI 92*
**Gray,** William Allan 1950- *WhoAmL 92*
**Gray,** William David 1916- *AmMWSc 92*
**Gray,** William Douglas 1941- *WhoAmL 92*
**Gray,** William Dudley 1912- *AmMWSc 92*
**Gray,** William Guerin 1948- *AmMWSc 92*
**Gray,** William H., III *NewYTBS 91 [port]*
**Gray,** William H., III 1941- *AlmAP 92 [port], WhoAmP 91, WhoBlA 92*
**Gray,** William H., Jr. 1927- *WhoRel 92*
**Gray,** William Harvey 1948- *AmMWSc 92*
**Gray,** William Mack 1944- *WhoMW 92*
**Gray,** William Martin, Jr. 1962- *WhoRel 92*
**Gray,** William Mason 1929- *AmMWSc 92*
**Gray,** William N 1949- *WhoAmP 91*
**Gray,** William Oxley 1914- *WhoAmL 92*
**Gray-Bussard,** Dolly H 1943- *IntAu&W 91*
**Gray Debros,** Winifred Marjorie *Who 92*
**Gray-Little,** Bernadette 1944- *WhoBlA 92*
**Gray of Contin,** Baron 1927- *Who 92*
**Graybeal,** Jack Daniel 1930- *AmMWSc 92*
**Graybeal,** Lynne Elizabeth 1956- *WhoAmL 92*
**Graybeal,** Walter Thomas 1918- *AmMWSc 92*
**Graybiel,** Ann M *AmMWSc 92*
**Graybiel,** Ashton 1902- *AmMWSc 92*
**Graybill,** Alicia Clare 1963- *WhoMW 92*
**Graybill,** Bruce Myron 1931- *AmMWSc 92*
**Graybill,** David Wesley 1949- *WhoWest 92*
**Graybill,** Donald Lee 1943- *AmMWSc 92*
**Graybill,** Franklin A 1921- *AmMWSc 92*
**Graybill,** Howard W 1915- *AmMWSc 92*
**Graydon,** Alexander 1752-1818 *BenetAL 91*
**Graydon,** Michael 1938- *Who 92*
**Graydon,** Ruth *DrAPF 91*
**Graydon,** Wasdon, Jr. 1950- *WhoBlA 92*
**Graydon,** William Frederick 1919- *AmMWSc 92*
**Grayer,** Jeff 1965- *BlkOlyM*
**Grayer,** Jeffrey 1965- *WhoBlA 92*
**Grayhack,** John Thomas 1923- *AmMWSc 92*
**Graylin,** John Cranmer 1921- *IntWW 91*
**Graylow,** Richard Vernon 1940- *WhoAmL 92*
**Grays,** Mattelia Bennett 1931- *WhoBlA 92*
**Grayson,** Barbara Ann 1954- *WhoBlA 92*
**Grayson,** Bette Rita 1947- *WhoAmL 92*
**Grayson,** Byron J., Sr. 1949- *WhoBlA 92*
**Grayson,** Cecil 1920- *IntWW 91, Who 92*
**Grayson,** D. W. *WhoRel 92*
**Grayson,** David *AmPeW, BenetAL 91*
**Grayson,** David S. 1943- *WhoMW 92*
**Grayson,** Deborah Eve *DrAPF 91*
**Grayson,** Dennis Michael 1944- *WhoEnt 92*
**Grayson,** Edward Davis 1938- *WhoAmL 92*
**Grayson,** Ellison Capers, Jr. 1928- *WhoWest 92*
**Grayson,** Elsie Michelle 1962- *WhoBlA 92*
**Grayson,** George W 1938- *WhoAmP 91*
**Grayson,** George Wallace 1938- *WhoAmP 91*
**Grayson,** George Welton 1938- *WhoBlA 92*
**Grayson,** Harry L. 1929- *WhoBlA 92*
**Grayson,** Herbert G 1926- *AmMWSc 92*
**Grayson,** Jennifer A. 1949- *WhoBlA 92*
**Grayson,** Jeremy 1933- *Who 92*
**Grayson,** John 1919- *AmMWSc 92*
**Grayson,** John Allan 1930- *WhoAmL 92*
**Grayson,** John Francis 1928- *AmMWSc 92*
**Grayson,** John Michael 1948- *WhoEnt 92*
**Grayson,** John N. 1932- *WhoBlA 92*
**Grayson,** John Wesley 1941- *WhoWest 92*
**Grayson,** Kathryn 1923- *IntMPA 92*
**Grayson,** Lawrence P 1937- *AmMWSc 92*
**Grayson,** Mark R. 1949- *WhoAmL 92*
**Grayson,** Martin *AmMWSc 92*
**Grayson,** Merrill 1919- *AmMWSc 92*
**Grayson,** Michael A 1941- *AmMWSc 92*
**Grayson,** N June 1927- *WhoAmP 91*
**Grayson,** Phillip Simon 1947- *WhoEnt 92*
**Grayson,** Richard *DrAPF 91*
**Grayson,** Richard Ethan 1948- *WhoAmL 92*
**Grayson,** Robert *WhoBlA 92*
**Grayson,** Rupert Stanley Harrington d1991 *Who 92N*
**Grayson,** Stanley Edward 1950- *WhoBlA 92*
**Grayson,** Walton George, III 1928- *WhoFI 92*
**Grayson,** William Curtis, Jr 1929- *AmMWSc 92*
**Grayson,** William John 1788-1863 *BenetAL 91*
**Grayston,** J Thomas 1924- *AmMWSc 92*
**Grayston,** Kenneth 1914- *Who 92*
**Grayzel,** Arthur I 1932- *AmMWSc 92*
**Grazer,** Brian 1951- *IntMPA 92*
**Graziadei,** Frank M. 1953- *WhoAmL 92*
**Graziani,** Edward C *WhoAmP 91*
**Graziani,** Rodolfo 1882-1955 *BiDExR, EncTR 91*
**Graziano,** Charles Dominic 1920- *WhoMW 92*
**Graziano,** Craig Frank 1950- *WhoAmL 92*
**Graziano,** Ernest Dennis 1942- *WhoIns 92*
**Graziano,** Frank *DrAPF 91*
**Graziano,** Frank M *AmMWSc 92*
**Graziano,** Rocky 1919?-1990 *AnObit 1990*
**Graziano,** Rocky 1921-1990 *FacFETw*
**Grazioli,** Albert John, Jr. 1954- *WhoWest 92*
**Grbac,** Nick Albert Arthur 1957- *WhoEnt 92*
**Grdina,** David John 1944- *AmMWSc 92, WhoMW 92*
**Grdis,** Enoch 1931- *AmMWSc 92*
**Greacen,** Sharon Hope O'Neal 1942- *WhoWest 92*
**Gread,** Joel J. 1956- *WhoEnt 92*
**Greager,** Oswald Herman 1905- *AmMWSc 92*
**Grean,** Stanley Vernon 1920- *WhoRel 92*
**Greaney,** James Robert 1922- *WhoFI 92*
**Greaney,** John Francis 1950- *WhoAmL 92*
**Greaney,** John M *WhoAmP 91*
**Greaney,** William A 1931- *AmMWSc 92*
**Greanias,** George 1948- *WhoAmP 91*
**Grear,** Effie C. 1927- *WhoBlA 92*
**Grear,** William A. 1923- *WhoBlA 92*
**Greaser,** Marion Lewis 1942- *AmMWSc 92*
**Greaser,** William Joseph 1926- *WhoMW 92*
**Greasham,** Randolph Louis 1942- *AmMWSc 92*
**Great,** Don Charles 1951- *WhoEnt 92, WhoWest 92*
**Greatbatch,** Wilson 1919- *AmMWSc 92*
**Greathead,** David John 1931- *Who 92*
**Greathouse,** Terrence Ray 1932- *AmMWSc 92*
**Greaux,** Cheryl Prejean 1949- *WhoBlA 92*
**Greaver,** Harry 1929- *WhoEnt 92*
**Greaves,** Bettina Bien 1917- *AmMWSc 92*
**Greaves,** Derrick 1927- *IntWW 91, TwCPaSc*
**Greaves,** Jeffrey 1926- *Who 92*
**Greaves,** Malcolm Watson 1933- *Who 92*
**Greaves,** Margaret 1914- *IntAu&W 91, WrDr 92*
**Greaves,** Walter 1846-1930 *TwCPaSc*
**Greaves,** Walter Stalker 1937- *AmMWSc 92*
**Greaves,** William *LesBEnT 92, WhoBlA 92*
**Greaves,** William Garfield *WhoEnt 92*
**Grebby,** Anne 1944- *TwCPaSc*
**Grebe,** Janice Durr 1940- *AmMWSc 92*
**Grebe,** Lynn Charles 1952- *WhoAmP 91*
**Grebe,** Michael W *WhoAmP 91*
**Grebenau,** Mark David 1951- *AmMWSc 92*
**Grebene,** Alan B 1939- *AmMWSc 92*
**Grebenik,** Eugene 1919- *Who 92*
**Grebenshchikov,** Boris 1953- *IntWW 91*
**Greber,** Isaac 1928- *AmMWSc 92*
**Grebner,** Eugene Ernest 1931- *AmMWSc 92*
**Grebner,** Georgy Eduardovich 1892-1954 *SovUnBD*
**Grebogi,** Celso 1947- *AmMWSc 92*
**Grebow,** Edward 1949- *WhoEnt 92, WhoFI 92*
**Grebow,** Peter Eric 1946- *AmMWSc 92*
**Grebstein,** Sheldon Norman 1928- *WrDr 92*
**Grecco,** William L 1924- *AmMWSc 92*
**Grech,** Joe Anthony 1950- *WhoMW 92*
**Grech,** Joe Debono 1941- *IntWW 91*
**Grech Orr,** Charles 1927- *IntWW 91*
**Grechaninov,** Alexander 1864-1956 *NewAmDM*
**Grechaninov,** Alexander Tikhonovich 1864-1956 *FacFETw*
**Grechko,** Andrey Antonovich 1903-1976 *SovUnBD*
**Grecian,** Phil Douglas 1948- *WhoEnt 92*
**Greco,** Claude Vincent 1930- *AmMWSc 92*
**Greco,** Edward Carl 1911- *AmMWSc 92*
**Greco,** Emilio 1913- *IntWW 91*
**Greco,** Giuseppe 1929- *IntWW 91*
**Greco,** Guy Benjamin 1951- *WhoAmL 92*
**Greco,** Ignazio J 1961- *WhoIns 92*
**Greco,** James Joseph 1958- *WhoAmL 92*
**Greco,** Jose 1918- *WhoEnt 92*
**Greco,** Jose 1919- *FacFETw*
**Greco,** Salvatore Joseph 1921- *AmMWSc 92*
**Greco,** Stephen *DrAPF 91*
**Greco,** Stephen R 1919- *WhoAmP 91*
**Greco,** William Robert 1951- *AmMWSc 92*
**Grecsek,** Matthew Thomas 1963- *WhoFI 92*
**Greden,** John F 1942- *AmMWSc 92*
**Greding,** Edward J, Jr 1940- *AmMWSc 92*
**Greear,** Philip French-Carson 1918- *AmMWSc 92*
**Greechie,** Richard Joseph 1941- *AmMWSc 92*
**Greedan,** John Edward 1942- *AmMWSc 92*
**Greeff,** Douglas Haven 1956- *WhoFI 92*
**Greek,** Gene Allen 1937- *WhoFI 92*
**Greeley,** Andrew 1928- *WrDr 92*
**Greeley,** Andrew Moran 1928- *WhoMW 92, WhoRel 92*
**Greeley,** Charles Matthew 1941- *WhoWest 92*
**Greeley,** Frederick 1919- *AmMWSc 92*
**Greeley,** George H, Jr 1947- *AmMWSc 92*
**Greeley,** Horace 1811-1872 *AmPolLe, BenetAL 91, RComAH*
**Greeley,** Richard Stiles 1927- *AmMWSc 92*
**Greeley,** Robert Charles 1948- *WhoWest 92*
**Greeley,** Ronald 1939- *AmMWSc 92, WhoWest 92*
**Greeley,** Sean McGovern 1961- *WhoFI 92*
**Greelish,** Thomas W. d1991 *NewYTBS 91*
**Greely,** Adolphus Washington 1844-1935 *BenetAL 91*
**Greely,** Michael T 1940- *WhoAmP 91*
**Greely,** Michael Truman 1940- *WhoWest 92*
**Green,** A. C. 1963- *WhoBlA 92*
**Green,** A Lincoln *ScFEYrs*
**Green,** Aaron Alphonso 1946- *WhoBlA 92*
**Green,** Adam *BenetAL 91*
**Green,** Adolph 1915- *IntMPA 92, WhoEnt 92*
**Green,** Al *WhoBlA 92*
**Green,** Al 1946- *WhoBlA 92, WhoEnt 92*
**Green,** Alan d1991 *Who 92N*
**Green,** Alan 1932- *TwCPaSc*
**Green,** Alan, Jr 1925- *WhoAmP 91*
**Green,** Alan Carroll 1952- *WhoMW 92*
**Green,** Albert Edward *IntWW 91, Who 92*
**Green,** Albert Wise 1938- *AmMWSc 92*
**Green,** Alex Edward Samuel 1919- *AmMWSc 92*
**Green,** Alfred Rozelaar 1917- *TwCPaSc*
**Green,** Allan 1935- *Who 92*
**Green,** Allan Wright 1949- *WhoWest 92*
**Green,** Allen T 1934- *AmMWSc 92*
**Green,** Allison Anne 1936- *WhoMW 92*
**Green,** Alvin 1931- *WhoAmL 92*
**Green,** Alwin Clark 1930- *AmMWSc 92*
**Green,** Andrew Curtis 1936- *Who 92*
**Green,** Andrew Fleming 1941- *Who 92*
**Green,** Andrew M 1927- *IntAu&W 91, WrDr 92*
**Green,** Angelo Gray 1950- *WhoBlA 92*
**Green,** Anna Katharine 1846-1935 *BenetAL 91*
**Green,** Anne 1899- *BenetAL 91*
**Green,** Anne Catherine Hoof 1720?-1775 *BlkwEAR*
**Green,** Anthony 1939- *TwCPaSc*
**Green,** Anthony Eric Sandall 1939- *IntWW 91, Who 92*
**Green,** Arthur 1928- *Who 92*
**Green,** Arthur 1941- *WhoRel 92*
**Green,** Arthur Edward Chase 1911- *Who 92*
**Green,** Arthur Jackson 1928- *Who 92*
**Green,** Arthur L. d1991 *NewYTBS 91*
**Green,** Arthur L. 1928- *WhoBlA 92*
**Green,** Arthur R 1934- *AmMWSc 92*
**Green,** Arthur Samuel 1951- *WhoRel 92*
**Green,** Asa *BenetAL 91*
**Green,** Barbara Beth 1962- *WhoEnt 92*
**Green,** Barbara Marie 1928- *WhoBlA 92*
**Green,** Barry 1940- *TwCPaSc*
**Green,** Barry A 1940- *AmMWSc 92*

Green, Barry George 1949- AmMWSc 92
Green, Barry Spencer 1932- Who 92
Green, Barry Steven 1957- WhoWest 92
Green, Barton Clark 1935- WhoAmL 92
Green, Benedict Who 92
Green, Benigna Regina 1956- WhoAmL 92
Green, Benjamin DrAPF 91
Green, Benjamin Daniel 1793-1862 BiInAmS
Green, Benny 1927- IntAu&W 91, Who 92, WrDr 92
Green, Bernard 1925- IntWW 91, Who 92
Green, Bernard Douglas 1940- WhoRel 92
Green, Bernard Lothair 1938- WhoRel 92
Green, Bernard Richardson 1843-1914 BiInAmS
Green, Betsy Ann 1963- WhoEnt 92
Green, Betsy M. 1930- WhoEnt 92
Green, Beverley R 1938- AmMWSc 92
Green, Beverly Robin 1956- WhoEnt 92
Green, Bill 1929- AlmAP 92 [port], WhoAmP 91
Green, Brenda Kay 1947- WhoBlA 92
Green, Brian WrDr 92
Green, Brian 1935- AmMWSc 92
Green, Brian Gerald 1954- WhoWest 92
Green, Bruce Allan 1948- WhoAmP 91
Green, Bryan Stuart Westmacott 1901- Who 92
Green, Brynmor Hugh 1941- Who 92
Green, Byron David 1950- AmMWSc 92
Green, Calvin Coolidge 1931- WhoBlA 92, WhoRel 92
Green, Carl Jay 1939- WhoAmL 92
Green, Carolyn Louise 1950- WhoBlA 92
Green, Cathy Jean 1953- WhoAmL 92
Green, Cecil WhoAmP 91
Green, Celia 1935- WrDr 92
Green, Charles A. WhoBlA 92
Green, Charles A. 1927- WhoBlA 92
Green, Charles E 1912- AmMWSc 92
Green, Charles Edward 1926- WhoRel 92
Green, Charles Frederick 1930- Who 92
Green, Charles Henry 1957- WhoFI 92
Green, Charles Raymond 1942- AmMWSc 92
Green, Charles Sylvester 1900-1980 DcNCBi 2
Green, Charles Thomas 1950- WhoFI 92
Green, Charles Wayne 1948- WhoRel 92
Green, Christina J. DrAPF 91
Green, Christopher Canfield 1940- WhoMW 92
Green, Christopher Edward Wastie 1943- Who 92
Green, Cicero M., Jr. 1930- WhoBlA 92
Green, Claire Magidovitch 1953- WhoRel 92
Green, Claude Cordell 1941- AmMWSc 92
Green, Clifford 1934- IntAu&W 91
Green, Clifford Scott 1923- WhoAmL 92, WhoBlA 92
Green, Clyde Octavious 1960- WhoBlA 92
Green, Consuella 1946- WhoBlA 92
Green, Curtis 1957- WhoBlA 92
Green, Curtis E. 1923- WhoBlA 92
Green, Cyril Kenneth 1931- WhoWest 92
Green, D. H. 1922- WrDr 92
Green, Dan 1935- IntWW 91
Green, Daniel F. 1947- WhoWest 92
Green, Daniel G 1937- AmMWSc 92
Green, Daniel Kevin 1955- WhoMW 92
Green, Darrell 1960- WhoBlA 92
Green, David Who 92
Green, David 1922- WhoFI 92, WhoMW 92
Green, David 1934- AmMWSc 92
Green, David Brian 1960- WhoWest 92
Green, David Charles 1953- WhoAmL 92
Green, David Claude 1945- AmMWSc 92
Green, David Ferrell 1935- WhoMW 92
Green, David Headley 1936- Who 92
Green, David J 1940- AmMWSc 92
Green, David Leo 1951- WhoAmP 91
Green, David M 1953- AmMWSc 92
Green, David Oliver, Jr. 1908- WhoWest 92
Green, David Wayne 1954- WhoRel 92
Green, David William 1942- AmMWSc 92
Green, David William 1951- WhoAmL 92
Green, Deborah Ann 1948- WhoFI 92
Green, Deborah Kennon 1951- WhoBlA 92
Green, Dennis 1949- WhoBlA 92
Green, Dennis Howard 1922- Who 92
Green, Dennis O. 1940- WhoBlA 92
Green, Detroy Edward 1930- AmMWSc 92
Green, Diana Florence 1950- WhoEnt 92
Green, Diane Patricia 1941- WhoAmP 91
Green, Don Wesley 1932- AmMWSc 92
Green, Donald Eugene 1926- AmMWSc 92
Green, Donald Hugh 1929- WhoAmL 92
Green, Donald MacDonald 1930- AmMWSc 92
Green, Donald Ross 1924- WrDr 92
Green, Donald Wayne 1924- AmMWSc 92
Green, Donna WhoAmP 91
Green, Dorothy 1915- IntAu&W 91
Green, Douglas D WhoAmP 91
Green, Douglas Foster 1947- WhoAmP 91
Green, Douglas R 1955- AmMWSc 92
Green, Edward Fairchild 1918- WhoAmL 92
Green, Edward Jewett 1937- AmMWSc 92
Green, Edward Joseph, Jr. 1963- WhoEnt 92
Green, Edward L. WhoBlA 92
Green, Edward Lewis 1946- AmMWSc 92
Green, Edward Michael 1930- Who 92
Green, Edward Stephen 1910- Who 92
Green, Edwin Alfred 1931- AmMWSc 92
Green, Edwin James 1954- AmMWSc 92
Green, Elizabeth A. H. 1906- WrDr 92
Green, Elizabeth Adine Herkimer 1906- IntAu&W 91
Green, Elizabeth Lee 1911- WhoBlA 92
Green, Eric 1967- WhoBlA 92
Green, Eric Douglas 1959- AmMWSc 92
Green, Erika Ana 1928- AmMWSc 92
Green, Ernest G. 1941- WhoBlA 92
Green, Eugene L 1927- AmMWSc 92
Green, Evanna E 1931- WhoAmP 91
Green, Farnifold 1674-1714 DcNCBi 2
Green, Fitzhugh 1888-1947 ScFEYrs
Green, Fitzhugh 1917- WhoAmP 91
Green, Fletcher Melvin 1895-1978 DcNCBi 2
Green, Floyd J 1917- AmMWSc 92
Green, Forrest F. 1915- WhoBlA 92
Green, Francis J. 1906- WhoRel 92
Green, Francis Mathews 1835-1902 BiInAmS
Green, Francis William 1920- WhoWest 92
Green, Frank Alan 1931- Who 92
Green, Frank Orville 1908- AmMWSc 92
Green, Franklin D. 1933- WhoBlA 92
Green, Fred Wallace 1945- WhoIns 92
Green, Freddie 1911-1987 NewAmDM
Green, Frederick Chapman 1920- WhoBlA 92
Green, Frederick Pratt 1903- WrDr 92
Green, Frederick Shepherd, Sr. 1923- WhoAmL 92
Green, G W 1857?-1902? BiInAmS
Green, G W 1927- AmMWSc 92
Green, Gabriel 1924- WhoWest 92
Green, Gabriel Marcus 1891-1919 BiInAmS
Green, Galen DrAPF 91
Green, Garrett 1941- WhoRel 92
Green, Gary Miller 1940- AmMWSc 92
Green, Gary Quentin 1942- WhoAmP 91
Green, Gaston Alfred, III 1966- WhoBlA 92
Green, Gene 1947- WhoAmP 91
Green, Geoffrey DrAPF 91
Green, Geoffrey Hugh 1920- Who 92
Green, George WhoWest 92
Green, George Ernest Who 92N
Green, George F WhoAmP 91
Green, George G 1922- AmMWSc 92
Green, George Howard 1948- WhoWest 92
Green, George Hugh 1911- Who 92
Green, George Norris 1939- WhoAmP 91
Green, Georgia Mae 1950- WhoBlA 92
Green, Gerald 1922- WrDr 92
Green, Gerald 1941- AmMWSc 92
Green, Gerald Walker 1945- WhoRel 92
Green, Geraldine D. 1938- WhoBlA 92
Green, Gerard Leo 1928- WhoRel 92
Green, Gerard Nicholas Valentine 1950- Who 92
Green, Gloria J. 1954- WhoBlA 92
Green, Gordon Ralph 1924- WhoEnt 92
Green, Gregory David 1948- Who 92
Green, Guy 1913- IntMPA 92
Green, Guy 1937- Who 92
Green, Guy Mervin Charles WhoEnt 92
Green, Guy Stephen Montague 1937- IntWW 91
Green, Hamilton 1934- IntWW 91
Green, Hannah DrAPF 91
Green, Harold D AmMWSc 92
Green, Harold Daniel 1934- WhoMW 92
Green, Harold Paul 1922- WhoAmL 92
Green, Harold Rugby 1926- AmMWSc 92
Green, Harry 1917- AmMWSc 92
Green, Harry J, Jr 1911- AmMWSc 92
Green, Harry Western, II 1940- AmMWSc 92
Green, Harry William 1932- WhoFI 92
Green, Henry 1905-1973 RfGEnL 91
Green, Henry 1905-1974 FacFETw
Green, Hilton A. 1929- WhoEnt 92
Green, Hope Stuart 1944- WhoEnt 92
Green, Horace Wade 1956- WhoAmL 92
Green, Howard 1925- AmMWSc 92, IntWW 91
Green, Howard Alan 1938- WhoFI 92
Green, Howard I. 1936- WhoEnt 92, WhoWest 92
Green, Hubert Gordon 1938- AmMWSc 92
Green, Hugh 1959- WhoBlA 92
Green, Humphrey Christian 1924- Who 92
Green, I. Bernard 1937- WhoEnt 92
Green, Ira AmMWSc 92
Green, Irving Morton 1925- WhoAmL 92
Green, J C R 1949- IntAu&W 91, WrDr 92
Green, Jack 1925- WhoWest 92
Green, Jack Peter 1925- AmMWSc 92
Green, Jacob 1790-1841 BiInAmS
Green, Jacob Carl 1957- WhoBlA 92
Green, James, Jr. 1737?-1784 DcNCBi 2
Green, James Collins 1921- WhoAmP 91
Green, James Craig 1933- WhoWest 92
Green, James Douglas 1921- WhoAmP 91
Green, James Henderson 1881-1955 DcNCBi 2
Green, James L. 1945- WhoBlA 92
Green, James P, Jr WhoAmP 91
Green, James Paul 1953- WhoAmL 92
Green, James Weston 1913- AmMWSc 92
Green, Jeffrey A. 1957- WhoFI 92
Green, Jeffrey C. 1941- WhoAmL 92
Green, Jeffrey David 1947- AmMWSc 92
Green, Jeffrey Scott 1947- AmMWSc 92
Green, Jeffrey Steven 1943- WhoAmL 92
Green, Jerie Ireland 1950- WhoMW 92
Green, Jerome 1953- AmMWSc 92
Green, Jerome George 1929- AmMWSc 92
Green, Jerome Joseph 1932- AmMWSc 92
Green, Jerrold David 1948- WhoWest 92
Green, Jerry Alan 1943- WhoWest 92
Green, Jerry Howard 1930- WhoFI 92, WhoMW 92
Green, Jerry Richard 1946- WhoFI 92
Green, Jersey Michael-Lee 1952- WhoAmL 92
Green, Jim 1936- WhoAmP 91
Green, Joan WhoAmP 91
Green, Joel Bennett 1956- WhoRel 92
Green, John 1807-1887 DcNCBi 2
Green, John 1932- TwCPaSc
Green, John Arthur Savage 1939- AmMWSc 92
Green, John Chandler 1932- AmMWSc 92
Green, John Dennis Fowler 1909- Who 92
Green, John Edward 1937- Who 92
Green, John F 1943- IntAu&W 91
Green, John Francis 1959- WhoFI 92
Green, John H 1929- AmMWSc 92
Green, John Irving 1924- AmMWSc 92
Green, John Joseph 1931- WhoFI 92
Green, John Kevin WhoAmP 91
Green, John Lafayette, Jr. 1933- WhoMW 92
Green, John M 1940- AmMWSc 92
Green, John Michael 1924- Who 92
Green, John Patterson 1845-1940 DcNCBi 2
Green, John Robert 1959- WhoRel 92
Green, John Root 1920- AmMWSc 92
Green, John Ruffin 1832-1869 DcNCBi 2
Green, John William 1935- AmMWSc 92
Green, John Willie 1914- AmMWSc 92
Green, Jonathan David 1946- WhoFI 92
Green, Jonathan P 1935- AmMWSc 92
Green, Jonathon 1948- ConAu 134
Green, Joseph 1706-1780 BenetAL 91
Green, Joseph 1905- IntMPA 92
Green, Joseph 1928- AmMWSc 92
Green, Joseph 1931- TwCSFW 91, WrDr 92
Green, Joseph 1938- IntMPA 92
Green, Joseph, Jr. 1950- WhoBlA 92
Green, Joseph G. 1934- WhoEnt 92
Green, Joseph Lee 1931- IntAu&W 91
Green, Joseph Martin 1925- WhoMW 92
Green, Joseph Matthew 1926- AmMWSc 92
Green, Josephine Wheeler 1942- WhoRel 92
Green, Joshua, III 1936- WhoFI 92, WhoWest 92
Green, Joyce 1928- WhoFI 92, WhoMW 92
Green, Joyce Hens 1928- WhoAmL 92
Green, Judith WrDr 92
Green, Judy 1943- AmMWSc 92
Green, Julian 1900- IntWW 91, LiExTwC
Green, Julian Hartridge 1900- IntAu&W 91, Who 92
Green, Julie Jayne WhoEnt 92
Green, Julien 1900- BenetAL 91, GuFrLit 1
Green, June Lazenby 1914- WhoAmL 92
Green, Karen Ann 1955- WhoEnt 92
Green, Kate DrAPF 91
Green, Keith 1940- AmMWSc 92
Green, Keith Malcolm 1954- WhoEnt 92
Green, Kenneth 1934- Who 92
Green, Kenneth David d1987 Who 92N
Green, Kenneth Harlon 1948- WhoWest 92
Green, Kenneth W WhoAmP 91
Green, Larry WhoRel 92
Green, Larry Anthony 1952- WhoMW 92
Green, Larry J 1931- AmMWSc 92
Green, Larry W. 1946- WhoBlA 92
Green, Lawrence 1937- AmMWSc 92
Green, Lawrence Jamalian 1945- WhoAmL 92
Green, Lawrence Raymond 1948- WhoAmL 92
Green, Lawrence Winter 1940- AmMWSc 92, WhoWest 92
Green, Leo Edward 1932- WhoAmP 91
Green, Leon William 1925- AmMWSc 92
Green, Leslie Claude 1920- WhoWest 92
Green, Leslie Leonard 1925- Who 92
Green, Lester L. 1941- WhoBlA 92
Green, Lila 1930- WhoMW 92
Green, Liller Bernice 1928- WhoBlA 92
Green, Linda Lou 1946- WhoFI 92
Green, Linda Luray Foster 1945- WhoMW 92
Green, Lisle Royal 1918- AmMWSc 92
Green, Lois Elaine 1953- WhoMW 92
Green, Louis Craig 1911- AmMWSc 92
Green, Louis Douglas 1916- AmMWSc 92
Green, Lowell Clark 1925- WhoRel 92
Green, Lucinda Jane 1953- Who 92
Green, Lynne 1944- WhoEnt 92
Green, Malcolm 1942- Who 92
Green, Malcolm C. 1925- IntMPA 92
Green, Malcolm Leslie Hodder 1936- Who 92
Green, Malcolm Robert 1943- Who 92
Green, Margaret TwCPaSc
Green, Margaret 1917- AmMWSc 92
Green, Marie Roder 1929- AmMWSc 92
Green, Mark 1917- Who 92
Green, Mark Alan 1956- AmMWSc 92
Green, Mark Lee 1947- AmMWSc 92
Green, Mark M 1937- AmMWSc 92
Green, Marshall 1916- IntWW 91, WhoAmP 91
Green, Martin 1927- IntAu&W 91, WrDr 92
Green, Martin David 1947- AmMWSc 92
Green, Martin Laurence 1949- AmMWSc 92
Green, Martin Sanford 1943- WhoEnt 92
Green, Martyn 1899-1975 NewAmDM
Green, Marvin Howe, Jr. 1935- WhoEnt 92
Green, Mary Eloise 1903- AmMWSc 92
Green, Mary Georgina 1913- Who 92
Green, Mary Michaeline WhoRel 92
Green, Mary Woodmansee 1946- WhoEnt 92
Green, Matthew 1696-1737 RfGEnL 91
Green, Maurice 1926- AmMWSc 92
Green, Maurice Spurgeon 1906- IntAu&W 91
Green, Maxine Wise 1917- WhoAmP 91
Green, Melvin Howard 1937- AmMWSc 92
Green, Melvin Martin 1916- AmMWSc 92
Green, Meyra Jeanne 1946- WhoFI 92
Green, Michael AmMWSc 92, Who 92
Green, Michael 1927- WrDr 92
Green, Michael Boris 1946- Who 92
Green, Michael Dale 1959- WhoMW 92
Green, Michael David 1950- WhoAmL 92
Green, Michael Dennis 1944- WhoMW 92
Green, Michael Enoch 1938- AmMWSc 92
Green, Michael Frederick 1927- IntAu&W 91
Green, Michael Frederick 1939- Who 92
Green, Michael H 1944- AmMWSc 92
Green, Michael Howard 1963- WhoFI 92
Green, Michael I. 1930- WhoWest 92
Green, Michael Ian 1958- WhoAmL 92
Green, Michael John 1941- Who 92
Green, Michael John 1942- AmMWSc 92
Green, Michael L. IntMPA 92
Green, Michael Paul 1951- WhoRel 92
Green, Michael Philip 1947- Who 92
Green, Michael Philip 1961- AmMWSc 92
Green, Milton 1912- AmMWSc 92
Green, Milton 1920- AmMWSc 92
Green, Mino 1927- Who 92
Green, Morris 1922- WhoMW 92
Green, Morris 1931- AmMWSc 92
Green, Morton 1917- AmMWSc 92
Green, Nancy Loughridge 1942- WhoMW 92
Green, Nancy R AmMWSc 92
Green, Nathaniel Charles 1903- IntMPA 92
Green, Norman WhoMW 92
Green, Norman Edward 1938- AmMWSc 92
Green, Norman Michael 1926- IntWW 91, Who 92
Green, O O IntAu&W 91X
Green, Oliver Winslow 1930- WhoBlA 92
Green, Orville 1926- AmMWSc 92
Green, Owen 1925- IntWW 91, Who 92
Green, Paul 1951- TwCPaSc
Green, Paul Allan 1950- WhoMW 92
Green, Paul Barnett 1931- AmMWSc 92
Green, Paul C 1919- WhoIns 92
Green, Paul Cecil 1919- WhoWest 92
Green, Paul E. 1894-1981 BenetAL 91
Green, Paul E, Jr 1924- AmMWSc 92
Green, Paul Eliot 1894-1981 DcNCBi 2
Green, Paul Warren 1952- WhoAmL 92
Green, Pauline 1948- Who 92
Green, Pearry Lee 1933- WhoRel 92
Green, Percy William Powlett 1912- Who 92

**Green,** Peter *TwCSFW 91, WhoWest 92*
**Green,** Peter 1924- *IntWW 91, Who 92, WrDr 92*
**Green,** Peter Morris 1924- *IntAu&W 91, Who 92*
**Green,** Philip Palmer 1891-1972 *DcNCBi 2*
**Green,** Philip S 1936- *AmMWSc 92*
**Green,** Phillip Dale 1940- *WhoWest 92*
**Green,** Phillip Joseph, II 1941- *AmMWSc 92*
**Green,** R V 1913- *AmMWSc 92*
**Green,** Ralph 1940- *AmMWSc 92*
**Green,** Ralph J, Jr 1923- *AmMWSc 92*
**Green,** Ray Charles 1930- *AmMWSc 92*
**Green,** Raymond A. 1944- *WhoBlA 92*
**Green,** Raymond Bert 1929- *WhoAmL 92, WhoFI 92*
**Green,** Raymond Silvernail 1915- *WhoEnt 92, WhoFI 92*
**Green,** Raymond William 1940- *WhoAmL 92*
**Green,** Rayna Diane 1942- *AmMWSc 92*
**Green,** Rebecca Lou 1948- *WhoAmL 92*
**Green,** Reuben H. 1934- *WhoBlA 92*
**Green,** Richard 1936- *AmMWSc 92, WhoAmL 92, WrDr 92*
**Green,** Richard Calvin, Jr. 1954- *WhoFI 92*
**Green,** Richard Carter 1947- *WhoBlA 92*
**Green,** Richard D 1940- *AmMWSc 92*
**Green,** Richard E 1931- *AmMWSc 92*
**Green,** Richard H 1936- *AmMWSc 92*
**Green,** Richard James 1928- *AmMWSc 92*
**Green,** Richard Nelson 1945- *WhoWest 92*
**Green,** Richard Stedman 1914- *AmMWSc 92*
**Green,** Rickey 1954- *WhoBlA 92*
**Green,** Robert A 1925- *AmMWSc 92*
**Green,** Robert Allen 1927- *WhoAmP 91*
**Green,** Robert B 1941- *WhoIns 92*
**Green,** Robert Bennett 1943- *AmMWSc 92*
**Green,** Robert Durham 1944- *WhoFI 92*
**Green,** Robert E, Jr 1932- *AmMWSc 92*
**Green,** Robert Gerard 1938- *WhoFI 92*
**Green,** Robert Glenn 1950- *WhoFI 92*
**Green,** Robert Hamilton 1935- *WhoFI 92*
**Green,** Robert I 1929- *AmMWSc 92*
**Green,** Robert James 1937- *Who 92*
**Green,** Robert L. 1933- *WhoBlA 92*
**Green,** Robert Lee, Jr 1921- *AmMWSc 92*
**Green,** Robert Leslie Stuart 1925- *Who 92*
**Green,** Robert M. 1953- *WhoFI 92*
**Green,** Robert Patrick 1925- *AmMWSc 92*
**Green,** Robert S 1914- *AmMWSc 92*
**Green,** Robert Scott 1953- *WhoWest 92*
**Green,** Robert Vincent 1957- *WhoAmL 92*
**Green,** Robert Wayne 1945- *WhoFI 92*
**Green,** Robert Wood 1922- *AmMWSc 92*
**Green,** Roger *DcNCBi 2*
**Green,** Roger Curtis 1932- *IntWW 91*
**Green,** Roger Harrison 1939- *AmMWSc 92*
**Green,** Roger James 1944- *WrDr 92*
**Green,** Roger L 1949- *WhoAmP 91*
**Green,** Roger Lancelyn 1918- *IntAu&W 91*
**Green,** Roger Oswald 1931- *WhoRel 92*
**Green,** Roland 1896-1972 *TwCPaSc*
**Green,** Roland, Sr. 1940- *WhoBlA 92*
**Green,** Ron *DrAPF 91*
**Green,** Ron Wayne 1962- *WhoRel 92*
**Green,** Ronald Elwood 1950- *WhoRel 92*
**Green,** Ronald Michael 1942- *WhoRel 92*
**Green,** Ronald W 1948- *AmMWSc 92*
**Green,** Roy 1957- *WhoBlA 92*
**Green,** Rudi 1935- *WhoWest 92*
**Green,** Russell Peter 1942- *WhoFI 92*
**Green,** Ruth A. 1917- *WhoBlA 92*
**Green,** Ruth Milton 1924- *WhoMW 92*
**Green,** RuthAnn 1935- *WhoMW 92*
**Green,** Sam 1907- *Who 92*
**Green,** Samuel *DrAPF 91*
**Green,** Samuel 1615-1702 *BenetAL 91*
**Green,** Samuel Bowdlear 1859-1910 *BiInAmS*
**Green,** Samuel L. *WhoRel 92*
**Green,** Sara Edmond 1954- *WhoMW 92*
**Green,** Saul 1925- *AmMWSc 92*
**Green,** Scott Elliott 1951- *WhoAmP 91*
**Green,** Seth 1817-1888 *BiInAmS*
**Green,** Sharon 1942- *IntAu&W 91*
**Green,** Shelley Z. *WhoAmL 92*
**Green,** Sheryl Anne 1952- *WhoWest 92*
**Green,** Shirley 1935-1983 *WhoBlA 92N*
**Green,** Sidney 1939- *AmMWSc 92*
**Green,** Sidney 1961- *WhoBlA 92*
**Green,** Sidney J 1937- *AmMWSc 92*
**Green,** Stanley 1923-1990 *ConAu 133*
**Green,** Stanley J 1920- *AmMWSc 92*
**Green,** Stephen *Who 92*
**Green,** Sterling 1946- *WhoBlA 92*
**Green,** Steven Hayes 1963- *WhoEnt 92*
**Green,** Steven Johnson 1952- *WhoFI 92*
**Green,** Steven Lee 1957- *WhoFI 92*
**Green,** Steven Ray 1956- *WhoAmP 91*
**Green,** Susan Ruth 1957- *WhoAmL 92*
**Green,** Ted *WhoWest 92*
**Green,** Terek Von 1964- *WhoWest 92*
**Green,** Terence Arthur 1934- *Who 92*
**Green,** Terry C 1935- *AmMWSc 92*
**Green,** Terry Raymond 1963- *WhoWest 92*
**Green,** Theodis Guy 1930- *WhoBlA 92*
**Green,** Theodore, III 1938- *AmMWSc 92*
**Green,** Theodore James 1935- *AmMWSc 92, WhoMW 92*
**Green,** Theodore Seth 1952- *WhoEnt 92*
**Green,** Thom Henning 1915- *AmMWSc 92*
**Green,** Thomas Alexander 1846-1932 *DcNCBi 2*
**Green,** Thomas Allen 1925- *AmMWSc 92*
**Green,** Thomas Andrew 1940- *WhoAmL 92*
**Green,** Thomas Charles 1915- *Who 92*
**Green,** Thomas Charles 1959- *WhoMW 92*
**Green,** Thomas Jefferson 1802-1863 *DcNCBi 2*
**Green,** Thomas L 1947- *AmMWSc 92*
**Green,** Thomas L., Sr. 1940- *WhoBlA 92*
**Green,** Timothy 1936- *IntAu&W 91, WrDr 92*
**Green,** Timothy P 1963- *WhoAmP 91*
**Green,** Timothy Paul 1949- *WhoRel 92*
**Green,** Toots *WhoAmP 91*
**Green,** Traill 1813-1897 *BiInAmS*
**Green,** Verna S. 1947- *WhoBlA 92*
**Green,** Vernon Albert 1921- *AmMWSc 92*
**Green,** Victor Eugene, Jr 1922- *AmMWSc 92*
**Green,** Vivian 1915- *WrDr 92*
**Green,** Vivian Hubert Howard 1915- *IntAu&W 91, Who 92*
**Green,** Wallace Dale 1927- *WhoAmP 91*
**Green,** Wallace Orphesus 1948- *WhoBlA 92*
**Green,** Walter 1924- *WhoBlA 92*
**Green,** Walter L 1934- *AmMWSc 92*
**Green,** Warren Ernest 1921- *WhoAmP 91*
**Green,** Warren Harold 1915- *WhoMW 92*
**Green,** Wharton Jackson 1831-1910 *DcNCBi 2*
**Green,** Willard Wynn 1910- *AmMWSc 92*
**Green,** William 1873-1952 *FacFETw*
**Green,** William A. 1951- *WhoFI 92*
**Green,** William Baillie 1927- *WhoRel 92*
**Green,** William Edward 1930- *WhoBlA 92*
**Green,** William Ernest 1936- *WhoBlA 92*
**Green,** William Fulton 1943- *WhoAmP 91*
**Green,** William Joseph 1938- *WhoAmP 91*
**Green,** William Lohr 1945- *AmMWSc 92*
**Green,** William M 1929- *ConAu 35NR*
**Green,** William Mark 1937- *WhoEnt 92*
**Green,** William Mercer 1798-1887 *DcNCBi 2*
**Green,** William Porter 1920- *WhoAmL 92, WhoFI 92, WhoWest 92*
**Green,** William Randolph 1959- *WhoRel 92*
**Green,** William Robert 1945- *WhoMW 92*
**Green,** William Robert 1950- *AmMWSc 92*
**Green,** William Scott 1946- *WhoRel 92*
**Green,** William Warden 1939- *AmMWSc 92*
**Green-Price,** Robert 1940- *Who 92*
**Green-Rick,** Nancy Carol 1961- *WhoFI 92*
**Greenacre,** David 1946- *IntAu&W 91*
**Greenall** *Who 92*
**Greenamyre,** John William 1929- *WhoRel 92*
**Greenawalt,** Peggy Freed Tomarkin 1942- *WhoFI 92*
**Greenawalt,** Robert Kent 1936- *WhoAmL 92*
**Greenawalt,** William Sloan 1934- *WhoAmL 92, WhoFI 92*
**Greenaway,** Alan Pearce 1913- *Who 92*
**Greenaway,** Derek 1910- *Who 92*
**Greenaway,** Frank 1917- *Who 92*
**Greenaway,** Frederick Thomas 1947- *AmMWSc 92*
**Greenaway,** Keith R 1916- *AmMWSc 92*
**Greenaway,** Leroy V. *WhoRel 92*
**Greenaway,** Peter 1942- *CurBio 91 [port], IntDcF 2-2 [port], IntMPA 92, IntWW 91*
**Greenaway,** Roy Francis 1929- *WhoAmP 91*
**Greenbaum,** Elias 1944- *AmMWSc 92*
**Greenbaum,** Frederick Joel 1952- *WhoAmL 92*
**Greenbaum,** Gary R. 1953- *WhoFI 92*
**Greenbaum,** Ira Fred 1951- *AmMWSc 92*
**Greenbaum,** James Richard, Jr. 1958- *WhoFI 92*
**Greenbaum,** James T. 1961- *WhoAmL 92*
**Greenbaum,** Jeffrey J. 1948- *WhoAmL 92*
**Greenbaum,** Kenneth 1944- *WhoAmL 92*
**Greenbaum,** Leon J, Jr 1923- *AmMWSc 92*
**Greenbaum,** Lowell Marvin 1928- *AmMWSc 92*
**Greenbaum,** Maurice C. 1918- *WhoAmL 92*
**Greenbaum,** Nathan Joel 1949- *WhoAmL 92*
**Greenbaum,** Sheldon Boris 1923- *AmMWSc 92*
**Greenbaum,** Sidney 1929- *IntAu&W 91, Who 92, WrDr 92*
**Greenbaum,** Steven Garry 1954- *AmMWSc 92*
**Greenberg,** Alan Courtney 1927- *WhoFI 92*
**Greenberg,** Allan S 1943- *AmMWSc 92*
**Greenberg,** Alvin *DrAPF 91*
**Greenberg,** Alvin 1932- *WrDr 92*
**Greenberg,** Alvin David 1932- *IntAu&W 91*
**Greenberg,** Arnold Elihu 1926- *WhoWest 92*
**Greenberg,** Arnold Harvey 1941- *AmMWSc 92*
**Greenberg,** Arthur 1946- *AmMWSc 92*
**Greenberg,** Arthur Bernard 1929- *AmMWSc 92*
**Greenberg,** Barbara L. *DrAPF 91*
**Greenberg,** Barry H 1944- *AmMWSc 92*
**Greenberg,** Bernard 1922- *AmMWSc 92, IntWW 91*
**Greenberg,** Bernard 1924- *AmMWSc 92*
**Greenberg,** Bernard Harley 1953- *WhoWest 92*
**Greenberg,** Charles Bernard 1939- *AmMWSc 92*
**Greenberg,** Clement 1909- *WrDr 92*
**Greenberg,** Daniel 1927- *AmMWSc 92*
**Greenberg,** Daniel Arthur 1931- *WhoEnt 92*
**Greenberg,** Danielle 1948- *AmMWSc 92*
**Greenberg,** David Arthur 1958- *WhoWest 92*
**Greenberg,** David B 1928- *AmMWSc 92*
**Greenberg,** David Morris 1895- *AmMWSc 92*
**Greenberg,** Donald P *AmMWSc 92*
**Greenberg,** Edward M. 1924- *ConTFT 9*
**Greenberg,** Elliott 1927- *AmMWSc 92*
**Greenberg,** Eva Mueller 1929- *WhoMW 92*
**Greenberg,** Everett Peter 1948- *AmMWSc 92*
**Greenberg,** Frank 1948- *AmMWSc 92*
**Greenberg,** Gerald Stephen 1951- *WhoAmL 92*
**Greenberg,** Glenn Hank 1947- *WhoFI 92*
**Greenberg,** Goodwin Robert 1918- *AmMWSc 92*
**Greenberg,** Hank 1911-1986 *FacFETw*
**Greenberg,** Harold 1938- *WhoAmL 92*
**Greenberg,** Harry *DrAPF 91*
**Greenberg,** Herbert Julius 1921- *AmMWSc 92*
**Greenberg,** Herman Samuel 1939- *AmMWSc 92*
**Greenberg,** Howard 1928- *AmMWSc 92*
**Greenberg,** Ira 1934- *WrDr 92*
**Greenberg,** Ira Arthur 1924- *WhoWest 92*
**Greenberg,** Irving 1933- *WhoRel 92*
**Greenberg,** Irwin 1935- *AmMWSc 92*
**Greenberg,** Jack 1924- *WhoAmL 92*
**Greenberg,** Jack Sam 1927- *AmMWSc 92*
**Greenberg,** Jacob 1929- *AmMWSc 92*
**Greenberg,** James M 1940- *AmMWSc 92*
**Greenberg,** Jay R 1943- *AmMWSc 92*
**Greenberg,** Jeff *WhoEnt 92*
**Greenberg,** Jeffrey W *WhoIns 92*
**Greenberg,** Jerome Herbert 1923- *AmMWSc 92*
**Greenberg,** Jerome Mayo 1922- *AmMWSc 92*
**Greenberg,** Jerrold 1947- *AmMWSc 92*
**Greenberg,** Joanne *DrAPF 91*
**Greenberg,** Joanne 1932- *IntAu&W 91, WrDr 92*
**Greenberg,** Joel Leonard 1950- *WhoFI 92*
**Greenberg,** Jonathan D. 1958- *ConAu 133*
**Greenberg,** Jonathan David 1957- *WhoAmL 92*
**Greenberg,** Joseph 1915- *WrDr 92*
**Greenberg,** Joseph Harold 1915- *IntWW 91*
**Greenberg,** Joseph J. d1991 *NewYTBS 91*
**Greenberg,** Joshua F. 1933- *WhoAmL 92*
**Greenberg,** Joyce Irene 1952- *WhoFI 92*
**Greenberg,** Judith Horovitz 1947- *AmMWSc 92*
**Greenberg,** Larry S 1942- *WhoAmP 91*
**Greenberg,** Leonard Jason 1926- *AmMWSc 92*
**Greenberg,** Les Paul 1946- *AmMWSc 92*
**Greenberg,** Mark Shiel 1948- *AmMWSc 92*
**Greenberg,** Martin *WhoFI 92*
**Greenberg,** Martin Herbert 1938- *WhoEnt 92*
**Greenberg,** Martin Jay 1945- *WhoAmL 92*
**Greenberg,** Marvin 1936- *WhoWest 92*
**Greenberg,** Marvin Jay 1935- *AmMWSc 92*
**Greenberg,** Marya Louise 1951- *WhoMW 92*
**Greenberg,** Maurice Raymond 1925- *WhoFI 92, WhoIns 92*
**Greenberg,** Max *DrAPF 91*
**Greenberg,** Maxwell Elfred 1922- *WhoAmL 92*
**Greenberg,** Meyer 1914- *WhoRel 92*
**Greenberg,** Michael D 1935- *AmMWSc 92*
**Greenberg,** Michael John 1931- *AmMWSc 92*
**Greenberg,** Milton 1918- *AmMWSc 92*
**Greenberg,** Morris 1908- *WhoAmL 92*
**Greenberg,** Morton I 1937- *WhoAmP 91*
**Greenberg,** Morton Ira 1933- *WhoAmL 92*
**Greenberg,** Morton Paul 1946- *WhoAmL 92, WhoFI 92*
**Greenberg,** Moshe 1928- *WhoRel 92*
**Greenberg,** Myron Silver 1945- *WhoAmL 92, WhoWest 92*
**Greenberg,** Nat 1918- *WhoEnt 92*
**Greenberg,** Nathan 1919- *WhoFI 92*
**Greenberg,** Neil 1941- *AmMWSc 92*
**Greenberg,** Newton Isaac 1936- *AmMWSc 92*
**Greenberg,** Noah 1919-1966 *NewAmDM*
**Greenberg,** Oscar Wallace 1932- *AmMWSc 92*
**Greenberg,** Paul Ernest 1962- *WhoFI 92*
**Greenberg,** Paul W. *LesBEnT 92*
**Greenberg,** Paul William 1933- *WhoEnt 92*
**Greenberg,** Philip Alan 1948- *WhoAmL 92*
**Greenberg,** Philip D 1946- *AmMWSc 92*
**Greenberg,** Ralph 1944- *AmMWSc 92*
**Greenberg,** Reuben M. 1944- *WhoBlA 92*
**Greenberg,** Richard A. 1931- *WhoFI 92*
**Greenberg,** Richard Aaron 1928- *AmMWSc 92*
**Greenberg,** Richard Allen 1947- *WhoEnt 92*
**Greenberg,** Richard Alvin 1927- *AmMWSc 92*
**Greenberg,** Richard Joseph 1947- *AmMWSc 92*
**Greenberg,** Robert A. 1939- *WhoFI 92*
**Greenberg,** Roger David 1944- *WhoEnt 92*
**Greenberg,** Roland 1935- *AmMWSc 92*
**Greenberg,** Ronald David 1939- *WhoAmL 92, WhoFI 92*
**Greenberg,** Ruven 1918- *AmMWSc 92*
**Greenberg,** Samuel 1893-1917 *BenetAL 91*
**Greenberg,** Seymour Samuel 1930- *AmMWSc 92*
**Greenberg,** Sherri 1958- *WhoAmP 91*
**Greenberg,** Sidney 1917- *WhoRel 92*
**Greenberg,** Sidney Abraham 1918- *AmMWSc 92*
**Greenberg,** Sidney S. d1991 *NewYTBS 91*
**Greenberg,** Simon 1901- *WhoRel 92*
**Greenberg,** Stanley 1945- *AmMWSc 92*
**Greenberg,** Stanley Irl 1941- *WhoAmL 92*
**Greenberg,** Stanley R. *LesBEnT 92*
**Greenberg,** Stanly Donald 1930- *AmMWSc 92*
**Greenberg,** Stephen B *AmMWSc 92*
**Greenberg,** Stephen Robert 1927- *AmMWSc 92*
**Greenberg,** Steven Morey 1949- *WhoAmL 92, WhoFI 92*
**Greenberg,** Steven Samuel 1946- *WhoAmL 92*
**Greenberg,** Suzanne Gabrielle Schlichtman 1961- *WhoMW 92*
**Greenberg,** William 1941- *AmMWSc 92*
**Greenberg,** William Michael 1938- *AmMWSc 92*
**Greenberger,** Allen Jay 1937- *WhoWest 92*
**Greenberger,** Daniel Mordecai 1933- *AmMWSc 92*
**Greenberger,** Howard *WrDr 92*
**Greenberger,** Howard 1924- *IntAu&W 91*
**Greenberger,** Howard Leroy 1929- *WhoAmL 92*
**Greenberger,** I. Michael 1945- *WhoAmL 92*
**Greenberger,** James Joseph 1958- *WhoMW 92*
**Greenberger,** Joel S 1946- *AmMWSc 92*
**Greenberger,** Lee M 1955- *AmMWSc 92*
**Greenberger,** Martin 1931- *AmMWSc 92*
**Greenberger,** Norton Jerald 1933- *AmMWSc 92*
**Greenblat,** Cathy S. 1940- *ConAu 133*
**Greenblatt,** Charles Leonard 1931- *AmMWSc 92*
**Greenblatt,** David J 1945- *AmMWSc 92*
**Greenblatt,** Deana Charlene 1948- *WhoMW 92*
**Greenblatt,** Edward Lande 1939- *WhoAmL 92*
**Greenblatt,** Eugene Newton 1923- *AmMWSc 92*
**Greenblatt,** Fred Harold 1938- *WhoFI 92*
**Greenblatt,** Gary Edward 1949- *WhoAmP 91*
**Greenblatt,** Gerald A 1932- *AmMWSc 92*
**Greenblatt,** Hellen Chaya 1947- *AmMWSc 92*
**Greenblatt,** Irwin M 1930- *AmMWSc 92*
**Greenblatt,** Jack Fred 1946- *AmMWSc 92*
**Greenblatt,** Jay Hersh 1936- *WhoAmL 92*
**Greenblatt,** Jayson Herschel 1922- *AmMWSc 92*
**Greenblatt,** Mark Leo 1947- *WhoMW 92*
**Greenblatt,** Marshal 1939- *AmMWSc 92*
**Greenblatt,** Martha 1941- *AmMWSc 92*

**Greenblatt,** Martin D. 1942- *WhoFI 92*
**Greenblatt,** Michael 1950- *WhoEnt 92*
**Greenblatt,** Michael Fred 1951- *WhoEnt 92*
**Greenblatt,** Milton 1914- *AmMWSc 92*
**Greenblatt,** Ray *DrAPF 91*
**Greenblatt,** Ray Harris 1931- *WhoAmL 92*
**Greenblatt,** Robert Harris 1961- *WhoFI 92*
**Greenblatt,** Samuel Harold 1939- *AmMWSc 92*
**Greenblatt,** Seth Alan 1960- *AmMWSc 92*
**Greenborough,** John Hedley 1922- *IntWW 91, Who 92*
**Greenburg,** Dan 1936- *WhoEnt 92*
**Greenburg,** Harold *LesBEnT 92*
**Greenburg,** Uri Zvi 1896-1981 *LiExTwC*
**Greenburg,** Virginia Hoff d1991 *NewYTBS 91*
**Greenbury,** Judith 1924- *TwCPaSc*
**Greenbury,** Richard 1936- *IntWW 91, Who 92*
**Greene** *Who 92*
**Greene,** A C 1923- *IntAu&W 91, WrDr 92*
**Greene,** Abigail 1955- *WhoEnt 92*
**Greene,** Abner Saul 1960- *WhoAmL 92*
**Greene,** Addison Kent 1941- *WhoAmL 92*
**Greene,** Alan Campbell 1935- *AmMWSc 92*
**Greene,** Allen Earl 1929- *WhoMW 92*
**Greene,** Alvin 1932- *WhoFI 92, WhoWest 92*
**Greene,** Arthur E 1923- *AmMWSc 92*
**Greene,** Arthur Edward 1945- *AmMWSc 92*
**Greene,** Arthur Franklin 1939- *AmMWSc 92*
**Greene,** Arthur Frederick, Jr 1927- *AmMWSc 92*
**Greene,** Asa 1789-1837? *BenetAL 91*
**Greene,** Aurelia 1934- *WhoAmP 91, WhoBlA 92*
**Greene,** Ava Danelle 1962- *WhoBlA 92*
**Greene,** Balcomb 1904-1990 *CurBio 91N*
**Greene,** Barbara E 1935- *AmMWSc 92*
**Greene,** Beatrice *DrAPF 91*
**Greene,** Bette *DrAPF 91*
**Greene,** Bette 1934- *Au&Arts 7 [port], WrDr 92*
**Greene,** Bettye Washington 1935- *AmMWSc 92*
**Greene,** Bill 1931- *WhoAmP 91*
**Greene,** Bob *SourALJ*
**Greene,** Bruce Edgar 1933- *AmMWSc 92*
**Greene,** Carla 1916- *SmATA 67*
**Greene,** Carol *ConAu 134*
**Greene,** Carol 19--?- *SmATA 66*
**Greene,** Carolyn Jetter 1942- *WhoBlA 92*
**Greene,** Cecil M., Jr. 1932- *WhoBlA 92*
**Greene,** Celene *WhoAmL 92, WhoWest 92*
**Greene,** Charles Andre 1939- *WhoBlA 92*
**Greene,** Charles Edward 1944- *BlkOlyM*
**Greene,** Charles Edward 1946- *WhoBlA 92*
**Greene,** Charles Edward Clarence 1921- *WhoBlA 92*
**Greene,** Charles Edwin 1919- *AmMWSc 92*
**Greene,** Charles Ezra 1842-1903 *BiInAmS*
**Greene,** Charles Lavant 1938- *WhoBlA 92*
**Greene,** Charles Richard 1923- *AmMWSc 92*
**Greene,** Charles Rodgers 1926- *WhoBlA 92*
**Greene,** Charles Sumner 1868-1957 *DcTwDes*
**Greene,** Charlotte Helen 1943- *AmMWSc 92*
**Greene,** Christopher Henry 1954- *AmMWSc 92*
**Greene,** Christopher Storm *AmMWSc 92*
**Greene,** Clarence 1918- *IntMPA 92*
**Greene,** Clifton M. 1916- *WhoBlA 92*
**Greene,** Clifton S. 1920- *WhoBlA 92*
**Greene,** Constance C. 1924- *Au&Arts 7 [port], IntAu&W 91, WrDr 92*
**Greene,** Craig Lee 1953- *WhoFI 92*
**Greene,** Curtis 1944- *AmMWSc 92*
**Greene,** Curtis Densmore 1929- *WhoIns 92*
**Greene,** Cynthia Lou 1950- *WhoAmL 92*
**Greene,** Daryle E 1932- *AmMWSc 92*
**Greene,** David 1921- *IntMPA 92*
**Greene,** David C 1922- *AmMWSc 92*
**Greene,** David Gorham 1915- *AmMWSc 92*
**Greene,** David Lee 1938- *AmMWSc 92*
**Greene,** David Lee 1944- *AmMWSc 92*
**Greene,** De Reef Anthony 1929- *WhoBlA 92*
**Greene,** Donald Miller 1949- *AmMWSc 92*
**Greene,** Dwight L. *WhoBlA 92*
**Greene,** Edith L. 1919- *WhoBlA 92*
**Greene,** Edward Forbes 1922- *AmMWSc 92*
**Greene,** Edward Lee 1843-1915 *BiInAmS*
**Greene,** Edward Reginald d1990 *Who 92N*
**Greene,** Elias Louis 1932- *AmMWSc 92*
**Greene,** Elizabeth A *WhoAmP 91*
**Greene,** Ellen *DrAPF 91, IntMPA 92*
**Greene,** Esther Rushford 1925- *WhoAmP 91*
**Greene,** F. Dennis 1949- *WhoBlA 92*
**Greene,** Ford 1952- *WhoAmL 92*
**Greene,** Frank Clemson 1939- *AmMWSc 92*
**Greene,** Frank Eugene *AmMWSc 92*
**Greene,** Frank S., Jr. 1938- *WhoBlA 92*
**Greene,** Frank Sullivan, Jr. 1938- *WhoFI 92, WhoWest 92*
**Greene,** Frank T 1932- *AmMWSc 92*
**Greene,** Franklin D. 1950- *WhoBlA 92*
**Greene,** Frederick Davis, II 1927- *AmMWSc 92*
**Greene,** Frederick Leslie 1944- *AmMWSc 92*
**Greene,** Gary Maynard, Sr. 1948- *WhoFI 92*
**Greene,** George C, III *AmMWSc 92*
**Greene,** George W, Jr 1919- *AmMWSc 92*
**Greene,** George Washington 1852-1911 *DcNCBi 2*
**Greene,** Gerald E *WhoAmP 91*
**Greene,** Gerald L 1937- *AmMWSc 92*
**Greene,** Glen Lee 1915-1991 *WhoRel 92*
**Greene,** Gordon William 1921- *AmMWSc 92*
**Greene,** Grace Randolph 1937- *WhoBlA 92*
**Greene,** Graham d1991 *Who 92N*
**Greene,** Graham 1904- *LiExTwC*
**Greene,** Graham 1904-1991 *CnDBLB 7 [port], ConAu 133, -35NR, CurBio 91N, DcLB Y91N [port], FacFETw, IntWW 91, -91N, NewYTBS 91 [port], News 91, RfGEnL 91*
**Greene,** Graham Carleton 1936- *IntWW 91, Who 92*
**Greene,** Gregory A. 1949- *WhoBlA 92*
**Greene,** Harold H. 1923- *WhoAmL 92*
**Greene,** Harry Lee *AmMWSc 92*
**Greene,** Helen 1923- *WhoAmP 91*
**Greene,** Henry L. *DrAPF 91*
**Greene,** Henry Mather 1870-1954 *DcTwDes*
**Greene,** Herbert Bruce 1934- *WhoFI 92*
**Greene,** Hoke Smith 1906- *AmMWSc 92*
**Greene,** Horace F. 1939- *WhoBlA 92*
**Greene,** Howard Lyman 1935- *AmMWSc 92*
**Greene,** Ian Rawdon 1909- *Who 92*
**Greene,** Ira S. 1946- *WhoAmL 92*
**Greene,** Jack Bruce 1915- *AmMWSc 92*
**Greene,** Jack Phillip 1931- *IntWW 91*
**Greene,** James 1926- *ConTFT 9*
**Greene,** James Fiedler 1958- *WhoWest 92*
**Greene,** James H 1915- *AmMWSc 92, IntAu&W 91, WrDr 92*
**Greene,** James L 1934- *WhoIns 92*
**Greene,** James R. 1958- *WhoAmL 92*
**Greene,** James R., III 1959- *WhoBlA 92*
**Greene,** James S., Jr. 1917- *WhoAmL 92*
**Greene,** James Young 1933- *WhoRel 92*
**Greene,** Janelle Langley 1940- *WhoFI 92*
**Greene,** Janice L 1930- *AmMWSc 92*
**Greene,** Jenny 1937- *IntAu&W 91, Who 92*
**Greene,** Jerome Alexander 1941- *WhoBlA 92, WhoRel 92*
**Greene,** JeRoyd X. 1940- *WhoBlA 92*
**Greene,** Joann Lavina *WhoBlA 92*
**Greene,** Joel Laurence 1947- *WhoAmL 92*
**Greene,** John 1947- *WhoAmP 91*
**Greene,** John Brian M. *Who 92*
**Greene,** John Clifford 1926- *AmMWSc 92*
**Greene,** John H. d1991 *NewYTBS 91*
**Greene,** John Joseph 1946- *WhoAmL 92*
**Greene,** John M 1928- *AmMWSc 92*
**Greene,** John O *ScFEYrs*
**Greene,** John Oscar 1954- *WhoMW 92*
**Greene,** John Philip 1955- *AmMWSc 92*
**Greene,** John Sullivan 1921- *WhoBlA 92*
**Greene,** John Thomas, Jr. 1929- *WhoAmL 92, WhoWest 92*
**Greene,** John W, Jr 1926- *AmMWSc 92*
**Greene,** John Warren 1950- *WhoRel 92*
**Greene,** Jonathan *DrAPF 91*
**Greene,** Jonathan 1943- *ConPo 91, IntAu&W 91, WrDr 92*
**Greene,** Joseph David 1940- *WhoBlA 92*
**Greene,** Joseph P. *WhoBlA 92*
**Greene,** Joshua Eli 1951- *WhoFI 92*
**Greene,** Judith *Who 92*
**Greene,** Judith 1936- *WrDr 92*
**Greene,** Kenneth Titsworth 1914- *AmMWSc 92*
**Greene,** Kenneth Vincent 1943- *WhoFI 92*
**Greene,** Kenneth Wayne 1947- *WhoRel 92*
**Greene,** Kevin Darwin 1962- *WhoBlA 92*
**Greene,** Kevin Thomas 1954- *WhoRel 92*
**Greene,** Kingsley L 1926- *AmMWSc 92*
**Greene,** Larry Joe 1949- *WhoRel 92*
**Greene,** Laura H 1952- *AmMWSc 92*
**Greene,** Laurence Whitridge, Jr. 1924- *WhoWest 92*
**Greene,** Lawrence William 1950- *WhoEnt 92*
**Greene,** Leo Charles 1945- *WhoEnt 92*
**Greene,** Leroy F 1918- *WhoAmP 91*
**Greene,** Lewis Joel 1934- *AmMWSc 92*
**Greene,** Lionel Oliver, Jr. 1948- *WhoBlA 92*
**Greene,** Lloyd A 1944- *AmMWSc 92*
**Greene,** Mamie Louise 1939- *WhoBlA 92*
**Greene,** Margaret McCaffrey *WhoEnt 92*
**Greene,** Marion O., Jr. *WhoBlA 92*
**Greene,** Mark Irwin 1948- *AmMWSc 92*
**Greene,** Marvin L. 1915- *WhoBlA 92*
**Greene,** Mean Joe 1946- *WhoBlA 92*
**Greene,** Michael E 1935- *WhoIns 92*
**Greene,** Michael Edward 1949- *WhoAmL 92*
**Greene,** Michael Harris 1933- *WhoEnt 92*
**Greene,** Michael Olin 1943- *WhoEnt 92*
**Greene,** Michael P 1938- *AmMWSc 92*
**Greene,** Michael Thornton 1941- *WhoWest 92*
**Greene,** Michele *WhoEnt 92*
**Greene,** Milton Louis 1912- *WhoEnt 92*
**Greene,** Mitchell Amos 1927- *WhoBlA 92*
**Greene,** Monroe Malcolm 1921- *WhoWest 92*
**Greene,** Nathan Doyle 1938- *AmMWSc 92*
**Greene,** Nathanael 1742-1786 *BlkwEAR*
**Greene,** Nathanael 1935- *WrDr 92*
**Greene,** Nathaniel D. *WhoBlA 92*
**Greene,** Neil E 1936- *AmMWSc 92*
**Greene,** Nelson E., Sr. 1914- *WhoBlA 92*
**Greene,** Nicholas Misplee 1922- *AmMWSc 92*
**Greene,** Nicholas Pond 1948- *WhoFI 92*
**Greene,** Norman L. 1948- *WhoAmL 92*
**Greene,** Percy 1900-1977 *WhoBlA 92N*
**Greene,** Peter Richard 1951- *AmMWSc 92*
**Greene,** R. W. *WhoBlA 92*
**Greene,** Ralph Vernon 1910- *WhoAmL 92*
**Greene,** Randall William 1963- *WhoRel 92*
**Greene,** Reginald 1934- *AmMWSc 92*
**Greene,** Richard *WhoAmP 91*
**Greene,** Richard L 1938- *AmMWSc 92*
**Greene,** Richard Larry 1947- *WhoAmP 91*
**Greene,** Richard Lorentz *AmMWSc 92*
**Greene,** Richard Martin 1953- *WhoWest 92*
**Greene,** Richard T. *WhoBlA 92*
**Greene,** Richard Thaddeus 1918- *WhoFI 92*
**Greene,** Richard Wallace 1941- *AmMWSc 92*
**Greene,** Robert 1558-1592 *RfGEnL 91*
**Greene,** Robert 1678?-1730 *BlkwCEP*
**Greene,** Robert Carl 1932- *AmMWSc 92*
**Greene,** Robert Everist 1943- *AmMWSc 92*
**Greene,** Robert Fisher 1948- *WhoFI 92*
**Greene,** Robert Michael 1945- *WhoAmL 92*
**Greene,** Robert Morris 1945- *AmMWSc 92*
**Greene,** Ronald Alexander 1945- *WhoBlA 92*
**Greene,** Ronald C 1928- *AmMWSc 92*
**Greene,** Samuel Stillman 1810-1883 *BiInAmS*
**Greene,** Sarah Moore 1917- *WhoBlA 92*
**Greene,** Shecky 1926- *WhoEnt 92*
**Greene,** Sheldon 1933- *WhoFI 92*
**Greene,** Stephen Craig 1946- *WhoAmL 92*
**Greene,** Steven 1956- *WhoEnt 92*
**Greene,** Steven Scott 1952- *WhoRel 92*
**Greene,** Stilson 1954- *WhoEnt 92*
**Greene,** Stuart C. 1955- *WhoRel 92*
**Greene,** Thomas A 1934- *WhoIns 92*
**Greene,** Thomas Ainsworth 1890-1951 *AmPeW*
**Greene,** Thomas Frederick 1938- *AmMWSc 92*
**Greene,** Tommy Clatus 1945- *WhoFI 92*
**Greene,** Velvl William 1928- *AmMWSc 92*
**Greene,** Victor 1933- *WrDr 92*
**Greene,** Virginia Carvel 1934- *AmMWSc 92*
**Greene,** Walter D. 1936- *WhoFI 92*
**Greene,** Ward 1892-1956 *BenetAL 91*
**Greene,** William 1933- *WhoBlA 92*
**Greene,** William Allan 1915- *AmMWSc 92*
**Greene,** William H 1855-1918 *ScFEYrs*
**Greene,** William H, II *WhoAmP 91*
**Greene,** William Henry L'Vel 1943- *WhoBlA 92*
**Greene,** William Houston 1853-1918 *BiInAmS*
**Greene,** William J. 1912- *WhoBlA 92*
**Greene,** Yvonne *WrDr 92*
**Greene Of Harrow Weald,** Baron 1910- *IntWW 91, Who 92*
**Greene-Thapedi,** Llwellyn L. *WhoBlA 92*
**Greenebaum,** Ben 1937- *AmMWSc 92*
**Greenebaum,** Leonard Charles 1934- *WhoAmL 92*
**Greenebaum,** Michael 1940- *AmMWSc 92*
**Greener,** Anthony Armitage 1940- *Who 92*
**Greener,** Evan H 1934- *AmMWSc 92*
**Greener,** Jay Leslie 1959- *WhoEnt 92*
**Greener,** Michael John 1931- *IntAu&W 91, WrDr 92*
**Greener,** Ralph Bertram 1940- *WhoAmL 92*
**Greenewalt,** Crawford Hallock 1902- *AmMWSc 92, Who 92*
**Greenewalt,** David 1931- *AmMWSc 92*
**Greenfeld,** Josh 1928- *WhoEnt 92*
**Greenfeld,** Sidney H 1923- *AmMWSc 92*
**Greenfelder,** Bernard *ScFEYrs*
**Greenfield,** Arthur Judah 1934- *AmMWSc 92*
**Greenfield,** David 1917- *Who 92*
**Greenfield,** David Wayne 1940- *AmMWSc 92*
**Greenfield,** Edward Harry 1928- *Who 92*
**Greenfield,** Elizabeth Taylor 1819?-1876 *NotBlAW 92 [port]*
**Greenfield,** Eloise 1929- *WhoBlA 92, WrDr 92*
**Greenfield,** Eugene W 1907- *AmMWSc 92, WhoWest 92*
**Greenfield,** George 1917- *DcLB Y91 [port]*
**Greenfield,** George B 1928- *AmMWSc 92*
**Greenfield,** Harold 1923- *AmMWSc 92*
**Greenfield,** Harvey Stanley 1924- *AmMWSc 92*
**Greenfield,** Helen Meyers 1908- *WhoFI 92*
**Greenfield,** Howard *Who 92*
**Greenfield,** Irwin G 1929- *AmMWSc 92*
**Greenfield,** James Lloyd 1924- *IntWW 91*
**Greenfield,** Jeanette *ConAu 134*
**Greenfield,** Jeff *LesBEnT 92*
**Greenfield,** Jerome *DrAPF 91*
**Greenfield,** Jerome 1923- *WrDr 92*
**Greenfield,** John Frederic 1943- *WhoAmP 91*
**Greenfield,** Joseph C, Jr 1931- *AmMWSc 92*
**Greenfield,** Julius Macdonald 1907- *IntWW 91, Who 92*
**Greenfield,** Larry Lee 1941- *WhoRel 92*
**Greenfield,** Lazar John 1934- *AmMWSc 92*
**Greenfield,** Leo 1916- *IntMPA 92*
**Greenfield,** Leon Edward 1941- *WhoAmP 91*
**Greenfield,** Leonard Julian 1926- *AmMWSc 92*
**Greenfield,** Manny Allison 1952- *WhoEnt 92*
**Greenfield,** Michael C. 1934- *WhoAmL 92*
**Greenfield,** Michael M. 1944- *WhoAmL 92*
**Greenfield,** Milton, Jr. 1910- *WhoAmL 92*
**Greenfield,** Peter Rex 1931- *Who 92*
**Greenfield,** Richard Sherman 1933- *AmMWSc 92*
**Greenfield,** Robert Howard 1927- *Who 92*
**Greenfield,** Robert Thomas, Jr. 1933- *WhoBlA 92*
**Greenfield,** Ronald Howard 1944- *WhoFI 92, WhoMW 92*
**Greenfield,** Roy Alonzo 1915- *WhoBlA 92*
**Greenfield,** Roy Jay 1936- *AmMWSc 92*
**Greenfield,** Seymour 1942- *AmMWSc 92*
**Greenfield,** Stanley Marshall 1927- *AmMWSc 92*
**Greenfield,** Sydney Stanley 1915- *AmMWSc 92*
**Greenfield,** W. M. 1944- *WhoFI 92*
**Greenfield,** Wilbert *WhoBlA 92*
**Greenfield,** Wilbert 1933- *AmMWSc 92*
**Greenfield,** William Russell, Jr. 1915- *WhoBlA 92*
**Greenfield-Marcus,** Margee Ann 1951- *WhoWest 92*
**Greengard,** Olga 1926- *AmMWSc 92*
**Greengard,** Paul 1925- *AmMWSc 92*
**Greenglass,** Alan B 1942- *WhoAmP 91*
**Greengrass,** Sarah 1951- *TwCPaSc*
**Greengross,** Alan 1929- *Who 92*
**Greengross,** Sally 1935- *Who 92*
**Greengus,** Samuel 1936- *WhoMW 92, WhoRel 92*
**Greenhalgh,** Jack 1926- *Who 92*
**Greenhalgh,** John Farr 1944- *WhoWest 92*
**Greenhalgh,** Roger Malcolm 1941- *Who 92*
**Greenhalgh,** Roy 1926- *AmMWSc 92*
**Greenhalgh,** Terry L. 1950- *WhoEnt 92*
**Greenhall,** Arthur Merwin 1911- *AmMWSc 92*
**Greenhall,** Charles August 1939- *AmMWSc 92, WhoWest 92*
**Greenham,** Peter 1909- *TwCPaSc*
**Greenham,** Peter George 1909- *Who 92*
**Greenham,** Robert 1906-1976 *TwCPaSc*
**Greenhaw,** Thomas Benton, IV 1925- *WhoEnt 92, WhoMW 92*
**Greenhill** *Who 92*
**Greenhill,** Baron 1924- *Who 92*
**Greenhill,** Basil Jack 1920- *IntAu&W 91, Who 92, WrDr 92*
**Greenhill,** Ira Judd 1921- *WhoAmL 92*
**Greenhill,** Joe R 1914- *WhoAmP 91*
**Greenhill,** Mina *TwCPaSc*
**Greenhill,** Mitchell Reed 1944- *WhoEnt 92*
**Greenhill,** Robert Foster 1936- *WhoFI 92*
**Greenhill,** Stanley E 1917- *AmMWSc 92*

**Greenhill**, William Duke 1946- *WhoAmL 92*
**Greenhill Of Harrow**, Baron 1913- *IntWW 91, Who 92*
**Greenhouse**, Dennis Edward 1950- *WhoAmP 91*
**Greenhouse**, Gerald Alan 1942- *AmMWSc 92*
**Greenhouse**, Harold Mitchell 1924- *AmMWSc 92*
**Greenhouse**, N Barry 1940- *WhoIns 92*
**Greenhouse**, Nathaniel Anthony 1940- *AmMWSc 92*
**Greenhouse**, Sally *DrAPF 91*
**Greenhouse**, Samuel William 1918- *AmMWSc 92*
**Greenhouse**, Steven Howard 1947- *AmMWSc 92*
**Greenhut**, Melvin Leonard 1921- *WhoFI 92*
**Greenhut**, Robert *IntMPA 92*
**Greenidge**, James Ernest 1949- *WhoBlA 92*
**Greenidge**, Kenneth Norman Haynes 1919- *AmMWSc 92*
**Greening**, Paul 1928- *Who 92*
**Greening**, Wilfrid Peter *Who 92*
**Greenkorn**, Robert A 1928- *AmMWSc 92*
**Greenkorn**, Robert Albert 1928- *WhoMW 92*
**Greenland**, Colin 1954- *IntAu&W 91, TwCSFW 91*
**Greenland**, Dennis James 1930- *Who 92*
**Greenlaw**, Edwin Almiron 1874-1931 *DcNCBi 2*
**Greenlaw**, Ernest Clifford *WhoAmP 91*
**Greenlaw**, Jon Stanley 1939- *AmMWSc 92*
**Greenlaw**, Roger Lee 1936- *WhoWest 92*
**Greenlaw**, William Allen 1943- *WhoRel 92*
**Greenlaw Ramonas**, Denise M 1953- *WhoAmP 91*
**Greenleaf**, Arthur Austin, III 1948- *WhoRel 92*
**Greenleaf**, Frederick P 1938- *AmMWSc 92*
**Greenleaf**, James Fowler *AmMWSc 92*
**Greenleaf**, John Edward 1932- *AmMWSc 92*
**Greenleaf**, Louis E. 1941- *WhoBlA 92*
**Greenleaf**, Richard Cranch 1809-1887 *BiInAmS*
**Greenleaf**, Robert Dale 1948- *AmMWSc 92*
**Greenleaf**, Stephen 1942- *IntAu&W 91, WrDr 92*
**Greenleaf**, Stewart John 1939- *WhoAmP 91*
**Greenleaf**, Sue *ScFEYrs*
**Greenleaf**, Vicki D. 1959- *WhoEnt 92*
**Greenleaf**, Walter Franklin 1946- *WhoAmL 92*
**Greenleaf**, Walter Helmuth 1912- *AmMWSc 92*
**Greenleaf**, William *IntAu&W 91, WrDr 92*
**Greenleaf**, William 1917- *TwCSFW 91*
**Greenlee**, George Gregory 1934- *WhoAmL 92*
**Greenlee**, Herbert Breckenridge 1927- *AmMWSc 92*
**Greenlee**, J. Harold 1918- *WrDr 92*
**Greenlee**, Jane Gill 1920- *WhoAmP 91*
**Greenlee**, John Edward 1940- *AmMWSc 92*
**Greenlee**, Kenneth William 1916- *AmMWSc 92, WhoMW 92*
**Greenlee**, Peter Anthony 1941- *WhoBlA 92*
**Greenlee**, Richard Dean 1953- *WhoEnt 92*
**Greenlee**, Robert Douglass 1940- *WhoBlA 92*
**Greenlee**, Robert Fargo, Jr. 1945- *WhoEnt 92*
**Greenlee**, Sam 1930- *WhoBlA 92*
**Greenlee**, Theodore K 1934- *AmMWSc 92*
**Greenlee**, Thomas Russell 1948- *AmMWSc 92*
**Greenler**, Kathleen Marie 1962- *WhoEnt 92*
**Greenler**, Robert George 1929- *AmMWSc 92, WhoMW 92*
**Greenley**, Robert Z 1934- *AmMWSc 92*
**Greenlick**, Merwyn Ronald 1935- *AmMWSc 92*
**Greenlick**, Vicki Ruth 1961- *WhoWest 92*
**Greenlief**, Charles M 1937- *AmMWSc 92*
**Greenlief**, Charles Michael 1961- *AmMWSc 92*
**Greenman**, David Lewis 1934- *AmMWSc 92*
**Greenman**, Frederic Edward 1936- *WhoAmL 92, WhoFI 92*
**Greenman**, Norman 1920- *AmMWSc 92*
**Greenoak**, Francesca Lavinia 1946- *IntAu&W 91*
**Greenock**, Lord 1952- *Who 92*
**Greenough**, Beverly *Who 92*
**Greenough**, Horatio 1805-1852 *BenetAL 91, DcTwDes*
**Greenough**, Peter B., Mrs. 1929- *WhoEnt 92*
**Greenough**, Ralph Clive 1932- *AmMWSc 92*
**Greenough**, William Tallant 1944- *AmMWSc 92*
**Greenshields**, John Bryce 1926- *AmMWSc 92*
**Greenshields**, Robert McLaren 1933- *Who 92*
**Greensides**, Ronald J 1941- *WhoAmP 91*
**Greenslade**, Forrest C 1939- *AmMWSc 92*
**Greenslade**, Roy 1946- *Who 92*
**Greenslade**, Thomas Boardman, Jr 1937- *AmMWSc 92, WhoMW 92*
**Greenslet**, Ferris 1875-1959 *BenetAL 91*
**Greensmith**, Edward William 1909- *Who 92*
**Greensmith**, Edwin Lloydd 1900- *Who 92*
**Greenspan**, Alan 1926- *IntWW 91, News 92-2 [port], Who 92, WhoAmP 91, WhoFI 92*
**Greenspan**, Barney *WhoMW 92*
**Greenspan**, Bernard 1914- *AmMWSc 92, WhoWest 92*
**Greenspan**, Bud *LesBEnT 92*
**Greenspan**, Bud 1926- *WhoEnt 92*
**Greenspan**, Cappy d1983 *LesBEnT 92*
**Greenspan**, Daniel S 1951- *AmMWSc 92, WhoMW 92*
**Greenspan**, David d1991 *NewYTBS 91*
**Greenspan**, David Ellison 1959- *WhoEnt 92*
**Greenspan**, Donald 1928- *AmMWSc 92*
**Greenspan**, Frank Philip 1917- *AmMWSc 92*
**Greenspan**, Harvey Philip 1933- *AmMWSc 92*
**Greenspan**, Jay Scott 1959- *WhoEnt 92*
**Greenspan**, Jeffrey Dov 1954- *WhoAmL 92*
**Greenspan**, John S. 1938- *WhoWest 92*
**Greenspan**, John Simon 1938- *AmMWSc 92*
**Greenspan**, Joseph 1909- *AmMWSc 92*
**Greenspan**, Kalman 1925- *AmMWSc 92*
**Greenspan**, Leon Joseph 1932- *WhoFI 92*
**Greenspan**, Michael Alan 1940- *WhoAmL 92*
**Greenspan**, Richard H 1925- *AmMWSc 92*
**Greenspan**, Stanley Ira 1941- *AmMWSc 92*
**Greenspon**, Jaq 1967- *WhoEnt 92*
**Greenspon**, Joshua Earl 1928- *AmMWSc 92*
**Greenspon**, Robert Alan 1947- *WhoAmL 92*
**Greenspoon**, Leonard Jay 1945- *WhoRel 92*
**Greenstadt**, Melvin 1918- *AmMWSc 92*
**Greenstein**, Benjamin Joel 1959- *AmMWSc 92*
**Greenstein**, David Snellenburg 1928- *AmMWSc 92*
**Greenstein**, George 1940- *AmMWSc 92*
**Greenstein**, Jeffrey Ian 1947- *AmMWSc 92*
**Greenstein**, Jesse Leonard 1909- *AmMWSc 92, IntWW 91*
**Greenstein**, Julia L 1956- *AmMWSc 92*
**Greenstein**, Julius S 1927- *AmMWSc 92*
**Greenstein**, Martin Richard 1944- *WhoAmL 92*
**Greenstein**, Merle Edward 1937- *WhoWest 92*
**Greenstein**, Neil David 1954- *WhoAmL 92*
**Greenstein**, Robert M 1946- *WhoAmP 91*
**Greenstein**, Robert Stanley 1955- *WhoEnt 92*
**Greenstein**, Shane W. 1960- *WhoFI 92*
**Greenstein**, Teddy 1937- *AmMWSc 92*
**Greenstock**, Clive Lewis 1939- *AmMWSc 92*
**Greenstock**, Jeremy Quentin 1943- *Who 92*
**Greenstone**, Reynold 1924- *AmMWSc 92*
**Greenstreet**, William LaVon 1925- *AmMWSc 92*
**Greentree**, Chris 1935- *Who 92*
**Greenwald**, A. Michael 1939- *WhoAmL 92*
**Greenwald**, David Mark 1961- *WhoAmL 92, WhoMW 92*
**Greenwald**, Edward Harris 1920- *WhoFI 92*
**Greenwald**, Gerald 1935- *IntWW 91, WhoFI 92*
**Greenwald**, Gilbert Saul 1927- *AmMWSc 92, WhoMW 92*
**Greenwald**, Harold Leopold 1917- *AmMWSc 92*
**Greenwald**, Jim 1938- *WhoFI 92*
**Greenwald**, Lewis 1943- *AmMWSc 92*
**Greenwald**, Maria Barnaby 1940- *WhoAmP 91*
**Greenwald**, Mathew Henry 1946- *WhoFI 92*
**Greenwald**, Peter 1936- *AmMWSc 92*
**Greenwald**, Robert 1945- *IntMPA 92*
**Greenwald**, Roger *DrAPF 91*
**Greenwald**, Stephen Mark 1947- *AmMWSc 92*
**Greenwald**, Susan 1949- *WhoMW 92*
**Greenwald**, Ted *DrAPF 91*
**Greenwalt**, Clifford Lloyd 1933- *WhoFI 92, WhoMW 92*
**Greenwalt**, Lynn Adams 1931- *WhoAmP 91*
**Greenwalt**, Roger Benson 1961- *WhoRel 92*
**Greenwalt**, Sandra Joyce 1962- *WhoEnt 92*
**Greenwalt**, Tibor J. 1914- *WrDr 92*
**Greenwalt**, Tibor Jack 1914- *AmMWSc 92, IntWW 91*
**Greenway** *Who 92*
**Greenway**, Baron 1941- *Who 92*
**Greenway**, Clive Victor 1937- *AmMWSc 92*
**Greenway**, Doug 1954- *WhoRel 92*
**Greenway**, George Rowland 1937- *WhoWest 92*
**Greenway**, Harry 1934- *Who 92*
**Greenway**, John Robert 1946- *Who 92*
**Greenway**, William *DrAPF 91*
**Greenwell**, Arthur Jeffrey 1931- *Who 92*
**Greenwell**, Edward 1948- *Who 92*
**Greenwell**, Jeffrey *Who 92*
**Greenwich**, Ellie *WhoEnt 92*
**Greenwood** *Who 92*
**Greenwood**, Viscount 1914- *Who 92*
**Greenwood**, Allan Nunns *AmMWSc 92*
**Greenwood**, Allen Harold Claude 1917- *Who 92*
**Greenwood**, Barbara 1940- *ConAu 134*
**Greenwood**, Betty May 1928- *WhoEnt 92*
**Greenwood**, Brian 1943- *AmMWSc 92*
**Greenwood**, Bruce *ConTFT 9*
**Greenwood**, Charles H. 1933- *WhoBlA 92*
**Greenwood**, Charles Huddie 1933- *WhoMW 92*
**Greenwood**, D T 1923- *AmMWSc 92*
**Greenwood**, Daphne T 1949- *WhoAmP 91*
**Greenwood**, David 1957- *WhoBlA 92*
**Greenwood**, David Christopher 1959- *WhoEnt 92*
**Greenwood**, David Ernest 1937- *Who 92*
**Greenwood**, Donald Dean 1931- *AmMWSc 92*
**Greenwood**, Dru Crigler 1946- *WhoRel 92*
**Greenwood**, Duncan 1919- *IntAu&W 91*
**Greenwood**, Duncan Joseph 1932- *IntWW 91, Who 92*
**Greenwood**, Frank 1924- *WhoFI 92, WhoMW 92*
**Greenwood**, Frederick C 1927- *AmMWSc 92*
**Greenwood**, George W 1929- *AmMWSc 92*
**Greenwood**, Gil Jay 1949- *AmMWSc 92*
**Greenwood**, Gordon H *WhoAmP 91*
**Greenwood**, Hugh J 1931- *AmMWSc 92*
**Greenwood**, Isaac 1702-1745 *BiInAmS*
**Greenwood**, Ivan Anderson 1921- *AmMWSc 92, WhoFI 92*
**Greenwood**, James, III 1936- *WhoAmP 91*
**Greenwood**, James Charles 1951- *WhoAmP 91*
**Greenwood**, James Gregory 1947- *WhoEnt 92*
**Greenwood**, James Robert 1943- *AmMWSc 92*
**Greenwood**, James Russell 1924- *Who 92*
**Greenwood**, Jeffrey Michael 1935- *Who 92*
**Greenwood**, Jeremy John Denis 1942- *Who 92*
**Greenwood**, Joan 1942- *WhoAmP 91*
**Greenwood**, John Arnold Charles 1914- *Who 92*
**Greenwood**, John E. 1922- *WhoMW 92*
**Greenwood**, John Edward Douglas 1923- *WhoFI 92*
**Greenwood**, John Frederic 1885-1954 *TwCPaSc*
**Greenwood**, John T. 1949- *WhoBlA 92*
**Greenwood**, Joseph Albert 1906- *AmMWSc 92*
**Greenwood**, Kenneth 1956- *WhoEnt 92*
**Greenwood**, L. C. Henderson 1946- *WhoBlA 92*
**Greenwood**, Lee Melvin 1942- *WhoEnt 92*
**Greenwood**, Lillian Bethel 1932- *IntAu&W 91*
**Greenwood**, Mark Lawrence 1951- *WhoAmL 92*
**Greenwood**, Mary Rita Cooke 1943- *AmMWSc 92*
**Greenwood**, Norman Neill 1925- *IntWW 91, Who 92, WrDr 92*
**Greenwood**, Paul Gene 1958- *AmMWSc 92*
**Greenwood**, Peter Bryan *Who 92*
**Greenwood**, Peter Humphry 1927- *Who 92*
**Greenwood**, Reginald Charles 1935- *AmMWSc 92*
**Greenwood**, Robert Ewing 1911- *AmMWSc 92*
**Greenwood**, Robin 1950- *TwCPaSc*
**Greenwood**, Ronald 1921- *Who 92*
**Greenwood**, Ted 1930- *IntAu&W 91, WrDr 92*
**Greenwood**, Theresa M. Winfrey 1936- *WhoBlA 92*
**Greenwood**, Tim *WhoAmP 91*
**Greenwood**, Walter 1903-1974 *RfGEnL 91*
**Greenwood**, William R 1938- *AmMWSc 92*
**Greep**, Linda Caryl 1947- *WhoWest 92*
**Greep**, Roy Orval 1905- *AmMWSc 92*
**Greer**, Albert H 1920- *AmMWSc 92*
**Greer**, Bayless Lynn 1941- *WhoAmP 91*
**Greer**, Carl Crawford 1940- *WhoMW 92*
**Greer**, Charles Eugene 1945- *WhoAmL 92*
**Greer**, Curtis William 1957- *WhoBlA 92*
**Greer**, Darrell Stephen 1949- *WhoWest 92*
**Greer**, David Clive 1937- *Who 92*
**Greer**, David Keith 1961- *WhoAmL 92*
**Greer**, David Steven 1925- *AmMWSc 92, IntWW 91*
**Greer**, Donald Lee 1936- *AmMWSc 92*
**Greer**, Donald Merrill 1936- *WhoFI 92*
**Greer**, Earl Vincent 1912- *AmMWSc 92*
**Greer**, Edward 1924- *WhoBlA 92*
**Greer**, Elizabeth F. *WhoRel 92*
**Greer**, Fred Jones 1916- *WhoIns 92*
**Greer**, George Gordon 1946- *AmMWSc 92*
**Greer**, Germaine 1939- *FacFETw, HanAmWH, IntAu&W 91, IntWW 91, Who 92, WrDr 92*
**Greer**, Gordon Bruce 1932- *WhoAmL 92*
**Greer**, Hal 1936- *WhoBlA 92*
**Greer**, Howard A L 1936- *AmMWSc 92*
**Greer**, Isaac Grafield 1881-1967 *DcNCBi 2*
**Greer**, J Ronnie 1952- *WhoAmP 91*
**Greer**, Jack *TwCWW 91*
**Greer**, James Walter 1946- *WhoAmL 92*
**Greer**, Jane 1924- *IntMPA 92*
**Greer**, Jean McDaniel 1917- *WhoRel 92*
**Greer**, Jerry Olin 1945- *WhoRel 92*
**Greer**, John W *WhoAmP 91*
**Greer**, Karyn Lynette 1962- *WhoBlA 92*
**Greer**, Linda Jean 1950- *WhoWest 92*
**Greer**, Michael 1956- *WhoBlA 92*
**Greer**, Monte Arnold 1922- *AmMWSc 92*
**Greer**, Pedro Jose, Jr. 1956- *WhoHisp 92*
**Greer**, Raymond T 1940- *AmMWSc 92*
**Greer**, Raymond Thomas 1940- *WhoMW 92*
**Greer**, Raymond White 1954- *WhoAmL 92, WhoFI 92*
**Greer**, Richard *ConAu 36NR, TwCSFW 91*
**Greer**, Robert O. *DrAPF 91*
**Greer**, Robert O. 1915- *WhoBlA 92N*
**Greer**, Robert O., Jr. 1944- *WhoBlA 92*
**Greer**, Robert William 1917- *WhoEnt 92*
**Greer**, Rowan A., III 1934- *WhoRel 92*
**Greer**, Sandra Charlene 1945- *AmMWSc 92*
**Greer**, Sheldon 1928- *AmMWSc 92*
**Greer**, Sonny 1903-1982 *NewAmDM*
**Greer**, Tee S., Jr. 1936- *WhoBlA 92*
**Greer**, William Louis 1943- *AmMWSc 92*
**Greeran**, Judith Rae 1939- *WhoWest 92*
**Greeson**, David Lloyd 1941- *WhoMW 92*
**Greeson**, Janet Rosemary 1943- *WhoFI 92*
**Greeson**, Phillip Edward 1940- *AmMWSc 92*
**Greet**, Kenneth Gerald 1918- *IntWW 91, Who 92, WrDr 92*
**Greetham**, Colin 1929- *Who 92*
**Greetham**, Geoffrey 1934- *TwCPaSc*
**Greever**, Joe Carroll 1944- *AmMWSc 92*
**Greever**, John 1934- *AmMWSc 92, WhoWest 92*
**Greeves**, Derrick Amphlet d1991 *Who 92N*
**Greeves**, Stuart d1989 *Who 92N*
**Greevy**, Bernadette *IntWW 91*
**Grefe**, Richard 1945- *WhoEnt 92*
**Grefe**, Robert Herman 1941- *WhoFI 92*
**Grefe**, William 1940- *WhoEnt 92*
**Greff**, Barry Steven 1957- *WhoAmL 92*
**Greg**, Barbara 1900- *TwCPaSc*
**Greg**, Percy 1836-1889 *ScFEYrs*
**Greger**, Debora *DrAPF 91*
**Greger**, Janet L 1948- *AmMWSc 92*
**Greger**, Janet Lee 1948- *WhoMW 92*
**Gregerman**, Robert Isaac 1930- *AmMWSc 92*
**Gregers-Hansen**, Vilhelm 1934 *AmMWSc 92*
**Gregersen**, Hans Miller 1938- *AmMWSc 92*
**Gregerson**, Byron Arnold 1942- *WhoIns 92*
**Gregerson**, Linda *DrAPF 91*
**Gregerson**, Richard O *WhoAmP 91*
**Gregg**, Charles T 1927- *SmATA 65*
**Gregg**, Charles Thornton 1927- *AmMWSc 92*
**Gregg**, Christine M 1938- *AmMWSc 92*
**Gregg**, Danny Earl 1948- *WhoFI 92*
**Gregg**, David, III 1933- *WhoFI 92*
**Gregg**, David Henry 1926- *AmMWSc 92*
**Gregg**, David Paul 1923- *WhoEnt 92*
**Gregg**, Davis Weinert 1918- *WrDr 92*
**Gregg**, Dick Hoskins, Jr 1939- *WhoAmP 91*
**Gregg**, Donald P 1927- *WhoAmP 91*
**Gregg**, Donna Coleman 1948- *WhoEnt 92*
**Gregg**, Harrison, Jr 1940- *WhoAmP 91*
**Gregg**, Harrison M., Jr. 1942- *WhoBlA 92*

**Gregg,** Hubert 1914- WrDr 92
**Gregg,** Hubert Robert Harry 1914- Who 92
**Gregg,** Hugh 1917- WhoAmP 91
**Gregg,** James Henderson 1920- AmMWSc 92
**Gregg,** James R 1914- AmMWSc 92
**Gregg,** John Bailey 1922- AmMWSc 92
**Gregg,** John Richard 1916- AmMWSc 92
**Gregg,** John Richard 1954- WhoAmP 91
**Gregg,** Jon Mann 1943- WhoAmL 92
**Gregg,** Josiah 1806-1850 BenetAL 91
**Gregg,** Judd 1947- AlmAP 92 [port], IntWW 91
**Gregg,** Judd Alan 1947- WhoAmP 91
**Gregg,** Linda DrAPF 91
**Gregg,** Lucius Perry 1933- WhoBlA 92
**Gregg,** Lucius Perry, Jr. 1933- WhoWest 92
**Gregg,** Mark Vaughan 1945- WhoFI 92
**Gregg,** Michael Charles 1939- AmMWSc 92
**Gregg,** Nadine Marie 1948- WhoRel 92
**Gregg,** Newton Dewitt 1923- WhoFI 92
**Gregg,** Pauline IntAu&W 91, WrDr 92
**Gregg,** Richard 1927- WrDr 92
**Gregg,** Richard Bartlett 1885-1974 AmPeW
**Gregg,** Robert E. 1960- WhoHisp 92
**Gregg,** Robert Edmond 1912- AmMWSc 92
**Gregg,** Robert Vincent 1928- AmMWSc 92
**Gregg,** Roger Allen 1938- AmMWSc 92
**Gregg,** Sidney John 1902- WrDr 92
**Gregg,** Thomas Allen 1942- WhoMW 92
**Gregg,** Thomas G 1931- AmMWSc 92
**Gregg,** William Henry 1830-1915 BiInAmS
**Greggs,** Elizabeth May Bushnell 1925- WhoWest 92
**Grego,** Nicholas John 1945- AmMWSc 92
**Grego,** Peter 1949- WhoEnt 92, WhoWest 92
**Gregoire,** Henri IntWW 91
**Gregoire,** Henri 1750-1831 BlkwCEP
**Gregoire,** Kent Joseph 1963- WhoFI 92
**Gregoire,** Paul 1911- IntWW 91, RelLAm 91, Who 92, WhoRel 92
**Gregoire,** Pierre 1907- IntWW 91
**Gregor,** Andrew, Jr. 1948- WhoFI 92
**Gregor,** Arthur DrAPF 91
**Gregor,** Arthur 1923- ConPo 91, LiExTwC, WrDr 92
**Gregor,** Clunie Bryan 1929- AmMWSc 92, WhoMW 92
**Gregor,** Harry Paul 1916- AmMWSc 92
**Gregor,** Jan 1923- IntWW 91
**Gregor,** William Edward 1948- WhoFI 92
**Gregor-Dellin,** Martin 1926-1988 LiExTwC
**Gregoratos,** Gabriel 1929- WhoWest 92
**Gregorek,** Richard James, Jr. 1954- WhoWest 92
**Gregorian,** Leon 1943- WhoEnt 92
**Gregorian,** Vartan 1934- IntWW 91
**Gregorich,** Barbara 1943- SmATA 66 [port]
**Gregorich,** David Tony 1937- AmMWSc 92
**Gregorie,** Alan Ross 1959- WhoEnt 92
**Gregorie,** Eugene 1908- DcTwDes
**Gregorie,** Richard Daniel 1947- WhoAmL 92
**Gregorio,** John T 1926- WhoAmP 91
**Gregorio,** William 1945- WhoAmP 91
**Gregorios** Who 92
**Gregorios,** Paulos 1922- IntWW 91
**Gregorios,** Paulos Mar 1922- DcEcMov, WhoRel 92
**Gregorsky,** Frank William 1955- WhoAmP 91
**Gregory,** Lady 1852-1932 RfGEnL 91
**Gregory of Agrigentum** EncEarC
**Gregory of Elvira** 320?-392? EncEarC
**Gregory of Nazianzus** 329?-390 EncEarC
**Gregory of Nyssa** 331?-395? EncEarC
**Gregory of Rimini** 1300?-1358 DcLB 115
**Gregory of Sitka,** Bishop WhoRel 92
**Gregory of Tours** 538-593? EncEarC
**Gregory Thaumaturgus** 210?-260 EncEarC
**Gregory I The Great** 540?-604 EncEarC
**Gregory,** A R 1915- AmMWSc 92
**Gregory,** Alan Thomas 1925- Who 92
**Gregory,** Alfred Thorne d1991 NewYTBS 91
**Gregory,** Annette Sharp 1937- WhoRel 92
**Gregory,** Arthur Robert 1925- AmMWSc 92
**Gregory,** Augusta 1852-1932 FacFETw
**Gregory,** Bernard Vincent 1926- WhoBlA 92
**Gregory,** Bill WhoAmP 91
**Gregory,** Bob Lee 1938- AmMWSc 92
**Gregory,** Brian Charles 1938- AmMWSc 92
**Gregory,** Brooke 1941- AmMWSc 92
**Gregory,** Calvin 1942- WhoFI 92, WhoWest 92
**Gregory,** Calvin Luther 1942- WhoIns 92
**Gregory,** Carole DrAPF 91
**Gregory,** Carolyn DrAPF 91
**Gregory,** Chester 1930- WhoAmP 91
**Gregory,** Christopher Michael 1961- WhoFI 92
**Gregory,** Claire Distelhorst 1926- WhoEnt 92
**Gregory,** Clarence Leslie, Jr 1930- AmMWSc 92
**Gregory,** Clifford 1924- Who 92
**Gregory,** Conal Robert 1947- Who 92
**Gregory,** Constantine J 1939- AmMWSc 92
**Gregory,** Cynde DrAPF 91
**Gregory,** Cynthia 1946- FacFETw
**Gregory,** Dale R 1934- AmMWSc 92
**Gregory,** Daniel Hayes 1933- AmMWSc 92
**Gregory,** David 1661-1708 BlkwCEP
**Gregory,** Dick 1932- ConBlB 1 [port], WhoAmP 91, WhoBlA 92, WhoEnt 92, WrDr 92
**Gregory,** Donald Clifford 1949- AmMWSc 92
**Gregory,** Donald W. 1957- WhoAmL 92
**Gregory,** Douglas Scott 1957- WhoAmL 92
**Gregory,** E. John, Sr. 1919- WhoHisp 92
**Gregory,** Edward Meeks 1922- WhoRel 92
**Gregory,** Eleanor Anne 1939- WhoWest 92
**Gregory,** Emily Lovira 1841-1897 BiInAmS
**Gregory,** Eric 1928- AmMWSc 92
**Gregory,** Eugene Michael 1945- AmMWSc 92
**Gregory,** Fletcher Harrison 1882-1970 DcNCBi 2
**Gregory,** Francis Joseph 1921- AmMWSc 92
**Gregory,** Frederick Drew 1941- WhoBlA 92
**Gregory,** Garold Fay 1926- AmMWSc 92
**Gregory,** Garry Allen 1941- AmMWSc 92
**Gregory,** George G. 1932- WhoAmL 92, WhoFI 92
**Gregory,** George T 1921- WhoAmP 91
**Gregory,** George Tillman, Jr. 1921- WhoAmL 92
**Gregory,** Gilbert E WhoAmP 91
**Gregory,** Hardy, Jr WhoAmP 91
**Gregory,** Hardy, Jr. 1936- WhoAmL 92
**Gregory,** Haskell Don 1959- WhoEnt 92
**Gregory,** Henry C., III 1935-1990 WhoBlA 92N
**Gregory,** Horace 1898-1982 BenetAL 91
**Gregory,** Ian 1926- AmMWSc 92
**Gregory,** Isaac 1737?-1800 DcNCBi 2
**Gregory,** J. S. ConAu 133
**Gregory,** Jackson 1882-1943 BenetAL 91, TwCWW 91
**Gregory,** Jackson V 1941- WhoAmP 91
**Gregory,** James S. 1912-1983 ConAu 133
**Gregory,** Janet Faye 1949- WhoRel 92
**Gregory,** Jennie Kane 1952- WhoRel 92
**Gregory,** Jesse Forrest, III 1950- AmMWSc 92
**Gregory,** Joel Edward 1939- WhoMW 92
**Gregory,** John IntAu&W 91X, TwCSFW 91, WrDr 92
**Gregory,** John Delafield 1923- AmMWSc 92
**Gregory,** John Peter 1925- Who 92
**Gregory,** John R. 1918- IntMPA 92
**Gregory,** Joseph Tracy 1914- AmMWSc 92
**Gregory,** Karl Dwight 1931- WhoBlA 92, WhoFI 92, WhoMW 92
**Gregory,** Kathrine Patricia 1952- WhoFI 92
**Gregory,** Keith Edward 1924- AmMWSc 92
**Gregory,** Kenneth Fowler 1926- AmMWSc 92
**Gregory,** Leslie Howard James 1915- Who 92
**Gregory,** Lester TwCWW 91
**Gregory,** Lewis Dean 1953- WhoAmL 92, WhoFI 92, WhoMW 92
**Gregory,** Louis George 1874-1951 RelLAm 91
**Gregory,** M Duane 1942- AmMWSc 92
**Gregory,** Mary Lloyd 1768-1858 DcNCBi 2
**Gregory,** Max Edwin 1931- AmMWSc 92
**Gregory,** Maxie David 1956- WhoMW 92
**Gregory,** Michael 1944- WhoEnt 92
**Gregory,** Michael Anthony 1925- Who 92
**Gregory,** Michael Baird 1944- AmMWSc 92
**Gregory,** Michael Lloyd 1954- WhoMW 92
**Gregory,** Michael Strietmann 1929- WhoWest 92
**Gregory,** Michael Vladimir 1945- AmMWSc 92
**Gregory,** Myra May 1912- WhoRel 92
**Gregory,** Nelson Bruce 1933- WhoFI 92, WhoWest 92
**Gregory,** Norman Wayne 1920- AmMWSc 92
**Gregory,** O. Grady 1895- WhoBlA 92
**Gregory,** Owen ScFEYrs
**Gregory,** Paul LesBEnT 92
**Gregory,** Paul Radcliffe 1920- WhoRel 92
**Gregory,** Paul Roderick 1941- WhoFI 92
**Gregory,** Peter 1947- AmMWSc 92
**Gregory,** Peter Roland 1946- Who 92
**Gregory,** R Lee 1936- AmMWSc 92
**Gregory,** Randy Alan 1952- WhoAmL 92
**Gregory,** Raymond 1901- AmMWSc 92
**Gregory,** Richard WhoRel 92
**Gregory,** Richard Alan, Jr 1943- AmMWSc 92
**Gregory,** Richard Claxton 1932- WhoBlA 92
**Gregory,** Richard Hyde 1960- WhoFI 92
**Gregory,** Richard Langton 1923- IntAu&W 91, Who 92, WrDr 92
**Gregory,** Richard Wallace 1936- AmMWSc 92
**Gregory,** Rick Dean 1954- WhoAmL 92
**Gregory,** Robert Aaron AmMWSc 92
**Gregory,** Robert Alphonso 1935- WhoBlA 92
**Gregory,** Robert D. DrAPF 91
**Gregory,** Robert Earle, Jr. 1942- WhoFI 92
**Gregory,** Robin Scott 1950- WhoFI 92
**Gregory,** Roderic Alfred d1990 IntWW 91N
**Gregory,** Roger Lee 1953- WhoBlA 92
**Gregory,** Roger Michael 1939- Who 92
**Gregory,** Roland Charles Leslie Who 92
**Gregory,** Ronald 1921- Who 92
**Gregory,** Roy 1916- Who 92
**Gregory,** Roy 1935- WrDr 92
**Gregory,** Roy George 1935- IntAu&W 91
**Gregory,** Stephan IntAu&W 91X, WrDr 92
**Gregory,** Stephen ConAu 35NR
**Gregory,** Stephen Albert 1948- AmMWSc 92
**Gregory,** Steven ConAu 134
**Gregory,** Susan 1954- WhoEnt 92
**Gregory,** Tenicia Ann 1933- WhoBlA 92
**Gregory,** Terence Van Buren 1950- WhoRel 92
**Gregory,** Theodore Morris 1952- WhoBlA 92
**Gregory,** Theopalis K 1952- WhoAmP 91
**Gregory,** Thomas Bradford 1944- AmMWSc 92, WhoMW 92
**Gregory,** Thomas Laurence Baker 1807-1859 DcNCBi 2
**Gregory,** Tim 1966- WhoAmP 91
**Gregory,** Vance Peter, Jr. 1943- WhoMW 92
**Gregory,** Wesley Wright, Jr 1942- AmMWSc 92
**Gregory,** William Edgar 1910- WhoWest 92
**Gregory,** William N., Jr. 1929- WhoIns 92
**Gregory,** William Scott 1942- WhoWest 92
**Gregory,** Wilton D. 1947- WhoBlA 92, WhoRel 92
**Gregotti,** Vittorio 1927- DcTwDes
**Gregson** Who 92
**Gregson,** Baron 1924- Who 92
**Gregson,** Lee F. TwCWW 91
**Gregson,** Mary Poage 1910- WhoAmP 91
**Gregson,** Peter 1936- Who 92
**Gregson,** Peter Lewis 1936- IntWW 91
**Gregson,** Stephen 1955- TwCPaSc
**Gregson,** William Derek Hadfield 1920- Who 92
**Gregus,** Daniel Ronald 1961- WhoAmL 92
**Gregware,** James Murray 1956- WhoFI 92
**Greher,** Gena R. 1951- WhoEnt 92
**Greibach,** Sheila Adele 1939- AmMWSc 92
**Greider,** Kenneth Randolph 1929- AmMWSc 92
**Greider,** Marie Helen 1922- AmMWSc 92
**Greider,** William WrDr 92
**Greif,** Edward Louis 1909- WhoFI 92
**Greif,** Lloyd 1955- WhoFI 92
**Greif,** Mortimer 1926- AmMWSc 92
**Greif,** Ralph 1935- AmMWSc 92
**Greif,** Robert 1938- AmMWSc 92
**Greif,** Roger Louis 1916- AmMWSc 92
**Greifer,** Aaron Philip 1919- AmMWSc 92
**Greiff,** Barrie S. 1935- ConAu 134
**Greiff,** Donald 1915- AmMWSc 92
**Greiffenhagen,** Maurice 1862-1931 TwCPaSc
**Greifinger,** Carl 1926- AmMWSc 92
**Greig,** Brian Strother 1950- WhoAmL 92
**Greig,** Carron 1925- Who 92
**Greig,** Doreen 1917- WrDr 92
**Greig,** Douglas Richard 1950- AmMWSc 92
**Greig,** Douglas Wylie 1944- WhoFI 92
**Greig,** Henry Louis Carron 1925- IntWW 91
**Greig,** J Robert 1938- AmMWSc 92
**Greig,** James 1903- Who 92
**Greig,** James Kibler, Jr 1923- AmMWSc 92
**Greig,** William Taber, Jr. 1924- WhoRel 92
**Greig of Eccles,** James Dennis 1926- Who 92
**Greigg,** Ronald Edwin 1946- WhoAmL 92
**Greigg,** Stanley Lloyd 1931- WhoAmP 91
**Greilsheimer,** James Gans 1937- WhoAmL 92
**Greim,** Barbara Ann AmMWSc 92
**Greim,** Robert, Ritter von 1892-1945 EncTR 91 [port]
**Greiman,** Alan J 1931- WhoAmP 91
**Greiman,** April 1948- WhoEnt 92
**Grein,** Friedrich 1929- AmMWSc 92
**Grein,** Richard Frank 1932- WhoRel 92
**Greindl,** Josef 1912- IntWW 91
**Greiner,** Dale L AmMWSc 92
**Greiner,** Douglas Earl 1939- AmMWSc 92
**Greiner,** G Roger 1942- WhoIns 92
**Greiner,** Keith Allen 1940- WhoAmP 91
**Greiner,** Morris Esty, Jr. 1920- WhoEnt 92
**Greiner,** Nicholas Frank 1947- Who 92
**Greiner,** Norman Roy 1938- AmMWSc 92
**Greiner,** Peter Charles 1938- AmMWSc 92
**Greiner,** Richard A 1931- AmMWSc 92
**Greiner,** Richard William 1932- AmMWSc 92
**Greiner,** Robert Frederic 1941- WhoMW 92
**Greiner,** Thomas H. 1945- WhoMW 92
**Greiner,** Walter Albin Erhard 1935- IntWW 91
**Greinke,** Arthur Joseph 1963- WhoEnt 92
**Greinke,** Eric DrAPF 91
**Greinke,** Everett D 1929- AmMWSc 92
**Greinke,** Ronald Alfred 1935- AmMWSc 92
**Greis,** Wayne Raymond 1942- WhoMW 92
**Greisen,** Eric Winslow 1944- AmMWSc 92
**Greisen,** Kenneth I 1918- AmMWSc 92
**Greiser,** Arthur 1897-1946 EncTR 91 [port]
**Greiser,** Arthur Karl 1897-1946 BiDExR
**Greisiger,** Arthur Eugene, Jr. 1954- WhoEnt 92
**Greisinger,** Ray John 1936- WhoMW 92
**Greisman,** Harvey William 1948- WhoFI 92
**Greisman,** Sheldon Edward 1928- AmMWSc 92
**Greiss,** Frank C, Jr 1928- AmMWSc 92
**Greist,** John Howard 1906- AmMWSc 92
**Greist,** Kim 1958- IntMPA 92
**Greitzer,** Carol WhoAmP 91
**Greitzer,** Edward Marc 1941- AmMWSc 92
**Greive,** Edward Gerhard 1942- WhoAmL 92
**Greive,** Tyrone Don 1943- WhoMW 92
**Greive,** William Henry 1933- WhoMW 92
**Greizerstein,** Hebe Beatriz AmMWSc 92
**Greizerstein,** Walter 1935- AmMWSc 92
**Grek,** Boris 1946- AmMWSc 92
**Grekov,** Leonid Ivanovich 1928- IntWW 91
**Grekov,** Mitrofan Borisovich 1882-1934 SovUnBD
**Grekova,** I. 1907- SovUnBD
**Grekova,** Irina Nikolaevna 1907- IntWW 91
**Grelecki,** Chester 1927- AmMWSc 92
**Grelen,** Harold Eugene 1929- AmMWSc 92
**Grelick,** Susan Joy 1954- WhoAmL 92
**Grell,** Mary Ellen 1930- WhoRel 92
**Grella,** Joseph John 1953- WhoMW 92
**Grella,** Robert Alan 1939- WhoIns 92
**Greller,** Andrew M 1941- AmMWSc 92
**Grelling,** Richard 1853-1929 EncTR 91
**Grembowski,** David Emil 1951- WhoWest 92
**Grembowski,** Eugene 1938- WhoFI 92, WhoWest 92
**Gremillon,** Jean 1901-1959 IntDcF 2-2
**Greminger,** George King, Jr 1916- AmMWSc 92
**Gremoli,** Bernardo Giovani WhoRel 92
**Gren,** Conrad Roger 1955- WhoWest 92
**Gren,** Jack E. 1923- WhoFI 92, WhoMW 92
**Grenander,** Ulf 1923- AmMWSc 92
**Grenard,** Jack 1933- WhoWest 92
**Grenchik,** Raymond Thomas 1922- AmMWSc 92
**Grenda,** Stanley C 1934- AmMWSc 92
**Grenda,** Victor J 1933- AmMWSc 92
**Grenda,** Walter Francis, Jr. 1957- WhoFI 92
**Grendell,** Timothy Joseph 1953- WhoAmL 92
**Grenemyer,** Timothy James 1960- WhoWest 92
**Grenesko,** Don WhoMW 92
**Grenfell** Who 92
**Grenfell,** Baron 1935- IntWW 91, Who 92
**Grenfell,** Andree 1940- Who 92
**Grenfell,** George Albert, Jr. 1941- WhoWest 92
**Grenfell,** James Byrnes 1952- WhoAmL 92
**Grenfell,** Joyce 1910-1979 FacFETw

**Grenfell**, Raymond Frederic 1917- *AmMWSc 92*
**Grenfell**, Simon Pascoe 1942- *Who 92*
**Grenfell**, Wilfred Thomason 1865-1940 *BenetAL 91*
**Grenfell-Baines**, George 1908- *Who 92*
**Grenga**, Helen E 1938- *AmMWSc 92*
**Grenier**, Claude Georges 1923- *AmMWSc 92*
**Grenier**, Edward Joseph, Jr. 1933- *WhoAmL 92*
**Grenier**, Henry R *WhoAmP 91*
**Grenier**, Jean-Marie Rene 1926- *IntWW 91*
**Grenier**, John Edward 1930- *WhoAmP 91*
**Grenier**, Judson A., Jr. 1930- *WhoWest 92*
**Grenier**, Peter Francis 1934- *Who 92*
**Grening**, L. Keith 1957- *WhoFI 92*
**Grenke**, David *WhoEnt 92*
**Grenley**, Philip 1912- *WhoWest 92*
**Grennan**, Eamon *DrAPF 91*
**Grennan**, Eamon 1941- *ConAu 133*
**Grenner**, William Bryan 1962- *WhoAmL 92*
**Grenney**, William James 1937- *AmMWSc 92*
**Grenside**, John 1921- *Who 92*
**Grensky**, Ronald D 1954- *WhoAmP 91*
**Grenvik**, Ake N A 1929- *AmMWSc 92*
**Grenville** *Who 92*
**Grenville**, George 1712-1770 *BlkwEAR*
**Grenville**, George 1920- *WhoEnt 92*
**Grenville**, John A S 1928- *IntAu&W 91, WrDr 92*
**Grenville**, John Ashley Soames 1928- *Who 92*
**Grenville-Grey**, Wilfrid Ernest 1930- *Who 92*
**Grenyer**, Herbert Charles 1913- *Who 92*
**Grenz**, Stanley J. 1950- *WhoRel 92*
**Gres**, Alix 1910- *DcTwDes*
**Greschuk**, Demetrius Martin 1923- *WhoRel 92*
**Gresens**, John Joseph 1959- *WhoAmL 92*
**Greseth**, Mona *WhoAmP 91*
**Gresh**, Dexter Perry, Jr. 1955- *WhoFI 92*
**Greshake**, Gisbert 1933- *WhoRel 92*
**Gresham**, Austin 1924- *Who 92*
**Gresham**, Donald 1956- *WhoBlA 92*
**Gresham**, John Kenneth *WhoAmP 91*
**Gresham**, Johnny, Jr *WhoAmP 91*
**Gresham**, Robert Coleman 1917- *WhoAmP 91*
**Gresham**, Robert Lambert, Jr. 1943- *WhoWest 92*
**Gresham**, Robert Marion 1943- *AmMWSc 92*
**Gresham**, Walter Quintin 1832-1895 *AmPolLe*
**Greshler**, Abner J. *IntMPA 92*
**Gresik**, Edward William 1939- *AmMWSc 92*
**Greskovich**, Charles David 1942- *AmMWSc 92*
**Gresley**, Herbert Nigel 1876-1941 *DcTwDes, FacFETw*
**Gress**, Edward Jules 1940- *WhoFI 92*
**Gress**, Esther *IntAu&W 91*
**Gress**, Mary Edith 1946- *AmMWSc 92*
**Gress**, Ronald E 1949- *AmMWSc 92*
**Gressel**, Jonathan Ben 1936- *AmMWSc 92*
**Gressens**, June P 1924- *WhoAmP 91*
**Gresser**, Ion 1928- *AmMWSc 92*
**Gresser**, Michael Joseph 1945- *AmMWSc 92*
**Gresser**, Seymour 1926- *WrDr 92*
**Gresser**, Seymour Gerald 1926- *IntAu&W 91*
**Gressle**, E. Mark 1950- *WhoFI 92*
**Gressle**, Lloyd Edward 1918- *WhoRel 92*
**Gressman**, Eugene 1917- *WhoAmL 92*
**Gresso**, Vernon Riddle 1927- *WhoFI 92*
**Grest**, Gary Stephen 1949- *AmMWSc 92*
**Gresty**, Hugh 1899-1958 *TwCPaSc*
**Greswell**, Jeaffreson Herbert 1916- *Who 92*
**Grethe**, Guenter 1933- *AmMWSc 92*
**Grether**, Henry Moroni, Jr. 1920- *WhoAmL 92*
**Gretry**, Andre-Ernest-Modeste 1741-1813 *BlkwCEP, NewAmDM*
**Gretsch**, Hermann 1895- *DcTwDes*
**Gretsky**, Neil E 1941- *AmMWSc 92*
**Grettie**, Donald Pomeroy 1900- *AmMWSc 92*
**Gretton** *Who 92*
**Gretton**, Baron 1975- *Who 92*
**Gretton**, Peter 1912- *Who 92*
**Gretzinger**, Ralph Edwin, III 1948- *WhoFI 92*
**Gretzky**, Wayne 1961- *FacFETw [port], WhoWest 92*
**Greub**, Louis John 1933- *AmMWSc 92*
**Greuer**, Rudolf E A 1927- *AmMWSc 92*
**Greule**, Alan L. 1956- *WhoEnt 92*
**Greulich**, Richard Curtice 1928- *AmMWSc 92*
**Greuze**, Jean Baptiste 1725-1805 *BlkwCEP*
**Greve**, Guy Robert 1947- *WhoMW 92*
**Greve**, J. William 1929- *WhoIns 92*
**Greve**, John 1927- *Who 92*
**Greve**, John Henry 1934- *AmMWSc 92*
**Greve**, Lucius, II 1915- *WhoFI 92, WhoMW 92*
**Greve**, Marilyn J. 1943- *WhoFI 92*
**Grever**, Jean Kempel 1926- *WhoMW 92*
**Greves**, Melvyn Francis 1941- *Who 92*
**Greville** *Who 92*
**Greville**, Fulke 1554-1628 *RfGEnL 91*
**Greville**, Phillip Jamieson 1925- *Who 92*
**Greville**, Thomas Nall Eden 1910- *AmMWSc 92*
**Grevisse**, Fernand 1924- *IntWW 91*
**Grew**, Edward Sturgis 1944- *AmMWSc 92*
**Grew**, Kimberly Ann 1962- *WhoMW 92*
**Grew**, Priscilla Croswell Perkins 1940- *AmMWSc 92*
**Grew**, Robert Ralph 1931- *WhoAmL 92, WhoFI 92*
**Grew**, Theophilus d1759 *BiInAmS*
**Grewal**, Harnam Singh 1937- *Who 92*
**Grewar**, David 1921- *AmMWSc 92*
**Grewe**, Alfred H, Jr 1926- *AmMWSc 92*
**Grewe**, John Mitchell 1938- *AmMWSc 92*
**Grewell**, Judith Lynn 1945- *WhoMW 92*
**Grey** *Who 92*
**Grey**, Earl 1939- *Who 92*
**Grey Owl** 1888-1938 *BenetAL 91*
**Grey**, Alan Hartley 1925- *Who 92*
**Grey**, Alan Hopwood 1932- *AmMWSc 92*
**Grey**, Anthony 1938- *WrDr 92*
**Grey**, Anthony 1949- *Who 92*
**Grey**, Anthony Keith 1938- *IntAu&W 91*
**Grey**, Beryl 1927- *Who 92, WrDr 92*
**Grey**, Beryl Elizabeth 1927- *IntAu&W 91, IntWW 91*
**Grey**, Brenda *IntAu&W 91X, WrDr 92*
**Grey**, Carol *TwCSFW 91*
**Grey**, Charles *IntAu&W 91X, TwCSFW 91, WrDr 92*
**Grey**, Edward 1862-1933 *FacFETw*
**Grey**, Francis Joseph 1931- *WhoFI 92*
**Grey**, Georgina *WrDr 92*
**Grey**, Gothard C 1957- *AmMWSc 92*
**Grey**, Howard M 1932- *AmMWSc 92*
**Grey**, Ian *WrDr 92*
**Grey**, Ian 1918- *IntAu&W 91*
**Grey**, J. David 1935- *ConAu 133*
**Grey**, James Tracy, Jr 1914- *AmMWSc 92*
**Grey**, Jason Wayne 1963- *WhoEnt 92*
**Grey**, Jennifer 1960- *IntMPA 92*
**Grey**, Jerry 1926- *AmMWSc 92, WrDr 92*
**Grey**, Joel 1932- *IntMPA 92, NewAmDM, WhoEnt 92*
**Grey**, John Egerton 1929- *Who 92*
**Grey**, John Franklin 1952- *WhoMW 92*
**Grey**, John St John 1934- *Who 92*
**Grey**, Linda *IntWW 91*
**Grey**, Paul Francis d1990 *Who 92N*
**Grey**, Peter 1938- *AmMWSc 92*
**Grey**, Robert Dean 1939- *AmMWSc 92*
**Grey**, Robert Waters *DrAPF 91*
**Grey**, Robin Douglas 1931- *Who 92*
**Grey**, Roger Allen 1947- *AmMWSc 92*
**Grey**, Romer Zane *TwCWW 91*
**Grey**, Ronald Brian 1962- *WhoWest 92*
**Grey**, Thomas C. 1941- *WhoAmL 92*
**Grey**, Virginia 1917- *IntMPA 92*
**Grey**, Wilfrid Ernest G. *Who 92*
**Grey**, Zane 1872-1939 *TwCWW 91*
**Grey**, Zane 1875-1939 *BenetAL 91, FacFETw*
**Grey Egerton**, John 1920- *Who 92*
**Grey of Codnor**, Baron 1903- *Who 92*
**Grey Of Naunton**, Baron 1910- *IntWW 91, Who 92*
**Grey-Wilson**, Christopher 1944- *IntAu&W 91, WrDr 92*
**Greyson**, Jerome 1927- *AmMWSc 92, WhoWest 92*
**Greyson**, Richard Irving 1932- *AmMWSc 92*
**Greytak**, David Edward 1941- *WhoFI 92*
**Greytak**, Lee Joseph 1949- *WhoFI 92*
**Greytak**, Thomas John 1940- *AmMWSc 92*
**Greywall**, Dennis Stanley 1943- *AmMWSc 92*
**Greywall**, Mahesh S 1934- *AmMWSc 92*
**Grezlak**, John Henry 1945- *AmMWSc 92*
**Grgurich**, Daniel F. 1954- *WhoFI 92*
**Gribachov**, Nikolay Matveyevich 1910- *IntWW 91*
**Gribbin**, David James 1939- *WhoAmP 91*
**Gribbin**, John *IntAu&W 91*
**Gribbin**, John R 1946- *TwCSFW 91*
**Gribble**, Arthur Stanley 1904- *Who 92*
**Gribble**, Carole L. 1940- *WhoFI 92, WhoWest 92*
**Gribble**, Charles Edward 1936- *WhoMW 92*
**Gribble**, David Harold 1932- *AmMWSc 92*
**Gribble**, Gordon W 1941- *AmMWSc 92*
**Gribble**, Leonard 1908- *IntAu&W 91*
**Gribble**, Leonard 1908-1953 *TwCWW 91*
**Gribble**, W George *ScFEYrs*
**Gribbon**, Edward John 1943- *Who 92*
**Gribbon**, Nigel St George 1917- *Who 92*
**Gribbons**, Michael Stanley 1953- *WhoRel 92*
**Gribkov**, Anatoliy Ivanovich 1919- *IntWW 91, SovUnBD*
**Griboval**, Paul 1925- *AmMWSc 92*
**Gribow**, Dale Seward 1943- *WhoFI 92*
**Grice**, George Daniel, Jr 1929- *AmMWSc 92*
**Grice**, Harvey H 1912- *AmMWSc 92*
**Gridban**, Volsted *IntAu&W 91X, TwCSFW 91, WrDr 92*
**Grider**, Jay *ConAu 133*
**Grider**, Joe Bob 1936- *WhoRel 92*
**Grider**, John Raymond 1952- *AmMWSc 92*
**Grider**, Joseph Kenneth 1921- *WhoRel 92*
**Grider**, Tommy Doyle 1949- *WhoEnt 92*
**Gridley** *Who 92*
**Gridley**, Baron 1906- *Who 92*
**Gridley**, Sam *DrAPF 91*
**Grieb**, Kenneth J. 1939- *WrDr 92*
**Grieb**, Merland William 1920- *AmMWSc 92*
**Grieb**, Robert William 1930- *WhoIns 92*
**Griebsch**, Linda 1948- *WhoAmP 91*
**Griech**, Frederick G. 1944- *WhoMW 92*
**Grieco**, Joseph V 1915- *WhoAmP 91*
**Grieco**, Michael H *AmMWSc 92*
**Grieco**, Paul Anthony 1944- *AmMWSc 92*
**Grieder**, Karen Suzanne 1957- *WhoEnt 92*
**Grieder**, Terence 1931- *ConAu 35NR*
**Grieg**, Edvard 1843-1907 *NewAmDM*
**Griege**, Mark Charles 1959- *WhoFI 92*
**Griego**, Adan 1959- *WhoHisp 92*
**Griego**, Alfred Anthony 1943- *WhoHisp 92*
**Griego**, Charles 1951- *WhoAmP 91*
**Griego**, Jose Sabino 1938- *WhoHisp 92*
**Griego**, Linda 1935- *WhoHisp 92*
**Griego**, Phil *WhoHisp 92*
**Griego**, Phillip Joseph 1951- *WhoAmL 92*
**Griego**, Richard Jerome 1939- *AmMWSc 92*
**Griego**, Vincent E. 1940- *WhoHisp 92*
**Griego Erwin**, Diana 1959- *WhoHisp 92*
**Griem**, Hans Rudolf 1928- *AmMWSc 92*
**Griem**, Helmut 1940- *IntMPA 92*
**Griem**, Melvin Luther 1925- *AmMWSc 92*
**Griem**, Sylvia F 1929- *AmMWSc 92*
**Grieman**, Frederick Joseph 1952- *AmMWSc 92*
**Grieninger**, Gerd *AmMWSc 92*
**Grier**, Albert Catton 1864-1941 *RelLAm 91*
**Grier**, Arthur E., Jr. 1943- *WhoBlA 92*
**Grier**, Bobby 1942- *WhoBlA 92*
**Grier**, Charles Crocker 1938- *AmMWSc 92, WhoWest 92*
**Grier**, David Alan 1956- *WhoBlA 92*
**Grier**, Eldon 1917- *IntAu&W 91, WrDr 92*
**Grier**, Francis Ebenezer 1948- *WhoAmP 91*
**Grier**, George Edward 1934- *WhoAmP 91*
**Grier**, Herbert E *AmMWSc 92*
**Grier**, Jack Wesley 1930- *WhoAmP 91*
**Grier**, James Edward 1935- *WhoAmL 92*
**Grier**, James William 1943- *AmMWSc 92*
**Grier**, John Bailey 1938- *WhoAmL 92*
**Grier**, John Richmond 1940- *WhoMW 92*
**Grier**, Johnny 1947- *WhoBlA 92*
**Grier**, Nathaniel 1918- *AmMWSc 92*
**Grier**, Pamala *WhoEnt 92*
**Grier**, Patricia Elizabeth Welch 1951- *WhoRel 92*
**Grier**, Patrick Arthur 1918- *Who 92*
**Grier**, Phillip Michael 1941- *WhoAmL 92*
**Grier**, Ronald Lee 1941- *AmMWSc 92*
**Grier**, Roosevelt 1932- *WhoBlA 92*
**Grier**, Rosey 1932- *WhoBlA 92*
**Grier**, Samuel Andrew 1841-1932 *DcNCBi 2*
**Grier**, Ted Charles 1954- *WhoRel 92*
**Grierson**, Francis 1848-1927 *BenetAL 91*
**Grierson**, Francis D 1888 *ScFEYrs*
**Grierson**, James Douglas 1931- *AmMWSc 92*
**Grierson**, John 1898-1972 *FacFETw, IntDcF 2-2 [port]*
**Grierson**, Michael 1921- *Who 92*
**Grierson**, Patricia Minter *DrAPF 91*
**Grierson**, Philip 1910- *IntWW 91, Who 92, WrDr 92*
**Grierson**, Ronald 1921- *Who 92*
**Grierson**, Ronald Hugh 1921- *IntWW 91*
**Gries**, David 1939- *AmMWSc 92*
**Gries**, George Alexander 1917- *AmMWSc 92*
**Gries**, John Charles 1940- *AmMWSc 92*
**Gries**, John Paul 1911- *AmMWSc 92*
**Gries**, Philip R. 1943- *WhoEnt 92*
**Gries**, Tom d1976 *LesBEnT 92*
**Griesa**, Thomas Poole 1930- *WhoAmL 92*
**Griesbach**, Robert Anthony 1924- *AmMWSc 92*
**Griesbach**, Robert James 1955- *AmMWSc 92*
**Griese**, Carol 1945- *Who 92*
**Griesedieck**, Edward Joseph, III 1958- *WhoAmL 92*
**Griesemer**, Allan David 1935- *WhoWest 92*
**Griesemer**, Omer Kenneth 1932- *WhoEnt 92*
**Griesemer**, Richard Allen 1929- *AmMWSc 92*
**Griesenauer**, Ronald Lee, Sr. 1947- *WhoMW 92*
**Grieser**, Daniel R 1926- *AmMWSc 92*
**Grieser**, Emil 1926- *WhoAmP 91*
**Grieshaber**, Charles K 1941- *AmMWSc 92*
**Grieshammer**, Lawrence Louis 1922- *AmMWSc 92*
**Griesheimer**, Ronald E 1936- *WhoAmP 91*
**Grieshober**, William Edward 1942- *WhoFI 92*
**Griesinger**, David Hadley 1944- *AmMWSc 92*
**Griesmann**, Donald Andre 1932- *WhoAmL 92*
**Griesmer**, James Hugo 1929- *AmMWSc 92*
**Griess**, John Christian, Jr 1922- *AmMWSc 92*
**Griess**, Robert Louis, Jr 1945- *AmMWSc 92*
**Grieve**, Lord 1917- *Who 92*
**Grieve**, Catherine Macy 1926- *AmMWSc 92*
**Grieve**, Christopher Murray *RfGEnL 91*
**Grieve**, Harold Walter 1901- *WhoWest 92*
**Grieve**, Leona Lee 1954- *WhoWest 92*
**Grieve**, Percy *Who 92*
**Grieve**, Peter 1936- *TwCPaSc*
**Grieve**, Pierson MacDonald 1927- *WhoFI 92, WhoMW 92*
**Grieve**, Richard Andrew 1943- *AmMWSc 92*
**Grieve**, Robert 1910- *Who 92*
**Grieve**, Robert 1939- *WhoAmP 91*
**Grieve**, Robert B 1951- *AmMWSc 92*
**Grieve**, Robert Burton 1951- *WhoWest 92*
**Grieve**, Walter Graham d1937 *TwCPaSc*
**Grieve**, William Percival 1915- *Who 92*
**Grieve**, William Robertson *Who 92*
**Grieves**, David 1933- *Who 92*
**Grieves**, John Kerr 1935- *Who 92*
**Grieves**, Robert Belanger 1935- *AmMWSc 92*
**Griew**, Stephen 1928- *Who 92*
**Grifalconi**, Ann 1929- *ConAu 35NR, SmATA 66 [port]*
**Griff**, James Joseph 1959- *WhoMW 92*
**Griffel**, Kay *WhoEnt 92*
**Griffel**, Maurice 1919- *AmMWSc 92*
**Griffen**, Dana Thomas 1943- *AmMWSc 92*
**Griffen**, Fred Andrew 1945- *WhoEnt 92*
**Griffen**, Ward O, Jr 1928- *AmMWSc 92*
**Griffenhagen**, George Bernard 1924- *AmMWSc 92*
**Griffes**, Charles T. 1884-1920 *NewAmDM*
**Griffes**, Charles Tomlinson 1884-1920 *FacFETw*
**Griffes**, Donald L 1931- *WhoAmP 91*
**Griffes**, James Elbridge 1927- *WhoRel 92*
**Griffey**, Dick 1943- *WhoBlA 92*
**Griffey**, Ken, Jr. 1969- *WhoBlA 92*
**Griffey**, Ken, Sr. 1950- *WhoBlA 92*
**Griffin**, Alfredo 1957- *WhoHisp 92*
**Griffin**, Allan 1939- *AmMWSc 92*
**Griffin**, Andrew *TwCWW 91*
**Griffin**, Anselm Clyde, III 1946- *AmMWSc 92*
**Griffin**, Anthony 1920- *IntWW 91, Who 92*
**Griffin**, Archie 1954- *WhoBlA 92*
**Griffin**, Arthur John 1924- *Who 92*
**Griffin**, Ben L., Jr. 1946- *WhoIns 92*
**Griffin**, Ben Lee 1946- *WhoFI 92*
**Griffin**, Benjamin Theodore 1940- *WhoRel 92*
**Griffin**, Bertha L. 1930- *WhoBlA 92*
**Griffin**, Betty Sue 1943- *WhoBlA 92*
**Griffin**, Bob Franklin 1935- *WhoAmP 91, WhoMW 92*
**Griffin**, Bobby L. 1938- *WhoBlA 92*
**Griffin**, Booker 1938- *WhoBlA 92*
**Griffin**, Bradney Beverley 1872?-1898 *BiInAmS*
**Griffin**, Bryant Wade 1915- *WhoAmL 92*
**Griffin**, Campbell Arthur, Jr. 1929- *WhoAmL 92*
**Griffin**, Charles 1679?-1720? *DcNCBi 2*
**Griffin**, Charles Campbell 1938- *AmMWSc 92*
**Griffin**, Charles Frank 1935- *AmMWSc 92*
**Griffin**, Charles Lawrence, III 1948- *WhoAmP 91*
**Griffin**, Charles Thomas 1942- *WhoMW 92*
**Griffin**, Claibourne Eugene, Jr 1929- *AmMWSc 92*
**Griffin**, Clarence Wilbur 1904-1958 *DcNCBi 2*
**Griffin**, Claude Lane 1937- *AmMWSc 92*
**Griffin**, Clayton Houstoun 1925- *AmMWSc 92*

**Griffin,** Dana Gove, III 1938- *AmMWSc 92*
**Griffin,** Daniel Joseph, Jr. 1947- *WhoAmL 92*
**Griffin,** David 1915- *Who 92*
**Griffin,** David H 1937- *AmMWSc 92*
**Griffin,** David William 1955- *AmMWSc 92*
**Griffin,** DeWitt James 1914- *WhoFI 92, WhoWest 92*
**Griffin,** Diane Edmund 1940- *AmMWSc 92*
**Griffin,** Donald 1915- *IntWW 91*
**Griffin,** Donald James 1958- *WhoRel 92*
**Griffin,** Donald Joe 1955- *WhoWest 92*
**Griffin,** Donald R 1915- *AmMWSc 92, WrDr 92*
**Griffin,** Donald Wayne 1937- *WhoFI 92*
**Griffin,** Edgar Allen 1907- *Who 92*
**Griffin,** Edmond Eugene 1930- *AmMWSc 92*
**Griffin,** Edna Westberry 1907- *WhoBlA 92*
**Griffin,** Edward L, Jr 1919- *AmMWSc 92*
**Griffin,** Ernest Lyle 1921- *AmMWSc 92*
**Griffin,** Ervin Verome 1949- *WhoBlA 92*
**Griffin,** Eurich Z. 1938- *WhoBlA 92*
**Griffin,** Frank M, Jr 1941- *AmMWSc 92*
**Griffin,** G. Edward 1931- *WhoEnt 92*
**Griffin,** Gail Carol 1953- *WhoWest 92*
**Griffin,** Gary Arthur 1937- *WhoFI 92*
**Griffin,** Gary J 1937- *AmMWSc 92*
**Griffin,** Gary Walter 1931- *AmMWSc 92*
**Griffin,** George Melvin, Jr 1928- *AmMWSc 92*
**Griffin,** Gerald 1803-1840 *RfGEnL 91*
**Griffin,** Gerald 1944- *WhoBlA 92*
**Griffin,** Gerald D 1927- *AmMWSc 92*
**Griffin,** Gregory Lee *AmMWSc 92*
**Griffin,** Gregory O. *WhoBlA 92*
**Griffin,** Guy David 1942- *AmMWSc 92*
**Griffin,** Hardy 1735?-1794 *DcNCBi 2*
**Griffin,** Harold Lee 1928- *AmMWSc 92*
**Griffin,** Harry 1911- *WrDr 92*
**Griffin,** Harry Frederick 1951- *WhoFI 92*
**Griffin,** Henry Claude 1937- *AmMWSc 92*
**Griffin,** J. Philip, Jr. 1932- *WhoIns 92*
**Griffin,** Jack Kennedy 1958- *WhoEnt 92*
**Griffin,** Jacqueline J 1942- *WhoAmP 91*
**Griffin,** James Alton 1956- *WhoEnt 92*
**Griffin,** James Anthony 1934- *WhoRel 92*
**Griffin,** James Bennett 1905- *IntWW 91*
**Griffin,** James D 1929- *WhoAmP 91*
**Griffin,** James Edward 1925- *AmMWSc 92*
**Griffin,** James Edward 1941- *WhoWest 92*
**Griffin,** James Emmett 1944- *AmMWSc 92*
**Griffin,** James J 1930- *AmMWSc 92*
**Griffin,** James Neil 1947- *WhoAmL 92*
**Griffin,** James Stafford 1917- *WhoBlA 92*
**Griffin,** Jane Flanigen 1933- *AmMWSc 92*
**Griffin,** Jasper 1937- *IntWW 91, Who 92*
**Griffin,** Jean 1931- *WhoEnt 92, WhoWest 92*
**Griffin,** Jean Thomas 1937- *WhoBlA 92*
**Griffin,** Jerry Howard 1945- *AmMWSc 92*
**Griffin,** Jerry Lynn 1949- *WhoRel 92*
**Griffin,** Jim Tyson *WhoAmP 91*
**Griffin,** Jo Ann Thomas 1933- *WhoFI 92*
**Griffin,** Joe Lee 1935- *AmMWSc 92*
**Griffin,** John *Who 92*
**Griffin,** John Bowes 1903- *Who 92*
**Griffin,** John Henry 1943- *AmMWSc 92, WhoWest 92*
**Griffin,** John Howard 1920-1980 *ConLC 68 [port], FacFETw*
**Griffin,** John James 1932- *WhoAmL 92*
**Griffin,** John James, Jr. 1943- *WhoAmL 92*
**Griffin,** John Leander 1923- *AmMWSc 92*
**Griffin,** John Parry 1938- *Who 92*
**Griffin,** John R 1936- *AmMWSc 92*
**Griffin,** Johnny 1928- *WhoBlA 92*
**Griffin,** Joseph Edward 1947- *WhoAmL 92*
**Griffin,** Joseph Lawrence 1951- *WhoMW 92*
**Griffin,** Justus Dale 1930- *WhoMW 92*
**Griffin,** Katherine L 1928- *WhoAmP 91*
**Griffin,** Kathleen 1943- *AmMWSc 92*
**Griffin,** Kathleen C. *DrAPF 91*
**Griffin,** Kathleen Mary 1943- *WhoFI 92*
**Griffin,** Keith B 1938- *IntAu&W 91, WrDr 92*
**Griffin,** Keith Broadwell 1938- *Who 92*
**Griffin,** Kenneth Adolphus 1926- *WhoAmL 92*
**Griffin,** Kenneth James 1928- *Who 92*
**Griffin,** L. Robert 1943- *WhoAmL 92*
**Griffin,** Larry 1935- *WhoWest 92*
**Griffin,** Larry Allen 1949- *WhoRel 92*
**Griffin,** Larry D. *DrAPF 91*
**Griffin,** Leonard James, Jr. 1962- *WhoBlA 92*
**Griffin,** Louis G., III 1943- *WhoBlA 92*
**Griffin,** Lula Bernice 1949- *WhoBlA 92*
**Griffin,** Madeline Sue 1951- *WhoAmL 92*
**Griffin,** Mario *WhoHisp 92*
**Griffin,** Martin Ignatius Joseph 1842-1911 *DcAmImH*
**Griffin,** Martin John 1933- *AmMWSc 92*
**Griffin,** Marvin A 1923- *AmMWSc 92*
**Griffin,** Mary A 1953- *WhoIns 92*
**Griffin,** Mary Brinson 1963- *WhoAmL 92*
**Griffin,** Merv *LesBEnT 92 [port]*
**Griffin,** Merv 1925- *IntMPA 92*
**Griffin,** Merv Edward 1925- *WhoEnt 92, WhoFI 92*
**Griffin,** Michael D. 1958- *WhoBlA 92*
**Griffin,** Michael Gary 1948- *WhoAmP 91*
**Griffin,** Michael Harold 1921- *Who 92*
**Griffin,** Michael J 1933- *WhoAmP 91*
**Griffin,** Moses 1753?-1816 *DcNCBi 2*
**Griffin,** Nancy Lien 1952- *WhoAmP 91*
**Griffin,** Nathaniel Moffitt 1941- *WhoMW 92*
**Griffin,** O. Daniel, Jr. 1960- *WhoEnt 92*
**Griffin,** Patrick J 1951- *AmMWSc 92*
**Griffin,** Patrick Joseph 1956- *WhoAmL 92*
**Griffin,** Paul 1922- *Who 92*
**Griffin,** Paul Joseph 1954- *AmMWSc 92*
**Griffin,** Peni R. 1961- *ConAu 134, SmATA 67 [port]*
**Griffin,** Percy Lee 1945- *WhoBlA 92*
**Griffin,** Peter J. 1943- *WhoFI 92*
**Griffin,** Ples Andrew 1929- *WhoBlA 92*
**Griffin,** Rachel 1962- *TwCPaSc*
**Griffin,** Ralph Hawkins 1921- *AmMWSc 92*
**Griffin,** Redd F 1938- *WhoAmP 91*
**Griffin,** Richard B 1942- *AmMWSc 92*
**Griffin,** Richard George, Jr. 1927- *WhoBlA 92*
**Griffin,** Richard Norman 1929- *AmMWSc 92*
**Griffin,** Richard Ray 1945- *WhoRel 92*
**Griffin,** Rick d1991 *NewYTBS 91*
**Griffin,** Robert Alfred 1944- *AmMWSc 92*
**Griffin,** Robert Gregory 1953- *WhoAmL 92*
**Griffin,** Robert H. 1960- *WhoAmL 92*
**Griffin,** Robert P. 1923- *IntWW 91, WhoAmL 92*
**Griffin,** Robert Paul 1923- *WhoAmP 91, WhoMW 92*
**Griffin,** Robert Thomas 1917- *WhoAmP 91*
**Griffin,** Ronald Charles 1943- *WhoBlA 92*
**Griffin,** Ronald Wayne 1953- *WhoEnt 92*
**Griffin,** Russell M 1943- *IntAu&W 91, TwCSFW 91*
**Griffin,** Ruth Lewin 1925- *WhoAmP 91*
**Griffin,** Sumner Albert 1922- *AmMWSc 92*
**Griffin,** Susan *DrAPF 91*
**Griffin,** Sylvia Gail 1935- *WhoWest 92*
**Griffin,** Thomas J. 1917- *WhoBlA 92*
**Griffin,** Thomas Lee, Jr. 1929- *WhoMW 92*
**Griffin,** Travis Barton 1934- *AmMWSc 92*
**Griffin,** Victor Gilbert Benjamin 1924- *IntWW 91, Who 92*
**Griffin,** Villard Stuart, Jr 1937- *AmMWSc 92*
**Griffin,** W. Boyd 1945- *WhoFI 92*
**Griffin,** W. C. *WhoRel 92*
**Griffin,** Walter *DrAPF 91*
**Griffin,** Walter Joseph 1926- *WhoAmP 91*
**Griffin,** Walter Roland 1942- *WhoAmP 91*
**Griffin,** Wilfred Lee 1939- *WhoAmP 91*
**Griffin,** William Albert 1939- *WhoRel 92*
**Griffin,** William Arthur 1936- *WhoRel 92*
**Griffin,** William Dallas 1925- *AmMWSc 92*
**Griffin,** William Mell, III 1957- *WhoAmL 92*
**Griffin,** William Stanley 1935- *WhoFI 92*
**Griffin,** William Thomas 1932- *AmMWSc 92*
**Griffin-Bernstorff,** Ann *TwCPaSc*
**Griffin-Johnson,** Lorraine Antionette 1951- *WhoBlA 92*
**Griffing,** David Francis 1926- *AmMWSc 92, WhoMW 92*
**Griffing,** George Warren 1921- *AmMWSc 92*
**Griffing,** J Bruce 1919- *AmMWSc 92*
**Griffing,** Josephine 1814-1872 *HanAmWH*
**Griffing,** Robert G 1927- *WhoIns 92*
**Griffing,** Thomas Mang 1933- *WhoFI 92*
**Griffing,** William James 1922- *AmMWSc 92*
**Griffinger,** Michael R. 1936- *WhoAmL 92*
**Griffioen,** Roger Duane 1934- *AmMWSc 92*
**Griffis,** Anthony Eric 1950- *WhoAmL 92*
**Griffis,** Curtis Raymond 1935- *WhoRel 92*
**Griffis,** Keith Newlon 1937- *WhoWest 92*
**Griffiss,** John McLeod 1940- *AmMWSc 92*
**Griffith,** Aaron B. *WhoEnt 92*
**Griffith,** Andy 1926- *IntMPA 92, WhoEnt 92*
**Griffith,** Arthur 1872-1922 *FacFETw*
**Griffith,** Arthur Leonard 1920- *IntAu&W 91, Who 92, WrDr 92*
**Griffith,** B Herold 1925- *AmMWSc 92*
**Griffith,** Barbara J. 1935- *WhoBlA 92*
**Griffith,** Bill *WrDr 92*
**Griffith,** Bonnie Kunis Kis 1947- *WhoFI 92*
**Griffith,** Calvin Grant, III 1927- *WhoAmP 91*
**Griffith,** Carl David 1937- *WhoWest 92*
**Griffith,** Cecil Baker 1923- *AmMWSc 92*
**Griffith,** Cecilia Girz 1949- *AmMWSc 92*
**Griffith,** Charles R 1931- *WhoIns 92*
**Griffith,** D W 1875-1948 *FacFETw, IntDcF 2-2 [port], RComAH*
**Griffith,** Darrell Steven 1958- *WhoBlA 92*
**Griffith,** David W. 1875-1948 *BenetAL 91*
**Griffith,** Donal Louis 1942- *AmMWSc 92*
**Griffith,** Donald Kendall 1933- *WhoAmL 92, WhoMW 92*
**Griffith,** Donald Nash 1935- *WhoRel 92*
**Griffith,** Edward *WhoAmP 91*
**Griffith,** Edward David 1944- *WhoAmL 92, WhoWest 92*
**Griffith,** Edward Jackson 1925- *AmMWSc 92*
**Griffith,** Edward Michael 1933- *Who 92*
**Griffith,** Elizabeth Ann Hall 1935- *AmMWSc 92*
**Griffith,** Elwin Jabez 1938- *WhoBlA 92*
**Griffith,** Emlyn Irving 1923- *WhoAmL 92, WhoFI 92*
**Griffith,** Ezra Edward 1942- *WhoBlA 92*
**Griffith,** G. Larry 1937- *WhoAmL 92*
**Griffith,** Gail Susan Tucker 1945- *AmMWSc 92*
**Griffith,** Garth Ellis 1928- *WhoAmL 92*
**Griffith,** George 1857-1906 *ScFEYrs, TwCSFW 91*
**Griffith,** Gordon Lamar 1921- *AmMWSc 92*
**Griffith,** Gregory Wood 1952- *WhoMW 92*
**Griffith,** Helen V. 1934- *WrDr 92*
**Griffith,** Herbert Eugene 1866-1920 *BiInAmS*
**Griffith,** J. Gordon 1931- *WhoWest 92*
**Griffith,** Jack Dee 1936- *AmMWSc 92*
**Griffith,** James Clifford 1948- *WhoFI 92*
**Griffith,** James H 1936- *AmMWSc 92*
**Griffith,** James Lewis 1940- *WhoAmL 92*
**Griffith,** James Raymond 1937- *WhoMW 92*
**Griffith,** Janice Clare 1940- *WhoAmL 92*
**Griffith,** John A. 1936- *WhoBlA 92*
**Griffith,** John Aneurin Grey 1918- *Who 92*
**Griffith,** John E 1927- *AmMWSc 92*
**Griffith,** John H. 1931- *WhoBlA 92*
**Griffith,** John Louis, Jr. 1947- *WhoFI 92*
**Griffith,** John Perry 1939- *WhoAmL 92*
**Griffith,** John Randall 1934- *AmMWSc 92*
**Griffith,** John Sidney 1935- *AmMWSc 92*
**Griffith,** John Spencer 1944- *AmMWSc 92*
**Griffith,** Katherine Scott 1942- *WhoFI 92*
**Griffith,** Kenneth 1921- *IntWW 91, Who 92*
**Griffith,** Leonard *Who 92*
**Griffith,** Linda M 1952- *AmMWSc 92*
**Griffith,** M S 1940- *AmMWSc 92*
**Griffith,** Mabel Maxine 1919- *WhoRel 92*
**Griffith,** Mark Reist 1955- *WhoFI 92*
**Griffith,** Mark Richard 1960- *WhoBlA 92, WhoEnt 92*
**Griffith,** Martin G 1939- *AmMWSc 92*
**Griffith,** Mary d1877 *ScFEYrs*
**Griffith,** Mearle Lee 1943- *WhoRel 92*
**Griffith,** Melanie 1957- *IntMPA 92, WhoEnt 92*
**Griffith,** Michael *Who 92*
**Griffith,** Michael Grey 1941- *AmMWSc 92*
**Griffith,** Michael James 1948- *AmMWSc 92*
**Griffith,** Michael John 1949- *WhoAmL 92*
**Griffith,** Michael Ted 1949- *WhoEnt 92*
**Griffith,** O Hayes 1938- *AmMWSc 92*
**Griffith,** Owen Glyn 1922- *Who 92*
**Griffith,** Owen Malcolm 1928- *AmMWSc 92*
**Griffith,** Owen Wendell 1946- *AmMWSc 92*
**Griffith,** Patricia Browning *DrAPF 91*
**Griffith,** Patricia Browning 1935- *ConAu 35NR*
**Griffith,** Paul *DrAPF 91*
**Griffith,** Peter 1927- *AmMWSc 92*
**Griffith,** Phillip A 1940- *AmMWSc 92*
**Griffith,** Prescott Friesth 1949- *WhoMW 92*
**Griffith,** Reginald Wilbert 1930- *WhoBlA 92*
**Griffith,** Richard Edward, Jr. 1956- *WhoEnt 92*
**Griffith,** Richard Lattimore 1939- *WhoAmL 92*
**Griffith,** Richard Lee 1930- *WhoFI 92*
**Griffith,** Robert E 1929- *WhoAmP 91*
**Griffith,** Robert Eglesfeld 1798-1850 *BiInAmS*
**Griffith,** Robert Frederick 1911- *WhoAmP 91*
**Griffith,** Robert W 1930- *AmMWSc 92*
**Griffith,** Scott Crandall 1957- *WhoMW 92*
**Griffith,** Steve Campbell, Jr. 1933- *WhoAmL 92, WhoFI 92*
**Griffith,** Steven Franklin, Sr. 1948- *WhoAmL 92, WhoFI 92*
**Griffith,** Stewart Cathie 1914- *Who 92*
**Griffith,** Thomas 1915- *IntAu&W 91, IntWW 91*
**Griffith,** Thomas 1930- *AmMWSc 92*
**Griffith,** Thomas Gwynfor 1926- *WrDr 92*
**Griffith,** Thomas Harvey 1947- *WhoRel 92*
**Griffith,** Thomas Ian 1960- *WhoEnt 92*
**Griffith,** Thomas Jefferson 1923- *WhoAmL 92*
**Griffith,** Thomas Lee, Jr. 1902- *WhoBlA 92*
**Griffith,** Vera Victoria 1920- *WhoBlA 92*
**Griffith,** Virgil Vernon 1928- *AmMWSc 92*
**Griffith,** W A 1922- *AmMWSc 92*
**Griffith,** Wayland C 1925- *AmMWSc 92*
**Griffith,** William Dudley 1930- *WhoRel 92*
**Griffith,** William E. 1920- *WrDr 92*
**Griffith,** William Henry 1944- *WhoEnt 92*
**Griffith,** William Kirk 1929- *AmMWSc 92*
**Griffith,** William Schuler 1949- *AmMWSc 92*
**Griffith,** William Thomas 1940- *AmMWSc 92*
**Griffith Edwards,** James *Who 92*
**Griffith-Jones,** George Chetwynd 1857-1906 *TwCSFW 91*
**Griffith-Jones,** Stephany 1947- *IntAu&W 91*
**Griffith Joyner,** Florence *IntWW 91*
**Griffith-Joyner,** Florence 1959- *BlkOlyM [port]*
**Griffith-Smith,** Bella De Leon *WhoEnt 92*
**Griffiths** *Who 92*
**Griffiths,** Baron 1923- *IntWW 91, Who 92*
**Griffiths,** Baron 1941- *IntWW 91*
**Griffiths,** Allen Phillips 1927- *Who 92*
**Griffiths,** Ambrose *Who 92*
**Griffiths,** Anthony F. 1930- *WhoFI 92*
**Griffiths,** Anthony J F 1940- *AmMWSc 92*
**Griffiths,** Arthur 1922- *Who 92*
**Griffiths,** Bede 1906- *IntWW 91*
**Griffiths,** Bertie Bernard 1930- *WhoBlA 92*
**Griffiths,** Bruce 1924- *Who 92*
**Griffiths,** Bryn 1933- *IntAu&W 91, WrDr 92*
**Griffiths,** Clifford H 1936- *AmMWSc 92*
**Griffiths,** David 1938- *AmMWSc 92*
**Griffiths,** David 1945- *WhoAmL 92*
**Griffiths,** David Howard 1922- *Who 92*
**Griffiths,** David Hubert 1940- *Who 92*
**Griffiths,** David Jeffery 1942- *AmMWSc 92*
**Griffiths,** David John 1931- *Who 92*
**Griffiths,** David John 1938- *AmMWSc 92*
**Griffiths,** David Laurence 1944- *Who 92*
**Griffiths,** David Nigel 1927- *Who 92*
**Griffiths,** David Warren 1944- *AmMWSc 92*
**Griffiths,** David William 1938- *WhoMW 92*
**Griffiths,** Edward 1929- *Who 92*
**Griffiths,** Eldon 1925- *Who 92*
**Griffiths,** Ernest Roy 1926- *Who 92*
**Griffiths,** Frank Harold 1938- *WhoEnt 92*
**Griffiths,** George Langford 1929- *WhoAmP 91*
**Griffiths,** George Motley 1923- *AmMWSc 92*
**Griffiths,** Harold Morris 1926- *Who 92*
**Griffiths,** Helen 1939- *IntAu&W 91, WrDr 92*
**Griffiths,** Howard 1938- *Who 92*
**Griffiths,** Howard 1947- *Who 92*
**Griffiths,** Islwyn Owen 1924- *Who 92*
**Griffiths,** James Edward 1931- *AmMWSc 92*
**Griffiths,** Jane Jackson 1932- *WhoAmP 91*
**Griffiths,** Joan Martha 1935- *AmMWSc 92*
**Griffiths,** John Calvert 1931- *Who 92*
**Griffiths,** John Cedric 1912- *AmMWSc 92*
**Griffiths,** John Charles 1934- *Who 92*
**Griffiths,** John Edward Seaton 1908- *Who 92*
**Griffiths,** John Frederick 1926- *AmMWSc 92*
**Griffiths,** John Gwyn 1911- *WrDr 92*
**Griffiths,** John N. *Who 92*
**Griffiths,** John Pankhurst 1930- *Who 92*
**Griffiths,** John William Roger 1921- *Who 92*
**Griffiths,** Joseph David Loftus 1931- *WhoWest 92*
**Griffiths,** Karen L 1953- *WhoAmP 91*
**Griffiths,** Lawrence 1933- *Who 92*
**Griffiths,** Leslie John 1942- *Who 92*
**Griffiths,** Lewis Gene, Jr. 1940- *WhoFI 92*
**Griffiths,** Linda Pauline 1957- *IntAu&W 91*
**Griffiths,** Lloyd Joseph 1941- *AmMWSc 92*
**Griffiths,** Lynn Christopher 1940- *WhoFI 92*
**Griffiths,** Martha 1912- *WhoAmP 91*
**Griffiths,** Michael Ambrose 1928- *Who 92*
**Griffiths,** Mike *TwCPaSc*

**Griffiths,** Nigel 1955- *Who 92*
**Griffiths,** Paul 1947- *WrDr 92*
**Griffiths,** Paul Anthony 1947- *Who 92*
**Griffiths,** Peggy Strauss 1925- *WhoBlA 92*
**Griffiths,** Percival Joseph 1899- *Who 92*
**Griffiths,** Peter Anthony 1945- *Who 92*
**Griffiths,** Peter Denham 1927- *Who 92*
**Griffiths,** Peter Harry Steve 1928- *Who 92*
**Griffiths,** Peter John 1944- *Who 92*
**Griffiths,** Philip A. 1938- *IntWW 91*
**Griffiths,** Phillip A 1938- *AmMWSc 92*
**Griffiths,** Raymond Bert 1915- *AmMWSc 92*
**Griffiths,** Reginald Ernest d1991 *Who 92N*
**Griffiths,** Richard 1935- *WrDr 92*
**Griffiths,** Robert Budington 1937- *AmMWSc 92*
**Griffiths,** Robert Pennell 1949- *WhoFI 92, WhoMW 92*
**Griffiths,** Roger Noel Price 1931- *Who 92*
**Griffiths,** Roland Redmond 1946- *AmMWSc 92*
**Griffiths,** Roy *Who 92*
**Griffiths,** Sally 1934- *WrDr 92*
**Griffiths,** Thomas Alan 1951- *AmMWSc 92*
**Griffiths,** Trevor 1913- *Who 92*
**Griffiths,** Trevor 1935- *IntAu&W 91, IntWW 91, Who 92, WrDr 92*
**Griffiths,** Vernon 1929- *AmMWSc 92*
**Griffiths,** William Arthur 1940- *Who 92*
**Griffiths,** William C 1939- *AmMWSc 92*
**Griffiths,** Winston James 1943- *Who 92*
**Griffiths of Fforestfach,** Baron 1941- *Who 92*
**Griffiths Ormhaug,** Ella 1926- *IntAu&W 91*
**Griffitts,** James John 1912- *AmMWSc 92*
**Griffitts,** Keith Loyd 1942- *WhoFI 92*
**Griffitts,** Wallace Rush 1919- *AmMWSc 92*
**Griffo,** Bob Charles 1956- *WhoAmL 92*
**Griffo,** James Vincent, Jr 1928- *AmMWSc 92*
**Griffo,** Joseph Salvatore 1927- *AmMWSc 92*
**Griffo,** Zora Jasincuk 1928- *AmMWSc 92*
**Griffy,** Thomas Alan 1936- *AmMWSc 92*
**Grigal,** David F 1941- *AmMWSc 92*
**Grigarick,** Albert Anthony, Jr 1927- *AmMWSc 92*
**Grigera Naon,** Horacio Alberto 1947- *WhoAmL 92*
**Grigg,** Eddie Garman 1957- *WhoRel 92*
**Grigg,** John 1924- *IntAu&W 91, Who 92, WrDr 92*
**Grigg,** Peter *AmMWSc 92*
**Grigg,** Richard Wyman 1937- *AmMWSc 92*
**Grigg,** William Humphrey 1932- *WhoFI 92*
**Grigger,** David John 1960- *AmMWSc 92*
**Griggs,** Allan Bingham 1909- *AmMWSc 92*
**Griggs,** Anthony 1946- *WhoBlA 92*
**Griggs,** Anthony 1960- *WhoBlA 92*
**Griggs,** Charles Wilfred 1942- *WhoRel 92*
**Griggs,** Douglas M, Jr 1928- *AmMWSc 92*
**Griggs,** Frederick Landseer 1876-1938 *TwCPaSc*
**Griggs,** Gary B 1943- *AmMWSc 92*
**Griggs,** Gary Bruce 1943- *WhoWest 92*
**Griggs,** Harry Kindell, Sr. 1910- *WhoBlA 92*
**Griggs,** Ian Macdonald *Who 92*
**Griggs,** James C. 1907- *WhoBlA 92*
**Griggs,** James Clifton, Jr. 1930- *WhoBlA 92*
**Griggs,** John d1991 *NewYTBS 91*
**Griggs,** John Robert 1949- *WhoMW 92*
**Griggs,** John W. 1924- *WhoBlA 92*
**Griggs,** John Wyeth 1947- *WhoAmL 92*
**Griggs,** Judith Ralph 1946- *WhoBlA 92*
**Griggs,** Leonard LeRoy, Jr. 1931- *WhoFI 92*
**Griggs,** Lillian Baker 1876-1955 *DcNCBi 2*
**Griggs,** Mildred Barnes 1942- *WhoBlA 92*
**Griggs,** Norman Edward 1916- *Who 92*
**Griggs,** Robert C 1925- *AmMWSc 92*
**Griggs,** Sutton Elbert 1872-1933 *RelLAm 91*
**Griggs,** Thomas Jay 1952- *WhoAmL 92*
**Griggs,** Thomas Russell 1943- *AmMWSc 92*
**Griggs,** William Holland 1916- *AmMWSc 92*
**Griglock,** William John 1948- *WhoIns 92*
**Grignard,** Francois Auguste Victor 1871-1935 *WhoNob 90*
**Grignaschi,** Giancarlo 1926- *IntWW 91*
**Grigorcea,** Adrian Gabriel 1965- *WhoFI 92*
**Grigorenko,** Petr Grigor'evich 1907-1986 *SovUnBD*
**Grigorenko,** Pyotr Grigorevich 1907-1987 *FacFETw*
**Grigorescu,** Dan 1931- *IntWW 91*
**Grigori,** Artur 1918- *AmMWSc 92*
**Grigoriu,** Mircea Dan 1943- *AmMWSc 92*
**Grigoropoulos,** Sotirios G 1933- *AmMWSc 92*
**Grigorovich,** Yuriy Nikolaevich 1927- *SovUnBD*
**Grigorovich,** Yuriy Nikolayevich 1927- *WhoEnt 92*
**Grigorovich,** Yuriy Vaganov Nikolayevich 1927- *IntWW 91*
**Grigsby,** Calvin Burchard 1946- *WhoBlA 92*
**Grigsby,** Charles T. *WhoBlA 92*
**Grigsby,** Chester Poole, Jr. 1929- *WhoFI 92*
**Grigsby,** David P. 1949- *WhoBlA 92*
**Grigsby,** F. Daniel 1956- *WhoEnt 92*
**Grigsby,** George Richard 1927- *WhoMW 92*
**Grigsby,** Gordon *DrAPF 91*
**Grigsby,** James 1944- *WhoMW 92*
**Grigsby,** James A 1942- *WhoIns 92*
**Grigsby,** Jefferson Eugene, Jr. 1918- *WhoBlA 92*
**Grigsby,** John Lynn 1924- *AmMWSc 92*
**Grigsby,** Laurie Henry 1961- *WhoEnt 92*
**Grigsby,** Leonard Lee 1929- *AmMWSc 92*
**Grigsby,** Lonnie Oscar 1939- *WhoFI 92*
**Grigsby,** Lucy Clemmons 1916- *WhoBlA 92*
**Grigsby,** Margaret Elizabeth 1923- *AmMWSc 92, WhoBlA 92*
**Grigsby,** Marshall C. 1946- *WhoBlA 92*
**Grigsby,** Phillip N. *WhoRel 92*
**Grigsby,** Ronald Davis 1936- *AmMWSc 92*
**Grigsby,** Troy L. 1934- *WhoBlA 92*
**Grigsby,** William Redman 1934- *AmMWSc 92*
**Grigson,** Geoffrey Douglas 1944- *Who 92*
**Grigson,** Jane 1928- *IntAu&W 91*
**Grigson,** Jane 1928-1990 *AnObit 1990*
**Grigull,** Ulrich 1912- *IntWW 91*
**Grijalva,** Carlos Vincent, Jr. 1950- *WhoHisp 92*
**Grijalva,** Joshua *WhoHisp 92*
**Grijalva,** Juan de 1489-1527 *HisDSpE*
**Grijalva,** Michelle Armijo 1953- *WhoHisp 92*
**Grijalva,** Raul M. *WhoHisp 92*
**Grika,** Larry Arnold 1932- *WhoEnt 92*
**Grile,** Dod *BenetAL 91*
**Griliches,** Zvi 1930- *IntWW 91, WhoFI 92*
**Grilikhes,** Alexandra *DrAPF 91*
**Grilione,** Patricia Louise 1935- *AmMWSc 92*
**Grill,** Herman, Jr 1936- *AmMWSc 92*
**Grill,** Linda 1938- *WhoHisp 92*
**Griller,** Sidney Aaron 1911- *Who 92*
**Grillet,** Alain R. *Who 92*
**Grillo,** Anival J. 1913- *WhoBlA 92*
**Grillo,** Basil F. 1910- *IntMPA 92*
**Grillo,** Joann Danielle 1939- *WhoEnt 92*
**Grillo,** Leo Francis 1949- *WhoWest 92*
**Grillo,** Ramon S 1931- *AmMWSc 92*
**Grillos,** Steve John 1928- *AmMWSc 92*
**Grillot,** Gerald Francis 1914- *AmMWSc 92*
**Grills,** Michael Geoffrey 1937- *Who 92*
**Grilly,** Edward Rogers 1917- *AmMWSc 92, WhoAmP 91, WhoWest 92*
**Grim,** Eugene 1922- *AmMWSc 92*
**Grim,** J Norman 1933- *AmMWSc 92*
**Grim,** John Norman 1933- *WhoWest 92*
**Grim,** Larry B 1945- *AmMWSc 92*
**Grim,** Patricia Ann 1940- *WhoFI 92*
**Grim,** Ralph Early 1902- *AmMWSc 92*
**Grim,** Samuel Oram 1935- *AmMWSc 92*
**Grim,** Wayne Martin 1930- *AmMWSc 92*
**Grima,** Andrew Peter 1921- *Who 92*
**Grimaldi,** Alberto 1927- *IntMPA 92*
**Grimaldi,** Edmond Anthony 1948- *WhoEnt 92*
**Grimaldi,** Frank 1924- *WhoMW 92*
**Grimaldi,** James Thomas 1928- *WhoFI 92*
**Grimaldi,** John Vincent 1916- *AmMWSc 92*
**Grimaldi,** Leonard Nicholas 1942- *WhoFI 92*
**Grimaldi,** Michael Francis 1949- *WhoMW 92*
**Grimalt,** Jose *WhoHisp 92*
**Grimble,** Ian 1921- *IntAu&W 91, WrDr 92*
**Grime,** Mark Stephen Eastburn 1948- *Who 92*
**Grimes,** Alan P. 1919- *WrDr 92*
**Grimes,** Barbara L 1945- *WhoAmP 91*
**Grimes,** Bill *LesBEnT 92*
**Grimes,** Bryan 1828-1880 *DcNCBi 2*
**Grimes,** Calvin M., Jr. *WhoBlA 92*
**Grimes,** Carol Jane Galles 1946- *AmMWSc 92*
**Grimes,** Carolyn E 1943- *AmMWSc 92*
**Grimes,** Charles B., Jr. 1927- *WhoFI 92*
**Grimes,** Charles Cullen 1931- *AmMWSc 92*
**Grimes,** Churchill Bragaw 1945- *AmMWSc 92*
**Grimes,** Craig Alan 1956- *AmMWSc 92*
**Grimes,** Dale M 1926- *AmMWSc 92*
**Grimes,** Darlene M. C. 1960- *WhoBlA 92*
**Grimes,** David 1948- *AmMWSc 92*
**Grimes,** Don 1937- *IntWW 91*
**Grimes,** Donald Wilburn 1932- *AmMWSc 92*
**Grimes,** Doreen 1932- *WhoEnt 92*
**Grimes,** Douglas M. 1942- *WhoBlA 92*
**Grimes,** Gary 1955- *IntMPA 92*
**Grimes,** Gary Wayne 1946- *AmMWSc 92*
**Grimes,** Gerald 1941- *WhoAmP 91*
**Grimes,** Howard Ray 1918- *WhoFI 92*
**Grimes,** Hubert Henry 1929- *AmMWSc 92*
**Grimes,** Hugh Gavin 1929- *WhoMW 92*
**Grimes,** James Joseph 1949- *WhoEnt 92*
**Grimes,** James Stanley 1807-1903 *BiInAmS*
**Grimes,** Jeff Dale 1948- *WhoEnt 92*
**Grimes,** Jesse 1781?-1866 *DcNCBi 2*
**Grimes,** John Bryan 1868-1923 *DcNCBi 2*
**Grimes,** John Edward, Jr. 1966- *WhoFI 92*
**Grimes,** John T. 1919-1990 *WhoBlA 92N*
**Grimes,** Joseph Edward 1941- *WhoWest 92*
**Grimes,** Joseph Rudolph 1923- *IntWW 91, WhoFI 92*
**Grimes,** Kevin Paul 1965- *WhoRel 92*
**Grimes,** L Nichols *AmMWSc 92*
**Grimes,** Larry Bruce 1940- *WhoAmL 92*
**Grimes,** Lawrence Lynn 1953- *WhoAmL 92*
**Grimes,** Lee 1920- *SmATA 68 [port]*
**Grimes,** Marilyn Kay 1942- *WhoRel 92*
**Grimes,** Martha *FacFETw, WrDr 92*
**Grimes,** Michael David 1948- *WhoWest 92*
**Grimes,** Nikki *DrAPF 91*
**Grimes,** Nikki 1950- *WhoBlA 92*
**Grimes,** Orville Frank 1916- *AmMWSc 92*
**Grimes,** Paul Wayne 1959- *WhoFI 92*
**Grimes,** Richard Allen 1929- *WhoFI 92*
**Grimes,** Richard Lee 1956- *WhoWest 92*
**Grimes,** Robert Lee 1946- *WhoAmL 92*
**Grimes,** Russell Newell 1935- *AmMWSc 92*
**Grimes,** Ruth Elaine 1949- *WhoWest 92*
**Grimes,** Samuel Joshua 1884-1967 *RelLAm 91*
**Grimes,** Sidney Ray, Jr 1947- *AmMWSc 92*
**Grimes,** Stephen F *WhoAmP 91*
**Grimes,** Stephen Henry 1927- *WhoAmL 92*
**Grimes,** Steven Munroe 1941- *AmMWSc 92, WhoMW 92*
**Grimes,** Tammy 1934- *ConTFT 9, IntMPA 92, WhoEnt 92*
**Grimes,** Voni B. 1922- *WhoBlA 92*
**Grimes,** William Thomas, Sr. 1909-1988 *WhoBlA 92N*
**Grimes,** William Winston 1927- *WhoBlA 92*
**Grimes-Farrow,** Dorothea D. 1952- *WhoFI 92*
**Griminger,** Paul 1920- *AmMWSc 92*
**Grimke,** Angelina 1805-1879 *RComAH*
**Grimke,** Angelina Emily 1805-1879 *BenetAL 91, HanAmWH*
**Grimke,** Angelina Weld 1880-1958 *NotBlAW 92 [port]*
**Grimke,** Sarah 1792-1873 *RComAH*
**Grimke,** Sarah Moore 1792-1873 *BenetAL 91, HanAmWH*
**Grimke,** Thomas S. 1786-1834 *AmPeW*
**Grimley,** Eugene Burhans, III 1941- *AmMWSc 92*
**Grimley,** Philip M 1935- *AmMWSc 92*
**Grimley,** Robert Thomas 1930- *AmMWSc 92*
**Grimley Evans,** John 1936- *Who 92*
**Grimm,** Arthur F 1931- *AmMWSc 92*
**Grimm,** Carl Albert 1926- *AmMWSc 92*
**Grimm,** Charles Henry 1911- *AmMWSc 92*
**Grimm,** Dan K. 1949- *WhoWest 92*
**Grimm,** Daniel K 1949- *WhoAmP 91*
**Grimm,** Douglas Montgomery 1940- *WhoEnt 92*
**Grimm,** Elizabeth Ann 1949- *AmMWSc 92*
**Grimm,** Friedrich 1888-1959 *EncTR 91*
**Grimm,** Friedrich Melchior 1723-1809 *BlkwCEP*
**Grimm,** Hans 1875-1959 *BiDExR, EncTR 91 [port]*
**Grimm,** Jakob Ludwig Carl 1785-1863 *BlkwCEP*
**Grimm,** James K 1930- *AmMWSc 92*
**Grimm,** Jay Vaughn 1926- *WhoFI 92*
**Grimm,** Larry Leon 1950- *WhoWest 92*
**Grimm,** Louis John 1933- *AmMWSc 92*
**Grimm,** Maria Teresa *WhoEnt 92*
**Grimm,** Robert Arthur 1937- *AmMWSc 92, WhoMW 92*
**Grimm,** Robert Blair 1930- *AmMWSc 92*
**Grimm,** Robert John 1933- *AmMWSc 92*
**Grimm,** Royden A 1953- *WhoIns 92*
**Grimm,** Stanley 1891-1966 *TwCPaSc*
**Grimm,** Terrence E. 1948- *WhoMW 92*
**Grimm,** Victor E. 1937- *WhoAmL 92*
**Grimm,** Wilhelm Carl 1786-1859 *BlkwCEP*
**Grimm,** William C 1907- *ConAu 34NR*
**Grimm,** William L. 1954- *WhoMW 92*
**Grimm-Jorgensen,** Yvonne 1942- *AmMWSc 92*
**Grimm-Richardson,** Anna Louise 1927- *IntAu&W 91*
**Grimmeiss,** Hermann Georg 1930- *IntWW 91*
**Grimmell,** William C 1941- *AmMWSc 92*
**Grimmer,** D. James 1941- *WhoMW 92*
**Grimmer,** Harry Clinton 1935- *WhoAmP 91*
**Grimmer,** Margot 1944- *WhoEnt 92*
**Grimmer,** Ronald Calvin 1941- *AmMWSc 92*
**Grimmet,** Alex J. 1928- *WhoRel 92*
**Grimmett,** Sadie A. 1932- *WhoBlA 92*
**Grimmett,** Shirley Sellers 1950- *WhoAmL 92*
**Grimmick,** Henry William 1945- *WhoWest 92*
**Grimmond,** Arlene Patricia 1944- *WhoBlA 92*
**Grimond** *Who 92*
**Grimond,** Baron 1913- *IntWW 91, Who 92*
**Grimond,** Jo 1913- *WrDr 92*
**Grimsal,** Edward George 1927- *AmMWSc 92*
**Grimsbo,** Raymond Allen 1948- *WhoWest 92*
**Grimsby,** Bishop Suffragan of 1935- *Who 92*
**Grimsby,** F Norman 1927- *AmMWSc 92*
**Grimsby,** Karen Sue 1950- *WhoRel 92*
**Grimsey,** J Herbert 1909- *WhoAmP 91*
**Grimshaw,** Donald Harvey 1923- *WhoWest 92*
**Grimshaw,** Ewing Henry Wrigley 1911- *Who 92*
**Grimshaw,** Nicholas Thomas 1939- *IntWW 91, Who 92*
**Grimshaw,** Paul *WhoEnt 92*
**Grimshaw,** Paul R 1922- *AmMWSc 92*
**Grimshaw,** Reginald 1910- *TwCPaSc*
**Grimshaw,** Robert 1850-1941 *ScFEYrs*
**Grimsley,** Ethelyne 1941- *WhoBlA 92*
**Grimsley,** George Adonijah 1862-1935 *DcNCBi 2*
**Grimson,** Baird Sanford 1943- *AmMWSc 92*
**Grimsrud,** David T 1938- *AmMWSc 92*
**Grimstad,** Paul Robert 1945- *AmMWSc 92*
**Grimstead,** Hettie *IntAu&W 91, WrDr 92*
**Grimsted,** Todd John 1951- *WhoEnt 92*
**Grimston** *Who 92*
**Grimston,** Viscount 1978- *Who 92*
**Grimston of Westbury,** Baron 1925- *Who 92*
**Grimthorpe,** Baron 1915- *Who 92*
**Grimthorpe,** Lady 1925- *Who 92*
**Grimwade,** Andrew 1930- *IntWW 91, Who 92*
**Grimwade,** Arthur Girling 1913- *WrDr 92*
**Grimwade,** John Girling 1920- *Who 92*
**Grimwood,** Brian 1948- *TwCPaSc*
**Grimwood,** Brian Gene 1940- *AmMWSc 92*
**Grimwood,** Charles 1931- *AmMWSc 92*
**Grin,** Aleksandr Stepanovich 1880-1932 *SovUnBD*
**Grin,** Alexander 1880-1932 *FacFETw*
**Grina,** Larry Dale 1943- *AmMWSc 92*
**Grinberg,** Eric L *AmMWSc 92*
**Grinberg,** Jan 1933- *AmMWSc 92*
**Grindal,** Gracia Marie 1943- *WhoRel 92*
**Grindall,** Emerson Leroy 1916- *AmMWSc 92*
**Grindberg,** Alan K 1932- *WhoAmP 91*
**Grindberg,** Thomas Carl 1957- *WhoAmP 91*
**Grinde,** Larry Hal 1948- *WhoAmP 91*
**Grindea,** Daniel 1924- *WhoFI 92*
**Grindea,** Miron 1909- *Who 92*
**Grindel,** John Anthony 1937- *WhoMW 92, WhoRel 92*
**Grindel,** Joseph Michael 1946- *AmMWSc 92*
**Grindeland,** Gary Allen 1954- *WhoRel 92*
**Grindeland,** Richard Edward 1929- *AmMWSc 92*
**Grindell,** Robert Maclean 1933- *WhoMW 92*
**Grindheim,** Diane Lee 1955- *WhoWest 92*
**Grindlay,** John 1933- *AmMWSc 92*
**Grindlay,** Jonathan Ellis 1944- *AmMWSc 92*
**Grindle,** Art 1923- *WhoAmP 91*
**Grindle,** John Annesley d1991 *Who 92N*
**Grindle,** Robert J 1934- *WhoAmP 91*
**Grindley,** Nigel David Forster 1945- *AmMWSc 92*
**Grindon,** John Evelyn 1917- *Who 92*
**Grindrod,** Helen Marjorie 1936- *Who 92*
**Grindrod,** John Basil Rowland 1919- *IntWW 91, Who 92*
**Grindrod,** Muriel 1902- *WrDr 92*
**Grindrod,** Paul 1925- *AmMWSc 92*

**Grindstaff,** Bob Reynolds 1934- *WhoAmP 91*
**Grindstaff,** Douglas Howard 1931- *WhoEnt 92*
**Grindstaff,** Roy Arthur 1946- *WhoRel 92*
**Grindstaff,** Teddy Hodge 1932- *AmMWSc 92*
**Grindstaff,** Thomas Howard 1942- *WhoMW 92*
**Grindstaff,** Wyman Keith 1939- *AmMWSc 92*
**Grine,** Donald Reaville 1930- *AmMWSc 92*
**Griner,** George F. 1948- *WhoEnt 92*
**Griner,** Paul F 1933- *AmMWSc 92*
**Grinevetsky,** Vasiliy Ignat'evich 1871-1919 *SovUnBD*
**Grinevsky,** Aleksandr Stepanovich 1880-1932 *SovUnBD*
**Gringauz,** Alex 1934- *AmMWSc 92*
**Gringo,** Harry *BenetAL 91*
**Grinker,** Joel A *AmMWSc 92*
**Grinker,** Morton *DrAPF 91*
**Grinker,** Ronald Lee 1939- *WhoEnt 92*
**Grinker,** Roy Richard, Jr. 1927- *WhoMW 92*
**Grinker,** Roy Richard, Sr 1900- *AmMWSc 92*
**Grin'ko,** Grigoriy Fedorovich 1890-1938 *SovUnBD*
**Grinling,** Anthony Gibbons 1896-1982 *TwCPaSc*
**Grinling,** Jasper Gibbons 1924- *Who 92*
**Grinnell,** Alan Dale 1936- *AmMWSc 92*
**Grinnell,** David *ConAu 135, TwCSFW 91*
**Grinnell,** Frederick 1945- *AmMWSc 92*
**Grinnell,** George Bird 1849-1938 *BenetAL 91*
**Grinnell,** John Michael 1957- *WhoRel 92*
**Grinnell,** Robin Roy 1932- *AmMWSc 92*
**Grinspoon,** Lester 1928- *AmMWSc 92*
**Grinstead,** Amelia Ann 1945- *WhoBlA 92*
**Grinstead,** Stanley 1924- *IntWW 91, Who 92*
**Grinstein,** Alexander 1918- *WhoMW 92*
**Grinstein,** Keith David 1960- *WhoFI 92*
**Grinstein,** Reuben H 1935- *AmMWSc 92*
**Grinstein,** Sergio 1950- *AmMWSc 92*
**Grint,** Edmund Thomas Charles 1904- *Who 92*
**Grinter,** Linton E 1902- *AmMWSc 92*
**Grinyer,** Peter Hugh 1935- *Who 92*
**Grip** 1855- *ScFEYrs*
**Grip,** Robert H 1929- *WhoAmP 91*
**Gripe,** Alan Gordon 1920- *WhoRel 92*
**Grippa,** Anthony John 1945- *WhoIns 92*
**Grippin,** Eugene Willard 1931- *WhoFI 92*
**Gris,** Juan *FacFETw*
**Grisafe,** David Anthony 1938- *AmMWSc 92*
**Grisaffe,** Salvatore J *AmMWSc 92*
**Grisaffe,** Salvatore John 1934- *WhoMW 92*
**Grisamore,** Nelson Thomas 1921- *AmMWSc 92*
**Grisanti,** Michael Alan 1957- *WhoRel 92*
**Grisar,** Johann Martin 1929- *AmMWSc 92*
**Grisaru,** Marcus Theodore 1929- *AmMWSc 92*
**Grischke,** Alan Edward 1945- *WhoAmL 92, WhoMW 92*
**Grischkowsky,** Daniel Richard 1940- *AmMWSc 92*
**Griscom,** Andrew 1928- *AmMWSc 92*
**Griscom,** David Lawrence 1938- *AmMWSc 92*
**Griscom,** John 1774-1852 *BiInAmS*
**Griscom,** Richard William 1926- *AmMWSc 92*
**Griseta,** Carlo Joseph 1960- *WhoRel 92*
**Grisewood,** Harman Joseph Gerard 1906- *Who 92*
**Grisewood,** R Norman 1876- *ScFEYrs*
**Grisey,** Gerard 1946- *ConCom 92*
**Grisez,** Germain 1929- *IntWW 91*
**Grisham,** Charles Milton 1947- *AmMWSc 92*
**Grisham,** Genevieve Dwyer 1927- *AmMWSc 92*
**Grisham,** Joe Wheeler 1931- *AmMWSc 92*
**Grisham,** Larry Richard 1949- *AmMWSc 92*
**Grisham,** Noel 1916- *WhoAmP 91*
**Grisham,** R B 1953- *WhoAmP 91*
**Grisham,** Robert Douglas 1926- *WhoAmL 92*
**Grisham,** Wayne Richard 1923- *WhoAmP 91*
**Grishchenko,** Anatoly 1935-1990 *FacFETw*
**Grishin,** Viktor Vasil'evich 1914- *SovUnBD*
**Grishin,** Yevgeniy Romanovich 1931- *SovUnBD*
**Grishkiavichus,** Pvatras Pyatrovich d1987 *IntWW 91N*
**Grisi,** Giuditta 1805-1840 *NewAmDM*
**Grisi,** Giulia 1811-1869 *NewAmDM*
**Grisim,** J. Terrence 1943- *WhoMW 92*
**Griskey,** R G 1931- *AmMWSc 92*
**Grismer,** Mark Edward 1958- *WhoWest 92*
**Grismore,** Roger 1924- *AmMWSc 92*
**Grisoli,** John Joseph 1925- *AmMWSc 92*
**Grisolia,** Santiago 1923- *AmMWSc 92*
**Grissell,** Edward Eric Fowler 1944- *AmMWSc 92*
**Grissett,** Willie James 1931- *WhoBlA 92*
**Grissinger,** Earl H 1931- *AmMWSc 92*
**Grissmer,** John 1933- *IntMPA 92*
**Grissmer,** John Michael 1933- *WhoEnt 92*
**Grisso,** Robert Dwight, Jr. 1956- *WhoMW 92*
**Grissom,** David 1935- *AmMWSc 92*
**Grissom,** Doug 1953- *WhoEnt 92*
**Grissom,** Eugene 1831-1902 *DcNCBi 2*
**Grissom,** Eugene Edward 1922- *WhoEnt 92*
**Grissom,** Fay *ConAu 133*
**Grissom,** Gerald Homer 1951- *WhoAmL 92*
**Grissom,** Joseph Carol 1931- *WhoMW 92*
**Grissom,** Ken 1945- *ConAu 135*
**Grissom,** Lee Alan 1942- *WhoWest 92*
**Grissom,** Robert Gilliam 1867-1955 *DcNCBi 2*
**Grissom,** Robert Leslie 1917- *AmMWSc 92*
**Grissom,** Virgil 1926-1967 *FacFETw*
**Grissom,** Willie Mae 1926- *WhoEnt 92*
**Grist,** Allen 1792-1866 *DcNCBi 2*
**Grist,** Arthur L. 1930- *WhoBlA 92*
**Grist,** Franklin Richard 1828-1912 *DcNCBi 2*
**Grist,** Ian 1938- *Who 92*
**Grist,** James Redding 1818-1876 *DcNCBi 2*
**Grist,** John 1928- *WhoFI 92*
**Grist,** John Frank 1924- *Who 92*
**Grist,** Norman Roy 1918- *IntWW 91, Who 92*
**Grist,** Raymond 1939- *WhoBlA 92*
**Grist,** Reri *WhoBlA 92*
**Grist,** Reri 1932- *NewAmDM*
**Grist,** Robin Digby 1940- *Who 92*
**Grist,** Ronald *WhoBlA 92*
**Grist,** William LaDon 1938- *WhoAmP 91*
**Griswell,** J Barry 1949- *WhoIns 92*
**Griswold,** A. J. 1905- *WhoBlA 92*
**Griswold,** Benjamin Howell, IV 1940- *WhoFI 92*
**Griswold,** Bernard Lee 1942- *AmMWSc 92*
**Griswold,** Daniel H 1909- *AmMWSc 92*
**Griswold,** Daniel Pratt, Jr 1928- *AmMWSc 92*
**Griswold,** David A 1954- *WhoAmP 91*
**Griswold,** Edward Mansfield 1905- *AmMWSc 92*
**Griswold,** Ernest 1905- *AmMWSc 92*
**Griswold,** Erwin Nathaniel 1904- *IntWW 91, WhoAmL 92, WhoAmP 91*
**Griswold,** Frank Tracy, III 1937- *WhoRel 92*
**Griswold,** Gary Norris 1947- *WhoFI 92*
**Griswold,** George B 1928- *AmMWSc 92*
**Griswold,** Gerald W 1938- *WhoIns 92*
**Griswold,** Joseph Garland 1943- *AmMWSc 92*
**Griswold,** Kenneth Edwin, Jr 1943- *AmMWSc 92*
**Griswold,** Martha Kerfoot 1930- *WhoWest 92*
**Griswold,** Michael David 1944- *AmMWSc 92*
**Griswold,** Norman Ernest 1935- *AmMWSc 92*
**Griswold,** Paul Michael 1945- *WhoMW 92*
**Griswold,** Philip Alan 1947- *WhoMW 92*
**Griswold,** Phillip Dwight 1948- *AmMWSc 92*
**Griswold,** Rufus W. 1815-1857 *BenetAL 91*
**Griswold del Castillo,** Richard A. 1942- *WhoHisp 92*
**Gritsai,** Alexei Michailovich 1914- *IntWW 91*
**Gritsay,** Aleksey Mikhailovich 1914- *SovUnBD*
**Gritsch,** Eric W. 1931- *WrDr 92*
**Grittinger,** Thomas Foster 1933- *AmMWSc 92*
**Grittinger,** William Paul 1959- *WhoEnt 92*
**Gritton,** Earl Thomas 1933- *AmMWSc 92*
**Gritton,** Eugene Charles 1941- *AmMWSc 92*
**Gritz,** Richard F. 1940- *WhoWest 92*
**Gritzmann,** Peter 1954- *AmMWSc 92*
**Gritzner,** Charles Frederick 1936- *WhoMW 92*
**Grivas,** George 1898-1974 *FacFETw*
**Griver,** Michael A 1942- *WhoIns 92*
**Grivet,** Pierre A. 1911- *IntWW 91*
**Grivetti,** Louis Evan 1938- *AmMWSc 92*
**Grivsky,** Eugene Michael 1911- *AmMWSc 92*
**Grizi,** Samir Amine 1942- *WhoFI 92*
**Grizzard,** George 1928- *IntMPA 92*
**Grizzard,** Lewis 1946- *WrDr 92*
**Grizzard,** Michael B 1945- *AmMWSc 92*
**Grizzard,** Robert Harold 1915- *WhoAmP 91*
**Grizzell,** Roy Ames, Jr 1918- *AmMWSc 92*
**Grizzle,** James Ennis 1930- *AmMWSc 92*
**Grizzle,** John Manuel 1949- *AmMWSc 92*
**Grizzle,** Mary R 1921- *WhoAmP 91*
**Grmela,** Miroslav 1939- *AmMWSc 92*
**Groa** *EncAmaz 91*
**Groark,** Eunice 1938- *WhoAmP 91*
**Groark,** Jerome Nicholas 1933- *WhoAmL 92*
**Groat,** Charles George 1940- *AmMWSc 92*
**Groat,** Linda Noel 1946- *WhoMW 92*
**Groat,** Richard Arnold *AmMWSc 92*
**Groat,** Robin R. 1930- *WhoWest 92*
**Grob,** David 1919- *AmMWSc 92*
**Grob,** Gerald N 1931- *AmMWSc 92, WrDr 92*
**Grob,** Howard Shea 1932- *AmMWSc 92*
**Grob,** Robert Lee 1927- *AmMWSc 92*
**Grob,** Steven Emil 1952- *WhoAmL 92*
**Groban,** Jack Louis 1945- *WhoFI 92*
**Grobar,** Lisa Morris 1961- *WhoFI 92*
**Grobe,** Charles Stephen 1935- *WhoAmL 92*
**Grobe,** James L *AmMWSc 92*
**Grobecker,** Alan J 1915- *AmMWSc 92*
**Grobelny,** Lori Jo-Ann 1954- *WhoFI 92*
**Grober,** Konrad 1872-1948 *EncTR 91*
**Grobler,** Richard Victor 1936- *Who 92*
**Groblewski,** Gerald Eugene 1926- *AmMWSc 92*
**Grobman,** Arnold Brams 1918- *AmMWSc 92*
**Grobman,** Warren David 1942- *AmMWSc 92*
**Grobner,** Paul Josef 1919- *AmMWSc 92*
**Grobowski,** John Vincent 1947- *WhoAmL 92*
**Grobschmidt,** Richard A 1948- *WhoAmP 91*
**Grobstein,** Clifford 1916- *AmMWSc 92*
**Grobstein,** Les Paul 1952- *WhoEnt 92*
**Grobstein,** Paul 1946- *AmMWSc 92*
**Grobstein,** Toni Lynn 1959- *WhoMW 92*
**Groce,** David Eiben 1936- *AmMWSc 92*
**Groce,** Herbert Monroe, Jr. 1929- *WhoBlA 92, WhoRel 92*
**Groce,** James Freelan 1948- *WhoFI 92*
**Groce,** John Wesley 1930- *AmMWSc 92*
**Groce,** William Henry 1940- *AmMWSc 92*
**Groch-Tochman,** David Antone 1963- *WhoWest 92*
**Grochoski,** Gregory T 1946- *AmMWSc 92*
**Grochowski,** Leon 1886-1969 *RelLAm 91*
**Grocock,** James Bennett 1958- *WhoAmL 92, WhoEnt 92*
**Grocock,** Robert Gordon 1925- *WhoEnt 92*
**Grocott,** Bruce Joseph 1940- *Who 92*
**Grodberg,** Marcus Gordon 1923- *AmMWSc 92*
**Grodberg,** Robert Samuel 1932- *WhoAmL 92*
**Grode,** Murray T *WhoIns 92*
**Grodecki,** Mary Reginella 1912- *WhoRel 92*
**Grodecki,** Wiktor 1960- *WhoEnt 92*
**Grodi,** Michael Edward 1951- *WhoFI 92*
**Grodin,** Charles 1935- *ConTFT 9, IntMPA 92, WhoEnt 92*
**Grodin,** Richard A *WhoAmP 91*
**Grodins,** Fred Sherman 1915- *AmMWSc 92*
**Grodner,** Mary Laslie 1935- *AmMWSc 92*
**Grodner,** Robert Maynard 1925- *AmMWSc 92*
**Grodnik,** Daniel Louis 1952- *WhoWest 92*
**Grodsky,** Gerold Morton 1927- *AmMWSc 92*
**Grody,** Wayne William 1952- *AmMWSc 92, WhoWest 92*
**Grodzicker,** Terri Irene 1942- *AmMWSc 92*
**Grodzins,** Lee 1926- *AmMWSc 92*
**Grodzinski,** Bernard 1946- *AmMWSc 92*
**Grodzinsky,** Alan J *AmMWSc 92*
**Groebe,** Hans 1916- *IntWW 91*
**Groeben,** Hans von der 1907- *IntWW 91*
**Groeger,** Theodore Oskar 1927- *AmMWSc 92*
**Groel,** John Trueman 1924- *AmMWSc 92*
**Groemer,** Helmut 1930- *AmMWSc 92*
**Groenekamp,** William A. 1933- *WhoFI 92*
**Groener,** Carl *TwCSFW 91*
**Groener,** Dick *WhoAmP 91*
**Groener,** Wilhelm 1867-1939 *EncTR 91 [port]*
**Groening,** Lucy Cotton 1934- *WhoRel 92*
**Groening,** Matt *WrDr 92*
**Groening,** Matt 1954- *Au&Arts 8 [port]*
**Groening,** Matthew Akbar 1954- *WhoEnt 92*
**Groenman,** Sjoerd 1913- *IntWW 91*
**Groennert,** Charles Willis 1937- *WhoFI 92*
**Groenweghe,** Leo Carl Denis 1925- *AmMWSc 92*
**Groer,** Hans Hermann 1919- *IntWW 91*
**Groer,** Hans Herrmann 1919- *WhoRel 92*
**Groer,** Maureen 1944- *AmMWSc 92*
**Groer,** Peter Gerold 1941- *AmMWSc 92*
**Groesbeck,** Mark Anton 1963- *WhoFI 92*
**Groesbeck,** Richard Lee 1951- *WhoFI 92*
**Groesch,** John William, Jr. 1923- *WhoMW 92*
**Groethe,** Reed 1952- *WhoAmL 92*
**Groetsch,** Charles William 1945- *AmMWSc 92*
**Grofe,** Ferde 1892-1972 *FacFETw, NewAmDM*
**Grofe,** Ferde, Jr 1930- *IntAu&W 91*
**Grofer,** Edward Joseph 1934- *WhoWest 92*
**Groff,** David Clark, Jr. 1946- *WhoAmL 92*
**Groff,** David Huston 1945- *WhoWest 92*
**Groff,** Donald William 1928- *AmMWSc 92*
**Groff,** Jo Ann 1956- *WhoAmP 91*
**Groff,** Raymond David 1933- *WhoFI 92*
**Groff,** Regis F 1935- *WhoAmP 91, WhoBlA 92*
**Groff,** Rodney R. 1950- *WhoRel 92*
**Groff,** Ronald Parke 1940- *AmMWSc 92*
**Groff,** Sidney Lavern 1919- *AmMWSc 92*
**Groffrey,** Frank Eden 1944- *WhoBlA 92*
**Grogan,** Alice Washington 1956- *WhoAmL 92, WhoFI 92*
**Grogan,** Allen R. 1953- *WhoAmL 92*
**Grogan,** Donald E 1938- *AmMWSc 92*
**Grogan,** Gerald 1884-1918 *ScFEYrs*
**Grogan,** James Bigbee 1932- *AmMWSc 92*
**Grogan,** Michael John 1938- *AmMWSc 92*
**Grogan,** Paul J 1918- *AmMWSc 92*
**Grogan,** Raymond Gerald 1920- *AmMWSc 92*
**Grogan,** Robert Harris 1933- *WhoAmL 92, WhoFI 92*
**Grogan,** Stanley Joseph, Jr. 1925- *WhoWest 92*
**Grogan,** Thomas Robert 1957- *WhoAmL 92*
**Grogan,** Tom *BenetAL 91*
**Grogan,** William McLean 1944- *AmMWSc 92*
**Grogan,** William Patrick 1949- *WhoAmL 92*
**Grogan,** William R *AmMWSc 92*
**Grogg,** Sylvia Kay 1941- *WhoEnt 92*
**Groginsky,** Herbert Leonard 1930- *AmMWSc 92*
**Groh,** Clifford John 1926- *WhoAmP 91*
**Groh,** Harold John 1928- *AmMWSc 92*
**Groh,** Lucille Sider 1946- *WhoRel 92*
**Groh,** Rupert James, Jr. 1933- *WhoAmL 92*
**Groh,** Theresa L. 1960- *WhoAmL 92*
**Grohe,** Josef 1902-1988 *BiDExR, EncTR 91*
**Grohse,** Edward William 1915- *AmMWSc 92*
**Grohskopf,** Bernice *DrAPF 91, WrDr 92*
**Groiss,** Fred George 1936- *WhoAmL 92*
**Grokoest,** Albert W. d1991 *NewYTBS 91*
**Grollman,** Arthur Patrick 1934- *AmMWSc 92*
**Grollman,** Sigmund 1923- *AmMWSc 92*
**Grollman,** Thomas B. 1939- *WhoWest 92*
**Grolnick,** Don *WhoEnt 92*
**Gromack,** Alexander J 1953- *WhoAmP 91*
**Gromacki,** Gary Robert 1958- *WhoRel 92*
**Groman,** Neal Benjamin 1921- *AmMWSc 92*
**Groman,** Richard Paul 1953- *WhoWest 92*
**Groman,** Vladimir Gustavovich 1874-1937? *SovUnBD*
**Gromashevsky,** Lev Vasil'evich 1887-1980 *SovUnBD*
**Grome,** Richard Stanley 1947- *WhoFI 92*
**Gromelski,** Stanley John, Jr 1942- *AmMWSc 92*
**Gromko,** Mark Hedges 1950- *AmMWSc 92*
**Gromme,** Charles Sherman 1933- *AmMWSc 92*
**Gromov,** Mikhael 1943- *IntWW 91*
**Gromyko,** Anatoly Andreyevich 1932- *IntWW 91*
**Gromyko,** Andrei 1909-1989 *ConAu 134*
**Gromyko,** Andrei Andreyevich 1909-1989 *FacFETw [port]*
**Gromyko,** Andrey Andreevich 1909-1989 *SovUnBD*
**Gron,** Poul 1927- *AmMWSc 92*
**Gronchi,** Giovanni 1887-1978 *FacFETw*
**Grondahl,** Carol Harriet 1940- *WhoAmP 91*
**Grondahl,** Jens Christian 1959- *IntAu&W 91*
**Grondahl,** Kirsti Kolle 1943- *IntWW 91*
**Grondal,** Benedikt 1924- *IntWW 91*
**Gronek,** Geoffrey Joseph 1952- *WhoMW 92*
**Gronek,** James Andrew 1950- *WhoWest 92*
**Gronemeyer,** Suzanne Alsop *AmMWSc 92*
**Gronemus,** Barbara 1931- *WhoAmP 91*
**Groner,** Augusta 1850-1929 *ScFEYrs*
**Groner,** Beverly Anne *WhoAmL 92*
**Groner,** Carl Fred 1942- *AmMWSc 92*
**Groner,** Gabriel F 1938- *AmMWSc 92*

**Groner,** Paul Stephen 1937- *AmMWSc 92*
**Groner,** Yoseph Y. 1955- *WhoRel 92*
**Gronhaug,** Arnold Conrad 1921- *Who 92*
**Groninga,** John Donald 1945- *WhoAmP 91*
**Groninger,** Joy Lynn 1946- *WhoMW 92*
**Groninger,** William Gene 1941- *WhoWest 92*
**Gronli,** John Victor 1932- *WhoWest 92*
**Gronlier,** Juan F. 1951- *WhoHisp 92*
**Gronneberg,** Arnold J 1912- *WhoAmP 91*
**Gronner,** A D 1913- *AmMWSc 92*
**Gronning,** Lloyd Joseph 1951- *WhoWest 92*
**Gronouski,** John Austin 1919- *IntWW 91*
**Gronow,** David Gwilym Colin 1929- *Who 92*
**Gronowetter,** Freda 1918- *WhoEnt 92*
**Gronowicz,** Antoni *DrAPF 91*
**Gronquist,** Carl Harry d1991 *NewYTBS 91*
**Gronsbell,** Charles Martin 1949- *WhoFI 92*
**Gronsky,** Ronald 1950- *AmMWSc 92*
**Gronstal,** Michael E 1950- *WhoAmP 91*
**Gronvall,** John Arnold 1931- *AmMWSc 92*
**Grood,** Edward S 1944- *AmMWSc 92*
**Groom,** Alan Clifford 1926- *AmMWSc 92*
**Groom,** Donald Eugene 1934- *AmMWSc 92*
**Groom,** Gary Lee 1946- *WhoFI 92*
**Groom,** James Haynes 1919- *WhoAmP 91*
**Groom,** Janet Marie 1953- *WhoEnt 92*
**Groom,** John Patrick 1929- *Who 92*
**Groom,** Jon 1953- *TwCPaSc*
**Groom,** Victor Emmanuel d1990 *Who 92N*
**Groom,** Winston 1943- *ConAu 34NR*
**Groome,** Reginald K. 1927- *WhoFI 92*
**Groomes,** Emrett W. 1930- *WhoBlA 92*
**Groomes,** Freddie Lang 1934- *WhoBlA 92*
**Grooms,** Charles Roger 1937- *FacFETw*
**Grooms,** Harlan Hobart d1991 *NewYTBS 91*
**Grooms,** Henry Randall 1944- *WhoBlA 92*
**Grooms,** James Trenton 1931- *WhoMW 92, WhoRel 92*
**Grooms,** Karen Victoria Morton 1956- *WhoBlA 92*
**Grooms,** Suzanne Simmons 1945- *WhoEnt 92*
**Grooms,** Thomas Albin 1943- *AmMWSc 92*
**Groopman,** John Davis 1952- *AmMWSc 92*
**Groot,** Cornelius 1919- *AmMWSc 92*
**Groot,** Per Soltoft 1924- *IntWW 91*
**Grootenhuis,** Peter 1924- *Who 92*
**Grootes,** Pieter Meiert 1944- *AmMWSc 92*
**Grootes-Reuvecamp,** Grada Alijda 1944- *AmMWSc 92*
**Groothaert,** Jacques 1922- *IntWW 91*
**Groothof Croddy,** Elisabeth Petra 1957- *WhoWest 92*
**Groothuis,** Douglas Richard 1957- *WhoRel 92*
**Groothuis,** Richard B 1937- *WhoIns 92*
**Groover,** Denmark, Jr *WhoAmP 91*
**Groover,** Gentle L. *WhoRel 92*
**Groover,** Marshall Eugene, Jr 1910- *AmMWSc 92*
**Groover,** Mikell 1939- *AmMWSc 92*
**Groover,** Pamela Jean 1957- *WhoMW 92*
**Gropen,** Arthur Louis 1932- *AmMWSc 92*
**Gropius,** Walter 1883-1969 *DcTwDes, EncTR 91 [port], FacFETw*
**Gropp,** Armin Henry 1915- *AmMWSc 92*
**Gropp,** Kenneth Ahlburn 1922- *WhoAmP 91*
**Gropper,** Allan Louis 1944- *WhoAmL 92*
**Gropper,** William 1897-1977 *FacFETw*
**Groppi,** James E 1931-1985 *FacFETw*
**Gros,** Andre 1908- *IntWW 91*
**Gros,** Francois 1925- *IntWW 91*
**Gros,** Jeffrey 1938- *WhoRel 92*
**Gros,** Marvin 1948- *WhoAmP 91*
**Gros Louis,** Kenneth Richard Russell 1936- *WhoMW 92*
**Grosbard,** Ulu 1929- *IntMPA 92, WhoEnt 92*
**Grosberg,** Percy 1925- *Who 92*
**Grosberg,** Sydnie 1953- *WhoEnt 92*
**Grosch,** Chester Enright 1934- *AmMWSc 92*
**Grosch,** Daniel Swartwood 1918- *AmMWSc 92*
**Groschel,** Deiter Hans Max 1931- *AmMWSc 92*
**Grose,** Alan 1937- *Who 92*
**Grose,** George Dennis 1953- *WhoWest 92*
**Grose,** Herschel Gene 1921- *AmMWSc 92*
**Grose,** Howard B. 1851-1939 *DcAmImH*
**Grose,** Peter 1934- *WrDr 92*
**Grose,** Peter Bolton 1934- *WhoFI 92*
**Grose,** Thomas Lucius Trowbridge 1924- *AmMWSc 92*
**Grose,** William Lyman 1939- *AmMWSc 92*
**Groseclose,** Barbara Diane 1944- *WhoMW 92*
**Groseclose,** Byron Clark 1934- *AmMWSc 92*
**Groseclose,** John Robert 1938- *WhoAmP 91*
**Groseclose,** William Buell, III 1959- *WhoWest 92*
**Grosenick,** Conrad *WhoRel 92*
**Grosewald,** Peter 1937- *AmMWSc 92*
**Grosfeld,** James 1938- *WhoFI 92*
**Grosfield,** Lorents 1944- *WhoAmP 91*
**Grosh,** Doris Lloyd 1924- *AmMWSc 92*
**Grosh,** Richard J 1927- *AmMWSc 92*
**Groshans,** David Edwin 1951- *WhoMW 92*
**Groshek,** Leonard Anthony 1913- *WhoAmP 91*
**Groshen,** Erica Lynn 1954- *WhoFI 92*
**Groshens,** Jean-Claude 1926- *IntWW 91*
**Grosholz,** Emily *DrAPF 91*
**Groshong,** Richard Hughes, Jr 1943- *AmMWSc 92*
**Grosklags,** James Henry 1929- *AmMWSc 92*
**Groskopf,** Aubrey Bud *WhoEnt 92*
**Groskopf,** John E 1945- *WhoIns 92*
**Grosky,** William Irvin 1944- *AmMWSc 92*
**Grosman,** Alan M. 1935- *WhoAmL 92*
**Grosman,** Louis Hirsch 1939- *AmMWSc 92*
**Grosof,** Miriam Schapiro 1932- *AmMWSc 92*
**Gross,** Abraham 1928- *WhoRel 92*
**Gross,** Alan John 1934- *AmMWSc 92*
**Gross,** Allen 1937- *WhoWest 92*
**Gross,** Anthony 1905-1984 *TwCPaSc*
**Gross,** Arthur Gerald 1935- *AmMWSc 92*
**Gross,** Benjamin Harrison 1930- *AmMWSc 92*
**Gross,** Benny J *WhoAmP 91*
**Gross,** Bernhard 1905- *IntWW 91*
**Gross,** Bryon William 1964- *WhoAmL 92*
**Gross,** Caroline Lord 1940- *WhoAmP 91*
**Gross,** Chaim 1904-1991 *CurBio 91N, NewYTBS 91*
**Gross,** Charles Gordon 1936- *AmMWSc 92*
**Gross,** Charles Meridith 1952- *WhoEnt 92*
**Gross,** Clark David 1952- *WhoAmL 92*
**Gross,** Darwin 1918- *RelLAm 91*
**Gross,** David 1941- *AmMWSc 92*
**Gross,** David Casper 1958- *WhoRel 92*
**Gross,** David John 1953- *AmMWSc 92*
**Gross,** David Lee 1943- *AmMWSc 92, WhoMW 92*
**Gross,** Delbert L 1950- *WhoAmP 91*
**Gross,** Delmer Ferd 1946- *AmMWSc 92*
**Gross,** Dennis Charles 1947- *AmMWSc 92*
**Gross,** Dennis Michael 1947- *AmMWSc 92*
**Gross,** Dodi Walker 1954- *WhoAmL 92*
**Gross,** Donald 1934- *AmMWSc 92*
**Gross,** Donald Richard, Jr. 1956- *WhoFI 92*
**Gross,** Edward Emanuel 1926- *AmMWSc 92*
**Gross,** Edward Niles 1954- *WhoRel 92*
**Gross,** Edward William 1956- *WhoMW 92*
**Gross,** Elizabeth Louise 1940- *AmMWSc 92*
**Gross,** Emma Rosalie 1943- *WhoWest 92*
**Gross,** Eric 1926- *ConCom 92*
**Gross,** Ernie 1913- *SmATA 67*
**Gross,** Eugene P. d1991 *NewYTBS 91*
**Gross,** Fletcher 1939- *AmMWSc 92*
**Gross,** Franz Lucretius 1937- *AmMWSc 92*
**Gross,** Fred 1933- *AmMWSc 92*
**Gross,** Fred W, Jr 1911- *WhoAmP 91*
**Gross,** Fritz A 1910- *AmMWSc 92*
**Gross,** Garrett John 1942- *AmMWSc 92*
**Gross,** George Alvin 1933- *AmMWSc 92*
**Gross,** George C 1914- *AmMWSc 92*
**Gross,** Gerardo Wolfgang 1923- *AmMWSc 92*
**Gross,** Guilford C 1917- *AmMWSc 92*
**Gross,** Hal Raymond 1914- *WhoRel 92*
**Gross,** Hanns 1928- *WhoMW 92*
**Gross,** Harriet P. Marcus 1934- *WhoRel 92*
**Gross,** Harry Douglass 1924- *AmMWSc 92*
**Gross,** Henry 1895-1986 *FacFETw*
**Gross,** Herbert Gerald 1916- *WhoWest 92*
**Gross,** Herbert Michael 1925- *AmMWSc 92*
**Gross,** Hilvie Olson 1926- *WhoAmP 91*
**Gross,** Ian 1943- *AmMWSc 92*
**Gross,** Irwin 1934- *WhoFI 92*
**Gross,** Jackie Louise 1956- *WhoAmL 92*
**Gross,** James Harrison 1942- *AmMWSc 92*
**Gross,** James Howard 1941- *WhoMW 92*
**Gross,** James Irvan, Jr. 1956- *WhoWest 92*
**Gross,** James Richard 1946- *AmMWSc 92*
**Gross,** Jeanne Bilger 1925- *WhoMW 92*
**Gross,** Jenard Morris 1929- *WhoFI 92*
**Gross,** Jerome 1917- *AmMWSc 92*
**Gross,** Joe L W *WhoAmP 91*
**Gross,** Joel 1951- *IntAu&W 91, WrDr 92*
**Gross,** Joel Edward 1939- *WhoFI 92*
**Gross,** Johannes 1932- *IntWW 91*
**Gross,** John 1935- *WrDr 92*
**Gross,** John Birney 1924- *WhoRel 92*
**Gross,** John Burgess 1920- *AmMWSc 92*
**Gross,** John Jacob 1935- *IntAu&W 91, IntWW 91, Who 92*
**Gross,** Jonathan Light 1941- *AmMWSc 92*
**Gross,** Joseph F 1932- *AmMWSc 92*
**Gross,** Justin Arthur 1932- *WhoFI 92*
**Gross,** Katherine Lynn 1953- *AmMWSc 92*
**Gross,** Kenneth Charles 1954- *AmMWSc 92*
**Gross,** Kenneth H. 1949- *IntMPA 92*
**Gross,** Kenneth Irwin 1938- *AmMWSc 92*
**Gross,** Lawrence Andrew 1953- *WhoEnt 92*
**Gross,** Leo 1915- *AmMWSc 92*
**Gross,** Leonard 1931- *AmMWSc 92*
**Gross,** Leonard 1941- *AmMWSc 92*
**Gross,** Leonard Edward 1951- *WhoAmL 92, WhoMW 92*
**Gross,** Leslie Jay 1944- *WhoAmL 92*
**Gross,** Liza Elisa 1957- *WhoHisp 92*
**Gross,** Lois Irene 1920- *WhoAmP 91*
**Gross,** Ludwik 1904- *AmMWSc 92, IntWW 91, WrDr 92*
**Gross,** Lynne Schafer 1937- *WhoEnt 92*
**Gross,** M Grant, Jr 1933- *AmMWSc 92*
**Gross,** Malcolm Edmund 1915- *AmMWSc 92*
**Gross,** Mark Warren 1956- *AmMWSc 92*
**Gross,** Martin 1942- *AmMWSc 92*
**Gross,** Martin Louis 1938- *WhoAmP 91*
**Gross,** Mary 1953- *IntMPA 92*
**Gross,** Melvin A. 1941- *WhoBlA 92*
**Gross,** Michael *WhoEnt 92*
**Gross,** Michael 1947- *IntMPA 92*
**Gross,** Michael 1948- *WhoRel 92*
**Gross,** Michael David 1946- *WhoAmL 92*
**Gross,** Michael Joseph 1953- *WhoAmL 92*
**Gross,** Michael Lawrence 1940- *AmMWSc 92, WhoMW 92*
**Gross,** Michael R 1934- *AmMWSc 92*
**Gross,** Mildred Lucile 1920- *AmMWSc 92*
**Gross,** Milt 1895-1953 *BenetAL 91*
**Gross,** Milton David 1948- *WhoMW 92*
**Gross,** Mircea Adrian 1923- *AmMWSc 92*
**Gross,** Nahum David 1923- *IntWW 91*
**Gross,** Nancy Lee 1950- *WhoFI 92*
**Gross,** Natan 1919- *IntAu&W 91*
**Gross,** Nikolaus 1898-1945 *EncTR 91 [port]*
**Gross,** Noel L *WhoAmP 91*
**Gross,** Oakford William, III 1956- *WhoFI 92*
**Gross,** Patrick Walter 1944- *WhoFI 92*
**Gross,** Paul 1902- *AmMWSc 92*
**Gross,** Paul Allan 1937- *WhoFI 92*
**Gross,** Paul Hans 1931- *AmMWSc 92*
**Gross,** Paul Magnus, Jr 1920- *AmMWSc 92*
**Gross,** Paul Randolph 1928- *AmMWSc 92*
**Gross,** Paul Stahl 1910- *WhoRel 92*
**Gross,** Peter A 1938- *AmMWSc 92*
**Gross,** Peter George 1947- *AmMWSc 92*
**Gross,** Richard 1920- *WrDr 92*
**Gross,** Richard Joseph 1947- *WhoAmL 92*
**Gross,** Richard Nick 1937- *WhoFI 92*
**Gross,** Richard Philip 1903- *WhoWest 92*
**Gross,** Richard Wilson 1948- *WhoAmL 92*
**Gross,** Robert Alfred 1927- *AmMWSc 92*
**Gross,** Robert Henry 1945- *AmMWSc 92*
**Gross,** Ronald *DrAPF 91*
**Gross,** Ronald Martin *WhoFI 92*
**Gross,** Ruth Chaiken 1941- *WhoRel 92*
**Gross,** Ruth T 1920- *AmMWSc 92*
**Gross,** Samson Richard 1926- *AmMWSc 92*
**Gross,** Shelly 1921- *WhoEnt 92*
**Gross,** Solomon Joseph 1920- *Who 92*
**Gross,** Stanley Burton 1931- *AmMWSc 92*
**Gross,** Stanley H 1923- *AmMWSc 92*
**Gross,** Stephen Richard 1943- *AmMWSc 92*
**Gross,** Steven Ross 1946- *WhoAmL 92*
**Gross,** Theodore Lawrence 1930- *WhoMW 92*
**Gross,** Thomas Alfred Otto 1918- *AmMWSc 92*
**Gross,** Thomas Lester 1945- *AmMWSc 92*
**Gross,** Victor 1921- *AmMWSc 92*
**Gross,** Walter 1904-1945 *EncTR 91*
**Gross,** Walter Burnham 1925- *AmMWSc 92*
**Gross,** William Allen 1924- *WhoWest 92*
**Gross,** William H 1944- *WhoIns 92*
**Gross,** William Joseph 1932- *WhoMW 92*
**Grossart,** Angus McFarlane McLeod 1937- *Who 92*
**Grossbart,** Jack Elliot 1948- *WhoEnt 92*
**Grossbeck,** John Arthur 1883-1914 *BiInAmS*
**Grossbeck,** Martin Lester 1944- *AmMWSc 92*
**Grossberg,** Arnold Lewis 1921- *AmMWSc 92*
**Grossberg,** David Alan 1950- *WhoAmL 92*
**Grossberg,** Jack 1927- *IntMPA 92*
**Grossberg,** Kenneth Alan 1946- *WhoFI 92*
**Grossberg,** Sidney Edward 1929- *AmMWSc 92*
**Grossberg,** Stephen 1939- *AmMWSc 92*
**Grosschmid-Zsogod,** Geza 1918- *Who 92*
**Grosse,** Russell Richard 1956- *WhoAmL 92*
**Grossenbacher,** Karl A 1910- *AmMWSc 92*
**Grosser,** Alfred 1925- *IntWW 91*
**Grosser,** Arthur Edward *WhoEnt 92*
**Grosser,** Arthur Edward 1934- *AmMWSc 92*
**Grosser,** Bernard Irving 1929- *AmMWSc 92, WhoWest 92*
**Grosser,** Daniel Robert 1961- *WhoFI 92*
**Grosser,** Elmer Joseph 1922- *WhoRel 92*
**Grosser,** Morton 1931- *WhoWest 92*
**Grossert,** James Stuart 1940- *AmMWSc 92*
**Grosset,** Alexander Donald, Jr. 1932- *WhoFI 92*
**Grosseteste,** Robert 1160?-1253 *DcLB 115 [port]*
**Grossetete,** Ginger Lee 1936- *WhoWest 92*
**Grossfeld,** Michael L. 1955- *WhoFI 92*
**Grossfield,** Joseph 1940- *AmMWSc 92*
**Grossi,** Carlo E 1927- *AmMWSc 92*
**Grossi,** Mario Dario 1925- *AmMWSc 92*
**Grossi,** Patrick S 1942- *WhoAmP 91*
**Grossi,** William Anthony 1953- *WhoMW 92*
**Grossie,** James Allen 1936- *AmMWSc 92*
**Grossinger,** Richard *DrAPF 91*
**Grossinger,** Tania 1937- *WrDr 92*
**Grossinger,** Tania Seifer 1937- *IntAu&W 91*
**Grosskreutz,** Joseph Charles 1922- *AmMWSc 92*
**Grosskurth,** Phyllis 1924- *WrDr 92*
**Grossling,** Bernardo Freudenburg 1918- *AmMWSc 92*
**Grossman,** Allen R. *DrAPF 91*
**Grossman,** Allen S 1938- *AmMWSc 92*
**Grossman,** Alvin Joseph 1934- *WhoMW 92*
**Grossman,** Andrew J. *DrAPF 91*
**Grossman,** Burton E. 1918- *WhoFI 92*
**Grossman,** Burton Jay 1924- *AmMWSc 92*
**Grossman,** Charles Jerome 1945- *AmMWSc 92*
**Grossman,** David 1954- *ConLC 67 [port]*
**Grossman,** David Benjamin 1951- *WhoAmL 92*
**Grossman,** David G 1941- *AmMWSc 92*
**Grossman,** Deborah Stone 1962- *WhoAmL 92*
**Grossman,** Debra A. 1951- *WhoAmL 92*
**Grossman,** Edith Searle 1863-1931 *RfGEnL 91*
**Grossman,** Elliot Sanford 1944- *WhoFI 92*
**Grossman,** Ernie 1924- *IntMPA 92*
**Grossman,** Florence *DrAPF 91*
**Grossman,** Gary 1941- *WhoFI 92*
**Grossman,** George 1914- *AmMWSc 92*
**Grossman,** George Stefan 1938- *WhoAmL 92*
**Grossman,** Herbert Daniel 1926- *WhoEnt 92*
**Grossman,** Herbert Jules 1923- *AmMWSc 92*
**Grossman,** Herman 1925- *AmMWSc 92*
**Grossman,** Herschel I. 1939- *WhoFI 92*
**Grossman,** Howard K. 1950- *IntMPA 92*
**Grossman,** I G 1917- *AmMWSc 92*
**Grossman,** Jack Joseph 1926- *AmMWSc 92*
**Grossman,** Jack Steven 1950- *WhoFI 92*
**Grossman,** Jacob 1916- *AmMWSc 92*
**Grossman,** Jeffrey N 1955- *AmMWSc 92*
**Grossman,** Jerome 1917- *WhoAmP 91*
**Grossman,** Jerome Barnett 1919- *WhoFI 92*
**Grossman,** Jerome H *AmMWSc 92*
**Grossman,** Jerome Kent 1953- *WhoAmL 92*
**Grossman,** Jerrold Wayne 1948- *WhoMW 92*
**Grossman,** Joanne Barbara 1949- *WhoAmL 92*
**Grossman,** John Mark 1954- *AmMWSc 92*
**Grossman,** Jon D. 1955- *WhoAmL 92*
**Grossman,** Julius 1912- *WhoEnt 92*
**Grossman,** Kenneth Cedric 1945- *WhoMW 92*
**Grossman,** Laura Anne 1946- *WhoAmL 92*
**Grossman,** Laurence Abraham 1916- *AmMWSc 92*
**Grossman,** Lawrence 1924- *AmMWSc 92*
**Grossman,** Lawrence 1946- *AmMWSc 92*
**Grossman,** Lawrence I 1939- *AmMWSc 92*
**Grossman,** Lawrence K. *LesBEnT 92 [port]*
**Grossman,** Lawrence M 1922- *AmMWSc 92*
**Grossman,** Leonard Edward 1935- *WhoFI 92*
**Grossman,** Leonard N 1936- *AmMWSc 92*

**Grossman,** Leonid Petrovich 1888-1965 *SovUnBD*
**Grossman,** Lisa Robbin 1952- *WhoMW 92*
**Grossman,** Marc A. 1956- *WhoWest 92*
**Grossman,** Marc Alan 1955- *WhoMW 92*
**Grossman,** Mark M. 1959- *WhoEnt 92*
**Grossman,** Mark Stanley 1957- *WhoAmL 92*
**Grossman,** Marshall Bruce 1939- *WhoAmL 92*
**Grossman,** Martin *DrAPF 91*
**Grossman,** Matthew Rodney 1948- *WhoEnt 92*
**Grossman,** Maurice 1907- *WhoWest 92*
**Grossman,** Michael 1940- *AmMWSc 92*
**Grossman,** Michael J. 1939- *WhoEnt 92*
**Grossman,** Nathaniel 1937- *AmMWSc 92*
**Grossman,** Norma 1941- *WhoEnt 92*
**Grossman,** Norman 1922- *AmMWSc 92*
**Grossman,** Pauline Fried 1916- *WhoMW 92*
**Grossman,** Perry L 1938- *AmMWSc 92*
**Grossman,** Richard *DrAPF 91*
**Grossman,** Richard 1952- *WhoMW 92*
**Grossman,** Robert Allen 1941- *WhoFI 92*
**Grossman,** Robert G 1933- *AmMWSc 92*
**Grossman,** Ron *DrAPF 91*
**Grossman,** Ronald H. 1926- *WhoAmL 92*
**Grossman,** Sanford 1929- *WhoAmL 92*
**Grossman,** Sanford Jay 1953- *WhoFI 92*
**Grossman,** Sebashau P 1934- *IntAu&W 91*
**Grossman,** Sebastian P. 1934- *WrDr 92*
**Grossman,** Sebastian Peter 1934- *AmMWSc 92*
**Grossman,** Stanley I 1942- *AmMWSc 92*
**Grossman,** Stephen Lewis 1954- *WhoFI 92*
**Grossman,** Steven *WhoAmP 91*
**Grossman,** Steven Harris 1945- *AmMWSc 92*
**Grossman,** Vasiliy Semenovich 1905-1964 *SovUnBD*
**Grossman,** Vasily Semyonovich 1905-1964 *FacFETw*
**Grossman,** William 1940- *AmMWSc 92*
**Grossman,** William Bernard Stewart 1941- *WhoRel 92*
**Grossman,** William Elderkin Leffingwell 1938- *AmMWSc 92*
**Grossmann,** Agnes *WhoEnt 92*
**Grossmann,** Elihu D 1927- *AmMWSc 92*
**Grossmann,** Hartmut Georg 1946- *WhoAmL 92*
**Grossmann,** Ignacio E 1949- *AmMWSc 92*
**Grossmann,** Reinhardt 1931- *WrDr 92*
**Grossmann,** William 1937- *AmMWSc 92*
**Grossmith,** George 1847-1912 *RfGEnL 91*
**Grossmith,** Robert 1954- *ConAu 134*
**Grossniklaus,** Albert H. 1953- *WhoEnt 92*
**Grosso,** Anthony J 1926- *AmMWSc 92*
**Grosso,** John A 1955- *AmMWSc 92*
**Grosso,** Judith Anne 1945- *WhoFI 92*
**Grosso,** Leonard 1922- *AmMWSc 92*
**Grosso,** Sandra Patricia 1957- *WhoAmL 92*
**Grosso-Jacobson** *LesBEnT 92*
**Grossse,** W. Jack 1923- *WhoAmL 92*
**Grossu,** Semen Kuz'mich 1934- *SovUnBD*
**Grosswald,** Emil 1912- *AmMWSc 92*
**Grossweiner,** Leonard Irwin 1924- *AmMWSc 92*
**Grostic,** Marvin Ford 1926- *AmMWSc 92*
**Grosvenor** *Who 92*
**Grosvenor,** Earl 1991- *Who 92*
**Grosvenor,** Clark Edward 1928- *AmMWSc 92*
**Grosvenor,** Craig Lusk 1950- *WhoWest 92*
**Grosvenor,** Gilbert H. 1875-1966 *BenetAL 91*
**Grosvenor,** Melville Bell 1901-1982 *ConAu 34NR*
**Grosvenor,** Niles E 1922- *AmMWSc 92*
**Grosvenor,** Verta Mae 1938- *NotBlAW 92, WhoBlA 92*
**Grosvenor,** Vertamae *DrAPF 91*
**Grosz,** George 1893-1959 *EncTR 91 [port], FacFETw*
**Grosz,** Hanus Jiri 1924- *AmMWSc 92*
**Grosz,** Karoly 1930- *IntWW 91*
**Grosz,** Mick *WhoAmP 91*
**Grosz,** Oliver 1906- *AmMWSc 92*
**Grosz,** Paul *WhoRel 92*
**Groszmann,** Roberto Jose 1939- *AmMWSc 92*
**Groszos,** Stephen Joseph 1920- *AmMWSc 92*
**Grot,** Walther Gustav Fredrich 1929- *AmMWSc 92*
**Grota,** Lee J 1937- *AmMWSc 92*
**Grotch,** Howard 1940- *AmMWSc 92*
**Grote,** Augustus Radcliffe 1841-1903 *BiInAmS*
**Grote,** Merwyn 1955- *WhoEnt 92*
**Grote,** Richard Eric 1959- *WhoMW 92*
**Grote,** Richard Tucker 1945- *WhoMW 92*
**Grote,** Royal U., Jr. *WhoRel 92*
**Grotefend,** Alan Charles 1942- *AmMWSc 92*
**Grotell,** Alfred 1946- *WhoAmL 92*
**Groteluschen,** Marelle Ellen 1939- *WhoMW 92*
**Groten,** Barney 1933- *AmMWSc 92*
**Groten,** Stuart *WhoFI 92*
**Grotenhuis,** Marshall 1918- *AmMWSc 92*
**Grotewiel,** Ken 1949- *WhoAmP 91*
**Grotewohl,** Otto 1894-1964 *FacFETw*
**Groth,** Brian J. *DrAPF 91*
**Groth,** Donald Paul 1928- *AmMWSc 92*
**Groth,** Edward John, III 1946- *AmMWSc 92*
**Groth,** James Arthur 1955- *WhoAmP 91*
**Groth,** James Vernon 1945- *AmMWSc 92*
**Groth,** Joyce Lorraine 1935- *AmMWSc 92*
**Groth,** Patricia Celley *DrAPF 91*
**Groth,** Richard Henry 1929- *AmMWSc 92*
**Groth,** Richard Lee 1946- *WhoAmP 91*
**Grothaus,** Clarence 1908- *AmMWSc 92*
**Grothaus,** Larry Henry 1930- *WhoMW 92*
**Grothaus,** Pamela Sue 1958- *WhoMW 92*
**Grothaus,** Roger Harry 1936- *AmMWSc 92*
**Grotheer,** Morris Paul 1928- *AmMWSc 92*
**Grother,** David Michael 1946- *WhoMW 92*
**Grotjahn,** Martin 1904- *WhoWest 92*
**Grotjan,** Harvey Edward, Jr 1947- *AmMWSc 92*
**Grotowski,** Jerzy 1933- *FacFETw, IntWW 91*
**Grotrian,** Dennis J. 1944- *WhoAmL 92*
**Grotrian,** Philip Christian Brent 1935- *Who 92*
**Grotta,** Henry Monroe 1923- *AmMWSc 92*
**Grotte,** Jeffrey Harlow 1947- *AmMWSc 92*
**Grottrup,** Helmut 1916-1981 *FacFETw*
**Grotz,** Leonard Charles 1927- *AmMWSc 92*
**Grotzinger,** Laurel Ann 1935- *WhoMW 92*
**Grotzinger,** Paul John 1918- *AmMWSc 92*
**Grouby,** E A, Jr *WhoAmP 91*
**Groues,** Henri 1912- *IntWW 91*
**Groues,** Henri Antoine *Who 92*
**Groult,** Benoite 1920- *FrenWW*
**Ground,** Patrick 1932- *Who 92*
**Ground,** Paul Elliot 1948- *WhoAmL 92*
**Grounds,** Roger 1938- *WrDr 92*
**Grounds,** Stanley Paterson 1904- *Who 92*
**Grounds,** Vernon Carl 1914- *WhoRel 92*
**Group,** Mitchell Hal 1952- *WhoEnt 92*
**Groupe,** Vincent 1918- *AmMWSc 92*
**Groussard,** Serge 1921- *IntWW 91*
**Groussman,** Raymond G. 1935- *WhoAmL 92*
**Groux,** Peter John 1960- *WhoFI 92*
**Grove,** Alvin Russell, Jr 1914- *AmMWSc 92*
**Grove,** Andrew S 1936- *AmMWSc 92, WhoWest 92*
**Grove,** Barry 1951- *WhoEnt 92*
**Grove,** Brandon H, Jr 1929- *WhoAmP 91*
**Grove,** Brian Allen 1960- *WhoFI 92*
**Grove,** Charles Gerald 1929- *Who 92*
**Grove,** Daniel 1923- *WhoBlA 92*
**Grove,** Denise Kathleen 1957- *WhoRel 92*
**Grove,** Dennis *Who 92*
**Grove,** Donald Jones 1919- *AmMWSc 92*
**Grove,** Edmund 1920- *Who 92*
**Grove,** Edwin Wiley 1850-1927 *DcNCBi 2*
**Grove,** Engelbertus Leonardus 1925- *IntWW 91*
**Grove,** Ewart Lester 1913- *AmMWSc 92, WhoMW 92*
**Grove,** Fred 1913- *IntAu&W 91, TwCWW 91, WrDr 92*
**Grove,** Frederick Philip 1879-1948 *BenetAL 91, RfGEnL 91, TwCWW 91*
**Grove,** Helen Harriet *WhoMW 92*
**Grove,** Henning 1932- *IntWW 91*
**Grove,** Jack Frederick 1953- *WhoAmL 92*
**Grove,** Jack Stein 1951- *WhoWest 92*
**Grove,** Jeffery Lynn 1941- *WhoMW 92, WhoRel 92*
**Grove,** John Amos 1938- *AmMWSc 92*
**Grove,** John Scott 1927- *Who 92*
**Grove,** Larry Charles 1938- *AmMWSc 92*
**Grove,** Mus 1933- *WhoEnt 92*
**Grove,** Patricia A 1952- *AmMWSc 92*
**Grove,** Richard Charles 1940- *WhoMW 92*
**Grove,** Richard Martin 1950- *WhoFI 92, WhoMW 92*
**Grove,** Robert Moses 1900-1975 *FacFETw*
**Grove,** Russell Sinclair, Jr. 1939- *WhoAmL 92*
**Grove,** Stanley Neal 1940- *AmMWSc 92*
**Grove,** Ted Russell 1961- *WhoRel 92*
**Grove,** Thurman Lee 1943- *AmMWSc 92*
**Grove,** Timothy Lynn 1949- *AmMWSc 92*
**Grove,** Trevor Charles 1945- *Who 92*
**Grove,** William Barry 1764-1818 *DcNCBi 2*
**Grove,** William Boyd 1929- *WhoRel 92*
**Grove,** William Dennis 1927- *Who 92*
**Grove-White,** Robin Bernard 1941- *Who 92*
**Grovenstein,** Erling, Jr 1924- *AmMWSc 92*
**Grover,** Amar Nath 1912- *IntWW 91*
**Grover,** Carole Lee 1948- *AmMWSc 92*
**Grover,** Derek James Langlands 1949- *Who 92*
**Grover,** Edward D. 1932- *WhoEnt 92*
**Grover,** Gary James 1954- *AmMWSc 92*
**Grover,** George Maurice 1915- *AmMWSc 92*
**Grover,** Herbert David 1951- *AmMWSc 92*
**Grover,** Herbert Joseph 1937- *WhoAmP 91*
**Grover,** James Robb 1928- *AmMWSc 92*
**Grover,** John Harris 1940- *AmMWSc 92*
**Grover,** John Wagner 1927- *WhoMW 92*
**Grover,** Leonard *ScFEYrs*
**Grover,** M Roberts, Jr 1927- *AmMWSc 92*
**Grover,** Marshall 1921- *TwCWW 91*
**Grover,** Norma Bence *WhoRel 92*
**Grover,** Norman LaMotte 1928- *WhoRel 92*
**Grover,** Paul L, Jr 1943- *AmMWSc 92*
**Grover,** Philip 1929- *WrDr 92*
**Grover,** Rajbans 1927- *AmMWSc 92*
**Grover,** Robert Frederic 1924- *AmMWSc 92*
**Grover-Haskin,** Kim Arleen 1960- *WhoEnt 92*
**Groves,** Charles 1915- *IntWW 91, Who 92*
**Groves,** Charles Barnard 1915- *WhoEnt 92*
**Groves,** Delores Ellis 1940- *WhoBlA 92*
**Groves,** Donald George *AmMWSc 92*
**Groves,** Eric Stedman 1942- *AmMWSc 92*
**Groves,** Franklin Nelson 1930- *WhoFI 92*
**Groves,** Georgina *WrDr 92*
**Groves,** Gordon William 1927- *AmMWSc 92*
**Groves,** Harold M. 1897-1969 *ConAu 134*
**Groves,** Harry Edward 1921- *WhoAmL 92, WhoBlA 92*
**Groves,** Ivor Durham, Jr 1919- *AmMWSc 92*
**Groves,** James Martin 1934- *WhoAmP 91*
**Groves,** John Dudley 1922- *Who 92*
**Groves,** John Taylor, III 1943- *AmMWSc 92*
**Groves,** Kenneth Cashman 1936- *WhoAmL 92*
**Groves,** Larry Gene 1950- *WhoEnt 92*
**Groves,** Leslie R 1896-1970 *FacFETw*
**Groves,** Marilyn Woislaw 1938- *WhoAmL 92*
**Groves,** Randall D. 1961- *WhoRel 92*
**Groves,** Ray John 1935- *WhoFI 92*
**Groves,** Richard Bebb 1933- *Who 92*
**Groves,** Ronald d1991 *Who 92N*
**Groves,** Ronald Edward 1920- *Who 92*
**Groves,** Steven H 1934- *AmMWSc 92*
**Groves,** Steven William 1957- *WhoWest 92*
**Groves,** Thomas Henry 1940- *WhoAmL 92*
**Groves,** Thomas Hoopes 1932- *AmMWSc 92*
**Groves,** William Craig 1941- *WhoAmP 91*
**Groves,** William Ernest 1935- *AmMWSc 92*
**Grow,** Galusha Aaron 1822-1907 *AmPolLe*
**Grow,** George Copernicus, Jr 1916- *AmMWSc 92*
**Grow,** John William 1932- *WhoAmL 92*
**Grow,** Lilly Yvonne 1944- *WhoAmP 91*
**Grow,** Richard W 1925- *AmMWSc 92*
**Growcock,** Frederick Bruce 1948- *AmMWSc 92*
**Growe,** Colleen Marie 1959- *WhoEnt 92*
**Growe,** Joan Anderson 1935- *WhoAmP 91, WhoMW 92*
**Growe,** Sarah Jane 1939- *ConAu 134*
**Grower,** John Marshall 1924- *WhoAmL 92*
**Growick,** Philip 1944- *WhoFI 92*
**Groza,** Joanna Raluca 1943- *WhoWest 92*
**Grozea,** Costel Bernard 1924- *WhoEnt 92*
**Grubaugh,** Stephen Gayle 1952- *WhoFI 92*
**Grubb,** Alan S 1939- *AmMWSc 92*
**Grubb,** Charles Carr 1946- *WhoAmL 92*
**Grubb,** David 1951- *WhoAmP 91*
**Grubb,** David H. 1936- *WhoFI 92, WhoWest 92*
**Grubb,** Floyd Dale 1949- *WhoAmP 91*
**Grubb,** George G. 1931- *WhoAmL 92*
**Grubb,** H V 1916- *AmMWSc 92*
**Grubb,** Kenneth 1900-1980 *DcEcMov*
**Grubb,** Lewis Craig 1954- *WhoFI 92*
**Grubb,** Lon A. 1953- *WhoFI 92*
**Grubb,** Norman Percy 1895- *WrDr 92*
**Grubb,** Randall Barth 1944- *AmMWSc 92*
**Grubb,** Robert Lee, Jr 1964- *AmMWSc 92*
**Grubb,** Stephen Bunyan 1945- *WhoFI 92*
**Grubb,** Thomas *WhoEnt 92*
**Grubb,** Willard Thomas 1923- *AmMWSc 92*
**Grubbs,** Bill G. 1929- *WhoFI 92*
**Grubbs,** Charles Leslie 1943- *AmMWSc 92*
**Grubbs,** Clinton Julian 1945- *AmMWSc 92*
**Grubbs,** David Edward 1943- *AmMWSc 92*
**Grubbs,** Donald Keeble 1938- *AmMWSc 92*
**Grubbs,** Donald Shaw, Jr. 1929- *WhoAmL 92, WhoFI 92*
**Grubbs,** Edward 1934- *AmMWSc 92*
**Grubbs,** Francis W. *WhoRel 92*
**Grubbs,** Frank Ephraim 1913- *AmMWSc 92*
**Grubbs,** Gerald Reid 1947- *WhoFI 92*
**Grubbs,** Robert Douglas 1958- *WhoRel 92*
**Grubbs,** Robert Howard 1942- *AmMWSc 92*
**Grubbs,** Rodney Paul 1966- *WhoEnt 92*
**Grubbs,** Steven E 1964- *WhoAmP 91*
**Grubbs,** Thomas Woodbury 1919- *WhoRel 92*
**Grubbs,** Wendy Joanne 1961- *WhoAmL 92*
**Grubbs,** William Eugene 1924- *WhoRel 92*
**Grube,** Elizabeth 1917- *WhoFI 92, WhoMW 92*
**Grube,** Ernst Theodore 1904- *WhoMW 92*
**Grube,** George Edward 1923- *AmMWSc 92*
**Grube,** Geraldine Joyce Terenzoni 1942- *AmMWSc 92*
**Grube,** James Richard 1947- *WhoMW 92*
**Grubel,** Albert 1918- *IntWW 91*
**Gruber,** Alan Richard 1927- *WhoFI 92*
**Gruber,** Arnold 1940- *AmMWSc 92*
**Gruber,** Aspasia 1948- *WhoIns 92*
**Gruber,** B A 1925- *AmMWSc 92*
**Gruber,** Carl L 1938- *AmMWSc 92*
**Gruber,** Charles W 1910- *AmMWSc 92*
**Gruber,** Elbert Egidius 1910- *AmMWSc 92*
**Gruber,** Eugene E, Jr 1933- *AmMWSc 92*
**Gruber,** Frank 1904-1969 *TwCWW 91*
**Gruber,** Gary John 1955- *WhoIns 92*
**Gruber,** George J 1936- *AmMWSc 92*
**Gruber,** Gerald William 1944- *AmMWSc 92*
**Gruber,** H Thomas 1929- *AmMWSc 92*
**Gruber,** Heinrich 1891-1975 *EncTR 91 [port]*
**Gruber,** Helen Elizabeth 1946- *AmMWSc 92*
**Gruber,** HK 1943- *ConCom 92*
**Gruber,** J. Mark 1954- *WhoAmL 92*
**Gruber,** J. Richard 1948- *WhoMW 92*
**Gruber,** Jack 1931- *AmMWSc 92*
**Gruber,** Jacques 1870-1936 *DcTwDes*
**Gruber,** John B 1935- *AmMWSc 92*
**Gruber,** John Edward 1936- *WhoMW 92*
**Gruber,** Karl J. 1909- *IntWW 91*
**Gruber,** Kenneth Allen 1948- *AmMWSc 92*
**Gruber,** Max 1921- *IntWW 91*
**Gruber,** Peter Johannes 1941- *AmMWSc 92*
**Gruber,** Richard Charles 1954- *WhoFI 92*
**Gruber,** Samuel Harvey 1938- *AmMWSc 92*
**Gruber,** Sheldon 1930- *AmMWSc 92*
**Gruber,** Terry 1953- *SmATA 66*
**Gruber,** Wilhelm F 1913- *AmMWSc 92*
**Gruberg,** Martin 1935- *WhoMW 92, WrDr 92*
**Gruberova,** Edita 1946- *NewAmDM*
**Grubich,** Donald Nicholas 1934- *WhoMW 92*
**Grubin,** David Robert 1944- *WhoEnt 92*
**Grubin,** Harold Lewis 1939- *AmMWSc 92*
**Grubman,** Marvin J 1945- *AmMWSc 92*
**Grubman,** Wallace Karl 1928- *AmMWSc 92*
**Gruca,** Christopher Francis 1959- *WhoEnt 92*
**Gruca,** W. Thomas 1943- *WhoMW 92*
**Gruccio-Thorman,** Lillian Joan 1927- *WhoAmL 92*
**Gruchalla,** Michael Emeric 1946- *WhoWest 92*
**Grudem,** Wayne Arden 1948- *WhoRel 92*
**Grue,** Eva Sue 1945- *WhoAmP 91*
**Grue,** Howard Wood 1927- *WhoFI 92*
**Grue,** Lee Meitzen *DrAPF 91*
**Gruelle,** Johnny 1880-1938 *BenetAL 91*
**Gruemer,** Hanns-Dieter 1924- *AmMWSc 92*
**Gruen,** Claude 1931- *WhoFI 92, WhoWest 92*
**Gruen,** Dieter Martin 1922- *AmMWSc 92*
**Gruen,** Erica Marlene 1951- *WhoEnt 92*
**Gruen,** Fred Martin 1915- *AmMWSc 92*
**Gruen,** H 1931- *AmMWSc 92*
**Gruen,** Hans Edmund 1925- *AmMWSc 92*
**Gruen,** Nina Jaffe 1933- *WhoWest 92*
**Gruen,** Robert 1913- *IntMPA 92*
**Gruen,** Victor 1903-1980 *FacFETw*
**Gruenbacher,** Kurt Eugene 1959- *WhoFI 92*
**Gruenbaum,** William Tod 1948- *AmMWSc 92*
**Gruenberg,** Erich 1924- *IntWW 91*
**Gruenberg,** Ernest Matsner d1991 *NewYTBS 91*
**Gruenberg,** Ernest Matsner 1915- *AmMWSc 92*
**Gruenberg,** Harry 1921- *AmMWSc 92*
**Gruenberg,** Jerry 1927- *IntMPA 92*
**Gruenberg,** Karl Walter 1928- *Who 92*

**Gruenberg**, Leonard S. 1913- *IntMPA 92*
**Gruenberg**, Louis 1884-1964 *NewAmDM*
**Gruenberg**, Max F, Jr 1943- *WhoAmP 91*
**Gruenberg**, Michael L. 1946- *WhoFI 92*
**Gruenberg**, Ralph Eberhardt 1930- *WhoRel 92*
**Gruenberger**, Fred J 1918- *AmMWSc 92*
**Gruener**, Raphael P 1939- *AmMWSc 92*
**Gruener**, William B 1944- *AmMWSc 92*
**Gruenes**, David B 1958- *WhoAmP 91*
**Gruenewald**, Patricia Mary 1953- *WhoFI 92*
**Gruenfeld**, Lee 1950- *WhoFI 92*
**Gruenhagen**, Richard Dale 1941- *AmMWSc 92*
**Gruening**, Ernest 1887-1974 *ConAu 34NR*
**Gruening**, Ernest Henry 1887-1974 *AmPeW*
**Gruenstein**, Eric Ian 1942- *AmMWSc 92*
**Gruentzig**, Andres 1939-1985 *FacFETw*
**Gruenwald**, George Henry 1922- *IntAu&W 91, WhoFI 92, WhoWest 92*
**Gruenwald**, Geza 1919- *AmMWSc 92*
**Gruenwald**, James Howard 1949- *WhoMW 92*
**Gruenwald**, Oskar 1941- *WhoWest 92*
**Gruenwedel**, Dieter Wolfgang *AmMWSc 92*
**Gruer**, William E. 1937- *WhoFI 92*
**Gruett**, Monte Deane 1933- *AmMWSc 92*
**Gruffydd**, Geraint 1928- *Who 92*
**Gruffydd**, Peter 1935- *IntAu&W 91*
**Gruffydd Jones**, Daniel *Who 92*
**Grugeon**, John 1928- *Who 92*
**Gruger**, Audrey Lindgren 1930- *WhoAmP 91*
**Gruger**, Edward H, Jr 1928- *AmMWSc 92*
**Gruhl**, James 1945- *WhoWest 92*
**Gruhl**, Robert H 1945- *WhoIns 92*
**Gruhl**, Suzanne Swiderski 1946- *WhoFI 92*
**Gruhn**, John George 1918- *AmMWSc 92*
**Gruhn**, Josephine 1927- *WhoAmP 91*
**Gruhn**, Robert Stephen 1938- *WhoMW 92*
**Gruhn**, Thomas Albin 1942- *AmMWSc 92*
**Gruijters**, Johannes Petrus Adrianus 1931- *IntWW 91*
**Gruits**, Patricia Beall 1923- *WhoRel 92*
**Gruitza**, Michael Cornell 1951- *WhoAmP 91*
**Grula**, Mary Muedeking 1920- *AmMWSc 92*
**Grum**, Allen Frederick 1931- *AmMWSc 92*
**Grum-Grzhimaylo**, Vladimir Yefimovich 1864-1928 *SovUnBD*
**Grumbach**, David William 1963- *WhoRel 92*
**Grumbach**, Doris *DrAPF 91*
**Grumbach**, Doris 1918- *IntAu&W 91, WrDr 92*
**Grumbach**, George Jacques, Jr. 1941- *WhoAmL 92*
**Grumbach**, Leonard 1914- *AmMWSc 92*
**Grumbach**, Melvin Malcolm 1925- *AmMWSc 92, IntWW 91*
**Grumbach**, Robert S 1925- *AmMWSc 92*
**Grumbacher**, John Richard 1950- *WhoAmL 92*
**Grumbine**, Edith Mae 1927- *WhoAmP 91*
**Grumbles**, Jim Bob 1928- *AmMWSc 92*
**Grumbo**, Howard *WhoAmP 91*
**Grumer**, Eugene Lawrence 1940- *AmMWSc 92*
**Grumer**, Joseph 1918- *AmMWSc 92*
**Grumet**, Alex 1919- *AmMWSc 92*
**Grumet**, Martin 1954- *AmMWSc 92*
**Grumette**, Stephen 1937- *WhoEnt 92*
**Grumiaux**, Arthur 1921-1986 *FacFETw, NewAmDM*
**Grumley**, Michael 1941- *IntAu&W 91, WrDr 92*
**Grumman**, Leroy 1901-1982 *FacFETw*
**Grummer**, Elisabeth 1921- *IntWW 91*
**Grummer**, Robert Henry 1916- *AmMWSc 92*
**Grummitt**, Oliver Joseph 1910- *AmMWSc 92*
**Grun**, Paul 1923- *AmMWSc 92*
**Grunbaum**, Adolf 1923- *WrDr 92*
**Grunbaum**, Branko 1929- *AmMWSc 92*
**Grunberg**, Emanuel 1922- *AmMWSc 92*
**Grunberg**, Neil Everett 1953- *AmMWSc 92*
**Grunberg**, Patrick Ramon 1941- *WhoHisp 92*
**Grunberg-Manago**, Marianne 1921- *IntWW 91*
**Grunberger**, Dezider 1922- *AmMWSc 92*
**Grund**, Francis Joseph 1798-1863 *BenetAL 91*
**Grund**, Richard Joseph 1955- *WhoEnt 92*
**Grund**, Vernon Roger 1946- *AmMWSc 92*
**Grundahl**, Kirk Henry 1956- *WhoFI 92, WhoMW 92*
**Grundbacher**, Frederick John 1926- *AmMWSc 92*
**Grundberg**, Andy *DrAPF 91*
**Grundberg**, Andy 1947- *WrDr 92*
**Grunder**, Allan Angus 1935- *AmMWSc 92*
**Grunder**, Arthur Neil 1936- *WhoFI 92*
**Grunder**, Fred Irwin 1940- *AmMWSc 92*
**Grunder**, Hermann August 1931- *AmMWSc 92*
**Grunder**, Robert Douglas 1953- *WhoWest 92*
**Grundfest**, Joseph A 1951- *WhoAmP 91*
**Grundfest**, Joseph Alexander 1951- *WhoFI 92*
**Grundgens**, Gustaf 1899-1963 *EncTR 91 [port]*
**Grundgens**, Gustav 1899-1963 *FacFETw*
**Grundhofer**, John F. 1939- *WhoMW 92*
**Grundig**, Max 1908-1989 *FacFETw*
**Grundleger**, Melvin Lewis 1947- *AmMWSc 92*
**Grundlehner**, Conrad Ernest 1942- *WhoFI 92*
**Grundman**, Valentine Rock, Jr. 1932- *WhoAmL 92*
**Grundmann**, Albert Wendell 1912- *AmMWSc 92*
**Grundmann**, Christoph Johann 1908- *AmMWSc 92*
**Grundmeier**, Ernest Winston 1929- *AmMWSc 92*
**Grundmeyer**, Douglas Lanaux 1948- *WhoAmL 92*
**Grundstein**, Nathan 1913- *WrDr 92*
**Grundstein**, Nathan David 1913- *IntAu&W 91*
**Grundtvig**, N.F.S. *DcAmImH*
**Grundy**, David Stanley 1943- *Who 92*
**Grundy**, James Caldwell, Jr 1923- *WhoAmP 91*
**Grundy**, Joan 1920- *WrDr 92*
**Grundy**, Milton 1926- *Who 92*
**Grundy**, Reg *LesBEnT 92*
**Grundy**, Roy Rawsthorne 1930- *WhoMW 92*
**Grundy**, Scott Montgomery 1933- *AmMWSc 92*
**Grundy**, Stephanie Christine 1958- *Who 92*
**Grundy**, Vincent Arthur 1931- *IntWW 91*
**Grune**, George Vincent 1929- *WhoFI 92*
**Gruner**, C. George 1946- *WhoFI 92*
**Gruner**, George *WhoAmP 91*
**Gruner**, Richard Steven 1953- *WhoAmL 92*
**Gruner**, Sol Michael 1950- *AmMWSc 92*
**Grunes**, David Leon 1921- *AmMWSc 92*
**Grunes**, Robert Lewis 1941- *AmMWSc 92*
**Grunewald**, Ann Mae 1933- *WhoAmP 91*
**Grunewald**, Gary Lawrence 1937- *AmMWSc 92, WhoMW 92*
**Grunewald**, Katharine Klevesahl 1952- *AmMWSc 92*
**Grunewald**, Ralph 1936- *AmMWSc 92*
**Grunewald**, Raymond Bernhard 1928- *WhoAmL 92*
**Grunewalt**, Pine *ConAu 134, SmATA 67*
**Grunfeld**, Cyril 1922- *Who 92*
**Grunfeld**, David I. 1943- *WhoAmL 92*
**Grunfeld**, Frederic V 1929- *IntAu&W 91, WrDr 92*
**Grunfeld**, Henry 1904- *IntWW 91, Who 92*
**Gruninger**, John E 1939- *WhoIns 92*
**Grunlan**, Stephen Arthur 1942- *WhoRel 92*
**Grunow**, William 1830-1917 *BiInAmS*
**Grunschlag**, Toni *WhoEnt 92*
**Grunsell**, Charles Stuart Grant 1915- *Who 92*
**Grunseth**, Jon Rieder 1945- *WhoAmP 91*
**Grunstein**, Leonard 1952- *WhoAmL 92*
**Grunstein**, Michael 1946- *AmMWSc 92*
**Grunstein**, Michael M 1947- *AmMWSc 92*
**Grunt**, Jerome Alvin 1923- *AmMWSc 92*
**Gruntfest**, Irving James 1917- *AmMWSc 92*
**Grunthal**, Ivar 1924- *LiExTwC*
**Grunthaner**, Frank John 1944- *AmMWSc 92*
**Grunwald**, Claus Hans 1934- *AmMWSc 92*
**Grunwald**, Ernest 1923- *IntWW 91*
**Grunwald**, Ernest Max 1923- *AmMWSc 92*
**Grunwald**, Gerald B 1954- *AmMWSc 92*
**Grunwald**, Henry A 1922- *WhoAmP 91*
**Grunwald**, Henry Anatole 1922- *IntWW 91*
**Grunwald**, Hubert Peter 1937- *AmMWSc 92*
**Grunwald**, John J 1931- *AmMWSc 92*
**Grunwald**, Joseph 1920- *WhoFI 92*
**Grunwald**, Linda Lisa 1956- *WhoRel 92*
**Grunwald**, Stefan *DrAPF 91*
**Gruny**, Charles Richard 1932- *WhoAmL 92*
**Gruoner**, David Frank 1953- *WhoRel 92*
**Grupen**, William Brightman 1930- *AmMWSc 92*
**Grupp**, Gunter 1920- *AmMWSc 92*
**Grupp**, Ingrid L 1928- *AmMWSc 92*
**Gruppo**, Leonard Quirico 1942- *WhoAmP 91*
**Grusa**, Jiri 1928- *LiExTwC*
**Gruse**, Gregory G *WhoAmP 91*
**Grusendorf**, Kent 1939- *WhoAmP 91*
**Grusenmeyer**, David Clouse 1953- *WhoWest 92*
**Grush**, Mary Ellen 1947- *WhoFI 92*
**Grushevoy**, Konstantin Stepanovich 1906-1982 *SovUnBD*
**Grushkin**, Bernard 1932- *AmMWSc 92*
**Grusin**, Dave 1934- *ConMus 7 [port], WhoEnt 92*
**Grusin**, David 1934- *IntMPA 92*
**Gruskin**, Felice Rhoda 1928- *WhoAmP 91*
**Grusky**, Robert R. 1957- *WhoFI 92*
**Gruson**, Michael 1936- *WhoAmL 92*
**Gruss**, Peter H 1949- *AmMWSc 92*
**Grussendorf**, Ben F 1942- *WhoAmP 91*
**Gruszczyk**, Jerome Henry 1915- *AmMWSc 92*
**Gruszecki**, Irene Monica 1954- *WhoMW 92*
**Gruszynski**, Stan 1949- *WhoAmP 91*
**Grutt**, Eugene Wadsworth, Jr 1916- *AmMWSc 92*
**Gruttadaurio**, John Joseph 1959- *WhoAmL 92*
**Grutz**, James Arthur 1940- *WhoAmL 92*
**Grutzner**, John Brandon 1941- *AmMWSc 92, WhoMW 92*
**Gruver**, Daryl Lee 1945- *WhoMW 92*
**Gruver**, Robert Martin 1921- *AmMWSc 92*
**Gruver**, William A 1941- *AmMWSc 92*
**Gruy**, Henry Jones 1915- *AmMWSc 92*
**Gruzalski**, Greg Robert 1948- *AmMWSc 92*
**Gruzin**, Boris 1937- *WhoEnt 92*
**Gruzynski**, William Michael 1952- *WhoMW 92*
**Gryc**, George 1919- *AmMWSc 92*
**Gryder**, John William 1926- *AmMWSc 92*
**Gryder**, Rosa Meyersburg 1926- *AmMWSc 92*
**Grylls**, Michael 1934- *Who 92*
**Gryn**, Hugo Gabriel 1930- *Who 92*
**Grynbaum**, Bruce B 1920- *AmMWSc 92*
**Grynberg**, Henryk 1936- *ConAu 34NR*
**Grynszpan**, Herschel 1921- *EncTR 91 [port]*
**Grynsztejn**, Madeleine 1962- *WhoWest 92*
**Gryte**, Rolf Edward 1945- *WhoMW 92*
**Gryting**, Harold Julian 1919- *AmMWSc 92*
**Grzebieniak**, John Francis 1949- *WhoMW 92*
**Grzesinski**, Albert 1879-1947 *EncTR 91*
**Grzimek**, Bernhard 1909-1987 *ConAu 133*
**Grzybowski**, Terry Lee 1956- *WhoRel 92*
**Grzymala-Busse**, Jerzy Witold 1942- *AmMWSc 92*
**Grzywa**, Edward Jan 1933- *IntWW 91*
**Gschneidner**, Karl A, Jr 1930- *AmMWSc 92*
**Gschneidner**, Karl Albert, Jr. 1930- *WhoMW 92*
**Gschwend**, Heinz W 1936- *AmMWSc 92*
**Gschwendtner**, Alfred Benedict 1936- *AmMWSc 92*
**Gschwind**, William Edward 1957- *WhoMW 92*
**Gu Changhe** 1938- *IntWW 91*
**Gu Chaohao** 1926- *IntWW 91*
**Gu Cheng** 1957- *LiExTwC*
**Gu Gongxu** 1908- *IntWW 91*
**Gu Hua** 1942- *IntWW 91*
**Gu Hui** 1930- *IntWW 91*
**Gu Jinchi** *IntWW 91*
**Gu Mu** 1914- *IntWW 91*
**Gu Xiulian** 1935- *IntWW 91*
**Gu Yingqi** 1930- *IntWW 91*
**Gu Zhuoxin** 1910- *IntWW 91*
**Gua de Malves**, Jean-Paul 1712-1786 *BlkwCEP*
**Guadagni**, Gaetano 1725-1792 *NewAmDM*
**Guadagnini** *NewAmDM*
**Guadalupe**, Robert 1942- *WhoHisp 92*
**Guadarrama**, Rosa Linda 1953- *WhoHisp 92*
**Guagnini**, Gloria Laura 1938- *WhoAmP 91*
**Guajardo**, Alfred S. 1951- *WhoHisp 92*
**Guajardo**, Larry 1943- *WhoHisp 92*
**Gualdoni**, Thomas Dale 1948- *WhoFI 92*
**Gualtieri**, Devlin Michael 1947- *AmMWSc 92*
**Guan Guangfu** 1931- *IntWW 91*
**Guan Junting** *IntWW 91*
**Guan Shanyue** 1912- *IntWW 91*
**Guan Sushuang** 1928- *IntWW 91*
**Guan Weiyan** 1928- *IntWW 91*
**Guanciale**, Patrick Donato 1951- *WhoMW 92*
**Guanhumara** *EncAmaz 91*
**Guanieri**, Terri *WhoEnt 92*
**Guard**, Dave *ConAu 134*
**Guard**, Dave d1991 *NewYTBS 91 [port]*
**Guard**, David 1934-1991 *ConAu 134*
**Guard**, Ray W 1927- *AmMWSc 92*
**Guardia**, Enrique J., Sr. 1933- *WhoHisp 92*
**Guardia-Granier**, Romulo Gonzalo 1961- *WhoEnt 92*
**Guardiani**, Joseph T. *WhoFI 92*
**Guardino**, Harry 1925- *ConTFT 9, IntMPA 92, WhoEnt 92*
**Guare**, John 1938- *BenetAL 91, ConLC 67 [port], FacFETw, IntAu&W 91, WhoEnt 92, WrDr 92*
**Guarini**, Frank J. 1924- *AlmAP 92 [port], WhoAmP 91*
**Guarino**, Anthony Michael 1934- *AmMWSc 92*
**Guarino**, Armand John 1926- *AmMWSc 92*
**Guarino**, Dagmar *SmATA 68*
**Guarino**, Deborah 1954- *SmATA 68 [port]*
**Guarino**, Ludwig Michael 1951- *WhoFI 92*
**Guarino**, Patricia Lamb 1952- *WhoWest 92*
**Guarino**, Philip Antonio 1907- *WhoAmP 91*
**Guarneri** *NewAmDM*
**Guarneri**, Andrea 1626?-1698 *NewAmDM*
**Guarneri**, Giuseppe 1698-1744 *NewAmDM*
**Guarnieri**, Camargo 1907- *NewAmDM*
**Guarnieri**, Johnny 1917-1985 *FacFETw*
**Guarnieri**, Raymond Louis 1939- *WhoFI 92*
**Guasco**, Ottaviano di 1715-1783 *BlkwCEP*
**Guastafeste**, Al Carmen 1932- *WhoEnt 92*
**Guastello**, Thomas 1943- *WhoAmP 91*
**Guay**, Gordon Hay 1948- *WhoWest 92*
**Guay**, Lawrence J 1931- *WhoAmP 91*
**Guay**, Reginald Joseph 1936- *WhoAmP 91*
**Guazzelli**, Victor 1920- *Who 92*
**Gubaidulina**, Sofia 1931- *ConCom 92*
**Gubaidullina**, Sofia Asgatovna 1931- *IntWW 91*
**Gubar**, Susan 1944- *WrDr 92*
**Gubaydulina**, Sofiya Asgatovna 1931- *SovUnBD*
**Gubbay**, Raymond Jonathan 1946- *Who 92*
**Gubbins**, Herbert *ScFEYrs*
**Gubbins**, Joan Margaret 1929- *WhoAmP 91*
**Gubbins**, Keith E 1937- *AmMWSc 92*
**Gubenko**, Nikolai 1941- *IntWW 91*
**Gubenko**, Nikolay Nikolaevich 1941- *SovUnBD*
**Guber**, Albert Lee 1935- *AmMWSc 92*
**Guber**, Peter 1942- *IntMPA 92, WhoEnt 92*
**Guber**, Susan 1938- *WhoAmP 91*
**Guberman**, David Aaron 1949- *WhoAmL 92*
**Guberman**, Jayseth *DrAPF 91*
**Gubernat**, Susan Anne *DrAPF 91*
**Gubernatis**, James Edward 1945- *AmMWSc 92*
**Gubersky**, Victor R 1935- *AmMWSc 92*
**Gubits**, David Barry 1941- *WhoAmL 92*
**Gubitz**, Linda Ann 1963- *WhoMW 92*
**Gubler**, Clark Johnson 1913- *AmMWSc 92*
**Gubler**, Duane J 1939- *AmMWSc 92*
**Gubler**, John Gray 1942- *WhoAmL 92*
**Gubner**, Richard S 1913- *AmMWSc 92*
**Gubow**, David M *WhoAmP 91*
**Gubrium**, Jaber F. 1943- *WrDr 92*
**Gubser**, Charles S 1916- *WhoAmP 91*
**Gubser**, Donald Urban 1940- *AmMWSc 92*
**Gucci**, Aldo 1905-1990 *AnObit 1990*
**Gucci**, Guccio 1881-1953 *DcTwDes, FacFETw*
**Guccione**, Anthony Joseph, III 1961- *WhoFI 92*
**Guccione**, Bob, Jr. 1956- *News 91 [port]*
**Guccione**, Robert Charles Joseph Edward 1930- *IntWW 91*
**Guccione**, Robert Charles Joseph Edward S 1930- *WhoEnt 92*
**Guccione**, Salvatore John 1962- *WhoFI 92*
**Guchhait**, Ras Bihari 1935- *AmMWSc 92*
**Guchkov**, Alexander Ivanovich 1862-1936 *FacFETw*
**Guckel**, Gunter 1935- *AmMWSc 92*
**Guckenheimer**, Daniel Paul 1943- *WhoFI 92*
**Guckenheimer**, John 1945- *AmMWSc 92*
**Gucker**, Gail 1942- *AmMWSc 92*
**Gucwa**, Paul Ramon 1947- *AmMWSc 92*
**Gudas**, Lorraine J *AmMWSc 92*
**Gudauskas**, Robert Thomas 1934- *AmMWSc 92*
**Guddat**, Allen Clifford 1930- *WhoWest 92*
**Gudder**, Stanley Phillip 1937- *AmMWSc 92*
**Gude**, Arthur James, III 1917- *AmMWSc 92*
**Gude**, Gilbert 1923- *WhoAmP 91*
**Gude**, John *LesBEnT 92*
**Gude**, Richard Hunter 1937- *AmMWSc 92*
**Gudehus**, Donald Henry 1939- *AmMWSc 92*
**Gudehus**, Lesley Jane 1956- *WhoEnt 92*
**Gudenius**, Carl Frederick 1957- *WhoEnt 92*
**Guder**, Darrell Likens 1939- *WhoRel 92*
**Guderian**, Heinz 1888-1954 *EncTR 91 [port], FacFETw*

**Guderley**, C., Mrs. *Who 92*
**Guderley**, Helga Elizabeth 1949- *AmMWSc 92*
**Guderley**, Karl Gottfried 1910- *AmMWSc 92*
**Gudger**, Eugene Willis 1866-1956 *DcNCBi 2*
**Gudger**, Hezekiah Alexander 1849-1917 *DcNCBi 2*
**Gudger**, James Madison, Jr. 1855-1920 *DcNCBi 2*
**Gudger**, Lamar 1919- *WhoAmP 91*
**Gudger**, Robert Harvey 1927- *WhoBlA 92*
**Gudim**, Steven Paul 1953- *WhoMW 92*
**Gudis**, Malcolm J. 1941- *WhoFI 92*
**Gudis**, Mark Elliot 1963- *WhoFI 92*
**Gudjonsson**, Halldor 1902- *WhoNob 90*
**Gudmestad**, Fern Lucille 1918- *WhoRel 92*
**Gudmundsen**, Richard Austin 1922- *AmMWSc 92*
**Gudmundsen-Holmgreen**, Pelle 1932- *ConCom 92*
**Gudmundsson**, Albert 1923- *IntWW 91*
**Gudmundsson**, Finnbogi 1924- *IntWW 91*
**Gudmundsson**, Gudmundur I. 1909- *IntWW 91, Who 92*
**Gudrun** *EncAmaz 91*
**Gudyashvili**, Lado Davidovich 1896-1980 *SovUnBD*
**Guedel**, John Bimel 1913- *WhoEnt 92*
**Gueden**, Hilde 1917-1988 *NewAmDM*
**Guedes**, Amancio d'Alpoim Miranda 1925- *IntWW 91*
**Guedes**, Antonio *WhoHisp 92*
**Guedron**, Pierre 1565-1621 *NewAmDM*
**Gueft**, Boris 1916- *AmMWSc 92*
**Guehler**, Paul Frederick 1938- *AmMWSc 92*
**Gueiler Tejada**, Lidia 1952- *IntWW 91*
**Guelar**, Diego Ramiro 1950- *IntWW 91*
**Guelich**, Robert Vernon 1917- *WhoMW 92*
**Guell**, David Lee 1938- *AmMWSc 92*
**Guemes**, Martin 1785-1821 *HisDSpE*
**Guemes Pacheco de Padilla**, Juan Vicente *HisDSpE*
**Guena**, Yves Rene Henri 1922- *IntWW 91*
**Guendelsberger**, Robert Joseph 1950- *WhoAmP 91*
**Guenee**, Bernard Marie Albert 1927- *IntWW 91*
**Guenette**, Robert Homer 1935- *WhoEnt 92*
**Guengerich**, Frederick Peter 1949- *AmMWSc 92*
**Guenin**, Marcel Andre 1937- *IntWW 91*
**Guennel**, Gottfried Kurt 1920- *AmMWSc 92*
**Guenter**, Raymond Albert 1932- *WhoAmL 92*
**Guentert**, Otto Johann 1924- *AmMWSc 92*
**Guentert**, Patrick Roman 1938- *WhoRel 92*
**Guenthardt**, Juanita 1951- *WhoAmP 91*
**Guenther**, Allen Robert 1938- *WhoRel 92*
**Guenther**, Arthur Henry 1931- *AmMWSc 92*
**Guenther**, Bobby Dean 1939- *AmMWSc 92*
**Guenther**, Charles *DrAPF 91*
**Guenther**, Charles 1920- *WrDr 92*
**Guenther**, Donna Marie 1938- *AmMWSc 92*
**Guenther**, Frederick Oliver 1919- *AmMWSc 92*
**Guenther**, Herb 1941- *WhoAmP 91*
**Guenther**, John James 1929- *AmMWSc 92*
**Guenther**, Kenneth Allen *WhoFI 92*
**Guenther**, Paul Bernard 1940- *WhoFI 92*
**Guenther**, Peter T 1935- *AmMWSc 92*
**Guenther**, R 1910- *AmMWSc 92*
**Guenther**, Raymond A 1932- *AmMWSc 92*
**Guenther**, Robert Anthony 1942- *WhoFI 92, WhoMW 92*
**Guenther**, Robert Stanley, II 1950- *WhoWest 92*
**Guenther**, Ronald Bernard 1937- *AmMWSc 92*
**Guenther**, Timothy Eric 1955- *WhoRel 92*
**Guenther**, William Benton 1928- *AmMWSc 92*
**Guenther**, William Charles 1921- *AmMWSc 92*
**Guentherman**, Robert Henry 1933- *AmMWSc 92*
**Guenthner**, Louis Robert, Jr 1944- *WhoAmP 91*
**Guentzel**, M Neal 1944- *AmMWSc 92*
**Guenzel**, Lawrence Martin 1947- *WhoRel 92*
**Guenzer**, Charles S P 1943- *AmMWSc 92*
**Guenzi**, Wayne D 1931- *AmMWSc 92*
**Guerard**, Albert 1914- *ConNov 91, WrDr 92*
**Guerard**, Albert J. *DrAPF 91*
**Guerard**, Michel Etienne 1933- *IntWW 91*
**Guerber**, Howard P 1926- *AmMWSc 92*
**Guerber**, Stephen Craig 1947- *WhoWest 92*
**Guerena**, Salvador 1952- *WhoHisp 92*
**Guerieri**, George Edward 1927- *WhoAmP 91*
**Gueriguian**, John Leo 1935- *AmMWSc 92*
**Guerin**, Charles Allan 1949- *WhoWest 92*
**Guerin**, Dean Patrick 1922- *WhoFI 92*
**Guerin**, Didier 1950- *WhoFI 92*
**Guerin**, Jean Louis 1935- *WhoFI 92*
**Guerin**, Jules-Napoleon 1860-1910 *BiDExR*
**Guerin**, Maurice de 1810-1839 *GuFrLit 1*
**Guerin**, Michael Richard 1941- *AmMWSc 92*
**Guerin**, Stacey Kay 1958- *WhoAmP 91*
**Gueritz**, Edward Findlay 1919- *Who 92*
**Guernica**, Antonio Jose 1951- *WhoHisp 92*
**Guernsey**, Dean of *Who 92*
**Guernsey**, Lord 1947- *Who 92*
**Guernsey**, Duane L *AmMWSc 92*
**Guernsey**, Edwin O 1920- *AmMWSc 92*
**Guernsey**, Janet Brown 1913- *AmMWSc 92*
**Guernsey**, Otis Love, Jr. 1918- *WhoEnt 92*
**Guernsey**, Paul *DrAPF 91*
**Guernsey**, Richard Montgomery 1937- *AmMWSc 92*
**Guernsey**, Roger Lewis 1920- *WhoAmP 91*
**Guernsey**, Sherwood 1946- *WhoAmP 91*
**Gueron**, Jules d1990 *IntWW 91N*
**Guerra**, Alicia R. 1960- *WhoHisp 92*
**Guerra**, Arturo 1948- *WhoHisp 92*
**Guerra**, Arturo Gregorio 1927- *WhoHisp 92*
**Guerra**, Berto *WhoHisp 92*
**Guerra**, Castulo 1945- *WhoEnt 92*
**Guerra**, Cesar A., Jr. 1958- *WhoHisp 92*
**Guerra**, Charles A. 1960- *WhoHisp 92*
**Guerra**, Charles Albert 1960- *WhoFI 92*
**Guerra**, Daniel J. 1955- *WhoHisp 92*
**Guerra**, Fernando J. 1958- *WhoHisp 92*
**Guerra**, Fred *WhoHisp 92*
**Guerra**, Ishmael 1932- *WhoHisp 92*
**Guerra**, John F. 1952- *WhoAmL 92*
**Guerra**, Jose O., Sr. *WhoHisp 92*
**Guerra**, Luis G., Jr. *WhoHisp 92*
**Guerra**, Michelle Dunham 1959- *WhoAmL 92*
**Guerra**, Norma Susan 1952- *WhoHisp 92*
**Guerra**, Prax *WhoHisp 92*
**Guerra**, R. David, Jr. *WhoHisp 92*
**Guerra**, Rene A. 1945- *WhoHisp 92*
**Guerra**, Ricardo 1950- *WhoHisp 92*
**Guerra**, Rodrigo *WhoHisp 92*
**Guerra**, Rolando, Jr. 1965- *WhoHisp 92*
**Guerra**, Russ, Jr 1924- *WhoAmP 91, WhoHisp 92*
**Guerra**, Ruy 1931- *IntDcF 2-2*
**Guerra**, Stella *WhoHisp 92*
**Guerra**, Veronica Amelia 1940- *WhoHisp 92*
**Guerra**, Victor Javier 1949- *WhoHisp 92*
**Guerra-Castro**, Jorge 1952- *WhoHisp 92*
**Guerra Gonzalez**, Alfonso 1940- *IntWW 91*
**Guerra-Hanson**, Imelda Celine 1953- *WhoHisp 92*
**Guerra Soria**, Armando *WhoRel 92*
**Guerra-Vela**, Claudio 1945- *WhoHisp 92*
**Guerrant**, Gordon Owen 1923- *AmMWSc 92*
**Guerrant**, John Lippincott 1910- *AmMWSc 92*
**Guerrant**, William Barnett, III 1949- *WhoAmL 92*
**Guerrant**, William Barnett, Jr 1922- *AmMWSc 92*
**Guerrera**, Eugene Rocco 1940- *WhoFI 92*
**Guerrera**, John F 1925- *WhoAmP 91*
**Guerrero**, Anthony R., Jr. 1945- *WhoHisp 92*
**Guerrero**, Antonio Moreno, Jr. 1950- *WhoHisp 92*
**Guerrero**, Ariel Heriberto 1922- *AmMWSc 92*
**Guerrero**, Carlos J. 1961- *WhoHisp 92*
**Guerrero**, Carlos Joel 1943- *WhoHisp 92*
**Guerrero**, Charles 1944- *WhoHisp 92*
**Guerrero**, Dan 1940- *WhoHisp 92*
**Guerrero**, Daniel G. 1951- *WhoHisp 92*
**Guerrero**, Dolores 1941- *WhoHisp 92*
**Guerrero**, E T 1924- *AmMWSc 92*
**Guerrero**, Edward Garcia 1932- *WhoAmP 91*
**Guerrero**, Fernando Moises 1962- *WhoFI 92*
**Guerrero**, Francisco 1528-1599 *NewAmDM*
**Guerrero**, Gilbert, Jr. 1960- *WhoHisp 92*
**Guerrero**, Guillermo E. 1946- *WhoHisp 92*
**Guerrero**, Herman R *WhoAmP 91*
**Guerrero**, Herman Rogolofoi 1939- *WhoWest 92*
**Guerrero**, Jorge 1942- *AmMWSc 92*
**Guerrero**, Jose Luis 1958- *WhoHisp 92*
**Guerrero**, Jose Miguel 1958- *WhoHisp 92*
**Guerrero**, Juan Manuel 1954- *WhoHisp 92*
**Guerrero**, Juan N. 1946- *WhoHisp 92*
**Guerrero**, Juan T *WhoAmP 91*
**Guerrero**, Lena 1957- *WhoAmP 91, WhoHisp 92*
**Guerrero**, Leo *WhoHisp 92*
**Guerrero**, Luis F. 1936- *WhoHisp 92*
**Guerrero**, Mario, Jr. 1962- *WhoHisp 92*
**Guerrero**, Pedro 1956- *WhoBlA 92, WhoHisp 92, WhoMW 92*
**Guerrero**, Roberto 1958- *WhoHisp 92*
**Guerrero**, Vicente 1783-1831 *HisDSpE*
**Guerrero-Anderson**, Esperanza 1944- *WhoMW 92*
**Guerrero-Munoz**, Frederico 1949- *AmMWSc 92*
**Guerri**, Sergio 1905- *IntWW 91, WhoRel 92*
**Guerri**, William Grant 1921- *WhoAmL 92*
**Guerrieri**, Joseph, Jr. 1947- *WhoAmL 92*
**Guerrieri**, Teresa Ellen 1934- *WhoWest 92*
**Guerriero**, Vincent, Jr 1952- *AmMWSc 92*
**Guerry**, Davenport, Jr 1917- *AmMWSc 92*
**Guertin**, Donald L. 1930- *WhoFI 92*
**Guertin**, Ralph Francis 1938- *AmMWSc 92*
**Guertin**, Robert Powell 1939- *AmMWSc 92*
**Guerttman**, Dan W. 1950- *WhoWest 92*
**Guess Who**, The *NewAmDM*
**Guess**, David Elwood 1960- *WhoRel 92*
**Guess**, Francis S 1946- *WhoAmP 91, WhoBlA 92*
**Guess**, George *BenetAL 91*
**Guess**, Gordon Blue 1936- *WhoAmP 91*
**Guess**, Harry Adelbert 1940- *AmMWSc 92*
**Guess**, James David 1941- *WhoAmL 92*
**Guess**, John Edwin 1951- *WhoFI 92*
**Guess**, Paul Richard 1945- *WhoWest 92*
**Guess**, Wallace Louis 1924- *AmMWSc 92*
**Guest** *Who 92*
**Guest**, Anthony Gordon 1930- *Who 92, WrDr 92*
**Guest**, Barbara *DrAPF 91*
**Guest**, Barbara 1920- *ConPo 91, WrDr 92*
**Guest**, Calvin Ray 1923- *WhoAmP 91*
**Guest**, Charles L., Sr. 1935- *WhoAmL 92*
**Guest**, Christopher 1948- *IntMPA 92*
**Guest**, Dean 1929- *WhoRel 92*
**Guest**, Don 1934- *WhoEnt 92*
**Guest**, Douglas 1916- *IntWW 91*
**Guest**, Douglas Albert 1916- *Who 92*
**Guest**, Edgar A. 1881-1959 *BenetAL 91*
**Guest**, Eric Ronald 1904- *Who 92*
**Guest**, Gareth E 1933- *AmMWSc 92*
**Guest**, George Howell 1924- *IntWW 91, Who 92*
**Guest**, Harry 1932- *ConPo 91, WrDr 92*
**Guest**, Henry Alan 1920- *Who 92*
**Guest**, Henry Bayly 1932- *IntAu&W 91*
**Guest**, Ivor 1920- *WrDr 92*
**Guest**, Ivor Forbes 1920- *Who 92*
**Guest**, John 1936- *WhoRel 92*
**Guest**, John Rodney 1935- *IntWW 91, Who 92*
**Guest**, Judith *DrAPF 91*
**Guest**, Judith 1936- *Au&Arts 7 [port], WrDr 92*
**Guest**, Lance 1960- *IntMPA 92*
**Guest**, Lynn Doremus 1939- *IntAu&W 91*
**Guest**, Mary Frances 1927- *AmMWSc 92*
**Guest**, Maurice Mason 1906- *AmMWSc 92*
**Guest**, Melville Richard John 1943- *Who 92*
**Guest**, Raymond Richard, Jr 1939- *WhoAmP 91*
**Guest**, Richard W 1932- *AmMWSc 92*
**Guest**, Robert H 1916- *WhoAmP 91*
**Guest**, Trevor George 1928- *Who 92*
**Guest**, Val *IntMPA 92*
**Guest**, William C 1925- *AmMWSc 92*
**Guethlein**, William O. 1927- *WhoAmL 92*
**Gueths**, James E 1939- *AmMWSc 92*
**Guettel**, Henry Arthur 1928- *WhoEnt 92, WhoFI 92*
**Guetter**, Harry Hendrik 1935- *AmMWSc 92*
**Guettgemanns**, Erhardt 1935- *WhoRel 92*
**Guetzloe**, Douglas Micheal 1954- *WhoAmP 91*
**Gueulette**, Michael James 1957- *WhoEnt 92*
**Guevara**, Alvaro 1894-1951 *TwCPaSc*
**Guevara**, Anne Marie 1949- *WhoWest 92*
**Guevara**, Daniel Luis 1947- *WhoHisp 92*
**Guevara**, Ernesto 1928-1967 *FacFETw [port]*
**Guevara**, Francisco A 1924- *AmMWSc 92*
**Guevara**, Francisco Antonio 1924- *WhoHisp 92*
**Guevara**, Gilberto 1942- *WhoHisp 92*
**Guevara**, Gustavo, Jr. 1949- *WhoHisp 92*
**Guevara**, Jacinto 1956- *WhoHisp 92*
**Guevara**, Jose Luis *WhoHisp 92*
**Guevara**, Juan G. *DrAPF 91*
**Guevara**, Meraud 1904- *TwCPaSc*
**Guevara**, Raul Rubio 1954- *WhoHisp 92*
**Guevara**, Roger 1954- *WhoAmL 92*
**Guevara**, Theresa Sabater 1947- *WhoHisp 92*
**Guevara**, Yingo 1931- *WhoHisp 92*
**Guevara Arze**, Walter 1911- *IntWW 91*
**Guevara Pinero**, Jose Luis 1931- *WhoHisp 92*
**Guevremont**, Roger M 1951- *AmMWSc 92*
**Guffey**, James Roger 1929- *WhoFI 92*
**Guffey**, Leo Wesley 1955- *WhoRel 92*
**Guffin**, Gilbert L. 1906- *WhoRel 92*
**Guffin**, Gilbert Lee 1906- *WrDr 92*
**Gugas**, Chris 1921- *WhoWest 92*
**Gugel**, Alexander 1961- *ConCom 92*
**Gugel**, Craig Thomas 1954- *WhoFI 92*
**Gugelot**, Hans 1920-1965 *DcTwDes*
**Gugelot**, Piet C 1918- *AmMWSc 92*
**Gugenheim**, Victor Kurt Alfred Morris 1923- *AmMWSc 92*
**Guger**, Charles Edmund, Jr 1942- *AmMWSc 92*
**Guggenberger**, Lloyd Joseph 1939- *AmMWSc 92*
**Guggenheim**, Alan Andre Albert Paul E. 1950- *WhoWest 92*
**Guggenheim**, Amy *DrAPF 91*
**Guggenheim**, Charles E. 1924- *WhoEnt 92*
**Guggenheim**, Martin Franklin 1946- *WhoAmL 92*
**Guggenheim**, Peggy 1898-1979 *FacFETw, RComAH*
**Guggenheim**, Ralph J. 1951- *WhoEnt 92*
**Guggenheim**, Robert Thomas 1953- *WhoAmL 92*
**Guggenheim**, Stephen 1948- *AmMWSc 92*
**Guggenheimer**, Heinrich Walter 1924- *AmMWSc 92*
**Guggenheimer**, James 1936- *AmMWSc 92*
**Guggenhime**, Richard Johnson 1940- *WhoWest 92*
**Guggino**, Anthony J. 1955- *WhoEnt 92*
**Guggino**, Thomas Anthony 1947- *WhoEnt 92*
**Gugig**, William 1914- *AmMWSc 92*
**Guglielmino**, Rosario Joseph 1911- *WhoAmL 92*
**Guglielmo**, Al Anthony 1950- *WhoEnt 92*
**Guha**, Phulrenu 1911- *IntWW 91*
**Guhl**, Richard Doehring 1949- *WhoRel 92*
**Guhse**, Mary Ann 1953- *WhoRel 92*
**Gui**, Luigi 1914- *IntWW 91*
**Gui**, Vittorio 1885-1975 *NewAmDM*
**Guibert**, Iliana *WhoHisp 92*
**Guice**, Daniel D, Jr 1953- *WhoAmP 91*
**Guice**, Gerald *WhoBlA 92*
**Guice**, Gregory Charles 1952- *WhoBlA 92*
**Guice**, Leroy 1944- *WhoBlA 92*
**Guice**, Raleigh Terry 1940- *WhoBlA 92*
**Guice**, Terry L 1955- *WhoAmP 91*
**Guichard**, Joseph-Benoit 1806-1880 *ThHElm*
**Guichard**, Olivier Marie Maurice 1920- *IntWW 91*
**Guida**, Vincent George 1948- *AmMWSc 92*
**Guida**, Wayne Charles 1946- *AmMWSc 92*
**Guidebeck**, Nanette Lynne 1962- *WhoEnt 92*
**Guidera**, George Clarence 1942- *WhoAmP 91*
**Guidera**, James F. 1953- *WhoFI 92*
**Guidera**, John Victor 1950- *WhoWest 92*
**Guideri**, Giancarlo 1931- *AmMWSc 92*
**Guidi**, John Neil 1954- *AmMWSc 92*
**Guidi**, Ronn *WhoEnt 92, WhoWest 92*
**Guidi**, Terrill Curtiss 1948- *WhoWest 92*
**Guidice**, Donald Anthony 1934- *AmMWSc 92*
**Guido d'Arezzo** 991?-1033? *NewAmDM*
**Guido**, Cecily Margaret 1912- *WrDr 92*
**Guido**, Michael Anthony 1915- *WhoRel 92*
**Guido**, Michael Anthony 1954- *WhoAmP 91*
**Guido**, Robert Norman 1935- *WhoAmP 91*
**Guidon**, Patrick *WhoRel 92*
**Guidotti**, Charles V 1935- *AmMWSc 92*
**Guidotti**, Guido 1933- *AmMWSc 92*
**Guidry**, Anne Mooney 1948- *WhoEnt 92*
**Guidry**, Arreader Pleanna *WhoBlA 92*
**Guidry**, Carlton Levon 1933- *AmMWSc 92*
**Guidry**, Clyde R 1956- *AmMWSc 92*
**Guidry**, Jessie P 1941- *WhoAmP 91*
**Guidry**, Marion Antoine 1925- *AmMWSc 92*
**Guidry**, Michele Dantin 1960- *WhoFI 92*
**Guidry**, Roman Antoine 1926- *WhoAmP 91*
**Guidry**, Stephen Allen 1958- *WhoEnt 92*
**Guiducci**, Mariano A 1930- *AmMWSc 92*
**Guier**, William Howard 1926- *AmMWSc 92*
**Guignabodet**, Liliane 1939- *IntWW 91*
**Guigou**, Elisabeth Alexandrine Marie 1946- *IntWW 91*
**Guigou**, Paul 1837-1871 *ThHElm*
**Guiher**, John Kenneth 1917- *AmMWSc 92*
**Guikema**, James Allen 1951- *AmMWSc 92*
**Guilarte**, Pedro M. 1952- *WhoHisp 92*
**Guilarte**, Pedro Manuel 1952- *WhoFI 92*
**Guilarte**, Tomas R 1953- *AmMWSc 92*
**Guilbault**, Lawrence James 1940- *AmMWSc 92*

**Guilbault**, Rose del Castillo 1952- WhoHisp 92
**Guilbeau**, Braxton H d1909 BiInAmS
**Guilbeau**, Eric J 1944- AmMWSc 92
**Guilbeau**, Jerry Bob 1935- WhoRel 92
**Guilbert**, John M 1931- AmMWSc 92
**Guilbert**, Lionel 1918- WhoAmP 91
**Guilboa**, Amos 1912- WhoHisp 92
**Guild**, Carol Elizabeth WhoEnt 92
**Guild**, Curtis 1827-1911 BenetAL 91
**Guild**, Ivor Reginald 1924- Who 92
**Guild**, Lloyd V 1920- AmMWSc 92
**Guild**, Lurelle 1898- DcTwDes, FacFETw
**Guild**, Philip White 1915- AmMWSc 92
**Guild**, Richard Samuel 1925- WhoFI 92
**Guild**, Roy Bergen 1871-1945 RelLAm 91
**Guild**, Walter Rufus 1923- AmMWSc 92
**Guild-Donovan**, Anne Louise 1932- WhoRel 92
**Guildford**, Bishop of 1929- Who 92
**Guildford**, Dean of Who 92
**Guile**, Donald Lloyd 1932- AmMWSc 92
**Guiles**, Fred Lawrence 1920- WrDr 92
**Guiles**, Fred Lawrence 1922- IntAu&W 91
**Guiles**, Jon Roger 1945- WhoAmP 91
**Guilfoil**, Thomas WhoAmP 91
**Guilford**, Earl of 1933- Who 92
**Guilford**, Andrew John 1950- WhoAmL 92
**Guilford**, Diane Patton 1949- WhoBlA 92
**Guilford**, Harry Garrett 1923- AmMWSc 92
**Guilfoyle**, George H. d1991 NewYTBS 91 [port]
**Guilfoyle**, James Joseph 1956- WhoMW 92
**Guilfoyle**, Margaret 1926- Who 92
**Guilfoyle**, Margaret Georgina Constance 1926- IntWW 91
**Guilfoyle**, Richard Howard 1939- AmMWSc 92
**Guilfoyle**, Richard J 1935- WhoIns 92
**Guilfoyle**, Thomas J 1946- AmMWSc 92
**Guilhamon**, Jean 1922- IntWW 91
**Guilhaume**, Philippe 1942- IntWW 91
**Guilinger**, James William 1930- WhoMW 92
**Guillabert**, Andre 1918- IntWW 91
**Guillard**, Robert Russell Louis 1921- AmMWSc 92
**Guillaud**, Jean Louis 1929- IntWW 91
**Guillaumat**, Pierre 1909-1991 NewYTBS 91 [port]
**Guillaumat**, Pierre L. J. 1909- IntWW 91
**Guillaume de Machaut** NewAmDM
**Guillaume**, Alfred Joseph, Jr. 1947- WhoBlA 92
**Guillaume**, Charles Edouard 1861-1938 WhoNob 90
**Guillaume**, Gilbert 1930- IntWW 91
**Guillaume**, Robert WhoBlA 92, WhoEnt 92
**Guillaume**, Robert 1937- ConTFT 9, IntMPA 92
**Guillaumin**, Armand 1841-1927 ThHEIm
**Guillaumont**, Antonie Jean-Baptiste 1915- IntWW 91
**Guillebeau**, Julie Graves 1948- WhoMW 92
**Guillebeaux**, Tamara Elise WhoBlA 92
**Guillem**, Sylvie WhoEnt 92
**Guillem**, Sylvie 1965- IntWW 91
**Guillemet**, Antoine 1843-1918 ThHEIm [port]
**Guillemette**, Eugene Joseph 1956- WhoFI 92
**Guillemin**, Henri 1903- IntWW 91
**Guillemin**, Roger 1924- AmMWSc 92, WhoNob 90, WhoWest 92
**Guillemin**, Roger Charles Louis 1924- IntWW 91, Who 92
**Guillemin**, Victor W 1937- AmMWSc 92
**Guillen**, Alfonso, Jr. 1949- WhoHisp 92
**Guillen**, Ana Magda WhoHisp 92
**Guillen**, Jorge 1893-1984 DcLB 108 [port], FacFETw, LiExTwC
**Guillen**, Manuel E. WhoHisp 92
**Guillen**, Mauro 1964- ConAu 134
**Guillen**, Nicholas 1902- IntAu&W 91
**Guillen**, Nicolas 1902- BenetAL 91
**Guillen**, Nicolas 1902-1989 BlkLC [port], LiExTwC
**Guillen**, Nicolas Batista 1904-1989 FacFETw
**Guillen**, Ozzie 1964- WhoHisp 92
**Guillen**, Tomas 1949- ConAu 134, WhoHisp 92
**Guillermin**, Armand Pierre 1936- WhoRel 92
**Guillermin**, John 1925- IntMPA 92, IntWW 91
**Guillery**, Rainer W. 1929- IntWW 91
**Guillery**, Rainer Walter 1929- AmMWSc 92, Who 92
**Guillet**, James Edwin 1927- AmMWSc 92
**Guillevic**, Eugene 1907- IntWW 91
**Guilliouma**, Larry Jay, Jr. 1950- WhoEnt 92
**Guillory**, Curtis J. 1943- WhoRel 92
**Guillory**, Elbert Lee 1944- WhoAmL 92
**Guillory**, Jack Paul 1938- AmMWSc 92
**Guillory**, James Keith 1935- AmMWSc 92
**Guillory**, John L. 1945- WhoBlA 92
**Guillory**, Julius James 1927- WhoBlA 92
**Guillory**, Keven 1953- WhoBlA 92
**Guillory**, Richard John 1930- AmMWSc 92
**Guillory**, Vivian Broussard 1953- WhoAmL 92
**Guillory**, William A. 1938- WhoBlA 92
**Guillory**, William Arnold 1938- AmMWSc 92
**Guillou**, Pierre John 1945- Who 92
**Guilly**, Richard Lester 1905- Who 92
**Guilmant**, Alexandre 1837-1911 NewAmDM
**Guilmenot**, Richard Arthur, III 1948- WhoBlA 92
**Guilmette**, Raymond Alfred 1946- AmMWSc 92, WhoWest 92
**Guiloff**, Jorge Francisco 1952- WhoHisp 92
**Guilton**, Henrietta Faye Brazelton 1941- WhoBlA 92
**Guimaraes**, Armenio Costa 1933- AmMWSc 92
**Guimaraes**, Romeu Cardoso 1943- AmMWSc 92
**Guimaraes Rosa**, Joao 1908-1967 BenetAL 91
**Guimard**, Hector 1867-1942 DcTwDes
**Guimond**, Robert Wilfrid 1938- AmMWSc 92
**Guin**, David Jonathan 1960- WhoAmL 92
**Guin**, Don Lester 1940- WhoFI 92
**Guin**, Junius Foy, Jr. 1924- WhoAmL 92
**Guin**, Wyman 1915- TwCSFW 91, WrDr 92
**Guinan**, Edward F 1942- AmMWSc 92
**Guinan**, Mary Elizabeth 1939- AmMWSc 92
**Guinan**, Michael Damon 1939- WhoRel 92
**Guinane**, James Edward 1932- AmMWSc 92
**Guinasso**, John David 1958- WhoAmL 92
**Guinasso**, Norman Louis, Jr 1943- AmMWSc 92
**Guinevere** EncAmaz 91
**Guiney**, Louise Imogen 1861-1920 BenetAL 91, TwCLC 41 [port]
**Guinier**, Andre Jean 1911- IntWW 91
**Guinier**, Ewart 1910-1990 WhoBlA 92N
**Guinn**, Gene 1928- AmMWSc 92
**Guinn**, John Rockne 1936- WhoEnt 92
**Guinn**, Kenny C. 1934- WhoWest 92
**Guinn**, Reuben Kent 1954- WhoFI 92
**Guinn**, Stanley Willis 1953- WhoFI 92, WhoMW 92
**Guinn**, Theodore 1924- AmMWSc 92
**Guinn**, Vincent Perry 1917- AmMWSc 92
**Guinness** Who 92
**Guinness**, Alec 1914- FacFETw [port], IntMPA 92, IntWW 91, Who 92, WhoEnt 92
**Guinness**, Bryan Who 92
**Guinness**, Bryan 1905- WrDr 92
**Guinness**, Bryan Walter 1905- IntAu&W 91
**Guinness**, Desmond 1931- Who 92
**Guinness**, Howard 1932- Who 92
**Guinness**, James Edward Alexander Rundell 1924- IntWW 91, Who 92
**Guinness**, John Ralph Sidney 1935- Who 92
**Guinness**, Jonathan Bryan 1930- Who 92
**Guinness**, Kenelm 1928- Who 92
**Guinotte**, Henry Paul 1930- WhoRel 92
**Guinouard**, Donald Edgar 1929- WhoWest 92
**Guinouard**, Philip Andre 1960- WhoWest 92
**Guinsberg**, Ilona TwCPaSc
**Guion**, Connie Myers 1882-1971 DcNCBi 2
**Guion**, Isaac 1740-1803 DcNCBi 2
**Guion**, Thomas Hyman 1919- AmMWSc 92
**Guira**, Marcelle Anne 1959- WhoFI 92
**Guiraldes**, Ricardo 1886-1927 BenetAL 91
**Guirande de Lavaur** EncAmaz 91
**Guirard**, Beverly Marie 1915- AmMWSc 92
**Guiraud**, Ernest 1837-1892 NewAmDM
**Guiraud**, Paul 1913- BiDExR
**Guirdham**, Arthur 1905- IntAu&W 91, WrDr 92
**Guirl**, James N., II 1960- WhoAmL 92
**Guise**, Elizabeth Mary Teresa de 1934- IntAu&W 91
**Guise**, John d1991 Who 92N
**Guise**, John 1914-1991 IntWW 91, -91N
**Guise**, John 1927- Who 92
**Guiseley**, Kenneth B 1933- AmMWSc 92
**Guist**, Fredric Michael 1946- WhoFI 92
**Guitano**, Anton W. 1950- WhoBlA 92
**Guitaras**, Ramon 1860?-1917 BiInAmS
**Guitart**, Agustin Ramon 1935- WhoHisp 92
**Guitart**, Jorge Miguel 1937- WhoHisp 92
**Guitart**, Michael Horacio 1935- WhoEnt 92, WhoFI 92
**Guitart**, William WhoHisp 92
**Guiterman**, Arthur 1871-1943 BenetAL 91
**Guitjens**, Johannes C 1935- AmMWSc 92
**Guiton**, Bonnie 1941- WhoBlA 92
**Guitry**, Sacha 1885-1957 IntDcF 2-2 [port]
**Guittar**, Lee John 1931- WhoFI 92
**Guitton**, Henri 1904- IntWW 91
**Guitton**, Jean Marie Pierre 1901- IntWW 91
**Guizar**, Ricardo Diaz 1933- WhoRel 92
**Guizar**, Tito Frederico 1908- WhoEnt 92
**Gujadhur**, Radhamohun 1909- Who 92
**Gujral**, Inder Kumar 1919- IntWW 91
**Gukovsky**, Grigoriy Aleksandrovich 1902-1950 SovUnBD
**Gula**, Allen Joseph, Jr. 1954- WhoFI 92
**Gula**, William Peter 1939- AmMWSc 92
**Gulager**, Clu 1928- IntMPA 92
**Gulari**, Esin 1946- WhoMW 92
**Gulati**, Adarsh Kumar 1956- AmMWSc 92
**Gulati**, Akhilesh 1954- WhoWest 92
**Gulati**, Subhash Chander 1950- AmMWSc 92
**Gulati**, Suresh T 1936- AmMWSc 92
**Gulbinowicz**, Henryk Roman 1928- IntWW 91, WhoRel 92
**Gulbis**, Modris Karlis 1927- WhoRel 92
**Gulbis**, Vitauts Modris 1955- WhoAmL 92
**Gulbrandsen**, Donald A. 1941- WhoMW 92
**Gulbrandsen**, G. Scott 1951- WhoEnt 92
**Gulbrandson**, L C 1922- WhoAmP 91
**Gulbransen**, Earl Alfred 1909- AmMWSc 92
**Gulbranson**, Roger L. 1952- WhoMW 92
**Gulda**, Edward James 1945- WhoFI 92, WhoMW 92
**Gulda**, Friedrich 1930- NewAmDM
**Guldberg**, Ove 1918- IntWW 91
**Gulden**, Terry Dale 1938- AmMWSc 92
**Guldin**, Samuel DcAmImH
**Guldner**, Harold W WhoAmP 91
**Guleke**, James O., II 1948- WhoAmL 92
**Gulens**, Janis 1944- AmMWSc 92
**Gulf**, Robert Charles 1955- WhoMW 92
**Guliano**, Alexandra 1952- WhoRel 92
**Gulick**, Bill 1916- TwCWW 91
**Gulick**, David Miller 1954- WhoMW 92
**Gulick**, Henry G WhoIns 92
**Gulick**, Luther Halsey 1865-1918 BiInAmS
**Gulick**, Peter VanDyke 1930- WhoAmL 92
**Gulick**, Sidney L, III 1936- AmMWSc 92
**Gulick**, Sidney Lewis 1860-1945 AmPeW
**Gulick**, Stephen Millard 1948- WhoAmP 91
**Gulick**, Walter Lawrence 1927- AmMWSc 92
**Gulick**, Wilson M, Jr 1939- AmMWSc 92
**Gulino**, Daniel Anthony 1957- WhoMW 92
**Gulino**, Frank 1954- WhoAmL 92
**Gulis**, Dean Alexander 1955- WhoFI 92
**Gulish**, Gary Byron 1957- WhoMW 92
**Gulkis**, Samuel 1937- AmMWSc 92
**Gulko**, Edward 1950- WhoFI 92
**Gull**, C. Ranger 1876-1923 ScFEYrs
**Gull**, Cloyd Dake 1915- AmMWSc 92
**Gull**, Dwain D 1923- AmMWSc 92
**Gull**, Paula Mae 1955- WhoWest 92
**Gull**, Rupert 1954- Who 92
**Gull**, Theodore Raymond 1944- AmMWSc 92
**Gulland**, Eugene D. 1947- WhoAmL 92
**Gullans**, Charles DrAPF 91
**Gullans**, Charles 1929- ConPo 91, WrDr 92
**Gullatt**, Jane WhoAmP 91
**Gullattee**, Alyce C. 1928- WhoBlA 92
**Gullberg**, William Karl 1925- WhoMW 92
**Gulledge**, Jerry Don 1952- WhoEnt 92
**Gulledge**, Michael Stanley 1950- WhoAmP 91
**Gulledge**, Robert Ivan 1932- WhoAmP 91
**Gulledge**, Yutana Ruth 1950- WhoAmP 91
**Gullekson**, Edwin Henry, Jr. 1935- WhoMW 92
**Gullen**, Warren Hartley AmMWSc 92
**Guller**, Todd Jaime 1960- WhoMW 92
**Gullers**, Karl Werner 1916- WhoWest 92
**Gulley**, Alfred Gurdon 1848-1917 BiInAmS
**Gulley**, David Lee, II 1953- WhoFI 92
**Gulley**, Frank 1930- WhoRel 92
**Gulley**, Girtha 1935- WhoAmP 91
**Gulley**, Needham Yancey 1855-1945 DcNCBi 2
**Gulley**, Norman Richard 1933- WhoRel 92
**Gulley**, Wilbur P 1948- WhoAmP 91
**Gulley**, Wilson 1937- WhoBlA 92
**Gullichsen**, Johan Erik 1936- IntWW 91
**Gullichsen**, Maire DcTwDes
**Gullickson**, Alvin WhoAmP 91
**Gullickson**, Dale Dean 1933- WhoAmP 91
**Gullickson**, Roger Wayne 1938- WhoAmP 91
**Gulliford**, Andrew Jellis 1953- WhoWest 92
**Gullikson**, Charles William 1928- AmMWSc 92
**Gullino**, Pietro M 1919- AmMWSc 92
**Gullion**, Gordon W 1923- AmMWSc 92
**Gulliver**, Frederic Putnam 1865-1919 BiInAmS
**Gulliver**, James Gerald 1930- Who 92
**Gulliver**, John Stephen 1950- AmMWSc 92, WhoMW 92
**Gulliver**, John William 1951- WhoAmL 92
**Gulliver**, Lemuel ScFEYrs
**Gulliver**, Lemuel, Jr ScFEYrs
**Gulliver**, Robert David, II 1945- AmMWSc 92, WhoMW 92
**Gullo**, Vincent Philip 1950- AmMWSc 92
**Gullotta**, Frank Paul 1942- AmMWSc 92
**Gullotti**, Antonio Pietro 1929- IntWW 91
**Gullstrand**, Allvar 1862-1930 WhoNob 90
**Gulluscio**, Ronald John 1937- WhoAmP 91
**Gully** Who 92
**Gully**, John Houston 1952- AmMWSc 92
**Gulotta**, Stephen Joseph 1933- AmMWSc 92
**Gulrajani**, Ramesh Mulchand 1944- AmMWSc 92
**Gulrich**, Leslie William, Jr 1933- AmMWSc 92
**Gulstrand**, Rudolph Elmer, Jr. 1939- WhoMW 92
**Gultekin**, N. Bulent 1947- WhoFI 92
**Gulyas**, Bela Janos 1938- AmMWSc 92
**Gulyas**, Denes 1954- IntWW 91
**Gulyassy**, Paul Francis 1928- AmMWSc 92
**Gum**, Donald Francis 1946- WhoRel 92
**Gum**, Ernest Kemp, Jr 1949- AmMWSc 92
**Gum**, James Raymond, Jr AmMWSc 92
**Gum**, Mary Lou 1948- AmMWSc 92
**Gum**, Oren Berkley 1919- AmMWSc 92
**Gum**, Wilson Franklin, Jr 1939- AmMWSc 92
**Guman**, William J 1929- AmMWSc 92
**Gumbaridze**, Givi 1945- IntWW 91
**Gumbaridze**, Givi Grigor'evich 1945- SovUnBD
**Gumbel**, Bryant LesBEnT 92
**Gumbel**, Bryant 1948- IntMPA 92
**Gumbel**, Bryant Charles 1948- WhoBlA 92, WhoEnt 92
**Gumbel**, Greg LesBEnT 92 [port]
**Gumbiner**, Barry M 1954- AmMWSc 92
**Gumbiner**, Kenneth Jay 1946- WhoAmL 92
**Gumble**, Arthur Robert 1920- WhoEnt 92
**Gumbleton**, Thomas J. 1930- WhoMW 92, WhoRel 92
**Gumbreck**, Laurence Gable 1904- AmMWSc 92
**Gumbs**, Godfrey Anthony 1948- AmMWSc 92
**Gumbs**, Oliver Sinclair 1913- WhoBlA 92
**Gumbs**, Philip N. 1923- WhoBlA 92
**Gumede**, Archiebald Jacob 1914- IntWW 91
**Gumfory**, Thomas Mac 1948- WhoAmL 92
**Gumilev**, Nikolai 1886-1921 FacFETw
**Gumilev**, Nikolay Stepanovich 1886-1921 SovUnBD
**Gumley**, Frances Jane 1955- Who 92
**Gummel**, Hermann K 1923- AmMWSc 92
**Gummer**, Ellis Norman 1915- Who 92
**Gummer**, John Selwyn 1939- IntWW 91, Who 92
**Gummer**, Peter Selwyn 1942- IntWW 91, Who 92
**Gummere**, John 1784-1845 BiInAmS
**Gummere**, John 1928- WhoIns 92
**Gummerus**, Herman Gregorius 1877-1948 BiDExR
**Gumms**, Emmanuel George, Sr. 1928- WhoBlA 92
**Gump**, Barry Hemphill 1940 AmMWSc 92
**Gump**, Dieter W 1933- AmMWSc 92
**Gump**, Frank E 1928- AmMWSc 92
**Gump**, J R 1921- AmMWSc 92
**Gumpert**, Jon IntMPA 92
**Gumpertz**, Werner H 1917- AmMWSc 92
**Gumpf**, David John 1942- AmMWSc 92
**Gumport**, Richard I 1937- AmMWSc 92, WhoMW 92
**Gumport**, Stephen Lawrence 1913- AmMWSc 92
**Gumprecht**, William Henry 1931- AmMWSc 92
**Gumrukcuoglu**, Rahmi Kamil 1927- Who 92
**Gums**, Reuben Henry 1927- WhoRel 92
**Gumucio-Granier**, Jorge IntWW 91
**Gun-Munro**, Sydney Douglas 1916- Who 92
**Guna**, Edward Francis 1948- WhoFI 92
**Guna-Kasem**, Pracha 1934- IntWW 91
**Gunar**, Lee Roy 1938- WhoIns 92

**Gunaratne**, Victor Thomas Herat 1912- *IntWW 91*
**Gunasekaran**, Muthukumaran 1942- *AmMWSc 92*
**Gunasekera**, Jay Sarath 1946- *WhoMW 92*
**Gunberg**, David Leo 1922- *AmMWSc 92*
**Gunberg**, Paul F 1917- *AmMWSc 92*
**Gunches**, Joseph Michael 1951- *WhoEnt 92*
**Gunckel**, Thomas L, II 1936- *AmMWSc 92*
**Gund**, George, III 1937- *WhoWest 92*
**Gund**, Gordon 1939- *WhoMW 92, WhoWest 92*
**Gund**, Peter Herman Lourie 1940- *AmMWSc 92*
**Gunder**, Henry 1837?-1916 *BiInAmS*
**Gunderman**, Joseph Charles 1957- *WhoEnt 92*
**Gundersen**, Beverley Joyce 1936- *WhoRel 92*
**Gundersen**, James Novotny 1925- *AmMWSc 92*
**Gundersen**, Larry Edward 1940- *AmMWSc 92*
**Gundersen**, Martin Adolph 1940- *AmMWSc 92*
**Gundersen**, Ralph Wilhelm 1938- *AmMWSc 92*
**Gundersen**, Roy Melvin 1930- *AmMWSc 92*
**Gundersheimer**, Karen 1939- *ConAu 133*
**Gunderson**, Cleon Henry 1932- *WhoWest 92*
**Gunderson**, Donald Raymond 1942- *AmMWSc 92*
**Gunderson**, Elmer Millard 1929- *WhoAmP 91, WhoWest 92*
**Gunderson**, Hans Magelssen 1938- *AmMWSc 92*
**Gunderson**, Harvey Lorraine 1913- *AmMWSc 92*
**Gunderson**, Joanna *DrAPF 91*
**Gunderson**, Judith Keefer 1939- *WhoFI 92*
**Gunderson**, Keith *DrAPF 91*
**Gunderson**, Leslie Charles 1935- *AmMWSc 92, WhoFI 92*
**Gunderson**, Norman Gustav 1917- *AmMWSc 92*
**Gunderson**, Norman O 1918- *AmMWSc 92*
**Gunderson**, Robert Gorman 1952- *WhoAmL 92*
**Gunderson**, Robert Vernon, Jr. 1951- *WhoAmL 92*
**Gunderson**, Stamy Sam 1963- *WhoWest 92*
**Gunderson**, Steve 1951- *AlmAP 92 [port]*
**Gunderson**, Steve Craig 1951- *WhoAmP 91, WhoMW 92*
**Gunderson**, Ted Lee 1928- *WhoWest 92*
**Gunderson**, William Mark 1955- *WhoFI 92*
**Gundlach**, Heinz Ludwig 1937- *WhoFI 92*
**Gundlach**, Robert William 1926- *AmMWSc 92*
**Gundlach**, Robert Wright, Jr. 1961- *WhoAmL 92*
**Gundolf**, Friedrich 1880-1931 *EncTR 91 [port]*
**Gundrum**, David Eugene 1952- *WhoRel 92*
**Gundrum**, James Richard 1929- *WhoRel 92*
**Gundy**, Jeff *DrAPF 91*
**Gundy**, Samuel Charles 1918- *AmMWSc 92*
**Guner**, Osman Fatih 1956- *WhoWest 92*
**Guney**, Yilmaz 1937-1984 *IntDcF 2-2*
**Gungaadorj**, Sharavyn 1935- *IntWW 91*
**Gungah**, Dwarkanath 1940- *IntWW 91*
**Gunion**, John Francis 1943- *AmMWSc 92*
**Gunji**, Hiroshi 1928- *AmMWSc 92*
**Gunjian**, Armen Garo 1936- *WhoFI 92*
**Gunkel**, Robert James 1925- *AmMWSc 92*
**Gunkel**, Wesley W 1921- *AmMWSc 92*
**Gunn**, Alan Richard 1936- *Who 92*
**Gunn**, Albert Edward 1933- *AmMWSc 92*
**Gunn**, Alex M., Jr. 1928- *WhoBlA 92*
**Gunn**, Arthur Clinton 1942- *WhoBlA 92*
**Gunn**, Bill 1934-1989 *WhoBlA 92N*
**Gunn**, Brooke *ConAu 135*
**Gunn**, Bunty Moffat 1923- *Who 92*
**Gunn**, Charles Robert 1927- *AmMWSc 92*
**Gunn**, Chesterfield Garvin, Jr 1920- *AmMWSc 92*
**Gunn**, Edwin Norman 1925- *WhoAmL 92*
**Gunn**, Frank Michael 1956- *WhoAmP 91*
**Gunn**, George F., Jr. 1927- *WhoAmL 92, WhoMW 92*
**Gunn**, Giles Buckingham 1938- *WhoRel 92*
**Gunn**, Gladys 1937- *WhoBlA 92*
**Gunn**, Hartford N., Jr. d1986 *LesBEnT 92*
**Gunn**, Herbert James 1893-1964 *TwCPaSc*
**Gunn**, Howard James 1945- *WhoMW 92*
**Gunn**, James *DrAPF 91*
**Gunn**, James 1923- *ScFEYrs*
**Gunn**, James E 1923- *TwCSFW 91, WrDr 92*
**Gunn**, James Edward 1938- *AmMWSc 92*
**Gunn**, James Edwin 1923- *IntAu&W 91*
**Gunn**, John Angus Livingston 1934- *Who 92*
**Gunn**, John Battiscombe 1928- *AmMWSc 92*
**Gunn**, John Charles 1937- *IntWW 91, Who 92*
**Gunn**, John Currie 1916- *Who 92*
**Gunn**, John Humphrey 1942- *Who 92*
**Gunn**, John Martyn 1945- *AmMWSc 92*
**Gunn**, John William, Jr 1928- *AmMWSc 92*
**Gunn**, Kenrick Lewis Stuart 1923- *AmMWSc 92*
**Gunn**, Lenton 1939- *WhoRel 92*
**Gunn**, Marion Ballantyne 1947- *Who 92*
**Gunn**, Mark Kevin 1963- *WhoAmL 92*
**Gunn**, Mary Elizabeth 1914- *WhoMW 92*
**Gunn**, Moses 1929- *IntMPA 92*
**Gunn**, Neil M. 1891-1973 *RfGEnL 91*
**Gunn**, Patricia Alice 1948- *WhoWest 92*
**Gunn**, Peter Nicholson 1914- *Who 92*
**Gunn**, Richard *Who 92*
**Gunn**, Robert Burns *AmMWSc 92*
**Gunn**, Robert Dewey 1928- *AmMWSc 92*
**Gunn**, Robert Kenneth 1952- *WhoAmL 92*
**Gunn**, Robert Louis 1931- *WhoAmP 91*
**Gunn**, Robert Norman 1925- *IntWW 91, Who 92*
**Gunn**, Roderick James 1945- *WhoEnt 92*
**Gunn**, Sandra Joyce 1951- *WhoRel 92*
**Gunn**, Thom *DrAPF 91*
**Gunn**, Thom 1929- *CnDBLB 8 [port], ConPo 91, IntAu&W 91, RfGEnL 91, WrDr 92*
**Gunn**, Thomas M. *WhoWest 92*
**Gunn**, Thomson William 1929- *Who 92*
**Gunn**, Vera 1925- *WhoBlA 92*
**Gunn**, Vonda 1920- *WhoAmP 91*
**Gunn**, Walter Joseph 1935- *AmMWSc 92*
**Gunn**, Wendell L 1932- *WhoIns 92*
**Gunn**, William 1914- *Who 92*
**Gunn**, William Archer 1914- *IntWW 91*
**Gunn**, William Harrison 1934-1989 *WhoBlA 92N*
**Gunn**, Willie Cosdena Thomas 1926- *WhoBlA 92*
**Gunnar**, Rolf McMillan 1926- *AmMWSc 92*
**Gunnars**, Kristjana 1948- *ConLC 69 [port]*
**Gunnarsson**, Birgir Isleifur 1936- *IntWW 91*
**Gunnarsson**, Gunnar 1889-1975 *FacFETw*
**Gunnel**, Joseph C., Sr. 1918- *WhoBlA 92*
**Gunnell**, James B. 1929- *WhoBlA 92*
**Gunnell**, John 1933- *Who 92*
**Gunnells**, Drew Jefferson 1932- *WhoRel 92*
**Gunnels**, Doug 1948- *WhoAmP 91*
**Gunner**, Haim Bernard 1924- *AmMWSc 92*
**Gunner**, Lawrence George 1939- *WhoAmP 91*
**Gunner**, Murray 1918- *WhoRel 92*
**Gunnerson**, Charles Gilbert 1920- *WhoFI 92*
**Gunnerson**, Kim Noreen 1965- *WhoWest 92*
**Gunness**, R C 1911- *AmMWSc 92*
**Gunness**, Robert Charles 1911- *IntWW 91*
**Gunning**, Brian Edgar Scourse 1934- *IntWW 91, Who 92*
**Gunning**, Charles Theodore 1935- *Who 92*
**Gunning**, Francis Patrick 1923- *WhoFI 92*
**Gunning**, Gerald Eugene 1932- *AmMWSc 92*
**Gunning**, Harry Emmet 1916- *AmMWSc 92*
**Gunning**, John Edward Maitland 1904- *Who 92*
**Gunning**, Lucille C. 1922- *NotBlAW 92*
**Gunning**, Robert Clifford 1931- *AmMWSc 92*
**Gunning**, William Dickey 1830-1888 *BiInAmS*
**Gunnings**, Thomas S. 1935- *WhoBlA 92*
**Gunnink**, Raymond 1932- *AmMWSc 92*
**Gunnison**, Albert Farrington 1939- *AmMWSc 92*
**Gunnoe**, Nancy Lavenia 1921- *WhoFI 92*
**Guns**, Ronald A 1948- *WhoAmP 91*
**Gunsalus**, Irwin Clyde 1912- *AmMWSc 92, IntWW 91*
**Gunsalus**, Robert Philip 1947- *AmMWSc 92*
**Gunsaulus**, Frank Wakeley 1856-1921 *RelLAm 91*
**Gunsberg**, Sheldon 1920- *IntMPA 92*
**Gunsch**, Ronald E *WhoAmP 91*
**Gunshor**, Robert Lewis 1935- *AmMWSc 92*
**Gunson**, Ameral Blanche Tregurtha 1948- *IntWW 91*
**Gunst**, Susan Jane *AmMWSc 92*
**Gunston**, Bill 1927- *WrDr 92*
**Gunston**, John 1962- *Who 92*
**Gunston**, Richard Wellesley d1991 *Who 92N*
**Gunston**, William Tudor 1927- *IntAu&W 91*
**Gunstone**, Frank Denby 1923- *WrDr 92*
**Gunstream**, Robby Dean 1951- *WhoWest 92*
**Gunsul**, Alan L. W. 1926- *WhoWest 92*
**Gunsul**, Craig J W 1937- *AmMWSc 92*
**Gunter**, Annie Laurie 1919- *WhoAmP 91*
**Gunter**, Archibald Clavering 1847-1907 *BenetAL 91*
**Gunter**, Bill 1934- *WhoAmP 91*
**Gunter**, Bobby J 1941- *AmMWSc 92*
**Gunter**, Bradley Hunt 1940- *WhoFI 92*
**Gunter**, Carl N, Jr 1938- *WhoAmP 91*
**Gunter**, Carolyn M 1931- *WhoAmP 91*
**Gunter**, Claude Ray 1939- *AmMWSc 92*
**Gunter**, Darrell Wayne 1959- *WhoMW 92*
**Gunter**, Deborah Ann *AmMWSc 92*
**Gunter**, Edgar Jackson, Jr 1934- *AmMWSc 92*
**Gunter**, Emily Diane 1948- *WhoFI 92*
**Gunter**, Gordon 1909- *AmMWSc 92*
**Gunter**, John Forsyth 1938- *Who 92*
**Gunter**, Karlene Klages 1939- *AmMWSc 92*
**Gunter**, Laurie 1922- *WhoBlA 92*
**Gunter**, Laurie M *AmMWSc 92*
**Gunter**, Michael Donwell 1947- *WhoAmL 92*
**Gunter**, Pete 1936- *WrDr 92*
**Gunter**, Pete A Y 1936- *ConAu 34NR, IntAu&W 91*
**Gunter**, Robert J. 1935- *WhoMW 92*
**Gunter**, Russell Allen 1950- *WhoAmL 92*
**Gunter**, Thomas E, Jr 1938- *AmMWSc 92*
**Gunter**, William D., Jr. 1934- *WhoIns 92*
**Guntharp**, Grady Elvis 1942- *WhoFI 92*
**Gunther**, Albert Everard 1903 *IntAu&W 91*
**Gunther**, Charles Frederick 1929- *WhoFI 92*
**Gunther**, Eberhard 1911- *IntWW 91*
**Gunther**, Gary Richard 1948- *AmMWSc 92*
**Gunther**, George Lackman 1919- *WhoAmP 91*
**Gunther**, Gerald 1927- *WhoAmL 92, WrDr 92*
**Gunther**, Greg 1951- *WhoEnt 92*
**Gunther**, Hans Friedrich Karl 1891-1968 *BiDExR, EncTR 91 [port]*
**Gunther**, Jay Kenneth 1938- *AmMWSc 92*
**Gunther**, John 1901-1970 *BenetAL 91, FacFETw*
**Gunther**, Leon 1939- *AmMWSc 92*
**Gunther**, Marian W J 1923- *AmMWSc 92*
**Gunther**, Richard S. 1925- *WhoWest 92*
**Gunther**, Ronald George 1933- *AmMWSc 92*
**Gunther**, Thomas Regis 1944- *WhoRel 92*
**Gunther**, Wolfgang Hans Heinrich 1931- *AmMWSc 92*
**Gunther-Mohr**, Gerard Robert 1922- *AmMWSc 92*
**Guntheroth**, Warren G 1927- *AmMWSc 92*
**Gunthorpe**, Uriel Derrick 1924- *WhoBlA 92*
**Guntly**, Gregory G. 1942- *WhoMW 92*
**Gunton**, James D 1937- *AmMWSc 92*
**Gunton**, Ramsay Willis 1922- *AmMWSc 92*
**Guntrum**, Suzanne Simmons 1946- *IntAu&W 91*
**Gunvara** *EncAmaz 91*
**Gunz**, Curt Gibson 1964- *WhoRel 92*
**Gunzburg**, David Micheal 1970- *WhoEnt 92*
**Gunzburger**, Max Donald 1945- *AmMWSc 92*
**Gunzenhauser**, Gerard Ralph, Jr. 1936- *WhoFI 92*
**Gunzenhauser**, Stephen Charles 1942- *WhoEnt 92*
**Guo Feng** *IntWW 91*
**Guo Fengmin** 1930- *IntWW 91*
**Guo Linxiang** 1914- *IntWW 91*
**Guo Liwen** 1920- *IntWW 91*
**Guo Musun** 1920- *IntWW 91*
**Guo Weicheng** 1912- *IntWW 91*
**Guo Yuehua** 1956- *IntWW 91*
**Guo Zhenqian** 1932- *IntWW 91*
**Guo**, Hua 1962- *AmMWSc 92*
**Guo**, Shumei 1954- *AmMWSc 92*
**Guo**, Yan-Shi 1943- *AmMWSc 92*
**Guppy**, Nicholas 1925- *WrDr 92*
**Gupta**, Ajaya Kumar 1944- *AmMWSc 92*
**Gupta**, Amitava 1947- *AmMWSc 92*
**Gupta**, Anil Kumar 1953- *WhoWest 92*
**Gupta**, Arjun Kumar 1938- *AmMWSc 92*
**Gupta**, Ashwani Kumar 1948- *AmMWSc 92*
**Gupta**, Ayodhya P 1928- *AmMWSc 92*
**Gupta**, Bhupender Singh 1937- *AmMWSc 92*
**Gupta**, Bhushan Brij 1951- *WhoWest 92*
**Gupta**, Bimleshwar Prasad 1946- *WhoWest 92*
**Gupta**, Brij Mohan 1947- *AmMWSc 92*
**Gupta**, Chaitan Prakash 1939- *AmMWSc 92*
**Gupta**, Devendra 1931- *AmMWSc 92*
**Gupta**, Dharam Vir 1945- *AmMWSc 92*
**Gupta**, Gian Chand 1939- *AmMWSc 92*
**Gupta**, Godaveri Rawat 1937- *AmMWSc 92*
**Gupta**, Goutam 1945- *AmMWSc 92*
**Gupta**, Jatinder Nath Dass 1942- *WhoMW 92*
**Gupta**, Kishan Chand 1932- *WhoMW 92*
**Gupta**, Krishana Chandara 1927- *AmMWSc 92*
**Gupta**, Krishna Chandra 1948- *AmMWSc 92*
**Gupta**, Krishna Murari 1949- *AmMWSc 92*
**Gupta**, Kuldip Chand 1940- *AmMWSc 92*
**Gupta**, Madan Mohan 1936- *AmMWSc 92*
**Gupta**, Madhu Sudan 1945- *AmMWSc 92*
**Gupta**, Manjula K 1942- *AmMWSc 92*
**Gupta**, Mona 1959- *WhoAmL 92*
**Gupta**, Naba K 1934- *AmMWSc 92*
**Gupta**, Nand K 1942- *AmMWSc 92*
**Gupta**, Narain Datt 1936- *AmMWSc 92*
**Gupta**, Om Prakash 1926- *AmMWSc 92*
**Gupta**, Prabodh Kumar 1937- *AmMWSc 92*
**Gupta**, Pradeep Kumar 1944- *AmMWSc 92*
**Gupta**, Radhey Shyam 1947- *AmMWSc 92*
**Gupta**, Raj K 1943- *AmMWSc 92*
**Gupta**, Rajendra 1943- *AmMWSc 92*
**Gupta**, Rajesh Kumar 1961- *WhoWest 92*
**Gupta**, Rakesh Kumar 1947- *AmMWSc 92*
**Gupta**, Ramesh 1947- *AmMWSc 92*
**Gupta**, Ramesh C 1944- *AmMWSc 92*
**Gupta**, Ramesh C 1949- *AmMWSc 92*
**Gupta**, Ramesh K 1953- *AmMWSc 92*
**Gupta**, Rishab Kumar 1943- *AmMWSc 92*
**Gupta**, Sanjeer 1954- *AmMWSc 92*
**Gupta**, Satish Chander 1945- *AmMWSc 92*
**Gupta**, Shanti Swarup 1925- *AmMWSc 92*
**Gupta**, Shyam Kirti 1942- *AmMWSc 92*
**Gupta**, Someshwar C 1935- *AmMWSc 92*
**Gupta**, Sudhir 1944- *AmMWSc 92*
**Gupta**, Sunil Kumar 1928- *IntWW 91*
**Gupta**, Suraj Narayan 1924- *AmMWSc 92, WhoFI 92*
**Gupta**, Surendra Mohan 1947- *AmMWSc 92*
**Gupta**, Tapan Kumar 1939- *AmMWSc 92*
**Gupta**, Udaiprakash I 1952- *AmMWSc 92*
**Gupta**, Umesh C 1937- *AmMWSc 92*
**Gupta**, Vaikunth N 1951- *AmMWSc 92*
**Gupta**, Vidya Sagar 1935- *AmMWSc 92*
**Gupta**, Vijai Prakash 1938- *AmMWSc 92*
**Gupta**, Vijay Kumar 1941- *AmMWSc 92*
**Gupta**, Virendra K 1932- *AmMWSc 92*
**Gupta**, Virendra Nath 1931- *AmMWSc 92*
**Gupta**, Vishnu Das 1931- *AmMWSc 92*
**Gupta**, Yogendra M 1949- *AmMWSc 92*
**Gupte**, Sharmila Shaila 1942- *AmMWSc 92*
**Gupte**, Shridhar 1933- *IntWW 91*
**Gupton**, Creighton Lee 1933- *AmMWSc 92*
**Gupton**, Guy Winfred, Jr 1926- *AmMWSc 92*
**Gupton**, John 1946- *AmMWSc 92*
**Gupton**, Oscar Wilmot 1924- *AmMWSc 92*
**Gupton**, Paul Stephen 1934- *AmMWSc 92*
**Gur**, David 1947- *AmMWSc 92*
**Gur**, Mordechai 1930- *IntWW 91*
**Gur**, Turgut M *AmMWSc 92*
**Gura**, Carol Ann 1941- *WhoRel 92*
**Gurak**, Kathleen Theresa 1943- *WhoEnt 92*
**Gurak**, Stanley Joseph 1949- *WhoWest 92*
**Guralnick**, Robert Michael 1950- *AmMWSc 92*
**Guralnick**, Walter *AmMWSc 92*
**Guram**, Malkiat Singh 1928- *AmMWSc 92*
**Gurarie**, David Eliezer 1948- *WhoMW 92*
**Gurash**, John Thomas 1910- *WhoFI 92, WhoWest 92*
**Gurau**, Yolanda Ileana 1946- *WhoWest 92*
**Gurbacki**, Robert Harry 1955- *WhoAmL 92*
**Gurbaxani**, Shyam H. M. 1928- *WhoWest 92*
**Gurbaxani**, Shyam Hassomal 1928- *AmMWSc 92*
**Gurchenko**, Ludmila Markovna 1935- *IntWW 91*
**Gurd**, Frank Ross Newman 1924- *AmMWSc 92*
**Gurd**, Fraser Newman 1914- *AmMWSc 92*
**Gurd**, Ruth Sights 1927- *AmMWSc 92*
**Gurdak**, John Anthony 1957- *WhoAmL 92*
**Gurdjieff**, Georgei Ivanovitch 1866?-1949 *RelLAm 91*
**Gurdjieff**, Georgei Ivanovitch 1877?-1949 *FacFETw*
**Gurdon** *Who 92*
**Gurdon**, John Bertrand 1933- *IntWW 91, Who 92*
**Gureckis**, Adam C, Sr 1924- *WhoAmP 91*
**Gurel**, Demet 1939- *AmMWSc 92*

Gurel, Okan 1931- *AmMWSc 92*
Gurenko, Stanislav Ivanovich 1936- *IntWW 91, SovUnBD A*
Gurer, Emir 1960- *AmMWSc 92*
Gurevich, G. I. 1917- *IntWW 91*
Gurevitch, Mark 1916- *AmMWSc 92*
Gurfein, Peter J. 1948- *WhoAmL 92*
Gurfein, Richard Alan 1946- *WhoAmL 92*
Gurfein, Stuart James 1947- *WhoFI 92*
Gurfinkel, German R 1932- *AmMWSc 92*
Gurganus, Allan *DrAPF 91*
Gurganus, Allan 1947- *ConAu 135, IntAu&W 91*
Gurganus, Kenneth Rufus 1948- *AmMWSc 92*
Gurgiolo, Glenn Arthur 1951- *WhoEnt 92*
Gurgulino de Souza, Heitor 1928- *IntWW 91*
Gurian, Paul R. 1946- *IntMPA 92*
Gurien, Harvey 1925- *AmMWSc 92*
Guries, Raymond Paul 1943- *AmMWSc 92*
Gurik, Diane Green 1949- *WhoFI 92, WhoMW 92*
Gurin, Meg *WhoEnt 92*
Gurin, Samuel 1905- *AmMWSc 92*
Gurinsky, David H 1914- *AmMWSc 92*
Gurion, Zev 1945- *WhoFI 92*
Gurk, Herbert Morton 1930- *AmMWSc 92*
Gurklis, John A 1921- *AmMWSc 92*
Gurland, John 1917- *AmMWSc 92*
Gurland, Joseph 1923- *AmMWSc 92*
Gurley, Dorothy J. 1931- *WhoBlA 92*
Gurley, Franklin Louis 1925- *WhoFI 92*
Gurley, Helen Ruth 1939- *WhoBlA 92*
Gurley, Joseph 1751-1816? *DcNCBi 2*
Gurley, Lawrence Ray 1935- *AmMWSc 92*
Gurley, Thomas Wood 1946- *AmMWSc 92*
Gurley, William R 1939- *WhoAmP 91*
Gurley Brown, Helen 1922- *IntAu&W 91, IntWW 91*
Gurll, Nelson 1942- *AmMWSc 92*
Gurnah, Abdulrazak 1948- *LiExTwC WrDr 92*
Gurnee, Hal *LesBEnT 92*
Gurnee, Hal 1935- *WhoEnt 92*
Gurnett, Donald Alfred 1940- *AmMWSc 92*
Gurney, A R, Jr 1930- *IntAu&W 91, WrDr 92*
Gurney, Albert Ramsdell 1930- *WhoEnt 92*
Gurney, Ashley Buell 1911- *AmMWSc 92*
Gurney, Christopher Scott 1965- *WhoAmP 91*
Gurney, Clifford W 1924- *AmMWSc 92*
Gurney, Daniel Sexton 1931- *WhoEnt 92, WhoWest 92*
Gurney, Edward John 1914- *WhoAmP 91*
Gurney, Elizabeth Tucker Guice 1941- *AmMWSc 92*
Gurney, Gene 1924- *SmATA 65 [port]*
Gurney, Ivor 1890-1937 *FacFETw, RfGEnL 91*
Gurney, James Thomas 1901- *WhoAmL 92*
Gurney, Nicholas Bruce Jonathan 1945- *Who 92*
Gurney, Oliver Robert 1911- *IntWW 91, Who 92*
Gurney, Pamela Kay 1948- *WhoMW 92*
Gurney, Ramsdell 1903- *AmMWSc 92*
Gurney, Theodore, Jr 1938- *AmMWSc 92*
Gurnsey, Kathleen W 1927- *WhoAmP 91*
Guro, Elena 1877-1910 *FacFETw*
Gurol, Mirat D 1951- *AmMWSc 92*
Gurowski, Adam G. de 1805-1866 *BenetAL 91*
Gurpide, Erlio 1927- *AmMWSc 92*
Gurr, A. J. 1936- *WrDr 92*
Gurr, Andrew 1936- *IntAu&W 91*
Gurr, Henry S 1937- *AmMWSc 92*
Gurr, Michael Ian 1939- *Who 92*
Gurrera, Vincent Sam 1963- *WhoAmL 92*
Gurrieri, Georgiana 1944- *WhoAmP 91*
Gurrola, Augustine E. *WhoHisp 92*
Gurrola, Robert James 1939- *WhoHisp 92*
Gurruchaga, Francisco de 1766-1846 *HisDSpE*
Gurry, Francis Gerard 1951- *WhoFI 92*
Gurry, Robert Wilton 1913- *AmMWSc 92*
Gursahaney, Kishin J. 1932- *WhoMW 92*
Gursey, Feza 1921- *AmMWSc 92*
Gurski, Thomas Richard 1940- *AmMWSc 92*
Gursky, Herbert 1930- *AmMWSc 92*
Gursky, Martin Lewis 1927- *AmMWSc 92*
Gurst, Jerome E 1938- *AmMWSc 92*
Gurstel, Norman Keith 1939- *WhoAmL 92*
Gursten, Lawrence Earl 1942- *WhoAmL 92*
Gurt, Elisabeth 1917- *IntAu&W 91*
Gurtin, Morton Edward 1934- *AmMWSc 92*
Gurtman, Bernard Paul 1931- *WhoEnt 92*
Gurtner, Franz 1881-1941 *EncTR 91 [port]*
Gurtner, Gail H 1938- *AmMWSc 92*
Gurucharri, Vincent Paul 1945- *WhoMW 92*
Gurudata, Neville 1937- *AmMWSc 92*
Gurule, Albert *WhoAmP 91*
Gurun, Kamuran 1924- *IntWW 91*
Gurusiddaiah, Sarangamat 1937- *AmMWSc 92*
Guruswamy, Vinodhini *AmMWSc 92*
Gurvich, Aleksandr Gavrilovich 1874-1954 *SovUnBD*
Gurvis, Eric Stuart 1956- *WhoRel 92*
Gurwin, Hanley M. 1934- *WhoAmL 92*
Gurwitch, Arnold Andrew 1925- *WhoEnt 92*
Gurwith, Marc Joseph 1939- *AmMWSc 92*
Gurzenda, Thaddeus J 1922- *WhoAmP 91*
Gus, Allan S. 1961- *WhoEnt 92*
Gusau, Sarkin Malamai Ibrahim 1925- *IntWW 91*
Gusberg, Saul Bernard 1913- *AmMWSc 92*
Gusciora, Audrey Joan 1950- *WhoFI 92*
Guscott, Charles Edgar 1928- *WhoMW 92*
Gusdon, John Paul 1931- *AmMWSc 92*
Guseman, Lawrence Frank, Jr 1938- *AmMWSc 92*
Gusenius, Edwin Maurtiz 1916- *AmMWSc 92*
Gusev, Petr Andreevich 1904- *SovUnBD*
Gusev, Vladimir Kuzmich 1932- *IntWW 91*
Gusewelle, C.W. *DrAPF 91*
Gush, Jean DiRezze *WhoAmP 91*
Gushee, Allison Taylor 1962- *WhoFI 92*
Gushee, Beatrice Eleanor 1918- *AmMWSc 92*
Gushiken, Elson Clyde 1950- *WhoFI 92*
Guskey, Louis Ernest 1942- *AmMWSc 92*
Guskin, Alan E. 1937- *WhoMW 92*
Gusovsky, Fabian 1957- *AmMWSc 92*
Guss, Cyrus Omar 1911- *AmMWSc 92*
Guss, Jonathan Samuel Gailey 1959- *WhoWest 92*
Guss, Maurice Louis 1922- *AmMWSc 92*
Guss, William C 1946- *AmMWSc 92*
Gusse, Brian Raymond 1948- *WhoWest 92*
Gussin, Arnold E S 1935- *AmMWSc 92*
Gussin, Gary Nathaniel 1939- *AmMWSc 92*
Gussin, Robert Z 1938- *AmMWSc 92*
Gussow, John Andrew 1946- *WhoAmL 92*
Gussow, Mel 1933- *WhoEnt 92*
Gussow, Wm C 1908- *AmMWSc 92*
Gust, Gerald N 1946- *WhoAmP 91*
Gust, J Devens, Jr 1944- *AmMWSc 92*
Gust, Lysle Arthur 1931- *WhoWest 92*
Gust, Robert Allan 1959- *WhoAmL 92*
Gusta, Lawrence V 1939- *AmMWSc 92*
Gustaferro, William R. 1929- *WhoFI 92*
Gustafson, Albert Katsuaki 1949- *WhoAmL 92, WhoFI 92*
Gustafson, Alvar Walter 1946- *AmMWSc 92*
Gustafson, Bill 1930- *WhoAmP 91*
Gustafson, Bo Ake Sture 1953- *AmMWSc 92*
Gustafson, Bruce LeRoy 1954- *AmMWSc 92*
Gustafson, Carl Gustaf, Jr 1925- *AmMWSc 92*
Gustafson, Carol Christine 1960- *WhoMW 92*
Gustafson, Cole Richard 1955- *WhoFI 92, WhoMW 92*
Gustafson, David Harold 1935- *AmMWSc 92*
Gustafson, David Harold 1940- *AmMWSc 92*
Gustafson, Donald Arvid 1913- *AmMWSc 92*
Gustafson, Donald F. 1934- *ConAu 36NR*
Gustafson, Donald Pink 1920- *AmMWSc 92*
Gustafson, Dwight Leonard 1930- *WhoEnt 92*
Gustafson, Grant Bernard 1944- *AmMWSc 92, WhoWest 92*
Gustafson, Henry Arnold 1924- *WhoMW 92, WhoRel 92*
Gustafson, Herold Richard 1937- *AmMWSc 92*
Gustafson, James E 1946- *WhoIns 92*
Gustafson, James M. 1925- *WhoRel 92*
Gustafson, Jeff F. 1945- *WhoWest 92*
Gustafson, Jim *DrAPF 91*
Gustafson, Jim 1938- *WhoAmP 91*
Gustafson, John Alvin 1932- *WhoWest 92*
Gustafson, John C 1944- *AmMWSc 92*
Gustafson, John Perry 1944- *AmMWSc 92*
Gustafson, Karl Edwin 1935- *AmMWSc 92*
Gustafson, Kay Alma 1936- *WhoEnt 92*
Gustafson, Keith Byron 1949- *WhoFI 92*
Gustafson, Lawrence Raymond 1918- *WhoAmL 92*
Gustafson, Lewis Brigham 1933- *AmMWSc 92*
Gustafson, Mark Edward 1952- *AmMWSc 92*
Gustafson, Paula 1941- *WhoWest 92*
Gustafson, Philip Felix 1924- *AmMWSc 92*
Gustafson, Ralph 1909- *BenetAL 91, ConPo 91, IntAu&W 91, RfGEnL 91, WrDr 92*
Gustafson, Ralph Alan 1939- *AmMWSc 92*
Gustafson, Ralph Wendell, Jr. 1951- *WhoRel 92*
Gustafson, Randall Lee 1947- *WhoWest 92*
Gustafson, Richard Paul 1957- *WhoWest 92*
Gustafson, Steven Carl 1945- *AmMWSc 92*
Gustafson, Terry Lee 1953- *AmMWSc 92*
Gustafson, Tom 1949- *WhoAmP 91*
Gustafson, William Howard 1944- *AmMWSc 92*
Gustafson, Winthrop A 1928- *AmMWSc 92*
Gustafsson, Carl Ake Torsten *IntWW 91N*
Gustafsson, Hans 1923- *IntWW 91*
Gustafsson, Jan-Ake 1943- *AmMWSc 92*
Gustafsson, Lars Erik Einar 1936- *IntAu&W 91, IntWW 91*
Gustafsson, Torgny Daniel 1946- *AmMWSc 92*
Gustainis, John Edward 1932- *WhoMW 92*
Gustav III 1746-1792 *BlkwCEP*
Gustav, Bonnie Lee 1944- *AmMWSc 92*
Gustavson, Dean Leonard 1924- *WhoWest 92*
Gustavson, Erick Brandt 1936- *WhoRel 92*
Gustavson, Fred Gehrung 1935- *AmMWSc 92*
Gustavson, Mark Steven 1951- *WhoAmL 92*
Gustavson, Marvin Ronald 1927- *AmMWSc 92*
Gustavson, Reuben Gilbert 1892-1974 *AmPeW*
Gustavson, Thomas Carl 1936- *AmMWSc 92*
Gustavson, Warner Hilmer 1933- *WhoIns 92*
Guste, William Joseph 1922- *WhoAmP 91*
Guste, William Joseph, Jr. 1922- *WhoAmL 92*
Gustin, Barry Enoch 1953- *WhoWest 92*
Gustin, Vaughn Kenneth 1936- *AmMWSc 92*
Gustine, David Lawrence 1941- *AmMWSc 92*
Gustine, Franklin Johns 1931- *WhoAmP 91*
Gustison, Robert Abdon 1920- *AmMWSc 92*
Gustloff, Wilhelm 1895-1936 *EncTR 91*
Gustus, Rudolph C. 1933- *WhoBlA 92*
Gusukuma, Meafelia Mina *WhoFI 92*
Gut, Gom *ConAu 35NR*
Gut, Rainer Emil 1932- *IntWW 91*
Gutay, Laszlo J 1935- *AmMWSc 92*
Gutberlet, Louis Charles 1928- *AmMWSc 92*
Gutbezahl, Boris 1927- *AmMWSc 92*
Gutcho, Sidney J 1919- *AmMWSc 92*
Gutek, Gerald Lee 1935- *WhoMW 92*
Gutelius, Edward Warner 1922- *WhoFI 92*
Gutelius, John Robert 1929- *AmMWSc 92*
Gutenberg, Rhonda Lynn 1957- *WhoMW 92*
Guterman, Donald Raymond 1955- *WhoRel 92*
Guterman, James Hans 1952- *WhoAmL 92*
Guterman, Martin Mayr 1941- *AmMWSc 92*
Guterman, Sheryl Levine *WhoEnt 92*
Guterman, Sonia Kosow 1944- *AmMWSc 92*
Gutermuth, Scott Alan 1953- *WhoFI 92, WhoMW 92*
Guterson, Eliot Bennett 1958- *WhoAmL 92*
Gutfinger, Dan Eli 1964- *AmMWSc 92*
Gutfreund, Herbert 1921- *IntWW 91, Who 92*
Gutfreund, John H. 1929- *WhoFI 92*
Gutfreund, John Halle 1929- *Who 92*
Gutfreund, Kurt 1924- *AmMWSc 92*
Guth, Alan Harvey 1947- *AmMWSc 92, IntWW 91*
Guth, Lloyd 1929- *AmMWSc 92*
Guth, Lorraine Joyce 1966- *WhoMW 92*
Guth, Paul 1910- *IntAu&W 91, IntWW 91*
Guth, Paul C. 1922- *WhoAmL 92*
Guth, Paul Henry 1927- *AmMWSc 92*
Guth, Paul Spencer 1931- *AmMWSc 92*
Guth, S Leon 1932- *AmMWSc 92*
Guth, Sylvester Karl 1908- *AmMWSc 92*
Guth, Wilfried 1919- *IntWW 91*
Guthals, Paul Robert 1929- *AmMWSc 92*
Guthardt, Helmut 1934- *IntWW 91*
Guthe, Karl Eugen 1866-1915 *BiInAmS*
Guthe, Karl Frederick 1918- *AmMWSc 92*
Gutheil, Thomas Gordon 1942- *AmMWSc 92*
Guthman, Jack 1938- *WhoAmL 92*
Guthman, Sandra Polk 1944- *WhoMW 92*
Guthmiller, John Harold 1951- *WhoEnt 92*
Guthrie, A.B. *DrAPF 91*
Guthrie, A. B., Jr. 1901-1991 *BenetAL 91, ConAu 134, CurBio 91N, NewYTBS 91 [port], SmATA 67, TwCWW 91*
Guthrie, Alan *IntAu&W 91X, TwCSFW 91*
Guthrie, Anne 1890-1979 *ConAu 134*
Guthrie, Arlo 1947- *BenetAL 91, ConMus 6 [port], FacFETw, NewAmDM*
Guthrie, Bert 1932- *WhoAmP 91*
Guthrie, Bradley Eugene 1962- *WhoRel 92*
Guthrie, Carlton Lyons 1952- *WhoBlA 92*
Guthrie, Charles 1938- *Who 92*
Guthrie, Charles Owen 1928- *WhoFI 92*
Guthrie, Christine 1945- *AmMWSc 92*
Guthrie, Daniel Albert 1939- *AmMWSc 92*
Guthrie, Daniel Vaughan 1943- *WhoMW 92*
Guthrie, David Burrell 1920- *AmMWSc 92*
Guthrie, Donald 1933- *AmMWSc 92*
Guthrie, Donald Angus 1931- *Who 92*
Guthrie, Donald Arthur 1926- *AmMWSc 92*
Guthrie, Eleanor Young 1915- *WhoAmL 92*
Guthrie, Eugene Harding 1924- *AmMWSc 92*
Guthrie, Frank Albert 1927- *AmMWSc 92, WhoMW 92*
Guthrie, Frank Edwin 1923- *AmMWSc 92*
Guthrie, Garth Michael 1941- *Who 92*
Guthrie, George D, Jr 1962- *AmMWSc 92*
Guthrie, George Drake 1932- *AmMWSc 92*
Guthrie, George Ralph 1928- *WhoFI 92*
Guthrie, Grant Williams 1949- *WhoEnt 92*
Guthrie, Harold Madison 1939- *WhoRel 92*
Guthrie, Harvey Henry, Jr. 1924- *WhoRel 92*
Guthrie, Helen A 1925- *AmMWSc 92*
Guthrie, Hugh D 1919- *AmMWSc 92*
Guthrie, James 1859-1930 *TwCPaSc*
Guthrie, James Bryan 1957- *WhoWest 92*
Guthrie, James Joshua 1874-1952 *TwCPaSc*
Guthrie, James Leverette 1931- *AmMWSc 92*
Guthrie, James Peter 1942- *AmMWSc 92*
Guthrie, James Warren 1923- *AmMWSc 92*
Guthrie, Jerry Ralph 1949- *WhoWest 92*
Guthrie, John Daulton 1903- *AmMWSc 92*
Guthrie, John Erskine 1926- *AmMWSc 92*
Guthrie, Joseph D 1942- *AmMWSc 92*
Guthrie, Kathleen 1905- *TwCPaSc*
Guthrie, Kenneth MacGregor 1900- *Who 92*
Guthrie, Kenneth Sylvan 1871-1940 *ScFEYrs*
Guthrie, Lynn H. 1946- *WhoEnt 92*
Guthrie, Malcolm 1942- *Who 92*
Guthrie, Marc D *WhoAmP 91*
Guthrie, Mark Claude 1955- *WhoEnt 92*
Guthrie, Marshall Beck 1919- *AmMWSc 92*
Guthrie, Mary Duncum 1923- *AmMWSc 92*
Guthrie, Michael *Who 92*
Guthrie, Michael J. 1950- *WhoBlA 92*
Guthrie, Randolph Hobson 1905- *IntWW 91*
Guthrie, Richard Alan 1950- *WhoEnt 92*
Guthrie, Richard Lafayette 1941- *AmMWSc 92*
Guthrie, Robert 1916- *AmMWSc 92*
Guthrie, Robert D 1936- *AmMWSc 92*
Guthrie, Robert Isles Loftus 1937- *Who 92*
Guthrie, Robin 1902-1971 *TwCPaSc*
Guthrie, Roger Thackston 1924- *AmMWSc 92*
Guthrie, Roland L 1928- *AmMWSc 92*
Guthrie, Roy David 1934- *IntWW 91, Who 92*
Guthrie, Rufus Kent 1923- *AmMWSc 92*
Guthrie, Russell Allen 1954- *WhoEnt 92*
Guthrie, Russell Dale 1936- *AmMWSc 92*
Guthrie, Samuel 1782-1848 *BiInAmS*
Guthrie, Shirley 1928- *WhoAmP 91*
Guthrie, Tyrone 1900-1971 *FacFETw*
Guthrie, Wilbur Dean 1924- *AmMWSc 92*
Guthrie, William Anthony 1949- *WhoRel 92*
Guthrie, Woody 1912-1967 *BenetAL 91, FacFETw [port], NewAmDM, RComAH*
Gutierrez, Albert Joseph 1962- *WhoFI 92*
Gutierrez, Alberto 1913- *WhoHisp 92*
Gutierrez, Alberto F. *WhoHisp 92*

**Gutierrez**, Alfredo WhoAmP 91, WhoHisp 92
**Gutierrez**, Alfredo, Jr. WhoHisp 92
**Gutierrez**, Ana Sol 1942- WhoHisp 92
**Gutierrez**, Andres 1953- WhoHisp 92
**Gutierrez**, Anthony 1961- WhoHisp 92
**Gutierrez**, Antonio 1939- WhoHisp 92
**Gutierrez**, Arturo F. WhoHisp 92
**Gutierrez**, Carl Tommy Cruz 1941- WhoAmP 91
**Gutierrez**, Carlos WhoHisp 92
**Gutierrez**, Carlos Jose 1927- IntWW 91
**Gutierrez**, Carlos M. WhoHisp 92
**Gutierrez**, David G. WhoHisp 92
**Gutierrez**, David Gregory 1954- WhoHisp 92
**Gutierrez**, David John 1963- WhoHisp 92
**Gutierrez**, Donald 1932- ConAu 36NR
**Gutierrez**, Donald Kenneth 1932- WhoHisp 92, WhoWest 92
**Gutierrez**, Eduardo BenetAL 91
**Gutierrez**, Emilio J. 1966- WhoHisp 92
**Gutierrez**, Felix Frank 1943- WhoHisp 92
**Gutierrez**, Fernando Jose WhoHisp 92
**Gutierrez**, Franklin 1948- WhoAmP 91
**Gutierrez**, Franklin Abel 1951- WhoHisp 92
**Gutierrez**, Fred A., Jr. 1951- WhoHisp 92
**Gutierrez**, Gabriel A. WhoHisp 92
**Gutierrez**, Gary George 1949- WhoHisp 92
**Gutierrez**, George A. 1954- WhoHisp 92
**Gutierrez**, George Armando 1932- WhoHisp 92
**Gutierrez**, Gerald A. 1954- WhoHisp 92
**Gutierrez**, Gerald Andrew 1952- WhoEnt 92
**Gutierrez**, Gerard V. 1924- WhoHisp 92
**Gutierrez**, Gloria 1943- WhoHisp 92
**Gutierrez**, Guillermo 1946- AmMWSc 92, WhoHisp 92
**Gutierrez**, Gustavo 1928- DcEcMov, IntWW 91, WhoRel 92
**Gutierrez**, Hector, Jr. 1947- WhoHisp 92
**Gutierrez**, Henry Florentino 1948- WhoHisp 92
**Gutierrez**, Horacio Tomas WhoHisp 92
**Gutierrez**, Horacio Tomas 1948- WhoEnt 92
**Gutierrez**, Irma Guadalupe 1951- WhoHisp 92
**Gutierrez**, Isidore Aragon, Sr. 1935- WhoHisp 92
**Gutierrez**, Jack Allen 1951- WhoHisp 92
**Gutierrez**, Jaime P WhoAmP 91
**Gutierrez**, Jaime P. 1949- WhoHisp 92
**Gutierrez**, Jay Jose 1951- WhoHisp 92
**Gutierrez**, Jesus 1928- WhoHisp 92
**Gutierrez**, John Michael 1947- WhoRel 92
**Gutierrez**, John R. 1952- WhoHisp 92
**Gutierrez**, Jose WhoHisp 92
**Gutierrez**, Jose Angel 1944- WhoHisp 92
**Gutierrez**, Jose Ramon 1936- WhoHisp 92
**Gutierrez**, Juan J. 1942- WhoHisp 92
**Gutierrez**, Julio Cesar 1920- IntWW 91
**Gutierrez**, Leonard Villapando, Jr 1932- AmMWSc 92
**Gutierrez**, Linda 1955- WhoHisp 92
**Gutierrez**, Lisa Jean 1962- WhoHisp 92
**Gutierrez**, Lorraine Padilla 1925- WhoHisp 92
**Gutierrez**, Luis V. 1953- WhoHisp 92
**Gutierrez**, Luis V 1956- WhoAmP 91
**Gutierrez**, Maria Lourdes WhoHisp 92
**Gutierrez**, Mario R. 1917- IntWW 91
**Gutierrez**, Max, Jr. 1930- WhoAmL 92
**Gutierrez**, Orlando WhoHisp 92
**Gutierrez**, Orlando A. WhoHisp 92
**Gutierrez**, Oswald WhoHisp 92
**Gutierrez**, Pamela Jean Holbrook 1956- WhoMW 92
**Gutierrez**, Paul WhoHisp 92
**Gutierrez**, Peter Luis 1939- AmMWSc 92, WhoHisp 92
**Gutierrez**, Ralph 1931- WhoHisp 92
**Gutierrez**, Ralph Joseph 1945- WhoHisp 92
**Gutierrez**, Ramon Arturo 1951- WhoHisp 92
**Gutierrez**, Raymond WhoHisp 92
**Gutierrez**, Robert P. WhoHisp 92
**Gutierrez**, Roberto WhoHisp 92
**Gutierrez**, Roberto 1936- WhoAmP 91
**Gutierrez**, Rodolfo V. 1951- WhoHisp 92
**Gutierrez**, Rosendo 1932- WhoAmP 91
**Gutierrez**, Rosie Maria 1949- WhoHisp 92
**Gutierrez**, Rudolfo C., Jr. 1947- WhoHisp 92
**Gutierrez**, Sally Valencia 1918- WhoHisp 92
**Gutierrez**, Sidney M. WhoHisp 92
**Gutierrez**, Sonia I. 1939- WhoHisp 92
**Gutierrez**, Ted A. 1940- WhoHisp 92
**Gutierrez**, Tony, III 1962- WhoRel 92
**Gutierrez**, Yezid 1936- WhoHisp 92, WhoMW 92
**Gutierrez Alea**, Tomas 1928- IntDcF 2-2
**Gutierrez Del Alamo**, Rosa Conde 1947- IntWW 91
**Gutierrez Mellado**, Manuel 1912- IntWW 91
**Gutierrez-Miravete**, Ernesto 1954- AmMWSc 92
**Gutierrez Najera**, Manuel 1859-1895 BenetAL 91
**Gutierrez-Revuelta**, Pedro 1949- WhoHisp 92
**Gutierrez-Sloan**, Esther 1953- WhoHisp 92
**Gutierrez-Spencer**, Maria E. 1919- WhoHisp 92
**Gutierrez-Witt**, Laura 1941- WhoHisp 92
**Gutin**, Irving 1932- WhoFI 92
**Gutis**, Mark Philip 1952- WhoAmL 92
**Gutjahr**, Allan L 1938- AmMWSc 92
**Gutkin**, Terry B. 1947- WhoMW 92
**Gutkind**, Lee DrAPF 91
**Gutknecht**, Gil 1951- WhoAmP 91
**Gutknecht**, Gilbert William, Jr. 1951- WhoMW 92
**Gutknecht**, James Evan 1950- WhoFI 92
**Gutknecht**, John William 1937- AmMWSc 92
**Gutman**, Alberto 1959- WhoAmP 91, WhoHisp 92
**Gutman**, Bill ConAu 135, SmATA 67
**Gutman**, D. Milton 1933- WhoFI 92
**Gutman**, Dan 1955- ConAu 133
**Gutman**, David 1934- AmMWSc 92
**Gutman**, George Andre 1945- AmMWSc 92
**Gutman**, George Garik 1953- AmMWSc 92
**Gutman**, Harry Largman 1942- WhoAmL 92
**Gutman**, Herbert G. 1928-1985 ConAu 36NR
**Gutman**, I. Cyrus 1912- WhoFI 92
**Gutman**, Judith Mara IntAu&W 91
**Gutman**, Judith Mara 1928- WrDr 92
**Gutman**, Natalia 1942- IntWW 91
**Gutman**, Richard Edward 1944- WhoAmL 92, WhoFI 92
**Gutman**, Robert W. 1925- WrDr 92
**Gutmann**, David L. 1925- ConAu 135
**Gutmann**, Francis Louis Alphonse Myrtil 1930- IntWW 91
**Gutmann**, Helmut Rudolph 1911- AmMWSc 92
**Gutmann**, Ludwig 1933- AmMWSc 92
**Gutmann**, Max 1922- WhoFI 92
**Gutmann**, Reinhart Bruno 1916- WhoRel 92
**Gutmann**, Ronald Jay 1940- AmMWSc 92
**Gutmann**, Viktor 1921- IntWW 91
**Gutnick**, Michael P. 1947- WhoFI 92
**Gutof**, Richard Stewart 1940- WhoMW 92
**Gutoff**, Edgar B 1930- AmMWSc 92
**Gutow**, Bernard Sidney 1939- WhoWest 92
**Gutowicz**, Matthew Francis, Jr. 1945- WhoMW 92
**Gutowski**, Gerald Edward 1941- AmMWSc 92
**Gutowski**, Paul Ramsden 1947- AmMWSc 92
**Gutowsky**, Herbert S 1919- AmMWSc 92
**Gutowsky**, Herbert Sander 1919- IntWW 91, WhoMW 92
**Gutsche**, Carl David 1921- AmMWSc 92
**Gutsche**, Graham Denton 1925- AmMWSc 92
**Gutschick**, Raymond Charles 1913- AmMWSc 92
**Gutshall**, Robert C. 1934- WhoFI 92
**Gutshall**, Thomas L. 1938- WhoFI 92, WhoWest 92
**Gutstadt**, Allan Morton 1926- AmMWSc 92
**Gutstein**, Solomon 1934- WhoAmL 92, WhoFI 92, WhoMW 92
**Gutstein**, William H 1922- AmMWSc 92
**Gutt**, Arthur 1891-1949 EncTR 91 [port]
**Gutt**, Phillip A. WhoWest 92
**Guttay**, Andrew John Robert 1924- AmMWSc 92
**Guttenberg**, Gustave d1895? BiInAmS
**Guttenberg**, Steve 1958- IntMPA 92, WhoEnt 92
**Guttenplan**, Jack David 1925- AmMWSc 92
**Guttenplan**, Joseph B AmMWSc 92
**Guttentag**, Joseph Harris 1929- WhoAmL 92
**Gutter**, Robert Harold 1938- WhoEnt 92
**Gutteridge**, Don 1937- ConAu 36NR, ConPo 91, WrDr 92
**Gutteridge**, Donald George 1937- IntAu&W 91
**Gutteridge**, Joyce Ada Cooke 1906- Who 92
**Gutteridge**, Lindsay 1923- TwCSFW 91
**Gutteridge**, William Frank 1919- WrDr 92
**Gutterman**, Alan Spencer 1955- WhoAmL 92
**Gutterman**, Jordan U 1938- AmMWSc 92
**Guttersen**, Laird 1925- WhoAmP 91
**Gutting**, David Alan 1950- WhoMW 92
**Guttlein**, Jorge de Jesus 1952- WhoAmL 92
**Guttman**, Burton Samuel 1936- AmMWSc 92
**Guttman**, Charles M 1939- AmMWSc 92
**Guttman**, Egon 1927- WhoAmL 92
**Guttman**, Frank Myron 1931- AmMWSc 92
**Guttman**, Gilda Rae 1951- WhoEnt 92
**Guttman**, Helene Augusta Nathan 1930- AmMWSc 92
**Guttman**, Irving Allen 1928- WhoEnt 92
**Guttman**, Lester 1919- AmMWSc 92
**Guttman**, Mark Alan 1951- WhoEnt 92
**Guttman**, Newman 1927- AmMWSc 92
**Guttman**, Sheldon 1941- AmMWSc 92
**Guttman**, Zoltan Lou 1949- WhoFI 92
**Guttmann**, Allen 1932- IntAu&W 91, WrDr 92
**Guttmann**, Mark 1924- AmMWSc 92
**Guttmann**, Ronald David 1936- AmMWSc 92
**Gutton**, Andre Henry Georges 1904- IntWW 91
**Guttormsson**, Stefan T. WhoMW 92, WhoRel 92
**Guttuso**, Renato 1912-1987 FacFETw
**Gutz**, Debra Ann 1958- WhoRel 92
**Gutzka**, David Ellwood 1952- WhoEnt 92
**Gutzke**, William H N 1950- AmMWSc 92
**Gutzman**, Philip Charles 1938- AmMWSc 92, WhoMW 92
**Gutzwiller**, Martin Charles 1925- AmMWSc 92
**Gutzwiller**, Peter Max 1941- IntWW 91
**Guven**, Necip 1936- AmMWSc 92
**Guy**, Addeliar Dell, III 1923- WhoBlA 92
**Guy**, Alexander 1962- TwCPaSc
**Guy**, Alexander Duke 1918- WhoAmP 91
**Guy**, Alice 1873-1968 IntDcF 2-2 [port]
**Guy**, Dorothy 1915- WhoAmP 91
**Guy**, Geoffrey Colin 1921- Who 92
**Guy**, George 1918- Who 92
**Guy**, George Anderson 1914- AmMWSc 92
**Guy**, George V. 1921- WhoBlA 92
**Guy**, Jasmine WhoEnt 92
**Guy**, Jasmine 1964?- ConBlB 2 [port], ConTFT 9, WhoBlA 92
**Guy**, Jeffrey Douglas 1965- WhoEnt 92
**Guy**, John Martin 1929- WhoAmP 91
**Guy**, John Willis 1941- WhoFI 92
**Guy**, Joseph Reid 1954- WhoAmL 92
**Guy**, Leona Ruth 1913- AmMWSc 92
**Guy**, Lygia Brown 1952- WhoBlA 92
**Guy**, Michel d1990 IntWW 91N
**Guy**, Mildred Dorothy 1929- WhoBlA 92, WhoWest 92
**Guy**, Ralph B, Jr WhoAmP 91
**Guy**, Ralph B., Jr. 1929- WhoAmL 92, WhoMW 92
**Guy**, Reed Augustus 1944- AmMWSc 92
**Guy**, Richard 1932- WhoAmL 92, WhoWest 92
**Guy**, Richard P WhoAmP 91
**Guy**, Robert Lincoln 1947- Who 92
**Guy**, Roland 1928- Who 92
**Guy**, Rosa DrAPF 91
**Guy**, Rosa 1928- ConAu 34NR, IntAu&W 91, NotBlAW 92, WrDr 92
**Guy**, Rosa Cuthbert 1925- WhoBlA 92
**Guy**, William Edwin, Jr. 1938- WhoAmL 92
**Guy**, William I. 1939- WhoBlA 92
**Guy**, William L 1919- WhoAmP 91
**Guy**, William Lewis, III 1946- WhoAmL 92
**Guy**, William Thomas, Jr 1919- AmMWSc 92
**Guy Blache**, Alice 1875-1968 ReelWom [port]
**Guyard**, Marius-Francois 1921- IntWW 91
**Guyatt**, Richard Gerald Talbot 1914- Who 92
**Guyda**, Harvey John 1938- AmMWSc 92
**Guyer**, Allen, Jr. 1967- WhoRel 92
**Guyer**, Cheryl Ann 1957- AmMWSc 92
**Guyer**, Gordon Earl 1926- AmMWSc 92
**Guyer**, Kenneth Eugene, Jr 1934- AmMWSc 92
**Guyer**, Paul Quentin 1923- AmMWSc 92
**Guyer**, Reynolds Winsor 1935- WhoEnt 92
**Guyer**, Roberto E. 1923- IntWW 91
**Guyerson**, Michael J. 1957- WhoAmL 92
**Guyett**, Robert Losee 1937- WhoFI 92, WhoWest 92
**Guyker**, William C, Jr 1933- AmMWSc 92
**Guynn**, Robert William 1942- AmMWSc 92
**Guyol**, William Benson 1924- WhoMW 92
**Guyon**, John Carl 1931- AmMWSc 92, WhoMW 92
**Guyot**, Arnold Henry 1807-1884 BiInAmS
**Guys**, Constantin 1805-1892 ThHEIm
**Guyselman**, John Bruce 1924- AmMWSc 92
**Guyton**, Alicia V. 1951- WhoBlA 92
**Guyton**, Arthur Clifton 1919- AmMWSc 92
**Guyton**, Booker T. 1944- WhoBlA 92
**Guyton**, James W 1932- AmMWSc 92
**Guyton**, Patsy 1949- WhoBlA 92
**Guyton**, Robert Pool 1937- WhoFI 92
**Guyton**, Samuel Percy 1937- WhoAmL 92
**Guyton**, Tyree 1955- WhoBlA 92
**Guyton**, William F 1917- AmMWSc 92
**Guyton de Morveau**, Louis-Bernard 1737-1816 BlkwCEP
**Guz**, Abraham 1929- Who 92
**Guze**, Carol 1935- AmMWSc 92
**Guze**, Samuel Barry 1923- AmMWSc 92, IntWW 91
**Guzek**, John Owen 1942- WhoMW 92
**Guzelian**, Philip Samuel 1941- AmMWSc 92
**Guziec**, Frank Stanley, Jr 1946- AmMWSc 92
**Guziec**, Lynn Erin 1951- AmMWSc 92
**Guzik**, Ronald Edward 1960- WhoMW 92
**Guzikowski**, Robert DrAPF 91
**Guzman**, Carlos E. 1945- WhoHisp 92
**Guzman**, Claudio 1927- ConTFT 9
**Guzman**, Claudio Elias 1927- WhoEnt 92
**Guzman**, Eddie Jose 1962- WhoWest 92
**Guzman**, Enrique Gonzales 1944- WhoHisp 92
**Guzman**, Fernando 1956- WhoHisp 92
**Guzman**, Gonzalo Nuno de 148-?-1558 HisDSpE
**Guzman**, Hector 1956- WhoHisp 92
**Guzman**, Isabel 1945- WhoHisp 92
**Guzman**, Jesse M. WhoHisp 92
**Guzman**, Jose 1963- WhoHisp 92
**Guzman**, Jose David 1958- WhoHisp 92
**Guzman**, Juan Andres Correa 1966- WhoHisp 92
**Guzman**, L. Philip 1946 WhoHisp 92
**Guzman**, Leonard Kenneth 1956- WhoWest 92
**Guzman**, Martin Luis 1887-1976 BenetAL 91
**Guzman**, Oscar L. 1945- WhoHisp 92
**Guzman**, Paschal WhoHisp 92
**Guzman**, Patricio 1941- IntDcF 2-2
**Guzman**, Ramiro WhoHisp 92
**Guzman**, Ruben Joseph 1957- WhoHisp 92
**Guzman**, Suzanna 1955- WhoHisp 92
**Guzman**, Victor Lionel 1914- AmMWSc 92
**Guzman Berrios**, Andrea 1929- WhoHisp 92
**Guzman de Garcia**, Lily 1952- WhoEnt 92, WhoHisp 92
**Guzman de Quirmbach**, Ana Maria Morales 1957- WhoHisp 92
**Guzman Foresti**, Miguel Angel 1925- AmMWSc 92
**Guzman Ocasio**, Enrique 1936- WhoHisp 92
**Guzy**, Marguerita Linnes 1938- WhoWest 92
**Guzzardo**, Buster J, Sr 1923- WhoAmP 91
**Guzzman**, Freddy 1939- WhoHisp 92
**Guzzo**, Lou 1919- ConAu 135
**Gvakhariya**, G.V. d1937? SovUnBD
**Gvishiani**, Dzhermen Mikhaylovich 1928- SovUnBD
**Gvishiani**, Jermen Mikhailovich 1928- IntWW 91
**Gvoyich**, George Paul 1936- WhoAmP 91
**Gvozdic**, Djordje A. 1953- WhoRel 92
**Gwadosky**, Dan A WhoAmP 91
**Gwadz**, Robert Walter 1940- AmMWSc 92
**Gwaltney**, Anne Brooks 1957- WhoAmP 91
**Gwaltney**, Eugene C. 1918- WhoFI 92
**Gwaltney**, Jack Merrit, Jr 1930- AmMWSc 92
**Gwaltney**, Javy Rudolph, III 1961- WhoFI 92
**Gwaltney**, John L. 1928- WhoBlA 92
**Gwaltney**, John Langston 1928- WrDr 92
**Gwaltney**, Lamar Edward 1933- WhoAmP 91
**Gwaltney**, Thomas Marion 1935- WhoMW 92
**Gwandu**, Emir of 1913- Who 92
**Gwartney**, John Michael 1941- WhoAmP 91
**Gwathmey**, Charles 1938- DcTwDes, IntWW 91
**Gwathmey**, Robert Ryland, III 1917- WhoAmP 91
**Gwatkin**, Ralph Buchanan Lloyd 1929- AmMWSc 92
**Gwazdauskas**, Francis Charles 1943- AmMWSc 92
**Gwenllian** EncAmaz 91
**Gwiazda**, S J 1922- AmMWSc 92
**Gwiazda**, Wladyslaw 1935- IntWW 91
**Gwilliam**, Gilbert Franklin 1925- AmMWSc 92
**Gwilliam**, John Albert 1923- Who 92
**Gwilliam**, Kenneth Mason 1937- Who 92
**Gwilliam**, Robert John 1943- Who 92
**Gwillim**, Russell Adams 1922- WhoFI 92, WhoMW 92
**Gwilt**, George David 1927- Who 92
**Gwin**, John Michael 1949- WhoFI 92
**Gwin**, Reginald 1924- AmMWSc 92

**Gwin,** Wiliviginia Faszhianato 1954- *WhoBlA 92*
**Gwinn,** James E 1923- *AmMWSc 92*
**Gwinn,** Joel Alderson 1929- *AmMWSc 92*
**Gwinn,** John Frederick 1942- *AmMWSc 92*
**Gwinn,** John W 1942- *WhoAmP 91*
**Gwinn,** Mary Ann 1951- *WhoWest 92*
**Gwinn,** Naomi Jean 1952- *WhoFI 92*
**Gwinn,** Paula 1923- *WhoEnt 92, WhoWest 92*
**Gwinn,** Robert P. 1907- *WhoFI 92, WhoMW 92*
**Gwinn,** William Dulaney 1916- *AmMWSc 92*
**Gwinn,** William Merritt 1954- *WhoMW 92*
**Gwinup,** Grant 1929- *AmMWSc 92*
**Gwinup,** Paul D 1931- *AmMWSc 92*
**Gwirtz,** Patricia Ann *AmMWSc 92*
**Gwozdziowski,** Joanna Monica 1959- *WhoFI 92*
**Gwyn,** Allen Hatchett 1893-1969 *DcNCBi 2*
**Gwyn,** Charles William 1936- *AmMWSc 92*
**Gwyn,** J E 1927- *AmMWSc 92*
**Gwyn,** W. B. 1927- *ConAu 36NR*
**Gwyn,** William Brent *WrDr 92*
**Gwyn Jones,** David 1942- *Who 92*
**Gwynedd,** Viscount 1951- *Who 92*
**Gwynn,** Anthony Keith 1960- *WhoWest 92*
**Gwynn,** Donald Eugene 1935- *AmMWSc 92*
**Gwynn,** Edgar Percival 1923- *AmMWSc 92*
**Gwynn,** Edward Harold 1912- *Who 92*
**Gwynn,** Florine Evayonne 1944- *WhoBlA 92*
**Gwynn,** Mary *DrAPF 91*
**Gwynn,** Robert H 1922- *AmMWSc 92*
**Gwynn,** Tony *NewYTBS 91 [port]*
**Gwynn,** Tony 1960- *WhoBlA 92*
**Gwynn,** Walter 1802-1882 *DcNCBi 2*
**Gwynn-Jones,** Peter Llewellyn 1940- *Who 92*
**Gwynne,** Fred 1926- *IntMPA 92, WhoEnt 92*
**Gwynne-Evans,** Francis Loring 1914- *Who 92*
**Gwynne Jones** *Who 92*
**Gwynne-Jones,** Allan 1892-1982 *TwCPaSc*
**Gwyther,** David 1924- *Who 92*
**Gyan,** Nanik D *AmMWSc 92*
**Gyberg,** Arlin Enoch 1938- *AmMWSc 92*
**Gyer,** Maurice Sanford 1933- *WhoWest 92*
**Gyftopolous,** Elias Panayiotis 1927- *ConAu 36NR*
**Gyftopoulos,** Elias P 1927- *AmMWSc 92*
**Gygax,** Gary 1938- *IntAu&W 91*
**Gyger,** Victoria Irene 1945- *WhoWest 92*
**Gygi,** George L 1924- *WhoAmP 91*
**Gygi,** Karen Maurine 1934- *WhoEnt 92*
**Gyibug Puncog Cedain** 1930- *IntWW 91*
**Gyldenvand,** Lily M. 1917- *WrDr 92*
**Gyle,** Norma *WhoAmP 91*
**Gyles,** C L 1940- *AmMWSc 92*
**Gyles,** Nicholas Roy 1922- *AmMWSc 92*
**Gyll,** John Soren 1940- *IntWW 91*
**Gyllenborg,** Gustave Fredrik 1731-1808 *BlkwCEP*
**Gyllenhammar,** Pehr Gustaf 1935- *IntWW 91, Who 92*
**Gyllensten,** Lars Johan Wictor 1921- *IntAu&W 91*
**Gylseth,** Doris Lillian Hanson 1934- *WhoWest 92*
**Gylys,** Jonas Antanas 1928- *AmMWSc 92*
**Gyngell,** Bruce 1929- *IntWW 91*
**Gyorey,** Geza Leslie 1933- *AmMWSc 92*
**Gyorgy,** Ernst Michael 1926- *AmMWSc 92*
**Gyorgyey,** Clara 1938- *LiExTwC*
**Gyorivanyi,** Sandor 1927- *IntWW 91*
**Gyorkey,** Ferenc *AmMWSc 92*
**Gyoury,** Chris John 1938- *WhoEnt 92*
**Gypsy Rose Lee** 1914-1970 *FacFETw*
**Gyrisco,** George Gordon 1920- *AmMWSc 92*
**Gysi,** Andrew Todd 1964- *WhoRel 92*
**Gysi,** Gregor 1948- *FacFETw*
**Gysin,** Brion *DrAPF 91*
**Gysling,** Henry J 1941- *AmMWSc 92*
**Gyulassy,** Miklos 1949- *AmMWSc 92*
**Gyure,** William Louis 1939- *AmMWSc 92*

# H

**H C M W** 1835- *ScFEYrs*
**H.D.** *BenetAL 91, ConAu 35NR, LiExTwC*
**H.H.** *BenetAL 91*
**Ha Van Lau** 1918- *IntWW 91*
**Ha**, Chong Wan 1938- *WhoFI 92, WhoWest 92*
**Ha**, Tai-You 1933- *AmMWSc 92*
**Haab**, Larry David 1937- *WhoFI 92, WhoMW 92*
**Haac**, Oscar A 1918- *IntAu&W 91, WrDr 92*
**Haack**, David Wilford 1945- *WhoWest 92*
**Haack**, Dieter 1934- *IntWW 91*
**Haack**, Donald C 1923- *AmMWSc 92*
**Haack**, Peter J., Jr. 1958- *WhoFI 92*
**Haack**, Randall Scott 1957- *WhoMW 92*
**Haack**, Richard Wilson 1935- *WhoMW 92*
**Haack**, Sharon Lorraine 1944- *WhoMW 92*
**Haacke**, Gottfried 1930- *AmMWSc 92*
**Haacke**, Hans Christoph Carl 1936- *IntWW 91*
**Haag**, Donald Lawrence 1923- *WhoMW 92*
**Haag**, Fred George 1931- *AmMWSc 92*
**Haag**, Joel Edward 1962- *WhoMW 92*
**Haag**, Lowell 1963- *WhoEnt 92*
**Haag**, Max Edwin 1929- *WhoMW 92*
**Haag**, Robert Edwin 1954- *AmMWSc 92*
**Haag**, Robert Marlay 1922- *AmMWSc 92*
**Haag**, Rudolf 1922- *IntWW 91*
**Haag**, Werner O 1926- *AmMWSc 92*
**Haag**, William Otto, Jr 1942- *WhoAmP 91*
**Haagenson**, Duard Dean 1941- *WhoAmP 91*
**Haak**, Frederik Albertus 1921- *AmMWSc 92*
**Haak**, Jan Friedrich Wilhelm 1917- *IntWW 91*
**Haak**, Richard Arlen 1944- *AmMWSc 92*
**Haak**, Robert Donel 1949- *WhoRel 92*
**Haakana**, Anna-Liisa 1937- *IntAu&W 91*
**Haake**, Catharine Ann 1954- *WhoAmL 92*
**Haake**, Eugene Vincent 1921- *AmMWSc 92*
**Haake**, F Peter 1934- *WhoIns 92*
**Haake**, Katharine *DrAPF 91*
**Haake**, Paul 1932- *AmMWSc 92*
**Haakenson**, Marlan Herman 1937- *WhoAmP 91*
**Haakenson**, Philip Niel 1924- *WhoMW 92*
**Haakonsen**, Harry Olav 1941- *AmMWSc 92*
**Haaland**, Carsten Meyer 1927- *AmMWSc 92*
**Haaland**, David Michael 1946- *AmMWSc 92*
**Haaland**, Douglas 1952- *WhoWest 92*
**Haaland**, John Edward 1935- *AmMWSc 92*
**Haaland**, Ronald L 1946- *AmMWSc 92*
**Haan**, Charles Thomas 1941- *AmMWSc 92*
**Haan**, Douglas Allyn 1957- *WhoMW 92*
**Haan**, James Warren 1956- *WhoRel 92*
**Haan**, Pieter de 1927- *IntWW 91*
**Haan**, Raymond Henry 1938- *WhoEnt 92*
**Haanstra**, Bert 1916- *IntDcF 2-2*
**Haar**, Ana Maria Fernandez 1951- *WhoFI 92*
**Haar**, Barbara Imler 1942- *WhoMW 92*
**Haar**, Charlene Kay 1941- *WhoAmP 91*
**Haar**, Charles M. 1920- *WrDr 92*
**Haar**, Charles Monroe 1920- *WhoAmL 92*
**Haar**, Gil 1930- *WhoEnt 92*
**Haar**, Jack Luther 1942- *AmMWSc 92*
**Haar**, James 1929- *WrDr 92*
**Haard**, Norman F 1941- *AmMWSc 92*
**Haarder**, Bertel 1944- *IntWW 91*
**Haarsager**, Dennis Lee 1947- *WhoEnt 92*
**Haas**, Albert B 1911- *AmMWSc 92*
**Haas**, Andreas Martin 1963- *WhoRel 92*
**Haas**, Anthony Joseph 1946- *WhoFI 92*
**Haas**, Anton Jacob, Jr. 1933- *WhoMW 92*
**Haas**, B. Randy 1952- *WhoFI 92*
**Haas**, Ben 1926-1977 *TwCWW 91*
**Haas**, Betty Jane 1924- *WhoAmP 91*
**Haas**, Bradley Dean 1957- *WhoWest 92*
**Haas**, Carol Kressler 1948- *AmMWSc 92*
**Haas**, Carolyn Buhai 1926- *IntAu&W 91*
**Haas**, Charles Friedman 1913- *WhoEnt 92*
**Haas**, Charles Gustavus, Jr 1923- *AmMWSc 92*
**Haas**, Charles John 1935- *AmMWSc 92*
**Haas**, Clyde Pinkney 1933- *WhoRel 92*
**Haas**, David Henry 1955- *WhoEnt 92*
**Haas**, David Jean 1939- *AmMWSc 92*
**Haas**, Deborah Lynn 1952- *WhoFI 92*
**Haas**, Dolly 1910- *WhoEnt 92*
**Haas**, Donald Ray 1930- *WhoEnt 92*
**Haas**, Edward Lee 1935- *WhoFI 92*
**Haas**, Eleanor A. 1932- *WhoFI 92*
**Haas**, Elena d1945 *EncAmaz 91*
**Haas**, Eric Thomas 1952- *WhoAmL 92*
**Haas**, Erwin 1906- *AmMWSc 92*
**Haas**, Felix 1921- *AmMWSc 92, WhoMW 92*
**Haas**, Francis Xavier, Jr 1938- *AmMWSc 92*
**Haas**, Frank C 1931- *AmMWSc 92*
**Haas**, Frederick Carl 1936- *AmMWSc 92*
**Haas**, George Arthur 1926- *AmMWSc 92*
**Haas**, Gerhard Julius 1917- *AmMWSc 92*
**Haas**, Gustav Frederick 1927- *AmMWSc 92*
**Haas**, Harold 1917- *WhoRel 92*
**Haas**, Harold Murray 1925- *WhoEnt 92, WhoFI 92*
**Haas**, Herbert 1934- *AmMWSc 92*
**Haas**, Herbert Frank 1914- *AmMWSc 92*
**Haas**, Howard Clyde 1920- *AmMWSc 92*
**Haas**, Jacqueline Crawford 1935- *WhoAmL 92*
**Haas**, James Wayne 1944- *WhoFI 92*
**Haas**, Jere Douglas 1945- *AmMWSc 92*
**Haas**, John Arthur *AmMWSc 92*
**Haas**, John William, Jr 1930- *AmMWSc 92*
**Haas**, Joseph Alan 1950- *WhoFI 92*
**Haas**, Kenneth Brooks, Jr 1928- *AmMWSc 92*
**Haas**, Kenneth Gregg 1943- *WhoEnt 92*
**Haas**, Larry Alfred 1935- *AmMWSc 92*
**Haas**, Lukas 1976- *IntMPA 92*
**Haas**, Marilyn Ann 1941- *WhoMW 92*
**Haas**, Mark 1955- *AmMWSc 92*
**Haas**, Merrill Wilber 1910- *AmMWSc 92*
**Haas**, Michael 1938- *WhoFI 92, WhoWest 92*
**Haas**, Michael John 1964- *AmMWSc 92*
**Haas**, Paul Arnold 1929- *AmMWSc 92*
**Haas**, Paul Robert 1936- *WhoMW 92*
**Haas**, Pavel 1899-1944 *NewAmDM*
**Haas**, Peter E. 1918- *WhoWest 92*
**Haas**, Peter E. 1919- *IntWW 91*
**Haas**, Peter Herbert 1921- *AmMWSc 92*
**Haas**, Peter Jerome 1947- *WhoRel 92*
**Haas**, Richard 1929- *AmMWSc 92*
**Haas**, Richard J 1937- *WhoIns 92*
**Haas**, Richard John 1936- *IntWW 91*
**Haas**, Robert 1949- *WhoMW 92*
**Haas**, Robert Douglas 1942- *WhoFI 92, WhoWest 92*
**Haas**, Robert James 1954- *WhoMW 92*
**Haas**, Ronald Henry 1937- *WhoMW 92*
**Haas**, Rose Nardi 1948- *WhoFI 92*
**Haas**, Suzanne Newhouse 1945- *WhoMW 92*
**Haas**, Terry Evans 1937- *AmMWSc 92*
**Haas**, Thomas Arthur 1946- *WhoMW 92*
**Haas**, Thomas J 1951- *AmMWSc 92*
**Haas**, Trice Walter 1932- *AmMWSc 92*
**Haas**, Violet Bushwick 1926- *AmMWSc 92*
**Haas**, Walter A., Jr. 1916- *WhoFI 92, WhoWest 92*
**Haas**, Walter J. *WhoWest 92*
**Haas**, Ward John 1921- *AmMWSc 92*
**Haas**, Werner E L 1928- *AmMWSc 92*
**Haas**, Zygmunt 1956- *AmMWSc 92*
**Haasch**, Mary Lynn 1954- *WhoMW 92*
**Haase**, Ashley Thomson 1939- *AmMWSc 92*
**Haase**, Bruce Lee 1938- *AmMWSc 92*
**Haase**, David Glen 1948- *AmMWSc 92*
**Haase**, Donald J 1938- *AmMWSc 92*
**Haase**, Edward Francis 1937- *AmMWSc 92*
**Haase**, Francis Philip 1953- *WhoFI 92*
**Haase**, Gunter R 1924- *AmMWSc 92*
**Haase**, Jan Raymond 1941- *AmMWSc 92*
**Haase**, John Peter 1961- *WhoFI 92*
**Haase**, Marilee Ellen 1947- *WhoFI 92, WhoWest 92*
**Haase**, Oswald 1925- *AmMWSc 92*
**Haase**, Richard Henry 1924- *AmMWSc 92*
**Haase**, Susan Jo 1942- *WhoAmP 91*
**Haasen**, Peter 1927- *IntWW 91*
**Haaser**, Norman Bray 1917- *AmMWSc 92*
**Haaseth**, Ronald Carl 1952- *WhoWest 92*
**Haavelmo**, Trygve *IntWW 91*
**Haavelmo**, Trygve 1911- *WhoFI 92, WhoNob 90*
**Haavik**, Coryce Ozanne 1933- *AmMWSc 92*
**Haavikko**, Paavo Juhani 1931- *IntWW 91*
**Haba**, Alois 1893-1973 *NewAmDM*
**Haba**, James *DrAPF 91*
**Habachy**, Nimet Saba 1944- *WhoEnt 92*
**Habakkuk**, Hrothgar John 1915- *IntWW 91*
**Habakkuk**, John Hrothgar 1915- *WrDr 92*
**Habal**, Mutaz 1938- *AmMWSc 92*
**Haban**, Tom 1948- *WhoEnt 92*
**Habash**, George 1925- *IntWW 91*
**Habashi**, Fathi 1928- *AmMWSc 92*
**Habashi**, Wagdi George 1946- *AmMWSc 92*
**Habbal**, Shadia Rifai 1948- *AmMWSc 92*
**Habbart**, Ellisa Opstbaum 1959- *WhoAmL 92*
**Habbel**, Wolfgang R. 1924- *IntWW 91*
**Habberton**, John 1842-1921 *BenetAL 91*
**Habe**, Hans 1911-1977 *LiExTwC*
**Habeck**, Dale Herbert 1931- *AmMWSc 92*
**Habeck**, Daniel Ernest 1932- *WhoRel 92*
**Habeck**, Fritz 1916- *IntAu&W 91, IntWW 91*
**Habeck**, James Robert 1932- *AmMWSc 92*
**Habeck**, Odo Georg 1959- *WhoFI 92*
**Habecker**, Eugene Brubaker 1946- *WhoMW 92, WhoRel 92*
**Habeeb**, Ahmed Fathi Sayed Ahmed 1928- *AmMWSc 92*
**Habeeb**, Tony G. 1927- *IntMPA 92*
**Habegger**, Alfred 1941- *WhoMW 92*
**Habel**, Robert Earl 1918- *AmMWSc 92*
**Haben**, John William 1956- *WhoMW 92*
**Haben**, Ralph H, Jr *WhoAmP 91*
**Habeneck**, Francois-Antoine 1781-1849 *NewAmDM*
**Habener**, Joel Francis 1937- *AmMWSc 92*
**Habenschuss**, Anton 1944- *AmMWSc 92*
**Haber**, Alan Howard 1930- *AmMWSc 92*
**Haber**, Alan J. d1991 *NewYTBS 91*
**Haber**, Bernard 1934- *AmMWSc 92*
**Haber**, Edgar 1932- *AmMWSc 92*
**Haber**, Fred 1921- *AmMWSc 92*
**Haber**, Fritz 1868-1934 *WhoNob 90*
**Haber**, Howard Eli 1952- *AmMWSc 92*
**Haber**, Irving *WhoAmL 92*
**Haber**, James Edward 1943- *AmMWSc 92*
**Haber**, Jeffry Robert 1960- *WhoFI 92*
**Haber**, Jerold Allan 1951- *WhoMW 92*
**Haber**, Joyce 1932- *IntMPA 92*
**Haber**, Kenneth Scott 1955- *WhoEnt 92*
**Haber**, Les Charles 1944- *WhoEnt 92*
**Haber**, Meryl H 1934- *AmMWSc 92*
**Haber**, Ralph Norman 1932- *WhoMW 92*
**Haber**, Richard Michael 1937- *WhoAmL 92*
**Haber**, Robert Morton 1932- *AmMWSc 92*
**Haber**, Seymour 1929- *AmMWSc 92*
**Haber**, Sonja B 1951- *AmMWSc 92*
**Haber**, Stephen B 1950- *AmMWSc 92*
**Haber-Schaim**, Uri 1926- *AmMWSc 92*
**Haberer**, Jean-Yves 1932- *IntWW 91*
**Haberer**, John Henry, Jr. 1955- *WhoRel 92*
**Haberfeld**, Gwyneth *Who 92*
**Haberfeld**, Joseph Lennard 1945- *AmMWSc 92, WhoMW 92*
**Haberfield**, Paul 1933- *AmMWSc 92*
**Haberland**, Margaret Elizabeth *AmMWSc 92*
**Haberle**, Joan *WhoAmP 91*
**Haberler**, Gottfried 1900- *WrDr 92*
**Haberman**, Charles Morris 1927- *AmMWSc 92*
**Haberman**, Daniel *DrAPF 91*
**Haberman**, Daniel 1933-1991 *ConAu 135*
**Haberman**, F. William 1940- *WhoAmL 92*
**Haberman**, Herbert Frederick 1934- *AmMWSc 92*
**Haberman**, Jacob 1930- *WhoRel 92*
**Haberman**, James Michael 1954- *WhoFI 92*
**Haberman**, John Phillip 1938- *AmMWSc 92*
**Haberman**, Joshua Oscar 1919- *WhoRel 92*
**Haberman**, Phyllis 1949- *WhoFI 92*
**Haberman**, Rex Stanley 1924- *WhoAmP 91*
**Haberman**, Richard 1945- *AmMWSc 92, WrDr 92*
**Haberman**, Warren Otto 1918- *AmMWSc 92*
**Haberman**, William L 1922- *AmMWSc 92*

**Habermann**, Arie Nicolaas 1932- *AmMWSc 92*
**Habermann**, Helen M 1927- *AmMWSc 92*
**Habermann**, Max 1885-1944 *EncTR 91*
**Habermann**, Michael R. 1950- *WhoEnt 92*
**Habermann**, Norman 1933- *WhoWest 92*
**Habermann**, Ted Richard 1957- *WhoAmL 92*
**Habermas**, Jurgen 1929- *IntWW 91*
**Habersham**, Robert 1929- *WhoBlA 92*
**Haberstich**, Albert 1927- *AmMWSc 92*
**Haberstroh**, Robert D 1928- *AmMWSc 92*
**Habetler**, George Joseph 1928- *AmMWSc 92*
**Habgood**, John Stapylton *Who 92*
**Habgood**, John Stapylton 1927- *IntAu&W 91, IntWW 91, WhoRel 92, WrDr 92*
**Habib**, Daniel 1936- *AmMWSc 92*
**Habib**, Edmund J 1927- *AmMWSc 92*
**Habib**, Edwin Emile 1927- *AmMWSc 92*
**Habib**, Gerald A. 1946- *WhoFI 92*
**Habib**, Izzeddin Salim 1934- *AmMWSc 92*
**Habib**, Philip Charles 1920- *IntWW 91, WhoAmP 91*
**Habib-Deloncle**, Michel 1921- *IntWW 91*
**Habibi**, Hassan Ebrahim *IntWW 91*
**Habibi**, Kamran 1937- *AmMWSc 92*
**Habicht**, Ernst Rollemann, Jr 1938- *AmMWSc 92*
**Habicht**, F Henry, II 1953- *WhoAmP 91*
**Habicht**, Frank Henry 1920- *WhoFI 92*
**Habicht**, Gail Sorem 1940- *AmMWSc 92*
**Habicht**, Jean-Pierre 1934- *AmMWSc 92*
**Habicht**, Kevin Blair 1959- *WhoFI 92*
**Habicht**, Theodor 1898-1944 *BiDExR*
**Habicht**, Werner 1930- *IntWW 91*
**Habif**, Isaac Nace 1922- *WhoAmL 92*
**Habig**, Robert L 1940- *AmMWSc 92*
**Habig**, William Henry *AmMWSc 92*
**Habington**, William 1605-1654 *RfGEnL 91*
**Habito**, Ruben Leodegario Flores 1947- *WhoRel 92*
**Hablutzel**, Nancy Zimmerman 1940- *WhoAmL 92*
**Hablutzel**, Philip Norman 1935- *WhoAmL 92, WhoFI 92, WhoMW 92*
**Hablutzel**, Rosalee Ann 1941- *WhoWest 92*
**Haboucha**, Bert Don 1955- *WhoFI 92*
**Haboush**, William Joseph 1942- *AmMWSc 92*
**Habowsky**, Joseph Edmund Johannes 1928- *AmMWSc 92*
**Habre**, Hissene *IntWW 91*
**Habsburg-Lothringen**, Otto von 1912- *IntWW 91*
**Habsburgo**, Inmaculada de *WhoHisp 92*
**Habte-Mariam**, Yitbarek 1949- *AmMWSc 92*
**Habtemariam**, Tsegaye 1942- *AmMWSc 92*
**Habush**, Robert Lee 1936- *WhoAmL 92*
**Haby**, Rene Jean 1919- *IntWW 91*
**Habyarimana**, Juvenal 1937- *IntWW 91*
**Habymana**, Bonaventure *IntWW 91*
**Hac**, Lucile R 1909- *AmMWSc 92*
**Hacanson**, Gordon LeRoy 1915- *WhoAmP 91*
**Hacault**, Antoine *Who 92*
**Hacault**, Antoine Joseph Leon 1926- *WhoRel 92*
**Hach**, Edwin E, Jr 1934- *AmMWSc 92*
**Hach**, Vladimir 1924- *AmMWSc 92*
**Hacha**, Emil 1872-1945 *EncTR 91 [port]*
**Hachette**, Jean-Louis 1925- *IntWW 91*
**Hachey**, Thomas Eugene 1938- *WhoMW 92*
**Hachigian**, Jack 1929- *AmMWSc 92*
**Hachinski**, Vladimir C 1941- *AmMWSc 92*
**Hachten**, Richard Arthur, II 1945- *WhoMW 92*
**Hack**, Jay Lawrence 1951- *WhoAmL 92*
**Hack**, John Tilton 1913- *AmMWSc 92*
**Hack**, Linda 1949- *WhoAmL 92*
**Hack**, Miriam Frances 1955- *WhoEnt 92*
**Hack**, Shelley *IntMPA 92*
**Hackam**, Reuben 1936- *AmMWSc 92*
**Hackbarth**, Dorothy Alice 1921- *WhoFI 92, WhoWest 92*
**Hackbarth**, Holly Lynn 1965- *WhoMW 92*
**Hackbarth**, Winston 1924- *AmMWSc 92*
**Hackbirth**, David William 1935- *WhoMW 92*
**Hackel**, Donald Benjamin 1921- *AmMWSc 92*
**Hackel**, Emanuel 1925- *AmMWSc 92, WhoMW 92*
**Hackel**, Lloyd Anthony 1949- *AmMWSc 92*
**Hackel**, Mary Roeper 1933- *WhoMW 92*
**Hackelman**, Thomas William 1965- *WhoRel 92*
**Hackeman**, Calvin Leslie 1953- *WhoFI 92*
**Hackenberg**, Robert Allan 1928- *AmMWSc 92*
**Hackenbrock**, Charles Robert 1929- *AmMWSc 92*
**Hacker**, Alan Ray 1938- *Who 92*
**Hacker**, Andrew 1929- *WrDr 92*
**Hacker**, Arthur 1858-1919 *TwCPaSc*
**Hacker**, Benjamin Thurman 1935- *WhoBlA 92*
**Hacker**, Carl Sidney 1941- *AmMWSc 92*
**Hacker**, Charles R. *IntMPA 92*
**Hacker**, David S 1925- *AmMWSc 92*
**Hacker**, George Lanyon *Who 92*
**Hacker**, Herbert, Jr 1930- *AmMWSc 92*
**Hacker**, Hilary Baumann 1913- *WhoRel 92*
**Hacker**, Joe 1930- *WhoRel 92*
**Hacker**, John 1936- *TwCPaSc*
**Hacker**, Marilyn *DrAPF 91*
**Hacker**, Marilyn 1942- *ConPo 91, IntAu&W 91, WrDr 92*
**Hacker**, Miles Paul *AmMWSc 92*
**Hacker**, Pat 1947- *WhoAmP 91*
**Hacker**, Peter Wolfgang 1942- *AmMWSc 92*
**Hacker**, Rose 1906- *WrDr 92*
**Hacker**, Sabina Ann Gonzales 1957- *WhoHisp 92*
**Hackerman**, Norman 1912- *AmMWSc 92*
**Hackert**, Marvin LeRoy 1944- *AmMWSc 92*
**Hackert**, Raymond L 1927- *AmMWSc 92*
**Hackes**, Peter Quinn 1957- *WhoEnt 92*
**Hackett**, Adeline J 1923- *AmMWSc 92*
**Hackett**, Albert 1900- *BenetAL 91*
**Hackett**, Barbara Kloka 1928- *WhoAmL 92, WhoMW 92*
**Hackett**, Barry Dean 1964- *WhoBlA 92*
**Hackett**, Bobby 1915-1976 *NewAmDM*
**Hackett**, Brian 1911- *Who 92*
**Hackett**, Buddy 1924- *IntMPA 92, WhoEnt 92*
**Hackett**, Carol Ann Hedden 1939- *WhoWest 92*
**Hackett**, Cecil Arthur 1908- *Who 92, WrDr 92*
**Hackett**, Charles 1950- *WhoMW 92*
**Hackett**, Colin Edwin 1943- *AmMWSc 92*
**Hackett**, Dennis William *IntAu&W 91*
**Hackett**, Dennis William 1929- *Who 92*
**Hackett**, Douglas Shane 1964- *WhoEnt 92*
**Hackett**, Earl Alan 1940- *WhoRel 92*
**Hackett**, Earl R 1932- *AmMWSc 92*
**Hackett**, Eric Dexter 1955- *WhoEnt 92*
**Hackett**, Frances Goodrich 1891-1984 *BenetAL 91*
**Hackett**, Francis 1883-1962 *BenetAL 91*
**Hackett**, George Whitehouse 1949- *WhoFI 92*
**Hackett**, Gregory Alan 1961- *WhoRel 92*
**Hackett**, Harry Leonard 1942- *WhoFI 92*
**Hackett**, James E 1936- *AmMWSc 92*
**Hackett**, James Edwin 1943- *WhoIns 92*
**Hackett**, James H. 1800-1871 *BenetAL 91*
**Hackett**, James K. 1869-1926 *BenetAL 91*
**Hackett**, Jean Marie 1956- *WhoEnt 92*
**Hackett**, Jeffrey Eugene 1956- *WhoEnt 92*
**Hackett**, John 1910- *WrDr 92*
**Hackett**, John Charles Thomas 1939- *Who 92*
**Hackett**, John Peter 1942- *WhoWest 92*
**Hackett**, John Taylor 1941- *AmMWSc 92*
**Hackett**, John Thomas 1932- *WhoMW 92*
**Hackett**, John Wilkings 1924- *Who 92*
**Hackett**, John Winthrop 1910- *IntAu&W 91, IntWW 91, SmATA 65, Who 92*
**Hackett**, Joseph Leo 1937- *AmMWSc 92*
**Hackett**, Le Roy Huntington, Jr 1944- *AmMWSc 92*
**Hackett**, Michael Joseph 1950- *WhoEnt 92*
**Hackett**, Nora Reed 1943- *AmMWSc 92*
**Hackett**, Obra V. 1937- *WhoBlA 92*
**Hackett**, Orwoll Milton 1920- *AmMWSc 92*
**Hackett**, Peter 1933- *Who 92*
**Hackett**, Peter Andrew 1948- *AmMWSc 92*
**Hackett**, Philip *DrAPF 91*
**Hackett**, Randall Scott 1943- *WhoWest 92*
**Hackett**, Raymond Lewis 1929- *AmMWSc 92*
**Hackett**, Richard C *WhoAmP 91*
**Hackett**, Richard Nathaniel 1866-1923 *DcNCBi 3*
**Hackett**, Robert C. 1938- *WhoAmL 92*
**Hackett**, Robert John 1943- *WhoWest 92*
**Hackett**, Robert N., Jr. 1942- *WhoAmL 92*
**Hackett**, Rufus E. 1910- *WhoBlA 92*
**Hackett**, Thomas Ross 1939- *WhoFI 92*
**Hackett**, Walter Paul 1941- *WhoMW 92*
**Hackett**, Wesley P 1930- *AmMWSc 92*
**Hackett**, Wilbur L., Jr. 1949- *WhoBlA 92*
**Hackey**, George Edward, Jr. 1948- *WhoBlA 92*
**Hackford**, Taylor 1944- *IntMPA 92, WhoEnt 92*
**Hacking** *Who 92*
**Hacking**, Baron 1938- *Who 92*
**Hacking**, Anthony Stephen 1941- *Who 92*
**Hackl**, Donald John 1934- *WhoMW 92*
**Hackland**, Sarah Ann *Who 92*
**Hackleman**, David E *AmMWSc 92*
**Hackler**, Lonnie Ross 1933- *AmMWSc 92*
**Hackler**, Robert Randolph 1935- *WhoRel 92*
**Hackler**, Ruth Ann 1924- *WhoAmP 91*
**Hackley**, Charles William 1809-1861 *BiInAmS*
**Hackley**, E. Azalia 1867-1922 *NotBlAW 92 [port]*
**Hackley**, Lloyd Vincent 1940- *WhoBlA 92*
**Hackman**, Elmer Ellsworth, III 1928- *AmMWSc 92*
**Hackman**, Gene 1930- *IntMPA 92, WhoEnt 92*
**Hackman**, Gene 1931- *IntWW 91*
**Hackman**, John Clement 1947- *AmMWSc 92*
**Hackman**, Karen Lee 1956- *WhoAmL 92*
**Hackman**, Martin Robert 1942- *AmMWSc 92*
**Hackman**, Robert J 1923- *AmMWSc 92*
**Hackman**, Robert M. 1953- *WhoWest 92*
**Hackman**, Robert Mark 1953- *AmMWSc 92*
**Hackmann**, Kathy Alene 1952- *WhoAmL 92*
**Hackmann**, Steven Mark 1964- *WhoRel 92*
**Hackney**, Archdeacon of *Who 92*
**Hackney**, Alfred 1926- *TwCPaSc*
**Hackney**, Arthur 1925- *TwCPaSc, Who 92*
**Hackney**, Cameron Ray 1951- *AmMWSc 92*
**Hackney**, Clinton Porter 1952- *WhoAmP 91*
**Hackney**, Courtney Thomas 1948- *AmMWSc 92*
**Hackney**, David Daniel 1948- *AmMWSc 92*
**Hackney**, Gary Ross 1948- *WhoMW 92*
**Hackney**, Henry 1953- *WhoMW 92*
**Hackney**, Howard Smith 1910- *WhoMW 92*
**Hackney**, Jack Dean 1924- *AmMWSc 92*
**Hackney**, Joe 1945- *WhoAmP 91*
**Hackney**, John Franklin 1945- *AmMWSc 92*
**Hackney**, Lucy Durr 1937- *WhoAmL 92*
**Hackney**, Robert Ward 1942- *AmMWSc 92, WhoWest 92*
**Hackney**, Rod 1942- *ConAu 135*
**Hackney**, Roderick Peter 1942- *IntWW 91, Who 92*
**Hackney**, William Pendleton 1924- *WhoAmL 92*
**Hacks**, Peter 1928- *LiExTwC*
**Hackwell**, Glenn Alfred 1931- *AmMWSc 92*
**Hackwell**, John Arthur 1947- *AmMWSc 92*
**Hackwood**, Susan 1955- *AmMWSc 92*
**Hackworth**, Donald E. 1937- *WhoFI 92*
**Hackworth**, John Dennis 1937- *WhoFI 92*
**Hackworth**, Theodore James, Jr. 1926- *WhoWest 92*
**Hacquebard**, Peter Albertus 1918- *AmMWSc 92*
**Hadamovsky**, Eugen 1904-1944 *EncTR 91 [port]*
**Hadas**, Julia Ann 1947- *WhoMW 92*
**Hadas**, Pamela White *DrAPF 91*
**Hadas**, Rachel *DrAPF 91*
**Hadas**, Rachel 1948- *WrDr 92*
**Hadaway**, Eileen 1949- *WhoRel 92*
**Hadba**, Carlos Benjamim 1960- *WhoWest 92*
**Hadd**, Harry Earle 1918- *AmMWSc 92*
**Haddad**, Benjamin Albert 1955- *WhoAmP 91*
**Haddad**, David John 1947- *WhoEnt 92*
**Haddad**, Edmonde Alex 1931- *WhoWest 92*
**Haddad**, Ernest Mudarri 1938- *WhoAmL 92*
**Haddad**, Eugene 1925- *AmMWSc 92*
**Haddad**, Fred 1946- *WhoAmL 92*
**Haddad**, George I 1935- *AmMWSc 92*
**Haddad**, George Richard 1918- *WhoEnt 92*
**Haddad**, Inad 1953- *WhoMW 92*
**Haddad**, James Brian 1942- *WhoAmL 92*
**Haddad**, Jerrier Abdo 1922- *AmMWSc 92*
**Haddad**, John George *AmMWSc 92*
**Haddad**, Louis Charles 1948- *AmMWSc 92, WhoMW 92*
**Haddad**, Michael D. *WhoFI 92*
**Haddad**, Richard A 1934- *AmMWSc 92*
**Haddad**, Robert Mitchell 1930- *WhoRel 92*
**Haddad**, Sulaiman Ahmed el 1930- *IntWW 91*
**Haddad**, Wadi 1928?-1978 *FacFETw*
**Haddad**, Zack H 1938- *AmMWSc 92*
**Haddaway**, James David 1933- *WhoFI 92*
**Haddeland**, Peter James 1956- *WhoAmP 91*
**Haddelsey**, Vincent 1934- *TwCPaSc*
**Hadden**, Arthur Roby 1929- *WhoAmL 92*
**Hadden**, Charles Thomas 1944- *AmMWSc 92*
**Hadden**, Earl French 1946- *WhoWest 92*
**Hadden**, Eddie Raynord 1943- *WhoBlA 92*
**Hadden**, John Winthrop 1939- *AmMWSc 92*
**Hadden**, Scott Robert 1952- *WhoEnt 92*
**Hadden**, Stuart Tracey 1911- *AmMWSc 92*
**Hadden**, William Joseph 1951- *WhoAmL 92*
**Hadden-Paton**, Adrian Gerard Nigel d1991 *Who 92N*
**Haddidi**, Helmi El- 1925- *IntWW 91*
**Haddington**, Earl of 1941- *Who 92*
**Haddix**, Charles E. 1915- *WhoWest 92*
**Haddix**, Michael 1961- *WhoBlA 92*
**Haddo**, Earl of 1955- *Who 92*
**Haddock**, Aldridge 1931- *TwCPaSc*
**Haddock**, Aubura Glen 1935- *AmMWSc 92*
**Haddock**, David 1944- *WhoAmL 92, WhoMW 92*
**Haddock**, Frederick Theodore, Jr 1919- *AmMWSc 92*
**Haddock**, Gerald Hugh 1929- *AmMWSc 92*
**Haddock**, John R *AmMWSc 92*
**Haddock**, Jorge 1955- *AmMWSc 92*
**Haddock**, Lillian 1929- *AmMWSc 92*
**Haddock**, Mable J. 1948- *WhoBlA 92*
**Haddock**, Philip George 1913- *AmMWSc 92*
**Haddock**, Robert Lynn 1945- *WhoFI 92*
**Haddock**, Roy P 1928- *AmMWSc 92*
**Haddon**, Barbara Jennie 1944- *WhoRel 92*
**Haddon**, Celia 1944- *WrDr 92*
**Haddon**, Harold Alan 1940- *WhoAmL 92*
**Haddon**, Jon Roger 1945- *WhoRel 92*
**Haddon**, Phoebe Anniese 1950- *WhoAmL 92*
**Haddon**, Robert Cort 1943- *AmMWSc 92*
**Haddon**, William F 1942- *AmMWSc 92*
**Haddon-Cave**, Philip 1925- *IntWW 91, Who 92*
**Haddox**, Charles Hugh, Jr 1921- *AmMWSc 92*
**Haddy**, Francis John 1922- *AmMWSc 92*
**Hadeen**, Kenneth Doyle 1931- *AmMWSc 92*
**Hadeishi**, Tetsuo *AmMWSc 92*
**Hadelman**, Stephen Bruce 1945- *WhoFI 92*
**Hademenos**, James George 1931- *AmMWSc 92*
**Haden**, Charles Edward 1959- *WhoAmL 92*
**Haden**, Charles H., II 1937- *WhoAmL 92*
**Haden**, Charles McIntyre 1923- *WhoAmL 92*
**Haden**, Clovis Roland 1940- *AmMWSc 92*
**Haden**, Jonathan Royen 1957- *WhoAmL 92*
**Haden**, Mabel D. *WhoBlA 92*
**Haden**, Walter Linwood, Jr 1915- *AmMWSc 92*
**Haden**, William Demmery 1909- *Who 92*
**Haden-Guest** *Who 92*
**Haden-Guest**, Baron 1913- *Who 92*
**Hader**, Robert John 1919- *AmMWSc 92*
**Hader**, Rodney N 1922- *AmMWSc 92*
**Haderlie**, Eugene Clinton 1921- *AmMWSc 92*
**Haderlie**, Lloyd Conn 1946- *AmMWSc 92*
**Hadermann**, Albert Felix 1938- *AmMWSc 92*
**Hades**, Edward *ScFEYrs*
**Hadfield**, Charles 1909- *Who 92*
**Hadfield**, Debra S. 1953- *WhoWest 92*
**Hadfield**, Esme Havelock 1921- *Who 92*
**Hadfield**, Geoffrey John 1923- *Who 92*
**Hadfield**, James Irvine Havelock 1930- *Who 92*
**Hadfield**, John Charles Heywood 1907- *IntAu&W 91, Who 92*
**Hadfield**, John Collingwood 1912- *Who 92*
**Hadfield**, Michael Gale 1937- *AmMWSc 92*
**Hadfield**, Robert L *ScFEYrs*
**Hadfield**, Robert L & Farncombe, Frank E *ScFEYrs*
**Hadfield**, Ronald 1939- *Who 92*
**Hadfield**, Tim 1953- *TwCPaSc*
**Hadfield**, Tomi Senger 1954- *WhoWest 92*
**Hadges**, Thomas Richard 1948- *WhoEnt 92, WhoWest 92*
**Hadidi**, Ahmed Fahmy 1937- *AmMWSc 92*
**Hadidian**, Dikran Yenovk 1920- *WhoRel 92*
**Hadidian**, Zareh 1911- *AmMWSc 92*
**Hadinata**, Rudy Bambang 1940- *WhoFI 92*
**Hadingham**, Evan 1951- *WrDr 92*
**Hadingham**, Reginald Edward Hawke 1915- *Who 92*
**Hadipriono**, Fabian Christy 1947- *WhoMW 92*
**Hadithi**, Murtada al- *IntWW 91*
**Hadiwijaya**, Toyib 1919- *IntWW 91*

**Hadjian,** Richard Albert 1949- *AmMWSc 92*
**Hadjimanolis,** John 1950- *WhoFI 92*
**Hadjimichael,** Evangelos 1937- *AmMWSc 92*
**Hadjopoulos,** Sue 1953- *WhoEnt 92*
**Hadlee,** Richard 1951- *Who 92*
**Hadlee,** Richard John 1951- *FacFETw, IntWW 91*
**Hadler,** Herbert Isaac 1920- *AmMWSc 92*
**Hadler,** Nortin M 1942- *AmMWSc 92*
**Hadley,** Anne Harris *ScFEYrs*
**Hadley,** Arthur Clayton 1938- *WhoRel 92*
**Hadley,** Bruce Alan 1950- *AmMWSc 92*
**Hadley,** Charles F 1914- *AmMWSc 92*
**Hadley,** Dale William 1949- *WhoFI 92*
**Hadley,** David Allen 1936- *Who 92*
**Hadley,** Donald G 1936- *AmMWSc 92*
**Hadley,** Drummond *DrAPF 91*
**Hadley,** Elbert Hamilton 1913- *AmMWSc 92*
**Hadley,** Elmer Burton 1936- *AmMWSc 92*
**Hadley,** Evan C 1947- *AmMWSc 92*
**Hadley,** Fred Judson 1946- *AmMWSc 92*
**Hadley,** George 1814?-1877 *BiInAmS*
**Hadley,** George Ronald 1946- *AmMWSc 92*
**Hadley,** Gilbert Gordon 1921- *AmMWSc 92*
**Hadley,** Graham Hunter 1944- *Who 92*
**Hadley,** Henry 1871-1937 *NewAmDM*
**Hadley,** Henry Hultman 1917- *AmMWSc 92*
**Hadley,** Henry Lee 1922- *AmMWSc 92*
**Hadley,** Howard Alva, Jr. 1941- *WhoBlA 92*
**Hadley,** James Warren 1924- *AmMWSc 92*
**Hadley,** Jeffery A 1958- *AmMWSc 92*
**Hadley,** Jerry 1952- *CurBio 91 [port]*
**Hadley,** Joan *ConAu 134, WrDr 92*
**Hadley,** John Bart 1942- *WhoFI 92*
**Hadley,** John Stephen 1942- *WhoMW 92*
**Hadley,** Joseph Edmund, Jr. 1943- *WhoAmL 92*
**Hadley,** Kate Hill 1950- *AmMWSc 92*
**Hadley,** Lawrence Hamilton 1945- *WhoFI 92*
**Hadley,** Lawrence Nathan 1916- *AmMWSc 92*
**Hadley,** Lee 1934- *ConAu 36NR, SmATA 14AS [port]*
**Hadley,** Leila 1929- *IntAu&W 91, WrDr 92*
**Hadley,** Leonard Albert 1911- *Who 92*
**Hadley,** Leonard Anson 1934- *WhoFI 92*
**Hadley,** Mac Eugene 1930- *AmMWSc 92*
**Hadley,** Neil F 1941- *AmMWSc 92*
**Hadley,** Neil Frederick 1941- *WhoWest 92*
**Hadley,** Philip Anson 1962- *WhoFI 92*
**Hadley,** Richard Frederick 1924- *AmMWSc 92*
**Hadley,** Robert Earl 1937- *WhoBlA 92*
**Hadley,** Robert James 1938- *WhoAmL 92*
**Hadley,** Steven George 1942- *AmMWSc 92*
**Hadley,** Susan Jane *AmMWSc 92*
**Hadley,** William Keith 1928- *AmMWSc 92, WhoWest 92*
**Hadley,** William Melvin 1942- *AmMWSc 92, WhoWest 92*
**Hadley,** William Owen 1939- *AmMWSc 92*
**Hadley,** William R. 1958- *WhoAmL 92*
**Hadley-Garcia,** George 1954- *WhoHisp 92*
**Hadlock,** Channing M. *IntMPA 92*
**Hadlock,** Charles Robert 1947- *AmMWSc 92*
**Hadlock,** Ronald K 1934- *AmMWSc 92*
**Hadlow,** Earl Bryce 1924- *WhoAmL 92, WhoFI 92*
**Hadlow,** William John 1921- *AmMWSc 92*
**Hadnot,** Thomas Edward 1944- *WhoBlA 92*
**Hadnott,** Bennie L. 1944- *WhoBlA 92*
**Hadnott,** Grayling 1950- *WhoBlA 92*
**Hadow,** Gordon 1908- *Who 92*
**Hadow,** Harlo Herbert 1945- *AmMWSc 92*
**Hadow,** Michael 1915- *Who 92*
**Hadrian** 76-138 *EncEarC*
**Hadsel,** Fred Latimer 1916- *WhoAmP 91*
**Hadwiger,** Lee A 1933- *AmMWSc 92*
**Hadzeriga,** Pablo 1929- *AmMWSc 92*
**Hadzija,** Bozena Wesley 1928- *AmMWSc 92*
**Hadziyev,** Dimitri 1929- *AmMWSc 92*
**Haeberle,** Frederick Roland 1919- *AmMWSc 92*
**Haeberle,** Warren Keith 1956- *WhoMW 92*
**Haeberle,** William Leroy 1922- *WhoFI 92, WhoMW 92*
**Haeberli,** Willy 1925- *AmMWSc 92*
**Haebler,** Ingrid 1926- *IntWW 91*
**Haeder,** Paul Albert 1915- *AmMWSc 92*
**Haedicke,** Paul *ScFEYrs*
**Haedo,** Jorge Alberto 1945- *WhoFI 92, WhoHisp 92*
**Haedrich,** Richard L 1938- *AmMWSc 92*
**Haefeli,** Robert J 1926- *AmMWSc 92*
**Haeff,** Andrew V 1904- *AmMWSc 92*
**Haeffner,** Johna B. 1954- *WhoMW 92*
**Haefliger,** Ernst 1919- *NewAmDM*
**Haefner,** A J 1923- *AmMWSc 92*
**Haefner,** George R. 1932- *WhoMW 92*
**Haefner,** James Charles 1956- *WhoFI 92*
**Haefner,** Paul Aloysius, Jr 1935- *AmMWSc 92*
**Haefner,** Richard Charles 1943- *AmMWSc 92*
**Haeften,** Hans-Bernd von 1905-1944 *EncTR 91 [port]*
**Haeften,** Werner von 1908-1944 *EncTR 91 [port]*
**Haegel,** Nancy M 1959- *AmMWSc 92*
**Haegele,** Klaus D 1941- *AmMWSc 92*
**Haegen,** Florence Virginia 1925- *WhoAmP 91*
**Haeger,** Beverly Jean *AmMWSc 92*
**Haehnle,** Clyde G. 1922- *WhoEnt 92*
**Haekenkamp,** Kevin Hubert 1958- *WhoMW 92*
**Haelterman,** Edward Omer 1918- *AmMWSc 92*
**Haemer,** Carl D 1946- *WhoAmP 91*
**Haemmel,** William Gordon 1924- *WhoAmL 92*
**Haemmelmann,** Keith Alan 1956- *WhoRel 92*
**Haen,** Peter John 1938- *AmMWSc 92, WhoWest 92*
**Haenchen,** Hartmut 1943- *WhoEnt 92*
**Haendel,** Georg Friederich *NewAmDM*
**Haendel,** Ida 1924- *NewAmDM*
**Haendel,** Ida 1928- *IntWW 91, Who 92*
**Haendel,** Richard Stone 1939- *AmMWSc 92*
**Haendler,** Blanca Louise 1948- *AmMWSc 92*
**Haendler,** Helmut Max 1913- *AmMWSc 92*
**Haenel,** Margaret Johanna 1955- *WhoWest 92*
**Haener,** Juan 1917- *AmMWSc 92*
**Haenisch,** Siegfried 1936- *AmMWSc 92*
**Haenlein,** George Friedrich Wilhelm 1927- *AmMWSc 92*
**Haenni,** David Richard 1947- *AmMWSc 92*
**Haenni,** Edward Otto 1907- *AmMWSc 92*
**Haensel,** Vladimir 1914- *AmMWSc 92*
**Haensly,** William Edward 1927- *AmMWSc 92*
**Haenszel,** William Manning 1910- *AmMWSc 92*
**Haerdtl,** Oswald 1889-1959 *DcTwDes*
**Haerer,** Armin Friedrich 1934- *AmMWSc 92*
**Haerer,** Deane Norman 1935- *WhoFI 92*
**Haering,** Edwin Raymond 1932- *AmMWSc 92*
**Haering,** George 1930- *AmMWSc 92*
**Haering,** Harold John 1930- *WhoAmP 91*
**Haering,** Rudolph Roland 1934- *AmMWSc 92*
**Haerle,** Paul Raymond 1932- *WhoAmP 91*
**Haerle,** Wilfried 1941- *WhoRel 92*
**Haertel,** Charles Wayne 1937- *WhoMW 92, WhoRel 92*
**Haertel,** John David 1937- *AmMWSc 92*
**Haertel,** Lois Steben 1939- *AmMWSc 92*
**Haertling,** Gene Henry 1932- *AmMWSc 92*
**Haertling,** Peter 1933- *SmATA 66*
**Haesche,** Arthur B, Jr 1932- *WhoAmP 91*
**Haeseler,** Carl W 1929- *AmMWSc 92*
**Haessler,** John F. 1936- *WhoFI 92*
**Haettenschwiller,** Alphonse 1925- *WhoAmP 91*
**Haeusgen,** Helmut *IntWW 91N*
**Haeussermann,** Walter 1914- *AmMWSc 92*
**Hafele,** Joseph Carl 1933- *AmMWSc 92*
**Hafeman,** Dean Gary 1949- *AmMWSc 92*
**Hafemeister,** David Walter 1934- *AmMWSc 92*
**Hafen,** Elizabeth Susan Scott 1946- *AmMWSc 92*
**Hafen,** Eric Carl 1955- *WhoEnt 92*
**Hafen,** Laurel Jean 1960- *WhoWest 92*
**Hafer,** Barbara *WhoAmP 91*
**Hafer,** John J *WhoAmP 91*
**Hafer,** Joseph Page 1941- *WhoAmL 92*
**Hafer,** Louis James 1955- *AmMWSc 92*
**Haferkamp,** Wilhelm 1923- *IntWW 91, Who 92*
**Hafets,** Richard Jay 1951- *WhoAmL 92*
**Hafetz,** Frederick P. 1939- *WhoAmL 92*
**Hafey,** Edward Earl Joseph 1917- *WhoWest 92*
**Hafez,** Amin El 1911- *IntWW 91*
**Haff,** Richard Francis 1929- *AmMWSc 92*
**Hafferman,** William F 1908- *WhoAmP 91*
**Haffey,** Jack 1945- *WhoAmP 91*
**Haffey,** Richard Arthur 1953- *WhoAmP 91*
**Haffley,** Philip Gene 1941- *AmMWSc 92*
**Haffner,** Albert Edward 1907- *Who 92*
**Haffner,** Alden Norman *AmMWSc 92*
**Haffner,** Alfred Loveland, Jr. 1925- *WhoAmL 92*
**Haffner,** Charles Christian, III 1928- *WhoFI 92*
**Haffner,** James Wilson 1929- *AmMWSc 92*
**Haffner,** Karl Mark 1961- *WhoRel 92*
**Haffner,** Richard William 1931- *AmMWSc 92*
**Haffner,** Rudolph Eric 1920- *AmMWSc 92*
**Haffner,** Steven Roger 1953- *WhoAmL 92*
**Hafford,** Arnold Albert 1957- *WhoAmL 92*
**Hafford,** Bradford C 1916- *AmMWSc 92*
**Hafft,** David Arnold 1956- *WhoMW 92*
**Hafley,** William LeRoy 1930- *AmMWSc 92*
**Hafner,** Erich 1928- *AmMWSc 92*
**Hafner,** Gary Stuart 1943- *AmMWSc 92*
**Hafner,** Lars A 1961- *WhoAmP 91*
**Hafner,** Theodore 1901- *AmMWSc 92*
**Hafs,** Harold David 1931- *AmMWSc 92*
**Hafstad,** Lawrence Randolph 1904- *AmMWSc 92*
**Haft,** Jacob I 1937- *AmMWSc 92*
**Haft,** Robert J. 1930- *WhoAmL 92*
**Haftel,** Michael Ivan 1943- *AmMWSc 92*
**Haftl,** Franklin Dale 1934- *WhoIns 92*
**Haftmann,** Werner 1912- *IntWW 91*
**Haga,** Enoch John 1931- *WhoWest 92, WrDr 92*
**Hagan,** Alfred Chris 1932- *WhoAmL 92, WhoWest 92*
**Hagan,** Barry Joseph 1931- *WhoRel 92*
**Hagan,** Dorothy Wermuth 1942- *WhoWest 92*
**Hagan,** James Francis 1936- *WhoRel 92*
**Hagan,** James Joyce 1926- *AmMWSc 92*
**Hagan,** John Charles, III 1943- *WhoMW 92*
**Hagan,** Melvin Roy 1934- *AmMWSc 92*
**Hagan,** Molly 1961- *WhoEnt 92*
**Hagan,** Patricia *DrAPF 91*
**Hagan,** Patricia Kittredge 1935- *WhoWest 92*
**Hagan,** Paul Wandel 1930- *WhoEnt 92*
**Hagan,** Richard Francies 1949- *WhoMW 92*
**Hagan,** Robert E *WhoAmP 91*
**Hagan,** Robert F *WhoAmP 91*
**Hagan,** Robert M 1916- *AmMWSc 92*
**Hagan,** Robert William 1948- *WhoFI 92*
**Hagan,** Thomas Marion 1944- *WhoAmP 91*
**Hagan,** Wallace Woodrow 1913- *AmMWSc 92*
**Hagan,** Wesley Dillard 1924- *WhoRel 92*
**Hagan,** William Aloysius, Jr. 1932- *WhoAmL 92*
**Hagan,** William John, Jr 1956- *AmMWSc 92*
**Hagan,** William Leonard 1936- *AmMWSc 92*
**Hagan,** Willie James 1950- *WhoBlA 92*
**Hagan-Harrell,** Mary M *WhoAmP 91*
**Hagans,** James Albert 1922- *AmMWSc 92*
**Hagar,** Charles Frederick 1930- *AmMWSc 92, WhoWest 92*
**Hagar,** Judith *WrDr 92*
**Hagar,** Lowell Paul 1926- *AmMWSc 92*
**Hagar,** Sammy 1947- *WhoEnt 92*
**Hagar,** Silas Stanley 1931- *AmMWSc 92*
**Hagard,** Spencer 1942- *Who 92*
**Hagart-Alexander,** Claud *Who 92*
**Hagarty,** Lois Sherman 1948- *WhoAmP 91*
**Hagberg,** Carl Thomas 1942- *WhoFI 92*
**Hagberg,** Chris Eric 1949- *WhoAmL 92*
**Hagberg,** Elroy Carl 1919- *AmMWSc 92*
**Hagberg,** Erik Gordon 1949- *AmMWSc 92*
**Hagberg,** Viola Wilgus 1952- *WhoAmL 92*
**Hage,** Keith Donald 1926- *AmMWSc 92*
**Hage,** Stephen John 1943- *WhoWest 92*
**Hageage,** George John, Jr 1935- *AmMWSc 92*
**Hagedorn,** Albert Berner 1915- *AmMWSc 92*
**Hagedorn,** Charles 1947- *AmMWSc 92*
**Hagedorn,** Christian Ludwig 1713-1780 *BlkwCEP*
**Hagedorn,** Dan Newman 1954- *WhoWest 92*
**Hagedorn,** Diana *DrAPF 91*
**Hagedorn,** Donald James 1919- *AmMWSc 92, WhoMW 92*
**Hagedorn,** Fred Bassett 1928- *AmMWSc 92*
**Hagedorn,** George Allan 1953- *AmMWSc 92*
**Hagedorn,** Henry Howard 1940- *AmMWSc 92, WhoWest 92*
**Hagedorn,** Hermann 1882-1964 *BenetAL 91*
**Hagedorn,** Jessica Tarahata *DrAPF 91*
**Hagedorn,** Jurgen 1933- *IntWW 91*
**Hagedorn,** Karl 1889- *TwCPaSc*
**Hagedorn,** Thomas M 1943- *WhoAmP 91*
**Hagee,** Charles Gilbert 1934- *WhoFI 92*
**Hagee,** George Richard 1925- *AmMWSc 92*
**Hagegard,** Hakan 1945- *NewAmDM*
**Hagel,** John, III 1950- *WhoFI 92*
**Hagel,** Karen Ann 1951- *WhoMW 92*
**Hagel,** Robert B 1943- *AmMWSc 92*
**Hagel,** William C 1927- *AmMWSc 92*
**Hagelbarger,** David William 1920- *AmMWSc 92*
**Hagelberg,** M Paul 1933- *AmMWSc 92*
**Hagelin,** Albert Viljam 1882-1946 *BiDExR*
**Hagelin,** John Samuel 1954- *AmMWSc 92*
**Hageman,** Donald Henry 1918- *AmMWSc 92*
**Hageman,** Fred Shaw 1928- *WhoWest 92*
**Hageman,** Gilbert Robert 1947- *AmMWSc 92*
**Hageman,** Gregory Scott *AmMWSc 92*
**Hageman,** Howard Garberich 1921- *WhoRel 92*
**Hageman,** James C 1930- *WhoAmP 91*
**Hageman,** James Howard 1942- *AmMWSc 92*
**Hageman,** Louis Alfred 1932- *AmMWSc 92*
**Hageman,** Paul Henry Kivett 1956- *WhoAmL 92*
**Hageman,** Richard Harry 1917- *AmMWSc 92*
**Hageman,** William E 1939- *AmMWSc 92*
**Hagemann,** Dolores Ann 1935- *WhoFI 92, WhoMW 92*
**Hagen,** Arnulf Peder 1942- *AmMWSc 92*
**Hagen,** Arthur Ainsworth 1933- *AmMWSc 92, WhoMW 92*
**Hagen,** Bruce 1930- *WhoAmP 91*
**Hagen,** Carl I. 1944- *IntWW 91*
**Hagen,** Carl Richard 1937- *AmMWSc 92*
**Hagen,** Cecelia *DrAPF 91*
**Hagen,** Charles Alfred 1925- *AmMWSc 92*
**Hagen,** Charles William, Jr 1918- *AmMWSc 92*
**Hagen,** Craig 1965- *WhoAmP 91*
**Hagen,** Daniel Russell 1952- *AmMWSc 92*
**Hagen,** Daniel Urban 1954- *WhoEnt 92*
**Hagen,** Donald E 1943- *AmMWSc 92*
**Hagen,** Donald Frederick 1932- *AmMWSc 92*
**Hagen,** Frederick J. 1951- *WhoWest 92*
**Hagen,** Glenn Arthur 1936- *WhoRel 92*
**Hagen,** Glenn W. 1948- *WhoAmL 92, WhoFI 92*
**Hagen,** Gretchen 1948- *AmMWSc 92*
**Hagen,** Harold Kolstoe 1924- *AmMWSc 92*
**Hagen,** Hermann August 1817-1893 *BiInAmS*
**Hagen,** Ione Carolyn 1924- *WhoRel 92*
**Hagen,** Jack Ingvald 1914- *AmMWSc 92*
**Hagen,** James Alfred 1932- *WhoFI 92*
**Hagen,** John Holte 1933- *WhoRel 92*
**Hagen,** John Peter d1990 *Who 92N*
**Hagen,** John William 1940- *AmMWSc 92*
**Hagen,** Jon Boyd 1940- *AmMWSc 92*
**Hagen,** Joseph Thaddeus 1945- *WhoAmL 92*
**Hagen,** Kennen Doyle 1958- *WhoAmL 92*
**Hagen,** Kenneth George 1936- *WhoRel 92*
**Hagen,** Kenneth Sverre 1919- *AmMWSc 92*
**Hagen,** Larry William 1945- *WhoWest 92*
**Hagen,** Lawrence J 1940- *AmMWSc 92*
**Hagen,** Linda S 1944- *WhoAmP 91*
**Hagen,** Mark Eric 1963- *WhoEnt 92*
**Hagen,** Nicholas Stewart 1942- *WhoWest 92*
**Hagen,** Orville West 1915- *WhoAmP 91*
**Hagen,** Oskar 1926- *AmMWSc 92*
**Hagen,** Paul Beo 1920- *AmMWSc 92*
**Hagen,** Richard E 1937- *WhoAmP 91*
**Hagen,** Richard Eugene 1937- *AmMWSc 92*
**Hagen,** Ross Lando *WhoEnt 92*
**Hagen,** Susan James 1953- *AmMWSc 92*
**Hagen,** Thomas Bailey 1935- *WhoFI 92, WhoIns 92*
**Hagen,** Uta 1919- *WrDr 92*
**Hagen,** Uta Thyra 1919- *IntWW 91, WhoEnt 92*
**Hagen,** Victor W. Von *Who 92*
**Hagen,** Walter 1892-1969 *FacFETw*
**Hagenauer,** Fedor 1920- *AmMWSc 92*
**Hagenbach,** W P 1922- *AmMWSc 92*
**Hagenbaugh,** Midge Ann 1941- *WhoRel 92*
**Hagenbuch,** John Jacob 1951- *WhoWest 92*
**Hagenbuch,** Rodney Dale *WhoWest 92*
**Hagenbuck,** Steven Wayne 1963- *WhoFI 92*
**Hagendorf,** Stanley 1930- *WhoAmL 92*
**Hagenlocher,** Arno Kurt 1928- *AmMWSc 92*
**Hagenlocker,** Edward Emerson 1939- *AmMWSc 92*
**Hagenmaier,** Robert Doller 1939- *AmMWSc 92*

**Hagens**, William Joseph 1942- *WhoWest 92*
**Hagenstein**, William David 1915- *WhoWest 92*
**Hager**, Albert David 1817-1888 *BiInAmS*
**Hager**, Anthony Wood 1939- *AmMWSc 92*
**Hager**, Bradford Hoadley 1950- *AmMWSc 92*
**Hager**, Charles Read 1937- *WhoAmL 92*
**Hager**, Chester Bradley 1938- *AmMWSc 92*
**Hager**, Douglas Eugene 1947- *WhoFI 92*
**Hager**, Douglas Francis 1949- *AmMWSc 92*
**Hager**, E Jant 1951- *AmMWSc 92*
**Hager**, Elizabeth Sears 1944- *WhoAmP 91*
**Hager**, George Philip, Jr 1916- *AmMWSc 92*
**Hager**, Gordon L 1942- *AmMWSc 92*
**Hager**, Henry G *WhoAmP 91*
**Hager**, Hettie J. 1961- *WhoMW 92*
**Hager**, James 1953- *WhoAmP 91*
**Hager**, Jean Carol *AmMWSc 92*
**Hager**, John Francis 1958- *WhoAmL 92*
**Hager**, John P 1936- *AmMWSc 92*
**Hager**, Joseph C. 1944- *WhoBlA 92*
**Hager**, Jutta Lore 1942- *AmMWSc 92*
**Hager**, Kurt 1912- *IntWW 91*
**Hager**, Leland Dale, Sr. 1947- *WhoFI 92*
**Hager**, Leopold 1935- *WhoEnt 92*
**Hager**, Lowell Paul 1926- *AmMWSc 92*
**Hager**, Marlene Joyce 1941- *WhoAmP 91*
**Hager**, Mary Hastings 1948- *AmMWSc 92*
**Hager**, Nathaniel Ellmaker, Jr 1922- *AmMWSc 92*
**Hager**, Richard Arnold 1932- *AmMWSc 92*
**Hager**, Robert B 1937- *AmMWSc 92*
**Hager**, Roscoe Franklin 1941- *WhoBlA 92*
**Hager**, Stanley Lee 1946- *AmMWSc 92*
**Hager**, Steven Ralph 1951- *AmMWSc 92*
**Hager**, Thomas Arthur 1953- *IntAu&W 91*
**Hager**, Tom 1938- *WhoAmP 91*
**Hager**, Trent J 1962- *WhoAmP 91*
**Hager**, Wayne R 1941- *AmMWSc 92*
**Hager**, William Ward 1948- *AmMWSc 92*
**Hagerla**, Mark R 1936- *WhoAmP 91*
**Hagerman**, Ann Elizabeth *AmMWSc 92*
**Hagerman**, Donald Charles 1929- *AmMWSc 92*
**Hagerman**, Dwain Douglas 1924- *AmMWSc 92*
**Hagerman**, John David 1941- *WhoAmL 92, WhoFI 92*
**Hagerman**, Larry M 1940- *AmMWSc 92*
**Hagerman**, Robert Lester 1940- *WhoFI 92*
**Hagerson**, John David 1966- *WhoWest 92*
**Hagerson**, Lawrence John 1931- *WhoFI 92*
**Hagerty**, James C. d1981 *LesBEnT 92*
**Hagerty**, John Joseph, Jr. 1952- *WhoWest 92*
**Hagerty**, Julie 1955- *IntMPA 92*
**Hagerty**, Michael Gerard 1954- *WhoEnt 92*
**Hagerty**, Michael Raymond 1950- *WhoFI 92*
**Hagerty**, Polly Martiel 1946- *WhoWest 92*
**Hagerty**, William John Gell 1939- *Who 92*
**Hagerup**, Henrik J 1932- *AmMWSc 92*
**Hageseth**, Gaylord Terrence 1935- *AmMWSc 92*
**Hagestadt**, John Valentine 1938- *Who 92*
**Hagey**, Walter Rex 1909- *WhoFI 92*
**Hagfors**, Tor 1930- *AmMWSc 92*
**Hagg**, Barbara Ann 1931- *WhoAmP 91*
**Hagg**, Rexford A *WhoAmP 91*
**Haggar**, Paul *IntMPA 92*
**Haggar**, Reginald George 1905- *TwCPaSc*
**Haggard**, Bruce Wayne 1943- *AmMWSc 92*
**Haggard**, Forrest Deloss 1925- *WhoMW 92, WhoRel 92*
**Haggard**, H. Rider 1856-1925 *RfGEnL 91, ScFEYrs, TwCSFW 91*
**Haggard**, J D 1917- *AmMWSc 92*
**Haggard**, James Herbert 1941- *AmMWSc 92*
**Haggard**, Joan Claire 1932- *WhoMW 92, WhoRel 92*
**Haggard**, Joel Edward 1939- *WhoAmL 92*
**Haggard**, Mary Ann 1935- *WhoMW 92*
**Haggard**, Mary Ellen 1924- *AmMWSc 92*
**Haggard**, Merle 1937- *NewAmDM*
**Haggard**, Merle Ronald 1937- *WhoEnt 92*
**Haggard**, Paul *IntAu&W 91X, WrDr 92*
**Haggard**, Paul Wintzel 1933- *AmMWSc 92*
**Haggard**, Piers 1939- *IntMPA 92*
**Haggard**, Richard Allan 1936- *AmMWSc 92*
**Haggard**, Stephan Mark 1952- *WhoFI 92*
**Haggard**, William *Who 92*
**Haggard**, William 1907- *ConNov 91, WrDr 92*
**Haggard**, William Henry 1920- *AmMWSc 92*
**Haggart**, Alastair Iain MacDonald 1915- *IntWW 91, Who 92*
**Haggart**, Mary Elizabeth *Who 92*
**Haggbom**, Nils-Ake 1942- *WhoEnt 92*
**Hagge**, John Bradley 1952- *WhoRel 92*
**Hagger**, Brian 1935- *TwCPaSc*
**Haggerston Gadsden**, Peter Drury *Who 92*
**Haggerty**, Brian John 1945- *WhoIns 92*
**Haggerty**, David M 1942- *WhoIns 92*
**Haggerty**, George Edgar 1949- *WhoWest 92*
**Haggerty**, James Francis 1916- *AmMWSc 92*
**Haggerty**, James J *WhoAmP 91*
**Haggerty**, James R. 1952- *WhoAmL 92*
**Haggerty**, John Richard 1935- *WhoFI 92*
**Haggerty**, John S *AmMWSc 92*
**Haggerty**, John S 1938- *AmMWSc 92*
**Haggerty**, Lawrence George 1916- *WhoFI 92*
**Haggerty**, Patrick B 1944- *WhoAmP 91*
**Haggerty**, Robert Johns 1925- *AmMWSc 92*
**Haggerty**, William Francis 1943- *WhoAmL 92*
**Haggerty**, William Joseph, Jr 1932- *AmMWSc 92*
**Haggett**, Peter 1933- *Who 92*
**Haggett**, Stuart John 1947- *Who 92*
**Haggins**, Jon 1943- *WhoBlA 92*
**Haggins**, Shelbra Jean 1957- *WhoMW 92*
**Haggis**, Arthur George, Jr. 1924- *WhoFI 92*
**Haggis**, Geoffrey Harvey 1924- *AmMWSc 92*
**Haggis**, Paul Edward 1953- *WhoEnt 92, WhoWest 92*
**Haggitt**, Rodger C 1942- *AmMWSc 92*
**Hagglof**, Gunnar 1904- *Who 92*
**Hagglund**, Clarance Edward 1927- *WhoAmL 92, WhoMW 92*
**Hagglund**, George S. 1929- *WhoMW 92*
**Haghiri**, Faz 1930- *AmMWSc 92*
**Hagie**, Leslie E. 1943- *WhoAmL 92*
**Hagin**, Kenneth Erwin, Sr. 1917- *RelLAm 91*
**Hagin**, Linwood Alton 1955- *WhoEnt 92*
**Hagino**, David M 1947- *WhoAmP 91*
**Hagino**, Gerald T 1949- *WhoAmP 91*
**Hagino**, Gerald Takao 1949- *WhoWest 92*
**Hagino**, Nobuyoshi 1932- *AmMWSc 92*
**Hagins**, Jean Arthur 1947- *WhoBlA 92*
**Hagins**, William *AmMWSc 92*
**Hagis**, Peter, Jr 1926- *AmMWSc 92*
**Hagiwara**, Kokichi 1924- *WhoFI 92*
**Hagiwara**, Susumu 1922- *AmMWSc 92*
**Hagler** d1763 *DcNCBi 3*
**Hagler**, Bill A. *WhoEnt 92*
**Hagler**, Jack Parnell 1960- *WhoEnt 92*
**Hagler**, James Neil 1945- *AmMWSc 92*
**Hagler**, Marion O 1939- *AmMWSc 92*
**Hagler**, Marvelous Marvin 1954- *IntWW 91, WhoBlA 92*
**Hagler**, Thomas Benjamin 1913- *AmMWSc 92*
**Hagley**, Douglas Allen 1952- *WhoMW 92*
**Hagley**, Terence Richard 1953- *WhoAmL 92*
**Hagloch**, Jennifer Kay 1954- *WhoWest 92*
**Haglund**, Bruce Thadd 1946- *WhoWest 92*
**Haglund**, John Richard 1931- *AmMWSc 92*
**Haglund**, Richard Forsberg, Jr 1942- *AmMWSc 92*
**Haglund**, William Arthur 1930- *AmMWSc 92*
**Hagman**, Donald Eric 1945- *AmMWSc 92*
**Hagman**, Larry *LesBEnT 92*
**Hagman**, Larry 1931- *IntMPA 92, WhoEnt 92*
**Hagmann**, Siegbert Johann 1948- *AmMWSc 92*
**Hagnauer**, Gary Lee 1943- *AmMWSc 92*
**Hagner**, Donald Alfred 1936- *WhoRel 92*
**Hagner**, Elmer F, Jr *WhoAmP 91*
**Hagni**, Richard D 1931- *AmMWSc 92*
**Hagni**, Richard Davis 1931- *WhoMW 92*
**Hagon**, Priscilla *IntAu&W 91X, WrDr 92*
**Hagood**, Margaret Jarman 1907-1963 *WomSoc*
**Hagood**, Mark William 1956- *WhoAmP 91*
**Hagoort**, Thomas Henry 1932- *WhoAmL 92*
**Hagopian**, Charles Lemuel 1940- *AmMWSc 92*
**Hagopian**, Miasnig 1927- *AmMWSc 92*
**Hagopian**, Michael Andrew 1951- *WhoFI 92*
**Hagopian**, Vasken 1937- *AmMWSc 92*
**Hagos**, Tecola Worq 1947- *WhoAmL 92*
**Hagrup**, Knut 1913- *IntWW 91, WhoFI 92*
**Hagsten**, Ib 1943- *WhoMW 92*
**Hagstrom**, Gerow Richard 1931- *AmMWSc 92*
**Hagstrom**, Jack Walter Carl 1933- *AmMWSc 92*
**Hagstrom**, Jane Stewart 1956- *WhoRel 92*
**Hagstrom**, Jerry 1947- *ConAu 34NR*
**Hagstrom**, Ray Theodore 1947- *AmMWSc 92*
**Hagstrom**, Stanley Alan 1930- *AmMWSc 92*
**Hagstrom**, Stig Bernt 1932- *AmMWSc 92*
**Hagstrum**, Homer Dupre 1915- *AmMWSc 92*
**Hague**, Alan Donald 1951- *WhoEnt 92*
**Hague**, Albert 1920- *WhoEnt 92*
**Hague**, Arnold 1840-1917 *BiInAmS*
**Hague**, David Michael 1963- *WhoRel 92*
**Hague**, Douglas 1926- *Who 92, WrDr 92*
**Hague**, Gregg Ross 1957- *WhoAmL 92*
**Hague**, James Duncan 1836-1908 *BiInAmS*
**Hague**, Michael R. 1948- *ConAu 36NR*
**Hague**, Paul Christian 1943- *WhoAmL 92*
**Hague**, Richard Norris 1934- *WhoMW 92*
**Hague**, William 1952- *WhoRel 92*
**Hague**, William Jefferson 1961- *Who 92*
**Hagura**, Nobuya 1919- *IntWW 91*
**Hagy**, David Lee 1953- *WhoEnt 92*
**Hagy**, George Washington 1923- *AmMWSc 92*
**Hahn**, Alexander J 1943- *AmMWSc 92*
**Hahn**, Allen W 1933- *AmMWSc 92*
**Hahn**, Anthony Wayne 1942- *WhoMW 92*
**Hahn**, Bevra H 1939- *AmMWSc 92*
**Hahn**, C Archie, Jr 1914- *AmMWSc 92*
**Hahn**, Carl Horst 1926- *IntWW 91, Who 92, WhoFI 92*
**Hahn**, Carol Kay 1940- *WhoMW 92*
**Hahn**, Celia Allison 1931- *WhoRel 92*
**Hahn**, Celia Ferner 1942- *WhoEnt 92*
**Hahn**, Charles Glenn, Jr. 1949- *WhoRel 92*
**Hahn**, Daniel Brase 1949- *WhoRel 92*
**Hahn**, David Bennett 1945- *WhoMW 92*
**Hahn**, DoWon 1931- *AmMWSc 92*
**Hahn**, Elliot F 1944- *AmMWSc 92*
**Hahn**, Elliott Julius 1949- *WhoAmL 92, WhoWest 92*
**Hahn**, Emily 1905- *IntAu&W 91, WrDr 92*
**Hahn**, Eric Walter 1932- *AmMWSc 92*
**Hahn**, Erwin Louis 1921- *AmMWSc 92, IntWW 91, WhoWest 92*
**Hahn**, Eugene H 1929- *WhoAmP 91*
**Hahn**, Fletcher Frederick 1939- *AmMWSc 92, WhoWest 92*
**Hahn**, Frank 1925- *IntWW 91*
**Hahn**, Frank H. 1925- *WrDr 92*
**Hahn**, Frank Horace 1925- *Who 92*
**Hahn**, Fred Ernst 1916- *AmMWSc 92*
**Hahn**, Galen Eugene 1947- *WhoRel 92*
**Hahn**, Gary Scott 1952- *WhoWest 92*
**Hahn**, George 1926- *AmMWSc 92*
**Hahn**, George Henkin 1949- *WhoMW 92*
**Hahn**, George LeRoy 1934- *AmMWSc 92*
**Hahn**, Gerald John 1930- *AmMWSc 92*
**Hahn**, Gilbert, Jr. 1921- *WhoAmL 92*
**Hahn**, Gregory Alan 1958- *WhoEnt 92*
**Hahn**, Gregory F 1949- *WhoAmP 91*
**Hahn**, Gregory James 1961- *WhoFI 92*
**Hahn**, H. Michael 1930- *WhoMW 92*
**Hahn**, Hannelore *DrAPF 91*
**Hahn**, Harold Thomas 1924- *AmMWSc 92, WhoWest 92*
**Hahn**, Heidi Herrera *WhoHisp 92*
**Hahn**, Heinz W. 1929- *IntWW 91*
**Hahn**, Helene *IntMPA 92*
**Hahn**, Helene B. *WhoEnt 92, WhoWest 92*
**Hahn**, Henry 1928- *AmMWSc 92*
**Hahn**, Hong Thomas 1942- *AmMWSc 92*
**Hahn**, Howard Clayton 1930- *WhoRel 92*
**Hahn**, Hwa Suk 1924- *AmMWSc 92*
**Hahn**, Jim 1935- *WhoAmP 91*
**Hahn**, Joan Christensen 1933- *WhoWest 92*
**Hahn**, John W 1940- *WhoIns 92*
**Hahn**, Julie Maya 1943- *WhoWest 92*
**Hahn**, Kimiko *DrAPF 91*
**Hahn**, Kyong T 1929- *AmMWSc 92*
**Hahn**, Kyoung-Dong 1954- *AmMWSc 92*
**Hahn**, Larry Alan 1940- *AmMWSc 92*
**Hahn**, Leo Bernard 1934- *WhoRel 92*
**Hahn**, Liang-Shin *AmMWSc 92*
**Hahn**, Linda Robb 1950- *WhoMW 92*
**Hahn**, Marjorie G 1948- *AmMWSc 92*
**Hahn**, Mark Stephen 1953- *WhoWest 92*
**Hahn**, Martin Earl 1943- *AmMWSc 92*
**Hahn**, Mary Downing 1937- *WrDr 92*
**Hahn**, Michael Jeffrey 1950- *WhoMW 92*
**Hahn**, Monte Andrea 1963- *WhoMW 92*
**Hahn**, Nicholas George, Jr. 1960- *WhoFI 92*
**Hahn**, Oscar 1938- *ConSpAP*
**Hahn**, Ottfried J 1935- *AmMWSc 92*
**Hahn**, Otto 1879-1968 *EncTR 91 [port], FacFETw, WhoNob 90*
**Hahn**, Peter 1923- *AmMWSc 92*
**Hahn**, Peter Mathias 1937- *AmMWSc 92*
**Hahn**, Reynaldo 1874-1947 *NewAmDM*
**Hahn**, Richard Allen 1938- *AmMWSc 92*
**Hahn**, Richard Balser 1913- *AmMWSc 92*
**Hahn**, Richard David 1912- *AmMWSc 92*
**Hahn**, Richard Ferdinand 1909- *WhoAmL 92*
**Hahn**, Richard Leonard 1934- *AmMWSc 92*
**Hahn**, Robert *DrAPF 91*
**Hahn**, Robert Gregory 1948- *WhoWest 92*
**Hahn**, Robert S 1916- *AmMWSc 92*
**Hahn**, Roger C 1932- *AmMWSc 92*
**Hahn**, S.C. *DrAPF 91*
**Hahn**, Samuel Wilfred 1921- *AmMWSc 92*
**Hahn**, Scott Walker 1957- *WhoRel 92*
**Hahn**, Steven William 1947- *WhoFI 92*
**Hahn**, Theodore John *AmMWSc 92*
**Hahn**, Thomas Andersen 1945- *WhoWest 92*
**Hahn**, Thomas Marshall, Jr. 1926- *IntWW 91*
**Hahn**, Timothy Duane 1962- *WhoMW 92*
**Hahn**, W C, Jr 1930- *AmMWSc 92*
**Hahn**, Walter I 1923- *AmMWSc 92*
**Hahn**, Walter Leopold 1926- *AmMWSc 92*
**Hahn**, William Eugene 1937- *AmMWSc 92, WhoWest 92*
**Hahn**, William Francis 1958- *WhoFI 92*
**Hahn**, Yu Hak 1934- *AmMWSc 92*
**Hahn**, Yukap 1932- *AmMWSc 92*
**Hahne**, C. E. 1940- *WhoFI 92*
**Hahne**, Henry V 1924- *AmMWSc 92*
**Hahne**, Rolf Mathieu August 1936- *AmMWSc 92*
**Hahnel**, Alwin 1912- *AmMWSc 92*
**Hahnert**, William Franklin 1901- *AmMWSc 92*
**Hahon**, Nicholas 1924- *AmMWSc 92*
**Hahs**, Sharon K 1947- *AmMWSc 92*
**Hai**, Chi-Ming 1955- *AmMWSc 92*
**Hai**, Francis 1937- *AmMWSc 92*
**Hai-Jew**, Shalin *DrAPF 91*
**Haiblum**, Isidore *DrAPF 91*
**Haiblum**, Isidore 1935- *IntAu&W 91, TwCSFW 91, WrDr 92*
**Haid**, Charles 1943- *IntMPA 92*
**Haid**, Charles M. 1943- *WhoEnt 92*
**Haid**, D A 1936- *AmMWSc 92*
**Haid**, Leo 1849-1924 *DcNCBi 3*
**Haidak**, Gerald Lewis 1917- *AmMWSc 92*
**Haidalla**, Mohamed Khouna Ould *IntWW 91*
**Haider**, Syed Farman 1946- *WhoFI 92*
**Haidet**, George Charles 1951- *WhoMW 92*
**Haidler**, William B 1926- *AmMWSc 92*
**Haig** *Who 92*
**Haig**, Earl 1918- *Who 92*
**Haig**, Al 1924-1982 *NewAmDM*
**Haig**, Alexander 1924- *FacFETw*
**Haig**, Alexander M, Jr 1924- *WhoAmP 91*
**Haig**, Alexander Meigs, Jr. 1924- *AmPolLe, IntWW 91, Who 92*
**Haig**, David M. 1951- *WhoWest 92*
**Haig**, Douglas 1861-1928 *FacFETw [port]*
**Haig**, Frank Rawle 1928- *AmMWSc 92*
**Haig**, George Alexander Eugene Douglas 1918- *TwCPaSc*
**Haig**, Ian Maurice 1936- *Who 92*
**Haig**, Janet 1925- *AmMWSc 92*
**Haig**, Mary Alison G. *Who 92*
**Haig**, Pierre Vahe 1917- *AmMWSc 92*
**Haig**, Robert Leighton 1947- *WhoAmL 92, WhoFI 92*
**Haig**, Theodor 1913- *WhoEnt 92*
**Haig**, Thomas O 1921- *AmMWSc 92*
**Haig-Brown**, Roderick 1908- *BenetAL 91*
**Haig-Brown**, Roderick 1908-1976 *TwCWW 91*
**Haigh**, Brian Roger 1931- *Who 92*
**Haigh**, Christopher 1944- *IntAu&W 91*
**Haigh**, Clement Percy 1920- *Who 92*
**Haigh**, Clifford 1906- *Who 92*
**Haigh**, Edward 1935- *Who 92*
**Haigh**, Jack 1910- *IntAu&W 91*
**Haigh**, Maurice Francis 1929- *Who 92*
**Haigh**, Paul 1949- *DcTwDes*
**Haigh**, William E 1937- *AmMWSc 92, WhoMW 92*
**Haigh**, William Francis 1937- *WhoEnt 92*
**Haight**, Bruce Marvin 1946- *WhoMW 92*
**Haight**, Charles Sherman, Jr. 1930- *WhoAmL 92*
**Haight**, Edward Allen 1910- *WhoAmL 92*
**Haight**, Frank Avery 1919- *AmMWSc 92*
**Haight**, Gilbert Pierce, Jr 1922- *AmMWSc 92*
**Haight**, James Theron 1924- *WhoAmL 92, WhoFI 92*
**Haight**, John Richard 1938- *AmMWSc 92*
**Haight**, Robert Cameron 1941- *AmMWSc 92*
**Haight**, Roger Dean 1936- *AmMWSc 92*
**Haight**, Scott Kerr 1961- *WhoAmL 92*
**Haight**, Thomas H 1936- *AmMWSc 92*
**Haight**, Timothy Robinson 1945- *WhoWest 92*
**Haight**, Warren Gazzam 1929- *WhoFI 92*
**Haighton**, Coenrad Alfred Augustus 1896-1943 *BiDExR*
**Haigler**, Boyd Frazier, Jr. 1945- *WhoFI 92*
**Haigler**, Henry James, Sr 1941- *AmMWSc 92*
**Haigler Ramirez**, Esteban Jose 1953- *WhoHisp 92*
**Haik**, George Michel 1910- *AmMWSc 92*
**Haik**, Richard T., Sr. 1950- *WhoAmL 92*
**Haik**, Theodore M, Jr 1945- *WhoAmP 91*
**Haikel**, Ahmed Abd al Maksoud 1922- *IntWW 91*
**Haile Selassie** 1892-1975 *FacFETw [port]*

**Haile,** Annette L. 1952- *WhoBlA 92*
**Haile,** Clarence Lee 1948- *AmMWSc 92*
**Haile,** James Mitchell 1946- *AmMWSc 92*
**Haile,** John Sanders 1956- *WhoAmL 92*
**Haile,** Lawrence Barclay 1938- *WhoAmL 92, WhoWest 92*
**Haile,** Marcus Alfred 1930- *WhoWest 92*
**Haile,** Richard H. 1910- *WhoBlA 92*
**Haile,** Sam 1909-1946 *TwCPaSc*
**Hailes,** Edward A. *WhoBlA 92*
**Hailes,** Edward Alexander 1925- *WhoRel 92*
**Hailey,** Arthur 1920- *BenetAL 91, ConAu 36NR, ConNov 91, IntAu&W 91, IntWW 91, Who 92, WhoEnt 92, WrDr 92*
**Hailey,** Elizabeth Forsythe 1938- *IntAu&W 91, WhoEnt 92, WrDr 92*
**Hailey,** Evelyn Momsen 1921- *WhoAmP 91*
**Hailey,** Frank William 1941- *WhoWest 92*
**Hailey,** James Douglas 1952- *WhoAmL 92*
**Hailey,** Oliver 1932- *IntAu&W 91, WhoEnt 92, WrDr 92*
**Hailey,** Priscilla W. 1947- *WhoBlA 92*
**Hailey,** Robert Carter 1926- *WhoEnt 92*
**Hailman,** Jack Parker 1936- *AmMWSc 92*
**Hailpern,** Raoul 1916- *AmMWSc 92*
**Hailsham,** Lord, of St. Marylebone *WrDr 92*
**Hailsham,** Viscount *Who 92*
**Hailsham of Saint Marylebone,** Baron 1907- *Who 92*
**Hailsham Of St. Marylebone,** Baron 1907- *IntWW 91*
**Hailsham of St Marylebone,** Quintin M 1907- *IntAu&W 91*
**Hailstone,** Bernard 1910-1987 *TwCPaSc*
**Haim,** Albert 1931- *AmMWSc 92*
**Haim,** Corey 1972- *IntMPA 92*
**Haiman,** Robert James 1936- *ConAu 133*
**Haimbaugh,** George Dow, Jr. 1916- *WhoAmL 92*
**Haime,** Nohra 1952- *WhoHisp 92*
**Haimendorf,** Christoph von F. *Who 92*
**Haimes,** Florence Catherine 1917- *AmMWSc 92*
**Haimes,** Howard B 1950- *AmMWSc 92*
**Haimes,** Terry Micheal 1946- *WhoAmP 91*
**Haimes,** Yacov Y 1936- *AmMWSc 92*
**Haimm,** Neil Keith 1955- *WhoAmL 92*
**Haimo,** Deborah Tepper 1921- *AmMWSc 92*
**Haimo,** Leah T *AmMWSc 92*
**Haimovich,** Beatrice 1958- *AmMWSc 92*
**Haimovitz,** Jules *LesBEnT 92 [port]*
**Haimovitz,** Jules 1950- *WhoEnt 92, WhoWest 92*
**Haimovitz,** Jules 1951- *IntMPA 92*
**Haims,** Bruce David 1940- *WhoAmL 92*
**Haimsohn,** Jana *DrAPF 91*
**Hain,** Fred Paul 1944- *AmMWSc 92*
**Hain,** Frederick Michael 1935- *WhoRel 92*
**Hain,** Peter Gerald 1950- *Who 92*
**Haindl,** Martin Wilhelm 1940- *AmMWSc 92*
**Haine van Ghizeghem** *NewAmDM*
**Haine,** James Moran 1943- *WhoMW 92*
**Haines,** Barry Gordon 1961- *WhoEnt 92*
**Haines,** Bernard A 1926- *AmMWSc 92*
**Haines,** C William 1928- *WhoAmP 91*
**Haines,** Charles Edward 1925- *WhoBlA 92*
**Haines,** Charles Wills 1939- *AmMWSc 92*
**Haines,** Christopher John Minton 1939- *Who 92*
**Haines,** Daniel Webster 1937- *AmMWSc 92*
**Haines,** David Clark 1942- *AmMWSc 92*
**Haines,** Donal Hamilton 1886-1951 *ScFEYrs*
**Haines,** Donald Arthur *AmMWSc 92*
**Haines,** Duane Edwin 1943- *AmMWSc 92*
**Haines,** Gail Kay 1943- *IntAu&W 91, WrDr 92*
**Haines,** Harry Caum 1914- *AmMWSc 92*
**Haines,** Helen Drake 1943- *WhoFI 92*
**Haines,** Helen E. 1872-1961 *BenetAL 91*
**Haines,** Howard Bodley 1935- *AmMWSc 92*
**Haines,** Jacque McCoy 1932- *WhoAmL 92*
**Haines,** James Richard 1938- *WhoMW 92*
**Haines,** Joan Renshaw 1934- *WhoAmP 91*
**Haines,** John *DrAPF 91, TwCWW 91*
**Haines,** John 1924- *ConAu 34NR, ConPo 91, WrDr 92*
**Haines,** John Haldor 1938- *AmMWSc 92*
**Haines,** John Meade 1924- *IntAu&W 91*
**Haines,** Joseph E 1923- *WhoAmP 91*
**Haines,** Joseph Thomas William 1928- *IntAu&W 91, Who 92*
**Haines,** Kenneth A 1907- *AmMWSc 92*
**Haines,** Larry E *WhoAmP 91*
**Haines,** Lee Mark, Jr. 1927- *WhoRel 92*
**Haines,** Michael Robert 1944- *WhoFI 92*
**Haines,** Pamela Mary 1929- *IntAu&W 91, WrDr 92*
**Haines,** Patrick A 1949- *AmMWSc 92*
**Haines,** Paul Lowell 1953- *WhoRel 92*
**Haines,** Perry Vansant 1944- *WhoFI 92*
**Haines,** Richard Foster 1937- *AmMWSc 92*
**Haines,** Richard Francis 1923- *AmMWSc 92*
**Haines,** Robert Gordon 1929- *AmMWSc 92*
**Haines,** Robert Ivor 1953- *AmMWSc 92*
**Haines,** Robert Taggart 1920- *WhoAmL 92*
**Haines,** Roland Arthur 1939- *AmMWSc 92*
**Haines,** Sigrid Cheryl 1959- *WhoAmL 92*
**Haines,** Stephen John 1949- *WhoMW 92*
**Haines,** Terry Alan 1943- *AmMWSc 92*
**Haines,** Thomas David, Jr. 1956- *WhoAmL 92*
**Haines,** Thomas Henry 1933- *AmMWSc 92*
**Haines,** Thomas W. W. 1941- *WhoAmL 92*
**Haines,** Thomas Walton 1917- *AmMWSc 92*
**Haines,** Walter Wells 1918- *WrDr 92*
**Haines,** William C 1942- *AmMWSc 92*
**Haines,** William Emerson 1917- *AmMWSc 92*
**Haines,** William Joseph 1919- *AmMWSc 92*
**Haines,** William Wister 1908- *BenetAL 91*
**Haining,** James *DrAPF 91*
**Haining,** Joseph Leo 1932- *AmMWSc 92*
**Haining,** Peter 1940- *ScFEYrs*
**Haining,** Peter Alexander 1940- *IntAu&W 91, WrDr 92*
**Haining,** Thomas Nivison 1927- *Who 92*
**Hainkel,** John Joseph, Jr 1938- *WhoAmP 91*
**Hainline,** Adrian, Jr 1921- *AmMWSc 92*
**Hainline,** Forrest Arthur, Jr. 1918- *WhoAmL 92, WhoFI 92*
**Hainline,** Louise 1947- *AmMWSc 92*
**Hainline,** Scott Eric 1963- *WhoEnt 92*
**Hains,** Thornton Jenkins 1866- *BenetAL 91*
**Hains,** Timothy G. 1948- *WhoAmL 92*
**Hainski,** Martha Barrionuevo 1932- *AmMWSc 92*
**Hainsworth,** Brad E. 1935- *WhoWest 92*
**Hainsworth,** Fenwick Reed 1941- *AmMWSc 92*
**Hainsworth,** Gordon 1934- *Who 92*
**Hainsworth,** John Raymond d1991 *Who 92N*
**Hainworth,** Henry Charles 1914- *IntWW 91, Who 92*
**Hair,** Jakie Alexander 1940- *AmMWSc 92*
**Hair,** Jennie *DrAPF 91*
**Hair,** John 1941- *WhoBlA 92*
**Hair,** Kittie Ellen 1948- *WhoWest 92*
**Hair,** Mattox Strickland 1938- *WhoAmP 91*
**Hair,** Michael L 1934- *AmMWSc 92*
**Haire,** James 1938- *WhoEnt 92*
**Haire,** James R 1947- *WhoIns 92*
**Haire,** Wilson John 1932- *IntAu&W 91, WrDr 92*
**Hairell,** Melvin L 1938- *WhoIns 92*
**Hairfield,** Harrell D, Jr 1930- *AmMWSc 92*
**Hairston,** Eddison R., Jr. 1933- *WhoBlA 92*
**Hairston,** James Christopher 1960- *WhoFI 92*
**Hairston,** Jay Timothy 1956- *WhoEnt 92*
**Hairston,** Jerry Wayne 1952- *WhoBlA 92*
**Hairston,** Jester *WhoBlA 92*
**Hairston,** Jester Joseph 1901- *WhoEnt 92*
**Hairston,** Joe Beck 1937- *WhoAmL 92*
**Hairston,** Joseph Henry 1922- *WhoBlA 92*
**Hairston,** Julie Janette 1963- *WhoMW 92*
**Hairston,** Nelson George 1917- *AmMWSc 92*
**Hairston,** Nelson George, Jr 1949- *AmMWSc 92*
**Hairston,** Oscar Grogan 1921- *WhoBlA 92*
**Hairston,** Otis L. 1918- *WhoBlA 92*
**Hairston,** Peter 1752-1832 *DcNCBi 3*
**Hairston,** Peter Wilson 1819-1886 *DcNCBi 3*
**Hairston,** Rowena L. 1928- *WhoBlA 92*
**Hairston,** William 1928- *WhoBlA 92*
**Hairston,** William Clifton 1921- *WhoRel 92*
**Hairstone,** Marcus A 1926- *AmMWSc 92, WhoBlA 92*
**Haisch,** Bernhard Michael 1949- *AmMWSc 92, WhoWest 92*
**Haisler,** Walter Ervin 1944- *AmMWSc 92*
**Haisley,** Fay Beverley 1933- *WhoWest 92*
**Haislip,** David Craig 1962- *WhoFI 92*
**Haislip,** John *DrAPF 91*
**Haissig,** Manfred 1942- *AmMWSc 92*
**Haist,** Dean Woodward 1953- *WhoEnt 92*
**Haithem,** Muhammad Ali 1940- *IntWW 91*
**Haitink,** Bernard 1929- *IntWW 91, NewAmDM, Who 92*
**Haitink,** Bernard J. H. 1929- *WhoEnt 92*
**Haitkin,** Jeffrey Marc 1944- *WhoFI 92*
**Haitko,** Deborah Ann 1951- *AmMWSc 92*
**Haitz,** Roland Hermann 1935- *AmMWSc 92*
**Haizlip,** Ellis B. d1991 *NewYTBS 91 [port]*
**Haizlip,** Ellis Benjamin 1929-1991 *WhoBlA 92N*
**Hajdu,** Joseph 1941- *AmMWSc 92*
**Hajdu,** Stephen 1916- *AmMWSc 92*
**Hajduk,** Stephen Louis 1952- *AmMWSc 92*
**Haje,** Peter Robert 1934- *WhoAmL 92*
**Hajek,** Anna Marie 1948- *WhoFI 92*
**Hajek,** Benjamin F 1931- *AmMWSc 92*
**Hajek,** Francis Paul 1958- *WhoAmL 92*
**Hajek,** Jiri 1913- *IntWW 91*
**Hajek,** Otomar 1930- *AmMWSc 92*
**Hajek,** Robert J. 1943- *WhoFI 92, WhoMW 92*
**Hajela,** Dan 1960- *AmMWSc 92*
**Hajela,** Prabhat 1956- *AmMWSc 92*
**Hajenian,** Florentia 1954- *WhoEnt 92*
**Haji-Sheikh,** Abdolhossein 1933- *AmMWSc 92*
**Hajian,** Arshag B 1930- *AmMWSc 92*
**Hajiyani,** Mehdi Hussain 1939- *AmMWSc 92*
**Hajj,** Ibrahim Nasri 1942- *AmMWSc 92*
**Hajjar,** Nicolas Philippe 1946- *AmMWSc 92*
**Hajnal,** John 1924- *IntWW 91, Who 92*
**Hajos,** Zoltan George 1926- *AmMWSc 92*
**Hajra,** Amiya Kumar 1935- *AmMWSc 92*
**Hajratwala,** Bhupendra R 1942- *AmMWSc 92*
**Hajratwala,** Bhupendra Ratanji 1942- *WhoMW 92*
**Hak,** Lawrence J 1944- *AmMWSc 92*
**Hakala,** Edith Marie 1942- *WhoAmP 91*
**Hakala,** Judyth Ann 1955- *WhoMW 92*
**Hakala,** Maire Tellervo 1917- *AmMWSc 92*
**Hakala,** Reino William 1923- *AmMWSc 92*
**Hakala,** William Walter 1935- *AmMWSc 92*
**Hakanoglu,** Erol 1957- *WhoFI 92*
**Hakansson,** Lars-Ove 1937- *IntWW 91*
**Hakansson,** Nils Hemming 1937- *WhoFI 92*
**Hake,** Carl 1927- *AmMWSc 92*
**Hake,** Richard Robb 1927- *AmMWSc 92*
**Hakel,** Edwin Henry 1909- *WhoRel 92*
**Haken,** Wolfgang 1928- *AmMWSc 92*
**Hakensen,** David Richard 1959- *WhoMW 92*
**Haker,** Franklin Arthur 1951- *WhoMW 92*
**Hakes,** Russell Alan 1947- *WhoAmL 92*
**Hakes,** Samuel D 1930- *AmMWSc 92*
**Hakewill,** Henry, Jr 1918- *AmMWSc 92*
**Hakim,** Ali Hussein 1943- *WhoFI 92*
**Hakim,** Edward Bernard 1936- *AmMWSc 92*
**Hakim,** George 1913- *IntWW 91*
**Hakim,** Louise Zalta 1922- *WhoFI 92*
**Hakim,** Margaret Heath 1938- *AmMWSc 92*
**Hakim,** Michel *WhoRel 92*
**Hakim,** Raziel Samuel 1947- *AmMWSc 92*
**Hakim,** S. *DrAPF 91*
**Hakim,** Seymour 1933- *IntAu&W 91*
**Hakim,** Tawfiq al 1898- *IntAu&W 91*
**Hakima,** Mala'ika 1950- *WhoBlA 92*
**Hakimi,** John 1950- *AmMWSc 92*
**Hakimi,** S L 1932- *AmMWSc 92*
**Hakkanen,** Matti Klaus Juhani 1936- *IntWW 91*
**Hakkila,** Eero Arnold 1931- *AmMWSc 92, WhoWest 92*
**Hakkila,** Jon Eric 1957- *AmMWSc 92*
**Hakkinen,** Raimo Jaakko 1926- *AmMWSc 92*
**Hakluyt,** Richard 1552?-1616 *BenetAL 91, RfGEnL 91*
**Hakomori,** Sen-Itiroh 1929- *AmMWSc 92*
**Haksar,** Ajit Narain 1925- *IntWW 91*
**Haksar,** Parmeshwar Narain 1913- *IntWW 91*
**Halaban,** Ruth 1938- *AmMWSc 92*
**Halabi,** Mohammed Ali el- 1937- *IntWW 91*
**Halabisky,** Lorne Stanley 1945- *AmMWSc 92*
**Halaby,** George Anton 1938- *AmMWSc 92*
**Halaby,** Najeeb Elias 1915- *Who 92*
**Halaby,** Sami Assad 1933- *AmMWSc 92*
**Halacsy,** Andrew A 1907- *AmMWSc 92*
**Halagera,** Raymond Thomas 1947- *WhoMW 92*
**Halam,** Ann *TwCSFW 91, WrDr 92*
**Halan,** John Paul 1928- *WhoFI 92*
**Halaris,** Angelos 1942- *AmMWSc 92*
**Halarnkar,** Premjit P 1959- *AmMWSc 92*
**Halas,** Cynthia Ann 1961- *WhoFI 92*
**Halas,** George 1895-1983 *FacFETw*
**Halas,** John 1912- *Who 92*
**Halasa,** Adel F 1933- *AmMWSc 92*
**Halasi,** Janos *EncAmaz 91*
**Halasi-Kun,** George Joseph 1916- *AmMWSc 92*
**Halasi-Kun,** Tibor d1991 *NewYTBS 91*
**Halasz,** Nicholas Alexis 1931- *AmMWSc 92*
**Halawi,** Ibrahim 1938- *IntWW 91*
**Halazon,** George Christ 1919- *AmMWSc 92*
**Halbach,** David Jerome 1958- *WhoMW 92*
**Halbach,** Edward Christian, Jr. 1931- *WhoAmL 92*
**Halbach,** Klaus 1925- *AmMWSc 92*
**Halbach,** Victor Marion, Jr. 1939- *WhoAmL 92*
**Halberg,** Charles C 1942- *WhoAmP 91*
**Halberg,** Charles John August, Jr 1921- *AmMWSc 92*
**Halberg,** Murray 1933- *Who 92*
**Halberstadt,** Marcel Leon 1937- *AmMWSc 92*
**Halberstam,** David 1934- *BenetAL 91, IntAu&W 91, WrDr 92*
**Halberstam,** Heini 1926- *AmMWSc 92*
**Halbert,** Edith Conrad 1931- *AmMWSc 92*
**Halbert,** John K. *WhoRel 92*
**Halbert,** Melvyn Leonard 1929- *AmMWSc 92*
**Halbert,** Robert Orlaf 1937- *WhoFI 92*
**Halbert,** Seymour Putterman 1917- *AmMWSc 92*
**Halbert,** Sheridan A 1943- *AmMWSc 92*
**Halbert,** Thomas Risher 1950- *AmMWSc 92*
**Halbig,** Joseph Benjamin 1938- *AmMWSc 92*
**Halbig,** Kimberly Deidre 1963- *WhoAmL 92*
**Halbleib,** John A 1936- *AmMWSc 92*
**Halbouty,** Michel Thomas 1909- *AmMWSc 92*
**Halbrendt,** Catherine Kwan-Yuk 1949- *WhoFI 92*
**Halbrendt,** John Marthon 1949- *AmMWSc 92*
**Halbritter,** Barry John 1943- *WhoFI 92*
**Halbritter,** Walter 1927- *IntWW 91*
**Halbrook,** David McCall 1927- *WhoAmP 91*
**Halby,** Anthony Wayne 1949- *WhoFI 92*
**Hald,** Edward 1883-1980 *DcTwDes*
**Haldane,** Charlotte 1898-1969 *ScFEYrs*
**Haldane,** Elizabeth Sanderson 1862-1937 *BiDBrF 2*
**Haldane,** John Burdon Sanderson 1892-1964 *FacFETw*
**Haldane,** Richard Burden 1856-1928 *FacFETw*
**Haldane-Stevenson,** James Patrick 1910- *WhoRel 92*
**Haldar,** Dipak 1937- *AmMWSc 92*
**Haldar,** Gopal 1902- *IntAu&W 91*
**Haldar,** Jaya 1939- *AmMWSc 92*
**Halde,** Carlyn Jean 1924- *AmMWSc 92*
**Haldeman,** Charles Edgar, Jr. 1948- *WhoFI 92*
**Haldeman,** Harry R. 1926- *IntWW 91*
**Haldeman,** Harry Robbins 1926- *AmPolLe*
**Haldeman,** Isaac Massey 1845-1933 *RelLAm 91*
**Haldeman,** Jack C 1941- *TwCSFW 91, WrDr 92*
**Haldeman,** Joe *DrAPF 91*
**Haldeman,** Joe 1943- *TwCSFW 91, WrDr 92*
**Haldeman,** Joe William 1943- *IntAu&W 91*
**Haldeman,** Samuel Steman 1812-1880 *BiInAmS*
**Haldeman-Julius,** E. 1889-1951 *BenetAL 91*
**Haldeman-Julius,** Emanuel 1889-1951 *RelLAm 91*
**Halden,** Frank 1929- *AmMWSc 92*
**Halder,** Franz 1884-1972 *EncTR 91 [port], FacFETw*
**Halder,** Narayan Chandra 1939- *AmMWSc 92*
**Haldimand,** Frederic *DcAmImH*
**Hale,** Alan, Jr. 1918?-1990 *AnObit 1990, ConTFT 9*
**Hale,** Allean Lemmon 1914- *WrDr 92*
**Hale,** Aurelia Ethel 1940- *WhoRel 92*
**Hale,** Barbara 1922- *IntMPA 92, WhoEnt 92*
**Hale,** Barbara Nelson 1938- *AmMWSc 92*
**Hale,** Beverly Ann 1939- *WhoMW 92*
**Hale,** Bob *ConAu 134*
**Hale,** Candace 1953- *WhoAmL 92*
**Hale,** Carl Dennis 1949- *WhoWest 92*
**Hale,** Carl Stanley 1965- *WhoMW 92*
**Hale,** Cecil Harrison 1919- *AmMWSc 92*
**Hale,** Cecil I., II 1945- *WhoBlA 92*
**Hale,** Charles Russell 1916- *WhoAmL 92*
**Hale,** Clara 1905- *NotBlAW 92*
**Hale,** Clara McBride *WhoBlA 92*
**Hale,** Clayton W 1941- *WhoAmP 91*
**Hale,** Creighton J 1924- *AmMWSc 92*
**Hale,** Cynthia Lynnette 1952- *WhoBlA 92*

**Hale**, Daniel Cudmore 1944- WhoAmL 92
**Hale**, Danny Lyman 1944- WhoFI 92
**Hale**, David C 1964- WhoAmP 91
**Hale**, David Glen 1952- WhoEnt 92
**Hale**, Dean Edward 1950- WhoWest 92
**Hale**, Diana 1933- WhoWest 92
**Hale**, Don WhoAmP 91
**Hale**, Edward Boyd 1938- AmMWSc 92
**Hale**, Edward Everett 1822-1909 BenetAL 91, RelLAm 91, ScFEYrs
**Hale**, Edward Everett, Jr. 1863-1932 BenetAL 91
**Hale**, Edward Harned 1923- WhoBlA 92
**Hale**, Edward Jones 1802-1883 DcNCBi 3
**Hale**, Edward Joseph 1835-1922 DcNCBi 3
**Hale**, Enoch 1790-1848 BiInAmS
**Hale**, Ernest A 1920- WhoAmP 91
**Hale**, Francis Joseph 1922- AmMWSc 92
**Hale**, Frank W., Jr. 1927- WhoBlA 92
**Hale**, Gary Allen 1954- WhoAmP 91
**Hale**, Gene WhoBlA 92
**Hale**, Gene 1946- WhoBlA 92
**Hale**, Gerald Albert 1927- WhoFI 92
**Hale**, Gerald G 1953- WhoAmP 91
**Hale**, Gerald Michael 1947- WhoEnt 92
**Hale**, Gina LaStelle 1959- WhoAmL 92
**Hale**, Glenn SmATA 66
**Hale**, Harold 1937- WhoAmP 91
**Hale**, Harry W 1920- AmMWSc 92
**Hale**, Harry W, Jr 1917- AmMWSc 92
**Hale**, Hilton Ingram 1956- WhoMW 92
**Hale**, Horatio Emmons 1817-1896 BiInAmS
**Hale**, Irving 1932- WhoFI 92, WhoWest 92
**Hale**, Jack Donald 1927- WhoEnt 92
**Hale**, Jack Kenneth 1928- AmMWSc 92
**Hale**, James Otis 1959- WhoAmL 92
**Hale**, James Russell 1918- WhoRel 92
**Hale**, James Thomas 1940- WhoAmL 92
**Hale**, Janice Ellen 1948- WhoBlA 92
**Hale**, Joe Allen 1954- WhoRel 92
**Hale**, John 1921- AmMWSc 92
**Hale**, John 1923- Who 92
**Hale**, John 1926- IntAu&W 91, WrDr 92
**Hale**, John Dewey 1937- AmMWSc 92
**Hale**, John Gregory 1960- WhoAmL 92
**Hale**, John Hampton 1924- IntWW 91, Who 92
**Hale**, John Mark 1955- WhoAmP 91
**Hale**, John Parker 1806-1873 AmPolLe
**Hale**, John Rigby 1923- IntWW 91
**Hale**, Joseph Rice 1935- WhoRel 92
**Hale**, Joseph Robert 1927- WhoAmP 91
**Hale**, Kathleen 1898- IntAu&W 91, SmATA 66 [port], TwCPaSc, Who 92
**Hale**, Keith 1955- IntAu&W 91
**Hale**, Kirk Kermit, Jr 1940- AmMWSc 92
**Hale**, Lance Mitchell 1956- WhoAmL 92
**Hale**, Lee Louis 1948- WhoAmL 92
**Hale**, Leonard Allen 1937- AmMWSc 92
**Hale**, Leonard Gerald 1939- WhoMW 92, WhoRel 92
**Hale**, Linda Adair 1956- WhoAmL 92
**Hale**, Louis Dewitt 1917- WhoAmP 91
**Hale**, Lucretia Peabody 1820-1900 BenetAL 91
**Hale**, Martha L 1946- AmMWSc 92
**Hale**, Mary Lynn 1956- WhoEnt 92
**Hale**, Mason Ellsworth, Jr 1928- AmMWSc 92
**Hale**, Maynard George 1920- AmMWSc 92
**Hale**, Michael WrDr 92
**Hale**, Millie E. 1881-1930 NotBlAW 92 [port]
**Hale**, Mona Walker WhoAmP 91
**Hale**, Monte 1919- WhoEnt 92
**Hale**, Nancy 1908-1988 BenetAL 91
**Hale**, Nathan 1755-1776 BenetAL 91, BlkwEAR
**Hale**, Nathan 1784-1863 BenetAL 91
**Hale**, Norman Morgan 1933- Who 92
**Hale**, Oron J. d1991 NewYTBS 91
**Hale**, Oron James 1902-1991 ConAu 135
**Hale**, Paul Edwards 1942- WhoFI 92
**Hale**, Peter Mallett 1829-1887 DcNCBi 3
**Hale**, Phale D. 1915- WhoBlA 92
**Hale**, Philip 1854-1934 NewAmDM
**Hale**, Raymond 1936- Who 92
**Hale**, Raymond Joseph 1918- AmMWSc 92
**Hale**, Richard Norman 1943- WhoAmL 92
**Hale**, Richard Stephen 1951- WhoAmP 91
**Hale**, Richard Thomas, Jr. 1945- WhoFI 92
**Hale**, Robert D. 1928- ConAu 134
**Hale**, Robert E 1929- AmMWSc 92
**Hale**, Robert Wesley 1949- WhoRel 92
**Hale**, Roger Loucks 1934- WhoMW 92
**Hale**, Ron L 1942- AmMWSc 92
**Hale**, Ronald F. 1943- WhoWest 92
**Hale**, Russell Dean 1944- WhoAmP 91
**Hale**, Samuel 1917- WhoAmP 91
**Hale**, Samuel Wesley, Jr. 1942- WhoRel 92
**Hale**, Sarah Josepha 1788-1879 HanAmWH
**Hale**, Sarah Josepha Buell 1788-1879 BenetAL 91
**Hale**, Seldon Houston 1948- WhoFI 92
**Hale**, Steven William 1953- WhoAmL 92
**Hale**, Susan 1833-1910 BenetAL 91
**Hale**, Violet Elaine WhoWest 92
**Hale**, Warren Frederick 1929- AmMWSc 92
**Hale**, William Bryan, Jr. 1933- WhoWest 92
**Hale**, William Harlan 1910-1974 BenetAL 91
**Hale**, William Harris 1920- AmMWSc 92
**Hale**, William Henry, Jr 1940- AmMWSc 92
**Hale-Robinson**, Lorraine Augusta 1948- WhoEnt 92
**Haleck**, Fiasili Puni WhoAmP 91
**Halefoglu**, Vahit M. 1919- IntWW 91
**Halegua**, Alfredo 1930- WhoHisp 92
**Halemane**, Thirumala Raya 1953- AmMWSc 92
**Haler**, Lawrence Eugene 1951- WhoWest 92
**Hales**, Alfred Washington 1938- AmMWSc 92
**Hales**, Antony John 1948- IntWW 91
**Hales**, Charles A 1941- AmMWSc 92
**Hales**, Charles Nicholas 1935- Who 92
**Hales**, Donald Caleb 1929- AmMWSc 92
**Hales**, Edward Everette 1932- WhoBlA 92
**Hales**, Edward John 1927- WhoRel 92
**Hales**, Frederick David 1930- Who 92
**Hales**, Hugh B 1940- AmMWSc 92
**Hales**, J Vern 1917- AmMWSc 92
**Hales**, Jack, Jr. 1933- WhoFI 92
**Hales**, Janette Callister 1933- WhoAmP 91
**Hales**, Jeremy M 1937- AmMWSc 92
**Hales**, Mary Ann 1953- WhoBlA 92
**Hales**, Milton Reynolds 1918- AmMWSc 92
**Hales**, Nicholas Who 92
**Hales**, Raleigh Stanton, Jr 1942- AmMWSc 92
**Hales**, Robert Lynn 1927- WhoWest 92
**Hales**, Stephen 1677-1761 BlkwCEP
**Hales**, William Roy 1934- WhoBlA 92
**Haletchko**, Sophie EncAmaz 91
**Halevy**, Daniel 1872-1962 GuFrLit 1
**Halevy**, Fromental 1799-1862 NewAmDM
**Halevy**, Ludovic 1833-1908 ThHEIm [port]
**Halevy**, Simon 1929- AmMWSc 92
**Haley**, Alex 1921- BenetAL 91, BlkLC [port], FacFETw [port], WrDr 92
**Haley**, Alexander Palmer 1921- WhoBlA 92
**Haley**, Bill 1925-1981 ConMus 6 [port], NewAmDM
**Haley**, Bill 1927-1981 FacFETw [port]
**Haley**, Boyd Eugene 1940- AmMWSc 92
**Haley**, Charles Lewis 1964- WhoBlA 92
**Haley**, Charlotte 1911- WhoMW 92
**Haley**, Donald C. 1928- WhoBlA 92
**Haley**, Earl Albert 1933- WhoBlA 92
**Haley**, Ed WhoAmP 91
**Haley**, Frances Shaller 1932- WhoAmP 91
**Haley**, Gail E 1939- ConAu 35NR, IntAu&W 91, SmATA 13AS [port], WrDr 92
**Haley**, George Williford Boyce 1925- WhoAmP 91, WhoBlA 92
**Haley**, Harold Bernard 1923- AmMWSc 92
**Haley**, Jack, Jr. ConAu 135, LesBEnT 92
**Haley**, Jack, Jr. 1933- IntMPA 92, WhoEnt 92
**Haley**, James Oliver 1912- WhoAmL 92
**Haley**, James William 1943- WhoAmP 91
**Haley**, Jean Rodger 1936- WhoMW 92
**Haley**, John C. 1929- IntWW 91
**Haley**, John Charles 1905- WhoWest 92
**Haley**, John David 1924- WhoWest 92
**Haley**, John J., Jr. 1933- ConAu 135
**Haley**, Johnetta Randolph WhoEnt 92, WhoMW 92
**Haley**, Johnetta Randolph 1923- WhoBlA 92
**Haley**, Keith Brian 1933- Who 92
**Haley**, Kenneth 1920- WrDr 92
**Haley**, Kenneth Harold Dobson 1920- IntAu&W 91, Who 92
**Haley**, Kenneth William 1939- AmMWSc 92
**Haley**, Leslie Ernest 1938- AmMWSc 92
**Haley**, Lucinda Jenkins 1956- WhoAmL 92
**Haley**, Margaret A. 1861-1939 HanAmWH
**Haley**, Michael Anslem 1952- WhoRel 92
**Haley**, Nancy Jean 1948- AmMWSc 92
**Haley**, Pat WhoAmP 91
**Haley**, Paul R 1953- WhoAmP 91
**Haley**, Rosemary Elizabeth 1926- WhoFI 92
**Haley**, Sally Fulton 1908- WhoWest 92
**Haley**, Samuel Randolph 1940- AmMWSc 92
**Haley**, Tenison WhoWest 92
**Haley**, Thomas John 1913- AmMWSc 92, WhoWest 92
**Haley**, Thomas Morrison 1952- WhoEnt 92
**Haley**, Vincent Peter 1931- WhoAmL 92
**Haley**, Wayne William 1947- WhoIns 92
**Haley**, William 1901-1987 FacFETw
**Haley**, William Francis 1952- WhoMW 92
**Half**, Robert 1918- WhoFI 92
**Halfacre**, Frank Edward 1936- WhoBlA 92
**Halfacre**, Robert Gordon 1941- AmMWSc 92
**Halfant**, Gary D. 1953- WhoWest 92
**Halfar**, Edwin 1917- AmMWSc 92
**Halferdahl**, Laurence Bowes 1930- AmMWSc 92
**Halferty**, James Burkhardt 1930- WhoMW 92
**Halff**, Albert Henry 1915- AmMWSc 92
**Halff**, Robert Hart 1908- WhoWest 92
**Halffter**, Cristobal 1930- ConCom 92
**Halffter**, Ernesto 1905- NewAmDM
**Halffter**, Rodolfo 1900- NewAmDM
**Halfhill**, John Eric 1932- AmMWSc 92
**Halfman**, Clarke Joseph 1941- AmMWSc 92
**Halfon**, Efraim 1948- AmMWSc 92
**Halfon**, Marc 1945- AmMWSc 92
**Halford**, Gary Ross 1937- AmMWSc 92
**Halford**, Jake Hallie 1941- AmMWSc 92
**Halford**, John Peter 1931- WhoEnt 92
**Halford**, Michael Charles Kirkpatrick 1914- Who 92
**Halford**, Richard W 1944- WhoAmP 91
**Halford-MacLeod**, Aubrey Seymour 1914- Who 92
**Halfpenny**, Brian Norman 1936- Who 92
**Halfpenny**, James C. 1947- WhoWest 92
**Halfvarson**, Lucille Robertson 1919- WhoEnt 92
**Halfyard**, Robert L. 1925- WhoAmL 92
**Halgren**, Lee A 1942- AmMWSc 92
**Halgren**, Thomas Arthur 1941- AmMWSc 92
**Haliburton**, Lawrence E. 1917- WhoBlA 92
**Haliburton**, T Allan 1938- AmMWSc 92
**Haliburton**, Thomas Chandler 1796-1865 BenetAL 91, RfGEnL 91
**Haliczer**, James Solomon 1952- WhoAmL 92, WhoFI 92
**Halifax** BlkwEAR
**Halifax**, Archbishop of 1924- Who 92
**Halifax**, Archdeacon of Who 92
**Halifax**, Earl of 1944- Who 92
**Halifax**, Edward F. L. Wood, Viscount 1881-1959 EncTR 91
**Halifax**, Edward Frederick Lindley Wood 1881-1959 FacFETw
**Halijak**, Charles A 1922- AmMWSc 92
**Halik**, Raymond R 1917- AmMWSc 92
**Halikas**, James Anastasio 1941- WhoMW 92
**Halisky**, Philip Michael 1924- AmMWSc 92
**Halitsky**, James 1919- AmMWSc 92
**Halivni**, David Weiss 1928- WhoRel 92
**Haliw**, Andrew Jerome, III 1946- WhoAmL 92
**Halket**, Thomas D 1948- AmMWSc 92, WhoAmL 92
**Halkett**, Alan Neilson 1931- WhoAmL 92
**Halkias**, Christos 1933- AmMWSc 92
**Halkias**, Christos Constantine 1933- WhoFI 92
**Halkias**, Demetrios 1932- AmMWSc 92
**Halkin**, Adele Diane 1931- WhoMW 92
**Halkin**, Hubert 1936- AmMWSc 92
**Halko**, Barbara Tomlonovic 1940- AmMWSc 92
**Halko**, David Joseph 1945- AmMWSc 92
**Halko**, Joseph Anthony 1940- WhoWest 92
**Hall & Oates** ConMus 6 [port], NewAmDM
**Hall**, A M 1948- WhoAmP 91
**Hall**, A S, Jr 1917- AmMWSc 92
**Hall**, Adam Who 92, WrDr 92
**Hall**, Adam Reid, Jr. 1938- WhoRel 92
**Hall**, Addie June 1930- WhoBlA 92
**Hall**, Adelaide 1895- NewAmDM
**Hall**, Adelaide 1904- NotBlAW 92
**Hall**, Adrian 1943- TwCPaSc
**Hall**, Alan 1939- WhoAmL 92
**Hall**, Alan H 1949- AmMWSc 92
**Hall**, Albert 1936- WhoAmP 91
**Hall**, Albert 1959- WhoBlA 92
**Hall**, Albert C 1914- AmMWSc 92
**Hall**, Albert M 1914- AmMWSc 92
**Hall**, Albert Mangold 1914- WhoMW 92
**Hall**, Albert Peter Who 92
**Hall**, Aleksander 1953- IntWW 91
**Hall**, Alfred Charles 1917- Who 92
**Hall**, Alfred Rupert 1920- IntWW 91, Who 92
**Hall**, Alfred Wayne 1947- WhoRel 92
**Hall**, Allmand 1772-1831 DcNCBi 3
**Hall**, Alton Jerome 1945- WhoBlA 92
**Hall**, Angus 1932- IntAu&W 91, WrDr 92
**Hall**, Anthony Elmitt 1940- AmMWSc 92, WhoWest 92
**Hall**, Anthony Michael 1968- IntMPA 92
**Hall**, Anthony Stewart 1945- Who 92, WrDr 92
**Hall**, Anthony Vincent 1936- IntWW 91
**Hall**, Anthony W., Jr. 1944- WhoBlA 92
**Hall**, Anthony William 1951- Who 92
**Hall**, Anthony William, Jr 1944- WhoAmP 91
**Hall**, Arnold 1915- Who 92
**Hall**, Arnold Alexander 1915- IntWW 91
**Hall**, Arsenio 1956- WhoBlA 92
**Hall**, Arsenio 1959- IntMPA 92
**Hall**, Arthur David, III 1924- AmMWSc 92
**Hall**, Arthur Eugene, Jr. 1955- WhoFI 92
**Hall**, Arthur Herbert 1901- Who 92
**Hall**, Arthur Raymond, Jr. 1922- WhoRel 92
**Hall**, Asaph 1829-1907 BiInAmS
**Hall**, Asaph Hale 1933- WhoMW 92
**Hall**, Austin 1882?-1933 TwCSFW 91
**Hall**, Austin 1885?-1933 ScFEYrs
**Hall**, Austin & Flint, Homer Eon ScFEYrs
**Hall**, Aylmer 1914- WrDr 92
**Hall**, Barbara 1960- ConAu 135, SmATA 68 [port]
**Hall**, Barry Dennis 1950- WhoEnt 92
**Hall**, Barry Gordon 1942- AmMWSc 92
**Hall**, Basil 1918- Who 92
**Hall**, Bayard Rush 1798-1863 BenetAL 91
**Hall**, Ben L WhoAmP 91
**Hall**, Benjamin Downs 1932- AmMWSc 92
**Hall**, Bennett Freeman 1914- WhoRel 92
**Hall**, Bernard 1921- Who 92
**Hall**, Bernice Lucia 1928- WhoRel 92
**Hall**, Betty 1921- Who 92
**Hall**, Betty B 1921- WhoAmP 91
**Hall**, Beverly Fenton 1955- AmMWSc 92
**Hall**, Beverly Field 1936- WhoWest 92
**Hall**, Blake G 1953- WhoAmP 91
**Hall**, Blanche Barbara 1928- WhoRel 92
**Hall**, Bobby Gene 1933- WhoWest 92
**Hall**, Bonnie Baker 1944- WhoFI 92
**Hall**, Bonnie Green 1941- WhoAmP 91
**Hall**, Bradley Douglas 1952- WhoFI 92
**Hall**, Brian Edward 1958- WhoBlA 92
**Hall**, Brian Howard 1947- WhoWest 92
**Hall**, Brian Keith 1941- AmMWSc 92
**Hall**, Bronwyn Hughes 1945- WhoFI 92
**Hall**, Carl Eldridge 1937- AmMWSc 92
**Hall**, Carl Franklin 1905- WhoRel 92
**Hall**, Carl W 1924- AmMWSc 92, ConAu 135
**Hall**, Carol Ann 1940- WhoWest 92
**Hall**, Carol Klein 1946- AmMWSc 92
**Hall**, Carole L AmMWSc 92
**Hall**, Carson Keith 1945- WhoRel 92
**Hall**, Catherine 1922- Who 92
**Hall**, Cecilia Vasquez 1947- WhoWest 92
**Hall**, Charles A 1920- AmMWSc 92
**Hall**, Charles A 1937- AmMWSc 92
**Hall**, Charles Adams 1949- WhoMW 92
**Hall**, Charles Addison Smith 1943- AmMWSc 92
**Hall**, Charles Allan 1941- AmMWSc 92
**Hall**, Charles E 1926- AmMWSc 92
**Hall**, Charles Eric 1916- AmMWSc 92
**Hall**, Charles Frederick 1920- AmMWSc 92
**Hall**, Charles Harold 1934- WhoBlA 92
**Hall**, Charles Mack 1941- AmMWSc 92
**Hall**, Charles Martin 1863-1914 BiInAmS
**Hall**, Charles Thomas 1929- AmMWSc 92
**Hall**, Charles Virdus 1923- AmMWSc 92
**Hall**, Charles W. 1944- WhoFI 92
**Hall**, Charles Washington 1930- WhoAmL 92
**Hall**, Charles William 1922- AmMWSc 92
**Hall**, Cherry Lynn 1953- WhoMW 92
**Hall**, Cheryl Ann 1954- WhoFI 92
**Hall**, Chesley Barker 1920- AmMWSc 92
**Hall**, Christine C. Iijima 1953- WhoBlA 92
**Hall**, Christopher 1930- TwCPaSc
**Hall**, Christopher Myles 1932- Who 92
**Hall**, Christopher Patrick 1954- WhoAmL 92
**Hall**, Christopher Webber 1845-1911 BiInAmS
**Hall**, Clarence Albert, Jr 1930- AmMWSc 92, WhoWest 92
**Hall**, Clarence Coney, Jr 1921- AmMWSc 92
**Hall**, Claudia IntAu&W 91X
**Hall**, Clement 1706-1759 DcNCBi 3
**Hall**, Clifford 1904-1973 TwCPaSc
**Hall**, Colby D, Jr 1919- AmMWSc 92
**Hall**, Conrad 1926- IntMPA 92, WhoEnt 92
**Hall**, Cynthia Holcomb WhoAmP 91
**Hall**, Cynthia Holcomb 1929- WhoAmL 92
**Hall**, Daisy WhoEnt 92
**Hall**, Dalale Diane 1949- WhoMW 92
**Hall**, Dale Emerson 1937- WhoWest 92
**Hall**, Daniel A. 1933- WhoBlA 92
**Hall**, Daniel G 1938- WhoIns 92

**Hall,** Daniel Ray Acomb 1927- *WhoFI 92*
**Hall,** Daryl 1948- *ConMus 6 [port]*
**Hall,** Daryl 1949- *WhoEnt 92*
**Hall,** David *DrAPF 91*
**Hall,** David 1928- *IntWW 91*
**Hall,** David 1930- *Who 92*
**Hall,** David 1938- *WhoRel 92*
**Hall,** David 1950- *WhoBlA 92*
**Hall,** David Alfred 1940- *AmMWSc 92*
**Hall,** David Anthony, Jr. 1945- *WhoBlA 92*
**Hall,** David Charles 1955- *WhoWest 92*
**Hall,** David Goodsell, III 1927- *AmMWSc 92*
**Hall,** David Goodsell, IV 1952- *AmMWSc 92*
**Hall,** David Goodsell, Sr 1903- *AmMWSc 92*
**Hall,** David Joseph 1943- *AmMWSc 92*
**Hall,** David Max 1949- *WhoAmL 92*
**Hall,** David McKee 1918-1960 *DcNCBi 3*
**Hall,** David McKenzie 1928- *WhoBlA 92, WhoFI 92*
**Hall,** David Michael 1936- *AmMWSc 92*
**Hall,** David Oakley 1935- *Who 92*
**Hall,** David Stanley 1935- *WhoWest 92*
**Hall,** David W 1947- *WhoIns 92*
**Hall,** David Warren 1935- *AmMWSc 92*
**Hall,** Delbert Louis 1954- *WhoEnt 92*
**Hall,** Delilah Ridley 1953- *WhoBlA 92*
**Hall,** Delores *WhoBlA 92*
**Hall,** Delton Dwayne 1965- *WhoBlA 92*
**Hall,** Denis C. *Who 92*
**Hall,** Denis Whitfield 1913- *Who 92*
**Hall,** Dennis Gene 1948- *AmMWSc 92*
**Hall,** Devra 1955- *WhoEnt 92*
**Hall,** Dewey Eugene 1932- *WhoMW 92*
**Hall,** Diana E 1938- *AmMWSc 92*
**Hall,** Dick 1938- *WhoAmP 91*
**Hall,** Dick Wick 1912- *AmMWSc 92*
**Hall,** Dolores Brown *WhoBlA 92*
**Hall,** Donald *DrAPF 91*
**Hall,** Donald 1928- *BenetAL 91, ConPo 91, IntWW 91, WrDr 92*
**Hall,** Donald 1930- *Who 92*
**Hall,** Donald D 1933- *AmMWSc 92*
**Hall,** Donald Eugene 1940- *AmMWSc 92*
**Hall,** Donald Herbert 1925- *AmMWSc 92*
**Hall,** Donald Joyce 1928- *WhoFI 92, WhoMW 92*
**Hall,** Donald M 1920- *WhoAmP 91*
**Hall,** Donald Norman Blake 1944- *AmMWSc 92*
**Hall,** Donald William 1942- *AmMWSc 92*
**Hall,** Douglas 1909- *Who 92*
**Hall,** Douglas E 1943- *WhoAmP 91*
**Hall,** Douglas Elliott Reed 1958- *WhoWest 92*
**Hall,** Douglas John 1928- *WhoRel 92*
**Hall,** Douglas N 1930- *WhoIns 92*
**Hall,** Douglas Scott 1940- *AmMWSc 92*
**Hall,** Duncan 1947- *Who 92*
**Hall,** Durward Gorham 1910- *WhoAmP 91*
**Hall,** Dwayne Allen 1958- *WhoFI 92*
**Hall,** Dwight Hubert 1940- *AmMWSc 92*
**Hall,** Edward d1991 *Who 92N*
**Hall,** Edward Clarence 1931- *WhoBlA 92*
**Hall,** Edward Dallas 1950- *AmMWSc 92*
**Hall,** Edward Dudley 1823-1896 *DcNCBi 3*
**Hall,** Edward Michael 1915- *Who 92*
**Hall,** Edward T 1914- *DcTwDes, FacFETw*
**Hall,** Edward Thomas 1924- *Who 92*
**Hall,** Edwin Huddleston, Jr. 1935- *WhoFI 92*
**Hall,** Edwin L 1949- *WhoAmP 91*
**Hall,** Elihu 1822-1882 *BiInAmS*
**Hall,** Elizabeth Rose 1914- *AmMWSc 92*
**Hall,** Elliott S. *WhoBlA 92*
**Hall,** Emmett Campbell *ScFEYrs*
**Hall,** Enoch d1753 *DcNCBi 3*
**Hall,** Eric John 1933- *AmMWSc 92*
**Hall,** Ernest 1930- *Who 92*
**Hall,** Ernest Lenard 1940- *AmMWSc 92*
**Hall,** Ervin 1947- *BlkOlyM*
**Hall,** Ethel Harris 1928- *WhoBlA 92*
**Hall,** Eugene Curtis 1958- *WhoBlA 92*
**Hall,** Evan *TwCWW 91, WrDr 92*
**Hall,** Evelyn Alice 1945- *WhoBlA 92*
**Hall,** Fergus 1947- *TwCPaSc*
**Hall,** Florence Marion Howe 1845-1922 *BenetAL 91*
**Hall,** Forrest G 1940- *AmMWSc 92*
**Hall,** Francis Ramey 1925- *AmMWSc 92*
**Hall,** Francis Woodall 1918- *Who 92*
**Hall,** Frank Foy 1940- *AmMWSc 92*
**Hall,** Frank Gregory 1896-1967 *DcNCBi 3*
**Hall,** Franklin Perkins 1938- *WhoAmP 91*
**Hall,** Franklin Robert 1934- *AmMWSc 92*
**Hall,** Fred, III 1945- *WhoBlA 92*
**Hall,** Frederick 1780-1843 *BiInAmS*
**Hall,** Frederick 1860-1948 *TwCPaSc*
**Hall,** Frederick Columbus 1927- *AmMWSc 92*
**Hall,** Frederick John 1931- *Who 92*
**Hall,** Frederick Keith 1930- *AmMWSc 92*
**Hall,** Frederick Theodore 1951- *WhoBlA 92*
**Hall,** Freeman Franklin, Jr 1928- *AmMWSc 92*
**Hall,** G. Stanley 1844-1924 *BenetAL 91, ScFEYrs*
**Hall,** Gary B. 1941- *WhoAmL 92*
**Hall,** Gary R 1944- *AmMWSc 92*
**Hall,** Gary Stephan 1957- *WhoMW 92*
**Hall,** Gene Stephen 1951- *AmMWSc 92*
**Hall,** Geoffrey Dana 1948- *WhoAmP 91*
**Hall,** Geoffrey Penrose Dickinson 1916- *Who 92*
**Hall,** Geoffrey Ronald 1928- *Who 92*
**Hall,** George *Who 92*
**Hall,** George Arthur, Jr 1920- *AmMWSc 92*
**Hall,** George E 1917- *AmMWSc 92*
**Hall,** George Frederick 1931- *AmMWSc 92*
**Hall,** George Lincoln 1926- *AmMWSc 92*
**Hall,** George Robert 1930- *WhoFI 92*
**Hall,** George Rumney 1937- *Who 92*
**Hall,** Gerald Farnham 1940- *WhoFI 92*
**Hall,** Gimone 1940- *IntAu&W 91, WrDr 92*
**Hall,** Glenn Eugene 1931- *AmMWSc 92*
**Hall,** Gordon 1926- *WhoAmP 91*
**Hall,** Gordon R. 1926- *WhoAmL 92, WhoWest 92*
**Hall,** Granville Stanley 1844-1924 *AmPeW*
**Hall,** Gretchen Randolph 1949- *AmMWSc 92*
**Hall,** Gus 1910- *FacFETw*
**Hall,** Gustav Wesley 1934- *AmMWSc 92*
**Hall,** Guy Herring 1927- *WhoFI 92*
**Hall,** H. Douglas *DrAPF 91*
**Hall,** Hal 1911- *WhoWest 92*
**Hall,** Hansel Crimiel 1929- *WhoBlA 92, WhoMW 92*
**Hall,** Harber Homer 1920- *WhoAmP 91*
**Hall,** Harlan Glenn *AmMWSc 92*
**Hall,** Harold Arthur 1938- *WhoRel 92*
**Hall,** Harold Edward 1951- *WhoMW 92*
**Hall,** Harold Eugene 1922- *WhoBlA 92*
**Hall,** Harold George 1920- *Who 92*
**Hall,** Harold Hershey 1924- *AmMWSc 92*
**Hall,** Harold L. *WhoBlA 92*
**Hall,** Harold Percival 1913- *Who 92*
**Hall,** Harold Robert 1935- *WhoWest 92*
**Hall,** Harvey 1904- *AmMWSc 92*
**Hall,** Henry Edgar 1928- *IntWW 91, Who 92*
**Hall,** Henry Kingston, Jr 1924- *AmMWSc 92*
**Hall,** Henry Lyon, Jr. 1931- *WhoAmL 92*
**Hall,** Herbert Glen 1933- *WhoAmL 92*
**Hall,** Herbert Joseph 1916- *AmMWSc 92*
**Hall,** Homer James 1911- *AmMWSc 92*
**Hall,** Homer L. 1939- *WhoMW 92*
**Hall,** Homer Richard *RelLAm 91*
**Hall,** Horathel 1926- *WhoBlA 92*
**Hall,** Howard Pickering 1915- *WhoWest 92*
**Hall,** Howard Ralph 1919- *WhoBlA 92*
**Hall,** Howard Tracy 1919- *AmMWSc 92*
**Hall,** Howard Wesley 1949- *WhoEnt 92*
**Hall,** Hubert Desmond 1925- *Who 92*
**Hall,** Hugh David 1931- *AmMWSc 92*
**Hall,** Huntz 1920- *IntMPA 92*
**Hall,** Hurley W 1935- *WhoAmP 91*
**Hall,** Ian Wavell *AmMWSc 92*
**Hall,** Ira DeVoyd 1905- *WhoBlA 92*
**Hall,** Iris Beryl Haddon 1937- *AmMWSc 92*
**Hall,** Ivan Victor 1927- *AmMWSc 92*
**Hall,** J A 1920- *AmMWSc 92*
**Hall,** J. C. 1920- *ConPo 91, WrDr 92*
**Hall,** J Gordon 1925- *AmMWSc 92*
**Hall,** J Herbert 1931- *AmMWSc 92*
**Hall,** James 1744-1826 *DcNCBi 3*
**Hall,** James 1793-1868 *BenetAL 91*
**Hall,** James 1811-1898 *BiInAmS*
**Hall,** James 1918- *WrDr 92*
**Hall,** James 1951- *WhoWest 92*
**Hall,** James B. 1918- *BenetAL 91, WrDr 92*
**Hall,** James Baker *DrAPF 91*
**Hall,** James Byron *DrAPF 91*
**Hall,** James Byron 1918- *IntAu&W 91*
**Hall,** James Conrad 1919- *AmMWSc 92*
**Hall,** James Dane 1933- *AmMWSc 92*
**Hall,** James Edison 1942- *AmMWSc 92*
**Hall,** James Emerson 1936- *AmMWSc 92*
**Hall,** James Ewbank 1941- *AmMWSc 92*
**Hall,** James King 1875-1948 *DcNCBi 3*
**Hall,** James Lawrence 1928- *AmMWSc 92*
**Hall,** James Lester 1910- *AmMWSc 92*
**Hall,** James Louis 1927- *AmMWSc 92*
**Hall,** James Norman 1887-1951 *BenetAL 91*
**Hall,** James Pierre 1848-1919 *BiInAmS*
**Hall,** James Randal 1958- *WhoAmL 92*
**Hall,** James Reginald 1936- *WhoBlA 92*
**Hall,** James Snowdon 1919- *Who 92*
**Hall,** James Stanley 1930- *WhoEnt 92*
**Hall,** James Timothy 1950- *AmMWSc 92*
**Hall,** James Wesley 1946- *WhoMW 92*
**Hall,** Jane Anna 1959- *IntAu&W 91*
**Hall,** Jason Yarwood 1945- *WhoAmP 91*
**Hall,** Jean Graham 1917- *Who 92*
**Hall,** Jeffrey Connor 1945- *AmMWSc 92*
**Hall,** Jennifer Dean 1944- *AmMWSc 92*
**Hall,** Jennifer Loie Pray 1951- *WhoEnt 92*
**Hall,** Jerome 1901- *WrDr 92*
**Hall,** Jerome William 1943- *AmMWSc 92*
**Hall,** Jerry 1956- *IntWW 91*
**Hall,** Jerry Lee 1938- *AmMWSc 92*
**Hall,** Jesse J. 1938- *WhoBlA 92*
**Hall,** Jessica Pincus 1951- *WhoAmL 92*
**Hall,** Jim *DrAPF 91*
**Hall,** Joan Joffe *DrAPF 91*
**Hall,** Joan M. 1939- *WhoAmL 92*
**Hall,** Joan Valerie 1935- *Who 92*
**Hall,** John *Who 92*
**Hall,** John 1767-1833 *DcNCBi 3*
**Hall,** John Anthony Sanderson 1921- *Who 92*
**Hall,** John B 1918- *AmMWSc 92*
**Hall,** John Bernard 1932- *Who 92*
**Hall,** John Bradley 1933- *AmMWSc 92*
**Hall,** John Daniel, II 1947- *WhoFI 92*
**Hall,** John Edgar 1929- *AmMWSc 92*
**Hall,** John Edward *AmMWSc 92*
**Hall,** John Edward 1959- *WhoAmL 92*
**Hall,** John Emmett 1925- *AmMWSc 92*
**Hall,** John Franklin, Jr. 1964- *WhoAmL 92*
**Hall,** John Frederick 1923- *AmMWSc 92*
**Hall,** John Herbert 1942- *WhoAmL 92*
**Hall,** John Hopkins 1925- *WhoAmL 92*
**Hall,** John Howland 1938- *WhoAmP 91*
**Hall,** John Jay 1931- *AmMWSc 92*
**Hall,** John L 1934- *AmMWSc 92*
**Hall,** John Noble, III 1945- *WhoEnt 92*
**Hall,** John Patrick, III 1963- *WhoEnt 92*
**Hall,** John R. 1932- *IntWW 91*
**Hall,** John Richard 1932- *WhoFI 92*
**Hall,** John Robert 1920- *WhoBlA 92*
**Hall,** John Ryder *WrDr 92*
**Hall,** John Scoville d1991 *NewYTBS 91*
**Hall,** John Stuart 1942- *WhoWest 92*
**Hall,** John Sylvester 1930- *AmMWSc 92*
**Hall,** John Thomas 1938- *WhoAmL 92*
**Hall,** John W 1929- *WhoIns 92*
**Hall,** John W 1939- *WhoAmP 91*
**Hall,** John Wesley, Jr. 1948- *WhoAmL 92, WhoFI 92*
**Hall,** John Wilfred 1941- *AmMWSc 92*
**Hall,** John William 1963- *WhoMW 92*
**Hall,** Jon K 1937- *AmMWSc 92*
**Hall,** Joseph 1574-1656 *RfGEnL 91*
**Hall,** Joseph A. 1908- *WhoBlA 92*
**Hall,** Joseph Albert 1931- *WhoMW 92*
**Hall,** Joseph Clemon 1955- *WhoBlA 92*
**Hall,** Joseph Glenn 1923- *AmMWSc 92*
**Hall,** Joseph L 1936- *AmMWSc 92*
**Hall,** Josephus Wells 1805-1873 *DcNCBi 3*
**Hall,** Joyce Clyde 1891-1982 *FacFETw*
**Hall,** Juanita 1901-1968 *NotBlAW 92*
**Hall,** Judd Lewis 1934- *AmMWSc 92*
**Hall,** Judith *DrAPF 91*
**Hall,** Judy Dale 1943- *AmMWSc 92*
**Hall,** Judy Kathryn 1953- *WhoEnt 92*
**Hall,** Julia Glover *WhoBlA 92*
**Hall,** Julian 1939- *Who 92*
**Hall,** Kate d1991 *NewYTBS 91*
**Hall,** Katherine Boussarie 1938- *WhoWest 92*
**Hall,** Kathleen 1924- *WrDr 92*
**Hall,** Katie 1938- *WhoAmP 91, WhoBlA 92*
**Hall,** Kenneth 1915- *WhoAmP 91, WhoBlA 92*
**Hall,** Kenneth Daland 1926- *AmMWSc 92*
**Hall,** Kenneth Franklin 1926- *WhoRel 92*
**Hall,** Kenneth K 1918- *WhoAmP 91*
**Hall,** Kenneth Keller 1918- *WhoAmL 92*
**Hall,** Kenneth Lynn 1927- *AmMWSc 92*
**Hall,** Kenneth Noble 1935- *AmMWSc 92*
**Hall,** Kenneth Richard 1939- *AmMWSc 92*
**Hall,** Kent D 1937- *AmMWSc 92*
**Hall,** Kent S, Sr 1928- *WhoAmP 91*
**Hall,** Kersh E, Jr 1947- *WhoAmP 91*
**Hall,** Kevin Patrick 1958- *WhoAmL 92*
**Hall,** Kim Felicia 1961- *WhoBlA 92*
**Hall,** Kimball Parker 1914- *AmMWSc 92*
**Hall,** Kirkwood Marshal 1944- *WhoBlA 92*
**Hall,** Kirsten Marie 1974- *ConAu 135, SmATA 67*
**Hall,** Kristin Kay 1967- *WhoMW 92*
**Hall,** Larry Bruce 1942- *WhoRel 92*
**Hall,** Larry Cully 1930- *AmMWSc 92*
**Hall,** Larry D. 1942- *WhoWest 92*
**Hall,** Larry Lamar 1948- *WhoMW 92*
**Hall,** Laura Margaret *Who 92*
**Hall,** Laurance David 1938- *Who 92*
**Hall,** Laurence Charles B. *Who 92*
**Hall,** Laurence Stanford 1929- *AmMWSc 92*
**Hall,** Lawrence H. 1944- *WhoBlA 92*
**Hall,** Lawrence John 1955- *AmMWSc 92*
**Hall,** Lawrence Sargent *DrAPF 91*
**Hall,** Leo McAloon 1929- *AmMWSc 92*
**Hall,** Leo Terry 1941- *AmMWSc 92*
**Hall,** Leon Morris, Jr 1946- *AmMWSc 92*
**Hall,** Leonard J 1943- *WhoAmP 91*
**Hall,** Leslie 1948- *IntAu&W 91*
**Hall,** Leslie North 1958- *WhoMW 92*
**Hall,** Leslie Warren 1962- *WhoFI 92*
**Hall,** Lilbourne Preston 1922- *WhoAmP 91*
**Hall,** Lloyd Eugene 1953- *WhoBlA 92*
**Hall,** Lois Riggs 1930- *WhoAmP 91, WhoEnt 92, WhoWest 92*
**Hall,** Lowell Headley, II 1937- *AmMWSc 92*
**Hall,** Luther Axtell Richard 1924- *AmMWSc 92*
**Hall,** Lyle Clarence 1935- *AmMWSc 92*
**Hall,** Lyman 1859-1905 *BiInAmS*
**Hall,** Lynn 1937- *IntAu&W 91, WrDr 92*
**Hall,** Lynnelle Marie Millard 1946- *WhoEnt 92*
**Hall,** Lysle Griffith, Jr. 1930- *WhoAmL 92*
**Hall,** Madeline Molnar 1936- *AmMWSc 92*
**Hall,** Manly Palmer 1901- *RelLAm 91*
**Hall,** Marcia Joy 1947- *WhoFI 92*
**Hall,** Margaret Dorothy 1936- *Who 92*
**Hall,** Marian Ella 1920- *WhoWest 92*
**Hall,** Marie Boas 1919- *IntAu&W 91, WrDr 92*
**Hall,** Marion H 1925- *WhoIns 92*
**Hall,** Marion Trufant 1920- *AmMWSc 92, WhoMW 92*
**Hall,** Marjory 1908- *IntAu&W 91, WrDr 92*
**Hall,** Mark Ronald 1941- *WhoWest 92*
**Hall,** Martin Hardwick 1925-1979? *ConAu 35NR*
**Hall,** Maureen 1936- *WhoEnt 92*
**Hall,** Melvin Curtis 1956- *WhoBlA 92*
**Hall,** Michael Alan 1950- *WhoFI 92*
**Hall,** Michael Kilgour H. *Who 92*
**Hall,** Michael Oakley 1936- *AmMWSc 92*
**Hall,** Michael Robert Pritchard 1922- *Who 92*
**Hall,** Michael Stephen 1958- *WhoAmL 92*
**Hall,** Michael Thurner 1949- *WhoAmL 92*
**Hall,** Mildred Martha 1949- *WhoBlA 92*
**Hall,** Miles Lewis, Jr. 1924- *WhoAmL 92, WhoFI 92*
**Hall,** Milton L. *WhoRel 92*
**Hall,** Monty *LesBEnT 92*
**Hall,** Monty 1925- *WhoEnt 92*
**Hall,** Munford Page, II 1948- *WhoAmL 92*
**Hall,** Nancy K 1947- *AmMWSc 92*
**Hall,** Nancy M. *WhoBlA 92*
**Hall,** Narrvel Elwin 1940- *WhoAmL 92*
**Hall,** Nathan Albert 1918- *AmMWSc 92*
**Hall,** Neal 1952- *ConAu 134*
**Hall,** Neil Robert 1953- *WhoWest 92*
**Hall,** Newman A 1913- *AmMWSc 92*
**Hall,** Nigel 1943- *TwCPaSc*
**Hall,** Nigel John 1943- *IntWW 91*
**Hall,** Oakley 1920- *BenetAL 91, IntAu&W 91, TwCWW 91, WrDr 92*
**Hall,** Oakley Maxwell 1920- *WhoWest 92*
**Hall,** Oliver 1869-1957 *TwCPaSc*
**Hall,** Otis F 1921- *AmMWSc 92*
**Hall,** Owen 1853-1903 *ScFEYrs*
**Hall,** Palmer Alohilani 1954- *WhoWest 92*
**Hall,** Pancho Delano 1960- *WhoFI 92*
**Hall,** Patricia Marty 1954- *WhoFI 92*
**Hall,** Patrick 1906- *TwCPaSc*
**Hall,** Patrick 1935- *TwCPaSc*
**Hall,** Perry Alonzo 1947- *WhoBlA 92*
**Hall,** Peter *Who 92*
**Hall,** Peter 1926- *AmMWSc 92*
**Hall,** Peter 1930- *ConAu 133, FacFETw*
**Hall,** Peter 1932- *IntAu&W 91, WrDr 92*
**Hall,** Peter Dalton 1924- *Who 92*
**Hall,** Peter Edward 1938- *Who 92*
**Hall,** Peter Francis 1924- *AmMWSc 92*
**Hall,** Peter Geoffrey 1932- *IntWW 91, Who 92*
**Hall,** Peter George 1924- *IntWW 91, Who 92*
**Hall,** Peter M 1934- *AmMWSc 92*
**Hall,** Peter Reginald Frederick 1930- *IntWW 91, Who 92, WhoEnt 92*
**Hall,** Phil 1964- *IntAu&W 91*
**Hall,** Philip George 1946- *WhoRel 92*
**Hall,** Philip Layton 1940- *AmMWSc 92*
**Hall,** Philip Logan 1930- *WhoMW 92*
**Hall,** Philip Wells, III 1925- *AmMWSc 92*
**Hall,** Phoebe Poulterer 1941- *WhoAmL 92*
**Hall,** Prescott F 1868-1920 *DcAmImH*
**Hall,** Prince *DcAmImH*
**Hall,** R Glenn, Jr 1921- *AmMWSc 92*
**Hall,** Radclyffe 1880-1943 *RfGEnL 91*
**Hall,** Ralph M. 1923- *AlmAP 92 [port], WhoAmP 91*
**Hall,** Rand 1945- *IntAu&W 91*
**Hall,** Randall Clark 1946- *AmMWSc 92*
**Hall,** Randall Steven 1954- *WhoMW 92, WhoRel 92*
**Hall,** Ray C 1944- *WhoIns 92*
**Hall,** Raymond A. 1914- *WhoBlA 92*
**Hall,** Raymond G, Jr 1937- *AmMWSc 92*
**Hall,** Reginald 1931- *Who 92*
**Hall,** Reginald Lawrence 1957- *WhoBlA 92*
**Hall,** Richard 1925- *WrDr 92*

Hall, Richard Brian 1947- AmMWSc 92
Hall, Richard Chandler 1939- AmMWSc 92
Hall, Richard Clyde, Jr. 1931- WhoRel 92
Hall, Richard Darrell 1953- WhoWest 92
Hall, Richard Dennis 1935- WhoWest 92
Hall, Richard Eugene 1936- AmMWSc 92, WhoWest 92
Hall, Richard Eugene 1943- AmMWSc 92
Hall, Richard Harold 1927- AmMWSc 92, WhoAmP 91
Hall, Richard L 1940- AmMWSc 92
Hall, Richard Leland 1923- AmMWSc 92
Hall, Richard Murray, Jr. 1947- WhoFI 92
Hall, Richard R 1932- WhoAmP 91
Hall, Richard Seymour 1925- IntAu&W 91
Hall, Richard Travis 1938- AmMWSc 92
Hall, Richard Wayne 1951- WhoEnt 92
Hall, Robert 1939- AmMWSc 92
Hall, Robert Alan 1958- WhoFI 92
Hall, Robert Carlton 1915- WhoFI 92
Hall, Robert de Zouche 1904- Who 92
Hall, Robert Dickinson 1947- AmMWSc 92
Hall, Robert Dilwyn 1929- AmMWSc 92
Hall, Robert Earl 1949- AmMWSc 92
Hall, Robert Emmett, Jr. 1936- WhoFI 92, WhoWest 92
Hall, Robert Everett 1924- AmMWSc 92
Hall, Robert Howell 1921- WhoAmL 92, WhoAmP 91
Hall, Robert Johnson 1937- WhoBlA 92
Hall, Robert Joseph 1926- AmMWSc 92
Hall, Robert Joseph 1929- WhoBlA 92
Hall, Robert L. d1991 NewYTBS 91
Hall, Robert L. 1937- WhoBlA 92
Hall, Robert Lester 1939- AmMWSc 92
Hall, Robert Lynn 1945- WhoMW 92
Hall, Robert Noel 1919- AmMWSc 92
Hall, Robert T 1933- WhoAmP 91
Hall, Rodney 1935- ConPo 91, IntAu&W 91, WrDr 92
Hall, Rodney 1955- WhoAmP 91
Hall, Roger 1939- ConAu 134, WrDr 92
Hall, Roger Dale 1955- WhoFI 92
Hall, Roger Lee 1942- WhoEnt 92
Hall, Roger Leighton 1939- IntAu&W 91
Hall, Ronald Henry 1930- AmMWSc 92, WhoMW 92
Hall, Ronald Lenard 1962- WhoMW 92
Hall, Ronald William 1946- WhoMW 92
Hall, Ross Hume 1926- AmMWSc 92
Hall, Rubye Maie 1912- WhoBlA 92
Hall, Russell P AmMWSc 92
Hall, Sam Blakeley, Jr. 1924- WhoAmL 92, WhoAmP 91
Hall, Sam S. 1838-1886 BenetAL 91
Hall, Samuel 1740-1809 BenetAL 91
Hall, Scott Michael 1950- WhoFI 92
Hall, Seymour Gerald 1940- AmMWSc 92
Hall, Sharon 1954- TwCPaSc
Hall, Shirley Robinson 1942- WhoAmP 91, WhoBlA 92
Hall, Simon Robert Dawson 1938- Who 92
Hall, Stan Stanley 1938- AmMWSc 92
Hall, Stanley Eckler 1934- WhoFI 92
Hall, Stanton Harris 1940- AmMWSc 92
Hall, Stephen Charles 1948- WhoAmL 92
Hall, Stephen Kenneth 1934- AmMWSc 92
Hall, Stephen Kenneth 1953- WhoAmL 92
Hall, Steve Henry 1954- WhoEnt 92
Hall, Steven Alan 1952- WhoWest 92
Hall, Stuart George 1928- Who 92, WhoRel 92
Hall, Stuart McPhail 1932- Who 92
Hall, Susan Jean 1951- WhoWest 92
Hall, T. Hartley, IV WhoRel 92
Hall, Talton 1958- WhoMW 92
Hall, TennieBee May 1940- WhoWest 92
Hall, Teresa Marie 1957- WhoWest 92
Hall, Theodore DrAPF 91
Hall, Theodore 1925- AmMWSc 92
Hall, Thomas Christopher 1921- AmMWSc 92
Hall, Thomas E 1919- WhoAmP 91
Hall, Thomas Emerson 1954- WhoFI 92
Hall, Thomas H., Jr. 1924- WhoRel 92
Hall, Thomas Harmison 1773-1853 DcNCBi 3
Hall, Thomas James 1957- WhoEnt 92
Hall, Thomas Jennings 1948- WhoAmL 92
Hall, Thomas Kenneth 1936- AmMWSc 92
Hall, Thomas Livingston 1931- AmMWSc 92
Hall, Thomas Munroe 1943- WhoEnt 92
Hall, Thomas Patrick 1954- WhoFI 92
Hall, Thomas William 1921- WhoRel 92
Hall, Thomas William 1931- Who 92
Hall, Thor 1927- WhoRel 92, WrDr 92
Hall, Tim L 1925- WhoAmP 91
Hall, Timothy 1956- WhoAmP 91
Hall, Timothy Arthur 1956- WhoFI 92
Hall, Timothy Couzens 1937- AmMWSc 92
Hall, Tom 1955- WhoEnt 92
Hall, Tom T. 1936- NewAmDM, WhoEnt 92
Hall, Tony P. 1942- AlmAP 92 [port], WhoAmP 91, WhoMW 92
Hall, Trevor H. 1910-1991 ConAu 134
Hall, Trevor Henry d1991 Who 92N
Hall, Trevor Henry 1910- IntAu&W 91, WrDr 92
Hall, Vernon F. 1904- Who 92
Hall, Virginia Duffer 1937- WhoAmP 91
Hall, Vivian Halpern 1922- WhoAmP 91
Hall, W J 1926- AmMWSc 92
Hall, W Keith 1918- AmMWSc 92
Hall, W M 1906- AmMWSc 92
Hall, Wade DrAPF 91
Hall, Wallace John 1934- Who 92
Hall, Warren A 1919- AmMWSc 92
Hall, Warren G 1948- AmMWSc 92
Hall, Wayne 1927- WhoAmP 91
Hall, Wayne Clark 1919- AmMWSc 92
Hall, Wayne Hawkins 1936- AmMWSc 92
Hall, Wendell Howard 1916- AmMWSc 92
Hall, Wesley Winfield 1937- IntWW 91
Hall, William 1775-1856 DcNCBi 3
Hall, William 1919- Who 92
Hall, William Andrew, Jr. 1962- WhoEnt 92
Hall, William Barkley, III 1933- WhoEnt 92
Hall, William Bartlett 1925- AmMWSc 92
Hall, William Bateman 1923- Who 92
Hall, William C 1922- WhoIns 92
Hall, William Charles 1940- AmMWSc 92
Hall, William Earl 1938- AmMWSc 92
Hall, William Edward, Jr. 1951- WhoFI 92
Hall, William Francis 1928- AmMWSc 92
Hall, William Heinlen 1910- AmMWSc 92
Hall, William Henry 1906- Who 92
Hall, William Jackson 1929- AmMWSc 92
Hall, William Joel 1926- AmMWSc 92
Hall, William K. 1943- IntWW 91
Hall, William King 1943- WhoFI 92, WhoMW 92
Hall, William N, Jr WhoAmP 91
Hall, William Pembroke 1929- WhoRel 92
Hall, William Spencer 1935- AmMWSc 92
Hall, William Wesley 1956- WhoAmP 91
Hall, Willie Green, Jr. 1947- WhoBlA 92
Hall, Willis 1929- ConAu 36NR, IntAu&W 91, SmATA 66, Who 92, WrDr 92
Hall, Wilson d1990 LesBEnT 92
Hall, Wilson 1922-1991 ConAu 133
Hall, Wilson D. d1991 NewYTBS 91
Hall, Wynn Ryle 1959- WhoWest 92
Hall, Yong Ok 1950- WhoWest 92
Hall, Yvonne WhoEnt 92
Hall, Yvonne Bonnie WhoBlA 92
Hall, Zach Winter 1937- AmMWSc 92
Hall-Keith, Jaqueline Yvonne 1953- WhoBlA 92
Hall-Matthews, Anthony Francis Who 92
Hall-Thompson, Lloyd 1920- Who 92
Hall Williams Who 92
Halla, Chris DrAPF 91
Hallada, Calvin James 1933- AmMWSc 92
Halladay, Eric 1930- Who 92
Halladay, Thomas Eugene 1954- WhoEnt 92
Hallahan, William H IntAu&W 91, WrDr 92
Hallahan, William Laskey 1946- AmMWSc 92
Hallam, Bishop of 1922- Who 92
Hallam, Elizabeth M. 1950- WrDr 92
Hallam, Everett Lee 1951- WhoMW 92
Hallam, Orval Keith, Jr. 1949- WhoAmL 92
Hallam, Robert J. WhoWest 92
Hallam, Robert J. 1952- WhoEnt 92
Hallam, Thomas Guy 1937- AmMWSc 92
Hallam Hipwell, H. Who 92
Hallanan, Elizabeth V. 1925- WhoAmL 92
Hallanan, Sharon Margaret 1961- WhoAmL 92
Hallanger, Lawrence William 1939- AmMWSc 92
Hallanger, Norman Lawrence 1912- AmMWSc 92
Hallard, Wayne Bruce 1951- WhoFI 92
Hallas, Laurence Edward 1954- AmMWSc 92
Hallas-Gottlieb, Lisa Gail 1950- WhoEnt 92
Hallatt, David Marrison 1937- Who 92
Hallauer, Arnel Roy 1932- AmMWSc 92
Hallbauer, Robert Edward 1930- WhoFI 92, WhoWest 92
Hallberg, Budd Jaye 1942- WhoFI 92
Hallberg, Carl William 1918- AmMWSc 92
Hallberg, Dale Merton 1927- WhoWest 92
Hallberg, Evelyne Anne 1946- WhoFI 92
Hallberg, Fred William 1935- WhoRel 92
Hallberg, George Robert 1946- AmMWSc 92
Hallberg, JoAnna Marie 1963- WhoMW 92
Hallberg, Paul Thure 1931- IntWW 91
Hallbom, Harold Raymond, Jr. 1951- WhoFI 92
Hallchurch, David Thomas 1929- Who 92
Halle, Adam de la NewAmDM
Halle, Charles 1819-1895 NewAmDM
Halle, Morris 1923- AmMWSc 92
Halle, Peter Edward 1944- WhoAmL 92
Halle, William 1912- TwCPaSc
Hallead, Glen James 1957- WhoRel 92
Halleck, Charles A 1900-1986 FacFETw
Halleck, Fitz-Greene 1790-1867 BenetAL 91
Halleck, Frank Eugene 1927- AmMWSc 92
Halleck, Margaret S 1937- AmMWSc 92
Halleck, Seymour Leon 1929- AmMWSc 92
Halleen, Robert M 1933- AmMWSc 92
Halleen, Shirley Kells 1935- WhoAmP 91
Hallen, A L ScFEYrs
Hallen, Kenneth Peter 1943- WhoIns 92
Hallenbeck, Gertrude Helene 1920- WhoEnt 92
Hallenbeck, Lane William 1955- WhoWest 92
Hallenbeck, Patrick Clark 1951- AmMWSc 92
Hallenbeck, Pomona Juanita 1938- WhoWest 92
Hallenbeck, William Hackett 1945- AmMWSc 92
Hallenberg, Robert Lewis 1948- WhoAmL 92
Haller, Albrecht von 1708-1777 BlkwCEP
Haller, Bill IntAu&W 91X, TwCWW 91, WrDr 92
Haller, Charles Regis 1931- AmMWSc 92
Haller, Edwin Wolfgang 1936- AmMWSc 92
Haller, Elden D 1909- AmMWSc 92
Haller, Eugene Ernest 1943- AmMWSc 92
Haller, Evelyn Harris 1937- WhoMW 92, WhoRel 92
Haller, Fritz 1924- DcTwDes, FacFETw
Haller, Gary Lee 1941- AmMWSc 92
Haller, Gary Louis 1936- WhoMW 92
Haller, Ivan 1934- AmMWSc 92
Haller, Kenneth E 1941- WhoIns 92
Haller, Kenneth Lawrence 1922- WhoAmP 91
Haller, Kurt 1928- AmMWSc 92
Haller, Pamela WhoRel 92
Haller, Peter J 1937- WhoIns 92
Haller, Scot DrAPF 91
Haller, William T 1947- AmMWSc 92
Haller, Wolfgang Karl 1922- AmMWSc 92
Halleran, E.E. 1905- TwCWW 91, WrDr 92
Halleran, Eugene Edward 1905- IntAu&W 91
Hallerman, Victoria DrAPF 91
Hallesy, Duane Wesley 1928- AmMWSc 92
Hallet, Bernard 1948- AmMWSc 92
Hallet, Raymon William, Jr 1920- AmMWSc 92
Hallet, Richard Matthews 1887-1967 BenetAL 91
Hallett, Carol 1937- WhoAmP 91
Hallett, Cecil Walter 1899- Who 92
Hallett, Charles Arthur, Jr. 1939- WhoEnt 92
Hallett, Dean Charles 1958- WhoWest 92
Hallett, Frederick Ross 1942- AmMWSc 92
Hallett, George Edward Maurice 1912- Who 92
Hallett, Graham 1929- WrDr 92
Hallett, Heather Carol 1949- Who 92
Hallett, John 1929- AmMWSc 92, WhoWest 92
Hallett, Laurence S 1957- WhoIns 92
Hallett, Mark 1943- AmMWSc 92
Hallett, Peter Edward 1937- AmMWSc 92
Hallett, Robin 1926- WrDr 92
Hallett, Victor George Henry 1921- Who 92
Hallett, Wilbur Y 1926- AmMWSc 92
Halleux, Albert Martin Julien 1920- WhoFI 92
Halley, Anne DrAPF 91
Halley, Edmond 1656-1742 BlkwCEP
Halley, James Woods 1938- AmMWSc 92
Halley, Laurence Who 92
Halley, Robert 1920- AmMWSc 92
Halley, Robert Bruce 1947- AmMWSc 92
Hallford, Dennis Murray 1948- AmMWSc 92
Hallfrisch, Judith AmMWSc 92
Hallgarten, Anthony Bernard Richard 1937- Who 92
Hallgarten, S. F. 1902- WrDr 92
Hallgren, Alvin Roland 1919- AmMWSc 92
Hallgren, Helen M 1940- AmMWSc 92
Hallgren, Richard E 1932- AmMWSc 92
Hallgrimsson, Geir 1925- IntWW 91
Hallgrimsson, Haflidi 1941- ConCom 92
Halliburton, Larry Eugene 1943- AmMWSc 92
Halliburton, Richard 1900-1939 BenetAL 91, ConAu 135
Halliburton, Robert John 1935- Who 92
Halliburton, Warren J. 1924- WhoBlA 92
Halliday, Brian 1966- WhoEnt 92
Halliday, Dorothy IntAu&W 91X
Halliday, Fred 1946- Who 92
Halliday, Ian 1928- AmMWSc 92
Halliday, Ian Francis 1927- IntWW 91, Who 92
Halliday, John Frederick 1942- Who 92
Halliday, John Meech 1936- WhoWest 92
Halliday, Joseph William 1938- WhoAmL 92
Halliday, Michael Alexander Kirkwood 1925- IntWW 91, Who 92
Halliday, Miriam DrAPF 91
Halliday, Norman Pryde 1932- Who 92
Halliday, Robert Taylor Who 92
Halliday, Robert William 1942- AmMWSc 92
Halliday, Roy 1923- Who 92
Halliday, S. F. P. Who 92
Halliday, Stephen Mills 1927- WhoFI 92
Halliday, William James, Jr. 1921- WhoFI 92
Halliday, William R. 1926- WrDr 92
Halliday, William Ross 1926- WhoWest 92
Halliday-Borkowski, Miriam DrAPF 91
Hallier, Hans-Joachim 1930- IntWW 91
Hallifax, David 1927- Who 92
Halligan, Buddy Emanuel 1964- WhoEnt 92
Halligan, James Edmund 1936- WhoWest 92
Halligan, Marion Mildred 1940- IntAu&W 91
Halligan, Mike Lewis 1949- WhoAmP 91
Halligan, Roger John, Jr. 1948- WhoMW 92
Hallin, Emily W IntAu&W 91
Hallin, Emily Watson 1919- WrDr 92
Hallinan, Adrian Lincoln 1922- Who 92
Hallinan, Hazel Hunkins 1891-1982 FacFETw
Hallinan, Lincoln Who 92
Hallinan, Mary Alethea Who 92
Hallinan, Nancy DrAPF 91
Hallinan, Thomas James 1941- AmMWSc 92
Halling, Beverly Jane 1931- WhoAmP 91
Halling, Jennifer Jane 1962- WhoRel 92
Halling, Solomon 1754?-1813 DcNCBi 3
Hallingby, Paul, Jr. 1919- WhoFI 92
Hallisey, Jeremiah F 1939- WhoAmP 91
Hallissey, Michael 1943- WhoFI 92
Halliwell, Brian 1930- Who 92
Halliwell, David 1936- IntAu&W 91, WrDr 92
Halliwell, Leslie 1929- IntAu&W 91
Halliwell, Richard Edward Winter 1937- Who 92
Halliwell, Robert Stanley 1931- AmMWSc 92
Hallman, Cloyce Eldon 1927- WhoFI 92
Hallman, Dwayne Duncan 1962- WhoIns 92
Hallman, Harry M, Jr 1934- WhoAmP 91
Hallman, Leroy 1915- WhoAmL 92
Hallman, Viola 1944- IntWW 91
Hallmark, Anne WhoEnt 92
Hallmundsson, Hallberg 1930- IntAu&W 91
Hallo, William W. 1928- WrDr 92
Hallock, Brook DrAPF 91
Hallock, Charles 1834-1917 BiInAmS
Hallock, Gilbert Vinton AmMWSc 92
Hallock, Harriett WhoEnt 92
Hallock, James A 1942- AmMWSc 92
Hallock, John Wallace, Jr 1946- WhoAmP 91
Hallock, Joseph Theodore 1921- WhoAmP 91
Hallock, Robert B 1943- AmMWSc 92
Hallock, Steve 1957- WhoEnt 92
Hallock, William 1857-1913 BiInAmS
Hallock, Zachariah R 1942- AmMWSc 92
Hallock-Muller, Pamela 1948- AmMWSc 92
Halloin, John McDonell 1938- AmMWSc 92
Halloin, Samuel 1923- WhoAmP 91
Halloran, Hobart Rooker 1916- AmMWSc 92
Halloran, James Vincent, III 1942- WhoWest 92
Halloran, Kevin Leo 1962- WhoWest 92
Halloran, Leo Augustine 1931- WhoFI 92
Halloran, Michael James 1941- WhoAmL 92, WhoWest 92
Halloran, Michael John 1957- WhoRel 92
Halloran, Patrick W., III 1943- WhoEnt 92
Halloran, Philip Francis 1944- AmMWSc 92

**Halloran**, Richard Colby 1930- *WhoWest 92*
**Halloran**, Thomas Giuld 1949- *WhoAmL 92*
**Halloran**, Victor David 1927- *WhoMW 92*
**Hallowell**, Benjamin 1799-1877 *BiInAmS*
**Hallowell**, Edward 1808-1860 *BiInAmS*
**Hallowell**, John H 1953- *WhoRel 92*
**Hallowell**, Susan Maria 1835-1911 *BiInAmS*
**Hallowell**, Tommy *ConAu 135*
**Hallowell**, Walter Henry 1943- *WhoFI 92*
**Hallowes**, Odette Marie Celine 1912- *IntWW 91, Who 92*
**Hallows**, Karen S. 1950- *WhoMW 92*
**Hallquist**, Allan Verner 1954- *WhoAmL 92*
**Halls**, Geraldine *IntAu&W 91X*
**Halls**, Lowell Keith 1918- *AmMWSc 92*
**Halls**, Wilfred Douglas 1918- *WrDr 92*
**Hallstein**, Walter 1901-1982 *FacFETw*
**Hallstrand**, Sarah Laymon 1944- *WhoRel 92*
**Hallstrom**, David Eric 1958- *WhoRel 92*
**Hallstrom**, Lasse 1946- *IntWW 91*
**Hallsworth**, Ernest Gordon 1913- *Who 92*
**Hallum**, Cecil Ralph 1944- *AmMWSc 92*
**Hallum**, Jules Verne 1925- *AmMWSc 92*
**Hallums**, Benjamin F. 1940- *WhoBlA 92*
**Hallward**, Bertrand Leslie 1901- *Who 92*
**Hallwas**, John Edward 1945- *WhoMW 92*
**Hallwood**, Clifford Paul 1946- *WhoFI 92*
**Hally**, Martha 1952- *WhoEnt 92*
**Halm**, Dan Robert 1955- *AmMWSc 92*
**Halm**, James Maurice *AmMWSc 92*
**Halmi**, Nicholas Stephen 1922- *AmMWSc 92*
**Halmi**, Robert *LesBEnT 92*
**Halmi**, Robert, Sr. 1924- *IntMPA 92*
**Halmos**, Paul Richard 1916- *AmMWSc 92*
**Halmos**, Steven J. 1948- *WhoFI 92*
**Halmrast**, Gerald A *WhoAmP 91*
**Halnan**, Patrick John 1925- *Who 92*
**Halonen**, Marilyn Jean 1941- *AmMWSc 92*
**Halonen**, Traja Kaarina 1943- *IntWW 91*
**Halopoff**, William Evon 1934- *WhoWest 92*
**Haloulakos**, Vassilios E 1931- *AmMWSc 92*
**Halpenny**, Diana Doris 1951- *WhoAmL 92*
**Halpenny**, Leonard Cameron 1915- *WhoWest 92*
**Halper**, Albert 1904-1984 *BenetAL 91*
**Halper**, Jaroslava 1953- *AmMWSc 92*
**Halperin**, Adam Michael 1966- *WhoFI 92*
**Halperin**, Bertrand Israel 1941- *AmMWSc 92, IntWW 91*
**Halperin**, David A. *WhoFI 92*
**Halperin**, Don A 1925- *AmMWSc 92*
**Halperin**, Donald Marc 1945- *WhoAmP 91*
**Halperin**, Herman 1898- *AmMWSc 92*
**Halperin**, Irving *DrAPF 91*
**Halperin**, Jerome Yale 1930- *WhoFI 92, WhoMW 92*
**Halperin**, Joan *DrAPF 91*
**Halperin**, John William 1941- *DcLB 111 [port]*
**Halperin**, Jonas Eli d1991 *NewYTBS 91*
**Halperin**, Joseph 1923- *AmMWSc 92*
**Halperin**, Mark W. *DrAPF 91*
**Halperin**, Mark Warren 1940- *WhoWest 92*
**Halperin**, Matthew Craig 1962- *WhoFI 92*
**Halperin**, Max 1917- *AmMWSc 92*
**Halperin**, Richard George 1948- *WhoFI 92*
**Halperin**, Robert Milton 1928- *WhoFI 92*
**Halperin**, Stephen 1942- *AmMWSc 92*
**Halperin**, Steven T. 1961- *WhoAmL 92*
**Halperin**, Tulio 1926- *IntWW 91*
**Halperin**, Walter 1932- *AmMWSc 92*
**Halperin**, Warren Leslie 1938- *WhoWest 92*
**Halperin**, William Paul 1945- *AmMWSc 92*
**Halperin-Maya**, Miriam Patricia 1945- *AmMWSc 92*
**Halpern**, Alvin M 1938- *AmMWSc 92*
**Halpern**, Arthur Merrill 1943- *AmMWSc 92*
**Halpern**, Belle Linda 1961- *WhoEnt 92*
**Halpern**, Benjamin David 1921- *AmMWSc 92*
**Halpern**, Bernard 1918- *AmMWSc 92*
**Halpern**, Bruce Peter 1933- *AmMWSc 92*
**Halpern**, Daniel *DrAPF 91*
**Halpern**, Daniel 1917- *AmMWSc 92*
**Halpern**, Daniel 1945- *BenetAL 91, ConPo 91, IntWW 91, WrDr 92*
**Halpern**, David 1942- *AmMWSc 92*
**Halpern**, David Seymour 1928- *WhoRel 92*
**Halpern**, Donald F 1936- *AmMWSc 92*
**Halpern**, Ephriam Philip 1922- *AmMWSc 92*
**Halpern**, Francis Robert 1929- *AmMWSc 92*
**Halpern**, Harold David *WhoRel 92*
**Halpern**, Henia *TwCPaSc*
**Halpern**, Howard S 1925- *AmMWSc 92*
**Halpern**, Isaac 1923- *AmMWSc 92*
**Halpern**, Jack 1925- *AmMWSc 92, IntWW 91, Who 92, WhoFI 92, WhoMW 92*
**Halpern**, James Bladen 1936- *WhoFI 92*
**Halpern**, James Daniel 1934- *AmMWSc 92*
**Halpern**, Jay *DrAPF 91*
**Halpern**, Joseph Yehuda 1953- *WhoWest 92*
**Halpern**, Joshua Baruch 1946- *AmMWSc 92*
**Halpern**, Keith Stacy 1956- *WhoAmL 92*
**Halpern**, Kenneth Jay 1942- *WhoAmL 92*
**Halpern**, Larry J. 1941- *WhoRel 92*
**Halpern**, Lawrence Mayer 1931- *AmMWSc 92*
**Halpern**, Leopold 1925- *AmMWSc 92*
**Halpern**, Martin 1929- *WhoEnt 92*
**Halpern**, Martin 1937- *AmMWSc 92*
**Halpern**, Martin B 1939- *AmMWSc 92*
**Halpern**, Mimi 1938- *AmMWSc 92*
**Halpern**, Mordecai Joseph 1920- *AmMWSc 92*
**Halpern**, Moyshe Leyb 1886-1932 *LiExTwC*
**Halpern**, Myron Herbert 1924- *AmMWSc 92*
**Halpern**, Nathan L 1914- *IntMPA 92*
**Halpern**, Ralph 1938- *IntWW 91, Who 92*
**Halpern**, Ralph Lawrence 1929- *WhoAmL 92*
**Halpern**, Salmon Reclus 1907- *AmMWSc 92*
**Halpern**, Seymour 1915- *WhoAmP 91*
**Halpern**, Steven Jason 1947- *WhoEnt 92*
**Halpern**, Teodoro 1931- *AmMWSc 92*
**Halpern**, Terry *WhoAmL 92*
**Halpern**, William 1923- *AmMWSc 92*
**Halpern**, Yuval 1940- *WhoMW 92*
**Halperson**, Michael Allen 1946- *WhoFI 92*
**Halpert**, James Robert 1949- *AmMWSc 92*
**Halpert**, Leonard 1922- *WhoBlA 92*
**Halpert**, Marc Wesley 1955- *WhoFI 92*
**Halpert**, Stephen Kirk 1951- *WhoAmL 92*
**Halpin**, Charles A. *Who 92*
**Halpin**, Charles Aime 1930- *WhoRel 92*
**Halpin**, Daniel William 1938- *AmMWSc 92, WhoMW 92*
**Halpin**, Joseph John 1939- *AmMWSc 92*
**Halpin**, Kathleen Mary 1903- *Who 92*
**Halpin**, Mary Elizabeth 1951- *WhoMW 92*
**Halpin**, Patrick Goodchild 1953- *WhoAmP 91*
**Halpin**, Zuleyma Tang 1945- *AmMWSc 92*
**Halpine**, Charles Graham 1829-1868 *BenetAL 91*
**Halprin**, Anna Schuman 1920- *WhoEnt 92*
**Halprin**, Arthur 1935- *AmMWSc 92*
**Halprin**, Kenneth M 1931- *AmMWSc 92*
**Halprin**, Lawrence 1916- *WhoWest 92*
**Halpryn**, Bruce 1957- *AmMWSc 92*
**Hals**, Finn 1924- *AmMWSc 92*
**Halsall**, Eric 1920- *IntAu&W 91, WrDr 92*
**Halsall**, H Brian 1943- *AmMWSc 92*
**Halsan**, Stuart A *WhoAmP 91*
**Halsbury**, Earl Of 1880-1943 *ScFEYrs*
**Halsbury**, Earl of 1908- *IntWW 91, Who 92*
**Halsey**, A. H. 1923- *WrDr 92*
**Halsey**, Albert Henry 1923- *IntWW 91, Who 92*
**Halsey**, Brenton S 1927- *AmMWSc 92*
**Halsey**, Brenton Shaw 1927- *WhoFI 92*
**Halsey**, David 1919- *Who 92*
**Halsey**, Dorris Maria *WhoEnt 92*
**Halsey**, George *WhoBlA 92*
**Halsey**, George Dawson, Jr 1925- *AmMWSc 92*
**Halsey**, James Albert 1930- *WhoEnt 92, WhoFI 92*
**Halsey**, James H, Jr 1933- *AmMWSc 92*
**Halsey**, John Frederick 1942- *AmMWSc 92*
**Halsey**, John Joseph 1918- *AmMWSc 92*
**Halsey**, John Walter Brooke 1933- *Who 92*
**Halsey**, Mark 1961- *TwCPaSc*
**Halsey**, Philip Hugh 1928- *Who 92*
**Halsey**, William F. 1882-1959 *FacFETw*
**Halstead**, Bruce W 1920- *AmMWSc 92*
**Halstead**, Charles Lemuel 1928- *AmMWSc 92*
**Halstead**, Dirck S. 1936- *ConAu 133*
**Halstead**, Eric Henry 1912- *IntWW 91*
**Halstead**, Joan Marie 1949- *WhoFI 92*
**Halstead**, John G. H. 1922- *IntWW 91*
**Halstead**, John Stanley 1958- *WhoRel 92*
**Halstead**, L. Lindsey 1930- *WhoMW 92*
**Halstead**, Lester Mark 1927- *WhoWest 92*
**Halstead**, Lester Mark, Jr. 1950- *WhoFI 92*
**Halstead**, Ronald 1927- *IntWW 91, Who 92*
**Halstead**, Ronald Lawrence 1923- *AmMWSc 92*
**Halstead**, Scott Barker 1930- *AmMWSc 92*
**Halstead**, Thora Waters *AmMWSc 92*
**Halsted**, A Stevens 1938- *AmMWSc 92*
**Halsted**, Byron David 1852-1918 *BiInAmS*
**Halsted**, Charles H 1936- *AmMWSc 92*
**Halsted**, Charles Hopkinson 1936- *WhoWest 92*
**Halston** 1932-1990 *AnObit 1990, DcTwDes, FacFETw*
**Halston**, Daniel William 1960- *WhoAmL 92*
**Halston Frowick**, Roy 1932-1990 *DcTwDes*
**Halstrom**, Frederic Norman 1944- *WhoAmL 92*
**Halstrom**, Lasse *IntMPA 92*
**Halt**, Alice 1925- *WhoMW 92*
**Halt**, Christine 1954- *TwCPaSc*
**Halt**, Karl, Ritter von 1891-1964 *EncTR 91 [port]*
**Halteman**, Beth 1957- *WhoAmP 91*
**Halter**, Gary 1941- *WhoAmP 91*
**Halter**, H. James, Jr. 1947- *WhoFI 92*
**Halter**, Jeffrey Brian 1945- *AmMWSc 92*
**Halterlein**, Anthony J *AmMWSc 92*
**Halterman**, Benjamin Ballard 1925- *WhoAmP 91*
**Halterman**, Jerry J 1922- *AmMWSc 92*
**Haltiner**, George Joseph 1918- *AmMWSc 92*
**Haltiwanger**, John D 1925- *AmMWSc 92*
**Haltner**, Arthur John 1927- *AmMWSc 92*
**Haltom**, Elbert Bertram, Jr. 1922- *WhoAmL 92*
**Halton**, John Henry 1931- *AmMWSc 92*
**Halton**, Mark Robert 1960- *WhoRel 92*
**Halton**, Robert d1749 *DcNCBi 3*
**Haltrecht**, Monty 1932- *WrDr 92*
**Halushka**, Perry Victor 1941- *AmMWSc 92*
**Haluska**, Edward J 1916- *WhoAmP 91*
**Halva**, Allen Keith 1913- *WhoAmL 92, WhoMW 92*
**Halver**, John Emil 1922- *AmMWSc 92, IntWW 91*
**Halverhout**, Winn William 1953- *WhoMW 92*
**Halverson**, Andrew Wayne 1920- *AmMWSc 92*
**Halverson**, Craig Richard 1942- *WhoMW 92*
**Halverson**, Dionne Porter 1947- *WhoAmP 91*
**Halverson**, Eric John, Jr. 1948- *WhoAmL 92*
**Halverson**, Frederick 1917- *AmMWSc 92*
**Halverson**, Harold Wendell 1926- *WhoAmP 91*
**Halverson**, Kenneth Shaffer 1933- *WhoAmP 91*
**Halverson**, Paul Kenneth 1959- *WhoMW 92*
**Halverson**, Rex Wenstrom 1952- *WhoFI 92*
**Halverson**, Richard Christian 1916- *WhoRel 92*
**Halverson**, Ronald T 1936- *WhoAmP 91*
**Halverson**, Steven Thomas 1954- *WhoAmL 92, WhoWest 92*
**Halverson**, Wendell Quelprud 1916- *WhoRel 92*
**Halverstadt**, Robert Dale 1920- *WhoFI 92*
**Halvorsen**, Einfrid 1937- *IntWW 91*
**Halvorsen**, John Paul 1946- *WhoAmL 92*
**Halvorson**, Alfred Rubin 1921- *WhoWest 92*
**Halvorson**, Ardell David 1945- *AmMWSc 92*
**Halvorson**, George Charles 1947- *WhoFI 92*
**Halvorson**, Harlyn Odell 1925- *AmMWSc 92*
**Halvorson**, Herbert Russell 1940- *AmMWSc 92*
**Halvorson**, Lloyd Chester 1918- *AmMWSc 92*
**Halvorson**, Lyndon Wade 1956- *WhoMW 92*
**Halvorson**, Marilyn 1948- *WrDr 92*
**Halvorson**, Newman Thorbus, Jr. 1936- *WhoAmL 92*
**Halvorson**, Rodney N 1949- *WhoAmP 91*
**Halvorson**, Roger A 1934- *WhoAmP 91*
**Halyard Harry** *BenetAL 91*
**Halyard**, Ardie Adlena d1989 *WhoBlA 92N*
**Halyard**, Michele Yvette 1961- *WhoBlA 92*
**Halzen**, Francis 1944- *AmMWSc 92*
**Ham**, Arlene Hansen 1936- *WhoAmP 91*
**Ham**, Arthur Worth 1902- *AmMWSc 92*
**Ham**, Caroline Richardson 1927- *WhoAmP 91*
**Ham**, David Kenneth R. *Who 92*
**Ham**, Debra Newman 1948- *WhoBlA 92*
**Ham**, Donald Jamieson 1934- *WhoAmP 91*
**Ham**, Frank Slagle 1928- *AmMWSc 92*
**Ham**, George Caverno 1912-1977 *DcNCBi 3*
**Ham**, George Edward 1931- *AmMWSc 92*
**Ham**, George Eldon 1939- *AmMWSc 92, WhoMW 92*
**Ham**, Inyong 1925- *AmMWSc 92*
**Ham**, James M 1920- *AmMWSc 92*
**Ham**, James Milton 1920- *IntWW 91, Who 92*
**Ham**, James Richard 1921- *WhoRel 92*
**Ham**, Jane Fay *WhoAmP 91*
**Ham**, Joe Strother 1928- *AmMWSc 92*
**Ham**, John Dudley Nelson 1902- *Who 92*
**Ham**, John Wilfred 1931- *WhoMW 92*
**Ham**, Lee Edward 1919- *AmMWSc 92*
**Ham**, Nancy Marie 1941- *WhoMW 92*
**Ham**, Richard 1923- *WhoAmP 91*
**Ham**, Richard George 1932- *AmMWSc 92*
**Ham**, Richard John 1946- *AmMWSc 92*
**Ham**, Russell Allen 1940- *AmMWSc 92*
**Ham**, Wayne Albert 1938- *IntAu&W 91, WrDr 92*
**Ham**, William Albert 1923- *WhoFI 92*
**Ham**, William Taylor, Jr 1908- *AmMWSc 92*
**Ham-Ying**, J. Michael 1956- *WhoBlA 92*
**Hama**, Francis R 1917- *AmMWSc 92*
**Hamachek**, Tod Russell 1946- *WhoWest 92*
**Hamacher**, Horst W 1951- *AmMWSc 92*
**Hamacher**, V Carl 1939- *AmMWSc 92*
**Hamad**, Abdul-Latif Yousef al- 1937- *IntWW 91*
**Hamada**, Harold Seichi 1935- *AmMWSc 92*
**Hamada**, Kiyoshi 1935- *WhoFI 92*
**Hamada**, Koichi 1936- *WhoFI 92*
**Hamada**, Mokhtar M 1935- *AmMWSc 92*
**Hamada**, Robert Seiji 1937- *WhoFI 92, WhoMW 92*
**Hamada**, Shoji 1894- *DcTwDes*
**Hamada**, Spencer Hiroshi 1943- *AmMWSc 92*
**Hamadanchi**, Mohsen 1960- *WhoMW 92*
**Hamady**, Ron 1947- *IntMPA 92*
**Hamai**, James Y 1926- *AmMWSc 92*
**Hamaker**, Frank Macklin 1934- *WhoWest 92*
**Hamaker**, John C, Jr 1924- *AmMWSc 92*
**Hamaker**, John Warren 1917- *AmMWSc 92*
**Hamamura Mariye**, Lily 1956- *WhoEnt 92*
**Hamani**, Ahmad *WhoRel 92*
**Hamann**, Donald Dale 1933- *AmMWSc 92*
**Hamann**, Donald Robert 1939- *AmMWSc 92*
**Hamann**, James Allen 1938- *WhoMW 92*
**Hamann**, Johann Georg 1730-1788 *BlkwCEP*
**Hamann**, Norman Lee, Sr. 1936- *WhoMW 92*
**Hamann**, Paul 1891-1973 *TwCPaSc*
**Hamann**, Sefton Davidson 1921- *IntWW 91*
**Hamar**, Dwayne Walter 1937- *AmMWSc 92*
**Hamar**, H. Jeffrey 1958- *WhoWest 92*
**Hamari**, Julia 1942- *IntWW 91*
**Hamarneh**, Sami K. 1925- *IntWW 91*
**Hamarneh**, Sami Khalaf 1925- *AmMWSc 92*
**Hamarstrom**, Patricia Ann 1952- *WhoEnt 92*
**Hamasaki**, Duco I 1929- *AmMWSc 92*
**Hamb**, Fredrick Lynn 1937- *AmMWSc 92*
**Hamberg**, Marcelle R. 1931- *WhoBlA 92*
**Hamberlin**, Emiel 1939- *WhoBlA 92*
**Hambidge**, Douglas Walter *Who 92*
**Hambidge**, Douglas Walter 1927- *IntWW 91, WhoRel 92, WhoWest 92*
**Hambidge**, K Michael 1932- *AmMWSc 92*
**Hambleden**, Dowager Viscountess 1904- *Who 92*
**Hambleden**, Viscount 1930- *Who 92*
**Hamblen**, Charles Hillen, Jr 1917- *WhoAmP 91*
**Hamblen**, David Gordon 1940- *AmMWSc 92*
**Hamblen**, David Philip 1928- *AmMWSc 92*
**Hamblen**, Derek Ivens Archibald 1917- *Who 92*
**Hamblen**, Donald Lee 1928- *WhoAmP 91*
**Hamblen**, Frank *WhoMW 92*
**Hamblen**, John Wesley 1924- *AmMWSc 92*
**Hamblen**, Lapsley Walker, Jr. 1926- *WhoAmL 92*
**Hamblen**, William Delano 1947- *WhoAmL 92*
**Hambleton**, Douglas McMurray 1955- *WhoAmL 92*
**Hambleton**, George Blow Elliott 1929- *WhoFI 92*

**Hambleton,** Kenneth George 1937- Who 92
**Hambleton,** Thomas Edward 1911- WhoEnt 92
**Hambleton,** William Weldon 1921- AmMWSc 92
**Hambley,** Egbert Barry Cornwall 1862-1906 DcNCBi 3
**Hambley,** Mark G 1948- WhoAmP 91
**Hamblin,** James R. 1936- WhoWest 92
**Hamblin,** Michael Wayne 1951- WhoEnt 92
**Hamblin,** William Kenneth 1928- AmMWSc 92
**Hambling,** Hugh 1919- Who 92
**Hambling,** Maggi 1945- IntWW 91, TwCPaSc
**Hambourger,** Paul David 1939- AmMWSc 92, WhoMW 92
**Hambraeus,** Bengt 1928- ConCom 92, WhoEnt 92
**Hambrecht,** Frederick Terry 1939- AmMWSc 92
**Hambrick,** George Walter, Jr 1922- AmMWSc 92
**Hambrick,** Harold E., Jr. 1943- WhoBlA 92
**Hambrick,** John William 1965- WhoEnt 92
**Hambrick-Stowe,** Charles Edwin 1948- WhoRel 92
**Hambright,** Frederick 1727-1817 DcNCBi 3
**Hambright,** Robert John 1956- WhoAmL 92
**Hambro,** Charles Eric Alexander 1930- IntWW 91, Who 92
**Hambro,** Jocelyn Olaf 1919- IntWW 91, Who 92
**Hambro,** Rupert Nicholas 1943- IntWW 91, Who 92
**Hamburg,** Beatrix A M 1923- AmMWSc 92
**Hamburg,** Charles Bruce 1939- WhoAmL 92
**Hamburg,** David Alan 1925- AmMWSc 92
**Hamburg,** Eileen Bajarski 1953- WhoIns 92
**Hamburg,** Joseph 1922- AmMWSc 92
**Hamburg,** Lynn Rae 1938- WhoRel 92
**Hamburg,** Roger Phillip 1934- WhoFI 92
**Hamburger,** Anne W 1947- AmMWSc 92
**Hamburger,** Christian 1904- IntWW 91
**Hamburger,** Edmund Anthony 1927- WhoEnt 92
**Hamburger,** Jean 1909- IntWW 91
**Hamburger,** Jeffrey Allen 1947- WhoFI 92
**Hamburger,** Kevin Edward 1954- WhoEnt 92, WhoWest 92
**Hamburger,** Michael 1924- ConPo 91, WrDr 92
**Hamburger,** Michael Peter Leopold 1924- IntWW 91, Who 92
**Hamburger,** Michael Wile 1953- AmMWSc 92
**Hamburger,** Philip 1914- IntAu&W 91, WrDr 92
**Hamburger,** Richard 1915- AmMWSc 92
**Hamburger,** Richard James 1937- WhoMW 92
**Hamburger,** Robert Newfield 1923- AmMWSc 92
**Hamburger,** Sidney 1914- Who 92
**Hamburger,** Viktor 1900- AmMWSc 92, IntWW 91
**Hamburgh,** Max 1922- AmMWSc 92
**Hamby,** Alonzo L. 1940- WrDr 92
**Hamby,** Dame Scott 1920- AmMWSc 92
**Hamby,** Drannan Carson 1933- AmMWSc 92
**Hamby,** Gene Malcolm, Jr. 1943- WhoAmL 92
**Hamby,** James A. DrAPF 91
**Hamby,** Jeannette K 1933- WhoAmP 91
**Hamby,** Jim Leon 1951- WhoRel 92
**Hamby,** John Arthur 1958- WhoEnt 92
**Hamby,** Michael E 1952- WhoIns 92
**Hamby,** Robert Jay 1932- AmMWSc 92
**Hamby,** Roscoe Jerome 1919- WhoBlA 92
**Hamdy,** Mohamed Yousry 1938- AmMWSc 92
**Hamdy,** Mostafa Kamal 1921- AmMWSc 92
**Hame,** Trevor Gordon 1927- WhoWest 92
**Hamed,** Awatef A 1944- AmMWSc 92, WhoMW 92
**Hamed,** Gary Ray 1950- AmMWSc 92
**Hamed,** Nihad Talaat 1924- WhoMW 92, WhoRel 92
**Hameed,** A. C. S. 1929- IntWW 91
**Hameed,** A. C. Shahul 1929- Who 92
**Hameed,** Sultan 1941- AmMWSc 92
**Hameedi,** Mohammad Jawed 1944- AmMWSc 92
**Hameister,** Lavon Louetta 1922- WhoFI 92, WhoMW 92
**Hameka,** Hendrik Frederik 1931- AmMWSc 92
**Hamel,** Aldona Mary 1946- WhoFI 92
**Hamel,** Coleman Rodney 1937- AmMWSc 92
**Hamel,** Earl Gregory, Jr 1928- AmMWSc 92
**Hamel,** Edward E 1926- AmMWSc 92
**Hamel,** Howard Neal 1953- WhoAmL 92
**Hamel,** James V 1944- AmMWSc 92
**Hamel,** Joseph Donat 1923- WhoRel 92
**Hamel,** Louis H., Jr. 1934- WhoAmL 92
**Hamel,** Louis Reginald 1945- WhoFI 92, WhoMW 92
**Hamel,** Mark Edwin 1953- WhoAmL 92
**Hamel,** Maurice 1941- WhoAmP 91
**Hamel,** Rodolphe 1929- WhoAmL 92
**Hamel,** Veronica 1943- IntMPA 92, WhoEnt 92
**Hamelin,** Claude 1943- AmMWSc 92
**Hamelin,** Jean-Guy 1925- WhoRel 92
**Hamelin,** Louis-Edmond 1923- IntWW 91
**Hamell,** Patrick Joseph 1910- WrDr 92
**Hament,** John Maxwell 1950- WhoAmL 92
**Hamer,** Christopher 1953- TwCPaSc
**Hamer,** David Allan 1938- ConAu 35NR
**Hamer,** Dean H 1951- AmMWSc 92
**Hamer,** Fanny Lou 1917-1977 NotBlAW 92 [port]
**Hamer,** Jan 1927- AmMWSc 92
**Hamer,** Jean Jerome 1916- IntWW 91, WhoRel 92
**Hamer,** Jeanne Huntington 1933- WhoEnt 92
**Hamer,** Jeffrey Michael 1949- WhoFI 92
**Hamer,** Judith Ann 1939- WhoBlA 92
**Hamer,** Justin Charles 1914- AmMWSc 92
**Hamer,** Marian E. 1947- WhoMW 92
**Hamer,** Martin 1928- AmMWSc 92
**Hamer,** Robert 1911-1963 IntDcF 2-2 [port]
**Hamer,** Rupert 1916- Who 92
**Hamer,** Rupert James 1916- IntWW 91
**Hamer,** Walter Jay 1907- AmMWSc 92
**Hamer-Tumaroff,** Yonit 1962- WhoEnt 92
**Hamerlik,** Michael Francis 1961- WhoAmP 91
**Hamerly,** Robert Glenn 1931- AmMWSc 92
**Hamerman,** David Jay 1925- AmMWSc 92
**Hamermesh,** Bernard 1919- AmMWSc 92
**Hamermesh,** Frances Witty 1943- WhoAmL 92
**Hamermesh,** Morton 1915- AmMWSc 92
**Hamerski,** Julian Joseph 1930- AmMWSc 92
**Hamerslough,** Walter Scott 1935- WhoWest 92
**Hamersma,** J Warren 1940- AmMWSc 92
**Hamerstrom,** Frances 1907- AmMWSc 92
**Hamerstrom,** Frederick Nathan 1909- AmMWSc 92
**Hamerton,** John Laurence 1929- AmMWSc 92
**Hamerton,** Philip Gilbert 1834-1894 ThHElm
**Hames,** F A 1919- AmMWSc 92
**Hames,** Frank 1951- WhoEnt 92
**Hames,** Gary Lawrence 1945- WhoMW 92
**Hames,** Leon H 1930- WhoIns 92
**Hames,** William Lester 1947- WhoAmL 92
**Hamet,** Pavel 1943- AmMWSc 92
**Hami,** Ghassan Jamil 1948- WhoMW 92
**Hamid,** Michael 1934- AmMWSc 92
**Hamid,** Salah 1924- IntWW 91
**Hamid,** Sarv 1956- WhoMW 92
**Hamideh,** Khalid Y. 1961- WhoAmL 92
**Hamidjaja,** Wiriadi 1962- WhoMW 92
**Hamielec,** Alvin Edward 1935- AmMWSc 92
**Hamil,** David Alexander 1908- WhoAmP 91
**Hamil,** Martha M 1939- AmMWSc 92
**Hamilin,** Conde ScFEYrs
**Hamill,** Allen William 1948- WhoFI 92
**Hamill,** Carol 1953- WhoWest 92
**Hamill,** Dennis W 1940- AmMWSc 92
**Hamill,** Ethel WrDr 92
**Hamill,** James Junior 1921- AmMWSc 92
**Hamill,** Janet DrAPF 91
**Hamill,** John P. 1940- WhoFI 92
**Hamill,** Margaret Hudgens 1937- WhoBlA 92
**Hamill,** Mark 1951- WhoEnt 92
**Hamill,** Mark 1952- IntMPA 92
**Hamill,** Nancy Lynn 1957- WhoMW 92
**Hamill,** Patrick 1930- Who 92
**Hamill,** Patrick James 1936- AmMWSc 92
**Hamill,** Paul 1930- WhoRel 92
**Hamill,** Pete 1935- IntMPA 92
**Hamill,** Peter Van Vechten 1926- AmMWSc 92
**Hamill,** Robert L 1927- AmMWSc 92
**Hamill,** Robert W 1942- AmMWSc 92
**Hamill,** Sam ConAu 15AS [port], DrAPF 91
**Hamill,** William Henry 1908- AmMWSc 92
**Hamilton** Who 92
**Hamilton,** Duke of 1938- Who 92
**Hamilton,** Marquess of 1969- Who 92
**Hamilton,** A C 1918- WhoAmP 91
**Hamilton,** A. C. 1921- ConAu 133
**Hamilton,** Adrian Walter 1923- Who 92
**Hamilton,** Adrianne Pauline U. Who 92
**Hamilton,** Alan 1943- ConAu 36NR, SmATA 66
**Hamilton,** Alexander 1755?-1804 AmPolLe [port], BenetAL 91, RComAH
**Hamilton,** Alexander 1757-1804 BlkwEAR [port]
**Hamilton,** Alexander Kenneth 1915- Who 92
**Hamilton,** Alexander Macdonald 1925- Who 92
**Hamilton,** Alfred Starr DrAPF 91
**Hamilton,** Alice 1869-1970 AmPeW, DcAmImH, HanAmWH, RComAH
**Hamilton,** Allan McLane 1848-1919 BiInAmS
**Hamilton,** Allen Emerson, Jr. 1935- WhoWest 92
**Hamilton,** Allen Philip 1937- WhoFI 92
**Hamilton,** Angus Cameron 1922- AmMWSc 92
**Hamilton,** Anthony Norris d1991 Who 92N
**Hamilton,** Archibald 1941- Who 92
**Hamilton,** Archie Clyde, Jr. 1942- WhoMW 92
**Hamilton,** Art WhoAmP 91, WhoBlA 92
**Hamilton,** Arthur Campbell 1942- Who 92
**Hamilton,** Arthur N. 1917- WhoBlA 92
**Hamilton,** Aubrey J. 1927- WhoBlA 92
**Hamilton,** Bernard 1932- WrDr 92
**Hamilton,** Beth Alleman 1927- WhoMW 92
**Hamilton,** Bobby Wayne 1946- WhoFI 92
**Hamilton,** Brent William 1957- WhoEnt 92
**Hamilton,** Brian Stuart 1964- WhoFI 92
**Hamilton,** Bruce King 1947- AmMWSc 92
**Hamilton,** Bruce M 1920- AmMWSc 92
**Hamilton,** Bruce Ross 1930- WhoAmP 91
**Hamilton,** Byron Bruce 1934- AmMWSc 92
**Hamilton,** C Howard 1935- AmMWSc 92
**Hamilton,** C. Wayne 1934- WhoMW 92
**Hamilton,** Carol Lee 1957- WhoAmL 92
**Hamilton,** Carole Lois 1937- AmMWSc 92
**Hamilton,** Catherine 1738-1782 NewAmDM
**Hamilton,** Charles 1913- IntAu&W 91, SmATA 65 [port], WrDr 92
**Hamilton,** Charles Howard 1935- WhoWest 92
**Hamilton,** Charles Leroy 1932- AmMWSc 92
**Hamilton,** Charles R 1935- AmMWSc 92
**Hamilton,** Charles S. 1927- WhoBlA 92
**Hamilton,** Charles Vernon 1929- WhoBlA 92
**Hamilton,** Charles William 1919- AmMWSc 92
**Hamilton,** Chico 1921- NewAmDM, WhoEnt 92
**Hamilton,** Christina Sundlof 1959- WhoAmL 92
**Hamilton,** Cicely 1872-1952 ScFEYrs
**Hamilton,** Clara Eddy 1923- AmMWSc 92
**Hamilton,** Clyde Henry 1934- WhoAmL 92
**Hamilton,** D C, Jr 1918- AmMWSc 92
**Hamilton,** Dagmar Strandberg 1932- WhoAmL 92
**Hamilton,** Daniel Stephen 1932- WhoRel 92
**Hamilton,** Darden Cole 1956- WhoWest 92
**Hamilton,** Darryl Quinn 1964- WhoBlA 92
**Hamilton,** David Foster 1946- AmMWSc 92
**Hamilton,** David Mike 1951- WhoWest 92
**Hamilton,** David Peter 1935- WhoEnt 92
**Hamilton,** David Whitman 1935- AmMWSc 92
**Hamilton,** Dennis Owen 1951- WhoMW 92
**Hamilton,** DeWayne 1951- WhoAmP 91
**Hamilton,** Don Foster 1937- WhoAmL 92
**Hamilton,** Donald 1916- TwCWW 91, WrDr 92
**Hamilton,** Donald B 1916- IntAu&W 91
**Hamilton,** Donald John 1941- WhoAmL 92
**Hamilton,** Douglas J 1930- AmMWSc 92
**Hamilton,** Douglas Owens 1931- Who 92
**Hamilton,** Douglas Stuart 1949- AmMWSc 92
**Hamilton,** Dundas Who 92
**Hamilton,** Dwight Alan 1928- WhoAmP 91
**Hamilton,** Eben William 1937- Who 92
**Hamilton,** Edith 1867-1963 BenetAL 91, RComAH
**Hamilton,** Edmond 1904-1973 ScFEYrs
**Hamilton,** Edmond 1904-1977 TwCSFW 91
**Hamilton,** Edward 1925- Who 92
**Hamilton,** Edward Marsh 1941- WhoFI 92, WhoMW 92
**Hamilton,** Edward N., Jr. 1947- WhoBlA 92
**Hamilton,** Edwin 1936- WhoBlA 92
**Hamilton,** Edwin Lee 1914- AmMWSc 92
**Hamilton,** Elizabeth 1906- WrDr 92
**Hamilton,** Ellen Littlefield 1955- WhoEnt 92
**Hamilton,** Ernest Scovell 1928- AmMWSc 92
**Hamilton,** Eugene Kenneth 1939- WhoAmP 91
**Hamilton,** Francis Hugh 1927- Who 92
**Hamilton,** Frank d1991 NewYTBS 91
**Hamilton,** Franklin ConAu 36NR
**Hamilton,** Franklin D 1942- AmMWSc 92, WhoBlA 92
**Hamilton,** Gail DrAPF 91, WrDr 92
**Hamilton,** Gale Wayne 1944- WhoMW 92
**Hamilton,** Gary Lee 1950- WhoFI 92
**Hamilton,** Gavin Francis 1930- WhoWest 92
**Hamilton,** George 1939- IntMPA 92
**Hamilton,** George Earl 1934- WhoWest 92
**Hamilton,** George Edmund 1961- WhoRel 92
**Hamilton,** George Heard 1910- FacFETw, Who 92
**Hamilton,** George Wayne 1957- WhoRel 92
**Hamilton,** Gordon 1892-1967 HanAmWH
**Hamilton,** Gordon Andrew 1935- AmMWSc 92
**Hamilton,** Gordon Wayne 1926- AmMWSc 92
**Hamilton,** Grace Towns 1907- NotBlAW 92 [port], WhoBlA 92
**Hamilton,** Graeme Montagu 1934- Who 92
**Hamilton,** Guy 1922- IntMPA 92, WhoEnt 92
**Hamilton,** H. J. Belton 1924- WhoBlA 92
**Hamilton,** Hamish d1988 DcLB 112 [port]
**Hamilton,** Harry E. 1962- WhoBlA 92
**Hamilton,** Harry Lemuel, Jr 1938- AmMWSc 92, WhoWest 92
**Hamilton,** Heidi Worley 1958- WhoEnt 92
**Hamilton,** Helen Packer 1927- WhoAmP 91
**Hamilton,** Henry 1734-1796 BlkwEAR
**Hamilton,** Henry Ronald 1932- WhoMW 92
**Hamilton,** Hobart Gordon, Jr 1939- AmMWSc 92
**Hamilton,** Howard Britton 1923- AmMWSc 92
**Hamilton,** Howard Laverne 1916- AmMWSc 92
**Hamilton,** Hugh 1847- BiInAmS
**Hamilton,** Hugh Gray Wybrants 1918- Who 92
**Hamilton,** Iain 1922- ConCom 92, NewAmDM
**Hamilton,** Iain Ellis 1922- Who 92, WhoEnt 92
**Hamilton,** Ian 1938- ConPo 91, IntAu&W 91, Who 92, WrDr 92
**Hamilton,** Ian Robert 1932- AmMWSc 92
**Hamilton,** Ian Robertson 1925- Who 92
**Hamilton,** J Hugh 1904- AmMWSc 92
**Hamilton,** Jack E. WhoRel 92
**Hamilton,** Jack H. 1941- WhoMW 92
**Hamilton,** Jackson Douglas 1949- WhoAmL 92
**Hamilton,** James 1918- Who 92
**Hamilton,** James 1923- Who 92
**Hamilton,** James 1938- WhoAmL 92
**Hamilton,** James 1939- WhoEnt 92
**Hamilton,** James Arthur 1947- AmMWSc 92
**Hamilton,** James Arthur Roy 1919- AmMWSc 92
**Hamilton,** James Beckham 1920- WhoAmP 91
**Hamilton,** James Beclone 1933- AmMWSc 92
**Hamilton,** James Douglas 1954- WhoFI 92
**Hamilton,** James Dundas 1919- IntWW 91, Who 92
**Hamilton,** James E 1935- WhoAmP 91
**Hamilton,** James F 1927- AmMWSc 92
**Hamilton,** James G. 1939- WhoBlA 92
**Hamilton,** James Guthrie 1923- AmMWSc 92
**Hamilton,** James Harold WhoAmP 91
**Hamilton,** James P 1946- WhoIns 92
**Hamilton,** James Robertson 1921- WrDr 92
**Hamilton,** James Whitelaw 1860-1932 TwCPaSc
**Hamilton,** James Wilburn 1936- AmMWSc 92
**Hamilton,** James William 1933- WhoWest 92
**Hamilton,** Janet V 1936- AmMWSc 92
**Hamilton,** Jeff 1934- WhoAmP 91
**Hamilton,** Jefferson Merritt, Jr 1918- AmMWSc 92

**Hamilton,** Jerald 1927- *WhoEnt 92, WhoWest 92*
**Hamilton,** Jimmy 1917- *NewAmDM*
**Hamilton,** Joan 1950- *WhoAmP 91*
**Hamilton,** Joe d1991 *LesBEnT 92, NewYTBS 91 [port]*
**Hamilton,** John d1816 *DcNCBi 3*
**Hamilton,** John 1827-1897 *BiInAmS*
**Hamilton,** John 1910- *Who 92*
**Hamilton,** John 1941- *Who 92*
**Hamilton,** John Brown 1847-1898 *BiInAmS*
**Hamilton,** John Dayton, Jr. 1934- *WhoAmL 92*
**Hamilton,** John Frederick 1928- *AmMWSc 92*
**Hamilton,** John Joslyn, Jr. 1949- *WhoBlA 92*
**Hamilton,** John M. *WhoBlA 92*
**Hamilton,** John Mark, Jr. 1931- *WhoBlA 92*
**Hamilton,** John Maxwell 1947- *IntAu&W 91, WrDr 92*
**Hamilton,** John Meacham 1912- *AmMWSc 92*
**Hamilton,** John Rasper, III 1947- *WhoMW 92*
**Hamilton,** John Robert 1925- *AmMWSc 92*
**Hamilton,** John Ross 1924- *WhoFI 92*
**Hamilton,** John Thomas, Jr. 1951- *WhoAmL 92*
**Hamilton,** Joseph Gregoire de Roulhac 1878-1961 *DcNCBi 3*
**Hamilton,** Joseph H, Jr 1932- *AmMWSc 92*
**Hamilton,** Joseph Henry Michael, Jr. 1929- *WhoEnt 92*
**Hamilton,** Joseph Willard 1922- *WhoBlA 92*
**Hamilton,** Judith Hall 1944- *WhoFI 92*
**Hamilton,** Kenneth 1917- *IntAu&W 91, WrDr 92*
**Hamilton,** Kenneth 1948- *WhoAmP 91*
**Hamilton,** Kenneth Gavin Andrew 1946- *AmMWSc 92*
**Hamilton,** Kevin 1956- *AmMWSc 92*
**Hamilton,** Kevin John 1957- *WhoAmL 92*
**Hamilton,** Kirk *TwCWW 91*
**Hamilton,** Lawrence Rice 1946- *WhoAmL 92*
**Hamilton,** Lawrence Stanley 1925- *AmMWSc 92*
**Hamilton,** Lee H. 1931- *AlmAP 92 [port]*
**Hamilton,** Lee Herbert 1931- *WhoAmP 91, WhoMW 92*
**Hamilton,** Leo Richard 1927- *WhoAmP 91*
**Hamilton,** Leonard *WhoBlA 92*
**Hamilton,** Leonard Derwent 1921- *AmMWSc 92*
**Hamilton,** Leroy Leslie 1934- *AmMWSc 92*
**Hamilton,** Lewis R 1941- *AmMWSc 92*
**Hamilton,** Linda *IntMPA 92*
**Hamilton,** Lonnie, III 1927- *WhoAmP 91*
**Hamilton,** Loudon Pearson 1932- *Who 92*
**Hamilton,** Louise Virginia 1913- *WhoAmP 91*
**Hamilton,** Lyle Howard 1924- *AmMWSc 92*
**Hamilton,** Lynn 1930- *WhoBlA 92*
**Hamilton,** Malcolm William Bruce S. *Who 92*
**Hamilton,** Marci A. 1957- *WhoAmL 92*
**Hamilton,** Margaret J. 1957- *WhoMW 92*
**Hamilton,** Martha *Who 92*
**Hamilton,** Martha Marti Lou 1942- *WhoWest 92*
**Hamilton,** Mary 1927- *WrDr 92*
**Hamilton,** Mary Agnes 1882-1966 *BiDBrF 2*
**Hamilton,** Mary Jane Gill 1925- *AmMWSc 92*
**Hamilton,** Mary Lucia Kerr 1926- *WhoFI 92*
**Hamilton,** Mary Margaret *Who 92*
**Hamilton,** McKinley John 1921- *WhoBlA 92*
**Hamilton,** Melinda R 1954- *WhoIns 92*
**Hamilton,** Michael Aubrey 1918- *Who 92*
**Hamilton,** Michael Scott 1953- *WhoMW 92*
**Hamilton,** Milo Charles 1945- *WhoFI 92*
**Hamilton,** Milton Holmes 1925- *WhoAmP 91*
**Hamilton,** Milton Hugh, Jr 1932- *WhoAmP 91*
**Hamilton,** Mollie *IntAu&W 91X*
**Hamilton,** Morse 1943- *IntAu&W 91*
**Hamilton,** Mostyn Neil 1949- *Who 92*
**Hamilton,** Myer Alan Barry K. *Who 92*
**Hamilton,** Nancy Jeanne 1959- *WhoWest 92*
**Hamilton,** Neil *Who 92*
**Hamilton,** Nigel John Mawdesley 1938- *Who 92*
**Hamilton,** North Edward Frederick D. *Who 92*
**Hamilton,** Orlando Nicholas, Jr. 1928- *WhoAmL 92*
**Hamilton,** Parkin Andrew 1959- *WhoAmL 92*
**Hamilton,** Pat Brooks 1930- *AmMWSc 92*
**Hamilton,** Pat R 1923- *WhoAmP 91*
**Hamilton,** Patrick 1923- *TwCPaSc*
**Hamilton,** Patrick George 1908- *Who 92*
**Hamilton,** Paul *IntAu&W 91X, WrDr 92*
**Hamilton,** Paul Barnard 1909- *AmMWSc 92*
**Hamilton,** Paul L. 1941- *WhoBlA 92*
**Hamilton,** Penny Rafferty 1948- *WhoMW 92*
**Hamilton,** Perrin C. 1921- *WhoAmL 92*
**Hamilton,** Peter Bannerman 1946- *WhoFI 92*
**Hamilton,** Phanuel J. 1929- *WhoBlA 92*
**Hamilton,** Phillip 1952- *WhoAmP 91*
**Hamilton,** Phillip Douglas 1954- *WhoAmL 92*
**Hamilton,** Priscilla *IntAu&W 91X, WrDr 92*
**Hamilton,** Rainy, Jr. 1956- *WhoBlA 92*
**Hamilton,** Ralph West 1933- *AmMWSc 92*
**Hamilton,** Raymond 1950- *WhoBlA 92*
**Hamilton,** Richard 1922- *FacFETw, IntWW 91, TwCPaSc, Who 92*
**Hamilton,** Richard Alfred 1941- *WhoMW 92*
**Hamilton,** Richard Caradoc *Who 92*
**Hamilton,** Richard Columbus 1943- *WhoAmP 91*
**Hamilton,** Richard Graham 1932- *Who 92*
**Hamilton,** Richard Lauren *WhoEnt 92*
**Hamilton,** Richard Nathaniel 1941- *WhoBlA 92*
**Hamilton,** Robert Appleby, Jr. 1940- *WhoFI 92, WhoMW 92*
**Hamilton,** Robert Bruce 1936- *AmMWSc 92*
**Hamilton,** Robert Charles Richard 1911- *Who 92*
**Hamilton,** Robert Duncan 1937- *AmMWSc 92*
**Hamilton,** Robert Hillery, Jr 1929- *AmMWSc 92*
**Hamilton,** Robert Houston 1906- *AmMWSc 92*
**Hamilton,** Robert L, Jr 1934- *AmMWSc 92*
**Hamilton,** Robert Milton Gregory 1939- *AmMWSc 92*
**Hamilton,** Robert Morrison 1936- *AmMWSc 92*
**Hamilton,** Robert Otte 1927- *WhoAmL 92*
**Hamilton,** Robert W 1939- *AmMWSc 92*
**Hamilton,** Robert William 1905- *Who 92*
**Hamilton,** Robert William 1930- *AmMWSc 92*
**Hamilton,** Robert Woodruff 1931- *WhoAmL 92*
**Hamilton,** Ron G. 1958- *WhoFI 92*
**Hamilton,** Ronald Ray 1932- *WhoRel 92*
**Hamilton,** Ross T. 1946- *WhoBlA 92*
**Hamilton,** Russell Lee 1936- *WhoRel 92*
**Hamilton,** Samuel Cartenius 1936- *WhoBlA 92*
**Hamilton,** Sandi Brown 1941- *WhoEnt 92*
**Hamilton,** Scott 1958- *FacFETw*
**Hamilton,** Scott Scovell 1958- *WhoEnt 92*
**Hamilton,** Stanley R 1948- *AmMWSc 92*
**Hamilton,** Stephen K 1946- *WhoIns 92*
**Hamilton,** Steve *DrAPF 91*
**Hamilton,** Steven J 1947- *AmMWSc 92*
**Hamilton,** Terrell Hunter 1935- *AmMWSc 92*
**Hamilton,** Theophilus Elliott 1923- *WhoBlA 92*
**Hamilton,** Thomas Alan 1950- *AmMWSc 92*
**Hamilton,** Thomas Charles 1947- *AmMWSc 92*
**Hamilton,** Thomas Dudley 1936- *AmMWSc 92*
**Hamilton,** Thomas J., Jr. 1933- *WhoWest 92*
**Hamilton,** Thomas Jeffrey 1943- *WhoEnt 92*
**Hamilton,** Thomas Reid 1911- *AmMWSc 92*
**Hamilton,** Thomas Woolman 1948- *WhoMW 92*
**Hamilton,** Virginia 1936- *NotBlAW 92, WhoBlA 92, WrDr 92*
**Hamilton,** Virginia Mae 1946- *WhoMW 92*
**Hamilton,** Wade *IntAu&W 91X, TwCWW 91*
**Hamilton,** Walter S 1931- *AmMWSc 92*
**Hamilton,** Warren Bell 1925- *AmMWSc 92*
**Hamilton,** Wilbur Wyatt 1931- *WhoBlA 92*
**Hamilton,** Willard Charlson 1942- *AmMWSc 92*
**Hamilton,** William *IntAu&W 91X*
**Hamilton,** William d1871 *BiInAmS*
**Hamilton,** William 1730-1803 *BlkwCEP*
**Hamilton,** William Baskerville 1908-1972 *DcNCBi 3*
**Hamilton,** William Donald 1936- *AmMWSc 92, IntWW 91, Who 92*
**Hamilton,** William Eugene, Jr 1942- *AmMWSc 92*
**Hamilton,** William Frederick, III 1943- *WhoWest 92*
**Hamilton,** William Howard 1918- *AmMWSc 92*
**Hamilton,** William J, Jr 1932- *WhoAmP 91*
**Hamilton,** William John, Jr 1902- *AmMWSc 92*
**Hamilton,** William Joseph 1930- *WhoMW 92*
**Hamilton,** William Kennon 1922- *AmMWSc 92*
**Hamilton,** William Lander 1943- *AmMWSc 92*
**Hamilton,** William McLean 1919- *IntWW 91*
**Hamilton,** William Milton 1925- *WhoFI 92, WhoMW 92*
**Hamilton,** William Nathan 1926- *WhoBlA 92*
**Hamilton,** William Oliver 1933- *AmMWSc 92*
**Hamilton,** William Riley 1952- *WhoRel 92*
**Hamilton,** William Thorne 1917- *AmMWSc 92*
**Hamilton,** William Winter 1917- *Who 92*
**Hamilton,** Willie L. 1941- *WhoMW 92*
**Hamilton-Dalrymple,** Hew *Who 92*
**Hamilton Depassier,** Juan *IntWW 91*
**Hamilton-Edwards,** Gerald 1906- *WrDr 92*
**Hamilton Fraser,** Donald *Who 92*
**Hamilton-Jones,** John 1926- *Who 92*
**Hamilton-Kemp,** Thomas Rogers 1942- *AmMWSc 92*
**Hamilton of Dalzell,** Baron 1938- *Who 92*
**Hamilton-Rahi,** Lynda Darlene 1950- *WhoBlA 92*
**Hamilton-Russell** *Who 92*
**Hamilton-Smith** *Who 92*
**Hamilton-Spencer-Smith,** John *Who 92*
**Hamilton-Steinraut,** Jean A 1938- *AmMWSc 92*
**Hamit,** Harold F 1913- *AmMWSc 92*
**Hamiyeh,** Adel 1940- *IntWW 91*
**Hamjian,** Harry J 1923- *AmMWSc 92*
**Hamkalo,** Barbara Ann 1944- *AmMWSc 92*
**Hamlar,** David Duffield, Sr. 1924- *WhoBlA 92*
**Hamlar,** Portia Y. T. 1932- *WhoBlA 92*
**Hamlet,** James Frank 1921- *WhoBlA 92*
**Hamlet,** Ova *TwCSFW 91*
**Hamlet,** Richard Graham 1938- *AmMWSc 92*
**Hamlet,** Zacharias 1930- *AmMWSc 92*
**Hamlett,** Dale Edward 1921- *WhoWest 92*
**Hamlett,** James Gordon 1923- *WhoFI 92*
**Hamlett,** Kenneth Lee 1962- *WhoEnt 92*
**Hamlett,** Leroy Reynolds, Jr. 1938- *WhoAmL 92*
**Hamlett,** Ray 1933- *WhoAmP 91*
**Hamlett,** William Cornelius 1948- *AmMWSc 92*
**Hamley,** Donald Alfred 1931- *Who 92*
**Hamlin,** Alan Russell 1948- *WhoFI 92*
**Hamlin,** Albert T. 1926- *WhoBlA 92*
**Hamlin,** Arthur Henry 1942- *WhoBlA 92*
**Hamlin,** Charles Edward 1825-1886 *BiInAmS*
**Hamlin,** Christopher Goddard 1951- *WhoMW 92*
**Hamlin,** Courtney Walker 1858-1950 *DcNCBi 3*
**Hamlin,** Daniel Allen 1926- *AmMWSc 92*
**Hamlin,** Don Auer 1934- *WhoFI 92*
**Hamlin,** Donald Walter 1936- *WhoWest 92*
**Hamlin,** Edmund Martin, Jr. 1949- *WhoWest 92*
**Hamlin,** Ernest Lee 1943- *WhoMW 92, WhoRel 92*
**Hamlin,** Griffith Askew 1919- *WhoRel 92*
**Hamlin,** Griffith Askew, Jr 1945- *AmMWSc 92*
**Hamlin,** Hannibal 1809-1891 *AmPolLe*
**Hamlin,** Harry 1951- *IntMPA 92*
**Hamlin,** Harry Robinson 1951- *WhoEnt 92*
**Hamlin,** Isadore d1991 *NewYTBS 91*
**Hamlin,** James T, III 1929- *AmMWSc 92*
**Hamlin,** John 1915- *WhoRel 92*
**Hamlin,** Joyce Libby 1939- *AmMWSc 92*
**Hamlin,** Kenneth Eldred, Jr 1917- *AmMWSc 92*
**Hamlin,** Michael John 1930- *Who 92*
**Hamlin,** Robert Louis 1933- *AmMWSc 92*
**Hamlin,** Roger Eugene 1945- *WhoMW 92*
**Hamlin,** Thomas 1930- *WhoMW 92*
**Hamlin,** Wayland 1949- *WhoRel 92*
**Hamlin,** William Earl 1922- *AmMWSc 92*
**Hamlin,** Winborne Leigh 1937- *WhoRel 92*
**Hamling,** Jerry Wayne 1951- *WhoMW 92*
**Hamlisch,** Marvin 1944- *IntMPA 92, IntWW 91, NewAmDM, WhoEnt 92*
**Hamlow,** Eugene Emanuel 1927- *AmMWSc 92*
**Hamlyn,** David Walter 1924- *Who 92*
**Hamlyn,** Paul 1926- *Who 92*
**Hamlyn,** Paul Bertrand 1926- *IntAu&W 91, IntWW 91*
**Hamm,** Barbara Lawanda 1957- *WhoBlA 92*
**Hamm,** Donald Ivan 1928- *AmMWSc 92*
**Hamm,** Eduard 1879-1944 *EncTR 91*
**Hamm,** Franklin Albert 1918- *AmMWSc 92*
**Hamm,** Fred P 1924- *WhoIns 92*
**Hamm,** George Ardeil 1934- *WhoWest 92*
**Hamm,** Harry Delmond 1940- *WhoMW 92*
**Hamm,** Joseph Nicholas 1915- *AmMWSc 92*
**Hamm,** Kenneth Lee 1923- *AmMWSc 92*
**Hamm,** Lee *WhoAmP 91*
**Hamm,** Michael Dennis 1936- *WhoMW 92, WhoRel 92*
**Hamm,** Patricia Ann 1943- *WhoMW 92*
**Hamm,** Randall Earl 1913- *AmMWSc 92*
**Hamm,** Thomas Edward, Jr 1942- *AmMWSc 92*
**Hamm,** Vernon Louis, Jr. 1951- *WhoMW 92*
**Hamm,** William Eugene 1944- *WhoMW 92*
**Hamm,** William Giles 1942- *WhoWest 92*
**Hamm,** William Joseph 1910- *AmMWSc 92*
**Hammack,** Henry Edgar 1928- *WhoEnt 92*
**Hammack,** Paul Willard, Jr. 1939- *WhoAmL 92*
**Hammack,** William Blaine 1943- *WhoFI 92*
**Hammad,** Alam E. 1943- *WhoFI 92*
**Hammadi,** Sadoon 1930- *IntWW 91*
**Hammaker,** Geneva Sinquefield 1936- *AmMWSc 92*
**Hammaker,** Robert Michael 1934- *AmMWSc 92*
**Hammam,** M Shawky *AmMWSc 92*
**Hamman,** Donald Jay 1929- *AmMWSc 92*
**Hamman,** Reg Duane 1945- *WhoRel 92*
**Hamman,** Steven Roger 1946- *WhoWest 92*
**Hammann,** Chester A 1948- *WhoIns 92*
**Hammann,** John William 1914- *AmMWSc 92*
**Hammann,** William Curl 1925- *AmMWSc 92*
**Hammar,** Allan H 1923- *AmMWSc 92*
**Hammar,** Kevin Douglas 1950- *WhoAmL 92*
**Hammar,** Richard Harry 1943- *WhoMW 92*
**Hammar,** Sherrel L 1931- *AmMWSc 92*
**Hammar,** Walton James 1941- *AmMWSc 92*
**Hammarlund,** Edwin Roy 1922- *AmMWSc 92*
**Hammarskjold,** Dag 1905-1961 *FacFETw [port]*
**Hammarskjold,** Dag Hjalmar Agne Carl 1905-1961 *WhoNob 90*
**Hammarskjold,** Knut 1922- *Who 92*
**Hammarskjold,** Knut Olof Hjalmar Akesson 1922- *IntWW 91*
**Hammarstrom,** Carl Arvid 1930- *WhoEnt 92*
**Hamme,** John Valentine 1919- *AmMWSc 92*
**Hamme,** Marc Milton 1959- *WhoFI 92*
**Hammel,** Edward Frederic 1918- *AmMWSc 92*
**Hammel,** Eric M 1946- *ConAu 35NR*
**Hammel,** Ernest Martin 1939- *WhoMW 92*
**Hammel,** Eugene A 1930- *AmMWSc 92*
**Hammel,** Eugene Alfred 1930- *IntWW 91*
**Hammel,** Harold Theodore 1921- *AmMWSc 92*
**Hammel,** Jay Edwin 1921- *AmMWSc 92*
**Hammel,** Jay Morris 1938- *AmMWSc 92*
**Hammel,** John Wingate 1943- *WhoAmL 92*
**Hammell,** Grandin Gaunt 1945- *WhoWest 92*
**Hammen,** Carl Schlee 1923- *AmMWSc 92*
**Hammen,** Donald G 1939- *WhoAmP 91*
**Hammen,** Susan Lum 1936- *AmMWSc 92*
**Hammer** *WhoEnt 92*
**Hammer,** Armand d1990 *IntWW 91N, Who 92N*
**Hammer,** Armand 1898-1990 *AnObit 1990, ConAu 134, CurBio 91N, FacFETw [port], News 91, -91-3*
**Hammer,** Ben *WhoEnt 92*
**Hammer,** Carl 1914- *AmMWSc 92*
**Hammer,** Carl Helman *AmMWSc 92*
**Hammer,** Charles F 1933- *AmMWSc 92*
**Hammer,** Charles Lawrence 1922- *AmMWSc 92*
**Hammer,** Charles Lawrence, Jr 1922- *WhoAmP 91*

**Hammer,** Charles Rankin 1927- *AmMWSc 92*
**Hammer,** Clarence Frederick, Jr 1919- *AmMWSc 92*
**Hammer,** David Andrew 1943- *AmMWSc 92*
**Hammer,** David Lindley 1929- *WhoAmL 92, WhoMW 92*
**Hammer,** Emanuel 1926- *IntAu&W 91*
**Hammer,** Emanuel F. 1926- *WrDr 92*
**Hammer,** Gary G 1934- *AmMWSc 92*
**Hammer,** Gregory John 1949- *WhoFI 92*
**Hammer,** Hali Diane 1948- *WhoEnt 92*
**Hammer,** Harold Harlan 1920- *WhoFI 92*
**Hammer,** Henry Felix 1921- *AmMWSc 92*
**Hammer,** Jacob 1950- *AmMWSc 92*
**Hammer,** Jacob Meyer 1927- *AmMWSc 92*
**Hammer,** James Dominic George 1929- *Who 92*
**Hammer,** Jan 1948- *WhoEnt 92*
**Hammer,** John A *AmMWSc 92*
**Hammer,** John Henry, II 1943- *WhoMW 92*
**Hammer,** Lawrence I. 1926- *WhoAmL 92*
**Hammer,** Louis *DrAPF 91*
**Hammer,** Lowell Clarke 1930- *AmMWSc 92*
**Hammer,** M. C. *News 91 [port]*
**Hammer,** M. C. 1962- *WhoBlA 92*
**Hammer,** M. C. 1963- *CurBio 91 [port]*
**Hammer,** Mark J 1931- *AmMWSc 92*
**Hammer,** Mary Lou Simpson 1934- *WhoAmP 91*
**Hammer,** Minnie Lee Hancock 1873-1959 *DcNCBi 3*
**Hammer,** Nathan Carlisle 1953- *WhoFI 92*
**Hammer,** Patrick, Jr. *DrAPF 91*
**Hammer,** Raymond Jack 1920- *Who 92*
**Hammer,** Richard 1928- *WhoEnt 92*
**Hammer,** Richard Benjamin 1943- *AmMWSc 92*
**Hammer,** Richard Hartman 1933- *AmMWSc 92*
**Hammer,** Robert Eugene 1931- *WhoMW 92*
**Hammer,** Robert Nelson 1924- *AmMWSc 92*
**Hammer,** Robert Russell 1936- *AmMWSc 92*
**Hammer,** Robert Wayne 1947- *WhoEnt 92*
**Hammer,** Roland Meredith 1928- *WhoMW 92*
**Hammer,** Ronald Page, Jr 1953- *AmMWSc 92*
**Hammer,** Sigmund Immanuel 1901- *AmMWSc 92*
**Hammer,** Susan *WhoAmP 91*
**Hammer,** Susan Berman H. 1950- *WhoFI 92*
**Hammer,** Ulrich Theodore 1924- *AmMWSc 92*
**Hammer,** William Cicero 1865-1930 *DcNCBi 3*
**Hammer,** Zevulun 1936- *IntWW 91*
**Hammerback,** John Clark 1938- *WhoWest 92*
**Hammerbeck,** Christopher John Anthony 1943- *Who 92*
**Hammerli,** Angela Mitchell 1950- *WhoEnt 92*
**Hammerli,** Martin 1938- *AmMWSc 92*
**Hammerling,** James Solomon 1907- *AmMWSc 92*
**Hammerling,** Robert Charles 1934- *WhoAmL 92*
**Hammerling,** Roy 1956- *WhoRel 92*
**Hammerling,** Ulrich *AmMWSc 92*
**Hammerly,** Harry Allan 1934- *WhoFI 92*
**Hammerman,** David Lewis 1935- *AmMWSc 92*
**Hammerman,** Ira Saul 1942- *AmMWSc 92*
**Hammerman,** Irving Harold, II 1920- *WhoFI 92*
**Hammerman,** Marc R 1947- *AmMWSc 92*
**Hammerman,** Stephen Lawrence 1938- *WhoAmL 92*
**Hammermeister,** Karl E 1939- *AmMWSc 92*
**Hammerness,** Francis Carl 1922- *AmMWSc 92*
**Hammerschlag,** Alice Berger 1917-1969 *TwCPaSc*
**Hammerschlag,** Richard 1939- *AmMWSc 92*
**Hammerschmidt,** Andreas 1611?-1675 *NewAmDM*
**Hammerschmidt,** John Paul 1922- *AlmAP 92 [port], WhoAmP 91*
**Hammerschmidt,** Judith L 1954- *WhoAmP 91*
**Hammersley,** John Michael 1920- *IntWW 91, Who 92*
**Hammersley,** Peter Gerald 1928- *Who 92*
**Hammersmith,** John L 1929- *AmMWSc 92*
**Hammerstedt,** Roy H 1941- *AmMWSc 92*
**Hammerstein,** Oscar 1846-1919 *NewAmDM*
**Hammerstein,** Oscar 1847?-1919 *BenetAL 91*
**Hammerstein,** Oscar, II 1895-1960 *BenetAL 91, FacFETw [port], NewAmDM*
**Hammerstein-Equord,** Kurt, Baron von 1878-1943 *EncTR 91 [port]*
**Hammerstrom,** Beverly Swoish 1944- *WhoAmP 91*
**Hammerstrom,** Harold Elmore 1927- *AmMWSc 92*
**Hammerstrom,** Norman Elwood & Searight, R *ScFEYrs*
**Hammerton,** Rolf Eric 1926- *Who 92*
**Hammes,** George Albert 1911- *WhoRel 92*
**Hammes,** Gordon G 1934- *AmMWSc 92, IntWW 91*
**Hammes,** John A. 1924- *WrDr 92*
**Hammes,** Michael Noel 1941- *IntWW 91*
**Hammes,** Terry Marie 1955- *WhoFI 92*
**Hammett,** Benjamin Cowles 1931- *WhoWest 92*
**Hammett,** Clifford 1917- *Who 92*
**Hammett,** Dashiell *DcLB Y91*
**Hammett,** Dashiell 1894-1961 *BenetAL 91, FacFETw [port], ScFEYrs*
**Hammett,** Edward Harold 1956- *WhoRel 92*
**Hammett,** Harold George 1906- *Who 92*
**Hammett,** Michael E 1937- *AmMWSc 92*
**Hammett,** Richard Maupin 1947- *WhoRel 92*
**Hammett,** Samuel Adams 1816-1865 *BenetAL 91*
**Hammett,** Seth *WhoAmP 91*
**Hammett,** William M. H. 1944- *WhoFI 92*
**Hammett,** Willie Anderson 1945- *WhoBlA 92*
**Hammick,** Georgina 1939- *IntAu&W 91*
**Hammick,** Stephen 1926- *Who 92*
**Hammill,** R Joseph 1942- *WhoAmP 91*
**Hammill,** Terrence Michael 1940- *AmMWSc 92*
**Hamming,** Kenneth W 1918- *AmMWSc 92*
**Hamming,** Mynard C 1921- *AmMWSc 92*
**Hamming,** Richard W 1915- *AmMWSc 92*
**Hamming,** Richard Wesley 1915- *WhoWest 92*
**Hammitt,** Frederick G 1923- *AmMWSc 92*
**Hammitt,** Jackson Lewis, III 1938- *WhoEnt 92*
**Hammitt,** James Gordon 1929- *WhoFI 92*
**Hammock,** Bruce Dupree 1947- *AmMWSc 92*
**Hammock,** Edward R. 1938- *WhoBlA 92*
**Hammock,** Elizabeth Catherine 1927- *IntAu&W 91*
**Hammock,** Jim 1933- *WhoAmP 91*
**Hammock,** Ted Lewis 1932- *WhoAmP 91*
**Hammon,** Briton *BenetAL 91*
**Hammon,** John 1760-1868 *DcNCBi 3*
**Hammon,** Jupiter 1711?-1800? *BlkLC*
**Hammon,** Jupiter 1720?-1800? *BenetAL 91*
**Hammon,** Patricia Jane 1946- *WhoWest 92*
**Hammon,** Thomas Frederick 1949- *WhoRel 92*
**Hammond,** Abner M, Jr 1939- *AmMWSc 92*
**Hammond,** Allen Lee 1943- *AmMWSc 92*
**Hammond,** Andrew Charles 1949- *AmMWSc 92*
**Hammond,** Anthony Hilgrove 1940- *Who 92*
**Hammond,** Benjamin Franklin 1934- *AmMWSc 92, WhoBlA 92*
**Hammond,** Bennie Eugene 1955- *WhoMW 92*
**Hammond,** Bill 1947- *WhoAmP 91*
**Hammond,** Blaine Randol 1946- *WhoRel 92*
**Hammond,** Brad 1947- *TwCWW 91*
**Hammond,** Brian Ralph 1934- *AmMWSc 92*
**Hammond,** Catherine Elizabeth 1909- *Who 92*
**Hammond,** Charles Ainley 1933- *WhoRel 92*
**Hammond,** Charles Bessellieu 1936- *AmMWSc 92*
**Hammond,** Charles E *AmMWSc 92*
**Hammond,** Charles Edgar 1943- *WhoWest 92*
**Hammond,** Charles Eugene 1940- *AmMWSc 92*
**Hammond,** Charles Thomas 1944- *AmMWSc 92*
**Hammond,** Chester Warren 1929- *WhoMW 92*
**Hammond,** David Alan 1948- *WhoEnt 92*
**Hammond,** David G 1913- *AmMWSc 92*
**Hammond,** Deborah Lynn 1958- *WhoRel 92*
**Hammond,** Debra Lauren 1957- *WhoBlA 92*
**Hammond,** Donald L 1927- *AmMWSc 92*
**Hammond,** Douglas Ellenwood 1946- *AmMWSc 92*
**Hammond,** Earl Edward 1957- *WhoRel 92*
**Hammond,** Earl Gullette 1926- *AmMWSc 92*
**Hammond,** Edward Clark 1959- *WhoAmL 92*
**Hammond,** Edward H. 1944- *WhoMW 92*
**Hammond,** Eric Albert Barratt 1929- *Who 92*
**Hammond,** Frank Jefferson, III 1953- *WhoAmL 92*
**Hammond,** Frank Joseph 1919- *WhoAmL 92*
**Hammond,** Geoffrey 1938- *TwCPaSc*
**Hammond,** George Denman 1923- *AmMWSc 92*
**Hammond,** George Simms 1921- *AmMWSc 92, IntWW 91*
**Hammond,** Gerald *WrDr 92*
**Hammond,** Glenn Barry, Sr. 1947- *WhoAmL 92*
**Hammond,** Gordon Leon 1931- *AmMWSc 92*
**Hammond,** Guyton Bowers 1930- *WhoRel 92*
**Hammond,** H David 1924- *AmMWSc 92*
**Hammond,** H W 1917- *WhoAmP 91*
**Hammond,** Harold Logan 1934- *AmMWSc 92, WhoMW 92*
**Hammond,** Hattie Philetta 1907- *WhoRel 92*
**Hammond,** James A. 1929- *WhoBlA 92*
**Hammond,** James Alexander, Jr 1936- *AmMWSc 92*
**Hammond,** James Anthony 1936- *Who 92*
**Hammond,** James B 1921- *AmMWSc 92*
**Hammond,** James Dillard 1933- *WhoFI 92*
**Hammond,** James Henry 1807-1864 *AmPolLe*
**Hammond,** James Herbert, Jr. 1940- *WhoFI 92*
**Hammond,** James Jacob 1941- *AmMWSc 92*
**Hammond,** James Matthew 1930- *WhoBlA 92*
**Hammond,** James W 1913- *AmMWSc 92*
**Hammond,** Jane *WrDr 92*
**Hammond,** Jane Laura *WhoAmL 92*
**Hammond,** Jay S. 1922- *IntWW 91*
**Hammond,** Jay Sterner 1922- *WhoAmP 91*
**Hammond,** Jeffrey Earl 1952- *WhoWest 92*
**Hammond,** Jimmy Martin 1944- *WhoAmP 91*
**Hammond,** Joan 1912- *IntWW 91, NewAmDM, Who 92*
**Hammond,** John *BenetAL 91, WhoBlA 92*
**Hammond,** John 1910-1987 *ConMus 6 [port], FacFETw*
**Hammond,** John Benedict 1960- *WhoEnt 92*
**Hammond,** John Moller 1944- *WhoEnt 92*
**Hammond,** John Pete, III 1936- *WhoRel 92*
**Hammond,** John R *WhoAmP 91*
**Hammond,** John William 1946- *WhoAmP 91*
**Hammond,** Johnie 1932- *WhoAmP 91*
**Hammond,** Joseph Langhorne, Jr 1927- *AmMWSc 92*
**Hammond,** Judy McLain 1956- *WhoWest 92*
**Hammond,** Kenneth Ray 1951- *WhoBlA 92*
**Hammond,** Kenneth T. 1926- *WhoBlA 92*
**Hammond,** Kenneth Winston 1955- *WhoMW 92*
**Hammond,** Laurens 1895-1973 *NewAmDM*
**Hammond,** Luther Carlisle 1921- *AmMWSc 92*
**Hammond,** Mac *DrAPF 91*
**Hammond,** Mac 1926- *WrDr 92*
**Hammond,** Mac Sawyer 1926- *IntAu&W 91*
**Hammond,** Margaret 1949- *WhoAmL 92*
**Hammond,** Martin 1944- *Who 92*
**Hammond,** Martin L 1936- *AmMWSc 92*
**Hammond,** Marvin H, Jr 1939- *AmMWSc 92*
**Hammond,** Mary Elizabeth Hale 1942- *AmMWSc 92*
**Hammond,** Max Dean 1946- *WhoRel 92*
**Hammond,** Melvin Alan Ray, Jr. 1949- *WhoBlA 92*
**Hammond,** Michael Harry Frank 1933- *Who 92*
**Hammond,** Michael Peter 1932- *WhoEnt 92*
**Hammond,** Nellie Handcock 1909- *WhoAmP 91*
**Hammond,** Nicholas 1907- *WrDr 92*
**Hammond,** Nicholas Geoffrey Lempriere 1907- *IntWW 91, Who 92*
**Hammond,** Norman David Curle 1944- *Who 92*
**Hammond,** Paul B 1923- *AmMWSc 92*
**Hammond,** Paul Ellsworth 1929- *AmMWSc 92*
**Hammond,** Paul Young 1929- *WhoFI 92*
**Hammond,** Peter 1923- *IntMPA 92*
**Hammond,** R Philip 1916- *AmMWSc 92*
**Hammond,** Ralph *WrDr 92*
**Hammond,** Ray Kenneth 1943- *AmMWSc 92*
**Hammond,** Richard A. 1947- *WhoFI 92*
**Hammond,** Ricky L 1951- *WhoIns 92*
**Hammond,** Robert Bruce 1948- *AmMWSc 92*
**Hammond,** Robert Grenfell 1917- *AmMWSc 92*
**Hammond,** Robert Hugh 1930- *AmMWSc 92*
**Hammond,** Ross William 1918- *WhoFI 92*
**Hammond,** Roy John William 1928- *Who 92*
**Hammond,** Russell Kenneth 1947- *WhoAmP 91*
**Hammond,** Ruth *DrAPF 91*
**Hammond,** Sally Katharine 1949- *AmMWSc 92*
**Hammond,** Sean Thomas 1946- *WhoMW 92*
**Hammond,** Sidney N *WhoAmP 91*
**Hammond,** Stephen J. *WhoRel 92*
**Hammond,** Stephen Van 1948- *WhoAmL 92*
**Hammond,** Terry Richard 1955- *WhoWest 92*
**Hammond,** Terry Wayne 1957- *WhoAmL 92*
**Hammond,** Ulysses Bernard 1951- *WhoBlA 92*
**Hammond,** Ulysses S., Jr. 1919- *WhoBlA 92*
**Hammond,** W. Rodney 1946- *WhoBlA 92*
**Hammond,** William Alexander 1828-1900 *BiInAmS*
**Hammond,** William Churchill, III 1947- *WhoFI 92*
**Hammond,** William Edward 1935- *AmMWSc 92*
**Hammond,** William Marion 1930- *AmMWSc 92*
**Hammond,** Willis Burdette 1942- *AmMWSc 92*
**Hammond Black,** Meryl Jean 1944- *WhoMW 92*
**Hammond-Chambers,** Alexander 1942- *Who 92*
**Hammond Innes,** Ralph 1913- *IntAu&W 91, IntWW 91, Who 92, WrDr 92*
**Hammond-Stroud,** Derek 1926- *Who 92*
**Hammond-Stroud,** Derek 1929- *NewAmDM*
**Hammonds,** Alfred 1937- *WhoBlA 92*
**Hammonds,** Cleveland, Jr. 1936- *WhoBlA 92*
**Hammonds,** Lloyd Harold 1952- *WhoMW 92*
**Hammonds,** Roger Kent 1948- *WhoRel 92*
**Hammonds,** Tom Edward 1967- *WhoBlA 92*
**Hammons,** Dennis Alvin 1956- *WhoRel 92*
**Hammons,** James Hutchinson 1934- *AmMWSc 92*
**Hammons,** Mark Edgar 1950- *WhoAmP 91*
**Hammons,** Paul Edward 1925- *AmMWSc 92*
**Hammons,** Ray Otto 1919- *AmMWSc 92*
**Hammontree,** Marie 1913- *WrDr 92*
**Hamner,** Charles Edward, Jr 1935- *AmMWSc 92*
**Hamner,** Earl 1923- *IntMPA 92*
**Hamner,** Earl, Jr. *LesBEnT 92*
**Hamner,** Martin E 1918- *AmMWSc 92*
**Hamner,** Reginald Turner 1939- *WhoAmL 92*
**Hamner,** William Frederick 1922- *AmMWSc 92*
**Hamnett,** Katharine 1948- *IntWW 91*
**Hamnett,** Nina 1890-1956 *TwCPaSc*
**Hamnett,** Thomas Orlando 1930- *Who 92*
**Hamod,** Sam *DrAPF 91*
**Hamolsky,** Milton William 1921- *AmMWSc 92*
**Hamon,** Avas Burdette 1940- *AmMWSc 92*
**Hamon,** Deborah Renee 1964- *WhoFI 92*
**Hamon,** J Hill 1931- *AmMWSc 92*
**Hamor,** Glenn Herbert 1920- *AmMWSc 92*
**Hamori,** Csaba 1948- *IntWW 91*
**Hamori,** Eugene 1933- *AmMWSc 92*
**Hamosh,** Margit 1933- *AmMWSc 92*
**Hamosh,** Paul 1931- *AmMWSc 92*
**Hamouris,** Richard David 1950- *WhoWest 92*
**Hamous,** Bruce Allan 1955- *WhoMW 92*
**Hampar,** Berge 1932- *AmMWSc 92*
**Hamparian,** Vincent 1927- *AmMWSc 92*
**Hampden** *Who 92*
**Hampden,** Viscount 1937- *Who 92*
**Hampe,** Michael 1935- *IntWW 91*
**Hampel,** Arnold E 1939- *AmMWSc 92*
**Hampel,** Clifford Allen 1912- *AmMWSc 92*
**Hamper,** Ben 1955- *NewYTBS 91 [port]*
**Hamper,** Nicholas 1956- *TwCPaSc*

**Hamper,** Robert Joseph 1956- *WhoFI 92, WhoMW 92*
**Hampl,** Patricia *DrAPF 91*
**Hampp,** Edward Gottlieb 1912- *AmMWSc 92*
**Hampsch,** George 1927- *WrDr 92*
**Hampshire,** Margaret Grace 1918- *Who 92*
**Hampshire,** Michael John 1939- *Who 92*
**Hampshire,** Stuart 1914- *FacFETw, IntWW 91, Who 92*
**Hampshire,** Stuart 1927- *WrDr 92*
**Hampshire,** Susan 1941- *IntMPA 92*
**Hampshire,** Susan 1942- *IntWW 91, Who 92, WhoEnt 92*
**Hampson,** Alfred Aubert 1920- *WhoAmL 92*
**Hampson,** Anne *IntAu&W 91, WrDr 92*
**Hampson,** Elwyn Lloyd 1916- *Who 92*
**Hampson,** Keith 1943- *Who 92*
**Hampson,** Michael Chisnall 1930- *AmMWSc 92*
**Hampson,** Norman 1922- *IntAu&W 91, IntWW 91, Who 92, WrDr 92*
**Hampson,** Robert 1948- *ConAu 135*
**Hampson,** Robert F, Jr 1930- *AmMWSc 92*
**Hampson,** Robert Gavin 1948- *IntAu&W 91*
**Hampson,** Robert George 1943- *WhoAmL 92*
**Hampson,** Thomas *NewYTBS 91 [port]*
**Hampson,** Thomas 1955- *CurBio 91 [port]*
**Hampson,** Thomas Lee 1948- *WhoRel 92*
**Hampson,** Wayne Scott 1957- *WhoEnt 92*
**Hampstead,** Archdeacon of *Who 92*
**Hampton,** Baron 1925- *Who 92*
**Hampton,** Antony Barmore 1919- *Who 92*
**Hampton,** Bryan 1938- *Who 92*
**Hampton,** Carol McDonald 1935- *WhoRel 92*
**Hampton,** Carolyn Hutchins 1936- *AmMWSc 92*
**Hampton,** Charles Edwin 1948- *WhoAmL 92*
**Hampton,** Charles Robert 1945- *AmMWSc 92, WhoMW 92*
**Hampton,** Christopher 1929- *IntAu&W 91*
**Hampton,** Christopher 1946- *IntAu&W 91, WrDr 92*
**Hampton,** Christopher James 1946- *FacFETw, IntWW 91, Who 92*
**Hampton,** David Clark 1934- *AmMWSc 92*
**Hampton,** Delon 1933- *AmMWSc 92, WhoBlA 92*
**Hampton,** Don Ameche 1941- *WhoMW 92*
**Hampton,** Edwin Harrell 1928- *WhoBlA 92*
**Hampton,** Elwood 1924- *WhoBlA 92*
**Hampton,** Frank, Sr. 1923- *WhoBlA 92*
**Hampton,** Gary Calvin 1953- *WhoRel 92*
**Hampton,** George Mervyn 1928- *WhoAmP 91*
**Hampton,** Glen Richard 1948- *WhoMW 92*
**Hampton,** Grace 1937- *WhoBlA 92*
**Hampton,** Henry *LesBEnT 92*
**Hampton,** Henry Eugene, Jr. 1940- *WhoBlA 92*
**Hampton,** James 1936- *IntMPA 92*
**Hampton,** James Wilburn 1931- *AmMWSc 92*
**Hampton,** Jeral L. 1921- *WhoFI 92*
**Hampton,** Jim *ConAu 133*
**Hampton,** John 1926- *Who 92*
**Hampton,** John Kyle, Jr 1923- *AmMWSc 92*
**Hampton,** John Lewis 1935- *ConAu 133*
**Hampton,** John Robinson 1807-1880 *DcNCBi 3*
**Hampton,** John Vernon 1929- *WhoAmP 91*
**Hampton,** Kenneth T *WhoAmP 91*
**Hampton,** Leroy 1927- *WhoBlA 92*
**Hampton,** Lionel 1909?- *ConMus 6 [port], FacFETw, NewAmDM*
**Hampton,** Lionel Leo 1908- *WhoBlA 92*
**Hampton,** Lionel Leo 1913- *WhoEnt 92*
**Hampton,** Lou *ScFEYrs*
**Hampton,** Loyd Donald 1930- *AmMWSc 92*
**Hampton,** Mark *IntAu&W 91X*
**Hampton,** Mark 1940- *DcTwDes*
**Hampton,** Michael Eugene 1955- *WhoBlA 92*
**Hampton,** Millard Frank 1956- *BlkOlyM*
**Hampton,** Opal Jewell 1942- *WhoBlA 92*
**Hampton,** Phillip Jewel 1922- *WhoBlA 92, WhoMW 92*
**Hampton,** Ralph Clayton, Jr. 1934- *WhoRel 92*
**Hampton,** Raymond Earl 1934- *AmMWSc 92*
**Hampton,** Richard Owen 1930- *AmMWSc 92*
**Hampton,** Robert K., Sr. 1919- *WhoFI 92*
**Hampton,** Robert L. 1947- *WhoBlA 92*
**Hampton,** Rodney 1969- *WhoBlA 92*
**Hampton,** Ronald Everett 1945- *WhoBlA 92*
**Hampton,** Sanford 1955- *WhoEnt 92*
**Hampton,** Slide 1932- *NewAmDM*
**Hampton,** Suzanne Harvey 1934- *AmMWSc 92*
**Hampton,** Thomas Earle 1950- *WhoBlA 92*
**Hampton,** Thurman B. 1949- *WhoBlA 92*
**Hampton,** Trevor Richard Walker 1930- *Who 92*
**Hampton,** Wade 1818-1902 *AmPolLe*
**Hampton,** Wanda Kay Baker *WhoBlA 92*
**Hampton,** Wayne *WhoAmP 91*
**Hampton,** William 1929- *WrDr 92*
**Hampton,** Willie L. 1933- *WhoBlA 92*
**Hamra,** Sam F, Jr 1932- *WhoAmP 91*
**Hamre,** Gary Leslie William 1939- *WhoMW 92*
**Hamre,** Harold Thomas 1910- *AmMWSc 92*
**Hamre,** James Stanley 1931- *WhoMW 92*
**Hamre,** Leif 1914- *WrDr 92*
**Hamre,** Melvin L 1932- *AmMWSc 92*
**Hamre,** Sverre Ludvig Borgund d1990 *IntWW 91N*
**Hamren,** Nancy Van Brasch 1947- *WhoWest 92*
**Hamric,** Peggy *WhoAmP 91*
**Hamrick,** Anna Katherine Barr 1947- *AmMWSc 92*
**Hamrick,** C. Page 1944- *WhoAmL 92*
**Hamrick,** Douglas Paul 1963- *WhoFI 92*
**Hamrick,** James Lewis 1942- *AmMWSc 92*
**Hamrick,** Joseph Eugene, Jr. 1954- *WhoWest 92*
**Hamrick,** Joseph Thomas 1921- *AmMWSc 92*
**Hamrick,** Joseph Thomas 1933- *AmMWSc 92*
**Hamrick,** Lewis Franklin 1938- *WhoRel 92*
**Hamrick,** Mark Alan 1960- *WhoEnt 92*
**Hamrin,** Charles E, Jr 1934- *AmMWSc 92*
**Hamrum,** Charles Lowell 1922- *AmMWSc 92*
**Hamsa,** William Rudolph 1903- *AmMWSc 92*
**Hamsher,** James J 1940- *AmMWSc 92*
**Hamsher,** Kerry de Sandoz 1946- *AmMWSc 92*
**Hamson,** Alvin Russell 1924- *AmMWSc 92*
**Hamstrom,** Mary-Elizabeth 1927- *AmMWSc 92*
**Hamsun,** Knut 1859-1952 *BiDExR, EncTR 91 [port], FacFETw, WhoNob 90*
**Hamsund,** Knud Pedersen 1859-1952 *WhoNob 90*
**Hamtil,** Charles Norbert 1913- *AmMWSc 92*
**Hamvas,** Lewis T. 1919- *WhoEnt 92*
**Hamwee,** Baroness 1947- *Who 92*
**Hamylton Jones,** Keith 1924- *Who 92*
**Hamza,** Mohamed Hamed 1936- *AmMWSc 92*
**Hamzaee,** Reza Gholi 1951- *WhoMW 92*
**Hamzah,** Razaleigh *IntWW 91*
**Hamzeh,** Zaid 1932- *IntWW 91*
**Hamzy,** Joseph Amin 1915- *WhoAmP 91*
**Han Boping** *IntWW 91*
**Han Guang** 1912- *IntWW 91*
**Han Huaizhi** *IntWW 91*
**Han Nianlong** 1910- *IntWW 91*
**Han Ningfu** *IntWW 91*
**Han Peixin** 1921- *IntWW 91*
**Han Shao Gong** 1953- *IntWW 91*
**Han Suyin** 1917- *IntWW 91, Who 92, WrDr 92*
**Han Tianshi** *IntWW 91*
**Han Xu** 1924- *IntWW 91*
**Han,** Byung Joon 1959- *AmMWSc 92*
**Han,** Chang Dae 1935- *AmMWSc 92*
**Han,** Charles Chih-Chao 1944- *AmMWSc 92*
**Han,** Chien-Pai 1936- *AmMWSc 92*
**Han,** Ittah 1939- *WhoFI 92, WhoWest 92*
**Han,** Jaok 1930- *AmMWSc 92*
**Han,** Kenneth N 1938- *AmMWSc 92*
**Han,** Ki Sup 1929- *AmMWSc 92*
**Han,** L S 1923- *AmMWSc 92*
**Han,** Moo-Young 1934- *AmMWSc 92*
**Han,** Seong S 1933- *AmMWSc 92*
**Han,** Shu-Tang 1913- *AmMWSc 92*
**Han,** Stephanie 1964- *WhoEnt 92*
**Han,** Suyin 1917- *IntAu&W 91*
**Han,** Tin 1933- *AmMWSc 92*
**Han,** Yuri Wha-Yul 1932- *AmMWSc 92*
**Hanable,** William Shannon 1938- *WhoWest 92*
**Hanafee,** James Eugene 1937- *AmMWSc 92*
**Hanafee,** William Norman 1926- *AmMWSc 92*
**Hanaford,** Phebe Ann Coffin 1829-1921 *RelLAm 91*
**Hanafusa,** Hidesaburo 1929- *AmMWSc 92*
**Hanahan,** Donald James 1919- *AmMWSc 92*
**Hanahan,** James Lake 1932- *WhoFI 92*
**Hanak,** Joseph J 1930- *AmMWSc 92*
**Hanaman,** David Blaine 1924- *WhoWest 92*
**Hanamirian,** Varujan 1952- *WhoFI 92*
**Hanan,** Barry Benton 1949- *AmMWSc 92*
**Hanan,** Joe John 1931- *AmMWSc 92*
**Hananiya,** Haldu A. 1942- *Who 92*
**Hanashi,** Nobuyuki 1928- *IntWW 91*
**Hanau,** Kenneth John, Jr. 1927- *WhoFI 92*
**Hanau,** Richard 1917- *AmMWSc 92*
**Hanauer,** Joe Franklin 1937- *WhoWest 92*
**Hanauer,** Richard 1943- *AmMWSc 92*
**Hanauer,** Stephen B 1952- *AmMWSc 92*
**Hanauer,** Stephen H 1927- *AmMWSc 92*
**Hanawalt,** Philip Courtland 1931- *AmMWSc 92*
**Hanaway,** Donald 1933- *WhoAmP 91*
**Hanaway,** Paul E 1932- *WhoAmP 91*
**Hanbauer,** Ingeborg 1943- *AmMWSc 92*
**Hanberry,** Annie E. 1903- *WhoBlA 92*
**Hanbury,** Hanmer 1916- *Who 92*
**Hanbury,** Harold Grenville 1898- *WrDr 92*
**Hanbury,** Harold Greville 1898- *Who 92*
**Hanbury,** John 1908- *Who 92*
**Hanbury,** Marshall Earl 1944- *WhoAmP 91*
**Hanbury-Tenison,** Airling Robin 1936- *Who 92*
**Hanbury-Tenison,** Richard 1925- *Who 92*
**Hanbury-Tenison,** Robin 1936- *IntAu&W 91, WrDr 92*
**Hanbury-Tracy** *Who 92*
**Hanby,** John Estes, Jr 1941- *AmMWSc 92*
**Hancarville,** Pierre-Francois Hugues d' 1719-1805 *BlkwCEP*
**Hance,** Anthony James 1932- *AmMWSc 92, WhoWest 92*
**Hance,** Clifford Joseph 1963- *WhoRel 92*
**Hance,** Harvey 1957- *WhoHisp 92*
**Hance,** James Henry, Jr. 1944- *WhoFI 92*
**Hance,** Kent 1942- *WhoAmP 91*
**Hance,** Robert Lee 1943- *AmMWSc 92*
**Hance,** Wiley Francis 1923- *WhoEnt 92*
**Hanchey,** Richard Howard 1913- *AmMWSc 92*
**Hanchuruck,** Stephen P 1955- *WhoAmP 91*
**Hanck,** Kenneth William 1942- *AmMWSc 92*
**Hanclosky,** Walter Vincent 1951- *WhoEnt 92*
**Hancock,** Allan G 1935- *WhoAmP 91*
**Hancock,** Allen C. 1908- *WhoBlA 92*
**Hancock,** Anthony John 1936- *AmMWSc 92*
**Hancock,** Beryl Lynette 1938- *IntAu&W 91*
**Hancock,** Bob 1909- *WhoFI 92*
**Hancock,** Charles M 1936- *WhoAmP 91*
**Hancock,** Charles Wilbourne 1924- *WhoRel 92*
**Hancock,** Christine *Who 92*
**Hancock,** Cyril Percy d1990 *Who 92N*
**Hancock,** David 1934- *Who 92*
**Hancock,** Deana Lori 1961- *AmMWSc 92*
**Hancock,** Don Edward 1952- *WhoEnt 92, WhoMW 92*
**Hancock,** Don Ray 1948- *WhoWest 92*
**Hancock,** Edward Lee 1873-1911 *BiInAmS*
**Hancock,** Elisabeth Joy 1947- *Who 92*
**Hancock,** Ellen Marie 1943- *WhoFI 92*
**Hancock,** Emily Stone 1945- *WhoWest 92*
**Hancock,** Eugene Wilson White 1929- *WhoBlA 92*
**Hancock,** Franklin Wills, Jr. 1894-1969 *DcNCBi 3*
**Hancock,** Gary C 1951- *WhoAmP 91*
**Hancock,** Geoffrey Francis 1926- *Who 92*
**Hancock,** Geoffrey White 1946- *IntAu&W 91*
**Hancock,** George Whitmore, Jr 1942- *AmMWSc 92*
**Hancock,** Gerre Edward 1934- *WhoEnt 92*
**Hancock,** Graeme Ernest Maxwell 1954- *WhoAmL 92*
**Hancock,** Gwendolyn Carter 1933- *WhoBlA 92*
**Hancock,** H Irving 1868-1922 *ScFEYrs*
**Hancock,** Harold E 1921- *AmMWSc 92*
**Hancock,** Henry Hervey 1928- *WhoAmL 92*
**Hancock,** Herbert Jeffrey 1940- *WhoBlA 92, WhoEnt 92*
**Hancock,** Herbie 1940- *FacFETw, NewAmDM*
**Hancock,** James Beaty *WhoMW 92*
**Hancock,** James Findley, Jr 1950- *AmMWSc 92*
**Hancock,** James Hughes 1931- *WhoAmL 92*
**Hancock,** Joan Herrin 1930- *WhoFI 92, WhoMW 92*
**Hancock,** John *WhoEnt 92, WhoRel 92*
**Hancock,** John 1737-1793 *AmPolLe [port], BlkwEAR [port], RComAH*
**Hancock,** John 1939- *IntMPA 92*
**Hancock,** John C 1929- *AmMWSc 92*
**Hancock,** John Charles 1938- *AmMWSc 92*
**Hancock,** John D. 1939- *WhoEnt 92*
**Hancock,** John Edward Herbert 1929- *AmMWSc 92*
**Hancock,** John Ray 1964- *WhoAmP 91*
**Hancock,** John Stephan 1943- *WhoEnt 92*
**Hancock,** John W. 1931- *WhoMW 92*
**Hancock,** John Walker, III 1937- *WhoFI 92*
**Hancock,** Joseph Griscom, Jr 1938- *AmMWSc 92*
**Hancock,** Keith Jackson 1935- *Who 92*
**Hancock,** Kenneth Farrell 1930- *AmMWSc 92*
**Hancock,** Kenneth George 1942- *AmMWSc 92*
**Hancock,** Langley George 1909- *IntWW 91*
**Hancock,** Loni 1940- *WhoWest 92*
**Hancock,** Loni 1950- *WhoAmP 91*
**Hancock,** Mary *EncAmaz 91*
**Hancock,** Mel 1929- *AlmAP 92 [port], WhoAmP 91, WhoMW 92*
**Hancock,** Michael B 1939- *AmMWSc 92*
**Hancock,** Michael Stephen 1917- *Who 92*
**Hancock,** Michael Thomas 1946- *Who 92*
**Hancock,** Molly McCoy 1863-1951 *DcNCBi 3*
**Hancock,** Newell Leslie 1943- *WhoWest 92*
**Hancock,** Norman 1916- *Who 92*
**Hancock,** P. E. Thompson 1904- *Who 92*
**Hancock,** Paul David 1958- *WhoEnt 92*
**Hancock,** Peter Adrian 1953- *AmMWSc 92, WhoMW 92*
**Hancock,** Robert Ernest William 1949- *AmMWSc 92*
**Hancock,** Ronald John 1934- *Who 92*
**Hancock,** Ronald Lee 1931- *AmMWSc 92*
**Hancock,** S. Lee 1955- *WhoAmL 92*
**Hancock,** Samuel Nathan 1883-1963 *RelLAm 91*
**Hancock,** Scott Courtney 1963- *WhoFI 92*
**Hancock,** Sheila *Who 92*
**Hancock,** Stewart Freeman, Jr 1923- *WhoAmP 91*
**Hancock,** Thomas Carlyle 1956- *WhoAmL 92*
**Hancock,** V Ray 1926- *AmMWSc 92*
**Hancock,** Valston Eldridge 1907- *Who 92*
**Hancock,** Vernon Ray 1926- *WhoAmP 91*
**Hancock,** William Frank, Jr. 1942- *WhoFI 92*
**Hancock,** William Geremain, Jr 1943- *WhoAmP 91*
**Hancock,** William Richard 1955- *WhoFI 92*
**Hancock,** Winfield Scott 1824-1886 *AmPolLe*
**Hancok,** Rick Dean 1952- *WhoMW 92*
**Hancox,** Robert Ernest 1943- *WhoFI 92*
**Hancox,** William Thomas 1940- *AmMWSc 92*
**Hand,** Arthur Ralph 1943- *AmMWSc 92*
**Hand,** Bethlyn J. *IntMPA 92*
**Hand,** Bryce Moyer 1936- *AmMWSc 92*
**Hand,** Cadet Hammond, Jr 1920- *AmMWSc 92*
**Hand,** Clifford Warren 1936- *AmMWSc 92*
**Hand,** Elaine 1934- *WhoAmP 91*
**Hand,** Elizabeth 1957- *TwCSFW 91*
**Hand,** Geoffrey David 1918- *Who 92*
**Hand,** Geoffrey Joseph Philip 1931- *Who 92, WrDr 92*
**Hand,** George Samuel, Jr 1936- *AmMWSc 92*
**Hand,** Herbert Hensley 1931- *WhoFI 92*
**Hand,** James Henry 1943- *AmMWSc 92*
**Hand,** Jehu 1956- *WhoAmL 92*
**Hand,** Joan Carole *DrAPF 91*
**Hand,** John Lester 1947- *Who 92*
**Hand,** Jon Thomas 1963- *WhoBlA 92*
**Hand,** Kernan K Skip 1945- *WhoAmP 91*
**Hand,** Learned 1872-1961 *FacFETw*
**Hand,** Lloyd N. 1929- *IntWW 91*
**Hand,** Louis Neff 1933- *AmMWSc 92*
**Hand,** Marcus Vernon 1937- *WhoRel 92*
**Hand,** Mickey Mary 1947- *WhoRel 92*
**Hand,** Paul Edgar 1931- *WhoFI 92*
**Hand,** Perry A 1945- *WhoAmP 91*
**Hand,** Peter James 1937- *AmMWSc 92*
**Hand,** Randall Eugene 1956- *WhoAmL 92*
**Hand,** Raymond W 1928- *WhoAmP 91*
**Hand,** Roger 1938- *AmMWSc 92*
**Hand,** Scott McKee 1942- *WhoFI 92*
**Hand,** Stephen Block 1942- *WhoAmL 92*
**Hand,** Steven Craig *AmMWSc 92*
**Hand,** Ted DeWitt 1959- *WhoEnt 92*
**Hand,** Thomas 1943- *AmMWSc 92*
**Hand,** William M *WhoAmP 91*
**Handa,** Paul 1950- *AmMWSc 92*
**Handa,** V K 1931- *AmMWSc 92*
**Handcock** *Who 92*
**Handel,** Darrell Dale 1933- *WhoEnt 92*
**Handel,** David 1938- *AmMWSc 92*

**Handel,** David Jonathan 1946- *WhoMW 92*
**Handel,** George Frederick 1685-1759 *BlkwCEP*
**Handel,** George Frideric 1685-1759 *NewAmDM*
**Handel,** Leo A. *IntMPA 92*
**Handel,** Mary Ann 1943- *AmMWSc 92*
**Handel,** Morton Emanuel 1935- *WhoFI 92*
**Handel,** Richard Craig 1945- *WhoAmL 92, WhoFI 92*
**Handel,** Rodney Robert 1957- *WhoAmL 92*
**Handel,** Steven Neil 1945- *AmMWSc 92*
**Handel,** William Keating 1935- *WhoFI 92, WhoWest 92*
**Handelman,** David Yale 1938- *WhoEnt 92*
**Handelman,** Eileen T 1928- *AmMWSc 92*
**Handelman,** George Herman 1921- *AmMWSc 92*
**Handelman,** Jay Harold 1958- *WhoEnt 92*
**Handelman,** William 1945- *WhoFI 92*
**Handelsman,** Harold S. 1946- *WhoAmL 92*
**Handelsman,** Jacob C 1919- *AmMWSc 92*
**Handelsman,** Jo 1959- *AmMWSc 92*
**Handelsman,** Morris 1917- *AmMWSc 92*
**Handford,** Clive *Who 92*
**Handford,** Jack 1917- *WhoWest 92*
**Handford,** Martin *News 91, -91-3*
**Handford,** Stanley Wing 1906- *AmMWSc 92*
**Handin,** John Walter 1919- *AmMWSc 92*
**Handin,** Robert I 1941- *AmMWSc 92*
**Handke,** Peter *DrAPF 91*
**Handke,** Peter 1942- *FacFETw, LiExTwC*
**Handl,** Irene 1902-1987 *FacFETw*
**Handl,** Jacob 1550-1591 *NewAmDM*
**Handler,** Alan B. 1931- *WhoAmL 92, WhoAmP 91*
**Handler,** Alfred Harris 1923- *AmMWSc 92*
**Handler,** Amy *WhoFI 92*
**Handler,** Arthur M. 1937- *WhoAmL 92*
**Handler,** Evelyn Erika 1933- *AmMWSc 92*
**Handler,** Harold Robert 1935- *WhoAmL 92*
**Handler,** Joel F. 1932- *WhoAmL 92*
**Handler,** Joseph S 1929- *AmMWSc 92*
**Handler,** Julian H. d1991 *NewYTBS 91*
**Handler,** Lawrence David 1945- *WhoFI 92*
**Handler,** Mark S. 1933- *WhoFI 92*
**Handler,** Milton 1903- *WhoAmL 92*
**Handler,** Paul 1929- *AmMWSc 92*
**Handler,** Shirley Wolz 1925- *AmMWSc 92*
**Handley,** Anthony Michael 1936- *Who 92*
**Handley,** Carol Margaret 1929- *Who 92*
**Handley,** David John D. *Who 92*
**Handley,** Dean A 1949- *AmMWSc 92*
**Handley,** Eric Walter 1926- *IntWW 91, Who 92, WrDr 92*
**Handley,** George E. *WhoRel 92*
**Handley,** George Warren, Jr. 1949- *WhoFI 92*
**Handley,** Gerald Matthew 1942- *WhoAmL 92*
**Handley,** Graham Roderick 1926- *IntAu&W 91, WrDr 92*
**Handley,** Helen M 1921- *WhoAmP 91*
**Handley,** Leon Hunter 1927- *WhoAmL 92*
**Handley,** Mike 1948- *WhoEnt 92*
**Handley,** Monte Wayne 1957- *WhoWest 92*
**Handley,** Ralph William 1913- *WhoWest 92*
**Handley,** Robert Harold 1925- *WhoMW 92*
**Handley,** Thomas Lange 1949- *WhoMW 92*
**Handley,** Vernon George 1930- *IntWW 91, Who 92*
**Handley-Taylor,** Geoffrey 1920- *Who 92*
**Handlin,** Dale L 1956- *AmMWSc 92*
**Handlin,** Jim *DrAPF 91*
**Handlin,** Oscar 1915- *BenetAL 91, IntWW 91, Who 92*
**Handman,** Barbara Ann 1928- *WhoAmP 91*
**Handman,** Marcus David 1950- *WhoEnt 92*
**Handman,** Stanley E 1923- *AmMWSc 92*
**Handon,** Marshall R., Jr. 1937- *WhoBlA 92*
**Handorf,** Charles Russell 1951- *AmMWSc 92*
**Handron,** Deanne Westfall 1955- *WhoWest 92*
**Hands,** David Richard Granville 1943- *Who 92*
**Hands,** Terence David 1941- *IntWW 91, Who 92*
**Handschuh,** G. Gregory 1941- *WhoAmL 92*
**Handschumacher,** Albert Gustave 1918- *WhoWest 92*
**Handschumacher,** Robert Edmund 1927- *AmMWSc 92*
**Handt,** Herbert 1926- *NewAmDM*
**Handwerger,** Barry S 1943- *AmMWSc 92*
**Handwerger,** Stuart 1938- *AmMWSc 92*
**Handwerker,** A. M. 1928- *WhoFI 92, WhoMW 92*
**Handwerker,** Thomas Samuel 1951- *AmMWSc 92*
**Handy,** Benny Ben 1937- *WhoAmP 91*
**Handy,** Carleton Thomas 1918- *AmMWSc 92*
**Handy,** Charles Brian 1932- *Who 92*
**Handy,** Deana Coble 1969- *WhoEnt 92*
**Handy,** Delores 1947- *WhoBlA 92*
**Handy,** Floyd E *WhoAmP 91*
**Handy,** James R 1954- *WhoAmP 91*
**Handy,** John Richard, III 1933- *WhoBlA 92*
**Handy,** John William, Jr. 1918- *WhoBlA 92*
**Handy,** Lowell Kent 1949- *WhoRel 92*
**Handy,** Lyman Lee 1919- *AmMWSc 92*
**Handy,** Michael Harold 1959- *WhoRel 92*
**Handy,** Nicholas Charles 1941- *Who 92*
**Handy,** Nixeon Civille *DrAPF 91*
**Handy,** Richard L 1929- *AmMWSc 92*
**Handy,** Richard Lincoln 1929- *WhoMW 92*
**Handy,** Robert M 1931- *AmMWSc 92*
**Handy,** Robert Theodore 1918- *WhoRel 92*
**Handy,** Rollo 1927- *WrDr 92*
**Handy,** Rollo Leroy 1927- *WhoFI 92*
**Handy,** Vera Sharp 1912- *WhoWest 92*
**Handy,** W. C. 1873-1958 *BenetAL 91, ConMus 7 [port], FacFETw, NewAmDM*
**Handy,** Wendell Taylor 1928- *WhoBlA 92*
**Handy,** William T., Jr. 1924- *WhoBlA 92*
**Handy,** William Talbot, Jr. 1924- *WhoMW 92, WhoRel 92*
**Handy-Miller,** D. Antoinette 1930- *WhoBlA 92*
**Handzel,** Patricia Reis 1936- *WhoAmP 91*
**Handzlik,** Jan Lawrence 1945- *WhoAmL 92*
**Hane,** Carl Edward 1943- *AmMWSc 92*
**Hane,** Guy Elliott 1952- *WhoEnt 92*
**Haneberg,** William Christopher 1959- *WhoWest 92*
**Hanebrink,** Earl L 1924- *AmMWSc 92*
**Hanegan,** James L 1944- *AmMWSc 92*
**Hanek,** Patricia Ann 1951- *WhoMW 92*
**Hanel,** Rudolf A 1922- *AmMWSc 92*
**Haneman,** Howard Frederick 1928- *WhoAmP 91*
**Haneman,** Vincent Siering, Jr. 1924- *WhoWest 92*
**Hanen,** Lynne Winters Sudranski 1945- *WhoMW 92*
**Hanen,** Mark Lee 1956- *WhoEnt 92*
**Hanenburg,** Kathleen Marie 1953- *WhoAmL 92*
**Hanenson,** Irwin Boris 1922- *AmMWSc 92*
**Haner,** Frederick Theodore 1929- *WhoFI 92*
**Hanerty,** Michael Joseph 1953- *WhoIns 92*
**Hanes,** Charles Samuel d1990 *Who 92N*
**Hanes,** Clifford Ronald 1952- *WhoRel 92*
**Hanes,** Dalibor 1914- *IntWW 91*
**Hanes,** Deanne Meredith 1942- *AmMWSc 92*
**Hanes,** Donald Dean 1926- *WhoAmP 91*
**Hanes,** Frank Borden *DrAPF 91*
**Hanes,** Frank Borden 1920- *WrDr 92*
**Hanes,** Frederick Moir 1883-1946 *DcNCBi 3*
**Hanes,** Harold 1931- *AmMWSc 92*
**Hanes,** James Gordon, Sr. 1886-1972 *DcNCBi 3*
**Hanes,** John Wesley 1850-1903 *DcNCBi 3*
**Hanes,** John Wesley, Jr. 1892-1987 *DcNCBi 3*
**Hanes,** Lewis 1826-1882 *DcNCBi 3*
**Hanes,** N Bruce 1934- *AmMWSc 92*
**Hanes,** Pleasant Henderson 1845-1925 *DcNCBi 3*
**Hanes,** Pleasant Huber, Sr. 1880-1967 *DcNCBi 3*
**Hanes,** Robert March 1890-1959 *DcNCBi 3*
**Hanes,** Ronnie Michael 1949- *AmMWSc 92*
**Hanes,** Ted L 1928- *AmMWSc 92*
**Hanesian,** Deran 1927- *AmMWSc 92*
**Hanessian,** Stephen 1935- *AmMWSc 92*
**Haney,** Alan William 1941- *AmMWSc 92*
**Haney,** Darnel L. 1937- *WhoBlA 92*
**Haney,** Don Lee 1934- *WhoBlA 92*
**Haney,** Donald C 1934- *AmMWSc 92*
**Haney,** Enoch Kelly 1940- *WhoAmP 91*
**Haney,** Gerald Lee 1925- *WhoRel 92*
**Haney,** James Filmore 1938- *AmMWSc 92*
**Haney,** James Stuart 1945- *WhoAmP 91*
**Haney,** Jim *WhoAmP 91*
**Haney,** Napoleon 1926- *WhoBlA 92*
**Haney,** Paul D 1911- *AmMWSc 92*
**Haney,** Robert Lee 1938- *AmMWSc 92*
**Haney,** Robert Locke 1928- *WhoFI 92, WhoWest 92*
**Haney,** Thomas Michael 1938- *WhoAmL 92*
**Haney,** William Raymond 1961- *WhoEnt 92*
**Haney,** William Valentine Patrick 1925- *WrDr 92*
**Hanf,** James Alphonso 1923- *IntAu&W 91, WhoWest 92*
**Hanff,** Ernest Salo 1940- *AmMWSc 92*
**Hanff,** Helene 1916- *Who 92, WrDr 92*
**Hanford,** Craig Bradley 1953- *WhoBlA 92*
**Hanford,** Mary *DrAPF 91*
**Hanford,** William Edward 1908- *AmMWSc 92*
**Hanfstaengl,** Ernst 1887-1975 *EncTR 91*
**Hanft,** John D 1943- *WhoIns 92*
**Hanft,** Ruth 1929- *IntWW 91*
**Hanft,** Ruth S 1929- *AmMWSc 92*
**Hang,** Daniel F 1918- *AmMWSc 92*
**Hang,** Hsueh-Ming 1956- *AmMWSc 92*
**Hang,** Yong Deng *AmMWSc 92*
**Hangaku** *EncAmaz 91*
**Hangen,** Welles *LesBEnT 92*
**Hanger,** Emmett Wilson, Jr 1948- *WhoAmP 91*
**Hanges,** James Constantine 1954- *WhoRel 92*
**Hangley,** William Thomas 1941- *WhoAmL 92*
**Hanham,** Harold John 1928- *IntWW 91, Who 92*
**Hanham,** Leonard Edward 1921- *Who 92*
**Hanham,** Michael 1922- *Who 92*
**Hani,** Chris 1942- *IntWW 91*
**Hani,** Susumi 1926- *IntDcF 2-2 [port]*
**Hanic,** Louis A 1928- *AmMWSc 92*
**Haniel,** Klaus 1916- *IntWW 91*
**Hanif Khan,** Rana Muhammad 1921- *IntWW 91*
**Hanifen,** Richard Charles 1931- *WhoRel 92, WhoWest 92*
**Hanifin,** Timothy John 1931- *WhoAmL 92*
**Hanig,** Joseph Peter 1941- *AmMWSc 92*
**Hanin,** Israel 1937- *AmMWSc 92, WhoMW 92*
**Haning,** Blanche Cournoyer 1943- *AmMWSc 92*
**Hanis,** Craig L 1952- *AmMWSc 92*
**Hank,** James Stephen 1946- *WhoEnt 92*
**Hanka,** Ladislav James 1920- *AmMWSc 92*
**Hankamer,** Jorge 1940- *WhoWest 92*
**Hankar,** Paul 1859-1901 *DcTwDes*
**Hanke,** Carl William 1943- *WhoMW 92*
**Hanke,** Karl 1903-1945 *EncTR 91 [port]*
**Hanke,** Karl William, III 1958- *WhoMW 92*
**Hanke,** Lewis Ulysses 1905- *IntWW 91*
**Hanke,** Mark Allen 1955- *WhoMW 92*
**Hanke,** Paul Augustus 1936- *WhoAmL 92*
**Hankel,** Ralph D *AmMWSc 92*
**Hankel,** Wilhelm 1929- *IntWW 91*
**Hanken,** James 1952- *AmMWSc 92*
**Hankenson,** Edward Craig, Jr. 1935- *WhoEnt 92*
**Hanker,** Jacob S 1925- *AmMWSc 92*
**Hankerson,** Elijah H. 1912- *WhoBlA 92*
**Hankerson,** Walter Leroy 1915- *WhoRel 92*
**Hankes,** Elmer Joseph 1913- *WhoMW 92*
**Hankes,** Gerald H 1936- *AmMWSc 92*
**Hankes,** Lawrence Valentine 1919- *AmMWSc 92*
**Hankes-Drielsma,** Claude Dunbar 1949- *IntWW 91, Who 92*
**Hankey** *Who 92*
**Hankey,** Baron 1905- *IntWW 91, Who 92*
**Hankey,** Henry Arthur Alers 1914- *Who 92*
**Hankey,** Wilbur Leason, Jr 1929- *AmMWSc 92*
**Hankin,** Jean H 1923- *AmMWSc 92*
**Hankin,** Lester 1926- *AmMWSc 92*
**Hankin,** Mitchell Robert 1949- *WhoAmL 92*
**Hankin,** Noel Newton 1946- *WhoBlA 92*
**Hankin,** St. John 1869-1909 *RfGEnL 91*
**Hankins,** Andrew Jay, Jr. 1942- *WhoBlA 92*
**Hankins,** B E 1929- *AmMWSc 92*
**Hankins,** David Joe 1957- *WhoMW 92, WhoRel 92*
**Hankins,** Freeman 1918- *WhoAmP 91*
**Hankins,** Freeman 1918-1988 *WhoBlA 92N*
**Hankins,** Geoffrey 1926- *Who 92*
**Hankins,** George Thomas 1925- *AmMWSc 92*
**Hankins,** Gerard S. *WhoBlA 92*
**Hankins,** Harold Charles Arthur 1930- *Who 92*
**Hankins,** Hesterly G., III 1950- *WhoWest 92*
**Hankins,** Hubert Allen 1938- *WhoAmP 91*
**Hankins,** Lewis Milton 1941- *WhoRel 92*
**Hankins,** Shirley Williams 1931- *WhoAmP 91*
**Hankins,** Timothy Hamilton 1941- *AmMWSc 92*
**Hankins,** Timothy Howard 1956- *WhoAmL 92*
**Hankins,** William Alfred 1934- *AmMWSc 92*
**Hankins,** Winston H. 1932- *WhoIns 92*
**Hankinson,** Denzel J 1915- *AmMWSc 92*
**Hankinson,** James F. 1943- *WhoFI 92*
**Hankinson,** Oliver 1946- *AmMWSc 92*
**Hankis,** Roy Allen 1943- *WhoMW 92*
**Hankla,** Cathryn *DrAPF 91*
**Hankla,** Susan 1951- *IntAu&W 91*
**Hankoff,** Leon Dudley 1927- *AmMWSc 92*
**Hanks,** Carl Thomas 1939- *AmMWSc 92*
**Hanks,** David L 1925- *AmMWSc 92*
**Hanks,** Edgar C 1921- *AmMWSc 92*
**Hanks,** Elbert Wayne, Sr. 1939- *WhoRel 92*
**Hanks,** Eugene Ralph 1918- *WhoWest 92*
**Hanks,** Henry Garber 1826-1907 *BiInAmS*
**Hanks,** James Elden 1924- *AmMWSc 92*
**Hanks,** John Dennis 1948- *WhoAmP 91*
**Hanks,** John Harold 1906- *AmMWSc 92*
**Hanks,** Kevin Marshall 1958- *WhoFI 92*
**Hanks,** Larry Lincoln 1943- *WhoAmP 91*
**Hanks,** Nancy 1784-1818 *DcNCBi 3*
**Hanks,** Patrick Wyndham 1940- *Who 92*
**Hanks,** Richard Donald 1918- *AmMWSc 92*
**Hanks,** Richard W 1935- *AmMWSc 92*
**Hanks,** Robert William 1915- *AmMWSc 92*
**Hanks,** Robert William 1928- *AmMWSc 92*
**Hanks,** Ronald John 1927- *AmMWSc 92*
**Hanks,** Thomas Colgrove 1944- *AmMWSc 92*
**Hanks,** Thomas Dixon 1934- *WhoRel 92*
**Hanks,** Thompson *WhoEnt 92*
**Hanks,** Tom *IntWW 91*
**Hanks,** Tom 1956- *IntMPA 92, WhoEnt 92*
**Hanle,** Paul Arthur 1947- *AmMWSc 92*
**Hanley,** Alyce A 1933- *WhoAmP 91*
**Hanley,** Arnold V 1927- *AmMWSc 92*
**Hanley,** Benjamin 1941- *WhoAmP 91*
**Hanley,** Boniface 1924- *SmATA 65*
**Hanley,** Clifford 1922- *ConNov 91, IntAu&W 91, WrDr 92*
**Hanley,** Dana Carlton 1962- *WhoAmP 91*
**Hanley,** Daniel F, Jr 1949- *AmMWSc 92*
**Hanley,** Gerald 1916- *ConNov 91, IntAu&W 91, WrDr 92*
**Hanley,** Gerald Anthony 1916- *Who 92*
**Hanley,** Howard Granville 1909- *Who 92*
**Hanley,** Howard James Mason 1937- *AmMWSc 92*
**Hanley,** J. Frank, II 1943- *WhoBlA 92*
**Hanley,** James 1901-1985 *ConAu 36NR, FacFETw, RfGEnL 91*
**Hanley,** James Michael 1920- *WhoAmP 91*
**Hanley,** James Richard, Jr 1929- *AmMWSc 92*
**Hanley,** Jeremy James 1945- *Who 92*
**Hanley,** John Francis 1955- *WhoAmP 91*
**Hanley,** John Gerald 1907- *WhoRel 92*
**Hanley,** John Herbert 1946- *AmMWSc 92*
**Hanley,** John Weller 1922- *IntWW 91*
**Hanley,** Keith Graham 1954- *WhoAmL 92*
**Hanley,** Kevin Joseph 1952- *AmMWSc 92*
**Hanley,** Liam 1933- *TwCPaSc*
**Hanley,** Mark Stephen 1958- *WhoAmP 91*
**Hanley,** Michael 1918- *Who 92*
**Hanley,** Priscilla Hobson 1950- *WhoAmP 91*
**Hanley,** Robert F. d1991 *NewYTBS 91*
**Hanley,** Thomas Andrew 1951- *AmMWSc 92*
**Hanley,** Thomas ODonnell 1923- *AmMWSc 92*
**Hanley,** Thomas Patrick 1951- *WhoMW 92*
**Hanley,** Thomas Richard 1945- *AmMWSc 92*
**Hanley,** Wayne Stewart 1945- *AmMWSc 92*
**Hanley,** William *DrAPF 91*
**Hanley,** William 1931- *BenetAL 91, WrDr 92*
**Hanlin,** John Gregory 1954- *WhoAmL 92*
**Hanlin,** Richard Thomas 1931- *AmMWSc 92*
**Hanlon,** C Rollins 1915- *AmMWSc 92*
**Hanlon,** Daniel Leo 1956- *WhoMW 92*
**Hanlon,** David G 1935- *WhoAmP 91*
**Hanlon,** Emily *DrAPF 91*
**Hanlon,** Gerald Richard 1933- *WhoEnt 92*
**Hanlon,** James Allison 1937- *WhoFI 92*
**Hanlon,** John Joseph 1912- *AmMWSc 92*
**Hanlon,** John William 1937- *WhoMW 92*
**Hanlon,** Lodge L. 1931- *WhoAmL 92*
**Hanlon,** Mary Sue 1933- *AmMWSc 92, WhoMW 92*
**Hanlon,** Neal B 1945- *WhoAmP 91*
**Hanlon,** Roger Thomas 1947- *AmMWSc 92*
**Hanlon,** Thomas Lee 1937- *AmMWSc 92*
**Hanlon,** Tom Allan 1945- *WhoAmP 91*
**Hanly,** W Carey 1936- *AmMWSc 92*

**Hanmer**, Daniel *DcNCBi 3*
**Hanmer**, John 1928- *Who 92*
**Hann**, Charles Reese 1926- *WhoAmL 92*
**Hann**, David William *AmMWSc 92*
**Hann**, Derek William 1935- *Who 92*
**Hann**, Eric Scott 1961- *WhoMW 92*
**Hann**, G C 1924- *AmMWSc 92*
**Hann**, Hie-Won L 1936- *AmMWSc 92*
**Hann**, James 1933- *Who 92*
**Hann**, Morag 1939- *WhoFI 92*
**Hann**, Roy William, Jr 1934- *AmMWSc 92*
**Hanna**, Adel 1943- *AmMWSc 92*
**Hanna**, Calvin 1923- *AmMWSc 92*
**Hanna**, Cassandria H. 1940- *WhoBlA 92*
**Hanna**, Colin Arthur 1946- *WhoFI 92*
**Hanna**, Edgar Ethelbert, Jr 1933- *AmMWSc 92*
**Hanna**, Ernest Royal 1930- *WhoEnt 92*
**Hanna**, Frank Joseph 1939- *WhoFI 92*
**Hanna**, Geoffrey Chalmers 1920- *AmMWSc 92*
**Hanna**, George P, Jr 1918- *AmMWSc 92*
**Hanna**, George R 1931- *AmMWSc 92*
**Hanna**, Harlington Leroy, Jr. 1951- *WhoBlA 92*
**Hanna**, Jerry Glenn 1946- *WhoAmP 91*
**Hanna**, Joel Michael 1938- *AmMWSc 92*
**Hanna**, John P 1918- *WhoIns 92*
**Hanna**, Judith Lynne 1936- *WhoEnt 92*
**Hanna**, Katherine Merritt 1953- *WhoAmP 91*
**Hanna**, Lavelle 1918- *AmMWSc 92*
**Hanna**, Marcus Alonzo 1837-1904 *AmPolLe, RComAH*
**Hanna**, Martin Shad 1940- *WhoAmP 91*
**Hanna**, Martin Slafter 1932- *AmMWSc 92*
**Hanna**, Mary Carr *DrAPF 91*
**Hanna**, Melvin Wesley 1932- *AmMWSc 92*
**Hanna**, Michael G, Jr 1936- *AmMWSc 92*
**Hanna**, Mike 1953- *WhoAmP 91*
**Hanna**, Milford A 1947- *AmMWSc 92*
**Hanna**, Nancy Magee 1951- *WhoFI 92*
**Hanna**, Owen Titus 1935- *AmMWSc 92*
**Hanna**, Pamela A. *WhoEnt 92*
**Hanna**, Patrick E 1940- *AmMWSc 92*
**Hanna**, Ralph Lynn 1919- *AmMWSc 92*
**Hanna**, Robert Cecil 1937- *WhoAmL 92, WhoWest 92*
**Hanna**, Roland *WhoBlA 92*
**Hanna**, Samir A 1934- *AmMWSc 92*
**Hanna**, Stanley Sweet 1920- *AmMWSc 92*
**Hanna**, Steven J 1937- *AmMWSc 92*
**Hanna**, Steven Rogers 1943- *AmMWSc 92*
**Hanna**, Suzanne Louise 1953- *WhoMW 92*
**Hanna**, Terry Ross 1947- *WhoAmL 92*
**Hanna**, Tom *DrAPF 91*
**Hanna**, Wayne William 1943- *AmMWSc 92*
**Hanna**, William 1911- *IntMPA 92*
**Hanna**, William Denby 1910- *WhoEnt 92*
**Hanna**, William F 1938- *AmMWSc 92*
**Hanna**, William J 1922- *AmMWSc 92*
**Hanna**, William Jefferson 1913- *AmMWSc 92*
**Hanna**, William Johnson 1922- *WhoWest 92*
**Hanna-Barbera** *LesBEnT 92*
**Hannafin**, James D. 1946- *WhoEnt 92*
**Hannaford**, Peter Dor 1932- *WhoFI 92*
**Hannaford**, Tom Dixon 1952- *WhoEnt 92*
**Hannaford**, William John 1943- *WhoMW 92*
**Hannah**, Barry *DrAPF 91*
**Hannah**, Barry 1942- *BenetAL 91, ConNov 91, IntAu&W 91, WrDr 92*
**Hannah**, Bruce 1941- *DcTwDes*
**Hannah**, Darrell Dale 1962- *WhoRel 92*
**Hannah**, Daryl 1960- *IntMPA 92, IntWW 91*
**Hannah**, Daryl 1961- *WhoEnt 92*
**Hannah**, Harold Winford 1911- *AmMWSc 92*
**Hannah**, Hubert H., Sr. 1920- *WhoBlA 92*
**Hannah**, John 1931- *AmMWSc 92*
**Hannah**, John A. 1902-1991 *CurBio 91N, NewYTBS 91 [port]*
**Hannah**, John H, Jr *WhoAmP 91*
**Hannah**, John Robert, Sr. 1939- *WhoFI 92*
**Hannah**, Lawrence Burlison 1943- *WhoAmL 92*
**Hannah**, Leslie 1947- *Who 92*
**Hannah**, Mack H., Jr. *WhoBlA 92*
**Hannah**, Marc Regis 1956- *WhoBlA 92*
**Hannah**, Melvin James 1938- *WhoBlA 92*
**Hannah**, Mosie R. 1949- *WhoBlA 92*
**Hannah**, Nicholas 1940- *IntWW 91*
**Hannah**, Selden J. d1991 *NewYTBS 91*
**Hannah**, Sidney Allison 1930- *AmMWSc 92*
**Hannah**, Thomas Edward 1949- *WhoFI 92*
**Hannah**, Tom 1948- *WhoAmP 91*
**Hannah**, Wayne Robertson, Jr. 1931- *WhoAmL 92*
**Hannah**, William 1929- *Who 92*
**Hannahs**, Raphael 1916- *WhoEnt 92*
**Hannam**, Charles Lewis *WrDr 92*
**Hannam**, John Gordon 1929- *Who 92*
**Hannam**, Michael Patrick Vivian 1920- *Who 92*
**Hannan**, Charles *ScFEYrs*
**Hannan**, David Carroll 1945- *WhoAmL 92*
**Hannan**, Edward James 1921- *WrDr 92*
**Hannan**, Greg *DrAPF 91*
**Hannan**, Herbert Herrick 1929- *AmMWSc 92*
**Hannan**, James Francis 1922- *AmMWSc 92*
**Hannan**, John Michael 1950- *WhoEnt 92*
**Hannan**, Mark C., III 1947- *WhoIns 92*
**Hannan**, Paul W 1949- *WhoAmP 91*
**Hannan**, Robert William 1939- *WhoFI 92*
**Hannan**, Roy Barton, Jr 1923- *AmMWSc 92*
**Hannan**, Steven Wayne 1957- *WhoMW 92*
**Hannan**, Thomas A. d1991 *NewYTBS 91*
**Hannan**, Wyota 1930- *WhoAmP 91*
**Hannan-Anton**, Laurie Casey 1956- *WhoEnt 92*
**Hannasch**, John Bernard 1965- *WhoFI 92*
**Hannawalt**, Willis Dale 1928- *WhoAmL 92*
**Hannaway**, David Bryon 1951- *AmMWSc 92*
**Hannaway**, Dorian Rae 1948- *WhoEnt 92*
**Hannay**, Alastair 1932- *WrDr 92*
**Hannay**, David 1935- *Who 92*
**Hannay**, David G 1945- *AmMWSc 92*
**Hannay**, David Hugh Alexander 1935- *IntWW 91*
**Hannay**, Elizabeth Anne Scott 1942- *Who 92*
**Hannay**, N. Bruce 1921- *IntWW 91*
**Hannay**, Norman Bruce 1921- *AmMWSc 92*
**Hannay**, William Mouat, III 1944- *WhoAmL 92*
**Hanne**, John R 1936- *AmMWSc 92*
**Hanneken**, Clemens 1923- *AmMWSc 92*
**Hanneline**, Richard Lee 1944- *WhoFI 92*
**Hannell**, John W, Jr 1923- *AmMWSc 92*
**Hanneman**, Paul A 1936- *WhoAmP 91*
**Hanneman**, Rodney E 1936- *AmMWSc 92*
**Hanneman**, Walter W 1927- *AmMWSc 92*
**Hannemann**, Daniel Paul 1951- *WhoRel 92*
**Hannemann**, Norman Albert 1924- *WhoRel 92*
**Hannemann**, Walter A. 1914- *IntMPA 92*
**Hannen**, John Edward *Who 92*
**Hannen**, John Edward 1937- *WhoRel 92, WhoWest 92*
**Hanner**, Bob *WhoAmP 91*
**Hannes**, James Alan 1943- *WhoIns 92*
**Hanni**, Don Lamar 1925- *WhoAmP 91*
**Hanni**, Philip Stanton 1932- *WhoRel 92*
**Hannibal**, Alice Priscilla 1916- *WhoBlA 92*
**Hannibal**, Edward *DrAPF 91*
**Hannibal**, Edward L. 1936- *WrDr 92*
**Hannibal**, Gary Eugene 1943- *WhoAmP 91*
**Hannibal**, Mark Victor 1958- *WhoAmL 92*
**Hannibalsson**, Jon Baldvin 1939- *IntWW 91*
**Hannig**, Gary 1952- *WhoAmP 91*
**Hannigan**, James *Who 92*
**Hannigan**, James Edgar 1928- *Who 92*
**Hannigan**, Joseph Clyde 1945- *WhoWest 92*
**Hannigan**, Paul *DrAPF 91*
**Hannigan**, Scott Reagen 1947- *WhoFI 92*
**Hannigan**, Thomas M 1940- *WhoAmP 91*
**Hanning**, Richard Alan 1944- *WhoAmL 92*
**Hannon**, Beverly A 1932- *WhoAmP 91, WhoMW 92*
**Hannon**, Brian Desmond Anthony *Who 92*
**Hannon**, Brian Owens 1959- *IntAu&W 91*
**Hannon**, Bruce Michael 1934- *AmMWSc 92*
**Hannon**, Donnie Lyn 1944- *WhoIns 92*
**Hannon**, Ezra *IntAu&W 91X, WrDr 92*
**Hannon**, James Patrick 1940- *AmMWSc 92*
**Hannon**, John Patrick 1927 *AmMWSc 92*
**Hannon**, John Robert 1945- *WhoFI 92*
**Hannon**, John W., Jr. 1922- *IntWW 91*
**Hannon**, Kemp *WhoAmP 91*
**Hannon**, Kitty Sue 1954- *WhoFI 92*
**Hannon**, Lenn Lamar 1943- *WhoAmP 91*
**Hannon**, Martin J 1942- *AmMWSc 92*
**Hannon**, Thomas A d1991 *NewYTBS 91*
**Hannon**, Thomas F. 1943- *WhoFI 92*
**Hannon**, Timothy Patrick 1948- *WhoAmL 92*
**Hannon**, Willard James, Jr 1938- *AmMWSc 92*
**Hannoosh**, James George 1948- *WhoFI 92*
**Hannover**, Georg Wilhelm, Prinz von 1915- *IntWW 91*
**Hannsgen**, Kenneth Bruce 1942- *AmMWSc 92*
**Hannum**, Gerald Luther 1915- *WhoAmP 91*
**Hannum**, John Thomas 1948- *WhoRel 92*
**Hannum**, Robert John 1921- *WhoAmP 91*
**Hannum**, Steven Earl 1941- *AmMWSc 92*
**Hanock**, James 1939- *WhoAmL 92*
**Hanon**, Bernard 1932- *IntWW 91, Who 92*
**Hanon**, Charles-Louis 1819-1900 *NewAmDM*
**Hanon**, Stephen Raymond 1962- *WhoMW 92*
**Hanor**, Charles Wayne 1947- *WhoAmL 92*
**Hanover**, Hollis Herbert 1938- *WhoAmL 92*
**Hanover**, James W 1930- *AmMWSc 92*
**Hanover**, John Allan 1953- *AmMWSc 92*
**Hanowell**, Ernest Goddin 1920- *WhoWest 92*
**Hanrahan**, Barbara 1939- *ConNov 91, WrDr 92*
**Hanrahan**, Brian 1949- *Who 92*
**Hanrahan**, Edward S 1929- *AmMWSc 92*
**Hanrahan**, John J 1932- *AmMWSc 92*
**Hanrahan**, Paul Martin 1930- *WhoAmL 92*
**Hanrahan**, Richard Andrew 1946- *WhoAmP 91*
**Hanrahan**, Robert Joseph 1932- *AmMWSc 92*
**Hanrahan**, Robert P 1934- *WhoAmP 91*
**Hanrahan**, Vincent Martin 1924- *WhoAmL 92*
**Hanrath**, Linda Carol 1949- *WhoMW 92*
**Hanratty**, Thomas J 1926- *AmMWSc 92*
**Hanreider**, Wolfram F. 1931- *WrDr 92*
**Hanrott**, Francis George Vivian 1921- *Who 92*
**Hans Adam II** 1945- *IntWW 91*
**Hans**, Paul Charles 1946- *WhoFI 92*
**Hansard**, Samuel L, II 1944- *AmMWSc 92*
**Hansard**, Samuel Leroy 1914- *AmMWSc 92*
**Hansberger**, Robert Vail 1920- *IntWW 91*
**Hansberry**, Lorraine 1930-1965 *AfrAmW, BenetAL 91, BlkLC [port], DramC 2 [port], FacFETw, HanAmWH, NotBlAW 92 [port]*
**Hansberry-Moore**, Virginia T. 1930- *WhoBlA 92*
**Hansburg**, Daniel *AmMWSc 92*
**Hansbury**, John Garfield 1940- *WhoAmP 91*
**Hansbury**, Stephan Charles 1946- *WhoAmL 92*
**Hansch**, Corwin Herman 1918- *AmMWSc 92*
**Hansch**, Diane Terrill 1961- *WhoAmP 91*
**Hansch**, Joachim Horst 1946- *WhoWest 92*
**Hansch**, Theodor Wolfgang 1941- *AmMWSc 92*
**Hanschen**, Peter Walter 1945- *WhoAmL 92*
**Hanscom**, Leslie Rutherford 1924- *ConAu 135*
**Hanscom**, Roger H 1944- *AmMWSc 92*
**Hanscome**, Thomas Chandler 1943- *WhoWest 92*
**Hansebout**, Robert Roger 1935- *AmMWSc 92*
**Hanseid**, Einar 1943- *IntWW 91*
**Hansel**, Pamela Kay 1942- *WhoWest 92*
**Hansel**, Paul G 1917- *AmMWSc 92*
**Hansel**, Stephen Arthur 1947- *WhoFI 92*
**Hansel**, William 1918- *AmMWSc 92*
**Hansel**, William Clayton 1917- *WhoAmP 91*
**Hansell**, Dean 1952- *WhoAmL 92*
**Hansell**, Edgar Frank 1937- *WhoAmL 92*
**Hansell**, George Ronald, Jr. 1955- *WhoRel 92*
**Hansell**, Jeffrey Elliott 1955- *WhoEnt 92*
**Hansell**, Margaret Mary 1941- *AmMWSc 92*
**Hansell**, Walter White 1959- *WhoAmL 92*
**Hanselman**, Gregory L 1952- *WhoAmP 91*
**Hanselman**, Raymond Bush 1932- *AmMWSc 92*
**Hanselman**, Richard Wilson 1927- *WhoFI 92*
**Hanselmann**, Fredrick Charles 1955- *WhoAmL 92*
**Hansen**, Adolf 1938- *WhoRel 92*
**Hansen**, Afton M 1925- *AmMWSc 92*
**Hansen**, Alicia 1952- *WhoAmP 91*
**Hansen**, Ann 1954- *WhoFI 92*
**Hansen**, Ann Natalie 1927- *IntAu&W 91, WrDr 92*
**Hansen**, Anthony David Anders 1951- *AmMWSc 92*
**Hansen**, Anton Juergen 1928- *AmMWSc 92*
**Hansen**, Arlen J. 1936- *ConAu 133*
**Hansen**, Arlen Jay 1936- *WhoWest 92*
**Hansen**, Arthur G 1925- *AmMWSc 92*
**Hansen**, Arthur Magne 1946- *WhoFI 92*
**Hansen**, Axel C 1919- *AmMWSc 92*
**Hansen**, Barbara *WrDr 92*
**Hansen**, Barbara C. 1941- *IntWW 91*
**Hansen**, Barbara Caleen 1941- *AmMWSc 92*
**Hansen**, Bent 1920- *IntWW 91*
**Hansen**, Bernard J 1944- *WhoAmP 91*
**Hansen**, Bernard Lyle 1916- *AmMWSc 92*
**Hansen**, Bev 1944- *WhoAmP 91*
**Hansen**, Bobby J. 1926- *WhoFI 92*
**Hansen**, Carl John 1933- *AmMWSc 92*
**Hansen**, Carl R 1926- *WhoAmP 91, WhoMW 92*
**Hansen**, Carl Tams 1929- *AmMWSc 92*
**Hansen**, Carol Baker *DrAPF 91*
**Hansen**, Chadwick 1926- *WrDr 92*
**Hansen**, Charles 1926- *WhoFI 92*
**Hansen**, Charles Brendan 1946- *WhoEnt 92*
**Hansen**, Christina Flores 1951- *WhoAmL 92*
**Hansen**, Christopher Agnew 1934- *WhoAmL 92*
**Hansen**, Clifford Peter 1912- *IntWW 91, WhoAmP 91, WhoWest 92*
**Hansen**, Darrel Chancy 1933- *WhoWest 92*
**Hansen**, David Dee 1947- *WhoAmP 91*
**Hansen**, David Elliott 1958- *AmMWSc 92*
**Hansen**, David Henry 1945- *AmMWSc 92*
**Hansen**, David Rasmussen 1938- *WhoAmL 92, WhoMW 92*
**Hansen**, Deborah Kay 1952- *AmMWSc 92*
**Hansen**, Dennis S 1942- *WhoAmP 91*
**Hansen**, Dixie 1952- *WhoEnt 92*
**Hansen**, Donald Curtis 1929- *WhoFI 92, WhoWest 92*
**Hansen**, Donald D 1928- *WhoIns 92*
**Hansen**, Donald Joseph 1932- *AmMWSc 92*
**Hansen**, Donald Vernon 1931- *AmMWSc 92*
**Hansen**, Donald Willis, Jr 1943- *AmMWSc 92*
**Hansen**, Douglas Brayshaw 1929- *AmMWSc 92*
**Hansen**, Eder Lindsay 1914- *AmMWSc 92*
**Hansen**, Edward Allen 1929- *WhoEnt 92*
**Hansen**, Edward Alvin Charles 1925- *WhoEnt 92*
**Hansen**, Edward Daniel 1939- *WhoAmP 91*
**Hansen**, Everett Mathew 1946- *AmMWSc 92*
**Hansen**, Florence Marie Congiolosi 1934- *WhoWest 92*
**Hansen**, Forest Warnyr 1931- *WhoMW 92*
**Hansen**, Francis Eugene 1925- *WhoRel 92*
**Hansen**, Frank *WhoAmP 91*
**Hansen**, Frederic J. 1946- *WhoWest 92*
**Hansen**, Gary Vaughn 1962- *WhoMW 92*
**Hansen**, Genevieve Evans 1931- *WhoFI 92*
**Hansen**, Geoffrey 1953- *WhoEnt 92*
**Hansen**, Geoffrey D. 1956- *WhoEnt 92*
**Hansen**, Gerald Delbert, Jr 1921- *AmMWSc 92*
**Hansen**, Grant Lewis 1921- *AmMWSc 92*
**Hansen**, Gunnar *DrAPF 91*
**Hansen**, Guttorm 1920- *IntWW 91*
**Hansen**, H. Jack 1922- *WhoFI 92, WhoMW 92*
**Hansen**, H. Reese 1942- *WhoAmL 92*
**Hansen**, Hans John *AmMWSc 92*
**Hansen**, Harold Westberg 1917- *AmMWSc 92*
**Hansen**, Harry 1884-1977 *CurBio 91N*
**Hansen**, Harry Louis 1924- *AmMWSc 92*
**Hansen**, Holger Victor 1935- *AmMWSc 92*
**Hansen**, Howard Edward 1923- *AmMWSc 92*
**Hansen**, Hugh J 1923- *AmMWSc 92*
**Hansen**, J Richard 1922- *AmMWSc 92*
**Hansen**, James Douglas 1954- *WhoWest 92*
**Hansen**, James E 1926- *AmMWSc 92*
**Hansen**, James Hans 1952- *WhoEnt 92*
**Hansen**, James V. 1932- *AlmAP 92 [port], WhoAmP 91, WhoWest 92*
**Hansen**, Jim 1959- *WhoAmP 91*
**Hansen**, Joe Bob 1933- *WhoFI 92*
**Hansen**, John Albert 1939- *WhoAmP 91*
**Hansen**, John C 1947- *AmMWSc 92*
**Hansen**, John D 1933- *WhoAmP 91*
**Hansen**, John Frederick 1942- *AmMWSc 92*
**Hansen**, John Herbert 1945- *WhoMW 92*
**Hansen**, John Norman 1942- *AmMWSc 92*
**Hansen**, John Paul 1928- *AmMWSc 92*
**Hansen**, John Theodore 1947- *AmMWSc 92*
**Hansen**, Jon *DrAPF 91*
**Hansen**, Joseph *DrAPF 91*
**Hansen**, Joseph 1923- *IntAu&W 91, WrDr 92*
**Hansen**, Joyce 1942- *WrDr 92*
**Hansen**, Joyce Viola 1942- *WhoBlA 92*
**Hansen**, Kathleen Greenlee 1957- *WhoMW 92*
**Hansen**, Kathryn Ann 1957- *WhoEnt 92*
**Hansen**, Kathryn Gertrude 1912- *WhoMW 92*
**Hansen**, Keith Leyton 1925- *AmMWSc 92*
**Hansen**, Kenneth Alan 1948- *WhoMW 92*
**Hansen**, Kent F 1931- *AmMWSc 92*

**Hansen,** Kent W 1936- *AmMWSc 92*
**Hansen,** Kurt 1910- *IntWW 91*
**Hansen,** Larry George 1941- *AmMWSc 92*
**Hansen,** Lars 1949- *WhoEnt 92*
**Hansen,** Lee Duane 1940- *AmMWSc 92*
**Hansen,** Leland Joe 1944- *WhoEnt 92, WhoFI 92*
**Hansen,** Leon A 1943- *AmMWSc 92*
**Hansen,** Leonard Joseph 1932- *WhoWest 92*
**Hansen,** Leslie Bennett 1951- *AmMWSc 92*
**Hansen,** Lisa Young 1957- *WhoWest 92*
**Hansen,** Louis Stephen 1918- *AmMWSc 92*
**Hansen,** Lowell C, II *WhoAmP 91*
**Hansen,** Lowell John 1941- *AmMWSc 92*
**Hansen,** Luisa Fernandez *AmMWSc 92*
**Hansen,** Lynn Marie 1954- *WhoMW 92*
**Hansen,** M Reed 1929- *WhoAmP 91*
**Hansen,** Marc F 1930- *AmMWSc 92*
**Hansen,** Marcus Lee 1892-1938 *DcAmImH*
**Hansen,** Matilda Anne 1929- *WhoAmP 91*
**Hansen,** Merle Fredrick 1917- *AmMWSc 92*
**Hansen,** Merrell S. 1951- *WhoMW 92*
**Hansen,** Mike 1931- *AmMWSc 92*
**Hansen,** Mogens Herman 1940- *IntWW 91*
**Hansen,** Morris H. 1910- *IntWW 91*
**Hansen,** Morris Howard 1910- *AmMWSc 92*
**Hansen,** Niels 1924- *IntWW 91*
**Hansen,** Niles Maurice 1937- *WhoFI 92*
**Hansen,** Ole 1934- *AmMWSc 92*
**Hansen,** Ole Viggo 1934- *WhoMW 92*
**Hansen,** Orval Howard 1926- *WhoAmP 91*
**Hansen,** P. Gregers 1933- *IntWW 91*
**Hansen,** Patricia Lea 1954- *WhoAmP 91*
**Hansen,** Patrick David 1958- *WhoAmL 92*
**Hansen,** Paul B 1913- *AmMWSc 92*
**Hansen,** Paul Gerhardt 1914- *WhoRel 92*
**Hansen,** Paul Vincent, Jr 1931- *AmMWSc 92*
**Hansen,** Per Kristian 1932- *WhoFI 92*
**Hansen,** Peter Gardner 1927- *AmMWSc 92*
**Hansen,** Peter Jacob 1939- *AmMWSc 92*
**Hansen,** Poul M T 1929- *AmMWSc 92*
**Hansen,** R. Christian 1943- *WhoRel 92*
**Hansen,** R J 1918- *AmMWSc 92*
**Hansen,** Ralph Holm 1923- *AmMWSc 92*
**Hansen,** Ralph W 1926- *AmMWSc 92*
**Hansen,** Raymond Edmund 1932- *WhoFI 92*
**Hansen,** Richard Arthur 1941- *WhoFI 92*
**Hansen,** Richard Lee 1950- *AmMWSc 92*
**Hansen,** Richard M 1924- *AmMWSc 92*
**Hansen,** Richard Olaf 1946- *AmMWSc 92*
**Hansen,** Richard Paul 1951- *WhoRel 92*
**Hansen,** Robert Arthur 1949- *WhoRel 92*
**Hansen,** Robert Blaine 1925- *WhoAmP 91*
**Hansen,** Robert C 1926- *AmMWSc 92*
**Hansen,** Robert Charles 1930- *WhoMW 92*
**Hansen,** Robert Conrad 1931- *AmMWSc 92*
**Hansen,** Robert Dennis 1945- *WhoWest 92*
**Hansen,** Robert Douglas 1929- *AmMWSc 92*
**Hansen,** Robert Gunnard 1939- *WhoWest 92*
**Hansen,** Robert J 1937- *AmMWSc 92*
**Hansen,** Robert J 1940- *AmMWSc 92*
**Hansen,** Robert Jack 1940- *AmMWSc 92*
**Hansen,** Robert John 1937- *AmMWSc 92*
**Hansen,** Robert M 1924- *AmMWSc 92*
**Hansen,** Robert Marshall 1949- *WhoAmL 92*
**Hansen,** Robert Suttle 1918- *AmMWSc 92*
**Hansen,** Rodney Harold 1944- *IntWW 91*
**Hansen,** Rodney Thor 1940- *AmMWSc 92*
**Hansen,** Roger D. 1935-1991 *ConAu 133*
**Hansen,** Roger Gaurth 1920- *AmMWSc 92*
**Hansen,** Roland Conrad 1949- *WhoMW 92*
**Hansen,** Rolf 1920- *IntWW 91*
**Hansen,** Ron 1947- *ConNov 91, TwCWW 91, WrDr 92*
**Hansen,** Ronald Garth 1954- *WhoEnt 92*
**Hansen,** Ronald Gregory 1929- *WhoWest 92*
**Hansen,** Rosanna Lee 1947- *WhoFI 92*
**Hansen,** Sigvard Theodore, Jr. 1935- *WhoWest 92*
**Hansen,** Stella Jean 1925- *WhoAmP 91*
**Hansen,** Steve D *WhoAmP 91*
**Hansen,** Ted Howard 1947- *AmMWSc 92*
**Hansen,** Thomas Dane 1956- *WhoAmL 92*
**Hansen,** Timothy Ray 1945- *AmMWSc 92*
**Hansen,** Tom *DrAPF 91*
**Hansen,** Torben Christen 1933- *AmMWSc 92*
**Hansen,** Uwe Jens 1933- *AmMWSc 92*
**Hansen,** Vaughn Ernest 1921- *AmMWSc 92*
**Hansen,** Vern *WrDr 92*
**Hansen,** W. Lee 1928- *WhoMW 92*
**Hansen,** Walter Eugene 1929- *WhoFI 92, WhoWest 92*
**Hansen,** Wayne Richard 1939- *AmMWSc 92, WhoWest 92*
**Hansen,** Wendell Jay 1910- *WhoBlA 92, WhoMW 92, WhoRel 92*
**Hansen,** Wilford Nels 1928- *AmMWSc 92*
**Hansen,** William Anthony 1948- *AmMWSc 92*
**Hansen,** William Freeman 1941- *WhoMW 92*
**Hansen-Rivera,** Carmen 1948- *WhoHisp 92*
**Hansen-Smith,** Feona May *AmMWSc 92*
**Hansenne,** Michel 1940- *IntWW 91, Who 92*
**Hanser,** Ronald Carl 1950- *WhoMW 92*
**Hansey,** Donald G 1929- *WhoAmP 91*
**Hansford,** John Edgar 1922- *Who 92*
**Hansford,** Larry Clarence 1945- *WhoFI 92*
**Hansford,** Richard Geoffrey 1944- *AmMWSc 92*
**Hansford,** Rowland Curtis 1912- *AmMWSc 92*
**Hansford,** Vernon Nathaniel 1943- *WhoAmL 92*
**Hanshaw,** Bruce Busser 1930- *AmMWSc 92*
**Hanshaw,** James Barry 1928- *AmMWSc 92*
**Hanshaw,** William 1953- *WhoAmL 92*
**Hansler,** Stephen Paul 1960- *WhoMW 92*
**Hanslick,** Eduard 1825-1904 *NewAmDM*
**Hansma,** Paul Kenneth 1946- *AmMWSc 92*
**Hansman,** Margaret Mary 1911- *AmMWSc 92*
**Hansman,** Robert H 1928- *AmMWSc 92*
**Hansmann,** Douglas R 1944- *AmMWSc 92*
**Hansmann,** Eugene William 1933- *AmMWSc 92*
**Hansmann,** Henry Baethke 1945- *WhoAmL 92, WhoFI 92*
**Hanson** *Who 92*
**Hanson,** Baron 1922- *IntWW 91, Who 92*
**Hanson,** Albert L 1952- *AmMWSc 92*
**Hanson,** Alfred Olaf 1914- *AmMWSc 92*
**Hanson,** Allen Dennis 1936- *WhoMW 92*
**Hanson,** Allen Louis 1915- *AmMWSc 92*
**Hanson,** Andrew Jorgen 1944- *AmMWSc 92*
**Hanson,** Angus Alexander 1922- *AmMWSc 92*
**Hanson,** Ann H 1935- *WhoAmP 91*
**Hanson,** Anthony 1934- *Who 92*
**Hanson,** Anthony Tyrrell 1916-1991 *ConAu 134*
**Hanson,** Austin Moe 1917- *AmMWSc 92*
**Hanson,** Barbara Ann 1948- *AmMWSc 92*
**Hanson,** Bernold M 1928- *AmMWSc 92*
**Hanson,** Bertram Speakman 1905- *Who 92*
**Hanson,** Beverly Faye 1929- *WhoMW 92*
**Hanson,** Brian John Taylor 1939- *Who 92*
**Hanson,** Bruce Eugene 1942- *WhoAmL 92, WhoFI 92, WhoMW 92*
**Hanson,** Bruce J 1942- *WhoAmP 91*
**Hanson,** Bruce Lloyd 1948- *WhoRel 92*
**Hanson,** Carl Veith 1943- *AmMWSc 92*
**Hanson,** Carol G 1934- *WhoAmP 91*
**Hanson,** Charles *DrAPF 91*
**Hanson,** Charles Allen 1926- *WhoAmP 91*
**Hanson,** Charles Easton, Jr. 1917- *WhoMW 92*
**Hanson,** Charles John 1919- *Who 92*
**Hanson,** Charles Richard 1948- *WhoFI 92*
**Hanson,** Christine Lynne 1947- *WhoWest 92*
**Hanson,** Clifford R 1936- *WhoIns 92*
**Hanson,** Craig Laverne 1952- *WhoMW 92*
**Hanson,** Curtis 1945- *WhoEnt 92*
**Hanson,** D N 1918- *AmMWSc 92*
**Hanson,** Dale S. 1938- *WhoFI 92*
**Hanson,** Daniel James 1928- *AmMWSc 92*
**Hanson,** Daniel Ralph 1947- *AmMWSc 92*
**Hanson,** Darrell Roy 1954- *WhoAmP 91*
**Hanson,** David Bigelow 1946- *WhoFI 92*
**Hanson,** David Lee 1935- *AmMWSc 92*
**Hanson,** David M 1942- *AmMWSc 92*
**Hanson,** David Scott, Jr 1946- *WhoAmP 91*
**Hanson,** David Warner 1944- *WhoMW 92*
**Hanson,** Dennis Wayne 1948- *WhoWest 92*
**Hanson,** Derrick George 1927- *Who 92*
**Hanson,** Diane Charske 1946- *WhoFI 92*
**Hanson,** Donald E 1926- *WhoAmP 91*
**Hanson,** Donald Farness 1946- *AmMWSc 92*
**Hanson,** Donald Wayne 1937- *AmMWSc 92*
**Hanson,** Donna McKinney 1940- *WhoRel 92*
**Hanson,** Duane 1925- *FacFETw, IntWW 91*
**Hanson,** Earl D. 1927- *WrDr 92*
**Hanson,** Earl Dorchester 1927- *AmMWSc 92, IntAu&W 91*
**Hanson,** Earle William 1910- *AmMWSc 92*
**Hanson,** Eric Alan 1953- *WhoFI 92*
**Hanson,** Erwin *WhoAmP 91*
**Hanson,** Floyd Bliss 1939- *AmMWSc 92*
**Hanson,** Frank *WhoEnt 92*
**Hanson,** Frank Edwin 1938- *AmMWSc 92*
**Hanson,** Frederick Douglas 1948- *WhoRel 92*
**Hanson,** Gail G 1947- *AmMWSc 92*
**Hanson,** Gary A. 1954- *WhoAmL 92*
**Hanson,** Gary W 1950- *WhoAmP 91*
**Hanson,** George H 1918- *AmMWSc 92*
**Hanson,** George Peter 1933- *AmMWSc 92, WhoWest 92*
**Hanson,** Gerald Warner 1938- *WhoWest 92*
**Hanson,** Gilbert N 1936- *AmMWSc 92*
**Hanson,** H S 1926- *WhoAmP 91*
**Hanson,** Harold Palmer 1921- *AmMWSc 92*
**Hanson,** Harry Thomas 1939- *AmMWSc 92*
**Hanson,** Harvey Myron 1931- *AmMWSc 92*
**Hanson,** Heidi Elizabeth 1954- *WhoAmL 92*
**Hanson,** Henry W A, III 1932- *AmMWSc 92*
**Hanson,** Hilary Ruth 1963- *WhoWest 92*
**Hanson,** Hiram Stanley 1923- *AmMWSc 92*
**Hanson,** Howard 1896-1981 *NewAmDM*
**Hanson,** Howard Grant 1920- *AmMWSc 92*
**Hanson,** Howard Harold 1896-1981 *FacFETw*
**Hanson,** Hugh 1915- *AmMWSc 92*
**Hanson,** James Carl 1962- *WhoMW 92*
**Hanson,** James Carter 1941- *WhoFI 92*
**Hanson,** James Charles 1931- *AmMWSc 92*
**Hanson,** James Donald 1935- *Who 92*
**Hanson,** James Edward 1927- *AmMWSc 92*
**Hanson,** James Edward 1962- *AmMWSc 92*
**Hanson,** James Richard 1943- *WhoWest 92*
**Hanson,** Jean Elizabeth 1949- *WhoAmL 92*
**Hanson,** Jeff O 1958- *WhoAmP 91*
**Hanson,** Jerry 1943- *WhoAmP 91*
**Hanson,** Jerry J *WhoAmP 91*
**Hanson,** Jerry Lee 1932- *AmMWSc 92*
**Hanson,** Jim *DrAPF 91*
**Hanson,** Joan 1938- *IntAu&W 91*
**Hanson,** Joe A 1928- *AmMWSc 92*
**Hanson,** John *Who 92*
**Hanson,** John Bernard 1918- *AmMWSc 92*
**Hanson,** John Elbert 1935- *AmMWSc 92, WhoMW 92*
**Hanson,** John Gilbert 1938- *Who 92*
**Hanson,** John J. 1922- *WhoAmL 92*
**Hanson,** John L. 1950- *WhoBlA 92*
**Hanson,** John M 1932- *AmMWSc 92*
**Hanson,** John R 1941- *WhoAmP 91*
**Hanson,** John Sherwood 1927- *AmMWSc 92*
**Hanson,** Jonathan C 1941- *AmMWSc 92*
**Hanson,** Kenneth *DrAPF 91*
**Hanson,** Kenneth Charles 1951- *WhoRel 92*
**Hanson,** Kenneth G. 1933- *WhoFI 92*
**Hanson,** Kenneth Hamilton 1919- *WhoAmL 92*
**Hanson,** Kenneth Marvin 1927- *AmMWSc 92*
**Hanson,** Kenneth Merrill 1940- *AmMWSc 92*
**Hanson,** Kenneth O 1922- *ConPo 91, WrDr 92*
**Hanson,** Kenneth Ralph 1930- *AmMWSc 92*
**Hanson,** Kenneth Warren 1922- *AmMWSc 92*
**Hanson,** Kent Bryan 1954- *WhoAmL 92*
**Hanson,** LaMont Dix 1954- *WhoWest 92*
**Hanson,** Lester Eugene 1912- *AmMWSc 92*
**Hanson,** Louise I Karle 1946- *AmMWSc 92*
**Hanson,** Lyle *WhoAmP 91*
**Hanson,** Lyle Eugene 1920- *AmMWSc 92*
**Hanson,** Marian W 1933- *WhoAmP 91*
**Hanson,** Marvin Wayne 1928- *AmMWSc 92*
**Hanson,** Merle Edwin 1934- *AmMWSc 92*
**Hanson,** Mervin Paul 1937- *AmMWSc 92*
**Hanson,** Milton Paul 1938- *AmMWSc 92*
**Hanson,** Morgan A 1930- *AmMWSc 92*
**Hanson,** Murray Lynn 1948- *WhoRel 92*
**Hanson,** Neil 1923- *Who 92*
**Hanson,** Noel Rodger 1942- *WhoFI 92, WhoWest 92*
**Hanson,** Norma Lee 1930- *WhoAmP 91*
**Hanson,** Norman 1916- *WhoAmL 92*
**Hanson,** Norman Walter 1925- *AmMWSc 92*
**Hanson,** Orlin 1930- *WhoAmP 91*
**Hanson,** Paul David 1939- *WhoRel 92*
**Hanson,** Paul David 1946- *WhoFI 92, WhoMW 92*
**Hanson,** Paul Eliot 1953- *AmMWSc 92*
**Hanson,** Paul R. 1952- *ConAu 134*
**Hanson,** Pauline *WrDr 92*
**Hanson,** Per Roland 1912- *AmMWSc 92*
**Hanson,** Peter 1935- *AmMWSc 92*
**Hanson,** Philip 1936- *WrDr 92*
**Hanson,** Philip Llewellyn 1961- *WhoEnt 92*
**Hanson,** Ray Lorain 1948- *WhoWest 92*
**Hanson,** Richard La Vern 1942- *WhoMW 92*
**Hanson,** Richard Steven 1935- *AmMWSc 92*
**Hanson,** Richard W 1935- *AmMWSc 92*
**Hanson,** Richard X. 1948- *WhoWest 92*
**Hanson,** Robert A. 1924- *IntWW 91*
**Hanson,** Robert Arthur 1924- *WhoFI 92, WhoMW 92*
**Hanson,** Robert Bruce 1947- *AmMWSc 92*
**Hanson,** Robert C 1944- *AmMWSc 92*
**Hanson,** Robert D 1935- *AmMWSc 92*
**Hanson,** Robert Eugene 1947- *WhoAmP 91, WhoMW 92*
**Hanson,** Robert Gordon 1944- *WhoMW 92*
**Hanson,** Robert Harold 1918- *AmMWSc 92*
**Hanson,** Robert Jack 1922- *AmMWSc 92*
**Hanson,** Robert Paul *IntWW 91N*
**Hanson,** Robert Paul 1918- *AmMWSc 92*
**Hanson,** Robin Grollmus 1953- *WhoMW 92*
**Hanson,** Roger Brian 1943- *AmMWSc 92*
**Hanson,** Roger James 1927- *AmMWSc 92*
**Hanson,** Roger Wayne 1922- *AmMWSc 92*
**Hanson,** Roland Clements 1934- *AmMWSc 92*
**Hanson,** Ronald Lee 1944- *AmMWSc 92*
**Hanson,** Ronald William 1950- *WhoAmL 92*
**Hanson,** Roy Eugene 1922- *AmMWSc 92*
**Hanson,** Russell Floyd 1939- *AmMWSc 92*
**Hanson,** Samuel Lee 1939- *WhoAmL 92*
**Hanson,** Selden Raymond 1918- *WhoAmP 91*
**Hanson,** Sherry Ballou 1944- *WhoMW 92*
**Hanson,** Thomas S 1939- *WhoAmP 91*
**Hanson,** Trevor Russell 1955- *AmMWSc 92*
**Hanson,** V. Joseph *TwCWW 91, WrDr 92*
**Hanson,** Vern *TwCWW 91, WrDr 92*
**Hanson,** Vic J *TwCWW 91, WrDr 92*
**Hanson,** Virgil 1920- *AmMWSc 92*
**Hanson,** Wallace B *WhoAmP 91*
**Hanson,** Wallace Raymond 1933- *WhoMW 92*
**Hanson,** Walter Raymond 1931- *WhoAmP 91*
**Hanson,** Warren Durward 1921- *AmMWSc 92*
**Hanson,** Wayne Carlyle 1923- *AmMWSc 92*
**Hanson,** William A *AmMWSc 92*
**Hanson,** William Bert 1923- *AmMWSc 92*
**Hanson,** William Lewis 1931- *AmMWSc 92*
**Hanson,** William Roderick 1918- *AmMWSc 92*
**Hanson,** Willis Dale 1926- *AmMWSc 92*
**Hansrote,** Charles Johnson, Jr 1930- *AmMWSc 92*
**Hanss,** Robert Edward 1933- *AmMWSc 92*
**Hanssen,** George Lyle 1927- *AmMWSc 92*
**Hansson,** Carolyn M 1941- *AmMWSc 92*
**Hansson,** Goran K 1951- *AmMWSc 92*
**Hansteen,** Henry B. d1991 *NewYTBS 91*
**Hanstein,** Otfrid Von 1869-1959 *ScFEYrs*
**Hanstein,** Penelope 1948- *WhoEnt 92*
**Hansvick,** Christine L. 1949- *WhoWest 92*
**Hantho,** Charles Harold 1931- *WhoFI 92*
**Hanthorn,** Dennis Wayne 1951- *WhoEnt 92*
**Hanthorn,** George Wilmot 1947- *WhoFI 92*
**Hanthorn,** Howard E 1909- *AmMWSc 92*
**Hantman,** Robert Gary 1941- *AmMWSc 92*
**Hanto,** Douglas W *AmMWSc 92*
**Hanton,** Alastair Kydd 1926- *Who 92*
**Hanton,** Emile Michael *WhoFI 92*
**Hanton,** John Patrick 1935- *AmMWSc 92*
**Hantz,** Anna Barbara *WhoAmP 91*
**Hanukoglu,** Israel 1952- *AmMWSc 92*
**Hanumara,** Ramachandra Choudary 1937- *AmMWSc 92*
**Hanus,** Frantisek 1943- *IntWW 91*
**Hanus,** Jerome 1940- *WhoRel 92*
**Hanus,** Paul 1855-1941 *DcAmImH*
**Hanushek,** Eric Alan 1943- *WhoFI 92*
**Hanussen,** Jan Erik 1889-1933 *EncTR 91*
**Hanuszkiewicz,** Adam 1924- *IntWW 91*
**Hanway,** Craig H. 1955- *WhoWest 92*
**Hanway,** Donald Grant 1918- *AmMWSc 92*

**Hanway**, H Edward 1952- *WhoIns 92*
**Hanway**, John, III 1952- *WhoFI 92*
**Hanway**, John E, Jr 1922- *AmMWSc 92*
**Hanway**, John Joseph 1920- *AmMWSc 92*
**Hanwell**, Robert Michael 1954- *WhoAmL 92*
**Hanworth**, Viscount 1916- *Who 92*
**Hanysak**, Denny Paul 1944- *WhoIns 92*
**Hanysz**, Eugene Arthur 1922- *AmMWSc 92*
**Hanzalek**, Astrid T 1928- *WhoAmP 91*
**Hanzel**, James Joseph 1949- *WhoMW 92*
**Hanzel**, Robert Stephen 1932- *AmMWSc 92*
**Hanzely**, Laszlo 1939- *AmMWSc 92*
**Hanzely**, Stephen 1940- *AmMWSc 92*
**Hanzlicek**, C.G. *DrAPF 91*
**Hanzlik**, Rayburn DeMara 1938- *WhoAmL 92, WhoAmP 91*
**Hanzlik**, Robert Paul 1943- *AmMWSc 92*
**Hao Jianxiu** 1935- *IntWW 91*
**Hao Ran** 1932- *IntWW 91*
**Hapai**, Marlene Nachbar 1948- *AmMWSc 92*
**Hapgood**, David 1926- *WrDr 92*
**Hapgood**, Hutchins *SourALJ*
**Hapgood**, Hutchins 1869-1944 *BenetAL 91, DcAmImH*
**Hapgood**, Norman 1868-1937 *BenetAL 91*
**Hapke**, Bern 1943- *AmMWSc 92*
**Hapke**, Bruce W 1931- *AmMWSc 92*
**Hapner**, Kenneth D 1939- *AmMWSc 92*
**Happ**, George Movius 1936- *AmMWSc 92*
**Happ**, Harvey Heinz 1928- *AmMWSc 92*
**Happ**, Stafford Coleman 1905- *AmMWSc 92*
**Happach**, Ronald Henry 1933- *WhoMW 92*
**Happel**, Dorothy 1927- *WhoEnt 92*
**Happel**, John 1908- *AmMWSc 92*
**Happel**, Leo Theodore, Jr 1943- *AmMWSc 92*
**Happer**, William, Jr 1939- *AmMWSc 92*
**Happold**, Edmund 1930- *Who 92*
**Happold**, Frank Charles d1991 *Who 92N*
**Happoldt**, Christopher 1823-1878 *DcNCBi 3*
**Haq**, Abaid-Ul 1953- *WhoWest 92*
**Haq**, Bilal U *AmMWSc 92*
**Haq**, M Safiul 1935- *AmMWSc 92*
**Haq**, Mohammad Zamir-ul 1936- *AmMWSc 92*
**Haqq**, Khalida Ismail 1946- *WhoBlA 92*
**Haque**, Azeez C 1933- *AmMWSc 92*
**Haque**, Malika Hakim *WhoMW 92*
**Haque**, Rizwanul 1940- *AmMWSc 92*
**Hara**, Bunbei 1913- *IntWW 91*
**Hara**, George 1952- *WhoWest 92*
**Hara**, Kenzaburo 1907- *IntWW 91*
**Hara**, Lloyd F. 1939- *WhoFI 92*
**Hara**, Saburo 1928- *AmMWSc 92*
**Hara**, Stanley Ikuo 1923- *WhoAmP 91*
**Hara**, Sumio 1911- *IntWW 91*
**Hara**, Toshiaki J 1932- *AmMWSc 92*
**Hara-Isa**, Nancy Jeanne 1961- *WhoEnt 92*
**Harab**, Elliot Peter 1948- *WhoAmL 92*
**Harad**, George Jay 1944- *WhoFI 92*
**Harada**, Shoza 1923?- *IntWW 91*
**Haragan**, Donald Robert 1936- *AmMWSc 92*
**Harahuc**, Donna Lee 1951- *WhoMW 92*
**Harakal**, Concetta 1923- *AmMWSc 92*
**Harakas**, N Konstantinos 1934- *AmMWSc 92*
**Harakas**, Stanley Samuel 1932- *ConAu 134*
**Harald V** 1937- *IntWW 91*
**Haraldseth**, Leif 1929- *IntWW 91*
**Haralick**, Robert M 1943- *AmMWSc 92*
**Haralick**, Robert Martin 1943- *WhoFI 92*
**Haralson**, Herndon 1757-1847 *DcNCBi 3*
**Haralson**, Larry L. *WhoBlA 92*
**Haramaki**, Chiko 1925- *AmMWSc 92*
**Harang**, Donald Francis, Jr. 1948- *WhoAmL 92*
**Harapiak**, John *WhoRel 92*
**Harare**, Archbishop of 1932- *Who 92*
**Harare**, Bishop of 1927- *Who 92*
**Harare**, Diocese *Who 92*
**Harary**, Donald Keith 1953- *WhoEnt 92*
**Harary**, Frank 1921- *AmMWSc 92, WhoWest 92*
**Harary**, Isaac 1923- *AmMWSc 92*
**Haraszthy**, Agoston *DcAmImH*
**Haraszty**, Eszter 1910?- *DcTwDes*
**Haray**, Richard John 1956- *WhoAmL 92*
**Harazin**, William Dennis 1953- *WhoAmL 92*
**Harb**, Joseph Marshall 1938- *AmMWSc 92*
**Harb**, Nidal 1955- *WhoMW 92*
**Harbach**, Barbara Carol 1946- *WhoEnt 92*
**Harbach**, Otto 1873-1963 *BenetAL 91*
**Harbach**, Ralph Edward 1948- *AmMWSc 92*
**Harbach**, William O. 1919- *IntMPA 92*
**Harbakkuk**, John 1915- *Who 92*
**Harbater**, David 1952- *AmMWSc 92*
**Harbaugh**, Allan Wilson 1926- *AmMWSc 92*
**Harbaugh**, Brent Kalen 1948- *AmMWSc 92*
**Harbaugh**, Daniel David 1942- *AmMWSc 92*
**Harbaugh**, Daniel Paul 1948- *WhoAmL 92, WhoWest 92*
**Harbaugh**, Gary L. 1936- *WhoRel 92*
**Harbaugh**, Henry 1817-1867 *BenetAL 91*
**Harbaugh**, John Warvelle 1926- *AmMWSc 92, WhoWest 92*
**Harbaugh**, Joseph Delbert 1939- *WhoAmL 92*
**Harbaugh**, Thomas Chalmers 1849-1924 *BenetAL 91*
**Harbaugh**, Thomas Edward 1940- *WhoMW 92*
**Harbeck**, Karen M. 1951- *WhoAmL 92*
**Harbeck**, Ronald Joseph 1942- *AmMWSc 92*
**Harbeck**, William James 1921- *WhoFI 92*
**Harben**, Will *ScFEYrs*
**Harben**, Will N. 1858-1919 *BenetAL 91*
**Harber**, Jerry Lance 1940- *WhoRel 92*
**Harber**, Leonard C 1927- *AmMWSc 92*
**Harberger**, Arnold C. 1924- *WrDr 92*
**Harberger**, Arnold Carl 1924- *WhoMW 92*
**Harbers**, Carole Ann Z 1943- *AmMWSc 92*
**Harbers**, Leniel H 1934- *AmMWSc 92*
**Harbert**, Charles A 1940- *AmMWSc 92*
**Harbert**, Edward Wesley, II 1923- *WhoEnt 92*
**Harbert**, Guy M., III 1958- *WhoAmL 92*
**Harbert**, Ted 1955- *IntMPA 92*
**Harbert**, Terry Lee 1947- *WhoMW 92*
**Harberton**, Viscount 1910- *Who 92*
**Harbeson**, John Willis 1938- *WhoFI 92*
**Harbig**, Rudolf 1913-1944 *EncTR 91 [port]*
**Harbin**, Charles Marvin 1939- *WhoMW 92*
**Harbin**, Harry Stephen 1951- *WhoAmL 92*
**Harbin**, John Pickens 1917- *WhoFI 92*
**Harbin**, Lawrence 1948- *WhoAmL 92*
**Harbin**, Michael Allen 1947- *WhoRel 92*
**Harbin**, Raymond 1948- *WhoAmP 91*
**Harbin**, Shirley Meverna 1931- *WhoEnt 92, WhoMW 92*
**Harbin**, William T 1908- *AmMWSc 92*
**Harbinson**, Joel Cline 1954- *WhoAmL 92*
**Harbison**, Earle Harrison, Jr. 1928- *IntWW 91, WhoFI 92, WhoMW 92*
**Harbison**, G Richard 1941- *AmMWSc 92*
**Harbison**, Gerard Stanislaus 1958- *AmMWSc 92*
**Harbison**, James Prescott 1951- *AmMWSc 92*
**Harbison**, John 1938- *ConCom 92, NewAmDM, WhoEnt 92, WhoMW 92*
**Harbison**, John Henry 1957- *WhoAmL 92*
**Harbison**, Marie Emma 1927- *WhoFI 92*
**Harbison**, Peter 1930- *IntWW 91*
**Harbison**, Raymond D 1943- *AmMWSc 92*
**Harbison**, S P 1952- *AmMWSc 92*
**Harbison**, Stephen Franklin 1943- *WhoAmL 92*
**Harbison**, William 1922- *Who 92*
**Harbison**, William J 1923- *WhoAmP 91*
**Harbison**, William James 1923- *WhoAmL 92*
**Harbo**, John Russell 1943- *AmMWSc 92*
**Harbold**, Mary Leah 1912- *AmMWSc 92*
**Harbor**, William H 1920- *WhoAmP 91*
**Harbord**, Anne Marie 1954- *WhoWest 92*
**Harbord-Hamond** *Who 92*
**Harbordt**, C Michael 1942- *AmMWSc 92*
**Harborne**, Peter Gale 1945- *Who 92*
**Harbottle**, Anthony Hall Harrison 1925- *Who 92*
**Harbottle**, Garman 1923- *AmMWSc 92*
**Harbottle**, George Laurence 1924- *Who 92*
**Harbottle**, Michael Neale 1917- *IntAu&W 91, Who 92, WrDr 92*
**Harbou**, Thea Von 1888-1953 *ScFEYrs*
**Harbour**, David Franklin, III 1942- *WhoAmP 91*
**Harbour**, Diane Rose 1961- *WhoMW 92*
**Harbour**, Jerry 1927- *AmMWSc 92*
**Harbour**, John Richard 1944- *AmMWSc 92*
**Harbourt**, Cyrus Oscar 1931- *AmMWSc 92*
**Harbron**, Garrett Lee 1940- *WhoMW 92*
**Harbron**, Thomas Richard 1937- *AmMWSc 92*
**Harbur**, Nathan Clayton 1951- *WhoMW 92*
**Harburg**, Edgar Y 1896-1981 *FacFETw*
**Harbury**, Colin 1922- *IntAu&W 91, WrDr 92*
**Harbury**, Henry Alexander 1927- *AmMWSc 92*
**Harbus**, Richard 1940- *WhoAmL 92*
**Harchalk**, Julie Ruth 1957- *WhoMW 92*
**Harchenhorn**, V Lanny *WhoAmP 91*
**Harclerode**, Jack E 1935- *AmMWSc 92*
**Harcombe**, Paul Albin 1945- *AmMWSc 92*
**Harcourt**, Barbara Arnold 1950- *WhoAmL 92*
**Harcourt**, Douglas George 1926- *AmMWSc 92*
**Harcourt**, Geoffrey Colin 1931- *IntAu&W 91, IntWW 91, Who 92, WrDr 92*
**Harcourt**, Geoffrey David 1935- *Who 92*
**Harcourt**, George 1868-1947 *TwCPaSc*
**Harcourt**, H Baxter 1924- *WhoAmP 91*
**Harcourt**, Michael Franklin 1943- *WhoWest 92*
**Harcourt**, Palma *IntAu&W 91, WrDr 92*
**Harcourt**, Robert Neff 1932- *WhoWest 92*
**Harcourt-Smith**, David 1931- *Who 92*
**Harcus**, Ronald Albert d1991 *Who 92N*
**Hard**, Cecil Gustav 1923- *AmMWSc 92*
**Hard**, Margaret McGregor 1919- *AmMWSc 92*
**Hard**, Richard C, Jr 1933- *AmMWSc 92*
**Hard**, Robert Paul 1944- *AmMWSc 92*
**Hard**, Thomas Michael 1937- *AmMWSc 92*
**Hard**, Walter 1882-1966 *BenetAL 91*
**Hard**, William *SourALJ*
**Hardage**, Bob Adrian 1939- *AmMWSc 92*
**Hardaker**, Charles 1934- *TwCPaSc*
**Hardaker**, Ian Alexander 1932- *Who 92*
**Hardaway**, Ernest, II 1934- *AmMWSc 92*
**Hardaway**, Ernest, II 1938- *WhoBlA 92*
**Hardaway**, Francine Olman 1941- *WhoWest 92*
**Hardaway**, Gregory Scott 1954- *WhoRel 92*
**Hardaway**, John E 1936- *AmMWSc 92*
**Hardaway**, Richard Travis, Jr. 1940- *WhoFI 92*
**Hardaway**, Robert M, III 1916- *AmMWSc 92*
**Hardaway**, Thomas C 1957- *WhoAmP 91*
**Hardaway**, Timothy Duane 1966- *WhoBlA 92*
**Hardaway**, Yvonne Veronica 1950- *WhoBlA 92*
**Hardberger**, Florian Max 1914- *AmMWSc 92*
**Hardcastle**, Alan John 1933- *Who 92*
**Hardcastle**, Donald Lee 1938- *AmMWSc 92*
**Hardcastle**, Jack Donald 1933- *Who 92*
**Hardcastle**, James C. 1914- *WhoBlA 92*
**Hardcastle**, James Edward 1932- *AmMWSc 92*
**Hardcastle**, Jesse Leslie 1926- *Who 92*
**Hardcastle**, Kenneth Irvin 1931- *AmMWSc 92*
**Hardcastle**, Michael 1933- *IntAu&W 91, WrDr 92*
**Hardcastle**, Robert Thomas 1949- *WhoAmL 92*
**Hardcastle**, Willis Santford 1921- *AmMWSc 92*
**Hardebeck**, Ellen Jean 1939- *AmMWSc 92*
**Hardee**, David Wyatt 1947- *WhoAmL 92, WhoFI 92*
**Hardee**, Dicky Dan 1938- *AmMWSc 92*
**Hardee**, Lewis Jefferson, Jr. 1937- *WhoEnt 92*
**Hardegree**, Mary Carolyn 1933- *AmMWSc 92*
**Hardekopf**, Robert Allen 1940- *AmMWSc 92*
**Hardell**, William John 1928- *AmMWSc 92*
**Hardeman**, Carole Hall *WhoBlA 92*
**Hardeman**, Donald Watson 1947- *WhoAmL 92*
**Hardeman**, James Anthony 1943- *WhoBlA 92*
**Hardeman**, Strotha E., Jr. 1929- *WhoBlA 92*
**Harden**, Alice Varnado 1948- *WhoAmP 91*
**Harden**, Arthur 1865-1940 *WhoNob 90*
**Harden**, Blaine 1952- *ConAu 135*
**Harden**, Bruce Donald Richard 1940- *WhoAmP 91*
**Harden**, Darrel Grover 1930- *AmMWSc 92*
**Harden**, Donald B. 1901- *WrDr 92*
**Harden**, Donald Benjamin 1901- *IntWW 91, Who 92*
**Harden**, James Richard Edwards 1916- *Who 92*
**Harden**, John William 1903-1985 *DcNCBi 3*
**Harden**, Marvin *WhoBlA 92, WhoWest 92*
**Harden**, Mary Louise 1942- *WhoMW 92*
**Harden**, O. Elizabeth 1935- *WrDr 92*
**Harden**, Patrick Alan 1936- *WhoWest 92*
**Harden**, Philip Howard 1908- *AmMWSc 92*
**Harden**, Robert James 1952- *WhoBlA 92*
**Harden**, Robert Neal 1952- *WhoRel 92*
**Harden**, Robert T 1960- *WhoAmP 91*
**Harden**, Vincent Louis 1955- *WhoMW 92*
**Hardenbrook**, Jim O 1951- *WhoRel 92*
**Hardenbrook**, Weldon Marshall 1939- *WhoRel 92*
**Hardenbrook**, Yvonne Moore *DrAPF 91*
**Hardenburg**, Robert Earle 1919- *AmMWSc 92*
**Harder**, Clark Andrew 1955- *WhoAmP 91*
**Harder**, David Rae 1950- *AmMWSc 92*
**Harder**, Donald Edwald 1939- *AmMWSc 92*
**Harder**, Edwin L 1905- *AmMWSc 92*
**Harder**, Gil J. 1951- *WhoRel 92*
**Harder**, Harold Cecil 1943- *AmMWSc 92*
**Harder**, James Albert 1926- *AmMWSc 92*
**Harder**, Jean 1931- *WhoRel 92*
**Harder**, Jesse J *WhoAmP 91*
**Harder**, John Dwight 1943- *AmMWSc 92*
**Harder**, John Jurgen 1919- *AmMWSc 92*
**Harder**, Joseph C 1916- *WhoAmP 91*
**Harder**, Manfred 1937- *IntWW 91*
**Harder**, Mark Allen 1960- *WhoMW 92*
**Harder**, Michael Upham 1953- *WhoWest 92*
**Harder**, Roger Wehe 1917- *AmMWSc 92*
**Harder**, Rolf Peter 1929- *WhoEnt 92*
**Harder**, Ronald R 1943- *WhoIns 92*
**Harders**, Clarence Waldemar 1915- *Who 92*
**Hardesty**, Boyd A 1932- *AmMWSc 92*
**Hardesty**, Christopher Scott 1945- *WhoFI 92*
**Hardesty**, Donald Lynn 1941- *WhoWest 92*
**Hardesty**, George Davis, III 1954- *WhoFI 92*
**Hardesty**, George K C 1909- *AmMWSc 92*
**Hardesty**, Patrick Thomas 1951- *AmMWSc 92*
**Hardesty**, Rodney d1991 *NewYTBS 91*
**Hardesty**, Thomas Fabian 1928- *WhoAmP 91*
**Hardeway**, Grant Ulysess 1945- *WhoAmL 92*
**Hardgrove**, George Lind, Jr 1933- *AmMWSc 92*
**Hardgrove**, James Alan 1945- *WhoAmL 92*
**Hardham**, William Morgan 1939- *AmMWSc 92*
**Hardie**, Andrew Rutherford 1946- *Who 92*
**Hardie**, Archibald George 1908- *Who 92*
**Hardie**, Charles 1910- *Who 92*
**Hardie**, Charles Edgar Mathewes 1910- *IntWW 91*
**Hardie**, Charles Jeremy 1938- *Who 92*
**Hardie**, Colin Graham 1906- *Who 92*
**Hardie**, Donald David Graeme 1936- *Who 92*
**Hardie**, Douglas 1923- *Who 92*
**Hardie**, Edith L 1931- *AmMWSc 92*
**Hardie**, Frank 1911- *WrDr 92*
**Hardie**, George Graham 1933- *WhoWest 92*
**Hardie**, Gerald 1931- *AmMWSc 92*
**Hardie**, Gwen 1962- *TwCPaSc*
**Hardie**, James 1938- *TwCPaSc*
**Hardie**, James Hiller 1929- *WhoAmL 92*
**Hardie**, Jeremy *Who 92*
**Hardie**, Keir 1856-1915 *FacFETw*
**Hardie**, Martin 1875-1952 *TwCPaSc*
**Hardie**, Miles Clayton 1924- *Who 92*
**Hardie**, Robert Howie 1923- *AmMWSc 92*
**Hardie**, Robert L., Jr. 1941- *WhoBlA 92*
**Hardie**, Sean 1947- *ConAu 135*
**Hardie**, William Francis Ross d1990 *Who 92N*
**Hardie**, William George 1958- *AmMWSc 92*
**Hardiman**, James W. 1926- *IntMPA 92*
**Hardiman**, Joseph Raymond 1937- *WhoFI 92*
**Hardiman**, Phillip Thomas 1935- *WhoBlA 92*
**Hardin**, Adlai Stevenson, Jr. 1937- *WhoAmL 92*
**Hardin**, Bobby Ott 1935- *AmMWSc 92*
**Hardin**, Boniface 1933- *WhoBlA 92*
**Hardin**, Bryan David 1944- *WhoMW 92*
**Hardin**, Charles Wheeler 1926- *WhoAmP 91*
**Hardin**, Clement *IntAu&W 91X, TwCWW 91, WrDr 92*
**Hardin**, Clifford M. 1915- *WrDr 92*
**Hardin**, Clifford Morris 1915- *AmMWSc 92, IntWW 91, WhoAmP 91, WhoFI 92, WhoMW 92*
**Hardin**, Clyde D 1925- *AmMWSc 92*
**Hardin**, Creighton A 1918- *AmMWSc 92*
**Hardin**, Dave *TwCWW 91*
**Hardin**, Edward Jackson 1943- *WhoAmL 92*
**Hardin**, Edwin M 1926- *AmMWSc 92*
**Hardin**, Eugene 1941- *WhoBlA 92*
**Hardin**, Garrett 1915- *AmMWSc 92*
**Hardin**, George C, Jr 1920- *AmMWSc 92*
**Hardin**, Henry E. 1912- *WhoBlA 92*
**Hardin**, Hilliard Frances 1917- *AmMWSc 92*
**Hardin**, Ian Russell 1944- *AmMWSc 92*
**Hardin**, J. D. *WrDr 92*
**Hardin**, James Carlisle, III 1948- *WhoAmL 92*
**Hardin**, James N 1939- *ConAu 35NR*

**Hardin,** James T 1934- *AmMWSc 92*
**Hardin,** James W 1946- *AmMWSc 92*
**Hardin,** James Walker 1929- *AmMWSc 92*
**Hardin,** James William 1943- *AmMWSc 92*
**Hardin,** Jay Charles 1942- *AmMWSc 92*
**Hardin,** John Alexander 1911- *WhoEnt 92*
**Hardin,** John Arthur 1948- *WhoBlA 92*
**Hardin,** John Avery 1943- *AmMWSc 92*
**Hardin,** Julia Patricia 1955- *WhoAmL 92*
**Hardin,** Linda Gay 1946- *WhoRel 92*
**Hardin,** Luther 1951- *WhoAmP 91*
**Hardin,** Mark Bernard 1838-1910 *BiInAmS*
**Hardin,** Martha Love Wood 1918- *WhoMW 92*
**Hardin,** Robert Allen 1934- *WhoEnt 92*
**Hardin,** Robert Calvin 1913- *AmMWSc 92*
**Hardin,** Robert Leon 1925- *WhoAmP 91*
**Hardin,** Robert Toombs 1931- *AmMWSc 92*
**Hardin,** Rodney Edward 1969- *WhoRel 92*
**Hardin,** Russell 1940- *WhoMW 92*
**Hardin,** Steve 1950- *WhoAmP 91*
**Hardin,** Terri *DrAPF 91*
**Hardin,** Thomas Jefferson, II 1945- *WhoFI 92*
**Harding** *Who 92*
**Harding,** Andrew Paul 1948- *WhoFI 92*
**Harding,** Anita Elizabeth 1952- *Who 92*
**Harding,** Anna Monroe 1933- *WhoEnt 92*
**Harding,** Boyd W 1926- *AmMWSc 92*
**Harding,** Bruce Alan 1947- *WhoMW 92*
**Harding,** Charles Enoch 1942- *AmMWSc 92*
**Harding,** Christopher George Francis 1939- *Who 92*
**Harding,** Christopher Philip 1944- *IntAu&W 91*
**Harding,** Clifford Vincent, III 1957- *AmMWSc 92*
**Harding,** Clifford Vincent, Jr 1925- *AmMWSc 92*
**Harding,** D. W. 1906- *WrDr 92*
**Harding,** David 1944- *TwCPaSc*
**Harding,** David Glenn 1954- *WhoAmL 92*
**Harding,** David Paul 1965- *WhoWest 92*
**Harding,** David S. 1956- *WhoEnt 92*
**Harding,** Debra Kathryn Anne 1957- *WhoMW 92*
**Harding,** Dennis William 1940- *Who 92*
**Harding,** Denys Wyatt 1906- *Who 92*
**Harding,** Derek William 1930- *Who 92*
**Harding,** Dorothy Hoxworth 1919- *WhoAmP 91*
**Harding,** Duane Douglas 1947- *AmMWSc 92*
**Harding,** Ed 1924- *WhoBlA 92*
**Harding,** Edmund Hoyt 1890-1970 *DcNCBi 3*
**Harding,** Ellison *ScFEYrs*
**Harding,** Ethel M 1927- *WhoAmP 91*
**Harding,** Fann 1930- *AmMWSc 92*
**Harding,** G. Homer *WhoMW 92*
**Harding,** G Homer 1925- *WhoAmP 91*
**Harding,** George William 1927- *Who 92*
**Harding,** Georgina 1955- *ConAu 133*
**Harding,** Gloria Mae 1940- *WhoRel 92*
**Harding,** Godfrey Kynard Matthew 1942- *AmMWSc 92*
**Harding,** Henry Patrick 1874-1959 *DcNCBi 3*
**Harding,** Homer Robert 1928- *AmMWSc 92*
**Harding,** Hugh Alastair 1917- *Who 92*
**Harding,** James 1929- *IntAu&W 91, WrDr 92*
**Harding,** James A 1935- *AmMWSc 92*
**Harding,** James George 1949- *WhoWest 92*
**Harding,** James Lombard 1929- *AmMWSc 92*
**Harding,** John 1896-1989 *FacFETw*
**Harding,** John 1948- *IntAu&W 91, WrDr 92*
**Harding,** John Edward 1938- *WhoBlA 92*
**Harding,** John Herbert 1914- *WhoMW 92*
**Harding,** John Joseph, Jr 1945- *WhoAmP 91*
**Harding,** John Philip 1911- *Who 92*
**Harding,** John Tisdale 1945- *WhoEnt 92*
**Harding,** John Walter 1947- *WhoEnt 92*
**Harding,** John Wesley 1965- *ConMus 6 [port]*
**Harding,** John Windsor 1933- *WhoFI 92*
**Harding,** Joseph Patrick 1959- *WhoAmL 92*
**Harding,** Joseph Warren, Jr 1948- *AmMWSc 92*
**Harding,** Karen Elaine 1949- *WhoWest 92*
**Harding,** Kenn E 1942- *AmMWSc 92*
**Harding,** Lee 1937- *IntAu&W 91, TwCSFW 91, WrDr 92*
**Harding,** Major B. 1935- *WhoAmL 92, WhoAmP 91*
**Harding,** Matt *IntAu&W 91X, TwCWW 91*
**Harding,** Matthew Whitman *IntAu&W 91X, TwCWW 91*
**Harding,** Maurice James Charles 1938- *AmMWSc 92*
**Harding,** Michael 1953- *WrDr 92*
**Harding,** Michael Allen 1959- *WhoMW 92*
**Harding,** Nancy *DrAPF 91*
**Harding,** Paul George Richard *AmMWSc 92*
**Harding,** Peter John 1940- *Who 92*
**Harding,** Peter Robin 1933- *IntWW 91, Who 92*
**Harding,** Peter Thomas 1930- *Who 92*
**Harding,** Philip Andreae 1938- *WhoEnt 92*
**Harding,** R H 1931- *AmMWSc 92*
**Harding,** Ray Murray, Jr. 1953- *WhoAmL 92*
**Harding,** Robert 1957- *TwCPaSc*
**Harding,** Robert Brooks 1942- *WhoAmL 92*
**Harding,** Robert E. 1930- *WhoBlA 92*
**Harding,** Roger John 1935- *Who 92*
**Harding,** Ross Philip 1921- *Who 92*
**Harding,** Rowe d1991 *Who 92N*
**Harding,** Roy 1924- *Who 92*
**Harding,** Roy Woodrow, Jr 1940- *AmMWSc 92*
**Harding,** Samuel William 1915- *AmMWSc 92*
**Harding,** Thomas Hague 1945- *AmMWSc 92*
**Harding,** Tommy Lee 1958- *WhoEnt 92*
**Harding,** Trewitt DeLano 1934- *WhoFI 92*
**Harding,** Vincent 1931- *WhoBlA 92*
**Harding,** W. M. 1934- *WhoWest 92*
**Harding,** Wallace Charles, Jr 1927- *AmMWSc 92*
**Harding,** Walter 1917- *DcLB 111 [port], WrDr 92*
**Harding,** Warren G. 1865-1923 *BenetAL 91, FacFETw [port], RComAH*
**Harding,** Warren Gamaliel 1865-1923 *AmPolLe [port]*
**Harding,** Wayne Edward, III 1954- *WhoWest 92*
**Harding,** Wes *TwCWW 91*
**Harding,** Wilfrid Gerald 1915- *Who 92*
**Harding,** William *Who 92*
**Harding,** William Alan 1944- *WhoMW 92*
**Harding,** Winfred Mood 1920- *AmMWSc 92*
**Harding-Barlow,** Ingeborg 1938- *AmMWSc 92*
**Harding of Petherton,** Baron 1928- *Who 92*
**Hardinge** *Who 92*
**Hardinge,** Viscount 1956- *Who 92*
**Hardinge,** Mervyn Gilbert *AmMWSc 92*
**Hardinge,** Robert Arnold 1914- *Who 92*
**Hardinge of Penshurst,** Baron 1921- *Who 92*
**Hardingham,** Robert 1903- *Who 92*
**Hardis,** Leonard 1916- *AmMWSc 92*
**Hardis,** Stephen Roger 1935- *WhoFI 92*
**Hardish,** Patrick Michael 1944- *WhoEnt 92*
**Hardison,** Harold Woodrow 1923- *WhoAmP 91*
**Hardison,** John Robert 1918- *AmMWSc 92*
**Hardison,** Joseph Hammond, III 1962- *WhoFI 92*
**Hardison,** Leslie Claire 1929- *WhoFI 92*
**Hardison,** O.B. *DrAPF 91*
**Hardison,** Osborne B. 1928- *WrDr 92*
**Hardison,** Osborne Bennett 1892-1959 *DcNCBi 3*
**Hardison,** Perry 1956- *WhoRel 92*
**Hardison,** Ross Cameron 1951- *AmMWSc 92*
**Hardison,** Roy Lewis 1929- *WhoWest 92*
**Hardison,** Ruth Inge 1914- *WhoBlA 92*
**Hardison,** Walter L., Jr. 1921- *WhoBlA 92*
**Hardison,** Wesley Aurel 1925- *AmMWSc 92*
**Hardisty,** Donald Mertz 1932- *WhoWest 92*
**Hardman,** Amy Elizabeth d1990 *Who 92N*
**Hardman,** Bruce Bertolette 1942- *AmMWSc 92*
**Hardman,** Carl Charles 1919- *AmMWSc 92*
**Hardman,** Della Brown 1922- *WhoBlA 92*
**Hardman,** Fred d1991 *Who 92N*
**Hardman,** Harold Francis 1927- *AmMWSc 92*
**Hardman,** Henry 1905- *Who 92*
**Hardman,** Ilene L 1937- *WhoAmP 91*
**Hardman,** James Arthur 1929- *Who 92*
**Hardman,** Joel G 1933- *AmMWSc 92*
**Hardman,** John Kemper 1934- *AmMWSc 92*
**Hardman,** John M 1933- *AmMWSc 92*
**Hardman,** John Michael 1947- *AmMWSc 92*
**Hardman,** John Nimrod 1939- *Who 92*
**Hardman-Cromwell,** Youtha Cordella 1941- *WhoBlA 92*
**Hardnett,** Carolyn Judy 1947- *WhoBlA 92*
**Hardon,** John A. 1914- *WrDr 92*
**Hardon,** John Anthony 1914- *WhoRel 92*
**Hardorp,** Johannes Christfried 1929- *AmMWSc 92*
**Hardrath,** Herbert Frank 1922- *AmMWSc 92*
**Hardt,** A V *WhoAmP 91*
**Hardt,** Alfred Black 1930- *AmMWSc 92*
**Hardt,** David Edgar 1950- *AmMWSc 92*
**Hardt,** Frederick William 1943- *WhoAmL 92*
**Hardt,** James Victor 1945- *AmMWSc 92*
**Hardt,** Jill Ann 1959- *WhoRel 92*
**Hardt,** John Wesley 1921- *WhoRel 92*
**Hardtke,** Fred Charles, Jr 1931- *AmMWSc 92*
**Hardtmann,** Goetz E 1932- *AmMWSc 92*
**Hardwick,** Charles Leighton 1941- *WhoAmP 91*
**Hardwick,** Christopher 1911- *Who 92*
**Hardwick,** Clifford E., III 1927- *WhoBlA 92*
**Hardwick,** David Francis 1934- *AmMWSc 92*
**Hardwick,** Donald 1926- *Who 92*
**Hardwick,** Elizabeth 1916- *BenetAL 91, ConNov 91, FacFETw, IntWW 91, ModAWWr, WrDr 92*
**Hardwick,** Gary Clifford 1960- *WhoAmL 92*
**Hardwick,** James Leslie 1913- *Who 92*
**Hardwick,** James Renfro 1940- *WhoRel 92*
**Hardwick,** Joan 1940- *ConAu 135*
**Hardwick,** John Lafayette 1944- *AmMWSc 92*
**Hardwick,** Leo Pliny 1930- *WhoMW 92*
**Hardwick,** Michael 1924- *WrDr 92*
**Hardwick,** Michael 1924-1991 *ConAu 134*
**Hardwick,** Michael John Drinkrow d1991 *Who 92N*
**Hardwick,** Mollie *IntAu&W 91, Who 92, WrDr 92*
**Hardwick,** R. Alan 1952- *WhoWest 92*
**Hardwick,** William Robert 1907- *WhoWest 92*
**Hardwicke,** Earl of 1971- *Who 92*
**Hardwicke,** James Ernest, Jr 1924- *AmMWSc 92*
**Hardwicke,** Norman Lawson 1924- *AmMWSc 92*
**Hardwidge,** Edward Albert 1946- *AmMWSc 92*
**Hardy** *Who 92*
**Hardy,** Adam *WrDr 92*
**Hardy,** Alan 1932- *Who 92*
**Hardy,** Alice Dale *SmATA 67*
**Hardy,** Anna Gwenllian *Who 92*
**Hardy,** Archie 1936- *WhoAmP 91*
**Hardy,** Arthur Sherburne 1847-1930 *BenetAL 91*
**Hardy,** Ashton Richard 1935- *WhoAmL 92*
**Hardy,** B Arthur d1991 *NewYTBS 91*
**Hardy,** Barbara *IntAu&W 91, WrDr 92*
**Hardy,** Barbara Gladys 1924- *Who 92*
**Hardy,** Benson B. 1920- *WhoWest 92*
**Hardy,** Beverley Jane 1944- *WhoFI 92*
**Hardy,** Bobbie 1913- *WrDr 92*
**Hardy,** Brian Albert 1931- *Who 92*
**Hardy,** Catherine 1930- *BlkOlyM*
**Hardy,** Cecil Ross 1908- *AmMWSc 92*
**Hardy,** Charles Exter, III 1960- *WhoRel 92, WhoWest 92*
**Hardy,** Charles Leach 1919- *WhoAmL 92*
**Hardy,** Charles Thomas 1941- *WhoAmL 92*
**Hardy,** Charlie Edward 1941- *WhoBlA 92*
**Hardy,** Christopher Robert 1952- *WhoMW 92*
**Hardy,** Clyde Thomas 1921- *AmMWSc 92*
**Hardy,** D Elmo 1914- *AmMWSc 92*
**Hardy,** Dale Deane 1947- *WhoRel 92*
**Hardy,** Daniel Wayne 1930- *Who 92, WhoRel 92*
**Hardy,** David William 1930- *Who 92*
**Hardy,** Donald McCoy, Jr. 1944- *WhoWest 92*
**Hardy,** Dorcas R 1946- *WhoAmP 91*
**Hardy,** Dorothy C. *WhoBlA 92*
**Hardy,** Duane Horace 1931- *WhoWest 92*
**Hardy,** Earle D 1907- *WhoAmP 91*
**Hardy,** Edgar Erwin 1913- *AmMWSc 92*
**Hardy,** Eursla Dickerson 1933- *WhoBlA 92*
**Hardy,** Flournoy Lane 1928- *AmMWSc 92*
**Hardy,** Frank 1917- *ConNov 91, WrDr 92*
**Hardy,** Freeman 1942- *WhoBlA 92*
**Hardy,** Gordon Alfred 1918- *WhoEnt 92, WhoWest 92*
**Hardy,** H Reginald, Jr 1931- *AmMWSc 92*
**Hardy,** Hagood 1937- *NewAmDM*
**Hardy,** Harvey Louchard 1914- *WhoAmL 92*
**Hardy,** Henry Benjamin, Jr 1925- *AmMWSc 92*
**Hardy,** Herbert Charles 1928- *Who 92*
**Hardy,** Hugh 1932- *DcTwDes*
**Hardy,** James 1932- *Who 92*
**Hardy,** James C 1930- *AmMWSc 92*
**Hardy,** James Chester 1930- *WhoMW 92*
**Hardy,** James D 1918- *AmMWSc 92*
**Hardy,** James Edward 1932- *AmMWSc 92*
**Hardy,** Jeremy Lawrence 1956- *WhoWest 92*
**Hardy,** John Campbell 1933- *Who 92*
**Hardy,** John Christopher 1941- *AmMWSc 92*
**Hardy,** John E., Jr. 1947- *WhoFI 92*
**Hardy,** John J 1937- *WhoIns 92*
**Hardy,** John Louis 1937- *WhoBlA 92*
**Hardy,** John Philips 1933- *IntAu&W 91, IntWW 91, WrDr 92*
**Hardy,** John Thomas 1938- *AmMWSc 92*
**Hardy,** John Thomas 1941- *AmMWSc 92*
**Hardy,** John W, Jr 1927- *AmMWSc 92*
**Hardy,** John William 1930- *AmMWSc 92*
**Hardy,** Joseph Johnston 1844-1915 *BiInAmS*
**Hardy,** Judson, Jr 1931- *AmMWSc 92*
**Hardy,** Kenneth Reginald 1929- *AmMWSc 92*
**Hardy,** Laura *WrDr 92*
**Hardy,** Laurence McNeil 1939- *AmMWSc 92*
**Hardy,** Lester B 1932- *AmMWSc 92*
**Hardy,** Linda B. 1955- *WhoWest 92*
**Hardy,** Lois Lynn 1928- *WhoWest 92*
**Hardy,** Lowell Richard 1953- *WhoRel 92, WhoWest 92*
**Hardy,** Marilyn Weiss 1948- *WhoEnt 92*
**Hardy,** Mark Richard 1957- *WhoWest 92*
**Hardy,** Mary Duffus 1825-1891 *DcAmImH*
**Hardy,** Matthew Phillip 1957- *AmMWSc 92*
**Hardy,** Michael James Langley 1933- *Who 92*
**Hardy,** Michael Leander 1945- *WhoBlA 92*
**Hardy,** Monika M. 1942- *WhoFI 92*
**Hardy,** Nancy Visser 1943- *WhoFI 92*
**Hardy,** Neal 1934- *WhoWest 92*
**Hardy,** Norman Edgar 1917- *IntWW 91*
**Hardy,** Oliver *FacFETw*
**Hardy,** Paul Jude 1942- *WhoAmP 91*
**Hardy,** Paul Wilson 1927- *AmMWSc 92*
**Hardy,** Peter 1931- *Who 92*
**Hardy,** Ralph W. F. 1934- *WhoFI 92*
**Hardy,** Ralph Wilbur Frederick 1934- *AmMWSc 92*
**Hardy,** Rene 1912-1987 *FacFETw*
**Hardy,** Richard Earl 1938- *WrDr 92*
**Hardy,** Richard G. 1953- *WhoAmL 92*
**Hardy,** Robert *Who 92*
**Hardy,** Robert 1925- *IntWW 91*
**Hardy,** Robert Eugene 1926- *WhoEnt 92, WhoWest 92*
**Hardy,** Robert J 1935- *AmMWSc 92*
**Hardy,** Robert James 1924- *Who 92*
**Hardy,** Robert Maynard *Who 92*
**Hardy,** Robert Paul 1958- *WhoAmL 92*
**Hardy,** Robert W 1952- *AmMWSc 92*
**Hardy,** Rolland L 1920- *AmMWSc 92*
**Hardy,** Ronald W *AmMWSc 92*
**Hardy,** Rupert 1902- *Who 92*
**Hardy,** Russ *TwCWW 91*
**Hardy,** Stephen D. 1949- *WhoAmL 92*
**Hardy,** Thomas 1839-1928 *FacFETw [port]*
**Hardy,** Thomas 1840-1928 *CnDBLB 5 [port], RfGEnL 91*
**Hardy,** Thomas Cresson 1942- *WhoFI 92, WhoIns 92*
**Hardy,** Thomas Tenney 1952- *WhoFI 92*
**Hardy,** Timothy Sydney Robert 1925- *Who 92*
**Hardy,** Todd 1949- *WhoEnt 92*
**Hardy,** Vernon E 1937- *AmMWSc 92*
**Hardy,** Victoria Elizabeth 1947- *WhoEnt 92, WhoFI 92*
**Hardy,** Walter Newbold 1940- *AmMWSc 92*
**Hardy,** Walter S. E. 1920- *WhoBlA 92*
**Hardy,** Warren B *WhoAmP 91*
**Hardy,** William Lyle 1936- *AmMWSc 92*
**Hardy,** Willie J. 1922- *WhoBlA 92*
**Hardy,** Yvan J 1941- *AmMWSc 92*
**Hardy-Henrion,** Daphne *TwCPaSc*
**Hardy-Hill,** Edna Mae 1943- *WhoBlA 92*
**Hardy-Roberts,** Geoffrey 1907- *Who 92*
**Hardy-Woolridge,** Karen E. 1951- *WhoBlA 92*
**Hardyman,** Norman Trenchard 1930- *Who 92*
**Hardymon,** David Wayne 1949- *WhoAmL 92*
**Hardymon,** James F. 1934- *WhoFI 92*
**Hare** *Who 92*
**Hare,** Alan Victor 1919- *Who 92*
**Hare,** Curtis R 1933- *AmMWSc 92*
**Hare,** David 1947- *FacFETw, IntAu&W 91, IntMPA 92, IntWW 91, Who 92, WhoEnt 92, WrDr 92*
**Hare,** Frederick Kenneth 1919- *AmMWSc 92, Who 92*
**Hare,** Georgia B 1946- *WhoAmP 91*
**Hare,** James Frederic 1945- *AmMWSc 92*
**Hare,** Joan Conway 1943- *AmMWSc 92*
**Hare,** John 1935- *IntAu&W 91*

**Hare,** John Daniel, III 1948- *AmMWSc 92*
**Hare,** John Donald 1928- *AmMWSc 92*
**Hare,** John Innes Clark 1816-1905 *BiInAmS*
**Hare,** Julia Reed 1942- *WhoBlA 92*
**Hare,** Kenneth *Who 92*
**Hare,** Kenneth 1919- *IntWW 91*
**Hare,** Leonard N 1921- *AmMWSc 92*
**Hare,** Linda Paskett 1948- *WhoBlA 92*
**Hare,** Mary Louise Eckles 1916- *AmMWSc 92*
**Hare,** Nathan 1933- *WhoBlA 92*
**Hare,** Paul Julian 1937- *WhoAmP 91*
**Hare,** Peter Edgar 1933- *AmMWSc 92*
**Hare,** Peter Hewitt 1935- *WhoRel 92*
**Hare,** R. M. 1919- *WrDr 92*
**Hare,** Raymond Arthur 1901- *IntWW 91*
**Hare,** Richard *Who 92*
**Hare,** Richard, Mrs. *Who 92*
**Hare,** Richard Mervyn 1919- *IntWW 91, Who 92*
**Hare,** Robert 1781-1858 *BenetAL 91, BiInAmS*
**Hare,** Robert Lee, Jr. 1920- *WhoRel 92*
**Hare,** Robert Ritzinger, Jr 1925- *AmMWSc 92*
**Hare,** Roger C 1927- *WhoAmP 91*
**Hare,** Ronald Ray 1947- *WhoAmP 91*
**Hare,** Sandra Florence 1952- *WhoMW 92*
**Hare,** Thomas 1930- *Who 92*
**Hare,** Thomas Richard *Who 92*
**Hare,** Walter Ben 1870-1950 *BenetAL 91*
**Hare,** William Currie Douglas 1925- *AmMWSc 92*
**Hare,** William Ray, Jr 1936- *AmMWSc 92*
**Hare Duke,** Michael 1925- *WrDr 92*
**Hare Duke,** Michael Geoffrey *Who 92*
**Hare Duke,** Michael Geoffrey 1925- *IntWW 91*
**Harein,** Phillip Keith 1928- *AmMWSc 92*
**Harel,** Yair H. 1954- *WhoFI 92*
**Hareld,** Gail B. 1954- *WhoBlA 92*
**Harelson,** Hugh 1930- *WhoWest 92*
**Harenberg,** Paul E *WhoAmP 91*
**Harendza-Harinxma,** Alfred Josef 1919- *AmMWSc 92*
**Harer,** Lisa *WhoEnt 92*
**Hares,** George Bigelow 1921- *AmMWSc 92*
**Hares,** Phillip Douglas George 1926- *Who 92*
**Haresign,** Thomas 1932- *AmMWSc 92*
**Hareven,** Tamara K. 1937- *WrDr 92*
**Harewood,** Earl of 1923- *IntWW 91, Who 92*
**Harewood,** Dorian *WhoBlA 92*
**Harewood,** Dorian 1950- *IntMPA 92*
**Harewood,** Ken Rupert *AmMWSc 92*
**Harfenist,** Morton 1922- *AmMWSc 92*
**Harff,** Charles Henry 1929- *WhoAmL 92, WhoFI 92*
**Harfield,** Alan 1929- *IntAu&W 91*
**Harford,** Agnes Gayler 1941- *AmMWSc 92*
**Harford,** Carl Gayler 1906- *AmMWSc 92*
**Harford,** James 1899- *Who 92*
**Harford,** James J 1924- *AmMWSc 92*
**Harford,** John Timothy 1932- *Who 92*
**Harford,** W G W 1825-1911 *BiInAmS*
**Hargens,** Charles William, III 1918- *AmMWSc 92*
**Harger,** Harold Hainsworth 1923- *WhoMW 92*
**Harger,** Mark Alan 1954- *WhoMW 92*
**Harger,** Oscar 1843-1887 *BiInAmS*
**Harger,** Robert Owens 1932- *AmMWSc 92*
**Hargesheimer,** Elbert, III 1944- *WhoAmL 92*
**Hargest,** Thomas Sewell 1925- *AmMWSc 92*
**Harget,** Frederick 1742?-1810 *DcNCBi 3*
**Hargett,** Frederick 1742?-1810 *DcNCBi 3*
**Hargett,** Louie Thomas 1932- *WhoFI 92*
**Hargis,** Betty Jean 1925- *AmMWSc 92*
**Hargis,** Billy James 1925- *RelLAm 91, WhoRel 92*
**Hargis,** Earl David 1942- *WhoRel 92*
**Hargis,** I Glen 1939- *AmMWSc 92*
**Hargis,** J Howard 1942- *AmMWSc 92*
**Hargis,** Joseph Paul 1948- *WhoWest 92*
**Hargis,** Larry G 1939- *AmMWSc 92*
**Hargis,** Philip Joseph, Jr 1944- *AmMWSc 92*
**Hargis,** Steve V. 1963- *WhoEnt 92*
**Hargis,** William Jennings, Jr 1923- *AmMWSc 92*
**Hargiss,** James Leonard 1921- *WhoWest 92*
**Hargitai,** Peter *DrAPF 91*
**Hargitay,** Bartholomew 1924- *AmMWSc 92*
**Hargrave,** Benjamin 1917- *WhoBlA 92*
**Hargrave,** Charles William 1929- *WhoBlA 92*
**Hargrave,** Irvin P. H., Jr. 1935- *WhoIns 92*
**Hargrave,** Janie Carlyle 1893-1975 *DcNCBi 3*
**Hargrave,** Leonie *ConAu 36NR, WrDr 92*
**Hargrave,** Paul Allan 1938- *AmMWSc 92*
**Hargrave,** Richard 1803-1879 *DcNCBi 3*
**Hargrave,** Robert 1938- *WhoWest 92*
**Hargrave,** Robert Warren 1944- *WhoFI 92*
**Hargrave,** Rudolph *WhoAmP 91*
**Hargrave,** Rudolph 1925- *WhoAmL 92*
**Hargrave,** Sharon K 1958- *WhoAmP 91*
**Hargrave,** Thomas Burkhardt, Jr. 1926- *WhoBlA 92*
**Hargraves,** Paul E 1941- *AmMWSc 92*
**Hargraves,** Peter Laurence 1944- *WhoFI 92*
**Hargraves,** Robert Bero 1928- *AmMWSc 92*
**Hargraves,** William Frederick, II 1932- *WhoBlA 92*
**Hargreaves,** Andrew Raikes 1955- *Who 92*
**Hargreaves,** David Harold 1939- *Who 92*
**Hargreaves,** David William 1943- *WhoFI 92*
**Hargreaves,** George H 1916- *AmMWSc 92*
**Hargreaves,** Ian Richard 1951- *Who 92*
**Hargreaves,** John *IntMPA 92*
**Hargreaves,** John D. 1924- *WrDr 92*
**Hargreaves,** John Desmond 1924- *Who 92*
**Hargreaves,** Kenneth 1939- *Who 92*
**Hargreaves,** Leon Abraham, Jr 1921- *AmMWSc 92*
**Hargreaves,** Robert 1914- *WhoEnt 92*
**Hargreaves,** Ronald Thomas 1946- *AmMWSc 92*
**Hargreaves,** William Herbert 1908- *Who 92*
**Hargrett,** James T, Jr 1942- *WhoAmP 91, WhoBlA 92*
**Hargrove,** Andrew 1922- *WhoBlA 92*
**Hargrove,** Clifford Kingston 1928- *AmMWSc 92*
**Hargrove,** David Lawrence 1953- *WhoWest 92*
**Hargrove,** David Lee 1959- *WhoAmL 92*
**Hargrove,** Dean *LesBEnT 92*
**Hargrove,** Elson Payne 1935- *WhoRel 92*
**Hargrove,** Erwin C. 1930- *WrDr 92*
**Hargrove,** Frank DuVal 1927- *WhoAmP 91*
**Hargrove,** George Lynn 1935- *AmMWSc 92*
**Hargrove,** Jere L *WhoAmP 91*
**Hargrove,** Jerry Edward, Jr. 1949- *WhoRel 92*
**Hargrove,** Jim *WhoAmP 91*
**Hargrove,** John E. 1903- *WhoBlA 92*
**Hargrove,** John R. 1923- *WhoAmL 92, WhoBlA 92*
**Hargrove,** Logan Ezral 1935- *AmMWSc 92*
**Hargrove,** Marion 1919- *BenetAL 91*
**Hargrove,** Mike 1949- *WhoMW 92*
**Hargrove,** Milton Beverly 1920- *WhoBlA 92*
**Hargrove,** Patsy Tunstall 1941- *WhoAmP 91*
**Hargrove,** Richard Lee 1931- *WhoMW 92*
**Hargrove,** Robert Clyde 1918- *WhoAmL 92*
**Hargrove,** Robert John 1942- *AmMWSc 92*
**Hargrove,** Thomas Stephen 1954- *WhoEnt 92*
**Hargrove,** Trent 1955- *WhoBlA 92*
**Hargroves,** Louis 1917- *Who 92*
**Harhoff,** Preben 1911- *IntWW 91*
**Hari Dass,** Baba 1921?- *RelLAm 91*
**Hari,** V 1936- *AmMWSc 92*
**Harig,** John Joseph 1951- *WhoMW 92*
**Harinck,** John Gordon 1939- *WhoMW 92*
**Harine,** Katherine Jane 1944- *WhoWest 92*
**Haring,** Bernard 1912- *WrDr 92*
**Haring,** Bernhard 1912- *IntWW 91*
**Haring,** Ernette Rae 1936- *WhoAmP 91*
**Haring,** Firth *DrAPF 91*
**Haring,** Joseph E. 1931- *WrDr 92*
**Haring,** Keith 1958-1990 *AnObit 1990, WorArt 1980 [port]*
**Haring,** Olga M 1917- *AmMWSc 92*
**Harington,** Charles 1910- *Who 92*
**Harington,** Charles Richard 1933- *AmMWSc 92*
**Harington,** Donald *DrAPF 91*
**Harington,** Edward Henry Vernon 1907- *Who 92*
**Harington,** John 1560-1612 *RfGEnL 91*
**Harington,** Joy 1914- *WrDr 92*
**Harington,** Kenneth Douglas Evelyn H 1911- *Who 92*
**Harington,** Nicholas 1942- *Who 92*
**Harington,** Vernon *Who 92*
**Hariot,** Thomas 1560-1621 *BenetAL 91*
**Hariri,** Rafic Bahaa Edine 1944- *IntWW 91*
**Haririan,** Mehdi 1950- *WhoFI 92*
**Haris,** Joseph Smith 1836-1910 *BiInAmS*
**Harish,** Michael 1936- *IntWW 91*
**Haritatos,** James Stephen 1948- *WhoMW 92*
**Haritatos,** Nicholas John 1931- *AmMWSc 92*
**Harjani,** Ramesh 1959- *WhoMW 92*
**Harjo,** Joy *DrAPF 91*
**Harjo,** Joy 1951- *BenetAL 91, ConAu 35NR*
**Harjo,** Suzan Shown *DrAPF 91*
**Harju,** Philip Herman 1930- *AmMWSc 92*
**Harkavy,** Allan Abraham 1925- *AmMWSc 92*
**Harkavy,** Ira Baer 1931- *WhoAmL 92*
**Harkaway,** Hal *ScFEYrs*
**Harkawik,** Dennis Paul 1950- *WhoAmL 92*
**Harke,** Douglas J 1942- *AmMWSc 92*
**Harke,** Gary Lee 1948- *WhoRel 92*
**Harker,** Charles Lewis, Jr. 1945- *WhoMW 92*
**Harker,** David d1991 *NewYTBS 91 [port]*
**Harker,** David 1906- *AmMWSc 92*
**Harker,** David 1906-1991 *IntWW 91, -91N*
**Harker,** J M 1926- *AmMWSc 92*
**Harker,** Kenneth James 1927- *AmMWSc 92*
**Harker,** Robert Ian 1926- *AmMWSc 92*
**Harker,** Roger George 1945- *WhoWest 92*
**Harker,** Yale Deon 1937- *AmMWSc 92*
**Harkess,** Nancy Robyn 1944- *WhoAmP 91*
**Harkey,** Ira Brown, Jr 1918- *IntAu&W 91, WrDr 92*
**Harkey,** Jack W 1921- *AmMWSc 92*
**Harkey,** John Norman 1933- *WhoAmL 92*
**Harkey,** Robert Shelton 1940- *WhoAmL 92*
**Harkin,** Brendan 1920- *Who 92*
**Harkin,** James C 1926- *AmMWSc 92*
**Harkin,** John McLay 1933- *AmMWSc 92*
**Harkin,** Thomas R. 1939- *IntWW 91*
**Harkin,** Thomas Richard 1939- *NewYTBS 91 [port], WhoMW 92*
**Harkin,** Tom 1939- *AlmAP 92 [port], WhoAmP 91*
**Harkins,** Bernard Joseph 1915- *WhoAmP 91*
**Harkins,** Bonnie Lu 1940- *WhoEnt 92*
**Harkins,** Carl Girvin 1939- *AmMWSc 92*
**Harkins,** Craig 1936- *WhoWest 92*
**Harkins,** Daniel Conger 1960- *WhoAmL 92*
**Harkins,** David P. 1937- *WhoMW 92*
**Harkins,** Edwin L. 1940- *WhoEnt 92*
**Harkins,** Francis Joseph, Jr. 1949- *WhoAmL 92*
**Harkins,** George F. d1991 *NewYTBS 91*
**Harkins,** Gerard Francis Robert 1936- *Who 92*
**Harkins,** James M 1953- *WhoAmP 91*
**Harkins,** John Graham, Jr. 1931- *WhoAmL 92*
**Harkins,** Kristi R *AmMWSc 92*
**Harkins,** Lida Eisenstadt *WhoAmP 91*
**Harkins,** Michael E 1941- *WhoAmP 91*
**Harkins,** Patrick Gregory 1944- *WhoMW 92*
**Harkins,** Richard Erle 1932- *WhoMW 92*
**Harkins,** Richard Wesley 1946- *WhoMW 92*
**Harkins,** Robert W 1935- *AmMWSc 92*
**Harkins,** Rosemary Knighton 1938- *AmMWSc 92, WhoBlA 92*
**Harkins,** Thomas Regis 1929- *AmMWSc 92*
**Harkless,** Lawrence Bernard 1951- *AmMWSc 92*
**Harkless-Webb,** Mildred 1935- *WhoBlA 92*
**Harkna,** Eric 1940- *WhoMW 92*
**Harkness,** Bernie Carroll 1945- *WhoRel 92*
**Harkness,** D W 1941- *WhoAmP 91*
**Harkness,** David W. 1937- *WrDr 92*
**Harkness,** Donald R 1932- *AmMWSc 92*
**Harkness,** Douglas Scott 1903- *Who 92*
**Harkness,** Edward *DrAPF 91*
**Harkness,** Georgia E 1891-1974 *FacFETw*
**Harkness,** Georgia Elma 1891-1974 *AmPeW, RelLAm 91*
**Harkness,** Jack *Who 92*
**Harkness,** James 1935- *Who 92*
**Harkness,** James Percy Knowles 1916- *Who 92*
**Harkness,** Jerry 1940- *WhoBlA 92*
**Harkness,** John Leigh 1918- *Who 92*
**Harkness,** Laurence Patrick 1941- *WhoMW 92*
**Harkness,** Laurie Anne 1952- *WhoEnt 92*
**Harkness,** Samuel Dacke 1940- *AmMWSc 92*
**Harkness,** William 1837-1903 *BiInAmS*
**Harkness,** William H 1821?-1901 *BiInAmS*
**Harkness,** William Leonard 1934- *AmMWSc 92*
**Harknett,** Terry *TwCWW 91*
**Harkrader,** Alan Dale, Jr. 1928- *WhoMW 92*
**Harkrider,** David Garrison 1931- *AmMWSc 92*
**Harl,** Marie Annette 1968- *WhoMW 92*
**Harlam,** Ruth 1924- *AmMWSc 92*
**Harlan,** Bruce Lovell 1959- *WhoAmL 92*
**Harlan,** Elizabeth 1945- *IntAu&W 91*
**Harlan,** Glen *WrDr 92*
**Harlan,** Horace David 1929- *AmMWSc 92*
**Harlan,** Ivan Clair 1929- *WhoMW 92*
**Harlan,** Jack Rodney 1917- *AmMWSc 92, IntWW 91*
**Harlan,** Jane Ann 1947- *WhoAmL 92*
**Harlan,** John Marshall 1833-1911 *AmPolLe, FacFETw, RComAH*
**Harlan,** John Marshall 1947- *AmMWSc 92, WhoWest 92*
**Harlan,** John Marshall, II 1899-1971 *FacFETw*
**Harlan,** Kathleen T. 1934- *WhoWest 92*
**Harlan,** Leonard Morton 1936- *WhoFI 92*
**Harlan,** Michael Burl 1951- *WhoEnt 92*
**Harlan,** Mitchele James 1960- *WhoAmL 92*
**Harlan,** Neil Eugene 1921- *WhoWest 92*
**Harlan,** Norman Ralph 1914- *WhoFI 92, WhoMW 92*
**Harlan,** Phillip Walker 1944- *AmMWSc 92*
**Harlan,** Raymond Carter 1943- *WhoWest 92*
**Harlan,** Richard 1796-1843 *BiInAmS*
**Harlan,** Robert Ernest 1936- *WhoMW 92*
**Harlan,** Robert Ridge 1953- *WhoEnt 92*
**Harlan,** Ronald A 1937- *AmMWSc 92*
**Harlan,** Ross *TwCWW 91*
**Harlan,** Stephen Donald 1933- *WhoFI 92*
**Harlan,** Susan N 1949- *WhoAmP 91*
**Harlan,** Veit 1899-1964 *EncTR 91 [port]*
**Harlan,** William R, Jr 1930- *AmMWSc 92*
**Harland,** Barbara Ferguson *AmMWSc 92*
**Harland,** Bryce *Who 92*
**Harland,** Bryce 1931- *IntWW 91*
**Harland,** Glen Eugene, Jr 1933- *AmMWSc 92*
**Harland,** Henry 1861-1905 *BenetAL 91*
**Harland,** Ian *Who 92*
**Harland,** Jane A 1948- *WhoAmP 91*
**Harland,** Marion *BenetAL 91*
**Harland,** Reginald 1920- *Who 92*
**Harland,** Ronald Scott 1962- *AmMWSc 92*
**Harland,** William Bryce 1931- *Who 92*
**Harle,** Elizabeth *WrDr 92*
**Harle,** James Coffin 1920- *Who 92*
**Harle,** John Crofton 1956- *Who 92*
**Harle,** Thomas Stanley 1932- *AmMWSc 92*
**Harlech,** Baron 1954- *Who 92*
**Harlech,** Lord 1918-1985 *FacFETw*
**Harlech,** Pamela 1934- *Who 92*
**Harleman,** Ann *DrAPF 91*
**Harleman,** Ann 1945- *IntAu&W 91*
**Harleman,** Donald R F 1922- *AmMWSc 92*
**Harless,** Shirley Kay 1948- *WhoAmP 91*
**Harleston,** Bernard Warren 1930- *WhoBlA 92*
**Harleston,** Robert Alonzo 1936- *WhoBlA 92*
**Harlett,** John Charles 1936- *AmMWSc 92*
**Harley,** Alexander George Hamilton 1941- *Who 92*
**Harley,** Betty 1930- *WhoAmP 91*
**Harley,** Bill *ConMus 7 [port]*
**Harley,** Colin Emile 1940- *WhoAmL 92*
**Harley,** Colin Kent 1953- *WhoAmL 92*
**Harley,** Daniel P., Jr. 1929- *WhoBlA 92*
**Harley,** Ellen A 1946- *WhoAmP 91*
**Harley,** George Way 1894-1966 *DcNCBi 3*
**Harley,** Halvor Larson 1948- *WhoAmL 92*
**Harley,** John Barker 1949- *AmMWSc 92*
**Harley,** John Brian d1991 *NewYTBS 91*
**Harley,** John Laker d1990 *IntWW 91N, Who 92N*
**Harley,** Legrand 1956- *WhoBlA 92*
**Harley,** Naomi Hallden *AmMWSc 92*
**Harley,** Peter W, III 1940- *AmMWSc 92*
**Harley,** Philip A. *WhoBlA 92*
**Harley,** Ralph Leroy, Jr. 1934- *WhoMW 92*
**Harley,** Robison Dooling 1911- *AmMWSc 92*
**Harley,** Robison Dooling, Jr. 1946- *WhoAmL 92, WhoWest 92*
**Harley,** Thomas Winlack d1991 *Who 92N*
**Harley,** William G. *LesBEnT 92*
**Harlib,** Joel Edwin 1942- *WhoMW 92*
**Harlin,** Marilyn Miler 1934- *AmMWSc 92*
**Harlin,** Vivian Krause 1924- *AmMWSc 92*
**Harling,** Carlos Gene 1946- *WhoMW 92*
**Harling,** Otto Karl 1931- *AmMWSc 92*
**Harling,** Robert 1910- *WrDr 92*
**Harling,** Simon 1950- *TwCPaSc*
**Harllee,** Frederick Earl, III 1945- *WhoFI 92*
**Harllee,** John 1914- *WhoAmP 91*
**Harllee,** John, Jr. 1941- *WhoAmL 92*
**Harlow,** Alison 1934- *RelLAm 91*
**Harlow,** Bryce Larimore 1949- *WhoAmP 91*
**Harlow,** Charles Alton 1940- *AmMWSc 92*
**Harlow,** Charles Vendale, Jr. 1931- *WhoWest 92*
**Harlow,** Enid *DrAPF 91*

**Harlow,** Francis Harvey, Jr 1928- *AmMWSc 92*
**Harlow,** H Gilbert 1914- *AmMWSc 92*
**Harlow,** James Gindling, Jr. 1934- *WhoFI 92*
**Harlow,** Jean 1911-1937 *FacFETw*
**Harlow,** John *TwCWW 91*
**Harlow,** Larry 1939- *WhoEnt 92*
**Harlow,** Michael 1937- *ConPo 91, WrDr 92*
**Harlow,** Richard Fessenden 1919- *AmMWSc 92*
**Harlow,** Richard Leslie 1942- *AmMWSc 92*
**Harlow,** Steven Mark 1954- *WhoWest 92*
**Harm,** Stephen Douglas 1964- *WhoEnt 92*
**Harman,** Avraham 1914- *IntWW 91*
**Harman,** Buddy 1928- *WhoEnt 92*
**Harman,** Charles M 1929- *AmMWSc 92*
**Harman,** Charlton Newton 1915- *WhoAmP 91*
**Harman,** David Rex 1948- *WhoEnt 92*
**Harman,** Denham 1916- *AmMWSc 92, WhoMW 92*
**Harman,** Gary Elvan 1944- *AmMWSc 92*
**Harman,** George Gibson, Jr 1924- *AmMWSc 92*
**Harman,** Gilbert Helms 1938- *IntWW 91*
**Harman,** Gill 1928- *TwCPaSc*
**Harman,** Harriet 1950- *Who 92*
**Harman,** Jack 1920- *Who 92*
**Harman,** Jane *WrDr 92*
**Harman,** Jane Lakes 1945- *WhoAmL 92*
**Harman,** Jeremiah 1930- *Who 92*
**Harman,** John Bishop 1907- *Who 92*
**Harman,** John Royden 1921- *WhoAmL 92*
**Harman,** Kenneth R. 1927- *WhoRel 92*
**Harman,** Leonard Charles 1947- *WhoEnt 92*
**Harman,** Robert Charles 1936- *WhoWest 92*
**Harman,** Robert Dale 1937- *WhoAmP 91*
**Harman,** Robert Donald 1928- *Who 92*
**Harman,** Robert John 1937- *WhoRel 92*
**Harman,** Rod 1942- *TwCPaSc*
**Harman,** Ronald Vern 1932- *WhoRel 92*
**Harman,** T C 1929- *AmMWSc 92*
**Harman,** Walter James 1928- *AmMWSc 92*
**Harman,** Willard Nelson 1937- *AmMWSc 92*
**Harman,** William Boys, Jr 1930- *WhoIns 92*
**Harmar,** Fairlie d1945 *TwCPaSc*
**Harmar-Nicholls** *Who 92*
**Harmar-Nicholls,** Baron 1912- *Who 92*
**Harmel,** Merel H 1917- *AmMWSc 92*
**Harmel,** Pierre Charles Jose Marie 1911- *IntWW 91*
**Harmelink,** Glenn William 1951- *WhoMW 92*
**Harmelink,** Herman, III 1933- *WhoRel 92*
**Harmen,** Raymond A 1917- *AmMWSc 92*
**Harmer,** Catherine Mary 1932- *WhoRel 92*
**Harmer,** David Edward 1929- *AmMWSc 92*
**Harmer,** Don Stutler 1928- *AmMWSc 92*
**Harmer,** Dudley d1991 *Who 92N*
**Harmer,** Ernest G *ScFEYrs*
**Harmer,** Frederic 1905- *Who 92*
**Harmer,** Martin Paul 1954- *AmMWSc 92*
**Harmer,** Michael Hedley 1912- *Who 92*
**Harmer,** Richard Sharpless 1941- *AmMWSc 92*
**Harmet,** Kenneth Herman 1924- *AmMWSc 92*
**Harmison,** Jerry Alva, Jr. 1962- *WhoAmL 92*
**Harmoko** 1939- *IntWW 91*
**Harmon,** Alan Dale 1944- *AmMWSc 92*
**Harmon,** Bruce Norman 1947- *AmMWSc 92*
**Harmon,** Bud Gene 1931- *AmMWSc 92*
**Harmon,** Cynthia Ann 1956- *WhoEnt 92*
**Harmon,** Dale Joseph 1927- *AmMWSc 92*
**Harmon,** Daniel Patrick 1938- *WhoRel 92*
**Harmon,** David Elmer, Jr 1932- *AmMWSc 92, WhoMW 92*
**Harmon,** David Michael 1947- *WhoRel 92*
**Harmon,** Eddie 1947- *WhoMW 92*
**Harmon,** Elaine 1939- *WhoAmL 92*
**Harmon,** Ellen Taubenblatt 1954- *WhoAmL 92*
**Harmon,** Ernest N 1894-1979 *FacFETw*
**Harmon,** Francis Eugene 1921- *WhoMW 92*
**Harmon,** G Lamar 1931- *AmMWSc 92*
**Harmon,** Gail McGreevy 1943- *WhoAmL 92*
**Harmon,** Gene Lane 1925- *WhoEnt 92*
**Harmon,** George Andrew 1923- *AmMWSc 92*
**Harmon,** Gil *TwCWW 91*
**Harmon,** Glynn 1933- *AmMWSc 92*
**Harmon,** H James 1946- *AmMWSc 92*
**Harmon,** J Frank 1939- *AmMWSc 92*
**Harmon,** James Allen 1935- *WhoFI 92*
**Harmon,** James F., Sr. 1932- *WhoBlA 92*
**Harmon,** Jeffrey Joseph 1958- *WhoAmL 92*
**Harmon,** Jerry *WhoAmP 91*
**Harmon,** Jessie Kate 1942- *WhoBlA 92*
**Harmon,** Joan T *AmMWSc 92*
**Harmon,** John H. 1942- *WhoBlA 92*
**Harmon,** John W 1943- *AmMWSc 92*
**Harmon,** Joseph Spencer 1942- *WhoAmL 92*
**Harmon,** Kenneth Millard 1929- *AmMWSc 92*
**Harmon,** Larry *WhoEnt 92*
**Harmon,** Laurence George 1913- *AmMWSc 92*
**Harmon,** Leon David 1922- *AmMWSc 92*
**Harmon,** M. Larry 1944- *WhoBlA 92*
**Harmon,** Mark *LesBEnT 92*
**Harmon,** Mark 1951- *IntMPA 92, WhoEnt 92*
**Harmon,** Maurice 1930- *IntAu&W 91, WrDr 92*
**Harmon,** Melva Jane 1947- *WhoAmL 92*
**Harmon,** Nolan Bailey, Jr. 1892- *RelLAm 91*
**Harmon,** Richard L. 1950- *WhoEnt 92*
**Harmon,** Richard Lincoln 1923- *WhoWest 92*
**Harmon,** Robert E 1931- *AmMWSc 92*
**Harmon,** Robert Lon 1938- *WhoAmL 92*
**Harmon,** Robert Wayne 1929- *AmMWSc 92*
**Harmon,** Ronnie Keith 1964- *WhoBlA 92*
**Harmon,** Scott McKneely 1951- *WhoWest 92*
**Harmon,** Sherman Allen 1916- *WhoBlA 92*
**Harmon,** Stephanie Methvin 1951- *WhoRel 92*
**Harmon,** Thomas Delano 1940- *WhoAmL 92*
**Harmon,** Thomas Dudley 1919-1990 *FacFETw*
**Harmon,** Tim James *WhoMW 92*
**Harmon,** Tom 1920-1990 *AnObit 1990*
**Harmon,** Verdell Thate 1937- *WhoFI 92*
**Harmon,** Victoria Tham 1956- *WhoFI 92*
**Harmon,** Wallace Morrow 1933- *AmMWSc 92*
**Harmon,** Warren Wayne 1936- *WhoWest 92*
**Harmon,** William *DrAPF 91*
**Harmon,** William 1938- *ConAu 35NR, SmATA 65 [port]*
**Harmon,** William Lewis 1928- *AmMWSc 92*
**Harmon,** William Wesley 1941- *WhoBlA 92*
**Harmon-Brown,** Carol Jean 1949- *WhoAmL 92*
**Harmony,** Judith A K 1943- *AmMWSc 92*
**Harmony,** Marlin D 1936- *AmMWSc 92*
**Harmood-Banner,** George Knowles d1990 *Who 92N*
**Harms,** Archie A 1934- *AmMWSc 92*
**Harms,** Benjamin C 1939- *AmMWSc 92*
**Harms,** Carl 1910- *WhoEnt 92*
**Harms,** Clarence Eugene 1934- *AmMWSc 92*
**Harms,** David Kent 1955- *WhoFI 92*
**Harms,** Forrest *WhoRel 92*
**Harms,** Hans Heinrich 1914- *IntWW 91*
**Harms,** John Conrad 1930- *AmMWSc 92*
**Harms,** John Kevin 1960- *WhoAmL 92*
**Harms,** Michael Dwain 1964- *WhoMW 92*
**Harms,** Paul G 1941- *AmMWSc 92*
**Harms,** Robert Henry 1923- *AmMWSc 92*
**Harms,** Robert W. 1955- *WhoAmL 92*
**Harms,** Steven Alan 1949- *WhoAmL 92*
**Harms,** Valerie *DrAPF 91*
**Harms,** Vernon Lee 1930- *AmMWSc 92*
**Harms,** Wendell G 1949- *WhoAmP 91*
**Harms,** William Otto 1923- *AmMWSc 92*
**Harmsen,** Larry James 1939- *WhoMW 92*
**Harmsen,** Ricardo Eduardo 1955- *WhoHisp 92*
**Harmsen,** Rudolf 1933- *AmMWSc 92*
**Harmsworth** *Who 92*
**Harmsworth,** Baron 1939- *Who 92*
**Harmsworth,** Alfred Charles William *FacFETw*
**Harmsworth,** Esmond Cecil 1898-1978 *FacFETw*
**Harmsworth,** Hildebrand Harold 1931- *Who 92*
**Harmsworth,** St John Bernard Vyvyan 1912- *Who 92*
**Harmuth,** Charles Moore 1922- *AmMWSc 92*
**Harmuth,** Henning Friedolf 1928- *AmMWSc 92*
**Harn,** Douglas Evans 1950- *WhoRel 92*
**Harn,** J Dixie 1912- *WhoAmP 91*
**Harn,** Stanton Douglas 1945- *AmMWSc 92*
**Harnack,** Adolf Von 1851-1930 *EncEarC*
**Harnack,** Arvid 1901-1942 *EncTR 91*
**Harnack,** Curtis *DrAPF 91*
**Harnack,** Curtis 1927- *WrDr 92*
**Harnack,** Curtis Arthur 1927- *WhoEnt 92*
**Harnack,** Don Steger 1928- *WhoAmL 92*
**Harnack,** Ernst von 1888-1945 *EncTR 91 [port]*
**Harnak,** Kenneth John 1943- *WhoMW 92*
**Harnapp,** Harlan Lucine 1932- *WhoRel 92*
**Harnden,** Arthur Baker 1909- *Who 92*
**Harnden,** David Gilbert 1932- *Who 92*
**Harnden,** John D, Jr 1928- *AmMWSc 92*
**Harne,** Eleanor Elizabeth 1941- *WhoFI 92*
**Harned,** Ben King *AmMWSc 92*
**Harned,** Danielle D'Ottavio *DrAPF 91*
**Harned,** David Baily 1932- *ConAu 135*
**Harned,** Herbert Spencer, Jr 1921- *AmMWSc 92*
**Harned,** Roger Kent 1934- *WhoMW 92*
**Harnell,** Stewart D. 1938- *IntMPA 92*
**Harner,** Carol O'Leary 1923- *WhoAmP 91*
**Harner,** Doris Wilhide 1927- *WhoAmP 91*
**Harner,** James Philip 1943- *AmMWSc 92*
**Harner,** L. Elizabeth 1941- *WhoWest 92*
**Harner,** Michael J. 1929- *ConAu 134*
**Harner,** Victor Emmanuel 1962- *WhoRel 92*
**Harness,** Charles L 1915- *IntAu&W 91, TwCSFW 91, WrDr 92*
**Harness,** J. Harold 1941- *WhoRel 92*
**Harness,** William Edward 1940- *WhoEnt 92*
**Harnest,** Grant Hopkins 1916- *AmMWSc 92*
**Harnett,** Cornelius d1742 *DcNCBi 3*
**Harnett,** Cornelius, Jr. 1723-1781 *DcNCBi 3*
**Harnett,** James Francis 1921- *WhoEnt 92*
**Harnett,** R Michael 1944- *AmMWSc 92*
**Harnett,** Thomas Aquinas 1924- *WhoIns 92*
**Harnetty,** Charles Samuel 1937- *WhoAmP 91*
**Harney,** Brian Michael 1944- *AmMWSc 92*
**Harney,** David Moran 1924- *WhoAmL 92, WhoWest 92*
**Harney,** David Thayer 1951- *WhoEnt 92*
**Harney,** John Thomas 1933- *WhoAmP 91*
**Harney,** Patricia Marie 1925- *AmMWSc 92*
**Harney,** Robert Charles 1949- *AmMWSc 92*
**Harnick,** Sheldon Mayer 1924- *IntWW 91, WhoEnt 92*
**Harnier,** Adolf von 1903-1945 *EncTR 91 [port]*
**Harnik,** Hans d1991 *NewYTBS 91*
**Harniman,** John Phillip 1939- *Who 92*
**Harno,** Raymond Theodore 1929- *WhoWest 92*
**Harnois,** Michael David 1956- *WhoRel 92*
**Harnoncourt,** Nikolaus 1929- *CurBio 91 [port], IntWW 91, NewAmDM*
**Harnoy,** Ofra 1965- *IntWW 91*
**Harnsberger,** Caroline Thomas 1902-1991 *ConAu 134*
**Harnsberger,** Hugh Francis 1924- *AmMWSc 92*
**Harnsberger,** Therese Coscarelli *WhoWest 92*
**Harnwell,** Gaylord P 1903-1982 *FacFETw*
**Haro** 1952- *WhoWest 92*
**Haro,** Jess D. *WhoHisp 92*
**Haro,** Sid 1931- *WhoHisp 92*
**Haroian,** Alan James 1950- *AmMWSc 92*
**Harold,** Franklin Marcel 1929- *AmMWSc 92*
**Harold,** Paul Dennis 1948- *WhoAmP 91*
**Harold,** Ruth L 1931- *AmMWSc 92*
**Harold,** Stephen 1928- *AmMWSc 92*
**Haroldsen,** Craig Grant 1952- *WhoWest 92*
**Haroldson,** Steven A 1946- *WhoIns 92*
**Haron,** David Lawrence 1944- *WhoAmL 92*
**Haronitis,** G Vassilios 1933- *IntAu&W 91*
**Harootunian,** Lee Craig 1957- *WhoFI 92*
**Harowitz,** Charles Lichtenberg 1926- *AmMWSc 92*
**Harp,** George Lemaul 1936- *AmMWSc 92*
**Harp,** James A *AmMWSc 92*
**Harp,** Jimmy Frank 1933- *AmMWSc 92*
**Harp,** John G 1952- *WhoAmP 91*
**Harp,** Peter Hayt 1899- *WhoAmL 92*
**Harp,** Robert George, Jr. 1959- *WhoRel 92, WhoWest 92*
**Harp,** Rufus William 1923- *WhoEnt 92, WhoWest 92*
**Harp,** William Arthur 1942- *WhoFI 92*
**Harp,** William R, Jr 1919- *AmMWSc 92*
**Harpavat,** Ganesh Lal 1944- *AmMWSc 92*
**Harpell,** Gary Allan 1937- *AmMWSc 92*
**Harpending,** Henry Cosad 1944- *AmMWSc 92*
**Harper,** Alan A. d1991 *NewYTBS 91*
**Harper,** Alan G. 1945- *WhoMW 92*
**Harper,** Alexander Maitland 1926- *AmMWSc 92*
**Harper,** Alfred Alexander 1907- *Who 92*
**Harper,** Alfred Edwin 1922- *AmMWSc 92*
**Harper,** Alfred John, II 1942- *WhoAmL 92*
**Harper,** Alphonza Vealvert, III 1948- *WhoBlA 92*
**Harper,** Andrew Henry 1935- *WhoEnt 92*
**Harper,** Anna Louise 1960- *WhoAmP 91*
**Harper,** Bernice Catherine *WhoBlA 92*
**Harper,** Betty J *WhoAmP 91*
**Harper,** Beverly A. 1942- *WhoBlA 92*
**Harper,** Billy 1943- *WhoEnt 92*
**Harper,** Bobby Joe 1955- *WhoRel 92*
**Harper,** Bradley Drake 1964- *WhoEnt 92*
**Harper,** C A 1926- *AmMWSc 92*
**Harper,** Charles *WhoAmP 91*
**Harper,** Charles Little 1930- *IntWW 91*
**Harper,** Charles Michel 1927- *IntWW 91, WhoFI 92, WhoMW 92*
**Harper,** Charles Woods, Jr 1938- *AmMWSc 92*
**Harper,** Clifton Stewart, Jr. 1958- *WhoMW 92*
**Harper,** Conrad Kenneth 1940- *WhoAmL 92, WhoBlA 92*
**Harper,** Curtis 1937- *AmMWSc 92, WhoBlA 92*
**Harper,** Daniel *IntAu&W 91X, WrDr 92*
**Harper,** David B. 1933- *WhoBlA 92*
**Harper,** Dean Owen 1934- *AmMWSc 92*
**Harper,** Delphine Bernice 1947- *WhoFI 92*
**Harper,** Denis Rawnsley 1907- *Who 92*
**Harper,** Derek Ricardo 1961- *WhoBlA 92*
**Harper,** Dixon Ladd 1922- *WhoEnt 92*
**Harper,** Donald Calvin 1942- *WhoWest 92*
**Harper,** Donald John 1923- *Who 92*
**Harper,** Doyal Alexander, Jr 1944- *AmMWSc 92*
**Harper,** Dwain Lockhart 1937- *WhoMW 92*
**Harper,** Dwayne Anthony 1966- *WhoBlA 92*
**Harper,** Earl 1929- *WhoBlA 92*
**Harper,** Edward 1941- *ConCom 92*
**Harper,** Edward James 1941- *IntWW 91*
**Harper,** Edwin Leland 1941- *WhoAmP 91, WhoFI 92*
**Harper,** Edwin T 1935- *AmMWSc 92*
**Harper,** Elizabeth 1922- *WhoBlA 92*
**Harper,** Elvin 1930- *AmMWSc 92*
**Harper,** Emery Walter 1936- *WhoAmL 92*
**Harper,** Frances E. W. 1825-1911 *NotBlAW 92 [port]*
**Harper,** Frances Ellen Watkins 1825-1911 *AfrAmW, AmPeW, BenetAL 91, BlkLC [port], HanAmWH, ModAWWr*
**Harper,** Francis Edward 1936- *AmMWSc 92*
**Harper,** Frank Richard 1929- *AmMWSc 92*
**Harper,** Gary Lee 1937- *WhoMW 92*
**Harper,** George Graham, Jr. 1924- *WhoMW 92*
**Harper,** George Mills 1914- *IntAu&W 91, WrDr 92*
**Harper,** George W. *DrAPF 91*
**Harper,** George Washington Finley 1834-1921 *DcNCBi 3*
**Harper,** Geraldine 1933- *WhoBlA 92*
**Harper,** Gerard E 1953- *WhoAmP 91*
**Harper,** Gordon L 1946- *WhoAmP 91*
**Harper,** Gregory William 1952- *WhoEnt 92*
**Harper,** Hal 1948- *WhoAmP 91*
**Harper,** Harold Anthony 1911- *AmMWSc 92*
**Harper,** Harry Dandridge 1934- *WhoBlA 92*
**Harper,** Heather 1930- *IntWW 91, NewAmDM, Who 92*
**Harper,** Henry Amos, Jr 1942- *AmMWSc 92*
**Harper,** Herbert Caldwell 1912- *WhoFI 92*
**Harper,** Howard 1904-1978 *ConAu 133*
**Harper,** Irving 1916- *DcTwDes*
**Harper,** James 1799-1879 *DcNCBi 3*
**Harper,** James, Jr. 1949- *WhoMW 92*
**Harper,** James Arthur 1916- *AmMWSc 92*
**Harper,** James Clarence 1819-1890 *DcNCBi 3*
**Harper,** James Douglas 1942- *AmMWSc 92*
**Harper,** James Eugene 1940- *AmMWSc 92*
**Harper,** James George 1934- *AmMWSc 92*
**Harper,** James Mitchell 1950- *WhoWest 92*
**Harper,** James Norman 1932- *Who 92*
**Harper,** James Roland 1918- *WhoAmL 92*
**Harper,** James Weldon, III 1937- *WhoFI 92*
**Harper,** Janet Sutherlin Lane 1940- *WhoEnt 92*
**Harper,** Jessica 1949- *IntMPA 92*
**Harper,** Joe 1941- *IntMPA 92*
**Harper,** Joe Steven 1947- *WhoRel 92*
**Harper,** John Brammer 1941- *WhoEnt 92*
**Harper,** John D 1930- *WhoAmP 91*
**Harper,** John David 1939- *AmMWSc 92*
**Harper,** John Harris 1938- *WhoAmL 92*
**Harper,** John Lander 1925- *IntWW 91, Who 92*
**Harper,** John Mansfield 1930- *Who 92*
**Harper,** John Martin 1947- *Who 92*

Harper, John Roy, II 1939- WhoAmP 91
Harper, Jon Jay 1941- AmMWSc 92
Harper, Joseph H, Jr 1948- WhoAmP 91
Harper, Joseph W., III 1931- WhoBlA 92
Harper, Judith Jean 1951- AmMWSc 92
Harper, Judson M 1936- AmMWSc 92
Harper, Judson Morse 1936- IntWW 91, WhoWest 92
Harper, Kendrick 1919- WhoBlA 92
Harper, Kennard W 1906- AmMWSc 92
Harper, Kenneth Charles 1946- WhoRel 92, WhoWest 92
Harper, Kenneth Franklin 1931- WhoAmP 91
Harper, Kenneth Marion 1948- WhoAmP 91
Harper, Kimball T 1931- AmMWSc 92
Harper, Kimball Taylor 1931- WhoWest 92
Harper, Laura Jane 1914- AmMWSc 92
Harper, Laurence Raymond, Jr 1929- AmMWSc 92
Harper, Lawrence Hueston 1938- AmMWSc 92
Harper, Leonard Alfred 1920-1991 WhoBlA 92N
Harper, Margaret Pease 1911- WhoEnt 92
Harper, Mary L. 1925- WhoBlA 92
Harper, Mary Starke 1919- WhoBlA 92
Harper, Michael John Kennedy 1935- AmMWSc 92
Harper, Michael S. DrAPF 91
Harper, Michael S 1928- IntAu&W 91
Harper, Michael S. 1938- BenetAL 91, ConPo 91, WrDr 92
Harper, Michael Steven 1938- WhoBlA 92
Harper, Mitchell Van 1956- WhoAmP 91
Harper, Neville W. WhoBlA 92
Harper, Oliver William, III 1953- WhoMW 92
Harper, Patricia Mullaney 1932- WhoAmP 91
Harper, Paul Alva 1904- AmMWSc 92
Harper, Paul Church, Jr. 1920- WhoFI 92
Harper, Paul Vincent 1915- AmMWSc 92
Harper, Pierre Paul 1942- AmMWSc 92
Harper, Richard A. IntMPA 92
Harper, Richard Allan AmMWSc 92
Harper, Richard Henry 1950- WhoEnt 92, WhoWest 92
Harper, Richard L WhoAmP 91
Harper, Richard Waltz 1943- AmMWSc 92
Harper, Robert WhoAmP 91
Harper, Robert Andrew 1954- WhoEnt 92
Harper, Robert Goodloe 1765-1825 DcNCBi 3
Harper, Robert John, Jr 1930- AmMWSc 92
Harper, Robert Lee 1920- WhoBlA 92
Harper, Robert Levell 1942- WhoWest 92
Harper, Ron 1951- WhoEnt 92
Harper, Ronald 1964- WhoBlA 92
Harper, Ronald Dean 1935- WhoRel 92
Harper, Ronald J. 1945- WhoBlA 92
Harper, Ross 1935- Who 92
Harper, Roy W. 1905- WhoAmL 92, WhoAmP 91, WhoMW 92
Harper, Ruth B. 1927- WhoBlA 92
Harper, Ruth Bebe 1927- WhoAmP 91
Harper, Ruth Elise 1951- WhoMW 92
Harper, Sara J. 1926- WhoBlA 92
Harper, Sarah Elizabeth WhoBlA 92
Harper, Stephen 1924- IntAu&W 91
Harper, T. Errol 1947- WhoBlA 92
Harper, Taylor F WhoAmP 91
Harper, Ted Alan 1947- WhoIns 92
Harper, Terry 1955- WhoBlA 92
Harper, Terry Layne 1948- WhoRel 92
Harper, Tess 1952- IntMPA 92
Harper, Thelma Marie 1940- WhoAmP 91, WhoBlA 92
Harper, Tommy 1940- WhoBlA 92
Harper, Valerie LesBEnT 92
Harper, Valerie 1940- IntMPA 92, WhoEnt 92
Harper, Verne Lester 1902- AmMWSc 92
Harper, Vincent ScFEYrs
Harper, Wallace George 1939- WhoEnt 92
Harper, Walter Edward, Jr. 1950- WhoBlA 92
Harper, Walter Joseph 1947- WhoFI 92
Harper, William A. 1915- IntMPA 92
Harper, William Hudson 1949- WhoEnt 92
Harper, William Robert 1952- WhoRel 92
Harper, William Ronald 1944- Who 92
Harper, Williard Flemmett 1924- WhoMW 92
Harper, Willis James 1923- AmMWSc 92
Harper Gow, Maxwell 1918- Who 92
Harpham, William 1906- Who 92
Harpley, Sydney 1927- TwCPaSc
Harpley, Sydney Charles 1927- IntWW 91, Who 92
Harpold, Michael Alan 1940- AmMWSc 92
Harpole, Wilma Kathryn 1933- WhoMW 92
Harpool, Doug 1956- WhoAmP 91
Harpp, David Noble 1937- AmMWSc 92
Harpprecht, Klaus Christoph 1927- IntWW 91
Harps, William S. 1916- WhoBlA 92
Harpst, Jerry Adams 1936- AmMWSc 92
Harpstead, Dale D 1926- AmMWSc 92
Harpstead, Dale Douglas 1926- WhoMW 92
Harpstead, Milo I 1930- AmMWSc 92
Harpster, James Erving 1923- WhoAmL 92
Harpster, Joseph 1932- AmMWSc 92
Harpster, Robert E 1930- AmMWSc 92
Harpur, Charles 1813-1868 RfGEnL 91
Harpur, Robert Peter 1921- AmMWSc 92
Harpur, Thomas William 1929- WhoRel 92
Harr, Barbara DrAPF 91
Harr, Dennis Gordon 1942- WhoMW 92
Harr, Joseph WhoRel 92
Harr, Lawrence F 1938- WhoIns 92
Harr, Robert Dennis 1941- AmMWSc 92
Harr, Sheldon Jay 1946- WhoRel 92
Harrach, Robert James 1937- AmMWSc 92
Harral, John Menteith 1948- WhoAmL 92
Harral, William Michael 1942- WhoFI 92, WhoMW 92
Harral McNally, Loretta Margaret 1957- WhoAmP 91
Harran, Bruce Foorde 1942- WhoMW 92
Harrap, George G. 1867-1938 DcLB 112 [port]
Harrar, Ellwood Scott, Jr. 1905-1975 DcNCBi 3
Harrar, Jackson Elwood 1930- AmMWSc 92
Harrawood, Paul 1928- AmMWSc 92
Harre, Alan Frederick 1940- WhoFI 92, WhoMW 92
Harre, Rom 1927- WrDr 92
Harre, T Everett 1884-1948 ScFEYrs
Harreld, James Bruce 1950- WhoFI 92
Harrell, Ann McKelvain 1952- WhoEnt 92
Harrell, Anthony James 1954- WhoBlA 92
Harrell, Byron Eugene 1924- AmMWSc 92
Harrell, Charles H. WhoBlA 92
Harrell, Costen Jordan 1885-1971 DcNCBi 3
Harrell, David Edwin, Jr. 1930- ConAu 34NR, WrDr 92
Harrell, Ernest James 1936- WhoBlA 92
Harrell, George T 1908- AmMWSc 92
Harrell, Gwendolyn Baumann 1958- WhoAmL 92
Harrell, H. Steve 1948- WhoBlA 92
Harrell, Irene Burk 1927- WrDr 92
Harrell, James Andrew, Sr. 1922- WhoRel 92
Harrell, James H 1937- WhoAmP 91
Harrell, James W, Jr 1942- AmMWSc 92
Harrell, Jerald Rice 1935- AmMWSc 92
Harrell, John 1806-1876 DcNCBi 3
Harrell, Limmie Lee, Jr. 1941- WhoAmL 92
Harrell, Linwood Parker, Jr. 1938- WhoFI 92
Harrell, Lynn 1944- IntWW 91, NewAmDM
Harrell, Lynn Morris 1944- WhoEnt 92, WhoWest 92
Harrell, Mack 1909-1960 NewAmDM
Harrell, Oscar W., Jr. WhoBlA 92
Harrell, Richard WhoEnt 92
Harrell, Robert L. 1930- WhoBlA 92
Harrell, Robert Wesley, Jr 1939- WhoAmP 91
Harrell, Ronald Earl 1944- AmMWSc 92
Harrell, Roy Harrison, Jr. 1928- WhoRel 92
Harrell, Ruth Flinn 1900- AmMWSc 92
Harrell, Samuel Macy 1931- WhoFI 92, WhoMW 92
Harrell, Shari Lynn 1958- WhoMW 92
Harrell, Stanley Maxie 1933- WhoFI 92
Harrell, Stephen Paul 1947- WhoRel 92
Harrell, Susan Wright 1956- WhoAmL 92
Harrell, T Gibson 1916- AmMWSc 92
Harrell, William Bernard 1823-1906 DcNCBi 3
Harrell, William Broomfield 1928- AmMWSc 92
Harrell, William Edwin 1962- WhoBlA 92
Harrelson, F. Daniel 1942- WhoAmL 92
Harrelson, John William 1885-1955 DcNCBi 3
Harrelson, Larry Eugene 1944- WhoRel 92
Harrelson, Walter Joseph 1919- WhoRel 92, WrDr 92
Harrelson, Woody WhoEnt 92
Harrelson, Woody 1961- IntMPA 92
Harren, Richard Edward 1922- AmMWSc 92
Harrenstien, Howard P 1931- AmMWSc 92
Harrer, Heinrich 1912- Who 92
Harrer, Karl 1890-1926 BiDExR
Harrhy, Eiddwen Mair 1949- Who 92
Harrice, Nicholas Cy 1915- WhoEnt 92
Harrienger, Tracy Scott 1962- WhoAmL 92
Harries, Hinrich 1928- AmMWSc 92
Harries, Richard Douglas Who 92
Harries, Richard Douglas 1936- IntWW 91
Harries, Wynford Lewis 1923- AmMWSc 92
Harriford, Daphne WrDr 92
Harrigan, Claire 1964- TwCPaSc
Harrigan, Edward 1845-1911 BenetAL 91, DcAmImH
Harrigan, John Frederick 1925- WhoWest 92
Harrigan, Kenneth William J. 1927- WhoFI 92
Harrigan, Lucille Frasca 1930- WhoAmP 91
Harrigan, Nancy Stafford 1941- WhoAmL 92
Harrigan, Rodney Emile 1945- WhoBlA 92
Harriger, Gary Carl 1940- WhoFI 92
Harrill, Bob E 1930- WhoAmP 91
Harrill, Fred Falls 1948- WhoAmP 91
Harrill, Inez Kemble 1917- AmMWSc 92
Harrill, Robert W 1941- AmMWSc 92
Harriman, Arthur J. d1991 NewYTBS 91
Harriman, Benjamin Ramage 1913- AmMWSc 92
Harriman, Craig Gordon 1950- WhoRel 92, WhoWest 92
Harriman, David Parker 1948- WhoAmL 92
Harriman, John E 1936- AmMWSc 92
Harriman, John Howland 1920- WhoAmP 91
Harriman, Katherine Jordan 1915- WhoAmP 91
Harriman, Leslie Oriseweyinmi 1930- IntWW 91
Harriman, Malcolm Bruce 1950- WhoFI 92
Harriman, Morril Hilton, Jr 1950- WhoAmP 91
Harriman, Neil Arthur 1938- AmMWSc 92
Harriman, Philip Darling 1937- AmMWSc 92
Harriman, Richard Lee 1932- WhoMW 92
Harriman, W Averell 1891-1986 FacFETw [port], RComAH
Harrington, Earl of 1922- Who 92
Harrington, Alan DrAPF 91
Harrington, Albert Blair 1914- Who 92
Harrington, Anthony Ross 1958- WhoEnt 92
Harrington, Bob 1950- WhoEnt 92
Harrington, Carol A. 1953- WhoAmL 92
Harrington, Charles 1856-1908 BiInAmS
Harrington, Charles E. 1923- WhoBlA 92
Harrington, Curtis 1928- IntMPA 92, WhoEnt 92
Harrington, Dalton 1934- AmMWSc 92
Harrington, Daniel Dale 1937- AmMWSc 92
Harrington, Daniel William 1938- WhoAmP 91
Harrington, David Daniel 1942- WhoFI 92
Harrington, David Holman 1937- AmMWSc 92
Harrington, David Rogers 1935- AmMWSc 92
Harrington, Dean Butler AmMWSc 92
Harrington, Deborah Kathleen 1960- WhoFI 92
Harrington, Donald James 1945- WhoRel 92
Harrington, Donald Szantho 1914- WhoAmP 91
Harrington, Edmund Aloysius, Jr 1943- AmMWSc 92
Harrington, Edward Dennis, Jr 1921- WhoAmP 91
Harrington, Edward F. 1933- WhoAmL 92
Harrington, Edward James 1926- AmMWSc 92
Harrington, Elaine Carolyn 1938- WhoBlA 92
Harrington, Ellis Jackson, Jr. 1944- WhoAmL 92
Harrington, Fred Haddox 1947- AmMWSc 92
Harrington, Fred Harvey 1912- IntWW 91
Harrington, Gary 1953- ConAu 135
Harrington, George William 1929- AmMWSc 92
Harrington, Gerald E. 1945- WhoBlA 92
Harrington, Glenn Lewis 1942- WhoFI 92, WhoWest 92
Harrington, Glenn William 1932- AmMWSc 92
Harrington, Hannah Karajian 1958- WhoRel 92
Harrington, Henry William 1747-1809 DcNCBi 3
Harrington, Herbert 1946- WhoFI 92
Harrington, Illtyd 1931- Who 92
Harrington, J. B. 1930- WhoRel 92
Harrington, J.G. 1960- WhoAmL 92
Harrington, James 1611-1677 BlkwCEP
Harrington, James Foster 1916- AmMWSc 92
Harrington, James Patrick 1939- AmMWSc 92
Harrington, James Thomas 1949- WhoAmP 91
Harrington, James Timothy 1942- WhoAmL 92
Harrington, Jan Donald 1943- WhoMW 92
Harrington, Jeremy Thomas 1932- WhoRel 92
Harrington, John B., Jr. d1973 LesBEnT 92
Harrington, John Charles 1929- WhoWest 92
Harrington, John Vincent 1919- AmMWSc 92
Harrington, John Wilbur 1918- AmMWSc 92
Harrington, Joseph Anthony 1939- AmMWSc 92
Harrington, Joseph D 1930- AmMWSc 92
Harrington, Joseph Donald 1926- AmMWSc 92
Harrington, Joseph Francis 1938- WhoFI 92
Harrington, Joseph Julian 1919- WhoAmP 91
Harrington, Kevin F. 1961- WhoEnt 92
Harrington, Larry David 1938- WhoMW 92
Harrington, Leonard 1922- WhoIns 92
Harrington, Louis Draper 1939- WhoAmL 92
Harrington, Malcolm W WhoAmP 91
Harrington, Marguerite Ann 1949- WhoFI 92
Harrington, Marian R WhoAmP 91
Harrington, Mark Garland 1953- WhoWest 92
Harrington, Marshall Cathcart 1904- AmMWSc 92
Harrington, Martin L 1929- WhoAmP 91
Harrington, Michael 1928- BenetAL 91
Harrington, Michael 1928-1989 AmPeW, FacFETw, RComAH
Harrington, Michael James, Sr 1945- WhoAmP 91
Harrington, Michael Joseph 1936- WhoAmP 91
Harrington, Michaele Mary 1946- WhoEnt 92
Harrington, Nathan Russell 1870-1899 BiInAmS
Harrington, Pat 1929- IntMPA 92
Harrington, Paul C 1950- WhoAmP 91
Harrington, Paul W 1934- WhoAmP 91
Harrington, Peter F 1936- WhoAmP 91
Harrington, Peter Tyrus 1951- WhoFI 92
Harrington, Philip Leroy 1946- WhoBlA 92
Harrington, Richard Arvin 1943- WhoWest 92
Harrington, Richart Hart 1936- WhoFI 92
Harrington, Robert D 1928- AmMWSc 92
Harrington, Robert Joseph 1941- AmMWSc 92
Harrington, Robert Sutton 1942- AmMWSc 92
Harrington, Rodney B 1931- AmMWSc 92
Harrington, Rodney E 1932- AmMWSc 92
Harrington, Roger F 1925- AmMWSc 92
Harrington, Roy Victor 1928- AmMWSc 92
Harrington, Sherman B. 1948- WhoMW 92
Harrington, Steven Jay 1947- AmMWSc 92
Harrington, Thomas Barrett 1936- WhoAmL 92
Harrington, Thomas Neal 1953- WhoAmL 92
Harrington, Timothy J. 1918- WhoRel 92
Harrington, Walter Howard, Jr. 1926- WhoWest 92
Harrington, Walter Joel 1916- AmMWSc 92
Harrington, William 1931- WhoEnt 92
Harrington, William Fields 1920- AmMWSc 92
Harrington, Zella Mason 1940- WhoBlA 92
Harrington-Lloyd, Jeanne Leigh WhoWest 92
Harriot, Thomas BenetAL 91
Harriot, Thomas 1560-1621 DcNCBi 3
Harriott, Esther WhoFI 92
Harriott, Peter 1927- AmMWSc 92
Harriott, Thomas 1560-1621 DcNCBi 3
Harris Who 92
Harris, Baron 1920- Who 92
Harris, Adrian Llewellyn 1950- Who 92
Harris, Al Carl 1956- WhoBlA 92
Harris, Alan 1916- Who 92
Harris, Alan William 1944- AmMWSc 92

**Harris,** Albert Edward 1927- IntWW 91
**Harris,** Albert Hall 1905- AmMWSc 92
**Harris,** Albert J. 1908- WrDr 92
**Harris,** Albert Kenneth, Jr 1943- AmMWSc 92
**Harris,** Albert Zeke 1938- AmMWSc 92
**Harris,** Alex L 1954- AmMWSc 92
**Harris,** Alexander L 1954- AmMWSc 92
**Harris,** Alfred DrAPF 91
**Harris,** Alfred 1930- TwCPaSc
**Harris,** Alfred Peter 1932- WhoMW 92
**Harris,** Alice Eaton 1924- WhoEnt 92
**Harris,** Allen 1929- WhoAmL 92
**Harris,** Alva H 1928- AmMWSc 92
**Harris,** Andrew Leonard 1951- AmMWSc 92
**Harris,** Andy Clay 1961- WhoRel 92
**Harris,** Angela P. 1961- WhoAmL 92
**Harris,** Anne Macintosh 1925- Who 92
**Harris,** Anthony 1918- Who 92
**Harris,** Anthony 1931- TwCPaSc
**Harris,** Anthony David 1941- Who 92
**Harris,** Anthony Geoffrey S. Who 92
**Harris,** Anthony Leonard 1935- Who 92
**Harris,** Archie Jerome 1950- WhoBlA 92
**Harris,** Arlo Dean 1934- AmMWSc 92
**Harris,** Arthur Brooks 1935- AmMWSc 92
**Harris,** Arthur Horne 1931- AmMWSc 92
**Harris,** Arthur Leonard, III 1949- WhoBlA 92
**Harris,** Arthur Travers 1892-1984 EncTR 91 [port], FacFETw
**Harris,** Augustine Who 92
**Harris,** Augustine 1917- IntWW 91
**Harris,** Aurand 1915- ConAu 36NR, IntAu&W 91, WhoEnt 92, WrDr 92
**Harris,** B L 1917- AmMWSc 92
**Harris,** Barbara 1930- NotBlAW 92 [port]
**Harris,** Barbara 1935- IntMPA 92, WhoEnt 92
**Harris,** Barbara 1951- FacFETw
**Harris,** Barbara Ann 1951- WhoBlA 92
**Harris,** Barbara Clemente 1931- WhoBlA 92
**Harris,** Barbara Clementine 1930- RelLAm 91, WhoRel 92
**Harris,** Barbara Hull 1921- WhoWest 92
**Harris,** Barney, Jr 1931- AmMWSc 92
**Harris,** Basil Vivian 1921- Who 92
**Harris,** Bayard Easter 1944- WhoAmL 92
**Harris,** Ben Gerald 1940- AmMWSc 92
**Harris,** Benjamin d1716? BenetAL 91
**Harris,** Benjamin Harte, Jr. 1937- WhoAmL 92
**Harris,** Bernard 1926- AmMWSc 92
**Harris,** Bernard 1927- AmMWSc 92
**Harris,** Bernice Eisen 1927- WhoFI 92
**Harris,** Bernice Kelly 1891-1973 DcNCBi 3
**Harris,** Bert J, Jr 1919- WhoAmP 91
**Harris,** Bertha DrAPF 91
**Harris,** Betty Wright 1940- WhoBlA 92
**Harris,** Beverly Howard 1927- AmMWSc 92
**Harris,** Bill 1916-1973 NewAmDM
**Harris,** Bill 1925-1988 WhoBlA 92N
**Harris,** Bill 1939- WhoAmP 91
**Harris,** Bravid Washington 1896-1965 DcNCBi 3
**Harris,** Brian Who 92
**Harris,** Brian Craig 1941- WhoAmL 92
**Harris,** Brian Nicholas 1931- Who 92
**Harris,** Brian Thomas 1932- Who 92
**Harris,** Bruce Eugene 1950- WhoFI 92
**Harris,** Bruce Fairgray 1921- WrDr 92
**Harris,** Bruno 1932- AmMWSc 92
**Harris,** Bryant G. 1916- WhoBlA 92
**Harris,** Burnell 1954- WhoBlA 92
**Harris,** Burt Mitchell 1930- WhoEnt 92
**Harris,** Burtt IntMPA 92
**Harris,** C Earl, Jr 1930- AmMWSc 92
**Harris,** Calvin D. 1941- WhoBlA 92
**Harris,** Carl Gordon 1936- WhoBlA 92
**Harris,** Carl Matthew 1940- AmMWSc 92
**Harris,** Carl Randall 1951- WhoFI 92
**Harris,** Carlton Phillip 1957- WhoRel 92
**Harris,** Carole Riggs 1939- WhoEnt 92
**Harris,** Caroline Aiken Jenkins 1847-1903? DcNCBi 3
**Harris,** Carolyn Ann 1953- WhoBlA 92
**Harris,** Caspa L., Jr. 1928- WhoBlA 92
**Harris,** Cassandra d1991 NewYTBS 91
**Harris,** Cecil Craig 1925- AmMWSc 92
**Harris,** Cecil Rhodes 1923- Who 92
**Harris,** Charles TwCPaSc, Who 92
**Harris,** Charles 1923- AmMWSc 92
**Harris,** Charles Albert 1952- WhoBlA 92
**Harris,** Charles Bonner 1940- AmMWSc 92
**Harris,** Charles Cornelius 1951- WhoBlA 92
**Harris,** Charles Cox 1952- WhoAmP 91
**Harris,** Charles Edison 1946- WhoFI 92
**Harris,** Charles Elmer 1922- WhoAmL 92, WhoMW 92
**Harris,** Charles F. 1934- WhoBlA 92
**Harris,** Charles Herbert S. Who 92
**Harris,** Charles Joseph 1853-1944 DcNCBi 3
**Harris,** Charles K. 1865-1930 BenetAL 91, NewAmDM
**Harris,** Charles Lawrence 1942- AmMWSc 92
**Harris,** Charles Leon 1943- AmMWSc 92
**Harris,** Charles Marcus 1943- WhoAmL 92
**Harris,** Charles Ronald 1932- AmMWSc 92
**Harris,** Charles S. 1950- WhoWest 92
**Harris,** Charles Somerville 1950- WhoBlA 92
**Harris,** Charles Wesley 1929- WhoBlA 92
**Harris,** Charles Wilson 1771-1804 DcNCBi 3
**Harris,** Chauncy D 1914- IntAu&W 91, WrDr 92
**Harris,** Chauncy Dennison 1914- IntWW 91, WhoMW 92
**Harris,** Chris 1948- WhoAmP 91
**Harris,** Christie 1907- IntAu&W 91, WrDr 92
**Harris,** Christie Lucy 1907- WhoWest 92
**Harris,** Christopher IntAu&W 91X
**Harris,** Christy Franklin 1945- WhoAmL 92
**Harris,** Clare I 1933- AmMWSc 92
**Harris,** Clare Winger 1891- ScFEYrs
**Harris,** Claude 1940- WhoAmP 91
**Harris,** Claude, Jr. 1940- AlmAP 92 [port]
**Harris,** Clifton L. 1938- WhoBlA 92
**Harris,** Colin C 1928- AmMWSc 92
**Harris,** Colin Grendon 1912- Who 92
**Harris,** Curtis Alexander 1956- WhoBlA 92
**Harris,** Curtis C 1943- AmMWSc 92
**Harris,** Cynthia Julian 1953- WhoBlA 92
**Harris,** Cyril Manton AmMWSc 92
**Harris,** D. George 1933- WhoFI 92
**Harris,** D Lee 1916- AmMWSc 92
**Harris,** Daisy 1931- WhoBlA 92
**Harris,** Dale Ray 1937- WhoAmL 92, WhoWest 92
**Harris,** Daniel Charles 1948- AmMWSc 92
**Harris,** Daniel Everett 1934- AmMWSc 92
**Harris,** Danny 1965- BlkOlyM
**Harris,** Darryl Lyndon 1951- WhoFI 92
**Harris,** David WhoAmP 91
**Harris,** David 1922- Who 92
**Harris,** David 1934- WhoRel 92
**Harris,** David, Jr. 1931- WhoBlA 92
**Harris,** David Anthony 1937- Who 92
**Harris,** David Christopher 1954- WhoFI 92
**Harris,** David Ellsworth 1934- WhoBlA 92
**Harris,** David Jack 1948- WhoWest 92
**Harris,** David Joel 1950- WhoFI 92
**Harris,** David L. 1952- WhoBlA 92
**Harris,** David Michael 1943- Who 92
**Harris,** David Michael 1947- WhoFI 92
**Harris,** David Owen 1939- AmMWSc 92
**Harris,** David Philip 1937- WhoMW 92
**Harris,** David R 1932- AmMWSc 92
**Harris,** David Russell 1930- Who 92
**Harris,** David Vernon 1910- AmMWSc 92
**Harris,** Deborah Turner 1951- ConAu 135
**Harris,** Debra Coral 1953- WhoWest 92
**Harris,** Del William WhoMW 92
**Harris,** Delbert Linn 1943- AmMWSc 92
**Harris,** DeLong d1985 WhoBlA 92N
**Harris,** Dennis George AmMWSc 92
**Harris,** Denny Olan 1937- AmMWSc 92
**Harris,** DeVerle Porter 1931- AmMWSc 92
**Harris,** Dewey Lynn 1933- AmMWSc 92
**Harris,** DeWitt O. 1944- WhoBlA 92
**Harris,** Diana DcNCBi 3
**Harris,** Diana R. Who 92
**Harris,** Dolores M. 1930- WhoBlA 92
**Harris,** Don Navarro 1929- AmMWSc 92, WhoBlA 92
**Harris,** Don Victor, Jr. 1921- WhoFI 92
**Harris,** Donald 1931- WhoEnt 92
**Harris,** Donald Bertram 1904- Who 92
**Harris,** Donald Blake 1954- WhoFI 92
**Harris,** Donald C 1936- AmMWSc 92
**Harris,** Donald J. WhoBlA 92
**Harris,** Donald James 1953- WhoMW 92
**Harris,** Donald R, Jr 1925- AmMWSc 92
**Harris,** Donald Stuart 1940- WhoBlA 92
**Harris,** Donald Wayne 1942- AmMWSc 92
**Harris,** Donnell Ray 1936- WhoRel 92
**Harris,** Dorothy Vilma 1936- WhoHisp 92
**Harris,** Dorothy Virginia 1931- AmMWSc 92
**Harris,** Douglas Allen 1942- WhoBlA 92
**Harris,** Douglas Allen 1954- WhoRel 92
**Harris,** Douglas Bryan 1954- WhoEnt 92
**Harris,** Douglas Clay 1939- WhoFI 92
**Harris,** Dudley Arthur 1925- WrDr 92
**Harris,** Durward Smith 1931- AmMWSc 92
**Harris,** Earl 1922- WhoBlA 92
**Harris,** Earl L WhoAmP 91
**Harris,** Earl L. 1941- WhoBlA 92
**Harris,** Ed 1950- IntMPA 92
**Harris,** Ed Jerome J 1920- WhoAmP 91
**Harris,** Edmund Leslie 1928- Who 92
**Harris,** Edward 1763-1813 DcNCBi 3
**Harris,** Edward 1799-1863 BiInAmS
**Harris,** Edward A. 1946- WhoEnt 92, WhoWest 92
**Harris,** Edward Allen 1950- WhoEnt 92
**Harris,** Edward David 1938- AmMWSc 92
**Harris,** Edward Day, Jr 1937- AmMWSc 92
**Harris,** Edward E. 1933- WhoBlA 92
**Harris,** Edward Grant 1924- AmMWSc 92
**Harris,** Edward Lyndol 1933- AmMWSc 92
**Harris,** Edward Paxton 1938- WhoFI 92, WhoMW 92
**Harris,** Edward Richard, Jr 1928- WhoAmP 91
**Harris,** Edwin 1891-1961 TwCPaSc
**Harris,** Edwin Cyrus 1940- WhoAmP 91
**Harris,** Edwin Everett 1952- WhoWest 92
**Harris,** Edwin Ledbetter, III 1950- WhoAmL 92
**Harris,** Edwin Randall 1932- AmMWSc 92
**Harris,** Elbert L. 1913- WhoBlA 92
**Harris,** Elihu Mason 1947- WhoAmP 91, WhoBlA 92, WhoWest 92
**Harris,** Elijah Paddock 1832-1920 BiInAmS
**Harris,** Elizabeth Forsyth 1935- AmMWSc 92
**Harris,** Elizabeth Holder 1944- AmMWSc 92
**Harris,** Elliott Stanley 1922- AmMWSc 92
**Harris,** Elmer Beseler 1939- WhoFI 92
**Harris,** Elroy 1966- WhoBlA 92
**Harris,** Emily Katharine DrAPF 91
**Harris,** Emma Earl 1936- WhoWest 92
**Harris,** Emmett Dewitt, Jr 1925- AmMWSc 92
**Harris,** Emmylou 1947- News 91 [port], -91-3 [port], WhoEnt 92
**Harris,** Emmylou 1949- NewAmDM
**Harris,** Emory Franklin 1937- WhoFI 92
**Harris,** Eric Albert 1920- WhoWest 92
**Harris,** Eric Nathan 1959- WhoWest 92
**Harris,** Erik Preston 1938- AmMWSc 92
**Harris,** Ernest James 1928- AmMWSc 92
**Harris,** Eugene Edward 1940- WhoBlA 92
**Harris,** F. Chandler 1914- WhoWest 92
**Harris,** Fletcher 1926- WhoAmP 91
**Harris,** Forest K 1902- AmMWSc 92
**Harris,** Forrest Joseph 1916- WhoAmP 91
**Harris,** Frances Alvord 1909- WhoEnt 92
**Harris,** Francis Laurie 1939- AmMWSc 92
**Harris,** Franco 1950- WhoBlA 92
**Harris,** Frank Who 92, WhoBlA 92
**Harris,** Frank 1854-1931 ScFEYrs
**Harris,** Frank 1856-1931 BenetAL 91, FacFETw, RfGEnL 91
**Harris,** Frank 1934- Who 92
**Harris,** Frank Bower, Jr 1927- AmMWSc 92
**Harris,** Frank Ephraim, Jr 1929- AmMWSc 92
**Harris,** Frank W 1920- WhoAmP 91
**Harris,** Frank Wayne 1942- AmMWSc 92
**Harris,** Franklin Stewart, Jr 1912- AmMWSc 92
**Harris,** Fred WhoBlA 92
**Harris,** Fred R 1930- WhoAmP 91, WrDr 92
**Harris,** Frederick Allan 1941- WhoWest 92
**Harris,** Freeman Cosmo 1935- WhoBlA 92
**Harris,** Gale Ion 1935- AmMWSc 92
**Harris,** Garry Preston 1949- WhoMW 92
**Harris,** Gary Lynn 1953- WhoBlA 92
**Harris,** Geoffrey 1928- TwCPaSc
**Harris,** Geoffrey Charles 1945- Who 92
**Harris,** Geoffrey Herbert 1914- Who 92
**Harris,** George Bryan 1964- WhoAmL 92
**Harris,** George Christe 1916- AmMWSc 92
**Harris,** George Clinton 1925- WhoRel 92, WhoWest 92
**Harris,** George Dea 1945- WhoBlA 92
**Harris,** George Emrick 1827-1911 DcNCBi 3
**Harris,** George H d1905 BiInAmS
**Harris,** George Washington 1814-1869 BenetAL 91
**Harris,** Geraldine 1951- WrDr 92
**Harris,** Geraldine E. WhoBlA 92
**Harris,** Gerard Francis 1957- WhoEnt 92
**Harris,** Gil W. 1946- WhoBlA 92
**Harris,** Gladys Bailey 1947- WhoAmL 92, WhoBlA 92
**Harris,** Gleason Ray 1952- WhoBlA 92
**Harris,** Glen WhoEnt 92
**Harris,** Glen Alan 1960- WhoRel 92
**Harris,** Glenn, Jr. 1929- WhoWest 92
**Harris,** Glenn H 1919- WhoAmP 91
**Harris,** Godfrey 1937- WhoFI 92, WhoWest 92
**Harris,** Gordon McLeod 1913- AmMWSc 92
**Harris,** Grant Anderson 1914- AmMWSc 92
**Harris,** Gregory George 1951- WhoAmL 92
**Harris,** Grover Cleveland, Jr 1931- AmMWSc 92
**Harris,** Guy H 1914- AmMWSc 92
**Harris,** H. S. 1926- WrDr 92
**Harris,** Harcourt Glenties 1928- WhoBlA 92
**Harris,** Harold H 1940- AmMWSc 92
**Harris,** Harold Joseph 1920- AmMWSc 92
**Harris,** Harry LesBEnT 92
**Harris,** Harry 1919- AmMWSc 92, IntWW 91, Who 92
**Harris,** Harwell 1903-1990 CurBio 91N
**Harris,** Harwell Hamilton d1990 IntWW 91N
**Harris,** Hassel B. 1931- WhoBlA 92
**Harris,** Helen 1927- WrDr 92
**Harris,** Helen B. 1925- WhoBlA 92
**Harris,** Henry 1925- IntWW 91, Who 92
**Harris,** Henry Earl 1936- AmMWSc 92
**Harris,** Henry Upham, Jr. 1926- WhoFI 92
**Harris,** Henry William 1919- AmMWSc 92
**Harris,** Henry Wood 1938- WhoEnt 92
**Harris,** Henson 1912- AmMWSc 92
**Harris,** Herbert 1911- WrDr 92
**Harris,** Herbert E, II 1926- WhoAmP 91
**Harris,** Herbert H 1906- AmMWSc 92
**Harris,** Holly Ann AmMWSc 92
**Harris,** Horatio Preston 1925- WhoBlA 92
**Harris,** Howard F. 1909- WhoBlA 92
**Harris,** Howard Jeffrey 1949- WhoWest 92
**Harris,** Hubert Andrew 1909- AmMWSc 92
**Harris,** Hugh Christopher Emlyn 1936- Who 92
**Harris,** Hugh Courtney 1947- AmMWSc 92
**Harris,** Hunter Lee 1866-1893 DcNCBi 3
**Harris,** Ian 1910- Who 92
**Harris,** Irene Joyce 1926- Who 92
**Harris,** Irving Brooks 1910- WhoFI 92
**Harris,** Isaac Foust 1879-1953 DcNCBi 3
**Harris,** Isadore 1927- AmMWSc 92
**Harris,** J Douglas 1939- AmMWSc 92
**Harris,** J Henry ScFEYrs
**Harris,** J Mervyn 1933- WhoAmP 91
**Harris,** J Ollie 1913- WhoAmP 91
**Harris,** J. Robert, II 1944- WhoBlA 92
**Harris,** J S 1920- AmMWSc 92
**Harris,** Jack WhoBlA 92
**Harris,** Jack H 1931- WhoAmP 91
**Harris,** Jack Howard, II 1945- WhoFI 92
**Harris,** Jack Kenyon 1945- AmMWSc 92
**Harris,** Jack R 1930- AmMWSc 92
**Harris,** Jack Wolfred Ashford 1906- Who 92
**Harris,** James 1709-1780 BlkwCEP
**Harris,** James, III WhoBlA 92
**Harris,** James A. 1926- WhoBlA 92
**Harris,** James Andrew 1932- WhoBlA 92
**Harris,** James B. 1928- IntMPA 92
**Harris,** James David 1953- WhoFI 92
**Harris,** James Douglas, Jr. 1943- WhoAmL 92
**Harris,** James E. 1946- WhoBlA 92
**Harris,** James Edward 1928- AmMWSc 92
**Harris,** James Edward 1947- WhoAmL 92
**Harris,** James Edward, III 1955- WhoWest 92
**Harris,** James G., Jr. 1931- WhoBlA 92
**Harris,** James Gordon 1940- WhoMW 92, WhoRel 92
**Harris,** James Harold, III 1943- WhoAmL 92
**Harris,** James Henry 1832-1891 DcNCBi 3
**Harris,** James Howard 1961- WhoEnt 92
**Harris,** James Joseph 1930- AmMWSc 92
**Harris,** James L. 1962- WhoAmL 92
**Harris,** James Ridout 1920- AmMWSc 92
**Harris,** James Stewart, Jr 1942- AmMWSc 92
**Harris,** James Thomas, III 1958- WhoMW 92
**Harris,** James Thornton 1951- WhoWest 92
**Harris,** James Wilbur 1948- WhoAmP 91
**Harris,** Jana DrAPF 91
**Harris,** Jana 1947- WrDr 92
**Harris,** Jana N 1947- IntAu&W 91
**Harris,** Jane E 1946- AmMWSc 92
**Harris,** Jasper William 1935- WhoBlA 92
**Harris,** Jay H 1936- AmMWSc 92
**Harris,** Jay Terrence 1948- WhoBlA 92
**Harris,** Jean Laney 1932- WhoAmP 91
**Harris,** Jean Louise 1931- AmMWSc 92, WhoBlA 92, WhoMW 92
**Harris,** Jeanette G. 1934- WhoBlA 92
**Harris,** Jed Gilbert, Jr 1954- WhoAmP 91
**Harris,** Jeffrey 1932- TwCPaSc
**Harris,** Jeffrey Mark 1946- WhoAmL 92
**Harris,** Jerome A. 1943- WhoMW 92
**Harris,** Jerome C., Jr. 1947- WhoBlA 92
**Harris,** Jerome Sylvan 1909- AmMWSc 92
**Harris,** Jesse Booker, Jr. 1943- WhoMW 92
**Harris,** Jesse Ray 1937- AmMWSc 92

Harris, Jimmie 1945- *WhoBlA 92*
Harris, Joan White 1931- *WhoEnt 92*
Harris, Joe Frank 1936- *WhoAmP 91*
Harris, Joe Newton 1946- *WhoWest 92*
Harris, Joel B. 1939- *WhoMW 92*
Harris, Joel Bruce 1941- *WhoAmL 92*
Harris, Joel Chandler 1848-1908 *BenetAL 91*
Harris, Joel Mark 1950- *AmMWSc 92*
Harris, John *WrDr 92*
Harris, John 1916- *IntAu&W 91*
Harris, John 1916-1991 *ConAu 134*
Harris, John Arland 1946- *WhoRel 92*
Harris, John Cebern Logan 1847-1918 *DcNCBi 3*
Harris, John Charles 1936- *Who 92*
Harris, John Clifton 1935- *WhoBlA 92*
Harris, John Colin 1943- *WhoRel 92*
Harris, John Edwin 1932- *Who 92*
Harris, John Everett 1930- *WhoBlA 92*
Harris, John F. 1931- *WrDr 92*
Harris, John Ferguson, Jr 1925- *AmMWSc 92*
Harris, John Frederick 1931- *Who 92*
Harris, John Frederick 1938- *Who 92*
Harris, John H. 1940- *WhoBlA 92*
Harris, John Hulme 1938- *Who 92*
Harris, John J. 1951- *WhoBlA 92*
Harris, John Kenneth 1934- *AmMWSc 92*
Harris, John Kenneth 1948- *WhoAmL 92*
Harris, John Michael 1942- *AmMWSc 92*
Harris, John Myron 1926- *WhoAmP 91*
Harris, John Percival 1925- *Who 92*
Harris, John Robert 1919- *IntWW 91, Who 92*
Harris, John Wallace 1941- *AmMWSc 92*
Harris, John Wayne 1937- *AmMWSc 92*
Harris, John William 1920- *AmMWSc 92*
Harris, John William 1949- *AmMWSc 92*
Harris, John William 1950- *WhoWest 92*
Harris, John Woods 1893- *WhoFI 92*
Harris, Jon 1943- *TwCPaSc*
Harris, Jonathan 1919- *WhoEnt 92*
Harris, Jonathan 1921- *WrDr 92*
Harris, Jonathan Toby 1953- *Who 92*
Harris, Jordan *WhoEnt 92*
Harris, Joseph *DrAPF 91*
Harris, Joseph 1919- *AmMWSc 92*
Harris, Joseph Belknap 1926- *AmMWSc 92, WhoMW 92*
Harris, Joseph Benjamin 1920- *WhoBlA 92*
Harris, Joseph Eugene, Sr. 1938- *WhoEnt 92*
Harris, Joseph Eugene, Sr. 1942- *WhoRel 92*
Harris, Joseph Henry 1959- *WhoRel 92*
Harris, Joseph John, III 1946- *WhoBlA 92*
Harris, Joseph McAllister 1929- *WhoMW 92*
Harris, Joseph P 1938- *WhoAmP 91*
Harris, Joseph Preston 1935- *WhoBlA 92*
Harris, Joseph R. 1937- *WhoBlA 92*
Harris, Joy *Who 92*
Harris, Joya Renee 1961- *WhoMW 92*
Harris, Judia C. Jackson 1873-19--? *NotBlAW 92*
Harris, Judith Anne Van Couvering 1938- *AmMWSc 92*
Harris, Jules Eli 1934- *AmMWSc 92*
Harris, Julie *IntMPA 92, NewYTBS 91 [port]*
Harris, Julie 1925- *FacFETw, IntMPA 92, IntWW 91, WhoEnt 92*
Harris, Julius 1940- *WhoBlA 92*
Harris, K. David 1927- *WhoAmL 92, WhoAmP 91, WhoMW 92*
Harris, Karen Kostock 1942- *WhoFI 92*
Harris, Katherine Leidel 1954- *WhoEnt 92*
Harris, Kathy Jean 1951- *WhoEnt 92*
Harris, Keith Murray 1932- *Who 92*
Harris, Keith Stell 1952- *WhoWest 92*
Harris, Kenneth 1919- *IntAu&W 91, IntWW 91*
Harris, Kenneth 1943- *AmMWSc 92*
Harris, Kenneth Alan 1955- *WhoFI 92*
Harris, Kenny D 1950- *WhoAmP 91*
Harris, Kerry Francis Patrick 1943- *AmMWSc 92*
Harris, Kevin Michael 1957- *WhoAmL 92*
Harris, Kim Sutherland 1952- *WhoFI 92*
Harris, King William 1943- *WhoMW 92*
Harris, Kip King 1945- *WhoWest 92*
Harris, Lara 1962- *WhoEnt 92*
Harris, Larry Eugene 1939- *WhoMW 92*
Harris, Larry Mark *WrDr 92*
Harris, Larry Vordell, Jr. 1954- *WhoBlA 92*
Harris, Lavinia *WrDr 92*
Harris, Lawren 1885-1970 *FacFETw*
Harris, Lawrence Dean 1942- *AmMWSc 92*
Harris, Lawrence Eugene 1956- *WhoFI 92*
Harris, Lawrence Kenneth 1935- *WhoWest 92*
Harris, Lawrence Peyton, Jr. 1947- *WhoFI 92*
Harris, Lawson P 1929- *AmMWSc 92*
Harris, Lee 1941- *WhoBlA 92*
Harris, Lee Andrew, II 1958- *WhoBlA 92*
Harris, Lee Errol 1953- *AmMWSc 92*
Harris, Leland 1924- *AmMWSc 92*
Harris, Leodis 1934- *WhoBlA 92*
Harris, Leon L. *WhoBlA 92*
Harris, Leonard 1929- *WrDr 92*
Harris, Leonard Andrew 1928- *AmMWSc 92*
Harris, Leonard Anthony 1966- *WhoBlA 92*
Harris, Leonard John 1941- *Who 92*
Harris, Leonard Milton 1960- *WhoBlA 92*
Harris, Leonard R. d1991 *NewYTBS 91 [port]*
Harris, Leonard R 1922- *IntAu&W 91*
Harris, Leonce Everett 1941- *AmMWSc 92*
Harris, Lester 1920- *WhoAmP 91*
Harris, Lester Earle, Jr 1922- *AmMWSc 92*
Harris, Lester L. *WhoBlA 92*
Harris, Lewis Eldon 1910- *AmMWSc 92*
Harris, Lewis John 1910- *Who 92*
Harris, Lewis Philip 1907- *AmMWSc 92*
Harris, Linda Kay 1947- *WhoEnt 92*
Harris, Linda Marie 1940- *WhoBlA 92*
Harris, Lloyd David 1940- *WhoRel 92*
Harris, Lorenzo W. 1921- *WhoBlA 92*
Harris, Loretta K. 1935- *WhoBlA 92*
Harris, Louis Selig 1927- *AmMWSc 92*
Harris, Lowell Dee 1943- *AmMWSc 92*
Harris, Loyd Ervin 1900- *AmMWSc 92*
Harris, Lucy Brown 1924- *WhoFI 92*
Harris, Lusia Mae 1955- *BlkOlyM*
Harris, Lyndon Goodwin 1928- *TwCPaSc, Who 92*
Harris, M. L. 1954- *WhoBlA 92*
Harris, MacDonald 1921- *WrDr 92*
Harris, Malcolm Stephen 1943- *WhoWest 92*
Harris, Marcelite J. 1943- *NotBlAW 92 [port], WhoBlA 92*
Harris, Marcella H. Eason 1925- *WhoMW 92*
Harris, Margaret 1943- *WhoEnt 92*
Harris, Margaret Frances 1904- *Who 92*
Harris, Margaret May 1929- *WhoMW 92*
Harris, Margaret R. 1943- *WhoBlA 92*
Harris, Marian L 1941- *WhoAmP 91*
Harris, Marie *DrAPF 91*
Harris, Marilyn 1931- *IntAu&W 91, WrDr 92*
Harris, Marilyn A *WhoAmP 91*
Harris, Marilyn L. 1950- *WhoMW 92*
Harris, Marilyn Rittenhouse 1935- *WhoWest 92*
Harris, Marion 1925- *WrDr 92*
Harris, Marion Hopkins 1938- *WhoBlA 92*
Harris, Marion Rex 1934- *WhoBlA 92*
Harris, Marion Rose 1925- *IntAu&W 91*
Harris, Marjorie Elizabeth 1924- *WhoBlA 92*
Harris, Marjorie Fields 1964- *WhoEnt 92*
Harris, Marjorie Iler 1925- *WhoAmP 91*
Harris, Mark *DrAPF 91*
Harris, Mark 1922- *BenetAL 91, ConNov 91, WrDr 92*
Harris, Mark 1943- *Who 92*
Harris, Mark 1954- *TwCPaSc*
Harris, Mark Hugh 1932- *WhoRel 92*
Harris, Mark Jonathan *DrAPF 91*
Harris, Mark O 1950- *WhoAmP 91*
Harris, Martha Ann 1946- *WhoRel 92*
Harris, Martin Best 1944- *IntWW 91, Who 92*
Harris, Martin H 1937- *AmMWSc 92*
Harris, Martin Richard 1922- *Who 92*
Harris, Martin Stephen 1939- *WhoWest 92*
Harris, Marvin Kirk 1943- *AmMWSc 92*
Harris, Mary 1943- *ConAu 135*
Harris, Mary Lorraine 1954- *WhoBlA 92*
Harris, Mary Styles 1949- *AmMWSc 92, WhoBlA 92*
Harris, MaryAnn 1946- *WhoBlA 92*
Harris, Matthew Lester 1956- *WhoEnt 92*
Harris, Matthew N 1931- *AmMWSc 92*
Harris, Mattie Pearle 1938- *WhoRel 92*
Harris, Maureen Isabelle 1943- *AmMWSc 92*
Harris, Maurice A. 1942- *WhoBlA 92*
Harris, Maurice Kingston 1916- *Who 92*
Harris, Maury Norton 1947- *WhoFI 92*
Harris, Mel *WhoEnt 92*
Harris, Mel 1957- *IntMPA 92*
Harris, Melvin 1953- *WhoBlA 92*
Harris, Melvyn H 1932- *AmMWSc 92*
Harris, Merry Baxter 1921- *IntAu&W 91*
Harris, Micalyn Shafer 1941- *WhoAmL 92, WhoFI 92*
Harris, Michael Christopher 1963- *WhoEnt 92*
Harris, Michael Dale 1963- *WhoRel 92*
Harris, Michael David 1950- *WhoWest 92*
Harris, Michael Gene 1942- *WhoAmL 92, WhoWest 92*
Harris, Michael George Temple 1941- *Who 92*
Harris, Michael James 1954- *WhoEnt 92*
Harris, Michael Richard 1936- *WhoWest 92*
Harris, Michael Robert 1940- *WhoAmL 92*
Harris, Michael Wesley 1945- *WhoBlA 92*
Harris, Michele Roles 1945- *WhoBlA 92*
Harris, Miles Fitzgerald 1913- *AmMWSc 92*
Harris, Milton d1991 *NewYTBS 91*
Harris, Milton 1906- *AmMWSc 92*
Harris, Morgan 1916- *AmMWSc 92*
Harris, Morton Allen 1934- *WhoAmL 92*
Harris, Morton E 1934- *AmMWSc 92*
Harris, Morton Edward 1934- *WhoMW 92*
Harris, Muriel Sheila 1937- *WhoMW 92*
Harris, Nancy C. *DrAPF 91*
Harris, Narvie J. *WhoBlA 92*
Harris, Nathaniel C., Jr. 1941- *WhoBlA 92*
Harris, Natholyn Dalton 1939- *AmMWSc 92*
Harris, Neil 1938- *WhoMW 92*
Harris, Neison 1915- *WhoMW 92*
Harris, Nellie Robbins 1917- *AmMWSc 92*
Harris, Nelson A. 1922- *WhoBlA 92*
Harris, Nelson George 1926- *WhoFI 92*
Harris, Nick A. 1952- *WhoMW 92, WhoRel 92*
Harris, Nigel John 1943- *Who 92*
Harris, Noah Alan, Sr. 1920- *WhoBlA 92*
Harris, Norman Oliver 1917- *AmMWSc 92*
Harris, Norman W., Jr. 1924- *WhoBlA 92*
Harris, Orene Elizabeth 1945- *WhoEnt 92*
Harris, Orland Harold 1932- *WhoAmP 91*
Harris, Oscar L., Jr. 1945- *WhoBlA 92*
Harris, Oscar Lewis 1943- *WhoBlA 92*
Harris, P J 1926- *AmMWSc 92*
Harris, Patricia 1924-1985 *NotBlAW 92 [port]*
Harris, Patricia Ann 1939- *Who 92*
Harris, Patricia J 1921- *AmMWSc 92*
Harris, Patricia Lea 1952- *WhoMW 92*
Harris, Patricia Roberts 1924-1985 *AmPolLe, ConBlB 2 [port], FacFETw*
Harris, Patrick Bradley 1911- *WhoAmP 91*
Harris, Patrick Burnet *Who 92*
Harris, Patrick Donald 1940- *AmMWSc 92*
Harris, Patrick Joseph, II 1964- *WhoEnt 92*
Harris, Pattie Lou 1934- *WhoEnt 92*
Harris, Paul Chappell 1930- *AmMWSc 92*
Harris, Paul E. *WhoBlA 92*
Harris, Paul Jonathan 1953- *AmMWSc 92*
Harris, Paul Percy 1868-1947 *AmPeW*
Harris, Paul Robert 1942- *AmMWSc 92*
Harris, Percy G. 1927- *WhoBlA 92*
Harris, Peter 1930- *AmMWSc 92*
Harris, Peter Bernard 1929- *WrDr 92*
Harris, Peter Charles 1923- *Who 92*
Harris, Peter J. 1955- *WhoBlA 92*
Harris, Peter Langridge 1929- *Who 92*
Harris, Peter Michael 1937- *Who 92*
Harris, Phil 1906- *IntMPA 92*
Harris, Phil B. 1918- *WhoAmL 92*
Harris, Philip 1915- *Who 92*
Harris, Philip 1942- *Who 92*
Harris, Philip Robert 1926- *IntAu&W 91, WrDr 92*
Harris, Phillip 1922- *Who 92*
Harris, Phyllis Irene 1927- *WhoMW 92*
Harris, R. Robert 1933- *WhoAmL 92*
Harris, Rae Lawrence, Jr 1926- *AmMWSc 92*
Harris, Ralph Rogers 1929- *AmMWSc 92*
Harris, Ramon Stanton 1926- *WhoBlA 92*
Harris, Randy *WhoFI 92*
Harris, Randy James 1964- *WhoRel 92*
Harris, Randy Jay 1946- *WhoFI 92*
Harris, Ransom Baine 1927- *WhoRel 92*
Harris, Ray, Sr. 1947- *WhoBlA 92*
Harris, Rayford Lee 1924- *WhoAmP 91*
Harris, Raymond 1919- *AmMWSc 92*
Harris, Reece Thomas 1932- *AmMWSc 92*
Harris, Reginald Brian 1934- *Who 92*
Harris, Reginald Lee 1890-1959 *DcNCBi 3*
Harris, Reuben Rivers 1867-1933 *DcNCBi 3*
Harris, Richard 1930- *IntMPA 92*
Harris, Richard 1933?- *ConTFT 9, WhoEnt 92*
Harris, Richard 1944- *AmMWSc 92*
Harris, Richard, Jr. 1923- *WhoBlA 92*
Harris, Richard Anthony Sidney 1940- *WhoFI 92*
Harris, Richard Elgin 1941- *AmMWSc 92*
Harris, Richard Foster, III 1942- *WhoAmL 92*
Harris, Richard Foster, Jr. 1918- *WhoFI 92*
Harris, Richard Franklin 1940- *WhoIns 92*
Harris, Richard Jacob 1945- *AmMWSc 92*
Harris, Richard Jerome 1940- *WhoWest 92*
Harris, Richard Lee 1934- *AmMWSc 92*
Harris, Richard Lee 1944- *WhoFI 92*
Harris, Richard Max 1935- *WhoFI 92*
Harris, Richard R. St. Johns 1933- *IntWW 91*
Harris, Richard Reader 1913- *Who 92*
Harris, Richard Steven 1949- *WhoMW 92*
Harris, Richard Travis 1919- *IntWW 91, Who 92*
Harris, Richard Vernon 1955- *WhoEnt 92*
Harris, Richard Wilson 1920- *AmMWSc 92*
Harris, Robert *IntMPA 92*
Harris, Robert 1900- *Who 92*
Harris, Robert A 1936- *AmMWSc 92*
Harris, Robert A. 1945- *IntMPA 92*
Harris, Robert Allen *WhoAmP 91*
Harris, Robert Allen 1938- *WhoBlA 92*
Harris, Robert Allison 1939- *AmMWSc 92*
Harris, Robert Alter 1955- *WhoMW 92*
Harris, Robert D. 1941- *WhoBlA 92*
Harris, Robert David 1948- *WhoEnt 92*
Harris, Robert Dennis 1957- *Who 92*
Harris, Robert Edward 1935- *WhoAmP 91*
Harris, Robert Eugene Peyton 1940- *WhoBlA 92*
Harris, Robert F. 1941- *WhoBlA 92*
Harris, Robert Franklin 1943- *WhoFI 92*
Harris, Robert George 1911- *WhoWest 92*
Harris, Robert Hutchison 1920- *AmMWSc 92*
Harris, Robert James 1940- *WhoFI 92*
Harris, Robert James 1950- *WhoAmP 91*
Harris, Robert L 1929- *AmMWSc 92*
Harris, Robert L. 1944- *WhoBlA 92*
Harris, Robert L, Jr 1924- *AmMWSc 92*
Harris, Robert L., Jr. 1943- *WhoBlA 92*
Harris, Robert Laird 1911- *WhoRel 92*
Harris, Robert Laurence 1923- *AmMWSc 92*
Harris, Robert Martin 1921- *AmMWSc 92*
Harris, Robert Ned 1961- *WhoEnt 92*
Harris, Robert Oberndoerfer 1929- *WhoAmP 91*
Harris, Robert Shields 1949- *WhoFI 92*
Harris, Robert Theodore 1945- *WhoAmP 91*
Harris, Robin 1949- *TwCPaSc*
Harris, Robin 1952- *Who 92*
Harris, Robin 1955-1990 *WhoBlA 92N*
Harris, Roger Mason 1946- *AmMWSc 92*
Harris, Rohan 1963- *TwCPaSc*
Harris, Rollin Arthur 1863-1918 *BiInAmS*
Harris, Ronald 1913- *Who 92*
Harris, Ronald Conrad 1950- *WhoRel 92*
Harris, Ronald David 1938- *AmMWSc 92*
Harris, Ronald L 1948- *AmMWSc 92*
Harris, Ronald Leon 1945- *WhoEnt 92*
Harris, Ronald W 1948- *BlkOlyM*
Harris, Ronald Walter 1916- *IntAu&W 91*
Harris, Ronald Wilbert 1938- *AmMWSc 92*
Harris, Ronney D 1932- *AmMWSc 92*
Harris, Rosemary 1923- *IntAu&W 91, WrDr 92*
Harris, Rosemary 1930- *IntMPA 92*
Harris, Rosemary Jeanne 1923- *Who 92*
Harris, Rosina Mary 1921- *Who 92*
Harris, Roy 1898-1979 *NewAmDM*
Harris, Roy 1931- *Who 92, WrDr 92*
Harris, Roy Ellsworth 1898-1979 *FacFETw*
Harris, Roy H 1928- *AmMWSc 92*
Harris, Rubie J. 1943- *WhoBlA 92*
Harris, Rudolph 1935- *AmMWSc 92*
Harris, Ruth B S 1955- *AmMWSc 92*
Harris, Ruth Cameron 1916- *AmMWSc 92*
Harris, Ruth Coles 1928- *WhoBlA 92*
Harris, Ryland Michael 1952- *WhoRel 92*
Harris, S Rex 1938- *WhoAmP 91*
Harris, S Richard 1932- *AmMWSc 92*
Harris, Samuel David 1903- *WhoMW 92*
Harris, Samuel Kent 1961- *WhoEnt 92*
Harris, Samuel M 1933- *AmMWSc 92*
Harris, Samuel William 1930- *AmMWSc 92*
Harris, Sarah Elizabeth 1937- *WhoBlA 92*
Harris, Scott Rodney 1951- *WhoMW 92*
Harris, Shari Lea 1964- *WhoMW 92*
Harris, Sheldon H 1928- *IntAu&W 91, WrDr 92*
Harris, Shirley O. 1937- *WhoWest 92*
Harris, Sidney E. 1949- *WhoBlA 92*
Harris, Sidney H. 1933- *WhoEnt 92*
Harris, Sidney Lewis 1927- *WhoRel 92*
Harris, Sigmund Paul 1921- *AmMWSc 92, WhoWest 92*
Harris, Stan *LesBEnT 92*
Harris, Stanley Austin 1882-1978 *DcNCBi 3*
Harris, Stanley Cyril 1916- *AmMWSc 92*
Harris, Stanley Edwards, Jr 1918- *AmMWSc 92*
Harris, Stanley Eugene 1953- *WhoFI 92*
Harris, Stanley Warren 1928- *AmMWSc 92*
Harris, Stephen 1936- *IntWW 91*
Harris, Stephen Dirk 1938- *WhoRel 92*

**Harris,** Stephen Ernest 1936- *AmMWSc 92*
**Harris,** Stephen Eubank 1942- *AmMWSc 92*
**Harris,** Stephen James 1955- *WhoWest 92*
**Harris,** Stephen Joel 1949- *AmMWSc 92*
**Harris,** Stephen LeRoy 1937- *WhoWest 92*
**Harris,** Steve Robert 1965- *WhoRel 92, WhoWest 92*
**Harris,** Steven Bradley 1955- *WhoAmL 92*
**Harris,** Steven H 1924- *AmMWSc 92*
**Harris,** Steven N. 1957- *WhoAmL 92*
**Harris,** Stewart 1937- *AmMWSc 92*
**Harris,** Stirlin 1941- *WhoEnt 92*
**Harris,** Susan *LesBEnT 92, WhoEnt 92*
**Harris,** Susan Elaine 1955- *WhoEnt 92*
**Harris,** Susan L. *WhoAmL 92*
**Harris,** Susanna 1919- *AmMWSc 92*
**Harris,** Suzanne Straight 1944- *AmMWSc 92, WhoAmP 91*
**Harris,** Terea Donnelle 1956- *WhoBlA 92*
**Harris,** Thaddeus William 1795-1856 *BiInAmS*
**Harris,** Theodore Clifford 1937- *WhoEnt 92*
**Harris,** Theodore Edward 1919- *AmMWSc 92*
**Harris,** Theodore Evans 1934- *WhoEnt 92*
**Harris,** Theodore Wilson 1921- *Who 92*
**Harris,** Thomas d1677 *DcNCBi 3*
**Harris,** Thomas 1940?- *ConAu 35NR, WrDr 92*
**Harris,** Thomas C. 1933- *WhoBlA 92*
**Harris,** Thomas David 1948- *AmMWSc 92*
**Harris,** Thomas George 1945- *Who 92*
**Harris,** Thomas L. 1931- *WhoMW 92*
**Harris,** Thomas Lake 1823-1906 *BenetAL 91, RelLAm 91*
**Harris,** Thomas Mason 1928- *AmMWSc 92*
**Harris,** Thomas Munson 1934- *AmMWSc 92*
**Harris,** Thomas R 1937- *AmMWSc 92*
**Harris,** Thomas Sarafen 1947- *WhoFI 92*
**Harris,** Thomas Waters, Jr. 1915- *WhoBlA 92*
**Harris,** Thomas West 1839-1888 *DcNCBi 3*
**Harris,** Timothy 1946- *IntMPA 92, WrDr 92*
**Harris,** Toby *Who 92*
**Harris,** Tom W. 1930- *WhoBlA 92*
**Harris,** Tomas 1908-1964 *TwCPaSc*
**Harris,** Trudier 1948- *NotBlAW 92, WhoBlA 92*
**Harris,** Tzvee N 1912- *AmMWSc 92*
**Harris,** Vander E. 1932- *WhoBlA 92*
**Harris,** Varno Arnello 1965- *WhoBlA 92*
**Harris,** Vera D. 1912- *WhoBlA 92*
**Harris,** Vernon Joseph 1926- *WhoBlA 92*
**Harris,** Vincent Crockett 1913- *AmMWSc 92*
**Harris,** Vivian Faye 1909- *WhoAmP 91*
**Harris,** W F *WhoAmP 91*
**Harris,** W. L. *WhoRel 92*
**Harris,** Wade Hampton 1858-1935 *DcNCBi 3*
**Harris,** Wallace Wayne 1925- *AmMWSc 92*
**Harris,** Walter, Jr. 1947- *WhoBlA 92*
**Harris,** Walter A. 1929- *WrDr 92*
**Harris,** Walter Edgar 1915- *AmMWSc 92*
**Harris,** Walter Edward 1904- *Who 92*
**Harris,** Walter Edward 1935- *WhoAmP 91*
**Harris,** Walter Frank 1920- *Who 92*
**Harris,** Walton Bryan 1949- *WhoRel 92*
**Harris,** Wardell Weldon 1941- *WhoRel 92*
**Harris,** Warren Edward 1961- *WhoWest 92*
**Harris,** Warren Wayne 1962- *WhoAmL 92*
**Harris,** Warren Whitman 1918- *AmMWSc 92*
**Harris,** Wayne G 1933- *AmMWSc 92*
**Harris,** Wayne Manley 1925- *WhoAmL 92*
**Harris,** Wesley L. 1941- *WhoBlA 92*
**Harris,** Wesley Lamar 1931- *AmMWSc 92*
**Harris,** Wesley Leroy 1941- *AmMWSc 92*
**Harris,** Wesley Young, Jr. 1925- *WhoBlA 92*
**Harris,** Wilhelmina d1991 *NewYTBS 91*
**Harris,** Willa Bing 1945- *WhoBlA 92*
**Harris,** William 1939- *WhoAmP 91*
**Harris,** William Albert 1949- *WhoEnt 92*
**Harris,** William Barclay 1911- *Who 92*
**Harris,** William Birch 1919- *AmMWSc 92*
**Harris,** William Burleigh 1943- *AmMWSc 92*
**Harris,** William Charles 1944- *AmMWSc 92*
**Harris,** William Cullen 1921- *WhoAmP 91*
**Harris,** William David 1954- *WhoRel 92*
**Harris,** William Edgar 1947- *AmMWSc 92*
**Harris,** William Franklin, III 1942- *AmMWSc 92*
**Harris,** William Fred 1928- *WhoMW 92*
**Harris,** William Gibson, II 1944- *WhoFI 92*
**Harris,** William Gordon 1912- *Who 92*
**Harris,** William H. 1944- *WhoBlA 92*
**Harris,** William H., Jr. 1942- *WhoBlA 92*
**Harris,** William Henry 1948- *WhoBlA 92*
**Harris,** William J. *DrAPF 91*
**Harris,** William J 1918- *AmMWSc 92*
**Harris,** William J. 1924- *WhoBlA 92*
**Harris,** William J. 1942- *WhoBlA 92*
**Harris,** William M. 1932- *WhoBlA 92*
**Harris,** William M 1940- *AmMWSc 92*
**Harris,** William McKinley, Sr. 1941- *WhoBlA 92*
**Harris,** William Merl 1931- *AmMWSc 92*
**Harris,** William Norman 1952- *WhoEnt 92*
**Harris,** William North 1938- *WhoFI 92*
**Harris,** William Owen 1929- *WhoRel 92*
**Harris,** William R. 1915- *WhoBlA 92*
**Harris,** William Shuler 1865- *ScFEYrs*
**Harris,** Willie Gray, Jr. 1945- *WhoRel 92*
**Harris,** Wilson *Who 92*
**Harris,** Wilson 1921- *ConNov 91, ConPo 91, IntAu&W 91, LiExTwC, RfGEnL 91, WrDr 92*
**Harris,** Winder Russell 1888-1973 *DcNCBi 3*
**Harris,** Winifred Clarke 1924- *WhoBlA 92*
**Harris,** Wynonie 1915-1969 *NewAmDM*
**Harris,** Zelema M. 1940- *WhoBlA 92*
**Harris,** Zellig S 1909- *AmMWSc 92*
**Harris-Burland,** J B *ScFEYrs*
**Harris-Ebohon,** Altheria Thyra 1948- *WhoBlA 92*
**Harris McKenzie,** Ruth Bates 1919- *WhoBlA 92*
**Harris-Noel,** Ann Graetsch 1934- *AmMWSc 92*
**Harris of Greenwich,** Baron 1930- *Who 92*
**Harris of High Cross,** Baron 1924- *Who 92*
**Harris-Warrick,** Ronald Morgan 1949- *AmMWSc 92*
**Harrisberger,** Edgar Lee 1924- *AmMWSc 92*
**Harrises,** Antonio Efthemios 1926- *AmMWSc 92*
**Harrison** *Who 92*
**Harrison,** A. B. 1909- *WhoBlA 92*
**Harrison,** Adlene 1923- *WhoAmP 91*
**Harrison,** Aix B 1925- *AmMWSc 92*
**Harrison,** Alastair Brian 1921- *Who 92*
**Harrison,** Albert Norman 1901- *Who 92*
**Harrison,** Albertis Sydney, Jr 1907- *WhoAmP 91*
**Harrison,** Alene *WhoWest 92*
**Harrison,** Alexander George 1931- *AmMWSc 92*
**Harrison,** Algea Othella 1936- *WhoBlA 92*
**Harrison,** Alice Willis 1929- *WhoRel 92*
**Harrison,** Aline Margaret 1940- *AmMWSc 92*
**Harrison,** Alonzo 1952- *WhoFI 92*
**Harrison,** Andrew 1947- *TwCPaSc*
**Harrison,** Ann Tukey 1938- *WhoMW 92*
**Harrison,** Anna Jane 1912- *AmMWSc 92*
**Harrison,** Anthony 1931- *TwCPaSc*
**Harrison,** Arnold Myron 1946- *AmMWSc 92*
**Harrison,** Arthur Desmond 1921- *AmMWSc 92*
**Harrison,** Arthur John 1919- *WhoFI 92*
**Harrison,** Arthur Pennoyer, Jr 1922- *AmMWSc 92*
**Harrison,** Benjamin 1833-1901 *AmPolLe [port], BenetAL 91, RComAH*
**Harrison,** Benjamin Keith 1947- *AmMWSc 92*
**Harrison,** Bernard 1933- *WrDr 92*
**Harrison,** Bertrand Fereday 1908- *AmMWSc 92*
**Harrison,** Bertrand Kent 1934- *AmMWSc 92*
**Harrison,** Bettina Hall *AmMWSc 92*
**Harrison,** Beverly E. 1948- *WhoBlA 92*
**Harrison,** Bob 1941- *WhoBlA 92*
**Harrison,** Booker David 1908- *WhoBlA 92*
**Harrison,** Boyd G., Jr. 1949- *WhoBlA 92*
**Harrison,** Brian *Who 92*
**Harrison,** Brian Fraser 1918- *WrDr 92*
**Harrison,** Bryan Desmond 1931- *IntWW 91, Who 92*
**Harrison,** C William *TwCWW 91*
**Harrison,** Carlos Enrique 1956- *WhoHisp 92*
**Harrison,** Carol L. 1946- *WhoBlA 92*
**Harrison,** Carole Alberta 1942- *WhoWest 92*
**Harrison,** Catherine Louise Rice 1945- *WhoRel 92*
**Harrison,** Chad Roger 1964- *WhoEnt 92*
**Harrison,** Charles Edward 1923- *WhoEnt 92*
**Harrison,** Charles Maurice 1927- *WhoAmL 92*
**Harrison,** Charles Victor 1907- *Who 92*
**Harrison,** Charles Wagner, Jr 1913- *AmMWSc 92, WhoWest 92*
**Harrison,** Charlie J., Jr. 1932- *WhoBlA 92*
**Harrison,** Charlie James, Jr 1932- *WhoAmP 91*
**Harrison,** Chip *WrDr 92*
**Harrison,** Christopher George Alick 1936- *AmMWSc 92*
**Harrison,** Claude *TwCPaSc*
**Harrison,** Claude 1922- *TwCPaSc*
**Harrison,** Claude William 1922- *Who 92*
**Harrison,** Colin *Who 92*
**Harrison,** Constance 1843-1920 *BenetAL 91*
**Harrison,** Craig Donald 1956- *WhoFI 92, WhoWest 92*
**Harrison,** Craig Royston 1933- *WhoWest 92*
**Harrison,** Dalton C 1953- *WhoAmP 91*
**Harrison,** Dalton S 1920- *AmMWSc 92*
**Harrison,** Daniel Edward 1955- *WhoRel 92*
**Harrison,** Daphne Duval 1932- *WhoBlA 92*
**Harrison,** David 1930- *IntWW 91, Who 92*
**Harrison,** David Brisco 1934- *WhoMW 92*
**Harrison,** David Carlton 1953- *WhoEnt 92*
**Harrison,** David Eldridge 1933- *WhoAmL 92*
**Harrison,** David Ellsworth 1942- *AmMWSc 92*
**Harrison,** David Kent 1931- *AmMWSc 92*
**Harrison,** David Lakin 1926- *WrDr 92*
**Harrison,** Delbert Eugene 1951- *WhoBlA 92*
**Harrison,** Denis Byrne 1917- *Who 92*
**Harrison,** Desmond Roger 1933- *Who 92*
**Harrison,** Dian Johnson 1948- *WhoBlA 92*
**Harrison,** Don Edmunds 1950- *AmMWSc 92, WhoWest 92*
**Harrison,** Don Edward 1928- *AmMWSc 92*
**Harrison,** Don Edward, Jr 1927- *AmMWSc 92*
**Harrison,** Don K., Sr. 1933- *WhoBlA 92*
**Harrison,** Donald 1925- *Who 92*
**Harrison,** Donald 1946- *WhoAmL 92*
**Harrison,** Donald C 1934- *AmMWSc 92*
**Harrison,** Donald Carey 1934- *WhoMW 92*
**Harrison,** Donald Richard 1947- *WhoAmP 91*
**Harrison,** Douglas Creese 1901- *Who 92*
**Harrison,** Douglas P 1937- *AmMWSc 92*
**Harrison,** Doyle 1939- *WhoRel 92*
**Harrison,** Earl David 1932- *WhoAmL 92, WhoFI 92*
**Harrison,** Earle 1903- *WhoFI 92, WhoWest 92*
**Harrison,** Edward Hardy 1926- *IntAu&W 91*
**Harrison,** Edward Joseph, III 1936- *WhoFI 92*
**Harrison,** Edward Peter Graham 1948- *Who 92*
**Harrison,** Edward Robert 1919- *AmMWSc 92*
**Harrison,** Edythe C 1937- *WhoAmP 91*
**Harrison,** Elizabeth Fancourt *WrDr 92*
**Harrison,** Elizabeth Fancourt 1921- *IntAu&W 91*
**Harrison,** Emma Louise 1918- *WhoBlA 92*
**Harrison,** Emmett Bruce, Jr. 1932- *WhoFI 92*
**Harrison,** Ernest 1926- *Who 92*
**Harrison,** Ernest Alexander 1937- *WhoBlA 92*
**Harrison,** Ernest Augustus, Jr 1934- *AmMWSc 92*
**Harrison,** Ernest Thomas 1926- *IntWW 91*
**Harrison,** Everett F. 1902- *WrDr 92*
**Harrison,** Florence Louise 1926- *AmMWSc 92*
**Harrison,** Floyd Perry 1927- *AmMWSc 92*
**Harrison,** Francis Alexander Lyle 1910- *Who 92*
**Harrison,** Francis Anthony Kitchener 1914- *Who 92*
**Harrison,** Frank *Who 92*
**Harrison,** Frank 1913- *AmMWSc 92*
**Harrison,** Frank 1940- *WhoAmP 91*
**Harrison,** Frank J. 1912- *WhoRel 92*
**Harrison,** Frank Joseph 1919- *WhoAmL 92*
**Harrison,** Fred *TwCWW 91*
**Harrison,** Fred Brian 1927- *Who 92*
**Harrison,** Frederick Joseph 1951- *WhoAmL 92, WhoAmP 91*
**Harrison,** Frederick Williams 1938- *AmMWSc 92*
**Harrison,** Gail Grigsby 1943- *AmMWSc 92*
**Harrison,** George 1943- *IntMPA 92, IntWW 91, WhoEnt 92*
**Harrison,** George Anthony 1930- *Who 92*
**Harrison,** George Bagshawe 1894- *Who 92*
**Harrison,** George Conrad, Jr 1929- *AmMWSc 92*
**Harrison,** George H 1943- *AmMWSc 92*
**Harrison,** George Michael 1925- *Who 92*
**Harrison,** Gloria *WhoHisp 92*
**Harrison,** Gordon R 1931- *AmMWSc 92*
**Harrison,** Gregory 1950- *IntMPA 92, WhoEnt 92*
**Harrison,** Gregory W. 1928- *WhoBlA 92*
**Harrison,** Gunyon M 1921- *AmMWSc 92*
**Harrison,** H Keith 1919- *AmMWSc 92*
**Harrison,** Halstead 1931- *AmMWSc 92*
**Harrison,** Harold Donald 1935- *WhoRel 92*
**Harrison,** Harold Edward 1908- *AmMWSc 92*
**Harrison,** Harry 1925- *TwCSFW 91, WrDr 92*
**Harrison,** Harry Paul 1923- *WhoAmP 91, WhoBlA 92*
**Harrison,** Hattie N 1928- *WhoAmP 91, WhoBlA 92*
**Harrison,** Hazel 1883-1969 *NotBlAW 92*
**Harrison,** Helen Connolly 1949- *AmMWSc 92*
**Harrison,** Helen Coplan 1911- *AmMWSc 92*
**Harrison,** Henry Sydnor 1880-1930 *BenetAL 91*
**Harrison,** Henry T. d1991 *NewYTBS 91*
**Harrison,** Ian Roland 1943- *AmMWSc 92*
**Harrison,** Ian Stewart 1919- *Who 92*
**Harrison,** Irene R 1952- *AmMWSc 92*
**Harrison,** J Berry 1939- *WhoAmP 91*
**Harrison,** J D 1930- *AmMWSc 92*
**Harrison,** J. Randall 1952- *WhoEnt 92*
**Harrison,** Jack Edward 1924- *AmMWSc 92*
**Harrison,** Jack Lamar 1927- *AmMWSc 92*
**Harrison,** James, Jr. 1930- *WhoBlA 92*
**Harrison,** James Beckman 1923- *AmMWSc 92*
**Harrison,** James Francis 1940- *AmMWSc 92, WhoMW 92*
**Harrison,** James H 1951- *WhoAmP 91*
**Harrison,** James Harvey, Jr. 1927- *WhoFI 92*
**Harrison,** James Merritt 1915- *AmMWSc 92, IntWW 91*
**Harrison,** James Ostelle 1920- *AmMWSc 92*
**Harrison,** James William, Jr 1932- *AmMWSc 92*
**Harrison,** Jeanette LaVerne 1948- *WhoBlA 92*
**Harrison,** Jeanne *WhoEnt 92*
**Harrison,** Jeffrey *DrAPF 91*
**Harrison,** Jeremy Thomas 1935- *WhoAmL 92*
**Harrison,** Jerry Wray, Jr. 1961- *WhoEnt 92*
**Harrison,** Jessel Anidjah 1923- *Who 92*
**Harrison,** Jim *DrAPF 91*
**Harrison,** Jim 1937- *BenetAL 91, ConLC 66 [port], ConNov 91, ConPo 91, IntAu&W 91, TwCWW 91, WrDr 92*
**Harrison,** Joan 1911- *ReelWom*
**Harrison,** John 1773-1833 *BiInAmS*
**Harrison,** John 1921- *Who 92*
**Harrison,** John Audley 1917- *Who 92*
**Harrison,** John Christopher 1929- *AmMWSc 92*
**Harrison,** John Clive 1937- *Who 92*
**Harrison,** John Conway 1913- *WhoAmL 92, WhoAmP 91, WhoWest 92*
**Harrison,** John F. C. 1921- *WrDr 92*
**Harrison,** John Fletcher Clews 1921- *Who 92*
**Harrison,** John H. *Who 92*
**Harrison,** John Henry, IV 1936- *AmMWSc 92*
**Harrison,** John Michael 1915- *AmMWSc 92*
**Harrison,** John Patrick 1940- *AmMWSc 92*
**Harrison,** John Philip 1949- *WhoRel 92*
**Harrison,** John Ray 1930- *WhoAmP 91*
**Harrison,** John Richard 1921- *Who 92*
**Harrison,** John William 1929- *AmMWSc 92*
**Harrison,** Jonas P 1928- *AmMWSc 92*
**Harrison,** Joseph, Jr 1810-1874 *BiInAmS*
**Harrison,** Joseph George, Jr. 1944- *WhoAmL 92*
**Harrison,** Joseph Gillis, Jr. 1950- *WhoHisp 92*
**Harrison,** Joseph Heavrin 1929- *WhoAmL 92*
**Harrison,** Joseph Horatio, Jr. 1950- *WhoAmL 92*
**Harrison,** Joseph William 1931- *WhoAmP 91*
**Harrison,** Joseph Wylie 1937- *WhoAmP 91*
**Harrison,** Joyce Virginia 1939- *WhoEnt 92*
**Harrison,** Julia 1920- *WhoAmP 91*
**Harrison,** Julian R, III 1934- *AmMWSc 92*
**Harrison,** Kathleen 1892- *Who 92*
**Harrison,** Keith 1932- *IntAu&W 91, WrDr 92*
**Harrison,** Keith Michaele 1956- *WhoWest 92*

**Harrison**, Ken L. 1942- WhoFI 92, WhoWest 92
**Harrison**, Kenneth 1915- IntAu&W 91, WrDr 92
**Harrison**, Kenneth Cecil 1915- Who 92
**Harrison**, Lillian 1899-1965 TwCPaSc
**Harrison**, Lionel George 1929- AmMWSc 92
**Harrison**, Liz 1947- TwCPaSc
**Harrison**, Lois Smith 1924- WhoFI 92
**Harrison**, Lou 1917- ConCom 92, NewAmDM
**Harrison**, Lou Silver 1917- WhoEnt 92
**Harrison**, Lowell H. 1922- WrDr 92
**Harrison**, Lura Ann 1942- AmMWSc 92
**Harrison**, Lyndon Henry Arthur 1947- Who 92
**Harrison**, M John 1945- IntAu&W 91, TwCSFW 91, WrDr 92
**Harrison**, Malcolm Charles 1937- AmMWSc 92
**Harrison**, Marc 1936- DcTwDes
**Harrison**, Margaret 1940- TwCPaSc
**Harrison**, Marion Edwyn 1931- WhoAmL 92
**Harrison**, Marion Fox 1911- WhoEnt 92
**Harrison**, Marjorie Freeman 1952- WhoAmP 91
**Harrison**, Marjorie Hall 1918- AmMWSc 92
**Harrison**, Marjorie Jeanne 1923- WhoMW 92
**Harrison**, Mark 1919- AmMWSc 92
**Harrison**, Mary Anne 1944- WhoEnt 92
**Harrison**, Mary Elizabeth 1959- WhoFI 92
**Harrison**, Melvin Arnold 1924- AmMWSc 92
**Harrison**, Merle E 1933- AmMWSc 92
**Harrison**, Mernoy Edward, Jr. 1947- WhoBlA 92, WhoWest 92
**Harrison**, Michael Who 92
**Harrison**, Michael 1907- IntAu&W 91, WrDr 92
**Harrison**, Michael 1939- Who 92
**Harrison**, Michael 1940- WhoEnt 92
**Harrison**, Michael 1945- TwCPaSc
**Harrison**, Michael A 1936- AmMWSc 92
**Harrison**, Michael Gregory 1941- WhoAmL 92
**Harrison**, Michael Guy Vicat 1939- Who 92
**Harrison**, Michael Jackson 1941- Who 92
**Harrison**, Michael James Harwood 1936- Who 92
**Harrison**, Michael Jay 1932- AmMWSc 92
**Harrison**, Michael R 1943- AmMWSc 92
**Harrison**, Molly 1909- Who 92
**Harrison**, Monty DeVerl 1934- AmMWSc 92
**Harrison**, Nancy Evelyn King 1943- AmMWSc 92
**Harrison**, Orval C 1940- WhoAmP 91
**Harrison**, Pamela DrAPF 91
**Harrison**, Patrick Kennard 1928- Who 92
**Harrison**, Paul C 1936- AmMWSc 92
**Harrison**, Paul Carter 1936- WhoBlA 92
**Harrison**, Paul Mansfield 1923- WhoRel 92
**Harrison**, Pearl Lewis 1932- WhoBlA 92
**Harrison**, Peyton Blanchard, Jr. 1956- WhoMW 92, WhoRel 92
**Harrison**, Philip 1946- WhoFI 92
**Harrison**, Philip Lewis 1945- IntAu&W 91
**Harrison**, R H 1927- AmMWSc 92
**Harrison**, R. Reed, III 1948- WhoFI 92
**Harrison**, Ralph Joseph 1924- AmMWSc 92
**Harrison**, Ray 1928- WhoAmP 91
**Harrison**, Raymond Vincent 1928- IntAu&W 91
**Harrison**, Rebecca Newth DrAPF 91
**Harrison**, Reginald Carey d1990 IntWW 91N
**Harrison**, Rex 1908-1990 AnObit 1990, ConTFT 9, FacFETw
**Harrison**, Richard Who 92
**Harrison**, Richard 1768-1856 DcNCBi 3
**Harrison**, Richard 1920- IntWW 91, Who 92, WrDr 92
**Harrison**, Richard Dean 1952- WhoRel 92
**Harrison**, Richard Gerald 1945- AmMWSc 92
**Harrison**, Richard Martin 1935- Who 92
**Harrison**, Richard Miller 1939- AmMWSc 92
**Harrison**, Richard Paul, Jr. 1960- WhoMW 92
**Harrison**, Richard Wayne 1944- WhoAmL 92
**Harrison**, Robert Cameron 1920- AmMWSc 92
**Harrison**, Robert Colin 1938- Who 92
**Harrison**, Robert Edwin 1947- AmMWSc 92
**Harrison**, Robert George 1943- WhoMW 92
**Harrison**, Robert J 1928- AmMWSc 92
**Harrison**, Robert Louis 1929- AmMWSc 92
**Harrison**, Robert Michael 1945- Who 92
**Harrison**, Robert W 1936- AmMWSc 92
**Harrison**, Robert Walker, III 1941- AmMWSc 92, WhoBlA 92
**Harrison**, Robert William 1915- AmMWSc 92
**Harrison**, Roger Who 92
**Harrison**, Roger 1938- WrDr 92
**Harrison**, Roger G WhoAmP 91
**Harrison**, Roland Kenneth 1920- WhoRel 92
**Harrison**, Ronald E. 1936- WhoBlA 92
**Harrison**, Ronald Gary 1941- WhoAmP 91
**Harrison**, Roscoe Conklin, Jr. 1944- WhoBlA 92
**Harrison**, Roslyn Siman 1935- WhoAmL 92
**Harrison**, Rowland John Hill 1943- IntWW 91
**Harrison**, Russell Edward 1921- IntWW 91
**Harrison**, Samuel Hughel 1956- WhoAmL 92
**Harrison**, Samuel S 1941- AmMWSc 92
**Harrison**, Sarah 1946- IntAu&W 91, WrDr 92
**Harrison**, Saul I 1925- AmMWSc 92
**Harrison**, Shari Lynne 1960- WhoAmL 92
**Harrison**, Shirley Dindy 1951- WhoBlA 92
**Harrison**, Shirley Wanda 1923- AmMWSc 92
**Harrison**, Stanley L 1935- AmMWSc 92
**Harrison**, Steadman Darnell, Jr 1947- AmMWSc 92
**Harrison**, Stephen Coplan 1943- AmMWSc 92
**Harrison**, Steven Dale 1958- WhoMW 92
**Harrison**, Stuart Amos 1912- AmMWSc 92
**Harrison**, Sue 1950- ConAu 135
**Harrison**, T Milner 1865- ScFEYrs
**Harrison**, Ted Who 92
**Harrison**, Terence 1931- WhoEnt 92
**Harrison**, Terence 1933- Who 92
**Harrison**, Theophilus George 1907- Who 92
**Harrison**, Thomas J 1935- AmMWSc 92
**Harrison**, Thomas Perrin 1864-1949 DcNCBi 3
**Harrison**, Timothy Stone 1927- AmMWSc 92
**Harrison**, Tommy Wayne 1949- WhoRel 92
**Harrison**, Tony 1937- ConPo 91, IntAu&W 91, IntWW 91, RfGEnL 91, Who 92, WrDr 92
**Harrison**, Virginia Ginny Elaine 1957- WhoWest 92
**Harrison**, W Craig 1940- AmMWSc 92
**Harrison**, Walter 1921- Who 92
**Harrison**, Walter Ashley 1930- AmMWSc 92
**Harrison**, Walter Kirby 1928- WhoWest 92
**Harrison**, Walter Lee 1946- WhoMW 92
**Harrison**, Warren 1951- WhoFI 92
**Harrison**, Wayne David 1953- IntWW 91
**Harrison**, Wilks Douglas 1932- AmMWSc 92
**Harrison**, Willard Wayne 1937- AmMWSc 92
**Harrison**, William DrAPF 91
**Harrison**, William Ashley 1933- AmMWSc 92
**Harrison**, William Donald 1934- WhoFI 92
**Harrison**, William Earl 1942- AmMWSc 92
**Harrison**, William Edgar 1912- WhoBlA 92N
**Harrison**, William Groce, III 1934- WhoFI 92
**Harrison**, William Henry 1773-1841 AmPolLe [port], BenetAL 91, RComAH
**Harrison**, William Henry 1924- AmMWSc 92
**Harrison**, William Henry, Jr 1950- WhoAmP 91
**Harrison**, William L 1936- WhoIns 92
**Harrison**, William Oliver, Jr 1945- WhoAmP 91, WhoFI 92
**Harrison**, William Paul 1920- AmMWSc 92
**Harrison**, William Wright, Jr. 1953- WhoAmL 92
**Harrison**, Wyman 1931- AmMWSc 92
**Harrison-Church**, Ronald James 1915- Who 92
**Harrison Dunlap**, Debra Louise 1956- WhoRel 92
**Harrison-Hall**, Michael Kilgour 1925- Who 92
**Harrison-Johnson**, Yvonne E AmMWSc 92
**Harriss**, C. Lowell 1912- WrDr 92
**Harriss**, Donald K 1934- AmMWSc 92
**Harriss**, Gerald Leslie 1925- IntWW 91, Who 92
**Harriss**, Thomas T 1918- AmMWSc 92
**Harrisse**, Henry 1830-1910 BenetAL 91
**Harrist**, Ronald Baxter 1936- AmMWSc 92
**Harristhal**, Christopher John 1961- WhoAmP 91
**Harroch**, Richard David 1953- WhoAmL 92
**Harrod**, C. Scott 1953- WhoWest 92
**Harrod**, Dominick Roy 1940- Who 92
**Harrod**, Howard Lee 1932- WhoRel 92
**Harrod**, John Frank 1934- AmMWSc 92
**Harrod**, Lionel Alexander Digby 1924- Who 92
**Harrod-Eagles**, Cynthia 1948- WrDr 92
**Harroff**, Stephen Creig 1942- WhoMW 92
**Harrold**, Austin Leroy 1942- WhoBlA 92
**Harrold**, Bernard 1925- WhoAmL 92
**Harrold**, Gordon Coleson 1906- AmMWSc 92
**Harrold**, Jeffery Deland 1956- WhoBlA 92
**Harrold**, Kathryn 1950- IntMPA 92
**Harrold**, Lawrence A. 1952- WhoBlA 92
**Harrold**, Pamela Kay 1947- WhoEnt 92
**Harrold**, Robert Edward 1945- WhoMW 92
**Harrold**, Robert Lee 1940- AmMWSc 92
**Harrold**, Ronald Thomas 1933- AmMWSc 92
**Harrold**, Roy Mealham 1928- Who 92
**Harrold**, William DrAPF 91
**Harrold**, William Eugene 1936- IntAu&W 91
**Harron**, Don 1924- WrDr 92
**Harrop**, Clayton Keith 1924- WhoRel 92
**Harrop**, Diane Glaser 1953- WhoWest 92
**Harrop**, Donald Bruce WhoWest 92
**Harrop**, Peter 1926- Who 92
**Harrop**, Robert Daniel 1950- WhoAmL 92
**Harrop**, Ronald 1926- AmMWSc 92
**Harrop**, William Caldwell 1929- WhoAmP 91
**Harroun**, Ann Patricia 1935- WhoAmP 91
**Harrow**, Judith S. 1945- RelLAm 91
**Harrow**, Lee Salem 1926- AmMWSc 92
**Harrow**, Nancy WhoEnt 92
**Harrowby**, Earl of 1922- Who 92
**Harrower**, Elizabeth 1928- ConNov 91, WrDr 92
**Harrower**, George Alexander 1924- AmMWSc 92
**Harrower**, Jack ScFEYrs
**Harrs**, Leland Allen 1936- WhoIns 92
**Harry**, Deborah Ann 1945- WhoEnt 92
**Harry**, George Yost 1919- AmMWSc 92
**Harry**, Harold William 1921- AmMWSc 92
**Harry**, J. S. 1939- ConPo 91, WrDr 92
**Harry**, Jackee WhoBlA 92
**Harry**, Phillip Brooks 1947- WhoEnt 92
**Harry**, Ralph Lindsay 1917- IntWW 91
**Harry**, Susan Elaine 1961- WhoFI 92
**Harry**, William, III 1955- WhoFI 92
**Harry**, William Thomas 1924- WhoEnt 92
**Harryhausen**, Ray IntWW 91
**Harryhausen**, Ray 1920- IntMPA 92
**Harryhausen**, Ray Frederick 1920- WhoEnt 92
**Harryman**, Eva Marie 1914- WhoAmP 91
**Harsanyi**, Andrew WhoRel 92
**Harsch**, Harold H 1950- AmMWSc 92
**Harsch**, Joseph Close 1905- IntAu&W 91, IntWW 91, Who 92
**Harsdorf**, James Ervin WhoAmP 91
**Harsdorf**, Sheila WhoAmP 91
**Harsent**, David 1942- ConPo 91, IntAu&W 91, WrDr 92
**Harsh**, George 1908-1980 FacFETw
**Harsh**, Vivian 1890-1960 NotBlAW 92
**Harsha**, William H 1921- WhoAmP 91
**Harshaw**, David Hare d1991 NewYTBS 91
**Harshaw**, Jay 1947- WhoEnt 92
**Harshaw**, Margaret 1909- NewAmDM
**Harshbarger**, Boyd 1906- AmMWSc 92
**Harshbarger**, John Carl, Jr 1936- AmMWSc 92
**Harshbarger**, Kenneth E 1914- AmMWSc 92
**Harshbarger**, Richard B. 1934- WhoFI 92
**Harshbarger**, Scott WhoAmP 91
**Harshbarger**, Scott 1941- WhoAmL 92
**Harshfield**, Edward Gordon 1937- WhoFI 92, WhoWest 92
**Harshman**, Elbert Nelson 1910- AmMWSc 92
**Harshman**, Jennifer Ione 1959- WhoRel 92
**Harshman**, Kemp Robert 1948- WhoAmP 91
**Harshman**, Marc DrAPF 91
**Harshman**, Raymond Brent 1948- WhoAmL 92
**Harshman**, Richard C 1922- AmMWSc 92
**Harshman**, Sidney 1930- AmMWSc 92
**Harsney**, Johanna Marie Offner 1914- WhoMW 92
**Harstad**, Kenneth Gunder 1939- WhoWest 92
**Harstad**, Ronald M. 1951- WhoFI 92
**Harston**, Julian John Robert Clive 1942- Who 92
**Hart** Who 92
**Hart**, Alan 1935- Who 92
**Hart**, Alan Edward 1935- Who 92
**Hart**, Alexander Hendry 1916- Who 92
**Hart**, Anelay Colton Wright 1934- Who 92
**Hart**, Anthony Who 92
**Hart**, Anthony Bernard 1917- Who 92
**Hart**, Anthony John 1923- Who 92
**Hart**, Anthony Ronald 1946- Who 92
**Hart**, Barbara McCollum 1937- WhoBlA 92
**Hart**, Benjamin 1958- IntAu&W 91
**Hart**, Benjamin Leslie 1935- AmMWSc 92
**Hart**, Boots Dale 1954- WhoEnt 92
**Hart**, Bret Sargent 1957- WhoEnt 92
**Hart**, Bruce 1938- WhoEnt 92
**Hart**, Carolyn G. 1936- WrDr 92
**Hart**, Cecil William Joseph 1931- WhoMW 92
**Hart**, Charles 1940- ConAu 133
**Hart**, Charles 1961- WhoEnt 92
**Hart**, Charles Arthur 1859-1918 BiInAmS
**Hart**, Charles Richard 1943- AmMWSc 92
**Hart**, Charles Willard, Jr 1928- AmMWSc 92
**Hart**, Christopher Alvin 1947- WhoBlA 92
**Hart**, Clarence Arthur 1927- AmMWSc 92
**Hart**, Clifford Harvey 1935- WhoAmL 92
**Hart**, Dabney Gardner 1940- AmMWSc 92
**Hart**, Daniel Anthony 1927- WhoRel 92
**Hart**, David A. 1947- WhoAmL 92
**Hart**, David Arthur 1942- AmMWSc 92
**Hart**, David Charles 1947- AmMWSc 92
**Hart**, David Churchill 1940- WhoAmL 92
**Hart**, David Dickinson 1952- AmMWSc 92
**Hart**, David Joel 1948- AmMWSc 92
**Hart**, David Lee 1950- WhoAmP 91
**Hart**, David Michael 1940- Who 92
**Hart**, David R 1926- AmMWSc 92
**Hart**, David Steven 1950- WhoRel 92
**Hart**, Derek 1951- WhoEnt 92
**Hart**, Dolores 1938- WhoEnt 92
**Hart**, Donald 1933- Who 92
**Hart**, Donald A. 1946- WhoWest 92
**Hart**, Donald Avery 1936- WhoFI 92
**Hart**, Donald John 1948- AmMWSc 92, WhoMW 92
**Hart**, Donald Larcum, Jr 1955- WhoAmP 91
**Hart**, Donald Purple 1937- WhoRel 92, WhoWest 92
**Hart**, Douglas Skinner 1951- WhoAmL 92
**Hart**, Earl W 1927- AmMWSc 92
**Hart**, Eddie James 1948- BlkOlyM
**Hart**, Eddie Lee 1932- WhoRel 92
**Hart**, Edward E. 1927- WhoBlA 92
**Hart**, Edward L. DrAPF 91
**Hart**, Edward Leon 1930- AmMWSc 92
**Hart**, Edward Richard 1945- WhoWest 92
**Hart**, Edward Walter 1918- AmMWSc 92
**Hart**, Elwood Roy 1938- AmMWSc 92
**Hart**, Emily 1940- WhoBlA 92
**Hart**, Eugene C. 1931- WhoRel 92
**Hart**, Everard Peter 1925- Who 92
**Hart**, Everett Martin 1918- WhoMW 92
**Hart**, Frances Noyes 1890-1943 BenetAL 91
**Hart**, Francis Dudley 1909- Who 92
**Hart**, Francis Edmund T. Who 92
**Hart**, Frank Donald Who 92
**Hart**, Frank James 1947- WhoWest 92
**Hart**, Frank Thomas 1911- Who 92
**Hart**, Fred H. BenetAL 91
**Hart**, Frederick Lewis 1945- AmMWSc 92
**Hart**, Garry Dewaine 1944- AmMWSc 92
**Hart**, Gary 1936- FacFETw, IntWW 91, WhoAmP 91
**Hart**, Gary Elwood 1934- AmMWSc 92
**Hart**, Gary K 1943- WhoAmP 91
**Hart**, Gary W. 1936- WhoWest 92
**Hart**, George 1927- WhoAmP 91
**Hart**, George Emerson, Jr 1929- AmMWSc 92
**Hart**, George Vaughan 1911- Who 92
**Hart**, Gerald Warren 1949- AmMWSc 92
**Hart**, Graham Allan 1940- Who 92
**Hart**, Guy William Pulbrook 1931- Who 92
**Hart**, H. L. A. 1907- WrDr 92
**Hart**, Harold 1922- AmMWSc 92
**Hart**, Harold Bird 1940- AmMWSc 92
**Hart**, Harold M 1913- AmMWSc 92
**Hart**, Harold Rudoff 1926- WhoBlA 92
**Hart**, Harvey 1928- IntMPA 92
**Hart**, Haskell Vincent 1943- AmMWSc 92
**Hart**, Herbert L 1907- FacFETw
**Hart**, Herbert Lionel Adolphus 1907- IntWW 91, Who 92
**Hart**, Hiram 1924- AmMWSc 92
**Hart**, Howard Franklin 1947- WhoWest 92

**Hart**, Howard Roscoe, Jr 1929- *AmMWSc 92*
**Hart**, Ila Jo 1928- *WhoAmP 91*
**Hart**, Irving Harlow, III 1938- *WhoWest 92*
**Hart**, Jacqueline D. *WhoBlA 92*
**Hart**, James D. 1911-1990 *AnObit 1990*
**Hart**, James Everett, III 1960- *WhoEnt 92*
**Hart**, James Harlan 1934- *WhoMW 92*
**Hart**, James R 1952- *WhoAmP 91*
**Hart**, James Russell 1957- *WhoRel 92*
**Hart**, James W. 1953- *WhoFI 92*
**Hart**, James Warren 1944- *WhoEnt 92*
**Hart**, Jay Albert Charles 1923- *WhoMW 92*
**Hart**, Jayne Thompson 1942- *AmMWSc 92*
**Hart**, Jean Macaulay *WhoWest 92*
**Hart**, Jeanne *IntAu&W 91*
**Hart**, Jerome Thomas 1932- *WhoAmP 91*
**Hart**, Joanne *DrAPF 91*
**Hart**, John *DrAPF 91, LesBEnT 92, WrDr 92*
**Hart**, John 1921- *TwCPaSc*
**Hart**, John 1924- *WhoWest 92*
**Hart**, John 1948- *IntAu&W 91*
**Hart**, John Birdsall 1924- *AmMWSc 92*
**Hart**, John Clifton 1945- *WhoAmL 92*
**Hart**, John Edward 1946- *WhoAmL 92*
**Hart**, John Edward 1959- *WhoAmL 92*
**Hart**, John Fraser 1924- *WrDr 92*
**Hart**, John Henderson 1936- *AmMWSc 92, WhoMW 92*
**Hart**, John Robert 1935- *AmMWSc 92*
**Hart**, John S. 1810-1877 *BenetAL 91*
**Hart**, John William 1943- *WhoRel 92*
**Hart**, Jonathan David 1956- *WhoAmL 92*
**Hart**, Joseph Anthony 1945- *WhoRel 92*
**Hart**, Joseph C. 1798-1855 *BenetAL 91*
**Hart**, Joseph H. 1931- *WhoRel 92, WhoWest 92*
**Hart**, Judith *IntWW 91*
**Hart**, Judith d1991 *NewYTBS 91*
**Hart**, Judith 1924- *WrDr 92*
**Hart**, Julian Deryl 1894-1980 *DcNCBi 3*
**Hart**, Kathleen Therese 1922- *AmMWSc 92*
**Hart**, Kathy Ann 1968- *WhoRel 92*
**Hart**, Kay M 1954- *WhoAmP 91*
**Hart**, Kenneth Howell 1924- *AmMWSc 92*
**Hart**, Kenneth Wayne 1955- *WhoAmL 92*
**Hart**, Kevin 1954- *ConAu 135, ConPo 91, WrDr 92*
**Hart**, Kim Patrick 1950- *WhoAmL 92*
**Hart**, Kitty Carlisle 1917- *WhoEnt 92*
**Hart**, Larry Edward 1945- *WhoFI 92*
**Hart**, Larry Glen 1932- *AmMWSc 92*
**Hart**, Lawrence Alan 1930- *AmMWSc 92*
**Hart**, LeRoy Banks 1954- *WhoFI 92*
**Hart**, Lewis Thomas 1933- *AmMWSc 92*
**Hart**, Lorenz 1895-1943 *BenetAL 91, FacFETw, NewAmDM*
**Hart**, Lyle Cordell 1931- *WhoEnt 92*
**Hart**, Lynn Patrick 1947- *AmMWSc 92*
**Hart**, Lynn W 1942- *AmMWSc 92*
**Hart**, Marian Griffith 1929- *WhoWest 92*
**Hart**, Marjorie Lynn 1964- *WhoRel 92*
**Hart**, Mark Dorsey 1956- *WhoRel 92*
**Hart**, Maurice I, Jr 1934- *AmMWSc 92*
**Hart**, Melissa A 1962- *WhoAmP 91*
**Hart**, Michael 1928- *Who 92*
**Hart**, Michael 1938- *IntWW 91, Who 92*
**Hart**, Michael Christopher Campbell 1948- *Who 92*
**Hart**, Michael Edward 1932- *WhoMW 92*
**Hart**, Michael H 1932- *AmMWSc 92*
**Hart**, Mickey 1944?- *News 91 [port]*
**Hart**, Mildred *WhoBlA 92*
**Hart**, Moss 1904-1961 *BenetAL 91, ConLC 66 [port], FacFETw*
**Hart**, N. Berne 1930- *WhoFI 92, WhoWest 92*
**Hart**, Nancy *EncAmaz 91*
**Hart**, Nancy 1755?-1840? *EncAmaz 91*
**Hart**, Nathan Hoult 1936- *AmMWSc 92*
**Hart**, Nathaniel 1734-1782 *DcNCBi 3*
**Hart**, Noel A. 1927- *WhoBlA 92*
**Hart**, Oliver Simon D'Arcy 1948- *Who 92*
**Hart**, Parker T. 1910- *IntWW 91*
**Hart**, Parker Thompson 1910- *WhoAmP 91*
**Hart**, Patrick E 1940- *AmMWSc 92*
**Hart**, Pearl 1872?- *EncAmaz 91*
**Hart**, Pembroke J 1929- *AmMWSc 92*
**Hart**, Percie W 1870- *ScFEYrs*
**Hart**, Peter *Who 92*
**Hart**, Peter E 1941- *AmMWSc 92*
**Hart**, Philip Donnell 1936- *WhoAmL 92*
**Hart**, Philip M. D'Arcy 1900- *Who 92*
**Hart**, Philip Ray 1925- *WhoRel 92*
**Hart**, Phillip A 1933- *AmMWSc 92*
**Hart**, Phyllis 1942- *WhoAmP 91*
**Hart**, Phyllis D. 1942- *WhoBlA 92*
**Hart**, Ray Lee 1929- *WhoRel 92*
**Hart**, Raymond 1913- *Who 92*
**Hart**, Raymond Kenneth 1928- *AmMWSc 92*
**Hart**, Richard Allen 1930- *AmMWSc 92, WhoMW 92*
**Hart**, Richard Cullen 1945- *AmMWSc 92*
**Hart**, Richard Harold 1933- *AmMWSc 92*
**Hart**, Richard LaVerne 1929- *WhoWest 92*
**Hart**, Richard Odum 1927- *WhoAmP 91*
**Hart**, Richard Royce 1933- *AmMWSc 92*
**Hart**, Richard Wesley 1933- *WhoFI 92*
**Hart**, Robert Camillus 1934- *WhoAmL 92, WhoFI 92*
**Hart**, Robert Carmon 1926- *WhoFI 92*
**Hart**, Robert Edward 1951- *WhoRel 92*
**Hart**, Robert Gerald 1937- *AmMWSc 92*
**Hart**, Robert John 1923- *AmMWSc 92*
**Hart**, Robert Mayes 1925- *IntWW 91*
**Hart**, Robert Thomas 1939- *WhoAmL 92*
**Hart**, Robert Warren 1922- *AmMWSc 92*
**Hart**, Robin Lee 1959- *WhoRel 92*
**Hart**, Ron 1947- *WhoEnt 92*
**Hart**, Ronald Leon 1937- *WhoRel 92, WhoWest 92*
**Hart**, Ronald O. 1942- *WhoBlA 92*
**Hart**, Ronald Wilson 1942- *AmMWSc 92*
**Hart**, Russ Allen 1946- *WhoEnt 92, WhoWest 92*
**Hart**, Rusty 1963- *WhoRel 92*
**Hart**, Samuel Steven 1962- *WhoEnt 92*
**Hart**, Stanley Robert 1935- *AmMWSc 92, IntWW 91*
**Hart**, Stephanie *DrAPF 91*
**Hart**, Stephen Albert 1946- *WhoRel 92*
**Hart**, Steven Weber 1956- *WhoFI 92*
**Hart**, Suzanne Marcella 1936- *WhoWest 92*
**Hart**, Thomas 1730?-1808 *DcNCBi 3*
**Hart**, Thomas Anthony 1940- *Who 92*
**Hart**, Thomas Daniel 1939- *WhoAmP 91*
**Hart**, Thomas Hughson, III 1955- *WhoAmL 92*
**Hart**, Thomas Mure 1909- *Who 92*
**Hart**, Thomas Paul 1951- *WhoFI 92*
**Hart**, Timothy Charles 1948- *WhoWest 92*
**Hart**, Timothy Ray 1942- *WhoWest 92*
**Hart**, Tony *BenetAL 91*
**Hart**, Tony 1954- *WhoBlA 92*
**Hart**, Trevor Stuart 1926- *Who 92*
**Hart**, Warren Craig 1951- *WhoMW 92*
**Hart**, William *DrAPF 91*
**Hart**, William Andrew 1904- *Who 92*
**Hart**, William C 1933- *WhoIns 92*
**Hart**, William D., Jr. 1950- *WhoFI 92*
**Hart**, William Forris 1906- *AmMWSc 92*
**Hart**, William Franklin 1945- *WhoRel 92*
**Hart**, William James, Jr 1923- *AmMWSc 92*
**Hart**, William Levata 1924- *WhoBlA 92*
**Hart**, William Thomas 1929- *WhoAmL 92*
**Hart-Davis**, Duff 1936- *IntAu&W 91, WrDr 92*
**Hart-Davis**, Rupert *DcLB 112 [port]*
**Hart-Davis**, Rupert 1907- *ConAu 134, IntAu&W 91, Who 92, WrDr 92*
**Hart Dyke**, David 1938- *Who 92*
**Hart Dyke**, David 1955- *Who 92*
**Hart-Kelly**, Lesly Margarita 1949- *WhoHisp 92*
**Hart-Leverton**, Colin Allen 1936- *Who 92*
**Hart-Nibbrig**, Harold C. 1938- *WhoBlA 92*
**Hart of South Lanark**, Baroness *Who 92*
**Hart Of South Lanark**, Baroness 1924- *IntWW 91*
**Hart-Smith**, William 1911- *IntAu&W 91*
**Hartack**, William John 1932- *FacFETw*
**Hartarto** 1932- *IntWW 91*
**Hartaway**, Thomas N., Jr. 1943- *WhoBlA 92*
**Hartberg**, Warren Keith 1941- *AmMWSc 92*
**Hartcup**, Adeline 1918- *IntAu&W 91, WrDr 92*
**Hartcup**, Guy 1919- *WrDr 92*
**Hartdagen**, Gerald Eugene 1931- *WhoMW 92*
**Hartdegen**, James Alan 1945- *WhoAmP 91*
**Hartdegen**, Stephen J 1907-1989 *FacFETw*
**Harte**, Bret 1836-1902 *BenetAL 91, ShSCr 8 [port]*
**Harte**, Christopher McCutcheon 1947- *WhoFI 92, WhoMW 92*
**Harte**, Houston Harriman 1927- *WhoFI 92*
**Harte**, John 1939- *AmMWSc 92*
**Harte**, John Joseph Meakin 1914- *WhoRel 92*
**Harte**, Julia Kathleen *Who 92*
**Harte**, Kenneth J 1935- *AmMWSc 92*
**Harte**, Marjorie *IntAu&W 91X, WrDr 92*
**Harte**, Michael John 1936- *Who 92*
**Hartel**, Arthur Paul, Jr. 1933- *WhoAmL 92*
**Hartel**, Stephen Allen 1957- *WhoFI 92*
**Hartenbach**, Stephen Charles 1943- *WhoMW 92*
**Hartenberg**, Richard S 1907- *AmMWSc 92*
**Hartenstein**, Roy 1932- *AmMWSc 92*
**Hartenstine**, Susanne Alicia 1964- *WhoEnt 92*
**Harter**, David John 1942- *WhoMW 92*
**Harter**, Donald Harry 1933- *AmMWSc 92*
**Harter**, George A *AmMWSc 92*
**Harter**, H Leon 1919- *AmMWSc 92*
**Harter**, James A 1922- *AmMWSc 92*
**Harter**, James Toshach 1958- *WhoFI 92*
**Harter**, Noble d1907 *BiInAmS*
**Harter**, Penny *DrAPF 91*
**Harter**, Robert Duane 1936- *AmMWSc 92*
**Harter**, Terry Price 1947- *WhoRel 92*
**Harter**, William George 1943- *AmMWSc 92*
**Hartfiel**, Darald Joe 1939- *AmMWSc 92*
**Hartford**, Carol Lynn 1962- *WhoRel 92*
**Hartford**, Huntington 1911- *IntWW 91*
**Hartford**, John Cowan 1937- *WhoEnt 92*
**Hartford**, K. 1922- *IntMPA 92*
**Hartford**, Kelly Sue 1964- *WhoMW 92*
**Hartford**, Kenneth 1922- *WhoEnt 92*
**Hartford**, Margaret Elizabeth 1917- *WhoWest 92*
**Hartford**, Winslow H 1910- *AmMWSc 92*
**Hartgen**, Stephen Anthony 1944- *WhoWest 92*
**Hartgerink**, Ronald Lee 1942- *AmMWSc 92*
**Hartgrove**, Bruce Norman 1949- *WhoRel 92*
**Harth**, Erich Martin 1919- *AmMWSc 92*
**Harth**, Larry John 1949- *WhoWest 92*
**Harth**, Raymond Earl 1929- *WhoBlA 92*
**Harth**, Robert James 1956- *WhoEnt 92*
**Harth**, Sidney 1929- *NewAmDM, WhoEnt 92*
**Harth**, Victor 1914- *IntWW 91*
**Harthan**, John Plant 1916- *Who 92*
**Harthun**, Luther Arthur 1935- *WhoAmL 92, WhoFI 92*
**Hartig**, Carl F., Jr. 1942- *WhoFI 92*
**Hartig**, Elmer Otto 1923- *AmMWSc 92*
**Hartig**, Gordon 1952- *WhoWest 92*
**Hartig**, Judith M 1938- *WhoAmP 91*
**Hartig**, Paul Richard 1949- *AmMWSc 92*
**Hartigan**, Grace 1922- *FacFETw*
**Hartigan**, James J. 1924- *IntWW 91*
**Hartigan**, John A 1937- *AmMWSc 92*
**Hartigan**, John D., Jr. 1945- *WhoAmL 92*
**Hartigan**, Martin Joseph 1943- *AmMWSc 92*
**Hartigan**, Neil F. 1938- *WhoAmL 92, WhoAmP 91, WhoMW 92*
**Hartill**, Donald L 1939- *AmMWSc 92*
**Hartill**, Edward Theodore 1943- *Who 92*
**Hartill**, Rosemary Jane 1949- *Who 92*
**Hartin**, William John 1962- *WhoWest 92*
**Harting**, Bruce Wilmer 1939- *WhoFI 92*
**Harting**, James W. 1958- *WhoFI 92*
**Hartinger**, John Michael 1955- *WhoAmP 91*
**Hartington**, Marquess of 1944- *Who 92*
**Hartje**, Robert W 1938- *WhoIns 92*
**Hartkamp**, Arthur Severijn 1945- *IntWW 91*
**Hartke**, Charles A 1944- *WhoAmP 91*
**Hartke**, Jerome L 1932- *AmMWSc 92*
**Hartke**, Vance 1919- *WhoAmP 91*
**Hartke**, Werner 1907- *IntWW 91*
**Hartkopf**, Arleigh Van 1942- *AmMWSc 92*
**Hartl**, Daniel L 1943- *AmMWSc 92*
**Hartl**, Donna Frances 1958- *WhoAmL 92*
**Hartl**, John George 1945- *WhoEnt 92*
**Hartl**, William Parker 1935- *WhoFI 92*
**Hartlage**, James Albert 1938- *AmMWSc 92*
**Hartlage**, Lawrence Clifton 1934- *AmMWSc 92*
**Hartland**, Michael 1941- *IntAu&W 91, WrDr 92*
**Hartland-Rowe**, Richard C B 1927- *AmMWSc 92*
**Hartland-Swann**, Julian Dana Nimmo 1936- *Who 92*
**Hartle**, Dean P 1931- *WhoAmP 91*
**Hartle**, James Burkett 1939- *AmMWSc 92*
**Hartle**, Kent Lewis 1952- *WhoMW 92*
**Hartle**, Mary Jean McCoy 1938- *IntAu&W 91*
**Hartle**, Michael Scott 1957- *WhoMW 92*
**Hartle**, Richard Eastham 1936- *AmMWSc 92*
**Hartley**, Albert Edward 1924- *WhoWest 92*
**Hartley**, Arnold Manchester 1926- *AmMWSc 92*
**Hartley**, Arthur Coulton 1906- *Who 92*
**Hartley**, Brian Joseph 1907- *Who 92*
**Hartley**, Brian Selby 1926- *IntWW 91, Who 92*
**Hartley**, Carl Ennis 1948- *WhoAmL 92*
**Hartley**, Charles LeRoy 1944- *AmMWSc 92*
**Hartley**, Christopher 1913- *Who 92*
**Hartley**, Craig Jay 1944- *AmMWSc 92*
**Hartley**, Craig Sheridan 1937- *AmMWSc 92*
**Hartley**, Danny L 1941- *AmMWSc 92*
**Hartley**, David 1705?-1757 *BlkwCEP*
**Hartley**, David 1942- *WhoAmP 91*
**Hartley**, David Fielding 1937- *Who 92*
**Hartley**, Duncan 1941- *WhoFI 92*
**Hartley**, Edward 1847?-1870 *BiInAmS*
**Hartley**, Elise Moore 1953- *WhoEnt 92*
**Hartley**, Elizabeth Jane 1952- *TwCPaSc*
**Hartley**, Francis d1691? *DcNCBi 3*
**Hartley**, Frank 1856-1913 *BiInAmS*
**Hartley**, Frank 1911- *Who 92*
**Hartley**, Frank Robinson 1942- *IntWW 91, Who 92*
**Hartley**, Fred L. d1990 *IntWW 91N*
**Hartley**, Fred L 1917- *AmMWSc 92*
**Hartley**, Gale Ray 1956- *WhoRel 92*
**Hartley**, Gilbert Hillard 1917- *Who 92*
**Hartley**, Grace Van Tine 1916- *WhoFI 92, WhoWest 92*
**Hartley**, Harold V, Jr 1931- *AmMWSc 92*
**Hartley**, Houston Lee 1921- *WhoFI 92*
**Hartley**, James Edward 1949- *WhoAmL 92*
**Hartley**, James Harrison 1946- *WhoWest 92*
**Hartley**, James Michaelis 1916- *WhoFI 92, WhoMW 92*
**Hartley**, Janet Wilson 1928- *AmMWSc 92*
**Hartley**, Jean 1933- *ConAu 135*
**Hartley**, Jeanne Louise 1921- *WhoAmP 91*
**Hartley**, Joan V *WhoAmP 91*
**Hartley**, John Edward 1940- *WhoRel 92*
**Hartley**, John T., Jr. 1930- *WhoFI 92*
**Hartley**, John Thomas 1930- *IntWW 91*
**Hartley**, Kenneth Russell 1961- *WhoFI 92*
**Hartley**, Kristin 1942- *WhoAmP 91*
**Hartley**, L.P. 1895-1972 *RfGEnL 91*
**Hartley**, Marie 1905- *WrDr 92*
**Hartley**, Mariette 1940- *IntMPA 92, WhoEnt 92*
**Hartley**, Marsden 1877-1943 *BenetAL 91*
**Hartley**, Marshall Wendell 1925- *AmMWSc 92*
**Hartley**, Michele Larie 1962- *WhoMW 92*
**Hartley**, Paul Richard 1944- *WhoAmP 91*
**Hartley**, Peter Harold Trahair 1909- *Who 92*
**Hartley**, Richard Leslie Clifford 1932- *Who 92*
**Hartley**, Robert Frederick, Sr 1930- *WhoAmP 91*
**Hartley**, Robert William, Jr 1927- *AmMWSc 92*
**Hartley**, Stuart Leslie 1938- *WhoFI 92*
**Hartley**, Terry L. 1947- *WhoMW 92*
**Hartley**, Walter Sinclair 1927- *WhoEnt 92*
**Hartley-Leonard**, Darryl *WhoMW 92*
**Hartley-Linse**, Bonnie Jean 1923- *WhoWest 92*
**Hartley-Urquhart**, William Roland 1958- *WhoFI 92*
**Hartline**, Beverly Karplus 1950- *AmMWSc 92*
**Hartline**, Daniel Keffer 1939- *AmMWSc 92*
**Hartline**, Darrell G. 1939- *WhoFI 92*
**Hartline**, Halden Keffer 1903-1983 *WhoNob 90*
**Hartline**, Jane A. 1950- *WhoWest 92*
**Hartline**, Mark Allen 1959- *WhoMW 92*
**Hartline**, Peter Haldan 1942- *AmMWSc 92*
**Hartline**, Richard 1932- *AmMWSc 92*
**Hartling**, Peter 1933- *IntWW 91*
**Hartling**, Poul 1914- *IntWW 91, Who 92*
**Hartlove**, Victoria Bernice 1962- *WhoEnt 92*
**Hartly**, Francis d1691? *DcNCBi 3*
**Hartman**, Albert William 1907- *AmMWSc 92*
**Hartman**, Angela 1959- *WhoEnt 92*
**Hartman**, Anne Carlton 1942- *WhoMW 92*
**Hartman**, Arthur A. 1926- *IntWW 91, WhoAmP 91*
**Hartman**, Arthur Dalton 1941- *AmMWSc 92*
**Hartman**, Barry David 1951- *WhoRel 92*
**Hartman**, Boyd Kent 1939- *AmMWSc 92*
**Hartman**, Burton Arthur 1924- *WhoAmL 92*
**Hartman**, Carl 1917- *WhoFI 92*
**Hartman**, Charles William 1932- *AmMWSc 92*
**Hartman**, Dan 1950- *WhoEnt 92*
**Hartman**, David *LesBEnT 92*
**Hartman**, David 1935- *IntMPA 92*
**Hartman**, David Downs 1935- *WhoEnt 92*
**Hartman**, David Elliott 1954- *WhoMW 92*
**Hartman**, David G 1942- *WhoIns 92*
**Hartman**, David Gardiner 1942- *WhoFI 92*
**Hartman**, David Robert 1940- *AmMWSc 92*
**Hartman**, Don Burton 1955- *WhoWest 92*
**Hartman**, Don Douglas 1930- *WhoFI 92*
**Hartman**, Don Lee 1935- *WhoAmL 92*
**Hartman**, Doris 1913- *WhoRel 92*
**Hartman**, Edward Arthur 1963- *WhoRel 92*
**Hartman**, Elizabeth *DrAPF 91*
**Hartman**, Emily Lou 1930- *AmMWSc 92*
**Hartman**, Fred Oscar 1915- *AmMWSc 92*
**Hartman**, Frederick Cooper 1939- *AmMWSc 92*

**Hartman,** Geoffrey H 1929- *IntAu&W 91, WrDr 92*
**Hartman,** Herbert Arthur, Jr. 1947- *WhoMW 92*
**Hartman,** Herman Bernard 1934- *AmMWSc 92*
**Hartman,** Hermene Demaris 1948- *WhoBlA 92*
**Hartman,** Hollister Anne 1955- *WhoWest 92*
**Hartman,** Iclal Sirel 1930- *AmMWSc 92*
**Hartman,** James Austin 1928- *AmMWSc 92*
**Hartman,** James Keith 1943- *AmMWSc 92*
**Hartman,** James Kern 1944- *AmMWSc 92*
**Hartman,** James Lowell 1953- *WhoMW 92*
**Hartman,** James T 1925- *AmMWSc 92*
**Hartman,** James Xavier 1942- *AmMWSc 92*
**Hartman,** Jan 1936- *IntAu&W 91*
**Hartman,** Jeffrey Edward 1959- *WhoRel 92*
**Hartman,** John Alan 1920- *AmMWSc 92*
**Hartman,** John David 1922- *AmMWSc 92*
**Hartman,** John E. 1941- *WhoAmL 92*
**Hartman,** John L 1930- *AmMWSc 92*
**Hartman,** John Paul 1936- *AmMWSc 92*
**Hartman,** John R 1950- *WhoIns 92*
**Hartman,** John Stephen 1938- *AmMWSc 92*
**Hartman,** Karl August 1935- *AmMWSc 92*
**Hartman,** Kenneth Dean 1954- *WhoMW 92*
**Hartman,** Kenneth Eugene 1942- *AmMWSc 92*
**Hartman,** Kenneth Owen 1939- *AmMWSc 92*
**Hartman,** Larry Eugene 1937- *WhoMW 92*
**Hartman,** Lawrence Mark 1943- *WhoFI 92*
**Hartman,** Lisa 1956- *ConTFT 9*
**Hartman,** M. Katrina 1940- *WhoMW 92*
**Hartman,** Marea 1920- *Who 92*
**Hartman,** Marvis Edgar 1940- *AmMWSc 92*
**Hartman,** Matthew Aloysius 1922- *WhoWest 92*
**Hartman,** Nile Franklin 1939- *AmMWSc 92*
**Hartman,** Patricia Anne 1950- *WhoMW 92*
**Hartman,** Patricia O *WhoAmP 91*
**Hartman,** Patrick James 1944- *AmMWSc 92*
**Hartman,** Paul Arthur 1926- *AmMWSc 92, WhoMW 92*
**Hartman,** Paul Leon 1913- *AmMWSc 92*
**Hartman,** Peter Arnold 1937- *WhoWest 92*
**Hartman,** Philip Emil 1926- *AmMWSc 92*
**Hartman,** Ralph D *WhoAmP 91, WhoHisp 92*
**Hartman,** Randall Lloyd 1952- *WhoAmP 91*
**Hartman,** Richard Leon 1937- *AmMWSc 92*
**Hartman,** Richard Michael 1958- *WhoMW 92*
**Hartman,** Richard Thomas 1921- *AmMWSc 92*
**Hartman,** Robert Charles 1938- *AmMWSc 92*
**Hartman,** Robert James 1937- *WhoIns 92*
**Hartman,** Robert John 1926- *AmMWSc 92*
**Hartman,** Robert Nelson d1903 *BiInAmS*
**Hartman,** Roger Duane 1935- *AmMWSc 92*
**Hartman,** Ronald G. 1950- *WhoAmL 92*
**Hartman,** Ross Andrew 1957- *WhoEnt 92*
**Hartman,** Standish Chard 1931- *AmMWSc 92*
**Hartman,** Steven Arthur 1954- *WhoRel 92*
**Hartman,** Suzanne *DrAPF 91*
**Hartman,** Wanda Fay 1940- *WhoRel 92*
**Hartman,** Warren Emery 1914- *AmMWSc 92*
**Hartman,** Wilbur Lee 1931- *AmMWSc 92*
**Hartman,** Willard Daniel 1921- *AmMWSc 92*
**Hartman,** William Charles 1955- *WhoWest 92*
**Hartman,** William Dell 1817-1899 *BiInAmS*
**Hartman,** Yuki *DrAPF 91*
**Hartmanis,** Juris 1928- *AmMWSc 92*
**Hartmann,** Alois J 1936- *AmMWSc 92*
**Hartmann,** Ann Wilson 1941- *WhoFI 92*
**Hartmann,** Bruce 1938- *AmMWSc 92*
**Hartmann,** Christopher Peter 1961- *WhoMW 92*
**Hartmann,** Dennis Lee 1949- *AmMWSc 92, WhoWest 92*
**Hartmann,** Donald Otto, Sr. 1934- *WhoMW 92*
**Hartmann,** Elizabeth 1951- *IntAu&W 91*
**Hartmann,** Erich 1922- *EncTR 91 [port]*
**Hartmann,** Ernest L. 1934- *WrDr 92*
**Hartmann,** Ernest Louis 1934- *AmMWSc 92*
**Hartmann,** Floyd Wellington 1913- *AmMWSc 92*
**Hartmann,** Francis Xavier 1953- *AmMWSc 92*
**Hartmann,** Frederick W 1940- *AmMWSc 92*
**Hartmann,** George Charles 1927- *AmMWSc 92*
**Hartmann,** George Cole 1940- *AmMWSc 92*
**Hartmann,** George Wilfried 1904-1955 *AmPeW*
**Hartmann,** Gregory Kemenyi 1911- *AmMWSc 92*
**Hartmann,** Hans S 1931- *AmMWSc 92*
**Hartmann,** Henrik Anton 1920- *AmMWSc 92*
**Hartmann,** Hudson Thomas 1914- *AmMWSc 92*
**Hartmann,** Judith Brown 1946- *AmMWSc 92*
**Hartmann,** Karl Amadeus 1905-1963 *NewAmDM*
**Hartmann,** Michael 1944- *WrDr 92*
**Hartmann,** Michael John 1944- *IntAu&W 91*
**Hartmann,** Richard Paul 1934- *WhoMW 92*
**Hartmann,** Richard W 1935- *AmMWSc 92*
**Hartmann,** Robert Carl 1919- *AmMWSc 92*
**Hartmann,** Robert Trowbridge 1917- *IntWW 91, WhoAmP 91*
**Hartmann,** Sadakichi 1867-1944 *BenetAL 91*
**Hartmann,** Sven Richard 1932- *AmMWSc 92*
**Hartmann,** William Herman 1931- *AmMWSc 92*
**Hartmann,** William K 1939- *AmMWSc 92*
**Hartmann,** William Morris 1939- *AmMWSc 92*
**Hartnack,** Carl Edward 1916- *IntWW 91*
**Hartnack,** Justus 1912- *WrDr 92*
**Hartnack,** Paul Richard Samuel 1942- *Who 92*
**Hartnedy,** John A 1939- *WhoIns 92*
**Hartner,** William Christopher 1939- *AmMWSc 92*
**Hartness,** Sandra Jean 1944- *WhoFI 92*
**Hartnett,** D Paul 1927- *WhoAmP 91*
**Hartnett,** David William 1952- *IntAu&W 91*
**Hartnett,** James P 1924- *AmMWSc 92*
**Hartnett,** John 1922- *AmMWSc 92*
**Hartnett,** John F. 1937- *WhoFI 92*
**Hartnett,** Marilyn Ann 1935- *WhoMW 92*
**Hartnett,** Michael 1941- *ConPo 91*
**Hartnett,** Thomas Forbes 1941- *WhoAmP 91*
**Hartnett,** Thomas Robert, III 1920- *WhoAmL 92*
**Hartnett,** Will Ford 1956- *WhoAmL 92, WhoAmP 91*
**Hartnett,** William Edward 1925- *AmMWSc 92*
**Hartney,** Joseph C., Jr. d1991 *NewYTBS 91*
**Hartocollis,** Peter 1922- *AmMWSc 92*
**Hartog,** Harold Samuel Arnold 1910- *IntWW 91, Who 92*
**Hartog,** Howard 1913-1990 *AnObit 1990*
**Hartog,** Jan de 1914- *FacFETw, IntWW 91, LiExTwC*
**Hartog,** John, II 1936- *WhoRel 92*
**Hartoko,** Dick 1922- *WhoRel 92*
**Harton,** Ernest H 1936- *WhoIns 92*
**Hartong,** Johan Sebastian 1947- *WhoEnt 92*
**Hartop,** William Lionel, Jr 1921- *AmMWSc 92*
**Hartopp,** John Edmund Cradock- 1912- *Who 92*
**Hartranft,** George Robert 1933- *AmMWSc 92*
**Hartrich,** Christopher David 1953- *WhoMW 92*
**Hartrick,** A.S. 1864-1950 *TwCPaSc*
**Hartroft,** Phyllis Merritt 1928- *AmMWSc 92*
**Hartrum,** Thomas Charles 1945- *AmMWSc 92*
**Hartsaw,** William O 1921- *AmMWSc 92*
**Hartse,** Denise Yvonne Durfee 1951- *WhoAmP 91*
**Hartsell,** Fletcher Lee, Jr 1947- *WhoAmP 91*
**Hartsfield,** Arnett L., Jr. 1918- *WhoBlA 92*
**Hartsfield,** Howard C. 1926- *WhoBlA 92*
**Hartsfield,** Nora Anne *WhoWest 92*
**Hartsfield,** Sandee Morris 1948- *AmMWSc 92*
**Hartshorn,** Herbert Hadley 1909- *WhoBlA 92*
**Hartshorn,** Joseph Harold 1922- *AmMWSc 92*
**Hartshorn,** Michael Philip 1936- *IntWW 91*
**Hartshorne,** Charles 1897- *IntAu&W 91, WrDr 92*
**Hartshorne,** Henry 1823-1897 *AmPeW, BiInAmS*
**Hartshorne,** Richard 1899- *WrDr 92*
**Hartshorne,** Robert Cope 1938- *AmMWSc 92*
**Hartshorne,** Thomas L. 1935- *WrDr 92*
**Hartsock,** Charles Patrick 1945- *WhoRel 92*
**Hartsock,** Darrell A. 1959- *WhoWest 92*
**Hartsoe,** James Russell 1934- *WhoRel 92*
**Hartsoe,** Joseph Robert 1954- *WhoAmL 92*
**Hartson,** Maurice J, III 1936- *WhoIns 92*
**Hartsook,** David L 1948- *WhoIns 92*
**Hartsook,** Joseph Thurman 1915- *AmMWSc 92*
**Hartsough,** Larry Dowd 1942- *AmMWSc 92*
**Hartsough,** Michael Thomas 1954- *WhoAmL 92*
**Hartsough,** Robert Ray 1957- *AmMWSc 92, WhoMW 92*
**Hartsough,** Walter Douglas 1924- *AmMWSc 92*
**Hartstein,** Allan Mark 1947- *AmMWSc 92*
**Hartstein,** Arthur M 1940- *AmMWSc 92*
**Hartstein,** Jacob I. d1991 *NewYTBS 91 [port]*
**Hartstirn,** Walter 1928- *AmMWSc 92*
**Hartston,** William Roland 1947- *IntAu&W 91, WrDr 92*
**Hartsuck,** Jean Ann 1939- *AmMWSc 92*
**Hartt,** Charles Frederick 1840-1878 *BiInAmS*
**Hartt,** Frederick 1914- *FacFETw*
**Hartt,** Frederick 1914-1991 *NewYTBS 91*
**Hartt,** Grover, III 1948- *WhoAmL 92*
**Hartt,** Julian Norris 1911- *WhoRel 92*
**Hartt,** Susan Kay 1948- *WhoAmL 92, WhoFI 92*
**Hartt,** William Handy 1939- *AmMWSc 92*
**Hartung,** Christin 1941- *WhoAmP 91*
**Hartung,** Frank Edwin 1940- *WhoAmP 91*
**Hartung,** G Harley 1933- *AmMWSc 92*
**Hartung,** Hans 1904- *FacFETw*
**Hartung,** Harald 1932- *IntWW 91*
**Hartung,** Homer Arthur 1927- *AmMWSc 92*
**Hartung,** Jack Burdair, Sr 1937- *AmMWSc 92*
**Hartung,** John 1951- *AmMWSc 92*
**Hartung,** John David 1947- *AmMWSc 92*
**Hartung,** Lorraine E. 1944- *WhoHisp 92*
**Hartung,** Mary *WhoAmP 91*
**Hartung,** Roderick Lee 1935- *WhoFI 92*
**Hartung,** Rolf 1935- *AmMWSc 92*
**Hartung,** Theodore Eugene 1929- *AmMWSc 92*
**Hartung,** Thomas Frederick 1927- *WhoAmP 91*
**Hartvig-Nielsen,** Niels 1956- *WhoEnt 92*
**Hartvigsen,** David Beesley 1959- *WhoAmL 92*
**Hartwell,** Baron 1911- *IntWW 91, Who 92*
**Hartwell,** Benjamin James 1908- *Who 92*
**Hartwell,** Brodrick William Charles Elwin 1909- *Who 92*
**Hartwell,** Charles 1825- *BiInAmS*
**Hartwell,** Charles Leonard 1873-1951 *TwCPaSc*
**Hartwell,** David 1942- *ScFEYrs*
**Hartwell,** David & Currey, Lloyd W *ScFEYrs*
**Hartwell,** Eric 1915- *Who 92*
**Hartwell,** George E, Jr 1940- *AmMWSc 92*
**Hartwell,** George Wilber 1881-1917 *BiInAmS*
**Hartwell,** Jonathan Lutton 1906- *AmMWSc 92*
**Hartwell,** Leland Harrison 1939- *AmMWSc 92*
**Hartwell,** Richard 1946- *TwCPaSc*
**Hartwell,** Robert Simpson 1952- *WhoEnt 92*
**Hartwell,** Samuel Adams 1930- *WhoFI 92*
**Hartwick,** Earl Brian 1942- *AmMWSc 92*
**Hartwick,** Frederick David Alfred 1941- *AmMWSc 92*
**Hartwick,** Richard Allen 1951- *AmMWSc 92*
**Hartwick,** Thomas Stanley 1934- *AmMWSc 92, WhoWest 92*
**Hartwig,** Curtis P 1939- *AmMWSc 92*
**Hartwig,** Harvey L 1943- *WhoIns 92*
**Hartwig,** John 1949- *AmMWSc 92*
**Hartwig,** Leonard John 1932- *WhoFI 92*
**Hartwig,** Nathan Leroy 1937- *AmMWSc 92*
**Hartwig,** Robert Allen, Jr. 1958- *WhoWest 92*
**Hartwig,** Robert Eduard 1941- *AmMWSc 92*
**Hartwig,** William Carl 1936- *WhoMW 92*
**Harty,** Belford Donald, Jr. 1928- *WhoBlA 92*
**Harty,** Bernard Peter 1943- *Who 92*
**Harty,** Donald K. *WhoBlA 92*
**Harty,** James Quinn 1925- *WhoAmL 92*
**Harty,** Michael *Who 92*
**Harty,** Michael 1912- *AmMWSc 92*
**Hartz,** Billy J 1926- *AmMWSc 92*
**Hartz,** Bradley Scott 1955- *WhoFI 92*
**Hartz,** Brendan Thomas 1956- *WhoEnt 92*
**Hartz,** Carroll Juan 1929- *WhoMW 92*
**Hartz,** Harry J. 1925- *WhoFI 92*
**Hartz,** Jim *LesBEnT 92*
**Hartz,** Jim 1940- *IntMPA 92*
**Hartz,** John William *AmMWSc 92*
**Hartz,** Roy Eugene 1940- *AmMWSc 92*
**Hartzell,** Andrew Cornelius, Jr. 1927- *WhoAmL 92*
**Hartzell,** Charles Ross, III 1941- *AmMWSc 92*
**Hartzell,** Kenneth R, Jr 1954- *AmMWSc 92*
**Hartzell,** Thomas H 1932- *AmMWSc 92*
**Hartzema,** Abraham Gijsbert 1947- *AmMWSc 92*
**Hartzen,** Richard I. 1936- *WhoMW 92*
**Hartzfeld,** Howard Alexander 1928- *AmMWSc 92*
**Hartzler,** Alfred James 1922- *AmMWSc 92*
**Hartzler,** Cheryl Elaine 1945- *WhoFI 92*
**Hartzler,** Eva Ruth 1911- *AmMWSc 92*
**Hartzler,** Harris Dale 1932- *AmMWSc 92*
**Hartzler,** Harrod Harold 1908- *AmMWSc 92*
**Hartzler,** Jon David 1941- *AmMWSc 92*
**Hartzler,** Stanley James 1947- *WhoMW 92*
**Hartzog,** Christopher Craig 1959- *WhoRel 92*
**Hartzog,** David G 1941- *AmMWSc 92*
**Hartzog,** Ernest E. 1928- *WhoBlA 92*
**Hartzog,** George B., Jr. 1920- *IntWW 91*
**Hartzog,** James Victor 1937- *AmMWSc 92*
**Hartzog,** Wendell L, Jr 1951- *WhoAmP 91*
**Haruda,** Fred David 1950- *WhoWest 92*
**Haruf,** Kent *DrAPF 91*
**Haruki,** Hiroshi 1918- *AmMWSc 92*
**Harun,** Joseph Stanley 1925- *AmMWSc 92*
**Haruna,** Alhaji *Who 92*
**Haruta,** Kyoichi 1931- *AmMWSc 92*
**Harutunian,** Albert Theodore, III 1955- *WhoAmL 92*
**Harvais,** Gaetan Hugues 1935- *AmMWSc 92*
**Harvalik,** Zaboj Vincent 1907- *AmMWSc 92*
**Harvard,** Beverly Bailey 1950- *WhoBlA 92*
**Harvard,** Jack *WhoAmP 91*
**Harvard,** Ronald Wilson 1943- *WhoRel 92*
**Harvarth,** Liana 1951- *AmMWSc 92*
**Harvath,** Liana 1951- *AmMWSc 92*
**Harvel,** Christopher Alvin 1944- *AmMWSc 92*
**Harvell,** Valeria Gomez 1958- *WhoBlA 92*
**Harves,** Duane Richard 1940- *WhoAmL 92*
**Harvest,** Ernest L., Jr. 1953- *WhoEnt 92*
**Harvey** *Who 92*
**Harvey,** A 1930- *AmMWSc 92*
**Harvey,** Abner McGehee 1911- *AmMWSc 92*
**Harvey,** Alan Eric 1938- *AmMWSc 92*
**Harvey,** Alan Frederick Ronald 1919- *Who 92*
**Harvey,** Albert Bigelow 1938- *AmMWSc 92*
**Harvey,** Albert Raymond 1921- *AmMWSc 92*
**Harvey,** Alexander 1868-1949 *ScFEYrs*
**Harvey,** Alexander, II 1923- *WhoAmL 92*
**Harvey,** Alexander Louis 1917- *AmMWSc 92*
**Harvey,** Alison Margaret 1950- *WhoAmP 91*
**Harvey,** Andrew 1952- *IntAu&W 91*
**Harvey,** Anne Berenice 1933- *IntAu&W 91*
**Harvey,** Anthony 1931- *ConTFT 9, IntMPA 92, IntWW 91*
**Harvey,** Anthony Ernest 1930- *Who 92*
**Harvey,** Anthony Peter 1940- *Who 92*
**Harvey,** Arthur Douglas 1916- *Who 92*
**Harvey,** Barbara Fitzgerald 1928- *IntWW 91, Who 92*
**Harvey,** Benjamin Hyde 1908- *Who 92*
**Harvey,** Beverly Ann 1957- *WhoBlA 92*
**Harvey,** Billy V 1932- *WhoAmP 91*
**Harvey,** Birt 1928- *AmMWSc 92*
**Harvey,** Bob *WhoAmP 91*
**Harvey,** Brett 1936- *IntAu&W 91*
**Harvey,** Brian Wilberforce 1936- *Who 92*
**Harvey,** Bryan Hugh 1914- *Who 92*
**Harvey,** Bryan Laurence 1937- *AmMWSc 92*
**Harvey,** C. Franklin, Jr. 1949- *WhoRel 92*
**Harvey,** Cameron 1948- *WhoEnt 92*
**Harvey,** Caroline *WrDr 92*
**Harvey,** Charles Arthur 1929- *AmMWSc 92*
**Harvey,** Charles P, II 1947- *WhoAmP 91*
**Harvey,** Charles Richard Musgrave 1937- *Who 92*
**Harvey,** Clarence Charles 1918- *AmMWSc 92*

**Harvey,** Clarie Collins 1916- *WhoBlA 92*
**Harvey,** Colin Stanley 1924- *Who 92*
**Harvey,** Crete Bowman 1929- *WhoAmP 91*
**Harvey,** Daniel 1959- *TwCPaSc*
**Harvey,** Daniel Richard 1930- *WhoRel 92*
**Harvey,** Darrel Lee 1962- *WhoRel 92*
**Harvey,** David 1935- *Who 92*
**Harvey,** David Christensen 1934- *WhoAmP 91*
**Harvey,** David Michael 1934- *WhoAmL 92*
**Harvey,** David Paul 1932- *WhoRel 92*
**Harvey,** David Pryor 1958- *WhoWest 92*
**Harvey,** Denise M. 1954- *WhoBlA 92*
**Harvey,** Dorothea S. 1928- *TwCPaSc*
**Harvey,** Douglas J 1924- *AmMWSc 92*
**Harvey,** Douglass Coate 1917- *AmMWSc 92*
**Harvey,** Edmund Lukens 1915- *WhoAmL 92*
**Harvey,** Edward Thomas 1948- *WhoFI 92*
**Harvey,** Elaine Louise 1936- *WhoWest 92*
**Harvey,** Elton Bartlett, III 1946- *WhoAmL 92*
**Harvey,** Everett H *AmMWSc 92*
**Harvey,** F Reese 1941- *AmMWSc 92*
**Harvey,** Frances J, II 1943- *AmMWSc 92*
**Harvey,** Francis Leroy 1850-1900 *BiInAmS*
**Harvey,** Frederick Parker 1920- *WhoFI 92*
**Harvey,** Gale Allen 1938- *AmMWSc 92*
**Harvey,** Gayle Ellen *DrAPF 91*
**Harvey,** George Ranson 1937- *AmMWSc 92*
**Harvey,** Gerald 1950- *WhoBlA 92*
**Harvey,** Gerald Paul 1956- *WhoRel 92*
**Harvey,** Gregory Alan 1949- *WhoWest 92*
**Harvey,** Harold 1874-1941 *TwCPaSc*
**Harvey,** Harold A. 1944- *WhoBlA 92*
**Harvey,** Harold H 1930- *AmMWSc 92*
**Harvey,** Herschel Ambrose, Jr. 1929- *WhoFI 92*
**Harvey,** J Bruce 1942- *WhoAmP 91*
**Harvey,** J Paul, Jr 1922- *AmMWSc 92*
**Harvey,** Jackson 1958- *WhoEnt 92*
**Harvey,** Jacqueline V. 1933- *WhoBlA 92*
**Harvey,** James 1922- *WhoAmP 91*
**Harvey,** James 1929- *ConAu 135*
**Harvey,** James Clement 1941- *WhoAmL 92*
**Harvey,** James Gerald 1934- *WhoWest 92*
**Harvey,** James Mathews, Jr. 1964- *WhoEnt 92*
**Harvey,** James Ross 1934- *WhoFI 92, WhoWest 92*
**Harvey,** Jeffrey Alan 1955- *AmMWSc 92*
**Harvey,** Joan *DrAPF 91*
**Harvey,** Joel 1938- *WhoRel 92*
**Harvey,** John d1679 *DcNCBi 3*
**Harvey,** John 1724?-1775 *DcNCBi 3*
**Harvey,** John 1911- *WrDr 92*
**Harvey,** John 1938- *TwCWW 91*
**Harvey,** John, Jr 1925- *AmMWSc 92*
**Harvey,** John Adriance 1930- *AmMWSc 92*
**Harvey,** John Arthur 1921- *AmMWSc 92*
**Harvey,** John B. 1938- *WrDr 92*
**Harvey,** John Barton 1938- *IntAu&W 91*
**Harvey,** John Collins 1923- *AmMWSc 92*
**Harvey,** John Edgar 1920- *Who 92*
**Harvey,** John F. 1921- *WrDr 92*
**Harvey,** John Frederick 1921- *WhoRel 92*
**Harvey,** John Grover 1934- *AmMWSc 92, WhoMW 92*
**Harvey,** John Hooper 1911- *IntAu&W 91*
**Harvey,** John Marshall 1921- *AmMWSc 92*
**Harvey,** John Randal 1964- *WhoMW 92*
**Harvey,** John Robert 1942- *IntAu&W 91*
**Harvey,** John Warren 1940- *AmMWSc 92*
**Harvey,** John Wilcox 1938- *AmMWSc 92*
**Harvey,** John Wynn 1923-1989 *TwCPaSc*
**Harvey,** Jonathan 1939- *ConCom 92*
**Harvey,** Jonathan Dean 1939- *IntWW 91, Who 92*
**Harvey,** Jonathan Paul 1941- *WhoAmL 92*
**Harvey,** Joseph Eldon 1927- *AmMWSc 92*
**Harvey,** Joseph K 1939- *WhoAmP 91*
**Harvey,** Katherine Abler 1946- *WhoMW 92*
**Harvey,** Kathryn Tinker 1924- *WhoAmP 91*
**Harvey,** Kenneth A 1951- *WhoAmP 91*
**Harvey,** Kenneth C 1947- *AmMWSc 92*
**Harvey,** Kenneth George 1940- *Who 92*
**Harvey,** Kenneth Ray 1965- *WhoBlA 92*
**Harvey,** Kenneth Ricardo 1956- *WhoWest 92*
**Harvey,** La Verne Deborah 1948- *WhoEnt 92*
**Harvey,** Lawrence Harmon 1930- *AmMWSc 92*
**Harvey,** Leonard Patrick 1929- *Who 92*
**Harvey,** Louis-Charles 1945- *WhoBlA 92, WhoRel 92*
**Harvey,** Mack Creede 1929- *AmMWSc 92*
**Harvey,** Malcolm 1936- *AmMWSc 92*
**Harvey,** Marc Sean 1960- *WhoAmL 92*
**Harvey,** Mark Charles 1953- *WhoRel 92*
**Harvey,** Mark Sumner 1946- *WhoEnt 92, WhoRel 92*
**Harvey,** Mary 1629-1704 *NewAmDM*
**Harvey,** Mary Frances Clare 1927- *Who 92*
**Harvey,** Michael John 1935- *AmMWSc 92*
**Harvey,** Michael Llewellyn Tucker 1943- *Who 92*
**Harvey,** Miles 1728-1776 *DcNCBi 3*
**Harvey,** Morris Lane 1950- *WhoAmL 92*
**Harvey,** Neil 1938- *Who 92*
**Harvey,** Nigel 1916- *IntAu&W 91, WrDr 92*
**Harvey,** Norma Baker 1943- *WhoBlA 92*
**Harvey,** Norman Ronald 1933- *WhoFI 92*
**Harvey,** P. D. A. 1930- *WrDr 92*
**Harvey,** Pamla 1963- *WhoWest 92*
**Harvey,** Patricia Jean 1931- *WhoWest 92*
**Harvey,** Paul *LesBEnT 92*
**Harvey,** Paul Dean Adshead 1930- *Who 92*
**Harvey,** Paul W. 1957- *WhoWest 92*
**Harvey,** Peter 1922- *Who 92*
**Harvey,** Peter 1951- *ConAu 135*
**Harvey,** Peter Francis 1933- *WhoEnt 92*
**Harvey,** Philip James Benedict 1915- *Who 92*
**Harvey,** Ralph d1991 *NewYTBS 91*
**Harvey,** Ralph 1901- *WhoAmP 91*
**Harvey,** Ralph Clayton 1952- *AmMWSc 92*
**Harvey,** Raymond 1950- *WhoBlA 92*
**Harvey,** Richard Alexander 1936- *AmMWSc 92*
**Harvey,** Richard David 1928- *AmMWSc 92*
**Harvey,** Richard Dudley 1923- *WhoFI 92, WhoWest 92*
**Harvey,** Richard R. *WhoBlA 92*
**Harvey,** Robert Gordon, Jr 1945- *AmMWSc 92*
**Harvey,** Robert J. *WhoWest 92*
**Harvey,** Robert Joseph 1938- *AmMWSc 92*
**Harvey,** Robert Lambart 1953- *Who 92*
**Harvey,** Ronald Gilbert 1927- *AmMWSc 92*
**Harvey,** Ross Buschlen 1917- *AmMWSc 92*
**Harvey,** Ruth Ann 1958- *WhoAmL 92*
**Harvey,** Stephen 1949- *ConAu 134*
**Harvey,** Stephen Craig 1940- *AmMWSc 92*
**Harvey,** Stewart Clyde 1921- *AmMWSc 92, WhoWest 92*
**Harvey,** Stuart Charles 1933- *WhoMW 92*
**Harvey,** Thomas d1699 *DcNCBi 3*
**Harvey,** Thomas, Jr. 1692-1729 *DcNCBi 3*
**Harvey,** Thomas Cockayne 1918- *Who 92*
**Harvey,** Thomas G 1907- *AmMWSc 92*
**Harvey,** Thomas J. 1939- *WhoRel 92*
**Harvey,** Thomas Larkin 1926- *AmMWSc 92*
**Harvey,** Thomas Stoltz 1912- *AmMWSc 92*
**Harvey,** Thomas William 1939- *WhoFI 92*
**Harvey,** Trice Jeraine 1936- *WhoAmP 91*
**Harvey,** Van Austin 1926- *WhoRel 92*
**Harvey,** Vaughn Robert 1955- *WhoEnt 92*
**Harvey,** Walter Robert 1919- *AmMWSc 92*
**Harvey,** Walter William 1925- *AmMWSc 92*
**Harvey,** Wardelle G. 1926- *WhoBlA 92*
**Harvey,** William 1957- *TwCPaSc*
**Harvey,** William Brantley, Jr 1930- *WhoAmP 91*
**Harvey,** William Daniel 1958- *WhoRel 92*
**Harvey,** William James, III 1912- *WhoBlA 92*
**Harvey,** William M. 1933- *WhoBlA 92*
**Harvey,** William R. 1941- *WhoBlA 92*
**Harvey,** William Ross 1930- *AmMWSc 92*
**Harvey-Bell,** Linda Jean 1960- *WhoRel 92*
**Harvey-Byrd,** Patricia Lynn 1954- *WhoBlA 92*
**Harvey-Jamieson,** Harvey Morro 1908- *Who 92*
**Harvey-Jones,** John 1924- *IntWW 91, Who 92*
**Harvey of Prestbury,** Baron 1906- *Who 92*
**Harvey of Tasburgh,** Baron 1921- *Who 92*
**Harveycutter,** Robert Carey, Jr 1952- *WhoAmP 91*
**Harvie-Clark,** Sidney d1991 *Who 92N*
**Harvie-Watt,** James 1940- *Who 92*
**Harville,** David Arthur 1940- *AmMWSc 92*
**Harville,** John Patrick 1918- *AmMWSc 92*
**Harvin,** Alvin 1937- *WhoBlA 92*
**Harvin,** C Alex, III 1950- *WhoAmP 91*
**Harvin,** David Tarleton 1945- *WhoAmL 92*
**Harvin,** James Shand 1929- *AmMWSc 92*
**Harvington,** Baron 1907- *Who 92*
**Harvith,** John Dana 1946- *WhoEnt 92*
**Harvith,** Susan Edwards 1946- *WhoEnt 92*
**Harvitt,** Adrianne Stanley 1954- *WhoAmL 92*
**Harvor,** Beth *ConAu 134*
**Harvor,** Elisabeth 1936- *ConAu 134*
**Harward,** Byron L 1949- *WhoAmP 91*
**Harward,** Gary John 1941- *WhoMW 92*
**Harwayne,** Frank 1920- *WhoIns 92*
**Harwell,** B Hicks 1933- *WhoAmP 91*
**Harwell,** Charles Larry 1953- *WhoAmL 92*
**Harwell,** David W 1932- *WhoAmP 91*
**Harwell,** David Walker 1932- *WhoAmL 92*
**Harwell,** Ernie *NewYTBS 91 [port]*
**Harwell,** Frances Olivia 1960- *WhoRel 92*
**Harwell,** Hugh Blake 1964- *WhoRel 92*
**Harwell,** James Henry 1953- *WhoFI 92*
**Harwell,** Janis Lauren 1954- *WhoAmL 92, WhoFI 92*
**Harwell,** Kenneth Edwin 1936- *AmMWSc 92*
**Harwell,** Kenneth Elzer 1921- *AmMWSc 92*
**Harwell,** Mark Alan 1947- *AmMWSc 92*
**Harwell,** Paul Lafayette 1930- *WhoRel 92*
**Harwell,** Thomas L. 1958- *WhoRel 92*
**Harwell,** William Earnest 1918- *WhoEnt 92*
**Harwell,** William Earnest 1935- *WhoMW 92*
**Harwich,** David Curtis 1955- *WhoEnt 92*
**Harwick,** Betty Corinne Burns 1926- *WhoRel 92, WhoWest 92*
**Harwick,** Dennis Patrick 1949- *WhoAmL 92*
**Harwick,** Lois Hoover 1924- *WhoRel 92*
**Harwick,** Maurice 1933- *WhoWest 92*
**Harwit,** Martin Otto 1931- *AmMWSc 92*
**Harwood,** Allan Dale 1939- *WhoEnt 92, WhoWest 92*
**Harwood,** Anne Elizabeth 1962- *WhoWest 92*
**Harwood,** Clare Theresa 1920- *AmMWSc 92*
**Harwood,** Clifford B *WhoAmP 91*
**Harwood,** Colin Frederick 1937- *AmMWSc 92*
**Harwood,** David 1938- *IntAu&W 91, WrDr 92*
**Harwood,** David Smith 1936- *AmMWSc 92*
**Harwood,** Don 1936- *WhoEnt 92*
**Harwood,** Donald *WhoEnt 92*
**Harwood,** Elisabeth 1938-1990 *NewAmDM*
**Harwood,** Elizabeth 1938-1990 *AnObit 1990*
**Harwood,** Elizabeth Jean d1990 *IntWW 91N*
**Harwood,** Gwen 1920- *ConPo 91, IntAu&W 91, WrDr 92*
**Harwood,** Harold James 1931- *AmMWSc 92*
**Harwood,** John B 1952- *WhoAmP 91*
**Harwood,** John Warwick 1946- *Who 92*
**Harwood,** Joseph 1952- *WhoMW 92*
**Harwood,** Julius J 1918- *AmMWSc 92*
**Harwood,** Lee 1939- *ConPo 91, IntAu&W 91, WrDr 92*
**Harwood,** Lucy 1893-1972 *TwCPaSc*
**Harwood,** Madeline Bailey 1914- *WhoAmP 91*
**Harwood,** Nevin Robert 1946- *WhoAmL 92*
**Harwood,** Philip Joseph 1938- *WhoMW 92*
**Harwood,** Raymond Charles 1906- *IntAu&W 91*
**Harwood,** Ronald 1934- *IntAu&W 91, IntMPA 92, LiExTwC, Who 92, WrDr 92*
**Harwood,** Stanley 1926- *WhoAmP 91*
**Harwood,** Thomas Riegel 1926- *AmMWSc 92*
**Harwood,** Vanessa Clare 1947- *WhoEnt 92*
**Harwood,** Virginia Ann 1925- *WhoMW 92*
**Harwood,** Warren Peter 1939- *WhoWest 92*
**Harwood,** William H 1922- *AmMWSc 92*
**Harwood,** William Sumner 1857-1908 *BiInAmS*
**Harwood-Nash,** Derek Clive 1936- *AmMWSc 92*
**Hary** 1440?-1495? *RfGEnL 91*
**Hary,** Guy William Pulbrook 1931- *IntWW 91*
**Haryett,** Rowland D 1923- *AmMWSc 92*
**Harz,** G. Michael 1951- *WhoWest 92*
**Hasan,** Abu Rashid 1949- *AmMWSc 92*
**Hasan,** Aqeel Khatib 1955- *WhoBlA 92*
**Hasan,** Iftekhar 1960- *WhoFI 92*
**Hasan,** Mahmudul 1936- *IntWW 91*
**Hasan,** Maria Rosaria 1947- *WhoIns 92*
**Hasan,** Mazhar 1927- *AmMWSc 92*
**Hasan,** Rabiul *DrAPF 91*
**Hasan,** Rashad 1954- *WhoBlA 92*
**Hasan,** Shah Mohammed 1957- *WhoMW 92*
**Hasan,** Syed Eqbal 1939- *AmMWSc 92*
**Hasan,** Waqar 1963- *WhoWest 92*
**Hasani,** Sinan 1922- *IntWW 91*
**Hasara,** Karen 1940- *WhoAmP 91*
**Hasay,** George C 1948- *WhoAmP 91*
**Hasbrook,** Arthur F 1913- *AmMWSc 92*
**Hasbrouck,** Ellsworth Eugene 1913- *WhoBlA 92*
**Hasbrouck,** Norman Gene 1952- *WhoRel 92*
**Hasbrouck,** Wilbert Roland 1931- *WhoMW 92*
**Hascall,** Gretchen Katharine 1941- *AmMWSc 92*
**Hascall,** Jane Marian 1938- *WhoWest 92*
**Hascall,** Vincent Charles, Jr 1940- *AmMWSc 92*
**Hasche,** Tilman 1950- *WhoAmL 92*
**Haschemeyer,** Audrey Elizabeth Veazie 1936- *AmMWSc 92*
**Haschke,** Ferdinand 1948- *AmMWSc 92*
**Haschke,** John Maurice 1941- *AmMWSc 92*
**Hasdal,** John Allan 1942- *AmMWSc 92*
**Hase,** David John 1940- *WhoAmL 92*
**Hase,** Karl-Gunther von 1917- *IntWW 91*
**Hase,** Paul von 1885-1944 *EncTR 91*
**Hase,** Thomas Carl 1962- *WhoEnt 92*
**Hase,** William Louis 1945- *AmMWSc 92*
**Haseeb,** Khair El-Din 1929- *IntWW 91*
**Hasegawa,** Ichiro 1915- *AmMWSc 92*
**Hasegawa,** Junji 1917- *AmMWSc 92*
**Hasegawa,** Kenko 1916- *IntWW 91*
**Hasegawa,** Lee Patton 1951- *WhoEnt 92, WhoMW 92*
**Hasegawa,** Norishige 1907- *IntWW 91*
**Hasegawa,** Ryusuke 1940- *AmMWSc 92*
**Hasegawa,** Taiji 1945- *WhoFI 92*
**Hasegawa,** Takashi 1912- *IntWW 91*
**Hasek,** Jaroslav 1883-1923 *FacFETw*
**Hasek,** Joseph Karel 1911- *WhoFI 92*
**Hasek,** Robert Hall 1918- *AmMWSc 92*
**Hasel,** Frank M. 1962- *WhoRel 92*
**Hasel,** Gerhard Franz 1935- *WhoRel 92*
**Hasel,** Michael Gerald 1968- *WhoRel 92*
**Haselbush,** Jack Garth 1947- *WhoWest 92*
**Haselden,** Geoffrey Gordon 1924- *Who 92*
**Haselden,** Ron 1944- *TwCPaSc*
**Haseldine,** Norman 1922- *Who 92*
**Haseler,** Stephen Michael Alan 1942- *Who 92*
**Haseley,** Edward Albert 1930- *AmMWSc 92*
**Haseley,** Susan L 1959- *WhoIns 92*
**Haselgrove,** Dennis Cliff 1914- *Who 92*
**Haselhurst,** Alan Gordon Barraclough 1937- *Who 92*
**Haselkorn,** Robert 1934- *AmMWSc 92*
**Hasell,** James d1785 *DcNCBi 3*
**Hasell,** William Soranzo 1780-1815 *DcNCBi 3*
**Haselmann,** John Philip 1940- *WhoFI 92*
**Haseloff,** Charles *DrAPF 91*
**Haseltine,** Florence Pat 1942- *AmMWSc 92*
**Haselton,** George Montgomery 1928- *AmMWSc 92*
**Haselton,** Judith Sidney 1954- *WhoFI 92*
**Haselton,** Rick Thomas 1953- *WhoAmL 92*
**Haselwood,** Eldon LaVerne 1933- *WhoMW 92*
**Haseman,** Joseph Fish 1914- *AmMWSc 92*
**Hasen,** Susan Katherine 1965- *WhoEnt 92, WhoMW 92*
**Hasenberg,** Werner 1928- *WhoFI 92*
**Hasenclever,** Walter 1890-1940 *FacFETw, LiExTwC*
**Hasenfus,** Harold J 1921- *AmMWSc 92*
**Hasenmiller,** Stephen J 1949- *WhoIns 92*
**Hasenoehrl,** Daniel Norbert Francis 1929- *WhoRel 92*
**Hasenohrl,** Donald W 1935- *WhoAmP 91*
**Hasford,** Gustav *DrAPF 91*
**Hash,** John Frank 1944- *WhoEnt 92*
**Hash,** John H 1929- *AmMWSc 92*
**Hashem,** Elaine M 1940- *WhoAmP 91*
**Hashim,** Jawad M. 1938- *IntWW 91*
**Hashim,** Mustafa 1935- *WhoBlA 92*
**Hashim,** Sami A 1929- *AmMWSc 92*
**Hashimi,** Abdul Razzak el- *IntWW 91*
**Hashimi,** Alamgir 1951- *WrDr 92*
**Hashimoto,** Clarice Y 1954- *WhoAmP 91*
**Hashimoto,** Ken 1931- *AmMWSc 92, WhoMW 92*
**Hashimoto,** Lloyd Ken 1944- *WhoWest 92*
**Hashimoto,** Masanori 1941- *WhoMW 92*
**Hashimoto,** Paulo Hitonari 1930- *AmMWSc 92*
**Hashimoto,** Richard Y. 1944- *WhoEnt 92*
**Hashimoto,** Ryutaro 1937- *IntWW 91*
**Hashin,** Zvi 1929- *AmMWSc 92*
**Hashmall,** Joseph Alan 1943- *AmMWSc 92*
**Hashmi,** Alamgir *DrAPF 91*
**Hashmi,** Alamgir 1951- *ConPo 91, IntAu&W 91*
**Hashmi,** Farrukh Siyar 1927- *IntWW 91, Who 92*
**Hashmi,** Mohammad Anaam 1957- *WhoMW 92*
**Hashmi,** Sajjad Ahmad 1933- *WhoIns 92, WhoMW 92*
**Hasinoff,** Brian Brennen 1944- *AmMWSc 92*

**Hasior,** Wladyslaw 1928- *IntWW 91*
**Haskale,** Hadassah *DrAPF 91*
**Haskard,** Cosmo 1916- *Who 92*
**Haskayne,** Richard Francis 1934- *WhoFI 92, WhoWest 92*
**Haske,** Bernard Joseph 1930- *AmMWSc 92*
**Haskell,** Barry G *AmMWSc 92*
**Haskell,** Benjamin Bruce 1953- *WhoRel 92*
**Haskell,** Betty Echternach 1925- *AmMWSc 92*
**Haskell,** Bob *WhoAmP 91*
**Haskell,** Charles Thomson 1924- *AmMWSc 92*
**Haskell,** David Andrew 1928- *AmMWSc 92*
**Haskell,** Donald Keith 1939- *Who 92*
**Haskell,** Donald McMillan 1932- *WhoAmL 92*
**Haskell,** Eric Todd 1950- *WhoWest 92*
**Haskell,** Evan Charles 1939- *WhoRel 92*
**Haskell,** Floyd K *WhoAmP 91*
**Haskell,** Francis 1928- *IntWW 91, WrDr 92*
**Haskell,** Francis James Herbert 1928- *Who 92*
**Haskell,** Harry 1954- *IntAu&W 91*
**Haskell,** John Henry Farrell, Jr. 1932- *WhoFI 92*
**Haskell,** Keith *Who 92*
**Haskell,** Molly 1939- *ConAu 135*
**Haskell,** Peter Abraham 1934- *WhoEnt 92*
**Haskell,** Peter Thomas 1923- *Who 92*
**Haskell,** Preston Hampton, III 1938- *WhoFI 92*
**Haskell,** Raymond H 1930- *WhoIns 92*
**Haskell,** Theodore Herbert, Jr 1921- *AmMWSc 92*
**Haskell,** Vernon Charles 1919- *AmMWSc 92*
**Haskell-Robinson,** Patricia Corbin 1931- *WhoFI 92*
**Haskett,** James Albert 1942- *WhoWest 92*
**Haskil,** Clara 1895-1960 *NewAmDM*
**Haskill,** John Stephen 1939- *AmMWSc 92*
**Haskin,** Harold H 1915- *AmMWSc 92*
**Haskin,** Larry A 1934- *AmMWSc 92*
**Haskin,** Lucille Arlepha 1926- *WhoRel 92*
**Haskin,** Marvin Edward 1930- *AmMWSc 92*
**Haskin,** Myra Ruth Singer 1935- *AmMWSc 92*
**Haskins,** Anne *DrAPF 91*
**Haskins,** Arthur L, Jr 1917- *AmMWSc 92*
**Haskins,** Caryl Davis 1867-1911 *BiInAmS*
**Haskins,** Caryl Parker 1908- *AmMWSc 92, IntWW 91, WhoFI 92*
**Haskins,** Cherry Anne *WhoAmP 91*
**Haskins,** Clem Smith 1943- *WhoBlA 92*
**Haskins,** Donald A 1931- *WhoAmP 91*
**Haskins,** Edward Frederick 1937- *AmMWSc 92*
**Haskins,** Francis Arthur 1922- *AmMWSc 92*
**Haskins,** George L. d1991 *NewYTBS 91*
**Haskins,** George Lee 1915- *IntAu&W 91, WhoAmL 92, WrDr 92*
**Haskins,** George Lee 1915-1991 *ConAu 135*
**Haskins,** Howard *ScFEYrs*
**Haskins,** James 1941- *IntAu&W 91*
**Haskins,** James George 1914- *IntWW 91*
**Haskins,** James S. 1941- *WhoBlA 92*
**Haskins,** James W., Jr. 1932- *WhoBlA 92*
**Haskins,** Jim 1941- *WrDr 92*
**Haskins,** Joseph, Jr. *WhoBlA 92*
**Haskins,** Joseph Richard 1926- *AmMWSc 92*
**Haskins,** Larry Wayne 1948- *WhoWest 92*
**Haskins,** Lola *DrAPF 91*
**Haskins,** Mark 1944- *AmMWSc 92*
**Haskins,** Michael A. d1991 *NewYTBS 91*
**Haskins,** Michael Kevin 1950- *WhoBlA 92*
**Haskins,** Morice Lee, Jr. 1947- *WhoBlA 92*
**Haskins,** Perry Glen 1938- *WhoMW 92*
**Haskins,** Reginald Hinton 1916- *AmMWSc 92*
**Haskins,** Richard E 1927 *WhoIns 92*
**Haskins,** Robert E 1952- *WhoAmP 91*
**Haskins,** Roger Allen 1951- *WhoWest 92*
**Haskins,** Sam 1926- *IntWW 91, Who 92*
**Haskins,** Scott David 1948- *WhoEnt 92*
**Haskins,** Terry E 1955- *WhoAmP 91*
**Haskins,** William J. 1930- *WhoBlA 92*
**Haskins,** Yvonne B. 1938- *WhoBlA 92*
**Haskowitz,** Howard 1947- *WhoIns 92*
**Haslam** *Who 92*
**Haslam,** Baron 1923- *IntWW 91, Who 92*
**Haslam,** Alec 1904- *Who 92*
**Haslam,** David William 1923- *Who 92*
**Haslam,** Geoffrey *Who 92*
**Haslam,** Gerald *DrAPF 91*
**Haslam,** Gerald 1937- *TwCWW 91*
**Haslam,** Gerald William 1937- *IntAu&W 91, WrDr 92*
**Haslam,** John Gordon 1932- *Who 92*
**Haslam,** John Lee 1939- *AmMWSc 92, WhoMW 92*
**Haslam,** William Geoffrey 1914- *Who 92*
**Haslanger,** Martha Louise 1947- *WhoEnt 92*
**Haslanger,** Martin Frederick 1947- *AmMWSc 92*
**Haslegrave,** Herbert Leslie 1902- *Who 92, WrDr 92*
**Haslegrave,** Neville Crompton 1914- *Who 92*
**Haslem,** William Joshua 1936- *AmMWSc 92*
**Hasler,** Arthur Davis 1908- *AmMWSc 92, IntWW 91*
**Hasler,** Arthur Frederick 1940- *AmMWSc 92*
**Hasler,** Marilyn Jean 1943- *AmMWSc 92*
**Haslett,** Caroline 1895-1957 *BiDBrF 2*
**Haslett,** James William 1944- *AmMWSc 92*
**Haslette,** John 1881- *ScFEYrs*
**Haslewood,** Geoffrey Arthur Dering 1910- *Who 92*
**Hasley,** Michael A 1941- *WhoIns 92*
**Hasley,** Ronald K. *WhoRel 92*
**Hasling,** Janie Barrios 1959- *WhoRel 92*
**Hasling,** Jill Freeman 1952- *AmMWSc 92*
**Haslip,** Joan 1912- *IntAu&W 91, Who 92*
**Hasluck,** Nicholas 1942- *ConNov 91, WrDr 92*
**Hasluck,** Paul 1905- *Who 92, WrDr 92*
**Hasluck,** Paul Meernaa Caedwalla 1905- *IntWW 91*
**Haslun,** Robert Alan 1945- *WhoEnt 92, WhoMW 92*
**Haslund,** R L 1932- *AmMWSc 92*
**Hasman,** Robert Henry 1935- *WhoMW 92*
**Hasner,** Rolf Kaare 1919- *WhoFI 92*
**Haspel,** Martin Victor 1945- *AmMWSc 92*
**Hasper,** John W 1935- *WhoAmP 91*
**Hasper,** Kurt T., Jr. 1946- *WhoWest 92*
**Haspiel,** Franklin 1927- *WhoMW 92*
**Hass,** Alvin A 1928- *AmMWSc 92*
**Hass,** Charles John William 1934- *WhoAmL 92*
**Hass,** Eric 1905-1980 *FacFETw*
**Hass,** Georg 1913- *AmMWSc 92*
**Hass,** George Marvin 1907- *AmMWSc 92*
**Hass,** George Michael 1943- *AmMWSc 92*
**Hass,** James Ronald 1945- *AmMWSc 92*
**Hass,** James W. 1948- *WhoMW 92*
**Hass,** Kenneth Philip 1934- *AmMWSc 92*
**Hass,** Louis F 1926- *AmMWSc 92*
**Hass,** Marvin 1930- *AmMWSc 92*
**Hass,** Michael A 1950- *AmMWSc 92*
**Hass,** Robert *DrAPF 91*
**Hass,** Robert 1941- *ConPo 91, WrDr 92*
**Hass,** Robert Henry 1922- *AmMWSc 92*
**Hass,** Robert Louis 1941- *IntAu&W 91*
**Hass,** William K 1929- *AmMWSc 92*
**Hassall,** Cedric Herbert 1919- *Who 92*
**Hassall,** Joan 1906- *TwCPaSc*
**Hassall,** John 1868-1948 *TwCPaSc*
**Hassall,** Tom Grafton 1943- *Who 92*
**Hassall,** William Owen 1912- *Who 92, WrDr 92*
**Hassam,** Childe 1859-1935 *FacFETw*
**Hassan II** 1929- *IntWW 91*
**Hassan Ibn Talal** 1947- *IntWW 91*
**Hassan,** Aftab Syed 1952- *WhoFI 92*
**Hassan,** Aslam Sultan *AmMWSc 92*
**Hassan,** Awatif E 1937- *AmMWSc 92*
**Hassan,** Hassan Ahmad 1931- *AmMWSc 92*
**Hassan,** Hosni Moustafa 1937- *AmMWSc 92*
**Hassan,** Ihab 1925- *WrDr 92*
**Hassan,** Jean-Claude Gaston 1954- *IntWW 91*
**Hassan,** Joshua 1915- *IntWW 91, Who 92*
**Hassan,** Mahmud 1947- *WhoFI 92*
**Hassan,** Mamoun Hamid 1937- *Who 92*
**Hassan,** Marwan *LiExTwC*
**Hassan,** Mohammad Zia 1933- *AmMWSc 92*
**Hassan,** Moulaye al- *IntWW 91*
**Hassan,** Sayed Abdullah El 1925- *Who 92*
**Hassan,** Tom Andrew 1964- *WhoFI 92*
**Hassan,** William Ephriam, Jr 1923- *AmMWSc 92, WhoAmL 92*
**Hassan Sharq,** Mohammad 1925- *IntWW 91*
**Hassanali,** Noor Mohamed 1918- *IntWW 91*
**Hassanein,** Richard C. 1951- *IntMPA 92*
**Hassanein,** Salah M. 1921- *IntMPA 92*
**Hasse,** Faustina *NewAmDM*
**Hasse,** Jean Louise 1958- *WhoEnt 92*
**Hasse,** Johann Adolf 1699?-1783 *BlkwCEP, NewAmDM*
**Hasse,** Margaret M. *DrAPF 91*
**Hasse,** Raymond William, Jr 1924- *AmMWSc 92*
**Hassel,** Kai-Uwe von 1913- *IntWW 91*
**Hassel,** Odd 1897-1981 *WhoNob 90*
**Hasselaar,** Amaron *EncAmaz 91*
**Hasselaar,** Kenau *EncAmaz 91*
**Hasselblad,** Victor 1906-1978 *FacFETw*
**Hasselbring,** Charles M., II 1963- *WhoRel 92*
**Hasselfeldt,** Gerda 1950- *IntWW 91*
**Hasselgren,** Per-Olof J 1947- *AmMWSc 92*
**Hasselgren,** Robert William 1949- *WhoFI 92, WhoIns 92*
**Hasselhoff,** David 1952- *IntMPA 92*
**Hasselkus,** Edward R 1932- *AmMWSc 92*
**Hassell,** Clinton Alton 1945- *AmMWSc 92*
**Hassell,** Cushing Biggs 1809-1880 *DcNCBi 3*
**Hassell,** Dennis Edward 1945- *WhoWest 92*
**Hassell,** Frances M. 1925- *WhoBlA 92*
**Hassell,** Frances Massey 1925- *WhoIns 92*
**Hassell,** H Paul, Jr 1928- *AmMWSc 92*
**Hassell,** Hugh Robert 1945- *WhoWest 92*
**Hassell,** James Thomas, Jr. 1959- *WhoRel 92*
**Hassell,** John Allen 1937- *AmMWSc 92, WhoMW 92*
**Hassell,** John David 1958- *WhoWest 92*
**Hassell,** John Robert 1943- *AmMWSc 92*
**Hassell,** Joyce Barnett 1932- *WhoAmP 91*
**Hassell,** Leroy R 1955- *WhoAmP 91*
**Hassell,** Leroy Rountree 1955- *WhoAmL 92*
**Hassell,** Leroy Rountree, Sr. 1955- *WhoBlA 92*
**Hassell,** Michael Patrick 1942- *IntWW 91, Who 92*
**Hassell,** Morris William 1916- *WhoAmL 92*
**Hassell,** Peter Albert 1916- *WhoMW 92*
**Hassell,** Sylvester 1842-1928 *DcNCBi 3*
**Hassell,** Thomas Michael 1945- *AmMWSc 92*
**Hassell,** Ulrich von 1881-1944 *EncTR 91 [port]*
**Hassell,** Wayne 1931- *WhoFI 92*
**Hasselman,** Didericus Petrus Hermannus 1931- *AmMWSc 92*
**Hasselmeyer,** Eileen Grace 1924- *AmMWSc 92*
**Hasselmo,** Nils 1931- *IntWW 91, WhoMW 92*
**Hasselquist,** Maynard Burton 1919- *WhoAmL 92, WhoFI 92, WhoMW 92*
**Hasselstrom,** Linda *DrAPF 91*
**Hasseman,** Dean Michael 1946- *WhoAmL 92*
**Hassena,** Baba Ould 1926- *HisDSpE*
**Hassenger,** Richard Mark 1944- *WhoFI 92*
**Hassert,** G Lee, Jr 1920- *AmMWSc 92*
**Hassett,** Charles Clifford 1905- *AmMWSc 92*
**Hassett,** Francis 1918- *Who 92*
**Hassett,** Francis George 1918- *IntWW 91*
**Hassett,** Jacquelyn Ann 1930- *WhoMW 92*
**Hassett,** Joseph Mark 1943- *WhoAmL 92*
**Hassett,** Raymond M 1932- *WhoIns 92*
**Hassett,** Ronald Douglas Patrick 1923- *Who 92*
**Hassey,** Catherine Ann 1964- *WhoFI 92*
**Hassfurder,** Leslie Jean 1943- *WhoMW 92*
**Hassialis,** Menelaos D 1909- *AmMWSc 92*
**Hassing,** William Joseph 1944- *WhoAmL 92*
**Hassinger,** Keith Byrd 1941- *WhoRel 92*
**Hassinger,** Mary Colleen 1953- *AmMWSc 92*
**Hasskamp,** Kris 1951- *WhoAmP 91*
**Hassler,** Alfred d1991 *NewYTBS 91*
**Hassler,** Craig Reinhold 1942- *AmMWSc 92*
**Hassler,** Donald M. *DrAPF 91*
**Hassler,** Donald M. 1937- *WrDr 92*
**Hassler,** Donald Mackey, II 1937- *WhoMW 92*
**Hassler,** Elaine *WhoAmP 91*
**Hassler,** F J 1921- *AmMWSc 92*
**Hassler,** Ferdinand Rudolph 1770-1843 *BiInAmS*
**Hassler,** Hans Leo 1564-1612 *NewAmDM*
**Hassler,** Jon 1933- *WrDr 92*
**Hassler,** Thomas J 1934- *AmMWSc 92*
**Hassler,** William Woods 1917- *AmMWSc 92, WhoRel 92*
**Hassner,** Alfred 1930- *AmMWSc 92*
**Hasso,** Signe Eleonora Cecilia 1915- *WhoEnt 92*
**Hassold,** Gregory Nahmen 1956- *AmMWSc 92*
**Hassold,** Terry Jon 1946- *AmMWSc 92*
**Hasson,** Dennis Francis 1934- *AmMWSc 92*
**Hasson,** Jack 1925- *AmMWSc 92*
**Hasson,** Joseph Albert 1921- *WhoFI 92*
**Hasson,** Maurice 1934- *IntWW 91*
**Hassoun,** Ghazi Qasim 1935- *AmMWSc 92*
**Hassoun,** Mohamad Hussein 1961- *AmMWSc 92*
**Hassouna,** Fred 1918- *WhoWest 92*
**Hassrick,** Peter Heyl 1941- *WhoWest 92*
**Hast,** Malcolm Howard 1931- *AmMWSc 92*
**Haste,** David 1938- *TwCPaSc*
**Hasted,** Michael 1946- *TwCPaSc*
**Hastenrath,** Stefan Ludwig 1934- *AmMWSc 92*
**Hasterlik,** Robert Joseph 1915- *AmMWSc 92*
**Hastert,** Dennis 1942- *AlmAP 92 [port], WhoAmP 91, WhoMW 92*
**Hastert,** Roger Joseph Leon 1929- *Who 92*
**Hastey,** Stanley LeRoy 1944- *WhoRel 92*
**Hastie,** John D. 1939- *WhoAmL 92*
**Hastie,** John William 1941- *AmMWSc 92*
**Hastie,** Robert Cameron 1933- *Who 92*
**Hastie,** Ronald Leslie 1941- *WhoMW 92*
**Hastie-Smith,** Richard Maybury 1931- *Who 92*
**Hastilow,** Michael Alexander 1923- *Who 92*
**Hastings** *Who 92*
**Hastings,** Baron 1912- *Who 92*
**Hastings,** Adrian Christopher 1929- *IntWW 91, Who 92*
**Hastings,** Alcee Lamar 1936- *WhoBlA 92*
**Hastings,** Alfred James 1938- *Who 92*
**Hastings,** Baird 1919- *WhoEnt 92*
**Hastings,** Beverly *ConAu 135, WrDr 92*
**Hastings,** Brooke 1946- *WrDr 92*
**Hastings,** Dan Thomas 1947- *WhoAmL 92*
**Hastings,** Deborah 1959- *WhoEnt 92*
**Hastings,** Don 1934- *IntMPA 92*
**Hastings,** Donald Francis 1934- *WhoEnt 92*
**Hastings,** Douglas Alfred 1949- *WhoAmL 92*
**Hastings,** Earl L 1928- *AmMWSc 92*
**Hastings,** Edmund Stuart 1924- *WhoFI 92*
**Hastings,** Edward Walton 1931- *WhoEnt 92, WhoWest 92*
**Hastings,** Edwin Hamilton 1917- *WhoAmL 92*
**Hastings,** Ellsworth 1910- *AmMWSc 92*
**Hastings,** Felton Leo 1938- *AmMWSc 92*
**Hastings,** George 1960- *TwCPaSc*
**Hastings,** George Gordon *ScFEYrs*
**Hastings,** Graham *IntAu&W 91X, WrDr 92*
**Hastings,** Harold Morris 1946- *AmMWSc 92*
**Hastings,** Honey Charlotte 1943- *WhoAmL 92*
**Hastings,** Ian James 1943- *AmMWSc 92*
**Hastings,** Joan King 1932- *WhoAmP 91*
**Hastings,** John 1907- *TwCPaSc*
**Hastings,** John A, Jr 1954- *WhoAmP 91*
**Hastings,** John Francis 1959- *WhoAmL 92*
**Hastings,** John Walter d1908 *BiInAmS*
**Hastings,** John Woodland 1927- *AmMWSc 92*
**Hastings,** Julius Mitchell 1920- *AmMWSc 92*
**Hastings,** Kathleen Agnes 1947- *WhoMW 92*
**Hastings,** Lansford Warren 1818?-1868 *BenetAL 91*
**Hastings,** Lawrence Vaeth 1919- *WhoAmL 92*
**Hastings,** Margaret Mitchell 1937- *WhoMW 92*
**Hastings,** Max M. 1945- *WrDr 92*
**Hastings,** Max Macdonald 1945- *IntAu&W 91, IntWW 91, Who 92*
**Hastings,** Merrill George, Jr. 1922- *WhoWest 92*
**Hastings,** Michael *ConAu 35NR*
**Hastings,** Michael 1938- *IntAu&W 91, Who 92, WrDr 92*
**Hastings,** Milo Milton 1884-1957 *ScFEYrs*
**Hastings,** Nancy Peters *DrAPF 91*
**Hastings,** Peter G *WhoAmP 91*
**Hastings,** Phyllis 1904- *IntAu&W 91, WrDr 92*
**Hastings,** Richard Norman 1941- *WhoAmP 91*
**Hastings,** Robert Clyde 1938- *AmMWSc 92*
**Hastings,** Robert Eugene 1932- *WhoMW 92*
**Hastings,** Robert Jean 1924- *WhoRel 92*
**Hastings,** Robert Paul 1933- *WrDr 92*
**Hastings,** Robert Pusey 1910- *WhoAmL 92*
**Hastings,** Robert Wayne 1943- *AmMWSc 92*
**Hastings,** Stephen 1921- *Who 92*
**Hastings,** Stuart 1937- *AmMWSc 92*
**Hastings,** Susan Kay 1952- *WhoFI 92*
**Hastings,** Thomas 1784-1872 *BenetAL 91, NewAmDM*
**Hastings,** William C 1921- *WhoAmP 91*
**Hastings,** William Charles 1921- *WhoAmL 92, WhoMW 92*
**Hastings Bass** *Who 92*
**Haston,** Raymond Curtiss, Jr. 1945- *WhoBlA 92*
**Hastreiter,** Alois Rudolf 1927- *AmMWSc 92*
**Hastrich,** Jerome Joseph 1914- *WhoRel 92, WhoWest 92*
**Hasty,** Christopher Spencer 1959- *WhoFI 92*

**Hasty,** David Long 1947- *AmMWSc 92*
**Hasty,** Gerald Richard 1926- *WhoAmL 92*
**Hasty,** John C 1930- *WhoAmP 91*
**Hasty,** Keith A. *WhoBlA 92*
**Hasty,** Noel Marion, Jr 1944- *AmMWSc 92*
**Hasty,** Robert Armistead 1936- *AmMWSc 92*
**Hasty,** Thomas Lloyd, III 1955- *WhoFI 92*
**Hasty,** Turner Elilah 1931- *AmMWSc 92*
**Hasty,** W G, Sr *WhoAmP 91*
**Hasty,** William Grady, Jr. 1947- *WhoAmL 92*
**Haswell,** Charles Haynes 1809-1907 *BiInAmS*
**Haswell,** Chetwynd John Drake 1919- *IntAu&W 91, WrDr 92*
**Haswell,** Frank I 1918- *WhoAmP 91*
**Haswell,** James 1922- *Who 92*
**Haswell,** Jock *WrDr 92*
**Haszeldine,** Robert Neville 1925- *IntWW 91, Who 92*
**Hatai,** Thomas Henry 1937- *WhoWest 92*
**Hatano,** Akira 1911- *IntWW 91*
**Hatch** *Who 92*
**Hatch,** Albert Jerold 1916- *AmMWSc 92*
**Hatch,** Ardis Messick *DrAPF 91*
**Hatch,** Charles Eldridge, III 1948- *AmMWSc 92*
**Hatch,** Daniel G d1895 *BiInAmS*
**Hatch,** David Edwin 1939- *Who 92*
**Hatch,** David Paul 1937- *WhoWest 92*
**Hatch,** Dorian Maurice 1940- *AmMWSc 92*
**Hatch,** Dorothy L. *DrAPF 91*
**Hatch,** Eastman Nibley 1927- *AmMWSc 92*
**Hatch,** Edward William 1952- *WhoMW 92*
**Hatch,** Francis Whiting, Jr 1925- *WhoAmP 91*
**Hatch,** Frederick Tasker 1924- *AmMWSc 92*
**Hatch,** Gary Ephraim 1947- *AmMWSc 92*
**Hatch,** George Clinton 1919- *WhoEnt 92*
**Hatch,** Henry Clifford, Jr. 1916- *IntWW 91*
**Hatch,** Jack Gilchrist 1950- *WhoAmP 91*
**Hatch,** Janet Maureen 1948- *WhoRel 92*
**Hatch,** John Phillip 1946- *AmMWSc 92*
**Hatch,** Kim Lanae 1965- *WhoWest 92*
**Hatch,** Linda *WhoAmP 91*
**Hatch,** Marshall Davidson 1932- *IntWW 91, Who 92*
**Hatch,** Melvin 1926- *AmMWSc 92*
**Hatch,** Michael Alan 1948- *WhoAmP 91*
**Hatch,** Norman Lowrie, Jr 1932- *AmMWSc 92*
**Hatch,** Orrin G. 1934- *AlmAP 92 [port]*
**Hatch,** Orrin Grant 1934- *IntWW 91, WhoAmP 91, WhoWest 92*
**Hatch,** Randolph Thomas 1945- *AmMWSc 92*
**Hatch,** Richard C 1936- *AmMWSc 92*
**Hatch,** Robert Alchin 1914- *AmMWSc 92*
**Hatch,** Robert Frederick 1934- *WhoWest 92*
**Hatch,** Roger Conant 1935- *AmMWSc 92*
**Hatch,** Ruth Cordle 1935- *WhoRel 92*
**Hatch,** Sherry Anne 1940- *WhoWest 92*
**Hatch,** Stephan LaVor 1945- *AmMWSc 92*
**Hatch,** Steven Graham 1951- *WhoFI 92, WhoWest 92*
**Hatch,** William H 1947- *WhoAmP 91*
**Hatch of Lusby,** Baron 1917- *Who 92*
**Hatch Of Lusby,** Lord 1917- *WrDr 92*
**Hatchadorian,** Matthew Jack 1941- *WhoAmP 91*
**Hatchard,** Frederick Henry 1923- *Who 92*
**Hatchard,** William Reginald 1919- *AmMWSc 92*
**Hatchel,** Robert Eugene 1937- *WhoAmP 91*
**Hatcher,** Baldwin 1953- *WhoRel 92*
**Hatcher,** Brian Paul 1957- *WhoAmL 92*
**Hatcher,** Charles F. 1939- *AlmAP 92 [port], WhoAmP 91*
**Hatcher,** Charles Richard 1932- *AmMWSc 92*
**Hatcher,** David Alton, Jr. 1946- *WhoWest 92*
**Hatcher,** E Porter, Jr 1936- *WhoAmP 91*
**Hatcher,** Ester L. 1933- *WhoBlA 92*
**Hatcher,** Harlan 1898- *BenetAL 91*
**Hatcher,** Herbert John 1926- *AmMWSc 92, WhoWest 92*
**Hatcher,** Jak P. 1928- *WhoFI 92*
**Hatcher,** James Donald 1923- *AmMWSc 92*
**Hatcher,** Jeffrey F. *WhoBlA 92*
**Hatcher,** John 1942- *WrDr 92*
**Hatcher,** John Bell 1861-1904 *BiInAmS*
**Hatcher,** John Burton 1909- *AmMWSc 92*
**Hatcher,** John Christopher 1946- *WhoWest 92*
**Hatcher,** John Woodville, Jr 1944- *WhoAmP 91*
**Hatcher,** LeAnna Jepson 1954- *WhoEnt 92, WhoRel 92*
**Hatcher,** Lillian 1915- *WhoBlA 92*
**Hatcher,** Lizzie R. 1954- *WhoBlA 92*
**Hatcher,** Lucia Corsiglia 1956- *WhoEnt 92*
**Hatcher,** Michael Robert 1962- *WhoAmL 92*
**Hatcher,** Milford Burriss, Jr. 1948- *WhoAmL 92*
**Hatcher,** Richard D., Sr. 1948- *WhoRel 92*
**Hatcher,** Richard G 1933- *WhoAmP 91*
**Hatcher,** Richard Gordon 1933- *WhoBlA 92*
**Hatcher,** Robert Dean, Jr 1940- *AmMWSc 92*
**Hatcher,** Robert Douglas 1924- *AmMWSc 92*
**Hatcher,** Robin Lee 1951- *IntAu&W 91*
**Hatcher,** S Ronald 1932- *AmMWSc 92*
**Hatcher,** Thomas Fountain 1931- *WhoMW 92*
**Hatcher,** Victor Bernard 1943- *AmMWSc 92*
**Hatcher,** William Julian, Jr 1935- *AmMWSc 92*
**Hatcher,** William S 1935- *AmMWSc 92, WrDr 92*
**Hatchett,** Edward Bryan, Jr. 1951- *WhoFI 92*
**Hatchett,** Elbert 1936- *WhoBlA 92*
**Hatchett,** Jimmy Howell 1935- *AmMWSc 92*
**Hatchett,** Joseph W 1932- *WhoAmP 91*
**Hatchett,** Joseph Woodrow 1932- *WhoAmL 92, WhoBlA 92*
**Hatchett,** Lloyd Ray 1937- *WhoRel 92*
**Hatchett,** Paul Andrew 1925- *WhoBlA 92*
**Hatchett,** Richard Jones, III 1945- *WhoFI 92*
**Hatchett,** William F. *WhoBlA 92*
**Hate Woman** *EncAmaz 91*
**Hatefi,** Youssef 1929- *AmMWSc 92*
**Hatem,** George 1910-1988 *FacFETw*
**Hatem,** Kristin Rene 1965- *WhoMW 92*
**Hatem,** Mohammed Abdel Kader 1917- *IntWW 91*
**Hatendi,** Ralph Peter *Who 92*
**Hater,** Robert James 1934- *WhoRel 92*
**Hatesohl,** Mark John 1960- *WhoMW 92*
**Hatfield,** Barbara Burruss 1935- *WhoAmP 91*
**Hatfield,** Bobby 1940- *IntMPA 92*
**Hatfield,** Charles, Jr 1920- *AmMWSc 92*
**Hatfield,** Charles Donald 1935- *WhoWest 92*
**Hatfield,** Charles Lee 1953- *WhoAmP 91, WhoMW 92*
**Hatfield,** Craig 1935- *AmMWSc 92*
**Hatfield,** David Alan 1961- *WhoFI 92*
**Hatfield,** Dolph Lee 1937- *AmMWSc 92*
**Hatfield,** Efton Everett 1919- *AmMWSc 92*
**Hatfield,** Frank *ScFEYrs*
**Hatfield,** G Wesley 1940- *AmMWSc 92*
**Hatfield,** Garry Kent 1934- *WhoMW 92*
**Hatfield,** Guy, III 1950- *WhoAmP 91*
**Hatfield,** Hurd 1918- *IntMPA 92*
**Hatfield,** Jack Kenton 1922- *WhoAmL 92, WhoFI 92*
**Hatfield,** James Allen 1953- *WhoEnt 92*
**Hatfield,** Jerry Lee 1949- *AmMWSc 92*
**Hatfield,** John Dempsey 1919- *AmMWSc 92*
**Hatfield,** Kevin 1951- *WhoAmP 91*
**Hatfield,** Leonard Fraser 1919- *Who 92, WhoRel 92*
**Hatfield,** Leslie Ruth Nohl 1954- *WhoAmP 91*
**Hatfield,** Lynn LaMar 1937- *AmMWSc 92*
**Hatfield,** Marcus Rankin 1909- *AmMWSc 92*
**Hatfield,** Mark O. *NewYTBS 91 [port]*
**Hatfield,** Mark O. 1922- *AlmAP 92 [port], IntWW 91, WhoWest 92*
**Hatfield,** Mark Odom 1922- *WhoAmP 91*
**Hatfield,** Mary Morozzo 1943- *WhoWest 92*
**Hatfield,** Paul Gerhart 1928- *WhoAmL 92, WhoWest 92*
**Hatfield,** Richard 1853- *ScFEYrs*
**Hatfield,** Richard Bennett d1991 *Who 92N*
**Hatfield,** Richard Bennett 1931- *IntWW 91*
**Hatfield,** Richard Eugene 1932- *WhoMW 92*
**Hatfield,** Roger Wayne 1948- *WhoEnt 92*
**Hatfield,** Roger William 1945- *WhoRel 92*
**Hatfield,** Ted 1936- *IntMPA 92*
**Hatfield,** William E 1937- *AmMWSc 92*
**Hatfield,** William Keith 1951- *WhoRel 92*
**Hatfield,** William Rukard Hurd 1920- *WhoEnt 92*
**Hatfull,** Alan Frederick 1927- *Who 92*
**Hatgidakis,** John Anthony 1946- *WhoRel 92*
**Hath,** David Collins 1944- *WhoWest 92*
**Hathaway,** Alden Moinet 1933- *WhoRel 92*
**Hathaway,** Anthony, Jr. 1921- *WhoBlA 92*
**Hathaway,** Brad Harding 1944- *WhoAmP 91*
**Hathaway,** Carmrid Glaston 1922- *WhoFI 92*
**Hathaway,** Charles Edward 1936- *AmMWSc 92*
**Hathaway,** Dale Ernest 1925- *WhoAmP 91*
**Hathaway,** Dale Kenneth 1961- *WhoMW 92*
**Hathaway,** David Henry 1951- *AmMWSc 92*
**Hathaway,** Gary Michael 1937- *AmMWSc 92*
**Hathaway,** Gerald Thomas 1954- *WhoAmL 92, WhoEnt 92*
**Hathaway,** Henry 1898-1985 *FacFETw, IntDcF 2-2 [port]*
**Hathaway,** James Robert Bent 1841-1904 *DcNCBi 3*
**Hathaway,** Jeanine *DrAPF 91*
**Hathaway,** Loline 1937- *WhoWest 92*
**Hathaway,** Maggie Mae 1925- *WhoBlA 92*
**Hathaway,** Michael David 1937- *WhoAmP 91*
**Hathaway,** Michael Jerry 1961- *IntAu&W 91*
**Hathaway,** Paul L., Jr. 1934- *WhoWest 92*
**Hathaway,** Ralph Robert 1928- *AmMWSc 92*
**Hathaway,** Robert J 1921- *AmMWSc 92*
**Hathaway,** Robert Richard 1930- *WhoAmP 91*
**Hathaway,** Ronald Philip 1943- *AmMWSc 92*
**Hathaway,** Stanley K 1924- *WhoAmP 91*
**Hathaway,** Stanley Knapp 1924- *WhoFI 92*
**Hathaway,** Stephen *DrAPF 91*
**Hathaway,** Susan Jane 1950- *AmMWSc 92*
**Hathaway,** Vaughn Edward, Jr. 1937- *WhoRel 92*
**Hathaway,** Wilfred Bostock 1919- *AmMWSc 92*
**Hathaway,** William *DrAPF 91*
**Hathaway,** William D 1924- *WhoAmP 91*
**Hathcoat,** Ronald Andrew 1949- *WhoRel 92*
**Hathcock,** Bobby Ray 1942- *AmMWSc 92*
**Hathcock,** John Nathan 1940- *AmMWSc 92*
**Hathcox,** Kyle Lee 1943- *AmMWSc 92*
**Hatherly,** John A. 1959- *WhoFI 92*
**Hatherton,** Baron 1950- *Who 92*
**Hatheway,** Allen Wayne 1937- *AmMWSc 92*
**Hatheway,** Charles Louis 1932- *AmMWSc 92*
**Hatheway,** Richard Brackett 1939- *AmMWSc 92*
**Hatheway,** William Howell 1923- *AmMWSc 92*
**Hathorne,** Alan M. 1953- *WhoAmL 92*
**Hathway,** Cedric Warren 1954- *WhoMW 92*
**Hatico,** Elliot Jose 1955- *WhoWest 92*
**Hatjis,** Christos George 1949- *WhoMW 92*
**Hatkin,** Leonard 1920- *AmMWSc 92*
**Hatoum,** Mona 1952- *TwCPaSc*
**Hatoyama,** Iichiro 1918- *IntWW 91*
**Hatschek,** Rudolf Alexander 1918- *WhoFI 92*
**Hatsell,** Charles Proctor 1944- *AmMWSc 92*
**Hatshepsut** d1479?BC *EncAmaz 91*
**Hatsopoulos,** George Nicholas 1927- *AmMWSc 92, WhoFI 92*
**Hatsopoulos,** John Nicholas 1934- *WhoFI 92*
**Hatsumura,** Takiichiro 1913- *IntWW 91*
**Hatt,** Robert Torrens 1902- *AmMWSc 92*
**Hatta,** Mohammed 1902-1980 *CurBio 91N*
**Hattala,** James Jeffery 1954- *WhoFI 92*
**Hattan,** David Gene 1942- *AmMWSc 92*
**Hattan,** Marie Candice 1951- *WhoAmL 92*
**Hattaway,** Bob 1936- *WhoAmP 91*
**Hattaway,** Herman Morell 1938- *WhoMW 92*
**Hattemer,** Jimmie Ray 1939- *AmMWSc 92*
**Hatten,** Betty Arlene 1929- *AmMWSc 92*
**Hatten,** Robert Lynn 1949- *WhoAmP 91*
**Hatten,** Robert Randolph 1948- *WhoAmL 92*
**Hatten,** Roger Lynn 1946- *WhoMW 92*
**Hattendorf,** John B. 1941- *ConAu 135*
**Hattenhauer,** Darryl Clyde 1948- *WhoWest 92*
**Hatter,** Henry 1935- *WhoAmP 91, WhoBlA 92*
**Hatter,** Terry Julius, Jr. 1933- *WhoAmL 92*
**Hattersley,** Edith Mary 1931- *Who 92*
**Hattersley,** Roy 1932- *IntAu&W 91, WrDr 92*
**Hattersley,** Roy Sydney George 1932- *IntWW 91, Who 92*
**Hattersley-Smith,** Geoffrey Francis 1923- *AmMWSc 92*
**Hattervig,** Robin Lynn 1958- *WhoMW 92*
**Hattery,** Thomas Harold 1954- *WhoAmP 91*
**Hattin,** Donald Edward 1928- *AmMWSc 92*
**Hattis,** Albert Daniel 1929- *WhoFI 92*
**Hattis,** Dale B 1946- *AmMWSc 92*
**Hattman,** Stanley 1938- *AmMWSc 92*
**Hattman,** Stephen Michael 1945- *WhoEnt 92*
**Hatto,** Arthur Thomas 1910- *Who 92*
**Hatton** *Who 92*
**Hatton,** Anne Kemble *BenetAL 91*
**Hatton,** Barbara R. 1941- *WhoBlA 92*
**Hatton,** Brian 1887-1916 *TwCPaSc*
**Hatton,** Bruce Nichols 1940- *WhoAmP 91*
**Hatton,** Glenn Irwin 1934- *AmMWSc 92*
**Hatton,** John Ernest 1938- *WhoFI 92*
**Hatton,** John Victor 1934- *AmMWSc 92*
**Hatton,** Ragnhild Marie 1913- *IntAu&W 91*
**Hatton,** Stephen 1961- *WhoEnt 92*
**Hatton,** Stephen Paul 1948- *IntWW 91*
**Hatton,** Thurman Timbrook, Jr 1922- *AmMWSc 92*
**Hattori,** Shoji 1937- *WhoFI 92*
**Hattori,** Todd Toshiharu 1962- *WhoWest 92*
**Hattori,** Toshiaki 1931- *AmMWSc 92*
**Hatty,** Cyril 1908- *Who 92*
**Hatvary,** George Egon *DrAPF 91*
**Hatwell,** Elizabeth 1937- *TwCPaSc*
**Hatwich,** Wayne Paul 1946- *WhoMW 92*
**Hatzai,** Glen Alan *WhoMW 92*
**Hatzakis,** Michael 1928- *AmMWSc 92*
**Hatzenbuhler,** Douglas Albert 1945- *AmMWSc 92*
**Hatzimichael,** Tasos Chris 1964- *WhoFI 92*
**Hatzios,** Kriton Kleanthis 1949- *AmMWSc 92*
**Hatzler,** Elizabeth *EncAmaz 91*
**Haubach,** Theodor 1896-1945 *EncTR 91 [port]*
**Haubein,** Albert Howard 1914- *AmMWSc 92*
**Haubenstock-Ramati,** Roman 1919- *NewAmDM*
**Hauber,** Janet Elaine 1937- *AmMWSc 92*
**Hauberg,** John Henry 1916- *WhoWest 92*
**Hauberg,** Robert Engelbrecht, Jr. 1943- *WhoAmL 92*
**Haubold,** Samuel Allen 1938- *WhoAmL 92*
**Haubrich,** Dean Robert 1943- *AmMWSc 92*
**Haubrich,** Michael Phillip 1956- *WhoFI 92*
**Haubrich,** Robert Rice 1923- *AmMWSc 92*
**Hauck,** Dennis William 1945- *WhoWest 92*
**Hauck,** George F W 1932- *AmMWSc 92*
**Haudenschild,** Christian C 1939- *AmMWSc 92*
**Haueisen,** Donald Carl 1945- *AmMWSc 92*
**Hauenstein,** Donald Herbert, Jr. 1942- *WhoWest 92*
**Hauenstein,** Jack David 1929- *AmMWSc 92*
**Hauenstein,** James George 1940- *WhoWest 92*
**Hauenstein,** Paul Edward 1943- *WhoRel 92*
**Hauer,** Gerald M. 1933- *WhoMW 92*
**Hauer,** Harvey Irwin 1940- *WhoAmL 92*
**Hauer,** Jakob Wilhelm 1881-1962 *EncTR 91*
**Hauer,** Josef Matthias 1883-1959 *NewAmDM*
**Hauer,** Rutger 1944- *IntMPA 92, IntWW 91*
**Hauerwas,** Stanley M. 1940- *WhoAmL 92, WhoRel 92*
**Hauff,** Volker 1940- *IntWW 91*
**Haufler,** Christopher Hardin 1950- *AmMWSc 92*
**Haufler,** Jonathan B 1952- *AmMWSc 92*
**Haufler,** Robert Christian, Jr. 1952- *WhoAmL 92*
**Haufrecht,** Herbert 1909- *WhoEnt 92*
**Haug,** Arthur John 1919- *AmMWSc 92*
**Haug,** Edward J, Jr 1940- *AmMWSc 92*
**Haug,** James *DrAPF 91*
**Haugaard,** Erik 1923- *WrDr 92*
**Haugaard,** Erik Christian 1923- *IntAu&W 91, SmATA 68 [port]*
**Haugaard,** Niels 1920- *AmMWSc 92*
**Hauge,** Hans Nilsen *DcAmImH*
**Hauge,** Jens Chr. 1915- *IntWW 91*
**Hauge,** Paul Stephen 1945- *AmMWSc 92*
**Hauge,** Richard A 1956- *WhoAmP 91*
**Haugeland,** John 1945- *ConAu 133*
**Haugen,** David Allen 1945- *AmMWSc 92*
**Haugen,** Einar 1906- *WrDr 92*
**Haugen,** Gilbert R 1930- *AmMWSc 92*
**Haugen,** James A *WhoAmP 91*

**Haugen**, Mary Margaret 1941- WhoAmP 91
**Haugen**, Orrin Millard 1927- WhoFI 92, WhoMW 92
**Haugen**, Paal-Helge 1945- IntAu&W 91
**Haugen**, Robert Kenneth 1947- AmMWSc 92
**Haugen**, Tormod 1945- ConAu 135, SmATA 66 [port]
**Haugen**, Wesley N. WhoRel 92
**Hauger**, James Scott 1949- WhoFI 92
**Haugh**, C Gene 1936- AmMWSc 92
**Haugh**, Charles Richard 1939- WhoMW 92
**Haugh**, Dan Anthony 1953- WhoMW 92
**Haugh**, Eugene 1929- AmMWSc 92
**Haugh**, John H 1910- WhoAmP 91
**Haugh**, John Richard 1940- AmMWSc 92
**Haugh**, Larry Douglas 1944- AmMWSc 92
**Haugh**, Robert James 1926- WhoFI 92
**Haugh**, Scott Charles 1957- WhoAmL 92
**Haughey**, Charles James 1925- IntWW 91, Who 92
**Haughey**, Francis James 1930- AmMWSc 92
**Haught**, Alan F 1936- AmMWSc 92
**Haught**, Jack Gregg 1958- WhoAmP 91
**Haught**, John Francis 1942- WhoRel 92
**Haught**, Robert L 1930- WhoAmP 91
**Haught**, William Dixon 1939- WhoAmL 92
**Haughton**, Daniel Jeremiah d1987 Who 92N
**Haughton**, David 1924- TwCPaSc
**Haughton**, Geoffrey 1932- AmMWSc 92
**Haughton**, James G. 1925- WhoBlA 92
**Haughton**, James Gray 1925- AmMWSc 92
**Haughton**, John Hooker 1810-1876 DcNCBi 3
**Haughton**, John Marsden 1924- Who 92
**Haughton**, Kenneth E 1928- AmMWSc 92
**Haughton**, Rosemary 1927- ConAu 35NR, WrDr 92
**Haughton**, Rosemary Elena Konradin 1927- IntWW 91
**Haughton**, Victor Mellet 1939- AmMWSc 92
**Haugland**, Aage IntWW 91
**Haugland**, Brynhild 1905- WhoAmP 91, WhoMW 92
**Haugland**, Jean 1927- WhoAmP 91
**Haugland**, Jens 1910- IntWW 91
**Haugland**, Richard Paul 1943- AmMWSc 92
**Haugo**, Roger Erling 1933- WhoAmP 91
**Haugsjaa**, Paul O 1942- AmMWSc 92
**Haugstad**, May Katheryn 1937- WhoBlA 92
**Hauk**, A. Andrew 1912- WhoAmL 92, WhoWest 92
**Hauk**, Barbara DrAPF 91
**Hauk**, Minnie 1851-1929 NewAmDM
**Hauk**, Peter 1937- AmMWSc 92
**Hauke**, Richard Louis 1930- AmMWSc 92
**Hauke**, Thomas 1938- WhoMW 92
**Hauke**, Thomas A 1938- WhoAmP 91
**Haukeness**, Helen DrAPF 91
**Haukoos**, Melvin Robert 1931- WhoAmP 91
**Hauksbee**, Francis d1713? BlkwCEP
**Haulenbeek**, Robert Bogle, Jr. 1941- WhoWest 92
**Haulica**, Dan 1932- IntWW 91
**Haumer**, Hans 1940- IntWW 91
**Haun**, Charles Kenneth 1930- AmMWSc 92
**Haun**, J W 1924- AmMWSc 92
**Haun**, James William 1924- WhoMW 92
**Haun**, John Daniel 1921- AmMWSc 92
**Haun**, Joseph Rhodes 1922- AmMWSc 92
**Haun**, Randy S 1956- AmMWSc 92
**Haun**, Robert Dee, Jr 1930- AmMWSc 92, WhoFI 92
**Haun**, Terry A 1957- WhoAmP 91
**Haun**, Tommy George 1950- WhoAmP 91
**Haunerland**, Norbert Heinrich 1955- AmMWSc 92
**Haunold**, Alfred 1929- AmMWSc 92, WhoWest 92
**Haunz**, Edgar Alfred 1910- AmMWSc 92
**Hau'ofa**, Epeli 1939- ConNov 91, WrDr 92
**Haupert**, John Edward 1938- WhoFI 92
**Haupt**, Carl P. 1940- WhoFI 92
**Haupt**, H. James 1940- WhoMW 92
**Haupt**, Herman 1817-1905 BiInAmS
**Haupt**, L M, Jr 1906- AmMWSc 92
**Haupt**, Ralph Freeman 1906- AmMWSc 92
**Hauptfuhrer**, Robert 1931- IntWW 91
**Hauptfuhrer**, Robert Paul 1931- WhoFI 92
**Hauptli**, Thomas 1956- WhoIns 92
**Hauptly**, Paul David 1944- WhoWest 92
**Hauptman**, Barbara Barbat 1946- WhoEnt 92
**Hauptman**, Herbert Aaron 1917- AmMWSc 92, Who 92, WhoNob 90
**Hauptman**, John Michael 1946- WhoMW 92
**Hauptman**, Michael 1933- WhoEnt 92
**Hauptman**, Stephen Phillip AmMWSc 92
**Hauptman**, William 1942- IntAu&W 91, WhoEnt 92
**Hauptmann**, Gerhart 1862-1946 EncTR 91 [port], FacFETw
**Hauptmann**, Gerhart Johann 1862-1946 WhoNob 90
**Hauptmann**, Moritz 1792-1868 NewAmDM
**Hauptmann**, Randal Mark 1956- AmMWSc 92
**Hauptmann**, William 1942- WrDr 92
**Hauptschein**, Murray 1923- AmMWSc 92
**Haurani**, Farid I 1928- AmMWSc 92
**Hauri**, Peter 1952- WhoEnt 92
**Haurin**, Donald Richard 1949- WhoFI 92
**Haurwitz**, Bernhard 1905- AmMWSc 92, IntWW 91
**Haury**, Emil W. 1904- IntWW 91
**Haury**, Loren Richard 1939- AmMWSc 92
**Haus**, Hermann A 1925- AmMWSc 92
**Haus**, Joseph Wendel 1948- AmMWSc 92
**Haus**, Thilo Enoch 1918- AmMWSc 92
**Hausam**, Neal Allen 1939- WhoWest 92
**Hausauer**, Alvin WhoAmP 91
**Hausauer**, Roy 1920- WhoAmP 91
**Hausberger**, Franz X 1908- AmMWSc 92
**Hausburg**, David Eugene 1925- WhoWest 92
**Hausch**, H George 1941- AmMWSc 92
**Hausch**, Walter Richard 1917- AmMWSc 92
**Hauschild**, Andreas H W 1929- AmMWSc 92
**Hauschild**, Raymond L. 1941- WhoMW 92
**Hauschild**, Wayne Arthur 1925- WhoAmP 91
**Hauschka**, Stephen D 1940- AmMWSc 92
**Hausdoerffer**, William H 1913- AmMWSc 92
**Hausdorfer**, Gary Lee 1946- WhoWest 92
**Hause**, Norman Laurance 1922- AmMWSc 92
**Hausel**, William Dan 1949- WhoWest 92
**Hauselt**, Denise Ann 1956- WhoAmL 92
**Hausen**, Jutta 1943- AmMWSc 92
**Hausenbuiller**, Robert Lee 1918- AmMWSc 92
**Hausenfluck**, Robert Dale 1947- WhoAmP 91
**Hauser**, Alan Jon 1945- WhoRel 92
**Hauser**, Charles Roy 1900-1970 DcNCBi 3
**Hauser**, Charlie Brady 1917- WhoAmP 91, WhoBlA 92
**Hauser**, Christopher George 1954- WhoAmL 92, WhoFI 92
**Hauser**, Clarence WhoRel 92
**Hauser**, Daniel Eugene 1942- WhoAmP 91
**Hauser**, Diana Louise 1964- WhoWest 92
**Hauser**, Edward J P 1938- AmMWSc 92
**Hauser**, Edward Russell 1942- AmMWSc 92
**Hauser**, Erich 1930- IntWW 91
**Hauser**, Frank Ivor 1922- Who 92
**Hauser**, Frank Marion 1943- AmMWSc 92
**Hauser**, George 1922- AmMWSc 92
**Hauser**, Gustave M. LesBEnT 92
**Hauser**, Gustave M. 1929- WhoEnt 92
**Hauser**, Helen Ann 1948- WhoAmL 92
**Hauser**, James Charles 1948- WhoAmL 92
**Hauser**, Jerry Lee 1950- WhoAmP 91
**Hauser**, John Reid 1938- AmMWSc 92
**Hauser**, Joyce Roberta WhoFI 92
**Hauser**, Karen Diane 1959- WhoFI 92
**Hauser**, Marianne DrAPF 91
**Hauser**, Marianne 1910- IntAu&W 91, WrDr 92
**Hauser**, Martin 1934- AmMWSc 92, WhoFI 92
**Hauser**, Michael George 1939- AmMWSc 92
**Hauser**, Norbert 1924- AmMWSc 92
**Hauser**, Philip M. 1909- IntWW 91, WrDr 92
**Hauser**, Ray Louis 1927- AmMWSc 92
**Hauser**, Richard Scott 1919- AmMWSc 92
**Hauser**, Rita Eleanore Abrams 1934- WhoAmL 92
**Hauser**, Robert J, Jr WhoAmP 91
**Hauser**, Robert Mason 1942- WhoMW 92
**Hauser**, Rolland Keith 1937- AmMWSc 92
**Hauser**, Rudolf 1909- IntWW 91
**Hauser**, Susan DrAPF 91
**Hauser**, Tim WhoEnt 92
**Hauser**, Victor La Vern 1929- AmMWSc 92
**Hauser**, Willard Allen 1937- AmMWSc 92
**Hauser**, William 1812-1880 DcNCBi 3
**Hauser**, William Joseph 1942- AmMWSc 92
**Hauser**, William P 1934- AmMWSc 92
**Hausfater**, Glenn 1947- AmMWSc 92
**Hausfeld**, James Frank 1955- WhoEnt 92
**Haushalter**, William R. 1948- WhoAmL 92
**Haushofer**, Albrecht 1903-1945 EncTR 91 [port]
**Haushofer**, Karl 1869-1946 EncTR 91 [port]
**Haushofer**, Karl Ernst 1869-1946 BiDExR
**Hausler**, Carl Louis 1941- AmMWSc 92
**Hausler**, Rudolf H 1934- AmMWSc 92
**Hausler**, William John, Jr 1926- AmMWSc 92
**Hausman**, Alice 1942- WhoAmP 91
**Hausman**, Arthur Herbert 1923- AmMWSc 92
**Hausman**, Daniel Murray 1947- WhoMW 92
**Hausman**, Gary J 1948- AmMWSc 92
**Hausman**, Gerald DrAPF 91
**Hausman**, Hershel J 1923- AmMWSc 92
**Hausman**, Howard 1945- WhoFI 92
**Hausman**, Jerry Allen 1946- WhoFI 92
**Hausman**, Michael IntMPA 92
**Hausman**, Richard Donald 1945- WhoAmP 91
**Hausman**, Robert 1914- AmMWSc 92
**Hausman**, Robert Edward 1947- AmMWSc 92
**Hausman**, Roberta Bernstein 1932- WhoMW 92
**Hausman**, Steven J 1945- AmMWSc 92
**Hausman**, Warren H AmMWSc 92
**Hausman**, William 1925- AmMWSc 92
**Hausman**, William John 1949- WhoFI 92
**Hausmann**, Christi Lyn 1968- WhoWest 92
**Hausmann**, Ernest 1929- AmMWSc 92
**Hausmann**, Werner Karl 1921- AmMWSc 92, WhoWest 92
**Hausmann**, Winifred Wilkinson 1922- WrDr 92
**Hausner**, Gideon d1990 IntWW 91N
**Hausner**, Gideon 1915-1990 FacFETw
**Hausner**, Henry H 1901- AmMWSc 92
**Hausner**, Melvin 1928- AmMWSc 92
**Hauspurg**, Arthur 1925- AmMWSc 92, IntWW 91
**Hausrath**, Alan Richard 1945- AmMWSc 92
**Haussamen**, Carol W WhoAmP 91
**Hausser**, Jack W 1935- AmMWSc 92
**Hausser**, Otto Friedrich 1937- AmMWSc 92
**Hausser**, Paul 1880-1972 EncTR 91 [port]
**Hausslein**, Robert William 1937- AmMWSc 92
**Haussler**, Willi 1907-1945 EncTR 91
**Haussling**, Henry Jacob 1945- AmMWSc 92
**Haussmann**, Helmut 1943- IntWW 91
**Haussmann**, Robert 1931- DcTwDes
**Haussmann**, Ulrich Gunther AmMWSc 92
**Haussmann**, Valentin 1570?-1614? NewAmDM
**Haust**, M Daria AmMWSc 92
**Haustein**, Peter Eugene 1944- AmMWSc 92
**Hauswirth**, Sandra Fay Marie 1939- WhoMW 92
**Hauswirth**, William Walter 1945- AmMWSc 92
**Haut**, Arthur 1927- AmMWSc 92
**Hautala**, Richard Roy 1943- AmMWSc 92
**Hautaluoma**, Jacob Edward 1933- WhoWest 92
**Hauth**, Willard E, III 1948- AmMWSc 92
**Hautzig**, Esther 1930- IntAu&W 91, WrDr 92
**Hautzig**, Esther Rudomin 1930- SmATA 68 [port]
**Hautzig**, Walter 1921- WhoEnt 92
**Hauxiku**, Bonifatius WhoRel 92
**Hauxwell**, Donald Lawrence 1938- AmMWSc 92
**Hauxwell**, Gerald Dean 1935- AmMWSc 92
**Hauxwell**, Hannah 1927- IntAu&W 91
**Hauxwell**, Ronald Earl 1946- AmMWSc 92
**Hava**, Milos 1927- AmMWSc 92
**Havard**, Bernard 1941- WhoEnt 92
**Havard**, Cyril 1925- WrDr 92
**Havard**, Francis T 1878?-1913 BiInAmS
**Havard**, John David Jayne 1924- Who 92
**Havard**, John Francis 1909- AmMWSc 92, WhoWest 92
**Havard**, Lisa Annette 1963- WhoMW 92
**Havard-Williams**, Peter 1922- Who 92
**Havas**, Helga Francis 1915- AmMWSc 92
**Havas**, Peter 1916- AmMWSc 92
**Havasy**, Edward Stephen 1925- WhoFI 92
**Havea**, Sione Amanaki 1922- WhoRel 92
**Havel**, Henry Acken 1954- AmMWSc 92
**Havel**, James Joseph 1947- AmMWSc 92
**Havel**, Richard Joseph 1925- AmMWSc 92, IntWW 91
**Havel**, Richard W. 1946- WhoAmL 92
**Havel**, Vaclav 1935- IntWW 91
**Havel**, Vaclav 1936- ConAu 36NR, ConLC 65 [port], ConTFT 9, FacFETw [port], IntAu&W 91, Who 92, WhoEnt 92
**Havelange**, Jean Marie Faustin Godefroid 1916- IntWW 91
**Havelka**, Thomas Edward 1947- WhoEnt 92, WhoMW 92
**Havelock**, Wilfrid 1912- Who 92
**Havelock-Allan**, Anthony James Allan 1904- Who 92
**Haveman**, Robert Henry 1936- WrDr 92
**Havemann**, Ernst 1918- ConAu 135
**Havemann**, Robert 1910-1982 FacFETw
**Havemeyer**, Henry Osborne 1847-1907 ThHEIm
**Havemeyer**, John Francis, III 1939- WhoFI 92
**Havemeyer**, Ruth Naomi 1932- AmMWSc 92
**Haven**, Dexter Stearns 1918- AmMWSc 92
**Haven**, Gilbert, Jr. 1821-1880 RelLAm 91
**Haven**, Kittredge 1921- WhoAmP 91
**Haven**, Thomas Edward 1920- WhoAmL 92
**Havener**, Robert D 1930- AmMWSc 92
**Havener**, William H 1927- AmMWSc 92
**Havenor**, Kay Charles 1931- AmMWSc 92
**Havens**, Abram Vaughn 1922- AmMWSc 92
**Havens**, Byron L 1914- AmMWSc 92
**Havens**, Candace Jean 1952- WhoWest 92
**Havens**, Charles W., III 1936- WhoAmL 92, WhoIns 92
**Havens**, James Meryle 1931- AmMWSc 92
**Havens**, Jerry Arnold 1939- AmMWSc 92
**Havens**, John Franklin 1927- WhoFI 92
**Havens**, Leston Laycock 1924- AmMWSc 92
**Havens**, Paul Franklin 1950- WhoMW 92
**Havens**, Thomas R. H. 1939- ConAu 34NR
**Havens**, Timothy Markle 1945- WhoFI 92
**Havens**, William Westerfield, Jr 1920- AmMWSc 92
**Havenstein**, Gerald B 1939- AmMWSc 92
**Haver**, Jurgen F. 1932- WhoFI 92
**Haver**, William Emery 1942- AmMWSc 92
**Haverkamp**, Robert James 1946- WhoAmL 92
**Haverkampf**, Christian Johann 1968- WhoEnt 92
**Haverland**, Gary Thomas 1940- WhoMW 92
**Haverland**, Mark A 1946- WhoAmP 91
**Haverland**, Richard Michael 1941- WhoIns 92
**Haverly**, Jeffrey Allen 1963- WhoMW 92
**Havern**, Robert A, III WhoAmP 91
**Havers** Who 92
**Havers**, Baron 1923- IntWW 91, Who 92
**Havers**, John Alan 1925- AmMWSc 92
**Havers**, Mandy 1953- TwCPaSc
**Havers**, Nigel 1949- IntMPA 92, IntWW 91
**Havers**, Robert William 1953- WhoMW 92
**Haverty**, Harold V. 1930- WhoMW 92
**Haverty**, Michael Irving 1946- AmMWSc 92
**Havertz**, David S 1931- AmMWSc 92
**Havery**, Richard Orbell 1934- Who 92
**Haviaras**, Stratis DrAPF 91
**Haviaras**, Stratis 1935- IntWW 91, WrDr 92
**Havice**, Bob J. 1945- WhoEnt 92
**Havighurst**, Alfred F. 1904- WrDr 92
**Havighurst**, Alfred F. 1904-1991 ConAu 133
**Havighurst**, Clark Canfield 1933- IntWW 91, WhoAmL 92
**Havighurst**, Robert J. d1991 NewYTBS 91
**Havighurst**, Robert J. 1900-1991 ConAu 133
**Havighurst**, Walter 1901- BenetAL 91
**Havil**, Anthony WrDr 92
**Haviland**, Brian Louis 1949- WhoEnt 92
**Haviland**, Camilla Klein 1926- WhoAmL 92
**Haviland**, Denis William Garstin Latimer 1910- IntWW 91, Who 92
**Haviland**, James West 1911- AmMWSc 92
**Haviland**, John Kenneth 1921- AmMWSc 92
**Haviland**, Merrill L 1933- AmMWSc 92, WhoMW 92
**Haviland**, Robert P 1913- AmMWSc 92
**Havill**, Juanita DrAPF 91
**Havill**, Nancy Ches 1945- WhoMW 92
**Havilland** Who 92
**Havinden**, Ashley 1903-1973 TwCPaSc
**Havir**, Evelyn A 1933- AmMWSc 92
**Havis**, John Ralph 1920- AmMWSc 92
**Havlicek**, Franklin J. 1947- WhoFI 92
**Havlicek**, Stephen 1941- AmMWSc 92
**Havlick**, Spenser Woodworth 1935- AmMWSc 92
**Havlik**, Patricia Jeanne 1956- WhoEnt 92
**Havner**, Kerry S 1934- AmMWSc 92
**Havnvik**, John Irwin 1942- WhoMW 92
**Havoc**, June 1916- IntMPA 92, WhoEnt 92
**Havran**, Martin Joseph 1929- WrDr 92

Havran, Wendy Lynn 1955- AmMWSc 92, WhoWest 92
Havrilesky, Thomas Michael 1939- WhoFI 92
Haw-Haw, Lord EncTR 91
Hawaii, Bishop of Who 92
Hawarden, Viscount d1991 Who 92N
Hawarden, Viscount 1961- Who 92
Hawaweeny, Raphael 1860-1915 RelLAm 91
Hawbecker, Byron L 1935- AmMWSc 92
Hawbecker, Byron Leon 1935- WhoMW 92
Hawe, David Lee 1938- WhoFI 92, WhoWest 92
Hawes, Bernadine Tinner 1950- WhoBlA 92
Hawes, Charles Boardman 1889-1923 BenetAL 91
Hawes, Debra Winifred 1958- WhoAmL 92
Hawes, Douglas Wesson 1932- WhoAmL 92
Hawes, Elizabeth 1903-1971 CurBio 91N
Hawes, George Wesson 1848-1882 BiInAmS
Hawes, Grace Maxcy 1926- WhoWest 92
Hawes, Hampton 1928-1977 NewAmDM
Hawes, Judy 1913- WrDr 92
Hawes, Robert Oscar 1935- AmMWSc 92
Hawes, Stephen 1475?-1523? LitC 17, RfGEnL 91
Hawes, Sue 1937- WhoAmL 92
Hawiger, Jack Jacek 1938- AmMWSc 92
Hawirko, Roma Zenovea 1919- AmMWSc 92
Hawk, Alex IntAu&W 91X, TwCWW 91, WrDr 92
Hawk, Caroline Winn 1933- WhoFI 92
Hawk, Charles N., Jr. 1931- WhoBlA 92
Hawk, Charles Nathaniel, III 1957- WhoBlA 92
Hawk, Donald Lee 1947- WhoFI 92
Hawk, Douglas James 1959- WhoWest 92
Hawk, Gary Lee 1947- WhoMW 92
Hawk, James Edward, Jr. 1926- WhoAmL 92
Hawk, Robert M 1924- WhoAmP 91
Hawk, Samuel Silas 1954- WhoEnt 92
Hawk, Timothy Carl 1962- WhoRel 92
Hawk, Virgil Brown 1908- AmMWSc 92
Hawk, William Andrew AmMWSc 92
Hawke Who 92
Hawke, Baron 1904- Who 92
Hawke, Ethan 1970- IntMPA 92
Hawke, Gary Richard 1942- WrDr 92
Hawke, John Daniel, Jr. 1933- WhoAmL 92
Hawke, Larry 1948- WhoAmP 91
Hawke, R Jack 1941- WhoAmP 91
Hawke, Robert 1929- FacFETw
Hawke, Robert D 1932- WhoAmP 91
Hawke, Robert James Lee 1929- IntWW 91, Who 92
Hawke, Ronald Samuel 1940- WhoWest 92
Hawke, Scott Dransfield 1942- AmMWSc 92
Hawke, Simon DrAPF 91, WrDr 92
Hawke, Simon 1951- TwCSFW 91
Hawke, W A 1906- AmMWSc 92
Hawken, Anthony 1948- TwCPaSc
Hawken, Lewis Dudley 1931- Who 92
Hawker, Albert Henry 1911- Who 92
Hawker, Cyril d1991 Who 92N
Hawker, Dennis Gascoyne 1921- Who 92
Hawker, Derrick 1936- TwCPaSc
Hawker, Marilyn Kay 1947- WhoWest 92
Hawker, Robert Stephen 1803-1875 RfGEnL 91
Hawker, Susan 1949- TwCPaSc
Hawkes, Christopher 1905- IntWW 91, Who 92
Hawkes, David 1923- Who 92
Hawkes, Diana R. 1947- WhoBlA 92
Hawkes, Glenn Rogers 1919- WhoWest 92
Hawkes, H Bowman 1907- AmMWSc 92
Hawkes, Herbert Edwin, Jr 1912- AmMWSc 92
Hawkes, J.G. 1915- ConAu 135
Hawkes, Jacquetta 1910- IntAu&W 91, IntWW 91, Who 92, WrDr 92
Hawkes, John DrAPF 91
Hawkes, John 1925- BenetAL 91, ConNov 91, IntAu&W 91, IntWW 91, WrDr 92
Hawkes, John Gregory 1915- Who 92
Hawkes, Joyce W AmMWSc 92
Hawkes, Julian 1944- TwCPaSc
Hawkes, Kevin 1959- ConAu 135
Hawkes, Michael John 1929- Who 92
Hawkes, Paul M 1957- WhoAmP 91
Hawkes, Raymond 1920- Who 92
Hawkes, Robert Lewis 1951- AmMWSc 92
Hawkes, Stephen J 1928- AmMWSc 92
Hawkes, Susan Patricia 1946- AmMWSc 92
Hawkes, Wayne Christian 1951- AmMWSc 92
Hawkes, Zachary WrDr 92
Hawkesbury, Viscount 1972- Who 92
Hawkesworth, Eric 1921- WrDr 92
Hawkesworth, John 1920- IntAu&W 91
Hawkesworth, John Stanley 1920- Who 92
Hawkesworth, Simon 1943- Who 92
Hawkey, Ernest Eric 1909- Who 92
Hawkey, Philip A. 1946- WhoWest 92
Hawking, Stephen W. 1942- WrDr 92
Hawking, Stephen William 1942- FacFETw, IntAu&W 91, IntWW 91, Who 92
Hawkings, Geoffrey d1990 Who 92N
Hawkins, A W 1912- AmMWSc 92
Hawkins, Alberta Lee 1947- WhoAmP 91
Hawkins, Alexander A. 1923-1989 WhoBlA 92N
Hawkins, Alma Mae 1904- WhoWest 92
Hawkins, Andre 1953- WhoBlA 92
Hawkins, Anthony Donald 1942- Who 92
Hawkins, Armis E WhoAmP 91
Hawkins, Armis Eugene 1920- WhoAmL 92
Hawkins, Arthur 1913- Who 92
Hawkins, Ashton 1937- WhoAmL 92
Hawkins, Augustus F 1907- WhoAmP 91, WhoBlA 92
Hawkins, Augustus Freeman 1907- WhoWest 92
Hawkins, Barton A WhoAmP 91
Hawkins, Benjamin 1754-1816 DcNCBi 3
Hawkins, Benjamin Sanford 1909- WhoEnt 92
Hawkins, Benny F., Sr. 1931- WhoBlA 92
Hawkins, Bobbie Louise DrAPF 91
Hawkins, Brett William 1937- WhoMW 92
Hawkins, Bruce 1930- AmMWSc 92
Hawkins, C Morton 1938- AmMWSc 92
Hawkins, Calvin D. 1945- WhoAmL 92, WhoBlA 92
Hawkins, Carmen Doloras 1955- WhoEnt 92
Hawkins, Catherine Eileen 1939- Who 92
Hawkins, Charles Edward 1941- AmMWSc 92
Hawkins, Charles Robert 1943- WhoAmP 91
Hawkins, Charles Thomas 1965- WhoRel 92
Hawkins, Christopher James 1937- Who 92
Hawkins, Coleman 1904-1969 FacFETw, NewAmDM
Hawkins, Connie 1942- WhoBlA 92
Hawkins, Crawford Walter 1933- WhoEnt 92
Hawkins, Cynthia Rayburn 1957- WhoAmL 92
Hawkins, Daniel Ballou 1934- AmMWSc 92, WhoWest 92
Hawkins, David Geoffrey 1937- AmMWSc 92
Hawkins, David Oliver 1945- WhoAmP 91
Hawkins, David Ramon 1927- WhoWest 92
Hawkins, David Richard 1937- Who 92
Hawkins, David Roger 1941- AmMWSc 92
Hawkins, Dennis 1925- TwCPaSc
Hawkins, Dennis Patrick 1945- WhoWest 92
Hawkins, Desmond 1908- Who 92
Hawkins, Desmond Ernest 1919- Who 92
Hawkins, Donald Bruce 1956- WhoAmP 91
Hawkins, Donna Black 1944- WhoAmP 91
Hawkins, Dorisula Wooten 1941- WhoBlA 92
Hawkins, Edward Jackson 1927- WhoAmL 92
Hawkins, Eldridge 1940- WhoBlA 92
Hawkins, Eldridge Thomas Enoch 1940- WhoAmP 91
Hawkins, Eliot Dexter 1932- WhoAmL 92
Hawkins, Elizabeth Anne 1957- WhoRel 92
Hawkins, Ellis Delano 1941- WhoMW 92
Hawkins, Eric William 1915- Who 92
Hawkins, Erskine 1914- NewAmDM
Hawkins, Erskine Ramsay 1914- WhoBlA 92
Hawkins, Falcon Black, Jr. 1927- WhoAmL 92
Hawkins, Francis Glenn 1917- WhoAmL 92
Hawkins, Frank Ernest 1904- Who 92
Hawkins, Frank Nelson, Jr. 1940- WhoFI 92
Hawkins, Gene WhoBlA 92
Hawkins, George Elliott, Jr 1919- AmMWSc 92
Hawkins, Gerald Stanley 1928- AmMWSc 92, WrDr 92
Hawkins, Gilbert Allan 1946- AmMWSc 92
Hawkins, Gordon Lee 1937- WhoRel 92
Hawkins, Harley Buford 1929- WhoAmP 91
Hawkins, Harold Stanley 1927- WhoRel 92
Hawkins, Hersey 1965- BlkOlyM
Hawkins, Hersey R., Jr. 1965- WhoBlA 92
Hawkins, Howard P. 1900- WhoBlA 92
Hawkins, Humphry Caesar 1923- Who 92
Hawkins, Hunt DrAPF 91
Hawkins, Isaac Kinney 1937- AmMWSc 92
Hawkins, J. D. 1943- WhoMW 92
Hawkins, James 1939- WhoBlA 92
Hawkins, James Barrett 1956- WhoAmL 92
Hawkins, James C. 1932- WhoBlA 92
Hawkins, James Lowell, Jr. 1950- WhoWest 92
Hawkins, James Wilbur, Jr 1932- AmMWSc 92
Hawkins, Jamesetta 1938- WhoBlA 92
Hawkins, Jeff Ray 1966- WhoMW 92
Hawkins, Jesse D. 1952- WhoRel 92
Hawkins, John d1717 DcNCBi 3
Hawkins, John 1719-1789 BlkwCEP, NewAmDM
Hawkins, John Davis 1781-1858 DcNCBi 3
Hawkins, John Donald, Jr. 1956- WhoAmL 92
Hawkins, John H, Jr WhoAmP 91
Hawkins, John Landrum 1954- WhoRel 92
Hawkins, John Morgan 1935- WhoAmP 91
Hawkins, John Russell, III 1949- WhoBlA 92
Hawkins, Joseph Elmer 1914- AmMWSc 92, WhoMW 92
Hawkins, Joyce H 1936- WhoAmP 91
Hawkins, Kenneth Bruce 1947- WhoAmP 91
Hawkins, Kenneth Lee 1951- WhoMW 92
Hawkins, Lawrence C. 1919- WhoBlA 92
Hawkins, Lawrence R 1943- WhoAmP 91
Hawkins, Linda Louise 1946- AmMWSc 92
Hawkins, Lionel Anthony 1933- WhoFI 92, WhoMW 92
Hawkins, Lorraine C. 1944- WhoEnt 92
Hawkins, Mary Ellen Higgins WhoAmP 91
Hawkins, Mary L. WhoBlA 92
Hawkins, Micajah Thomas 1790-1858 DcNCBi 3
Hawkins, Michael D 1945- WhoAmP 91
Hawkins, Michael John 1947- AmMWSc 92
Hawkins, Morris, Jr 1944- AmMWSc 92
Hawkins, Morris M. 1920- WhoBlA 92
Hawkins, Muriel A. 1946- WhoBlA 92
Hawkins, Nansi Hughes 1958- WhoRel 92
Hawkins, Neil Middleton 1935- AmMWSc 92
Hawkins, Osie Penman, Jr. 1913- WhoEnt 92
Hawkins, Paul 1912- Who 92
Hawkins, Paula IntWW 91
Hawkins, Paula F 1927- WhoAmP 91
Hawkins, Peter TwCPaSc
Hawkins, Philemon, II 1717-1801 DcNCBi 3
Hawkins, Philemon, III 1752-1833 DcNCBi 3
Hawkins, Reginald A. 1923- WhoBlA 92
Hawkins, Richard Albert 1940- AmMWSc 92
Hawkins, Richard Graeme 1941- Who 92
Hawkins, Richard Holmes 1934- AmMWSc 92
Hawkins, Richard Horace 1922- AmMWSc 92
Hawkins, Richard L 1954- AmMWSc 92
Hawkins, Richard Michael 1949- WhoAmL 92
Hawkins, Richard Stephen Who 92
Hawkins, Richard Thomas 1929- AmMWSc 92
Hawkins, Richard Thurber 1933- WhoRel 92
Hawkins, Robert 1939- WhoAmP 91
Hawkins, Robert C AmMWSc 92
Hawkins, Robert Drake 1946- AmMWSc 92
Hawkins, Robert Garvin 1936- WhoFI 92
Hawkins, Robert Lee 1938- WhoAmP 91, WhoFI 92, WhoWest 92
Hawkins, Robert Lewis, Jr. 1922- WhoAmL 92
Hawkins, Robert S 1938- WhoAmP 91
Hawkins, Ronald Cletus 1952- WhoMW 92
Hawkins, Russell Balthis 1948- WhoFI 92
Hawkins, Scott Alexis 1954- WhoAmL 92
Hawkins, Stan 1955- WhoAmP 91
Hawkins, Steven Wayne 1962- WhoBlA 92
Hawkins, Theo M 1928- AmMWSc 92
Hawkins, Theodore F. 1908- WhoBlA 92
Hawkins, Thomas William, Jr 1938- AmMWSc 92
Hawkins, Tom DrAPF 91
Hawkins, W Bruce 1930- AmMWSc 92
Hawkins, Walter Lenell 1948- WhoMW 92
Hawkins, Walter Lincoln 1911- AmMWSc 92, WhoBlA 92
Hawkins, Willard Royce 1922- AmMWSc 92
Hawkins, William 1777-1819 DcNCBi 3
Hawkins, William Andrew 1938- WhoAmP 91
Hawkins, William Douglas 1946- WhoBlA 92
Hawkins, William Joseph 1819-1894 DcNCBi 3
Hawkins, William M, Jr 1909- AmMWSc 92
Hawkins, William Max 1926- AmMWSc 92
Hawkins, William R WhoIns 92
Hawkins, Willis M 1913- AmMWSc 92
Hawkinson, Carl E 1947- WhoAmP 91
Hawkinson, Marie C 1927- WhoAmP 91
Hawkinson, Stuart Winfield 1943- AmMWSc 92
Hawkinson, Thomas Edwin 1952- WhoMW 92
Hawkland, William Dennis 1920- WhoAmL 92
Hawkridge, Fred Martin 1944- AmMWSc 92
Hawks, Barrett Kingsbury 1938- WhoAmL 92
Hawks, Byron Lovejoy 1909- AmMWSc 92
Hawks, Cicero Stephens 1811-1868 DcNCBi 3
Hawks, Francis Lister 1798-1866 DcNCBi 3
Hawks, George H, III 1938- AmMWSc 92
Hawks, Howard 1896-1977 BenetAL 91, IntDcF 2-2 [port]
Hawks, Howard Winchester 1896-1977 FacFETw
Hawks, John 1731-1790 DcNCBi 3
Hawks, Keith Harold 1941- AmMWSc 92
Hawks, William Harry, Jr WhoAmP 91
Hawksley, Alan J. 1955- WhoAmL 92
Hawksley, John Callis 1903- Who 92
Hawksley, Oscar 1920- AmMWSc 92
Hawksley, Warren 1943- Who 92
Hawksley, William J 1919- WhoAmP 91
Hawksmoor, Nicholas 1661?-1736 BlkwCEP
Hawksworth, David Leslie 1946- Who 92
Hawksworth, Frank Goode 1926- AmMWSc 92
Hawksworth, Marjorie DrAPF 91
Hawksworth, Paul D 1934- WhoIns 92
Hawley, Bernard Russell 1926- WhoRel 92
Hawley, Charles Caldwell 1929- WhoWest 92
Hawley, Donald 1921- Who 92
Hawley, Donald Frederick 1921- IntWW 91
Hawley, Frank Jordan, Jr. 1927- WhoFI 92
Hawley, Frederick William, III 1931- WhoFI 92
Hawley, Helen 1937- TwCPaSc
Hawley, Henry Nicholas Who 92
Hawley, James F. 1938- WhoMW 92
Hawley, John Follen 1954- WhoWest 92
Hawley, John William 1932- AmMWSc 92
Hawley, Joseph Roswell 1826-1905 DcNCBi 3
Hawley, Mabel C. SmATA 67
Hawley, Martin C 1939- AmMWSc 92
Hawley, Merle Dale 1939- AmMWSc 92
Hawley, Nanci Elizabeth 1942- WhoFI 92, WhoWest 92
Hawley, Newton Seymour, Jr 1925- AmMWSc 92
Hawley, Paul F 1910- AmMWSc 92
Hawley, Philip Lines 1928- AmMWSc 92
Hawley, Philip Metschan 1925- WhoFI 92, WhoWest 92
Hawley, Phillip Eugene 1940- WhoFI 92
Hawley, R Stephen WhoAmP 91
Hawley, Richard A. 1945- WrDr 92
Hawley, Robert 1936- IntWW 91
Hawley, Robert Cross 1920- WhoWest 92
Hawley, Robert John 1940- AmMWSc 92
Hawley, Thomas Alan 1955- WhoAmP 91
Hawn, Goldie 1945- IntMPA 92, IntWW 91, WhoEnt 92
Hawn, Thomas R. 1953- WhoMW 92
Haworth, Betsy Ellen 1924- Who 92
Haworth, Byron Allen 1907- WhoAmP 91
Haworth, D R 1928- AmMWSc 92
Haworth, Daniel Thomas 1928- AmMWSc 92, WhoMW 92
Haworth, Gerrard Wendell 1911- WhoFI 92
Haworth, James C 1923- AmMWSc 92
Haworth, Jann 1942- TwCPaSc
Haworth, John Liegh W. Who 92
Haworth, Lionel 1912- IntWW 91, Who 92
Haworth, Patricia Anne 1951- WhoFI 92

**Haworth**, Philip 1927- *Who 92*
**Haworth**, Richard Thomas 1944- *AmMWSc 92*
**Haworth**, Robert Downs d1990 *IntWW 91N*
**Haworth**, Walter Norman 1883-1950 *WhoNob 90*
**Haworth**, William Lancelot 1941- *AmMWSc 92*
**Haworth**, William Royal 1944- *WhoRel 92*
**Hawran**, Paul William 1952- *WhoFI 92*
**Hawrylewicz**, Ervin J *AmMWSc 92*
**Hawrylko**, Eugenia Anna 1942- *AmMWSc 92*
**Hawryluk**, Andrew Michael 1954- *AmMWSc 92*
**Hawryluk**, Richard Janusz 1950- *AmMWSc 92*
**Hawrylyshyn**, Bohdan Wolodymyr 1926- *WhoFI 92*
**Hawrysh**, Zenia Jean 1938- *AmMWSc 92*
**Haws**, Byron Austin 1921- *AmMWSc 92*
**Haws**, Henry H 1934- *WhoAmP 91*
**Haws**, Lyle Clinton 1950- *WhoMW 92*
**Haws**, Robert John 1947- *WhoAmL 92*
**Hawse**, Thomas J, III 1945- *WhoAmP 91*
**Hawthorn**, Christopher John 1936- *Who 92*
**Hawthorne**, Angel L. 1959- *WhoBlA 92*
**Hawthorne**, Betty Eileen 1920- *AmMWSc 92*
**Hawthorne**, Donald Bruce 1955- *WhoWest 92*
**Hawthorne**, Donald Clair 1926- *AmMWSc 92*
**Hawthorne**, Douglas Bruce 1948- *WhoWest 92*
**Hawthorne**, Edward I 1921- *AmMWSc 92*
**Hawthorne**, Frank Christopher 1946- *AmMWSc 92*
**Hawthorne**, Gerald Foster 1925- *WhoRel 92*
**Hawthorne**, Harry David 1918- *WhoRel 92*
**Hawthorne**, Hildegarde 1871-1952 *BenetAL 91*
**Hawthorne**, James Burns 1930- *Who 92*
**Hawthorne**, James Donald 1961- *WhoEnt 92*
**Hawthorne**, John William 1941- *WhoMW 92*
**Hawthorne**, Julian 1846-1934 *BenetAL 91, ScFEYrs, -A*
**Hawthorne**, Kenneth L. *WhoBlA 92*
**Hawthorne**, Lucia Shelia *WhoBlA 92*
**Hawthorne**, Marion Frederick 1928- *AmMWSc 92*
**Hawthorne**, Marla Kay 1955- *WhoMW 92*
**Hawthorne**, Minnie Bell 1945- *WhoRel 92*
**Hawthorne**, Nan Louise 1952- *WhoWest 92*
**Hawthorne**, Nathaniel 1804-1864 *BenetAL 91, RComAH, ScFEYrs*
**Hawthorne**, Nathaniel 1943- *WhoBlA 92*
**Hawthorne**, Nigel 1929- *IntMPA 92*
**Hawthorne**, Nigel Barnard 1929- *IntWW 91, Who 92*
**Hawthorne**, Robert Alexander, Jr. 1937- *WhoAmL 92, WhoAmP 91*
**Hawthorne**, Robert Montgomery, Jr 1929- *AmMWSc 92*
**Hawthorne**, Timothy Robert 1950- *WhoEnt 92, WhoMW 92*
**Hawthorne**, Victor Morrison 1921- *AmMWSc 92*
**Hawthorne**, William 1913- *IntWW 91, Who 92*
**Hawtin**, Brian Richard 1946- *Who 92*
**Hawtin**, David Christopher 1943- *Who 92*
**Hawtin**, Michael Victor 1942- *Who 92*
**Hawton**, Larry David 1937- *AmMWSc 92*
**Hawton**, Margaret H 1942- *AmMWSc 92*
**Hawtrey**, John Havilland Procter 1905- *Who 92*
**Hawtrey**, Stephen Charles d1990 *Who 92N*
**Hawxby**, Keith William 1940- *AmMWSc 92*
**Haxby**, B V 1921- *AmMWSc 92*
**Haxby**, Donald Leslie 1928- *Who 92*
**Haxel**, Otto Philipp Leonhard 1909- *IntWW 91*
**Haxell**, Frank 1913-1988 *FacFETw*
**Haxhiu**, Musa A 1939- *AmMWSc 92*
**Haxo**, Francis Theodore 1921- *AmMWSc 92*
**Haxo**, Henry Emile, Jr 1918- *AmMWSc 92*
**Haxton**, Brooks *DrAPF 91*
**Haxton**, Brooks 1950- *WrDr 92*
**Haxton**, David 1943- *WhoEnt 92*
**Haxton**, Richard Kenneth, Jr. 1919- *WhoEnt 92*
**Haxton**, Richardson Ayres 1948- *WhoAmP 91*
**Haxton**, Wick Christopher 1949- *AmMWSc 92*
**Hay** *Who 92*
**Hay**, Lord 1984- *Who 92*
**Hay**, Alexandre 1919- *IntWW 91*
**Hay**, Alexandre 1919-1991 *NewYTBS 91*
**Hay**, Allan Stuart 1929- *AmMWSc 92, IntWW 91, Who 92*
**Hay**, Andrew Mackenzie 1928- *WhoFI 92, WhoWest 92*
**Hay**, Andrew Osborne 1945- *IntWW 91*
**Hay**, Arthur Thomas Erroll 1909- *Who 92*
**Hay**, David 1916- *Who 92*
**Hay**, David 1927- *Who 92*
**Hay**, David McKechnie 1935- *WhoRel 92*
**Hay**, David Russell 1927- *IntWW 91*
**Hay**, Dennis Lee 1958- *WhoAmL 92*
**Hay**, Denys 1915- *Who 92, WrDr 92*
**Hay**, Donald Ian 1933- *AmMWSc 92*
**Hay**, Donald Robert 1939- *AmMWSc 92*
**Hay**, Edward Craig 1921- *WhoRel 92*
**Hay**, Elizabeth Dexter 1927- *AmMWSc 92*
**Hay**, Frances Mary *Who 92*
**Hay**, George Adam 1930- *Who 92*
**Hay**, George Alan 1942- *WhoAmL 92*
**Hay**, George Austin 1915- *WhoEnt 92, WhoFI 92*
**Hay**, George Edward 1914- *AmMWSc 92*
**Hay**, George Norman 1928- *WhoRel 92*
**Hay**, George William 1929- *AmMWSc 92*
**Hay**, Gyula 1900-1975 *FacFETw*
**Hay**, Hamish 1927- *Who 92*
**Hay**, Ian Leslie 1934- *AmMWSc 92*
**Hay**, James, Jr. 1881-1936 *DcNCBi 3*
**Hay**, James B. D. *Who 92*
**Hay**, James Robert 1925- *AmMWSc 92*
**Hay**, Janet S 1933- *WhoAmP 91*
**Hay**, Jess Thomas 1931- *WhoAmP 91*
**Hay**, John 1757?-1809 *DcNCBi 3*
**Hay**, John 1838-1905 *BenetAL 91*
**Hay**, John Albert 1919- *Who 92*
**Hay**, John Duncan 1909- *Who 92*
**Hay**, John Leonard 1940- *WhoAmL 92, WhoWest 92*
**Hay**, John Milton 1838-1905 *AmPolLe*
**Hay**, John Woods, Jr. 1905- *WhoFI 92, WhoWest 92*
**Hay**, Julius 1900-1975 *LiExTwC*
**Hay**, Louise 1926- *WhoRel 92, WhoWest 92*
**Hay**, Louise 1935- *AmMWSc 92*
**Hay**, Melba Porter 1949- *ConAu 133*
**Hay**, Peter Marsland 1921- *AmMWSc 92*
**Hay**, Philip Jeffrey 1945- *AmMWSc 92*
**Hay**, Raymond A. *IntWW 91*
**Hay**, Richard 1942- *Who 92*
**Hay**, Richard Laurence 1929- *WhoEnt 92*
**Hay**, Richard Le Roy 1926- *AmMWSc 92*
**Hay**, Robert 1835-1895 *BiInAmS*
**Hay**, Robert Arthur 1920- *Who 92*
**Hay**, Robert Colquhoun 1933- *Who 92*
**Hay**, Robert E 1937- *AmMWSc 92*
**Hay**, Robert J 1938- *AmMWSc 92*
**Hay**, Robert Pettus 1941- *WhoMW 92*
**Hay**, Robin William Patrick Hamilton 1939- *Who 92*
**Hay**, Ronald Frederick Hamilton 1941- *Who 92*
**Hay**, Russell Earl, Jr 1918- *AmMWSc 92*
**Hay**, Russell J 1940- *WhoAmP 91*
**Hay**, William Charles 1935- *WhoWest 92*
**Hay**, William Delisle *ScFEYrs*
**Hay**, William Walter 1908- *AmMWSc 92*
**Hay**, William Winn 1934- *AmMWSc 92*
**Hay Davison**, Ian Frederic *Who 92*
**Hay-Roe**, Hugh 1928- *AmMWSc 92*
**Haya**, Katsuji 1943- *AmMWSc 92*
**Haya de la Torre**, Victor Raul 1894-1979 *FacFETw*
**Hayaishi**, Osamu 1920- *IntWW 91*
**Hayakawa**, Kan-Ichi 1931- *AmMWSc 92*
**Hayakawa**, S. I. 1906- *BenetAL 91*
**Hayakawa**, Samuel Ichiye 1906- *IntWW 91, WhoAmP 91*
**Hayakawa**, Satio 1923- *IntWW 91*
**Hayasaka**, Steven S 1947- *AmMWSc 92*
**Hayase**, Kozo 1954- *WhoFI 92*
**Hayashi**, Edwin Kenichi 1942- *WhoAmP 91*
**Hayashi**, Eiichi Ed 1945- *WhoMW 92*
**Hayashi**, Fumihiko 1930- *AmMWSc 92*
**Hayashi**, Izumi 1948- *AmMWSc 92*
**Hayashi**, James Akira 1926- *AmMWSc 92*
**Hayashi**, Keiichiro 1929- *WhoFI 92*
**Hayashi**, Ko 1947- *WhoWest 92*
**Hayashi**, Leslie Ann 1954- *WhoAmL 92*
**Hayashi**, Masao 1947- *AmMWSc 92*
**Hayashi**, Richard Keiji 1947- *WhoWest 92*
**Hayashi**, Teru 1914- *AmMWSc 92*
**Hayashi**, Teruo Terry 1921- *AmMWSc 92*
**Hayashi**, Tetsumaro 1929- *WhoMW 92, WrDr 92*
**Hayashi**, Yoshikazu 1943- *AmMWSc 92*
**Hayashi**, Yoshimi 1922- *WhoAmL 92, WhoAmP 91, WhoWest 92*
**Hayashi**, Yoshiro 1927- *IntWW 91*
**Hayashi**, Yuko *WhoEnt 92*
**Hayashida**, Frank 1933- *WhoEnt 92, WhoMW 92*
**Hayashida**, Larry W. 1944- *WhoRel 92*
**Hayashida**, Tetsuo 1917- *AmMWSc 92*
**Hayashida**, Yukio 1915- *IntWW 91*
**Hayasi**, Nisiki 1929- *WhoFI 92*
**Hayat**, M A 1938- *AmMWSc 92*
**Hayatsu**, Ryoichi 1928- *AmMWSc 92*
**Hayball**, Frederick Ronald 1914- *Who 92*
**Haybron**, Ronald M 1934- *AmMWSc 92*
**Haycock**, Dean A 1952- *AmMWSc 92*
**Haycock**, Ernest William 1927- *AmMWSc 92*
**Haycock**, John Winthrop 1949- *AmMWSc 92*
**Haycox**, Ernest 1899-1950 *BenetAL 91, TwCWW 91*
**Haycraft**, Anna *WrDr 92*
**Haycraft**, Anna Margaret 1932- *IntWW 91, Who 92*
**Haycraft**, Colin Berry 1929- *Who 92*
**Haycraft**, Howard d1991 *NewYTBS 91 [port]*
**Haycraft**, Howard 1905- *IntAu&W 91, IntWW 91*
**Haycraft**, John 1926- *ConAu 133*
**Haycraft**, John Stacpoole 1926- *Who 92*
**Haydar**, Loutof Allah 1940- *Who 92*
**Haydar**, Mohammad Haydar 1931- *IntWW 91*
**Hayday**, Anthony Victor 1930- *Who 92*
**Hayday**, Frederick d1990 *Who 92N*
**Haydee**, Marcia 1937- *FacFETw, WhoEnt 92*
**Haydel**, James V., Sr. *WhoBlA 92*
**Hayden**, Carla Diane 1952- *WhoBlA 92*
**Hayden**, Cedric 1934- *WhoAmP 91*
**Hayden**, Della Irving 1851-1924 *NotBlAW 92*
**Hayden**, Dolores *DrAPF 91*
**Hayden**, Dolores 1945- *IntAu&W 91*
**Hayden**, Donald E 1915- *IntAu&W 91, WrDr 92*
**Hayden**, Edgar C 1922- *AmMWSc 92*
**Hayden**, Eric William 1919- *IntAu&W 91, WrDr 92*
**Hayden**, Ferdinand Vandiveer 1829-1887 *BiInAmS*
**Hayden**, Frank *WhoBlA 92*
**Hayden**, Gary Lynn 1950- *WhoAmL 92*
**Hayden**, George A 1928- *AmMWSc 92*
**Hayden**, Harold 1947- *WhoAmP 91*
**Hayden**, Horace H 1769-1844 *BiInAmS*
**Hayden**, Howard Corwin 1940- *AmMWSc 92*
**Hayden**, Jay *TwCWW 91*
**Hayden**, Jeffrey *LesBEnT 92*
**Hayden**, Jeffrey 1926- *WhoEnt 92*
**Hayden**, Jess, Jr *AmMWSc 92*
**Hayden**, John Carleton 1933- *WhoBlA 92*
**Hayden**, John Michael 1944- *IntWW 91*
**Hayden**, Joseph P, Jr 1929- *WhoIns 92*
**Hayden**, Julian Howard 1930- *WhoAmL 92*
**Hayden**, Lawrence Marie 1925- *WhoRel 92*
**Hayden**, Leroy Austin 1927- *WhoAmP 91*
**Hayden**, Leroy Robert, Jr 1935- *WhoIns 92*
**Hayden**, Marshall Wayne 1941- *WhoRel 92*
**Hayden**, Martin S *WhoAmP 91*
**Hayden**, Michael Allen 1958- *WhoWest 92*
**Hayden**, Mike 1944- *WhoAmP 91*
**Hayden**, Paul M. 1956- *WhoMW 92*
**Hayden**, Paul Thomas 1956- *WhoAmL 92*
**Hayden**, Ralph Frederick 1922- *WhoFI 92*
**Hayden**, Raymond Paul 1939- *WhoAmL 92*
**Hayden**, Richard 1956- *WhoAmP 91*
**Hayden**, Richard Amherst 1928- *AmMWSc 92*
**Hayden**, Richard John 1922- *AmMWSc 92*
**Hayden**, Robert 1913-1980 *AfrAmW, BlkLC [port]*
**Hayden**, Robert C., Jr. 1937- *WhoBlA 92*
**Hayden**, Robert E. 1913-1980 *BenetAL 91, FacFETw*
**Hayden**, Ron L. 1948- *WhoWest 92*
**Hayden**, Roy Edmund 1932- *WhoRel 92*
**Hayden**, Spencer James 1922- *WhoFI 92*
**Hayden**, Susan Marie Liebich 1957- *WhoEnt 92*
**Hayden**, Thomas Day 1944- *AmMWSc 92*
**Hayden**, Thomas Lee 1932- *AmMWSc 92*
**Hayden**, Tom 1939- *WhoAmP 91, WhoWest 92, WrDr 92*
**Hayden**, Torey L 1951- *ConAu 35NR, SmATA 65 [port]*
**Hayden**, Vern Clarence 1937- *WhoFI 92*
**Hayden**, William George 1933- *IntWW 91, Who 92*
**Hayden**, William Hughes 1940- *WhoBlA 92*
**Hayden**, William Joseph 1929- *Who 92, WhoFI 92*
**Hayden**, William Robert 1947- *WhoAmL 92*
**Hayden-Wing**, Larry Dean 1935- *AmMWSc 92*
**Haydn**, Hiram 1907-1973 *BenetAL 91*
**Haydn**, Joseph 1732-1809 *BlkwCEP, NewAmDM*
**Haydn**, Michael 1737-1806 *NewAmDM*
**Haydock**, Paul Vincent *AmMWSc 92*
**Haydock**, Roger Silve 1945- *WhoAmL 92*
**Haydock**, Walter James 1947- *WhoMW 92*
**Haydon**, Benjamin Robert 1786-1846 *DcLB 110 [port]*
**Haydon**, Francis Edmund Walter 1928- *Who 92*
**Haydon**, George William 1914- *AmMWSc 92*
**Haydon**, Robin 1920- *IntWW 91*
**Haydon**, Walter Robert 1920- *Who 92*
**Haydu**, Juan B 1930- *AmMWSc 92*
**Haydu**, Peter Edmund 1948- *WhoEnt 92*
**Hayduk**, Michael 1951- *WhoRel 92*
**Hayduk**, Walter 1931- *AmMWSc 92*
**Haye**, Clifford S. 1942- *WhoBlA 92*
**Haye**, Colvyn Hugh 1925- *IntWW 91, Who 92*
**Haye**, Keith R 1953- *AmMWSc 92*
**Haye**, Nicolaa de la 1160?-1218 *EncAmaz 91*
**Hayek**, Carolyn Jean 1948- *WhoAmL 92*
**Hayek**, Dean Harrison 1931- *AmMWSc 92*
**Hayek**, Friedrich August 1899- *IntWW 91, Who 92*
**Hayek**, Friedrich August Von 1899- *WhoNob 90*
**Hayek**, Grace M. 1962- *WhoMW 92*
**Hayek**, Ignace Antoine, II 1910- *IntWW 91*
**Hayek**, Lee-Ann Collins 1943- *AmMWSc 92*
**Hayek**, Mason 1920- *AmMWSc 92*
**Hayek**, Nicholas G. 1928- *IntWW 91*
**Hayek**, Sabih I 1938- *AmMWSc 92*
**Hayes**, Agnes Thresa 1919- *WhoAmP 91*
**Hayes**, Alan Lauffer 1946- *WhoRel 92*
**Hayes**, Albertine Brannum *WhoBlA 92*
**Hayes**, Alfred 1911-1985 *BenetAL 91*
**Hayes**, Alice Bourke 1937- *AmMWSc 92*
**Hayes**, Alvin, Jr. 1932- *WhoBlA 92*
**Hayes**, Andrew Wallace 1939- *AmMWSc 92*
**Hayes**, Ann *DrAPF 91*
**Hayes**, Annamarie Gillespie 1931- *WhoBlA 92*
**Hayes**, Arthur C *WhoAmP 91*
**Hayes**, Arthur Chester 1918- *WhoMW 92*
**Hayes**, Augustus Allen 1806-1882 *BiInAmS*
**Hayes**, Barbara Anne 1951- *WhoMW 92*
**Hayes**, Barbara Lynn 1942- *WhoFI 92*
**Hayes**, Bernardine Frances 1939- *WhoFI 92*
**Hayes**, Bettine J. 1928- *WhoFI 92*
**Hayes**, Bonaventure Francis 1941- *WhoRel 92*
**Hayes**, Brenda Sue 1941- *WhoMW 92*
**Hayes**, Brian 1929- *IntWW 91, Who 92*
**Hayes**, Brian 1940- *Who 92*
**Hayes**, Byron Jackson, Jr. 1934- *WhoAmL 92, WhoWest 92*
**Hayes**, Carol J 1940- *AmMWSc 92*
**Hayes**, Charles 1943- *WhoBlA 92*
**Hayes**, Charles 1950- *WhoMW 92, WhoRel 92*
**Hayes**, Charles A. 1918- *AlmAP 92 [port], WhoAmP 91, WhoBlA 92, WhoMW 92*
**Hayes**, Charles Amos, Jr 1916- *AmMWSc 92*
**Hayes**, Charles Franklin 1941- *AmMWSc 92*
**Hayes**, Charles L. *DrAPF 91*
**Hayes**, Charles Leonard 1921- *WhoBlA 92*
**Hayes**, Charles Parker 1938- *WhoRel 92*
**Hayes**, Charles Willard 1858-1916 *BiInAmS*
**Hayes**, Cheryl Davis 1950- *IntWW 91*
**Hayes**, Claude 1912- *Who 92*
**Hayes**, Claude Q C 1945- *AmMWSc 92*
**Hayes**, Claude Quinten Christopher 1945- *WhoWest 92*
**Hayes**, Colin 1919- *TwCPaSc*
**Hayes**, Colin Graham Frederick 1919- *Who 92*
**Hayes**, Curtiss Leo 1931- *WhoBlA 92*
**Hayes**, Cynthia Lela 1949- *WhoFI 92*
**Hayes**, D. Thomas 1954- *WhoEnt 92*
**Hayes**, Dallas T 1931- *AmMWSc 92*
**Hayes**, David J. 1953- *WhoAmL 92*
**Hayes**, David Lloyd 1956- *WhoAmL 92*
**Hayes**, David Michael 1943- *WhoAmL 92, WhoFI 92*
**Hayes**, David R 1937- *AmMWSc 92*
**Hayes**, David Sayre 1941- *WhoAmP 91*
**Hayes**, David Wayne 1936- *AmMWSc 92*
**Hayes**, Dennis C. 1951- *WhoAmL 92*
**Hayes**, Dennis E 1938- *AmMWSc 92*
**Hayes**, Donald Charles 1932- *AmMWSc 92*
**Hayes**, Donald H 1937- *AmMWSc 92*
**Hayes**, Donald LeRaye 1939- *WhoAmP 91*
**Hayes**, Donald M 1928- *AmMWSc 92*
**Hayes**, Donald Scott 1939- *AmMWSc 92*
**Hayes**, Dora Kruse 1931- *AmMWSc 92*
**Hayes**, Dorsha *DrAPF 91*
**Hayes**, Dorsha 1897?-1990 *ConAu 133*
**Hayes**, Douglas Martin 1943- *WhoFI 92*
**Hayes**, Earl T 1912- *AmMWSc 92*

**Hayes**, Edward, Jr. 1947- *WhoAmL 92, WhoBlA 92*
**Hayes**, Edward C 1937- *ConAu 35NR*
**Hayes**, Edward Francis 1941- *AmMWSc 92*
**Hayes**, Edward J 1924- *AmMWSc 92*
**Hayes**, Edwin Junius, Jr. 1932- *WhoWest 92*
**Hayes**, Eleanor Maxine 1954- *WhoBlA 92*
**Hayes**, Elizabeth A 1957- *WhoAmP 91*
**Hayes**, Elvin E., Sr. 1945- *WhoBlA 92*
**Hayes**, Ernest M. 1946- *WhoWest 92*
**Hayes**, Everett Russell 1917- *AmMWSc 92*
**Hayes**, Floyd Windom, III 1942- *WhoBlA 92*
**Hayes**, Francis Wingate, Jr. 1914- *WhoRel 92*
**Hayes**, Frank N. 1938- *WhoFI 92*
**Hayes**, Gene Leroy 1940- *WhoMW 92*
**Hayes**, Geoffrey Leigh 1947- *WhoRel 92*
**Hayes**, George J 1918- *AmMWSc 92*
**Hayes**, George Nicholas 1928- *WhoAmL 92*
**Hayes**, George Oliver 1924- *WhoRel 92*
**Hayes**, George Stephen 1947- *WhoFI 92*
**Hayes**, Gerald Joseph 1950- *WhoAmL 92*
**Hayes**, Giles Peter 1939- *WhoRel 92*
**Hayes**, Gordon Glenn 1936- *WhoWest 92*
**Hayes**, Graham Edmondson 1929- *WhoBlA 92*
**Hayes**, Gregory Andrew 1962- *WhoAmL 92*
**Hayes**, Gregory Michael 1954- *WhoWest 92*
**Hayes**, Guy Scull 1912- *AmMWSc 92*
**Hayes**, Harold O., Jr 1929- *WhoFI 92*
**Hayes**, Helen 1900- *FacFETw, IntMPA 92, IntWW 91, Who 92, WhoEnt 92*
**Hayes**, Helen 1923- *WhoMW 92, WhoRel 92*
**Hayes**, Helen Young 1962- *WhoFI 92*
**Hayes**, Henry Clifton 1942- *WhoAmP 91*
**Hayes**, Hubert Harrison 1901-1964 *DcNCBi 3*
**Hayes**, Isaac 1938- *NewAmDM*
**Hayes**, Isaac 1942- *WhoBlA 92, WhoEnt 92*
**Hayes**, Isaac I. 1832-1881 *BenetAL 91*
**Hayes**, Isaac Israel *ScFEYrs B*
**Hayes**, Isaac Israel 1832-1881 *BiInAmS*
**Hayes**, J Edmund 1910- *AmMWSc 92*
**Hayes**, J. Harold, Jr. 1953- *WhoBlA 92*
**Hayes**, J Hurst 1875- *ScFEYrs*
**Hayes**, J Scott 1946- *AmMWSc 92*
**Hayes**, Jackie Rhea 1954- *WhoRel 92*
**Hayes**, Jacqueline Crement 1941- *WhoMW 92*
**Hayes**, James A. 1946- *AlmAP 92 [port]*
**Hayes**, James Alison 1946- *WhoAmP 91*
**Hayes**, James Mark 1958- *WhoAmL 92*
**Hayes**, James Martin *Who 92*
**Hayes**, James Michael 1939- *WhoAmL 92*
**Hayes**, James Patrick 1938- *WhoAmL 92*
**Hayes**, James Robert 1929- *WhoRel 92*
**Hayes**, Janan Mary 1942- *AmMWSc 92*
**Hayes**, Janet Gray 1926- *WhoAmP 91*
**Hayes**, Jeffrey Charles 1954- *AmMWSc 92*
**Hayes**, Jeremiah Francis 1934- *AmMWSc 92*
**Hayes**, Jeremy Joseph James 1953- *Who 92*
**Hayes**, Joan Eames 1916- *WhoAmP 91*
**Hayes**, Joe Black 1915- *WhoAmP 91*
**Hayes**, John 1913- *Who 92*
**Hayes**, John 1929- *WrDr 92*
**Hayes**, John A 1929- *AmMWSc 92*
**Hayes**, John Bernard 1934- *AmMWSc 92*
**Hayes**, John Bruton, Jr. 1942- *WhoFI 92*
**Hayes**, John C, III 1945- *WhoAmP 91*
**Hayes**, John Edward 1941- *WhoEnt 92*
**Hayes**, John Edward, Jr. 1937- *WhoMW 92*
**Hayes**, John Francis 1919- *WhoAmL 92, WhoAmP 91*
**Hayes**, John Lord 1812-1887 *BiInAmS*
**Hayes**, John Michael 1919- *IntMPA 92*
**Hayes**, John Michael 1940- *AmMWSc 92*
**Hayes**, John Patrick 1921- *WhoFI 92*
**Hayes**, John Patrick, Jr. 1949- *WhoEnt 92*
**Hayes**, John Philip 1924- *IntWW 91, Who 92*
**Hayes**, John Terrence 1928- *AmMWSc 92*
**Hayes**, John Thompson 1940- *AmMWSc 92*
**Hayes**, John Trevor 1929- *IntWW 91, Who 92*
**Hayes**, John William 1944- *AmMWSc 92*
**Hayes**, John William 1945- *Who 92*
**Hayes**, Johnnie Ray 1942- *AmMWSc 92*
**Hayes**, Johnson Jay 1886-1970 *DcNCBi 3*
**Hayes**, Jonathan Michael 1962- *WhoBlA 92*
**Hayes**, Joseph 1918- *BenetAL 91, WhoEnt 92, WrDr 92*
**Hayes**, Joseph Clay 1920- *WhoEnt 92*
**Hayes**, Joseph Edward, Jr 1927- *AmMWSc 92*
**Hayes**, Judith Slayden 1947- *WhoRel 92*
**Hayes**, Karen Wood 1935- *WhoAmP 91*
**Hayes**, Kenneth Cronise 1939- *AmMWSc 92*
**Hayes**, Kenneth Edward 1928- *AmMWSc 92*
**Hayes**, Kirby Maxwell 1922- *AmMWSc 92*
**Hayes**, Kirk M 1936- *WhoIns 92*
**Hayes**, Larry B. 1939- *WhoAmL 92*
**Hayes**, Leola G. *WhoBlA 92*
**Hayes**, Lester 1955- *WhoBlA 92*
**Hayes**, Lewis Mifflin, Jr. 1941- *WhoAmL 92*
**Hayes**, Lisa Helene Rice 1958- *WhoAmL 92*
**Hayes**, Marion LeRoy 1931- *WhoBlA 92*
**Hayes**, Mark Allan 1914- *AmMWSc 92*
**Hayes**, Mark Wayne 1962- *WhoRel 92*
**Hayes**, Martin Joseph 1932- *WhoAmP 91*
**Hayes**, Mary Phyllis 1921- *WhoFI 92, WhoMW 92*
**Hayes**, Michael Cecil 1946- *WhoAmL 92*
**Hayes**, Michael D 1951- *WhoAmP 91*
**Hayes**, Michael Joseph 1963- *WhoAmL 92*
**Hayes**, Miles O 1934- *AmMWSc 92*
**Hayes**, Miles V 1911- *AmMWSc 92*
**Hayes**, Murray Lawrence 1929- *AmMWSc 92*
**Hayes**, Neil John 1951- *WhoAmL 92*
**Hayes**, Nicholas 1947- *WhoAmP 91*
**Hayes**, Norman Robert, Jr. 1948- *WhoAmL 92*
**Hayes**, Orlando Dewayne 1958- *WhoFI 92*
**Hayes**, Patricia Ann *WhoEnt 92*
**Hayes**, Patrick Joseph 1867-1938 *RelLAm 91*
**Hayes**, Paul Gordon 1934- *WhoMW 92*
**Hayes**, Paul Martin 1942- *WrDr 92*
**Hayes**, Percy B. 1936- *WhoMW 92*
**Hayes**, Peter John 1942- *WhoFI 92*
**Hayes**, Peter Lind 1915- *IntMPA 92*
**Hayes**, Philip Harold 1940- *WhoAmP 91*
**Hayes**, Randy Alan 1950- *WhoMW 92*
**Hayes**, Rawlene Briar Watters *WhoFI 92*
**Hayes**, Raymond L, Jr 1938- *AmMWSc 92*
**Hayes**, Raymond Leroy 1923- *AmMWSc 92*
**Hayes**, Raymond Leroy 1953- *WhoRel 92*
**Hayes**, Rebecca Anne 1950- *WhoFI 92*
**Hayes**, Richard C. 1938- *WhoBlA 92*
**Hayes**, Richard J 1932- *AmMWSc 92*
**Hayes**, Richard Johnson 1933- *WhoAmL 92*
**Hayes**, Robert Allen 1939- *WhoAmP 91*
**Hayes**, Robert Arthur 1920- *AmMWSc 92*
**Hayes**, Robert C 1936- *WhoAmP 91*
**Hayes**, Robert Charles 1966- *WhoRel 92*
**Hayes**, Robert E 1933- *WhoAmP 91*
**Hayes**, Robert Emmet 1951- *WhoAmP 91*
**Hayes**, Robert Green 1936- *AmMWSc 92*
**Hayes**, Robert L 1942- *BlkOlyM*
**Hayes**, Robert M 1945- *AmMWSc 92*
**Hayes**, Robert Mayo 1926- *AmMWSc 92*
**Hayes**, Robert Wesley, Jr 1952- *WhoAmP 91*
**Hayes**, Roger Peter 1945- *IntWW 91*
**Hayes**, Roland 1887-1977 *NewAmDM*
**Hayes**, Roland Harris 1931- *WhoBlA 92*
**Hayes**, Ronald George 1936- *WhoFI 92*
**Hayes**, Russell E 1935- *AmMWSc 92*
**Hayes**, Rutherford B. 1822-1893 *BenetAL 91, RComAH*
**Hayes**, Rutherford Birchard 1822-1893 *AmPolLe [port]*
**Hayes**, Samuel E, Jr 1940- *WhoAmP 91*
**Hayes**, Samuel Perkins 1910- *WrDr 92*
**Hayes**, Sheldon P 1913- *AmMWSc 92*
**Hayes**, Sherill D. *WhoRel 92*
**Hayes**, Stephen Kurtz 1949- *WhoMW 92*
**Hayes**, Stephen Matthew 1950- *WhoMW 92*
**Hayes**, Stephen Thorne 1952- *WhoAmL 92*
**Hayes**, Susan Seaforth *WhoEnt 92*
**Hayes**, Terence James 1941- *AmMWSc 92*
**Hayes**, Terrill Grant 1948- *WhoRel 92*
**Hayes**, Thomas A 1943- *WhoIns 92*
**Hayes**, Thomas B *AmMWSc 92*
**Hayes**, Thomas Clark 1950- *WhoFI 92*
**Hayes**, Thomas G 1936- *AmMWSc 92*
**Hayes**, Thomas Jay, III 1914- *AmMWSc 92*
**Hayes**, Thomas L 1927- *AmMWSc 92*
**Hayes**, Thomas W *WhoAmP 91*
**Hayes**, Thomas William *WhoWest 92*
**Hayes**, Timothy *TwCWW 91*
**Hayes**, Timothy Lee 1955- *WhoMW 92*
**Hayes**, Timothy Mitchell 1941- *AmMWSc 92*
**Hayes**, Vertis 1911- *WhoBlA 92*
**Hayes**, Wallace D 1918- *AmMWSc 92*
**Hayes**, Walter 1924- *Who 92*
**Hayes**, Wayland Jackson, Jr 1917- *AmMWSc 92*
**Hayes**, Webb Cook, III 1920- *WhoAmL 92*
**Hayes**, Wilbur Frank 1936- *AmMWSc 92*
**Hayes**, William 1913- *Who 92*
**Hayes**, William 1930- *Who 92*
**Hayes**, William Kenneth 1928- *WhoFI 92*
**Hayes**, Willis B 1942- *AmMWSc 92*
**Hayes**, Zachary Jerome 1932- *WhoRel 92*
**Hayes-Giles**, Joyce V. 1948- *WhoBlA 92*
**Hayet**, Leonard 1932- *WhoFI 92*
**Hayflick**, Leonard 1928- *AmMWSc 92*
**Hayford**, Dale N. 1944- *WhoRel 92*
**Hayford**, Jack W. *WhoRel 92*
**Haygarth**, John Charles 1940- *AmMWSc 92*
**Haygood**, Atticus Greene 1839-1896 *RelLAm 91*
**Haygood**, Margo Genevieve 1954- *AmMWSc 92*
**Haygood**, Wil 1954- *WhoBlA 92*
**Haygreen**, John G 1930- *AmMWSc 92*
**Hayhoe**, Bernard John 1925- *Who 92*
**Hayhoe**, Frank George James 1920- *Who 92*
**Hayhurst**, Richard Allen 1948- *WhoAmP 91*
**Hayle**, Claudette Frederica 1955- *WhoFI 92*
**Hayles**, William Joseph 1927- *AmMWSc 92*
**Haylett**, Margaret Wendy 1953- *WhoEnt 92*
**Hayling**, William H. 1925- *WhoBlA 92*
**Haylock**, John 1918- *ConAu 133*
**Haylock**, John Mervyn 1918- *IntAu&W 91*
**Haymaker**, Gideon Timberlake 1958- *WhoFI 92*
**Haymaker**, Richard Webb 1940- *AmMWSc 92*
**Hayman**, Alan Conrad 1947- *AmMWSc 92*
**Hayman**, Carol Bessant *DrAPF 91*
**Hayman**, Carol Bessent 1927- *WrDr 92*
**Hayman**, David 1927- *IntAu&W 91, WrDr 92*
**Hayman**, Ernest Paul 1946- *AmMWSc 92*
**Hayman**, Helene 1949- *Who 92*
**Hayman**, Jane *DrAPF 91*
**Hayman**, Jeffrey Lloyd 1955- *WhoAmL 92*
**Hayman**, John David Woodburn 1918- *Who 92*
**Hayman**, Patrick d1988 *IntWW 91N*
**Hayman**, Patrick 1915-1988 *TwCPaSc*
**Hayman**, Peter 1914- *Who 92*
**Hayman**, Peter Telford 1914- *IntWW 91*
**Hayman**, Richard Warren Joseph 1920- *WhoEnt 92*
**Hayman**, Ronald 1932- *IntAu&W 91, WrDr 92*
**Hayman**, Selma 1931- *AmMWSc 92*
**Hayman**, Walter Kurt 1926- *IntWW 91, Who 92, WrDr 92*
**Hayman**, Warren C. 1932- *WhoBlA 92*
**Hayman**, William Samuel 1903- *Who 92*
**Hayman-Joyce**, Robert John 1940- *Who 92*
**Haymer**, John *ConTFT 9*
**Haymer**, Johnny 1920-1989 *ConTFT 9*
**Haymerle**, Heinrich 1910- *IntWW 91*
**Haymes**, Don 1940- *WhoRel 92*
**Haymes**, Edward A. 1940- *WhoFI 92*
**Haymes**, Peggy A. 1960- *WhoRel 92*
**Haymes**, Robert C 1931- *AmMWSc 92*
**Haymet**, Anthony Douglas-John 1956- *AmMWSc 92*
**Haymon**, Gregory L. 1955- *WhoFI 92*
**Haymon**, S. T. 1918- *WrDr 92*
**Haymond**, Herman Ralph 1924- *AmMWSc 92*
**Haymond**, J Brent 1936- *WhoAmP 91*
**Haymond**, Rufus 1805?-1886 *BiInAmS*
**Haymore**, Barry Lant 1945- *AmMWSc 92*
**Haymore**, Tyrone 1947- *WhoBlA 92*
**Haymovits**, Asher 1933- *AmMWSc 92*
**Hayn**, Annette *DrAPF 91*
**Hayn**, Carl Hugo 1916- *AmMWSc 92*
**Hayna**, Lois Beebe *DrAPF 91*
**Hayne van Ghizeghem** 1445?-1472? *NewAmDM*
**Hayne**, Don William 1911- *AmMWSc 92*
**Hayne**, Harriet 1922- *WhoAmP 91*
**Hayne**, Jack McVicar 1920- *WhoAmP 91*
**Hayne**, Paul Hamilton 1830-1886 *BenetAL 91*
**Hayne**, Robert Young 1791-1839 *AmPolLe*
**Hayner**, David William 1959- *WhoWest 92*
**Hayner**, Herman Henry 1916- *WhoAmL 92*
**Hayner**, Jeannette C 1919- *WhoAmP 91*
**Hayner**, Jeannette Clare 1919- *WhoWest 92*
**Hayner**, Stephen A. *WhoRel 92*
**Haynes**, Alfred 1921- *AmMWSc 92*
**Haynes**, Alphonso Worden *WhoBlA 92*
**Haynes**, Arden R. *WhoFI 92*
**Haynes**, Arden Ramon 1927- *IntWW 91*
**Haynes**, Arthur Edwin 1849-1915 *BiInAmS*
**Haynes**, Barbara Asche 1935- *WhoBlA 92*
**Haynes**, Boyd W, Jr 1917- *AmMWSc 92*
**Haynes**, Bradley 1954- *WhoAmP 91*
**Haynes**, Caleb Vance, Jr 1928- *AmMWSc 92, WhoWest 92*
**Haynes**, Clarence E *WhoAmP 91*
**Haynes**, David Francis 1926- *Who 92*
**Haynes**, Dean L 1932- *AmMWSc 92*
**Haynes**, Denys Eyre Lankester 1913- *Who 92*
**Haynes**, Douglas Martin 1922- *AmMWSc 92*
**Haynes**, Duncan Harold 1945- *AmMWSc 92*
**Haynes**, Edwin William George 1911- *Who 92*
**Haynes**, Eleanor Louise *WhoBlA 92*
**Haynes**, Eleanor Louise 1929- *WhoFI 92*
**Haynes**, Elizabeth Ross 1883-1953 *NotBlAW 92 [port]*
**Haynes**, Elwood 1857-1925 *FacFETw*
**Haynes**, Emanuel 1916- *AmMWSc 92*
**Haynes**, Emmit Howard 1926- *AmMWSc 92*
**Haynes**, Ernest Anthony 1922- *Who 92*
**Haynes**, Eugene, Jr. *WhoBlA 92, WhoEnt 92*
**Haynes**, Frank *Who 92*
**Haynes**, Frank L., Jr. 1944- *WhoBlA 92*
**Haynes**, Frank Lloyd, Jr 1920- *AmMWSc 92*
**Haynes**, Frank Maurice 1935- *WhoFI 92*
**Haynes**, Gene A *WhoAmP 91*
**Haynes**, George E., Jr. 1920- *WhoBlA 92*
**Haynes**, George Edmund, Jr. 1912- *WhoBlA 92*
**Haynes**, George Rufus 1928- *AmMWSc 92*
**Haynes**, Henry William, Jr 1942- *AmMWSc 92*
**Haynes**, Henry Williamson 1831-1912 *BiInAmS*
**Haynes**, Jacquelyn Carol 1952- *WhoAmL 92*
**Haynes**, James Earl, Jr. 1943- *WhoWest 92*
**Haynes**, James H. 1953- *WhoBlA 92*
**Haynes**, James Kay 1937- *WhoRel 92*
**Haynes**, James Mitchell 1951- *AmMWSc 92*
**Haynes**, Jean Reed 1949- *WhoAmL 92*
**Haynes**, Joe M 1936- *WhoAmP 91*
**Haynes**, John J 1925- *AmMWSc 92*
**Haynes**, John K. *WhoBlA 92*
**Haynes**, John Kermit 1943- *AmMWSc 92, WhoBlA 92*
**Haynes**, John Lenneis 1934- *AmMWSc 92*
**Haynes**, Jorge *WhoHisp 92*
**Haynes**, Leonard L., III 1947- *WhoBlA 92*
**Haynes**, Leonard L., Jr. 1923- *WhoBlA 92*
**Haynes**, LeRoy Wilbur 1934- *AmMWSc 92*
**Haynes**, Linda Jean 1954- *WhoWest 92*
**Haynes**, Marcia Margaret 1931- *WhoMW 92*
**Haynes**, Margaret Campbell 1956- *WhoAmL 92*
**Haynes**, Mark Edward 1953- *WhoAmL 92*
**Haynes**, Martha Patricia 1951- *AmMWSc 92*
**Haynes**, Marti 1947- *WhoFI 92*
**Haynes**, Mary *DrAPF 91*
**Haynes**, Mary 1938- *ConAu 35NR, SmATA 65*
**Haynes**, Mary L. 1942- *WhoMW 92*
**Haynes**, Mary Rapstine 1945- *WhoAmP 91*
**Haynes**, Michael E. 1927- *WhoBlA 92*
**Haynes**, Michael James 1953- *WhoBlA 92*
**Haynes**, Munro K 1923- *AmMWSc 92*
**Haynes**, N Bruce 1926- *AmMWSc 92*
**Haynes**, Neal J. 1912- *WhoBlA 92*
**Haynes**, Ora Lee 1925- *WhoBlA 92*
**Haynes**, Patricia Somerville 1956- *WhoBlA 92*
**Haynes**, Peter 1925- *Who 92*
**Haynes**, Raleigh Rutherford 1851-1917 *DcNCBi 3*
**Haynes**, Ralph Edwards *AmMWSc 92*
**Haynes**, Renee 1906- *ConAu 34NR*
**Haynes**, Renee Oriana *WrDr 92*
**Haynes**, Renee Oriana Tickell 1906- *IntAu&W 91*
**Haynes**, Richard L 1934- *WhoAmP 91*
**Haynes**, Robert *DrAPF 91*
**Haynes**, Robert Brian 1947- *AmMWSc 92*
**Haynes**, Robert C 1938- *AmMWSc 92*
**Haynes**, Robert Clark, Jr 1925- *AmMWSc 92*
**Haynes**, Robert Hall 1931- *AmMWSc 92*
**Haynes**, Robert Ralph 1945- *AmMWSc 92*
**Haynes**, Ronald Eugene 1927- *WhoWest 92*
**Haynes**, Ronnie J 1944- *AmMWSc 92*
**Haynes**, Roy Owen 1926- *NewAmDM*
**Haynes**, Samuel Lloyd 1934- *WhoBlA 92*
**Haynes**, Scott Kendall 1964- *WhoAmL 92*
**Haynes**, Sherwood Kimball 1910- *AmMWSc 92*
**Haynes**, Simon John 1944- *AmMWSc 92*
**Haynes**, Sophy Pellegrini-Quarantotti 1928- *WhoEnt 92*
**Haynes**, Sue Blood 1939- *WhoBlA 92*
**Haynes**, Suzanne G *AmMWSc 92*
**Haynes**, Sybille 1926- *WrDr 92*
**Haynes**, Thomas Beranek 1956- *WhoAmL 92, WhoEnt 92*
**Haynes**, Tiger 1914- *IntMPA 92*

**Haynes**, Todd 1961- *WhoEnt 92*
**Haynes**, Tony Eugene 1960- *AmMWSc 92*
**Haynes**, Tyler Henry, Jr. 1930- *WhoMW 92*
**Haynes**, Ulric St. Clair, Jr. 1931- *WhoBlA 92*
**Haynes**, Walter Wesley 1919- *WhoBlA 92*
**Haynes**, William Ernest 1936- *WhoFI 92*
**Haynes**, William J., Jr. 1949- *WhoBlA 92*
**Haynes**, William Miller 1936- *AmMWSc 92*
**Haynes**, William P 1921- *AmMWSc 92*
**Haynes**, William S. 1864-1939 *NewAmDM*
**Haynes**, Willie C., III 1951- *WhoBlA 92*
**Haynes**, Worth Edward 1942- *WhoBlA 92*
**Haynes-Dixon**, Margaret Rumer *Who 92*
**Haynie**, Fred Hollis 1932- *AmMWSc 92*
**Haynie**, Howard Edward 1928- *WhoAmL 92*
**Haynie**, Kenneth Harlan 1933- *WhoAmL 92*
**Haynie**, Mary Donaldson 1923- *WhoAmP 91*
**Haynie**, Thomas Powell, III 1932- *AmMWSc 92*
**Haynie**, Tony Wayne 1955- *WhoAmL 92*
**Haynsworth**, Harry Jay, IV 1938- *WhoAmL 92*
**Hayon**, Elie M 1932- *AmMWSc 92*
**Hayr**, Kenneth 1935- *Who 92*
**Hayre**, Harbhajan Singh 1929- *AmMWSc 92*
**Hayre**, Ruth Wright *WhoBlA 92*
**Hayry**, Pekka J 1939- *AmMWSc 92*
**Hays**, Brad L 1947- *WhoAmP 91*
**Hays**, Byron G 1937- *AmMWSc 92*
**Hays**, Charles Ray 1957- *WhoMW 92*
**Hays**, Cindy Shelton 1949- *WhoAmP 91*
**Hays**, Dan Andrew 1939- *AmMWSc 92*
**Hays**, Daniel Mauger 1919- *AmMWSc 92*
**Hays**, David Arthur 1930- *WhoEnt 92*
**Hays**, David Eugene 1951- *WhoMW 92*
**Hays**, Diana Joyce Watkins 1945- *WhoFI 92*
**Hays**, Donald Brooks 1939- *AmMWSc 92*
**Hays**, Donald F 1929- *AmMWSc 92*
**Hays**, Donald R 1929- *AmMWSc 92*
**Hays**, Donald Ralph 1929- *WhoMW 92*
**Hays**, Elizabeth Teuber 1940- *AmMWSc 92*
**Hays**, Esther Fincher 1927- *AmMWSc 92*
**Hays**, Frank Drury 1912- *WhoFI 92*
**Hays**, Franklin Ernest 1947- *WhoRel 92*
**Hays**, George E 1921- *AmMWSc 92*
**Hays**, George Vincent 1932- *WhoWest 92*
**Hays**, George Waight Secrest 1954- *WhoMW 92*
**Hays**, Herschel Martin 1920- *WhoFI 92*
**Hays**, Horace Albennie 1914- *AmMWSc 92*
**Hays**, Isaac 1796-1879 *BiInAmS*
**Hays**, J Jefferson 1929- *WhoAmP 91*
**Hays**, James D 1933- *AmMWSc 92*
**Hays**, James Fred 1933- *AmMWSc 92*
**Hays**, Janice *DrAPF 91*
**Hays**, John *WhoAmP 91*
**Hays**, John Bruce 1937- *AmMWSc 92, WhoWest 92*
**Hays**, John Thomas 1914- *AmMWSc 92*
**Hays**, John W. 1956- *WhoRel 92*
**Hays**, Julian Brite, Jr. 1954- *WhoRel 92*
**Hays**, Kirby Lee 1928- *AmMWSc 92*
**Hays**, Larry Weldon 1936- *WhoAmL 92*
**Hays**, Louis Anthony, Jr. 1954- *WhoMW 92*
**Hays**, Marilyn Patricia 1935- *WhoFI 92, WhoMW 92*
**Hays**, Marion Steele 1925- *WhoAmP 91*
**Hays**, Mary *EncAmaz 91*
**Hays**, Mary 1760-1843 *BlkwCEP, RfGEnL 91*
**Hays**, Mary 1943- *WhoEnt 92*
**Hays**, Patrick Gregory 1942- *WhoWest 92*
**Hays**, Patrick Henry *WhoAmP 91*
**Hays**, Paul M 1946- *WhoAmP 91*
**Hays**, Peter L 1938- *IntAu&W 91, WrDr 92*
**Hays**, Richard Bevan 1948- *WhoRel 92*
**Hays**, Richard Martin 1927- *WhoAmL 92, WhoFI 92*
**Hays**, Richard Mortimer 1927- *AmMWSc 92*
**Hays**, Richard Secrest 1951- *WhoRel 92*
**Hays**, Rick F. 1952- *WhoWest 92*
**Hays**, Robert *DrAPF 91*
**Hays**, Robert 1947- *IntMPA 92, WhoEnt 92*
**Hays**, Roger L. 1954- *WhoMW 92*
**Hays**, Ron d1991 *NewYTBS 91*
**Hays**, Ronald Jackson 1928- *IntWW 91*
**Hays**, Ruth Lanier 1940- *AmMWSc 92*
**Hays**, Sidney Brooks 1931- *AmMWSc 92*
**Hays**, Sorrel 1941- *ConCom 92*
**Hays**, Steele 1925- *WhoAmL 92*
**Hays**, Thomas A. 1932- *WhoFI 92*
**Hays**, Thomas Chandler 1935- *WhoFI 92*
**Hays**, Thomas R. 1915- *WhoFI 92*
**Hays**, Virgil Wilford 1928- *AmMWSc 92*
**Hays**, William Harrison 1879-1954 *AmPolLe*
**Hays**, William Henry 1922- *AmMWSc 92*
**Hays**, Wilma Pitchford 1909- *IntAu&W 91, WrDr 92*
**Haysbert**, Raymond Victor, Sr. 1920- *WhoBlA 92*
**Hayslett**, John P 1935- *AmMWSc 92*
**Hayt**, William H, Jr 1920- *AmMWSc 92*
**Haytaian**, Garabed 1938- *WhoAmP 91*
**Hayter**, Baron 1911- *Who 92*
**Hayter**, Alethea 1911- *WrDr 92*
**Hayter**, Alethea Catharine 1911- *IntAu&W 91*
**Hayter**, Dianne 1949- *Who 92*
**Hayter**, John Bingley 1945- *AmMWSc 92*
**Hayter**, Karen Johnson 1943- *WhoEnt 92*
**Hayter**, Paul David Grenville 1942- *Who 92*
**Hayter**, Roy G 1932- *AmMWSc 92*
**Hayter**, Stanley William 1901-1988 *FacFETw*
**Hayter**, Stanley William 1901-1989 *TwCPaSc*
**Hayter**, Teresa *WrDr 92*
**Hayter**, Walter R, Jr 1923- *AmMWSc 92*
**Hayter**, William 1906- *WrDr 92*
**Hayter**, William Goodenough 1906- *IntWW 91, Who 92*
**Haythorn**, J. Denny 1947- *WhoAmL 92*
**Haythorne**, George Vickers 1909- *WrDr 92*
**Haythorne**, Harry 1926- *WhoEnt 92*
**Haythorne**, John *Who 92*
**Haythorne**, Naomi Christine *Who 92*
**Haythornthwaite**, Philip John 1951- *IntAu&W 91, WrDr 92*
**Haythornthwaite**, Robert M 1922- *AmMWSc 92*
**Hayton**, Bernard Quentin, Jr. 1942- *WhoMW 92*
**Hayton**, William Leroy 1944- *AmMWSc 92*
**Hayward**, Abraham 1801-1884 *ScFEYrs*
**Hayward**, Alfred 1875-1971 *TwCPaSc*
**Hayward**, Ann Stewart 1944- *WhoBlA 92*
**Hayward**, Anthony 1927- *Who 92*
**Hayward**, Anthony R *AmMWSc 92*
**Hayward**, Brian Robin 1937- *Who 92*
**Hayward**, Bruce Jolliffe 1928- *AmMWSc 92*
**Hayward**, Charles Lynn 1903- *AmMWSc 92*
**Hayward**, Derek *Who 92*
**Hayward**, Evans Vaughan 1922- *AmMWSc 92*
**Hayward**, Fredric Mark 1946- *WhoWest 92*
**Hayward**, George Ernest 1923- *WhoWest 92*
**Hayward**, George Victor 1918- *Who 92*
**Hayward**, Gerald William 1927- *Who 92*
**Hayward**, Harold 1920- *WhoFI 92*
**Hayward**, Jack 1923- *Who 92*
**Hayward**, Jack Ernest Shalom 1931- *Who 92*
**Hayward**, Jacqueline C. 1944- *WhoBlA 92*
**Hayward**, James Lloyd 1948- *AmMWSc 92*
**Hayward**, James Rogers 1920- *AmMWSc 92*
**Hayward**, Jeffery J 1960- *WhoAmP 91*
**Hayward**, John Derek 1923- *Who 92*
**Hayward**, John S 1937- *AmMWSc 92*
**Hayward**, John T 1910- *AmMWSc 92*
**Hayward**, Lance d1991 *NewYTBS 91*
**Hayward**, Lloyl Douglas 1919- *AmMWSc 92*
**Hayward**, Max 1924-1979 *FacFETw*
**Hayward**, Oliver Thomas 1921- *AmMWSc 92*
**Hayward**, Raymond ebster 1921- *AmMWSc 92*
**Hayward**, Raymond Lee 1949- *WhoRel 92*
**Hayward**, Richard 1910- *Who 92*
**Hayward**, Robert Antony 1949- *Who 92*
**Hayward**, Ronald 1917- *IntWW 91*
**Hayward**, Ronald George 1917- *Who 92*
**Hayward**, Stephen 1954- *ConAu 133*
**Hayward**, Thomas B. 1924- *IntWW 91*
**Hayward**, Thomas Doyle 1940- *AmMWSc 92*
**Hayward**, Timothy Yeatman 1941- *WhoAmP 91*
**Hayward Ellen**, Patricia Mae *Who 92*
**Hayward Smith**, Rodger 1943- *Who 92*
**Haywood**, Anne Mowbray 1935- *AmMWSc 92*
**Haywood**, Bertron Don 1934- *WhoBlA 92*
**Haywood**, Carolyn 1898- *IntAu&W 91*
**Haywood**, Charles 1904- *IntAu&W 91, WrDr 92*
**Haywood**, Edmund Burke 1825-1894 *DcNCBi 3*
**Haywood**, Edmund Burke 1953- *WhoAmL 92*
**Haywood**, Egbert 1730-1801 *DcNCBi 3*
**Haywood**, Eliza 1693?-1756 *BlkwCEP, RfGEnL 91*
**Haywood**, Emmett L. 1937- *WhoBlA 92*
**Haywood**, Ernest 1860-1946 *DcNCBi 3*
**Haywood**, Fabius Julius 1803-1880 *DcNCBi 3*
**Haywood**, Frederick F 1936- *AmMWSc 92*
**Haywood**, Garfield Thomas 1880-1931 *RelLAm 91*
**Haywood**, H Carl 1931- *AmMWSc 92*
**Haywood**, Harold 1923- *Who 92*
**Haywood**, Hiram H., Jr. 1921- *WhoBlA 92*
**Haywood**, Hubert Benbury, Sr. 1883-1961 *DcNCBi 3*
**Haywood**, John 1685-1758 *DcNCBi 3*
**Haywood**, John 1755-1827 *DcNCBi 3*
**Haywood**, John 1762-1826 *DcNCBi 3*
**Haywood**, L. Julian *WhoBlA 92*
**Haywood**, L Julian 1927- *AmMWSc 92*
**Haywood**, Margaret A. 1912- *WhoBlA 92*
**Haywood**, Marshall De Lancey 1871-1933 *DcNCBi 3*
**Haywood**, Norcell D. 1935- *WhoBlA 92*
**Haywood**, Richard Bennehan 1819-1889 *DcNCBi 3*
**Haywood**, Richard Mowbray 1933- *WrDr 92*
**Haywood**, Robert Carroll 1950- *WhoWest 92*
**Haywood**, Roosevelt V., Jr. 1929- *WhoBlA 92*
**Haywood**, Sherwood 1762-1829 *DcNCBi 3*
**Haywood**, Spencer 1949- *BlkOlyM, WhoBlA 92*
**Haywood**, Theodore J 1929- *AmMWSc 92*
**Haywood**, Thomas Charles Stanley 1911- *Who 92*
**Haywood**, Wardell 1928- *WhoBlA 92*
**Haywood**, William 1730-1779 *DcNCBi 3*
**Haywood**, William 1869-1928 *RComAH*
**Haywood**, William Dudley 1869-1928 *BenetAL 91*
**Haywood**, William H. 1942- *WhoBlA 92*
**Haywood**, William Henry, Jr. 1801-1852 *DcNCBi 3*
**Haywoode**, M. Douglas 1938- *WhoBlA 92*
**Hayworth**, Curtis B 1920- *AmMWSc 92*
**Hayworth**, Rita 1918-1987 *FacFETw [port]*
**Hayworth**, Ruth A 1930- *WhoAmP 91*
**Hayzlett**, Gary Keith 1941- *WhoAmP 91*
**Hazam**, Lou d1983 *LesBEnT 92*
**Hazam**, Louis 1911-1983 *FacFETw*
**Hazama**, Chuck 1932- *WhoAmP 91*
**Hazama**, Yoshikazu 1948- *WhoFI 92*
**Hazard**, Ebenezer 1744-1817 *BenetAL 91*
**Hazard**, Evan Brandao 1929- *AmMWSc 92*
**Hazard**, Geoffrey Cornell, Jr. 1929- *WhoAmL 92*
**Hazard**, Herbert Ray 1917- *AmMWSc 92*
**Hazard**, Jack *IntAu&W 91X, TwCWW 91, WrDr 92*
**Hazard**, John Beach 1905- *AmMWSc 92*
**Hazard**, John Newbold 1909- *WhoAmL 92, WrDr 92*
**Hazard**, Joseph Taylor 1879- *ScFEYrs*
**Hazard**, Katharine Elizabeth 1915- *AmMWSc 92*
**Hazard**, Laurence *IntAu&W 91X*
**Hazard**, Leland 1893-1980 *ConAu 133*
**Hazard**, Michael David 1952- *WhoEnt 92*
**Hazard**, Rowland 1829-1898 *BiInAmS*
**Hazard**, Shepherd Tom 1797-1886 *BenetAL 91*
**Hazdra**, James Joseph 1933- *AmMWSc 92*
**Hazekamp**, Nancy H 1926- *WhoAmP 91*
**Hazel**, Charles Richard 1929- *AmMWSc 92*
**Hazel**, Gerald Vernon 1931- *WhoFI 92*
**Hazel**, J. Patrick 1933- *WhoAmL 92*
**Hazel**, James R. C., Jr. 1940- *WhoMW 92*
**Hazel**, Jeffrey Ronald 1945- *AmMWSc 92*
**Hazel**, Joanie Beverly 1946- *WhoWest 92*
**Hazel**, Joseph Ernest 1933- *AmMWSc 92*
**Hazel**, Myrthie 1959- *WhoRel 92*
**Hazel**, Richard Melvin 1958- *WhoEnt 92*
**Hazel**, Robert *DrAPF 91*
**Hazelbauer**, Gerald Lee 1944- *AmMWSc 92, WhoWest 92*
**Hazelett**, Samuel Richard 1923- *WhoRel 92*
**Hazelhoff**, Robertus 1930- *IntWW 91*
**Hazell**, Bertie 1907- *Who 92*
**Hazell**, Clive Garrad 1947- *WhoMW 92*
**Hazell**, Frederick Roy 1930- *Who 92*
**Hazell**, Quinton 1920- *Who 92*
**Hazell**, Robert John Davidge 1948- *Who 92*
**Hazelrig**, Jane 1937- *AmMWSc 92*
**Hazelrigg**, Charles Richard 1933- *WhoFI 92, WhoWest 92*
**Hazelrigg**, George Arthur, Jr 1939- *AmMWSc 92*
**Hazeltine**, Barrett 1931- *AmMWSc 92*
**Hazeltine**, Gerald Lester 1924- *WhoMW 92*
**Hazeltine**, Horace 1858-1920 *ScFEYrs*
**Hazeltine**, James Ezra, Jr 1916- *AmMWSc 92*
**Hazeltine**, Joyce *WhoAmP 91, WhoMW 92*
**Hazeltine**, Richard Deimel 1942- *AmMWSc 92*
**Hazelton**, Bonni Jane *AmMWSc 92*
**Hazelton**, Penny Ann 1947- *WhoAmL 92*
**Hazelton**, Russell Frank 1914- *AmMWSc 92*
**Hazelwood**, Donald Hill 1931- *AmMWSc 92*
**Hazelwood**, Harry, Jr. 1921- *WhoBlA 92*
**Hazelwood**, Rachel *AmPeW*
**Hazelwood**, Robert Leonard 1927- *AmMWSc 92*
**Hazelwood**, Robert Nichols 1928- *AmMWSc 92*
**Hazen**, Annette 1929- *AmMWSc 92*
**Hazen**, Carl Raymond 1932- *WhoFI 92*
**Hazen**, David Comstock 1927- *AmMWSc 92*
**Hazen**, Donald Emerson 1939- *WhoMW 92*
**Hazen**, Eleanor Franklin 1939- *WhoAmP 91*
**Hazen**, Gary Alan 1950- *AmMWSc 92*
**Hazen**, George Gustave 1923- *AmMWSc 92*
**Hazen**, Glenn Alan 1938- *WhoMW 92*
**Hazen**, Henry Allen 1849-1900 *BiInAmS*
**Hazen**, John Vose 1850-1919 *BiInAmS*
**Hazen**, Joseph H 1898- *IntMPA 92*
**Hazen**, Lee d1991 *NewYTBS 91*
**Hazen**, Martha L 1931- *AmMWSc 92*
**Hazen**, Paul Mandeville 1941- *WhoFI 92, WhoWest 92*
**Hazen**, Richard 1911- *AmMWSc 92*
**Hazen**, Richard R 1925- *AmMWSc 92*
**Hazen**, Robert Miller 1948- *AmMWSc 92*
**Hazen**, Terry Clyde 1951- *AmMWSc 92*
**Hazen**, Wayne Eskett 1914- *AmMWSc 92*
**Hazen**, William Babcock 1830-1887 *BiInAmS*
**Hazen**, William Eugene 1925- *AmMWSc 92*
**Hazewinkel**, Van 1943- *WhoWest 92*
**Hazeyama**, Yuji 1943- *AmMWSc 92*
**Hazi**, Andrew Udvar 1941- *AmMWSc 92*
**Hazi**, Vencel 1925- *Who 92*
**Hazim**, Ignace 1921- *IntWW 91*
**Hazirjian**, Dikran Michael 1949- *WhoEnt 92*
**Hazlegrove**, Leven S 1924- *AmMWSc 92*
**Hazlehurst**, Cameron 1941- *WrDr 92*
**Hazlehurst**, David Anthony 1930- *AmMWSc 92*
**Hazlerigg** *Who 92*
**Hazlerigg**, Baron 1910- *Who 92*
**Hazleton**, Lesley 1945- *IntAu&W 91*
**Hazlett**, David Richard 1932- *AmMWSc 92*
**Hazlett**, Paul Edward 1937- *WhoMW 92*
**Hazlett**, Robert Neil 1924- *AmMWSc 92*
**Hazlewood**, Arthur Dennis 1921- *Who 92*
**Hazlewood**, Carlton Frank 1935- *AmMWSc 92*
**Hazlewood**, Donald Gene *AmMWSc 92*
**Hazlewood**, Frederick Samuel 1921- *Who 92*
**Hazlewood**, John *Who 92*
**Hazlewood-Brady**, Anne *DrAPF 91*
**Hazlitt**, Henry 1894- *IntAu&W 91, IntWW 91*
**Hazlitt**, William 1778-1830 *BlkwCEP, DcLB 110 [port], RfGEnL 91*
**Hazo**, Samuel *DrAPF 91*
**Hazo**, Samuel 1928- *ConPo 91, IntAu&W 91, WrDr 92*
**Hazou**, Peter J. 1916-1991 *NewYTBS 91*
**Hazouri**, Cathryn Lynn 1948- *WhoAmL 92*
**Hazouri**, Louis A, Jr 1948- *WhoIns 92*
**Hazouri**, Louis Abraham, Jr. 1948- *WhoFI 92*
**Hazouri**, Thomas L 1944- *WhoAmP 91*
**Hazra**, Bilas Kumar 1946- *WhoFI 92*
**Hazrat Mahal** *EncAmaz 91*
**Hazuda**, Daria Jean *AmMWSc 92*
**Hazy**, Andrew Christopher 1938- *AmMWSc 92*
**Hazzard**, DeWitt George 1932- *AmMWSc 92*
**Hazzard**, Frances Jane Osborn 1925- *WhoFI 92*
**Hazzard**, Guy Chase *ScFEYrs*
**Hazzard**, James 1955- *WhoAmP 91*
**Hazzard**, Mary *DrAPF 91*
**Hazzard**, Robert Charles 1935- *WhoMW 92*
**Hazzard**, Shirley *DrAPF 91*
**Hazzard**, Shirley 1931- *BenetAL 91, ConNov 91, CurBio 91 [port], IntAu&W 91, IntWW 91, WrDr 92*
**Hazzard**, Terry Louis 1957- *WhoBlA 92*
**Hazzard**, Walter R. 1942- *WhoBlA 92*
**Hazzard**, Walter Raphael 1942- *BlkOlyM*
**Hazzard**, William Russell 1936- *AmMWSc 92*
**He Dongchang** 1923- *IntWW 91*
**He Guangyu** 1910- *IntWW 91*
**He Guangyuan** 1930- *IntWW 91*
**He Hai Xia** 1908- *IntWW 91*

**He Jingzhi** 1924- *IntWW 91*
**He Jinheng** *IntWW 91*
**He Kang** 1923- *IntWW 91*
**He Lu-ting** 1903- *ConCom 92*
**He Luting** 1903- *IntWW 91*
**He Qizong** 1943- *IntWW 91*
**He Xiaohua** 1950- *IntWW 91*
**He Ying** 1915- *IntWW 91*
**He Yixiang** 1911- *IntWW 91*
**He Youfa** 1920- *IntWW 91*
**He Zehui** 1914- *IntWW 91*
**He Zhengwen** 1917- *IntWW 91*
**He Zhenliang** 1930- *IntWW 91*
**He Zhiyuan** 1912- *IntWW 91*
**He Zhukang** 1932- *IntWW 91*
**He Zuoxiu** 1927- *IntWW 91*
**He-e-e** *EncAmaz 91*
**Heacock,** Craig S *AmMWSc 92*
**Heacock,** Don Roland 1928- *WhoBlA 92*
**Heacock,** Grace Anne 1943-1990 *WhoWest 92*
**Heacock,** Richard Ralph 1920- *AmMWSc 92*
**Heacock,** Ronald A 1928- *AmMWSc 92*
**Heacock,** Steven Robert 1956- *WhoAmL 92*
**Heacox,** William Dale 1942- *AmMWSc 92*
**Head** *Who 92*
**Head,** Viscount 1937- *Who 92*
**Head,** Adrian Herbert 1923- *Who 92*
**Head,** Alan Kenneth 1925- *IntWW 91, Who 92*
**Head,** Anita Kessler *WhoAmL 92*
**Head,** Audrey May 1924- *Who 92*
**Head,** Barbara Gamwell 1918- *WhoAmP 91*
**Head,** Ben Thomas 1920- *WhoAmL 92*
**Head,** Bessie 1937-1986 *BlkLC [port], ConLC 67 [port], LiExTwC*
**Head,** Charles Everett 1941- *AmMWSc 92*
**Head,** Dennis Alec 1925- *Who 92*
**Head,** Earl S. 1931- *WhoMW 92*
**Head,** Edith 1907-1981 *FacFETw, ReelWom [port]*
**Head,** Edith 1927- *WhoBlA 92*
**Head,** Edward Dennis 1919- *WhoRel 92*
**Head,** Evelyn Harris Shields 1944- *WhoBlA 92, WhoFI 92, WhoMW 92*
**Head,** Francis 1916- *Who 92*
**Head,** George Lewis 1941- *WhoIns 92*
**Head,** Glenn O 1925- *WhoIns 92*
**Head,** Gwen *DrAPF 91*
**Head,** H Herbert 1935- *AmMWSc 92*
**Head,** Hayden Wilson, Jr. 1944- *WhoAmL 92*
**Head,** Helaine *WhoBlA 92*
**Head,** Howard d1991 *NewYTBS 91*
**Head,** James Thomas 1945- *WhoAmP 91*
**Head,** James William, III 1941- *AmMWSc 92*
**Head,** Janet Allan 1946- *WhoMW 92*
**Head,** Joanne Crane 1930- *WhoAmP 91*
**Head,** Joseph Henry, Jr. 1932- *WhoAmL 92*
**Head,** Laura Dean 1948- *WhoBlA 92*
**Head,** Martha E Moore 1941- *AmMWSc 92*
**Head,** Michael Edward 1936- *Who 92*
**Head,** Mildred Eileen 1911- *Who 92*
**Head,** Patrick James 1932- *WhoAmL 92, WhoFI 92*
**Head,** Philip John 1951- *Who 92*
**Head,** Ralph H 1913- *WhoIns 92*
**Head,** Raymond, Jr. 1921- *WhoBlA 92*
**Head,** Richard G 1938- *ConAu 35NR*
**Head,** Ronald Alan 1930- *AmMWSc 92*
**Head,** Roy Joe *WhoAmP 91*
**Head,** Samuel 1948- *WhoBlA 92*
**Head,** Thomas Floyd 1937- *WhoIns 92*
**Head,** Thomas James 1934- *AmMWSc 92*
**Head,** Tim 1946- *TwCPaSc*
**Head,** Tim David 1946- *IntWW 91*
**Head,** Verna Silva 1914- *WhoAmP 91*
**Head,** W R 1829?-1910 *BiInAmS*
**Head,** William Carl 1951- *WhoAmL 92*
**Head,** William Iverson, Sr. 1925- *WhoFI 92*
**Head-Gordon,** Martin Paul 1962- *AmMWSc 92*
**Head-Gordon,** Teresa Lyn 1960- *AmMWSc 92*
**Headding,** Lillian Susan 1944- *WhoFI 92, WhoWest 92*
**Headfort,** Marquis of 1932- *Who 92*
**Headings,** Verle Emery 1935- *AmMWSc 92*
**Headington,** Christopher 1930- *WrDr 92*
**Headington,** Christopher John Magenis 1930- *IntWW 91*
**Headington,** John Terrence 1930- *AmMWSc 92*
**Headlam,** Mary 1874-1959 *TwCPaSc*
**Headlee,** Joseph L. 1934- *WhoEnt 92*
**Headlee,** Kent Baker 1944- *WhoWest 92*
**Headlee,** Raymond 1917- *AmMWSc 92*
**Headlee,** Richard Harold 1930- *WhoIns 92*
**Headlee,** Rolland Dockeray 1916- *WhoWest 92*
**Headlee,** William Hugh 1907- *AmMWSc 92*
**Headley,** Baron 1902- *Who 92*
**Headley,** Allan Dave 1955- *AmMWSc 92*
**Headley,** Anne Renouf 1937- *WhoFI 92*
**Headley,** Barbara Eyvonne 1955- *WhoRel 92*
**Headley,** Barbara Joan 1946- *WhoMW 92*
**Headley,** De Costa Oneal 1946- *WhoBlA 92*
**Headley,** Glenne 1955- *WhoEnt 92*
**Headley,** John M. 1929- *WrDr 92*
**Headley,** Joseph Charles 1930- *AmMWSc 92*
**Headley,** Kathryn Wilma 1940- *WhoMW 92*
**Headley,** Robert N 1932- *AmMWSc 92*
**Headley,** Velmer Bentley 1934- *AmMWSc 92*
**Headley-Neave,** Alice *TwCPaSc*
**Headly,** Derek 1908- *Who 92*
**Headly,** Glenne 1957- *IntMPA 92*
**Headly,** Glenne Aimee 1958- *WhoEnt 92*
**Headman,** Arlan Osmond, Jr. 1952- *WhoAmL 92*
**Headrick,** Elida 1958- *WhoMW 92*
**Headrick,** Jerry Willard 1942- *WhoRel 92*
**Headrick,** John Anderson 1931- *WhoFI 92, WhoMW 92*
**Headrick,** Jon C 1943- *WhoIns 92*
**Headrick,** Randall L 1960- *AmMWSc 92*
**Headstrom,** Richard 1902- *WrDr 92*
**Heady,** Harold F. 1916- *WrDr 92*
**Heady,** Harold Franklin 1916- *AmMWSc 92*
**Heady,** Judith E 1939- *AmMWSc 92*
**Heaf,** Peter Julius Denison 1922- *Who 92*
**Heagarty,** Margaret Caroline 1934- *AmMWSc 92*
**Heagle,** Allen Streeter 1938- *AmMWSc 92*
**Heagler,** John B, Jr 1924- *AmMWSc 92*
**Heagy,** Fred Clark 1919- *AmMWSc 92*
**Heal,** Ambrose 1872-1959 *DcTwDes*
**Heal,** Anthony Standerwick 1907- *Who 92*
**Heal,** Geoffrey Martin 1944- *WhoFI 92*
**Heal,** Oliver Standerwick 1949- *Who 92*
**Heal,** Sylvia Lloyd 1942- *Who 92*
**Heald,** Anthony 1944- *IntMPA 92*
**Heald,** Charles William 1942- *AmMWSc 92*
**Heald,** Emerson Francis 1934- *AmMWSc 92*
**Heald,** Felix Pierpont, Jr 1921- *AmMWSc 92*
**Heald,** Henry 1779- *BenetAL 91*
**Heald,** Jack Wendell 1935- *WhoWest 92*
**Heald,** Mark Aiken 1929- *AmMWSc 92*
**Heald,** Mervyn 1930- *Who 92*
**Heald,** Milton Tidd 1919- *AmMWSc 92*
**Heald,** Pamela 1950- *AmMWSc 92*
**Heald,** Thomas Routledge 1923- *Who 92*
**Heald,** Tim 1944- *WrDr 92*
**Heald,** Timothy Villiers 1944- *IntAu&W 91*
**Heald,** Walter Roland 1920- *AmMWSc 92*
**Heale,** David 1954- *TwCPaSc*
**Heale,** Jonathan 1949- *TwCPaSc*
**Healey,** Ann Ruston 1939- *WhoRel 92*
**Healey,** Anne *WhoAmP 91*
**Healey,** Anthony J 1940- *AmMWSc 92*
**Healey,** Arthur H *WhoAmP 91*
**Healey,** Arthur H. 1920- *WhoAmL 92*
**Healey,** Ben 1908- *IntAu&W 91, WrDr 92*
**Healey,** Charles Edward C. *Who 92*
**Healey,** Denis 1917- *FacFETw, IntAu&W 91, WrDr 92*
**Healey,** Denis Winston 1917- *IntWW 91, Who 92*
**Healey,** Derek Edward 1936- *WhoEnt 92*
**Healey,** Deryck John 1937- *Who 92*
**Healey,** E J 1924- *WhoAmP 91*
**Healey,** Edna May 1918- *Who 92*
**Healey,** Edward Hopkins 1925- *WhoMW 92*
**Healey,** Frank Henry 1924- *AmMWSc 92*
**Healey,** John 1894- *TwCPaSc*
**Healey,** John Edward, Jr 1922- *AmMWSc 92*
**Healey,** Kerry Murphy 1960- *WhoFI 92*
**Healey,** Laurette Ann 1954- *WhoWest 92*
**Healey,** Linda Pamela Nielsen 1948- *WhoWest 92*
**Healey,** Mark Calvin 1947- *AmMWSc 92*
**Healey,** Michael Charles 1942- *AmMWSc 92*
**Healey,** Myron Daniel 1923- *WhoEnt 92*
**Healey,** Patrick Leonard 1936- *AmMWSc 92*
**Healey,** Philip B 1921- *WhoAmP 91*
**Healey,** Robert Mathieu 1921- *WhoRel 92*
**Healey,** Robert William 1947- *WhoMW 92*
**Healey,** Skip 1934- *WhoAmP 91*
**Healey,** Thomas J. 1942- *WhoFI 92*
**Healey,** Thomas Spencer 1930- *WhoEnt 92*
**Healey,** William John, III 1940- *WhoFI 92*
**Healton,** Bruce Carney 1955- *WhoMW 92*
**Healy,** Barbara Anne 1951- *WhoFI 92, WhoWest 92*
**Healy,** Bernadine P *AmMWSc 92, NewYTBS 91 [port]*
**Healy,** Bernard Patrick 1948- *WhoRel 92*
**Healy,** Daniel Francis 1954- *WhoMW 92*
**Healy,** Daniel J 1908- *WhoAmP 91*
**Healy,** David Frank 1926- *IntAu&W 91, WrDr 92*
**Healy,** Eliza 1846-1918 *RelLAm 91*
**Healy,** Eliza 1846-1919 *NotBlAW 92*
**Healy,** Elizabeth Irene 1961- *WhoMW 92*
**Healy,** Eloise Klein *DrAPF 91*
**Healy,** George Richard 1924- *AmMWSc 92*
**Healy,** George W 1909- *AmMWSc 92*
**Healy,** George William, III 1930- *WhoAmL 92*
**Healy,** James A. d1991 *NewYTBS 91*
**Healy,** James Augustine 1830-1900 *RelLAm 91*
**Healy,** James Bruce 1947- *WhoWest 92*
**Healy,** James Casey 1956- *WhoAmL 92*
**Healy,** James Gerard 1957- *WhoAmL 92*
**Healy,** Janet *WhoEnt 92*
**Healy,** Jeremiah 1948- *WrDr 92*
**Healy,** Jeremiah Francis, III 1948- *WhoAmL 92*
**Healy,** John Carleton 1924- *WhoAmL 92*
**Healy,** John Francis 1926- *Who 92*
**Healy,** John H 1929- *AmMWSc 92*
**Healy,** John Joseph 1943- *AmMWSc 92*
**Healy,** John Patrick 1959- *WhoAmL 92*
**Healy,** John T. *IntMPA 92*
**Healy,** Jonathan Lee 1945- *WhoAmP 91*
**Healy,** Joseph Francis, Jr. 1930- *WhoAmL 92, WhoFI 92*
**Healy,** Kieran John Patrick 1957- *WhoEnt 92, WhoWest 92*
**Healy,** Martin Russell 1950- *WhoAmL 92*
**Healy,** Mary 1918- *WhoEnt 92*
**Healy,** Mary Coleen Quirk *WhoRel 92*
**Healy,** Maurice Eugene 1933- *Who 92*
**Healy,** Michael 1948- *WhoEnt 92*
**Healy,** Michael L 1936- *AmMWSc 92*
**Healy,** Michael Patrick 1966- *WhoMW 92*
**Healy,** Michael W 1946- *WhoAmP 91*
**Healy,** Nicholas Joseph 1910- *WhoAmL 92*
**Healy,** Patricia Colleen 1935- *WhoMW 92*
**Healy,** Patrick Francis 1834-1910 *RelLAm 91*
**Healy,** Paul John 1963- *WhoAmL 92*
**Healy,** Paul William 1915- *AmMWSc 92*
**Healy,** Philip Francis 1928- *WhoRel 92*
**Healy,** Steven Michael 1949- *WhoFI 92, WhoMW 92*
**Healy,** Theresa Ann 1932- *WhoAmP 91*
**Healy,** Theresa M 1946- *WhoAmP 91*
**Healy,** Thomas Martin 1921- *WhoFI 92*
**Healy,** Thomas William 1937- *IntWW 91*
**Healy,** Tim T. *Who 92*
**Healy,** Timothy Stafford 1923- *WhoEnt 92*
**Healy,** Walter 1910- *WhoAmP 91*
**Healy,** Walter F. X. 1941- *WhoAmL 92*
**Healy,** William Carleton, Jr 1925- *AmMWSc 92*
**Healy,** William James 1939- *WhoAmP 91*
**Healy,** William Ryder 1938- *AmMWSc 92*
**Healy,** Winston, Jr. 1937- *WhoWest 92*
**Heaney,** David Paul 1927- *AmMWSc 92*
**Heaney,** Gerald William 1918- *WhoAmL 92*
**Heaney,** Henry Joseph 1935- *Who 92*
**Heaney,** James Patrick 1940- *AmMWSc 92*
**Heaney,** John Joseph 1925- *WhoRel 92*
**Heaney,** Lawrence R 1952- *AmMWSc 92*
**Heaney,** Leonard Martin 1906- *Who 92*
**Heaney,** Robert John 1922- *AmMWSc 92*
**Heaney,** Robert Proulx 1927- *AmMWSc 92*
**Heaney,** Robert S. d1991 *NewYTBS 91*
**Heaney,** Seamus 1939- *CnDBLB 8 [port], ConPo 91, FacFETw, IntAu&W 91, IntWW 91, RfGEnL 91, WrDr 92*
**Heaney,** Seamus Justin 1939- *Who 92*
**Heaney,** Sheila Anne Elizabeth d1991 *Who 92N*
**Heaney,** William Joseph 1943- *WhoAmP 91*
**Heanley,** Charles Laurence 1907- *Who 92*
**Heap,** Desmond 1907- *Who 92, WrDr 92*
**Heap,** Douglas 1934- *ConTFT 9*
**Heap,** James C 1935- *WhoAmP 91*
**Heap,** James Clarence *WhoMW 92*
**Heap,** John Arnfield 1932- *Who 92*
**Heap,** Peter William 1935- *IntWW 91, Who 92*
**Heap,** Robert Brian 1935- *Who 92*
**Heaphy,** James Cullen, III 1952- *WhoWest 92*
**Heaphy,** John Merrill 1927- *WhoAmL 92*
**Heaps,** Melvin George *AmMWSc 92*
**Heard,** Andrew 1958- *TwCPaSc*
**Heard,** Anthony Hazlitt 1937- *ConAu 134*
**Heard,** Fred W 1940- *WhoAmP 91*
**Heard,** Gerald *TwCSFW 91*
**Heard,** H F 1889-1971 *TwCSFW 91*
**Heard,** Harry Gordon 1922- *AmMWSc 92*
**Heard,** Herman Willie, Jr. 1961- *WhoBlA 92*
**Heard,** John 1946- *IntMPA 92*
**Heard,** John 1947- *WhoEnt 92*
**Heard,** John Len 1935- *WhoWest 92*
**Heard,** John Thibaut, Jr 1940- *AmMWSc 92*
**Heard,** Josephine D. 1861-1921? *NotBlAW 92*
**Heard,** Lonear Windham *WhoBlA 92*
**Heard,** Nathan Cliff 1936- *WhoBlA 92*
**Heard,** Paul W, Jr *WhoAmP 91*
**Heard,** Peter 1939- *TwCPaSc*
**Heard,** Peter Graham 1929- *Who 92*
**Heard,** Ronald Roy 1947- *WhoEnt 92, WhoWest 92*
**Heard,** William Herman 1935- *AmMWSc 92*
**Heard,** William Robert 1925- *WhoFI 92, WhoIns 92*
**Hearing,** Vincent Joseph, Jr 1945- *AmMWSc 92*
**Hearn,** Anthony Clem 1937- *AmMWSc 92, WhoWest 92*
**Hearn,** Barry Maurice William 1948- *Who 92*
**Hearn,** Bernard Carter, Jr 1933- *AmMWSc 92*
**Hearn,** Charles Jackson 1936- *AmMWSc 92*
**Hearn,** Charles Virgil 1930- *WhoRel 92, WhoWest 92*
**Hearn,** Clifford Burton, Jr 1937- *WhoAmP 91*
**Hearn,** David Anthony 1929- *Who 92*
**Hearn,** David Russell 1942- *AmMWSc 92*
**Hearn,** Donald Peter 1947- *Who 92*
**Hearn,** Dwight D 1933- *AmMWSc 92*
**Hearn,** Frank Wright 1919- *Who 92*
**Hearn,** George Arthur *Who 92*
**Hearn,** Henry James, Jr 1927- *AmMWSc 92*
**Hearn,** James Woodrow 1931- *WhoMW 92, WhoRel 92*
**Hearn,** John Patrick 1943- *Who 92*
**Hearn,** Joyce Camp *WhoAmP 91*
**Hearn,** Lafcadio 1850-1904 *BenetAL 91*
**Hearn,** Michael Joseph 1949- *AmMWSc 92*
**Hearn,** Robert Henderson 1940- *AmMWSc 92*
**Hearn,** Rosamond Ernst 1924- *WhoEnt 92*
**Hearn,** Rosemary 1929- *WhoBlA 92, WhoMW 92*
**Hearn,** Ruby Puryear 1940- *AmMWSc 92*
**Hearn,** Walter Russell 1926- *AmMWSc 92*
**Hearn,** Wendy Lee 1958- *WhoEnt 92*
**Hearn-Haynes,** Theresa 1954- *WhoAmL 92*
**Hearne,** Betsy Gould 1942- *ConAu 35NR*
**Hearne,** Earl 1956- *WhoBlA 92*
**Hearne,** Graham James 1937- *IntWW 91, Who 92*
**Hearne,** Horace Clark, Jr 1930- *AmMWSc 92*
**Hearne,** John 1926- *ConNov 91, IntAu&W 91, WrDr 92*
**Hearne,** Peter Ambrose 1927- *Who 92*
**Hearne,** Reginald 1929- *WrDr 92*
**Hearne,** Samuel 1745-1792 *BenetAL 91*
**Hearne,** Stephen Zachary 1952- *WhoRel 92*
**Hearnes,** Betty 1927- *WhoAmP 91*
**Hearnes,** Warren Eastman 1923- *IntWW 91, WhoAmP 91*
**Hearney,** Elaine Schmidt 1944- *AmMWSc 92*
**Hearns,** Thomas 1958- *IntWW 91, WhoBlA 92*
**Hearnshaw,** Leslie Spencer d1991 *Who 92N*
**Hearon,** Dennis James 1941- *WhoBlA 92*
**Hearon,** Shelby *DrAPF 91*
**Hearon,** Shelby 1931- *WrDr 92*
**Hearon,** William Montgomery 1914- *AmMWSc 92*
**Hearsey,** Bryan Vandiver 1942- *AmMWSc 92*
**Hearst,** Austine McDonnell d1991 *NewYTBS 91*
**Hearst,** Bella Rachael *WhoMW 92*
**Hearst,** George Randolph, Jr. 1927- *IntWW 91*
**Hearst,** John Eugene 1935- *AmMWSc 92*
**Hearst,** Joseph R 1931- *AmMWSc 92*
**Hearst,** Patricia 1954- *FacFETw*
**Hearst,** Peter Jacob 1923- *AmMWSc 92*
**Hearst,** Randolph Apperson 1915- *IntWW 91, WhoFI 92*
**Hearst,** Stephen 1919- *Who 92*
**Hearst,** William Randolph 1863-1951 *BenetAL 91, FacFETw, RComAH*
**Hearst,** William Randolph, III 1949- *WhoWest 92*
**Hearst,** William Randolph, Jr. 1908- *IntWW 91, Who 92*
**Heartfield,** John 1891-1968 *DcTwDes, EncTR 91, FacFETw*

**Hearth,** Donald Payne 1928- *AmMWSc 92*
**Hearth,** John Dennis Miles 1929- *Who 92*
**Heartt,** Dennis 1783-1870 *DcNCBi 3*
**Heartz,** Daniel Leonard 1928- *WhoEnt 92*
**Heasel,** John Frederick 1934- *WhoMW 92*
**Heasell,** E L 1931- *AmMWSc 92*
**Heasley,** Gene 1932- *AmMWSc 92*
**Heasley,** James Henry 1927- *AmMWSc 92*
**Heasley,** Victor Lee 1937- *AmMWSc 92*
**Heaslip,** Richard George 1932- *Who 92*
**Heaslip,** Richard Joseph 1955- *AmMWSc 92*
**Heaslip,** William Graham 1928- *AmMWSc 92*
**Heaston,** Robert Joseph 1931- *AmMWSc 92*
**Heaston,** Ted R. 1947- *WhoRel 92*
**Heat-Moon,** William Least 1939- *BenetAL 91*
**Heater,** Derek Benjamin 1931- *IntAu&W 91, WrDr 92*
**Heater,** Kevin Edward 1956- *WhoFI 92*
**Heater,** William Henderson 1928- *WhoMW 92*
**Heath,** Adrian 1920- *TwCPaSc*
**Heath,** Adrian Lewis Ross 1920- *IntWW 91*
**Heath,** Al 1935- *NewAmDM*
**Heath,** Alan Gard 1935- *AmMWSc 92*
**Heath,** Annie P. 1964- *WhoMW 92*
**Heath,** Barry Bruce 1946- *WhoRel 92*
**Heath,** Bernard Oliver 1925- *Who 92*
**Heath,** Bertha Clara 1909- *WhoBlA 92*
**Heath,** Bradley Webster 1947- *WhoEnt 92*
**Heath,** Carl E, Jr 1930- *AmMWSc 92*
**Heath,** Catherine 1924- *WrDr 92*
**Heath,** Catherine Judith 1924- *IntAu&W 91*
**Heath,** Charles Chastain 1921- *WhoAmP 91, WhoFI 92*
**Heath,** Charles Dickinson 1941- *WhoAmL 92*
**Heath,** Clark Wright, Jr 1933- *AmMWSc 92*
**Heath,** Comer, III 1935- *WhoBlA 92*
**Heath,** D P 1919- *AmMWSc 92*
**Heath,** David Clay 1942- *AmMWSc 92*
**Heath,** Donald Wayne 1942- *WhoWest 92*
**Heath,** Dwight B 1930- *IntAu&W 91, WrDr 92*
**Heath,** Edith 1911- *DcTwDes*
**Heath,** Edward 1916- *FacFETw [port], IntAu&W 91, WrDr 92*
**Heath,** Edward Peter 1914- *Who 92*
**Heath,** Edward Richard George 1916- *IntWW 91, Who 92*
**Heath,** Eugene Cartmill 1943- *AmMWSc 92*
**Heath,** Everett 1935- *AmMWSc 92*
**Heath,** G Ross 1939- *AmMWSc 92*
**Heath,** Gary Brian 1954- *WhoWest 92*
**Heath,** George A 1927- *AmMWSc 92*
**Heath,** George Edmund, Jr. 1965- *WhoMW 92*
**Heath,** George L 1924- *AmMWSc 92*
**Heath,** George Ross 1939- *WhoWest 92*
**Heath,** Gordon d1991 *NewYTBS 91*
**Heath,** Gordon Glenn 1922- *AmMWSc 92*
**Heath,** Harrison Duane 1923- *AmMWSc 92*
**Heath,** Henry Wylde Edwards 1912- *Who 92*
**Heath,** Honor Southard 1958- *WhoAmL 92*
**Heath,** Hunter, III 1942- *WhoMW 92*
**Heath,** Ian Brent 1945- *AmMWSc 92*
**Heath,** James E. 1926- *WhoBlA 92*
**Heath,** James Edward 1935- *AmMWSc 92*
**Heath,** James Erven 1952- *WhoRel 92*
**Heath,** James Eugene 1942- *AmMWSc 92*
**Heath,** James Ewell 1792-1862 *BenetAL 91*
**Heath,** James Lee 1939- *AmMWSc 92*
**Heath,** James Milton 1948- *WhoIns 92*
**Heath,** Jeffrey Dale 1962- *WhoRel 92*
**Heath,** Jerome Bruce 1939- *WhoEnt 92*
**Heath,** Jimmy 1926- *NewAmDM*
**Heath,** John Baldwin 1924- *Who 92*
**Heath,** John Charles 1947- *WhoAmL 92*
**Heath,** John Moore 1922- *Who 92*
**Heath,** John Vance, II 1949- *WhoEnt 92*
**Heath,** Larman Jefferson 1916- *AmMWSc 92*
**Heath,** Larry Francis 1938- *AmMWSc 92*
**Heath,** Lenwood S 1953- *AmMWSc 92*
**Heath,** Linden Weimer 1921- *WhoRel 92*
**Heath,** Malcolm 1957- *WrDr 92*
**Heath,** Mariwyn Dwyer 1935- *WhoMW 92*
**Heath,** Mark 1927- *Who 92*
**Heath,** Martha Ellen 1952- *AmMWSc 92*
**Heath,** Maurice 1909- *Who 92*
**Heath,** Michael John 1935- *Who 92*
**Heath,** Michael Stuart 1940- *Who 92*
**Heath,** Michele Christine 1945- *AmMWSc 92*
**Heath,** Norman Edward 1947- *WhoMW 92*
**Heath,** Oscar Victor Sayer 1903- *Who 92*
**Heath,** Percy 1923- *NewAmDM*
**Heath,** Ralph Carr 1925- *AmMWSc 92*
**Heath,** Richard Eddy 1930- *WhoAmL 92*
**Heath,** Richard Raymond 1929- *WhoFI 92*
**Heath,** Robert 1575-1649 *DcNCBi 3*
**Heath,** Robert Bruce 1936- *AmMWSc 92*
**Heath,** Robert Galbraith 1915- *AmMWSc 92*
**Heath,** Robert Gardner 1924- *AmMWSc 92*
**Heath,** Robert Louis 1940- *AmMWSc 92*
**Heath,** Robert Thornton 1942- *AmMWSc 92, WhoMW 92*
**Heath,** Robert Winship 1933- *AmMWSc 92*
**Heath,** Roger Charles 1943- *WhoAmP 91*
**Heath,** Roy A. K. 1926- *ConNov 91, IntAu&W 91, WrDr 92*
**Heath,** Roy Elmer 1915- *AmMWSc 92*
**Heath,** Russell La Verne 1926- *AmMWSc 92*
**Heath,** Sandra *WrDr 92*
**Heath,** Sharon Lynne 1961- *WhoAmL 92*
**Heath,** Terrence 1936- *ConAu 36NR*
**Heath,** Timothy Douglas *AmMWSc 92*
**Heath,** Vernon H. 1929- *WhoMW 92*
**Heath,** Veronica 1927- *WrDr 92*
**Heath,** William *DrAPF 91*
**Heath,** William W. 1929- *WrDr 92*
**Heath-Stubbs,** John 1918- *ConPo 91, IntAu&W 91, IntWW 91, Who 92, WrDr 92*
**Heathcoat-Amory,** David Philip 1949- *Who 92*
**Heathcoat Amory,** Ian 1942- *Who 92*
**Heathcock,** Clayton Howell 1936- *AmMWSc 92*
**Heathcock,** John Edwin 1937- *WhoMW 92, WhoRel 92*
**Heathcock,** John Herman 1943- *WhoFI 92*
**Heathcote,** Frederic Roger 1944- *Who 92*
**Heathcote,** Gilbert 1913- *Who 92*
**Heathcote,** Michael Perryman 1927- *Who 92*
**Heathcote,** Nancy Dodd 1939- *WhoAmL 92*
**Heathcote,** Phillips Elis, Jr. 1960- *WhoAmL 92*
**Heathcote-Drummond-Willoughby** *Who 92*
**Heathcote-Smith,** Clifford Bertram Bruce 1912- *Who 92*
**Heathcott,** Mary *IntAu&W 91X*
**Heather,** James Brian 1944- *AmMWSc 92*
**Heather,** Stanley Frank 1917- *Who 92*
**Heatherly,** David A 1950- *WhoIns 92*
**Heatherly,** Henry Edward 1936- *AmMWSc 92*
**Heatherton,** Joey 1944- *IntMPA 92*
**Heathfield,** Cecil *TwCPaSc*
**Heatly,** Peter 1924- *Who 92*
**Heaton,** Adna 1786?-1858 *AmPeW*
**Heaton,** Charles Daniel 1921- *AmMWSc 92*
**Heaton,** Charles Lloyd 1935- *WhoMW 92*
**Heaton,** David 1823-1870 *DcNCBi 3*
**Heaton,** David 1923- *Who 92*
**Heaton,** Doreen 1930- *TwCPaSc*
**Heaton,** E Henry, Jr 1954- *WhoAmP 91*
**Heaton,** Eric William 1920- *IntWW 91, Who 92, WrDr 92*
**Heaton,** Fritz Charles 1954- *WhoWest 92*
**Heaton,** Hannah 1721-1794 *HanAmWH*
**Heaton,** Howard S 1935- *AmMWSc 92*
**Heaton,** Jane 1931- *WhoRel 92*
**Heaton,** Joe L 1951- *WhoAmP 91*
**Heaton,** John Busby 1953- *WhoAmP 91*
**Heaton,** Ken L *WhoAmP 91*
**Heaton,** Larry Cadwalder, II 1956- *WhoFI 92*
**Heaton,** LeRoy 1924- *AmMWSc 92*
**Heaton,** Maria Malachowski 1932- *AmMWSc 92*
**Heaton,** Marieta Barrow *AmMWSc 92*
**Heaton,** Ralph Neville 1912- *Who 92*
**Heaton,** Richard Clawson 1946- *AmMWSc 92*
**Heaton,** Thomas Peter Starke 1928- *ConAu 134*
**Heaton,** Tom *ConAu 134*
**Heaton,** William Andrew Lambert 1947- *AmMWSc 92*
**Heaton,** Yvo Henniker- 1954- *Who 92*
**Heaton-Ward,** William Alan 1919- *Who 92, WrDr 92*
**Heatwole,** Harold Franklin 1934- *AmMWSc 92*
**Heatwole,** Mark M. 1948- *WhoAmL 92*
**Heatwole,** Thomas Cromer 1948- *WhoFI 92*
**Heaven,** Constance 1911- *IntAu&W 91, WrDr 92*
**Heavener,** Robert William 1906- *Who 92*
**Heavey,** Michael *WhoAmP 91*
**Heavilin,** John Keith 1929- *WhoRel 92*
**Heavner,** James E 1944- *AmMWSc 92*
**Heavner,** Robert Owen 1941- *WhoWest 92*
**Heavysege,** Charles 1816-1876 *BenetAL 91*
**Heazel,** Francis James 1891-1977 *DcNCBi 3*
**Hebald,** Carol *DrAPF 91*
**Hebald,** Carol 1934- *IntAu&W 91*
**Hebard,** Arthur Foster 1940- *AmMWSc 92*
**Hebard,** Emory 1917- *WhoAmP 91*
**Hebb,** Brian Robert Royce 1949- *WhoEnt 92*
**Hebb,** Maurice F, Jr 1924- *AmMWSc 92*
**Hebbard,** Don William 1957- *WhoRel 92*
**Hebbard,** Frederick Worthman 1923- *AmMWSc 92*
**Hebbard,** Leigh G. 1940- *WhoRel 92*
**Hebbel,** Robert P *AmMWSc 92*
**Hebben,** Nancy *AmMWSc 92*
**Hebblethwaite,** Brian Leslie 1939- *Who 92*
**Hebblethwaite,** Peter *IntAu&W 91*
**Hebblethwaite,** Peter 1930- *Who 92, WrDr 92*
**Hebborn,** Eric 1934- *TwCPaSc*
**Hebborn,** Nigel Peter 1958- *WhoIns 92*
**Hebborn,** Peter 1932- *AmMWSc 92*
**Hebda,** Lawrence John 1954- *WhoMW 92*
**Hebda,** Richard Joseph 1950- *AmMWSc 92*
**Hebda,** Robert Edward 1946- *WhoAmL 92*
**Hebden,** Mark *ConAu 134, WrDr 92*
**Hebden,** Rosemary 1924- *TwCPaSc*
**Hebditch,** Maxwell Graham 1937- *Who 92*
**Hebel,** Doris A. 1935- *WhoMW 92*
**Hebel,** George 1948- *WhoIns 92*
**Hebel,** John Richard 1935- *AmMWSc 92*
**Hebel,** Louis Charles 1930- *AmMWSc 92*
**Hebeler,** Henry K 1933- *AmMWSc 92*
**Hebenstreit,** Jean Estill Stark *WhoRel 92*
**Hebenstreit,** Stephen Louis 1940- *WhoIns 92*
**Heber,** David 1948- *AmMWSc 92*
**Heber-Percy,** Algernon Eustace Hugh 1944- *Who 92*
**Heberer,** Thomas 1947- *ConAu 135*
**Heberger,** John M 1944- *AmMWSc 92*
**Heberle,** Juergen 1925- *AmMWSc 92*
**Heberlein,** Douglas Garavel 1916- *AmMWSc 92*
**Heberlein,** Gary T 1939- *AmMWSc 92*
**Heberlein,** Joachim Viktor Rudolf 1939- *AmMWSc 92*
**Heberlig,** Harold Dean, Jr. 1944- *WhoAmL 92*
**Heberling,** Jack Waugh, Jr 1928- *AmMWSc 92*
**Heberling,** Richard Leon 1926- *AmMWSc 92*
**Hebert,** Anne 1916- *BenetAL 91, FacFETw, GuFrLit 1*
**Hebert,** Archille William 1909- *WhoWest 92*
**Hebert,** Bliss Edmund 1930- *WhoEnt 92*
**Hebert,** Budd Hansel 1941- *WhoAmP 91*
**Hebert,** Clarence Louis 1912- *AmMWSc 92*
**Hebert,** Curt, Jr 1962- *WhoAmP 91*
**Hebert,** David Paul 1947- *WhoEnt 92*
**Hebert,** Dennis P 1926- *WhoAmP 91*
**Hebert,** Gerard Rosaire 1924- *AmMWSc 92*
**Hebert,** Joel J 1939- *AmMWSc 92*
**Hebert,** Leonard Bernard, Jr. 1924- *WhoFI 92*
**Hebert,** Mary Olivia 1921- *WhoMW 92*
**Hebert,** Melvin Roy 1935- *WhoFI 92*
**Hebert,** Normand Claude 1930- *AmMWSc 92*
**Hebert,** Robert Francis 1943- *WhoFI 92*
**Hebert,** Stanley Paul 1922- *WhoBlA 92*
**Hebert,** Teddy T 1914- *AmMWSc 92*
**Hebert,** Zenebework Teshome 1942- *WhoBlA 92*
**Hebner,** Charles L 1926- *WhoAmP 91*
**Hebner,** Paul Chester 1919- *IntWW 91, WhoFI 92, WhoWest 92*
**Hebrank,** Roger A. 1932- *WhoFI 92, WhoMW 92*
**Hebson,** Robert Tadd 1938- *WhoWest 92*
**Hechemy,** Karim E 1938- *AmMWSc 92*
**Hechenbleikner,** Ingenuin Albin 1911- *AmMWSc 92*
**Hechinger,** Fred 1920- *WrDr 92*
**Hechinger,** John W 1920- *WhoAmP 91*
**Hechler,** Ken 1914- *WhoAmP 91*
**Hechler,** Stephen Herman 1939- *AmMWSc 92*
**Hecht,** Abraham Berl 1922- *WhoRel 92*
**Hecht,** Adolph 1914- *AmMWSc 92*
**Hecht,** Alan David 1944- *AmMWSc 92*
**Hecht,** Albert 1842-1894 *ThHEIm*
**Hecht,** Anthony *DrAPF 91*
**Hecht,** Anthony 1923- *BenetAL 91, ConPo 91, WrDr 92*
**Hecht,** Anthony Evan 1923- *IntAu&W 91, IntWW 91*
**Hecht,** Ben 1893-1964 *BenetAL 91, FacFETw*
**Hecht,** Charles Edward 1930- *AmMWSc 92*
**Hecht,** Chic 1928- *WhoAmP 91, WhoWest 92*
**Hecht,** Deborah C. *DrAPF 91*
**Hecht,** Donald Stuart 1941- *WhoAmL 92*
**Hecht,** Eli Charles 1921- *WhoFI 92*
**Hecht,** Elizabeth Anne 1939- *AmMWSc 92*
**Hecht,** Eugene 1938- *AmMWSc 92*
**Hecht,** Frank Thomas 1944- *WhoAmL 92*
**Hecht,** Frederick 1930- *AmMWSc 92*
**Hecht,** Gerald 1934- *AmMWSc 92*
**Hecht,** Harold 1907-1985 *FacFETw*
**Hecht,** Harold Arthur 1921- *WhoMW 92*
**Hecht,** Harold Michael 1939- *WhoWest 92*
**Hecht,** Harry George 1936- *AmMWSc 92*
**Hecht,** Henry William 1932- *WhoEnt 92*
**Hecht,** Herbert 1922- *AmMWSc 92, WhoFI 92*
**Hecht,** J L 1926- *AmMWSc 92*
**Hecht,** Karl Eugene 1956- *WhoFI 92, WhoWest 92*
**Hecht,** Max Knobler 1925- *AmMWSc 92*
**Hecht,** Michael 1940- *WhoRel 92*
**Hecht,** Michael James 1956- *WhoFI 92*
**Hecht,** Myron J 1954- *AmMWSc 92*
**Hecht,** Nathan L 1949- *WhoAmP 91*
**Hecht,** Nathan Lincoln 1949- *WhoAmL 92*
**Hecht,** Norman B 1940- *AmMWSc 92*
**Hecht,** Norman Seymour 1938- *WhoEnt 92*
**Hecht,** Ralph J 1942- *AmMWSc 92*
**Hecht,** Ralph Martin 1943- *AmMWSc 92*
**Hecht,** Richard Gregory 1954- *WhoMW 92*
**Hecht,** Sidney Michael 1944- *AmMWSc 92*
**Hecht,** Stephen Samuel 1942- *AmMWSc 92*
**Hecht,** Susan Elizabeth 1942- *WhoRel 92*
**Hecht,** Toby T *AmMWSc 92*
**Hecht,** W. Arthur 1923- *WhoFI 92*
**Hechter,** Daniel 1938- *IntWW 91*
**Hechter,** Michael 1943- *WrDr 92*
**Hechter,** Oscar Milton 1916- *AmMWSc 92*
**Heck,** Cathy Laura 1966- *WhoWest 92*
**Heck,** Daniel Curtis, Jr. 1951- *WhoMW 92*
**Heck,** David Alan 1952- *WhoMW 92*
**Heck,** Edward Timmel 1909- *AmMWSc 92*
**Heck,** Fannie Exile Scudder 1862-1915 *DcNCBi 3*
**Heck,** Fred Carl 1930- *AmMWSc 92*
**Heck,** Gary B. *WhoWest 92*
**Heck,** Glenn Eugene 1929- *WhoEnt 92*
**Heck,** Henry d'Arcy 1939- *AmMWSc 92*
**Heck,** Homer 1936- *WhoAmP 91*
**Heck,** James Virgil 1952- *AmMWSc 92*
**Heck,** Jonathan Daniel 1952- *AmMWSc 92*
**Heck,** Jonathan McGee 1831-1894 *DcNCBi 3*
**Heck,** Joseph Gerard 1926- *AmMWSc 92*
**Heck,** Kathleen 1954- *WhoMW 92*
**Heck,** Larry Lee 1940- *WhoFI 92*
**Heck,** Margaret Mathilde Sophie 1959- *AmMWSc 92*
**Heck,** Norma Jean 1931- *WhoAmP 91*
**Heck,** Oscar Benjamin 1927- *AmMWSc 92*
**Heck,** Richard Fred 1931- *AmMWSc 92*
**Heck,** Richard T. 1924- *WhoMW 92*
**Heck,** Robert Skinrood 1929- *AmMWSc 92*
**Heck,** Ronald Marshall 1943- *AmMWSc 92*
**Heck,** Rose *WhoAmP 91*
**Heck,** Walter Webb 1926- *AmMWSc 92*
**Heckard,** David Custer 1922- *AmMWSc 92*
**Heckard,** Donald Harvey 1924- *WhoAmP 91*
**Heckard,** Lawrence Ray 1923- *AmMWSc 92*
**Heckard,** William Norman 1922- *WhoAmP 91*
**Heckart,** Eileen 1919- *IntMPA 92, WhoEnt 92*
**Heckathorn,** Harry Mervin, III 1944- *AmMWSc 92*
**Heckel,** Daniel Maurice 1958- *WhoRel 92*
**Heckel,** Edgar 1936- *AmMWSc 92*
**Heckel,** Erich 1883-1970 *EncTR 91, FacFETw*
**Heckel,** Johann Adam 1812?-1877 *NewAmDM*
**Heckel,** John Louis 1931- *WhoFI 92, WhoMW 92*
**Heckel,** Philip Henry 1938- *AmMWSc 92*
**Heckel,** Richard W 1934- *AmMWSc 92*
**Heckel,** Thomas Joseph 1964- *WhoEnt 92*
**Heckel,** Wilhelm 1856-1909 *NewAmDM*
**Heckel,** Wilhelm Hermann 1879-1952 *NewAmDM*
**Heckelmann,** Charles N 1913- *IntAu&W 91, TwCWW 91, WrDr 92*
**Heckelsberg,** Louis Fred 1922- *AmMWSc 92*
**Heckendorf,** Allen Harvey 1941- *WhoMW 92*
**Heckendorn,** Larry Clark 1946- *WhoMW 92*
**Heckenkamp,** Robert Glenn 1923- *WhoAmL 92*
**Hecker,** Art L 1944- *AmMWSc 92*

**Hecker**, Barry WhoBlA 92
**Hecker**, David Alan 1939- WhoWest 92
**Hecker**, Dustin Frederick 1956- WhoAmL 92
**Hecker**, Francois 1919- IntWW 91
**Hecker**, George Ernst 1939- AmMWSc 92
**Hecker**, George Sprake 1922- WhoAmL 92
**Hecker**, Isaac Thomas 1819-1888 RelLAm 91
**Hecker**, Mel Jason 1946- WhoMW 92
**Hecker**, Richard 1930- WhoFI 92
**Hecker**, Richard Jacob 1928- AmMWSc 92, WhoWest 92
**Hecker**, Robert J. 1937- WhoAmL 92
**Hecker**, Siegfried Stephen 1943- AmMWSc 92, WhoWest 92
**Heckerling**, Amy 1954- IntMPA 92, WhoEnt 92
**Heckerman**, Raymond Otto 1924- AmMWSc 92
**Heckert**, David Clinton 1939- AmMWSc 92
**Heckert**, Lloyd Randall 1954- WhoRel 92
**Heckert**, Richard Edwin 1924- IntWW 91
**Heckewelder**, John Gottlieb 1743-1823 BenetAL 91
**Hecklefield**, John d1721 DcNCBi 3
**Heckler**, David W 1947- WhoAmP 91
**Heckler**, Donna A. 1963- WhoMW 92
**Heckler**, George Earl 1920- AmMWSc 92
**Heckler**, Gerard Vincent 1941- WhoAmL 92
**Heckler**, John Maguire 1927- WhoFI 92
**Heckler**, Jonellen DrAPF 91
**Heckler**, Margaret M 1932- WhoAmP 91
**Heckly**, Robert Joseph 1920- AmMWSc 92
**Heckman**, Carol A 1944- AmMWSc 92, WhoMW 92
**Heckman**, Craig Douglas 1951- WhoAmL 92
**Heckman**, Harry Hughes 1923- AmMWSc 92
**Heckman**, Henry Trevennen Shick 1918- WhoFI 92, WhoMW 92
**Heckman**, James Joseph 1944- WhoFI 92, WhoMW 92
**Heckman**, Jerome Harold 1927- WhoAmL 92
**Heckman**, Richard Ainsworth 1929- AmMWSc 92, WhoFI 92, WhoWest 92
**Heckman**, Richard Cooper 1928- AmMWSc 92
**Heckman**, Robert Arthur 1937- AmMWSc 92
**Heckman**, Timothy Martin 1951- AmMWSc 92
**Heckman**, Warren Leslie 1937- WhoRel 92
**Heckmann**, Richard Anderson 1931- AmMWSc 92
**Heckrotte**, Carlton 1929- AmMWSc 92
**Heckscher**, August 1913- ConAu 35NR, IntWW 91
**Heckscher**, Eric Ely 1923- WhoEnt 92
**Heckscher**, Stevens 1930- AmMWSc 92
**Heckscher**, William 1904- WrDr 92
**Heckscher**, William S 1904- IntAu&W 91
**Hecky**, Robert Eugene 1944- AmMWSc 92
**Hecox**, Bernadette WhoEnt 92
**Hector**, David Lawrence 1939- AmMWSc 92
**Hector**, Gordon Matthews 1918- Who 92
**Hector**, Mina Fisher 1947- AmMWSc 92
**Hector**, Robert C 1918- WhoAmP 91
**Hector-Harris**, Carol Ann 1950- WhoMW 92
**Hectus**, Charles Thomas 1949- WhoAmL 92
**Hedahl**, Gorden Orlin 1946- WhoEnt 92, WhoMW 92
**Hedayat**, A Samad 1937- AmMWSc 92
**Hedayat**, Sadeq 1903-1951 FacFETw
**Hedayat**, Sadeyh LiExTwC
**Hedberg**, Art 1929- WhoAmP 91
**Hedberg**, Dale Terry 1942- WhoMW 92
**Hedberg**, Hollis D. IntWW 91N
**Hedberg**, Hollis Dow 1903- AmMWSc 92
**Hedberg**, Karen K AmMWSc 92
**Hedberg**, Kenneth Wayne 1920- AmMWSc 92
**Hedberg**, Marguerite Zeigel 1907- AmMWSc 92
**Hedberg**, Paul Clifford 1939- WhoEnt 92
**Hedbor**, James David 1943- WhoAmP 91
**Hedde**, Richard Duane 1945- AmMWSc 92
**Hedden**, Gregory Dexter 1919- AmMWSc 92
**Hedden**, Kenneth Forsythe 1941- AmMWSc 92
**Hedden**, Sheila Pohlman 1962- WhoWest 92
**Hedderwick**, Mairi 1939- WrDr 92
**Heddinger**, Frederick Martin, Sr. 1917- WhoFI 92
**Heddle**, John A M 1938- AmMWSc 92
**Heddleson**, Milford Raynord 1921- AmMWSc 92
**Heddleston**, Kenneth Luther 1916- AmMWSc 92
**Heddy**, Brian Huleatt 1916- Who 92
**Hedea** EncAmaz 91
**Hedelius**, Tom Christer 1939- IntWW 91
**Hedelman**, Harold 1950- WhoEnt 92
**Hedemann**, Justus Wilhelm 1878-1963 EncTR 91
**Heden**, Carl-Goran 1920- IntWW 91
**Hedenburg**, John Frederick 1924- AmMWSc 92
**Heder Bai** 1930- IntWW 91
**Hederich**, Karlheinz 1902- EncTR 91 [port]
**Hedgcock**, Frank A 1875- ScFEYrs
**Hedgcock**, Frederick Thomas 1924- AmMWSc 92
**Hedgcoth**, Charlie, Jr 1936- AmMWSc 92
**Hedge**, Arthur Joseph, Jr. 1936- WhoFI 92
**Hedge**, Douglas Clarence 1955- WhoMW 92
**Hedge**, George Albert 1939- AmMWSc 92
**Hedge**, H Kay 1928- WhoAmP 91
**Hedge**, Henry 1805-1890 BenetAL 91
**Hedge**, Jeanne Colleen 1960- WhoFI 92
**Hedge**, William Arthur 1952- WhoMW 92
**Hedgecock**, Dennis 1949- AmMWSc 92
**Hedgecock**, Le Roy Darien 1913- AmMWSc 92
**Hedgecock**, Nigel Edward 1934- AmMWSc 92
**Hedgecoe**, John 1937- Who 92
**Hedgeland**, Philip Michael Sweatman 1922- Who 92
**Hedgeman**, Anna Arnold 1899-1990 NotBlAW 92 [port]
**Hedgepath**, Leslie Eugene 1922- WhoBlA 92
**Hedgepeth**, Chester Melvin, Jr. 1937- WhoBlA 92
**Hedgepeth**, John M 1926- AmMWSc 92
**Hedgepeth**, Leonard WhoBlA 92
**Hedgepeth**, Royster Cromwell 1944- WhoWest 92
**Hedger**, Cecil Raymond 1947- WhoFI 92, WhoWest 92
**Hedger**, Eric Frank 1919- Who 92
**Hedger**, John Clive 1942- Who 92
**Hedger**, Thomas Charles 1953- WhoFI 92
**Hedges**, Anthony 1931- Who 92
**Hedges**, Carl Devon 1924- WhoWest 92
**Hedges**, Charles Eugene, Jr. 1953- WhoRel 92
**Hedges**, Dorothea Huseby 1928- AmMWSc 92
**Hedges**, Georganne Combs 1921- WhoAmP 91
**Hedges**, Harry G 1923- AmMWSc 92
**Hedges**, James Robert 1959- WhoFI 92
**Hedges**, Janet 1955- TwCPaSc
**Hedges**, John Ivan 1946- AmMWSc 92
**Hedges**, Joseph WrDr 92
**Hedges**, Kenneth William 1949- WhoFI 92
**Hedges**, Mark Stephen 1950- WhoMW 92
**Hedges**, Richard H. 1952- WhoMW 92
**Hedges**, Richard Marion 1927- AmMWSc 92
**Hedges**, Robert J 1948- WhoIns 92
**Hedges**, Thomas Reed, Jr 1923- AmMWSc 92
**Hedgespeth**, George T., Jr. 1949- WhoBlA 92
**Hedgley**, David R. 1907- WhoBlA 92
**Hedgley**, David Rice, Jr. 1937- WhoBlA 92
**Hedglin**, Walter L 1942- AmMWSc 92
**Hedgspeth**, Adrienne Cassandra 1959- WhoBlA 92
**Hedien**, Colette Johnston 1939- WhoAmL 92
**Hedien**, Wayne Evans 1934- WhoFI 92, WhoIns 92, WhoMW 92
**Hediger**, Robert Thomas 1963- WhoMW 92
**Hedilla Larrey**, Manuel 1902-1970 BiDExR
**Hedin**, Alan Edgar 1935- AmMWSc 92
**Hedin**, David Robert 1954- AmMWSc 92
**Hedin**, Mary DrAPF 91
**Hedin**, Mary Ann 1929- IntAu&W 91
**Hedin**, Paul A 1926- AmMWSc 92
**Hedin**, Robert DrAPF 91
**Hedine**, Kristian Einar 1956- WhoAmL 92
**Hedley**, Ann DrAPF 91
**Hedley**, Anthony Johnson 1941- Who 92
**Hedley**, David Van Houten 1945- WhoFI 92
**Hedley**, Leslie Woolf DrAPF 91
**Hedley**, Mary Katherine 1950- WhoAmL 92
**Hedley**, Olwen 1912- IntAu&W 91, WrDr 92
**Hedley**, Robert Griffith 1956- WhoFI 92
**Hedley**, Robert Peveril 1937- WhoFI 92
**Hedley**, Ronald 1917- Who 92
**Hedley**, Ronald Henderson 1928- Who 92
**Hedley**, William H 1930- AmMWSc 92
**Hedley**, William Henby 1930- WhoFI 92, WhoMW 92
**Hedley-Miller**, Mary 1923- Who 92
**Hedley-Whyte**, Elizabeth Tessa 1937- AmMWSc 92
**Hedley-Whyte**, John 1933- AmMWSc 92
**Hedlin**, Charles P 1927- AmMWSc 92
**Hedlin**, Robert Arthur 1921- AmMWSc 92
**Hedlund**, Carel Theilgard 1948- WhoAmL 92
**Hedlund**, Dennis 1946- IntMPA 92, WhoEnt 92
**Hedlund**, Donald A 1924- AmMWSc 92
**Hedlund**, Gustav Arnold 1904- AmMWSc 92
**Hedlund**, James Howard 1941- AmMWSc 92
**Hedlund**, James L 1928- AmMWSc 92
**Hedlund**, John Kendell 1961- WhoMW 92
**Hedlund**, Laurence William 1937- AmMWSc 92
**Hedlund**, Richard Warren 1935- AmMWSc 92
**Hedlund**, Robert L 1961- WhoAmP 91
**Hedlund**, Ronald 1934- WhoEnt 92
**Hedlund**, Ronald David 1941- AmMWSc 92
**Hedman**, Bruce Alden 1953- WhoRel 92
**Hedman**, Dale E 1935- AmMWSc 92
**Hedman**, Frederick Alvin 1937- WhoFI 92
**Hedman**, Fritz Algot 1906- AmMWSc 92
**Hedman**, Stephen Clifford 1941- AmMWSc 92
**Hedquist**, Jeffrey Paul 1945- WhoEnt 92
**Hedrich**, Loren Wesley 1929- AmMWSc 92
**Hedrick**, Basil Calvin 1932- WhoMW 92
**Hedrick**, Benjamin Sherwood 1827-1886 DcNCBi 3
**Hedrick**, Charles Lynnwood 1934- WhoFI 92
**Hedrick**, Charles Webster 1934- WhoRel 92
**Hedrick**, Clyde Lewis, Jr 1939- AmMWSc 92
**Hedrick**, David Ward 1953- WhoFI 92
**Hedrick**, David Warrington 1917- WhoAmL 92
**Hedrick**, Geary Dean 1940- WhoMW 92
**Hedrick**, George Ellwood, III 1943- AmMWSc 92
**Hedrick**, Harold Burdette 1924- AmMWSc 92
**Hedrick**, Harold Gilman 1924- AmMWSc 92
**Hedrick**, Ira Grant 1913- AmMWSc 92
**Hedrick**, Jack LeGrande 1937- AmMWSc 92
**Hedrick**, Jacob Thomas 1934- WhoAmP 91
**Hedrick**, Jerry Leo 1936- AmMWSc 92
**Hedrick**, John Charles, Jr. 1940- WhoRel 92
**Hedrick**, John Leonard 1946- WhoMW 92
**Hedrick**, John Warrington 1955- WhoAmL 92
**Hedrick**, Joseph Watson, Jr. 1924- WhoWest 92
**Hedrick**, Laura Anne 1954- WhoRel 92
**Hedrick**, Lois Jean 1927- WhoFI 92
**Hedrick**, Mary Carde 1922- WhoAmP 91
**Hedrick**, Peggy Shepherd 1936- WhoAmL 92
**Hedrick**, Philip William 1942- AmMWSc 92
**Hedrick**, Ralph 1925- WhoAmP 91
**Hedrick**, Ronald Paul 1950- AmMWSc 92
**Hedrick**, Ross Melvin 1921- AmMWSc 92
**Hedrick**, Sarah Carmella 1951- WhoRel 92
**Hedrick**, Sue Goforth 1939- WhoAmP 91
**Hedrick**, Theodore Isaac 1912- AmMWSc 92
**Hedrick**, Wallace Edward 1947- WhoWest 92
**Hedstrom**, Arvid E 1928- WhoAmP 91
**Hedstrom**, Ase 1950- ConCom 92
**Hedstrom**, Gerald Walter 1933- AmMWSc 92
**Hedstrom**, John Richard 1937- AmMWSc 92
**Hedstrom**, Kenneth Gerald 1939- WhoWest 92
**Hedstrom**, Mitchell Warren 1951- WhoFI 92
**Hedstrom**, Ruth Elaine 1925- WhoEnt 92
**Hedtke**, James Lee 1943- AmMWSc 92
**Hee**, Christopher Edward 1939- AmMWSc 92
**Heeb**, Louis F. WhoAmL 92
**Heebe**, Frederick Jacob Regan 1922- WhoAmL 92
**Heebner**, Charles Frederick 1938- AmMWSc 92
**Heebner**, David Richard 1927- AmMWSc 92, WhoFI 92
**Heed**, Joseph James 1931- AmMWSc 92
**Heed**, William Battles 1926- AmMWSc 92
**Heede**, Burchard Heinrich 1918- AmMWSc 92
**Heege**, Robert Charles 1922- WhoAmL 92
**Heeger**, Alan J 1936- AmMWSc 92
**Heeger**, Jack Jay 1930- WhoWest 92
**Heeke**, Bernard Allen, Jr. 1963- WhoAmL 92
**Heeke**, Dennis Henry 1927- WhoAmP 91
**Heekin**, Valerie Anne 1953- WhoWest 92
**Heeks**, R E 1928- AmMWSc 92
**Heeley**, David Ernest 1940- WhoEnt 92
**Heeling**, Hendrik Aaltinus 1955- WhoWest 92
**Heelis**, Roderick Antony 1948- AmMWSc 92
**Heemstra**, Daniel Craig 1966- WhoRel 92
**Heen**, Leslie Alan 1961- WhoMW 92
**Heen**, Mary L. 1949- WhoAmL 92
**Heenan**, Cindy Christ 1959- WhoAmL 92
**Heenan**, David A. 1940- WhoWest 92
**Heenan**, Greg Stephen 1950- WhoRel 92
**Heenan**, Mary Anne WhoRel 92
**Heenan**, Maurice 1912- Who 92
**Heenan**, William A 1941- AmMWSc 92
**Heeps**, William 1929- Who 92
**Heer**, Clifford V 1920- AmMWSc 92, WhoMW 92
**Heer**, David MacAlpine 1930- WrDr 92
**Heer**, Edwin LeRoy 1938- WhoFI 92
**Heer**, Ewald 1930- AmMWSc 92
**Heerema**, Nickolas 1922- AmMWSc 92
**Heerema**, Ruurd Herre 1943- AmMWSc 92
**Heeren**, Fredric Jon 1953- WhoEnt 92
**Heeren**, James Kenneth 1929- AmMWSc 92
**Heerman**, William R 1933- WhoIns 92
**Heermann**, Dale F 1937- AmMWSc 92
**Heermann**, Ruben Martin 1921- AmMWSc 92
**Heers**, Arthur Frank 1944- WhoWest 92
**Heerwagen**, Elwood J., Jr. 1934- WhoAmL 92
**Heerwagen**, Paul K. 1895- WrDr 92
**Heery**, Michael Anthony 1966- WhoRel 92
**Hees**, George H. 1910- Who 92
**Hees**, George Harris 1910- IntWW 91
**Heesch**, Cheryl Miller 1948- AmMWSc 92
**Heeschen**, Barbara Ann 1931- WhoEnt 92, WhoMW 92
**Heeschen**, Conrad WhoAmP 91
**Heeschen**, David Sutphin 1926- AmMWSc 92, IntWW 91
**Heeschen**, Jerry Parker 1932- AmMWSc 92
**Heese**, William John 1936- WhoEnt 92
**Heeson**, Crispin 1950- TwCPaSc
**Heestand**, Glenn Martin 1942- AmMWSc 92
**Heetderks**, William John 1948- AmMWSc 92
**Hefestay**, Jack 1947- WhoAmP 91
**Heffelfinger**, Carl John 1924- AmMWSc 92
**Heffer**, Eric Samuel d1991 Who 92N
**Hefferlin**, Ray 1929- AmMWSc 92
**Heffern**, Clara Bernard 1910- WhoWest 92
**Heffern**, Richard Charles 1944- WhoAmL 92
**Heffernan**, Gerald R 1919- AmMWSc 92
**Heffernan**, James Scott 1953- WhoEnt 92
**Heffernan**, James Vincent 1926- WhoAmL 92
**Heffernan**, John 1934- WhoEnt 92
**Heffernan**, John A 1871-1952 ScFEYrs
**Heffernan**, Laurel Grace 1945- AmMWSc 92
**Heffernan**, Michael DrAPF 91
**Heffernan**, Nathan Stewart 1920- WhoAmL 92, WhoAmP 91, WhoMW 92
**Heffernan**, Thomas DrAPF 91
**Heffernan**, Thomas 1939- IntAu&W 91
**Hefferren**, John James 1928- AmMWSc 92
**Heffes**, Harry 1939- AmMWSc 92
**Heffington**, Jack Grisham 1944- WhoAmL 92
**Heffler**, Curt Lewis 1960- WhoAmL 92
**Heffley**, James D 1941- AmMWSc 92
**Hefflinger**, LeRoy Arthur 1935- WhoWest 92
**Heffner**, Daniel Jason 1956- WhoEnt 92
**Heffner**, Elizabeth Summers 1959- WhoRel 92
**Heffner**, John Howard 1947- WhoRel 92
**Heffner**, Mark B WhoAmP 91
**Heffner**, Reid Russell, Jr 1938- AmMWSc 92
**Heffner**, Richard 1925- IntMPA 92
**Heffner**, Richard Douglas 1925- WhoWest 92
**Heffner**, Richard Louis 1933- WhoFI 92
**Heffner**, Thomas G 1949- AmMWSc 92
**Heffron**, Dorris 1944- ConAu 36NR, SmATA 68, WrDr 92
**Heffron**, Dorris M 1944- IntAu&W 91
**Heffron**, Mary J. 1935- ConAu 135
**Heffron**, Peter John 1943- AmMWSc 92
**Heffron**, Richard T. 1930- IntMPA 92
**Heffron**, W Gordon 1925- AmMWSc 92
**Heffter**, Jerome L AmMWSc 92

**Hefler**, William Louis *WhoMW 92*
**Hefley**, Alta Jean 1941- *AmMWSc 92*
**Hefley**, Joel 1935- *AlmAP 92 [port]*
**Hefley**, Joel M. *WhoWest 92*
**Hefley**, Joel Maurice 1935- *WhoAmP 91*
**Heflich**, Robert Henry 1946- *AmMWSc 92*
**Heflin**, Alan Michael 1939- *WhoAmP 91*
**Heflin**, Donald *ConAu 35NR*
**Heflin**, Howell T. 1921- *AlmAP 92 [port]*
**Heflin**, Howell Thomas 1921- *WhoAmP 91*
**Heflin**, John F. 1941- *WhoBlA 92*
**Heflin**, Leland Earl 1946- *WhoMW 92*
**Heflin**, Mary Frances 1923- *WhoEnt 92*
**Heflin**, Talmadge Loraine 1940- *WhoAmP 91*
**Heflinger**, Lee Opert 1927- *AmMWSc 92*
**Hefner**, Cassandra Jewell 1956- *WhoWest 92*
**Hefner**, Christie *NewYTBS 91 [port]*
**Hefner**, Christie Ann 1952- *WhoEnt 92, WhoFI 92*
**Hefner**, Elroy M 1923- *WhoAmP 91, WhoMW 92*
**Hefner**, Hugh Marston 1926- *IntWW 91, WhoEnt 92*
**Hefner**, James A. 1941- *WhoBlA 92*
**Hefner**, Jerry W 1949- *WhoAmP 91*
**Hefner**, Lloyd Lee 1923- *AmMWSc 92*
**Hefner**, Philip James 1932- *WhoMW 92, WhoRel 92*
**Hefner**, Robert Alan 1929- *WhoAmL 92, WhoWest 92*
**Hefner**, W. G. 1930- *AlmAP 92 [port], WhoAmP 91*
**Heft**, Carolyn Mae 1942- *WhoAmL 92*
**Heft**, James Lewis 1943- *WhoRel 92*
**Heftel**, Cecil 1924- *WhoAmP 91*
**Hefter**, Laurence Roy 1935- *WhoAmL 92*
**Hefti**, Franz F 1947- *AmMWSc 92*
**Hefti**, Neal 1922- *NewAmDM*
**Heftmann**, Erich 1918- *AmMWSc 92*
**Hefty**, Duane Seymore 1923- *WhoFI 92*
**Hegan**, Alice *BenetAL 91*
**Hegarty**, Anthony Francis 1942- *IntWW 91*
**Hegarty**, Frances 1948- *ConAu 135*
**Hegarty**, George John 1948- *WhoMW 92*
**Hegarty**, Mary Frances 1950- *WhoAmL 92, WhoMW 92*
**Hegarty**, Patrick Vincent 1939- *AmMWSc 92*
**Hegarty**, Seamus *Who 92*
**Hegarty**, William Edward 1926- *WhoAmL 92*
**Hegazy**, Abdel Aziz Muhammad 1923- *IntWW 91*
**Hegberg**, Dennis Carl 1947- *WhoFI 92*
**Hegde**, Kawdoor Sadanand 1909- *IntWW 91*
**Hegde**, Rama Krishna 1927- *IntWW 91*
**Hege**, Constantine Alexander 1843-1914 *DcNCBi 3*
**Hege**, E K *AmMWSc 92*
**Hege**, Joe H, Jr 1926- *WhoAmP 91*
**Hegedus**, L Louis 1941- *AmMWSc 92*
**Hegedus**, Louis Stevenson 1943- *AmMWSc 92*
**Hegedus**, Steven Scott 1955- *AmMWSc 92*
**Hegel**, Eduard 1911- *IntWW 91*
**Hegele**, Robert A 1957- *AmMWSc 92*
**Hegeman**, Charles Oxford 1940- *WhoBlA 92*
**Hegeman**, George D 1938- *AmMWSc 92*
**Hegeman**, James Alan 1943- *WhoFI 92*
**Hegeman**, Mary Theodore 1907- *WrDr 92*
**Hegemier**, Eugene Earl 1933- *WhoRel 92*
**Hegemonius** *EncEarC*
**Hegenauer**, Jack C 1939- *AmMWSc 92*
**Hegenberger**, John 1947- *ConAu 135*
**Heger**, Frederick Louis 1930- *WhoMW 92*
**Heger**, James J 1918- *AmMWSc 92*
**Hegerhorst**, Pat *WhoWest 92*
**Hegesippus** 110?-180 *EncEarC*
**Hegge**, Carolyn Ann 1954- *WhoAmL 92*
**Heggemeier**, Lyle M. 1956- *WhoRel 92*
**Heggen**, Arthur W 1945- *WhoIns 92*
**Heggen**, Ivar Nelson 1954- *WhoAmL 92*
**Heggen**, Thomas 1919-1949 *BenetAL 91*
**Hegger**, Wilber L. 1936- *WhoBlA 92*
**Heggers**, John Paul 1933- *AmMWSc 92*
**Heggestad**, Carl B 1930- *AmMWSc 92*
**Heggestad**, Howard Edwin 1915- *AmMWSc 92*
**Heggestad**, John Richard 1936- *WhoFI 92*
**Heggie**, Robah Gray, Jr 1929- *WhoIns 92*
**Heggie**, Robert 1909- *AmMWSc 92*
**Heggie**, Robert Murray 1927- *AmMWSc 92*
**Heggs**, Geoffrey Ellis 1928- *Who 92*
**Heggs**, Renee Fanny Madeleine 1929- *Who 92*
**Heggtveit**, Halvor Alexander 1933- *AmMWSc 92*
**Hegi**, Ursula *DrAPF 91*
**Hegi**, Ursula Johanna 1946- *IntAu&W 91*
**Heginbotham**, Christopher John 1948- *Who 92*
**Heginbotham**, Wilfred Brooks 1924- *Who 92*
**Hegland**, David Leroy 1919- *Who 92*
**Heglund**, Norman C 1949- *AmMWSc 92*
**Hegmann**, Joseph Paul 1940- *AmMWSc 92*
**Hegmon**, Oliver Louis 1907- *WhoBlA 92*
**Hegre**, Carman Stanford 1937- *AmMWSc 92*
**Hegre**, Orion Donald 1943- *AmMWSc 92*
**Hegrenes**, Jack Richard 1929- *WhoWest 92*
**Hegsted**, David Mark 1914- *AmMWSc 92*
**Hegsted**, Maren 1950- *AmMWSc 92*
**Hegstrom**, Roger Allen 1941- *AmMWSc 92*
**Hegwood**, Donald Augustine 1931- *AmMWSc 92*
**Hegwood**, Gordon F. 1935- *WhoBlA 92*
**Hegwood**, William Lewis 1918- *WhoBlA 92*
**Hegyeli**, Ruth I E J 1931- *AmMWSc 92*
**Hegyi**, Dennis 1942- *AmMWSc 92*
**Hegyi**, Julius 1923- *WhoEnt 92*
**Hegyvary**, Csaba 1938- *AmMWSc 92*
**Hegyvary**, Sue Thomas 1943- *AmMWSc 92*
**Hehemann**, Robert F 1921- *AmMWSc 92*
**Hehl**, Lambert *WhoAmL 92*
**Hehl**, Lambert Lawrence 1924- *WhoAmP 91*
**Hehman**, Roger G. 1944- *WhoMW 92*
**Hehmsoth**, Henry 1952- *WhoEnt 92*
**Hehre**, Edward James 1912- *AmMWSc 92*
**Hehre**, Edward James, Jr 1940- *AmMWSc 92*
**Hei Boli** 1918- *IntWW 91*
**Heiba**, El-Ahmadi Ibrahim 1926- *AmMWSc 92*
**Heibel**, John T 1943- *AmMWSc 92*
**Heiber**, Robert Jay 1951- *WhoEnt 92*
**Heiberg**, Harold Willard 1922- *WhoEnt 92*
**Heiberg**, Peter Andreas 1758-1841 *BlkwCEP*
**Heiberg**, Robert Alan 1943- *WhoAmL 92*
**Heiberger**, Philip 1919- *AmMWSc 92*
**Heiblum**, Mordehai 1947- *AmMWSc 92*
**Heichel**, Gary Harold 1940- *AmMWSc 92*
**Heichelheim**, Hubert Reed 1931- *AmMWSc 92*
**Heicklen**, Julian Phillip 1932- *AmMWSc 92*
**Heid** *EncAmaz 91*
**Heid**, Lisa Josephine 1955- *WhoMW 92*
**Heid**, Roland Leo 1914- *AmMWSc 92*
**Heid**, Walter W. 1954- *WhoEnt 92*
**Heidbreder**, Edna 1890-1985 *WomPsyc*
**Heidbreder**, Glenn R 1929- *AmMWSc 92*
**Heidcamp**, William H 1944- *AmMWSc 92*
**Heide**, Beth Vivian 1906- *WhoAmP 91*
**Heide**, Florence Parry 1919- *IntAu&W 91, WrDr 92*
**Heide**, Gary Howard 1940- *WhoRel 92, WhoWest 92*
**Heide**, Jan Brede 1958- *WhoFI 92*
**Heide**, John Halloran 1962- *WhoAmL 92*
**Heide**, Ola Mikal 1931- *IntWW 91*
**Heide**, Richard Thomas 1931- *WhoAmP 91*
**Heide**, Thomas Robert 1949- *WhoFI 92*
**Heideger**, William J 1932- *AmMWSc 92*
**Heidegger**, Martin 1889-1976 *BiDExR, ConAu 34NR, FacFETw [port]*
**Heidegger**, Martin 1899-1976 *EncTR 91 [port]*
**Heidelbaugh**, Norman Dale 1927- *AmMWSc 92*
**Heidelberg**, Helen Susan Hatvani 1957- *WhoMW 92*
**Heidelberger**, Michael d1991 *NewYTBS 91 [port]*
**Heidelberger**, Michael 1888- *AmMWSc 92, IntWW 91*
**Heidelberger**, Philip 1951- *AmMWSc 92*
**Heideman**, Gerald Ned 1931- *WhoMW 92*
**Heideman**, John Mark 1960- *WhoRel 92*
**Heideman**, Richard Dennis 1947- *WhoFI 92*
**Heideman**, William Robert 1933- *WhoEnt 92*
**Heidemann**, Otto 1842-1916 *BiInAmS*
**Heidemann**, Steven Richard 1949- *AmMWSc 92*
**Heiden**, Eric Arthur 1958- *FacFETw*
**Heiden**, Jeri McManus 1959- *WhoEnt 92*
**Heidenreich**, Charles John 1927- *AmMWSc 92*
**Heidenriech**, Edward E. 1938- *WhoMW 92*
**Heidenstam**, Verner Von 1859-1940 *FacFETw*
**Heidenthal**, Gertrude Antoinette 1908- *AmMWSc 92*
**Heidepriem**, Scott Nelson 1956- *WhoAmP 91*
**Heider**, David Arthur 1941- *WhoFI 92*
**Heider**, Frederick *IntMPA 92*
**Heider**, George Charles 1953- *WhoMW 92, WhoRel 92*
**Heider**, Jon Vinton 1934- *WhoAmL 92, WhoFI 92*
**Heider**, Shirley A 1912- *AmMWSc 92*
**Heidger**, Paul McClay, Jr 1941- *AmMWSc 92*
**Heidig**, Elizabeth Anne 1959- *WhoAmL 92*
**Heidkamp**, Patricia Jean 1951- *WhoFI 92*
**Heidler**, Robert Daniel 1948- *WhoRel 92*
**Heidner**, Robert Hubbard 1919- *AmMWSc 92*
**Heidrich**, William A. 1954- *WhoAmL 92*
**Heidrick**, Gardner Wilson 1911- *WhoFI 92, WhoMW 92*
**Heidrick**, Lee E 1921- *AmMWSc 92*
**Heidrick**, Margaret Louise 1938- *AmMWSc 92*
**Heidrick**, Robert Lindsay 1941- *WhoFI 92*
**Heidrick**, Steven Andrew 1960- *WhoAmL 92*
**Heidt**, Ellen Virginia *WhoBlA 92*
**Heidt**, Gary A 1942- *AmMWSc 92*
**Heidt**, Horace Hamilton, Jr. 1946- *WhoEnt 92*
**Heidt**, Raymond Joseph 1933- *WhoWest 92*
**Heiduck**, Donald Fred 1956- *WhoWest 92*
**Heieck**, Paul Jay 1937- *WhoFI 92, WhoWest 92*
**Heien**, Sharon Fay Carey 1941- *WhoRel 92*
**Heier**, David Scott 1953- *WhoAmL 92*
**Heifetz**, Carl Louis 1935- *AmMWSc 92, WhoMW 92*
**Heifetz**, Hank *DrAPF 91*
**Heifetz**, Harold 1919- *IntAu&W 91*
**Heifetz**, Jascha 1901-1987 *FacFETw [port], NewAmDM*
**Heifetz**, Jonathan 1956- *AmMWSc 92*
**Heifetz**, Michael Ruvimovitch 1934- *LiExTwC*
**Heifetz**, Milton David 1921- *AmMWSc 92*
**Heiffer**, Melvin Harold 1927- *AmMWSc 92*
**Heifitz**, Josef 1905- *IntDcF 2-2*
**Heifner**, Richard Glenn 1934- *WhoFI 92*
**Heigaard**, William S 1938- *WhoAmP 91*
**Heigert**, Hans A 1925- *IntAu&W 91, IntWW 91*
**Heiges**, Jesse G. d1991 *NewYTBS 91*
**Height**, Dorothy 1912- *NotBlAW 92 [port]*
**Height**, Dorothy I. 1912- *ConBlB 2 [port], WhoBlA 92*
**Heigl**, Alan Lee 1944- *WhoEnt 92*
**Heigl**, Friedrich 1947- *WhoFI 92*
**Heigold**, Paul C 1936- *AmMWSc 92*
**Heijermans**, Herman 1864-1924 *FacFETw*
**Heikal**, Muhammed Hassanein 1923- *IntWW 91*
**Heiken**, Grant Harvey 1942- *AmMWSc 92*
**Heiken**, Jay Paul 1952- *WhoMW 92*
**Heikenen**, Charles Edward 1950- *WhoFI 92*
**Heikkenen**, Herman John 1930- *AmMWSc 92*
**Heikkila**, John J 1950- *AmMWSc 92*
**Heikkila**, Richard Elmer 1942- *AmMWSc 92*
**Heikkila**, Walter John 1928- *AmMWSc 92*
**Heikkinen**, Dale William 1938- *AmMWSc 92*
**Heikkinen**, Donald D 1932- *AmMWSc 92*
**Heikkinen**, Henry Wendell 1935- *AmMWSc 92*
**Heil**, Ed 1921- *WhoWest 92*
**Heil**, John F, Jr 1936- *AmMWSc 92*
**Heil**, John P. 1948- *WhoAmL 92*
**Heil**, Michael Duane 1947- *WhoFI 92*
**Heil**, Paul Samuel 1947- *WhoEnt 92, WhoRel 92*
**Heil**, Richard Wendell 1926- *AmMWSc 92*
**Heil**, Robert Dean 1932- *AmMWSc 92*
**Heil**, Wolfgang Heinrich 1940- *AmMWSc 92*
**Heiland**, Juanita Marie 1942- *WhoHisp 92*
**Heilborn**, George Heinz 1935- *WhoFI 92*
**Heilbron**, Gail 1951- *WhoEnt 92*
**Heilbron**, Hilary Nora Burstein 1949- *Who 92*
**Heilbron**, Rose 1914- *Who 92*
**Heilbroner**, Robert L. *WrDr 92*
**Heilbroner**, Robert L. 1919- *IntWW 91*
**Heilbrun**, Carolyn G. 1926- *WrDr 92*
**Heilbrun**, Carolyn Gold 1926- *IntWW 91*
**Heilbrunn**, Jeffrey 1950- *WhoMW 92*
**Heilenday**, Anita Richard 1927- *WhoRel 92*
**Heilenday**, Frank W 1927- *AmMWSc 92*
**Heiles**, Carl 1939- *AmMWSc 92*
**Heilicser**, Bernard Jay 1947- *WhoMW 92*
**Heilig**, George Harris, Jr 1942- *WhoAmP 91*
**Heiligenstein**, Christian E. 1929- *WhoAmL 92*
**Heiliger**, Bernhard 1915- *IntWW 91*
**Heilker**, Vincent de Paul 1924- *WhoEnt 92*
**Heiller**, Anton 1923-1979 *NewAmDM*
**Heilman**, Alan Smith 1927- *AmMWSc 92*
**Heilman**, Carl Edwin 1911- *WhoAmL 92, WhoFI 92*
**Heilman**, Carol A *AmMWSc 92*
**Heilman**, Caryn *WhoEnt 92*
**Heilman**, Claude 1927- *IntMPA 92*
**Heilman**, Edna May 1938- *WhoRel 92*
**Heilman**, Joan Rattner *IntAu&W 91*
**Heilman**, Paul E 1931- *AmMWSc 92*
**Heilman**, Richard Dean 1937- *AmMWSc 92*
**Heilman**, Robert B. 1906- *WrDr 92*
**Heilman**, Robert Bechtold 1906- *IntAu&W 91*
**Heilman**, William Joseph 1930- *AmMWSc 92*
**Heilman**, William Paul 1948- *AmMWSc 92*
**Heilmann**, Ernst 1881-1940 *EncTR 91 [port]*
**Heilmeier**, George Harry 1936- *AmMWSc 92, WhoFI 92*
**Heilprin**, Angelo 1853-1907 *BenetAL 91, BiInAmS*
**Heilprin**, Laurence Bedford 1906- *AmMWSc 92*
**Heilprin**, Michael 1823-1888 *BenetAL 91*
**Heilweil**, Israel Joel 1924- *AmMWSc 92*
**Heim**, Alice W. 1913- *WrDr 92*
**Heim**, Alice Winifred 1913- *IntAu&W 91*
**Heim**, Bruno Bernard 1911- *Who 92, WhoRel 92*
**Heim**, Carol Elizabeth 1955- *WhoFI 92*
**Heim**, Charles W 1936- *WhoAmP 91*
**Heim**, David Michael 1952- *WhoAmL 92*
**Heim**, Donald John 1927- *WhoFI 92*
**Heim**, Joel James 1958- *WhoRel 92*
**Heim**, Joseph Peter 1942- *WhoMW 92*
**Heim**, Kathryn Marie 1952- *WhoMW 92*
**Heim**, Lyle Raymond 1933- *AmMWSc 92*
**Heim**, Michael Carl 1963- *WhoFI 92*
**Heim**, Paul Emil 1932- *Who 92*
**Heim**, Ralph D. 1895-1983 *ConAu 133*
**Heim**, Robert Charles 1942- *WhoAmL 92*
**Heim**, Werner George 1929- *AmMWSc 92*
**Heiman**, David Gilbert 1945- *WhoAmL 92, WhoFI 92*
**Heiman**, Donald Eugene 1947- *AmMWSc 92*
**Heiman**, Mark Louis 1952- *AmMWSc 92*
**Heiman**, Marvin Stewart 1945- *WhoFI 92, WhoMW 92*
**Heiman**, Maxwell 1932- *WhoAmL 92*
**Heiman**, Thomas Leon 1956- *WhoEnt 92*
**Heimann**, Betsy Faith *WhoEnt 92*
**Heimann**, Janet Barbara 1931- *WhoWest 92*
**Heimann**, John G 1929- *WhoAmP 91*
**Heimann**, John Gaines 1929- *WhoFI 92*
**Heimann**, Judith Moscow 1936- *WhoAmP 91*
**Heimann**, Jurgen Steffen 1965- *WhoEnt 92*
**Heimann**, Peter Aaron 1949- *AmMWSc 92*
**Heimann**, Robert B 1938- *AmMWSc 92*
**Heimann**, Robert L 1946- *AmMWSc 92*
**Heimann**, Sandra Woeste 1943- *WhoIns 92*
**Heimbach**, David M *AmMWSc 92*
**Heimbach**, David Tucker 1950- *WhoAmL 92*
**Heimbach**, Richard Dean 1935- *AmMWSc 92*
**Heimbecker**, Raymond Oliver 1922- *AmMWSc 92*
**Heimberg**, Murray 1925- *AmMWSc 92*
**Heimberger**, Mable Alice 1924- *WhoAmP 91*
**Heimbinder**, Isaac 1943- *WhoAmL 92, WhoFI 92*
**Heimbold**, Charles Andreas, Jr. 1933- *WhoFI 92*
**Heimburg**, Richard W 1938- *AmMWSc 92*
**Heimer**, Edgar P 1937- *AmMWSc 92*
**Heimer**, Norman Eugene 1940- *AmMWSc 92*
**Heimer**, Ralph 1921- *AmMWSc 92*
**Heimerdinger**, John Frederick 1932- *WhoFI 92*
**Heimerl**, John Jules 1950- *WhoEnt 92*
**Heimerl**, Joseph Mark 1940- *AmMWSc 92*
**Heimerman**, Dennis Joseph 1954- *WhoMW 92*
**Heimlich**, Ellen Kramer 1942- *WhoAmL 92*
**Heimlich**, Richard Allen 1932- *AmMWSc 92*
**Heimlich**, Richard William 1941- *WhoFI 92*
**Heimo**, Marcel 1917- *IntWW 91*
**Heimsch**, Charles 1914- *WhoMW 92*
**Heimsch**, Charles W 1914- *AmMWSc 92*
**Heimsch**, Richard Charles 1942- *AmMWSc 92*
**Hein**, Dale Arthur 1933- *AmMWSc 92*
**Hein**, David William 1955- *AmMWSc 92*
**Hein**, Denise Cooper 1958- *WhoMW 92*
**Hein**, Helmut *WhoEnt 92*
**Hein**, James R 1947- *AmMWSc 92*
**Hein**, James Rodney 1947- *WhoWest 92*
**Hein**, John William 1920- *AmMWSc 92*

**Hein**, Kenneth Charles Lawrence 1938- *WhoRel 92, WhoWest 92*
**Hein**, Lucille Eleanor 1915- *WrDr 92*
**Hein**, Peter Charles 1952- *WhoAmP 91*
**Hein**, Peter Leo, Jr 1930- *AmMWSc 92*
**Hein**, Piet 1905- *DcTwDes, FacFETw*
**Hein**, R F 1923- *AmMWSc 92*
**Hein**, Richard Earl 1919- *AmMWSc 92*
**Hein**, Richard William 1934- *AmMWSc 92*
**Hein**, Rolland Neal 1932- *WhoMW 92, WhoRel 92*
**Hein**, Ronald Reed 1949- *WhoAmP 91*
**Hein**, Rosemary Ruth 1924- *AmMWSc 92*
**Hein**, Todd Jonathan 1960- *WhoFI 92*
**Hein**, Warren Walter 1944- *AmMWSc 92*
**Heinberg**, Milton 1928- *AmMWSc 92*
**Heindel**, Max 1865-1919 *RelLAm 91*
**Heindel**, Ned Duane 1937- *AmMWSc 92*
**Heindl**, Clifford Joseph 1926- *AmMWSc 92, WhoWest 92*
**Heindl**, Gottfried 1924- *IntWW 91*
**Heindl**, Phares Matthews 1949- *WhoAmL 92*
**Heindsmann**, T E 1925- *AmMWSc 92*
**Heine**, George Winfield, III 1949- *AmMWSc 92, WhoWest 92*
**Heine**, Gunter Karl 1941- *WhoWest 92*
**Heine**, Harold Warren 1922- *AmMWSc 92*
**Heine**, Helme 1941- *ConAu 135, SmATA 67 [port]*
**Heine**, Leonard M., Jr. 1924- *WhoFI 92*
**Heine**, Melvin Wayne 1933- *AmMWSc 92*
**Heine**, Raymond Arnold Carl 1922- *WhoRel 92*
**Heine**, Richard W 1918- *AmMWSc 92*
**Heine**, Robert Jan 1952- *WhoEnt 92*
**Heine**, Spencer H. 1942- *WhoAmL 92*
**Heine**, Ursula Ingrid 1926- *AmMWSc 92*
**Heine**, Volker 1930- *IntWW 91, Who 92*
**Heine**, William A. 1940- *WhoFI 92*
**Heineback**, Barbara Taylor 1951- *WhoBlA 92*
**Heineken**, Alfred Henry 1923- *IntWW 91*
**Heineken**, Frederick George 1939- *AmMWSc 92*
**Heineman**, Adam John 1924- *WhoWest 92*
**Heineman**, Andrew David 1928- *WhoAmL 92*
**Heineman**, Benjamin Walter, Jr. 1944- *WhoAmL 92, WhoAmP 91*
**Heineman**, William Richard 1942- *AmMWSc 92*
**Heinemann**, Alexanna Padilla 1959- *WhoHisp 92*
**Heinemann**, David 1947- *WhoRel 92*
**Heinemann**, David John 1945- *WhoAmP 91*
**Heinemann**, Edward H 1908- *AmMWSc 92*
**Heinemann**, George *LesBEnT 92*
**Heinemann**, George Alfred 1918- *WhoEnt 92*
**Heinemann**, Guy Leo 1944- *WhoAmL 92*
**Heinemann**, Heinz 1913- *AmMWSc 92*
**Heinemann**, Katherine *DrAPF 91*
**Heinemann**, Larry *DrAPF 91*
**Heinemann**, Larry 1944- *DcLB DS9 [port]*
**Heinemann**, Larry C. 1944- *WrDr 92*
**Heinemann**, Richard Leslie 1931- *AmMWSc 92*
**Heinemann**, William 1863-1920 *DcLB 112 [port]*
**Heinemann**, Wilton Walter 1920- *AmMWSc 92*
**Heinen**, James Albin 1943- *AmMWSc 92, WhoMW 92*
**Heinen**, Mary Florita 1933- *WhoRel 92*
**Heinen**, Paul Abelardo 1930- *WhoAmL 92*
**Heiner**, Dennis Grant 1943- *WhoFI 92*
**Heiner**, Douglas C 1925- *AmMWSc 92*
**Heiner**, Douglas Cragun 1925- *WhoWest 92*
**Heiner**, Lawrence Elden 1938- *WhoWest 92*
**Heiner**, Robert T. 1925- *WhoWest 92*
**Heiner**, Terry Charles 1941- *AmMWSc 92*
**Heinerman**, John 1946- *IntAu&W 91*
**Heinert**, Dale Mathew 1951- *WhoMW 92*
**Heines**, Edmund 1897-1934 *EncTR 91 [port]*
**Heines**, Thomas Samuel 1927- *AmMWSc 92*
**Heinesen**, Knud 1932- *IntWW 91*
**Heinesen**, William 1900-1991 *IntWW 91, -91N*
**Heiney**, Terry Leigh 1946- *WhoWest 92*
**Heinichen**, Jeffrey Kirk 1952- *WhoMW 92*
**Heinicke**, Herbert Raymond 1927- *AmMWSc 92, WhoMW 92*
**Heinicke**, Peter Hart 1956- *AmMWSc 92*
**Heinicke**, Ralph Martin 1914- *AmMWSc 92*
**Heinig**, Hans Paul 1931- *AmMWSc 92*
**Heinig**, Ruth Beall 1936- *WhoEnt 92*
**Heiniger**, Hans-Jorg 1938- *AmMWSc 92*
**Heininen**, Paavo 1938- *ConCom 92*
**Heining**, James William 1950- *WhoRel 92*
**Heininger**, Clarence George, Jr 1928- *AmMWSc 92*
**Heininger**, Erwin Carl 1921- *WhoAmL 92*
**Heininger**, S Allen 1925- *AmMWSc 92*
**Heinis**, Julius Leo 1926- *AmMWSc 92*
**Heinisch**, Roger Paul 1938- *AmMWSc 92, WhoFI 92*
**Heinitz**, Kenneth Lawrence 1926- *WhoRel 92*
**Heinitz**, O J 1921- *WhoAmP 91*
**Heinke**, Clarence Henry 1912- *AmMWSc 92*
**Heinke**, Gerhard William 1932- *AmMWSc 92*
**Heinke**, Rex S. 1950- *WhoAmL 92*
**Heinkel**, Ernst 1888-1958 *EncTR 91 [port]*
**Heinle**, Donald Roger *AmMWSc 92*
**Heinle**, Preston Joseph 1924- *AmMWSc 92*
**Heinlein**, Gregory John 1963- *WhoMW 92*
**Heinlein**, Oscar Allen 1911- *WhoWest 92*
**Heinlein**, Robert A. 1907-1988 *BenetAL 91, FacFETw, TwCSFW 91*
**Heinlen**, Daniel Lee 1937- *WhoMW 92*
**Heinlen**, Ronald Eugene 1937- *WhoAmL 92*
**Heino**, Charles H *WhoAmP 91*
**Heino**, Walden Leo 1930- *AmMWSc 92*
**Heinold**, Robert H 1931- *AmMWSc 92*
**Heinrich**, Anthony Philip 1781-1861 *NewAmDM*
**Heinrich**, Bernd 1940- *AmMWSc 92*
**Heinrich**, Bonnie Miller *WhoAmP 91*
**Heinrich**, Eberhardt William 1918- *AmMWSc 92*
**Heinrich**, Elmer G. 1934- *WhoFI 92*
**Heinrich**, Gerhard *AmMWSc 92*
**Heinrich**, Janet *AmMWSc 92*
**Heinrich**, John Joseph 1934- *WhoRel 92*
**Heinrich**, Kevin Randall 1959- *WhoAmP 91*
**Heinrich**, Kurt Francis Joseph 1921- *AmMWSc 92*
**Heinrich**, Max Alfred, Jr 1924- *AmMWSc 92*
**Heinrich**, Milton Rollin 1919- *AmMWSc 92, WhoWest 92*
**Heinrich**, Peggy *DrAPF 91*
**Heinrich**, R L 1911- *AmMWSc 92*
**Heinrich**, Ross Raymond 1915- *AmMWSc 92*
**Heinrichs**, Andrew Chris 1949- *WhoAmL 92*
**Heinrichs**, Donald Frederick 1938- *AmMWSc 92*
**Heinrichs**, Donna Boccar 1950- *WhoAmL 92*
**Heinrichs**, W LeRoy 1932- *AmMWSc 92*
**Heinrikson**, Robert L 1935- *AmMWSc 92*
**Heins**, Albert Edward 1912- *AmMWSc 92, WhoMW 92*
**Heins**, Conrad F 1939- *AmMWSc 92*
**Heins**, Conrad P, Jr 1937- *AmMWSc 92*
**Heins**, Henry L., Jr. 1931- *WhoBlA 92*
**Heins**, Marilyn 1930- *WhoWest 92*
**Heins**, Marjorie 1946- *WhoAmL 92*
**Heins**, Maurice Haskell 1915- *AmMWSc 92*
**Heins**, Robert W 1924- *AmMWSc 92*
**Heins**, Roger Gordon 1939- *WhoWest 92*
**Heinselman**, Miron L 1920- *AmMWSc 92*
**Heinsohn**, Elisa M. 1962- *WhoEnt 92*
**Heinsohn**, George Edwin 1933- *WrDr 92*
**Heinsohn**, Robert J 1932- *AmMWSc 92*
**Heinssen**, Betty Julia 1942- *WhoAmP 91*
**Heinstein**, Peter 1935- *AmMWSc 92*
**Heintel**, Erich 1912- *IntWW 91*
**Heintz**, Carolinea Cabaniss 1920- *WhoMW 92*
**Heintz**, Edward Allein 1931- *AmMWSc 92*
**Heintz**, Julia Anne 1957- *WhoAmL 92*
**Heintz**, Roger Lewis 1937- *AmMWSc 92*
**Heintz**, Sarah Ellen 1961- *WhoAmL 92*
**Heintz**, Wulff Dieter 1930- *AmMWSc 92*
**Heintze**, Gerhard 1912- *IntWW 91*
**Heintzelman**, Richard Wayne 1947- *AmMWSc 92*
**Heintzleman**, Walter Gray 1935- *WhoFI 92*
**Heiny**, James Ray 1928- *WhoAmL 92*
**Heiny**, Robert Lowell 1942- *AmMWSc 92*
**Heinz**, Don J 1931- *AmMWSc 92, WhoWest 92*
**Heinz**, Elise Brookfield 1935- *WhoAmP 91*
**Heinz**, Erich *AmMWSc 92*
**Heinz**, Hanspeter 1939- *WhoRel 92*
**Heinz**, Henry John, III 1938-1991 *IntWW 91, -91N*
**Heinz**, John 1938-1991 *CurBio 91N, NewYTBS 91 [port], News 91*
**Heinz**, John Michael 1933- *AmMWSc 92*
**Heinz**, John Peter 1936- *WhoAmL 92*
**Heinz**, Otto 1924- *AmMWSc 92*
**Heinz**, Richard Meade 1939- *AmMWSc 92*
**Heinz**, Tony F 1956- *AmMWSc 92*
**Heinz**, Ulrich Walter 1955- *AmMWSc 92*
**Heinz**, W. C. 1915- *WrDr 92*
**Heinze**, Jeffrey Ronald 1958- *WhoAmL 92*
**Heinze**, Ruth-Inge 1919- *WhoWest 92*
**Heinze**, William Daniel 1948- *AmMWSc 92*
**Heinzen**, Bernard George 1930- *WhoAmL 92, WhoFI 92*
**Heiple**, Clinton R 1939- *AmMWSc 92*
**Heiple**, James D 1933- *WhoAmP 91*
**Heiple**, James Dee 1933- *WhoAmL 92, WhoMW 92*
**Heiple**, Loren Ray 1918- *AmMWSc 92*
**Heir**, Douglas 1960- *WhoAmL 92*
**Heir**, Phil *WhoAmP 91*
**Heirman**, Donald N 1940- *AmMWSc 92*
**Heirtzler**, James Ransom 1925- *AmMWSc 92*
**Heisbourg**, Francois 1949- *Who 92*
**Heisbourg**, Georges 1918- *IntWW 91, Who 92*
**Heise**, Eugene Royce 1932- *AmMWSc 92*
**Heise**, Fred Henry, Jr. 1935- *WhoMW 92*
**Heise**, John J 1931- *AmMWSc 92*
**Heise**, Marilyn Beardsley 1935- *WhoMW 92*
**Heisel**, Ralph Arthur 1935- *WhoFI 92*
**Heisenberg**, Werner 1901-1976 *EncTR 91 [port]*
**Heisenberg**, Werner Karl 1901-1976 *FacFETw, WhoNob 90*
**Heiser**, Arnold M 1933- *AmMWSc 92*
**Heiser**, Charles B., Jr. 1920- *WrDr 92*
**Heiser**, Charles Bixler, Jr 1920- *AmMWSc 92, WhoMW 92*
**Heiser**, Michael J. 1954- *WhoWest 92*
**Heiser**, Rolland Valentine 1925- *WhoFI 92*
**Heiser**, Terence Michael 1932- *Who 92*
**Heiser**, Walter Charles 1922- *WhoRel 92*
**Heiserman**, Frederick Von 1927- *WhoWest 92*
**Heiserman**, Robert Gifford 1946- *WhoAmL 92*
**Heisermann**, Gary J *AmMWSc 92*
**Heisey**, Lowell Vernon 1919- *AmMWSc 92*
**Heisey**, S Richard 1928- *AmMWSc 92*
**Heishman**, James Branson 1955- *WhoMW 92*
**Heisig**, Charles G 1924- *AmMWSc 92*
**Heisinger**, James Fredrick 1935- *AmMWSc 92*
**Heiskell**, Andrew 1915- *IntWW 91, Who 92, WhoEnt 92*
**Heiskell**, Edgar Frank, III 1940- *WhoAmP 91*
**Heiskell**, Henry Lee 1850-1914 *BiInAmS*
**Heiskell**, Michael Porter 1951- *WhoBlA 92*
**Heisler**, Charles Rankin 1924- *AmMWSc 92*
**Heisler**, Christopher Joseph 1965- *WhoMW 92*
**Heisler**, Elwood Douglas 1935- *WhoFI 92*
**Heisler**, Harold Reinhart *WhoFI 92, WhoMW 92*
**Heisler**, John Columbus 1926- *WhoFI 92*
**Heisler**, Joseph Patrick 1934- *AmMWSc 92*
**Heisler**, Leslie 1928- *WhoAmP 91*
**Heisler**, Quentin George, Jr. 1943- *WhoAmL 92, WhoMW 92*
**Heisler**, Rodney 1942- *AmMWSc 92*
**Heisler**, Seymour 1943- *AmMWSc 92*
**Heisler**, Stanley Dean 1946- *WhoAmL 92*
**Heiss**, John 1938- *WhoEnt 92*
**Heiss**, John F 1920- *AmMWSc 92*
**Heiss**, Michael Harris 1949- *WhoEnt 92*
**Heiss**, Richard Walter 1930- *WhoFI 92*
**Heissenbuttel**, Helmut 1921- *IntWW 91*
**Heissmeyer**, August 1897-1979 *EncTR 91*
**Heist**, Herbert Ernest 1924- *AmMWSc 92*
**Heist**, Paulus A. 1917- *WhoWest 92*
**Heistad**, Donald Dean 1940- *AmMWSc 92*
**Heistand**, Joseph Thomas 1924- *WhoRel 92, WhoWest 92*
**Heister**, Robert John, Jr. 1953- *WhoAmL 92*
**Heitkamp**, Heidi *WhoAmP 91*
**Heitkamp**, Norman Denis 1940- *AmMWSc 92*
**Heitkamp**, Richard Renfrew 1925- *WhoWest 92*
**Heitkemper**, Margaret M 1951- *AmMWSc 92*
**Heitler**, Bruce F. 1945- *WhoWest 92*
**Heitman**, Betty Green 1929- *WhoAmP 91*
**Heitman**, Gregory Erwin 1947- *WhoWest 92*
**Heitman**, Hubert, Jr 1917- *AmMWSc 92, WhoWest 92*
**Heitman**, John Franklin 1840-1904 *DcNCBi 3*
**Heitman**, Richard Edgar 1930- *AmMWSc 92*
**Heitmann**, Adair Wilson 1953- *WhoEnt 92*
**Heitmann**, George Joseph 1933- *WhoFI 92*
**Heitmeier**, Donald Elmer 1926- *AmMWSc 92*
**Heitmeier**, Francis C 1950- *WhoAmP 91*
**Heitner**, Cyril 1941- *AmMWSc 92*
**Heitner**, Robert R. 1920- *WrDr 92*
**Heitsch**, Charles Weyand 1931- *AmMWSc 92*
**Heitsch**, Ernst 1928- *IntWW 91*
**Heitsch**, James Lawrence 1946- *AmMWSc 92, WhoMW 92*
**Heitschmidt**, Rodney Keith 1944- *AmMWSc 92*
**Heitz**, James Robert 1941- *AmMWSc 92*
**Heitz**, Mark V. 1952- *WhoFI 92*
**Heitzenrater**, Richard Paul 1939- *WhoRel 92*
**Heitzman**, Charles 1836-1896 *BiInAmS*
**Heizer**, Edgar Francis, Jr. 1929- *WhoFI 92*
**Heizer**, Kenneth W 1923- *AmMWSc 92*
**Heizer**, Michael 1944- *WorArt 1980 [port]*
**Heizer**, William David 1937- *AmMWSc 92*
**Hejhal**, Dennis Arnold 1948- *AmMWSc 92, WhoMW 92*
**Hejhall**, Roy Charles 1932- *WhoWest 92*
**Hejinian**, Lyn *ConPo 91, DrAPF 91*
**Hejinian**, Lyn 1941- *WrDr 92*
**Hejlik**, Cheryl Regina 1966- *WhoMW 92*
**Hejna**, William Frank 1932- *AmMWSc 92*
**Hejtmancik**, Kelly Erwin 1948- *AmMWSc 92*
**Hejtmancik**, Milton R 1919- *AmMWSc 92*
**Hejtmanek**, Danton Charles 1951- *WhoAmL 92, WhoFI 92, WhoMW 92*
**Hekal**, Ihab M 1938- *AmMWSc 92*
**Hekker**, Roeland M T 1953- *AmMWSc 92*
**Hekmat**, Hamid Moayed 1940- *AmMWSc 92*
**Hekmatpanah**, Javad 1934- *AmMWSc 92*
**Helaissi**, Abdulrahman Al- 1922- *IntWW 91, Who 92*
**Helander**, Christine Marie 1956- *WhoFI 92*
**Helander**, Donald P 1931- *AmMWSc 92*
**Helander**, Herbert Dick Ferdinand 1935- *AmMWSc 92*
**Helander**, John Winston 1961- *WhoFI 92*
**Helander**, Martin E. Gustav 1943- *WhoFI 92*
**Helander**, Martin Erik Gustav 1943- *AmMWSc 92*
**Helander**, Robert Charles 1932- *WhoAmL 92*
**Helander**, Robert E. 1930- *WhoWest 92*
**Helanen**, Vilho Veikko Paivio 1899-1952 *BiDExR*
**Helava**, U V 1923- *AmMWSc 92*
**Helbach**, David W 1948- *WhoAmP 91, WhoMW 92*
**Helbert**, James Raymond 1918- *AmMWSc 92*
**Helbert**, John N 1946- *AmMWSc 92*
**Helbig**, Herbert Frederick 1934- *AmMWSc 92*
**Helbing**, Reinhard Karl Bodo 1935- *AmMWSc 92*
**Helburn**, Theresa 1887?-1959 *BenetAL 91*
**Held**, Abraham Albert 1934- *AmMWSc 92*
**Held**, Al 1928- *IntWW 91*
**Held**, Berel 1938- *AmMWSc 92*
**Held**, David *IntMPA 92*
**Held**, Harold Frederick Theadore 1912- *WhoRel 92*
**Held**, Heinrich 1868-1938 *EncTR 91 [port]*
**Held**, Heinz Joachim 1928- *IntWW 91, WhoRel 92*
**Held**, Irene Rita *AmMWSc 92*
**Held**, Isaac Meyer 1948- *AmMWSc 92*
**Held**, James Robert 1961- *WhoFI 92*
**Held**, Jay Allen 1961- *WhoRel 92*
**Held**, Joe R 1931- *AmMWSc 92*
**Held**, John, Jr. 1889-1958 *BenetAL 91*
**Held**, Judith Raye 1938- *WhoEnt 92*
**Held**, Martin 1908- *IntWW 91*
**Held**, Michael Charles *WhoAmP 91*
**Held**, Nancy Jean 1932- *WhoMW 92*
**Held**, Peter *WrDr 92*
**Held**, Richard M. 1922- *IntWW 91*
**Held**, Robert Paul 1939- *AmMWSc 92*
**Held**, Serge *ScFEYrs*
**Held**, Virginia P. 1929- *WrDr 92*
**Held**, Walter W. 1954- *WhoEnt 92*
**Held**, William Allen 1940- *AmMWSc 92*
**Helder**, Bruce Alan 1953- *WhoMW 92*
**Helder**, Karen Fay 1952- *WhoMW 92*
**Helderman**, J Harold 1945- *AmMWSc 92*
**Helders**, Gerardus Philippus 1905- *IntWW 91*
**Heldman**, Dennis Ray 1938- *AmMWSc 92*
**Heldman**, James Gardner 1949- *WhoAmL 92*
**Heldman**, Julius David 1919- *AmMWSc 92*
**Heldman**, Morris J 1914- *AmMWSc 92*
**Heldman**, Paul W. *WhoAmL 92*
**Heldreth**, Leonard Guy 1939- *IntAu&W 91, WhoMW 92*
**Heldt**, Lloyd A 1934- *AmMWSc 92*
**Heldt**, Marilyn Rae 1959- *WhoFI 92*
**Heldt**, Walter Z 1928- *AmMWSc 92*
**Hele**, Desmond George K. *Who 92*
**Hele**, Ivor 1912- *Who 92*
**Hele**, James Warwick 1926- *Who 92*

**Hele**, Priscilla 1920- AmMWSc 92
**Helen**, Nils Gunnar 1918- IntWW 91
**Helena** 250?-330? EncEarC
**Heleniak**, David William 1945- WhoAmL 92
**Heleringer**, Bob 1951- WhoAmP 91
**Helfand**, David John 1950- AmMWSc 92
**Helfand**, Eugene 1934- AmMWSc 92
**Helfand**, Leonard T. 1943- WhoAmL 92
**Helfand**, Margaret 1947- WhoFI 92
**Helfand**, William S. 1962- WhoAmL 92
**Helfer**, Erwin Albert 1936- WhoEnt 92
**Helfer**, Herman Lawrence 1929- AmMWSc 92
**Helfer**, Jeffrey Joseph 1943- WhoFI 92
**Helfert**, Erich Anton 1931- WhoWest 92
**Helfet**, Arthur 1907- IntWW 91
**Helfferich**, Friedrich G 1922- AmMWSc 92
**Helfgott**, Benjamin Wolf 1908- WhoRel 92
**Helfgott**, Cecil 1926- AmMWSc 92
**Helfgott**, Daniel 1952- WhoEnt 92
**Helfgott**, Michael WhoAmP 91
**Helfgott**, Roy B. 1925- WhoFI 92
**Helfinstine**, Kelly Ann 1957- WhoFI 92
**Helfman**, Bradley David 1961- WhoMW 92
**Helfman**, Elizabeth S 1911- IntAu&W 91, WrDr 92
**Helfman**, Howard N 1920- AmMWSc 92
**Helfond**, Wendy Worrall 1963- WhoWest 92
**Helford**, Paul Quinn 1947- WhoEnt 92, WhoWest 92
**Helforth**, John ConAu 35NR
**Helfrich**, Bernard D. WhoRel 92
**Helfrich**, Charles Thomas 1932- AmMWSc 92
**Helfrich**, Paul Michael 1955- WhoEnt 92
**Helfrich**, Peter Brigham 1957- WhoWest 92
**Helfrich**, Philip 1927- AmMWSc 92
**Helfrich**, Thomas E 1950- WhoIns 92
**Helfrich**, Wayne J 1933- AmMWSc 92
**Helfrick**, Edward W 1928- WhoAmP 91
**Helft**, Jorge Santiago 1934- IntWW 91
**Helgadottir**, Ragnhildur 1930- IntWW 91
**Helgason**, Dean Eugene 1940- WhoWest 92
**Helgason**, Hordur 1923- IntWW 91
**Helgason**, Ingi Ragnar 1924- IntWW 91
**Helgason**, Jon 1931- IntWW 91
**Helgason**, Sigurdur 1927- AmMWSc 92
**Helgason**, Sigurdur Bjorn 1913- AmMWSc 92
**Helgerson**, Henry M, Jr 1952- WhoAmP 91
**Helgerson**, Richard 1940- WhoWest 92
**Helgesen**, Robert Gordon 1942- AmMWSc 92
**Helgeson**, Duane Marcellus 1930- WhoWest 92
**Helgeson**, Harold Charles 1931- AmMWSc 92
**Helgeson**, James Daniel 1941- WhoFI 92, WhoWest 92
**Helgeson**, John Paul 1935- AmMWSc 92
**Helin**, Eleanor Kay AmMWSc 92
**Helin**, James Dennis 1942- WhoWest 92
**Helinski**, Donald Raymond 1933- AmMWSc 92, IntWW 91
**Helis**, Howard Morrell 1952- WhoMW 92
**Helitzer**, Jack Bernard 1933- WhoAmL 92
**Helke**, Cinda Jane 1951- AmMWSc 92
**Helke**, Fritz 1905-1967 EncTR 91
**Helker**, Keith Philip 1952- WhoMW 92
**Hell Cat Maggie** EncAmaz 91
**Hell**, Richard DrAPF 91
**Hellaby**, Alan 1926- Who 92
**Hellack**, Jenna Jo 1945- AmMWSc 92
**Hellam**, Robert Wayne 1947- WhoRel 92
**Helland**, George Archibald, Jr. 1937- WhoFI 92
**Helland**, Mark Duane 1949- WhoMW 92
**Helland**, Vivian 1921- WhoAmP 91
**Hellbaum**, Harold 1926- WhoAmP 91
**Hellberg**, Richard Alan 1951- WhoFI 92
**Helldorf**, Wolf Heinrich, Count von 1896-1944 EncTR 91 [port]
**Helldorfer**, Bernard George 1955- WhoAmL 92
**Helle**, John Harold 1935- AmMWSc 92
**Hellebust**, Johan Arnvid 1933- AmMWSc 92
**Helleiner**, Christopher Walter 1930- AmMWSc 92
**Hellems**, Harper Keith 1920- AmMWSc 92
**Hellen**, Mary Ardith 1952- WhoFI 92
**Hellenga**, Robert R. DrAPF 91
**Hellenthal**, Ronald Allen 1945- AmMWSc 92
**Hellenthal**, S. Ronald 1949- WhoWest 92
**Helleny**, Edward Joseph 1955- WhoEnt 92
**Heller**, Abraham 1917- AmMWSc 92
**Heller**, Adam 1933- AmMWSc 92
**Heller**, Agnes S AmMWSc 92
**Heller**, Alex 1925- AmMWSc 92
**Heller**, Alfred 1930- AmMWSc 92
**Heller**, Alfred 1931- WhoEnt 92
**Heller**, Barbara Ruth 1931- AmMWSc 92, WhoMW 92
**Heller**, Carol Ruth 1960- WhoEnt 92
**Heller**, Charles O 1936- AmMWSc 92
**Heller**, Dean WhoAmP 91
**Heller**, Donald Herbert 1943- WhoAmL 92
**Heller**, Douglas Max 1918- AmMWSc 92
**Heller**, Douglas Paul 1947- WhoAmL 92
**Heller**, Edward Lincoln 1912- AmMWSc 92
**Heller**, Edward Michael 1958- WhoFI 92
**Heller**, Edwin 1929- WhoAmL 92
**Heller**, Eric Johnson 1946- AmMWSc 92
**Heller**, Franklin IntMPA 92
**Heller**, Fred 1924- WhoFI 92
**Heller**, Gerald S 1920- AmMWSc 92
**Heller**, H Robert 1940- WhoAmP 91
**Heller**, Hanan Chonon 1930- AmMWSc 92
**Heller**, Heinz Robert 1940- WhoFI 92, WhoWest 92
**Heller**, Henry B 1941- WhoAmP 91
**Heller**, Hiram Daniel 1953- WhoMW 92
**Heller**, Horace Craig 1943- AmMWSc 92
**Heller**, Irving Henry 1926- AmMWSc 92
**Heller**, Jack 1922- AmMWSc 92
**Heller**, Jack Bernard 1919- WhoWest 92
**Heller**, James Stephen 1950- WhoAmL 92
**Heller**, Jan K 1951- WhoAmP 91
**Heller**, Janet Ruth DrAPF 91
**Heller**, John Herbert 1921- AmMWSc 92
**Heller**, John L., II 1953- WhoFI 92, WhoMW 92
**Heller**, John Philip 1923- AmMWSc 92
**Heller**, John Roderick 1905- AmMWSc 92
**Heller**, John Roderick, III 1937- WhoAmL 92
**Heller**, Jorge 1927- AmMWSc 92
**Heller**, Joseph DrAPF 91
**Heller**, Joseph 1923- BenetAL 91, ConNov 91, FacFETw, IntAu&W 91, IntWW 91, WrDr 92
**Heller**, Kenneth Jeffrey 1943- AmMWSc 92
**Heller**, Leon 1929- AmMWSc 92
**Heller**, Lois Jane 1942- AmMWSc 92, WhoMW 92
**Heller**, Mark 1914- WrDr 92
**Heller**, Mark 1955- WhoEnt 92
**Heller**, Marlene Ann 1953- IntAu&W 91
**Heller**, Marvin W 1926- AmMWSc 92
**Heller**, Max M 1919- WhoAmP 91
**Heller**, Melvin S 1922- AmMWSc 92
**Heller**, Meyer 1921- WhoRel 92
**Heller**, Michael DrAPF 91
**Heller**, Michael 1937- ConPo 91
**Heller**, Michael D. 1937- WrDr 92
**Heller**, Michael David 1937- IntAu&W 91
**Heller**, Milton David 1921- AmMWSc 92
**Heller**, Morgan Silliman 1925- AmMWSc 92
**Heller**, Norman Scott 1952- WhoAmL 92
**Heller**, Orlo DcTwDes
**Heller**, Paul 1914- AmMWSc 92
**Heller**, Paul 1927- ConTFT 9
**Heller**, Paul M. ConTFT 9
**Heller**, Paul M. 1927- IntMPA 92
**Heller**, Paul Michael 1927- WhoEnt 92
**Heller**, Paul R 1948- AmMWSc 92
**Heller**, Pauline Berman 1911- WhoAmL 92
**Heller**, Peter 1920- IntAu&W 91
**Heller**, Philip 1952- WhoAmL 92
**Heller**, Ralph 1914- AmMWSc 92
**Heller**, Randee 1947- WhoEnt 92
**Heller**, Robert 1899-1973 DcTwDes, FacFETw
**Heller**, Robert, Jr 1931- AmMWSc 92
**Heller**, Robert A 1928- AmMWSc 92
**Heller**, Robert Leo 1919- AmMWSc 92
**Heller**, Ronald Ian 1956- WhoAmL 92, WhoFI 92
**Heller**, Ruth M. 1924- SmATA 66 [port]
**Heller**, Stephen 1813-1888 NewAmDM
**Heller**, Stephen Richard 1943- AmMWSc 92
**Heller**, Steve F. DrAPF 91
**Heller**, Steven Nelson 1950- AmMWSc 92
**Heller**, Terry Lynn 1947- WhoMW 92
**Heller**, Theodore F 1942- WhoIns 92
**Heller**, Thomas C. 1944- WhoAmL 92
**Heller**, Walter W 1915-1987 FacFETw
**Heller**, Warren Herbert 1935- WhoAmL 92
**Heller**, Wendell Thurlo 1930- WhoRel 92
**Heller**, William Benjamin d1991 NewYTBS 91
**Heller**, William F., II WhoAmL 92
**Heller**, William Mohn 1926- AmMWSc 92
**Heller**, William R 1920- AmMWSc 92
**Heller**, Zachary I. WhoRel 92
**Heller**, Zindel Herbert 1927- AmMWSc 92
**Hellerman**, Fred 1927- WhoEnt 92
**Hellerman**, Herbert 1927- AmMWSc 92
**Hellermann**, William David 1939- WhoEnt 92
**Hellerstein**, Alvin Kenneth 1933- WhoAmL 92
**Hellerstein**, Herman Kopel 1916- AmMWSc 92
**Hellerstein**, Stanley 1926- AmMWSc 92
**Hellerstein**, Walter 1946- WhoAmL 92
**Hellesen**, Gunnar 1913- IntWW 91
**Hellew**, J.V. DrAPF 91
**Hellewell**, Gloria J 1951- WhoAmP 91
**Hellickson**, Kazuko Sato 1947- WhoWest 92
**Hellickson**, Martin Leon 1945- AmMWSc 92
**Hellickson**, Mylo A 1942- AmMWSc 92
**Hellie**, Richard 1937- ConAu 36NR, IntAu&W 91, WrDr 92
**Hellier**, Eric Jim 1927- Who 92
**Hellier**, Thomas Robert, Jr 1928- AmMWSc 92
**Hellige**, Gene Raymond 1951- WhoMW 92
**Helliker**, Adam Andrew Alexander 1958- IntAu&W 91
**Helliker**, Steven A. 1948- WhoEnt 92
**Helling**, Charles Siver 1940- AmMWSc 92
**Helling**, John Frederic 1933- AmMWSc 92
**Helling**, Robert Bruce 1936- AmMWSc 92
**Hellinga**, Lotte 1932- Who 92
**Hellinger**, Mark 1903-1947 BenetAL 91
**Hellings**, Brian Aliol 1936- WhoFI 92
**Hellings**, Peter William Cradock d1990 Who 92N
**Helliwell**, R A 1920- AmMWSc 92
**Helliwell**, Robert A. 1920- IntWW 91
**Helliwell**, Thomas McCaffree 1936- AmMWSc 92
**Hellman**, Alfred 1931- AmMWSc 92
**Hellman**, Barnet Richard 1956- WhoWest 92
**Hellman**, Frances 1956- AmMWSc 92
**Hellman**, Frederick Warren 1934- WhoFI 92, WhoWest 92
**Hellman**, Hal 1927- WrDr 92
**Hellman**, Henry Martin 1920- AmMWSc 92
**Hellman**, Herbert Martin 1943- WhoAmL 92, WhoFI 92
**Hellman**, Jerome 1928- IntMPA 92
**Hellman**, Kenneth P 1934- AmMWSc 92
**Hellman**, Lillian 1905-1984 BenetAL 91, DramC 1 [port], FacFETw [port], HanAmWH, ModAWWr, ReelWom
**Hellman**, Louis M 1908- AmMWSc 92
**Hellman**, Marcia Joan 1935- WhoMW 92
**Hellman**, Martin Edward 1945- AmMWSc 92
**Hellman**, Monte 1932- IntMPA 92, WhoEnt 92
**Hellman**, Nison Norman 1920- AmMWSc 92
**Hellman**, Samuel 1934- AmMWSc 92
**Hellman**, Sheila DrAPF 91
**Hellman**, Theodore Albert, Jr. 1946- WhoAmL 92
**Hellman**, Ursula Sylvia 1911- WhoRel 92
**Hellman**, William S 1931- AmMWSc 92
**Hellmann**, Max 1919- AmMWSc 92
**Hellmann**, Robert F WhoAmP 91
**Hellmer**, Brian Allen 1964- WhoFI 92
**Hellmers**, Henry 1915- AmMWSc 92
**Hellmold**, Ralph O. 1940- WhoFI 92
**Hellmuth**, C T 1926- WhoIns 92
**Hellmuth**, George Francis 1907- IntWW 91
**Hellmuth**, James Grant 1923- WhoFI 92
**Hellmuth**, James Grant 1925- WhoAmP 91
**Hellmuth**, Theodore Henning 1949- WhoAmL 92, WhoMW 92
**Hellmuth**, Walter Wilhelm 1938- AmMWSc 92
**Hellmuth**, William Frederick, Jr. 1920- WhoFI 92
**Hellring**, Bernard d1991 NewYTBS 91
**Hellrung**, Stephen Andrew 1947- WhoAmL 92
**Hellstrom**, Harold Richard 1928- AmMWSc 92
**Hellstrom**, Ingegerd Elisabet 1932- AmMWSc 92
**Hellstrom**, Karl Erik Lennart 1934- AmMWSc 92
**Hellstrom**, Mats 1942- IntWW 91
**Hellstrom**, Pamela Donworth 1948- WhoFI 92, WhoWest 92
**Hellstrom**, Ward 1930- IntAu&W 91, WrDr 92
**Hellums**, Jesse David 1929- AmMWSc 92
**Hellwarth**, Robert Willis 1930- AmMWSc 92
**Hellwege**, Herbert Elmore 1921- AmMWSc 92
**Hellwig**, Fritz 1912- IntWW 91
**Hellwig**, Helmut Wilhelm 1938- AmMWSc 92
**Hellwig**, L R 1928- AmMWSc 92
**Hellwig**, Monika Konrad 1929- WhoRel 92
**Helly**, Walter S 1930- AmMWSc 92
**Hellyer**, Arthur George Lee 1902- IntAu&W 91, Who 92, WrDr 92
**Hellyer**, Constance Anne 1937- WhoWest 92
**Hellyer**, Jill 1925- IntAu&W 91, WrDr 92
**Hellyer**, Paul T. 1923- WrDr 92
**Hellyer**, Paul Theodore 1923- IntWW 91, Who 92
**Hellyer**, Timothy Michael 1954- WhoMW 92
**Helm**, Donald Cairney 1937- AmMWSc 92
**Helm**, Gary Stewart 1956- WhoRel 92
**Helm**, George Neville, III 1954- WhoFI 92
**Helm**, Gladys Maxine 1941- WhoMW 92
**Helm**, Hugh Barnett 1914- WhoAmL 92
**Helm**, James Leroy 1932- AmMWSc 92
**Helm**, Joan Mary 1934- WhoFI 92
**Helm**, Joseph Burge 1931- WhoAmL 92
**Helm**, Lewis Marshall 1931- WhoAmP 91
**Helm**, Percy Ralph 1926- WhoMW 92
**Helm**, Raymond E 1930- AmMWSc 92
**Helm**, Richard H 1922- AmMWSc 92
**Helm**, Robert Albert 1921- AmMWSc 92
**Helm**, Robert G 1949- WhoAmP 91
**Helm**, Thomas Eugene 1943- WhoRel 92
**Helm**, Timothy J. 1957- WhoRel 92
**Helm**, Todd Norman 1962- WhoMW 92
**Helm**, William C. 1925- WhoBlA 92
**Helm**, William Thomas 1923- AmMWSc 92
**Helman**, Nathan W. 1907- WhoFI 92
**Helman**, Robert Alan 1934- WhoAmL 92
**Helman**, Sandy I 1939- AmMWSc 92
**Helman**, William Phillip 1936- AmMWSc 92
**Helmbold**, William Ross 1947- WhoAmL 92
**Helmbrecht**, Glen Vincent 1952- WhoFI 92
**Helmer**, David Alan 1946- WhoAmL 92, WhoAmP 91
**Helmer**, John 1926- AmMWSc 92
**Helmer**, LaVonne Jones 1928- WhoAmP 91
**Helmer**, Richard Guy 1934- AmMWSc 92
**Helmer**, Robert L 1930- WhoAmP 91
**Helmer**, Yaron 1955- WhoAmL 92
**Helmerich**, Peggy Varnadow 1928- WhoEnt 92
**Helmerick**, Robert Howard 1926- AmMWSc 92
**Helmers**, Donald Jacob 1917- AmMWSc 92
**Helmers**, Robert Glee 1952- WhoEnt 92
**Helmes**, Leslie Scott 1945- WhoMW 92
**Helmes**, Scott DrAPF 91
**Helmfrid**, Staffan 1927- IntWW 91
**Helmholdt**, Gerald R 1934- WhoAmP 91
**Helmholtz**, Hermann von 1821-1894 NewAmDM
**Helmholz**, August Carl 1915- AmMWSc 92
**Helmholz**, Richard Henry 1940- WhoAmL 92
**Helmick**, Aileen Barnett 1930- WhoMW 92
**Helmick**, Larry Scott 1941- AmMWSc 92
**Helmick**, Walter Dolph 1945- WhoAmP 91
**Helminen**, Jussi 1947- IntAu&W 91
**Helminger**, Paul Andrew 1941- AmMWSc 92
**Helminiak**, Daniel Albert 1942- WhoRel 92
**Helminiak**, Thaddeus Edmund 1935- AmMWSc 92
**Helmkamp**, George Kenneth 1921- AmMWSc 92
**Helmkamp**, George Merlin, Jr 1943- AmMWSc 92
**Helmke**, Kenneth Jon 1949- WhoMW 92
**Helmke**, Paul 1948- WhoAmP 91
**Helmker**, Judith A 1940- IntAu&W 91, WrDr 92
**Helmly**, Robert L 1927- WhoAmP 91
**Helmond**, Katherine 1934- IntMPA 92, WhoEnt 92
**Helmore**, Roy Lionel 1926- Who 92
**Helmreich**, Ernst Christian 1902- WrDr 92
**Helmreich**, Ernst J M 1922- AmMWSc 92, IntWW 91
**Helmrich**, Joel Marc 1953- WhoAmL 92
**Helms**, Boyce Dewayne 1937- AmMWSc 92
**Helms**, Carl Wilbert 1933- AmMWSc 92
**Helms**, David Alonzo 1934- WhoAmL 92, WhoBlA 92
**Helms**, J. Mark 1955- WhoRel 92
**Helms**, James Marvin, Jr 1927- WhoAmP 91
**Helms**, Jesse 1921- IntWW 91, WhoAmP 91
**Helms**, Jesse A. 1921- AlmAP 92 [port], AmPolLe
**Helms**, John Andrew 1931- AmMWSc 92
**Helms**, John F 1919- AmMWSc 92
**Helms**, Lester LaVerne 1927- AmMWSc 92

**Helms**, Ned James 1945- *WhoAmP 91*
**Helms**, Parks 1935- *WhoAmP 91*
**Helms**, Randel 1942- *IntAu&W 91, WrDr 92*
**Helms**, Richard Lynn 1946- *WhoMW 92*
**Helms**, Richard M. 1913- *IntWW 91*
**Helms**, Ruth Helms 1941- *WhoAmP 91*
**Helms**, Thomas Joseph 1939- *AmMWSc 92*
**Helms**, Ward Julian 1938- *AmMWSc 92*
**Helmsen**, Ralph John 1932- *AmMWSc 92*
**Helmsing**, Charles H. 1908- *Who 92*
**Helmsing**, Frederick George 1940- *WhoAmL 92*
**Helmstetter**, Charles E 1933- *AmMWSc 92*
**Helmsworth**, James Alexander 1915- *AmMWSc 92*
**Helmuth**, Hermann Siegfried 1939- *AmMWSc 92*
**Helmuth**, John William 1944- *WhoFI 92*
**Helmuth**, Ned D 1928- *WhoFI 92*
**Helmuth**, Ricky Jay 1949- *WhoAmL 92*
**Heloe**, Leif Arne 1932- *IntWW 91*
**Helou**, Charles 1911- *IntWW 91*
**Helpap**, John Frederick 1940- *WhoMW 92*
**Helper**, Hardie Hogan 1822-1899 *DcNCBi 3*
**Helper**, Hinton Rowan 1829-1909 *BenetAL 91, DcNCBi 3*
**Helphrey**, David Bryan 1944- *WhoFI 92*
**Helphrey**, Gloria Suzanne 1943- *WhoAmP 91*
**Helpmann**, Robert 1909-1986 *FacFETw*
**Helppie**, Charles Everett, III 1952- *WhoMW 92*
**Helprin**, Mark *NewYTBS 91 [port]*
**Helprin**, Mark 1947- *BenetAL 91, CurBio 91 [port], IntAu&W 91, WrDr 92*
**Helps**, Robert 1928- *NewAmDM*
**Helps**, Robert Eugene 1928- *WhoEnt 92*
**Helquist**, Paul M 1947- *AmMWSc 92*
**Helrich**, Carl Sanfrid, Jr 1941- *AmMWSc 92, WhoMW 92*
**Helrich**, Martin 1922- *AmMWSc 92*
**Hels**, Sharon Jean 1953- *WhoRel 92*
**Helsdon**, John H, Jr 1948- *AmMWSc 92*
**Helsel**, Larry Allen 1943- *WhoIns 92*
**Helsel**, Zane Roger 1949- *AmMWSc 92*
**Helser**, Daniel Corey 1962- *WhoEnt 92*
**Helseth**, Donald Lawrence, Jr 1953- *AmMWSc 92*
**Helsley**, Charles Everett 1934- *AmMWSc 92*
**Helsley**, Grover Cleveland 1926- *AmMWSc 92*
**Helsley**, Marvin Edward 1922- *WhoWest 92*
**Helsom**, Frank Elliott 1942- *WhoFI 92*
**Helson**, Henry 1927- *AmMWSc 92*
**Helson**, Lawrence 1931- *AmMWSc 92*
**Helson**, Ravenna 1925- *WomPsyc*
**Helstrom**, Carl Wilhelm 1925- *AmMWSc 92*
**Heltau**, Michael 1938- *IntWW 91*
**Heltemes**, Eugene Casmir 1934- *AmMWSc 92*
**Heltne**, Paul Gregory 1941- *AmMWSc 92, WhoMW 92*
**Helton**, Arthur Henry, Jr 1937- *WhoAmP 91*
**Helton**, Audus Winzle 1922- *AmMWSc 92*
**Helton**, Barbara Joanne 1952- *WhoMW 92*
**Helton**, F Joanne 1945- *AmMWSc 92*
**Helton**, James Carter 1927- *WhoAmP 91*
**Helton**, Jeffrey Albert 1956- *WhoFI 92*
**Helton**, Jerry William 1950- *WhoRel 92*
**Helton**, John W 1944- *AmMWSc 92*
**Helton**, Max Edward 1940- *WhoRel 92*
**Helton**, Richard Lance 1944- *WhoEnt 92*
**Helton**, Robert Bruce 1963- *WhoRel 92*
**Helton**, Sandra Lynn 1949- *WhoFI 92*
**Helton**, Thomas Joe 1944- *WhoMW 92*
**Helton**, Thomas Oswald 1940- *WhoAmL 92*
**Helton**, Walter Lee 1933- *AmMWSc 92*
**Helton**, William Stokely, Jr. 1943- *WhoMW 92*
**Helvenston**, Brantly Walker, III 1928- *WhoAmP 91*
**Helvetius**, Claude-Adrien 1715-1771 *BlkwCEP*
**Helvey**, Edward Douglas 1956- *WhoMW 92*
**Helvidius** *EncEarC*
**Helweg**, Otto Jennings 1936- *AmMWSc 92*
**Helwig**, David 1938- *ConNov 91, ConPo 91, IntAu&W 91, WrDr 92*
**Helwig**, Harold Lavern 1917- *AmMWSc 92*
**Helwig**, James A 1941- *AmMWSc 92*
**Helwig**, John, Jr 1927- *AmMWSc 92*
**Helwig**, Ted S. 1954- *WhoAmL 92*
**Hely**, Arthur Hubert McMath 1909- *Who 92*
**Hely**, James 1950- *WhoAmL 92*
**Hely-Hutchinson** *Who 92*
**Helyar**, Jane Penelope Josephine 1933- *IntAu&W 91*
**Helyer**, Larry Randall 1942- *WhoMW 92, WhoRel 92*
**Helz**, George Rudolph 1942- *AmMWSc 92*
**Helz**, Rosalind Tuthill 1944- *AmMWSc 92*
**Helzer**, Gerry A 1937- *AmMWSc 92*
**Helzer**, James Albert 1946- *WhoFI 92, WhoWest 92*
**Helzer**, James Dennis 1938- *WhoWest 92*
**Hem**, John David 1916- *AmMWSc 92, WhoWest 92*
**Hem**, Stanley L 1939- *AmMWSc 92*
**Hemami**, Hooshang 1936- *AmMWSc 92*
**Heman**, Bob *DrAPF 91*
**Heman-Ackah**, Samuel Monie 1926- *AmMWSc 92*
**Hemann**, Raymond Glenn 1933- *WhoFI 92, WhoWest 92*
**Hemans**, Felicia 1793-1835 *RfGEnL 91*
**Hemans**, Simon Nicholas Peter 1940- *Who 92*
**Hembree**, Carolyn Joan 1955- *WhoFI 92*
**Hembree**, George Hunt 1930- *AmMWSc 92*
**Hembrough**, Frederick B 1924- *AmMWSc 92*
**Hembry**, Foster Glen 1941- *AmMWSc 92*
**Hemby**, Dorothy Jean *WhoBlA 92*
**Hemby**, Dorothy Jean 1940- *WhoFI 92*
**Hemdal**, John Frederick 1934- *AmMWSc 92*
**Hemen**, Lee Howard 1953- *WhoRel 92*
**Hemenway**, Joan Elizabeth 1938- *WhoRel 92*
**Hemenway**, Mary-Kay Meacham 1943- *AmMWSc 92*
**Hemenway**, Russell Douglas 1925- *WhoAmP 91*
**Hemenway**, Stephen James 1955- *WhoEnt 92*
**Hemesath**, James B. *DrAPF 91*
**Hemily**, Philip Wright 1922- *AmMWSc 92*
**Heming**, Arthur Edward 1913- *AmMWSc 92*
**Heming**, Bruce Sword 1939- *AmMWSc 92*
**Hemingford**, Baron *Who 92*
**Heminghous**, William Wayne 1945- *WhoMW 92*
**Heminghous**, William Wayne, Sr 1945- *AmMWSc 92*
**Hemings**, Sally 1773-1836 *NotBlAW 92*
**Hemingway**, Albert 1902- *Who 92*
**Hemingway**, Alfred Henry, Jr. 1942- *WhoAmL 92*
**Hemingway**, Bruce Sherman 1939- *AmMWSc 92*
**Hemingway**, Ernest d1961 *SourALJ*
**Hemingway**, Ernest 1898-1961 *FacFETw*
**Hemingway**, Ernest 1899-1961 *BenetAL 91, ConAu 34NR, RComAH*
**Hemingway**, Ernest Miller 1899-1961 *LiExTwC, WhoNob 90*
**Hemingway**, George Thomson 1940- *AmMWSc 92*
**Hemingway**, Margaux 1955- *IntMPA 92*
**Hemingway**, Mariel 1961- *IntMPA 92, WhoEnt 92*
**Hemingway**, Peter 1926- *Who 92*
**Hemingway**, Richard William 1927- *WhoAmL 92*
**Hemingway**, William David 1947- *WhoFI 92*
**Heminway**, John Hylan, Jr. 1944- *WhoEnt 92, WrDr 92*
**Hemion**, Dwight *LesBEnT 92*
**Hemion**, Dwight Arlington 1926- *WhoEnt 92, WhoWest 92*
**Hemion**, Mac *LesBEnT 92*
**Hemken**, Roger Wayne 1928- *AmMWSc 92*
**Hemker**, Elizabeth Jean 1944- *WhoRel 92*
**Hemler**, John Vaughn, Jr 1929- *WhoAmP 91*
**Hemley**, Elaine G. *DrAPF 91*
**Hemley**, Eugene Adams 1918- *WhoFI 92*
**Hemley**, John Julian 1926- *AmMWSc 92*
**Hemley**, Robin *DrAPF 91*
**Hemlow**, Joyce 1906- *IntAu&W 91, Who 92, WrDr 92*
**Hemm**, Robert Virgil 1921- *AmMWSc 92*
**Hemmat**, Steven Amir *WhoAmL 92*
**Hemmendinger**, Arthur 1912- *AmMWSc 92*
**Hemmendinger**, Henry 1915- *AmMWSc 92*
**Hemmer**, Paul Edward 1944- *WhoEnt 92*
**Hemmerdinger**, H. Dale 1944- *WhoFI 92*
**Hemmerechts**, Kristien 1955- *ConAu 133*
**Hemmerle**, William J 1927- *AmMWSc 92*
**Hemmert**, Max L. 1945- *WhoWest 92*
**Hemmes**, Don E 1942- *AmMWSc 92*
**Hemmes**, Paul Richard 1944- *AmMWSc 92*
**Hemming**, Adrian 1945- *TwCPaSc*
**Hemming**, Idris George Selvin 1911- *Who 92*
**Hemming**, John Henry 1935- *IntAu&W 91, IntWW 91, Who 92, WrDr 92*
**Hemming**, Lindy 1948- *ConTFT 9*
**Hemminger**, Allen Edward 1933- *WhoMW 92*
**Hemminger**, John Charles 1949- *AmMWSc 92*
**Hemmings**, David 1938- *IntMPA 92*
**Hemmings**, David Leslie Edward 1941- *IntWW 91, Who 92, WhoEnt 92*
**Hemmings**, Fred, Jr 1946- *WhoAmP 91*
**Hemmings**, Peter William 1934- *WhoEnt 92, WhoWest 92*
**Hemmings**, Raymond Thomas 1948- *AmMWSc 92*
**Hemmings**, Terry Allen 1959- *WhoEnt 92*
**Hemmingsen**, Barbara Bruff 1941- *AmMWSc 92*
**Hemmingsen**, Edvard A 1932- *AmMWSc 92*
**Hemmingsen**, Erik 1917- *AmMWSc 92*
**Hemmingway**, Beulah S. 1943- *WhoBlA 92*
**Hemmy**, Mary Louise 1914- *WhoWest 92*
**Hemon**, Louis 1880-1913 *BenetAL 91*
**Hemond**, Conrad J, Jr 1916- *AmMWSc 92*
**Hemp**, Gene Willard 1938- *AmMWSc 92*
**Hemp**, Ralph C 1936- *WhoIns 92*
**Hemp**, William Spooner 1916- *Who 92*
**Hempe**, Cornelia Gordon 1942- *WhoMW 92*
**Hempeck**, Matthew Paul 1964- *WhoRel 92*
**Hempel**, Carl G 1905- *FacFETw*
**Hempel**, Eldon Robert 1932- *WhoRel 92*
**Hempel**, Franklin Glenn 1939- *AmMWSc 92*
**Hempel**, Frieda 1885-1955 *NewAmDM*
**Hempel**, Johannes 1929- *IntWW 91, WhoRel 92*
**Hempel**, John Paul 1935- *AmMWSc 92*
**Hempel**, Judith Cato 1941- *AmMWSc 92*
**Hempelmann**, L. Dean 1939- *WhoMW 92*
**Hemperly**, John Jacob 1951- *AmMWSc 92*
**Hempfling**, Gregory Jay 1961- *WhoFI 92*
**Hempfling**, Walter Pahl 1938- *AmMWSc 92*
**Hemphill**, Baron 1928- *Who 92*
**Hemphill**, Adley W 1925- *AmMWSc 92*
**Hemphill**, Alan Polk 1933- *WhoWest 92*
**Hemphill**, Andrea Renea 1967- *WhoWest 92*
**Hemphill**, Andrew Frederick 1927- *AmMWSc 92*
**Hemphill**, Barbara J. 1941- *WhoMW 92*
**Hemphill**, Darrell Lee 1913- *WhoAmP 91*
**Hemphill**, Delbert Dean 1918- *AmMWSc 92*
**Hemphill**, Frank 1943- *WhoBlA 92*
**Hemphill**, Garth Leonard 1966- *WhoEnt 92*
**Hemphill**, Gwendolyn 1941- *WhoBlA 92*
**Hemphill**, Henry 1830-1914 *BilnAmS*
**Hemphill**, Horace David 1933- *WhoWest 92*
**Hemphill**, Jo 1930- *WhoFI 92, WhoWest 92*
**Hemphill**, Kenneth S. 1948- *ConAu 134*
**Hemphill**, Louis 1927- *AmMWSc 92*
**Hemphill**, Miley Mae 1914- *WhoBlA 92*
**Hemphill**, Paul 1930- *WrDr 92*
**Hemphill**, Paul W. *WhoBlA 92*
**Hemphill**, William Alfred, III 1949- *WhoWest 92*
**Hempling**, Harold George 1926- *AmMWSc 92*
**Hempstead**, Charles Francis 1925- *AmMWSc 92*
**Hempstead**, George H., III 1943- *WhoAmL 92*
**Hempstead**, J C 1904- *AmMWSc 92*
**Hempstead**, Robert Douglas 1943- *AmMWSc 92*
**Hempstone**, Smith, Jr *WhoAmP 91*
**Hempton**, Paul 1946- *TwCPaSc*
**Hemry**, Larry Harold 1941- *WhoWest 92*
**Hemschemeyer**, Judith *DrAPF 91*
**Hemsing**, Josephine Claudia 1953- *WhoEnt 92*
**Hemsky**, Joseph William 1936- *AmMWSc 92*
**Hemsley**, Lawrence E. 1950- *WhoRel 92*
**Hemsley**, Sherman 1938- *IntMPA 92, WhoBlA 92, WhoEnt 92*
**Hemsley**, Thomas Jeffrey 1927- *Who 92*
**Hemsoll**, Eileen Mary 1924- *TwCPaSc*
**Hemstad**, Richard 1933- *WhoAmP 91*
**Hemsterhuys**, Francois 1721-1790 *BlkwCEP*
**Hemsworth**, Gerard 1945- *TwCPaSc*
**Hemsworth**, Martin C 1918- *AmMWSc 92*
**Hemwall**, Edwin Lyman *AmMWSc 92*
**Hen**, John 1941- *AmMWSc 92*
**Henager**, Charles Henry 1927- *WhoWest 92*
**Henahan**, Donal 1921- *WhoEnt 92*
**Henao**, Ravu 1927- *Who 92*
**Henard**, Elizabeth Ann 1947- *WhoFI 92*
**Henault**, Marie 1921- *WrDr 92*
**Henbest**, Harold Bernard *Who 92*
**Henbest**, Nigel 1951- *WrDr 92*
**Henbos** *ConAu 135*
**Hence**, Marie J. 1936- *WhoBlA 92*
**Hench**, David Le Roy 1941- *AmMWSc 92*
**Hench**, Larry Leroy 1938- *AmMWSc 92*
**Hench**, Miles Ellsworth 1919- *AmMWSc 92*
**Hench**, Philip Kahler 1930- *WhoWest 92*
**Hench**, Philip Showalter 1896-1965 *FacFETw, WhoNob 90*
**Henchman**, Michael J 1935- *AmMWSc 92*
**Henck**, John Benjamin 1815-1903 *BilnAmS*
**Hencke**, Paul Gerard 1927- *WhoEnt 92*
**Hendee**, John Clare 1938- *AmMWSc 92*
**Hendee**, William Richard 1938- *AmMWSc 92*
**Hendel**, Alfred Z 1916- *AmMWSc 92*
**Hendel**, Hans William 1922- *AmMWSc 92*
**Hendel**, Patricia Thall 1932- *WhoAmP 91*
**Hender**, John Derrik 1926- *Who 92*
**Henderek**, Michael Frank 1944- *WhoFI 92*
**Henderlong**, Paul Robert 1937- *AmMWSc 92*
**Hendershot**, Carl H. *WrDr 92*
**Hendershot**, William Fred 1930- *AmMWSc 92*
**Hendershott**, Charles Henry, Jr 1923- *AmMWSc 92*
**Hendershott Love**, Arles June 1956- *WhoEnt 92, WhoMW 92*
**Henderson** *Who 92*
**Henderson**, Alan 1925- *WhoAmP 91*
**Henderson**, Alan Charless 1946- *WhoFI 92*
**Henderson**, Albert John 1920- *WhoAmL 92*
**Henderson**, Alex 1924- *AmMWSc 92*
**Henderson**, Alfred James, Jr. 1943- *WhoMW 92*
**Henderson**, Alice Corbin 1881-1949 *BenetAL 91*
**Henderson**, Archibald 1768-1822 *DcNCBi 3*
**Henderson**, Archibald 1877-1963 *DcNCBi 3*
**Henderson**, Arn *DrAPF 91*
**Henderson**, Arnold Richard 1932- *AmMWSc 92*
**Henderson**, Arthur 1863-1935 *FacFETw, WhoNob 90*
**Henderson**, Australia Tarver 1942- *WhoBlA 92*
**Henderson**, B. Alex 1957- *WhoFI 92*
**Henderson**, Barbara Bynum 1880-1955 *DcNCBi 3*
**Henderson**, Barry *Who 92*
**Henderson**, Beauford Earl 1939- *AmMWSc 92*
**Henderson**, Bernard Levie, Jr 1950- *WhoAmP 91*
**Henderson**, Bernard Vere 1928- *Who 92*
**Henderson**, Bert Thomas 1949- *WhoAmP 91*
**Henderson**, Billy Joe 1937- *AmMWSc 92*
**Henderson**, Bradley Lawrence 1963- *WhoRel 92*
**Henderson**, Butler Thomas 1919-1990 *WhoBlA 92N*
**Henderson**, C. Nell 1959- *ConAu 135*
**Henderson**, Carl L., Jr. 1945- *WhoBlA 92*
**Henderson**, Carlota Nuanez 1933- *WhoHisp 92*
**Henderson**, Charles 1937- *WhoBlA 92*
**Henderson**, Charles B 1929- *AmMWSc 92*
**Henderson**, Charles Edward 1939- *Who 92*
**Henderson**, Charles Ira 1947- *WhoAmL 92*
**Henderson**, Charles Joseph 1924- *Who 92*
**Henderson**, Charles Linscott, Jr 1928- *WhoAmP 91*
**Henderson**, Charles R 1848-1915 *DcAmImH*
**Henderson**, Charles R 1911- *AmMWSc 92*
**Henderson**, Charles W. 1948- *ConAu 135*
**Henderson**, Clayton P 1954- *WhoAmP 91*
**Henderson**, Clayton Wilson 1936- *WhoEnt 92*
**Henderson**, Courtland M 1915- *AmMWSc 92*
**Henderson**, Crawford, Sr. 1931- *WhoBlA 92*
**Henderson**, D. Rudolph 1921- *WhoBlA 92*
**Henderson**, D W 1919- *AmMWSc 92*
**Henderson**, Dale Barlow 1941- *AmMWSc 92*
**Henderson**, Dan Fenno 1921- *WhoAmL 92, WrDr 92*
**Henderson**, Daniel 1880-1955 *BenetAL 91*
**Henderson**, Daniel McIntyre 1851-1906 *BenetAL 91*
**Henderson**, David *DrAPF 91, Who 92, WhoBlA 92, WrDr 92*
**Henderson**, David 1945- *WhoWest 92*
**Henderson**, David Andrew 1948- *AmMWSc 92*
**Henderson**, David Bremner 1840-1906 *AmPolLe*
**Henderson**, David Edward 1946- *AmMWSc 92*
**Henderson**, David Kroner 1951- *WhoFI 92*
**Henderson**, David Lee 1958- *WhoBlA 92*
**Henderson**, David Martin 1946- *WhoFI 92*

**Henderson**, David Michael 1940- *AmMWSc 92*
**Henderson**, David Richard 1950- *WhoFI 92*
**Henderson**, David Wilson 1939- *AmMWSc 92*
**Henderson**, Deirdre Healy 1942- *WhoMW 92*
**Henderson**, Dennis Roger 1939- *WhoMW 92*
**Henderson**, Denys 1932- *IntWW 91, Who 92*
**Henderson**, Derek 1935- *Who 92*
**Henderson**, Derek Scott 1929- *Who 92*
**Henderson**, Donald 1938- *AmMWSc 92*
**Henderson**, Donald Ainslie 1928- *AmMWSc 92, IntWW 91*
**Henderson**, Donald Blanton 1949- *WhoAmP 91*
**Henderson**, Donald Kirk 1961- *WhoRel 92*
**Henderson**, Donald Lee 1933- *AmMWSc 92*
**Henderson**, Donald Munro 1920- *AmMWSc 92*
**Henderson**, Donald Wayne 1951- *WhoWest 92*
**Henderson**, Douglas Bruce 1946- *WhoMW 92*
**Henderson**, Douglas J 1934- *AmMWSc 92*
**Henderson**, Douglas John 1949- *Who 92*
**Henderson**, Douglas Mackay 1927- *Who 92*
**Henderson**, Douglass Miles 1938- *AmMWSc 92*
**Henderson**, E. Hope *TwCPaSc*
**Henderson**, Earl Erwin 1946- *AmMWSc 92*
**Henderson**, Eddie L. 1932- *WhoBlA 92*
**Henderson**, Edward Chance 1916- *Who 92*
**Henderson**, Edward Firth 1917- *Who 92*
**Henderson**, Edward George 1935- *AmMWSc 92*
**Henderson**, Edward Hugh 1939- *WhoRel 92*
**Henderson**, Edward S 1932- *AmMWSc 92*
**Henderson**, Edwin 1883-1977 *FacFETw*
**Henderson**, Edwin Harold 1927- *WhoRel 92*
**Henderson**, Ellen Jane 1940- *AmMWSc 92*
**Henderson**, Elmer W. 1913- *WhoBlA 92*
**Henderson**, Elsie 1880-1967 *TwCPaSc*
**Henderson**, Erma 1917- *WhoAmP 91*
**Henderson**, Erma L. 1917- *WhoBlA 92*
**Henderson**, Eugene F 1920- *WhoAmP 91*
**Henderson**, Eugene Leroy 1925- *WhoAmL 92*
**Henderson**, Evelyn Berry 1927- *WhoRel 92*
**Henderson**, Ewen 1934- *TwCPaSc*
**Henderson**, F. M. 1921- *WrDr 92*
**Henderson**, Fletcher 1897-1952 *FacFETw, NewAmDM*
**Henderson**, Florence 1934- *WhoEnt 92*
**Henderson**, Floyd M 1946- *AmMWSc 92*
**Henderson**, Frank E 1928- *WhoAmP 91*
**Henderson**, Frank Ellis 1928- *WhoAmL 92, WhoMW 92*
**Henderson**, Frank S., Jr. 1958- *WhoBlA 92*
**Henderson**, Freddye Scarborough 1917- *WhoBlA 92*
**Henderson**, Frederick Bishop 1941- *WhoFI 92*
**Henderson**, Frederick Bradley, III 1935- *AmMWSc 92*
**Henderson**, Gary Borgar 1946- *AmMWSc 92*
**Henderson**, Gary Lee 1938- *AmMWSc 92*
**Henderson**, George 1932- *WhoBlA 92*
**Henderson**, George Asa 1940- *AmMWSc 92*
**Henderson**, George David Smith 1931- *Who 92*
**Henderson**, George Edwin 1906- *AmMWSc 92*
**Henderson**, George I 1943- *AmMWSc 92*
**Henderson**, George Kennedy Buchanan *Who 92*
**Henderson**, George Patrick 1915- *Who 92, WrDr 92*
**Henderson**, George Richard 1945- *AmMWSc 92*
**Henderson**, Gerald 1956- *WhoBlA 92*
**Henderson**, Gerald Eugene 1928- *WhoBlA 92*
**Henderson**, Gerald Gordon Lewis 1926- *AmMWSc 92*
**Henderson**, Gerald Vernon 1931- *AmMWSc 92*
**Henderson**, Giles Lee 1943- *AmMWSc 92*
**Henderson**, Glenn Vale, Jr. 1940- *WhoFI 92*
**Henderson**, Gordon Desmond 1930- *WhoAmL 92*
**Henderson**, Gray Stirling 1941- *AmMWSc 92*
**Henderson**, Greer F 1932- *WhoIns 92*
**Henderson**, H Thurman 1932- *AmMWSc 92*
**Henderson**, Hala Zawawi 1931- *AmMWSc 92*
**Henderson**, Hamish 1919- *ConPo 91, WrDr 92*
**Henderson**, Harold Douglas 1959- *WhoRel 92*
**Henderson**, Harold Richard, Jr. 1942- *WhoAmL 92*
**Henderson**, Henry Fairfax, Jr. 1928- *WhoBlA 92*
**Henderson**, Herbert Bernard 1911- *WhoWest 92*
**Henderson**, Herbert H. *WhoBlA 92*
**Henderson**, Horace Edward 1917- *IntWW 91*
**Henderson**, Hugh C. 1930- *WhoBlA 92*
**Henderson**, I. D., Jr. 1929- *WhoBlA 92*
**Henderson**, Ian Dalton 1918- *Who 92*
**Henderson**, Isabelle Bowen 1899-1969 *DcNCBi 3*
**Henderson**, Isaiah Hilkiah, Jr. *WhoBlA 92*
**Henderson**, Jacob R. 1911- *WhoBlA 92*
**Henderson**, James, Jr *WhoAmP 91*
**Henderson**, James A., Jr. 1938- *WhoAmL 92*
**Henderson**, James Alan 1934- *WhoFI 92, WhoMW 92*
**Henderson**, James B 1926- *AmMWSc 92*
**Henderson**, James Ewart 1923- *Who 92*
**Henderson**, James H. 1937- *WhoBlA 92*
**Henderson**, James H. M. 1917- *WhoBlA 92*
**Henderson**, James Harold 1948- *WhoFI 92, WhoMW 92*
**Henderson**, James Henry, Sr. 1925- *WhoBlA 92*
**Henderson**, James Henry Meriwether 1917- *AmMWSc 92*
**Henderson**, James J., Sr. 1908- *WhoBlA 92*
**Henderson**, James Jackson, Jr. *WhoEnt 92*
**Henderson**, James Maddock *TwCWW 91*
**Henderson**, James Matthew, Sr. 1958- *WhoAmL 92*
**Henderson**, James Monroe 1921- *AmMWSc 92*
**Henderson**, James Pinckney 1809-1858 *DcNCBi 3*
**Henderson**, James R. 1919- *WhoBlA 92*
**Henderson**, James Robert *WhoBlA 92*
**Henderson**, James Stewart Barry 1936- *Who 92*
**Henderson**, James Stuart 1928- *AmMWSc 92*
**Henderson**, James Thyne 1901- *Who 92*
**Henderson**, Janet Lee 1957- *WhoFI 92*
**Henderson**, Joan *Who 92*
**Henderson**, Joel Andrew 1953- *WhoAmL 92*
**Henderson**, John 1943- *TwCPaSc*
**Henderson**, John A. 1946- *WhoRel 92*
**Henderson**, John Frederick 1933- *AmMWSc 92*
**Henderson**, John L. 1932- *WhoBlA 92*
**Henderson**, John Nicholas 1919- *IntWW 91, Who 92*
**Henderson**, John Ronald 1920- *Who 92*
**Henderson**, John Steele 1846-1916 *DcNCBi 3*
**Henderson**, John Stuart Wilmot 1919- *Who 92*
**Henderson**, John Tamblyn, Jr. 1939- *WhoEnt 92*
**Henderson**, John Warren 1912- *AmMWSc 92*
**Henderson**, John Woodworth 1916- *AmMWSc 92*
**Henderson**, Jon Loren 1951- *WhoFI 92*
**Henderson**, Joyce Ann 1947- *WhoBlA 92*
**Henderson**, Julia 1915- *IntWW 91*
**Henderson**, Julie Kay 1950- *WhoMW 92*
**Henderson**, Karen LeCraft *WhoAmP 91*
**Henderson**, Karen LeCraft 1944- *WhoAmL 92*
**Henderson**, Keith Pernell 1966- *WhoBlA 92*
**Henderson**, Kenneth Atwood 1905- *WhoFI 92*
**Henderson**, Kevin 1963- *TwCPaSc*
**Henderson**, Larry Ray 1950- *WhoFI 92*
**Henderson**, Larry W. 1954- *WhoBlA 92*
**Henderson**, Laurence 1928- *IntAu&W 91*
**Henderson**, Lavell Merl 1917- *AmMWSc 92, WhoWest 92*
**Henderson**, Lawrence J 1952- *AmMWSc 92*
**Henderson**, LeMon *WhoBlA 92*
**Henderson**, Lenneal Joseph, Jr. 1946- *WhoBlA 92*
**Henderson**, Leon 1895-1986 *AmPolLe*
**Henderson**, Leonard 1772-1833 *DcNCBi 3*
**Henderson**, Leroy W., Jr. 1936- *WhoBlA 92*
**Henderson**, Leslie Edwin 1922- *Who 92*
**Henderson**, Linda Shlatz 1946- *AmMWSc 92*
**Henderson**, Lloyd D. 1945- *WhoBlA 92*
**Henderson**, Lon 1958- *WhoWest 92*
**Henderson**, Louis E 1934- *AmMWSc 92*
**Henderson**, Madeleine 1938- *TwCPaSc*
**Henderson**, Madeline M Berry 1922- *AmMWSc 92*
**Henderson**, Marilyn Ann 1949- *WhoFI 92*
**Henderson**, Martha Louise 1952- *WhoMW 92*
**Henderson**, Mary Ferrand 1887-1965 *DcNCBi 3*
**Henderson**, Maureen McGrath 1926- *AmMWSc 92*
**Henderson**, Maurice Brian 1961- *IntAu&W 91*
**Henderson**, Merlin Theodore 1914- *AmMWSc 92*
**Henderson**, Michael Dean 1961- *WhoMW 92*
**Henderson**, Michael John Glidden 1938- *Who 92*
**Henderson**, Michael L. 1957- *WhoRel 92*
**Henderson**, Moses, Jr. 1941- *WhoWest 92*
**Henderson**, Nannette S. 1946- *WhoBlA 92*
**Henderson**, Nannette Smith 1946- *AmMWSc 92*
**Henderson**, Nathan H. *WhoRel 92*
**Henderson**, Nicholas *IntWW 91, Who 92*
**Henderson**, Nigel Stuart 1909- *Who 92*
**Henderson**, Norman Leo 1932- *AmMWSc 92*
**Henderson**, Patricia McGovern 1940- *WhoWest 92*
**Henderson**, Patrick David 1927- *IntWW 91, Who 92, WrDr 92*
**Henderson**, Patrick Moran 1946- *WhoAmP 91*
**Henderson**, Paul 1940- *Who 92*
**Henderson**, Philip George 1936- *WhoMW 92*
**Henderson**, Philo P. 1823-1852 *DcNCBi 3*
**Henderson**, Pleasant 1756-1840 *DcNCBi 3*
**Henderson**, Ralph Joseph, Jr 1940- *AmMWSc 92*
**Henderson**, Ramona Estelle 1952- *WhoBlA 92*
**Henderson**, Ray 1896-1970 *NewAmDM*
**Henderson**, Remond 1952- *WhoBlA 92*
**Henderson**, Richard 1735-1785 *DcNCBi 3*
**Henderson**, Richard 1924- *IntAu&W 91, WrDr 92*
**Henderson**, Richard 1928- *WhoAmP 91*
**Henderson**, Richard 1945- *IntWW 91, Who 92*
**Henderson**, Richard Elliott Lee 1945- *AmMWSc 92*
**Henderson**, Richard Wayne *AmMWSc 92*
**Henderson**, Richard Yates 1931- *Who 92*
**Henderson**, Rickey Henley 1958- *WhoBlA 92, WhoWest 92*
**Henderson**, Robb Alan 1956- *WhoRel 92*
**Henderson**, Robbye R. 1937- *WhoBlA 92*
**Henderson**, Robert Alistair 1917- *IntWW 91, Who 92*
**Henderson**, Robert Brumwell 1929- *Who 92*
**Henderson**, Robert Burr 1919- *AmMWSc 92*
**Henderson**, Robert E 1935- *AmMWSc 92*
**Henderson**, Robert Edward 1925- *AmMWSc 92*
**Henderson**, Robert Ewart 1937- *Who 92*
**Henderson**, Robert G 1918- *WhoAmP 91*
**Henderson**, Robert Vann, Sr. 1925- *WhoFI 92*
**Henderson**, Robert Waugh 1920- *WhoRel 92*
**Henderson**, Robert Wesley 1914- *AmMWSc 92*
**Henderson**, Rogene Faulkner 1933- *AmMWSc 92*
**Henderson**, Roger Anthony 1943- *Who 92*
**Henderson**, Romeo Clanton 1915- *WhoBlA 92*
**Henderson**, Rosemary 1936- *WhoMW 92*
**Henderson**, Roy 1899- *Who 92*
**Henderson**, Salathiel James 1944- *WhoRel 92*
**Henderson**, Sammy Wayne 1957- *WhoWest 92*
**Henderson**, Samuel 1746-1816 *DcNCBi 3*
**Henderson**, Schuyler Kent 1945- *WhoAmL 92*
**Henderson**, Sheri Dawn 1953- *AmMWSc 92*
**Henderson**, Skitch 1918- *IntMPA 92, NewAmDM, WhoEnt 92*
**Henderson**, Stanley Dale 1935- *WhoAmL 92*
**Henderson**, Stanley L. 1909- *WhoBlA 92*
**Henderson**, Stephen Douglas 1942- *WhoMW 92*
**Henderson**, Stephen E. 1925- *WhoBlA 92*
**Henderson**, Stephen John 1947- *WhoAmL 92*
**Henderson**, Stephen Paul 1949- *WhoAmL 92*
**Henderson**, Steven Lee 1948- *WhoWest 92*
**Henderson**, Surena Bissette 1935- *WhoAmP 91*
**Henderson**, Thelton Eugene 1933- *WhoAmL 92, WhoBlA 92*
**Henderson**, Thomas 1752-1821 *DcNCBi 3*
**Henderson**, Thomas, Jr. 1787-1835 *DcNCBi 3*
**Henderson**, Thomas Dean 1959- *WhoWest 92*
**Henderson**, Thomas E 1934- *AmMWSc 92*
**Henderson**, Thomas Edward 1952- *BlkOlyM*
**Henderson**, Thomas James 1931- *WhoWest 92*
**Henderson**, Thomas Otis 1937- *AmMWSc 92*
**Henderson**, Thomas Ranney 1941- *AmMWSc 92*
**Henderson**, Thomas Richard 1932- *AmMWSc 92*
**Henderson**, Tony Curtis 1955- *WhoMW 92, WhoRel 92*
**Henderson**, Ulysses Virgil, Jr 1926- *AmMWSc 92*
**Henderson**, Verne Eugene 1929- *WhoRel 92*
**Henderson**, Veryl Floyd 1943- *WhoRel 92*
**Henderson**, Victor Warren 1951- *WhoWest 92*
**Henderson**, Virginia Ruth McKinney 1932- *WhoBlA 92*
**Henderson**, W Lecil, II 1958- *WhoAmP 91*
**Henderson**, W Loy 1892-1986 *FacFETw*
**Henderson**, Walter J *WhoAmP 91*
**Henderson**, Warren Robert 1927- *AmMWSc 92*
**Henderson**, Wilburn Allen 1953- *WhoRel 92*
**Henderson**, William 1913- *Who 92*
**Henderson**, William 1941- *TwCPaSc*
**Henderson**, William Arthur, Jr 1932- *AmMWSc 92*
**Henderson**, William B. *DcNCBi 3*
**Henderson**, William C. *DrAPF 91*
**Henderson**, William C., II 1941- *WhoBlA 92*
**Henderson**, William Crichton 1931- *Who 92*
**Henderson**, William J. 1925- *WhoMW 92*
**Henderson**, William L. 1927- *WrDr 92*
**Henderson**, William MacGregor 1913- *IntWW 91*
**Henderson**, William Otto 1904- *WrDr 92*
**Henderson**, William Ross 1936- *Who 92*
**Henderson**, Zenna 1917-1983 *ConAu 133, TwCSFW 91*
**Henderson-Holmes**, Safiya *DrAPF 91*
**Henderson-Howat**, Gerald *WrDr 92*
**Henderson-Hudson**, Brenda Dianne 1964- *WhoEnt 92*
**Henderson-Mowat**, Gerald *IntAu&W 91X*
**Henderson-Nocho**, Audrey J. 1959- *WhoBlA 92*
**Henderson of Brompton**, Baron 1922- *Who 92*
**Henderson Smith**, Stephen Lane 1919- *WrDr 92*
**Henderson-Stewart**, David 1941- *Who 92*
**Hendl**, Walter 1917- *NewAmDM, WhoEnt 92*
**Hendler**, Edwin 1922- *AmMWSc 92*
**Hendler**, Ernesto Danilo 1935- *AmMWSc 92*
**Hendler**, Gordon Lee 1946- *AmMWSc 92*
**Hendler**, Nelson Howard 1944- *AmMWSc 92*
**Hendler**, Richard Wallace 1927- *AmMWSc 92*
**Hendley**, Dan Lunsford 1938- *WhoFI 92*
**Hendley**, Edith Di Pasquale 1927- *AmMWSc 92*
**Hendley**, Joseph Owen 1937- *AmMWSc 92*
**Hendlin**, David 1920- *AmMWSc 92*
**Hendon**, Donald W *IntAu&W 91*
**Hendon**, Joseph C 1938- *AmMWSc 92*
**Hendon**, Lea Alpha 1953- *WhoBlA 92*
**Hendon**, Rickey *WhoAmP 91*
**Hendon**, William S 1933- *ConAu 35NR*
**Hendrawan**, Frans 1936- *WhoFI 92*
**Hendren**, Gary E. 1943- *WhoFI 92*
**Hendren**, Richard Wayne 1948- *AmMWSc 92*
**Hendren**, Robert Lee 1930- *WhoRel 92*
**Hendren**, Robert Lee, Jr. 1925- *WhoWest 92*
**Hendren**, William Mayhew 1871-1939 *DcNCBi 3*
**Hendrey**, George Rummens 1940- *AmMWSc 92*
**Hendrich**, Chester Eugene 1935- *AmMWSc 92*
**Hendrick**, Brice *WhoRel 92*
**Hendrick**, Howard Hamlin 1954- *WhoAmP 91*
**Hendrick**, John Kerr 1847-1921 *DcNCBi 3*
**Hendrick**, Keith Coleman 1926- *WhoFI 92*
**Hendrick**, Larry Eugene, Jr. 1957- *WhoRel 92*
**Hendrick**, Lynn Denson 1937- *AmMWSc 92*
**Hendrick**, Michael Ezell 1945- *AmMWSc 92*

**Hendrick,** Ronald Lynn 1946- *WhoWest 92*
**Hendricker,** David George 1938- *AmMWSc 92*
**Hendricks,** Albert Cates 1937- *AmMWSc 92*
**Hendricks,** Arthur Donald 1947- *WhoMW 92*
**Hendricks,** B L, Jr 1918- *WhoAmP 91*
**Hendricks,** Barbara 1948- *IntWW 91, WhoBlA 92*
**Hendricks,** Barkley L. 1945- *WhoBlA 92*
**Hendricks,** Beatrice E. *WhoBlA 92*
**Hendricks,** Bill L. *IntMPA 92*
**Hendricks,** Bob 1925- *WhoAmL 92*
**Hendricks,** Charles D, Jr 1926- *AmMWSc 92*
**Hendricks,** Charles Henning 1917- *AmMWSc 92*
**Hendricks,** Clare Joseph 1938- *WhoRel 92*
**Hendricks,** David Warren 1931- *AmMWSc 92*
**Hendricks,** Deloy G 1938- *AmMWSc 92*
**Hendricks,** Donovan Edward 1940- *AmMWSc 92*
**Hendricks,** Edward David 1946- *WhoFI 92*
**Hendricks,** Elrod Jerome 1940- *WhoBlA 92*
**Hendricks,** Evan Daniel 1955- *WhoEnt 92*
**Hendricks,** Fanny-Dell 1939- *WhoWest 92*
**Hendricks,** Geoffrey *DrAPF 91*
**Hendricks,** George David, Sr 1913- *IntAu&W 91, WrDr 92*
**Hendricks,** George Lorimer, Jr. 1945- *WhoMW 92*
**Hendricks,** Grant Walstein 1916- *AmMWSc 92*
**Hendricks,** J Edwin 1935- *ConAu 34NR*
**Hendricks,** James Earnest 1944- *WhoMW 92*
**Hendricks,** James Owen 1909- *AmMWSc 92*
**Hendricks,** James Patrick 1939- *WhoEnt 92*
**Hendricks,** James Richard 1920- *AmMWSc 92*
**Hendricks,** James Vance 1936- *WhoWest 92*
**Hendricks,** James W. 1924- *WhoAmL 92*
**Hendricks,** Jerry Dean 1944- *AmMWSc 92*
**Hendricks,** John *LesBEnT 92*
**Hendricks,** Jon 1912- *NewAmDM*
**Hendricks,** Jon 1921- *WhoBlA 92*
**Hendricks,** Juanita 1935- *WhoBlA 92*
**Hendricks,** Kathleen 1939- *IntAu&W 91*
**Hendricks,** Larry 1936- *WhoAmP 91*
**Hendricks,** Lawrence Joseph 1919- *AmMWSc 92*
**Hendricks,** Leta 1954- *WhoBlA 92*
**Hendricks,** Lewis T 1940- *AmMWSc 92*
**Hendricks,** Lewis Talbot 1940- *WhoMW 92*
**Hendricks,** Lloyd I *WhoAmP 91*
**Hendricks,** Malvin Leon, Sr 1921- *WhoAmP 91*
**Hendricks,** Mark Kenneth 1952- *WhoEnt 92*
**Hendricks,** Marvin B. 1951- *WhoBlA 92*
**Hendricks,** Randal Arlan 1945- *WhoAmL 92*
**Hendricks,** Richard D. 1937- *WhoBlA 92*
**Hendricks,** Robert Michael 1943- *WhoFI 92, WhoIns 92*
**Hendricks,** Robert Wayne 1937- *AmMWSc 92*
**Hendricks,** Robert William 1929- *AmMWSc 92*
**Hendricks,** Stanley Marshall, II 1952- *WhoFI 92*
**Hendricks,** Steven Aaron 1960- *WhoBlA 92*
**Hendricks,** Terence Eugene 1952- *WhoRel 92*
**Hendricks,** Thomas Andrews 1819-1885 *AmPolLe*
**Hendricks,** Thomas Lee, II 1956- *WhoRel 92*
**Hendricks,** Walter James 1935- *AmMWSc 92*
**Hendricks,** William Lawrence 1929- *WhoRel 92*
**Hendricks,** William Leon, Jr. 1959- *WhoAmL 92*
**Hendricks,** William Nels 1949- *WhoFI 92, WhoMW 92*
**Hendricks-Verdejo,** Carlos Doel, Sr. 1959- *WhoHisp 92*
**Hendrickse,** Helenard Joe 1927- *IntWW 91*
**Hendrickse,** Ralph George 1926- *IntWW 91, Who 92*
**Hendrickson,** Adolph C 1927- *AmMWSc 92*
**Hendrickson,** Alfred A 1929- *AmMWSc 92*
**Hendrickson,** Anita Elizabeth 1936- *AmMWSc 92*
**Hendrickson,** Bruce C 1930- *WhoIns 92*
**Hendrickson,** Chris Thompson 1950- *AmMWSc 92, WhoFI 92*
**Hendrickson,** Constance McRight 1949- *AmMWSc 92*
**Hendrickson,** David Burton 1937- *WhoAmL 92*
**Hendrickson,** David Norman 1943- *AmMWSc 92*
**Hendrickson,** Donald Allen 1942- *AmMWSc 92*
**Hendrickson,** Elizabeth Ann 1936- *WhoWest 92*
**Hendrickson,** Frank R 1926- *AmMWSc 92*
**Hendrickson,** G. Paul 1950- *WhoFI 92*
**Hendrickson,** Herbert T 1940- *AmMWSc 92*
**Hendrickson,** Herman Stewart, II 1937- *AmMWSc 92*
**Hendrickson,** James Briggs 1928- *AmMWSc 92*
**Hendrickson,** James E 1932- *IntAu&W 91*
**Hendrickson,** Jerome Orland 1918- *WhoFI 92*
**Hendrickson,** John Alfred, Jr 1941- *AmMWSc 92*
**Hendrickson,** John Robert 1944- *AmMWSc 92*
**Hendrickson,** John Roscoe 1921- *AmMWSc 92*
**Hendrickson,** John T, Jr *WhoAmP 91*
**Hendrickson,** Kenneth Elton, Jr. 1936- *WhoWest 92*
**Hendrickson,** Kevin Hugh 1953- *WhoAmL 92*
**Hendrickson,** Lester Ellsworth 1941- *AmMWSc 92*
**Hendrickson,** Mary Rachel 1957- *WhoEnt 92*
**Hendrickson,** Mona Lynn 1951- *WhoFI 92*
**Hendrickson,** Neal B 1949- *WhoAmP 91*
**Hendrickson,** Olaf Knute 1961- *WhoFI 92*
**Hendrickson,** Richard A 1933- *AmMWSc 92*
**Hendrickson,** Richard Eugene 1957- *WhoAmL 92*
**Hendrickson,** Robert A. 1923- *WrDr 92*
**Hendrickson,** Robert Augustus 1923- *WhoAmL 92*
**Hendrickson,** Robert Frederick 1933- *WhoFI 92*
**Hendrickson,** Robert Mark, Jr 1938- *AmMWSc 92*
**Hendrickson,** Steven Dale 1953- *WhoEnt 92*
**Hendrickson,** Thomas Atherton 1927- *WhoAmL 92, WhoMW 92*
**Hendrickson,** Thomas James 1926- *AmMWSc 92*
**Hendrickson,** Tom A 1935- *AmMWSc 92*
**Hendrickson,** Tom Allen 1935- *WhoFI 92*
**Hendrickson,** W F 1876?-1902 *BiInAmS*
**Hendrickson,** Waldemar Forrsel 1934- *AmMWSc 92*
**Hendrickson,** Wayne Arthur 1941- *AmMWSc 92*
**Hendrickson,** Willard James 1916- *AmMWSc 92*
**Hendrickson,** William George 1918- *WhoFI 92*
**Hendrickson,** William Richard 1948- *WhoEnt 92*
**Hendrickson,** William Woodbury 1844-1920 *BiInAmS*
**Hendrickson,** Yngve Gust 1927- *AmMWSc 92*
**Hendrickx,** Andrew George 1933- *AmMWSc 92*
**Hendrickx,** Leonard Henry 1953- *WhoWest 92*
**Hendrie,** David Lowery 1932- *AmMWSc 92*
**Hendrie,** Don, Jr. *DrAPF 91*
**Hendrie,** Gerald Mills 1935- *Who 92*
**Hendrie,** Joseph Mallam 1925- *AmMWSc 92, WhoAmP 91*
**Hendrieth,** Brenda Lucille 1955- *WhoBlA 92*
**Hendriks,** A. L. 1922- *ConPo 91, IntAu&W 91, WrDr 92*
**Hendriks,** Herbert Edward 1918- *AmMWSc 92*
**Hendriksen,** Hans d1989 *IntWW 91N*
**Hendrix,** B G 1922- *WhoAmP 91*
**Hendrix,** C E 1924- *AmMWSc 92*
**Hendrix,** Daniel W. 1922- *WhoBlA 92*
**Hendrix,** Deborah Lynne 1961- *WhoBlA 92*
**Hendrix,** Donald Louis 1942- *AmMWSc 92*
**Hendrix,** Eugene Russell 1847-1927 *RelLAm 91*
**Hendrix,** Floyd Fuller, Jr 1933- *AmMWSc 92*
**Hendrix,** James 1920- *WhoEnt 92*
**Hendrix,** James Easton 1941- *AmMWSc 92*
**Hendrix,** James Harvey, Jr 1920- *AmMWSc 92*
**Hendrix,** James Lauris 1943- *AmMWSc 92*
**Hendrix,** James Lee 1961- *WhoMW 92*
**Hendrix,** James Walter, Jr. 1958- *WhoFI 92*
**Hendrix,** James William 1937- *AmMWSc 92*
**Hendrix,** Jimi 1942-1970 *FacFETw [port], NewAmDM*
**Hendrix,** John Edwin 1930- *AmMWSc 92*
**Hendrix,** John Walter 1915- *AmMWSc 92*
**Hendrix,** Lance Allen 1963- *WhoEnt 92*
**Hendrix,** Louise Butts 1911- *WhoWest 92*
**Hendrix,** Lynn Parker 1951- *WhoAmL 92*
**Hendrix,** Martha Raye 1939- *WhoBlA 92*
**Hendrix,** Mary J C 1953- *AmMWSc 92*
**Hendrix,** Roger Walden 1943- *AmMWSc 92*
**Hendrix,** Ronald Wayne 1943- *WhoMW 92*
**Hendrix,** Sherman Samuel 1939- *AmMWSc 92*
**Hendrix,** Stephen C. 1941- *WhoFI 92*
**Hendrix,** Stephen Joseph 1956- *WhoEnt 92*
**Hendrix,** Thomas Eugene 1933- *AmMWSc 92*
**Hendrix,** Thomas Russell 1920- *AmMWSc 92*
**Hendrix,** Walker A 1949- *WhoAmP 91*
**Hendrix,** Walter Newton, Jr. 1955- *WhoRel 92*
**Hendrix,** William George 1951- *WhoFI 92*
**Hendron,** Alfred J, Jr 1937- *AmMWSc 92*
**Hendry,** Andrew D. *WhoAmL 92*
**Hendry,** Anne Teresa 1936- *AmMWSc 92*
**Hendry,** Archibald Wagstaff 1936- *AmMWSc 92, WhoMW 92*
**Hendry,** Arnold William 1921- *Who 92*
**Hendry,** David Forbes 1944- *Who 92*
**Hendry,** Diana 1941- *SmATA 68 [port]*
**Hendry,** George Orr 1937- *AmMWSc 92*
**Hendry,** Gloria *WhoBlA 92*
**Hendry,** Hugh Edward 1944- *AmMWSc 92*
**Hendry,** James E. 1912- *WhoFI 92*
**Hendry,** Joy 1953- *ConAu 133*
**Hendry,** Joy McLaggan 1953- *IntAu&W 91*
**Hendry,** Linda May 1957- *WhoWest 92*
**Hendry,** Richard Allan 1929- *AmMWSc 92*
**Hendry,** Robert Ryon 1936- *WhoAmL 92*
**Hendry,** Samuel Aldridge, Jr. 1948- *WhoRel 92*
**Hendry,** Thomas 1929- *IntAu&W 91, WrDr 92*
**Hendryx,** James B 1880-1963 *TwCWW 91*
**Hendryx,** Michael Shawn 1960- *WhoMW 92*
**Hendy,** John Giles 1948- *Who 92*
**Henebry,** Michael Stevens 1946- *WhoMW 92*
**Henegan,** John Clark 1950- *WhoAmL 92*
**Henegar,** Dale L *WhoAmP 91*
**Heneghan,** James Beyer 1935- *AmMWSc 92*
**Henein,** Naeim A *AmMWSc 92*
**Henery,** Daniel M. 1947- *WhoMW 92*
**Henery,** James Daniel 1940- *AmMWSc 92*
**Henery-Logan,** Kenneth Robert 1921- *AmMWSc 92*
**Henes,** Donna *DrAPF 91*
**Henes,** Donna 1945- *WhoEnt 92*
**Henes,** John Derek 1937- *Who 92*
**Heney,** Joseph Edward 1927- *WhoFI 92*
**Heney,** Lysle Joseph, Jr 1923- *AmMWSc 92*
**Heng Samrin** 1934- *IntWW 91*
**Heng,** Donald James, Jr. 1944- *WhoAmL 92*
**Heng,** Gerald C-W 1941- *WhoAmL 92*
**Heng,** Samrin 1934- *FacFETw*
**Heng,** Stanley Mark 1937- *WhoMW 92*
**Hengehold,** Robert Leo 1936- *AmMWSc 92*
**Hengel,** Martin 1926- *WhoRel 92*
**Hengesbaugh,** Bernard L 1946- *WhoIns 92*
**Hengesh,** Donald James 1944- *WhoMW 92*
**Hengsbach,** Franz 1910- *IntWW 91*
**Hengstler,** Gary Ardell 1947- *WhoAmL 92*
**Henham,** John Alfred 1924- *Who 92*
**Henican,** Caswell Ellis 1905- *WhoAmL 92*
**Henick,** Alfred 1925- *WhoFI 92*
**Henie,** Sonja 1912-1969 *FacFETw*
**Henig,** John Alec, Jr. 1949- *WhoAmL 92*
**Henig,** Stanley 1939- *Who 92*
**Henika,** Richard Grant 1921- *AmMWSc 92*
**Henikoff,** Leo M., Jr. 1939- *WhoMW 92*
**Heningburg,** Gustav 1930- *WhoBlA 92*
**Heninger,** George Robert 1934- *AmMWSc 92*
**Heninger,** Kurt Allen 1950- *WhoMW 92*
**Heninger,** Richard Wilford 1931- *AmMWSc 92*
**Heninger,** Ronald Lee 1944- *AmMWSc 92*
**Henins,** Ivars 1933- *AmMWSc 92*
**Henion,** Kristine Rose 1950- *WhoMW 92*
**Henion,** Richard S 1939- *AmMWSc 92*
**Henis,** Jay Myls Stuart 1938- *AmMWSc 92*
**Henisch,** Heinz Kurt 1922- *AmMWSc 92*
**Henissart,** Paul 1923- *IntAu&W 91*
**Henisz,** Jerzy Emil 1937- *AmMWSc 92*
**Henize,** Karl Gordon 1926- *AmMWSc 92*
**Henk,** Floyd Henry 1929- *WhoFI 92*
**Henkart,** Pierre 1941- *AmMWSc 92*
**Henke,** Burton Lehman 1922- *AmMWSc 92*
**Henke,** Dan 1924- *WhoAmL 92*
**Henke,** Frank Paul 1939- *WhoMW 92*
**Henke,** Janice Carine 1938- *WhoMW 92*
**Henke,** Marilyn D. 1951- *WhoMW 92*
**Henke,** Michael John 1940- *WhoAmL 92*
**Henke,** Mitchell C 1949- *AmMWSc 92*
**Henke,** Randolph Ray 1948- *AmMWSc 92*
**Henke,** Richard Stewart 1948- *WhoFI 92*
**Henke,** Russell W 1924- *AmMWSc 92*
**Henke,** Theodore R. 1952- *WhoFI 92*
**Henke,** Theodore Robert 1952- *WhoIns 92*
**Henke,** Werner d1991 *NewYTBS 91*
**Henkel,** Arthur John, Jr. 1945- *WhoFI 92*
**Henkel,** Barbara Jane 1940- *WhoMW 92*
**Henkel,** Daniel James 1951- *WhoEnt 92*
**Henkel,** David 1795-1831 *DcNCBi 3*
**Henkel,** Elmer Thomas 1936- *AmMWSc 92*
**Henkel,** James Gregory 1945- *AmMWSc 92*
**Henkel,** Jenny Marie 1952- *WhoAmP 91*
**Henkel,** John Harmon 1924- *AmMWSc 92*
**Henkel,** Konrad 1915- *IntWW 91*
**Henkel,** Lee H, Jr 1928- *WhoAmP 91*
**Henkel,** Paul 1754-1825 *DcNCBi 3*
**Henkel,** Richard Luther 1921- *AmMWSc 92*
**Henkel,** Steve 1933- *IntAu&W 91, WrDr 92*
**Henkel,** Zane Grey 1937- *WhoFI 92, WhoMW 92*
**Henkels,** Mark *WhoWest 92*
**Henkels,** Walter Harvey 1944- *AmMWSc 92*
**Henkemans,** Hans 1913- *ConCom 92*
**Henkens,** Robert William *AmMWSc 92*
**Henker,** Fred Oswald, III 1922- *AmMWSc 92*
**Henkes,** Robert 1922- *WrDr 92*
**Henkin,** Howard H. 1926- *IntMPA 92*
**Henkin,** Hyman 1915- *AmMWSc 92*
**Henkin,** Jack 1947- *AmMWSc 92, WhoMW 92*
**Henkin,** Leon 1921- *AmMWSc 92*
**Henkin,** Louis 1917- *IntAu&W 91, WrDr 92*
**Henkin,** Robert I 1930- *AmMWSc 92*
**Henkin,** Stephen Morgan 1947- *WhoEnt 92*
**Henkind,** Paul 1932- *AmMWSc 92*
**Henkle,** William Randolph, Jr. 1947- *WhoWest 92*
**Henle,** Christian-Peter 1938- *IntWW 91*
**Henle,** James Marston 1946- *AmMWSc 92*
**Henle,** Jorg Alexander 1934- *IntWW 91*
**Henle,** Mary 1913- *WomPsyc*
**Henle,** Robert A 1924- *AmMWSc 92*
**Henlein,** Konrad 1898-1945 *BiDExR, EncTR 91 [port]*
**Henley,** Baron 1953- *Who 92*
**Henley,** Arthur *WrDr 92*
**Henley,** Arthur 1921- *WhoEnt 92*
**Henley,** Beth 1952- *BenetAL 91, WhoEnt 92, WrDr 92*
**Henley,** Carl R. 1955- *WhoBlA 92*
**Henley,** Charles *DrAPF 91*
**Henley,** Don 1948- *WhoEnt 92*
**Henley,** Douglas 1919- *Who 92*
**Henley,** Douglas Owen 1919- *IntWW 91*
**Henley,** Edgar Floyd, Jr 1940- *WhoAmP 91*
**Henley,** Elizabeth Becker 1952- *IntAu&W 91, IntWW 91*
**Henley,** Ernest J 1926- *AmMWSc 92*
**Henley,** Ernest M. 1924- *IntWW 91*
**Henley,** Ernest Mark 1924- *AmMWSc 92*
**Henley,** Jane Ellen 1947- *WhoRel 92*
**Henley,** John Irving 1955- *WhoAmL 92*
**Henley,** John Tannery 1921- *WhoAmP 91*
**Henley,** Joseph 1909- *Who 92*
**Henley,** Joseph Oliver 1949- *WhoFI 92*
**Henley,** Keith Stuart 1924- *AmMWSc 92, WhoMW 92*
**Henley,** Melvin Brent, Jr 1935- *AmMWSc 92*
**Henley,** Michael Harry George 1938- *Who 92*
**Henley,** Patricia *DrAPF 91*
**Henley,** Peter 1724-1758 *DcNCBi 3*
**Henley,** Preston vanFleet 1913- *WhoFI 92*
**Henley,** Robert Lee 1934- *WhoMW 92*
**Henley,** Rod Kinder 1946- *WhoEnt 92*
**Henley,** Terry Lew 1940- *WhoFI 92*
**Henley,** Vernard W. 1929- *WhoBlA 92*
**Henley,** W.E. 1849-1903 *RfGEnL 91*
**Henley,** Walter L *AmMWSc 92*
**Henley,** Wanda G. 1953- *WhoMW 92*
**Henley,** William Armstrong 1934- *WhoFI 92*

**Henley**, William Ballentine 1905- IntWW 91
**Henly**, Robert Stuart 1931- AmMWSc 92
**Henn**, Charles Herbert 1931- Who 92
**Henn**, Daniel Joseph 1960- WhoEnt 92
**Henn**, Eugene E. WhoAmL 92
**Henn**, Fritz Albert 1941- AmMWSc 92
**Henn**, Harry George 1919- ConAu 36NR, WhoAmL 92
**Henn**, Mary Ann DrAPF 91
**Henn**, Steven Michael 1962- WhoWest 92
**Henn**, Walter 1912- IntWW 91
**Hennacy**, Ammon 1893-1970 AmPeW
**Henne**, Rolf 1901-1966 BiDExR
**Henneberg**, Gerd Michael 1922- IntWW 91
**Henneberger**, Lawrence Francis 1938- WhoAmL 92
**Henneberger**, Walter Carl 1930- AmMWSc 92
**Henneberry**, Kirk Stephen 1960- WhoRel 92
**Henneberry**, Richard Christopher 1937- AmMWSc 92
**Henneberry**, Thomas James 1929- AmMWSc 92
**Hennedy**, Hugh DrAPF 91
**Hennefer**, David Arthur 1948- WhoFI 92
**Henneike**, Henry Fred 1939- AmMWSc 92
**Henneke**, Edmund George, II 1941- AmMWSc 92
**Henneke**, Edward G. 1940- WhoAmL 92
**Hennel**, Nancy Lee 1936- WhoFI 92
**Hennell**, Michael Murray 1918- Who 92
**Hennell**, Thomas 1903-1945 TwCPaSc
**Hennelly**, Edmund Paul 1923- WhoAmL 92, WhoFI 92
**Hennelly**, Edward Joseph 1923- AmMWSc 92
**Hennelly**, John Joseph 1943- WhoAmL 92
**Henneman**, Elwood 1915- AmMWSc 92
**Henneman**, Harold Albert 1918- AmMWSc 92
**Henneman**, Scott Alan 1960- WhoMW 92
**Hennen**, Joe Fleetwood 1928- AmMWSc 92
**Hennen**, Sally 1935- AmMWSc 92
**Hennen**, Tom DrAPF 91
**Hennepin**, Louis 1640-1701? BenetAL 91
**Henner**, Marilu 1952- IntMPA 92, WhoEnt 92
**Henner**, William David 1949- WhoWest 92
**Hennes**, Peter Michael 1954- WhoEnt 92
**Hennes**, Robert G 1905- AmMWSc 92
**Hennesey**, James 1926- WhoRel 92
**Hennessee**, E. Lee 1953- WhoFI 92
**Hennessee**, Elizabeth Lee 1955- WhoFI 92
**Hennessey**, Audrey Kathleen 1936- AmMWSc 92
**Hennessey**, Colleen WhoRel 92
**Hennessey**, David Patrick 1950- WhoFI 92
**Hennessey**, Edward F 1919- WhoAmP 91
**Hennessey**, Edward Francis 1919- WhoAmL 92
**Hennessey**, Hugh IntAu&W 91X
**Hennessey**, Jean Lande 1927- WhoAmP 91
**Hennessey**, Jevera Kaye 1960- WhoAmL 92
**Hennessey**, Kevin 1920- TwCPaSc
**Hennessey**, Maurice Vincent 1927- WhoAmP 91
**Hennessey**, Peter J, Jr 1920- WhoIns 92
**Hennessey**, Peter John, III 1943- WhoFI 92
**Hennessey**, Raymond Frank 1925- WhoAmP 91, WhoFI 92
**Hennessey**, William John 1948- WhoMW 92
**Hennessy** Who 92
**Hennessy**, Arthur Leo, Jr 1925- WhoAmP 91
**Hennessy**, Christopher 1909- Who 92
**Hennessy**, Dean McDonald 1923- WhoAmL 92
**Hennessy**, Edward L., Jr. 1928- IntWW 91
**Hennessy**, Edward Lawrence, Jr. 1928- WhoFI 92
**Hennessy**, Ellen Anne 1949- WhoAmL 92
**Hennessy**, Francis Xavier 1930- WhoAmL 92
**Hennessy**, James 1923- Who 92
**Hennessy**, James Ernest 1933- WhoFI 92
**Hennessy**, James Patrick Ivan 1923- IntWW 91
**Hennessy**, John Basil 1925- IntWW 91
**Hennessy**, John Francis 1961- WhoEnt 92
**Hennessy**, John Francis, III 1955- WhoFI 92
**Hennessy**, John Francis, Jr. 1961- WhoAmL 92
**Hennessy**, John LeRoy 1952- AmMWSc 92
**Hennessy**, John Wyndham P. Who 92
**Hennessy**, Madeleine DrAPF 91
**Hennessy**, Mary Brigid Teresa 1933- Who 92
**Hennessy**, Max ConAu 134, WrDr 92
**Hennessy**, Patricia Marie 1959- WhoFI 92
**Hennessy**, Paul Kevin 1932- WhoRel 92
**Hennessy**, Peter 1947- WrDr 92
**Hennessy**, Peter John 1947- Who 92
**Hennessy**, Rose Marie WhoRel 92
**Hennessy**, Thomas Christopher 1916- WhoRel 92
**Hennessy**, Wesley J. d1991 NewYTBS 91
**Hennesy**, James Leon 1934- WhoRel 92
**Henney**, Christopher Scot 1941- AmMWSc 92
**Henney**, Dagmar Renate AmMWSc 92
**Henney**, Henry Russell, Jr 1934- AmMWSc 92
**Henney**, Robert Charles 1925- AmMWSc 92
**Henney**, William Henry 1956- WhoAmL 92
**Hennig**, Harvey 1919- AmMWSc 92
**Hennig**, V. WhoRel 92
**Hennigan**, James Michael 1943- WhoAmL 92
**Hennigan**, Mickey Lee 1943- WhoWest 92
**Hennigan**, Robert Dwyer 1925- AmMWSc 92
**Hennigar**, Curtis Alan 1959- WhoFI 92
**Hennigar**, David J. 1939- WhoFI 92
**Hennigar**, Gordon Ross, Jr 1919- AmMWSc 92
**Hennigar**, Richard A. WhoRel 92
**Henniger**, Bernard Robert 1934- AmMWSc 92
**Henniger**, David Thomas 1936- WhoAmL 92
**Henniger**, James Perry 1938- AmMWSc 92
**Henniger**, James Ray 1946- WhoRel 92
**Hennighausen**, Fred H. 1924- WhoFI 92
**Henniker**, Baron 1916- IntWW 91, Who 92
**Henniker**, Mark Chandos Auberon 1906- Who 92
**Henniker Heaton**, Yvo Robert Who 92
**Henniker-Major** Who 92
**Henning**, Andrea Alison 1965- WhoMW 92
**Henning**, Barbara DrAPF 91
**Henning**, Carl Douglas 1939- AmMWSc 92
**Henning**, Dan 1942- WhoWest 92
**Henning**, Doug 1947- WhoEnt 92
**Henning**, Emilie D 1930- AmMWSc 92
**Henning**, George Thomas, Jr. 1941- WhoFI 92
**Henning**, Geraldo de Azevedo 1917- IntWW 91
**Henning**, Hans Helmut Fritz 1927- IntAu&W 91
**Henning**, Harley Barry 1931- AmMWSc 92
**Henning**, Joel Frank 1939- WhoAmL 92
**Henning**, Josephine Terrell 1914- WhoAmP 91
**Henning**, Judy WhoAmP 91
**Henning**, Lester Allan 1939- AmMWSc 92
**Henning**, Linda Kaye 1944- IntMPA 92
**Henning**, Paul LesBEnT 92
**Henning**, Paul 1911- IntMPA 92
**Henning**, Robert Joseph 1941- WhoMW 92
**Henning**, Rudolf E 1923- AmMWSc 92
**Henning**, Sandra Jean 1940- WhoMW 92
**Henning**, Susan June 1946- AmMWSc 92
**Henning**, Walter Friedrich 1939- AmMWSc 92
**Henning**, William A. 1938- WhoFI 92
**Henning**, William Demmler, Jr. 1949- WhoRel 92
**Henning**, William Harrold 1931- WhoMW 92
**Henning-Guria**, Beth Anne 1964- WhoAmL 92
**Henning-Jensen**, Astrid 1914- IntDcF 2-2
**Henning-Jensen**, Bjarne 1908- IntDcF 2-2
**Henninger**, Ann Louise 1946- AmMWSc 92, WhoMW 92
**Henninger**, Charlene Dianne 1953- WhoEnt 92
**Henninger**, Daniel Paul 1946- WhoFI 92
**Henninger**, Derek Philip 1962- WhoWest 92
**Henninger**, Ernest Herman 1932- AmMWSc 92
**Henninger**, Francis Joseph 1935- WhoMW 92
**Henninger**, Kathy Jean 1957- WhoEnt 92
**Henningfield**, Mary Frances 1961- AmMWSc 92
**Hennings**, Deirdre Ellen 1951- WhoWest 92
**Hennings**, Dorothy Ann 1937- WhoFI 92
**Hennings**, George 1922- AmMWSc 92
**Hennings**, Henry 1941- AmMWSc 92
**Hennings**, Kenneth Milton 1943- WhoBlA 92
**Hennings**, Richard Owen 1911- Who 92
**Hennings**, Sam WhoEnt 92
**Henningsen**, Poul 1895-1967 DcTwDes
**Hennion**, Carolyn Laird 1943- WhoFI 92
**Hennion**, George Felix 1910- AmMWSc 92
**Hennion**, Reeve Lawrence 1941- WhoEnt 92
**Hennis**, Henry Emil 1925- AmMWSc 92
**Hennock**, Frieda B. d1960 LesBEnT 92
**Hennon**, David Kent 1933- AmMWSc 92, WhoMW 92
**Hennrich**, Carl Potter 1947- WhoWest 92
**Henny**, Charles Joseph 1943- AmMWSc 92
**Henreid**, Paul WhoEnt 92
**Henreid**, Paul 1908- IntMPA 92
**Henrey**, Madeleine 1906- WrDr 92
**Henrey**, Robert, Mrs. 1906- Who 92
**Henri**, Adrian 1932- ConAu 34NR, ConPo 91, IntAu&W 91, TwCPaSc, WrDr 92
**Henri**, Adrian Maurice 1932- Who 92
**Henri**, Lise Marie 1962- WhoEnt 92
**Henri**, Robert 1865-1929 FacFETw
**Henrich**, Christopher John 1942- AmMWSc 92
**Henrich**, Curtis J AmMWSc 92
**Henrich**, Dieter 1927- IntWW 91
**Henrich**, Victor E 1939- AmMWSc 92
**Henrich**, Williams Lloyd AmMWSc 92
**Henrichs**, Paul Mark 1943- AmMWSc 92
**Henrici**, Carl Ressler 1915- AmMWSc 92
**Henrick**, Clive Arthur 1941- AmMWSc 92
**Henrick**, Michael Francis 1948- WhoAmL 92
**Henricks**, Donald Maurice 1936- AmMWSc 92
**Henricks**, Kaw ConAu 34NR
**Henricksen**, Thomas Alva AmMWSc 92
**Henrickson**, Charles Henry 1938- AmMWSc 92
**Henrickson**, Eiler Leonard 1920- AmMWSc 92
**Henrickson**, James Solberg 1940- AmMWSc 92
**Henrickson**, Pamela Quigg 1958- WhoAmL 92
**Henrickson**, Paul Robert 1928- WhoWest 92
**Henrickson**, Richard Ralph 1948- WhoEnt 92
**Henrickson**, Robert Lee 1920- AmMWSc 92
**Henrie**, Kim Barton 1951- WhoWest 92
**Henriksen**, Lance IntMPA 92
**Henriksen**, Melvin 1927- AmMWSc 92, WhoWest 92
**Henriksen**, Richard Norman 1940- AmMWSc 92
**Henriksen**, Roger D. 1955- WhoAmL 92
**Henrikson**, Ernest Hilmer 1903- AmMWSc 92
**Henrikson**, Katherine Pointer 1939- AmMWSc 92
**Henrikson**, Lois Elizabeth 1921- WhoFI 92
**Henrikson**, Pamela Smith 1940- WhoFI 92
**Henrikson**, Ray Charles 1937- AmMWSc 92
**Henriksson**, Thomas Martin 1951- WhoWest 92
**Henrion**, Henri Kay Frederick 1914- DcTwDes
**Henrion**, Robert 1915- IntWW 91
**Henriot**, Philippe 1889-1944 BiDExR
**Henriques**, Richard Henry Quixano 1943- Who 92
**Henriques**, Rose L. TwCPaSc
**Henriquez**, Andres Antonio 1947- WhoHisp 92
**Henriquez**, Francis WhoHisp 92
**Henriquez**, Manuel Armando 1963- WhoFI 92
**Henriquez**, Nelson 1941- WhoHisp 92
**Henriquez**, Theodore Aurelio 1934- AmMWSc 92
**Henriquez Gonzalez**, Camilo 1769-1825 HisDSpE
**Henrison**, Rosina 1902- Who 92
**Henrix**, Hans Hermann 1941- WhoRel 92
**Henry VIII** 1491-1547 NewAmDM
**Henry of Ghent** 1217?-1293 DcLB 115
**Henry The Minstrel** RfGEnL 91
**Henry**, Aaron E. 1922- WhoBlA 92
**Henry**, Aaron Edd 1922- WhoAmP 91
**Henry**, Alberta 1920- WhoBlA 92
**Henry**, Alberta Hill 1920- WhoAmP 91
**Henry**, Alice 1857-1943 DcAmImH
**Henry**, Allan Francis 1925- AmMWSc 92
**Henry**, Andre Armand 1934- IntWW 91
**Henry**, Arnold William 1938- AmMWSc 92
**Henry**, Billy Wendell 1929- AmMWSc 92
**Henry**, Bob LesBEnT 92
**Henry**, Boyd 1925- AmMWSc 92
**Henry**, Brent Lee 1947- WhoBlA 92
**Henry**, Bruce Edward 1952- WhoMW 92
**Henry**, Bryan Roger 1941- AmMWSc 92
**Henry**, Buck 1930- ConTFT 9, IntMPA 92, WhoEnt 92
**Henry**, Caleb Sprague 1804-1884 AmPeW
**Henry**, Calvin O. L. 1940- WhoBlA 92
**Henry**, Carl F. H. 1913- IntWW 91
**Henry**, Carl Ferdinand Howard 1913- RelLAm 91, WhoRel 92
**Henry**, Carol DrAPF 91
**Henry**, Carol 1930- WhoAmP 91
**Henry**, Cecil James, Jr. 1937- WhoMW 92
**Henry**, Charles D., II 1923-1982 WhoBlA 92N
**Henry**, Charles E. 1935- WhoBlA 92
**Henry**, Charles E 1958- WhoAmP 91
**Henry**, Charles H 1937- AmMWSc 92
**Henry**, Charles Patrick 1947- WhoBlA 92
**Henry**, Charles Stuart 1946- AmMWSc 92
**Henry**, Christopher Duval 1946- AmMWSc 92
**Henry**, Claudette 1947- WhoAmP 91
**Henry**, Claudia 1931- AmMWSc 92
**Henry**, Clay Allen 1932- AmMWSc 92
**Henry**, Clifford, Jr 1928- WhoAmP 91
**Henry**, Cyrus A, Jr 1931- WhoIns 92
**Henry**, Dana Senit 1946- WhoAmL 92
**Henry**, Daniel Joseph 1945- WhoBlA 92
**Henry**, David 1925- Who 92
**Henry**, David Allen 1950- WhoWest 92
**Henry**, David Arnold 1949- WhoRel 92
**Henry**, David Carl 1960- WhoFI 92
**Henry**, David Greer, Sr. 1957- WhoAmL 92
**Henry**, David P, II 1942- AmMWSc 92
**Henry**, David Paul 1948- WhoRel 92
**Henry**, David Reid 1919- TwCPaSc
**Henry**, David Weston 1932- AmMWSc 92
**Henry**, Deborah Jane 1952- WhoMW 92
**Henry**, DeLysle Leon 1935- WhoAmL 92, WhoMW 92
**Henry**, Denis 1917- Who 92
**Henry**, Denis 1931- Who 92
**Henry**, DeWitt DrAPF 91
**Henry**, Donald J 1910- AmMWSc 92
**Henry**, Donald Lee 1942- AmMWSc 92
**Henry**, Dora Priaulx 1904- AmMWSc 92
**Henry**, Doreen 1906-1990 AnObit 1990
**Henry**, Douglas Selph, Jr 1926- WhoAmP 91
**Henry**, E. William LesBEnT 92
**Henry**, Edgar 1838-1905 ScFEYrs
**Henry**, Edgar Robert 1937- WhoEnt 92
**Henry**, Edgerton L 1936- WhoAmP 91
**Henry**, Edward Frank 1923- WhoFI 92, WhoMW 92
**Henry**, Edwin Maurice, Jr. 1930- WhoAmL 92
**Henry**, Egbert Winston 1931- AmMWSc 92, WhoBlA 92
**Henry**, Eugene W 1932- AmMWSc 92
**Henry**, Forest T., Jr. 1937- WhoBlA 92
**Henry**, Frank Haywood 1913- WhoBlA 92
**Henry**, Frederick Edward 1947- WhoAmL 92
**Henry**, Frederick Porteous 1844- BiInAmS
**Henry**, George 1858-1943 TwCPaSc
**Henry**, George Mark 1955- WhoAmP 91
**Henry**, Gerrit DrAPF 91
**Henry**, Harold Robert 1928- AmMWSc 92
**Henry**, Harry James 1917- AmMWSc 92
**Henry**, Helen L 1944- AmMWSc 92
**Henry**, Herman Luther, Jr 1918- AmMWSc 92
**Henry**, Homer C. 1950- WhoMW 92
**Henry**, Hugh Fort 1916- AmMWSc 92
**Henry**, Jack Leland 1918- AmMWSc 92
**Henry**, Jacob 1775?-1847 DcNCBi 3
**Henry**, James Carlton, Jr. 1926- WhoFI 92
**Henry**, James H 1922- AmMWSc 92
**Henry**, James Holmes 1911- Who 92
**Henry**, James M 1945- WhoAmP 91
**Henry**, James Paget 1914- AmMWSc 92
**Henry**, James R WhoAmP 91
**Henry**, James R 1959- WhoIns 92
**Henry**, James T., Sr. 1910- WhoBlA 92
**Henry**, James William 1945- WhoRel 92
**Henry**, Janice Schoen 1946- WhoMW 92
**Henry**, Jay Edward 1950- WhoEnt 92
**Henry**, Jimmy Russell 1943- WhoRel 92
**Henry**, John Bernard 1928- AmMWSc 92
**Henry**, John Patrick, Jr 1935- AmMWSc 92
**Henry**, John Philip 1946- Who 92
**Henry**, John W., Jr. 1929- WhoBlA 92
**Henry**, Jonathan Flake 1951- AmMWSc 92
**Henry**, Joseph 1797-1878 BiInAmS
**Henry**, Joseph A. 1917- WhoBlA 92
**Henry**, Joseph King 1948- WhoBlA 92
**Henry**, Joseph L 1924- AmMWSc 92
**Henry**, Joseph Louis 1924- IntWW 91, WhoBlA 92
**Henry**, Joseph Patrick 1925- WhoMW 92
**Henry**, Joseph Patrick 1947- AmMWSc 92
**Henry**, Joseph Peter 1921- AmMWSc 92
**Henry**, Joseph R. 1945- WhoWest 92
**Henry**, Joseph W 1916- WhoAmP 91
**Henry**, Joyce WhoAmP 91
**Henry**, Justin 1971- IntMPA 92
**Henry**, Justin Worthington 1971- WhoEnt 92
**Henry**, Karen Hawley 1943- WhoAmL 92, WhoWest 92
**Henry**, Karl H. 1936- WhoBlA 92
**Henry**, Kenneth Albin 1923- AmMWSc 92

**Henry,** Laurie DrAPF 91
**Henry,** Leonard Francis, III 1942- AmMWSc 92
**Henry,** Lester Franklin 1948- WhoFI 92
**Henry,** Louis Debonair 1788-1846 DcNCBi 3
**Henry,** Lowman Scott 1957- WhoAmP 91
**Henry,** Marcelett Campbell 1928- WhoBlA 92
**Henry,** Marguerite WrDr 92
**Henry,** Marie H 1935- SmATA 65 [port]
**Henry,** Marion Wetmore 1925- WhoRel 92
**Henry,** Mark Alan 1958- WhoAmP 91
**Henry,** Mary Gerard 1954- AmMWSc 92
**Henry,** Matthew George 1910-1974 DcNCBi 3
**Henry,** Merton Goodell 1926- WhoAmP 91
**Henry,** Mildred M. Dalton WhoBlA 92
**Henry,** Morriss M 1931- WhoAmP 91
**Henry,** Myron S 1941- AmMWSc 92
**Henry,** Nancy L. 1940- WhoBlA 92
**Henry,** Nancy Louise 1940- WhoAmP 91
**Henry,** Neil Wylie 1937- AmMWSc 92
**Henry,** Nelson Charles 1955- WhoMW 92
**Henry,** Norma Kay WhoMW 92
**Henry,** O. 1862-1910 BenetAL 91, TwCWW 91
**Henry,** Patricia Ann WhoEnt 92
**Henry,** Patrick 1736-1799 AmPolLe [port], BenetAL 91, BlkwEAR, RComAH
**Henry,** Patrick G. 1939- WhoRel 92
**Henry,** Patrick M 1928- AmMWSc 92
**Henry,** Paul 1876-1958 TwCPaSc
**Henry,** Paul B. 1942- AlmAP 92 [port]
**Henry,** Paul Brentwood 1942- WhoAmP 91, WhoMW 92
**Henry,** Paul Eugene, Jr. 1941- WhoRel 92
**Henry,** Paul Raleigh 1928- WhoFI 92
**Henry,** Peter York 1951- WhoAmL 92, WhoFI 92
**Henry,** Philip Lawrence 1940- WhoWest 92
**Henry,** Pierre 1927- NewAmDM
**Henry,** Ragan A. 1934- WhoBlA 92, WhoEnt 92
**Henry,** Raymond Leo 1930- AmMWSc 92
**Henry,** Richard Conn 1940- AmMWSc 92
**Henry,** Richard Joseph 1918- AmMWSc 92
**Henry,** Richard Lynn 1948- AmMWSc 92
**Henry,** Richard Warfield 1932- AmMWSc 92
**Henry,** Robert C. 1951- WhoAmL 92
**Henry,** Robert Charles 1929- WhoAmP 91
**Henry,** Robert Clayton 1923- WhoBlA 92
**Henry,** Robert David 1927- AmMWSc 92
**Henry,** Robert Edwin 1911- AmMWSc 92
**Henry,** Robert Francis 1956- WhoAmL 92, WhoFI 92
**Henry,** Robert H. 1953- WhoAmL 92, WhoAmP 91
**Henry,** Robert John 1950- WhoAmL 92, WhoRel 92
**Henry,** Robert Ledyard 1920- AmMWSc 92
**Henry,** Robert R 1955- AmMWSc 92
**Henry,** Rodney WhoRel 92
**Henry,** Roger P 1938- AmMWSc 92
**Henry,** Ronald Alton 1940- AmMWSc 92
**Henry,** Ronald Andrew 1916- AmMWSc 92
**Henry,** Ronald James Whyte 1940- AmMWSc 92
**Henry,** Roy Monroe 1939- WhoMW 92
**Henry,** Samuel Dudley 1947- WhoBlA 92
**Henry,** Shirley Ann 1937- WhoWest 92
**Henry,** Susan Armstrong 1946- AmMWSc 92
**Henry,** Sydney Mark 1930- AmMWSc 92
**Henry,** Sylvia Diane 1938- WhoAmP 91
**Henry,** Thomas 1934- WhoBlA 92
**Henry,** Thomas Charlton 1825-1877 BiInAmS
**Henry,** Thomas Cradock 1910- Who 92
**Henry,** Thornton Montagu 1943- WhoAmL 92
**Henry,** Timothy James 1939- AmMWSc 92
**Henry,** Trevor 1902- Who 92
**Henry,** Vaughn William 1951- WhoWest 92
**Henry,** Vernon James, Jr 1931- AmMWSc 92
**Henry,** Vic Houston 1958- WhoAmL 92
**Henry,** Virgil Dwight 1953- WhoAmP 91
**Henry,** Walter Lester, Jr 1915- AmMWSc 92, WhoBlA 92
**Henry,** Warren Elliott 1909- WhoBlA 92
**Henry,** Wendy Ann Who 92
**Henry,** Will BenetAL 91, ConAu 135, IntAu&W 91X, TwCWW 91, WrDr 92
**Henry,** William 1729-1786 BiInAmS
**Henry,** William Arthur, II 1939- WhoBlA 92
**Henry,** William C WhoAmP 91
**Henry,** William Cameron, Jr. 1964- WhoEnt 92
**Henry,** William Mellinger 1918- AmMWSc 92
**Henry,** William Robert 1915- IntWW 91, Who 92
**Henry,** William Thomas 1950- WhoAmP 91
**Henry,** Zachary Adolphus 1930- AmMWSc 92
**Henry de Villeneuve,** Xavier 1932- IntWW 91
**Henry-Fairhurst,** Ellenae L. 1943- WhoBlA 92
**Henry-John,** Emmanuel Sylvester 1949- WhoRel 92, WhoWest 92
**Henry-Thiel,** Lois Hollender 1941- WhoFI 92
**Henryson,** Robert 1436?-1504? RfGEnL 91
**Henschel,** Austin 1906- AmMWSc 92
**Henschel,** Elizabeth Georgie IntAu&W 91, WrDr 92
**Henschel,** George 1850-1934 NewAmDM
**Henschel,** John James 1954- WhoAmL 92
**Henschel,** Ruth Mary Who 92
**Henschell,** Todd Edward 1954- WhoEnt 92
**Henschen,** Keith Page 1943- WhoWest 92
**Henschen,** Lawrence Joseph 1944- AmMWSc 92
**Hensel,** Clair Olen 1936- WhoMW 92
**Hensel,** Dale Robert 1931- AmMWSc 92
**Hensel,** Donald N 1926- WhoAmP 91
**Hensel,** Donna Mae 1929- WhoAmP 91
**Hensel,** Fanny NewAmDM
**Hensel,** Gustav 1934- AmMWSc 92
**Hensel,** H. Struve d1991 NewYTBS 91 [port]
**Hensel,** H. Struve 1901-1991 CurBio 91N
**Hensel,** Jeffrey 1962- WhoWest 92
**Hensel,** John Charles 1930- AmMWSc 92
**Hensel,** Katherine Ruth 1959- WhoFI 92
**Hensel,** Mitzi Lisa 1961- WhoMW 92
**Hensel,** Walther 1887-1956 EncTR 91
**Hensel,** Witold 1917- IntWW 91
**Henseler,** Suzanne M 1942- WhoAmP 91
**Hensell,** Eugene Merrill 1942- WhoRel 92
**Henselmeier,** Sandra Nadine 1937- WhoMW 92
**Hensens,** Otto Derk 1940- AmMWSc 92
**Hensgen,** M. Caroleen WhoRel 92
**Henshall,** Michael Who 92
**Henshaw,** Clement Long 1906- AmMWSc 92
**Henshaw,** Edgar Cummings 1929- AmMWSc 92
**Henshaw,** Edmund Lee, Jr 1925- WhoAmP 91
**Henshaw,** Elizabeth Donaldson 1946- WhoAmP 91
**Henshaw,** Frank Charles 1930- Who 92
**Henshaw,** James Ene 1924- IntAu&W 91, WrDr 92
**Henshaw,** James Ernest 1931- WhoAmP 91
**Henshaw,** Jere C. 1932- WhoEnt 92
**Henshaw,** Kenneth Ralph 1918- IntWW 91
**Henshaw,** Marshall 1820-1900 BiInAmS
**Henshaw,** Paul Carrington 1913- AmMWSc 92
**Henshaw,** Paul Stewart 1902- AmMWSc 92
**Henshaw,** Robert Eugene 1934- AmMWSc 92
**Henshaw,** Samuel d1907 BiInAmS
**Henshel,** Diane S. Walden 1955- WhoWest 92
**Henslee,** William Douglas 1954- WhoEnt 92
**Hensleigh,** Howard Edgar 1920- WhoAmL 92
**Hensler,** Carol Sue 1950- WhoAmP 91
**Hensler,** Charles Morris 1924- WhoAmP 91
**Hensler,** Donald H 1933- AmMWSc 92
**Hensler,** Gary Lee 1945- AmMWSc 92
**Hensler,** Guenter Manfred 1939- WhoEnt 92
**Hensler,** Joseph Raymond 1924- AmMWSc 92
**Hensler,** Ronald Fred 1944- AmMWSc 92
**Hensley,** Albert Lloyd, Jr. 1928- WhoMW 92
**Hensley,** Anthony Marc 1953- WhoAmP 91
**Hensley,** Bob WhoAmP 91
**Hensley,** Chad L 1924- WhoIns 92
**Hensley,** David Lee 1944- WhoEnt 92
**Hensley,** Douglas Austin 1949- AmMWSc 92
**Hensley,** Dwight Stoner 1952- WhoEnt 92
**Hensley,** Eugene Benjamin 1918- AmMWSc 92
**Hensley,** George Went d1955 RelLAm 91
**Hensley,** Gordon Randolph 1952- WhoRel 92
**Hensley,** Hal Darrell 1934- WhoAmP 91
**Hensley,** Joe L. DrAPF 91
**Hensley,** Joe L 1926- TwCSFW 91, WrDr 92
**Hensley,** John 1910- Who 92
**Hensley,** John Clark 1912- WhoRel 92
**Hensley,** John Coleman, II 1933- AmMWSc 92
**Hensley,** John Terry 1953- WhoMW 92
**Hensley,** Ken 1945- WhoEnt 92
**Hensley,** Louis Samuel, III 1955- WhoMW 92
**Hensley,** Louis Samuel, Jr. 1926- WhoFI 92
**Hensley,** Marble John, Sr 1922- AmMWSc 92
**Hensley,** R. Keith 1956- WhoRel 92
**Hensley,** Robert Paul 1931- WhoMW 92
**Hensley,** Sam P WhoAmP 91
**Hensley,** Sess D 1920- AmMWSc 92
**Hensley,** Teresa Louise 1952- WhoAmL 92
**Henslin,** James M 1937- ConAu 34NR
**Henson,** Anna Miriam 1935- AmMWSc 92
**Henson,** Arnold 1931- WhoFI 92
**Henson,** Bob Londes 1935- AmMWSc 92, WhoMW 92
**Henson,** Brian WhoEnt 92
**Henson,** Brian 1964?- News 92-1 [port]
**Henson,** C Ward 1940- AmMWSc 92
**Henson,** Carl P 1938- AmMWSc 92
**Henson,** Carol Kennemer 1954- WhoFI 92
**Henson,** Charles A. 1915- WhoBlA 92
**Henson,** Daniel Phillip, III 1943- WhoBlA 92
**Henson,** David DrAPF 91
**Henson,** David Bernard 1938- WhoBlA 92
**Henson,** Donald E 1935- AmMWSc 92
**Henson,** Earl Bennette 1925- AmMWSc 92
**Henson,** Ernest Paul 1924- WhoFI 92
**Henson,** Gerald L 1926- WhoAmP 91
**Henson,** Howard Kirk 1956- WhoAmL 92
**Henson,** James 1939-1990 FacFETw
**Henson,** James Bond 1933- AmMWSc 92
**Henson,** James Maury 1936-1990 SmATA 65
**Henson,** James Wesley 1929- AmMWSc 92
**Henson,** Jim SmATA 65
**Henson,** Jim d1990 LesBEnT 92 [port]
**Henson,** Jim 1936-1990 AnObit 1990
**Henson,** John Douglas 1950- WhoRel 92
**Henson,** Jonathan Ross 1964- WhoEnt 92
**Henson,** Joseph Lawrence 1932- AmMWSc 92
**Henson,** Josiah 1789-1881 BenetAL 91
**Henson,** Lance DrAPF 91
**Henson,** Lisa IntMPA 92
**Henson,** Louise Adrieanne Van Emden 1929- WhoAmP 91
**Henson,** Marguerite Ann Who 92
**Henson,** Matthew 1866-1955 ConBlB 2 [port]
**Henson,** Michael Brent 1959- WhoRel 92
**Henson,** Michele 1946- WhoAmP 91
**Henson,** Nicholas Victor Leslie 1945- Who 92
**Henson,** O'Dell Williams, Jr 1934- AmMWSc 92
**Henson,** Pamela Jane Carlin 1957- WhoMW 92
**Henson,** Paul D 1937- AmMWSc 92
**Henson,** Paul Harry 1925- WhoFI 92, WhoMW 92
**Henson,** Peter Mitchell 1940- AmMWSc 92
**Henson,** Richard Nelson 1941- AmMWSc 92
**Henson,** Robert Thomas 1929- WhoRel 92
**Henson,** Ronald Alfred 1915- Who 92
**Henson,** Steve 1959- WhoAmP 91
**Henson,** W H, Jr 1928- AmMWSc 92
**Henson,** William Francis 1933- WhoBlA 92
**Henson,** William L. 1934- WhoBlA 92
**Henson,** William Michael 1939- WhoMW 92
**Henstell,** Bruce Michael 1945- WhoEnt 92
**Henstell,** Diana ConAu 134
**Henstock,** Thomas Raymond 1936- WhoRel 92
**Henstra,** Friso 1928- SmATA 14AS [port]
**Hensz,** Richard Albert 1929- AmMWSc 92
**Henszey,** Michael Meagher 1964- WhoEnt 92
**Hente,** Sandra Lorraine 1946- WhoRel 92
**Hentel,** Nat Herbert 1919- WhoAmL 92
**Hentges,** David John 1928- AmMWSc 92
**Hentges,** Diane Kathryn 1946- WhoMW 92
**Hentges,** James Franklin, Jr 1925- AmMWSc 92
**Hentges,** Lynnette S W AmMWSc 92
**Hentisberus,** Guillelmus 1310?-1372? DcLB 115
**Hentoff,** Nat WrDr 92
**Hentoff,** Nat 1925- BenetAL 91
**Henton,** Willis Ryan 1925- WhoRel 92
**Hentrel,** Bobbie Kuykendall 1938- WhoBlA 92
**Hentrich,** Helmut 1905- IntWW 91
**Hentschel,** Robert A A 1910- AmMWSc 92
**Hentschell,** James Sheryl 1939- WhoMW 92
**Henty,** G.A. 1832-1902 RfGEnL 91
**Hentz,** Caroline Lee 1800-1856 BenetAL 91
**Hentz,** Caroline Lee Whiting 1800-1856 DcNCBi 3
**Hentz,** Forrest Clyde, Jr 1933- AmMWSc 92
**Hentz,** Nicholas Marcellus 1797-1856 BenetAL 91, BiInAmS, DcNCBi 3
**Hentz,** Robert R. DrAPF 91
**Hentzel,** Irvin Roy 1943- AmMWSc 92, WhoMW 92
**Henwood,** Douglas Francis 1952- WhoFI 92
**Henych,** Ivo 1935- WhoFI 92
**Henze,** Hans Werner 1926- ConCom 92, FacFETw, IntWW 91, Who 92
**Henze,** Hanz Werner 1926- NewAmDM
**Henzel,** John Russell, Jr. 1953- WhoFI 92
**Henzel,** Richard Paul 1945- AmMWSc 92
**Henzl,** Milan Rastislav 1928- AmMWSc 92
**Henzlik,** Raymond Eugene 1926- AmMWSc 92, WhoMW 92
**Hepburn,** Andrew Dousa 1830-1921 DcNCBi 3
**Hepburn,** Audrey 1929- IntMPA 92, IntWW 91, Who 92, WhoEnt 92
**Hepburn,** Bryan Audley St John d1991 Who 92N
**Hepburn,** Davidson Lincoln 1932- IntWW 91
**Hepburn,** Frank 1922- AmMWSc 92
**Hepburn,** James 1752?-1798 DcNCBi 3
**Hepburn,** John Christopher 1942- AmMWSc 92
**Hepburn,** John Duncan 1944- AmMWSc 92
**Hepburn,** John William 1938- Who 92
**Hepburn,** Katharine 1907- FacFETw [port], HanAmWH, IntMPA 92, NewYTBS 91 [port]
**Hepburn,** Katharine 1909- IntWW 91, News 91 [port], Who 92
**Hepburn,** Katharine Houghton 1907- WhoEnt 92
**Hepburn,** Michael F WhoAmP 91
**Hepburn,** Nicol Sinclair 1913- Who 92
**Hepburn,** Ninian B. A. J. B. Who 92
**Hepburn,** Ronald William 1927- Who 92, WrDr 92
**Hepburn,** Ted 1931- WhoEnt 92
**Hepburne-Scott** Who 92
**Hepfer,** Cheryl Lynn 1946- WhoAmL 92
**Hepfinger,** Norbert Francis 1932- AmMWSc 92
**Hepher,** David 1935- TwCPaSc
**Hepher,** Michael Leslie 1944- Who 92
**Hephner,** Gervase A 1936- WhoAmP 91
**Hepler,** Charles Douglas 1938- AmMWSc 92
**Hepler,** Kenneth Russel 1926- WhoFI 92, WhoWest 92
**Hepler,** Loren George 1928- AmMWSc 92
**Hepler,** Merlin Judson, Jr. 1929- WhoFI 92, WhoWest 92
**Hepler,** Opal Elsie 1899- AmMWSc 92
**Hepler,** Paul Raymond 1925- AmMWSc 92
**Hepler,** Peter Klock 1936- AmMWSc 92
**Hepler,** Robert S 1934- AmMWSc 92
**Hepner,** Abe 1931- WhoWest 92
**Hepner,** Charles Edward 1925- WhoAmL 92
**Hepner,** Irv 1950- WhoAmL 92
**Hepner,** Lee 1920- NewAmDM
**Hepner,** Marcia Anne 1957- WhoMW 92
**Hepner,** Martin Douglas 1963- WhoWest 92
**Hepner,** Ronald Allen 1938- WhoMW 92
**Heppa,** Douglas Van 1945- AmMWSc 92
**Heppe,** R Richard 1923- AmMWSc 92
**Heppel,** Alan IntMPA 92
**Heppel,** Leon A. 1912- IntWW 91
**Heppel,** Leon Alma 1912- AmMWSc 92
**Heppell,** Strachan 1935- Who 92
**Heppenheimer,** Thomas A. 1947- WrDr 92
**Hepper,** Anthony Evelyn 1923- Who 92
**Hepper,** Douglas Clifford 1950- WhoMW 92
**Hepple,** Bob Alexander 1934- Who 92
**Hepple,** Jeanne Marion 1936- WhoEnt 92
**Hepple,** Norman 1908- TwCPaSc, Who 92
**Hepple,** Robert Norman 1908- IntWW 91
**Heppleston,** Alfred Gordon 1915- Who 92
**Hepplewhite,** Rosalind Mary Joy 1952- Who 92
**Heppner,** Frank Henry 1940- AmMWSc 92
**Heppner,** Gloria Hill 1940- AmMWSc 92
**Heppner,** James P 1927- AmMWSc 92
**Heppner,** John Bernhard 1947- AmMWSc 92
**Heppner,** Puncky Paul 1951- WhoMW 92
**Heppner,** Richard Alan 1962- WhoRel 92

**Hepting,** George Henry *IntWW 91N*
**Hepting,** George Henry 1907- *AmMWSc 92*
**Heptinstall,** Leslie George 1919- *Who 92*
**Heptinstall,** Robert Hodgson 1920- *AmMWSc 92*
**Hepton,** Anthony 1936- *AmMWSc 92*
**Hepworth,** Barbara 1903-1975 *FacFETw, ModArCr 2 [port], TwCPaSc*
**Hepworth,** Cecil 1874-1953 *FacFETw, IntDcF 2-2 [port]*
**Hepworth,** David 1923- *Who 92*
**Hepworth,** H Kent 1942- *AmMWSc 92*
**Hepworth,** Lorne 1947- *WhoWest 92*
**Hepworth,** Malcolm T 1932- *AmMWSc 92*
**Hepworth,** Mike 1938- *WrDr 92*
**Hepworth,** Noel P. 1934- *WrDr 92*
**Hepworth,** Noel Peers 1934- *Who 92*
**Heracleon** *EncEarC*
**Herakovich,** Carl Thomas 1937- *AmMWSc 92, WhoFI 92*
**Herald,** Cherry Lou 1940- *AmMWSc 92*
**Herald,** Delbert Leon, Jr 1941- *AmMWSc 92*
**Herald,** John Patrick 1947- *WhoAmL 92*
**Herald,** Peter *IntMPA 92*
**Herald,** Robert Merl 1959- *WhoMW 92*
**Herald,** William Joseph 1954- *WhoMW 92*
**Herat,** Harold 1930- *Who 92*
**Heraud,** Javier 1942-1963 *ConSpAP*
**Herb,** Edmund Michael 1942- *WhoWest 92*
**Herb,** John A 1946- *AmMWSc 92*
**Herb,** Raymond George 1908- *AmMWSc 92, IntWW 91*
**Herb,** Samuel Martin 1938- *WhoFI 92*
**Herb,** Thomas *IntMPA 92*
**Herbach,** Leon Howard 1923- *AmMWSc 92*
**Herbecq,** John 1922- *Who 92*
**Herbein,** Joseph Henry, Jr 1943- *AmMWSc 92*
**Herbel,** Carlton Homer 1927- *AmMWSc 92*
**Herbelin,** Thomas N. 1956- *WhoAmL 92*
**Herbener,** George Henry 1929- *AmMWSc 92*
**Herbener,** Mark Basil 1932- *WhoRel 92*
**Herbener,** Roland Eugene 1923- *AmMWSc 92*
**Herber,** John Frederick 1933- *AmMWSc 92*
**Herber,** Lawrence Justin 1937- *AmMWSc 92*
**Herber,** Lewis *WrDr 92*
**Herber,** Raymond 1932- *AmMWSc 92*
**Herber,** Rolfe H 1927- *AmMWSc 92*
**Herberman,** Ronald Bruce 1940- *AmMWSc 92*
**Herbert** *Who 92*
**Herbert,** Lord 1978- *Who 92*
**Herbert,** Alfred James 1924- *Who 92*
**Herbert,** Arthur *TwCWW 91*
**Herbert,** Benne S. 1946- *WhoBlA 92*
**Herbert,** Brian 1947- *ConAu 133*
**Herbert,** Brian Douglas 1930- *Who 92*
**Herbert,** Brian Patrick 1947- *IntAu&W 91*
**Herbert,** Christopher William 1944- *Who 92*
**Herbert,** Damon Charles 1945- *AmMWSc 92*
**Herbert,** David Lee 1948- *WhoMW 92*
**Herbert,** David Niten 1945- *WhoAmP 91*
**Herbert,** Dennis Nicholas 1934- *IntWW 91, Who 92*
**Herbert,** Don *LesBEnT 92*
**Herbert,** Dorothy Fess 1917- *WhoAmP 91*
**Herbert,** Edward Franklin 1946- *WhoMW 92*
**Herbert,** Elton Warren, Jr 1943- *AmMWSc 92*
**Herbert,** Emily Grifo 1917- *WhoAmP 91*
**Herbert,** Eugenia W 1929- *ConAu 35NR*
**Herbert,** Floyd Leigh 1942- *AmMWSc 92*
**Herbert,** Frank 1910-1986 *FacFETw*
**Herbert,** Frank 1920-1986 *BenetAL 91, TwCSFW 91*
**Herbert,** Frederick William 1922- *Who 92*
**Herbert,** Gavin Shearer, Jr. 1932- *WhoWest 92*
**Herbert,** George 1593-1633 *CnDBLB 1 [port], PoeCrit 4 [port], RfGEnL 91*
**Herbert,** Gilbert 1924- *WrDr 92*
**Herbert,** Harold Bernard 1924- *Who 92*
**Herbert,** Henry William 1807-1858 *BenetAL 91*
**Herbert,** Ivor 1925- *IntAu&W 91, WrDr 92*
**Herbert,** Jack Durnin 1940- *AmMWSc 92*
**Herbert,** James 1943- *IntAu&W 91, TwCSFW 91, WrDr 92*
**Herbert,** Jean Jules 1905- *IntWW 91*
**Herbert,** Jocelyn 1917- *Who 92*
**Herbert,** John 1926- *WrDr 92*
**Herbert,** John Frank, IV 1955- *WhoRel 92*
**Herbert,** John Travis, Jr. 1943- *WhoBlA 92*
**Herbert,** Marc L 1948- *AmMWSc 92*
**Herbert,** Michael 1928- *AmMWSc 92*
**Herbert,** Morley Allen 1944- *AmMWSc 92*
**Herbert,** Nicholas *Who 92*
**Herbert,** Peter 1929- *Who 92*
**Herbert,** Robert L. 1929- *ConAu 36NR*
**Herbert,** Robert Louis 1929- *Who 92*
**Herbert,** Robin Arthur Elidyr 1934- *Who 92*
**Herbert,** Samuel Alfred 1943- *WhoWest 92*
**Herbert,** Stephen Aven 1923- *AmMWSc 92*
**Herbert,** Suzi 1943- *WhoAmP 91*
**Herbert,** Thomas James 1942- *AmMWSc 92*
**Herbert,** Thorwald 1937- *AmMWSc 92*
**Herbert,** Victor 1859-1924 *BenetAL 91, FacFETw [port], NewAmDM*
**Herbert,** Victor 1927- *AmMWSc 92*
**Herbert,** Walter William 1934- *IntWW 91, Who 92*
**Herbert,** William Penry Millwarden 1921- *Who 92*
**Herbert,** William Valentine 1936- *IntWW 91*
**Herbert,** Xavier 1901-1984 *RfGEnL 91*
**Herbert,** Zbigniew 1924- *ConAu 36NR, FacFETw, IntAu&W 91, IntWW 91, LiExTwC*
**Herbert-Jones,** Hugh Jarrett 1922- *Who 92*
**Herbert of Cherbury,** Lord 1582-1648 *RfGEnL 91*
**Herbette,** Leo G 1953- *AmMWSc 92*
**Herbich,** John Bronislaw 1922- *AmMWSc 92*
**Herbig,** George Howard 1920- *AmMWSc 92, IntWW 91*
**Herbig,** Gunther 1931- *IntWW 91, NewAmDM, WhoEnt 92*
**Herbison,** Gerald J 1937- *AmMWSc 92*
**Herbison,** Jean 1923- *Who 92*
**Herbison,** John Steve 1939- *WhoWest 92*
**Herbison,** Margaret McCrorie 1907- *Who 92*
**Herbison,** Priscilla Joan 1943- *WhoMW 92*
**Herbits,** Stephen Edward 1942- *WhoFI 92*
**Herblin,** William Fitts 1937- *AmMWSc 92*
**Herbolsheimer,** Glenn 1912- *AmMWSc 92*
**Herbolsheimer,** Robert Tilton 1954- *WhoAmL 92*
**Herbrandson,** Harry Fred 1921- *AmMWSc 92*
**Herbst,** Anthony F 1941- *ConAu 35NR*
**Herbst,** Axel 1918- *IntWW 91*
**Herbst,** Della Mae 1935- *WhoAmP 91*
**Herbst,** Edward John 1918- *AmMWSc 92*
**Herbst,** Eric 1946- *AmMWSc 92*
**Herbst,** Hartwig Martin 1945- *WhoFI 92*
**Herbst,** Jan Francis 1947- *AmMWSc 92*
**Herbst,** Johannes 1735-1812 *DcAmImH, DcNCBi 3, NewAmDM*
**Herbst,** John A *AmMWSc 92*
**Herbst,** John J 1935- *AmMWSc 92*
**Herbst,** Josephine 1897-1969 *BenetAL 91*
**Herbst,** Jurgen 1928- *WrDr 92*
**Herbst,** Lawrence Robert 1946- *WhoEnt 92, WhoFI 92*
**Herbst,** Marcia Anne 1948- *WhoAmP 91*
**Herbst,** Marie A 1928- *WhoAmP 91*
**Herbst,** Mark Joseph *AmMWSc 92*
**Herbst,** Noel Martin 1937- *AmMWSc 92*
**Herbst,** Richard Peter 1940- *AmMWSc 92*
**Herbst,** Robert LeRoy 1935- *WhoAmP 91*
**Herbst,** Robert Max 1904- *AmMWSc 92*
**Herbst,** Robert Taylor 1926- *AmMWSc 92*
**Herbst,** Todd Leslie 1952- *WhoAmL 92*
**Herbst,** Walter Brown 1937- *WhoMW 92*
**Herbst,** William 1947- *AmMWSc 92*
**Herbstman,** Sheldon 1931- *AmMWSc 92*
**Herbuveaux,** Jules d1990 *LesBEnT 92*
**Hercer,** Mark Stephen 1960- *WhoEnt 92*
**Herch,** Frank Alan 1949- *WhoAmL 92*
**Hercules,** David Michael 1932- *AmMWSc 92*
**Hercules,** Frank E. M. 1917- *WhoBlA 92*
**Hercus,** Ann 1942- *Who 92*
**Hercus,** Luise Anna 1926- *IntWW 91*
**Hercus,** Margaret Ann 1942- *IntWW 91*
**Herczeg,** John W 1942- *AmMWSc 92*
**Herczfeld,** Peter Robert 1936- *AmMWSc 92*
**Herczog,** Andrew 1917- *AmMWSc 92*
**Herczynski,** Andrzej 1956- *AmMWSc 92*
**Herd** *NewAmDM*
**Herd,** Charmian June 1930- *WhoEnt 92*
**Herd,** Darrell Gilbert 1949- *AmMWSc 92*
**Herd,** Frederick Charles 1915- *Who 92*
**Herd,** Harold S 1918- *WhoAmP 91*
**Herd,** Harold Shields 1918- *WhoAmL 92, WhoMW 92*
**Herd,** James Alan 1932- *AmMWSc 92*
**Herd,** John E. 1932- *WhoBlA 92*
**Herd,** Shirley Mae Deal 1935- *IntAu&W 91*
**Herda,** Hans-Heinrich Wolfgang 1938- *AmMWSc 92*
**Herda,** Thilo H 1949- *WhoIns 92*
**Herdeg,** Howard Brian 1929- *WhoWest 92*
**Herdendorf,** Charles Edward, III 1939- *AmMWSc 92*
**Herder,** Johann Gottfried 1744-1803 *EncEarC*
**Herder,** Johann Gottfried von 1744-1803 *BlkwCEP*
**Herder,** Robert H. *WhoRel 92*
**Herder,** W. Ed *IntMPA 92*
**Herdklotz,** John Key 1943- *AmMWSc 92*
**Herdklotz,** Richard James 1940- *AmMWSc 92*
**Herdle,** Lloyd Emerson 1913- *AmMWSc 92*
**Herdman,** Mark 1932- *Who 92*
**Herdman,** Terry Lee 1945- *AmMWSc 92*
**Herdman,** William James 1848-1906 *BiInAmS*
**Herdon,** Christopher de Lancy 1928- *Who 92*
**Herdt,** Robert William 1939- *AmMWSc 92*
**Heredia,** Jose Maria de 1803-1839 *BenetAL 91, HisDSpE*
**Heredia,** Jose-Maria de 1842-1905 *GuFrLit 1*
**Heredia,** Luis 1951- *WhoHisp 92*
**Heredia,** Pedro de 149-?-1554 *HisDSpE*
**Heredy,** Laszlo A. 1921- *WhoWest 92*
**Hereford,** Archdeacon of *Who 92*
**Hereford,** Bishop of 1935- *Who 92*
**Hereford,** Dean of *Who 92*
**Hereford,** Viscount 1932- *Who 92*
**Hereford,** Frank Loucks, Jr 1923- *AmMWSc 92*
**Hereford,** Sonnie Wellington, III 1931- *WhoBlA 92*
**Hereman,** Willy Alois Maria 1954- *WhoWest 92*
**Heremans,** Joseph P 1953- *AmMWSc 92*
**Heren,** Louis 1919- *WrDr 92*
**Heren,** Louis Philip 1919- *IntAu&W 91, Who 92*
**Herendeen,** Robert Albert 1940- *AmMWSc 92*
**Herendeen,** Steven Joe 1947- *WhoMW 92*
**Herenton,** Willie W. 1940- *WhoBlA 92*
**Herford,** Geoffrey Vernon Brooke 1905- *Who 92*
**Herford,** Oliver 1863-1935 *BenetAL 91*
**Herforth,** Lieselott 1916- *IntWW 91*
**Herforth,** Robert S 1939- *AmMWSc 92*
**Herft,** Roger Adrian *Who 92*
**Herge,** J. Curtis 1938- *WhoAmL 92*
**Hergenrader,** Gary Lee 1939- *AmMWSc 92*
**Hergenroeder,** Gerard 1949- *WhoFI 92*
**Hergenroeder,** Henry Robert, Jr 1943- *WhoAmP 91*
**Hergenrother,** William Lee 1938- *AmMWSc 92*
**Herger,** Wally 1945- *AlmAP 92 [port]*
**Herger,** Wally W, Jr 1945- *WhoAmP 91, WhoWest 92*
**Hergert,** Herbert L 1927- *AmMWSc 92*
**Hergert,** Richard Gary 1949- *WhoWest 92*
**Hergesheimer,** Joseph 1880-1954 *BenetAL 91*
**Herget,** Charles John 1937- *AmMWSc 92*
**Herget,** William F 1931- *AmMWSc 92*
**Herget,** Harold Douglas 1938- *WhoRel 92*
**Herglotz,** Heribert Karl Josef 1919- *AmMWSc 92*
**Heric,** Eugene LeRoy 1924- *AmMWSc 92*
**Herin,** David V. 1944- *WhoAmL 92*
**Herin,** Reginald Augustus 1924- *AmMWSc 92*
**Herincx,** Raimund 1927- *IntWW 91*
**Hering,** Doris Minnie 1920- *WhoEnt 92*
**Hering,** Eberhard Arnulf 1936- *WhoRel 92*
**Hering,** Gerhard F. 1908- *IntWW 91*
**Hering,** Gottlieb 1887-1945 *EncTR 91*
**Hering,** Henry A 1864- *ScFEYrs*
**Hering,** Juergen 1937- *IntWW 91*
**Hering,** Robert Gustave 1934- *AmMWSc 92*
**Hering,** Thomas M 1952- *AmMWSc 92*
**Hering,** William Marshall 1940- *WhoWest 92*
**Heringer,** Michael A. 1950- *WhoMW 92*
**Herion,** Gary Alan 1954- *WhoRel 92*
**Herion,** John Carroll 1927- *AmMWSc 92*
**Heriot,** Alexander John 1914- *Who 92*
**Herip,** Walter Michael 1947- *WhoEnt 92*
**Heritage,** John Langdon 1931- *Who 92*
**Heritage,** Robert 1927- *Who 92*
**Heritage,** Thomas Charles 1908- *Who 92*
**Herk,** Leonard Frank 1931- *AmMWSc 92*
**Herke,** Horst W. 1931- *IntWW 91*
**Herkes,** Frank Edward 1939- *AmMWSc 92*
**Herkes,** Robert N 1931- *WhoAmP 91*
**Herko,** Mark Stephen 1952- *WhoEnt 92*
**Herkstroeter,** William G 1938- *AmMWSc 92*
**Herl,** Rose Ann 1942- *WhoMW 92*
**Herlad,** Kathleen *IntAu&W 91X*
**Herlands,** Charles William *AmMWSc 92*
**Herlands,** E. Ward *DrAPF 91*
**Herley,** Patrick James 1934- *AmMWSc 92*
**Herliczek,** Siegfried H 1940- *AmMWSc 92*
**Herlie,** Eileen 1920- *Who 92*
**Herlihy,** David 1930-1991 *ConAu 133*
**Herlihy,** James Leo *DrAPF 91*
**Herlihy,** James Leo 1927- *BenetAL 91, ConNov 91, WhoEnt 92, WrDr 92*
**Herlihy,** Jeremiah Timothy *AmMWSc 92*
**Herlihy,** John Francis 1949- *WhoAmL 92*
**Herlihy,** Linda Jolley 1960- *WhoWest 92*
**Herlihy,** Thomas Mortimer 1953- *WhoAmL 92*
**Herlin,** Melvin Arnold 1923- *AmMWSc 92*
**Herling,** Michael James 1957- *WhoAmL 92*
**Herlinger,** Albert William 1943- *AmMWSc 92*
**Herlinger,** Daniel Robert 1946- *WhoWest 92*
**Herlocker,** John Robert 1935- *WhoRel 92, WhoWest 92*
**Herlong,** Albert Sydney, Jr 1909- *WhoAmP 91*
**Herlow,** Erik 1913- *DcTwDes*
**Herlyn,** Dorothee Maria 1945- *AmMWSc 92*
**Herm,** Ronald Richard 1940- *AmMWSc 92*
**Hermach,** Francis L 1917- *AmMWSc 92*
**Hermalin,** Albert Isaac 1928- *WhoMW 92*
**Herman,** Bishop *WhoRel 92*
**Herman of Philadelphia,** Bishop *WhoRel 92*
**Herman,** Alan Harvey 1950- *WhoFI 92*
**Herman,** Alexis M 1947- *WhoAmP 91, WhoBlA 92*
**Herman,** Andrea Maxine 1938- *WhoWest 92*
**Herman,** Arthur Ludwig 1930- *WhoRel 92*
**Herman,** Barbara Helen 1950- *AmMWSc 92*
**Herman,** Benjamin Morris 1929- *AmMWSc 92*
**Herman,** Bernard Albert 1910- *WhoFI 92*
**Herman,** Bertram 1935- *AmMWSc 92*
**Herman,** Brett P. 1955- *WhoAmL 92*
**Herman,** Brian *AmMWSc 92*
**Herman,** Ceil Ann 1946- *AmMWSc 92*
**Herman,** Charlotte 1937- *ConAu 34NR*
**Herman,** Chester Joseph 1941- *AmMWSc 92*
**Herman,** Daniel Francis 1919- *AmMWSc 92*
**Herman,** David S 1936- *AmMWSc 92*
**Herman,** Dennis Andrew 1946- *WhoIns 92*
**Herman,** E E 1921- *AmMWSc 92*
**Herman,** Eliot Mark 1952- *AmMWSc 92*
**Herman,** Eugene Alexander 1937- *AmMWSc 92, WhoMW 92*
**Herman,** Eugene H 1936- *AmMWSc 92*
**Herman,** Floyd Lehman 1937- *WhoRel 92*
**Herman,** Frank 1926- *AmMWSc 92*
**Herman,** Fred L. 1950- *WhoAmL 92*
**Herman,** Frederick Louis 1951- *AmMWSc 92*
**Herman,** Georg Nicholas 1954- *WhoAmL 92*
**Herman,** George 1922- *AmMWSc 92*
**Herman,** George Richard 1925- *WrDr 92*
**Herman,** Gerald 1944- *WhoEnt 92*
**Herman,** Grace *DrAPF 91*
**Herman,** Harley Scott 1953- *WhoAmL 92*
**Herman,** Harvey Bruce 1936- *AmMWSc 92*
**Herman,** Herbert 1934- *AmMWSc 92*
**Herman,** Ira Marc 1952- *AmMWSc 92*
**Herman,** Irving Philip 1951- *AmMWSc 92*
**Herman,** Jan Aleksander 1923- *AmMWSc 92*
**Herman,** Jerome Herbert 1934- *AmMWSc 92*
**Herman,** Jerry *WhoEnt 92*
**Herman,** Jerry 1933- *NewAmDM*
**Herman,** Joan E 1953- *WhoIns 92*
**Herman,** Joanna *DrAPF 91*
**Herman,** John Edward 1938- *AmMWSc 92*
**Herman,** John Henry 1939- *WhoWest 92*
**Herman,** Jonathan Michael 1947- *WhoAmL 92*
**Herman,** Josef 1911- *TwCPaSc, Who 92*
**Herman,** Josh Seth 1957- *WhoEnt 92*
**Herman,** Kathleen Virgil 1942- *WhoBlA 92*
**Herman,** Kathy Ellen 1962- *WhoAmL 92*
**Herman,** Kurt 1930- *WhoFI 92*
**Herman,** Lawrence 1924- *AmMWSc 92*
**Herman,** Lawrence 1929- *WhoAmL 92*
**Herman,** Lee Merideth 1954- *WhoAmL 92*
**Herman,** Leslie Jo 1955- *WhoMW 92*
**Herman,** Lynn Briggs 1956- *WhoAmP 91*
**Herman,** Mark B 1933- *WhoAmP 91*
**Herman,** Martin *AmMWSc 92*
**Herman,** Marvin 1927- *AmMWSc 92*
**Herman,** Mary M 1935- *AmMWSc 92*
**Herman,** Michael Alan 1945- *WhoWest 92*
**Herman,** Michelle *DrAPF 91*
**Herman,** Norman 1924- *IntMPA 92*
**Herman,** Paul Theodore 1939- *AmMWSc 92*

**Herman,** Pee-Wee 1952- *ConTFT 9, IntMPA 92*
**Herman,** Pinky 1905- *IntMPA 92*
**Herman,** Ray Michael 1949- *AmMWSc 92*
**Herman,** Richard Gerald 1944- *AmMWSc 92*
**Herman,** Richard Howard 1941- *AmMWSc 92*
**Herman,** Robert 1914- *AmMWSc 92*
**Herman,** Robert 1925-1991 *NewYTBS 91 [port]*
**Herman,** Robert Lewis 1927- *WhoFI 92*
**Herman,** Roger Eliot 1943- *WhoMW 92*
**Herman,** Roger Myers 1934- *AmMWSc 92*
**Herman,** Ronald Charles 1948- *WhoWest 92*
**Herman,** Ross Neil 1956- *WhoAmL 92*
**Herman,** Roy Alan 1943- *WhoMW 92*
**Herman,** Russ Michel 1942- *WhoAmL 92*
**Herman,** Samuel Sidney 1917- *AmMWSc 92*
**Herman,** Sidney N. 1953- *WhoAmL 92*
**Herman,** Sidney Samuel 1930- *AmMWSc 92*
**Herman,** Stephen Allen 1943- *WhoAmL 92*
**Herman,** Stephen Charles 1951- *WhoAmL 92, WhoMW 92*
**Herman,** Stephen Edward 1949- *WhoEnt 92*
**Herman,** Stewart Winfield 1948- *WhoRel 92*
**Herman,** Sumner Wilfred 1928- *WhoFI 92*
**Herman,** Theodore L 1936- *WhoIns 92*
**Herman,** Timothy Daniel 1964- *WhoEnt 92*
**Herman,** Warren Nevin 1948- *AmMWSc 92*
**Herman,** William 1926- *IntAu&W 91*
**Herman,** William S 1931- *AmMWSc 92*
**Herman,** Woody 1913-1987 *FacFETw, NewAmDM*
**Herman,** Zelek Seymour 1945- *AmMWSc 92*
**Hermance,** C E 1936- *AmMWSc 92*
**Hermance,** John Francis 1939- *AmMWSc 92*
**Hermangarde** *EncAmaz 91*
**Hermanies,** John Hans 1922- *WhoAmP 91*
**Hermaniuk,** Maxim 1911- *IntWW 91, WhoRel 92*
**Hermann,** Alexander Henry Baxter 1917- *Who 92*
**Hermann,** Allen Max 1938- *AmMWSc 92*
**Hermann,** Betty Jo 1934- *WhoAmP 91*
**Hermann,** Dale Milton 1942- *WhoAmL 92, WhoFI 92*
**Hermann,** Donald F 1921- *WhoAmP 91*
**Hermann,** Donald Harold James 1943- *WhoAmL 92, WhoFI 92, WhoMW 92*
**Hermann,** Edward Robert 1920- *AmMWSc 92*
**Hermann,** Eric Rudolf 1953- *WhoFI 92*
**Hermann,** Georg 1871-1943 *EncTR 91*
**Hermann,** Henry Remley, Jr 1935- *AmMWSc 92*
**Hermann,** Howard T 1925- *AmMWSc 92*
**Hermann,** Irene Irma 1914- *WhoFI 92*
**Hermann,** James Ray 1946- *WhoFI 92*
**Hermann,** Jane Pomerance 1935- *WhoEnt 92*
**Hermann,** John Alexander 1921- *AmMWSc 92*
**Hermann,** John Harlow 1960- *WhoWest 92*
**Hermann,** Joseph N *WhoAmP 91*
**Hermann,** Philip J. 1916- *WhoAmL 92, WhoMW 92*
**Hermann,** R 1904- *AmMWSc 92*
**Hermann,** Richard Karl 1924- *AmMWSc 92*
**Hermann,** Robert J *AmMWSc 92*
**Hermann,** Robert Jay 1933- *WhoAmP 91*
**Hermann,** Robert John 1944- *WhoFI 92*
**Hermann,** Robert Ringen 1923- *WhoFI 92*
**Hermann,** Steven Istvan 1934- *WhoFI 92*
**Hermann,** William Darrell 1924- *WhoFI 92*
**Hermannsson,** Steingrimur 1928- *IntWW 91*
**Hermano Pedro** *HisDSpE*
**Herman's Hermits** *NewAmDM*
**Hermans,** Christopher 1936- *IntWW 91*
**Hermans,** Colin Olmsted 1936- *AmMWSc 92*
**Hermans,** Cornelius Eduardus 1897- *BiDExR*
**Hermans,** Hans J 1938- *AmMWSc 92*
**Hermans,** Jan Joseph 1909- *AmMWSc 92*
**Hermans,** Paul E 1927- *AmMWSc 92*
**Hermanson,** Gordon Edward 1942- *WhoMW 92*
**Hermanson,** Harvey Philip 1932- *AmMWSc 92*
**Hermanson,** John Carl 1940- *AmMWSc 92*
**Hermanson,** Ronald Eldon 1933- *AmMWSc 92*
**Hermanuz,** Ghislaine *WhoBlA 92*
**Hermas** *EncEarC*
**Hermaszewski,** Miroslaw 1941- *IntWW 91*
**Hermening,** Kevin J 1959- *WhoAmP 91*
**Hermening,** Kevin Jay 1959- *WhoMW 92*
**Hermens,** Richard Anthony 1935- *AmMWSc 92*
**Hermer,** Julius 1933- *Who 92*
**Hermes** *IntAu&W 91X*
**Hermes** 1811-1875 *ScFEYrs*
**Hermes,** Andreas 1878-1964 *EncTR 91 [port]*
**Hermes,** David Paul 1954- *WhoMW 92*
**Hermes,** Gertrude 1901-1983 *TwCPaSc*
**Hermes,** Henry 1933- *AmMWSc 92*
**Hermes,** Marjory Ruth 1931- *WhoMW 92*
**Hermes,** O Don 1939- *AmMWSc 92*
**Hermes,** Theresa Margaret 1906- *WhoRel 92*
**Hermida,** Israel Octavio 1940- *WhoHisp 92*
**Hermione of Argos** *EncAmaz 91*
**Hermlin,** Stephan 1915- *LiExTwC*
**Hermo,** Alfonso Davila 1931- *WhoHisp 92*
**Hermodson,** Mark Allen 1942- *AmMWSc 92*
**Hermon,** Bev 1933- *WhoAmP 91*
**Hermon,** John 1928- *IntWW 91, Who 92*
**Hermon,** Peter Michael Robert 1928- *Who 92*
**Hermon-Hodge** *Who 92*
**Hermon-Taylor,** John 1936- *Who 92*
**Hermosillo,** Danny James 1962- *WhoHisp 92*
**Hermosillo,** Jaime Humberto 1942- *IntDcF 2-2*
**Hermreck,** Arlo Scott *AmMWSc 92*
**Herms,** Eilert Franz Martin 1940- *WhoRel 92*
**Hermsen,** Richard J 1928- *AmMWSc 92*
**Hermsen,** Robert W 1934- *AmMWSc 92*
**Hermsen,** Terry *DrAPF 91*
**Hermsmeier,** Lee F 1917- *AmMWSc 92*
**Hermsmeyer,** David Carl 1950- *WhoMW 92*
**Hermsmeyer,** Ralph Kent 1942- *AmMWSc 92*
**Hern,** Oliver, Jr. *WhoHisp 92*
**Hern,** Thomas Albert 1941- *AmMWSc 92*
**Hern,** William Richard 1921- *Who 92*
**Hernamann-Johnson,** Francis 1879-1949 *ScFEYrs*
**Hernandez,** Aileen 1926- *NotBlAW 92*
**Hernandez,** Aileen Clarke 1926- *WhoBlA 92*
**Hernandez,** Al 1955- *WhoEnt 92*
**Hernandez,** Albert L. 1924- *WhoHisp 92*
**Hernandez,** Albert P. 1948- *WhoHisp 92*
**Hernandez,** Alex *WhoHisp 92*
**Hernandez,** Alfonso V. 1937- *WhoHisp 92*
**Hernandez,** Andrew *WhoHisp 92*
**Hernandez,** Antonia 1948- *WhoHisp 92*
**Hernandez,** Antonio 1938- *WhoHisp 92*
**Hernandez,** Arturo 1947- *WhoHisp 92*
**Hernandez,** Augustin 1937- *WhoHisp 92*
**Hernandez,** Barbara *DrAPF 91*
**Hernandez,** Barbara Lorraine Michiels 1948- *WhoEnt 92*
**Hernandez,** Benigno Carlos 1917- *WhoHisp 92*
**Hernandez,** Berta Esperanza 1952- *WhoAmL 92*
**Hernandez,** Carlos 1967- *WhoHisp 92*
**Hernandez,** Christine 1951- *WhoAmP 91, WhoHisp 92*
**Hernandez,** Cirilo C. 1929- *WhoHisp 92*
**Hernandez,** Colleen Dalton *WhoMW 92*
**Hernandez,** Cruz Guajardo 1942- *WhoAmP 91*
**Hernandez,** David Andrade 1935- *WhoHisp 92*
**Hernandez,** David P. 1936- *WhoHisp 92*
**Hernandez,** Diego Edyl 1934- *WhoHisp 92*
**Hernandez,** Edward 1946- *WhoHisp 92*
**Hernandez,** Elia 1969- *WhoHisp 92*
**Hernandez,** Encarnacion 1946- *WhoHisp 92*
**Hernandez,** Enrique 1951- *WhoHisp 92*
**Hernandez,** Ernest G. 1931- *WhoHisp 92*
**Hernandez,** Evelio Joseph 1922- *WhoRel 92*
**Hernandez,** Evelyn 1958- *WhoHisp 92*
**Hernandez,** Fernando Vargas 1939- *WhoAmL 92*
**Hernandez,** Frances 1926- *WhoHisp 92*
**Hernandez,** Francis Xavier 1965- *WhoHisp 92*
**Hernandez,** Gary *WhoHisp 92*
**Hernandez,** Gary J. 1953- *WhoHisp 92*
**Hernandez,** George S. 1934- *WhoHisp 92*
**Hernandez,** George Stephen, Jr 1934- *WhoAmP 91*
**Hernandez,** Gladys 1951- *WhoHisp 92*
**Hernandez,** Gonzalez Jose Maria 1927- *WhoRel 92*
**Hernandez,** Gonzalo J 1936- *AmMWSc 92*
**Hernandez,** Guillermo Villanueva 1954- *WhoHisp 92*
**Hernandez,** Hector *WhoHisp 92*
**Hernandez,** Hector Rene 1953- *WhoHisp 92*
**Hernandez,** Henry O., Jr. 1956- *WhoHisp 92*
**Hernandez,** Hilda 1947- *WhoHisp 92*
**Hernandez,** Humberto *WhoHisp 92*
**Hernandez,** Irene Beltran 1945- *WhoHisp 92*
**Hernandez,** Irene C. *WhoHisp 92*
**Hernandez,** Isabel C. 1959- *WhoHisp 92*
**Hernandez,** Jacqueline Charmaine 1960- *WhoAmL 92*
**Hernandez,** James, Jr. 1942- *WhoHisp 92*
**Hernandez,** Jay 1957- *WhoFI 92*
**Hernandez,** Jesus Navarro 1935- *WhoHisp 92*
**Hernandez,** Jesus Ramon 1938- *WhoHisp 92*
**Hernandez,** Jo Farb 1952- *WhoWest 92*
**Hernandez,** Joe George 1946- *WhoHisp 92*
**Hernandez,** Joe L 1933- *WhoAmP 91*
**Hernandez,** Joe V. *WhoHisp 92*
**Hernandez,** John Peter 1940- *AmMWSc 92*
**Hernandez,** John R. 1955- *WhoHisp 92*
**Hernandez,** John S 1945- *WhoAmP 91*
**Hernandez,** John Stephen 1945- *WhoHisp 92*
**Hernandez,** John W 1929- *AmMWSc 92*
**Hernandez,** John Whitlock 1929- *WhoAmP 91, WhoHisp 92*
**Hernandez,** Jorge *BlkOlyM*
**Hernandez,** Jose 1834-1886 *BenetAL 91*
**Hernandez,** Jose 1935- *WhoHisp 92*
**Hernandez,** Jose Amaro 1930- *WhoHisp 92*
**Hernandez,** Jose Antonio 1951- *WhoHisp 92*
**Hernandez,** Jose E. 1957- *WhoHisp 92*
**Hernandez,** Jose Manuel 1925- *WhoHisp 92*
**Hernandez,** Joseph 1935- *WhoHisp 92*
**Hernandez,** Joseph Anthony 1950- *WhoHisp 92*
**Hernandez,** Juan *BlkOlyM*
**Hernandez,** Juan Antonio 1929- *AmMWSc 92*
**Hernandez,** Juan Donaldo 1933- *WhoHisp 92*
**Hernandez,** Juan Jose 1956- *WhoRel 92*
**Hernandez,** Juana Amelia *WhoHisp 92*
**Hernandez,** Julio, Jr. 1920- *WhoHisp 92*
**Hernandez,** Julio R 1931- *WhoIns 92*
**Hernandez,** Justin Joseph 1952- *WhoHisp 92*
**Hernandez,** Keith 1953- *WhoHisp 92*
**Hernandez,** Leodoro 1930- *WhoHisp 92*
**Hernandez,** Librada 1955- *WhoHisp 92*
**Hernandez,** Lillian A. 1959- *WhoWest 92*
**Hernandez,** Lisa 1962- *WhoHisp 92*
**Hernandez,** Louis Fernando 1952- *WhoHisp 92*
**Hernandez,** Luis Garcia 1941- *WhoHisp 92*
**Hernandez,** Luisa Josefina 1928- *SpAmWW*
**Hernandez,** Luz Corpi 1945- *WhoHisp 92*
**Hernandez,** Mack Ray 1944- *WhoAmL 92, WhoHisp 92*
**Hernandez,** Malu *WhoHisp 92*
**Hernandez,** Manny *WhoHisp 92*
**Hernandez,** Manuel 1936- *WhoHisp 92*
**Hernandez,** Manuel, Jr. 1951- *WhoHisp 92*
**Hernandez,** Marcos, Jr. 1950- *WhoHisp 92*
**Hernandez,** Maria *HanAmWH, WhoHisp 92*
**Hernandez,** Maria A. 1949- *WhoHisp 92*
**Hernandez,** Marie-Theresa 1952- *WhoHisp 92*
**Hernandez,** Mary N. 1940- *WhoBlA 92*
**Hernandez,** Michael A. *WhoHisp 92*
**Hernandez,** Michael Bruington 1960- *WhoHisp 92*
**Hernandez,** Miguel Angel, Jr. 1941- *WhoHisp 92*
**Hernandez,** Mike *WhoHisp 92*
**Hernandez,** Mike A. *WhoHisp 92*
**Hernandez,** Milagros 1938- *WhoHisp 92*
**Hernandez,** Nicolas, Jr. 1953- *WhoHisp 92*
**Hernandez,** Noel *WhoHisp 92*
**Hernandez,** Norma 1934- *AmMWSc 92*
**Hernandez,** Onesimo 1925- *WhoHisp 92*
**Hernandez,** Patrick Jerry 1968- *WhoEnt 92*
**Hernandez,** Paul F. 1954- *WhoHisp 92*
**Hernandez,** Philip Anthony 1940- *WhoAmP 91, WhoHisp 92*
**Hernandez,** Ramon R. *WhoHisp 92*
**Hernandez,** Randal J. 1959- *WhoHisp 92*
**Hernandez,** Raoul Emilio 1955- *WhoHisp 92*
**Hernandez,** Raul Antonio 1962- *WhoHisp 92*
**Hernandez,** Richard Froylan 1943- *WhoHisp 92*
**Hernandez,** Richard G. 1953- *WhoHisp 92*
**Hernandez,** Rita Rios 1953- *WhoHisp 92*
**Hernandez,** Robert Louis 1947- *WhoHisp 92*
**Hernandez,** Robert Michael 1945- *WhoAmP 91, WhoHisp 92*
**Hernandez,** Roberto F. 1948- *WhoHisp 92*
**Hernandez,** Roger Emilio 1955- *WhoHisp 92*
**Hernandez,** Ronald J. *WhoHisp 92*
**Hernandez,** Ruben 1949- *WhoHisp 92*
**Hernandez,** Sam 1948- *WhoHisp 92*
**Hernandez,** Samuel E. 1935- *WhoHisp 92*
**Hernandez,** Santiago 1947- *WhoHisp 92*
**Hernandez,** Sergio Anthony 1946- *WhoHisp 92*
**Hernandez,** Sigfredo Augusto 1954- *WhoHisp 92*
**Hernandez,** Susan 1960- *WhoHisp 92*
**Hernandez,** Teme P 1919- *AmMWSc 92*
**Hernandez,** Teme Paul 1919- *WhoHisp 92*
**Hernandez,** Thomas 1914- *AmMWSc 92*
**Hernandez,** Tony *WhoHisp 92*
**Hernandez,** Tony 1951- *WhoAmP 91*
**Hernandez,** Victoria 1948- *WhoHisp 92*
**Hernandez,** William 1948- *WhoFI 92*
**Hernandez,** William Hector, Jr. 1930- *WhoHisp 92*
**Hernandez,** Xavier 1965- *WhoHisp 92*
**Hernandez,** Zaida *WhoAmP 91*
**Hernandez Agosto,** Miguel A 1927- *WhoAmP 91*
**Hernandez-Agosto,** Miguel Angel 1927- *WhoHisp 92*
**Hernandez Albalate,** Emilio J. *WhoRel 92*
**Hernandez Alcerro,** Jorge Ramon 1948- *IntWW 91*
**Hernandez Avila,** Manuel Luis 1935- *AmMWSc 92, WhoHisp 92*
**Hernandez Cervantes,** Hector 1923- *IntWW 91*
**Hernandez Colon,** Rafael 1936- *IntWW 91, WhoAmP 91, WhoHisp 92*
**Hernandez Cruz,** Victor *DrAPF 91*
**Hernandez de Cordoba,** Francisco 1475-1518 *HisDSpE*
**Hernandez-Delgado,** Julio Luis 1953- *WhoHisp 92*
**Hernandez de Lopez,** Ana Maria 1930- *WhoHisp 92*
**Hernandez-Denton,** Federico 1944- *WhoAmP 91*
**Hernandez-Denton,** Federico 1954- *WhoAmL 92*
**Hernandez-G.,** Manuel de Jesus 1949- *WhoHisp 92*
**Hernandez Jimenez,** Consuelo *WhoHisp 92*
**Hernandez Jove,** Francis F *WhoAmP 91*
**Hernandez Mancha,** Antonio *IntWW 91*
**Hernandez-Miyares,** Julio Enrique 1931- *WhoHisp 92*
**Hernandez-Morales,** Roberto Eduardo 1931- *WhoHisp 92*
**Hernandez Ochoa,** Rafael 1915- *IntWW 91*
**Hernandez-Pinero,** Sally *WhoHisp 92*
**Hernandez-Prewitt,** Rufina Ann 1955- *WhoWest 92*
**Hernandez-Ramos,** Florence Dolores 1950- *WhoHisp 92*
**Hernandez-Rivera,** Andres 1935- *WhoHisp 92*
**Hernandez-Serna,** Isabel 1945- *WhoHisp 92*
**Hernandez Toledo,** Rene Antonio 1943- *WhoHisp 92*
**Hernandez Torres,** Zaida *WhoHisp 92*
**Hernandez-Vallejo,** Evelyn 1954- *WhoHisp 92*
**Hernandez von Hoff,** Gladys Amanda *WhoHisp 92*
**Herndobler,** Robin T. 1935- *WhoMW 92*
**Herndon,** Charles Harbison 1915- *AmMWSc 92*
**Herndon,** Charles L 1921- *AmMWSc 92*
**Herndon,** Craig Garris 1947- *WhoBlA 92*
**Herndon,** D. Blake 1960- *WhoFI 92*
**Herndon,** David N *AmMWSc 92*
**Herndon,** David Richard 1953- *WhoAmL 92*
**Herndon,** Gloria E. 1950- *WhoBlA 92*
**Herndon,** Hunter Venable 1927- *WhoEnt 92*
**Herndon,** James 1925- *WhoBlA 92*
**Herndon,** James Henry, Jr 1939- *AmMWSc 92*
**Herndon,** James W 1957- *AmMWSc 92*
**Herndon,** Lance H. 1955- *WhoBlA 92*
**Herndon,** Larry Lee 1953- *WhoBlA 92*
**Herndon,** Mark Steven 1947- *WhoWest 92*
**Herndon,** Noah Twist 1932- *WhoFI 92*
**Herndon,** Phillip George 1951- *WhoBlA 92*
**Herndon,** Robert McCulloch 1935- *AmMWSc 92, WhoWest 92*
**Herndon,** Roy C 1934- *AmMWSc 92*
**Herndon,** Walter Roger 1926- *AmMWSc 92*
**Herndon,** William Cecil 1932- *AmMWSc 92*
**Herndon,** William Henry 1818-1891 *BenetAL 91*
**Herne,** James A. 1839-1901 *BenetAL 91*
**Herne,** Mary *LesBEnT 92*
**Hernelius,** Allan 1911- *IntWW 91*
**Herner,** Albert Erwin 1931- *AmMWSc 92*

**Herniman**, Ronald George 1923- Who 92
**Hernqvist**, Karl Gerhard 1922- AmMWSc 92
**Hernried**, Robert 1883-1951 NewAmDM
**Hernstadt**, William H 1935- WhoAmP 91, WhoEnt 92
**Hernton**, Calvin DrAPF 91
**Hernton**, Calvin C. 1933- ConPo 91, WrDr 92
**Hernton**, Calvin Coolidge WhoBlA 92
**Hernu**, Charles 1923-1990 AnObit 1990
**Herochik**, Priscilla Andrea WhoAmL 92
**Herod**, James, Jr WhoAmP 91
**Herod**, James Victor 1937- AmMWSc 92
**Herold**, Cynthia Diane 1965- WhoWest 92
**Herold**, Don 1889-1966 BenetAL 91
**Herold**, E W 1907- AmMWSc 92
**Herold**, Ferdinand 1791-1833 NewAmDM
**Herold**, John Downs 1941- WhoMW 92
**Herold**, Karl Guenter 1947- WhoAmL 92
**Herold**, Paula M. WhoEnt 92
**Herold**, Richard Carl 1927- AmMWSc 92
**Herold**, Robert Johnston 1920- AmMWSc 92
**Herold**, William J 1930- WhoIns 92
**Herold-Paquis**, Jean 1912-1945 BiDExR
**Heron**, Benjamin 1722-1770 DcNCBi 3
**Heron**, Conrad 1916- Who 92
**Heron**, Hilary 1923- TwCPaSc
**Heron**, Julian Briscoe, Jr. 1939- WhoAmL 92
**Heron**, Patrick 1920- IntWW 91, TwCPaSc, Who 92, WrDr 92
**Heron**, Raymond 1924- Who 92
**Heron**, Robert 1927- Who 92
**Heron**, S Duncan 1926- AmMWSc 92
**Heron**, Susanna 1949- TwCPaSc
**Heron**, Timothy Edward 1948- WhoMW 92
**Heron**, Wesley David 1949- WhoFI 92
**Heron-Allen**, Edward TwCSFW 91
**Heron-Maxwell**, Nigel 1944- Who 92
**Herout**, Vlastimil 1921- IntWW 91
**Heroux**, Claude 1942- IntMPA 92
**Heroux**, Leon J 1927- AmMWSc 92
**Herowitz**, Alma Maxine 1919- WhoMW 92
**Heroy**, Susan DrAPF 91
**Heroy**, William Bayard, Jr 1915- AmMWSc 92
**Herpel**, Coleman 1911- AmMWSc 92
**Herr**, Dan 1917- IntWW 91
**Herr**, David Guy 1937- AmMWSc 92
**Herr**, Donald Edward 1926- AmMWSc 92
**Herr**, Earl Binkley, Jr 1928- AmMWSc 92, WhoMW 92
**Herr**, Frank Leaman, Jr 1948- AmMWSc 92
**Herr**, Harry Wallace 1943- AmMWSc 92
**Herr**, James Michael 1943- WhoAmL 92
**Herr**, John Christian 1948- AmMWSc 92
**Herr**, John Mervin, Jr 1930- AmMWSc 92
**Herr**, Kent Robert 1949- WhoFI 92
**Herr**, Leonard Jay 1928- AmMWSc 92
**Herr**, Michael SourALJ
**Herr**, Michael 1940?- BenetAL 91, WrDr 92
**Herr**, Monty LeRoy 1938- WhoWest 92
**Herr**, Pamela 1939- IntAu&W 91
**Herr**, Philip Michael 1955- WhoAmL 92
**Herr**, Richard 1922- WhoWest 92
**Herr**, Richard Baessler 1936- AmMWSc 92
**Herr**, Ross Robert 1926- AmMWSc 92
**Herr**, Stanley Sholom 1945- WhoAmL 92
**Herran**, Manuel A. WhoHisp 92
**Herregat**, Guy-Georges Jacques 1939- WhoFI 92
**Herreid**, Clyde F, II 1934- AmMWSc 92
**Herrell**, Astor Y 1935- AmMWSc 92
**Herrell**, Astor Yeary 1935- WhoBlA 92
**Herrell**, David Joy 1936- WhoRel 92
**Herrell**, Joseph Brett 1963- WhoRel 92
**Herrell**, Roger Wayne 1938- WhoAmL 92
**Herrema**, Donald James 1952- WhoFI 92
**Herren**, Albert R WhoAmP 91
**Herren**, Donald Ray 1930- WhoRel 92
**Herren**, Philip Curtis, Jr. 1930- WhoMW 92
**Herrera**, Albert A. 1950- WhoHisp 92
**Herrera**, Alfred J. WhoHisp 92
**Herrera**, Angel 1952- BlkOlyM [port]
**Herrera**, Bertha Garza de 1927- WhoHisp 92
**Herrera**, C. Andrea 1959- WhoHisp 92
**Herrera**, Carl WhoHisp 92
**Herrera**, Carlos d1992 WhoHisp 92N
**Herrera**, Carlos E. 1957- WhoHisp 92
**Herrera**, Carolina WhoHisp 92
**Herrera**, David Patrick 1944- WhoWest 92
**Herrera**, Eduardo Antonio 1953- WhoHisp 92
**Herrera**, Esau Ruiz 1950- WhoHisp 92
**Herrera**, Estela Maris 1943- WhoHisp 92
**Herrera**, Eusebio Stenio 1945- WhoWest 92
**Herrera**, Fidel Michael 1939- WhoHisp 92
**Herrera**, Francisco Rafael 1943- WhoWest 92
**Herrera**, Frank 1942- WhoHisp 92
**Herrera**, Frank G. 1943- WhoHisp 92
**Herrera**, George 1957- WhoHisp 92
**Herrera**, Guillermo Osvaldo 1952- WhoWest 92
**Herrera**, Herman Richard 1940- WhoHisp 92
**Herrera**, Jose 1973- WhoEnt 92
**Herrera**, Joseph Q. 1949- WhoHisp 92
**Herrera**, Juan de 1665?-1738 NewAmDM
**Herrera**, Lorenzo, Jr. 1948- WhoHisp 92
**Herrera**, Luis WhoHisp 92
**Herrera**, Luis Alberto 1944- WhoHisp 92
**Herrera**, Luis Felipe 1922- IntWW 91
**Herrera**, Manuel G. WhoHisp 92
**Herrera**, Marina A. 1942- WhoHisp 92
**Herrera**, Mario A. 1948- WhoHisp 92
**Herrera**, Monica Maria 1944- WhoHisp 92
**Herrera**, Peter 1953- WhoHisp 92
**Herrera**, Rafael C. 1934- WhoHisp 92
**Herrera**, Rene J. 1953- WhoHisp 92
**Herrera**, Richard Leo Salaz 1942- WhoHisp 92
**Herrera**, Robert Bennett 1913- WhoWest 92
**Herrera**, Rodimiro, Jr. 1944- WhoHisp 92
**Herrera**, Rosalinda G. 1948- WhoHisp 92
**Herrera**, Ruperto BlkOlyM
**Herrera**, Shirley Mae 1942- WhoFI 92, WhoWest 92
**Herrera**, Steve 1949- WhoHisp 92
**Herrera**, Steve J. 1943- WhoHisp 92
**Herrera**, Tomas BlkOlyM
**Herrera-Baez**, Porfiro 1915- IntWW 91
**Herrera Caceres**, Hector Roberto 1943- IntWW 91
**Herrera Campins**, Luis 1925- IntWW 91
**Herrera-Lavan**, Mario Antonio 1931- WhoHisp 92
**Herrera y Reissig**, Julio 1875-1910 BenetAL 91
**Herrera y Tordesillas**, Antonio 1559-1625 HisDSpE
**Herrerias**, Catalina 1948- WhoHisp 92
**Herrero**, Carmen A. 1960- WhoHisp 92
**Herrero**, Federico Antonio 1941- AmMWSc 92
**Herrero**, Van James, III 1949- WhoAmL 92
**Herrero-Kunhardt**, Susana 1945- WhoHisp 92
**Herrero Rodriguez De Minon**, Miguel 1940- IntWW 91
**Herres**, Robert T 1932- WhoIns 92
**Herres**, Ron P. 1952- WhoEnt 92
**Herreshoff**, Nathanael Greene 1848-1938 DcTwDes
**Herrett**, Richard Allison 1932- AmMWSc 92
**Herrick**, Bruce W 1944- WhoIns 92
**Herrick**, Clarence Luther 1858-1904 BiInAmS
**Herrick**, Claude Cummings 1927- AmMWSc 92
**Herrick**, David Rawls 1947- AmMWSc 92
**Herrick**, Earl George 1938- WhoWest 92
**Herrick**, Edward Claudius 1811-1862 BiInAmS
**Herrick**, Elbert Charles 1919- AmMWSc 92
**Herrick**, Franklin Willard 1922- AmMWSc 92
**Herrick**, Gerald D. 1934- WhoWest 92
**Herrick**, Glenn Arthur 1945- AmMWSc 92
**Herrick**, Irving Weymouth, Jr. 1932- WhoRel 92
**Herrick**, John Berne 1919- AmMWSc 92
**Herrick**, Joseph Raymond 1932- AmMWSc 92
**Herrick**, Kenneth Gilbert 1921- WhoFI 92, WhoMW 92
**Herrick**, Kristine Ford 1947- WhoEnt 92
**Herrick**, Peter 1926- WhoFI 92
**Herrick**, Robert 1591?-1674 RfGEnL 91
**Herrick**, Robert 1868-1938 BenetAL 91
**Herrick**, Robert Michael 1951- WhoFI 92
**Herrick**, Stewart Thurston 1945- WhoAmL 92
**Herrick**, Thomas J 1913- AmMWSc 92
**Herrick**, Todd W. 1942- WhoFI 92, WhoMW 92
**Herrick**, Tracy Grant 1933- WhoWest 92
**Herrick**, William DrAPF 91
**Herrick**, William 1915- IntAu&W 91, WrDr 92
**Herricks**, Edwin E 1946- AmMWSc 92
**Herridge**, Geoffrey Howard 1904- IntWW 91, Who 92
**Herries**, Michael Alexander Robert Young- 1923- Who 92
**Herries of Terregles**, Lady 1938- Who 92
**Herriford**, Merle Baird 1919- WhoBlA 92
**Herriman**, George 1880-1944 BenetAL 91
**Herrin**, Burley Francis 1944- WhoRel 92
**Herrin**, Charles Selby 1939- AmMWSc 92
**Herrin**, Eugene Thornton, Jr 1929- AmMWSc 92
**Herrin**, Moreland 1922- AmMWSc 92
**Herring**, Bernard Duane WhoBlA 92
**Herring**, Bernard Duane 1929- WhoAmL 92
**Herring**, Carey Reuben 1943- AmMWSc 92
**Herring**, Charles 1945- WhoAmP 91
**Herring**, Charles David 1943- WhoWest 92
**Herring**, Conyers 1914- IntWW 91
**Herring**, Cyril Alfred 1915- Who 92
**Herring**, David John 1958- WhoAmL 92
**Herring**, David Mayo 1929- WhoFI 92
**Herring**, Grover Cleveland 1925- WhoAmL 92
**Herring**, H James 1939- AmMWSc 92
**Herring**, Harold Keith 1939- AmMWSc 92
**Herring**, Harriet Laura 1892-1976 DcNCBi 3
**Herring**, Herbert James 1899-1966 DcNCBi 3
**Herring**, Jackson Rea 1931- AmMWSc 92
**Herring**, Jerone Carson 1938- WhoAmL 92
**Herring**, John Wesley, Jr 1927- AmMWSc 92
**Herring**, Joseph Dahlet 1934- WhoRel 92
**Herring**, Larry Windell 1946- WhoBlA 92
**Herring**, Laura WhoHisp 92
**Herring**, Leonard, Jr. 1934- WhoBlA 92
**Herring**, Patricia LeBlanc 1944- WhoFI 92
**Herring**, Raymond Mark 1952- WhoMW 92
**Herring**, Richard Norman 1938- AmMWSc 92
**Herring**, Susan Weller 1947- AmMWSc 92
**Herring**, Thomas A. 1942- WhoMW 92
**Herring**, Victoria L. 1947- WhoFI 92
**Herring**, Wade Wilkes, II 1958- WhoAmL 92
**Herring**, William Arthur 1945- WhoMW 92
**Herring**, William Benjamin 1928- AmMWSc 92
**Herring**, William Conyers 1914- AmMWSc 92
**Herring**, William F. 1932- WhoBlA 92
**Herring-Davis**, Denise 1957- WhoMW 92
**Herringer**, Frank Casper 1942- WhoFI 92, WhoWest 92
**Herrington**, Alex P. 1907- WhoFI 92
**Herrington**, Bryan David 1956- WhoRel 92
**Herrington**, Curtis Leo 1938- WhoRel 92
**Herrington**, Dale Elizabeth 1913- WhoRel 92
**Herrington**, Janet Eileen Rew 1954- WhoEnt 92
**Herrington**, John 1939- WhoAmP 91
**Herrington**, John S. 1939- IntWW 91
**Herrington**, Kermit 1923- AmMWSc 92
**Herrington**, Lee Pierce 1933- AmMWSc 92
**Herrington**, Neva DrAPF 91
**Herrington**, Perry Lee 1951- WhoBlA 92
**Herrington**, Robert Kingdon 1914- WhoEnt 92
**Herrington**, Walter John 1928- Who 92
**Herrington**, William D. 1841- DcNCBi 3
**Herrinton**, Paul Matthew 1957- AmMWSc 92
**Herriot**, Edouard 1872-1957 FacFETw
**Herriot**, Edouard Marie 1872-1957 EncTR 91 [port]
**Herriot**, James IntAu&W 91, Who 92, WrDr 92
**Herriot**, James 1916- IntWW 91
**Herriot**, John George 1916- AmMWSc 92
**Herriott**, Arthur W 1941- AmMWSc 92
**Herriott**, Donald R 1928- AmMWSc 92
**Herriott**, Jon R 1937- AmMWSc 92
**Herriott**, Roger Moss 1908- AmMWSc 92
**Herritage**, William 1707?-1769 DcNCBi 3
**Herrity**, Andrew Charles 1948- WhoWest 92
**Herrman**, Augustine 1605-1686 BiInAmS
**Herrman**, Esther 1822?-1911 BiInAmS
**Herrman**, John Henry 1960- WhoWest 92
**Herrman**, Marcia Kutz 1927- WhoWest 92
**Herrmann**, Arthur L 1926- WhoAmP 91
**Herrmann**, Bernard 1911-1975 FacFETw, NewAmDM
**Herrmann**, Cal C. 1930- WhoWest 92
**Herrmann**, Christian, Jr 1921- AmMWSc 92
**Herrmann**, Diana Chang DrAPF 91
**Herrmann**, Edward 1943- IntMPA 92
**Herrmann**, Edward Kirk 1943- WhoEnt 92
**Herrmann**, Ernest Carl, Jr 1925- AmMWSc 92
**Herrmann**, George 1921- AmMWSc 92
**Herrmann**, Heinz 1911- AmMWSc 92
**Herrmann**, Helen d1991 NewYTBS 91
**Herrmann**, John Bellows 1932- AmMWSc 92
**Herrmann**, Kenneth L 1934- AmMWSc 92
**Herrmann**, Kenneth Walter 1929- AmMWSc 92
**Herrmann**, Klaus Manfred 1937- AmMWSc 92
**Herrmann**, Lacy Bunnell 1929- WhoFI 92
**Herrmann**, Leo Anthony 1925- AmMWSc 92
**Herrmann**, Leonard R 1936- AmMWSc 92
**Herrmann**, Lorena Joyce 1925- WhoMW 92
**Herrmann**, Luke John 1932- WrDr 92
**Herrmann**, Raymond 1941- AmMWSc 92
**Herrmann**, Raymond Pahl 1951- WhoMW 92
**Herrmann**, Rebecca Garrou 1964- WhoAmL 92
**Herrmann**, Robert Arthur 1934- AmMWSc 92
**Herrmann**, Robert Bernard 1944- AmMWSc 92
**Herrmann**, Robert Lawrence 1928- AmMWSc 92
**Herrmann**, Roy G 1920- AmMWSc 92
**Herrmann**, Sandra Sue 1944- WhoRel 92
**Herrmann**, Scott Joseph 1942- AmMWSc 92
**Herrmann**, Siegfried 1926- IntWW 91
**Herrmann**, Steven H AmMWSc 92
**Herrmann**, Thomas Anthony 1928- WhoMW 92
**Herrmann**, Thomas Francis 1951- WhoMW 92
**Herrmann**, Ulrich Otto 1925- AmMWSc 92
**Herrmann**, Walter 1930- AmMWSc 92
**Herrmann**, Walter L 1923- AmMWSc 92
**Herrmann**, Wyatt D. 1956- WhoEnt 92
**Herrmanns**, Ralph 1933- IntAu&W 91, WrDr 92
**Herrmannsfeldt**, William Bernard 1931- AmMWSc 92
**Herrnkind**, William Frank 1940- AmMWSc 92
**Herrnstein**, Barbara WrDr 92
**Herro**, David Gregory 1960- WhoFI 92
**Herrod**, Donald 1930- Who 92
**Herrod**, Henry Grady AmMWSc 92
**Herron**, Andrew 1909- IntWW 91, Who 92
**Herron**, Bill DrAPF 91
**Herron**, Bruce Wayne 1954- WhoBlA 92
**Herron**, David Kent 1942- AmMWSc 92
**Herron**, Edwin Hunter, Jr. 1938- WhoFI 92
**Herron**, Elizabeth C. DrAPF 91
**Herron**, Ellen Patricia 1927- WhoWest 92
**Herron**, George Davis 1862-1925 RelLAm 91
**Herron**, George M 1925- AmMWSc 92
**Herron**, Henry 1911- Who 92
**Herron**, Isom H 1946- AmMWSc 92
**Herron**, James Dudley 1936- AmMWSc 92
**Herron**, James M. 1934- WhoAmL 92
**Herron**, James Watt 1920- AmMWSc 92
**Herron**, James Wayne 1955- WhoRel 92
**Herron**, John Thomas 1931- AmMWSc 92
**Herron**, Michael Myrl 1949- AmMWSc 92
**Herron**, Norman 1954- AmMWSc 92
**Herron**, Orley R. 1933- WhoMW 92
**Herron**, Orley Rufus 1933- WrDr 92
**Herron**, Ronald James 1930- Who 92
**Herron**, Roy B 1953- WhoAmP 91
**Herron**, Shaun IntAu&W 91
**Herron**, Sidney Earl 1952- WhoFI 92
**Herron**, Vernon M. 1928- WhoBlA 92
**Herron**, William 1933- WrDr 92
**Herrstrom**, David Sten DrAPF 91
**Herrup**, Cynthia B. 1950- WhoAmL 92
**Herrup**, Karl Franklin 1948- AmMWSc 92
**Hersant**, Robert Joseph Emile 1920- IntWW 91, WhoEnt 92
**Hersch**, Dennis Steven 1947- WhoAmL 92
**Hersch**, Eugen 1887-1967 TwCPaSc
**Herschbach**, Dudley Robert 1932- AmMWSc 92, IntWW 91, Who 92, WhoNob 90
**Herschberger**, Ruth DrAPF 91
**Herschberger**, Ruth 1917- BenetAL 91
**Herschel**, John DrAPF 91
**Herschel**, William 1738-1822 BlkwCEP, NewAmDM
**Herschell** Who 92
**Herschell**, Baron 1923- Who 92
**Herschensohn**, Bruce 1932- WhoEnt 92
**Herscher**, Uri David 1941- WhoWest 92
**Herschfus**, Leon WhoAmP 91
**Herschler**, Elijah David 1940- WhoWest 92
**Herschler**, Leslie Norman 1958- WhoWest 92
**Herschler**, Michael Saul 1936- AmMWSc 92
**Herschman**, Arthur d1991 NewYTBS 91
**Herschman**, Arthur 1929- AmMWSc 92
**Herschman**, Harvey R 1940- AmMWSc 92
**Herschorn**, Michael 1933- AmMWSc 92
**Herscovics**, Annette Antoinette 1938- AmMWSc 92
**Herscowitz**, Herbert Bernard 1939- AmMWSc 92
**Herseth**, Adolph 1921- NewAmDM
**Herseth**, Ralph Lars WhoAmP 91
**Hersey**, David Kenneth 1939- Who 92, WhoEnt 92

**Hersey,** Harold Brainerd 1893-1956 *BenetAL 91*
**Hersey,** John *DrAPF 91*
**Hersey,** John 1914- *BenetAL 91, ConNov 91, FacFETw, SourALJ, Who 92, WrDr 92*
**Hersey,** John B 1913- *AmMWSc 92*
**Hersey,** John Richard 1914- *IntAu&W 91, IntWW 91*
**Hersey,** Stephen J 1943- *AmMWSc 92*
**Hersh,** Barry Fred 1947- *WhoFI 92*
**Hersh,** Burton David 1933- *IntAu&W 91*
**Hersh,** Charles K 1924- *AmMWSc 92*
**Hersh,** Evan Manuel 1935- *AmMWSc 92*
**Hersh,** Herbert N 1923- *AmMWSc 92*
**Hersh,** John Franklin 1920- *AmMWSc 92*
**Hersh,** Leroy S 1931- *AmMWSc 92*
**Hersh,** Louis Barry 1940- *AmMWSc 92*
**Hersh,** Phyllis Janet 1965- *WhoFI 92*
**Hersh,** Reuben 1927- *AmMWSc 92*
**Hersh,** Robert Michael 1940- *WhoAmL 92*
**Hersh,** Robert Tweed 1927- *AmMWSc 92*
**Hersh,** Solomon Philip 1929- *AmMWSc 92*
**Hersh,** Stephen I. 1956- *WhoMW 92*
**Hersh,** Stuart Allen 1934- *WhoEnt 92*
**Hersh,** Sylvan David 1940- *AmMWSc 92*
**Hersh,** Theodore *AmMWSc 92*
**Hersha,** Alexander Joseph 1929- *WhoAmL 92*
**Hershan,** Stella K. *DrAPF 91, LiExTwC*
**Hershatter,** Richard Lawrence 1923- *WhoAmL 92*
**Hershberg,** David Stephen 1941- *WhoFI 92*
**Hershberg,** Philip I 1935- *AmMWSc 92*
**Hershberger,** Charles Lee 1942- *AmMWSc 92, WhoMW 92*
**Hershberger,** Ervin N. 1914- *WhoRel 92*
**Hershberger,** Jerry Richard 1951- *WhoMW 92*
**Hershberger,** John Wayne, II 1946- *WhoIns 92*
**Hershberger,** Larry D 1944- *WhoIns 92*
**Hershberger,** Robert Glen 1936- *WhoWest 92*
**Hershberger,** Truman Verne 1927- *AmMWSc 92*
**Hershenov,** B 1927- *AmMWSc 92*
**Hershenov,** Joseph 1935- *AmMWSc 92*
**Hershenson,** Benjamin R 1940- *AmMWSc 92*
**Hershenson,** Herbert Malcolm 1929- *AmMWSc 92*
**Hersher,** Kurt Bernard 1928- *WhoFI 92*
**Hershey,** Alfred D 1908- *AmMWSc 92*
**Hershey,** Alfred Day 1908- *IntWW 91, Who 92, WhoNob 90*
**Hershey,** Allen Vincent 1910- *AmMWSc 92*
**Hershey,** Amos Shartle 1867-1933 *AmPeW*
**Hershey,** Arthur Duane 1937- *WhoAmP 91*
**Hershey,** Barbara *IntWW 91*
**Hershey,** Barbara 1948- *IntMPA 92, WhoEnt 92*
**Hershey,** Colin Harry 1935- *WhoFI 92*
**Hershey,** Daniel 1931- *AmMWSc 92, WhoMW 92*
**Hershey,** Falls Bacon 1918- *AmMWSc 92*
**Hershey,** Franklin Quick 1907- *DcTwDes, FacFETw*
**Hershey,** H Garland 1905- *AmMWSc 92*
**Hershey,** Harry Chenault 1938- *AmMWSc 92*
**Hershey,** Jane 1961- *WhoAmP 91*
**Hershey,** John Landis 1935- *AmMWSc 92*
**Hershey,** John William Baker 1934- *AmMWSc 92*
**Hershey,** Linda Ann 1947- *AmMWSc 92*
**Hershey,** Nathan 1930- *AmMWSc 92*
**Hershey,** Robert Lewis 1941- *AmMWSc 92*
**Hershey,** Roger W. 1945- *WhoAmL 92*
**Hershey,** Solomon George 1914- *AmMWSc 92*
**Hershfield,** Earl S 1934- *AmMWSc 92*
**Hershfield,** Michael Steven 1942- *AmMWSc 92*
**Hershiser,** Orel Leonard, IV 1958- *WhoWest 92*
**Hershkowitz,** Noah 1941- *AmMWSc 92*
**Hershkowitz,** Robert L 1938- *AmMWSc 92*
**Hershman,** James Howard, Jr 1947- *WhoAmP 91*
**Hershman,** Jerome Marshall 1932- *AmMWSc 92*
**Hershman,** Mendes 1911- *WhoIns 92*
**Hershman,** Scott Edward 1958- *WhoAmL 92*
**Hershner,** Ivan Raymond, Jr 1916- *AmMWSc 92*
**Hershon,** Robert *DrAPF 91*
**Hersi,** Abdurahman Nur 1934- *IntWW 91*
**Herskovits,** Theodore Tibor 1928- *AmMWSc 92*
**Herskovitz,** Arthur M. 1920- *IntMPA 92*
**Herskovitz,** Arthur Maurice 1920- *WhoEnt 92*
**Herskovitz,** Marshall 1952- *IntMPA 92*
**Herskovitz,** Marshall, and Zwick, Edward *LesBEnT 92*
**Herskovitz,** Marshall Schreiber 1952- *WhoEnt 92*
**Herskovitz,** Melville Jean 1895-1963 *BenetAL 91*
**Herskovitz,** Sam Marc 1949- *WhoAmL 92*
**Herskovitz,** Thomas 1947- *AmMWSc 92*
**Herskowitz,** Carol A *WhoAmP 91*
**Herskowitz,** Gerald Joseph 1936- *AmMWSc 92*
**Herskowitz,** Ira 1946- *AmMWSc 92*
**Herskowitz,** Irwin Herman 1920- *AmMWSc 92*
**Herskowitz,** Jon Michael 1964- *WhoAmL 92*
**Herslip,** Larry 1945- *WhoAmP 91*
**Hersman,** Ferd William 1922- *WhoFI 92*
**Hersom,** Naomi Louisa 1927- *IntWW 91*
**Herson,** Arlene Rita *WhoEnt 92*
**Herson,** Diane S 1944- *AmMWSc 92*
**Hersov,** Basil Edward 1926- *IntWW 91*
**Hersrud,** James Robert 1946- *WhoAmP 91*
**Herst,** Douglas Julian 1943- *WhoFI 92*
**Herstam,** Chris 1949- *WhoAmP 91*
**Herstand,** Theodore 1930- *WhoEnt 92*
**Herstek,** Maureen Crook 1948- *WhoAmP 91*
**Hertel,** Curtis A 1953- *WhoAmP 91*
**Hertel,** Dennis M. 1948- *AlmAP 92 [port], WhoAmP 91*
**Hertel,** Dennis Mark 1948- *WhoMW 92*
**Hertel,** George Robert 1934- *AmMWSc 92*
**Hertel,** Paul R, Jr 1928- *WhoIns 92*
**Hertelendy,** Frank 1931- *AmMWSc 92*
**Herter,** Christian Archibald 1865-1910 *BiInAmS*
**Herter,** Christian Archibald 1895-1966 *AmPolLe*
**Herter,** Frederic P 1920- *AmMWSc 92*
**Hertford,** Bishop Suffragan of 1936- *Who 92*
**Hertford,** Marquess of 1930- *Who 92*
**Hertfordshire,** Bishop in *Who 92*
**Herther,** Nancy K. 1951- *WhoFI 92*
**Hertig,** Arthur Tremain 1904- *AmMWSc 92*
**Herting,** Claireen LaVern 1929- *WhoAmL 92*
**Herting,** David Clair 1928- *AmMWSc 92*
**Herting,** Robert Leslie 1929- *AmMWSc 92*
**Hertl,** Regina M. 1959- *WhoFI 92*
**Hertl,** William 1932- *AmMWSc 92*
**Hertle,** Frank *DrAPF 91*
**Hertlein,** Fred, III 1933- *AmMWSc 92, WhoWest 92*
**Hertler,** Walter Raymond 1933- *AmMWSc 92*
**Hertling,** Viktoria *WhoWest 92*
**Hertneky,** Randy Lee 1955- *WhoWest 92*
**Hertsgaard,** Doris M Fisher 1939- *AmMWSc 92*
**Hertweck,** E. Romayne 1928- *WhoWest 92*
**Hertweck,** Galen Fredric 1946- *WhoRel 92*
**Hertweck,** Gerald 1934- *AmMWSc 92*
**Hertwig,** Waldemar R 1920- *AmMWSc 92*
**Herty,** Charles Holmes 1867-1938 *DcNCBi 3*
**Herty,** Charles Holmes, Jr. 1896-1953 *DcNCBi 3*
**Hertz,** Alfred 1872-1942 *NewAmDM*
**Hertz,** Bradley William 1963- *WhoAmL 92*
**Hertz,** David Bendel 1919- *AmMWSc 92*
**Hertz,** Friedrich Otto 1878-1964 *EncTR 91*
**Hertz,** Gustav 1887-1975 *EncTR 91 [port], FacFETw*
**Hertz,** Gustav Ludwig 1887-1975 *WhoNob 90*
**Hertz,** Harry Steven 1947- *AmMWSc 92*
**Hertz,** Howard 1949- *WhoAmL 92, WhoEnt 92*
**Hertz,** John Atlee 1945- *AmMWSc 92*
**Hertz,** Kenneth Theodore 1951- *WhoEnt 92*
**Hertz,** Leonard B 1924- *AmMWSc 92*
**Hertz,** Michael Terry 1944- *WhoAmL 92*
**Hertz,** Paul 1888-1961 *EncTR 91*
**Hertz,** Paul Eric 1951- *AmMWSc 92*
**Hertz,** Richard Cornell 1916- *WhoRel 92*
**Hertz,** Roy 1909- *AmMWSc 92, IntWW 91*
**Hertz,** William 1923- *IntMPA 92*
**Hertzberg,** Abraham 1922- *AmMWSc 92*
**Hertzberg,** Arthur 1921- *WhoRel 92, WrDr 92*
**Hertzberg,** Harold Joel 1922- *WhoWest 92*
**Hertzberg,** Hendrik 1943- *IntAu&W 91*
**Hertzberg,** Martin 1930- *AmMWSc 92*
**Hertzberg,** Paul Stuart 1949- *WhoEnt 92*
**Hertzberg,** Richard Lloyd 1963- *WhoAmL 92*
**Hertzberg,** Richard Warren 1937- *AmMWSc 92*
**Hertzberg,** Robert Steven 1954- *WhoAmL 92*
**Hertzberg,** Stuart E 1926- *WhoAmP 91*
**Hertzberger,** Herman 1932- *IntWW 91*
**Hertzel,** Brian James 1954- *WhoFI 92*
**Hertzenberg,** Elliot Paul 1938- *AmMWSc 92*
**Hertzig,** David 1932- *AmMWSc 92, WhoFI 92*
**Hertzler,** Barry Lee 1947- *AmMWSc 92*
**Hertzler,** Donald Vincent 1938- *AmMWSc 92*
**Hertzler,** Emanuel Cassel 1917- *AmMWSc 92*
**Hertzman,** Phillip Alan 1946- *WhoWest 92*
**Hertzmark,** Donald Ian 1949- *WhoFI 92*
**Herum,** Floyd L 1928- *AmMWSc 92*
**Herum,** Steven A. *WhoAmL 92*
**Herve** 1825-1892 *NewAmDM*
**Herve,** Edmond 1942- *IntWW 91*
**Herve,** Gustave 1871-1944 *EncTR 91*
**Herve-Bazin,** Jean-Pierre Marie 1911- *IntWW 91*
**Hervey** *Who 92*
**Hervey,** Billy T. 1937- *WhoBlA 92*
**Hervey,** Evelyn *ConAu 34NR*
**Hervey,** Harry C. 1900-1951 *BenetAL 91*
**Hervey,** Jack L. 1938- *WhoFI 92, WhoMW 92*
**Hervey,** John Bethell 1928- *Who 92*
**Hervey,** Ramon Triche, II 1950- *WhoBlA 92*
**Hervey-Bathurst,** F. *Who 92*
**Herwald,** Seymour W 1917- *AmMWSc 92*
**Herwarth Von Bittenfeld,** Hans 1904- *IntWW 91*
**Herwarth von Bittenfeld,** Hans Heinrich 1904- *Who 92*
**Herwig,** Lloyd Otto 1921- *AmMWSc 92*
**Herwig,** Rob 1935- *WrDr 92*
**Herwig,** Steven Roger 1948- *WhoMW 92*
**Herwitz,** David Richard 1925- *WhoAmL 92*
**Herwitz,** Paul Stanley 1923- *AmMWSc 92*
**Herz,** Andrew Lee 1946- *WhoAmL 92*
**Herz,** Arthur H 1921- *AmMWSc 92*
**Herz,** Carl Samuel 1930- *AmMWSc 92*
**Herz,** David Stanley 1946- *WhoEnt 92*
**Herz,** Fritz 1930- *AmMWSc 92*
**Herz,** Henri 1803-1888 *NewAmDM*
**Herz,** Jack L 1938- *AmMWSc 92*
**Herz,** Marvin Ira 1927- *AmMWSc 92*
**Herz,** Matthew Lawrence 1941- *AmMWSc 92*
**Herz,** Michael Joseph 1936- *WhoWest 92*
**Herz,** Norman 1923- *AmMWSc 92*
**Herz,** Werner 1921- *AmMWSc 92*
**Herzberg,** Charles Francis 1924- *Who 92*
**Herzberg,** Dorothy Crews 1935- *WhoWest 92*
**Herzberg,** Gerhard 1904- *AmMWSc 92, IntWW 91, Who 92, WhoNob 90, WrDr 92*
**Herzberg,** Max J. 1886-1958 *BenetAL 91*
**Herzberger,** Arthur Conrad 1917- *WhoAmP 91*
**Herzeca,** Lois Friedman 1954- *WhoAmL 92*
**Herzel,** Leo 1923- *WhoAmL 92*
**Herzenberg,** Arvid 1925- *AmMWSc 92*
**Herzenberg,** Caroline Stuart Littlejohn 1932- *AmMWSc 92*
**Herzenberg,** Leonard Arthur 1931- *AmMWSc 92*
**Herzer,** Richard Kimball 1931- *WhoFI 92*
**Herzfeld,** Charles Maria 1925- *AmMWSc 92*
**Herzfeld,** Garson 1951- *WhoRel 92*
**Herzfeld,** Helmut *DcTwDes*
**Herzfeld,** Judith 1948- *AmMWSc 92*
**Herzfeld,** Julian 1958- *WhoEnt 92*
**Herzfeld,** Valerius E 1921- *AmMWSc 92*
**Herzfeld,** Will Lawrence 1937- *WhoBlA 92*
**Herzig,** Charles E. 1929- *WhoRel 92*
**Herzig,** Christopher 1926- *Who 92*
**Herzig,** David Jacob 1936- *AmMWSc 92*
**Herzig,** Geoffrey Peter 1941- *AmMWSc 92*
**Herzl,** Theodor 1860-1904 *EncTR 91 [port], FacFETw [port]*
**Herzlich,** Harold Joel 1934- *AmMWSc 92*
**Herzlinger,** George Arthur 1943- *AmMWSc 92*
**Herzog,** Arthur 1927- *WrDr 92*
**Herzog,** Bertram 1929- *AmMWSc 92*
**Herzog,** Brigitte 1943- *WhoAmL 92*
**Herzog,** Chaim 1918- *FacFETw, IntWW 91, Who 92*
**Herzog,** Emil Rudolph 1917- *AmMWSc 92*
**Herzog,** Fritz 1902- *AmMWSc 92*
**Herzog,** Gary Drew 1964- *WhoWest 92*
**Herzog,** Gerald B 1927- *AmMWSc 92*
**Herzog,** Gregory F 1944- *AmMWSc 92*
**Herzog,** H. Donald 1942- *WhoFI 92*
**Herzog,** Hershel Leon 1924- *AmMWSc 92*
**Herzog,** James Herman 1939- *AmMWSc 92*
**Herzog,** John L 1938- *WhoAmP 91*
**Herzog,** John Orlando 1935- *AmMWSc 92*
**Herzog,** Karl A 1940- *AmMWSc 92*
**Herzog,** Leonard Frederick, II 1926- *AmMWSc 92*
**Herzog,** Lester Barry 1953- *WhoAmL 92*
**Herzog,** Maurice 1919- *IntWW 91*
**Herzog,** Raymond Harry 1915- *IntWW 91*
**Herzog,** Richard 1911- *AmMWSc 92*
**Herzog,** Richard Barnard 1939- *WhoAmL 92*
**Herzog,** Scott McComb 1953- *WhoEnt 92*
**Herzog,** Steven Craig 1962- *WhoAmL 92*
**Herzog,** Steven Paul 1960- *WhoFI 92*
**Herzog,** Werner 1942- *FacFETw, IntDcF 2-2, IntMPA 92, IntWW 91*
**Herzog,** Whitey 1931- *WhoWest 92*
**Herzstein,** Robert Erwin 1931- *WhoAmL 92*
**Hesburgh,** Theodore M 1917- *FacFETw, IntWW 91*
**Hesburgh,** Theodore Martin 1917- *RelLAm 91, WhoRel 92*
**Heschel,** Abraham Joshua 1907-1972 *RelLAm 91*
**Heschong,** Gregg 1949- *WhoEnt 92*
**Heseltine,** John *TwCPaSc*
**Heseltine,** Michael 1933- *FacFETw, Who 92*
**Heseltine,** Michael Ray Dibdin 1933- *IntWW 91*
**Heseltine,** Philip Arnold 1894-1930 *NewAmDM*
**Heseltine,** William 1930- *Who 92*
**Heselton,** Corys M 1905- *WhoAmP 91*
**Hesen,** Mitchell Huto 1957- *WhoFI 92*
**Hesh,** Joseph McLean 1954- *WhoRel 92, WhoWest 92*
**Heskes,** Scott Earle 1952- *WhoWest 92*
**Hesketh,** Baron 1950- *Who 92*
**Hesketh,** Howard E 1931- *AmMWSc 92*
**Hesketh,** J D 1935- *AmMWSc 92*
**Hesketh,** Phoebe 1909- *ConPo 91, IntAu&W 91, WrDr 92*
**Heskin,** Thomas M *WhoAmP 91*
**Heskins-Lazar,** Susan Michelle 1960- *WhoRel 92*
**Hesla,** Stephen *DrAPF 91*
**Heslam,** Janet Vernon 1940- *WhoRel 92*
**Heslam,** Noelle *Who 92*
**Heslep,** Robert Durham 1930- *WrDr 92*
**Heslin,** James William, Jr 1944- *WhoIns 92*
**Heslop,** Marvin S *WhoAmP 91*
**Heslop,** Philip Linnell 1948- *Who 92*
**Heslop,** Van Christopher 1955- *WhoRel 92*
**Heslop-Harrison,** John 1920- *IntWW 91, Who 92*
**Hespenheide,** Henry August, III 1942- *AmMWSc 92*
**Hespers,** Theo 1903-1943 *EncTR 91*
**Hess,** Adrien LeRoy 1908- *AmMWSc 92*
**Hess,** Allan Duane *AmMWSc 92*
**Hess,** Arin Lynd 1956- *WhoAmP 91*
**Hess,** Arthur 1927- *AmMWSc 92*
**Hess,** Barbara M. 1952- *WhoFI 92*
**Hess,** Bartlett Leonard 1910- *WhoMW 92, WhoRel 92*
**Hess,** Benno 1922- *IntWW 91*
**Hess,** Bernard Andes, Jr 1940- *AmMWSc 92*
**Hess,** Carol E 1942- *WhoAmP 91*
**Hess,** Carroll V 1923- *AmMWSc 92*
**Hess,** Charles 1931- *AmMWSc 92*
**Hess,** Charles Thomas 1940- *AmMWSc 92*
**Hess,** Daniel Bartlett 1940- *WhoAmP 91*
**Hess,** Daniel Nicholas 1920- *AmMWSc 92*
**Hess,** David C. 1963- *WhoFI 92*
**Hess,** David Clarence 1916- *AmMWSc 92*
**Hess,** David Filbert 1940- *AmMWSc 92, WhoMW 92*
**Hess,** David Graham 1957- *WhoFI 92*
**Hess,** David L. 1941- *WhoWest 92*
**Hess,** David W 1942- *WhoAmP 91*
**Hess,** Delbert Coy 1936- *AmMWSc 92*
**Hess,** Dennis John 1940- *WhoFI 92*
**Hess,** Dennis William 1947- *AmMWSc 92*
**Hess,** Dexter Winfield 1927- *AmMWSc 92*
**Hess,** Dick L 1938- *WhoAmP 91*
**Hess,** Donald F. 1919- *WhoFI 92*
**Hess,** Douglas M. 1948- *WhoAmL 92*
**Hess,** Earl Hollinger 1928- *AmMWSc 92*
**Hess,** Ellen Elizabeth 1908- *Who 92*
**Hess,** Emerson Garfield 1914- *WhoAmL 92*
**Hess,** Errol *DrAPF 91*
**Hess,** Eugene Lyle 1914- *AmMWSc 92*
**Hess,** Evelyn V 1926- *AmMWSc 92*
**Hess,** Frederick Dan 1946- *AmMWSc 92*
**Hess,** Frederick J. 1941- *WhoAmL 92*
**Hess,** Gary Charles 1948- *WhoRel 92*
**Hess,** Gary R. 1937- *WrDr 92*
**Hess,** Geoffrey LaVerne 1949- *WhoFI 92*
**Hess,** George Burns 1936- *AmMWSc 92*
**Hess,** George Franklin, II 1939- *WhoAmL 92*
**Hess,** George G 1938- *AmMWSc 92*
**Hess,** George Griffith 1938- *WhoMW 92*
**Hess,** George Paul 1926- *AmMWSc 92*

**Hess**, Hans-Jurgen Ernst 1930- *AmMWSc 92*
**Hess**, Helen Hope 1923- *AmMWSc 92*
**Hess**, Hermann 1877-1962 *LiExTwC*
**Hess**, Howard Drysdale 1872?-1916 *BiInAmS*
**Hess**, Howard M 1908- *AmMWSc 92*
**Hess**, Joan *WrDr 92*
**Hess**, Joan 1949- *ConAu 134*
**Hess**, John Berger 1942- *AmMWSc 92*
**Hess**, John Lloyd 1939- *AmMWSc 92*
**Hess**, John Monroe Converse 1931- *AmMWSc 92*
**Hess**, John Philip 1954- *WhoMW 92*
**Hess**, John Stephen 1958- *WhoEnt 92*
**Hess**, John Warren 1947- *AmMWSc 92*
**Hess**, Jonathan Louis 1940- *WhoMW 92*
**Hess**, Joseph W, Jr 1926- *AmMWSc 92*
**Hess**, Karl 1923- *WhoAmP 91*
**Hess**, Karl 1945- *AmMWSc 92*
**Hess**, Karsten 1930- *WhoFI 92*
**Hess**, Larry Lee 1939- *WhoRel 92*
**Hess**, LaVerne Derryl 1933- *AmMWSc 92*
**Hess**, Lawrence Eugene, Jr. 1923- *WhoAmL 92*
**Hess**, Lawrence George 1916- *AmMWSc 92*
**Hess**, Lee Howard 1947- *WhoFI 92*
**Hess**, Leon 1914- *WhoFI 92*
**Hess**, Lindsay LaRoy 1940- *AmMWSc 92*
**Hess**, Lucille Jane 1945- *WhoMW 92*
**Hess**, Lynn *DrAPF 91*
**Hess**, Margaret Johnston 1915- *WhoMW 92, WhoRel 92*
**Hess**, Marilyn E 1924- *AmMWSc 92*
**Hess**, Melvin 1925- *AmMWSc 92*
**Hess**, Michael L *AmMWSc 92*
**Hess**, Myra 1890-1965 *FacFETw, NewAmDM*
**Hess**, Patrick Henry 1931- *AmMWSc 92*
**Hess**, Paul C 1940- *AmMWSc 92*
**Hess**, R A 1942- *AmMWSc 92*
**Hess**, Ralph W 1939- *WhoAmP 91*
**Hess**, Richard Alfred 1926- *WhoWest 92*
**Hess**, Richard C. d1991 *NewYTBS 91*
**Hess**, Richard Lowell 1951- *WhoWest 92*
**Hess**, Richard William 1944- *AmMWSc 92*
**Hess**, Robert, Jr. 1957- *WhoFI 92*
**Hess**, Robert B. 1959- *WhoEnt 92*
**Hess**, Robert Haldeman 1937- *WhoMW 92*
**Hess**, Robert L 1924- *AmMWSc 92*
**Hess**, Robert L. 1932- *WrDr 92*
**Hess**, Robert Pratt 1942- *WhoAmL 92*
**Hess**, Roger Leroy 1914- *WhoAmP 91*
**Hess**, Ronald Eugene 1938- *AmMWSc 92*
**Hess**, Ronald L. 1942- *WhoWest 92*
**Hess**, Rudolf 1894-1987 *EncTR 91 [port], FacFETw [port]*
**Hess**, Sonya *DrAPF 91*
**Hess**, Ted Harold 1932- *WhoWest 92*
**Hess**, Victor Franz 1883-1964 *WhoNob 90*
**Hess**, Walter Richard Rudolf 1894-1987 *BiDExR*
**Hess**, Walter Rudolph 1881-1973 *WhoNob 90*
**Hess**, Wendell Wayne 1935- *AmMWSc 92*
**Hess**, Werner 1914- *IntWW 91*
**Hess**, Wilford Moser 1934- *WhoWest 92*
**Hess**, Wilford Moser Bill 1934- *AmMWSc 92*
**Hess**, William E 1898- *WhoAmP 91*
**Hess**, Wilmot Norton 1926- *AmMWSc 92*
**Hessayon**, David Gerald 1928- *Who 92*
**Hessayon**, Joan Parker 1932- *IntAu&W 91*
**Hesse**, Christian August *AmMWSc 92*
**Hesse**, Christian August 1925- *WhoWest 92*
**Hesse**, Conrad E 1866-1910 *BiInAmS*
**Hesse**, Daniel Ryan 1953- *WhoFI 92*
**Hesse**, Eva 1936-1970 *WorArt 1980 [port]*
**Hesse**, Gerhard Edmund 1908- *IntWW 91*
**Hesse**, Helmut 1916-1943 *EncTR 91*
**Hesse**, Herman 1877-1962 *ShSCr 9 [port], WhoNob 90*
**Hesse**, Hermann 1877-1962 *ConLC 69 [port], FacFETw*
**Hesse**, M H 1927- *AmMWSc 92*
**Hesse**, Martha 1942- *WhoAmP 91*
**Hesse**, Mary Brenda 1924- *Who 92, WrDr 92*
**Hesse**, Nancy Jane 1948- *WhoFI 92*
**Hesse**, Reinhard 1936- *AmMWSc 92*
**Hesse**, Robert Louis 1930- *WhoAmL 92*
**Hesse**, Walter Herman 1920- *AmMWSc 92*
**Hesse**, Walter J 1923- *AmMWSc 92*
**Hesse**, William R. 1914- *WhoFI 92*
**Hesse**, Zora *WhoAmP 91*
**Hessel**, Alexander 1916- *AmMWSc 92*
**Hessel**, Arthur Richard 1942- *WhoAmL 92*
**Hessel**, Donald Wesley 1922- *AmMWSc 92*
**Hessel**, Kenneth Neal 1960- *WhoRel 92*
**Hessel**, Kenneth Ray 1939- *AmMWSc 92*
**Hessel**, Merrill 1933- *AmMWSc 92*
**Hessel**, Phoebe 1713-1821 *EncAmaz 91*
**Hessel**, Rudolph 1825-1900 *BiInAmS*
**Hessel**, Stephane F. 1917- *IntWW 91*
**Hesselbach**, Walter 1915- *IntWW 91*
**Hesselfeld**, Heinrich Josef 1930- *WhoRel 92*
**Hesselink**, Ira John, Jr. 1928- *WhoMW 92, WhoRel 92*
**Hesselink**, Lambertus 1948- *AmMWSc 92*
**Hessellund-Jensen**, Peter Lykke 1945- *WhoAmL 92*
**Hesseltine**, Clifford William 1917- *AmMWSc 92, WhoMW 92*
**Hesseltine**, Wilbur R 1919- *AmMWSc 92*
**Hesseman**, Howard 1940- *IntMPA 92, WhoEnt 92*
**Hessemer**, Robert A, Jr 1923- *AmMWSc 92*
**Hessen**, Stephen Jeffrey 1963- *WhoAmL 92*
**Hesser**, James Edward 1941- *AmMWSc 92*
**Hesser**, Woodrow Cleveland 1918- *WhoAmP 91*
**Hessert**, Paul 1925- *IntAu&W 91, WrDr 92*
**Hessing**, Dennis *IntAu&W 91X*
**Hessinger**, Carl John William 1915- *WhoAmL 92*
**Hessinger**, David Alwyn 1942- *AmMWSc 92*
**Hession**, Thomas D *WhoAmP 91*
**Hessler**, Gary Lee 1943- *WhoMW 92*
**Hessler**, Gordon 1930- *IntMPA 92*
**Hessler**, Jack Ronald 1939- *AmMWSc 92*
**Hessler**, Jan Paul 1944- *AmMWSc 92*
**Hessler**, Janet Pratt 1937- *WhoMW 92*
**Hessler**, Robert Raymond 1932- *AmMWSc 92*
**Hessler**, Robert Roamie 1918- *WhoMW 92*
**Hessler**, William Gerhard 1926- *WhoMW 92*
**Hessley**, Rita Kathleen 1946- *AmMWSc 92*
**Hesslund**, Bradley Harry 1958- *WhoFI 92, WhoMW 92*
**Hesson**, John Edward 1938- *WhoWest 92*
**Hestad**, Bjorn Mark 1926- *WhoFI 92, WhoMW 92*
**Hestand**, Cynthia Ann 1955- *WhoEnt 92*
**Hestand**, Joel Dwight 1939- *WhoRel 92*
**Hestenes**, David 1933- *AmMWSc 92*
**Hestenes**, Roberta *WhoHisp 92*
**Hester**, Arthur C. 1942- *WhoBlA 92*
**Hester**, Bruce Edward 1956- *WhoRel 92*
**Hester**, Donald Denison 1935- *WhoFI 92, WhoMW 92*
**Hester**, Donald L 1934- *AmMWSc 92*
**Hester**, Douglas Ansley 1951- *WhoWest 92*
**Hester**, Edward John 1938- *WhoMW 92*
**Hester**, Eva B *WhoAmP 91*
**Hester**, Forrest Glenn 1946- *WhoMW 92*
**Hester**, Gerald LeRoy 1928- *WhoWest 92*
**Hester**, Harris Ryland 1942- *WhoFI 92*
**Hester**, Jack W 1929- *WhoAmP 91*
**Hester**, Jackson Boling, Jr 1933- *AmMWSc 92*
**Hester**, James David 1931- *WhoRel 92*
**Hester**, James Dwight 1939- *WhoRel 92*
**Hester**, James Herbert, Jr. 1948- *WhoRel 92*
**Hester**, James McNaughton 1924- *IntWW 91*
**Hester**, Jarrett Charles 1938- *AmMWSc 92*
**Hester**, Joan L 1932- *WhoAmP 91*
**Hester**, John Edward 1950- *WhoRel 92*
**Hester**, John Frear 1927- *Who 92*
**Hester**, John Nelson 1930- *AmMWSc 92*
**Hester**, Karlton Edward 1949- *WhoEnt 92*
**Hester**, Lawrence Lamar, Jr 1920- *AmMWSc 92*
**Hester**, M.L. *DrAPF 91*
**Hester**, Melvyn Francis 1938- *WhoBlA 92*
**Hester**, Norman Eric 1946- *AmMWSc 92*
**Hester**, Norman Lawrence 1935- *WhoRel 92*
**Hester**, Patrick Joseph 1951- *WhoAmL 92*
**Hester**, Paul Finley 1935- *WhoAmP 91*
**Hester**, Randolph Thompson, Jr. 1944- *ConAu 34NR*
**Hester**, Richard Kelly 1947- *AmMWSc 92*
**Hester**, Robert Leslie 1953- *AmMWSc 92*
**Hester**, Ronald Ernest 1936- *Who 92*
**Hester**, Steven Michael 1961- *WhoEnt 92*
**Hester**, Thomas Patrick 1937- *WhoAmL 92, WhoFI 92*
**Hester**, William 1933- *IntAu&W 91*
**Hester-Lunt**, Jean 1953- *WhoEnt 92*
**Hesterberg**, Gene Arthur 1918- *AmMWSc 92*
**Hesterberg**, Thomas William 1950- *AmMWSc 92*
**Hesterman**, Wilfred Otto 1927- *WhoAmP 91*
**Heston**, Charlton 1923- *FacFETw*
**Heston**, Charlton 1924- *IntMPA 92, IntWW 91, Who 92, WhoEnt 92A*
**Heston**, Leonard L 1930- *AmMWSc 92*
**Heston**, William May, Jr 1922- *AmMWSc 92*
**Hesychius of Egypt** *EncEarC*
**Hesychius of Jerusalem** d451? *EncEarC*
**Hetebrink**, Darrow 1952- *WhoRel 92, WhoWest 92*
**Hetenhouser**, Leland Sherman 1930- *WhoMW 92*
**Hetenyi**, Geza Joseph 1923- *AmMWSc 92*
**Heterick**, Robert Cary, Jr 1936- *AmMWSc 92, WhoAmP 91*
**Heth**, Diana Sue 1948- *WhoMW 92*
**Heth**, Michael Lewis 1951- *WhoMW 92*
**Hetha** *EncAmaz 91*
**Hethcote**, Herbert Wayne 1941- *AmMWSc 92, WhoMW 92*
**Hetherington**, Alastair *Who 92*
**Hetherington**, Alastair 1919- *IntAu&W 91*
**Hetherington**, Arthur Carleton 1916- *Who 92*
**Hetherington**, Arthur Ford 1911- *IntWW 91, Who 92*
**Hetherington**, Burton Lee 1928- *WhoAmP 91*
**Hetherington**, Carleton *Who 92*
**Hetherington**, Cheryl Keiko 1952- *WhoWest 92*
**Hetherington**, Derick Henry Fellowes 1911- *Who 92*
**Hetherington**, Donald Wordsworth 1945- *AmMWSc 92*
**Hetherington**, Guy 1948- *TwCPaSc*
**Hetherington**, Hector Alastair 1919- *IntWW 91, Who 92*
**Hetherington**, John 1930- *WhoWest 92*
**Hetherington**, John Alan Crawford 1928- *WhoAmL 92*
**Hetherington**, John Joseph 1947- *WhoAmL 92*
**Hetherington**, Norriss Swigart 1942- *IntAu&W 91*
**Hetherington**, Thomas Chalmers 1926- *Who 92*
**Hetherwick**, Gilbert Lewis 1952- *WhoEnt 92, WhoMW 92*
**Hetlage**, Robert Owen 1931- *WhoMW 92*
**Hetland**, John Robert 1930- *WhoAmL 92, WhoFI 92, WhoWest 92*
**Hetnarski**, Richard Bozyslaw 1928- *AmMWSc 92*
**Hetrick**, Barbara Ann 1951- *AmMWSc 92*
**Hetrick**, David LeRoy 1927- *AmMWSc 92*
**Hetrick**, Frank M 1932- *AmMWSc 92*
**Hetrick**, John Henry 1916- *AmMWSc 92*
**Hetrick**, Lawrence Andrew 1910- *AmMWSc 92*
**Hetrick**, Lisa Kay 1959- *WhoMW 92*
**Hetsko**, Cyril Francis 1911- *WhoAmL 92, WhoFI 92*
**Hetsko**, Cyril Michael 1942- *WhoMW 92*
**Hett**, Joan Margaret 1936- *WhoWest 92*
**Hett**, John Henry 1909- *AmMWSc 92*
**Hettche**, Leroy Raymond 1938- *AmMWSc 92*
**Hettich**, Michael *DrAPF 91*
**Hettinger**, Deborah D R *AmMWSc 92*
**Hettinger**, Robert James 1930- *WhoIns 92*
**Hettinger**, Stephen Ray 1945- *WhoAmP 91*
**Hettinger**, William Peter, Jr 1922- *AmMWSc 92*
**Hettlage**, Karl Maria 1902- *IntWW 91*
**Hettler**, Paul *WhoEnt 92*
**Hettmansperger**, Thomas Philip 1939- *AmMWSc 92*
**Hettrick**, William Eugene 1939- *WhoEnt 92*
**Hetu**, Jacques 1938- *NewAmDM*
**Hetu**, Pierre 1936- *NewAmDM*
**Hetzel**, Donald Stanford 1941- *AmMWSc 92*
**Hetzel**, Howard Roy 1931- *AmMWSc 92*
**Hetzel**, Otto Joseph 1933- *WhoAmL 92*
**Hetzel**, Paula Rae 1951- *WhoAmL 92*
**Hetzel**, Phyllis Bertha Mabel 1918- *Who 92*
**Hetzel**, Ralph D. 1912- *IntMPA 92*
**Hetzel**, Richard Ernest 1935- *AmMWSc 92*
**Hetzel**, Richard Lee 1952- *WhoWest 92*
**Hetzel**, Theodore B 1906- *AmMWSc 92*
**Hetzler**, Bruce Edward 1948- *AmMWSc 92*
**Hetzler**, Donald F. 1923- *WhoRel 92*
**Hetzler**, Morris Clifford, Jr 1937- *AmMWSc 92*
**Hetzron**, Robert 1937- *WrDr 92*
**Heuberger**, Oscar 1924- *AmMWSc 92*
**Heuchling**, Theodore P 1925- *AmMWSc 92*
**Heuer**, Ann Elizabeth 1930- *AmMWSc 92*
**Heuer**, Ann Foster 1934- *WhoAmP 91*
**Heuer**, Arthur Harold 1936- *AmMWSc 92*
**Heuer**, Charles Vernon 1937- *AmMWSc 92*
**Heuer**, Gerald Arthur 1930- *AmMWSc 92*
**Heuer**, Margaret B. 1935- *WhoFI 92*
**Heuer**, Michael Alexander 1932- *WhoMW 92*
**Heuer**, Robert Maynard, II 1944- *WhoEnt 92*
**Heuertz**, John Anthony 1949- *WhoEnt 92*
**Heugly**, Mark H. 1946- *WhoFI 92*
**Heuman**, Donna Rena 1949- *WhoWest 92*
**Heuman**, William 1912-1971 *TwCWW 91*
**Heumann**, Karl Fredrich 1921- *AmMWSc 92*
**Heunis**, Christiaan 1927- *IntWW 91*
**Heusch**, Clemens August 1932- *AmMWSc 92*
**Heuschele**, Ann 1938- *AmMWSc 92*
**Heuschele**, Otto 1900- *EncTR 91*
**Heuschele**, Werner Paul 1929- *AmMWSc 92, WhoWest 92*
**Heuser**, Eva T 1932- *AmMWSc 92*
**Heuser**, Gunnar 1927- *AmMWSc 92*
**Heusinger**, Adolf 1897-1982 *EncTR 91*
**Heusinger**, Hans-Joachim 1925- *IntWW 91*
**Heusinkveld**, Frances Mary 1926- *WhoEnt 92*
**Heusinkveld**, Myron Ellis 1921- *AmMWSc 92*
**Heusner**, Alfred August *AmMWSc 92*
**Heuss**, Theodor 1884-1963 *EncTR 91 [port]*
**Heusser**, Calvin John 1924- *AmMWSc 92*
**Heusser**, Linda Olga 1932- *AmMWSc 92*
**Heustis**, Albert Edward 1913- *AmMWSc 92*
**Heuston**, Robert Francis Vere 1923- *Who 92*
**Heutger**, Nicolaus Carl 1932- *WhoRel 92*
**Heuvers**, Konrad John 1940- *AmMWSc 92, WhoMW 92*
**Heuze**, Francois E 1941- *AmMWSc 92*
**Hevel**, David Roger 1950- *WhoAmL 92*
**Heveran**, John Edward 1938- *AmMWSc 92*
**Heverly**, Richard Charles 1928- *WhoFI 92*
**Hevesi**, Alan G 1940- *WhoAmP 91*
**Hevesy**, George Charles von 1885-1966 *WhoNob 90*
**Hevey**, Ronald William 1941- *WhoFI 92*
**Hevier**, Richard Scott 1957- *WhoAmP 91*
**Hevner**, Alan Raymond 1950- *AmMWSc 92*
**Hew**, Choy-Leong 1942- *AmMWSc 92*
**Hewak**, Benjamin 1935- *WhoMW 92*
**Heward**, Anthony Wilkinson 1918- *Who 92*
**Heward**, Edmund Rawlings 1912- *Who 92*
**Hewat**, Alan V. *DrAPF 91*
**Hewat**, Alexander 1745?-1829 *BenetAL 91*
**Hewat**, William Brian 1936- *WhoFI 92*
**Hewel**, Walther 1904-1945 *EncTR 91*
**Hewer**, Gary Arthur 1940- *AmMWSc 92*
**Hewer**, Thomas Frederick 1903- *Who 92*
**Hewes**, Amy 1877-1970 *WomSoc*
**Hewes**, Dorothy Walker 1922- *WhoWest 92*
**Hewes**, George Poindexter, III 1928- *WhoAmL 92*
**Hewes**, Henry 1917- *WhoEnt 92*
**Hewes**, Joseph 1730-1779 *DcNCBi 3*
**Hewes**, Ralph Allan 1939- *AmMWSc 92*
**Hewes**, Richard David 1926- *WhoAmP 91*
**Hewes**, Robert Charles 1953- *WhoMW 92*
**Hewes**, Robin Anthony Charles 1945- *Who 92*
**Hewetson**, Christopher 1929- *Who 92*
**Hewetson**, John Francis 1939- *AmMWSc 92*
**Hewetson**, Reginald 1908- *Who 92*
**Hewett**, Arthur Edward 1935- *WhoAmL 92*
**Hewett**, Dennis W 1947- *AmMWSc 92*
**Hewett**, Dorothy 1923- *ConPo 91, IntAu&W 91, WrDr 92*
**Hewett**, James Veith 1921- *AmMWSc 92*
**Hewett**, Joanne Lea 1960- *AmMWSc 92*
**Hewett**, John Earl 1937- *AmMWSc 92*
**Hewett**, John George d1990 *Who 92N*
**Hewett**, Lionel Donnell 1938- *AmMWSc 92*
**Hewett**, Ouida Hewett 1933- *WhoAmP 91*
**Hewett**, Peter 1931- *Who 92*
**Hewett**, Richard William 1923- *Who 92*
**Hewett'Emmett**, David 1946- *AmMWSc 92*
**Hewgill**, Denton Elwood 1940- *AmMWSc 92*
**Hewing**, Margaret Susan 1962- *WhoAmL 92*
**Hewing**, Pernell Hayes 1933- *WhoBlA 92*
**Hewins**, Caroline Maria 1846-1926 *HanAmWH*
**Hewins**, Roger Herbert 1940- *AmMWSc 92*
**Hewinson**, Morgan 1913- *TwCPaSc*
**Hewish**, Antony 1924- *AmMWSc 92, IntWW 91, Who 92, WhoNob 90*
**Hewitson**, Walter Milton 1933- *AmMWSc 92*
**Hewitt** *Who 92*
**Hewitt**, Alison Hope 1915- *WrDr 92*
**Hewitt**, Allan A 1934- *AmMWSc 92*

**Hewitt**, Anthony Victor 1943- AmMWSc 92
**Hewitt**, Arthur Tyl AmMWSc 92
**Hewitt**, Basil 1926- WhoBlA 92
**Hewitt**, Carl Herbert 1952- WhoAmL 92
**Hewitt**, Cecil Rolph Who 92
**Hewitt**, Charles Hayden 1929- AmMWSc 92
**Hewitt**, Charles Walworth 1943- WhoFI 92
**Hewitt**, Charles William 1953- WhoWest 92
**Hewitt**, Cynthia Dawn 1957- WhoWest 92
**Hewitt**, Cyrus Lenox 1917- Who 92
**Hewitt**, David 1927- AmMWSc 92
**Hewitt**, Dennis Edwin 1944- WhoFI 92
**Hewitt**, Don LesBEnT 92 [port]
**Hewitt**, Don S. 1922- WhoEnt 92
**Hewitt**, Edwin 1920- AmMWSc 92, WhoWest 92
**Hewitt**, Eric John 1919- IntWW 91, Who 92
**Hewitt**, Francis Anthony 1943- Who 92
**Hewitt**, Frankie Lea 1931- WhoEnt 92
**Hewitt**, Frederick George 1929- AmMWSc 92
**Hewitt**, Gaelynne Joy WhoFI 92
**Hewitt**, Gavin Wallace 1944- Who 92
**Hewitt**, Geof DrAPF 91
**Hewitt**, Geof 1943- IntAu&W 91, WrDr 92
**Hewitt**, Geoffrey 1930- TwCPaSc
**Hewitt**, Geoffrey Frederick 1934- Who 92
**Hewitt**, George Berlyn 1930- AmMWSc 92
**Hewitt**, George Henry Gordon 1912- Who 92
**Hewitt**, Graves Desha 1928- WhoIns 92
**Hewitt**, Harold 1908- Who 92
**Hewitt**, Harold 1917- Who 92
**Hewitt**, Harry Ronald 1920- IntWW 91, Who 92
**Hewitt**, Hudy C, Jr 1937- AmMWSc 92
**Hewitt**, James 1770-1827 BenetAL 91, NewAmDM
**Hewitt**, James Watt 1932- WhoAmL 92, WhoMW 92
**Hewitt**, Jerene Cline 1917- WhoWest 92
**Hewitt**, Jess Paul, III 1957- WhoFI 92
**Hewitt**, Joe B. 1931- WhoRel 92
**Hewitt**, John 1907- IntAu&W 91
**Hewitt**, John Graham d1991 Who 92N
**Hewitt**, John H., Jr. 1924- WhoBlA 92
**Hewitt**, John Hill 1801-1890 BenetAL 91
**Hewitt**, Lenox Who 92
**Hewitt**, Margaret d1991 Who 92N
**Hewitt**, Martha Ann 1961- WhoEnt 92
**Hewitt**, Michael Earling 1936- Who 92
**Hewitt**, Nicholas Charles Joseph 1947- Who 92
**Hewitt**, Patricia Hope 1948- Who 92
**Hewitt**, Paul Buck 1949- WhoAmL 92
**Hewitt**, Penelope Ann 1932- Who 92
**Hewitt**, Peter McGregor 1929- Who 92
**Hewitt**, Philip Cooper 1925- AmMWSc 92
**Hewitt**, Richard Arnold 1939- WhoMW 92
**Hewitt**, Richard Thornton 1917- Who 92
**Hewitt**, Robert Lee 1934- AmMWSc 92
**Hewitt**, Robert T 1909- AmMWSc 92
**Hewitt**, Roger R 1937- AmMWSc 92
**Hewitt**, Ronald Jerome 1932- WhoBlA 92
**Hewitt**, Thomas Edward 1939- WhoFI 92, WhoMW 92
**Hewitt**, Vivian Davidson WhoBlA 92
**Hewitt**, William Alexander 1914- IntWW 91
**Hewitt**, William Boright 1908- AmMWSc 92
**Hewitt**, William Francis 1914- WhoWest 92
**Hewitt**, William Harley 1954- WhoFI 92
**Hewitt**, William Lane 1916- AmMWSc 92
**Hewkin**, Andrew 1949- TwCPaSc
**Hewko**, Eric 1955- WhoAmL 92
**Hewko**, John Steven 1954- WhoRel 92
**Hewlett**, Antoinette Payne WhoBlA 92
**Hewlett**, Dial, Jr. 1948- WhoBlA 92
**Hewlett**, Everett Augustus, Jr. 1943- WhoBlA 92
**Hewlett**, Francis 1930- TwCPaSc
**Hewlett**, John David 1922- AmMWSc 92
**Hewlett**, Martinez Joseph 1942- AmMWSc 92
**Hewlett**, Stephen Owen 1944- WhoAmP 91
**Hewlett**, Sylvia Ann 1946- WrDr 92
**Hewlett**, T.J. 1941- WhoWest 92
**Hewlett**, W R 1913- AmMWSc 92
**Hewlett**, William Redington 1913- WhoWest 92
**Hewlett-Davies**, Janet Mary 1938- Who 92
**Hewlings**, Charles 1948- TwCPaSc
**Hewson**, Ann 1933- TwCPaSc
**Hewson**, Donna Walters 1947- WhoFI 92
**Hewson**, Edgar Wendell 1910- AmMWSc 92
**Hewson**, John 1930- IntAu&W 91, WrDr 92
**Hewson**, John 1946- IntWW 91
**Hewson**, John Robert 1946- Who 92
**Hewston**, John G 1923- AmMWSc 92
**Hexham & Newcastle**, Auxiliary Bishop of Who 92
**Hexham And Newcastle**, Bishop of 1927- Who 92
**Hext**, Gregory Wayne 1955- WhoFI 92
**Hext**, Harrington 1862-1960 ScFEYrs
**Hext**, Kathleen Florence 1941- WhoWest 92
**Hexter**, Daniel Jonathan 1955- WhoEnt 92
**Hexter**, Robert Maurice 1925- AmMWSc 92
**Hexter**, William Michael 1927- AmMWSc 92
**Hexum**, Terry Donald 1941- AmMWSc 92
**Hey**, Cicely 1896- TwCPaSc
**Hey**, Ernest 1912- Who 92
**Hey**, James Stanley 1909- Who 92
**Hey**, John Anthony 1959- AmMWSc 92
**Hey**, John Denis 1944- Who 92
**Hey**, Keith Joseph 1934- WhoMW 92
**Hey**, Nigel Stewart 1936- WhoWest 92
**Hey**, Phillip H. DrAPF 91
**Hey**, Richard N 1947- AmMWSc 92
**Hey**, Robert P. 1935- ConAu 133
**Heybach**, John Peter 1950- AmMWSc 92, WhoFI 92
**Heybey**, Otfried Willibald Georg 1938- AmMWSc 92
**Heyborne**, Robert L 1923- AmMWSc 92
**Heyck**, Theodore Daly 1941- WhoAmL 92, WhoWest 92
**Heyd**, Allen 1935- AmMWSc 92
**Heyd**, Charles E 1928- AmMWSc 92
**Heyd**, William Ernst 1945- AmMWSc 92
**Heyda**, Donald William 1946- AmMWSc 92
**Heydanek**, Menard George, Jr 1942- AmMWSc 92
**Heyde**, Christopher Charles 1939- IntWW 91
**Heyde**, James Wallace 1933- WhoMW 92
**Heyde**, Werner 1902-1964 EncTR 91 [port]
**Heydegger**, Helmut Roland 1935- AmMWSc 92
**Heydemann**, Peter Ludwig Martin 1928- AmMWSc 92
**Heyden**, Francis Joseph 1907- AmMWSc 92
**Heyden**, Francis Joseph 1907-1991 NewYTBS 91
**Heyden**, Haye van der 1957- IntAu&W 91
**Heyderman**, Arthur Jerome 1946- WhoMW 92
**Heyding**, Robert Donald 1925- AmMWSc 92
**Heydinger**, Andrew Gerard 1951- WhoMW 92
**Heydman**, Abby Maria 1943- WhoWest 92
**Heydorn**, William Edward 1954- WhoMW 92
**Heydrich**, Reinhard 1904-1942 EncTR 91 [port]
**Heydrich**, Reinhard Tristan Eugen 1904-1942 BiDExR
**Heydrick**, Fred Painter 1934- AmMWSc 92
**Heydron**, Vicki Ann 1945- IntAu&W 91
**Heydt**, Gerald Thomas 1943- AmMWSc 92
**Heyen**, William DrAPF 91
**Heyen**, William 1940- BenetAL 91, ConPo 91, WrDr 92
**Heyen**, William H 1940- IntAu&W 91
**Heyer**, Carol Ann 1950- WhoWest 92
**Heyer**, John Hajdu 1945- WhoEnt 92
**Heyer**, Paul 1936- WrDr 92
**Heyerdahl**, Eugene Gerhardt 1940- AmMWSc 92
**Heyerdahl**, Thor 1914- FacFETw, IntAu&W 91, IntWW 91, Who 92, WrDr 92
**Heyert**, Martin David 1934- WhoAmL 92
**Heyes**, Gerald Bernard 1954- WhoEnt 92, WhoMW 92
**Heygate**, George Lloyd Who 92
**Heyhoe**, David Charles Ross 1938- Who 92
**Heyhoe Flint**, Rachael 1939- Who 92
**Heying**, Theodore Louis 1927- AmMWSc 92
**Heyl**, Allen Van, Jr 1918- AmMWSc 92, WhoWest 92
**Heyl**, George Richard AmMWSc 92
**Heyland**, Michael 1940- WhoEnt 92
**Heyler**, Grover Ross 1926- WhoAmL 92
**Heylin**, Angela Christine 1943- IntWW 91
**Heylin**, Clinton 1960- ConAu 135
**Heym**, Stefan 1913- BenetAL 91, IntWW 91, LiExTwC
**Heyman**, Abigail 1942- WrDr 92
**Heyman**, Albert 1916- AmMWSc 92
**Heyman**, Allan 1921- Who 92
**Heyman**, Barton Spenser 1937- WhoEnt 92
**Heyman**, Duane Allan 1941- AmMWSc 92
**Heyman**, Harry Clinton 1924- WhoAmP 91
**Heyman**, Horace 1912- Who 92
**Heyman**, Ira Michael 1930- IntWW 91, WhoAmL 92, WhoWest 92
**Heyman**, Jacques 1925- Who 92, WrDr 92
**Heyman**, John 1933- IntMPA 92
**Heyman**, Joseph Saul 1943- AmMWSc 92
**Heyman**, Karl 1904- AmMWSc 92
**Heyman**, Laurel Elaine 1941- AmMWSc 92
**Heyman**, Louis 1923- AmMWSc 92
**Heyman**, Philip WhoAmP 91
**Heyman**, Samuel J. 1939- WhoFI 92
**Heyman**, Stanley Edward 1959- WhoAmL 92
**Heyman**, William Herbert 1948- WhoFI 92
**Heymann**, Dieter 1927- AmMWSc 92
**Heymann**, Franz Ferdinand 1924- Who 92
**Heymann**, Michael Alexander 1937- AmMWSc 92
**Heymann**, Philip B. 1932- WhoAmL 92
**Heymann**, S. Richard 1944- WhoAmL 92
**Heymann**, Thomas N. 1958- ConAu 135
**Heymann**, Tom ConAu 135
**Heymann**, Werner H. 1910- WhoRel 92
**Heymans**, Corneille Jean Francois 1892-1968 WhoNob 90
**Heymont**, George Adam 1947- WhoEnt 92
**Heymsfeld**, David Alan 1938- WhoFI 92
**Heymsfield**, Andrew Joel 1947- AmMWSc 92
**Heymsfield**, Gerald M 1949- AmMWSc 92
**Heymsfield**, Steven B 1944- AmMWSc 92
**Heyn**, Anton Nicolaas Johannes 1906- AmMWSc 92
**Heyn**, Arno Harry Albert 1918- AmMWSc 92
**Heyn**, Ernest V. 1904- ConAu 134
**Heyn**, Gerald Henry 1936- WhoEnt 92
**Heyn**, William Carveth WhoFI 92
**Heyn-Cubacub**, Jan Judith 1956- WhoEnt 92
**Heyne**, Christian Gottlob 1729-1812 BlkwCEP
**Heyne**, Elmer George 1912- AmMWSc 92
**Heyne**, Roland Maywood, Sr. 1933- WhoMW 92
**Heyneman**, Donald 1925- AmMWSc 92
**Heynen**, A. James 1945- WhoMW 92
**Heynen**, James 1940- WrDr 92
**Heynen**, Jim DrAPF 91
**Heynen**, Jim 1940- TwCWW 91
**Heyner**, Susan 1936- AmMWSc 92
**Heynick**, Louis Norman 1919- AmMWSc 92
**Heyns**, J. A. WhoRel 92
**Heyrovsky**, Jaroslav 1890-1967 WhoNob 90
**Heys**, John Richard 1947- AmMWSc 92
**Heyse**, Hans 1891-1976 EncTR 91
**Heyse**, Paul 1830-1914 FacFETw
**Heyse**, Paul Johann Ludwig von 1830-1914 WhoNob 90
**Heyse**, Stephen P 1948- AmMWSc 92
**Heyse**, Warren John 1923- WhoFI 92, WhoMW 92
**Heyser**, William H. 1928- WhoFI 92
**Heyssel**, Robert M 1928- AmMWSc 92
**Heyssel**, Robert Morris 1928- IntWW 91
**Heystek**, Hendrik 1924- AmMWSc 92
**Heytesbury**, Baron 1931- Who 92
**Heytesbury**, William 1310?-1372? DcLB 115
**Heytler**, Peter George 1930- AmMWSc 92
**Heyward**, Andrew LesBEnT 92 [port]
**Heyward**, Andrew John 1950- WhoEnt 92
**Heyward**, Craig W. 1966- WhoBlA 92
**Heyward**, Don H. 1931- WhoBlA 92
**Heyward**, Dorothy 1890-1961 BenetAL 91
**Heyward**, DuBose 1885-1940 BenetAL 91
**Heyward**, Ilene Patricia 1948- WhoBlA 92
**Heyward**, Isaac 1935- WhoBlA 92
**Heyward**, James Oliver 1930- WhoBlA 92
**Heyward**, John Wesley, Jr. 1934- WhoRel 92
**Heyward**, Louis Mortimere 1920- WhoEnt 92
**Heyward**, Oliver Spencer 1926- Who 92
**Heywood**, Anne 1931- IntMPA 92
**Heywood**, Eddie 1915-1989 FacFETw, NewAmDM
**Heywood**, Ezra Hervey 1829-1893 AmPeW
**Heywood**, Francis Melville 1908- Who 92
**Heywood**, Geoffrey 1916- Who 92
**Heywood**, Joe T. ConAu 134
**Heywood**, John 1497?-1580? RfGEnL 91
**Heywood**, John Benjamin 1938- AmMWSc 92
**Heywood**, Joseph 1943- ConAu 134
**Heywood**, Max 1950- WhoEnt 92
**Heywood**, Oliver Kerr 1920- Who 92
**Heywood**, Peter 1943- AmMWSc 92
**Heywood**, Robert Gilmour 1949- WhoAmL 92
**Heywood**, Robert Wales 1933- WhoMW 92
**Heywood**, Sally 1964- TwCPaSc
**Heywood**, Stuart Mackenzie 1934- AmMWSc 92
**Heywood**, Thomas 1573?-1641? RfGEnL 91
**Heywood**, Vernon Hilton 1927- Who 92
**Heywood-Lonsdale**, Robert Henry 1919- Who 92
**Heywood Thomas**, John 1926- WhoRel 92, WrDr 92
**Heyworth**, James O. 1942- WhoEnt 92, WhoFI 92
**Heyworth**, Laurence 1955- ConAu 134
**Heyworth**, Peter 1921- IntAu&W 91
**Heyworth**, Peter 1921-1991 ConAu 135, NewYTBS 91
**Heyworth**, Peter Lawrence Frederick 1921- Who 92
**Hezlep**, William Earl 1936- WhoEnt 92, WhoMW 92
**Hezlet**, Arthur Richard 1914- Who 92
**Hezzelwood**, William L 1947- WhoIns 92
**Hiaasen**, Carl 1953- WrDr 92
**Hiam**, Alexander Watson 1957- WhoFI 92
**Hiapo**, Patricia Kamaka 1943- WhoRel 92
**Hiat**, Elchik ConAu 134, IntAu&W 91X
**Hiatt**, Andrew Jackson 1932- AmMWSc 92
**Hiatt**, Arnold 1927- WhoFI 92
**Hiatt**, Caspar Wistar, III 1919- AmMWSc 92
**Hiatt**, Charles Milton 1949- WhoRel 92
**Hiatt**, Dana Sims WhoBlA 92
**Hiatt**, Dietrah 1944- WhoBlA 92
**Hiatt**, Duane Evan 1937- WhoEnt 92
**Hiatt**, Florence Ellen WhoEnt 92
**Hiatt**, Harold 1921- AmMWSc 92
**Hiatt**, Houston Boyd 1886-1941 DcNCBi 3
**Hiatt**, Howard H. 1925- ConAu 133
**Hiatt**, Howard Haym 1925- AmMWSc 92
**Hiatt**, J M ScFEYrs
**Hiatt**, James Lee 1934- AmMWSc 92
**Hiatt**, Jane Crater 1944- WhoEnt 92
**Hiatt**, John David 1949- WhoEnt 92
**Hiatt**, Norman Arthur 1937- AmMWSc 92
**Hiatt**, Peter 1930- WhoWest 92
**Hiatt**, Ralph Ellis 1910- AmMWSc 92
**Hiatt**, Robert Burritt 1917- AmMWSc 92
**Hiatt**, Steven Lee 1958- WhoWest 92
**Hiatt**, William Seth 1932- WhoAmP 91
**Hibbard**, Aubrey D 1908- AmMWSc 92
**Hibbard**, Bryan Montague 1926- Who 92
**Hibbard**, Dave Westby 1949- WhoAmP 91
**Hibbard**, David Andrew 1946- WhoEnt 92
**Hibbard**, Judith Hoffman 1948- WhoWest 92
**Hibbard**, Malcolm Jackman 1936- AmMWSc 92
**Hibbard**, Richard Paul 1923- WhoWest 92
**Hibbard**, Roger Williams, III 1942- WhoAmL 92
**Hibbard**, Walter Rollo, Jr 1918- AmMWSc 92
**Hibbeler**, Russell Charles 1944- AmMWSc 92
**Hibben**, Craig Rittenhouse 1930- AmMWSc 92
**Hibberd**, Jack 1940- IntAu&W 91, WrDr 92
**Hibberd**, Roy Wayne 1952- WhoAmL 92
**Hibberd**, Steven 1961- TwCPaSc
**Hibberd**, William James 1952- WhoIns 92
**Hibbert** Who 92
**Hibbert**, Alun 1949- WrDr 92
**Hibbert**, Alun James 1949- IntAu&W 91
**Hibbert**, Barrie Edward 1935- Who 92
**Hibbert**, Christopher 1924- IntAu&W 91, Who 92, WrDr 92
**Hibbert**, Dorothy Lasalle 1923- WhoBlA 92
**Hibbert**, Eleanor IntAu&W 91, Who 92
**Hibbert**, Eleanor Alice Burford WrDr 92
**Hibbert**, Jack 1932- IntWW 91, Who 92
**Hibbert**, Julia Hegsted 1938- WhoWest 92
**Hibbert**, Larry Eugene 1937- AmMWSc 92
**Hibbert**, Reginald 1922- Who 92
**Hibbert**, Reginald Alfred 1922- IntWW 91
**Hibbett**, Howard 1920- WrDr 92
**Hibbits**, James Oliver, Jr 1924- AmMWSc 92
**Hibbitts**, James R 1935- WhoIns 92
**Hibbs**, Andrew D AmMWSc 92
**Hibbs**, Clair Maurice 1923- AmMWSc 92
**Hibbs**, Dale W 1940- WhoAmP 91
**Hibbs**, Jack Duane, Jr. 1956- WhoRel 92
**Hibbs**, John 1925- WrDr 92
**Hibbs**, John Alfred Blyth 1925- IntAu&W 91
**Hibbs**, John Burnham AmMWSc 92
**Hibbs**, John David 1948- WhoWest 92
**Hibbs**, John Stanley 1934- WhoAmL 92, WhoFI 92
**Hibbs**, John William 1917- AmMWSc 92
**Hibbs**, Loyal Robert 1925- WhoAmL 92
**Hibbs**, Richard Guythal 1922- AmMWSc 92
**Hibbs**, Robert A 1923- AmMWSc 92
**Hibbs**, Roger Franklin 1921- AmMWSc 92
**Hibbs**, Tim 1962- WhoEnt 92
**Hibbs**, William Ernest, III 1950- WhoRel 92

**Hibdon,** James E. 1924- *WrDr 92*
**Hibler,** Charles Phillip 1930- *AmMWSc 92*
**Hibler,** William David, III 1943- *AmMWSc 92*
**Hibner,** Janet Louise 1935- *WhoAmP 91*
**Hibner,** Paul D 1939- *WhoAmP 91*
**Hibner,** Rae Anne 1956- *WhoMW 92*
**Hichar,** Joseph Kenneth 1928- *AmMWSc 92*
**Hichborn,** Clyde Austin 1910- *WhoAmP 91*
**Hichens,** Antony Peverell 1936- *Who 92*
**Hichens,** Walter Wilson 1917- *WhoAmP 91*
**Hick,** Graeme Ashley 1966- *IntWW 91*
**Hick,** John 1922- *WrDr 92*
**Hick,** John Harwood 1922- *IntAu&W 91, IntWW 91, Who 92, WhoRel 92*
**Hick,** Kenneth William 1946- *WhoFI 92, WhoWest 92*
**Hickam,** Jean Anne 1931- *WhoMW 92*
**Hickel,** Walter J. 1919- *AlmAP 92 [port]*
**Hickel,** Walter Joseph 1919- *IntWW 91, WhoAmP 91, WhoWest 92*
**Hicken,** Mandy *ConAu 135*
**Hicken,** Marilyn E. 1937- *ConAu 135*
**Hicken,** Victor 1921- *WrDr 92*
**Hickenbottom,** John Powell 1938- *AmMWSc 92*
**Hickernell,** Fred Slocum 1932- *AmMWSc 92*
**Hickernell,** Frederick Slocum 1932- *WhoWest 92*
**Hickernell,** Gary L 1942- *AmMWSc 92*
**Hickerson,** Glenn Lindsey 1937- *WhoWest 92*
**Hickerson,** Janet L. 1955- *WhoFI 92*
**Hickerson,** Jay Allen 1934- *WhoEnt 92*
**Hickerson,** Mary 1943- *WhoMW 92*
**Hickerson,** O. B. 1936- *WhoBlA 92*
**Hickerson,** Thomas Felix 1882-1968 *DcNCBi 3*
**Hickey,** Barbara Mary 1945- *AmMWSc 92*
**Hickey,** Barbara Standish 1946- *WhoFI 92*
**Hickey,** Catherine Josephine 1936- *WhoRel 92*
**Hickey,** Dale Eugene 1942- *WhoRel 92*
**Hickey,** David Hugh 1950- *WhoAmL 92*
**Hickey,** Dennis Walter 1914- *WhoRel 92*
**Hickey,** Donal Aloysius 1948- *AmMWSc 92*
**Hickey,** E. Lawrence 1959- *WhoFI 92*
**Hickey,** Eugene Francis 1926- *WhoAmP 91*
**Hickey,** Gordon R. 1950- *WhoMW 92*
**Hickey,** Gregory Joseph 1947- *WhoRel 92*
**Hickey,** Harrison R., Jr. 1925- *WhoWest 92*
**Hickey,** Howard Wesley 1930- *WhoMW 92*
**Hickey,** James Aloysius 1920- *IntWW 91, RelLAm 91, WhoRel 92*
**Hickey,** James Clyde 1936- *WhoAmP 91*
**Hickey,** James Paul, Jr. 1946- *WhoEnt 92*
**Hickey,** Janet E 1963- *WhoAmP 91*
**Hickey,** Jimmy Ray 1929- *AmMWSc 92*
**Hickey,** John Edmund 1943- *WhoFI 92*
**Hickey,** John Heyward 1954- *WhoAmL 92*
**Hickey,** John M 1944- *WhoIns 92*
**Hickey,** John Michael 1936- *WhoFI 92*
**Hickey,** John R 1936- *WhoAmP 91*
**Hickey,** John Thomas, Jr. 1952- *WhoAmL 92*
**Hickey,** Joseph Francis 1958- *WhoFI 92*
**Hickey,** Joseph James 1907- *AmMWSc 92*
**Hickey,** Joseph Michael, Jr. 1940- *WhoFI 92*
**Hickey,** Justin 1925- *Who 92*
**Hickey,** Kenneth Dyer 1933- *AmMWSc 92*
**Hickey,** Leo Joseph 1940- *AmMWSc 92*
**Hickey,** Liliam Lujan *WhoHisp 92*
**Hickey,** Martha Lee 1931- *WhoAmP 91*
**Hickey,** Michael Kevin 1938- *WhoFI 92*
**Hickey,** Patrick J *WhoAmP 91*
**Hickey,** Paul Joseph 1950- *WhoAmL 92*
**Hickey,** Richard James 1913- *AmMWSc 92*
**Hickey,** Robert Cornelius 1917- *AmMWSc 92*
**Hickey,** Robert Edward, Jr 1949- *WhoAmP 91*
**Hickey,** Robert Joseph *AmMWSc 92*
**Hickey,** Roger 1942- *AmMWSc 92*
**Hickey,** Ruth Cecelia 1914- *WhoRel 92*
**Hickey,** Thomas J 1930- *WhoAmP 91*
**Hickey,** Vivian Veach 1916- *WhoAmP 91*
**Hickey,** William August 1936- *AmMWSc 92*
**Hickey,** Winifred *WhoAmP 91*
**Hickey,** Winifred Espy *WhoWest 92*
**Hickey Green,** Mary E 1907- *WhoAmP 91*
**Hickie,** Melvin Russell 1949- *WhoWest 92*
**Hickie,** Robert Allan 1936- *AmMWSc 92*
**Hickinbotham,** Letha Belle 1935- *WhoMW 92*
**Hickle,** Ralph 1904- *WhoAmP 91*
**Hicklin,** Denis Raymond 1918- *Who 92*
**Hicklin,** Fannie *WhoBlA 92*
**Hicklin,** Ronald Lee 1937- *WhoEnt 92, WhoWest 92*
**Hicklin,** Walker 1952- *WhoEnt 92*
**Hickling,** Colin John Anderson 1931- *Who 92*
**Hickling,** Reginald Hugh 1920- *Who 92*
**Hickman,** Bert G., Jr. 1924- *WrDr 92*
**Hickman,** Bert George, Jr. 1924- *WhoFI 92, WhoWest 92*
**Hickman,** Carole Stentz 1942- *AmMWSc 92*
**Hickman,** Carolyn Burrell Granger 1920- *WhoRel 92*
**Hickman,** Carter Malcolm 1910- *WhoAmP 91*
**Hickman,** Charles Wallace 1952- *WhoMW 92*
**Hickman,** Cleveland Pendleton, Jr 1928- *AmMWSc 92*
**Hickman,** Darrell *WhoAmP 91*
**Hickman,** Darryl 1930- *IntMPA 92*
**Hickman,** David Francis 1947- *WhoWest 92*
**Hickman,** David Scott 1940- *WhoFI 92*
**Hickman,** Eugene, Sr 1928- *AmMWSc 92*
**Hickman,** Franklin Simpson 1886-1965 *DcNCBi 3*
**Hickman,** Gail Morgan 1948- *WhoEnt 92*
**Hickman,** Garrison M. 1945- *WhoBlA 92*
**Hickman,** Glenn *Who 92*
**Hickman,** Howard Minor 1925- *AmMWSc 92*
**Hickman,** Hoyt Leon 1927- *WhoRel 92*
**Hickman,** J. Kenneth 1928- *WhoFI 92*
**Hickman,** Jack Walter 1931- *AmMWSc 92*
**Hickman,** James Blake 1921- *AmMWSc 92*
**Hickman,** James Charles 1927- *AmMWSc 92, WhoFI 92*
**Hickman,** James Joseph 1942- *AmMWSc 92*
**Hickman,** Jerry A. 1946- *WhoBlA 92*
**Hickman,** Joe Eugene 1951- *WhoEnt 92*
**Hickman,** John Hampton, III 1937- *WhoFI 92*
**Hickman,** John Kyrle 1927- *Who 92*
**Hickman,** John Roy 1934- *AmMWSc 92*
**Hickman,** Lucille 1949- *WhoMW 92*
**Hickman,** Marjorie Ruth 1918- *WhoFI 92*
**Hickman,** Michael 1943- *AmMWSc 92*
**Hickman,** Michael Ranulf 1922- *Who 92*
**Hickman,** Richard Glenn 1949- *Who 92*
**Hickman,** Richard Hulett 1950- *WhoMW 92*
**Hickman,** Roy D 1932- *AmMWSc 92*
**Hickman,** Roy Scott 1934- *AmMWSc 92*
**Hickman,** Ruth Virginia 1931- *WhoRel 92*
**Hickman,** Thomas Carlyle 1932- *WhoBlA 92*
**Hickman,** Timothy Mark 1961- *WhoRel 92*
**Hickman,** Timothy Ricktor 1946- *WhoAmP 91*
**Hickman,** Tracy Raye 1955- *IntAu&W 91*
**Hickman,** Warren David 1941- *AmMWSc 92*
**Hickmet,** Richard Saladin 1947- *Who 92*
**Hickmon,** Ned 1934- *WhoBlA 92*
**Hickmott,** Thomas Ward 1929- *AmMWSc 92*
**Hickner,** Richard Allan 1932- *AmMWSc 92*
**Hickner,** Thomas L 1954- *WhoAmP 91*
**Hickock,** Will *TwCWW 91*
**Hickok,** David Keith 1936- *WhoMW 92*
**Hickok,** Leslie George 1946- *AmMWSc 92*
**Hickok,** Robert Baker 1910- *AmMWSc 92*
**Hickok,** Robert L, Jr 1929- *AmMWSc 92*
**Hickok,** Robert Lee 1929- *AmMWSc 92*
**Hickok,** Thomas Alan 1952- *WhoFI 92*
**Hickok,** Wild Bill 1837-1876 *BenetAL 91*
**Hickory,** John Edward 1943- *WhoMW 92*
**Hickox,** A. C. 1959- *WhoEnt 92*
**Hickox,** George Keyes, Jr. 1958- *WhoFI 92*
**Hickox,** Philip Homer 1949- *WhoRel 92*
**Hickox,** Richard Sidney 1948- *IntWW 91, Who 92, WhoEnt 92*
**Hickox,** William Horace, III 1941- *WhoFI 92*
**Hickrod,** George Alan Karnes Wallis 1930- *WhoMW 92*
**Hicks** *Who 92*
**Hicks,** Arthur James 1938- *WhoBlA 92*
**Hicks,** Arthur M 1917- *AmMWSc 92*
**Hicks,** Arthur Wesley, Jr. 1958- *WhoFI 92*
**Hicks,** Barbara *ConTFT 9*
**Hicks,** Barbara Alice 1933- *WhoRel 92*
**Hicks,** Bethany Gribben 1951- *WhoAmL 92, WhoWest 92*
**Hicks,** Bruce Boundy 1940- *AmMWSc 92*
**Hicks,** C. Flippo 1929- *WhoAmL 92*
**Hicks,** C. J. *WhoRel 92*
**Hicks,** Catherine 1951- *IntMPA 92*
**Hicks,** Charles Robert 1920- *AmMWSc 92*
**Hicks,** Christopher 1950- *WhoAmP 91*
**Hicks,** Clarence Flippo 1929- *WhoAmP 91*
**Hicks,** Clayton Nathaniel 1943- *WhoBlA 92*
**Hicks,** Clifford Wendell, Jr. 1964- *WhoBlA 92*
**Hicks,** Colin Peter 1946- *Who 92*
**Hicks,** Cullen L. *WhoRel 92*
**Hicks,** Daisy C. 1919- *WhoBlA 92*
**Hicks,** Dale R 1938- *AmMWSc 92*
**Hicks,** Dan 1941- *WhoEnt 92*
**Hicks,** Darrell Lee 1937- *AmMWSc 92, WhoMW 92*
**Hicks,** D'Atra *WhoBlA 92*
**Hicks,** David *Who 92*
**Hicks,** David 1929- *DcTwDes, IntWW 91, Who 92*
**Hicks,** David Earl 1931- *WhoWest 92*
**Hicks,** David Gregory 1958- *WhoRel 92*
**Hicks,** David Harold 1949- *WhoFI 92*
**Hicks,** David L 1935- *AmMWSc 92*
**Hicks,** Delphus Van, Jr. 1939- *WhoBlA 92*
**Hicks,** Donald Gail 1934- *AmMWSc 92*
**Hicks,** Doris Askew 1926- *WhoBlA 92*
**Hicks,** Doris Morrison 1933- *WhoBlA 92*
**Hicks,** E. B. 1907- *WhoBlA 92*
**Hicks,** Edith A. 1939- *WhoBlA 92*
**Hicks,** Edward James 1936- *AmMWSc 92*
**Hicks,** Eleanor *IntAu&W 91X, WrDr 92*
**Hicks,** Eleanor 1943- *WhoBlA 92*
**Hicks,** Eleanor B. *SmATA 67*
**Hicks,** Elias 1748-1830 *BenetAL 91*
**Hicks,** Elija Maxie, Jr 1920- *AmMWSc 92*
**Hicks,** Ellen Thompson 1866-1951 *DcNCBi 3*
**Hicks,** Ellis Arden 1915- *AmMWSc 92*
**Hicks,** Floyd V 1915- *WhoAmP 91*
**Hicks,** Garland Fisher, Jr 1945- *AmMWSc 92*
**Hicks,** Granville 1901-1982 *BenetAL 91*
**Hicks,** Gregory Steven 1959- *WhoFI 92*
**Hicks,** H. Beecher, Jr. 1944- *WhoBlA 92*
**Hicks,** Harold E 1919- *AmMWSc 92*
**Hicks,** Harry David 1923- *Who 92*
**Hicks,** Harry Gross 1922- *AmMWSc 92*
**Hicks,** Harvey *SmATA 67*
**Hicks,** Henderson 1930- *WhoBlA 92*
**Hicks,** Henry Beecher, Sr. 1912- *WhoBlA 92*
**Hicks,** Henry Davies 1915- *IntWW 91*
**Hicks,** Heraline Elaine 1951- *AmMWSc 92*
**Hicks,** Herbert Ray 1939- *WhoRel 92*
**Hicks,** Hilly Gene 1950- *WhoBlA 92*
**Hicks,** Howard Victor Stephen 1936- *WhoMW 92*
**Hicks,** Irvin 1938- *WhoAmP 91*
**Hicks,** Israel *WhoEnt 92*
**Hicks,** J. Portis 1938- *WhoAmL 92*
**Hicks,** Jackson Earl 1934- *AmMWSc 92*
**Hicks,** James Earl 1951- *WhoMW 92*
**Hicks,** James Thomas *WhoAmL 92*
**Hicks,** James Thomas 1924- *AmMWSc 92, WhoFI 92*
**Hicks,** Jerry 1927- *TwCPaSc*
**Hicks,** Jim Ray 1935- *WhoAmP 91*
**Hicks,** Jimmie Lee 1936- *AmMWSc 92, WhoWest 92*
**Hicks,** John 1904- *WrDr 92*
**Hicks,** John Charles 1928- *Who 92*
**Hicks,** John F d1903 *BiInAmS*
**Hicks,** John J. 1916-1983 *WhoBlA 92N*
**Hicks,** John Mark 1957- *WhoRel 92*
**Hicks,** John O, III 1943- *WhoAmP 91*
**Hicks,** John Richard 1904- *Who 92*
**Hicks,** John Richard 1904-1989 *WhoNob 90*
**Hicks,** John Robert 1961- *WhoWest 92*
**Hicks,** John T *AmMWSc 92*
**Hicks,** John T 1925- *WhoAmP 91*
**Hicks,** John Victor 1907- *IntWW 91, WhoWest 92*
**Hicks,** John W, III 1921- *AmMWSc 92*
**Hicks,** Judith Eileen 1947- *WhoMW 92*
**Hicks,** Ken Carlyle 1953- *WhoFI 92*
**Hicks,** Kenneth Ward 1940- *AmMWSc 92*
**Hicks,** Kenneth William 1923- *WhoRel 92*
**Hicks,** Kevin B 1952- *AmMWSc 92*
**Hicks,** Larry W 1948- *WhoAmP 91*
**Hicks,** Leon Nathaniel 1933- *WhoBlA 92*
**Hicks,** Lisa Lee 1963- *WhoMW 92*
**Hicks,** Louis Charles, Jr. 1951- *WhoBlA 92*
**Hicks,** Lucile P 1938- *WhoAmP 91*
**Hicks,** Marilyn Sue 1949- *WhoRel 92*
**Hicks,** Mark C, Jr 1927- *WhoAmP 91*
**Hicks,** Maryellen 1949- *WhoBlA 92*
**Hicks,** Maryellen Whitlock 1949- *WhoAmL 92*
**Hicks,** Maureen Patricia 1948- *Who 92*
**Hicks,** Michael *Who 92*
**Hicks,** Michael Dewayne 1961- *WhoEnt 92*
**Hicks,** Morris Alvin 1936- *WhoWest 92*
**Hicks,** Nicola 1960- *TwCPaSc*
**Hicks,** Patricia Fain 1927- *AmMWSc 92*
**Hicks,** Paul B, III 1956- *WhoAmP 91*
**Hicks,** Paul B., Jr. 1925- *WhoFI 92*
**Hicks,** Ralph William, Jr. 1942- *WhoWest 92*
**Hicks,** Richard A 1941- *WhoIns 92*
**Hicks,** Richard Hilton, Jr. 1945- *WhoAmL 92*
**Hicks,** Richard Louis, Jr. 1921-1977 *WhoBlA 92N*
**Hicks,** Richard R. 1931- *WhoBlA 92*
**Hicks,** Robert 1938- *Who 92*
**Hicks,** Robert Alvin 1932- *WhoWest 92*
**Hicks,** Robert Eugene 1943- *AmMWSc 92*
**Hicks,** Robert Michael 1945- *WhoRel 92*
**Hicks,** Robert Miller 1925- *WhoAmP 91*
**Hicks,** Robin Edgcumbe 1942- *Who 92*
**Hicks,** Roger Andrew 1957- *WhoRel 92*
**Hicks,** Samuel Pendleton 1913- *AmMWSc 92*
**Hicks,** Sheila 1934- *DcTwDes*
**Hicks,** Sherman Gregory 1946- *WhoMW 92, WhoRel 92*
**Hicks,** Sonja Elaine 1940- *AmMWSc 92*
**Hicks,** Steacy Dopp 1925- *AmMWSc 92*
**Hicks,** Stephen Dale 1956- *WhoFI 92*
**Hicks,** Susan Adelia 1947- *WhoMW 92*
**Hicks,** T Philip 1952- *AmMWSc 92*
**Hicks,** Terrence Henry 1952- *WhoFI 92*
**Hicks,** Thomas *Who 92*
**Hicks,** Thurston Titus 1857-1927 *DcNCBi 3*
**Hicks,** Timothy Gerald 1952- *WhoAmP 91*
**Hicks,** Troy L 1932- *AmMWSc 92*
**Hicks,** Veronica Abena 1949- *WhoBlA 92*
**Hicks,** W.B. Dub 1911- *WhoWest 92*
**Hicks,** William B 1925- *AmMWSc 92*
**Hicks,** William H. 1925- *WhoBlA 92*
**Hicks,** William Hampton 1956- *WhoEnt 92*
**Hicks,** William J. 1948- *WhoBlA 92*
**Hicks,** William Jackson 1827-1911 *DcNCBi 3*
**Hicks,** William L. 1928- *WhoBlA 92*
**Hicks,** William Michael 1928- *Who 92*
**Hicks,** William Paul, III 1957- *WhoFI 92*
**Hicks,** Willie Lee 1931- *WhoBlA 92*
**Hicks-Bartlett,** Sharon Theresa 1951- *WhoBlA 92*
**Hicks Beach** *Who 92*
**Hickson,** Donald Andrew 1931- *AmMWSc 92*
**Hickson,** Eugene, Sr. 1930- *WhoBlA 92*
**Hickson,** James Forbes 1954- *AmMWSc 92*
**Hickson,** John LeFever 1916- *AmMWSc 92*
**Hickson,** Sherman Ruben 1950- *WhoBlA 92*
**Hickson,** William F., Jr. 1936- *WhoBlA 92*
**Hicyilmaz,** Gay 1947- *ConAu 133*
**Hida** *EncAmaz 91*
**Hidaka,** Yuji 1952- *WhoMW 92*
**Hidalgo,** Alberto 1935- *WhoHisp 92*
**Hidalgo,** Carlos Alberto 1955- *WhoHisp 92*
**Hidalgo,** David *WhoHisp 92*
**Hidalgo,** Edward 1912- *WhoAmL 92, WhoHisp 92*
**Hidalgo,** Hector J 1954- *WhoAmP 91*
**Hidalgo,** Henry 1922- *AmMWSc 92*
**Hidalgo,** Hilda *WhoHisp 92*
**Hidalgo,** James Michael 1951- *WhoHisp 92*
**Hidalgo,** John 1916- *AmMWSc 92*
**Hidalgo,** Jose Luis 1919-1947 *DcLB 108 [port]*
**Hidalgo,** Juan 1612?-1685 *NewAmDM*
**Hidalgo,** Manuel T *WhoIns 92*
**Hidalgo,** Michel Joseph 1955- *WhoEnt 92*
**Hidalgo,** Miguel 1958- *WhoFI 92*
**Hidalgo,** Nitza Mercedes 1951- *WhoHisp 92*
**Hidalgo,** Rodrigo 1940- *WhoHisp 92*
**Hidalgo,** Stanley Peter, II 1943- *WhoFI 92*
**Hidalgo de Cisneros,** Baltasar *HisDSpE*
**Hidalgo-De Jesus,** Amarilis 1962- *WhoHisp 92*
**Hidalgo y Castilla,** Miguel 1753-1811 *HisDSpE*
**Hiday,** Lanny L. 1944- *WhoAmL 92*
**Hidayatullah,** Mohammed 1905- *IntWW 91, Who 92*
**Hidden,** Anthony Brian 1936- *Who 92*
**Hidden,** Norman 1913- *WrDr 92*
**Hidden,** William Earl 1853-1918 *BiInAmS*
**Hiddleston,** Ronal Eugene 1939- *WhoWest 92*
**Hide,** Raymond 1929- *IntWW 91, Who 92*
**Hiden,** Robert Battaile, Jr. 1933- *WhoAmL 92*
**Hider,** William Oliver 1946- *WhoFI 92*
**Hidore,** John J 1932- *AmMWSc 92*
**Hidu,** Herbert 1931- *AmMWSc 92*
**Hidy,** George Martel 1935- *AmMWSc 92*
**Hidy,** Phil Harter 1915- *AmMWSc 92*
**Hieatt,** Constance B. 1928- *WrDr 92*
**Hieatt,** Constance Bartlett 1928- *IntAu&W 91*
**Hieb,** Marianne 1946- *WhoRel 92*
**Hieb,** Mario Kirk 1958- *WhoEnt 92*
**Hiebaum,** Kurt Georg 1946- *WhoFI 92*
**Hieber,** George Frederick, II 1942- *WhoAmP 91*
**Hieber,** Thomas Eugene 1936- *AmMWSc 92*

**Hieber**, William George, Jr. 1937- *WhoFI 92*
**Hieber**, William Ralph 1934- *WhoMW 92*
**Hiebert**, Allen G 1941- *AmMWSc 92*
**Hiebert**, Clarence Roy 1927- *WhoRel 92*
**Hiebert**, D. Edmond 1910- *WrDr 92*
**Hiebert**, Donald Lee 1943- *WhoMW 92*
**Hiebert**, Elizabeth Blake 1910- *WhoMW 92*
**Hiebert**, Ernest 1941- *AmMWSc 92*
**Hiebert**, Erwin Nick 1919- *AmMWSc 92, IntWW 91*
**Hiebert**, Gordon Lee 1927- *AmMWSc 92*
**Hiebert**, John Covell 1934- *AmMWSc 92*
**Hiebert**, Lindsay Darrell 1958- *WhoMW 92*
**Hiebert**, Paul 1892- *BenetAL 91*
**Hiebert**, Peter Nicholas 1949- *WhoAmL 92*
**Hiebert**, William John 1938- *WhoMW 92*
**Hieble**, J Paul 1948- *AmMWSc 92*
**Hieftje**, Gary Martin 1942- *AmMWSc 92*
**Hiegel**, Frank S. 1946- *WhoFI 92*
**Hieken**, Charles 1928- *WhoAmL 92*
**Hiel**, Darrel Thomas *WhoMW 92*
**Hielscher**, Frank Henning 1938- *AmMWSc 92*
**Hielscher**, Leo 1926- *Who 92*
**Hielscher**, Udo Artur 1939- *WhoFI 92*
**Hiemenz**, Paul C 1936- *AmMWSc 92*
**Hienton**, James Robert 1951- *WhoFI 92*
**Hienz**, Robert Douglas 1944- *AmMWSc 92*
**Hier**, Marshall David 1945- *WhoAmL 92*
**Hier**, Perry O *WhoAmP 91*
**Hiergeist**, Franz Xavier 1938- *AmMWSc 92*
**Hierholzer**, John Charles 1938- *AmMWSc 92*
**Hierl**, Konstantin 1875-1955 *EncTR 91 [port]*
**Hierl**, Peter Marston 1941- *AmMWSc 92*
**Hierocles** *EncEarC*
**Hieronymus**, Clara Booth Wiggins 1913- *WhoEnt 92*
**Hierro**, Jose 1922- *DcLB 108 [port]*
**Hiers**, Richard Hyde 1932- *WhoRel 92*
**Hiesberger**, Jean-Marie 1941- *WhoRel 92*
**Hieser**, Rex Arthur 1952- *WhoMW 92*
**Hieserman**, Clarence Edward 1917- *AmMWSc 92*
**Hiesiger**, Barbara *DrAPF 91*
**Hiestand**, Emily 1947- *ConAu 134*
**Hiestand**, Everett Nelson 1920- *AmMWSc 92, WhoMW 92*
**Hietanen-Makela**, Anna 1909- *AmMWSc 92*
**Hietbrink**, Bernard Edward 1930- *AmMWSc 92*
**Hietbrink**, Earl Henry 1930- *AmMWSc 92*
**Hift**, Fred 1924- *IntMPA 92*
**Higa**, Harry Hiroshi *AmMWSc 92*
**Higa**, Leslie Hideyasu 1925- *AmMWSc 92*
**Higa**, Walter Hiroichi 1919- *AmMWSc 92*
**Higa**, Wayne Hajime 1954- *WhoFI 92*
**Higaki**, Tokutaro 1916- *IntWW 91*
**Higashi**, Gene Isao 1938- *AmMWSc 92*
**Higashikuni**, Naruhiko 1887-1990 *FacFETw*
**Higashiyama**, Tadayoshi 1933- *AmMWSc 92*
**Higbe**, Henry Fraser, Jr. 1950- *WhoFI 92*
**Higbee**, Donald William 1931- *WhoFI 92*
**Higbee**, James Franklin, III 1947- *WhoEnt 92*
**Higbee**, John P 1933- *WhoAmP 91*
**Higbie**, Leslie Wilson 1914- *WhoEnt 92*
**Higby**, Edward Julian 1939- *WhoFI 92*
**Higby**, Gregory James 1953- *WhoMW 92*
**Higby**, Lynn Carlton 1938- *WhoAmL 92*
**Higdem**, Roger Leon 1933- *AmMWSc 92*
**Higdon**, Archie 1905- *AmMWSc 92*
**Higdon**, Bernice Cowan 1918- *WhoWest 92*
**Higdon**, C. Mark 1952- *WhoRel 92*
**Higdon**, Charles Gregory 1947- *WhoAmP 91*
**Higdon**, Hal 1931- *IntAu&W 91, WrDr 92*
**Higdon**, James Noel 1944- *WhoAmL 92*
**Higdon**, Leo I. *WhoFI 92*
**Higdon**, Robert Jack, Jr. 1963- *WhoAmL 92*
**Higdon**, William Michael 1962- *WhoMW 92*
**Higdon**, William Vitas 1944- *WhoMW 92*
**Higdon**, Willie Junior 1924- *WhoAmP 91*
**Higerd**, Thomas Braden 1942- *AmMWSc 92*
**Higginbotham**, A. Leon, Jr. 1928- *WhoAmL 92, WhoAmP 91, WhoBlA 92*
**Higginbotham**, Don *WhoAmP 91*
**Higginbotham**, G J *WhoAmP 91*
**Higginbotham**, J.C. 1906-1973 *NewAmDM*
**Higginbotham**, Jay 1937- *WrDr 92*
**Higginbotham**, John Burnell 1955- *WhoFI 92*
**Higginbotham**, John Taylor 1947- *WhoAmL 92*
**Higginbotham**, Kenneth Day, Sr. 1928- *WhoBlA 92*
**Higginbotham**, Lloyd William 1934- *WhoWest 92*
**Higginbotham**, Patrick Errol 1938- *WhoAmL 92, WhoAmP 91*
**Higginbotham**, Peyton Randolph 1902- *WhoBlA 92*
**Higginbotham**, Prieur Jay 1937- *IntAu&W 91*
**Higginbotham**, Robert David 1921- *AmMWSc 92*
**Higginbotham**, Samuel Page 1916- *WhoAmP 91*
**Higginbotham**, Timothy Borden 1954- *WhoMW 92*
**Higginbottom**, Donald Noble 1925- *Who 92*
**Higgins** *Who 92*
**Higgins**, Aidan 1927- *ConNov 91, WrDr 92*
**Higgins**, Alec Wilfred 1914- *Who 92*
**Higgins**, Andrew J 1921- *WhoAmP 91*
**Higgins**, Andrew Jackson 1921- *WhoAmL 92, WhoMW 92*
**Higgins**, Andrew James 1948- *Who 92*
**Higgins**, Bennett Edward 1931- *WhoBlA 92*
**Higgins**, Bill Edward 1961- *WhoWest 92*
**Higgins**, Brian Alton 1930- *WhoEnt 92*
**Higgins**, Brian Gavin 1948- *AmMWSc 92*
**Higgins**, Charles Graham 1925- *AmMWSc 92*
**Higgins**, Chester A., Sr. 1917- *WhoBlA 92*
**Higgins**, Chester Archer, Jr. 1946- *WhoBlA 92*
**Higgins**, Christopher 1914- *Who 92*
**Higgins**, Clarence R., Jr. 1927- *WhoBlA 92*
**Higgins**, Cleo Surry 1923- *WhoBlA 92*
**Higgins**, Daryl Clyde 1948- *WhoRel 92*
**Higgins**, Dennis Roy 1937- *WhoWest 92*
**Higgins**, Dick *DrAPF 91*
**Higgins**, Dick 1938- *WrDr 92*
**Higgins**, Donald George 1914- *WhoAmP 91*
**Higgins**, Donald Steven 1946- *WhoFI 92*
**Higgins**, Dorothy 1930- *AmMWSc 92*
**Higgins**, E Arnold 1930- *AmMWSc 92*
**Higgins**, Edwin Stanley 1925- *AmMWSc 92*
**Higgins**, Eoin *Who 92*
**Higgins**, Francis Edward 1935- *WhoMW 92*
**Higgins**, Frank *DrAPF 91*
**Higgins**, Frank 1927- *Who 92*
**Higgins**, Frederick 1918- *WhoRel 92*
**Higgins**, Frederick B, Jr 1936- *AmMWSc 92*
**Higgins**, George A, Jr 1917- *AmMWSc 92*
**Higgins**, George Gilmary 1916- *IntWW 91*
**Higgins**, George V. *DrAPF 91*
**Higgins**, George V. 1939- *BenetAL 91, ConNov 91, IntAu&W 91, WrDr 92*
**Higgins**, George Vincent 1939- *IntWW 91*
**Higgins**, Harrison Scott 1945- *WhoFI 92*
**Higgins**, Ian T 1919- *AmMWSc 92*
**Higgins**, Irwin Raymond 1919- *AmMWSc 92*
**Higgins**, Jack *IntAu&W 91X, IntWW 91, Who 92, WrDr 92*
**Higgins**, Jack 1954- *WhoMW 92*
**Higgins**, James Edward 1961- *WhoFI 92*
**Higgins**, James Jacob 1943- *AmMWSc 92*
**Higgins**, James McCoy 1954- *WhoFI 92*
**Higgins**, James Robert, Jr. 1943- *WhoAmL 92*
**Higgins**, James Thaddeus 1954- *WhoEnt 92*
**Higgins**, James Thomas, Jr 1934- *AmMWSc 92*
**Higgins**, James Victor 1933- *AmMWSc 92*
**Higgins**, James Woodrow 1921- *AmMWSc 92*
**Higgins**, Jay Francis 1945- *WhoFI 92*
**Higgins**, Jeff Kent 1954- *WhoEnt 92*
**Higgins**, Jerry Mitchell 1930- *AmMWSc 92*
**Higgins**, Jim S 1932- *WhoAmP 91*
**Higgins**, Joel Franklin 1943- *WhoEnt 92*
**Higgins**, John Andrew 1940- *Who 92*
**Higgins**, John Christopher 1932- *Who 92*
**Higgins**, John Clayborn 1934- *AmMWSc 92*
**Higgins**, John Dalby 1934- *IntAu&W 91*
**Higgins**, John J 1943- *AmMWSc 92*
**Higgins**, John Patrick Basil 1927- *Who 92*
**Higgins**, Joseph John 1932- *AmMWSc 92*
**Higgins**, Judith *DrAPF 91*
**Higgins**, Kenneth Milton 1936- *WhoWest 92*
**Higgins**, Larry Charles 1936- *AmMWSc 92*
**Higgins**, Leslie Bradbury 1919- *WhoAmP 91*
**Higgins**, Linwood McIntire 1948- *WhoAmP 91*
**Higgins**, Margaret Tullar 1930- *WhoAmP 91*
**Higgins**, Marge 1931- *WhoAmP 91*
**Higgins**, Marion West 1915- *WhoFI 92*
**Higgins**, Michael John 1935- *Who 92*
**Higgins**, Michael Joseph 1951- *WhoRel 92*
**Higgins**, Michael Lee 1940- *AmMWSc 92*
**Higgins**, Millicent Williams Payne 1928- *AmMWSc 92*
**Higgins**, Milton Prince 1842-1912 *BiInAmS*
**Higgins**, N Patrick 1946- *AmMWSc 92*
**Higgins**, Ora A. 1919- *WhoBlA 92*
**Higgins**, Paul Anthony 1964- *WhoMW 92*
**Higgins**, Paul Daniel 1946- *AmMWSc 92*
**Higgins**, Paul R 1944- *WhoAmP 91*
**Higgins**, Peter Matthew 1923- *Who 92*
**Higgins**, Reynold Alleyne 1916- *IntAu&W 91, Who 92, WrDr 92*
**Higgins**, Richard C 1938- *IntAu&W 91*
**Higgins**, Richard J 1939- *AmMWSc 92*
**Higgins**, Robert Arthur 1924- *AmMWSc 92*
**Higgins**, Robert Arthur, Jr. 1952- *WhoEnt 92*
**Higgins**, Robert Gerard 1952- *WhoMW 92*
**Higgins**, Robert H 1942- *AmMWSc 92*
**Higgins**, Robert Price 1932- *AmMWSc 92*
**Higgins**, Rod Dwayne 1960- *WhoBlA 92*
**Higgins**, Rosalyn 1937- *IntWW 91, Who 92, WrDr 92*
**Higgins**, Ruth Ann 1944- *WhoWest 92*
**Higgins**, Ruth Ellen 1945- *WhoEnt 92, WhoMW 92*
**Higgins**, Sammie L. 1923- *WhoBlA 92*
**Higgins**, Sean Marielle 1968- *WhoBlA 92*
**Higgins**, Shaun O'Leary 1948- *WhoWest 92*
**Higgins**, Stann 1952- *WhoBlA 92*
**Higgins**, Stephen Boyd 1946- *WhoAmL 92*
**Higgins**, Terence 1928- *Who 92*
**Higgins**, Terry Jay 1947- *AmMWSc 92*
**Higgins**, Theodore Parker 1920- *AmMWSc 92*
**Higgins**, Thomas A. 1932- *WhoAmL 92*
**Higgins**, Thomas Ernest 1948- *AmMWSc 92*
**Higgins**, Thomas James 1911- *AmMWSc 92*
**Higgins**, Thomas James 1945- *WhoAmP 91*
**Higgins**, Thomas Joseph 1899- *WrDr 92*
**Higgins**, Verna Jessie 1943- *AmMWSc 92*
**Higgins**, W F 1920- *AmMWSc 92*
**Higgins**, Wallace Winfield 1931- *WhoAmP 91*
**Higgins**, Wilfred Frank *Who 92*
**Higgins**, William Alleyne 1928- *Who 92*
**Higgins**, William Hubert 1946- *WhoWest 92*
**Higgins**, William Joseph 1947- *AmMWSc 92*
**Higgins**, William Russell 1951- *WhoWest 92*
**Higgins**, William Waugh 1935- *WhoFI 92*
**Higginsen**, Vy *WhoBlA 92*
**Higginson**, Francis 1586-1630 *BenetAL 91*
**Higginson**, George W, Jr 1923- *AmMWSc 92*
**Higginson**, Gordon Robert 1929- *Who 92*
**Higginson**, Jerry Alden, Jr. 1957- *WhoFI 92*
**Higginson**, Jerry Cassim 1938- *WhoAmP 91*
**Higginson**, John 1922- *AmMWSc 92, IntWW 91*
**Higginson**, John 1932- *WhoWest 92*
**Higginson**, Mehetabel Robie 1727-1818 *BlkwEAR*
**Higginson**, Thomas Joseph 1940- *WhoFI 92*
**Higginson**, Thomas Wentworth 1823-1911 *BenetAL 91, BiInAmS*
**Higginson**, William J. *DrAPF 91*
**Higgs**, Barry 1934- *Who 92*
**Higgs**, Brian James 1930- *Who 92*
**Higgs**, Charles Edward 1950- *WhoRel 92*
**Higgs**, Frederick C. 1935- *WhoBlA 92*
**Higgs**, Hubert Laurence 1911- *Who 92*
**Higgs**, Jeffrey Brent 1945- *WhoMW 92*
**Higgs**, John H. 1934- *WhoAmL 92*
**Higgs**, John Michael 1912- *Who 92*
**Higgs**, Lloyd Albert 1937- *AmMWSc 92*
**Higgs**, Mary Ann Spicer 1951- *WhoBlA 92*
**Higgs**, Michael *Who 92*
**Higgs**, Peter Ware 1929- *IntWW 91, Who 92*
**Higgs**, Robert Hughes 1932- *AmMWSc 92*
**Higgs**, Roger L 1938- *AmMWSc 92*
**High**, Charles Victor 1957- *WhoMW 92*
**High**, Denny F. 1939- *WhoFI 92*
**High**, Edward Garfield 1918- *AmMWSc 92*
**High**, Freida 1946- *WhoBlA 92*
**High**, Lee Rawdon, Jr 1941- *AmMWSc 92*
**High**, LeRoy Bertolet 1914- *AmMWSc 92*
**High**, Monique Raphel 1949- *IntAu&W 91*
**High**, Philip E 1914- *IntAu&W 91, TwCSFW 91, WrDr 92*
**High**, S. Dale 1942- *WhoFI 92*
**High**, Suzanne Irene 1946- *WhoAmL 92, WhoMW 92*
**High**, Thomas W. 1947- *WhoWest 92*
**Higham**, Charles 1931- *WrDr 92*
**Higham**, Geoffrey Arthur 1927- *Who 92*
**Higham**, John 1920- *IntWW 91*
**Higham**, John Drew 1914- *Who 92*
**Higham**, Norman 1924- *Who 92*
**Higham**, Philip Roger Canning 1920- *Who 92*
**Higham**, Robert R. A. 1935- *WrDr 92*
**Higham**, Robin 1925- *IntAu&W 91, WhoMW 92, WrDr 92*
**Higham**, Roger Stephen *WrDr 92*
**Highberger**, Craig Bender 1953- *WhoEnt 92*
**Highberger**, Mary Kohring 1940- *WhoMW 92*
**Highberger**, William Foster 1950- *WhoAmL 92*
**Highers**, Alan Edward 1937- *WhoAmL 92*
**Highet**, David Allan 1913- *IntWW 91*
**Highet**, Gilbert 1906-1978 *BenetAL 91*
**Highet**, Helen Clark *Who 92*
**Highet**, John 1918- *WrDr 92*
**Highet**, Robert John 1925- *AmMWSc 92*
**Highfield**, Ronald Curtis 1951- *WhoRel 92*
**Highfill**, Robert Steven 1951- *WhoRel 92, WhoWest 92*
**Highgate**, Edmonia 1844-1870 *HanAmWH*
**Highland**, Dora *WrDr 92*
**Highland**, Henry Arthur 1924- *AmMWSc 92*
**Highland**, Marilyn Rae Schnell 1956- *WhoWest 92*
**Highland**, Monica *IntAu&W 91X, WrDr 92*
**Highland**, Virgil Lee 1935- *AmMWSc 92*
**Highlander**, Richard William 1940- *WhoWest 92*
**Highlands**, Matthew Edward 1905- *AmMWSc 92*
**Highlen**, Larry Wade 1936- *WhoMW 92*
**Highley**, Terry L 1940- *AmMWSc 92*
**Highleyman**, Samuel Locke, III 1928- *WhoAmL 92*
**Highman**, Benjamin 1909- *AmMWSc 92*
**Highsmith**, Alonzo Walter 1965- *WhoBlA 92*
**Highsmith**, Carlton L. *WhoBlA 92*
**Highsmith**, Charles Albert 1921- *WhoBlA 92*
**Highsmith**, Jacob Franklin 1868-1939 *DcNCBi 3*
**Highsmith**, John Henry 1877-1953 *DcNCBi 3*
**Highsmith**, Patricia 1921- *BenetAL 91, ConNov 91, FacFETw, IntAu&W 91, IntWW 91, Who 92, WrDr 92*
**Highsmith**, Phillip E 1925- *AmMWSc 92*
**Highsmith**, Robert F 1945- *AmMWSc 92*
**Highsmith**, Robert M. 1950- *WhoAmL 92*
**Highsmith**, Ronald Earl 1939- *AmMWSc 92*
**Highstein**, Stephen Morris 1939- *AmMWSc 92*
**Hight**, Donald Wayne 1931- *AmMWSc 92*
**Hight**, Harold Philip 1924- *WhoWest 92*
**Hight**, Ralph Dale 1945- *AmMWSc 92*
**Hight**, Robert 1930- *AmMWSc 92*
**Hight Hellens**, Lawrence Othello 1922- *WhoEnt 92*
**Highton**, Richard 1927- *AmMWSc 92*
**Hightower**, Allen Ross, Jr 1946- *WhoAmP 91*
**Hightower**, Anthony *WhoBlA 92*
**Hightower**, Anthony 1961- *WhoAmP 91*
**Hightower**, Charles H., III 1934- *WhoBlA 92*
**Hightower**, Collin James 1936- *AmMWSc 92*
**Hightower**, Dan 1925- *AmMWSc 92*
**Hightower**, Dennis Fowler 1941- *WhoBlA 92*
**Hightower**, Edward Stewart 1940- *WhoBlA 92*
**Hightower**, Felda 1909- *AmMWSc 92*
**Hightower**, Florence Cole 1916-1981 *ConAu 35NR*
**Hightower**, Foyle Robert, Jr 1941- *WhoAmP 91*
**Hightower**, Herma J. *WhoBlA 92*
**Hightower**, Jack English 1926- *WhoAmL 92, WhoAmP 91*
**Hightower**, James Howard *WhoBlA 92*
**Hightower**, James K 1937- *AmMWSc 92*
**Hightower**, James Robert, Jr. 1954- *WhoRel 92*
**Hightower**, Jana Lynn 1958- *WhoEnt 92*
**Hightower**, Jesse Robert 1939- *AmMWSc 92*
**Hightower**, Jim 1943- *WhoAmP 91*
**Hightower**, Joe W 1936- *AmMWSc 92*
**Hightower**, John B. 1933- *IntWW 91*

**Hightower**, Kenneth Ralph 1947- *AmMWSc 92*
**Hightower**, Lawrence Edward 1946- *AmMWSc 92*
**Hightower**, Michael *WhoBlA 92*
**Hightower**, Monteria 1929- *WhoBlA 92*
**Hightower**, Nicholas Carr, Jr 1918- *AmMWSc 92*
**Hightower**, Thomas Reginald, Jr. 1958- *WhoAmL 92*
**Hightower**, Willar H., Jr. 1943- *WhoBlA 92*
**Hights**, William E. *WhoBlA 92*
**Highwater**, Jamake *DrAPF 91*
**Highwater**, Jamake 1942?- *Au&Arts 7 [port], BenetAL 91, ConAu 34NR, IntAu&W 91, WrDr 92*
**Higi**, William L. 1933- *WhoRel 92*
**Higinbotham**, Harlow Niles 1946- *WhoFI 92*
**Higinbotham**, William Alfred 1910- *AmMWSc 92*
**Higle**, Tommy Charles 1949- *WhoRel 92*
**Higley**, David L 1952- *WhoIns 92*
**Higley**, Leon George 1958- *AmMWSc 92*
**Higley**, William John 1960- *WhoRel 92*
**Higman**, Donald Gordon 1928- *AmMWSc 92*
**Higman**, Graham 1917- *Who 92*
**Higman**, Henry Booth 1927- *AmMWSc 92*
**Higman**, James B 1922- *AmMWSc 92*
**Hignett**, John Mulock 1934- *Who 92*
**Hignett**, Peter George 1925- *Who 92*
**Hignett**, Sean 1934- *IntAu&W 91, WrDr 92*
**Hignett**, Travis P 1907- *AmMWSc 92*
**Hignight**, Sherrill Grant 1957- *WhoRel 92*
**Higonnet**, Patrice 1938- *WrDr 92*
**Higson**, Gordon Robert 1932- *Who 92*
**Higton**, Dennis John 1921- *Who 92*
**Higuchi**, Hiroshi *AmMWSc 92*
**Higuchi**, Shinpei 1923- *WhoRel 92*
**Higuchi**, William Iyeo 1931- *AmMWSc 92*
**Higuera**, April Dawne 1962- *WhoEnt 92*
**Higuera**, Jesus 1950- *WhoHisp 92*
**Higuera**, Jesus R 1950- *WhoAmP 91*
**Higuera**, Ted 1958- *WhoHisp 92*
**Higuera**, Teodoro Ted 1958- *WhoMW 92*
**Hihara**, Lloyd Hiromi 1961- *AmMWSc 92*
**Hihara-Endo**, Linda Masae 1956- *WhoFI 92*
**Hijikata**, Takeshi 1915- *IntWW 91*
**Hijuelos**, Oscar 1951- *ConLC 65 [port], IntAu&W 91*
**Hijuelos**, Oscar J. 1951- *WhoHisp 92*
**Hiken**, Nat d1968 *LesBEnT 92*
**Hikida**, Robert Seiichi 1941- *AmMWSc 92, WhoMW 92*
**Hikind**, Dov 1950- *WhoAmP 91*
**Hikmet**, Nazim 1902-1963 *LiExTwC*
**Hilal**, Ahmed Izzedin 1924- *IntWW 91*
**Hilal**, Sadek K 1930- *AmMWSc 92*
**Hilaly**, Agha 1911- *IntWW 91, Who 92*
**Hilarion**, His Grace Bishop 1948- *WhoRel 92*
**Hilary** *EncEarC*
**Hilary of Arles** 401-449 *EncEarC*
**Hilary of Poitiers** 315?-367? *EncEarC*
**Hilary**, David Henry Jephson 1932- *Who 92*
**Hilbe**, Alfred J. 1928- *IntWW 91*
**Hilbe**, Joseph Michael 1944- *WhoWest 92*
**Hilberdink**, Fred Joannes 1942- *WhoEnt 92*
**Hilberg**, Albert William 1922- *AmMWSc 92*
**Hilberg**, Raul 1926- *WrDr 92*
**Hilberry**, Conrad *DrAPF 91*
**Hilberry**, Conrad Arthur 1928- *WrDr 92*
**Hilbersheimer**, Ludwig Karl 1885-1967 *DcTwDes, FacFETw*
**Hilbert**, David 1862-1943 *FacFETw*
**Hilbert**, Morton S 1917- *AmMWSc 92*
**Hilbert**, Paul J 1949- *WhoAmP 91*
**Hilbert**, Peter Louis, Jr. 1952- *WhoAmL 92*
**Hilbert**, Robert S 1941- *AmMWSc 92*
**Hilbert**, Stephen Russell 1942- *AmMWSc 92*
**Hilboldt**, James Sonnemann 1929- *WhoAmL 92, WhoFI 92*
**Hilborn**, David Alan 1945- *AmMWSc 92*
**Hilborn**, John R. 1928- *WhoFI 92*
**Hilborn**, Robert Clarence 1943- *AmMWSc 92*
**Hilbrecht**, Norman Ty 1933- *WhoAmP 91, WhoWest 92*
**Hilburg**, Alan Jay 1948- *WhoFI 92*
**Hilburn**, John Charles 1946- *WhoFI 92*
**Hilburn**, John L 1938- *AmMWSc 92*
**Hilby**, Bruce Titus 1944- *WhoWest 92*
**Hilchey**, Harry St. Clair 1922- *WhoRel 92*
**Hilchie**, Douglas Walter 1930- *AmMWSc 92*
**Hilcken**, John Allen 1916- *AmMWSc 92*
**Hild** *EncAmaz 91*
**Hild**, John Henry 1931- *Who 92*
**Hild**, Walter J 1919- *AmMWSc 92*
**Hild**, William Howard 1955- *WhoRel 92*
**Hilda**, Roland 1946- *WhoWest 92*
**Hilde**, Thomas Wayne Clark 1938- *AmMWSc 92*
**Hildebidle**, John *DrAPF 91*
**Hildebolt**, William Morton 1943- *AmMWSc 92*
**Hildebrand**, Adolf J 1956- *AmMWSc 92*
**Hildebrand**, Adolf Joseph 1956- *WhoMW 92*
**Hildebrand**, Bernard 1924- *AmMWSc 92*
**Hildebrand**, Bernard Percy 1930- *AmMWSc 92*
**Hildebrand**, Carl Edgar 1944- *AmMWSc 92*
**Hildebrand**, David Kent 1940- *AmMWSc 92*
**Hildebrand**, Don Cecil 1943- *WhoWest 92*
**Hildebrand**, Donald Clair 1932- *AmMWSc 92*
**Hildebrand**, Francis Begnaud 1915- *AmMWSc 92*
**Hildebrand**, Friedrich 1898-1948 *BiDExR, EncTR 91 [port]*
**Hildebrand**, Henry H 1922- *AmMWSc 92*
**Hildebrand**, Henry Peter 1911- *WhoRel 92*
**Hildebrand**, John Grant, III 1942- *AmMWSc 92*
**Hildebrand**, Milton 1918- *AmMWSc 92*
**Hildebrand**, Richard Allen 1916- *WhoBlA 92, WhoRel 92*
**Hildebrand**, Roger Henry 1922- *AmMWSc 92*
**Hildebrand**, Stephen George 1944- *AmMWSc 92*
**Hildebrand**, Verna 1924- *WrDr 92*
**Hildebrand**, Verna Lee 1924- *IntAu&W 91*
**Hildebrandt**, Alvin Frank 1925- *AmMWSc 92*
**Hildebrandt**, Frederick Dean, Jr. 1933- *WhoFI 92*
**Hildebrandt**, Greg Alan 1950- *WhoMW 92*
**Hildebrandt**, Jacob 1930- *AmMWSc 92*
**Hildebrandt**, Lanny Ross 1954- *WhoAmP 91*
**Hildebrandt**, Paul John 1929- *WhoFI 92*
**Hildebrandt**, Paul Knud *AmMWSc 92*
**Hildebrandt**, Theodore Alexander 1951- *WhoRel 92*
**Hildebrandt**, Theodore Ware 1922- *AmMWSc 92*
**Hildebrandt**, Thomas 1950- *WhoIns 92*
**Hildebrandt**, Wayne Arthur 1947- *AmMWSc 92*
**Hildebrant**, Andy McClellan 1929- *WhoWest 92*
**Hildebrant**, John A 1935- *AmMWSc 92*
**Hildegard of Bingen** 1098-1179 *NewAmDM*
**Hildeman**, Gregory John 1947- *AmMWSc 92*
**Hilden**, Shirley Ann 1940- *AmMWSc 92*
**Hilder**, F F 1827?-1901 *BiInAmS*
**Hilder**, Rowland 1905- *TwCPaSc, Who 92*
**Hilderbran**, Harvey 1960- *WhoAmP 91*
**Hilderbrand**, David Curtis 1946- *AmMWSc 92*
**Hildesheimer**, Wolfgang 1916- *IntWW 91*
**Hildesheimer**, Wolfgang 1916-1991 *ConAu 135, NewYTBS 91 [port]*
**Hildick**, E.W. *SmATA 68*
**Hildick**, E. W. 1925- *WrDr 92*
**Hildick**, Edmund Wallace 1925- *IntAu&W 91*
**Hildick**, Wallace *WrDr 92*
**Hildick**, Wallace 1925- *SmATA 68 [port]*
**Hilding**, Jerel Lee 1949- *WhoEnt 92*
**Hilding**, Stephen R 1936- *AmMWSc 92*
**Hilditch**, Clifford Arthur d1991 *Who 92N*
**Hildner**, Ernest Gotthold, III 1940- *AmMWSc 92, WhoWest 92*
**Hildner**, Phillips Brooks, II 1944- *WhoAmL 92*
**Hildreth**, Charles Lotin 1856-1892 *ScFEYrs*
**Hildreth**, Charles Steven 1949- *WhoWest 92*
**Hildreth**, Eugene A. *IntWW 91*
**Hildreth**, Eugene Augustus 1924- *AmMWSc 92*
**Hildreth**, Gladys Johnson 1933- *WhoBlA 92*
**Hildreth**, Harold John 1908- *Who 92*
**Hildreth**, Jan 1932- *Who 92*
**Hildreth**, Michael B 1955- *AmMWSc 92*
**Hildreth**, Patricia Yvonne 1934- *WhoMW 92*
**Hildreth**, Philip Elwin 1923- *AmMWSc 92*
**Hildreth**, Richard 1807-1865 *BenetAL 91*
**Hildreth**, Robert Claire 1924- *AmMWSc 92*
**Hildreth**, Samuel Prescott 1783-1863 *BiInAmS*
**Hildrew**, Bryan 1920- *IntWW 91, Who 92*
**Hildt**, Barbara A 1946- *WhoAmP 91*
**Hildyard**, David 1916- *Who 92*
**Hile**, Mahlon Malcolm Schallig 1946- *AmMWSc 92*
**Hileman**, Andrew R 1926- *AmMWSc 92*
**Hileman**, Byron Paxson, Jr. 1943- *WhoAmL 92*
**Hileman**, Orville Edwin, Jr 1936- *AmMWSc 92*
**Hileman**, Robert E 1929- *AmMWSc 92*
**Hiler**, Edward Allan 1939- *AmMWSc 92*
**Hiler**, John Patrick 1953- *WhoAmP 91*
**Hiler**, Julia Evans 1950- *WhoFI 92*
**Hiles**, Bradley Stephen 1955- *WhoAmL 92*
**Hiles**, Maurice 1936- *AmMWSc 92*
**Hiles**, Richard Allen 1943- *AmMWSc 92*
**Hiley**, Thomas 1905- *Who 92*
**Hilf**, Russell 1931- *AmMWSc 92*
**Hilfer**, Richard James 1947- *WhoAmL 92*
**Hilfer**, Saul Robert 1931- *AmMWSc 92*
**Hilferding**, Rudolf 1877-1941 *EncTR 91 [port]*
**Hilferty**, Frank Joseph 1920- *AmMWSc 92*
**Hilferty**, Susan *ConTFT 9*
**Hilfiger**, Roger Henry 1945- *WhoAmL 92*
**Hilfiker**, Franklin Roberts 1943- *AmMWSc 92*
**Hilford**, Lawrence B. 1934- *WhoEnt 92*
**Hilgar**, Arthur Gilbert 1926- *AmMWSc 92*
**Hilgard**, Ernest 1904- *WrDr 92*
**Hilgard**, Ernest Ropiequet 1904- *IntWW 91*
**Hilgard**, Eugene Woldemar 1833-1916 *BiInAmS*
**Hilgard**, Henry Rohrs *AmMWSc 92*
**Hilgard**, Julius Erasmus 1825-1891 *BiInAmS*
**Hilgard**, Theodore Charles 1828-1875 *BiInAmS*
**Hilgart**, Arthur A., Jr. 1936- *WhoMW 92*
**Hilgeman**, Georgia Kay 1950- *WhoWest 92*
**Hilgenfeldt**, Erich 1897-1969 *EncTR 91 [port]*
**Hilgenreiner**, Karl 1867-1948 *EncTR 91*
**Hilger**, Anthony Edward 1944- *AmMWSc 92*
**Hilger**, Frederick Lee, Jr. 1946- *WhoFI 92, WhoWest 92*
**Hilger**, James Eugene *AmMWSc 92*
**Hilger**, Wolfgang 1929- *IntWW 91*
**Hilgers**, DeAnne Marie 1965- *WhoRel 92*
**Hilibrand**, J 1930- *AmMWSc 92*
**Hilken**, E Gene *WhoAmP 91*
**Hilken**, Glen A. 1936-1976 *ConAu 134*
**Hilker**, Doris M 1923- *AmMWSc 92*
**Hilker**, Harry Van Der Veer, Jr 1925- *AmMWSc 92*
**Hilker**, Walter Robert, Jr. 1921- *WhoAmL 92*
**Hill** *Who 92*
**Hill**, Viscount 1931- *Who 92*
**Hill**, A Alan 1938- *WhoAmP 91*
**Hill**, Aaron 1685-1750 *RfGEnL 91*
**Hill**, Adrian Keith Graham 1895- *TwCPaSc*
**Hill**, Alan Geoffrey 1931- *Who 92*
**Hill**, Alan John Wills 1912- *Who 92*
**Hill**, Alastair Malcolm 1936- *Who 92*
**Hill**, Albert Bernard 1928- *WhoAmP 91*
**Hill**, Alette Olin 1933- *WhoWest 92*
**Hill**, Alexis *ConAu 133, SmATA 65*
**Hill**, Alfred 1925- *WhoBlA 92*
**Hill**, Alfred, Jr 1919- *AmMWSc 92*
**Hill**, Allen *Who 92*
**Hill**, Amy Wilmer 1961- *WhoFI 92*
**Hill**, Andrew Warren 1951- *WhoEnt 92*
**Hill**, Andrew William 1937- *WhoBlA 92, WhoEnt 92*
**Hill**, Anita Carraway 1928- *WhoAmP 91*
**Hill**, Anita Faye 1956- *NewYTBS 91*
**Hill**, Ann Gertrude 1922- *AmMWSc 92*
**Hill**, Anna Marie 1938- *WhoWest 92*
**Hill**, Anne Pendergrass 1954- *WhoAmL 92*
**Hill**, Annette Tillman 1937- *WhoBlA 92*
**Hill**, Annlia Paganini 1946- *AmMWSc 92*
**Hill**, Anthony 1930- *IntWW 91*
**Hill**, Antony James de Villiers 1940- *Who 92*
**Hill**, Archibald G 1950- *AmMWSc 92*
**Hill**, Archibald Vivian 1886-1977 *WhoNob 90*
**Hill**, Archie Clyde 1922- *AmMWSc 92*
**Hill**, Armin John 1912- *AmMWSc 92*
**Hill**, Arthur 1920- *Who 92*
**Hill**, Arthur 1922- *IntMPA 92, WhoEnt 92*
**Hill**, Arthur Burit 1922- *WhoBlA 92*
**Hill**, Arthur Derek 1916- *IntWW 91, Who 92*
**Hill**, Arthur James 1948- *WhoBlA 92, WhoFI 92*
**Hill**, Arthur Joseph, Jr 1918- *AmMWSc 92*
**Hill**, Arthur S 1941- *AmMWSc 92*
**Hill**, Arthur Thomas 1920- *AmMWSc 92*
**Hill**, Austin Bradford d1991 *NewYTBS 91, Who 92N*
**Hill**, Austin Bradford 1897-1991 *IntWW 91, -91N*
**Hill**, Avery 1924- *WhoBlA 92*
**Hill**, Barbara Ann 1950- *WhoBlA 92*
**Hill**, Benjamin 1925- *IntMPA 92*
**Hill**, Bennett David 1934- *WhoBlA 92*
**Hill**, Benny Joe 1935- *AmMWSc 92*
**Hill**, Bernard 1944- *IntMPA 92*
**Hill**, Bernard Dale 1948- *AmMWSc 92*
**Hill**, Bettie L 1935- *WhoAmP 91*
**Hill**, Betty J. 1948- *WhoBlA 92*
**Hill**, Beverly Ellen 1937- *WhoMW 92*
**Hill**, Billy 1898-1940 *BenetAL 91*
**Hill**, Billy 1947- *WhoBlA 92*
**Hill**, Bobby L. 1941- *WhoBlA 92*
**Hill**, Boyd *WhoAmP 91*
**Hill**, Brandon T. *WhoBlA 92*
**Hill**, Brent David 1964- *WhoFI 92*
**Hill**, Brian 1930- *Who 92*
**Hill**, Brian 1932- *Who 92*
**Hill**, Brian 1938- *AmMWSc 92*
**Hill**, Brian Kellogg 1943- *AmMWSc 92*
**Hill**, Brice Alan 1966- *WhoWest 92*
**Hill**, Bruce Colman 1948- *AmMWSc 92*
**Hill**, Bruce Edward 1964- *WhoBlA 92*
**Hill**, Bruce M 1935- *AmMWSc 92*
**Hill**, Calvin 1947- *WhoBlA 92*
**Hill**, Carl M. *WhoBlA 92*
**Hill**, Carl McClellan 1907- *AmMWSc 92*
**Hill**, Carl Richard, Jr. 1941- *WhoRel 92*
**Hill**, Carol *DrAPF 91*
**Hill**, Carol 1942- *ConNov 91, WrDr 92*
**Hill**, Carol Lynne 1956- *WhoAmL 92*
**Hill**, Carolyn Ann 1945- *WhoRel 92*
**Hill**, Charles 1904-1989 *FacFETw*
**Hill**, Charles Applewhite 1784-1831 *DcNCBi 3*
**Hill**, Charles Barton 1863?-1910 *BiInAmS*
**Hill**, Charles Earl 1935- *AmMWSc 92*
**Hill**, Charles Evan 1956- *WhoMW 92, WhoRel 92*
**Hill**, Charles Graham, Jr 1937- *AmMWSc 92*
**Hill**, Charles Horace, Jr 1921- *AmMWSc 92*
**Hill**, Charles Lester 1941- *WhoEnt 92*
**Hill**, Charles Whitacre 1940- *AmMWSc 92*
**Hill**, Charlie H. 1926- *WhoBlA 92*
**Hill**, Chesley R. 1934- *WhoRel 92*
**Hill**, Christopher *IntWW 91, Who 92*
**Hill**, Christopher 1912- *IntAu&W 91, WrDr 92*
**Hill**, Christopher John 1945- *IntWW 91, Who 92*
**Hill**, Christopher T 1951- *AmMWSc 92*
**Hill**, Christopher Thomas 1942- *AmMWSc 92*
**Hill**, Clara Grant 1928- *WhoBlA 92*
**Hill**, Clarence *BlkOlyM*
**Hill**, Cliff Otis 1941- *AmMWSc 92*
**Hill**, Colin Arnold Clifford 1929- *Who 92*
**Hill**, Curtis T., Sr. 1929- *WhoBlA 92*
**Hill**, Cynthia D. 1952- *WhoBlA 92*
**Hill**, D W R *TwCSFW 91*
**Hill**, Dale Eugene 1931- *AmMWSc 92*
**Hill**, Dale Richard 1939- *WhoWest 92*
**Hill**, Daniel George 1956- *WhoIns 92*
**Hill**, Daniel Harvey 1821-1889 *DcNCBi 3*
**Hill**, Daniel Harvey, Jr. 1859-1924 *DcNCBi 3*
**Hill**, Daniel Milton 1956- *WhoWest 92*
**Hill**, Danny Edward 1947- *WhoAmL 92, WhoAmP 91*
**Hill**, David 1946- *IntWW 91*
**Hill**, David 1954- *WhoBlA 92*
**Hill**, David Allan 1942- *AmMWSc 92, WhoWest 92*
**Hill**, David Byrne 1938- *AmMWSc 92*
**Hill**, David Easton 1929- *AmMWSc 92*
**Hill**, David G 1937- *AmMWSc 92*
**Hill**, David James 1948- *WhoAmL 92*
**Hill**, David Jayne 1850-1932 *AmPeW*
**Hill**, David Keynes 1915- *Who 92*
**Hill**, David Kimball 1910- *WhoMW 92*
**Hill**, David Lawrence 1919- *AmMWSc 92, WhoFI 92*
**Hill**, David Neil 1957- *Who 92*
**Hill**, David Paul 1935- *AmMWSc 92*
**Hill**, David Thomas 1947- *AmMWSc 92*
**Hill**, David W 1936- *AmMWSc 92*
**Hill**, David William 1949- *WhoMW 92*
**Hill**, Dean Allen 1934- *WhoWest 92*
**Hill**, DeAnn Gail 1953- *WhoFI 92*
**Hill**, Deborah 1944- *WhoBlA 92*
**Hill**, Debra *IntMPA 92*
**Hill**, Dennis Odell 1953- *WhoBlA 92*
**Hill**, Dennis Patrick 1960- *WhoFI 92, WhoMW 92*
**Hill**, Derek *Who 92*
**Hill**, Derek 1916- *TwCPaSc*
**Hill**, Derek Keith 1967- *WhoBlA 92*
**Hill**, Derek Leonard 1930- *AmMWSc 92*
**Hill**, Diana Joan 1936- *WhoRel 92*
**Hill**, Dianne 1955- *WhoBlA 92*
**Hill**, Donald Gardner 1941- *AmMWSc 92*
**Hill**, Donald Louis 1921- *AmMWSc 92*
**Hill**, Donald Lynch 1937- *AmMWSc 92*
**Hill**, Donald P 1929- *AmMWSc 92*
**Hill**, Donald V. 1954- *WhoRel 92*
**Hill**, Donna *DrAPF 91*
**Hill**, Donna Marie 1957- *WhoFI 92*
**Hill**, Dorothy 1907- *Who 92*
**Hill**, Douglas 1935- *WrDr 92*
**Hill**, Douglas Arthur 1935- *IntAu&W 91*
**Hill**, Douglas E 1939- *WhoAmP 91*
**Hill**, Douglas Wayne 1927- *AmMWSc 92*
**Hill**, Douglas Whittier 1927- *WhoRel 92*

Hill, Doyle Eugene 1946- AmMWSc 92
Hill, Drew 1956- WhoBlA 92
Hill, E. Shelton 1903- WhoBlA 92
Hill, Earl McColl 1926- WhoAmL 92, WhoWest 92
Hill, Earlene H WhoAmP 91
Hill, Eddie P 1930- AmMWSc 92
Hill, Edward Burlingame 1872-1960 NewAmDM
Hill, Edward C 1920- AmMWSc 92
Hill, Edward Jeffrey 1953- WhoWest 92
Hill, Edward Roderick 1904- Who 92
Hill, Edward T 1938- AmMWSc 92
Hill, Edwin C 1884-1957 FacFETw
Hill, Eldon G 1918- AmMWSc 92
Hill, Elgin Alexander 1935- AmMWSc 92
Hill, Eliot Michael 1935- Who 92
Hill, Elizabeth 1900- Who 92
Hill, Elizabeth K 1917- WhoAmP 91
Hill, Elizabeth Starr 1925- IntAu&W 91, WrDr 92
Hill, Ellsworth Jerome 1833-1917 BiInAmS
Hill, Ellyn Askins 1907- WhoBlA 92
Hill, Elwood Fayette 1939- AmMWSc 92
Hill, Emery Folsom 1943- WhoFI 92
Hill, Eric 1927- ConAu 134, SmATA 66 [port]
Hill, Eric 1966- WhoBlA 92
Hill, Eric Dale 1952- WhoRel 92
Hill, Eric Stanley 1925- AmMWSc 92
Hill, Ernest E 1922- AmMWSc 92
Hill, Errol 1921- WrDr 92
Hill, Errol Gaston 1921- IntAu&W 91, WhoBlA 92, WhoEnt 92
Hill, Esther P. 1922- WhoBlA 92
Hill, Fannie E. WhoBlA 92
Hill, Felicity 1915- Who 92
Hill, Florence Bernice 1938- WhoAmP 91
Hill, Floyd Isom 1921- AmMWSc 92
Hill, Floyd Randall 1941- WhoRel 92, WhoWest 92
Hill, Ford Dale 1939- WhoWest 92
Hill, Frank 1954- WhoAmP 91
Hill, Frank B 1924- AmMWSc 92
Hill, Franklin D 1933- AmMWSc 92
Hill, Fred 1939- WhoAmP 91
Hill, Frederic Stanhope 1805-1851 BenetAL 91
Hill, Frederick Burns, Jr 1913- AmMWSc 92
Hill, Frederick Conrad 1943- AmMWSc 92
Hill, Frederick Jones 1792-1861 DcNCBi 3
Hill, Fredric William 1918- AmMWSc 92
Hill, Fredrick J 1936- AmMWSc 92
Hill, Gale Bartholomew 1936- AmMWSc 92
Hill, Gary Martin 1946- AmMWSc 92
Hill, Geoffrey 1932- CnDBLB 8 [port], ConPo 91, FacFETw, IntWW 91, RfGEnL 91, Who 92, WrDr 92
Hill, Geoffrey Guild 1946- WhoFI 92
Hill, George Anthony 1842-1916 BiInAmS
Hill, George C 1938- WhoIns 92
Hill, George C. 1939- WhoBlA 92
Hill, George Calvin 1925- WhoBlA 92
Hill, George Carver 1939- AmMWSc 92
Hill, George Geoffrey David 1911- Who 92
Hill, George Handel 1809-1848 BenetAL 91
Hill, George Hiram 1940- WhoBlA 92
Hill, George Jackson, III 1932- WhoFI 92
Hill, George James, II 1932- AmMWSc 92
Hill, George Raymond 1925- Who 92
Hill, George Richard 1921- AmMWSc 92
Hill, George Roy WhoEnt 92
Hill, George Roy 1921- IntDcF 2-2, IntMPA 92, IntWW 91
Hill, George William 1838-1914 BiInAmS
Hill, Gerald Wayne 1947- WhoAmP 91
Hill, Gertrude Beatrice 1943- WhoBlA 92
Hill, Gideon D 1922- AmMWSc 92
Hill, Gilbert 1932- WhoBlA 92
Hill, Gladys 1894- Who 92
Hill, Gordon R. 1950- WhoWest 92
Hill, Grace Brooks SmATA 67
Hill, Grace Livingston 1865-1947 BenetAL 91
Hill, Graham Starforth 1927- IntWW 91, Who 92
Hill, Green, Jr. 1741-1826 DcNCBi 3
Hill, Gretchen Myers 1942- AmMWSc 92
Hill, Hamilton Stanton 1911- AmMWSc 92
Hill, Hampden 1886-1918 BiInAmS
Hill, Harold Eugene 1918- WhoRel 92
Hill, Harold Woodrow, Jr. 1942- WhoFI 92
Hill, Harry 1924- Who 92
Hill, Harry David 1944- WhoWest 92
Hill, Harry Gilbert 1946- WhoAmP 91
Hill, Harry James, Jr 1943- WhoAmP 91
Hill, Harry Raymond 1941- AmMWSc 92
Hill, Helen LeHew 1913- WhoWest 92
Hill, Helene Zimmermann 1929- AmMWSc 92
Hill, Henry WhoBlA 92
Hill, Henry, Jr. 1935- WhoBlA 92
Hill, Henry Allen 1933- AmMWSc 92
Hill, Henry Barker 1849-1903 BiInAmS
Hill, Henry Gordon 1921- Who 92
Hill, Henry Harrington 1894-1987 DcNCBi 3
Hill, Herbert Henderson, Jr 1945- AmMWSc 92
Hill, Herbert Hewett 1933- AmMWSc 92
Hill, Howard Earl 1952- WhoFI 92
Hill, Howard Hampton 1915- WhoBlA 92
Hill, Hubert Mack 1918- AmMWSc 92
Hill, Hugh Allen 1937- Who 92
Hill, Hugh Francis, III 1949- WhoAmL 92
Hill, Hyacinthe 1920- IntAu&W 91
Hill, Ian Macdonald 1919- Who 92
Hill, Ian Starforth 1921- Who 92
Hill, Isabel Morrison 1954- WhoEnt 92
Hill, Ivan Conrad 1906- Who 92
Hill, Jack 1933- WhoEnt 92
Hill, Jack 1944- WhoAmP 91
Hill, Jack Douglas 1937- AmMWSc 92
Hill, Jack Filson 1926- AmMWSc 92
Hill, Jackson 1941- WhoEnt 92
Hill, Jacqueline R. 1940- WhoBlA 92
Hill, James DcNCBi 3, IntMPA 92, Who 92
Hill, James, Jr. 1941- WhoBlA 92
Hill, James A., Jr. 1947- WhoBlA 92
Hill, James A., Sr. 1934- WhoBlA 92
Hill, James C, Jr 1947- WhoAmP 91
Hill, James Carroll 1941- AmMWSc 92
Hill, James Clinkscales 1924- WhoAmL 92
Hill, James D. 1948- WhoMW 92
Hill, James Dean 1923- WhoAmP 91
Hill, James Edward 1926- WhoFI 92
Hill, James Edward 1942- AmMWSc 92
Hill, James Frederick 1943- Who 92
Hill, James H. 1947- WhoBlA 92
Hill, James L. 1928- WhoBlA 92
Hill, James L. 1936- WhoBlA 92
Hill, James Lafe 1937- AmMWSc 92
Hill, James Lee 1941- WhoBlA 92
Hill, James Leslie 1940- AmMWSc 92
Hill, James Milton 1944- AmMWSc 92
Hill, James O. 1937- WhoBlA 92
Hill, James P WhoAmP 91
Hill, James Paul 1954- WhoAmP 91
Hill, James Stewart 1912- AmMWSc 92
Hill, James Stewart 1946- WhoEnt 92
Hill, James Tomilson 1948- WhoFI 92
Hill, James Wagy 1942- AmMWSc 92
Hill, James Walter, IV 1951- WhoEnt 92
Hill, James William Thomas Who 92
Hill, Jane Virginia Foster 1946- AmMWSc 92
Hill, Jayne Lilles 1948- WhoWest 92
Hill, Jeffrey J 1948- WhoAmP 91
Hill, Jeffrey John 1948- WhoWest 92
Hill, Jeffrey Robert 1960- WhoAmL 92
Hill, Jeffrey Ronald 1948- WhoBlA 92
Hill, Jeffrey W. 1955- WhoAmL 92
Hill, Jerome 1937- WhoAmP 91
Hill, Jesse, Jr. WhoBlA 92
Hill, Jesse King 1947- AmMWSc 92
Hill, Jim 1947- WhoAmP 91
Hill, Jim Edwin 1969- WhoRel 92
Hill, Jim T 1939- AmMWSc 92
Hill, Jimmy Who 92
Hill, Joan Ruth Armstrong 1929- WhoEnt 92
Hill, Joe 1879-1915 BenetAL 91
Hill, John ConAu 36NR, TwCSFW 91, WrDr 92
Hill, John 1797-1861 DcNCBi 3
Hill, John 1922- Who 92
Hill, John Alexander 1858-1916 BenetAL 91
Hill, John Alexander 1907- IntWW 91
Hill, John C. 1926- WhoBlA 92
Hill, John Cameron 1927- Who 92
Hill, John Campbell 1938- AmMWSc 92
Hill, John Christian 1936- AmMWSc 92
Hill, John Donald 1930- AmMWSc 92
Hill, John Earl 1953- WhoWest 92
Hill, John-Edward 1947- WhoEnt 92
Hill, John Edward Bernard 1912- Who 92
Hill, John Edward Christopher 1912- IntWW 91, Who 92
Hill, John Frederick Rowland d1991 Who 92N
Hill, John Hamon Massey 1932- AmMWSc 92
Hill, John Howard 1940- WhoAmL 92
Hill, John Joseph 1921- AmMWSc 92
Hill, John L 1923- WhoAmP 91
Hill, John Lawrence 1934- Who 92
Hill, John Ledyard 1919- AmMWSc 92
Hill, John Luke, Jr. 1923- WhoAmL 92
Hill, John Maxwell 1914- Who 92
Hill, John Mayes, Jr 1938- AmMWSc 92
Hill, John McGregor 1921- IntWW 91, Who 92
Hill, John Millard 1956- WhoRel 92
Hill, John Richard 1929- Who 92
Hill, John Roger 1912- AmMWSc 92
Hill, John Sprunt 1869-1961 DcNCBi 3
Hill, John Wesley 1863-1936 AmPeW
Hill, John William 1933- AmMWSc 92
Hill, Johnny R. 1944- WhoBlA 92
Hill, Johnny Ray 1944- WhoMW 92
Hill, Johnson ConAu 134, SmATA 67
Hill, Jon Hurd 1940- WhoAmL 92
Hill, Joseph Allen 1924- WhoRel 92
Hill, Joseph Alston 1800-1835 DcNCBi 3
Hill, Joseph Havord 1940- WhoBlA 92
Hill, Joseph MacGlashan 1905- AmMWSc 92
Hill, Joseph Paul 1947- AmMWSc 92
Hill, Judith C WhoAmP 91
Hill, Judith Deegan 1940- WhoWest 92
Hill, Judy Ellen 1955- WhoFI 92
Hill, Julia A WhoAmP 91
Hill, Julia H. WhoBlA 92
Hill, Julius W. 1917- WhoBlA 92
Hill, Kathleen DrAPF 91
Hill, Keith J. 1925- WhoRel 92
Hill, Kenneth 1937- WhoAmP 91
Hill, Kenneth Clyde 1953- WhoRel 92
Hill, Kenneth D. 1938- WhoBlA 92
Hill, Kenneth Lee 1931- AmMWSc 92
Hill, Kenneth Randal 1952- WhoBlA 92
Hill, Kenneth Richard 1930- AmMWSc 92, WhoMW 92
Hill, Kenneth Wayne 1945- AmMWSc 92
Hill, Kent 1957- WhoBlA 92
Hill, L Leighton 1928- AmMWSc 92
Hill, Larkin Payne 1954- WhoFI 92
Hill, Larry Kyle 1950- WhoAmP 91
Hill, Laurette Hurd 1958- WhoRel 92
Hill, Laurie Ann 1944- WhoMW 92
Hill, Lawrence Sidney 1923- WhoFI 92
Hill, Lawrence Thorne 1947- WhoBlA 92
Hill, Lee Edward 1948- WhoMW 92
Hill, Lemmuel Leroy 1933- AmMWSc 92
Hill, Len Who 92
Hill, Leo 1937- WhoBlA 92
Hill, Leslie Francis 1936- Who 92
Hill, Lewis Allan 1950- WhoWest 92
Hill, Leyla Rael 1948- WhoEnt 92
Hill, Lonzell Ramon 1965- WhoBlA 92
Hill, Loren Gilbert 1940- AmMWSc 92
Hill, Loren Wallace 1939- AmMWSc 92
Hill, Louis A, Jr 1927- AmMWSc 92
Hill, Louis G 1924- WhoAmP 91
Hill, Lowell Dean 1930- WhoMW 92
Hill, Lynn 1961?- News 91
Hill, Lynn Michael 1941- AmMWSc 92
Hill, Malcolm R. 1942- WrDr 92
Hill, Marcus Edward 1947- WhoIns 92
Hill, Margaret C 1924- WhoAmP 91
Hill, Marion Elzie 1920- AmMWSc 92
Hill, Marquita K 1938- AmMWSc 92
Hill, Martha WhoEnt 92
Hill, Martha Adele 1922- AmMWSc 92
Hill, Martyn Geoffrey 1944- Who 92
Hill, Marvin Francis 1925- AmMWSc 92
Hill, Mary Alice 1938- WhoBlA 92
Hill, Mary Rae 1923- AmMWSc 92
Hill, Mason Lowell 1904- AmMWSc 92
Hill, Max W 1930- AmMWSc 92
Hill, Meredith ConAu 133, SmATA 65
Hill, Merton Earle, III 1947- AmMWSc 92
Hill, Mervyn E., Jr. 1947- WhoBlA 92
Hill, Michael Who 92
Hill, Michael 1945- WhoAmP 91
Hill, Michael Carroll 1949- WhoAmL 92
Hill, Michael Edward 1943- WhoBlA 92
Hill, Michael J. 1943- WrDr 92
Hill, Michael J. 1958- WhoRel 92
Hill, Michael John 1954- WhoMW 92
Hill, Michael Richard 1948- WhoAmP 91
Hill, Michael William 1928- IntWW 91, Who 92
Hill, Mike WhoAmP 91
Hill, Milton King, Jr. 1926- WhoAmL 92
Hill, Miriam Helen 1953- WhoMW 92
Hill, Nancy Lou 1949- WhoAmP 91
Hill, Nathaniel Peter 1832-1900 BiInAmS
Hill, Nellie DrAPF 91
Hill, Nicole F. 1955- WhoFI 92
Hill, Niki 1938- IntAu&W 91
Hill, Nolanda Sue 1944- WhoEnt 92
Hill, Norman A. Who 92
Hill, Norman S. 1933- WhoBlA 92
Hill, Oliver F. 1887-1968 DcTwDes
Hill, Oliver W. 1907- WhoBlA 92
Hill, Oliver White, Sr. 1907- WhoAmL 92
Hill, Orville Farrow 1919- AmMWSc 92
Hill, Pam LesBEnT 92
Hill, Pamela 1920- IntAu&W 91, WrDr 92
Hill, Pamela 1938- WhoEnt 92
Hill, Pamela Jean 1958- WhoMW 92
Hill, Pati DrAPF 91
Hill, Patricia Ellen 1945- WhoAmP 91
Hill, Patricia Liggins 1942- WhoBlA 92
Hill, Patrick Arthur 1922- AmMWSc 92
Hill, Patrick Ray 1950- WhoWest 92
Hill, Paul Daniel 1933- AmMWSc 92
Hill, Paul David 1924- WhoIns 92
Hill, Paul Drennen 1941- WhoFI 92
Hill, Paul Gordon 1933- WhoBlA 92
Hill, Paul Mark 1953- WhoMW 92, WhoRel 92
Hill, Pearl M. 1949- WhoBlA 92
Hill, Percy Holmes 1923- AmMWSc 92
Hill, Peter Waverly 1953- WhoAmL 92, WhoAmP 91
Hill, Philip 1917- WhoAmL 92
Hill, Philip G 1932- AmMWSc 92
Hill, Polly 1914- IntWW 91, Who 92
Hill, Prescott F 1934- WhoIns 92
Hill, Ralph Nading 1917-1987 SmATA 65
Hill, Ray 1959- WhoAmP 91
Hill, Ray Allen 1942- AmMWSc 92, WhoBlA 92
Hill, Ray Thomas, Jr. 1926- WhoFI 92, WhoWest 92
Hill, Raymond A. d1991 NewYTBS 91
Hill, Raymond A. 1922- WhoBlA 92
Hill, Raymond Dunlap, Jr. 1947- WhoFI 92
Hill, Raymond Joseph 1935- WhoMW 92
Hill, Reba Michels 1930- AmMWSc 92
Hill, Rebecca DrAPF 91
Hill, Reginald 1936- IntAu&W 91, WrDr 92
Hill, Reuben Benjamin 1938- WhoBlA 92
Hill, Richard 1925- Who 92
Hill, Richard A 1932- AmMWSc 92
Hill, Richard C 1918- AmMWSc 92
Hill, Richard F. DrAPF 91
Hill, Richard Fontaine 1941- IntAu&W 91
Hill, Richard Keith 1928- AmMWSc 92
Hill, Richard L 1919- WhoAmP 91
Hill, Richard Lee 1931- WhoMW 92
Hill, Richard M 1934- AmMWSc 92
Hill, Richard Nathaniel 1930- WhoBlA 92
Hill, Richard Norman 1937- AmMWSc 92
Hill, Richard Peter 1942- AmMWSc 92
Hill, Richard Ray, Jr 1936- AmMWSc 92
Hill, Richard William 1925- AmMWSc 92
Hill, Richard William 1942- AmMWSc 92
Hill, Rick WhoAmP 91
Hill, Robb B 1957- WhoIns 92
Hill, Robert d1991 Who 92N
Hill, Robert 1899-1991 IntWW 91, -91N
Hill, Robert 1922- AmMWSc 92
Hill, Robert 1937- Who 92
Hill, Robert Andrews 1811-1900 DcNCBi 3
Hill, Robert Arthur 1961- WhoEnt 92
Hill, Robert Benjamin 1930- AmMWSc 92
Hill, Robert Bernard 1938- WhoBlA 92
Hill, Robert Colgrove, Jr. 1963- WhoWest 92
Hill, Robert D 1937- AmMWSc 92
Hill, Robert Dickson 1913- AmMWSc 92
Hill, Robert F 1929- AmMWSc 92
Hill, Robert F. 1945- WhoAmL 92
Hill, Robert George, Jr 1922- AmMWSc 92
Hill, Robert J., Jr. 1943- WhoBlA 92
Hill, Robert Jackson 1921- WhoEnt 92
Hill, Robert James 1929- AmMWSc 92
Hill, Robert Joe 1930- AmMWSc 92
Hill, Robert John 1932- WhoMW 92
Hill, Robert K. 1917- WhoBlA 92
Hill, Robert Larry 1946- WhoWest 92
Hill, Robert Lee 1928- AmMWSc 92, IntWW 91
Hill, Robert Lewis 1934- WhoBlA 92
Hill, Robert Martin 1949- WhoWest 92
Hill, Robert Mathew 1922- AmMWSc 92
Hill, Robert Matteson 1926- AmMWSc 92
Hill, Robert Michael 1943- WhoAmP 91
Hill, Robert Nyden 1935- AmMWSc 92
Hill, Robert Thomas 1940- WhoMW 92
Hill, Robert W. DrAPF 91
Hill, Robert Wayne 1927- WhoFI 92
Hill, Robert William 1927- AmMWSc 92
Hill, Robert Williamson 1936- Who 92
Hill, Robyn Lesley 1942- WhoMW 92
Hill, Roderick Who 92
Hill, Rodney 1921- IntWW 91, Who 92
Hill, Rodney E. 1938- WhoMW 92, WhoRel 92
Hill, Roger TwCWW 91
Hill, Roger W 1919- AmMWSc 92
Hill, Rolla B, Jr 1929- AmMWSc 92
Hill, Ronald Ames 1934- AmMWSc 92
Hill, Ronald Stewart 1951- AmMWSc 92
Hill, Rosalie A. 1933- WhoBlA 92
Hill, Rosalind Mary Theodosia 1908- WrDr 92
Hill, Roy Kenneth Leonard 1924- Who 92
Hill, Rufus S. 1923- WhoBlA 92
Hill, Russell John 1934- AmMWSc 92
Hill, S. Richardson, Jr. 1923- IntWW 91
Hill, Sally L. WhoRel 92
Hill, Sam 1918- WhoBlA 92
Hill, Samuel Richardson, Jr 1923- AmMWSc 92
Hill, Sandra Patricia 1943- WhoBlA 92
Hill, Scott Alan 1954- WhoMW 92
Hill, Selima 1945- ConPo 91, WrDr 92
Hill, Shirley Ann 1927- AmMWSc 92
Hill, Shirley Yarde 1941- AmMWSc 92
Hill, Sonny 1936- WhoBlA 92
Hill, Stan Wayne 1945- WhoEnt 92
Hill, Stanley James Allen 1926- Who 92
Hill, Stanley James Ledger 1911- Who 92
Hill, Starforth Who 92
Hill, Stephanie Jean 1956- WhoRel 92
Hill, Stephen James 1943- AmMWSc 92
Hill, Steve C. 1949- WhoEnt 92
Hill, Steve Edward 1949- WhoEnt 92

**Hill**, Steven Phillips 1936- WhoMW 92
**Hill**, Stuart Baxter 1943- AmMWSc 92
**Hill**, Stuart C 1926- WhoAmP 91
**Hill**, Susan 1942- ConNov 91, WrDr 92
**Hill**, Susan Chidester 1951- WhoRel 92
**Hill**, Susan Douglas 1940- AmMWSc 92
**Hill**, Susan Elizabeth 1942- IntAu&W 91, IntWW 91, Who 92
**Hill**, Sylvia Ione-Bennett 1940- WhoBlA 92
**Hill**, Terence 1941- IntMPA 92
**Hill**, Terrell Leslie 1917- AmMWSc 92, IntWW 91
**Hill**, Terry S. 1946- WhoEnt 92
**Hill**, Thelma W. 1933- WhoBlA 92
**Hill**, Theophilus 1741-1790 DcNCBi 3
**Hill**, Theophilus Hunter 1836-1901 DcNCBi 3
**Hill**, Thomas 1818-1891 BiInAmS
**Hill**, Thomas 1960- ConAu 135
**Hill**, Thomas Allen 1958- WhoAmL 92, WhoMW 92
**Hill**, Thomas Bowen, III 1929- WhoAmL 92
**Hill**, Thomas Clark 1946- WhoMW 92
**Hill**, Thomas Dawson 1955- WhoMW 92
**Hill**, Thomas Lionel 1949- BlkOlyM
**Hill**, Thomas Morgan 1938- WhoRel 92
**Hill**, Thomas Norfleet 1838-1904 DcNCBi 3
**Hill**, Thomas Stewart 1936- WhoMW 92
**Hill**, Thomas Westfall 1945- AmMWSc 92
**Hill**, Thomas William, Jr. 1924- WhoAmL 92
**Hill**, Tony 1956- WhoBlA 92
**Hill**, Trevor Bruce 1928- AmMWSc 92
**Hill**, Tyrone 1968- WhoBlA 92
**Hill**, Ureli Corelli 1802-1875 NewAmDM
**Hill**, Uri K. 1780-1844 NewAmDM
**Hill**, Velma Murphy 1938- WhoBlA 92
**Hill**, Victor Ernst, IV 1939- AmMWSc 92
**Hill**, Virgil 1964- BlkOlyM
**Hill**, Vonciel Jones 1948- WhoBlA 92
**Hill**, W. Clayton 1916- WhoFI 92
**Hill**, W Ryland 1911- AmMWSc 92
**Hill**, Walter 1942- IntDcF 2-2 [port], IntMPA 92
**Hill**, Walter Andrew 1946- AmMWSc 92
**Hill**, Walter Earl 1941- WhoAmP 91
**Hill**, Walter Edward, Jr 1931- AmMWSc 92
**Hill**, Walter Ensign 1937- AmMWSc 92
**Hill**, Walter Ernest 1945- AmMWSc 92
**Hill**, Walter Nickerson 1846-1884 BiInAmS
**Hill**, Wendell T., Jr. 1924- WhoBlA 92
**Hill**, Whitmel 1743-1797 DcNCBi 3
**Hill**, William 1737-1783 DcNCBi 3
**Hill**, William 1773-1857 DcNCBi 3
**Hill**, William Bradley, Jr. 1952- WhoBlA 92
**Hill**, William Charles 1917- WhoAmP 91
**Hill**, William Geddy 1806-1877 DcNCBi 3
**Hill**, William George 1940- Who 92
**Hill**, William H. 1930- WhoEnt 92
**Hill**, William Henry 1767-1808 DcNCBi 3
**Hill**, William Joseph 1924- WrDr 92
**Hill**, William Joseph 1940- AmMWSc 92
**Hill**, William Preston 1939- WhoMW 92
**Hill**, William Randolph, Jr. 1936- WhoBlA 92
**Hill**, William Sephton 1926- Who 92
**Hill**, William T 1925- AmMWSc 92
**Hill**, William Thomas 1952- WhoFI 92
**Hill**, Willie Ray 1962- WhoRel 92
**Hill**, Wills 1718-1793 BlkwEAR
**Hill**, Wilmer Bailey 1928- WhoAmL 92
**Hill**, XaCadene Averyllis 1909- WhoBlA 92
**Hill-Lubin**, Mildred Anderson 1933- WhoBlA 92
**Hill-Norton** Who 92
**Hill-Norton**, Baron 1915- IntWW 91, Who 92
**Hill-Norton**, Nicholas John 1939- Who 92
**Hill-Rice**, Janet Sue 1957- WhoEnt 92
**Hill-Smith**, Derek Edward 1922- Who 92
**Hill Smith**, Marilyn 1952- IntWW 91
**Hill-Trevor** Who 92
**Hill-Wood**, David 1926- Who 92
**Hillabrandt**, Larry Lee 1947- WhoFI 92
**Hillaby**, John 1917- IntWW 91, Who 92, WrDr 92
**Hillaire-Marcel**, Claude 1944- AmMWSc 92
**Hillaker**, Harry J 1919- AmMWSc 92
**Hillam**, Bruce Parks 1945- AmMWSc 92
**Hillam**, Kenneth L 1927- AmMWSc 92
**Hillar**, Marian 1938- AmMWSc 92
**Hillard**, Carole WhoAmP 91
**Hillard**, Cecilia Jane AmMWSc 92
**Hillard**, Darla 1946- ConAu 135
**Hillard**, Richard Arthur Loraine 1906- Who 92
**Hillary**, Edmund 1919- FacFETw, IntAu&W 91, Who 92, WrDr 92
**Hillary**, Edmund Percival 1919- IntWW 91
**illborg**, Anders 1954- ConCom 92
**Hillcoat**, Brian Leslie 1932- AmMWSc 92
**Hilldrup**, David J 1936- AmMWSc 92
**Hille**, Bertil 1940- AmMWSc 92
**Hille**, Kenneth R 1927- AmMWSc 92
**Hille**, Merrill Burr 1939- AmMWSc 92
**Hille**, Robert John 1953- WhoAmL 92
**Hilleary**, Daniel John 1956- WhoFI 92
**Hilleboe**, Carla Jean 1953- WhoEnt 92
**Hillebrecht**, Rudolf Friedrich Heinrich 1910- IntWW 91
**Hillegas**, Shawn 1964- WhoHisp 92
**Hillegas**, William Joseph 1937- AmMWSc 92
**Hillegonds**, Paul Christie 1949- WhoAmP 91
**Hillel**, Daniel 1930- AmMWSc 92
**Hillel**, Shlomo 1923- IntWW 91
**Hillelson**, Jeffrey P 1919- WhoAmP 91
**Hilleman**, Maurice Ralph 1919- AmMWSc 92, IntWW 91
**Hillenbrand**, Martin Joseph 1915- IntWW 91
**Hillenkoetter**, Roscoe Henry 1897-1982 FacFETw
**Hiller**, Arthur 1923- IntMPA 92, WhoEnt 92
**Hiller**, Catherine DrAPF 91
**Hiller**, Dale Murray 1924- AmMWSc 92
**Hiller**, David D. 1953- WhoAmL 92
**Hiller**, Eric DrAPF 91
**Hiller**, Ferdinand 1811-1885 NewAmDM
**Hiller**, Frederick Charles 1942- AmMWSc 92
**Hiller**, Frederick W 1927- AmMWSc 92
**Hiller**, George C 1958- WhoIns 92
**Hiller**, Howard Lyn 1953- WhoFI 92
**Hiller**, Jacob Moses 1939- AmMWSc 92
**Hiller**, Joan Vitek 1960- WhoMW 92
**Hiller**, Johann Adam 1728-1804 BlkwCEP, NewAmDM
**Hiller**, Larry Keith 1941- AmMWSc 92
**Hiller**, Lejaren 1924- NewAmDM, WrDr 92
**Hiller**, Lejaren A, Jr 1924- ConCom 92
**Hiller**, Lejaren Arthur 1924- AmMWSc 92
**Hiller**, Michael James 1952- WhoRel 92
**Hiller**, Robert Ellis 1927- AmMWSc 92
**Hiller**, Stanley, Jr. 1924- WhoFI 92
**Hiller**, Susan 1940- IntWW 91
**Hiller**, Thomas Carl 1950- WhoRel 92
**Hiller**, Wendy IntWW 91, Who 92, WhoEnt 92
**Hiller**, Wendy 1912- IntMPA 92
**Hiller**, William Arlington 1928- WhoFI 92
**Hillerbrand**, Hans J. 1931- ConAu 134
**Hillerman**, John 1932- IntMPA 92
**Hillerman**, John Benedict WhoEnt 92
**Hillerman**, Tony 1925- BenetAL 91, IntAu&W 91, TwCWW 91, WhoWest 92, WrDr 92
**Hillers**, Joe Karl 1938- AmMWSc 92
**Hillert**, Gloria Bonnin 1930- WhoMW 92
**Hillert**, Margaret 1920- IntAu&W 91
**Hillery**, Herbert Vincent 1924- AmMWSc 92
**Hillery**, Patrick John 1923- IntWW 91, Who 92
**Hillery**, Paul Stuart 1941- AmMWSc 92
**Hillestad**, Charles Andrew 1945- WhoAmL 92
**Hilley**, Donna WhoEnt 92
**Hillgarth**, J. N. 1929- WrDr 92
**Hillhouse**, James A. 1789-1841 BenetAL 91
**Hillhouse**, John Morgan 1947- WhoMW 92
**Hillhouse**, Russell 1938- Who 92
**Hilliard**, Asa Grant, III 1933- WhoBlA 92
**Hilliard**, Craig Sterling 1955- WhoAmP 91
**Hilliard**, Dalton 1964- WhoBlA 92
**Hilliard**, Danny C 1957- WhoAmP 91
**Hilliard**, David Craig 1937- WhoAmL 92
**Hilliard**, Delories WhoBlA 92
**Hilliard**, Donnie Ray 1950- WhoRel 92
**Hilliard**, Earl Frederick 1942- WhoAmP 91, WhoBlA 92
**Hilliard**, Garrison L. DrAPF 91
**Hilliard**, General K. 1940- WhoBlA 92
**Hilliard**, Henry Washington 1808-1892 DcNCBi 3
**Hilliard**, John E 1926- AmMWSc 92
**Hilliard**, John Roy, Jr 1924- AmMWSc 92
**Hilliard**, Kirk Loveland, Jr. 1941- WhoMW 92
**Hilliard**, Landon 1939- WhoFI 92
**Hilliard**, Louis 1837-1894 DcNCBi 3
**Hilliard**, Nancy Ann Segur 1798-1873 DcNCBi 3
**Hilliard**, Noel 1929- ConNov 91, IntAu&W 91, WrDr 92
**Hilliard**, R Glenn 1943- WhoIns 92
**Hilliard**, Robert Glenn 1943- WhoAmL 92
**Hilliard**, Robert Lee Moore 1931- WhoBlA 92
**Hilliard**, Ronnie Lewis 1937- AmMWSc 92
**Hilliard**, Roy C 1931- AmMWSc 92
**Hilliard**, Stephen Dale 1939- AmMWSc 92
**Hilliard**, Thomas Eugene 1948- WhoRel 92
**Hilliard**, Wallace J. 1932- WhoFI 92
**Hilliard**, William Alexander WhoBlA 92
**Hillidge**, Christopher James 1944- AmMWSc 92
**Hillier**, Bevis 1940- IntAu&W 91, IntWW 91, Who 92, WrDr 92
**Hillier**, Donald Edward 1947- WhoIns 92
**Hillier**, Frederick Stanton 1936- AmMWSc 92
**Hillier**, Jack Ronald 1912- Who 92, WrDr 92
**Hillier**, James 1915- AmMWSc 92
**Hillier**, Jim 1941- WrDr 92
**Hillier**, Malcolm Dudley 1936- Who 92
**Hillier**, Paul Douglas 1949- Who 92
**Hillier**, Richard David 1938- AmMWSc 92
**Hillier**, Tristram 1905-1983 TwCPaSc
**Hillier**, William Edward 1936- Who 92
**Hillier-Fry**, Norman 1923- Who 92
**Hillier-Fry**, William Norman 1923- IntWW 91
**Hillig**, Kurt Walter, II 1954- AmMWSc 92
**Hillig**, William Bruno 1924- AmMWSc 92
**Hilliker**, David Lee 1935- AmMWSc 92
**Hillin**, Wayne Kirby 1942- WhoAmL 92
**Hillis**, Argye Briggs 1933- AmMWSc 92
**Hillis**, Arthur Henry Macnamara 1905- Who 92
**Hillis**, David Mark 1958- AmMWSc 92
**Hillis**, Elwood Haynes 1926- WhoAmP 91
**Hillis**, Ivory V, Jr 1930- WhoAmP 91
**Hillis**, Jeffrey DeLair 1948- WhoMW 92
**Hillis**, Llewellya 1930- AmMWSc 92
**Hillis**, Margaret 1921- NewAmDM, WhoEnt 92
**Hillis**, Mary Olive 1919- AmMWSc 92
**Hillis**, Newell Dwight 1858-1929 RelLAm 91
**Hillis**, Richard K. 1936- WhoWest 92
**Hillis**, Rick 1956- ConAu 134, ConLC 66 [port]
**Hillis**, Stephen Kendall 1942- WhoAmP 91
**Hillis**, William Daniel, Sr 1933- AmMWSc 92
**Hillison**, John Howard 1944- WhoFI 92
**Hillman**, Abraham P 1918- AmMWSc 92
**Hillman**, Adria Sue 1947- WhoAmL 92
**Hillman**, Barry 1942- WrDr 92
**Hillman**, Barry Leslie 1945- IntAu&W 91
**Hillman**, Bessie Abramowitz 1895-1970 DcAmImH
**Hillman**, Bill 1922- WhoWest 92
**Hillman**, Brenda DrAPF 91
**Hillman**, Bruce John, Sr. 1938- WhoFI 92
**Hillman**, Charlene Hamilton WhoMW 92
**Hillman**, Chris 1944- WhoEnt 92
**Hillman**, Constance Pappas 1948- WhoEnt 92
**Hillman**, Cris Timothy 1955- WhoMW 92
**Hillman**, David McLeod 1953- WhoFI 92
**Hillman**, Dean Elof 1936- AmMWSc 92
**Hillman**, Donald 1929- AmMWSc 92
**Hillman**, Donald Arthur 1925- AmMWSc 92
**Hillman**, Donald Earl 1928- WhoFI 92
**Hillman**, Douglas Woodruff 1922- WhoAmL 92, WhoMW 92
**Hillman**, Elizabeth S AmMWSc 92
**Hillman**, Ellis Simon 1928- Who 92
**Hillman**, Elsie Hilliard 1925- WhoAmP 91
**Hillman**, Gilbert R 1943- AmMWSc 92
**Hillman**, Gracia 1949- WhoBlA 92
**Hillman**, Harry W 1870- ScFEYrs
**Hillman**, John Richard 1944- Who 92
**Hillman**, Joyce 1936- WhoAmP 91
**Hillman**, M. Renee 1966- WhoWest 92
**Hillman**, Manny 1928- AmMWSc 92
**Hillman**, Morton C 1926- WhoAmP 91
**Hillman**, Pearl Elizabeth 1907- WhoRel 92
**Hillman**, Ralph 1929- AmMWSc 92
**Hillman**, Richard Ephraim 1940- AmMWSc 92
**Hillman**, Robert Andrew 1946- WhoAmL 92
**Hillman**, Robert B 1930- AmMWSc 92
**Hillman**, Robert Daniel 1962- WhoAmL 92
**Hillman**, Robert Edward 1933- AmMWSc 92
**Hillman**, Roger Lewis 1944- WhoFI 92
**Hillman**, Sidney 1887-1946 DcAmImH, FacFETw
**Hillman**, Stanley Eric Gordon 1911- WhoMW 92
**Hillman**, Stanley Severin 1948- AmMWSc 92
**Hillman**, Thomas J. 1955- WhoFI 92
**Hillman**, William Bryon IntMPA 92
**Hillman**, William Chernick 1935- WhoAmL 92
**Hillman**, William Sermolino 1929- AmMWSc 92
**Hillner**, Edward 1929- AmMWSc 92
**Hillock**, Gerald A WhoAmP 91
**Hilloowala**, Rumy Ardeshir 1935- AmMWSc 92
**Hillquit**, Morris 1869-1933 AmPeW
**Hillringhouse**, Mark DrAPF 91
**Hills**, Alan Lee 1954- WhoWest 92
**Hills**, Albert Freeman, III 1961- WhoFI 92
**Hills**, Andrew Worth 1949- Who 92
**Hills**, Carla Anderson 1934- IntWW 91, WhoAmP 91, WhoFI 92
**Hills**, Claude Hibbard 1912- AmMWSc 92
**Hills**, David Graeme Muspratt 1925- Who 92
**Hills**, David Henry 1933- Who 92
**Hills**, Denis 1913- WrDr 92
**Hills**, Eric Donald 1917- Who 92
**Hills**, F Jackson 1919- AmMWSc 92
**Hills**, Francis Allan 1934- AmMWSc 92
**Hills**, Frank Stanley 1935- WhoAmL 92
**Hills**, George 1918- WrDr 92
**Hills**, Graham 1926- Who 92
**Hills**, Graham William 1949- AmMWSc 92
**Hills**, Howard Kent 1938- AmMWSc 92
**Hills**, Jack Gilbert 1943- AmMWSc 92
**Hills**, James Bricky 1944- WhoBlA 92
**Hills**, John Moore 1910- AmMWSc 92
**Hills**, Lawrence D. 1911-1990 AnObit 1990
**Hills**, Lawrence Donegan d1990 Who 92N
**Hills**, Leonard Vincent 1933- AmMWSc 92
**Hills**, Linda Launey 1947- WhoWest 92
**Hills**, Loran C 1925- AmMWSc 92
**Hills**, Michael 1958- WhoWest 92
**Hills**, Philip James 1933- WrDr 92
**Hills**, Richard Edwin 1945- Who 92
**Hills**, Robert, Jr 1922- AmMWSc 92
**Hills**, Roderick Maltman 1931- IntWW 91
**Hills**, Stanley 1930- AmMWSc 92
**Hillsborough**, Earl of 1959- Who 92
**Hillsman**, Gerald C. 1926- WhoBlA 92
**Hillsman**, John Edward 1958- WhoEnt 92
**Hillsman**, Matthew Jerome 1935- AmMWSc 92
**Hillsman**, William Gerard 1953- WhoEnt 92
**Hillson**, Charles James 1926- AmMWSc 92
**Hillstrom**, Thomas Peter 1943- WhoFI 92
**Hillstrom**, Warren W 1935- AmMWSc 92
**Hilly**, John C. d1991 NewYTBS 91
**Hillyard**, Ira William 1924- AmMWSc 92
**Hillyard**, Lawrence R 1909- AmMWSc 92
**Hillyard**, Lyle William 1940- WhoAmP 91, WhoWest 92
**Hillyard**, Patrick Cyril Henry d1991 Who 92N
**Hillyard**, Stanley Donald AmMWSc 92
**Hillyard**, Steven Allen 1942- AmMWSc 92
**Hillyer**, George Vanzandt 1943- AmMWSc 92
**Hillyer**, Irvin George 1927- AmMWSc 92
**Hillyer**, Janet Ann 1954- WhoWest 92
**Hillyer**, John Whitfield 1936- WhoWest 92
**Hillyer**, Robert 1895-1961 BenetAL 91
**Hillyer**, William Hudson 1928- WhoAmP 91
**Hilmas**, Duane Eugene 1938- AmMWSc 92, WhoMW 92
**Hilmoe**, Russell J 1921- AmMWSc 92
**Hilpert**, Bruce Emil 1950- WhoWest 92
**Hilpert**, Brunette Kathleen Powers 1909- WhoMW 92
**Hilpert**, Edward Theodore, Jr. 1928- WhoAmL 92
**Hilpman**, Paul Lorenz 1932- AmMWSc 92
**Hils**, Dana Sue 1963- WhoMW 92
**Hilsenhoff**, William Leroy 1929- AmMWSc 92
**Hilsenrath**, Joel Alan 1965- WhoFI 92
**Hilsinger**, Harold W 1932- AmMWSc 92
**Hilsinger**, Judith Louise 1942- WhoWest 92
**Hilsman**, Hoyt Roger 1948- WhoEnt 92
**Hilsman**, Roger 1919- IntWW 91, WrDr 92
**Hilson**, Arthur Lee 1936- WhoBlA 92
**Hilst**, Arvin Rudolph 1924- AmMWSc 92
**Hilst**, Glenn Rudolph 1923- AmMWSc 92
**Hilston**, Thomas Allan 1947- WhoAmL 92
**Hilsum**, Cyril 1925- IntWW 91, Who 92
**Hilt**, Richard Leighton 1936- AmMWSc 92
**Hilt**, Thomas Harry 1947- WhoRel 92
**Hiltbold**, Arthur Edward, Jr 1925- AmMWSc 92
**Hilterman**, Fred John 1941- AmMWSc 92
**Hiltibran**, Robert Comegys 1920- AmMWSc 92
**Hiltl**, Hermann 1872-1930 BiDExR
**Hiltner**, William Albert 1914- AmMWSc 92
**Hilton**, Alan John Howard 1942- Who 92
**Hilton**, Andrew Carson 1928- WhoFI 92
**Hilton**, Anthony Victor 1946- Who 92
**Hilton**, Ashley Stewart 1940- AmMWSc 92
**Hilton**, Barron 1927- WhoFI 92, WhoWest 92

**Hilton,** Boyd 1944- *WrDr 92*
**Hilton,** Brian James George 1940- *Who 92*
**Hilton,** Claude Meredith 1940- *WhoAmL 92*
**Hilton,** Clifford Thomas 1934- *WhoRel 92*
**Hilton,** Conrad 1887-1979 *FacFETw*
**Hilton,** David *DrAPF 91*
**Hilton,** Donald Frederick James 1944- *AmMWSc 92*
**Hilton,** Donnette Louise 1935- *WhoAmP 91*
**Hilton,** Dorothy *ScFEYrs*
**Hilton,** Ernest Auburn 1879-1948 *DcNCBi 3*
**Hilton,** Frederic H. 1924- *WhoAmL 92*
**Hilton,** Frederick Kelker 1926- *AmMWSc 92*
**Hilton,** George Woodman 1925- *WrDr 92*
**Hilton,** H Wayne 1923- *AmMWSc 92*
**Hilton,** Hart Dale 1913- *WhoWest 92*
**Hilton,** Horace Gill 1932- *AmMWSc 92*
**Hilton,** James 1900-1954 *BenetAL 91, FacFETw*
**Hilton,** James Gorton 1923- *AmMWSc 92*
**Hilton,** James Lee 1930- *AmMWSc 92*
**Hilton,** Janet 1945- *IntWW 91*
**Hilton,** John Howard *Who 92*
**Hilton,** John L 1927- *AmMWSc 92*
**Hilton,** John Millard Thomas 1934- *Who 92*
**Hilton,** John Robert 1908- *Who 92*
**Hilton,** Kenneth M 1926- *WhoIns 92*
**Hilton,** Lester Elliot 1923- *WhoAmP 91*
**Hilton,** Margaret Lynette 1946- *SmATA 68 [port]*
**Hilton,** Margery *WrDr 92*
**Hilton,** Margot Pamela 1947 *IntAu&W 91*
**Hilton,** Mary Anderson 1926- *AmMWSc 92*
**Hilton,** Matthew 1948- *TwCPaSc*
**Hilton,** Nette *SmATA 68*
**Hilton,** Nette 1946- *ChlLR 25 [port]*
**Hilton,** Nicola Mary *Who 92*
**Hilton,** Paul Edgar 1927- *WhoMW 92*
**Hilton,** Peter 1919- *Who 92*
**Hilton,** Peter 1923- *WrDr 92*
**Hilton,** Peter John 1923- *AmMWSc 92, Who 92*
**Hilton,** R. H. *ConAu 134*
**Hilton,** Ray 1930- *AmMWSc 92*
**Hilton,** Robert L *WhoIns 92*
**Hilton,** Rodney 1916- *ConAu 134*
**Hilton,** Rodney Howard 1916- *Who 92*
**Hilton,** Roger 1911-1975 *TwCPaSc*
**Hilton,** Ronald 1911- *WrDr 92*
**Hilton,** Rose 1931- *TwCPaSc*
**Hilton,** Stanley William, Jr. *WhoBlA 92, WhoEnt 92*
**Hilton,** Stephen Homer 1944- *WhoWest 92*
**Hilton,** Suzanne 1922- *WrDr 92*
**Hilton,** Suzanne McLean 1922- *IntAu&W 91*
**Hilton,** Wallace Atwood 1911- *AmMWSc 92*
**Hilton,** Walter 1343?-1396 *RfGEnL 91*
**Hilton,** Wendy *WhoEnt 92*
**Hilton,** William 1617-1675 *DcNCBi 3*
**Hilton,** William 1926- *Who 92*
**Hilton,** William Howard 1949- *WhoMW 92*
**Hilton of Eggardon,** Baroness 1936- *Who 92*
**Hilts,** Earl T. 1946- *WhoAmL 92*
**Hiltscher,** John David 1944- *WhoMW 92*
**Hiltunen,** Jarl Kalervo 1933- *AmMWSc 92*
**Hilty,** James Willard 1936- *AmMWSc 92*
**Hilty,** Peter Daniel *DrAPF 91*
**Hiltz,** Arnold Aubrey 1924- *AmMWSc 92*
**Hiltz,** Paul Christopher 1959- *WhoMW 92*
**Hilu,** Khidir Wanni 1946- *AmMWSc 92*
**Hilyard,** Judith Elaine *WhoFI 92*
**Hilyard,** Tommy Lee 1948- *WhoBlA 92*
**Hilyer,** Amanda Gray 1870-1957 *NotBlAW 92*
**Hime,** Martin 1928- *Who 92*
**Hime,** William Gene 1925- *AmMWSc 92*
**Himebaugh,** Arthur Elliott 1925- *WhoFI 92*
**Himegarner,** Albert 1937- *WhoMW 92*
**Himel,** Chester Mora 1916- *AmMWSc 92*
**Himelein,** Larry M. 1949- *WhoAmL 92*
**Himelfarb,** Richard Jay 1942- *WhoFI 92*
**Himelfarb,** Stephen Roy 1954- *WhoAmL 92*
**Himelick,** Eugene Bryson 1926- *AmMWSc 92*
**Himelstein,** Morgan Y. 1926- *WrDr 92*
**Himes,** Charles Francis 1838-1918 *BiInAmS*
**Himes,** Chester 1909-1984 *BenetAL 91, BlkLC [port], LiExTwC*
**Himes,** Craig L 1927- *AmMWSc 92*
**Himes,** Frank Lawrence 1927- *AmMWSc 92, WhoMW 92*
**Himes,** Geoffrey *DrAPF 91*
**Himes,** Geoffrey Charles 1952- *WhoEnt 92*
**Himes,** George Elliott 1922- *WhoMW 92*
**Himes,** James Albert 1919- *AmMWSc 92*
**Himes,** John Harter 1947- *AmMWSc 92*
**Himes,** Joshua Vaughan 1805-1895 *AmPeW*
**Himes,** Kenneth Alan 1937- *WhoFI 92*
**Himes,** Laurence Austin 1940- *WhoMW 92*
**Himes,** Marion 1923- *AmMWSc 92*
**Himes,** Richard H 1935- *AmMWSc 92*
**Himes,** Robert Lynn 1945- *WhoMW 92*
**Himes,** Tim A. 1948- *WhoEnt 92*
**Himle,** Erik 1924- *IntWW 91*
**Himle,** John 1954- *WhoAmP 91*
**Himler,** Robert J. 1926- *WhoFI 92*
**Himmel,** Leon 1921- *AmMWSc 92*
**Himmel,** Martin Richard d1991 *NewYTBS 91 [port]*
**Himmel,** Robert Louis 1939- *WhoMW 92*
**Himmelberg,** Charles John 1931- *AmMWSc 92*
**Himmelberg,** Charles John, III 1931- *WhoFI 92*
**Himmelberg,** Glen Ray 1937- *AmMWSc 92*
**Himmelberger,** Irene Ursula 1945- *WhoWest 92*
**Himmelblau,** Bruce Allen 1958- *WhoEnt 92*
**Himmelblau,** David M 1923- *AmMWSc 92*
**Himmelfarb,** Gertrude 1922- *IntWW 91, WrDr 92*
**Himmelfarb,** Milton 1918- *WhoRel 92, WrDr 92*
**Himmelman,** Robert Francis 1950- *WhoAmL 92*
**Himmelreich,** David Baker 1954- *WhoAmL 92*
**Himmelsbach,** Clifton Keck 1907- *AmMWSc 92*
**Himmelstein,** Sydney 1927- *AmMWSc 92*
**Himmler,** Heinrich 1900-1945 *BiDExR, EncTR 91 [port], FacFETw [port]*
**Himms-Hagen,** Jean 1933- *AmMWSc 92*
**Himoe,** Albert 1938- *AmMWSc 92*
**Himonas,** James Demosthenes, Jr. 1932- *WhoWest 92*
**Himpsel,** Franz J 1949- *AmMWSc 92*
**Himschoot,** James Anthony 1965- *WhoMW 92*
**Himsl,** Mathias A 1912- *WhoAmP 91*
**Himsl,** Mathias Alfred 1912- *WhoWest 92*
**Himsworth,** Eric d1991 *Who 92N*
**Himsworth,** Harold 1905- *Who 92*
**Himsworth,** Harold Percival 1905- *IntWW 91*
**Himsworth,** Richard Lawrence 1937- *Who 92*
**Himwich,** Williamina Armstrong 1912- *AmMWSc 92*
**Hinata,** Satoshi 1944- *AmMWSc 92*
**Hinault,** Bernard 1954- *IntWW 91*
**Hinch,** Andrew Lewis, Sr. 1919- *WhoBlA 92*
**Hinch,** Stephen Walter 1951- *WhoWest 92*
**Hinch,** William Harry 1919- *WhoWest 92*
**Hincha,** Richard Emil 1954- *WhoMW 92*
**Hinchcliff,** Richard Henry, Jr 1948- *WhoIns 92*
**Hinchcliff,** Woodbine K. *TwCPaSc*
**Hinchcliffe,** Peter Robert Mossom 1937- *IntWW 91, Who 92*
**Hinchcliffe,** Richard George 1868-1942 *TwCPaSc*
**Hinchen,** John J 1926- *AmMWSc 92*
**Hinchey,** Bruce Alan 1949- *WhoAmP 91, WhoWest 92*
**Hinchey,** John William 1941- *WhoAmL 92*
**Hinchey,** Maurice D 1938- *WhoAmP 91*
**Hinchingbrooke,** Viscount *Who 92*
**Hinchliff,** James Thomas 1939- *WhoAmL 92*
**Hinchliff,** Peter Bingham 1929- *Who 92, WrDr 92*
**Hinchliff,** Stephen 1926- *Who 92*
**Hinchliffe,** David Martin 1948- *Who 92*
**Hinchman,** Ray Richard 1937- *AmMWSc 92*
**Hinck,** Lawrence Wilson 1940- *AmMWSc 92*
**Hinck,** Vincent C 1926- *AmMWSc 92*
**Hinck,** Walter 1922- *IntWW 91*
**Hinckle,** Warren James, III 1938- *WhoWest 92*
**Hinckley,** Alden Dexter 1931- *AmMWSc 92*
**Hinckley,** Barbara 1937- *WrDr 92*
**Hinckley,** Conrad Cutler 1934- *AmMWSc 92, WhoMW 92*
**Hinckley,** Frank T 1913- *WhoAmP 91*
**Hinckley,** Gordon B. 1910- *WhoRel 92, WhoWest 92*
**Hinckley,** Gregory Keith 1946- *WhoWest 92*
**Hinckley,** Helen 1903- *IntAu&W 91, WrDr 92*
**Hinckley,** John Paul, Jr. 1941- *WhoMW 92*
**Hinckley,** Stuart Wadsworth 1953- *WhoAmP 91*
**Hind al-Hunud** *EncAmaz 91*
**Hind,** Alfred Thomas, Jr 1914- *AmMWSc 92*
**Hind,** Geoffrey 1937- *AmMWSc 92*
**Hind,** Greg William 1946- *WhoFI 92, WhoWest 92*
**Hind,** Harry William 1915- *WhoWest 92*
**Hind,** John William *Who 92*
**Hind,** Joseph Edward 1923- *AmMWSc 92*
**Hind,** Kenneth 1920- *Who 92*
**Hind,** Kenneth Harvard 1949- *Who 92*
**Hind,** Stephen Robert 1952- *WhoRel 92*
**Hind,** Steven *DrAPF 91*
**Hindal,** Dale Frank 1938- *AmMWSc 92*
**Hinde,** Robert Aubrey 1923- *IntWW 91, Who 92*
**Hinde,** Thomas *IntAu&W 91X, IntWW 91, Who 92*
**Hinde,** Thomas 1926- *ConNov 91, WrDr 92*
**Hinde,** Wendy 1919- *IntAu&W 91, WrDr 92*
**Hindemith,** Paul 1895-1963 *EncTR 91, FacFETw, NewAmDM*
**Hindenburg,** Oskar von 1883-1960 *EncTR 91*
**Hindenburg,** P. von Beneckendorff und von 1846-1934 *EncTR 91 [port]*
**Hindenburg,** Paul von 1847-1934 *FacFETw [port]*
**Hinder,** Ronald Albert 1942- *AmMWSc 92*
**Hinderas,** Natalie 1927-1987 *NewAmDM, NotBlAW 92*
**Hindermann,** Richard L *WhoIns 92*
**Hindersinn,** Raymond Richard 1918- *AmMWSc 92*
**Hindin,** David A. 1958- *WhoAmL 92*
**Hindin,** Nathan *IntAu&W 91X*
**Hindle,** Brooke 1918- *AmMWSc 92*
**Hindle,** Timothy Simon 1946- *IntAu&W 91*
**Hindle,** Winston Russell, Jr. 1930- *WhoFI 92*
**Hindley,** Colin Boothman 1923- *Who 92*
**Hindley,** Michael John 1947- *Who 92*
**Hindley,** Norman *DrAPF 91*
**Hindley-Smith,** David Dury 1916- *Who 92*
**Hindlian,** Richard James 1946- *WhoAmL 92*
**Hindlip,** Baron 1912- *Who 92*
**Hindman,** Don J. 1926- *WhoMW 92*
**Hindman,** Edward Evans 1942- *AmMWSc 92*
**Hindman,** Joseph Lee 1933- *AmMWSc 92*
**Hindman,** Kyle *WhoAmP 91*
**Hindman,** Larrie C. 1937- *WhoAmL 92*
**Hindman,** Lloyd Stephenson 1914- *WhoRel 92*
**Hindmarsh,** Frederick Bell 1919- *Who 92*
**Hindmarsh,** Irene 1923- *Who 92*
**Hinds,** David Rodney 1961- *WhoMW 92*
**Hinds,** David Stewart 1939- *AmMWSc 92, WhoWest 92*
**Hinds,** Douglas L 1933- *WhoAmP 91*
**Hinds,** Edward C 1917- *AmMWSc 92*
**Hinds,** Frank Crossman 1930- *AmMWSc 92*
**Hinds,** Harold Earl, Jr. 1941- *WhoMW 92*
**Hinds,** Howard Rand 1942- *WhoFI 92*
**Hinds,** James Wadsworth 1941- *AmMWSc 92*
**Hinds,** Lennox S. *WhoBlA 92*
**Hinds,** Marvin Harold 1928- *AmMWSc 92*
**Hinds,** Nancy Webb 1947- *AmMWSc 92*
**Hinds,** Robert James 1931- *WhoWest 92*
**Hinds,** Robert Taylor, Jr. 1940- *WhoAmL 92*
**Hinds,** Sterling 1961- *BlkOlyM*
**Hinds,** Thomas Edward 1922- *AmMWSc 92*
**Hinds,** William Alfred 1833-1910 *AmPeW*
**Hindson,** William Stanley 1920- *Who 92*
**Hindus,** Maurice 1891-1969 *BenetAL 91*
**Hindus,** Milton 1916- *IntAu&W 91, WrDr 92*
**Hine,** Darlene Clark 1947- *WhoBlA 92*
**Hine,** Daryl *DrAPF 91*
**Hine,** Daryl 1936- *BenetAL 91, ConAu 15AS [port], ConPo 91, IntAu&W 91, WrDr 92*
**Hine,** Edward, Jr 1952- *WhoAmP 91*
**Hine,** Frederick Roy 1925- *AmMWSc 92*
**Hine,** Gerald John 1916- *AmMWSc 92*
**Hine,** Jack 1923- *AmMWSc 92*
**Hine,** John Maynard 1920- *AmMWSc 92*
**Hine,** Lewis 1874-1940 *DcTwDes, FacFETw*
**Hine,** Lewis W 1874-1940 *DcAmImH*
**Hine,** Lorraine A *WhoAmP 91*
**Hine,** Maynard Kiplinger 1907- *AmMWSc 92, IntWW 91*
**Hine,** Patrick 1932- *IntWW 91, Who 92*
**Hine,** Richard Bates 1929- *AmMWSc 92*
**Hine,** Robert V. 1921- *WrDr 92*
**Hine,** Robert Van Norden 1921- *IntAu&W 91*
**Hine,** Robert Walter 1924- *WhoAmP 91*
**Hine,** Ruth Louise 1923- *AmMWSc 92*
**Hine,** William Clyde 1944- *WhoMW 92*
**Hinegardner,** Ralph 1931- *AmMWSc 92*
**Hineman,** Kalo A 1922- *WhoAmP 91*
**Hineman,** William Carl 1942- *WhoEnt 92*
**Hiner,** Calvin Albert, Jr. 1945- *WhoMW 92*
**Hiner,** Leslie Davis 1957- *WhoAmL 92, WhoMW 92*
**Hinerman,** Charles Ovalee 1928- *AmMWSc 92*
**Hinerman,** Dorin Lee 1914- *AmMWSc 92*
**Hines,** Alan *DrAPF 91*
**Hines,** Andrew Hampton, Jr. 1923- *WhoFI 92*
**Hines,** Angus Irving, Jr. 1923- *WhoFI 92*
**Hines,** Anna G. 1946- *ConAu 36NR*
**Hines,** Anson Hemingway 1947- *AmMWSc 92*
**Hines,** Anthony Loring 1941- *AmMWSc 92*
**Hines,** Barry 1939- *ConNov 91, WrDr 92*
**Hines,** Barry Melvin 1939- *IntAu&W 91, Who 92*
**Hines,** Bedford Forrest 1945- *WhoMW 92*
**Hines,** Carl R, Sr 1931- *WhoAmP 91, WhoBlA 92*
**Hines,** Charles Alfonso 1935- *WhoBlA 92*
**Hines,** Colin 1919- *Who 92*
**Hines,** Earl 1905-1983 *NewAmDM*
**Hines,** Earl 1907-1983 *FacFETw*
**Hines,** Edward Francis, Jr. 1945- *WhoAmL 92*
**Hines,** Gregory 1946- *ConBlB 1 [port], IntMPA 92, WhoBlA 92*
**Hines,** Gregory Oliver 1946- *WhoEnt 92*
**Hines,** Harold C 1937- *AmMWSc 92*
**Hines,** J. Edward, Jr. 1908- *WhoBlA 92*
**Hines,** James R 1923- *AmMWSc 92*
**Hines,** James R 1946- *BlkOlyM*
**Hines,** James Robert 1937- *WhoEnt 92*
**Hines,** James William 1950- *WhoMW 92*
**Hines,** Jeffrey Alan 1954- *WhoAmL 92*
**Hines,** Jerome 1921- *NewAmDM, WhoEnt 92*
**Hines,** John Elbridge 1910- *RelLAm 91*
**Hines,** John J 1936- *WhoAmP 91*
**Hines,** Kingsley B. 1944- *WhoBlA 92*
**Hines,** Laura M. 1922- *WhoBlA 92*
**Hines,** Leonard Russell 1913- *AmMWSc 92*
**Hines,** Lovit 1852-1921 *DcNCBi 3*
**Hines,** Margaret H 1923- *AmMWSc 92*
**Hines,** Mark Edward 1950- *AmMWSc 92*
**Hines,** Morgan B. 1946- *WhoBlA 92*
**Hines,** N. William 1936- *WhoAmL 92*
**Hines,** Naomi 1965- *TwCPaSc*
**Hines,** Neal *WhoAmP 91*
**Hines,** Pamela Jean 1952- *AmMWSc 92*
**Hines,** Paul Steward 1940- *AmMWSc 92*
**Hines,** Peter Evans 1828-1908 *DcNCBi 3*
**Hines,** Ralph Howard 1927- *WhoBlA 92*
**Hines,** Randy Lee 1959- *WhoFI 92*
**Hines,** Richard 1792-1851 *DcNCBi 3*
**Hines,** Robert S. 1926- *WrDr 92*
**Hines,** Roderick Ludlow 1925- *AmMWSc 92*
**Hines,** Thomas S. 1936- *WrDr 92*
**Hines,** Warren Ashley 1951- *WhoAmP 91*
**Hines,** Wiley Earl 1942- *WhoBlA 92*
**Hines,** William Curtis 1940- *AmMWSc 92*
**Hines,** William E. 1958- *WhoBlA 92*
**Hines,** William Everett 1923- *WhoWest 92*
**Hines,** William Grant 1916- *AmMWSc 92*
**Hines,** William Jay 1930- *WhoMW 92*
**Hines,** William John 1956- *WhoFI 92*
**Hines,** William Joseph 1951- *WhoAmL 92*
**Hines,** William W 1932- *AmMWSc 92*
**Hines-Hayward,** Olga Loretta *WhoBlA 92*
**Hinesley,** Carl Phillip 1944- *AmMWSc 92*
**Hinesly,** James Arturo *WhoMW 92*
**Hinestrosa,** Dukardo 1933- *WhoHisp 92*
**Hinga,** John James 1923- *WhoMW 92*
**Hingamire,** Buddanna 1933- *IntAu&W 91*
**Hingerty,** Brian Edward 1948- *AmMWSc 92*
**Hingle,** Pat 1924- *IntMPA 92, WhoEnt 92*
**Hingorani,** Narain G 1931- *AmMWSc 92*
**Hingorani,** Sanjiv Gopal 1960- *WhoFI 92*
**Hingsbergen,** John Edward 1950- *WhoEnt 92*
**Hingson,** John Henry, III 1946- *WhoAmL 92*
**Hingst,** Lawrence W 1940- *WhoIns 92*
**Hingston,** Walter George 1905- *Who 92*
**Hinich,** Melvin Jay 1939- *WhoFI 92*
**Hinig,** William E 1919- *WhoAmP 91*
**Hinish,** Wilmer Wayne 1925- *AmMWSc 92*
**Hink,** Heinz R 1927- *WhoAmP 91*
**Hink,** Walter Fredric 1938- *AmMWSc 92*
**Hinkamp,** James Benjamin 1919- *AmMWSc 92*
**Hinkamp,** Paul Eugene 1925- *AmMWSc 92*
**Hinke,** Joseph Anthony Michael 1931- *AmMWSc 92*
**Hinke,** Norlan Lynn 1950- *WhoFI 92*

**Hinkebein**, John Arnold 1931- *AmMWSc 92*
**Hinkel**, Hans 1901- *EncTR 91 [port]*
**Hinkel**, Robert Dale 1914- *AmMWSc 92*
**Hinkelman**, Ruth A 1949- *WhoIns 92*
**Hinkelmann**, Klaus Heinrich 1932- *AmMWSc 92*
**Hinkemeyer**, Michael T 1940- *ConAu 34NR*
**Hinkemeyer**, Michael Thomas *DrAPF 91*
**Hinken**, Christopher Thomas 1950- *WhoMW 92*
**Hinkes**, Thomas Michael 1929- *AmMWSc 92*
**Hinkfuss**, Rosemary 1931- *WhoAmP 91*
**Hinkle**, Allan Eugene 1960- *WhoMW 92*
**Hinkle**, Ann M. 1952- *WhoMW 92*
**Hinkle**, Barton L 1925- *AmMWSc 92*
**Hinkle**, Charles Frederick 1942- *WhoAmL 92*
**Hinkle**, Charles N 1930- *AmMWSc 92*
**Hinkle**, Charles Robert 1945- *WhoEnt 92*
**Hinkle**, Dale Albert 1911- *AmMWSc 92*
**Hinkle**, David Currier 1944- *AmMWSc 92*
**Hinkle**, George Henry 1952- *AmMWSc 92*
**Hinkle**, Jackson Herbert 1943- *WhoBlA 92*
**Hinkle**, James Alton 1940- *WhoMW 92, WhoRel 92*
**Hinkle**, Jill Elaine 1956- *WhoRel 92*
**Hinkle**, Lawrence Earl, Jr 1918- *AmMWSc 92*
**Hinkle**, Mark Wilson Argee 1951- *WhoAmP 91*
**Hinkle**, Patricia M 1943- *AmMWSc 92*
**Hinkle**, Peter Currier 1940- *AmMWSc 92*
**Hinkle**, Robert *IntMPA 92*
**Hinkle**, Samuel F 1900-1984 *FacFETw*
**Hinkle**, Thomas C. 1876-1949 *BenetAL 91*
**Hinkle**, Winton Marshall 1942- *WhoAmL 92*
**Hinkley**, David Victor 1944- *AmMWSc 92, Who 92*
**Hinkley**, Everett David 1936- *AmMWSc 92*
**Hinkley**, Mark W 1945- *WhoIns 92*
**Hinkley**, Robert Edwin, Jr 1943- *AmMWSc 92*
**Hinkley**, Scott Williams, Sr. 1949- *WhoMW 92*
**Hinkley**, Stanley S *WhoAmP 91*
**Hinks**, David George 1939- *AmMWSc 92*
**Hinkson**, Jimmy Wilford 1931- *AmMWSc 92*
**Hinkson**, Thomas Clifford 1939- *AmMWSc 92*
**Hinlicky**, Paul Richard 1952- *WhoRel 92*
**Hinman**, Alanson 1921- *AmMWSc 92*
**Hinman**, Channing L 1943- *AmMWSc 92*
**Hinman**, Charles Wiley 1927- *AmMWSc 92*
**Hinman**, Chester Arthur 1939- *AmMWSc 92*
**Hinman**, Edward John 1931- *AmMWSc 92*
**Hinman**, Eugene Edward 1930- *AmMWSc 92*
**Hinman**, George L 1905- *WhoAmP 91*
**Hinman**, George Wheeler 1927- *AmMWSc 92*
**Hinman**, Harvey DeForest 1940- *WhoAmL 92*
**Hinman**, Jack Wiley 1919- *AmMWSc 92*
**Hinman**, Myra Mahlow 1926- *WhoMW 92*
**Hinman**, Norman Dean 1944- *AmMWSc 92*
**Hinman**, Peter Greayer 1937- *AmMWSc 92*
**Hinman**, Richard Leslie 1927- *AmMWSc 92*
**Hinman**, Wallace Porter 1914- *WhoAmP 91*
**Hinn**, Benny 1952- *RelLAm 91*
**Hinnant**, Clarence Henry, III 1938- *WhoFI 92*
**Hinnant**, Ollen B. 1931- *WhoBlA 92*
**Hinnebusch**, Paul 1917- *ConAu 35NR*
**Hinners**, Noel W 1935- *AmMWSc 92*
**Hinnov**, Einar 1930- *AmMWSc 92*
**Hinnrichs-Dahms**, Holly Beth 1945- *WhoMW 92*
**Hinojos**, Alfred 1941- *WhoHisp 92*
**Hinojosa**, Albino R. 1943- *WhoHisp 92*
**Hinojosa**, Carlos M. 1944- *WhoHisp 92*
**Hinojosa**, David Andres 1959- *WhoHisp 92*
**Hinojosa**, Federico Gustavo, Jr. 1947- *WhoHisp 92*
**Hinojosa**, Gilberto *WhoHisp 92*
**Hinojosa**, Gilberto Miguel 1942- *WhoHisp 92*
**Hinojosa**, Hector Oscar 1950- *WhoHisp 92*
**Hinojosa**, Jesus Hector 1935- *WhoHisp 92*
**Hinojosa**, Juan 1946- *WhoHisp 92*
**Hinojosa**, Juan J 1946- *WhoAmP 91*
**Hinojosa**, Liborio *WhoHisp 92*
**Hinojosa**, Luis Sainz *WhoRel 92*
**Hinojosa**, Maria de Lourdes 1961- *WhoHisp 92*
**Hinojosa**, Mariano G. 1946- *WhoHisp 92*
**Hinojosa**, R. Marie 1940- *WhoHisp 92*
**Hinojosa**, Rafael, Jr. 1933- *WhoHisp 92*
**Hinojosa**, Ricardo H. 1950- *WhoAmL 92, WhoHisp 92*
**Hinojosa**, Rogelio H. 1954- *WhoHisp 92*
**Hinojosa**, Rolando *DrAPF 91*
**Hinojosa**, Tony, Jr. 1944- *WhoHisp 92*
**Hinojosa**, Troy 1960- *WhoHisp 92*
**Hinojosa Berrones**, Alfonso 1924- *WhoRel 92*
**Hinojosa-Smith**, R. Rolando 1929- *WhoHisp 92*
**Hinote**, Samuel I. 1942- *WhoFI 92*
**Hinrichs**, Clarence H 1935- *AmMWSc 92*
**Hinrichs**, Edgar Neal 1922- *WhoWest 92*
**Hinrichs**, James Victor 1941- *WhoMW 92*
**Hinrichs**, Karl 1925- *AmMWSc 92*
**Hinrichs**, Katrin 1954- *AmMWSc 92*
**Hinrichs**, Lowell A 1935- *AmMWSc 92*
**Hinrichs**, Mark Christian 1953- *WhoWest 92*
**Hinrichs**, Paul Rutland 1928- *AmMWSc 92*
**Hinrichs**, Wayne Eldon 1931- *WhoWest 92*
**Hinrichsen**, John James Luett 1903- *AmMWSc 92*
**Hinrichsen**, Keith L 1951- *WhoAmP 91*
**Hinsch**, Gertrude Wilma 1932- *AmMWSc 92*
**Hinsch**, James E 1937- *AmMWSc 92*
**Hinsch**, William Paul 1910- *WhoIns 92*
**Hinsche**, William Ernest 1951- *WhoEnt 92*
**Hinsdale**, John Wetmore 1843-1921 *DcNCBi 3*
**Hinsdill**, Ronald D 1933- *AmMWSc 92*
**Hinshaw**, Ada Sue 1939- *AmMWSc 92*
**Hinshaw**, Charles Theron, Jr 1932- *AmMWSc 92*
**Hinshaw**, Chester John 1941- *WhoAmL 92*
**Hinshaw**, David B 1923- *AmMWSc 92*
**Hinshaw**, David B., Jr. 1945- *WhoWest 92*
**Hinshaw**, Donald Gray 1934- *WhoEnt 92*
**Hinshaw**, J Raymond 1923- *AmMWSc 92*
**Hinshaw**, Jerald Clyde 1944- *AmMWSc 92*
**Hinshaw**, Jerry E 1917- *WhoAmP 91*
**Hinshaw**, Lerner Brady 1921- *AmMWSc 92*
**Hinshaw**, Sheryl Kay 1958- *WhoAmP 91*
**Hinshaw**, Verlin Orville 1925- *WhoRel 92*
**Hinshaw**, Virginia Snyder 1944- *AmMWSc 92*
**Hinshelwood**, Cyril Norman 1897-1967 *WhoNob 90*
**Hinsley**, Harry 1918- *IntWW 91, Who 92, WrDr 92*
**Hinsman**, Edward James 1934- *AmMWSc 92, WhoMW 92*
**Hinson**, Caldwell Thomas 1920- *WhoAmP 91*
**Hinson**, David Chandler 1939- *AmMWSc 92*
**Hinson**, E. Glenn 1931- *WrDr 92*
**Hinson**, Edward Glenn 1931- *IntAu&W 91*
**Hinson**, Jack Allsbrook 1944- *AmMWSc 92*
**Hinson**, Kuell 1924- *AmMWSc 92*
**Hinson**, Robert Evans 1945- *WhoRel 92*
**Hinson**, Roy Manus 1961- *WhoBlA 92*
**Hintch**, Elizabeth Mary 1963- *WhoMW 92*
**Hinterberger**, Henry 1921- *AmMWSc 92*
**Hinterbuchner**, Catherine Nicolaides 1926- *AmMWSc 92*
**Hinterbuchner**, Ladislav Paul 1922- *AmMWSc 92*
**Hinteregger**, Gerald *IntWW 91*
**Hinteregger**, Hans Erich 1919- *AmMWSc 92*
**Hinterscheid**, Mathias 1931- *IntWW 91*
**Hinthorne**, James Roscoe 1942- *AmMWSc 92*
**Hintikka**, Harri Juhani 1937- *WhoFI 92*
**Hintikka**, Jaakko 1929- *WrDr 92*
**Hinton**, Alfred Fontaine 1940- *WhoBlA 92*
**Hinton**, Anita Marie 1946- *WhoRel 92*
**Hinton**, Barry Thomas 1950- *AmMWSc 92*
**Hinton**, Charles Franklin 1932- *WhoAmL 92*
**Hinton**, Charles H 1844-1907 *BiInAmS*
**Hinton**, Charles Howard 1853-1907 *ScFEYrs*
**Hinton**, Charles Lewis 1793-1861 *DcNCBi 3*
**Hinton**, Chris 1961- *WhoBlA 92*
**Hinton**, Christopher Jerome 1952- *WhoBlA 92*
**Hinton**, Claude Willey 1928- *AmMWSc 92*
**Hinton**, David Earl 1942- *AmMWSc 92*
**Hinton**, Deane R 1923- *WhoAmP 91*
**Hinton**, Deborah M 1953- *AmMWSc 92*
**Hinton**, Denys James 1921- *Who 92*
**Hinton**, Don Barker 1937- *AmMWSc 92*
**Hinton**, Floyd 1924- *WhoBlA 92*
**Hinton**, Frederick Lee 1939- *AmMWSc 92*
**Hinton**, George Greenough 1925- *AmMWSc 92*
**Hinton**, Gerry Earl 1930- *WhoAmP 91*
**Hinton**, Gregory Tyrone 1949- *WhoBlA 92*
**Hinton**, Hortense Beck 1950- *WhoBlA 92*
**Hinton**, James 1750?-1794 *DcNCBi 3*
**Hinton**, James Faulk 1938- *AmMWSc 92*
**Hinton**, James Forrest, Jr. 1951- *WhoAmL 92*
**Hinton**, John 1718?-1784 *DcNCBi 3*
**Hinton**, John 1748-1818 *DcNCBi 3*
**Hinton**, John Philip 1947- *WhoWest 92*
**Hinton**, Jonathan Wayne 1944- *AmMWSc 92*
**Hinton**, Mary Hilliard 1869-1961 *DcNCBi 3*
**Hinton**, Michael Herbert 1934- *Who 92*
**Hinton**, Milt *ConAu 134*
**Hinton**, Milton John 1910- *ConAu 134*
**Hinton**, Nelda Ruth 1937- *WhoAmP 91*
**Hinton**, Nicholas John 1942- *Who 92*
**Hinton**, Paula Weems 1954- *WhoAmL 92*
**Hinton**, Raymond Price 1925- *AmMWSc 92*
**Hinton**, S. E. 1948- *BenetAL 91, WrDr 92*
**Hinton**, Warren Miles 1920- *WhoBlA 92*
**Hinton**, Wayne Kendall 1940- *WhoAmP 91*
**Hintz**, Bernd Jurgen 1942- *WhoFI 92*
**Hintz**, Harold Franklin 1937- *AmMWSc 92*
**Hintz**, Howard William 1921- *AmMWSc 92*
**Hintz**, John Arnold 1945- *WhoWest 92*
**Hintz**, Norton Mark 1922- *AmMWSc 92*
**Hintz**, Richard Lee 1949- *AmMWSc 92*
**Hintze**, Lehi Ferdinand 1921- *AmMWSc 92*
**Hintze**, Thomas Henry *AmMWSc 92*
**Hintzen**, Paul Michael 1950- *AmMWSc 92*
**Hintzen**, Percy Claude 1947- *WhoBlA 92*
**Hinz**, Carl Frederick, Jr 1927- *AmMWSc 92*
**Hinz**, Dorothy Elizabeth *WhoFI 92*
**Hinz**, Gerald *WhoRel 92*
**Hinz**, Leo *WhoRel 92*
**Hinz**, Paul Norman 1935- *AmMWSc 92*
**Hinze**, Harry Clifford 1930- *AmMWSc 92*
**Hinze**, William James 1930- *AmMWSc 92*
**Hinze**, Willie Lee 1949- *AmMWSc 92*
**Hiort**, Esbjorn 1912- *IntWW 91*
**Hipel**, Keith William 1946- *AmMWSc 92*
**Hipkin**, John 1935- *Who 92*
**Hipkins**, James Richard 1927- *WhoRel 92*
**Hipp**, Billy Wayne 1933- *AmMWSc 92*
**Hipp**, Kenneth Byron 1945- *WhoAmL 92*
**Hipp**, Sally Sloan 1937- *AmMWSc 92*
**Hipp**, Van 1960- *WhoAmP 91*
**Hippard**, Raymond Avery, Jr. 1941- *WhoMW 92*
**Hippe**, Anne Elaine 1951- *WhoMW 92*
**Hippisley-Cox**, Peter Denzil John 1921- *Who 92*
**Hippius**, Zinaida 1869-1945 *LiExTwC*
**Hipple**, Robert Craig 1944- *WhoWest 92*
**Hippo** *EncAmaz 91*
**Hippodameia** *EncAmaz 91*
**Hippolytus** 170?-236? *EncEarC [port]*
**Hippopotamus**, Eugene H *IntAu&W 91X, SmATA 65*
**Hipps**, Charles W *WhoAmP 91*
**Hipps**, Diana L. 1951- *WhoRel 92*
**Hipps**, Kerry W 1948- *AmMWSc 92*
**Hipps**, Larry Clay 1953- *WhoRel 92*
**Hipwell**, Hermine H. *Who 92*
**Hirabayashi**, Dean I. 1962- *WhoWest 92*
**Hirabayashi**, Kazuko *WhoEnt 92*
**Hirahara**, Patti 1955- *WhoFI 92*
**Hirahara**, Tsuyoshi 1920- *IntWW 91, Who 92*
**Hirai**, Denitsu 1943- *WhoMW 92*
**Hirai**, Takushi 1931- *IntWW 91*
**Hiraki**, Kenneth T 1960- *WhoAmP 91*
**Hiramatsu**, Morihiko 1924- *IntWW 91*
**Hiramoto**, Raymond Natsuo 1930- *AmMWSc 92*
**Hirano**, Asao 1926- *AmMWSc 92*
**Hirano**, Cathy 1957- *SmATA 68 [port]*
**Hirano**, Ken-ichi 1927- *WhoFI 92*
**Hirano**, Toshio 1947- *AmMWSc 92*
**Hirao**, Teruo 1925- *IntWW 91*
**Hiraoka**, Hiroyuki 1932- *AmMWSc 92*
**Hiraoka**, William T 1917- *WhoIns 92*
**Hirasaki**, George J 1939- *AmMWSc 92*
**Hirasawa**, Ko 1900- *IntWW 91*
**Hirasuna**, Alan Ryo 1939- *AmMWSc 92*
**Hirata**, Arthur Atsunobu 1924- *AmMWSc 92*
**Hirata**, Fusao 1941- *AmMWSc 92*
**Hirata**, Gary Dean 1954- *WhoFI 92*
**Hirata**, Yutaka 1925- *IntWW 91*
**Hiratsuka**, Yasuyuki 1933- *AmMWSc 92*
**Hirayama**, Chikara 1924- *AmMWSc 92*
**Hirayama**, Fred 1934- *WhoAmP 91*
**Hirbe**, Richard Andrew, Jr. 1952- *WhoRel 92*
**Hird**, David William 1942- *AmMWSc 92*
**Hird**, Thora 1911- *Who 92*
**Hird**, Thora 1914- *IntMPA 92*
**Hiregowdara**, Dananagoud *AmMWSc 92*
**Hiremath**, Shivanand T 1952- *AmMWSc 92*
**Hires**, Jack Merle 1932- *WhoAmL 92*
**Hires**, Richard Ives 1939- *AmMWSc 92*
**Hirko**, Ronald John 1943- *AmMWSc 92*
**Hirleman**, Edwin Daniel, Jr 1951- *AmMWSc 92*
**Hirn**, Richard Joseph 1954- *WhoAmL 92*
**Hirnbock**, August *WhoRel 92*
**Hirning**, Lane D 1958- *AmMWSc 92*
**Hiro**, Dilip *IntAu&W 91, WrDr 92*
**Hiro**, Keitaro 1908- *IntWW 91*
**Hirohata**, Laurie Ann 1958- *WhoWest 92*
**Hirohito** 1901-1989 *FacFETw [port]*
**Hirokawa**, Katsuiku 1939- *AmMWSc 92*
**Hirokawa**, Michael Isamu 1946- *WhoWest 92*
**Hiromoto**, Robert Etsuo 1946- *WhoWest 92*
**Hirono**, Mazie 1947- *WhoAmP 91*
**Hirons**, Montague 1916- *WrDr 92*
**Hirooka**, Tomoo 1907- *IntWW 91*
**Hirose**, Akira 1941- *AmMWSc 92*
**Hirose**, Shin-ichi 1913- *IntWW 91*
**Hirota**, Jed 1943- *AmMWSc 92*
**Hirozawa**, Shurei 1919- *WhoWest 92*
**Hirrel**, Michael John 1951- *WhoAmL 92*
**Hirs**, Christophe Henri Werner 1923- *AmMWSc 92*
**Hirsch**, Albert Edgar 1924- *AmMWSc 92*
**Hirsch**, Allen Frederick 1935- *AmMWSc 92*
**Hirsch**, Ann Mary 1947- *AmMWSc 92*
**Hirsch**, Arthur 1921- *AmMWSc 92*
**Hirsch**, Barbara Ann 1953- *WhoEnt 92*
**Hirsch**, Barry 1933- *WhoEnt 92, WhoFI 92*
**Hirsch**, Carl Alvin 1929- *AmMWSc 92*
**Hirsch**, Carl E. 1946- *WhoEnt 92*
**Hirsch**, Carl Herbert 1934- *WhoFI 92*
**Hirsch**, Charles Bronislaw 1919- *WhoRel 92*
**Hirsch**, Daniel 1940- *WhoAmL 92*
**Hirsch**, David Alan 1947- *WhoAmL 92*
**Hirsch**, David Alan 1959- *WhoAmL 92*
**Hirsch**, David L. *WhoAmL 92*
**Hirsch**, Donald Earl 1924- *AmMWSc 92*
**Hirsch**, E. D., Jr. 1928- *WrDr 92*
**Hirsch**, Edward *DrAPF 91*
**Hirsch**, Edward 1950- *IntAu&W 91, WrDr 92*
**Hirsch**, Ellen Gail 1946- *WhoAmL 92*
**Hirsch**, Georges-Francois 1944- *IntWW 91*
**Hirsch**, Helmut V B 1943- *AmMWSc 92*
**Hirsch**, Henry Richard 1933- *AmMWSc 92*
**Hirsch**, Horst Eberhard 1933- *AmMWSc 92*
**Hirsch**, Jacob Irwin 1926- *AmMWSc 92*
**Hirsch**, Jay G 1930- *AmMWSc 92*
**Hirsch**, Jerome Seth 1948- *WhoAmL 92*
**Hirsch**, Jerry 1922- *AmMWSc 92*
**Hirsch**, Jerry Allan 1941- *AmMWSc 92*
**Hirsch**, Joel Stephen 1941- *WhoMW 92*
**Hirsch**, John Emile 1944- *WhoEnt 92*
**Hirsch**, John Michele 1947- *AmMWSc 92*
**Hirsch**, Jorge E 1951- *AmMWSc 92*
**Hirsch**, Judd *LesBEnT 92*
**Hirsch**, Judd 1935- *IntMPA 92, IntWW 91, WhoEnt 92*
**Hirsch**, Judith Ann *AmMWSc 92*
**Hirsch**, Jules 1927- *AmMWSc 92*
**Hirsch**, June *DrAPF 91*
**Hirsch**, June Schaut 1925- *WhoMW 92, WhoRel 92*
**Hirsch**, Laurence E. 1945- *WhoFI 92*
**Hirsch**, Lawrence Leonard 1922- *AmMWSc 92*
**Hirsch**, Leonard Stanley 1932- *WhoFI 92*
**Hirsch**, Les J 1947- *WhoAmP 91*
**Hirsch**, Martin Stanley 1939- *AmMWSc 92*
**Hirsch**, Milton *WhoAmP 91*
**Hirsch**, Milton Charles 1952- *WhoAmL 92*
**Hirsch**, Morris William 1933- *AmMWSc 92*
**Hirsch**, Otto 1885-1941 *EncTR 91*
**Hirsch**, Peter 1925- *Who 92*
**Hirsch**, Peter Bernhard 1925- *IntWW 91*
**Hirsch**, Peter M 1939- *AmMWSc 92*
**Hirsch**, Philip 1945- *WhoFI 92*
**Hirsch**, Philip Francis 1925- *AmMWSc 92*
**Hirsch**, Raymond Robert 1936- *WhoAmL 92*
**Hirsch**, Richard George 1926- *WhoRel 92*
**Hirsch**, Robert 1912- *IntWW 91*
**Hirsch**, Robert Allen 1946- *WhoAmL 92*
**Hirsch**, Robert George 1946- *AmMWSc 92*
**Hirsch**, Robert L *AmMWSc 92*
**Hirsch**, Robert Louis 1935- *AmMWSc 92*
**Hirsch**, Robert Mackin 1937- *WhoEnt 92*
**Hirsch**, Robert Paul 1925- *IntWW 91*
**Hirsch**, Robert William 1925- *WhoAmL 92*
**Hirsch**, Roland Felix 1939- *AmMWSc 92*
**Hirsch**, Samuel Roger 1930- *AmMWSc 92*
**Hirsch**, Seev 1931- *WrDr 92*
**Hirsch**, Solomon 1926- *AmMWSc 92*
**Hirsch**, Stephen Charles 1941- *WhoIns 92*
**Hirsch**, Stephen Simeon 1937- *AmMWSc 92*
**Hirsch**, Steven Richard 1937- *Who 92*

**Hirsch**, Steven Richard 1949- *WhoEnt 92*
**Hirsch**, Teddy James 1929- *AmMWSc 92*
**Hirsch**, Thomas Edward, III 1953- *WhoAmL 92*
**Hirsch**, Walter 1917- *WhoFI 92*, *WhoWest 92*
**Hirsch**, Warren Maurice 1923- *AmMWSc 92*
**Hirsch**, Werner Z. 1920- *WrDr 92*
**Hirsch**, Werner Zvi 1920- *WhoFI 92*
**Hirsch Ballin**, Ernst 1950- *IntWW 91*
**Hirsch Butler**, Carol Ann 1946- *WhoWest 92*
**Hirsch-Fikejs**, Judith Ann 1939- *WhoRel 92*
**Hirschberg**, Albert I 1934- *AmMWSc 92*
**Hirschberg**, Carlos Benjamin 1943- *AmMWSc 92*
**Hirschberg**, Erich 1921- *AmMWSc 92*
**Hirschberg**, Joseph Gustav 1921- *AmMWSc 92*
**Hirschberg**, Rona L 1943- *AmMWSc 92*
**Hirschel**, Ronald Melvin 1950- *WhoAmL 92*
**Hirschfeld**, Albert 1903- *WhoEnt 92*
**Hirschfeld**, Alec Evan 1947- *WhoEnt 92*
**Hirschfeld**, Burt 1923- *ConAu 134*
**Hirschfeld**, Daniel Allen 1957- *WhoFI 92*
**Hirschfeld**, Gerald Joseph 1921- *WhoEnt 92*
**Hirschfeld**, Magnus 1868-1935 *EncTR 91 [port]*
**Hirschfeld**, Michael 1950- *WhoAmL 92*
**Hirschfeld**, Ronald Colman 1930- *AmMWSc 92*
**Hirschfeld**, Stephen Jay 1957- *WhoAmL 92*
**Hirschfeld**, Sue Ellen 1941- *AmMWSc 92*
**Hirschfeld**, Tomas Beno 1939- *AmMWSc 92*
**Hirschfeld**, William Jacob 1938- *WhoRel 92*
**Hirschfelder**, John Joseph 1943- *AmMWSc 92*
**Hirschfelder**, Joseph Oakland d1990 *IntWW 91N*
**Hirschfelder**, Joseph Oakland 1854-1920 *BiInAmS*
**Hirschfelder**, Joseph Oakland 1911- *AmMWSc 92*
**Hirschfield**, Alan J. *IntWW 91*, *WhoEnt 92*, *WhoFI 92*, *WhoWest 92*
**Hirschfield**, Alan J. 1935- *IntMPA 92*
**Hirschhorn**, Clive 1940- *WrDr 92*
**Hirschhorn**, Clive Errol 1940- *IntAu&W 91*
**Hirschhorn**, Fred, Jr. 1919- *WhoFI 92*
**Hirschhorn**, Joel S 1939- *AmMWSc 92*
**Hirschhorn**, Kurt 1926- *AmMWSc 92*
**Hirschhorn**, Rochelle 1932- *AmMWSc 92*
**Hirschi**, David Price 1951- *WhoAmL 92*
**Hirschi**, John 1933- *WhoAmP 91*
**Hirschkop**, Philip Jay 1936- *WhoAmL 92*
**Hirschman**, Albert 1921- *AmMWSc 92*
**Hirschman**, Albert Otto 1915- *IntWW 91*
**Hirschman**, Charles, Jr. 1943- *WhoWest 92*
**Hirschman**, Herbert *LesBEnT 92*
**Hirschman**, Isidore Isaac, Jr 1922- *AmMWSc 92*
**Hirschman**, Jack *DrAPF 91*
**Hirschman**, Jack 1933- *ConPo 91*, *IntAu&W 91*, *WrDr 92*
**Hirschman**, Lynette 1945- *AmMWSc 92*
**Hirschman**, Shalom Zarach 1936- *AmMWSc 92*
**Hirschman**, Sherman Joseph 1935- *WhoAmL 92*, *WhoMW 92*
**Hirschmann**, Erwin 1924- *AmMWSc 92*
**Hirschmann**, Franz Gottfried 1945- *WhoWest 92*
**Hirschmann**, Hans 1909- *AmMWSc 92*
**Hirschmann**, James William, III 1960- *WhoFI 92*
**Hirschmann**, Ralph Franz 1922- *AmMWSc 92*
**Hirschmann**, Robert P 1934- *AmMWSc 92*
**Hirschowitz**, Basil Isaac 1925- *AmMWSc 92*
**Hirschson**, Linda Benjamin 1941- *WhoAmL 92*
**Hirschtritt**, Geri R. 1947- *WhoMW 92*
**Hirsh**, Allen Gene 1947- *AmMWSc 92*
**Hirsh**, Barry 1933- *WhoAmL 92*
**Hirsh**, Carl Stuart 1955- *WhoEnt 92*, *WhoFI 92*
**Hirsh**, Dwight Charles, III 1938- *AmMWSc 92*
**Hirsh**, Eva Maria Hauptmann 1928- *AmMWSc 92*
**Hirsh**, Ira Jean 1922- *AmMWSc 92*
**Hirsh**, Mary Elizabeth 1947- *IntAu&W 91*
**Hirsh**, Merle Norman 1931- *AmMWSc 92*
**Hirsh**, Norman Barry 1935- *WhoFI 92*
**Hirsh**, Richard Allan 1953- *WhoRel 92*
**Hirsh**, Robert Joel 1935- *WhoAmL 92*
**Hirsh**, Theodore William 1934- *WhoAmL 92*
**Hirshan**, Leonard 1927- *IntMPA 92*, *WhoEnt 92*
**Hirshaut**, Yashar 1938- *AmMWSc 92*
**Hirshbein**, Omus 1934- *WhoEnt 92*
**Hirshberg**, William Mark 1957- *WhoAmL 92*
**Hirshburg**, Robert Ivan 1949- *AmMWSc 92*
**Hirshenson**, Janet Kathleen 1947- *WhoEnt 92*
**Hirshfeld**, Fred Lurie 1927- *AmMWSc 92*
**Hirshfield** *Who 92*
**Hirshfield**, Baron 1913- *Who 92*
**Hirshfield**, James Albert, Jr. 1939- *WhoWest 92*
**Hirshfield**, Jane *DrAPF 91*
**Hirshfield**, Jay Leonard 1931- *AmMWSc 92*
**Hirshfield**, Morris 1872-1946 *FacFETw*
**Hirshfield**, Stuart 1941- *WhoAmL 92*
**Hirshleifer**, David Adam 1958- *WhoWest 92*
**Hirshman**, Carol A 1944- *AmMWSc 92*
**Hirshman**, Justin Leonard 1930- *AmMWSc 92*
**Hirshman**, Linda R. *WhoAmL 92*
**Hirshon**, Jack Thomas 1931- *WhoAmL 92*
**Hirshon**, Jordon Barry 1939- *AmMWSc 92*
**Hirshon**, Ronald 1939- *AmMWSc 92*
**Hirshorn**, Anne Sue *DrAPF 91*
**Hirsley**, Michael 1942- *WhoRel 92*
**Hirson**, Denis 1951- *LiExTwC*
**Hirson**, Estelle *WhoWest 92*
**Hirst**, Albert Edmund 1915- *AmMWSc 92*
**Hirst**, Barry 1934- *TwCPaSc*
**Hirst**, David 1925- *Who 92*
**Hirst**, David Michael Geoffrey 1933- *Who 92*
**Hirst**, Derek 1930- *TwCPaSc*
**Hirst**, George Keble 1909- *AmMWSc 92*
**Hirst**, Henry Beck 1817-1874 *BenetAL 91*
**Hirst**, John Malcolm 1921- *IntWW 91*, *Who 92*
**Hirst**, Jonathan William 1953- *Who 92*
**Hirst**, Maurice 1940- *AmMWSc 92*
**Hirst**, Michael William 1946- *Who 92*
**Hirst**, Omer Lee 1913- *WhoAmP 91*
**Hirst**, Paul Heywood 1927- *IntAu&W 91*, *IntWW 91*, *Who 92*
**Hirst**, Paul Quentin 1946- *IntAu&W 91*, *WrDr 92*
**Hirst**, Robert Charles 1932- *AmMWSc 92*
**Hirst**, Rodney Julian 1920- *Who 92*
**Hirst**, Wilma Elizabeth *WhoWest 92*
**Hirsty**, Drew J. 1956- *WhoMW 92*
**Hirsty**, Sylvain Max 1925- *AmMWSc 92*
**Hirt**, Al 1922- *IntMPA 92*, *NewAmDM*
**Hirt**, Andrew Michael 1955- *AmMWSc 92*
**Hirt**, Cyril William, Jr 1936- *AmMWSc 92*
**Hirt**, Thomas J 1931- *AmMWSc 92*
**Hirtenstein**, Daniel J 1931- *WhoIns 92*
**Hirth**, Harold Frederick 1932- *AmMWSc 92*
**Hirth**, John P 1930- *AmMWSc 92*
**Hirth**, Robert Stephen 1935- *AmMWSc 92*
**Hirth**, Russell Julius 1924- *WhoWest 92*
**Hirthe**, Walter M 1927- *AmMWSc 92*
**Hirtsiefer**, Heinrich 1876-1941 *EncTR 91*
**Hirtzel**, Cynthia S *AmMWSc 92*
**Hirvonen**, Raymond Matt 1928- *WhoFI 92*
**Hirwe**, Ashalata Shyamsunder 1938- *AmMWSc 92*
**Hirzebruch**, Friedrich Ernst Peter 1927- *IntWW 91*
**Hirzel**, James Charles 1954- *WhoMW 92*
**Hirzy**, John William 1936- *AmMWSc 92*
**Hisada**, Mituhiko 1929- *AmMWSc 92*
**Hisatsune**, Isamu Clarence 1924- *AmMWSc 92*
**Hisaw**, Frederick Lee, Jr 1927- *AmMWSc 92*
**Hiscock**, William Allen 1951- *AmMWSc 92*
**Hiscocks**, Charles Richard 1907- *Who 92*
**Hiscocks**, Richard 1907- *WrDr 92*
**Hiscoe**, Helen Brush 1919- *AmMWSc 92*
**Hiscott**, Richard Nicholas 1951- *AmMWSc 92*
**Hise**, Mark Allen 1950- *WhoWest 92*
**Hisek**, Dennis Dale 1949- *WhoRel 92*
**Hiser**, Harold Russell, Jr. 1931- *WhoFI 92*
**Hiser**, Homer Wendell 1924- *AmMWSc 92*
**Hisey**, Robert Warren 1931- *AmMWSc 92*
**Hishon**, Robert Harold 1941- *WhoAmL 92*
**Hiskes**, John Robert 1928- *AmMWSc 92*
**Hiskes**, Ronald 1941- *AmMWSc 92*
**Hiskey**, Clarence Francis 1912- *AmMWSc 92*
**Hiskey**, J Brent 1944- *AmMWSc 92*
**Hiskey**, Richard Grant 1929- *AmMWSc 92*
**Hisle**, Lorraine Pearl 1957- *WhoMW 92*
**Hislop**, George Steedman 1914- *Who 92*
**Hislop**, Helen Jean 1929- *AmMWSc 92*
**Hislop**, Ian David 1960- *Who 92*
**Hisrich**, Joseph C *WhoAmP 91*
**Hiss**, Alger 1904- *FacFETw [port]*, *Who 92*
**Hiss**, Philip Hanson, Jr 1868-1913 *BiInAmS*
**Hisserich**, John Charles 1939- *AmMWSc 92*
**Hissong**, Todd Michael 1955- *WhoMW 92*
**Histake**, Suafaase'e Faipa *WhoAmP 91*
**Histand**, Michael B 1942- *AmMWSc 92*
**Histed**, John Allan 1929- *AmMWSc 92*
**Hitam**, Mohd. Yusof 1936- *IntWW 91*
**Hitam**, Musa bin 1934- *IntWW 91*
**Hitch**, Brian 1932- *IntWW 91*, *Who 92*
**Hitch**, Charles Johnston 1910- *IntWW 91*
**Hitch**, Horace 1921- *WhoAmL 92*
**Hitch**, Robert Landis 1947- *WhoMW 92*
**Hitchcock**, Adam Percival 1951- *AmMWSc 92*
**Hitchcock**, Alfred d1980 *LesBEnT 92 [port]*
**Hitchcock**, Alfred 1899-1980 *BenetAL 91*, *FacFETw [port]*, *IntDcF 2-2 [port]*
**Hitchcock**, Anthony John Michael 1929- *Who 92*
**Hitchcock**, Bion Earl 1942- *WhoAmL 92*
**Hitchcock**, Charles Henry 1836-1919 *BiInAmS*
**Hitchcock**, Christopher Brian 1947- *WhoFI 92*
**Hitchcock**, Claude Raymond 1917- *AmMWSc 92*
**Hitchcock**, Daniel Augustus 1947- *AmMWSc 92*
**Hitchcock**, Dorothy Jean *AmMWSc 92*
**Hitchcock**, Edward 1793-1864 *BiInAmS*
**Hitchcock**, Edward 1828-1911 *BiInAmS*
**Hitchcock**, Edward Keith 1941- *WhoIns 92*
**Hitchcock**, Edward Robert 1929- *IntWW 91*, *Who 92*
**Hitchcock**, Eldon Titus 1924- *AmMWSc 92*
**Hitchcock**, Enos 1744-1803 *BenetAL 91*
**Hitchcock**, Ethan Allen 1798-1870 *BenetAL 91*, *BiInAmS*
**Hitchcock**, George *DrAPF 91*
**Hitchcock**, George 1914- *ConPo 91*, *WrDr 92*
**Hitchcock**, George Parks 1914- *IntAu&W 91*
**Hitchcock**, Harold 1914- *TwCPaSc*
**Hitchcock**, Harold Bradford 1903- *AmMWSc 92*
**Hitchcock**, Henry-Russell 1903-1987 *FacFETw*
**Hitchcock**, Hugh Wiley 1923- *WhoEnt 92*
**Hitchcock**, J. Gareth 1914- *WhoAmL 92*, *WhoMW 92*
**Hitchcock**, John David 1909- *WhoWest 92*
**Hitchcock**, John Lathrop 1936- *WhoRel 92*
**Hitchcock**, John Paul 1945- *AmMWSc 92*
**Hitchcock**, John Robert 1951- *WhoMW 92*
**Hitchcock**, Malcolm Franklin 1940- *WhoMW 92*
**Hitchcock**, Margaret 1940- *AmMWSc 92*
**Hitchcock**, Pamela Azilee 1950- *WhoFI 92*
**Hitchcock**, Raymond John 1922- *IntAu&W 91*, *WrDr 92*
**Hitchcock**, Robert Brian 1944- *WhoWest 92*
**Hitchcock**, Vernon Thomas 1919- *WhoWest 92*
**Hitchcock-DeGregori**, Sarah Ellen 1943- *AmMWSc 92*
**Hitchen**, Brian 1936- *Who 92*
**Hitchen**, Harold, Jr 1934- *WhoIns 92*
**Hitchen**, John David 1935- *Who 92*
**Hitchen**, Stephen 1953- *TwCPaSc*
**Hitchens**, Christopher 1949- *WrDr 92*
**Hitchens**, Christopher Eric 1949- *WhoAmP 91*
**Hitchens**, David William 1955- *WhoWest 92*
**Hitchens**, Gilbert Archibald Ford 1932- *Who 92*
**Hitchens**, Ivon 1893-1979 *TwCPaSc*
**Hitchens**, John 1940- *TwCPaSc*
**Hitchens**, Robert Joseph 1942- *WhoRel 92*
**Hitchin**, Aylwin Drakeford 1907- *Who 92*
**Hitchin**, Nigel James 1946- *Who 92*
**Hitching**, Alan Norman 1941- *Who 92*
**Hitchings**, David Allyn 1964- *WhoEnt 92*
**Hitchings**, George H 1905- *FacFETw*
**Hitchings**, George Herbert 1905- *AmMWSc 92*, *IntWW 91*, *Who 92*, *WhoNob 90*
**Hitchins**, Diddy R. M. 1945- *WhoWest 92*
**Hitchins**, Ron 1926- *TwCPaSc*
**Hitchman**, James Harold 1932- *WhoWest 92*
**Hitchman**, Terry D. 1957- *WhoAmL 92*
**Hitchmough**, Colin 1943- *TwCPaSc*
**Hitchner**, Stephen B., Jr. d1991 *NewYTBS 91*
**Hitchner**, Stephen Ballinger 1916- *AmMWSc 92*
**Hitchon**, Brian 1930- *AmMWSc 92*
**Hite**, Catharine Leavey 1924- *WhoEnt 92*
**Hite**, Gilbert J 1931- *AmMWSc 92*
**Hite**, J Roger 1939- *AmMWSc 92*
**Hite**, Joseph Pierce 1957- *WhoRel 92*
**Hite**, Mark 1935- *AmMWSc 92*
**Hite**, Nancy Ursula 1956- *WhoBlA 92*
**Hite**, Richard Rutledge 1959- *WhoFI 92*
**Hite**, Robert Wesley 1936- *WhoWest 92*
**Hite**, S C 1922- *AmMWSc 92*
**Hite**, Shere D. *IntWW 91*
**Hite**, William Richard, Jr. 1950- *WhoMW 92*
**Hites**, Ronald Atlee 1942- *AmMWSc 92*, *WhoMW 92*
**Hitler**, Adolf 1889-1945 *BiDExR*, *EncTR 91 [port]*, *FacFETw [port]*
**Hitler**, Alois 1837-1903 *EncTR 91*
**Hitler**, Eva *EncTR 91*
**Hitler**, Klara 1860-1907 *EncTR 91 [port]*
**Hitlin**, David G 1942- *AmMWSc 92*
**Hitlin**, David George 1942- *WhoWest 92*
**Hitner**, Henry William 1939- *AmMWSc 92*
**Hitpas**, Robert E. 1938- *WhoMW 92*
**Hitrec**, Hrvoje 1943- *IntAu&W 91*
**Hitschfeld**, Walter 1922- *AmMWSc 92*
**Hitt**, Danny Leon 1931- *WhoAmL 92*
**Hitt**, Ellis Francis 1938- *WhoMW 92*
**Hitt**, John Burton 1931- *AmMWSc 92*
**Hitt**, Leo N. 1955- *WhoAmL 92*
**Hitt**, Mary Barton 1936- *WhoAmP 91*
**Hitt**, Patricia Reilly 1918- *WhoAmP 91*
**Hittelman**, Allen M 1945- *AmMWSc 92*
**Hittelman**, Walter Nathan 1944- *AmMWSc 92*
**Hitter**, Joseph Ira 1944- *WhoAmL 92*
**Hittinger**, Raymond Clayton 1942- *WhoRel 92*
**Hittinger**, Richard Charles 1951- *WhoFI 92*
**Hittinger**, William C 1922- *AmMWSc 92*
**Hittle**, Carl Nelson 1922- *AmMWSc 92*
**Hittle**, David William 1947- *WhoAmL 92*
**Hittle**, Douglas Carl 1947- *AmMWSc 92*
**Hittle**, Larry Glenn 1933- *WhoAmL 92*
**Hittle**, Leroy Michael 1912- *WhoWest 92*
**Hittle**, Richard Howard 1923- *WhoFI 92*
**Hittmair**, Hans Christoph 1928- *IntWW 91*
**Hittmair**, Otto 1924- *IntWW 91*
**Hittner**, David 1939- *WhoAmL 92*
**Hitz**, Chester W 1912- *AmMWSc 92*
**Hitz**, Demi 1942- *ConAu 35NR*, *SmATA 66*
**Hitz**, Duane E. 1939- *WhoMW 92*
**Hitz**, John *DcAmImH*
**Hitzeman**, Jean Walter 1926- *AmMWSc 92*
**Hitzig**, Rupert *IntMPA 92*
**Hitzke**, Ronald Scott 1950- *WhoMW 92*
**Hitzman**, Donald Oliver 1926- *AmMWSc 92*
**Hiu**, Dawes Nyukleu 1927- *AmMWSc 92*
**Hively**, Neal Otto 1950- *WhoRel 92*
**Hively**, Robert Arland 1921- *AmMWSc 92*
**Hives** *Who 92*
**Hives**, Baron 1913- *Who 92*
**Hivnor**, Robert 1916- *IntAu&W 91*
**Hix**, Elliott Lee 1925- *AmMWSc 92*
**Hix**, H. Edgar *DrAPF 91*
**Hix**, Homer Bennett 1920- *AmMWSc 92*
**Hixon**, James Edward 1938- *WhoMW 92*
**Hixon**, Mark A 1951- *AmMWSc 92*
**Hixon**, Sumner B 1930- *AmMWSc 92*
**Hixson**, Elmer LaVerne 1924- *AmMWSc 92*
**Hixson**, Floyd Marcus 1918- *AmMWSc 92*
**Hixson**, James Elmer 1952- *AmMWSc 92*
**Hixson**, Judson Lemoine 1950- *WhoBlA 92*
**Hixson**, Keith Evan 1945- *WhoRel 92*
**Hixson**, Sheila Ellis 1933- *WhoAmP 91*
**Hixson**, Stephen Sherwin 1943- *AmMWSc 92*
**Hixson**, Susan Harvill 1944- *AmMWSc 92*
**Hiyama**, Tetsuo 1939- *AmMWSc 92*
**Hiza**, Michael John, Jr 1931- *AmMWSc 92*
**Hjelle**, Joseph Thomas 1949- *AmMWSc 92*
**Hjelm**, Andrea Marie 1943- *WhoMW 92*
**Hjelm**, Howard F 1927- *WhoAmP 91*
**Hjelm-Wallen**, Lena 1943- *IntWW 91*
**Hjelme**, Dag Roar 1959- *AmMWSc 92*
**Hjelmeland**, Leonard M *AmMWSc 92*
**Hjelmesaeth**, Frode Sture 1959- *WhoWest 92*
**Hjelmfelt**, Allen T, Jr 1937- *AmMWSc 92*
**Hjelmstad**, William David 1954- *WhoWest 92*
**Hjerpe**, Edward Alfred, III 1959- *WhoFI 92*
**Hjorne**, Lars Goran 1929- *IntWW 91*
**Hjort**, Johan Bernhard 1895-1969 *BiDExR*
**Hjorth**, Poul Lindegard 1927- *IntWW 91*
**Hjorth-Nielsen**, Henning d1990 *IntWW 91N*
**Hjortsberg**, William *DrAPF 91*
**Hjortsberg**, William 1941- *BenetAL 91*, *WrDr 92*
**Hjortsberg**, William Reinhold 1941- *IntAu&W 91*, *WhoEnt 92*

**Hla Han** 1918- *IntWW 91*
**Hladky,** Joseph F., Jr. 1910- *WhoMW 92*
**Hlasko,** Marek 1934-1969 *LiExTwC*
**Hlasta,** Dennis John 1953- *AmMWSc 92*
**Hlavacek,** Robert Allen 1949- *AmMWSc 92*
**Hlavacek,** Robert John 1923- *AmMWSc 92*
**Hlavacek,** Vladimir 1939- *AmMWSc 92*
**Hlavay,** Jay Alan 1956- *WhoFI 92*
**Hlavka,** Joseph John 1927- *AmMWSc 92*
**Hlavsa,** David Anton 1961- *WhoEnt 92*
**Hlawitschka,** Eduard 1928- *IntWW 91*
**Hlawka,** Edmund 1916- *IntWW 91*
**Hlubek,** Jeffry Joseph 1946- *WhoWest 92*
**Hmurovic,** John Michael 1952- *WhoEnt 92*
**Hnat,** Marsha Ann 1950- *WhoRel 92*
**Hnatiuk,** Bohdan T 1915- *AmMWSc 92*
**Hnatow,** Miquel Alexander 1942- *AmMWSc 92*
**Hnatowich,** Donald John 1940- *AmMWSc 92*
**Hnatyshyn,** Ramon John 1934- *IntWW 91, Who 92*
**Ho Chi Minh** 1890-1969 *FacFETw [port]*
**Ho Dam** d1991 *NewYTBS 91*
**Ho Te Que** d1965 *EncAmaz 91*
**Ho Ying-chin** 1889-1987 *FacFETw*
**Ho,** Alexander Kitman 1950- *WhoEnt 92*
**Ho,** Alfred K 1919- *ConAu 35NR*
**Ho,** Andrew Kong-Sun 1939- *AmMWSc 92*
**Ho,** Anna Shao-Fu 1946- *WhoAmL 92*
**Ho,** Begonia Y 1962- *AmMWSc 92*
**Ho,** Beng Thong 1932- *AmMWSc 92*
**Ho,** Bong 1931- *AmMWSc 92*
**Ho,** Chee Sin 1935- *WhoRel 92*
**Ho,** Chi-Tang 1944- *AmMWSc 92*
**Ho,** Chien 1934- *AmMWSc 92*
**Ho,** Cho-Yen 1928- *AmMWSc 92*
**Ho,** Chong Cheong 1938- *AmMWSc 92*
**Ho,** Christopher Gene 1954- *WhoWest 92*
**Ho,** Chung-Wu *AmMWSc 92*
**Ho,** Chung-wu 1938- *WhoMW 92*
**Ho,** Chung You 1933- *AmMWSc 92*
**Ho,** Clara Lin 1932- *AmMWSc 92*
**Ho,** Dah-Hsi 1931- *AmMWSc 92*
**Ho,** Dar-Veig 1931- *AmMWSc 92*
**Ho,** David K. 1948- *WhoMW 92*
**Ho,** David Tuan-hua 1948- *AmMWSc 92*
**Ho,** Donald Tai Loy 1930- *WhoWest 92*
**Ho,** Eric Peter 1927- *Who 92*
**Ho,** Fanghuai H 1934- *AmMWSc 92*
**Ho,** Floyd Fong-Lok *AmMWSc 92*
**Ho,** Grace Ping-Poo *AmMWSc 92*
**Ho,** Guan Lim 1925- *IntWW 91*
**Ho,** Henry Sokore 1942- *AmMWSc 92*
**Ho,** Hon Hing 1939- *AmMWSc 92*
**Ho,** Hung-Ta 1921- *AmMWSc 92*
**Ho,** Ing Kang 1939- *AmMWSc 92*
**Ho,** Iwan 1925- *AmMWSc 92, WhoWest 92*
**Ho,** James Chien Ming 1937- *AmMWSc 92*
**Ho,** James Kai 1952- *WhoFI 92*
**Ho,** John Ting-Sum 1942- *AmMWSc 92*
**Ho,** Ju-Shey 1935- *AmMWSc 92*
**Ho,** Kang-Jey 1937- *AmMWSc 92*
**Ho,** Keh Ming 1936- *AmMWSc 92*
**Ho,** Leo Chi Chien 1940- *WhoFI 92, WhoMW 92*
**Ho,** Louis T 1930- *AmMWSc 92*
**Ho,** Lydia Su-yong 1939- *AmMWSc 92*
**Ho,** Mat H 1951- *AmMWSc 92*
**Ho,** May-Kin 1952- *AmMWSc 92*
**Ho,** Monto 1927- *AmMWSc 92*
**Ho,** Nancy Wang-Yang *AmMWSc 92*
**Ho,** Pak Tae *WhoRel 92*
**Ho,** Patience Ching-Ru *AmMWSc 92*
**Ho,** Paul Siu-Chung 1936- *AmMWSc 92*
**Ho,** Peng-Yoke 1926- *IntWW 91*
**Ho,** Peter Peck Koh 1937- *AmMWSc 92*
**Ho,** Ping-Pei 1949- *AmMWSc 92*
**Ho,** Ren-jye *AmMWSc 92*
**Ho,** Robert En Ming 1942- *WhoMW 92*
**Ho,** Robert P. 1949- *WhoFI 92*
**Ho,** Rodney Jin Yong 1959- *WhoWest 92*
**Ho,** S 1931- *AmMWSc 92*
**Ho,** Stuart Tse Kong 1935- *WhoWest 92*
**Ho,** Tao 1936- *IntWW 91*
**Ho,** Thomas Inn Min 1948- *AmMWSc 92*
**Ho,** Thomas Tong-Yun 1931- *AmMWSc 92*
**Ho,** Yew Kam 1946- *AmMWSc 92*
**Ho,** Yu-Chi 1934- *AmMWSc 92*
**Ho-Kim,** Quang 1938- *AmMWSc 92*
**Hoa,** Suong Van 1948- *AmMWSc 92*
**Hoad,** Norman Edward 1923- *Who 92*
**Hoadley,** Alfred Warner 1934- *AmMWSc 92*
**Hoadley,** Douglas Andrew 1952- *WhoFI 92*
**Hoadley,** George B 1909- *AmMWSc 92*
**Hoadley,** Robert Bruce 1933- *AmMWSc 92*
**Hoadley,** Walter Evans 1916- *WhoFI 92, WhoRel 92*
**Hoadly,** Benjamin 1676-1761 *BlkwCEP*
**Hoag,** Arthur Allen 1921- *AmMWSc 92*
**Hoag,** Bonnie Elizabeth *DrAPF 91*
**Hoag,** Charles Kelso 1931- *WhoEnt 92*
**Hoag,** David Garratt 1925- *AmMWSc 92*
**Hoag,** Roland Boyden, Jr 1945- *AmMWSc 92*
**Hoag,** Terry S 1942- *WhoIns 92*
**Hoagberg,** Rudolph Karl 1930- *AmMWSc 92*
**Hoage,** Terrell Rudolph 1934- *AmMWSc 92*
**Hoagenson,** Connie Lou 1937- *WhoMW 92*
**Hoagland,** A S 1926- *AmMWSc 92*
**Hoagland,** Alan D 1911- *AmMWSc 92*
**Hoagland,** Albert Joseph, Jr. 1939- *WhoWest 92*
**Hoagland,** Edward *DrAPF 91*
**Hoagland,** Edward 1932- *BenetAL 91, ConNov 91, IntWW 91, TwCWW 91, WrDr 92*
**Hoagland,** Everett H., III 1942- *WhoBlA 92*
**Hoagland,** G William *WhoAmP 91*
**Hoagland,** Gordon W. 1936- *WhoWest 92*
**Hoagland,** Gordon Wood 1936- *AmMWSc 92*
**Hoagland,** Jack Charles 1918- *AmMWSc 92*
**Hoagland,** K Elaine 1947- *AmMWSc 92*
**Hoagland,** Karl King, Jr. 1933- *WhoAmL 92*
**Hoagland,** Lawrence Clay 1931- *AmMWSc 92*
**Hoagland,** Mahlon Bush 1921- *AmMWSc 92*
**Hoagland,** Peter 1941- *AlmAP 92 [port], WhoAmP 91*
**Hoagland,** Peter Jackson 1941- *WhoMW 92*
**Hoagland,** Robert Edward 1942- *AmMWSc 92*
**Hoagland,** Samuel Albert 1953- *WhoAmL 92, WhoWest 92*
**Hoagland,** Steven William 1948- *WhoFI 92*
**Hoagland,** Vincent DeForest, Jr 1940- *AmMWSc 92*
**Hoaglin,** David Caster 1944- *AmMWSc 92*
**Hoaglund,** Hudson 1899-1982 *FacFETw*
**Hoaglund,** Ronald John 1951- *WhoMW 92*
**Hoagstrom,** Carl William 1940- *AmMWSc 92*
**Hoak,** James McClain, Jr. 1944- *WhoEnt 92*
**Hoak,** John C *AmMWSc 92*
**Hoan,** Daniel W. 1881-1961 *DcAmImH*
**Hoang Van Hoan** d1991 *NewYTBS 91 [port]*
**Hoang,** Duc Van 1926- *WhoWest 92*
**Hoang,** Minh Co 1931- *WhoWest 92*
**Hoar,** George Frisbie 1826-1904 *AmPolLe*
**Hoar,** John, Jr 1917- *WhoAmP 91*
**Hoar,** Richard Morgan 1927- *AmMWSc 92*
**Hoar,** Ronald William Cecil 1931- *Who 92*
**Hoar,** Samuel 1927- *WhoAmL 92*
**Hoar,** Warren Thomas 1927- *WhoWest 92*
**Hoar,** William Stewart 1913- *AmMWSc 92, IntWW 91*
**Hoard,** Donald Ellsworth 1928- *AmMWSc 92*
**Hoard,** Elmer David 1947- *WhoAmL 92*
**Hoard,** James Lynn 1905- *AmMWSc 92*
**Hoard,** Leroy 1968- *WhoBlA 92*
**Hoare,** Charles Antony Richard 1934- *IntWW 91, Who 92*
**Hoare,** James Patrick 1921- *AmMWSc 92, WhoMW 92*
**Hoare,** Jeff *TwCPaSc*
**Hoare,** John Michael 1932- *Who 92*
**Hoare,** Marcus Bertram 1910- *Who 92*
**Hoare,** Merval Hannah 1914- *IntAu&W 91, WrDr 92*
**Hoare,** Peter Richard David 1932- *Who 92*
**Hoare,** Philip 1958- *ConAu 134*
**Hoare,** Richard David 1927- *AmMWSc 92*
**Hoare,** Rupert William Noel 1940- *Who 92*
**Hoare,** Samuel 1880-1959 *EncTR 91*
**Hoare,** Timothy Edward Charles 1934- *Who 92*
**Hoare,** Tyler James 1940- *WhoWest 92*
**Hoback,** John Holland 1920- *AmMWSc 92*
**Hoback,** John Thomas 1940- *WhoFI 92*
**Hoban,** Brian Michael Stanislaus 1921- *Who 92*
**Hoban,** Russell 1925- *BenetAL 91, ConNov 91, LiExTwC, TwCSFW 91, WrDr 92*
**Hoban,** Russell Conwell 1925- *IntAu&W 91, IntWW 91, Who 92*
**Hobart,** Alice Tisdale 1882-1967 *BenetAL 91*
**Hobart,** Anne Moore 1929- *WhoAmP 91*
**Hobart,** David Edward 1949- *AmMWSc 92*
**Hobart,** Donald Bayne *TwCWW 91*
**Hobart,** Everett W 1931- *AmMWSc 92*
**Hobart,** Garret Augustus 1844-1899 *AmPolLe*
**Hobart,** John Donald, Jr. 1960- *WhoAmL 92*
**Hobart,** John Vere 1945- *Who 92*
**Hobart,** Peter Merrill 1946- *AmMWSc 92*
**Hobart,** Robert H 1932- *AmMWSc 92*
**Hobart,** Rose Bosworth 1906- *WhoEnt 92*
**Hobart-Hampden** *Who 92*
**Hobbes,** Thomas 1588-1679 *BlkwCEP, RfGEnL 91*
**Hobbie,** A. Clark, Jr. 1941- *WhoFI 92*
**Hobbie,** John Eyres 1935- *AmMWSc 92*
**Hobbie,** Russell Klyver 1934- *AmMWSc 92*
**Hobbins,** Barry John 1951- *WhoAmP 91*
**Hobbins,** John Clark 1936- *AmMWSc 92*
**Hobbs,** Allan Wilson 1885-1960 *DcNCBi 3*
**Hobbs,** Ann Snow 1945- *AmMWSc 92*
**Hobbs,** Anne Stevenson 1942- *ConAu 133*
**Hobbs,** Anson Parker 1915- *AmMWSc 92*
**Hobbs,** Benjamin F 1954- *AmMWSc 92*
**Hobbs,** Billy Frankel 1931- *AmMWSc 92*
**Hobbs,** Caswell O., III 1941- *WhoAmL 92*
**Hobbs,** Cecil 1907- *WrDr 92*
**Hobbs,** Charles Clifton, Jr 1927- *AmMWSc 92*
**Hobbs,** Charles Floyd 1935- *AmMWSc 92*
**Hobbs,** Charles Henry 1942- *AmMWSc 92*
**Hobbs,** Charles Roderick Bruce, Jr 1929- *AmMWSc 92*
**Hobbs,** Christopher 1950- *ConCom 92*
**Hobbs,** Clifford Dean 1933- *AmMWSc 92*
**Hobbs,** Clinton Howard 1915- *AmMWSc 92*
**Hobbs,** Donald Clifford 1930- *AmMWSc 92*
**Hobbs,** Fred R 1947- *WhoAmP 91*
**Hobbs,** G. Warfield, III d1991 *NewYTBS 91*
**Hobbs,** George Edgar 1907- *AmMWSc 92*
**Hobbs,** Guy Stephen 1955- *WhoWest 92*
**Hobbs,** Herbert Harry 1912- *Who 92*
**Hobbs,** Herman Hedberg 1927- *AmMWSc 92*
**Hobbs,** Herschel 1907- *RelLAm 91*
**Hobbs,** Herschel H. 1907- *WrDr 92*
**Hobbs,** Herschel Harold 1907- *WhoRel 92*
**Hobbs,** Horton Holcombe, III 1944- *AmMWSc 92*
**Hobbs,** Horton Holcombe, Jr 1914- *AmMWSc 92*
**Hobbs,** J. Kline *DrAPF 91*
**Hobbs,** J. Timothy, Sr. 1941- *WhoAmL 92*
**Hobbs,** James Arthur 1914- *AmMWSc 92*
**Hobbs,** John Charles 1917- *Who 92*
**Hobbs,** John Daniel 1931- *WhoBlA 92*
**Hobbs,** John Robert 1941- *AmMWSc 92*
**Hobbs,** Joseph 1948- *WhoBlA 92*
**Hobbs,** Keith 1925- *Who 92*
**Hobbs,** Kenneth Burkett 1930- *WhoWest 92*
**Hobbs,** Kenneth Edward Frederick 1936- *Who 92*
**Hobbs,** Lewis Lyndon 1849-1932 *DcNCBi 3*
**Hobbs,** Lewis Mankin 1937- *AmMWSc 92*
**Hobbs,** Lyndel Erin 1958- *WhoRel 92*
**Hobbs,** M Floyd 1924- *AmMWSc 92*
**Hobbs,** Marcus Edwin 1909- *AmMWSc 92*
**Hobbs,** Marvin 1912- *WhoFI 92*
**Hobbs,** Mary Mendenhall 1852-1930 *DcNCBi 3*
**Hobbs,** Michael Arthur 1947- *WhoBlA 92*
**Hobbs,** Michael Dickinson 1941- *WhoAmP 91*
**Hobbs,** Michael Edward 1950- *WhoAmL 92*
**Hobbs,** Michael Edwin 1940- *WhoEnt 92*
**Hobbs,** Michael Frederick 1937- *Who 92*
**Hobbs,** Milford Leroy 1904- *AmMWSc 92*
**Hobbs,** Perry Lynes 1861-1912 *BiInAmS*
**Hobbs,** Peter Victor 1936- *AmMWSc 92*
**Hobbs,** R. Dee 1956- *WhoAmL 92*
**Hobbs,** Rebecca Ann 1950- *WhoEnt 92*
**Hobbs,** Richard Junius Mendenhall 1888-1967 *DcNCBi 3*
**Hobbs,** Robert Wesley 1938- *AmMWSc 92*
**Hobbs,** Samuel Huntington, Jr. 1895-1969 *DcNCBi 3*
**Hobbs,** Samuel Warren 1911- *AmMWSc 92*
**Hobbs,** Stanley Young 1944- *AmMWSc 92*
**Hobbs,** Steven Leonard 1962- *WhoWest 92*
**Hobbs,** Suzanne Marie *DrAPF 91*
**Hobbs,** Thadeaus H. 1924- *WhoBlA 92*
**Hobbs,** Truman McGill 1921- *WhoAmL 92*
**Hobbs,** Wilbur E. 1921- *WhoBlA 92*
**Hobby,** Charles R 1930- *AmMWSc 92*
**Hobby,** Elaine 1956- *WrDr 92*
**Hobby,** Gladys Lounsbury 1910- *AmMWSc 92*
**Hobby,** Oveta Culp 1905- *AmPolLe, IntWW 91*
**Hobby,** William Pettus 1932- *WhoAmP 91, WhoEnt 92, WhoFI 92*
**Hobday,** Gordon 1916- *IntWW 91, Who 92*
**Hobden,** Dennis Harry 1920- *Who 92*
**Hobden,** Reginald Herbert 1919- *Who 92*
**Hobdy,** Clarence Chester 1902- *WhoAmP 91*
**Hobeika,** Antoine George 1943- *AmMWSc 92*
**Hobelman,** Carl Donald 1931- *WhoAmL 92*
**Hobelman,** Margaret Ellen 1926- *WhoAmP 91*
**Hoben,** Sandra *DrAPF 91*
**Hoberman,** Alfred Elliott 1939- *AmMWSc 92*
**Hoberman,** David *IntMPA 92, WhoEnt 92*
**Hoberman,** Henry Don 1914- *AmMWSc 92*
**Hoberman,** Stuart A. 1946- *WhoAmL 92*
**Hobey,** William David 1935- *AmMWSc 92*
**Hobgood,** Burnet M. 1922- *WhoEnt 92*
**Hobgood,** Franklin P. 1847-1924 *DcNCBi 3*
**Hobgood,** Richard Troy, Jr 1939- *AmMWSc 92*
**Hobgood,** Robert H *WhoAmP 91*
**Hobhouse,** Charles Chisholm d1991 *Who 92N*
**Hobhouse,** Charles John Spinney 1962- *Who 92*
**Hobhouse,** Hermione *Who 92*
**Hobhouse,** Hermione 1934- *IntAu&W 91, WrDr 92*
**Hobhouse,** Janet d1991 *NewYTBS 91*
**Hobhouse,** Janet 1948-1991 *ConAu 133*
**Hobhouse,** Mary Hermione *Who 92*
**Hobhouse,** Penelope 1929- *Who 92*
**Hobin,** Bill *LesBEnT 92*
**Hobin,** Bill 1923- *IntMPA 92*
**Hobkirk,** Elspeth 1903-1990 *AnObit 1990*
**Hobkirk,** Michael Dalgliesh 1924- *Who 92*
**Hobkirk,** Ronald 1930- *AmMWSc 92*
**Hobler,** John Forde 1907- *Who 92*
**Hobley,** Brian 1930- *Who 92*
**Hobley,** John William Dixon 1929- *Who 92*
**Hoblin,** Philip J., Jr. 1929- *WhoFI 92*
**Hoblit,** Louis Douglas 1919- *AmMWSc 92*
**Hoblitt,** Richard Patrick 1944- *AmMWSc 92*
**Hoblitzell,** John R 1948- *WhoAmP 91*
**Hoblitzelle,** George Knapp 1921- *WhoAmP 91*
**Hoblock,** Michael J, Jr 1942- *WhoAmP 91*
**Hobman,** David Burton 1927- *Who 92*
**Hoboken,** Anthony van 1887-1983 *NewAmDM*
**Hobrock,** Don Leroy 1936- *AmMWSc 92*
**Hobsbaum,** Philip 1932- *ConPo 91, WrDr 92*
**Hobsbaum,** Philip Dennis 1932- *IntAu&W 91*
**Hobsbawm,** Eric 1917- *WrDr 92*
**Hobsbawm,** Eric John Ernest 1917- *IntWW 91, Who 92*
**Hobsley,** Michael 1929- *Who 92*
**Hobson,** Anthony Robert Alwyn 1921- *Who 92, WrDr 92*
**Hobson,** Arthur Stanley 1934- *AmMWSc 92*
**Hobson,** Calvin Jackson, III 1945- *WhoAmP 91*
**Hobson,** Carol J. 1923- *WhoBlA 92*
**Hobson,** Charles Blagrove 1936- *WhoBlA 92, WhoEnt 92*
**Hobson,** David 1936- *WhoAmP 91*
**Hobson,** David Constable 1922- *Who 92*
**Hobson,** David L. 1936- *AlmAP 92 [port]*
**Hobson,** David Lee 1936- *WhoMW 92*
**Hobson,** Donald Lewis 1935- *WhoBlA 92*
**Hobson,** Edmund Schofield 1931- *AmMWSc 92*
**Hobson,** Fred Colby 1943- *WrDr 92*
**Hobson,** Fred Colby, Jr 1943- *IntAu&W 91*
**Hobson,** Geary *DrAPF 91*
**Hobson,** Harold 1904- *IntAu&W 91, Who 92, WrDr 92*
**Hobson,** Harry E., Jr. 1948- *WhoMW 92*
**Hobson,** Harry Lee, Jr. 1929- *WhoAmL 92*
**Hobson,** Howard d1991 *NewYTBS 91*
**Hobson,** James Richmond 1937- *WhoAmL 92, WhoFI 92*
**Hobson,** Jay Damon 1942- *WhoFI 92*
**Hobson,** John 1946- *Who 92*
**Hobson,** John Allan 1933- *AmMWSc 92*
**Hobson,** John Peter 1924- *AmMWSc 92*
**Hobson,** John Richard 1931- *WhoRel 92*
**Hobson,** Laura Z. 1900-1986 *BenetAL 91*
**Hobson,** Lawrence John 1921- *Who 92*
**Hobson,** Mary 1926- *IntAu&W 91*
**Hobson,** Melvin Clay, Jr 1926- *AmMWSc 92*
**Hobson,** Patricia Pinnix 1947- *WhoBlA 92*
**Hobson,** Phillip Maurice 1942- *WhoAmP 91*
**Hobson,** Richard R G 1931- *WhoAmP 91*
**Hobson,** Robert Marshall 1926- *AmMWSc 92*

**Hobson,** Robert R. 1930- *WhoBlA 92*
**Hobson,** Valerie Babette Louise *Who 92*
**Hobson,** Walter Edmund 1949- *WhoFI 92*
**Hobson,** William D. 1908- *WhoBlA 92*
**Hobson-Pilot,** Ann *WhoEnt 92*
**Hobson-Simmons,** Joyce Ann 1947- *WhoBlA 92*
**Hobstetter,** John Norman 1917- *AmMWSc 92*
**Hoburg,** James Frederick 1946- *AmMWSc 92*
**Hobus,** Robert Allen 1924- *WhoRel 92*
**Hobuss,** Jim J. 1955- *WhoWest 92*
**Hoccleve,** Thomas 1368?-1426? *RfGEnL 91*
**Hocevar,** Gary 1951- *WhoAmP 91*
**Hoch,** Alan Randall 1948- *WhoWest 92*
**Hoch,** August 1868-1919 *BiInAmS*
**Hoch,** Edward D. *DrAPF 91*
**Hoch,** Edward D 1930- *IntAu&W 91, TwCSFW 91, WrDr 92*
**Hoch,** Frederic Louis 1920- *AmMWSc 92*
**Hoch,** Gary W. 1943- *WhoAmL 92*
**Hoch,** George Edward 1931- *AmMWSc 92*
**Hoch,** Harvey C *AmMWSc 92*
**Hoch,** Ivan Stewart 1935- *WhoEnt 92*
**Hoch,** James Alfred 1939- *AmMWSc 92*
**Hoch,** Margaret Ellen 1957- *WhoAmL 92*
**Hoch,** Michael 1923- *AmMWSc 92*
**Hoch,** Orion 1928- *IntWW 91*
**Hoch,** Orion L 1928- *AmMWSc 92*
**Hoch,** Orion Lindel 1928- *WhoFI 92, WhoWest 92*
**Hoch,** Paul Edwin 1920- *AmMWSc 92*
**Hoch,** Rand 1955- *WhoAmL 92, WhoAmP 91*
**Hoch,** Richmond Joel 1935- *AmMWSc 92*
**Hoch,** Sallie O'Neil 1941- *AmMWSc 92*
**Hoch,** William Henry 1944- *WhoWest 92*
**Hochachka,** Peter William 1937- *AmMWSc 92*
**Hochanadel,** Clarence Joseph 1916- *AmMWSc 92*
**Hochberg,** David Michael 1966- *WhoMW 92*
**Hochberg,** Frederick George 1913- *WhoFI 92, WhoWest 92*
**Hochberg,** Irving 1934- *AmMWSc 92*
**Hochberg,** Jerome 1925- *AmMWSc 92*
**Hochberg,** Joel Morton 1939- *WhoEnt 92, WhoFI 92, WhoMW 92*
**Hochberg,** Kenneth J 1950- *AmMWSc 92*
**Hochberg,** Melvin 1920- *AmMWSc 92*
**Hochberg,** Murray 1943- *AmMWSc 92*
**Hochberg,** Philip Robert 1940- *WhoAmL 92*
**Hochberg,** Victoria Greene 1952- *WhoEnt 92*
**Hochberg,** William David 1958- *WhoAmL 92*
**Hochberger,** John Richard 1960- *WhoWest 92*
**Hochbrueckner,** George 1938- *AlmAP 92 [port]*
**Hochbrueckner,** George Joseph 1938- *WhoAmP 91*
**Hoche,** Alfred 1865-1943 *EncTR 91*
**Hoche,** Philip A 1906- *WhoIns 92*
**Hochel,** Robert Charles 1944- *AmMWSc 92*
**Hochella,** Norman Joseph 1930- *AmMWSc 92*
**Hochgesang,** Michael John 1942- *WhoFI 92*
**Hochhalter,** Gordon Ray 1946- *WhoMW 92*
**Hochhaus,** Larry 1942- *AmMWSc 92*
**Hochhaus,** Pernola Jean 1944- *WhoAmP 91*
**Hochhauser,** Sheila 1951- *WhoAmP 91*
**Hochhauser,** Victor 1923- *Who 92*
**Hochheimer,** Bernard Ford 1929- *AmMWSc 92*
**Hochheimer,** Frank Leo 1943- *WhoFI 92*
**Hochheimer,** Laura 1933- *WhoEnt 92*
**Hochhuth,** Rolf 1931- *IntAu&W 91, IntWW 91*
**Hochman,** Alan Robert 1950- *WhoAmL 92*
**Hochman,** Barry David 1948- *WhoMW 92*
**Hochman,** Benjamin 1925- *AmMWSc 92*
**Hochman,** Harold Marvin 1936- *WhoFI 92*
**Hochman,** Jack M 1939- *AmMWSc 92*
**Hochman,** Jeffrey J. 1952- *WhoAmL 92*
**Hochman,** Kenneth George 1947- *WhoAmL 92*
**Hochman,** Larry 1953- *WhoEnt 92*
**Hochman,** Mark Nelson 1936- *WhoFI 92*
**Hochman,** Paula S 1953- *AmMWSc 92*
**Hochman,** Robert F 1928- *AmMWSc 92*
**Hochman,** Sandra *DrAPF 91*
**Hochman,** Sandra 1936- *ConPo 91, IntAu&W 91, WrDr 92*
**Hochmeister,** Angela Beth 1958- *WhoAmL 92*
**Hochmuth,** Robert Milo 1939- *AmMWSc 92*
**Hochschild,** Adam 1942- *IntAu&W 91*
**Hochschild,** Carroll Shepherd 1935- *WhoWest 92*
**Hochschild,** Gerhard P *AmMWSc 92*
**Hochschwender,** Herman Karl 1920- *WhoFI 92*
**Hochschwender,** Karl Albert 1927- *WhoFI 92*
**Hochstadt,** Harry 1925- *AmMWSc 92*
**Hochstadt,** Joy 1939- *AmMWSc 92*
**Hochstatter,** Harold *WhoAmP 91*
**Hochstein,** Herbert Donald 1929- *AmMWSc 92*
**Hochstein,** Lawrence I 1928- *AmMWSc 92*
**Hochstein,** Paul Eugene 1926- *AmMWSc 92*
**Hochstein,** Rolaine *DrAPF 91*
**Hochster,** Melvin 1943- *AmMWSc 92*
**Hochstetler,** Alan Ray 1939- *AmMWSc 92*
**Hochstetler,** Douglass Clifford 1952- *WhoAmL 92*
**Hochstetler,** Greg A. 1946- *WhoEnt 92*
**Hochstim,** Adolf R 1928- *AmMWSc 92*
**Hochstrasser,** Donald Lee 1927- *AmMWSc 92*
**Hochstrasser,** Robin 1931- *AmMWSc 92*
**Hochstrasser,** Robin Main 1931- *IntWW 91*
**Hochuli,** Urs Erwin 1927- *AmMWSc 92*
**Hochwald,** Gerald Martin 1932- *AmMWSc 92*
**Hochwalder,** Fritz 1911- *LiExTwC*
**Hochwalt,** Carroll Alonzo 1899- *AmMWSc 92*
**Hochwalt,** William Joseph 1955- *WhoFI 92*
**Hock,** Arthur George 1941- *AmMWSc 92*
**Hock,** Delwin D. 1935- *WhoWest 92*
**Hock,** Donald Charles 1929- *AmMWSc 92*
**Hock,** Frederick Wyeth 1924- *WhoAmL 92*
**Hock,** Mort 1929- *IntMPA 92*
**Hock,** Morton 1929- *WhoFI 92*
**Hock,** Robert Leroy, Jr. 1933- *WhoRel 92*
**Hock,** Ronald Francis 1944- *WhoRel 92*
**Hock,** Thomas Paul 1947- *WhoAmL 92*
**Hockaday,** Arthur 1926- *Who 92*
**Hockaday,** Irvine O., Jr. 1936- *WhoFI 92, WhoMW 92*
**Hocke,** Jean-Pierre 1938- *IntWW 91, Who 92*
**Hockel,** Gregory Martin 1950- *AmMWSc 92*
**Hockemeier,** J. Curt 1948- *WhoEnt 92*
**Hocken,** Robert John 1944- *AmMWSc 92*
**Hockenberry,** Terry Oliver 1938- *AmMWSc 92*
**Hockenbury,** Robert Wesley 1928- *AmMWSc 92*
**Hockenhull,** Arthur James Weston 1915- *Who 92*
**Hockensmith,** Robert Franklin, Jr. 1955- *WhoFI 92*
**Hocker,** Alexander *Who 92*
**Hocker,** Earl Wesley 1927- *WhoEnt 92*
**Hocker,** George Benjamin 1942- *AmMWSc 92*
**Hockert,** Barbara 1932- *WhoAmP 91*
**Hockett,** Bob 1925- *WhoAmP 91*
**Hockett,** Charles F. 1916- *IntWW 91, WrDr 92*
**Hockett,** Curtis Fredrick 1934- *WhoFI 92*
**Hockett,** Edwin Ralph 1950- *WhoMW 92*
**Hockey,** Elizabeth Greenslade 1958- *WhoMW 92*
**Hockin,** Thomas 1938- *IntWW 91*
**Hocking,** Anthony 1938- *WrDr 92*
**Hocking,** Drake 1940- *AmMWSc 92*
**Hocking,** Frederick Denison Maurice 1899- *Who 92*
**Hocking,** George Macdonald 1908- *AmMWSc 92*
**Hocking,** John Gilbert 1920- *AmMWSc 92*
**Hocking,** Martin Blake 1938- *AmMWSc 92*
**Hocking,** Mary 1921- *IntAu&W 91, WrDr 92*
**Hocking,** Philip Norman 1925- *Who 92*
**Hocking,** Ronald Raymond 1932- *AmMWSc 92*
**Hockle,** M. Henrietta *WhoRel 92*
**Hockley,** Anthony Heritage F. *Who 92*
**Hockley,** Raymond Alan 1929- *Who 92*
**Hockley,** Thomas d1892 *BiInAmS*
**Hockman,** Charles Henry 1923- *AmMWSc 92*
**Hockman,** Deborah C 1955- *AmMWSc 92*
**Hockman,** Deborah Charmaine 1955- *WhoMW 92*
**Hockman,** Karl Kalevi 1924- *WhoFI 92, WhoWest 92*
**Hockman,** Stephen Alexander 1947- *Who 92*
**Hockney,** David 1937- *FacFETw, IntWW 91, TwCPaSc, Who 92, WhoEnt 92, WhoWest 92*
**Hockney,** Richard L *AmMWSc 92*
**Hockstra,** Dale Jon 1948- *AmMWSc 92*
**Hocog,** Victor B *WhoAmP 91*
**Hocott,** C R 1909- *AmMWSc 92*
**Hocott,** Joe Bill 1921- *WhoFI 92*
**Hocq,** Nathalie 1951- *IntWW 91*
**Hocter,** William Joseph, Sr. 1934- *WhoMW 92*
**Hocutt,** Betty E 1939- *WhoAmP 91*
**Hocutt,** Charles H 1944- *AmMWSc 92*
**Hodam,** Helen *WhoEnt 92*
**Hodapp,** Larry Frank 1956- *WhoMW 92*
**Hodapp,** Leroy Charles 1923- *WhoMW 92, WhoRel 92*
**Hodapp,** Paul Francis 1943- *WhoWest 92*
**Hodde,** Melvin Dee 1960- *WhoMW 92*
**Hodder and Stoughton** *DcLB 106 [port]*
**Hodder,** Bramwell William 1923- *Who 92*
**Hodder,** Edwin Clifton 1955- *WhoWest 92*
**Hodder,** Kent Holmes 1956- *WhoEnt 92*
**Hodder,** Robert William 1932- *AmMWSc 92*
**Hodder,** Vincent MacKay 1927- *AmMWSc 92*
**Hodder-Williams,** Christopher 1926- *IntAu&W 91, TwCSFW 91, WrDr 92*
**Hodder-Williams,** Paul 1910- *Who 92*
**Hoddinott,** Alun 1929- *ConCom 92, IntWW 91, Who 92*
**Hoddinott,** Anthony Paul 1942- *Who 92*
**Hoddinott,** R. F. 1913- *WrDr 92*
**Hodeir,** Andre 1921- *ConAu 34NR*
**Hodel,** Donald Paul 1935- *IntWW 91, WhoAmP 91*
**Hodel,** Margaret Jones 1941- *AmMWSc 92*
**Hodel,** Richard Earl 1937- *AmMWSc 92*
**Hodemart,** Peter *IntAu&W 91X*
**Hodenpyl,** Eugene 1863-1910 *BiInAmS*
**Hodes,** Abram 1922- *WhoWest 92*
**Hodes,** Art 1904- *NewAmDM*
**Hodes,** Barbara 1941- *WhoMW 92*
**Hodes,** Louis 1934- *AmMWSc 92*
**Hodes,** Marion Edward 1925- *AmMWSc 92, WhoMW 92*
**Hodes,** Mel 1943- *WhoAmP 91*
**Hodes,** Paul William 1951- *WhoEnt 92*
**Hodes,** Philip J 1906- *AmMWSc 92*
**Hodes,** Richard S 1924- *WhoAmP 91*
**Hodes,** Robert Bernard 1925- *WhoAmL 92*
**Hodes,** Scott 1937- *WhoAmP 91, WhoFI 92*
**Hodes,** W. William 1943- *WhoAmL 92*
**Hodes,** William 1925- *AmMWSc 92*
**Hodes,** Zachary Isaac 1953- *WhoMW 92*
**Hodgart,** Matthew 1916- *WrDr 92*
**Hodgart,** Matthew John Caldwell 1916- *Who 92*
**Hodgden,** Lavinia Richards 1920- *WhoAmP 91*
**Hodgdon,** F E 1915- *AmMWSc 92*
**Hodgdon,** Harry Edward 1946- *AmMWSc 92*
**Hodgdon,** Russell Bates, Jr 1924- *AmMWSc 92*
**Hodgdon,** Shirley Lamson 1921- *WhoAmP 91*
**Hodge,** A Winston *WhoAmP 91*
**Hodge,** Abraham 1755-1805 *DcNCBi 3*
**Hodge,** Adele P. 1942- *WhoBlA 92*
**Hodge,** Al d1979 *LesBEnT 92*
**Hodge,** Alexander Mitchell 1916- *Who 92*
**Hodge,** Bartow 1920- *AmMWSc 92*
**Hodge,** Bobby Lynn 1956- *WhoFI 92*
**Hodge,** Charles 1797-1878 *BenetAL 91*
**Hodge,** Charles Forrest, III 1944- *WhoMW 92*
**Hodge,** Charles Mason 1938- *WhoBlA 92*
**Hodge,** Cynthia Elois 1947- *WhoBlA 92*
**Hodge,** Daniel B 1938- *AmMWSc 92*
**Hodge,** David 1909- *Who 92*
**Hodge,** David Charles 1931- *AmMWSc 92*
**Hodge,** David Phillips *WhoEnt 92*
**Hodge,** Dennis 1939- *AmMWSc 92*
**Hodge,** Derek M. 1941- *WhoBlA 92*
**Hodge,** Derek Michael 1941- *WhoAmP 91*
**Hodge,** Donald Ray 1939- *AmMWSc 92*
**Hodge,** Ernest M. *WhoBlA 92*
**Hodge,** Francis 1915- *WrDr 92*
**Hodge,** Frederick Allen 1939- *AmMWSc 92*
**Hodge,** Frederick Webb 1864-1956 *BenetAL 91*
**Hodge,** Harold Carpenter 1904- *AmMWSc 92*
**Hodge,** Ian Moir 1946- *AmMWSc 92*
**Hodge,** J. Lonnie *DrAPF 91*
**Hodge,** James Dwight 1933- *AmMWSc 92*
**Hodge,** James Edgar 1929- *AmMWSc 92*
**Hodge,** James Robert 1927- *WhoMW 92*
**Hodge,** James Thatcher 1816-1871 *BiInAmS*
**Hodge,** James William 1943- *Who 92*
**Hodge,** Jane Aiken 1917- *IntAu&W 91, WrDr 92*
**Hodge,** Janice Constance *WhoRel 92*
**Hodge,** Jesse Lynn 1942- *WhoRel 92*
**Hodge,** Jimmy L. 1947- *WhoRel 92*
**Hodge,** John Dennis 1929- *Who 92*
**Hodge,** John Edward 1914- *AmMWSc 92, WhoBlA 92*
**Hodge,** John Rowland 1913- *Who 92*
**Hodge,** Julian Stephen Alfred 1904- *Who 92*
**Hodge,** Marguerite V. 1920- *WhoBlA 92*
**Hodge,** Mary Ann 1941- *WhoWest 92*
**Hodge,** Norris 1927- *WhoBlA 92*
**Hodge,** Paget T. *WhoBlA 92*
**Hodge,** Patricia *IntWW 91*
**Hodge,** Patricia 1946- *IntMPA 92, Who 92*
**Hodge,** Paul William 1934- *AmMWSc 92, IntAu&W 91, WrDr 92*
**Hodge,** Philip G, Jr 1920- *AmMWSc 92*
**Hodge,** Ralph Wayne 1943- *WhoRel 92*
**Hodge,** Randall Ross 1956- *WhoAmL 92*
**Hodge,** Raymond 1922- *AmMWSc 92*
**Hodge,** Raymond Douglas 1951- *WhoRel 92*
**Hodge,** Regina Hazel 1963- *WhoRel 92*
**Hodge,** Robert White 1939- *WhoMW 92*
**Hodge,** Rusty Harvey 1962- *WhoWest 92*
**Hodge,** Steven McNiven 1942- *AmMWSc 92*
**Hodge,** T Shirby 1841-1926 *ScFEYrs*
**Hodge,** Thomas E *WhoAmP 91*
**Hodge,** W. J. *WhoBlA 92*
**Hodge,** William 1747?-1819? *DcNCBi 3*
**Hodge,** William Anthony 1962- *WhoBlA 92*
**Hodgen,** Gary Dean 1943- *AmMWSc 92*
**Hodgen,** John Thompson 1826-1882 *BiInAmS*
**Hodgen,** Mathew Earl 1964- *WhoRel 92*
**Hodges,** Agil Earl 1933- *WhoAmL 92*
**Hodges,** Albert Willfred 1914- *WhoEnt 92*
**Hodges,** Ann *WhoEnt 92*
**Hodges,** Billy Gene 1929- *AmMWSc 92*
**Hodges,** C Walter 1909- *IntAu&W 91, Who 92, WrDr 92*
**Hodges,** Carl Norris 1937- *AmMWSc 92*
**Hodges,** Carolyn Richardson 1947- *WhoBlA 92*
**Hodges,** Carroll Ann 1936- *AmMWSc 92*
**Hodges,** Charles Thomas 1951- *AmMWSc 92*
**Hodges,** Clarence Eugene 1939- *WhoAmP 91, WhoBlA 92*
**Hodges,** Clinton Frederick 1939- *AmMWSc 92*
**Hodges,** Cother L. 1920- *WhoBlA 92*
**Hodges,** Craig Anthony 1960- *WhoBlA 92*
**Hodges,** David A 1937- *AmMWSc 92*
**Hodges,** David Julian 1944- *WhoBlA 92*
**Hodges,** Dean T, Jr 1944- *AmMWSc 92*
**Hodges,** Donald Clark 1923- *WrDr 92*
**Hodges,** Doris M. 1915- *WrDr 92*
**Hodges,** Edward N., III 1920- *WhoBlA 92*
**Hodges,** Edwin Clair 1940- *WhoFI 92*
**Hodges,** Elaine Mary 1928- *Who 92*
**Hodges,** Elizabeth *DrAPF 91*
**Hodges,** Fletcher, III 1933- *WhoFI 92*
**Hodges,** Floyd Norman 1939- *AmMWSc 92*
**Hodges,** Gerald 1925- *Who 92*
**Hodges,** Gil 1924-1972 *FacFETw*
**Hodges,** Glenn R 1941- *AmMWSc 92*
**Hodges,** H Gaylord, Jr 1941- *WhoIns 92*
**Hodges,** Hardy M 1963- *AmMWSc 92*
**Hodges,** Harold Earl 1934- *WhoBlA 92*
**Hodges,** Harold T 1936- *WhoAmP 91*
**Hodges,** Harry Franklin 1933- *AmMWSc 92*
**Hodges,** Helen Leslie 1945- *AmMWSc 92*
**Hodges,** Helene 1949- *WhoBlA 92*
**Hodges,** Hollis *DrAPF 91*
**Hodges,** J. Alex 1941- *WhoEnt 92*
**Hodges,** James Hovis 1956- *WhoAmP 91*
**Hodges,** John Deavours 1937- *AmMWSc 92*
**Hodges,** John Hendricks 1914- *AmMWSc 92*
**Hodges,** John Herbert 1928- *AmMWSc 92*
**Hodges,** John O. 1944- *WhoBlA 92*
**Hodges,** John Oliver 1944- *WhoRel 92*
**Hodges,** Johnny 1906-1970 *NewAmDM*
**Hodges,** Joseph Lawson, Jr 1922- *AmMWSc 92*
**Hodges,** Joseph Thomas Charles 1932- *Who 92*
**Hodges,** Jot Holiver, Jr. 1932- *WhoAmL 92*
**Hodges,** Joy 1915- *WhoEnt 92*
**Hodges,** Joyce E *WhoAmP 91*
**Hodges,** Kaneaster, Jr *WhoAmP 91*
**Hodges,** Kristin Henderson 1962- *WhoEnt 92*
**Hodges,** Lance Thomas 1934- *AmMWSc 92*
**Hodges,** Laurent 1940- *AmMWSc 92*
**Hodges,** Lawrence H *AmMWSc 92*
**Hodges,** Lew 1956- *Who 92*
**Hodges,** Lewis 1918- *Who 92*
**Hodges,** Lillian Bernice 1939- *WhoBlA 92*
**Hodges,** Linda Carol 1951- *AmMWSc 92*
**Hodges,** Louis Wendell 1933- *WhoRel 92*
**Hodges,** Luther Hartwell 1898-1974 *DcNCBi 3*
**Hodges,** Margaret 1911- *IntAu&W 91, WrDr 92*
**Hodges,** Mark Willie 1923- *Who 92*
**Hodges,** Melvin Sancho 1940- *WhoBlA 92*

**Hodges**, Nancy Hutton 1933- *WhoAmP 91*
**Hodges**, Neal Howard, II 1948- *AmMWSc 92*
**Hodges**, Paul 1950- *TwCPaSc*
**Hodges**, Paul Joseph 1959- *WhoFI 92*
**Hodges**, Paul V, Jr 1913- *WhoAmP 91*
**Hodges**, Ralph B. 1930- *WhoAmL 92*
**Hodges**, Ralph Byron 1930- *WhoAmP 91*
**Hodges**, Ralph Richard, Jr 1933- *AmMWSc 92*
**Hodges**, Richard Andrew 1952- *Who 92*
**Hodges**, Richard Edwin 1928- *WhoWest 92*
**Hodges**, Robert Edgar 1922- *AmMWSc 92*
**Hodges**, Robert Stanley 1943- *AmMWSc 92*
**Hodges**, Ronald William 1934- *AmMWSc 92*
**Hodges**, Scott Dean 1952- *WhoMW 92*
**Hodges**, Sidney Edward 1924- *AmMWSc 92*
**Hodges**, Thomas Kent 1936- *AmMWSc 92*
**Hodges**, Virgil Hall 1936- *WhoBlA 92*
**Hodges**, Warner, III 1951- *WhoAmL 92*
**Hodges**, William Terrell 1934- *WhoAmL 92*
**Hodgetts**, Richard M. 1942- *WrDr 92*
**Hodgetts**, Robert Bartley 1918- *Who 92*
**Hodgetts**, Ross Birnie 1941- *AmMWSc 92*
**Hodgin**, Ezra Clay 1947- *AmMWSc 92*
**Hodgins**, Daniel Stephen 1939- *AmMWSc 92*
**Hodgins**, Eric 1899-1971 *BenetAL 91*
**Hodgins**, George Raymond 1926- *AmMWSc 92*
**Hodgins**, Grant Milton 1955- *WhoWest 92*
**Hodgins**, Jack 1938- *BenetAL 91, ConNov 91, WrDr 92*
**Hodgins**, Jack Stanley 1938- *WhoWest 92*
**Hodgins**, John Stanley 1938- *IntAu&W 91*
**Hodgins**, Michael Minden 1912- *Who 92*
**Hodgins**, Theodore Sylvester, III 1966- *WhoEnt 92*
**Hodgkin**, Alan 1914- *Who 92*
**Hodgkin**, Alan Lloyd 1914- *IntWW 91, WhoNob 90*
**Hodgkin**, Brian Charles 1941- *AmMWSc 92*
**Hodgkin**, C. Eliot 1905-1987 *TwCPaSc*
**Hodgkin**, Dorothy Crowfoot 1910- *IntWW 91, WhoNob 90*
**Hodgkin**, Dorothy Mary Crowfoot 1910- *Who 92*
**Hodgkin**, Douglas Irving 1939- *WhoAmP 91*
**Hodgkin**, Howard 1932- *CurBio 91 [port], FacFETw, IntWW 91, TwCPaSc, Who 92, WorArt 1980*
**Hodgkin**, Jonathan Alan 1949- *Who 92*
**Hodgkin**, Robin A. 1916- *WrDr 92*
**Hodgkins**, Christopher Joseph 1957- *WhoAmP 91*
**Hodgkins**, David John 1934- *Who 92*
**Hodgkins**, Earl Joseph 1916- *AmMWSc 92*
**Hodgkins**, Frances 1869-1947 *TwCPaSc*
**Hodgkins**, Henry Follett, Jr. 1928- *WhoFI 92*
**Hodgkins**, Russell Dearborn, Jr. 1958- *WhoWest 92*
**Hodgkinson**, Arthur Edward 1913- *Who 92*
**Hodgkinson**, Derek *Who 92*
**Hodgkinson**, Randall *WhoEnt 92*
**Hodgkinson**, Terence William Ivan 1913- *Who 92*
**Hodgkinson**, William Derek 1917- *Who 92*
**Hodgkinson**, William James 1939- *WhoFI 92*
**Hodgkiss**, Alan Geoffrey 1921- *IntAu&W 91, WrDr 92*
**Hodgkiss**, Anita Sue 1960- *WhoAmL 92*
**Hodgman**, David Renwick 1947- *WhoAmL 92*
**Hodgman**, Joan Elizabeth 1923- *AmMWSc 92*
**Hodgman**, Vicki Jean 1933- *WhoMW 92*
**Hodgson**, Adam Robin 1937- *Who 92*
**Hodgson**, Alfreda Rose 1940- *IntWW 91, Who 92*
**Hodgson**, Allan Archibald 1937- *WhoFI 92*
**Hodgson**, Arthur Brian 1916- *Who 92*
**Hodgson**, Arthur Clay 1907- *WhoAmL 92, WhoMW 92*
**Hodgson**, Carlton Roy 1930- *WhoBlA 92*
**Hodgson**, Carole 1940- *TwCPaSc*
**Hodgson**, Clive 1953- *TwCPaSc*
**Hodgson**, Derek *Who 92*
**Hodgson**, Derek John 1942- *AmMWSc 92*
**Hodgson**, Edward Shilling 1926- *AmMWSc 92*
**Hodgson**, Ernest 1932- *AmMWSc 92*
**Hodgson**, Esther Naomi 1915- *WhoAmP 91*
**Hodgson**, George Charles Day 1913- *Who 92*
**Hodgson**, Gordon Hewett 1929- *Who 92*
**Hodgson**, Gordon Wesley 1924- *AmMWSc 92*
**Hodgson**, Gregory Bernard 1946- *WhoWest 92*
**Hodgson**, Howard Osmond Paul 1950- *Who 92*
**Hodgson**, J William 1940- *AmMWSc 92*
**Hodgson**, Jacqueline Lou 1927- *WhoFI 92*
**Hodgson**, James 1925- *Who 92*
**Hodgson**, James B, Jr 1920- *AmMWSc 92*
**Hodgson**, James Day 1915- *IntWW 91, WhoAmP 91*
**Hodgson**, James Russell 1942- *AmMWSc 92*
**Hodgson**, John 1705?-1747 *DcNCBi 3*
**Hodgson**, John, II 1740?-1774 *DcNCBi 3*
**Hodgson**, John Bury 1912- *Who 92*
**Hodgson**, John Derek 1931- *Who 92*
**Hodgson**, John Lawrence *ScFEYrs*
**Hodgson**, Jonathan Peter Edward 1942- *AmMWSc 92*
**Hodgson**, Keith Owen 1947- *AmMWSc 92*
**Hodgson**, Kenneth P. 1945- *WhoWest 92*
**Hodgson**, Lynn Morrison 1948- *AmMWSc 92*
**Hodgson**, Maurice 1919- *Who 92*
**Hodgson**, Maurice Arthur Eric 1919- *IntWW 91*
**Hodgson**, Norman Donald 1946- *WhoMW 92*
**Hodgson**, Patricia Anne 1947- *Who 92*
**Hodgson**, Paul Edmund 1921- *AmMWSc 92*
**Hodgson**, Peter C. 1934- *WrDr 92*
**Hodgson**, Peter Crafts 1934- *IntAu&W 91, WhoRel 92*
**Hodgson**, Peter Edward 1928- *WrDr 92*
**Hodgson**, Phyllis 1909- *Who 92*
**Hodgson**, Ralph 1871-1962 *RfGEnL 91*
**Hodgson**, Richard 1855-1905 *BiInAmS*
**Hodgson**, Richard Holmes 1929- *AmMWSc 92*
**Hodgson**, Richard John Wesley 1941- *AmMWSc 92*
**Hodgson**, Robert Arnold 1924- *AmMWSc 92*
**Hodgson**, Robin Granville 1942- *Who 92*
**Hodgson**, Rodney 1939- *AmMWSc 92*
**Hodgson**, Stanley Ernest 1918- *Who 92*
**Hodgson**, Stephen Frederic 1938- *WhoMW 92*
**Hodgson**, Steven Sargeant 1956- *WhoRel 92*
**Hodgson**, Terence Harold Henry 1916- *Who 92*
**Hodgson**, Thom Joel 1938- *AmMWSc 92*
**Hodgson**, Thomas Richard 1941- *WhoFI 92, WhoMW 92*
**Hodgson**, Thomas Richard Burnham 1926- *Who 92*
**Hodgson**, Trevor 1931- *TwCPaSc*
**Hodgson**, Voigt R 1923- *AmMWSc 92*
**Hodgson**, Walter Derek 1917- *Who 92*
**Hodgson**, William Donald John 1923- *Who 92*
**Hodgson**, William Gordon 1929- *AmMWSc 92*
**Hodgson**, William Hope 1877-1918 *FacFETw, ScFEYrs, TwCSFW 91*
**Hodgson-Brooks**, Gloria J. 1942- *WhoBlA 92*
**Hodgson Steele**, Hilda Berneice 1911- *WhoMW 92*
**Hodin**, Josef Paul 1905- *IntAu&W 91, IntWW 91, Who 92, WrDr 92*
**Hodjat**, Yahya 1950- *WhoMW 92*
**Hodkin**, Hedley 1902- *Who 92*
**Hodkinson**, Henry Malcolm 1931- *Who 92*
**Hodkinson**, Judith Marie *Who 92*
**Hodkinson**, Sydney Phillip 1934- *WhoEnt 92*
**Hodkinson**, William d1991 *Who 92N*
**Hodnett**, Ernest Matelle 1914- *AmMWSc 92*
**Hodsden**, Albert Edward, III 1947- *WhoFI 92*
**Hodsdon**, Anne Collins 1953- *WhoFI 92*
**Hodsoll**, Francis S M 1938- *WhoAmP 91*
**Hodson**, Arthur *TwCWW 91*
**Hodson**, Charles Andrew 1947- *AmMWSc 92*
**Hodson**, Denys Fraser 1928- *Who 92*
**Hodson**, Frank 1921- *Who 92*
**Hodson**, Harold H, Jr 1939- *AmMWSc 92*
**Hodson**, Henry Vincent 1906- *IntAu&W 91, IntWW 91, Who 92, WrDr 92*
**Hodson**, Jean Turnbaugh 1920- *AmMWSc 92*
**Hodson**, Jimmy 1962- *WhoEnt 92*
**Hodson**, John 1946- *Who 92*
**Hodson**, Kenneth Allan 1954- *WhoAmL 92*
**Hodson**, Michael 1932- *Who 92*
**Hodson**, Phillip Harvey 1931- *AmMWSc 92, WhoMW 92*
**Hodson**, Robert Cleaves 1937- *AmMWSc 92*
**Hodson**, Thomas David Tattersall 1942- *Who 92*
**Hodson**, Thomas William 1946- *WhoMW 92*
**Hodson**, William Myron 1943- *AmMWSc 92*
**Hodur**, Francis 1866-1953 *RelLAm 91*
**Hodur**, Franciszek *DcAmImH*
**Hodza**, Fadil 1916- *IntWW 91*
**Hoe**, Richard March 1939- *WhoFI 92*
**Hoeben**, Richard Francis 1941- *WhoMW 92*
**Hoeberichts**, Joan Backer 1942- *WhoFI 92*
**Hoefakker**, Gilbert, Jr. 1933- *WhoMW 92, WhoRel 92*
**Hoefelmeyer**, Albert Bernard 1928- *AmMWSc 92*
**Hoefer**, Jacob A 1915- *AmMWSc 92*
**Hoefer**, Raymond H 1952- *AmMWSc 92*
**Hoefer**, Wolfgang Johannes Reinhard 1941- *AmMWSc 92*
**Hoefert**, Lynn Lucretia 1935- *AmMWSc 92*
**Hoeffding**, Wassily 1914- *AmMWSc 92*
**Hoeffe**, Dietmar 1942- *WhoRel 92*
**Hoeffel**, Joseph M, III 1950- *WhoAmP 91*
**Hoefflin**, Richard Michael 1949- *WhoAmL 92*
**Hoeffner**, Karol Ann 1952- *WhoEnt 92*
**Hoeffner**, William Karl 1965- *WhoFI 92*
**Hoefle**, Milton Louis 1922- *AmMWSc 92*
**Hoeflich**, Michael Harlan 1952- *WhoAmL 92*
**Hoefling**, Rudolf Joachim 1942- *WhoFI 92*
**Hoefling**, Virginia Ann 1931- *WhoAmL 92*
**Hoeflinger**, Norman Charles 1925- *WhoRel 92*
**Hoeft**, Arthur Peter 1945- *WhoWest 92*
**Hoeft**, Julius Albert 1946- *WhoFI 92*
**Hoeft**, Lothar Otto 1931- *AmMWSc 92*
**Hoeft**, Robert D. *DrAPF 91*
**Hoeft**, Robert Gene 1944- *AmMWSc 92*
**Hoeg**, Donald Francis 1931- *AmMWSc 92*
**Hoeg**, Jeffrey Michael *AmMWSc 92*
**Hoeg**, Thomas E 1953- *WhoIns 92*
**Hoegberg**, Lon Richard 1963- *WhoEnt 92*
**Hoegerman**, Stanton Fred 1944- *AmMWSc 92*
**Hoegger**, Erhard Fritz 1924- *AmMWSc 92*
**Hoegh**, Leo Arthur 1908- *WhoAmP 91*
**Hoeh**, Theodore J 1946- *WhoIns 92*
**Hoehn**, A J 1919- *AmMWSc 92*
**Hoehn**, G L 1925- *AmMWSc 92*
**Hoehn**, Harvey Herbert 1914- *AmMWSc 92*
**Hoehn**, Martha Vaughan 1951- *AmMWSc 92*
**Hoehn**, Marvin Martin 1920- *AmMWSc 92*
**Hoehn-Saric**, Rudolf 1929- *AmMWSc 92*
**Hoehne**, William Hermann, Jr. 1948- *WhoEnt 92*
**Hoehner**, Harold W. 1935- *WrDr 92*
**Hoehner**, Harold Walter 1935- *WhoRel 92*
**Hoehns**, Kenneth Wayne 1927- *WhoRel 92*
**Hoek**, Joannes Bernardus 1942- *AmMWSc 92*
**Hoekenga**, Mark T 1920- *AmMWSc 92*
**Hoekman**, Alvin James 1935- *WhoAmP 91*
**Hoekman**, Johan Bernard 1931- *IntWW 91, Who 92*
**Hoekman**, Theodore Bernard 1939- *AmMWSc 92*
**Hoeksema**, Herman, Jr 1920- *AmMWSc 92*
**Hoeksema**, Walter David 1942- *AmMWSc 92*
**Hoekstra**, John Junior 1929- *AmMWSc 92*
**Hoekstra**, Karl Egmond 1935- *AmMWSc 92*
**Hoekstra**, Paul Douglas 1961- *WhoEnt 92*
**Hoekstra**, William George 1928- *AmMWSc 92*
**Hoel**, David Gerhard 1939- *AmMWSc 92*
**Hoel**, Lester A 1935- *AmMWSc 92*
**Hoel**, Paul Gerhard 1905- *AmMWSc 92*
**Hoel**, Roger Satrang 1938- *WhoEnt 92, WhoMW 92*
**Hoel**, Sigurd 1890-1960 *LiExTwC*
**Hoelldobler**, Bert 1936- *ConAu 134*
**Hoellen**, John James 1914- *WhoAmL 92, WhoAmP 91*
**Hoelscher**, Gregory Paul 1955- *WhoFI 92*
**Hoelscher**, Ludwig 1907- *IntWW 91*
**Hoelzel**, Charles Bernard 1932- *AmMWSc 92*
**Hoelzel**, Kathleen M 1943- *WhoAmP 91*
**Hoelzeman**, Ronald G 1940- *AmMWSc 92*
**Hoen**, August 1817-1886 *BiInAmS*
**Hoene**, Robert Edward 1920- *WhoRel 92*
**Hoener**, Betty-ann 1946- *AmMWSc 92*
**Hoener**, Gordon J. 1931- *WhoMW 92*
**Hoener**, Walter Frederick, Jr. 1927- *WhoMW 92*
**Hoenes**, Delores M. 1945- *WhoFI 92*
**Hoenig**, Alan 1949- *AmMWSc 92*
**Hoenig**, Clarence L 1931- *AmMWSc 92*
**Hoenig**, Gerald Jay 1944- *WhoAmL 92*
**Hoenig**, J. 1916- *WrDr 92*
**Hoenig**, Michael Alexander 1952- *WhoEnt 92*
**Hoenig**, Scott 1957- *WhoFI 92*
**Hoenig**, Stuart Alfred 1928- *AmMWSc 92*
**Hoenigswald**, Henry M. 1915- *WrDr 92*
**Hoepfinger**, Lynn Morris 1941- *AmMWSc 92*
**Hoepner**, Erich 1886-1944 *EncTR 91 [port]*
**Hoeppner**, Conrad Henry 1928- *AmMWSc 92*
**Hoeppner**, David William 1935- *AmMWSc 92*
**Hoeppner**, Gerard Anthony 1953- *WhoEnt 92*
**Hoeppner**, Jerome John, Jr. 1922- *WhoMW 92*
**Hoeprich**, Paul Daniel 1924- *AmMWSc 92*
**Hoercher**, Henry E 1930- *AmMWSc 92*
**Hoerger**, Fred Donald 1929- *AmMWSc 92, WhoMW 92*
**Hoering**, Thomas Carl 1925- *AmMWSc 92*
**Hoerl**, Bryan G 1921- *AmMWSc 92*
**Hoerlein**, Alvin Bernard 1917- *AmMWSc 92*
**Hoerman**, Kirk Conklin 1924- *AmMWSc 92*
**Hoermann**, Edward Richard 1926- *WhoMW 92*
**Hoerneman**, Calvin A., Jr. 1940- *WhoFI 92, WhoMW 92*
**Hoerner**, George M, Jr 1929- *AmMWSc 92*
**Hoerner**, Robert Jack 1931- *WhoAmL 92*
**Hoerni**, Jean Amedee 1924- *WhoWest 92*
**Hoerr**, Frederic John 1952- *AmMWSc 92*
**Hoerr**, John P. 1930- *ConAu 135*
**Hoerr**, Lucile Marie *DcNCBi 3*
**Hoertz**, Charles David, Jr 1926- *AmMWSc 92*
**Hoerz**, Barry Scott 1956- *WhoRel 92*
**Hoeschele**, Guenther Kurt 1925- *AmMWSc 92*
**Hoeschele**, James David 1937- *WhoMW 92*
**Hoeschele**, Patrice Goeller 1959- *WhoMW 92*
**Hoese**, Hinton Dickson 1935- *AmMWSc 92*
**Hoesing**, Barbara Joan 1932- *WhoAmP 91*
**Hoesman**, Cindy Len 1958- *WhoMW 92*
**Hoess**, Rudolf Franz Ferdinand 1900-1947 *BiDExR*
**Hoessle**, Charles Herman 1931- *WhoMW 92*
**Hoets**, Pieter August 1946- *WhoFI 92*
**Hoetzsch**, Otto 1876-1946 *EncTR 91*
**Hoeve**, Cornelis Abraham Jacob 1924- *AmMWSc 92*
**Hoeve**, Heikobus Johannes Hubertus 1882-1918 *BiInAmS*
**Hoevel**, Michael James 1944- *WhoWest 92*
**Hoeveler**, William M. 1922- *WhoAmL 92*
**Hoewing**, Mark Wesley 1956- *WhoFI 92*
**Hoey**, Allen *DrAPF 91*
**Hoey**, Brian *IntAu&W 91*
**Hoey**, Catharine Letitia 1946- *Who 92*
**Hoey**, Clyde Roark 1877-1954 *DcNCBi 3*
**Hof**, Liselotte Bertha 1937- *AmMWSc 92*
**Hofacker**, Casar von 1896-1944 *EncTR 91 [port]*
**Hofeldt**, Fred Dan 1936- *AmMWSc 92*
**Hofer**, Charles Warren 1940- *WhoFI 92*
**Hofer**, Clifford Andrew 1911- *WhoAmP 91*
**Hofer**, Franz 1902-1975 *EncTR 91*
**Hofer**, Kenneth Emil 1934- *AmMWSc 92*
**Hofer**, Kurt Gabriel 1939- *AmMWSc 92*
**Hofer**, Lawrence John Edward 1915- *AmMWSc 92*
**Hofer**, Peter *ConAu 133*
**Hofer**, Robert D 1932- *WhoAmP 91*
**Hoferer**, Jeanne *WhoAmP 91*
**Hofert**, Edward Charles 1926- *WhoAmL 92*
**Hofert**, Jack 1930- *WhoWest 92*
**Hofert**, John Frederick 1935- *AmMWSc 92*
**Hoff**, Bert John 1934- *AmMWSc 92*
**Hoff**, Charles Jay 1937- *AmMWSc 92*
**Hoff**, Dale Richard 1927- *AmMWSc 92*
**Hoff**, Darrel Barton 1932- *AmMWSc 92*
**Hoff**, David Foster 1950- *WhoMW 92*
**Hoff**, David Lee 1942- *WhoMW 92*
**Hoff**, Gary Leroy 1946- *WhoMW 92*
**Hoff**, Gerhardt Michael 1930- *WhoIns 92*
**Hoff**, Gloria Thelma 1930- *AmMWSc 92*
**Hoff**, Harry Summerfield *Who 92, WrDr 92*
**Hoff**, Henry Frederick 1938- *AmMWSc 92*
**Hoff**, James Gaven 1935- *AmMWSc 92*
**Hoff**, Joan *ConAu 134*
**Hoff**, John C 1928- *AmMWSc 92*
**Hoff**, Jonathan Morind 1955- *WhoAmL 92*
**Hoff**, Kenneth Michael 1934- *AmMWSc 92*
**Hoff**, Lawrence Conrad 1929- *IntWW 91*
**Hoff**, Marcian Edward, Jr 1937- *AmMWSc 92*

**Hoff,** Margo 1912- *WorArt 1980 [port]*
**Hoff,** Marvin Dean 1936- *WhoRel 92*
**Hoff,** Michael Robert 1940- *WhoAmL 92*
**Hoff,** N J 1906- *AmMWSc 92*
**Hoff,** Nathaniel Hawthorne 1929- *WhoBlA 92*
**Hoff,** Philip Henderson 1924- *WhoAmP 91*
**Hoff,** Raymond E 1934- *AmMWSc 92*
**Hoff,** Richard William 1930- *AmMWSc 92*
**Hoff,** Robert Arthur 1957- *WhoWest 92*
**Hoff,** Syd 1912- *IntAu&W 91, WrDr 92*
**Hoff,** Timothy 1941- *WhoAmL 92*
**Hoff,** Victor John 1929- *AmMWSc 92*
**Hoff,** Wilford J, Jr 1928- *AmMWSc 92*
**Hoff,** William John 1926- *WhoMW 92*
**Hoff-Ginsberg,** Erika 1951- *WhoMW 92*
**Hoff-Wilson,** Joan *ConAu 134*
**Hoffa,** James R 1913-1975 *FacFETw*
**Hoffart,** Larry James 1946- *WhoWest 92*
**Hoffbeck,** Loren John 1932- *AmMWSc 92*
**Hoffberg,** Judith A. 1934- *WhoWest 92*
**Hoffberger,** Bruce Silver 1948- *WhoIns 92*
**Hoffbrand,** Victor 1935- *Who 92*
**Hoffecker,** Pamela Ruth Hobbs 1942- *IntAu&W 91*
**Hoffee,** Patricia Anne 1937- *AmMWSc 92*
**Hoffeld,** J Terrell 1946- *AmMWSc 92*
**Hoffelder,** Ann McIntosh 1935- *AmMWSc 92*
**Hoffenberg,** Raymond 1923- *IntWW 91, Who 92*
**Hoffenblum,** Allan Ernest 1940- *WhoWest 92*
**Hoffenstein,** Samuel 1890-1947 *BenetAL 91*
**Hoffer,** Abby 1918- *WhoEnt 92*
**Hoffer,** Abraham *AmMWSc 92*
**Hoffer,** Alan R *AmMWSc 92*
**Hoffer,** J A 1946- *AmMWSc 92*
**Hoffer,** Jerry M 1934- *AmMWSc 92*
**Hoffer,** Paul B 1939- *AmMWSc 92*
**Hoffer,** Roger M 1937- *AmMWSc 92*
**Hoffer,** Thomas Edward 1927- *AmMWSc 92*
**Hoffer,** Thomas Wayne 1963- *WhoMW 92*
**Hoffer,** Thomas William 1938- *WhoEnt 92*
**Hoffert,** J Stanley 1947- *WhoIns 92*
**Hoffert,** Jack Russell 1935- *AmMWSc 92*
**Hofferth,** Burt Frederick 1922- *AmMWSc 92*
**Hoffheimer,** Daniel Joseph 1950- *WhoMW 92*
**Hoffland,** Dorinda Ruth 1961- *WhoEnt 92*
**Hoffleit,** Ellen Dorrit 1907- *AmMWSc 92*
**Hoffler,** Richard Winfred, Jr. 1944- *WhoBlA 92*
**Hofflund,** Paul 1928- *WhoAmL 92*
**Hoffman,** Abbie 1936-1989 *ConAu 35NR, FacFETw, RComAH*
**Hoffman,** Adonis Edward 1954- *WhoAmL 92*
**Hoffman,** Alan Bruce 1941- *AmMWSc 92*
**Hoffman,** Alan Craig 1944- *WhoAmL 92*
**Hoffman,** Alan Jay 1948- *WhoAmL 92*
**Hoffman,** Alan Jerome 1924- *AmMWSc 92, IntWW 91*
**Hoffman,** Albert Charles 1938- *AmMWSc 92*
**Hoffman,** Alexander A J 1931- *AmMWSc 92*
**Hoffman,** Alice 1952- *ConAu 34NR, ConNov 91, IntAu&W 91, WrDr 92*
**Hoffman,** Allan Jordan 1925- *AmMWSc 92*
**Hoffman,** Allan Richard 1937- *AmMWSc 92*
**Hoffman,** Allan Sachs 1932- *AmMWSc 92, WhoWest 92*
**Hoffman,** Allan Stuart 1945- *WhoAmL 92*
**Hoffman,** Allen Herbert 1942- *AmMWSc 92*
**Hoffman,** Ann Marie 1958- *WhoMW 92*
**Hoffman,** Arlene Faun 1941- *AmMWSc 92*
**Hoffman,** Art *TwCWW 91*
**Hoffman,** Arthur W. 1921- *WrDr 92*
**Hoffman,** Barbara A 1940- *WhoAmP 91*
**Hoffman,** Basil 1941- *WhoEnt 92*
**Hoffman,** Bernard H. 1933- *WhoAmL 92*
**Hoffman,** Beth Lynn 1943- *WhoAmL 92*
**Hoffman,** Brian Mark 1941- *AmMWSc 92*
**Hoffman,** Bruce Perry 1957- *WhoWest 92*
**Hoffman,** C. Fenno, III 1958- *WhoWest 92*
**Hoffman,** Charles Fenno 1806-1884 *BenetAL 91*
**Hoffman,** Charles John 1918- *AmMWSc 92*
**Hoffman,** Chuck 1938- *WhoAmP 91*
**Hoffman,** Clark Samuel, Jr 1938- *AmMWSc 92*
**Hoffman,** Claud Milton 1931- *WhoWest 92*
**Hoffman,** Clyde Harris 1925- *WhoMW 92*
**Hoffman,** Craig Allan 1955- *WhoFI 92*
**Hoffman,** Cynthia L 1949- *WhoAmP 91*
**Hoffman,** Cyrus Miller 1942- *AmMWSc 92*
**Hoffman,** Dale A 1930- *AmMWSc 92*
**Hoffman,** Dan Clayton 1943- *WhoRel 92*
**Hoffman,** Daniel *DrAPF 91*
**Hoffman,** Daniel 1923- *BenetAL 91, ConPo 91, IntAu&W 91, WrDr 92*
**Hoffman,** Daniel A., III 1941- *WhoMW 92*
**Hoffman,** Daniel Lewis 1938- *AmMWSc 92*
**Hoffman,** Darleane Christian 1926- *AmMWSc 92, WhoWest 92*
**Hoffman,** David 1957- *WhoAmP 91*
**Hoffman,** David Allen 1944- *AmMWSc 92*
**Hoffman,** David J 1944- *AmMWSc 92*
**Hoffman,** David Llewellyn 1949- *WhoMW 92*
**Hoffman,** David Pollock 1934- *WhoRel 92*
**Hoffman,** David Robert 1954- *WhoMW 92*
**Hoffman,** Debra Carin 1960- *WhoEnt 92*
**Hoffman,** Dennis Mark 1947- *AmMWSc 92*
**Hoffman,** Dolores Garcia 1936- *WhoHisp 92*
**Hoffman,** Donald Alfred 1936- *WhoAmL 92*
**Hoffman,** Donald Bertrand 1939- *AmMWSc 92*
**Hoffman,** Donald David 1955- *WhoWest 92*
**Hoffman,** Donald Oliver 1916- *AmMWSc 92*
**Hoffman,** Donald Richard 1943- *AmMWSc 92*
**Hoffman,** Donald Stuart 1931- *WhoEnt 92*
**Hoffman,** Dorothea Heyl 1919- *AmMWSc 92*
**Hoffman,** Douglas Eric 1959- *WhoAmL 92*
**Hoffman,** Douglas Weir 1920- *AmMWSc 92*
**Hoffman,** Doyt K, Jr 1943- *AmMWSc 92*
**Hoffman,** Dustin 1937- *FacFETw, IntMPA 92*
**Hoffman,** Dustin Lee 1937- *IntWW 91, Who 92, WhoEnt 92*
**Hoffman,** Edward Fenno, III d1991 *NewYTBS 91*
**Hoffman,** Edward Jack 1925- *AmMWSc 92*
**Hoffman,** Edward Leland 1928- *WhoMW 92*
**Hoffman,** Edward Richard, III 1928- *WhoFI 92*
**Hoffman,** Edwin Philip 1942- *WhoFI 92, WhoMW 92*
**Hoffman,** Elaine Janet 1925- *WhoWest 92*
**Hoffman,** Elliot Lee 1930- *WhoEnt 92*
**Hoffman,** Emil 1866-1926 *RelLAm 91*
**Hoffman,** Eric Alfred 1951- *AmMWSc 92*
**Hoffman,** Eugene James 1935- *AmMWSc 92*
**Hoffman,** Eva 1945- *LiExTwC*
**Hoffman,** Everett John 1908- *AmMWSc 92*
**Hoffman,** F E 1927- *AmMWSc 92*
**Hoffman,** Frank Lloyd 1956- *WhoWest 92*
**Hoffman,** Frank Thomas 1958- *WhoMW 92*
**Hoffman,** Frederick 1937- *AmMWSc 92*
**Hoffman,** Frederick William, IV 1951- *WhoAmP 91*
**Hoffman,** G W 1928- *AmMWSc 92*
**Hoffman,** Gary Michael 1946- *WhoEnt 92*
**Hoffman,** Gene Louis 1932- *WhoAmP 91*
**Hoffman,** George Alan 1937- *WhoWest 92*
**Hoffman,** George Henry, Jr. 1924- *WhoRel 92*
**Hoffman,** George Michael 1943- *WhoMW 92*
**Hoffman,** George R 1935- *AmMWSc 92*
**Hoffman,** George Seixas 1941- *WhoFI 92*
**Hoffman,** Gerald Leon 1947- *WhoMW 92*
**Hoffman,** Gerald M 1926- *AmMWSc 92*
**Hoffman,** Glenn Lyle 1918- *AmMWSc 92*
**Hoffman,** Gloria Levy 1933- *IntAu&W 91, WhoFI 92*
**Hoffman,** Grace 1925- *IntWW 91*
**Hoffman,** H W 1923- *AmMWSc 92*
**Hoffman,** Harold A 1930- *AmMWSc 92*
**Hoffman,** Harold Maurice 1929- *WhoAmL 92*
**Hoffman,** Heiner 1919- *AmMWSc 92*
**Hoffman,** Henry Allen, Jr 1920- *AmMWSc 92*
**Hoffman,** Henry Harland 1922- *AmMWSc 92*
**Hoffman,** Henry Tice, Jr 1925- *AmMWSc 92*
**Hoffman,** Herbert I 1925- *AmMWSc 92*
**Hoffman,** Howard Edgar 1926- *AmMWSc 92*
**Hoffman,** Howard Torrens 1923- *AmMWSc 92*
**Hoffman,** Ira Eliot 1952- *WhoAmL 92*
**Hoffman,** Irwin 1924- *WhoEnt 92*
**Hoffman,** Jack J. 1935- *WhoWest 92*
**Hoffman,** Jacob Matthew, Jr 1944- *AmMWSc 92*
**Hoffman,** Jacqueline Louise 1952- *AmMWSc 92*
**Hoffman,** James Irvie 1941- *AmMWSc 92*
**Hoffman,** James Irvie, III 1941- *WhoMW 92*
**Hoffman,** James Paul 1943- *WhoAmL 92, WhoMW 92*
**Hoffman,** James R. 1932- *WhoMW 92, WhoRel 92*
**Hoffman,** James Tracy 1935- *AmMWSc 92*
**Hoffman,** Jane *WhoEnt 92*
**Hoffman,** Janet N. 1936- *WhoMW 92*
**Hoffman,** Jay C *WhoAmP 91*
**Hoffman,** Jeffrey Alan 1944- *AmMWSc 92*
**Hoffman,** Jerry C 1943- *AmMWSc 92*
**Hoffman,** Jerry Irwin 1935- *WhoMW 92*
**Hoffman,** Jill *DrAPF 91*
**Hoffman,** Joan Bentley 1946- *WhoMW 92*
**Hoffman,** Joe Douglas 1934- *AmMWSc 92*
**Hoffman,** Joel Elihu 1937- *WhoAmL 92*
**Hoffman,** Joel Harvey 1953- *WhoEnt 92*
**Hoffman,** John D 1922- *AmMWSc 92*
**Hoffman,** John Ernest, Jr. 1934- *WhoAmL 92*
**Hoffman,** John Fletcher 1946- *WhoAmL 92*
**Hoffman,** John Harold 1929- *AmMWSc 92*
**Hoffman,** John Harry 1913- *WhoMW 92*
**Hoffman,** John L 1930- *WhoIns 92*
**Hoffman,** John Raleigh 1926- *AmMWSc 92*
**Hoffman,** John Robert 1920- *WhoAmL 92*
**Hoffman,** John Russell 1953- *WhoWest 92*
**Hoffman,** John Wayne 1947- *WhoWest 92*
**Hoffman,** Jonathan Marshall 1948- *WhoAmL 92*
**Hoffman,** Joseph 1909- *IntMPA 92*
**Hoffman,** Joseph Ellsworth, Jr 1935- *AmMWSc 92*
**Hoffman,** Joseph Frederick 1925- *AmMWSc 92*
**Hoffman,** Joseph Irvine, Jr. 1939- *WhoBlA 92*
**Hoffman,** Joyce N 1952- *WhoIns 92*
**Hoffman,** Julien Ivor Ellis 1925- *AmMWSc 92*
**Hoffman,** Julius 1921- *AmMWSc 92*
**Hoffman,** Julius R 1919- *AmMWSc 92*
**Hoffman,** Karla Leigh 1948- *AmMWSc 92*
**Hoffman,** Kenneth Charles 1933- *AmMWSc 92*
**Hoffman,** Kenneth Myron 1930- *AmMWSc 92*
**Hoffman,** Kenneth Wayne 1955- *AmMWSc 92*
**Hoffman,** Lance J 1942- *AmMWSc 92*
**Hoffman,** Larry J. 1930- *WhoAmL 92*
**Hoffman,** Larry Ronald 1936- *AmMWSc 92*
**Hoffman,** Lee 1932- *IntAu&W 91, TwCSFW 91, TwCWW 91, WrDr 92*
**Hoffman,** Linda M 1939- *AmMWSc 92*
**Hoffman,** Lois Wladis 1929- *WhoMW 92*
**Hoffman,** Loren Harold 1941- *AmMWSc 92*
**Hoffman,** Lyman F 1950- *WhoAmP 91*
**Hoffman,** Malvina 1887-1966 *FacFETw*
**Hoffman,** Malvina Cornell 1887-1966 *HanAmWH*
**Hoffman,** Manny *WhoAmP 91*
**Hoffman,** Marion Marie 1934- *WhoAmP 91*
**Hoffman,** Mark Leslie 1952- *WhoEnt 92*
**Hoffman,** Mark Peter 1941- *AmMWSc 92, WhoMW 92*
**Hoffman,** Marvin Morrison 1925- *AmMWSc 92*
**Hoffman,** Michael Charles 1947- *WhoMW 92*
**Hoffman,** Michael Duncan 1945- *WhoAmL 92*
**Hoffman,** Michael G 1952- *AmMWSc 92*
**Hoffman,** Michael J. 1939- *WrDr 92*
**Hoffman,** Michael Jerome 1939- *WhoWest 92*
**Hoffman,** Michael K 1941- *AmMWSc 92*
**Hoffman,** Michael Richard 1939- *IntWW 91, Who 92*
**Hoffman,** Michael William 1955- *WhoAmL 92*
**Hoffman,** Milton Bernard 1946- *WhoEnt 92, WhoFI 92, WhoWest 92*
**Hoffman,** Mitchell Wade 1954- *WhoFI 92*
**Hoffman,** Morton Z 1935- *AmMWSc 92*
**Hoffman,** Myron A 1930- *AmMWSc 92*
**Hoffman,** Nancy 1933- *WhoAmL 92*
**Hoffman,** Nancy E. 1944- *WhoAmL 92*
**Hoffman,** Nelson Miles, III 1948- *AmMWSc 92*
**Hoffman,** Norman 1922- *WhoIns 92*
**Hoffman,** Norman Edwin 1928- *AmMWSc 92, WhoMW 92*
**Hoffman,** Patricia Ann 1953- *WhoFI 92*
**Hoffman,** Patricia Patrick 1925- *WhoMW 92*
**Hoffman,** Paul Gray 1891-1974 *AmPeW*
**Hoffman,** Paul Maxim Laurence 1942- *Who 92*
**Hoffman,** Paul Ned 1947- *AmMWSc 92*
**Hoffman,** Paul Roger 1934- *AmMWSc 92*
**Hoffman,** Peter Toll 1946- *WhoAmL 92*
**Hoffman,** Philip Andrew 1931- *WhoMW 92*
**Hoffman,** Philip Donald 1932- *WhoMW 92*
**Hoffman,** Philip E 1951- *WhoAmP 91*
**Hoffman,** Philip Edward 1951- *WhoMW 92*
**Hoffman,** Rand 1954- *WhoEnt 92*
**Hoffman,** Richard *DrAPF 91*
**Hoffman,** Richard 1831-1909 *NewAmDM*
**Hoffman,** Richard Bruce 1936- *AmMWSc 92*
**Hoffman,** Richard George 1949- *WhoMW 92*
**Hoffman,** Richard Laird 1939- *AmMWSc 92*
**Hoffman,** Richard Lawrence 1927- *AmMWSc 92*
**Hoffman,** Richard M. 1942- *WhoAmL 92*
**Hoffman,** Richard Otto 1939- *AmMWSc 92*
**Hoffman,** Richard Wagner 1927- *AmMWSc 92*
**Hoffman,** Roald 1937- *WhoNob 90*
**Hoffman,** Robert *WhoAmP 91*
**Hoffman,** Robert 1928- *AmMWSc 92*
**Hoffman,** Robert A 1919- *AmMWSc 92*
**Hoffman,** Robert A 1934- *AmMWSc 92*
**Hoffman,** Robert B 1947- *WhoIns 92*
**Hoffman,** Robert E 1924- *WhoAmP 91*
**Hoffman,** Robert Frank 1935- *AmMWSc 92*
**Hoffman,** Robert M 1944- *AmMWSc 92*
**Hoffman,** Robert Vernon 1944- *AmMWSc 92*
**Hoffman,** Rodney Joseph 1950- *WhoWest 92*
**Hoffman,** Roger Alan 1924- *AmMWSc 92*
**Hoffman,** Roger Allen 1915- *AmMWSc 92*
**Hoffman,** Ronald 1941- *ConAu 133*
**Hoffman,** Ruth I 1925- *AmMWSc 92*
**Hoffman,** S. Mark 1953- *WhoEnt 92*
**Hoffman,** Stanley Harold 1917- *Who 92*
**Hoffman,** Stanley John 1935- *WhoFI 92*
**Hoffman,** Sue Ellen 1945- *WhoMW 92*
**Hoffman,** Susan Katz 1949- *WhoAmL 92*
**Hoffman,** Suzanne Elizabeth 1963- *WhoMW 92*
**Hoffman,** T W 1931- *AmMWSc 92*
**Hoffman,** Theodore P 1929- *AmMWSc 92*
**Hoffman,** Thomas 1947- *AmMWSc 92*
**Hoffman,** Thomas R 1923- *AmMWSc 92*
**Hoffman,** Valerie Jane 1953- *WhoAmL 92*
**Hoffman,** Walter Edward 1907- *WhoAmL 92*
**Hoffman,** Walter James 1846-1899 *BiInAmS*
**Hoffman,** Warren E 1923- *AmMWSc 92*
**Hoffman,** Warren Eugene, II 1954- *WhoWest 92*
**Hoffman,** Wayne Larry 1937- *AmMWSc 92*
**Hoffman,** Wayne Melvin 1923- *WhoWest 92*
**Hoffman,** William *DrAPF 91*
**Hoffman,** William Andrew, Jr 1928- *AmMWSc 92*
**Hoffman,** William Brian 1951- *WhoAmL 92*
**Hoffman,** William Charles 1919- *AmMWSc 92, WhoWest 92*
**Hoffman,** William E 1946- *AmMWSc 92*
**Hoffman,** William F 1929- *AmMWSc 92*
**Hoffman,** William G 1937- *WhoIns 92*
**Hoffman,** William George 1939- *WhoFI 92*
**Hoffman,** William Hubert *AmMWSc 92*
**Hoffman,** William Kenneth 1924- *WhoMW 92*
**Hoffman,** William M. *DrAPF 91*
**Hoffman,** William M 1939- *IntAu&W 91, WhoEnt 92, WrDr 92*
**Hoffman,** William Marvin 1939- *WhoAmL 92*
**Hoffman-Biegel,** Sharon Irene 1965- *WhoFI 92*
**Hoffman-Bright,** Betty Ann 1921- *WhoAmP 91*
**Hoffman-Goetz,** Laurie *AmMWSc 92*
**Hoffman-Ladd,** Valerie Jon 1954- *WhoRel 92*
**Hoffmann,** Andrew W. *WhoRel 92*
**Hoffmann,** Ann Marie 1930- *WrDr 92*
**Hoffmann,** Arnold, Jr. d1991 *NewYTBS 91*
**Hoffmann,** Bob 1960- *WhoEnt 92*
**Hoffmann,** Bruce 1947- *WhoAmP 91*
**Hoffmann,** Carol Tomb 1952- *WhoFI 92*
**Hoffmann,** Christoph Ludwig 1944- *WhoFI 92*
**Hoffmann,** Conrad Edmund 1920- *AmMWSc 92*
**Hoffmann,** Daniel 1912- *IntAu&W 91*
**Hoffmann,** Dietrich 1924- *AmMWSc 92*
**Hoffmann,** Donald 1933- *IntAu&W 91, WrDr 92*
**Hoffmann,** E.T.A. 1776-1822 *NewAmDM, ScFEYrs*
**Hoffmann,** Edward Marker 1934- *AmMWSc 92*

**Hoffmann,** Evan Keith 1960- *WhoFI 92*
**Hoffmann,** Friedrich 1832-1904 *BiInAmS*
**Hoffmann,** Geoffrey William 1944- *AmMWSc 92*
**Hoffmann,** George Robert 1946- *AmMWSc 92*
**Hoffmann,** Harrison Adolph 1910- *AmMWSc 92*
**Hoffmann,** Heather Lynn 1961- *WhoMW 92*
**Hoffmann,** Heinrich 1885-1957 *EncTR 91 [port]*
**Hoffmann,** James *WhoEnt 92*
**Hoffmann,** Joan Carol 1934- *AmMWSc 92*
**Hoffmann,** Jon Arnold 1942- *AmMWSc 92, WhoWest 92*
**Hoffmann,** Josef 1870-1956 *DcTwDes, FacFETw*
**Hoffmann,** Joseph John 1950- *AmMWSc 92*
**Hoffmann,** Kathleen Ruth 1949- *WhoFI 92*
**Hoffmann,** Leonard Hubert 1934- *Who 92*
**Hoffmann,** Linda 1959- *WhoAmL 92*
**Hoffmann,** Louis Gerhard 1932- *AmMWSc 92*
**Hoffmann,** Malcolm A. 1912- *WrDr 92*
**Hoffmann,** Malcolm Arthur 1912- *WhoAmL 92*
**Hoffmann,** Manfred Walter 1938- *WhoFI 92*
**Hoffmann,** Martin R. 1932- *IntWW 91, WhoAmL 92*
**Hoffmann,** Martin Richard 1932- *WhoFI 92*
**Hoffmann,** Michael K 1939- *AmMWSc 92*
**Hoffmann,** Michael Richard 1947- *WhoAmL 92*
**Hoffmann,** Michael Robert 1946- *AmMWSc 92*
**Hoffmann,** Nancy Larraine 1947- *WhoAmP 91*
**Hoffmann,** Oswald Carl Julius 1913- *WhoRel 92*
**Hoffmann,** Peggy 1910- *WrDr 92*
**Hoffmann,** Peter 1930- *WrDr 92*
**Hoffmann,** Philip Craig 1936- *AmMWSc 92*
**Hoffmann,** Richard John 1946- *AmMWSc 92*
**Hoffmann,** Roald *DrAPF 91*
**Hoffmann,** Roald 1937- *AmMWSc 92, IntWW 91, Who 92*
**Hoffmann,** Robert Millard 1946- *WhoRel 92*
**Hoffmann,** Robert Shaw 1929- *AmMWSc 92*
**Hoffmann,** Stanley 1928- *WrDr 92*
**Hoffmann,** Thomas Russell 1933- *AmMWSc 92*
**Hoffmann,** Wayne Thomas 1955- *WhoMW 92*
**Hoffmann,** William Frederick 1933- *AmMWSc 92, WhoWest 92*
**Hoffmann-Pinther,** Peter Hugo 1935- *AmMWSc 92*
**Hoffmaster,** Donald Edeburn 1911- *AmMWSc 92*
**Hoffmaster,** Nancy Jo Clement 1940- *WhoWest 92*
**Hoffmeister,** Bertram Meryl 1907- *Who 92*
**Hoffmeister,** Donald F 1916- *IntAu&W 91*
**Hoffmeister,** Donald Frederick 1916- *AmMWSc 92, WrDr 92*
**Hoffmeister,** Franz Anton 1754-1812 *NewAmDM*
**Hoffmeister,** Gerhart 1936- *WhoWest 92*
**Hoffmeyer,** Erik 1924- *IntWW 91*
**Hoffmeyer,** William Frederick 1936- *WhoAmL 92*
**Hoffner,** David Michael 1956- *WhoEnt 92*
**Hoffner,** Serenus Paul 1946- *WhoAmP 91*
**Hoffnung,** Gerard 1925-1959 *NewAmDM, TwCPaSc*
**Hoffsommer,** John C 1932- *AmMWSc 92*
**Hoffstein,** Victor 1942- *AmMWSc 92*
**Hofhaimer,** Paul 1459-1537 *NewAmDM*
**Hofland,** John Allen 1947- *WhoMW 92*
**Hoflehner,** Rudolf 1916- *IntWW 91*
**Hofling,** Charles K 1920-1980 *ConAu 34NR*
**Hofman,** Elaine 1937- *WhoAmP 91*
**Hofman,** Emil Thomas 1921- *AmMWSc 92*
**Hofman,** Leonard John 1928- *WhoMW 92, WhoRel 92*
**Hofman,** Pieter A. 1946- *WhoEnt 92*
**Hofman,** Sam 1928- *WhoAmP 91*
**Hofman,** Wendell Fey 1942- *AmMWSc 92*
**Hofmann,** Alan Frederick 1931- *AmMWSc 92, WhoWest 92*
**Hofmann,** Albrecht Werner 1939- *AmMWSc 92*
**Hofmann,** Bo 1953- *AmMWSc 92*
**Hofmann,** Charles Bartholomew 1939- *AmMWSc 92*
**Hofmann,** Corris Mabelle 1915- *AmMWSc 92*
**Hofmann,** David John 1937- *AmMWSc 92*
**Hofmann,** Frederick Gustave 1923- *AmMWSc 92*
**Hofmann,** George Michael 1958- *WhoFI 92*
**Hofmann,** Gunter August George 1935- *AmMWSc 92*
**Hofmann,** Hans 1923- *WhoRel 92*
**Hofmann,** James Gerard 1952- *WhoFI 92*
**Hofmann,** John Richard, Jr. 1922- *WhoAmL 92*
**Hofmann,** Josef 1876-1957 *NewAmDM*
**Hofmann,** Julius Valentine 1882-1965 *DcNCBi 3*
**Hofmann,** Karl Heinrich 1932- *AmMWSc 92*
**Hofmann,** Klaus 1911- *IntWW 91*
**Hofmann,** Klaus Heinrich 1911- *AmMWSc 92*
**Hofmann,** Lenat 1934- *AmMWSc 92*
**Hofmann,** Lorenz M 1937- *AmMWSc 92*
**Hofmann,** Michael 1957- *ConPo 91, IntAu&W 91, WrDr 92*
**Hofmann,** Peter 1944- *IntWW 91*
**Hofmann,** Peter L 1925- *AmMWSc 92*
**Hofmann,** Peter Ludwig 1925- *WhoMW 92*
**Hofmann,** Theo 1924- *AmMWSc 92*
**Hofmann,** Werner 1928- *IntWW 91*
**Hofmannsthal,** Hugo von 1874-1929 *FacFETw, NewAmDM*
**Hofmaster,** Richard Namon 1915- *AmMWSc 92*
**Hofmeister,** Paul Emil Julius 1909- *IntWW 91*
**Hofmekler,** Ori 1952- *IntWW 91*
**Hofmeyr,** Murray 1925- *IntWW 91*
**Hofmeyr,** Murray Bernard 1925- *Who 92*
**Hofreiter,** Bernard T 1924- *AmMWSc 92*
**Hofreiter,** Bernard Theodore 1924- *WhoMW 92*
**Hofrenning,** Daniel James Brown 1958- *WhoMW 92*
**Hofrenning,** James Bernard 1926- *WhoRel 92*
**Hofrichter,** Charles Henry 1914- *AmMWSc 92*
**Hofrichter,** David Alan 1948- *WhoMW 92*
**Hofrichter,** Harry James 1943- *AmMWSc 92*
**Hofslund,** Pershing Benard 1918- *AmMWSc 92*
**Hofsommer,** Donovan Lowell 1938- *WhoMW 92*
**Hofstadter,** Douglas 1945- *WrDr 92*
**Hofstadter,** Richard 1916-1970 *RComAH*
**Hofstadter,** Robert d1990 *IntWW 91N, Who 92N*
**Hofstadter,** Robert 1915- *AmMWSc 92, WhoNob 90*
**Hofstadter,** Robert 1915-1990 *AnObit 1990, CurBio 91N, FacFETw*
**Hofstatter,** Peter R. 1913- *IntWW 91*
**Hofstead,** James Warner 1913- *WhoFI 92*
**Hofstede,** Geert *ConAu 35NR*
**Hofstede,** Geert H. *ConAu 35NR*
**Hofstede,** Gerard H 1928- *ConAu 35NR*
**Hofstein,** David Neal 1951- *WhoAmL 92*
**Hofstetter,** Benita 1955- *WhoEnt 92*
**Hofstetter,** Edward 1932- *AmMWSc 92*
**Hofstetter,** Henry W 1914- *AmMWSc 92, WrDr 92*
**Hofstetter,** Kenneth John 1940- *AmMWSc 92*
**Hofstetter,** Ronald Harold 1939- *AmMWSc 92*
**Hofstra,** Gerald 1938- *AmMWSc 92*
**Hofstra,** Hendrik Jan 1904- *IntWW 91*
**Hoft,** Richard Gibson 1926- *AmMWSc 92*
**Hoga,** Takashi *LesBEnT 92*
**Hogaboam,** George Joseph 1919- *AmMWSc 92*
**Hogan,** Aden Ellsworth, Jr. 1951- *WhoWest 92*
**Hogan,** Aloysius Joseph, Jr 1928- *AmMWSc 92*
**Hogan,** Arthur James 1940- *WhoFI 92*
**Hogan,** Ben 1912- *FacFETw*
**Hogan,** Ben W. 1912- *IntWW 91*
**Hogan,** Beverly Wade 1951- *WhoBlA 92*
**Hogan,** Carolyn Ann 1944- *WhoBlA 92*
**Hogan,** Christopher James 1957- *AmMWSc 92*
**Hogan,** Clarence Lester 1920- *AmMWSc 92, WhoWest 92*
**Hogan,** Claude Hollis 1920- *WhoAmL 92*
**Hogan,** Cliff *DrAPF 91*
**Hogan,** Curtis Jule 1926- *WhoFI 92, WhoWest 92*
**Hogan,** Dennis Charles 1964- *WhoAmP 91*
**Hogan,** Desmond 1950- *ConNov 91, IntAu&W 91, WrDr 92*
**Hogan,** Edward L 1932- *AmMWSc 92*
**Hogan,** Edward Patrick 1939- *WhoMW 92*
**Hogan,** Eileen 1946- *TwCPaSc*
**Hogan,** Ernest 1865-1909 *NewAmDM*
**Hogan,** Fannie Burrell *WhoBlA 92*
**Hogan,** G W *WhoAmP 91*
**Hogan,** Gary D 1949- *AmMWSc 92*
**Hogan,** Guy T 1933- *AmMWSc 92*
**Hogan,** Harlan Robert 1946- *WhoEnt 92*
**Hogan,** Henry Algernon Vickers 1909- *Who 92*
**Hogan,** James B 1919- *WhoAmP 91*
**Hogan,** James C 1939- *AmMWSc 92*
**Hogan,** James Carroll, Jr. 1939- *WhoBlA 92*
**Hogan,** James J 1937- *AmMWSc 92*
**Hogan,** James Joseph 1941- *AmMWSc 92*
**Hogan,** James Michael 1946- *WhoFI 92*
**Hogan,** James P 1941- *IntAu&W 91, TwCSFW 91, WrDr 92*
**Hogan,** John A. *WhoBlA 92*
**Hogan,** John D 1927- *WhoIns 92*
**Hogan,** John Donald 1927- *WhoFI 92*
**Hogan,** John Edward *WhoAmP 91*
**Hogan,** John Frederick 1951- *WhoFI 92*
**Hogan,** John Paul 1919- *AmMWSc 92*
**Hogan,** John Thomas 1941- *AmMWSc 92*
**Hogan,** John Wesley 1936- *AmMWSc 92*
**Hogan,** Joseph C 1922- *AmMWSc 92*
**Hogan,** Judy *DrAPF 91*
**Hogan,** Katherine A. 1951- *WhoAmL 92*
**Hogan,** Kay *DrAPF 91*
**Hogan,** Le Moyne 1926- *AmMWSc 92*
**Hogan,** Linda *DrAPF 91*
**Hogan,** Linda 1947- *BenetAL 91, TwCWW 91, WrDr 92*
**Hogan,** Michael *DrAPF 91*
**Hogan,** Michael 1943- *ConAu 34NR*
**Hogan,** Michael Arthur 1931- *WhoMW 92*
**Hogan,** Michael Edward 1951- *AmMWSc 92*
**Hogan,** Michael Henry 1927- *Who 92*
**Hogan,** Michael Ray 1953- *WhoMW 92*
**Hogan,** Molly 1945- *WhoEnt 92*
**Hogan,** Morris Bernard 1902- *WhoAmP 91*
**Hogan,** Ogelia M. 1904- *WhoBlA 92*
**Hogan,** Patrick Colm 1957- *ConAu 134*
**Hogan,** Paul *IntWW 91, WhoEnt 92*
**Hogan,** Paul 1939- *IntMPA 92*
**Hogan,** Paul Francis 1950- *WhoFI 92*
**Hogan,** Pendleton 1907- *IntAu&W 91*
**Hogan,** Philip 1925- *AmMWSc 92*
**Hogan,** Ray 1908- *IntAu&W 91, TwCWW 91, WrDr 92*
**Hogan,** Robert 1930- *IntAu&W 91, WrDr 92*
**Hogan,** Ronald P. 1940- *WhoFI 92*
**Hogan,** Roscoe Benjamin, Jr. 1921- *WhoAmL 92*
**Hogan,** Rosemarie 1924- *WhoAmP 91*
**Hogan,** Sheila Maureen 1958- *WhoMW 92*
**Hogan,** Steven Ryan 1946- *WhoAmP 91*
**Hogan,** Thomas Dennis, III 1930- *WhoFI 92*
**Hogan,** Thomas E *WhoAmP 91*
**Hogan,** Thomas Francis 1938- *WhoAmL 92*
**Hogan,** Thomas V. 1936- *WhoFI 92*
**Hogan,** William 1923- *AmMWSc 92*
**Hogan,** William E. 1928- *WhoAmL 92*
**Hogan,** William E., II 1942- *WhoBlA 92*
**Hogan,** William John 1940- *AmMWSc 92*
**Hogan,** William LeGrange 1934- *WhoRel 92*
**Hogans,** William Robertson, III 1945- *WhoBlA 92*
**Hogarth,** Arthur Paul 1917- *Who 92*
**Hogarth,** Burne 1911- *WhoWest 92*
**Hogarth,** Grace 1905- *WrDr 92*
**Hogarth,** Jacke Edwin 1923- *AmMWSc 92*
**Hogarth,** James 1914- *Who 92*
**Hogarth,** John M. 1931- *IntMPA 92*
**Hogarth,** Paul *Who 92*
**Hogarth,** Paul 1917- *IntWW 91, TwCPaSc*
**Hogarth,** Ronald Phillip 1949- *WhoFI 92*
**Hogarth,** William 1697-1764 *BlkwCEP*
**Hogben,** Charles Adrian Michael 1921- *AmMWSc 92*
**Hogben,** David 1929- *AmMWSc 92*
**Hogben,** Leslie 1952- *AmMWSc 92*
**Hogben,** Peter Graham 1925- *Who 92*
**Hogben,** Philip 1945- *TwCPaSc*
**Hogberg,** Carl Gustav 1913- *WhoFI 92*
**Hogberg,** Robert James 1959- *WhoFI 92*
**Hoge,** Harold James 1907- *AmMWSc 92*
**Hoge,** Harry Porter 1936- *AmMWSc 92*
**Hoge,** James Cleo 1916- *WhoRel 92*
**Hoge,** James Fulton, Jr. 1935- *WhoFI 92*
**Hoge,** Phyllis *ConAu 36NR, DrAPF 91*
**Hogeboom,** Robert Wood 1947- *WhoAmL 92*
**Hogen,** Marvis Thomas 1923- *WhoAmP 91*
**Hogen,** Philip N 1944- *WhoAmP 91*
**Hogen,** Philip Nere 1944- *WhoAmL 92*
**Hogen-Esch,** Thieo Eltjo 1936- *AmMWSc 92*
**Hogenboom,** David L 1936- *AmMWSc 92*
**Hogenboom,** Marion Jennie 1937- *WhoMW 92*
**Hogendorn,** Jan Stafford 1937- *WrDr 92*
**Hogenkamp,** Henricus Petrus C 1925- *AmMWSc 92*
**Hogenkamp,** Henricus Petrus Cornelis 1925- *WhoMW 92*
**Hogerheide,** Ric Arlen 1953- *WhoMW 92*
**Hogg** *Who 92*
**Hogg,** Alan Mitchell 1936- *AmMWSc 92*
**Hogg,** Arthur 1896- *Who 92*
**Hogg,** Christopher 1936- *Who 92*
**Hogg,** Christopher Anthony 1936- *IntWW 91*
**Hogg,** David Clarence 1921- *AmMWSc 92*
**Hogg,** David Edward 1936- *AmMWSc 92*
**Hogg,** Douglas Martin 1945- *Who 92*
**Hogg,** Edward William L. *Who 92*
**Hogg,** Gary Lynn 1946- *AmMWSc 92*
**Hogg,** Gavin 1788-1835 *DcNCBi 3*
**Hogg,** Gilbert Charles 1933- *Who 92*
**Hogg,** Helen Sawyer 1905- *AmMWSc 92*
**Hogg,** Ian 1911- *Who 92*
**Hogg,** Ian Vernon 1926- *IntAu&W 91*
**Hogg,** James 1729-1804 *DcNCBi 3*
**Hogg,** James 1770-1835 *RfGEnL 91*
**Hogg,** James Cameron *AmMWSc 92*
**Hogg,** James Felter 1918- *AmMWSc 92*
**Hogg,** John *DcNCBi 3*
**Hogg,** John 1765-1826 *DcNCBi 3*
**Hogg,** John 1912- *Who 92*
**Hogg,** John Leslie 1948- *AmMWSc 92*
**Hogg,** John Nicholson 1912- *IntWW 91*
**Hogg,** Mary Claire 1947- *Who 92*
**Hogg,** Norman 1938- *Who 92*
**Hogg,** Peter Beauchamp 1924- *Who 92*
**Hogg,** Quintin 1907- *WrDr 92*
**Hogg,** Richard 1938- *AmMWSc 92*
**Hogg,** Robert d1780 *DcNCBi 3*
**Hogg,** Robert Vincent, Jr 1924- *AmMWSc 92*
**Hogg,** Robert W 1938- *AmMWSc 92*
**Hogg,** Robin Ivor Trower 1932- *Who 92*
**Hogg,** Samuel E. 1783-1842 *DcNCBi 3*
**Hogg,** Sarah Elizabeth Mary 1946- *Who 92*
**Hogg,** Thomas Devereux 1823-1904 *DcNCBi 3*
**Hoggan,** Daniel Hunter 1929- *AmMWSc 92*
**Hoggan,** Malcolm David 1930- *AmMWSc 92*
**Hoggan,** Roger D 1940- *AmMWSc 92*
**Hoggard,** James 1941- *WrDr 92*
**Hoggard,** James Clinton 1916- *WhoRel 92*
**Hoggard,** James Martin 1941- *IntAu&W 91*
**Hoggard,** Lara Guldmar 1915- *WhoEnt 92*
**Hoggard,** Patrick Earle 1944- *AmMWSc 92*
**Hoggart,** Richard 1918- *IntWW 91, Who 92, WrDr 92*
**Hoggart,** Simon David 1946- *IntAu&W 91, Who 92*
**Hoggatt,** Clela Allphin 1932- *WhoWest 92*
**Hoggatt,** Vern Eugene 1948- *WhoWest 92*
**Hogge,** Michael 1925- *Who 92*
**Hogges,** Ralph 1947- *WhoBlA 92*
**Hoggett,** Anthony John Christopher 1940- *Who 92*
**Hoggett,** Bernda Marjorie 1945- *Who 92*
**Hogle,** Donald Hugh 1924- *AmMWSc 92*
**Hoglund,** Annette M *WhoAmP 91*
**Hoglund,** John Andrew 1945- *WhoAmL 92*
**Hoglund,** William Elis 1934- *WhoFI 92*
**Hogness,** David Swenson 1925- *AmMWSc 92*
**Hogness,** John Rusten 1922- *AmMWSc 92*
**Hognestad,** Eivind 1921- *AmMWSc 92*
**Hogoboom,** Belford E 1926- *WhoIns 92*
**Hogsett,** Joseph *WhoMW 92*
**Hogsett,** Joseph H 1956- *WhoAmP 91*
**Hogu,** Barbara J. Jones 1938- *WhoBlA 92*
**Hogue,** Bobby L 1939- *WhoAmP 91*
**Hogue,** Carol Jane Rowland 1945- *AmMWSc 92*
**Hogue,** Charles Leonard 1935- *AmMWSc 92*
**Hogue,** Cynthia *DrAPF 91*
**Hogue,** Cynthia A. 1960- *WhoAmL 92*
**Hogue,** Douglas Emerson 1931- *AmMWSc 92*
**Hogue,** James Lawrence 1923- *WhoRel 92*
**Hogue,** James Roland 1948- *WhoEnt 92*
**Hogue,** Terry Glynn 1944- *WhoAmL 92*
**Hogue,** Wilson Thomas 1852-1920 *RelLAm 91*
**Hoguet,** Geoffrey Robert 1950- *WhoFI 92*
**Hoguet,** Robert Gerard 1948- *AmMWSc 92*
**Hogun,** James d1781 *DcNCBi 3*
**Hogwood,** Christopher 1941- *NewAmDM*
**Hogwood,** Christopher Jarvis Haley 1941- *IntWW 91, Who 92, WhoEnt 92, WhoMW 92*
**Hoh,** George Lok Kwong 1935- *AmMWSc 92*
**Hoham,** Ronald William 1942- *AmMWSc 92*
**Hoheisel,** Peter *DrAPF 91*
**Hohenberg,** Charles Morris 1940- *AmMWSc 92*
**Hohenberg,** John 1906- *IntAu&W 91, WrDr 92*
**Hohenberg,** Pierre Claude 1934- *AmMWSc 92*

**Hohenboken**, William Daniel 1941- *AmMWSc 92*
**Hohenemser**, Christoph 1937- *AmMWSc 92*
**Hohenemser**, Kurt Heinrich 1906- *AmMWSc 92*
**Hohenfellner**, Peter 1939- *IntWW 91*
**Hohimer**, A Roger *AmMWSc 92*
**Hohl**, Frank 1934- *AmMWSc 92*
**Hohl**, Jakob Hans 1930- *AmMWSc 92*
**Hohl**, Joan M. *WrDr 92*
**Hohlbaum**, Robert 1886-1955 *EncTR 91*
**Hohler**, Henry Arthur Frederick 1911- *Who 92*
**Hohlmayer**, Earl J. 1921- *WhoWest 92*
**Hohman**, A. J., Jr. 1934- *WhoAmL 92*
**Hohman**, Richard Burton, Jr. 1955- *WhoMW 92*
**Hohman**, Walter Robert 1964- *WhoFI 92*
**Hohman**, William H 1939- *AmMWSc 92*
**Hohmann**, John Edward 1941- *WhoMW 92*
**Hohmann**, Philip George 1943- *AmMWSc 92*
**Hohn**, Arno R 1931- *AmMWSc 92*
**Hohn**, Edward Lewis 1933- *WhoWest 92*
**Hohn**, Emil Otto 1919- *AmMWSc 92*
**Hohn**, Harry G 1932- *WhoIns 92*
**Hohn**, Harry George 1932- *WhoFI 92*
**Hohn**, Matthew Henry 1920- *AmMWSc 92*
**Hohn**, Reinhard 1904- *EncTR 91*
**Hohn**, Richard G 1936- *WhoIns 92*
**Hohnadel**, David Charles 1941- *AmMWSc 92*
**Hohner**, Kenneth Dwayne 1934- *WhoFI 92, WhoWest 92*
**Hohnke**, Dieter Karl 1936- *AmMWSc 92*
**Hohnstedt**, Leo Frank 1924- *AmMWSc 92*
**Hohnstein**, William Conrad, Jr. 1952- *WhoEnt 92*
**Hohnstreiter**, Glenn Fredrick 1937- *WhoWest 92*
**Hohoff**, Curt 1913- *IntWW 91*
**Hohulin**, Martin 1964- *WhoAmP 91*
**Hoiby**, Lee 1926- *NewAmDM, WhoEnt 92*
**Hoiness**, David Eldon 1935- *AmMWSc 92*
**Hoinka**, Sandra Lea 1942- *WhoMW 92*
**Hoisie**, Adolfy 1957- *AmMWSc 92*
**Hoisington**, David B 1920- *AmMWSc 92*
**Hoitink**, Harry A J 1938- *AmMWSc 92*
**Hojdahl**, Odd 1921- *IntWW 91*
**Hojeda**, Diego de 1571-1615 *HisDSpE*
**Hojnacki**, Jerome Louis 1947- *AmMWSc 92*
**Hojvat**, Carlos F 1939- *AmMWSc 92*
**Hokama**, Takeo 1931- *AmMWSc 92*
**Hokama**, Yoshitsugi 1926- *AmMWSc 92*
**Hokana**, Gregory Howard 1944- *WhoWest 92*
**Hokana**, John M 1953- *WhoAmP 91*
**Hokanson**, Alicia *DrAPF 91*
**Hokanson**, Gerard Clifford 1949- *AmMWSc 92*
**Hokanson**, Kenneth Eric Fabian 1941- *AmMWSc 92*
**Hokanson**, Rona Wolk 1940- *WhoEnt 92*
**Hokanson**, Shirley Ann 1936- *WhoAmP 91*
**Hoke**, Donald Edwin 1919- *WhoRel 92*
**Hoke**, Donald I 1930- *AmMWSc 92*
**Hoke**, Donald Irvin 1930- *WhoMW 92*
**Hoke**, Glenn Dale 1952- *AmMWSc 92*
**Hoke**, Helen 1903-1990 *SmATA 65*
**Hoke**, James Richard 1946- *WhoFI 92*
**Hoke**, John Franklin 1820-1888 *DcNCBi 3*
**Hoke**, John Henry 1922- *AmMWSc 92*
**Hoke**, John Humphreys 1926- *AmMWSc 92*
**Hoke**, Kenneth Olan 1949- *WhoRel 92*
**Hoke**, Michael 1810-1844 *DcNCBi 3*
**Hoke**, Michael 1874-1944 *DcNCBi 3*
**Hoke**, Robert Frederick 1837-1912 *DcNCBi 3*
**Hoke**, Stephen Turner 1949- *WhoRel 92*
**Hoke**, William Alexander 1851-1925 *DcNCBi 3*
**Hokenson**, Earl Godfrey 1937- *WhoMW 92*
**Hokin**, Lowell Edward 1924- *AmMWSc 92*
**Hokin-Neaverson**, Mabel *AmMWSc 92*
**Hokr**, Dorothy Irene 1923- *WhoAmP 91*
**Hoks**, Barbara L. 1955- *WhoHisp 92*
**Holabird**, John Augur, Jr. 1920- *WhoMW 92*
**Holabird**, Robin Piard 1954- *WhoEnt 92*
**Holaday**, Duncan Asa 1916- *AmMWSc 92*
**Holaday**, John W 1945- *AmMWSc 92*
**Holaday**, William J 1928- *AmMWSc 92*
**Holahan**, Susan *DrAPF 91*
**Holanek**, Adam M F 1922- *IntAu&W 91*
**Holbach**, Paul Henri Thiry, Baron d' 1723-1789 *BlkwCEP*
**Holbein**, Susan Joy 1948- *WhoEnt 92*
**Holben**, Douglas Eric 1946- *WhoRel 92*
**Holben**, Ralph Erdman 1916- *WhoFI 92*
**Holberg**, Ludvig 1684-1754 *BlkwCEP, ScFEYrs*
**Holberg**, Ralph Gans, Jr. 1908- *WhoAmL 92*
**Holbert**, Donald 1941- *AmMWSc 92*
**Holbert**, Gene W 1948- *AmMWSc 92*
**Holbert**, John Charles 1946- *WhoRel 92*
**Holbert**, Josef Paul 1936- *WhoWest 92*
**Holbert**, Raymond Ray 1945- *WhoBlA 92*
**Holberton**, Philip Vaughan 1942- *WhoEnt 92*
**Holbik**, Karel 1920- *WrDr 92*
**Holbo**, Paul Sothe 1929- *WhoWest 92, WrDr 92*
**Holborow**, Eric John 1918- *Who 92*
**Holborow**, Leslie Charles 1941- *IntWW 91, Who 92*
**Holbrook**, A. C. 1938- *WhoRel 92*
**Holbrook**, Charles R, III 1938- *WhoAmP 91*
**Holbrook**, David 1923- *ConPo 91, WrDr 92*
**Holbrook**, David A. 1967- *WhoFI 92*
**Holbrook**, David D *WhoIns 92*
**Holbrook**, David James, Jr 1933- *AmMWSc 92*
**Holbrook**, David Kenneth 1923- *IntAu&W 91, Who 92*
**Holbrook**, Donald Benson 1925- *WhoAmL 92, WhoFI 92*
**Holbrook**, Frank Malvin 1952- *WhoAmL 92*
**Holbrook**, Frederick R 1935- *AmMWSc 92*
**Holbrook**, Gabriel Peter 1957- *AmMWSc 92*
**Holbrook**, Hal *LesBEnT 92*
**Holbrook**, Hal 1925- *IntMPA 92, WhoEnt 92*
**Holbrook**, James Robert 1956- *WhoWest 92*
**Holbrook**, James Russell 1944- *WhoWest 92*
**Holbrook**, John *DrAPF 91*
**Holbrook**, John Edwards 1794-1871 *BiInAmS*
**Holbrook**, Josiah 1788-1854 *BenetAL 91*
**Holbrook**, Karen Ann 1942- *AmMWSc 92*
**Holbrook**, Lanny Robert 1946- *WhoAmP 91*
**Holbrook**, Martin Luther 1831-1902 *BiInAmS*
**Holbrook**, Nikki J *AmMWSc 92*
**Holbrook**, Robert G 1917- *WhoAmP 91*
**Holbrook**, Robert Sumner 1932- *WhoFI 92, WhoMW 92*
**Holbrook**, Sidney John 1950- *WhoAmP 91*
**Holbrook**, Steven Charles 1952- *WhoRel 92*
**Holbrook**, Stewart H. 1893-1964 *BenetAL 91*
**Holbrook**, William Michael 1958- *WhoEnt 92*
**Holbrooke**, Richard 1941- *ConAu 135, WhoAmP 91*
**Holbrooke**, Richard Charles Albert 1941- *WhoFI 92*
**Holbrow**, Charles H 1935- *AmMWSc 92*
**Holby**, Grethe Barrett 1948- *WhoEnt 92*
**Holcenberg**, John Stanley 1935- *AmMWSc 92*
**Holck**, Frederick H. George 1927- *WhoRel 92*
**Holck**, Gary LeRoy 1938- *AmMWSc 92*
**Holck**, Manfred, Jr. 1930- *WrDr 92*
**Holcomb**, Amasa 1787-1875 *BiInAmS*
**Holcomb**, C E *WhoAmP 91*
**Holcomb**, Carla 1963- *WhoWest 92*
**Holcomb**, Charles Edward 1924- *AmMWSc 92*
**Holcomb**, Constance L. 1942- *WhoFI 92*
**Holcomb**, Craig 1948- *WhoAmP 91*
**Holcomb**, David Nelson 1936- *AmMWSc 92, WhoMW 92*
**Holcomb**, Donald Frank 1925- *AmMWSc 92*
**Holcomb**, George Ruhle 1927- *AmMWSc 92*
**Holcomb**, Gordon Ernest 1932- *AmMWSc 92*
**Holcomb**, Gordon Randolph 1960- *WhoWest 92*
**Holcomb**, Herman Perry 1934- *AmMWSc 92*
**Holcomb**, Ira James 1934- *AmMWSc 92*
**Holcomb**, Jim 1945- *WhoAmP 91*
**Holcomb**, Lyle Donald, Jr. 1929- *WhoAmL 92*
**Holcomb**, M Staser 1932- *WhoIns 92*
**Holcomb**, Philo 1936- *WhoFI 92*
**Holcomb**, Robert M 1916- *AmMWSc 92*
**Holcomb**, Robin Terry 1943- *AmMWSc 92*
**Holcomb**, W R *WhoAmP 91*
**Holcombe**, Arthur Norman 1884-1977 *AmPeW*
**Holcombe**, Cressie Earl, Jr 1945- *AmMWSc 92*
**Holcombe**, George Roland 1933- *WhoRel 92*
**Holcombe**, Henry 1762-1824 *AmPeW*
**Holcombe**, James Andrew 1948- *AmMWSc 92*
**Holcombe**, Randall Gregory 1950- *WhoFI 92*
**Holcombe**, Sandra 1962- *WhoEnt 92*
**Holcombe**, Troy Leon 1940- *AmMWSc 92*
**Holcombre**, Paul A., Jr. *WhoAmL 92*
**Holcroft**, Peter 1931- *Who 92*
**Holcroft**, Thomas 1745-1809 *RfGEnL 91*
**Holcslaw**, Terry Lee 1946- *AmMWSc 92*
**Holczer**, Geoffrey M. 1949- *WhoFI 92*
**Holdaway**, Michael Jon 1936- *AmMWSc 92*
**Holdcroft**, Leslie Thomas 1922- *WhoRel 92, WhoWest 92*
**Holdeman**, James F., Jr. 1946- *WhoAmL 92*
**Holdeman**, John 1832-1900 *AmPeW, RelLAm 91*
**Holdeman**, Jonas Tillman, Jr 1937- *AmMWSc 92*
**Holdeman**, Louis Brian 1938- *AmMWSc 92*
**Holden**, A C 1935- *WhoAmP 91*
**Holden**, Aaron Charles 1942- *WhoBlA 92*
**Holden**, Alistair David Craig 1928- *AmMWSc 92*
**Holden**, Ann 1954- *WhoMW 92*
**Holden**, Anthony 1947- *WrDr 92*
**Holden**, Anthony Ivan 1947- *Who 92*
**Holden**, Basil Munroe 1913- *Who 92*
**Holden**, Carol Helen 1942- *WhoAmP 91*
**Holden**, Cliff 1919- *TwCPaSc*
**Holden**, Dalby *WrDr 92*
**Holden**, David 1915- *Who 92*
**Holden**, David Powell 1927- *WhoRel 92*
**Holden**, Denis *TwCPaSc*
**Holden**, Derek 1935- *Who 92*
**Holden**, Dorothy M. 1928-1988 *WhoBlA 92N*
**Holden**, Edgar Howard 1914- *WhoAmP 91*
**Holden**, Edward 1916- *Who 92*
**Holden**, Edward F 1930- *WhoIns 92*
**Holden**, Edward Singleton 1846-1914 *BiInAmS*
**Holden**, Elizabeth Rhoda *WrDr 92*
**Holden**, Ernest Lloyd 1941- *WhoWest 92*
**Holden**, Frank C 1921- *AmMWSc 92*
**Holden**, Frederick Douglass, Jr. 1949- *WhoAmL 92*
**Holden**, Frederick Thompson 1915- *AmMWSc 92*
**Holden**, George Fredric 1937- *WhoFI 92, WhoWest 92*
**Holden**, Glen A *WhoAmP 91*
**Holden**, Harold William 1929- *AmMWSc 92*
**Holden**, Howard T *AmMWSc 92*
**Holden**, J. Milnes 1918- *WrDr 92*
**Holden**, James Edward 1944- *AmMWSc 92*
**Holden**, James Phillip 1932- *WhoAmL 92*
**Holden**, James Richard 1928- *AmMWSc 92*
**Holden**, James Stuart 1914- *WhoAmL 92*
**Holden**, Joan 1939- *IntAu&W 91, WrDr 92*
**Holden**, John B, Jr 1935- *AmMWSc 92*
**Holden**, John David 1967- *Who 92*
**Holden**, John Reid 1913- *Who 92*
**Holden**, Jonathan *DrAPF 91*
**Holden**, Joseph Larry 1935- *WhoWest 92*
**Holden**, Joseph Thaddeus 1925- *AmMWSc 92*
**Holden**, Joseph William 1844-1875 *DcNCBi 3*
**Holden**, Kenneth George 1934- *AmMWSc 92*
**Holden**, Kenneth Graham d1990 *Who 92N*
**Holden**, Kip 1952- *WhoBlA 92*
**Holden**, Lily B. *TwCPaSc*
**Holden**, Lyle Wilson *ScFEYrs*
**Holden**, Mark Raymond 1956- *WhoRel 92*
**Holden**, Mary Lynn 1945- *WhoMW 92*
**Holden**, Matthew, Jr. 1931- *WrDr 92*
**Holden**, Melvin Lee *WhoAmP 91*
**Holden**, Melvin Lee 1952- *WhoBlA 92*
**Holden**, Michael Lloyd 1947- *WhoEnt 92*
**Holden**, Michelle Y. 1954- *WhoBlA 92*
**Holden**, Mickey C. 1955- *WhoEnt 92*
**Holden**, Molly 1927-1981 *ConAu 133*
**Holden**, Norman Edward 1936- *AmMWSc 92*
**Holden**, Palmer Joseph 1943- *AmMWSc 92*
**Holden**, Patrick Brian 1937- *Who 92*
**Holden**, Raymond 1894-1972 *BenetAL 91*
**Holden**, Robert *DcNCBi 3*
**Holden**, Roberto 1925- *IntWW 91*
**Holden**, Ronald Michael 1942- *WhoWest 92*
**Holden**, Sandra Sue 1938- *WhoFI 92*
**Holden**, Thomas More *AmMWSc 92*
**Holden**, William Douglas 1912- *AmMWSc 92*
**Holden**, William Melville 1923- *IntAu&W 91*
**Holden**, William R 1928- *AmMWSc 92*
**Holden**, William Vaughn 1949- *WhoFI 92*
**Holden**, William Ward 1952- *WhoFI 92*
**Holden**, William Willard 1958- *WhoWest 92*
**Holden**, William Woods 1818-1892 *DcNCBi 3*
**Holden-Brown**, Derrick 1923- *IntWW 91, Who 92*
**Holder**, Arthur Glenn 1952- *WhoRel 92*
**Holder**, Barbara *DrAPF 91*
**Holder**, Charles Burt, Jr 1914- *AmMWSc 92*
**Holder**, Charles Frederick 1851-1915 *BiInAmS*
**Holder**, Christopher Peirce 1947- *WhoEnt 92*
**Holder**, Cleo W. 1957- *WhoFI 92*
**Holder**, David Gordon 1943- *AmMWSc 92*
**Holder**, David Hugh 1964- *WhoRel 92*
**Holder**, Douglas Richard 1959- *WhoRel 92*
**Holder**, Geoffrey 1930- *WhoBlA 92, WhoEnt 92*
**Holder**, Gerald D 1950- *AmMWSc 92*
**Holder**, Gregory Paul 1953- *WhoAmL 92*
**Holder**, Harold Douglas 1939- *AmMWSc 92*
**Holder**, Harold Douglas, Sr. 1931- *WhoFI 92*
**Holder**, Henry 1928- *Who 92*
**Holder**, Howard Randolph, Sr. 1916- *WhoFI 92*
**Holder**, Ian Alan 1934- *AmMWSc 92*
**Holder**, Idalia 1947- *WhoBlA 92*
**Holder**, Joseph Bassett 1824-1888 *BiInAmS*
**Holder**, Julius H. 1918- *WhoBlA 92*
**Holder**, Leonard Irvin 1923- *AmMWSc 92*
**Holder**, Paul 1911- *Who 92*
**Holder**, Reuben D. 1923- *WhoBlA 92*
**Holder**, Richard G. *WhoFI 92*
**Holder**, Sandra Sue 1938- *WhoWest 92*
**Holder**, Thomas M 1926- *AmMWSc 92*
**Holder**, Virginia Mary 1942- *WhoEnt 92*
**Holder**, William Dunbar 1929- *WhoAmL 92, WhoFI 92*
**Holderbaum**, Daniel *AmMWSc 92*
**Holderlin**, Friedrich 1770-1843 *PoeCrit 4 [port]*
**Holderman**, Conni Ann 1950- *WhoWest 92*
**Holderness**, Baron 1920- *IntWW 91, Who 92*
**Holderness**, Algernon Sidney, Jr. 1938- *WhoAmL 92*
**Holderness**, George Allen 1867-1947 *DcNCBi 3*
**Holderness**, George Malcolm 1937- *WhoAmL 92*
**Holderness**, Grizelda 1953- *TwCPaSc*
**Holderness**, Helen *TwCPaSc*
**Holderness**, Richard William 1927- *Who 92*
**Holderness**, Susan Rutherford 1941- *WhoMW 92, WhoRel 92*
**Holderness**, William Henry 1904-1965 *DcNCBi 3*
**Holdgate**, Martin W. 1931- *WrDr 92*
**Holdgate**, Martin Wyatt 1931- *IntWW 91, Who 92*
**Holdgrafer**, Marian Helen 1927- *WhoAmP 91*
**Holdgrive**, David Russell 1958- *WhoEnt 92*
**Holdheim**, William 1926- *WrDr 92*
**Holdhusen**, James S 1925- *AmMWSc 92*
**Holding**, Clyde 1931- *IntWW 91*
**Holding**, John Francis 1936- *Who 92*
**Holding**, Malcolm Alexander 1932- *Who 92*
**Holding**, Robert Powell 1896-1957 *DcNCBi 3*
**Holdredge**, Russell M 1933- *AmMWSc 92*
**Holdren**, John Paul 1944- *AmMWSc 92*
**Holdridge**, John H 1924- *WhoAmP 91*
**Holdridge**, Lee 1944- *IntMPA 92*
**Holdstock**, Robert 1948- *IntAu&W 91, TwCSFW 91, WrDr 92*
**Holdsworth**, Albert Edward 1909- *Who 92*
**Holdsworth**, Arthur John 1915- *Who 92*
**Holdsworth**, Carole Adele 1936- *WhoMW 92*
**Holdsworth**, David Jay 1956- *WhoAmL 92*
**Holdsworth**, George Trevor 1927- *Who 92*
**Holdsworth**, Janet Nott 1941- *WhoWest 92*
**Holdsworth**, John *Who 92*
**Holdsworth**, Robert Leo, Jr. 1959- *WhoFI 92*
**Holdsworth**, Robert Powell 1915- *AmMWSc 92*
**Holdsworth**, Trevor *Who 92*
**Holdsworth**, Trevor 1927- *IntWW 91*
**Holdt**, David *DrAPF 91*
**Holdwick**, Frances Lillian 1947- *WhoAmP 91*
**Hole**, Derek Norman 1933- *Who 92*
**Hole**, Dorothy *ConAu 135*
**Hole**, Francis Doan 1913- *AmMWSc 92*
**Hole**, Richard Douglas 1949- *WhoAmL 92*

**Hole**, Richard Eugene, II 1937- *WhoAmP 91*
**Holec**, James Michael, Jr. 1949- *WhoFI 92*
**Holechek**, Jerry Lee 1948- *AmMWSc 92*
**Holeman**, Dennis Leigh 1946- *AmMWSc 92*
**Holeman**, Marilyn Batey 1938- *IntAu&W 91*
**Holeman**, Mark Melvin 1920- *WhoMW 92*
**Holen**, Arlene *WhoAmP 91*
**Holender**, Barbara D. *DrAPF 91*
**Holender**, Barbara D 1927- *IntAu&W 91*
**Holeski**, Paul Michael 1943- *AmMWSc 92*
**Holewinski**, Michael S 1947- *WhoAmP 91*
**Holey**, Brett Allen 1960- *WhoEnt 92*
**Holfeld**, Winfried Thomas 1926- *AmMWSc 92*
**Holford**, Castello N *ScFEYrs*
**Holford**, Frank Douglas d1991 *Who 92N*
**Holford**, Ingrid 1920- *WrDr 92*
**Holford**, John Morley 1909- *Who 92*
**Holford**, Richard L 1937- *AmMWSc 92*
**Holford**, Richard Moore 1938- *AmMWSc 92*
**Holford**, Theodore Richard 1947- *AmMWSc 92*
**Holgate**, Harold Norman 1933- *Who 92*
**Holgate**, Sidney 1918- *Who 92*
**Holgate**, William 1906- *Who 92*
**Holger**, David Kermit 1948- *WhoMW 92*
**Holger-Madsen** 1878-1943 *IntDcF 2-2*
**Holguin**, Alfonso Hudson 1931- *AmMWSc 92*
**Holguin**, Cesar Alfonso 1958- *WhoHisp 92*
**Holguin**, Guillermo 1944- *WhoFI 92*
**Holguin**, Hector 1935- *WhoHisp 92*
**Holick**, Michael Francis 1946- *AmMWSc 92*
**Holick**, Sally Ann 1948- *AmMWSc 92*
**Holiday**, Billie 1915-1959 *ConBlB 1 [port], ConMus 6 [port], FacFETw [port], HanAmWH, NewAmDM, NotBlAW 92*
**Holiday**, Doc 1943- *WhoEnt 92*
**Holiday**, Harry, Jr. 1923- *IntWW 91*
**Holiday**, James Ernest 1953- *WhoAmL 92*
**Holiday**, Martha 1926- *WhoEnt 92*
**Holiday**, Michael 1954- *WhoAmL 92*
**Holiday**, Patrick James 1947- *WhoEnt 92, WhoMW 92*
**Holien**, Kim Bernard 1948- *WhoFI 92*
**Holifield**, Charles Leslie 1940- *AmMWSc 92*
**Holifield**, E. Brooks 1942- *WhoRel 92*
**Holifield**, Kam *DrAPF 91*
**Holiman**, William Jess 1958- *WhoRel 92*
**Holinger**, Richard *DrAPF 91*
**Holinger**, William *DrAPF 91*
**Holinshed**, Raphael *RfGEnL 91*
**Holkeboer**, Paul Edward 1928- *AmMWSc 92*
**Holkeri**, Harri Hermanni 1937- *IntWW 91*
**Holl**, Edwin G *WhoAmP 91*
**Holl**, Frederick Brian 1944- *AmMWSc 92*
**Holl**, J William 1928- *AmMWSc 92*
**Holl**, Manfred Matthias 1928- *AmMWSc 92*
**Holl**, Mary Katherine 1958- *WhoWest 92*
**Holl**, Shelley Nannette Cloete 1952- *WhoMW 92*
**Hollaar**, Lee Allen 1947- *AmMWSc 92*
**Holladay**, Alexander Quarles 1839-1909 *DcNCBi 3*
**Holladay**, Cleo Call 1932- *WhoEnt 92*
**Holladay**, Hugh Edwin 1923- *WhoAmP 91*
**Holladay**, James Franklin, Jr. 1951- *WhoRel 92*
**Holladay**, Kenneth Richard 1952- *WhoRel 92*
**Holladay**, Waller 1840- *BiInAmS*
**Hollahan**, John Ronald 1936- *AmMWSc 92*
**Hollamby**, Edward Ernest 1921- *Who 92*
**Hollamon**, Elizabeth Erskine 1930- *WhoRel 92*
**Hollan**, R. Susan 1920- *IntWW 91*
**Holland**, Alfred Charles *Who 92*
**Holland**, Andrew Brian 1940- *AmMWSc 92*
**Holland**, Anita Carol 1963- *WhoRel 92*
**Holland**, Annie Wealthy 1871-1934 *DcNCBi 3, NotBlAW 92 [port]*
**Holland**, Anthony *Who 92*
**Holland**, Arthur David 1913- *Who 92*
**Holland**, Bernard George 1948- *WhoWest 92*
**Holland**, Beth *WhoEnt 92*
**Holland**, Bobby Ray, Jr 1952- *WhoAmP 91*
**Holland**, Brian Arthur 1935- *Who 92*
**Holland**, Bruce *WhoAmP 91*
**Holland**, Cecelia *DrAPF 91*
**Holland**, Cecelia 1943- *IntAu&W 91, WrDr 92*
**Holland**, Charles 1909-1987 *NewAmDM*
**Holland**, Charles D 1921- *AmMWSc 92*
**Holland**, Charles Edward 1940- *WhoFI 92*
**Holland**, Charles Hepworth 1923- *IntWW 91*
**Holland**, Charles Jordan 1948- *AmMWSc 92*
**Holland**, Charles Joseph 1949- *WhoAmL 92*
**Holland**, Charles Lee 1941- *WhoFI 92*
**Holland**, Christie Anna 1950- *AmMWSc 92*
**Holland**, Christine Elizabeth 1958- *WhoAmL 92*
**Holland**, Christopher John 1937- *Who 92*
**Holland**, Clarence A 1929- *WhoAmP 91*
**Holland**, Clifton Vaughan 1914- *Who 92*
**Holland**, Daniel Stephen 1955- *WhoAmP 91*
**Holland**, Darrell Wendell 1932- *WhoRel 92*
**Holland**, David Cuthbert Lyall 1915- *Who 92*
**Holland**, David George 1925- *Who 92*
**Holland**, David Michael 1946- *WhoIns 92*
**Holland**, David Ray 1939- *WhoFI 92*
**Holland**, David Vernon 1954- *WhoRel 92*
**Holland**, Dena 1941- *WhoEnt 92*
**Holland**, Derek 1927- *TwCPaSc*
**Holland**, Derek 1950- *WhoAmP 91*
**Holland**, Dewey G 1937- *AmMWSc 92*
**Holland**, Dewey George 1937- *WhoMW 92*
**Holland**, Donald Harry 1928- *WhoAmP 91*
**Holland**, Edward *Who 92*
**Holland**, Edward James, Jr. 1943- *WhoAmL 92*
**Holland**, Edward McHarg 1939- *WhoAmP 91*
**Holland**, Edward Richard Charles 1925- *Who 92*
**Holland**, Edwin Clifford 1794?-1824 *BenetAL 91*
**Holland**, Einion *Who 92*
**Holland**, Elizabeth Anne 1928- *IntAu&W 91, WrDr 92*
**Holland**, Endesha Ida Mae 1944- *WhoEnt 92*
**Holland**, Ethel M. 1946- *WhoBlA 92*
**Holland**, Eugene Paul 1935- *AmMWSc 92*
**Holland**, F D, Jr 1924- *AmMWSc 92*
**Holland**, Francis, Jr. *WrDr 92*
**Holland**, Frank Robert Dacre 1924- *Who 92*
**Holland**, Fred Anthony 1955- *WhoAmL 92*
**Holland**, Gail Bernice 1940- *IntAu&W 91*
**Holland**, Gary Alexander 1933- *WhoFI 92*
**Holland**, Gary L. 1953- *WhoEnt 92*
**Holland**, Geoffrey 1938- *Who 92*
**Holland**, Gerald Fagan 1931- *AmMWSc 92*
**Holland**, Gilbert Strom 1918- *WhoAmP 91*
**Holland**, Graham Rex 1946- *AmMWSc 92*
**Holland**, Guy 1918- *Who 92*
**Holland**, H. Russel 1936- *WhoAmL 92, WhoWest 92*
**Holland**, Hans J 1929- *AmMWSc 92*
**Holland**, Harold Edward 1924- *WhoWest 92*
**Holland**, Harold Herbert 1932- *WhoMW 92*
**Holland**, Harry 1941- *TwCPaSc*
**Holland**, Heinrich Dieter 1927- *AmMWSc 92, IntWW 91*
**Holland**, Herbert Leslie 1947- *AmMWSc 92*
**Holland**, Iris K 1920- *WhoAmP 91*
**Holland**, Isabelle 1920- *IntAu&W 91, WrDr 92*
**Holland**, Israel Irving 1915- *AmMWSc 92*
**Holland**, J. Archibald *WhoBlA 92*
**Holland**, Jack Calvin 1925- *AmMWSc 92*
**Holland**, Jack Henry 1922- *WhoRel 92*
**Holland**, James 1754-1823 *DcNCBi 3*
**Holland**, James 1948- *TwCPaSc*
**Holland**, James Frederick 1925- *AmMWSc 92*
**Holland**, James M 1928- *WhoAmP 91*
**Holland**, James Paul 1948- *WhoFI 92*
**Holland**, James Philip 1934- *AmMWSc 92*
**Holland**, James R. 1944- *WrDr 92*
**Holland**, James Read 1930- *AmMWSc 92*
**Holland**, Jeffrey R. 1940- *WhoRel 92, WhoWest 92*
**Holland**, Jo Anne 1942- *WhoAmL 92*
**Holland**, John *Who 92*
**Holland**, John 1943- *WhoEnt 92*
**Holland**, John Anthony 1938- *Who 92*
**Holland**, John Deal 1937- *WhoFI 92, WhoMW 92*
**Holland**, John Henry 1929- *AmMWSc 92*
**Holland**, John Joseph 1929- *AmMWSc 92*
**Holland**, John Lewis 1937- *Who 92*
**Holland**, John Michael 1950- *WhoFI 92*
**Holland**, John Philip 1840-1914 *BiInAmS*
**Holland**, John Philip 1841-1914 *DcAmImH*
**Holland**, John Ray 1933- *WhoRel 92*
**Holland**, John Tristram d1990 *Who 92N*
**Holland**, Joseph Robert 1936- *WhoAmP 91*
**Holland**, Joshua Zalman 1921- *AmMWSc 92*
**Holland**, Josiah Gilbert 1819-1881 *BenetAL 91*
**Holland**, Joy 1946- *WhoMW 92*
**Holland**, Judith Rawie 1942- *WhoEnt 92, WhoWest 92*
**Holland**, Julie Frances 1955- *WhoAmL 92*
**Holland**, Ken 1934- *WhoAmP 91*
**Holland**, Kenneth 1918- *Who 92*
**Holland**, Kevin John William C *Who 92*
**Holland**, Laurence H. 1926- *WhoBlA 92*
**Holland**, Lewis 1925- *AmMWSc 92*
**Holland**, Louis Edward, II 1948- *AmMWSc 92*
**Holland**, Lyman Faith, Jr. 1931- *WhoAmL 92*
**Holland**, Lyman Lyle 1940- *AmMWSc 92*
**Holland**, Marjorie Miriam 1947- *AmMWSc 92*
**Holland**, Mary Jean Carey 1942- *AmMWSc 92*
**Holland**, Max 1950- *ConAu 135*
**Holland**, Merritt L. 1961- *WhoEnt 92*
**Holland**, Michael James 1950- *WhoWest 92*
**Holland**, Monte W 1938- *AmMWSc 92*
**Holland**, Nancy H *AmMWSc 92*
**Holland**, Neal Stewart 1929- *AmMWSc 92*
**Holland**, Nicholas Drew 1938- *AmMWSc 92*
**Holland**, Norman James Abbott 1927- *Who 92*
**Holland**, Norman N 1927- *IntAu&W 91, WrDr 92*
**Holland**, Paul Richard 1948- *WhoMW 92*
**Holland**, Paul Vincent 1937- *AmMWSc 92*
**Holland**, Paul William 1940- *AmMWSc 92*
**Holland**, Philip 1917- *Who 92*
**Holland**, Randy *WhoAmP 91*
**Holland**, Randy James 1947- *WhoAmL 92*
**Holland**, Ray W 1924- *AmMWSc 92*
**Holland**, Redus Foy 1930- *AmMWSc 92*
**Holland**, Richard 1420?- *RfGEnL 91*
**Holland**, Richard Edward 1935- *WhoFI 92*
**Holland**, Richard Eugene 1951- *WhoRel 92*
**Holland**, Richard Joyner 1925- *WhoAmP 91*
**Holland**, Robert *DrAPF 91*
**Holland**, Robert Campbell 1923- *AmMWSc 92*
**Holland**, Robert Carl 1925- *WhoFI 92*
**Holland**, Robert Dale 1928- *WhoWest 92*
**Holland**, Robert Einion 1927- *Who 92*
**Holland**, Robert Emmett 1920- *AmMWSc 92*
**Holland**, Robert Eonion 1927- *IntWW 91*
**Holland**, Robert Francis 1908- *AmMWSc 92*
**Holland**, Robert Michael *WhoAmP 91*
**Holland**, Robert Vance, Jr. 1946- *WhoAmL 92*
**Holland**, Robin Jean 1942- *WhoWest 92*
**Holland**, Robin W. 1953- *WhoBlA 92*
**Holland**, Rupert Sargent 1878-1952 *BenetAL 91*
**Holland**, Russell Sedgwick 1929- *AmMWSc 92*
**Holland**, Samuel S, Jr 1928- *AmMWSc 92*
**Holland**, Sheila 1937- *IntAu&W 91, WrDr 92*
**Holland**, Spencer H. 1939- *WhoBlA 92*
**Holland**, Steven William 1951- *AmMWSc 92*
**Holland**, Stuart 1940- *Who 92*
**Holland**, Thomas 1908- *Who 92*
**Holland**, Tim Ray 1959- *WhoRel 92*
**Holland**, Toby J J, Jr 1928- *WhoAmP 91*
**Holland**, Tom *TwCWW 91*
**Holland**, Tom 1936- *WhoEnt 92*
**Holland**, Tom 1947- *IntAu&W 91*
**Holland**, Walter Werner 1929- *Who 92*
**Holland**, Wilbur Charles 1935- *AmMWSc 92*
**Holland**, William Frederick 1914- *AmMWSc 92*
**Holland**, William John 1920 *AmMWSc 92*
**Holland**, William Meredith *WhoBlA 92*
**Holland**, William Robert 1938- *AmMWSc 92*
**Holland-Beeton**, Ruth Elizabeth 1936- *AmMWSc 92*
**Holland-Calbert**, Mary Ann 1941- *WhoBlA 92*
**Holland-Hibbert** *Who 92*
**Holland-Martin**, Robert George 1939- *Who 92*
**Holland-Martin**, Rosamund Mary 1914- *Who 92*
**Hollander**, Adrian Willoughby 1941- *WhoMW 92*
**Hollander**, David 1949- *WhoAmL 92*
**Hollander**, George Mitchell 1934- *WhoAmL 92*
**Hollander**, Gerhard Ludwig 1922- *AmMWSc 92*
**Hollander**, Herbert I. 1924- *WhoFI 92*
**Hollander**, Jack Marvin 1927- *AmMWSc 92*
**Hollander**, Jean *DrAPF 91*
**Hollander**, John *DrAPF 91*
**Hollander**, John 1929- *BenetAL 91, ConPo 91, CurBio 91 [port], IntAu&W 91, IntWW 91, WrDr 92*
**Hollander**, Jonathan 1951- *WhoEnt 92*
**Hollander**, Joseph Lee 1910- *AmMWSc 92*
**Hollander**, Joshua 1936- *AmMWSc 92*
**Hollander**, Lawrence Jay 1940- *WhoFI 92*
**Hollander**, Leonore 1906- *AmMWSc 92*
**Hollander**, Max Leo 1923- *AmMWSc 92*
**Hollander**, Milton B 1928- *AmMWSc 92*
**Hollander**, Myles 1941- *AmMWSc 92*
**Hollander**, Paul *ConAu 36NR*
**Hollander**, Philip B 1924- *AmMWSc 92*
**Hollander**, Philip Ben 1924- *WhoMW 92*
**Hollander**, Samuel 1937- *WrDr 92*
**Hollander**, Stanley C. 1919- *WrDr 92*
**Hollander**, Stanley Charles 1919- *WhoFI 92*
**Hollander**, Vincent Paul 1917- *AmMWSc 92*
**Hollander**, Walter, Jr 1922- *AmMWSc 92*
**Hollander**, William 1925- *AmMWSc 92*
**Hollands**, Roy Derrick 1924- *IntAu&W 91*
**Hollandsworth**, Clinton E 1930- *AmMWSc 92*
**Hollandsworth**, James G., Jr. 1944- *ConAu 135*
**Hollandsworth**, Kenneth Peter 1934- *WhoFI 92*
**Hollandsworth**, Marla Jean 1956- *WhoAmL 92*
**Hollanek**, Adam Michal Franciszek 1922- *IntAu&W 91*
**Hollar**, Milton Conover 1930- *WhoBlA 92*
**Hollard**, Florian 1926- *WhoEnt 92*
**Hollas**, Eric M. 1948- *WhoRel 92*
**Hollatz**, Sarah Schoales 1944- *WhoWest 92*
**Hollbach**, Natasha Coffin 1933- *AmMWSc 92*
**Holldobler**, Bert *ConAu 134*
**Holldobler**, Bert 1936- *WrDr 92*
**Holldobler**, Berthold Karl 1936- *AmMWSc 92, IntWW 91*
**Holle**, Miguel 1937- *AmMWSc 92*
**Holle**, Paul August 1923- *AmMWSc 92*
**Holle**, Reginald Henry 1925- *WhoMW 92, WhoRel 92*
**Holleb**, Doris B. 1922- *WhoMW 92*
**Hollein**, Hans 1934- *DcTwDes*
**Hollein**, Helen Conway Faris 1943- *AmMWSc 92*
**Holleman**, Carl Partin 1921- *WhoAmL 92*
**Holleman**, Frank Sharp, III 1954- *WhoAmP 91*
**Holleman**, Kendrick Alfred 1934- *AmMWSc 92*
**Holleman**, Robert Dunn 1914- *WhoAmL 92*
**Holleman**, Robert Wood, Jr. 1931- *WhoWest 92*
**Holleman**, Sandy Lee 1940- *WhoRel 92*
**Holleman**, Warren Lee 1955- *WhoRel 92*
**Holleman**, William H 1940- *AmMWSc 92*
**Hollen**, Arlene P 1932- *WhoAmP 91*
**Hollenbach**, Edwin 1918- *AmMWSc 92*
**Hollenbach**, Mark Harold 1954- *WhoRel 92*
**Hollenbach**, Ruth *WhoRel 92*
**Hollenbaugh**, Henry Ritchey 1947- *WhoMW 92*
**Hollenbaugh**, Kenneth Malcolm 1934- *AmMWSc 92*
**Hollenbeck**, Clarie Beall 1947- *AmMWSc 92*
**Hollenbeck**, Don d1954 *LesBEnT 92*
**Hollenbeck**, Harold Capistran 1938- *WhoAmP 91*
**Hollenbeck**, Karen Fern 1943- *WhoMW 92*
**Hollenbeck**, L D 1939- *WhoAmP 91*
**Hollenbeck**, Mark John 1960- *WhoAmP 91*
**Hollenbeck**, Marynell 1939- *WhoMW 92*
**Hollenbeck**, Robert Gary 1949- *AmMWSc 92*
**Hollenberg**, Charles H 1930- *AmMWSc 92*
**Hollenberg**, David Henry 1946- *AmMWSc 92*
**Hollenberg**, J Leland 1926- *AmMWSc 92*
**Hollenberg**, Joel Warren 1938- *AmMWSc 92*
**Hollenberg**, Martin James 1934- *AmMWSc 92*
**Hollenberg**, Milton 1930- *AmMWSc 92*
**Hollenberg**, Morley Donald 1942- *AmMWSc 92*
**Hollenberg**, Paul Frederick 1942- *AmMWSc 92, WhoMW 92*
**Hollenden**, Baron 1914- *Who 92*
**Hollender**, Alfred L. *IntMPA 92*
**Hollender**, John Edward 1941- *WhoFI 92*
**Hollender**, Louis Francois 1922- *IntWW 91*
**Hollender**, Marc Hale 1916- *AmMWSc 92*

**Hollenhorst,** Robert William 1913- *AmMWSc 92*
**Hollensen,** Raymond Hans 1931- *AmMWSc 92*
**Hollenshead,** Robert Earl 1940- *WhoMW 92*
**Hollenweger,** Walter Jacob 1927- *Who 92*
**Holleque,** Kathryn Louise 1946- *WhoMW 92*
**Holler,** Adlai Cornwell, Jr. 1925- *WhoRel 92*
**Holler,** Albert Cochran 1921- *AmMWSc 92*
**Holler,** Floyd James 1946- *AmMWSc 92*
**Holler,** Jacob William 1912- *AmMWSc 92*
**Holler,** Joseph 1932- *WhoMW 92*
**Holler,** Nicholas Robert 1939- *AmMWSc 92*
**Holler,** Robert Keath 1931- *WhoRel 92*
**Holler,** York 1944- *ConCom 92*
**Holleran,** Eugene Martin 1922- *AmMWSc 92*
**Holleran,** Sheila 1939- *WhoRel 92*
**Holleran-Rivera,** Maria *WhoHisp 92*
**Hollerer,** Walter Friedrich 1922- *IntWW 91*
**Holles,** Robert 1926- *IntAu&W 91, WrDr 92*
**Holleweg dit Wegman,** Willy 1934- *WhoFI 92*
**Holley,** Alexander Lyman 1832-1882 *BiInAmS*
**Holley,** Audrey Rodgers 1939- *WhoAmL 92*
**Holley,** Charles H 1919- *AmMWSc 92*
**Holley,** Charles Hardin 1936-1959 *FacFETw*
**Holley,** Daniel Charles 1949- *AmMWSc 92*
**Holley,** Edward Gailon 1927- *WrDr 92*
**Holley,** Frieda Koster 1944- *AmMWSc 92*
**Holley,** Gregory Lee 1954- *WhoRel 92*
**Holley,** Horace Hotchkiss 1887-1960 *RelLAm 91*
**Holley,** Howard Lamar 1914- *AmMWSc 92*
**Holley,** Irving Brinton, Jr. 1919- *WrDr 92*
**Holley,** James W, III *WhoAmP 91*
**Holley,** James W., III 1926- *WhoBlA 92*
**Holley,** Jim 1943- *WhoBlA 92*
**Holley,** Jimmy W *WhoAmP 91*
**Holley,** Major 1924-1990 *AnObit 1990*
**Holley,** Marietta 1836-1926 *BenetAL 91*
**Holley,** Mary 1784-1846 *BenetAL 91*
**Holley,** Richard Andrew 1943- *AmMWSc 92*
**Holley,** Richard Howard 1943- *AmMWSc 92*
**Holley,** Robert Paul 1944- *WhoMW 92*
**Holley,** Robert W. 1922- *IntWW 91, Who 92*
**Holley,** Robert William 1922- *AmMWSc 92, WhoNob 90, WhoWest 92*
**Holley,** Ronald Victor 1931- *Who 92*
**Holley,** Sandra Cavanaugh 1943- *WhoBlA 92*
**Holley,** Sharon Yvonne 1949- *WhoBlA 92*
**Holley,** Stephen 1920- *Who 92*
**Holli,** Melvin George 1933- *IntAu&W 91, WrDr 92*
**Hollibaugh,** William Calvert 1916- *AmMWSc 92*
**Hollick** *Who 92*
**Hollick,** Baron 1945- *Who 92*
**Holliday,** Alfonso David 1931- *WhoBlA 92*
**Holliday,** Anne Elaine 1962- *WhoFI 92*
**Holliday,** Bertha Garrett 1947- *WhoBlA 92*
**Holliday,** Billie *WhoBlA 92*
**Holliday,** Charles Walter 1946- *AmMWSc 92*
**Holliday,** Dale Vance 1940- *AmMWSc 92*
**Holliday,** Frances B. *WhoBlA 92*
**Holliday,** Frederick 1935- *Who 92*
**Holliday,** Gay 1936- *WhoAmP 91*
**Holliday,** George Hayes 1922- *AmMWSc 92*
**Holliday,** Jennifer *WhoBlA 92*
**Holliday,** Jennifer 1960- *NotBlAW 92*
**Holliday,** Jennifer Yvette 1960- *WhoEnt 92*
**Holliday,** Leslie John 1921- *Who 92*
**Holliday,** Leslie Talbott 1948- *WhoEnt 92*
**Holliday,** Linda L. 1951- *WhoAmL 92*
**Holliday,** Malcolm A 1924- *AmMWSc 92*
**Holliday,** Patricia Ruth McKenzie 1935- *WhoRel 92*
**Holliday,** Prince E. 1935- *WhoBlA 92*
**Holliday,** Robert Kelvin 1933- *WhoAmP 91*
**Holliday,** Robin 1932- *IntWW 91, Who 92*
**Holliday,** Thomas Edgar 1948- *WhoAmL 92*
**Holliday-Hayes,** Wilhelmina Evelyn *WhoBlA 92*
**Hollien,** Harry 1926- *AmMWSc 92*
**Hollies,** Linda Hall 1943- *WhoRel 92*
**Hollies,** Norman Robert Stanley 1922- *AmMWSc 92*
**Hollifield,** Gordon R *WhoAmP 91*
**Holliger,** Heinz 1939- *ConCom 92, IntWW 91, NewAmDM, Who 92*
**Hollihan,** John Philip, III 1950- *WhoFI 92*
**Holliman,** Dan Clark 1932- *AmMWSc 92*
**Holliman,** David L. 1929- *WhoBlA 92*
**Holliman,** Earl 1928- *IntMPA 92, WhoEnt 92*
**Holliman,** Margaret Cloud 1930- *WhoAmP 91*
**Holliman,** Mary Constance 1930- *IntAu&W 91*
**Holliman,** Rhodes Burns 1928- *AmMWSc 92*
**Hollin,** Kenneth Ronald 1948- *WhoBlA 92*
**Hollin,** Shelby W. 1925- *WhoAmL 92*
**Hollindale,** Peter 1936- *WrDr 92*
**Holling,** Crawford Stanley 1930- *AmMWSc 92*
**Holling,** Herbert Edward 1908- *AmMWSc 92*
**Hollingdale,** Michael Richard 1946- *AmMWSc 92*
**Hollingdale,** Reginald John 1930- *IntAu&W 91, WrDr 92*
**Hollinger,** F Blaine 1935- *AmMWSc 92*
**Hollinger,** Henry Boughton 1933- *AmMWSc 92*
**Hollinger,** James Pippert 1933- *AmMWSc 92*
**Hollinger,** Mannfred Alan 1939- *AmMWSc 92*
**Hollinger,** Paula Colodny 1940- *WhoAmP 91*
**Hollinger,** Thomas Garber 1942- *AmMWSc 92*
**Hollinghurst,** Alan 1954- *ConNov 91*
**Hollings,** Ernest F. 1922- *AlmAP 92 [port], IntWW 91*
**Hollings,** Ernest Frederick 1922- *WhoAmP 91*
**Hollings,** Kenneth 1918- *Who 92*
**Hollings,** Leslie 1923- *IntWW 91*
**Hollings,** Michael Richard 1921- *IntWW 91, Who 92*
**Hollingshaus,** John *WhoAmP 91*
**Hollingshead,** Jonathan Charles 1954- *WhoAmL 92*
**Hollingsworth,** Alfred Delano 1942- *WhoBlA 92*
**Hollingsworth,** Charles Alvin 1917- *AmMWSc 92*
**Hollingsworth,** Charles Glenn 1946- *AmMWSc 92*
**Hollingsworth,** Charles Ray 1938- *WhoFI 92*
**Hollingsworth,** Cornelia Ann 1957- *AmMWSc 92*
**Hollingsworth,** David Royce 1946- *WhoRel 92*
**Hollingsworth,** David S *AmMWSc 92*
**Hollingsworth,** Devon Glenn 1946- *WhoRel 92*
**Hollingsworth,** Dorothy Frances 1916- *Who 92*
**Hollingsworth,** Gary Mayes 1944- *WhoMW 92*
**Hollingsworth,** Jack W 1924- *AmMWSc 92*
**Hollingsworth,** James W 1926- *AmMWSc 92*
**Hollingsworth,** John Alexander 1925- *WhoBlA 92*
**Hollingsworth,** John Gressett 1938- *AmMWSc 92*
**Hollingsworth,** Joseph Pettus 1922- *AmMWSc 92*
**Hollingsworth,** Joseph Rogers 1932- *WhoMW 92*
**Hollingsworth,** Leslie Anne 1946- *WhoEnt 92*
**Hollingsworth,** Margaret 1940- *IntAu&W 91, WrDr 92*
**Hollingsworth,** Margaret Camille 1929- *WhoWest 92*
**Hollingsworth,** Mary Carolyn 1947- *WhoRel 92*
**Hollingsworth,** Meredith Beaton 1941- *WhoWest 92*
**Hollingsworth,** Meredith Theodore 1916- *WhoEnt 92*
**Hollingsworth,** Michael Charles 1946- *Who 92*
**Hollingsworth,** Paul M 1932- *IntAu&W 91, WhoWest 92, WrDr 92*
**Hollingsworth,** Perlesta A. 1936- *WhoBlA 92*
**Hollingsworth,** Perlesta Arthur 1936- *WhoAmL 92*
**Hollingsworth,** Pierre 1931- *WhoBlA 92*
**Hollingsworth,** Ralph George 1947- *AmMWSc 92*
**Hollingsworth,** Ruth *TwCPaSc*
**Hollingsworth,** Samuel Hawkins, Jr. 1922- *WhoEnt 92*
**Hollington,** Richard R, Jr 1932- *WhoAmP 91*
**Hollington,** Richard Rings, Jr. 1932- *WhoAmL 92*
**Hollingworth,** Beverly 1935- *WhoAmP 91*
**Hollingworth,** Clare 1911- *Who 92*
**Hollingworth,** John Harold 1930- *Who 92*
**Hollingworth,** Leta Stetter 1886-1939 *WomPsyc, WomSoc*
**Hollingworth,** Mick 1945- *TwCPaSc*
**Hollingworth,** Peter John *Who 92*
**Hollingworth,** Robert Michael 1939- *AmMWSc 92*
**Hollins,** Harry B. d1991 *NewYTBS 91*
**Hollins,** Hubert Walter Elphinstone 1923- *Who 92*
**Hollins,** Joseph Edward 1927- *WhoBlA 92*
**Hollins,** Leroy 1945- *WhoBlA 92*
**Hollins,** Mitchell Leslie 1947- *WhoAmL 92*
**Hollins,** Robert Alphonso 1915- *WhoBlA 92*
**Hollins,** Robert Edward 1940- *AmMWSc 92*
**Hollinshead,** Ariel Cahill 1929- *AmMWSc 92*
**Hollinshead,** Earl Darnell, Jr. 1927- *WhoAmL 92, WhoFI 92*
**Hollinshead,** May B 1913- *AmMWSc 92*
**Hollinshead,** Peter Donald 1952- *WhoFI 92*
**Hollis** *Who 92*
**Hollis,** Allen 1932- *WhoRel 92*
**Hollis,** Anthony Barnard 1927- *Who 92*
**Hollis,** Bruce Warren 1951- *AmMWSc 92*
**Hollis,** Cecil George 1924- *AmMWSc 92*
**Hollis,** Charles Hatfield 1956- *WhoAmL 92*
**Hollis,** Clarence O. 1913- *WhoBlA 92N*
**Hollis,** Crispian *Who 92*
**Hollis,** Daniel Ayrton 1925- *Who 92*
**Hollis,** Daniel Lester, Jr 1924- *AmMWSc 92*
**Hollis,** Daryl Joseph 1946- *WhoAmL 92*
**Hollis,** Dean 1960- *WhoWest 92*
**Hollis,** Donald Roger 1936- *WhoFI 92*
**Hollis,** Gerald 1919- *Who 92*
**Hollis,** Gilbert Ray 1939- *AmMWSc 92*
**Hollis,** J Searcy 1918- *AmMWSc 92*
**Hollis,** James Martin 1938- *Who 92*
**Hollis,** Jan Michael 1941- *AmMWSc 92*
**Hollis,** Jesse Kendrick, Jr 1942- *WhoAmP 91*
**Hollis,** Jocelyn *DrAPF 91*
**Hollis,** John E 1931- *WhoIns 92*
**Hollis,** John Lee 1943- *WhoAmL 92*
**Hollis,** Joseph William 1922- *WhoMW 92*
**Hollis,** Kathleen Sue 1955- *WhoFI 92, WhoMW 92*
**Hollis,** Lanny Keith 1957- *WhoRel 92*
**Hollis,** Mark Dexter 1908- *AmMWSc 92*
**Hollis,** Mary Lee 1942- *WhoBlA 92*
**Hollis,** Meldon S., Jr. 1945- *WhoBlA 92*
**Hollis,** Meldon Stonewall Jackson 1945- *WhoAmL 92*
**Hollis,** Michael R. *WhoBlA 92*
**Hollis,** Posy *Who 92*
**Hollis,** Reginald 1932- *Who 92, WhoRel 92*
**Hollis,** Richard Whittington, Jr. 1954- *WhoWest 92*
**Hollis,** Roger Francis Crispian *Who 92*
**Hollis,** Sheila Slocum 1948- *WhoAmL 92*
**Hollis,** Susan Tower 1939- *WhoRel 92*
**Hollis,** Theodore M 1939- *AmMWSc 92*
**Hollis,** Walter Jesse 1921- *AmMWSc 92*
**Hollis,** William Frederick 1954- *AmMWSc 92*
**Hollis-Allbritton,** Cheryl Dawn 1959- *WhoMW 92*
**Hollis of Heigham,** Baroness 1941- *Who 92*
**Hollister,** Alan Scudder 1947- *AmMWSc 92*
**Hollister,** Charles Davis 1936- *AmMWSc 92*
**Hollister,** Charlotte Ann 1940- *AmMWSc 92*
**Hollister,** David Clinton 1942- *WhoAmP 91*
**Hollister,** David Manship 1929- *WhoEnt 92*
**Hollister,** Gideon Hiram 1817-1881 *BenetAL 91*
**Hollister,** Gloria 1902-1988 *FacFETw*
**Hollister,** John Baker, Jr. 1925- *WhoFI 92*
**Hollister,** Leo E 1920- *AmMWSc 92*
**Hollister,** Lincoln Steffens 1938- *AmMWSc 92*
**Hollister,** Ripley Robert 1955- *WhoWest 92*
**Hollister,** Victor F 1925- *AmMWSc 92*
**Hollister,** Walter M 1930- *AmMWSc 92*
**Holliway,** John Harold 1927- *WhoWest 92*
**Hollman,** Arthur 1923- *Who 92*
**Hollmann,** Stanley Edward *WhoMW 92*
**Hollo,** Anselm *DrAPF 91*
**Hollo,** Anselm 1934- *ConPo 91, IntAu&W 91, WrDr 92*
**Hollo,** Janos 1919- *IntWW 91*
**Hollocher,** Thomas Clyde, Jr 1931- *AmMWSc 92*
**Hollom,** Jasper 1917- *IntWW 91, Who 92*
**Holloman,** Charles James 1926- *WhoFI 92*
**Holloman,** George Vernon 1902-1946 *DcNCBi 3*
**Holloman,** James Horace, Jr. 1946- *WhoAmL 92*
**Holloman,** John L S, Jr 1919- *AmMWSc 92, WhoBlA 92*
**Holloman,** Robert C 1928- *WhoIns 92*
**Holloman,** Thaddeus Bailey 1955- *WhoBlA 92*
**Hollon,** Herbert Holstein 1936- *WhoBlA 92*
**Holloran,** Lori Jean 1956- *WhoRel 92*
**Holloszy,** John O 1933- *AmMWSc 92*
**Holloway,** Albert Curtis 1931- *WhoBlA 92*
**Holloway,** Anne Forrester 1941- *WhoBlA 92*
**Holloway,** Arthur D. 1931-1978 *WhoBlA 92N*
**Holloway,** Arthur Lee 1957- *WhoMW 92*
**Holloway,** Barry 1934- *Who 92*
**Holloway,** Benjamin Duke 1925- *WhoFI 92*
**Holloway,** Brian Douglass 1959- *WhoBlA 92*
**Holloway,** Bruce William 1928- *IntWW 91*
**Holloway,** Callon Wesley, Jr. 1953- *WhoBlA 92*
**Holloway,** Carl Maurice 1947- *WhoFI 92*
**Holloway,** Carlton Lawrence 1938- *WhoRel 92*
**Holloway,** Caroline T 1937- *AmMWSc 92*
**Holloway,** Cindy 1960- *WhoFI 92, WhoWest 92*
**Holloway,** Clarke L 1926- *AmMWSc 92*
**Holloway,** Clive Edward 1938- *AmMWSc 92*
**Holloway,** Clyde 1943- *AlmAP 92 [port]*
**Holloway,** Clyde C 1943- *WhoAmP 91*
**Holloway,** David 1924- *WrDr 92*
**Holloway,** David James 1943- *WhoWest 92*
**Holloway,** David Richard 1924- *IntAu&W 91, Who 92*
**Holloway,** Dennis Michael 1940- *AmMWSc 92*
**Holloway,** Derrick Robert Le Blond 1917- *Who 92*
**Holloway,** Donald Phillip 1928- *WhoAmL 92, WhoFI 92, WhoMW 92*
**Holloway,** Douglas Patrick 1938- *WhoFI 92*
**Holloway,** Edgar 1914- *TwCPaSc [port]*
**Holloway,** Edward L *WhoAmP 91*
**Holloway,** Ernest Leon 1930- *WhoBlA 92*
**Holloway,** Ernestine 1930- *WhoBlA 92*
**Holloway,** Frank 1924- *Who 92*
**Holloway,** Frank A 1940- *AmMWSc 92*
**Holloway,** Frederic Ancrum Lord 1914- *AmMWSc 92*
**Holloway,** Frederic Masters, Jr. 1939- *WhoFI 92*
**Holloway,** G Allen, Jr 1938- *AmMWSc 92*
**Holloway,** Gary Nelson 1956- *WhoRel 92*
**Holloway,** Geoffrey 1918- *ConPo 91, WrDr 92*
**Holloway,** George Allen, Jr. 1938- *WhoWest 92*
**Holloway,** Glenna Rose 1928- *IntAu&W 91*
**Holloway,** Harris M. 1949- *WhoBlA 92*
**Holloway,** Harry 1925- *WrDr 92*
**Holloway,** Harry Charles 1933- *AmMWSc 92*
**Holloway,** Harry Lee, Jr 1926- *AmMWSc 92*
**Holloway,** Herman M., Sr. 1922- *WhoBlA 92*
**Holloway,** Herman Monwell, Sr 1922- *WhoAmP 91*
**Holloway,** Hiliary H. 1928- *WhoBlA 92*
**Holloway,** Hiliary Hamilton 1928- *WhoFI 92*
**Holloway,** J. Mills 1924- *WhoBlA 92*
**Holloway,** James Ashley 1936- *AmMWSc 92*
**Holloway,** James D 1931- *WhoAmP 91*
**Holloway,** James L. 1927- *WhoBlA 92*
**Holloway,** James Lemuel, III 1922- *IntWW 91*
**Holloway,** Jerry 1941- *WhoBlA 92*
**Holloway,** Joaquin Miller, Jr. 1937- *WhoBlA 92*
**Holloway,** John 1920- *IntAu&W 91, IntWW 91, Who 92, WrDr 92*
**Holloway,** John Leith, Jr 1927- *AmMWSc 92*
**Holloway,** John Requa 1940- *AmMWSc 92*
**Holloway,** John Thomas 1922- *AmMWSc 92*
**Holloway,** Joseph 1951- *WhoEnt 92*
**Holloway,** Leland Edgar 1936- *AmMWSc 92*
**Holloway,** Mark 1917- *WrDr 92*

**Holloway,** Mark Albert 1961- *WhoAmP 91*
**Holloway,** Mark Graham 1917- *IntAu&W 91*
**Holloway,** Muriel 1927- *WhoAmP 91*
**Holloway,** Nathaniel Overton, Jr. 1926- *WhoBlA 92*
**Holloway,** Nigel 1953- *ConAu 135*
**Holloway,** Paul Howard 1943- *AmMWSc 92*
**Holloway,** Percival Geoffrey 1918- *IntAu&W 91*
**Holloway,** Peter William 1938- *AmMWSc 92*
**Holloway,** Ralph L, Jr 1935- *AmMWSc 92*
**Holloway,** Red 1927- *WhoBlA 92*
**Holloway,** Reginald Eric 1932- *Who 92*
**Holloway,** Richard Frederick *Who 92*
**Holloway,** Richard Frederick 1933- *IntWW 91*
**Holloway,** Richard George 1951- *AmMWSc 92*
**Holloway,** Robert Anthony 1946- *WhoWest 92*
**Holloway,** Robert Charles 1927- *WhoEnt 92*
**Holloway,** Robert Wester 1945- *WhoWest 92*
**Holloway,** Robin 1943- *ConCom 92*
**Holloway,** Robin Greville 1943- *IntWW 91, Who 92*
**Holloway,** Robin Hugh Ferguson 1922- *Who 92*
**Holloway,** Stanley 1890-1982 *FacFETw*
**Holloway,** Sterling 1905- *IntMPA 92*
**Holloway,** Sterling Price *WhoEnt 92*
**Holloway,** Thomas Thornton 1944- *AmMWSc 92*
**Holloway,** Wendell Mondoza 1933- *WhoFI 92*
**Holloway,** William J, Jr *WhoAmP 91*
**Holloway,** William J., Jr. 1923- *WhoAmL 92, WhoWest 92*
**Hollowell,** Bill 1928- *WhoAmP 91*
**Hollowell,** Donald L. 1917- *WhoBlA 92*
**Hollowell,** Johnny Laveral 1951- *WhoBlA 92*
**Hollowell,** Joseph Gurney, Jr 1932- *AmMWSc 92*
**Hollowell,** Kenneth Lawrence 1945- *WhoBlA 92*
**Hollowell,** Melvin L. 1930- *WhoBlA 92*
**Hollrah,** David 1948- *WhoAmL 92*
**Hollstein,** Ulrich 1927- *AmMWSc 92*
**Hollub,** Raymond M 1928- *AmMWSc 92*
**Hollwedel,** Charles Nicholas, Jr. 1923- *WhoWest 92*
**Hollweg,** Alexander 1936- *TwCPaSc*
**Hollweg,** Arnd 1927- *WhoRel 92*
**Hollweg,** Joseph Vincent 1944- *AmMWSc 92*
**Holly,** Buddy 1936-1959 *FacFETw*
**Holly,** Buddy 1938-1959 *NewAmDM*
**Holly,** Ella Louise 1949- *WhoBlA 92*
**Holly,** Frank Joseph 1934- *AmMWSc 92*
**Holly,** J. Hunter 1932- *WrDr 92*
**Holly,** John 1944- *WhoEnt 92*
**Hollyday,** Christopher 1970- *WhoEnt 92*
**Hollyday,** Guy T.O. d1991 *NewYTBS 91*
**Hollyer,** Arthur Rene 1938- *WhoAmL 92*
**Hollyer,** Richard Vervaet 1934- *WhoAmL 92*
**Hollyfield,** Joe G 1938- *AmMWSc 92*
**Hollyfield,** John S. 1939- *WhoAmL 92*
**Hollywood,** John M 1910- *AmMWSc 92*
**Holm,** Barbara J *WhoAmP 91*
**Holm,** Bart Edward 1925- *WhoFI 92*
**Holm,** Carl Henry 1915- *Who 92*
**Holm,** Carol 1943- *WhoWest 92*
**Holm,** Celeste 1919- *IntMPA 92, WhoEnt 92*
**Holm,** Dale M 1924- *AmMWSc 92*
**Holm,** David Garth 1950- *AmMWSc 92*
**Holm,** David George 1935- *AmMWSc 92*
**Holm,** Duane *WhoRel 92*
**Holm,** Edith Muriel 1921- *WhoAmP 91*
**Holm,** Elisabeth 1917- *IntWW 91*
**Holm,** Hanya 1898- *FacFETw*
**Holm,** Harvey William 1941- *AmMWSc 92*
**Holm,** Ian 1931- *ConTFT 9, IntMPA 92, IntWW 91, Who 92, WhoEnt 92*
**Holm,** John Cecil 1904-1981 *BenetAL 91*
**Holm,** L W 1923- *AmMWSc 92*
**Holm,** LeRoy George 1917- *AmMWSc 92, WhoMW 92*
**Holm,** Lloyd David 1953- *WhoMW 92*
**Holm,** Melvin C. 1916-1991 *NewYTBS 91*
**Holm,** Myron James 1930- *AmMWSc 92*
**Holm,** Peter Rowde 1931- *IntAu&W 91*
**Holm,** Richard H 1933- *AmMWSc 92, IntWW 91*
**Holm,** Robert Anton 1938- *WhoMW 92*
**Holm,** Robert E 1940- *AmMWSc 92*
**Holm,** Thomas Russell 1949- *WhoMW 92*
**Holm,** Tryggve O. A. 1905- *IntWW 91*
**Holm-Hansen,** Osmund 1928- *AmMWSc 92*
**Holm-Kennedy,** James William 1939- *AmMWSc 92*
**Holm Patrick,** Baron d1991 *Who 92N*
**Holman,** Alvin T. 1948- *WhoBlA 92*
**Holman,** Arthur Stearns 1926- *WhoWest 92*
**Holman,** B Leonard 1941- *AmMWSc 92*
**Holman,** Benjamin F. 1930- *WhoBlA 92*
**Holman,** Bob *DrAPF 91*
**Holman,** Bud George 1929- *WhoAmL 92*
**Holman,** Calvin Morns 1931- *WhoAmP 91*
**Holman,** Cheri Lynn 1956- *WhoMW 92*
**Holman,** Clarence Hugh 1914-1981 *DcNCBi 3*
**Holman,** Clyde Charles 1952- *WhoAmP 91*
**Holman,** Cranston William 1907- *AmMWSc 92*
**Holman,** David Calvin 1937- *WhoEnt 92*
**Holman,** David Shepard d1901 *BiInAmS*
**Holman,** Dennis Clark 1945- *WhoMW 92*
**Holman,** Doris Ann 1924- *WhoBlA 92*
**Holman,** Felice 1919- *WrDr 92*
**Holman,** Forest H. 1942- *WhoBlA 92*
**Holman,** Frank B 1930- *WhoAmP 91*
**Holman,** Gerald Hall 1929- *AmMWSc 92*
**Holman,** Gordon Dean 1949- *AmMWSc 92*
**Holman,** Halsted Reid 1925- *AmMWSc 92, WhoWest 92*
**Holman,** J Alan 1931- *AmMWSc 92*
**Holman,** Jack Philip 1934- *AmMWSc 92*
**Holman,** James 1947- *Who 92*
**Holman,** James Lewis 1926- *WhoMW 92*
**Holman,** John 1951- *ConAu 133*
**Holman,** John Ervin, Jr 1933- *AmMWSc 92*
**Holman,** John Foster 1946- *WhoFI 92, WhoWest 92*
**Holman,** Kingsley David 1922- *WhoAmP 91*
**Holman,** Larry Dean 1940- *WhoFI 92*
**Holman,** M Carl 1919-1988 *FacFETw*
**Holman,** Miriam Burton d1991 *NewYTBS 91*
**Holman,** Newton 1946- *WhoAmP 91*
**Holman,** Norman Frederick 1914- *Who 92*
**Holman,** Paul David 1943- *WhoWest 92*
**Holman,** Ralph Theodore 1918- *AmMWSc 92, IntWW 91, WhoMW 92*
**Holman,** Richard Bruce 1943- *AmMWSc 92*
**Holman,** Robert 1936- *IntAu&W 91, WrDr 92*
**Holman,** Rodney A. 1960- *WhoBlA 92*
**Holman,** Scott White, III 1957- *WhoFI 92*
**Holman,** Silas Whitcomb 1856-1900 *BiInAmS*
**Holman,** Thomas A 1948- *WhoAmP 91*
**Holman,** Wayne J, Jr 1907- *AmMWSc 92*
**Holman,** William Baker 1925- *WhoMW 92*
**Holman-Hoepfner,** Kristina Sue 1958- *WhoAmL 92*
**Holmberg,** Bo 1942- *IntWW 91*
**Holmberg,** Branton Keith 1936- *WhoFI 92*
**Holmberg,** Charles Arthur 1944- *AmMWSc 92*
**Holmberg,** Eric Robert Reginald 1917- *Who 92*
**Holmberg,** Joyce *WhoAmP 91*
**Holmberg,** Raymon E 1943- *WhoAmP 91*
**Holmberg,** Ronald Keith 1932- *WhoIns 92*
**Holmboe,** Vagn 1909- *ConCom 92, IntWW 91*
**Holmdahl,** John W 1924- *WhoAmP 91*
**Holme** *Who 92*
**Holme,** Barbara Shaw 1946- *WhoAmP 91*
**Holme,** Bryan 1913-1990 *SmATA 66*
**Holme,** Howard Kelley 1945- *WhoAmL 92*
**Holme,** K. E. *WrDr 92*
**Holme,** Michael Walter 1918- *Who 92*
**Holme,** Thomas 1624-1695 *BiInAmS*
**Holme,** Thomas T 1913- *AmMWSc 92*
**Holme of Cheltenham,** Baron 1936- *Who 92*
**Holmen,** Reynold Emanuel 1916- *AmMWSc 92*
**Holmer,** Alan F 1949- *WhoAmP 91*
**Holmer,** Alan Freeman 1949- *WhoAmL 92*
**Holmer,** Donald A 1934- *AmMWSc 92*
**Holmer,** Freeman 1917- *WhoWest 92*
**Holmer,** Mark Edwin 1942- *WhoRel 92*
**Holmer,** Paul Cecil Henry 1923- *Who 92*
**Holmer,** Paul L. 1916- *WrDr 92*
**Holmer,** Ralph Carrol 1916- *AmMWSc 92*
**Holmes,** Abiel 1763-1837 *BenetAL 91*
**Holmes,** Albert William, Jr 1932- *AmMWSc 92, WhoWest 92*
**Holmes,** Alfred 1939- *WhoRel 92*
**Holmes,** Alvin A *WhoAmP 91*
**Holmes,** Alvin Adolf 1939- *WhoBlA 92*
**Holmes,** Alvin W 1901- *AmMWSc 92*
**Holmes,** Anna-Marie 1946- *WhoEnt 92*
**Holmes,** Anthony 1931- *Who 92*
**Holmes,** Arthur F. 1924- *WrDr 92*
**Holmes,** Arthur Frank 1924- *WhoMW 92*
**Holmes,** Augusta 1847-1903 *NewAmDM*
**Holmes,** B.J. 1939- *TwCWW 91, WrDr 92*
**Holmes,** Barbara J. 1934- *WhoBlA 92*
**Holmes,** Barbara Ware 1945- *SmATA 65*
**Holmes,** Barry Trevor 1933- *Who 92*
**Holmes,** Brian 1920- *Who 92*
**Holmes,** Broox Garrett 1932- *WhoAmL 92*
**Holmes,** Bryan David 1962- *WhoMW 92*
**Holmes,** Calvin Virgil 1924- *AmMWSc 92*
**Holmes,** Carl 1925- *WhoBlA 92*
**Holmes,** Carl 1929- *WhoBlA 92*
**Holmes,** Carl Dean 1940- *WhoMW 92*
**Holmes,** Carl Dean 1944- *WhoAmP 91*
**Holmes,** Carlton 1951- *WhoBlA 92*
**Holmes,** Carol Ann 1944- *WhoMW 92*
**Holmes,** Charles 1868-1936 *TwCPaSc*
**Holmes,** Charles Everett 1931- *WhoAmL 92, WhoFI 92*
**Holmes,** Charles Robert 1918- *AmMWSc 92*
**Holmes,** Charlotte *DrAPF 91*
**Holmes,** Christian R 1946- *WhoAmP 91*
**Holmes,** Christopher Edward 1963- *WhoEnt 92*
**Holmes,** Christopher Francis 1959- *WhoFI 92*
**Holmes,** Claire Coleman 1931- *WhoFI 92*
**Holmes,** Clara *ScFEYrs*
**Holmes,** Clayton Ernest 1904- *AmMWSc 92*
**Holmes,** Clellon 1926- *BenetAL 91*
**Holmes,** Clifford Newton 1922- *AmMWSc 92*
**Holmes,** Clifton 1932- *WhoAmP 91*
**Holmes,** Cloyd James 1939- *WhoBlA 92*
**Holmes,** Curtis Frank 1943- *AmMWSc 92*
**Holmes,** D Brainerd 1921- *AmMWSc 92*
**Holmes,** Dale Arthur 1937- *AmMWSc 92*
**Holmes,** Dallas Scott 1940- *WhoAmL 92, WhoWest 92*
**Holmes,** Daniel Wyandt, Jr. 1938- *WhoMW 92*
**Holmes,** Darrell E 1934- *WhoAmP 91*
**Holmes,** David 1935- *Who 92*
**Holmes,** David G 1943- *AmMWSc 92*
**Holmes,** David Lee 1955- *WhoWest 92*
**Holmes,** David Richard 1940- *WhoFI 92, WhoMW 92*
**Holmes,** David S, Jr 1914- *WhoAmP 91, WhoBlA 92*
**Holmes,** David Vivian 1926- *Who 92*
**Holmes,** David Wesley 1953- *WhoAmL 92*
**Holmes,** David Willis 1914- *AmMWSc 92*
**Holmes,** Deborah L. 1946- *WhoMW 92*
**Holmes,** Doloris *DrAPF 91*
**Holmes,** Donald Eugene 1934- *AmMWSc 92*
**Holmes,** Donald G *WhoAmP 91*
**Holmes,** Dorothy E. 1943- *WhoBlA 92*
**Holmes,** Douglas Burnham 1938- *AmMWSc 92*
**Holmes,** Douglas J 1932- *WhoAmP 91*
**Holmes,** Douglas Quirk 1956- *WhoFI 92*
**Holmes,** Dyer Brainerd 1921- *IntWW 91*
**Holmes,** Edward Bruce 1927- *AmMWSc 92*
**Holmes,** Edward Lawson 1909- *AmMWSc 92*
**Holmes,** Edward Warren 1941- *AmMWSc 92*
**Holmes,** Eileen Martinez 1952- *WhoHisp 92*
**Holmes,** Eric Harmon 1951- *WhoWest 92*
**Holmes,** Ernest Shurtleff 1887-1960 *RelLAm 91*
**Holmes,** Everlena M. 1934- *WhoBlA 92*
**Holmes,** Ezekiel 1801-1865 *BiInAmS*
**Holmes,** Francis Simmons 1815-1882 *BiInAmS*
**Holmes,** Francis W 1929- *AmMWSc 92*
**Holmes,** Frank 1924- *Who 92*
**Holmes,** Gabriel 1769-1829 *DcNCBi 3*
**Holmes,** Gary Mayo 1943- *WhoBlA 92*
**Holmes,** Geoffrey Shorter 1928- *IntAu&W 91, IntWW 91, Who 92, WrDr 92*
**Holmes,** George Arthur 1927- *IntWW 91, Who 92*
**Holmes,** George Dennis 1926- *Who 92*
**Holmes,** George Edward 1937- *AmMWSc 92*
**Holmes,** George M 1929- *WhoAmP 91*
**Holmes,** Hamilton Earl 1941- *WhoBlA 92*
**Holmes,** Hardin 1926- *WhoAmL 92*
**Holmes,** Harry Dadisman 1944- *WhoFI 92*
**Holmes,** Helen 1892-1950 *ReelWom*
**Holmes,** Helen Bequaert 1929- *AmMWSc 92*
**Holmes,** Helen Juanita 1940- *IntAu&W 91*
**Holmes,** Henry Sidney, III 1944- *WhoBlA 92*
**Holmes,** Herbert 1932- *WhoBlA 92*
**Holmes,** Howard Frank 1931- *AmMWSc 92*
**Holmes,** Ivan Gregory 1935- *AmMWSc 92*
**Holmes,** Jack Edward 1941- *WhoMW 92*
**Holmes,** James Arthur, Jr. 1954- *WhoBlA 92*
**Holmes,** James Franklin 1945- *WhoBlA 92*
**Holmes,** James Frederick 1937- *AmMWSc 92*
**Holmes,** James Parker 1940- *WhoFI 92*
**Holmes,** Jay Thorpe 1942- *WhoFI 92*
**Holmes,** Jerry 1957- *WhoBlA 92*
**Holmes,** Jerry Dell 1935- *AmMWSc 92*
**Holmes,** John *WrDr 92*
**Holmes,** John 1904-1962 *BenetAL 91*
**Holmes,** John 1913- *IntAu&W 91, WrDr 92*
**Holmes,** John A 1949- *WhoAmP 91*
**Holmes,** John Carl 1932- *AmMWSc 92*
**Holmes,** John Charles 1934- *WhoAmL 92*
**Holmes,** John Ernest Raymond 1925- *Who 92*
**Holmes,** John Haynes 1879-1964 *AmPeW, BenetAL 91, RelLAm 91*
**Holmes,** John Leonard 1931- *AmMWSc 92*
**Holmes,** John Richard 1917- *AmMWSc 92*
**Holmes,** John Robert 1955- *WhoMW 92*
**Holmes,** John Sharp, Jr *WhoAmP 91*
**Holmes,** John Thomas 1936- *AmMWSc 92*
**Holmes,** John W. 1910-1989 *ConAu 134*
**Holmes,** John Wentworth 1925- *Who 92*
**Holmes,** Joseph Austin 1859-1915 *BiInAmS, DcNCBi 3*
**Holmes,** Joseph Charles 1925- *AmMWSc 92*
**Holmes,** Karen Frances 1955- *WhoEnt 92*
**Holmes,** Kathryn Voelker 1940- *AmMWSc 92*
**Holmes,** Kenneth Charles 1934- *IntWW 91, Who 92*
**Holmes,** Kenneth E 1942- *WhoIns 92*
**Holmes,** Kenneth Robert 1937- *AmMWSc 92*
**Holmes,** Kenneth Soar 1912- *Who 92*
**Holmes,** King Kennard 1937- *AmMWSc 92*
**Holmes,** Kirby Garrett 1933- *WhoAmP 91*
**Holmes,** L B 1932- *AmMWSc 92*
**Holmes,** L.P. 1895-1988 *TwCWW 91*
**Holmes,** Larry 1949- *IntWW 91, WhoBlA 92*
**Holmes,** Larry A 1941- *AmMWSc 92*
**Holmes,** Leo S. 1919- *WhoBlA 92*
**Holmes,** Lester Allan 1930- *WhoWest 92*
**Holmes,** Litdell Melvin, Jr. 1944- *WhoBlA 92*
**Holmes,** Lorene B. 1937- *WhoBlA 92*
**Holmes,** Louyco W. 1924- *WhoBlA 92*
**Holmes,** Lowell D. 1925- *WrDr 92*
**Holmes,** Margaret Cardozo 1898- *NotBlAW 92*
**Holmes,** Marion 1940- *WhoBlA 92*
**Holmes,** Marjorie 1910- *WrDr 92*
**Holmes,** Marjorie Rose *IntAu&W 91*
**Holmes,** Mark Lawrence 1938- *AmMWSc 92*
**Holmes,** Martin 1905- *IntAu&W 91, WrDr 92*
**Holmes,** Mary Brown 1950- *WhoBlA 92*
**Holmes,** Mary C *WhoAmP 91*
**Holmes,** Mary E 1945- *WhoAmP 91*
**Holmes,** Mary Emilee 1849-1906 *BiInAmS*
**Holmes,** Mary Jane 1825-1907 *BenetAL 91*
**Holmes,** Maurice 1911- *Who 92*
**Holmes,** Maurice Colston 1935- *Who 92*
**Holmes,** Michael 1936- *WhoWest 92*
**Holmes,** Michael Gene 1937- *WhoAmL 92*
**Holmes,** Michael William 1950- *WhoRel 92*
**Holmes,** Michael Wilson 1961- *WhoFI 92*
**Holmes,** Moses L. 1817-1889 *DcNCBi 3*
**Holmes,** Neal Jay 1931- *AmMWSc 92, WhoMW 92*
**Holmes,** Norman Leonard 1928- *WhoAmL 92*
**Holmes,** Oliver Wendell 1809-1894 *ScFEYrs*
**Holmes,** Oliver Wendell 1841-1935 *AmPolLe [port]*
**Holmes,** Oliver Wendell, Jr. 1841-1935 *BenetAL 91, FacFETw [port], RComAH*
**Holmes,** Oliver Wendell, Sr. 1809-1894 *BenetAL 91*
**Holmes,** Owen Gordon 1929- *AmMWSc 92*
**Holmes,** Patrick 1939- *Who 92*
**Holmes,** Paul 1954- *WhoRel 92*
**Holmes,** Paul Kinloch, III 1951- *WhoAmP 91*
**Holmes,** Paul Luther 1919- *WhoWest 92*
**Holmes,** Paul Thayer 1935- *AmMWSc 92*
**Holmes,** Peter 1932- *Who 92*
**Holmes,** Peter Douglas 1948- *WhoAmL 92*
**Holmes,** Peter F. 1932- *IntWW 91*
**Holmes,** Peter Sloan 1942- *Who 92*
**Holmes,** Philip Alan 1946- *WhoFI 92*
**Holmes,** Philip John 1945- *AmMWSc 92*
**Holmes,** Polly Mudge 1923- *WhoAmP 91*
**Holmes,** Presley Dixon 1929- *WhoEnt 92*
**Holmes,** R H Lavergne 1911- *AmMWSc 92*
**Holmes,** Randall Kent 1940- *AmMWSc 92*
**Holmes,** Raymond *WrDr 92*
**Holmes,** Reed M. 1917- *WhoRel 92*
**Holmes,** Richard 1912- *AmMWSc 92*
**Holmes,** Richard 1945- *ConAu 133, IntAu&W 91, WrDr 92*
**Holmes,** Richard Bruce 1939- *AmMWSc 92*

Holmes, Richard Gordon Heath 1945- Who 92
Holmes, Richard Turner 1936- AmMWSc 92
Holmes, Richard W 1923- WhoAmP 91
Holmes, Richard Winn 1923- WhoAmL 92, WhoMW 92
Holmes, Robert A 1943- WhoAmP 91, WhoBlA 92
Holmes, Robert Allen 1947- WhoAmL 92, WhoMW 92
Holmes, Robert B, Jr 1946- WhoAmP 91
Holmes, Robert C. 1945- WhoBlA 92
Holmes, Robert Edward 1922- WhoAmL 92, WhoAmP 91, WhoMW 92
Holmes, Robert Ernest 1943- WhoBlA 92
Holmes, Robert Kathrone, Jr. 1952- WhoBlA 92
Holmes, Robert L., Jr. 1934- WhoBlA 92
Holmes, Robert Lewis 1926- WrDr 92
Holmes, Robert Richard 1928- AmMWSc 92
Holmes, Robert V 1938- WhoAmP 91
Holmes, Robert W 1925- AmMWSc 92
Holmes, Robert Wayne 1950- WhoWest 92
Holmes, Robin Edmond Kendall 1938- Who 92
Holmes, Roger Arnold 1931- AmMWSc 92
Holmes, Shelly WhoEnt 92
Holmes, Stephen T. 1948- WhoAmL 92
Holmes, Stewart 1947- WhoWest 92
Holmes, Stewart Quentin 1929- IntAu&W 91
Holmes, Theodore Neal 1939- WhoBlA 92
Holmes, Theophilus Hunter 1804-1880 DcNCBi 3
Holmes, Thomas Ewen 1954- WhoRel 92
Holmes, Thomas Joseph 1953- WhoWest 92
Holmes, Thomas Leroy 1953- WhoWest 92
Holmes, Urban Tigner, III 1930-1981 DcNCBi 3
Holmes, Urban Tigner, Jr. 1900-1972 DcNCBi 3
Holmes, Wendell P., Jr. 1922- WhoBlA 92
Holmes, Wesley C. 1916- WhoRel 92
Holmes, Willard WhoWest 92
Holmes, William 1922- Who 92
Holmes, William 1940- WhoBlA 92
Holmes, William B. 1937- WhoBlA 92
Holmes, William D. 1945- WhoEnt 92
Holmes, William Ernest 1947- WhoIns 92
Holmes, William Farrar 1932- AmMWSc 92
Holmes, William H. 1960- WhoAmL 92
Holmes, William Henry 1846-1933 BenetAL 91
Holmes, William James 1955- WhoAmL 92
Holmes, William Leighton 1918- AmMWSc 92
Holmes, William Neil 1927- AmMWSc 92, Who 92
Holmes, Willie A. 1928- WhoBlA 92
Holmes, Willynda 1944- WhoAmP 91
Holmes, Wilma K. 1933- WhoBlA 92
Holmes, Zan W., Jr. WhoBlA 92
Holmes, Zoe Ann 1942- AmMWSc 92
Holmes, Zoe Ann Kerbey 1949- WhoAmL 92
Holmes a Court Who 92
Holmes a Court, Robert d1990 IntWW 91N
Holmes a Court, Robert 1937-1990 AnObit 1990
Holmes a Court, Robert Hamilton 1937-1990 FacFETw
Holmes Sellors, Patrick John Who 92
Holmgren, Arthur Herman 1912- AmMWSc 92
Holmgren, Fred WhoEnt 92
Holmgren, Fredrick Carlson 1926- WhoRel 92
Holmgren, Harry D 1928- AmMWSc 92
Holmgren, John P 1933- WhoAmP 91
Holmgren, Laton Earle 1915- WhoRel 92
Holmgren, Mark DrAPF 91
Holmgren, Noel Herman 1937- AmMWSc 92
Holmgren, Patricia Kern 1940- AmMWSc 92
Holmgren, Paul 1937- AmMWSc 92
Holmlund, Chester Eric 1921- AmMWSc 92
Holmlund, Lisa Lynne 1960- WhoWest 92
Holmpatrick, Baron 1955- Who 92
Holmquist, Barton 1943- AmMWSc 92
Holmquist, Carl Edward 1943- WhoFI 92
Holmquist, John Edward 1955- WhoEnt 92
Holmquist, John William 1960- WhoFI 92
Holmquist, Nelson D 1924- AmMWSc 92
Holmquist, Paul R 1943- WhoIns 92
Holmquist, Walter Richard 1934- AmMWSc 92, WhoWest 92
Holmsen, Theodore Waage 1930- AmMWSc 92
Holmstedt, Jan Olle Valter 1933- AmMWSc 92
Holmstrom, Frank Ross 1936- AmMWSc 92
Holmstrom, Fred Edward 1927- AmMWSc 92
Holmstrom, Gustaf Werner 1923- WhoRel 92
Holmstrom, Lynda Lytle 1939- WrDr 92
Holness, Gordon Victor Rix 1939- WhoFI 92
Holob, Gary M 1947- AmMWSc 92
Holohan, William A 1928- WhoAmP 91
Holoien, Martin O 1928- AmMWSc 92
Holonyak, N, Jr 1928- AmMWSc 92
Holorenshaw, Henry IntAu&W 91X
Holoubek, Gustaw 1923- IntWW 91
Holoubek, Viktor 1928- AmMWSc 92
Holowaty, Michael O 1922- AmMWSc 92
Holowenko, A R 1916- AmMWSc 92
Holowinsky, Andrew Wolodymyr 1936- AmMWSc 92
Holowka, David Allan 1948- AmMWSc 92
Holper, Jacob Charles 1924- AmMWSc 92
Holperin, James C 1950- WhoAmP 91
Holroyd, Emilie Adams 1931- WhoAmP 91
Holroyd, Frank 1935- Who 92
Holroyd, John Hepworth 1935- Who 92
Holroyd, Louis Vincent 1925- AmMWSc 92
Holroyd, Margaret Who 92
Holroyd, Michael 1935- ConAu 35NR, IntAu&W 91, IntWW 91, Who 92, WrDr 92
Holroyd, Richard Allan 1930- AmMWSc 92
Holroyd, William Arthur Hepworth 1938- Who 92
Holroyd, William Casper WhoAmP 91
Holroyde, Christopher Peter 1941- AmMWSc 92
Holroyde, Geoffrey Vernon 1928- Who 92
Holsapple, Dan Edward 1951- WhoWest 92
Holsapple, Keith Alan 1938- WhoWest 92
Holschbach, Vernon W 1926- WhoAmP 91
Holscher, Richard Harry 1928- WhoFI 92
Holschuh, John David 1926- WhoAmL 92, WhoMW 92
Holschuh, John David, Jr. 1955- WhoAmL 92
Holsclaw, Douglas S, Jr 1934- AmMWSc 92
Holsen, James N 1924- AmMWSc 92
Holsen, James Noble, Jr. 1924- WhoMW 92
Holsen, Thomas Michael 1959- AmMWSc 92
Holsendolph, Ernest 1935- WhoBlA 92
Holser, William Thomas 1920- AmMWSc 92
Holsey, Lilla G. 1941- WhoBlA 92
Holsey, Lucius H. 1842-1920 RelLAm 91
Holsey, William Fleming, Jr. 1923- WhoBlA 92
Holshevnikoff, Bill 1959- WhoEnt 92
Holshouser, Don F 1920- AmMWSc 92
Holshouser, James E., Jr. 1934- IntWW 91
Holshouser, James Eubert, Jr 1934- WhoAmP 91
Holshouser, Marion S WhoAmP 91
Holshouser, W L 1911- AmMWSc 92
Holsinger, Henry Ritz 1833-1905 AmPeW, RelLAm 91
Holsinger, John Robert 1934- AmMWSc 92
Holsinger, Kent Eugene 1956- AmMWSc 92
Holsinger, Ralph Lee 1918- WhoMW 92
Holsinger, Virginia Harris AmMWSc 92
Holsinger, William H 1952- WhoAmP 91
Holske, Robin Maule 1941- WhoEnt 92
Holson, Ralph Robert 1941- AmMWSc 92
Holsopple, Curtis Royer 1951- WhoRel 92
Holst, Edward Harland 1930- AmMWSc 92
Holst, Ernst Frederick 1934- WhoRel 92
Holst, Gerald Carl 1942- AmMWSc 92
Holst, Gustav 1874-1934 FacFETw, NewAmDM
Holst, Imogen 1907-1984 NewAmDM
Holst, Jewel Magee AmMWSc 92
Holst, Johan Jorgen 1937- IntWW 91
Holst, Mary-Ella 1934- WhoRel 92
Holst, Per 1939- IntWW 91
Holst, Sanford 1946- WhoWest 92
Holst, Spencer DrAPF 91
Holst, Timothy Bailey 1951- AmMWSc 92
Holst, William Frederick AmMWSc 92
Holstead, George B 1924- WhoAmP 91
Holstead, John Burnham 1938- WhoAmL 92
Holsted, James Leon 1944- WhoAmP 91
Holstein, Arthur G 1911- AmMWSc 92
Holstein, Arthur George, III 1939- WhoMW 92
Holstein, Barry Ralph 1943- AmMWSc 92
Holstein, Jay Allen 1938- WhoRel 92
Holstein, Jens Christian 1930- WhoFI 92
Holstein, John C. 1945- WhoAmL 92, WhoAmP 91, WhoMW 92
Holstein, Michael DrAPF 91
Holstein, Richard Alan 1954- WhoMW 92
Holstein, Thomas James 1943- AmMWSc 92
Holsten, John Robert 1931- AmMWSc 92
Holsten, Richard David 1937- AmMWSc 92
Holstener-Jorgensen, Helge 1924- IntWW 91
Holsti, Kalevi J. 1935- WrDr 92
Holsti, Ole Rudolf 1933- IntAu&W 91, WrDr 92
Holstius, Elvin Albert 1921- AmMWSc 92
Holston, James Benjamin, III 1958- WhoEnt 92
Holston, James Eugene 1951- WhoRel 92
Holston, James L 1942- AmMWSc 92
Holston, John Curtis 1939- WhoAmP 91
Holsztynski, Wlodzimierz 1942- AmMWSc 92
Holt, Alan Craig 1945- AmMWSc 92
Holt, Alex A. 1936- WhoWest 92
Holt, Aline G. 1942- WhoBlA 92
Holt, Arthur Frederick 1914- Who 92
Holt, Arthur H., Jr. 1931- WhoEnt 92
Holt, Ben Dance 1919- AmMWSc 92
Holt, Bertha Marian 1904- WhoRel 92
Holt, Bertha Merrill 1916- WhoAmP 91
Holt, Calvin L d1991 NewYTBS 91
Holt, Charlene Poland 1938- AmMWSc 92
Holt, Charles A 1921- AmMWSc 92
Holt, Charles Lee Roy, Jr 1924- AmMWSc 92
Holt, Charles Steele 1937- AmMWSc 92
Holt, Christopher Robert Vesey 1915- Who 92
Holt, Constance 1924- Who 92
Holt, David Lowell 1961- AmMWSc 92
Holt, David Simon 1935- WhoMW 92
Holt, Deloris Lenette WhoBlA 92
Holt, Dennis F. WhoWest 92
Holt, Donald Alexander 1932- AmMWSc 92
Holt, Donald H. 1941- WhoBlA 92
Holt, Donnell Shaw 1908-1982 DcNCBi 3
Holt, Dorothy L. 1930- WhoBlA 92
Holt, Douglas Emerson 1944- WhoAmP 91
Holt, Drawdy Norton, Jr 1922- WhoAmP 91
Holt, Earl Kendall, III 1945- WhoRel 92
Holt, Edgar Joe, Jr. 1955- WhoRel 92
Holt, Edward C, Jr 1923- AmMWSc 92
Holt, Edward James 1942- WhoRel 92
Holt, Edwin Duane 1951- WhoEnt 92
Holt, Edwin J. WhoBlA 92
Holt, Edwin Michael 1807-1884 DcNCBi 3
Holt, Eleanor Louise 1928- WhoAmP 91
Holt, Emily Newman DrAPF 91
Holt, Emogene 1927- WhoAmP 91
Holt, Eric 1944- TwCPaSc
Holt, Essie W. WhoBlA 92
Holt, Ethan Cleddy 1921- AmMWSc 92
Holt, Fred D. 1931- WhoBlA 92
Holt, Frederick Sheppard 1920- AmMWSc 92
Holt, George IntAu&W 91X
Holt, George Chandler 1907-1969 AmPeW
Holt, Gila TwCPaSc
Holt, Glen Edward 1939- WhoMW 92
Holt, Gordon Arthur 1951- WhoFI 92
Holt, Grace S. 1922- WhoBlA 92
Holt, Gregory Allan 1956- WhoRel 92
Holt, Hamilton 1872-1951 AmPeW
Holt, Harold 1926- WhoAmP 91
Holt, Harriette Lucille 1926- WhoAmL 92, WhoWest 92
Holt, Harvey Allen 1943- AmMWSc 92
Holt, Helen Keil 1937- AmMWSc 92
Holt, Herbert d1991 NewYTBS 91
Holt, Imy Vincent 1919- AmMWSc 92
Holt, Ivan Lee 1886-1967 RelLAm 91
Holt, Jack Who 92
Holt, Jack, Jr WhoAmP 91
Holt, Jack Wilson, Jr. 1929- WhoAmL 92
Holt, Jacob Farnum d1908 BiInAmS
Holt, Jacob W. 1811-1880 DcNCBi 3
Holt, James 1922- Who 92
Holt, James Allen 1934- AmMWSc 92
Holt, James Clarke 1922- IntWW 91, WrDr 92
Holt, James D 1940- WhoAmP 91
Holt, James Franklin 1924- AmMWSc 92
Holt, James Franklin 1927- WhoWest 92
Holt, James Henry 1833-1897 DcNCBi 3
Holt, James Richard d1990 Who 92N
Holt, James Richard 1931- Who 92
Holt, James Stokes, III 1927- WhoBlA 92
Holt, Jeanne Gleason 1937- WhoAmP 91
Holt, Jeffery Thomas 1959- WhoRel 92
Holt, Jeremy 1931-1965 TwCPaSc
Holt, Joe D 1940- WhoAmP 91
Holt, John 1923-1985 FacFETw
Holt, John Allen 1852-1915 DcNCBi 3
Holt, John Anthony L. Who 92
Holt, John B. 1915- WhoRel 92
Holt, John Bayley 1912- Who 92
Holt, John C. 1940- WhoFI 92
Holt, John Dominis, IV 1919- WhoWest 92
Holt, John Floyd 1915- AmMWSc 92
Holt, John Gilbert 1929- AmMWSc 92
Holt, John J. 1931- WhoBlA 92
Holt, John Lapworth 1912- Who 92
Holt, John Michael 1935- Who 92
Holt, John Riley 1918- Who 92
Holt, Joseph Paynter, Sr 1911- AmMWSc 92
Holt, Kathleen Magouirk 1947- WhoEnt 92
Holt, Kenneth Charles 1948- WhoBlA 92
Holt, Kevin Warren 1950- WhoWest 92
Holt, L Emmett 1855-1924 DcAmImH
Holt, Lawrence Shackleford 1851-1937 DcNCBi 3
Holt, Lee WhoAmP 91
Holt, Leigh Ann 1963- WhoAmL 92
Holt, Leo E. 1927- WhoBlA 92
Holt, Leon Conrad, Jr. 1925- WhoFI 92
Holt, Leroy 1967- WhoBlA 92
Holt, Lilian 1898-1983 TwCPaSc
Holt, Lynn Banks 1842-1920 DcNCBi 3
Holt, Marcia Chadwick 1936- WhoAmL 92
Holt, Maria Glen WhoAmP 91
Holt, Marjorie Sewell 1920- WhoAmP 91
Holt, Martin Hicks 1855-1914 DcNCBi 3
Holt, Mary Who 92
Holt, Matthew Leslie 1904- AmMWSc 92
Holt, Maurice 1918- AmMWSc 92
Holt, Michael 1929- WrDr 92
Holt, Michael, III 1778-1842 DcNCBi 3
Holt, Michael, Jr. 1723-1799 DcNCBi 3
Holt, Michael L. 1952- WhoBlA 92
Holt, Milton 1952- WhoAmP 91
Holt, Myron Charles 1925- WhoMW 92
Holt, Noel Clark 1935- WhoMW 92, WhoRel 92
Holt, Nora 1885?-1974 NotBlAW 92
Holt, Norman Barry 1949- WhoRel 92
Holt, Patrick Bryan 1953- WhoEnt 92
Holt, Perry Cecil 1912- AmMWSc 92
Holt, Peter Malcolm 1918- IntWW 91, Who 92
Holt, Peter Stephen 1951- AmMWSc 92
Holt, Richard Who 92
Holt, Richard A 1942- AmMWSc 92
Holt, Richard Anthony Appleby 1920- Who 92
Holt, Richard E 1923- AmMWSc 92
Holt, Richard Spencer 1942- WhoAmL 92
Holt, Richard Thomas 1938- AmMWSc 92
Holt, Robert Louis 1921- AmMWSc 92
Holt, Robert R 1917- ConAu 35NR
Holt, Rochelle Lynn DrAPF 91
Holt, Rochelle Lynn 1946- IntAu&W 91
Holt, Ronald Lee 1952- WhoAmL 92
Holt, Roy James 1947- AmMWSc 92
Holt, Rush Dew, Jr 1948- AmMWSc 92
Holt, Scott W 1948- WhoAmP 91
Holt, Simon 1958- ConCom 92
Holt, Smith Lewis, Jr 1938- AmMWSc 92
Holt, Sondra S. 1944- WhoAmL 92
Holt, Stephen S 1940- AmMWSc 92
Holt, Tex TwCWW 91
Holt, Thomas Charles Louis 1961- ConAu 135
Holt, Thomas Manning 1943- AmMWSc 92
Holt, Thomas Michael 1831-1896 DcNCBi 3
Holt, Tim 1945- WhoAmP 91
Holt, Timothy A 1953- WhoIns 92
Holt, Timothy Arthur 1953- WhoFI 92
Holt, Tom ConAu 135
Holt, Veitya Eileene 1962- WhoBlA 92
Holt, Vernon Emerson 1930- AmMWSc 92
Holt, Victoria IntAu&W 91X, Who 92
Holt, Victoria 1906- FacFETw, WrDr 92
Holt, Walter Lawrence 1859-1913 DcNCBi 3
Holt, William Anthony 1934- WhoWest 92
Holt, William Edwin 1839-1917 DcNCBi 3
Holt, William Harold, Jr. 1949- WhoEnt 92
Holt, William Henry 1939- AmMWSc 92
Holt, William Rainey 1798-1868 DcNCBi 3
Holt, William Robert 1930- AmMWSc 92
Holt-White, William Edward Bradden 1878- ScFEYrs
Holtam, Brenda 1960- TwCPaSc
Holtan, Heggie Nordahl 1909- AmMWSc 92
Holtan, Ruth Iona Tweeten 1924- WhoAmP 91
Holtan, Stanford Eugene 1921- WhoAmP 91
Holtby, Douglas Martin 1947- WhoEnt 92
Holtby, Kenneth F 1922- AmMWSc 92

**Holtby**, Robert Tinsley 1921- Who 92, WrDr 92
**Holtby**, Winifred 1898-1935 BiDBrF 2, FacFETw, RfGEnL 91
**Holte**, James Edward 1931- AmMWSc 92
**Holte**, Karl E 1931- AmMWSc 92
**Holten**, Bo 1948- ConCom 92
**Holten**, Darold Duane 1935- AmMWSc 92
**Holten**, James Joseph 1940- WhoMW 92
**Holten**, Virginia Zewe 1938- AmMWSc 92
**Holter**, Arlen Rolf 1946- WhoMW 92
**Holter**, Don Wendell 1905- WhoRel 92
**Holter**, Heinz 1904- IntWW 91
**Holter**, James Burgess 1934- AmMWSc 92
**Holter**, Marvin Rosenkrantz 1922- AmMWSc 92
**Holter**, Norman Jefferis 1914- AmMWSc 92
**Holtermann**, Karl 1894-1955 EncTR 91
**Holtfreter**, Johannes F. C. 1901- IntWW 91
**Holtfreter**, Johannes Friedrich Karl 1901- AmMWSc 92
**Holtgrewe**, Karen June 1952- WhoRel 92
**Holth**, Fredrik Davidson 1940- WhoAmL 92
**Holth**, Henry Albert 1927- WhoWest 92
**Holtham**, Carmen Gloria 1922- Who 92
**Holthaus**, Thomas Anthony 1941- WhoMW 92
**Holthus**, Rita May 1928- WhoAmP 91
**Holthusen**, Hans Egon 1913- IntWW 91
**Holtkamp**, Dorsey Emil 1919- AmMWSc 92, WhoMW 92
**Holtkamp**, Freddy Henry 1934- AmMWSc 92
**Holtkamp**, James Arnold 1949- WhoAmL 92
**Holtkamp**, Ronald W 1952- WhoIns 92
**Holtkamp**, Ronald Walter 1952- WhoFI 92
**Holtman**, Darlington Frank 1903- AmMWSc 92
**Holtman**, Mark Steven 1949- AmMWSc 92
**Holtmann**, Wilfried 1939- AmMWSc 92
**Holtmyer**, Marlin Dean 1937- AmMWSc 92
**Holton**, A. Linwood, Jr. 1923- IntWW 91, WhoAmP 91
**Holton**, Adolphus 1912- AmMWSc 92
**Holton**, Alfred Eugene 1852-1928 DcNCBi 3
**Holton**, Gerald 1922- AmMWSc 92, IntWW 91
**Holton**, Holland 1888-1947 DcNCBi 3
**Holton**, Isaac Farwell 1812-1874 BiInAmS
**Holton**, James R 1938- AmMWSc 92
**Holton**, Michael 1927- Who 92
**Holton**, Michael David 1961- WhoBlA 92
**Holton**, Nina d1908 BiInAmS
**Holton**, Priscilla Browne 1921- WhoBlA 92
**Holton**, Raymond William 1929- AmMWSc 92
**Holton**, Richard Henry 1926- WhoFI 92
**Holton**, Robert Lawrence 1928- AmMWSc 92
**Holton**, Tabitha Anne 1854-1886 DcNCBi 3
**Holton**, Thomas Ashley 1941- WhoAmL 92
**Holton**, William Chester 1939- WhoWest 92
**Holton**, William Coffeen 1930- AmMWSc 92
**Holtrop**, Philip Cornelius 1934- WhoRel 92
**Holtsinger**, Edgar M 1922- WhoAmP 91
**Holtslander**, William John 1937- AmMWSc 92
**Holttum**, Eric 1895-1990 AnObit 1990
**Holttum**, Richard Eric d1990 Who 92N
**Holtum**, Alfred G 1918- AmMWSc 92
**Holtvedt**, John R 1920- WhoAmP 91
**Holty**, Ludwig Heinrich Cristoph 1748-1776 BlkwCEP
**Holtz**, Abel WhoHisp 92
**Holtz**, Alan Edward 1932- WhoRel 92
**Holtz**, Alan Steffen, Sr. 1922- WhoMW 92
**Holtz**, Carl Frederick 1940- AmMWSc 92
**Holtz**, Daniel Martin 1959- WhoFI 92
**Holtz**, David 1942- AmMWSc 92
**Holtz**, Edgar Wolfe 1922- WhoAmL 92
**Holtz**, Gilbert Joseph 1924- WhoFI 92
**Holtz**, Glenn Edward 1938- WhoFI 92, WhoMW 92
**Holtz**, Paul Roscoe 1933- WhoAmP 91
**Holtz**, Sam 1942- WhoEnt 92
**Holtz**, Wesley G 1911- AmMWSc 92
**Holtzapfel**, Patricia Kelly 1948- WhoWest 92
**Holtzberg**, Frederic 1922- AmMWSc 92
**Holtzclaw**, Henry Fuller, Jr 1921- AmMWSc 92
**Holtzclaw**, Joyce Madelyn Irene 1956- WhoWest 92
**Holtzer**, Alfred Melvin 1929- AmMWSc 92
**Holtzer**, Howard 1923- AmMWSc 92
**Holtzer**, Marilyn Emerson 1938- AmMWSc 92
**Holtzman**, Abraham 1921- IntAu&W 91, WrDr 92
**Holtzman**, Alexander 1924- WhoFI 92
**Holtzman**, Andrew Jay 1953- WhoEnt 92
**Holtzman**, Eric 1939- AmMWSc 92
**Holtzman**, Golde Ivan 1946- AmMWSc 92
**Holtzman**, Jerome Joseph 1930- WhoRel 92
**Holtzman**, Jordan L 1933- AmMWSc 92
**Holtzman**, Julian Charles 1935- AmMWSc 92
**Holtzman**, Neil Anton 1934- AmMWSc 92
**Holtzman**, Richard Beves 1927- AmMWSc 92
**Holtzman**, Robert Arthur 1929- WhoAmL 92
**Holtzman**, Samuel 1955- AmMWSc 92
**Holtzman**, Seymour 1934- AmMWSc 92
**Holtzman**, Wayne H 1923- ConAu 34NR, IntWW 91
**Holtzman**, Wayne Harold 1923- WrDr 92
**Holtzman**, William Scott 1951- WhoEnt 92
**Holtzmann**, Howard Marshall 1921- WhoAmL 92
**Holtzmann**, Oliver Vincent 1922- AmMWSc 92
**Holtzschue**, Karl Bressem 1938- WhoAmL 92
**Holub**, Bruce John 1944- AmMWSc 92
**Holub**, Donald Arthur 1928- AmMWSc 92
**Holub**, Elaine Nathanson 1949- WhoWest 92
**Holub**, Fred F 1921- AmMWSc 92
**Holub**, Gregory Steven 1950- WhoMW 92
**Holub**, James Robert 1942- AmMWSc 92
**Holub**, Miroslav 1923- IntAu&W 91, IntWW 91
**Holub**, Robert C 1949- ConAu 35NR
**Holubec**, Zenowie Michael 1937- AmMWSc 92
**Holubka**, Joseph Walter 1950- AmMWSc 92
**Holuj**, Frank 1927- AmMWSc 92
**Holum**, John Robert 1928- AmMWSc 92, WhoMW 92
**Holve**, Leslie Martin 1926- WhoWest 92
**Holveck**, Jack 1943- WhoAmP 91
**Holverson**, Edwin LeRoy 1934- AmMWSc 92
**Holvey**, Samuel Boyer 1935- WhoEnt 92
**Holway**, James Colin 1927- WhoFI 92
**Holway**, James Gary 1931- AmMWSc 92
**Holway**, Lowell Hoyt, Jr 1931- AmMWSc 92
**Holwell**, Peter 1936- Who 92
**Holwerda**, David Earl 1932- WhoRel 92
**Holwerda**, James G 1925- AmMWSc 92
**Holwerda**, Robert Alan 1947- AmMWSc 92
**Holwill**, Richard N 1945- WhoAmP 91
**Holy**, Norman Lee 1941- AmMWSc 92
**Holyer**, Erna Maria 1925- IntAu&W 91
**Holyer**, Ernie 1925- WrDr 92
**Holyer**, Robert Kent 1946- WhoRel 92
**Holyfield**, Evander NewYTBS 91, WhoBlA 92
**Holyfield**, Evander 1962- BlkOlyM, News 91 [port], -91-3 [port]
**Holyoake**, Keith Jacka 1904-1983 FacFETw
**Holyoke**, Caleb William, Jr 1943- AmMWSc 92
**Holyoke**, Edward Augustus 1728-1829 BiInAmS
**Holyoke**, Edward Augustus 1908- AmMWSc 92
**Holyoke**, Samuel 1762-1820 NewAmDM
**Holyoke**, Thomas Campbell 1922- AmMWSc 92
**Holz**, Anthony David 1942- WhoRel 92
**Holz**, George Gilbert, Jr 1922- AmMWSc 92
**Holz**, Harry George 1934- WhoAmL 92
**Holz**, Max 1889-1933 EncTR 91 [port]
**Holz**, Michael Harold 1942- WhoMW 92
**Holzach**, Robert 1922- IntWW 91, Who 92
**Holzapfel**, Christina Marie 1942- AmMWSc 92
**Holzapfel**, George Stephen 1951- WhoAmL 92
**Holzapfel**, James William 1944- WhoAmL 92
**Holzbach**, R Thomas 1929- AmMWSc 92
**Holzbauer**, Dale Lee 1947- WhoRel 92
**Holzbecher**, Jiri 1943- AmMWSc 92
**Holzberlein**, Thomas M 1926- AmMWSc 92
**Holzel**, Robert William 1933- WhoWest 92
**Holzemer**, Robert Liszt 1913- WhoMW 92
**Holzendorf**, Betty S 1939- WhoAmP 91, WhoBlA 92
**Holzer**, Alfred 1925- AmMWSc 92
**Holzer**, Arnim S. 1959- WhoFI 92
**Holzer**, Gunther Ulrich 1942- AmMWSc 92
**Holzer**, Harry Joseph 1957- WhoMW 92
**Holzer**, Jenny 1950- IntWW 91, WorArt 1980 [port]
**Holzer**, John Michael, Jr. 1952- WhoMW 92
**Holzer**, Robert Edward 1906- AmMWSc 92
**Holzer**, Robert Lee 1938- WhoMW 92
**Holzer**, Siegfried Mathias 1936- AmMWSc 92
**Holzer**, Thomas Edward 1944- AmMWSc 92
**Holzer**, Thomas Lequear 1944- AmMWSc 92, WhoWest 92
**Holzer**, Timothy J 1951- AmMWSc 92
**Holzhandler**, Dora 1928- TwCPaSc
**Holzheauser**, Steve 1953- WhoAmP 91
**Holzhey**, Charles Steven 1936- AmMWSc 92
**Holzinger**, Joseph Rose 1914- AmMWSc 92
**Holzinger**, Thomas Walter 1930- AmMWSc 92
**Holzman**, Albert G 1921- AmMWSc 92
**Holzman**, D. Keith 1936- WhoEnt 92
**Holzman**, Dennis Tilden DrAPF 91
**Holzman**, Franklyn D. 1918- WrDr 92
**Holzman**, George 1920- AmMWSc 92
**Holzman**, George Robert 1919- AmMWSc 92
**Holzman**, Gerald Bruce 1933- AmMWSc 92
**Holzman**, James Louis 1949- WhoAmL 92
**Holzman**, Lew DrAPF 91
**Holzman**, Malcolm DcTwDes
**Holzman**, Philip S 1922- AmMWSc 92
**Holzman**, Robert Stephen 1940- AmMWSc 92
**Holzman**, Sheridan Verne 1930- WhoMW 92
**Holzmann**, Ernest G 1921- AmMWSc 92
**Holzmann**, Gerard J 1951- AmMWSc 92
**Holzmann**, Richard Thomas 1927- AmMWSc 92
**Holzmeister**, Alicia Lynn 1954- WhoAmL 92
**Holzrichter**, John Frederick 1941- AmMWSc 92
**Holzwarth**, George Michael 1937- AmMWSc 92
**Holzwarth**, James C 1924- AmMWSc 92
**Holzworth**, Jean 1915- AmMWSc 92
**Holzworth**, Robert H, II 1950- AmMWSc 92
**Hom**, Ben Lin 1936- AmMWSc 92
**Hom**, Foo Song 1929- AmMWSc 92
**Hom**, Richard Yee 1950- WhoWest 92
**Hom**, Theresa Maria 1957- WhoMW 92
**Homa**, John, Jr. 1951- WhoFI 92
**Homan**, Benjamin Keith 1959- WhoRel 92
**Homan**, Clarke Gilbert 1931- AmMWSc 92
**Homan**, Delmar Charles 1927- WhoMW 92
**Homan**, Elton Richard 1932- AmMWSc 92
**Homan**, John Vincent 1927- Who 92
**Homan**, Kenneth B. 1953- WhoRel 92
**Homan**, Martin J. 1953- WhoRel 92
**Homan**, Mildred Haerther 1922- WhoAmP 91
**Homan**, Ralph D 1928- WhoAmP 91
**Homan**, Ralph William 1951- WhoFI 92, WhoWest 92
**Homan**, Richard F 1924- WhoAmP 91
**Homan**, Ruth Elizabeth 1944- AmMWSc 92
**Homan**, Thomas Buckhurst 1921- Who 92
**Homan**, William E. d1991 NewYTBS 91
**Homann**, Frederick Anthony 1929- AmMWSc 92
**Homann**, H Robert 1937- AmMWSc 92
**Homann**, Peter H 1933- AmMWSc 92
**Homans**, George Caspar 1910- Who 92
**Homans**, Peter 1930- WrDr 92
**Homberg**, Otto Albert 1931- AmMWSc 92
**Homberg**, Robert H. 1935- WhoEnt 92
**Homberger**, Dominique Gabrielle 1948- AmMWSc 92
**Homberger**, Eric 1942- IntAu&W 91, WrDr 92
**Hombs**, Margaret Mavourneen 1934- WhoWest 92
**Homburger**, Freddy 1916- AmMWSc 92
**Homburger**, Henry A 1940- AmMWSc 92
**Homburger**, Walter Fritz 1924- WhoEnt 92
**Home** Who 92
**Home**, Earl of Who 92
**Home**, Lord FacFETw
**Home**, Alex Douglas 1903- WrDr 92
**Home**, Anna Margaret 1938- Who 92
**Home**, David George 1904- Who 92
**Home**, George 1920- Who 92
**Home**, John 1722-1808 RfGEnL 91
**Home**, William Douglas 1912- IntAu&W 91, Who 92, WrDr 92
**Home Of The Hirsel**, Baron 1903- IntWW 91, Who 92
**Home Robertson**, John David 1948- Who 92
**Homeier**, Edwin H, Jr 1937- AmMWSc 92
**Homeier**, Skip 1930- IntMPA 92
**Homelson**, Rochelle 1954- WhoAmP 91
**Homer**, Arthur DrAPF 91
**Homer**, Arthur Thomas 1951- WhoMW 92
**Homer**, Barry Wayne 1950- WhoAmL 92
**Homer**, Bruce Arthur 1931- WhoFI 92
**Homer**, George Mohn 1924- AmMWSc 92
**Homer**, Louis David 1935- AmMWSc 92
**Homer**, Paul Bruce 1939- AmMWSc 92
**Homer**, Raymond Rodney 1926- WhoEnt 92
**Homer**, Roger Harry 1924- AmMWSc 92
**Homer**, Ronald A. 1947- WhoBlA 92
**Homer**, Sidney 1864-1953 BenetAL 91
**Homer**, Steven Elliott 1952- AmMWSc 92
**Homer**, Thomas J 1947- WhoAmP 91
**Homer**, William Innes 1929- WrDr 92
**Homer**, Winslow 1836-1910 RComAH
**Homes**, A.M. DrAPF 91
**Homestead**, Susan 1937- WhoWest 92
**Homeyer**, August Henry 1908- AmMWSc 92, WhoMW 92
**Homeyer**, Howard C. 1933- WhoFI 92
**Homiak**, Albert S 1949- WhoIns 92
**Hommel**, Nicolas 1915- IntWW 91
**Hommel**, William Sam, Jr. 1960- WhoAmL 92
**Hommen**, Jan H. M. 1943- WhoFI 92
**Hommersand**, Max Hoyt 1930- AmMWSc 92
**Hommes**, Frits A 1934- AmMWSc 92
**Hommrich**, Denis E 1945- WhoAmP 91
**Homolka**, Calvin Dean, II 1950- WhoMW 92
**Hompertz**, Melba Ann 1936- WhoFI 92
**Homsher**, Earl Edwin, II 1942- AmMWSc 92
**Homsher**, Paul John 1931- AmMWSc 92
**Homsy**, Charles Albert 1932- AmMWSc 92
**Hon**, David Nyok-Sai 1947- AmMWSc 92
**Hon**, Edward Harry Gee 1917- AmMWSc 92
**Hon**, Jackson P. 1932- WhoRel 92
**Hon**, Ralph Clifford 1903- WhoAmL 92
**Hon**, Wilma Joy 1934- WhoAmP 91
**Hon-cho Lo** EncAmaz 91
**Honablue**, Richard Riddick 1948- WhoBlA 92
**Honaker**, Carl Boggess 1926- AmMWSc 92
**Honaker**, Jimmie Joe 1939- WhoAmL 92
**Honaker**, Richard Henderson 1951- WhoAmP 91
**Honaman**, June N 1920- WhoAmP 91
**Honan**, Kevin G WhoAmP 91
**Honan**, Park 1928- DcLB 111 [port], IntAu&W 91, WrDr 92
**Honan**, William Holmes 1930- IntAu&W 91
**Honchi** EncAmaz 91
**Honda**, Barry Marvin 1950- AmMWSc 92
**Honda**, Carol A. WhoEnt 92
**Honda**, Herbert Junji 1927- WhoAmP 91
**Honda**, Kazuo AmMWSc 92
**Honda**, Shigeru Irwin 1927- AmMWSc 92
**Honda**, Soichiro 1906- IntWW 91
**Honda**, Soichiro 1906-1991 NewYTBS 91 [port], News 92-1
**Hondeghem**, Luc M 1944- AmMWSc 92
**Honderich**, Edgar Dawn Ross 1933- Who 92
**Honderich**, Ted 1933- ConAu 35NR, WrDr 92
**Hondo**, Med 1936- IntDcF 2-2
**Hondros**, Ernest Demetrios 1930- IntWW 91, Who 92
**Hone**, Daniel W 1937- AmMWSc 92
**Hone**, David 1928- Who 92
**Hone**, Evie 1894-1955 FacFETw, TwCPaSc
**Hone**, Joseph 1937- ConAu 35NR, IntAu&W 91, WrDr 92
**Hone**, Louis Raymond 1950- WhoEnt 92
**Hone**, Philip 1780-1851 BenetAL 91
**Hone**, Ralph 1896- IntWW 91, Who 92
**Hone**, Robert Monro 1923- Who 92
**Hone**, William 1780-1842 DcLB 110 [port]
**Honea**, Franklin Ivan 1931- AmMWSc 92
**Honea**, Glenn Dale 1953- WhoWest 92
**Honeck**, Henry Charles 1930- AmMWSc 92
**Honecker**, Erich 1912- FacFETw, IntWW 91
**Honecker**, George J. DrAPF 91
**Honecker**, Margot 1927- IntWW 91
**Honegger**, Arthur 1892-1955 FacFETw, NewAmDM
**Honegger**, Fritz 1917- IntWW 91
**Honegger**, Gottfried 1917- WorArt 1980
**Honer**, Paul Edward WhoFI 92
**Hones**, Michael J 1942- AmMWSc 92
**Honey**, Michael 1941- Who 92
**Honey**, Richard Churchill 1924- AmMWSc 92
**Honey**, Robert John 1936- Who 92

**Honeychurch,** Denis Arthur 1946- *WhoAmL 92*
**Honeycombe,** Gordon *Who 92*
**Honeycombe,** Gordon 1936- *ConAu 34NR, IntAu&W 91, WrDr 92*
**Honeycombe,** Robert 1921- *Who 92*
**Honeycombe,** Robert William Kerr 1921- *IntWW 91*
**Honeycombe,** Ronald Gordon 1936- *Who 92*
**Honeycutt,** Roy Lee *WhoRel 92*
**Honeycutt,** Thomas Lynn 1942- *AmMWSc 92*
**Honeyman,** Brenda *IntAu&W 91X, WrDr 92*
**Honeyman,** Janice Lynne 1949- *IntWW 91*
**Honeyman,** Merton Seymour 1925- *AmMWSc 92*
**Honeysett,** Martin 1943- *Who 92*
**Honeywell,** Larry Gene 1935- *WhoFI 92, WhoMW 92*
**Honeywell,** Wallace I 1936- *AmMWSc 92*
**Hong Qian** *IntWW 91*
**Hong Xuezhi** 1913- *IntWW 91*
**Hong,** Bor-Shyue *AmMWSc 92*
**Hong,** Chung Il 1938- *AmMWSc 92*
**Hong,** Donald David *AmMWSc 92*
**Hong,** Francis *WhoRel 92*
**Hong,** Howard V. 1912- *WrDr 92*
**Hong,** James 1929?- *ConTFT 9*
**Hong,** Jau-Shyong 1943- *AmMWSc 92*
**Hong,** Jen Shiang 1939- *AmMWSc 92*
**Hong,** Keelung 1943- *AmMWSc 92*
**Hong,** Ki C 1936- *AmMWSc 92*
**Hong,** Kuochih *AmMWSc 92*
**Hong,** Norman G. Y. 1947- *WhoWest 92*
**Hong,** Perry 1965- *WhoEnt 92*
**Hong,** Pill Whoon 1921- *AmMWSc 92*
**Hong,** Richard 1929- *AmMWSc 92*
**Hong,** Se June 1944- *AmMWSc 92*
**Hong,** Suk Ki 1928- *AmMWSc 92*
**Hong,** Sun Il 1952- *WhoWest 92*
**Hong,** Wen-Hai 1934- *AmMWSc 92*
**Hong,** Wilson S. 1934- *IntMPA 92*
**Hong Young,** Arabella 1927- *WhoEnt 92*
**Hongen,** Elisabeth 1906- *NewAmDM*
**Hongladarom,** Sunthorn 1912- *IntWW 91, Who 92*
**Hongo,** Garrett 1951- *ConPo 91, WrDr 92*
**Hongo,** Garrett Kaoru *DrAPF 91*
**Hongo,** Garrett Kaoru 1951- *ConAu 133*
**Honhart,** Barbara Ann Baker 1942- *WhoMW 92*
**Honhon,** Paul-Marie Joseph Alexandre J. 1948- *WhoWest 92*
**Honig,** Arnold 1928- *AmMWSc 92*
**Honig,** Barbara J 1933- *WhoAmP 91*
**Honig,** Bill 1937- *WhoAmP 91, WhoWest 92*
**Honig,** Carl Robert 1925- *AmMWSc 92*
**Honig,** David Herman 1928- *AmMWSc 92*
**Honig,** Donald *DrAPF 91*
**Honig,** Edwin *DrAPF 91*
**Honig,** Edwin 1919- *ConPo 91, IntAu&W 91, IntWW 91, WrDr 92*
**Honig,** Emanuel M. 1915- *WhoRel 92*
**Honig,** Frederick 1912- *Who 92*
**Honig,** George Raymond *AmMWSc 92*
**Honig,** George Raymond 1936- *WhoMW 92*
**Honig,** John Gerhart 1923- *AmMWSc 92*
**Honig,** Lawrence Edward 1948- *WhoFI 92, WhoMW 92*
**Honig,** Lucy *DrAPF 91*
**Honig,** Martin 1941- *WhoAmL 92*
**Honig,** Milton Leslie 1944- *AmMWSc 92*
**Honig,** Richard Edward 1917- *AmMWSc 92*
**Honig,** Robyn Frye 1960- *WhoAmL 92*
**Honigberg,** Bronislaw Mark 1920- *AmMWSc 92*
**Honigberg,** Irwin Leon 1930- *AmMWSc 92*
**Honigman,** David M 1955- *WhoAmP 91*
**Honigmann,** Ernst Anselm Joachim 1927- *Who 92*
**Honkala,** Fred Saul 1919- *AmMWSc 92*
**Honkanen,** Pentti A 1932- *AmMWSc 92*
**Honkisz,** James Edward 1948- *WhoAmL 92*
**Honma,** Shigemi 1920- *AmMWSc 92*
**Honn,** Michael Alan 1956- *WhoMW 92*
**Honnell,** Martial A 1910- *AmMWSc 92*
**Honnell,** Pierre M 1908- *AmMWSc 92*
**Honnert,** Gary Thomas 1952- *WhoMW 92*
**Honnold,** Vincent Richard 1924- *AmMWSc 92*
**Honoratus of Lerins** 350?-430? *EncEarC*
**Honore,** Antony Maurice 1921- *Who 92*
**Honore,** Stephan LeRoy 1938- *WhoBlA 92*
**Honore,** Tony 1921- *WrDr 92*
**Honorius** 384-423 *EncEarC*
**Honoroff,** Richard Alan 1951- *WhoEnt 92*
**Honour,** Hugh 1927- *Who 92, WrDr 92*
**Honour,** Scott Michael 1966- *WhoFI 92*
**Honri,** Peter 1929- *WrDr 92*
**Honri,** Peter Roger Baynham 1929- *IntAu&W 91*
**Honrubia,** Vicente 1934- *AmMWSc 92*
**Honsaker,** John Leonard 1934- *AmMWSc 92*
**Honsberg,** Wolfgang 1929- *AmMWSc 92*
**Honsinger,** Harvey Paul 1960- *WhoAmL 92*
**Honsinger,** Vernon Bertram *AmMWSc 92*
**Honstead,** William Henry 1916- *AmMWSc 92*
**Honton,** Edward Jude 1955- *WhoMW 92*
**Honton,** Margaret *DrAPF 91*
**Honts,** George Edward, III 1940- *WhoAmL 92*
**Hontzeas,** S 1923- *AmMWSc 92*
**Honwana,** Luis Bernardo 1942- *LiExTwC*
**Honywood,** Filmer 1930- *Who 92*
**Honzatko,** George Joseph 1926- *WhoMW 92*
**Hoo,** Cheong Seng 1938- *AmMWSc 92, WhoWest 92*
**Hoo,** Joe Jie 1944- *AmMWSc 92, WhoMW 92*
**Hoober,** John Kenneth 1938- *AmMWSc 92*
**Hoobing,** Stanley Carl 1942- *WhoRel 92*
**Hoobler,** Elizabeth Ulrich 1928- *WhoMW 92*
**Hoobler,** James Ferguson 1938- *WhoAmP 91*
**Hoobler,** Sibley Worth 1911- *AmMWSc 92*
**Hood** *Who 92*
**Hood,** Viscount 1914- *Who 92*
**Hood,** Ann 1956- *IntAu&W 91*
**Hood,** Boyde W. 1939- *WhoEnt 92*
**Hood,** Carroll V 1936- *WhoAmP 91*
**Hood,** Christopher 1943- *WrDr 92*
**Hood,** Claude Ian 1925- *AmMWSc 92*
**Hood,** Donald C 1942- *AmMWSc 92*
**Hood,** Donald Wilbur 1918- *AmMWSc 92*
**Hood,** Douglas Crary 1932- *WhoMW 92*
**Hood,** E James 1947- *WhoAmP 91*
**Hood,** Earl James 1947- *WhoMW 92*
**Hood,** Edward E, Jr 1930- *AmMWSc 92*
**Hood,** Edward Exum, Jr. 1930- *WhoFI 92*
**Hood,** Elizabeth 1930- *WhoBlA 92*
**Hood,** Fred H 1926- *WhoAmP 91*
**Hood,** George Ezekiel 1875-1960 *DcNCBi 3*
**Hood,** Gurney Pope 1884-1962 *DcNCBi 3*
**Hood,** Harold 1916- *Who 92*
**Hood,** Harold 1931- *WhoAmP 91, WhoBlA 92*
**Hood,** Harvey 1946- *TwCPaSc*
**Hood,** Horace Edward 1923- *AmMWSc 92*
**Hood,** Hugh 1928- *BenetAL 91, ConNov 91, FacFETw, WrDr 92*
**Hood,** Hugh John 1928- *IntAu&W 91*
**Hood,** James 1948- *Who 92*
**Hood,** James B 1937- *WhoIns 92*
**Hood,** James Calton 1947- *WhoAmL 92*
**Hood,** James Matthew, Jr 1934- *WhoAmP 91*
**Hood,** James Walker 1831-1918 *DcNCBi 3, RelLAm 91*
**Hood,** James Warren 1925- *AmMWSc 92*
**Hood,** Jerry A 1934- *AmMWSc 92*
**Hood,** Joe Don 1936- *WhoWest 92*
**Hood,** John 1924- *Who 92*
**Hood,** John Bell 1831-1879 *BenetAL 91*
**Hood,** John Mack, Jr 1925- *AmMWSc 92*
**Hood,** Joseph 1924- *AmMWSc 92*
**Hood,** Kenneth Dean 1953- *WhoAmP 91*
**Hood,** Kregg Russell 1956- *WhoRel 92*
**Hood,** Lamartine Frain 1937- *AmMWSc 92*
**Hood,** Larry Lee 1944- *AmMWSc 92*
**Hood,** Leonard Paul, Jr. 1960- *WhoEnt 92*
**Hood,** Leroy E 1938- *AmMWSc 92*
**Hood,** Leroy Edward 1938- *IntWW 91*
**Hood,** Leslie Lynn 1948- *WhoRel 92*
**Hood,** Lois Sage 1933- *WhoAmP 91*
**Hood,** Lonnie Lamar 1949- *AmMWSc 92*
**Hood,** Louise B 1916- *WhoAmP 91*
**Hood,** Lynley 1942- *ConAu 135*
**Hood,** Martin Sinclair 1917- *Who 92*
**Hood,** Martin Sinclair Frankland 1917- *WrDr 92*
**Hood,** Michael James 1946- *WhoWest 92*
**Hood,** Morris, Jr 1934- *WhoAmP 91, WhoBlA 92*
**Hood,** Neil 1943- *Who 92*
**Hood,** Nicholas *Who 92, WhoAmP 91*
**Hood,** Nicholas 1923- *WhoBlA 92*
**Hood,** Norman Arthur d1990 *Who 92N*
**Hood,** Peter *DrAPF 91*
**Hood,** Raymond M. 1881-1934 *DcTwDes, FacFETw*
**Hood,** Raymond W. 1936- *WhoBlA 92*
**Hood,** Raymond Walter 1936- *WhoAmP 91*
**Hood,** Richard Fred 1926- *AmMWSc 92*
**Hood,** Robert Holmes 1944- *WhoAmL 92*
**Hood,** Robert L 1929- *AmMWSc 92*
**Hood,** Robin James 1942- *AmMWSc 92*
**Hood,** Rodney Taber 1924- *AmMWSc 92, WhoMW 92*
**Hood,** Roger Grahame 1936- *Who 92*
**Hood,** Ronald David 1941- *AmMWSc 92*
**Hood,** Ronald Lee 1945- *WhoMW 92*
**Hood,** Ruth P *WhoAmP 91*
**Hood,** Samuel Harold 1926- *Who 92*
**Hood,** Samuel Lowry 1918- *AmMWSc 92*
**Hood,** Sinclair *Who 92*
**Hood,** Stuart 1915- *IntAu&W 91*
**Hood,** Thomas 1799-1845 *RfGEnL 91*
**Hood,** Thomas Edward 1941- *WhoAmL 92*
**Hood,** Thomas Gregory 1948- *WhoRel 92*
**Hood,** William Acland 1901- *Who 92*
**Hood,** William Boyd, Jr 1932- *AmMWSc 92, WhoFI 92*
**Hood,** William Calvin 1937- *AmMWSc 92*
**Hood,** William Clarence 1921- *IntWW 91, WhoFI 92*
**Hood,** William Nicholas 1935- *Who 92*
**Hood,** William R 1923- *WhoAmP 91*
**Hood,** William Wayne, Jr. 1941- *WhoAmL 92*
**Hooe,** John Robert, III 1952- *WhoAmP 91*
**Hoofman,** Cliff 1943- *WhoAmP 91*
**Hoofnagle,** Jay H 1943- *AmMWSc 92*
**Hooft,** Gerardus 't 1946- *IntWW 91*
**Hoog,** Thomas William 1939- *WhoAmP 91*
**Hoogenboom,** Gerrit 1955- *AmMWSc 92*
**Hoogestraat,** Jane *DrAPF 91*
**Hoogeveen,** Kim 1953- *WhoMW 92*
**Hoogheem,** Thomas John 1951- *AmMWSc 92*
**Hoogland,** Robert Frederics 1955- *WhoAmL 92*
**Hooglandt,** Jan Daniel 1926- *IntWW 91*
**Hoogsteden,** Aloysius Franciscus 1936- *WhoFI 92*
**Hoogstraal,** Harry 1917- *AmMWSc 92*
**Hoogstraten,** Harry 1941- *IntAu&W 91*
**Hoogstraten,** Jan 1917- *AmMWSc 92*
**Hook,** David Morgan Alfred 1931- *Who 92*
**Hook,** Derek John 1947- *AmMWSc 92*
**Hook,** Donal D 1933- *AmMWSc 92*
**Hook,** Edward Watson, Jr 1924- *AmMWSc 92*
**Hook,** Ernest *AmMWSc 92*
**Hook,** Gary Edward Raumati 1942- *AmMWSc 92*
**Hook,** George Matthew Verity 1917- *WhoFI 92*
**Hook,** Harold Swanson 1931- *WhoFI 92, WhoIns 92*
**Hook,** James Edward 1947- *AmMWSc 92*
**Hook,** Jerry Bruce 1937- *AmMWSc 92*
**Hook,** John W 1922- *AmMWSc 92*
**Hook,** Jonathan David 1957- *WhoFI 92*
**Hook,** Magnus Ao 1946- *AmMWSc 92*
**Hook,** Ralph Clifford, Jr. 1923- *WhoWest 92*
**Hook,** Richard Alan 1951- *WhoEnt 92*
**Hook,** Rollin Earl 1934- *AmMWSc 92*
**Hook,** Ross Sydney 1917- *Who 92*
**Hook,** Sidney 1902- *IntAu&W 91*
**Hook,** Sidney 1902-1989 *FacFETw*
**Hook,** Theodore 1788-1841 *RfGEnL 91*
**Hook,** William Arthur 1930- *AmMWSc 92*
**Hook,** William Franklin 1935- *WhoMW 92*
**Hooke,** Robert 1918- *AmMWSc 92*
**Hooke,** Roger LeBaron 1939- *AmMWSc 92*
**Hooke,** William Hines 1943- *AmMWSc 92*
**Hooker,** Arthur Lee 1924- *AmMWSc 92*
**Hooker,** Billie June 1938- *WhoFI 92*
**Hooker,** Brian 1880-1946 *BenetAL 91*
**Hooker,** Charles W 1883?-1913 *BiInAmS*
**Hooker,** Charlie 1953- *IntWW 91*
**Hooker,** David Nicholas 1949- *WhoFI 92*
**Hooker,** Douglas Randolf 1954- *WhoBlA 92*
**Hooker,** Eric H. *WhoBlA 92*
**Hooker,** James Todd 1946- *WhoMW 92*
**Hooker,** Jeremy 1941- *ConPo 91, IntAu&W 91, WrDr 92*
**Hooker,** John 1932- *IntAu&W 91, WrDr 92*
**Hooker,** John Daggett 1838-1911 *BiInAmS*
**Hooker,** John Lee 1917- *NewAmDM, WhoBlA 92, WhoEnt 92*
**Hooker,** John Wesley 1932- *WhoMW 92*
**Hooker,** Mark L 1947- *AmMWSc 92*
**Hooker,** Michael Ayerst 1923- *Who 92*
**Hooker,** Morna Dorothy 1931- *Who 92, WhoRel 92, WrDr 92*
**Hooker,** Odessa Walker 1930- *WhoBlA 92*
**Hooker,** Richard 1554-1600 *RfGEnL 91*
**Hooker,** Ronald George 1921- *Who 92*
**Hooker,** Thomas 1586-1647 *BenetAL 91*
**Hooker,** Thomas M, Jr 1936- *AmMWSc 92*
**Hooker,** Wade Stuart, Jr. 1941- *WhoAmL 92*
**Hooker,** William *DrAPF 91*
**Hooker,** William James 1914- *AmMWSc 92*
**Hooker,** William Mead 1942- *AmMWSc 92*
**Hooker,** Worthington 1806-1867 *BiInAmS*
**Hooks,** Benjamin L. *LesBEnT 92*
**Hooks,** Benjamin L. 1925- *ConBlB 2 [port]*
**Hooks,** Benjamin Lawson *WhoAmP 91*
**Hooks,** Benjamin Lawson 1925- *WhoBlA 92*
**Hooks,** Charles 1768-1843 *DcNCBi 3*
**Hooks,** Frances Dancy 1927- *WhoBlA 92*
**Hooks,** George Bardin 1945- *WhoAmP 91*
**Hooks,** James Byron, Jr. 1933- *WhoBlA 92*
**Hooks,** Julia 1852-1942 *NotBlAW 92 [port]*
**Hooks,** Kevin 1958- *ConTFT 9, IntMPA 92, WhoEnt 92*
**Hooks,** Michael Anthony 1950- *WhoBlA 92*
**Hooks,** Mose Yvonne Brooks *WhoBlA 92*
**Hooks,** Robert 1937- *IntMPA 92*
**Hooks,** Robert Keith 1929- *Who 92*
**Hooks,** Ronald Fred 1941- *AmMWSc 92*
**Hooks,** Tommy Louis 1936- *WhoAmP 91*
**Hooks,** William Gary 1927- *AmMWSc 92*
**Hookstratten,** Edward Gregory 1932- *WhoFI 92*
**Hookway,** Harry 1921- *Who 92*
**Hookway,** Harry Thurston 1921- *IntWW 91*
**Hookway,** Hugh Eaton, Jr. 1944- *WhoRel 92*
**Hool,** James N 1938- *AmMWSc 92*
**Hool,** Lance 1948- *IntMPA 92*
**Hool,** Lance Winston 1948- *WhoEnt 92*
**Hoolahan,** Anthony Terence 1925- *Who 92*
**Hoole,** Alan Norman 1942- *Who 92*
**Hoole,** Arthur 1924- *Who 92*
**Hooley,** Christopher 1928- *IntWW 91, Who 92*
**Hooley,** Darlene 1939- *WhoAmP 91*
**Hooley,** Frank Oswald 1923- *Who 92*
**Hooley,** John Francis 1952- *WhoAmL 92*
**Hooley,** John Rouse 1927- *Who 92*
**Hooley,** Joseph Gilbert 1914- *AmMWSc 92*
**Hooley,** Michael 1944- *WhoMW 92*
**Hoon,** Geoffrey William 1953- *Who 92*
**Hoon,** Paul Waitman 1910- *WhoRel 92*
**Hoonan,** Kelly Martin 1961- *WhoWest 92*
**Hoontrakul,** Sommai 1918- *IntWW 91*
**Hoop,** Bernard, Jr 1939- *AmMWSc 92*
**Hoop,** Rita Caporicci 1963- *WhoWest 92*
**Hoopengardner,** Stanley Joseph 1947- *WhoRel 92*
**Hooper** *Who 92*
**Hooper,** Baroness 1939- *Who 92*
**Hooper,** Alan Bacon 1937- *AmMWSc 92*
**Hooper,** Anne Caroline Dodge 1926- *AmMWSc 92*
**Hooper,** Anthony 1937- *Who 92*
**Hooper,** Anthony Sidney Colchester 1943- *IntWW 91*
**Hooper,** Archibald Maclaine 1775-1853 *DcNCBi 3*
**Hooper,** Ben Walter, II 1939- *WhoAmL 92, WhoAmP 91*
**Hooper,** Biff 1964- *ConAu 135*
**Hooper,** Billy Ernest 1931- *AmMWSc 92*
**Hooper,** Catherine Evelyn 1939- *AmMWSc 92, WhoWest 92*
**Hooper,** Charles Frederick, Jr 1932- *AmMWSc 92*
**Hooper,** Charles German 1911- *Who 92*
**Hooper,** Charles Newton 1933- *WhoAmL 92*
**Hooper,** David Dean 1957- *WhoEnt 92*
**Hooper,** Davis Lee 1943- *WhoFI 92*
**Hooper,** Don 1945- *WhoAmP 91*
**Hooper,** Donald Lloyd 1938- *AmMWSc 92*
**Hooper,** Edwin Bickford 1937- *WhoWest 92*
**Hooper,** Edwin Bickford, Jr 1937- *AmMWSc 92*
**Hooper,** Ellen 1812?-1848 *BenetAL 91*
**Hooper,** Emmet Thurman, Jr 1911- *AmMWSc 92*
**Hooper,** F C 1924- *AmMWSc 92*
**Hooper,** Frank Fincher 1918- *AmMWSc 92*
**Hooper,** Franklin William 1851-1914 *BiInAmS*
**Hooper,** Gary Raymond 1946- *WhoBlA 92*
**Hooper,** George 1744?-1821 *DcNCBi 3*
**Hooper,** George 1910- *TwCPaSc*
**Hooper,** George Bates 1924- *AmMWSc 92*
**Hooper,** Gerald F. 1923- *WhoBlA 92*
**Hooper,** Henry Olcott 1935- *AmMWSc 92, WhoWest 92*
**Hooper,** Irvin P 1914- *AmMWSc 92*
**Hooper,** Irving R 1921- *AmMWSc 92*
**Hooper,** James E. 1933- *WhoEnt 92*
**Hooper,** James Fullerton, III 1915- *WhoAmP 91*
**Hooper,** James R 1915- *AmMWSc 92*
**Hooper,** John De Berniere 1811-1886 *DcNCBi 3*
**Hooper,** John William 1931- *AmMWSc 92*
**Hooper,** Johnson Jones 1815-1862 *BenetAL 91, DcNCBi 3*
**Hooper,** Josh 1952- *WhoEnt 92*
**Hooper,** Kay *WrDr 92*
**Hooper,** Kevin Cameron 1955- *WhoEnt 92*
**Hooper,** Kevin Lee 1959- *WhoMW 92*
**Hooper,** Leo Duane *WhoMW 92*

**Hooper,** Leonard 1914- *Who 92*
**Hooper,** Meredith Jean 1939- *WrDr 92*
**Hooper,** Michele J. 1951- *WhoBlA 92*
**Hooper,** Nigel 1961- *AmMWSc 92*
**Hooper,** Noel Barrie 1931- *Who 92*
**Hooper,** Patricia *DrAPF 91*
**Hooper,** Perry O 1925- *WhoAmP 91*
**Hooper,** Peter 1919- *ConPo 91, IntAu&W 91, WrDr 92*
**Hooper,** Richard 1939- *Who 92*
**Hooper,** Robert Alexander 1947- *WhoEnt 92*
**Hooper,** Robert John 1931- *AmMWSc 92*
**Hooper,** Roy B, Jr 1947- *WhoAmP 91*
**Hooper,** Susan Jeanne 1950- *WhoMW 92*
**Hooper,** Thomas 1746?-1821? *DcNCBi 3*
**Hooper,** Thomas Fredrick, III 1958- *WhoAmP 91*
**Hooper,** Tobe *IntMPA 92*
**Hooper,** Virginia R Fite 1917- *WhoAmP 91*
**Hooper,** William 1742-1790 *DcNCBi 3*
**Hooper,** William 1792-1876 *DcNCBi 3*
**Hooper,** William John, Jr 1935- *AmMWSc 92*
**Hooper,** William Leslie 1855-1918 *BiInAmS*
**Hooper-Todd,** Nita LaVone 1952- *WhoRel 92*
**Hoopes,** David Craig 1942- *WhoAmP 91*
**Hoopes,** John A 1936- *AmMWSc 92*
**Hoopes,** John Eugene 1931- *AmMWSc 92*
**Hoopes,** John L. 1946- *WhoWest 92*
**Hoopes,** John W, Jr 1922- *AmMWSc 92*
**Hoopes,** Joshua 1788?-1874 *BiInAmS*
**Hoopes,** Josiah 1832-1904 *BiInAmS*
**Hoopes,** Keith Hale 1930- *AmMWSc 92*
**Hoopes,** Laura Livingston Mays 1942- *AmMWSc 92*
**Hoopes,** Lauren Mattleman 1960- *WhoAmL 92*
**Hoopes,** Lyn Littlefield 1953- *IntAu&W 91*
**Hoopes,** Sidney Lou 1944- *WhoWest 92*
**Hoopes,** Spencer Wendell 1947- *WhoWest 92*
**Hoopingarner,** Doyle Anson 1930- *WhoMW 92*
**Hoopingarner,** Roger A 1933- *AmMWSc 92*
**Hoopis,** Harry Peter 1947- *WhoMW 92*
**Hoopman,** Harold DeWaine 1920- *IntWW 91*
**Hoops,** Christopher Rory 1950- *WhoRel 92*
**Hoops,** Richard Allen 1933- *AmMWSc 92, WhoMW 92*
**Hoops,** Stephen C 1940- *AmMWSc 92*
**Hoornaert,** Paul 1888-1944 *BiDExR*
**Hoornbeek,** Frank Kent 1928- *AmMWSc 92*
**Hoornstra,** Paul Zenas 1920- *WhoRel 92*
**Hoort,** Steven Thomas 1949- *WhoAmL 92*
**Hoorwitz,** Mark Ira 1961- *WhoFI 92*
**Hoory,** Shlomo 1935- *AmMWSc 92*
**Hoose,** Alfred Julius 1918- *WhoEnt 92*
**Hooseinny,** Lloyd Michael 1949- *WhoRel 92*
**Hooson** *Who 92*
**Hooson,** Baron 1925- *Who 92*
**Hooten,** William Foster, Jr. 1926- *WhoMW 92*
**Hootman,** Harry Edward 1933- *AmMWSc 92*
**Hooton,** E. A. 1887-1954 *BenetAL 91*
**Hoots,** Felix R 1947- *AmMWSc 92*
**Hoover,** Annette Louise 1944- *WhoFI 92*
**Hoover,** Carl Franklin 1957- *WhoEnt 92*
**Hoover,** Charles Wilson, Jr 1925- *AmMWSc 92*
**Hoover,** Cynthia Adams 1934- *WhoEnt 92*
**Hoover,** Dallas Gene 1951- *AmMWSc 92*
**Hoover,** David 1781-1866 *DcNCBi 3*
**Hoover,** David A 1939- *WhoAmP 91*
**Hoover,** David Carlson 1950- *WhoAmL 92*
**Hoover,** Donald Barry 1950- *AmMWSc 92*
**Hoover,** Donald Brunton 1930- *AmMWSc 92, WhoWest 92*
**Hoover,** Donald Leroy 1952- *WhoFI 92*
**Hoover,** Dwight 1926- *IntAu&W 91*
**Hoover,** Dwight Wesley 1926- *WrDr 92*
**Hoover,** Felix A. 1949- *WhoBlA 92*
**Hoover,** Fred Wayne 1914- *AmMWSc 92*
**Hoover,** Gary McClellan 1939- *AmMWSc 92*
**Hoover,** H. M. 1935- *ConAu 36NR, TwCSFW 91, WrDr 92*
**Hoover,** Helen Mary 1935- *IntAu&W 91*
**Hoover,** Herbert 1874-1964 *BenetAL 91, FacFETw [port], RComAH*
**Hoover,** Herbert Allen 1957- *WhoRel 92*
**Hoover,** Herbert Clark 1874-1964 *AmPeW, AmPolLe [port], EncTR 91 [port]*
**Hoover,** Herbert William, Jr. 1918- *IntWW 91, Who 92*
**Hoover,** Howard S., Jr. *WhoAmL 92*
**Hoover,** J Edgar 1895-1972 *FacFETw [port], RComAH*
**Hoover,** James Lloyd 1945- *WhoAmL 92*
**Hoover,** James M 1928- *AmMWSc 92*
**Hoover,** Jerri 1950- *WhoAmP 91*
**Hoover,** Jesse 1918- *WhoBlA 92*
**Hoover,** John Edgar 1895-1972 *AmPolLe*
**Hoover,** John Ross 1946- *WhoFI 92*
**Hoover,** John Russel Eugene 1925- *AmMWSc 92*
**Hoover,** John W 1916- *AmMWSc 92*
**Hoover,** Kenneth Edward 1907- *WhoRel 92*
**Hoover,** L Ronald 1940- *AmMWSc 92*
**Hoover,** Linn 1923- *AmMWSc 92*
**Hoover,** Lon Ahlers 1930- *WhoMW 92*
**Hoover,** Loretta White *AmMWSc 92*
**Hoover,** M Frederick 1938- *AmMWSc 92*
**Hoover,** Mae 1938- *WhoAmP 91*
**Hoover,** Mark Douglas 1948- *AmMWSc 92*
**Hoover,** Mary Nell 1946- *WhoMW 92*
**Hoover,** Odie Millard, Jr. 1921-1973 *WhoBlA 92N*
**Hoover,** Paul *DrAPF 91*
**Hoover,** Pearl Rollings 1924- *WhoWest 92*
**Hoover,** Peter Redfield 1939- *AmMWSc 92*
**Hoover,** Ray Allen 1932- *WhoIns 92*
**Hoover,** Richard *WhoEnt 92*
**Hoover,** Richard Brice 1943- *AmMWSc 92*
**Hoover,** Robert Cleary 1928- *WhoWest 92*
**Hoover,** Robert Lloyd 1933- *WhoEnt 92*
**Hoover,** Robert Milton 1926- *WhoFI 92*
**Hoover,** Roderick P, Jr 1954- *WhoIns 92*
**Hoover,** Roy William 1932- *WhoRel 92, WhoWest 92*
**Hoover,** Susan *DrAPF 91*
**Hoover,** Theressa 1925- *WhoBlA 92*
**Hoover,** Thomas Burdett 1920- *AmMWSc 92*
**Hoover,** Thomas Earl 1941- *AmMWSc 92*
**Hoover,** Thomas Jude 1958- *WhoMW 92*
**Hoover,** Thomas Warren 1932- *WhoAmP 91*
**Hoover,** William G 1906- *AmMWSc 92*
**Hoover,** William Graham 1936- *AmMWSc 92*
**Hoover,** William Jay 1928- *AmMWSc 92*
**Hoover,** William L 1924- *AmMWSc 92*
**Hoover,** William Ray 1930- *WhoFI 92, WhoWest 92*
**Hoover,** William Walter 1932- *WhoAmP 91*
**Hooykaas,** Reijer 1906- *IntWW 91*
**Hooz,** John 1935- *AmMWSc 92*
**Hopcraft,** Arthur 1932- *ConAu 35NR, WrDr 92*
**Hopcraft,** Arthur Edward 1932- *IntAu&W 91*
**Hopcroft,** George William 1927- *Who 92*
**Hopcroft,** John E 1939- *AmMWSc 92*
**Hope** *Who 92*
**Hope,** Lord 1938- *IntWW 91, Who 92*
**Hope,** A. D. 1907- *ConPo 91, RfGEnL 91, WrDr 92*
**Hope,** A. Guy 1914-1982 *ConAu 133*
**Hope,** Adrian Price Webley 1911- *Who 92*
**Hope,** Akua Lezli *DrAPF 91*
**Hope,** Alan 1933- *Who 92*
**Hope,** Alec Derwent 1907- *IntAu&W 91, IntWW 91*
**Hope,** Anthony 1863-1933 *RfGEnL 91*
**Hope,** Bob *LesBEnT 92 [port]*
**Hope,** Bob 1903- *FacFETw [port], IntMPA 92, IntWW 91, Who 92, WhoEnt 92, WrDr 92*
**Hope,** Brian Bradshaw 1936- *AmMWSc 92*
**Hope,** Charles Peter 1912- *Who 92*
**Hope,** Christopher 1944- *ConNov 91, LiExTwC, Who 92, WrDr 92*
**Hope,** Christopher David Tully 1944- *IntAu&W 91*
**Hope,** Colin Frederick Newton 1932- *Who 92*
**Hope,** Craig Allen 1964- *WhoWest 92*
**Hope,** David *Who 92*
**Hope,** David Michael *Who 92*
**Hope,** Eleanor 1946- *WhoEnt 92*
**Hope,** Elizabeth Greeley 1943- *AmMWSc 92*
**Hope,** George Marion 1938- *AmMWSc 92*
**Hope,** Gerri Danette 1956- *WhoWest 92*
**Hope,** Hakon 1930- *AmMWSc 92*
**Hope,** Harry 1926- *IntMPA 92, WhoEnt 92*
**Hope,** Hugh Johnson 1938- *AmMWSc 92*
**Hope,** Jack Irvin 1928- *WhoMW 92*
**Hope,** James Arthur David *Who 92*
**Hope,** Jimmy Milton 1944- *WhoRel 92*
**Hope,** John 1939- *Who 92*
**Hope,** Judith H 1939- *WhoAmP 91*
**Hope,** Julius Caesar 1932- *WhoBlA 92*
**Hope,** Laura Lee *BenetAL 91, SmATA 67*
**Hope,** Laurence 1928- *TwCPaSc*
**Hope,** Laurence Frank 1918- *Who 92*
**Hope,** Lawrence Latimer 1939- *AmMWSc 92*
**Hope,** Leslie Townes 1903- *IntAu&W 91*
**Hope,** Lugenia Burns 1871-1947 *HanAmWH, NotBlAW 92*
**Hope,** Marcus Laurence Hulbert 1942- *Who 92*
**Hope,** Margaret *WrDr 92*
**Hope,** Marjorie 1923- *WrDr 92*
**Hope,** Mark Alan 1960- *WhoFI 92*
**Hope,** Maurice 1951- *IntWW 91*
**Hope,** Michael S. 1942- *WhoEnt 92*
**Hope,** Patricia Harriet 1935- *WhoMW 92*
**Hope,** Peter *Who 92*
**Hope,** Polly 1933- *TwCPaSc*
**Hope,** Richard Oliver 1939- *WhoBlA 92*
**Hope,** Robert Holms-Kerr 1900- *Who 92*
**Hope,** Ronald 1921- *IntAu&W 91, WrDr 92*
**Hope,** Ronald Richmond 1943- *AmMWSc 92*
**Hope,** Roy Norris 1940- *WhoMW 92*
**Hope,** Thomas Walker 1920- *WhoEnt 92*
**Hope,** Warren T 1944- *WhoIns 92*
**Hope,** William Duane 1935- *AmMWSc 92*
**Hope-Dunbar,** David 1941- *Who 92*
**Hope Johnstone** *Who 92*
**Hope-Jones,** Ronald Christopher 1920- *Who 92*
**Hope-Morley** *Who 92*
**Hope-Simpson,** Jacynth 1930- *IntAu&W 91, WrDr 92*
**Hope-Wallace,** Jaqueline 1909- *Who 92*
**Hopekirk,** Helen 1856-1945 *NewAmDM*
**Hopen,** Herbert 1934- *AmMWSc 92*
**Hopen,** Herbert John 1934- *WhoMW 92*
**Hopenfield,** Joram 1934- *AmMWSc 92*
**Hopes,** David Brendan *DrAPF 91*
**Hopetoun,** Earl of 1969- *Who 92*
**Hopewell,** John Prince 1920- *Who 92*
**Hopewell,** Luz Araoz *WhoHisp 92*
**Hopf,** Frederic A 1942- *AmMWSc 92*
**Hopf,** James F. 1961- *WhoAmL 92*
**Hopfenbeck,** George Martin, Jr. 1929- *WhoAmL 92*
**Hopfenberg,** Harold Bruce 1938- *AmMWSc 92*
**Hopfer,** Roy L 1944- *AmMWSc 92*
**Hopfer,** Samuel 1914- *AmMWSc 92*
**Hopfer,** Ulrich 1939- *AmMWSc 92*
**Hopfield,** John Joseph 1933- *AmMWSc 92, WhoWest 92*
**Hopfinger,** J Anthony 1951- *AmMWSc 92*
**Hopke,** Philip Karl 1944- *AmMWSc 92*
**Hopkin,** A M 1919- *AmMWSc 92*
**Hopkin,** Bryan *Who 92*
**Hopkin,** Bryan 1914- *IntWW 91*
**Hopkin,** David 1922- *Who 92*
**Hopkin,** Elizabeth 1920- *TwCPaSc*
**Hopkin,** John Raymond 1935- *Who 92*
**Hopkin,** William Aylsham Bryan 1914- *Who 92*
**Hopkins,** A. R. *WhoRel 92*
**Hopkins,** Alan Cripps Nind 1926- *Who 92*
**Hopkins,** Albert 1807-1872 *BiInAmS*
**Hopkins,** Albert E., Sr. 1928- *WhoBlA 92*
**Hopkins,** Albert Lafayette, Jr 1931- *AmMWSc 92*
**Hopkins,** Allen Arthur, Jr. 1930- *WhoEnt 92*
**Hopkins,** Allen John 1942- *AmMWSc 92*
**Hopkins,** Amos Lawrence 1926- *AmMWSc 92*
**Hopkins,** Anthony 1937- *IntMPA 92, IntWW 91*
**Hopkins,** Anthony Philip 1937- *Who 92, WhoEnt 92*
**Hopkins,** Anthony Strother 1940- *Who 92*
**Hopkins,** Antony 1921- *IntAu&W 91, IntWW 91, Who 92, WrDr 92*
**Hopkins,** Barry L. 1943- *WhoBlA 92*
**Hopkins,** Betty Jo Henderson *AmMWSc 92*
**Hopkins,** Bo *WhoEnt 92*
**Hopkins,** Bo 1942- *IntMPA 92*
**Hopkins,** Bonnie Jean 1954- *WhoMW 92*
**Hopkins,** Bruce Wallace 1945- *WhoEnt 92*
**Hopkins,** Carl Douglas 1944- *AmMWSc 92*
**Hopkins,** Cecilia Ann 1922- *WhoWest 92*
**Hopkins,** Charles B, Jr 1922- *AmMWSc 92*
**Hopkins,** Charles Peter, II 1953- *WhoAmL 92, WhoFI 92*
**Hopkins,** Charmaine L. 1946- *WhoBlA 92*
**Hopkins,** Clarence Yardley 1903- *AmMWSc 92*
**Hopkins,** Clyde 1946- *TwCPaSc*
**Hopkins,** Colin Russell 1939- *AmMWSc 92*
**Hopkins,** Cyril George 1866-1919 *BiInAmS*
**Hopkins,** Daniel T 1932- *AmMWSc 92*
**Hopkins,** David Alan 1942- *AmMWSc 92*
**Hopkins,** David L., Jr. 1928- *WhoFI 92*
**Hopkins,** David Moody 1921- *AmMWSc 92*
**Hopkins,** David Rex Eugene 1930- *Who 92*
**Hopkins,** David Roger 1941- *WhoRel 92*
**Hopkins,** Dianne McAfee 1944- *WhoBlA 92*
**Hopkins,** Don Carlos 1936- *AmMWSc 92*
**Hopkins,** Donald Lee 1943- *AmMWSc 92*
**Hopkins,** Donald R 1941- *AmMWSc 92*
**Hopkins,** Donald Ray 1936- *WhoAmL 92, WhoBlA 92*
**Hopkins,** Douglas Edward 1902- *Who 92*
**Hopkins,** Dwight Nathaniel 1953- *WhoRel 92*
**Hopkins,** Edna J. 1924- *WhoBlA 92*
**Hopkins,** Edward Curtis 1922- *WhoAmP 91*
**Hopkins,** Edward Donald 1937- *WhoMW 92*
**Hopkins,** Edwina Weiskittel 1947- *WhoWest 92*
**Hopkins,** Elizabeth Anna 1958- *WhoAmL 92*
**Hopkins,** Emma Curtis 1849-1925 *RelLAm 91*
**Hopkins,** Ernest Loyd 1930- *WhoBlA 92*
**Hopkins,** Esek 1718-1802 *BlkwEAR*
**Hopkins,** Esther Arvilla 1926- *WhoBlA 92*
**Hopkins,** Esther Arvilla Harrison 1926- *AmMWSc 92*
**Hopkins,** Frederick Gowland 1861-1947 *WhoNob 90*
**Hopkins,** Frederick Sherman, Jr 1922- *AmMWSc 92*
**Hopkins,** Gary Wayne 1942- *WhoMW 92*
**Hopkins,** Gayle P. 1941- *WhoBlA 92*
**Hopkins,** George 1958- *WhoAmP 91*
**Hopkins,** George C 1935- *AmMWSc 92*
**Hopkins,** George Emil 1937- *WrDr 92*
**Hopkins,** George H, Jr 1933- *AmMWSc 92*
**Hopkins,** George Mathews Marks 1923- *WhoAmL 92*
**Hopkins,** George Milton 1842-1902 *BiInAmS*
**Hopkins,** George Robert 1928- *AmMWSc 92*
**Hopkins,** George William, II 1947- *AmMWSc 92*
**Hopkins,** Gerald Frank 1943- *WhoWest 92*
**Hopkins,** Gerard Manley 1844-1889 *CnDBLB 5 [port], RfGEnL 91*
**Hopkins,** Ginny *WhoEnt 92*
**Hopkins,** Glen Eugene, Jr 1949- *WhoAmP 91*
**Hopkins,** Godfrey Thurston 1913- *IntWW 91*
**Hopkins,** Gordon Bruce *AmMWSc 92*
**Hopkins,** Grace Francesca 1973- *WhoEnt 92*
**Hopkins,** Grover Prevatte 1933- *WhoAmP 91*
**Hopkins,** Harlow Eugene 1931- *WhoEnt 92*
**Hopkins,** Harold Anthony, Jr. *WhoRel 92*
**Hopkins,** Harold Horace 1918- *IntWW 91, Who 92*
**Hopkins,** Harrison *DrAPF 91*
**Hopkins,** Harry 1890-1946 *FacFETw [port]*
**Hopkins,** Harry 1913- *IntAu&W 91, WrDr 92*
**Hopkins,** Harry Dean 1952- *WhoFI 92*
**Hopkins,** Harry Lloyd 1890-1946 *AmPolLe*
**Hopkins,** Harry P, Jr 1939- *AmMWSc 92*
**Hopkins,** Hiram *TwCWW 91*
**Hopkins,** Homer Thawley 1913- *AmMWSc 92*
**Hopkins,** Horace H, Jr 1922- *AmMWSc 92*
**Hopkins,** Jack Walker 1930- *WhoAmP 91*
**Hopkins,** James Clarence 1930- *WhoFI 92*
**Hopkins,** James Melvin, II 1954- *WhoRel 92*
**Hopkins,** James Michael 1946- *WhoMW 92*
**Hopkins,** James S. R. S. *Who 92*
**Hopkins,** Jasper 1936- *WrDr 92*
**Hopkins,** Jerry 1935- *WhoEnt 92*
**Hopkins,** Jerry Berl 1945- *WhoRel 92*
**Hopkins,** John 1931- *IntAu&W 91, Who 92, WrDr 92*
**Hopkins,** John Chapman 1933- *AmMWSc 92*
**Hopkins,** John David 1933- *WhoBlA 92*
**Hopkins,** John David 1938- *WhoAmL 92*
**Hopkins,** John Orville 1930- *WhoBlA 92*
**Hopkins,** John Raymond 1944- *AmMWSc 92*
**Hopkins,** John Taylor 1956- *WhoMW 92*
**Hopkins,** Johns Wilson 1933- *AmMWSc 92*
**Hopkins,** Joseph W. 1949- *WhoAmL 92*
**Hopkins,** Julian *Who 92*
**Hopkins,** Karen *WhoEnt 92*
**Hopkins,** Keith *Who 92*
**Hopkins,** Kenneth Arthur, Jr. 1962- *WhoRel 92*
**Hopkins,** Kevin R 1954- *WhoAmP 91*
**Hopkins,** Larry J. 1933- *AlmAP 92 [port]*
**Hopkins,** Larry Jones 1933- *WhoAmP 91*
**Hopkins,** Lee Bennett 1938- *IntAu&W 91, SmATA 68 [port], WrDr 92*
**Hopkins,** Lemuel 1750-1801 *BenetAL 91*
**Hopkins,** Leon Lorraine 1935- *AmMWSc 92*
**Hopkins,** Leroy Taft, Jr. 1942- *WhoBlA 92*
**Hopkins,** Lightnin' 1912-1982 *NewAmDM*

**Hopkins,** Lisa Love *WhoFI 92*
**Hopkins,** Lyman *IntAu&W 91X, WrDr 92*
**Hopkins,** M E 1928- *AmMWSc 92*
**Hopkins,** Mansell Herbert, Jr 1927- *AmMWSc 92*
**Hopkins,** Mark 1802-1887 *BenetAL 91*
**Hopkins,** Matthew John 1963- *WhoMW 92*
**Hopkins,** Michael F. *DrAPF 91*
**Hopkins,** Michael John 1935- *IntWW 91, Who 92*
**Hopkins,** Morris Keith 1934- *Who 92*
**Hopkins,** Muriel-Beth Norbrey 1951- *WhoAmL 92*
**Hopkins,** Myrtle B 1933- *WhoAmP 91*
**Hopkins,** Nathan Thomas 1852-1927 *DcNCBi 3*
**Hopkins,** Nigel John 1922- *AmMWSc 92*
**Hopkins,** Patrick Joseph 1950- *WhoAmL 92*
**Hopkins,** Paul Brink 1956- *AmMWSc 92*
**Hopkins,** Paul Donald 1935- *AmMWSc 92*
**Hopkins,** Paul Jeffrey 1940- *WhoRel 92*
**Hopkins,** Paul Nathan 1952- *WhoWest 92*
**Hopkins,** Paulene A. 1919-1990 *WhoBlA 92N*
**Hopkins,** Pauline 1859-1930 *BenetAL 91, NotBlAW 92*
**Hopkins,** Pauline Elizabeth 1859-1930 *BlkLC [port]*
**Hopkins,** Perea M. 1931- *WhoBlA 92*
**Hopkins,** Philip Joseph 1954- *WhoWest 92*
**Hopkins,** Phill 1961- *TwCPaSc*
**Hopkins,** R Howard 1939- *WhoIns 92*
**Hopkins,** Richard 1948- *WhoEnt 92*
**Hopkins,** Richard Allen 1943- *AmMWSc 92*
**Hopkins,** Richard H 1940- *AmMWSc 92*
**Hopkins,** Richard Julian 1940- *Who 92*
**Hopkins,** Robert Arthur 1920- *WhoWest 92*
**Hopkins,** Robert Charles 1937- *AmMWSc 92*
**Hopkins,** Robert E 1929- *WhoAmP 91*
**Hopkins,** Robert Earl 1915- *AmMWSc 92*
**Hopkins,** Robert Elliott 1931- *WhoEnt 92, WhoMW 92*
**Hopkins,** Robert West 1924- *AmMWSc 92*
**Hopkins,** Ronald Murray 1942- *AmMWSc 92*
**Hopkins,** Ronald Nicholas Lamond d1990 *Who 92N*
**Hopkins,** Roy *WhoAmP 91*
**Hopkins,** Russell Harold 1958- *WhoEnt 92*
**Hopkins,** Sam 1912-1982 *FacFETw*
**Hopkins,** Samuel 1721-1803 *BenetAL 91*
**Hopkins,** Sarah Winnemucca 1844-1891 *BenetAL 91, HanAmWH*
**Hopkins,** Shelley A. 1950- *WhoAmL 92*
**Hopkins,** Sidney Arthur 1932- *Who 92*
**Hopkins,** Speed Elliott 1948- *WhoEnt 92*
**Hopkins,** Stephen 1707-1785 *BenetAL 91, BlkwEAR*
**Hopkins,** Theodore Emo 1929- *AmMWSc 92*
**Hopkins,** Theodore Louis 1929- *AmMWSc 92*
**Hopkins,** Theodore Mark 1926- *WhoRel 92*
**Hopkins,** Thomas Arscott 1931- *WhoAmL 92*
**Hopkins,** Thomas Franklin *WhoBlA 92*
**Hopkins,** Thomas Franklin 1924- *AmMWSc 92*
**Hopkins,** Thomas Moore 1952- *WhoFI 92*
**Hopkins,** Thomas R 1938- *AmMWSc 92*
**Hopkins,** Vashti Edythe Johnson 1924- *WhoBlA 92*
**Hopkins,** Wes 1961- *WhoBlA 92*
**Hopkins,** William A. 1943- *WhoBlA 92*
**Hopkins,** William Benjamin 1922- *WhoAmP 91*
**Hopkins,** William Francis 1962- *WhoEnt 92*
**Hopkins,** William George 1937- *AmMWSc 92*
**Hopkins,** William Stephen 1931- *AmMWSc 92*
**Hopkins,** Woodrow Justin 1957- *WhoEnt 92*
**Hopkinson** *Who 92*
**Hopkinson,** Albert Cyril 1911- *Who 92*
**Hopkinson,** Barnabas John 1939- *Who 92*
**Hopkinson,** David Hugh 1930- *IntAu&W 91, Who 92*
**Hopkinson,** David Hugh Laing 1926- *Who 92*
**Hopkinson,** Francis 1737-1791 *BenetAL 91, NewAmDM*
**Hopkinson,** Giles 1931- *Who 92*
**Hopkinson,** H T 1905- *IntAu&W 91*
**Hopkinson,** John 1941- *TwCPaSc*
**Hopkinson,** John Charles Oswald Rooke 1931- *Who 92*
**Hopkinson,** John Edmund 1924- *Who 92*
**Hopkinson,** Joseph 1770-1842 *BenetAL 91*
**Hopkinson,** Ralph Galbraith 1913- *Who 92*
**Hopkinson,** Shirley Lois 1924- *WhoWest 92*
**Hopkinson,** Thomas d1990 *IntWW 91N*
**Hopkinson,** Tom *IntAu&W 91X*
**Hopkinson,** Tom 1905-1990 *AnObit 1990*
**Hopkirk,** Joyce *Who 92*
**Hopla,** Cluff Earl 1917- *AmMWSc 92*
**Hopman,** Harry 1906-1985 *FacFETw*
**Hopp,** Daniel Frederick 1947- *WhoAmL 92*
**Hopp,** Donald L 1945- *WhoAmP 91*
**Hopp,** Nancy Smith 1943- *WhoMW 92*
**Hopp,** William Beecher 1917- *AmMWSc 92*
**Hoppa,** Donald 1945- *WhoMW 92*
**Hoppe,** Allen Earl 1953- *WhoFI 92*
**Hoppe,** Arthur 1925- *WrDr 92*
**Hoppe,** Arthur Watterson 1925- *IntAu&W 91*
**Hoppe,** Charles W. 1935- *WhoFI 92*
**Hoppe,** David Matthew 1942- *AmMWSc 92*
**Hoppe,** Iver 1920- *IntWW 91, Who 92*
**Hoppe,** John Cameron 1943- *AmMWSc 92*
**Hoppe,** Kathleen Murphy *WhoMW 92*
**Hoppe,** Leslie John 1944- *WhoRel 92*
**Hoppe,** Manley Robert 1910- *WhoMW 92*
**Hoppe,** Paul-Werner 1920-1974 *EncTR 91*
**Hoppe,** Peter Christian 1942- *AmMWSc 92*
**Hoppe,** Thomas J 1957- *WhoAmP 91*
**Hoppe,** Wolfgang 1933- *WhoAmL 92*
**Hoppel,** Robert Gerald, Jr. 1921- *WhoAmL 92*
**Hoppenjans,** Donald William 1941- *AmMWSc 92*
**Hopper,** Anita Klein 1945- *AmMWSc 92*
**Hopper,** Arthur Frederick 1917- *AmMWSc 92*
**Hopper,** Cecil Harold *WhoMW 92*
**Hopper,** Chris A. 1952- *WhoWest 92*
**Hopper,** Cornelius Lenard 1934- *WhoBlA 92*
**Hopper,** Dale Francis 1941- *WhoEnt 92*
**Hopper,** David Henry 1927- *WhoRel 92*
**Hopper,** David Lee 1953- *WhoWest 92*
**Hopper,** Dennis 1936- *IntMPA 92, IntWW 91, WhoEnt 92*
**Hopper,** E. Kent 1946- *WhoEnt 92*
**Hopper,** Edward 1882-1967 *FacFETw, ModArCr 2 [port]*
**Hopper,** Frederick Ernest 1919- *Who 92*
**Hopper,** George Drew 1950- *WhoRel 92*
**Hopper,** Grace Murray 1906- *AmMWSc 92*
**Hopper,** Hedda 1890-1966 *ReelWom*
**Hopper,** Jack Pollard 1958- *WhoEnt 92*
**Hopper,** Jack R 1937- *AmMWSc 92*
**Hopper,** James Ernest 1942- *AmMWSc 92*
**Hopper,** John D 1923- *WhoAmP 91*
**Hopper,** John Dowl, Jr. 1946- *WhoBlA 92*
**Hopper,** John Henry 1925- *AmMWSc 92*
**Hopper,** Mary Alice 1942- *WhoWest 92*
**Hopper,** Mary Elizabeth 1962- *WhoMW 92*
**Hopper,** Michael James 1940- *AmMWSc 92*
**Hopper,** Norman Wayne 1943- *AmMWSc 92*
**Hopper,** Paul Frederick 1924- *AmMWSc 92*
**Hopper,** Rea d1991 *NewYTBS 91*
**Hopper,** Robert William *AmMWSc 92*
**Hopper,** Sally *WhoWest 92*
**Hopper,** Sally H 1934- *WhoAmP 91*
**Hopper,** Samuel Hersey 1911- *AmMWSc 92*
**Hopper,** Sarah Priestly 1925- *AmMWSc 92*
**Hopper,** Stephen Raymond 1951- *WhoRel 92*
**Hopper,** Stephen Rodger 1949- *WhoMW 92*
**Hopper,** Steven Phillip 1945- *AmMWSc 92*
**Hopper,** Taylor Lincoln 1933- *WhoAmP 91*
**Hopper,** Thomas A, Jr 1959- *WhoAmP 91*
**Hopper,** W. David 1927- *IntWW 91*
**Hopper,** Walter Everett 1915- *WhoAmL 92, WhoFI 92*
**Hopper,** Wilbert Hill 1933- *IntWW 91, WhoFI 92, WhoWest 92*
**Hopper,** William Joseph 1929- *Who 92*
**Hoppert,** Earl William 1939- *WhoRel 92*
**Hoppes,** Alice Faye 1939- *WhoBlA 92*
**Hoppes,** Brian Henry 1946- *WhoMW 92*
**Hoppes,** Dale DuBois 1928- *AmMWSc 92*
**Hoppes,** Harrison Neil 1935- *WhoFI 92*
**Hoppin,** Richard Arthur 1921- *AmMWSc 92*
**Hopping,** Richard Lee 1928- *AmMWSc 92*
**Hopping,** Robert Daniel 1949- *WhoWest 92*
**Hopping,** William Russell 1947- *WhoWest 92*
**Hopple,** Richard Van Tromp, Jr. 1947- *WhoFI 92*
**Hoppmann,** Barbara Elsie 1953- *WhoAmL 92*
**Hoppmann,** William Henry, II 1908- *AmMWSc 92*
**Hoppmeyer,** Warren Herbert, Jr. 1950- *WhoMW 92*
**Hoppock,** Robert 1901- *WrDr 92*
**Hopponen,** Jerry Dale 1946- *AmMWSc 92*
**Hopps,** Hope Elizabeth Byrne 1926- *AmMWSc 92*
**Hopps,** Howard Carl 1914- *AmMWSc 92*
**Hopps,** John Alexander 1919- *AmMWSc 92*
**Hopps,** Raymond, Jr. 1949- *WhoFI 92*
**Hopps,** Sidney Bryce 1934- *WhoAmL 92*
**Hopson,** Clifford Andrae 1928- *AmMWSc 92*
**Hopson,** Dennis 1965- *WhoBlA 92*
**Hopson,** Edwin Sharp 1945- *WhoAmL 92*
**Hopson,** Harold Theodore, II 1937- *WhoBlA 92*
**Hopson,** James A 1935- *AmMWSc 92*
**Hopson,** John Wilbur, Jr 1940- *AmMWSc 92*
**Hopson,** Joyce Sue 1950- *WhoAmP 91*
**Hopson,** Judy Alice 1947- *WhoAmL 92*
**Hopson,** Melvin Clarence 1937- *WhoBlA 92*
**Hopson,** Ricky 1957- *WhoEnt 92*
**Hopson,** William 1907- *TwCWW 91*
**Hopthrow,** Harry Ewart 1896- *Who 92*
**Hoptman,** Julian 1925- *AmMWSc 92*
**Hopton,** Frederick James 1936- *AmMWSc 92*
**Hopwood** *Who 92*
**Hopwood,** Anthony George 1944- *Who 92*
**Hopwood,** Avery 1882-1928 *BenetAL 91*
**Hopwood,** David Alan 1933- *IntWW 91, Who 92*
**Hopwood,** Howard H. 1945- *WhoAmL 92*
**Hopwood,** Larry Eugene 1945- *AmMWSc 92*
**Hor Lhamo** *EncAmaz 91*
**Horackova,** Magda 1940- *AmMWSc 92*
**Horad,** Sewell D., Sr. 1922- *WhoBlA 92*
**Horadam,** Alwyn Francis 1923- *WrDr 92*
**Horahan,** Edward Bernard, III 1951- *WhoAmL 92*
**Horai,** Ki-iti 1934- *AmMWSc 92*
**Horak,** Donald L 1937- *AmMWSc 92*
**Horak,** Gerry 1949- *WhoAmP 91*
**Horak,** James Albert 1931- *AmMWSc 92*
**Horak,** Martin George 1936- *AmMWSc 92*
**Horak,** Vaclav 1922- *AmMWSc 92*
**Horakova,** Zdenka 1925- *AmMWSc 92*
**Horam,** John Rhodes 1939- *Who 92*
**Horan,** Brien Purcell 1953- *WhoAmL 92*
**Horan,** Clark J., III 1950- *WhoRel 92*
**Horan,** Forbes Trevor 1905- *Who 92*
**Horan,** Francis E 1914- *AmMWSc 92*
**Horan,** John Rogers 1938- *WhoAmL 92*
**Horan,** Judith Kay *WhoEnt 92*
**Horan,** Mary Ann Theresa 1936- *WhoWest 92*
**Horan,** Michael 1945- *AmMWSc 92*
**Horan,** Michael Francis 1942- *WhoAmP 91*
**Horan,** Patrick Joseph 1957- *WhoFI 92*
**Horan,** Paul Karl 1942- *AmMWSc 92*
**Horan,** R Kevin 1950- *WhoAmP 91*
**Horan,** Robert Bailey, Jr. 1952- *WhoWest 92*
**Horan,** Stephen Francis 1933- *WhoWest 92*
**Horan,** Terence Lee 1951- *WhoMW 92*
**Horan,** William F, Jr *WhoAmP 91*
**Horbal,** Koryne Emily 1937- *WhoAmP 91*
**Horbatsch,** Marko M 1954- *AmMWSc 92*
**Horbett,** Thomas Alan 1943- *AmMWSc 92*
**Horch,** Kenneth William 1942- *AmMWSc 92, WhoWest 92*
**Horch,** Nettie S. d1991 *NewYTBS 91*
**Horcher,** Paul V *WhoAmP 91*
**Hord,** Brian Howard 1934- *Who 92*
**Hord,** Charles W 1937- *AmMWSc 92*
**Hord,** Frederick Lee 1941- *WhoBlA 92*
**Hord,** Noel Edward 1946- *WhoBlA 92*
**Hord,** William Eugene *AmMWSc 92*
**Horde,** Gaither Wilson 1926- *WhoAmP 91*
**Hordeman,** Agnes Marie 1929- *WhoFI 92*
**Horden,** John Robert Backhouse *Who 92*
**Horder** *Who 92*
**Horder,** Baron 1910- *Who 92*
**Horder,** John Plaistowe 1919- *Who 92*
**Horder,** Mervyn 1910- *WrDr 92*
**Hordern,** Christopher *Who 92*
**Hordern,** Michael 1911- *IntMPA 92, Who 92*
**Hordern,** Michael Murray 1911- *IntWW 91*
**Hordern,** Peter 1929- *Who 92*
**Hordon,** Robert M 1936- *AmMWSc 92*
**Hordt,** Philipp 1891-1933 *EncTR 91*
**Hore,** John Edward 1929- *WhoFI 92*
**Hore,** Marlene Carole 1944- *WhoFI 92*
**Hore-Belisha,** Leslie 1893-1957 *EncTR 91*
**Hore-Ruthven** *Who 92*
**Horecka,** Richard Robert 1952- *WhoMW 92*
**Horecker,** Bernard L. 1914- *IntWW 91*
**Horecker,** Bernard Leonard 1914- *AmMWSc 92*
**Horecky,** Paul L. 1913- *WrDr 92*
**Horeczy,** Joseph Thomas 1913- *AmMWSc 92*
**Horel,** James Alan 1931- *AmMWSc 92*
**Horel,** Martha Travis 1955- *WhoAmP 91*
**Horelick,** Brindell 1932- *AmMWSc 92*
**Horen,** Daniel J 1928- *AmMWSc 92*
**Horenstein,** Evelyn Anne 1924- *AmMWSc 92*
**Horenstein,** Jascha 1898-1973 *FacFETw*
**Horenstein,** Jascha 1899-1973 *NewAmDM*
**Horenstein,** Muriel Catherine 1919- *WhoEnt 92*
**Horenstein,** Simon 1924- *AmMWSc 92*
**Horevay,** Duane Joseph 1955- *WhoRel 92*
**Horevitz,** Richard Paul 1945- *WhoMW 92*
**Horgan,** Cornelius Oliver 1944- *AmMWSc 92*
**Horgan,** Dean K 1944- *WhoAmP 91*
**Horgan,** James D 1922- *AmMWSc 92*
**Horgan,** James Edward 1953- *WhoFI 92*
**Horgan,** James Kevin 1952- *WhoAmL 92*
**Horgan,** Paul *DrAPF 91*
**Horgan,** Paul 1903- *BenetAL 91, ConAu 35NR, ConNov 91, IntAu&W 91, IntWW 91, TwCWW 91, WrDr 92*
**Horgan,** Stephen William 1942- *AmMWSc 92*
**Horgan,** Susan Bedsow 1947- *WhoEnt 92*
**Horgan,** Thomas R 1953- *WhoAmP 91*
**Horgen,** Paul Arthur 1944- *AmMWSc 92*
**Horger,** Edgar Olin, III 1937- *AmMWSc 92*
**Horger,** Lewis Milton 1927- *AmMWSc 92*
**Horgos,** Gyula 1920- *IntWW 91*
**Horgos,** Robert P *WhoAmP 91*
**Horhota,** Stephen Thomas 1950- *AmMWSc 92*
**Hori,** Kosuke *IntWW 91*
**Horie,** Yasuyuki 1937- *AmMWSc 92*
**Horikoshi,** Teizo 1898- *IntWW 91*
**Horine,** John William 1929- *WhoMW 92*
**Horine,** Paul Arlington 1921- *WhoRel 92*
**Horing,** Sheldon 1936- *AmMWSc 92*
**Horisberger,** Don Hans 1951- *WhoEnt 92, WhoMW 92*
**Horita,** Akira 1928- *AmMWSc 92*
**Horita,** Karen Keiko 1952- *WhoAmP 91*
**Horita,** Robert Eiji 1937- *AmMWSc 92*
**Horiuchi,** Kensuke 1933- *AmMWSc 92*
**Horiuchi,** Randy 1954- *WhoAmP 91*
**Horiuchi,** Toshio 1918- *IntWW 91*
**Horky,** Reginald Patrick 1952- *WhoFI 92, WhoMW 92*
**Horlander,** Nelle P 1929- *WhoAmP 91*
**Horlander,** Walter Franklin 1932- *WhoRel 92*
**Horlick,** Edwin John 1925- *Who 92*
**Horlick,** Gary 1944- *AmMWSc 92*
**Horlick,** Gary Norman 1947- *WhoAmL 92*
**Horlick,** John 1922- *Who 92*
**Horlick,** Louis 1921- *AmMWSc 92*
**Horlick,** Ted *Who 92*
**Horlock,** Henry Wimburn Sudell 1915- *Who 92*
**Horlock,** John Harold 1928- *IntWW 91, Who 92, WrDr 92*
**Hormats,** Ellis Irving 1919- *AmMWSc 92*
**Hormats,** Robert David 1943- *WhoAmP 91*
**Hormisdas** *EncEarC*
**Horn,** Alan *WhoEnt 92A*
**Horn,** Alan 1943- *IntMPA 92*
**Horn,** Alan Bowes 1917- *Who 92*
**Horn,** Alexander Grice 1817-1886 *DcNCBi 3*
**Horn,** Alfred 1918- *AmMWSc 92*
**Horn,** Allen Frederick, Jr 1929- *AmMWSc 92*
**Horn,** Andrew Warren 1946- *WhoAmL 92*
**Horn,** Bonnie Phyllis 1951- *WhoAmL 92*
**Horn,** Carl Lewis 1928- *WhoAmL 92*
**Horn,** Charles Frederick 1924- *WhoAmP 91*
**Horn,** Charles G. 1939- *WhoFI 92*
**Horn,** Chris 1940- *WhoEnt 92*
**Horn,** Chris Wayne 1965- *WhoRel 92*
**Horn,** Christian Friedrich 1927- *AmMWSc 92, WhoFI 92*
**Horn,** Dag 1950- *AmMWSc 92*
**Horn,** Daniel d1991 *NewYTBS 91*
**Horn,** Daniel 1934-1991 *ConAu 134*
**Horn,** David D 1941- *WhoIns 92*
**Horn,** David Jacobs 1943- *AmMWSc 92*
**Horn,** David Nicholas 1944- *AmMWSc 92*
**Horn,** Diane *AmMWSc 92*
**Horn,** Donald H 1945- *WhoAmP 91*
**Horn,** Edward Gustav 1942- *AmMWSc 92*
**Horn,** Eugene Harold 1926- *AmMWSc 92*
**Horn,** Evelyn B. 1953- *WhoBlA 92*
**Horn,** Everett Byron, Jr. 1927- *WhoFI 92, WhoIns 92*
**Horn,** Francis H. 1908- *IntWW 91*
**Horn,** Friedemann Hans Christian 1921- *WhoRel 92*
**Horn,** Gabriel 1927- *IntWW 91, Who 92*

**Horn**, George Henry 1840-1897 *BiInAmS*
**Horn**, Gilbert *WhoRel 92*
**Horn**, Gyula 1932- *IntWW 91*
**Horn**, Harry Moore 1931- *AmMWSc 92*
**Horn**, Heinz 1930- *IntWW 91*
**Horn**, Henry Stainken 1941- *AmMWSc 92*
**Horn**, Hoye 1934- *WhoAmP 91*
**Horn**, J W 1929- *AmMWSc 92*
**Horn**, James Charles 1950- *WhoRel 92*
**Horn**, James H 1919- *WhoIns 92*
**Horn**, James Nathan 1941- *WhoAmP 91*
**Horn**, Jan Kurt 1950- *WhoWest 92*
**Horn**, Jerry Eugene 1938- *WhoRel 92*
**Horn**, Jim *WhoAmP 91*
**Horn**, Joan Kelly *WhoMW 92*
**Horn**, Joan Kelly 1936- *AlmAP 92 [port], WhoAmP 91*
**Horn**, Joanne Gabrielle 1929- *WhoRel 92*
**Horn**, John F. 1941- *WhoFI 92*
**Horn**, John Harold 1927- *WhoAmL 92*
**Horn**, John J 1917- *WhoAmP 91*
**Horn**, Karen Gail 1953- *WhoAmL 92*
**Horn**, Karen Nicholson 1943- *WhoMW 92*
**Horn**, Keith Donald 1958- *WhoFI 92*
**Horn**, Kenneth Porter 1937- *AmMWSc 92*
**Horn**, Lawrence Charles 1938- *WhoBlA 92*
**Horn**, Leif 1925- *AmMWSc 92*
**Horn**, Lois Burley 1928- *WhoEnt 92*
**Horn**, Lyle Henry 1924- *AmMWSc 92*
**Horn**, Lyle William 1943- *AmMWSc 92*
**Horn**, Marian Blank 1943- *WhoAmL 92*
**Horn**, Maury Ronald 1949- *WhoEnt 92*
**Horn**, Michael Hastings 1942- *AmMWSc 92*
**Horn**, Myron K 1930- *AmMWSc 92*
**Horn**, Nicholas Johnson 1945- *WhoAmP 91*
**Horn**, Paul Ervin 1919- *WhoRel 92*
**Horn**, Paul Joseph 1930- *WhoEnt 92*
**Horn**, Raymond O. 1916- *WhoFI 92*
**Horn**, Rebecca 1944- *WorArt 1980*
**Horn**, Richard Michael 1954- *WhoAmL 92*
**Horn**, Roger Alan 1942- *AmMWSc 92*
**Horn**, Ronald C 1936- *WhoIns 92*
**Horn**, Shirley *WhoEnt 92*
**Horn**, Shirley 1934- *ConMus 7 [port]*
**Horn**, Siegfried H. 1908- *WrDr 92*
**Horn**, Stephen 1931- *WhoAmP 91, WrDr 92*
**Horn**, Susan Dadakis 1943- *AmMWSc 92*
**Horn**, Wally E 1933- *WhoAmP 91*
**Horn**, William Everett 1928- *AmMWSc 92*
**Horn**, William F. *BenetAL 91*
**Horn**, William Fred 1925- *WhoAmP 91*
**Horn-Dalton**, Kathy Ellen 1952- *WhoWest 92*
**Horna**, Otakar Anthony 1922- *AmMWSc 92*
**Hornack**, Frederick Mathew 1929- *AmMWSc 92*
**Hornaday**, Aline Grandier 1923- *WhoWest 92*
**Hornaday**, Jeffrey *WhoEnt 92*
**Hornak**, Mark Raymond 1956- *WhoAmL 92*
**Hornak**, Thomas 1924- *AmMWSc 92*
**Hornback**, Joseph Michael 1943- *AmMWSc 92*
**Hornback**, Vernon T., Jr. 1931- *WhoWest 92*
**Hornbaker**, Edwin Dale 1929- *AmMWSc 92*
**Hornbaker**, Larry Douglas 1934- *WhoWest 92*
**Hornbeck**, David Arthur 1943- *WhoAmL 92*
**Hornbeck**, John A 1918- *AmMWSc 92*
**Hornbein**, Thomas F 1930- *AmMWSc 92*
**Hornbein**, Victor 1913- *WhoWest 92*
**Hornberger**, Carl Stanley, Jr 1923- *AmMWSc 92*
**Hornberger**, George Milton 1942- *AmMWSc 92*
**Hornberger**, Lee 1946- *WhoAmL 92*
**Hornblass**, Jerome 1941- *WhoAmL 92*
**Hornblower**, Augusta 1948- *WhoAmP 91*
**Hornbostel**, Joel Scott 1963- *WhoEnt 92*
**Hornbostel**, Peter Anthony 1936- *WhoAmL 92*
**Hornbrook**, K Roger 1936- *AmMWSc 92*
**Hornbrooke**, Obadiah *IntAu&W 91X*
**Hornbuckle**, Franklin L 1941- *AmMWSc 92*
**Hornbuckle**, Napoleon 1942- *WhoBlA 92*
**Hornbuckle**, Phyllis Ann 1938- *AmMWSc 92*
**Hornby**, D Brock *WhoAmP 91*
**Hornby**, David Brock 1944- *WhoAmL 92*
**Hornby**, Derek 1930- *Who 92*
**Hornby**, Derrick Richard 1926- *Who 92*
**Hornby**, Frank *DcTwDes*
**Hornby**, James Angus 1922- *Who 92*
**Hornby**, Lesley *Who 92*
**Hornby**, Lesley 1949- *WhoEnt 92*
**Hornby**, Richard Phipps 1922- *Who 92*
**Hornby**, Simon 1934- *IntWW 91, Who 92*
**Hornby**, William Harry 1923- *WhoWest 92*
**Horne**, Alan Gray 1948- *Who 92*
**Horne**, Alexander John *AmMWSc 92*
**Horne**, Alistair 1925- *WrDr 92*
**Horne**, Alistair Allan 1925- *IntAu&W 91, Who 92*
**Horne**, Alvin Matthew 1947- *WhoRel 92*
**Horne**, Ashley 1841-1913 *DcNCBi 3*
**Horne**, Charles E, III 1932- *WhoIns 92*
**Horne**, Chuck *WhoAmP 91*
**Horne**, Colin James 1912- *IntWW 91*
**Horne**, David Oliver 1932- *Who 92*
**Horne**, Deborah Jean 1953- *WhoBlA 92*
**Horne**, Dennis LaFon 1954- *WhoRel 92*
**Horne**, Donald Richmond 1921- *IntAu&W 91, IntWW 91, WrDr 92*
**Horne**, Edwin Clay 1924- *WhoBlA 92*
**Horne**, Francis R 1939- *AmMWSc 92*
**Horne**, Frank *WhoAmP 91*
**Horne**, Frederic Thomas 1917- *Who 92*
**Horne**, Frederick Herbert 1934- *AmMWSc 92, WhoWest 92*
**Horne**, G T 1924- *AmMWSc 92*
**Horne**, Gayle Brenda 1962- *WhoEnt 92*
**Horne**, Gene-Ann P. 1926- *WhoBlA 92*
**Horne**, Gerald C. 1949- *WhoBlA 92*
**Horne**, Gray *Who 92*
**Horne**, Gregory Stuart 1935- *AmMWSc 92*
**Horne**, Herman Harrell 1874-1946 *DcNCBi 3*
**Horne**, James Grady, Jr 1926- *AmMWSc 92*
**Horne**, Joshua Lawrence 1887-1974 *DcNCBi 3*
**Horne**, June C. 1952- *WhoBlA 92*
**Horne**, June Merideth 1936- *WhoBlA 92*
**Horne**, Katharyn 1932- *WhoEnt 92*
**Horne**, Lena 1917- *FacFETw, IntMPA 92, NewAmDM, NotBlAW 92 [port], WhoBlA 92, WhoEnt 92*
**Horne**, Lewis *DrAPF 91*
**Horne**, Marilyn *NewYTBS 91 [port]*
**Horne**, Marilyn 1934- *ConAu 133, IntWW 91, NewAmDM, WhoEnt 92*
**Horne**, Mark J. 1960- *WhoAmL 92*
**Horne**, Marvin L. R., Jr. 1936- *WhoBlA 92*
**Horne**, Michael Rex 1921- *IntWW 91, Who 92*
**Horne**, Michael Stewart 1938- *WhoAmL 92*
**Horne**, Milton Parnell 1956- *WhoRel 92*
**Horne**, Nigel William 1940- *Who 92*
**Horne**, R. A. 1929- *WrDr 92*
**Horne**, Ralph Albert 1929- *AmMWSc 92, IntAu&W 91*
**Horne**, Robert D 1935- *AmMWSc 92*
**Horne**, Robert Drake 1945- *Who 92*
**Horne**, Roland Nicholas 1952- *AmMWSc 92*
**Horne**, Samuel Emmett, Jr 1924- *AmMWSc 92*
**Horne**, Semmion N. *WhoBlA 92*
**Horne**, T. G. *WrDr 92*
**Horne**, Terry 1948- *WhoWest 92*
**Horne**, Tom Lee, III 1950- *WhoFI 92*
**Horne**, Tommy Arthur 1936- *WhoAmP 91*
**Horne**, Westry Grover 1913- *WhoBlA 92*
**Horne**, William S 1936- *WhoAmP 91*
**Horne-McGee**, Patricia J. 1946- *WhoBlA 92*
**Hornecker**, Wendell E. 1941- *WhoFI 92*
**Hornel**, Edward Atkinson 1864-1933 *TwCPaSc*
**Hornemann**, Ulfert 1939- *AmMWSc 92*
**Horner**, Alan Alfred 1934- *AmMWSc 92*
**Horner**, Althea Jane 1926- *WhoWest 92*
**Horner**, Arthur William 1909- *Who 92*
**Horner**, B Elizabeth 1917- *AmMWSc 92*
**Horner**, Charles Albert 1936- *NewYTBS 91 [port]*
**Horner**, Chester Ellsworth 1925- *AmMWSc 92*
**Horner**, Constance Joan 1942- *WhoAmP 91*
**Horner**, David Norman 1939- *WhoWest 92*
**Horner**, Donald *ScFEYrs*
**Horner**, Donald Gordon 1950- *WhoWest 92*
**Horner**, Donald Ray 1935- *AmMWSc 92*
**Horner**, Douglas George 1917- *Who 92*
**Horner**, Earl Stewart 1918- *AmMWSc 92*
**Horner**, Evan Wayne 1950- *WhoRel 92*
**Horner**, Frederick 1918- *Who 92*
**Horner**, George John 1923- *AmMWSc 92*
**Horner**, Harry 1910- *IntMPA 92, WhoEnt 92*
**Horner**, Harry Charles, Jr. 1937- *WhoWest 92*
**Horner**, Harry Theodore 1936- *AmMWSc 92*
**Horner**, James *IntMPA 92*
**Horner**, James Hunter 1822-1892 *DcNCBi 3*
**Horner**, James M 1935- *AmMWSc 92*
**Horner**, James William, Jr 1914- *AmMWSc 92*
**Horner**, Jerome Channing 1853-1951 *DcNCBi 3*
**Horner**, Jerry Wade 1936- *WhoRel 92*
**Horner**, Jocelyn 1902-1973 *TwCPaSc*
**Horner**, John 1911- *Who 92*
**Horner**, John Henry 1927- *IntWW 91*
**Horner**, John Richard 1936- *WhoMW 92*
**Horner**, John Robert 1946- *WhoWest 92*
**Horner**, John Robert 1949- *WhoAmP 91*
**Horner**, Junius Moore 1859-1933 *DcNCBi 3*
**Horner**, Kenneth Allen 1951- *WhoMW 92*
**Horner**, Larry Dean 1934- *WhoFI 92*
**Horner**, Margo Elizabeth 1947- *WhoAmP 91*
**Horner**, Matina S 1939- *WhoIns 92*
**Horner**, Maxine Edwyna 1933- *WhoAmP 91*
**Horner**, Nadine Dawn 1940- *WhoRel 92*
**Horner**, Norman Aste 1913- *WhoRel 92*
**Horner**, Norman V 1942- *AmMWSc 92*
**Horner**, Richard E 1917- *AmMWSc 92*
**Horner**, Richard Elmer 1917- *IntWW 91*
**Horner**, Russell G., Jr. *WhoAmL 92*
**Horner**, Sally Melvin 1935- *AmMWSc 92*
**Horner**, Theodore Wright 1924- *AmMWSc 92*
**Horner**, Vivian *LesBEnT 92*
**Horner**, William Edmonds 1793-1853 *BiInAmS*
**Horner**, William Harry 1923- *AmMWSc 92*
**Horner**, William Wesley 1930- *AmMWSc 92*
**Horness**, Cindy Kay 1959- *WhoEnt 92*
**Horney**, Amos Grant 1907- *AmMWSc 92*
**Horney**, Brigitte 1911-1988 *EncTR 91 [port]*
**Horney**, Karen 1885-1952 *FacFETw, HanAmWH, RComAH, WomPsyc*
**Horney**, Samuel Iradell, III 1952- *WhoWest 92*
**Horney**, Stephen Henry 1946- *WhoFI 92*
**Hornfeck**, Anthony J 1912- *AmMWSc 92*
**Horng**, Liou Liang 1955- *WhoMW 92*
**Horng**, Shi-Jinn 1957- *AmMWSc 92*
**Horng**, Wayne J *AmMWSc 92*
**Hornibrook**, Wallace 1925- *WhoRel 92*
**Hornibrook**, Walter J. d1991 *NewYTBS 91*
**Hornibrook**, Walter John 1916- *AmMWSc 92*
**Hornick**, Joshua 1959- *WhoAmL 92*
**Hornick**, Richard B 1929- *AmMWSc 92*
**Hornick**, Sharon B 1948- *AmMWSc 92*
**Hornig**, Donald Frederick 1920- *AmMWSc 92, IntWW 91, WhoAmP 91*
**Hornig**, Doug *DrAPF 91*
**Hornig**, George Ronald 1954- *WhoFI 92*
**Hornig**, Howard Chester 1924- *AmMWSc 92*
**Hornig**, James Frederick 1929- *AmMWSc 92*
**Horniman**, Annie 1860-1937 *FacFETw*
**Horniman**, Roy 1874-1930 *ScFEYrs*
**Horning**, Evan Charles 1916- *AmMWSc 92*
**Horning**, Marjorie G 1917- *AmMWSc 92*
**Horning**, Robert Alan 1954- *WhoWest 92*
**Hornor**, Sally Graham 1949- *AmMWSc 92*
**Hornsby**, Alton, Jr. 1940- *WhoBlA 92, WrDr 92*
**Hornsby**, Arthur Grady 1940- *AmMWSc 92*
**Hornsby**, B. Kay 1906- *WhoBlA 92*
**Hornsby**, Ben F *WhoAmP 91*
**Hornsby**, Bruce Randall 1954- *WhoEnt 92*
**Hornsby**, E C 1936- *WhoAmP 91*
**Hornsby**, Herbert Lewis, Jr. 1949- *WhoFI 92*
**Hornsby**, Rogers 1896-1963 *FacFETw*
**Hornsby**, Sonny *WhoAmL 92*
**Hornsby**, Timothy Richard 1940- *Who 92*
**Hornsby**, Walter Spurgeon, III 1941- *WhoBlA 92*
**Hornsby-Smith**, Baroness 1914-1985 *FacFETw*
**Hornsey**, Edward Eugene 1937- *AmMWSc 92*
**Hornstein**, Irwin 1917- *AmMWSc 92*
**Hornstein**, John Stanley 1941- *AmMWSc 92*
**Hornstein**, Mark 1947- *WhoFI 92*
**Hornthal**, Louis Philip, Jr. 1936- *WhoAmL 92*
**Horntvedt**, Earl W 1948- *AmMWSc 92*
**Hornuff**, Lothar Edward, Jr 1928- *AmMWSc 92*
**Hornung**, Christian 1845-1918 *BiInAmS*
**Hornung**, David Eugene 1945- *AmMWSc 92*
**Hornung**, Erwin William 1919- *AmMWSc 92*
**Hornung**, Jim Lee 1960- *WhoMW 92*
**Hornung**, Mark Andrew 1957- *WhoFI 92*
**Hornung**, Paul Vernon 1935- *FacFETw*
**Hornung**, Thomas A. 1943- *WhoWest 92*
**Hornyak**, Eugene Augustine 1919- *WhoRel 92*
**Hornyak**, William Frank 1922- *AmMWSc 92*
**Hornyik**, Karl 1926- *AmMWSc 92*
**Horodyski**, Robert Joseph 1943- *AmMWSc 92*
**Horoshko**, Roger N 1937- *AmMWSc 92*
**Horovitz**, Israel *DrAPF 91*
**Horovitz**, Israel 1939- *BenetAL 91, WrDr 92*
**Horovitz**, Israel Arthur 1939- *WhoEnt 92*
**Horovitz**, Joseph 1926- *IntWW 91*
**Horovitz**, Michael 1935- *ConPo 91, IntAu&W 91, TwCPaSc, WrDr 92*
**Horovitz**, Richard Allen d1991 *NewYTBS 91*
**Horovitz**, Zola Phillip 1934- *AmMWSc 92*
**Horowicz**, Paul 1931- *AmMWSc 92*
**Horowitz**, Alan Stanley 1930- *AmMWSc 92*
**Horowitz**, Avery Mark 1949- *WhoFI 92*
**Horowitz**, Barney Louis 1938- *WhoFI 92*
**Horowitz**, Ben 1914- *WhoFI 92, WhoWest 92*
**Horowitz**, Carl 1923- *AmMWSc 92*
**Horowitz**, David Allen 1942- *WhoAmL 92*
**Horowitz**, David Charles 1937- *WhoEnt 92*
**Horowitz**, David Morris 1942- *WhoMW 92, WhoRel 92*
**Horowitz**, Donald Leonard 1939- *IntAu&W 91, WhoAmL 92*
**Horowitz**, Donna Beth 1962- *WhoFI 92*
**Horowitz**, Ellis 1944- *AmMWSc 92*
**Horowitz**, Emanuel 1923- *AmMWSc 92*
**Horowitz**, Esther 1920- *AmMWSc 92*
**Horowitz**, Evan Joshua 1961- *WhoWest 92*
**Horowitz**, Fred L. 1954- *WhoMW 92*
**Horowitz**, Gary T 1955- *AmMWSc 92*
**Horowitz**, Harold W. 1923- *WhoAmL 92*
**Horowitz**, Herbert E 1930- *WhoAmP 91*
**Horowitz**, Howard Joel 1947- *WhoEnt 92*
**Horowitz**, Hugh H 1928- *AmMWSc 92*
**Horowitz**, Irving Louis 1929- *IntAu&W 91, WhoFI 92, WrDr 92*
**Horowitz**, Isaac 1920- *AmMWSc 92*
**Horowitz**, Jack 1931- *AmMWSc 92*
**Horowitz**, Joel Lawrence 1941- *WhoFI 92, WhoMW 92*
**Horowitz**, John M 1934- *AmMWSc 92*
**Horowitz**, Kenneth Paul 1956- *WhoEnt 92*
**Horowitz**, Larry Lowell 1949- *AmMWSc 92*
**Horowitz**, Lewis Jay 1935- *WhoFI 92*
**Horowitz**, Mardi J *AmMWSc 92*
**Horowitz**, Mark Charles 1950- *AmMWSc 92*
**Horowitz**, Martin I 1929- *AmMWSc 92*
**Horowitz**, Michael 1943- *Who 92*
**Horowitz**, Michael Joshua 1938- *WhoAmP 91*
**Horowitz**, Mikhail *DrAPF 91*
**Horowitz**, Myer 1932- *Who 92, WhoWest 92*
**Horowitz**, Myer George 1924- *AmMWSc 92*
**Horowitz**, Norman *LesBEnT 92*
**Horowitz**, Norman Harold 1915- *AmMWSc 92, IntWW 91*
**Horowitz**, Paul Martin 1939- *AmMWSc 92*
**Horowitz**, Rachelle 1939- *WhoAmP 91*
**Horowitz**, Richard E 1931- *AmMWSc 92*
**Horowitz**, Robert 1944- *WhoMW 92*
**Horowitz**, Robert Miller 1921- *AmMWSc 92*
**Horowitz**, Samuel Boris 1927- *AmMWSc 92*
**Horowitz**, Shel *DrAPF 91*
**Horowitz**, Sidney Lester 1921- *AmMWSc 92*
**Horowitz**, Stephen Paul 1943- *WhoAmL 92, WhoWest 92*
**Horowitz**, Steven Gary 1950- *WhoAmL 92*
**Horowitz**, Sylvia Teich *AmMWSc 92*
**Horowitz**, Vladimir 1904-1989 *NewAmDM*
**Horowitz**, Vladimir Samoylovich 1903-1989 *FacFETw [port]*
**Horowitz**, Zachary I. 1953- *WhoEnt 92, WhoWest 92*
**Horr**, David James 1955- *WhoAmL 92*
**Horrall**, Robert Louis 1942- *WhoEnt 92*
**Horrell**, John Ray 1929- *Who 92*
**Horrell**, Karen Holley 1952- *WhoIns 92*
**Horrell**, Roger William 1935- *Who 92*
**Horres**, Alan Dixon 1929- *AmMWSc 92*
**Horres**, Charles Russell, Jr 1945- *AmMWSc 92*
**Horridge**, Adrian 1927- *Who 92*
**Horridge**, G. Adrian 1927- *IntWW 91*
**Horridge**, Patricia Emily 1937- *AmMWSc 92*
**Horrigan**, Alfred Frederic 1914- *WhoRel 92*
**Horrigan**, Brian Richard 1951- *WhoFI 92*
**Horrigan**, Frank Anthony 1933- *AmMWSc 92*
**Horrigan**, Philip Archibald 1928- *AmMWSc 92*
**Horrigan**, Robert V 1924- *AmMWSc 92*
**Horrigan**, Terrence John 1945- *WhoMW 92*
**Horrobin**, David Frederick 1939- *AmMWSc 92*

**Horrocks**, Brian 1895-1985 *FacFETw*
**Horrocks**, Lloyd Allen 1932- *AmMWSc 92*
**Horrocks**, Nancy *TwCPaSc*
**Horrocks**, Norman 1927- *WhoFI 92*
**Horrocks**, Raymond 1930- *IntWW 91, Who 92*
**Horrocks**, Robert H 1928- *AmMWSc 92*
**Horrocks**, Rodney Dwain 1938- *AmMWSc 92*
**Horrocks**, William DeWitt, Jr 1934- *AmMWSc 92*
**Horsbrugh**, Ian Robert 1941- *Who 92*
**Horsbrugh-Porter**, John 1938- *Who 92*
**Horsburgh**, Iain Lockhart 1951- *WhoFI 92*
**Horsburgh**, John Millar Stewart 1938- *Who 92*
**Horsburgh**, Robert Laurie 1931- *AmMWSc 92*
**Horsch**, James Everett 1939- *WhoRel 92*
**Horsch**, John 1867-1941 *AmPeW*
**Horsch**, John 1867-1942 *RelLAm 91*
**Horsch**, Robert Bruce 1952- *AmMWSc 92*
**Horsefield**, John Keith 1901- *Who 92*
**Horsell**, Mary Kay 1917- *WhoWest 92*
**Horseman**, Barbara Ann 1935- *WhoRel 92*
**Horseman**, Nelson Douglas 1951- *AmMWSc 92*
**Horsey**, Gordon 1926- *Who 92*
**Horsey**, Henry R 1924- *WhoAmP 91*
**Horsey**, Henry Ridgely 1924- *WhoAmL 92*
**Horsfall**, James Gordon 1905- *AmMWSc 92, IntWW 91*
**Horsfall**, John 1915- *Who 92*
**Horsfall**, William Robert 1908- *AmMWSc 92, WhoMW 92*
**Horsfield**, David Ralph 1916- *Who 92*
**Horsfield**, Nicholas 1917- *TwCPaSc*
**Horsfield**, Peter Muir Francis 1932- *Who 92*
**Horsfield**, Susan 1928- *TwCPaSc*
**Horsfield**, Thomas 1773-1859 *BilnAmS*
**Horsford**, Alan Arthur 1927- *Who 92*
**Horsford**, Anna Maria 1949- *WhoBlA 92*
**Horsford**, Derek Gordon Thomond 1917- *Who 92*
**Horsford**, Eben Norton 1818-1893 *BilnAmS*
**Horsham**, Archdeacon of *Who 92*
**Horsham**, Bishop Suffragan of 1945- *Who 92*
**Horsham**, Jean 1922- *Who 92*
**Horsing**, Otto 1874-1937 *EncTR 91*
**Horsley**, Alan Avery 1936- *Who 92*
**Horsley**, Beresford Peter 1921- *Who 92*
**Horsley**, Colin 1920- *Who 92*
**Horsley**, David *IntAu&W 91X, TwCWW 91*
**Horsley**, Jack Everett 1915- *WhoAmL 92, WhoFI 92, WhoMW 92*
**Horsley**, John Anthony 1943- *AmMWSc 92*
**Horsley**, John Shelton, III 1927- *AmMWSc 92*
**Horsley**, Lee 1955- *IntMPA 92*
**Horsley**, Nicholas 1934- *Who 92*
**Horsley**, Peter *Who 92*
**Horsley**, Stephen Daril 1947- *Who 92*
**Horsley**, Waller Holladay 1931- *WhoAmL 92*
**Horsma**, David August 1940- *AmMWSc 92, WhoWest 92*
**Horsman**, David A. Elliott 1932- *WhoFI 92*
**Horsman**, Dorothea 1918- *Who 92*
**Horsman**, James Deverell 1935- *WhoWest 92*
**Horsman**, Malcolm 1933- *Who 92*
**Horsman**, Reginald 1931- *WrDr 92*
**Horsnell**, Christian Alan 1949- *WhoAmL 92*
**Horst**, Bruce Everett 1921- *WhoMW 92*
**Horst**, David Michael 1955- *WhoEnt 92*
**Horst**, G Roy 1933- *AmMWSc 92*
**Horst**, Ralph Kenneth 1935- *AmMWSc 92*
**Horst**, Ralph L, Jr 1925- *AmMWSc 92*
**Horst**, Richard Harley 1958- *WhoMW 92*
**Horst**, Ronald Lee 1949- *AmMWSc 92*
**Horstadius**, Sven 1898- *IntWW 91*
**Horsting**, Walter Johnson 1951- *WhoEnt 92*
**Horstman**, Arden William 1930- *AmMWSc 92*
**Horstman**, Donald H 1939- *AmMWSc 92*
**Horstman**, Patrice Marie 1953- *WhoAmL 92*
**Horstmann**, Dorothy Millicent 1911- *AmMWSc 92*
**Horstmann**, Mark Steven 1958- *WhoFI 92*
**Horszowski**, Mieczyslaw 1892- *NewAmDM*
**Hort**, Eugene Victor 1921- *AmMWSc 92*
**Hort**, James Fenton 1926- *Who 92*
**Horta**, Adolfo 1957- *BlkOlyM*
**Horta**, Victor 1861-1947 *DcTwDes*
**Horthy**, Miklos 1868-1957 *EncTR 91 [port]*
**Horthy de Nagybanya**, Miklos 1868-1957 *FacFETw*
**Hortick**, Harvey J 1935- *AmMWSc 92*
**Hortillosa**, Raul Pamplona 1941- *WhoFI 92*
**Hortin**, Glen Lee 1954- *WhoMW 92*
**Hortmann**, Alfred Guenther 1937- *AmMWSc 92*
**Horton**, Aaron Wesley 1919- *AmMWSc 92*
**Horton**, Alexander Romeo 1923- *IntWW 91*
**Horton**, Arthur MacNeill, Jr. 1947- *ConAu 35NR*
**Horton**, Billy D 1930- *AmMWSc 92*
**Horton**, Billy Mitchusson 1918- *AmMWSc 92*
**Horton**, Bruce M 1934- *WhoIns 92*
**Horton**, Carrell Peterson 1928- *WhoBlA 92*
**Horton**, Charles Abell 1918- *AmMWSc 92*
**Horton**, Clarence Pennington 1910- *WhoBlA 92*
**Horton**, Claude Wendell, Jr 1942- *AmMWSc 92*
**Horton**, Claude Wendell, Sr 1915- *AmMWSc 92*
**Horton**, Clifford E 1922- *AmMWSc 92*
**Horton**, David Alan 1957- *WhoRel 92*
**Horton**, Derek 1932- *AmMWSc 92*
**Horton**, Dollie Bea Dixon 1942- *WhoBlA 92*
**Horton**, Douglas 1891-1968 *RelLAm 91*
**Horton**, Douglas Jay 1945- *WhoMW 92*
**Horton**, Earle C. 1943- *WhoBlA 92*
**Horton**, Edward S *AmMWSc 92*
**Horton**, Eldon Arvid 1942- *WhoMW 92*
**Horton**, Eric William 1929- *Who 92*
**Horton**, Felix Lee *IntAu&W 91X, TwCWW 91*
**Horton**, Finis Gene 1953- *WhoFI 92*
**Horton**, Frank 1919- *AlmAP 92 [port], WhoAmP 91*
**Horton**, Frank E. 1939- *WrDr 92*
**Horton**, Frank Elba 1939- *IntWW 91, WhoMW 92*
**Horton**, Gary Bruce 1943- *WhoFI 92*
**Horton**, Gary William 1940- *WhoAmP 91*
**Horton**, George Moses 1797?-1883? *DcNCBi 3*
**Horton**, George Moses 1798?-1880? *BenetAL 91*
**Horton**, Glyn Michael John 1942- *AmMWSc 92*
**Horton**, Gretchen Mary 1941- *WhoEnt 92*
**Horton**, Herschella *WhoAmP 91*
**Horton**, Horace Robert 1935- *AmMWSc 92*
**Horton**, Howard Franklin 1926- *AmMWSc 92*
**Horton**, Jack 1955- *WhoAmP 91*
**Horton**, Jack King 1916- *IntWW 91, WhoWest 92*
**Horton**, James Charles 1927- *AmMWSc 92*
**Horton**, James Heathman 1931- *AmMWSc 92*
**Horton**, James Jay 1937- *WhoIns 92*
**Horton**, James O 1943- *ConAu 35NR*
**Horton**, James T. 1918- *WhoBlA 92*
**Horton**, James V. 1948- *TwCPaSc*
**Horton**, James Wright, Jr 1950- *AmMWSc 92*
**Horton**, Janice S 1945- *WhoAmP 91*
**Horton**, Jerry Lee 1944- *WhoAmP 91*
**Horton**, Jerry Smith 1941- *WhoRel 92*
**Horton**, John 1934- *AmMWSc 92*
**Horton**, John Edward 1930- *AmMWSc 92*
**Horton**, Joseph Arno, Jr 1951- *AmMWSc 92*
**Horton**, Joseph William 1929- *AmMWSc 92*
**Horton**, Jureta 1941- *AmMWSc 92*
**Horton**, Kenneth Edwin 1932- *AmMWSc 92*
**Horton**, Larkin, Jr. 1939- *WhoBlA 92*
**Horton**, Larnie G. *WhoBlA 92*
**Horton**, Larry Bruce 1942- *WhoAmL 92, WhoFI 92*
**Horton**, Larry David 1948- *WhoMW 92*
**Horton**, Lawrence Stanley 1926- *WhoWest 92*
**Horton**, Lemuel Leonard 1936- *WhoBlA 92*
**Horton**, Louise *DrAPF 91*
**Horton**, Lynn C *WhoAmP 91*
**Horton**, M Duane 1935- *AmMWSc 92*
**Horton**, Madeline Mary 1939- *WhoFI 92*
**Horton**, Matthew Bethell 1946- *Who 92*
**Horton**, Maurice Lee 1931- *AmMWSc 92*
**Horton**, Michael Scott 1964- *ConAu 135*
**Horton**, O. Charles 1937- *WhoRel 92*
**Horton**, Odell 1929- *WhoAmL 92, WhoBlA 92*
**Horton**, Otis Howard 1917- *AmMWSc 92*
**Horton**, Patricia Sandra 1947- *WhoRel 92*
**Horton**, Paul B. 1916- *WrDr 92*
**Horton**, Paul Bradfield 1920- *WhoAmL 92, WhoFI 92*
**Horton**, Percy 1897-1970 *TwCPaSc*
**Horton**, Peter William *WhoEnt 92*
**Horton**, Philip Bish 1926- *AmMWSc 92*
**Horton**, Ralph Lee 1921- *WhoMW 92*
**Horton**, Ralph M 1934- *AmMWSc 92*
**Horton**, Raymond Anthony 1960- *WhoBlA 92*
**Horton**, Richard 1932- *AmMWSc 92*
**Horton**, Richard E 1940- *AmMWSc 92*
**Horton**, Richard Greenfield 1912- *AmMWSc 92*
**Horton**, Robert 1924- *IntMPA 92*
**Horton**, Robert, Jr 1954- *AmMWSc 92*
**Horton**, Robert Baynes 1939- *IntWW 91, Who 92*
**Horton**, Robert Carlton 1926- *AmMWSc 92, WhoAmP 91*
**Horton**, Robert J *IntAu&W 91X*
**Horton**, Robert Louis 1920- *AmMWSc 92*
**Horton**, Robert Louis 1944- *AmMWSc 92*
**Horton**, Roger Francis 1943- *AmMWSc 92*
**Horton**, Ronald Lee 1948- *WhoEnt 92*
**Horton**, Sherman D *WhoAmP 91*
**Horton**, Stanley Monroe 1916- *WhoRel 92*
**Horton**, Stella Jean 1944- *WhoBlA 92*
**Horton**, Thomas Edward, Jr 1935- *AmMWSc 92*
**Horton**, Thomas Frederick 1926- *WhoEnt 92*
**Horton**, Thomas R. 1926- *WhoFI 92*
**Horton**, Thomas Roscoe 1926- *AmMWSc 92*
**Horton**, Walter James 1913- *AmMWSc 92*
**Horton**, Wilkins Perryman 1889-1950 *DcNCBi 3*
**Horton**, William d1845 *BilnAmS*
**Horton**, William A *AmMWSc 92*
**Horton**, William Pharis 1934- *WhoAmL 92*
**Horton**, William Russell 1931- *WhoFI 92*
**Horton**, William Wiley 1959- *WhoAmL 92*
**Horton**, Willie Wattison 1942- *WhoBlA 92*
**Horvat**, Branko 1928- *IntWW 91*
**Horvat**, Michel Daniel 1961- *WhoEnt 92*
**Horvat**, Robert Emil 1940- *AmMWSc 92*
**Horvath**, Betty 1927- *WrDr 92*
**Horvath**, Csaba Gyula 1930- *AmMWSc 92*
**Horvath**, Donald James 1929- *AmMWSc 92*
**Horvath**, Fred Ernest 1924- *AmMWSc 92*
**Horvath**, Imre Gabor 1940- *WhoEnt 92*
**Horvath**, John, Jr. *DrAPF 91*
**Horvath**, John Michael 1924- *AmMWSc 92*
**Horvath**, Juliana 1948- *WhoMW 92*
**Horvath**, Kalman 1940- *AmMWSc 92*
**Horvath**, Louis J 1928- *WhoAmP 91*
**Horvath**, Michael John 1948- *WhoMW 92*
**Horvath**, Odon von 1901-1938 *FacFETw, LiExTwC*
**Horvath**, Paul Douglas 1967- *WhoFI 92*
**Horvath**, Peter Joseph 1952- *WhoEnt 92*
**Horvath**, Ralph S 1936- *AmMWSc 92*
**Horvath**, Ralph Steve 1936- *WhoMW 92*
**Horvath**, Steven Michael 1911- *AmMWSc 92*
**Horvath**, Terrence Michael 1961- *WhoWest 92*
**Horvath**, Theodore James 1928- *WhoAmL 92*
**Horvath**, William John 1917- *AmMWSc 92*
**Horve**, Leslie A 1938- *AmMWSc 92*
**Horvit**, Michael M. 1932- *WhoEnt 92*
**Horvitz**, Daniel Goodman 1921- *AmMWSc 92*
**Horvitz**, Howard Robert 1947- *AmMWSc 92*
**Horvitz**, Paul Michael 1935- *WhoFI 92*
**Horwedel**, Charles Richard 1902- *AmMWSc 92*
**Horwich**, Alan 1948- *Who 92*
**Horwich**, George 1924- *WhoFI 92, WhoMW 92*
**Horwin**, Leonard 1913- *WhoAmL 92, WhoWest 92*
**Horwitch**, Elaine d1991 *NewYTBS 91*
**Horwitch**, Richard 1945- *WhoFI 92*
**Horwitt**, Max Kenneth 1908- *AmMWSc 92, WhoMW 92*
**Horwitt**, Nathan George 1898-1990 *DcTwDes*
**Horwitz**, Alan Fredrick 1944- *AmMWSc 92*
**Horwitz**, Allan Barry 1947- *WhoFI 92*
**Horwitz**, Barbara Ann 1940- *AmMWSc 92, WhoWest 92*
**Horwitz**, David Larry 1942- *AmMWSc 92*
**Horwitz**, Donald Paul 1936- *WhoAmL 92*
**Horwitz**, Earl Philip 1930- *AmMWSc 92*
**Horwitz**, Edwin M 1959- *AmMWSc 92*
**Horwitz**, Harry 1927- *AmMWSc 92, WhoMW 92*
**Horwitz**, Howie d1976 *LesBEnT 92*
**Horwitz**, James David 1957- *WhoAmL 92*
**Horwitz**, Jeffrey Alan 1959- *WhoAmL 92*
**Horwitz**, Jerome Philip 1919- *AmMWSc 92*
**Horwitz**, Joseph 1936- *AmMWSc 92*
**Horwitz**, Kathryn Bloch *AmMWSc 92*
**Horwitz**, Larry Stuckey 1949- *WhoWest 92*
**Horwitz**, Lawrence D 1939- *AmMWSc 92*
**Horwitz**, Lawrence H. 1946- *WhoMW 92*
**Horwitz**, Lawrence Paul 1930- *AmMWSc 92*
**Horwitz**, Marcus Aaron 1946- *AmMWSc 92*
**Horwitz**, Marshall Sydney 1937- *AmMWSc 92*
**Horwitz**, Mayer 1939- *WhoAmL 92*
**Horwitz**, Melvin 1926- *WhoAmL 92*
**Horwitz**, Morton J. 1938- *WhoAmL 92*
**Horwitz**, Murray 1949- *WhoEnt 92*
**Horwitz**, Murray Lee 1957- *WhoFI 92*
**Horwitz**, Nahmin 1927- *AmMWSc 92*
**Horwitz**, Orville 1858?-1913 *BilnAmS*
**Horwitz**, Orville 1909- *AmMWSc 92*
**Horwitz**, Paul 1938- *AmMWSc 92*
**Horwitz**, Ralph Irving 1947- *AmMWSc 92*
**Horwitz**, Samuel 1918- *WhoAmP 91*
**Horwitz**, Sol 1920- *IntMPA 92*
**Horwitz**, Susan Band *AmMWSc 92*
**Horwitz**, William 1918- *AmMWSc 92*
**Horwood**, Edgar M 1919- *AmMWSc 92*
**Horwood**, Harold 1923- *ConAu 15AS [port]*
**Horwood**, Owen Pieter Faure 1916- *IntWW 91, Who 92*
**Horwood**, William *IntAu&W 91*
**Horz**, Friedrich 1940- *AmMWSc 92*
**Horzempa**, Lewis Michael 1949- *AmMWSc 92*
**Horzepa**, John Philip 1943- *AmMWSc 92*
**Horzewski**, Jerome Charles 1933- *WhoMW 92*
**Hosack**, David 1769-1835 *BilnAmS*
**Hosack**, Robert E 1911- *WhoAmP 91*
**Hosain**, Fazle 1932- *AmMWSc 92*
**Hosain**, Mahbub Ul 1938- *AmMWSc 92*
**Hosansky**, Norman Leon 1924- *AmMWSc 92*
**Hoschede**, Alice 1841-1911 *ThHEIm*
**Hoschede**, Ernest 1838-1890 *ThHEIm*
**Hose**, John Horsley 1928- *Who 92*
**Hose**, Richard K 1920- *AmMWSc 92*
**Hosea**, Joel Carlton 1938- *AmMWSc 92*
**Hosein**, Esau Abbas 1922- *AmMWSc 92*
**Hosek**, James Robert 1944- *WhoFI 92*
**Hoselton**, Steven Dale 1961- *WhoAmL 92*
**Hoseman**, Daniel 1935- *WhoAmL 92*
**Hosenball**, S. Neil *WhoAmL 92*
**Hoseney**, Russell Carl 1934- *AmMWSc 92*
**Hosey**, M Marlene *AmMWSc 92*
**Hosfield**, George W. 1957- *WhoFI 92*
**Hosford**, John Percival d1991 *Who 92N*
**Hosford**, Robert Morgan, Jr 1933- *AmMWSc 92*
**Hosford**, William Fuller, Jr 1928- *AmMWSc 92*
**Hoshaw**, Robert William 1921- *AmMWSc 92*
**Hoshiko**, Michael S *AmMWSc 92*
**Hoshiko**, Tomuo 1927- *AmMWSc 92*
**Hoshino**, Kenji Phillip 1954- *WhoAmL 92*
**Hosick**, Howard Lawrence 1943- *AmMWSc 92*
**Hosie**, David 1962- *TwCPaSc*
**Hosie**, James Findlay 1913- *Who 92*
**Hosie**, Stanley William 1922- *WhoEnt 92, WhoFI 92, WhoWest 92*
**Hosie**, William Carlton 1936- *WhoWest 92*
**Hosier**, Gerald Douglas 1941- *WhoAmL 92*
**Hosier**, John 1928- *Who 92*
**Hosier**, Peter *WrDr 92*
**Hosinski**, Peter Mitten 1954- *WhoAmL 92*
**Hosinski**, Thomas Edmund 1946- *WhoRel 92*
**Hosius of Cordova** 257?-357? *EncEarC*
**Hosken**, William H 1937- *AmMWSc 92*
**Hosker**, Gerald Albery 1933- *Who 92*
**Hosker**, Rayford Peter, Jr 1943- *AmMWSc 92*
**Hoskin**, Anne Eleanore 1924- *WhoAmP 91*
**Hoskin**, Francis Clifford George 1922- *AmMWSc 92*
**Hoskin**, George Perry 1941- *AmMWSc 92*
**Hoskin**, John 1921- *TwCPaSc*
**Hosking**, Barbara Nancy 1926- *Who 92*
**Hosking**, Eric John d1991 *Who 92N*
**Hosking**, Geoffrey Alan 1942- *Who 92*
**Hosking**, John Everard 1929- *Who 92*
**Hosking**, Knighton 1944- *TwCPaSc*
**Hoskins**, Alan Lloyd 1936- *WhoMW 92*
**Hoskins**, Barbara Bruno 1948- *WhoWest 92*
**Hoskins**, Beth *AmMWSc 92*
**Hoskins**, Bob 1942- *IntMPA 92, IntWW 91, WhoEnt 92*
**Hoskins**, Brian John 1945- *Who 92*
**Hoskins**, Charles W. 1818-1846 *DcNCBi 3*
**Hoskins**, Cortez William 1930- *AmMWSc 92*
**Hoskins**, Curtis Lynn 1937- *WhoFI 92*
**Hoskins**, Dale Douglas 1928- *AmMWSc 92*
**Hoskins**, Donald Martin 1930- *AmMWSc 92*
**Hoskins**, Earl R, Jr 1934- *AmMWSc 92*

**Hoskins,** Frederick Hall 1936- *AmMWSc 92*
**Hoskins,** Hartley 1938- *AmMWSc 92*
**Hoskins,** John Richard 1919- *AmMWSc 92*
**Hoskins,** Leo Claron 1940- *AmMWSc 92*
**Hoskins,** Ned 1939- *TwCPaSc*
**Hoskins,** Robert 1933- *IntAu&W 91, ScFEYrs, TwCSFW 91, WrDr 92*
**Hoskins,** Robert William 1942- *Who 92*
**Hoskins,** Sam Whitworth, Jr 1921- *AmMWSc 92*
**Hoskins,** Thomas H 1828?-1902 *BiInAmS*
**Hoskins,** W. Lee *NewYTBS 91 [port]*
**Hoskins,** William George 1908- *IntWW 91, Who 92*
**Hoskins Clark,** Tempy M. 1938- *WhoBlA 92*
**Hoskyns,** Benedict 1928- *Who 92*
**Hoskyns,** John 1927- *Who 92*
**Hoskyns,** John Austin Hungerford Leigh 1927- *IntWW 91*
**Hosler,** Charles Frederick, Jr 1939- *AmMWSc 92*
**Hosler,** Charles Luther, Jr 1924- *AmMWSc 92*
**Hosler,** E Ramon 1935- *AmMWSc 92*
**Hosler,** John Frederick 1920- *AmMWSc 92*
**Hosler,** Mary Margaret 1938- *WhoMW 92*
**Hosler,** Peter 1927- *AmMWSc 92*
**Hosley,** David Henry 1949- *WhoWest 92*
**Hosley,** Robert James 1923- *AmMWSc 92*
**Hosman,** Glenn B., Jr. 1937- *WhoRel 92*
**Hosmane,** Narayan Sadashiv 1948- *AmMWSc 92*
**Hosmane,** Ramachandra Sadashiv 1944- *AmMWSc 92*
**Hosmanek,** Jane Elizabeth 1956- *WhoAmL 92*
**Hosmer,** Bradley Clark 1937- *WhoWest 92*
**Hosmer,** Craig 1959- *WhoAmP 91*
**Hosmer,** Harriet Goodhue 1830-1908 *HanAmWH*
**Hosmer,** LaRue Tone 1927- *WhoMW 92*
**Hosmer,** William Howe Cuyler 1814-1877 *BenetAL 91*
**Hosner,** James Robert 1944- *WhoEnt 92*
**Hosner,** John Frank 1925- *AmMWSc 92*
**Hosni,** Naguib 1928- *IntWW 91*
**Hosni,** Yasser Ali 1941- *AmMWSc 92*
**Hosoda,** Junko *AmMWSc 92*
**Hosoda,** Kichizo 1912- *IntWW 91*
**Hosokawa,** Keiichi 1929- *AmMWSc 92*
**Hosokawa,** Toshio 1955- *ConCom 92*
**Hosono,** Erwin 1960- *WhoFI 92*
**Hospelhorn,** Verne D 1922- *AmMWSc 92*
**Hospital,** Janette Turner 1942- *ConNov 91*
**Hospital,** Maria Carolina 1957- *WhoHisp 92*
**Hoss,** Donald Adron 1940- *WhoMW 92*
**Hoss,** Donald Earl 1936- *AmMWSc 92*
**Hoss,** Eric Christopher 1965- *WhoMW 92*
**Hoss,** Granville *ScFEYrs*
**Hoss,** Rudolf 1900-1947 *EncTR 91 [port]*
**Hoss,** Selim al- 1930- *IntWW 91*
**Hoss,** Wayne Paul 1943- *AmMWSc 92, WhoMW 92*
**Hossack,** George William 1926- *WhoWest 92*
**Hossain,** Anwar 1944- *IntWW 91*
**Hossain,** Kemaluddin 1923- *IntWW 91*
**Hossain,** Shafi Ul 1926- *AmMWSc 92*
**Hossain,** Shah Moazzem 1939- *IntWW 91*
**Hossaini,** Ali A 1928- *AmMWSc 92*
**Hossbach,** Friedrich 1894-1980 *EncTR 91*
**Hossein,** Robert 1927- *IntWW 91*
**Hossfeld,** Walter Edward, Jr. 1932- *WhoFI 92*
**Hossler,** David J 1940- *WhoAmP 91*
**Hossler,** David Joseph 1940- *WhoAmL 92, WhoWest 92*
**Hossler,** Fred E 1941- *AmMWSc 92*
**Hossner,** Lloyd Richard 1936- *AmMWSc 92*
**Hosten,** Adrian *WhoBlA 92*
**Hoster,** Donald Paul 1941- *AmMWSc 92*
**Hoster,** Fred William 1939- *WhoEnt 92*
**Hoster,** William Henry, Jr. 1912- *WhoFI 92*
**Hosterman,** John W 1923- *AmMWSc 92*
**Hostetler,** Emory Leon 1950- *WhoMW 92*
**Hostetler,** H Richard 1942- *WhoAmP 91*
**Hostetler,** Jeptha Ray 1939- *AmMWSc 92*
**Hostetler,** Karl Yoder 1939- *AmMWSc 92*
**Hostetler,** N. Douglas 1956- *WhoFI 92*
**Hostetler,** Robert Paul 1937- *AmMWSc 92*
**Hostetler,** Roy Ivan 1916- *AmMWSc 92*
**Hostetter,** Amos, Jr. *LesBEnT 92*
**Hostetter,** Donald Lee 1941- *AmMWSc 92*
**Hostetter,** Iris Adrian 1912- *WhoEnt 92*
**Hostetter,** James William 1948- *WhoMW 92*
**Hostetter,** Mark David 1959- *WhoAmL 92*
**Hostetter,** William Wallace 1945- *WhoRel 92*
**Hostettler,** Dorie McFetridge 1910- *WhoAmP 91*
**Hostettler,** John Davison 1941- *AmMWSc 92*
**Hosticka,** Carl 1944- *WhoAmP 91*
**Hostler,** Charles Warren 1919- *WhoAmP 91*
**Hostnik,** Charles Rivoire 1954- *WhoAmL 92*
**Hoston,** Germaine A. 1954- *WhoBlA 92*
**Hostos,** Eugenio Maria de 1839- *HisDSpE*
**Hostos,** Eugenio Maria de 1839-1903 *BenetAL 91*
**Hostrop,** Richard W. 1925- *WrDr 92*
**Hotaling,** Ada E. 1953- *WhoHisp 92*
**Hotaling,** John James 1947- *WhoAmP 91*
**Hotchin,** John Elton 1921- *AmMWSc 92*
**Hotchkin,** John Francis 1935- *WhoRel 92*
**Hotchkiss,** Bill *DrAPF 91*
**Hotchkiss,** Bruce A 1935- *WhoAmP 91*
**Hotchkiss,** Daniel Delos 1955- *WhoRel 92*
**Hotchkiss,** Donald K 1928- *AmMWSc 92*
**Hotchkiss,** Frank Root 1942- *WhoFI 92*
**Hotchkiss,** Henry 1909- *AmMWSc 92*
**Hotchkiss,** Henry Washington 1937- *WhoFI 92*
**Hotchkiss,** Jedediah 1828-1899 *BiInAmS*
**Hotchkiss,** Judy Cohen 1940- *WhoAmP 91*
**Hotchkiss,** Julane 1934- *AmMWSc 92*
**Hotchkiss,** Paul A. 1951- *WhoEnt 92*
**Hotchkiss,** Rollin Douglas 1911- *AmMWSc 92, IntWW 91*
**Hotchkiss,** Sanford Norman 1923- *WhoMW 92*
**Hotchkiss,** Sharon K 1942- *AmMWSc 92*
**Hotchkiss,** Wesley Akin 1919- *WhoBlA 92, WhoRel 92*
**Hotchkiss,** William Rouse 1937- *AmMWSc 92, WhoWest 92*
**Hotchner,** A E 1920- *IntAu&W 91, WrDr 92*
**Hotchner,** Beverly June 1928- *WhoMW 92*
**Hotelling,** Addyson Harold 1895-1973 *DcNCBi 3*
**Hotelling,** Eric Bell 1923- *AmMWSc 92*
**Hoth,** Daniel F 1946- *AmMWSc 92*
**Hoth,** Steven Sergey 1941- *WhoAmL 92*
**Hotham** *Who 92*
**Hotham,** Baron 1940- *Who 92*
**Hotham,** Gary *DrAPF 91*
**Hothfield,** Baron d1991 *Who 92N*
**Hothfield,** Baron 1939- *Who 92*
**Hotle,** Jackie Lee 1939- *WhoWest 92*
**Hotot,** Agnes *EncAmaz 91*
**Hotson,** John Hargrove 1930- *WrDr 92*
**Hotson,** Leslie 1897- *IntWW 91, Who 92*
**Hotta,** Shoichi Steven 1929- *AmMWSc 92*
**Hotta,** Yasuo 1932- *AmMWSc 92*
**Hottel,** Hoyt C 1903- *AmMWSc 92*
**Hottel,** Hoyt Clarke 1903- *IntWW 91*
**Hottelet,** Richard C. *LesBEnT 92*
**Hottenstein,** Evelyn Jeanette Kenny 1948- *WhoFI 92*
**Hotter,** Hans *Who 92*
**Hotter,** Hans 1909- *IntWW 91, NewAmDM*
**Hotteterre,** Jaques 1674-1763? *NewAmDM*
**Hottinger,** George Charles 1953- *WhoAmL 92*
**Hottinger,** John Creighton 1945- *WhoAmP 91*
**Hottman,** Carol Lee 1949- *WhoMW 92*
**Hotton,** Nicholas, III 1921- *AmMWSc 92*
**Hotung,** Joseph Edward 1930- *Who 92*
**Hotvedt,** Kris Joanna 1943- *WhoWest 92*
**Hotz,** Henry Palmer 1925- *AmMWSc 92, WhoWest 92*
**Hotz,** Jimmy Christian 1953- *WhoEnt 92*
**Hotz,** Preston Enslow 1913- *AmMWSc 92*
**Hotz,** V. Joseph 1949- *WhoMW 92*
**Hou Guangjiong** 1905- *IntWW 91*
**Hou Hsiao-Hsien** 1948- *IntDcF 2-2*
**Hou Jie** *IntWW 91*
**Hou Jingru** 1902- *IntWW 91*
**Hou Runyu** 1945- *IntWW 91*
**Hou Zongbin** *IntWW 91*
**Hou,** Ching-Tsang 1935- *AmMWSc 92*
**Hou,** Gene Jean-Win 1952- *AmMWSc 92*
**Hou,** Hsiao-hsien 1947- *IntWW 91*
**Hou,** Kenneth C 1929- *AmMWSc 92*
**Hou,** Roger Hsiang-Dah 1936- *AmMWSc 92*
**Hou,** William Chen-nan 1955- *WhoAmL 92*
**Houbolt,** John C 1919- *AmMWSc 92*
**Houchen,** Gil Ray 1961- *WhoMW 92*
**Houchen,** Joan Carol 1930- *WhoAmP 91*
**Houchens,** David Paul 1937- *AmMWSc 92*
**Houchins,** Daniel Thomas 1955- *WhoMW 92*
**Houchins,** Karen Kay 1942- *WhoFI 92*
**Houck,** C T 1930- *WhoAmP 91*
**Houck,** Charles Weston 1933- *WhoAmL 92*
**Houck,** Cory-Jeanne 1960- *WhoAmP 91*
**Houck,** David R 1956- *AmMWSc 92*
**Houck,** Frank Scanland 1930- *AmMWSc 92*
**Houck,** James Richard 1940- *AmMWSc 92*
**Houck,** John Bunn 1936- *WhoMW 92*
**Houck,** John Burton 1928- *WhoAmL 92*
**Houck,** John Candee 1931- *AmMWSc 92*
**Houck,** John Roland 1923- *WhoRel 92*
**Houck,** Laurie Gerald 1928- *AmMWSc 92*
**Houck,** Lewis Daniel, Jr. 1932- *WhoFI 92*
**Houck,** Mark Hedrich 1951- *AmMWSc 92, WhoMW 92*
**Houck,** Mary Catherine 1960- *WhoWest 92*
**Houck,** R Edward 1950- *WhoAmP 91*
**Houck,** William Russell 1926- *WhoRel 92*
**Houck,** William S, Jr 1929- *WhoAmP 91*
**Houde,** Edward Donald 1941- *AmMWSc 92*
**Houde,** John Michael 1959- *WhoEnt 92*
**Houde,** Raymond Wilfred 1916- *AmMWSc 92*
**Houde,** Robert A 1931- *AmMWSc 92*
**Houdek,** Robert G *WhoAmP 91*
**Houdini** *ConAu 133*
**Houdini,** Harry 1874-1926 *FacFETw [port]*
**Houdon,** Jean-Antoine 1741-1828 *BlkwCEP*
**Houedard,** Sylvester 1924- *ConPo 91, IntAu&W 91, WrDr 92*
**Hougan,** Carolyn Aileen 1943- *WhoRel 92*
**Hougas,** Robert Wayne 1918- *AmMWSc 92*
**Hougen,** Everett Douglas 1916- *WhoFI 92*
**Hougen,** Frithjof W 1920- *AmMWSc 92*
**Hougen,** Joel O 1914- *AmMWSc 92*
**Hougen,** Jon T 1936- *AmMWSc 92*
**Hough,** Bruce *WhoAmP 91*
**Hough,** Bruce Harold 1944- *WhoRel 92*
**Hough,** Charlotte 1924- *IntAu&W 91, WrDr 92*
**Hough,** Eldred W 1916- *AmMWSc 92*
**Hough,** Emerson 1857-1923 *BenetAL 91, TwCWW 91*
**Hough,** Francis Madison, Jr. 1949- *WhoEnt 92*
**Hough,** Franklin Benjamin 1822-1885 *BiInAmS*
**Hough,** George Hubert 1921- *Who 92*
**Hough,** George Washington 1836-1909 *BiInAmS*
**Hough,** Henry Beetle 1896-1985 *BenetAL 91*
**Hough,** Hugh Walter 1922- *AmMWSc 92*
**Hough,** James Thomas 1956- *WhoEnt 92*
**Hough,** Jane Linscott *AmMWSc 92*
**Hough,** Jane Ruth Elder 1923- *WhoEnt 92*
**Hough,** John 1941- *IntMPA 92*
**Hough,** John Patrick 1928- *Who 92*
**Hough,** Julia Marie *Who 92*
**Hough,** Lawrence A. *WhoFI 92*
**Hough,** Lindsay B 1950- *AmMWSc 92*
**Hough,** Lindy *DrAPF 91*
**Hough,** Mark Mason 1945- *WhoAmL 92*
**Hough,** Mark Paul 1957- *WhoEnt 92*
**Hough,** Maxine *WhoAmP 91*
**Hough,** Michael 1928- *ConAu 133*
**Hough,** Nanette 1933- *WhoWest 92*
**Hough,** Paul Van Campen 1925- *AmMWSc 92*
**Hough,** Ralph Degnan 1943- *WhoAmP 91*
**Hough,** Ralph L 1930- *AmMWSc 92*
**Hough,** Richard 1922- *IntWW 91, WrDr 92*
**Hough,** Richard Alexander 1922- *IntAu&W 91, Who 92*
**Hough,** Richard Anton 1942- *AmMWSc 92, WhoMW 92*
**Hough,** Richard R 1917- *AmMWSc 92*
**Hough,** S B *TwCSFW 91*
**Hough,** S. B. 1917- *WrDr 92*
**Hough,** Stanley Bennett 1917- *IntAu&W 91*
**Hough,** Stephen 1961- *Who 92*
**Hough,** Stephen Andrew Gill 1961- *IntWW 91*
**Hough,** Steven Hedges 1938- *WhoAmL 92*
**Hough,** Thomas Bryant 1903- *WhoRel 92*
**Hough,** Thomas Henry Michael 1933- *WhoAmL 92*
**Hough,** Walter Andrew 1932- *AmMWSc 92*
**Hough,** Williston Samuel 1860-1912 *BiInAmS*
**Hough-Dunnette,** Leaetta Marie 1947- *WhoMW 92*
**Hough-Goldstein,** Judith Anne 1950- *AmMWSc 92*
**Hougham,** Norman Russell 1937- *WhoMW 92*
**Houghtaling,** Colleen J. *DrAPF 91*
**Houghtaling,** Pamela Ann 1949- *WhoFI 92*
**Houghton** *Who 92*
**Houghton,** Alan N 1947- *AmMWSc 92*
**Houghton,** Alfred Thomas 1896- *Who 92*
**Houghton,** Amo 1926- *AlmAP 92 [port]*
**Houghton,** Amory, Jr. 1926- *IntWW 91, WhoAmP 91*
**Houghton,** Arthur, Jr. 1906-1990 *AnObit 1990*
**Houghton,** Arthur Vincent, III 1926- *AmMWSc 92*
**Houghton,** Brian Thomas 1931- *Who 92*
**Houghton,** Charles Joseph 1932- *AmMWSc 92*
**Houghton,** Charles Norris 1909- *WhoEnt 92*
**Houghton,** David Drew 1938- *AmMWSc 92*
**Houghton,** Douglass 1809-1845 *BiInAmS*
**Houghton,** Eric 1930- *IntAu&W 91, WrDr 92*
**Houghton,** George Knight 1929- *WhoFI 92*
**Houghton,** Herbert 1920- *Who 92*
**Houghton,** James Richard 1936- *AmMWSc 92*
**Houghton,** James Richardson 1936- *IntWW 91, WhoFI 92*
**Houghton,** Janet Anne 1952- *AmMWSc 92*
**Houghton,** John 1922- *Who 92*
**Houghton,** John M 1941- *AmMWSc 92*
**Houghton,** John Theodore 1931- *IntWW 91, Who 92*
**Houghton,** Judith Dean 1939- *WhoEnt 92*
**Houghton,** Katharine 1945- *WhoEnt 92*
**Houghton,** Kenneth Sinclair, Sr 1940- *AmMWSc 92*
**Houghton,** Robert Dyer 1912- *Who 92*
**Houghton,** Robert W 1941- *AmMWSc 92*
**Houghton,** Stanley 1881-1913 *RfGEnL 91*
**Houghton,** Timothy *DrAPF 91*
**Houghton,** William Henry 1887-1947 *RelLAm 91*
**Houghton,** William I *WhoAmP 91*
**Houghton Of Sowerby,** Baron 1898- *IntWW 91, Who 92*
**Hougie,** Cecil 1922- *AmMWSc 92*
**Hougland,** Arthur Eldon 1935- *AmMWSc 92*
**Hougland,** Patricia A. 1945- *WhoWest 92*
**Hougron,** Jean 1923- *IntAu&W 91, IntWW 91*
**Houh,** Chorng Shi 1926- *AmMWSc 92*
**Houk,** Albert Edward Hennessee 1914- *AmMWSc 92*
**Houk,** Billie Gene 1948- *WhoAmP 91*
**Houk,** Clifford C 1933- *AmMWSc 92*
**Houk,** Howard Franklin 1914- *WhoAmL 92*
**Houk,** James Charles 1939- *AmMWSc 92, WhoMW 92*
**Houk,** Kendall N 1943- *AmMWSc 92*
**Houk,** Larry Wayne 1941- *AmMWSc 92*
**Houk,** Nancy 1940- *AmMWSc 92*
**Houk,** Richard Duncan 1933- *AmMWSc 92*
**Houk,** Robert Samuel 1952- *AmMWSc 92*
**Houk,** Thomas William 1944- *AmMWSc 92*
**Houlden,** Leslie 1929- *Who 92*
**Houlder,** John Maurice 1916- *Who 92*
**Houlding,** Virginia H. 1953- *WhoWest 92*
**Houldsworth,** Richard 1947- *Who 92*
**Houle,** Cyril O. 1913- *WrDr 92*
**Houle,** Frances Anne 1952- *AmMWSc 92*
**Houle,** George Louis 1927- *WhoWest 92*
**Houle,** James Alfred 1948- *WhoAmL 92*
**Houle,** Joseph Adrien 1928- *WhoWest 92*
**Houle,** Joseph E 1930- *AmMWSc 92*
**Houley,** Robert D 1927- *WhoAmP 91*
**Houlihan,** Charles Daniel, Jr. 1953- *WhoAmL 92*
**Houlihan,** Christopher Michael 1949- *WhoAmL 92*
**Houlihan,** David Paul 1937- *WhoAmL 92*
**Houlihan,** Dennis J 1949- *WhoAmP 91*
**Houlihan,** Dennis James 1949- *WhoFI 92*
**Houlihan,** Francis Robert, Jr. 1944- *WhoAmL 92*
**Houlihan,** John Frank 1942- *AmMWSc 92*
**Houlihan,** Kevin John 1948- *WhoMW 92*
**Houlihan,** Patricia Powell 1947- *WhoFI 92*
**Houlihan,** Robert Alan 1938- *WhoIns 92*
**Houlihan,** Rodney T 1926- *AmMWSc 92*
**Houlihan,** William J 1930- *AmMWSc 92*
**Houlne,** Paul Joseph 1931- *WhoFI 92*
**Houlsby,** Guy Tinmouth 1954- *Who 92*
**Hoult,** Peter John 1943- *WhoFI 92*
**Houlton,** Loyce J. 1926- *WhoMW 92*
**Houlton,** Peggy Mann 1925?-1990 *ConAu 35NR*
**Houmann,** Borge Kruuse 1902- *IntWW 91*
**Houn,** Franklin W. 1920- *WrDr 92*
**Hounsell,** Mark 1952- *WhoAmP 91*
**Hounsell,** Morris Reuben 1945- *WhoEnt 92*
**Hounsell,** William J 1943- *WhoAmP 91*
**Hounsfield,** G Newbold 1919- *AmMWSc 92*
**Hounsfield,** Godfrey 1919- *FacFETw, Who 92*
**Hounsfield,** Godfrey Newbold 1919- *IntWW 91, WhoNob 90*
**Hounshell,** David A 1950- *AmMWSc 92*
**Hounshell,** Michael Drew 1960- *WhoEnt 92*
**Hounshell,** William Douglas 1951- *AmMWSc 92*
**Hounslow,** Arthur William 1933- *AmMWSc 92*
**Houphouet-Boigny,** Felix 1905?- *CurBio 91 [port], FacFETw, IntWW 91*

**Houpis**, Constantine H 1922- *AmMWSc 92*
**Houpis**, Constantine Harry 1922- *WhoMW 92*
**Houpis**, Harry Louis Francis 1954- *WhoWest 92*
**Houpis**, James Louis Joseph 1956- *AmMWSc 92*
**Houpt**, Katherine Albro 1939- *AmMWSc 92*
**Houpt**, Thomas Richard 1925- *AmMWSc 92*
**Hourigan**, David R 1947- *WhoAmP 91*
**Hourigan**, Michael James, Jr. 1953- *WhoFI 92*
**Hourigan**, Stephen Roy 1949- *WhoFI 92*
**Hourigan**, William R 1929- *AmMWSc 92*
**Hourston**, Alan Stewart 1926- *AmMWSc 92*
**Housch**, Paul Toby 1956- *WhoAmL 92*
**Housden**, James Alan George 1904- *Who 92*
**Housden**, Peter James 1950- *Who 92*
**House**, Abby 1796?-1881 *DcNCBi 3*
**House**, Arthur Stephen 1921- *AmMWSc 92*
**House**, Briane Maynard 1957- *WhoAmL 92*
**House**, Carleen Faye 1950- *WhoMW 92*
**House**, Carolyn Joyce 1952- *WhoBlA 92*
**House**, Charles Raymond 1945- *WhoAmP 91*
**House**, Charles Staver 1908- *WhoAmL 92*
**House**, David 1922- *Who 92*
**House**, David George 1922- *IntWW 91*
**House**, Delpha LeAnn 1953- *WhoEnt 92*
**House**, Donald Victor 1900- *Who 92*
**House**, Edward Holcombe 1929- *AmMWSc 92*
**House**, Edward Mandell 1858-1938 *AmPolLe, BenetAL 91, FacFETw, ScFEYrs*
**House**, Edwin W 1939- *AmMWSc 92*
**House**, Ernest Robert 1937- *WhoWest 92*
**House**, Francis Harry 1908- *Who 92*
**House**, Gary Lawrence 1947- *AmMWSc 92*
**House**, George Michael 1955- *WhoWest 92*
**House**, Herbert Otis 1929- *AmMWSc 92*
**House**, Howard Leslie 1918- *AmMWSc 92*
**House**, James E. *WhoBlA 92*
**House**, James Evan, Jr 1936- *AmMWSc 92*
**House**, James Stephen 1944- *AmMWSc 92*
**House**, Jay Wesley *WhoRel 92*
**House**, Jesse O. 1935- *WhoBlA 92*
**House**, John Peter Humphry 1945- *Who 92*
**House**, Joseph W 1931- *WhoIns 92*
**House**, Juliette Alane 1963- *WhoAmL 92*
**House**, Kelly Ross 1962- *WhoMW 92*
**House**, Kevin N. 1957- *WhoBlA 92*
**House**, Leland Richmond 1908- *AmMWSc 92*
**House**, Lewis Lundberg 1933- *AmMWSc 92*
**House**, Mark Aaron 1953- *WhoRel 92*
**House**, Mary Corbin 1925- *WhoAmP 91*
**House**, Millard L. 1944- *WhoBlA 92*
**House**, Robert Burton 1892-1987 *DcNCBi 3*
**House**, Robert W 1927- *AmMWSc 92*
**House**, Ronald Edward 1939- *WhoEnt 92*
**House**, Royal Earl 1814-1895 *BiInAmS*
**House**, Son 1902-1988 *NewAmDM*
**House**, Stanley Curtis 1947- *WhoAmL 92*
**House**, Ted 1959- *WhoAmP 91*
**House**, Verl Lee 1919- *AmMWSc 92*
**House**, Vincent F 1938- *WhoAmP 91*
**House**, William Burtner 1918- *AmMWSc 92*
**House**, William Michael 1945- *WhoAmP 91*
**Houseal**, John Irving, Jr. 1945- *WhoAmL 92*
**Housecroft**, Catherine Elizabeth 1955- *AmMWSc 92*
**Household**, Geoffrey Edward West 1900- *IntAu&W 91*
**Household**, Geoffrey Edward West 1900-1988 *FacFETw*
**Household**, Humphrey 1906- *WrDr 92*
**Householder**, Alston Scott 1904- *AmMWSc 92*
**Householder**, James Earl 1916- *AmMWSc 92*
**Householder**, Michael K 1941- *AmMWSc 92*
**Householder**, William Allen 1921- *AmMWSc 92*
**Houseknecht**, David Wayne 1951- *AmMWSc 92*
**Housel**, Jerry Winters 1912- *WhoAmL 92, WhoAmP 91*
**Houseman**, Alan William 1943- *WhoAmL 92*
**Houseman**, Alexander Randolph 1920- *Who 92*
**Houseman**, Barton L 1933- *AmMWSc 92*
**Houseman**, Gerald L. 1935- *WhoMW 92*
**Houseman**, John d1988 *LesBEnT 92*
**Houseman**, John 1902- *IntAu&W 91*
**Houseman**, John 1902-1988 *FacFETw*
**Housen**, Sevrin *DrAPF 91*
**Housepian**, Edgar M 1928- *AmMWSc 92*
**Houser**, Donald Eugene 1948- *WhoFI 92*
**Houser**, Franklin Delano 1934- *WhoAmL 92*
**Houser**, Harold Byron 1921- *AmMWSc 92*
**Houser**, John J 1939- *AmMWSc 92*
**Houser**, Peggy Carter 1932- *WhoFI 92*
**Houser**, Robert Erle 1947- *WhoRel 92*
**Houser**, Thomas J. *LesBEnT 92*
**Houser**, Thomas J 1930- *AmMWSc 92*
**Houseweart**, Mark Wayne 1946- *AmMWSc 92*
**Housewright**, Riley Dee 1913- *AmMWSc 92*
**Housewright**, Wiley Lee 1913- *WhoEnt 92*
**Houshiary**, Shirazeh 1955- *IntWW 91, TwCPaSc*
**Housholder**, Glenn Etta 1925- *AmMWSc 92*
**Houska**, Charles Robert 1927- *AmMWSc 92*
**Houslanger**, William *WhoAmL 92*
**Houslay**, Miles Douglas 1950- *IntWW 91*
**Housley**, Robert Melvin 1934- *AmMWSc 92*
**Housley**, Thomas Lee 1942- *AmMWSc 92*
**Housman**, A. E. 1859-1936 *CnDBLB 5 [port], RfGEnL 91*
**Housman**, Alfred Edward 1859-1936 *FacFETw*
**Housman**, Clemence Annie 1861-1955 *BiDBrF 2*
**Housman**, Laurence 1865-1959 *BiDBrF 2, RfGEnL 91*
**Housmans**, Philippe Robert H P 1953- *AmMWSc 92*
**Housmyer**, Carl Leonidas 1936- *AmMWSc 92*
**Housner**, George W 1910- *AmMWSc 92*
**Houssay**, Bernardo Alberto 1887-1971 *WhoNob 90*
**Houssaye**, Arsene 1825-1896 *ThHElm*
**Houssemayne du Boulay**, George 1922- *Who 92*
**Houssemayne du Boulay**, Roger 1922- *Who 92*
**Houstecky**, Miroslav 1926- *IntWW 91, Who 92*
**Houstis**, Elias N 1945- *AmMWSc 92*
**Houston**, Agnes Wood 1920- *WhoBlA 92*
**Houston**, Alfred Dearborn 1940- *WhoFI 92*
**Houston**, Alice V. *WhoBlA 92*
**Houston**, Arthur Hillier 1931- *AmMWSc 92*
**Houston**, Aubrey Claud D. *Who 92*
**Houston**, Birgie Ann 1951- *WhoMW 92*
**Houston**, Bland Bryan, Jr 1926- *AmMWSc 92*
**Houston**, Bruce 1937- *WhoWest 92*
**Houston**, Cecil J. 1943- *ConAu 135*
**Houston**, Charles Snead 1913- *AmMWSc 92*
**Houston**, Christopher 1744-1837 *DcNCBi 3*
**Houston**, Cissy *ConMus 6 [port]*
**Houston**, Clarence Stuart 1927- *AmMWSc 92*
**Houston**, Clyde Erwin 1914- *AmMWSc 92*
**Houston**, Corinne P. 1922- *WhoBlA 92*
**Houston**, Dale M. 1937- *WhoWest 92*
**Houston**, David 1929- *Who 92*
**Houston**, David Franklin 1886-1940 *DcNCBi 3*
**Houston**, David John 1952- *WhoAmL 92*
**Houston**, David R. 1936- *WhoBlA 92*
**Houston**, David Royce 1932- *AmMWSc 92*
**Houston**, E. James, Jr. 1939- *WhoFI 92*
**Houston**, Edwin James 1847-1914 *BiInAmS*
**Houston**, Elizabeth Reece Manasco 1935- *WhoWest 92*
**Houston**, Feather O'Connor 1946- *WhoAmP 91*
**Houston**, Forrest Gish 1916- *AmMWSc 92*
**Houston**, Geary DeWayne 1953- *WhoFI 92*
**Houston**, Harry Rollins 1928- *WhoWest 92*
**Houston**, Heather Ann 1955- *WhoAmL 92*
**Houston**, Herbert Sherman 1866-1956 *AmPeW*
**Houston**, Ian 1934- *TwCPaSc*
**Houston**, Ivan J. 1925- *WhoBlA 92, WhoIns 92*
**Houston**, J Gorman, Jr 1933- *WhoAmP 91*
**Houston**, Jack E 1933- *AmMWSc 92*
**Houston**, James 1933- *BenetAL 91*
**Houston**, James A 1921- *IntAu&W 91, WrDr 92*
**Houston**, James Archibald 1921- *WhoEnt 92*
**Houston**, James Caldwell 1917- *Who 92*
**Houston**, James D. *DrAPF 91*
**Houston**, James D. 1933- *WrDr 92*
**Houston**, James Grey 1938- *AmMWSc 92*
**Houston**, James Robert 1947- *AmMWSc 92*
**Houston**, Jane Hunt 1919- *WhoWest 92*
**Houston**, Jeanne Wakatsuki 1934- *BenetAL 91*
**Houston**, John 1930- *TwCPaSc*
**Houston**, John Michael 1944- *WhoAmP 91*
**Houston**, John Patrick *WhoAmP 91*
**Houston**, Johnny L. 1941- *WhoBlA 92*
**Houston**, Johnny Lee 1941- *AmMWSc 92*
**Houston**, Kenneth Ray 1944- *WhoBlA 92*
**Houston**, L L 1940- *AmMWSc 92*
**Houston**, Les *WhoAmP 91*
**Houston**, Lillian S. 1946- *WhoBlA 92*
**Houston**, Marsh S. 1918- *WhoBlA 92*
**Houston**, Marshall Lee 1938- *AmMWSc 92*
**Houston**, Neal J 1926- *WhoAmP 91*
**Houston**, Norman Oliver 1893- *WhoBlA 92*
**Houston**, Paul David 1944- *WhoWest 92*
**Houston**, Paul Lyon 1947- *AmMWSc 92*
**Houston**, Peyton *DrAPF 91*
**Houston**, R B *IntAu&W 91X, WrDr 92*
**Houston**, Robert *DrAPF 91*
**Houston**, Robert Edgar, Jr 1924- *AmMWSc 92*
**Houston**, Robert S 1923- *AmMWSc 92*
**Houston**, Roy Seamands 1942- *AmMWSc 92*
**Houston**, Sally 1954- *TwCPaSc*
**Houston**, Sam 1793-1863 *BenetAL 91, RComAH*
**Houston**, Samuel 1793-1863 *AmPolLe*
**Houston**, Samuel Robert 1935- *AmMWSc 92*
**Houston**, Scott William 1960- *WhoEnt 92*
**Houston**, Seawadon Lee 1942- *WhoBlA 92*
**Houston**, Tex *TwCWW 91*
**Houston**, Vern Lynn 1947- *AmMWSc 92*
**Houston**, W. Eugene 1920- *WhoBlA 92*
**Houston**, W. Robert 1928- *WrDr 92*
**Houston**, Wade *WhoBlA 92*
**Houston**, Walter Scott 1912- *AmMWSc 92*
**Houston**, Whitney 1963- *WhoBlA 92, WhoEnt 92*
**Houston**, Will *TwCWW 91*
**Houston**, William, Sr. d1795? *DcNCBi 3*
**Houston**, William Bernard, Jr 1929- *AmMWSc 92*
**Houston**, William Churchill 1746-1788 *DcNCBi 3*
**Houston**, William DeBoise 1940- *WhoBlA 92*
**Houston**, William John Ballantyne d1991 *Who 92N*
**Houston**, William Joseph 1961- *WhoFI 92*
**Houston**, William Robert Montgomery 1922- *WhoMW 92*
**Houston**, Willie Walter, Jr 1951- *AmMWSc 92*
**Houstoun-Boswall**, Alford 1947- *Who 92*
**Houtepen**, Anton Willem Joseph 1940- *WhoRel 92*
**Houthakker**, Hendrik Samuel 1924- *IntWW 91, WhoFI 92*
**Houthuesen**, Albert 1903-1979 *TwCPaSc*
**Houtman**, Thomas, Jr 1918- *AmMWSc 92*
**Houts**, Dan Mason 1947- *WhoMW 92*
**Houts**, Garnette Edwin 1936- *AmMWSc 92*
**Houts**, Larry Lee 1942- *AmMWSc 92*
**Houts**, Peter Stevens 1933- *AmMWSc 92*
**Houts**, Ronald C 1937- *AmMWSc 92*
**Houtte**, Jean van 1907- *IntWW 91*
**Houvouras**, Richard Paul 1949- *WhoAmP 91*
**Houze**, Jeneice Carmel 1938- *WhoBlA 92*
**Houze**, Richard Neal 1938- *AmMWSc 92*
**Hovanec**, B Michael 1952- *AmMWSc 92*
**Hovanesian**, Joseph Der 1930- *AmMWSc 92, WhoMW 92*
**Hovanessian**, Shahen Alexander 1931- *AmMWSc 92*
**Hovanessian**, Simon 1940- *ConCom 92*
**Hovannisian**, Richard G 1932- *IntAu&W 91, WrDr 92*
**Hovatter**, Kurt Eugene 1954- *WhoWest 92*
**Hovda**, Theodore J 1951- *WhoAmP 91*
**Hovde**, A.J. *DrAPF 91*
**Hovde**, Christian Arneson 1922- *AmMWSc 92*
**Hovde**, F. Boyd 1934- *WhoAmL 92*
**Hovde**, Frederick Russell 1955- *WhoAmL 92*
**Hovde**, Ruth Frances 1917- *AmMWSc 92*
**Hovdesven**, Arne 1928- *WhoAmL 92*
**Hove**, Howard Joseph 1925- *WhoAmP 91*
**Hove**, John Edward 1924- *AmMWSc 92*
**Hovee**, Gene Herbert 1930- *WhoMW 92*
**Hovel**, Harold John 1942- *AmMWSc 92*
**Hoveland**, Carl Soren 1927- *AmMWSc 92*
**Hovell-Thurlow-Cumming-Bruce** *Who 92*
**Hoven**, Helmert Frans van den 1923- *Who 92*
**Hover**, Charles S, Jr *WhoAmP 91*
**Hover**, John Charles 1935- *WhoAmL 92*
**Hovermale**, John Bruce 1938- *AmMWSc 92*
**Hoversland**, Arthur Stanley 1922- *AmMWSc 92*
**Hoversland**, Roger Carl 1951- *AmMWSc 92*
**Hoverson**, Ronald Andrew 1937- *WhoMW 92*
**Hoverson**, Sigmund John 1941- *AmMWSc 92*
**Hoversten**, Omar Henry 1922- *WhoFI 92*
**Hovestol**, Mark *WhoRel 92*
**Hovey**, Alan Edwin, Jr. 1933- *WhoFI 92*
**Hovey**, E. Paul 1908- *WrDr 92*
**Hovey**, Harry Henry, Jr 1930- *AmMWSc 92*
**Hovey**, Horace Carter 1833-1914 *BiInAmS*
**Hovey**, James Clark 1948- *WhoAmP 91*
**Hovey**, Ralph Wayne 1926- *WhoRel 92*
**Hovey**, Richard 1864-1900 *BenetAL 91*
**Hoveyda**, Fereydoun 1924- *IntWW 91*
**Hovhaness**, Alan 1911- *ConCom 92, FacFETw, WhoEnt 92*
**Hovhaness**, Alan Scott 1911- *NewAmDM*
**Hovhanissian**, Hratchia 1919- *IntWW 91*
**Hovijitra**, Suteera Tantiteerachart 1944- *WhoMW 92*
**Hovin**, Arne William 1922- *AmMWSc 92*
**Hoving**, John Hannes Forester 1923- *WhoFI 92*
**Hoving**, Thomas 1931- *IntWW 91, Who 92*
**Hovingh**, Jack 1935- *AmMWSc 92*
**Hovingh**, Morris Frank 1928- *WhoRel 92*
**Hovis**, Lorraine June 1924- *WhoAmP 91*
**Hovis**, Louis Samuel 1926- *AmMWSc 92*
**Hovland**, Daniel Lee 1954- *WhoAmL 92*
**Hovland**, Egil 1924- *ConCom 92*
**Hovmand**, Svend 1939- *AmMWSc 92*
**Hovnanian**, H Philip 1920- *AmMWSc 92*
**Hovorka**, John 1921- *AmMWSc 92*
**Hovorka**, Robert Bartlett 1936- *AmMWSc 92*
**Hovorre**, M Auburre *ScFEYrs*
**Hovsepian**, Vatche 1930- *WhoRel 92*
**How**, Stanley John 1928- *WhoMW 92*
**How-Martyn**, Edith 1875-1954 *BiDBrF 2*
**Howadji**, The *BenetAL 91*
**Howald**, Jeremiah Mark 1927- *AmMWSc 92*
**Howald**, John William 1935- *WhoAmL 92*
**Howald**, Reed Anderson 1930- *AmMWSc 92*
**Howard** *Who 92*
**Howard**, A. E. Dick 1933- *WrDr 92*
**Howard**, Alan 1937- *Who 92*
**Howard**, Alan Charles 1944- *WhoMW 92*
**Howard**, Alan Mackenzie 1937- *IntWW 91*
**Howard**, Alex T., Jr. 1924- *WhoAmL 92*
**Howard**, Alexander Edward 1909- *Who 92*
**Howard**, Allan Clark 1950- *WhoMW 92*
**Howard**, Allan D 1949- *WhoAmP 91*
**Howard**, Angela Kay 1964- *WhoAmL 92*
**Howard**, Anita 1926- *TwCPaSc*
**Howard**, Ann 1936- *IntWW 91*
**Howard**, Anthony Michell 1934- *IntAu&W 91, IntWW 91, Who 92*
**Howard**, Arthur Ellsworth Dick 1933- *WhoAmL 92*
**Howard**, Aubrey J. 1945- *WhoBlA 92*
**Howard**, Aughtum Smith 1906- *AmMWSc 92*
**Howard**, Barbara June 1957- *WhoMW 92*
**Howard**, Barbara V 1941- *AmMWSc 92*
**Howard**, Barry C. 1960- *WhoRel 92*
**Howard**, Bart 1915- *WhoEnt 92*
**Howard**, Ben *DrAPF 91*
**Howard**, Bernard Eufinger 1920- *AmMWSc 92*
**Howard**, Betty 1923- *AmMWSc 92*
**Howard**, Billie Jean 1950- *WhoBlA 92*
**Howard**, Bradford Reuel 1957- *WhoWest 92*
**Howard**, Bronson 1842-1908 *BenetAL 91*
**Howard**, Bruce David 1937- *AmMWSc 92*
**Howard**, C. Jeriel 1939- *WhoMW 92*
**Howard**, Caleb D. *DcNCBi 3*
**Howard**, Calvin Johnson 1947- *WhoBlA 92*
**Howard**, Carleton James 1944- *AmMWSc 92*
**Howard**, Charles 1899-1978 *TwCPaSc*
**Howard**, Charles 1919- *AmMWSc 92*
**Howard**, Charles Frank, Jr 1932- *AmMWSc 92*
**Howard**, Charles Marion 1933- *AmMWSc 92*
**Howard**, Charles Preston, Jr. 1921- *WhoBlA 92*
**Howard**, Christian *Who 92*
**Howard**, Christopher Anthony 1950- *WhoFI 92*
**Howard**, Christopher John 1932- *Who 92*
**Howard**, Chubby 1926- *WhoEnt 92*
**Howard**, Clarence Edward 1929- *AmMWSc 92*
**Howard**, Clark *DrAPF 91*

**Howard,** Clark 1934- *IntAu&W 91, WrDr 92*
**Howard,** Clifford 1868- *ScFEYrs*
**Howard,** Clyde Thomas, III 1959- *WhoRel 92*
**Howard,** Constance 1910- *IntAu&W 91, WrDr 92*
**Howard,** Corliss Mays 1927- *WhoBlA 92*
**Howard,** Cy 1915- *IntMPA 92*
**Howard,** Cyril *IntMPA 92*
**Howard,** Daggett Horton 1917- *WhoAmL 92*
**Howard,** Dalton J., Jr. *WhoBlA 92*
**Howard,** Darnley William 1957- *WhoBlA 92*
**Howard,** David 1937- *WhoEnt 92*
**Howard,** David K 1949- *AmMWSc 92*
**Howard,** David M 1928- *IntAu&W 91, WrDr 92*
**Howard,** David Morris 1928- *WhoRel 92*
**Howard,** Dean Denton 1927- *AmMWSc 92*
**Howard,** Denean 1964- *BlkOlyM*
**Howard,** Dexter Herbert 1927- *AmMWSc 92*
**Howard,** Don *ScFEYrs*
**Howard,** Donald 1927- *Who 92*
**Howard,** Donald Grant 1937- *AmMWSc 92*
**Howard,** Donald John 1935- *WhoAmL 92*
**Howard,** Donald R. 1927-1987 *DcLB 111 [port]*
**Howard,** Donald R. 1928- *WhoBlA 92*
**Howard,** Donald Ray 1945- *WhoRel 92*
**Howard,** Donald Robert 1940- *AmMWSc 92*
**Howard,** Donald Searcy 1928- *WhoFI 92*
**Howard,** Donavan Craig 1967- *WhoRel 92*
**Howard,** Douglas Brian 1956- *WhoMW 92*
**Howard,** Earle 1926- *WhoAmP 91*
**Howard,** Edgar, Jr 1922- *AmMWSc 92*
**Howard,** Edmund Bernard Carlo 1909- *Who 92*
**Howard,** Edward *Who 92*
**Howard,** Edward George, Jr 1921- *AmMWSc 92*
**Howard,** Edward L 1926- *WhoAmP 91*
**Howard,** Edward T., III 1942- *WhoBlA 92*
**Howard,** Elizabeth Fitzgerald 1927- *WhoBlA 92*
**Howard,** Elizabeth Jane 1923- *ConNov 91, IntAu&W 91, IntWW 91, Who 92, WrDr 92*
**Howard,** Ellen 1943- *SmATA 67 [port], WrDr 92*
**Howard,** Ellen D. 1929- *WhoBlA 92*
**Howard,** Ernest E., III 1943- *WhoFI 92*
**Howard,** Eugene Frank 1938- *AmMWSc 92*
**Howard,** Forrest Hayden 1908- *WhoWest 92*
**Howard,** Forrest William 1936- *AmMWSc 92*
**Howard,** Frances Drake 1912- *WhoEnt 92*
**Howard,** Frances Minturn *DrAPF 91*
**Howard,** Francis Alex 1922- *Who 92*
**Howard,** Frank Leslie 1903- *AmMWSc 92*
**Howard,** Frederic Koch 1939- *WhoAmL 92*
**Howard,** Fredric Timothy 1939- *AmMWSc 92*
**Howard,** G Michael 1935- *AmMWSc 92*
**Howard,** Gary Scott 1951- *WhoEnt 92*
**Howard,** Gene C 1926- *WhoAmP 91*
**Howard,** Gene Claude 1926- *WhoAmL 92*
**Howard,** George 1935- *WrDr 92*
**Howard,** George, Jr. 1829-1905 *DcNCBi 3*
**Howard,** George, Jr. 1924- *WhoAmL 92, WhoBlA 92*
**Howard,** George Bronson 1884-1922 *BenetAL 91*
**Howard,** George Bronson & Dillon, Robert *ScFEYrs*
**Howard,** George Eulan 1935- *WhoRel 92*
**Howard,** George Harmon 1934- *WhoWest 92*
**Howard,** George Sallade 1903- *WhoEnt 92*
**Howard,** George Thomas 1929- *WhoEnt 92*
**Howard,** Gerald Kenneth 1938- *WhoRel 92*
**Howard,** Gilbert Thoreau 1941- *AmMWSc 92*
**Howard,** Glen 1942- *WhoBlA 92*
**Howard,** Glen 1956- *WhoBlA 92*
**Howard,** Glenn Willard, Jr 1939- *AmMWSc 92*
**Howard,** Gregory Charles 1947- *WhoAmL 92*
**Howard,** Gregory Steven 1966- *WhoEnt 92*
**Howard,** Guy Allen *AmMWSc 92*
**Howard,** Gwendolyn Julius 1932- *WhoBlA 92*
**Howard,** H Taylor 1932- *AmMWSc 92*
**Howard,** Hamilton Edward 1915- *Who 92*
**Howard,** Harlan Perry 1927- *WhoEnt 92*
**Howard,** Harold Henry 1928- *AmMWSc 92*
**Howard,** Harold Lloyd 1927- *WhoAmP 91*
**Howard,** Harriette Ella Pierce 1954- *AmMWSc 92*
**Howard,** Harry Nicholas 1902- *IntWW 91*
**Howard,** Harry Nicholas 1902-1987 *ConAu 34NR*
**Howard,** Helen Addison 1904- *WrDr 92*
**Howard,** Henry *RfGEnL 91, WhoAmP 91*
**Howard,** Henry Cobourn 1928- *AmMWSc 92*
**Howard,** Henry Frederick 1608-1652 *DcNCBi 3*
**Howard,** Henry L. 1930- *WhoBlA 92*
**Howard,** Herbert Hoover 1928- *WhoFI 92*
**Howard,** Hildegarde 1901- *AmMWSc 92*
**Howard,** Howell J., Jr. 1938- *WhoBlA 92*
**Howard,** Humbert Lincoln 1915- *WhoBlA 92*
**Howard,** Ian 1952- *TwCPaSc*
**Howard,** Ian Porteous 1920- *AmMWSc 92*
**Howard,** Iris Anne 1953- *AmMWSc 92*
**Howard,** Irmgard Matilda Keeler 1941- *AmMWSc 92*
**Howard,** J Daniel 1943- *WhoAmP 91*
**Howard,** J T 1936- *WhoAmP 91*
**Howard,** J. Woodford, Jr. 1931- *WrDr 92*
**Howard,** Jack *Who 92*
**Howard,** Jack Benny 1937- *AmMWSc 92*
**Howard,** Jack Rohe 1910- *IntWW 91*
**Howard,** James Anthony 1937- *AmMWSc 92*
**Howard,** James Boag 1915- *Who 92*
**Howard,** James Bryant 1942- *AmMWSc 92*
**Howard,** James D 1932- *WhoAmP 91*
**Howard,** James Dolan 1934- *AmMWSc 92*
**Howard,** James Griffiths 1927- *Who 92*
**Howard,** James Hatten, III 1939- *AmMWSc 92*
**Howard,** James Joseph, III 1935- *WhoFI 92, WhoMW 92*
**Howard,** James Kenneth 1932- *Who 92*
**Howard,** James L. 1918- *WhoBlA 92*
**Howard,** James Lawrence 1941- *AmMWSc 92*
**Howard,** James Ward 1955- *WhoAmL 92*
**Howard,** James Webb 1925- *WhoFI 92, WhoWest 92*
**Howard,** Jane 1935- *WrDr 92*
**Howard,** Jane Osburn 1926- *WhoWest 92*
**Howard,** Jane R. *DrAPF 91*
**Howard,** Jasper Byron 1933- *WhoFI 92*
**Howard,** Jean C. *DrAPF 91*
**Howard,** Jeffrey C. 1954- *WhoAmL 92*
**Howard,** Jeffrey Hjalmar 1944- *WhoAmL 92*
**Howard,** Jeffrey R. *WhoAmL 92*
**Howard,** Jerome Edward 1933- *WhoFI 92*
**Howard,** Jill Roberta 1954- *WhoAmL 92*
**Howard,** Jo Ann 1937- *WhoWest 92*
**Howard,** John *WhoAmP 91*
**Howard,** John 1726-1790 *BlkwCEP*
**Howard,** John 1902- *TwCPaSc*
**Howard,** John 1933- *AmMWSc 92*
**Howard,** John Addison 1946- *WhoAmL 92*
**Howard,** John Charles 1924- *AmMWSc 92*
**Howard,** John Hall 1934- *AmMWSc 92*
**Howard,** John James 1923- *Who 92*
**Howard,** John L. 1957- *WhoAmL 92*
**Howard,** John Lindsay 1931- *WhoFI 92*
**Howard,** John Loring 1935- *WhoFI 92*
**Howard,** John Malone 1919- *AmMWSc 92*
**Howard,** John Nelson 1921- *AmMWSc 92*
**Howard,** John Philip 1934- *Who 92*
**Howard,** John Robert 1933- *WhoBlA 92*
**Howard,** John William 1925- *AmMWSc 92*
**Howard,** John Winston 1939- *IntWW 91, Who 92*
**Howard,** Joseph Clemens 1922- *WhoAmL 92, WhoBlA 92*
**Howard,** Joseph H. 1912- *WhoBlA 92*
**Howard,** Joseph H 1931- *AmMWSc 92*
**Howard,** Joseph H G 1933- *AmMWSc 92*
**Howard,** Joseph Kinsey 1906-1951 *BenetAL 91*
**Howard,** Julia Craven 1944- *WhoAmP 91*
**Howard,** Kathleen 1947- *WhoFI 92, WhoMW 92*
**Howard,** Keith Arthur 1939- *AmMWSc 92*
**Howard,** Keith L. 1940- *WhoBlA 92*
**Howard,** Ken 1932- *TwCPaSc*
**Howard,** Ken 1944- *IntMPA 92*
**Howard,** Kenneth *Who 92*
**Howard,** Kenneth Calvin, Jr. 1947- *WhoAmL 92*
**Howard,** Kenneth Joseph, Jr. 1944- *WhoEnt 92*
**Howard,** Laurence Edward 1934- *WhoMW 92*
**Howard,** Lawrence Cabot 1925- *WhoBlA 92*
**Howard,** Lee 1931- *WhoEnt 92*
**Howard,** Lee Scott 1959- *WhoEnt 92*
**Howard,** Leon *WhoBlA 92*
**Howard,** Leon W., Jr. 1935- *WhoBlA 92*
**Howard,** Leonard Henry 1904- *Who 92*
**Howard,** Leslie 1893-1943 *FacFETw*
**Howard,** Leslie Kenyatta 1950- *WhoBlA 92*
**Howard,** Lillie Pearl 1949- *WhoBlA 92, WhoMW 92*
**Howard,** Linda 1950- *WrDr 92*
**Howard,** Lorn Lambier 1917- *AmMWSc 92*
**Howard,** Louis Norberg 1929- *AmMWSc 92*
**Howard,** Louis T 1923- *WhoAmP 91*
**Howard,** Lytia Ramani 1950- *WhoBlA 92*
**Howard,** M. W., Jr. 1946- *WhoBlA 92*
**Howard,** Malcolm Jones 1939- *WhoAmL 92, WhoAmP 91*
**Howard,** Mamie R. 1946- *WhoBlA 92*
**Howard,** Margaret 1938- *Who 92*
**Howard,** Marguerite Charlotte 1932- *WhoWest 92*
**Howard,** Marie *ConAu 134*
**Howard,** Mark Edwin 1954- *WhoRel 92*
**Howard,** Martin d1781 *BenetAL 91*
**Howard,** Martin 1725?-1781 *DcNCBi 3*
**Howard,** Mary *IntAu&W 91X*
**Howard,** Mary 1907- *WrDr 92*
**Howard,** Maureen 1930- *ConNov 91, IntAu&W 91, WrDr 92*
**Howard,** Mel 1935- *WhoEnt 92*
**Howard,** Melvin 1935- *WhoFI 92*
**Howard,** Melvyn Lawrence 1948- *WhoFI 92*
**Howard,** Michael 1922- *Who 92, WrDr 92*
**Howard,** Michael 1941- *IntWW 91, Who 92*
**Howard,** Michael Anthony 1962- *WhoMW 92*
**Howard,** Michael E. 1942- *WhoAmL 92*
**Howard,** Michael Eliot 1922- *IntWW 91*
**Howard,** Michael Joseph 1951- *WhoMW 92*
**Howard,** Michael Newman 1947- *Who 92*
**Howard,** Michael R 1945- *WhoIns 92*
**Howard,** Michael Stockwin 1922- *Who 92*
**Howard,** Milfred Earl 1947- *WhoFI 92*
**Howard,** Milton L. 1927- *WhoBlA 92*
**Howard,** Moses William, Jr. 1946- *WhoRel 92*
**Howard,** Murray 1914- *WhoFI 92*
**Howard,** Neil 1940- *WhoEnt 92*
**Howard,** Noni *DrAPF 91*
**Howard,** Norman 1947- *WhoBlA 92*
**Howard,** Norman Leroy 1930- *WhoBlA 92*
**Howard,** Oliver Otis 1830-1909 *BenetAL 91*
**Howard,** Osbie L., Jr. 1943- *WhoBlA 92*
**Howard,** Patricia 1937- *IntAu&W 91, WrDr 92*
**Howard,** Patricia Arlene 1951- *WhoMW 92*
**Howard,** Patricia D. *TwCPaSc*
**Howard,** Paul Edward 1943- *AmMWSc 92*
**Howard,** Peter *WhoEnt 92*
**Howard,** Peter 1925- *Who 92*
**Howard,** Peter J. 1943- *WhoFI 92*
**Howard,** Philip 1933- *WrDr 92*
**Howard,** Philip Hall 1943- *AmMWSc 92*
**Howard,** Philip Martin 1939- *WhoFI 92, WhoMW 92*
**Howard,** Philip Nicholas Charles 1933- *IntAu&W 91, Who 92*
**Howard,** Phillenore Drummond 1941- *AmMWSc 92*
**Howard,** Pierre 1943- *WhoAmP 91*
**Howard,** Randy DeWayne 1934- *WhoWest 92*
**Howard,** Ray F. 1945- *WhoBlA 92*
**Howard,** Raymond Ballew 1936- *WhoFI 92*
**Howard,** Raymond Monroe, Sr. 1921- *WhoBlA 92*
**Howard,** Richard *DrAPF 91*
**Howard,** Richard 1929- *BenetAL 91, ConPo 91, IntAu&W 91, WhoEnt 92, WrDr 92*
**Howard,** Richard Alden 1917- *AmMWSc 92*
**Howard,** Richard James 1952- *AmMWSc 92*
**Howard,** Richard John 1924- *AmMWSc 92*
**Howard,** Richard W 1935- *BlkOlyM*
**Howard,** Rio Cecily 1943- *WhoWest 92*
**Howard,** Robert 1626-1698 *RfGEnL 91*
**Howard,** Robert 1939- *Who 92*
**Howard,** Robert Adrian 1913- *AmMWSc 92*
**Howard,** Robert Allen 1944- *WhoAmP 91*
**Howard,** Robert Berry, Jr. 1916- *WhoBlA 92*
**Howard,** Robert Bruce 1920- *AmMWSc 92*
**Howard,** Robert Campbell, Jr. 1951- *WhoWest 92*
**Howard,** Robert Clark 1931- *WhoFI 92*
**Howard,** Robert E. 1906-1936 *TwCWW 91*
**Howard,** Robert Ernest 1947- *AmMWSc 92*
**Howard,** Robert Ervin 1906-1936 *ScFEYrs*
**Howard,** Robert Eugene 1937- *AmMWSc 92*
**Howard,** Robert Franklin 1932- *AmMWSc 92*
**Howard,** Robert Lawrence 1948- *WhoAmL 92*
**Howard,** Robert Matthew 1956- *WhoAmL 92*
**Howard,** Robert Murn 1950- *WhoMW 92*
**Howard,** Robert Palmer 1912- *AmMWSc 92*
**Howard,** Robert T. *LesBEnT 92*
**Howard,** Robert T 1920- *AmMWSc 92*
**Howard,** Robert T 1927- *IntMPA 92*
**Howard,** Robert Thornton 1927- *WhoEnt 92*
**Howard,** Robert William 1954- *WhoWest 92*
**Howard,** Robin Jared Stanley 1924- *FacFETw*
**Howard,** Roger 1935- *AmMWSc 92*
**Howard,** Roger 1938- *IntAu&W 91, WrDr 92*
**Howard,** Ron *LesBEnT 92*
**Howard,** Ron 1954- *Au&Arts 8 [port], IntMPA 92, IntWW 91, WhoEnt 92*
**Howard,** Ronald A 1934- *AmMWSc 92*
**Howard,** Ronald Claude 1902- *Who 92*
**Howard,** Ronald Eugene 1955- *WhoRel 92*
**Howard,** Ronald M 1920- *AmMWSc 92*
**Howard,** Rosalind Frances 1845-1921 *BiDBrF 2*
**Howard,** Rosemary Christian 1916- *Who 92*
**Howard,** Rowland Bailey 1837-1892 *AmPeW*
**Howard,** Roy 1883-1964 *FacFETw*
**Howard,** Roy Siefert 1940- *WhoAmL 92*
**Howard,** Rufus Oliver 1929- *AmMWSc 92*
**Howard,** Russell Alfred 1941- *AmMWSc 92*
**Howard,** Russell John 1950- *AmMWSc 92*
**Howard,** Sally Purnell 1943- *WhoAmP 91*
**Howard,** Samuel H. 1939- *WhoBlA 92*
**Howard,** Samuel Houston 1939- *WhoEnt 92, WhoFI 92*
**Howard,** Samuel Hunter, Jr 1953- *WhoAmP 91*
**Howard,** Sandy 1927- *IntMPA 92, WhoEnt 92*
**Howard,** Sethanne 1944- *AmMWSc 92*
**Howard,** Sherri 1962- *BlkOlyM*
**Howard,** Shirley M. 1935- *WhoBlA 92*
**Howard,** Sidney 1891-1939 *BenetAL 91*
**Howard,** Stephen Arthur 1941- *AmMWSc 92*
**Howard,** Stephen Michael 1951- *WhoAmL 92*
**Howard,** Susan *WhoEnt 92*
**Howard,** Susan Carol Pearcy 1954- *AmMWSc 92*
**Howard,** Susan E. 1961- *WhoBlA 92*
**Howard,** Suzanne Marie 1941- *WhoFI 92*
**Howard,** Tanya Millicent 1968- *WhoBlA 92*
**Howard,** Thomas E 1919- *AmMWSc 92*
**Howard,** Thomas Hyland 1945- *AmMWSc 92*
**Howard,** Thomas Keith 1955- *WhoEnt 92*
**Howard,** Thomas Smith 1950- *WhoAmL 92*
**Howard,** Timothy Lee 1955- *WhoWest 92*
**Howard,** Trevor 1916-1988 *FacFETw*
**Howard,** Troy *TwCWW 91*
**Howard,** Vance F 1937- *WhoIns 92*
**Howard,** Vechel *TwCWW 91*
**Howard,** Vera Gouke *WhoBlA 92*
**Howard,** Victor 1923- *WhoWest 92*
**Howard,** Victor Carl 1952- *WhoAmP 91*
**Howard,** Vivian Gordon 1923- *WhoBlA 92*
**Howard,** Volney Ward, Jr 1941- *AmMWSc 92, WhoWest 92*
**Howard,** W O *WhoAmP 91*
**Howard,** W Terry 1936- *AmMWSc 92*
**Howard,** Walter B 1916- *AmMWSc 92*
**Howard,** Walter Boivin 1927- *WhoAmP 91*
**Howard,** Walter Egner 1917- *AmMWSc 92*
**Howard,** Walter Stewart 1888- *Who 92*
**Howard,** Warren Keith 1958- *WhoAmL 92*
**Howard,** Webster Eugene 1934- *AmMWSc 92*
**Howard,** William 1793-1834 *BiInAmS*
**Howard,** William Brian 1926- *Who 92*
**Howard,** William Daniel 1945- *WhoMW 92*
**Howard,** William Dotson 1964- *WhoBlA 92*
**Howard,** William Eager, III 1932- *AmMWSc 92*
**Howard,** William Gates, Jr 1941- *AmMWSc 92*
**Howard,** William Jack 1922- *AmMWSc 92*
**Howard,** William K. 1899-1954 *IntDcF 2-2 [port]*
**Howard,** William Travis 1821-1907 *DcNCBi 3*
**Howard,** William Weaver 1922- *AmMWSc 92*
**Howard,** Wilmont Frederick, Jr 1946- *AmMWSc 92*
**Howard,** Wm Leslie 1958- *WhoEnt 92*

**Howard De Walden**, Baron 1912- *Who 92*
**Howard-Dobson**, Patrick John 1921- *Who 92*
**Howard-Drake**, Jack Thomas Arthur 1919- *Who 92*
**Howard-Flanders**, Paul 1919- *AmMWSc 92*
**Howard-Johnston**, Clarence Dinsmore 1903- *Who 92*
**Howard-Jones**, Ray 1903- *TwCPaSc*
**Howard-Lawson**, John *Who 92*
**Howard-Lock**, Helen Elaine 1938- *AmMWSc 92*
**Howard of Penrith**, Baron 1905- *Who 92*
**Howard-Peebles**, Patricia Nell 1941- *AmMWSc 92*
**Howard-Vyse**, Edward 1905- *Who 92*
**Howard-Williams**, Jeremy 1922- *WrDr 92*
**Howards**, Stuart S 1937- *AmMWSc 92*
**Howarth**, Alan Thomas 1944- *Who 92*
**Howarth**, Birkett, Jr 1936- *AmMWSc 92*
**Howarth**, Clifford 1925- *WhoAmP 91*
**Howarth**, David 1912- *WrDr 92*
**Howarth**, David 1912-1991 *ConAu 134, SmATA 68*
**Howarth**, David Armine d1991 *Who 92N*
**Howarth**, David Armine 1912- *IntAu&W 91*
**Howarth**, Donald 1931- *WrDr 92*
**Howarth**, Elgar 1935- *IntWW 91, Who 92*
**Howarth**, Francis Gard 1940- *AmMWSc 92*
**Howarth**, George Edward 1949- *Who 92*
**Howarth**, Gerald 1947- *Who 92*
**Howarth**, Leslie 1911- *IntWW 91, Who 92*
**Howarth**, Patrick 1916- *WrDr 92*
**Howarth**, Robert Lever 1927- *Who 92*
**Howarth**, Robert Lewis *WhoAmP 91*
**Howarth**, Robert Ruell 1931- *WhoFI 92*
**Howarth**, Robert W 1952- *AmMWSc 92*
**Howarth**, Ronald Edward 1940- *AmMWSc 92*
**Howarth**, Thomas 1914- *IntWW 91*
**Howarth**, W D 1922- *ConAu 35NR*
**Howarth**, William 1940- *WrDr 92*
**Howat**, Gerald 1928- *WrDr 92*
**Howat**, Gerald Malcolm David Henderson 1928- *IntAu&W 91*
**Howat**, Henry Taylor 1911- *Who 92*
**Howatch**, Susan 1940- *IntAu&W 91, IntWW 91, WrDr 92*
**Howatson**, John 1920- *AmMWSc 92*
**Howatt**, Helen Clare 1927- *WhoWest 92*
**Howatt**, William Frederick 1929- *AmMWSc 92*
**Howcroft**, Wilbur Gordon 1917- *IntAu&W 91*
**Howd**, Frank Hawver 1924- *AmMWSc 92*
**Howd**, Isobel 1928- *Who 92*
**Howd**, Robert A 1944- *AmMWSc 92*
**Howd**, Robert Allen 1944- *WhoWest 92*
**Howden**, David Gordon 1937- *AmMWSc 92*
**Howden**, Henry Fuller 1925- *AmMWSc 92*
**Howden**, Timothy Simon 1937- *IntWW 91, Who 92*
**Howder**, Deloris Jean 1926- *WhoEnt 92*
**Howe**, Earl 1951- *Who 92*
**Howe Yoon Chong** 1923- *IntWW 91*
**Howe**, Albert Berry, Jr 1917- *WhoAmP 91*
**Howe**, Allen 1918- *Who 92*
**Howe**, Beatrice 1867-1932 *TwCPaSc*
**Howe**, Ben Steventon 1935- *WhoAmP 91*
**Howe**, Brian Leslie 1936- *IntWW 91*
**Howe**, Calderon 1916- *AmMWSc 92*
**Howe**, Carroll Victor 1923- *WhoFI 92*
**Howe**, Charles Bryan 1935- *WhoAmP 91*
**Howe**, Chin Chen 1933- *AmMWSc 92*
**Howe**, Christopher Barry 1937- *Who 92*
**Howe**, David Allan 1949- *AmMWSc 92*
**Howe**, David Allen 1935- *AmMWSc 92*
**Howe**, David Nathan 1941- *WhoMW 92*
**Howe**, Denis 1927- *Who 92*
**Howe**, Dennis 1940- *WhoAmP 91*
**Howe**, Dennis George 1943- *AmMWSc 92*
**Howe**, Derek Andrew 1934- *Who 92*
**Howe**, Dianne Shelden 1949- *WhoEnt 92*
**Howe**, Doris *IntAu&W 91, WrDr 92*
**Howe**, Douglas Paul 1959- *WhoRel 92*
**Howe**, Drayton Ford, Jr. 1931- *WhoAmL 92, WhoWest 92*
**Howe**, E. Margaret *WhoRel 92*
**Howe**, E. W. 1853-1937 *BenetAL 91*
**Howe**, Edwin Alberts, Jr. 1939- *WhoAmL 92*
**Howe**, Elias 1820-1895 *NewAmDM*
**Howe**, Ellic 1910-1991 *ConAu 135*
**Howe**, Elliot C 1828-1899 *BiInAmS*
**Howe**, Elspeth Rosamund Morton 1932- *Who 92*
**Howe**, Eric James 1931- *Who 92*
**Howe**, Eugene Everett 1912- *AmMWSc 92*
**Howe**, Eunice Dunster 1947- *IntAu&W 91*
**Howe**, Everett D 1903- *AmMWSc 92*
**Howe**, Fanny *DrAPF 91*
**Howe**, Fanny 1940- *WrDr 92*
**Howe**, Frederick C. 1867-1940 *DcAmImH*
**Howe**, Geoffrey *Who 92*
**Howe**, Geoffrey 1926- *FacFETw*
**Howe**, Geoffrey Leslie 1924- *Who 92*
**Howe**, Geoffrey Richard 1942- *AmMWSc 92*
**Howe**, George 1876-1936 *DcNCBi 3*
**Howe**, George 1886-1955 *DcTwDes, FacFETw*
**Howe**, George Edward 1925- *Who 92*
**Howe**, George Franklin 1931- *AmMWSc 92*
**Howe**, George Melvyn 1920- *Who 92*
**Howe**, George R 1933- *AmMWSc 92*
**Howe**, Gilbert Paul 1951- *WhoEnt 92*
**Howe**, Gordon 1928- *FacFETw [port]*
**Howe**, Harold, II 1918- *IntWW 91*
**Howe**, Helen 1905-1975 *BenetAL 91*
**Howe**, Henry Branch, Jr 1924- *AmMWSc 92*
**Howe**, Henry Franklin 1946- *AmMWSc 92*
**Howe**, Herbert James 1931- *AmMWSc 92*
**Howe**, Hubert S., Jr. *WhoEnt 92*
**Howe**, Irving 1920- *BenetAL 91, FacFETw, WhoRel 92, WrDr 92*
**Howe**, Jack 1911- *Who 92*
**Howe**, James 1946- *IntAu&W 91, WrDr 92*
**Howe**, James Everett 1930- *WhoFI 92*
**Howe**, James Murray 1924- *WhoAmL 92*
**Howe**, James Tarsicius 1924- *WhoFI 92*
**Howe**, John A 1927- *AmMWSc 92*
**Howe**, John A 1933- *AmMWSc 92*
**Howe**, John Francis 1944- *Who 92*
**Howe**, John Frederick George 1930- *Who 92*
**Howe**, John Kingman 1945- *WhoMW 92*
**Howe**, John P 1910- *AmMWSc 92*
**Howe**, John Prentice, III 1943- *WhoFI 92*
**Howe**, John Thomas 1926- *WhoWest 92*
**Howe**, John Wadsworth 1942- *WhoRel 92*
**Howe**, John William Alexander 1920- *Who 92*
**Howe**, Jonathan Thomas 1940- *WhoAmL 92*
**Howe**, Joseph 1804-1873 *BenetAL 91*
**Howe**, Joseph William 1930- *WhoWest 92*
**Howe**, Josephine Mary O'C. *Who 92*
**Howe**, Julia Ward 1819-1910 *AmPeW, BenetAL 91, HanAmWH*
**Howe**, Juliette Coupain 1944- *AmMWSc 92*
**Howe**, Kenneth Jesse 1923- *AmMWSc 92*
**Howe**, King Lau 1928- *AmMWSc 92*
**Howe**, Linda Moulton 1942- *WhoEnt 92*
**Howe**, M. A. DeWolfe 1864-1960 *BenetAL 91*
**Howe**, Marie Elizabeth 1939- *WhoAmP 91*
**Howe**, Marshall Atherton 1944- *AmMWSc 92*
**Howe**, Martha Morgan 1945- *AmMWSc 92*
**Howe**, Martin 1936- *Who 92*
**Howe**, Mary Jane 1964- *WhoRel 92*
**Howe**, Michael William 1948- *WhoMW 92*
**Howe**, Muriel *WrDr 92*
**Howe**, Norman Elton, Jr 1946- *AmMWSc 92*
**Howe**, Philip Sherwood 1947- *WhoMW 92*
**Howe**, Ralph W, III 1954- *WhoAmP 91*
**Howe**, Ramona E *WhoAmP 91*
**Howe**, Reuel Lanphier, Jr. 1943- *WhoRel 92*
**Howe**, Richard 1726-1799 *BlkwEAR*
**Howe**, Richard Cuddy 1924- *WhoAmL 92, WhoAmP 91, WhoWest 92*
**Howe**, Richard Edward Geoffrey 1926- *IntWW 91, Who 92*
**Howe**, Richard Esmond, Jr. 1927- *WhoEnt 92*
**Howe**, Richard Hildreth 1927- *AmMWSc 92*
**Howe**, Richard J. 1928- *IntWW 91*
**Howe**, Richard Karl 1943- *WhoAmL 92*
**Howe**, Richard Rives 1942- *WhoAmL 92*
**Howe**, Richard Samuel 1936- *AmMWSc 92*
**Howe**, Robert 1732-1786 *DcNCBi 3*
**Howe**, Robert 1945- *TwCPaSc*
**Howe**, Robert Blaine, Jr. 1943- *WhoEnt 92*
**Howe**, Robert C 1939- *AmMWSc 92*
**Howe**, Robert Crombie 1939- *WhoMW 92*
**Howe**, Robert George 1926- *AmMWSc 92*
**Howe**, Robert H L 1922- *AmMWSc 92*
**Howe**, Robert Johnston 1936- *AmMWSc 92*
**Howe**, Robert Kenneth 1939- *AmMWSc 92*
**Howe**, Robert T 1920- *AmMWSc 92*
**Howe**, Robin 1908- *WrDr 92*
**Howe**, Roger 1945- *AmMWSc 92*
**Howe**, Ronald Evans 1945- *WhoRel 92*
**Howe**, Ronald William 1932- *Who 92*
**Howe**, Rosethel 1924- *WhoMW 92*
**Howe**, Ruth-Arlene W. 1933- *WhoBlA 92*
**Howe**, Samuel Gridley 1801-1876 *BenetAL 91*
**Howe**, Stanley Merrill 1924- *WhoMW 92*
**Howe**, Susan *ConPo 91, DrAPF 91, WrDr 92*
**Howe**, Tina 1937- *IntAu&W 91, WhoEnt 92, WrDr 92*
**Howe**, Virgil K 1931- *AmMWSc 92*
**Howe**, Wallace Brady 1926- *AmMWSc 92*
**Howe**, Wesley Jackson 1921- *WhoFI 92*
**Howe**, William 1729-1814 *BenetAL 91, BlkwEAR [port]*
**Howe**, William Edward 1948- *AmMWSc 92*
**Howe**, William Jeffrey 1946- *AmMWSc 92*
**Howe**, William Wirt 1833-1909 *ScFEYrs*
**Howe-Weintraub**, Melody RaeDell 1959- *WhoAmP 91*
**Howell**, Alan Peter 1927- *WhoAmL 92, WhoWest 92*
**Howell**, Alvin H 1908- *AmMWSc 92*
**Howell**, Amaziah, III 1948- *WhoBlA 92*
**Howell**, Anthony 1945- *ConPo 91, WrDr 92*
**Howell**, Arthur 1918- *WhoAmL 92*
**Howell**, Barbara *DrAPF 91*
**Howell**, Barbara Fennema 1924- *AmMWSc 92*
**Howell**, Barbara Jane 1927- *AmMWSc 92*
**Howell**, Barton John 1917- *AmMWSc 92*
**Howell**, Benjamin F, Jr 1917- *AmMWSc 92*
**Howell**, Bob A 1942- *AmMWSc 92*
**Howell**, Bruce Inman 1942- *WhoFI 92*
**Howell**, C. Thomas 1966- *IntMPA 92*
**Howell**, Carolyn Thomas 1958- *WhoAmL 92*
**Howell**, Chandler F. 1959- *WhoEnt 92*
**Howell**, Charles Frederick 1932- *AmMWSc 92*
**Howell**, Charles Maitland 1914- *AmMWSc 92*
**Howell**, Chester Thomas 1937- *WhoBlA 92*
**Howell**, Christopher *DrAPF 91*
**Howell**, Clinton T. 1913-1981 *ConAu 133*
**Howell**, Daniel Bunce 1937- *AmMWSc 92*
**Howell**, Danny S. 1951- *WhoEnt 92*
**Howell**, David 1936- *WrDr 92*
**Howell**, David Abel, Jr. 1950- *WhoEnt 92*
**Howell**, David Arthur Russell 1936- *IntWW 91, Who 92*
**Howell**, David Brian 1956- *WhoRel 92*
**Howell**, David Dwight, Jr. 1965- *WhoRel 92*
**Howell**, David McBrier 1933- *AmMWSc 92*
**Howell**, David Moore 1925- *AmMWSc 92*
**Howell**, David Sanders 1923- *AmMWSc 92*
**Howell**, Denis Herbert 1923- *Who 92*
**Howell**, Dillon Lee 1927- *AmMWSc 92*
**Howell**, Donald Lee 1935- *WhoAmL 92, WhoFI 92*
**Howell**, Doris Ahlee 1923- *AmMWSc 92*
**Howell**, Edward Tillson 1897- *AmMWSc 92*
**Howell**, Edward Vernon 1872-1931 *DcNCBi 3*
**Howell**, Edwin Eugene 1845-1911 *BiInAmS*
**Howell**, Elizabeth E 1951- *AmMWSc 92*
**Howell**, Embry Martin 1945- *AmMWSc 92*
**Howell**, Evelyn Anne 1947- *AmMWSc 92*
**Howell**, Evelyn Michael Thomas 1913- *Who 92*
**Howell**, Everette Irl 1914- *AmMWSc 92*
**Howell**, F. Clark 1925- *WrDr 92*
**Howell**, Francine Louise 1955- *WhoWest 92*
**Howell**, Francis Clark 1925- *AmMWSc 92, IntWW 91*
**Howell**, Francis V 1923- *AmMWSc 92*
**Howell**, Gareth 1935- *Who 92*
**Howell**, George F. *DrAPF 91*
**Howell**, Gerald T. 1914- *WhoBlA 92*
**Howell**, Golden Leon 1928- *AmMWSc 92*
**Howell**, Gordon Stanley, Jr 1941- *AmMWSc 92*
**Howell**, Gregory A 1943- *AmMWSc 92*
**Howell**, Gwynne Richard 1938- *Who 92*
**Howell**, Harley Thomas 1937- *WhoAmL 92, WhoFI 92*
**Howell**, Henry Evans, Jr 1920- *WhoAmP 91*
**Howell**, Honor Sharon 1947- *WhoRel 92*
**Howell**, James Arnold 1932- *AmMWSc 92*
**Howell**, James Burt, III 1933- *WhoFI 92*
**Howell**, James F 1934- *WhoAmP 91*
**Howell**, James Levert 1917- *AmMWSc 92*
**Howell**, James MacGregor 1942- *AmMWSc 92*
**Howell**, James Milton 1944- *AmMWSc 92*
**Howell**, James Stewart 1941- *WhoFI 92*
**Howell**, Janice Hopkins 1942- *WhoWest 92*
**Howell**, Jeanne Harriet 1922- *WhoFI 92*
**Howell**, Jerry Fonce 1941- *AmMWSc 92*
**Howell**, Jo Ann Shaw 1945- *AmMWSc 92*
**Howell**, Joan *TwCPaSc*
**Howell**, John Anthony 1939- *AmMWSc 92*
**Howell**, John Bernard Lloyd *Who 92*
**Howell**, John Christian 1924- *IntAu&W 91, WrDr 92*
**Howell**, John Emory 1938- *AmMWSc 92*
**Howell**, John Frederick 1941- *Who 92*
**Howell**, John H 1913- *AmMWSc 92*
**Howell**, John N 1940- *AmMWSc 92*
**Howell**, John Paul 1952- *WhoRel 92*
**Howell**, John Reid 1936- *AmMWSc 92*
**Howell**, Joseph L. 1930- *WhoBlA 92*
**Howell**, Joyce Ann 1955- *WhoAmL 92*
**Howell**, Kenneth Walter 1909- *Who 92*
**Howell**, Larry James 1943- *AmMWSc 92*
**Howell**, Laurence A. 1943- *WhoBlA 92*
**Howell**, Leon *WhoRel 92*
**Howell**, Leonard Rudolph, Jr 1925- *AmMWSc 92*
**Howell**, Lloyd 1923- *Who 92*
**Howell**, Malqueen 1949- *WhoBlA 92*
**Howell**, Margaret 1946- *IntWW 91*
**Howell**, Maribeth Anne 1949- *WhoRel 92*
**Howell**, Mary Elizabeth 1942- *WhoFI 92*
**Howell**, Mary Gertrude 1932- *AmMWSc 92*
**Howell**, Max 1915- *WhoAmP 91*
**Howell**, Michael Edward 1933- *IntWW 91, Who 92*
**Howell**, Norbert Allen 1951- *WhoMW 92*
**Howell**, Norman Gary 1949- *AmMWSc 92*
**Howell**, Orvie Leon 1931- *WhoMW 92*
**Howell**, Patricia Hagan *DrAPF 91*
**Howell**, Patrick Leonard 1942- *Who 92*
**Howell**, Paul 1917- *ConAu 135*
**Howell**, Paul Frederic 1951- *Who 92*
**Howell**, Paul Philip 1917- *Who 92*
**Howell**, Paul Raymond 1946- *AmMWSc 92*
**Howell**, Peter Adam 1928- *AmMWSc 92*
**Howell**, Peter Adrian 1941- *Who 92*
**Howell**, Rachel 1961- *WhoBlA 92*
**Howell**, Ralph Frederic 1923- *Who 92*
**Howell**, Ralph Rodney 1931- *AmMWSc 92*
**Howell**, Raymond Gary 1947- *WhoMW 92*
**Howell**, Rednap d1787 *DcNCBi 3*
**Howell**, Richard S 1935- *WhoAmP 91*
**Howell**, Robert Boyte Crawford 1801-1868 *DcNCBi 3*
**Howell**, Robert J., Jr. 1935- *WhoBlA 92*
**Howell**, Robert Richard 1952- *AmMWSc 92*
**Howell**, Robert T 1927- *AmMWSc 92*
**Howell**, Robert Thomas, Jr. 1942- *WhoAmL 92*
**Howell**, Robert Wayne 1916- *AmMWSc 92*
**Howell**, Ronald Hunter 1935- *AmMWSc 92*
**Howell**, Rose Cole 1949- *WhoBlA 92*
**Howell**, Sandy Lu 1948- *WhoMW 92*
**Howell**, Scott Newell 1953- *WhoAmP 91*
**Howell**, Sharon Marie 1950- *WhoBlA 92*
**Howell**, Stephen Barnard 1944- *WhoWest 92*
**Howell**, Stephen Herbert 1941- *AmMWSc 92*
**Howell**, Stephen Quincy 1937- *WhoWest 92*
**Howell**, Thomas Howard 1945- *AmMWSc 92*
**Howell**, Thomas Jefferson 1842-1912 *BiInAmS*
**Howell**, Thomas Patrick 1962- *WhoMW 92*
**Howell**, Thomas Raymond 1924- *AmMWSc 92*
**Howell**, Vincent Wyatt 1953- *WhoBlA 92*
**Howell**, Virginia Tier *IntAu&W 91X, WrDr 92*
**Howell**, W Nathaniel 1939- *WhoAmP 91*
**Howell**, Wallace Egbert 1914- *AmMWSc 92*
**Howell**, William Ashley, III 1949- *WhoAmL 92, WhoFI 92*
**Howell**, William B. 1932- *WhoBlA 92*
**Howell**, William Edwin 1923- *AmMWSc 92*
**Howell**, William J 1946- *WhoIns 92*
**Howell**, William James 1943- *WhoAmP 91*
**Howell**, William Robert 1936- *WhoFI 92*
**Howell**, Willie R. 1926- *WhoBlA 92*
**Howell**, Wilson Nathaniel 1939- *IntWW 91*
**Howells**, Anne 1941- *Who 92*
**Howells**, Anne Elizabeth 1941- *IntWW 91*
**Howells**, Geraint Wyn 1925- *Who 92*
**Howells**, Gwyn 1918- *IntWW 91, Who 92*
**Howells**, Herbert 1892-1983 *NewAmDM*
**Howells**, John Gwilym 1918- *WrDr 92*
**Howells**, Kim Scott 1946- *Who 92*
**Howells**, R. Tim *WhoWest 92*
**Howells**, Thomas Alfred 1911- *AmMWSc 92*
**Howells**, Ursula 1922- *ConTFT 9, IntMPA 92*
**Howells**, W. D. *ConAu 134*
**Howells**, William D. *ConAu 134*
**Howells**, William Dean 1837-1920 *BenetAL 91, ConAu 134, RComAH, ScFEYrs, TwCLC 41 [port], TwCSFW 91*

**Howells**, William White 1908- *AmMWSc 92, IntWW 91, WrDr 92*
**Howenstine**, E. Jay 1914- *WhoFI 92*
**Hower**, Arthur Aaron, Jr 1937- *AmMWSc 92*
**Hower**, Charles Oliver 1935- *AmMWSc 92*
**Hower**, Edward *DrAPF 91*
**Hower**, Glen L 1934- *AmMWSc 92*
**Hower**, John, Jr 1927- *AmMWSc 92*
**Hower**, Meade M 1925- *AmMWSc 92*
**Hower**, Timothy James 1966- *WhoEnt 92*
**Howerd**, Frankie *Who 92*
**Howerd**, Frankie 1921- *IntMPA 92*
**Howerton**, Charles C. 1938- *WhoEnt 92*
**Howerton**, Herman Hugh 1943- *WhoAmL 92*
**Howerton**, Murlin T 1920- *AmMWSc 92*
**Howerton**, Robert James 1923- *AmMWSc 92*
**Howery**, Darryl Gilmer 1936- *AmMWSc 92*
**Howery**, Donald E. 1941- *WhoFI 92*
**Howes**, Alfred S 1917- *WhoIns 92*
**Howes**, Alfred Spencer 1917- *WhoFI 92*
**Howes**, Allan John 1916- *WhoRel 92*
**Howes**, Barbara *DrAPF 91*
**Howes**, Barbara 1914- *BenetAL 91, ConPo 91, IntAu&W 91, WrDr 92*
**Howes**, Brian Thomas 1957- *WhoAmL 92, WhoMW 92*
**Howes**, Bruce Becker 1953- *WhoRel 92*
**Howes**, Cecil Edgar 1918- *AmMWSc 92*
**Howes**, Christopher Kingston 1942- *Who 92*
**Howes**, Dwight Alexander 1958- *WhoAmL 92*
**Howes**, Franklin J. 1921- *WhoFI 92*
**Howes**, Gloria *WhoAmP 91*
**Howes**, Harold, Jr 1930- *AmMWSc 92*
**Howes**, John Francis 1943- *AmMWSc 92*
**Howes**, Kenneth Ronald 1935- *WhoMW 92*
**Howes**, Ralph Orvel, Jr. 1943- *WhoMW 92*
**Howes**, Robert Ingersoll, Jr 1941- *AmMWSc 92*
**Howes**, Ruth Hege 1944- *AmMWSc 92, WhoMW 92*
**Howes**, Sally Ann *Who 92*
**Howgate**, David W 1932- *AmMWSc 92*
**Howgill**, Martyn W. C., Sr. 1946- *WhoMW 92*
**Howick**, Lester Carl 1928- *AmMWSc 92*
**Howick of Glendale**, Baron 1937- *Who 92*
**Howie** *Who 92*
**Howie**, Archibald 1934- *IntWW 91, Who 92*
**Howie**, Donald Lavern 1924- *AmMWSc 92*
**Howie**, J. Robert 1929- *IntWW 91*
**Howie**, James 1907- *Who 92*
**Howie**, James 1931- *TwCPaSc*
**Howie**, John 1929- *WhoMW 92*
**Howie**, John Garvie Robertson 1937- *Who 92*
**Howie**, John Mackintosh 1936- *Who 92*
**Howie**, John Robert 1946- *WhoAmL 92*
**Howie**, Robert Andrew 1923- *Who 92*
**Howie**, Tomas Vincent 1957- *WhoEnt 92*
**Howie of Troon**, Baron 1924- *Who 92*
**Howington**, Linda S. *WrDr 92*
**Howison**, George Holmes 1834-1916 *BiInAmS*
**Howith**, Harry 1934- *IntAu&W 91*
**Howitt**, Angus Joseph 1919- *AmMWSc 92*
**Howitt**, Anthony Wentworth 1920- *Who 92*
**Howitt**, Mary 1799-1888 *DcLB 110 [port]*
**Howitt**, W. Fowler 1924- *Who 92*
**Howitt**, William 1792-1879 *DcLB 110 [port]*
**Howker**, Janni 1957- *SmATA 13AS [port]*
**Howkins**, Colin *TwCPaSc*
**Howkins**, John 1907- *Who 92*
**Howkins**, John Anthony 1945- *Who 92*
**Howkins**, John Blair 1932- *WhoFI 92*
**Howkins**, Stuart D 1938- *AmMWSc 92*
**Howland**, Lord 1962- *Who 92*
**Howland**, Allen Hathaway 1921- *WhoFI 92*
**Howland**, Beth *WhoEnt 92*
**Howland**, Bette *DrAPF 91*
**Howland**, Frank L 1926- *AmMWSc 92*
**Howland**, George Russell 1932- *AmMWSc 92*
**Howland**, Grafton Dulany 1943- *WhoFI 92*
**Howland**, Howard Chase 1933- *AmMWSc 92*
**Howland**, James Lucien 1929- *AmMWSc 92*
**Howland**, James Secord 1937- *AmMWSc 92*
**Howland**, Jay Allen 1943- *WhoWest 92*
**Howland**, John Hudson, Sr 1915- *WhoAmP 91*
**Howland**, John LaFollette 1935- *AmMWSc 92*
**Howland**, Joseph E 1918- *AmMWSc 92*
**Howland**, Joseph Emery 1918- *WhoWest 92*
**Howland**, Joyce Elizabeth 1946- *WhoFI 92*
**Howland**, Louis Philip 1929- *AmMWSc 92*
**Howland**, Peter McKinnon 1956- *WhoWest 92*
**Howland**, Richard 1934- *WhoAmP 91*
**Howland**, Richard A 1942- *AmMWSc 92*
**Howland**, Richard David 1942- *AmMWSc 92*
**Howland**, Richard Moulton 1940- *WhoAmL 92*
**Howland**, Willard J 1927- *AmMWSc 92*
**Howland**, William G. C. 1915- *IntWW 91*
**Howland**, William Goldwin Carrington 1915- *Who 92*
**Howland**, William Stapleton 1919- *AmMWSc 92*
**Howlett**, Allyn C 1950- *AmMWSc 92*
**Howlett**, Anthony Douglas 1924- *Who 92*
**Howlett**, D. Roger 1945- *ConAu 135*
**Howlett**, Dale L *WhoAmP 91*
**Howlett**, Duncan 1906- *WrDr 92*
**Howlett**, Geoffrey 1930- *Who 92*
**Howlett**, Jack 1912- *Who 92*
**Howlett**, Joan *DrAPF 91*
**Howlett**, John d1991 *NewYTBS 91*
**Howlett**, John David 1952- *WhoWest 92*
**Howlett**, John Reginald 1940- *IntAu&W 91*
**Howlett**, Joseph 1943- *WhoAmP 91*
**Howlett**, Leland Carl 1943- *WhoWest 92*
**Howlett**, Neville Stanley 1927- *Who 92*
**Howlett**, Ronald William 1928- *Who 92*
**Howlett**, Susan Ellen 1957- *AmMWSc 92*
**Howley**, James McAndrew 1928- *WhoAmL 92*
**Howley**, Kevin Richard 1959- *WhoMW 92*
**Howley**, Peter Maxwell 1946- *AmMWSc 92*
**Howlin' Wolf** 1910-1976 *ConMus 6 [port], NewAmDM*
**Howlin**, John 1941- *TwCPaSc*
**Howman**, John Hartley 1918- *IntWW 91*
**Howren**, Charles Gresham 1941- *WhoAmP 91*
**Howrigan**, D Francis 1917- *WhoAmP 91*
**Howsden**, Arley Levern 1926- *WhoAmP 91*
**Howse**, Benjamin Tommy 1952- *WhoFI 92*
**Howse**, Ernest Marshall 1902- *WrDr 92*
**Howse**, Harold Darrow 1928- *AmMWSc 92*
**Howse**, Humphrey Derek 1919- *Who 92*
**Howsley**, Richard Thornton 1948- *WhoWest 92*
**Howsmon**, John Arthur 1919- *AmMWSc 92*
**Howson**, John 1908- *Who 92*
**Howson**, Peter 1958- *TwCPaSc*
**Howton**, David Ronald 1920- *AmMWSc 92*
**Howze**, Dorothy J. 1923- *WhoBlA 92*
**Howze**, Joseph Lawson 1923- *WhoBlA 92*
**Howze**, Joseph Lawson Edward 1923- *WhoRel 92*
**Howze**, Karen Aileen 1950- *WhoBlA 92*
**Hoxha**, Enver 1908-1985 *FacFETw*
**Hoxie**, Vinnie 1847-1914 *HanAmWH*
**Hoxit-Smith**, Linda Caroline 1953- *WhoEnt 92*
**Hoxsey**, Betty June 1923- *WhoAmP 91*
**Hoxter**, Curtis Joseph 1922- *WhoFI 92*
**Hoy**, Casey William 1954- *AmMWSc 92*
**Hoy**, David 1913- *Who 92*
**Hoy**, David Couzens 1944- *WrDr 92*
**Hoy**, George Philip 1937- *WhoMW 92, WhoRel 92*
**Hoy**, Gilbert Richard 1932- *AmMWSc 92*
**Hoy**, James Benjamin 1935- *AmMWSc 92*
**Hoy**, Linda 1946- *SmATA 65*
**Hoy**, Marjorie Ann *AmMWSc 92*
**Hoy**, Michael Charles 1953- *WhoRel 92*
**Hoy**, Philo Romayne 1816-1892 *BiInAmS*
**Hoy**, Rex Bruce 1928- *WhoAmP 91*
**Hoy**, Robert C 1933- *AmMWSc 92*
**Hoy**, Ronald Raymond 1939- *AmMWSc 92*
**Hoy**, William Glenn 1961- *WhoRel 92, WhoWest 92*
**Hoy**, William Ivan 1915- *WhoRel 92*
**Hoye**, Daniel Francis 1946- *WhoRel 92*
**Hoye**, John T *WhoAmP 91*
**Hoye**, Thomas Robert 1950- *AmMWSc 92*
**Hoye**, Walter B. 1930- *WhoBlA 92*
**Hoye**, Walter B., II 1956- *WhoBlA 92*
**Hoye**, Walter Brisco 1930- *WhoWest 92*
**Hoyem**, Andrew *DrAPF 91*
**Hoyem**, Andrew 1935- *WrDr 92*
**Hoyem**, Tom 1941- *IntWW 91*
**Hoyer**, Bill Henriksen 1921- *AmMWSc 92*
**Hoyer**, Carl Ivan 1930- *WhoIns 92*
**Hoyer**, David Ralph 1931- *WhoFI 92, WhoWest 92*
**Hoyer**, Eugene Richard 1940- *WhoAmP 91*
**Hoyer**, Leon William 1936- *AmMWSc 92*
**Hoyer**, Steny H. 1939- *AlmAP 92 [port]*
**Hoyer**, Steny Hamilton 1939- *WhoAmP 91*
**Hoyer-Ellefsen**, Sigurd 1932- *AmMWSc 92*
**Hoyes**, Thomas 1935- *Who 92*
**Hoying**, Timothy Joseph 1962- *WhoFI 92*
**Hoyland**, Francis 1930- *TwCPaSc*
**Hoyland**, Janet Louise 1940- *WhoRel 92*
**Hoyland**, John 1934- *IntWW 91, TwCPaSc, Who 92*
**Hoyland**, Michael 1925- *IntAu&W 91, WrDr 92*
**Hoyland**, Philippa 1924- *TwCPaSc*
**Hoyland**, Vic 1945- *ConCom 92*
**Hoyle**, Classie 1936- *WhoBlA 92*
**Hoyle**, Eric 1931- *Who 92*
**Hoyle**, Eric Douglas 1930- *Who 92*
**Hoyle**, Fred 1915- *FacFETw, IntAu&W 91, IntWW 91, TwCSFW 91, Who 92, WrDr 92*
**Hoyle**, Frederick James 1918- *Who 92*
**Hoyle**, Geoffrey 1942- *IntAu&W 91, TwCSFW 91, WrDr 92*
**Hoyle**, Hughes Bayne, Jr 1909- *AmMWSc 92*
**Hoyle**, Susan 1953- *Who 92*
**Hoyle**, Trevor 1940- *TwCSFW 91, WrDr 92*
**Hoyle**, William Vinton, Jr. 1949- *WhoAmL 92*
**Hoyles**, J. Arthur 1908- *WrDr 92*
**Hoyne**, Thomas Temple 1935- *WhoMW 92*
**Hoynes**, Louis LeNoir, Jr. 1935- *WhoAmL 92*
**Hoyos**, Alexander 1912- *Who 92*
**Hoyt**, Bradley Arthur 1953- *WhoFI 92*
**Hoyt**, Bradley James 1949- *WhoFI 92*
**Hoyt**, Charlee Ildora 1936- *WhoFI 92*
**Hoyt**, Charles D, Jr 1912- *AmMWSc 92*
**Hoyt**, Charles Hale 1860-1900 *BenetAL 91*
**Hoyt**, Charles Orcutt 1929- *WhoFI 92*
**Hoyt**, David Lemire 1951- *WhoEnt 92*
**Hoyt**, Don A. *DrAPF 91*
**Hoyt**, Donald Frank 1945- *AmMWSc 92*
**Hoyt**, Earle B, Jr 1937- *AmMWSc 92*
**Hoyt**, Edwin P. *DrAPF 91*
**Hoyt**, Erich 1950- *IntAu&W 91, SmATA 65 [port]*
**Hoyt**, Harry Charles 1924- *AmMWSc 92*
**Hoyt**, Harry E *WhoIns 92*
**Hoyt**, Herbert Austin Aikins 1937- *WhoEnt 92*
**Hoyt**, Herman Arthur 1909- *RelLAm 91*
**Hoyt**, Jack W 1922- *AmMWSc 92*
**Hoyt**, Jack Wallace 1922- *WhoWest 92*
**Hoyt**, James Edward 1955- *WhoRel 92*
**Hoyt**, John d1991 *NewYTBS 91*
**Hoyt**, John Manson 1919- *AmMWSc 92*
**Hoyt**, Kathleen Clark 1942- *WhoAmP 91*
**Hoyt**, Kenneth M. 1948- *WhoAmL 92*
**Hoyt**, Linda Jane 1955- *WhoAmP 91*
**Hoyt**, Merrill Craig 1942- *WhoAmL 92*
**Hoyt**, Mont Powell 1940- *WhoAmL 92*
**Hoyt**, Nelson *TwCWW 91*
**Hoyt**, Norris 1935- *WhoAmP 91*
**Hoyt**, Paul John 1937- *WhoFI 92*
**Hoyt**, Richard 1941- *WrDr 92*
**Hoyt**, Robert Dan 1941- *AmMWSc 92*
**Hoyt**, Roger Alan 1952- *WhoMW 92*
**Hoyt**, Rosalie Chase 1914- *AmMWSc 92*
**Hoyt**, Samuel LeRoy 1947- *WhoRel 92*
**Hoyt**, Scott McNair 1960- *WhoFI 92*
**Hoyt**, Scott Randall 1952- *WhoAmL 92*
**Hoyt**, Stanley Charles 1929- *AmMWSc 92*
**Hoyt**, Thomas L., Jr. 1941- *WhoBlA 92*
**Hoyt**, William B 1937- *WhoAmP 91*
**Hoyt**, William F 1926- *AmMWSc 92*
**Hoyt**, William Lind 1928- *AmMWSc 92*
**Hoyt**, William Russell, III 1924- *WhoRel 92*
**Hoyte**, Arthur Hamilton 1938- *WhoBlA 92*
**Hoyte**, Hugh Desmond 1929- *IntWW 91, Who 92*
**Hoyte**, James Sterling 1944- *WhoBlA 92*
**Hoyte**, Lenon Holder 1905- *WhoBlA 92*
**Hoyte**, Robert Mikell 1943- *AmMWSc 92*
**Hoyte-Smith**, Joslyn Y 1954- *BlkOlyM*
**Hoyton**, Edward Bouverie 1900-1988 *TwCPaSc*
**Hoyumpa**, Anastacio Maningo 1937- *AmMWSc 92*
**Hozeski**, Bruce William 1941- *WhoMW 92*
**Hozumi**, Nobumichi 1943- *AmMWSc 92*
**Hraba**, John Burnett 1921- *AmMWSc 92*
**Hrabal**, Bohumil 1914- *ConLC 67 [port], IntWW 91*
**Hrabovsky**, Joseph Emil 1942- *WhoFI 92*
**Hrabovsky**, Leonid 1935- *ConCom 92*
**Hrabowski**, Freeman Alphonsa, III 1950- *WhoBlA 92*
**Hracho**, Lawrence John 1948- *WhoAmL 92*
**Hrawi**, Elias *IntWW 91*
**Hrazanek**, Richard J 1937- *WhoIns 92*
**Hrazdina**, Geza 1939- *AmMWSc 92*
**Hrbek**, George W 1927- *AmMWSc 92*
**Hrdina**, Pavel Dusan 1929- *AmMWSc 92*
**Hrdy**, Sarah Blaffer 1946- *AmMWSc 92, ConAu 35NR*
**Hren**, John J 1933- *AmMWSc 92*
**Hrescak**, Victor John 1953- *WhoFI 92*
**Hreshchyshyn**, Myroslaw M 1927- *AmMWSc 92*
**Hribal**, C.J. *DrAPF 91*
**Hribar**, John Anthony 1934- *AmMWSc 92*
**Hribar**, John Peter, Sr. 1936- *WhoWest 92*
**Hric**, Paul J 1926- *WhoAmP 91*
**Hrinko**, Daniel Dean 1955- *WhoMW 92*
**Hrishko**, Daniel George 1947- *WhoWest 92*
**Hriskevich**, Michael Edward 1926- *AmMWSc 92*
**Hritz**, George F. 1948- *WhoAmL 92*
**Hrivnak**, Bruce John 1949- *AmMWSc 92*
**Hrivnak**, Pavel 1931- *IntWW 91*
**Hrkel**, Edward James 1942- *AmMWSc 92*
**Hromadka**, Josef Lukl 1889-1970 *DcEcMov [port]*
**Hromatko**, Wesley Vinton 1947- *WhoRel 92*
**Hron**, Frederic James 1954- *WhoMW 92*
**Hrones**, John Anthony 1912- *AmMWSc 92*
**Hrones**, Stephen Baylis 1942- *WhoAmL 92*
**Hrouda**, Barthel 1929- *IntWW 91*
**Hrovat**, Davorin 1949- *AmMWSc 92*
**Hruban**, Zdenek 1921- *AmMWSc 92*
**Hrubant**, Henry Everett 1929- *AmMWSc 92*
**Hrubesh**, Lawrence Wayne 1940- *AmMWSc 92*
**Hruby**, Frank M. 1918- *WhoEnt 92*
**Hruby**, Paul James 1927- *WhoMW 92*
**Hruby**, Victor J 1938- *AmMWSc 92*
**Hruschka**, Howard Wilbur 1915- *AmMWSc 92*
**Hrushesky**, William John Michael 1947- *AmMWSc 92*
**Hruska**, Alan J. 1933- *WhoAmL 92*
**Hruska**, Antonin 1934- *AmMWSc 92*
**Hruska**, Elias N. *DrAPF 91*
**Hruska**, Elias N. 1943- *IntAu&W 91*
**Hruska**, Roman Lee 1904- *WhoAmP 91*
**Hruska**, Samuel Joseph 1936- *AmMWSc 92*
**Hrut**, Christopher Boleslaw 1958- *WhoWest 92*
**Hrutfiord**, Bjorn F 1932- *AmMWSc 92*
**Hruza**, Zdenek 1926- *AmMWSc 92*
**Hrycak**, Peter 1923- *AmMWSc 92, WhoFI 92*
**Hrydziusko**, Wesley J 1931- *WhoAmP 91*
**Hryniuk**, William 1939- *AmMWSc 92*
**Hsi**, Bartholomew P 1925- *AmMWSc 92*
**Hsi**, David Ching Heng 1928- *AmMWSc 92*
**Hsi**, Denise Chur-Yee Tso 1958- *WhoWest 92*
**Hsi**, Edward Yang 1957- *WhoAmL 92*
**Hsi**, Richard S P 1933- *AmMWSc 92*
**Hsia**, Henry Tao-Sze 1923- *AmMWSc 92*
**Hsia**, Hsiao *IntAu&W 91X*
**Hsia**, Jack Jinn-Goe 1937- *AmMWSc 92*
**Hsia**, John S 1938- *AmMWSc 92*
**Hsia**, Judo J. D. 1947- *WhoEnt 92*
**Hsia**, Mong Tseng Stephen 1946- *AmMWSc 92*
**Hsia**, Richard C 1948- *WhoIns 92*
**Hsia**, Sung Lan 1920- *AmMWSc 92*
**Hsia**, Yu-Ping 1936- *AmMWSc 92*
**Hsia**, Yukun 1941- *AmMWSc 92*
**Hsiang**, Thomas Y 1948- *AmMWSc 92*
**Hsiao**, Benjamin S 1958- *AmMWSc 92*
**Hsiao**, Chih Chun 1919- *AmMWSc 92*
**Hsiao**, George Chia-Chu 1934- *AmMWSc 92*
**Hsiao**, Henry Shih-Chan 1943- *AmMWSc 92*
**Hsiao**, Hsia *WrDr 92*
**Hsiao**, Mu-Yue 1933- *AmMWSc 92*
**Hsiao**, Roger Chenfang 1955- *WhoFI 92*
**Hsiao**, Sidney Chihti 1905- *AmMWSc 92*
**Hsiao**, Theodore Ching-Teh 1931- *AmMWSc 92*
**Hsiao**, Ting Huan 1936- *AmMWSc 92*
**Hsiaw**, Henry Ching-Ye 1955- *WhoFI 92*
**Hsie**, Abraham Wuhsiung 1940- *AmMWSc 92*
**Hsieh**, Chung Kuo 1932- *AmMWSc 92*
**Hsieh**, David Arthur 1953- *WhoFI 92*
**Hsieh**, Dennis P H 1937- *AmMWSc 92*
**Hsieh**, Din-Yu 1933- *AmMWSc 92*
**Hsieh**, Henry Lien 1930- *AmMWSc 92*
**Hsieh**, Hsung-Cheng 1929- *AmMWSc 92*
**Hsieh**, Hui-Kuang 1944- *AmMWSc 92*
**Hsieh**, Jui Sheng 1921- *AmMWSc 92*
**Hsieh**, Ke Chiang 1940- *AmMWSc 92*
**Hsieh**, Michael Thomas 1958- *WhoFI 92*
**Hsieh**, Monica C *AmMWSc 92*
**Hsieh**, Paul Yao Tong 1927- *AmMWSc 92*
**Hsieh**, Philip Kwok-Young *AmMWSc 92*
**Hsieh**, Po-Fang 1934- *AmMWSc 92*
**Hsieh**, Richard Kuochi 1932- *AmMWSc 92*
**Hsieh**, Rudy Ru-Pin 1950- *WhoFI 92*

**Hsieh**, Tom WhoAmP 91
**Hsieh**, You-Lo 1953- AmMWSc 92
**Hsieh**, Yu-Nian 1942- AmMWSc 92
**Hsien**, Lady EncAmaz 91
**Hsin**, Victor Jun-Kuan 1945- WhoFI 92
**Hsiung Shih-I** 1902- IntWW 91
**Hsiung**, Andrew K 1920- AmMWSc 92
**Hsiung**, Chi-Hua Wu 1930- AmMWSc 92
**Hsiung**, Chuan Chih 1916- AmMWSc 92
**Hsiung**, Gueh Djen 1918- AmMWSc 92
**Hsiung**, Shih I. d1991 Who 92N
**Hsu Ching-Chung** 1907- IntWW 91
**Hsu Shui-Teh** 1931- IntWW 91
**Hsu Tsang-houei** 1929- ConCom 92
**Hsu Tzu-Chiu** 1920- IntWW 91
**Hsu**, Andrew C T 1916- AmMWSc 92
**Hsu**, C C 1923- AmMWSc 92
**Hsu**, Chao Kuang 1939- AmMWSc 92
**Hsu**, Charles Ching-Hsiang 1959- AmMWSc 92
**Hsu**, Charles Fu-Jen 1920- AmMWSc 92
**Hsu**, Charles Jui-cheng 1930- WhoFI 92
**Hsu**, Charles Teh-Ching 1935- AmMWSc 92
**Hsu**, Chen C 1940- AmMWSc 92
**Hsu**, Chen-Hsing 1937- AmMWSc 92
**Hsu**, Cheng-Ting 1923- AmMWSc 92
**Hsu**, Chieh-Su 1922- AmMWSc 92, WhoWest 92
**Hsu**, Chin-Fei 1947- AmMWSc 92
**Hsu**, Chin Shung 1948- AmMWSc 92
**Hsu**, Ching-Hsin 1956- WhoEnt 92
**Hsu**, Clement C S 1937- AmMWSc 92
**Hsu**, David Kuei-Yu 1941- AmMWSc 92
**Hsu**, David Shiao-Yo 1944- AmMWSc 92
**Hsu**, Deh Yuan 1943- AmMWSc 92
**Hsu**, Edward Ching-Sheng 1942- AmMWSc 92
**Hsu**, Frank Hsiao-Hua 1935- AmMWSc 92
**Hsu**, H P 1930- AmMWSc 92
**Hsu**, Howard Huai Ta 1938- AmMWSc 92
**Hsu**, Hsi Fan 1906- AmMWSc 92
**Hsu**, Hsien-Wen 1928- AmMWSc 92
**Hsu**, Hsiu-Sheng 1931- AmMWSc 92
**Hsu**, Hsiung 1920- AmMWSc 92
**Hsu**, Jang-Yu 1949- AmMWSc 92
**Hsu**, Jay C 1934- AmMWSc 92
**Hsu**, Jeng Mein 1920- AmMWSc 92
**Hsu**, John Tseng Hsin 1931- WhoEnt 92
**Hsu**, John Y 1938- AmMWSc 92
**Hsu**, K. ConAu 135
**Hsu**, K.J. ConAu 135
**Hsu**, K. Jinghwa ConAu 135
**Hsu**, Katharine Han Kuang 1914- AmMWSc 92
**Hsu**, Kenneth Hsuehchia 1950- AmMWSc 92
**Hsu**, Kenneth J. 1929- ConAu 135
**Hsu**, Kenneth Jinghwa 1929- AmMWSc 92, IntWW 91
**Hsu**, Konrad Chang 1901- AmMWSc 92
**Hsu**, Kwan 1913- AmMWSc 92
**Hsu**, Laura Hwei-Nien Ling 1939- AmMWSc 92
**Hsu**, Liang-Chi 1931- AmMWSc 92
**Hsu**, Linda 1944- AmMWSc 92
**Hsu**, Michael Kingman 1948- WhoFI 92
**Hsu**, Ming-Ta 1944- AmMWSc 92
**Hsu**, Ming-Ta Sung 1937- AmMWSc 92
**Hsu**, Nai-Chao AmMWSc 92
**Hsu**, Nelson Nae-Ching 1934- AmMWSc 92
**Hsu**, Paul L. 1922- WhoWest 92
**Hsu**, Robert Ying 1926- AmMWSc 92
**Hsu**, Roger Y. K. 1927- WhoAmL 92
**Hsu**, Samuel 1947- WhoEnt 92
**Hsu**, Shaw Ling 1948- AmMWSc 92
**Hsu**, Sheng Teng 1934- AmMWSc 92
**Hsu**, Shih-Ang 1936- AmMWSc 92
**Hsu**, Shu-Dean 1943- WhoWest 92
**Hsu**, Shu Ying Li 1920- AmMWSc 92
**Hsu**, Stephen M 1943- AmMWSc 92
**Hsu**, Su-Ming 1949- AmMWSc 92
**Hsu**, Susan Hu 1943- AmMWSc 92
**Hsu**, Tsong-Han 1922- AmMWSc 92
**Hsu**, Walter Haw 1946- AmMWSc 92
**Hsu**, Wen-Tah 1930- AmMWSc 92
**Hsu**, William Yang-Hsing 1948- AmMWSc 92
**Hsu**, Y C 1935- AmMWSc 92
**Hsu**, Yu Kao 1922- AmMWSc 92
**Hsu**, Yu-Sheng 1945- AmMWSc 92
**Hsuan**, Hulbert C S 1939- AmMWSc 92
**Hsueh**, Aaron Jen Wang 1948- AmMWSc 92
**Hsueh**, Andie M 1940- AmMWSc 92
**Hsueh**, Chun-tu 1922- ConAu 34NR
**Hsueh**, Ya 1936- AmMWSc 92
**Hsui**, Albert Tong-Kwan 1945- AmMWSc 92
**Htoo**, Maung Shwe 1927- AmMWSc 92
**Hu Bingyun** 1911- IntWW 91
**Hu Dingyi** 1922- Who 92
**Hu Fuguo** 1938- IntWW 91
**Hu Han** IntWW 91
**Hu Hong** 1918- IntWW 91
**Hu Jintao** 1942- IntWW 91
**Hu Jiwei** 1916- IntWW 91
**Hu Lijiao** 1914- IntWW 91
**Hu Ping** 1930- IntWW 91
**Hu Qiaomu** 1912- IntWW 91
**Hu Qili** 1929- IntWW 91
**Hu Sheng** 1918- IntWW 91
**Hu Yaobang** 1915-1989 FacFETw
**Hu Yizhou** 1927- IntWW 91
**Hu**, Alfred Soy Lan 1928- AmMWSc 92
**Hu**, Bambi 1945- AmMWSc 92
**Hu**, Bei 1962- WhoMW 92
**Hu**, Bei-Lok Bernard 1947- AmMWSc 92
**Hu**, Chenming 1947- AmMWSc 92
**Hu**, Chi-Yu 1933- AmMWSc 92
**Hu**, Chia-Ren 1939- AmMWSc 92
**Hu**, Ching-Yeh 1937- AmMWSc 92
**Hu**, Funan 1919- AmMWSc 92
**Hu**, Hopin 1954- WhoMW 92
**Hu**, James Tsu-Cheng 1948- WhoFI 92
**Hu**, Jimmy WhoHisp 92
**Hu**, Jing-Shan 1963- AmMWSc 92
**Hu**, John Chih-An 1922- WhoWest 92
**Hu**, John Nan-Hai 1936- AmMWSc 92
**Hu**, Joseph Chi-Ping 1946- WhoFI 92
**Hu**, L W 1922- AmMWSc 92
**Hu**, Mary Lee 1943- WhoWest 92
**Hu**, Ming-Kuei 1918- AmMWSc 92
**Hu**, Pung Nien 1926- AmMWSc 92
**Hu**, Richard Tachi 1925- WhoWest 92
**Hu**, Sheng-Cheng 1940- WhoFI 92
**Hu**, Shiu-Lok 1949- AmMWSc 92
**Hu**, Steve Seng-Chiu AmMWSc 92
**Hu**, Sung Chiao 1942- AmMWSc 92
**Hu**, Tao 1964- WhoWest 92
**Hu**, Te Chiang 1930- AmMWSc 92
**Hu**, Wei-Shou 1951- AmMWSc 92
**Hu**, William H 1927- AmMWSc 92
**Hu Tsu Tau**, Richard 1926- IntWW 91
**Hua Guofeng** 1920- FacFETw, IntWW 91
**Hua**, Duy Huu 1952- AmMWSc 92
**Hua**, Hsuan 1908- RelLAm 91
**Hua**, Ping 1963- AmMWSc 92
**Huaco**, George Arthur 1927- WhoWest 92
**Huacuja**, Yvonne Tamara 1948- WhoHisp 92
**Huang An-Lun** 1949- IntWW 91
**Huang Anren** 1924- IntWW 91
**Huang Bingwei** 1913- IntWW 91
**Huang Da** 1925- IntWW 91
**Huang Demao** 1919- IntWW 91
**Huang Dufeng** 1913- IntWW 91
**Huang Ganying** 1921- IntWW 91
**Huang Hou** 1913- IntWW 91
**Huang Hua** 1913- IntWW 91
**Huang Huang** 1933- IntWW 91
**Huang Jingbo** 1919- IntWW 91
**Huang Ju** 1938- IntWW 91
**Huang Kewei** 1907- IntWW 91
**Huang Kun** 1919- IntWW 91
**Huang Luobin** IntWW 91
**Huang Mingda** IntWW 91
**Huang Pemei** EncAmaz 91
**Huang Rong** IntWW 91
**Huang Shao-Ku** 1901- IntWW 91
**Huang Shu** IntWW 91
**Huang Weilu** 1916- IntWW 91
**Huang Xinting** 1913- IntWW 91
**Huang Yongyu** 1924- IntWW 91
**Huang Yukun** 1920- IntWW 91
**Huang Zhizhen** 1920- IntWW 91
**Huang Zhou** 1925- IntWW 91
**Huang Zongying** 1925- IntWW 91
**Huang**, Alice Shih-Hou 1939- AmMWSc 92
**Huang**, Anthony Hwoon Chung 1945- AmMWSc 92
**Huang**, Barney K 1931- AmMWSc 92
**Huang**, C Yuan 1935- AmMWSc 92
**Huang**, Cham-Ber 1925- NewAmDM
**Huang**, Chaofu 1959- AmMWSc 92
**Huang**, Charles T L 1938- AmMWSc 92
**Huang**, Charles Y AmMWSc 92
**Huang**, Chau-Ting 1939- AmMWSc 92
**Huang**, Che C AmMWSc 92
**Huang**, Cheng-Cher 1947- AmMWSc 92
**Huang**, Cheng-Chun 1938- AmMWSc 92
**Huang**, Chester Chen-Chiu 1927- AmMWSc 92
**Huang**, Chi-Lung Dominic 1930- AmMWSc 92
**Huang**, Chien Chang 1931- WhoWest 92
**Huang**, Chin Pao 1941- AmMWSc 92
**Huang**, Ching-hsien 1935- AmMWSc 92
**Huang**, Ching-Rong 1932- AmMWSc 92
**Huang**, Denis K 1925- AmMWSc 92
**Huang**, Eng-Shang 1940- AmMWSc 92
**Huang**, Eugene Yuching 1917- AmMWSc 92
**Huang**, Fan-Hsiung Frank 1940- AmMWSc 92
**Huang**, Fan-Zhang 1931- IntWW 91
**Huang**, Francis F 1922- AmMWSc 92
**Huang**, Francis Fu-Tse 1922- WhoWest 92
**Huang**, H T 1921- AmMWSc 92
**Huang**, Haitao 1962- WhoMW 92
**Huang**, Henry Hung-Chang 1939- AmMWSc 92
**Huang**, Huey Wen 1940- AmMWSc 92
**Huang**, Jack Shih Ta 1933- AmMWSc 92
**Huang**, Jacob Wen-Kuang 1935- AmMWSc 92
**Huang**, Jamin 1951- AmMWSc 92
**Huang**, Jen-Tzaw 1938- WhoWest 92
**Huang**, Jeng-Sheng 1940- AmMWSc 92
**Huang**, Jennming Stephen 1947- AmMWSc 92
**Huang**, John S 1940- AmMWSc 92
**Huang**, Joseph Chi Kan 1938- AmMWSc 92
**Huang**, Ju-Chang 1941- AmMWSc 92
**Huang**, Jung-Chang 1935- AmMWSc 92
**Huang**, Jung San AmMWSc 92
**Huang**, Justin C 1935- AmMWSc 92
**Huang**, Kai-Loo 1909- WhoRel 92
**Huang**, Kechang 1903-1986 FacFETw
**Huang**, Kee-Chang 1917- AmMWSc 92
**Huang**, Keh-Ning 1947- AmMWSc 92
**Huang**, Kerson 1928- AmMWSc 92
**Huang**, Kun-Yen 1933- AmMWSc 92
**Huang**, Kuo-Ping 1942- AmMWSc 92
**Huang**, Laura Chi 1937- AmMWSc 92
**Huang**, Leaf 1946- AmMWSc 92
**Huang**, Leo W 1942- AmMWSc 92
**Huang**, Liang Hsiung 1939- AmMWSc 92
**Huang**, Mou-Tuan AmMWSc 92
**Huang**, Nai-Chien 1932- AmMWSc 92
**Huang**, P M 1934- AmMWSc 92
**Huang**, Pien-Chien 1931- AmMWSc 92
**Huang**, Rayson Lisung 1920- IntWW 91, Who 92
**Huang**, Robert Y M 1930- AmMWSc 92
**Huang**, Ru-Chih Chow 1932- AmMWSc 92
**Huang**, Samuel J 1937- AmMWSc 92
**Huang**, Shao-nan AmMWSc 92
**Huang**, Shaw-Guang 1949- AmMWSc 92
**Huang**, Shu-Jen Wu 1945- AmMWSc 92
**Huang**, Suei-Rong 1932- AmMWSc 92
**Huang**, Sung-Cheng 1944- AmMWSc 92
**Huang**, Sylvia Lee 1930- AmMWSc 92
**Huang**, T C AmMWSc 92
**Huang**, Thomas Shi-Tao 1936- AmMWSc 92
**Huang**, Thomas Tao Shing 1939- AmMWSc 92
**Huang**, Thomas Tsung-Tse 1938- AmMWSc 92
**Huang**, Thomas Weishing 1941- WhoAmL 92
**Huang**, Tiao-yuan 1949- AmMWSc 92
**Huang**, Tseng 1925- AmMWSc 92
**Huang**, Victor Tsangmin 1951- WhoMW 92
**Huang**, Vivian Wenhuey Chen 1942- WhoAmL 92
**Huang**, Wai Mun AmMWSc 92
**Huang**, Wann Sheng 1939- AmMWSc 92
**Huang**, Wei-Chiao 1955- WhoFI 92, WhoMW 92
**Huang**, Wei-Feng 1930- AmMWSc 92
**Huang**, Wen Hsing 1936- AmMWSc 92
**Huang**, Y T 1927- AmMWSc 92
**Huant**, Ernest Albin Camille 1909- IntWW 91
**Huard**, Joseph R., Jr. 1957- WhoFI 92
**Huascar** 1495-1533 HisDSpE
**Huayna Capac** 1450?-1525 HisDSpE
**Huayta Nunez**, Wilfredo IntWW 91
**Huba**, Francis 1920- AmMWSc 92
**Huba**, Mikulas d1986 IntWW 91N
**Hubatka**, Milton Anthony WhoEnt 92
**Hubay**, Charles Alfred 1918- AmMWSc 92
**Hubback**, David Francis d1991 Who 92N
**Hubbard** Who 92
**Hubbard**, Alan R 1944- WhoAmP 91
**Hubbard**, Amos B. 1930- WhoBlA 92
**Hubbard**, Ann Louise 1943- AmMWSc 92
**Hubbard**, Arnette Rhinehart WhoBlA 92
**Hubbard**, Arthur T 1941- AmMWSc 92
**Hubbard**, Bertie Earl 1928- AmMWSc 92
**Hubbard**, Bruce d1991 NewYTBS 91
**Hubbard**, Bruce Alan 1948- WhoBlA 92
**Hubbard**, Calvin L. 1940- WhoBlA 92
**Hubbard**, Carroll, Jr. 1937- AlmAP 92 [port], WhoAmP 91
**Hubbard**, Charles Richard 1954- WhoFI 92
**Hubbard**, Charles Ronald 1933- WhoWest 92
**Hubbard**, Charles W 1943- WhoIns 92
**Hubbard**, Colin D 1939- AmMWSc 92
**Hubbard**, Darrell 1966- WhoBlA 92
**Hubbard**, David Who 92
**Hubbard**, David Allan 1928- WhoRel 92
**Hubbard**, Dean Leon 1939- WhoMW 92
**Hubbard**, Donald 1900- AmMWSc 92
**Hubbard**, Donald 1926- WhoWest 92
**Hubbard**, Donald 1943- WhoBlA 92
**Hubbard**, Doris Jones 1950- WhoAmP 91
**Hubbard**, Dorthy Stuart 1925- WhoAmP 91
**Hubbard**, Edward Leonard 1921- AmMWSc 92
**Hubbard**, Elbert 1856-1915 BenetAL 91, DcTwDes
**Hubbard**, Elizabeth WhoEnt 92
**Hubbard**, Eric Hesketh 1892-1957 TwCPaSc
**Hubbard**, Eric R 1943- AmMWSc 92
**Hubbard**, Fordyce Mitchell 1809-1888 DcNCBi 3
**Hubbard**, Francis Patrick 1944- WhoAmL 92
**Hubbard**, Frank 1920-1976 NewAmDM
**Hubbard**, Fred Leonhardt 1940- WhoAmL 92
**Hubbard**, Freddie 1938- NewAmDM, WhoBlA 92
**Hubbard**, Frederick Dewayne 1938- WhoEnt 92
**Hubbard**, G C d1902 BiInAmS
**Hubbard**, Gardiner Greene 1822-1897 BiInAmS
**Hubbard**, Grant Robert, II 1950- WhoMW 92
**Hubbard**, Gregory Scott 1948- WhoWest 92
**Hubbard**, Harmon William 1923- AmMWSc 92
**Hubbard**, Harry 1924- WhoAmP 91
**Hubbard**, Harvey Hart 1921- AmMWSc 92
**Hubbard**, Henry Guernsey 1850-1899 BiInAmS
**Hubbard**, Herbert Hendrix 1922- WhoFI 92
**Hubbard**, Howard James 1938- WhoRel 92
**Hubbard**, Hylan T., III 1947- WhoBlA 92
**Hubbard**, Hylan Thomas, III 1947- WhoFI 92
**Hubbard**, James Madison, Jr. WhoBlA 92
**Hubbard**, James Stuart 1954- AmMWSc 92
**Hubbard**, Jean P. 1917- WhoBlA 92
**Hubbard**, Jeremiah 1777-1849 DcNCBi 3
**Hubbard**, Jerry S 1932- AmMWSc 92
**Hubbard**, Joan Laird 1935- WhoFI 92
**Hubbard**, Joan Moody 1941- WhoMW 92
**Hubbard**, John 1931- IntWW 91, TwCPaSc
**Hubbard**, John Castleman 1922- AmMWSc 92
**Hubbard**, John Edward 1933- AmMWSc 92
**Hubbard**, John Ingram 1930- IntWW 91
**Hubbard**, John Lewis 1947- AmMWSc 92
**Hubbard**, John Morris 1916- WhoMW 92
**Hubbard**, John Patrick 1935- AmMWSc 92
**Hubbard**, John W 1956- AmMWSc 92
**Hubbard**, Joseph Stillman 1823-1863 BiInAmS
**Hubbard**, Josephine Brodie 1938- WhoBlA 92
**Hubbard**, Kenneth Dean, Jr. 1959- WhoEnt 92
**Hubbard**, Kin 1868-1930 BenetAL 91
**Hubbard**, L. Ron 1911-1986 BenetAL 91, FacFETw, RelLAm 91, TwCSFW 91
**Hubbard**, Lincoln Beals 1940- AmMWSc 92
**Hubbard**, M M 1906- AmMWSc 92
**Hubbard**, Marilyn French 1946- WhoBlA 92
**Hubbard**, Michael Joseph 1942- Who 92
**Hubbard**, Nettie LaRue Fallin 1921- WhoWest 92
**Hubbard**, Oliver Payson 1809-1900 BiInAmS
**Hubbard**, Paul Leonard 1942- WhoBlA 92
**Hubbard**, Paul Stancyl, Jr 1931- AmMWSc 92
**Hubbard**, Peter Lawrence 1946- WhoAmL 92
**Hubbard**, Phil 1956- WhoBlA 92
**Hubbard**, Philip G 1921- AmMWSc 92
**Hubbard**, Phillip WhoAmP 91, WhoHisp 92
**Hubbard**, Phillip Gregory 1956- BlkOlyM
**Hubbard**, Reginald T. WhoBlA 92
**Hubbard**, Richard Alexander, II 1926- AmMWSc 92
**Hubbard**, Richard David 1936- Who 92
**Hubbard**, Richard Forest 1948- AmMWSc 92
**Hubbard**, Richard M 1941- WhoAmP 91
**Hubbard**, Richard W 1929- AmMWSc 92
**Hubbard**, Robert Glenn 1958- WhoFI 92
**Hubbard**, Robert Louis, Jr. 1943- WhoRel 92
**Hubbard**, Robert Phillip 1943- AmMWSc 92
**Hubbard**, Roger W 1939- AmMWSc 92
**Hubbard**, Ruth 1924- AmMWSc 92
**Hubbard**, Scott David 1957- WhoAmL 92
**Hubbard**, Stanley, Sr. 1940- WhoBlA 92
**Hubbard**, Stanley Eugene 1897- WhoEnt 92
**Hubbard**, Stanley S. LesBEnT 92
**Hubbard**, Stanley Stub 1933- WhoEnt 92, WhoFI 92, WhoMW 92
**Hubbard**, Susan DrAPF 91
**Hubbard**, T Brannon, Jr 1918- AmMWSc 92
**Hubbard**, Thomas Edwin 1944- WhoAmL 92, WhoFI 92
**Hubbard**, Timothy J. 1945- WhoWest 92

**Hubbard**, Van Saxton 1945- AmMWSc 92
**Hubbard**, Walter T. 1924- WhoBlA 92
**Hubbard**, Willard Dwight 1924- AmMWSc 92
**Hubbard**, William 1621-1704 BenetAL 91
**Hubbard**, William Bogel 1940- AmMWSc 92
**Hubbard**, William DeHart 1903- BlkOlyM
**Hubbard**, William Jack 1943- AmMWSc 92
**Hubbard**, William Marshall 1935- AmMWSc 92
**Hubbard**, William Neill, Jr 1919- AmMWSc 92
**Hubbard**, Z. Dianne 1950- WhoMW 92
**Hubbard-Miles**, Peter Charles 1927- Who 92
**Hubbart**, James E 1925- AmMWSc 92
**Hubbartt**, Ramona A. 1952- WhoMW 92
**Hubbe**, Henry Ernest 1932- WhoFI 92
**Hubbe**, Nikolaj WhoEnt 92
**Hubbel**, Michael Robert 1954- WhoFI 92
**Hubbell**, Billy James 1949- WhoAmL 92
**Hubbell**, Carl 1903-1988 FacFETw
**Hubbell**, Corinne Mallen 1928- WhoAmP 91
**Hubbell**, D S 1904- AmMWSc 92
**Hubbell**, David Heuston 1937- AmMWSc 92
**Hubbell**, Douglas Osborne 1942- AmMWSc 92
**Hubbell**, Ernest 1914- WhoAmL 92
**Hubbell**, Harry Hopkins, Jr 1914- AmMWSc 92
**Hubbell**, James Wallace 1955- WhoAmL 92
**Hubbell**, John Howard 1925- AmMWSc 92
**Hubbell**, Raymond 1879-1954 NewAmDM
**Hubbell**, Robert Newell 1931- WhoWest 92
**Hubbell**, Roger Sherman 1916- WhoMW 92
**Hubbell**, Stephen Philip 1942- AmMWSc 92
**Hubbell**, Wayne Charles 1943- AmMWSc 92
**Hubben**, Klaus 1930- AmMWSc 92
**Hubbert**, Marion King 1903- AmMWSc 92
**Hubbert**, Mark William WhoFI 92
**Hubble**, Billy Ray 1944- AmMWSc 92
**Hubble**, Edwin Powell 1889-1953 FacFETw
**Hubbs**, Clark 1921- AmMWSc 92
**Hubbs**, Orlando 1840-1930 DcNCBi 3
**Hubbs**, Robert A 1935- AmMWSc 92
**Hubbs**, Ronald M. 1908- WhoFI 92, WhoMW 92
**Hubbuch**, Theodore N 1902- AmMWSc 92
**Hubbuck**, Rodney 1940- TwCPaSc
**Hubby**, John L 1932- AmMWSc 92
**Hube**, Douglas Peter 1941- AmMWSc 92
**Hubel**, David Hunter 1926- AmMWSc 92, IntWW 91, Who 92, WhoNob 90
**Hubel**, Dennis James 1947- WhoAmL 92
**Hubel**, Kenneth Andrew 1927- AmMWSc 92
**Huben**, Brian David 1962- WhoAmL 92
**Huben**, Dolores Quevedo 1951- WhoHisp 92
**Hubener**, Helmut 1925-1942 EncTR 91
**Huber**, Antje Charlotte 1924- IntWW 91
**Huber**, Blake 1950- WhoAmP 91
**Huber**, Brigitte T 1948- AmMWSc 92
**Huber**, Calvin 1932- AmMWSc 92
**Huber**, Carol 1937- AmMWSc 92
**Huber**, Clayton Lloyd 1955- WhoFI 92
**Huber**, Clayton Shirl 1938- AmMWSc 92
**Huber**, Colleen Adlene 1927- WhoWest 92
**Huber**, Constance Lynn 1951- WhoMW 92
**Huber**, David Lawrence 1937- AmMWSc 92
**Huber**, Don Morgan 1935- AmMWSc 92
**Huber**, Donald John 1951- AmMWSc 92
**Huber**, Donald Lester 1940- WhoRel 92
**Huber**, Edward Allen 1929- AmMWSc 92
**Huber**, Ernst Rudolf 1903- EncTR 91
**Huber**, Floyd Milton 1937- AmMWSc 92
**Huber**, Francie WhoEnt 92
**Huber**, Gary Louis 1939- AmMWSc 92
**Huber**, Gregory B 1956- WhoAmP 91
**Huber**, Harold E 1925- AmMWSc 92
**Huber**, Ivan 1931- AmMWSc 92
**Huber**, Jack T. WrDr 92
**Huber**, Joan 1925- WomSoc
**Huber**, Joan MacMonnies 1927- WhoFI 92
**Huber**, Joe Roger 1957- WhoMW 92
**Huber**, Joel E 1936- AmMWSc 92
**Huber**, John Michael 1958- WhoFI 92
**Huber**, John Talmage 1931- AmMWSc 92
**Huber**, Joseph William, III 1944- AmMWSc 92
**Huber**, Karl 1915- IntWW 91
**Huber**, Katherine Jeanne 1958- WhoMW 92
**Huber**, Klaus 1924- NewAmDM
**Huber**, Kurt 1893-1943 EncTR 91 [port]
**Huber**, Margaret Ann 1949- WhoRel 92
**Huber**, Melvin Lefever 1922- AmMWSc 92
**Huber**, Michel Thomas 1931- WhoFI 92
**Huber**, Nicolaus A 1939- ConCom 92
**Huber**, Norman Fred 1935- WhoWest 92
**Huber**, Norman King 1926- AmMWSc 92, WhoWest 92
**Huber**, Oren John 1917- AmMWSc 92
**Huber**, Paul W 1920- AmMWSc 92
**Huber**, Peter William 1952- AmMWSc 92
**Huber**, Raymond C 1917- AmMWSc 92
**Huber**, Raymond Stewart 1957- WhoAmP 91
**Huber**, Richard Glen 1937- WhoMW 92
**Huber**, Richard Leslie 1936- WhoMW 92
**Huber**, Richard Miller 1922- WrDr 92
**Huber**, Richard V 1948- AmMWSc 92
**Huber**, Rita Norma 1931- WhoAmP 91
**Huber**, Robert 1937- AmMWSc 92, IntWW 91, Who 92, WhoNob 90
**Huber**, Robert Daniel 1922- WhoAmP 91
**Huber**, Robert John 1935- AmMWSc 92
**Huber**, Robert T 1920- WhoAmP 91
**Huber**, Roger Thomas 1934- AmMWSc 92
**Huber**, Rudolf Paul 1954- WhoFI 92
**Huber**, Rueben Eugene 1940- AmMWSc 92
**Huber**, Samuel G 1918- AmMWSc 92
**Huber**, Thomas Albert 1957- WhoEnt 92
**Huber**, Thomas Lee 1935- AmMWSc 92
**Huber**, Thomas Wayne 1942- AmMWSc 92
**Huber**, W Frederick 1918- AmMWSc 92
**Huber**, Wayne Charles 1941- AmMWSc 92
**Huber**, William Richard, III 1941- AmMWSc 92
**Huberman**, Bernardo Abel 1943- AmMWSc 92
**Huberman**, Bronislaw 1882-1947 NewAmDM
**Huberman**, Eliezer 1939- AmMWSc 92
**Huberman**, Jeffrey Howard 1948- WhoEnt 92
**Huberman**, Joel Anthony 1941- AmMWSc 92
**Huberman**, Marshall Norman 1932- AmMWSc 92
**Hubert**, Becky Bryant 1951- WhoMW 92
**Hubert**, Bernard 1929- WhoRel 92
**Hubert**, Dick LesBEnT 92
**Hubert**, Helen Betty 1950- AmMWSc 92
**Hubert**, Janette Louise 1962- WhoEnt 92
**Hubert**, Jay Marvin 1944- AmMWSc 92
**Hubert**, Jean-Loup 1949- WhoEnt 92
**Hubert**, Jean-Luc 1960- WhoFI 92, WhoMW 92
**Hubert**, Jim DrAPF 91
**Hubert**, John Frederick 1930- AmMWSc 92
**Hubert**, Richard Frank 1938- WhoEnt 92
**Huberty**, Carl J 1934- AmMWSc 92
**Hubiak**, Daniel 1926- WhoRel 92
**Hubin**, Wilbert N 1938- AmMWSc 92
**Hubing**, Leone X 1912- WhoAmP 91
**Hubins**, Arlie Karen 1953- WhoWest 92
**Hubisz**, John Lawrence, Jr 1938- AmMWSc 92
**Hubka**, William Frank 1939- AmMWSc 92
**Hubler**, Bruce Albert 1944- WhoFI 92
**Hubler**, David E. DrAPF 91
**Hubler**, Graham Kelder, Jr 1944- AmMWSc 92
**Hubler**, James Terrence 1943- WhoFI 92
**Hubler**, Mary 1952- WhoAmP 91
**Hubler**, Myron J., Jr. 1928- WhoRel 92
**Hubler**, Richard G. DrAPF 91
**Hubler**, Richard G 1912- IntAu&W 91
**Hubler**, Shane Lauson 1964- WhoMW 92
**Hubley**, Faith LesBEnT 92
**Hubley**, John d1977 LesBEnT 92
**Hubley**, Season WhoEnt 92
**Hublitz**, Sue 1940- WhoFI 92
**Hubner**, David Peter 1940- WhoRel 92
**Hubner**, Karl Franz 1934- AmMWSc 92
**Hubred**, Gale L 1939- AmMWSc 92
**Hubscher**, Arthur Ronald 1933- WhoAmP 91
**Hubschman**, Henry Allan 1947- WhoAmL 92
**Hubschman**, Jerry Henry 1929- AmMWSc 92, WhoMW 92
**Hubschman**, Thomas DrAPF 91
**Hubsher**, Muriel WhoAmL 92
**Huby**, Pamela Margaret 1922- IntAu&W 91, WrDr 92
**Huby**, Peter 1946- TwCPaSc
**Hucbald** 840?-930 NewAmDM
**Huch**, Ricarda 1864-1947 EncTR 91 [port]
**Huchel**, Peter 1903-1981 LiExTwC
**Huchital**, Daniel H 1940- AmMWSc 92
**Huchra**, John P 1948- AmMWSc 92
**Huchteman**, Ralph Douglas 1946- WhoAmL 92
**Huck**, Arthur 1926- WrDr 92
**Huck**, Edward Joseph 1949- WhoAmP 91
**Huck**, John Lloyd 1922- IntWW 91, WhoFI 92
**Huck**, L. Francis 1947- WhoAmL 92
**Huck**, Larry Ralph 1942- WhoWest 92
**Huck**, Matthew L. 1961- WhoWest 92
**Huck**, Michael Vette 1956- WhoFI 92
**Huck**, Morris Glen 1937- AmMWSc 92
**Huck**, Richard Felix, III 1957- WhoAmL 92
**Hucka**, Vladimir Joseph 1925- AmMWSc 92
**Huckaba**, Charles Edwin 1922- AmMWSc 92
**Huckaba**, Frank J 1934- WhoAmP 91
**Huckaba**, James Albert 1936- AmMWSc 92
**Huckaba**, James Allen 1946- WhoRel 92
**Huckabay**, Houston Keller 1932- AmMWSc 92
**Huckabay**, John Porter 1928- AmMWSc 92
**Huckabee**, Michael Dale 1955- WhoRel 92
**Huckabee**, Phyllis 1963- WhoWest 92
**Huckabee**, Thomas Eric 1952- WhoFI 92
**Huckaby**, Dale Alan 1944- AmMWSc 92
**Huckaby**, David George 1942- AmMWSc 92
**Huckaby**, Henry Lafayette 1934- WhoBlA 92
**Huckaby**, Hilry, III 1944- WhoBlA 92
**Huckaby**, Jerry 1941- AlmAP 92 [port]
**Huckaby**, Teri Lynn 1962- WhoRel 92
**Huckaby**, Thomas J 1941- WhoAmP 91
**Hucke**, Dorothy Marie 1927- AmMWSc 92
**Hucke**, Edward E 1930- AmMWSc 92
**Huckeby**, Karen Marie 1957- WhoWest 92
**Hucker**, Howard B 1926- AmMWSc 92
**Hucker**, Michael Frederick 1933- Who 92
**Huckfield**, Leslie 1942- Who 92
**Huckins**, Vernon Dale 1944- WhoFI 92
**Huckins**, William Judd 1927- WhoAmL 92
**Huckle**, George 1914- Who 92
**Hucko**, Michael 1918- WhoEnt 92
**Huckstep**, Ronald Lawrie 1926- IntWW 91, Who 92
**Hucles**, Henry B., III 1923- WhoBlA 92
**Huda**, Mirza Nurul 1919- IntWW 91
**Hudak**, George 1935- WhoAmP 91
**Hudak**, Michael J 1952- AmMWSc 92
**Hudak**, Norman John 1933- AmMWSc 92
**Hudak**, Paul Raymond 1952- AmMWSc 92
**Hudak**, William John 1929- AmMWSc 92
**Hudale**, James Scott 1965- WhoFI 92
**Hudd**, Roy 1936- Who 92
**Hudde**, Andries 1608-1663 BiInAmS
**Huddie**, David 1916- Who 92
**Huddle**, Benjamin Paul, Jr 1941- AmMWSc 92
**Huddle**, David DrAPF 91
**Huddle**, David 1942- WrDr 92
**Huddle**, Donald Leroy 1933- WhoFI 92
**Huddleson**, Edwin Emmett, III 1945- WhoAmL 92
**Huddleston**, Charles Martin 1925- AmMWSc 92
**Huddleston**, David 1930- IntMPA 92
**Huddleston**, David Winfield 1943- WhoRel 92
**Huddleston**, Ellis Wright 1935- AmMWSc 92
**Huddleston**, George Richmond, Jr 1921- AmMWSc 92
**Huddleston**, Jackson Noyes, Jr. 1938- WhoWest 92
**Huddleston**, James Herbert 1942- AmMWSc 92
**Huddleston**, John Derek 1934- IntAu&W 91
**Huddleston**, John Henry 1864-1915 BiInAmS
**Huddleston**, John Vincent 1928- AmMWSc 92
**Huddleston**, Joseph Russell 1937- WhoAmL 92
**Huddleston**, Joseph Wayne 1948- WhoMW 92, WhoRel 92
**Huddleston**, Philip Lee 1947- AmMWSc 92
**Huddleston**, Richard Elbert 1950- WhoMW 92
**Huddleston**, Robert E 1939- AmMWSc 92
**Huddleston**, Trevor 1913- IntWW 91, Who 92, WrDr 92
**Huddleston**, Walter D. 1926- IntWW 91
**Huddleston**, Walter Darlington 1926- WhoAmP 91
**Huddlestone**, Richard H 1926- AmMWSc 92
**Hudecek**, Vaclav 1952- IntWW 91
**Hudecki**, Michael Stephen 1943- AmMWSc 92
**Hudgens**, Richard Watts 1931- AmMWSc 92, WhoMW 92
**Hudgens**, Richard Wayne 1955- WhoRel 92
**Hudgeons**, Louise Taylor 1931- WhoBlA 92
**Hudgik**, Steven C. 1951- WhoFI 92
**Hudgin**, Donald Edward 1917- AmMWSc 92
**Hudgins**, Andrew DrAPF 91
**Hudgins**, Arthur Judson 1920- AmMWSc 92
**Hudgins**, Aubrey C, Jr 1935- AmMWSc 92
**Hudgins**, Bonnie Jenell 1949- WhoFI 92
**Hudgins**, Catherine Harding 1913- WhoFI 92
**Hudgins**, David Drake 1955- WhoAmL 92
**Hudgins**, Dudley Rodger 1937- WhoRel 92
**Hudgins**, Gary A. 1953- WhoAmL 92
**Hudgins**, Patricia Montague 1938- AmMWSc 92
**Hudgins**, Robert R 1937- AmMWSc 92
**Hudiak**, David Michael 1953- WhoAmL 92
**Hudiburg**, John Justus, Jr. 1928- WhoFI 92
**Hudik**, Martin Francis 1949- WhoFI 92, WhoMW 92
**Hudis**, Jerome 1925- AmMWSc 92
**Hudis**, Jonathan 1963- WhoAmL 92
**Hudkins**, John Wayne 1946- WhoAmL 92
**Hudler**, George William 1947- AmMWSc 92
**Hudleston**, Edmund C. 1908- Who 92
**Hudleston**, Peter John 1944- AmMWSc 92
**Hudley**, James C. 1943- WhoRel 92
**Hudlicky**, Milos 1919- AmMWSc 92
**Hudlicky**, Tomas 1949- AmMWSc 92
**Hudlin**, Reginald NewYTBS 91
**Hudlin**, Reginald Alan 1961- WhoBlA 92, WhoEnt 92
**Hudlin**, Richard A. 1934- WhoBlA 92
**Hudlin**, Warrington NewYTBS 91, WhoBlA 92, WhoEnt 92
**Hudlow**, Michael Dale 1940- AmMWSc 92
**Hudlun**, Anna 1819-1914 NotBlAW 92
**Hudnall**, David Harrison 1948- WhoFI 92
**Hudnall**, Phillip Montgomery 1944- AmMWSc 92
**Hudner**, Philip 1931- WhoAmL 92
**Hudnut**, Robert K. 1934- WrDr 92
**Hudnut**, Robert Kilborne 1934- WhoRel 92
**Hudnut**, William Herbert, III 1932- WhoAmP 91, WhoMW 92
**Hudock**, George Anthony 1937- AmMWSc 92
**Hudock**, Joseph Andrew, Sr. 1937- WhoAmL 92
**Hudock**, William J 1950- WhoAmP 91
**Hudome**, Michael J 1962- WhoAmP 91
**Hudon**, L. Denis 1924- IntWW 91
**Hudrlik**, Anne Marie 1941- AmMWSc 92
**Hudrlik**, Paul Frederick 1941- AmMWSc 92
**Hudson**, Alan P 1948- AmMWSc 92
**Hudson**, Albert Berry 1929- AmMWSc 92
**Hudson**, Alice Marilyn 1930- WhoFI 92
**Hudson**, Alice Peterson 1942- AmMWSc 92
**Hudson**, Alvin Maynard 1922- AmMWSc 92
**Hudson**, Andrew Harold 1915- WhoBlA 92
**Hudson**, Anne Lester 1932- AmMWSc 92
**Hudson**, Anne Mary 1938- Who 92
**Hudson**, Anthony Hugh 1928- Who 92
**Hudson**, Anthony Webster 1937- WhoBlA 92
**Hudson**, Arthur Palmer 1892-1978 DcNCBi 3
**Hudson**, Barbara Jayne 1962- WhoMW 92
**Hudson**, Barbara T 1952- WhoIns 92
**Hudson**, Betty 1931- WhoAmP 91
**Hudson**, Bill WhoAmP 91
**Hudson**, Billy Gerald 1941- AmMWSc 92
**Hudson**, Bruce William 1928- AmMWSc 92
**Hudson**, C B WhoIns 92
**Hudson**, Cecil Ivan, Jr 1937- AmMWSc 92
**Hudson**, Charles 1932- WrDr 92
**Hudson**, Charles Daugherty 1927- WhoFI 92
**Hudson**, Charles Franklin, III 1953- WhoWest 92
**Hudson**, Charles Lynn 1959- WhoBlA 92
**Hudson**, Charles Michael 1935- AmMWSc 92
**Hudson**, Christopher 1946- IntAu&W 91
**Hudson**, Christopher John 1948- WhoWest 92
**Hudson**, Cola H 1926- WhoAmP 91
**Hudson**, David Darrell 1952- WhoWest 92
**Hudson**, David Frank 1937- AmMWSc 92
**Hudson**, Dennis Lee 1936- WhoAmL 92
**Hudson**, Derek 1911- IntAu&W 91, WrDr 92
**Hudson**, Derek Fernando 1952- WhoFI 92
**Hudson**, Donald E 1916- AmMWSc 92
**Hudson**, Donald Edwin 1921- AmMWSc 92

**Hudson,** Donald J. 1930- *WhoFI 92, WhoWest 92*
**Hudson,** Donna Lee 1946- *WhoWest 92*
**Hudson,** Edward Voyle 1915- *WhoWest 92*
**Hudson,** Elbert T. *WhoBlA 92*
**Hudson,** Eleanor Erlund 1912- *Who 92*
**Hudson,** Erlund *Who 92*
**Hudson,** Ernie *IntMPA 92*
**Hudson,** Fleeta Cain 1935- *WhoAmP 91*
**Hudson,** Frank Alden 1923- *AmMWSc 92*
**Hudson,** Frank M 1935- *AmMWSc 92*
**Hudson,** Frank Michael Stanislaus 1916- *Who 92*
**Hudson,** Frederick Bernard 1947- *WhoBlA 92*
**Hudson,** Frederick Douglass 1928- *WhoBlA 92*
**Hudson,** Frederick Mitchell 1934- *AmMWSc 92*
**Hudson,** George 1919- *WhoAmP 91*
**Hudson,** George 1924- *Who 92*
**Hudson,** George Elbert 1916- *AmMWSc 92*
**Hudson,** H Claude 1886-1989 *FacFETw*
**Hudson,** Harold Don 1943- *WhoMW 92*
**Hudson,** Havelock 1919- *Who 92*
**Hudson,** Havelock Henry Trevor 1919- *IntWW 91*
**Hudson,** Helen 1920- *WrDr 92*
**Hudson,** Henry d1611? *BenetAL 91*
**Hudson,** Herman C. 1923- *WhoBlA 92*
**Hudson,** Hilliard Clyde 1954- *WhoRel 92*
**Hudson,** Hosea Peter 1932- *WhoMW 92*
**Hudson,** Hugh *IntMPA 92, IntWW 91*
**Hudson,** Hugh T 1933- *AmMWSc 92*
**Hudson,** Ian Francis 1925- *Who 92*
**Hudson,** J L 1937- *AmMWSc 92*
**Hudson,** Jack William, Jr 1926- *AmMWSc 92*
**Hudson,** James Blaine, III 1949- *WhoBlA 92*
**Hudson,** James Bloomer 1927- *AmMWSc 92*
**Hudson,** James Gary 1946- *AmMWSc 92*
**Hudson,** James Ralph 1916- *Who 92*
**Hudson,** James Wesley, Jr. 1946- *WhoWest 92*
**Hudson,** Jan *WrDr 92*
**Hudson,** Jeffrey *IntAu&W 91X, WrDr 92*
**Hudson,** Jeffrey Foster 1949- *WhoFI 92*
**Hudson,** Jeffrey Reid 1952- *WhoAmL 92*
**Hudson,** Jerome William 1953- *WhoBlA 92*
**Hudson,** John Arthur 1920- *Who 92*
**Hudson,** John B 1934- *AmMWSc 92*
**Hudson,** John Boswell 1930- *WhoFI 92*
**Hudson,** John D. 1927- *WhoBlA 92*
**Hudson,** John Pilkington 1910- *Who 92*
**Hudson,** Joseph Charles 1943- *WhoMW 92*
**Hudson,** Juley 1963- *TwCPaSc*
**Hudson,** Keith 1954- *WhoBlA 92*
**Hudson,** Keith Henry 1939- *WhoFI 92*
**Hudson,** Keith William 1928- *Who 92*
**Hudson,** Les Eugene 1961- *WhoRel 92*
**Hudson,** Lester Darnell 1949- *WhoBlA 92*
**Hudson,** Liam 1933- *IntAu&W 91, Who 92, WrDr 92*
**Hudson,** Lincoln Theodore 1916-1988 *WhoBlA 92N*
**Hudson,** Lois Phillips 1927- *TwCWW 91, WrDr 92*
**Hudson,** Lou 1944- *WhoBlA 92*
**Hudson,** Lynn Diane 1953- *AmMWSc 92*
**Hudson,** Manley Ottmer 1886-1960 *AmPeW*
**Hudson,** Marc *DrAPF 91*
**Hudson,** Marisu 1958- *WhoEnt 92*
**Hudson,** Martha 1939- *BlkOlyM*
**Hudson,** Mary Katherine 1949- *AmMWSc 92*
**Hudson,** Maurice William Petre 1901- *Who 92*
**Hudson,** Merry C. 1943- *WhoBlA 92*
**Hudson,** Michael *TwCSFW 91*
**Hudson,** Michael Elliott, Sr. 1955- *WhoWest 92*
**Hudson,** Myra Linden Frank 1950- *WhoFI 92*
**Hudson,** Newt 1926- *WhoAmP 91*
**Hudson,** Nora Malliene 1955- *WhoAmP 91*
**Hudson,** Norman Barrie 1937- *Who 92*
**Hudson,** Page 1931- *AmMWSc 92*
**Hudson,** Pamela May *Who 92*
**Hudson,** Paul Stephen 1947- *WhoAmL 92*
**Hudson,** Peggy R 1947- *AmMWSc 92*
**Hudson,** Peter 1923- *Who 92*
**Hudson,** Peter Geoffrey 1926- *Who 92*
**Hudson,** Peter John 1919- *Who 92*
**Hudson,** Ralph P 1924- *AmMWSc 92*
**Hudson,** Rebekah Jane 1962- *WhoRel 92*
**Hudson,** Reggie Lester 1952- *AmMWSc 92*
**Hudson,** Repps Bedford 1946- *WhoMW 92*
**Hudson,** Richard Delano, Jr 1924- *AmMWSc 92*
**Hudson,** Richard Lloyd 1920- *WhoRel 92*
**Hudson,** Robert B 1920- *AmMWSc 92*
**Hudson,** Robert Douglas 1931- *AmMWSc 92*
**Hudson,** Robert Francis 1922- *IntWW 91, Who 92*
**Hudson,** Robert Frank *AmMWSc 92*
**Hudson,** Robert Franklin, Jr. 1946- *WhoAmL 92*
**Hudson,** Robert L. 1939- *WhoBlA 92*
**Hudson,** Robert McKim 1926- *AmMWSc 92*
**Hudson,** Robert Y 1912- *AmMWSc 92*
**Hudson,** Rock 1925-1985 *FacFETw*
**Hudson,** Rodney Merrell 1957- *WhoEnt 92*
**Hudson,** Ronald Morgan 1954- *WhoMW 92*
**Hudson,** Roy 1925- *WhoAmP 91*
**Hudson,** Roy Davage 1930- *AmMWSc 92, WhoBlA 92*
**Hudson,** Samuel W, III *WhoAmP 91*
**Hudson,** Samuel William, III 1940- *WhoBlA 92*
**Hudson,** Sidney Allen 1954- *WhoAmP 91*
**Hudson,** Sigmund Nyrop 1936- *AmMWSc 92*
**Hudson,** Sterling Henry, III 1950- *WhoBlA 92*
**Hudson,** Steven David 1961- *AmMWSc 92*
**Hudson,** Terry V 1944- *WhoIns 92*
**Hudson,** Theodore R. *WhoBlA 92*
**Hudson,** Thomas Charles 1915- *IntWW 91, Who 92*
**Hudson,** Thomas H 1946- *WhoAmP 91*
**Hudson,** Thomson Jay 1834-1903 *BiInAmS*
**Hudson,** Tom 1922- *TwCPaSc*
**Hudson,** Victor Talmage 1943- *WhoAmL 92*
**Hudson,** W.H. 1841-1922 *RfGEnL 91, ScFEYrs*
**Hudson,** William H 1841-1922 *FacFETw*
**Hudson,** William L. *WhoEnt 92*
**Hudson,** William Meredith Fisher 1916- *Who 92*
**Hudson,** William Nathaniel *AmMWSc 92*
**Hudson,** William Ronald 1933- *AmMWSc 92*
**Hudson,** William Rucker 1925- *AmMWSc 92*
**Hudson,** William Thomas 1929- *WhoBlA 92*
**Hudson,** Wilma Jones 1916- *WrDr 92*
**Hudson,** Winson *WhoBlA 92*
**Hudson,** Winson 1916- *WhoAmP 91*
**Hudson,** Winthrop S. 1911- *WrDr 92*
**Hudson,** Winthrop Still 1911- *WhoRel 92*
**Hudson,** Yeager 1931- *WhoRel 92*
**Hudson-Bendersky,** Pamela May 1931- *Who 92*
**Hudson Davies,** Ednyfed *Who 92*
**Hudson-Knapp,** Marshall Ralph 1949- *WhoRel 92*
**Hudson-Weems,** Clenora Frances 1945- *WhoBlA 92*
**Hudson-Williams,** Harri Llwyd 1911- *Who 92*
**Hudspeth,** Albert James 1945- *AmMWSc 92*
**Hudspeth,** Emmett Leroy 1916- *AmMWSc 92*
**Hudspeth,** Gregory Charles, Sr. 1947- *WhoBlA 92*
**Hudspeth,** Harry Lee 1935- *WhoAmL 92*
**Hudspeth,** Stephen Mason 1947- *WhoAmL 92*
**Hudspith,** Vicki *DrAPF 91*
**Hueber,** W. Graham 1959- *WhoFI 92*
**Huebert,** Barry Joe 1945- *AmMWSc 92*
**Huebner,** Albert Louis 1931- *AmMWSc 92*
**Huebner,** Clarence R 1888-1972 *FacFETw*
**Huebner,** Donald Frank 1925- *WhoFI 92, WhoMW 92*
**Huebner,** Erwin 1943- *AmMWSc 92*
**Huebner,** Fredrick D. 1955- *ConAu 133*
**Huebner,** George J 1910- *AmMWSc 92*
**Huebner,** George L, Jr 1918- *AmMWSc 92*
**Huebner,** Gregory Karl 1953- *WhoMW 92*
**Huebner,** Jay Stanley 1939- *AmMWSc 92*
**Huebner,** John Stephen 1940- *AmMWSc 92*
**Huebner,** Judith Dee 1947- *AmMWSc 92*
**Huebner,** Kathleen Mary 1945- *WhoRel 92*
**Huebner,** Michael Denis 1941- *Who 92*
**Huebner,** Paul John 1959- *WhoMW 92*
**Huebner,** Robert Joseph 1914- *AmMWSc 92*
**Huebner,** Russell Henry, Sr 1941- *AmMWSc 92*
**Huebner,** Walter F 1928- *AmMWSc 92*
**Huebsch,** Ian O 1927- *AmMWSc 92*
**Huebsch,** Tony Louis 1929- *WhoMW 92*
**Huebschman,** Eugene Carl 1919- *AmMWSc 92*
**Huebschman,** Paula JoAnn 1964- *WhoRel 92*
**Huebschmann,** John W 1924- *AmMWSc 92*
**Hueca,** La Nina de la *EncAmaz 91*
**Hueckels,** Jack G *ScFEYrs*
**Hueg,** William Frederick, Jr 1924- *AmMWSc 92*
**Huege,** Fred Robert 1943- *AmMWSc 92*
**Huegel,** Virginia Lee 1949- *WhoMW 92*
**Huegel,** William A. 1943- *WhoRel 92*
**Hueglin,** Steven J. d1991 *NewYTBS 91 [port]*
**Huehner,** Martin Klaus 1948- *WhoMW 92*
**Huelke,** Donald Fred 1930- *AmMWSc 92*
**Huellen,** Juergen 1956- *WhoMW 92*
**Huels,** Patrick 1949- *WhoAmP 91*
**Huelsman,** Joanne B 1938- *WhoAmP 91*
**Huelsman,** Lawrence Paul 1926- *AmMWSc 92*
**Huenefeld,** Fred, Jr 1929- *WhoAmP 91*
**Huenefeld,** Thomas Ernst 1937- *WhoFI 92*
**Hueneke,** Terry A. 1942- *WhoFI 92*
**Huenemann,** Edward Martin 1920- *WhoRel 92*
**Huenemann,** Joel *WhoRel 92*
**Huenemann,** Ruben Henry 1909- *WhoRel 92*
**Huenemann,** Ruth L 1910- *AmMWSc 92*
**Huening,** Walter C, Jr 1923- *AmMWSc 92*
**Huenink,** Jeffrey C 1956- *WhoAmP 91*
**Huennekens,** Frank Matthew, Jr 1923- *AmMWSc 92*
**Huennekens,** John Patrick 1952- *AmMWSc 92*
**Huereque,** Cynthia Patricia 1947- *WhoHisp 92*
**Huerner,** Martin Richard 1946- *WhoMW 92*
**Huerta,** Albert 1943- *WhoHisp 92*
**Huerta,** David 1949- *ConSpAP*
**Huerta,** Dolores 1930- *HanAmWH*
**Huerta,** Dolores Fernandez 1930- *WhoHisp 92*
**Huerta,** Efrain 1914-1982 *ConSpAP*
**Huerta,** John Edmund 1943- *WhoAmL 92*
**Huerta,** Jorge Alfonso 1942- *WhoEnt 92*
**Huerta,** Manuel Andres 1943- *AmMWSc 92*
**Huerta,** Michael Peter 1956- *WhoHisp 92*
**Huerta,** Ramon 1924- *WhoAmP 91, WhoHisp 92*
**Huerta,** Ventura Perez 1933- *WhoHisp 92*
**Huerta Diaz,** Ismael 1916- *IntWW 91*
**Huertas,** Jorge 1924- *AmMWSc 92*
**Huerter,** Regina Marie 1960- *WhoWest 92*
**Huesca,** Robert Thomas 1959- *WhoHisp 92*
**Huesca Pacheco,** Rosendo 1932- *WhoRel 92*
**Hueser,** Roberta Jean 1932- *WhoMW 92*
**Huesmann,** Louis MacDonald 1957- *WhoRel 92*
**Huessy,** Hans Rosenstock 1921- *AmMWSc 92*
**Huestis,** David Lee 1946- *AmMWSc 92*
**Huestis,** Douglas William 1925- *AmMWSc 92*
**Huestis,** Laurence Dean 1934- *AmMWSc 92*
**Huestis,** Stephen Porter 1946- *AmMWSc 92*
**Hueston,** Oliver David 1941- *WhoBlA 92*
**Huet,** Philippe Emile Jean 1920- *IntWW 91*
**Huet,** Pierre 1920- *IntWW 91*
**Huet,** Thomas Victor 1955- *WhoEnt 92*
**Huete,** Stephen Marc 1955- *WhoHisp 92*
**Hueter,** Francis Gordon 1929- *AmMWSc 92*
**Hueter,** James Warren 1925- *WhoWest 92*
**Hueter,** Richard George 1935- *WhoRel 92*
**Hueter,** Theodor Friedrich 1917- *AmMWSc 92*
**Huether,** Carl Albert 1937- *AmMWSc 92*
**Huether,** Robert *WhoAmP 91*
**Huetig,** Roger Dean 1947- *WhoAmP 91*
**Huettner,** David Joseph 1938- *AmMWSc 92*
**Huettner,** Richard Alfred 1927- *WhoAmL 92, WhoFI 92*
**Huey,** Edmund Burke 1870-1913 *BiInAmS*
**Huey,** F. B., Jr. 1925- *WhoRel 92*
**Huey,** Mark C. *DrAPF 91*
**Huey,** Raymond Brunson 1944- *AmMWSc 92*
**Huey,** William S 1925- *AmMWSc 92*
**Hufana,** Alejandrino G. 1926- *ConPo 91, IntAu&W 91, WrDr 92*
**Huff,** Albert Keith 1942- *AmMWSc 92*
**Huff,** Barbara A. 1929- *ConAu 135, SmATA 67 [port]*
**Huff,** Brett Eugene 1960- *WhoRel 92*
**Huff,** Charles William 1920- *AmMWSc 92*
**Huff,** Dale Duane 1939- *AmMWSc 92*
**Huff,** Dale Eugene 1930- *WhoWest 92*
**Huff,** David Lawrence 1957- *WhoRel 92*
**Huff,** David Richard 1948- *WhoMW 92*
**Huff,** Dennis Karl 1940- *AmMWSc 92*
**Huff,** Douglas Lee 1944- *WhoMW 92*
**Huff,** Edgar R. 1919- *WhoBlA 92*
**Huff,** Gayle Compton 1956- *WhoMW 92*
**Huff,** Gene 1929- *WhoAmP 91*
**Huff,** George Franklin 1923- *AmMWSc 92*
**Huff,** H. Stanley 1925- *WhoMW 92*
**Huff,** Helen Schaeffer 1883-1913 *BiInAmS*
**Huff,** James Eli 1928- *AmMWSc 92*
**Huff,** Janice Wages 1960- *WhoBlA 92*
**Huff,** Jesse William 1916- *AmMWSc 92*
**Huff,** John David 1952- *WhoMW 92, WhoRel 92*
**Huff,** John Gardner 1951- *WhoAmP 91*
**Huff,** Kenneth O 1926- *AmMWSc 92, WhoWest 92*
**Huff,** Larry Waldo 1953- *WhoRel 92*
**Huff,** Laura Weaver 1930- *WhoEnt 92*
**Huff,** Leon Alexander 1942- *WhoBlA 92*
**Huff,** Louis Andrew 1949- *WhoBlA 92*
**Huff,** Lula Lunsford 1949- *WhoBlA 92*
**Huff,** Marilyn L. 1951- *WhoAmL 92*
**Huff,** Norman Leroy 1921- *WhoRel 92*
**Huff,** Norman Nelson 1933- *WhoFI 92, WhoWest 92*
**Huff,** Norman Thomas 1940- *AmMWSc 92*
**Huff,** Ocie Burgess 1935- *WhoWest 92*
**Huff,** Ralph Richard 1944- *WhoAmP 91*
**Huff,** Robert *DrAPF 91*
**Huff,** Robert 1924- *IntAu&W 91*
**Huff,** Thomas Allen 1935- *AmMWSc 92*
**Huff,** Thomas Ellis 1949- *WhoAmP 91*
**Huff,** W Ray 1935- *WhoAmP 91*
**Huff,** Warren D 1937- *AmMWSc 92*
**Huff,** William 1920- *WhoBlA 92*
**Huff,** William Henry, III 1937- *WhoIns 92*
**Huff,** William J 1919- *AmMWSc 92*
**Huff,** William Nathan 1912- *AmMWSc 92*
**Huffaker,** Carl Barton 1914- *AmMWSc 92*
**Huffaker,** Clair 1928-1990 *TwCWW 91*
**Huffaker,** James Neal 1937- *AmMWSc 92*
**Huffaker,** John Boston 1925- *WhoAmL 92*
**Huffaker,** Ray C 1929- *AmMWSc 92*
**Huffine,** Coy L 1924- *AmMWSc 92*
**Huffine,** Virginia Elizabeth 1922- *WhoEnt 92*
**Huffine,** Wayne Winfield 1919- *AmMWSc 92*
**Huffines,** William Davis 1927- *AmMWSc 92*
**Huffington,** Arianna Stassinopoulos *WrDr 92*
**Huffington,** Norris J, Jr 1921- *AmMWSc 92*
**Huffington,** Roy Michael 1917- *AmMWSc 92, WhoAmP 91, WhoFI 92*
**Huffinley,** Beryl 1926- *Who 92*
**Huffman,** Alice A 1936- *WhoAmP 91*
**Huffman,** Allan Murray 1936- *AmMWSc 92*
**Huffman,** Arlie Curtis, Jr. 1942- *WhoWest 92*
**Huffman,** Bill S 1924- *WhoAmP 91*
**Huffman,** Dale L 1931- *AmMWSc 92*
**Huffman,** David A 1925- *AmMWSc 92*
**Huffman,** David Curtis 1950- *WhoRel 92*
**Huffman,** David George 1941- *AmMWSc 92*
**Huffman,** Dayon Lee 1944- *WhoRel 92*
**Huffman,** Delia Gonzalez 1953- *WhoHisp 92*
**Huffman,** Dennis Don 1942- *WhoMW 92*
**Huffman,** Donald Marion 1929- *AmMWSc 92*
**Huffman,** Donald Ray 1935- *AmMWSc 92*
**Huffman,** Donald Wise 1927- *WhoAmP 91*
**Huffman,** Doris R *WhoAmP 91*
**Huffman,** Edgar Joseph 1939- *WhoFI 92, WhoWest 92*
**Huffman,** Ernest Otto 1911- *AmMWSc 92*
**Huffman,** Fred Norman 1932- *AmMWSc 92*
**Huffman,** George Garrett 1916- *AmMWSc 92*
**Huffman,** George Wallen 1921- *AmMWSc 92*
**Huffman,** Gerald P 1938- *AmMWSc 92*
**Huffman,** Gordon Seth, Jr. 1943- *WhoRel 92*
**Huffman,** Harry Dale 1943- *WhoAmP 91*
**Huffman,** Jacob Brainard 1919- *AmMWSc 92*
**Huffman,** James Thomas William 1947- *WhoFI 92*
**Huffman,** Jasper Jefferson, III 1944- *WhoBlA 92*
**Huffman,** John Abram, Jr. 1940- *WhoRel 92*
**Huffman,** John Curtis 1941- *AmMWSc 92*
**Huffman,** John William 1903- *AmMWSc 92*
**Huffman,** John William, Jr 1932- *AmMWSc 92*
**Huffman,** John William, Jr. 1953- *WhoRel 92*
**Huffman,** K Robert 1933- *AmMWSc 92*
**Huffman,** Louie Clarence 1926- *AmMWSc 92*
**Huffman,** Margaret Ann 1955- *WhoRel 92*
**Huffman,** Nona Gay 1942- *WhoWest 92*
**Huffman,** Odell Hampton 1923- *WhoAmP 91*
**Huffman,** Phyllis *ConAu 133*

**Huffman**, Robert Allen, Jr. 1950- *WhoAmL 92*
**Huffman**, Robert Eugene 1931- *AmMWSc 92*
**Huffman**, Robert Obediah 1890-1978 *DcNCBi 3*
**Huffman**, Robert Wesly 1932- *AmMWSc 92*
**Huffman**, Ronald Dean 1937- *AmMWSc 92*
**Huffman**, Rufus C. 1927- *WhoBlA 92*
**Huffman**, Samuel Floyd 1936- *WhoMW 92*
**Huffman**, T. Brent 1944- *WhoWest 92*
**Huffman**, Ted E. 1953- *WhoRel 92*
**Huffman**, Thomas Alexander 1927- *WhoWest 92*
**Huffman**, Tommie Ray 1929- *AmMWSc 92*
**Huffman**, Vernon 1955- *WhoEnt 92*
**Huffman**, Willard Keith 1939- *WhoRel 92*
**Huffman**, William C. 1955- *WhoAmL 92*
**Huffnagle**, Norman Parmley 1941- *WhoFI 92, WhoWest 92*
**Hufford**, Charles David 1944- *AmMWSc 92*
**Hufford**, George 1927- *AmMWSc 92*
**Hufford**, Scott Alan 1959- *WhoMW 92*
**Hufford**, Terry Lee 1935- *AmMWSc 92*
**Huffstetler**, Palmer Eugene 1937- *WhoAmL 92, WhoFI 92*
**Huffstutler**, Edgar Lane 1920- *WhoRel 92, WhoWest 92*
**Hufham**, Barbara Frances 1939- *WhoAmL 92*
**Hufham**, James Birk 1935- *AmMWSc 92*
**Hufham**, James Dunn 1834-1921 *DcNCBi 3*
**Hufker**, Barry Eugene 1954- *WhoMW 92*
**Hufnagel**, Charles Anthony 1916- *AmMWSc 92*
**Hufnagel**, Charles Anthony 1916-1989 *FacFETw*
**Hufnagel**, Henry Bernhardt 1942- *WhoFI 92*
**Hufnagel**, Linda Ann 1939- *AmMWSc 92*
**Hufnagel**, Robert Ernest 1932- *AmMWSc 92*
**Hufnagle**, Paul C 1936- *WhoAmP 91*
**Hufschmidt**, Maynard Michael 1912- *AmMWSc 92*
**Hufstedler**, Robert Sloan 1924- *AmMWSc 92*
**Hufstedler**, Shirley Mount 1925- *WhoAmL 92*
**Huft**, Michael John 1949- *AmMWSc 92*
**Huft**, Randall A. *WhoEnt 92*
**Huftalen**, Lisa Freeman 1953- *WhoFI 92*
**Hufton**, Olwen *Who 92*
**Hug**, Carl Casimir, Jr 1936- *AmMWSc 92*
**Hug**, Daniel Hartz 1927- *AmMWSc 92*
**Hug**, George 1931- *AmMWSc 92*
**Hug**, Michel 1930- *IntWW 91*
**Hug**, Procter, Jr 1931- *WhoAmP 91*
**Hug**, Procter Ralph, Jr. 1931- *WhoAmL 92, WhoWest 92*
**Hug**, Verena 1941- *AmMWSc 92*
**Hugdahl**, Scott Steven 1958- *WhoMW 92*
**Huge**, Arthur William 1945- *WhoFI 92*
**Huge**, Thomas Arnold 1944- *WhoEnt 92*
**Hugel**, Charles E. 1928- *IntWW 91*
**Hugel**, Philip Rudolph, IV 1940- *WhoRel 92*
**Hugelman**, Rodney D 1934- *AmMWSc 92*
**Hugenberg**, Alfred 1865-1951 *BiDExR, EncTR 91 [port]*
**Huger**, Francis P 1947- *AmMWSc 92*
**Huger**, James E. *WhoBlA 92*
**Huggans**, James Lee 1933- *AmMWSc 92*
**Huggard**, John Parker 1945- *WhoAmL 92*
**Huggett Family** *NewAmDM*
**Huggett**, Clayton 1917- *AmMWSc 92*
**Huggett**, Frank Edward 1924- *IntAu&W 91, WrDr 92*
**Huggett**, Joyce 1937- *IntAu&W 91*
**Huggett**, Richard 1929- *WrDr 92*
**Huggett**, Richard William, Jr 1930- *AmMWSc 92*
**Huggett**, Robert James 1942- *AmMWSc 92*
**Hugghins**, Ernest Jay 1920- *AmMWSc 92*
**Huggins** *Who 92*
**Huggins**, Alan 1921- *Who 92*
**Huggins**, Charles B. 1901- *IntWW 91, Who 92*
**Huggins**, Charles Brenton 1901- *AmMWSc 92, WhoMW 92, WhoNob 90*
**Huggins**, Charles Edward 1929- *AmMWSc 92*
**Huggins**, Charlotte Susan Harrison 1933- *WhoMW 92*
**Huggins**, Clarence L. 1926- *WhoBlA 92*
**Huggins**, Clyde Griffin 1922- *AmMWSc 92*
**Huggins**, Dawn 1937- *TwCPaSc*
**Huggins**, Elisha R 1934- *AmMWSc 92*
**Huggins**, Frank Norris 1926- *AmMWSc 92*
**Huggins**, Harry Legette, Jr. 1948- *WhoFI 92*
**Huggins**, Hazel Renfroe 1908- *WhoBlA 92*
**Huggins**, Hosiah, Jr. 1950- *WhoBlA 92*
**Huggins**, James Anthony 1953- *AmMWSc 92*
**Huggins**, James Bernard 1950- *WhoAmP 91*
**Huggins**, James Dwyre, Sr. 1874-1932 *DcNCBi 3*
**Huggins**, Jeffrey Jon 1963- *WhoMW 92*
**Huggins**, John 1938- *TwCPaSc*
**Huggins**, John Joseph 1958- *WhoWest 92*
**Huggins**, Kenneth Herbert 1908- *Who 92*
**Huggins**, Kenneth Millard 1932- *WhoFI 92*
**Huggins**, Larry Francis 1937- *AmMWSc 92*
**Huggins**, Linda Johnson 1950- *WhoBlA 92*
**Huggins**, Maloy Alton 1890-1971 *DcNCBi 3*
**Huggins**, Nathan Irvin 1927-1989 *WhoBlA 92N*
**Huggins**, Patrick John 1948- *AmMWSc 92*
**Huggins**, Peter Jeremy William *Who 92*
**Huggins**, Randall D. 1959- *WhoFI 92*
**Huggins**, Richard Collier 1946- *WhoMW 92*
**Huggins**, Robert A 1929- *AmMWSc 92*
**Huggins**, Robert Gene 1938- *WhoAmP 91*
**Huggins**, Roy *LesBEnT 92*
**Huggins**, Roy 1914- *IntMPA 92*
**Huggins**, Sara Espe 1913- *AmMWSc 92*
**Huggins**, Tim Edward 1959- *WhoWest 92*
**Huggins**, W H 1919- *AmMWSc 92*
**Huggins**, Waymond C *WhoAmP 91*
**Huggins**, William Lawrence 1948- *WhoWest 92*
**Hugh**, Gregory Joseph 1942- *WhoMW 92*
**Hugh**, Rudolph 1923- *AmMWSc 92*
**Hugh-Jones**, Wynn Normington 1923- *Who 92*
**Hugh Smith**, Andrew Colin 1931- *IntWW 91, Who 92*
**Hugh Smith**, Henry Owen 1937- *Who 92*
**Hughan**, Jessie Wallace 1875-1955 *AmPeW, HanAmWH*
**Hughart**, Barry 1934- *TwCSFW 91*
**Hughart**, Stanley Parlett 1918- *AmMWSc 92*
**Hughart**, Thomas Arthur 1932- *WhoRel 92*
**Hughbanks**, Robert Allen 1944- *WhoRel 92*
**Hughbanks**, Woodard Monroe 1928- *WhoRel 92*
**Hughel**, Thomas J 1919- *AmMWSc 92*
**Hughes** *Who 92*
**Hughes**, Baron 1911- *Who 92*
**Hughes**, Abbie Angharad 1940- *AmMWSc 92*
**Hughes**, Albert Hilliard 1928- *WhoEnt 92*
**Hughes**, Alexandra Ormond 1954- *WhoEnt 92*
**Hughes**, Alfred Clifton 1932- *WhoRel 92*
**Hughes**, Allan Bebout 1924- *WhoWest 92*
**Hughes**, Allen 1921- *WhoEnt 92*
**Hughes**, Allen Lee 1949- *WhoEnt 92*
**Hughes**, Andrew Anderson 1915- *Who 92*
**Hughes**, Aneurin Rhys 1937- *Who 92*
**Hughes**, Anita Lillian 1938- *WhoBlA 92*
**Hughes**, Anthony Philip Gilson 1948- *Who 92*
**Hughes**, Anthony Vernon 1936- *IntWW 91*
**Hughes**, Antony Elwyn 1941- *Who 92*
**Hughes**, Arthur D 1909- *AmMWSc 92*
**Hughes**, Author E. 1929- *WhoWest 92*
**Hughes**, Barbara Bradford 1941- *WhoMW 92*
**Hughes**, Barbara Lynn 1961- *WhoEnt 92*
**Hughes**, Barnard 1915- *IntMPA 92, WhoEnt 92*
**Hughes**, Benjamin G 1937- *AmMWSc 92*
**Hughes**, Blyth Alvin 1936- *AmMWSc 92*
**Hughes**, Bradley James 1940- *WhoFI 92*
**Hughes**, Bradley Richard 1954- *WhoFI 92, WhoWest 92*
**Hughes**, Brenda *IntAu&W 91X, WrDr 92*
**Hughes**, Buddy Lee 1942- *AmMWSc 92*
**Hughes**, Byron William 1945- *WhoAmL 92*
**Hughes**, C. Don 1935- *WhoRel 92*
**Hughes**, Carl D. *WhoBlA 92*
**Hughes**, Carolyn J. Fairweather *DrAPF 91*
**Hughes**, Carolyn S. 1921- *WhoHisp 92*
**Hughes**, Carolyn Sue 1945- *WhoWest 92*
**Hughes**, Carrie Ann 1960- *WhoMW 92*
**Hughes**, Catherine Liggins 1947- *WhoBlA 92*
**Hughes**, Charles E 1931- *WhoIns 92*
**Hughes**, Charles Edward 1943- *AmMWSc 92*
**Hughes**, Charles Evans 1862-1948 *AmPolLe [port], BenetAL 91, FacFETw, RComAH*
**Hughes**, Charles James 1931- *AmMWSc 92*
**Hughes**, Charles Richard 1955- *WhoRel 92*
**Hughes**, Charles W., Jr. 1942- *WhoBlA 92*
**Hughes**, Charles Wilson 1946- *WhoWest 92*
**Hughes**, Cledwyn *IntWW 91*
**Hughes**, Colin Anfield 1930- *IntAu&W 91, WrDr 92*
**Hughes**, Daniel *DrAPF 91*
**Hughes**, Daniel Richard 1927- *AmMWSc 92*
**Hughes**, Daniel Webster 1926- *WhoBlA 92*
**Hughes**, David 1930- *ConNov 91, IntAu&W 91, WrDr 92*
**Hughes**, David 1936- *Who 92*
**Hughes**, David Edward 1922- *AmMWSc 92*
**Hughes**, David Evan Peter 1932- *Who 92*
**Hughes**, David Glyn 1928- *Who 92*
**Hughes**, David H. 1928- *WhoFI 92*
**Hughes**, David John 1930- *Who 92*
**Hughes**, David John 1942- *WhoFI 92*
**Hughes**, David John 1954- *WhoWest 92*
**Hughes**, David Knox 1940- *AmMWSc 92*
**Hughes**, David Michael 1952- *WhoRel 92*
**Hughes**, David Morgan 1926- *Who 92*
**Hughes**, David William 1933- *AmMWSc 92*
**Hughes**, Davis 1910- *Who 92*
**Hughes**, Deborah Lee 1954- *WhoMW 92*
**Hughes**, Debra Lynn 1955- *WhoMW 92*
**Hughes**, Derek 1934- *WhoIns 92*
**Hughes**, Desmond *Who 92*
**Hughes**, Dickson 1922- *WhoEnt 92*
**Hughes**, Donald Kenneth 1933- *WhoAmP 91*
**Hughes**, Donald Lewellyn 1957- *WhoWest 92*
**Hughes**, Dorothy B. 1904- *WrDr 92*
**Hughes**, Dusty 1947- *WrDr 92*
**Hughes**, Edsel 1923- *WhoAmP 91*
**Hughes**, Edward Joseph 1937- *WhoAmP 91*
**Hughes**, Edward Marshall 1913- *Who 92*
**Hughes**, Edward Stuart Reginald 1919- *IntWW 91, Who 92, WrDr 92*
**Hughes**, Edward T. 1920- *WhoRel 92*
**Hughes**, Edwin Holt 1866-1950 *RelLAm 91*
**Hughes**, Edwin Lawson 1924- *WhoFI 92*
**Hughes**, Edwin R 1928- *AmMWSc 92*
**Hughes**, Eleanor Mary 1882-1959 *TwCPaSc*
**Hughes**, Eleanor Pollock d1991 *NewYTBS 91*
**Hughes**, Elinor Lambert 1906- *WhoEnt 92*
**Hughes**, Elizabeth *WrDr 92*
**Hughes**, Ernelle Combs 1918- *WhoBlA 92*
**Hughes**, Essie Meade 1908- *WhoBlA 92*
**Hughes**, Estelene Dial 1936- *WhoAmP 91*
**Hughes**, Ethel Lena 1933- *WhoFI 92*
**Hughes**, Eugene Morgan 1934- *AmMWSc 92, WhoFI 92, WhoWest 92*
**Hughes**, Everett C 1904- *AmMWSc 92*
**Hughes**, Fiona-Anne 1960- *WhoFI 92*
**Hughes**, Frances 1905- *TwCPaSc*
**Hughes**, Francis Norman 1908- *AmMWSc 92*
**Hughes**, Frederick Desmond 1919- *Who 92*
**Hughes**, George 1937- *Who 92*
**Hughes**, George Farant, Jr. 1923- *WhoFI 92*
**Hughes**, George Melvin 1938- *WhoBlA 92*
**Hughes**, George Morgan 1925- *Who 92*
**Hughes**, George Muggah 1929- *AmMWSc 92*
**Hughes**, George Vincent 1930- *WhoBlA 92*
**Hughes**, Gilbert C 1933- *AmMWSc 92*
**Hughes**, Glyn 1935- *ConAu 35NR, ConPo 91, IntAu&W 91, WrDr 92*
**Hughes**, Glyn Tegai 1923- *Who 92*
**Hughes**, Gordon Frierson 1937- *AmMWSc 92*
**Hughes**, Grace-Flores 1946- *WhoAmL 92*
**Hughes**, H. Hasbrock, Jr. *WhoRel 92*
**Hughes**, H. Richard 1926- *IntWW 91*
**Hughes**, H Stuart 1916- *IntAu&W 91, WrDr 92*
**Hughes**, Harold Everett 1922- *WhoAmP 91*
**Hughes**, Harold Hasbrouck, Jr. 1930- *WhoRel 92*
**Hughes**, Harold K 1911- *AmMWSc 92*
**Hughes**, Harold Paul 1926- *Who 92*
**Hughes**, Harold Victor 1926- *Who 92*
**Hughes**, Harrison Gilliatt 1948- *AmMWSc 92*
**Hughes**, Harry Roe 1926- *WhoAmP 91*
**Hughes**, Harry Wayne 1951- *WhoMW 92*
**Hughes**, Harvey L. 1909- *WhoBlA 92*
**Hughes**, Hatcher 1881-1945 *BenetAL 91, DcNCBi 3*
**Hughes**, Heather 1954- *ConAu 133*
**Hughes**, Helen Elizabeth 1922- *WhoMW 92*
**Hughes**, Helen MacGill 1903- *WomSoc*
**Hughes**, Herbert Delauney 1914- *Who 92*
**Hughes**, Herschel Austin 1921- *WhoRel 92*
**Hughes**, Hollis Eugene, Jr. 1943- *WhoBlA 92*
**Hughes**, Howard 1938- *Who 92*
**Hughes**, Howard Robard 1869-1924 *FacFETw*
**Hughes**, Howard Robard 1905-1976 *FacFETw [port]*
**Hughes**, Ian 1958- *TwCPaSc*
**Hughes**, Ieuan Arwel 1944- *Who 92*
**Hughes**, Ingrid *DrAPF 91*
**Hughes**, Isaac Sunny 1944- *WhoBlA 92*
**Hughes**, Jack 1916- *Who 92*
**Hughes**, James Alton 1962- *WhoAmL 92*
**Hughes**, James Arthur 1929- *AmMWSc 92*
**Hughes**, James Arthur 1939- *WhoFI 92, WhoWest 92*
**Hughes**, James Ernest 1927- *IntWW 91, Who 92*
**Hughes**, James F *WhoAmP 91*
**Hughes**, James Gilliam 1910- *AmMWSc 92*
**Hughes**, James John 1942- *WhoFI 92*
**Hughes**, James Mitchell 1945- *AmMWSc 92*
**Hughes**, James P 1920- *AmMWSc 92*
**Hughes**, James Sinclair 1934- *AmMWSc 92*
**Hughes**, Janice S 1937- *AmMWSc 92*
**Hughes**, Jay Melvin 1930- *AmMWSc 92*
**Hughes**, Jeffrey Graham 1953- *WhoEnt 92*
**Hughes**, Jerome Michael 1929- *WhoAmP 91, WhoMW 92*
**Hughes**, Jerry M 1944- *WhoAmP 91*
**Hughes**, Jimmy Franklin, Sr. 1952- *WhoBlA 92*
**Hughes**, John *IntMPA 92, NewYTBS 91 [port], Who 92*
**Hughes**, John 1677-1720 *RfGEnL 91*
**Hughes**, John 1797-1864 *DcAmImH*
**Hughes**, John 1925- *Who 92*
**Hughes**, John 1930- *IntAu&W 91*
**Hughes**, John 1937- *IntDcF 2-2*
**Hughes**, John 1950?- *Au&Arts 7 [port], CurBio 91 [port]*
**Hughes**, John A. 1941- *WrDr 92*
**Hughes**, John Bradford 1955- *WhoMW 92*
**Hughes**, John Chester 1924- *Who 92*
**Hughes**, John David 1935- *WhoAmL 92*
**Hughes**, John Dennis 1927- *Who 92*
**Hughes**, John Farrell 1946- *WhoFI 92*
**Hughes**, John G 1930- *WhoIns 92*
**Hughes**, John George *Who 92*
**Hughes**, John Gilliam 1921- *WhoEnt 92*
**Hughes**, John Harold 1936- *WhoWest 92*
**Hughes**, John I 1919- *AmMWSc 92*
**Hughes**, John Lawrence 1925- *IntWW 91*
**Hughes**, John Lawrence 1928- *AmMWSc 92*
**Hughes**, John P 1922- *AmMWSc 92*
**Hughes**, John Pinnington- 1942- *Who 92*
**Hughes**, John Richard Poulton 1920- *Who 92*
**Hughes**, John Robert 1920- *WhoWest 92*
**Hughes**, John Russell 1928- *AmMWSc 92*
**Hughes**, John Russell 1949- *AmMWSc 92*
**Hughes**, John Taylor 1908- *Who 92*
**Hughes**, John W. *WhoEnt 92*
**Hughes**, John William 1926- *WhoAmP 91*
**Hughes**, Johnnie Lee 1924- *WhoBlA 92*
**Hughes**, Jon Christopher 1945- *IntAu&W 91, WhoMW 92*
**Hughes**, Jonah 1938- *WhoMW 92*
**Hughes**, Jonathan Philip 1947-1991 *WhoRel 92*
**Hughes**, Joyce A. 1940- *WhoAmL 92, WhoBlA 92*
**Hughes**, Judith M. 1941- *WrDr 92*
**Hughes**, Judith Markham 1941- *IntAu&W 91, WhoWest 92*
**Hughes**, Judy Lynne 1939- *WhoAmP 91*
**Hughes**, Julie *WhoEnt 92*
**Hughes**, Karen Lu 1947- *WhoAmL 92*
**Hughes**, Karen Woodbury 1940- *AmMWSc 92*
**Hughes**, Kathleen 1928- *IntMPA 92, WhoEnt 92*
**Hughes**, Kathleen Allison Barnhart 1955- *WhoAmL 92*
**Hughes**, Ken 1922- *IntMPA 92*
**Hughes**, Kenneth 1927- *TwCPaSc*
**Hughes**, Kenneth D. 1960- *WhoAmL 92*
**Hughes**, Kenneth E 1939- *AmMWSc 92*
**Hughes**, Kenneth Graham 1922- *WhoEnt 92*
**Hughes**, Kenneth James 1921- *AmMWSc 92*
**Hughes**, Kenneth Ray 1961- *WhoEnt 92*
**Hughes**, Kenneth Russell 1925- *WhoAmL 92*
**Hughes**, Kenneth Russell 1933- *AmMWSc 92*
**Hughes**, Kevin John 1962- *WhoAmL 92*
**Hughes**, Kevin Peter 1943- *WhoAmL 92*
**Hughes**, Kimberly Arden 1960- *WhoEnt 92*
**Hughes**, Langston *DcAmImH*

**Hughes,** Langston 1902-1967 *AfrAmW, BenetAL 91, BlkLC [port], ConAu 34NR, FacFETw [port], LiExTwC, RComAH*
**Hughes,** Laurie 1955- *WhoAmL 92, WhoEnt 92*
**Hughes,** Lawrence Edward 1922- *WhoAmP 91*
**Hughes,** Leonard S., Jr. 1926- *WhoBlA 92*
**Hughes,** Leslie Ernest 1932- *IntWW 91, Who 92*
**Hughes,** Linda J. 1950- *WhoWest 92*
**Hughes,** Linda Renate 1947- *WhoAmL 92*
**Hughes,** Lisa Lynn 1964- *WhoRel 92*
**Hughes,** Louis Eugene 1920- *WhoAmP 91*
**Hughes,** Louis R. 1949- *IntWW 91*
**Hughes,** Louis Ralph 1949- *Who 92*
**Hughes,** Lynn Nettleton 1941- *WhoAmL 92*
**Hughes,** Malcolm 1920- *TwCPaSc*
**Hughes,** Malcolm Kenneth 1943- *AmMWSc 92*
**Hughes,** Mamie F. 1929- *WhoBlA 92*
**Hughes,** Marcia Marie 1949- *WhoAmL 92*
**Hughes,** Margaret 1930- *TwCPaSc*
**Hughes,** Margaret Eileen 1943- *WhoWest 92*
**Hughes,** Marija Matich *WhoAmL 92*
**Hughes,** Mark *Who 92*
**Hughes,** Mark 1931- *AmMWSc 92*
**Hughes,** Mark 1953- *WhoAmP 91*
**Hughes,** Mark Edward 1949- *WhoMW 92*
**Hughes,** Mark Lee 1960- *WhoMW 92*
**Hughes,** Martin *WhoHisp 92*
**Hughes,** Martin 1922- *WhoAmP 91*
**Hughes,** Mary Elizabeth 1841-1888 *DcNCBi 3*
**Hughes,** Mary Gray *DrAPF 91*
**Hughes,** Mary Katherine 1949- *WhoWest 92*
**Hughes,** Maryanne Robinson 1930- *AmMWSc 92*
**Hughes,** Matilda *IntAu&W 91X, WrDr 92*
**Hughes,** Maysie J H 1918- *AmMWSc 92*
**Hughes,** Michael Charles 1942- *AmMWSc 92*
**Hughes,** Michael H 1954- *WhoIns 92*
**Hughes,** Michaela Kelly *WhoEnt 92*
**Hughes,** Monica 1925- *IntAu&W 91, TwCSFW 91, WrDr 92*
**Hughes,** Nicholas Collin 1822-1893 *DcNCBi 3*
**Hughes,** Nigel 1940- *TwCPaSc*
**Hughes,** Nigel Howard 1937- *Who 92*
**Hughes,** Norman 1932- *AmMWSc 92*
**Hughes,** O Richard 1938- *AmMWSc 92*
**Hughes,** Patrick 1939- *TwCPaSc*
**Hughes,** Patrick 1964- *WhoMW 92*
**Hughes,** Patrick Henry 1934- *AmMWSc 92*
**Hughes,** Patrick Henry 1942- *WhoIns 92*
**Hughes,** Patrick Richard 1943- *AmMWSc 92*
**Hughes,** Paul *Who 92*
**Hughes,** Paul Anthony 1957- *WhoRel 92*
**Hughes,** Peter *Who 92*
**Hughes,** Peter C 1940- *AmMWSc 92*
**Hughes,** Philip Arthur Booley *Who 92*
**Hughes,** Phillip William 1926- *WrDr 92*
**Hughes,** Quentin 1920- *WrDr 92*
**Hughes,** R. John 1930- *WrDr 92*
**Hughes,** Ralph M *WhoAmP 91*
**Hughes,** Randy *WhoAmP 91*
**Hughes,** Ray Harrison 1924- *WhoRel 92*
**Hughes,** Raymond Hargett 1927- *AmMWSc 92*
**Hughes,** Reuben Paul d1990 *NewYTBS 91*
**Hughes,** Richard 1900-1976 *FacFETw, RfGEnL 91, ScFEYrs*
**Hughes,** Richard 1906-1984 *FacFETw*
**Hughes,** Richard Charles 1915- *Who 92*
**Hughes,** Richard David 1919- *AmMWSc 92*
**Hughes,** Richard Douglas 1951- *WhoWest 92*
**Hughes,** Richard Lawrence 1936- *AmMWSc 92*
**Hughes,** Richard Roberts 1921- *AmMWSc 92*
**Hughes,** Richard Thomas 1943- *WhoRel 92*
**Hughes,** Richard V 1900- *AmMWSc 92*
**Hughes,** Robert 1932- *Who 92*
**Hughes,** Robert 1938- *WrDr 92*
**Hughes,** Robert Alan 1938- *AmMWSc 92*
**Hughes,** Robert Clark 1940- *AmMWSc 92*
**Hughes,** Robert David 1943- *AmMWSc 92*
**Hughes,** Robert Davis, III 1943- *WhoRel 92*
**Hughes,** Robert Edward 1924- *AmMWSc 92*
**Hughes,** Robert Edwin 1931- *WhoFI 92*
**Hughes,** Robert Evans 1928- *WhoAmP 91*
**Hughes,** Robert Gurth 1951- *Who 92*
**Hughes,** Robert John 1930- *Who 92*
**Hughes,** Robert Louis 1926- *WhoAmL 92*
**Hughes,** Robert Merrill 1936- *WhoFI 92, WhoWest 92*
**Hughes,** Robert N 1938- *WhoIns 92*
**Hughes,** Robert Powell 1940- *WhoIns 92*
**Hughes,** Robert Saunders, Jr. 1948- *WhoWest 92*
**Hughes,** Robert Scott 1958- *WhoMW 92*
**Hughes,** Robert Studley Forrest 1938- *Who 92*
**Hughes,** Robert William 1935- *WhoEnt 92*
**Hughes,** Rochford *Who 92*
**Hughes,** Rodney H 1925- *WhoAmP 91*
**Hughes,** Ronald Frederick 1927- *Who 92*
**Hughes,** Royston John 1925- *Who 92*
**Hughes,** Rupert 1872-1956 *BenetAL 91*
**Hughes,** Russell Profit 1946- *AmMWSc 92*
**Hughes,** Samuel Wellwood 1815-1884 *DcNCBi 3*
**Hughes,** Sean Patrick Francis 1941- *IntWW 91, Who 92*
**Hughes,** Shirley 1927- *IntAu&W 91, Who 92, WrDr 92*
**Hughes,** Sidney Weetman Rochford 1914- *Who 92*
**Hughes,** Simon Henry Ward 1951- *Who 92*
**Hughes,** Sophie *DrAPF 91*
**Hughes,** Stanley John 1918- *AmMWSc 92*
**Hughes,** Stella 1916- *IntAu&W 91*
**Hughes,** Stephen Edward 1953- *AmMWSc 92*
**Hughes,** Stephen Phillip 1948- *WhoRel 92*
**Hughes,** Stephen Skipsey 1952- *Who 92*
**Hughes,** Steve Michael 1942- *WhoAmP 91*
**Hughes,** Steven Jay 1948- *WhoAmL 92*
**Hughes,** Susan Kay Tauscher 1962- *WhoWest 92*
**Hughes,** Suzanne Helen 1944- *WhoAmP 91*
**Hughes,** Ted 1930- *ConPo 91, FacFETw, IntAu&W 91, IntWW 91, RfGEnL 91, Who 92, WrDr 92*
**Hughes,** Teresa P 1932- *WhoAmP 91*
**Hughes,** Thomas 1822-1896 *RfGEnL 91*
**Hughes,** Thomas Clayton 1962- *WhoRel 92*
**Hughes,** Thomas Gerald, Jr 1942- *WhoAmP 91*
**Hughes,** Thomas Joseph 1926- *WhoFI 92*
**Hughes,** Thomas Joseph 1943- *AmMWSc 92*
**Hughes,** Thomas Lowe 1925- *Who 92*
**Hughes,** Thomas Rogers, Jr 1931- *AmMWSc 92*
**Hughes,** Thomas Russell 1940- *WhoRel 92*
**Hughes,** Travis Hubert 1937- *AmMWSc 92*
**Hughes,** Trevor 1925- *Who 92*
**Hughes,** Trevor Denby L. *Who 92*
**Hughes,** Vernon Willard 1921- *AmMWSc 92*
**Hughes,** Vester Thomas, Jr. 1928- *WhoAmL 92*
**Hughes,** Victor *Who 92*
**Hughes,** Victor A 1925- *AmMWSc 92*
**Hughes,** Vince *WhoBlA 92*
**Hughes,** Vincent 1956- *WhoAmP 91*
**Hughes,** W. James 1944- *WhoWest 92*
**Hughes,** Walter Jay, Sr 1942- *IntAu&W 91*
**Hughes,** Walter Lee, Jr 1915- *AmMWSc 92*
**Hughes,** Walter Llewellyn 1910- *IntAu&W 91*
**Hughes,** Walter T 1930- *AmMWSc 92*
**Hughes,** Walter William, III 1951- *AmMWSc 92*
**Hughes,** William 1910- *Who 92*
**Hughes,** William 1926- *AmMWSc 92*
**Hughes,** William 1936- *WrDr 92*
**Hughes,** William Anthony 1921- *WhoRel 92*
**Hughes,** William Carroll 1938- *AmMWSc 92*
**Hughes,** William Dillon 1900- *Who 92*
**Hughes,** William E 1932- *AmMWSc 92*
**Hughes,** William F 1930- *AmMWSc 92*
**Hughes,** William J. 1932- *AlmAP 92 [port]*
**Hughes,** William James 1935- *WhoAmP 91*
**Hughes,** William John 1932- *WhoAmP 91*
**Hughes,** William L. 1952- *WhoFI 92, WhoWest 92*
**Hughes,** William Mark 1932- *Who 92*
**Hughes,** William Morris 1864-1952 *FacFETw*
**Hughes,** William Reginald Noel d1990 *Who 92N*
**Hughes,** William Taylor 1936- *AmMWSc 92*
**Hughes,** William Young 1940- *Who 92*
**Hughes,** Zach *WrDr 92*
**Hughes,** Zach 1928- *TwCSFW 91*
**Hughes Jones,** Nevin Campbell 1923- *Who 92*
**Hughes-Morgan,** David 1925- *Who 92*
**Hughes-Stanton,** Blair 1902- *TwCPaSc*
**Hughes-Stanton,** Herbert Edwin Pelham 1870-1937 *TwCPaSc*
**Hughes-Young** *Who 92*
**Hughesdon,** Charles Frederick 1909- *Who 92*
**Hughett,** Paul William 1950- *AmMWSc 92, WhoWest 92*
**Hughey,** David V. *DrAPF 91*
**Hughey,** Mark William 1957- *WhoRel 92*
**Hughey,** Wilbur Lewis 1925- *WhoRel 92*
**Hughff,** Victor William 1931- *Who 92*
**Hughitt,** Jeremiah Keefe 1930- *WhoFI 92*
**Hughs,** Mary Geraldine 1929- *WhoWest 92*
**Hughston,** Jess 1923- *WhoAmP 91, WhoWest 92*
**Hughston,** Thomas Leslie, Jr 1943- *WhoAmP 91*
**Hugill,** John 1930- *Who 92*
**Hugill,** Michael James 1918- *Who 92*
**Hugill,** Stan 1906- *WrDr 92*
**Hugin,** Adolph Charles Eugene 1907- *WhoAmL 92, WhoFI 92, WhoRel 92*
**Hugli,** Tony Edward 1941- *AmMWSc 92*
**Hugo,** Bruce 1945- *WhoAmP 91*
**Hugo,** David 1958- *TwCPaSc*
**Hugo,** John 1899- *Who 92*
**Hugo,** Norman Eliot 1933- *AmMWSc 92*
**Hugo,** Randall Warren 1950- *WhoAmL 92*
**Hugo,** Richard 1923-1982 *BenetAL 91*
**Hugo,** Victor 1802-1885 *GuFrLit 1*
**Hugo Cabeza de Vaca,** James 1948- *WhoHisp 92*
**Hugoson,** Gene 1945- *WhoAmP 91*
**Huguenard,** James Aaron 1954- *WhoAmL 92*
**Huguenin,** George Richard 1937- *AmMWSc 92*
**Huguez,** Michael D. *WhoHisp 92*
**Huguley,** Charles Mason, Jr 1918- *AmMWSc 92*
**Hugunin,** Alan Godfrey 1945- *AmMWSc 92*
**Hugus,** Z Zimmerman, Jr 1923- *AmMWSc 92*
**Huh,** Oscar Karl 1935- *AmMWSc 92*
**Huheey,** James Edward 1935- *AmMWSc 92*
**Huhn,** David Raymond 1937- *WhoFI 92*
**Huhne,** Christopher 1954- *ConAu 133*
**Huhnlein,** Adolf 1881-1942 *EncTR 91 [port]*
**Huhs,** John I. 1944- *WhoAmL 92*
**Huhs,** Roy Elbert, Jr. 1948- *WhoAmL 92*
**Hui Po Yung** *EncAmaz 91*
**Hui Yuyu** 1906- *IntWW 91*
**Hui,** Chiu Shuen 1942- *AmMWSc 92*
**Hui,** Koon-Sea 1948- *AmMWSc 92*
**Hui,** Norman Hung 1944- *WhoWest 92*
**Hui,** Sek Wen 1935- *AmMWSc 92*
**Hui,** Siu Lui 1948- *AmMWSc 92*
**Huiatt,** Ted W *AmMWSc 92*
**Huidobro,** Vicente 1893-1948 *BenetAL 91*
**Huie,** Bill Wayne 1933- *WhoEnt 92*
**Huie,** John M. 1938- *WhoMW 92*
**Huie,** Robert Elliott 1945- *AmMWSc 92*
**Huie,** William Bradford 1910-1986 *FacFETw*
**Huie,** William Orr 1911- *WhoAmL 92*
**Huie,** William Stell 1930- *WhoAmL 92*
**Huijing,** Frans 1936- *AmMWSc 92*
**Huijsman,** Nicolaas Basil Jacques 1915- *Who 92*
**Huisenga,** Kelly Regine 1963- *WhoMW 92*
**Huisgen,** Rolf 1920- *IntWW 91*
**Huisinga,** Alan D 1945- *WhoIns 92*
**Huisingh,** Donald 1937- *AmMWSc 92*
**Huisjen,** Martin Albert 1944- *AmMWSc 92*
**Huisman,** Titus Hendrik Jan 1923- *AmMWSc 92*
**Huismans,** Sipko 1940- *Who 92*
**Huitema,** Bradley Eugene 1938- *AmMWSc 92*
**Huitink,** Geraldine M 1942- *AmMWSc 92*
**Huitric,** Alain Corentin 1911- *AmMWSc 92*
**Huitt,** Jimmie L. 1923- *WhoFI 92*
**Huizenga,** H. Wayne 1937- *WhoFI 92*
**Huizenga,** John R. 1921- *IntWW 91*
**Huizenga,** John Robert 1921- *AmMWSc 92*
**Huizenga,** Wayne 1938?- *News 92-1 [port]*
**Huizinga,** Harry William 1934- *AmMWSc 92*
**Huizinga,** William Arys, III 1942- *WhoFI 92*
**Hujer,** Adolf 1921- *IntAu&W 91*
**Hujio,** Masayuki 1917- *IntWW 91*
**Huke,** Bob 1920- *IntMPA 92*
**Hukill,** Peter Biggs 1927- *AmMWSc 92*
**Hulan,** Howard Winston 1941- *AmMWSc 92*
**Hulbert,** Bruce Walker 1937- *WhoFI 92*
**Hulbert,** Edwin James 1829-1910 *BiInAmS*
**Hulbert,** Lewis E 1924- *AmMWSc 92*
**Hulbert,** Lloyd Clair 1918- *AmMWSc 92*
**Hulbert,** Matthew H 1942- *AmMWSc 92*
**Hulbert,** Richard Wilks 1951- *WhoWest 92*
**Hulbert,** Richard Woodward 1929- *WhoAmL 92*
**Hulbert,** Samuel Foster 1936- *AmMWSc 92, WhoMW 92*
**Hulbert,** Thelma 1913- *TwCPaSc*
**Hulbert,** Thomas Eugene 1935- *AmMWSc 92*
**Hulbert,** Victoria Springer 1946- *WhoAmP 91*
**Hulce,** Jerry Ted 1942- *IntWW 91*
**Hulce,** Thomas 1953- *ConTFT 9*
**Hulce,** Tom *ConTFT 9*
**Hulce,** Tom 1953- *IntMPA 92, IntWW 91, WhoEnt 92*
**Hulcher,** Frank H 1926- *AmMWSc 92*
**Huldeen,** John 1926- *WhoAmP 91*
**Hulet,** Clarence Veloid 1924- *AmMWSc 92*
**Hulet,** Ervin Kenneth 1926- *AmMWSc 92*
**Hulet,** Randall Gardner 1956- *AmMWSc 92*
**Hulet,** William Henry 1925- *AmMWSc 92*
**Hulett,** Rosemary D. 1954- *WhoBlA 92*
**Hulett,** Susan 1944- *WhoWest 92*
**Huling,** Bertha Anne 1943- *WhoEnt 92*
**Hulka,** Barbara Sorenson 1931- *AmMWSc 92*
**Hulka,** Jaroslav Fabian 1930- *AmMWSc 92*
**Hulko,** Robert Lee 1941- *WhoEnt 92*
**Hull,** Bishop Suffragan of 1925- *Who 92*
**Hull,** Alvin C, Jr 1909- *AmMWSc 92*
**Hull,** Andrew P 1920- *AmMWSc 92*
**Hull,** Ann Remington 1925- *WhoAmP 91*
**Hull,** Barbara *DrAPF 91*
**Hull,** Bernard S. 1929- *WhoBlA 92*
**Hull,** Brett *NewYTBS 91 [port]*
**Hull,** Brett 1964- *News 91 [port], WhoMW 92*
**Hull,** Bruce Lansing 1941- *AmMWSc 92*
**Hull,** Carl Ellis 1943- *WhoAmP 91*
**Hull,** Carl Max 1908- *AmMWSc 92*
**Hull,** Carroll G 1920- *WhoAmP 91*
**Hull,** Charles William 1936- *WhoMW 92*
**Hull,** Clarence Joseph 1919- *AmMWSc 92*
**Hull,** Cordell 1871-1955 *AmPeW, AmPolLe, EncTR 91 [port], FacFETw, WhoNob 90*
**Hull,** Cordell William 1933- *WhoFI 92, WhoWest 92*
**Hull,** Dale O 1912- *AmMWSc 92*
**Hull,** David G 1937- *AmMWSc 92*
**Hull,** David Lee 1939- *AmMWSc 92*
**Hull,** David Stewart 1938- *WrDr 92*
**Hull,** Derek 1931- *Who 92*
**Hull,** Donald Albert 1938- *AmMWSc 92*
**Hull,** Donald R 1911- *AmMWSc 92*
**Hull,** Eleanor 1913- *IntAu&W 91, WrDr 92*
**Hull,** Ellis L., Sr. 1928- *WhoBlA 92*
**Hull,** Everson Warren 1943- *WhoBlA 92*
**Hull,** Frank M. 1948- *WhoAmL 92*
**Hull,** Frederick Charles 1915- *AmMWSc 92*
**Hull,** Garrison Allan 1955- *WhoEnt 92*
**Hull,** George, Jr 1921- *AmMWSc 92*
**Hull,** George, Jr. 1922- *WhoBlA 92*
**Hull,** Gloria T. *WhoBlA 92*
**Hull,** Gloria T. 1944- *NotBlAW 92*
**Hull,** Gordon Ferrie, Jr 1912- *AmMWSc 92*
**Hull,** Grafton Hazard, Jr. 1943- *WhoMW 92*
**Hull,** Gregory Stewart 1950- *WhoWest 92*
**Hull,** Gretchen Gaebelein 1930- *WhoRel 92*
**Hull,** Harry H 1911- *AmMWSc 92*
**Hull,** Harvard Leslie 1906- *AmMWSc 92*
**Hull,** Herbert Mitchell 1919- *AmMWSc 92*
**Hull,** Hugh Boden 1920- *AmMWSc 92*
**Hull,** James 1921-1990 *TwCPaSc*
**Hull,** James Clark 1945- *AmMWSc 92*
**Hull,** James Ernest 1928- *WhoRel 92*
**Hull,** James Richard 1933- *WhoAmL 92, WhoFI 92*
**Hull,** Jan Gunnar 1939- *WhoWest 92*
**Hull,** Jane Dee 1935- *WhoAmP 91*
**Hull,** Jerome, Jr 1930- *AmMWSc 92*
**Hull,** John Daniel, IV 1953- *WhoAmL 92*
**Hull,** John Doster 1924- *WhoFI 92*
**Hull,** John Folliott Charles 1925- *IntWW 91, Who 92*
**Hull,** John Grove 1931- *Who 92*
**Hull,** John Laurence 1924- *AmMWSc 92, WhoFI 92*
**Hull,** John R 1949- *AmMWSc 92*
**Hull,** John Ralph 1949- *WhoMW 92*
**Hull,** Joseph A 1925- *AmMWSc 92*
**Hull,** Joseph L 1945- *WhoAmP 91*
**Hull,** Joseph Poyer Deyo, Jr 1931- *AmMWSc 92*
**Hull,** Larry Allen 1950- *AmMWSc 92*
**Hull,** Maurice Walter 1922- *AmMWSc 92*
**Hull,** McAllister Hobart, Jr 1923- *AmMWSc 92*
**Hull,** Michael Earl 1961- *WhoEnt 92*
**Hull,** Michael Neill 1942- *AmMWSc 92*
**Hull,** Moses 1835-1907 *RelLAm 91*
**Hull,** N. E. H. 1949- *WhoAmL 92*

**Hull**, Richard Amyatt 1907-1989 *FacFETw*
**Hull**, Richard F 1931- *WhoIns 92*
**Hull**, Richard James 1934- *AmMWSc 92*
**Hull**, Robert Dale 1946- *WhoMW 92*
**Hull**, Robert Glenn 1929- *WhoFI 92*
**Hull**, Robert Joseph 1936- *AmMWSc 92*
**Hull**, Robert Marvin 1939- *FacFETw*
**Hull**, Robert Richard, Jr. 1944- *WhoRel 92*
**Hull**, Roger Harold 1942- *WhoMW 92*
**Hull**, Roger Kermit 1946- *WhoWest 92*
**Hull**, T Clark 1921- *WhoAmP 91*
**Hull**, Thomas Edward 1922- *AmMWSc 92*
**Hull**, Thomas Gray 1926- *WhoAmL 92*
**Hull**, Treat Clark 1921- *WhoAmL 92*
**Hull**, William E. 1930- *WrDr 92*
**Hull**, William Edward 1930- *WhoRel 92*
**Hull**, William I. 1868-1939 *AmPeW*
**Hull**, William L 1913- *AmMWSc 92*
**Hull**, Zenda *WhoAmP 91*
**Hull-Itkin**, Nicole Karol 1964- *WhoFI 92*
**Hulland**, Thomas John 1930- *AmMWSc 92*
**Hullar**, Theodore Lee 1935- *AmMWSc 92, WhoWest 92*
**Hulleberg**, Brian Elvis 1970- *WhoMW 92*
**Hullett**, John Wayne 1942- *WhoMW 92*
**Hulley**, Clair Montrose 1925- *AmMWSc 92*
**Hulley**, William Christopher 1958- *WhoFI 92*
**Hullinger**, Ronald Loral 1941- *AmMWSc 92*
**Hullinghorst**, Dickey Lee 1943- *WhoAmP 91*
**Hulm**, John Kenneth 1923- *AmMWSc 92*
**Hulme**, Bishop Suffragan of 1933- *Who 92*
**Hulme**, Bernie Lee 1939- *AmMWSc 92*
**Hulme**, David Lee 1957- *WhoEnt 92*
**Hulme**, Geoffrey Gordon 1931- *Who 92*
**Hulme**, Henry Rainsford d1991 *Who 92N*
**Hulme**, Jerrie Anthony 1935- *Who 92*
**Hulme**, Keri 1947- *ConNov 91, IntAu&W 91, IntWW 91, WrDr 92*
**Hulme**, Norman Arthur 1924- *AmMWSc 92*
**Hulme**, Paul 1942- *Who 92*
**Hulme**, T E 1883-1917 *FacFETw*
**Hulme-Beaman**, Emeric *ScFEYrs*
**Huls**, Judith Anne 1949- *WhoWest 92*
**Hulsbos**, C 1920- *AmMWSc 92*
**Hulse**, Arthur Charles 1945- *AmMWSc 92*
**Hulse**, Charles O 1928- *AmMWSc 92*
**Hulse**, Clinton Vennoy 1922- *WhoAmP 91*
**Hulse**, Dexter Curtis 1952- *WhoMW 92*
**Hulse**, Hamilton Westrow 1909- *Who 92*
**Hulse**, James Warren 1930- *WrDr 92*
**Hulse**, Jesse Gifford 1955- *WhoFI 92*
**Hulse**, Michael 1955- *ConPo 91, WrDr 92*
**Hulse**, Michael William 1955- *IntAu&W 91*
**Hulse**, Ralph Robert 1935- *WhoWest 92*
**Hulse**, Russell Alan 1950- *AmMWSc 92*
**Hulse**, Westrow *Who 92*
**Hulsey**, J Leroy 1941- *AmMWSc 92*
**Hulsey**, Ruth Lenora 1927- *WhoWest 92*
**Hulsey**, Sam Byron 1932- *WhoRel 92*
**Hulsey**, Wilda Jean 1937- *WhoRel 92*
**Hulsizer**, Robert Inslee, Jr 1919- *AmMWSc 92*
**Hulst**, Dale Allen 1964- *WhoMW 92*
**Hulst**, George Duryea 1846-1900 *BiInAmS*
**Hulst**, Hendrik Christoffel van de 1918- *IntWW 91*
**Hulstrand**, George Eugene 1918- *WhoAmL 92*
**Hult**, John Luther 1916- *AmMWSc 92*
**Hult**, Richard Lee 1945- *AmMWSc 92*
**Hultberg**, David Godfrey 1951- *WhoRel 92*
**Hulten**, John James 1913- *WhoAmP 91*
**Hulteng**, John L. 1921- *WrDr 92*
**Hulterstrom**, Sven Ake 1938- *IntWW 91*
**Hultgren**, Arland John 1939- *WhoRel 92*
**Hultgren**, David 1951- *WhoAmP 91*
**Hultgren**, David D 1959- *WhoAmP 91*
**Hultgren**, Dennis Eugene 1929- *WhoMW 92*
**Hultgren**, Frank Alexander 1936- *AmMWSc 92*
**Hultgren**, Herbert Nils 1917- *AmMWSc 92*
**Hultgren**, Ralph Raymond 1905- *AmMWSc 92*
**Hultin**, Herbert Oscar 1934- *AmMWSc 92*
**Hultin**, Pamela Nagle 1945- *WhoMW 92*
**Hultin**, Sven Olof 1920- *IntWW 91*
**Hultman**, Bertha *WhoAmP 91*
**Hultman**, Calvin O 1941- *WhoAmP 91*
**Hultman**, Paul C. 1962- *WhoEnt 92*
**Hulton**, Ann d1779 *BenetAL 91*
**Hulton**, Geoffrey 1920- *Who 92*
**Hulton**, John 1915- *Who 92*
**Hultquist**, Donald Elliott 1934- *AmMWSc 92*
**Hultquist**, Martin Everett 1910- *AmMWSc 92*
**Hultquist**, Paul F 1920- *AmMWSc 92*
**Hultquist**, Robert Allan 1929- *AmMWSc 92*
**Hultquist**, Robert Charles 1931- *WhoMW 92*
**Hultquist**, Stephen Robert 1947- *WhoWest 92*
**Hultquist**, Timothy Allen 1950- *WhoFI 92*
**Hultqvist**, Bengt Karl Gustaf 1927- *IntWW 91*
**Hults**, Malcom E 1926- *AmMWSc 92*
**Hultsch**, Roland Arthur 1931- *AmMWSc 92*
**Hultstrand**, Donald Maynard 1927- *WhoMW 92, WhoRel 92*
**Hulyalkar**, Ramchandra K 1929- *AmMWSc 92*
**Hum**, Christopher Owen 1946- *Who 92*
**Hum**, Richard Clark 1945- *WhoFI 92*
**Human**, Cornelis J. F. 1922- *IntWW 91*
**Humann**, Kirstin L. 1965- *WhoAmL 92*
**Humar**, Jagmohan Lal 1937- *AmMWSc 92*
**Humaydan**, Hasib Shaheen 1945- *AmMWSc 92*
**Humayun**, Mir Z 1949- *AmMWSc 92*
**Humbach**, John Albert 1943- *WhoAmL 92*
**Humbach**, Robert Frederick 1958- *WhoWest 92*
**Humbard**, Rex 1919- *RelLAm 91*
**Humber**, Leslie George 1931- *AmMWSc 92*
**Humber**, Richard Alan 1947- *AmMWSc 92*
**Humber**, Robert Lee 1898-1970 *DcNCBi 3*
**Humber**, Wilbur J. 1911- *WhoMW 92*
**Humberd**, Jesse David 1921- *AmMWSc 92*
**Humberger**, Frank Edward 1914- *WhoRel 92*
**Humbertson**, Albert O, Jr 1933- *AmMWSc 92*
**Humble**, James Kenneth 1936- *Who 92*
**Humble**, Jimmy Logan 1944- *WhoMW 92*
**Humble**, Keith 1927- *ConCom 92*
**Humble**, Monty Garfield 1951- *WhoAmL 92*
**Humboldt**, Alexander Von 1769-1859 *HisDSpE*
**Humboldt**, Wilhelm, Freiherr von 1767-1835 *BlkwCEP*
**Humburg**, Neil Edward 1933- *AmMWSc 92*
**Hume**, Alan 1913- *Who 92*
**Hume**, Alexander 1560?-1609 *RfGEnL 91*
**Hume**, Arthur Scott 1928- *AmMWSc 92*
**Hume**, Basil *Who 92*
**Hume**, Basil 1923- *IntWW 91, WhoRel 92*
**Hume**, Brit *LesBEnT 92*
**Hume**, Brit 1943- *IntAu&W 91*
**Hume**, Cyril 1900-1966 *ScFEYrs*
**Hume**, David 1711-1776 *BlkwCEP, BlkwEAR*
**Hume**, David John 1940- *AmMWSc 92*
**Hume**, David Newton 1917- *AmMWSc 92*
**Hume**, Donald E 1926- *WhoAmP 91*
**Hume**, Fergus 1859-1932 *ScFEYrs*
**Hume**, Gary 1962- *TwCPaSc*
**Hume**, George Basil *FacFETw*
**Hume**, George Haliburton 1923- *IntAu&W 91*
**Hume**, Harold Frederick *AmMWSc 92*
**Hume**, Horace Delbert 1898- *WhoFI 92, WhoMW 92*
**Hume**, James Bell 1923- *Who 92*
**Hume**, James David 1923- *AmMWSc 92*
**Hume**, James Nairn Patterson 1923- *AmMWSc 92*
**Hume**, Jaquelin Holliday d1991 *NewYTBS 91*
**Hume**, John 1937- *IntWW 91, Who 92*
**Hume**, John Chandler 1911- *AmMWSc 92*
**Hume**, John Robert 1939- *IntAu&W 91, WrDr 92*
**Hume**, L. J. 1926- *ConAu 135*
**Hume**, Lindel O *WhoAmP 91*
**Hume**, Merril Wayne 1939- *AmMWSc 92*
**Hume**, Michael 1924- *AmMWSc 92*
**Hume**, Patsy Ruth 1929- *WhoAmP 91*
**Hume**, Robert D. 1944- *WrDr 92*
**Hume**, Sandy Gwenne Estona 1942- *WhoAmP 91*
**Hume**, Thomas 1836-1912 *DcNCBi 3*
**Hume**, Thomas Andrew 1917- *Who 92*
**Hume**, Tobias 1570?-1645 *NewAmDM*
**Hume**, Wayne C 1936- *AmMWSc 92*
**Hume**, William 1801-1870 *BiInAmS*
**Humenick**, Michael John, II 1936- *AmMWSc 92*
**Humenik**, Frank James 1937- *AmMWSc 92*
**Humenik**, Michael, Jr 1924- *AmMWSc 92*
**Humer**, Philip Wilson 1932- *AmMWSc 92*
**Humerickhouse**, Steven Edward 1955- *WhoEnt 92*
**Humes**, Arthur Grover 1916- *AmMWSc 92*
**Humes**, Emanuel I., Sr. 1928- *WhoBlA 92*
**Humes**, Gary Edward 1950- *WhoAmL 92*
**Humes**, H. L. 1926- *BenetAL 91*
**Humes**, John Leroy 1936- *AmMWSc 92*
**Humes**, Paul Edwin 1942- *AmMWSc 92*
**Humes**, Robert Ernest 1943- *WhoFI 92*
**Humes**, Vera B *WhoAmP 91*
**Humfrey**, Pelham 1647-1674 *NewAmDM*
**Humi**, Mayer 1944- *AmMWSc 92*
**Humick**, Thomas Charles Campbell 1947- *WhoAmL 92*
**Humiec**, Frank S, Jr 1933- *AmMWSc 92*
**Humiston**, David Michael 1954- *WhoAmL 92*
**Humita**, Tiberius Ted 1913- *WhoMW 92*
**Humke**, David E 1948- *WhoAmP 91*
**Humke**, Paul Daniel 1945- *AmMWSc 92*
**Humke**, Steven Keith 1960- *WhoAmL 92*
**Huml**, Frank *WhoMW 92*
**Humleker**, Peter Dahl, III 1946- *WhoAmL 92*
**Humm**, Douglas George 1917- *AmMWSc 92*
**Humm**, Harold Judson 1912- *AmMWSc 92*
**Humm**, Roger Frederick 1937- *Who 92*
**Hummel**, Arthur William, Jr. 1920- *IntWW 91*
**Hummel**, Donald George 1925- *AmMWSc 92*
**Hummel**, Doris Jane 1918- *WhoAmP 91*
**Hummel**, F A 1915- *AmMWSc 92*
**Hummel**, Frederick Cornelius 1915- *Who 92*
**Hummel**, Frederick Eugene 1935- *WhoRel 92*
**Hummel**, Gene Maywood 1926- *WhoRel 92*
**Hummel**, Gregory William 1949- *WhoAmL 92, WhoMW 92*
**Hummel**, Hans Eckhardt 1939- *AmMWSc 92*
**Hummel**, Jackson Lowe 1933- *WhoAmL 92*
**Hummel**, James Alexander 1927- *AmMWSc 92*
**Hummel**, Johann Nepomuk 1778-1837 *NewAmDM*
**Hummel**, John Philip 1931- *AmMWSc 92*
**Hummel**, John Richard 1951- *AmMWSc 92*
**Hummel**, John William 1940- *AmMWSc 92*
**Hummel**, Kyle 1935- *WhoAmP 91*
**Hummel**, Monte 1946- *ConAu 135*
**Hummel**, Richard Line 1928- *AmMWSc 92*
**Hummel**, Robert P 1928- *AmMWSc 92*
**Hummel**, Robert Paul 1928- *WhoMW 92*
**Hummel**, Rolf Erich 1934- *AmMWSc 92*
**Hummel**, Steven G 1958- *AmMWSc 92*
**Hummel**, Steven Gregg 1958- *WhoWest 92*
**Hummeler**, Klaus 1922- *AmMWSc 92*
**Hummels**, Donald Ray 1936- *AmMWSc 92*
**Hummer**, David Graybill 1934- *AmMWSc 92*
**Hummer**, James Knight 1926- *AmMWSc 92*
**Hummer**, Robert Harrison, Jr. 1944- *WhoFI 92*
**Hummer**, T.R. *DrAPF 91*
**Hummer**, Thomas William 1937- *WhoMW 92*
**Hummers**, Edward William, Jr. 1936- *WhoAmL 92*
**Hummers**, JoAnn 1939- *WhoMW 92*
**Hummers**, William Strong, Jr 1917- *AmMWSc 92*
**Hummert**, George Thomas 1938- *AmMWSc 92*
**Hummon**, William Dale 1932- *AmMWSc 92*
**Humpage**, John Cornelius 1928- *WhoMW 92*
**Humperdinck**, Engelbert 1854-1921 *NewAmDM*
**Humperdinck**, Engelbert 1936- *WhoEnt 92*
**Humpherys**, Alfred Glen 1939- *WhoWest 92*
**Humpherys**, Allan S 1926- *AmMWSc 92*
**Humpherys**, LeGrande Rich 1949- *WhoAmL 92*
**Humphreville**, John David 1953- *WhoAmL 92*
**Humphrey**, Albert S 1926- *AmMWSc 92*
**Humphrey**, Ann Wickett d1991 *NewYTBS 91 [port]*
**Humphrey**, Arthur *WhoBlA 92*
**Humphrey**, Arthur E 1927- *AmMWSc 92*
**Humphrey**, Arthur Hugh Peters 1911- *Who 92*
**Humphrey**, Basil 1918- *Who 92*
**Humphrey**, Bingham Johnson 1906- *AmMWSc 92, WhoFI 92*
**Humphrey**, Bobby 1966- *WhoBlA 92*
**Humphrey**, Charles Harve 1925- *AmMWSc 92*
**Humphrey**, Donald Glen 1927- *AmMWSc 92*
**Humphrey**, Donald R 1935- *AmMWSc 92*
**Humphrey**, Edward William 1926- *AmMWSc 92, WhoMW 92*
**Humphrey**, Floyd Bernard 1925- *AmMWSc 92*
**Humphrey**, George Louis 1921- *AmMWSc 92*
**Humphrey**, Gordon J 1940- *WhoAmP 91*
**Humphrey**, Gordon John 1940- *IntWW 91*
**Humphrey**, Gordon Laird 1940- *AmMWSc 92*
**Humphrey**, Harold Edward Burton, Jr 1940- *AmMWSc 92*
**Humphrey**, Howard Clark *WhoIns 92*
**Humphrey**, Howard John 1940- *WhoBlA 92*
**Humphrey**, Howard S, Sr 1905- *WhoAmP 91*
**Humphrey**, Hubert Grant 1910- *WhoBlA 92*
**Humphrey**, Hubert Horatio 1911-1978 *AmPolLe [port]*
**Humphrey**, Hubert Horatio, III 1942- *WhoAmL 92, WhoAmP 91, WhoMW 92*
**Humphrey**, Hubert Horatio, Jr 1911-1978 *FacFETw [port]*
**Humphrey**, J Richard 1942- *AmMWSc 92*
**Humphrey**, James 1939- *WrDr 92*
**Humphrey**, James A *WhoAmP 91*
**Humphrey**, James Ellis 1861-1897 *BiInAmS*
**Humphrey**, James Philip 1921- *WhoBlA 92*
**Humphrey**, Jennifer *DrAPF 91*
**Humphrey**, Jimmy Luther 1936- *AmMWSc 92*
**Humphrey**, John Julius 1926- *WhoWest 92*
**Humphrey**, John Peters 1905- *IntWW 91*
**Humphrey**, Karen 1945- *WhoAmP 91*
**Humphrey**, Karen Michael 1945- *WhoWest 92*
**Humphrey**, Kathryn Britt 1923- *WhoBlA 92*
**Humphrey**, Lloyd Ray 1951- *WhoRel 92*
**Humphrey**, Lucie King 1911- *WhoAmP 91*
**Humphrey**, Margo 1942- *WhoBlA 92*
**Humphrey**, Marian J. *WhoBlA 92*
**Humphrey**, Mary Ann 1943- *ConAu 134*
**Humphrey**, Melvin 1921-1988 *WhoBlA 92N*
**Humphrey**, N. Jean 1933- *WhoRel 92*
**Humphrey**, Neil Darwin 1928- *WhoMW 92*
**Humphrey**, Paul *DrAPF 91*
**Humphrey**, Philip Strong 1926- *AmMWSc 92*
**Humphrey**, Ray Eicken 1931- *AmMWSc 92*
**Humphrey**, Richard Pryor, Jr *WhoAmP 91*
**Humphrey**, Robert Charles 1961- *WhoBlA 92*
**Humphrey**, Robert Thomas 1957- *WhoWest 92*
**Humphrey**, Ronald DeVere 1938- *AmMWSc 92*
**Humphrey**, Ronald Mack 1932- *AmMWSc 92*
**Humphrey**, S Bruce 1927- *AmMWSc 92*
**Humphrey**, Shirley J 1937- *WhoAmP 91*
**Humphrey**, Sonnie *WhoBlA 92*
**Humphrey**, Thomas Milton, Jr 1924- *AmMWSc 92*
**Humphrey**, Watts S 1927- *AmMWSc 92*
**Humphrey**, Willard Edward, Jr. 1945- *WhoRel 92*
**Humphrey**, William *DrAPF 91*
**Humphrey**, William 1924- *BenetAL 91, ConNov 91, TwCWW 91, WrDr 92*
**Humphrey**, William Albert 1927- *WhoFI 92*
**Humphrey**, William Gerald 1904- *Who 92*
**Humphreys**, Andrew Atkinson 1810-1883 *BiInAmS*
**Humphreys**, Arthur Leslie Charles 1917- *Who 92*
**Humphreys**, B. V. *WrDr 92*
**Humphreys**, Beverley Joan 1939- *WhoRel 92*
**Humphreys**, Colin John 1941- *Who 92*
**Humphreys**, David 1752-1818 *BenetAL 91*
**Humphreys**, David 1937- *TwCPaSc*
**Humphreys**, David Colin 1925- *IntWW 91, Who 92*
**Humphreys**, E Norman 1927- *WhoIns 92*
**Humphreys**, Edward Maurice 1952- *WhoMW 92*
**Humphreys**, Edwin Coleman, Jr 1919- *WhoAmP 91*
**Humphreys**, Emyr 1919- *ConNov 91, WrDr 92*
**Humphreys**, Emyr Owen 1919- *IntAu&W 91, Who 92*
**Humphreys**, George Charles d1991 *Who 92N*
**Humphreys**, J.R. *DrAPF 91*
**Humphreys**, Jack Bishop 1933- *AmMWSc 92*
**Humphreys**, James Charles 1934- *IntWW 91*
**Humphreys**, James F 1948- *WhoAmP 91*

**Humphreys**, Jan Gordon 1941- AmMWSc 92
**Humphreys**, John Henry 1917- Who 92
**Humphreys**, Josephine DrAPF 91
**Humphreys**, Josephine 1945- IntAu&W 91
**Humphreys**, Keith Wood 1934- Who 92
**Humphreys**, Kenneth Jerome 1944- WhoFI 92
**Humphreys**, Kenneth K 1938- AmMWSc 92
**Humphreys**, Kenneth William 1916- Who 92
**Humphreys**, Kent Jack 1946- WhoRel 92
**Humphreys**, Lynn Marie 1962- WhoWest 92
**Humphreys**, Mabel Gweneth 1911- AmMWSc 92
**Humphreys**, Mildred WhoAmP 91
**Humphreys**, Myles Who 92
**Humphreys**, Olliver 1902- Who 92
**Humphreys**, Olliver William 1902- IntWW 91
**Humphreys**, Priscilla Faith 1912- WhoAmP 91
**Humphreys**, Raymond Evelyn Myles 1925- Who 92
**Humphreys**, Robert, Jr 1932- WhoIns 92
**Humphreys**, Robert Arthur 1907- Who 92
**Humphreys**, Robert Edward 1942- AmMWSc 92
**Humphreys**, Robert Lee 1924- WhoFI 92
**Humphreys**, Robert William Riley 1951- AmMWSc 92
**Humphreys**, Roberta Marie 1944- AmMWSc 92
**Humphreys**, Susie Hunt 1939- AmMWSc 92
**Humphreys**, Thomas Elder 1924- AmMWSc 92
**Humphreys**, Tom Daniel 1936- AmMWSc 92
**Humphreys**, Wallace F 1927- AmMWSc 92
**Humphreys**, Walter James 1922- AmMWSc 92
**Humphries**, Arthur Lee, Jr 1928- AmMWSc 92
**Humphries**, Asa Alan, Jr 1924- AmMWSc 92
**Humphries**, Barry Who 92
**Humphries**, Barry 1934- IntAu&W 91, IntWW 91
**Humphries**, Charles, Jr. 1943- WhoBlA 92
**Humphries**, David Ernest 1937- Who 92
**Humphries**, Edward Francis 1957- WhoAmL 92
**Humphries**, Ervin G 1936- AmMWSc 92
**Humphries**, Frederick S. 1935- WhoBlA 92
**Humphries**, Gerard William 1928- Who 92
**Humphries**, J O'Neal 1931- AmMWSc 92
**Humphries**, Jack Thomas 1929- AmMWSc 92
**Humphries**, James Donald, III 1944- WhoAmL 92
**Humphries**, James Edward, Jr 1940- AmMWSc 92
**Humphries**, Jay 1962- WhoBlA 92
**Humphries**, Jefferson 1955- ConAu 36NR
**Humphries**, John Anthony Charles 1925- Who 92
**Humphries**, John Barry 1934- Who 92
**Humphries**, John Charles Freeman 1937- Who 92
**Humphries**, Laurie Lee 1944- AmMWSc 92
**Humphries**, Lawrence 1926- WhoEnt 92
**Humphries**, Michael Lawrence 1953- WhoRel 92
**Humphries**, Robert Gordon 1945- AmMWSc 92
**Humphries**, Rolfe 1894-1969 BenetAL 91
**Humphries**, Romilly Helfenstein 1930- WhoFI 92
**Humphries**, Stanley, Jr. 1946- WhoWest 92
**Humphries**, T W WhoAmP 91
**Humphries**, William Darlington 1927- WhoFI 92
**Humphries**, William R WhoAmP 91
**Humphris**, Robert R 1928- AmMWSc 92
**Humphriss**, Helen Marie 1961- WhoMW 92
**Humphry**, Ann Wickett d1991 NewYTBS 91 [port]
**Humphry**, Derek 1931?- News 92-2 [port]
**Humphry**, Derek John 1930- IntAu&W 91, WhoWest 92
**Humphrys**, Geoffrey WrDr 92
**Humphrys**, John 1943- Who 92
**Humphrys**, Leslie George 1921- WrDr 92
**Humpleby**, Twyla Jean 1933- WhoAmP 91
**Hun Sen** 1950- IntWW 91
**Hunciker**, Kurt Michael 1953- WhoAmL 92
**Hund**, Friedrich 1896- IntWW 91
**Hund**, Robert Arthur 1927- WhoMW 92
**Hundal**, Mahendra S 1934- AmMWSc 92
**Hunderfund**, Richard C 1929- AmMWSc 92
**Hundert**, Irwin 1925- AmMWSc 92
**Hundert**, Murray Bernard 1919- AmMWSc 92
**Hundertmark**, Charles A. 1940- WhoFI 92
**Hundertwasser**, Friedensreich 1928- IntWW 91
**Hundhausen**, Arthur James 1936- AmMWSc 92
**Hundhausen**, David Frank 1939- WhoEnt 92
**Hundhausen**, Joan Rohrer AmMWSc 92
**Hundley**, Charles Morgan 1942- WhoFI 92
**Hundley**, John Gower 1929- AmMWSc 92
**Hundley**, Louis Reams 1926- AmMWSc 92
**Hundley**, Norris C., Jr. WrDr 92
**Hundley**, Richard O'Neil 1935- AmMWSc 92
**Hundt**, Barbara Ann 1953- WhoMW 92
**Hune**, Floyd Edward 1946- WhoMW 92
**Huneke**, Harold Vernon 1917- AmMWSc 92
**Huneke**, John George 1931- WhoRel 92
**Huneke**, John Philip 1942- AmMWSc 92
**Huneke**, William Lester 1954- WhoAmP 91
**Huneker**, James Gibbons 1860-1921 BenetAL 91
**Hunerberg**, David W. 1943- WhoMW 92
**Huneycutt**, Alice Ruth 1951- WhoAmL 92, WhoFI 92
**Huneycutt**, James Ernest, Jr 1942- AmMWSc 92
**Huneycutt**, Maeburn Bruce 1923- AmMWSc 92
**Hung**, George Wen-Chi 1932- AmMWSc 92
**Hung**, James Chen 1929- AmMWSc 92
**Hung**, James Y 1935- AmMWSc 92
**Hung**, John Hui-Hsiung 1937- AmMWSc 92
**Hung**, Kuen-Shan 1938- AmMWSc 92
**Hung**, Mimi Wong WhoFI 92
**Hung**, Paul P 1933- AmMWSc 92
**Hung**, Rham 1913-1988 FacFETw
**Hung**, Ru J 1934- AmMWSc 92
**Hung**, Tonney H M 1932- AmMWSc 92
**Hung**, William Mo-Wei 1940- AmMWSc 92
**Hung**, You-Tsai Joseph 1932- AmMWSc 92
**Hungate**, Frank Porter 1918- AmMWSc 92
**Hungate**, Robert Edward 1906- AmMWSc 92
**Hungate**, William Leonard 1922- WhoAmL 92, WhoAmP 91, WhoMW 92
**Hunger**, Herbert 1914- IntWW 91
**Hunger**, Herbert Ferdinand 1927- AmMWSc 92
**Hunger**, John David 1941- WhoFI 92
**Hunger**, Robert Marvin 1954- AmMWSc 92
**Hungerford**, Ed Vernon, III 1939- AmMWSc 92
**Hungerford**, Gary A. 1948- WhoFI 92, WhoIns 92
**Hungerford**, Gerald Fred 1923- AmMWSc 92
**Hungerford**, Herbert Eugene 1918- AmMWSc 92
**Hungerford**, Kenneth Eugene 1916- AmMWSc 92
**Hungerford**, Robert L, Sr 1916- WhoAmP 91
**Hungerford**, Thomas W 1936- AmMWSc 92
**Hungerford**, Thomas William 1936- WhoMW 92
**Hunicke**, Henry August 1861-1909 BiInAmS
**Hunig**, Siegfried Helmut 1921- IntWW 91
**Hunigan**, Earl 1929- WhoBlA 92
**Huning**, Deborah Gray 1950- WhoEnt 92
**Hunke**, William Allen 1950- AmMWSc 92
**Hunker**, Henry L 1924- IntAu&W 91, WrDr 92
**Hunkin**, Tim Mark Trelawney 1950- WrDr 92
**Hunking**, Loila Belcher 1939- WhoAmP 91
**Hunkins**, Kenneth 1928- AmMWSc 92
**Hunkins**, Raymond Breedlove 1939- WhoAmL 92
**Hunkins-Hallinan**, Hazel 1890-1982 BiDBrF 2
**Hunkler**, James Richard 1928- WhoMW 92
**Hunlede**, Ayi Houenou 1925- IntWW 91
**Hunley**, Jearl Dean 1938- WhoRel 92
**Hunley**, W. Helen 1920- WhoWest 92
**Hunn**, Dorothy Fegan 1928- WhoBlA 92
**Hunn**, Douglas Arthur 1954- WhoFI 92
**Hunn**, Jack 1906- Who 92
**Hunn**, John Murray 1937- IntWW 91
**Hunn**, Joseph Bruce 1933- AmMWSc 92
**Hunn**, Myron Vernon 1926- WhoBlA 92
**Hunnell**, John Wesley 1932- AmMWSc 92
**Hunnicut**, Gayle 1943- IntMPA 92
**Hunnicutt**, Benjamin Kline 1943- WhoMW 92
**Hunnicutt**, Charles Alvin 1950- WhoAmL 92, WhoAmP 91
**Hunnicutt**, Ellen DrAPF 91
**Hunnicutt**, Richard P 1926- AmMWSc 92
**Hunnicutt**, Richard Pearce 1926- WhoWest 92
**Hunnicutt**, Robert William 1954- WhoWest 92
**Hunnicutt**, V. Gayle 1945- WhoEnt 92
**Hunninghake**, Gary W 1946- AmMWSc 92
**Hunningher**, Benjamin d1991 NewYTBS 91
**Hunnings**, Neville March 1929- WrDr 92
**Hunnings**, Thomas Neville March 1929- IntAu&W 91
**Hunnisett**, Roy Frank 1928- Who 92
**Hunsaker**, Don, II 1930- AmMWSc 92
**Hunsaker**, Fred R 1939- WhoAmP 91
**Hunsaker**, Neville Carter 1907- WhoWest 92
**Hunsaker**, Richard Kendall 1960- WhoAmL 92
**Hunsaker**, Worthen Neville 1939- WhoMW 92
**Hunsaker-Howard**, Marla Elaine 1955- WhoFI 92
**Hunsberger**, Bruce DrAPF 91
**Hunsberger**, Charles Wesley 1929- WhoWest 92
**Hunsberger**, Donald Ross 1932- WhoEnt 92
**Hunsberger**, Ken Duane 1953- WhoRel 92
**Hunsberger**, Robert Earl 1947- WhoWest 92
**Hunsberger**, Ruby Moore 1913- WhoRel 92
**Hunscher**, William Homer, Sr. 1938- WhoFI 92
**Hunsdon of Hunsdon**, Baron Who 92
**Hunsicker**, Harold Yundt 1914- AmMWSc 92
**Hunsinger**, Bill Jo 1939- AmMWSc 92
**Hunsinger**, Doyle J. 1947- WhoFI 92
**Hunsinger**, Edward Eugene 1945- WhoRel 92
**Hunsley**, Roger Eugene 1938- AmMWSc 92, WhoMW 92
**Hunsperger**, Robert G 1940- AmMWSc 92
**Hunstad**, Norman A 1924- AmMWSc 92
**Hunstad**, Norman Allen 1924- WhoMW 92
**Hunstad**, Robert Edward 1940- WhoIns 92, WhoMW 92
**Hunston**, Donald Lee 1943- AmMWSc 92
**Hunsucker**, Robert Dudley 1930- AmMWSc 92
**Hunsworth**, John Alfred 1921- Who 92
**Hunt** Who 92
**Hunt**, Baron 1910- IntWW 91, Who 92
**Hunt**, A. Thomas 1940- WhoAmL 92
**Hunt**, Abby Campbell 1933?-1985 ConAu 135
**Hunt**, Alan Charles 1941- Who 92
**Hunt**, Albert Melvin 1929- AmMWSc 92
**Hunt**, Alfred Ephraim 1855-1899 BiInAmS
**Hunt**, Andrew Dickson 1915- AmMWSc 92
**Hunt**, Angus Lamar 1925- AmMWSc 92
**Hunt**, Ann Hampton 1942- AmMWSc 92
**Hunt**, Arlon Jason 1939- AmMWSc 92
**Hunt**, Arthur James 1915- Who 92
**Hunt**, Barbara Ann 1931- WhoBlA 92
**Hunt**, Barnabas John 1937- WhoRel 92
**Hunt**, Bernice Kohn 1920- WrDr 92
**Hunt**, Betty Syble 1919- WhoBlA 92
**Hunt**, Billie Jean 1926- WhoFI 92
**Hunt**, Bobby Ray 1941- AmMWSc 92
**Hunt**, Bryan 1947- WorArt 1980 [port]
**Hunt**, C Warren 1924- AmMWSc 92
**Hunt**, Carl E AmMWSc 92
**Hunt**, Carlton Cuyler 1918- AmMWSc 92
**Hunt**, Caroline Rose 1923- IntWW 91
**Hunt**, Cecil Arthur 1873-1965 TwCPaSc
**Hunt**, Charles Amoes 1950- WhoBlA 92
**Hunt**, Charles E 1935- AmMWSc 92
**Hunt**, Charles Edmund Laurence 1935- AmMWSc 92
**Hunt**, Charles Maxwell 1911- AmMWSc 92
**Hunt**, Charles Ronald 1941- WhoAmL 92
**Hunt**, Charlotte WrDr 92
**Hunt**, Christina Lee 1959- WhoAmL 92
**Hunt**, Constance Darlene 1950- IntWW 91
**Hunt**, Daniel Stevenson, Sr. 1947- WhoRel 92
**Hunt**, Darrold Victor 1941- WhoBlA 92, WhoEnt 92
**Hunt**, David 1913- WrDr 92
**Hunt**, David Ford 1931- WhoAmL 92
**Hunt**, David James Fletcher 1942- IntWW 91, Who 92
**Hunt**, David Roderic Notley 1947- Who 92
**Hunt**, David Wathen Stather 1913- IntWW 91, Who 92
**Hunt**, Derek Simpson 1939- Who 92
**Hunt**, Desmond Charles 1918- Who 92
**Hunt**, Dominic Joseph 1922- AmMWSc 92
**Hunt**, Donald F 1925- AmMWSc 92
**Hunt**, Donald F 1941- AmMWSc 92
**Hunt**, Donald Frederick 1930- Who 92
**Hunt**, Donald Samuel 1938- WhoFI 92
**Hunt**, Donnell Ray 1926- AmMWSc 92
**Hunt**, Douglas A 1945- WhoAmP 91
**Hunt**, E Howard 1918- IntAu&W 91, WrDr 92
**Hunt**, Earle Raymond 1936- AmMWSc 92
**Hunt**, Edgar Hubert 1909- WrDr 92
**Hunt**, Edward Bissell 1822-1863 BiInAmS
**Hunt**, Edward Eyre 1922- AmMWSc 92
**Hunt**, Edward H. 1939- WrDr 92
**Hunt**, Edwin Fitzgerald 1928- WhoAmL 92
**Hunt**, Ernest 1878-1967 RelLAm 91
**Hunt**, Ernest Edward, III 1934- WhoRel 92
**Hunt**, Eugene 1948- WhoBlA 92
**Hunt**, Eugene B 1923- AmMWSc 92
**Hunt**, Evelyn Phyllis 1925- WhoMW 92
**Hunt**, Everett Clair 1928- AmMWSc 92
**Hunt**, Fern Ensminger 1926- AmMWSc 92
**Hunt**, Francesca WrDr 92
**Hunt**, Frederick Talley Drum, Jr. 1947- WhoFI 92
**Hunt**, Gary W 1942- AmMWSc 92
**Hunt**, George Andrew 1949- WhoAmL 92
**Hunt**, George G 1935- WhoIns 92
**Hunt**, George Glen 1935- WhoMW 92
**Hunt**, George Lester, Jr 1942- AmMWSc 92
**Hunt**, George Nelson 1931- WhoRel 92
**Hunt**, George P. d1991 NewYTBS 91
**Hunt**, George William 1937- WhoRel 92
**Hunt**, Georgina TwCPaSc
**Hunt**, Gil TwCSFW 91
**Hunt**, Gilbert Adams 1914- Who 92
**Hunt**, Gill IntAu&W 91X, WrDr 92
**Hunt**, Gladys M. 1926- WrDr 92
**Hunt**, Gordon 1934- WhoAmL 92
**Hunt**, Graham Hugh 1930- AmMWSc 92
**Hunt**, Gregory Lynn 1954- WhoRel 92
**Hunt**, Guy Marion, Jr 1915- AmMWSc 92
**Hunt**, H Guy 1933- WhoAmP 91
**Hunt**, Harold Guy 1933- AlmAP 92 [port]
**Hunt**, Harold Russell, Jr 1932- AmMWSc 92
**Hunt**, Harry Bass, Jr. 1944- WhoRel 92
**Hunt**, Helen BenetAL 91
**Hunt**, Helen 1963- IntMPA 92
**Hunt**, Heman Dowd 1919- AmMWSc 92
**Hunt**, Holman 1924- Who 92
**Hunt**, Howard Beeman 1902- AmMWSc 92
**Hunt**, Hugh 1911- Who 92
**Hunt**, Hugh Sydney 1911- IntWW 91
**Hunt**, Hurshell Harvey 1930- AmMWSc 92
**Hunt**, Irene 1907- IntAu&W 91, WrDr 92
**Hunt**, Isaac 1742?-1809 BenetAL 91
**Hunt**, Isaac Cosby, Jr. 1937- WhoAmL 92, WhoBlA 92
**Hunt**, Isabelle F 1929- AmMWSc 92
**Hunt**, J. McVicker d1991 NewYTBS 91
**Hunt**, J. McVicker 1906- WrDr 92
**Hunt**, J. McVicker 1906-1991 ConAu 133
**Hunt**, James Who 92
**Hunt**, James, Jr. 1944- WhoBlA 92
**Hunt**, James Barton 1943- WhoWest 92
**Hunt**, James Baxter, Jr 1937- WhoAmP 91
**Hunt**, James Calvin 1925- AmMWSc 92
**Hunt**, James Dennis 1931- WhoRel 92
**Hunt**, James Gibbons 1826?-1893 BiInAmS
**Hunt**, James Gregory 1962- WhoAmL 92
**Hunt**, James Howell 1944- AmMWSc 92
**Hunt**, James L 1933- AmMWSc 92
**Hunt**, James Leonard 1938- WhoAmP 91
**Hunt**, James Robert 1925- WhoMW 92
**Hunt**, James Simon Wallis 1947- IntWW 91, Who 92
**Hunt**, James Vaughn 1941- WhoFI 92
**Hunt**, Janell E 1950- WhoAmP 91
**Hunt**, Janet R 1952- AmMWSc 92
**Hunt**, Jasper Stewart 1953- WhoMW 92
**Hunt**, Jeffrey Brian 1958- WhoMW 92
**Hunt**, Jerald Francis 1936- WhoMW 92
**Hunt**, Jerry Donald 1938- AmMWSc 92
**Hunt**, Jerry Eugene 1953- WhoMW 92
**Hunt**, John TwCWW 91
**Hunt**, John 1644?-1710 DcNCBi 3
**Hunt**, John 1929- Who 92
**Hunt**, John A 1935- AmMWSc 92
**Hunt**, John Baker 1933- AmMWSc 92
**Hunt**, John Bankson 1956- WhoAmP 91
**Hunt**, John Clifton 1946- WhoMW 92
**Hunt**, John Edwin 1918- WhoFI 92
**Hunt**, John J 1922- WhoAmP 91
**Hunt**, John Maitland 1932- Who 92
**Hunt**, John Meacham 1918- AmMWSc 92
**Hunt**, John Philip 1923- AmMWSc 92
**Hunt**, John R 1928- AmMWSc 92
**Hunt**, John Wilfred 1930- AmMWSc 92
**Hunt**, Jonathan Lucas 1938- IntWW 91
**Hunt**, Joyce 1927- IntAu&W 91

**Hunt**, Judy WhoAmP 91
**Hunt**, Julian Charles Roland 1941- Who 92
**Hunt**, June Dawn 1951- WhoAmP 91
**Hunt**, Kenneth 1914- Who 92
**Hunt**, Kenneth Charles 1949- WhoAmL 92
**Hunt**, Kenneth Whitten 1909- AmMWSc 92
**Hunt**, Kenton Lloyd 1960- WhoRel 92
**Hunt**, Lamar 1932- WhoMW 92
**Hunt**, Lawrence Barrie 1932- AmMWSc 92
**Hunt**, Lawrence Halley, Jr. 1943- WhoAmL 92
**Hunt**, Lee McCaa 1926- AmMWSc 92
**Hunt**, Leigh 1784-1859 DcLB 110 [port], RfGEnL 91
**Hunt**, Leon Gibson 1931- AmMWSc 92
**Hunt**, Linda 1945- ConTFT 9, IntMPA 92, WhoEnt 92
**Hunt**, Linda Margaret 1947- AmMWSc 92
**Hunt**, Lindsay McLaurin, Jr 1939- AmMWSc 92
**Hunt**, Lois Turpin 1933- AmMWSc 92
**Hunt**, Mahlon Seymour 1925- AmMWSc 92
**Hunt**, Malcolm Peter John 1938- Who 92
**Hunt**, Marsha 1917- ConTFT 9, IntMPA 92
**Hunt**, Marsha A. ConTFT 9
**Hunt**, Martin Robert 1942- Who 92
**Hunt**, Mary Hannah Hanchett 1830-1906 BiInAmS
**Hunt**, Mary Reilly 1921- WhoMW 92
**Hunt**, Maurice 1943- WhoBlA 92
**Hunt**, Maurice William 1936- Who 92
**Hunt**, Memucan 1729-1808 DcNCBi 3
**Hunt**, Michael O'Leary 1935- AmMWSc 92
**Hunt**, Morton 1920- IntAu&W 91
**Hunt**, Nan DrAPF 91
**Hunt**, Nathan 1758-1853 DcNCBi 3
**Hunt**, Nicholas 1930- Who 92
**Hunt**, Nicholas Streynsham 1930- IntWW 91
**Hunt**, Norman C. ConAu 133
**Hunt**, Norman Charles 1918- Who 92
**Hunt**, O'Neal 1914- WhoBlA 92
**Hunt**, Patricia Joan WrDr 92
**Hunt**, Patricia Stanford 1928- WhoAmL 92, WhoAmP 91
**Hunt**, Patrick James 1943- Who 92
**Hunt**, Paul Payson 1930- AmMWSc 92
**Hunt**, Peter 1928- IntMPA 92
**Hunt**, Peter 1945- WrDr 92
**Hunt**, Peter H. 1938- IntMPA 92
**Hunt**, Peter Huls 1938- WhoEnt 92
**Hunt**, Peter John 1933- IntWW 91, Who 92
**Hunt**, Peter Roger 1925- WhoEnt 92, WhoWest 92
**Hunt**, Pfilip Gardnyr 1935- WhoAmL 92
**Hunt**, Philip Alexander 1949- Who 92
**Hunt**, Philip Bodley 1916- Who 92
**Hunt**, Pierre 1925- IntWW 91
**Hunt**, Portia L. 1947- WhoBlA 92
**Hunt**, R Samuel, III 1941- WhoAmP 91
**Hunt**, Ralph WhoAmP 91
**Hunt**, Ray NewYTBS 91 [port]
**Hunt**, Rex 1926- Who 92
**Hunt**, Rex Masterman 1926- IntWW 91
**Hunt**, Richard 1935- WhoMW 92
**Hunt**, Richard Bruce 1927- Who 92
**Hunt**, Richard Henry 1912- Who 92
**Hunt**, Richard Henry 1925- AmMWSc 92
**Hunt**, Richard Howard 1935- WhoBlA 92
**Hunt**, Richard Lee 1936- AmMWSc 92
**Hunt**, Richard Stanley 1944- AmMWSc 92
**Hunt**, Richard Tim 1943- Who 92
**Hunt**, Robert 1918- Who 92
**Hunt**, Robert 1923- WrDr 92
**Hunt**, Robert 1929- TwCPaSc
**Hunt**, Robert Alan 1935- Who 92
**Hunt**, Robert Gordon 1927- WhoWest 92
**Hunt**, Robert Harry 1932- AmMWSc 92
**Hunt**, Robert L 1933- AmMWSc 92
**Hunt**, Robert M, Jr 1941- AmMWSc 92
**Hunt**, Robert Nelson 1946- AmMWSc 92
**Hunt**, Robert S. 1951- WhoBlA 92
**Hunt**, Robert Weldon 1935- AmMWSc 92
**Hunt**, Robert William 1947- WhoEnt 92, WhoWest 92
**Hunt**, Robert William Gainer 1923- IntAu&W 91
**Hunt**, Roger WhoAmP 91
**Hunt**, Roger 1935- Who 92
**Hunt**, Roland Charles Colin 1916- Who 92
**Hunt**, Ronald Duncan 1935- AmMWSc 92
**Hunt**, Ronald Forrest 1943- WhoAmL 92
**Hunt**, Ronald Joseph 1951- WhoBlA 92
**Hunt**, Ross Stuart 1959- WhoFI 92
**Hunt**, Roy Edward 1918- AmMWSc 92
**Hunt**, Sam 1946- ConPo 91, IntAu&W 91, WrDr 92
**Hunt**, Samuel D. 1933- WhoBlA 92
**Hunt**, Samuel Pancoast, III 1943- WhoAmL 92
**Hunt**, Samuel William 1942- WhoAmP 91
**Hunt**, Steven Charles 1953- AmMWSc 92
**Hunt**, Steven James 1954- WhoRel 92
**Hunt**, Stuart W, Sr 1927- WhoAmP 91
**Hunt**, Sue Whittington 1952- WhoFI 92
**Hunt**, Terence 1943- Who 92
**Hunt**, Terry Griffith 1940- WhoMW 92
**Hunt**, Thomas Chester 1947- WhoEnt 92
**Hunt**, Thomas Kintzing 1937- AmMWSc 92, WhoMW 92
**Hunt**, Thomas Knight 1930- AmMWSc 92
**Hunt**, Thomas Sterry 1826-1892 BiInAmS
**Hunt**, Thomas Webb 1929- WhoRel 92
**Hunt**, Tim Who 92
**Hunt**, Timothy Arthur 1949- WhoWest 92
**Hunt**, Timothy Earle 1942- WhoEnt 92
**Hunt**, Timothy J. 1931- WhoFI 92
**Hunt**, Timothy Jon 1968- WhoRel 92
**Hunt**, V Daniel 1939- AmMWSc 92
**Hunt**, Vincent E. 1941- WhoFI 92
**Hunt**, Virgil 1911- WhoMW 92
**Hunt**, Virginia 1935- WhoWest 92
**Hunt**, Walter Andrew AmMWSc 92
**Hunt**, Wanda 1944- WhoAmP 91
**Hunt**, Warren Who 92
**Hunt**, William DrAPF 91
**Hunt**, William 1733-1772 DcNCBi 3
**Hunt**, William A 1930- AmMWSc 92
**Hunt**, William B, Jr 1927- AmMWSc 92
**Hunt**, William Cecil 1923- AmMWSc 92
**Hunt**, William Daniel 1954- AmMWSc 92
**Hunt**, William E WhoAmP 91
**Hunt**, William E., Sr. 1923- WhoWest 92
**Hunt**, William Edward 1921- AmMWSc 92
**Hunt**, William Gibbes 1791-1833 BenetAL 91
**Hunt**, William H. 1942- WhoRel 92
**Hunt**, William J 1946- WhoIns 92
**Hunt**, William Lynn 1928- WhoFI 92
**Hunt**, William Robert 1913- WhoAmP 91
**Hunt**, William Warren 1909- Who 92
**Hunt**, Willie 1941- IntMPA 92
**Hunt**, Willie Wayne 1943- WhoRel 92
**Hunt**, Willis B, Jr WhoAmP 91
**Hunt Of Tanworth**, Baron 1919- IntWW 91, Who 92
**Hunte**, Beryl Eleanor AmMWSc 92
**Hunte**, Joseph Alexander 1917- Who 92
**Hunten**, Donald Mount 1925- AmMWSc 92, IntWW 91
**Hunter** Who 92
**Hunter**, Lord 1913- Who 92
**Hunter**, Aaron Burtis 1854-1933 DcNCBi 3
**Hunter**, Adam d1991 Who 92N
**Hunter**, Adam Kenneth 1920- Who 92
**Hunter**, Alan 1912- Who 92
**Hunter**, Alan 1922- WrDr 92
**Hunter**, Alan Graham 1934- AmMWSc 92
**Hunter**, Alan James Herbert 1922- IntAu&W 91
**Hunter**, Albert Sinclair 1908- AmMWSc 92
**Hunter**, Alberta 1895-1984 ConMus 7 [port], NotBlAW 92 [port]
**Hunter**, Alexander 1920- Who 92
**Hunter**, Alexander Freeland Cairns 1939- Who 92
**Hunter**, Alexander Watson 1950- WhoRel 92
**Hunter**, Alexis 1948- TwCPaSc
**Hunter**, Alice S 1923- AmMWSc 92
**Hunter**, Alistair John 1936- Who 92
**Hunter**, Andrew Robert Frederick 1943- Who 92
**Hunter**, Anson ConAu 35NR
**Hunter**, Anthony George Weaver 1916- Who 92
**Hunter**, Anthony Rex Who 92
**Hunter**, Archibald Macbride d1991 Who 92N
**Hunter**, Archibald MacBride 1906- WrDr 92
**Hunter**, Archie Louis 1925- WhoBlA 92
**Hunter**, Arvel Hatch 1921- AmMWSc 92
**Hunter**, Barry B 1939- AmMWSc 92
**Hunter**, Barry Russell Who 92
**Hunter**, Blake 1934- WhoEnt 92
**Hunter**, Bonnie L. 1951- WhoMW 92
**Hunter**, Bruce F 1933- WhoAmP 91
**Hunter**, Burton Douglas 1941- WhoAmL 92
**Hunter**, Byron Alexander 1910- AmMWSc 92
**Hunter**, Carol Margaret 1948- WhoRel 92
**Hunter**, Cecil Thomas 1925- WhoBlA 92
**Hunter**, Charles A. 1926- WhoBlA 92
**Hunter**, Charles Alvin 1926- WhoRel 92
**Hunter**, Charles David 1929- WhoFI 92
**Hunter**, Charles Norfleet 1852?-1931 DcNCBi 3
**Hunter**, Charmaine WhoEnt 92
**Hunter**, Christopher 1934- AmMWSc 92
**Hunter**, Christopher Mark 1959- WhoFI 92
**Hunter**, Clarence WhoAmP 91
**Hunter**, Clarence Cal 1927- WhoRel 92
**Hunter**, Clarence Henry 1925- WhoBlA 92
**Hunter**, Clementine 1886-1988 NotBlAW 92 [port]
**Hunter**, Colin Graeme 1913- Who 92
**Hunter**, Conrad James 1960- WhoEnt 92
**Hunter**, Cynthia L 1954- AmMWSc 92
**Hunter**, Cyrus Lee 1807-1881 DcNCBi 3
**Hunter**, Dard 1883-1966 BenetAL 91
**Hunter**, Dard 1886-1966 DcTwDes
**Hunter**, David 1941- WhoBlA 92
**Hunter**, David A 1951- WhoIns 92
**Hunter**, David Austin 1951- WhoFI 92
**Hunter**, David George 1954- WhoRel 92
**Hunter**, David Lee 1933- WhoBlA 92
**Hunter**, David Stronach 1926- Who 92
**Hunter**, Deanna Lorraine 1946- WhoBlA 92
**Hunter**, Donald H 1911- WhoAmP 91
**Hunter**, Douglas Lee 1948- WhoFI 92, WhoMW 92
**Hunter**, Douglas Lyle 1940- AmMWSc 92
**Hunter**, Duncan 1948- AlmAP 92 [port], WhoAmP 91
**Hunter**, Duncan Lee 1948- WhoWest 92
**Hunter**, Durant Adams 1949- WhoFI 92
**Hunter**, Earle Leslie, III 1929- WhoMW 92
**Hunter**, Edward Brian 1925- WhoAmL 92
**Hunter**, Edwin Ford, Jr. 1911- WhoAmL 92
**Hunter**, Edwina Earle 1943- WhoBlA 92
**Hunter**, Elizabeth WrDr 92
**Hunter**, Elmo Bolton 1915- WhoAmL 92
**Hunter**, Elza Harris 1908- WhoBlA 92
**Hunter**, Emmett Marshall 1913- WhoAmL 92
**Hunter**, Eric 1948- AmMWSc 92
**Hunter**, Eric E. 1960- WhoBlA 92
**Hunter**, Eric J. 1930- WrDr 92
**Hunter**, Evan DrAPF 91
**Hunter**, Evan 1916- IntAu&W 91
**Hunter**, Evan 1926- BenetAL 91, ConNov 91, FacFETw, IntWW 91, TwCSFW 91, Who 92, WrDr 92
**Hunter**, Everest Carlton 1939- WhoFI 92
**Hunter**, Ezekiel d1773 DcNCBi 3
**Hunter**, Frances S. 1928- WhoBlA 92
**Hunter**, Francis Edmund, Jr 1916- AmMWSc 92
**Hunter**, Fred WhoAmP 91, WhoWest 92
**Hunter**, Frederick Douglas 1940- WhoBlA 92
**Hunter**, Frissell Roy 1924- AmMWSc 92
**Hunter**, Garrett Bell 1937- WhoFI 92
**Hunter**, Geoffrey 1934- AmMWSc 92
**Hunter**, George 1927- WhoIns 92
**Hunter**, George L 1932- WhoAmP 91
**Hunter**, George L K 1922- AmMWSc 92
**Hunter**, George Truman 1918- AmMWSc 92
**Hunter**, George William 1911- AmMWSc 92
**Hunter**, George William, III 1902- AmMWSc 92
**Hunter**, Georgia L. 1938- WhoRel 92
**Hunter**, Gertrude T. 1926- WhoBlA 92
**Hunter**, Glenn R. H. 1949- WhoWest 92
**Hunter**, Gordon Eugene 1930- AmMWSc 92
**Hunter**, Guy 1911- Who 92
**Hunter**, Hal Edward, Jr 1921- WhoAmP 91
**Hunter**, Harold V 1917- WhoAmP 91
**Hunter**, Harriet Louise 1917- WhoBlA 92
**Hunter**, Hiram Tyram 1883-1947 DcNCBi 3
**Hunter**, Holly 1958- IntMPA 92, WhoEnt 92
**Hunter**, Howard J, Jr 1946- WhoAmP 91
**Hunter**, Howard Jacque, Jr. 1946- WhoBlA 92
**Hunter**, Howard William 1907- WhoWest 92
**Hunter**, Hugh Wylie 1911- AmMWSc 92
**Hunter**, Ian 1919- Who 92
**Hunter**, Ian Gerald Adamson 1944- Who 92
**Hunter**, Ian McLellan d1991 NewYTBS 91
**Hunter**, Ian Murray 1917- Who 92
**Hunter**, Irby B. 1940- WhoBlA 92
**Hunter**, Isaac 1745?-1823 DcNCBi 3
**Hunter**, Ivory Joe 1914-1974 NewAmDM
**Hunter**, Ivy Joe 1966- WhoBlA 92
**Hunter**, J Paul 1934- IntAu&W 91, WrDr 92
**Hunter**, Jack Corbett 1930- WhoAmP 91
**Hunter**, Jack D. 1921- WrDr 92
**Hunter**, Jack Duval 1937- WhoAmL 92, WhoFI 92
**Hunter**, Jack Duval, II 1959- WhoFI 92
**Hunter**, James 1735?-1783? DcNCBi 3
**Hunter**, James 1740-1821 DcNCBi 3
**Hunter**, James 1767-1831 DcNCBi 3
**Hunter**, James Austen, Jr. 1941- WhoAmL 92
**Hunter**, James Bruce 1915- AmMWSc 92
**Hunter**, James Charles 1946- AmMWSc 92
**Hunter**, James Edward 1935- AmMWSc 92
**Hunter**, James Edward 1945- AmMWSc 92
**Hunter**, James Galbraith, Jr. 1942- WhoAmL 92, WhoMW 92
**Hunter**, James H 1931- AmMWSc 92
**Hunter**, James Hardin, Jr 1938- AmMWSc 92
**Hunter**, James Mackiell 1946- WhoBlA 92
**Hunter**, James Paul 1963- WhoRel 92
**Hunter**, Jane Edna 1882-1971 NotBlAW 92 [port]
**Hunter**, Jeffrey Charles 1938- WhoWest 92
**Hunter**, Jehu Callis 1922- AmMWSc 92
**Hunter**, Jerry Don 1935- AmMWSc 92
**Hunter**, Jerry L. 1942- WhoBlA 92
**Hunter**, Jim 1939- SmATA 65, WrDr 92
**Hunter**, Joel A 1951- WhoAmP 91
**Hunter**, John TwCWW 91
**Hunter**, John 1728-1793 BlkwCEP
**Hunter**, John 1915- Who 92
**Hunter**, John 1921- Who 92
**Hunter**, John Davidson WhoBlA 92
**Hunter**, John Earl 1929- AmMWSc 92
**Hunter**, John Garvin 1947- Who 92
**Hunter**, John Harnden 1934- WhoWest 92
**Hunter**, John Logan 1959- WhoAmL 92
**Hunter**, John Murray 1920- Who 92
**Hunter**, John Nathaniel 1929- WhoWest 92
**Hunter**, John Oswald Mair Who 92
**Hunter**, John Robert, Jr 1936- WhoAmP 91
**Hunter**, John Roe 1934- AmMWSc 92
**Hunter**, John Stuart 1923- AmMWSc 92
**Hunter**, John W. 1934- WhoBlA 92
**Hunter**, Joseph Lawrence 1913- AmMWSc 92
**Hunter**, Joseph Vincent 1925- AmMWSc 92
**Hunter**, Judith Ann 1947- WhoMW 92
**Hunter**, Katherine Morton 1939- AmMWSc 92
**Hunter**, Keith Robert 1936- Who 92
**Hunter**, Kenneth Who 92
**Hunter**, Kenneth Eugene 1943- WhoFI 92
**Hunter**, Kenneth F 1926- WhoAmP 91
**Hunter**, Kenneth James 1944- WhoFI 92
**Hunter**, Kenneth W, Jr AmMWSc 92
**Hunter**, Kennith George 1955- WhoMW 92
**Hunter**, Kim 1922- IntMPA 92, WhoEnt 92
**Hunter**, Kristin DrAPF 91
**Hunter**, Kristin 1931- BenetAL 91, ConNov 91, IntAu&W 91, WrDr 92
**Hunter**, Larry Dean 1950- WhoAmL 92
**Hunter**, Larry Lee 1938- WhoFI 92
**Hunter**, Larry Russel 1953- AmMWSc 92
**Hunter**, Laurence Colvin 1934- Who 92
**Hunter**, Lawrence J WhoAmP 91
**Hunter**, Lawrence Wilbert 1945- AmMWSc 92
**Hunter**, Leslie 1879-1931 TwCPaSc
**Hunter**, Lloyd Philip 1916- AmMWSc 92
**Hunter**, Lloyd Thomas 1936- WhoBlA 92
**Hunter**, Madeline 1916?- News 91 [port]
**Hunter**, Margaret 1948- TwCPaSc
**Hunter**, Margaret Blake 1913- WhoAmP 91
**Hunter**, Martin 1950- WhoEnt 92
**Hunter**, Mic 1957- WhoMW 92
**Hunter**, Michael 1949- WrDr 92
**Hunter**, Michael James 1956- WhoAmP 91
**Hunter**, Mollie 1922- ChlLR 25 [port], IntAu&W 91, WrDr 92
**Hunter**, Muir Vane Skerrett 1913- Who 92
**Hunter**, N.C. 1908-1971 RfGEnL 91
**Hunter**, Neil TwCWW 91
**Hunter**, Norman 1899- WrDr 92
**Hunter**, Norman George Lorimer 1899- IntAu&W 91
**Hunter**, Norman L. 1932- WhoBlA 92
**Hunter**, Norman Robert 1941- AmMWSc 92
**Hunter**, Norman W 1931- AmMWSc 92
**Hunter**, Oliver Clifford, Jr. 1935- WhoBlA 92
**Hunter**, Orville, Jr 1938- AmMWSc 92
**Hunter**, Oscar Benwood, Jr 1915- AmMWSc 92
**Hunter**, Pamela 1919- Who 92
**Hunter**, Patrick J. 1929- WhoBlA 92
**Hunter**, Paul DrAPF 91
**Hunter**, Philip Brown 1909- Who 92
**Hunter**, Philip John 1939- Who 92
**Hunter**, Preston Eugene 1927- AmMWSc 92
**Hunter**, R Haze 1924- WhoAmP 91
**Hunter**, Ralph Eugene 1935- AmMWSc 92
**Hunter**, Raymond Eugene 1935- AmMWSc 92, WhoWest 92
**Hunter**, Raymond Joseph 1942- WhoFI 92
**Hunter**, Reese 1927- WhoAmP 91
**Hunter**, Richard C. 1939- WhoBlA 92
**Hunter**, Richard Edmund 1923- AmMWSc 92
**Hunter**, Richard Samford, Jr. 1954- WhoAmL 92
**Hunter**, Rita 1933- NewAmDM, Who 92
**Hunter**, Robert BenetAL 91
**Hunter**, Robert 1874-1942 DcAmImH
**Hunter**, Robert 1920- TwCPaSc
**Hunter**, Robert Blaine 1955- WhoAmL 92

**Hunter,** Robert C 1944- *WhoAmP 91*
**Hunter,** Robert Charles 1948- *WhoFI 92*
**Hunter,** Robert Dean 1928- *WhoAmP 91*
**Hunter,** Robert Dean 1951- *WhoAmL 92*
**Hunter,** Robert Douglas 1944- *AmMWSc 92*
**Hunter,** Robert E 1940- *WhoAmP 91*
**Hunter,** Robert J. 1934- *WhoBlA 92*
**Hunter,** Robert John 1933- *IntWW 91*
**Hunter,** Robert L 1921- *AmMWSc 92*
**Hunter,** Robert L 1939- *AmMWSc 92*
**Hunter,** Robert Mercer Taliaferro 1809-1887 *AmPolLe*
**Hunter,** Robert P 1933- *AmMWSc 92*
**Hunter,** Robert Shannon 1919- *WhoMW 92*
**Hunter,** Rodney John 1940- *WhoRel 92*
**Hunter,** Ronald Lee 1949- *WhoWest 92*
**Hunter,** Ronald R. 1938- *WhoMW 92*
**Hunter,** Ronald V. 1944- *WhoFI 92*
**Hunter,** Ross 1916- *IntMPA 92*
**Hunter,** Ross 1926- *WhoEnt 92*
**Hunter,** Roy, Jr 1930- *AmMWSc 92*
**Hunter,** Royce Glenn 1938- *WhoIns 92*
**Hunter,** Sally Irene 1936- *WhoMW 92*
**Hunter,** Sam 1923- *WrDr 92*
**Hunter,** Samuel W 1921- *AmMWSc 92*
**Hunter,** Stanley Dean 1954- *AmMWSc 92*
**Hunter,** Susan Julia *AmMWSc 92*
**Hunter,** Susan Martin *WhoEnt 92*
**Hunter,** Tab 1931- *IntMPA 92*
**Hunter,** Teola P 1923- *WhoAmP 91*
**Hunter,** Teola P. 1933- *WhoBlA 92*
**Hunter,** Terryl *DrAPF 91*
**Hunter,** Theodore Paul 1951- *WhoWest 92*
**Hunter,** Theophilus 1727?-1798 *DcNCBi 3*
**Hunter,** Thomas 1735?-1784 *DcNCBi 3*
**Hunter,** Thomas Harrison 1913- *AmMWSc 92*
**Hunter,** Tim *IntMPA 92*
**Hunter,** Todd 1953- *WhoAmP 91*
**Hunter,** Todd Ames 1953- *WhoAmL 92*
**Hunter,** Tonia Jean 1945- *WhoMW 92*
**Hunter,** Tony 1943- *AmMWSc 92, IntWW 91, Who 92*
**Hunter,** Tony Wayne 1960- *WhoBlA 92*
**Hunter,** Tricia *WhoAmP 91*
**Hunter,** Willard Bowen 1944- *WhoMW 92*
**Hunter,** William Andrew 1913- *WhoBlA 92*
**Hunter,** William Armstrong 1953- *WhoAmL 92, WhoAmP 91*
**Hunter,** William G 1937- *AmMWSc 92*
**Hunter,** William Hal 1919- *WhoRel 92*
**Hunter,** William Hill 1916- *Who 92*
**Hunter,** William John 1937- *Who 92*
**Hunter,** William L. 1936- *WhoBlA 92*
**Hunter,** William Leslie 1928- *AmMWSc 92*
**Hunter,** William Louis 1942- *WhoFI 92*
**Hunter,** William Ray 1924- *AmMWSc 92*
**Hunter,** William Sam 1940- *AmMWSc 92*
**Hunter,** William Schmidt 1931- *WhoFI 92*
**Hunter,** William Stuart 1927- *AmMWSc 92*
**Hunter,** William Winslow, Jr 1930- *AmMWSc 92*
**Hunter,** Wood E 1940- *AmMWSc 92*
**Hunter-Blair,** Edward 1920- *Who 92*
**Hunter Blair,** Pauline *IntAu&W 91*
**Hunter-Gault,** Charlayne *WhoBlA 92*
**Hunter-Gault,** Charlayne 1942- *NotBlAW 92*
**Hunter Johnston,** David Alan 1915- *Who 92*
**Hunter-Lattany,** Kristin Eggleston 1931- *WhoBlA 92*
**Hunter Of Newington,** Baron 1915- *IntWW 91, Who 92*
**Hunter Smart,** Norman *Who 92*
**Hunter Smart,** William Norman 1921- *Who 92*
**Hunter-Tod,** John 1917- *Who 92*
**Hunthausen,** Raymond Gerhardt 1921- *WhoRel 92, WhoWest 92*
**Hunting,** Alfred Curtis 1928- *AmMWSc 92*
**Hunting,** Anne Ritchie 1944- *WhoWest 92*
**Hunting,** Charles Patrick 1910- *Who 92*
**Hunting,** Clive 1925- *Who 92*
**Hunting,** Constance Coulter 1925- *WhoFI 92*
**Hunting,** David D., Jr. 1926- *WhoMW 92*
**Hunting,** Gardner 1872-1958 *ScFEYrs*
**Hunting,** Leonard 1951- *TwCPaSc*
**Hunting,** Patrick *Who 92*
**Hunting,** Richard Hugh 1946- *Who 92*
**Hunting,** Ward Martin 1923- *WhoAmP 91*
**Hunting,** Wesley Jay 1958- *WhoRel 92*
**Huntingdon,** Archdeacon of *Who 92*
**Huntingdon,** Bishop Suffragan of 1932- *Who 92*
**Huntingdon,** Earl of 1948- *Who 92*
**Huntingfield,** Baron 1915- *Who 92*
**Huntington,** Anna Hyatt 1876-1973 *FacFETw*
**Huntington,** Archer M. 1870-1955 *BenetAL 91*
**Huntington,** Charles Ellsworth 1919- *AmMWSc 92*
**Huntington,** Collis P. 1821-1900 *BenetAL 91*
**Huntington,** Cynthia *DrAPF 91*
**Huntington,** David Hans 1926- *AmMWSc 92*
**Huntington,** Earl Lloyd 1929- *WhoAmL 92*
**Huntington,** Henry E. 1850-1927 *BenetAL 91*
**Huntington,** Hillard Bell 1910- *AmMWSc 92*
**Huntington,** Hillard Griswold 1944- *WhoFI 92*
**Huntington,** Robert, Jr 1907- *AmMWSc 92*
**Huntington,** Robert Hubbard 1937- *WhoFI 92*
**Huntington,** Roswell 1763-1836 *DcNCBi 3*
**Huntington,** Samuel Phillips 1927- *IntAu&W 91, WrDr 92*
**Huntington,** William 1792-1874 *DcNCBi 3*
**Huntington,** William Reed 1838-1909 *RelLAm 91*
**Huntington-Whiteley,** Hugo 1924- *Who 92*
**Huntley,** Chet d1974 *LesBEnT 92*
**Huntley,** Chet 1911-1974 *FacFETw*
**Huntley,** Dan *DrAPF 91*
**Huntley,** David 1950- *AmMWSc 92*
**Huntley,** Donald Wayne 1942- *WhoAmL 92*
**Huntley,** Douglas Spencer 1947- *WhoAmP 91*
**Huntley,** Harvey Lewis, Jr. 1945- *WhoRel 92*
**Huntley,** James Robert 1923- *WrDr 92*
**Huntley,** Jimmy Charles 1946- *AmMWSc 92*
**Huntley,** Mark Edward 1950- *WhoWest 92*
**Huntley,** Raymond 1904-1990 *AnObit 1990*
**Huntley,** Richard Frank 1926- *WhoBlA 92*
**Huntley,** Robert C, Jr 1932- *WhoAmP 91*
**Huntley,** Robert Carson, Jr. 1932- *WhoWest 92*
**Huntley,** Robert Ross 1926- *AmMWSc 92*
**Huntley James,** Ladonna *WhoMW 92*
**Huntly,** Marquess of 1944- *Who 92*
**Huntly,** Gibbs *ScFEYrs*
**Hunton,** Addie W. 1875-1943 *NotBlAW 92 [port]*
**Hunton,** Jerry Floyd 1950- *WhoAmP 91*
**Hunton,** Richard Edwin 1924- *WrDr 92*
**Huntoon,** Jacqueline E 1959- *AmMWSc 92*
**Huntoon,** Robert Brian 1927- *WhoFI 92*
**Huntress,** Betty Ann 1932- *WhoMW 92*
**Huntress,** Wesley Theodore, Jr 1942- *AmMWSc 92*
**Hunts,** Barney Dean 1936- *AmMWSc 92*
**Huntsberger,** David Vernon 1917- *AmMWSc 92*
**Huntsberger,** James Robert 1921- *AmMWSc 92*
**Huntsman,** Gene Raymond 1940- *AmMWSc 92*
**Huntsman,** Jon M 1937- *WhoAmP 91, WhoWest 92*
**Huntsman,** Lee L 1941- *AmMWSc 92*
**Huntsman,** Peter William 1935- *Who 92*
**Huntsman,** William Duane 1925- *AmMWSc 92*
**Huntwork,** John C 1948- *WhoAmP 91*
**Huntzicker,** James John 1941- *AmMWSc 92*
**Huntziger,** Charles 1880-1941 *EncTR 91*
**Hunzeker,** Hubert La Von 1920- *WhoMW 92*
**Hunzeker,** Hubert LaVon 1920- *AmMWSc 92*
**Hunzicker,** Warren John 1920- *WhoIns 92*
**Hunzicker-Dunn,** Mary *AmMWSc 92*
**Hunziker,** Heinrich Erwin 1934- *AmMWSc 92*
**Hunziker,** Rodney William 1922- *AmMWSc 92*
**Huo Shilian** 1911- *IntWW 91*
**Huong,** Tran Van *IntWW 91*
**Huotari,** Bernice M 1940- *WhoAmP 91*
**Hupalo,** Kathleen Fixsen 1945- *WhoAmL 92*
**Hupalowski,** Tadeusz 1922- *IntWW 91*
**Hupcey,** Joseph Vincent, Jr. 1944- *WhoEnt 92*
**Hupe,** Donald John 1944- *AmMWSc 92*
**Hupert,** Julius Jan Marian 1910- *AmMWSc 92*
**Hupka,** Arthur Lee 1940- *AmMWSc 92*
**Hupp,** Dennis Lee 1951- *WhoAmP 91*
**Hupp,** Eugene Wesley 1933- *AmMWSc 92*
**Hupp,** Harry L. 1929- *WhoAmL 92*
**Hupp,** Jack S 1930- *WhoIns 92*
**Hupp,** Patricia Ellen 1950- *WhoMW 92*
**Hupp,** Robert Craig 1949- *WhoAmL 92*
**Hupp,** Terrance Paul 1954- *WhoMW 92*
**Huppe,** Francis Frowin 1934- *AmMWSc 92*
**Huppert,** Herbert Eric 1943- *IntWW 91, Who 92*
**Huppert,** Irwin Neil 1938- *AmMWSc 92*
**Huppert,** Isabelle 1955- *IntMPA 92*
**Huppert,** Isabelle Anne 1953- *IntWW 91*
**Hupy,** Art 1924- *WhoWest 92*
**Huq,** Muhammad Shamsul 1910- *IntWW 91*
**Huq,** Shamsul 1931- *IntWW 91*
**Hur,** J James 1920- *AmMWSc 92*
**Hur,** Stephen Ponyi 1947- *WhoWest 92*
**Hura,** Gurdeep Singh 1950- *AmMWSc 92*
**Hurabiell,** John Philip, Sr. 1947- *WhoWest 92*
**Huras,** William David 1932- *WhoRel 92*
**Huray,** Paul Gordon 1941- *AmMWSc 92*
**Hurches,** Carlos E. *WhoHisp 92*
**Hurd,** Albert Edward 1940- *WhoRel 92*
**Hurd,** Albert Emerson *AmMWSc 92*
**Hurd,** Bruce Edward 1954- *WhoMW 92*
**Hurd,** Byron Thomas 1933- *WhoMW 92*
**Hurd,** Colin Michael 1937- *AmMWSc 92*
**Hurd,** Cuthbert Corwin 1911- *AmMWSc 92*
**Hurd,** David James, Jr. 1950- *WhoBlA 92*
**Hurd,** Douglas 1930- *IntAu&W 91, Who 92*
**Hurd,** Douglas Richard 1930- *IntWW 91*
**Hurd,** Dwight Irvin 1932- *WhoAmL 92*
**Hurd,** Edith Thacher *IntAu&W 91*
**Hurd,** Edith Thacher 1910- *SmATA 13AS [port]*
**Hurd,** Eric R 1936- *AmMWSc 92*
**Hurd,** G. David 1929- *WhoFI 92, WhoIns 92, WhoMW 92*
**Hurd,** Gale Anne 1955- *ConTFT 9, IntMPA 92, WhoEnt 92*
**Hurd,** James L. P. 1945- *WhoBlA 92*
**Hurd,** James William 1951- *AmMWSc 92*
**Hurd,** Jeffery L 1954- *AmMWSc 92*
**Hurd,** Jerrie W. *DrAPF 91*
**Hurd,** John Gavin 1914- *WhoAmP 91*
**Hurd,** Jon Rickey 1945- *AmMWSc 92*
**Hurd,** Joseph Kindall, Jr. 1938- *WhoBlA 92*
**Hurd,** Lawrence Edward 1947- *AmMWSc 92*
**Hurd,** Maggie Patricianne 1940- *AmMWSc 92*
**Hurd,** Michael 1928- *ConCom 92*
**Hurd,** Michael John 1928- *IntAu&W 91, WrDr 92*
**Hurd,** Paul DeHart 1905- *AmMWSc 92*
**Hurd,** Paul Gemmill 1946- *WhoAmL 92*
**Hurd,** Ralph Eugene 1950- *AmMWSc 92*
**Hurd,** Richard Nelson 1926- *AmMWSc 92*
**Hurd,** Robert Charles 1922- *AmMWSc 92*
**Hurd,** Suzanne Sheldon 1939- *AmMWSc 92*
**Hurd,** Thacher 1949- *ConAu 36NR*
**Hurd,** William Charles 1947- *WhoBlA 92*
**Hurdis,** Everett Cushing 1918- *AmMWSc 92*
**Hurdle,** Burton Garrison 1918- *AmMWSc 92*
**Hurdle,** Edmund Stephenson 1925- *WhoBlA 92*
**Hurdle,** Hortense O. McNeil 1925- *WhoBlA 92*
**Hurdle,** Robert 1918- *TwCPaSc*
**Hurdle,** Velma B. Brooks 1931- *WhoBlA 92*
**Huret,** Barry S. 1938- *WhoFI 92*
**Hurewitz,** Lane Steven 1962- *WhoAmL 92*
**Hurford,** Christopher John 1931- *IntWW 91*
**Hurford,** David Phelps 1959- *WhoMW 92*
**Hurford,** Peter 1930- *Who 92*
**Hurford,** Peter John 1930- *IntWW 91*
**Hurford,** Thomas Rowland 1941- *AmMWSc 92*
**Hurgerford,** Pixie *IntAu&W 91X*
**Hurkman,** Diane Lee 1950- *WhoMW 92*
**Hurlbert,** Bernard Stuart 1930- *AmMWSc 92*
**Hurlbert,** Robert Boston 1926- *AmMWSc 92*
**Hurlbert,** Roger William 1941- *WhoWest 92*
**Hurlbert,** Stuart Hartley 1939- *AmMWSc 92*
**Hurlburt,** David Arthur 1950- *WhoAmL 92*
**Hurlburt,** Douglas Herendeen 1941- *AmMWSc 92*
**Hurlburt,** H Zeh 1921- *AmMWSc 92*
**Hurlbut,** Cornelius Searle, Jr 1906- *AmMWSc 92, WrDr 92*
**Hurlbut,** Franklin Charles 1920- *AmMWSc 92*
**Hurlbut,** Jesse Lyman 1843-1930 *RelLAm 91*
**Hurlbut,** Robert Harold 1935- *WhoFI 92*
**Hurlbut,** Ronald Leon 1941- *WhoFI 92*
**Hurlbutt,** Henry Winthrop 1934- *AmMWSc 92*
**Hurlbutt,** Robert Harris, III 1924- *WhoMW 92*
**Hurley,** Alfred Francis 1928- *IntWW 91*
**Hurley,** Charles 1958- *WhoAmP 91*
**Hurley,** Christian Riblet 1956- *WhoFI 92*
**Hurley,** Denis Eugene 1915- *IntWW 91*
**Hurley,** Edmund Michael 1934- *WhoAmL 92*
**Hurley,** Forrest Reyburn 1921- *AmMWSc 92*
**Hurley,** Francis Joseph 1927- *AmMWSc 92*
**Hurley,** Francis T. 1927- *WhoRel 92, WhoWest 92*
**Hurley,** Frank Leo 1944- *AmMWSc 92*
**Hurley,** Frank Thomas, Jr. 1924- *WhoFI 92*
**Hurley,** George Willie 1884-1943 *RelLAm 91*
**Hurley,** Harry James 1926- *AmMWSc 92*
**Hurley,** Jack *WhoAmP 91*
**Hurley,** James Donald, Jr. 1935- *WhoFI 92*
**Hurley,** James Edgar 1929- *AmMWSc 92*
**Hurley,** James Edward, Jr. 1952- *WhoBlA 92*
**Hurley,** James Frederick 1941- *AmMWSc 92*
**Hurley,** James Joseph 1961- *WhoMW 92*
**Hurley,** James P 1932- *AmMWSc 92*
**Hurley,** James R 1931- *AmMWSc 92*
**Hurley,** James Richardson 1932- *WhoAmP 91*
**Hurley,** James Vincent 1934- *WhoAmL 92*
**Hurley,** John 1928- *WrDr 92*
**Hurley,** John Anthony 1945- *WhoMW 92*
**Hurley,** John Garling d1990 *Who 92N*
**Hurley,** John Kenneth 1931- *WhoFI 92*
**Hurley,** John Philip 1939- *WhoAmL 92*
**Hurley,** John W 1933- *WhoAmP 91*
**Hurley,** John William 1929- *WhoFI 92*
**Hurley,** Katherine Torkelsen 1921- *WhoAmP 91*
**Hurley,** Kevin James 1944- *WhoFI 92*
**Hurley,** Laurence Harold 1944- *AmMWSc 92*
**Hurley,** Lawrence Eugene 1925- *WhoAmP 91*
**Hurley,** Lawrence Joseph 1946- *WhoAmL 92*
**Hurley,** Margaret E *WhoAmP 91*
**Hurley,** Mark Joseph 1919- *WhoRel 92*
**Hurley,** Marlene Emogene 1938- *WhoWest 92*
**Hurley,** Mary E *WhoAmP 91*
**Hurley,** Maureen *AmMWSc 92, DrAPF 91*
**Hurley,** Michael Anthony 1923- *IntWW 91*
**Hurley,** Neal Lilburn 1928- *AmMWSc 92*
**Hurley,** Patrick J 1883-1963 *FacFETw*
**Hurley,** Patrick Joseph 1941- *WhoAmP 91*
**Hurley,** Patrick Mason 1912- *AmMWSc 92*
**Hurley,** Patrick W. 1937- *WhoAmL 92*
**Hurley,** Robert Edward 1911- *AmMWSc 92, WhoMW 92*
**Hurley,** Robert Joseph 1929- *AmMWSc 92*
**Hurley,** Robert Landon, Jr. 1948- *WhoEnt 92, WhoFI 92*
**Hurley,** Rosalinde 1929- *IntWW 91, Who 92*
**Hurley,** Ruby 1909-1980 *FacFETw, WhoBlA 92N*
**Hurley,** Ruby 1913?- *NotBlAW 92*
**Hurley,** Samuel Clay, III 1936- *WhoFI 92*
**Hurley,** Thomas G. *DrAPF 91*
**Hurley,** Willard Lee 1926- *WhoFI 92*
**Hurley,** William Charles 1931- *AmMWSc 92*
**Hurley,** William James, Jr. 1924- *WhoMW 92*
**Hurley,** William Jordan 1943- *AmMWSc 92*
**Hurley,** William Joseph 1926- *WhoAmL 92*
**Hurley,** William Joseph 1939- *WhoFI 92*
**Hurley,** William Joseph 1940- *AmMWSc 92*
**Hurlich,** Marshall Gerald 1946- *AmMWSc 92*
**Hurlimann,** Hans 1918- *IntWW 91*
**Hurll,** Alfred William d1991 *Who 92N*
**Hurlock,** James Bickford 1933- *WhoAmL 92*
**Hurlock,** Roger W. 1912- *IntMPA 92*
**Hurmence,** Belinda 1921- *ChILR 25 [port]*
**Hurn,** David 1934- *IntWW 91*
**Hurn,** R W 1919- *AmMWSc 92*
**Hurn,** Raymond Walter 1921- *WhoRel 92*
**Hurn,** Roger 1938- *Who 92*
**Hurney,** Kate 1940- *WhoEnt 92*
**Hurnik,** Ilja 1922- *IntWW 91*
**Hurok,** Sol 1888-1974 *FacFETw*
**Huron,** Bishop of 1938- *Who 92*
**Huron,** James Raymond 1936- *WhoMW 92, WhoRel 92*
**Huron,** Roderick Eugene 1934- *WhoRel 92*
**Hurrell,** Ann Patricia 1942- *WhoWest 92*
**Hurrell,** Anthony 1927- *Who 92*
**Hurrell,** Frederick Charles 1928- *Who 92*
**Hurrell,** John Patrick 1938- *AmMWSc 92*
**Hurren,** Eric 1922- *TwCPaSc*
**Hurren,** Weiler R 1935- *AmMWSc 92*
**Hurry,** Leslie 1909-1978 *TwCPaSc*
**Hursey,** James Samuel 1931- *WhoBlA 92*
**Hursey,** Ralph Michael 1951- *WhoAmL 92*

**Hursh,** John R 1943- *WhoAmP 91*
**Hursh,** John W 1920- *AmMWSc 92*
**Hursh,** Judy Ann Lopez 1945- *WhoAmP 91*
**Hursh,** Robert W 1916- *AmMWSc 92*
**Hurson,** John Adams *WhoAmP 91*
**Hurst and Blackett** *DcLB 106*
**Hurst,** Angas 1923- *IntWW 91*
**Hurst,** Beverly J. 1933- *WhoBlA 92*
**Hurst,** Bobby 1953- *WhoAmP 91*
**Hurst,** Charles Wilson 1957- *WhoAmL 92*
**Hurst,** Cleveland, Jr. 1939- *WhoBlA 92*
**Hurst,** Dave N. 1933- *WhoMW 92*
**Hurst,** David Charles 1928- *AmMWSc 92*
**Hurst,** Dennis Michael 1951- *WhoAmP 91*
**Hurst,** Donald D 1929- *AmMWSc 92*
**Hurst,** Edith Marie Maclennan 1926- *AmMWSc 92*
**Hurst,** Elaine H 1920- *AmMWSc 92*
**Hurst,** Ernest Connor 1926- *WhoAmL 92*
**Hurst,** Fannie 1889-1968 *BenetAL 91, DcAmImH, FacFETw*
**Hurst,** G Samuel 1927- *AmMWSc 92*
**Hurst,** George 1926- *NewAmDM, Who 92*
**Hurst,** Gerald Barry 1933- *WhoAmP 91*
**Hurst,** Gregory Squire 1947- *WhoEnt 92*
**Hurst,** H Rex 1939- *WhoIns 92*
**Hurst,** Harrell Emerson 1949- *AmMWSc 92*
**Hurst,** Henry Ronald Grimshaw 1919- *Who 92*
**Hurst,** Homer T 1919- *AmMWSc 92*
**Hurst,** James Kendall 1940- *AmMWSc 92*
**Hurst,** Janet Leigh 1950- *WhoEnt 92*
**Hurst,** Jeffrey Marshall 1956- *WhoFI 92*
**Hurst,** Jerry G 1932- *AmMWSc 92*
**Hurst,** John Gilbert 1927- *Who 92*
**Hurst,** Josephine M 1938- *AmMWSc 92*
**Hurst,** Lee Edwin, III 1956- *WhoAmP 91*
**Hurst,** Lionel Alexander 1950- *IntWW 91*
**Hurst,** Lorin Winslow, Jr. 1941- *WhoWest 92*
**Hurst,** Margaret Anne 1957- *WhoAmL 92*
**Hurst,** Mark W 1951- *WhoAmP 91*
**Hurst,** Peggy Morison 1925- *AmMWSc 92*
**Hurst,** Peter Thomas 1942- *Who 92*
**Hurst,** Rex LeRoy 1923- *AmMWSc 92*
**Hurst,** Richard Maurice 1938- *WhoMW 92*
**Hurst,** Richard William 1948- *AmMWSc 92*
**Hurst,** Robert 1915- *Who 92*
**Hurst,** Robert Jay 1945- *WhoFI 92*
**Hurst,** Robert Nelson 1930- *AmMWSc 92*
**Hurst,** Robert Philip 1930- *AmMWSc 92*
**Hurst,** Robert R 1937- *AmMWSc 92*
**Hurst,** Robert Thomas, Jr 1953- *WhoAmP 91*
**Hurst,** Rodney Lawrence 1944- *WhoBlA 92*
**Hurst,** S B H 1876-1937 *ScFEYrs*
**Hurst,** Sharleene Page 1959- *WhoAmP 91*
**Hurst,** Steve 1932- *TwCPaSc*
**Hurst,** Vernon James 1923- *AmMWSc 92*
**Hurst,** Wilbur Scott 1939- *AmMWSc 92*
**Hurst,** William Jeffrey 1948- *AmMWSc 92*
**Hurston,** Zora Neale 1891-1960 *AfrAmW, BenetAL 91, ModAWWr, NotBlAW 92 [port], RComAH*
**Hurston,** Zora Neale 1901?-1960 *BlkLC [port], FacFETw, HanAmWH*
**Hurt,** Alfred B, Jr 1920- *AmMWSc 92*
**Hurt,** Allen Frank 1946- *WhoEnt 92*
**Hurt,** Charlie Deuel, III 1950- *WhoWest 92*
**Hurt,** Daniel I. 1951- *WhoFI 92*
**Hurt,** David T. 1940- *WhoMW 92*
**Hurt,** H David 1941- *AmMWSc 92*
**Hurt,** Hubert Olyn 1925- *WhoRel 92*
**Hurt,** James E. 1928- *WhoBlA 92*
**Hurt,** James Edward 1935- *AmMWSc 92*
**Hurt,** James Joseph 1939- *AmMWSc 92, WhoMW 92*
**Hurt,** James Riggins 1934- *WhoMW 92*
**Hurt,** Jennings Laverne, III 1952- *WhoAmL 92*
**Hurt,** John 1940- *IntMPA 92, IntWW 91, Who 92*
**Hurt,** John Calvin 1941- *AmMWSc 92*
**Hurt,** John Vincent 1940- *WhoEnt 92*
**Hurt,** Joseph Richard 1953- *WhoAmL 92*
**Hurt,** Katha 1947- *WhoAmP 91*
**Hurt,** Larry Emery 1944- *WhoRel 92*
**Hurt,** Louis T., Sr. 1938- *WhoBlA 92*
**Hurt,** Marcia Ellen 1946- *WhoMW 92*
**Hurt,** Mark Albert 1956- *WhoMW 92*
**Hurt,** Mary Beth *WhoEnt 92*
**Hurt,** Mary Beth 1948- *IntMPA 92*
**Hurt,** Mississippi John 1894-1966 *NewAmDM*
**Hurt,** Robert Glenn 1919- *WhoFI 92, WhoWest 92*
**Hurt,** Robert H 1943- *WhoAmP 91*
**Hurt,** Steven Eugene 1947- *WhoMW 92*
**Hurt,** Susan Schilt 1947- *AmMWSc 92*
**Hurt,** Verner C 1929- *AmMWSc 92*
**Hurt,** Waverly Glenn 1938- *AmMWSc 92*
**Hurt,** William 1950- *IntMPA 92, IntWW 91, WhoEnt 92*
**Hurt,** William C, Jr 1907- *AmMWSc 92*
**Hurt,** William Clarence 1922- *AmMWSc 92*
**Hurt-Bacchetti,** Pamela Denise 1964- *WhoMW 92*
**Hurtado,** Ciro 1954- *WhoHisp 92*
**Hurtado,** I. Jay 1943- *WhoHisp 92*
**Hurtado de Mendoza,** Garcia 1535-1609 *HisDSpE*
**Hurtado Larrea,** Oswaldo 1940- *IntWW 91*
**Hurtarte,** Susana Penalosa 1946- *WhoHisp 92*
**Hurte,** Leroy E. 1915- *WhoBlA 92*
**Hurter,** Arthur P 1936- *AmMWSc 92*
**Hurter,** Arthur Patrick *WhoFI 92, WhoMW 92*
**Hurtes,** Hettie Lynne 1952- *WhoEnt 92*
**Hurtgen,** Peter Joseph 1941- *WhoAmL 92*
**Hurtig,** Anita Landau 1932- *WhoMW 92*
**Hurto,** Kirk Allen 1951- *AmMWSc 92*
**Hurtt,** Woodland 1932- *AmMWSc 92*
**Hurtubise,** Mark 1948- *WhoWest 92*
**Hurtubise,** Robert John 1941- *AmMWSc 92*
**Hurvich,** Leo M. 1910- *IntWW 91*
**Hurvich,** Leo Maurice 1910- *AmMWSc 92*
**Hurvitz,** Arthur Isaac 1939- *AmMWSc 92*
**Hurwicz,** Leonid 1917- *AmMWSc 92*
**Hurwitz,** Abraham B. 1905-1981 *ConAu 133*
**Hurwitz,** Alexander 1937- *AmMWSc 92*
**Hurwitz,** Charles E 1937- *AmMWSc 92*
**Hurwitz,** David Allan 1938- *AmMWSc 92*
**Hurwitz,** David Louis 1967- *WhoWest 92*
**Hurwitz,** Emanuel 1919- *IntWW 91*
**Hurwitz,** Henry, Jr 1918- *AmMWSc 92*
**Hurwitz,** Holly Ann 1955- *WhoWest 92*
**Hurwitz,** Irving Leonard 1941- *WhoAmL 92*
**Hurwitz,** Jan Krosst 1924- *AmMWSc 92*
**Hurwitz,** Jeffrey Stephen 1950- *WhoFI 92*
**Hurwitz,** Jerard 1928- *AmMWSc 92, IntWW 91*
**Hurwitz,** Johanna *DrAPF 91*
**Hurwitz,** Johanna 1937- *WrDr 92*
**Hurwitz,** Lawrence Neal 1939- *WhoFI 92*
**Hurwitz,** Leo d1991 *NewYTBS 91*
**Hurwitz,** Leon *AmMWSc 92*
**Hurwitz,** Melvin David 1917- *AmMWSc 92*
**Hurwitz,** Michael 1956- *WhoEnt 92*
**Hurwitz,** Michele Leslie Weber 1959- *WhoMW 92*
**Hurwitz,** Robert Irving 1939- *WhoEnt 92*
**Hurwitz,** Shawn Michael 1965- *WhoFI 92*
**Hurwitz,** Solomon 1907- *AmMWSc 92*
**Hurwitz,** Victor 1926- *WhoEnt 92*
**Hurwitz,** Vivian Ronald 1926- *Who 92*
**Hury,** James 1946- *WhoAmP 91*
**Hurych,** Zdenek 1941- *AmMWSc 92*
**Husa,** Donald L 1940- *AmMWSc 92*
**Husa,** Karel 1921- *ConCom 92, NewAmDM*
**Husa,** Karel Jaroslav 1921- *WhoEnt 92*
**Husa,** William John, Jr 1927- *AmMWSc 92*
**Husain,** Abul Basher M. *Who 92*
**Husain,** Ansar 1923- *AmMWSc 92*
**Husain,** Liaquat 1942- *AmMWSc 92*
**Husain,** Maqbool Fida 1915- *IntWW 91*
**Husain,** Mazhar 1949- *WhoFI 92*
**Husain,** Syed 1939- *AmMWSc 92*
**Husain,** Syed Alamdar 1931- *AmMWSc 92*
**Husain,** Taqdir 1929- *AmMWSc 92*
**Husaini,** Saeed A 1926- *AmMWSc 92*
**Husak,** Emil J 1930- *WhoAmP 91*
**Husak,** Gustav 1913- *FacFETw, IntWW 91*
**Husak,** Gustav 1913-1991 *NewYTBS 91 [port]*
**Husar,** John Paul 1937- *WhoMW 92*
**Husar,** Rudolf Bertalan 1941- *AmMWSc 92*
**Husarik,** Ernest Alfred 1941- *WhoMW 92*
**Husarik,** Stephen 1944- *WhoEnt 92, WhoMW 92*
**Husband,** David Dwight 1939- *AmMWSc 92*
**Husband,** Herman 1724-1795? *DcNCBi 3*
**Husband,** J. D. *WhoRel 92*
**Husband,** John Frederick 1949- *WhoMW 92*
**Husband,** John Michael 1952- *WhoAmL 92*
**Husband,** Richard Lorin, Sr. 1931- *WhoFI 92*
**Husband,** Rick Douglas 1957- *WhoWest 92*
**Husband,** Robert Murray 1919- *AmMWSc 92*
**Husband,** Robert W 1931- *AmMWSc 92*
**Husband,** Robert Wayne 1931- *WhoMW 92*
**Husband,** Thomas Mutrie 1936- *Who 92*
**Husband,** Thomas Paul 1950- *AmMWSc 92*
**Husband,** William Swire 1939- *WhoMW 92*
**Husbands,** Herman 1724-1795? *DcNCBi 3*
**Husby,** David Michael 1943- *WhoWest 92*
**Husby,** Fredric Martin 1943- *AmMWSc 92*
**Husby,** John Richard 1950- *WhoMW 92*
**Husch,** Lawrence S 1942- *AmMWSc 92*
**Huschilt,** John 1931- *AmMWSc 92*
**Huschke,** Ralph Ernest 1925- *AmMWSc 92*
**Huse,** Eugene Franklin 1927- *WhoMW 92*
**Huse,** Howard Russel 1890-1977 *DcNCBi 3*
**Huseboe,** Doris Louise 1933- *WhoMW 92*
**Husemann,** Friedrich 1873-1935 *EncTR 91*
**Husemoller,** Roger P 1939- *WhoIns 92*
**Husen,** Torsten 1916- *IntWW 91*
**Huset,** Richard Alfred 1947- *WhoMW 92*
**Huseyin,** Koncay 1936- *AmMWSc 92*
**Hush,** Noel Sydney 1924- *IntWW 91, Who 92*
**Hushak,** Leroy J 1939- *AmMWSc 92*
**Husick,** Lawrence Alan 1958- *WhoAmL 92*
**Husimi,** Kodi 1909- *IntWW 91*
**Husk,** Donald Estel 1925- *WhoMW 92*
**Husk,** George Ronald 1937- *AmMWSc 92*
**Huske,** John d1792 *DcNCBi 3*
**Huskey,** Glen E 1931- *AmMWSc 92*
**Huskey,** Harry D 1916- *AmMWSc 92*
**Huskey,** Harry Douglas 1916- *WhoWest 92*
**Huskey,** Herbert 1916- *WhoAmP 91*
**Huskey,** Larry C 1944- *WhoAmP 91*
**Huskey,** Robert John 1938- *AmMWSc 92*
**Huskey,** William Jerome 1936- *WhoAmP 91*
**Huskins,** Amelia Hughes 1959- *WhoAmL 92*
**Huskins,** Chester Walker 1921- *AmMWSc 92*
**Huskins,** Joseph Patterson 1908- *WhoAmP 91*
**Huskisson,** Robert Andrews 1923- *Who 92*
**Husman,** Catherine Bigot 1943- *WhoIns 92*
**Husmann,** George 1827-1902 *BiInAmS*
**Husni,** Elias A 1924- *AmMWSc 92*
**Huson,** Christopher John 1958- *WhoMW 92*
**Huson,** Frederick Russell 1936- *AmMWSc 92*
**Huson,** Paul 1942- *WrDr 92*
**Huson,** Paul Anthony 1942- *WhoEnt 92*
**Huss,** Betty Jo 1932- *WhoMW 92*
**Huss,** Charles Maurice 1946- *WhoWest 92*
**Huss,** Edward Adolf 1926- *WhoWest 92*
**Huss,** Glenn I 1921- *AmMWSc 92*
**Huss,** Harry O 1912- *AmMWSc 92*
**Huss,** Harry Otto 1912- *WhoMW 92*
**Huss,** Ronald John 1953- *AmMWSc 92*
**Huss,** Walter 1918- *WhoAmP 91*
**Huss,** William Lee 1956- *WhoMW 92*
**Hussa,** Robert Oscar 1941- *AmMWSc 92*
**Hussain,** A K M Fazle 1943- *AmMWSc 92*
**Hussain,** Kabir 1960- *TwCPaSc*
**Hussain,** Karamat 1926- *Who 92*
**Hussain,** Malek Gholoum Malek 1953- *AmMWSc 92*
**Hussain,** Moayyed A 1937- *AmMWSc 92*
**Hussain,** Mohammed Mustafa 1948- *IntWW 91*
**Hussain,** Nayyer 1954- *WhoFI 92*
**Hussain,** Nihad A 1941- *AmMWSc 92*
**Hussain,** Riaz 1937- *AmMWSc 92*
**Hussain,** Syed Taseer 1943- *AmMWSc 92*
**Hussak,** Robert Edward 1961- *AmMWSc 92*
**Hussamy,** Samir 1935- *AmMWSc 92*
**Hussar,** Daniel Alexander 1941- *AmMWSc 92*
**Hussein** 1952- *FacFETw [port]*
**Hussein bin Dato Onn** 1922-1990 *FacFETw*
**Hussein Bin Onn** d1990 *IntWW 91N*
**Hussein bin Talal** 1935- *Who 92*
**Hussein Ibn Talal** 1935- *IntWW 91*
**Hussein,** Abdirizak Haji 1924- *IntWW 91*
**Hussein,** Abdul-Aziz 1921- *IntWW 91*
**Hussein,** Carlessia Amanda 1936- *WhoBlA 92*
**Hussein,** Hamzah Abbas 1934- *IntWW 91*
**Hussein,** Mansour 1923- *IntWW 91*
**Hussein,** Saddam *IntWW 91*
**Hussein,** Saddam 1937- *FacFETw [port], News 91 [port]*
**Hussein,** Uday *NewYTBS 91 [port]*
**Hussein,** Waris 1938- *IntMPA 92, WhoEnt 92*
**Husserl,** Consuelo R. 1948- *WhoHisp 92*
**Husserl,** E. G. *ConAu 133*
**Husserl,** Edmund 1859-1938 *ConAu 133, FacFETw*
**Husserl,** Fred E. 1946- *WhoHisp 92*
**Hussey,** Arthur M, II 1931- *AmMWSc 92*
**Hussey,** Charles Logan 1947- *AmMWSc 92*
**Hussey,** Clara Veronica 1920- *AmMWSc 92*
**Hussey,** Daniel James 1947- *WhoAmP 91*
**Hussey,** Edward Walter 1938- *AmMWSc 92*
**Hussey,** Elisabeth 1929- *IntAu&W 91*
**Hussey,** Gemma 1938- *IntWW 91*
**Hussey,** Joan Mervyn *Who 92*
**Hussey,** John B *WhoAmP 91*
**Hussey,** Keith Morgan 1908- *AmMWSc 92*
**Hussey,** Leonard *IntAu&W 91X*
**Hussey,** Mark 1956- *ConAu 135*
**Hussey,** Marmaduke James 1923- *IntWW 91, Who 92*
**Hussey,** Olivia 1951- *IntMPA 92*
**Hussey,** Richard Sommers 1942- *AmMWSc 92*
**Hussey,** Robert D *WhoAmP 91*
**Hussey,** Robert E, Jr *WhoAmP 91*
**Hussey,** Robert Gregory 1935- *AmMWSc 92*
**Hussey,** Ruth *WhoEnt 92*
**Hussey,** Susan Katharine 1939- *Who 92*
**Hussey,** Walter 1909-1985 *ConAu 133*
**Hussian,** Richard A 1952- *AmMWSc 92*
**Hussingtree,** Martin 1899- *ScFEYrs*
**Husson,** Philippe Jean Louis Marie 1927- *IntWW 91*
**Husson,** Samir S 1934- *AmMWSc 92*
**Hussong,** Donald MacGregor 1942- *AmMWSc 92*
**Hussung,** Alleen Mosette 1934- *WhoEnt 92*
**Hussung,** Karl Frederick 1931- *AmMWSc 92*
**Hust,** Bruce Kevin 1957- *WhoAmL 92*
**Hust,** Jerome Gerhardt 1932- *AmMWSc 92*
**Hustad,** Carolyn Marziasz 1963- *WhoWest 92*
**Hustad,** Dianne Michelle 1960- *WhoFI 92*
**Hustad,** Thomas Pegg 1945- *WhoFI 92, WhoMW 92*
**Husted,** Albert N 1833-1912 *BiInAmS*
**Husted,** Clinton Chandler, Jr. 1950- *WhoFI 92*
**Husted,** John E 1915- *AmMWSc 92*
**Husted,** Russell Forest 1950- *AmMWSc 92*
**Hustoles,** Paul John 1952- *WhoEnt 92, WhoMW 92*
**Huston,** Anjelica *FacFETw*
**Huston,** Anjelica 1951- *IntMPA 92, WhoEnt 92*
**Huston,** Anjelica 1952- *IntWW 91*
**Huston,** Danny 1962- *IntMPA 92*
**Huston,** DeVerille Anne 1947- *WhoAmL 92*
**Huston,** Ernest Lee 1940- *AmMWSc 92*
**Huston,** Harriette Irene Otwell *WhoWest 92*
**Huston,** James Webb 1953- *WhoAmL 92*
**Huston,** Jeffrey Charles 1951- *AmMWSc 92, WhoMW 92*
**Huston,** Jimmy 1947- *WhoEnt 92*
**Huston,** John 1906- *IntAu&W 91*
**Huston,** John 1906-1987 *BenetAL 91, ConAu 34NR, FacFETw, IntDcF 2-2 [port]*
**Huston,** John Charles 1927- *WhoWest 92*
**Huston,** John Lewis 1919- *AmMWSc 92*
**Huston,** John Richard 1920- *WhoWest 92*
**Huston,** Joyce W. 1940- *WhoMW 92*
**Huston,** Keith Arthur 1926- *AmMWSc 92*
**Huston,** Mervyn J. 1912- *WrDr 92*
**Huston,** Mervyn James 1912- *AmMWSc 92*
**Huston,** Michael E 1948- *WhoIns 92*
**Huston,** Norman Earl 1919- *AmMWSc 92*
**Huston,** Robert James 1931- *AmMWSc 92*
**Huston,** Ronald L 1937- *AmMWSc 92*
**Huston,** Scott 1916- *NewAmDM*
**Huston,** Scott Alan 1960- *WhoEnt 92*
**Huston,** Sterling Wendell 1936- *WhoRel 92*
**Huston,** Thelma Diane 1956- *WhoHisp 92*
**Huston,** Walter *FacFETw*
**Huston,** William Alvin 1939- *WhoWest 92*
**Hustrulid,** William A 1940- *AmMWSc 92*
**Huszar,** Arlene Celia 1952- *WhoAmL 92*
**Huszar,** Gabor *AmMWSc 92*
**Huszar,** Marta Jean 1953- *WhoEnt 92*
**Huszti,** Joseph Bela 1936- *WhoWest 92*
**Hut,** Piet 1952- *AmMWSc 92*
**Huta,** Henry Nicholaus 1947- *WhoFI 92*
**Hutasingh,** Prakob 1912- *IntWW 91*
**Hutchcraft,** A. Stephens, Jr. 1930- *WhoWest 92*
**Hutchcroft,** Alan Charles 1941- *AmMWSc 92*
**Hutchcroft,** Charles Dennett 1918- *AmMWSc 92*
**Hutchcroft,** John Carter 1941- *WhoEnt 92*
**Hutchcroft,** Kevin 1964- *WhoAmP 91*
**Hutchenrider,** Clarence B. d1991 *NewYTBS 91*
**Hutchens,** Ann 1936- *WhoAmP 91*
**Hutchens,** Don Derrel 1948- *WhoAmP 91*
**Hutchens,** John Oliver 1914- *AmMWSc 92*
**Hutchens,** Tyra Thornton 1921- *AmMWSc 92*
**Hutcheon,** Cifford Robert 1913- *WhoFI 92*

**Hutcheon,** Duncan Elliot 1922- *AmMWSc 92*
**Hutcherson,** Bernice B. R. 1925- *WhoBlA 92*
**Hutcherson,** Joseph William 1940- *AmMWSc 92*
**Hutcheson,** David Paul 1941- *AmMWSc 92*
**Hutcheson,** Eldridge Tilmon, III 1942- *AmMWSc 92*
**Hutcheson,** Francis 1694-1746 *BlkwCEP*
**Hutcheson,** Harvie Leon, Jr 1937- *AmMWSc 92*
**Hutcheson,** J A 1905- *AmMWSc 92*
**Hutcheson,** James Sterling 1919- *WhoAmL 92*
**Hutcheson,** Jere Trent 1938- *WhoEnt 92*
**Hutcheson,** Jerry Dee 1932- *WhoWest 92*
**Hutcheson,** Kermit 1929- *AmMWSc 92*
**Hutcheson,** Kevin Scott 1959- *WhoAmL 92*
**Hutcheson,** Paul Henry 1928- *AmMWSc 92*
**Hutcheson,** Philo Allen 1951- *WhoMW 92*
**Hutcheson,** Thomas Barksdale, Jr 1926- *AmMWSc 92*
**Hutcheson,** Zenas Willard, III 1953- *WhoFI 92*
**Hutcheson-Tipton,** David Quinn 1962- *WhoRel 92*
**Hutchey,** Brenda Jean 1952- *WhoEnt 92*
**Hutchin,** Kenneth Charles 1908- *WrDr 92*
**Hutchin,** Maxine E 1922- *AmMWSc 92*
**Hutchin,** Richard Ariel 1946- *AmMWSc 92*
**Hutchings,** Andrew William Seymour 1907- *Who 92*
**Hutchings,** Brian Lamar 1915- *AmMWSc 92*
**Hutchings,** Donald Edward 1934- *AmMWSc 92*
**Hutchings,** Gregory Frederick *Who 92*
**Hutchings,** John Barrie 1941- *AmMWSc 92*
**Hutchings,** L E 1920- *AmMWSc 92*
**Hutchings,** Marjorie Clyde 1922- *WhoAmP 91*
**Hutchings,** Peter Lounsbery 1943- *WhoFI 92*
**Hutchings,** Vernon Michael 1955- *WhoAmP 91*
**Hutchings,** William A. 1952- *WhoRel 92*
**Hutchings,** William Frank 1938- *AmMWSc 92*
**Hutchins,** Bertha 1938- *WhoBlA 92*
**Hutchins,** C W 1931- *WhoAmP 91*
**Hutchins,** Charles Larry 1938- *WhoWest 92*
**Hutchins,** Christine Burbank 1919- *WhoAmP 91*
**Hutchins,** Dexter Carleton 1938- *WhoFI 92*
**Hutchins,** Donovan Bartlett 1955- *WhoAmL 92*
**Hutchins,** Earl Leroy 1908- *WhoWest 92*
**Hutchins,** Elizabeth Leigh 1858-1935 *BiDBrF 2*
**Hutchins,** Francis Gilman 1939- *WrDr 92*
**Hutchins,** Francis L., Jr. 1943- *WhoBlA 92*
**Hutchins,** Fred S, Jr 1932- *WhoAmP 91*
**Hutchins,** Grace 1885-1969 *AmPeW*
**Hutchins,** Gregory Ray 1955- *WhoEnt 92, WhoRel 92*
**Hutchins,** Grover MacGregor 1932- *AmMWSc 92*
**Hutchins,** Hastings Harold, Sr 1922- *AmMWSc 92*
**Hutchins,** Hazel J. 1952- *WrDr 92*
**Hutchins,** Henry T. 1931-1987 *WhoBlA 92N*
**Hutchins,** Jan Darwin 1949- *WhoBlA 92*
**Hutchins,** Jeffrey Carlton 1959- *WhoWest 92*
**Hutchins,** John R, III 1934- *AmMWSc 92*
**Hutchins,** Joshua I., Jr. 1937- *WhoBlA 92*
**Hutchins,** Lawrence G., Sr. 1931- *WhoBlA 92*
**Hutchins,** MaryGail Kinzer 1940- *AmMWSc 92*
**Hutchins,** Maude *DrAPF 91, IntAu&W 91*
**Hutchins,** Pat 1942- *IntAu&W 91, WrDr 92*
**Hutchins,** Phillip Michael 1942- *AmMWSc 92*
**Hutchins,** Robert Ayer 1940- *WhoFI 92, WhoMW 92*
**Hutchins,** Robert Maynard 1899-1977 *BenetAL 91, FacFETw, RComAH*
**Hutchins,** Robert Owen, Sr 1939- *AmMWSc 92*
**Hutchins,** Robert S. d1990 *NewYTBS 91*
**Hutchins,** Robert Wendel 1945- *WhoAmP 91*
**Hutchins,** Ronald Edward 1912- *Who 92*
**Hutchins,** Sandra Elaine 1946- *WhoWest 92*
**Hutchins,** Susan Louise 1953- *WhoAmP 91*
**Hutchins,** Thomas 1730-1789 *BiInAmS*
**Hutchins,** William Bruce, III 1943- *WhoFI 92*
**Hutchins,** William R 1919- *AmMWSc 92*
**Hutchinson** *DcLB 112, Who 92*
**Hutchinson Family** *NewAmDM*
**Hutchinson,** Alan Bradford 1927- *WhoRel 92*
**Hutchinson,** Alfred 1924- *LiExTwC*
**Hutchinson,** Amos K 1920- *WhoAmP 91*
**Hutchinson,** Anne 1591-1643 *BenetAL 91, PorAmW [port], RComAH*
**Hutchinson,** Anne Marbury 1591-1643 *HanAmWH*
**Hutchinson,** Arno Merton, Jr. 1924- *WhoRel 92*
**Hutchinson,** Arthur Edward 1934- *Who 92*
**Hutchinson,** Bennett B 1942- *AmMWSc 92*
**Hutchinson,** Betty Jo 1933- *WhoAmP 91*
**Hutchinson,** Bruce Neil 1945- *WhoWest 92*
**Hutchinson,** C. Alan 1914-1981 *ConAu 133*
**Hutchinson,** Carell, Jr. 1930- *WhoBlA 92*
**Hutchinson,** Carroll R 1933- *WhoIns 92*
**Hutchinson,** Charles E 1935- *AmMWSc 92*
**Hutchinson,** Charles F 1946- *AmMWSc 92*
**Hutchinson,** Charles Kimball 1928- *WhoFI 92*
**Hutchinson,** Charles Percy, Jr. 1935- *WhoFI 92*
**Hutchinson,** Charles S, Jr 1930- *AmMWSc 92*
**Hutchinson,** Chester R. 1950- *WhoBlA 92*
**Hutchinson,** Christopher Haynes d1990 *Who 92N*
**Hutchinson,** Deborah Gibson 1956- *WhoFI 92*
**Hutchinson,** Donald Patrick 1947- *AmMWSc 92*
**Hutchinson,** Donald Paul 1945- *WhoAmP 91*
**Hutchinson,** Dorothy Hewitt 1905-1984 *AmPeW*
**Hutchinson,** Eric 1920- *AmMWSc 92*
**Hutchinson,** Everett 1915- *WhoAmL 92*
**Hutchinson,** Franklin 1920- *AmMWSc 92*
**Hutchinson,** Frederick Edward 1930- *AmMWSc 92*
**Hutchinson,** G. Evelyn 1903-1991 *ConAu 134*
**Hutchinson,** George 1938- *WhoBlA 92*
**Hutchinson,** George Allen 1936- *AmMWSc 92*
**Hutchinson,** George Evelyn 1903- *AmMWSc 92*
**Hutchinson,** George J. 1937- *WhoFI 92, WhoIns 92*
**Hutchinson,** George Keating 1932- *AmMWSc 92*
**Hutchinson,** George Malcolm 1935- *Who 92*
**Hutchinson,** George William 1921- *Who 92*
**Hutchinson,** Gordon Lee 1943- *AmMWSc 92*
**Hutchinson,** Gradystein Williams 1933- *NewYTBS 91 [port]*
**Hutchinson,** Harold David 1931- *AmMWSc 92*
**Hutchinson,** Harold Lee 1939- *AmMWSc 92*
**Hutchinson,** Harry F 1919- *WhoFI 92*
**Hutchinson,** James Herbert, Jr 1933- *AmMWSc 92*
**Hutchinson,** James J., Jr. 1947- *WhoBlA 92*
**Hutchinson,** James R 1932- *AmMWSc 92*
**Hutchinson,** James Richard 1936- *WhoMW 92*
**Hutchinson,** Jerome 1926- *WhoBlA 92*
**Hutchinson,** Joan Prince 1945- *AmMWSc 92*
**Hutchinson,** John 1674-1737 *BlkwCEP*
**Hutchinson,** John Maxwell 1948- *Who 92*
**Hutchinson,** John W 1927- *AmMWSc 92*
**Hutchinson,** John William 1938- *WhoFI 92*
**Hutchinson,** Joseph Candler 1920- *WhoWest 92*
**Hutchinson,** Joseph Wood, III 1953- *WhoAmL 92*
**Hutchinson,** Julius Steven 1952- *WhoFI 92*
**Hutchinson,** Kenneth A 1932- *AmMWSc 92*
**Hutchinson,** Kirk 1956- *WhoEnt 92*
**Hutchinson,** Leslie *WhoAmP 91*
**Hutchinson,** Louise *TwCPaSc*
**Hutchinson,** Louise Daniel 1928- *WhoBlA 92*
**Hutchinson,** Malcolm *Who 92*
**Hutchinson,** Mark Christopher 1962- *WhoMW 92*
**Hutchinson,** Maxwell *Who 92*
**Hutchinson,** Maxwell 1948- *IntWW 91*
**Hutchinson,** Nancy Anne 1947- *WhoWest 92*
**Hutchinson,** Orion Neely, Jr. 1928- *WhoRel 92*
**Hutchinson,** Patricia Margaret 1926- *Who 92*
**Hutchinson,** Paul Bryant 1959- *WhoEnt 92*
**Hutchinson,** Paul R, Jr 1937- *WhoAmP 91*
**Hutchinson,** Pearse 1927- *IntAu&W 91, WrDr 92*
**Hutchinson,** Pemberton 1931- *WhoFI 92*
**Hutchinson,** Philip 1938- *Who 92*
**Hutchinson,** Richard Allen 1942- *AmMWSc 92*
**Hutchinson,** Richard Hampson 1927- *Who 92*
**Hutchinson,** Richard Jerome 1958- *WhoMW 92*
**Hutchinson,** Richard William 1928- *AmMWSc 92*
**Hutchinson,** Robert B. *DrAPF 91*
**Hutchinson,** Robert Maskiell 1928- *AmMWSc 92*
**Hutchinson,** Ron *IntAu&W 91, WrDr 92*
**Hutchinson,** Ross 1914- *Who 92*
**Hutchinson,** Suzanne 1957- *TwCPaSc*
**Hutchinson,** Thomas 1711-1780 *AmPolLe, BenetAL 91, BlkwEAR, RComAH*
**Hutchinson,** Thomas C 1939- *AmMWSc 92*
**Hutchinson,** Thomas Eugene 1936- *AmMWSc 92*
**Hutchinson,** Tom *WhoEnt 92*
**Hutchinson,** W Asa 1950- *WhoAmP 91*
**Hutchinson,** Warren B *ScFEYrs*
**Hutchinson,** William Burke 1909- *AmMWSc 92*
**Hutchinson,** William D 1932- *WhoAmP 91*
**Hutchinson,** William David 1932- *WhoAmL 92*
**Hutchinson,** William Oliphant 1889-1970 *TwCPaSc*
**Hutchinson,** Y Tim 1949- *WhoAmP 91*
**Hutchinson of Lullington,** Baron 1915- *Who 92*
**Hutchison,** A. Michael Clark 1914- *Who 92*
**Hutchison,** Agnes Diana 1953- *WhoEnt 92*
**Hutchison,** Andrew *Who 92*
**Hutchison,** Bruce *Who 92*
**Hutchison,** Clyde A., Jr. 1913- *IntWW 91*
**Hutchison,** Clyde Allen, III 1938- *AmMWSc 92*
**Hutchison,** Clyde Allen, Jr 1913- *AmMWSc 92*
**Hutchison,** Craig Austin 1952- *WhoMW 92*
**Hutchison,** David Allan 1947- *AmMWSc 92*
**Hutchison,** David M 1935- *AmMWSc 92*
**Hutchison,** Dorris Jeannette 1918- *AmMWSc 92*
**Hutchison,** Douglas *Who 92*
**Hutchison,** Douglas Paul 1939- *WhoAmL 92*
**Hutchison,** Geordie Oliphant 1934- *Who 92*
**Hutchison,** George B 1922- *AmMWSc 92*
**Hutchison,** George Ian Clark 1903- *Who 92*
**Hutchison,** Harry Greene, IV 1948- *WhoBlA 92*
**Hutchison,** Helena Ann *Who 92*
**Hutchison,** Henry 1923- *WrDr 92*
**Hutchison,** Humphrey Gray 1919- *WhoFI 92*
**Hutchison,** Ian Clark *Who 92*
**Hutchison,** James A 1930- *AmMWSc 92*
**Hutchison,** James Robert 1940- *AmMWSc 92*
**Hutchison,** Jane Campbell 1932- *WhoMW 92*
**Hutchison,** Janie Ruth 1943- *WhoEnt 92*
**Hutchison,** Jeanne S 1942- *AmMWSc 92*
**Hutchison,** John Howard 1939- *AmMWSc 92*
**Hutchison,** John Joseph 1939- *AmMWSc 92*
**Hutchison,** Joseph *DrAPF 91*
**Hutchison,** Joseph Douglas 1918- *Who 92*
**Hutchison,** Kathryn Lee 1945- *WhoRel 92*
**Hutchison,** Kay Bailey 1943- *WhoAmP 91*
**Hutchison,** Kenneth James 1936- *AmMWSc 92*
**Hutchison,** Loyal Dwayne 1933- *WhoWest 92*
**Hutchison,** Michael 1933- *Who 92*
**Hutchison,** Nancy Jean 1950- *AmMWSc 92*
**Hutchison,** Pearse 1927- *ConPo 91*
**Hutchison,** Peter 1907- *Who 92*
**Hutchison,** Peter Craft 1935- *Who 92*
**Hutchison,** Peyton S. 1925- *WhoBlA 92*
**Hutchison,** Richard Connor 1933- *WhoRel 92*
**Hutchison,** Richard David 1957- *WhoRel 92*
**Hutchison,** Robert B 1935- *AmMWSc 92*
**Hutchison,** Robert Edward 1922- *Who 92*
**Hutchison,** Ronald Blaine 1950- *WhoFI 92*
**Hutchison,** Sidney Charles 1912- *Who 92, WrDr 92*
**Hutchison,** Terence Wilmot 1912- *Who 92*
**Hutchison,** Theodore M 1932- *WhoIns 92*
**Hutchison,** Thomas Oliver 1931- *Who 92*
**Hutchison,** Thomas Sherret 1921- *AmMWSc 92*
**Hutchison,** Victor Hobbs 1931- *AmMWSc 92*
**Hutchison,** Warner 1930- *WhoEnt 92*
**Hutchison,** William Bruce 1901- *Who 92*
**Hutchison,** William Forrest 1925- *AmMWSc 92*
**Hutchison,** William Marwick 1919- *AmMWSc 92*
**Hutchison,** William McPhee 1924- *Who 92*
**Hutchison,** William Robert 1930- *WhoRel 92*
**Hutchison,** William Watt 1935- *AmMWSc 92*
**Hutchison-Hall,** William Ellsworth H., IV 1963- *WhoFI 92*
**Hutckins,** Sherman H *WhoAmP 91*
**Huth,** Edward J 1923- *AmMWSc 92*
**Huth,** James J. 1967- *WhoEnt 92*
**Huth,** William L. 1950- *WhoFI 92*
**Huthmacher,** J Joseph 1929- *IntAu&W 91*
**Huthmacher,** Marilyn Anne 1930- *WhoAmP 91*
**Huthnance,** Edward Dennis, Jr 1942- *AmMWSc 92*
**Hutjens,** Michael Francis 1945- *AmMWSc 92*
**Hutler,** David 1935- *TwCPaSc*
**Hutner,** Herbert L. *WhoWest 92*
**Hutner,** Seymour Herbert 1911- *AmMWSc 92*
**Hutnik,** Russell James 1924- *AmMWSc 92*
**Hutoron,** Adam Nathan 1965- *WhoWest 92*
**Hutson,** Andrew Rhodes 1926- *AmMWSc 92*
**Hutson,** AnnMarie 1965- *WhoRel 92*
**Hutson,** Arthur James 1947- *WhoMW 92*
**Hutson,** Danny James 1957- *WhoEnt 92*
**Hutson,** Francis 1895- *Who 92*
**Hutson,** Henry Porter Wolseley 1893- *Who 92*
**Hutson,** Jean Blackwell 1914- *NotBlAW 92, WhoBlA 92*
**Hutson,** Jeffrey Woodward 1941- *WhoAmL 92, WhoMW 92*
**Hutson,** John Whiteford 1927- *Who 92*
**Hutson,** Julie Wildes 1964- *WhoEnt 92*
**Hutson,** Richard Lee 1936- *AmMWSc 92*
**Hutson,** Ronald Alan 1942- *WhoRel 92*
**Hutson,** Rutledge Quillian 1962- *WhoAmL 92*
**Hutson,** Shaun *TwCWW 91*
**Hutt,** David Handley 1938- *Who 92*
**Hutt,** Eric John Villette 1915- *WhoFI 92*
**Hutt,** Frederick Bruce 1897- *AmMWSc 92*
**Hutt,** Martin P 1926- *AmMWSc 92*
**Hutt,** Monroe L. 1920- *WhoBlA 92*
**Hutt,** Peter Barton 1934- *IntWW 91, WhoAmL 92*
**Hutt,** Randy 1947- *AmMWSc 92*
**Hutt,** William Ian DeWitt 1920- *WhoEnt 92*
**Hutt-Fletcher,** Lindsey Marion 1947- *AmMWSc 92*
**Hutta,** Paul John 1946- *AmMWSc 92*
**Hutte,** Robert E. 1917- *IntMPA 92*
**Hutten,** Philipp d1546 *HisDSpE*
**Hutten,** Ulrich von 1488-1523 *LitC 16*
**Huttenlocher,** Dietrich F 1928- *AmMWSc 92*
**Hutter,** Bruce Allen 1957- *WhoEnt 92*
**Hutter,** David 1930-1990 *TwCPaSc*
**Hutter,** Edwin Christian 1918- *AmMWSc 92*
**Hutter,** George Frederick 1943- *AmMWSc 92*
**Hutter,** Heidi E 1957- *WhoIns 92*
**Hutter,** James Risque 1924- *WhoAmL 92, WhoWest 92*
**Hutter,** Otto Fred 1924- *Who 92*
**Hutter,** Robert V P 1929- *AmMWSc 92*
**Hutterer,** Ferenc 1929- *AmMWSc 92*
**Huttlin,** George Anthony 1947- *AmMWSc 92*
**Huttner,** Richard M. 1947- *WhoFI 92*
**Hutto,** Earl 1926- *AlmAP 92 [port], WhoAmP 91*
**Hutto,** Francis Baird, Jr 1926- *AmMWSc 92*
**Hutto,** Jerry W *WhoAmP 91*
**Hutto,** Terrell Don 1935- *WhoFI 92*
**Hutto,** Thomas Augustus 1932- *WhoAmP 91*
**Hutton,** Alasdair Henry 1940- *Who 92*
**Hutton,** Anthony Charles 1941- *Who 92*
**Hutton,** Betty 1921- *IntMPA 92*
**Hutton,** Brian Edward 1931- *IntWW 91*
**Hutton,** Brian G. 1935- *IntMPA 92*
**Hutton,** Brian Gerald 1933- *Who 92*
**Hutton,** Christopher Wilson 1950- *WhoAmP 91*
**Hutton,** David Lavon *WhoBlA 92*

Hutton, Edward Luke 1919- WhoFI 92, WhoMW 92
Hutton, Elaine Myrtle 1940- AmMWSc 92
Hutton, Frederick Remsen 1853-1918 BiInAmS
Hutton, Gabriel Bruce 1932- Who 92
Hutton, George Thompson 1946- WhoAmL 92
Hutton, Gerald L. WhoBlA 92
Hutton, Harold M 1937- AmMWSc 92
Hutton, Herbert J. 1937- WhoAmL 92
Hutton, Hubert Robin 1933- Who 92
Hutton, James 1726-1797 BlkwCEP
Hutton, James Brian 1931- Who 92
Hutton, James Robert 1943- AmMWSc 92
Hutton, James Robert 1947- WhoFI 92
Hutton, Janet 1938- Who 92
Hutton, John 1928- WrDr 92
Hutton, John Harwood 1928- IntAu&W 91
Hutton, John James, Jr 1936- AmMWSc 92
Hutton, John Philip 1940- Who 92
Hutton, Joseph 1787-1828 BenetAL 91
Hutton, Kenneth 1931- Who 92
Hutton, Kenneth Earl 1928- AmMWSc 92
Hutton, Lauren 1943- IntMPA 92
Hutton, Lauren 1944- WhoEnt 92
Hutton, Laurence 1843-1904 BenetAL 91
Hutton, Len 1916-1990 AnObit 1990
Hutton, Leonard d1990 IntWW 91N
Hutton, Leonard 1916-1990 FacFETw
Hutton, Lewis Joseph 1921- WhoRel 92
Hutton, Lucreda Ann 1926- AmMWSc 92
Hutton, Marilyn Adele 1950- WhoBlA 92
Hutton, Paul Andrew 1949- ConAu 133
Hutton, Robert 1920- ConTFT 9, IntMPA 92
Hutton, Robert Allen 1943- WhoFI 92
Hutton, Robin Who 92
Hutton, Ronald I. 1949- WhoBlA 92
Hutton, Sheila Rae 1965- WhoFI 92
Hutton, Thomas Joseph 1956- WhoAmL 92
Hutton, Thomas Watkins 1927- AmMWSc 92
Hutton, Timothy 1960- IntMPA 92, IntWW 91
Hutton, Timothy 1961- WhoEnt 92
Hutton, Walter Morland 1912- Who 92
Hutton, Warwick 1939- WrDr 92
Hutton, Wilbert, Jr 1927- AmMWSc 92
Hutton, William S 1943- WhoIns 92
Hutton, Winfield Travis 1935- WhoFI 92
Hutton-Williams, Derek Alfred 1914- Who 92
Hutzell, Jeffrey Scott 1949- WhoAmL 92
Hutzell, Robert Raymond 1948- WhoMW 92
Hutzelman, Stephen Howard 1942- WhoAmL 92
Hutzenlaub, John F 1918- AmMWSc 92
Hutzinger, Otto 1933- AmMWSc 92
Hutzler, John R 1929- AmMWSc 92
Hutzler, Leroy, III 1921- AmMWSc 92
Huva, David Wayne 1942- WhoMW 92
Huval, Lee Roy 1923- WhoAmP 91
Huvelin, Paul 1902- IntWW 91
Huwe, Darrell O 1932- AmMWSc 92
Huwe, Franklin 1934- WhoAmP 91
Huws, Bethan 1961- TwCPaSc
Huws Jones, Robin Who 92
Hux, George A WhoAmP 91
Huxford, John Calvitt 1931- WhoEnt 92
Huxley, Aldous 1894-1963 CnDBLB 6 [port], FacFETw, RfGEnL 91, TwCSFW 91
Huxley, Andrew Fielding 1917- FacFETw, IntWW 91, Who 92, WhoNob 90
Huxley, Anthony Julian 1920- IntAu&W 91, Who 92, WrDr 92
Huxley, Brian 1931- Who 92
Huxley, Elspeth 1907- WrDr 92
Huxley, Elspeth Josceline 1907- IntAu&W 91, IntWW 91, Who 92
Huxley, George Leonard 1932- IntWW 91, Who 92, WrDr 92
Huxley, Gervas, Mrs. Who 92
Huxley, Hugh E 1924- AmMWSc 92
Huxley, Hugh Esmor 1924- IntWW 91, Who 92
Huxley, Julian 1887-1975 ScFEYrs
Huxley, Julian Sorell 1887-1975 FacFETw
Huxley, Keith 1933- Who 92
Huxley, Paul 1938- TwCPaSc, Who 92
Huxley, Peter Arthur 1926- Who 92
Huxsoll, David Leslie 1936- AmMWSc 92
Huxstep, Emily Mary 1906- Who 92
Huxtable, Ada Louise IntWW 91, WhoEnt 92
Huxtable, Ada Louise 1921- WrDr 92
Huxtable, Ada Louse IntAu&W 91
Huxtable, Charles Richard 1931- Who 92
Huxtable, John d1990 Who 92N
Huxtable, John 1912- WrDr 92
Huxtable, L. Garth 1911-1989 DcTwDes
Huxtable, Ryan James 1943- AmMWSc 92
Huybregts, Pierre Philomene 1932- WhoEnt 92
Huyck, Margaret Hellie 1939- WhoMW 92
Huyck, Willard IntMPA 92
Huydecoper, Jonkheer Reinier 1922- IntWW 91, Who 92
Huyer, Adriana 1945- AmMWSc 92
Huyett, Daniel Henry, III 1921- WhoAmL 92
Huygens, Robert Burchard Constantijn 1931- IntWW 91
Huyghe, Patrick 1952- ConAu 135
Huyghe, Rene 1906- IntWW 91, Who 92
Huyghues-des-Etages, Jacques 1923- IntWW 91
Huyler, Jean Wiley 1935- ConAu 35NR, IntAu&W 91
Huynh, Son Xuan 1951- WhoMW 92
Huyser, Earl Stanley 1929- AmMWSc 92
Huysmans, Joris-Karl 1848-1907 GuFrLit 1, ThHEIm
Huzinaga, Sigeru 1926- AmMWSc 92
Hvass, Charles Thomas, Jr. 1950- WhoAmL 92
Hvatum, Hein 1923- AmMWSc 92
Hveding, Vidkunn 1921- IntWW 91
Hvidding, James Milton 1945- WhoFI 92
Hvidt, Peter 1916- DcTwDes
Hvoslef, Ketil 1939- ConCom 92
Hwa, Jesse Chia Hsi 1924- AmMWSc 92
Hwa, Rudolph Chia-Chao 1931- AmMWSc 92
Hwang Byung-ki 1936- ConCom 92
Hwang, Bruce You-Huei 1936- AmMWSc 92
Hwang, Cherng-Jia 1937- AmMWSc 92
Hwang, Ching-Lai 1929- AmMWSc 92
Hwang, Cordelia Jong 1942- WhoWest 92
Hwang, David Henry 1957- BenetAL 91, IntAu&W 91, WhoEnt 92, WrDr 92
Hwang, Evelyn 1935- WhoRel 92
Hwang, Frank K 1940- AmMWSc 92
Hwang, Hu Hsien 1923- AmMWSc 92
Hwang, Jennie S. WhoFI 92
Hwang, John Dzen 1941- AmMWSc 92
Hwang, Kai 1943- AmMWSc 92
Hwang, Li-San 1935- AmMWSc 92
Hwang, Neddy H C 1934- AmMWSc 92
Hwang, S Steve 1938- AmMWSc 92
Hwang, San-Bao 1946- AmMWSc 92
Hwang, Shy-Shung 1938- AmMWSc 92
Hwang, Sun-Tak 1935- AmMWSc 92
Hwang, Tzu-Yang 1953- WhoRel 92
Hwang, William Gaong 1949- AmMWSc 92
Hwang, Yu-Tang 1930- AmMWSc 92
Hwang-Shum, Jen-Jen 1957- WhoWest 92
Hway, Philip Joseph 1946- WhoFI 92
Hwong, Lucia Han-Chi 1953- WhoEnt 92
Hwu, Mark Chung-Kong 1926- AmMWSc 92
Hyam, Michael Joshua 1938- Who 92
Hyam, Ronald 1936- WrDr 92
Hyams, Andrew Leon 1954- WhoAmL 92
Hyams, Charles Walter 1863-1941 DcNCBi 3
Hyams, Daisy Deborah 1912- Who 92
Hyams, Harold 1943- WhoAmL 92
Hyams, Joe 1923- WhoEnt 92, WrDr 92
Hyams, Joseph 1926- IntMPA 92
Hyams, Mordecai E. 1819-1891 DcNCBi 3
Hyams, Peter 1943- IntMPA 92
Hyatali, Isaac 1917- Who 92
Hyatt, Abraham 1910- AmMWSc 92
Hyatt, Alpheus 1838-1902 BiInAmS
Hyatt, Anna Vaughn 1876-1973 HanAmWH
Hyatt, Asher Angel 1930- AmMWSc 92
Hyatt, David Ernest 1942- AmMWSc 92
Hyatt, Derek 1931- TwCPaSc
Hyatt, Donald B. LesBEnT 92
Hyatt, Donald Bishop 1924- WhoEnt 92
Hyatt, Edmond Preston 1923- AmMWSc 92
Hyatt, George, Jr 1914- AmMWSc 92
Hyatt, Herman Wilbert, Sr. 1926- WhoBlA 92
Hyatt, J. Philip 1909-1972 ConAu 134
Hyatt, James Lewis, Jr. 1938- WhoRel 92
Hyatt, Jerry Herbert 1940- WhoAmP 91
Hyatt, John Anthony 1948- AmMWSc 92
Hyatt, John Wesley 1837-1920 BiInAmS
Hyatt, Jonathan Deuel 1825-1912 BiInAmS
Hyatt, Kenneth Ernest 1940- WhoFI 92
Hyatt, Raymond R, Jr 1950- AmMWSc 92
Hyatt, Robert Eliot 1925- AmMWSc 92
Hyatt, Robert Monroe 1943- AmMWSc 92
Hyatt King, Alexander Who 92
Hybl, Albert 1932- AmMWSc 92
Hybl, William Joseph 1942- WhoAmL 92, WhoFI 92, WhoWest 92
Hybner, Mark Joseph 1957- WhoEnt 92
Hybridge, John 1948- WhoWest 92
Hyde, Lord 1976- Who 92
Hyde, Beal Baker 1923- AmMWSc 92
Hyde, Charles E. 1950- WhoEnt 92
Hyde, Dallas Melvin 1945- AmMWSc 92
Hyde, Dayton O. 1925- WrDr 92
Hyde, Dayton Ogden 1925- IntAu&W 91
Hyde, Douglas 1860-1949 FacFETw
Hyde, Earl K 1920- AmMWSc 92
Hyde, Edward 1667-1712 DcNCBi 3
Hyde, Eleanor DrAPF 91, WrDr 92
Hyde, Geoffrey 1930- AmMWSc 92
Hyde, George Charles, Jr. 1947- WhoEnt 92
Hyde, George E. 1882-1968 ConAu 133
Hyde, H Montgomery 1907- IntAu&W 91
Hyde, Henry J. 1924- AlmAP 92 [port]
Hyde, Henry John 1924- WhoAmP 91, WhoMW 92
Hyde, Henry Van Zile 1906- AmMWSc 92
Hyde, Henry Van Zile, Jr 1936- WhoAmP 91
Hyde, Herbert Lee 1925- WhoAmP 91
Hyde, Howard Laurence 1957- WhoAmL 92
Hyde, James Nevins 1840-1910 BiInAmS
Hyde, James Stewart 1932- AmMWSc 92
Hyde, John W. IntMPA 92
Hyde, John Welford 1910- AmMWSc 92
Hyde, Kendell Heman AmMWSc 92
Hyde, Kenneth E 1941- AmMWSc 92
Hyde, Kenneth Martin 1943- AmMWSc 92
Hyde, Lawrence Layton 1930- WhoMW 92
Hyde, Margaret O. 1917- ConAu 36NR
Hyde, Margaret Sheila 1945- Who 92
Hyde, Mark Anthony 1952- WhoRel 92
Hyde, Mark Powell ScFEYrs
Hyde, Michael 1908- WrDr 92
Hyde, Noel Spencer 1954- WhoAmL 92
Hyde, Norris J 1924- WhoAmP 91
Hyde, Paul Martin 1923- AmMWSc 92
Hyde, Richard Moorehead 1933- AmMWSc 92
Hyde, Richard Witherington 1929- AmMWSc 92
Hyde, Robin 1906-1939 RfGEnL 91
Hyde, Rosel H. LesBEnT 92
Hyde, Shelley ConAu 36NR, TwCSFW 91
Hyde, Stephen WhoEnt 92
Hyde, Tommy 1916- IntMPA 92
Hyde, W. Leonard Who 92
Hyde, Wallace Nathaniel 1923- WhoAmP 91
Hyde, Walter Lewis 1919- AmMWSc 92
Hyde, William R. 1923- WhoBlA 92
Hyde, William W 1946- AmMWSc 92
Hyde-Jackson, Maxine Deborah 1949- WhoBlA 92
Hyde-Parker, Richard William Who 92
Hyde-White, Wilfred 1903-1991 IntWW 91
Hyde-White, Wilfrid d1991 NewYTBS 91 [port], Who 92N
Hyde-White, Wilfrid 1903-1991 IntWW 91N
Hyden, Dorothy Louise 1948- WhoMW 92
Hyden, Elaine 1949- WhoFI 92
Hyden, Glen Warren 1961- WhoAmP 91
Hyden, Joe Bailey 1939- WhoAmL 92
Hyder, Donald N 1921- AmMWSc 92
Hyder, Monte Lee 1936- AmMWSc 92
Hyder, Robert Lee 1910- WhoAmP 91
Hyder, Stephen Talbert WhoAmL 92
Hydler, Glenda DrAPF 91
Hydock, Joseph J 1918- AmMWSc 92
Hydok, Joseph Thomas 1928- WhoFI 92
Hyer, Douglas Keith 1943- WhoFI 92
Hyer, Frederick L, Jr 1940- WhoIns 92
Hyer, Frederick Lewis, Jr. 1940- WhoFI 92
Hyer, Laura Jane 1956- WhoFI 92
Hyer, Martha 1924- IntMPA 92
Hyers Sisters, The NotBlAW 92
Hyers, Anna Madah 1856?-193-? NotBlAW 92
Hyers, Conrad 1933- WhoRel 92
Hyers, Donald Holmes 1913- AmMWSc 92
Hyers, Emma Louise 1858?-1899? NotBlAW 92
Hyers, Judith Gegenheimer 1945- WhoFI 92
Hyers, Thomas Morgan 1943- AmMWSc 92
Hyett, Barbara Helfgott DrAPF 91
Hyett, Doyle Gregory 1948- WhoFI 92
Hygh, Earl Hampton 1933- AmMWSc 92
Hyken, Shepard Alan 1960- WhoEnt 92
Hykes, David 1953- NewAmDM
Hyland, Edward Bernard 1942- WhoFI 92
Hyland, John P 1928- WhoIns 92
Hyland, John R 1925- AmMWSc 92
Hyland, John Roth, Jr. 1950- WhoWest 92
Hyland, Kathy Ruth 1950- WhoEnt 92
Hyland, Kerwin Ellsworth, Jr 1924- AmMWSc 92
Hyland, L A 1897-1989 FacFETw
Hyland, Mike Joseph 1949- WhoEnt 92
Hyland, Paul 1947- IntAu&W 91
Hyland, Richard Stephen 1935- WhoAmL 92
Hyland, Stanley 1914- WrDr 92
Hyland, Thomas Sheridan, Jr. 1943- WhoFI 92
Hyland, William Francis 1923- WhoAmP 91
Hyland, William G. 1929- IntWW 91
Hyland, William H. LesBEnT 92
Hylander, David Peter 1924- AmMWSc 92
Hylander, William Leroy 1938- AmMWSc 92
Hyle, Matthew R. 1955- WhoMW 92
Hyler, Lora Lee 1959- WhoBlA 92
Hylin, John Walter 1929- AmMWSc 92
Hylton, Baron 1932- Who 92
Hylton, Alvin Roy 1924- AmMWSc 92
Hylton, Andrea Lamarr 1965- WhoBlA 92
Hylton, Joseph Gordon 1952- WhoAmL 92
Hylton, Kenneth N. 1929- WhoBlA 92
Hylton, Taft H. 1936- WhoBlA 92
Hylton, Tracy 1922- WhoAmP 91
Hylton-Foster Who 92
Hylton-Foster, Baroness 1908- Who 92
Hyman, Abraham 1924- AmMWSc 92
Hyman, Arthur Bernard 1905- AmMWSc 92
Hyman, Bradley Clark 1952- AmMWSc 92
Hyman, Earle 1926- WhoBlA 92, WhoEnt 92
Hyman, Edward Sidney 1925- AmMWSc 92
Hyman, Flo 1954- BlkOlyM
Hyman, George E. 1938- WhoBlA 92
Hyman, Harold M 1924- IntAu&W 91, WrDr 92
Hyman, James Macklin 1950- AmMWSc 92
Hyman, Jerome Elliot 1923- WhoAmL 92, WhoFI 92
Hyman, Joe 1921- IntWW 91, Who 92
Hyman, John Adams 1840-1891 DcNCBi 3
Hyman, Jonathan Morris 1943- WhoAmL 92
Hyman, Kevin Michael 1950- WhoFI 92
Hyman, Lawrence 1940- WhoMW 92
Hyman, Leonard Stephen 1940- WhoFI 92
Hyman, Lloyd George 1928- AmMWSc 92
Hyman, Melvin 1927- AmMWSc 92
Hyman, Montague Allan 1941- WhoAmL 92
Hyman, Morton Peter 1936- WhoFI 92
Hyman, Richard W 1941- AmMWSc 92
Hyman, Robert Scott 1953- WhoRel 92
Hyman, Robin Philip 1931- Who 92
Hyman, Roger David 1957- WhoAmL 92
Hyman, Ronald T. 1933- WrDr 92
Hyman, Ronald Terry 1933- IntAu&W 91
Hyman, Seymour C 1919- AmMWSc 92
Hyman, Sigmund M. 1921- WhoFI 92
Hyman, Terry Mac 1951- WhoAmP 91
Hyman, Timothy 1946- IntWW 91, TwCPaSc
Hyman, Trina Schart 1939- ConAu 36NR
Hymans, William E 1940- AmMWSc 92
Hymer, Wesley C 1935- AmMWSc 92
Hymers, Robert Leslie, Jr. 1941- WhoRel 92
Hymes, Jesse 1939- WhoBlA 92
Hymes, William Henry 1921- WhoBlA 92
Hymmen, Friedrich Wilhelm 1913- EncTR 91
Hymowitz, Theodore 1934- AmMWSc 92
Hynd, Noel 1947- WhoEnt 92
Hynd, Ronald 1931- Who 92
Hynd, Ronald, Mrs. Who 92
Hynde, Chrissie 1951- News 91 [port]
Hyndman, Arnold Gene 1952- AmMWSc 92
Hyndman, Donald William 1936- AmMWSc 92
Hyndman, Harry Lester 1940- AmMWSc 92, WhoMW 92
Hyndman, John Robert 1920- AmMWSc 92
Hyndman, Roy D 1940- AmMWSc 92
Hyne, C J Cutcliffe 1865-1944 TwCSFW 91
Hyne, C J Cutcliffe 1866-1944 ScFEYrs
Hyne, James Bissett 1929- AmMWSc 92
Hyne, Norman John 1939- AmMWSc 92
Hynek, Frederick James 1944- WhoWest 92
Hynek, J Allen 1910-1986 FacFETw
Hynek, Robert James 1927- AmMWSc 92
Hyneman, Donald Lee 1953- WhoWest 92
Hyneman, James Richard 1957- WhoWest 92
Hyneman, John George 1927- WhoMW 92
Hynes, Carolyn E 1925- WhoAmP 91
Hynes, Charles J. 1936- WhoAmL 92
Hynes, Frank M 1940- WhoAmP 91
Hynes, Garry 1953- IntWW 91
Hynes, Gladys 1888-1958 TwCPaSc
Hynes, Hugh Bernard Noel 1917- AmMWSc 92
Hynes, James 1956?- ConLC 65 [port]
Hynes, John Barry 1936- AmMWSc 92
Hynes, John Dennis 1936- WhoAmL 92
Hynes, John Edward 1940- AmMWSc 92
Hynes, John Thomas 1933- AmMWSc 92
Hynes, Martin Dennis, III 1949- AmMWSc 92
Hynes, Mary Ann 1947- WhoAmL 92

**Hynes,** Michael Thomas 1956- *WhoFI 92*
**Hynes,** Richard Olding 1944- *AmMWSc 92, Who 92*
**Hynes,** Samuel 1924- *WrDr 92*
**Hynes,** Terence Michael 1954- *WhoAmL 92*
**Hynes,** Thomas Vincent 1938- *AmMWSc 92*
**Hynson,** Carroll Henry, Jr. 1936- *WhoBlA 92*
**Hynson,** Richard Washburn 1926- *WhoFI 92*
**Hypatia** d415 *EncEarC*
**Hypatius** d537 *EncEarC*
**Hypsicratea** *EncAmaz 91*
**Hysell,** Hugh David 1965- *WhoEnt 92*
**Hyslop,** David Johnson 1942- *WhoEnt 92, WhoMW 92*
**Hyslop,** James Hervey 1854-1920 *BiInAmS*
**Hyslop,** James Telfer 1916- *Who 92*
**Hyslop,** Newton Everett, Jr 1935- *AmMWSc 92*
**Hyslop,** Paul A 1952- *AmMWSc 92*
**Hyslop,** Robert John M. *Who 92*
**Hyslop,** Wade A, Jr *WhoAmP 91*
**Hyson,** Archibald Miller 1921- *AmMWSc 92*
**Hyson,** Kevin 1951- *IntMPA 92*
**Hysong,** James W. 1947- *WhoFI 92*
**Hytche,** William P. 1927- *WhoBlA 92*
**Hytner,** Benet Alan 1927- *Who 92*
**Hytner,** Nicholas 1956- *ConTFT 9*
**Hytner,** Nicholas Robert 1956- *IntWW 91, Who 92*
**Hyuga,** Hosai 1906- *IntWW 91*
**Hyun,** Christopher Charles 1962- *WhoAmL 92*
**Hyun,** Kun Sup 1937- *AmMWSc 92*
**Hyzer,** William Gordon 1925- *AmMWSc 92, WhoMW 92*

# I

**I,** Ting-Po 1941- *AmMWSc 92*
**I S** 1896-1977 *ScFEYrs*
**Iacangelo,** Peter August 1948- *WhoEnt 92*
**Iachetti,** Rose Maria Anne 1931- *WhoWest 92*
**Iacobelli,** John Louis 1931- *WhoFI 92, WhoMW 92*
**Iacobelli,** Mark Anthony 1957- *WhoMW 92*
**Iacobucci,** Guillermo Arturo 1927- *AmMWSc 92, WhoFI 92*
**Iacocca,** Lee *IntAu&W 91*
**Iacocca,** Lee 1924- *FacFETw, WrDr 92*
**Iacocca,** Lee A 1924- *AmMWSc 92, IntWW 91*
**Iacocca,** Lido Anthony Lee 1924- *WhoFI 92, WhoMW 92*
**Iacona,** Nicholas Lawrence 1968- *WhoEnt 92*
**Iacone,** Marge 1943- *WhoFI 92*
**Iacono,** Charles Paul 1954- *WhoEnt 92*
**Iacono,** George Dante 1922- *WhoWest 92*
**Iacono,** James M 1925- *AmMWSc 92*
**Iacono,** John 1941- *WhoEnt 92*
**Iacopino,** Michael Joseph 1958- *WhoAmL 92*
**Iacovou,** Georgios 1938- *IntWW 91*
**Iadanza,** Eugene Anthony 1948- *WhoAmL 92*
**Iadavaia,** Elizabeth Ann 1960- *WhoFI 92*
**Iadecola,** Costantino 1953- *AmMWSc 92*
**Iafrate,** Gerald Joseph 1941- *AmMWSc 92*
**Iakovos,** Archbishop 1911- *IntWW 91, RelLAm 91, WhoRel 92*
**Iakovos,** Bishop *WhoMW 92, WhoRel 92*
**Iamblichus** 245?-330 *EncEarC*
**Iamele,** Arthur L. 1946- *WhoMW 92*
**Iamele,** Richard Thomas 1942- *WhoAmL 92, WhoWest 92*
**Iammarino,** Richard Michael 1926- *AmMWSc 92*
**Iampietro,** P F 1925- *AmMWSc 92*
**Ian,** Janis 1951- *NewAmDM*
**Iandolo,** John Joseph 1938- *AmMWSc 92*
**Iannaccone,** Anthony 1943- *NewAmDM, WhoEnt 92, WhoMW 92*
**Iannaccone,** Michael 1962- *WhoFI 92*
**Iannacone,** Randolph Frank 1953- *WhoAmL 92*
**Iannarone,** Michael 1916- *AmMWSc 92*
**Iannella,** Egidio 1921- *IntWW 91*
**Iannetta,** Scott Kimon 1943- *WhoWest 92*
**Ianni,** Lawrence Albert 1930- *WhoMW 92*
**Ianni,** Ronald William 1935- *IntWW 91*
**Iannicelli,** Joseph 1929- *AmMWSc 92*
**Iannocci,** Robert 1962- *WhoAmL 92*
**Iannone,** James R 1947- *WhoAmP 91*
**Iannone,** Rosemarie Alexandria 1958- *WhoFI 92*
**Iannoni,** F. Joseph, Jr. 1952- *WhoFI 92*
**Iannucci,** Salvatore J. 1927- *IntMPA 92*
**Iannucci,** Salvatore Joseph 1927- *WhoEnt 92*
**Iannuzzi,** John Nicholas 1935- *WhoAmL 92, WrDr 92*
**Ianuzzo,** C David 1938- *AmMWSc 92*
**Ianziti,** Adelbert John 1927- *WhoFI 92*
**Iapoce,** Michael Anthony 1950- *WhoWest 92*
**Iaquinta,** Leonard Phillip 1944- *WhoMW 92*
**Iarezza,** Juan Carlos 1942- *IntWW 91*
**Iasiello,** Ray Louis 1952- *WhoEnt 92*
**Iason,** Lawrence 1945- *WhoAmL 92*
**Iatauro,** Michael Anthony 1943- *WhoEnt 92*
**Iatesta,** John Michael 1944- *WhoAmL 92*
**Iatropoulos,** Michael John 1938- *AmMWSc 92*
**Iatrou,** Kostas 1946- *AmMWSc 92*
**Iavicoli,** Mario Anthony 1939- *WhoAmP 91*
**Ibaceta,** Herminia D. 1933- *WhoHisp 92*
**Ibach,** Douglas Theodore 1925- *WhoRel 92*
**Ibach,** Johannes Adolph 1766-1848 *NewAmDM*
**Ibach,** Robert Daniel, Jr. 1940- *WhoRel 92*
**Ibanez,** Manuel L. 1935- *WhoHisp 92*
**Ibanez,** Manuel Luis 1935- *AmMWSc 92*
**Ibanez,** Maria Elena *WhoHisp 92*
**Ibanez,** Michael Louis 1916- *AmMWSc 92*
**Ibanez,** Ramon Medina *WhoRel 92*
**Ibanez,** Richard *WhoHisp 92*
**Ibanez,** Sara de 1909-1971 *SpAmWW*
**Ibarbourou,** Juana de 1892-1979 *SpAmWW*
**Ibarguen,** Alberto 1944- *WhoHisp 92*
**Ibarguren,** Carlos 1877-1956 *BiDExR*
**Ibarra,** Enrique 1957- *WhoHisp 92*
**Ibarra,** Francisco de 1539-1575 *HisDSpE*
**Ibarra,** Jesse Daniel, Jr. 1918- *WhoHisp 92*
**Ibarra,** Oscar 1952- *WhoHisp 92*
**Ibarria,** Antonio *WhoHisp 92*
**Ibarruri,** Dolores Gomez 1895-1989 *FacFETw*
**Ibas** d457 *EncEarC*
**Ibbeken,** David H. 1941- *WhoAmL 92*
**Ibberson,** Vincent *TwCPaSc*
**Ibbetson,** Arthur 1922- *ConTFT 9, IntMPA 92*
**Ibbetson,** Edwin Thornton 1923- *WhoWest 92*
**Ibbotson,** Eva 1925- *WrDr 92*
**Ibbotson,** Lancelot William Cripps 1909- *Who 92*
**Ibbotson,** Peter Stamford 1943- *Who 92*
**Ibbott,** Alec 1930- *Who 92*
**Ibbs,** Robin 1926- *IntWW 91, Who 92*
**Ibekwe,** Dan Onwura 1919- *IntWW 91*
**Ibekwe,** Lawrence Anene 1952- *WhoBlA 92*
**Ibele,** Warren Edward 1924- *AmMWSc 92*
**Ibelema,** Minabere 1952- *WhoBlA 92*
**Iben,** Icko, Jr 1931- *AmMWSc 92*
**Iber,** Frank Lynn 1928- *AmMWSc 92*
**Iberall,** Arthur Saul 1918- *AmMWSc 92, WhoWest 92*
**Ibers,** James Arthur 1930- *AmMWSc 92*
**Ibert,** Jacques 1890-1962 *FacFETw, NewAmDM*
**Ibert,** Lloyd *IntMPA 92*
**Iberville,** Sieur d' 1661-1706 *BenetAL 91*
**Ibiam,** Akanu 1906- *Who 92*
**Ibiam,** Francis Akanu 1906- *DcEcMov, IntWW 91*
**Ibieta,** Gabriella 1953- *WhoHisp 92*
**Ibn Bajja** 1077?-1138 *DcLB 115*
**Ibn Gabirol,** Solomon 1021?-1058? *DcLB 115 [port]*
**Ibn Saud,** Abd al-Aziz 1880?-1953 *FacFETw*
**Ibrahim,** A Mahammad 1953- *AmMWSc 92*
**Ibrahim,** Abdullah 1934- *NewAmDM, WhoBlA 92*
**Ibrahim,** Abu al-Qassim Mohammed 1937- *IntWW 91*
**Ibrahim,** Adly N 1917- *AmMWSc 92*
**Ibrahim,** Ashfaq 1948- *WhoFI 92*
**Ibrahim,** Baky Badie 1947- *AmMWSc 92*
**Ibrahim,** Encik Anwar bin 1947- *IntWW 91*
**Ibrahim,** Fayez Fares 1941- *WhoMW 92*
**Ibrahim,** Hassan Hamdi 1925- *IntWW 91*
**Ibrahim,** Ibrahim N. 1940- *WhoRel 92*
**Ibrahim,** Izzat 1942- *IntWW 91*
**Ibrahim,** Kashim 1910- *IntWW 91, Who 92*
**Ibrahim,** Medhat Ahmed Helmy 1939- *AmMWSc 92*
**Ibrahim,** Michel A 1934- *AmMWSc 92*
**Ibrahim,** Ragai Kamel 1929- *AmMWSc 92*
**Ibrahim,** Sid Moulay Abdullah 1918- *IntWW 91*
**Ibrahimov,** Mirza Azhdar Oglu 1911- *IntAu&W 91, IntWW 91*
**Ibsen,** Henrik 1828-1906 *DramC 2 [port]*
**Ibsen,** Kenneth Howard 1931- *AmMWSc 92, WhoWest 92*
**Ibser,** Homer Wesley 1920- *AmMWSc 92*
**Ibuka,** Masaru 1908- *IntWW 91*
**Ibur,** Jane Ellen *DrAPF 91*
**Icahn,** Carl C. 1936- *IntWW 91, WhoFI 92*
**Icard,** Timothy Lee 1958- *WhoWest 92*
**Icaza,** Jorge 1906-1979 *BenetAL 91*
**Ice,** Anne-Mare 1945- *WhoBlA 92*
**Ice,** David Robert 1936- *WhoFI 92*
**Ice,** George Gary 1950- *WhoWest 92*
**Ice,** Marie 1938- *WhoWest 92*
**Ice,** Richard Eugene 1930- *WhoRel 92*
**Ice,** Rodney D 1937- *AmMWSc 92*
**Ice,** Ruth *DrAPF 91*
**Ice,** Sue Harper 1934- *WhoAmP 91*
**Ice-T** 195-?- *ConMus 7 [port]*
**Iceland,** William Frederick 1924- *WhoWest 92*
**Iceman,** The *WhoEnt 92*
**Icenogle,** Phillip Lee 1943- *WhoMW 92, WhoRel 92*
**Icenogle,** Ronald Dean 1951- *WhoWest 92*
**Icerman,** Larry 1945- *AmMWSc 92*
**Ichaso,** Leon *WhoHisp 92*
**Ichazo,** Oscar 1931- *RelLAm 91*
**Ichel,** David W. 1953- *WhoAmL 92*
**Ichida,** Allan A 1929- *AmMWSc 92*
**Ichiishi,** Tatsuro 1943- *WhoFI 92, WhoMW 92*
**Ichikawa,** Kon 1915- *IntDcF 2-2 [port], IntWW 91*
**Ichikawa,** Satomi 1949- *IntAu&W 91*
**Ichikawa,** Shuichi 1943- *AmMWSc 92*
**Ichikawa,** Wayne 1954- *WhoWest 92*
**Ichikawa,** Yoshio 1914- *WhoFI 92*
**Ichiki,** Albert Tatsuo 1936- *AmMWSc 92*
**Ichinohe,** Saeko *WhoEnt 92*
**Ichinose,** Herbert 1931- *AmMWSc 92*
**Ichinose,** Susan M. 1944- *WhoAmL 92*
**Ichiyama,** Dennis Yoshihide 1944- *WhoEnt 92, WhoMW 92*
**Ichiyanagi,** Toshi 1933- *ConCom 92*
**Ichiye,** Takashi 1921- *AmMWSc 92*
**Ichniowski,** Casimir Thaddeus 1909- *AmMWSc 92*
**Ichniowski,** Thaddeus Casimir 1933- *AmMWSc 92*
**Ichord,** Richard Howard 1926- *WhoAmP 91*
**Icke,** Gillian *TwCPaSc*
**Icke,** Harold James 1944- *WhoWest 92*
**Icke,** Vincent 1946- *AmMWSc 92*
**Ickes,** Gary R 1944- *WhoAmP 91*
**Ickes,** Harold 1874-1952 *FacFETw*
**Ickes,** Harold Le Claire 1874-1952 *AmPolLe*
**Ickes,** Harold McEwen 1939- *WhoAmP 91*
**Ickes,** William K 1926- *AmMWSc 92*
**Idalie,** Heinric, Mme *Who 92*
**Idavoy,** Connie 1949- *WhoHisp 92*
**Iddesleigh,** Earl of 1932- *Who 92*
**Iddings,** Carl Kenneth 1933- *AmMWSc 92*
**Iddings,** Frank Allen 1933- *AmMWSc 92*
**Iddings,** Joseph Paxson 1857-1920 *BiInAmS*
**Iddings,** Kathleen *DrAPF 91, IntAu&W 91*
**Ide,** Carl Heinz 1928- *AmMWSc 92*
**Ide,** Hiroyuki 1933- *AmMWSc 92*
**Ide,** Judith Hope 1943- *WhoAmP 91*
**Ide,** Roger Henry 1937- *AmMWSc 92*
**Ide,** Simeon 1794-1889 *BenetAL 91*
**Ideler Tonelli,** Santiago 1924- *IntWW 91*
**Idell,** Albert E. 1901-1958 *BenetAL 91*
**Idell-Wenger,** Jane Arlene *AmMWSc 92*
**Idelsohn,** Sergio Rodolfo 1947- *AmMWSc 92*
**Idelson,** Martin 1928- *AmMWSc 92*
**Idemitsu,** Keisuke 1900- *IntWW 91*
**Iden,** Charles R 1942- *AmMWSc 92*
**Iden,** William *ConAu 35NR*
**Idham Chalid,** Kyai Haji 1922- *IntWW 91*
**Idiens,** Dale 1942- *Who 92*
**Iding,** Allan Earl 1939- *WhoAmL 92*
**Idle,** Eric 1943- *ConAu 35NR, IntMPA 92, WhoEnt 92*
**Idleman,** Kenneth Darrell 1947- *WhoRel 92*
**Idleman,** Lee Hillis 1933- *WhoFI 92*
**Idler,** David Richard 1923- *AmMWSc 92*
**Idol,** Billy 1955- *WhoEnt 92*
**Idol,** James Daniel, Jr 1928- *AmMWSc 92*
**Idoux,** John Paul 1941- *AmMWSc 92*
**Idowu,** Elayne Arrington 1940- *AmMWSc 92*
**Idris Shah,** Sultan 1924-1984 *FacFETw*
**Idris,** Yusuf 1927-1991 *NewYTBS 91*
**Idriss,** Izzat M *AmMWSc 92*
**Idso,** Sherwood B 1942- *AmMWSc 92*
**Idson,** Bernard 1919- *AmMWSc 92*
**Idziak,** Edmund Stefan 1935- *AmMWSc 92*
**Idzik,** Frank Michael 1927- *WhoAmP 91*
**Idzik,** Mark Michael 1954- *WhoAmP 91*
**Idzik,** Martin Francis 1942- *WhoAmL 92*
**Idzkowsky,** Henry Joseph 1908- *AmMWSc 92*
**Ieng Sary** *IntWW 91*
**Ierardi,** Stephen John 1960- *WhoWest 92*
**Ievers,** Frank George Eyre 1910- *Who 92*
**Ievers,** John Augustine 1912- *Who 92*
**Ievlev,** Aleksandr Ivanovich 1926- *IntWW 91*
**Ieyoub,** Kalil Phillip 1935- *AmMWSc 92*
**Iezman,** Alan H. 1950- *WhoEnt 92*
**Iezzi,** Jacinta Marie 1959- *WhoAmL 92*
**Iezzi,** Robert Aldo 1944- *AmMWSc 92*
**Ifediora,** John Obi 1957- *WhoMW 92*
**Iffland,** Don Charles 1921- *AmMWSc 92*
**Ifft,** Edward M 1937- *AmMWSc 92*
**Ifill,** O. Urcille, Sr. 1921-1991 *NewYTBS 91 [port]*
**Ifju,** Geza 1931- *AmMWSc 92*

**Iford,** Robert 1948- *WhoAmP 91, WhoBlA 92*
**Ige,** David Y 1957- *WhoAmP 91*
**Ige,** Marshall Kaoru 1954- *WhoAmP 91*
**Igel,** Howard Joseph 1934- *AmMWSc 92*
**Iger,** Robert 1951- *IntMPA 92*
**Iger,** Robert A. *LesBEnT 92 [port], WhoEnt 92*
**Igesz,** Bodo 1935- *WhoEnt 92*
**Iggers,** Georg G. 1926- *WrDr 92*
**Iggers,** Georg Gerson 1926- *IntAu&W 91*
**Iggo,** Ainsley 1924- *IntWW 91, Who 92*
**Iggulden,** John Manners 1917- *IntAu&W 91, WrDr 92*
**Ighner,** Benard T. 1945- *WhoBlA 92*
**Igl,** David Herman 1949- *WhoEnt 92*
**Iglar,** Albert Francis, Jr 1939- *AmMWSc 92*
**Iglauer,** Bruce *WhoEnt 92, WhoMW 92*
**Iglehart,** Donald Lee 1933- *AmMWSc 92*
**Iglehart,** Lloyd D. 1938- *WhoBlA 92*
**Iglehart,** T. D. *WhoRel 92*
**Igler,** Hans 1920- *IntWW 91*
**Iglesia,** Enrique 1954- *AmMWSc 92*
**Iglesias,** Abel L. *WhoHisp 92*
**Iglesias,** Doris T. *WhoHisp 92*
**Iglesias,** Elizabeth Ivette 1951- *WhoHisp 92*
**Iglesias,** Enrique V. *WhoHisp 92*
**Iglesias,** Enrique V. 1930- *WhoFI 92*
**Iglesias,** Enrique V. 1931- *IntWW 91*
**Iglesias,** Estrella Maria 1953- *WhoHisp 92*
**Iglesias,** Julio 1943- *WhoEnt 92, WhoHisp 92*
**Iglesias,** Mario 1924- *WhoHisp 92*
**Iglesias,** Mario A. 1957- *WhoAmL 92*
**Iglesias Pantin,** Santiago 1872-1939 *HisDSpE*
**Igleski,** Thomas Robert 1934- *WhoFI 92, WhoIns 92*
**Iglewicz,** Boris 1939- *AmMWSc 92*
**Iglewicz,** Raja 1945- *AmMWSc 92*
**Iglewski,** Barbara Hotham 1938- *AmMWSc 92*
**Iglewski,** Wallace 1938- *AmMWSc 92*
**Iglowski,** Rudolph Alexander 1950- *WhoMW 92*
**Ignacio,** Joselyn *DrAPF 91*
**Ignarro,** Louis Joseph 1941- *AmMWSc 92*
**Ignat'ev,** Semen Denisovich 1904-1983 *SovUnBD*
**Ignatiev,** Alex 1945- *AmMWSc 92*
**Ignatios IV** 1920- *DcEcMov*
**Ignatios IV,** Patriarch *WhoRel 92*
**Ignatius of Antioch** *EncEarC*
**Ignatius Zakkal Iwas** 1933- *IntWW 91*
**Ignatov,** Nikolay Grigor'evich 1901-1966 *SovUnBD*
**Ignatov,** Vadim Nikolaevich 1931- *IntWW 91*
**Ignatow,** David *DrAPF 91*
**Ignatow,** David 1914- *BenetAL 91, ConPo 91, IntAu&W 91, WrDr 92*
**Ignatow,** Rose Graubart *DrAPF 91*
**Ignizio,** James Paul 1939- *AmMWSc 92*
**Ignoffo,** Carlo Michael 1928- *AmMWSc 92*
**Igo,** Donald James 1926- *WhoFI 92*
**Igo,** George 1925- *AmMWSc 92*
**Igo,** John 1927- *IntAu&W 91, WrDr 92*
**Igoe,** Daniel James 1943- *WhoAmL 92*
**Igras,** Henry 1952- *WhoRel 92*
**Igrunov,** Nikolai Stefanovich 1932- *IntWW 91*
**Igrunov,** Nikolay Stefanovich 1932- *SovUnBD*
**Igusa,** Jun-Ichi 1924- *AmMWSc 92*
**Igwebuike,** Donald Amechi 1960- *WhoBlA 92*
**Ih,** Charles Chung-Sen 1933- *AmMWSc 92*
**Iha,** Franklin Takashi 1937- *AmMWSc 92*
**Ihaka,** Kingi 1921- *Who 92*
**Ihamuotila,** Jaakko 1939- *IntWW 91*
**Ihara,** Les, Jr 1951- *WhoAmP 91*
**Ihas,** Gary Gene 1945- *AmMWSc 92*
**Ihde,** Aaron John 1909- *AmMWSc 92*
**Ihde,** Daniel Carlyle 1943- *AmMWSc 92*
**Ihde,** Don 1934- *WrDr 92*
**Iheagwara,** Charles Mbadiwe 1959- *WhoMW 92*
**Ihimaera,** Witi 1944- *ConNov 91, IntAu&W 91, WrDr 92*
**Ihlanfeldt,** William 1936- *WhoMW 92*
**Ihle,** Herbert Duane 1939- *WhoFI 92*
**Ihlenfeld,** William C. 1945- *WhoFI 92*
**Ihler,** Garret Martin 1939- *AmMWSc 92*
**Ihling,** Charles Hubbard 1953- *WhoWest 92*
**Ihnat,** Milan 1941- *AmMWSc 92*
**Ihndris,** Raymond Will 1920- *AmMWSc 92*
**Ihrig,** Edwin Charles, Jr. 1947- *WhoWest 92*
**Ihrig,** Judson La Moure 1925- *AmMWSc 92*
**Ihrke,** Charles A. 1938- *WhoMW 92*
**Ihrke,** Charles Albert 1938- *AmMWSc 92*
**Ihrman,** Kryn George 1930- *AmMWSc 92*
**Ihsanoglu,** Ekmeleddin 1943- *IntWW 91*
**Ihssen,** Peter Edowald 1939- *AmMWSc 92*
**Ii,** Jack Morito 1926- *WhoWest 92*
**Iiams,** Thomas M., Jr. 1928- *ConAu 35NR*
**Iida,** John 1962- *WhoRel 92*
**Iida,** Keizo 1900- *IntWW 91*
**Iida,** Yotaro 1920- *IntWW 91*
**Ijams,** Charles Carroll 1913- *AmMWSc 92*
**Ijaz,** Lubna Razia 1940- *AmMWSc 92*
**Ijaz,** Mujaddid A 1937- *AmMWSc 92*
**Ik,** Kim Yong *DrAPF 91*
**Ika,** Prasad Venkata 1958- *AmMWSc 92*
**Ikard,** Frank N d1991 *NewYTBS 91 [port]*
**Ikard,** Frank Neville, Jr. 1942- *WhoAmL 92*
**Ikawa,** Miyoshi 1919- *AmMWSc 92*
**Ike Gozen** *EncAmaz 91*
**Ike,** Rev. 1935- *WhoBlA 92*
**Ike,** Reverend 1935- *WhoRel 92*
**Ike,** Albert Francis 1932- *AmMWSc 92*
**Ikeda,** Daisaku 1928- *IntWW 91, RelLAm 91*
**Ikeda,** Donna Rika 1939- *WhoAmP 91, WhoWest 92*
**Ikeda,** George J 1935- *AmMWSc 92*
**Ikeda,** Kikuei 1947- *WhoEnt 92*
**Ikeda,** Moss Marcus Masanobu 1931- *WhoWest 92*
**Ikeda,** Richard Masayoshi 1934- *AmMWSc 92*
**Ikeda,** Robert Mitsuru 1925- *AmMWSc 92*
**Ikeda,** Suzee Wendy 1947- *WhoEnt 92*
**Ikeda,** Tatsuya 1940- *AmMWSc 92*
**Ikeda,** Tsuguo 1924- *WhoWest 92*
**Ikeda-Saito,** Masao *AmMWSc 92*
**Ikegawa,** Shiro 1933- *WhoWest 92*
**Ikegaya,** Takashi 1930- *WhoFI 92*
**Ikeguchi,** Nobuo 1934- *WhoEnt 92*
**Ikehara,** Yukio 1939- *AmMWSc 92*
**Ikeler,** Herman Howard 1936- *WhoAmP 91*
**Ikenberry,** Dennis L 1939- *AmMWSc 92*
**Ikenberry,** Gilford John, Jr 1929- *AmMWSc 92*
**Ikenberry,** Henry Cephas, Jr. 1920- *WhoAmL 92*
**Ikenberry,** Luther Curtis 1917- *AmMWSc 92*
**Ikenberry,** Oliver Samuel 1908-1978 *ConAu 134*
**Ikenberry,** Richard W 1937- *AmMWSc 92*
**Ikenberry,** Roy Dewayne 1940- *AmMWSc 92*
**Ikenberry,** Stanley Oliver 1935- *WhoMW 92*
**Ikerman,** Ruth C. 1910- *WrDr 92*
**Ikerrin,** Viscount 1953- *Who 92*
**Ikeura,** Kisaburo 1916- *IntWW 91*
**Ikezi,** Hiroyuki 1937- *AmMWSc 92*
**Ikezoe-Halevi,** Jean Marie 1953- *WhoEnt 92*
**Ikhouria,** Isaac *BlkOlyM*
**Ikle,** Fred C. 1924- *WrDr 92*
**Ikle,** Fred Charles 1924- *IntWW 91, WhoAmP 91*
**Iko,** Momoko *DrAPF 91*
**Ikonne,** Justus Uzoma 1949- *AmMWSc 92*
**Ikuma,** Hiroshi 1932- *AmMWSc 92*
**Ilacqua,** Rosario S. 1927- *WhoFI 92*
**Ilan,** Aviv M. 1970- *WhoEnt 92*
**Ilangaratne,** Tikiri Bandara 1913- *IntWW 91*
**Ilangyi,** Bya'ene Akulu *WhoRel 92*
**Ilao,** Tom Javate 1941- *WhoRel 92*
**Ilar,** Craig Scott 1966- *WhoEnt 92*
**Ilardi,** Joseph Michael 1939- *AmMWSc 92*
**Ilchester,** Earl of 1920- *Who 92*
**Ilchuk,** Frank H. d1991 *NewYTBS 91*
**Ilchuk,** Peter Kenneth 1947- *WhoAmP 91*
**Ildefonsus of Toledo** 610?-667 *EncEarC*
**Ildico** *EncAmaz 91*
**Ileana of Romania,** Princess 1909-1991 *NewYTBS 91*
**Ileo Songoamba** 1921- *IntWW 91*
**Iler,** Ralph Kingsley 1909- *AmMWSc 92*
**Ilerio,** Pedro Julio 1920- *WhoHisp 92*
**Ilersic,** Alfred Roman 1920- *Who 92, WrDr 92*
**Iles,** Delma Ann 1954- *WhoEnt 92*
**Iles,** Edgar Milton 1927- *WhoAmP 91*
**Iles,** Jane 1954- *ConAu 135*
**Iles,** Kenneth William 1946- *WhoAmL 92*
**Ileto,** Rafael M. 1920- *IntWW 91*
**Ilf and Petrov** *FacFETw*
**Ilf,** Ilya 1897-1937 *SovUnBD*
**Ilf,** Ilya, and Petrov, Yevgeniy *SovUnBD*
**Ilg,** Harald Karl 1961- *WhoWest 92*
**Ilg,** Harold Franz 1947- *WhoFI 92*
**Iliadis,** Nick 1951- *WhoMW 92*
**Ilic,** Marija 1951- *AmMWSc 92*
**Ilic,** Pedro D. 1944- *WhoHisp 92*
**Ilich,** Richard J. 1959- *WhoFI 92*
**Il'ichev,** Leonid Fedorovich 1906- *SovUnBD*
**Ilie,** Paul 1932- *WrDr 92*
**Iliescu,** Ion 1930- *IntWW 91*
**Iliff,** Jann Marie 1952- *WhoAmL 92*
**Iliffe** *Who 92*
**Iliffe,** Baron 1908- *Who 92*
**Iliffe,** Barrie John 1925- *Who 92*
**Iliffe,** John 1939- *Who 92*
**Iliffe,** Robert Peter Richard 1944- *Who 92*
**Il'insky,** Igor' Vladimirovich 1901-1987 *SovUnBD*
**Iliya II** *WhoRel 92*
**Ilko,** Donald W. 1943- *WhoEnt 92*
**Illangasekare,** Tissa H 1949- *AmMWSc 92*
**Ille,** Bernard G 1927- *WhoIns 92*
**Illia,** Arturo 1900-1986 *FacFETw*
**Illian,** Carl Richard 1941- *AmMWSc 92*
**Illich,** Ivan 1926- *ConAu 35NR, FacFETw, IntWW 91, WrDr 92*
**Illick,** J Rowland 1919- *AmMWSc 92*
**Illig,** Alvin A. d1991 *NewYTBS 91*
**Illing,** Joseph Raymond 1943- *WhoWest 92*
**Illinger,** Joyce Lefever 1937- *AmMWSc 92*
**Illinger,** Karl Heinz 1934- *AmMWSc 92*
**Illingworth,** Charles Frederick William d1991 *Who 92N*
**Illingworth,** David Gordon 1921- *Who 92*
**Illingworth,** George Ernest 1935- *AmMWSc 92*
**Illingworth,** Juan 1786-1853 *HisDSpE*
**Illingworth,** Keith 1932- *AmMWSc 92*
**Illingworth,** Raymond 1932- *Who 92*
**Illingworth,** Ronald 1909-1990 *AnObit 1990*
**Illion,** Larry Steven 1949- *WhoFI 92*
**Illis,** Alexander 1917- *AmMWSc 92*
**Illman,** William Irwin 1921- *AmMWSc 92*
**Illmann,** Margaret Louise 1965- *WhoEnt 92*
**Illsley,** Bryan 1937- *TwCPaSc*
**Illsley,** Eric Evlyn 1955- *Who 92*
**Illsley,** Raymond 1919- *Who 92*
**Illson,** James Elias 1953- *WhoMW 92*
**Illston,** John Michael 1928- *Who 92*
**Illueca,** Jorge E. 1918- *IntWW 91*
**Illuzzi,** Michael Chambers 1956- *WhoMW 92*
**Illuzzi,** Vincent 1953- *WhoAmP 91*
**Ilmet,** Ivor 1930- *AmMWSc 92*
**Ilnicki,** Richard Demetry 1928- *AmMWSc 92*
**Iloff,** Phillip Murray, Jr 1921- *AmMWSc 92*
**Ilogu,** Edmund Christopher Onyedum 1920- *WhoRel 92*
**Ilott,** Pamela *LesBEnT 92*
**Ilsley,** Velma E. 1918- *WrDr 92*
**Ilson,** Bernard 1932- *WhoEnt 92*
**Ilson,** Robert Frederick 1937- *IntAu&W 91*
**Ilson,** Saul, and Chambers, Ernest *LesBEnT 92*
**Ilstad,** Geir Are 1955- *WhoFI 92, WhoWest 92*
**Ilten,** David Frederick 1938- *AmMWSc 92*
**Iltis,** Donald Richard 1936- *AmMWSc 92*
**Iltis,** Hugh Hellmut 1925- *AmMWSc 92*
**Iltis,** John Frederic 1940- *WhoEnt 92*
**Iltis,** Wilfred Gregor 1923- *AmMWSc 92*
**Iltner,** Edgar Karlovich 1925-1983 *SovUnBD*
**Ilyenko,** Yuriy Gerasimovich 1936- *IntWW 91*
**Ilyichev,** Leonid Fyodorovich 1906- *IntAu&W 91, IntWW 91*
**Ilyichev,** Victor Ivanovich 1932- *IntWW 91*
**Ilyushin,** Sergei Vladimirovich 1894-1977 *FacFETw*
**Il'yushin,** Sergey Vladimirovich 1894-1977 *SovUnBD*
**Im,** Jang Hi 1942- *AmMWSc 92*
**Im,** Un Kyung 1934- *AmMWSc 92*
**Imady,** Mohammed 1930- *IntWW 91*
**Imaeda,** Tamotsu 1927- *AmMWSc 92*
**Imagawa,** David Tadashi 1922- *AmMWSc 92*
**Imai,** Hideshige 1923- *AmMWSc 92*
**Imai,** Nobuko 1943- *IntWW 91*
**Imai,** Tadashi 1912- *IntDcF 2-2, IntWW 91*
**Imam,** Zafar 1940- *IntWW 91*
**Imamura,** Shohei 1926- *IntDcF 2-2, IntMPA 92, IntWW 91*
**Imamura,** Yemyo 1867-1932 *RelLAm 91*
**Imana,** Jorge Garron 1930- *WhoWest 92*
**Imanaga,** Fumio 1928- *IntWW 91*
**Imanaka,** Mitchell Akio 1954- *WhoAmL 92*
**Imas,** Silvio Cesar 1949- *WhoHisp 92*
**Imathiu,** Lawi *WhoRel 92*
**Imber,** Murray *AmMWSc 92*
**Imberski,** Richard Bernard 1935- *AmMWSc 92*
**Imbert,** Bertrand Sainclair Maire 1924- *IntWW 91*
**Imbert,** Jean Raoul Leon 1919- *IntWW 91*
**Imbert,** Peter 1933- *Who 92*
**Imbert,** Peter Michael 1933- *IntWW 91*
**Imbert,** Rafael A. 1950- *WhoHisp 92*
**Imbert-Terry,** Michael Edward Stanley 1950- *Who 92*
**Imbler,** C Clarke 1933- *WhoIns 92*
**Imbler,** John Mark 1945- *WhoRel 92*
**Imboden,** John Baskerville 1925- *AmMWSc 92*
**Imbriano,** Robert J. 1944- *WhoBlA 92*
**Imbrie,** Andrew 1921- *ConCom 92, NewAmDM*
**Imbrie,** Andrew Welsh 1921- *WhoEnt 92*
**Imbrie,** John 1925- *AmMWSc 92*
**Imbrie,** John Z 1956- *AmMWSc 92*
**Imbrie,** Theron David 1959- *WhoFI 92*
**Imbrogno,** James Joseph 1955- *WhoMW 92*
**Imbruce,** Richard Peter 1942- *AmMWSc 92*
**Imbusch,** George Francis 1935- *IntWW 91*
**Imbusch,** Heinrich 1878-1945 *EncTR 91*
**Imel,** Arthur Madison 1932- *AmMWSc 92*
**Imel,** Gary Lee 1941- *WhoWest 92*
**Imel,** John Michael 1932- *WhoAmL 92*
**Imershein,** Robert A. 1957- *WhoFI 92*
**Imes,** Kenneth Churchill 1947- *WhoAmP 91*
**Imesch,** Joseph Leopold 1931- *WhoRel 92*
**Imeson,** Kenneth Robert 1908- *Who 92*
**Imhof,** William Lowell 1929- *AmMWSc 92*
**Imhoff,** Donald Wilbur 1939- *AmMWSc 92*
**Imhoff,** John Leonard 1923- *AmMWSc 92*
**Imhoff,** Michael Andrew 1942- *AmMWSc 92*
**Imhoff,** Phyllis E. 1947- *WhoEnt 92*
**Imhoff,** Richard James 1958- *WhoFI 92*
**Imi,** Tony 1937- *ConTFT 9, IntMPA 92*
**Imig,** Charles Joseph 1922- *AmMWSc 92*
**Imig,** Thomas Jacob 1945- *AmMWSc 92*
**Imirzian,** Marlene Siroun 1958- *WhoWest 92*
**Imlay,** Gilbert 1754-1828? *BenetAL 91*
**Imlay,** Gordon Lake 1937- *WhoWest 92*
**Imlay,** Richard Larry 1940- *AmMWSc 92*
**Imle,** Ernest Paul 1910- *AmMWSc 92*
**Immediata,** Tony Michael 1913- *AmMWSc 92*
**Immenschuh,** William Taber 1917- *WhoWest 92*
**Immergut,** Edmund H 1928- *AmMWSc 92*
**Immerman,** Mark D. 1950- *WhoAmL 92*
**Immerman,** William J. 1937- *IntMPA 92*
**Immesberger,** Helmut 1934- *WhoFI 92*
**Imming,** Daniel Cornell 1951- *WhoMW 92*
**Imming,** Harry S 1918- *AmMWSc 92*
**Immke,** Keith Henry 1953- *WhoAmL 92*
**Immoos,** Thomas 1918- *ConAu 35NR*
**Imms,** David 1945- *TwCPaSc*
**Imms,** George 1911- *Who 92*
**Imondi,** Anthony Rocco 1940- *AmMWSc 92*
**Imp,** Raymond A. *WhoMW 92*
**Impagliazzo,** John 1941- *AmMWSc 92*
**Imparato,** Anthony Michael 1922- *AmMWSc 92*
**Impastato,** Fred John 1929- *AmMWSc 92*
**Impellizzeri,** Richard 1950- *WhoRel 92*
**Imperato,** Carlo 1963- *WhoEnt 92*
**Imperato,** Pascal James 1937- *AmMWSc 92*
**Imperatore,** Luke Edward 1960- *WhoFI 92*
**Imperial,** George Romero 1929- *AmMWSc 92*
**Imperial,** Robert Salvadore 1945- *WhoWest 92*
**Imperiale,** Michael Angelo 1950- *WhoFI 92*
**Imperiale,** Michael James 1952- *WhoRel 92*
**Imperiali,** Beatrice 1957- *WhoFI 92*
**Impink,** Albert J, Jr 1931- *AmMWSc 92*
**Impraim,** Chaka Cetewayo 1951- *AmMWSc 92*
**Impressions,** The *NewAmDM*
**Impreveduto,** Anthony Neil 1948- *WhoAmP 91*
**Imran Khan** 1952- *Who 92*
**Imran Tuanku Jaafar** *IntWW 91*
**Imray,** Colin Henry 1933- *IntWW 91, Who 92*
**Imredy,** Bela 1891-1946 *BiDExR*
**Imrie,** Jeffrey Neal 1965- *WhoFI 92*
**Imru Haile Selassie,** Lij Mikhail 1930- *IntWW 91*
**Imsande,** John 1931- *AmMWSc 92*
**Imse,** Robert A *WhoIns 92*
**Imus,** John Franklin 1958- *WhoMW 92*
**Imus,** Russel Walter 1935- *WhoFI 92*
**Inaba,** Lawrence A. 1932- *WhoWest 92*
**Inaba,** Minoru 1904- *WhoAmP 91*
**Inada,** Hitoshi 1937- *AmMWSc 92*
**Inada,** Lawson Fusao *DrAPF 91*
**Inada,** Minoru 1930- *WhoRel 92*
**Inagaki,** Masao *IntWW 91*
**Inagami,** Tadashi 1931- *AmMWSc 92*
**Inai,** Yoshihiro 1911- *IntWW 91*
**Inamine,** Edward S 1926- *AmMWSc 92*
**Inamine,** Gail Tamae 1951- *WhoRel 92*
**Inamura,** Sakonshiro *IntWW 91*
**Inamura,** Toshiyuki 1935- *IntWW 91*
**Inana,** George 1947- *AmMWSc 92*
**Inatome,** Rick 1953- *WhoFI 92*
**Inbal,** Eliahu 1936- *IntWW 91*
**Inbau,** Fred E. 1909- *WrDr 92*

**Inber,** Vera Mikhaylovna 1890-1972 *SovUnBD*
**Inbody,** Dale Dewayne 1925- *WhoMW 92*
**Inbody,** Tyron Lee 1940- *WhoRel 92*
**Inborden,** Thomas Sewell 1865-1951 *DcNCBi 3*
**Incandela,** Sal 1950- *WhoMW 92*
**Incardona,** Antonino L 1936- *AmMWSc 92*
**Ince,** A Nejat 1928- *AmMWSc 92*
**Ince,** Basil Andre 1933- *IntWW 91, Who 92*
**Ince,** Harold S. 1930- *WhoBlA 92*
**Ince,** Simon 1921- *AmMWSc 92*
**Ince,** Thomas Harper 1882-1924 *FacFETw*
**Ince,** Wesley Armstrong 1893- *Who 92*
**Ince,** William J 1933- *AmMWSc 92*
**Incera,** Alfred J. 1946- *WhoHisp 92*
**Inch,** John Ritchie 1911- *Who 92*
**Inch,** Morris Alton 1925- *IntAu&W 91, WhoRel 92, WrDr 92*
**Inch,** William Rodger 1928- *AmMWSc 92*
**Inchbald,** Elizabeth 1753-1821 *RfGEnL 91*
**Inchbald,** Michael John Chantrey 1920- *Who 92*
**Inchcape,** Earl of 1917- *IntWW 91, Who 92*
**Inchiosa,** Mario Anthony, Jr 1929- *AmMWSc 92*
**Inchiquin,** Baron of 1943- *Who 92*
**Inchyra,** Baron 1935- *Who 92*
**Incledon,** Philip *IntAu&W 91X, WrDr 92*
**Incropera,** Frank P 1939- *AmMWSc 92*
**Ind,** Jack Kenneth 1935- *Who 92*
**Ind,** William *Who 92*
**Indeck,** Ronald S 1958- *AmMWSc 92*
**Indeglia,** Gilbert 1941- *WhoAmP 91*
**Indelicato,** Joseph Michael 1941- *AmMWSc 92*
**Inderbitzen,** Anton Louis, Jr 1935- *AmMWSc 92*
**Inderfurth,** Karl Frederick 1946- *WhoAmP 91*
**India,** Sigismondo d' 1582?-1629 *NewAmDM*
**Indian Ocean,** Archbishop of the *Who 92*
**Indiana,** Robert 1928- *IntWW 91*
**Indictor,** Norman 1932- *AmMWSc 92*
**Indra,** Alois d1990 *IntWW 91N*
**Indrani** *WhoEnt 92*
**Indresano,** Albert Thomas 1945- *WhoMW 92*
**Indursky,** Arthur 1943- *WhoEnt 92*
**Indusi,** Joseph Paul 1942- *AmMWSc 92*
**Indy,** Vincent d' 1851-1931 *FacFETw, NewAmDM*
**Inez,** Colette *DrAPF 91*
**Inez,** Colette 1931- *IntAu&W 91, WrDr 92*
**Infanger,** Ann 1933- *AmMWSc 92*
**Infanger,** Ray E 1924- *WhoAmP 91*
**Infante,** Anthony A 1938- *AmMWSc 92*
**Infante,** Donald Richard 1937- *WhoWest 92*
**Infante,** E. Anthony *WhoHisp 92*
**Infante,** Ettore F 1938- *AmMWSc 92*
**Infante,** Ettore Ferrari 1938- *WhoMW 92*
**Infante,** Gabriel A 1945- *AmMWSc 92, WhoHisp 92*
**Infante,** Lindy 1940- *WhoMW 92*
**Infante,** Ronald Peter 1940- *AmMWSc 92*
**Infante-Arana,** Frantsisko 1943- *SovUnBD*
**Infeld,** Martin Howard 1940- *AmMWSc 92*
**Infield,** Marthea Mae 1929- *WhoMW 92*
**Infiesta,** Felix *WhoHisp 92*
**Infusino,** Achille Francis 1953- *WhoMW 92*
**Infuso,** Joseph 1927- *WhoEnt 92, WhoFI 92*
**Ing,** Dean 1931- *IntAu&W 91, TwCSFW 91, WrDr 92*
**Ing,** Dennis Roy 1947- *WhoWest 92*
**Ing,** Harry 1940- *AmMWSc 92*
**Ing,** Samuel W, Jr 1932- *AmMWSc 92*
**Ing,** Wendell Yin You 1945- *WhoEnt 92*
**Inga,** Kandra Joyce 1959- *WhoEnt 92*
**Ingall,** Carol Krepon 1940- *WhoRel 92*
**Ingalls,** Don *IntMPA 92*
**Ingalls,** Donald George *WhoEnt 92*
**Ingalls,** James Warren, Jr 1919- *AmMWSc 92*
**Ingalls,** Jeremy *DrAPF 91*
**Ingalls,** Jeremy 1911- *BenetAL 91, IntAu&W 91, WhoWest 92, WrDr 92*
**Ingalls,** Jesse Ray 1936- *AmMWSc 92*
**Ingalls,** Kenneth Robert 1950- *WhoWest 92*
**Ingalls,** Marie C *WhoAmP 91*
**Ingalls,** Paul D 1944- *AmMWSc 92*
**Ingalls,** Rachel 1941- *BenetAL 91, WrDr 92*
**Ingalls,** Redfield *ScFEYrs*
**Ingalls,** Robert L 1934- *AmMWSc 92*
**Ingalls,** Theodore Hunt 1908- *AmMWSc 92*
**Ingalls,** William Lisle 1918- *AmMWSc 92*
**Ingals,** Ephraim Fletcher 1848-1918 *BiInAmS*
**Ingalsbe,** David Weeden 1927- *AmMWSc 92*
**Ingamells,** John 1934- *IntWW 91*
**Ingamells,** John Anderson Stuart 1934- *Who 92*
**Ingard,** Karl Uno 1921- *AmMWSc 92*
**Ingate,** Mary 1912- *WrDr 92*
**Ingber,** Abie Isaac 1950- *WhoMW 92, WhoRel 92*
**Ingber,** Jeffrey Roy 1943- *WhoEnt 92*
**Inge,** George Patrick Francis 1941- *Who 92*
**Inge,** M. Thomas 1936- *WrDr 92*
**Inge,** Peter 1935- *Who 92*
**Inge,** Samuel Williams 1817-1868 *DcNCBi 3*
**Inge,** Theodore R. 1901- *WhoBlA 92*
**Inge,** Walter Herndon, Jr 1933- *AmMWSc 92*
**Inge,** William 1913-1973 *BenetAL 91, FacFETw*
**Inge,** William Marshall 1802-1846 *DcNCBi 3*
**Inge,** William R 1860-1954 *FacFETw*
**Inge-Innes-Lillingston,** George David 1923- *Who 92*
**Ingebretsen,** Charles M. 1959- *WhoWest 92*
**Ingebretson,** Gary Duane 1943- *WhoFI 92*
**Ingegneri,** Marc' Antonio 1545?-1592 *NewAmDM*
**Ingelman-Sundberg,** Axel 1910- *IntWW 91*
**Ingels,** Franklin M 1937- *AmMWSc 92*
**Ingels,** Harold Clayton 1941- *WhoWest 92*
**Ingels,** Jack Edward 1942- *WhoFI 92*
**Ingels,** Marty 1936- *IntMPA 92, WhoEnt 92*
**Ingels,** Neil Barton, Jr 1937- *AmMWSc 92*
**Ingeman,** Jerry Andrew 1950- *WhoMW 92*
**Ingemunson,** Dallas C 1938- *WhoAmP 91*
**Ingen-Housz,** Jan 1730-1799 *BlkwCEP*
**Ingenito,** Alphonse J 1932- *AmMWSc 92*
**Ingenito,** Frank Leo 1932- *AmMWSc 92*
**Ingerman,** Michael Leigh 1937- *WhoFI 92, WhoWest 92*
**Ingersol,** Robert Harding 1921- *AmMWSc 92*
**Ingersoll,** Andrew Perry 1940- *AmMWSc 92, WhoWest 92*
**Ingersoll,** Charles Jared 1782-1862 *BenetAL 91*
**Ingersoll,** Edwin Marvin 1919- *AmMWSc 92*
**Ingersoll,** Ernest 1852-1946 *BenetAL 91*
**Ingersoll,** Henry Gilbert 1915- *AmMWSc 92*
**Ingersoll,** John Gregory 1948- *WhoWest 92*
**Ingersoll,** Ralph McAllister 1900-1985 *FacFETw*
**Ingersoll,** Raymond Vail 1947- *AmMWSc 92*
**Ingersoll,** Richard King 1944- *WhoAmL 92*
**Ingersoll,** Robert G. 1833-1899 *BenetAL 91*
**Ingersoll,** Robert Green 1833-1899 *RelLAm 91*
**Ingersoll,** William Boley 1938- *WhoAmL 92*
**Ingersoll,** William Franklin 1955- *WhoMW 92*
**Ingerson,** Fred Earl 1906- *AmMWSc 92*
**Ingestre,** Viscount 1978- *Who 92*
**Ingham,** Bernard 1932- *IntWW 91, Who 92*
**Ingham,** Bryan 1936- *TwCPaSc*
**Ingham,** Cranford A. *WhoAmL 92*
**Ingham,** Daniel *IntAu&W 91X, WrDr 92*
**Ingham,** George Alexander 1936- *WhoFI 92*
**Ingham,** Herbert Smith, Jr 1931- *AmMWSc 92*
**Ingham,** John Henry 1910- *Who 92*
**Ingham,** Kenneth 1921- *IntAu&W 91, Who 92, WrDr 92*
**Ingham,** Kenneth Culver 1942- *AmMWSc 92*
**Ingham,** Kenneth R 1938- *AmMWSc 92*
**Ingham,** Merton Charles 1930- *AmMWSc 92*
**Ingham,** Norman William 1934- *WhoMW 92*
**Ingham,** R. A. 1935- *WrDr 92*
**Ingham,** Robert Edwin 1944- *WhoWest 92*
**Ingham,** Robert Kelly 1926- *AmMWSc 92*
**Ingham,** Stanley Ainsworth 1920- *Who 92*
**Ingham,** Steven Charles 1961- *AmMWSc 92*
**Inghram,** Mark Gordon 1919- *AmMWSc 92, IntWW 91*
**Ingibergsson,** Asgeir 1928- *WhoRel 92*
**Ingilby,** Joan Alicia 1911- *WrDr 92*
**Ingilby,** Thomas 1955- *Who 92*
**Ingle,** Clifford 1915-1977 *ConAu 134*
**Ingle,** Clyde *WhoMW 92*
**Ingle,** Cress Stuart *WhoAmP 91*
**Ingle,** Donald Lee 1936- *AmMWSc 92*
**Ingle,** George William 1917- *AmMWSc 92*
**Ingle,** James Chesney, Jr 1935- *AmMWSc 92, WhoWest 92*
**Ingle,** James Davis 1913- *AmMWSc 92*
**Ingle,** James Davis, Jr 1946- *AmMWSc 92*
**Ingle,** John Ide 1919- *AmMWSc 92*
**Ingle,** L Morris 1929- *AmMWSc 92*
**Ingle,** Morton Blakeman 1942- *AmMWSc 92*
**Ingle,** Robert D. 1939- *WhoWest 92*
**Ingleby,** Viscount 1926- *Who 92*
**Ingledew,** William Michael 1942- *AmMWSc 92*
**Ingledow,** Anthony Brian 1928- *Who 92*
**Ingledue,** Scott Leroy 1949- *WhoMW 92*
**Inglefield,** Gilbert 1909- *Who 92*
**Inglefield-Watson,** John 1926- *Who 92*
**Ingles,** Charles James 1942- *AmMWSc 92*
**Ingles,** Jose D. 1912- *IntWW 91*
**Ingles,** Joseph Legrand 1939- *WhoWest 92*
**Inglessis,** Criton George S 1930- *AmMWSc 92*
**Inglett,** George Everett 1928- *AmMWSc 92*
**Inglewood,** Baron 1951- *Who 92*
**Inglis,** Brian 1916- *IntAu&W 91, Who 92, WrDr 92*
**Inglis,** Brian Scott 1924- *Who 92*
**Inglis,** George Bruton 1933- *Who 92*
**Inglis,** Ian Grahame 1929- *Who 92*
**Inglis,** Jack Morton 1923- *AmMWSc 92*
**Inglis,** James *WhoFI 92*
**Inglis,** James 1945- *AmMWSc 92*
**Inglis,** James Craufuird Roger 1925- *Who 92*
**Inglis,** Judy 1952- *TwCPaSc*
**Inglis,** Kenneth Stanley 1929- *IntWW 91, Who 92*
**Inglis,** Robert Alexander 1918- *Who 92*
**Inglis-Jones,** Nigel John 1935- *Who 92*
**Inglis of Glencorse,** Roderick 1936- *Who 92*
**Ingman,** David Charles 1928- *Who 92*
**Ingman,** Nicholas 1948- *ConAu 134, WrDr 92*
**Ingman,** Richard Wilson 1944- *WhoMW 92*
**Ingoglia,** Nicholas Andrew *AmMWSc 92*
**Ingold,** Cecil Terence 1905- *Who 92*
**Ingold,** Donald Alfred 1934- *AmMWSc 92*
**Ingold,** Gerard 1922- *IntAu&W 91*
**Ingold,** Keith Usherwood 1929- *AmMWSc 92, IntWW 91, Who 92*
**Ingold,** Klara 1913-1980 *ConAu 134*
**Ingraham,** David Wood 1942- *WhoEnt 92, WhoFI 92*
**Ingraham,** John Charles 1936- *AmMWSc 92*
**Ingraham,** John Lyman 1924- *AmMWSc 92*
**Ingraham,** John Wright 1930- *WhoFI 92*
**Ingraham,** Joseph Holt 1809-1860 *BenetAL 91*
**Ingraham,** Joseph Sterling 1920- *AmMWSc 92*
**Ingraham,** Kimberlee DeAnn 1955- *WhoRel 92*
**Ingraham,** Lloyd Lewis 1920- *AmMWSc 92*
**Ingraham,** Prentiss 1843-1904 *BenetAL 91*
**Ingraham,** Richard Lee 1923- *AmMWSc 92*
**Ingraham,** Thomas Robert 1920- *AmMWSc 92*
**Ingraham Dietzen,** Carolyn Anne 1947- *WhoAmL 92*
**Ingram** *Who 92*
**Ingram,** Adam Paterson 1947- *Who 92*
**Ingram,** Adell, Jr. 1948- *WhoBlA 92*
**Ingram,** Alvin John 1914- *AmMWSc 92, IntWW 91*
**Ingram,** Alvin Richard 1918- *AmMWSc 92*
**Ingram,** Alyce *DrAPF 91*
**Ingram,** Barbara Averett 1960- *WhoRel 92*
**Ingram,** Charles William 1956- *WhoAmP 91*
**Ingram,** Daniel Trombley 1934- *WhoEnt 92*
**Ingram,** David Christopher 1953- *AmMWSc 92*
**Ingram,** David John Edward 1927- *IntWW 91, Who 92*
**Ingram,** David Stanley 1941- *Who 92*
**Ingram,** Denny Ouzts, Jr. 1929- *WhoAmL 92*
**Ingram,** Derek Thynne 1925- *WrDr 92*
**Ingram,** Earl Girardeau 1936- *WhoBlA 92*
**Ingram,** Edith J. 1942- *NotBlAW 92*
**Ingram,** Eldridge B. 1949- *WhoBlA 92*
**Ingram,** Forrest Duane 1938- *AmMWSc 92, WhoMW 92*
**Ingram,** Gary John 1933- *WhoAmP 91*
**Ingram,** George Conley 1930- *WhoAmL 92*
**Ingram,** George Mason, IV 1944- *WhoFI 92*
**Ingram,** Gerald E 1928- *AmMWSc 92*
**Ingram,** Glenn R 1928- *AmMWSc 92*
**Ingram,** Helen Q 1932- *WhoAmP 91*
**Ingram,** Hunter *TwCWW 91*
**Ingram,** James *WhoBlA 92*
**Ingram,** James 1966- *Who 92*
**Ingram,** James Charles 1928- *IntWW 91*
**Ingram,** James Franklin 1937- *WhoAmL 92*
**Ingram,** James William, Jr. 1938- *WhoBlA 92*
**Ingram,** Jeffrey Charles 1953- *WhoAmL 92*
**Ingram,** John, Jr 1924- *AmMWSc 92*
**Ingram,** John Gerard 1943- *WhoAmL 92*
**Ingram,** Jordan Miles 1936- *AmMWSc 92*
**Ingram,** Kathleen Annie *Who 92*
**Ingram,** Kenneth F 1929- *WhoAmP 91*
**Ingram,** Kenneth Frank 1929- *WhoAmL 92*
**Ingram,** Lafayette N, III 1940- *WhoAmP 91*
**Ingram,** LaVerne Dorothy 1955- *WhoBlA 92*
**Ingram,** Lonnie O'Neal 1947- *AmMWSc 92*
**Ingram,** Margaret Lucille 1949- *IntAu&W 91*
**Ingram,** Maria *DrAPF 91*
**Ingram,** Marylou 1920- *AmMWSc 92*
**Ingram,** Nathaniel Hawthorne 1918- *WhoAmP 91*
**Ingram,** Osmond Carraway, Jr. 1952- *WhoRel 92*
**Ingram,** Paul 1934- *Who 92*
**Ingram,** Peggy Joyce 1943- *WhoWest 92*
**Ingram,** Peter 1938- *AmMWSc 92*
**Ingram,** Phillip M. 1945- *WhoBlA 92*
**Ingram,** Rex 1893-1950 *IntDcF 2-2 [port]*
**Ingram,** Richard Grant 1945- *AmMWSc 92*
**Ingram,** Robert B. 1936- *WhoBlA 92*
**Ingram,** Robert Bruce 1940- *WhoAmL 92*
**Ingram,** Robert Edward Lee 1932- *WhoWest 92*
**Ingram,** Robert John 1926- *WhoMW 92*
**Ingram,** Robert L 1930- *WhoAmP 91*
**Ingram,** Robina Elaine 1956- *WhoWest 92*
**Ingram,** Roland Harrison 1935- *AmMWSc 92*
**Ingram,** Ross 1935- *WhoEnt 92*
**Ingram,** Roy Lee 1921- *AmMWSc 92*
**Ingram,** Sammy Walker, Jr 1933- *AmMWSc 92*
**Ingram,** Samuel William, Jr. 1933- *WhoAmL 92*
**Ingram,** Sheila Rena 1957- *BlkOlyM*
**Ingram,** Stanley Edward 1922- *Who 92*
**Ingram,** Steven Craig 1959- *WhoMW 92*
**Ingram,** Valerie J. 1959- *WhoBlA 92*
**Ingram,** Vernon M. 1924- *IntWW 91*
**Ingram,** Vernon Martin 1924- *AmMWSc 92, Who 92, WrDr 92*
**Ingram,** W Kent 1942- *WhoAmP 91*
**Ingram,** William Austin 1924- *WhoAmL 92*
**Ingram,** William B. 1935- *WhoBlA 92*
**Ingram,** William Thomas 1937- *AmMWSc 92*
**Ingram,** William Thomas, III 1937- *WhoMW 92*
**Ingram,** Winifred 1913- *WhoBlA 92*
**Ingram-Grant,** Edith Jacqueline 1942- *WhoBlA 92*
**Ingrams** *Who 92*
**Ingrams,** Doreen 1906- *WrDr 92*
**Ingrams,** Richard 1937- *WrDr 92*
**Ingrams,** Richard Reid 1937- *IntAu&W 91, IntWW 91, Who 92*
**Ingrand,** Henry 1908- *IntWW 91*
**Ingrao,** Charles William 1948- *WhoMW 92*
**Ingrao,** Pietro 1915- *IntWW 91*
**Ingratta,** Frank Jerry 1949- *AmMWSc 92*
**Ingress Bell,** Philip *Who 92*
**Ingrey,** Paul Bosworth 1939- *WhoIns 92*
**Ingrow,** Baron 1917- *Who 92*
**Ingruber,** Otto Vincent 1919- *AmMWSc 92*
**Ingrum,** Adrienne G. 1954- *WhoBlA 92*
**Ingstad,** Helge Marcus 1899- *IntWW 91*
**Ingstad,** Jack W *WhoAmP 91*
**Ingster,** Boris 1913- *IntMPA 92*
**Ingulli,** Alfred Francis 1941- *WhoFI 92*
**Inguva,** Ramarao 1941- *AmMWSc 92*
**Ingvarsson,** Ingvi S. 1924- *IntWW 91*
**Ingvoldstad,** D F 1912- *AmMWSc 92*
**Ingwall,** Joanne S 1941- *AmMWSc 92*
**Ingwalson,** Raymond Wesley 1912- *AmMWSc 92*
**Ingwer,** Mark 1952- *WhoMW 92*
**Ingwersen,** Martin Lewis 1919- *WhoFI 92*
**Inhaber,** Herbert 1941- *AmMWSc 92*
**Inhelder,** Barbel 1913- *WomPsyc*
**Inhofe,** James M. 1934- *AlmAP 92 [port]*
**Inhofe,** James Mountain 1934- *WhoAmP 91*
**Inhorn,** Stanley L 1928- *AmMWSc 92*
**Inigo,** Rafael Madrigal 1932- *AmMWSc 92*
**Ink Spots,** The *NewAmDM*
**Ink,** Claude 1928- *IntWW 91*

**Inkeles**, Alex 1920- *IntWW 91, WhoWest 92*
**Inkin**, Geoffrey David 1934- *Who 92*
**Inkley**, John James, Jr. 1945- *WhoAmL 92*
**Inkley**, Scott Russell 1921- *AmMWSc 92*
**Inlander**, Henry 1925- *TwCPaSc*
**Inlow**, Rush Osborne 1944- *WhoWest 92*
**Inman**, Bobby Ray 1931- *WhoAmP 91*
**Inman**, Charles Gordon 1929- *AmMWSc 92*
**Inman**, Christopher Crosby 1941- *WhoWest 92*
**Inman**, Claudia Jean 1942- *WhoWest 92*
**Inman**, Douglas Lamar 1920- *AmMWSc 92*
**Inman**, Edward Oliver 1948- *Who 92*
**Inman**, Edward S, III 1960- *WhoAmP 91*
**Inman**, Franklin Pope, Jr 1937- *AmMWSc 92*
**Inman**, Fred Winston 1931- *AmMWSc 92*
**Inman**, Henry 1801-1846 *BenetAL 91*
**Inman**, Henry 1837-1899 *BenetAL 91*
**Inman**, Herbert 1917- *Who 92*
**Inman**, John Keith 1928- *AmMWSc 92*
**Inman**, Mary Lou 1925- *WhoAmP 91*
**Inman**, Peter & Tina Darragh *DrAPF 91*
**Inman**, Robert 1931- *IntAu&W 91, WrDr 92*
**Inman**, Robert Davies 1949- *AmMWSc 92*
**Inman**, Robert Frederick 1943- *WhoEnt 92*
**Inman**, Roger 1915- *Who 92*
**Inman**, Ross 1931- *AmMWSc 92*
**Inman**, Samuel Guy 1877-1965 *AmPeW*
**Inman**, Will *DrAPF 91*
**Innamorato**, Anthony John 1936- *WhoFI 92*
**Innanen**, Kimmo A 1937- *AmMWSc 92*
**Innaurato**, Albert 1947- *IntAu&W 91*
**Innaurato**, Albert 1948- *WrDr 92*
**Innerarity**, Tom L 1943- *AmMWSc 92*
**Innerbichler**, Nicholas R. *WhoHisp 92*
**Inners**, Jon David 1942- *AmMWSc 92*
**Innerst**, J. Stuart 1894-1975 *AmPeW*
**Innes**, Alan *TwCSFW 91*
**Innes**, Brian 1928- *IntAu&W 91*
**Innes**, Callum 1962- *TwCPaSc*
**Innes**, Charles 1946- *TwCPaSc*
**Innes**, David Charles 1940- *WhoRel 92*
**Innes**, David Lyn 1941- *AmMWSc 92*
**Innes**, Evan *WrDr 92*
**Innes**, Fergus Munro 1903- *Who 92*
**Innes**, George 1913-1970 *TwCPaSc*
**Innes**, Georgette Meyer 1918- *WhoFI 92*
**Innes**, Hammond *IntWW 91, Who 92, WrDr 92*
**Innes**, Hammond 1913- *ConNov 91*
**Innes**, James 1700?-1759 *DcNCBi 3*
**Innes**, James Dickson 1887-1914 *TwCPaSc*
**Innes**, Jean *WrDr 92*
**Innes**, John Edwin 1938- *AmMWSc 92*
**Innes**, Kenneth Frederick, III 1950- *WhoAmL 92*
**Innes**, Kenneth Keith 1928- *AmMWSc 92*
**Innes**, Maughan William 1922- *Who 92*
**Innes**, Michael *Who 92, WrDr 92*
**Innes**, Peter 1937- *Who 92*
**Innes**, Peter Bruce 1941- *WhoWest 92*
**Innes**, Richard Wilson 1933- *WhoRel 92*
**Innes**, Sheila Miriam 1931- *Who 92*
**Innes**, Walter Rundle 1945- *AmMWSc 92*
**Innes**, William Alexander Disney 1910- *Who 92*
**Innes**, William Beveridge 1913- *AmMWSc 92*
**Innes**, William Henry 1905- *TwCPaSc*
**Innes**, William James Alexander 1934- *Who 92*
**Innes-Ker** *Who 92*
**Innes of Coxton**, Charles Kenneth Gordon d1990 *Who 92N*
**Innes of Coxton**, David 1940- *Who 92*
**Innes Of Edingight**, Malcolm Rognvald 1938- *IntWW 91, Who 92*
**Inness-Brown**, Elizabeth *DrAPF 91*
**Innis**, Chris Jean 1966- *WhoEnt 92*
**Innis**, Eileen Scheffler 1929- *WhoWest 92*
**Innis**, George Seth 1937- *AmMWSc 92*
**Innis**, Richard Joseph 1946- *WhoAmL 92*
**Innis**, Robert E. 1941- *WrDr 92*
**Innis**, Roy Emile Alfredo 1934- *IntWW 91, WhoBlA 92*
**Inniss**, Charles Evans 1935- *WhoBlA 92*
**Inniss**, Clifford 1910- *Who 92*
**Inniss**, Daryl 1961- *AmMWSc 92*
**Inniss**, William Edgar 1936- *AmMWSc 92*
**Innitzer**, Theodor 1875-1955 *EncTR 91 [port]*
**Innocent I** *EncEarC*
**Innocenti**, Antonio 1915- *IntWW 91, WhoRel 92*
**Innocenti**, Luigi 1923- *IntWW 91*
**Inokuti**, Mitio 1933- *AmMWSc 92*
**Inomata**, Akira 1931- *AmMWSc 92*
**Inomata**, Yoshio 1934- *WhoEnt 92*
**Inonu** 1884-1973 *EncTR 91*
**Inonu**, Ismet 1884-1973 *FacFETw*
**Inos**, Joseph S 1947- *WhoAmP 91*
**Inose**, Hiroshi 1927- *IntWW 91*
**Inoue**, Hisashi 1947- *WhoFI 92*
**Inoue**, Michael Shigeru 1936- *AmMWSc 92*
**Inoue**, Michi Yoshi 1946- *WhoEnt 92*
**Inoue**, Shinya 1921- *AmMWSc 92*
**Inouye**, Daniel K. 1924- *AlmAP 92 [port]*
**Inouye**, Daniel Ken 1924- *IntWW 91, WhoAmP 91, WhoWest 92*
**Inouye**, David William 1950- *AmMWSc 92*
**Inouye**, Greg Alan 1956- *WhoWest 92*
**Inouye**, Kaoru 1906- *IntWW 91*
**Inouye**, Masayori *AmMWSc 92*
**Inouye**, Minoru 1924- *IntWW 91*
**Insalata**, Nino F 1926- *AmMWSc 92*
**Insall**, Donald William 1926- *Who 92*
**Insall**, Eugene Madison, Jr. 1961- *WhoMW 92*
**Insana**, Sam Frank 1949- *WhoAmL 92*
**Insanally**, Samuel Rudolph 1936- *IntWW 91*
**Insani**, John Louis 1925- *WhoFI 92*
**Insch**, James Ferguson 1911- *Who 92*
**Insco**, Michael Andrew 1950- *WhoAmL 92*
**Inscoe**, May Nilson 1925- *AmMWSc 92*
**Insdorf**, Annette 1950- *IntMPA 92*
**Insel**, Arnold J 1940- *AmMWSc 92*
**Insel**, Arnold Joseph 1940- *WhoMW 92*
**Insel**, Paul Anthony 1945- *AmMWSc 92*
**Inselberg**, Alfred 1936- *AmMWSc 92, WhoWest 92*
**Inselberg**, Edgar 1930- *AmMWSc 92*
**Inserra**, Donna Louise 1948- *WhoEnt 92*
**Inshaw**, David 1943- *TwCPaSc*
**Insinna**, Paul William 1958- *WhoAmL 92, WhoEnt 92*
**Inskeep**, Emmett Keith 1938- *AmMWSc 92*
**Inskeep**, George Esler 1918- *AmMWSc 92*
**Inskeep**, Jill Roake 1950- *WhoWest 92*
**Inskeep**, Richard Guy 1923- *AmMWSc 92*
**Inskeep**, Robert Forman 1944- *WhoWest 92*
**Inskip** *Who 92*
**Inskip**, Ervin Basil 1941- *AmMWSc 92*
**Inskip**, Harold Kirkwood 1922- *AmMWSc 92*
**Inskip**, John Hampden 1924- *Who 92*
**Inslee**, Jay R *WhoAmP 91*
**Insley**, Earl Glendon 1907- *AmMWSc 92*
**Insley**, Lillian Dorothy 1929- *WhoAmP 91*
**Insley**, Richard Wallace 1918- *WhoFI 92*
**Insley**, Robert H 1923- *AmMWSc 92*
**Insley**, Will 1929- *WorArt 1980 [port]*
**Insole**, Douglas John 1926- *Who 92*
**Insolia**, Robert Spencer 1957- *WhoAmL 92*
**Intaglietta**, Marcos 1935- *AmMWSc 92, WhoWest 92*
**Intemann**, Gerald William 1943- *AmMWSc 92*
**Intemann**, Robert Louis 1938- *AmMWSc 92*
**Interlandi**, Telesio 1894-1965 *BiDExR*
**Interrante**, Leonard V 1939- *AmMWSc 92*
**Intilli**, Sharon Marie 1950- *WhoEnt 92*
**Intorre**, Benjamin Joseph, Sr. 1929- *WhoEnt 92*
**Intres**, Richard *AmMWSc 92*
**Intriere**, Anthony Donald 1920- *WhoWest 92*
**Intriligator**, Devrie Shapiro *AmMWSc 92*
**Intriligator**, Marc Steven 1952- *WhoAmL 92*
**Intriligator**, Michael David 1938- *WhoFI 92*
**Inturrisi**, Charles E 1941- *AmMWSc 92*
**Intzes**, Vassilios 1929- *IntWW 91*
**Inui**, Thomas S 1943- *AmMWSc 92*
**Inui**, Thomas Spencer 1943- *WhoWest 92*
**Inverforth**, Baron 1966- *Who 92*
**Inverness**, Provost of *Who 92*
**Invernon**, Louis Alcocer 1936- *WhoEnt 92*
**Inverso**, Marlene Joy 1942- *WhoWest 92*
**Inverurie**, Lord 1976- *Who 92*
**Inwood**, Mary Ruth Brink 1928- *WhoEnt 92*
**Inyamah**, Nathaniel Ginikanwa N. 1934- *WhoBlA 92*
**Inzetta**, Mark Stephen 1956- *WhoAmL 92*
**Inzunza**, Ralph *WhoHisp 92*
**Ioachim**, Harry L 1924- *AmMWSc 92*
**Ioannides**, George X. 1924- *IntWW 91*
**Ioannides**, I D 1931- *IntAu&W 91*
**Ioannidis**, Yannis 1930- *NewAmDM*
**Ioannou**, Susan 1944- *IntAu&W 91*
**Iodice**, Arthur Alfonso 1928- *AmMWSc 92*
**Iodice**, Ruth G. *DrAPF 91*
**Iodice**, Ruth Genevieve 1925- *IntAu&W 91*
**Ioean**, Boris Mikhailovich *IntWW 91N*
**Iofan**, Boris Mikhaylovich 1891-1976 *SovUnBD*
**Ioffe**, Adolf Abrahmovich 1883-1927 *FacFETw*
**Ioganson**, Boris Valdimirovich 1893-1973 *SovUnBD*
**Iola** *AmPeW*
**Iona**, Mario 1917- *AmMWSc 92*
**Ione**, Carole *DrAPF 91*
**Ionesco**, Eugene 1912- *FacFETw [port], GuFrLit 1, IntWW 91, LiExTwC, Who 92, WhoEnt 92*
**Ionescu**, Dan 1943- *AmMWSc 92*
**Ionescu**, George Ghita 1913- *Who 92*
**Ionescu**, Ghita 1913- *WrDr 92*
**Ionescu**, Lavinel G 1943- *AmMWSc 92*
**Ionescu Tulcea**, Cassius 1923- *AmMWSc 92*
**Ioor**, William 1780?-1830 *BenetAL 91*
**Iorgulescu**, Jorge 1935- *WhoFI 92*
**Iorillo**, Anthony J 1938- *AmMWSc 92*
**Iorio**, Theodore *WhoAmL 92*
**Iorns**, Martin Joshua d1909 *BiInAmS*
**Iorns**, Terry Vern 1944- *AmMWSc 92*
**Ioseliani**, Otar 1934- *IntDcF 2-2, SovUnBD*
**Iosifescu**, Marius Vicentiu Viorel 1936- *IntWW 91*
**Iovino**, Anthony Joseph 1925- *AmMWSc 92*
**Iozzo**, Anne Marie Wilchek 1945- *WhoRel 92*
**Ip**, Clement Cheung-Yung 1947- *AmMWSc 92*
**Ip**, Margot Morris 1943- *AmMWSc 92*
**Ip**, Stephen H 1949- *AmMWSc 92*
**Ip**, Wallace 1948- *AmMWSc 92*
**Ipatieff**, Vladimir Nikolaevich 1867-1952 *SovUnBD*
**Ipatyeff**, Vladimir Nikolayevich 1867-1952 *FacFETw*
**Ipema**, William Bernard 1938- *WhoMW 92, WhoRel 92*
**Iphianassa** *EncAmaz 91*
**Iphinoe** *EncAmaz 91*
**Ippel**, Larry Peter 1947- *WhoEnt 92*
**Ippen**, Erich Peter 1940- *AmMWSc 92*
**Ippen-Ihler**, Karin Ann 1942- *AmMWSc 92*
**Ippolito**, Donna *DrAPF 91*
**Ippolito**, Mark Edward 1947- *WhoMW 92*
**Ippolitov-Ivanov**, Mikhail 1859-1935 *NewAmDM*
**Ipsen**, D. C. 1921- *WrDr 92*
**Ipsen**, David Carl 1921- *IntAu&W 91*
**Ipsen**, Diana 1950- *WhoFI 92*
**Ipser**, James Reid 1942- *AmMWSc 92*
**Ipswich**, Archdeacon of *Who 92*
**Ipswich**, Bishop of *Who 92*
**Ipswich**, Viscount 1978- *Who 92*
**Iqbal**, Khalid 1949- *WhoMW 92*
**Iqbal**, Mohammed Omer 1953- *WhoMW 92*
**Iqbal**, Zafar 1946- *AmMWSc 92*
**Iradier y Bulfy**, Manuel 1854-1911 *HisDSpE*
**Irahola**, Rene C. 1928- *WhoHisp 92*
**Irala**, Domingo Martinez de *HisDSpE*
**Iralu**, Vichazelhu 1924- *AmMWSc 92*
**Iran**, Empress of *IntWW 91*
**Irani**, Jamshed Jiji 1936- *IntWW 91*
**Irani**, Keki B *AmMWSc 92*
**Irani**, N F 1934- *AmMWSc 92*
**Irani**, Ray R. 1935- *IntWW 91, WhoFI 92, WhoWest 92*
**Irani**, Riyad Ray 1935- *AmMWSc 92*
**Iranpour**, Maria Fatima 1963- *WhoFI 92*
**Irausquin**, Hiltje 1937- *AmMWSc 92*
**Irazusta**, Julio Alberto Gustavo 1899-1982 *BiDExR*
**Irazusta**, Rodolfo 1897-1967 *BiDExR*
**Irby** *Who 92*
**Irby**, Bobby Newell 1932- *AmMWSc 92*
**Irby**, Holt 1937- *WhoAmL 92*
**Irby**, Kenneth *DrAPF 91*
**Irby**, Kenneth 1936- *ConPo 91, IntAu&W 91, WrDr 92*
**Irby**, Nathan C, Jr 1931- *WhoAmP 91*
**Irby**, Ray 1918- *WhoBlA 92*
**Irby**, William Robert 1923- *AmMWSc 92*
**Ircink**, Gregory Francis 1960- *WhoAmL 92*
**Iredale**, Eugene Gerald 1951- *WhoAmL 92*
**Iredale**, Peter 1932- *Who 92*
**Iredale**, Randle W. 1929- *IntWW 91*
**Iredale**, Roger Oliver 1934- *Who 92*
**Iredell**, James 1751-1799 *BlkwEAR*
**Iredell**, James, Jr. 1788-1853 *DcNCBi 3*
**Iredell**, James, Sr. 1751-1799 *DcNCBi 3*
**Ireijo**, James Satoru 1946- *WhoAmL 92*
**Irelan**, Robert Withers 1937- *WhoFI 92*
**Ireland**, Andrew P 1930- *WhoAmP 91*
**Ireland**, Andy 1930- *AlmAP 92 [port]*
**Ireland**, Barbara M *WhoAmP 91*
**Ireland**, Carol Beard 1948- *AmMWSc 92*
**Ireland**, Charles T., Jr. d1972 *LesBEnT 92*
**Ireland**, David 1927- *ConNov 91, IntAu&W 91, WrDr 92*
**Ireland**, Donovan Edward 1913- *WhoAmP 91*
**Ireland**, Frank Edward 1913- *Who 92*
**Ireland**, Gordon Alexander 1944- *AmMWSc 92*
**Ireland**, Herbert O 1919- *AmMWSc 92*
**Ireland**, James 1947- *AmMWSc 92*
**Ireland**, James Duane, III 1950- *WhoEnt 92*
**Ireland**, Jill 1936-1990 *AnObit 1990, ConAu 135*
**Ireland**, Jill 1941-1990 *ConTFT 9*
**Ireland**, John 1838-1918 *DcAmImH, RelLAm 91*
**Ireland**, John 1879-1962 *FacFETw*
**Ireland**, John 1916- *IntMPA 92*
**Ireland**, Kevin 1933- *ConPo 91, WrDr 92*
**Ireland**, Kevin Mark 1933- *IntAu&W 91*
**Ireland**, Lynda 1950- *WhoBlA 92*
**Ireland**, Marvin Edwin 1947- *WhoFI 92*
**Ireland**, Norman Charles 1927- *IntWW 91, Who 92*
**Ireland**, Patricia *NewYTBS 91 [port]*
**Ireland**, Patricia 1946?- *News 92-2 [port]*
**Ireland**, Patrick 1934- *TwCPaSc*
**Ireland**, Patrick Gault de C. *Who 92*
**Ireland**, Robert Ellsworth 1929- *AmMWSc 92*
**Ireland**, Robert Livingston, III 1920- *WhoFI 92*
**Ireland**, Roderick Louis 1944- *WhoBlA 92*
**Ireland**, Ronald David 1925- *Who 92*
**Ireland**, Timothy F 1958- *WhoAmP 91*
**Ireland**, William Henry 1777-1835 *BlkwCEP*
**Irell**, Lawrence Elliott 1912- *WhoAmL 92*
**Iremonger**, Lucille *IntAu&W 91*
**Iremonger**, Thomas Lascelles Isa Shandon *Who 92*
**Irenaeus** 115?-202? *EncEarC*
**Irene**, Eugene Arthur 1941- *AmMWSc 92*
**Ireney**, Metropolitan 1892-1981 *RelLAm 91*
**Irens**, Alfred Norman 1911- *Who 92*
**Ireson**, Gordon Worley 1906- *Who 92*
**Ireson**, Roger William 1939- *WhoRel 92*
**Ireson**, W Grant 1915- *AmMWSc 92*
**Ireton**, Barrie Rowland 1944- *Who 92*
**Ireton**, Kikuko Monica 1929- *IntMPA 92*
**Irey**, Charlotte York 1918- *WhoEnt 92*
**Irey**, Nelson Sumner 1911- *AmMWSc 92*
**Irey**, Richard Kenneth 1936- *AmMWSc 92*
**Irfan**, Muhammad 1933- *AmMWSc 92*
**Irgens**, Roar L 1930- *AmMWSc 92*
**Irgolic**, Kurt Johann 1938- *AmMWSc 92*
**Irgon**, Joseph 1919- *AmMWSc 92*
**Iriani**, Abdul Karim al- *IntWW 91*
**Iribarne**, Julio Victor 1916- *AmMWSc 92*
**Iribarren**, Norma Carmen 1938- *WhoHisp 92*
**Iribarren Borges**, Ignacio 1912- *IntWW 91*
**Irick**, Gether, Jr 1936- *AmMWSc 92*
**Irick**, Paul Eugene 1918- *AmMWSc 92*
**Irie**, Reiko Furuse 1940- *AmMWSc 92*
**Irigaray**, Luce 193-?- *FrenWW*
**Irigoin**, Jean 1920- *IntWW 91*
**Irigonegaray**, Pedro Luis 1948- *WhoHisp 92*
**Irigoyen**, Fructuoso Rascon 1949- *WhoHisp 92*
**Irigoyen**, Matilde M. 1949- *WhoHisp 92*
**Irigoyen**, Sal A. 1954- *WhoHisp 92*
**Irimescu**, Ion 1903- *IntWW 91*
**Irion**, Mary Jean *DrAPF 91*
**Irion**, Mary Jean 1922- *WrDr 92*
**Irish**, Donald Edward 1932- *AmMWSc 92*
**Irish**, Douglas Lynn 1939- *WhoAmL 92*
**Irish**, Hugh *ScFEYrs*
**Irish**, James David 1943- *AmMWSc 92*
**Irish**, James McCredie, III 1943- *AmMWSc 92*
**Irish**, James Richard 1946- *WhoFI 92*
**Irish**, Jerry Arthur 1936- *WhoRel 92*
**Irish**, Leon Eugene 1938- *WhoAmL 92*
**Irish**, Ronald 1913- *Who 92*
**Irish**, Terry Lee 1951- *WhoRel 92*
**Iritani**, W M 1923- *AmMWSc 92*
**Irizarry**, Balvino *WhoHisp 92*
**Irizarry**, Carmen 1956- *WhoHisp 92*
**Irizarry**, Herminio 1952- *WhoHisp 92*
**Irizarry**, John 1946- *WhoHisp 92*
**Irizarry**, Victor *WhoHisp 92*
**Irizarry-Graziani**, Carmen 1948- *WhoHisp 92*
**Irizarry-Paoli**, Julio A. 1955- *WhoHisp 92*
**Irmagean** 1947- *WhoBlA 92*
**Irmak**, Sadi 1904- *IntWW 91*
**Irmas**, Sydney Milton, Jr. 1925- *WhoFI 92*
**Irmer**, Douglas Daryl 1959- *WhoRel 92*
**Irminger**, Eugene Herman 1929- *WhoFI 92, WhoMW 92*
**Irmiter**, Theodore Ferer 1922- *AmMWSc 92*
**Irmscher**, Scott William 1951- *WhoAmL 92*
**Irobe**, Yoshiaki 1911- *IntWW 91*
**Irok**, Leo Moggie Anak 1941- *IntWW 91*
**Irom**, Joseph M. 1931- *WhoAmL 92*
**Iron Thunderhorse** *ConAu 133*
**Ironbiter**, Suzanne Potter *DrAPF 91*
**Ironquill** *BenetAL 91*
**Irons**, David 1870-1907 *BiInAmS*
**Irons**, Edgar T 1936- *AmMWSc 92*
**Irons**, Edward D. *WhoBlA 92*
**Irons**, Jeremy 1948- *IntMPA 92, IntWW 91, News 91 [port], Who 92*
**Irons**, Jeremy John 1948- *WhoEnt 92*
**Irons**, Margaret Jean 1951- *AmMWSc 92*

**Irons**, Mark William 1962- *WhoRel 92*
**Irons**, Neil L. 1936- *WhoRel 92*
**Irons**, Richard Davis 1947- *AmMWSc 92*
**Irons**, Sandra Jean 1940- *WhoBlA 92*
**Irons**, Sue 1943- *WhoBlA 92*
**Irons**, William V 1943- *WhoAmP 91*
**Ironside** *Who 92*
**Ironside**, Baron 1924- *Who 92*
**Ironside**, Christopher 1913- *Who 92*
**Ironside**, Derek *ScFEYrs*
**Ironside**, Harry 1876-1951 *RelLAm 91*
**Ironside**, Robin 1912-1965 *TwCPaSc*
**Irr**, Joseph David 1934- *AmMWSc 92*
**Irrthum**, Henri Emile 1947- *WhoFI 92*
**Irsa**, Adolph Peter 1922- *AmMWSc 92*
**Irsay**, James Steven 1959- *WhoMW 92*
**Irsay**, Robert 1923- *WhoMW 92*
**Irsfeld**, John H. *DrAPF 91*
**Irsfeld**, John Henry 1937- *IntAu&W 91, WhoWest 92*
**Irshaidat**, Salah 1919- *IntWW 91*
**Irvan**, Robert P *WhoIns 92*
**Irvin**, Albert 1922- *TwCPaSc*
**Irvin**, Ben Leroy 1935- *WhoAmL 92*
**Irvin**, Byron Edward 1966- *WhoBlA 92*
**Irvin**, Charles Leslie 1935- *WhoBlA 92*
**Irvin**, Constance Olivia 1940- *WhoEnt 92*
**Irvin**, Howard Brownlee 1919- *AmMWSc 92*
**Irvin**, Howard H 1918- *AmMWSc 92*
**Irvin**, James Duard 1942- *AmMWSc 92*
**Irvin**, James Kee 1941- *WhoAmL 92*
**Irvin**, John 1940- *IntMPA 92*
**Irvin**, LeRoy 1957- *WhoBlA 92*
**Irvin**, Maurice Ray 1930- *WhoRel 92*
**Irvin**, Melvin, Jr 1942- *WhoAmP 91*
**Irvin**, Monford Merrill 1919- *WhoBlA 92*
**Irvin**, Patricia Louise 1955- *WhoAmL 92*
**Irvin**, Robert Andrew 1948- *WhoAmP 91*
**Irvin**, Sally A. 1949- *WhoAmL 92*
**Irvin**, Thomas *WhoAmP 91*
**Irvin**, Tinsley H 1933- *WhoIns 92*
**Irvine** *Who 92*
**Irvine**, Alan Montgomery 1926- *Who 92*
**Irvine**, Bruce Alan 1961- *WhoEnt 92*
**Irvine**, Bryant Godman 1909- *Who 92*
**Irvine**, Carolyn Lenette 1947- *WhoBlA 92*
**Irvine**, Cynthia Emberson 1948- *AmMWSc 92*
**Irvine**, David Robert 1943- *WhoAmP 91*
**Irvine**, Donald Grant 1930- *AmMWSc 92*
**Irvine**, Donald Hamilton 1935- *Who 92*
**Irvine**, Donald McLean 1920- *AmMWSc 92*
**Irvine**, Frances L 1940- *WhoAmP 91*
**Irvine**, Francis Sprague 1923- *WhoAmL 92*
**Irvine**, Freeman Raymond, Jr. 1931- *WhoBlA 92*
**Irvine**, George Norman 1922- *AmMWSc 92*
**Irvine**, Gerard Sutherland 1913- *Who 92*
**Irvine**, James Bosworth 1914- *AmMWSc 92*
**Irvine**, James Eccles Malise 1925- *Who 92*
**Irvine**, James Estill 1928- *AmMWSc 92*
**Irvine**, Janice M. 1951- *ConAu 135*
**Irvine**, Jerry Gerald Andrew 1958- *WhoWest 92*
**Irvine**, John 1914- *Who 92*
**Irvine**, John Ferguson 1920- *Who 92*
**Irvine**, John Maxwell 1939- *IntWW 91, Who 92*
**Irvine**, John Murray 1924- *Who 92*
**Irvine**, John Withers, Jr 1913- *AmMWSc 92*
**Irvine**, Kevin Michael 1950- *WhoEnt 92*
**Irvine**, Mary Elizabeth 1913- *WhoAmP 91*
**Irvine**, Merle M 1924- *AmMWSc 92*
**Irvine**, Michael Fraser 1939- *Who 92*
**Irvine**, Murray *Who 92*
**Irvine**, Norman Forrest 1922- *Who 92*
**Irvine**, Reed John 1922- *WhoEnt 92*
**Irvine**, Richard H. 1942- *IntMPA 92*
**Irvine**, Robert Gerald 1931- *WhoWest 92*
**Irvine**, Robin 1929- *Who 92*
**Irvine**, Robin Orlando Hamilton 1929- *IntWW 91*
**Irvine**, Stuart James Curzon 1953- *AmMWSc 92*
**Irvine**, T Neil 1933- *AmMWSc 92*
**Irvine**, Thomas A. 1955- *WhoEnt 92*
**Irvine**, Thomas Francis 1922- *AmMWSc 92*
**Irvine**, Vernon Bruce 1943- *WhoWest 92*
**Irvine**, William 1743-1787 *BlkwCEP*
**Irvine**, William Burriss 1925- *WhoFI 92*
**Irvine**, William Michael 1936- *AmMWSc 92*
**Irvine of Lairg**, Baron 1940- *Who 92*
**Irving**, Amy 1953- *IntMPA 92, IntWW 91, WhoEnt 92*
**Irving**, Charles *Who 92*
**Irving**, Charles Clayton 1932- *AmMWSc 92*
**Irving**, Clarence Larry, Jr. 1955- *WhoBlA 92*
**Irving**, Clifford *Who 92*
**Irving**, Clifford 1930- *FacFETw, IntAu&W 91, WrDr 92*
**Irving**, David Gerow 1935- *WhoEnt 92*
**Irving**, Edmund 1910-1990 *AnObit 1990*
**Irving**, Edmund George d1990 *Who 92N*
**Irving**, Edward 1927- *AmMWSc 92, IntWW 91, Who 92*
**Irving**, Edward Clifford 1914- *Who 92*
**Irving**, Frank Dunham 1923- *AmMWSc 92*
**Irving**, Frederick 1921- *WhoAmP 91*
**Irving**, George Steven 1922- *WhoEnt 92*
**Irving**, George Washington, Jr 1910- *AmMWSc 92*
**Irving**, Harry Munroe Napier Hetherington 1905- *Who 92*
**Irving**, Henry E., II 1937- *WhoBlA 92*
**Irving**, James P 1936- *AmMWSc 92*
**Irving**, James Tutin 1902- *AmMWSc 92, Who 92*
**Irving**, John *DrAPF 91*
**Irving**, John 1920- *Who 92*
**Irving**, John 1942- *Au&Arts 8 [port], BenetAL 91, ConNov 91, FacFETw, WrDr 92*
**Irving**, John Duer 1874-1918 *BiInAmS*
**Irving**, John Stiles, Jr. 1940- *WhoAmL 92*
**Irving**, John Treat 1812-1906 *BenetAL 91*
**Irving**, John Winslow 1942- *IntWW 91*
**Irving**, Miles Horsfall 1935- *Who 92*
**Irving**, Ophelia McAlpin 1929- *WhoBlA 92*
**Irving**, Patricia Marie 1950- *AmMWSc 92*
**Irving**, Peter 1771-1838 *BenetAL 91*
**Irving**, Pierre 1803-1876 *BenetAL 91*
**Irving**, Richard d1991 *LesBEnT 92*
**Irving**, Robert *IntAu&W 91X*
**Irving**, Robert 1913-1991 *NewYTBS 91 [port]*
**Irving**, Robert Augustine d1991 *Who 92N*
**Irving**, Robert Augustine 1913- *IntWW 91*
**Irving**, Robert Churchill 1928- *WhoFI 92*
**Irving**, Roland Duer 1847-1888 *BiInAmS*
**Irving**, Terry 1951- *WhoEnt 92*
**Irving**, Thomas Pitts d1818 *DcNCBi 3*
**Irving**, Washington 1783-1859 *BenetAL 91*
**Irving**, William 1766-1821 *BenetAL 91*
**Irving-Swift**, Charles Edward 1954- *WhoFI 92*
**Irvis**, K Leroy 1919- *WhoAmP 91, WhoBlA 92*
**Irwin**, Lord 1977- *Who 92*
**Irwin**, Ann 1915- *ConAu 36NR, SmATA 14AS [port]*
**Irwin**, Arthur S 1912- *AmMWSc 92*
**Irwin**, Benjamin Hardin 1854- *RelLAm 91*
**Irwin**, Bill 1950- *IntMPA 92*
**Irwin**, Blair Garnett 1945- *WhoEnt 92*
**Irwin**, Brian St George 1917- *Who 92*
**Irwin**, Byron 1941- *WhoFI 92*
**Irwin**, Charles 1940- *WhoEnt 92*
**Irwin**, Charles Edwin, Jr 1945- *AmMWSc 92*
**Irwin**, Christopher 1948- *IntMPA 92*
**Irwin**, Constance 1913- *IntAu&W 91, WrDr 92*
**Irwin**, Darlene Muriel 1946- *WhoRel 92*
**Irwin**, David 1945- *AmMWSc 92*
**Irwin**, David B *WhoAmP 91*
**Irwin**, David George 1933- *WrDr 92*
**Irwin**, Deborah Jo 1952- *WhoWest 92*
**Irwin**, Don d1991 *NewYTBS 91*
**Irwin**, Donald Jay 1926- *WhoAmP 91*
**Irwin**, Frances Mary 1932- *WhoEnt 92*
**Irwin**, G H *TwCSFW 91*
**Irwin**, George Rankin 1907- *AmMWSc 92*
**Irwin**, Glenn Ward, Jr 1920- *AmMWSc 92*
**Irwin**, Grace Lilian 1907- *WrDr 92*
**Irwin**, Graham W. d1991 *NewYTBS 91*
**Irwin**, Graham W. 1920-1991 *ConAu 135*
**Irwin**, Gwyther 1931- *TwCPaSc*
**Irwin**, Hadley *ConAu 36NR, SmATA 14AS [port]*
**Irwin**, Hampton William 1930- *WhoWest 92*
**Irwin**, Henry 1725?-1777 *DcNCBi 3*
**Irwin**, Howard Samuel 1928- *AmMWSc 92*
**Irwin**, Ian Sutherland 1933- *Who 92*
**Irwin**, Inez Haynes 1873-1970 *BenetAL 91*
**Irwin**, James 1930- *FacFETw*
**Irwin**, James 1930-1991 *News 92-1*
**Irwin**, James Alfred 1949- *WhoEnt 92*
**Irwin**, James B. 1930-1991 *NewYTBS 91 [port]*
**Irwin**, James Campbell d1990 *Who 92N*
**Irwin**, James Joseph 1958- *AmMWSc 92*
**Irwin**, Jared 1750-1818 *DcNCBi 3*
**Irwin**, Joe Robert 1936- *WhoFI 92*
**Irwin**, John 1926- *WhoAmP 91*
**Irwin**, John Barrows 1909- *AmMWSc 92*
**Irwin**, John Charles 1935- *AmMWSc 92*
**Irwin**, John Conran 1917- *Who 92*
**Irwin**, John David 1939- *AmMWSc 92*
**Irwin**, John McCormick 1929- *AmMWSc 92*
**Irwin**, John N, II 1913- *WhoAmP 91*
**Irwin**, John W 1914- *WhoAmP 91*
**Irwin**, Karen Osborne *WhoAmP 91*
**Irwin**, Lafayette K 1922- *AmMWSc 92*
**Irwin**, Louis Neal 1943- *AmMWSc 92*
**Irwin**, Lynne Howard 1941- *AmMWSc 92*
**Irwin**, Margaret 1889-1967 *CurBio 91N*
**Irwin**, Margaret Hardinge d1940 *BiDBrF 2*
**Irwin**, Mark *DrAPF 91*
**Irwin**, Mary Frances 1925- *WhoWest 92*
**Irwin**, May 1862-1938 *NewAmDM*
**Irwin**, Michael Edward 1940- *AmMWSc 92*
**Irwin**, Michael Henry Knox 1931- *Who 92*
**Irwin**, Miriam Dianne Owen 1930- *WhoFI 92*
**Irwin**, Mitch 1952- *WhoAmP 91*
**Irwin**, P K *IntAu&W 91X*
**Irwin**, Pat 1921- *WhoAmP 91*
**Irwin**, Paul Garfield 1937- *WhoRel 92*
**Irwin**, Peter Anthony 1945- *AmMWSc 92*
**Irwin**, Peter George 1925- *WrDr 92*
**Irwin**, Philip Donnan 1933- *WhoAmL 92*
**Irwin**, Philip George 1934- *AmMWSc 92*
**Irwin**, R. Neil 1941- *WhoAmL 92*
**Irwin**, R. Robert 1933- *WhoAmL 92, WhoWest 92*
**Irwin**, Richard Leslie 1917- *AmMWSc 92*
**Irwin**, Richard Stephen 1942- *AmMWSc 92*
**Irwin**, Robert 1946- *WrDr 92*
**Irwin**, Robert Cook 1929- *AmMWSc 92*
**Irwin**, Ronald Gilbert 1933- *WhoRel 92*
**Irwin**, Scott Hal 1958- *WhoMW 92*
**Irwin**, Stanley Roy 1941- *WhoMW 92*
**Irwin**, Steven Arnold 1966- *WhoEnt 92*
**Irwin**, Wallace 1875-1959 *BenetAL 91*
**Irwin**, Will 1873-1948 *BenetAL 91*
**Irwin**, William Arthur 1898- *IntWW 91*
**Irwin**, William Edward 1926- *AmMWSc 92*
**Irwin**, William Elliot 1928- *AmMWSc 92*
**Irwin**, William Henry 1873-1948 *AmPeW*
**Irwin**, William Rankin 1940- *WhoAmL 92*
**Iryani**, Qadi Abdul Rahman 1917- *IntWW 91*
**Isa Bin Sulman Al-Khalifa** *IntWW 91*
**Isa**, Abdallah Mohammad 1938- *AmMWSc 92*
**Isaac** *EncEarC*
**Isaac of Antioch** d460? *EncEarC*
**Isaac of Nineveh** d700? *EncEarC*
**Isaac**, Alfred James 1919- *Who 92*
**Isaac**, Annette Louise 1946- *WhoAmP 91*
**Isaac**, Anthony John Gower 1931- *Who 92*
**Isaac**, Bina Susan 1958- *WhoMW 92*
**Isaac**, Brian Jeffrey 1959- *WhoAmL 92*
**Isaac**, Brian Wayne *WhoBlA 92*
**Isaac**, Cecil 1930- *WhoEnt 92*
**Isaac**, Earlean 1950- *WhoBlA 92*
**Isaac**, Ephraim 1936- *WhoBlA 92*
**Isaac**, Eugene Leonard 1915- *WhoBlA 92*
**Isaac**, Heinrich 1450?-1517 *NewAmDM*
**Isaac**, James Keith 1932- *Who 92*
**Isaac**, Jim L 1936- *WhoAmP 91*
**Isaac**, Joseph William Alexander 1935- *WhoBlA 92*
**Isaac**, Luis *WhoHisp 92*
**Isaac**, Maurice Laurence Reginald 1928- *Who 92*
**Isaac**, Peter Ashley Hammond 1945- *AmMWSc 92*
**Isaac**, Peter Charles Gerald 1921- *Who 92*
**Isaac**, Richard Eugene 1934- *AmMWSc 92*
**Isaac**, Robert A 1936- *AmMWSc 92*
**Isaac**, Robert Arthur 1933- *Who 92*
**Isaac**, Robert M 1928- *WhoAmP 91*
**Isaac**, Robert Michael 1928- *WhoWest 92*
**Isaac**, Walter 1927- *AmMWSc 92*
**Isaac**, William Michael 1943- *WhoFI 92*
**Isaac**, Yvonne Renee 1948- *WhoBlA 92*
**Isaacks**, Russell Ernest 1935- *AmMWSc 92*
**Isaackson**, Larry Dean 1951- *WhoIns 92*
**Isaacs** *Who 92*
**Isaacs**, Alan 1925- *IntAu&W 91*
**Isaacs**, Albertha Madeline 1900- *Who 92*
**Isaacs**, Andrea 1952- *WhoEnt 92*
**Isaacs**, Anthony John 1942- *Who 92*
**Isaacs**, Bernard 1924- *WrDr 92*
**Isaacs**, Brenda Gail 1958- *WhoEnt 92*
**Isaacs**, Charles Edward 1811-1860 *BiInAmS*
**Isaacs**, Charles Edward 1949- *AmMWSc 92*
**Isaacs**, Cheryl Boone *IntMPA 92*
**Isaacs**, Damon Lynn 1962- *WhoRel 92*
**Isaacs**, Doris C. 1939- *WhoBlA 92*
**Isaacs**, Earle Lofland 1930- *WhoAmP 91*
**Isaacs**, Edith J. R. 1878-1956 *BenetAL 91*
**Isaacs**, Gerald W 1927- *AmMWSc 92*
**Isaacs**, Godfrey Leonard 1924- *AmMWSc 92*
**Isaacs**, Gregory Sullivan 1947- *WhoEnt 92*
**Isaacs**, Hugh Solomon 1936- *AmMWSc 92*
**Isaacs**, I Martin 1940- *AmMWSc 92*
**Isaacs**, Jeremy Israel 1932- *IntWW 91, Who 92*
**Isaacs**, John David 1945- *WhoAmP 91*
**Isaacs**, Jonathan Mark 1961- *WhoFI 92*
**Isaacs**, Jorge 1837-1895 *BenetAL 91*
**Isaacs**, Kenneth Sidney 1920- *WhoFI 92, WhoMW 92*
**Isaacs**, Leslie Laszlo 1933- *AmMWSc 92*
**Isaacs**, Pamela Kay 1957- *WhoMW 92*
**Isaacs**, Patricia 1949- *WhoBlA 92*
**Isaacs**, Phil 1922- *IntMPA 92, WhoEnt 92*
**Isaacs**, Philip Klein 1927- *AmMWSc 92*
**Isaacs**, Robert Charles 1919- *WhoAmL 92*
**Isaacs**, Robert Wolfe 1931- *WhoFI 92*
**Isaacs**, S. Fred 1937- *WhoFI 92*
**Isaacs**, S. Ted 1914- *WhoFI 92, WhoMW 92*
**Isaacs**, Stanley 1944- *WhoEnt 92*
**Isaacs**, Stephen D. 1944- *WhoBlA 92*
**Isaacs**, Stuart Lindsay 1952- *Who 92*
**Isaacs**, Susan *DrAPF 91*
**Isaacs**, Susan 1943- *IntAu&W 91, WhoEnt 92, WrDr 92*
**Isaacs**, Tami Yvette 1952- *AmMWSc 92*
**Isaacs**, Vernon A., Jr. *WhoFI 92*
**Isaacs-Lowe**, Arlene Elizabeth 1959- *WhoBlA 92*
**Isaacson**, Allen 1932- *AmMWSc 92*
**Isaacson**, Allen Ira 1938- *WhoAmL 92, WhoFI 92*
**Isaacson**, Boris 1926- *WhoFI 92, WhoWest 92*
**Isaacson**, Clifford Edwin 1934- *WhoRel 92*
**Isaacson**, David 1948- *AmMWSc 92*
**Isaacson**, Dennis Lee 1942- *AmMWSc 92*
**Isaacson**, Eugene 1919- *AmMWSc 92*
**Isaacson**, Eugene I 1933- *AmMWSc 92*
**Isaacson**, Gary Alan 1952- *WhoFI 92*
**Isaacson**, Gerald Sidney 1927- *WhoFI 92*
**Isaacson**, Henry Verschay 1939- *AmMWSc 92*
**Isaacson**, Judith Magyar 1925- *ConAu 133*
**Isaacson**, Lavar King 1934- *AmMWSc 92*
**Isaacson**, Mae Deloris 1924- *WhoAmP 91*
**Isaacson**, Michael Saul 1942- *AmMWSc 92*
**Isaacson**, Peter Edwin 1946- *AmMWSc 92*
**Isaacson**, Raymond E 1928- *WhoAmP 91*
**Isaacson**, Robert B 1936- *AmMWSc 92*
**Isaacson**, Robert John 1932- *AmMWSc 92*
**Isaacson**, Robert Lee 1928- *AmMWSc 92*
**Isaacson**, Robert Louis 1944- *WhoWest 92*
**Isaacson**, Ruby May 1940- *WhoFI 92*
**Isaacson**, Stanley Leonard 1927- *AmMWSc 92*
**Isaacson**, Thomas Adam 1958- *WhoAmL 92*
**Isaak**, Chris 1956- *ConMus 6 [port]*
**Isaak**, Dale Darwin 1948- *AmMWSc 92*
**Isaak**, Gotthilf Eugene 1937- *WhoFI 92*
**Isaak**, Robert D 1921- *AmMWSc 92*
**Isaaman**, Gerald Michael 1933- *Who 92*
**Isabella I** 1451-1504 *EncAmaz 91*
**Isabella Clara Eugenia** *EncAmaz 91*
**Isabella de Lorraine** 1410?-1453 *EncAmaz 91*
**Isabella Leonarda** 1620-1704 *NewAmDM*
**Isabella of Castile** 1451-1504 *HisDSpE*
**Isabella**, Mary Margaret 1947- *WhoAmL 92*
**Isabella**, Rande Brian 1956- *WhoEnt 92*
**Isabelle of England** 1285?-1313? *EncAmaz 91*
**Isachenko**, Boris Lavrent'evich 1871-1948 *SovUnBD*
**Isachsen**, Yngvar William 1920- *AmMWSc 92*
**Isacks**, Bryan L 1936- *AmMWSc 92*
**Isackson**, Doran *WhoAmP 91*
**Isada**, Nelson M 1923- *AmMWSc 92*
**Isadore**, Harold W. *WhoBlA 92*
**Isai**, Hekuran 1933- *IntWW 91*
**Isaiah** *EncEarC*
**Isaki**, Lucy Power Slyngstad 1945- *WhoAmL 92*
**Isakoff**, Louis Alan 1954- *WhoAmL 92, WhoEnt 92*
**Isakoff**, Sheldon Erwin 1925- *AmMWSc 92*
**Isakov**, Ivan Stepanovich 1894-1967 *SovUnBD*
**Isakov**, Victor Fyodorovich 1932- *IntWW 91*
**Isakov**, Victor Michael 1947- *WhoMW 92*
**Isakova**, Bayan Seikhanovna 1957- *IntWW 91*
**Isakova**, Bayan Seilkhanovna 1957- *SovUnBD*
**Isakovsky**, Mikhail Vasil'evich 1900-1973 *SovUnBD*
**Isakow**, Selwyn 1952- *WhoFI 92*
**Isaks**, Martin 1935- *AmMWSc 92*
**Isaksen**, Robert L. *WhoRel 92*
**Isakson**, Hans Robert 1944- *WhoMW 92*
**Isakson**, Johnny 1944- *WhoAmP 91*
**Isakson**, Joseph Leroy 1931- *WhoMW 92*
**Isaman**, Francis 1930- *AmMWSc 92*
**Isarangkun Na Ayuthaya**, Charunphan 1914- *IntWW 91*
**Isarangkun Na Ayuthaya**, Chirayu 1942- *IntWW 91*
**Isard**, Harold Joseph 1910- *AmMWSc 92*
**Isard**, Walter 1919- *IntWW 91*
**Isasi-Diaz**, Ada Maria 1943- *WhoHisp 92*
**Isayev**, Aleksandr Sergeyevich *IntWW 91*
**Isayev**, Vasiliy Yakovlevich 1917- *IntWW 91*
**Isban**, Mary Gervase 1958- *WhoAmL 92*

**Isbasescu**, Mihai 1915- IntWW 91
**Isbell**, Arthur Furman 1917- AmMWSc 92
**Isbell**, Charles Lester 1936- WhoRel 92
**Isbell**, David Bradford 1929- WhoAmL 92
**Isbell**, Harold Max 1936- WhoWest 92
**Isbell**, Horace Smith 1898- AmMWSc 92
**Isbell**, James S. 1918- WhoBlA 92
**Isbell**, John Rolfe 1930- AmMWSc 92
**Isbell**, Raymond Eugene 1932- AmMWSc 92
**Isbell**, Sheila Dianne 1958- WhoAmL 92
**Isbell**, Virginia 1932- WhoAmP 91
**Isberg**, Clifford A 1935- AmMWSc 92
**Isberg**, Larry Alger 1948- WhoMW 92
**Isbin**, Herbert S 1919- AmMWSc 92
**Isbin**, Sharon 1956- WhoEnt 92
**Isbister**, Claude Malcolm 1914- IntWW 91
**Isbister**, David Kent 1940- WhoFI 92
**Isbister**, Roger John 1942- AmMWSc 92
**Isbrandt**, Lester Reinhardt 1946- AmMWSc 92
**Isby**, David Carpenter 1953- WhoAmP 91
**Iscaro**, Robert 1955- WhoAmL 92
**Isch**, Helen A 1907- WhoAmP 91
**Isdaner**, Lawrence Arthur 1934- WhoFI 92
**Isebrands**, Judson G 1943- AmMWSc 92
**Isele**, William Paul 1949- WhoAmL 92
**Iseler**, Elmer 1927- NewAmDM
**Iseler**, Gerald William 1938- AmMWSc 92
**Iselin**, Donald G 1922- AmMWSc 92
**Iselin**, John Jay LesBEnT 92
**Isely**, Duane 1918- AmMWSc 92, WhoMW 92
**Isely**, Henry Philip 1915- WhoFI 92, WhoWest 92
**Iseman**, Stephen Dane 1948- WhoMW 92
**Isenberg**, Allen 1938- AmMWSc 92
**Isenberg**, George Raymond, Jr 1929- AmMWSc 92
**Isenberg**, Henry David 1922- AmMWSc 92
**Isenberg**, Irving Harry 1909- AmMWSc 92
**Isenberg**, James Allen 1951- WhoWest 92
**Isenberg**, Lionel 1925- AmMWSc 92
**Isenberg**, Norbert 1923- AmMWSc 92
**Isenberg**, Peter James 1966- WhoRel 92
**Isenberg**, Phillip Lee 1939- WhoAmP 91
**Isenberg**, Seymour 1930- WhoEnt 92, WrDr 92
**Isenbergh**, Joseph 1945- WhoAmL 92
**Isenecker**, Lawrence Elmer 1924- AmMWSc 92
**Isenhour**, Thomas Lee 1939- AmMWSc 92
**Isenhower**, W Stine WhoAmP 91
**Isenor**, Neil R 1932- AmMWSc 92
**Isensee**, Allan Robert 1939- AmMWSc 92
**Isensee**, Robert William 1919- AmMWSc 92
**Isepp**, Martin Johannes Sebastian 1930- Who 92
**Iseri**, Lloyd T 1917- AmMWSc 92
**Iseri**, Oscar Akio 1927- AmMWSc 92
**Iserson**, Kenneth Victor 1949- AmMWSc 92
**Isett**, Robert David 1942- AmMWSc 92
**Isgur**, Benjamin 1911- AmMWSc 92
**Isgur**, Nathan 1947- AmMWSc 92
**Ish**, Carl Jackson 1919- AmMWSc 92
**Isham**, Bernice Jean 1929- WhoEnt 92
**Isham**, Elmer Rex 1935- AmMWSc 92
**Isham**, Ian 1923- Who 92
**Isham**, Quentin Delbert, Jr 1944- WhoAmP 91
**Isham**, Richard Basil 1939- WhoAmL 92
**Ishaq**, Khalid Sulaiman 1933- AmMWSc 92
**Ishay**, Ram Raymond 1931- IntWW 91
**Isherwood**, Benjamin Franklin 1822-1915 BiInAmS
**Isherwood**, Christopher 1904-1986 BenetAL 91, ConAu 35NR, FacFETw, LiExTwC, RfGEnL 91
**Isherwood**, Dana Joan AmMWSc 92
**Isherwood**, William Frank 1941- AmMWSc 92
**Isherwood**, William Thomas 1951- WhoMW 92
**Ishiba**, Jiro 1908- IntWW 91
**Ishibashi**, Kanichiro 1920- IntWW 91
**Ishibashi**, Kazuya 1922- IntWW 91
**Ishida**, Hatsuo 1948- AmMWSc 92
**Ishida**, Hirohide 1914- IntWW 91
**Ishida**, Takanobu 1931- AmMWSc 92
**Ishida**, Yukisato 1948- AmMWSc 92
**Ishiguro**, Kazuo 1954- ConNov 91, IntAu&W 91, IntWW 91, LiExTwC, Who 92, WrDr 92
**Ishihara**, Kohei 1941- AmMWSc 92
**Ishihara**, Matthew Masamitsu 1933- WhoMW 92
**Ishihara**, Shintaro 1932- IntWW 91
**Ishihara**, Takashi 1912- IntWW 91, Who 92
**Ishihara**, Teruo 1927- AmMWSc 92
**Ishii**, Douglas Nobuo 1942- AmMWSc 92
**Ishii**, Hajime 1935- IntWW 91
**Ishii**, T Koryu 1927- AmMWSc 92
**Ishii**, Thomas Koryu 1927- WhoMW 92
**Ishii-Kuntz**, Masako 1954- WhoWest 92
**Ishikawa**, Hiroshi 1941- AmMWSc 92, WhoFI 92
**Ishikawa**, Sadamu 1932- AmMWSc 92
**Ishikawa**, Shigeru 1918- IntWW 91
**Ishikawa**, Tadao 1922- IntWW 91
**Ishikawa**, Yozo IntWW 91
**Ishimaru**, Akira 1928- AmMWSc 92, WhoWest 92
**Ishimoto**, Kathy Anne Keiko 1955- WhoWest 92
**Ishimoto**, Shigeru 1913- IntWW 91
**Ishino**, Catherine Jo 1952- WhoEnt 92
**Ishino**, Shinichi IntWW 91
**Ishisaki**, Ben T. 1962- WhoWest 92
**Ishizaka**, Jiro 1927- WhoFI 92
**Ishizaka**, Kimishige 1925- AmMWSc 92
**Ishizaka**, Teruko 1926- AmMWSc 92
**Ishler**, Michael William 1952- WhoWest 92
**Ishler**, Norman Hamilton 1914- AmMWSc 92
**Ishlinsky**, Aleksandr Yulevich 1913- IntWW 91
**Ishmael**, William Earl 1946- WhoWest 92
**Ishman**, Sybil R. 1946- WhoBlA 92
**Ishwaran**, K. 1922- WrDr 92
**Ishwaran**, Karigoudar 1922- IntAu&W 91
**Isibor**, Edward Iroguehi 1940- WhoBlA 92
**Isidore** EncEarC
**Isidore of Pelusium** 360?-435? EncEarC
**Isidore of Seville** 560?-636? EncEarC
**Isidoro**, Edith Annette 1957- WhoWest 92
**Isied**, Stephan Saleh 1946- AmMWSc 92
**Isihara**, Akira AmMWSc 92
**Isik**, Hasan Esat 1916- IntWW 91
**Iskander**, Fazil 1929- FacFETw
**Iskander**, Fazil Abdulovich 1929- IntWW 91, SovUnBD
**Iskander**, Felib Youssef 1949- AmMWSc 92
**Iskander**, Shafik Kamel 1934- AmMWSc 92
**Iskrant**, John Dermot 1943- WhoAmL 92
**Islam**, A K M Nurul 1925- IntWW 91
**Islam**, Mir Nazrul 1947- AmMWSc 92
**Islam**, Muhammad Munirul 1936- AmMWSc 92
**Islam**, Nurul 1929- IntWW 91
**Islam**, Nurul 1939- AmMWSc 92
**Islam**, Shahidul 1948- IntWW 91
**Islan**, Gregory deFontaine 1947- WhoEnt 92
**Islas**, Arturo 1938- IntAu&W 91
**Islas**, Arturo 1938-1991 WhoHisp 92N
**Islas**, E. Michelle 1953- WhoHisp 92
**Islas**, Maya DrAPF 91
**Islas**, Maya C. 1947- WhoHisp 92
**Isle of Wight**, Archdeacon of Who 92
**Isleib**, Donald Richard 1927- AmMWSc 92
**Isler**, Gene A 1940- AmMWSc 92
**Isler**, Henri Gustave 1920- AmMWSc 92
**Isler**, Marshall A., III 1939- WhoBlA 92
**Isler**, Ralph Charles 1933- AmMWSc 92
**Isler**, Vicki Jan 1955- WhoAmL 92
**Isles**, David Frederick 1935- AmMWSc 92
**Isles**, Donald Edward 1924- Who 92
**Isley**, Constance Marie 1952- WhoMW 92
**Isley**, James Don 1928- AmMWSc 92
**Ismach**, Arnold Harvey 1930- WhoWest 92
**Ismael**, Julius Emanuel 1927- IntWW 91
**Ismael Manigra**, Aboobacar WhoRel 92
**Ismail Amat** 1934- IntWW 91
**Ismail**, Abdul Malek 1937- IntWW 91
**Ismail**, Ahmed Sultan 1923- IntWW 91
**Ismail**, Amin Rashid 1958- AmMWSc 92
**Ismail**, Mohamed Ali 1918- IntWW 91
**Ismail**, Mourad E H 1944- AmMWSc 92
**Ismail**, Razali 1939- IntWW 91
**Ismail**, Rocket 1969- WhoBlA 92
**Ismay**, Walter Nicholas 1921- Who 92
**Ismial**, Salaam Ibn WhoBlA 92
**Isnard**, Arnaud Joseph 1956- WhoFI 92
**Isnardi**, Michael Anthony 1960- WhoEnt 92
**Isobel**, Countess of Buchan 1296-1358 EncAmaz 91
**Isoda**, Ichiro 1913- IntWW 91
**Isokallio**, Kaarlo 1948- IntWW 91
**Isokane**, Sam Setsuo 1925- WhoWest 92
**Isola**, Maija 1927- DcTwDes
**Isolani**, Casimiro Peter Hugh Tomasi 1917- Who 92
**Isoldi**, Donna Jane 1959- WhoMW 92
**Isoltsev**, Apollovna EncAmaz 91
**Isom**, Billy Gene 1932- AmMWSc 92
**Isom**, Dotcy Ivertus, Jr. 1931- WhoRel 92
**Isom**, Gary E 1946- AmMWSc 92
**Isom**, Gerald Adrian 1938- WhoIns 92
**Isom**, Glen David 1959- WhoEnt 92
**Isom**, Harriet C 1947- AmMWSc 92
**Isom**, Harriet W 1936- WhoAmP 91
**Isom**, John B 1925- AmMWSc 92
**Isom**, Lloyd Warren 1928- WhoFI 92, WhoWest 92
**Isom**, Morris P 1928- AmMWSc 92
**Isom**, Sam 1942- WhoWest 92
**Isom**, William Howard 1917- AmMWSc 92
**Ison**, Gordon 1966- WhoEnt 92
**Ison-Franklin**, Eleanor Lutia 1929- AmMWSc 92
**Isong**, Clement Nyong 1920- IntWW 91
**Isoye**, Steven Tsutomu 1963- WhoMW 92
**Isozaki**, Arata 1931- DcTwDes, IntWW 91
**Isphording**, Wayne Carter 1937- AmMWSc 92
**Isquith**, Fred Taylor 1947- WhoAmL 92, WhoFI 92
**Isquith**, Irwin R 1942- AmMWSc 92
**Israel**, Adrian C. d1991 NewYTBS 91 [port]
**Israel**, Allen D. 1946- WhoAmL 92
**Israel**, Barry John 1946- WhoAmL 92
**Israel**, Charles DrAPF 91
**Israel**, David Hutchins 1951- WhoAmP 91
**Israel**, David Oliver 1942- WhoEnt 92
**Israel**, George M, III WhoAmP 91
**Israel**, Harold L 1909- AmMWSc 92
**Israel**, Harry, III 1934- AmMWSc 92
**Israel**, Herbert William 1931- AmMWSc 92
**Israel**, Joan 1943- WhoWest 92
**Israel**, John 1935- WrDr 92
**Israel**, Larry H. LesBEnT 92
**Israel**, Lesley Lowe 1938- WhoAmP 91
**Israel**, Martin Henry 1941- AmMWSc 92, WhoMW 92
**Israel**, Martin Spencer 1927- IntAu&W 91, Who 92
**Israel**, Neal IntMPA 92
**Israel**, Neal 1945?- ConTFT 9
**Israel**, Peter DrAPF 91
**Israel**, Philip 1935- ConAu 133
**Israel**, Richard Jerome 1930- WhoAmP 91
**Israel**, Richard Stanley 1931- WhoWest 92
**Israel**, Rucker L. 1927- WhoRel 92
**Israel**, Stanley C 1942- AmMWSc 92
**Israel**, Steven Max 1953- WhoEnt 92
**Israel**, Theodore 1927- WhoEnt 92
**Israel**, Vivianne Winters 1954- WhoFI 92, WhoWest 92
**Israel**, Warthen Talmadge 1932- WhoRel 92
**Israel**, Werner 1931- AmMWSc 92, IntWW 91, Who 92
**Israel**, Yedy 1939- AmMWSc 92
**Israelachvili**, Jacob Nissim 1944- IntWW 91, Who 92
**Israelievitch**, Jacques 1948- WhoEnt 92
**Israels**, Lyonel Garry 1926- AmMWSc 92
**Israels**, Michael Jozef 1949- WhoAmL 92
**Israelsen**, C Earl 1928- AmMWSc 92
**Israelstam**, Gerald Frank 1929- AmMWSc 92
**Israelyan**, Martin 1938- ConCom 92
**Israili**, Zafar Hasan 1934- AmMWSc 92
**Israni**, Kim 1935- WhoMW 92
**Issa**, Aswad Hashim Asim 1948- WhoMW 92, WhoRel 92
**Issa**, Daniel 1952- WhoAmP 91
**Issajenko**, Angella 1958- BlkOlyM
**Issaq**, Haleem Jeries 1936- AmMWSc 92
**Issari**, Mohammad Ali 1921- WhoEnt 92, WhoWest 92
**Issayi**, Youhannan Semaan WhoRel 92
**Issekutz**, Bela, Jr 1912- AmMWSc 92
**Issel**, Charles John 1943- AmMWSc 92
**Isselbacher**, Kurt Julius 1925- AmMWSc 92, IntWW 91
**Isselbacher**, Rhoda Solin 1932- WhoAmL 92
**Isselhard**, Donald Edward 1941- WhoMW 92
**Issenberg**, Phillip 1936- AmMWSc 92
**Isserlis**, Steven 1958- Who 92
**Isserman**, Andrew Mark 1947- WhoFI 92
**Isserman**, Joan Louise 1952- WhoAmL 92
**Isseroff**, Hadar 1938- AmMWSc 92
**Isserow**, Saul 1922- AmMWSc 92
**Issigonis**, Alec 1906- DcTwDes, FacFETw
**Issitt**, Peter David 1933- AmMWSc 92
**Issler**, Harry 1935- WhoAmL 92
**Istead**, Peter Walter Ernest 1935- Who 92
**Istock**, Conrad Alan 1936- AmMWSc 92
**Istock**, Verne George 1940- WhoFI 92
**Istomin**, Eugene 1925- NewAmDM
**Istomin**, Eugene George 1925- IntWW 91
**Istomin**, Marta Casals 1936- WhoEnt 92, WhoHisp 92
**Istook**, Ernest James, Jr 1950- WhoAmP 91
**Istrati**, Panait 1884-1935 GuFrLit 1
**Istre**, Clifton O, Jr 1932- AmMWSc 92
**Iszard**, Calvin Oscar, Jr. 1943- WhoEnt 92
**Iszler**, Harry Eugene 1930- WhoAmP 91
**Ita**, Lawrence Eyo 1939- WhoBlA 92
**Itabashi**, Hideo Henry 1926- AmMWSc 92
**Itagaki** EncAmaz 91
**Itakura**, Keiichi 1942- AmMWSc 92
**Italiaander**, Rolf Bruno Maximilian 1913- IntWW 91
**Italiano**, Julia Anne 1958- WhoWest 92
**Itami**, Juzo 1933- IntDcF 2-2 [port], IntMPA 92, IntWW 91
**Itano**, Harvey Akio 1920- AmMWSc 92
**Itano**, Wayne Masao 1951- AmMWSc 92, WhoWest 92
**Itard**, Jean-Marc-Gaspard 1775-1838 BlkwCEP
**Itatani**, Michiko WhoMW 92
**Iten**, Jonathan David 1957- WhoAmL 92, WhoFI 92
**Iten**, Laurie Elaine 1947- AmMWSc 92
**Itiaba**, Kibe 1931- AmMWSc 92
**Itil**, Turan M 1924- AmMWSc 92
**Itin**, James Richard 1933- WhoFI 92
**Itin**, Thomas William 1934- WhoMW 92
**Itkin**, Irving Herbert 1917- AmMWSc 92
**Itkin**, Ivan 1936- WhoAmP 91
**Itkin**, Iza 1930- WhoEnt 92
**Itkin**, Michael Francis Augustine 1936-1989 RelLAm 91
**Itkin**, Robert Jeffrey 1956- WhoAmL 92
**Itkoff**, David F. 1953- WhoAmL 92
**Ito**, Junetsu AmMWSc 92
**Ito**, Keith A 1939- AmMWSc 92
**Ito**, Masayoshi 1913- IntWW 91
**Ito**, Midori 1969- NewYTBS 91 [port]
**Ito**, Philip J 1932- AmMWSc 92
**Ito**, Soichiro 1924- IntWW 91
**Ito**, Susumu 1919- AmMWSc 92
**Ito**, Takeru 1928- AmMWSc 92
**Ito**, Y Marvin 1940- AmMWSc 92
**Itoga**, Stephen Yukio AmMWSc 92
**Itoh**, Junji 1922- IntWW 91
**Itoh**, Kyoichi 1914- IntWW 91
**Itoh**, Tatsuo 1940- AmMWSc 92
**Itokawa**, Hideo 1912- IntWW 91
**Iton**, Lennox Elroy 1949- AmMWSc 92
**Its**, Rudolph Ferdinandovich d1990 IntWW 91N
**Itta**, Paul d1991 NewYTBS 91
**Ittel**, Steven Dale 1946- AmMWSc 92
**Itten**, Johannes 1888-1967 DcTwDes
**Itule-Martin**, Margo 1953- WhoWest 92
**Iturbi**, Jose 1895-1980 FacFETw, NewAmDM
**Iturbide**, Agustin de 1783-1824 HisDSpE
**Iturrian**, William Ben 1939- AmMWSc 92
**Iturrigaray y Arostegui**, Jose Joaquin De 1742-1815 HisDSpE
**Iturrino**, Fernando L 1924- WhoAmP 91, WhoHisp 92
**Itwaru**, Arnold 1942- ConAu 134
**Itzen**, Monty Keefe 1951- WhoAmP 91
**Itzin**, Charles F. DrAPF 91
**Itzkan**, Irving 1929- AmMWSc 92
**Itzkoff**, Donald Martin 1961- WhoAmL 92
**Itzkoff**, Seymour William WrDr 92
**Itzkowich**, Carla Allida 1961- WhoHisp 92
**Itzkowitz**, Gerald Lee 1938- AmMWSc 92
**Iuanow**, Nicholas James 1960- WhoFI 92
**Iuli**, Opa Iosefo WhoAmP 91
**Iuli**, Vincent Kapeli 1958- WhoEnt 92
**Iuliano**, James P. 1959- WhoWest 92
**Iuliucci**, John Domenic AmMWSc 92
**Iuppa**, Nicholas Victor 1942- WhoWest 92
**Iuvone**, Paul Michael 1951- AmMWSc 92
**Ivamy**, Edward 1920- WrDr 92
**Ivamy**, Edward Richard Hardy 1920- Who 92
**Ivan IV** 1530-1584 LitC 17 [port]
**Ivan**, Martin 1945- WhoAmP 91
**Ivan**, Michael 1938- AmMWSc 92
**Ivancie**, Francis James 1924- WhoAmP 91
**Ivanek**, Zeljko 1957- IntMPA 92
**Ivanetich**, Richard John 1941- AmMWSc 92
**Ivanick**, Daniel Mark 1957- WhoEnt 92
**Ivanier**, Isin 1906- WhoFI 92
**Ivanier**, Paul 1932- WhoFI 92
**Ivankovich**, Anthony D 1939- AmMWSc 92
**Ivanov**, Anatoliy Stepanovich 1928- IntWW 91, SovUnBD
**Ivanov**, Il'ya Ivanovich 1870-1932 SovUnBD
**Ivanov**, Ivan Minchev 1940- IntWW 91
**Ivanov**, Konstantin Konstantinovich 1907- SovUnBD
**Ivanov**, Modest Vasil'evich 1875-1942 SovUnBD
**Ivanov**, Nikolay Veniaminovich 1952- SovUnBD
**Ivanov**, V.I. 1885- SovUnBD
**Ivanov**, Vladimir 1923- IntWW 91
**Ivanov**, Vsevolod Vyacheslavovich 1895-1963 FacFETw, SovUnBD
**Ivanov**, Vyacheslav Ivanovich 1866-1949 FacFETw, LiExTwC
**Ivanov**, Vyacheslav Nikolaevich 1938- SovUnBD
**Ivanov**, Yuriy Aleksandrovich 1928- IntWW 91
**Ivanov-Razumnik** 1878-1946 FacFETw
**Ivanov-Razumnik**, Razumnik Vasilievich 1878-1946 SovUnBD
**Ivanova**, Tatyana Georgiyevna 1940- IntWW 91
**Ivanovitch**, Michael Stevo 1939- WhoFI 92
**Ivanovna**, Liza EncAmaz 91
**Ivanovs**, Janis 1906- SovUnBD
**Ivanovsky**, Aleksandr Viktorovich 1881-1967 SovUnBD

**Ivanovsky,** Yevgeniy Filippovich 1918- *IntWW 91*
**Ivanovsky,** Yevgeny Filippovich 1918- *SovUnBD*
**Ivans,** Dainis 1954- *IntWW 91*
**Ivans,** Daynis 1954- *SovUnBD*
**Ivanso,** Eugene V 1908- *AmMWSc 92*
**Ivantsov,** Anatoliy Ivanovich 1922- *IntWW 91*
**Ivany,** J. W. George 1938- *WhoWest 92*
**Ivanyi,** Thomas Peter 1944- *WhoFI 92*
**Ivash,** Eugene V 1925- *AmMWSc 92*
**Ivashkiv,** Eugene 1923- *AmMWSc 92*
**Ivashko,** Vladimir Antonovich 1932- *IntWW 91, SovUnBD*
**Ivask,** Ivar 1927- *LiExTwC*
**Ivatt,** Raymond John 1949- *AmMWSc 92*
**Ivaturi,** Rao Venkata Krishna 1960- *AmMWSc 92, WhoMW 92*
**Iveagh,** Earl of 1937- *IntWW 91, Who 92*
**Ivener,** Mark Alan 1942- *WhoAmL 92*
**Ivens,** Joris 1898-1989 *FacFETw, IntDcF 2-2*
**Ivens,** Mary Sue 1929- *AmMWSc 92*
**Ivens,** Michael William 1924- *Who 92, WrDr 92*
**Iveroth,** C. Axel 1914- *IntWW 91*
**Ivers,** Donald L 1941- *WhoAmP 91*
**Ivers,** Drew Russell 1946- *AmMWSc 92*
**Ivers,** Irving N. 1939- *IntMPA 92*
**Ivers,** Julia Crawford d1930 *ReelWom*
**Iversen,** Edwin Severin 1922- *AmMWSc 92*
**Iversen,** Gudmund R 1934- *AmMWSc 92*
**Iversen,** James D 1933- *AmMWSc 92*
**Iversen,** Leslie Lars 1937- *IntWW 91, Who 92*
**Iverson,** A Evan *AmMWSc 92*
**Iverson,** Dennis D 1943- *WhoAmP 91*
**Iverson,** F Kenneth 1925- *AmMWSc 92*
**Iverson,** Francis Kenneth 1925- *WhoFI 92*
**Iverson,** Janice 1941- *WhoRel 92*
**Iverson,** John Burton 1949- *AmMWSc 92*
**Iverson,** John Charles 1944- *WhoWest 92*
**Iverson,** Jon Kermit 1956- *WhoMW 92*
**Iverson,** Kenneth Eugene 1920- *AmMWSc 92*
**Iverson,** Kenneth John 1957- *WhoMW 92*
**Iverson,** Laura Himes 1960- *AmMWSc 92*
**Iverson,** Lois O 1922- *WhoAmP 91*
**Iverson,** Lucille *DrAPF 91*
**Iverson,** Marlowe Wendell 1925- *WhoRel 92*
**Iverson,** Patricia Darlene 1948- *WhoMW 92*
**Iverson,** Ray Mads 1927- *AmMWSc 92*
**Iverson,** Robert Louis, Jr. 1944- *WhoMW 92*
**Iverson,** Stewart Eldridge, Jr 1950- *WhoAmP 91*
**Iverson,** Stuart Leroy 1939- *AmMWSc 92*
**Iverson,** Willard F 1935- *WhoIns 92*
**Ivery,** Eddie Lee 1957- *WhoBlA 92*
**Ivery,** James A. 1950- *WhoBlA 92*
**Ives,** Alden Allen 1925- *WhoAmP 91*
**Ives,** Arthur Glendinning Loveless 1904- *Who 92*
**Ives,** Burl 1909- *FacFETw, IntMPA 92, NewAmDM, WhoEnt 92*
**Ives,** Burl Icle Ivanhoe 1909- *IntWW 91*
**Ives,** Charles 1874-1954 *FacFETw [port], NewAmDM, RComAH*
**Ives,** Charles Edward 1874-1954 *BenetAL 91*
**Ives,** David Homer 1933- *AmMWSc 92*
**Ives,** Eli 1778-1861 *BiInAmS*
**Ives,** George 1845-1894 *NewAmDM*
**Ives,** George Skinner 1922- *WhoAmP 91*
**Ives,** J. Atwood 1936- *WhoFI 92*
**Ives,** James Merritt 1824-1895 *BenetAL 91*
**Ives,** Jeffrey Lee 1951- *AmMWSc 92*
**Ives,** John David 1931- *AmMWSc 92*
**Ives,** Kenneth James 1926- *Who 92*
**Ives,** Levi Silliman 1797-1867 *DcNCBi 3*
**Ives,** Michael Brian 1934- *AmMWSc 92*
**Ives,** Morgan *WrDr 92*
**Ives,** Norton C 1917- *AmMWSc 92*
**Ives,** Philip Truman 1909- *AmMWSc 92*
**Ives,** Richard *DrAPF 91*
**Ives,** Robert Blackman 1936- *WhoRel 92*
**Ives,** Robert Southwick 1913- *AmMWSc 92*
**Ives,** S. Clifton 1937- *WhoRel 92*
**Ives,** Stephen Bradshaw, Jr. 1924- *WhoAmL 92*
**Ives,** Timothy Read 1928- *WhoAmP 91*
**Ives,** Victor Milo 1935- *WhoEnt 92*
**Ives,** William Charles 1933- *WhoAmP 91*
**Iveson,** Herbert Todd 1915- *AmMWSc 92*
**Ivester,** Melvin Douglas 1947- *WhoFI 92*
**Ivett,** Reginald William 1915- *AmMWSc 92*
**Ivey,** Charles Wray 1936- *WhoRel 92*
**Ivey,** Don Louis 1935- *AmMWSc 92*
**Ivey,** Donald Glenn 1922- *AmMWSc 92*
**Ivey,** E H, Jr 1921- *AmMWSc 92*
**Ivey,** Elizabeth Spencer 1935- *AmMWSc 92*
**Ivey,** George Franks 1870-1952 *DcNCBi 3*
**Ivey,** Henry Franklin 1921- *AmMWSc 92*
**Ivey,** Horace Spencer 1931- *WhoBlA 92*
**Ivey,** Jean Eichelberger 1923- *WhoEnt 92*
**Ivey,** Jerry Lee 1942- *AmMWSc 92*
**Ivey,** Joseph Benjamin 1864-1958 *DcNCBi 3*
**Ivey,** Judith 1951- *IntMPA 92, WhoEnt 92*
**Ivey,** Mark, III 1935- *WhoBlA 92*
**Ivey,** Marvin 1932- *AmMWSc 92*
**Ivey,** Michael Hamilton 1930- *AmMWSc 92*
**Ivey,** Rachel Shoaf 1908- *WhoRel 92*
**Ivey,** Rebecca 1965- *WhoBlA 92*
**Ivey,** Robert Carl 1939- *WhoEnt 92*
**Ivey,** Robert Charles 1943- *AmMWSc 92*
**Ivey,** Thaddeus 1855-1933 *DcNCBi 3*
**Ivey,** Thomas Neal 1860-1923 *DcNCBi 3*
**Ivey,** William James 1944- *WhoEnt 92*
**Ivie,** Allan Denny 1873-1927 *DcNCBi 3*
**Ivie,** Evan Leon 1931- *WhoFI 92*
**Ivie,** Glen Wayne 1944- *AmMWSc 92*
**Ivie,** Leslie Todd 1960- *WhoFI 92*
**Ivins,** Anthony Woodward 1852-1934 *RelLAm 91*
**Ivins,** Richard O 1934- *AmMWSc 92*
**Ivison,** David Malcolm 1936- *Who 92*
**Ivnev,** Ryurik 1893- *FacFETw*
**Ivon,** Louis W 1934- *WhoAmP 91*
**Ivory,** Brian Gammell 1949- *Who 92*
**Ivory,** Carolyn Kay 1944- *WhoBlA 92*
**Ivory,** Eric William 1961- *WhoWest 92*
**Ivory,** James 1928- *IntDcF 2-2 [port], IntMPA 92*
**Ivory,** James Francis 1928- *IntWW 91, Who 92, WhoEnt 92*
**Ivory,** John Edward 1929- *AmMWSc 92*
**Ivory,** John Joseph 1962- *WhoMW 92*
**Ivory,** Larry R. 1950- *WhoMW 92*
**Ivory,** Lee Allen 1910- *WhoBlA 92*
**Ivory,** Thomas Martin, III 1943- *AmMWSc 92*
**Ivsic,** Mathieu Michel 1934- *WhoFI 92*
**Ivy,** Bob 1964- *WhoEnt 92*
**Ivy,** Conway Gayle 1941- *WhoFI 92, WhoMW 92*
**Ivy,** James E. 1937- *WhoBlA 92*
**Ivy,** L H 1930- *WhoAmP 91*
**Iwai,** Thomas Yoshio, Jr. 1949- *WhoWest 92*
**Iwai,** Wilfred Kiyoshi 1941- *WhoAmL 92*
**Iwamoto,** Reynold Toshiaki 1928- *AmMWSc 92*
**Iwamoto,** Tomio 1939- *AmMWSc 92*
**Iwamura,** Eiro 1915- *IntWW 91*
**Iwan,** Dafydd 1943- *IntWW 91*
**Iwan,** DeAnn Colleen 1950- *AmMWSc 92*
**Iwaniec,** Tadeusz 1947- *AmMWSc 92*
**Iwanski,** Marie Ida 1948- *WhoMW 92*
**Iwanski,** Ruth Ann 1946- *WhoRel 92*
**Iwao,** Wayne Haruto 1957- *WhoWest 92*
**Iwasa,** Kunihiko 1944- *AmMWSc 92*
**Iwasa,** Yukikazu 1938- *AmMWSc 92*
**Iwasaki,** Iwao 1929- *AmMWSc 92, WhoMW 92*
**Iwasawa,** Kenkichi 1917- *AmMWSc 92*
**Iwase,** Randy 1947- *WhoAmP 91*
**Iwata,** Masakazu 1917- *WrDr 92*
**Iwig,** Mark Michael 1951- *AmMWSc 92*
**Iwinski,** James Phillip 1960- *WhoMW 92*
**Ix,** Robert Edward 1929- *WhoFI 92*
**Iyanaga,** Shokichi 1906- *IntWW 91*
**Iyayi,** Festus 1947- *ConNov 91*
**Iyengar,** Doreswamy Raghavachar 1930- *AmMWSc 92*
**Iyengar,** Raja M 1927- *AmMWSc 92*
**Iyer,** B. Rajam 1922- *WhoEnt 92*
**Iyer,** Hariharaiyer Mahadeva 1931- *AmMWSc 92, WhoWest 92*
**Iyer,** Rajul V 1930- *AmMWSc 92*
**Iyer,** Ram R 1953- *AmMWSc 92*
**Iyer,** Ravi 1958- *AmMWSc 92*
**Iyer,** Ravishankar Krishnan 1949- *WhoMW 92*
**Iyer,** Vijay Kumar 1962- *WhoMW 92*
**Iyomasa,** Aaron Bruce 1960- *WhoEnt 92*
**Iype,** Pullolickal Thomas *AmMWSc 92*
**Izant,** Robert James, Jr 1921- *AmMWSc 92*
**Izard,** John 1923- *WhoAmL 92*
**Izatt,** Jerald Ray 1928- *AmMWSc 92*
**Izatt,** Reed McNeil 1926- *AmMWSc 92*
**Izay,** Jo Roybal *WhoHisp 92*
**Izen,** Joseph N 1956- *AmMWSc 92*
**Izen,** Raymond Larry 1941- *WhoEnt 92*
**Izenour,** George C 1912- *AmMWSc 92*
**Izenzon,** David 1932-1979 *NewAmDM*
**Izmerov,** Nikolay Fedotovich 1927- *IntWW 91*
**Izod,** Thomas Paul John 1945- *AmMWSc 92*
**Izquierdo,** Ricardo 1962- *AmMWSc 92*
**Izquierdo-Mora,** Luis A 1931- *WhoAmP 91, WhoHisp 92*
**Izquierdo Stella,** Jose *WhoAmP 91*
**Izquierdo Stella,** Jose G. *WhoHisp 92*
**Izrael,** Yuri Antonovich 1930- *IntWW 91*
**Izui,** Shozo 1946- *AmMWSc 92*
**Izvolsky,** Alexander Petrovich 1856-1919 *FacFETw*
**Izydore,** Robert Andrew 1943- *AmMWSc 92*
**Izziddin,** Ibrahim 1934- *IntWW 91*
**Izzo,** Donatella 1956- *IntAu&W 91*
**Izzo,** Joseph Anthony, Jr 1917- *AmMWSc 92*
**Izzo,** Lucio 1932- *IntWW 91*
**Izzo,** Mary Alice 1953- *WhoWest 92*
**Izzo,** Patrick Thomas 1918- *AmMWSc 92*
**Izzo,** Thomas J *WhoAmP 91*

# J

**J. Geils Band** *NewAmDM*
**J. A. A.** *ScFEYrs*
**J C T** *IntAu&W 91X*
**J F B** *ScFEYrs*
**J G M** *ScFEYrs*
**J J** *IntAu&W 91X*
**J.S. of Dale** *BenetAL 91*
**Ja,** William Yin 1936- *AmMWSc 92*
**Jaacks,** John William 1928- *WhoWest 92*
**Jaanus,** Siret Desiree *AmMWSc 92*
**Jabali,** Habib Hilmi 1943- *WhoFI 92*
**Jabalpurwala,** Kaizer E 1932- *AmMWSc 92*
**Jabara,** Harvey F. G. 1965- *WhoMW 92*
**Jabara,** Michael Dean 1952- *WhoWest 92*
**Jabarin,** Saleh Abd El Karim 1939- *AmMWSc 92*
**Jabbar,** Gina Marie *AmMWSc 92*
**Jabbour,** George Moussa 1949- *WhoFI 92*
**Jabbour,** J T 1927- *AmMWSc 92*
**Jabbour,** Kahtan Nicolas 1934- *AmMWSc 92*
**Jabbour,** Richard Turner 1962- *WhoFI 92*
**Jabbra,** Joseph George 1938- *WhoWest 92*
**Jabbur,** Ramzi Jibrail 1937- *AmMWSc 92*
**Jaberg,** Alan Dean 1948- *WhoMW 92*
**Jaberg,** Eugene Carl 1927- *WhoMW 92, WhoRel 92*
**Jabes,** Edmond 1912- *LiExTwC*
**Jabes,** Edmond 1912-1991 *ConAu 133, NewYTBS 91*
**Jabez** *ConAu 36NR*
**Jabin,** Marvin Mark 1929- *WhoFI 92*
**Jabine,** Thomas Boyd 1925- *AmMWSc 92*
**Jablon,** Barry Peter 1940- *WhoAmL 92*
**Jablon,** Brian Seth 1960- *WhoAmL 92*
**Jablon,** Seymour 1918- *AmMWSc 92*
**Jabloner,** Harold 1937- *AmMWSc 92*
**Jablons,** Beverly *DrAPF 91*
**Jablons,** Jane Ellen 1953- *WhoAmL 92*
**Jablonski,** Daniel Gary 1954- *AmMWSc 92*
**Jablonski,** David 1953- *AmMWSc 92*
**Jablonski,** Felix Joseph 1925- *AmMWSc 92*
**Jablonski,** Frank Edward 1915- *AmMWSc 92*
**Jablonski,** Henryk 1909- *IntWW 91*
**Jablonski,** Louis John, Jr. 1950- *WhoFI 92*
**Jablonski,** Mark Steven 1961- *WhoEnt 92*
**Jablonski,** Werner Louis 1924- *AmMWSc 92*
**Jablonsky,** David 1938- *ConAu 133*
**Jabour,** Paul V 1956- *WhoAmP 91*
**Jabra,** Jabra Ibrahim 1920- *IntAu&W 91*
**Jac,** F P 1955- *IntAu&W 91*
**Jaccarino,** Vincent 1924- *AmMWSc 92*
**Jacchia,** Luigi Giuseppe 1910- *AmMWSc 92*
**Jaccottet,** Philippe 1925- *FacFETw, GuFrLit 1*
**Jacey,** Charles Frederick, Jr. 1936- *WhoFI 92*
**Jach,** Joseph 1929- *AmMWSc 92*
**Jache,** Albert William 1924- *AmMWSc 92*
**Jachens,** Robert C 1939- *AmMWSc 92*
**Jaches de Wert** *NewAmDM*
**Jachimowicz,** Christopher Scott 1963- *WhoEnt 92*
**Jachimowicz,** Felek 1947- *AmMWSc 92*
**Jacinto,** Emilio 1857- *HisDSpE*
**Jack Downing** *BenetAL 91*
**Jack,** Alieu 1922- *Who 92*
**Jack,** Andrew John 1967- *WhoFI 92*
**Jack,** Bonnie Lee 1945- *WhoAmP 91*
**Jack,** David 1918- *Who 92*
**Jack,** David M. *Who 92*
**Jack,** Homer Alexander 1916- *AmPeW, WhoRel 92*
**Jack,** Hulan E, Jr 1935- *AmMWSc 92*
**Jack,** Ian 1923- *IntAu&W 91, WrDr 92*
**Jack,** Ian Robert James 1923- *Who 92*
**Jack,** James 1731-1822 *DcNCBi 3*
**Jack,** John James 1943- *AmMWSc 92*
**Jack,** John Michael 1946- *Who 92*
**Jack,** Kelli Jeanette 1965- *WhoFI 92*
**Jack,** Kenneth Henderson 1918- *IntWW 91, Who 92*
**Jack,** Malcolm Roy 1946- *Who 92*
**Jack,** Michael *Who 92*
**Jack,** Raymond Evan 1942- *Who 92*
**Jack,** Robert Barr 1928- *Who 92*
**Jack,** Robert Cecil Milton 1929- *AmMWSc 92*
**Jack,** Stephanie C. 1950- *WhoBlA 92*
**Jack,** Thomas Richard 1947- *AmMWSc 92*
**Jack,** Tom E 1935- *WhoIns 92*
**Jack,** William Hugh 1929- *Who 92*
**Jack,** William Irvine 1935- *WhoAmL 92*
**Jackall,** Robert *ConAu 135*
**Jackaman,** Michael Clifford John 1935- *Who 92*
**Jackanicz,** Theodore Michael 1938- *AmMWSc 92*
**Jacke,** Hurdle Clay, II 1958- *WhoAmL 92*
**Jackee** *WhoBlA 92*
**Jackel,** Lawrence David 1948- *AmMWSc 92*
**Jackel,** Simon Samuel 1917- *AmMWSc 92, WhoFI 92*
**Jackelen,** Henry Richard 1952- *WhoFI 92*
**Jackels,** Charles Frederick 1946- *AmMWSc 92*
**Jackels,** Susan Carol 1946- *AmMWSc 92*
**Jacker,** Corinne *LesBEnT 92*
**Jacker,** Corinne 1933- *WrDr 92*
**Jacker,** Corinne Litvin 1933- *WhoEnt 92*
**Jackisch,** Philip Frederick 1935- *AmMWSc 92*
**Jackiw,** Roman Wladimir 1939- *AmMWSc 92*
**Jacklet,** Jon Willis 1935- *AmMWSc 92*
**Jacklich,** Joel 1948- *WhoWest 92*
**Jacklin,** Anthony 1944- *Who 92*
**Jacklin,** Bill 1943- *TwCPaSc*
**Jacklin,** Tony 1944- *IntWW 91*
**Jacklin,** William 1943- *Who 92*
**Jacklin,** William Thomas 1940- *WhoMW 92*
**Jackling,** Roger Tustin 1943- *Who 92*
**Jackman,** Alonzo 1809-1879 *BiInAmS*
**Jackman,** Brian 1935- *IntAu&W 91*
**Jackman,** Christopher J. 1916-1991 *NewYTBS 91*
**Jackman,** Donald Coe 1940- *AmMWSc 92*
**Jackman,** Douglas 1902- *Who 92*
**Jackman,** Francis Sweet 1921- *WhoFI 92*
**Jackman,** Lloyd Miles 1926- *AmMWSc 92*
**Jackman,** Lora Ann 1965- *WhoWest 92*
**Jackman,** Michele 1944- *WhoWest 92*
**Jackman,** Stuart 1922- *IntAu&W 91, WrDr 92*
**Jackman,** Sydney Wayne 1925- *WrDr 92*
**Jackman,** Thomas Edward 1951- *AmMWSc 92*
**Jackman,** Wilbur Samuel 1855-1907 *BiInAmS*
**Jacknow,** Joel 1937- *AmMWSc 92*
**Jacko,** George G *WhoAmP 91*
**Jacko,** Michael George 1938- *AmMWSc 92*
**Jackobs,** John Joseph 1939- *AmMWSc 92, WhoMW 92*
**Jackobs,** Joseph Alden 1917- *AmMWSc 92*
**Jackovitz,** John Franklin 1939- *AmMWSc 92*
**Jackowiak,** Patricia 1959- *WhoAmL 92, WhoMW 92*
**Jackowska,** Nicki 1942- *IntAu&W 91*
**Jacks,** Benjamin Barend 1939- *WhoRel 92*
**Jacks,** Brian Paul 1943- *WhoWest 92*
**Jacks,** Hector Beaumont 1903- *Who 92*
**Jacks,** Oliver *IntAu&W 91X, WrDr 92*
**Jacks,** Thomas Jerome 1938- *AmMWSc 92*
**Jacks,** Thomas Mauro 1941- *AmMWSc 92*
**Jacks,** Thomas Richard 1946- *WhoFI 92*
**Jacks,** Ulysses 1937- *WhoAmL 92, WhoBlA 92*
**Jackson 5,** The *ConMus 7 [port]*
**Jackson,** Abbie Clement 1899- *WhoBlA 92*
**Jackson,** Acy Lee 1937- *WhoBlA 92*
**Jackson,** Ada Jean Work 1935- *WhoBlA 92*
**Jackson,** Adele Martin 1918- *WhoBlA 92*
**Jackson,** Agnes Moreland 1930- *WhoBlA 92*
**Jackson,** Alan 1938- *ConPo 91*
**Jackson,** Alan 1958- *ConMus 7 [port]*
**Jackson,** Alan Robert 1936- *Who 92*
**Jackson,** Albert Leslie Samuel 1918- *Who 92*
**Jackson,** Albert S 1927- *AmMWSc 92*
**Jackson,** Albert Smith 1927- *WhoWest 92*
**Jackson,** Albert Stanton, Jr 1949- *WhoAmP 91*
**Jackson,** Alexander Cosby Fishburn 1903- *Who 92*
**Jackson,** Alexander Young 1882-1973 *FacFETw*
**Jackson,** Alexis Camille *WhoBlA 92*
**Jackson,** Alfred, Jr. 1959- *WhoEnt 92*
**Jackson,** Alfred Thomas 1937- *WhoBlA 92*
**Jackson,** Alphonse, Jr 1927- *WhoAmP 91, WhoBlA 92*
**Jackson,** Alterman 1948- *WhoBlA 92*
**Jackson,** Althea 1922- *WhoRel 92*
**Jackson,** Alvin B., Jr. 1961- *WhoBlA 92*
**Jackson,** Amy Berman 1954- *WhoAmL 92*
**Jackson,** Andrew 1767-1845 *AmPolLe [port], BenetAL 91, DcNCBi 3, RComAH*
**Jackson,** Andrew 1945- *WhoBlA 92*
**Jackson,** Andrew 1948- *AmMWSc 92*
**Jackson,** Andrew D, Jr 1941- *AmMWSc 92*
**Jackson,** Andrew Dudley 1943- *WhoAmL 92*
**Jackson,** Andrew Otis 1941- *AmMWSc 92*
**Jackson,** Andrew Preston 1947- *WhoBlA 92*
**Jackson,** Anna Mae 1934- *WhoBlA 92*
**Jackson,** Anne *WhoEnt 92*
**Jackson,** Anne 1926- *IntMPA 92*
**Jackson,** Anne Louise *AmMWSc 92*
**Jackson,** Anne McEwen 1956- *WhoMW 92*
**Jackson,** Anthony 1926- *WrDr 92*
**Jackson,** Anthony Brian 1943- *WhoEnt 92*
**Jackson,** Archie Kim 1954- *WhoRel 92*
**Jackson,** Art Eugene, Sr. 1941- *WhoBlA 92*
**Jackson,** Arthur D., Jr. 1942- *WhoBlA 92*
**Jackson,** Arthur Gilbert 1949- *WhoFI 92*
**Jackson,** Arthur James 1943- *WhoBlA 92*
**Jackson,** Arthur Mells, II 1915-1975 *WhoBlA 92N*
**Jackson,** Arthur Roszell 1949- *WhoBlA 92*
**Jackson,** Aubrey N. 1926- *WhoBlA 92*
**Jackson,** Audrey Muriel W. *Who 92*
**Jackson,** Audrey Nabors 1926- *WhoBlA 92*
**Jackson,** Barbara Loomis 1928- *WhoBlA 92*
**Jackson,** Barry Trevor 1936- *Who 92*
**Jackson,** Barry Wendell 1930- *WhoAmP 91*
**Jackson,** Benita Marie 1956- *WhoBlA 92*
**Jackson,** Benjamin A 1929- *AmMWSc 92*
**Jackson,** Benjamin T 1929- *AmMWSc 92*
**Jackson,** Bennie, Jr. 1947- *WhoMW 92*
**Jackson,** Bernard H. *WhoBlA 92*
**Jackson,** Bernard Vernon 1942- *AmMWSc 92*
**Jackson,** Betty 1947- *Who 92*
**Jackson,** Betty 1949- *IntWW 91*
**Jackson,** Betty Eileen 1925- *WhoEnt 92, WhoWest 92*
**Jackson,** Betty Jane 1925- *WhoAmP 91*
**Jackson,** Betty L. Deason 1927- *WhoFI 92, WhoMW 92*
**Jackson,** Beverley Joy Jacobson 1928- *WhoWest 92*
**Jackson,** Beverly Anne 1947- *WhoBlA 92*
**Jackson,** Beverly Joyce 1955- *WhoBlA 92*
**Jackson,** Blyden 1910- *WhoBlA 92*
**Jackson,** Bo 1962- *CurBio 91 [port], WhoBlA 92*
**Jackson,** Bobby L. 1945- *WhoBlA 92*
**Jackson,** Bobby Rand 1931- *WhoRel 92*
**Jackson,** Brandon Donald 1934- *Who 92*
**Jackson,** Brendan 1935- *Who 92*
**Jackson,** Brian 1931- *IntMPA 92*
**Jackson,** Bruce Campbell, Jr. 1960- *WhoAmL 92*
**Jackson,** Burnett Lamar, Jr. 1928- *WhoBlA 92*
**Jackson,** Byron Haden 1943- *WhoRel 92*
**Jackson,** C. Bernard 1927- *WhoBlA 92*
**Jackson,** C Ian 1935- *AmMWSc 92*
**Jackson,** Cameron W. 1939- *WhoBlA 92*
**Jackson,** Carl Eugene 1953- *WhoEnt 92*
**Jackson,** Carl Wayne 1942- *AmMWSc 92*
**Jackson,** Carlton Darnell 1938- *AmMWSc 92*
**Jackson,** Carmault B, Jr 1924- *AmMWSc 92*
**Jackson,** Caroline Frances 1946- *Who 92*
**Jackson,** Cedric Douglas Tyrone, Sr. 1962- *WhoRel 92*
**Jackson,** Celia S. 1958- *WhoHisp 92*
**Jackson,** Charles 1903-1968 *BenetAL 91*
**Jackson,** Charles Benjamin 1952- *WhoRel 92*
**Jackson,** Charles E. 1944- *WhoBlA 92*
**Jackson,** Charles E., Sr. 1938- *WhoBlA 92*
**Jackson,** Charles Edward 1943- *WhoAmP 91*
**Jackson,** Charles Edward, Sr. 1938- *WhoMW 92*
**Jackson,** Charles Ellis 1930- *WhoBlA 92*

Jackson, Charles Lewis WhoRel 92
Jackson, Charles Loring 1847-1935 ScFEYrs
Jackson, Charles N., II 1931- WhoBlA 92
Jackson, Charles Ray 1927- WhoMW 92
Jackson, Charles Richard, Jr. 1929- WhoBlA 92
Jackson, Charles Thomas 1805-1880 BiInAmS
Jackson, Charles Wayne 1930- WhoFI 92
Jackson, Chris Wayne 1969- WhoBlA 92
Jackson, Christopher Murray 1935- Who 92
Jackson, Christopher Paul 1949- WhoRel 92
Jackson, Clarence H. 1924- WhoBlA 92
Jackson, Claude 1942- WhoBlA 92
Jackson, Cleo Eugene, III 1961- WhoRel 92
Jackson, Clinton 1954- WhoBlA 92
Jackson, Clyde O. 1928- WrDr 92
Jackson, Clyde Wilson 1936- WhoAmP 91
Jackson, Colin 1967- BlkOlyM
Jackson, Cora May 1928- WhoAmP 91
Jackson, Cordell 1923- WhoEnt 92
Jackson, Cornelia Pinkney WhoBlA 92
Jackson, Craig Merton 1941- AmMWSc 92
Jackson, Crawford Gardner, Jr 1931- AmMWSc 92
Jackson, Curtis M 1933- AmMWSc 92
Jackson, Curtis M. 1938- WhoBlA 92
Jackson, Curtis Maitland 1933- WhoMW 92
Jackson, Curtis Rukes 1927- AmMWSc 92
Jackson, D. Brooks 1941- WhoEnt 92
Jackson, Dakota 1949- DcTwDes
Jackson, Dale Latham 1932- AmMWSc 92
Jackson, Dana Leigh 1968- WhoMW 92
Jackson, Daniel ConAu 133
Jackson, Daniel Francis 1925- AmMWSc 92
Jackson, Daphne Diana 1933- Who 92
Jackson, Daphne Frances d1991 Who 92N
Jackson, Darryl Dean 1932- AmMWSc 92
Jackson, Daryl Sanders 1937- IntWW 91
Jackson, David A. 1924- WhoMW 92
Jackson, David Archer 1942- AmMWSc 92
Jackson, David Cooper 1931- Who 92, WrDr 92
Jackson, David Diether 1943- AmMWSc 92
Jackson, David E. 1933- WhoMW 92
Jackson, David Gordon 1936- WhoRel 92
Jackson, David Henry 1917- WhoRel 92
Jackson, David Lee 1946- WhoMW 92
Jackson, David M. 1935- WhoBlA 92
Jackson, David M 1944- WhoIns 92
Jackson, David Phillip 1940- AmMWSc 92
Jackson, David Samuel 1940- WhoBlA 92
Jackson, David Warren 1955- WhoAmL 92
Jackson, Denise Suzanne 1951- WhoEnt 92
Jackson, Dennis Lee 1937- WhoBlA 92
Jackson, Dennis R. 1946- WhoMW 92
Jackson, Derrah Eugene 1948- WhoRel 92
Jackson, Derrick Alfonso 1964- WhoMW 92
Jackson, Derrick Zane 1955- WhoBlA 92
Jackson, Don Cecil 1931- WhoFI 92
Jackson, Don Edward 1954- WhoRel 92
Jackson, Donald WhoRel 92
Jackson, Donald Cargill 1937- AmMWSc 92
Jackson, Donald Clifton, Jr. 1946- WhoBlA 92
Jackson, Donald J. 1943- WhoBlA 92
Jackson, Donald Richard 1938- WhoFI 92
Jackson, Donald Thomas 1959- WhoFI 92
Jackson, Donna Ann 1951- WhoEnt 92
Jackson, Dorothea E. WhoBlA 92
Jackson, Dorothy W. WhoMW 92
Jackson, Douglas Stanley 1954- WhoAmP 91
Jackson, Drel Michael Kenneth 1955- WhoEnt 92
Jackson, Dudley Pennington 1924- AmMWSc 92
Jackson, Durward P 1940- AmMWSc 92
Jackson, E F IntAu&W 91X, WrDr 92
Jackson, E Sydney 1922- WhoIns 92
Jackson, Earl, Jr. 1938- WhoBlA 92
Jackson, Earl C. 1933- WhoBlA 92
Jackson, Earl Graves 1920- AmMWSc 92
Jackson, Earl J. 1943- WhoBlA 92
Jackson, Earl K., Sr. 1938- WhoBlA 92
Jackson, Earl Rogers 1930- AmMWSc 92
Jackson, Earline 1943- WhoBlA 92
Jackson, Earnest 1959- WhoBlA 92
Jackson, Edgar Newton, Jr. 1959- WhoBlA 92
Jackson, Edward Who 92
Jackson, Edward Gardner 1942- WhoAmP 91
Jackson, Edward Milton 1938- WhoMW 92
Jackson, Edward Payson 1840-1906 ScFEYrs
Jackson, Edward R. 1942- WhoBlA 92
Jackson, Edward W. 1915- WhoBlA 92
Jackson, Edwin Atlee 1931- AmMWSc 92
Jackson, Edwin Kerry 1952- AmMWSc 92
Jackson, Edwin Sydney 1922- IntWW 91
Jackson, Elaine WrDr 92
Jackson, Elijah, Jr. 1959- WhoEnt 92
Jackson, Elizabeth Burger 1914- AmMWSc 92
Jackson, Ellen Swepson 1935- WhoBlA 92
Jackson, Elmer Carter, Jr. 1912- WhoBlA 92
Jackson, Emil A. 1911- WhoBlA 92
Jackson, Emory Napoleon 1937- WhoBlA 92
Jackson, Eric Stead d1991 Who 92N
Jackson, Eric Stead 1909- IntWW 91
Jackson, Ernest Baker 1914- AmMWSc 92
Jackson, Esther Cooper 1917- WhoBlA 92
Jackson, Ethel Noland 1944- AmMWSc 92
Jackson, Eugene Bernard 1915- AmMWSc 92
Jackson, Eugene D. 1943- WhoBlA 92
Jackson, Eugene L. 1939- WhoBlA 92
Jackson, Everatt WrDr 92
Jackson, Felix W. 1920- WhoBlA 92
Jackson, Fleda Brown DrAPF 91
Jackson, Francis Alan 1917- IntWW 91, Who 92
Jackson, Francis Charles 1917- AmMWSc 92
Jackson, Francis Earnest 1872-1945 TwCPaSc
Jackson, Francis J 1932- AmMWSc 92
Jackson, Frank 1941- WhoRel 92
Jackson, Frank Cameron 1943- IntWW 91
Jackson, Frank Donald 1951- WhoBlA 92
Jackson, Frank Hardin 1939- WhoAmL 92
Jackson, Frank Thomas 1934- WhoWest 92
Jackson, Franklin DB 1934- WhoBlA 92
Jackson, Fred 1886-1959 ScFEYrs
Jackson, Fred H., Jr. 1933- WhoBlA 92
Jackson, Freda 1907-1990 AnObit 1990
Jackson, Freda Lucille 1928- WhoRel 92
Jackson, Freddie 1958- WhoBlA 92
Jackson, Frederick 1928- WhoBlA 92
Jackson, Frederick Hume 1918- Who 92
Jackson, Frederick Leon 1934- WhoBlA 92
Jackson, Gail P. 1960- WhoBlA 92
Jackson, Gail Patricia 1960- WhoFI 92
Jackson, Gary E 1951- WhoAmP 91
Jackson, Gary Leslie 1945- AmMWSc 92
Jackson, Gary Loucks 1938- AmMWSc 92
Jackson, Gary Michael 1951- WhoFI 92
Jackson, Gene Franklin 1929- WhoFI 92
Jackson, George 1931- WhoEnt 92
Jackson, George 1942- WhoBlA 92
Jackson, George Frederic Clarence d1990 Who 92N
Jackson, George Frederick, III 1943- AmMWSc 92
Jackson, George G 1920- AmMWSc 92
Jackson, George John 1931- AmMWSc 92
Jackson, George K. 1757-1822 NewAmDM
Jackson, George K. 1919- WhoBlA 92
Jackson, George Pullen 1874-1953 BenetAL 91, NewAmDM
Jackson, George Richard 1920- AmMWSc 92
Jackson, George Terry 1943- WhoAmL 92
Jackson, George Thomas 1852-1916 BiInAmS
Jackson, George W 1924- WhoAmP 91
Jackson, George Winfield 1937- WhoAmP 91
Jackson, Georgina 1957- WhoBlA 92
Jackson, Gerald Breck 1916- Who 92
Jackson, Gerald E. 1949- WhoBlA 92, WhoMW 92
Jackson, Gerald Milton 1943- WhoBlA 92
Jackson, Giles B. 1924- WhoBlA 92
Jackson, Glenda 1936- FacFETw, IntMPA 92, IntWW 91, Who 92, WhoEnt 92
Jackson, Gloria June 1940- WhoAmP 91
Jackson, Gordon 1923-1990 AnObit 1990, ConTFT 9
Jackson, Gordon Alexander 1913- WhoFI 92
Jackson, Gordon Noel 1913- Who 92, WrDr 92
Jackson, Governor Eugene, Jr. 1951- WhoBlA 92
Jackson, Grace 1961- BlkOlyM
Jackson, Grandvel Andrew 1910- WhoBlA 92
Jackson, Grant D 1945- AmMWSc 92
Jackson, Grant Dwight 1942- WhoBlA 92
Jackson, Gregory Allen 1956- WhoRel 92
Jackson, Gregory Wayne 1950- WhoMW 92
Jackson, Guida DrAPF 91
Jackson, Hal 1922- WhoBlA 92
Jackson, Harold 1937- AmMWSc 92
Jackson, Harold Baron, Jr. 1939- WhoBlA 92
Jackson, Harold E, Jr 1933- AmMWSc 92
Jackson, Harold Hobson 1932- IntAu&W 91
Jackson, Harold Jerome 1953- WhoBlA 92
Jackson, Harold Leonard 1923- AmMWSc 92
Jackson, Harold Leonard, Jr. 1955- WhoBlA 92
Jackson, Harold Woodworth 1928- AmMWSc 92
Jackson, Harry Andrew 1924- WhoWest 92
Jackson, Haywood DrAPF 91
Jackson, Hazel Brill d1991 NewYTBS 91
Jackson, Helen Hunt 1830-1885 BenetAL 91
Jackson, Helen Maria Hunt 1830-1885 HanAmWH
Jackson, Henry F. 1939-1991 ConAu 135
Jackson, Henry M 1912-1983 FacFETw
Jackson, Henry Martin 1912-1983 AmPolLe
Jackson, Henry Ralph 1915- WhoBlA 92
Jackson, Herbert C. 1941- WhoFI 92, WhoWest 92
Jackson, Herbert Cross 1917- WhoRel 92
Jackson, Herbert Lewis 1921- AmMWSc 92
Jackson, Herbert William 1911- AmMWSc 92
Jackson, Herbert Worth 1865-1936 DcNCBi 3
Jackson, Hermoine Prestine 1945- WhoBlA 92
Jackson, Hope Erna 1922- WhoRel 92
Jackson, Horace 1935- WhoBlA 92
Jackson, Horace Franklin 1934- WhoFI 92
Jackson, Ian 1914- Who 92
Jackson, Ida Louise WhoBlA 92
Jackson, Ira L 1930- WhoAmP 91
Jackson, Isaiah 1945- NewAmDM, WhoEnt 92, WhoMW 92
Jackson, Isaiah Allen 1945- WhoBlA 92
Jackson, Ivor Michael David 1936- AmMWSc 92
Jackson, J Elvin 1938- WhoAmP 91
Jackson, Jack C WhoAmP 91
Jackson, Jacqueline 1928- SmATA 65 [port]
Jackson, Jacquelyne Johnson 1932- NotBlAW 92, WhoBlA 92
Jackson, James Alan 1952- WhoMW 92
Jackson, James Conroy 1913- WhoBlA 92
Jackson, James Edward 1925- AmMWSc 92
Jackson, James F AmMWSc 92
Jackson, James H. 1939- WhoBlA 92
Jackson, James Holmen 1949- WhoBlA 92
Jackson, James Jeffrey 1958- WhoAmL 92
Jackson, James Karl 1949- WhoAmL 92
Jackson, James Larry 1940- WhoRel 92
Jackson, James M 1943- WhoIns 92
Jackson, James Oliver 1939- AmMWSc 92
Jackson, James Oswald 1940- WhoWest 92
Jackson, James Sidney 1944- WhoBlA 92, WhoMW 92
Jackson, James Talmadge 1921- WhoBlA 92
Jackson, James Theodore, Jr. 1944- WhoAmL 92
Jackson, James W ScFEYrs
Jackson, James Wesley 1952- WhoRel 92
Jackson, Jane 1944- IntAu&W 91
Jackson, Jane W. 1944- WhoWest 92
Jackson, Janet 1966- CurBio 91 [port], WhoBlA 92
Jackson, Janet Damita 1966- WhoEnt 92
Jackson, Janice Tudy 1945- WhoBlA 92
Jackson, Jasper Andrew, Jr 1923- AmMWSc 92
Jackson, Jeanette Bucklin 1946- WhoAmP 91
Jackson, Jeremy Bradford Cook 1942- AmMWSc 92
Jackson, Jerome Alan 1943- AmMWSc 92
Jackson, Jerry Dwayne 1941- WhoAmP 91
Jackson, Jesse 1941- ConBlB 1 [port], RComAH, RelLAm 91
Jackson, Jesse L. 1928- WhoBlA 92
Jackson, Jesse Louis 1941- FacFETw [port], IntWW 91, WhoAmP 91, WhoBlA 92, WhoRel 92
Jackson, Jesse Luther, III 1947- WhoRel 92
Jackson, Jewel 1942- WhoWest 92
Jackson, Jo-Anne Alice 1951- AmMWSc 92
Jackson, Joe WhoEnt 92
Jackson, John 1948- WhoBlA 92
Jackson, John Barnard Swett 1806-1879 BiInAmS
Jackson, John Berrye 1919- WhoBlA 92
Jackson, John Brinckerhoff 1909- WhoWest 92
Jackson, John Charles 1939- WhoMW 92
Jackson, John David 1925- AmMWSc 92
Jackson, John Earnest 1941- WhoEnt 92
Jackson, John Edward 1917- AmMWSc 92
Jackson, John Edward 1925- Who 92
Jackson, John Elwin, Jr 1948- AmMWSc 92
Jackson, John Eric 1937- AmMWSc 92
Jackson, John Fenwick 1928- AmMWSc 92
Jackson, John H. 1943- WhoBlA 92
Jackson, John Henry 1838-1908 BiInAmS
Jackson, John Henry 1916- IntMPA 92
Jackson, John Henry 1922- WhoMW 92
Jackson, John Henry 1948- Who 92
Jackson, John Hollis, Jr. 1941- WhoAmL 92
Jackson, John Howard 1932- WhoAmL 92
Jackson, John Jay 1961- WhoRel 92
Jackson, John Mathews 1908- AmMWSc 92
Jackson, John N. 1925- WrDr 92
Jackson, John Robert 1946- WhoFI 92
Jackson, John Sterling 1922- AmMWSc 92
Jackson, Johnny, Jr WhoAmP 91
Jackson, Johnny, Jr. 1943- WhoBlA 92
Jackson, Johnny W. 1933- WhoRel 92
Jackson, Joni Bradley 1932- WhoAmP 91
Jackson, Joseph Brian 1946- WhoWest 92
Jackson, Joseph H. d1990 WhoBlA 92N
Jackson, Joseph Harrison 1900- RelLAm 91
Jackson, Joseph Henry 1894-1955 BenetAL 91
Jackson, Joseph T. 1916- WhoBlA 92
Jackson, Judge 1883-1958 NewAmDM
Jackson, Julia Carolyn 1934- WhoAmP 91
Jackson, Julian Curley 1933- WhoRel 92
Jackson, Julius 1916- AmMWSc 92
Jackson, Julius Hamilton 1944- WhoBlA 92
Jackson, Julius Lee 1938- WhoRel 92
Jackson, Karen Louise 1961- WhoEnt 92
Jackson, Karl Don 1947- WhoBlA 92
Jackson, Kate 1949- IntMPA 92, WhoEnt 92
Jackson, Keith LesBEnT 92
Jackson, Keith A. 1958- WhoFI 92
Jackson, Keith Hunter 1953- WhoBlA 92
Jackson, Keith M. 1948- WhoBlA 92
Jackson, Kelvin Purnell 1959- WhoRel 92
Jackson, Kennell A., Jr. 1942- WhoBlA 92
Jackson, Kenneth Hurlstone d1991 Who 92N
Jackson, Kenneth Lee 1926- AmMWSc 92
Jackson, Kenneth Ronald 1951- AmMWSc 92
Jackson, Kenneth T 1939- IntAu&W 91, WrDr 92
Jackson, Kenneth William 1924- WhoBlA 92
Jackson, Kenny 1962- WhoBlA 92
Jackson, Kent Phillips 1949- WhoRel 92
Jackson, Kern Chandler 1920- AmMWSc 92
Jackson, Kevin Gray 1962- WhoRel 92
Jackson, Laban Phelps 1914- WhoAmP 91
Jackson, Larron Deonne 1949- WhoBlA 92
Jackson, Larry Eugene 1943- WhoBlA 92
Jackson, Larry LaVern 1942- AmMWSc 92
Jackson, Larry Lee 1940- AmMWSc 92
Jackson, Larry Lynn 1940- AmMWSc 92
Jackson, Larry R. 1941- WhoMW 92
Jackson, Laura IntWW 91, WrDr 92
Jackson, Laura 1901-1991 ConAu 135
Jackson, Laura Riding BenetAL 91
Jackson, Laura Riding d1991 Who 92N
Jackson, Lawrence 1913- Who 92
Jackson, Lawrence 1926- Who 92
Jackson, Lee F 1950- WhoAmP 91
Jackson, Lee Frazer 1958- WhoFI 92
Jackson, Leland Brooks 1940- AmMWSc 92
Jackson, Lenwood A. 1944- WhoBlA 92
Jackson, Leo A. 1920- WhoBlA 92
Jackson, Leo Edwin 1925- WhoBlA 92
Jackson, Leon 1944- WhoBlA 92
Jackson, Leroy Anthony, Jr. 1935- WhoBlA 92
Jackson, LeRoy Warren 1936- WhoAmP 91
Jackson, Lillian WhoBlA 92
Jackson, Lillian Ann 1956- WhoMW 92
Jackson, Linda Dianne 1953- WhoEnt 92
Jackson, Lionel Eric, Jr 1947- AmMWSc 92
Jackson, Lloyd G, II 1952- WhoAmP 91
Jackson, Lloyd K 1922- AmMWSc 92
Jackson, Loretta Y Blunt 1935- WhoAmP 91
Jackson, Lucius Brown 1941- BlkOlyM
Jackson, Luke 1919- WhoBlA 92
Jackson, Luther Porter, Jr. 1925- WhoBlA 92
Jackson, Lynda Kay 1949- WhoFI 92
Jackson, M Kate 1938- WhoAmP 91
Jackson, M L 1915- AmMWSc 92

**Jackson**, Mabel I. 1907- WhoBlA 92
**Jackson**, Mae DrAPF 91
**Jackson**, Mae Howard 1877-1931 NotBlAW 92
**Jackson**, Mahalia 1911-1972 FacFETw, NewAmDM, NotBlAW 92 [port], RelLAm 91
**Jackson**, Margaret E 1928- AmMWSc 92
**Jackson**, Margaret Myfanwy Wood Who 92
**Jackson**, Maria Pilar 1949- WhoHisp 92
**Jackson**, Marian Ruck 1922- WhoAmP 91
**Jackson**, Marion Leroy 1914- AmMWSc 92
**Jackson**, Marion T 1933- AmMWSc 92
**Jackson**, Marion Thomas 1933- WhoMW 92
**Jackson**, Marjorie WhoEnt 92
**Jackson**, Mark A. 1965- WhoBlA 92
**Jackson**, Marlin James 1953- WhoEnt 92
**Jackson**, Martin Patrick Arden 1947- AmMWSc 92
**Jackson**, Marvin Alexander 1927- AmMWSc 92, WhoBlA 92
**Jackson**, Mary 1910- WhoEnt 92
**Jackson**, Mary 1932- WhoBlA 92
**Jackson**, Mary Anna Morrison 1831-1915 DcNCBi 3
**Jackson**, Matthew Paul 1959- AmMWSc 92
**Jackson**, Mattie J. 1921- WhoBlA 92
**Jackson**, Mattie Lee 1924- WhoBlA 92
**Jackson**, Maxie C. 1939- WhoBlA 92
**Jackson**, Maynard 1938- ConBlB 2 [port]
**Jackson**, Maynard Holbrook 1938- WhoAmP 91, WhoBlA 92
**Jackson**, Mel Clinton 1962- AmMWSc 92
**Jackson**, Melodee Sue 1947- WhoAmP 91
**Jackson**, Melvin Robert 1943- AmMWSc 92
**Jackson**, Meyer B 1951- AmMWSc 92
**Jackson**, Michael 1940- ConPo 91, WrDr 92
**Jackson**, Michael 1958- FacFETw, IntMPA 92, NewAmDM, Who 92, WhoBlA 92, WhoEnt 92A
**Jackson**, Michael Charles 1940- WhoFI 92
**Jackson**, Michael J 1938- AmMWSc 92
**Jackson**, Michael Joseph 1958- IntWW 91
**Jackson**, Michael R. 1946- WhoEnt 92
**Jackson**, Michael Rodney 1935- Who 92
**Jackson**, Michael Roland 1919- Who 92
**Jackson**, Michael Scott 1952- WhoRel 92
**Jackson**, Michele 1945- WhoRel 92
**Jackson**, Mike 1953- WhoAmP 91
**Jackson**, Milt 1923- NewAmDM
**Jackson**, Milton 1923- WhoBlA 92, WhoEnt 92
**Jackson**, Milton Reed 1942- WhoAmP 91
**Jackson**, Morton Barrows 1921- WhoAmL 92
**Jackson**, Muriel W. Who 92
**Jackson**, Murray Earl 1926- WhoAmP 91, WhoBlA 92
**Jackson**, Nagle 1936- ConTFT 9, WhoEnt 92
**Jackson**, Nathaniel G. 1942- WhoBlA 92
**Jackson**, Neal A. 1943- WhoAmL 92
**Jackson**, Nell 1929-1988 NotBlAW 92
**Jackson**, Neville WrDr 92
**Jackson**, Nicholas 1934- Who 92
**Jackson**, Noel 1931- AmMWSc 92
**Jackson**, Norlishia A. 1942- WhoBlA 92
**Jackson**, Norman A. 1932- WhoBlA 92
**Jackson**, Ocie 1904- WhoBlA 92
**Jackson**, Oliver James V. Who 92
**Jackson**, Oscar Jerome 1929- WhoBlA 92
**Jackson**, Patrick Who 92
**Jackson**, Paul Ernest 1956- WhoEnt 92
**Jackson**, Paul Howard 1952- WhoRel 92
**Jackson**, Paul L. 1907- WhoBlA 92
**Jackson**, Paul Trescott 1935- WhoMW 92
**Jackson**, Paulina Ruth 1932- WhoAmP 91
**Jackson**, Pazel 1932- WhoBlA 92
**Jackson**, Peter 1926- WrDr 92
**Jackson**, Peter John Edward 1944- Who 92
**Jackson**, Peter Michael 1928- Who 92
**Jackson**, Peter Richard 1948- AmMWSc 92
**Jackson**, Peter Vorious, III 1927- WhoWest 92
**Jackson**, Philip C WhoAmP 91
**Jackson**, Philip Douglas WhoMW 92
**Jackson**, Philip Larkin 1921- AmMWSc 92
**Jackson**, Price Arthur, Jr 1952- WhoAmP 91
**Jackson**, Prince A, Jr 1925- AmMWSc 92
**Jackson**, Prince Albert, Jr. 1925- WhoBlA 92
**Jackson**, R. Bryan 1951- WhoEnt 92
**Jackson**, Ralph 1914- Who 92
**Jackson**, Randall W. 1954- WhoFI 92
**Jackson**, Randolph 1943- WhoBlA 92
**Jackson**, Randon Howard 1951- WhoRel 92
**Jackson**, Rashleigh Esmond 1929- IntWW 91
**Jackson**, Ray Dean 1929- AmMWSc 92
**Jackson**, Ray Weldon 1921- AmMWSc 92
**Jackson**, Raymond Allen 1927- Who 92
**Jackson**, Raymond Carl 1928- AmMWSc 92
**Jackson**, Raymond Sidney, Jr. 1938- WhoAmL 92
**Jackson**, Raymond T. 1933- WhoBlA 92
**Jackson**, Raynard 1960- WhoBlA 92
**Jackson**, Rebecca Cox 1795-1871 NotBlAW 92
**Jackson**, Reggie Martinez 1946- WhoBlA 92
**Jackson**, Reginald Leo 1945- WhoBlA 92
**Jackson**, Reginald Sherman, Jr. 1946- WhoAmL 92, WhoFI 92, WhoMW 92
**Jackson**, Renard I. 1946- WhoBlA 92
**Jackson**, Richard DrAPF 91
**Jackson**, Richard Brinkley 1929- WhoFI 92
**Jackson**, Richard Brooke 1947- WhoAmL 92
**Jackson**, Richard E., Jr. 1945- WhoBlA 92
**Jackson**, Richard Edward 1950- WhoAmP 91
**Jackson**, Richard Eli 1946- WhoAmL 92
**Jackson**, Richard Eugene 1941- WhoEnt 92
**Jackson**, Richard H. 1933- WhoBlA 92
**Jackson**, Richard H. 1941- WhoWest 92
**Jackson**, Richard H F 1947- AmMWSc 92
**Jackson**, Richard Lee 1939- AmMWSc 92
**Jackson**, Richard Leon 1948- WhoFI 92
**Jackson**, Richard Michael 1940- Who 92
**Jackson**, Richard Seymour 1915- WhoEnt 92
**Jackson**, Richard Thomas 1930- AmMWSc 92
**Jackson**, Richard W AmMWSc 92
**Jackson**, Rick Alan 1955- WhoFI 92
**Jackson**, Rickey Anderson 1958- WhoBlA 92
**Jackson**, Robert 1910- Who 92
**Jackson**, Robert 1911-1991 NewYTBS 91 [port]
**Jackson**, Robert, Jr. 1936- WhoBlA 92
**Jackson**, Robert Andrew 1959- WhoBlA 92
**Jackson**, Robert Bruce, Jr 1929- AmMWSc 92
**Jackson**, Robert C AmMWSc 92
**Jackson**, Robert E. 1937- WhoBlA 92
**Jackson**, Robert Edgar 1931- WhoAmL 92
**Jackson**, Robert Emerson 1926- WhoMW 92
**Jackson**, Robert Gillman Allen d1991 IntWW 91N, Who 92N
**Jackson**, Robert H. 1892-1954 EncTR 91 [port], FacFETw
**Jackson**, Robert J. 1936- WrDr 92
**Jackson**, Robert John 1922- WhoFI 92, WhoWest 92
**Jackson**, Robert L. 1962- WhoFI 92
**Jackson**, Robert Loring 1926- WhoMW 92
**Jackson**, Robert Louis 1923- IntAu&W 91
**Jackson**, Robert Preston, III 1953- WhoEnt 92
**Jackson**, Robert Sherwood 1945- WhoFI 92
**Jackson**, Robert Victor 1946- Who 92
**Jackson**, Robert W AmMWSc 92
**Jackson**, Robert W 1936- WhoIns 92
**Jackson**, Robert Walter 1943- WhoAmP 91
**Jackson**, Robert William 1930- WhoMW 92
**Jackson**, Rodney Who 92
**Jackson**, Roland Lewis 1925- WhoWest 92
**Jackson**, Ronald 1957- WhoMW 92
**Jackson**, Ronald G. 1952- WhoBlA 92
**Jackson**, Ronald Gordon 1924- IntWW 91, Who 92
**Jackson**, Ronald Lee 1943- WhoBlA 92
**Jackson**, Ronald Shannon 1940- WhoEnt 92
**Jackson**, Roscoe George, II 1948- AmMWSc 92
**Jackson**, Rose Valdez 1953- WhoHisp 92
**Jackson**, Rosemary Elizabeth 1917- WrDr 92
**Jackson**, Roswell F. 1922- WhoBlA 92
**Jackson**, Roy 1931- AmMWSc 92
**Jackson**, Roy Arthur 1928- Who 92
**Jackson**, Roy J., Jr. 1944- WhoBlA 92
**Jackson**, Roy Joseph 1944- AmMWSc 92
**Jackson**, Roy Lee 1954- WhoBlA 92
**Jackson**, Rudolph Ellsworth 1935- WhoBlA 92
**Jackson**, Rupert Matthew 1948- Who 92
**Jackson**, Russell A. 1934- WhoBlA 92
**Jackson**, Rusty 1953- WhoBlA 92
**Jackson**, Ruth Farrier 1923- WhoAmP 91
**Jackson**, Ruth Moore 1938- WhoBlA 92
**Jackson**, Samuel 1787-1872 BiInAmS
**Jackson**, Samuel Macauley 1851-1912 RelLAm 91
**Jackson**, Samuel S., Jr. 1934- WhoBlA 92
**Jackson**, Sandei Jean 1940- WhoWest 92
**Jackson**, Sara ConAu 133
**Jackson**, Sarah Mindwell 1957- WhoAmL 92
**Jackson**, Seaton J. 1914- WhoBlA 92
**Jackson**, Sharon Juanita 1938- WhoFI 92
**Jackson**, Sharon Wesley 1936- AmMWSc 92
**Jackson**, Sheila Benson 1956- WhoWest 92
**Jackson**, Sheila Cathryn DrAPF 91
**Jackson**, Sheldon 1834-1909 RelLAm 91
**Jackson**, Shirley 1919-1965 BenetAL 91, FacFETw, ShSCr 9 [port]
**Jackson**, Shirley Ann WhoBlA 92
**Jackson**, Shirley Ann 1946- AmMWSc 92, NotBlAW 92
**Jackson**, Sonia WhoEnt 92
**Jackson**, Spencer 1910-1990 WhoBlA 92N
**Jackson**, Steve Eric 1961- WhoEnt 92
**Jackson**, Stuart Wayne 1955- WhoBlA 92
**Jackson**, Terrence Michael 1946- WhoWest 92
**Jackson**, Thelma Conley 1934- WhoBlA 92
**Jackson**, Theodore Roosevelt 1913- WhoAmP 91
**Jackson**, Thomas Who 92
**Jackson**, Thomas 1925- Who 92
**Jackson**, Thomas A J 1942- AmMWSc 92
**Jackson**, Thomas Edwin 1944- AmMWSc 92
**Jackson**, Thomas Edwin 1955- WhoFI 92
**Jackson**, Thomas F 1927- WhoAmP 91
**Jackson**, Thomas Francis, III 1940- WhoAmL 92
**Jackson**, Thomas Gene 1949- WhoAmL 92
**Jackson**, Thomas Gerald 1936- AmMWSc 92
**Jackson**, Thomas Humphrey 1950- WhoAmL 92
**Jackson**, Thomas J 1824-1863 RComAH
**Jackson**, Thomas Jonathan 1824-1863 BenetAL 91
**Jackson**, Thomas Lloyd 1922- AmMWSc 92
**Jackson**, Thomas Micajah, Jr 1957- WhoAmP 91
**Jackson**, Thomas Mitchell 1932- WhoBlA 92
**Jackson**, Thomas Penfield 1937- WhoAmL 92
**Jackson**, Tiffany Christina 1970- WhoMW 92
**Jackson**, Timm C. 1945- WhoRel 92
**Jackson**, Togwell Alexander 1939- AmMWSc 92
**Jackson**, Tom 1951- WhoBlA 92
**Jackson**, Tomi L. 1923- WhoBlA 92
**Jackson**, Tommie Lee 1951- WhoMW 92
**Jackson**, Tommy L. 1914- WhoBlA 92
**Jackson**, Vanessa 1953- TwCPaSc
**Jackson**, Velma Louise 1945- WhoAmL 92
**Jackson**, Vera Ruth 1912- WhoBlA 92
**Jackson**, Victoria Lynn 1959- WhoEnt 92
**Jackson**, W. Sherman 1939- WhoBlA 92
**Jackson**, Walter Clinton 1879-1959 DcNCBi 3
**Jackson**, Walter Coleman, III 1933- WhoRel 92
**Jackson**, Walter K. 1914- WhoBlA 92
**Jackson**, Walter Patrick 1929- Who 92
**Jackson**, Warren, Jr 1922- AmMWSc 92
**Jackson**, Warren G. 1929- WhoBlA 92
**Jackson**, Warren Garrison WhoBlA 92
**Jackson**, William 1917- Who 92, WrDr 92
**Jackson**, William 1918- WrDr 92
**Jackson**, William Addison 1926- AmMWSc 92
**Jackson**, William Bruce 1926- AmMWSc 92
**Jackson**, William David 1927- AmMWSc 92
**Jackson**, William E. 1936- WhoBlA 92
**Jackson**, William Ed 1932- WhoBlA 92
**Jackson**, William Eldred 1919- WhoAmL 92
**Jackson**, William Elmer, Jr. 1935- WhoFI 92
**Jackson**, William F 1952- AmMWSc 92
**Jackson**, William Fred 1938- WhoBlA 92
**Jackson**, William G 1919- AmMWSc 92
**Jackson**, William Gene 1946- WhoMW 92
**Jackson**, William Godfrey Fothergill 1917- IntAu&W 91, IntWW 91
**Jackson**, William James 1940- AmMWSc 92
**Jackson**, William Joseph 1943- WhoRel 92
**Jackson**, William Keith 1928- IntAu&W 91, WrDr 92
**Jackson**, William Lawrence 1954- WhoEnt 92
**Jackson**, William Lynn 1919- WhoAmL 92
**Jackson**, William Morgan 1936- AmMWSc 92
**Jackson**, William Morrison 1926- AmMWSc 92
**Jackson**, William Roy, Jr 1936- AmMWSc 92
**Jackson**, William S WhoAmP 91
**Jackson**, William Theodore 1906- Who 92
**Jackson**, William Thomas 1923- AmMWSc 92
**Jackson**, William Thomas 1927- Who 92
**Jackson**, William Unsworth 1926- Who 92
**Jackson**, William Vernon 1926- WhoMW 92
**Jackson**, Willis Randell, II 1945- WhoBlA 92
**Jackson**, Wilma Littlejohn WhoBlA 92
**Jackson**, Winston Burleigh 1927- WhoBlA 92
**Jackson**, Winston Jerome, Jr 1926- AmMWSc 92
**Jackson**, Wynn 1952- WhoEnt 92
**Jackson**, Yvette P. 1953- WhoBlA 92
**Jackson**, Yvonne Brenda 1920- Who 92
**Jackson-Foy**, Lucy Maye 1919- WhoBlA 92
**Jackson-Lipkin**, Miles Henry Who 92
**Jackson-Ransom**, Bunnie 1940- WhoBlA 92
**Jackson-Sirls**, Mary Louise 1944- WhoBlA 92
**Jackson-Smith**, Princess Nadine 1946- WhoWest 92
**Jackson-Stops**, Gervase Frank Ashworth 1947- Who 92
**Jackson-Stops**, Timothy William Ashworth 1942- Who 92
**Jackson-Teal**, Rita F. 1949- WhoBlA 92
**Jackson-Thompson**, Marie O. 1947- WhoBlA 92
**Jacksons**, The ConMus 7 [port]
**Jaclot**, Francois Charles 1949- WhoFI 92
**Jaco**, Charles M, Jr 1924- AmMWSc 92
**Jaco**, E. Gartly 1923- WrDr 92
**Jaco**, James Harold, Jr. 1941- WhoRel 92
**Jaco**, William Howard 1940- AmMWSc 92
**Jacob Baradaeus** 500?-578 EncEarC
**Jacob de Senleches** NewAmDM
**Jacob of Sarug** 451?-521 EncEarC
**Jacob**, Abe John 1944- WhoEnt 92
**Jacob**, Bernard Victor 1921- Who 92
**Jacob**, Bruce Robert 1935- WhoAmL 92
**Jacob**, Chaim O 1951- AmMWSc 92
**Jacob**, David Oliver Ll. Who 92
**Jacob**, Edward Ian 1899- Who 92
**Jacob**, Edward Ian Claud 1899- IntWW 91
**Jacob**, Edwin J. 1927- WhoAmL 92
**Jacob**, Fielden Emmitt 1910- AmMWSc 92
**Jacob**, Francois 1920- IntWW 91, Who 92, WhoNob 90
**Jacob**, Frederick Henry 1915- Who 92
**Jacob**, Gary Steven 1947- AmMWSc 92
**Jacob**, George Korathu 1959- AmMWSc 92
**Jacob**, Gordon 1895-1984 NewAmDM
**Jacob**, Harry S 1933- AmMWSc 92
**Jacob**, Henry George, Jr 1922- AmMWSc 92
**Jacob**, Horace S 1931- AmMWSc 92
**Jacob**, Ian Who 92
**Jacob**, Isaac Hai 1908- Who 92
**Jacob**, John DrAPF 91
**Jacob**, John 1950- IntAu&W 91
**Jacob**, John DeWitt 1938- WhoMW 92
**Jacob**, John E. 1934- ConBlB 2 [port]
**Jacob**, John Edward 1934- WhoBlA 92
**Jacob**, Jonah Hye 1943- AmMWSc 92
**Jacob**, K Thomas 1944- AmMWSc 92
**Jacob**, Ken 1949- WhoAmP 91
**Jacob**, Klaus H 1936- AmMWSc 92
**Jacob**, Leonard Steven 1949- AmMWSc 92
**Jacob**, Marvin Eugene 1935- WhoAmL 92
**Jacob**, Mary 1933- AmMWSc 92
**Jacob**, Max 1876-1944 GuFrLit 1
**Jacob**, Nancy Louise 1943- WhoWest 92
**Jacob**, Paul B, Jr 1922- AmMWSc 92
**Jacob**, Peyton, III 1947- AmMWSc 92
**Jacob**, Richard John 1937- AmMWSc 92
**Jacob**, Richard L 1932- AmMWSc 92
**Jacob**, Robert Allen 1942- AmMWSc 92
**Jacob**, Robert Edward 1954- WhoMW 92
**Jacob**, Robert J K 1950- AmMWSc 92
**Jacob**, Robert Raphael Hayim 1941- Who 92
**Jacob**, Samson T AmMWSc 92
**Jacob**, Stanley W 1924- AmMWSc 92
**Jacob**, Ted WhoAmP 91
**Jacob**, Theodore August 1919- AmMWSc 92
**Jacob**, William Burkley 1954- WhoWest 92
**Jacob**, William Mungo 1944- Who 92
**Jacob**, William Ungoed d1990 Who 92N
**Jacob**, Willis Harvey 1943- WhoBlA 92
**Jacober**, William John 1917- AmMWSc 92
**Jacobetti**, Dominic J 1920- WhoAmP 91
**Jacobi**, Abraham 1830-1919 BiInAmS
**Jacobi**, Allen L. 1947- WhoEnt 92
**Jacobi**, Derek 1938- IntMPA 92

**Jacobi**, Derek George 1938- *IntWW 91, Who 92, WhoEnt 92*
**Jacobi**, Frederick 1891-1952 *NewAmDM*
**Jacobi**, Friedrich Heinrich 1743-1819 *BlkwCEP*
**Jacobi**, George 1922- *AmMWSc 92*
**Jacobi**, James 1925- *Who 92*
**Jacobi**, Jan de Greeff 1944- *WhoMW 92*
**Jacobi**, Jeffrey Ernest 1958- *WhoEnt 92*
**Jacobi**, John Albert 1947- *WhoAmL 92*
**Jacobi**, Lotte 1896-1990 *AnObit 1990, FacFETw*
**Jacobi**, Lou 1913- *WhoEnt 92*
**Jacobi**, Mary Corinna Putnam 1842-1906 *BiInAmS*
**Jacobi**, Mary Putnam 1842-1906 *RComAH*
**Jacobi**, Peter Alan 1945- *AmMWSc 92*
**Jacobi**, Robert V., Jr. 1958- *WhoMW 92*
**Jacobi**, Roger Edgar 1924- *WhoEnt 92*
**Jacobi**, Ronald N. 1947- *WhoEnt 92*
**Jacobi**, W M 1930- *AmMWSc 92*
**Jacobi**, William G. *LesBEnT 92*
**Jacobik**, Gray *DrAPF 91*
**Jacobitti**, Suzanne Duvall 1940- *WhoMW 92*
**Jacobo**, Esperanza Delao 1944- *WhoHisp 92*
**Jacobo**, John Rodriguez 1942- *WhoHisp 92*
**Jacobowitz**, David 1931- *AmMWSc 92*
**Jacobowitz**, Diane Beth 1952- *WhoEnt 92*
**Jacobowitz**, Harold Saul 1950- *WhoAmL 92*
**Jacobowitz**, Judah *DrAPF 91*
**Jacobowitz**, Lisa Ann 1957- *WhoAmL 92*
**Jacobowitz**, Ronald 1934- *AmMWSc 92*
**Jacobowitz**, Ruth Scherr *WhoMW 92*
**Jacobs**, Abigail Conway 1942- *AmMWSc 92*
**Jacobs**, Alan 1947- *WhoAmL 92*
**Jacobs**, Alan M 1932- *AmMWSc 92*
**Jacobs**, Alan Martin 1942- *AmMWSc 92*
**Jacobs**, Allan Edward 1938- *AmMWSc 92*
**Jacobs**, Allen Leon 1931- *AmMWSc 92*
**Jacobs**, Allen Wayne 1942- *AmMWSc 92, WhoMW 92*
**Jacobs**, Allyn 1953- *WhoWest 92*
**Jacobs**, Alma Rau 1924- *WhoAmP 91*
**Jacobs**, Andrew, Jr 1932- *WhoAmP 91, WhoMW 92*
**Jacobs**, Andy, Jr. 1932- *AlmAP 92 [port]*
**Jacobs**, Anita Isaacson 1948- *WhoMW 92*
**Jacobs**, Ann Elizabeth 1950- *WhoAmL 92*
**Jacobs**, Anthony *Who 92*
**Jacobs**, Anthony Becket 1965- *WhoRel 92*
**Jacobs**, Arthur David 1922- *IntAu&W 91, Who 92, WrDr 92*
**Jacobs**, Arthur Dietrich 1933- *WhoFI 92, WhoWest 92*
**Jacobs**, Barbara B 1929- *AmMWSc 92*
**Jacobs**, Barbara Frank 1942- *WhoFI 92*
**Jacobs**, Barry 1924- *IntMPA 92*
**Jacobs**, Barry Leonard *AmMWSc 92*
**Jacobs**, Bernard B. 1916- *WhoEnt 92*
**Jacobs**, Carl Eugene 1942- *WhoMW 92*
**Jacobs**, Carl Henry 1948- *AmMWSc 92*
**Jacobs**, Caryn Leslie 1958- *WhoAmL 92*
**Jacobs**, Charles Warren 1954- *AmMWSc 92*
**Jacobs**, Cheryl Lee 1961- *WhoEnt 92*
**Jacobs**, Christopher Paul 1954- *WhoEnt 92*
**Jacobs**, Clyde 1925- *WrDr 92*
**Jacobs**, Dan N. 1924- *WrDr 92*
**Jacobs**, Daniel Wesley, Sr. 1933- *WhoBlA 92*
**Jacobs**, David *LesBEnT 92*
**Jacobs**, David 1939- *WhoEnt 92*
**Jacobs**, David Anthony 1931- *Who 92*
**Jacobs**, David Lewis 1926- *Who 92*
**Jacobs**, David R, Jr 1945- *AmMWSc 92*
**Jacobs**, Delton Lowell 1951- *WhoMW 92*
**Jacobs**, Denny 1937- *WhoAmP 91*
**Jacobs**, Diane Margaret 1940- *AmMWSc 92*
**Jacobs**, Dick Morrell 1938- *WhoMW 92*
**Jacobs**, Donald Gustavus 1916- *WhoRel 92*
**Jacobs**, Donald P. 1927- *WhoFI 92, WhoMW 92*
**Jacobs**, Donald Phillip 1924- *WhoMW 92*
**Jacobs**, Donald Seyler 1945- *WhoMW 92*
**Jacobs**, Donald Thomas 1949- *AmMWSc 92, WhoMW 92*
**Jacobs**, Douglas George 1939- *WhoAmP 91*
**Jacobs**, Edward James 1932- *WhoMW 92*
**Jacobs**, Elliott Warren 1950- *AmMWSc 92*
**Jacobs**, Emmett S 1926- *AmMWSc 92*
**Jacobs**, Francis Albin 1918- *AmMWSc 92*
**Jacobs**, Francis G. 1939- *WrDr 92*
**Jacobs**, Francis Geoffrey 1939- *IntWW 91, Who 92*
**Jacobs**, Gary Wayne 1961- *WhoRel 92*
**Jacobs**, George Joseph 1917- *AmMWSc 92*
**Jacobs**, Gerald Daniel 1935- *AmMWSc 92*
**Jacobs**, Gerard Anthony 1952- *WhoMW 92*
**Jacobs**, H Kurt 1943- *AmMWSc 92*
**Jacobs**, Harold Robert 1936- *AmMWSc 92*
**Jacobs**, Harriet 1815-1897 *DcNCBi 3*
**Jacobs**, Harriet A. 1813-1897 *BenetAL 91*
**Jacobs**, Harriet Ann 1813-1897 *NotBlAW 92*
**Jacobs**, Harry Allan, Jr. 1921- *WhoFI 92*
**Jacobs**, Harry David, Jr. 1928- *WhoMW 92*
**Jacobs**, Harry Lewis 1925- *AmMWSc 92*
**Jacobs**, Harry Milburn, Jr. 1928- *WhoEnt 92*
**Jacobs**, Harvey 1928- *AmMWSc 92*
**Jacobs**, Harvey Collins 1915- *WhoMW 92*
**Jacobs**, Hazel A. 1948- *WhoBlA 92*
**Jacobs**, Helen Hull 1908- *WrDr 92*
**Jacobs**, Henry Eyster 1844-1932 *RelLAm 91*
**Jacobs**, Hyde Spencer 1926- *AmMWSc 92*
**Jacobs**, Ilene B. 1947- *WhoFI 92*
**Jacobs**, Ira 1931- *AmMWSc 92*
**Jacobs**, Irwin Mark 1933- *AmMWSc 92*
**Jacobs**, Israel S 1925- *AmMWSc 92*
**Jacobs**, J H 1916- *AmMWSc 92*
**Jacobs**, Jack Bernard 1942- *WhoAmL 92*
**Jacobs**, Jacqueline E 1923- *AmMWSc 92*
**Jacobs**, Jacqueline Minette 1936- *WhoBlA 92*
**Jacobs**, James B. 1947- *WhoAmL 92*
**Jacobs**, James Ethan 1940- *WhoAmL 92*
**Jacobs**, James Michael 1947- *WhoWest 92*
**Jacobs**, James Paul 1930- *WhoFI 92*
**Jacobs**, James Walter 1945- *WhoMW 92*
**Jacobs**, Jane 1916- *WrDr 92*
**Jacobs**, Janelle Marie 1966- *WhoMW 92*
**Jacobs**, Jeffrey Lee 1951- *WhoAmL 92*
**Jacobs**, Jeffrey Lyndon 1961- *WhoMW 92*
**Jacobs**, Jeffrey P *WhoAmP 91*
**Jacobs**, Jerold Lance 1943- *WhoAmL 92*
**Jacobs**, Jerome Barry 1942- *AmMWSc 92*
**Jacobs**, Jim 1942- *WhoEnt 92*
**Jacobs**, Joel *WhoAmP 91*
**Jacobs**, John *IntMPA 92*
**Jacobs**, John 1916- *WrDr 92*
**Jacobs**, John Allen 1939- *AmMWSc 92*
**Jacobs**, John Arthur 1916- *Who 92*
**Jacobs**, John Edward 1920- *AmMWSc 92*
**Jacobs**, John Howard 1925- *WhoWest 92*
**Jacobs**, John Robert Maurice 1925- *Who 92*
**Jacobs**, Jonathan Martin 1956- *WhoWest 92*
**Jacobs**, Joseph Donovan 1908- *AmMWSc 92*
**Jacobs**, Joseph James 1925- *WhoAmL 92*
**Jacobs**, Joseph John 1916- *AmMWSc 92, WhoFI 92, WhoWest 92*
**Jacobs**, Joseph M. 1959- *WhoAmL 92*
**Jacobs**, Joseph Martin 1911- *WhoAmL 92*
**Jacobs**, Judyth L. 1942- *WhoMW 92*
**Jacobs**, Julian I. 1937- *WhoAmL 92*
**Jacobs**, Julyette Gail 1946- *WhoMW 92*
**Jacobs**, Karen Folger 1940- *WhoEnt 92*
**Jacobs**, Kenneth 1917- *Who 92*
**Jacobs**, Kenneth A. 1948- *WhoEnt 92*
**Jacobs**, Kenneth Charles 1942- *AmMWSc 92*
**Jacobs**, Kent Frederick 1938- *WhoWest 92*
**Jacobs**, Kimberly Hague 1961- *WhoMW 92*
**Jacobs**, Larry Ben 1959- *WhoBlA 92*
**Jacobs**, Laurence Alan 1949- *AmMWSc 92*
**Jacobs**, Laurence Stanton 1940- *AmMWSc 92*
**Jacobs**, Lawrence Ronald d1991 *NewYTBS 91*
**Jacobs**, Leah *IntAu&W 91X, WrDr 92*
**Jacobs**, Leo Herman 1902- *WhoFI 92*
**Jacobs**, Leslie William 1944- *WhoMW 92*
**Jacobs**, Libby 1947- *WhoEnt 92*
**Jacobs**, Lloydstone Leonard Fitzmorgan 1937- *IntWW 91*
**Jacobs**, Lois Jean 1947- *AmMWSc 92*
**Jacobs**, Louis 1920- *Who 92, WrDr 92*
**Jacobs**, Louis John 1943- *AmMWSc 92*
**Jacobs**, Loyd Donald 1932- *AmMWSc 92*
**Jacobs**, Lucky *DrAPF 91*
**Jacobs**, Marc Quillen 1938- *AmMWSc 92*
**Jacobs**, Mark 1950- *AmMWSc 92*
**Jacobs**, Martin Irwin 1943- *AmMWSc 92*
**Jacobs**, Martin John 1944- *AmMWSc 92*
**Jacobs**, Mary Margaret 1939- *WhoWest 92*
**Jacobs**, Maryce Mercedes 1944- *AmMWSc 92*
**Jacobs**, Melvin 1926- *WhoFI 92*
**Jacobs**, Merle Emmor 1918- *AmMWSc 92*
**Jacobs**, Michael 1808-1871 *BiInAmS*
**Jacobs**, Michael Allen 1955- *WhoAmL 92*
**Jacobs**, Michael Craig 1961- *WhoFI 92*
**Jacobs**, Michael Frederick 1958- *WhoFI 92*
**Jacobs**, Michael Moises 1950- *AmMWSc 92*
**Jacobs**, Mike 1932- *WhoFI 92*
**Jacobs**, Morton Howard 1924- *AmMWSc 92*
**Jacobs**, Myron Samuel 1922- *AmMWSc 92*
**Jacobs**, Ned L. 1949- *WhoWest 92*
**Jacobs**, Nicholas Joseph 1933- *AmMWSc 92*
**Jacobs**, Norma Morris 1949- *WhoBlA 92*
**Jacobs**, Norman Allan 1937- *WhoFI 92*
**Jacobs**, Patricia Ann 1934- *AmMWSc 92*
**Jacobs**, Patricia Anne 1947- *AmMWSc 92*
**Jacobs**, Patricia Dianne 1950- *WhoBlA 92*
**Jacobs**, Patrick W M 1923- *AmMWSc 92*
**Jacobs**, Patrick William McCarthy 1923- *IntWW 91*
**Jacobs**, Paul 1930-1983 *NewAmDM*
**Jacobs**, Paul Alan 1940- *WhoAmL 92, WhoWest 92*
**Jacobs**, Peter Alan 1943- *IntWW 91*
**Jacobs**, Piers 1933- *IntWW 91, Who 92*
**Jacobs**, Ralph, Jr. 1940- *WhoWest 92*
**Jacobs**, Ralph R 1942- *AmMWSc 92*
**Jacobs**, Randall Brian 1951- *WhoWest 92*
**Jacobs**, Randall Charles 1947- *WhoMW 92*
**Jacobs**, Raymond Andrew 1955- *WhoMW 92*
**Jacobs**, Reuven 1956- *WhoAmL 92*
**Jacobs**, Rhoda S *WhoAmP 91*
**Jacobs**, Richard Dearborn 1920- *WhoMW 92*
**Jacobs**, Richard L 1930- *AmMWSc 92*
**Jacobs**, Richard Lee 1931- *AmMWSc 92*
**Jacobs**, Richard Lewis 1927- *AmMWSc 92*
**Jacobs**, Richard Lewis 1950- *WhoAmP 91*
**Jacobs**, Richard M 1924- *AmMWSc 92*
**Jacobs**, Richard Oliver 1931- *WhoAmL 92*
**Jacobs**, Robert Alan 1937- *WhoAmL 92*
**Jacobs**, Robert Alan 1948- *WhoAmL 92*
**Jacobs**, Robert Allan 1905- *IntWW 91*
**Jacobs**, Robert Cooper 1939- *WhoWest 92*
**Jacobs**, Robert Marion 1938- *WhoEnt 92*
**Jacobs**, Robert Noel *WhoAmL 92*
**Jacobs**, Robert Saul *AmMWSc 92*
**Jacobs**, Roger Francis 1937- *WhoAmL 92*
**Jacobs**, Ronald Nicholas *WhoEnt 92*
**Jacobs**, Ronald S. *WhoEnt 92*
**Jacobs**, Rosetta 1932- *WhoEnt 92*
**Jacobs**, Ross 1925- *AmMWSc 92*
**Jacobs**, Rudolf Antonius Maria 1948- *WhoEnt 92*
**Jacobs**, S Lawrence 1929- *AmMWSc 92*
**Jacobs**, Scott William 1950- *WhoEnt 92*
**Jacobs**, Sharon Nan 1961- *WhoAmL 92*
**Jacobs**, Sigmund James 1912- *AmMWSc 92*
**Jacobs**, Simone 1966- *BlkOlyM*
**Jacobs**, Stanley J 1936- *AmMWSc 92*
**Jacobs**, Stanley S 1940- *AmMWSc 92*
**Jacobs**, Stephen 1954- *WhoAmL 92*
**Jacobs**, Stephen Frank 1928- *AmMWSc 92*
**Jacobs**, Stephen Louis 1953- *WhoAmL 92*
**Jacobs**, Steven Paul 1953- *WhoEnt 92*
**Jacobs**, Susan 1945- *WhoAmL 92*
**Jacobs**, Suzan Jon 1957- *WhoAmL 92*
**Jacobs**, Sylvia Marie 1946- *WhoBlA 92*
**Jacobs**, Tamara 1951- *WhoAmL 92*
**Jacobs**, Theodore Alan 1927- *AmMWSc 92*
**Jacobs**, Thomas Edward, III 1949- *WhoFI 92*
**Jacobs**, Thomas Linwood 1933- *WhoBlA 92*
**Jacobs**, Thomas Lloyd 1908- *AmMWSc 92*
**Jacobs**, Timothy Ward 1951- *WhoMW 92*
**Jacobs**, Verne Louis 1941- *AmMWSc 92*
**Jacobs**, Virgil Leon 1935- *AmMWSc 92*
**Jacobs**, W.W. 1863-1943 *RfGEnL 91*
**Jacobs**, Walter Darnell 1922- *WrDr 92*
**Jacobs**, Walter L 1896-1985 *FacFETw*
**Jacobs**, Walter W. 1932- *WhoRel 92*
**Jacobs**, Wendell Early, Jr. 1945- *WhoAmL 92*
**Jacobs**, Wesley D. 1946- *WhoEnt 92*
**Jacobs**, Wilbur R. 1918- *WrDr 92*
**Jacobs**, Wilbur Ripley *WhoWest 92*
**Jacobs**, Wilfred 1919- *Who 92*
**Jacobs**, Wilfred Ebenezer 1919- *IntWW 91*
**Jacobs**, William Donald 1928- *AmMWSc 92*
**Jacobs**, William Paul 1919- *AmMWSc 92*
**Jacobs**, William Randall 1959- *WhoMW 92*
**Jacobs**, William Stephen 1772-1843 *BiInAmS*
**Jacobs**, William Thomas 1958- *WhoEnt 92*
**Jacobs**, William Wescott 1943- *AmMWSc 92*
**Jacobs**, William Wood, Jr 1947- *AmMWSc 92*
**Jacobs**, Woodrow Cooper 1908- *AmMWSc 92*
**Jacobs-Lorena**, Marcelo 1942- *AmMWSc 92*
**Jacobsen**, Alf G. 1937- *WhoEnt 92*
**Jacobsen**, Arne 1902-1971 *DcTwDes*
**Jacobsen**, Barry James 1947- *AmMWSc 92*
**Jacobsen**, Bruce Frederik 1946- *WhoFI 92*
**Jacobsen**, Chris J 1960- *AmMWSc 92*
**Jacobsen**, Donald Weldon 1939- *AmMWSc 92*
**Jacobsen**, Douglas Andrew 1928- *WhoAmL 92*
**Jacobsen**, Edward Hastings 1926- *AmMWSc 92*
**Jacobsen**, Eric Kasner 1932- *WhoFI 92, WhoMW 92, WhoWest 92*
**Jacobsen**, Fred Marius 1925- *AmMWSc 92*
**Jacobsen**, Frederick Marius 1954- *AmMWSc 92*
**Jacobsen**, Frithjof Halfdan 1914- *Who 92*
**Jacobsen**, Glenn Eugene 1928- *WhoAmP 91*
**Jacobsen**, Hazel Catherine 1909- *WhoMW 92*
**Jacobsen**, Jack Ellsworth 1923- *WhoRel 92*
**Jacobsen**, James Conrad 1935- *WhoFI 92*
**Jacobsen**, Jens Peter 1847-1885 *NinCLC 34 [port]*
**Jacobsen**, Joel Kenton 1959- *WhoAmL 92*
**Jacobsen**, Josephine *DrAPF 91*
**Jacobsen**, Josephine 1908- *ConPo 91, IntAu&W 91, WrDr 92*
**Jacobsen**, Joyce Penelope 1961- *WhoFI 92*
**Jacobsen**, Judith Eva 1952- *WhoWest 92*
**Jacobsen**, K. C. 1939- *ConAu 133*
**Jacobsen**, Ken *WhoAmP 91*
**Jacobsen**, Kim Andrew 1952- *WhoWest 92*
**Jacobsen**, Laren 1937- *WhoWest 92*
**Jacobsen**, Lawrence E 1921- *WhoAmP 91*
**Jacobsen**, Lynn C 1918- *AmMWSc 92*
**Jacobsen**, Nadine Klecha 1941- *AmMWSc 92*
**Jacobsen**, Neil Soren 1930- *AmMWSc 92*
**Jacobsen**, Nelson Robert, III 1964- *WhoFI 92*
**Jacobsen**, Paul Douglas 1952- *WhoMW 92*
**Jacobsen**, Raymond Alfred, Jr. 1949- *WhoAmL 92*
**Jacobsen**, Rebecca Hanson 1949- *WhoWest 92*
**Jacobsen**, Richard T 1941- *AmMWSc 92*
**Jacobsen**, Roger Craig 1945- *WhoIns 92*
**Jacobsen**, Stein Bjornar 1950- *AmMWSc 92*
**Jacobsen**, Stephen C *AmMWSc 92*
**Jacobsen**, Stephen Charles *WhoWest 92*
**Jacobsen**, Terry Dale 1950- *AmMWSc 92*
**Jacobsen**, Thomas Herbert 1939- *WhoMW 92*
**Jacobsen**, Thorkild 1904- *WhoRel 92*
**Jacobsen**, William E 1912- *AmMWSc 92*
**Jacobsen**, William L, Jr 1936- *WhoAmP 91*
**Jacobsmeyer**, Jay Michael 1959- *WhoWest 92*
**Jacobsmeyer**, Vincent Paul 1906- *AmMWSc 92*
**Jacobsohn**, Gert Max 1929- *AmMWSc 92*
**Jacobsohn**, Myra K 1939- *AmMWSc 92*
**Jacobsohn**, Richard Harvey 1944- *WhoFI 92*
**Jacobson**, Abram Robert *AmMWSc 92*
**Jacobson**, Ada Leah 1933- *AmMWSc 92*
**Jacobson**, Albert H, Jr 1917- *AmMWSc 92*
**Jacobson**, Albert Herman, Jr. 1917- *WhoWest 92*
**Jacobson**, Alexander Donald 1933- *AmMWSc 92*
**Jacobson**, Alf Edgar 1924- *WhoAmP 91*
**Jacobson**, Alfred Thurl 1919- *IntWW 91*
**Jacobson**, Allan Joseph 1944- *AmMWSc 92*
**Jacobson**, Allan Stanley 1932- *AmMWSc 92*
**Jacobson**, Allen F 1926- *AmMWSc 92*
**Jacobson**, Allen Frank 1926- *WhoFI 92, WhoMW 92*
**Jacobson**, Allen H. 1939- *WhoFI 92*
**Jacobson**, Ann Beatrice 1938- *AmMWSc 92*
**Jacobson**, Anna Sue 1940- *WhoFI 92, WhoMW 92*
**Jacobson**, Antone Gardner 1929- *AmMWSc 92*
**Jacobson**, Arland Dean 1941- *WhoRel 92*
**Jacobson**, Arnold P 1932- *AmMWSc 92*
**Jacobson**, Arthur 1924- *WhoWest 92*
**Jacobson**, Arthur E 1928- *AmMWSc 92*
**Jacobson**, Arvid Victor 1947- *WhoAmL 92*
**Jacobson**, Barry Martin 1945- *WhoMW 92*
**Jacobson**, Barry Stephen 1955- *WhoAmL 92, WhoFI 92*
**Jacobson**, Baruch S 1925- *AmMWSc 92*
**Jacobson**, Bernard 1928- *AmMWSc 92*
**Jacobson**, Bertil 1923- *AmMWSc 92*
**Jacobson**, Bonnie *DrAPF 91*
**Jacobson**, Bruce John 1949- *WhoMW 92*
**Jacobson**, Bruce Shell 1940- *AmMWSc 92*
**Jacobson**, Charles May 1941- *WhoFI 92*
**Jacobson**, Clarence E 1912- *WhoAmP 91*
**Jacobson**, Craig Lowell 1955- *WhoFI 92, WhoWest 92*
**Jacobson**, D. Blaine 1955- *WhoWest 92*
**Jacobson**, Dale *DrAPF 91*

**Jacobson**, Dan 1929- *ConNov 91, IntAu&W 91, IntWW 91, LiExTwC, WrDr 92*
**Jacobson**, Daniel P 1961- *WhoAmP 91*
**Jacobson**, David 1909- *WhoRel 92*
**Jacobson**, Donald Thomas 1932- *WhoWest 92*
**Jacobson**, Elaine Louise 1945- *AmMWSc 92*
**Jacobson**, Elaine Zeporah 1942- *WhoMW 92*
**Jacobson**, Eli Asher 1947- *WhoFI 92*
**Jacobson**, Elliott Roy 1942- *WhoMW 92*
**Jacobson**, Eric Scott 1952- *WhoAmL 92*
**Jacobson**, Eugene Donald 1930- *AmMWSc 92*
**Jacobson**, Florence Dorfman 1918- *AmMWSc 92*
**Jacobson**, Frank Henry 1915- *AmMWSc 92*
**Jacobson**, Frank Joel 1948- *WhoWest 92*
**Jacobson**, Gail M 1938- *AmMWSc 92*
**Jacobson**, Gilbert H. 1956- *WhoAmL 92, WhoRel 92*
**Jacobson**, Glen Arthur 1926- *AmMWSc 92*
**Jacobson**, Gunnard Kenneth 1947- *AmMWSc 92*
**Jacobson**, Harold 1929- *AmMWSc 92*
**Jacobson**, Harold Gordon 1912- *AmMWSc 92*
**Jacobson**, Harold Karan 1929- *WhoMW 92*
**Jacobson**, Harry C 1931- *AmMWSc 92*
**Jacobson**, Harry R 1947- *AmMWSc 92*
**Jacobson**, Henning *WhoAmP 91*
**Jacobson**, Herbert 1923- *AmMWSc 92*
**Jacobson**, Homer 1922- *AmMWSc 92*
**Jacobson**, Howard 1942- *ConNov 91*
**Jacobson**, Howard Christian 1935- *WhoAmP 91*
**Jacobson**, Howard Newman 1923- *AmMWSc 92*
**Jacobson**, Ira David 1942- *AmMWSc 92*
**Jacobson**, Irven Allan, Jr 1928- *AmMWSc 92*
**Jacobson**, James Bassett 1922- *WhoFI 92*
**Jacobson**, James Lamma, Jr. 1946- *WhoFI 92*
**Jacobson**, Jay Stanley 1934- *AmMWSc 92*
**Jacobson**, Jeffrey Eli 1956- *WhoAmL 92, WhoEnt 92*
**Jacobson**, Jimmy Joe 1937- *AmMWSc 92*
**Jacobson**, Joan 1924- *AmMWSc 92*
**Jacobson**, John Christian 1795-1870 *DcNCBi 3*
**Jacobson**, John Howard, Jr. 1933- *WhoMW 92*
**Jacobson**, John Obert 1939- *AmMWSc 92*
**Jacobson**, Jon Obert *WhoWest 92*
**Jacobson**, Jon Stanley 1938- *WhoWest 92*
**Jacobson**, Jonathan G 1953- *WhoAmP 91*
**Jacobson**, Jonathan M. 1952- *WhoAmL 92*
**Jacobson**, Judith Helen 1939- *WhoAmP 91*
**Jacobson**, Julia Ann 1963- *WhoAmL 92*
**Jacobson**, Karl Bruce 1928- *AmMWSc 92*
**Jacobson**, Keith Hazen 1918- *AmMWSc 92*
**Jacobson**, Kenneth Alan 1953- *AmMWSc 92*
**Jacobson**, Kenneth Allan 1941- *AmMWSc 92*
**Jacobson**, L. Dale 1957- *WhoEnt 92*
**Jacobson**, Larry A 1940- *AmMWSc 92*
**Jacobson**, Lawrence Seymour *WhoEnt 92*
**Jacobson**, Leon Orris 1911- *AmMWSc 92, IntWW 91*
**Jacobson**, Leslie Bravman 1948- *WhoEnt 92*
**Jacobson**, Lewis A 1942- *AmMWSc 92*
**Jacobson**, Lloyd Eldred 1923- *WhoMW 92*
**Jacobson**, Louis 1915- *AmMWSc 92*
**Jacobson**, Marc 1952- *WhoEnt 92*
**Jacobson**, Marcus 1930- *AmMWSc 92*
**Jacobson**, Mark Alan 1961- *WhoAmL 92*
**Jacobson**, Martha Edelstein 1938- *WhoEnt 92*
**Jacobson**, Martin 1919- *AmMWSc 92*
**Jacobson**, Martin Michael 1934- *AmMWSc 92*
**Jacobson**, Marvin 1921- *AmMWSc 92*
**Jacobson**, Melvin Joseph 1928- *AmMWSc 92*
**Jacobson**, Michael F 1943- *AmMWSc 92*
**Jacobson**, Michael M. 1959- *WhoEnt 92*
**Jacobson**, Michael Ray 1950- *AmMWSc 92*
**Jacobson**, Murray M 1915- *AmMWSc 92*
**Jacobson**, Myron Kenneth 1943- *AmMWSc 92*
**Jacobson**, Nathan 1910- *AmMWSc 92, IntWW 91*
**Jacobson**, Norman Leonard 1918- *AmMWSc 92*
**Jacobson**, Paul Wayne 1948- *WhoAmL 92*
**Jacobson**, Peter A. 1944- *WhoAmL 92*
**Jacobson**, Ralph Allen 1940- *AmMWSc 92*
**Jacobson**, Raymond E 1922- *AmMWSc 92*
**Jacobson**, Raymond Earl 1922- *WhoFI 92, WhoWest 92*
**Jacobson**, Richard Joseph 1943- *WhoAmL 92*
**Jacobson**, Richard Lee 1942- *WhoAmL 92*
**Jacobson**, Richard Martin 1947- *AmMWSc 92*
**Jacobson**, Robert Andrew 1932- *AmMWSc 92, WhoMW 92*
**Jacobson**, Robert Leroy 1932- *AmMWSc 92*
**Jacobson**, Stanley 1937- *AmMWSc 92*
**Jacobson**, Stephen Ernest 1945- *AmMWSc 92*
**Jacobson**, Stephen Richard 1944- *AmMWSc 92*
**Jacobson**, Steve Evan 1955- *WhoWest 92*
**Jacobson**, Steven Blair 1945- *WhoAmL 92*
**Jacobson**, Stuart Lee 1934- *AmMWSc 92*
**Jacobson**, Susan S. *DrAPF 91*
**Jacobson**, Sverre Theodore 1922- *WhoRel 92*
**Jacobson**, Thomas Ernest 1931- *WhoWest 92*
**Jacobson**, Wayne Lee 1953- *WhoRel 92*
**Jacobson**, Willard James 1922- *AmMWSc 92*
**Jacobson**, William Jay, II 1940- *WhoEnt 92*
**Jacobson-Wolf**, Joan Elizabeth 1949- *WhoRel 92*
**Jacobus**, Brent Arlyn 1961- *WhoMW 92*
**Jacobus**, Charles Joseph 1947- *WhoAmL 92*
**Jacobus**, Cheri Christine 1947- *WhoAmP 91*
**Jacobus**, David Penman 1927- *AmMWSc 92*
**Jacobus**, Lee A 1935- *IntAu&W 91*
**Jacobus**, Mary 1944- *IntAu&W 91, WrDr 92*
**Jacobus**, Otha John 1939- *AmMWSc 92*
**Jacobus**, Terry 1948- *IntAu&W 91*
**Jacobus**, William Edward 1942- *AmMWSc 92*
**Jacobvits De Szeged**, Adriaan Pieter R. 1935- *IntWW 91*
**Jacoby**, Alexander Robb 1922- *AmMWSc 92*
**Jacoby**, Andrea 1945- *WhoFI 92*
**Jacoby**, Coleman *WhoEnt 92*
**Jacoby**, Doris Faith 1926- *WhoEnt 92*
**Jacoby**, Ellen Rae *WhoEnt 92*
**Jacoby**, Erika 1928- *WhoWest 92*
**Jacoby**, Frank 1925- *WhoEnt 92*
**Jacoby**, Frank David 1925- *IntMPA 92*
**Jacoby**, Henry I 1936- *AmMWSc 92*
**Jacoby**, Jay 1917- *AmMWSc 92*
**Jacoby**, Jim d1991 *NewYTBS 91 [port]*
**Jacoby**, John Primm 1941- *WhoAmL 92*
**Jacoby**, Joseph 1942- *IntMPA 92, WhoEnt 92*
**Jacoby**, Lawrence John 1943- *AmMWSc 92*
**Jacoby**, Leo Peter 1949- *WhoRel 92*
**Jacoby**, Peter Fredrickson 1947- *WhoWest 92*
**Jacoby**, Robert Ottinger 1939- *AmMWSc 92*
**Jacoby**, Ronald Lee 1943- *AmMWSc 92*
**Jacoby**, Russell Stephen 1939- *AmMWSc 92*
**Jacoby**, Sanford Mark 1953- *WhoWest 92*
**Jacoby**, Scott 1956- *IntMPA 92*
**Jacoby**, Stewart William 1938- *WhoEnt 92*
**Jacoby**, William R 1926- *AmMWSc 92*
**Jacocks**, Henry Miller 1953- *WhoFI 92*
**Jacocks**, William Picard 1877-1965 *DcNCBi 3*
**Jacolev**, Leon 1914- *AmMWSc 92*
**Jacomb**, Charles E 1888- *ScFEYrs*
**Jacomb**, Martin 1929- *Who 92*
**Jacomb**, Martin Wakefield 1929- *IntWW 91*
**Jacomb-Hood**, George Percy 1857-1929 *TwCPaSc*
**Jacon**, Bernard *IntMPA 92*
**Jacopo da Bologna** *NewAmDM*
**Jacover**, Jerold Alan 1945- *WhoAmL 92, WhoMW 92*
**Jacovides**, Linos J 1940- *AmMWSc 92*
**Jacovides**, Linos Jacovou 1940- *WhoMW 92*
**Jacox**, Ada K *AmMWSc 92*
**Jacox**, John William 1938- *WhoFI 92, WhoMW 92*
**Jacox**, Marilyn Esther 1929- *AmMWSc 92*
**Jacox**, Ralph Franklin 1913- *AmMWSc 92*
**Jacquard**, Marie 1752-1834 *DcTwDes*
**Jacqueline of Bavaria** 1402-1437 *EncAmaz 91*
**Jacquemard**, Simonne 1924- *IntWW 91*
**Jacquemin**, John Michael 1946- *WhoFI 92*
**Jacquemin**, Robert *IntMPA 92*
**Jacqueney**, Stephanie Alice *WhoAmL 92*
**Jacques** *Who 92*
**Jacques**, Baron 1905- *Who 92*
**Jacques de Liege** 1260?-1330? *NewAmDM*
**Jacques**, Emile J 1925- *WhoAmP 91*
**Jacques**, Felix Anthony 1924- *AmMWSc 92*
**Jacques**, Jean-Guy 1930- *WhoEnt 92*
**Jacques**, Joseph William 1953- *WhoFI 92*
**Jacques**, Paul F *WhoAmP 91*
**Jacques**, Peter Roy Albert 1939- *Who 92*
**Jacques**, Reginald 1894-1969 *NewAmDM*
**Jacques**, Robert C. 1919- *IntMPA 92*
**Jacques**, Robin 1920- *Who 92*
**Jacques**, William Lowell, II 1966- *WhoWest 92*
**Jacques**, Yves Henri 1929- *IntWW 91*
**Jacquet of Mantua** 1483-1559 *NewAmDM*
**Jacquet**, Herve 1939- *AmMWSc 92*
**Jacquet**, Illinois 1922- *NewAmDM*
**Jacquet**, Jean Baptiste Illinois 1922- *WhoBlA 92*
**Jacquet**, Yasuko F *AmMWSc 92*
**Jacquet de la Guerre**, Elisabeth-Claude 1666?-1729 *NewAmDM*
**Jacquez**, Albert S. *WhoHisp 92*
**Jacquez**, John Alfred 1922- *AmMWSc 92, WhoMW 92*
**Jacquin**, Arnaud Eric 1964- *AmMWSc 92*
**Jacquinot**, Pierre 1910- *IntWW 91*
**Jacquot**, Raymond G 1938- *AmMWSc 92*
**Jad al-Haq**, Jad al-Haq Ali *WhoRel 92*
**Jadiker**, Mary D 1937- *WhoAmP 91*
**Jadlow**, Joseph Martin 1942- *WhoFI 92*
**Jadlowiec**, Kenneth M 1951- *WhoAmP 91*
**Jadoo**, Ramduthsirg 1937- *IntWW 91*
**Jadot**, Jean Lambert Octave 1909- *WhoRel 92*
**Jadra**, Ramon *WhoHisp 92*
**Jaduszliwer**, Bernardo 1943- *AmMWSc 92*
**Jadwin**, Todd *WhoFI 92*
**Jaeckel**, Richard 1926- *IntMPA 92, WhoEnt 92*
**Jaecker**, John Alvin 1945- *AmMWSc 92*
**Jaecks**, Duane H 1935- *AmMWSc 92*
**Jaecks**, Lenard Dale 1932- *WhoRel 92*
**Jaeger**, Charles Herman 1930- *WhoIns 92*
**Jaeger**, Charles Wayne 1943- *AmMWSc 92*
**Jaeger**, David Allen 1944- *AmMWSc 92*
**Jaeger**, Don Theodore 1936- *WhoEnt 92*
**Jaeger**, Gerard A 1952- *IntAu&W 91*
**Jaeger**, Gregory Gerald 1951- *WhoAmL 92*
**Jaeger**, Herbert Karl 1931- *AmMWSc 92*
**Jaeger**, Ina Claire 1929- *WhoEnt 92*
**Jaeger**, James J *AmMWSc 92*
**Jaeger**, Klaus Bruno 1938- *AmMWSc 92*
**Jaeger**, Leslie Gordon 1926- *Who 92*
**Jaeger**, Lowell *DrAPF 91*
**Jaeger**, Marc Jules 1929- *AmMWSc 92*
**Jaeger**, Muriel *ScFEYrs*
**Jaeger**, Ralph R 1940- *AmMWSc 92*
**Jaeger**, Richard 1913- *IntWW 91*
**Jaeger**, Richard Charles 1944- *AmMWSc 92*
**Jaeger**, Robert Corwin 1941- *WhoEnt 92*
**Jaeger**, Robert Gordon 1937- *AmMWSc 92*
**Jaeger**, Rudolph John 1944- *AmMWSc 92*
**Jaeger**, Sharon Ann *DrAPF 91*
**Jaeger**, Sharon Ann 1945- *WhoWest 92*
**Jaeger**, Vernon Paul 1906- *WhoRel 92*
**Jaehn**, Sigmund 1937- *FacFETw*
**Jaehning**, Judith A 1950- *AmMWSc 92*
**Jaekle**, Robert George 1951- *WhoAmP 91*
**Jael** *EncAmaz 91*
**Jaenicke**, Lothar 1923- *IntWW 91*
**Jaenike**, John Robert 1926- *AmMWSc 92*
**Jaenisch**, Rudolf *AmMWSc 92*
**Jaeschke**, Walter Henry 1909- *AmMWSc 92*
**Jafek**, Bev *DrAPF 91*
**Jafek**, Bruce William 1941- *AmMWSc 92*
**Jaffa**, George 1916- *WrDr 92*
**Jaffa**, Robert E 1935- *AmMWSc 92*
**Jaffar**, Khalid Mohammad 1922- *IntWW 91*
**Jaffe**, Alan Steven 1939- *WhoAmL 92*
**Jaffe**, Andrew Mark 1938- *WhoEnt 92, WhoFI 92*
**Jaffe**, Andrew Michael 1923- *IntWW 91*
**Jaffe**, Annette Bronkesh 1946- *AmMWSc 92*
**Jaffe**, Arthur Michael 1937- *AmMWSc 92*
**Jaffe**, Bernard Mordecai 1917- *AmMWSc 92*
**Jaffe**, Betsy *ConAu 135*
**Jaffe**, Bruce M. 1944- *WhoFI 92*
**Jaffe**, Dan *DrAPF 91*
**Jaffe**, David Bigman 1956- *WhoAmL 92*
**Jaffe**, Donald 1931- *AmMWSc 92*
**Jaffe**, Donald Nolan 1938- *WhoAmL 92*
**Jaffe**, Edward E 1928- *AmMWSc 92*
**Jaffe**, Eileen Karen 1954- *AmMWSc 92*
**Jaffe**, Elaine Sarkin 1943- *AmMWSc 92*
**Jaffe**, Elizabeth Latimer 1935- *ConAu 135*
**Jaffe**, Eric Allen 1942- *AmMWSc 92*
**Jaffe**, Ernst Richard 1925- *AmMWSc 92*
**Jaffe**, F. Filmore 1918- *WhoAmL 92*
**Jaffe**, Fred 1930- *AmMWSc 92*
**Jaffe**, Hans 1919- *AmMWSc 92*
**Jaffe**, Harold *DrAPF 91*
**Jaffe**, Harold 1930- *AmMWSc 92*
**Jaffe**, Herb *IntMPA 92*
**Jaffe**, Herb d1991 *NewYTBS 91*
**Jaffe**, Howard Lawrence 1955- *WhoRel 92*
**Jaffe**, Howard William 1919- *AmMWSc 92*
**Jaffe**, Ira Hugh 1945- *WhoEnt 92*
**Jaffe**, Ira Sheldon 1943- *WhoEnt 92*
**Jaffe**, Irving 1913- *WhoAmP 91*
**Jaffe**, Israeli Aaron 1927- *AmMWSc 92*
**Jaffe**, James Mark 1943- *AmMWSc 92*
**Jaffe**, James Martin 1949- *WhoEnt 92*
**Jaffe**, Jerry 1946- *WhoEnt 92*
**Jaffe**, Joan Feldgoise 1932- *WhoAmL 92*
**Jaffe**, Jonah 1929- *AmMWSc 92*
**Jaffe**, Julian Joseph 1926- *AmMWSc 92*
**Jaffe**, Karen Leslie 1952- *WhoMW 92*
**Jaffe**, Laurinda A 1952- *AmMWSc 92*
**Jaffe**, Lawrence Edward 1939- *WhoAmL 92, WhoFI 92*
**Jaffe**, Leo 1909- *IntMPA 92, WhoEnt 92*
**Jaffe**, Leonard 1926- *AmMWSc 92*
**Jaffe**, Leonard David 1919- *AmMWSc 92*
**Jaffe**, Lionel F 1927- *AmMWSc 92*
**Jaffe**, Louise *DrAPF 91*
**Jaffe**, Maggie *DrAPF 91*
**Jaffe**, Mark Lester 1958- *WhoEnt 92*
**Jaffe**, Mark M. 1941- *WhoAmL 92*
**Jaffe**, Marlyn Bloch 1964- *WhoRel 92*
**Jaffe**, Martin Steven 1948- *WhoMW 92*
**Jaffe**, Marvin Richard 1938- *AmMWSc 92*
**Jaffe**, Matthew Ely 1941- *WhoAmL 92*
**Jaffe**, Michael 1923- *Who 92, WrDr 92*
**Jaffe**, Michael 1942- *AmMWSc 92*
**Jaffe**, Miriam Walther 1922- *AmMWSc 92*
**Jaffe**, Mordecai J 1933- *AmMWSc 92*
**Jaffe**, Morry 1940- *AmMWSc 92*
**Jaffe**, Patricia Lewis 1924- *WhoEnt 92*
**Jaffe**, Paul Lawrence 1928- *WhoAmL 92*
**Jaffe**, Philip Monlane 1927- *AmMWSc 92*
**Jaffe**, Randal Craig 1947- *AmMWSc 92*
**Jaffe**, Richard Paul 1946- *WhoAmL 92*
**Jaffe**, Robert B 1933- *AmMWSc 92*
**Jaffe**, Robert Loren 1946- *AmMWSc 92*
**Jaffe**, Robert Mark 1953- *WhoEnt 92*
**Jaffe**, Robert Murray 1951- *WhoFI 92*
**Jaffe**, Rona *IntAu&W 91, WrDr 92*
**Jaffe**, Russell M 1947- *AmMWSc 92*
**Jaffe**, Samuel Zelmen 1922- *WhoRel 92*
**Jaffe**, Sigmund 1921- *AmMWSc 92*
**Jaffe**, Sol Samson 1920- *AmMWSc 92*
**Jaffe**, Stanley R. 1940- *IntMPA 92*
**Jaffe**, Stanley Richard 1940- *WhoEnt 92*
**Jaffe**, Steven-Charles 1954- *IntMPA 92*
**Jaffe**, Susan *DrAPF 91, WhoEnt 92*
**Jaffe**, Suzanne Denbo 1943- *WhoFI 92*
**Jaffe**, Werner G 1914- *AmMWSc 92*
**Jaffe**, William J 1910- *AmMWSc 92*
**Jaffe-Notier**, Peter Andrew 1947- *WhoMW 92*
**Jaffee**, Al 1921- *ConAu 135, SmATA 66*
**Jaffee**, Annette Williams *DrAPF 91*
**Jaffee**, Dwight M. 1943- *WhoFI 92*
**Jaffee**, Michael 1938- *WhoEnt 92*
**Jaffee**, Oscar Charles 1916- *AmMWSc 92*
**Jaffee**, Robert I 1917- *AmMWSc 92*
**Jaffee**, Sandra Schuyler 1943- *WhoFI 92*
**Jaffer**, Adrian Michael 1943- *WhoWest 92*
**Jaffer**, Frances *DrAPF 91*
**Jaffer**, Rashida Amin *WhoAmL 92*
**Jaffey**, Arthur Harold 1914- *AmMWSc 92*
**Jaffey**, Herbert *IntMPA 92*
**Jaffin**, David 1937- *ConAu 34NR, ConPo 91, WrDr 92*
**Jaffray**, Alistair Robert Morton 1925- *Who 92*
**Jaffray**, William Otho 1951- *Who 92*
**Jagadeesh**, Gowra G 1949- *AmMWSc 92*
**Jagan**, Cheddi 1918- *IntWW 91, Who 92*
**Jagan**, Janet 1920- *IntWW 91*
**Jagannath**, Sitaraman *WhoFI 92*
**Jagannathan**, Kannan 1954- *AmMWSc 92*
**Jagannathan**, S. 1914- *IntWW 91*
**Jagannathan**, Singanallur N 1934- *AmMWSc 92*
**Jagel**, Frederick 1897-1982 *NewAmDM*
**Jagel**, Kenneth I, Jr 1927- *AmMWSc 92*
**Jagendorf**, Andre Tridon 1926- *AmMWSc 92, IntWW 91*
**Jager**, Fred Gerrit 1938- *WhoFI 92*
**Jager**, Karl 1888-1959 *EncTR 91*
**Jager**, Martin Otto 1925- *WrDr 92*
**Jager**, Merle LeRoy 1942- *WhoWest 92*
**Jager**, Tammy Sue 1963- *WhoWest 92*
**Jagerman**, David Lewis 1923- *AmMWSc 92*
**Jaggard**, Dwight Lincoln 1948- *AmMWSc 92*
**Jagger**, Bianca 1950- *WhoEnt 92*
**Jagger**, Charles Sargeant 1885-1934 *TwCPaSc*
**Jagger**, Dean 1903-1991 *NewYTBS 91 [port]*
**Jagger**, John 1924- *AmMWSc 92*
**Jagger**, Mick 1943- *ConMus 7 [port], FacFETw [port], IntMPA 92, IntWW 91, NewAmDM, WhoEnt 92*
**Jagger**, Peter 1938- *WrDr 92*
**Jagger**, Peter John 1938- *WhoRel 92*

Jaggers, George Henry, Jr. 1926- WhoBlA 92
Jaggers, Steven Bryan 1962- WhoRel 92
Jaggi, Arvind 1960- WhoFI 92
Jaggs, Steve IntMPA 92
Jagiello, Appolonia 1825- EncAmaz 91
Jagiello, Georgiana Mary 1927- AmMWSc 92
Jagiello, Walter Edward 1930- WhoEnt 92
Jaglan, Prem S 1929- AmMWSc 92
Jaglom, Andre Richard 1953- WhoAmL 92
Jaglom, Henry 1943- IntMPA 92
Jaglom, Henry David 1941- WhoEnt 92
Jagnandan, Wilfred Lilpersaud 1920- WhoBlA 92
Jagner, Ronald Paul 1942- WhoMW 92
Jago, David Edgar John 1937- Who 92
Jagoda, Barry LesBEnT 92
Jagoda, Deborah Sheila Kavesh 1959- WhoAmL 92
Jagoda, Robert DrAPF 91
Jagodka, Paul Joseph 1957- WhoMW 92
Jagodzinski, Michael Norbert 1959- WhoFI 92
Jagow, Charles Herman 1910- WhoFI 92
Jahan, Marine 1958- WhoEnt 92
Jahan-Parwar, Behrus 1938- AmMWSc 92
Jaher, Frederic Cople 1934- WhoMW 92
Jaher, John d1991 NewYTBS 91
Jahiel, Rene 1928- AmMWSc 92
Jahier, Piero 1884-1966 DcLB 114 [port]
Jahn, Edwin Cornelius 1902- AmMWSc 92
Jahn, Ernesto 1942- AmMWSc 92
Jahn, Friedrich Ludwig 1778-1852 EncTR 91
Jahn, Gerhard 1927 IntWW 91
Jahn, Helmut 1940- WhoMW 92
Jahn, J Russell 1926- AmMWSc 92
Jahn, Laurence R 1926- AmMWSc 92
Jahn, Lawrence A 1941- AmMWSc 92
Jahn, Robert F WhoAmP 91
Jahn, Robert G 1930- AmMWSc 92
Jahn, Warren Thomas 1951- WhoMW 92
Jahn, Wolfgang 1918- Who 92
Jahngen, Edwin Georg Emil, Jr 1946- AmMWSc 92
Jahnke, Eric Richard 1954- WhoFI 92
Jahnke, John Curtis 1929- WhoMW 92
Jahnke, Monte Douglas 1946- WhoAmL 92
Jahnn, Hans Henny 1894-1959 EncTR 91, LiExTwC
Jahns, Fred H. 1956- WhoMW 92
Jahns, Hans O 1931- AmMWSc 92
Jahns, Jeffrey 1946- WhoAmL 92
Jahns, Monroe Frank 1928- AmMWSc 92
Jahns, T.R. DrAPF 91
Jahoda, Franz C 1930- AmMWSc 92
Jahoda, Fritz 1909- WhoEnt 92
Jahoda, Gerald 1925- AmMWSc 92
Jahoda, Gustav 1920- ConAu 135, Who 92
Jahoda, John C 1944- AmMWSc 92
Jahoda, Marie 1907- Who 92, WomPsyc
Jahr, Clifford d1991 NewYTBS 91
Jahr, John d1991 NewYTBS 91
Jahsman, William Edward 1926- AmMWSc 92
Jaicks, Frederick G AmMWSc 92
Jaicomo, Ronald James 1932- WhoAmL 92, WhoMW 92
Jaidah, Ali Mohammed 1941- IntWW 91
Jaikrishnan, Kadambi Rajgopal AmMWSc 92
Jaime, Francisco 1960- WhoHisp 92
Jaime, Gerardo Martin 1967- WhoHisp 92
Jaime, Kalani 1961- WhoHisp 92
Jaimovich, David Gerard 1954- WhoMW 92
Jain, Anant Vir 1940- AmMWSc 92
Jain, Anil Kumar 1946- AmMWSc 92
Jain, Anrudh Kumar 1941- AmMWSc 92
Jain, Aridaman Kumar 1938- AmMWSc 92
Jain, Duli Chandra 1929- AmMWSc 92
Jain, Girilal 1923- IntAu&W 91, IntWW 91
Jain, Himanshu 1955- AmMWSc 92
Jain, Kailash Chandra 1943- AmMWSc 92
Jain, Lalit K. 1944- WhoAmL 92
Jain, Mahavir 1941- AmMWSc 92
Jain, Mahendra Kumar 1929- AmMWSc 92
Jain, Mahendra Kumar 1938- AmMWSc 92
Jain, Naresh C 1932- AmMWSc 92
Jain, Nemichand B 1951- AmMWSc 92
Jain, Piyare Lal 1921- AmMWSc 92
Jain, Rajendra K. 1951- ConAu 134
Jain, Rakesh 1956- WhoFI 92
Jain, Rakesh Kumar 1950- AmMWSc 92
Jain, Ravinder Kumar 1935- AmMWSc 92
Jain, Subodh K 1934- AmMWSc 92
Jain, Surender K 1938- AmMWSc 92
Jain, Surendra Kumar 1922- IntWW 91
Jain, Sushil C 1939- AmMWSc 92
Jain, Sushil Kumar 1950- AmMWSc 92
Jain, Vijay Kumar 1937- AmMWSc 92
Jain, Vinod K. 1943- WhoMW 92
Jain, Vinod Kumar AmMWSc 92
Jainchill, Jerome 1932- AmMWSc 92
Jaine, Tom William Mahony 1943- Who 92
Jaisingh, Hari 1941- IntWW 91
Jaisinghani, Rajan A 1945- AmMWSc 92
Jaiswal, Arvind Kumar Jay 1943- WhoFI 92
Jaiswal, Gopaljee 1937- WhoAmL 92
Jajuga, James P WhoAmP 91
JAK Who 92
Jakab, George Joseph 1939- AmMWSc 92
Jakacky, John M 1956- AmMWSc 92
Jakala, Stanley H. 1926- WhoAmL 92
Jakeman, Eric 1939- Who 92
Jakes, Frank R. 1958- WhoAmL 92, WhoEnt 92
Jakes, Gerald Allan 1930- WhoMW 92
Jakes, John 1932- BenetAL 91, TwCSFW 91, TwCWW 91, WrDr 92
Jakes, Karen Sorkin 1947- AmMWSc 92
Jakes, Peter H. 1946- WhoAmL 92
Jakes, W C 1922- AmMWSc 92
Jakeway, Derek 1915- Who 92
Jakhar, Bal Ram 1923- IntWW 91
Jaki, Stanley L. 1924- IntWW 91
Jakins, Alan Richard 1951- WhoWest 92
Jakle, Kenneth Richard 1942- WhoEnt 92
Jaklevic, Joseph Michael 1941- AmMWSc 92
Jaklevic, Robert C 1934- AmMWSc 92
Jaklitsch, Joseph John, Jr. 1919- WhoEnt 92
Jaklitsch, Richard Louis 1958- WhoAmL 92
Jakmauh, Edward 1942- WhoFI 92
Jako, Geza Julius 1930- WhoAmP 91
Jakob, Fredi 1934- AmMWSc 92
Jakob, Karl Michael 1921- AmMWSc 92
Jakobiec, Frederick Albert AmMWSc 92
Jakobovits Who 92
Jakobovits, Baron 1921- IntWW 91, Who 92
Jakobovits, Immanuel 1921- WhoRel 92
Jakobsen, Frode 1906- IntWW 91
Jakobsen, Johan J. 1937- IntWW 91
Jakobsen, Mimi 1948- IntWW 91
Jakobsen, Robert John 1929- AmMWSc 92
Jakobson, Mark John 1923- AmMWSc 92
Jakobson, Max 1923- IntWW 91
Jakobsson, Eric Gunnar, Sr 1938- AmMWSc 92
Jakoby, William Bernard 1928- AmMWSc 92
Jakoi, Emma Raff 1946- AmMWSc 92
Jakosa, Jody Young 1957- WhoAmL 92
Jakowatz, Charles V 1920- AmMWSc 92
Jakowska, Sophie 1922- AmMWSc 92
Jaksy, Joseph J d1991 NewYTBS 91
Jakubauskas, Edward Benedict 1930- WhoMW 92
Jakubiec, Robert Joseph 1941- AmMWSc 92
Jakubowicz, Robert F 1932- WhoAmP 91
Jakubowski, Gerald S 1949- AmMWSc 92
Jakubowski, Hieronim Zbigniew 1946- AmMWSc 92
Jakubowski, Janusz Lech 1905- IntWW 91
Jakubowski, Thad J. WhoRel 92
Jakus, Karl 1938- AmMWSc 92
Jakus, Marie A 1914- AmMWSc 92
Jakvani, Shoukat Majid 1955- WhoWest 92
Jakway, George Elmer 1931- AmMWSc 92
Jakway, Jacqueline Sinks 1928- AmMWSc 92
Jalajas, Emil Walter Peter 1960- WhoWest 92
Jalal, Mahsoun B. 1936- IntWW 91
Jalal, Syed M 1938- AmMWSc 92
Jalan, Bimal IntWW 91
Jalan, Vinod Motilal 1943- AmMWSc 92
Jalan-Aajav, Sampilyn 1923- IntWW 91
Jalbert, Jeffrey Scott 1940- AmMWSc 92
Jalbert, Joe Jay IntMPA 92
Jalbert, John 1925- WhoAmP 91
Jalbert, Michael Joseph 1951- WhoAmL 92
Jalife, Jose 1947- AmMWSc 92
Jalil, Mazhar 1938- AmMWSc 92
Jalland, Pat 1941- ConAu 133
Jalland, William Herbert Wainwright 1922- Who 92
Jallins, Richard David 1957- WhoAmL 92
Jalloud, Abdul Salam Ahmed 1944- IntWW 91
Jalonen, Nancy Lee 1927- WhoEnt 92
Jalufka, Nelson Wayne 1932- AmMWSc 92
Jaluria, Yogesh 1949- AmMWSc 92
Jam, Jimmy WhoBlA 92
Jamail, Joseph Dahr, Jr. 1925- WhoAmL 92
Jamail, Randall WhoEnt 92
Jamal, Ahmad WhoEnt 92
Jamal, Ahmad 1930- NewAmDM, WhoBlA 92
Jamal, Amir Habib 1922- IntWW 91
Jamal, Jasim Yousif 1940- IntWW 91
Jamal, Moez Ahamed 1955- WhoFI 92
Jamaludeen, Abdul Hamid 1945- WhoBlA 92
Jamalzade, Mohammed Ali 1895?- FacFETw
Jamar, John Philip 1961- WhoMW 92
Jamar, Peter Norton 1957- WhoWest 92
Jamar, Steven Dwight 1953- WhoAmL 92
Jamasbi, Roudabeh J AmMWSc 92
Jamba, Sousa 1966- ConAu 134
Jambor, Agi 1909- IntWW 91
Jambor, David Freeman 1954- WhoMW 92
Jambor, Louise Irma WhoAmP 91
Jambor, Paul Emil 1937- AmMWSc 92
Jamerson, Doug 1947- WhoAmP 91
Jamerson, Frank Edward 1927- AmMWSc 92
Jamerson, Jerome Donnell 1950- WhoBlA 92
Jamerson, John William, Jr. 1910- WhoBlA 92
James EncEarC, Who 92
James I 1394-1437 RfGEnL 91
James, A. Lincoln, Sr. WhoRel 92
James, Advergus Dell, Jr. 1944- WhoBlA 92
James, Alan 1943- IntAu&W 91, WrDr 92
James, Alexander, Jr. 1933- WhoBlA 92
James, Alice 1848-1892 BenetAL 91, HanAmWH
James, Allix Bledsoe 1922- WhoBlA 92, WhoRel 92
James, Alton Everette, Jr 1938- AmMWSc 92
James, Andrew IntAu&W 91X
James, Anne Eleanor S. Who 92
James, Anthony Trafford 1922- IntWW 91, Who 92
James, Arlo D 1931- WhoAmP 91
James, Arminta Susan 1924- WhoBlA 92
James, Arthur Walter 1912- Who 92
James, Aubrey Graham Wallen 1918- Who 92
James, Barbara Ann 1951- WhoMW 92
James, Barry Ray 1956- WhoFI 92, WhoMW 92
James, Basil 1918- Who 92
James, Bela Michael 1940- AmMWSc 92
James, Betty Harris 1932- WhoBlA 92
James, Betty L. 1921- WhoMW 92
James, Betty Nowlin 1936- WhoBlA 92
James, Bill ConAu 35NR, WrDr 92
James, Bill 1949- WrDr 92
James, Bill 1951- WhoEnt 92
James, Bob 1939- WhoEnt 92
James, Bobby Charles 1946- WhoBlA 92
James, Brian Robert 1936- AmMWSc 92
James, Bushrod Washington 1836-1903 BiInAmS
James, C L R 1901-1989 FacFETw, LiExTwC
James, Carlos Adrian 1946- WhoBlA 92
James, Carolyne Faye 1945- WhoEnt 92
James, Carrie Houser 1949- WhoBlA 92
James, Cary TwCWW 91
James, Cecil Who 92
James, Charles Alexander 1922- WhoBlA 92
James, Charles Edwin Frederic 1943- Who 92
James, Charles Ford 1935- WhoBlA 92
James, Charles Franklin, Jr 1931- AmMWSc 92
James, Charles Howell, II 1930- WhoBlA 92
James, Charles L. 1934- WhoBlA 92
James, Charles William 1929- AmMWSc 92
James, Christopher John 1932- Who 92
James, Christopher Philip 1934- Who 92
James, Christopher Robert 1935- AmMWSc 92
James, Clarence L., Jr. 1933- WhoBlA 92
James, Clifton 1925- IntMPA 92
James, Clive 1939- WrDr 92
James, Clive Vivian Leopold 1939- IntAu&W 91, IntWW 91, Who 92
James, Colin Clement Walter Who 92
James, Connie Sue 1947- WhoRel 92
James, Craig T. 1941- AlmAP 92 [port], WhoAmP 91
James, Cy TwCWW 91
James, Cynlais Morgan 1926- IntWW 91, Who 92
James, Cynthia Ann 1954- WhoMW 92
James, Dan TwCWW 91
James, Dan 1951- WhoEnt 92
James, Daniel Shaw 1933- AmMWSc 92
James, Daryl Edward 1958- WhoMW 92
James, Dava Paulette WhoBlA 92
James, David DrAPF 91
James, David Edward 1937- Who 92, WrDr 92
James, David Eugene 1945- AmMWSc 92
James, David Evan 1939- AmMWSc 92
James, David F 1939- AmMWSc 92
James, David Geraint 1922- Who 92, WrDr 92
James, David Gwynfor 1925- Who 92
James, David Harold 1942- WhoFI 92
James, David Lee 1933- WhoWest 92
James, David Phillip 1940- WhoBlA 92
James, David William Francis 1929- Who 92
James, David Winston 1929- AmMWSc 92
James, Dean B 1934- AmMWSc 92
James, Dennis LesBEnT 92
James, Dennis 1917- IntMPA 92
James, Derek Claude 1929- Who 92
James, Dion 1962- WhoBlA 92
James, Donald Gordon 1938- AmMWSc 92
James, Dorothy 1901-1982 NewAmDM
James, Dorothy Marie 1936- WhoBlA 92
James, Douglas Craig 1938- WhoEnt 92
James, Douglas Garfield Limbrey 1924- AmMWSc 92
James, Dynely SmATA 68
James, E Pendleton 1929- WhoAmP 91
James, Earl Eugene, Jr. 1923- WhoFI 92
James, Eddie William 1939- WhoRel 92
James, Edgar 1915- Who 92
James, Edgar C. 1933- WhoMW 92, WhoRel 92
James, Edith Joyce 1926- WhoFI 92
James, Edmund Purcell S. Who 92
James, Edward, Jr 1917- AmMWSc 92
James, Edward Foster 1917- Who 92
James, Edwin 1797-1861 BenetAL 91, BiInAmS
James, Edwin Kenneth George 1916- Who 92
James, Eleanor Mary 1935- Who 92
James, Elizabeth 1945- WrDr 92
James, Elridge M. 1942- WhoBlA 92
James, Eric Arthur 1925- Who 92
James, Ernest Gethin 1925- Who 92
James, Ernest Wilbur 1931- WhoMW 92
James, Estelle 1935- WhoFI 92
James, Etta 1938- ConMus 6 [port], NewAmDM, WhoBlA 92
James, Evan Maitland 1911- Who 92
James, Felix 1937- WhoBlA 92
James, Forrest Hood, Jr. 1934- IntWW 91
James, Frances Crews 1930- AmMWSc 92
James, Francis Edward 1849-1920 TwCPaSc
James, Francis Edward, Jr. 1931- WhoFI 92
James, Frank Samuel, III 1945- WhoBlA 92
James, Franklin Ward 1922- AmMWSc 92
James, Frederick C. 1922- WhoBlA 92
James, Frederick Calhoun 1922- WhoRel 92
James, Frederick John 1938- WhoBlA 92
James, Garth A 1926- AmMWSc 92
James, Gary Miles 1962- WhoEnt 92
James, George Barker, II 1937- WhoFI 92, WhoWest 92
James, George Ellert 1917- AmMWSc 92
James, George Lawrence 1947- BlkOlyM
James, George W 1949- ConAu 35NR
James, George Watson, III 1918- AmMWSc 92
James, Geraint Who 92
James, Geraldine 1950- IntWW 91, Who 92
James, Gethin Who 92
James, Gideon T 1927- AmMWSc 92
James, Gillette Oriel 1935- WhoBlA 92
James, Gordon, III 1947- WhoAmL 92
James, Gordon Thomas 1940- AmMWSc 92
James, Gregory Creed 1956- WhoBlA 92
James, Gregory Michael 1966- WhoFI 92
James, Gregory Robert, Jr. 1959- WhoAmL 92
James, Gus John, II 1938- WhoAmL 92
James, H Grady, III 1945- WhoAmP 91
James, H. Rhett 1928- WhoBlA 92
James, Hamice R., Jr. 1929- WhoBlA 92
James, Harold 1942- WhoAmP 91
James, Harold 1956- IntWW 91
James, Harold L. 1912- IntWW 91
James, Harold Lee 1939- AmMWSc 92
James, Harold Lloyd 1912- AmMWSc 92
James, Harry 1916-1983 FacFETw, NewAmDM
James, Harry 1931- WhoAmP 91
James, Helen Jane 1943- AmMWSc 92
James, Henry 1843-1916 FacFETw [port], LiExTwC, RComAH, RfGEnL 91, ShSCr 8 [port], ThHElm [port]
James, Henry, Jr. 1843-1916 BenetAL 91
James, Henry, Sr. 1811-1882 BenetAL 91
James, Henry Grady, III 1945- WhoBlA 92
James, Henry Gray DrAPF 91
James, Henry Leonard 1919- Who 92
James, Henry Nathaniel 1908- WhoBlA 92
James, Herb Mark 1936- WhoWest 92

**James**, Herbert I 1933- *AmMWSc 92, WhoBlA 92*
**James**, Herman Delano 1943- *WhoBlA 92*
**James**, Hinton 1776-1847 *DcNCBi 3*
**James**, Hinton 1884-1948 *DcNCBi 3*
**James**, Horace 1818-1875 *DcNCBi 3*
**James**, Howard Oland, Sr. 1941- *WhoRel 92*
**James**, Howell Malcolm Plowden 1954- *Who 92*
**James**, Hugh Neal 1952- *WhoEnt 92*
**James**, Hugo A 1930- *AmMWSc 92*
**James**, Hytolia Roberts 1928- *WhoBlA 92*
**James**, Ioan Mackenzie 1928- *IntWW 91, Who 92*
**James**, Isaac 1914- *WhoBlA 92*
**James**, Jack N 1920- *AmMWSc 92*
**James**, Jefferson Ann 1943- *WhoEnt 92*
**James**, Jeffrey 1944- *AmMWSc 92*
**James**, Jeffrey Allen 1962- *WhoAmL 92*
**James**, Jennifer Austin 1943- *WhoFI 92*
**James**, Jennifer Siboney *WhoEnt 92*
**James**, Jerry Lee 1945- *WhoRel 92*
**James**, Jesse 1847-1882 *BenetAL 91*
**James**, Jesse 1937- *AmMWSc 92*
**James**, Jessica 1929- *WhoEnt 92*
**James**, Jessica 1931?-1990 *ConTFT 9*
**James**, Joan Noble Grace 1960- *WhoAmL 92*
**James**, John 1906- *Who 92*
**James**, John A. *Who 92*
**James**, John Alan 1927- *WhoFI 92*
**James**, John Anthony 1913- *Who 92*
**James**, John Cary 1926- *AmMWSc 92*
**James**, John Christopher Urmston 1937- *Who 92*
**James**, John Douglas 1949- *Who 92*
**James**, John Henry 1944- *Who 92*
**James**, John Ivor Pulsford 1913- *Who 92, WrDr 92*
**James**, John Jocelyn S. *Who 92*
**James**, John Morrice Cairns *IntWW 91*
**James**, John Nigel Courtenay 1935- *Who 92*
**James**, John Sullivan 1957- *WhoEnt 92*
**James**, John Warren 1944- *WhoWest 92*
**James**, Jonathan Elwyn Rayner 1950- *Who 92*
**James**, Joni *WhoEnt 92*
**James**, Joseph Francis 1857-1897 *BiInAmS*
**James**, Josephine *AmPeW*
**James**, Joyce L. 1950- *WhoBlA 92*
**James**, Juanita T. 1952- *WhoBlA 92*
**James**, June, III 1934- *WhoBlA 92*
**James**, Karen K 1944- *AmMWSc 92*
**James**, Kay C. 1949- *WhoBlA 92*
**James**, Keith Alan 1957- *WhoAmL 92*
**James**, Kelvin Christopher *DrAPF 91*
**James**, Kenneth *Who 92*
**James**, Kenneth Eugene 1942- *AmMWSc 92*
**James**, L Allan 1949- *AmMWSc 92*
**James**, Larry George 1947- *AmMWSc 92*
**James**, Larry Michael 1950- *WhoMW 92*
**James**, Laurence 1942- *TwCWW 91*
**James**, Laurence Beresford 1916- *AmMWSc 92*
**James**, Laurence Joseph 1934- *WhoMW 92, WhoRel 92*
**James**, Laurie Harper 1930- *WhoEnt 92*
**James**, Laylin Knox, Jr 1927- *AmMWSc 92*
**James**, Lee Morton 1916- *AmMWSc 92*
**James**, Lionel Frederic Edward 1912- *Who 92*
**James**, Livia *TwCWW 91*
**James**, Lorene 1945- *WhoMW 92*
**James**, Louis 1933- *WrDr 92*
**James**, Luther 1928- *WhoBlA 92, WhoEnt 92*
**James**, M R 1862-1936 *FacFETw, RfGEnL 91*
**James**, Marie Moody 1928- *WhoMW 92, WhoRel 92*
**James**, Marilyn Shaw 1926- *WhoMW 92*
**James**, Marion Ray 1940- *WhoFI 92*
**James**, MarLynn Rees 1933- *AmMWSc 92*
**James**, Marquis 1891-1955 *BenetAL 91*
**James**, Marquita L. 1932- *WhoBlA 92*
**James**, Martin *ConAu 35NR, DrAPF 91*
**James**, Mary *WrDr 92*
**James**, Mary F 1915- *WhoAmP 91*
**James**, Mary Frances 1913- *AmMWSc 92*
**James**, Matthew *WrDr 92*
**James**, Merlin Lehn 1922- *AmMWSc 92*
**James**, Michael *Who 92*
**James**, Michael Leonard 1941- *IntWW 91, Who 92*
**James**, Michael Norman George 1940- *Who 92*
**James**, Michael Royston 1950- *AmMWSc 92*
**James**, Michael Thames 1949- *WhoFI 92*
**James**, Nancy Esther *DrAPF 91*
**James**, Naomi 1949- *Who 92*
**James**, Naomi Ellen 1927- *WhoBlA 92*
**James**, Noel David Glaves 1911- *IntAu&W 91, Who 92, WrDr 92*
**James**, Odette Bricmont 1942- *AmMWSc 92*
**James**, P. D. *Who 92*
**James**, P.D. 1920- *CnDBLB 8 [port], ConNov 91, IntAu&W 91, WrDr 92*
**James**, P D 1923- *FacFETw*
**James**, Patrick Leonard 1926- *Who 92*
**James**, Peggi C. 1940- *WhoBlA 92*
**James**, Peter Maunde Coram 1922- *Who 92*
**James**, Philip *Who 92*
**James**, Philip 1890-1975 *NewAmDM*
**James**, Philip Benjamin 1940- *AmMWSc 92*
**James**, Philip J. 1938- *WhoWest 92*
**James**, Philip Nickerson 1932- *AmMWSc 92*
**James**, Philip Seaforth 1914- *Who 92, WrDr 92*
**James**, Polly *IntMPA 92*
**James**, R V Rhodes 1933- *IntAu&W 91, WrDr 92*
**James**, Ralph Boyd 1953- *AmMWSc 92*
**James**, Ralph L 1941- *AmMWSc 92*
**James**, Ray 1948- *WhoMW 92*
**James**, Raymond N. 1933- *WhoBlA 92*
**James**, Richard Austin 1920- *Who 92*
**James**, Richard L. 1926- *WhoBlA 92*
**James**, Richard M. 1946- *WhoFI 92*
**James**, Richard Stephen 1940- *AmMWSc 92*
**James**, Rick *WhoBlA 92*
**James**, Rick 1955- *WhoEnt 92*
**James**, Robert Brian 1950- *WhoEnt 92*
**James**, Robert Clarke 1918- *AmMWSc 92*
**James**, Robert D. 1950- *WhoBlA 92*
**James**, Robert Earl 1946- *WhoBlA 92*
**James**, Robert Leo 1936- *WhoFI 92*
**James**, Robert Michael 1934- *Who 92*
**James**, Robert Scott 1943- *WhoMW 92*
**James**, Robert Vidal R. *Who 92*
**James**, Robin 1953- *IntAu&W 91*
**James**, Robison Brown 1931- *WhoAmP 91*
**James**, Roland Orlando 1958- *WhoBlA 92*
**James**, Ronald 1950- *WhoBlA 92*
**James**, Ronald Albert 1945- *WhoMW 92*
**James**, Ronald Harvey 1948- *WhoAmP 91*
**James**, Ronald J. 1937- *WhoBlA 92*
**James**, Ronald Valdemar 1943- *AmMWSc 92*
**James**, Sandra Elaine 1956- *WhoWest 92*
**James**, Sharpe *WhoAmP 91*
**James**, Sharpe 1936- *WhoBlA 92*
**James**, Sheila *Who 92*
**James**, Sherman Athonia 1943- *AmMWSc 92*
**James**, Sibyl *DrAPF 91*
**James**, Sidney J. 1935- *WhoBlA 92*
**James**, Sidney Lorraine 1906- *WhoEnt 92*
**James**, Sondra Diane 1952- *WhoEnt 92, WhoWest 92*
**James**, Stanley D 1932- *AmMWSc 92*
**James**, Stanley Francis 1927- *Who 92*
**James**, Stephanie *WrDr 92*
**James**, Stephanie Lynn *AmMWSc 92*
**James**, Stephen Elisha 1942- *WhoBlA 92, WhoMW 92*
**James**, Stephen Lawrence 1930- *Who 92*
**James**, Stephen P 1947- *AmMWSc 92*
**James**, Steven Wynne Lloyd 1934- *Who 92*
**James**, Susannah *WrDr 92*
**James**, Sydney V. 1929- *WrDr 92*
**James**, Ted Ralph 1936- *AmMWSc 92*
**James**, Theodore, Jr. 1934- *WrDr 92*
**James**, Thomas Arthur, Jr. 1948- *WhoAmL 92*
**James**, Thomas Cecil 1918- *Who 92*
**James**, Thomas Garnet Henry 1923- *IntWW 91, Who 92*
**James**, Thomas Geraint Illtyd 1900- *Who 92*
**James**, Thomas Larry 1944- *AmMWSc 92*
**James**, Thomas Naum 1925- *AmMWSc 92*
**James**, Thomas Potts 1803-1882 *BiInAmS*
**James**, Thomas Ray 1946- *AmMWSc 92*
**James**, Thomas Stuart 1930- *WhoAmL 92*
**James**, Thomas William 1918- *AmMWSc 92*
**James**, Tim 1942- *WhoAmL 92*
**James**, Timothy Arcee 1962- *WhoBlA 92*
**James**, Troy Lee *WhoAmP 91*
**James**, Troy Lee 1924- *WhoBlA 92*
**James**, Uriah Pierson 1811-1889 *BiInAmS*
**James**, V Eugene 1929- *AmMWSc 92*
**James**, Vanessa *ConAu 134*
**James**, Vernon G 1910- *WhoAmP 91*
**James**, Vivian Hector Thomas 1924- *Who 92*
**James**, W Gerald 1922- *AmMWSc 92*
**James**, Walter *Who 92*
**James**, Walter 1915- *WhoMW 92*
**James**, Walter 1924- *Who 92*
**James**, Warren A. 1960- *ConAu 133*
**James**, Wayne Edward 1950- *WhoWest 92*
**James**, Will 1892-1942 *BenetAL 91, TwCWW 91*
**James**, William *FacFETw, WhoRel 92*
**James**, William 1842-1910 *AmPeW, BiInAmS, RComAH*
**James**, William 1910- *BenetAL 91*
**James**, William 1945- *WhoBlA 92*
**James**, William Albert 1947- *WhoMW 92*
**James**, William Holden 1909- *AmMWSc 92*
**James**, William Joseph 1922- *AmMWSc 92*
**James**, William Langford 1939- *WhoWest 92*
**James**, William M. *TwCWW 91, WrDr 92*
**James**, William M. 1916- *WhoBlA 92*
**James**, William Philip 1938- *Who 92*
**James**, William Ramsay 1933- *WhoEnt 92, WhoFI 92*
**James**, William Thomas 1950- *WhoMW 92*
**James**, William W. 1931- *WhoFI 92, WhoMW 92*
**James-Jensen**, Laura Ann 1961- *WhoMW 92*
**James-Moore**, Jonathan Guy 1946- *Who 92*
**James Of Holland Park**, Baroness 1920- *IntWW 91, Who 92*
**James Of Rusholme**, Baron 1909- *IntWW 91, Who 92*
**James-Strand**, Nancy Kay Leabhard 1943- *WhoMW 92*
**Jameson**, A Keith 1933- *AmMWSc 92*
**Jameson**, Arthur Gregory 1915- *AmMWSc 92*
**Jameson**, Charles Scott Kennedy 1925- *WhoWest 92*
**Jameson**, Charles William 1948- *AmMWSc 92*
**Jameson**, David Lee 1927- *AmMWSc 92*
**Jameson**, Derek 1929- *Who 92*
**Jameson**, Donald Albert 1929- *AmMWSc 92*
**Jameson**, Dorothea 1920- *AmMWSc 92*
**Jameson**, Eric *WrDr 92*
**Jameson**, Everett Williams, Jr 1921- *AmMWSc 92*
**Jameson**, Grace Klein 1924- *WhoAmP 91*
**Jameson**, James Larry 1937- *WhoFI 92*
**Jameson**, James Larry 1954- *AmMWSc 92*
**Jameson**, Jay Marshall 1943- *WhoFI 92*
**Jameson**, Jerry *IntMPA 92*
**Jameson**, Patricia Madoline 1939- *AmMWSc 92*
**Jameson**, Patrick Geraint 1912- *Who 92*
**Jameson**, Paula Ann 1945- *WhoAmL 92*
**Jameson**, Ray Brent 1964- *WhoWest 92*
**Jameson**, Richard 1944- *WhoEnt 92*
**Jameson**, Richard P. *WhoRel 92*
**Jameson**, Robert A 1937- *AmMWSc 92*
**Jameson**, Storm 1891-1986 *FacFETw*
**Jameson**, Susan Peter 1955- *WhoEnt 92*
**Jameson**, Victor Loyd 1924- *WhoRel 92*
**Jameson**, William J, Jr 1930- *AmMWSc 92*
**Jamie**, Kathleen 1962- *ConPo 91, WrDr 92*
**Jamieson**, Alexander MacRae 1944- *AmMWSc 92*
**Jamieson**, Brian George 1943- *Who 92*
**Jamieson**, D Donald 1926- *WhoAmP 91*
**Jamieson**, David Auldjo 1920- *Who 92*
**Jamieson**, David Ewan 1930- *Who 92*
**Jamieson**, Derek Maitland 1930- *AmMWSc 92*
**Jamieson**, Ewan *Who 92*
**Jamieson**, Glen Stewart *AmMWSc 92*
**Jamieson**, Graham Archibald 1929- *AmMWSc 92*
**Jamieson**, Hamish Thomas Umphelby *Who 92*
**Jamieson**, Harvey Morro H. *Who 92*
**Jamieson**, Ian Wyndham 1920- *Who 92*
**Jamieson**, J A 1929- *AmMWSc 92*
**Jamieson**, James C 1939- *AmMWSc 92*
**Jamieson**, James Douglas 1934- *AmMWSc 92*
**Jamieson**, John Edward, Jr. 1945- *WhoRel 92*
**Jamieson**, John Kenneth 1910- *IntWW 91, Who 92*
**Jamieson**, Kenneth Douglas 1921- *Who 92*
**Jamieson**, Leah H 1949- *AmMWSc 92*
**Jamieson**, Leland, Jr. *DrAPF 91*
**Jamieson**, Mary Jeanette *WhoAmP 91*
**Jamieson**, Michael Lawrence 1940- *WhoAmL 92*
**Jamieson**, Norman Clark 1935- *AmMWSc 92*
**Jamieson**, Penelope Ann Bansall *Who 92*
**Jamieson**, R Bruce 1935- *WhoIns 92*
**Jamieson**, Reginald Mac 1927- *WhoIns 92*
**Jamieson**, Robert Kirkland 1881-1950 *TwCPaSc*
**Jamieson**, Stephen Allen 1958- *WhoWest 92*
**Jamieson**, William David 1929- *AmMWSc 92*
**Jamieson-Magathan**, Esther R 1937- *AmMWSc 92*
**Jamil Rais**, Abdul *Who 92*
**Jamin**, Matthew Daniel 1947- *WhoAmL 92*
**Jamir**, S. C. 1931- *IntWW 91*
**Jamison**, Birdie Hairston 1957- *WhoBlA 92*
**Jamison**, David W. 1939- *WhoWest 92*
**Jamison**, H F *ScFEYrs*
**Jamison**, Homer Claude 1921- *AmMWSc 92*
**Jamison**, James Hardie 1913- *Who 92*
**Jamison**, James Kenneth 1931- *Who 92*
**Jamison**, Joel Dexter 1932- *AmMWSc 92*
**Jamison**, John Ambler 1916- *WhoAmL 92*
**Jamison**, Joseph Vanjamin 1933- *WhoRel 92*
**Jamison**, Judith 1943- *WhoBlA 92*
**Jamison**, Judith 1944- *NotBlAW 92 [port], WhoEnt 92*
**Jamison**, King W, Jr 1931- *AmMWSc 92*
**Jamison**, Lafayette 1926- *WhoBlA 92*
**Jamison**, Leila Duncan 1932- *WhoBlA 92*
**Jamison**, Mark Allen 1956- *WhoMW 92*
**Jamison**, Marshall Shipman 1918- *WhoEnt 92*
**Jamison**, Michael Howard 1950- *WhoRel 92*
**Jamison**, Nadine 1938- *WhoAmP 91*
**Jamison**, Richard Melvin 1938- *AmMWSc 92*
**Jamison**, Robert Edward 1948- *AmMWSc 92*
**Jamison**, Robin Ralph d1991 *Who 92N*
**Jamison**, Robin Ralph 1912- *IntWW 91*
**Jamison**, Roger W. 1937- *WhoEnt 92, WhoMW 92*
**Jamison**, Ronald D 1931- *AmMWSc 92*
**Jamison**, Sheila Ann English 1950- *WhoFI 92*
**Jamison**, William H 1932- *AmMWSc 92*
**Jammal**, A. Salah 1940- *WhoEnt 92*
**Jammes**, Francis 1868-1938 *GuFrLit 1*
**Jammu**, K S 1935- *AmMWSc 92*
**Jamnback**, Hugo Andrew, Jr 1926- *AmMWSc 92*
**Jampala**, Sadasiva B. 1951- *WhoMW 92*
**Jampel**, Robert Steven 1926- *AmMWSc 92*
**Jamplis**, Robert W 1920- *AmMWSc 92*
**Jampol**, Craig Brian 1957- *WhoFI 92*
**Jampolis**, Neil Peter 1943- *WhoEnt 92*
**Jampolsky**, Arthur 1919- *AmMWSc 92*
**Jamrich**, John Xavier 1920- *AmMWSc 92*
**Jamshidi**, Mohammad Mo 1944- *AmMWSc 92*
**Jan**, George Pokung 1925- *WhoMW 92*
**Jan**, Kung-Ming *AmMWSc 92*
**Janabil** 1934- *IntWW 91*
**Janac**, Lou *DrAPF 91*
**Janacek**, Leos 1854-1928 *FacFETw, NewAmDM*
**Janak**, James Francis 1938- *AmMWSc 92*
**Janakananda**, Swami Rajasi 1892-1955 *RelLAm 91*
**Janakidevi**, K *AmMWSc 92*
**Janas**, Gregory 1949- *WhoAmP 91*
**Janaszek**, Barbara Jessie 1950- *WhoAmL 92*
**Janata**, Jiri 1939- *AmMWSc 92*
**Janatova**, Jarmila 1929- *AmMWSc 92*
**Janauer**, Gilbert E 1931- *AmMWSc 92*
**Janavaras**, Basil John 1943- *WhoMW 92*
**Janca**, Frank Charles 1946- *AmMWSc 92*
**Jancarik**, Jiri 1941- *AmMWSc 92*
**Janco**, Marcel 1895-1984 *FacFETw*
**Jancso**, Miklos 1921- *IntDcF 2-2 [port], IntWW 91*
**Janda**, Bruce Willis 1954- *WhoMW 92*
**Janda**, John Michael 1949- *AmMWSc 92*
**Janda**, Kenneth Carl 1950- *AmMWSc 92*
**Janda**, Michael Lawrence 1954- *WhoAmL 92*
**Janda**, Richard Charles 1964- *WhoFI 92*
**Jandacek**, Ronald James 1942- *AmMWSc 92*
**Jande**, Sohan Singh 1933- *AmMWSc 92*
**Jandl**, Ernst 1925- *IntAu&W 91, IntWW 91*
**Jandl**, James Harriman 1925- *AmMWSc 92*
**Jandorf**, Bernard Joseph 1915- *AmMWSc 92*
**Jandro**, Luis Allan 1918- *WhoWest 92*
**Jandura**, Louise 1962- *WhoWest 92*
**Jane**, Countess of Montfort *EncAmaz 91*
**Jane**, Alexander Lesole 1945- *IntWW 91*
**Jane**, Fred 1865-1916 *ScFEYrs*
**Jane**, John Anthony 1931- *AmMWSc 92*
**Janecke**, Joachim Wilhelm 1929- *AmMWSc 92, WhoMW 92*
**Janecky**, David Richard 1953- *WhoWest 92*
**Janek**, Adeline 1942- *WhoFI 92*
**Janequin**, Clement 1485?-1558 *NewAmDM*
**Jane's Addiction** *ConMus 6 [port]*
**Janes**, Alfred 1911- *TwCPaSc*
**Janes**, Brandon Chaison 1951- *WhoAmL 92*

Janes, Donald Lucian 1939- AmMWSc 92
Janes, Donald Wallace 1929- AmMWSc 92
Janes, Douglas 1918- Who 92
Janes, George Sargent 1927- AmMWSc 92
Janes, J. Robert 1935- WrDr 92
Janes, Loren 1931- WhoEnt 92
Janes, Mervyn 1920- Who 92
Janes, Norman 1892-1980 TwCPaSc
Janes, Robert James 1925- WhoAmP 91
Janes, William Michael 1940- WhoFI 92
Janes, William Sargent 1953- WhoFI 92
Janeski, William Louis 1932- WhoWest 92
Janet, Lillian WrDr 92
Janet, Pierre 1859-1947 FacFETw
Janetatos, Jack Peter 1934- WhoAmL 92
Janetzke, Douglas Kirk 1948- WhoRel 92
Janeway, Charles Alderson, Jr 1943- AmMWSc 92
Janeway, Edward Gamaliel 1841-1911 BiInAmS
Janeway, Eliot 1913- IntWW 91, WrDr 92
Janeway, Elizabeth DrAPF 91
Janeway, Elizabeth 1913- BenetAL 91
Janeway, Elizabeth Hall 1913- IntWW 91
Janeway, Richard 1933- AmMWSc 92, IntWW 91
Janeway, Theodore Caldwell 1872-1917 BiInAmS
Janezich, Jerry R 1950- WhoAmP 91
Jang, Sei Joo 1947- AmMWSc 92
Jangaard, Norman Olaf 1941- AmMWSc 92
Jangdharrie, Wycliffe K. 1926- WhoBlA 92
Janger, Allen R. 1932- WrDr 92
Janger, Allen Robert 1932- IntAu&W 91
Janger, Kathleen N. 1940- SmATA 66
Janghorbani, Morteza 1943- AmMWSc 92
Janiak, Anthony Richard, Jr. 1946- WhoFI 92
Janiak, Thomas Anthony 1949- WhoEnt 92
Janich, George Peter 1929- WhoIns 92
Janick, Herbert Frederick, III 1959- WhoAmL 92
Janick, Jules 1931- AmMWSc 92, WhoMW 92
Janicki, Bernard William 1931- AmMWSc 92
Janicki, Casimir A 1934- AmMWSc 92
Janicki, Czeslaw 1926- IntWW 91
Janicki, Jerzy 1928- IntAu&W 91
Janicki, Steven George 1953- WhoEnt 92
Janiczek, Paul Michael 1937- AmMWSc 92
Janifer, Laurence M 1933- IntAu&W 91, TwCSFW 91, WrDr 92
Janigian, Bruce Jasper 1950- WhoWest 92
Janigro, Antonio 1918-1989 NewAmDM
Janik, Borek 1933- AmMWSc 92
Janik, Gerald S 1940- AmMWSc 92
Janik, Phyllis DrAPF 91
Janine-Marie de Foix EncAmaz 91
Janion, Hugh 1923- Who 92
Janis, Allen Ira 1930- AmMWSc 92
Janis, Barbara 1942- WhoAmP 91
Janis, Brian Charles 1959- WhoWest 92
Janis, Byron 1928- NewAmDM, WhoEnt 92
Janis, Christine Marie 1950- AmMWSc 92
Janis, Conrad WhoEnt 92
Janis, F Timothy 1940- AmMWSc 92
Janis, Robert Samuel 1958- WhoFI 92
Janis, Ronald Allen 1943- AmMWSc 92
Janischewskyj, W 1925- AmMWSc 92
Janiszewski, Michal 1926- IntWW 91
Janiw, Wolodymyr 1908- IntAu&W 91
Janke, Kenneth 1934- WhoFI 92
Janke, Lynn M. 1955- WhoMW 92
Janke, Norman C 1923- AmMWSc 92
Janke, Norman Charles 1923- WhoWest 92
Janke, Robert A 1922- AmMWSc 92
Janke, Robert Arthur 1922- WhoMW 92
Janke, Roger Alvin 1938- WhoRel 92
Janke, Ronald Robert 1947- WhoAmL 92
Janke, Wilfred Edwin 1932- AmMWSc 92
Janklow, William John 1939- IntWW 91, WhoAmP 91
Janko, Paul von 1856-1919 NewAmDM
Jankovic, Tomislav 1933- IntWW 91
Jankowitsch, Peter 1933- IntWW 91
Jankowski, Christopher K 1940- AmMWSc 92
Jankowski, Conrad M 1928- AmMWSc 92
Jankowski, Francis James 1922- AmMWSc 92
Jankowski, Gene F. LesBEnT 92
Jankowski, Gene F. 1934- IntMPA 92
Jankowski, Paul G. 1966- WhoEnt 92
Jankowski, Peter M 1962- WhoAmP 91
Jankowski, Robert John 1941- WhoFI 92
Jankowski, Stanley John 1928- AmMWSc 92
Jankowsky, Joel WhoAmL 92
Jankura, Donald Eugene 1929- WhoWest 92
Jankus, Edward Francis 1930- AmMWSc 92
Jankus, Vytautas Zachary 1919- AmMWSc 92
Janky, Douglas Michael 1946- AmMWSc 92
Janky, Gladyce O. 1953- WhoFI 92
Janman, Timothy Simon 1956- Who 92
Jann, Donn Gerard 1929- WhoRel 92
Janna, William Sied 1949- AmMWSc 92
Jannarone, Mike S. 1963- WhoEnt 92
Jannasch, Holger Windekilde 1927- AmMWSc 92
Janneh, Bocar Ousman S. Who 92
Jannelli, Tony 1950- WhoEnt 92
Jannequin, Clement NewAmDM
Janner, Lady Who 92
Janner, Greville Ewan 1928- Who 92
Jannes, Christopher Peter 1963- WhoAmL 92
Jannett, Frederick Joseph, Jr 1946- AmMWSc 92
Jannetta, Peter Joseph 1932- AmMWSc 92
Janney, Clinton Dales 1920- AmMWSc 92
Janney, Donald Herbert 1931- AmMWSc 92
Janney, Donald Wayne 1952- WhoAmL 92
Janney, Gareth Maynard 1934- AmMWSc 92
Janni, Joseph 1916- IntMPA 92
Janning, Mary Bernadette 1917- WhoRel 92
Jannings, Emil 1884-1950 EncTR 91 [port]
Jannotti, Harry Peter 1924- WhoAmP 91
Janoff, Aaron 1930- AmMWSc 92
Janoff, Ronald Wiley DrAPF 91
Janofsky, Bonnie Ruth 1953- WhoEnt 92
Janos, David Paul 1947- AmMWSc 92
Janos, Joseph John, III 1953- WhoAmL 92
Janos, Ludvik 1922- AmMWSc 92, WhoWest 92
Janos, William Augustus 1926- AmMWSc 92
Janosch 1931- ChlLR 26 [port]
Janoski, Henry Valentine 1933- WhoFI 92
Janosko, Linda 1949- WhoEnt 92
Janot, Raymond Marcel Louis 1917- IntWW 91
Janota, Harvey Franklin 1935- AmMWSc 92
Janousek, Arnold Lee 1930- WhoMW 92
Janov, Lauren Lynn 1958- WhoAmL 92
Janover, Robert H. 1930- WhoMW 92
Janovy, John, Jr 1937- AmMWSc 92
Janowicz, Peter Francis 1940- WhoWest 92
Janowitz, Gerald S 1943- AmMWSc 92
Janowitz, Gundula 1937- IntWW 91
Janowitz, Gundula 1939- NewAmDM
Janowitz, Henry David 1915- AmMWSc 92
Janowitz, Melvin Fiva 1929- AmMWSc 92
Janowitz, Phyllis DrAPF 91
Janowitz, Phyllis 1940- IntAu&W 91
Janowitz, Tama DrAPF 91
Janowitz, Tama 1957- ConNov 91, WrDr 92
Janowski, Jan Stanislaw 1928- IntWW 91
Janowski, Marek IntWW 91
Janowski, Marek 1940- NewAmDM
Janowski, Marek G. 1939- WhoEnt 92
Janowski, Max 1912-1991 NewYTBS 91
Janowski, Thaddeus-Marian 1923- WrDr 92
Janowsky, David Steffan 1939- AmMWSc 92
Janowsky, Oscar I. 1900- WrDr 92
Jans, James Patrick 1927- AmMWSc 92
Jansen, A M d1914 BiInAmS
Jansen, Ann Kealey 1959- WhoAmL 92
Jansen, Bernard Joseph 1927- AmMWSc 92
Jansen, Cornelius 1586-1638 BlkwCEP
Jansen, Daniel Ervin 1965- WhoMW 92
Jansen, Dennis William 1956- WhoFI 92
Jansen, Donald Orville 1939- WhoAmL 92
Jansen, E. Harold 1930- WhoRel 92
Jansen, Elly 1929- Who 92
Jansen, Frank 1946- AmMWSc 92
Jansen, Gail 1946- WhoEnt 92
Jansen, George, Jr 1934- AmMWSc 92
Jansen, George James 1925- AmMWSc 92
Jansen, Gustav Richard 1930- AmMWSc 92, WhoWest 92
Jansen, Hank IntAu&W 91X
Jansen, Hendrik 1742-1812 BlkwCEP
Jansen, Henricus Cornelis 1942- AmMWSc 92
Jansen, Ivan John 1941- AmMWSc 92
Jansen, Jan Kristian Schoning 1931- IntWW 91
Jansen, Jared WrDr 92
Jansen, John Carl 1947- WhoEnt 92
Jansen, Marius B. 1922- WrDr 92
Jansen, Michael 1956- AmMWSc 92
Jansen, Michael E. 1946- WrDr 92
Jansen, Peter Johan 1940- IntWW 91, Who 92
Jansen, Robert Bruce 1922- AmMWSc 92
Jansen, Ross 1932- Who 92
Jansing, Jo Ann 1938- AmMWSc 92
Janski, Alvin Michael 1949- AmMWSc 92
Jansky, Sandra W. 1949- WhoFI 92
Jansma, Theodore John, Jr. 1943- WhoMW 92
Janson, Agnes WhoWest 92
Janson, Blair F 1918- AmMWSc 92
Janson, H W 1913-1982 FacFETw
Janson, Marilyn 1936- WhoRel 92
Janson, Richard Wilford 1926- WhoMW 92
Janson, Teunis Nicolaas Hendrik 1919- IntWW 91
Janson, Thomas 1947- WhoMW 92
Jansons, Andrejs 1938- WhoEnt 92
Jansons, Maris Arvidovich 1943- IntWW 91
Jansons, Mariss 1943- WhoEnt 92
Jansons, Vilma Karina AmMWSc 92
Janssen, Allen S 1907- AmMWSc 92
Janssen, Charles Albert 1954- WhoAmL 92
Janssen, Daniel 1936- IntWW 91
Janssen, Frank Walter 1926- AmMWSc 92
Janssen, Jerry Frederick 1936- AmMWSc 92
Janssen, Michael Allen 1937- AmMWSc 92
Janssen, Orville Henry 1926- WhoRel 92
Janssen, Paul-Emmanuel 1931- IntWW 91
Janssen, Richard William 1940- AmMWSc 92
Janssen, Robert J 1931- AmMWSc 92
Janssen, Werner 1899- NewAmDM
Janssen, Werner 1899-1990 FacFETw
Jansson, Birger 1921- AmMWSc 92
Jansson, David Guild AmMWSc 92
Jansson, Erik DcAmImH
Jansson, Jan-Magnus 1922- IntWW 91
Jansson, Peter Allan 1942- AmMWSc 92
Jansson, Peter N 1944- WhoAmP 91
Jansz, Hendrik Simon 1927- IntWW 91
Jantz, Harold David 1937- WhoRel 92
Jantz, O K 1934- AmMWSc 92
Jantz, Paul Richard 1952- WhoEnt 92
Jantz, Waldemar 1955- WhoFI 92
Jantz, William Ernest 1953- WhoFI 92
Jantzen, Jens Carsten 1948- WhoWest 92
Jantzen, John Marc 1908- WhoWest 92
January, Lewis Edward 1910- AmMWSc 92
Janura, Jan Arol 1949- WhoFI 92, WhoWest 92
Janus, Alan Robert 1937- AmMWSc 92
Janus, Julie WhoEnt 92
Janus, Sam 1930- ConAu 134
Janusek, Linda Witek 1952- AmMWSc 92
Janusz, Gerald Joseph 1940- AmMWSc 92
Janusz, Michael John 1954- AmMWSc 92
Janutolo, Delano Blake 1952- AmMWSc 92
Janutolo, Sarah Catherine 1935- WhoMW 92
Janvier, Thomas A. 1849-1913 BenetAL 91, ScFEYrs
Janvrin, Richard Benest 1915- Who 92
Janvrin, Robin Berry 1946- Who 92
Janway, Jack Lee 1954- WhoEnt 92
Janz, George John 1917- AmMWSc 92
Janzen, Alexander Frank 1940- AmMWSc 92
Janzen, Betty Lou 1922- WhoAmP 91
Janzen, Daniel Hunt 1939- AmMWSc 92, IntWW 91
Janzen, Edward George 1932- AmMWSc 92
Janzen, Jacob John 1919- WhoAmP 91
Janzen, Jay 1940- AmMWSc 92
Janzen, Jean DrAPF 91
Janzen, John Gerald 1932- WhoRel 92
Janzen, Norine Madelyn Quinlan 1943- WhoMW 92
Janzon, Bengt, Mrs. Who 92
Janzow, Edward F 1941- AmMWSc 92
Jaouni, Katherine Cook 1929- AmMWSc 92
Jaouni, Taysir M 1924- AmMWSc 92
Japan, Emperor of IntWW 91, Who 92
Japar, Steven Martin 1944- AmMWSc 92
Japp, Darsie 1883-1973 TwCPaSc
Jaqua, Frederick William 1921- WhoAmL 92
Jaques, Carlos Eduardo 1946- WhoHisp 92
Jaques, Elliott 1917- Who 92, WrDr 92
Jaques, Louis Barker 1911- AmMWSc 92, WrDr 92
Jaques, Robert Paul 1931- AmMWSc 92
Jaques, William Everett 1917- AmMWSc 92
Jaques, William Henry 1848-1916 BiInAmS
Jaques-Dalcroze, Emile 1865-1950 NewAmDM
Jaquette, Peter Barnes 1952- WhoFI 92
Jaquiss, Donald B G 1929- AmMWSc 92
Jaquith, George Oakes 1916- WhoWest 92
Jaquith, Richard Herbert 1919- AmMWSc 92
Jarabo, Jose R 1944- WhoAmP 91
Jaramillo, Ann WhoHisp 92
Jaramillo, Annabelle E. 1940- WhoHisp 92
Jaramillo, Anthony B. 1959- WhoHisp 92
Jaramillo, Arthur Lewis 1949- WhoAmL 92
Jaramillo, Debbie WhoHisp 92
Jaramillo, Delio Arturo, Jr. 1965- WhoHisp 92
Jaramillo, Ellen M. 1952- WhoHisp 92
Jaramillo, Ernesto 1963- WhoHisp 92
Jaramillo, George WhoHisp 92
Jaramillo, Henry, Jr. 1928- WhoHisp 92
Jaramillo, Jeannine D. 1960- WhoHisp 92
Jaramillo, Jorge 1934- AmMWSc 92
Jaramillo, Mari-Luci 1928- WhoHisp 92
Jaramillo, Rudy WhoHisp 92
Jaramillo de Estrada, Cleopatra Marie 1951- WhoHisp 92
Jaray, Paul 1889-1974 DcTwDes, FacFETw
Jaray, Tess 1937- IntWW 91, TwCPaSc
Jarboe, Charles Harry 1928- AmMWSc 92
Jarboe, John A 1933- WhoIns 92
Jarboe, Mark Alan 1951- WhoAmL 92
Jarboe, Robert Steven 1951- WhoRel 92
Jarboe, Thomas Richard 1945- AmMWSc 92
Jarbola, Andrew John, III 1959- WhoAmL 92
Jarboro, Caterina 1903-1986 NewAmDM
Jarc, Frank Robert 1942- WhoFI 92
Jarcho, Leonard W. 1916- WhoWest 92
Jarcho, Leonard Wallenstein 1916- AmMWSc 92
Jarcho, Saul 1906- AmMWSc 92
Jarchow, Homer E WhoAmP 91
Jardetzky, Oleg 1929- AmMWSc 92
Jardim, Oswaldo Veiga 1959- WhoEnt 92
Jardine, Andrew 1955- Who 92
Jardine, Andrew Rupert Buchanan- 1923- Who 92
Jardine, D A 1930- AmMWSc 92
Jardine, Don Leroy 1926- WhoMW 92
Jardine, George 1920- TwCPaSc
Jardine, Ian 1948- AmMWSc 92
Jardine, James Christopher Macnaughton 1930- Who 92
Jardine, John Frederick James d1990 Who 92N
Jardine, John McNair 1919- AmMWSc 92
Jardine, John Scott 1955- WhoWest 92
Jardine, Leslie James 1945- WhoWest 92
Jardine, Ronald Charles C. Who 92
Jardine, Rupert Buchanan- Who 92
Jardine of Applegirth, Alexander Maule 1947- Who 92
Jardine Paterson, John 1920- Who 92
Jardon, John Raymond 1948- WhoFI 92, WhoMW 92
Jared, Alva Harden 1934- AmMWSc 92
Jared, Jerry A WhoAmP 91
Jarem, John 1921- AmMWSc 92
Jares, Joe 1937- WrDr 92
Jares, Joseph Frank 1937- IntAu&W 91
Jaress, Jill Ann 1952- WhoEnt 92
Jarett, Leonard 1936- AmMWSc 92
Jargiello, Patricia 1944- AmMWSc 92
Jargon, Jerry Robert 1939- AmMWSc 92
Jariwala, Sharad Lallubhai 1940- AmMWSc 92
Jariwalla, Raxit Jayantilal 1949- AmMWSc 92
Jarke, Frank Henry 1946- AmMWSc 92
Jarkovsky, Isaac 1926- WhoAmL 92
Jarmakani, Jay M AmMWSc 92
Jarman, Claude, Jr. 1934- IntMPA 92
Jarman, Claude Miller, Jr. 1934- WhoEnt 92
Jarman, Derek 1942- ConTFT 9, IntDcF 2-2 [port], IntWW 91, TwCPaSc, Who 92
Jarman, Douglas 1942- ConAu 133
Jarman, Franklin Maxey 1931- IntWW 91
Jarman, Joseph 1937- NewAmDM
Jarman, Mark DrAPF 91
Jarman, Mark Foster 1952- IntAu&W 91
Jarman, Martha Foley 1927- WhoAmP 91
Jarman, Nicholas Francis Barnaby 1938- Who 92
Jarman, Roger Whitney 1935- Who 92
Jarman, Rosemary Hawley 1935- WrDr 92
Jarmer, Gary Edward 1941- WhoMW 92
Jarmick, Christopher James 1956- WhoEnt 92
Jarmie, Nelson 1928- AmMWSc 92
Jarmolowski, Jerzy 1940- IntAu&W 91
Jarmon, James Henry, Jr. 1942- WhoBlA 92
Jarmus, Stephan Onysym 1925- WhoRel 92
Jarmusch, Jim WhoEnt 92
Jarmusch, Jim 1953- ConTFT 9, IntDcF 2-2, IntMPA 92, IntWW 91
Jarmusz, Diane 1952- WhoFI 92

**Jarnach,** Philipp 1892-1982 *NewAmDM*
**Jarnagan,** Harry William, Jr. 1953- *WhoFI 92*
**Jarnagin,** Richard Calvin 1930- *AmMWSc 92*
**Jarnes,** Benjamin 1888-1949 *LiExTwC*
**Jarocki,** Jerzy 1929- *IntWW 91*
**Jaroff,** Leon Morton 1927- *ConAu 135*
**Jarolin,** Stanley J 1933- *WhoAmP 91*
**Jarolmen,** Howard 1937- *AmMWSc 92*
**Jaron,** Dov 1935- *AmMWSc 92*
**Jaros,** Arthur George 1922- *WhoFI 92*
**Jaros,** Jerome Edward 1944- *WhoFI 92*
**Jaros,** Mike 1944- *WhoAmP 91*
**Jaros,** Peter 1940- *IntAu&W 91*
**Jaros,** Robert James 1939- *WhoFI 92*
**Jaros,** Stanley E 1919- *AmMWSc 92*
**Jaroska,** Faythe Ann 1945- *WhoAmP 91*
**Jaroski,** Edward L 1946- *WhoIns 92*
**Jaroski,** Edward Leonard 1946- *WhoFI 92*
**Jaroslawicz,** David 1947- *WhoAmL 92*
**Jaross,** Andor 1896-1946 *BiDExR*
**Jarosz,** Frederick John 1929- *WhoIns 92*
**Jaroudi,** Saeb 1929- *IntWW 91*
**Jarowinsky,** Werner 1927- *IntWW 91*
**Jarowski,** Charles I 1917- *AmMWSc 92*
**Jarratt,** Alexander Anthony 1924- *IntWW 91, Who 92*
**Jarratt,** Peter 1935- *Who 92*
**Jarre,** Jean-Michel Andre 1948- *IntWW 91*
**Jarre,** Maurice 1924- *IntMPA 92, NewAmDM*
**Jarre,** Maurice Alexis 1924- *WhoEnt 92*
**Jarreau,** Al 1940- *WhoBlA 92, WhoEnt 92*
**Jarrell,** Benjamin Franklin 1880-1946 *DcNCBi 3*
**Jarrell,** John W. *WhoMW 92*
**Jarrell,** Joseph Andy 1950- *AmMWSc 92*
**Jarrell,** Mack 1926- *WhoAmP 91*
**Jarrell,** Mary Long 1929- *WhoAmP 91*
**Jarrell,** Randall 1914-1965 *BenetAL 91, ConAu 34NR, DcNCBi 3, FacFETw*
**Jarrell,** Thomas Jefferson 1901-1985 *DcNCBi 3*
**Jarrell,** Wesley Michael 1948- *AmMWSc 92*
**Jarres,** Karl 1874-1951 *EncTR 91*
**Jarret,** Ronald Marcel 1960- *AmMWSc 92*
**Jarrett,** Alexis 1948- *WhoFI 92, WhoMW 92*
**Jarrett,** Charles E. 1957- *WhoAmL 92*
**Jarrett,** Charles William 1948- *WhoMW 92*
**Jarrett,** Clifford 1909- *Who 92*
**Jarrett,** Derek 1928- *WrDr 92*
**Jarrett,** Diana Louise *WhoEnt 92*
**Jarrett,** Emmett *DrAPF 91*
**Jarrett,** Harry Wellington, III 1950- *AmMWSc 92*
**Jarrett,** Hobart Sidney 1915- *WhoBlA 92*
**Jarrett,** Howard Starke, Jr 1927- *AmMWSc 92*
**Jarrett,** Jeffrey E 1940- *AmMWSc 92*
**Jarrett,** Keith 1945- *IntWW 91, NewAmDM, WhoEnt 92*
**Jarrett,** Mary Olive 1947- *WhoFI 92*
**Jarrett,** Mitzi Marie 1961- *WhoRel 92*
**Jarrett,** Noel 1921- *AmMWSc 92*
**Jarrett,** Ronald Douglas 1952- *WhoWest 92*
**Jarrett,** Roxanne *ConAu 34NR*
**Jarrett,** Steven Michael 1936- *AmMWSc 92*
**Jarrett,** Susan 1948- *WhoEnt 92*
**Jarrett,** Sylvester 1926- *IntWW 91*
**Jarrett,** Thomas D. 1912- *WhoBlA 92*
**Jarrett,** Vernon D. 1921- *WhoBlA 92*
**Jarrett,** William Fleming Hoggan 1928- *IntWW 91, Who 92*
**Jarrico,** Paul 1915- *IntMPA 92, WhoEnt 92*
**Jarriel,** Tom *LesBEnT 92*
**Jarrin,** Jaime 1935- *WhoHisp 92*
**Jarring,** Gunnar 1907- *IntWW 91, Who 92*
**Jarrold and Sons** *DcLB 106*
**Jarrold,** Kenneth Wesley 1948- *Who 92*
**Jarrold,** Nicholas Robert 1946- *Who 92*
**Jarroll,** Edward Lee, Jr 1948- *AmMWSc 92*
**Jarrott,** Charles 1927- *IntMPA 92*
**Jarrow,** Bishop Suffragan of 1936- *Who 92*
**Jarry,** Alfred 1873-1907 *FacFETw, GuFrLit 1*
**Jaruzelski,** Janina Anne 1958- *WhoAmL 92*
**Jaruzelski,** John Janusz 1926- *AmMWSc 92*
**Jaruzelski,** Wojciech 1923- *IntWW 91*
**Jaruzelski,** Wojciech 1923- *FacFETw*
**Jarves,** Deming 1790-1869 *BiInAmS*
**Jarves,** James Jackson 1818-1888 *BenetAL 91*
**Jarvey,** Paulette Sue 1945- *WhoFI 92*
**Jarvi,** Dennis Wade 1941- *WhoMW 92*
**Jarvi,** Esa Tero 1954- *AmMWSc 92*
**Jarvi,** Neeme 1937- *FacFETw, IntWW 91, Who 92, WhoEnt 92, WhoMW 92*
**Jarvi,** Osmo Henrik 1911- *IntWW 91*
**Jarvik,** Jonathan Wallace 1945- *AmMWSc 92*
**Jarvik,** Lissy F *AmMWSc 92*
**Jarvik,** Murray Elias 1923- *AmMWSc 92*
**Jarvik,** Robert Koffler 1946- *IntWW 91*
**Jarvinen,** Richard Dalvin 1938- *AmMWSc 92, WhoAmP 91*
**Jarvis,** Barbara Ann 1946- *WhoFI 92*
**Jarvis,** Bruce B 1942- *AmMWSc 92*
**Jarvis,** Charlene Drew 1941- *WhoAmP 91*
**Jarvis,** Charlene Marie 1964- *WhoWest 92*
**Jarvis,** Charles Windle 1950- *WhoAmP 91*
**Jarvis,** Christine Woodruff 1949- *AmMWSc 92*
**Jarvis,** Donald Bertram 1928- *WhoWest 92*
**Jarvis,** E. K. *ConAu 36NR*
**Jarvis,** Edward 1803-1884 *BiInAmS*
**Jarvis,** Edward Curtis 1951- *WhoFI 92*
**Jarvis,** Floyd Eldridge, Jr 1921- *AmMWSc 92*
**Jarvis,** Frederick Frank 1924- *Who 92*
**Jarvis,** Gary Lee 1949- *WhoRel 92*
**Jarvis,** Gary Lee 1955- *WhoFI 92*
**Jarvis,** Graham Powley 1930- *WhoEnt 92*
**Jarvis,** Gregory 1941-1986 *FacFETw*
**Jarvis,** Harold Lewis 1930- *WhoRel 92*
**Jarvis,** Howard 1902-1986 *FacFETw*
**Jarvis,** Hugh John 1930- *Who 92*
**Jarvis,** Jack Reynolds 1915- *AmMWSc 92*
**Jarvis,** James Gordon 1924- *AmMWSc 92*
**Jarvis,** James Howard, II 1937- *WhoAmL 92*
**Jarvis,** Jeffrey Scott 1952- *WhoEnt 92*
**Jarvis,** John Cecil 1949- *WhoAmL 92*
**Jarvis,** John Frederick 1941- *AmMWSc 92*
**Jarvis,** John J 1941- *AmMWSc 92*
**Jarvis,** John Manners 1947- *Who 92*
**Jarvis,** Kent Graham 1942- *WhoWest 92*
**Jarvis,** Lactance Aubrey 1921- *AmMWSc 92*
**Jarvis,** Lucy *LesBEnT 92*
**Jarvis,** Martin 1941- *IntAu&W 91, Who 92*
**Jarvis,** Neldon Lynn 1935- *AmMWSc 92*
**Jarvis,** Patrick William 1926- *Who 92*
**Jarvis,** Polly Stevens 1939- *WhoRel 92*
**Jarvis,** Richard S 1949- *AmMWSc 92*
**Jarvis,** Robert Mark 1959- *WhoAmL 92*
**Jarvis,** Roger George 1928- *AmMWSc 92*
**Jarvis,** Roland 1926- *TwCPaSc*
**Jarvis,** Sharon 1943- *IntAu&W 91*
**Jarvis,** Simon Michael *AmMWSc 92*
**Jarvis,** Susan D. 1955- *WhoFI 92*
**Jarvis,** Thomas d1694 *DcNCBi 3*
**Jarvis,** Thomas Jordan 1836-1915 *DcNCBi 3*
**Jarvis,** William Chapman 1855-1895 *BiInAmS*
**Jarvis,** William Robert 1927- *AmMWSc 92*
**Jarvis,** William Tyler 1935- *AmMWSc 92*
**Jarzebski,** Stefan 1917- *IntWW 91*
**Jarzen,** David MacArthur 1941- *AmMWSc 92*
**Jarzynski,** Jacek 1935- *AmMWSc 92*
**Jasanoff,** Sheila Sen 1944- *AmMWSc 92*
**Jasch,** Laura Gwendolyn 1945- *AmMWSc 92*
**Jasek,** Diane Martha 1955- *WhoAmP 91*
**Jaselskis,** Bruno 1924- *AmMWSc 92*
**Jasen,** Matthew Joseph 1915- *WhoAmP 91*
**Jashnani,** Indru 1944- *AmMWSc 92*
**Jasica,** Andrea Lynn 1945- *WhoFI 92*
**Jasien,** Deborah Anne 1954- *WhoEnt 92*
**Jasin,** Hugo E 1933- *AmMWSc 92*
**Jasinski,** Donald Robert 1938- *AmMWSc 92*
**Jasinski,** George John 1954- *WhoAmL 92*
**Jasinski,** Jerry Peter 1940- *AmMWSc 92*
**Jasinski,** Roman 1907-1991 *NewYTBS 91*
**Jaske,** Carl Edward 1943- *WhoMW 92*
**Jaskiernia,** Jerzy 1950- *IntWW 91*
**Jaskoski,** Benedict Jacob 1915- *AmMWSc 92*
**Jaskowiak,** Robert Bryan 1959- *WhoAmL 92*
**Jaskulski,** Robert W 1926- *WhoAmP 91*
**Jaskwhich,** Michael F 1942- *WhoAmP 91*
**Jasmin,** Ernest Augustus 1934- *WhoAmL 92*
**Jasmin,** Gaetan 1924- *AmMWSc 92*
**Jasmund,** Elizabeth Donlin 1959- *WhoAmL 92*
**Jasny,** George R 1924- *AmMWSc 92*
**Jason,** Andrew John 1938- *AmMWSc 92*
**Jason,** Emil Fred 1927- *AmMWSc 92*
**Jason,** Henry Thomas 1921- *WhoBlA 92*
**Jason,** J. Julie 1949- *WhoAmL 92*
**Jason,** J. Paul 1955- *WhoFI 92*
**Jason,** Jeanne 1934- *WhoBlA 92*
**Jason,** Jerry *TwCSFW 91, WrDr 92*
**Jason,** Johnny *IntAu&W 91X*
**Jason,** Judy B. *DrAPF 91*
**Jason,** Katherine 1953- *IntAu&W 91*
**Jason,** Mark Edward 1949- *AmMWSc 92*
**Jason,** Michael *DrAPF 91*
**Jason,** Philip K. *DrAPF 91*
**Jason,** Philip K 1941- *ConAu 35NR*
**Jason,** Rick 1926- *IntMPA 92*
**Jason,** Stuart *IntAu&W 91X*
**Jason,** Sybil *WhoEnt 92*
**Jason,** Veronica *WrDr 92*
**Jasper,** Barry Lewis 1939- *WhoMW 92*
**Jasper,** Christopher Howard 1951- *WhoEnt 92*
**Jasper,** David 1951- *WhoRel 92*
**Jasper,** Donald Edward 1918- *AmMWSc 92*
**Jasper,** Donald K *AmMWSc 92*
**Jasper,** Doris Jean Berry 1933- *WhoMW 92*
**Jasper,** Heinrich 1875-1945 *EncTR 91*
**Jasper,** Herbert Henry 1906- *AmMWSc 92*
**Jasper,** John J. 1812-1901 *BenetAL 91*
**Jasper,** Joseph J. 1927- *WhoAmL 92*
**Jasper,** Lawrence E. 1946- *WhoBlA 92*
**Jasper,** Margaret Catherine 1954- *WhoEnt 92*
**Jasper,** Martin Theophilus 1934- *AmMWSc 92*
**Jasper,** Robert Lawrence 1918- *AmMWSc 92*
**Jasper,** Robin Leslie Darlow 1914- *Who 92*
**Jasper,** Samuel Jacob 1921- *AmMWSc 92*
**Jasper,** Seymour 1919- *WhoAmL 92*
**Jasper,** Shawn N 1959- *WhoAmP 91*
**Jaspers,** Karl 1883-1969 *EncTR 91 [port], FacFETw*
**Jaspers,** Louis J. 1928- *WhoRel 92*
**Jasperse,** Craig Peter 1960- *AmMWSc 92*
**Jasperse,** John Milton 1922- *WhoFI 92*
**Jasperse,** John R 1935- *AmMWSc 92*
**Jaspersen,** Frederick Zarr 1938- *WhoFI 92*
**Jasperson,** Stephen Newell 1941- *AmMWSc 92*
**Jasrai,** Puntsagiin 1933- *IntWW 91*
**Jass,** Herman Earl 1918- *AmMWSc 92*
**Jassby,** Daniel Lewis 1942- *AmMWSc 92*
**Jasso,** Hermilo 1959- *WhoHisp 92*
**Jasso,** Paula Inosencia 1951- *WhoHisp 92*
**Jasso,** William Gattis 1953- *WhoMW 92*
**Jassy,** Everett Lewis 1937- *WhoAmL 92*
**Jastak,** J Theodore 1936- *AmMWSc 92*
**Jastrab,** Kathleen Marie 1958- *WhoRel 92*
**Jastram,** Daniel Norman 1955- *WhoRel 92*
**Jastram,** Philip Sheldon 1920- *AmMWSc 92*
**Jastram,** Roy W. d1991 *NewYTBS 91*
**Jastrow,** Joseph 1863-1944 *BenetAL 91*
**Jastrow,** Marie d1991 *NewYTBS 91*
**Jastrow,** Robert 1925- *AmMWSc 92, IntWW 91, WrDr 92*
**Jaswal,** Sitaram Singh 1937- *AmMWSc 92*
**Jaszberenyi,** Joseph C 1948- *AmMWSc 92*
**Jaszczak,** Ronald Jack 1942- *AmMWSc 92*
**Jatlow,** J L 1903- *AmMWSc 92*
**Jatoi,** Ghulam Mustafa *IntWW 91*
**Jatti,** Basappa Danappa 1912- *IntWW 91*
**Jauch,** Robert 1945- *WhoAmP 91*
**Jauchem,** Esquire 1947- *WhoEnt 92*
**Jauchem,** James Robert 1951- *AmMWSc 92*
**Jaucourt,** Louis, chevalier de 1704-1780 *BlkwCEP*
**Jaudel,** Jean Emmanuel 1910- *IntWW 91*
**Jaudes,** Richard Edward 1943- *WhoAmL 92*
**Jaudes,** William E. 1937- *WhoAmL 92*
**Jauhar,** Prem P 1939- *AmMWSc 92*
**Jauho,** Pekka Antti Olavi 1923- *IntWW 91*
**Jaume,** William 1954- *WhoHisp 92*
**Jaumot,** Frank Edward, Jr 1923- *AmMWSc 92*
**Jaumotte,** Andre 1919- *IntWW 91*
**Jaunarena,** Jose Horacio 1942- *IntWW 91*
**Jauncey** *Who 92*
**Jauncey of Tullichettle,** Baron 1925- *Who 92*
**Jauquet-Kalinoski,** Barbara 1948- *WhoMW 92*
**Jauregui,** Gabriel Ruben, Sr. 1941- *WhoHisp 92*
**Jauregui,** Gaston A. 1943- *WhoHisp 92*
**Jaures,** Jean 1859-1914 *FacFETw*
**Jauss,** Anne Marie d1991 *NewYTBS 91*
**Jauss,** Anne Marie 1902?-1991 *ConAu 135*
**Jauss,** David *DrAPF 91*
**Jaussi,** August Wilhelm 1925- *AmMWSc 92*
**Javadpour,** Nasser 1937- *AmMWSc 92*
**Javaher,** James N 1924- *AmMWSc 92*
**Javaid,** Javaid Iqbal 1942- *AmMWSc 92*
**Javalera,** Elizabeth Rico 1934- *WhoRel 92*
**Javan,** Ali 1926- *AmMWSc 92*
**Javel,** Eric 1947- *AmMWSc 92*
**Javick,** Richard Anthony 1932- *AmMWSc 92*
**Javid,** Mansour 1919- *AmMWSc 92*
**Javid,** Manucher J 1922- *AmMWSc 92*
**Javidi,** Bahram 1959- *AmMWSc 92*
**Javier,** Rafael Art 1948- *WhoHisp 92*
**Javier,** Stan 1965- *WhoHisp 92*
**Javierre Ortas,** Antonio Maria 1921- *IntWW 91, WhoRel 92*
**Javits,** Jacob 1904-1986 *FacFETw*
**Javits,** Joshua Moses 1950- *WhoFI 92*
**Javitt,** Norman B 1928- *AmMWSc 92*
**Javor,** Frank A. 1916- *ConAu 135*
**Javor,** Kenneth D 1948- *WhoIns 92*
**Javorsky,** Henry V. 1912- *WhoEnt 92*
**Jawa,** Manjit S 1934- *AmMWSc 92*
**Jawad,** Maan Hamid 1943- *AmMWSc 92*
**Jawara,** Dawda 1924- *IntWW 91*
**Jawara,** Dawda Kairaba 1924- *Who 92*
**Jawed,** Inam 1947- *AmMWSc 92*
**Jaweed,** Mazher *AmMWSc 92*
**Jawetz,** Ernest 1916- *AmMWSc 92*
**Jawien,** Andrzej *ConAu 133*
**Jaworowski,** Andrzej Edward 1942- *AmMWSc 92*
**Jaworowski,** Jan W 1928- *AmMWSc 92*
**Jaworski,** Casimir A 1930- *AmMWSc 92*
**Jaworski,** David Joseph 1952- *WhoFI 92*
**Jaworski,** Ernest George 1926- *AmMWSc 92*
**Jaworski,** Francis Anthony *ConAu 135*
**Jaworski,** Jan Guy 1946- *AmMWSc 92*
**Jaworski,** Leon 1905-1982 *FacFETw*
**Jaworski,** Rosanne 1952- *WhoRel 92*
**Jay** *Who 92*
**Jay and the Americans** *NewAmDM*
**Jay,** Baron 1907- *IntWW 91, Who 92*
**Jay,** Allen 1831-1910 *DcNCBi 3*
**Jay,** Antony 1930- *Who 92, WrDr 92*
**Jay,** Antony Rupert 1930- *IntAu&W 91*
**Jay,** Barrie Samuel 1929- *Who 92*
**Jay,** Bernard 1946- *WhoEnt 92*
**Jay,** Burton Dean 1937- *WhoIns 92*
**Jay,** Carol Ann 1950- *WhoFI 92*
**Jay,** Charles Douglas 1925- *WhoRel 92*
**Jay,** Charlotte *IntAu&W 91X*
**Jay,** Daniel Graham 1952- *WhoMW 92*
**Jay,** Daniel Joseph 1954- *WhoAmP 91*
**Jay,** David Gerald 1938- *WhoAmL 92*
**Jay,** David Jakubowicz 1925- *WhoFI 92, WhoWest 92*
**Jay,** Douglas Patrick Thomas 1907- *IntAu&W 91*
**Jay,** Geraldine Mary 1919- *IntAu&W 91*
**Jay,** James Albert 1916- *WhoFI 92*
**Jay,** James M. 1927- *WhoBlA 92*
**Jay,** James Monroe 1927- *AmMWSc 92*
**Jay,** Jeffrey Robert 1958- *WhoFI 92*
**Jay,** John 1745-1829 *AmPolLe, BenetAL 91, RComAH*
**Jay,** John 1754-1829 *BlkwEAR*
**Jay,** Joyce Williams 1942- *WhoMW 92*
**Jay,** Leslie *IntMPA 92*
**Jay,** Marion *WrDr 92*
**Jay,** Mel *TwCSFW 91, WrDr 92*
**Jay,** Michael Hastings 1946- *Who 92*
**Jay,** Nancy 1955- *WhoEnt 92*
**Jay,** Peter 1937- *IntAu&W 91, IntWW 91, Who 92, WrDr 92*
**Jay,** Peter 1945- *WrDr 92*
**Jay,** William 1789-1858 *AmPeW*
**Jay,** William Walton 1943- *WhoAmL 92*
**Jayachandran,** Toke *AmMWSc 92*
**Jayadev,** T S *AmMWSc 92*
**Jayakumar,** Shunmugam 1939- *IntWW 91*
**Jayant,** Nuggehally S 1946- *AmMWSc 92*
**Jayaram,** Susan Ann 1930- *WhoWest 92*
**Jayaraman,** Aiyasami 1926- *AmMWSc 92*
**Jayaraman,** H 1936- *AmMWSc 92*
**Jayaraman,** Narayanan 1948- *AmMWSc 92*
**Jayas,** Digvir Singh 1958- *AmMWSc 92*
**Jayaswal,** Radheshyam K 1949- *AmMWSc 92*
**Jayawardana,** Christopher Allan Hector P 1898- *Who 92*
**Jayawardene,** Junius Richard 1906- *IntWW 91*
**Jayaweera,** Kolf 1938- *AmMWSc 92*
**Jaycox,** Elbert Ralph 1923- *AmMWSc 92*
**Jaycox,** Mary Irine 1939- *WhoBlA 92*
**Jaye,** Dave 1958- *WhoAmP 91*
**Jaye,** Miles *WhoBlA 92*
**Jaye,** Murray Joseph 1937- *AmMWSc 92*
**Jaye,** Peter 1946- *WhoEnt 92*
**Jaye,** Seymour 1931- *AmMWSc 92*
**Jayes,** Percy Harris 1915- *Who 92*
**Jayewardene,** Hector Wilfred 1916- *IntWW 91*
**Jayewardene,** Junius Richard 1906- *FacFETw, Who 92*
**Jayme,** David Woodward 1950- *AmMWSc 92*
**Jayme,** William North 1925- *WhoWest 92*
**Jaymes,** Dorothy L. 1934- *WhoWest 92*
**Jaymes,** Kenny 1967- *WhoEnt 92*
**Jayne,** Benjamin A 1928- *AmMWSc 92*
**Jayne,** Edward Randolph, II 1944- *WhoMW 92*
**Jayne,** Harry Walker 1857-1910 *BiInAmS*
**Jayne,** Horace Fort 1859-1913 *BiInAmS*
**Jayne,** Jack Edgar 1925- *AmMWSc 92*
**Jayne,** Jerrold Clarence 1931- *AmMWSc 92*
**Jayne,** Theodore D 1929- *AmMWSc 92*
**Jaynes,** Edwin Thompson 1922- *AmMWSc 92*
**Jaynes,** Gerald David 1947- *WhoBlA 92*

**Jaynes**, Hugh Oliver 1931- *AmMWSc 92*
**Jaynes**, John Alva 1929- *AmMWSc 92*
**Jaynes**, Marlin Sanders, Jr. 1942- *WhoRel 92*
**Jaynes**, Phil 1923- *WhoWest 92*
**Jaynes**, Richard Andrus 1935- *AmMWSc 92*
**Jaynes**, Steven Mark 1958- *WhoWest 92*
**Jayroe**, Aubrey L. 1952- *WhoRel 92*
**Jayson**, Christopher Paul 1960- *WhoAmL 92*
**Jayson**, Malcolm Irving Vivian 1937- *Who 92*
**Jayson**, Melinda Gayle 1956- *WhoAmL 92*
**Jayson**, Ronald Paul 1948- *WhoAmL 92*
**Jayston**, Michael 1935- *IntMPA 92, IntWW 91, Who 92*
**Jaywork**, John Terence 1947- *WhoAmL 92*
**Jazairy**, Idriss 1936- *IntWW 91*
**JB** 1951- *WhoEnt 92*
**Jeaffreson**, David Gregory 1931- *Who 92*
**Jeal**, Tim 1945- *IntAu&W 91, WrDr 92*
**Jean Benoit Guillaume Marie Robert Louis** 1921- *IntWW 91*
**Jean**, George Noel 1929- *AmMWSc 92*
**Jean**, Robert R 1926- *WhoAmP 91*
**Jean**, Robert W 1957- *WhoAmP 91*
**Jean**, Roger Lucien 1947- *WhoIns 92*
**Jean**, Romeo W 1907- *WhoAmP 91*
**Jean**, Sylvio Herve 1926- *WhoRel 92*
**Jean-Baptiste**, Emile 1947- *AmMWSc 92*
**JeanBaptiste**, Carl S. 1930- *WhoBlA 92*
**Jeanblanc**, Dean Baylor 1933- *WhoRel 92*
**Jeancourt-Galignani**, Antoine 1937- *IntWW 91*
**Jeanes**, Jack Kenneth 1923- *AmMWSc 92*
**Jeanes**, Leslie Edwin Elloway 1920- *Who 92*
**Jeanes**, Ronald Eric 1926- *Who 92*
**Jeanes**, Samuel Arthur 1912- *WhoRel 92*
**Jeanloz**, Raymond 1952- *AmMWSc 92, WhoWest 92*
**Jeanloz**, Roger William 1917- *AmMWSc 92*
**Jeanmaire**, Renee Marcelle 1924- *IntWW 91*
**Jeanmaire**, Robert L 1920- *AmMWSc 92*
**Jeanne de Belleville** *EncAmaz 91*
**Jeanne de Montfort** *EncAmaz 91*
**Jeanne de Penthierre** *EncAmaz 91*
**Jeanne des Armoises** *EncAmaz 91*
**Jeanne Hachette** 1454- *EncAmaz 91*
**Jeanne La Ferone** *EncAmaz 91*
**Jeanne of Navarre** 1271-1304 *EncAmaz 91*
**jeanne**, ave *DrAPF 91*
**Jeanneney**, Jean-Marcel 1910- *IntWW 91*
**Jeanneney**, Jean-Noel 1942- *IntWW 91*
**Jeanneret** *DcTwDes*
**Jeanneret**, John Joseph 1958- *WhoMW 92*
**Jeanneret**, Pierre 1896-1967 *DcTwDes*
**Jeanniot**, Pierre Jean 1933- *WhoFI 92*
**Jeanrenaud**, Joan Dutcher 1956- *WhoEnt 92*
**Jeans**, Francis *TwCPaSc*
**Jeanson**, John Bouduin 1927- *WhoMW 92*
**Jeansonne**, John Allen, Jr. 1945- *WhoAmL 92*
**Jeansonne**, Vernon Joseph 1924- *WhoAmL 92*
**Jeantet**, Claude 1902-1982 *BiDExR*
**Jeapes**, Anthony Showan 1935- *Who 92*
**Jearld**, Ambrose, Jr 1944- *AmMWSc 92*
**Jeas**, William C. 1938- *WhoFI 92*
**Jeavons**, John Campbell 1942- *WhoFI 92, WhoWest 92*
**Jeavons**, Norman Stone 1930- *WhoAmL 92*
**Jebb** *Who 92*
**Jebb**, Philip 1932- *Who 92*
**Jebe**, Emil H 1909- *AmMWSc 92*
**Jebsen**, Atle 1935- *IntWW 91*
**Jebsen**, Robert H 1931- *AmMWSc 92*
**Jech**, Thomas J 1944- *AmMWSc 92*
**Jecius**, Kestutis Povilas 1961- *WhoMW 92*
**Jeck**, Richard Kahr 1938- *AmMWSc 92*
**Jeckel**, Robert Francis 1947- *WhoAmL 92*
**Jecklin**, Lois Underwood 1934- *WhoEnt 92*
**Jeddere-Fisher**, Arthur 1924- *Who 92*
**Jedenoff**, George Alexander 1917- *WhoWest 92*
**Jedinak**, Thomas Joseph 1947- *WhoAmL 92*
**Jedlicka**, Judith Ann 1944- *WhoEnt 92, WhoFI 92*
**Jedlicka**, William Joseph 1947- *WhoFI 92*
**Jedlicka**, Woodrow William 1945- *WhoMW 92*
**Jedlinski**, Henryk 1924- *AmMWSc 92*
**Jedlinski**, Ronald Thomas 1939- *WhoMW 92*
**Jedruch**, Jacek 1927- *AmMWSc 92*
**Jedynak**, Leo 1928- *AmMWSc 92*
**Jedynak**, Michael Alan 1958- *WhoAmL 92*
**Jee**, Webster Shew Shun 1925- *AmMWSc 92*
**Jeejeebhoy**, Khursheed Nowrojee 1935- *AmMWSc 92*
**Jeelof**, Gerrit 1927- *IntWW 91, Who 92*
**Jeeps**, Richard Eric Gautrey 1931- *Who 92*
**Jeevanandam**, Malayappa 1931- *AmMWSc 92*
**Jeeves**, Malcolm 1926- *WrDr 92*
**Jeeves**, Malcolm Alexander 1926- *Who 92*
**Jeewoolall**, Ramesh *IntWW 91*
**Jeewoolall**, Ramesh 1940- *Who 92*
**Jefcoate**, Colin R 1942- *AmMWSc 92*
**Jeff**, Gloria Jean 1952- *WhoBlA 92*
**Jeffares**, A. Norman 1920- *WrDr 92*
**Jeffares**, Alexander Norman 1920- *IntWW 91, Who 92*
**Jeffay**, Henry 1927- *AmMWSc 92*
**Jeffcoat**, Cleaties Harriel 1948- *WhoRel 92*
**Jeffcoat**, James Wilson, Jr. 1961- *WhoBlA 92*
**Jeffcoat**, Marjorie K 1951- *AmMWSc 92*
**Jeffcoat**, Mark Randall 1950- *WhoRel 92*
**Jeffcoat**, Otis Allen, III 1948- *WhoAmL 92*
**Jeffcoate**, Norman 1907- *Who 92, WrDr 92*
**Jeffcott**, Leo Broof 1942- *Who 92*
**Jeffee**, Saul d1991 *NewYTBS 91*
**Jefferies**, Charlotte S. 1944- *WhoBlA 92*
**Jefferies**, David George 1933- *Who 92*
**Jefferies**, Jack P. 1928- *WhoAmL 92*
**Jefferies**, John D 1928- *WhoAmP 91*
**Jefferies**, John Trevor 1925- *AmMWSc 92, WhoWest 92*
**Jefferies**, Michael John 1941- *AmMWSc 92*
**Jefferies**, Richard 1838-1887 *ScFEYrs*
**Jefferies**, Richard 1848-1887 *RfGEnL 91*
**Jefferies**, Roger David 1939- *Who 92*
**Jefferies**, Sheelagh 1926- *Who 92*
**Jefferies**, Stephen 1951- *Who 92*
**Jefferies**, Steven 1951- *AmMWSc 92*
**Jefferis**, D Allen 1937- *WhoAmP 91*
**Jefferis**, Frank Dodgson 1952- *WhoFI 92, WhoMW 92*
**Jefferis**, Paul Bruce 1952- *WhoAmL 92*
**Jeffers**, Arnold P 1929- *WhoAmP 91*
**Jeffers**, Ben L. 1944- *WhoBlA 92*
**Jeffers**, Clifton R. 1934- *WhoBlA 92*
**Jeffers**, Crystal Lee 1938- *WhoAmP 91*
**Jeffers**, Donald E 1925- *WhoIns 92*
**Jeffers**, E.L. *DrAPF 91*
**Jeffers**, Gary Edwin 1946- *WhoMW 92*
**Jeffers**, Grady Rommel 1943- *WhoBlA 92*
**Jeffers**, H. Paul *TwCWW 91, WrDr 92*
**Jeffers**, Jack 1928- *WhoBlA 92*
**Jeffers**, John Henry, Jr. 1948- *WhoWest 92*
**Jeffers**, John Norman Richard 1926- *Who 92*
**Jeffers**, John William 1936- *WhoAmL 92*
**Jeffers**, Kevin Allen 1961- *WhoEnt 92*
**Jeffers**, Mark John 1958- *WhoEnt 92*
**Jeffers**, Mary L *WhoAmP 91*
**Jeffers**, Robinson 1887-1962 *BenetAL 91, ConAu 35NR, FacFETw*
**Jeffers**, Ronald Joseph 1939- *WhoRel 92*
**Jeffers**, Steven Nye 1953- *WhoMW 92*
**Jeffers**, Suzanne 1949- *WhoEnt 92*
**Jeffers**, Thomas Kirk 1941- *AmMWSc 92*
**Jeffers**, Wayne Thomas 1951- *WhoFI 92*
**Jeffers**, William Allen, Jr 1936- *AmMWSc 92*
**Jeffers**, William Nicholson 1824-1883 *BiInAmS*
**Jeffers Wikle**, Margaret Alison 1961- *WhoAmL 92*
**Jefferson Airplane** *FacFETw, NewAmDM*
**Jefferson Starship** *FacFETw*
**Jefferson**, Alan 1918- *TwCPaSc*
**Jefferson**, Alan 1921- *IntAu&W 91, WrDr 92*
**Jefferson**, Alphine Wade 1950- *WhoBlA 92*
**Jefferson**, Andrew L., Jr. 1934- *WhoBlA 92*
**Jefferson**, Arthur 1938- *WhoBlA 92*
**Jefferson**, Austin, Jr. *WhoBlA 92*
**Jefferson**, Blind Lemon 1897?-1930 *NewAmDM*
**Jefferson**, Bryan *Who 92*
**Jefferson**, Carol Annette 1948- *AmMWSc 92*
**Jefferson**, Charles Edward 1860-1937 *RelLAm 91*
**Jefferson**, Charmain 1963- *WhoBlA 92*
**Jefferson**, Cheryl May 1954- *WhoEnt 92*
**Jefferson**, Clifton 1928- *WhoBlA 92*
**Jefferson**, David Kenoss 1938- *AmMWSc 92*
**Jefferson**, Donald Earl 1927- *AmMWSc 92*
**Jefferson**, Doris Vernice 1924- *WhoAmP 91, WhoMW 92*
**Jefferson**, Douglas Ray 1962- *WhoEnt 92*
**Jefferson**, E. Kenneth, Jr. 1952- *WhoMW 92*
**Jefferson**, Edward G 1921- *AmMWSc 92*
**Jefferson**, Fredrick Carl, Jr. 1934- *WhoBlA 92*
**Jefferson**, Gary Scott 1945- *WhoBlA 92*
**Jefferson**, George Rowland 1921- *IntWW 91, Who 92*
**Jefferson**, Hilda Hutchinson 1920- *WhoBlA 92*
**Jefferson**, Horace Lee 1924- *WhoBlA 92*
**Jefferson**, James, Jr. 1951- *WhoAmL 92*
**Jefferson**, James E. 1922- *WhoBlA 92*
**Jefferson**, James Walter 1937- *AmMWSc 92, WhoMW 92*
**Jefferson**, Joan Ena 1946- *Who 92*
**Jefferson**, John Bryan 1928- *Who 92*
**Jefferson**, John Daniel 1948- *WhoWest 92*
**Jefferson**, Joseph 1829-1905 *BenetAL 91*
**Jefferson**, Joseph L. 1940- *WhoBlA 92*
**Jefferson**, June L., Jr. 1924- *WhoBlA 92*
**Jefferson**, Karen L. 1952- *WhoBlA 92*
**Jefferson**, Leonard Shelton 1939- *AmMWSc 92*
**Jefferson**, Lucy C. 1866-1953 *NotBlAW 92*
**Jefferson**, M. Ivory 1924- *WhoBlA 92*
**Jefferson**, Marcia D. 1935- *WhoBlA 92*
**Jefferson**, Marcus Devon 1960- *WhoAmP 91*
**Jefferson**, Margaret Correan 1947- *AmMWSc 92*
**Jefferson**, Mervyn Stewart D. *Who 92*
**Jefferson**, Myra LaVerne Tull *WhoWest 92*
**Jefferson**, Nancy B. 1923- *WhoBlA 92*
**Jefferson**, Nancy Zanders 1936- *WhoFI 92*
**Jefferson**, Overton C. *WhoBlA 92*
**Jefferson**, Patricia Ann 1951- *WhoBlA 92*
**Jefferson**, Richard 1931- *WhoAmP 91*
**Jefferson**, Robert R. 1932- *WhoBlA 92*
**Jefferson**, Roland Newton 1911- *AmMWSc 92*
**Jefferson**, Roland S. 1939- *ConAu 35NR*
**Jefferson**, Roland Spratlin 1939- *WhoBlA 92, WhoEnt 92*
**Jefferson**, Roy Lee, Jr. 1943- *WhoBlA 92*
**Jefferson**, Sandra Traylor 1942- *WhoEnt 92*
**Jefferson**, Sandra Williamson 1948- *WhoBlA 92*
**Jefferson**, Shirley Almira 1929- *WhoAmP 91*
**Jefferson**, Thomas 1743-1826 *AmPolLe [port], BenetAL 91, BiInAmS, BlkwCEP, BlkwEAR [port], RComAH*
**Jefferson**, Thomas 1962- *BlkOlyM*
**Jefferson**, Thomas Bradley 1924- *AmMWSc 92*
**Jefferson**, Thomas Hutton, Jr 1941- *AmMWSc 92*
**Jefferson**, William Emmett, Jr 1925- *AmMWSc 92*
**Jefferson**, William J. 1947- *AlmAP 92 [port], WhoAmP 91, WhoBlA 92*
**Jefferson-Moss**, Carolyn 1945- *WhoBlA 92*
**Jefferson Smith**, Peter 1939- *Who 92*
**Jefferts**, Keith Bartlett 1931- *AmMWSc 92*
**Jeffery**, David Henry 1963- *WhoEnt 92*
**Jeffery**, David John 1936- *Who 92*
**Jeffery**, Duane Eldro 1937- *AmMWSc 92*
**Jeffery**, Geoffrey Marron 1919- *AmMWSc 92*
**Jeffery**, Harley Bradley 1872-1954 *RelLAm 91*
**Jeffery**, James Nels 1944- *WhoWest 92*
**Jeffery**, Larry S 1936- *AmMWSc 92*
**Jeffery**, Lawrence R 1927- *AmMWSc 92*
**Jeffery**, Maria Aoling Chea 1962- *WhoFI 92*
**Jeffery**, Michael Ives 1944- *WhoAmL 92*
**Jeffery**, Robert Martin Colquhoun 1935- *Who 92*
**Jeffery**, Rondo Nelden 1940- *AmMWSc 92*
**Jeffery**, Thomas Kirkendall 1942- *WhoMW 92*
**Jeffery**, William Richard 1944- *AmMWSc 92*
**Jefferys**, William H, III 1940- *AmMWSc 92*
**Jefford**, Barbara Mary 1930- *Who 92*
**Jefford**, Bat *IntAu&W 91X, TwCWW 91*
**Jefford**, Clayton Nance 1955- *WhoRel 92*
**Jeffords**, Edward Alan 1945- *WhoAmL 92*
**Jeffords**, James M. 1934- *AlmAP 92 [port]*
**Jeffords**, James Merrill 1934- *IntWW 91, WhoAmP 91*
**Jeffords**, Lynn Redding 1957- *WhoEnt 92*
**Jeffords**, Russell MacGregor 1918- *AmMWSc 92*
**Jeffredo**, John Victor 1927- *WhoFI 92, WhoWest 92*
**Jeffress**, Edwin Bedford, Sr. 1887-1961 *DcNCBi 3*
**Jeffress**, Robert J. 1955- *WhoRel 92*
**Jeffrey**, Charles Alan 1950- *WhoFI 92*
**Jeffrey**, Charles James, Jr. 1925- *WhoBlA 92*
**Jeffrey**, David Gordon 1946- *WhoWest 92*
**Jeffrey**, Francis 1773-1850 *DcLB 107 [port], NinCLC 33 [port]*
**Jeffrey**, Francis 1950- *ConAu 135*
**Jeffrey**, George Alan 1915- *AmMWSc 92*
**Jeffrey**, Graham 1935- *WrDr 92*
**Jeffrey**, Jackson Eugene 1931- *AmMWSc 92*
**Jeffrey**, Jacqueline Elaine 1943- *WhoFI 92*
**Jeffrey**, James E. 1951- *WhoRel 92*
**Jeffrey**, John E 1938- *WhoAmP 91*
**Jeffrey**, John J 1937- *AmMWSc 92*
**Jeffrey**, John Orval 1963- *WhoAmL 92*
**Jeffrey**, Kenneth Robert 1941- *AmMWSc 92*
**Jeffrey**, Llewelyn 1917- *WhoAmP 91*
**Jeffrey**, Mildred M. *DrAPF 91*
**Jeffrey**, Pamela Kunatz 1949- *WhoMW 92*
**Jeffrey**, Ronald James 1949- *WhoWest 92*
**Jeffrey**, Ronnald James 1949- *WhoBlA 92*
**Jeffrey**, William *ConAu 35NR*
**Jeffreys** *Who 92*
**Jeffreys**, Baron 1957- *Who 92*
**Jeffreys**, Albert Leonidas *WhoAmL 92*
**Jeffreys**, Alec John 1950- *Who 92*
**Jeffreys**, Anne 1923- *IntMPA 92*
**Jeffreys**, David Alfred 1934- *Who 92*
**Jeffreys**, Donald Bearss 1925- *AmMWSc 92*
**Jeffreys**, Elystan Geoffrey 1926- *WhoFI 92*
**Jeffreys**, George 1610?-1685 *NewAmDM*
**Jeffreys**, George Washington 1793?-1848 *DcNCBi 3*
**Jeffreys**, J. G. *WrDr 92*
**Jeffreys**, John H. 1940- *WhoBlA 92*
**Jeffreys**, Judith Diana 1927- *Who 92*
**Jeffreys**, Marcel 1872-1924 *TwCPaSc*
**Jeffreys**, Ron Bruce 1958- *WhoEnt 92*
**Jeffries**, Benjamin Joy 1833-1915 *BiInAmS*
**Jeffries**, Carson Dunning 1922- *AmMWSc 92, IntWW 91*
**Jeffries**, Charles Dean 1929- *AmMWSc 92, WhoMW 92*
**Jeffries**, Georgia Thomas 1951- *WhoEnt 92*
**Jeffries**, Graham Harry 1929- *AmMWSc 92*
**Jeffries**, Harry Perry 1929- *AmMWSc 92*
**Jeffries**, Haywood Franklin 1964- *WhoBlA 92*
**Jeffries**, James E 1925- *WhoAmP 91*
**Jeffries**, James J. 1875-1953 *FacFETw*
**Jeffries**, Jay B 1947- *AmMWSc 92*
**Jeffries**, John 1744?-1819 *BiInAmS*
**Jeffries**, John Amory 1859-1892 *BiInAmS*
**Jeffries**, John Calvin, Jr. 1948- *WhoAmL 92*
**Jeffries**, LeRoy William 1912- *WhoBlA 92*
**Jeffries**, Lionel 1926- *ConTFT 9, IntMPA 92, IntWW 91*
**Jeffries**, Lionel Charles 1926- *Who 92*
**Jeffries**, McChesney Hill 1922- *WhoAmL 92*
**Jeffries**, Neal Powell 1935- *AmMWSc 92*
**Jeffries**, Neil 1959- *TwCPaSc*
**Jeffries**, Quentin Ray 1920- *AmMWSc 92*
**Jeffries**, Robert Alan 1933- *AmMWSc 92*
**Jeffries**, Roderic 1926- *WrDr 92*
**Jeffries**, Rosalind R. 1936- *WhoBlA 92*
**Jeffries**, Thomas William 1947- *AmMWSc 92*
**Jeffries**, William Bowman 1926- *AmMWSc 92*
**Jeffries**, William Patrick 1945- *IntWW 91*
**Jeffs**, George W 1925- *AmMWSc 92*
**Jeffs**, James 1900- *Who 92*
**Jeffs**, Julian 1931- *IntAu&W 91, Who 92, WrDr 92*
**Jeffs**, Kenneth Peter 1931- *Who 92*
**Jeffs**, Peter W 1933- *AmMWSc 92*
**Jeffs**, Rae 1921- *IntAu&W 91, WrDr 92*
**Jeffs**, Thomas Hamilton, II 1938- *WhoFI 92*
**Jeffs**, Wallace E 1926- *WhoIns 92*
**Jeffus**, Maggie 1934- *WhoAmP 91*
**Jefimenko**, Oleg D 1922- *AmMWSc 92*
**Jegasothy**, Brian V 1943- *AmMWSc 92*
**Jegede**, Emmanuel 1943- *TwCPaSc*
**Jegen**, Carol Frances 1925- *WhoRel 92*
**Jegen**, Lawrence A., III 1934- *WhoAmL 92*
**Jeger**, Baroness 1915- *Who 92*
**Jeghers**, Sanderson John 1945- *WhoFI 92*
**Jegi**, John I 1866-1904 *BiInAmS*
**Jegla**, Dorothy Eldredge 1939- *AmMWSc 92*
**Jegla**, Thomas Cyril 1935- *AmMWSc 92*
**Jeglum**, John Karl 1938- *AmMWSc 92*
**Jehan des Murs** 1300?-1350? *NewAmDM*
**Jehangir**, Hirji 1915- *Who 92*
**Jehle**, Michael Edward 1954- *WhoAmL 92*
**Jehlen**, Patricia D *WhoAmP 91*
**Jehlweiser**, Olga *EncAmaz 91*
**Jehn**, Betty L. 1921- *WhoMW 92*
**Jehn**, Lawrence A 1921- *AmMWSc 92*
**Jehn**, Lawrence Andrew 1921- *WhoMW 92*
**Jehnsen**, David Charles 1943- *WhoAmP 91*
**Jehue**, Richard James 1964- *WhoWest 92*
**Jeillison-Knock**, Randy Wayne 1959- *WhoRel 92*
**Jejeebhoy**, Jamsetjee 1913- *Who 92*
**Jekel**, Eugene Carl 1930- *AmMWSc 92*

**Jekel**, James Franklin 1934- *AmMWSc 92*
**Jekel**, Pam *DrAPF 91*
**Jekel**, Pamela 1948- *ConAu 135*
**Jekel**, Pamela Lee 1948- *WrDr 92*
**Jekeli**, Christopher 1953- *AmMWSc 92*
**Jeker**, Robert A. 1935- *IntWW 91*
**Jelavich**, Barbara 1923- *WhoMW 92*
**Jelen**, Frederic Charles 1910- *AmMWSc 92*
**Jelen**, Jaroslaw Andrzej 1943- *WhoWest 92*
**Jelenko**, Carl, III 1931- *AmMWSc 92*
**Jelf**, Richard William 1904- *Who 92*
**Jelinek**, Arthur Gilbert 1917- *AmMWSc 92*
**Jelinek**, Bohdan 1910- *AmMWSc 92*
**Jelinek**, Charles Frank 1917- *AmMWSc 92*
**Jelinek**, Frederick 1932- *AmMWSc 92*
**Jelinek**, Hanns 1901-1969 *NewAmDM*
**Jelinek**, James L. 1942- *WhoRel 92*
**Jelinek**, Otto John 1940- *IntWW 91, WhoFI 92*
**Jelinek**, Robert V 1926- *AmMWSc 92*
**Jelinek**, Susan Lynn 1960- *WhoRel 92*
**Jelinski**, Lynn W 1949- *AmMWSc 92*
**Jelinski**, Richard James 1952- *WhoMW 92*
**Jeljaszewicz**, Janusz 1930- *IntWW 91*
**Jellard**, Charles H 1916- *AmMWSc 92*
**Jellema**, Rod *DrAPF 91*
**Jellett**, Mainie 1877-1944 *TwCPaSc*
**Jelley**, Francis D 1918- *WhoAmP 91*
**Jellico**, John Anthony 1914- *WhoWest 92*
**Jellico**, Nancy Rose 1939- *WhoWest 92*
**Jellicoe** *Who 92*
**Jellicoe**, Earl 1918- *IntWW 91, Who 92*
**Jellicoe**, Ann *Who 92*
**Jellicoe**, Ann 1927- *IntAu&W 91, WrDr 92*
**Jellicoe**, Colin 1942- *TwCPaSc*
**Jellicoe**, Geoffrey 1900- *IntWW 91, Who 92, WrDr 92*
**Jellicoe**, John Rushworth 1859-1935 *FacFETw*
**Jellicoe**, Patricia Ann 1927- *Who 92*
**Jelliffe**, Derrick Brian 1921- *AmMWSc 92*
**Jelliffe**, Roger Woodham 1929- *AmMWSc 92*
**Jellinck**, Peter Harry 1928- *AmMWSc 92*
**Jellinek**, George 1919- *WhoEnt 92*
**Jellinek**, Hans Helmut Gunter 1917- *AmMWSc 92*
**Jellinek**, Max 1929- *AmMWSc 92*
**Jelling**, Murray 1918- *AmMWSc 92*
**Jellinger**, Thomas Christian 1923- *AmMWSc 92*
**Jellison**, Gerald Earle, Jr 1946- *AmMWSc 92*
**Jellison**, James Logan, II 1922- *WhoMW 92*
**Jellum**, Milton Delbert 1934- *AmMWSc 92*
**Jelusich**, Mirko 1886-1969 *EncTR 91 [port]*
**Jemal**, Mohammed *AmMWSc 92*
**Jemelian**, Joni Lee 1964- *WhoRel 92*
**Jemian**, Wartan A 1925- *AmMWSc 92*
**Jemielity**, Thomas John 1933- *WhoMW 92*
**Jemison**, John Snow, III 1949- *WhoFI 92*
**Jemison**, Mae C. 1956- *NotBlAW 92 [port], WhoBlA 92*
**Jemison**, Mae C. 1957?- *ConBlB 1 [port]*
**Jemison**, Mary 1743-1833 *BenetAL 91*
**Jemison**, Theodore Judson 1918- *WhoBlA 92, WhoRel 92*
**Jemison-Renner**, Lynn *WhoEnt 92*
**Jemmerson**, Ronald Renomer Weaver 1951- *AmMWSc 92*
**Jemmott**, Hensley B. 1947- *WhoBlA 92*
**Jemski**, Joseph Victor 1920- *AmMWSc 92*
**Jen**, Chih Kung 1906- *AmMWSc 92*
**Jen**, Gish *ConAu 135*
**Jen**, Joseph Jwu-Shan 1939- *AmMWSc 92*
**Jen**, Kai-Lin Catherine 1949- *AmMWSc 92*
**Jen**, Lillian 1956?- *ConAu 135*
**Jen**, Philip Hungsun 1944- *AmMWSc 92*
**Jen**, Shen 1947- *AmMWSc 92*
**Jen**, Yun 1927- *AmMWSc 92*
**Jen-Jacobson**, Linda 1941- *AmMWSc 92*
**Jena**, Purusottam 1943- *AmMWSc 92*
**Jencks**, Charles 1939- *WrDr 92*
**Jencks**, Charles Alexander 1939- *IntAu&W 91, Who 92*
**Jencks**, Richard W. *LesBEnT 92*
**Jencks**, William Platt 1927- *AmMWSc 92, IntWW 91*
**Jenden**, Donald James 1926- *AmMWSc 92*
**Jendrek**, Eugene Francis, Jr 1949- *AmMWSc 92*
**Jendresen**, Malcolm Dan 1933- *AmMWSc 92*
**Jenefsky**, Jack 1919- *WhoFI 92, WhoMW 92*
**Jenen**, Paul Raymond 1949- *WhoAmL 92*
**Jenerick**, Howard Peter 1923- *AmMWSc 92*
**Jenest**, Jeffrey Mark 1952- *WhoEnt 92*
**Jeney**, Peggy Jean 1934- *WhoAmP 91*
**Jeng**, Duen-Ren 1932- *AmMWSc 92*
**Jeng**, Raymond Ing-Song 1940- *AmMWSc 92*
**Jenicek**, John Andrew 1922- *AmMWSc 92*
**Jenifer**, Franklyn G. 1939- *ConBlB 2 [port]*
**Jenifer**, Franklyn Green 1939- *WhoBlA 92*
**Jenike**, Andrew W 1914- *AmMWSc 92*
**Jeniker**, Charles J 1924- *WhoAmP 91*
**Jenings**, William d1687 *DcNCBi 3*
**Jenison**, William d1853 *BiInAmS*
**Jenkin** *Who 92*
**Jenkin**, Conrad *Who 92*
**Jenkin**, David Conrad 1928- *Who 92*
**Jenkin**, Howard M 1925- *AmMWSc 92*
**Jenkin**, Ian Tregarthen 1920- *Who 92*
**Jenkin**, Len 1941- *IntAu&W 91, WrDr 92*
**Jenkin**, Simon William Geoffrey 1943- *Who 92*
**Jenkin Of Roding**, Baron 1926- *IntWW 91, Who 92*
**Jenkin Yepez**, Deborah Rae 1957- *WhoAmL 92*
**Jenkins** *Who 92*
**Jenkins**, Lord *WrDr 92*
**Jenkins**, Adam, Jr. 1942- *WhoBlA 92*
**Jenkins**, Adelbert Howard 1934- *WhoBlA 92*
**Jenkins**, Agnes Elizabeth 1947- *WhoRel 92*
**Jenkins**, Ainslee *ScFEYrs*
**Jenkins**, Alan 1914- *IntAu&W 91, WrDr 92*
**Jenkins**, Alan Roberts 1926- *IntAu&W 91, Who 92*
**Jenkins**, Albert Felton, Jr. 1941- *WhoAmL 92*
**Jenkins**, Alfred Martin 1917- *AmMWSc 92*
**Jenkins**, Alice 1887-1967 *BiDBrF 2*
**Jenkins**, Alonzo Clark 1953- *WhoBlA 92*
**Jenkins**, Althea H. 1941- *WhoBlA 92*
**Jenkins**, Alvin Wilkins, Jr 1928- *AmMWSc 92*
**Jenkins**, Andrew 1936- *WhoBlA 92*
**Jenkins**, Andrew 1941- *WhoAmP 91*
**Jenkins**, Andrew James 1941- *WhoBlA 92*
**Jenkins**, Aubrey Dennis 1927- *Who 92*
**Jenkins**, Augustus G., Jr. 1943- *WhoBlA 92*
**Jenkins**, Barbara Alexander 1942- *WhoRel 92*
**Jenkins**, Barbara Williams 1934- *WhoBlA 92*
**Jenkins**, Benjamin Larry 1938- *WhoIns 92*
**Jenkins**, Betty Jean 1940- *WhoWest 92*
**Jenkins**, Bobby G. 1939- *WhoBlA 92*
**Jenkins**, Bonnie Denise 1960- *WhoAmL 92*
**Jenkins**, Brian 1935- *Who 92*
**Jenkins**, Bruce Armand 1933- *WhoFI 92*
**Jenkins**, Bruce Sterling 1927- *WhoAmL 92*
**Jenkins**, Bunny Gloria 1953- *WhoMW 92*
**Jenkins**, Burke *ScFEYrs*
**Jenkins**, Burton Charles 1920- *AmMWSc 92*
**Jenkins**, Carl Scarborough 1916- *WhoBlA 92*
**Jenkins**, Carle Frederick 1931- *WhoRel 92*
**Jenkins**, Carol Ann 1944- *WhoBlA 92*
**Jenkins**, Cecil R, Jr *WhoAmP 91*
**Jenkins**, Charles 1941- *IntMPA 92*
**Jenkins**, Charles Christopher *ScFEYrs*
**Jenkins**, Charles E., Sr. 1928- *WhoBlA 92*
**Jenkins**, Charles Francis d1934 *LesBEnT 92*
**Jenkins**, Charles Lamont 1934- *BlkOlyM*
**Jenkins**, Charles Peter de Brisay 1925- *Who 92*
**Jenkins**, Charles Robert 1930- *AmMWSc 92*
**Jenkins**, Chester *WhoBlA 92*
**Jenkins**, Chester L *WhoAmP 91*
**Jenkins**, Christopher *Who 92*
**Jenkins**, Clara Barnes *WhoBlA 92*
**Jenkins**, Clive *Who 92*
**Jenkins**, Clive 1926- *IntWW 91*
**Jenkins**, Curtis S *WhoAmP 91*
**Jenkins**, Cynthia 1924- *WhoBlA 92*
**Jenkins**, Cynthia Ann Latiolais 1952- *WhoAmP 91*
**Jenkins**, D. Patrick 1945- *WhoMW 92*
**Jenkins**, Dale Wilson 1918- *AmMWSc 92*
**Jenkins**, Dan 1916- *IntMPA 92*
**Jenkins**, Dan 1929- *IntAu&W 91*
**Jenkins**, Daniel Thomas 1914- *IntAu&W 91*
**Jenkins**, David 1912- *Who 92*
**Jenkins**, David 1937- *ConTFT 9*
**Jenkins**, David A. *WhoAmL 92*
**Jenkins**, David A 1937- *AmMWSc 92*
**Jenkins**, David Aaron 1822-1886 *DcNCBi 3*
**Jenkins**, David Alan 1952- *WhoMW 92*
**Jenkins**, David Clive 1926- *Who 92*
**Jenkins**, David Edward *Who 92*
**Jenkins**, David Edward 1925- *IntWW 91*
**Jenkins**, David Edward Stewart 1949- *Who 92*
**Jenkins**, David Graham 1933- *IntWW 91*
**Jenkins**, David Isaac 1935- *AmMWSc 92*
**Jenkins**, David John 1948- *Who 92*
**Jenkins**, David John Anthony *AmMWSc 92*
**Jenkins**, David R 1924- *AmMWSc 92*
**Jenkins**, Derek 1937- *TwCPaSc*
**Jenkins**, Drewie Gutrimez 1915- *WhoBlA 92*
**Jenkins**, E Cynthia 1921- *WhoAmP 91*
**Jenkins**, Ed 1933- *AlmAP 92 [port]*
**Jenkins**, Edgar Lanier 1933- *WhoAmP 91, WhoFI 92*
**Jenkins**, Edgar William 1933- *AmMWSc 92*
**Jenkins**, Edmond Thomas 1930- *WhoBlA 92*
**Jenkins**, Edward Beynon 1939- *AmMWSc 92*
**Jenkins**, Edward Felix 1906- *AmMWSc 92*
**Jenkins**, Edwin Fred 1948- *WhoRel 92*
**Jenkins**, Elaine B. 1916- *WhoBlA 92*
**Jenkins**, Elizabeth *IntAu&W 91, IntWW 91, Who 92, WrDr 92*
**Jenkins**, Elizabeth Ameta 1929- *WhoBlA 92*
**Jenkins**, Ella Louise 1924- *WhoBlA 92*
**Jenkins**, Emmanuel Lee 1934- *WhoBlA 92*
**Jenkins**, Ernest Alfred 1926- *WhoRel 92*
**Jenkins**, Everett Wilbur, Jr. 1953- *WhoAmL 92*
**Jenkins**, Farish Alston, Jr 1940- *AmMWSc 92*
**Jenkins**, Ferguson 1943- *WhoBlA 92*
**Jenkins**, Florence Foster 1868-1944 *NewAmDM*
**Jenkins**, Floyd Albert 1916- *AmMWSc 92*
**Jenkins**, Frank Graham 1923- *Who 92*
**Jenkins**, Frank Shockley 1925- *WhoBlA 92*
**Jenkins**, Garth John 1933- *Who 92*
**Jenkins**, Gary 1928- *WrDr 92*
**Jenkins**, Gayle Expose 1927- *WhoBlA 92*
**Jenkins**, George 1908- *IntMPA 92, WhoEnt 92*
**Jenkins**, George Arthur, Jr. 1955- *WhoBlA 92*
**Jenkins**, George Charles 1927- *Who 92*
**Jenkins**, George Henry 1929- *WhoMW 92*
**Jenkins**, George Robert 1914- *AmMWSc 92*
**Jenkins**, George W. 1907- *WhoFI 92*
**Jenkins**, Gilbert Kenneth 1918- *Who 92*
**Jenkins**, Graeme James 1958- *WhoEnt 92*
**Jenkins**, Harold 1909- *IntAu&W 91, IntWW 91, Who 92, WrDr 92*
**Jenkins**, Harry Lancaster 1932- *WhoBlA 92*
**Jenkins**, Helen Ann 1945- *WhoFI 92*
**Jenkins**, Henry Alfred 1925- *Who 92*
**Jenkins**, Herbert d1923 *DcLB 112*
**Jenkins**, Herbert 1907-1990 *FacFETw*
**Jenkins**, Herman Lee 1940- *WhoBlA 92*
**Jenkins**, Howard, Jr. 1915- *WhoBlA 92*
**Jenkins**, Howard Bryner 1928- *AmMWSc 92*
**Jenkins**, Howard J. *WhoRel 92*
**Jenkins**, Howard Jones 1916- *AmMWSc 92*
**Jenkins**, Howard Malcolm 1842-1902 *AmPeW*
**Jenkins**, Hugh Royston 1933- *Who 92*
**Jenkins**, Hughes Brantley, Jr 1927- *AmMWSc 92*
**Jenkins**, Ivor 1913- *Who 92*
**Jenkins**, James Allister 1923- *AmMWSc 92, WhoMW 92*
**Jenkins**, James Christopher 1939- *Who 92*
**Jenkins**, James E. 1939- *WhoBlA 92*
**Jenkins**, James Lineberry 1883-1973 *DcNCBi 3*
**Jenkins**, James Michael 1933- *WhoAmL 92*
**Jenkins**, James Vandiver 1950- *WhoEnt 92*
**Jenkins**, James William 1921- *AmMWSc 92*
**Jenkins**, James William 1953- *WhoMW 92*
**Jenkins**, Jane 1943- *WhoEnt 92*
**Jenkins**, Janet Ann 1950- *WhoAmP 91*
**Jenkins**, Janet Elaine 1941- *WhoAmP 91*
**Jenkins**, Jeff Harlin 1937- *AmMWSc 92*
**Jenkins**, Jennifer *Who 92*
**Jenkins**, Jennifer 1921- *IntWW 91*
**Jenkins**, Jennifer Jill 1962- *WhoEnt 92*
**Jenkins**, Jimmy Raymond 1943- *AmMWSc 92, WhoBlA 92*
**Jenkins**, Joe Wiley 1941- *AmMWSc 92*
**Jenkins**, John d1681 *DcNCBi 3*
**Jenkins**, John 1592-1678 *NewAmDM*
**Jenkins**, John Akins 1953- *WhoRel 92*
**Jenkins**, John Bruner 1941- *AmMWSc 92*
**Jenkins**, John Clack 1951- *WhoRel 92*
**Jenkins**, John George 1919- *Who 92*
**Jenkins**, John Geraint 1929- *IntAu&W 91, WrDr 92*
**Jenkins**, John Owen 1922- *Who 92*
**Jenkins**, John Robin 1912- *Who 92*
**Jenkins**, John Smith 1932- *WhoAmL 92*
**Jenkins**, Johnie Norton 1934- *AmMWSc 92*
**Jenkins**, Jon Keith 1945- *WhoAmL 92*
**Jenkins**, Joseph A *WhoAmP 91*
**Jenkins**, Joseph Walter, Jr. 1941- *WhoBlA 92*
**Jenkins**, Joyce L. 1953- *WhoRel 92*
**Jenkins**, Julius *WhoBlA 92*
**Jenkins**, Katharine Mary 1945- *Who 92*
**Jenkins**, Kay Elizabeth 1964- *WhoMW 92*
**Jenkins**, Ken Lawrence 1947- *WhoEnt 92*
**Jenkins**, Kenneth Dunning 1944- *AmMWSc 92*
**Jenkins**, Kenneth James William 1929- *AmMWSc 92*
**Jenkins**, Kenneth Vincent *WhoBlA 92*
**Jenkins**, Kevin Lynn 1955- *WhoRel 92*
**Jenkins**, Kirk Christopher 1961- *WhoAmL 92*
**Jenkins**, Lamont Joseph 1935- *WhoFI 92*
**Jenkins**, Lawrence E 1933- *AmMWSc 92*
**Jenkins**, Leo Donald 1932- *WhoAmP 91*
**Jenkins**, Leonard Cecil 1926- *AmMWSc 92*
**Jenkins**, Leroy 1935- *RelLAm 91*
**Jenkins**, Leslie Hugh 1924- *AmMWSc 92*
**Jenkins**, Lew 1916-1981 *CurBio 91N*
**Jenkins**, Linda Walsh 1944- *WhoWest 92*
**Jenkins**, Loren 1941- *WhoAmP 91*
**Jenkins**, Louis *DrAPF 91*
**Jenkins**, Louis 1947- *WhoAmP 91*
**Jenkins**, Louis E. 1931- *WhoBlA 92*
**Jenkins**, Lozelle DeLuz *WhoBlA 92*
**Jenkins**, Madge Marie 1938- *WhoMW 92*
**Jenkins**, Mamie Leah Young 1940- *AmMWSc 92*
**Jenkins**, Margaret Aikens 1925- *WhoWest 92*
**Jenkins**, Marilyn Joyce 1943- *WhoBlA 92*
**Jenkins**, Martha 1961- *WhoAmP 91*
**Jenkins**, Mary 1939- *WhoAmP 91*
**Jenkins**, Mary Jennifer 1921- *Who 92*
**Jenkins**, Matthew Grady 1950- *WhoFI 92*
**Jenkins**, Melvin E., Jr. 1923- *WhoBlA 92*
**Jenkins**, Melvin Earl 1923- *AmMWSc 92*
**Jenkins**, Melvin L. 1947- *WhoBlA 92*
**Jenkins**, Michael 1936- *WrDr 92*
**Jenkins**, Michael Nicholas Howard 1932- *Who 92*
**Jenkins**, Michael Romilly Heald 1936- *IntWW 91, Who 92*
**Jenkins**, Monica 1961- *WhoBlA 92*
**Jenkins**, Myra Ellen 1916- *WhoWest 92*
**Jenkins**, Neil Edmund 1949- *WhoAmL 92*
**Jenkins**, Newell 1915- *NewAmDM, WhoEnt 92*
**Jenkins**, Nigel 1949- *IntAu&W 91*
**Jenkins**, O. Randall 1964- *WhoRel 92*
**Jenkins**, Orville Wesley 1913- *WhoRel 92*
**Jenkins**, Owain 1907- *Who 92*
**Jenkins**, Ozella 1945- *WhoBlA 92*
**Jenkins**, Pamela Gardner 1950- *WhoAmP 91*
**Jenkins**, Paul *DrAPF 91*
**Jenkins**, Paul LeRoy 1947- *WhoEnt 92*
**Jenkins**, Peter 1934- *ConAu 135, Who 92*
**Jenkins**, Peter Edwin 1940- *WhoMW 92*
**Jenkins**, Peter George James 1934- *IntAu&W 91*
**Jenkins**, Peter White 1937- *Who 92*
**Jenkins**, Philip Winder 1933- *AmMWSc 92*
**Jenkins**, Phillip Lane 1923- *WhoFI 92*
**Jenkins**, Ray 1935- *WrDr 92*
**Jenkins**, Richard Lee 1931- *WhoFI 92*
**Jenkins**, Richard Leos 1903- *AmMWSc 92*
**Jenkins**, Richard Peter Vellacott 1943- *Who 92*
**Jenkins**, Robert 1945- *TwCPaSc*
**Jenkins**, Robert Allan 1934- *AmMWSc 92*
**Jenkins**, Robert Berryman 1950- *WhoFI 92*
**Jenkins**, Robert Brian 1955- *AmMWSc 92*
**Jenkins**, Robert Edward 1938- *AmMWSc 92*
**Jenkins**, Robert Ellsworth, Jr 1942- *AmMWSc 92*
**Jenkins**, Robert George 1944- *AmMWSc 92*
**Jenkins**, Robert Kenneth, Jr. 1947- *WhoBlA 92*
**Jenkins**, Robert M 1923- *AmMWSc 92*
**Jenkins**, Robert Rowe 1933- *WhoAmL 92*
**Jenkins**, Robert Walls, Jr 1936- *AmMWSc 92*
**Jenkins**, Robin *Who 92*
**Jenkins**, Robin 1912- *ConNov 91, IntAu&W 91, WrDr 92*
**Jenkins**, Roger J. 1939- *WhoBlA 92*
**Jenkins**, Ronald Lee 1952- *AmMWSc 92*
**Jenkins**, Ronald Patrick 1960- *WhoWest 92*
**Jenkins**, Roy 1920- *FacFETw, WrDr 92*
**Jenkins**, Roy Harris 1920- *IntAu&W 91*
**Jenkins**, Ruben Lee 1929- *WhoAmL 92*

**Jenkins,** Russell Willis, III 1951- *WhoFI 92*
**Jenkins,** Samuel Forest, Jr 1930- *AmMWSc 92*
**Jenkins,** Shirley Lymons 1936- *WhoBlA 92*
**Jenkins,** Simon 1943- *WrDr 92*
**Jenkins,** Simon David 1943- *IntAu&W 91, IntWW 91, Who 92*
**Jenkins,** Speight 1937- *WhoWest 92*
**Jenkins,** Stanley Kenneth 1920- *Who 92*
**Jenkins,** Stanley Michael 1940- *WhoFI 92*
**Jenkins,** Stephen Reginald Martin 1915- *Who 92*
**Jenkins,** Stephen Robert 1952- *WhoMW 92*
**Jenkins,** Terry Lloyd 1935- *AmMWSc 92*
**Jenkins,** Thomas Edward 1902- *Who 92*
**Jenkins,** Thomas Gordon 1947- *AmMWSc 92*
**Jenkins,** Thomas Harris 1920- *Who 92*
**Jenkins,** Thomas Llewellyn 1927- *AmMWSc 92*
**Jenkins,** Thomas M. *WhoBlA 92*
**Jenkins,** Thomas M. 1921- *WhoAmL 92*
**Jenkins,** Thomas O. 1926- *WhoBlA 92*
**Jenkins,** Thomas William 1922- *AmMWSc 92*
**Jenkins,** Van 1911- *WhoBlA 92*
**Jenkins,** Vernon Kelly 1932- *AmMWSc 92*
**Jenkins,** Vivian Evan 1918- *Who 92*
**Jenkins,** Walter Donald *WhoMW 92*
**Jenkins,** Walter Leon 1930- *WhoFI 92*
**Jenkins,** Warren Charles 1925- *WhoIns 92*
**Jenkins,** Will F *TwCSFW 91*
**Jenkins,** Will F. 1896-1975 *TwCWW 91*
**Jenkins,** William Ferrell 1936- *WhoRel 92*
**Jenkins,** William Kenneth 1947- *AmMWSc 92*
**Jenkins,** William L 1937- *AmMWSc 92*
**Jenkins,** William Robert 1927- *AmMWSc 92*
**Jenkins,** William Schley, III 1957- *WhoEnt 92*
**Jenkins,** William Wesley 1917- *AmMWSc 92*
**Jenkins,** Wilmer Atkinson, II 1928- *AmMWSc 92*
**Jenkins,** Winborne Terry 1932- *AmMWSc 92*
**Jenkins,** Woodie R., Jr. 1940- *WhoBlA 92*
**Jenkins,** Yolanda L. 1945- *WhoBlA 92*
**Jenkins Of Hillhead,** Baron 1920- *IntWW 91, Who 92*
**Jenkins of Hillhead,** Lady *Who 92*
**Jenkins of Putney,** Baron 1908- *Who 92*
**Jenkins-Scott,** Jackie 1949- *WhoBlA 92*
**Jenkinson,** David Stewart 1928- *Who 92*
**Jenkinson,** Edith 1893-1975 *TwCPaSc*
**Jenkinson,** Jeffrey Charles 1939- *Who 92*
**Jenkinson,** John 1945- *Who 92*
**Jenkinson,** Marion Anne 1937- *AmMWSc 92*
**Jenkinson,** Stephen G 1947- *AmMWSc 92*
**Jenkis,** Robert Elmar 1954- *WhoEnt 92*
**Jenks,** Downing Bland 1915- *IntWW 91*
**Jenks,** George C 1850-1929 *TwCWW 91*
**Jenks,** George Charles 1850-1929 *BenetAL 91*
**Jenks,** Glenn Herbert 1916- *AmMWSc 92*
**Jenks,** Jeremiah W 1856-1929 *DcAmImH*
**Jenks,** John Whipple Potter 1819-1895 *BiInAmS*
**Jenks,** Randolph 1912- *IntAu&W 91*
**Jenks,** Richard Atherley 1906- *Who 92*
**Jenks,** Richard D 1937- *AmMWSc 92*
**Jenks,** Ronald H. 1945- *WhoFI 92*
**Jenks,** Stephen 1772-1856 *NewAmDM*
**Jenks,** Tudor 1857-1922 *BenetAL 91*
**Jenks,** William Elliott 1946- *WhoEnt 92*
**Jenks,** William Furness 1909- *AmMWSc 92*
**Jenkyns,** Henry Leigh 1917- *Who 92*
**Jenne,** Carole Seegert 1942- *WhoRel 92*
**Jenne,** Eldred Llewellyn 1885-1912 *BiInAmS*
**Jenne,** Everett A 1930- *AmMWSc 92*
**Jenne,** Kenneth C 1946- *WhoAmP 91*
**Jennemann,** Karen Sue 1955- *WhoAmL 92*
**Jennemann,** Vincent Francis 1921- *AmMWSc 92*
**Jenner,** Ann Maureen 1944- *Who 92*
**Jenner,** Charles Edwin 1919- *AmMWSc 92*
**Jenner,** David Charles 1943- *AmMWSc 92*
**Jenner,** Edward 1749-1823 *BlkwCEP*
**Jenner,** Edward Baker, Jr. 1948- *WhoFI 92*
**Jenner,** Edward L 1918- *AmMWSc 92*
**Jenner,** William Alexander 1915- *WhoMW 92*
**Jenness,** Eugene Ray, Jr. 1966- *WhoRel 92*
**Jenness,** Jeanette Marie 1950- *WhoWest 92*
**Jenness,** Linda Jane 1941- *WhoAmP 91*
**Jenness,** Robert 1917- *AmMWSc 92*
**Jenness,** Stuart Edward 1925- *AmMWSc 92*
**Jennett,** Frederick Stuart 1924- *Who 92*
**Jennett,** Joseph Charles 1940- *AmMWSc 92*
**Jennett,** Norman Ethre 1877-1970 *DcNCBi 3*
**Jennett,** Shirley Shimmick 1937- *WhoWest 92*
**Jennett,** William Bryan 1926- *Who 92*
**Jennette,** Noble Stevenson, III 1953- *WhoAmL 92*
**Jennewein,** James Joseph 1929- *WhoFI 92*
**Jenney,** David S 1931- *AmMWSc 92*
**Jenney,** Elizabeth Holden 1912- *AmMWSc 92*
**Jenney,** Neil 1945- *WorArt 1980*
**Jenney,** Timothy Paul 1956- *WhoRel 92*
**Jenni,** Donald Alison 1932- *AmMWSc 92, WhoWest 92*
**Jenni,** Donald Martin 1937- *WhoEnt 92*
**Jennifer,** Susan *IntAu&W 91X, WrDr 92*
**Jennings,** A. Drue *WhoMW 92*
**Jennings,** Albert 1896- *Who 92*
**Jennings,** Albert Ray 1926- *AmMWSc 92*
**Jennings,** Alfred Roy, Jr 1945- *AmMWSc 92*
**Jennings,** Alfred S 1925- *AmMWSc 92*
**Jennings,** Allen Lee 1943- *AmMWSc 92*
**Jennings,** Alston, Jr. 1947- *WhoAmL 92*
**Jennings,** Arnold Harry 1915- *Who 92*
**Jennings,** Audrey Mary 1928- *Who 92*
**Jennings,** Bennie Alfred 1933- *WhoBlA 92*
**Jennings,** Bernard Waylon-Handel 1968- *WhoBlA 92*
**Jennings,** Bojan Hamlin 1920- *AmMWSc 92*
**Jennings,** Burgess H 1903- *AmMWSc 92*
**Jennings,** Byron Kent 1951- *AmMWSc 92*
**Jennings,** Carl Anthony 1944- *AmMWSc 92*
**Jennings,** Charles David 1939- *AmMWSc 92*
**Jennings,** Charles Warren 1918- *AmMWSc 92*
**Jennings,** Charles Wayne 1944- *WhoWest 92*
**Jennings,** Chris 1949- *TwCPaSc*
**Jennings,** Coleman Alonzo 1933- *WhoEnt 92*
**Jennings,** Dana Andrew *DrAPF 91*
**Jennings,** Daniel Thomas 1935- *AmMWSc 92*
**Jennings,** David Phipps 1941- *AmMWSc 92*
**Jennings,** Dean *TwCWW 91, WrDr 92*
**Jennings,** Dennis Raymond 1942- *WhoFI 92*
**Jennings,** Donald B 1932- *AmMWSc 92*
**Jennings,** Donald Edward 1948- *AmMWSc 92*
**Jennings,** Edward Payson 1853-1915 *BiInAmS*
**Jennings,** Elizabeth 1926- *ConPo 91, IntAu&W 91, IntWW 91, SmATA 66, Who 92, WrDr 92*
**Jennings,** Eugene Emerson 1953- *WhoWest 92*
**Jennings,** Frank Lamont 1921- *AmMWSc 92*
**Jennings,** G *IntAu&W 91X*
**Jennings,** Grover Cullen 1939- *WhoAmP 91*
**Jennings,** Harley Young, Jr 1926- *AmMWSc 92*
**Jennings,** Harry 1917- *WhoAmP 91*
**Jennings,** Humphrey 1907-1950 *IntDcF 2-2 [port], TwCPaSc*
**Jennings,** James 1925- *Who 92*
**Jennings,** James 1949- *WhoHisp 92*
**Jennings,** James Burnett 1940- *WhoFI 92*
**Jennings,** James Francis, Jr. 1933- *WhoWest 92*
**Jennings,** James Murray 1924- *WhoFI 92, WhoMW 92*
**Jennings,** Jay Bradford 1957- *WhoWest 92*
**Jennings,** Jeanette 1945- *WhoBlA 92*
**Jennings,** Jeffrey Howells 1919- *WhoAmL 92, WhoFI 92*
**Jennings,** Jesse David 1909- *IntWW 91*
**Jennings,** John Baker 1943- *WhoFI 92*
**Jennings,** John Edward, Jr. 1906-1973 *BenetAL 91*
**Jennings,** John R. R. 1937- *IntWW 91*
**Jennings,** John Southwood 1937- *IntWW 91, Who 92*
**Jennings,** Joseph Wallace 1938- *WhoEnt 92*
**Jennings,** Karla 1956- *ConAu 134*
**Jennings,** Kate *DrAPF 91*
**Jennings,** Keith Lynden 1932- *IntWW 91*
**Jennings,** Kenneth Neal 1930- *Who 92*
**Jennings,** Lane *DrAPF 91*
**Jennings,** Laurence Duane 1929- *AmMWSc 92*
**Jennings,** Lillian Pegues *WhoBlA 92*
**Jennings,** Lisa Helen Kyle 1955- *AmMWSc 92*
**Jennings,** Loren G 1951- *WhoAmP 91*
**Jennings,** M. David, Jr. 1935- *WhoMW 92*
**Jennings,** Madelyn Pulver 1934- *WhoFI 92*
**Jennings,** Marcella Grady 1920- *WhoFI 92, WhoWest 92*
**Jennings,** Margaret Elaine 1943- *WhoBlA 92*
**Jennings,** Marie Patricia 1930- *IntAu&W 91*
**Jennings,** Mark Edward 1962- *WhoFI 92*
**Jennings,** Michael Leon 1948- *AmMWSc 92*
**Jennings,** Paul 1918- *IntAu&W 91*
**Jennings,** Paul Bernard, Jr 1938- *AmMWSc 92*
**Jennings,** Paul C 1936- *AmMWSc 92*
**Jennings,** Paul Christian 1936- *WhoWest 92*
**Jennings,** Paul H. 1938- *WhoMW 92*
**Jennings,** Paul Harry 1938- *AmMWSc 92*
**Jennings,** Paul W 1936- *AmMWSc 92*
**Jennings,** Percival Henry 1903- *Who 92*
**Jennings,** Peter *LesBEnT 92 [port]*
**Jennings,** Peter 1937- *Who 92*
**Jennings,** Peter 1938- *ConAu 134, IntMPA 92*
**Jennings,** Peter Nevile Wake 1934- *Who 92*
**Jennings,** Phillip C 1946- *IntAu&W 91*
**Jennings,** Ralph Merwin 1938- *WhoEnt 92*
**Jennings,** Raymond 1897- *Who 92*
**Jennings,** Renz D 1941- *WhoAmP 91*
**Jennings,** Richard Alan 1943- *WhoEnt 92*
**Jennings,** Richard Louis 1933- *AmMWSc 92*
**Jennings,** Robert 1913- *Who 92*
**Jennings,** Robert Burgess 1926- *AmMWSc 92*
**Jennings,** Robert Lee 1942- *WhoMW 92*
**Jennings,** Robert Martin, Jr. 1953- *WhoMW 92*
**Jennings,** Robert Ray 1950- *WhoBlA 92*
**Jennings,** Robert Yewdall 1913- *IntWW 91*
**Jennings,** Rudolph Dillon 1923- *WhoAmP 91*
**Jennings,** Sharon 1954- *ConAu 134*
**Jennings,** Stephen Grant 1946- *WhoMW 92*
**Jennings,** Sylvesta Lee 1933- *WhoBlA 92*
**Jennings,** Thomas Parks 1947- *WhoAmL 92*
**Jennings,** Timothy James 1961- *WhoFI 92*
**Jennings,** Timothy William 1961- *WhoMW 92*
**Jennings,** Timothy Zeph 1950- *WhoAmP 91*
**Jennings,** Toni 1949- *WhoAmP 91*
**Jennings,** Vivan M 1936- *AmMWSc 92*
**Jennings,** Vivien Ann 1934- *WhoRel 92*
**Jennings,** Wallace, Jr *WhoAmP 91*
**Jennings,** Walter Goodrich 1922- *AmMWSc 92*
**Jennings,** Warren E, Jr 1928- *WhoIns 92*
**Jennings,** William Harney, Jr 1931- *AmMWSc 92*
**Jennings,** William Randall 1954- *WhoMW 92*
**Jennison,** Beverly Petersen 1952- *WhoAmL 92*
**Jennison,** Brian L. 1950- *WhoWest 92*
**Jennison,** Dwight Richard 1943- *AmMWSc 92*
**Jennison,** Harold Stewart 1922- *WhoAmP 91*
**Jennison,** Robin 1954- *WhoAmP 91*
**Jennrich,** Ellen Coutlee 1939- *WhoAmP 91*
**Jennrich,** Robert I 1932- *AmMWSc 92*
**Jenny,** Hans K 1919- *AmMWSc 92*
**Jenny,** Neil Allan 1936- *AmMWSc 92*
**Jenny,** Patrick Duncan 1964- *WhoWest 92*
**Jenour,** Maynard 1905- *Who 92*
**Jenoure,** Joseph d1732 *DcNCBi 3*
**Jenrette,** Richard Hampton 1929- *IntWW 91, WhoFI 92*
**Jenrich,** Charles Lester 1947- *WhoMW 92*
**Jens,** Elizabeth Lee Shafer 1915- *WhoMW 92*
**Jens,** Salome 1935- *IntMPA 92, WhoEnt 92*
**Jens,** Walter 1923- *IntWW 91*
**Jens,** Wayne H 1921- *AmMWSc 92*
**Jenschke,** Tanis J 1939- *WhoIns 92*
**Jensen,** Adolph Robert 1915- *AmMWSc 92*
**Jensen,** Albert Christian 1924- *AmMWSc 92*
**Jensen,** Aldon Homan 1922- *AmMWSc 92*
**Jensen,** Alfred Julio 1903-1981 *FacFETw*
**Jensen,** Arnold William 1928- *AmMWSc 92*
**Jensen,** Arthur Robert 1923- *IntWW 91, WrDr 92*
**Jensen,** Arthur Seigfried 1917- *AmMWSc 92*
**Jensen,** Barbara Lynne *AmMWSc 92*
**Jensen,** Barbara Wood 1927- *WhoWest 92*
**Jensen,** Bess T 1924- *WhoAmP 91*
**Jensen,** Betty Klainminc 1949- *AmMWSc 92*
**Jensen,** Bo Green 1955- *IntAu&W 91*
**Jensen,** Bob 1928- *WhoAmP 91*
**Jensen,** Bruce A 1930- *AmMWSc 92*
**Jensen,** Bruce David 1954- *AmMWSc 92*
**Jensen,** Bruce L 1944- *AmMWSc 92*
**Jensen,** Bruce Merritt 1953- *WhoMW 92*
**Jensen,** Carl Martin 1929- *WhoWest 92*
**Jensen,** Christian Reid 1940- *WhoFI 92*
**Jensen,** Christopher Lars 1961- *WhoWest 92*
**Jensen,** Clayne 1930- *WrDr 92*
**Jensen,** Clayton Everett 1920- *AmMWSc 92*
**Jensen,** Clyde B 1948- *AmMWSc 92*
**Jensen,** Craig Leebens 1950- *AmMWSc 92*
**Jensen,** Creighton Randall 1929- *AmMWSc 92*
**Jensen,** Cynthia Ann 1953- *WhoWest 92*
**Jensen,** Cynthia G 1938- *AmMWSc 92*
**Jensen,** D. Lowell 1928- *WhoAmL 92, WhoWest 92*
**Jensen,** Dallin W. 1932- *WhoAmL 92*
**Jensen,** David 1926- *AmMWSc 92*
**Jensen,** David Allen 1948- *WhoWest 92*
**Jensen,** David Arel 1950- *WhoEnt 92*
**Jensen,** David Bernard 1938- *WhoAmL 92*
**Jensen,** David Elmer Thure 1947- *WhoFI 92*
**Jensen,** David Gram 1955- *WhoWest 92*
**Jensen,** David James 1935- *AmMWSc 92*
**Jensen,** David William 1943- *WhoFI 92*
**Jensen,** De Lamar 1925- *IntAu&W 91, WrDr 92*
**Jensen,** Dennis Mark 1946- *WhoFI 92*
**Jensen,** Dick Leroy 1930- *WhoAmL 92*
**Jensen,** Donald Ray 1932- *AmMWSc 92*
**Jensen,** Donald Reed 1931- *AmMWSc 92*
**Jensen,** Doris Bernice 1922- *WhoEnt 92*
**Jensen,** Douglas Andrew 1940- *AmMWSc 92*
**Jensen,** Douglas Blaine 1943- *WhoAmL 92*
**Jensen,** Douglas Glen 1957- *WhoWest 92*
**Jensen,** Douglas W 1950- *WhoAmP 91*
**Jensen,** Edmund Paul 1937- *WhoFI 92, WhoWest 92*
**Jensen,** Edwin Harry 1922- *AmMWSc 92*
**Jensen,** Eldon S 1942- *WhoAmP 91*
**Jensen,** Elwood V. 1920- *IntWW 91*
**Jensen,** Elwood Vernon 1920- *AmMWSc 92, WhoMW 92*
**Jensen,** Emron Alfred 1925- *AmMWSc 92*
**Jensen,** Erik Hugo 1924- *AmMWSc 92*
**Jensen,** Erik Michael 1945- *WhoMW 92*
**Jensen,** Erling 1919- *IntWW 91*
**Jensen,** Erling N 1908- *AmMWSc 92*
**Jensen,** Gary Jon 1949- *WhoWest 92*
**Jensen,** Gary Lee 1933- *AmMWSc 92*
**Jensen,** Gary Richard 1941- *AmMWSc 92*
**Jensen,** Georg Arthur 1866-1935 *DcTwDes, FacFETw*
**Jensen,** George R. 1948- *WhoFI 92*
**Jensen,** Georgia Caye 1947- *WhoAmP 91*
**Jensen,** Gordon D 1926- *AmMWSc 92*
**Jensen,** Gordon Lloyd 1943- *WhoAmL 92*
**Jensen,** H L 1928- *WhoAmP 91*
**Jensen,** Hanne Margrete 1935- *AmMWSc 92*
**Jensen,** Hans Peter 1943- *IntWW 91*
**Jensen,** Harbo Peter 1948- *AmMWSc 92*
**Jensen,** Harold James 1921- *AmMWSc 92*
**Jensen,** Helen 1919- *WhoWest 92*
**Jensen,** Herluf Matthias 1923- *WhoRel 92*
**Jensen,** Homer d1991 *NewYTBS 91 [port]*
**Jensen,** J H, Jr 1916- *AmMWSc 92*
**Jensen,** Jack Albert 1928- *WhoAmL 92*
**Jensen,** Jacob 1926- *DcTwDes*
**Jensen,** Jakki Renee 1959- *WhoWest 92*
**Jensen,** James Burt 1943- *AmMWSc 92*
**Jensen,** James Le Roy 1915- *AmMWSc 92*
**Jensen,** James Leslie 1939- *AmMWSc 92, WhoWest 92*
**Jensen,** Jane Mary 1951- *WhoMW 92*
**Jensen,** Jennifer Jo 1960- *WhoMW 92*
**Jensen,** Jens Alford 1948- *WhoWest 92*
**Jensen,** Jens Peder 1947- *WhoFI 92*
**Jensen,** Jerrold S 1945- *WhoAmP 91*
**Jensen,** Jerry Kirtland 1947- *WhoFI 92*
**Jensen,** Johannes 1873-1950 *FacFETw*
**Jensen,** Johannes Hans Daniel 1907-1973 *WhoNob 90*
**Jensen,** Johannes V. 1873-1950 *TwCLC 41 [port]*
**Jensen,** Johannes Vilhelm 1873-1950 *WhoNob 90*
**Jensen,** John Bruno 1964- *WhoMW 92*
**Jensen,** John Robert 1946- *WhoAmL 92*
**Jensen,** John W 1926- *WhoAmP 91*
**Jensen,** John Warner 1944- *WhoEnt 92*
**Jensen,** Joseph Norman 1924- *WhoRel 92*
**Jensen,** Judy Dianne 1948- *WhoWest 92*
**Jensen,** Kai Arne 1908- *IntWW 91*
**Jensen,** Katherine Kemp 1955- *WhoFI 92*
**Jensen,** Keith Edwin 1924- *AmMWSc 92*
**Jensen,** Keith Frank 1938- *AmMWSc 92*
**Jensen,** Laura *DrAPF 91*
**Jensen,** Laura Linnea 1948- *IntAu&W 91*
**Jensen,** Lawrence Craig-Winston 1936- *AmMWSc 92*
**Jensen,** Lawrence Robert 1959- *WhoWest 92*
**Jensen,** Leo Stanley 1925- *AmMWSc 92*

**Jensen**, Loren Ann 1953- *WhoWest 92*
**Jensen**, Louis Richard 1940- *WhoMW 92*
**Jensen**, Lyle Howard 1915- *AmMWSc 92*
**Jensen**, Marcus Martin 1929- *AmMWSc 92*
**Jensen**, Marvin E 1926- *AmMWSc 92*
**Jensen**, Mead LeRoy 1925- *AmMWSc 92*
**Jensen**, Melvin George 1948- *WhoMW 92*
**Jensen**, Milton G *WhoAmP 91*
**Jensen**, Nels Nordy, Jr. 1942- *WhoWest 92*
**Jensen**, Norman P 1938- *AmMWSc 92*
**Jensen**, Ole Vig 1936- *IntWW 91*
**Jensen**, Paul Allen 1936- *AmMWSc 92*
**Jensen**, Paul Edward T 1926- *AmMWSc 92*
**Jensen**, Paul Timothy 1950- *WhoRel 92*
**Jensen**, Peter *ConAu 35NR*
**Jensen**, Randolph A 1919- *AmMWSc 92*
**Jensen**, Reed Jerry 1936- *AmMWSc 92*
**Jensen**, Regina Brunhild 1951- *WhoWest 92*
**Jensen**, Renaldo Mario 1934- *WhoBlA 92*
**Jensen**, Richard 1941- *WrDr 92*
**Jensen**, Richard Arthur 1936- *AmMWSc 92*
**Jensen**, Richard Currie 1939- *WhoAmL 92*
**Jensen**, Richard Donald 1936- *AmMWSc 92*
**Jensen**, Richard Erling 1938- *AmMWSc 92*
**Jensen**, Richard Eugene 1927- *AmMWSc 92*
**Jensen**, Richard Grant 1936- *AmMWSc 92*
**Jensen**, Richard Grover 1942- *WhoAmP 91*
**Jensen**, Richard Harvey 1941- *AmMWSc 92*
**Jensen**, Richard Jorg 1947- *AmMWSc 92, WhoMW 92*
**Jensen**, Richard Wayne 1946- *WhoFI 92*
**Jensen**, Robert Alan 1940- *AmMWSc 92*
**Jensen**, Robert Allen 1947- *WhoFI 92*
**Jensen**, Robert Gordon 1926- *AmMWSc 92*
**Jensen**, Robert Neal 1947- *WhoAmL 92*
**Jensen**, Roland Jens 1929- *WhoFI 92, WhoMW 92*
**Jensen**, Ronald Harry 1938- *AmMWSc 92*
**Jensen**, Ronnie Blaine 1950- *WhoFI 92*
**Jensen**, Roxanne 1938- *WhoAmP 91*
**Jensen**, Roy A 1936- *AmMWSc 92*
**Jensen**, Ruby Jean 1930- *IntAu&W 91*
**Jensen**, Rue 1911- *AmMWSc 92*
**Jensen**, Scott L. 1948- *WhoEnt 92*
**Jensen**, Soren Georg 1917- *DcTwDes*
**Jensen**, Stanley George 1934- *AmMWSc 92*
**Jensen**, Susan Elaine 1950- *AmMWSc 92*
**Jensen**, Teresa Elaine 1948- *WhoFI 92*
**Jensen**, Thomas E 1932- *AmMWSc 92*
**Jensen**, Thomas Edward 1945- *WhoAmL 92*
**Jensen**, Thomas Lee 1934- *WhoAmP 91*
**Jensen**, Thorkil 1919- *AmMWSc 92*
**Jensen**, Timothy B 1939- *AmMWSc 92*
**Jensen**, Timothy Ward 1956- *WhoRel 92*
**Jensen**, Tom 1948- *WhoAmP 91*
**Jensen**, Tommy Gert 1954- *WhoWest 92*
**Jensen**, Torkil Hesselberg 1932- *AmMWSc 92*
**Jensen**, Wallace M. 1947- *WhoWest 92*
**Jensen**, Wallace Norup 1921- *AmMWSc 92*
**Jensen**, Walter Edward 1937- *WhoAmL 92, WhoFI 92*
**Jensen**, William August 1927- *AmMWSc 92*
**Jensen**, William Neale 1939- *WhoAmL 92*
**Jensen**, William Phelps 1937- *AmMWSc 92*
**Jensen-Reinke**, Clemens Immanuel 1961- *WhoRel 92*
**Jensh**, Ronald Paul 1938- *AmMWSc 92*
**Jenski**, Laura Jean 1952- *AmMWSc 92*
**Jenson**, A Bennett *AmMWSc 92*
**Jenson**, Charles David 1952- *WhoWest 92*
**Jenson**, Douglas D. 1956- *WhoWest 92*
**Jenson**, Ronald Allen 1948- *WhoRel 92*
**Jenson**, Scott L. 1944- *WhoFI 92*
**Jenson**, Thomas Lowell 1950- *WhoFI 92*
**Jenssen**, Thomas Alan 1939- *AmMWSc 92*
**Jenstad**, Nels Linden 1956- *WhoWest 92*
**Jenstrom**, Eino Emil 1921- *WhoAmL 92*
**Jent**, George Larry 1951- *WhoAmL 92*
**Jent**, Glenn Alvin 1944- *WhoRel 92*
**Jentes**, William Robert 1932- *WhoAmL 92*
**Jentner**, Norman Raben 1954- *WhoMW 92*
**Jentoft**, Joyce Eileen 1945- *AmMWSc 92*
**Jentoft**, Ralph Eugene, Jr 1918- *AmMWSc 92*
**Jentsch**, William August, Jr. 1958- *WhoFI 92, WhoWest 92*
**Jentz**, Gaylord Adair 1931- *WhoAmL 92*
**Jenyns**, Soame 1704-1787 *BlkwCEP*
**Jenzano**, Anthony Francis 1919- *AmMWSc 92*
**Jeon**, Bang Nam 1954- *WhoFI 92*
**Jeon**, Kwang Wu 1934- *AmMWSc 92*
**Jeong**, Tung Hon 1935- *AmMWSc 92*
**Jephcott**, Anthony 1924- *Who 92*
**Jephcott**, Samuel C. 1944- *IntMPA 92*
**Jeppesen**, Gordon Lutz 1913- *WhoMW 92*
**Jeppesen**, Laura *WhoEnt 92*
**Jeppesen**, Randolph H *AmMWSc 92*
**Jeppson**, J. O. *ConAu 36NR*
**Jeppson**, John 1916- *WhoFI 92*
**Jeppson**, Lee Ralph 1910- *AmMWSc 92*
**Jeppson**, Robert Baird, Jr. 1920- *WhoWest 92*
**Jeppson**, Roger Wayne 1936- *WhoAmL 92*
**Jeppson**, Roland W 1933- *AmMWSc 92*
**Jepsen**, Carl H. 1940- *WhoWest 92*
**Jepsen**, Charles Terral 1952- *WhoEnt 92*
**Jepsen**, Donald William 1932- *AmMWSc 92*
**Jepsen**, George C *WhoAmP 91*
**Jepsen**, Roger W. 1928- *IntWW 91*
**Jepsen**, Roger William 1928- *WhoAmP 91, WhoFI 92*
**Jepson**, Charles Warren 1946- *WhoWest 92*
**Jepson**, Edgar 1863-1938 *ScFEYrs*
**Jepson**, Hans Godfrey 1936- *WhoFI 92*
**Jepson**, Robert Scott, Jr. 1942- *WhoFI 92, WhoMW 92*
**Jepson**, Selwyn 1899- *IntAu&W 91*
**Jepson**, Steven Baker 1960- *WhoEnt 92*
**Jepson**, William W 1926- *AmMWSc 92*
**Jeralds**, Luther R 1938- *WhoAmP 91*
**Jerdan**, William H. S., Jr. *WhoRel 92*
**Jereb**, Brian James 1958- *WhoAmL 92*
**Jeremia**, Michael Francis 1950- *WhoMW 92*
**Jeremiah** *EncEarC*
**Jeremiah**, Jeremiah Simon, Jr. 1935- *WhoAmL 92*
**Jeremiah**, Lester Earl 1941- *AmMWSc 92*
**Jeremiah**, Melvyn Gwynne 1939- *Who 92*
**Jeremias**, Charles George 1920- *AmMWSc 92*
**Jeremias**, Otakar 1892-1962 *NewAmDM*
**Jeren**, John Anthony, Jr. 1946- *WhoAmL 92*
**Jerez**, Francisco de 1497?-1563? *HisDSpE*
**Jerez-Farran**, Carlos 1950- *WhoHisp 92*
**Jerez Garcia**, Cesar A. 1936- *IntWW 91*
**Jerge**, Marie Charlotte 1952- *WhoRel 92*
**Jergens**, Adele 1922- *IntMPA 92*
**Jergens**, Andrew MacAdidh 1935- *WhoRel 92*
**Jergensen**, Dirk Orme 1950- *WhoWest 92*
**Jerger**, E W 1922- *AmMWSc 92*
**Jergeson**, Greg 1950- *WhoAmP 91*
**Jeria**, Jorge 1947- *WhoHisp 92*
**Jerina**, Carol 1947- *IntAu&W 91*
**Jerina**, Donald M 1940- *AmMWSc 92*
**Jeris**, John S 1930- *AmMWSc 92*
**Jerison**, Harry Jacob 1925- *AmMWSc 92, WhoWest 92*
**Jerison**, Meyer 1922- *AmMWSc 92*
**Jeritza**, Maria 1887-1982 *FacFETw, NewAmDM*
**Jerke**, William H 1955- *WhoAmP 91*
**Jerkins**, Alonzo Thomas 1807-1895 *DcNCBi 3*
**Jerkins**, Jerry Gaines *WhoBlA 92*
**Jerkofsky**, Maryann 1943- *AmMWSc 92*
**Jerman**, Cornelia Petty 1874-1946 *DcNCBi 3*
**Jermann**, William Howard 1935- *AmMWSc 92*
**Jermier**, Donald Alfred 1930- *WhoFI 92*
**Jerne**, Niels Kaj 1911- *AmMWSc 92, IntWW 91, Who 92, WhoNob 90*
**Jerner**, R Craig 1938- *AmMWSc 92*
**Jernigan**, Alicia 1944- *WhoHisp 92*
**Jernigan**, C.B. 1863-1930 *RelLAm 91*
**Jernigan**, Candy d1991 *NewYTBS 91*
**Jernigan**, Curtis Dean 1945- *WhoBlA 92*
**Jernigan**, Eddie Dean 1956- *WhoFI 92*
**Jernigan**, Finith Ewin, II 1952- *WhoFI 92*
**Jernigan**, Gerald D 1943- *WhoAmP 91*
**Jernigan**, Homer Large 1922- *WhoRel 92*
**Jernigan**, Howard Maxwell, Jr 1943- *AmMWSc 92*
**Jernigan**, James Earl 1925- *WhoAmP 91*
**Jernigan**, James Leroy 1936- *WhoWest 92*
**Jernigan**, Malcolm Lathon 1937- *WhoMW 92*
**Jernigan**, Robert Lee 1941- *AmMWSc 92*
**Jernigan**, Thomas Roberts 1847-1920 *DcNCBi 3*
**Jernow**, Jane L *AmMWSc 92*
**Jernstedt**, Kenneth A 1917- *WhoAmP 91*
**Jernstedt**, Kenneth Elliott 1944- *WhoAmL 92*
**Jernstedt**, Richard Don 1947- *WhoFI 92*
**Jerome** 347?-419? *EncEarC [port]*
**Jerome of Moravia** *NewAmDM*
**Jerome**, Bette *WhoEnt 92*
**Jerome**, Cecilia Anne 1961- *WhoMW 92*
**Jerome**, Dan *WhoAmP 91*
**Jerome**, Harry Winston 1940-1982 *BlkOlyM*
**Jerome**, James Alexander 1933- *IntWW 91, Who 92*
**Jerome**, Jerome K. 1859-1927 *RfGEnL 91, ScFEYrs*
**Jerome**, Jerrold Vincent 1929- *WhoIns 92*
**Jerome**, John 1932- *WrDr 92*
**Jerome**, John James 1933- *WhoAmL 92*
**Jerome**, Joseph *WrDr 92*
**Jerome**, Joseph Walter 1939- *AmMWSc 92, WhoMW 92*
**Jerome**, Judson *DrAPF 91*
**Jerome**, Judson d1991 *NewYTBS 91*
**Jerome**, Judson 1927- *ConPo 91, WrDr 92*
**Jerome**, Judson Blair 1927- *IntAu&W 91*
**Jerome**, Norge Winifred 1930- *AmMWSc 92, WhoBlA 92*
**Jeronimo**, Lawrence J 1947- *WhoIns 92*
**Jeroski**, Anthony Joseph, Jr. 1948- *WhoMW 92*
**Jeroslow**, Robert G 1942- *AmMWSc 92*
**Jerousek**, William Fred 1920- *WhoMW 92*
**Jerow**, John F. 1944- *WhoFI 92*
**Jerram**, Richard Martyn 1928- *Who 92*
**Jerrard**, Richard Patterson 1925- *AmMWSc 92*
**Jerrells**, Thomas Ray 1944- *AmMWSc 92*
**Jerrett**, Nathaniel *WhoRel 92*
**Jerri**, Abdul J 1932- *AmMWSc 92*
**Jerritts**, Stephen G. 1925- *WhoFI 92*
**Jerrold**, Douglas William 1803-1857 *RfGEnL 91*
**Jerry**, Robert Howard, II 1953- *WhoAmL 92*
**Jerrytone**, Samuel Joseph 1947- *WhoWest 92*
**Jersevic**, Roland Joseph 1952- *WhoAmL 92*
**Jersey**, Dean of *Who 92*
**Jersey**, Earl of 1910- *Who 92*
**Jersey**, George Carl 1940- *AmMWSc 92*
**Jersey**, William Clifford 1927- *WhoEnt 92*
**Jersild**, Per Christian 1935- *IntAu&W 91*
**Jersild**, Ralph Alvin, Jr 1931- *AmMWSc 92*
**Jersild**, Thomas Nielsen 1936- *WhoAmL 92, WhoMW 92*
**Jersin**, Edward Anthony 1920- *WhoAmL 92*
**Jersin**, Wayne Neal 1938- *WhoFI 92*
**Jeruchim**, Michel Claude 1937- *AmMWSc 92*
**Jerue**, James Louis 1956- *WhoAmL 92*
**Jerus**, Robert George 1955- *WhoMW 92*
**Jerusalem**, Siegfried 1940- *IntWW 91*
**Jerusalem & The Middle East**, Bishop of *Who 92*
**Jervay**, Marion White 1948- *WhoBlA 92*
**Jervay**, Paul Reginald, Jr. 1949- *WhoBlA 92*
**Jervay**, Thomas Clarence, Sr. 1914- *WhoBlA 92*
**Jervey**, Edward D. 1929- *ConAu 133*
**Jerving**, John Wesley 1950- *WhoMW 92, WhoRel 92*
**Jervis** *Who 92*
**Jervis**, Charles Elliott 1907- *Who 92*
**Jervis**, Herbert Hunter 1942- *AmMWSc 92*
**Jervis**, John Bloomfield 1795-1885 *BiInAmS*
**Jervis**, Robert 1940- *WrDr 92*
**Jervis**, Robert Alfred 1938- *AmMWSc 92*
**Jervis**, Robert E 1927- *AmMWSc 92*
**Jervis**, Roger P. *Who 92*
**Jervis**, Sally Ann 1937- *WhoEnt 92*
**Jervis**, Simon Swynfen 1943- *IntWW 91, Who 92*
**Jesaitis**, Algirdas Joseph 1945- *AmMWSc 92*
**Jesaitis**, Raymond G 1943- *AmMWSc 92*
**Jeschke**, Marlin 1929- *WhoRel 92*
**Jeschke**, Wolfgang 1936- *TwCSFW 91A*
**Jeschonnek**, Hans 1899-1943 *EncTR 91 [port]*
**Jesernig**, Jim *WhoAmP 91*
**Jeseseke**, Ellen Frances 1954- *WhoFI 92*
**Jesewitz**, Larry 1943- *WhoMW 92*
**Jesih**, Boris 1943- *IntWW 91*
**Jeska**, Edward Lawrence 1923- *AmMWSc 92*
**Jeskey**, Harold Alfred 1912- *AmMWSc 92*
**Jesky**, T. J. 1947- *WhoFI 92*
**Jesmok**, Gary J 1947- *AmMWSc 92*
**Jespersen**, James 1934- *AmMWSc 92*
**Jespersen**, Neil David 1946- *AmMWSc 92*
**Jespersen**, Nils Vidar 1951- *AmMWSc 92*
**Jess**, Edward Orland 1917- *AmMWSc 92*
**Jesse**, Glen D 1943- *WhoAmP 91*
**Jesse**, H. William, Jr. 1951- *WhoFI 92*
**Jesse**, Kenneth Edward 1933- *AmMWSc 92, WhoMW 92*
**Jesse**, Norman Gale 1937- *WhoAmP 91*
**Jessel**, Charles 1924- *Who 92*
**Jessel**, Ian 1939- *IntMPA 92*
**Jessel**, Oliver Richard 1929- *Who 92*
**Jessel**, Penelope 1920- *Who 92*
**Jessel**, Toby Francis Henry 1934- *Who 92*
**Jessen**, Borge 1907- *IntWW 91*
**Jessen**, Carl Roger 1933- *AmMWSc 92*
**Jessen**, Daryl Lee 1960- *WhoMW 92*
**Jessen**, Del 1948- *WhoEnt 92*
**Jessen**, Nicholas C, Jr 1944- *AmMWSc 92*
**Jessen**, Nicholas C, Sr 1913- *AmMWSc 92*
**Jesser**, William Augustus 1939- *AmMWSc 92*
**Jessie**, Waymon Thomas 1945- *WhoBlA 92*
**Jessing**, Theodore Charles 1949- *WhoWest 92*
**Jessner**, Leopold 1878-1945 *FacFETw*
**Jessop**, Alan Michael 1934- *AmMWSc 92*
**Jessop**, Alexander Smethurst 1943- *Who 92*
**Jessop**, Nancy Meyer 1926- *AmMWSc 92*
**Jessop**, Reuben Theodore Carl 1962- *WhoFI 92*
**Jessup**, Ann Matthews 1738-1822 *DcNCBi 3*
**Jessup**, Darinda Jane 1962- *WhoMW 92*
**Jessup**, Gayle Louise 1957- *WhoBlA 92*
**Jessup**, Gordon L, Jr 1922- *AmMWSc 92*
**Jessup**, Harley 1954- *WhoEnt 92*
**Jessup**, Joe Lee 1913- *WhoFI 92*
**Jessup**, Lynne Katie 1951- *WhoRel 92*
**Jessup**, Marsha Edwina 1944- *WhoBlA 92*
**Jessup**, Philip Caryl, Jr. 1926- *WhoAmL 92*
**Jessup**, Richard 1925-1982 *TwCWW 91*
**Jessup**, Richard Edward 1932- *WhoRel 92*
**Jessup**, Roger L 1929- *WhoAmP 91*
**Jessup**, W. Edgar, Jr. 1922- *WhoAmL 92*
**Jessup**, William Walker 1938- *WhoFI 92*
**Jessye**, Eva 1895- *NewAmDM, NotBlAW 92*
**Jester**, Guy Earlscort 1929- *AmMWSc 92*
**Jester**, Guy Earlscourt *WhoFI 92*
**Jester**, James Vincent 1950- *AmMWSc 92*
**Jester**, John Selby 1942- *WhoRel 92*
**Jester**, Katharine M 1928- *WhoAmP 91*
**Jester**, Royston, III 1913- *WhoAmP 91*
**Jester**, William A 1934- *AmMWSc 92*
**Jesup**, Henry Griswold 1826-1903 *BiInAmS*
**Jesup**, Morris Ketchum 1830-1908 *BiInAmS*
**Jesus** *EncEarC, EncTR 91*
**Jeswiet**, Jacob 1946- *AmMWSc 92*
**Jeszenszky**, Geza 1941- *IntWW 91*
**Jet**, Jimmy 1950- *WhoEnt 92*
**Jeter**, Clifton B., Jr. 1944- *WhoBlA 92*
**Jeter**, Delores DeAnn 1949- *WhoBlA 92*
**Jeter**, Felicia Rene 1948- *WhoBlA 92*
**Jeter**, Frank Hamilton, Jr 1918- *WhoAmP 91*
**Jeter**, Hewitt Webb 1941- *AmMWSc 92*
**Jeter**, James Rolater, Jr 1940- *AmMWSc 92*
**Jeter**, Jeff F., III 1965- *WhoEnt 92*
**Jeter**, Jennifer Kay 1962- *WhoEnt 92*
**Jeter**, Joseph C., Jr. 1961- *WhoBlA 92*
**Jeter**, Joseph Roscoe, Jr. 1943- *WhoRel 92*
**Jeter**, K W 1950- *TwCSFW 91, WrDr 92*
**Jeter**, Katherine Leslie Brash 1921- *WhoAmL 92, WhoFI 92*
**Jeter**, Loren Eugene, Sr. 1909- *WhoWest 92*
**Jeter**, Michael *WhoEnt 92*
**Jeter**, Michael 1952- *IntMPA 92*
**Jeter**, Raphael Garland 1909- *WhoFI 92*
**Jeter**, Sheila Ann 1952- *WhoBlA 92*
**Jeter**, Thomas Elliott 1929- *WhoBlA 92*
**Jeter**, Velma Marjorie Dreyfus 1906- *WhoBlA 92*
**Jeter**, Wayburn Stewart 1926- *AmMWSc 92*
**Jethro Tull** *NewAmDM*
**Jetson**, Raymond 1956- *WhoAmP 91*
**Jett**, Arthur Victor, Sr. 1906- *WhoBlA 92*
**Jett**, Charles Cranston 1941- *WhoFI 92, WhoMW 92*
**Jett**, James Hubert 1938- *AmMWSc 92*
**Jett**, Richard James 1940- *WhoFI 92*
**Jett**, Stephen Clinton 1938- *WrDr 92*
**Jett**, Steven Adrian 1952- *WhoRel 92*
**Jett-Tilton**, Marti 1941- *AmMWSc 92*
**Jette**, Archelle Norman 1934- *AmMWSc 92*
**Jette**, Ernest Arthur 1945- *WhoAmL 92*
**Jetten**, Anton Marinus 1946- *AmMWSc 92*
**Jetter**, Arthur Carl, Jr. 1947- *WhoMW 92*
**Jetter**, John Alan 1950- *WhoFI 92*
**Jettke**, Harry Jerome 1925- *WhoMW 92*
**Jeudy**, Luc Marie Antoine 1947- *WhoWest 92*
**Jeune**, Claude le *NewAmDM*
**Jeury**, Michel 1934- *TwCSFW 91A*
**Jeutter**, Dean Curtis 1944- *AmMWSc 92*
**Jevning**, Ron 1942- *AmMWSc 92*
**Jevons**, Frederic Raphael 1929- *Who 92*
**Jewel**, Julie S 1953- *WhoAmP 91*
**Jewell**, David John 1934- *Who 92*
**Jewell**, Dorothy Althea 1923- *WhoWest 92*
**Jewell**, Frederick Forbes, Sr 1928- *AmMWSc 92*
**Jewell**, George Benson 1944- *WhoAmL 92*

**Jewell,** George Hiram 1922- *WhoAmL 92*
**Jewell,** Jack Lee 1954- *AmMWSc 92*
**Jewell,** Janice Marie 1940- *WhoAmL 92*
**Jewell,** Jerry D 1930- *WhoAmP 91*
**Jewell,** Jerry Donal 1930- *WhoBlA 92*
**Jewell,** Lewis Ellsworth *BiInAmS*
**Jewell,** Nicholas Patrick 1952- *AmMWSc 92*
**Jewell,** Paula L. 1943- *WhoBlA 92*
**Jewell,** Peter Arundel 1925- *Who 92*
**Jewell,** Terri L. *DrAPF 91*
**Jewell,** Tommy Edward, III 1954- *WhoBlA 92*
**Jewell,** William R 1935- *AmMWSc 92*
**Jewell,** William S 1932- *AmMWSc 92*
**Jewers,** William George 1921- *Who 92*
**Jewett,** Charlie Ruth 1936- *WhoBlA 92*
**Jewett,** Don L 1931- *AmMWSc 92*
**Jewett,** Ezekiel 1791-1877 *BiInAmS*
**Jewett,** Hugh Judge 1903- *AmMWSc 92*
**Jewett,** Jack B 1946- *WhoAmP 91*
**Jewett,** John Gibson 1937- *AmMWSc 92*
**Jewett,** Lucille McIntyre 1929- *WhoWest 92*
**Jewett,** Paul King 1919-1991 *ConAu 135*
**Jewett,** Robert 1933- *WhoRel 92*
**Jewett,** Robert Elwin 1934- *AmMWSc 92*
**Jewett,** Sally Jean 1953- *WhoEnt 92*
**Jewett,** Sandra Lynne 1945- *AmMWSc 92*
**Jewett,** Sarah Orne 1849-1909 *BenetAL 91, HanAmWH, ModAWWr*
**Jewison,** Norman *LesBEnT 92*
**Jewison,** Norman 1926- *IntDcF 2-2*
**Jewison,** Norman Frederick 1926- *IntWW 91, WhoEnt 92*
**Jewison,** Norman P. 1926- *IntMPA 92*
**Jewkes,** Gordon 1931- *Who 92*
**Jewkes,** Gordon Wesley 1931- *IntWW 91*
**Jewsbury,** Wilbur 1906- *AmMWSc 92*
**Jewson,** Richard Wilson 1944- *Who 92*
**Jex,** Robert F. 1946- *WhoWest 92*
**Jeyapalan,** Kandiah 1938- *AmMWSc 92*
**Jeyaretnam,** J. B. 1926- *IntWW 91*
**Jeydel,** Richard K. 1950- *WhoAmL 92*
**Jeye,** Peter Austin 1959- *WhoFI 92*
**Jezak,** Edward V 1934- *AmMWSc 92*
**Jezebel** d884BC *EncAmaz 91*
**Jezerinac,** Raymond Felix 1940- *WhoMW 92*
**Jezeski,** James John 1918- *AmMWSc 92*
**Jezioro,** Therese Marie 1948- *WhoFI 92*
**Jezl,** James Louis 1918- *AmMWSc 92*
**Jezorek,** John Robert 1942- *AmMWSc 92*
**Jezyk,** Peter Franklin 1939- *AmMWSc 92*
**Jha,** Akhilshwar 1932- *WrDr 92*
**Jha,** Mahesh Chandra 1945- *AmMWSc 92*
**Jha,** Shacheenatha 1918- *AmMWSc 92*
**Jha,** Shyam Chandra 1959- *WhoFI 92, WhoWest 92*
**Jhabvala,** Ruth Prawer *DrAPF 91*
**Jhabvala,** Ruth Prawer 1927- *ConNov 91, FacFETw, IntAu&W 91, IntMPA 92, IntWW 91, LiExTwC, RfGEnL 91, Who 92, WrDr 92*
**Jhamandas,** Khem 1939- *AmMWSc 92*
**Jhanwar,** Suresh Chandra *AmMWSc 92*
**Jhirad,** David John 1939- *AmMWSc 92*
**Jhon,** Myung S *AmMWSc 92*
**Ji Chaozhu** 1929- *IntWW 91, Who 92*
**Ji Pengfei** 1910- *IntWW 91*
**Ji Xianlin** 1911- *IntWW 91*
**Ji,** Chueng Ryong 1954- *AmMWSc 92*
**Ji,** Guangda Winston *AmMWSc 92*
**Ji,** Inhae 1938- *AmMWSc 92*
**Ji,** Ronghui 1957- *WhoMW 92*
**Ji,** Sungchul 1937- *AmMWSc 92*
**Ji,** Tae H 1941- *AmMWSc 92*
**Jia Chunwang** 1938- *IntWW 91*
**Jia Lanpo** 1908- *IntWW 91*
**Jia Pingwa** 1953- *IntWW 91*
**Jia Zhijie** 1936- *IntWW 91*
**Jiagge,** Annie R. 1918- *DcEcMov*
**Jiagge,** Annie Ruth 1918- *IntWW 91*
**Jiampietro,** Joseph Richard 1941- *WhoAmP 91*
**Jiang Baolin** 1942- *IntWW 91*
**Jiang Chunyun** *IntWW 91*
**Jiang Hongquan** *IntWW 91*
**Jiang Hua** 1907- *IntWW 91*
**Jiang Jialiang** 1963- *IntWW 91*
**Jiang Lijin** 1919- *IntWW 91*
**Jiang Ming** *IntWW 91*
**Jiang Minkuan** 1930- *IntWW 91*
**Jiang Qing** 1914- *IntWW 91*
**Jiang Qing** 1914-1991 *NewYTBS 91 [port], News 92-1*
**Jiang Qingxiang** 1918- *IntWW 91*
**Jiang Shengjie** 1913- *IntWW 91*
**Jiang Weiqing** 1907- *IntWW 91*
**Jiang Wen** 1914- *IntWW 91*
**Jiang Xiesheng** *IntWW 91*
**Jiang Xinxiong** 1931- *IntWW 91*
**Jiang Yiwei** 1920- *IntWW 91*
**Jiang Yizhen** *IntWW 91*
**Jiang Yonghui** 1916- *IntWW 91*
**Jiang Zemin** 1926- *IntWW 91*
**Jiang Zilong** 1941- *IntWW 91*
**Jiang,** Jack Bau-Chien 1947- *AmMWSc 92*
**Jiang,** Nai-Siang 1931- *AmMWSc 92*
**Jiao Linyi** 1920- *IntWW 91*
**Jiao Ruoyu** 1616- *IntWW 91*
**Jibben,** Laura Ann 1949- *WhoMW 92*
**Jibson,** Randall W 1956- *AmMWSc 92*
**Jicha,** Henry Louis, Jr 1928- *AmMWSc 92, WhoFI 92*
**Jicinsky,** Zdenek 1929- *IntWW 91*
**Jie,** Zhang *ConAu 133*
**Jiganti,** Mel Richard 1932- *WhoAmL 92*
**Jiggetts,** Danny Marcellus 1954- *WhoBlA 92*
**Jigme Singye Wangchuk** 1955- *FacFETw*
**Jilani,** Asaf 1934- *Who 92*
**Jilek,** Ray R 1933- *WhoAmP 91*
**Jiles,** Charles William 1927- *AmMWSc 92*
**Jiles,** Dwayne 1961- *WhoBlA 92*
**Jiles,** Pamela Theresa 1955- *BlkOlyM*
**Jiles,** Paulette 1943- *ConPo 91*
**Jilhewar,** Ashok 1947- *WhoMW 92*
**Jilka,** Robert Laurence 1948- *AmMWSc 92*
**Jillian,** Ann 1951- *IntMPA 92*
**Jillie,** Don W 1948- *AmMWSc 92*
**Jillings,** Godfrey Frank 1940- *Who 92*
**Jillson,** Kenneth R 1932- *WhoIns 92*
**Jim,** Kam Fook 1953- *AmMWSc 92*
**Jimbow,** Kowichi 1941- *AmMWSc 92*
**Jimeez,** Francisco 1943- *WhoWest 92*
**Jimenez,** A. Jimmy *WhoHisp 92*
**Jimenez,** Agnes E 1943- *AmMWSc 92*
**Jimenez,** Andres Eugenio 1953- *WhoHisp 92*
**Jimenez,** Angel F. *WhoHisp 92*
**Jimenez,** Bettie Eileen 1932- *WhoMW 92*
**Jimenez,** Cristobal 1932- *WhoHisp 92*
**Jimenez,** Daniel 1936- *WhoHisp 92*
**Jimenez,** David 1961- *WhoHisp 92*
**Jimenez,** Donna 1961- *WhoHisp 92*
**Jimenez,** Eduardo 1959- *WhoHisp 92*
**Jimenez,** Eradio T. *WhoHisp 92*
**Jimenez,** Felix J. 1949- *WhoHisp 92*
**Jimenez,** Francisco *DrAPF 91*
**Jimenez,** Francisco 1943- *WhoHisp 92*
**Jimenez,** Francisco J. 1940- *WhoHisp 92*
**Jimenez,** Iris C. 1951- *WhoHisp 92*
**Jimenez,** Javier 1961- *WhoHisp 92*
**Jimenez,** Joaquin Bernardo, II 1955- *WhoHisp 92*
**Jimenez,** Jose Mariano 1781-1811 *HisDSpE*
**Jimenez,** Jose Olivio *WhoHisp 92*
**Jimenez,** Josephine Santos 1954- *WhoFI 92*
**Jimenez,** Juan Carlos 1952- *WhoHisp 92*
**Jimenez,** Juan Ramon 1881-1958 *FacFETw, LiExTwC, WhoNob 90*
**Jimenez,** Luis A., Jr. 1940- *WhoHisp 92*
**Jimenez,** Luis Alexander 1954- *WhoHisp 92*
**Jimenez,** Maria C. *WhoHisp 92*
**Jimenez,** Maria De Los Angeles 1950- *WhoHisp 92*
**Jimenez,** Maria J. 1964- *WhoHisp 92*
**Jimenez,** Marie John 1932- *WhoHisp 92*
**Jimenez,** Matt *WhoHisp 92*
**Jimenez,** Raul, Jr. *WhoHisp 92*
**Jimenez,** Sergio 1942- *AmMWSc 92*
**Jimenez,** Sergio A. 1942- *WhoHisp 92*
**Jimenez,** Steven *WhoHisp 92*
**Jimenez,** Susan Ann 1943- *WhoHisp 92*
**Jimenez,** Tony *WhoHisp 92*
**Jimenez,** Victorino 1915- *WhoHisp 92*
**Jimenez,** Vita Marie *DrAPF 91*
**Jimenez De Arechaga,** Eduardo 1918- *IntWW 91, Who 92*
**Jimenez de Encino,** Salvador 1765-1841 *HisDSpE*
**Jimenez de Quesada,** Gonzalo 1509-1579 *HisDSpE*
**Jimenez Hyre,** Silvia 1950- *WhoHisp 92*
**Jimenez-Mabarak,** Carlos 1916- *ConCom 92*
**Jimenez-Ortiz,** Roberto 1948- *WhoFI 92*
**Jimenez P.,** Rodrigo *WhoHisp 92*
**Jimenez-Penaloza,** Rosa 1955- *WhoHisp 92*
**Jimenez-Velez,** Jose L. 1927- *WhoHisp 92*
**Jimenez-Wagenheim,** Olga 1941- *WhoHisp 92*
**Jimeno,** Philip C 1947- *WhoAmP 91*
**Jimerson,** George David 1944- *AmMWSc 92*
**Jimerson,** Royal W *ScFEYrs*
**Jimerson,** William Allen 1950- *WhoEnt 92*
**Jimeson,** Robert M, Jr 1921- *AmMWSc 92*
**Jimirro,** James P. 1937- *WhoEnt 92*
**Jimmerson,** William Allen, Jr. 1954- *WhoFI 92*
**Jimmink,** Glenda Lee 1935- *WhoWest 92*
**Jin Baosheng** 1927- *IntWW 91*
**Jin Jian** *IntWW 91*
**Jin Ming** 1908- *IntWW 91*
**Jin Shanbao** 1895- *IntWW 91*
**Jin Shangyi** 1934- *IntWW 91*
**Jin Shui** 1951- *IntWW 91*
**Jin,** Rong-Sheng 1933- *AmMWSc 92*
**Jin,** Sungho 1945- *AmMWSc 92*
**Jin Luxian,** Louis 1944- *IntWW 91*
**Jinadasa,** Kankanam Gamage 1950- *WhoMW 92*
**Jindrak,** Karel 1926- *AmMWSc 92*
**Jinga** *EncAmaz 91*
**Jingo Kogo** *EncAmaz 91*
**Jinkens,** Robert Carl 1945- *WhoFI 92*
**Jinkinson,** Alan Raymond 1935- *Who 92*
**Jinnah,** Muhammad Ali 1876-1948 *FacFETw [port]*
**Jinnett,** Robert Jefferson 1949- *WhoAmL 92*
**Jipcho,** Benjamin W 1943- *BlkOlyM*
**Jipson,** Eugene Edward 1955- *WhoRel 92*
**Jirak,** K. B. 1891-1972 *NewAmDM*
**Jires,** Jaromil 1935- *IntDcF 2-2 [port]*
**Jirgensons,** Arnold 1906- *AmMWSc 92*
**Jiricna,** Eva Magdalena 1939- *Who 92*
**Jirik,** David T. 1950- *WhoEnt 92*
**Jirkans,** Maribeth Joie 1945- *WhoMW 92*
**Jirkovsky,** Ivo 1935- *AmMWSc 92*
**Jirmanus,** Munir N 1944- *AmMWSc 92*
**Jiron,** Arnoldo Jose 1946- *WhoHisp 92*
**Jiron,** E. Charles *WhoHisp 92*
**Jiron,** Herardo A. 1926- *WhoHisp 92*
**Jiroudek,** Frantisek 1914- *IntWW 91*
**Jirovec,** Ronald Arthur 1948- *WhoFI 92*
**Jirsa,** James O 1938- *AmMWSc 92*
**Jirsa,** Robert Joseph 1955- *WhoFI 92*
**Jischke,** Martin C 1941- *AmMWSc 92, WhoMW 92*
**Jittlov,** Mike 1948- *WhoEnt 92*
**Jiu,** James 1929- *AmMWSc 92*
**Jiusto,** James E 1929- *AmMWSc 92*
**Jivan,** Suzan *DrAPF 91*
**Jizba,** Zdenek Vaclav 1927- *AmMWSc 92*
**Jnah-Pis,** Edwige Claudia 1946- *WhoEnt 92*
**Jo-Mo,** Dr. *DrAPF 91*
**Joachim** *DrAPF 91*
**Joachim,** Frank G 1920- *AmMWSc 92*
**Joachim,** Joseph 1831-1907 *NewAmDM*
**Joachim,** Margaret Jane 1949- *Who 92*
**Joachim,** Otto 1910- *NewAmDM*
**Joachim,** Raymond John, Jr 1948- *WhoAmP 91*
**Joan Beaufort,** Queen of Scotland 1405?-1445 *EncAmaz 91*
**Joan of Arc** 1412-1431 *EncAmaz 91*
**Joan the Maid of Sarmaize** *EncAmaz 91*
**Joan,** Polly *DrAPF 91*
**Joannopoulos,** John Dimitris 1947- *AmMWSc 92*
**Joannou,** Johnny Savas 1940- *WhoAmP 91*
**Joanou,** Phil 1961- *WhoEnt 92*
**Joanou,** Phillip 1933- *WhoFI 92, WhoWest 92*
**Joans,** Ted *DrAPF 91*
**Joans,** Ted 1928- *WhoBlA 92*
**Joao V** 1689-1750 *BlkwCEP*
**Joaquim,** Richard Ralph 1936- *WhoFI 92, WhoWest 92*
**Joaquin,** Albert, Jr. 1960- *WhoHisp 92*
**Job of Hartford,** Bishop *WhoRel 92*
**Job,** Reuben Philip 1928- *WhoRel 92*
**Job,** Robert Charles 1943- *AmMWSc 92*
**Job,** Roger 1936- *Who 92*
**Jobe,** Edward Blinn 1929- *WhoIns 92*
**Jobe,** Frank Wilson 1925- *WhoWest 92*
**Jobe,** Jan S 1950- *WhoIns 92*
**Jobe,** John M 1933- *AmMWSc 92*
**Jobe,** Lowell A 1914- *AmMWSc 92*
**Jobe,** Muriel Ida 1931- *WhoMW 92*
**Jobe,** Phillip Carl 1940- *AmMWSc 92*
**Jobe,** Robert Welty 1951- *WhoRel 92*
**Jobe,** Shirley A. 1946- *WhoBlA 92*
**Jobe,** Warren Yancey 1940- *WhoFI 92*
**Jobert,** Michel 1921- *IntWW 91, Who 92*
**Jobes,** Forrest Crossett, Jr 1935- *AmMWSc 92*
**Jobes,** Patrick Clark 1941- *WhoWest 92*
**Jobim,** Antonio Carlos 1927- *CurBio 91 [port]*
**Jobin,** Andre 1933- *NewAmDM*
**Jobin,** Kenneth Joseph 1965- *WhoMW 92*
**Jobin,** Raoul 1906-1974 *NewAmDM*
**Jobling,** James Hobson 1921- *Who 92*
**Joblove,** George *WhoEnt 92*
**Jobs,** Steven P 1955- *AmMWSc 92*
**Jobs,** Steven Paul 1955- *IntWW 91, WhoFI 92, WhoWest 92*
**Jobsis,** Frans Frederik 1929- *AmMWSc 92*
**Jobson,** Roy 1947- *Who 92*
**Jobst,** Joel Edward 1936- *AmMWSc 92*
**Jocelyn** *Who 92*
**Jocelyn,** Henry David 1933- *IntWW 91, Who 92*
**Jocelyn,** Richard *IntAu&W 91X*
**Jocher,** Katharine 1888-1983 *DcNCBi 3*
**Jochim,** Kenneth Erwin 1911- *AmMWSc 92*
**Jochle,** Wolfgang 1927- *AmMWSc 92*
**Jochman,** Richard Lee 1948- *AmMWSc 92*
**Jochsberger,** Theodore 1940- *AmMWSc 92*
**Jochum,** Eugen 1902-1987 *FacFETw, NewAmDM*
**Jochum,** Lester H. 1929- *WhoWest 92*
**Jochum,** Thomas J 1951- *WhoAmP 91*
**Jochum,** Veronica *WhoEnt 92*
**Jock,** Paul F., II 1943- *WhoAmL 92*
**Jockers,** Laurens R 1940- *WhoIns 92*
**Jockusch,** Carl Groos, Jr 1941- *AmMWSc 92*
**Jocoy,** Edward Henry 1933- *AmMWSc 92*
**Jodeit,** Max A, Jr 1937- *AmMWSc 92*
**Jodl,** Alfred 1890-1946 *EncTR 91 [port]*
**Jodock,** Darrell Harland 1941- *WhoRel 92*
**Jodry,** Richard L 1922- *AmMWSc 92*
**Jodsaas,** Larry Elvin 1935- *WhoFI 92*
**Joe,** Isaac C 1915- *WhoAmP 91*
**Joebstl,** Johann Anton 1927- *AmMWSc 92*
**Joedicke,** Ingo Bernd 1948- *AmMWSc 92*
**Joel,** Amos Edward, Jr 1918- *AmMWSc 92*
**Joel,** Asher 1912- *Who 92*
**Joel,** Billy 1949- *WhoEnt 92*
**Joel,** Cliffe David 1932- *AmMWSc 92*
**Joel,** Darrel Dean 1933- *AmMWSc 92*
**Joel,** Harry Joel 1894- *Who 92*
**Joel,** Lawrence 1928-1984 *DcNCBi 3*
**Joell,** Pamela S. 1961- *WhoBlA 92*
**Joelson,** Jack Bernard 1927- *WhoMW 92*
**Joelson,** Mark Rene 1934- *WhoAmL 92*
**Joensuu,** Oiva I 1915- *AmMWSc 92*
**Joerg,** Charles William 1942- *WhoAmP 91*
**Joergensen,** Robert *ScFEYrs*
**Joerling,** Dale Raymond 1949- *WhoAmL 92*
**Joern,** Anthony 1948- *AmMWSc 92*
**Joern,** Charles Edward, Jr. 1951- *WhoAmL 92*
**Joesten,** Melvin D 1932- *AmMWSc 92*
**Joesten,** Raymond 1944- *AmMWSc 92*
**Joesting,** Linden Hi'ileiali'i 1958- *WhoAmL 92*
**Joffe,** Anatole 1932- *AmMWSc 92*
**Joffe,** Charles H. 1929- *ConTFT 9, IntMPA 92*
**Joffe,** Edward *IntMPA 92*
**Joffe,** Frederick M 1936- *AmMWSc 92*
**Joffe,** Hal *WhoRel 92*
**Joffe,** Joseph 1909- *AmMWSc 92*
**Joffe,** Robert David 1943- *WhoAmL 92*
**Joffe,** Roland 1945- *IntMPA 92*
**Joffe,** Roland I. V. 1945- *IntWW 91*
**Joffe,** Stephen N 1943- *AmMWSc 92*
**Joffe,** Stephen Neal 1943- *WhoFI 92*
**Joffe,** William Irving 1931- *WhoRel 92*
**Joffee,** Irving Brian 1946- *AmMWSc 92*
**Joffrey,** Robert 1930-1989 *FacFETw*
**Joftes,** David Lion 1924- *AmMWSc 92*
**Joh,** Erik Edward 1945- *WhoAmP 91*
**Joh,** Tong Hyub *AmMWSc 92*
**Joham,** Howard Ernest 1919- *AmMWSc 92*
**Johanes,** Jaromir 1933- *IntWW 91*
**Johann,** Joan Carol 1934- *WhoAmP 91*
**Johannes de Dumbleton** 1310?-1349? *DcLB 115*
**Johannes de Garlandia** *NewAmDM*
**Johannes de Muris** *NewAmDM*
**Johannes,** Herman 1913- *IntWW 91*
**Johannes,** James Michael 1950- *WhoFI 92, WhoMW 92*
**Johannes,** Robert 1927- *AmMWSc 92*
**Johannes,** Robert Earl 1936- *AmMWSc 92*
**Johannes,** Virgil Ivancich 1930- *AmMWSc 92*
**Johannesburg,** Bishop of 1935- *Who 92*
**Johannesen,** Irene Rose 1947- *WhoHisp 92*
**Johanneson,** Gerald B. 1940- *WhoFI 92*
**Johannessen,** Carl L 1924- *AmMWSc 92*
**Johannessen,** George Andrew 1919- *AmMWSc 92*
**Johannessen,** Jack 1915- *AmMWSc 92*
**Johannessen,** Paul Romberg 1926- *AmMWSc 92*
**Johannessen,** V Maurice 1934- *WhoAmP 91*
**Johanning,** Daniel Joseph 1960- *WhoMW 92*
**Johanningsmeier,** Arthur George 1930- *AmMWSc 92*
**Johanns,** Charles F 1936- *WhoIns 92*
**Johannsen,** Chris Jakob 1937- *WhoMW 92*
**Johannsen,** Christian Jakob 1937- *AmMWSc 92*
**Johannsen,** David Charles 1957- *WhoWest 92*
**Johannsen,** Frederick Richard 1946- *AmMWSc 92*
**Johannsen,** Kenneth Ludwig 1930- *WhoMW 92*
**Johannson,** Kjartan 1939- *IntWW 91*
**Johanos,** Donald 1928- *WhoEnt 92, WhoWest 92*
**Johansen,** Arnold Edward 1938- *WhoWest 92*
**Johansen,** David 1950- *ConMus 7 [port]*
**Johansen,** Elmer L 1930- *AmMWSc 92*
**Johansen,** Erling 1923- *AmMWSc 92*
**Johansen,** Gunnar 1906-1991 *NewYTBS 91 [port]*
**Johansen,** Hans Christian 1935- *IntWW 91*

**Johansen**, Hans William 1932- *AmMWSc 92*
**Johansen**, Holger Friis 1927- *IntWW 91*
**Johansen**, Jim Eric 1964- *WhoEnt 92*
**Johansen**, John MacLane 1916- *IntWW 91*
**Johansen**, Nils Ivar 1941- *AmMWSc 92, WhoWest 92*
**Johansen**, Peter 1938- *IntWW 91*
**Johansen**, Peter Herman 1939- *AmMWSc 92*
**Johansen**, Robert H 1922- *AmMWSc 92*
**Johansen**, Ruth Lynne 1944- *WhoMW 92*
**Johansen**, Thomas Clay 1958- *WhoFI 92*
**Johansen**, Wilford Woodruff 1928- *WhoAmP 91*
**Johansen-Berg**, John 1935- *Who 92*
**Johanson**, Brian 1929- *Who 92*
**Johanson**, Chris Ellyn 1945- *AmMWSc 92*
**Johanson**, Donald C. 1943- *WrDr 92*
**Johanson**, Donald Carl 1943- *IntWW 91, WhoWest 92*
**Johanson**, Jerry Ray 1937- *AmMWSc 92, WhoWest 92*
**Johanson**, L N 1921- *AmMWSc 92*
**Johanson**, Lamar 1935- *AmMWSc 92*
**Johanson**, Lynn Steven 1950- *WhoMW 92*
**Johanson**, Richard Arthur 1925- *WhoFI 92*
**Johanson**, Robert Gail 1936- *AmMWSc 92*
**Johanson**, Waldemar Gustave, Jr 1937- *AmMWSc 92*
**Johanson**, William Richard 1948- *AmMWSc 92*
**Johansson**, Bengt K. A. 1937- *IntWW 91*
**Johansson**, Jan Gunnar 1952- *WhoAmL 92*
**Johansson**, Karl Richard 1920- *AmMWSc 92*
**Johansson**, Lennart Valdemar 1921- *IntWW 91*
**Johansson**, Marie Elsa 1949- *WhoEnt 92*
**Johansson**, Markku 1949- *WhoEnt 92*
**Johansson**, Mats W 1958- *AmMWSc 92*
**Johansson**, Robert John 1936- *WhoRel 92*
**Johansson**, Sune 1928- *AmMWSc 92*
**Johansson**, Tage Sigvard Kjell 1919- *AmMWSc 92*
**Johansson-Backe**, Karl Erik 1914- *IntAu&W 91*
**Johar**, J S 1935- *AmMWSc 92*
**Johari**, Om 1940- *AmMWSc 92*
**Johler**, Joseph Ralph 1919- *WhoFI 92, WhoWest 92*
**John** *EncEarC*
**John II** *EncEarC*
**John V** 1689-1750 *BlkwCEP*
**John XXIII** 1881-1963 *DcEcMov, FacFETw [port]*
**John**, Bishop 1836-1914 *RelLAm 91*
**John Charles**, Brother *Who 92*
**John Chrysostom** 347?-407 *EncEarC [port]*
**John Climacus** 579?-649 *EncEarC*
**John Malalas** *EncEarC*
**John Maxentius** *EncEarC*
**John Moschus** 550?-619 *EncEarC*
**John of Afflighem** *NewAmDM*
**John of Antioch** d441 *EncEarC*
**John of Caesarea** *EncEarC*
**John of Carpathus** *EncEarC*
**John of Damascus** 650?-749? *EncEarC*
**John of Dumbleton** 1310?-1349? *DcLB 115*
**John of Ephesus** 507?-589 *EncEarC*
**John of Euboea** *EncEarC*
**John of Gaza** *EncEarC*
**John of Scythopolis** *EncEarC*
**John of the Cross**, St. 1542-1591 *LitC 18 [port]*
**John Paul I** 1912-1978 *FacFETw*
**John Paul II** *FacFETw [port]*
**John Paul II** 1920- *DcEcMov, IntWW 91*
**John Paul II**, His Holiness Pope 1920- *Who 92, WhoRel 92*
**John Paul II**, Pope 1920- *ConAu 133*
**John Philoponus** 490?-57-? *EncEarC*
**John XXIII**, Pope 1881-1963 *ConAu 134*
**John The Baptist** *EncEarC*
**John**, Andrew 1934- *AmMWSc 92*
**John**, Anthony 1950- *WhoBlA 92*
**John**, Arthur Walwyn *Who 92*
**John**, Augustus 1878-1961 *TwCPaSc*
**John**, Augustus 1879-1961 *FacFETw*
**John**, Christopher Charles 1960- *WhoAmP 91*
**John**, David Dilwyn 1901- *IntWW 91, Who 92*
**John**, David Thomas 1941- *AmMWSc 92*
**John**, Donas *DrAPF 91*
**John**, E Roy 1924- *AmMWSc 92*
**John**, Elton 1947- *FacFETw, NewAmDM*
**John**, Elton Hercules 1947- *IntWW 91, Who 92, WhoEnt 92*
**John**, Fritz 1910- *AmMWSc 92, IntWW 91*
**John**, Geoffrey Richards 1934- *Who 92*
**John**, George 1921- *AmMWSc 92*
**John**, Gerald Warren 1947- *WhoMW 92*
**John**, Gwen 1876-1939 *TwCPaSc*
**John**, Hugo Herman 1929- *AmMWSc 92*
**John**, James Edward Albert 1933- *AmMWSc 92*
**John**, John Price Durbin 1843-1916 *BiInAmS*
**John**, Joseph 1938- *AmMWSc 92*
**John**, K. K. 1936- *WhoMW 92, WhoRel 92*
**John**, Kavanakuvhiy V *AmMWSc 92*
**John**, Maldwyn Noel 1929- *Who 92*
**John**, Maliyakal Eappen *AmMWSc 92*
**John**, Mertis, Jr. 1932- *WhoEnt 92, WhoMW 92*
**John**, Michael Louis 1942- *WhoEnt 92*
**John**, Michael M. *Who 92*
**John**, Nancy *WrDr 92*
**John**, Patrick 1937- *IntWW 91*
**John**, Peter William Meredith 1923- *AmMWSc 92*
**John**, Robert *WrDr 92*
**John**, Robert McClintock 1947- *WhoAmL 92*
**John**, Ronald David 1948- *WhoWest 92*
**John**, Rupert 1916- *Who 92*
**John**, Russell T 1946- *WhoIns 92*
**John**, Susan V 1957- *WhoAmP 91*
**John**, Vivien 1915- *TwCPaSc*
**John**, Walter 1924- *AmMWSc 92*
**John-Mackie**, Baron 1909- *Who 92*
**John-Sandy**, Rene Emanuel 1945- *WhoBlA 92*
**Johncock**, Lynda Marie 1948- *WhoWest 92*
**Johnican**, Minerva Jane 1939- *WhoAmP 91, WhoBlA 92*
**Johnk**, Carl T A 1919- *AmMWSc 92*
**Johnke**, Torben V. 1922- *WhoEnt 92*
**Johnny Appleseed** *BenetAL 91*
**Johns**, Alan Wesley 1931- *Who 92*
**Johns**, Alison I. 1960- *WhoEnt 92*
**Johns**, Althea Patricia *WhoAmL 92*
**Johns**, Anthony Hearle 1928- *IntWW 91*
**Johns**, Avery *WrDr 92*
**Johns**, Betty Jo 1932- *WhoMW 92*
**Johns**, David Garrett 1929- *AmMWSc 92*
**Johns**, David John 1931- *IntWW 91, Who 92*
**Johns**, Donald Arvid 1953- *WhoRel 92*
**Johns**, Donna J 1945- *WhoIns 92*
**Johns**, Emerson Thomas 1947- *WhoFI 92*
**Johns**, Glynis *Who 92*
**Johns**, Glynis 1923- *IntMPA 92*
**Johns**, Harold E 1915- *AmMWSc 92*
**Johns**, Jackie C. 1953- *WhoBlA 92*
**Johns**, Jasper 1930- *FacFETw, IntWW 91, RComAH*
**Johns**, Kenneth *IntAu&W 91X, TwCSFW 91*
**Johns**, Kenneth Charles 1944- *AmMWSc 92*
**Johns**, Lewis E, Jr 1935- *AmMWSc 92*
**Johns**, Margy 1931- *WhoAmP 91*
**Johns**, Marston *TwCSFW 91, WrDr 92*
**Johns**, Martin Wesley 1913- *AmMWSc 92*
**Johns**, Michael Alan 1946- *Who 92*
**Johns**, Michael E 1946- *WhoAmP 91*
**Johns**, Michael Earl 1945- *WhoBlA 92*
**Johns**, Milton Vernon, Jr 1925- *AmMWSc 92*
**Johns**, Patricia Holly 1933- *Who 92*
**Johns**, Paul 1934- *Who 92*
**Johns**, Paul V. 1958- *WhoBlA 92*
**Johns**, Philip Timothy 1943- *AmMWSc 92*
**Johns**, Richard A. 1929- *WrDr 92*
**Johns**, Richard Edward 1939- *Who 92*
**Johns**, Richard James 1925- *AmMWSc 92*
**Johns**, Richard Seth Ellis 1946- *WhoAmL 92*
**Johns**, Robert Alan 1959- *WhoEnt 92*
**Johns**, Robert William 1954- *WhoFI 92*
**Johns**, Roy 1929- *WhoWest 92*
**Johns**, Sonja Maria 1953- *WhoBlA 92*
**Johns**, Stephen Arnold 1920- *WhoBlA 92*
**Johns**, Susan D 1954- *WhoAmP 91*
**Johns**, Thomas H. 1931- *WhoMW 92*
**Johns**, Thomas Richards, II 1924- *AmMWSc 92*
**Johns**, Varner Jay, Jr 1921- *AmMWSc 92*
**Johns**, W E 1893-1968 *TwCSFW 91*
**Johns**, William Campbell 1925- *WhoAmP 91*
**Johns**, William Davis 1925- *AmMWSc 92*
**Johns**, William E *AmMWSc 92*
**Johns**, William Francis 1930- *AmMWSc 92*
**Johns**, William Howard 1941- *WhoMW 92*
**Johns**, William Patrick 1941- *WhoFI 92*
**Johnsen**, Dennis O 1937- *AmMWSc 92*
**Johnsen**, Eugene Carlyle 1932- *AmMWSc 92*
**Johnsen**, Gretchen *DrAPF 91*
**Johnsen**, John Herbert 1923- *AmMWSc 92*
**Johnsen**, Marlene Helen 1936- *WhoAmP 91*
**Johnsen**, Peter Berghsey 1950- *AmMWSc 92*
**Johnsen**, Rainer 1940- *AmMWSc 92*
**Johnsen**, Ray V 1927- *WhoAmP 91*
**Johnsen**, Richard Emanuel 1936- *AmMWSc 92*
**Johnsen**, Roger Craig 1938- *AmMWSc 92*
**Johnsen**, Russell Harold 1922- *AmMWSc 92*
**Johnsen**, Thomas Norman, Jr 1929- *AmMWSc 92*
**Johnsen**, Walter Craig 1950- *WhoFI 92*
**Johnsgard**, Paul A. 1931- *WrDr 92*
**Johnsgard**, Paul Austin 1931- *AmMWSc 92, IntAu&W 91*
**Johnson** *Who 92*
**Johnson**, A Burtron, Jr 1929- *AmMWSc 92*
**Johnson**, A E *IntAu&W 91X, WrDr 92*
**Johnson**, A. Ross 1939- *WrDr 92*
**Johnson**, A. Thomas 1952- *WhoAmL 92*
**Johnson**, A Visanio 1941- *WhoAmP 91, WhoBlA 92*
**Johnson**, A William 1933- *AmMWSc 92*
**Johnson**, Aaron LaVoie 1957- *WhoBlA 92*
**Johnson**, Abigail Ridley 1945- *WhoEnt 92*
**Johnson**, Addie Collins *WhoBlA 92*
**Johnson**, Adrian Earl, Jr 1928- *AmMWSc 92*
**Johnson**, Al *WhoBlA 92*
**Johnson**, Alan *ConTFT 9*
**Johnson**, Alan Arthur 1930- *AmMWSc 92*
**Johnson**, Alan B. 1939- *WhoAmL 92*
**Johnson**, Alan Campbell *Who 92*
**Johnson**, Alan J 1919- *AmMWSc 92*
**Johnson**, Alan Keith 1964- *WhoEnt 92*
**Johnson**, Alan Kim 1942- *AmMWSc 92*
**Johnson**, Alan Roberts 1943- *WhoAmL 92*
**Johnson**, Alan Taylor 1931- *Who 92*
**Johnson**, Albert 1869-1957 *DcAmImH*
**Johnson**, Albert J. 1910- *WhoBlA 92*
**Johnson**, Albert James 1943- *WhoBlA 92*
**Johnson**, Albert Lee, Sr. 1923- *WhoBlA 92*
**Johnson**, Albert M 1926- *WhoAmP 91*
**Johnson**, Albert Sydney, III 1933- *AmMWSc 92*
**Johnson**, Albert W 1906- *WhoAmP 91*
**Johnson**, Albert W 1926- *AmMWSc 92*
**Johnson**, Albert Wayne 1944- *AmMWSc 92*
**Johnson**, Albert William, Sr. 1926- *WhoBlA 92*
**Johnson**, Alcee LaBranche 1905- *WhoBlA 92*
**Johnson**, Alex Moore 1953- *WhoAmL 92*
**Johnson**, Alexander Bryan 1860-1917 *BiInAmS*
**Johnson**, Alexander Charles 1948- *WhoAmL 92*
**Johnson**, Alexander Hamilton, Jr. 1924- *WhoBlA 92*
**Johnson**, Alexander Lawrence 1931- *AmMWSc 92*
**Johnson**, Alexander Smith 1817-1878 *BiInAmS*
**Johnson**, Alfred Theodore, Jr 1941- *AmMWSc 92*
**Johnson**, Alice Elaine 1929- *WhoRel 92, WhoWest 92*
**Johnson**, Alice M *WhoAmP 91*
**Johnson**, Alice Ruffin 1936- *AmMWSc 92*
**Johnson**, Allan Alexander *AmMWSc 92*
**Johnson**, Allen Neill 1944- *AmMWSc 92*
**Johnson**, Almeta Ann 1947- *WhoBlA 92*
**Johnson**, Alva William 1936- *AmMWSc 92*
**Johnson**, Alvan Nathaniel 1916- *WhoAmP 91*
**Johnson**, Alvin Harold 1914- *WhoEnt 92*
**Johnson**, Alvin Roscoe 1942- *WhoBlA 92*
**Johnson**, Alvin S. 1874-1971 *BenetAL 91*
**Johnson**, Amos Neill 1908-1975 *DcNCBi 3*
**Johnson**, Amy 1903-1941 *FacFETw*
**Johnson**, Andi T 1953- *WhoAmP 91*
**Johnson**, Andrea 1947- *WhoRel 92*
**Johnson**, Andrew 1808-1875 *AmPolLe [port], BenetAL 91, DcNCBi 3, RComAH*
**Johnson**, Andrew 1946- *WhoBlA 92*
**Johnson**, Andrew L. 1911- *WhoBlA 92*
**Johnson**, Andrew L., Jr. 1931- *WhoBlA 92*
**Johnson**, Andrew L., Sr. 1905- *WhoBlA 92*
**Johnson**, Andy J. 1961- *WhoMW 92*
**Johnson**, Angel Patricia 1942- *WhoBlA 92*
**Johnson**, Anita Marie 1927- *WhoWest 92*
**Johnson**, Anita Watson 1949- *WhoFI 92*
**Johnson**, Ann Braden 1945- *ConAu 135*
**Johnson**, Ann Swepson Boyd Hawkins R. 1788-1861? *DcNCBi 3*
**Johnson**, Annabel 1921- *WrDr 92*
**Johnson**, Annabell 1921- *IntAu&W 91*
**Johnson**, Anne Bradstreet 1927- *AmMWSc 92*
**Johnson**, Anne-Marie *WhoBlA 92*
**Johnson**, Anne Montgomrey 1922- *Who 92*
**Johnson**, Anne Murray 1960- *WhoFI 92*
**Johnson**, Anthony Michael 1954- *WhoBlA 92*
**Johnson**, Anthony Richardo *WhoWest 92*
**Johnson**, Archibald 1859-1934 *DcNCBi 3*
**Johnson**, Arlo F 1915- *AmMWSc 92*
**Johnson**, Armead 1942- *AmMWSc 92*
**Johnson**, Arnold *AmMWSc 92*
**Johnson**, Arnold Burges 1834-1915 *BiInAmS*
**Johnson**, Arnold Cale 1925- *WhoAmL 92*
**Johnson**, Arnold Gordon 1936- *WhoRel 92*
**Johnson**, Arnold Hjalmer 1920- *WhoRel 92*
**Johnson**, Arnold I 1919- *AmMWSc 92*
**Johnson**, Arnold Richard, Jr 1929- *AmMWSc 92*
**Johnson**, Arnold William 1916- *WhoMW 92*
**Johnson**, Arte 1934- *IntMPA 92*
**Johnson**, Arthur Albin 1925- *AmMWSc 92*
**Johnson**, Arthur Curtis 1928- *WhoAmL 92*
**Johnson**, Arthur Edward 1942- *AmMWSc 92*
**Johnson**, Arthur Franklin 1917- *AmMWSc 92*
**Johnson**, Arthur Gilbert 1926- *AmMWSc 92*
**Johnson**, Arthur J. *WhoBlA 92*
**Johnson**, Arthur L. *WhoBlA 92*
**Johnson**, Arthur Lyman 1918- *WhoBlA 92*
**Johnson**, Arthur Stanton Eric 1934- *WhoWest 92*
**Johnson**, Arthur T. 1947- *WhoBlA 92*
**Johnson**, Arthur Thomas 1941- *AmMWSc 92*
**Johnson**, Arthur William, Jr. 1949- *WhoWest 92*
**Johnson**, Audrey Jackson 1936- *WhoRel 92*
**Johnson**, Audreye Earle 1929- *WhoBlA 92*
**Johnson**, Augustus Clark 1914- *WhoAmP 91*
**Johnson**, Avery 1965- *WhoBlA 92*
**Johnson**, Ayubu 1943- *WhoBlA 92*
**Johnson**, B. A. 1925- *WhoBlA 92*
**Johnson**, B Connor 1911- *AmMWSc 92*
**Johnson**, B Lamar, Jr 1930- *AmMWSc 92*
**Johnson**, B M 1930- *AmMWSc 92*
**Johnson**, B.S. 1933-1973 *RfGEnL 91*
**Johnson**, Badri Nahvi 1934- *WhoMW 92*
**Johnson**, Barbara Ann 1944- *WhoAmP 91*
**Johnson**, Barbara C. 1931- *WhoBlA 92*
**Johnson**, Barbara Ferry 1923- *IntAu&W 91, WrDr 92*
**Johnson**, Barbara Jean 1932- *WhoAmL 92*
**Johnson**, Barnabas David 1943- *WhoAmL 92*
**Johnson**, Barry 1952- *Who 92*
**Johnson**, Barry Edward 1937- *IntWW 91, Who 92*
**Johnson**, Barry Lee 1938- *AmMWSc 92*
**Johnson**, Beatrice Marian 1930- *WhoAmP 91*
**Johnson**, Becky Beard 1942- *AmMWSc 92*
**Johnson**, Ben 1918- *IntMPA 92*
**Johnson**, Ben 1946- *TwCPaSc*
**Johnson**, Ben 1961- *ConBlB 1 [port], FacFETw, IntWW 91*
**Johnson**, Ben Batchelor 1921- *WhoWest 92*
**Johnson**, Ben Butler 1920- *AmMWSc 92*
**Johnson**, Ben D. *WhoBlA 92*
**Johnson**, Ben E. 1937- *WhoBlA 92*
**Johnson**, Ben Francis 1943- *AmMWSc 92*
**Johnson**, Ben S, Jr 1917- *AmMWSc 92*
**Johnson**, Ben Sigel 1929- *WhoEnt 92*
**Johnson**, Benjamin, Jr. 1950- *WhoBlA 92*
**Johnson**, Benjamin Earl 1943- *WhoBlA 92*
**Johnson**, Benjamin Edgar 1921- *WhoRel 92*
**Johnson**, Benjamin Franklin, III 1943- *WhoAmL 92*
**Johnson**, Benjamin Freeman 1956- *WhoWest 92*
**Johnson**, Benjamin Washington 1914- *WhoBlA 92*
**Johnson**, Benjamine Sinclair, Jr 1961- *BlkOlyM*
**Johnson**, Bernard 1936- *WhoBlA 92*
**Johnson**, Bertil Lennart 1909- *AmMWSc 92*
**Johnson**, Beth Exum 1952- *WhoAmL 92*
**Johnson**, Betty Jo 1940- *WhoBlA 92*
**Johnson**, Betty Jo 1943- *WhoEnt 92*
**Johnson**, Beulah C. 1909- *WhoBlA 92*
**Johnson**, Beverley Ernestine 1953- *WhoBlA 92*
**Johnson**, Beverley Peck *WhoEnt 92*
**Johnson**, Beverly *WhoBlA 92*
**Johnson**, Beverly 1952- *ConBlB 2 [port], NotBlAW 92*
**Johnson**, Bill Wade 1943- *WhoBlA 92*
**Johnson**, Blind Willie 1902?-1950? *NewAmDM*
**Johnson**, Bob d1991 *NewYTBS 91 [port]*
**Johnson**, Bob 1945- *WhoAmP 91*
**Johnson**, Bob Duell 1936- *AmMWSc 92*
**Johnson**, Bobbie Gene 1941- *WhoBlA 92*
**Johnson**, Bobby *DrAPF 91*
**Johnson**, Bobby JoJo 1947- *WhoBlA 92*
**Johnson**, Bobby Ray 1941- *AmMWSc 92*
**Johnson**, Bolley L 1951- *WhoAmP 91*
**Johnson**, Bonnie *DrAPF 91*

**Johnson,** Brad Keith 1958- *WhoFI 92*
**Johnson,** Bradley S 1951- *WhoAmP 91*
**Johnson,** Bradley T 1935- *WhoAmP 91*
**Johnson,** Brann 1946- *AmMWSc 92*
**Johnson,** Brant Montgomery 1949- *AmMWSc 92*
**Johnson,** Brent E. 1947- *WhoBlA 92*
**Johnson,** Brian *Who 92*
**Johnson,** Brian A 1944- *WhoIns 92*
**Johnson,** Brian Frederick Gilbert 1938- *Who 92*
**Johnson,** Brian John 1938- *AmMWSc 92*
**Johnson,** Brian Keith 1956- *WhoWest 92*
**Johnson,** Brooke Bailey 1951- *WhoEnt 92*
**Johnson,** Bruce 1932- *AmMWSc 92*
**Johnson,** Bruce 1936- *WhoAmL 92*
**Johnson,** Bruce Edward 1959- *WhoFI 92*
**Johnson,** Bruce Fletcher 1956- *AmMWSc 92*
**Johnson,** Bruce Joseph F. *Who 92*
**Johnson,** Bruce McDougall 1943- *AmMWSc 92*
**Johnson,** Bruce Paul 1938- *AmMWSc 92, WhoWest 92*
**Johnson,** Bryan 1948- *ConAu 133*
**Johnson,** Bryan Hugh 1940- *AmMWSc 92*
**Johnson,** Bryce Vincent 1949- *AmMWSc 92*
**Johnson,** Buck 1964- *WhoBlA 92*
**Johnson,** Bunk 1889-1949 *NewAmDM*
**Johnson,** Burges 1877-1963 *BenetAL 91*
**Johnson,** Byron Eugene 1936- *WhoMW 92*
**Johnson,** Byron F 1928- *AmMWSc 92*
**Johnson,** Byron Jerald 1937- *WhoAmL 92, WhoAmP 91, WhoWest 92*
**Johnson,** Byron John 1944- *WhoAmL 92*
**Johnson,** Byron Lindberg 1917- *WhoAmP 91*
**Johnson,** C Bruce 1935- *AmMWSc 92*
**Johnson,** C. Christine 1928- *WhoBlA 92*
**Johnson,** C Farrell 1925- *WhoAmP 91*
**Johnson,** C Scott 1932- *AmMWSc 92*
**Johnson,** C. Terry 1937- *WhoAmL 92*
**Johnson,** C Walter 1910- *AmMWSc 92*
**Johnson,** C William 1925- *WhoAmP 91*
**Johnson,** Cage Saul 1941- *WhoBlA 92, WhoWest 92*
**Johnson,** Caliph 1938- *WhoBlA 92*
**Johnson,** Calvert Berry 1949- *WhoEnt 92*
**Johnson,** Calvin Harsha 1944- *WhoAmL 92*
**Johnson,** Calvin Keith 1937- *AmMWSc 92*
**Johnson,** Calvin P. 1946- *WhoBlA 92*
**Johnson,** Candace Sue 1949- *AmMWSc 92*
**Johnson,** Carl Albert 1930- *WhoMW 92*
**Johnson,** Carl Arnold 1925- *AmMWSc 92*
**Johnson,** Carl Boone 1938- *AmMWSc 92*
**Johnson,** Carl Edward 1946- *AmMWSc 92*
**Johnson,** Carl Edwin 1917- *AmMWSc 92*
**Johnson,** Carl Elliott 1956- *WhoBlA 92*
**Johnson,** Carl Emil, Jr 1921- *AmMWSc 92*
**Johnson,** Carl Erick 1914- *AmMWSc 92*
**Johnson,** Carl J. 1911- *WhoBlA 92*
**Johnson,** Carl J 1929- *AmMWSc 92*
**Johnson,** Carl Josephs 1911- *WhoEnt 92*
**Johnson,** Carl Lee 1928- *WhoBlA 92*
**Johnson,** Carl Lynn 1941- *AmMWSc 92*
**Johnson,** Carl R 1922- *WhoAmP 91*
**Johnson,** Carl Randolph 1937- *AmMWSc 92*
**Johnson,** Carl Thomas 1914- *WhoBlA 92*
**Johnson,** Carl William 1942- *AmMWSc 92*
**Johnson,** Carlos *DrAPF 91*
**Johnson,** Carlton E 1917- *AmMWSc 92*
**Johnson,** Carlton Robert 1926- *AmMWSc 92*
**Johnson,** Carol A *WhoAmP 91*
**Johnson,** Carol Alfred 1903- *Who 92*
**Johnson,** Carol Ann 1941- *WhoRel 92*
**Johnson,** Carol F 1937- *WhoAmP 91*
**Johnson,** Carol Wilson 1942- *WhoMW 92*
**Johnson,** Caroline Janice 1941- *WhoMW 92*
**Johnson,** Carolyn Elizabeth 1921- *WhoWest 92*
**Johnson,** Carolyn Jean 1938- *WhoAmL 92*
**Johnson,** Carrie Clements 1931- *WhoBlA 92*
**Johnson,** Carroll Jones 1948- *WhoBlA 92*
**Johnson,** Carroll Kenneth 1929- *AmMWSc 92*
**Johnson,** Carter Samuel 1961- *WhoEnt 92*
**Johnson,** Cato, II 1947- *WhoBlA 92*
**Johnson,** Cecil Gray 1922- *AmMWSc 92*
**Johnson,** Cecil L. *WhoAmL 92*
**Johnson,** Celia 1908-1982 *FacFETw*
**Johnson,** Charles *DrAPF 91, IntWW 91*
**Johnson,** Charles d1802 *DcNCBi 3*
**Johnson,** Charles 1927- *WhoBlA 92*
**Johnson,** Charles 1948- *BlkLC [port], ConLC 65 [port], ConNov 91, CurBio 91 [port]*
**Johnson,** Charles Albert 1954- *WhoAmP 91*
**Johnson,** Charles Andrew 1915- *AmMWSc 92*
**Johnson,** Charles Bernard 1954- *WhoBlA 92*
**Johnson,** Charles Beverly *WhoBlA 92*
**Johnson,** Charles Birkery 1932- *WhoRel 92*
**Johnson,** Charles C, Jr *AmMWSc 92*
**Johnson,** Charles Clinton 1946- *WhoRel 92*
**Johnson,** Charles E. 1946- *WhoBlA 92*
**Johnson,** Charles E. Memusi 1933- *WhoBlA 92*
**Johnson,** Charles Earl 1851-1923 *DcNCBi 3*
**Johnson,** Charles Edward 1938- *WhoBlA 92*
**Johnson,** Charles Edward 1940- *AmMWSc 92*
**Johnson,** Charles Emil 1959- *WhoRel 92*
**Johnson,** Charles Ernest 1918- *Who 92*
**Johnson,** Charles F 1927- *AmMWSc 92*
**Johnson,** Charles Floyd *WhoBlA 92, WhoEnt 92*
**Johnson,** Charles Foreman 1929- *WhoFI 92, WhoWest 92*
**Johnson,** Charles George 1954- *WhoEnt 92*
**Johnson,** Charles H. 1932- *WhoBlA 92*
**Johnson,** Charles Haggard 1925- *WhoAmP 91*
**Johnson,** Charles Harley 1947- *WhoAmL 92*
**Johnson,** Charles Henry 1925- *AmMWSc 92*
**Johnson,** Charles Henry 1946- *WhoBlA 92*
**Johnson,** Charles Henry, Jr. 1946- *WhoAmL 92*
**Johnson,** Charles Jerome 1942- *WhoFI 92*
**Johnson,** Charles Lee 1941- *WhoBlA 92*
**Johnson,** Charles M. 1941- *WhoFI 92*
**Johnson,** Charles Marion 1891-1964 *DcNCBi 3*
**Johnson,** Charles Minor 1923- *AmMWSc 92*
**Johnson,** Charles Nelson, Jr 1915- *AmMWSc 92*
**Johnson,** Charles R. 1948- *ConBlB 1 [port], WrDr 92*
**Johnson,** Charles Reginald 1965- *WhoRel 92, WhoWest 92*
**Johnson,** Charles Richard 1912- *WhoMW 92*
**Johnson,** Charles Richard 1948- *WhoBlA 92*
**Johnson,** Charles Richard 1958- *WhoEnt 92*
**Johnson,** Charles Richard, Jr 1950- *AmMWSc 92*
**Johnson,** Charles Robert 1941- *AmMWSc 92*
**Johnson,** Charles Ronald 1951- *WhoAmP 91*
**Johnson,** Charles Ronald, Sr. 1951- *WhoBlA 92*
**Johnson,** Charles Royal 1948- *AmMWSc 92*
**Johnson,** Charles Sidney, Jr 1936- *AmMWSc 92*
**Johnson,** Charles Simons 1940- *WhoFI 92*
**Johnson,** Charles Spurgeon 1893-1956 *BenetAL 91*
**Johnson,** Charles V. 1928- *WhoBlA 92*
**Johnson,** Charles W. *WhoAmL 92, WhoAmP 91*
**Johnson,** Charles W. 1929- *WhoBlA 92*
**Johnson,** Charles Wayne 1921- *WhoFI 92, WhoWest 92*
**Johnson,** Charles Wesley 1931- *WhoMW 92*
**Johnson,** Charles William 1922- *AmMWSc 92, WhoBlA 92*
**Johnson,** Charlie James 1923- *WhoRel 92*
**Johnson,** Chloe Rene 1939- *WhoFI 92*
**Johnson,** Chris Alan 1949- *AmMWSc 92*
**Johnson,** Christina Ardell 1963- *WhoEnt 92*
**Johnson,** Christine 1946- *WhoBlA 92*
**Johnson,** Christine Ann 1951- *WhoMW 92*
**Johnson,** Christopher Edmund 1934- *Who 92*
**Johnson,** Christopher L. 1949- *WhoMW 92*
**Johnson,** Christopher Louis McIntosh 1931- *IntWW 91*
**Johnson,** Christopher Paul 1960- *WhoAmL 92*
**Johnson,** Christopher Ray 1960- *WhoWest 92*
**Johnson,** Christopher Thomas 1965- *WhoFI 92, WhoMW 92*
**Johnson,** Clarence Daniel 1931- *AmMWSc 92*
**Johnson,** Clarence Eugene 1941- *AmMWSc 92*
**Johnson,** Clarence L 1910- *AmMWSc 92, DcTwDes, FacFETw*
**Johnson,** Clarence L. 1910-1990 *CurBio 91N*
**Johnson,** Clarence Ray 1943- *WhoRel 92*
**Johnson,** Clarissa 1913- *WhoBlA 92*
**Johnson,** Clark E, Jr 1930- *AmMWSc 92*
**Johnson,** Clark Hughes 1935- *WhoFI 92*
**Johnson,** Claudia Jean 1952- *WhoWest 92*
**Johnson,** Clayton Errold 1921- *WhoFI 92, WhoWest 92*
**Johnson,** Clayton Henry, Jr 1916- *AmMWSc 92*
**Johnson,** Cleland Howard 1922- *AmMWSc 92*
**Johnson,** Clemon 1956- *WhoBlA 92*
**Johnson,** Cleo M. *WhoBlA 92*
**Johnson,** Cleveland, Jr. 1934- *WhoBlA 92*
**Johnson,** Cliff 1951- *WhoAmP 91*
**Johnson,** Clifford Gilbert 1921- *WhoEnt 92*
**Johnson,** Clifton 1865-1940 *BenetAL 91*
**Johnson,** Clifton E. *WhoBlA 92*
**Johnson,** Clifton Herman 1921- *WhoBlA 92*
**Johnson,** Clifton W 1924- *AmMWSc 92*
**Johnson,** Clinisson Anthony 1947- *WhoBlA 92*
**Johnson,** Clinton Lamont 1953- *WhoAmP 91*
**Johnson,** Clinton Lee 1947- *WhoAmP 91*
**Johnson,** Clinton Lee, Sr. 1947- *WhoBlA 92*
**Johnson,** Colin 1938- *WrDr 92*
**Johnson,** Colin 1939- *ConNov 91*
**Johnson,** Colin T. 1942- *TwCPaSc*
**Johnson,** Collis, Jr. 1946- *WhoBlA 92*
**Johnson,** Conor Deane 1943- *AmMWSc 92*
**Johnson,** Constance Ada 1934- *WhoAmP 91*
**Johnson,** Corey Benett 1948- *WhoWest 92*
**Johnson,** Corinne Lessig 1938- *AmMWSc 92*
**Johnson,** Cornelius 1913- *BlkOlyM*
**Johnson,** Corwin McGillivray 1924- *AmMWSc 92*
**Johnson,** Curt *DrAPF 91, WhoAmP 91*
**Johnson,** Curtis Alan 1948- *AmMWSc 92*
**Johnson,** Curtis Allen 1917- *AmMWSc 92*
**Johnson,** Curtis Eduard 1941- *WhoAmP 91*
**Johnson,** Cynthia Elaine 1953- *WhoFI 92*
**Johnson,** Cynthia Le Mae 1952- *WhoAmL 92*
**Johnson,** Cyrus Edwin 1929- *WhoBlA 92*
**Johnson,** D. Gale 1916- *WrDr 92*
**Johnson,** D Lynn 1934- *AmMWSc 92*
**Johnson,** Dale A 1937- *AmMWSc 92, WhoFI 92, WhoMW 92*
**Johnson,** Dale Arthur 1936- *WhoRel 92*
**Johnson,** Dale Baker 1935- *WhoRel 92*
**Johnson,** Dale Howard 1945- *AmMWSc 92*
**Johnson,** Dale Richard *AmMWSc 92*
**Johnson,** Dale Waldo 1915- *AmMWSc 92*
**Johnson,** Dallas Eugene 1938- *AmMWSc 92*
**Johnson,** Dan *DrAPF 91*
**Johnson,** Dana Kay 1940- *WhoWest 92*
**Johnson,** Daniel, Jr. 1948- *WhoAmL 92*
**Johnson,** Daniel Arthur 1963- *WhoMW 92*
**Johnson,** Daniel Lee, Sr. 1936- *WhoWest 92*
**Johnson,** Darell James 1949- *AmMWSc 92*
**Johnson,** Darlene Ann 1949- *WhoMW 92*
**Johnson,** Darlene Anne 1952- *WhoEnt 92*
**Johnson,** Daryle G 1936- *WhoIns 92*
**Johnson,** Dave *WhoAmP 91*
**Johnson,** David *DrAPF 91*
**Johnson,** David 1944- *AmMWSc 92*
**Johnson,** David Alfred 1938- *AmMWSc 92*
**Johnson,** David Allen 1944- *WhoAmL 92*
**Johnson,** David Allen 1954- *WhoEnt 92, WhoMW 92*
**Johnson,** David Ashby 1943- *AmMWSc 92*
**Johnson,** David B 1940- *AmMWSc 92*
**Johnson,** David Barton 1946- *AmMWSc 92*
**Johnson,** David Burnham 1930- *Who 92*
**Johnson,** David Carl 1942- *WhoAmL 92*
**Johnson,** David Chester 1933- *WhoMW 92*
**Johnson,** David Christopher 1968- *WhoEnt 92*
**Johnson,** David Curtis 1953- *WhoWest 92*
**Johnson,** David Douglas 1955- *WhoMW 92*
**Johnson,** David Edsel 1927- *AmMWSc 92*
**Johnson,** David Elliot 1933- *WhoRel 92*
**Johnson,** David Freeman 1925- *AmMWSc 92, WhoBlA 92*
**Johnson,** David Gale 1916- *IntWW 91*
**Johnson,** David Gregory 1940- *AmMWSc 92*
**Johnson,** David Harlan 1949- *WhoMW 92*
**Johnson,** David Harley 1941- *AmMWSc 92*
**Johnson,** David Horace 1925- *WhoBlA 92*
**Johnson,** David Hugh Nevil 1920- *Who 92*
**Johnson,** David John 1938- *Who 92*
**Johnson,** David L 1929- *WhoIns 92*
**Johnson,** David L. 1941- *WhoRel 92*
**Johnson,** David Lee 1946- *AmMWSc 92*
**Johnson,** David Leroy 1947- *AmMWSc 92*
**Johnson,** David Lincoln 1929- *WhoAmL 92*
**Johnson,** David Linton 1945- *AmMWSc 92*
**Johnson,** David Norseen 1938- *AmMWSc 92*
**Johnson,** David Raymond 1946- *WhoAmL 92*
**Johnson,** David Raymond 1952- *WhoAmL 92*
**Johnson,** David Reynold 1945- *WhoAmL 92*
**Johnson,** David Robert W. *Who 92*
**Johnson,** David Russell 1945- *AmMWSc 92*
**Johnson,** David Sellie 1935- *WhoWest 92*
**Johnson,** David Simonds 1924- *AmMWSc 92*
**Johnson,** David W, Jr 1942- *AmMWSc 92*
**Johnson,** David Wayne 1958- *WhoAmL 92*
**Johnson,** David Wesley 1955- *WhoEnt 92*
**Johnson,** David Willis 1932- *WhoFI 92*
**Johnson,** Davis 1934- *WhoBlA 92*
**Johnson,** Dean E 1931- *WhoIns 92*
**Johnson,** Dean Elton 1947- *WhoAmP 91*
**Johnson,** Delwin Phelps 1926- *AmMWSc 92*
**Johnson,** Denis 1949- *ConNov 91, IntAu&W 91, WrDr 92*
**Johnson,** Denis Gordon 1911- *Who 92*
**Johnson,** Denise R 1947- *WhoAmP 91*
**Johnson,** Dennis 1954- *WhoBlA 92*
**Johnson,** Dennis Allen 1949- *AmMWSc 92*
**Johnson,** Dennis Anthony 1960- *WhoFI 92*
**Johnson,** Dennis Duane 1938- *AmMWSc 92*
**Johnson,** Dennis Robert 1946- *WhoAmL 92*
**Johnson,** Derwood 1929- *WhoAmL 92*
**Johnson,** DeWayne Carl 1935- *AmMWSc 92*
**Johnson,** Dewey, Jr 1926- *AmMWSc 92*
**Johnson,** Diane *DrAPF 91*
**Johnson,** Diane 1929- *WhoBlA 92*
**Johnson,** Diane 1934- *ConNov 91, WrDr 92*
**Johnson,** Diane Harvey *WhoAmP 91*
**Johnson,** Dick *ConAu 135*
**Johnson,** Dolores DeBower 1932- *WhoEnt 92*
**Johnson,** Don 1950- *IntMPA 92*
**Johnson,** Don Edwin 1939- *WhoAmL 92*
**Johnson,** Don Frederick 1953- *WhoWest 92*
**Johnson,** Don Robert 1942- *WhoRel 92*
**Johnson,** Don Wayne 1949- *WhoEnt 92*
**Johnson,** Donal Dabell 1922- *AmMWSc 92*
**Johnson,** Donald, Jr *WhoAmP 91*
**Johnson,** Donald Charles 1927- *AmMWSc 92*
**Johnson,** Donald Curtis 1935- *AmMWSc 92*
**Johnson,** Donald Edward 1924- *WhoAmP 91*
**Johnson,** Donald Edwin 1920- *Who 92*
**Johnson,** Donald Elwood 1935- *AmMWSc 92*
**Johnson,** Donald Eugene 1938- *AmMWSc 92*
**Johnson,** Donald Glen 1931- *AmMWSc 92*
**Johnson,** Donald L 1927- *AmMWSc 92*
**Johnson,** Donald L 1931- *WhoAmP 91*
**Johnson,** Donald R 1930- *AmMWSc 92*
**Johnson,** Donald Ralph 1931- *AmMWSc 92*
**Johnson,** Donald Rex 1938- *AmMWSc 92, WhoAmP 91*
**Johnson,** Donald Richard 1929- *AmMWSc 92*
**Johnson,** Donald Ross 1920- *AmMWSc 92*
**Johnson,** Donald W 1929- *AmMWSc 92*
**Johnson,** Donald Wayne 1950- *WhoAmL 92*
**Johnson,** Donn S. 1947- *WhoBlA 92*
**Johnson,** Donna Alligood 1956- *WhoBlA 92*
**Johnson,** Donna Mae 1931- *WhoRel 92*
**Johnson,** Donovan Earl 1942- *AmMWSc 92*
**Johnson,** Doris Elayne 1954- *WhoBlA 92*
**Johnson,** Dorothy Almyra 1916- *WhoRel 92*
**Johnson,** Dorothy M. 1905-1984 *TwCWW 91*
**Johnson,** Dorothy Phyllis 1925- *WhoMW 92*
**Johnson,** Dorothy Turner 1915- *WhoBlA 92*
**Johnson,** Douglas Alan 1949- *WhoMW 92*
**Johnson,** Douglas Allan 1949- *AmMWSc 92*
**Johnson,** Douglas H. 1943- *WhoBlA 92*
**Johnson,** Douglas J 1942- *WhoAmP 91*
**Johnson,** Douglas L 1925- *AmMWSc 92*

**Johnson,** Douglas Thomas 1957- *WhoAmL 92*
**Johnson,** Douglas Walter 1946- *WhoWest 92*
**Johnson,** Douglas Wayne 1934- *WhoRel 92*
**Johnson,** Douglas Wells 1949- *WhoAmL 92*
**Johnson,** Douglas William 1953- *AmMWSc 92, WhoFI 92*
**Johnson,** Douglas William John 1925- *IntWW 91, Who 92*
**Johnson,** Dudley Paul 1940- *AmMWSc 92*
**Johnson,** Durward Elton 1932- *WhoAmP 91*
**Johnson,** E Calvin 1926- *AmMWSc 92*
**Johnson,** E E *ScFEYrs*
**Johnson,** E. Eric 1927- *WhoWest 92*
**Johnson,** E G 1925- *WhoAmP 91*
**Johnson,** E O 1919- *AmMWSc 92*
**Johnson,** E Richard 1938- *IntAu&W 91*
**Johnson,** E. Scott 1951- *WhoEnt 92*
**Johnson,** Earl, Jr. 1933- *WhoAmL 92*
**Johnson,** Earl E. 1926- *WhoBlA 92*
**Johnson,** Earle Bertrand 1914- *WhoFI 92*
**Johnson,** Earle David 1943- *WhoMW 92*
**Johnson,** Earnest J 1931- *AmMWSc 92*
**Johnson,** Earvin *NewYTBS 91 [port]*
**Johnson,** Earvin 1959- *WhoWest 92*
**Johnson,** Earvin, Jr. 1959- *WhoBlA 92*
**Johnson,** Ed F. 1937- *WhoBlA 92*
**Johnson,** Eddie A. 1959- *WhoBlA 92*
**Johnson,** Eddie Bernice 1935- *WhoAmP 91*
**Johnson,** Eddie C. 1920- *WhoBlA 92*
**Johnson,** Edgar Gustav 1922- *AmMWSc 92*
**Johnson,** Edmond R. 1937- *WhoBlA 92*
**Johnson,** Edna DeCoursey 1922- *WhoBlA 92*
**Johnson,** Edna Ruth 1918- *WhoRel 92*
**Johnson,** Edward 1598-1672 *BenetAL 91*
**Johnson,** Edward 1878-1959 *NewAmDM*
**Johnson,** Edward, Jr. 1955- *WhoBlA 92*
**Johnson,** Edward A. 1940- *WhoBlA 92*
**Johnson,** Edward Austin 1860-1944 *DcNCBi 3*
**Johnson,** Edward Elemuel *WhoBlA 92*
**Johnson,** Edward Lee 1931- *WhoWest 92*
**Johnson,** Edward M. 1943- *WhoBlA 92*
**Johnson,** Edward Michael 1944- *WhoAmL 92*
**Johnson,** Edward Michael 1945- *AmMWSc 92*
**Johnson,** Edwin Ferry 1803-1872 *BiInAmS*
**Johnson,** Edwin George 1922- *WhoAmP 91*
**Johnson,** Edwin Wallace 1923- *AmMWSc 92*
**Johnson,** Einar William 1955- *WhoAmL 92*
**Johnson,** Einer Wesley, Jr 1919- *AmMWSc 92*
**Johnson,** Elaine McDowell 1942- *WhoBlA 92*
**Johnson,** Eldon 1930- *WhoAmP 91*
**Johnson,** Eleanor Mae 1925- *WhoMW 92*
**Johnson,** Elijah 1948- *AmMWSc 92*
**Johnson,** Elizabeth Briggs 1921- *AmMWSc 92*
**Johnson,** Elizabeth Diane Long 1945- *WhoAmL 92*
**Johnson,** Elizabeth Hill 1913- *WhoWest 92*
**Johnson,** Elizabeth Katharine 1951- *WhoWest 92*
**Johnson,** Elizabeth M 1931- *WhoAmP 91*
**Johnson,** Ellen Christine 1948- *WhoFI 92, WhoMW 92*
**Johnson,** Ellen Schultz 1918- *WhoEnt 92*
**Johnson,** Elliott Amos 1907- *WhoAmL 92*
**Johnson,** Ellis Lane 1938- *AmMWSc 92*
**Johnson,** Elmer Hubert 1917- *WrDr 92*
**Johnson,** Elmer Marshall 1930- *AmMWSc 92*
**Johnson,** Elmer Roger 1911- *AmMWSc 92*
**Johnson,** Elmer William 1932- *WhoAmL 92*
**Johnson,** Elmore W. 1944- *WhoBlA 92*
**Johnson,** Elsie Ernest *AmMWSc 92*
**Johnson,** Elwin L Pete 1935- *AmMWSc 92*
**Johnson,** Emil Richard 1937- *WrDr 92*
**Johnson,** Emmett John 1929- *AmMWSc 92*
**Johnson,** Emory Emanuel 1914- *AmMWSc 92*
**Johnson,** Enid C. 1931- *WhoBlA 92*
**Johnson,** Eric 1944- *WhoAmL 92*
**Johnson,** Eric Alfred George 1911- *Who 92*
**Johnson,** Eric Carl 1951- *WhoMW 92*
**Johnson,** Eric Elliott *WhoWest 92*
**Johnson,** Eric G. 1951- *WhoBlA 92*
**Johnson,** Eric G, Jr 1936- *AmMWSc 92*
**Johnson,** Eric Kai 1950- *WhoMW 92*
**Johnson,** Eric Norman 1952- *WhoAmP 91*
**Johnson,** Eric Richard 1947- *AmMWSc 92*
**Johnson,** Eric Robert 1947- *AmMWSc 92*
**Johnson,** Eric Van 1943- *AmMWSc 92*
**Johnson,** Eric W. 1918- *WrDr 92*
**Johnson,** Erma Chansler 1942- *WhoBlA 92*
**Johnson,** Ernest Dwain 1947- *WhoWest 92*
**Johnson,** Ernest F 1918- *AmMWSc 92*
**Johnson,** Ernest Kaye, III 1950- *WhoBlA 92*
**Johnson,** Ernest Walter 1943- *AmMWSc 92*
**Johnson,** Ervin Willard 1916- *WhoMW 92*
**Johnson,** Eugene A 1925- *AmMWSc 92*
**Johnson,** Eugene Laurence 1936- *WhoAmL 92*
**Johnson,** Eugene Malcolm, Jr 1943- *AmMWSc 92*
**Johnson,** Eugene W 1939- *AmMWSc 92*
**Johnson,** Eunice Marian 1927- *WhoMW 92*
**Johnson,** Eunice Walker *NotBlAW 92, WhoBlA 92*
**Johnson,** Evelyn F. 1925- *WhoBlA 92*
**Johnson,** Evelyn Marie *WhoAmP 91*
**Johnson,** Evert William 1921- *AmMWSc 92*
**Johnson,** Eyvind 1900-1976 *ConAu 34NR, FacFETw*
**Johnson,** Eyvind Olof Verner 1900-1976 *WhoNob 90*
**Johnson,** Ezra 1955- *WhoBlA 92*
**Johnson,** F Brent 1942- *AmMWSc 92*
**Johnson,** F Clifford 1932- *AmMWSc 92*
**Johnson,** F. J., Jr. 1930- *WhoBlA 92*
**Johnson,** F. Michael 1953- *WhoWest 92*
**Johnson,** F. Raymond 1920- *WhoBlA 92*
**Johnson,** Falk S. 1913- *WrDr 92*
**Johnson,** Fannie Miriam Harris 1938- *WhoEnt 92*
**Johnson,** Fatima Nunes 1939- *AmMWSc 92*
**Johnson,** Faye *WhoAmP 91*
**Johnson,** Fenton *DrAPF 91*
**Johnson,** Fenton 1888-1958 *BlkLC [port]*
**Johnson,** Ferd 1905- *WhoEnt 92*
**Johnson,** Florence N. 1956- *WhoEnt 92*
**Johnson,** Francis 1930- *AmMWSc 92*
**Johnson,** Francis Edward, Jr. 1948- *WhoBlA 92*
**Johnson,** Francis Rea 1921- *Who 92*
**Johnson,** Francis Severin 1918- *AmMWSc 92*
**Johnson,** Francis Willard 1920- *WhoRel 92*
**Johnson,** Frank *WhoRel 92*
**Johnson,** Frank 1792-1844 *NewAmDM*
**Johnson,** Frank 1958- *WhoBlA 92*
**Johnson,** Frank Anthony 1962- *WhoMW 92*
**Johnson,** Frank Arthur 1938- *WhoRel 92*
**Johnson,** Frank B, Jr *WhoAmP 91*
**Johnson,** Frank Bacchus 1919- *AmMWSc 92*
**Johnson,** Frank Harris 1908- *AmMWSc 92*
**Johnson,** Frank J. 1939- *WhoBlA 92*
**Johnson,** Frank Junior 1930- *AmMWSc 92*
**Johnson,** Frank M, Jr 1918- *WhoAmP 91*
**Johnson,** Frank Minis, Jr. 1918- *WhoAmL 92*
**Johnson,** Frank Robert 1943- *Who 92*
**Johnson,** Frank Scott 1956- *WhoFI 92*
**Johnson,** Frank Sidney Roland 1917- *Who 92*
**Johnson,** Frank Walker 1909- *AmMWSc 92*
**Johnson,** Frank William 1948- *WhoFI 92*
**Johnson,** Frankie, Jr. 1952- *WhoEnt 92*
**Johnson,** Franklin M 1940- *AmMWSc 92*
**Johnson,** Franklin Ridgway 1912- *WhoAmL 92*
**Johnson,** Franklin William 1931- *WhoWest 92*
**Johnson,** Fred D. 1933- *WhoBlA 92*
**Johnson,** Fred Lee 1931- *WhoAmP 91*
**Johnson,** Fred Lowery, Jr 1927- *AmMWSc 92*
**Johnson,** Fred Richard 1915- *WhoMW 92*
**Johnson,** Frederic Allan 1932- *AmMWSc 92*
**Johnson,** Frederic Duane 1925- *AmMWSc 92*
**Johnson,** Frederick, Jr. 1940- *WhoBlA 92*
**Johnson,** Frederick Alistair 1928- *Who 92*
**Johnson,** Frederick Allan 1923- *AmMWSc 92*
**Johnson,** Frederick Arthur, Jr 1923- *AmMWSc 92*
**Johnson,** Frederick Carroll 1940- *AmMWSc 92*
**Johnson,** Frederick Douglass 1946- *WhoBlA 92*
**Johnson,** Frederick E. 1941- *WhoBlA 92*
**Johnson,** Frederick Ross 1931- *IntWW 91, WhoFI 92*
**Johnson,** Fredrick Bolan 1935- *WhoEnt 92*
**Johnson,** G Allan 1947- *AmMWSc 92*
**Johnson,** G. Edwin 1949- *WhoFI 92*
**Johnson,** G. Eric 1941- *WhoWest 92*
**Johnson,** G. Griffith 1912- *IntMPA 92*
**Johnson,** G. Matthew 1950- *WhoMW 92*
**Johnson,** G. R. Hovey 1930- *WhoBlA 92*
**Johnson,** G. Roberts 1940- *WhoAmL 92*
**Johnson,** Gabriel Ampah 1930- *IntWW 91*
**Johnson,** Gage 1924- *WhoBlA 92*
**Johnson,** Gage Randolph 1961- *WhoAmL 92*
**Johnson,** Galen Leslie 1952- *WhoEnt 92*
**Johnson,** Gardiner 1905- *WhoAmP 91*
**Johnson,** Garey A. 1947- *WhoBlA 92*
**Johnson,** Garland A 1936- *AmMWSc 92*
**Johnson,** Garrett Bruce 1946- *WhoAmL 92*
**Johnson,** Garry 1937- *Who 92*
**Johnson,** Gary Allen 1954- *WhoRel 92*
**Johnson,** Gary Brian 1947- *WhoFI 92*
**Johnson,** Gary Charles 1946- *WhoAmP 91*
**Johnson,** Gary David 1945- *WhoEnt 92*
**Johnson,** Gary Dean 1942- *AmMWSc 92*
**Johnson,** Gary Harold 1943- *WhoFI 92, WhoWest 92*
**Johnson,** Gary Keith 1951- *WhoMW 92*
**Johnson,** Gary Kenneth 1939- *WhoAmP 91*
**Johnson,** Gary Kent 1936- *WhoWest 92*
**Johnson,** Gary Lee 1938- *AmMWSc 92*
**Johnson,** Gary Lee 1955- *WhoRel 92*
**Johnson,** Gary Leonard 1953- *WhoAmL 92*
**Johnson,** Gary Leroy 1938- *WhoRel 92*
**Johnson,** Gary M. 1947- *WhoAmL 92*
**Johnson,** Gary Neil 1951- *WhoAmP 91*
**Johnson,** Gary R 1956- *WhoAmP 91*
**Johnson,** Gearold Robert 1940- *AmMWSc 92*
**Johnson,** Gene C. 1941- *WhoBlA 92*
**Johnson,** Gene Randolph 1937- *WhoAmL 92*
**Johnson,** Geneva B. *WhoBlA 92*
**Johnson,** Genevieve N. 1899- *WhoBlA 92*
**Johnson,** George 1920- *WhoMW 92*
**Johnson,** George 1952- *ConAu 133, WrDr 92*
**Johnson,** George, Jr 1926- *AmMWSc 92*
**Johnson,** George, Jr. 1934- *WhoBlA 92*
**Johnson,** George Andrew 1914- *AmMWSc 92*
**Johnson,** George Ellis 1927- *WhoBlA 92*
**Johnson,** George F *WhoAmP 91*
**Johnson,** George Frederick 1916- *AmMWSc 92*
**Johnson,** George H. 1941- *WhoFI 92*
**Johnson,** George Leonard 1931- *AmMWSc 92*
**Johnson,** George M. 1900- *WhoBlA 92*
**Johnson,** George Patrick 1932- *AmMWSc 92*
**Johnson,** George Philip 1926- *AmMWSc 92*
**Johnson,** George Robert 1917- *AmMWSc 92*
**Johnson,** George Robert 1927- *WhoMW 92*
**Johnson,** George S 1943- *AmMWSc 92*
**Johnson,** George Taylor 1930- *WhoMW 92*
**Johnson,** George Thomas 1916- *AmMWSc 92*
**Johnson,** George Weldon 1930- *WhoAmL 92, WhoMW 92*
**Johnson,** George Wilfred 1956- *WhoRel 92*
**Johnson,** Georgia Anna 1930- *WhoBlA 92*
**Johnson,** Georgia Douglas 1877-1966 *NotBlAW 92 [port]*
**Johnson,** Georgianna 1930- *WhoBlA 92*
**Johnson,** Gerald D 1931- *WhoIns 92*
**Johnson,** Gerald Glenn, Jr 1939- *AmMWSc 92*
**Johnson,** Gerald Lynn 1950- *WhoAmP 91*
**Johnson,** Gerald Thomas 1954- *WhoWest 92*
**Johnson,** Gerald W. 1890-1980 *BenetAL 91*
**Johnson,** Gerald White 1890-1980 *DcNCBi 3*
**Johnson,** Gerald Winford 1932- *AmMWSc 92*
**Johnson,** Geraldine Ross 1946- *WhoBlA 92*
**Johnson,** Glade 1946- *WhoWest 92*
**Johnson,** Glen D, Jr 1954- *WhoAmP 91*
**Johnson,** Glen Eric 1951- *AmMWSc 92*
**Johnson,** Glendon E 1924- *WhoIns 92*
**Johnson,** Glenn M *AmMWSc 92*
**Johnson,** Glenn Richard 1938- *AmMWSc 92*
**Johnson,** Glenn T. 1917- *WhoBlA 92*
**Johnson,** Glenn Thompson 1917- *WhoAmL 92*
**Johnson,** Gloria Dean 1948- *WhoBlA 92*
**Johnson,** Golden Elizabeth 1944- *WhoBlA 92*
**Johnson,** Gordon *Who 92*
**Johnson,** Gordon Carlton 1929- *AmMWSc 92*
**Johnson,** Gordon E 1934- *AmMWSc 92*
**Johnson,** Gordon Gilbert 1919- *WhoRel 92*
**Johnson,** Gordon Gustav 1936- *AmMWSc 92*
**Johnson,** Gordon Lee 1932- *AmMWSc 92*
**Johnson,** Gordon Oliver 1944- *AmMWSc 92*
**Johnson,** Gordon V 1940- *AmMWSc 92*
**Johnson,** Gordon Verle 1933- *AmMWSc 92*
**Johnson,** Grace Manchester 1907- *WhoAmP 91*
**Johnson,** Graham Rhodes 1950- *Who 92*
**Johnson,** Grant Lester 1929- *WhoAmL 92, WhoFI 92*
**Johnson,** Greg *DrAPF 91*
**Johnson,** Gregory Conrad 1963- *AmMWSc 92*
**Johnson,** Gregory L. *WhoAmL 92*
**Johnson,** Gregory Wayne 1953- *WhoBlA 92*
**Johnson,** Grover Leon 1931- *AmMWSc 92*
**Johnson,** Gus, Jr. 1938-1987 *WhoBlA 92N*
**Johnson,** Guy, Jr 1922- *AmMWSc 92*
**Johnson,** Guy B. d1991 *NewYTBS 91 [port]*
**Johnson,** Guy Charles 1933- *WhoEnt 92*
**Johnson,** Guy Charles 1946- *WhoBlA 92*
**Johnson,** Gwenavere Anelisa 1909- *WhoWest 92*
**Johnson,** H. Arvid 1936- *WhoAmL 92, WhoFI 92*
**Johnson,** H. Webster 1906- *WrDr 92*
**Johnson,** Hal G 1915- *AmMWSc 92*
**Johnson,** Hall 1888-1970 *NewAmDM*
**Johnson,** Halle Tanner Dillon 1864-1901 *NotBlAW 92 [port]*
**Johnson,** Halvard *DrAPF 91*
**Johnson,** Hamilton McKee 1915- *AmMWSc 92*
**Johnson,** Harlan Bruce 1922- *AmMWSc 92*
**Johnson,** Harlan C. 1919- *WhoBlA 92*
**Johnson,** Harlan Paul 1939- *AmMWSc 92*
**Johnson,** Harmer Frederik 1943- *WhoFI 92*
**Johnson,** Harold Arthur 1924- *WhoFI 92*
**Johnson,** Harold Cumings 1933- *WhoEnt 92*
**Johnson,** Harold David 1924- *AmMWSc 92*
**Johnson,** Harold E.B. 1918- *WhoBlA 92*
**Johnson,** Harold Earl 1939- *WhoFI 92*
**Johnson,** Harold Gene 1934- *WhoAmL 92*
**Johnson,** Harold Hazen 1936- *WhoRel 92*
**Johnson,** Harold Hunt 1929- *AmMWSc 92*
**Johnson,** Harold J. 1948- *WhoAmL 92*
**Johnson,** Harold R. 1926- *WhoBlA 92*
**Johnson,** Harold Stephens 1928- *WhoRel 92*
**Johnson,** Harold Thomas 1938- *WhoFI 92*
**Johnson,** Harry A. 1920- *WhoBlA 92*
**Johnson,** Harry A., III 1949- *WhoAmL 92*
**Johnson,** Harry Dean 1930- *WhoMW 92*
**Johnson,** Harry McClure 1925- *AmMWSc 92*
**Johnson,** Harry Sterling 1954- *WhoAmL 92*
**Johnson,** Harry William, Jr 1927- *AmMWSc 92*
**Johnson,** Hayman 1912- *Who 92*
**Johnson,** Heidi Smith 1946- *WhoWest 92*
**Johnson,** Helen Chaffin 1905- *WhoAmP 91*
**Johnson,** Helen Jeannette 1951- *WhoAmP 91*
**Johnson,** Helen M 1928- *WhoAmP 91*
**Johnson,** Helene 1906- *NotBlAW 92*
**Johnson,** Henderson A., III 1929- *WhoBlA 92*
**Johnson,** Henry *DrAPF 91*
**Johnson,** Henry 1937- *WhoBlA 92*
**Johnson,** Henry Arna 1919- *WhoFI 92*
**Johnson,** Henry Leslie d1991 *Who 92N*
**Johnson,** Henry Stanley, Jr 1926- *AmMWSc 92*
**Johnson,** Herbert Gardner 1933- *AmMWSc 92*
**Johnson,** Herbert Gordon 1916- *AmMWSc 92*
**Johnson,** Herbert Harrison 1931- *AmMWSc 92*
**Johnson,** Herbert Lavern 1936- *WhoEnt 92*
**Johnson,** Herbert M. 1941- *WhoBlA 92*
**Johnson,** Herbert Windal 1920- *AmMWSc 92*
**Johnson,** Herman Leonall 1935- *AmMWSc 92*
**Johnson,** Hermon M., Sr. 1929- *WhoBlA 92*
**Johnson,** Herschel Lee 1948- *WhoBlA 92*
**Johnson,** Herschel Vespasian 1894-1966 *DcNCBi 3*
**Johnson,** Hilding Reynold 1920- *AmMWSc 92*
**Johnson,** Hiram 1866-1945 *FacFETw*
**Johnson,** Hiram Warren 1866-1945 *AmPolLe*
**Johnson,** Hollis Ralph 1928- *AmMWSc 92, WhoMW 92*
**Johnson,** Hollister, Jr 1929- *AmMWSc 92*
**Johnson,** Homer F, Jr 1920- *AmMWSc 92*

Johnson, Horace Richard 1926- AmMWSc 92
Johnson, Horton Anton 1926- AmMWSc 92
Johnson, Howard 1933- AmMWSc 92
Johnson, Howard Arthur, Jr. 1952- WhoFI 92
Johnson, Howard Arthur, Sr 1923- AmMWSc 92
Johnson, Howard B 1936- AmMWSc 92
Johnson, Howard Deering 1896-1972 FacFETw
Johnson, Howard Ernest 1935- AmMWSc 92
Johnson, Howard Eugene 1915- WhoFI 92
Johnson, Howard Marcellus AmMWSc 92
Johnson, Howard P 1923- AmMWSc 92
Johnson, Howard R. 1942- WhoBlA 92
Johnson, Howard Sydney 1911- Who 92
Johnson, Howard Wesley 1922- IntWW 91
Johnson, Hugh Eric Allan 1939- IntAu&W 91, IntWW 91, Who 92
Johnson, Hugh Mitchell 1923- AmMWSc 92
Johnson, Hunter 1906- NewAmDM
Johnson, Hymon T., Jr. 1919-1982 WhoBlA 92N
Johnson, I Birger 1913- AmMWSc 92
Johnson, I S Leevy 1942- WhoAmP 91, WhoBlA 92
Johnson, Ina Phay Roberts 1944- WhoRel 92
Johnson, Iola Vivian 1947- WhoBlA 92
Johnson, Irene L 1918- WhoAmP 91
Johnson, Irma Maria Z. 1930- WhoHisp 92
Johnson, Irving 1918- AmMWSc 92, WhoMW 92
Johnson, Irving M. 1905-1991 NewYTBS 91
Johnson, Irving McClure 1905-1991 ConAu 133
Johnson, Irving Stanley 1925- AmMWSc 92
Johnson, Ivan M 1940- AmMWSc 92
Johnson, Iver Christian 1928- WhoFI 92
Johnson, Ivory 1938- WhoBlA 92
Johnson, J Alan 1933- AmMWSc 92
Johnson, J. Albert 1933- WhoAmL 92
Johnson, J. Bond 1926- IntMPA 92
Johnson, J David AmMWSc 92
Johnson, J. Dennis 1950- WhoFI 92
Johnson, J Donald 1935- AmMWSc 92
Johnson, J.J. 1924- NewAmDM
Johnson, J. M. 1940- WhoRel 92
Johnson, J. Mitchell 1951- WhoFI 92
Johnson, J R 1923- AmMWSc 92
Johnson, J. Rosamond 1873-1954 NewAmDM
Johnson, J Stuart 1912- AmMWSc 92
Johnson, J. Wayne 1941- WhoFI 92
Johnson, Jack 1930- AmMWSc 92
Johnson, Jack Donald 1931- AmMWSc 92
Johnson, Jack Leo 1933- WhoIns 92
Johnson, Jack Leroy 1944- WhoMW 92
Johnson, Jack Stoddard 1932- WhoWest 92
Johnson, Jack Wayne 1950- AmMWSc 92
Johnson, Jackson Melvin 1940- WhoWest 92
Johnson, Jacob Edwards, III 1922- WhoBlA 92
Johnson, James WhoAmP 91
Johnson, James 1811-1891 DcNCBi 3
Johnson, James 1908- Who 92
Johnson, James 1955- WhoEnt 92
Johnson, James, Jr. 1933- WhoBlA 92
Johnson, James A. WhoBlA 92, WhoRel 92
Johnson, James A. 1943- WhoFI 92
Johnson, James Allen, Jr 1954- AmMWSc 92
Johnson, James Brooks 1919- WhoMW 92
Johnson, James C, Jr WhoAmP 91
Johnson, James Carl AmMWSc 92
Johnson, James Clyde 1957- WhoAmP 91
Johnson, James Daniel 1944- AmMWSc 92, WhoWest 92
Johnson, James David 1948- WhoWest 92
Johnson, James Dow 1934- WhoEnt 92
Johnson, James Dwight 1932- WhoRel 92
Johnson, James E. 1927- WhoMW 92
Johnson, James Edgar Who 92
Johnson, James Edward 1931- WhoBlA 92
Johnson, James Edward 1936- AmMWSc 92
Johnson, James Edward 1940- AmMWSc 92
Johnson, James Edwin 1917- AmMWSc 92
Johnson, James Elver 1937- AmMWSc 92
Johnson, James Erling 1942- WhoFI 92
Johnson, James G. 1935- WhoRel 92
Johnson, James Gibson, Jr. 1938- WhoWest 92
Johnson, James H. 1932- WhoBlA 92
Johnson, James Harmon 1943- AmMWSc 92
Johnson, James Harold 1944- WhoAmL 92
Johnson, James Henry 1930- IntAu&W 91, WrDr 92
Johnson, James Hervey 1901-1988 RelLAm 91
Johnson, James Jim T. 1939- WhoEnt 92
Johnson, James Kenneth 1942- WhoBlA 92
Johnson, James LaMont 1941- WhoEnt 92
Johnson, James Lawrence 1927- WhoFI 92
Johnson, James Lawrence 1953- WhoWest 92
Johnson, James Leslie 1921- AmMWSc 92
Johnson, James M 1915- AmMWSc 92
Johnson, James Nathaniel 1932- Who 92
Johnson, James Norman 1939- AmMWSc 92
Johnson, James P. 1894-1955 NewAmDM
Johnson, James P 1930- WhoAmP 91
Johnson, James Patrick 1953- WhoEnt 92
Johnson, James R. 1934- WhoBlA 92
Johnson, James Ralph 1922- IntAu&W 91, WhoWest 92, WrDr 92
Johnson, James Randall 1951- WhoAmL 92
Johnson, James Robert 1947- WhoFI 92
Johnson, James S. 1918- WhoBlA 92
Johnson, James W 1930- AmMWSc 92
Johnson, James W., Jr. WhoBlA 92
Johnson, James W, Jr 1951- WhoAmP 91
Johnson, James Walter, Jr. 1941- WhoBlA 92
Johnson, James Weldon 1871-1938 AfrAmW, BenetAL 91, BlkLC [port], FacFETw, NewAmDM, RComAH
Johnson, James William, III 1938- WhoWest 92
Johnson, James Wilson 1942- WhoRel 92
Johnson, Jane 1951- TwCPaSc
Johnson, Jane Claudia Saunders 1832-1899 DcNCBi 3
Johnson, Janet 1940- WhoAmP 91
Johnson, Janice Kay 1946- AmMWSc 92
Johnson, Janice Marie 1954- WhoBlA 92
Johnson, Jay 1947- WhoBlA 92
Johnson, Jay Allan 1941- AmMWSc 92
Johnson, Jay William 1964- WhoEnt 92
Johnson, Jay Withington 1943- WhoMW 92
Johnson, Jean 1937- IntAu&W 91
Johnson, Jean DeWitt 1923- WhoMW 92
Johnson, Jean Elaine 1925- AmMWSc 92
Johnson, Jean Louise 1947- AmMWSc 92
Johnson, Jeannette Fay 1957- WhoFI 92
Johnson, Jed, Jr 1939- WhoAmP 91
Johnson, Jeff Deems 1900-1960 DcNCBi 3
Johnson, Jeffalyn Brown WhoBlA 92
Johnson, Jeffery Lee 1941- AmMWSc 92
Johnson, Jeffrey Allan 1956- WhoRel 92
Johnson, Jeffrey D 1958- WhoAmP 91
Johnson, Jeffrey Donald 1968- WhoEnt 92
Johnson, Jeffry Lynn 1961- WhoMW 92
Johnson, Jeh Vincent 1931- WhoBlA 92
Johnson, Jennifer J. 1962- WhoWest 92
Johnson, Jennifer Lea-Bates 1970- WhoEnt 92
Johnson, Jenyce WhoFI 92
Johnson, Jerald Arthur 1943- WhoFI 92
Johnson, Jerald D. WhoRel 92
Johnson, Jerome WhoRel 92
Johnson, Jerome Ben 1950- WhoWest 92
Johnson, Jerome H 1918- AmMWSc 92
Johnson, Jerome Linne 1929- WhoWest 92
Johnson, Jerry Calvin 1920- WhoBlA 92
Johnson, Jerry Carl 1951- WhoRel 92
Johnson, Jerry K 1933- WhoAmP 91
Johnson, Jerry L. 1947- WhoBlA 92
Johnson, Jerry Wayne 1948- AmMWSc 92
Johnson, Jesse J. 1914- WhoBlA 92, WrDr 92
Johnson, Jesse J. 1921- WhoBlA 92
Johnson, Jimmie Ron 1943- WhoMW 92
Johnson, Jimmy Ray 1943- WhoEnt 92
Johnson, Joan 1943- WhoAmP 91
Johnson, Joan B. 1929- WhoBlA 92
Johnson, Joan J. 1942- WrDr 92
Johnson, Joan Kiff 1929- WhoAmP 91
Johnson, Joanne Mary 1947- WhoFI 92
Johnson, Joe AmMWSc 92, DrAPF 91, IntWW 91
Johnson, Joe 1940- WhoBlA 92
Johnson, Joe Arley 1930- WhoAmP 91
Johnson, Joe C. 1926- WhoHisp 92
Johnson, Joe W 1908- AmMWSc 92
Johnson, Joel Patrick 1956- WhoEnt 92
Johnson, John 1922- WhoAmP 91
Johnson, John Alan 1943- AmMWSc 92
Johnson, John Alexander 1924- AmMWSc 92
Johnson, John Allen 1950- WhoFI 92
Johnson, John Andrew 1942- WhoMW 92
Johnson, John Arnold 1924- AmMWSc 92
Johnson, John Arthur 1878-1946 FacFETw [port]
Johnson, John Arthur 1934- WhoAmL 92
Johnson, John Arvid 1953- WhoMW 92
Johnson, John Butler 1850-1902 BiInAmS
Johnson, John C 1944- WhoAmP 91
Johnson, John Christopher, Jr 1924- AmMWSc 92
Johnson, John Clark 1919- AmMWSc 92
Johnson, John David 1938- WhoWest 92
Johnson, John E 1931- AmMWSc 92
Johnson, John E, Jr 1860?-1919 BiInAmS
Johnson, John E, Jr 1945- AmMWSc 92
Johnson, John Edwin 1931- WhoMW 92
Johnson, John Frank 1942- WhoFI 92, WhoMW 92
Johnson, John H. 1918- ConAu 135, IntAu&W 91, IntWW 91, WhoBlA 92, WhoFI 92, WhoIns 92, WhoMW 92
Johnson, John Hal 1930- AmMWSc 92
Johnson, John Harold AmMWSc 92
Johnson, John Harold 1918- FacFETw
Johnson, John Harold 1946- WhoMW 92
Johnson, John Harris 1937- AmMWSc 92
Johnson, John Henry 1951- WhoEnt 92
Johnson, John Irwin, Jr 1931- AmMWSc 92
Johnson, John J. WhoBlA 92
Johnson, John LeRoy 1936- AmMWSc 92
Johnson, John Lewis 1818-1900 DcNCBi 3
Johnson, John Lowell 1926- AmMWSc 92
Johnson, John Mark 1961- WhoEnt 92
Johnson, John Marshall 1944- AmMWSc 92
Johnson, John Morris 1937- AmMWSc 92
Johnson, John Philip 1949- WhoWest 92
Johnson, John Randall, Sr. 1945- WhoRel 92
Johnson, John Raymond 1905- AmMWSc 92
Johnson, John Recter 1923- WhoWest 92
Johnson, John Richard 1942- AmMWSc 92
Johnson, John Richard 1949- WhoWest 92
Johnson, John Robin 1927- Who 92
Johnson, John Rodney 1930- IntWW 91, Who 92
Johnson, John Thomas 1942- WhoBlA 92
Johnson, John W. 1934- WhoBlA 92
Johnson, John Webster, Jr 1925- AmMWSc 92
Johnson, Johnnie Who 92, WhoRel 92
Johnson, Johnnie 1956- WhoBlA 92
Johnson, Johnnie D. 1938- WhoFI 92
Johnson, Johnnie L., Jr. 1946- WhoBlA 92
Johnson, Johnny Albert 1938- AmMWSc 92
Johnson, Johnny B. 1920- WhoBlA 92
Johnson, Johnny Burl 1944- WhoFI 92
Johnson, Johnny R 1929- AmMWSc 92
Johnson, Jon D 1948- WhoAmP 91, WhoBlA 92
Johnson, Jondelle H. 1924- WhoBlA 92
Johnson, Joscelyn Andrea 1966- WhoBlA 92
Johnson, Joseph WhoAmP 91
Johnson, Joseph 1751-1776? BlkwEAR
Johnson, Joseph A. 1925- WhoBlA 92
Johnson, Joseph Andrew, III 1940- AmMWSc 92
Johnson, Joseph B. 1934- WhoBlA 92
Johnson, Joseph Bernard 1919- WhoAmL 92
Johnson, Joseph Charles 1968- WhoEnt 92
Johnson, Joseph Clayton, Jr. 1943- WhoAmL 92
Johnson, Joseph David 1945- WhoBlA 92
Johnson, Joseph E WhoAmP 91
Johnson, Joseph E. 1906-1990 CurBio 91N
Johnson, Joseph Earl 1946- WhoAmP 91
Johnson, Joseph Edward 1934- WhoBlA 92
Johnson, Joseph Edward 1955- WhoAmL 92
Johnson, Joseph Eggleston, III 1930- AmMWSc 92, IntWW 91
Johnson, Joseph Ernest 1942- WhoIns 92
Johnson, Joseph H. d1991 NewYTBS 91 [port]
Johnson, Joseph H., Jr. 1925- WhoAmL 92
Johnson, Joseph Harvey 1916- WhoBlA 92
Johnson, Joseph L AmMWSc 92
Johnson, Joseph Leslie 1925- WhoRel 92
Johnson, Joseph P, Jr 1931- WhoAmP 91
Johnson, Joseph Richard 1922- AmMWSc 92
Johnson, Joseph Richardson 1945- WhoAmL 92
Johnson, Josephine 1910- ConNov 91, IntAu&W 91
Johnson, Josephine W. 1910- BenetAL 91
Johnson, Joshua 1949- WhoBlA 92
Johnson, Joy J. 1921- WhoBlA 92
Johnson, Joy Joseph 1922- WhoAmP 91
Johnson, Joyce 1935- WrDr 92
Johnson, Joyce Colleen 1939- WhoBlA 92
Johnson, Joyce M 1952- WhoAmP 91
Johnson, Joyce Sandeen DrAPF 91
Johnson, Juanita B. 1927- WhoBlA 92
Johnson, Judith DrAPF 91
Johnson, Judith Ekberg 1949- WhoEnt 92
Johnson, Judith Martha Darrow 1942- WhoAmL 92
Johnson, Judy 1900-1989 WhoBlA 92N
Johnson, Juel S 1923- WhoAmP 91
Johnson, Julian Frank 1923- AmMWSc 92
Johnson, Juliana Cornish 1957- WhoBlA 92
Johnson, Julie Marie 1953- WhoMW 92
Johnson, Justin Morris 1933- WhoAmL 92, WhoBlA 92
Johnson, Karen Ann 1941- WhoAmP 91
Johnson, Karen B 1942- WhoAmP 91
Johnson, Karen Brown 1943- WhoRel 92
Johnson, Karen Elise 1950- AmMWSc 92
Johnson, Karen Louise 1941- AmMWSc 92
Johnson, Karl Clinthorne, Jr. 1957- WhoFI 92
Johnson, Karmen Denise 1960- WhoAmL 92
Johnson, Kate Ancrum Burr 1881-1968 DcNCBi 3
Johnson, Kate Knapp DrAPF 91
Johnson, Katherine Anne 1947- WhoAmL 92
Johnson, Katherine Grace 1960- WhoMW 92
Johnson, Keith 1921- IntWW 91
Johnson, Keith Edward 1935- AmMWSc 92
Johnson, Keith Edwin 1948- WhoRel 92
Johnson, Keith Huber 1936- AmMWSc 92
Johnson, Keith Leonard 1952- WhoAmL 92
Johnson, Keith O. 1938- WhoEnt 92
Johnson, Keith Ronald 1929- WhoWest 92
Johnson, Keith Windsor 1952- WhoFI 92
Johnson, Kelley Antonio 1962- WhoBlA 92
Johnson, Kelly 1910-1990 AnObit 1990
Johnson, Kenneth 1907- AmMWSc 92
Johnson, Kenneth Alan 1931- AmMWSc 92
Johnson, Kenneth Allen 1949- AmMWSc 92
Johnson, Kenneth C. 1942- WhoEnt 92
Johnson, Kenneth Delford 1911- AmMWSc 92
Johnson, Kenneth Duane 1944- AmMWSc 92
Johnson, Kenneth E. 1964- WhoEnt 92
Johnson, Kenneth Earl 1921- AmMWSc 92
Johnson, Kenneth George 1930- AmMWSc 92
Johnson, Kenneth Gerald 1925- AmMWSc 92
Johnson, Kenneth Harvey 1936- AmMWSc 92
Johnson, Kenneth James 1926- Who 92
Johnson, Kenneth Lance 1963- WhoBlA 92
Johnson, Kenneth Langstreth 1925- IntWW 91, Who 92
Johnson, Kenneth Lavon 1937- WhoBlA 92
Johnson, Kenneth Lee 1959- WhoMW 92
Johnson, Kenneth Maurice, Jr 1944- AmMWSc 92
Johnson, Kenneth Myron 1967- WhoEnt 92
Johnson, Kenneth Odell 1922- WhoFI 92, WhoMW 92
Johnson, Kenneth Olafur AmMWSc 92
Johnson, Kenneth Oscar 1920- WhoFI 92
Johnson, Kenneth Peter 1930- WhoBlA 92
Johnson, Kenneth Peter, Sr 1930- WhoAmP 91
Johnson, Kenneth Ray 1941- WhoRel 92
Johnson, Kenneth Stanley 1950- WhoFI 92
Johnson, Kenneth Stuart 1928- WhoFI 92, WhoMW 92
Johnson, Kenneth Sutherland 1934- AmMWSc 92
Johnson, Kenneth Thorwald 1944- WhoMW 92
Johnson, Kent J 1946- AmMWSc 92
Johnson, Kent L 1949- WhoAmP 91
Johnson, Kent Laurel 1934- WhoRel 92
Johnson, Kenwin N. WhoRel 92
Johnson, Kermit Douglas 1928- WhoRel 92
Johnson, Kevin 1964- WhoWest 92
Johnson, Kevin 1966?- News 91 [port]
Johnson, Kevin Blaine 1956- WhoAmL 92
Johnson, Kevin Maurice 1966- WhoBlA 92
Johnson, Kevin Raymond 1958- WhoAmL 92, WhoHisp 92
Johnson, Kim 1955- ConAu 133
Johnson, Kim Howard ConAu 133
Johnson, Kurt Boyd 1960- WhoWest 92
Johnson, Kurt Edward 1943- AmMWSc 92
Johnson, Kurt P 1938- AmMWSc 92
Johnson, L D 1937- AmMWSc 92
Johnson, L Ensign 1931- AmMWSc 92
Johnson, L. J. 1935- WhoFI 92
Johnson, L. Ronald 1938- WhoMW 92

**Johnson,** LaDon Jerome 1934- AmMWSc 92
**Johnson,** Lael Frederic 1938- WhoAmL 92, WhoFI 92
**Johnson,** Lamont 1922- IntMPA 92
**Johnson,** Lance Conrad 1945- WhoMW 92
**Johnson,** Lance Franklin 1938- WhoAmP 91
**Johnson,** Larenda Renee 1957- WhoMW 92
**Johnson,** Larry 1949- AmMWSc 92
**Johnson,** Larry Alan 1935- WhoAmP 91
**Johnson,** Larry Arnold 1950- WhoMW 92
**Johnson,** Larry Claud 1936- AmMWSc 92
**Johnson,** Larry Dean 1943- WhoRel 92
**Johnson,** Larry Dean 1945- WhoAmL 92
**Johnson,** Larry Don 1940- AmMWSc 92
**Johnson,** Larry K 1936- AmMWSc 92
**Johnson,** Larry Ray 1935- AmMWSc 92
**Johnson,** Larry Reidar 1945- AmMWSc 92
**Johnson,** Larry Robert 1943- WhoMW 92
**Johnson,** Larry Walter 1934- WhoAmL 92
**Johnson,** Larry Wayne 1952- WhoFI 92
**Johnson,** Larry Wilson 1938- WhoRel 92
**Johnson,** Laurie 1927- IntMPA 92
**Johnson,** LaVell R 1935- AmMWSc 92
**Johnson,** Lawrence Alan 1947- AmMWSc 92
**Johnson,** Lawrence Allan, Sr. 1943- WhoWest 92
**Johnson,** Lawrence Arthur 1936- AmMWSc 92
**Johnson,** Lawrence Clement 1822- BiInAmS
**Johnson,** Lawrence E., Sr. 1948- WhoBlA 92
**Johnson,** Lawrence H 1926- WhoAmP 91
**Johnson,** Lawrence Lloyd 1941- AmMWSc 92
**Johnson,** Lawrence M. 1940- WhoWest 92
**Johnson,** Lawrence Robert 1931- AmMWSc 92
**Johnson,** Lawrence Washington 1901- WhoBlA 92
**Johnson,** Lawrence Wilbur, Jr. 1955- WhoAmL 92
**Johnson,** Laymon, Jr. 1948- WhoWest 92
**Johnson,** Layne Mark 1953- AmMWSc 92
**Johnson,** Leander Floyd 1926- AmMWSc 92
**Johnson,** Leardrew L. 1921- WhoBlA 92
**Johnson,** Leary J 1934- WhoAmP 91
**Johnson,** Lectoy Tarlington 1931- WhoBlA 92
**Johnson,** Lee Carroll 1933- WhoWest 92
**Johnson,** Lee Frederick 1946- AmMWSc 92
**Johnson,** Lee H 1909- AmMWSc 92
**Johnson,** Lee Murphy 1934- AmMWSc 92
**Johnson,** Lee W 1938- AmMWSc 92
**Johnson,** Leigh Thornton 1943- WhoWest 92
**Johnson,** Leland Gilbert 1937- AmMWSc 92
**Johnson,** Lemuel A. 1941- WhoBlA 92
**Johnson,** Lennart Ingemar 1924- AmMWSc 92, WhoMW 92
**Johnson,** Leo Francis 1928- AmMWSc 92
**Johnson,** Leon 1930- WhoBlA 92
**Johnson,** Leon, Jr. 1946- WhoBlA 92
**Johnson,** Leon Joseph 1929- AmMWSc 92
**Johnson,** Leonard Evans 1940- AmMWSc 92
**Johnson,** Leonard Hjalma 1957- WhoAmL 92
**Johnson,** Leonard Roy 1942- AmMWSc 92
**Johnson,** Leonidas Alexander 1959- WhoWest 92
**Johnson,** Leroy WhoBlA 92
**Johnson,** Leroy 1928- WhoBlA 92
**Johnson,** LeRoy C 1937- IntAu&W 91
**Johnson,** Leroy Dennis 1908- AmMWSc 92
**Johnson,** LeRoy Franklin 1933- AmMWSc 92
**Johnson,** Leroy Reginald WhoBlA 92
**Johnson,** Leroy Ronald 1944- WhoBlA 92
**Johnson,** Leslie Kilham 1945- AmMWSc 92
**Johnson,** Leslie Royston 1924- IntWW 91
**Johnson,** Leslie Whiting 1943- WhoAmP 91
**Johnson,** Leslye AmMWSc 92
**Johnson,** Lester 1947- WhoBlA 92
**Johnson,** Lester Deane 1932- WhoFI 92
**Johnson,** Linda Arlene 1946- WhoMW 92
**Johnson,** Linda C. 1945- WhoBlA 92
**Johnson,** Linn Valen 1942- WhoWest 92
**Johnson,** Linton Kwesi 1952- ConPo 91, WrDr 92
**Johnson,** Lionel 1867-1902 RfGEnL 91
**Johnson,** Lionel Washington 1923- WhoAmP 91
**Johnson,** Lissa H 1955- SmATA 65 [port]
**Johnson,** Littleton Wales 1929- AmMWSc 92
**Johnson,** Livingston 1857-1931 DcNCBi 3
**Johnson,** Livingstone M. 1927- WhoBlA 92
**Johnson,** Lloyd A. 1932- WhoBlA 92
**Johnson,** Lloyd N 1921- AmMWSc 92
**Johnson,** Lloyd Peter 1930- WhoFI 92, WhoMW 92
**Johnson,** Loering M 1926- AmMWSc 92
**Johnson,** Lois Jean 1950- WhoWest 92
**Johnson,** Lonnie 1899?-1970 NewAmDM
**Johnson,** Lonnie C 1947- WhoAmP 91
**Johnson,** Lonnie L. 1932- WhoBlA 92
**Johnson,** Lorenzo N d1897 BiInAmS
**Johnson,** Loretta Turner 1940- WhoMW 92
**Johnson,** Lorna Karen 1958- WhoBlA 92
**Johnson,** Lorraine Jefferson 1918- WhoBlA 92
**Johnson,** Lorretta 1938- WhoBlA 92
**Johnson,** Louis 1933- WhoBlA 92
**Johnson,** Louis 1937- WhoAmP 91
**Johnson,** Louis Albert 1924- IntAu&W 91
**Johnson,** Louis W. 1903- WhoBlA 92
**Johnson,** Louise H 1927- AmMWSc 92
**Johnson,** Louise Mason 1917- WhoBlA 92
**Johnson,** Louise Napier 1940- Who 92
**Johnson,** Lovell, Sr. 1925- WhoRel 92
**Johnson,** Lowell Boyden 1935- AmMWSc 92
**Johnson,** Lowell C. 1920- WhoMW 92
**Johnson,** Lowell Curtis 1920- WhoAmP 91
**Johnson,** Loyd 1927- AmMWSc 92
**Johnson,** Lucien Love 1941- WhoBlA 92
**Johnson,** Lucy Black 1924- WhoAmP 91
**Johnson,** Luther Elman 1910- AmMWSc 92
**Johnson,** Luther Mason, Jr. 1930- WhoBlA 92
**Johnson,** Luvern Charles, III 1954- WhoAmL 92
**Johnson,** Lyman Keating 1951- WhoEnt 92
**Johnson,** Lyndon B 1908-1973 RComAH
**Johnson,** Lyndon Baines 1908-1973 AmPolLe [port], BenetAL 91, FacFETw [port]
**Johnson,** Lynn H. 1957- WhoFI 92
**Johnson,** Lynn-Holly 1958- WhoEnt 92
**Johnson,** Lynn Smith 1956- WhoAmL 92
**Johnson,** Lynn Thomas 1958- WhoAmL 92
**Johnson,** Lynwood Albert 1933- AmMWSc 92
**Johnson,** Mable Jean 1920- WhoAmP 91
**Johnson,** Mack Evans 1942- WhoAmP 91
**Johnson,** Magic 1959- WhoBlA 92, WhoWest 92
**Johnson,** Mal 1924- WhoBlA 92
**Johnson,** Malcolm Julius 1917- AmMWSc 92
**Johnson,** Malcolm Pratt 1941- AmMWSc 92
**Johnson,** Malcolm R 1930- WhoIns 92
**Johnson,** Manuel H., Jr. 1949- IntWW 91
**Johnson,** Manuel Holman, Jr. 1949- WhoFI 92
**Johnson,** Marc 1943- WhoWest 92
**Johnson,** Marc Anton 1948- WhoFI 92
**Johnson,** Marc B. 1947- WhoWest 92
**Johnson,** Marcia Beth 1942- WhoAmP 91
**Johnson,** Margaret Bourns 1938- WhoMW 92
**Johnson,** Margaret Douglas 1951- WhoMW 92
**Johnson,** Margaret Helen 1933- WhoFI 92, WhoMW 92
**Johnson,** Margaret L WhoAmP 91
**Johnson,** Marguerite M. 1948- WhoBlA 92
**Johnson,** Marie C. Bellamy 1911- WhoAmL 92
**Johnson,** Marie Elizabeth 1948- WhoBlA 92
**Johnson,** Marie-Louise T 1927- AmMWSc 92
**Johnson,** Marie Love 1925- WhoBlA 92
**Johnson,** Marijo Anne 1935- WhoEnt 92
**Johnson,** Marion I. 1915- WhoBlA 92
**Johnson,** Marion T. 1948- WhoBlA 92
**Johnson,** Mark WhoAmL 92
**Johnson,** Mark 1949- WhoAmP 91
**Johnson,** Mark Alan 1952- WhoWest 92
**Johnson,** Mark Andrew 1959- WhoAmL 92
**Johnson,** Mark Edward 1952- AmMWSc 92
**Johnson,** Mark Eugene 1951- WhoAmL 92
**Johnson,** Mark Harold 1956- WhoAmL 92
**Johnson,** Mark Henry 1953- WhoWest 92
**Johnson,** Mark Hunt 1964- WhoMW 92
**Johnson,** Mark Leonard 1954- WhoFI 92
**Johnson,** Mark Mathis 1945- WhoEnt 92
**Johnson,** Mark Scott 1951- AmMWSc 92
**Johnson,** Mark Stephen 1960- WhoRel 92
**Johnson,** Mark Wallace 1958- WhoFI 92
**Johnson,** Marlene 1946- WhoAmP 91, WhoMW 92
**Johnson,** Marlene E. 1936- WhoBlA 92
**Johnson,** Marlin Duane 1934- WhoEnt 92
**Johnson,** Marques Kevin 1956- WhoBlA 92
**Johnson,** Marshall Duane 1935- WhoRel 92
**Johnson,** Martha Celestia Koutz 1903- WhoMW 92
**Johnson,** Martha Ellen McArthur 1926- WhoAmP 91
**Johnson,** Martin 1884-1937 BenetAL 91, FacFETw
**Johnson,** Martin 1962- WhoRel 92
**Johnson,** Martin Clyde-Vandivort 1959- WhoFI 92
**Johnson,** Martin Leroy 1941- WhoBlA 92
**Johnson,** Martin Timothy 1950- WhoAmL 92
**Johnson,** Marvin Elroy 1945- AmMWSc 92
**Johnson,** Marvin Francis Linton 1920- AmMWSc 92
**Johnson,** Marvin L 1954- BlkOlyM
**Johnson,** Marvin M 1928- AmMWSc 92
**Johnson,** Marvin Melrose 1925- AmMWSc 92, WhoMW 92
**Johnson,** Mary Anne 1954- WhoAmP 91
**Johnson,** Mary Beatrice 1942- WhoRel 92
**Johnson,** Mary Beatrice 1952- WhoBlA 92
**Johnson,** Mary Blow 1925- WhoAmP 91
**Johnson,** Mary Elizabeth 1933- WhoEnt 92
**Johnson,** Mary Frances 1940- AmMWSc 92
**Johnson,** Mary Frances 1951- AmMWSc 92
**Johnson,** Mary Ida 1942- AmMWSc 92
**Johnson,** Mary Ignacia 1933- WhoHisp 92
**Johnson,** Mary Jane 1952- WhoAmP 91
**Johnson,** Mary Knettles 1929- AmMWSc 92
**Johnson,** Mary Lee Alexander 1944- WhoAmP 91
**Johnson,** Mary Lou 1923- WhoRel 92
**Johnson,** Mary Lynn Miller 1938- AmMWSc 92
**Johnson,** Mary Susan 1937- WhoFI 92, WhoMW 92
**Johnson,** Mary Teel 1921- WhoEnt 92
**Johnson,** Maryann WhoAmP 91
**Johnson,** Matthew Brian 1957- WhoEnt 92
**Johnson,** Mattiedna 1918- WhoBlA 92
**Johnson,** Maxine Frahm 1939- WhoFI 92
**Johnson,** Maynard DrAPF 91
**Johnson,** Maynard Reuben 1939- WhoMW 92
**Johnson,** Mel WrDr 92
**Johnson,** Melinda 1936- WhoWest 92
**Johnson,** Melvin Andrew 1929- AmMWSc 92
**Johnson,** Melvin Clark 1938- AmMWSc 92
**Johnson,** Melvin Russell 1946- WhoBlA 92
**Johnson,** Melvin Walter, Jr 1928- AmMWSc 92
**Johnson,** Mertha Ruth WhoBlA 92
**Johnson,** Mervil V. 1953- WhoBlA 92
**Johnson,** Merwyn Who 92
**Johnson,** Merwyn Stratford 1938- WhoRel 92
**Johnson,** Micah William 1963- WhoEnt 92
**Johnson,** Michael 1937- TwCPaSc
**Johnson,** Michael Almer 1944- WhoAmL 92
**Johnson,** Michael Anthony 1951- WhoBlA 92
**Johnson,** Michael Charles 1947- WhoAmL 92
**Johnson,** Michael David 1945- AmMWSc 92
**Johnson,** Michael Evart 1945- AmMWSc 92
**Johnson,** Michael Howard 1930- Who 92
**Johnson,** Michael Jay 1961- WhoRel 92
**Johnson,** Michael Jerome 1955- WhoEnt 92
**Johnson,** Michael Kevin 1960- WhoBlA 92
**Johnson,** Michael L. DrAPF 91
**Johnson,** Michael L 1947- AmMWSc 92
**Johnson,** Michael Nicholas 1959- WhoFI 92
**Johnson,** Michael Paul 1937- AmMWSc 92
**Johnson,** Michael Ross 1944- AmMWSc 92
**Johnson,** Michael Scott Herbert 1962- WhoFI 92
**Johnson,** Michael William 1953- WhoWest 92
**Johnson,** Michael York- Who 92
**Johnson,** Michele 1959- WhoBlA 92
**Johnson,** Michele Nicole 1966- WhoBlA 92
**Johnson,** Mike IntAu&W 91X, WrDr 92
**Johnson,** Mikkel Borlaug 1943- AmMWSc 92
**Johnson,** Mildred WhoEnt 92
**Johnson,** Miles F 1936- AmMWSc 92
**Johnson,** Millard Wallace, Jr 1928- AmMWSc 92
**Johnson,** Miller Alanson, II 1933- WhoFI 92
**Johnson,** Milton D. 1928- WhoBlA 92
**Johnson,** Milton Lee 1931- WhoFI 92
**Johnson,** Milton R, Jr 1919- AmMWSc 92
**Johnson,** Minnie Redmond 1910- WhoBlA 92
**Johnson,** Miriam B. WhoBlA 92
**Johnson,** Miriam Massey 1928- WhoWest 92
**Johnson,** Monica Who 92
**Johnson,** Montgomery Hunt 1907- AmMWSc 92
**Johnson,** Morris Alfred 1937- AmMWSc 92
**Johnson,** Murray Leathers 1914- AmMWSc 92
**Johnson,** Myrle F 1918- AmMWSc 92
**Johnson,** Nancy L. 1935- AlmAP 92 [port], WhoAmP 91
**Johnson,** Nancy M 1947- WhoIns 92
**Johnson,** Nancy Raynor 1930- WhoAmP 91
**Johnson,** Nathan 1944- WhoBlA 92
**Johnson,** Nathaniel J., Sr. 1940- WhoBlA 92
**Johnson,** Neal Sox 1933- WhoAmP 91
**Johnson,** Ned Keith 1932- AmMWSc 92
**Johnson,** Neil Francis 1948- AmMWSc 92
**Johnson,** Nellie Stone WhoAmP 91
**Johnson,** Nevil 1929- Who 92
**Johnson,** Newell Walter 1938- Who 92
**Johnson,** Nicholas LesBEnT 92
**Johnson,** Nicholas 1934- WrDr 92
**Johnson,** Nick DrAPF 91
**Johnson,** Nickolas O 1935- WhoAmP 91
**Johnson,** Niel Melvin 1931- WhoMW 92
**Johnson,** Nina Sidler 1927- WhoAmP 91
**Johnson,** Noah R 1928- AmMWSc 92
**Johnson,** Nora DrAPF 91
**Johnson,** Norbert Edwin 1925- WhoMW 92, WhoRel 92
**Johnson,** Norma Holloway NotBlAW 92, WhoAmL 92, WhoBlA 92
**Johnson,** Norman 1928- WhoEnt 92
**Johnson,** Norman 1938- WhoFI 92
**Johnson,** Norman B. WhoBlA 92
**Johnson,** Norman Elden 1933- AmMWSc 92
**Johnson,** Norman Huff 1880-1943 DcNCBi 3
**Johnson,** Norman J. 1919- WhoBlA 92
**Johnson,** Norman L 1939- AmMWSc 92
**Johnson,** Norman Lloyd 1917- AmMWSc 92
**Johnson,** Norris Brock 1942- WhoBlA 92
**Johnson,** Nunnally 1897-1977 BenetAL 91
**Johnson,** Odell 1936- WhoAmP 91
**Johnson,** Ogden Carl 1929- AmMWSc 92
**Johnson,** Olendruff Lerey 1956- WhoBlA 92
**Johnson,** Oliver 1919- AmMWSc 92
**Johnson,** Oliver Thomas, Jr. 1946- WhoAmL 92
**Johnson,** Oliver William 1930- AmMWSc 92
**Johnson,** Omotunde Evan George 1941- WhoFI 92
**Johnson,** Onette E. WhoBlA 92
**Johnson,** Ora J. 1932- WhoRel 92
**Johnson,** Orland Eugene 1923- AmMWSc 92
**Johnson,** Orson Bennett 1848?-1917 BiInAmS
**Johnson,** Osa 1894-1953 BenetAL 91
**Johnson,** Oscar Hugo 1914- AmMWSc 92
**Johnson,** Oscar Walter 1935- AmMWSc 92
**Johnson,** Otis Coe 1839-1912 BiInAmS
**Johnson,** Otis Samuel 1942- WhoAmP 91, WhoBlA 92
**Johnson,** Owen 1878-1952 BenetAL 91
**Johnson,** Owen H 1929- WhoAmP 91
**Johnson,** Owen Verne 1946- IntAu&W 91
**Johnson,** Owen W 1931- AmMWSc 92
**Johnson,** Pam McAllister 1945- WhoBlA 92
**Johnson,** Pamela Hansford 1912-1981 FacFETw, RfGEnL 91
**Johnson,** Parker Collins 1961- WhoBlA 92
**Johnson,** Patrice Doreen 1952- WhoBlA 92
**Johnson,** Patricia Anita 1944- WhoBlA 92
**Johnson,** Patricia Ann J 1943- AmMWSc 92
**Johnson,** Patricia Dumas 1950- WhoBlA 92
**Johnson,** Patricia Duren 1943- WhoBlA 92
**Johnson,** Patricia Gayle 1947- WhoWest 92
**Johnson,** Patricia L. 1956- WhoBlA 92
**Johnson,** Patricia Lyn 1957- WhoMW 92
**Johnson,** Patricia R 1931- AmMWSc 92
**Johnson,** Patrick 1904- Who 92
**Johnson,** Paul WhoWest 92
**Johnson,** Paul 1928- ConAu 34NR, IntAu&W 91, IntWW 91, Who 92, WrDr 92
**Johnson,** Paul 1959- WhoAmP 91
**Johnson,** Paul Christian 1928- AmMWSc 92

**Johnson,** Paul E. 1898-1974 *ConAu 134*
**Johnson,** Paul Edwin 1933- *WhoBlA 92*
**Johnson,** Paul Edwin 1934- *WhoAmP 91*
**Johnson,** Paul Eugene 1959- *WhoEnt 92*
**Johnson,** Paul H 1916- *AmMWSc 92*
**Johnson,** Paul Hickok 1943- *AmMWSc 92*
**Johnson,** Paul L 1900- *AmMWSc 92*
**Johnson,** Paul L. 1943- *WhoBlA 92*
**Johnson,** Paul Lawrence 1931- *WhoBlA 92*
**Johnson,** Paul Lorentz 1941- *AmMWSc 92*
**Johnson,** Paul Oren 1937- *WhoFI 92*
**Johnson,** Paul Owen 1919- *WhoAmL 92*
**Johnson,** Paul Ronald 1955- *WhoWest 92*
**Johnson,** Paul W 1941- *WhoAmP 91*
**Johnson,** Pauline 1861-1913 *BenetAL 91, TwCWW 91*
**Johnson,** Pearl M. 1942- *WhoRel 92*
**Johnson,** Pete *WhoAmP 91*
**Johnson,** Peter 1930- *Who 92, WrDr 92*
**Johnson,** Peter Dexter 1921- *AmMWSc 92*
**Johnson,** Peter Graham 1945- *AmMWSc 92*
**Johnson,** Peter Neils 1944- *WhoEnt 92*
**Johnson,** Philander Chase 1866-1939 *BenetAL 91*
**Johnson,** Philip 1906- *CurBio 91 [port], FacFETw, RComAH*
**Johnson,** Philip A. d1991 *NewYTBS 91*
**Johnson,** Philip A. 1915-1991 *ConAu 133*
**Johnson,** Philip Ashley 1949- *WhoAmP 91*
**Johnson,** Philip C 1906- *DcTwDes*
**Johnson,** Philip Charles 1943- *WhoFI 92*
**Johnson,** Philip Cortelyou 1906- *IntWW 91, Who 92*
**Johnson,** Philip Douglas 1954- *WhoWest 92*
**Johnson,** Philip L 1931- *AmMWSc 92*
**Johnson,** Philip M 1940- *AmMWSc 92*
**Johnson,** Philip Martin 1940- *WhoFI 92*
**Johnson,** Philip McBride 1938- *WhoAmL 92*
**Johnson,** Philip Otho 1955- *WhoFI 92*
**Johnson,** Philip Wayne 1944- *WhoAmL 92*
**Johnson,** Phillip E. 1940- *WhoAmL 92*
**Johnson,** Phillip Eugene 1937- *AmMWSc 92*
**Johnson,** Phyllis Campbell 1954- *WhoBlA 92*
**Johnson,** Phyllis Elaine 1949- *AmMWSc 92*
**Johnson,** Phyllis Marie 1918- *WhoRel 92, WhoWest 92*
**Johnson,** Phyllis Mercedes 1919- *WhoBlA 92*
**Johnson,** Phyllis Truth 1926- *AmMWSc 92*
**Johnson,** Pierre Marc 1946- *IntWW 91*
**Johnson,** Pompie Louis, Jr 1926- *WhoAmP 91, WhoBlA 92*
**Johnson,** Porter W 1942- *AmMWSc 92*
**Johnson,** Preston Benton 1932- *AmMWSc 92*
**Johnson,** Quincy Lindell 1954- *WhoMW 92*
**Johnson,** Quintin C 1935- *AmMWSc 92*
**Johnson,** Qulan Adrian 1942- *WhoFI 92, WhoWest 92*
**Johnson,** R A 1932- *AmMWSc 92*
**Johnson,** R. Benjamin 1944- *WhoBlA 92*
**Johnson,** R Earl *BlkOlyM*
**Johnson,** R. V. 1927- *WrDr 92*
**Johnson,** Rachel Ramirez 1937- *WhoHisp 92*
**Johnson,** Rafer Lewis 1934- *BlkOlyM [port]*
**Johnson,** Rafer Lewis 1935- *WhoBlA 92*
**Johnson,** Raleigh Francis, Jr 1941- *AmMWSc 92*
**Johnson,** Raleigh West 1934- *WhoAmP 91*
**Johnson,** Ralph Alton 1919- *AmMWSc 92*
**Johnson,** Ralph C. 1941- *WhoBlA 92*
**Johnson,** Ralph Edson 1919- *WhoAmP 91*
**Johnson,** Ralph Glassgow 1913- *WhoRel 92*
**Johnson,** Ralph H 1923- *WhoAmP 91*
**Johnson,** Ralph Howard 1949- *WhoAmL 92*
**Johnson,** Ralph Hudson 1933- *Who 92*
**Johnson,** Ralph M, Jr 1918- *AmMWSc 92*
**Johnson,** Ralph Sterling, Jr 1926- *AmMWSc 92*
**Johnson,** Ralph T, Jr 1935- *AmMWSc 92*
**Johnson,** Ralph V. *WhoBlA 92*
**Johnson,** Randall Morris 1936- *WhoBlA 92, WhoMW 92*
**Johnson,** Randolph Mellus 1950- *AmMWSc 92*
**Johnson,** Randy Allan 1947- *AmMWSc 92*
**Johnson,** Ray 1935- *WhoBlA 92*
**Johnson,** Ray Edwin 1936- *AmMWSc 92*
**Johnson,** Ray Leland 1939- *AmMWSc 92*
**Johnson,** Ray O 1955- *AmMWSc 92*
**Johnson,** Raymond Allen Constan 1923- *WhoAmP 91*
**Johnson,** Raymond C. 1923- *WhoAmL 92*
**Johnson,** Raymond C, Jr 1922- *AmMWSc 92*
**Johnson,** Raymond Earl 1914- *AmMWSc 92*
**Johnson,** Raymond Erick, II 1952- *WhoAmL 92*
**Johnson,** Raymond L. 1936- *WhoBlA 92*
**Johnson,** Raymond L., Sr. 1922- *WhoBlA 92*
**Johnson,** Raymond Lewis 1943- *AmMWSc 92, WhoBlA 92*
**Johnson,** Raymond Nils 1941- *AmMWSc 92*
**Johnson,** Raymond Roy 1932- *AmMWSc 92, WhoWest 92*
**Johnson,** Raymond W. 1934- *WhoWest 92*
**Johnson,** Rebecca L. 1956- *SmATA 67*
**Johnson,** Rebecca M. 1905- *WhoBlA 92*
**Johnson,** Reginald Stuart 1933- *Who 92*
**Johnson,** Revery Dean 1961- *WhoWest 92*
**Johnson,** Rex 1921- *Who 92*
**Johnson,** Reynold B 1906- *AmMWSc 92*
**Johnson,** Rheuben C 1937- *WhoIns 92*
**Johnson,** Rhoda E. 1946- *WhoBlA 92*
**Johnson,** Richard *WhoAmP 91*
**Johnson,** Richard 1927- *IntMPA 92*
**Johnson,** Richard 1963- *WhoBlA 92*
**Johnson,** Richard A. 1955- *ConAu 135*
**Johnson,** Richard A. 1961- *WhoAmL 92*
**Johnson,** Richard Allen 1945- *AmMWSc 92*
**Johnson,** Richard Arlo 1952- *WhoAmL 92*
**Johnson,** Richard Arthur 1950- *WhoEnt 92*
**Johnson,** Richard Clayton 1930- *AmMWSc 92*
**Johnson,** Richard Craig 1937- *WhoAmL 92*
**Johnson,** Richard D 1934- *AmMWSc 92*
**Johnson,** Richard D 1935- *WhoAmP 91*
**Johnson,** Richard Dean 1936- *AmMWSc 92*
**Johnson,** Richard Duane 1935- *WhoMW 92*
**Johnson,** Richard E. 1945- *WhoRel 92*
**Johnson,** Richard Evan 1936- *AmMWSc 92*
**Johnson,** Richard Fred 1944- *WhoAmL 92*
**Johnson,** Richard G. 1941- *WhoMW 92*
**Johnson,** Richard H 1930- *WhoAmP 91*
**Johnson,** Richard Harlan 1945- *AmMWSc 92*
**Johnson,** Richard Howard 1931- *WhoBlA 92*
**Johnson,** Richard Karl 1947- *WhoWest 92*
**Johnson,** Richard Keith 1927- *IntWW 91, Who 92*
**Johnson,** Richard Lawrence 1939- *AmMWSc 92*
**Johnson,** Richard Leon 1938- *AmMWSc 92*
**Johnson,** Richard Lloyd 1918- *WhoWest 92*
**Johnson,** Richard Mentor 1781-1850 *AmPolLe*
**Johnson,** Richard Noring 1934- *AmMWSc 92*
**Johnson,** Richard Ray 1947- *AmMWSc 92*
**Johnson,** Richard T 1931- *AmMWSc 92*
**Johnson,** Richard T 1939- *AmMWSc 92*
**Johnson,** Richard T. 1955- *WhoFI 92*
**Johnson,** Richard Tenney 1930- *WhoAmL 92, WhoAmP 91, WhoFI 92*
**Johnson,** Richard Turner 1933- *WhoEnt 92*
**Johnson,** Richard W. 1937- *WhoMW 92*
**Johnson,** Richard Walter 1928- *WhoMW 92*
**Johnson,** Richard Wayne 1933- *WhoRel 92*
**Johnson,** Richard William 1950- *AmMWSc 92*
**Johnson,** Richie 1932- *WhoEnt 92*
**Johnson,** Ricky Leon 1952- *WhoRel 92*
**Johnson,** Rita *DrAPF 91*
**Johnson,** Rita Falkener *WhoBlA 92*
**Johnson,** Rita Nielsen *WhoAmP 91*
**Johnson,** Riva Taft 1955- *WhoAmL 92*
**Johnson,** Rob 1955- *WhoAmP 91*
**Johnson,** Robert *LesBEnT 92*
**Johnson,** Robert 1500?-1560? *NewAmDM*
**Johnson,** Robert 1583?-1633? *NewAmDM*
**Johnson,** Robert 1911-1938 *ConBlB 2 [port], ConMus 6 [port]*
**Johnson,** Robert 1912-1938 *FacFETw, NewAmDM*
**Johnson,** Robert 1937- *WhoBlA 92*
**Johnson,** Robert A 1919- *WhoAmP 91*
**Johnson,** Robert A 1932- *AmMWSc 92*
**Johnson,** Robert A. 1948- *WhoWest 92*
**Johnson,** Robert Alan 1923- *WhoWest 92*
**Johnson,** Robert Alan 1933- *AmMWSc 92*
**Johnson,** Robert Alan 1944- *WhoAmL 92*
**Johnson,** Robert Aylwin 1928- *WhoAmP 91*
**Johnson,** Robert B. 1928- *WhoBlA 92*
**Johnson,** Robert Brian 1932- *Who 92*
**Johnson,** Robert Britten 1924- *AmMWSc 92, WhoWest 92*
**Johnson,** Robert Bruce 1912- *WhoMW 92*
**Johnson,** Robert C. 1945- *WhoBlA 92*
**Johnson,** Robert Chandler 1930- *AmMWSc 92*
**Johnson,** Robert Clyde 1919- *WhoRel 92, WrDr 92*
**Johnson,** Robert Dale 1943- *WhoAmP 91, WhoMW 92*
**Johnson,** Robert Dale 1965- *WhoMW 92*
**Johnson,** Robert David 1957- *WhoFI 92*
**Johnson,** Robert Dewey 1952- *WhoMW 92*
**Johnson,** Robert E. 1923- *WrDr 92*
**Johnson,** Robert Ed 1942- *AmMWSc 92*
**Johnson,** Robert Edward 1922- *WhoBlA 92*
**Johnson,** Robert Edward 1939- *AmMWSc 92*
**Johnson,** Robert Edward 1950- *WhoRel 92*
**Johnson,** Robert Eugene 1911- *AmMWSc 92*
**Johnson,** Robert F 1929- *AmMWSc 92*
**Johnson,** Robert Francis 1957- *WhoFI 92*
**Johnson,** Robert Glenn 1922- *AmMWSc 92*
**Johnson,** Robert Grady 1895-1951 *DcNCBi 3*
**Johnson,** Robert Gudwin 1927- *AmMWSc 92*
**Johnson,** Robert H 1936- *AmMWSc 92*
**Johnson,** Robert H. 1938- *WhoBlA 92*
**Johnson,** Robert Henry 1916- *WhoAmP 91*
**Johnson,** Robert Hoyt 1939- *WhoRel 92*
**Johnson,** Robert Joseph 1915- *AmMWSc 92*
**Johnson,** Robert Karl 1944- *AmMWSc 92*
**Johnson,** Robert Kent 1953- *WhoMW 92*
**Johnson,** Robert L. *WhoBlA 92, WhoRel 92*
**Johnson,** Robert L 1919- *AmMWSc 92*
**Johnson,** Robert L 1920- *AmMWSc 92*
**Johnson,** Robert L. 1946- *WhoBlA 92*
**Johnson,** Robert Lee 1926- *AmMWSc 92*
**Johnson,** Robert Leonard 1930- *WhoAmP 91*
**Johnson,** Robert Leroy 1940- *AmMWSc 92*
**Johnson,** Robert Leslie 1923- *WhoWest 92*
**Johnson,** Robert Lewis, Jr. 1935- *WhoFI 92*
**Johnson,** Robert Lionel 1933- *Who 92*
**Johnson,** Robert Louis 1946- *WhoEnt 92, WhoFI 92*
**Johnson,** Robert M 1934- *WhoAmP 91*
**Johnson,** Robert M 1939- *AmMWSc 92*
**Johnson,** Robert Maurice 1945- *WhoFI 92*
**Johnson,** Robert Max 1942- *WhoAmL 92*
**Johnson,** Robert Melvin 1956- *WhoFI 92*
**Johnson,** Robert Michael *AmMWSc 92*
**Johnson,** Robert Milton 1962- *WhoMW 92*
**Johnson,** Robert Oscar 1926- *AmMWSc 92*
**Johnson,** Robert P 1945- *WhoIns 92*
**Johnson,** Robert R 1928- *AmMWSc 92*
**Johnson,** Robert Reiner 1932- *AmMWSc 92*
**Johnson,** Robert Ronald 1949- *WhoFI 92*
**Johnson,** Robert Ross 1920- *WhoRel 92*
**Johnson,** Robert S 1937- *AmMWSc 92*
**Johnson,** Robert Shepard 1928- *AmMWSc 92*
**Johnson,** Robert T. *WhoAmL 92, WhoBlA 92*
**Johnson,** Robert Thane 1945- *WhoAmP 91*
**Johnson,** Robert Underwood 1853-1937 *BenetAL 91*
**Johnson,** Robert Veiling, II 1939- *WhoAmL 92*
**Johnson,** Robert W. 1921- *WrDr 92*
**Johnson,** Robert W 1931- *WhoAmP 91*
**Johnson,** Robert W, Jr 1924- *AmMWSc 92*
**Johnson,** Robert Walter 1930- *AmMWSc 92*
**Johnson,** Robert Ward 1929- *AmMWSc 92*
**Johnson,** Robert Wells 1938- *AmMWSc 92*
**Johnson,** Robert White 1912- *Who 92*
**Johnson,** Robert William 1955- *WhoEnt 92*
**Johnson,** Robert William, Jr 1927- *AmMWSc 92*
**Johnson,** Robin *DrAPF 91*
**Johnson,** Robin C *WhoAmP 91*
**Johnson,** Robin Eliot 1929- *Who 92*
**Johnson,** Robin Stewart 1944- *WhoWest 92*
**Johnson,** Rod 1953- *WhoAmP 91*
**Johnson,** Rod 1957- *WhoAmP 91*
**Johnson,** Rodney Dale 1944- *WhoWest 92*
**Johnson,** Rodney Gardner 1942- *WhoAmL 92*
**Johnson,** Rodney L *AmMWSc 92*
**Johnson,** Rodney Wayne 1953- *WhoEnt 92*
**Johnson,** Roger Christie 1925- *WhoAmP 91*
**Johnson,** Roger D, Jr 1930- *AmMWSc 92*
**Johnson,** Roger Dean 1935- *WhoIns 92*
**Johnson,** Roger Lee 1937- *WhoMW 92*
**Johnson,** Roger Lee 1941- *WhoRel 92*
**Johnson,** Roger Paul 1931- *Who 92*
**Johnson,** Roger Truman 1927- *WhoMW 92*
**Johnson,** Roger W 1929- *AmMWSc 92*
**Johnson,** Roger W. 1935- *WhoWest 92*
**Johnson,** Roland A. *WhoEnt 92*
**Johnson,** Rolland Paul 1941- *AmMWSc 92*
**Johnson,** Ron 1958- *WhoBlA 92*
**Johnson,** Ronald *DrAPF 91*
**Johnson,** Ronald 1913- *Who 92*
**Johnson,** Ronald 1935- *ConPo 91, WrDr 92*
**Johnson,** Ronald 1936- *WhoBlA 92*
**Johnson,** Ronald C 1941- *WhoIns 92*
**Johnson,** Ronald Carl 1935- *AmMWSc 92*
**Johnson,** Ronald Clyde 1949- *WhoAmP 91*
**Johnson,** Ronald Cornelius 1946- *WhoBlA 92*
**Johnson,** Ronald Douglas 1949- *WhoWest 92*
**Johnson,** Ronald Ernest 1939- *AmMWSc 92*
**Johnson,** Ronald G *WhoAmP 91*
**Johnson,** Ronald Gene 1941- *AmMWSc 92*
**Johnson,** Ronald Glenn 1949- *WhoEnt 92*
**Johnson,** Ronald N 1933- *WhoAmP 91*
**Johnson,** Ronald Roy 1928- *AmMWSc 92*
**Johnson,** Ronald Sanders 1952- *AmMWSc 92*
**Johnson,** Ronald Webster 1948- *WhoWest 92*
**Johnson,** Ronnie 1948- *WhoFI 92*
**Johnson,** Roosevelt, Jr. 1924- *WhoBlA 92*
**Johnson,** Roosevelt Young 1946- *WhoBlA 92*
**Johnson,** Rose Mary 1927- *AmMWSc 92*
**Johnson,** Ross 1939- *WhoAmP 91*
**Johnson,** Ross Byron 1919- *AmMWSc 92*
**Johnson,** Ross Glenn 1942- *AmMWSc 92*
**Johnson,** Rother Rodenious 1918- *AmMWSc 92*
**Johnson,** Roy Allen 1937- *AmMWSc 92*
**Johnson,** Roy Andrew 1939- *AmMWSc 92*
**Johnson,** Roy Edward 1959- *WhoBlA 92*
**Johnson,** Roy Lee 1955- *WhoBlA 92*
**Johnson,** Roy Lynn 1954- *WhoBlA 92*
**Johnson,** Roy Ragnar 1932- *AmMWSc 92, WhoMW 92*
**Johnson,** Roy Steven 1956- *WhoBlA 92*
**Johnson,** Roy W, Jr *WhoAmP 91*
**Johnson,** Royal C 1925- *WhoAmP 91*
**Johnson,** Royal M. 1944- *WhoWest 92*
**Johnson,** Rudolph *WhoAmP 91*
**Johnson,** Rulon Edward, Jr 1929- *AmMWSc 92*
**Johnson,** Russell 1924- *IntMPA 92*
**Johnson,** Russell Allan 1947- *WhoWest 92*
**Johnson,** Russell Clarence 1930- *AmMWSc 92*
**Johnson,** Russell Dee, Jr 1928- *AmMWSc 92*
**Johnson,** Ruth Ann 1947- *WhoFI 92*
**Johnson,** Ruth Anna 1950- *WhoWest 92*
**Johnson,** Ruth M. 1919-1989 *WhoBlA 92N*
**Johnson,** Ruthie 1924- *WhoAmP 91*
**Johnson,** Sam *WhoBlA 92*
**Johnson,** Sam 1930- *AlmAP 92 [port]*
**Johnson,** Sam D. 1920- *WhoAmL 92, WhoAmP 91*
**Johnson,** Sam R 1930- *WhoAmP 91*
**Johnson,** Samuel 1696-1772 *BenetAL 91*
**Johnson,** Samuel 1709-1784 *BlkwCEP, CnDBLB 2 [port], RfGEnL 91*
**Johnson,** Samuel Britton 1926- *AmMWSc 92*
**Johnson,** Samuel Curtis 1928- *WhoFI 92, WhoMW 92*
**Johnson,** Samuel Edgar, II 1944- *AmMWSc 92*
**Johnson,** Samuel Harrison 1916- *WhoBlA 92*
**Johnson,** Samuel Q, III 1939- *WhoAmP 91*
**Johnson,** Samuel William 1830-1909 *BiInAmS*
**Johnson,** Sandra Hanneken 1952- *WhoAmL 92*
**Johnson,** Sandra Lee 1952- *AmMWSc 92*
**Johnson,** Sandra Olivia 1953- *WhoEnt 92*
**Johnson,** Sandra Virginia *WhoBlA 92*
**Johnson,** Sarah H. 1938- *WhoBlA 92*
**Johnson,** Sarah Yvonne 1950- *WhoBlA 92*
**Johnson,** Scott Edwin 1894- *WhoBlA 92*
**Johnson,** Scott Lee 1949- *WhoEnt 92*
**Johnson,** Scott Leon 1952- *WhoFI 92*
**Johnson,** Scott Nels 1954- *WhoMW 92*
**Johnson,** Scott William 1940- *WhoAmL 92*
**Johnson,** Sean Andre 1968- *WhoWest 92*
**Johnson,** Sergio Davide 1962- *WhoEnt 92*
**Johnson,** Sharisse Lyn 1962- *WhoWest 92*
**Johnson,** Sharon Kay Haneroff *WhoMW 92*

**Johnson,** Sharon Marie Blom 1937- *WhoFI 92*
**Johnson,** Sharon Reed 1944- *WhoBlA 92*
**Johnson,** Sheila Monroe 1957- *WhoBlA 92*
**Johnson,** Shelli Wright 1953- *WhoAmL 92*
**Johnson,** Sherrel Edmund 1945- *WhoEnt 92, WhoFI 92, WhoWest 92*
**Johnson,** Sherrod C. 1899-1961 *RelLAm 91*
**Johnson,** Shirley 1937- *WhoAmP 91*
**Johnson,** Shirley Ann 1944- *WhoFI 92*
**Johnson,** Shirley Elaine 1941- *WhoBlA 92*
**Johnson,** Shirley Elaine 1946- *WhoFI 92, WhoMW 92*
**Johnson,** Shirley Mae 1940- *AmMWSc 92*
**Johnson,** Sidney *WhoAmP 91*
**Johnson,** Solomon Tilewa *WhoRel 92*
**Johnson,** Sondra Lea 1952- *WhoMW 92*
**Johnson,** Stafford Quincy 1948- *WhoBlA 92*
**Johnson,** Stanley 1912- *Who 92*
**Johnson,** Stanley C *WhoAmP 91*
**Johnson,** Stanley E 1934- *WhoAmP 91*
**Johnson,** Stanley F 1927- *WhoAmP 91*
**Johnson,** Stanley Harris 1938- *AmMWSc 92*
**Johnson,** Stanley O 1930- *AmMWSc 92*
**Johnson,** Stanley Patrick 1940- *Who 92*
**Johnson,** Stanley R. 1938- *WhoFI 92*
**Johnson,** Stephanye 1959- *WhoBlA 92*
**Johnson,** Stephen 1947- *IntAu&W 91, WrDr 92*
**Johnson,** Stephen Allen 1948- *AmMWSc 92*
**Johnson,** Stephen Bruce 1956- *WhoFI 92*
**Johnson,** Stephen Charles 1950- *WhoWest 92*
**Johnson,** Stephen Curtis 1944- *AmMWSc 92*
**Johnson,** Stephen L. 1944- *WhoBlA 92*
**Johnson,** Stephen Michael 1962- *WhoWest 92*
**Johnson,** Stephen Monroe 1949- *WhoRel 92*
**Johnson,** Stephen Randall 1957- *WhoRel 92*
**Johnson,** Stephen Thomas 1954- *AmMWSc 92*
**Johnson,** Stephen Wendell 1947- *WhoRel 92*
**Johnson,** Sterling 1934- *WhoBlA 92*
**Johnson,** Steve 1957- *WhoBlA 92*
**Johnson,** Steve Kenneth 1942- *WhoAmP 91*
**Johnson,** Steven B. 1962- *WhoMW 92*
**Johnson,** Steven Douglas 1950- *WhoFI 92*
**Johnson,** Steven Kenneth 1960- *WhoEnt 92*
**Johnson,** Steven R *WhoAmP 91*
**Johnson,** Stewart Willard 1933- *WhoWest 92*
**Johnson,** Stowers *IntAu&W 91, WrDr 92*
**Johnson,** Stuart *Who 92*
**Johnson,** Sture Archie Mansfield 1907- *AmMWSc 92*
**Johnson,** Suellen O 1942- *WhoAmP 91*
**Johnson,** Susan 1939- *WrDr 92*
**Johnson,** Susan Bissette 1951- *AmMWSc 92*
**Johnson,** Sylvia Marian 1954- *AmMWSc 92*
**Johnson,** Sylvia Sue 1940- *WhoWest 92*
**Johnson,** Tammy Adele 1965- *WhoBlA 92*
**Johnson,** Tance 1925- *WhoEnt 92*
**Johnson,** Ted H. 1948- *WhoRel 92*
**Johnson,** Terrell Kent 1947- *AmMWSc 92*
**Johnson,** Terrence Lamond 1959- *WhoMW 92*
**Johnson,** Terri Lynn 1947- *WhoMW 92*
**Johnson,** Terry 1955- *IntAu&W 91, WrDr 92*
**Johnson,** Terry Charles 1936- *AmMWSc 92*
**Johnson,** Terry R 1932- *AmMWSc 92*
**Johnson,** Terry Robert 1932- *WhoMW 92*
**Johnson,** Terry Walter, Jr 1923- *AmMWSc 92*
**Johnson,** Tesla Francis 1934- *WhoFI 92*
**Johnson,** Theodore, Sr. 1920- *WhoBlA 92*
**Johnson,** Theodore A. *WhoBlA 92*
**Johnson,** Theodore Armand 1924- *WhoAmP 91*
**Johnson,** Theodore L. 1929- *WhoBlA 92*
**Johnson,** Theodore Marvin, Jr. 1947- *WhoFI 92, WhoWest 92*
**Johnson,** Theodore Mebane 1934- *WhoFI 92*
**Johnson,** Theodore Oliver, Jr. 1929- *WhoEnt 92*
**Johnson,** Theodore Reynold 1946- *AmMWSc 92, WhoMW 92*
**Johnson,** Theodore Thomas 1949- *WhoBlA 92*
**Johnson,** Therese Myers 1926- *WhoAmP 91*
**Johnson,** Thomas *BenetAL 91*
**Johnson,** Thomas 1936- *AmMWSc 92*
**Johnson,** Thomas 1964- *WhoBlA 92*
**Johnson,** Thomas Aldrige 1928- *WhoBlA 92*
**Johnson,** Thomas Allibone Budd 1955- *WhoFI 92*
**Johnson,** Thomas Charles 1944- *AmMWSc 92*
**Johnson,** Thomas E. *DrAPF 91*
**Johnson,** Thomas E. 1948- *WhoAmL 92*
**Johnson,** Thomas Eugene 1948- *AmMWSc 92*
**Johnson,** Thomas F 1917- *AmMWSc 92*
**Johnson,** Thomas Floyd 1943- *WhoRel 92*
**Johnson,** Thomas H. 1932- *WhoBlA 92*
**Johnson,** Thomas Hawkins 1943- *AmMWSc 92*
**Johnson,** Thomas Humrickhouse 1841-1914 *BiInAmS*
**Johnson,** Thomas Jerald 1953- *WhoAmL 92, WhoMW 92*
**Johnson,** Thomas Lee 1949- *WhoAmL 92*
**Johnson,** Thomas Lynn 1919- *AmMWSc 92*
**Johnson,** Thomas Nick 1923- *AmMWSc 92*
**Johnson,** Thomas Norman 1956- *WhoFI 92*
**Johnson,** Thomas O. 1893- *WhoBlA 92*
**Johnson,** Thomas R. 1946- *WhoAmL 92*
**Johnson,** Thomas Raymond 1944- *AmMWSc 92*
**Johnson,** Thomas S. 1940- *IntWW 91*
**Johnson,** Thomas Stephen 1940- *WhoFI 92*
**Johnson,** Thomas Stuart 1942- *WhoAmL 92, WhoMW 92*
**Johnson,** Thomas Webber, Jr. 1941- *WhoAmL 92*
**Johnson,** Thor Martin 1913-1975 *DcNCBi 3*
**Johnson,** Thruston Charles 1914- *WhoEnt 92*
**Johnson,** Thys B 1934- *AmMWSc 92*
**Johnson,** Tim 1946- *AlmAP 92 [port]*
**Johnson,** Timothy Allen 1948- *WhoRel 92*
**Johnson,** Timothy Daniel 1949- *WhoFI 92*
**Johnson,** Timothy John Albert *AmMWSc 92*
**Johnson,** Timothy Julius, Jr. 1935- *WhoBlA 92*
**Johnson,** Timothy Neil 1959- *WhoRel 92*
**Johnson,** Timothy P 1946- *WhoAmP 91*
**Johnson,** Timothy Peter 1946- *WhoMW 92*
**Johnson,** Timothy Vincent 1946- *WhoAmP 91*
**Johnson,** Timothy Walter 1941- *AmMWSc 92*
**Johnson,** Tobe 1929- *WhoBlA 92*
**Johnson,** Tom *DrAPF 91, LesBEnT 92*
**Johnson,** Tom 1939- *NewAmDM*
**Johnson,** Tom 1949- *WhoAmP 91*
**Johnson,** Tom Milroy 1935- *AmMWSc 92*
**Johnson,** Tommie Ulmer 1925- *WhoBlA 92*
**Johnson,** Torrence Vaino 1944- *AmMWSc 92*
**Johnson,** Troy Dwan 1962- *WhoBlA 92*
**Johnson,** Trudy Oulliber 1952- *WhoWest 92*
**Johnson,** U. Alexis 1908- *IntWW 91, WhoAmP 91*
**Johnson,** Ulysses Johann, Jr. 1929- *WhoBlA 92*
**Johnson,** Una E. *ConAu 134*
**Johnson,** Uwe 1934-1984 *LiExTwC*
**Johnson,** Vahe Duncan 1938- *WhoAmL 92*
**Johnson,** Valerie Sharon 1950- *WhoMW 92*
**Johnson,** Valrie E. *WhoBlA 92*
**Johnson,** Van 1916- *IntMPA 92*
**Johnson,** Vannette William 1930- *WhoAmP 91, WhoBlA 92*
**Johnson,** Vard 1939- *WhoAmP 91*
**Johnson,** Vard Hayes 1909- *AmMWSc 92*
**Johnson,** Vaughan Monroe 1962- *WhoBlA 92*
**Johnson,** Vaughn Arzah 1951- *WhoBlA 92*
**Johnson,** Velma Jean 1937- *WhoWest 92*
**Johnson,** Verdia Earline 1950- *WhoBlA 92*
**Johnson,** Vermelle Jamison 1933- *WhoBlA 92*
**Johnson,** Vern Ray 1937- *AmMWSc 92*
**Johnson,** Verner Carl 1943- *AmMWSc 92, WhoWest 92*
**Johnson,** Vernon A. *WhoAmL 92*
**Johnson,** Vernon Eugene 1930- *WhoWest 92*
**Johnson,** Victor Lawrence 1928- *WhoFI 92*
**Johnson,** Vincent Arnold 1928- *AmMWSc 92, WhoMW 92*
**Johnson,** Vincent L. 1931- *WhoBlA 92*
**Johnson,** Vinnie 1956- *WhoBlA 92*
**Johnson,** Violet Erosemond 1915- *WhoAmP 91*
**Johnson,** Virgil Allen 1921- *AmMWSc 92*
**Johnson,** Virgil Joel 1932- *WhoAmP 91*
**Johnson,** Virginia 1925- *WrDr 92*
**Johnson,** Virginia 1937- *WhoAmP 91*
**Johnson,** Virginia Alma Fairfax 1950- *WhoBlA 92, WhoEnt 92*
**Johnson,** Virginia E. 1925- *ConAu 34NR*
**Johnson,** Virginia O. 1917- *WhoBlA 92*
**Johnson,** Viteria Copeland 1941- *WhoBlA 92*
**Johnson,** W C 1927- *AmMWSc 92*
**Johnson,** W. Lloyd 1951- *WhoMW 92*
**Johnson,** W. Michael 1942- *WhoWest 92*
**Johnson,** W Reed 1931- *AmMWSc 92*
**Johnson,** W Thomas 1945- *AmMWSc 92*
**Johnson,** Waldo Emerson, Jr. 1955- *WhoBlA 92*
**Johnson,** Wallace Darnell 1956- *WhoBlA 92*
**Johnson,** Wallace Delmar 1939- *AmMWSc 92*
**Johnson,** Wallace E 1925- *AmMWSc 92*
**Johnson,** Wallace Harold 1939- *WhoAmL 92*
**Johnson,** Wallace W 1926- *AmMWSc 92*
**Johnson,** Walter 1887-1946 *FacFETw*
**Johnson,** Walter C 1913- *AmMWSc 92*
**Johnson,** Walter Curtis, Jr 1939- *AmMWSc 92, WhoWest 92*
**Johnson,** Walter Earl 1942- *WhoWest 92*
**Johnson,** Walter Felix 1961- *WhoEnt 92*
**Johnson,** Walter Frank, Jr. 1945- *WhoAmL 92*
**Johnson,** Walter Hamlet 1917- *Who 92*
**Johnson,** Walter Heinrick, Jr 1928- *AmMWSc 92*
**Johnson,** Walter J. 1957- *WhoBlA 92*
**Johnson,** Walter K 1923- *AmMWSc 92*
**Johnson,** Walter Lee 1918- *AmMWSc 92, WhoBlA 92*
**Johnson,** Walter Louis, Sr. 1949- *WhoBlA 92*
**Johnson,** Walter Richard 1929- *AmMWSc 92*
**Johnson,** Walter Rogers 1794-1852 *BiInAmS*
**Johnson,** Walter Roland 1927- *AmMWSc 92*
**Johnson,** Walter Stanley 1945- *WhoRel 92*
**Johnson,** Walter Thaniel, Jr. 1940- *WhoBlA 92*
**Johnson,** Walton Richard 1909- *WhoBlA 92*
**Johnson,** Warren 1922- *WhoAmP 91*
**Johnson,** Warren A 1937- *IntAu&W 91, WrDr 92*
**Johnson,** Warren Richard 1928- *WhoFI 92*
**Johnson,** Warren S. 1947- *WhoBlA 92*
**Johnson,** Warren Stofflet 1911- *WhoFI 92*
**Johnson,** Warren Thurston 1925- *AmMWSc 92*
**Johnson,** Warren Victor 1951- *AmMWSc 92, WhoMW 92*
**Johnson,** Warren W 1923- *AmMWSc 92*
**Johnson,** Wayne 1956- *ConAu 135*
**Johnson,** Wayne Alan 1961- *WhoBlA 92*
**Johnson,** Wayne Douglas *AmMWSc 92*
**Johnson,** Wayne Eaton 1930- *WhoEnt 92*
**Johnson,** Wayne Gustave 1930- *WhoRel 92*
**Johnson,** Wayne H. 1942- *WhoEnt 92*
**Johnson,** Wayne Jon 1939- *AmMWSc 92*
**Johnson,** Wayne Lee 1953- *WhoBlA 92*
**Johnson,** Wayne Orrin 1942- *AmMWSc 92*
**Johnson,** Wayne Richard 1951- *WhoFI 92*
**Johnson,** Wayne Wright, III 1953- *WhoBlA 92*
**Johnson,** Weldon Howard 1937- *WhoFI 92*
**Johnson,** Wendel J 1941- *AmMWSc 92*
**Johnson,** Wendell Gilbert 1922- *AmMWSc 92*
**Johnson,** Wendell L., Jr. 1922- *WhoBlA 92*
**Johnson,** Wendell Louis 1944- *WhoBlA 92*
**Johnson,** Wendell Norman, Sr. 1933- *WhoBlA 92*
**Johnson,** Wendell Stacy 1927- *IntAu&W 91*
**Johnson,** Wendy Robin 1956- *WhoBlA 92, WhoFI 92*
**Johnson,** Wenner Dudley 1930- *WhoMW 92*
**Johnson,** Wesley Earl 1931- *WhoRel 92*
**Johnson,** Weyman Thompson, Jr. 1951- *WhoAmL 92*
**Johnson,** Whitney Larsen 1927- *AmMWSc 92*
**Johnson,** Wilbur Eugene 1954- *WhoBlA 92*
**Johnson,** Wilbur Vance 1931- *AmMWSc 92*
**Johnson,** Wiley Carroll, Jr 1930- *AmMWSc 92*
**Johnson,** Wilhelmina Lashaun 1950- *WhoBlA 92*
**Johnson,** Willard Drake 1859-1917 *BiInAmS*
**Johnson,** Willard Raymond 1935- *WhoBlA 92*
**Johnson,** William 1715-1774 *BenetAL 91, BlkwEAR*
**Johnson,** William 1903- *Who 92*
**Johnson,** William 1922- *IntWW 91, Who 92*
**Johnson,** William 1941- *AmMWSc 92*
**Johnson,** William A. 1917- *WhoBlA 92*
**Johnson,** William A., II 1952- *WhoBlA 92*
**Johnson,** William A., Jr. 1942- *WhoBlA 92*
**Johnson,** William Alexander 1922- *AmMWSc 92*
**Johnson,** William Alexander 1934- *WhoRel 92*
**Johnson,** William Arthur 1950- *WhoMW 92*
**Johnson,** William Arthur 1952- *WhoBlA 92*
**Johnson,** William Arvill 1924- *WhoAmP 91*
**Johnson,** William Bowie 1954- *AmMWSc 92*
**Johnson,** William Buhmann 1944- *AmMWSc 92*
**Johnson,** William C. 1930- *WhoBlA 92*
**Johnson,** William C. 1940- *WhoRel 92*
**Johnson,** William Cone 1926- *AmMWSc 92*
**Johnson,** William Dale 1952- *WhoMW 92*
**Johnson,** William Douglas, Jr. 1958- *WhoFI 92*
**Johnson,** William E. 1936- *WhoBlA 92*
**Johnson,** William E, Jr 1930- *AmMWSc 92*
**Johnson,** William Everett 1921- *AmMWSc 92*
**Johnson,** William G. 1934- *WhoFI 92*
**Johnson,** William Hall 1960- *WhoAmL 92*
**Johnson,** William Harold Barrett 1916- *Who 92*
**Johnson,** William Harry 1941- *WhoWest 92*
**Johnson,** William Herbert 1928- *WhoMW 92*
**Johnson,** William Hilton 1935- *AmMWSc 92, WhoMW 92*
**Johnson,** William Howard 1922- *AmMWSc 92*
**Johnson,** William Hugh 1932- *AmMWSc 92*
**Johnson,** William Hugh, Jr. 1935- *WhoWest 92*
**Johnson,** William J *WhoAmP 91*
**Johnson,** William Jacob 1914- *AmMWSc 92*
**Johnson,** William Jennings 1955- *WhoFI 92*
**Johnson,** William Julius 1900-1989 *WhoBlA 92N*
**Johnson,** William K 1927- *AmMWSc 92*
**Johnson,** William Kelly 1943- *WhoFI 92*
**Johnson,** William L. 1932- *WhoBlA 92*
**Johnson,** William Larry 1923- *WhoMW 92*
**Johnson,** William Lawrence 1936- *AmMWSc 92*
**Johnson,** William Lee, Jr. 1927-1987 *WhoBlA 92N*
**Johnson,** William Lewis 1940- *AmMWSc 92*
**Johnson,** William Lewis 1948- *AmMWSc 92*
**Johnson,** William Paul, Jr. 1963- *WhoBlA 92*
**Johnson,** William Potter 1935- *WhoFI 92, WhoWest 92*
**Johnson,** William R. 1930- *WhoAmL 92, WhoAmP 91*
**Johnson,** William Randolph 1930- *WhoBlA 92*
**Johnson,** William Randolph, Jr 1930- *AmMWSc 92*
**Johnson,** William Ransom 1782-1849 *DcNCBi 3*
**Johnson,** William Ray 1930- *WhoFI 92*
**Johnson,** William Robert 1939- *AmMWSc 92*
**Johnson,** William Roy 1947- *WhoMW 92*
**Johnson,** William S 1939- *AmMWSc 92*
**Johnson,** William Smith 1941- *WhoBlA 92*
**Johnson,** William Summer 1913- *AmMWSc 92, IntWW 91*
**Johnson,** William T. M. 1921- *WhoBlA 92*
**Johnson,** William Theolious 1943- *WhoBlA 92, WhoEnt 92*
**Johnson,** William Thomas 1930-1989 *WhoBlA 92N*
**Johnson,** William Thomas 1960- *WhoBlA 92*
**Johnson,** William W 1934- *AmMWSc 92*
**Johnson,** William Wayne 1934- *AmMWSc 92*
**Johnson,** William Weber 1909- *IntAu&W 91, WrDr 92*
**Johnson,** Willie 1925- *WhoBlA 92*
**Johnson,** Willie 1954- *WhoMW 92*
**Johnson,** Willie Earman 1933- *WhoRel 92*
**Johnson,** Willie F. 1939- *WhoBlA 92*
**Johnson,** Willis Grant 1866-1908 *BiInAmS*
**Johnson,** Willis Hugh 1902- *AmMWSc 92*
**Johnson,** Willis Merwyn 1923- *Who 92*

**Johnson,** Wingate Memory 1885-1963 *DcNCBi 3*
**Johnson,** Woodrow Eldred 1917- *AmMWSc 92*
**Johnson,** Wylie Pierson 1919- *WhoFI 92*
**Johnson,** Wyneva 1948- *WhoBlA 92*
**Johnson,** Zodie Anderson 1920- *WhoBlA 92*
**Johnson-Bennett,** Margaret Jane 1939- *WhoWest 92*
**Johnson-Blount,** Theresa 1952- *WhoBlA 92*
**Johnson-Brown,** Hazel Winfred 1927- *WhoBlA 92*
**Johnson-Carson,** Linda D. 1954- *WhoBlA 92*
**Johnson-Crockett,** Mary Alice 1937- *WhoBlA 92*
**Johnson-Crosby,** Deborah A. 1951- *WhoBlA 92*
**Johnson-Dismukes,** Karen 1947- *WhoBlA 92*
**Johnson-Ferguson,** Neil 1905- *Who 92*
**Johnson-Gilbert,** Ronald Stuart 1925- *Who 92*
**Johnson-Gilbert,** Thomas Ian 1923- *Who 92*
**Johnson-Glebe,** David Curtis 1952- *WhoAmL 92*
**Johnson-Hamilton,** Joyce *WhoEnt 92*
**Johnson-Laird,** Philip Nicholas 1936- *IntWW 91, Who 92*
**Johnson-Lesson,** Charleen Ann 1949- *WhoMW 92*
**Johnson-Lussenburg,** Christine Margaret 1931- *AmMWSc 92*
**Johnson-Marshall,** Percy Edwin Alan 1915- *Who 92*
**Johnson-Odim,** Cheryl 1948- *WhoBlA 92*
**Johnson-Sadur,** Kristina Joy 1953- *WhoAmP 91*
**Johnson-Scott,** Jerodene Patrice 1952- *WhoBlA 92*
**Johnson Smith,** Geoffrey 1924- *Who 92*
**Johnson-Tanis,** Pamela Sue 1946- *WhoEnt 92*
**Johnson-Winegar,** Anna 1945- *AmMWSc 92*
**Johnson-Wint,** Barbara Paule *AmMWSc 92*
**Johnson-Wolff,** Christina Marie 1950- *WhoFI 92*
**Johnsrud,** Duwayne 1943- *WhoAmP 91*
**Johnsrude,** Junne Margarette 1920- *WhoAmP 91*
**Johnsson,** Hillary Crute 1959- *WhoEnt 92*
**Johnston** *Who 92*
**Johnston Smith** *BenetAL 91*
**Johnston,** A Sidney 1937- *AmMWSc 92*
**Johnston,** Alan 1942- *WrDr 92*
**Johnston,** Alan 1945- *TwCPaSc*
**Johnston,** Alan Charles Macpherson 1942- *Who 92*
**Johnston,** Alan Cope 1946- *WhoAmL 92*
**Johnston,** Alan Robert 1931- *AmMWSc 92*
**Johnston,** Alexander 1905- *Who 92*
**Johnston,** Alexander Graham 1944- *Who 92*
**Johnston,** Alistair D 1937- *WhoIns 92*
**Johnston,** Allen Howard 1912- *IntWW 91, Who 92*
**Johnston,** Andrea 1921- *AmMWSc 92*
**Johnston,** Andrew William 1932- *WhoAmP 91*
**Johnston,** Annie Fellows 1863-1931 *BenetAL 91*
**Johnston,** Barrance V. 1942- *WhoMW 92*
**Johnston,** Ben 1926- *NewAmDM*
**Johnston,** Betty Joan 1916- *Who 92*
**Johnston,** Brian 1912- *Who 92*
**Johnston,** Bruce 1905- *AmMWSc 92*
**Johnston,** C Edward *AmMWSc 92*
**Johnston,** Carmon 1947- *WhoEnt 92*
**Johnston,** Carol Strickland 1957- *WhoWest 92*
**Johnston,** Carole Anne 1944- *IntAu&W 91*
**Johnston,** Charles Hughes 1877-1917 *BiInAmS*
**Johnston,** Charles Lamb 1928- *WhoFI 92*
**Johnston,** Charlie Gymann 1915- *WhoFI 92*
**Johnston,** Christian William 1911- *AmMWSc 92*
**Johnston,** Christina Jane 1952- *WhoFI 92*
**Johnston,** Christopher 1822-1891 *BiInAmS*
**Johnston,** Clair C 1899- *AmMWSc 92*
**Johnston,** Clarence Dinsmore H. *Who 92*
**Johnston,** Colin Deane 1940- *AmMWSc 92*
**Johnston,** Colleen Kelly 1932- *WhoAmP 91*
**Johnston,** Craig Alan 1955- *WhoWest 92*
**Johnston,** Craig Dean 1948- *WhoEnt 92*
**Johnston,** Cyrus Conrad, Jr 1929- *AmMWSc 92*
**Johnston,** David 1936- *Who 92*
**Johnston,** David Alan H. *Who 92*
**Johnston,** David Glen 1952- *WhoEnt 92*
**Johnston,** David Hervey 1951- *AmMWSc 92*
**Johnston,** David Lawrence 1936- *Who 92*
**Johnston,** David Lloyd 1941- *IntWW 91, Who 92*
**Johnston,** David Lloyd 1942- *WhoMW 92*
**Johnston,** David Owen 1930- *AmMWSc 92*
**Johnston,** David Russell 1932- *Who 92*
**Johnston,** David Ware 1926- *AmMWSc 92*
**Johnston,** Dean 1947- *AmMWSc 92*
**Johnston,** Denis 1901- *LiExTwC*
**Johnston,** Denis 1901-1984 *RfGEnL 91*
**Johnston,** Dennis Addington 1944- *AmMWSc 92*
**Johnston,** Dennis Roy 1937- *WhoFI 92*
**Johnston,** Dennis W 1942- *WhoAmP 91*
**Johnston,** Don 1927- *IntWW 91*
**Johnston,** Don Richard 1937- *AmMWSc 92*
**Johnston,** Donald Gerard 1962- *WhoMW 92*
**Johnston,** Donald Robert 1926- *WhoAmL 92*
**Johnston,** Donna Faye 1941- *WhoFI 92*
**Johnston,** Douglas Frederick 1930- *WhoFI 92*
**Johnston,** Douglas Scott 1947- *WhoRel 92*
**Johnston,** E Russell, Jr 1925- *AmMWSc 92*
**Johnston,** Edward 1929- *Who 92*
**Johnston,** Elizabeth Johnston Evans 1851-1934 *DcNCBi 3*
**Johnston,** Ernest Raymond 1907- *AmMWSc 92*
**Johnston,** Faber Laine, Jr. 1927- *WhoAmL 92*
**Johnston,** Frances Benjamin 1864-1952 *HanAmWH*
**Johnston,** Francis Claiborne, Jr. 1943- *WhoAmL 92*
**Johnston,** Francis E 1931- *AmMWSc 92*
**Johnston,** Francis J 1924- *AmMWSc 92*
**Johnston,** Frederick Mervyn Kieran 1911- *Who 92*
**Johnston,** Frederick Patrick Mair 1935- *Who 92*
**Johnston,** G W 1926- *AmMWSc 92*
**Johnston,** Gabriel 1698?-1752 *DcNCBi 3*
**Johnston,** Gary *DrAPF 91*
**Johnston,** George 1912-1970 *LiExTwC*
**Johnston,** George 1913- *BenetAL 91, ConPo 91, IntAu&W 91, WhoRel 92, WrDr 92*
**Johnston,** George Doherty 1832-1910 *DcNCBi 3*
**Johnston,** George Elmer 1927- *WhoFI 92*
**Johnston,** George I 1929- *AmMWSc 92*
**Johnston,** George Lawrence 1932- *AmMWSc 92*
**Johnston,** George Robert 1934- *AmMWSc 92*
**Johnston,** George Sim d1991 *NewYTBS 91 [port]*
**Johnston,** George Taylor 1942- *AmMWSc 92*
**Johnston,** Gerald Samuel 1930- *AmMWSc 92*
**Johnston,** Gladys Styles 1942- *WhoBlA 92*
**Johnston,** Gordon 1874-1934 *DcNCBi 3*
**Johnston,** Gordon Howard 1959- *WhoRel 92*
**Johnston,** Gordon Robert 1928- *AmMWSc 92*
**Johnston,** Gordon Wolf 1951- *WhoAmL 92*
**Johnston,** Gwinavere Adams 1943- *WhoWest 92*
**Johnston,** H. Robert 1956- *WhoEnt 92*
**Johnston,** Harlin Dee 1942- *AmMWSc 92*
**Johnston,** Harold S. 1920- *IntWW 91*
**Johnston,** Harold Sledge 1920- *AmMWSc 92*
**Johnston,** Harry A. 1931- *AlmAP 92 [port]*
**Johnston,** Harry A, II 1931- *WhoAmP 91*
**Johnston,** Harry Henry 1929- *AmMWSc 92*
**Johnston,** Henrietta 1670?-1728? *HanAmWH*
**Johnston,** Henry Bruce 1927- *WhoBlA 92*
**Johnston,** Henry Butler M. *Who 92*
**Johnston,** Herbert Norris 1928- *AmMWSc 92*
**Johnston,** Herman Justin 1962- *WhoFI 92*
**Johnston,** Hugh Francis 1961- *WhoFI 92*
**Johnston,** Hugh Philip 1927- *Who 92*
**Johnston,** Ian Alistair 1944- *Who 92*
**Johnston,** Ian Henderson 1925- *Who 92*
**Johnston,** J. Bennett 1932- *AlmAP 92 [port]*
**Johnston,** J Bennett, Jr 1932- *WhoAmP 91*
**Johnston,** J. Phillips L. *WhoFI 92*
**Johnston,** Jacqueline Rose 1946- *WhoAmP 91*
**Johnston,** James Baker 1946- *AmMWSc 92*
**Johnston,** James Bennett 1943- *AmMWSc 92*
**Johnston,** James Campbell 1912- *Who 92*
**Johnston,** James Cathcart 1782-1865 *DcNCBi 3*
**Johnston,** James D. 1930- *WhoFI 92*
**Johnston,** James Frederick Junor 1939- *Who 92*
**Johnston,** James Kirkland 1956- *WhoRel 92*
**Johnston,** James P 1931- *AmMWSc 92*
**Johnston,** Jean Vance 1912- *AmMWSc 92*
**Johnston,** Jennifer 1930- *ConNov 91, IntAu&W 91, Who 92, WrDr 92*
**Johnston,** Jill 1929- *IntAu&W 91, WrDr 92*
**Johnston,** Jocelyn Elaine 1954- *WhoAmL 92*
**Johnston,** John 1806-1879 *BiInAmS*
**Johnston,** John 1918- *IntWW 91, Who 92*
**Johnston,** John 1925- *AmMWSc 92*
**Johnston,** John Alexander 1927- *WhoRel 92*
**Johnston,** John B 1929- *AmMWSc 92*
**Johnston,** John Bennett, Jr. 1932- *IntWW 91*
**Johnston,** John Devereaux, Jr. 1932- *WhoAmL 92*
**Johnston,** John Douglas Hartley 1935- *Who 92*
**Johnston,** John Eric 1948- *AmMWSc 92*
**Johnston,** John Frederick Dame 1922- *Who 92*
**Johnston,** John Marshall 1928- *AmMWSc 92*
**Johnston,** John O'Neal 1939- *AmMWSc 92*
**Johnston,** John Paul 1948- *WhoFI 92*
**Johnston,** John Spencer 1944- *AmMWSc 92*
**Johnston,** John Wayne 1943- *WhoMW 92*
**Johnston,** Johnie Edward, Jr. 1946- *WhoRel 92*
**Johnston,** Jonas 1740-1779 *DcNCBi 3*
**Johnston,** Joseph Forney 1843-1913 *DcNCBi 3*
**Johnston,** Julia Mayo 1926- *WhoBlA 92*
**Johnston,** Kaarin Spencer 1950- *WhoMW 92*
**Johnston,** Karen Lang 1949- *WhoAmP 91*
**Johnston,** Katharine Gentry 1921- *AmMWSc 92*
**Johnston,** Kathleen Ann 1959- *WhoEnt 92*
**Johnston,** Kathryn 1957- *WhoAmL 92*
**Johnston,** Kenneth John 1941- *AmMWSc 92*
**Johnston,** Kenneth Robert Hope 1905- *Who 92*
**Johnston,** Kevin P 1950- *WhoAmP 91*
**Johnston,** L.V., Jr. 1958- *WhoEnt 92*
**Johnston,** La Verne Albert 1930- *AmMWSc 92*
**Johnston,** Lancelot 1748-1832 *DcNCBi 3*
**Johnston,** Laurance S 1950- *AmMWSc 92*
**Johnston,** Lawrence Harding 1918- *AmMWSc 92*
**Johnston,** Lloyd Allan 1953- *WhoRel 92*
**Johnston,** Logan Truax, III 1947- *WhoAmL 92*
**Johnston,** Lorene Gayle 1952- *WhoAmP 91*
**Johnston,** Lorne Carlyle 1950- *WhoFI 92*
**Johnston,** Lynn H 1931- *WhoIns 92*
**Johnston,** Malcolm Campbell 1931- *AmMWSc 92*
**Johnston,** Manley Roderick 1942- *AmMWSc 92*
**Johnston,** Margaret *IntMPA 92, Who 92*
**Johnston,** Marilyn Frances Meyers 1937- *AmMWSc 92*
**Johnston,** Marjorie Diane 1943- *WhoWest 92*
**Johnston,** Marshall Conring 1930- *AmMWSc 92*
**Johnston,** Mary 1870-1936 *BenetAL 91*
**Johnston,** Maryann 1939- *WhoRel 92*
**Johnston,** Maurice 1929- *Who 92*
**Johnston,** Melvin Roscoe 1921- *AmMWSc 92*
**Johnston,** Michael Alexander Ninian C. *Who 92*
**Johnston,** Michael Errington 1916- *Who 92*
**Johnston,** Michael J. 1938- *WhoFI 92*
**Johnston,** Michael L 1945- *WhoAmP 91*
**Johnston,** Michael O'Neill 1935- *WhoAmP 91*
**Johnston,** Miles Gregory *AmMWSc 92*
**Johnston,** Milton Dwynell, Jr 1943- *AmMWSc 92*
**Johnston,** Ninian Rutherford Jamieson d1990 *Who 92N*
**Johnston,** Norma *WrDr 92*
**Johnston,** Norman Joseph 1934- *AmMWSc 92*
**Johnston,** Norman Lloyd 1933- *WhoRel 92*
**Johnston,** Norman Paul 1941- *AmMWSc 92*
**Johnston,** Norman Wilson 1942- *AmMWSc 92*
**Johnston,** Patrick 1946- *WhoAmP 91*
**Johnston,** Paul Bruns 1927- *AmMWSc 92*
**Johnston,** Paula P 1945- *WhoAmP 91*
**Johnston,** Perry Max 1921- *AmMWSc 92*
**Johnston,** Peter Barbour, IV 1966- *WhoWest 92*
**Johnston,** Peter Ramsey 1926- *AmMWSc 92*
**Johnston,** Peter William 1943- *Who 92*
**Johnston,** Philip Crater 1943- *WhoAmL 92*
**Johnston,** Philip William 1944- *WhoAmP 91*
**Johnston,** R. J. 1941- *WrDr 92*
**Johnston,** Ralph Kennedy, Sr. 1942- *WhoWest 92*
**Johnston,** Raymond F 1913- *AmMWSc 92*
**Johnston,** Richard Alan 1950- *WhoAmL 92*
**Johnston,** Richard B *WhoAmP 91*
**Johnston,** Richard Boles, Jr 1935- *AmMWSc 92*
**Johnston,** Richard Fourness 1925- *AmMWSc 92*
**Johnston,** Richard H 1929- *AmMWSc 92*
**Johnston,** Richard Malcolm 1822-1898 *BenetAL 91*
**Johnston,** Rita Margaret 1935- *Who 92, WhoWest 92*
**Johnston,** Robert Alan 1924- *IntWW 91, Who 92*
**Johnston,** Robert Benjamin 1922- *AmMWSc 92*
**Johnston,** Robert Daniel 1837-1919 *DcNCBi 3*
**Johnston,** Robert Donaghy 1929- *WhoEnt 92*
**Johnston,** Robert E 1942- *AmMWSc 92*
**Johnston,** Robert Edward 1947- *AmMWSc 92*
**Johnston,** Robert Gordon Scott 1933- *Who 92*
**Johnston,** Robert Howard 1924- *AmMWSc 92*
**Johnston,** Robert Kent 1945- *WhoRel 92*
**Johnston,** Robert Morris 1930- *WhoRel 92*
**Johnston,** Robert R 1929- *AmMWSc 92*
**Johnston,** Robert Smith *Who 92*
**Johnston,** Robert Ward 1925- *AmMWSc 92*
**Johnston,** Robert William Fairfield 1895- *Who 92*
**Johnston,** Robin W. *WhoRel 92*
**Johnston,** Roger Glenn 1954- *AmMWSc 92, WhoWest 92*
**Johnston,** Ronald 1926- *IntAu&W 91, WrDr 92*
**Johnston,** Ronald Harvey 1939- *AmMWSc 92*
**Johnston,** Ronald John 1941- *IntAu&W 91*
**Johnston,** Ronald Vernon 1942- *WhoFI 92*
**Johnston,** Ross W. 1947- *WhoWest 92*
**Johnston,** Roy G 1914- *AmMWSc 92*
**Johnston,** Rufus Zenas 1874-1959 *DcNCBi 3*
**Johnston,** Russell *Who 92*
**Johnston,** Russell 1932- *WrDr 92*
**Johnston,** Russell Shayne 1948- *AmMWSc 92*
**Johnston,** Samuel 1733-1816 *DcNCBi 3*
**Johnston,** Samuel Iredell 1806-1865 *DcNCBi 3*
**Johnston,** Samuel Thomas, Jr. 1964- *WhoEnt 92*
**Johnston,** Sheryl L. 1944- *WhoMW 92*
**Johnston,** Stephen Charles 1950- *AmMWSc 92*
**Johnston,** Taylor Jimmie 1940- *AmMWSc 92*
**Johnston,** Terry C 1947- *TwCWW 91, WrDr 92*
**Johnston,** Terry D 1947- *WhoAmP 91*
**Johnston,** Terry L. 1946- *WhoRel 92*
**Johnston,** Thomas Alexander 1956- *Who 92*
**Johnston,** Thomas Dillard 1840-1902 *DcNCBi 3*
**Johnston,** Thomas John 1922- *WhoFI 92*
**Johnston,** Thomas Lothian 1927- *IntWW 91, Who 92*
**Johnston,** Thomas M 1921- *AmMWSc 92*
**Johnston,** Thomas Pinkney 1808-1883 *DcNCBi 3*
**Johnston,** Thomas Watts 1936- *WhoAmL 92*
**Johnston,** Tudor Wyatt 1932- *AmMWSc 92*
**Johnston,** Velda *WrDr 92*
**Johnston,** Virgil Lloyd 1928- *WhoWest 92*
**Johnston,** Virginia Evelyn 1933- *WhoWest 92*
**Johnston,** W Cairns *ScFEYrs*
**Johnston,** Wallace O. 1929- *WhoBlA 92*
**Johnston,** Walter Edward 1939- *AmMWSc 92*
**Johnston,** Walter Eugene, III 1936- *WhoAmP 91*
**Johnston,** Warren E 1933- *AmMWSc 92*

**Johnston,** Wilbur Dexter, Jr 1940- *AmMWSc 92*
**Johnston,** William 1737-1785 *DcNCBi 3*
**Johnston,** William 1817-1896 *DcNCBi 3*
**Johnston,** William 1925- *IntAu&W 91, WrDr 92*
**Johnston,** William Arnold 1942- *WhoEnt 92*
**Johnston,** William Bryce 1921- *IntWW 91, Who 92*
**Johnston,** William Cargill 1917- *AmMWSc 92*
**Johnston,** William David 1944- *WhoMW 92*
**Johnston,** William Dwight 1928- *AmMWSc 92*
**Johnston,** William Francis 1930- *Who 92*
**Johnston,** William James 1919- *Who 92*
**Johnston,** William James 1942- *WhoAmP 91*
**Johnston,** William Murray 1936- *WrDr 92*
**Johnston,** William Robert Patrick K. *Who 92*
**Johnston,** William V 1927- *AmMWSc 92*
**Johnston,** William Webb 1933- *AmMWSc 92*
**Johnston-Calati,** Kathleen Louise *WhoAmP 91*
**Johnston-Feller,** Ruth M 1923- *AmMWSc 92*
**Johnston of Rockport,** Baron 1915- *Who 92*
**Johnstone** *Who 92*
**Johnstone,** Lord 1971- *Who 92*
**Johnstone,** Vanden-Bempde- *Who 92*
**Johnstone,** Alan Stewart d1990 *Who 92N*
**Johnstone,** Alexander Vallance Riddell 1916- *Who 92*
**Johnstone,** C Wilkin 1916- *AmMWSc 92*
**Johnstone,** Chauncey Olcott 1943- *WhoFI 92*
**Johnstone,** D. Bruce 1941- *IntWW 91*
**Johnstone,** David 1926- *IntMPA 92*
**Johnstone,** David Kirkpatrick 1926- *Who 92*
**Johnstone,** David Lawson *ScFEYrs*
**Johnstone,** Deborah Blackmon 1953- *WhoAmL 92*
**Johnstone,** Donald Boyes 1919- *AmMWSc 92*
**Johnstone,** Donald Lee 1939- *AmMWSc 92*
**Johnstone,** Douglas Inge 1941- *WhoAmL 92, WhoAmP 91*
**Johnstone,** Edward H. 1922- *WhoAmL 92*
**Johnstone,** Frederic 1906- *Who 92*
**Johnstone,** Gregg Martin 1947- *WhoEnt 92*
**Johnstone,** H L *ScFEYrs*
**Johnstone,** Iain Gilmour 1943- *IntAu&W 91*
**Johnstone,** Irvine Blakeley, III 1948- *WhoAmL 92*
**Johnstone,** Isobel Theodora 1944- *Who 92*
**Johnstone,** James G 1920- *AmMWSc 92*
**Johnstone,** John Raymond 1929- *Who 92*
**Johnstone,** John W., Jr. 1932- *IntWW 91*
**Johnstone,** John William, Jr. 1932- *WhoFI 92*
**Johnstone,** Keith *WrDr 92*
**Johnstone,** Kenneth Ernest 1929- *WhoWest 92*
**Johnstone,** L Craig *WhoAmP 91*
**Johnstone,** Larry Anthony 1958- *WhoAmL 92*
**Johnstone,** Michael Anthony 1936- *Who 92*
**Johnstone,** Pat M. 1958- *WhoEnt 92*
**Johnstone,** Philip MacLaren 1961- *WhoAmL 92, WhoFI 92*
**Johnstone,** Raymond *Who 92*
**Johnstone,** Robert 1951- *IntAu&W 91*
**Johnstone,** Robert Edgeworth 1900- *Who 92*
**Johnstone,** Robert Milton 1944- *WhoAmL 92*
**Johnstone,** Rose M 1928- *AmMWSc 92*
**Johnstone,** Terry Lynn 1947- *WhoMW 92*
**Johnstone,** William 1897-1981 *TwCPaSc*
**Johnstone,** William 1915- *Who 92*
**Johnstone,** William 1936- *Who 92*
**Johnstone,** William Mervyn 1946- *WhoWest 92*
**Johore,** Sultan of 1932- *IntWW 91*
**Johst,** Hanns 1890-1978 *EncTR 91 [port]*
**Joice,** Johnny 1943- *WhoFI 92*
**Joicey** *Who 92*
**Joicey,** Baron 1925- *Who 92*
**Joicey,** Richard *TwCPaSc*
**Joiner,** Burnett 1941- *WhoBlA 92*
**Joiner,** C. Raymond, Jr. 1952- *WhoRel 92*
**Joiner,** Charles, Jr. 1947- *WhoBlA 92*
**Joiner,** Edward Earl 1924- *WhoRel 92*
**Joiner,** Jasper Newton 1921- *AmMWSc 92*
**Joiner,** Larry J. 1939- *WhoMW 92*
**Joiner,** R Gracen 1933- *AmMWSc 92*
**Joiner,** Robert Russell 1916- *AmMWSc 92*
**Joiner,** Stephen Neal 1957- *WhoAmL 92*
**Joiner,** Steven Craig 1958- *WhoRel 92*
**Joiner,** William Cornelius Henry 1936- *AmMWSc 92*
**Joio,** Norman Dello *NewAmDM*
**Jokanovic,** Vukasin 1939- *IntWW 91*
**Jokela,** Jalmer John 1921- *AmMWSc 92*
**Jokerst,** Carol Ann 1939- *WhoRel 92*
**Jokerst,** Nan Marie 1961- *AmMWSc 92*
**Jokinen,** Eileen Hope 1943- *AmMWSc 92*
**Jokipii,** Jack Randolph 1939- *AmMWSc 92*
**Jokipii,** Liisa 1943- *IntWW 91*
**Jokl,** Ernst 1907- *AmMWSc 92*
**Jokl,** Miloslav Vladimir 1933- *AmMWSc 92*
**Joklik,** G Frank 1928- *AmMWSc 92*
**Joklik,** Wolfgang Karl 1926- *AmMWSc 92, IntWW 91*
**Jokostra,** Peter 1912- *IntAu&W 91*
**Jokubaitis,** Lisa Marie 1966- *WhoMW 92*
**Jolas,** Betsy 1926- *ConCom 92, NewAmDM*
**Jolicoeur,** Pierre 1934- *AmMWSc 92*
**Joliet,** Rene 1938- *IntWW 91*
**Jolin,** Peg 1952- *WhoAmP 91*
**Jolin,** Peggy 1952- *WhoWest 92*
**Joliot,** Pierre Adrien 1932- *IntWW 91*
**Joliot-Curie,** Frederic 1900-1958 *FacFETw, WhoNob 90*
**Joliot-Curie,** Irene 1897-1956 *FacFETw, WhoNob 90*
**Jolissaint,** Mark Alan 1949- *WhoAmP 91*
**Jolivet,** Andre 1905-1974 *NewAmDM*
**Jolivet,** Jo Ann Collins *WhoWest 92*
**Jolivet,** Linda Catherine 1950- *WhoBlA 92*
**Jolivet,** Vincent Michel 1930- *WhoFI 92*
**Jolivette,** Peter Lauson 1941- *AmMWSc 92*
**Joll,** James 1918- *IntAu&W 91, WrDr 92*
**Joll,** James Bysse 1918- *Who 92*
**Jolles,** Ira Hervey 1938- *WhoAmL 92*
**Jolles,** Mitchell Ira 1953- *AmMWSc 92*
**Jolles,** Paul Rodolphe 1919- *IntWW 91*
**Jolley,** David 1942- *WhoFI 92*
**Jolley,** David Kent 1944- *AmMWSc 92*
**Jolley,** Donal Clark 1933- *WhoWest 92*
**Jolley,** Elizabeth 1923- *ConNov 91, IntAu&W 91, WrDr 92*
**Jolley,** Homer Richard 1916- *AmMWSc 92*
**Jolley,** John Eric 1929- *AmMWSc 92*
**Jolley,** Robert Louis 1929- *AmMWSc 92*
**Jolley,** Ronald Swapp 1936- *WhoRel 92*
**Jolley,** Stan 1926- *IntMPA 92, WhoEnt 92*
**Jolley,** Weldon Bosen 1926- *AmMWSc 92*
**Jollick,** Joseph Darryl 1941- *AmMWSc 92*
**Jollie,** Malcolm Thomas 1919- *AmMWSc 92*
**Jollie,** William Pucette 1928- *AmMWSc 92*
**Jolliff,** Robert Allen 1943- *WhoFI 92*
**Jolliffe** *Who 92*
**Jolliffe,** Alfred Walton 1907- *AmMWSc 92*
**Jolliffe,** Anthony 1938- *Who 92*
**Jolliffe,** Christopher 1912- *Who 92*
**Jolliffe,** John 1935- *ConAu 133*
**Jolliffe,** Ronald Lynn 1949- *WhoRel 92*
**Jolliffe,** William d1902 *BiInAmS*
**Jolliffe,** William Orlando 1925- *Who 92*
**Jolls,** Claudia Lee 1953- *AmMWSc 92*
**Jolls,** Kenneth Robert 1933- *AmMWSc 92*
**Jolly,** Alison Bishop 1937- *AmMWSc 92*
**Jolly,** Anthony Charles 1932- *Who 92*
**Jolly,** Arthur Richard 1934- *Who 92, WhoFI 92*
**Jolly,** Charles Nelson 1942- *WhoFI 92*
**Jolly,** Clayton Leon, III 1959- *WhoAmL 92*
**Jolly,** Clifford J 1939- *AmMWSc 92*
**Jolly,** Daniel Ehs 1952- *WhoMW 92*
**Jolly,** E Grady *WhoAmP 91*
**Jolly,** E. Grady 1937- *WhoAmL 92*
**Jolly,** Elton 1931- *WhoBlA 92*
**Jolly,** James A. 1921- *WhoWest 92*
**Jolly,** Janice Laurene Willard 1931- *AmMWSc 92*
**Jolly,** Marva Lee 1937- *WhoBlA 92*
**Jolly,** Mary B. 1940- *WhoBlA 92*
**Jolly,** Michael John 1960- *WhoWest 92*
**Jolly,** Richard *Who 92*
**Jolly,** Richard Donald 1956- *WhoWest 92*
**Jolly,** Robert Dudley 1930- *IntWW 91*
**Jolly,** Robert Malcolm 1920- *Who 92*
**Jolly,** Stuart Martin 1946- *AmMWSc 92*
**Jolly,** W. P. 1922- *WrDr 92*
**Jolly,** Wayne Travis 1940- *AmMWSc 92*
**Jolly,** William Lee 1927- *AmMWSc 92*
**Jolovitz,** Herbert Allen 1930- *WhoAmP 91*
**Jolowicz,** J. A. 1926- *WrDr 92*
**Jolowicz,** John Anthony 1926- *Who 92*
**Jolson,** Al 1886-1950 *FacFETw [port], NewAmDM*
**Jolson,** Alfred James 1928- *WhoRel 92*
**Joly,** Alain 1938- *IntWW 91*
**Joly,** Cyril Matthew, Jr 1925- *WhoAmP 91*
**Joly,** Daniel Jose 1921- *AmMWSc 92*
**Joly,** George W 1917- *AmMWSc 92*
**Joly,** Louis Philippe 1928- *AmMWSc 92*
**Joly,** Olga G *AmMWSc 92*
**Joly de Lotbiniere,** Edmond 1903- *Who 92*
**Jommelli,** Niccolo 1714-1774 *NewAmDM*
**Jona,** Franco Paul 1922- *AmMWSc 92*
**Jonah** *EncEarC*
**Jonah,** Charles D 1943- *AmMWSc 92*
**Jonah,** Margaret Martin 1942- *AmMWSc 92, WhoMW 92*
**Jonas,** Albert Moshe 1931- *AmMWSc 92*
**Jonas,** Ana 1943- *AmMWSc 92*
**Jonas,** Ann *DrAPF 91*
**Jonas,** Ann 1919- *IntAu&W 91*
**Jonas,** Carl 1913-1976 *BenetAL 91*
**Jonas,** Charles Andrew 1876-1955 *DcNCBi 3*
**Jonas,** David A. 1964- *WhoFI 92*
**Jonas,** Edward Charles 1924- *AmMWSc 92*
**Jonas,** Ernesto A. 1939- *WhoBlA 92*
**Jonas,** Gary Fred 1945- *WhoFI 92*
**Jonas,** George *DrAPF 91*
**Jonas,** George 1935- *WrDr 92*
**Jonas,** Gerald *DrAPF 91*
**Jonas,** Harry 1893-1990 *TwCPaSc*
**Jonas,** Herbert 1915- *AmMWSc 92*
**Jonas,** Jiri 1932- *AmMWSc 92, WhoMW 92*
**Jonas,** Joan 1936- *WhoWest 92*
**Jonas,** John Joseph 1914- *AmMWSc 92*
**Jonas,** John Joseph 1932- *AmMWSc 92*
**Jonas,** Johnny 1948- *TwCPaSc*
**Jonas,** Leonard Abraham 1920- *AmMWSc 92*
**Jonas,** Manfred 1927- *IntAu&W 91, WrDr 92*
**Jonas,** Peter 1946- *IntWW 91, Who 92, WhoEnt 92*
**Jonas,** Robert James 1926- *AmMWSc 92*
**Jonas,** Royal Flagg 1922- *WhoAmL 92*
**Jonassen,** Hans Boegh 1912- *AmMWSc 92*
**Jonasson,** Timothy Robert 1962- *WhoWest 92*
**Jonatansson,** Halldor 1932- *WhoFI 92*
**Jonathan,** Brother *BenetAL 91*
**Joncas,** Grace Lucille 1923- *WhoAmP 91*
**Joncas,** Jean Harry 1930- *AmMWSc 92*
**Jondahl,** H Lynn *WhoAmP 91*
**Jondahl,** Terri Elise 1959- *WhoFI 92*
**Jondorf,** W Robert 1928- *AmMWSc 92*
**Joneja,** Madan Gopal 1936- *AmMWSc 92*
**Jones** *Who 92*
**Jones,** Mother 1830-1930 *HanAmWH*
**Jones,** Mother 1837-1930 *RComAH*
**Jones,** Prophet 1908-1971 *RelLAm 91*
**Jones,** A Clifford 1921- *WhoAmP 91*
**Jones,** A R 1921- *AmMWSc 92*
**Jones,** Aaron Delmas, II 1966- *WhoBlA 92*
**Jones,** Abeodu Bowen *IntWW 91*
**Jones,** Absalom 1746-1818 *RComAH*
**Jones,** Addie D. 1951- *WhoMW 92*
**Jones,** Adrian 1845-1938 *TwCPaSc*
**Jones,** Adrienne 1915- *WrDr 92*
**Jones,** Alan A 1944- *AmMWSc 92*
**Jones,** Alan C. 1942- *WhoWest 92*
**Jones,** Alan Griffith 1943- *WrDr 92*
**Jones,** Alan Lee 1939- *AmMWSc 92*
**Jones,** Alan Payan P. *Who 92*
**Jones,** Alan Porter, Jr. 1925- *WhoMW 92*
**Jones,** Alan Richard 1939- *AmMWSc 92*
**Jones,** Alan Robert 1945- *WhoAmP 91*
**Jones,** Alan Stanley 1946- *IntWW 91*
**Jones,** Alan William 1940- *WhoRel 92*
**Jones,** Alan Wingate 1939- *Who 92*
**Jones,** Albert 1929- *WhoAmP 91*
**Jones,** Albert Allen 1913- *WhoBlA 92*
**Jones,** Albert Arthur 1915- *Who 92*
**Jones,** Albert Cleveland 1929- *AmMWSc 92*
**Jones,** Albert J. 1928- *WhoBlA 92*
**Jones,** Albert L. 1945- *WhoBlA 92*
**Jones,** Albert Pearson 1907- *WhoAmL 92*
**Jones,** Albert Stanley 1925- *Who 92*
**Jones,** Alex S. 1946- *ConAu 135*
**Jones,** Alexander 1802-1863 *DcNCBi 3*
**Jones,** Alexander Hamilton 1822-1901 *DcNCBi 3*
**Jones,** Alexander R. 1952- *WhoBlA 92*
**Jones,** Alfred 1932- *AmMWSc 92*
**Jones,** Alfred 1946- *BlkOlyM*
**Jones,** Alfred A. *WhoBlA 92*
**Jones,** Alfredean 1940- *WhoBlA 92*
**Jones,** Alister Vallance 1924- *AmMWSc 92*
**Jones,** Allan Barry 1936- *WhoRel 92*
**Jones,** Allan W 1929- *WhoIns 92*
**Jones,** Allan W 1937- *AmMWSc 92*
**Jones,** Allen 1739-1798 *DcNCBi 3*
**Jones,** Allen 1937- *IntWW 91, Who 92*
**Jones,** Allen, Jr. 1930- *WhoAmL 92*
**Jones,** Almut Gitter 1923- *AmMWSc 92*
**Jones,** Alphonzo James 1946- *WhoBlA 92*
**Jones,** Alun *Who 92*
**Jones,** Alun Denry Wynn 1939- *Who 92*
**Jones,** Alun Richard 1928- *AmMWSc 92*
**Jones,** Alwyn Rice *Who 92*
**Jones,** Ammia W. 1910- *WhoBlA 92*
**Jones,** Amy Holden 1953- *IntMPA 92*
**Jones,** Andrew Jackson 1826-1873 *DcNCBi 3*
**Jones,** Anita Katherine *AmMWSc 92*
**Jones,** Ann Maret 1937- *IntAu&W 91*
**Jones,** Ann R. 1921- *WhoBlA 92*
**Jones,** Annabel Marie 1953- *WhoAmL 92*
**Jones,** Anne 1935- *Who 92*
**Jones,** Anne Hudson 1944- *ConAu 135*
**Jones,** Anne P. *LesBEnT 92*
**Jones,** Anne P 1935- *WhoAmP 91*
**Jones,** Annette *WhoAmP 91*
**Jones,** Annette 1944- *WhoFI 92*
**Jones,** Annette Merritt 1946- *WhoBlA 92*
**Jones,** Anthony, Jr. 1933- *WhoBlA 92*
**Jones,** Anthony Edward 1944- *WhoMW 92*
**Jones,** Anthony George Clifford 1923- *Who 92*
**Jones,** Anthony R. 1953- *WhoEnt 92*
**Jones,** Anthony Talbot 1956- *WhoWest 92*
**Jones,** Anthony W. *Who 92*
**Jones,** Aquilla 1811-1891 *DcNCBi 3*
**Jones,** Archie Herbert, III 1971- *WhoEnt 92*
**Jones,** Arlender *WhoBlA 92*
**Jones,** Armistead 1846-1925 *DcNCBi 3*
**Jones,** Arnold Pearson *WhoBlA 92*
**Jones,** Arthur *Who 92*
**Jones,** Arthur L. 1922- *WhoBlA 92*
**Jones,** Arthur Stanley 1932- *Who 92*
**Jones,** Arves E 1925- *WhoAmP 91*
**Jones,** Asbury Paul 1914- *WhoBlA 92*
**Jones,** Aubrey 1911- *IntAu&W 91, IntWW 91, Who 92, WrDr 92*
**Jones,** Aubrey Lee, Jr 1953- *WhoAmP 91*
**Jones,** Audrey Boswell *WhoBlA 92*
**Jones,** B. Calvin 1925- *WhoEnt 92*
**Jones,** B Rees 1937- *WhoIns 92*
**Jones,** Barbara d1978 *TwCPaSc*
**Jones,** Barbara A. P. 1943- *WhoFI 92*
**Jones,** Barbara Ann Posey 1943- *WhoBlA 92*
**Jones,** Barbara Christine 1942- *WhoWest 92*
**Jones,** Barbara Ellen 1944- *AmMWSc 92*
**Jones,** Barbara Pearl 1937- *BlkOlyM*
**Jones,** Barclay G 1931- *AmMWSc 92*
**Jones,** Barclay Gibbs, III 1960- *WhoFI 92*
**Jones,** Barry *Who 92*
**Jones,** Barry Owen 1932- *IntWW 91*
**Jones,** Basil Douglas 1903- *Who 92*
**Jones,** Beatrice Eleanor 1904- *WhoAmP 91*
**Jones,** Beau *WhoAmP 91*
**Jones,** Ben 1941- *AlmAP 92 [port], WhoAmP 91*
**Jones,** Ben 1947- *TwCPaSc*
**Jones,** Ben F. 1942- *WhoBlA 92*
**Jones,** Ben Joseph 1924- *IntWW 91*
**Jones,** Benjamin A, Jr 1926- *AmMWSc 92*
**Jones,** Benjamin E. 1935- *WhoBlA 92*
**Jones,** Benjamin Franklin, Jr 1936- *AmMWSc 92*
**Jones,** Benjamin Lewis 1952- *AmMWSc 92*
**Jones,** Bernard H., Sr. 1931- *WhoBlA 92*
**Jones,** Berne Lee 1941- *AmMWSc 92*
**Jones,** Bernie 1952- *WhoBlA 92*
**Jones,** Bertha Diggs *WhoBlA 92*
**Jones,** Bertha H. 1918- *WhoBlA 92*
**Jones,** Berwyn E 1937- *AmMWSc 92*
**Jones,** Beti 1919- *Who 92*
**Jones,** Betsy 1926- *AmMWSc 92*
**Jones,** Betty *WhoEnt 92*
**Jones,** Betty Harris 1937-1989 *WhoBlA 92N*
**Jones,** Betty Jean T. 1943- *WhoBlA 92*
**Jones,** Betty Ruth 1951- *AmMWSc 92*
**Jones,** Bill T. *News 91 [port]*
**Jones,** Bill T. 1952?- *ConBlB 1 [port]*
**Jones,** Billy Emanuel 1938- *WhoBlA 92*
**Jones,** Billy Mac 1925- *WhoMW 92, WrDr 92*
**Jones,** Blair Francis 1934- *AmMWSc 92*
**Jones,** Blanche Calloway 1902-1978 *FacFETw*
**Jones,** Bob, Jr. 1911- *WrDr 92*
**Jones,** Bob Gordon 1932- *WhoRel 92, WhoWest 92*
**Jones,** Bobby 1902-1971 *FacFETw*
**Jones,** Bobby 1933- *WhoBlA 92*
**Jones,** Bobby Truesdell 1933- *WhoAmP 91*
**Jones,** Bonnie Louise 1952- *WhoBlA 92*
**Jones,** Booker Tee 1939- *WhoBlA 92*
**Jones,** Bradford B. 1951- *WhoEnt 92*
**Jones,** Bradford Clay 1959- *WhoMW 92*
**Jones,** Brent M. 1946- *WhoBlA 92*
**Jones,** Brent R. 1963- *WhoMW 92*
**Jones,** Brereton C 1939- *WhoAmP 91*
**Jones,** Brian 1938- *ConPo 91, IntAu&W 91, WrDr 92*
**Jones,** Brian Harrison 1951- *WhoMW 92*
**Jones,** Brian Herbert 1937- *AmMWSc 92*
**Jones,** Brian Keith 1943- *WhoRel 92*
**Jones,** Brian Kevin 1956- *WhoFI 92*
**Jones,** Brian Leslie 1930- *Who 92*
**Jones,** Brinley *Who 92*
**Jones,** Bryn 1927- *TwCPaSc*
**Jones,** Buck 1940- *WhoBlA 92*
**Jones,** Burton Fredrick 1942- *AmMWSc 92*
**Jones,** Burton Ira 1934- *WhoRel 92*

**Jones,** Butler Alfonso 1916- *WhoBlA 92*
**Jones,** C. David 1939- *WhoMW 92*
**Jones,** C Goodman *WhoIns 92*
**Jones,** C. J. 1943- *WhoEnt 92*
**Jones,** C. Kingsley 1926- *TwCPaSc*
**Jones,** C Robert 1933- *AmMWSc 92*
**Jones,** Cadwallader 1813-1899 *DcNCBi 3*
**Jones,** Caldwell 1950- *WhoBlA 92*
**Jones,** Calico *TwCWW 91*
**Jones,** Calvin 1775-1846 *DcNCBi 3*
**Jones,** Calvin Bell 1934- *WhoBlA 92*
**Jones,** Carl Joseph 1949- *AmMWSc 92*
**Jones,** Carl L. 1933- *WhoBlA 92*
**Jones,** Carl Trainer 1910- *AmMWSc 92*
**Jones,** Carol A 1936- *AmMWSc 92*
**Jones,** Carol Adaire 1951- *WhoFI 92*
**Jones,** Carol Joyce 1938- *WhoBlA 92*
**Jones,** Carol Leigh 1949- *WhoEnt 92*
**Jones,** Carol Wells 1944- *WhoMW 92*
**Jones,** Caroline Robinson 1942- *WhoBlA 92*
**Jones,** Carolyn G. 1943- *WhoBlA 92*
**Jones,** Carolyn Jane 1937- *WhoRel 92*
**Jones,** Casey *BenetAL 91*
**Jones,** Casey C 1915- *WhoAmP 91, WhoBlA 92*
**Jones,** Cedric Decorrus 1960- *WhoBlA 92*
**Jones,** Charisse Monsio 1965- *WhoBlA 92*
**Jones,** Charles 1910- *NewAmDM*
**Jones,** Charles 1926- *AmMWSc 92*
**Jones,** Charles 1962- *WhoBlA 92*
**Jones,** Charles, Jr. 1946- *WhoBlA 92*
**Jones,** Charles A. 1934- *WhoBlA 92*
**Jones,** Charles Beynon Lloyd 1932- *Who 92*
**Jones,** Charles Calhoun 1940- *WhoMW 92*
**Jones,** Charles D 1950- *WhoAmP 91*
**Jones,** Charles Davis 1917- *WhoFI 92*
**Jones,** Charles E 1920- *AmMWSc 92*
**Jones,** Charles E 1928- *AmMWSc 92*
**Jones,** Charles Edward 1936- *Who 92*
**Jones,** Charles Edward 1956- *WhoRel 92*
**Jones,** Charles Edwin 1932- *WhoRel 92*
**Jones,** Charles Eric, Jr. 1957- *WhoAmL 92*
**Jones,** Charles Fred 1930- *WhoAmP 91*
**Jones,** Charles Gregory 1950- *WhoMW 92*
**Jones,** Charles Ian McMillan 1934- *Who 92*
**Jones,** Charles Irving 1943- *WhoRel 92, WhoWest 92*
**Jones,** Charles J. 1940- *WhoWest 92*
**Jones,** Charles Leonard 1949- *WhoRel 92, WhoWest 92*
**Jones,** Charles Martin 1912- *WhoEnt 92*
**Jones,** Charles Miller, Jr 1935- *AmMWSc 92*
**Jones,** Charles Price 1865-1949 *RelLAm 91*
**Jones,** Charles R 1944- *WhoAmP 91*
**Jones,** Charles S. 1941- *WhoRel 92*
**Jones,** Charles Sam 1956- *WhoAmP 91*
**Jones,** Charles W. 1923- *WhoMW 92*
**Jones,** Charlie *LesBEnT 92*
**Jones,** Charlotte Schiff *LesBEnT 92*
**Jones,** Chester George 1936- *AmMWSc 92*
**Jones,** Chester Ray 1946- *WhoBlA 92*
**Jones,** Christine Miller *WhoBlA 92*
**Jones,** Christine Miller 1929- *WhoAmP 91*
**Jones,** Christopher 1937- *WrDr 92*
**Jones,** Christopher 1958- *TwCPaSc*
**Jones,** Christopher Dennis 1949- *IntAu&W 91*
**Jones,** Christopher Ernest 1952- *WhoMW 92*
**Jones,** Christopher Kent 1959- *WhoWest 92*
**Jones,** Christopher L. *Who 92*
**Jones,** Chuck *IntMPA 92, LesBEnT 92, WhoEnt 92*
**Jones,** Chuck 1912- *IntMPA 92*
**Jones,** Cindy 1949- *WhoMW 92*
**Jones,** Claiborne Stribling 1914- *AmMWSc 92*
**Jones,** Clara Padilla 1940- *WhoAmP 91*
**Jones,** Clara Stanton 1913- *NotBlAW 92 [port]*
**Jones,** Clarance J. 1943- *WhoBlA 92*
**Jones,** Clarance W. 1938- *WhoBlA 92*
**Jones,** Clarence J., Jr. 1933- *WhoBlA 92*
**Jones,** Clarence S 1926- *AmMWSc 92*
**Jones,** Clark R. 1920- *IntMPA 92*
**Jones,** Claudella Archambeault 1938- *WhoMW 92*
**Jones,** Claudia Ann 1954- *WhoMW 92*
**Jones,** Clement *Who 92*
**Jones,** Cleon Boyd 1961- *WhoWest 92*
**Jones,** Clifford Aaron 1912- *WhoAmL 92*
**Jones,** Clifford Anthony, Sr. 1943- *WhoBlA 92*
**Jones,** Clifford Kenneth 1932- *AmMWSc 92*
**Jones,** Clifford L 1927- *WhoAmP 91*
**Jones,** Clifford M. 1902- *WrDr 92*
**Jones,** Clifton Patrick 1927- *WhoBlA 92*
**Jones,** Clifton Ralph 1910- *WhoBlA 92*
**Jones,** Clive Gareth 1951- *AmMWSc 92*
**Jones,** Clive Lawson 1937- *Who 92*
**Jones,** Cloyzelle Karrelle *WhoBlA 92*
**Jones,** Clyde Bruce 1944- *WhoFI 92*
**Jones,** Clyde Eugene 1954- *WhoBlA 92*
**Jones,** Clyde Joe 1935- *AmMWSc 92*
**Jones,** Colin 1934- *TwCPaSc*
**Jones,** Cornell 1923- *WhoBlA 92*
**Jones,** Craig 1945- *ConAu 34NR*
**Jones,** Craig Robert 1946- *WhoWest 92*
**Jones,** Cranston E. 1918-1991 *ConAu 134, NewYTBS 91*
**Jones,** Creighton Clinton 1913- *AmMWSc 92*
**Jones,** Curley C. 1941- *WhoBlA 92*
**Jones,** Curtis H *WhoAmP 91*
**Jones,** Cynthia Jane 1963- *WhoAmL 92*
**Jones,** D F *IntAu&W 91*
**Jones,** D F d1981 *TwCSFW 91*
**Jones,** D. G. 1929- *BenetAL 91, ConPo 91, WrDr 92*
**Jones,** D Lee 1903- *WhoAmP 91*
**Jones,** D. Michael 1942- *WhoFI 92, WhoWest 92*
**Jones,** Dale Edwin 1948- *WhoAmL 92*
**Jones,** Dale P. 1936- *WhoFI 92*
**Jones,** Dale Robert 1924- *AmMWSc 92*
**Jones,** Dallas Wayne 1938- *AmMWSc 92*
**Jones,** Dane Robert 1947- *AmMWSc 92*
**Jones,** Daniel 1912- *ConCom 92*
**Jones,** Daniel David 1943- *AmMWSc 92*
**Jones,** Daniel Elven 1943- *AmMWSc 92*
**Jones,** Daniel Gruffydd 1933- *Who 92*
**Jones,** Daniel Jenkyn 1912- *IntWW 91*
**Jones,** Daniel Patrick 1941- *AmMWSc 92*
**Jones,** Daniel Silas, Jr 1943- *AmMWSc 92*
**Jones,** Danny 1950- *WhoAmP 91*
**Jones,** Daryl *WhoAmP 91*
**Jones,** Daryl 1946- *ConAu 134*
**Jones,** Daryl Emrys 1946- *WhoWest 92*
**Jones,** David 1895-1974 *CnDBLB 7 [port], FacFETw, RfGEnL 91, TwCPaSc*
**Jones,** David 1934- *IntMPA 92*
**Jones,** David 1940- *Who 92*
**Jones,** David A. *Who 92*
**Jones,** David A, Jr 1937- *AmMWSc 92*
**Jones,** David Alan 1954- *WhoRel 92*
**Jones,** David Allen 1931- *WhoFI 92*
**Jones,** David Arthur 1961- *WhoAmL 92*
**Jones,** David B 1921- *AmMWSc 92*
**Jones,** David Charles 1921- *IntWW 91*
**Jones,** David Charles 1935- *WhoFI 92*
**Jones,** David Charles 1943- *Who 92*
**Jones,** David Colin 1943- *WhoRel 92*
**Jones,** David Evan Alun 1925- *Who 92*
**Jones,** David F. 1934- *WhoMW 92*
**Jones,** David G. *Who 92*
**Jones,** David George 1941- *Who 92*
**Jones,** David Hartley 1939- *AmMWSc 92*
**Jones,** David Hay 1959- *ConAu 133*
**Jones,** David Hugh 1934- *Who 92, WhoEnt 92*
**Jones,** David Ian Stewart 1934- *Who 92*
**Jones,** David John 1933- *WhoIns 92*
**Jones,** David John 1934- *WhoWest 92*
**Jones,** David L. 1948- *WhoFI 92*
**Jones,** David Lawrence 1930- *AmMWSc 92*
**Jones,** David le Brun 1923- *Who 92*
**Jones,** David Lee 1948- *WhoFI 92*
**Jones,** David Lee 1956- *WhoRel 92*
**Jones,** David Leigh 1954- *WhoRel 92*
**Jones,** David Lloyd 1919- *AmMWSc 92*
**Jones,** David M. *Who 92*
**Jones,** David M 1951- *WhoAmP 91*
**Jones,** David Martin 1944- *Who 92*
**Jones,** David Morgan 1915- *Who 92*
**Jones,** David Norris 1948- *WhoAmP 91*
**Jones,** David Phillips 1841-1903 *BiInAmS*
**Jones,** David Robert 1941- *AmMWSc 92*
**Jones,** David Russell 1948- *WhoBlA 92*
**Jones,** David Vernon 1950- *WhoAmL 92*
**Jones,** David Wayne 1948- *WhoEnt 92*
**Jones,** Davy 1946- *ConTFT 9*
**Jones,** Deacon 1934- *WhoBlA 92*
**Jones,** Dean 1931- *IntMPA 92*
**Jones,** Dean Carroll *WhoEnt 92*
**Jones,** Dean Clarence 1932- *WhoWest 92*
**Jones,** Dean Paul 1949- *AmMWSc 92*
**Jones,** Debora Elaine 1959- *WhoBlA 92*
**Jones,** Deborah *TwCPaSc*
**Jones,** Dee R. 1939- *WhoRel 92*
**Jones,** Della *Who 92*
**Jones,** Delmos J. 1936- *WhoBlA 92*
**Jones,** Delna L 1940- *WhoAmP 91*
**Jones,** Delores 1954- *WhoBlA 92*
**Jones,** Delwin 1924- *WhoAmP 91*
**Jones,** Dennis Edmund 1943- *WhoEnt 92*
**Jones,** Dennis L 1941- *WhoAmP 91*
**Jones,** Dennis Neil 1946- *WhoRel 92*
**Jones,** Dennis Pierce 1940- *WhoFI 92, WhoWest 92*
**Jones,** Denzil Eugene 1910- *WhoAmP 91*
**Jones,** Derek A. *Who 92*
**Jones,** Derek Charles 1946- *WhoFI 92*
**Jones,** Derek John Claremont 1927- *Who 92*
**Jones,** Derek R. *Who 92*
**Jones,** Derek William 1933- *AmMWSc 92*
**Jones,** Derwyn Dixon 1925- *Who 92, WhoRel 92*
**Jones,** Desmond V. *Who 92*
**Jones,** DeVerges Booker 1950- *WhoBlA 92*
**Jones,** Diana Wynne 1934- *IntAu&W 91, WrDr 92*
**Jones,** Don *DrAPF 91*
**Jones,** Don E 1949- *WhoAmP 91*
**Jones,** Donald 1931- *ConAu 34NR*
**Jones,** Donald Akers 1930- *AmMWSc 92*
**Jones,** Donald Barry 1939- *WhoRel 92*
**Jones,** Donald Eugene 1934- *AmMWSc 92*
**Jones,** Donald Forsyth 1942- *WhoWest 92*
**Jones,** Donald L. *WhoWest 92*
**Jones,** Donald Ray 1947- *WhoFI 92, WhoWest 92*
**Jones,** Donald W. 1939- *WhoBlA 92*
**Jones,** Donlan F 1930- *AmMWSc 92*
**Jones,** Donna M 1939- *WhoAmP 91*
**Jones,** Dorinda A. 1926- *WhoBlA 92*
**Jones,** Dorothy Fuller 1946- *WhoMW 92*
**Jones,** Dorothy Holder 1925?-1991 *ConAu 134*
**Jones,** Dorsey W. 1939- *WhoMW 92*
**Jones,** Doug Keith 1948- *WhoEnt 92*
**Jones,** Douglas 1949- *WhoHisp 92*
**Jones,** Douglas C 1924- *TwCWW 91, WrDr 92*
**Jones,** Douglas Emron 1930- *AmMWSc 92*
**Jones,** Douglas Epps 1930- *AmMWSc 92*
**Jones,** Douglas L 1948- *AmMWSc 92*
**Jones,** Douglas Linwood 1937- *AmMWSc 92*
**Jones,** Douglas R *WhoAmP 91*
**Jones,** Douglas Rawlinson 1919- *Who 92*
**Jones,** Douglas Samuel 1922- *IntWW 91, Who 92*
**Jones,** Duane L. 1937- *WhoBlA 92*
**Jones,** Duvall Albert 1933- *AmMWSc 92*
**Jones,** Dwight Elmo 1952- *BlkOlyM*
**Jones,** E. Bradley 1927- *IntWW 91*
**Jones,** E. Bruce 1933- *WhoFI 92*
**Jones,** E. Fay *NewYTBS 91*
**Jones,** E M T 1924- *AmMWSc 92*
**Jones,** E. Stewart, Jr. 1941- *WhoAmL 92, WhoFI 92*
**Jones,** E. Thomas 1950- *WhoAmL 92*
**Jones,** Earl 1925- *WhoWest 92*
**Jones,** Earl 1964- *BlkOlyM*
**Jones,** Earl Frederick 1949- *WhoBlA 92*
**Jones,** Earle Douglas 1931- *AmMWSc 92*
**Jones,** Eben Lee 1949- *WhoFI 92*
**Jones,** Ebenezer 1820-1860 *RfGEnL 91*
**Jones,** Ebon Richard 1944- *WhoFI 92, WhoWest 92*
**Jones,** Ed 1912- *WhoAmP 91*
**Jones,** Eddie, Jr. 1950- *WhoRel 92*
**Jones,** Edgar Allan, Jr. 1921- *WhoAmL 92*
**Jones,** Edgar DeWitt 1876-1956 *RelLAm 91*
**Jones,** Edgar Stafford 1909- *Who 92*
**Jones,** Edith H *WhoAmP 91*
**Jones,** Edith Hollan 1949- *WhoAmL 92*
**Jones,** Edith Irby 1927- *WhoBlA 92*
**Jones,** Edmund 1848-1920 *DcNCBi 3*
**Jones,** Edmund Samuel Philip 1934- *WhoRel 92*
**Jones,** Edward *Who 92*
**Jones,** Edward 1762-1841 *DcNCBi 3*
**Jones,** Edward A. 1903-1981 *ConAu 134*
**Jones,** Edward Ames 1952- *WhoFI 92*
**Jones,** Edward David 1920- *AmMWSc 92*
**Jones,** Edward Francis 1932- *WhoEnt 92*
**Jones,** Edward G. *Who 92*
**Jones,** Edward George 1939- *AmMWSc 92*
**Jones,** Edward Grant 1942- *AmMWSc 92*
**Jones,** Edward Lee 1951- *WhoBlA 92*
**Jones,** Edward Louis 1922- *WhoBlA 92, WhoWest 92*
**Jones,** Edward Martin F. *Who 92*
**Jones,** Edward Norman 1914- *WhoBlA 92*
**Jones,** Edward O, Jr 1922- *AmMWSc 92*
**Jones,** Edward Raymond 1943- *AmMWSc 92*
**Jones,** Edward Stephen 1931- *AmMWSc 92*
**Jones,** Edward W. *Who 92*
**Jones,** Edward Warburton 1912- *Who 92*
**Jones,** Edward White, II 1921- *WhoAmL 92*
**Jones,** Edward Witker 1929- *WhoRel 92*
**Jones,** Edwin C 1903- *AmMWSc 92*
**Jones,** Edwin C, Jr 1934- *AmMWSc 92*
**Jones,** Edwin Rudolph, Jr 1938- *AmMWSc 92*
**Jones,** Effie Hall 1928- *WhoBlA 92*
**Jones,** Eifion 1912- *Who 92*
**Jones,** Elaine R. 1944- *WhoBlA 92*
**Jones,** Eldon Melton 1914- *AmMWSc 92*
**Jones,** Eleanor Green Dawley 1929- *AmMWSc 92*
**Jones,** Eleri Wynne 1933- *Who 92*
**Jones,** Elizabeth Selle 1926- *WhoRel 92*
**Jones,** Elizabeth W 1939- *AmMWSc 92*
**Jones,** Elmer Everett 1926- *AmMWSc 92*
**Jones,** Elnetta Griffin 1934- *WhoBlA 92*
**Jones,** Elvin 1927- *NewAmDM*
**Jones,** Emil, Jr 1935- *WhoAmP 91, WhoBlA 92, WhoMW 92*
**Jones,** Emlyn Bartley *Who 92*
**Jones,** Emma Pettway 1945- *WhoBlA 92*
**Jones,** Emrys *Who 92*
**Jones,** Emrys 1920- *Who 92, WrDr 92*
**Jones,** Emrys Lloyd 1931- *Who 92*
**Jones,** Endsley Terrence 1941- *WhoMW 92*
**Jones,** Enoch 1922- *WhoBlA 92*
**Jones,** Eric 1904-1963 *TwCPaSc*
**Jones,** Eric Daniel 1936- *AmMWSc 92*
**Jones,** Eric Lionel 1936- *WrDr 92*
**Jones,** Eric Louis 1948- *WhoBlA 92*
**Jones,** Eric Manning 1944- *AmMWSc 92*
**Jones,** Eric Phillip 1947- *WhoEnt 92*
**Jones,** Eric S. *Who 92*
**Jones,** Eric Thomas 1961- *WhoMW 92*
**Jones,** Eric Wynn 1924- *AmMWSc 92*
**Jones,** Ernest 1923- *WhoBlA 92*
**Jones,** Ernest Addison 1918- *AmMWSc 92*
**Jones,** Ernest Austin, Jr 1960- *AmMWSc 92*
**Jones,** Ernest Edward 1931- *Who 92, WhoRel 92*
**Jones,** Ernest Edward 1944- *WhoBlA 92*
**Jones,** Ernest Olin 1923- *AmMWSc 92*
**Jones,** Ervin Edward 1938- *WhoBlA 92*
**Jones,** Ethelene Dyer 1930- *IntAu&W 91*
**Jones,** Etta *WhoEnt 92*
**Jones,** Eugene Gordon 1929- *WhoMW 92*
**Jones,** Eugene Laverne 1928- *AmMWSc 92*
**Jones,** Eurfron Gwynne 1934- *Who 92*
**Jones,** Eva 1931- *WhoBlA 92*
**Jones,** Evan *WhoAmP 91*
**Jones,** Evan 1931- *ConPo 91, WrDr 92*
**Jones,** Evan 1957- *WhoFI 92*
**Jones,** Evan Earl 1935- *AmMWSc 92*
**Jones,** Everet Clyde 1923- *AmMWSc 92*
**Jones,** Everett 1930- *AmMWSc 92*
**Jones,** Everett Bruce 1933- *AmMWSc 92*
**Jones,** Everett Le Roi 1934- *IntWW 91*
**Jones,** Ewan Perrins W. *Who 92*
**Jones,** Ewart 1911- *Who 92*
**Jones,** Ewart Ray Herbert 1911- *IntWW 91*
**Jones,** Ezell 1947- *WhoFI 92, WhoMW 92*
**Jones,** F. Ben 1932- *WhoFI 92*
**Jones,** Faber Benjamin 1932- *AmMWSc 92*
**Jones,** Farrell 1926- *WhoBlA 92*
**Jones,** Ferdinand Taylor, Jr. 1932- *WhoBlA 92*
**Jones,** Fernando 1964- *WhoMW 92*
**Jones,** Fielding *Who 92*
**Jones,** Floresta Deloris 1950- *WhoBlA 92*
**Jones,** Floyd Burton 1910- *AmMWSc 92*
**Jones,** Francis 1908- *Who 92*
**Jones,** Francis A, III 1935- *WhoAmP 91*
**Jones,** Francis Clark 1933- *WhoWest 92*
**Jones,** Francis Dunn 1923- *WhoMW 92*
**Jones,** Francis John 1928- *Who 92*
**Jones,** Francis Thomas 1933- *AmMWSc 92*
**Jones,** Francis Tucker 1905- *AmMWSc 92*
**Jones,** Frank 1950- *WhoBlA 92*
**Jones,** Frank Benson 1938- *WhoBlA 92*
**Jones,** Frank Culver 1932- *AmMWSc 92*
**Jones,** Frank Griffith 1941- *WhoAmL 92*
**Jones,** Frank Lancaster 1937- *WrDr 92*
**Jones,** Frank Llewellyn- 1907- *Who 92*
**Jones,** Frank Norton 1936- *AmMWSc 92*
**Jones,** Frank S. 1928- *WhoBlA 92*
**Jones,** Frank Stephen 1949- *IntAu&W 91*
**Jones,** Franklin 1939- *RelLAm 91*
**Jones,** Franklin Allan 1932- *WhoRel 92*
**Jones,** Franklin D. 1935- *WhoBlA 92*
**Jones,** Franklin D. 1939- *WhoBlA 92*
**Jones,** Franklin Del 1935- *AmMWSc 92*
**Jones,** Franklin M 1933- *AmMWSc 92*
**Jones,** Fred 1920- *Who 92*
**Jones,** Fred Cecil 1891-1956 *TwCPaSc*
**Jones,** Fred Reese 1935- *WhoAmP 91*
**Jones,** Frederick 1680?-1722 *DcNCBi 3*
**Jones,** Frederick Douglass, Jr. 1955- *WhoBlA 92*
**Jones,** Frederick Goodwin 1935- *AmMWSc 92*
**Jones,** Frederick Stanley 1953- *WhoRel 92*
**Jones,** Fredrick E. *WhoBlA 92*
**Jones,** Furman Madison, Jr. 1927- *WhoBlA 92*
**Jones,** G. Daniel *WhoBlA 92, WhoRel 92*
**Jones,** G. Marcus 1919- *WhoRel 92*
**Jones,** Galen Everts 1928- *AmMWSc 92*
**Jones,** Galen Ray 1948- *WhoWest 92*
**Jones,** Gareth *Who 92*
**Jones,** Gareth 1930- *Who 92, WrDr 92*
**Jones,** Gareth 1941- *TwCPaSc*
**Jones,** Garry A. 1943- *TwCPaSc*
**Jones,** Garth 1932- *AmMWSc 92*
**Jones,** Garth Wicks 1940- *AmMWSc 92*
**Jones,** Gary 1942- *WhoBlA 92*
**Jones,** Gary Edward 1940- *AmMWSc 92*
**Jones,** Gary Leland 1944- *WhoAmP 91*
**Jones,** Gary Lewis 1961- *WhoFI 92*
**Jones,** Gayl 1949- *AfrAmW, BenetAL 91, BlkLC [port], ConNov 91, IntAu&W 91, WhoBlA 92, WrDr 92*
**Jones,** Gemma 1942- *IntMPA 92*
**Jones,** Gene Kerry 1928- *WhoFI 92*
**Jones,** Gene Stanley 1951- *WhoEnt 92*
**Jones,** Genevieve 1906- *WhoEnt 92*
**Jones,** Geoffrey *Who 92*

Jones, Geoffrey M. Who 92
Jones, Geoffrey Melvill 1923- AmMWSc 92
Jones, Geoffrey Rippon R. Who 92
Jones, George 1800-1870 BiInAmS
Jones, George 1896- Who 92
Jones, George 1931- WhoEnt 92
Jones, George Albert 1904- WhoBlA 92
Jones, George Briscoe 1929- Who 92
Jones, George H. 1942- WhoBlA 92
Jones, George Henry 1942- AmMWSc 92
Jones, George Humphrey 1923- WhoMW 92
Jones, George R 1930- AmMWSc 92
Jones, George Tallmon 1897- WhoMW 92
Jones, George W. 1924- WhoBlA 92
Jones, George Washington, Jr. 1953- WhoAmL 92
Jones, George William 1837-1911 BiInAmS
Jones, George William 1930- WhoMW 92, WhoRel 92
Jones, George William 1938- Who 92
Jones, George Williams 1931- WhoBlA 92
Jones, George Wilson 1926- WhoAmP 91
Jones, Geraint Iwan 1917- IntWW 91, Who 92
Jones, Geraint Stanley 1936- Who 92
Jones, Gerald 1939- Who 92
Jones, Gerald E. 1937- WhoBlA 92
Jones, Gerald Joseph 1920- WhoWest 92
Jones, Gerald Murray 1941- AmMWSc 92
Jones, Gerald Walter 1942- AmMWSc 92
Jones, Gerald Winfield 1931- WhoBlA 92
Jones, Geraldine J. 1939- WhoBlA 92
Jones, Geraldine W 1929- WhoAmP 91
Jones, Gerallt Who 92
Jones, Geri Duncan 1958- WhoMW 92
Jones, Gerre Lyle 1926- WhoFI 92, WhoWest 92
Jones, Giffin Denison 1918- AmMWSc 92
Jones, Gilbert Fred 1930- AmMWSc 92
Jones, Gilda Lynn 1927- AmMWSc 92
Jones, Glendell Asbury, Jr 1939- WhoAmP 91
Jones, Glenn Clark 1935- AmMWSc 92
Jones, Glenn Williamson, Jr. 1948- WhoFI 92
Jones, Gloria Lee 1923- WhoAmP 91
Jones, Glower Whitehead 1936- WhoAmL 92
Jones, Glyn 1905- ConNov 91, ConPo 91, IntAu&W 91, WrDr 92
Jones, Glyn 1908- Who 92
Jones, Glyn 1930- TwCPaSc
Jones, Glyn 1936- TwCPaSc
Jones, Glyndwr 1935- Who 92
Jones, Glynn 1933- Who 92
Jones, Gordon Ervin 1936- AmMWSc 92
Jones, Gordon Frederick 1929- Who 92
Jones, Gordon Henry 1940- AmMWSc 92
Jones, Gordon Kempton 1946- WhoMW 92
Jones, Gordon Pearce 1927- Who 92
Jones, Gordon Wayne 1930- WhoFI 92
Jones, Grace WhoEnt 92
Jones, Grace 1952- IntMPA 92, IntWW 91
Jones, Grace 1954- WhoBlA 92
Jones, Graham Alfred 1935- AmMWSc 92
Jones, Graham Edward 1944- Who 92
Jones, Graham Julian 1936- Who 92
Jones, Graham Wyn 1943- Who 92
Jones, Grandpa 1913- NewAmDM
Jones, Grant 1922- WhoAmP 91
Jones, Gregg R IntAu&W 91
Jones, Gregory Lawing 1960- WhoAmL 92
Jones, Greta Waller 1939- WhoAmP 91
Jones, Griffith 1910- IntMPA 92
Jones, Griffith R. Who 92
Jones, Griffith Winston Guthrie 1914- Who 92
Jones, Grover William 1934- WhoBlA 92
Jones, Guilford, II 1943- AmMWSc 92
Jones, Guy Langston 1923- AmMWSc 92
Jones, Gwendolyn J. 1953- WhoBlA 92
Jones, Gwilym Haydn Who 92
Jones, Gwilym Strong 1942- AmMWSc 92
Jones, Gwilym Wyn 1926- Who 92
Jones, Gwyn Who 92
Jones, Gwyn 1907- ConNov 91, IntAu&W 91, Who 92, WrDr 92
Jones, Gwyn Idris M. Who 92
Jones, Gwyn Owain 1917- Who 92, WrDr 92
Jones, Gwyneth 1936- IntWW 91, NewAmDM, Who 92, WhoEnt 92
Jones, Gwyneth A 1952- TwCSFW 91, WrDr 92
Jones, Gwynoro Glyndwr 1942- Who 92
Jones, H. Douglas 1955- WhoAmL 92
Jones, H. Milton 1932- WhoFI 92
Jones, H. Thomas, II 1944- WhoBlA 92
Jones, H. W. Kasey 1942- WhoMW 92
Jones, Hamilton Chamberlain 1798-1868 DcNCBi 3
Jones, Hamilton Chamberlain, Jr. 1837-1904 DcNCBi 3
Jones, Hank 1918- NewAmDM
Jones, Hardi Liddell 1942- WhoBlA 92
Jones, Harley M. 1936- WhoBlA 92
Jones, Harold 1904- TwCPaSc
Jones, Harold Calvert, II 1949- WhoRel 92
Jones, Harold Lester 1943- AmMWSc 92
Jones, Harold M. 1934- WhoBlA 92
Jones, Harold Roger 1947- WhoWest 92
Jones, Harold Trainer 1925- AmMWSc 92, WhoMW 92
Jones, Harry 1911- Who 92
Jones, Harry Austin TwCWW 91
Jones, Harry Clary 1865-1916 BiInAmS
Jones, Hawatthia 1960- WhoRel 92
Jones, Haydn Harold 1920- Who 92
Jones, Hayes Wendell 1938- BlkOlyM
Jones, Helen WrDr 92
Jones, Helen Hampton 1941- WhoBlA 92
Jones, Helen M 1924- WhoAmP 91
Jones, Helena Speiser 1940- AmMWSc 92
Jones, Henry 1912- IntMPA 92, WhoEnt 92
Jones, Henry Alphonso 1936- WhoWest 92
Jones, Henry Arthur 1851-1929 RfGEnL 91
Jones, Henry Arthur 1917- Who 92
Jones, Henry John 1924- Who 92
Jones, Henry Vinton 1938- WhoIns 92
Jones, Herbert WhoAmP 91
Jones, Herbert, Jr 1930- WhoAmP 91
Jones, Herbert C. 1936- WhoBlA 92
Jones, Herbert Lyon 1866?-1898 BiInAmS
Jones, Herman Harvey, Jr. 1925- WhoBlA 92
Jones, Hettie DrAPF 91
Jones, Hilary Pollard 1863-1938 FacFETw
Jones, Hobart Wayne 1921- AmMWSc 92
Jones, Homer Daniel, Jr. 1917- WhoRel 92
Jones, Hortense 1918- WhoBlA 92
Jones, Howard 1937- AmMWSc 92
Jones, Howard James 1944- WhoBlA 92
Jones, Howard Mumford 1892-1980 BenetAL 91
Jones, Howard St Claire, Jr 1921- AmMWSc 92
Jones, Hugh Who 92
Jones, Hugh 1670?-1760 BenetAL 91
Jones, Hugh 1692?-1760 BiInAmS
Jones, Hugh Alan 1950- WhoAmP 91
Jones, Hugh Jarrett H. Who 92
Jones, Hugh Richard, Jr. 1938- WhoAmL 92
Jones, Hughie Who 92
Jones, Hywel Francis 1928- Who 92
Jones, Hywel Glyn 1948- Who 92
Jones, Hywel James 1918- Who 92
Jones, I. Gene WhoBlA 92
Jones, Ian 1947- TwCPaSc
Jones, Ian C. Who 92
Jones, Ian E. Who 92
Jones, Ida Kilpatrick 1924- WhoBlA 92
Jones, Ida M. 1953- WhoBlA 92
Jones, Idus, Jr. 1927- WhoBlA 92
Jones, Idwal 1892-1964 BenetAL 91
Jones, Ieuan Wyn 1949- Who 92
Jones, Ilston Percival Ll. Who 92
Jones, Ina DrAPF 91
Jones, Ingrid Saunders 1945- WhoBlA 92
Jones, Inigo 1573?-1652 NewAmDM
Jones, Ira 1934- AmMWSc 92
Jones, Irving Wendell AmMWSc 92
Jones, Isaac, Jr. 1933- WhoBlA 92
Jones, Isham Russell, II 1942- WhoEnt 92
Jones, Ivan Dunlavy 1903- AmMWSc 92
Jones, Ivor R. Who 92
Jones, J B 1923- AmMWSc 92
Jones, J Benton, Jr 1930- AmMWSc 92
Jones, J.E.M. DrAPF 91
Jones, J. Gilbert 1922- WhoFI 92, WhoWest 92
Jones, J Knox, Jr 1929- AmMWSc 92
Jones, J L, Jr 1918- AmMWSc 92
Jones, J P 1941- AmMWSc 92
Jones, J. Raymond d1991 NewYTBS 91 [port]
Jones, J. William 1929- WhoRel 92
Jones, Jack 1938- WhoEnt 92
Jones, Jack Bristol 1931- WhoWest 92
Jones, Jack E. 1919- WhoRel 92
Jones, Jack Earl 1925- AmMWSc 92
Jones, Jack Edenfield 1929- AmMWSc 92
Jones, Jack L. Who 92
Jones, Jack W. 1940- WhoEnt 92
Jones, Jacqueline 1948- WrDr 92
Jones, Jacqueline Yvonne 1928- WhoAmP 91
Jones, James 1914- Who 92
Jones, James 1921-1977 BenetAL 91, FacFETw, LiExTwC
Jones, James 1961- WhoBlA 92
Jones, James A. 1932- WhoBlA 92
Jones, James Addison 1869-1950 DcNCBi 3
Jones, James Alonzo 1933- WhoRel 92
Jones, James Alton 1956- WhoAmL 92
Jones, James Athearn 1791-1854 BenetAL 91
Jones, James Bennett 1931- WhoBlA 92
Jones, James C. 1913- WhoBlA 92
Jones, James Darren 1959- AmMWSc 92
Jones, James Donald 1930- AmMWSc 92
Jones, James Earl 1931- FacFETw, IntMPA 92, WhoBlA 92, WhoEnt 92
Jones, James Edward 1896- WhoBlA 92
Jones, James Edward 1924- AmMWSc 92
Jones, James Edward 1934- WhoRel 92
Jones, James Edward 1939- WhoMW 92
Jones, James Edward, Jr. 1924- WhoBlA 92
Jones, James Eirug Thomas 1927- Who 92
Jones, James Francis, Jr 1934- WhoAmP 91
Jones, James G. 1936- WhoBlA 92
Jones, James Gary 1950- WhoAmP 91
Jones, James Graham 1948- WhoFI 92, WhoMW 92
Jones, James H. 1831-1921 DcNCBi 3
Jones, James Harold 1930- WhoWest 92
Jones, James Henry 1952- AmMWSc 92
Jones, James Holden 1928- AmMWSc 92
Jones, James Howard 1940- WhoMW 92
Jones, James Jordan 1938- AmMWSc 92, WhoWest 92
Jones, James L 1926- AmMWSc 92
Jones, James Lamar 1958- WhoMW 92
Jones, James Larkin 1913- IntWW 91, Who 92
Jones, James McCoy 1941- WhoBlA 92
Jones, James Ogden AmMWSc 92
Jones, James P. 1914- WhoBlA 92
Jones, James Parker 1940- WhoAmP 91
Jones, James R. 1939- WhoFI 92
Jones, James Randall 1925- WhoBlA 92
Jones, James Robert 1931- AmMWSc 92
Jones, James Robert 1939- IntWW 91, WhoAmP 91
Jones, James Robert 1952- WhoEnt 92
Jones, James Roger 1952- Who 92
Jones, James Thomas 1942- WhoAmP 91, WhoWest 92
Jones, James Thomas 1949- WhoFI 92
Jones, James Thomas, Jr. 1946- WhoFI 92
Jones, James V. 1942- WhoBlA 92
Jones, James Wesley 1935- WhoBlA 92
Jones, Jan Laverty WhoWest 92
Jones, Janet Benson J.B. 1952- WhoWest 92
Jones, Janet Dulin 1957- WhoEnt 92
Jones, Janice Lorraine 1943- AmMWSc 92
Jones, Janis Laverty 1949- WhoFI 92, WhoWest 92
Jones, Jean DrAPF 91
Jones, Jean 1927- TwCPaSc
Jones, Jeanette 1950- AmMWSc 92
Jones, Jeffrey 1947- IntMPA 92
Jones, Jeffrey Foster 1944- WhoAmL 92
Jones, Jeffrey Gordon 1954- WhoMW 92
Jones, Jeffrey Richard 1921- Who 92
Jones, Jeffrey Thad 1954- WhoAmL 92
Jones, Jenkin Lloyd 1843-1918 AmPeW
Jones, Jennie Y. 1921- WhoBlA 92
Jones, Jennifer Who 92, WhoBlA 92
Jones, Jennifer 1919- IntMPA 92, WhoEnt 92
Jones, Jennings Hinch 1913- AmMWSc 92
Jones, Jerold W 1937- AmMWSc 92
Jones, Jerome B. 1947- WhoBlA 92
Jones, Jerrauld Cory 1954- WhoAmP 91
Jones, Jerry D. 1951- WhoRel 92
Jones, Jerry Earl 1955- WhoFI 92
Jones, Jerry Latham 1946- AmMWSc 92
Jones, Jerry Lynn 1933- AmMWSc 92
Jones, Jerry T. 1936- WhoBlA 92
Jones, Jess Harold 1935- AmMWSc 92
Jones, Jesse Holman 1874-1956 FacFETw
Jones, Jesse J., Jr. d1990 WhoBlA 92N
Jones, Jesse W 1931- AmMWSc 92, WhoAmP 91, WhoBlA 92
Jones, Jesse Weimar 1895-1968 DcNCBi 3
Jones, Jim 1931-1978 RelLAm 91
Jones, Jim Belton 1940- WhoAmP 91
Jones, Jimmie Dene 1939- WhoBlA 92
Jones, Jimmy Barthel 1933- AmMWSc 92
Jones, Jingo ScFEYrs
Jones, Jo TwCPaSc
Jones, Jo 1911-1985 NewAmDM
Jones, Joan Ann 1942- WhoWest 92
Jones, Joanna IntAu&W 91X, WrDr 92
Jones, Joe Maxey 1942- AmMWSc 92
Jones, John Who 92
Jones, John 1817-1879 DcNCBi 3
Jones, John 1924- WrDr 92
Jones, John 1926- TwCPaSc
Jones, John, Jr 1917- AmMWSc 92
Jones, John A 1932- AmMWSc 92
Jones, John Ackland 1934- AmMWSc 92
Jones, John Bailey 1927- WhoAmL 92, WhoMW 92
Jones, John Barclay, Jr. 1928- WhoAmL 92
Jones, John Beauchamp 1810-1866 BenetAL 91
Jones, John Bryan 1934- AmMWSc 92
Jones, John Clement 1915- Who 92
Jones, John Dewi 1926- AmMWSc 92
Jones, John Edward 1914- Who 92
Jones, John Elfed 1933- Who 92
Jones, John Emrys 1914- Who 92
Jones, John Ernest A. Who 92
Jones, John Ernest P. Who 92
Jones, John Evan 1930- AmMWSc 92
Jones, John F 1932- AmMWSc 92
Jones, John Finbar 1929- WhoWest 92
Jones, John Frank 1922- WhoAmL 92
Jones, John Gareth 1936- Who 92
Jones, John Geoffrey 1928- Who 92
Jones, John H. Who 92
Jones, John H, Jr 1944- WhoIns 92
Jones, John Henry H. Who 92
Jones, John Hubert E. Who 92
Jones, John J. ConAu 133
Jones, John Kenneth 1910- Who 92
Jones, John Knighton C. Who 92
Jones, John L. 1939- WhoBlA 92
Jones, John Lewis 1923- Who 92
Jones, John Maurice 1931- Who 92
Jones, John Murray R. Who 92
Jones, John P. 1915- WhoBlA 92
Jones, John Paul 1747-1792 BenetAL 91, BlkwEAR, RComAH
Jones, John Paul 1924- AmMWSc 92
Jones, John Paul 1932- AmMWSc 92
Jones, John Paul 1940- AmMWSc 92
Jones, John Paul 1944- WhoAmL 92
Jones, John Prichard Who 92
Jones, John Richard 1947- AmMWSc 92
Jones, John Stephen Langton 1889- Who 92
Jones, John T 1940- WhoIns 92
Jones, John Taylor 1932- AmMWSc 92
Jones, John Verrier 1930- AmMWSc 92
Jones, John Wesley 1942- WhoWest 92
Jones, John Wesley 1958- BlkOlyM
Jones, John William 1961- WhoWest 92
Jones, John Winston 1791-1848 AmPolLe
Jones, Johnnie A., III 1953- WhoAmL 92
Jones, Johnnie Anderson 1919- WhoBlA 92
Jones, Johnny L. 1933- WhoBlA 92
Jones, Johnnye M 1943- AmMWSc 92
Jones, Johnston Blakeley 1814-1889 DcNCBi 3
Jones, Joie Pierce 1941- AmMWSc 92
Jones, Jonah 1919- TwCPaSc
Jones, Joni Lou 1932- WhoBlA 92
Jones, Joseph 1833-1896 BiInAmS
Jones, Joseph 1928- WhoBlA 92
Jones, Joseph Brent 1955- WhoAmL 92
Jones, Joseph Louis 1923- WhoFI 92
Jones, Joseph Seawell 1806?-1855 DcNCBi 3
Jones, Joseph Stevens 1809-1877 BenetAL 91
Jones, Joyce Howell 1944- AmMWSc 92
Jones, Judy Ann 1935- WhoAmP 91
Jones, Julia 1923- IntAu&W 91, WrDr 92
Jones, Julia Coleman 1919- WhoAmP 91
Jones, Julia Hughes 1939- WhoAmP 91
Jones, Julius Gamble, III 1952- WhoFI 92
Jones, Justin 1961- TwCPaSc
Jones, K C 1932- BlkOlyM, WhoBlA 92, WhoWest 92
Jones, Kaplin S. 1953- WhoAmL 92
Jones, Katharine Jean 1940- WhoFI 92
Jones, Katherine Borst 1948- WhoEnt 92
Jones, Katherine Elizabeth Butler 1936- WhoBlA 92
Jones, Kathleen 1922- Who 92
Jones, Kathryn Ann 1950- WhoMW 92
Jones, Kathryn Cherie 1955- WhoRel 92
Jones, Kathryn Kristy 1958- WhoMW 92
Jones, Kathy IntMPA 92
Jones, Kathy Rambus 1950- WhoRel 92
Jones, Kay H 1935- AmMWSc 92
Jones, Kaylie 1960- WrDr 92
Jones, Keith Alden 1941- WhoAmL 92
Jones, Keith H. Who 92
Jones, Keith Marshall, III 1945- WhoFI 92
Jones, Keith Stephen 1911- Who 92
Jones, Keith Warlow 1928- AmMWSc 92
Jones, Kelsey A. 1933- WhoBlA 92
Jones, Kelvin Samuel 1947- WhoRel 92
Jones, Ken 1938- WhoBlA 92
Jones, Ken Paul 1959- WhoAmL 92
Jones, Ken Wayne 1951- WhoRel 92
Jones, Kenn D. 1956- WhoEnt 92
Jones, Kenneth Who 92
Jones, Kenneth 1921- Who 92
Jones, Kenneth C. WhoRel 92
Jones, Kenneth Charles 1934- AmMWSc 92
Jones, Kenneth Edward 1952- WhoFI 92
Jones, Kenneth Leroy WhoBlA 92
Jones, Kenneth Lester 1905- AmMWSc 92
Jones, Kenneth Merle 1937- WhoWest 92
Jones, Kenneth Sheldon, II 1968- WhoAmP 91
Jones, Kenneth Wayne 1946- AmMWSc 92
Jones, Kenneth Westcott 1921- IntAu&W 91
Jones, Kent Albert 1953- WhoFI 92
Jones, Kevin McDill 1955- AmMWSc 92
Jones, Kevin Michael 1963- WhoFI 92
Jones, Kevin Scott 1958- AmMWSc 92
Jones, King Solomon WhoBlA 92
Jones, Kirkland C. 1938- WhoBlA 92

Jones, Kirkland Lee 1941- AmMWSc 92
Jones, L E 1910- AmMWSc 92
Jones, L. Q. 1927- WhoEnt 92
Jones, Lafayette Glenn 1944- WhoBlA 92
Jones, Landon Y. 1943- WrDr 92
Jones, Larri Sue 1966- WhoEnt 92
Jones, Larry DrAPF 91
Jones, Larry Currell 1948- WhoAmL 92
Jones, Larry David 1956- WhoRel 92
Jones, Larry E. 1938- WhoRel 92
Jones, Larry Earl 1946- WhoBlA 92
Jones, Larry Hudson 1948- AmMWSc 92
Jones, Larry Mallory 1939- WhoAmP 91
Jones, Larry Philip 1934- AmMWSc 92
Jones, Larry T. 1934- WhoFI 92
Jones, Larry Warner 1934- AmMWSc 92
Jones, Larry Wayne 1950- WhoBlA 92
Jones, Laura Mae 1949- WhoBlA 92
Jones, Lauren Denise 1964- WhoEnt 92
Jones, Laurence 1933- Who 92
Jones, Laurie Ganong 1954- WhoFI 92
Jones, Lawrence Edward 1952- WhoMW 92
Jones, Lawrence Kelly 1953- WhoAmL 92
Jones, Lawrence N. 1921- WhoBlA 92
Jones, Lawrence Neale 1921- WhoRel 92
Jones, Lawrence Ryman 1921- AmMWSc 92
Jones, Lawrence Tunnicliffe 1950- WhoAmL 92
Jones, Lawrence W. 1942- WhoBlA 92
Jones, Lawrence William 1925- AmMWSc 92
Jones, Le Roi BenetAL 91, IntWW 91
Jones, Leander Corbin 1934- WhoBlA 92, WhoMW 92
Jones, Lee Bennett 1938- AmMWSc 92, WhoMW 92
Jones, LeeAnn 1961- WhoAmL 92
Jones, Leeland Newton, Jr. 1921- WhoBlA 92
Jones, LeeRoy G 1929- AmMWSc 92
Jones, Lemuel B. 1929- WhoBlA 92
Jones, Leon 1936- WhoAmL 92
Jones, Leon C. 1919- WhoBlA 92
Jones, Leon Lamont 1930- WhoWest 92
Jones, Leon P. 1940- WhoBlA 92
Jones, Leonade Diane 1947- WhoBlA 92
Jones, Leonard Virgil 1921- WhoBlA 92
Jones, Leonidas John 1937- AmMWSc 92
Jones, Leroi DrAPF 91
Jones, LeRoi 1934- WhoBlA 92, WrDr 92
Jones, Leslie 1917- Who 92
Jones, Leslie F 1965- AmMWSc 92
Jones, Lester Tyler 1939- AmMWSc 92
Jones, Leticia Rene 1961- WhoFI 92
Jones, Lewis Bevel, III 1926- WhoRel 92
Jones, Lewis C. Who 92
Jones, Lewis Hammond, IV 1941- AmMWSc 92
Jones, Lewis William 1906- AmMWSc 92
Jones, Lilian Pauline N. Who 92
Jones, Lillie Agnes 1910- WhoWest 92
Jones, Lily Ann 1938- AmMWSc 92
Jones, Lincoln D 1923- AmMWSc 92
Jones, Lisa 1961- WrDr 92
Jones, Lisa Payne 1958- WhoBlA 92
Jones, Llewellyn Claiborne, Jr 1919- AmMWSc 92
Jones, Lloyd WhoAmP 91
Jones, Lloyd George 1919- AmMWSc 92
Jones, Lloyd K ScFEYrs
Jones, Lloyd O. 1944- WhoBlA 92
Jones, Lois M. 1905- NotBlAW 92
Jones, Lois Mailou 1905- WhoBlA 92
Jones, Lois Marilyn 1934- AmMWSc 92
Jones, Lonzie L. 1912-1973 WhoBlA 92N
Jones, Lorean Electa 1938- WhoBlA 92
Jones, Lorella Margaret 1943- AmMWSc 92
Jones, Louis B. ConLC 65 [port]
Jones, Louis C. 1908-1990 ConAu 133
Jones, Louis Clayton 1935- WhoBlA 92
Jones, Louis Woodard 1932- BlkOlyM
Jones, Louise Hinrichsen 1930- AmMWSc 92
Jones, Lovana S 1938- WhoAmP 91
Jones, Lucian Cox 1942- WhoAmL 92
Jones, Lucius 1918- WhoBlA 92
Jones, Lucy 1955- TwCPaSc
Jones, Luke TwCWW 91
Jones, Lyle Vincent 1924- AmMWSc 92, IntWW 91
Jones, Mack H. 1937- WhoBlA 92
Jones, Madison 1925- ConNov 91, WrDr 92
Jones, Madison Percy 1925- IntAu&W 91
Jones, Madonna Mary 1940- WhoMW 92
Jones, Maitland, Jr 1937- AmMWSc 92
Jones, Major J. 1918- WhoRel 92
Jones, Major Joseph BenetAL 91
Jones, Malcolm David 1923- AmMWSc 92
Jones, Malcolm V. 1940- WrDr 92
Jones, Malcolm Vince 1940- IntAu&W 91
Jones, Malinda Thiessen 1947- WhoFI 92
Jones, Mallory 1939- WhoEnt 92
Jones, Marcia Mae 1924- WhoEnt 92
Jones, Marcus Earl 1943- WhoBlA 92
Jones, Marcus Edmund 1960- WhoBlA 92
Jones, Margaret E. W. 1938- WrDr 92
Jones, Margaret Zee 1936- AmMWSc 92
Jones, Marguerite Margie Rose 1938- WhoWest 92
Jones, Marian Ilene 1929- WhoWest 92
Jones, Marilyn Elaine WhoBlA 92
Jones, Marilyn Gibson 1934- WhoAmP 91
Jones, Marion WrDr 92
Jones, Marion Patrick ConNov 91
Jones, Marjorie Ann 1944- AmMWSc 92
Jones, Mark 1942- TwCPaSc
Jones, Mark Allen 1953- WhoRel 92
Jones, Mark E. 1920- WhoBlA 92
Jones, Mark Ellis Powell 1951- Who 92
Jones, Mark Logan 1950- WhoFI 92
Jones, Mark Martin 1928- AmMWSc 92
Jones, Mark Perrin, III 1932- WhoAmP 91
Jones, Mark Wallon 1916- AmMWSc 92
Jones, Mark Wayne 1958- WhoMW 92
Jones, Mark William 1960- WhoRel 92
Jones, Marlene Wiseman 1939- WhoMW 92
Jones, Marmaduke 1724?-1787 DcNCBi 3
Jones, Marnie 1948- WhoEnt 92
Jones, Marsha Regina 1962- WhoBlA 92
Jones, Marshall William, Jr 1932- WhoAmP 91
Jones, Martha E. 1926- WhoBlA 92
Jones, Martha Jean 1935- WhoAmP 91
Jones, Martha Ownbey 1940- AmMWSc 92
Jones, Martin Kenneth 1951- Who 92
Jones, Martyn David 1947- Who 92
Jones, Marvin O 1923- WhoAmP 91
Jones, Marvin Richard 1914- AmMWSc 92
Jones, Marvin Thomas 1936- AmMWSc 92, WhoMW 92
Jones, Mary Della 1949- WhoFI 92
Jones, Mary Ellen 1922- AmMWSc 92, IntWW 91
Jones, Mary Harris 1830-1930 DcAmImH
Jones, Mary Harris 1837-1930 RComAH
Jones, Mary L 1934- WhoAmP 91
Jones, Mary Lloyd 1934- TwCPaSc
Jones, Mary M. 1967- WhoFI 92
Jones, Mary Voell 1933- WrDr 92
Jones, Mason 1919- WhoEnt 92
Jones, Matt 1955- WhoAmP 91
Jones, Matthew Lincoln 1945- WhoRel 92
Jones, Maude Elizabeth 1921- Who 92
Jones, Maurice Harry 1927- AmMWSc 92
Jones, Mavis N. 1918- WhoBlA 92
Jones, McKinley WhoRel 92
Jones, Medford Herbert 1919- WhoRel 92
Jones, Melody Ann 1964- WhoMW 92
Jones, Melton Rodney 1945- AmMWSc 92, WhoBlA 92
Jones, Melvin D 1943- AmMWSc 92
Jones, Merle S. d1976 LesBEnT 92
Jones, Merrell Robert 1938- AmMWSc 92
Jones, Merrill C 1925- AmMWSc 92
Jones, Mervyn 1922- ConNov 91, IntAu&W 91, Who 92, WrDr 92
Jones, Miah Gwynfor 1948- Who 92
Jones, Michael Abbott 1944- Who 92
Jones, Michael Allen 1947- WhoMW 92
Jones, Michael Andrea 1937- WhoBlA 92
Jones, Michael Barry 1932- Who 92
Jones, Michael Baxter 1944- AmMWSc 92
Jones, Michael E 1950- WhoAmP 91
Jones, Michael Earl 1950- WhoEnt 92
Jones, Michael Lee 1957- WhoAmP 91
Jones, Michael Owen 1942- WhoWest 92
Jones, Michael Roy 1958- WhoRel 92
Jones, Michael Ward 1949- WhoAmL 92
Jones, Michele Woods 1945- WhoBlA 92
Jones, Michelle Lynn 1964- WhoMW 92
Jones, Mickey Wayne 1941- WhoEnt 92
Jones, Miles James 1952- WhoBlA 92
Jones, Millard Lawrence, Jr 1933- AmMWSc 92
Jones, Miller, Mrs. Who 92
Jones, Milton Bennion 1926- AmMWSc 92
Jones, Milton David, Jr. 1942- WhoFI 92
Jones, Milton Lee 1953- WhoRel 92
Jones, Morris Thompson 1916- AmMWSc 92
Jones, Morton Edward 1928- AmMWSc 92
Jones, Myra Lee 1936- WhoAmP 91
Jones, Myron 1925- WhoAmP 91
Jones, Nancy C. 1942- WhoWest 92
Jones, Nancy Glen 1944- WhoRel 92
Jones, Nancy Lynne 1938- WhoWest 92
Jones, Napoleon A., Jr. 1940- WhoBlA 92
Jones, Nard 1904-1972 BenetAL 91, TwCWW 91
Jones, Nathan William 1952- WhoBlA 92
Jones, Nathaniel WhoRel 92
Jones, Nathaniel, Sr. 1948- WhoBlA 92
Jones, Nathaniel R WhoAmP 91
Jones, Nathaniel R. 1926- WhoBlA 92
Jones, Nathaniel Raphael 1926- WhoAmL 92
Jones, Neal T 1950- WhoAmP 91
Jones, Ned 1944- WhoAmP 91
Jones, Neil Calvin 1963- WhoAmL 92
Jones, Neil R 1909-1988 TwCSFW 91
Jones, Nellie L. 1933- WhoBlA 92
Jones, Nellie Rowe 1887-1960 DcNCBi 3
Jones, Nettie Pearl 1941- WhoBlA 92
Jones, Nevin Campbell H. Who 92
Jones, Nigel John I. Who 92
Jones, Nina F. 1918- WhoBlA 92
Jones, Noel Debroy Who 92
Jones, Noel Duane 1937- AmMWSc 92
Jones, Nolan E. 1944- WhoBlA 92
Jones, Nolan T 1927- AmMWSc 92
Jones, Norma Louise WhoMW 92
Jones, Norman Arthur W. Who 92
Jones, Norman Fielding 1931- Who 92
Jones, Norman Henry 1941- Who 92
Jones, Norman M. 1930- WhoMW 92
Jones, Norman Stewart C. Who 92
Jones, Norman Thomas 1936- WhoFI 92
Jones, Norman William 1923- IntWW 91, Who 92
Jones, Norvela Who 92
Jones, O. T. WhoRel 92
Jones, Odell 1932- WhoRel 92
Jones, Olga Unita 1928- WhoBlA 92
Jones, Oliver, Jr. 1947- WhoBlA 92
Jones, Oliver Perry 1906- AmMWSc 92
Jones, Oliver William 1932- AmMWSc 92
Jones, Ordie Reginal 1937- AmMWSc 92
Jones, Oris Pinckney 1903-1989 WhoBlA 92N
Jones, Orton Alan 1938- WhoAmP 91
Jones, Orval Edwin 1959- WhoAmL 92
Jones, Orval Elmer 1934- AmMWSc 92
Jones, Oscar C., Jr. 1932- WhoBlA 92
Jones, Oscar Calvin 1932- WhoRel 92
Jones, Otha Clyde 1908- AmMWSc 92
Jones, Owaiian Maurice 1961- WhoAmL 92
Jones, Owen John, III 1949- WhoFI 92
Jones, Owen Lloyd 1935- AmMWSc 92
Jones, Owen Rogers WrDr 92
Jones, Owen Trevor 1927- Who 92
Jones, Ozro T., Jr. WhoBlA 92
Jones, Ozro Thurston, Sr. 1891-1972 RelLAm 91
Jones, P H 1931- AmMWSc 92
Jones, Patricia 1951- WhoBlA 92
Jones, Patricia H 1938- AmMWSc 92
Jones, Patricia Pearce AmMWSc 92
Jones, Patricia Spears DrAPF 91
Jones, Patricia Thuner DrAPF 91
Jones, Patricia Yvonne 1956- WhoBlA 92
Jones, Patrick 1948- TwCPaSc
Jones, Patrick Louis 1940- WhoMW 92
Jones, Patrick P. 1928- WhoBlA 92
Jones, Patrick Ray 1943- AmMWSc 92
Jones, Patty Sue 1949- WhoWest 92
Jones, Paul DrAPF 91, WhoAmP 91
Jones, Paul 1951- WhoFI 92
Jones, Paul Griffin, II 1942- WhoRel 92
Jones, Paul Harvey 1943- WhoWest 92
Jones, Paul Hastings 1918- AmMWSc 92
Jones, Paul Kenneth 1943- AmMWSc 92
Jones, Paul R. 1928- WhoBlA 92
Jones, Paul Raymond 1930- AmMWSc 92
Jones, Paul Ronald 1940- AmMWSc 92
Jones, Peaches 1952-1988 ReelWom
Jones, Pearl Pullins 1915- WhoBlA 92
Jones, Pembroke 1858-1919 DcNCBi 3
Jones, Penry 1922- Who 92
Jones, Percival de Courcy 1913- Who 92
Jones, Percy Elwood 1940- WhoBlA 92
Jones, Peter 1917- TwCPaSc
Jones, Peter 1929- IntAu&W 91, WrDr 92
Jones, Peter 1930-1990 FacFETw
Jones, Peter A 1941- WhoIns 92
Jones, Peter Benjamin Gurner 1932- Who 92
Jones, Peter C. 1960- WhoWest 92
Jones, Peter D 1940- AmMWSc 92
Jones, Peter Derek 1932- Who 92
Jones, Peter Eldon 1927- Who 92
Jones, Peter Ferry 1920- Who 92
Jones, Peter Frank 1937- AmMWSc 92
Jones, Peter George Edward Fitzgerald 1925- Who 92
Jones, Peter Hadley 1934- AmMWSc 92
Jones, Peter Lawson 1952- WhoBlA 92
Jones, Peter Llewellyn G. Who 92
Jones, Peter Lloyd 1932- TwCPaSc
Jones, Peter Michael 1952- WhoAmL 92
Jones, Peter Trevor S. Who 92
Jones, Philip Who 92
Jones, Philip 1933- TwCPaSc
Jones, Philip Arthur 1924- AmMWSc 92
Jones, Philip Graham 1937- Who 92
Jones, Philip James 1921- IntWW 91, Who 92
Jones, Philip Mark 1928- IntWW 91, Who 92
Jones, Phillip C. 1950- WhoRel 92
Jones, Phillip Erskine 1940- WhoBlA 92
Jones, Phillip Sanford 1912- AmMWSc 92
Jones, Phillips Russell 1930- AmMWSc 92
Jones, Philly Joe 1923-1985 NewAmDM
Jones, Phyllis Edith 1924- AmMWSc 92
Jones, Piers Nicholas L. Who 92
Jones, Quincy 1933- IntMPA 92, IntWW 91, NewAmDM, WhoEnt 92
Jones, Quincy Delight, Jr. 1933- WhoBlA 92
Jones, R E Douglas 1933- AmMWSc 92
Jones, R James 1921- AmMWSc 92
Jones, R Norman 1913- AmMWSc 92
Jones, R.P. DrAPF 91
Jones, Rachel 1908- Who 92
Jones, Radford Wedgewood 1939- WhoMW 92
Jones, Ralph Darrell 1936- WhoWest 92
Jones, Ralph William 1921- AmMWSc 92
Jones, Randall Dean 1953- WhoIns 92
Jones, Randall Jefferies 1915- AmMWSc 92
Jones, Randy Kane 1957- WhoBlA 92
Jones, Ray 1949- TwCPaSc
Jones, Raymond, Sr. 1925- WhoBlA 92
Jones, Raymond Dean 1945- WhoBlA 92
Jones, Raymond E 1941- WhoIns 92
Jones, Raymond Edgar 1919- Who 92
Jones, Raymond Edward 1949- WhoRel 92
Jones, Raymond Eugene 1941- WhoFI 92
Jones, Raymond F 1915- TwCSFW 91, WrDr 92
Jones, Raymond Jackson, Jr. 1959- WhoRel 92
Jones, Raymond Morris 1922- WhoBlA 92
Jones, Rebecca Anne 1951- AmMWSc 92
Jones, Reese Tasker 1932- AmMWSc 92
Jones, Regina Nickerson 1942- WhoBlA 92
Jones, Reginald Ernest 1904- Who 92
Jones, Reginald L WhoAmP 91
Jones, Reginald L. 1931- WhoBlA 92
Jones, Reginald Lorrin 1951- WhoMW 92
Jones, Reginald Nash 1943- WhoAmL 92
Jones, Reginald Victor 1911- IntWW 91, Who 92
Jones, Rena Talley 1937- AmMWSc 92, WhoBlA 92
Jones, Renee Kauerauf 1949- WhoFI 92
Jones, Rhona Mary 1921- Who 92
Jones, Rhydderch Thomas 1935- IntAu&W 91
Jones, Rhys Tudor Brackley 1925- Who 92
Jones, Richard DrAPF 91
Jones, Richard 1784-1860 DcNCBi 3
Jones, Richard 1926- WrDr 92
Jones, Richard Alan 1948- WhoWest 92
Jones, Richard Allan 1943- WrDr 92
Jones, Richard Allan 1947- WhoEnt 92
Jones, Richard Benjamin 1933- WrDr 92
Jones, Richard Bradley 1947- AmMWSc 92
Jones, Richard Conrad 1916- AmMWSc 92
Jones, Richard Cyrus 1928- WhoAmL 92, WhoFI 92
Jones, Richard Dell AmMWSc 92
Jones, Richard Earl 1944- WhoMW 92
Jones, Richard Elmore 1944- AmMWSc 92
Jones, Richard Evan 1940- AmMWSc 92
Jones, Richard Evan, Jr 1940- AmMWSc 92
Jones, Richard Granville 1926- Who 92, WrDr 92
Jones, Richard Herbert 1930- WhoAmL 92
Jones, Richard Hunn 1934- AmMWSc 92
Jones, Richard Ian Who 92
Jones, Richard K. Who 92
Jones, Richard L 1923- WhoAmP 91
Jones, Richard Lamar 1939- AmMWSc 92
Jones, Richard Lawrence 1933- WhoWest 92
Jones, Richard Lee 1929- AmMWSc 92
Jones, Richard Lee 1944- AmMWSc 92
Jones, Richard M. Who 92, WhoAmL 92
Jones, Richard M. 1926- IntWW 91
Jones, Richard Merritt 1958- WhoRel 92
Jones, Richard Michael 1952- WhoAmL 92
Jones, Richard Nelson 1950- WhoRel 92
Jones, Richard S. Who 92
Jones, Richard Theodore 1929- AmMWSc 92, WhoWest 92
Jones, Richard Victor 1929- AmMWSc 92
Jones, Richard Watson 1837-1914 BiInAmS
Jones, Richmond Addison 1937- WhoBlA 92, WhoEnt 92, WhoMW 92
Jones, Rick Lee 1957- WhoMW 92
Jones, Rickie Lee 1954- WhoEnt 92
Jones, Robbie Neely 1940- WhoBlA 92
Jones, Robert NewAmDM
Jones, Robert, Jr. 1718-1766 DcNCBi 3
Jones, Robert, Sr. 1883-1968 RelLAm 91
Jones, Robert A 1939- WhoAmP 91
Jones, Robert Allan 1938- AmMWSc 92
Jones, Robert Alonzo 1937- WhoFI 92, WhoWest 92
Jones, Robert Alton 1944- WhoBlA 92
Jones, Robert Alun 1949- Who 92
Jones, Robert Beasley 1939- WhoAmP 91
Jones, Robert Brannock 1950- Who 92
Jones, Robert Brinley 1929- Who 92
Jones, Robert C. 1943- WhoEnt 92

**Jones**, Robert Calvin 1958- *WhoRel 92*
**Jones**, Robert Carlisle 1956- *WhoFI 92*
**Jones**, Robert Clark 1916- *AmMWSc 92*
**Jones**, Robert Drake 1941- *WhoWest 92*
**Jones**, Robert E 1927- *WhoAmP 91*
**Jones**, Robert Earl 1942- *WhoBlA 92*
**Jones**, Robert Edmond 1887-1954 *BenetAL 91*
**Jones**, Robert Edward 1923- *AmMWSc 92*
**Jones**, Robert Edward 1927- *WhoWest 92*
**Jones**, Robert Edward 1939- *Who 92*
**Jones**, Robert Elijah 1872-1960 *DcNCBi 3, RelLAm 91*
**Jones**, Robert Emmett, II 1912- *WhoAmP 91*
**Jones**, Robert Eugene 1923- *WhoWest 92*
**Jones**, Robert F 1926- *AmMWSc 92*
**Jones**, Robert G 1936- *WhoAmP 91, WhoBlA 92*
**Jones**, Robert Gean 1925- *WhoRel 92*
**Jones**, Robert Gerallt 1934- *Who 92*
**Jones**, Robert Gwilym L. *Who 92*
**Jones**, Robert Hefin 1932- *Who 92*
**Jones**, Robert James 1951- *AmMWSc 92*
**Jones**, Robert Jeffries 1939- *WhoAmL 92*
**Jones**, Robert L. *DrAPF 91*
**Jones**, Robert L 1936- *AmMWSc 92*
**Jones**, Robert L., III 1944- *WhoAmL 92*
**Jones**, Robert Lee 1920- *WhoRel 92*
**Jones**, Robert Lee 1958- *WhoFI 92*
**Jones**, Robert Leonard 1928- *WhoAmP 91*
**Jones**, Robert Leroy 1939- *AmMWSc 92*
**Jones**, Robert Lloyd 1929- *WhoAmP 91*
**Jones**, Robert Lyle 1959- *WhoMW 92*
**Jones**, Robert Maynard 1929- *IntAu&W 91*
**Jones**, Robert McKittrick, III 1933- *WhoMW 92*
**Jones**, Robert Millard 1939- *AmMWSc 92*
**Jones**, Robert Sidney 1936- *AmMWSc 92*
**Jones**, Robert Stanley 1936- *WhoMW 92*
**Jones**, Robert Thomas 1910- *AmMWSc 92, IntWW 91*
**Jones**, Robert Wesley 1929- *WhoBlA 92*
**Jones**, Robert William 1927- *AmMWSc 92*
**Jones**, Robert William 1940- *AmMWSc 92*
**Jones**, Robert William 1944- *AmMWSc 92*
**Jones**, Robert William, III 1944- *WhoMW 92*
**Jones**, Robert William Hugh 1911- *Who 92*
**Jones**, Roberts Titus 1940- *WhoFI 92*
**Jones**, Robin Francis McN *Who 92*
**Jones**, Robin Huws 1909- *Who 92*
**Jones**, Robin L 1940- *AmMWSc 92*
**Jones**, Robin Richard 1937- *AmMWSc 92*
**Jones**, Rodney 1950- *ConAu 133, WrDr 92*
**Jones**, Roger *DrAPF 91, Who 92*
**Jones**, Roger 1940- *AmMWSc 92*
**Jones**, Roger Alan 1947- *AmMWSc 92*
**Jones**, Roger C 1919- *AmMWSc 92*
**Jones**, Roger Clyde 1919- *WhoWest 92*
**Jones**, Roger Eugene 1928- *WhoRel 92*
**Jones**, Roger Franklin 1930- *AmMWSc 92*
**Jones**, Roger L 1949- *AmMWSc 92*
**Jones**, Roger Stanley 1934- *AmMWSc 92*
**Jones**, Roger W. *DrAPF 91*
**Jones**, Roger Warren 1908- *IntWW 91*
**Jones**, Roger Wayne 1939- *WhoWest 92*
**Jones**, Roland 1813-1869 *DcNCBi 3*
**Jones**, Roland Manning 1932- *WhoRel 92*
**Jones**, Ronald Christopher H. *Who 92*
**Jones**, Ronald Dale 1932- *AmMWSc 92*
**Jones**, Ronald David 1930- *WhoAmL 92*
**Jones**, Ronald Edward 1958- *WhoRel 92*
**Jones**, Ronald Goldin 1933- *AmMWSc 92*
**Jones**, Ronald H. 1938- *WhoWest 92*
**Jones**, Ronald M. *Who 92*
**Jones**, Ronald McClung 1951- *AmMWSc 92*
**Jones**, Ronald Vance 1946- *WhoMW 92*
**Jones**, Roscoe T., Jr. 1935- *WhoBlA 92*
**Jones**, Rosemary 1941- *AmMWSc 92*
**Jones**, Roxanne H 1928- *WhoAmP 91*
**Jones**, Roy 1969- *BlkOlyM*
**Jones**, Roy Carl, Jr 1939- *AmMWSc 92*
**Jones**, Roy Junios 1925- *WhoBlA 92*
**Jones**, Royden Anthony 1925- *Who 92*
**Jones**, Ruby W 1932- *WhoAmP 91*
**Jones**, Rufus 1936- *NewAmDM*
**Jones**, Rufus Elmer 1940- *WhoAmP 91*
**Jones**, Rufus Matthew 1863-1948 *AmPeW, RelLAm 91*
**Jones**, Rufus Sidney 1940- *AmMWSc 92*
**Jones**, Russ L. 1963- *WhoRel 92*
**Jones**, Russel C 1935- *AmMWSc 92*
**Jones**, Russel Clyde 1921- *WhoAmL 92*
**Jones**, Russell Dean 1933- *WhoWest 92*
**Jones**, Russell Howard 1944- *AmMWSc 92*
**Jones**, Russell K 1922- *AmMWSc 92*
**Jones**, Russell Lewis 1941- *AmMWSc 92*
**Jones**, Russell Stine 1914- *AmMWSc 92*
**Jones**, Ruth Braswell 1914- *WhoBlA 92*
**Jones**, Ruth Elayne 1920- *WhoWest 92*
**Jones**, Sadie Waterford 1889- *WhoBlA 92*
**Jones**, Sally Roberts 1935- *IntAu&W 91, WrDr 92*
**Jones**, Sam H., Sr. 1938- *WhoBlA 92*
**Jones**, Sam Houston 1898?-1978 *CurBio 91N*
**Jones**, Sam J. 1954- *IntMPA 92*
**Jones**, Sammy Ray 1941- *WhoRel 92*
**Jones**, Samuel 1933- *WhoBlA 92*
**Jones**, Samuel 1935- *WhoEnt 92*
**Jones**, Samuel 1939- *Who 92*
**Jones**, Samuel, Jr. 1944- *WhoRel 92*
**Jones**, Samuel B, Jr 1933- *AmMWSc 92*
**Jones**, Samuel J 1836-1901 *BiInAmS*
**Jones**, Samuel M. 1936- *WhoAmL 92*
**Jones**, Samuel O'Brien 1911- *AmMWSc 92*
**Jones**, Samuel Porter 1847-1906 *RelLAm 91*
**Jones**, Samuel Stimpson 1923- *AmMWSc 92*
**Jones**, Sandra 1946- *WhoMW 92*
**Jones**, Sandra Lou 1944- *WhoWest 92*
**Jones**, Sanford L 1925- *AmMWSc 92*
**Jones**, Sarah Garland 18--?-1905 *NotBlAW 92*
**Jones**, Schuyler 1930- *Who 92*
**Jones**, Scott Austin 1962- *WhoWest 92*
**Jones**, Seaborn *DrAPF 91*
**Jones**, Seymour 1931- *WhoFI 92*
**Jones**, Sharon Davis 1961- *WhoFI 92*
**Jones**, Sharon Diana 1948- *WhoBlA 92*
**Jones**, Sharon Elaine 1955- *WhoAmL 92*
**Jones**, Sharon Lynn 1960- *AmMWSc 92*
**Jones**, Shelby L 1936- *WhoIns 92*
**Jones**, Sheldon Atwell 1938- *WhoAmL 92*
**Jones**, Sherman Jarvis 1935- *WhoAmP 91, WhoBlA 92*
**Jones**, Sheryl Cassandra 1947- *WhoFI 92*
**Jones**, Shirley *WhoEnt 92*
**Jones**, Shirley 1934- *IntMPA 92*
**Jones**, Shirley Ann *Who 92*
**Jones**, Shirley Joan 1931- *WhoBlA 92*
**Jones**, Shirley M *WhoAmP 91*
**Jones**, Shirley Machocky 1937- *WhoAmP 91*
**Jones**, Sidney A., Jr. 1909- *WhoBlA 92*
**Jones**, Sidney Alexander 1934- *WhoBlA 92*
**Jones**, Sidney Eugene 1936- *WhoBlA 92*
**Jones**, Sidney Lewis 1933- *WhoFI 92*
**Jones**, Sidney Pope, Jr *WhoAmP 91*
**Jones**, Silas *DrAPF 91*
**Jones**, Simon Benton 1941- *Who 92*
**Jones**, Sissieretta 1868-1933 *NewAmDM*
**Jones**, Sissieretta 1869-1933 *NotBlAW 92 [port]*
**Jones**, Sondra Michelle 1948- *WhoBlA 92*
**Jones**, Sonia Josephine 1945- *WhoFI 92*
**Jones**, Spencer 1946- *WhoBlA 92, WhoRel 92*
**Jones**, Spike 1911-1964 *FacFETw*
**Jones**, Spike 1911-1965 *NewAmDM*
**Jones**, Stanley B 1938- *AmMWSc 92*
**Jones**, Stanley Bennett 1922- *AmMWSc 92*
**Jones**, Stanley Bernard 1961- *WhoBlA 92*
**Jones**, Stanley C 1933- *AmMWSc 92*
**Jones**, Stanley E 1939- *AmMWSc 92*
**Jones**, Stanley Leslie 1919- *AmMWSc 92*
**Jones**, Stanley Tanner 1945- *AmMWSc 92*
**Jones**, Stella Marie 1947- *WhoMW 92*
**Jones**, Stephan L 1935- *WhoIns 92*
**Jones**, Stephanie Tubbs 1949- *WhoBlA 92*
**Jones**, Stephen 1940- *WhoAmL 92, WhoAmP 91*
**Jones**, Stephen 1953- *ConAu 134*
**Jones**, Stephen Barry 1938- *Who 92*
**Jones**, Stephen Bender 1945- *AmMWSc 92*
**Jones**, Stephen Graf 1947- *WhoEnt 92*
**Jones**, Stephen James 1945- *WhoIns 92*
**Jones**, Stephen Morris 1948- *Who 92*
**Jones**, Stephen R. *DrAPF 91*
**Jones**, Stephen Richard Maurice 1950- *WhoRel 92*
**Jones**, Stephen Thomas 1942- *AmMWSc 92*
**Jones**, Stephen Wallace 1953- *AmMWSc 92*
**Jones**, Steven Earl 1949- *WhoWest 92*
**Jones**, Steven Emrys 1957- *WhoAmL 92*
**Jones**, Steven Matthew 1950- *WhoRel 92*
**Jones**, Stewart 1919- *WhoMW 92*
**Jones**, Stuart Lloyd 1917- *Who 92*
**Jones**, Sumie Amikura 1937- *WhoMW 92*
**Jones**, Susan *TwCPaSc*
**Jones**, Susan Eileen 1951- *WhoEnt 92*
**Jones**, Susan Kraus 1949- *WhoMW 92*
**Jones**, Susan Muriel *AmMWSc 92*
**Jones**, Susan Short 1953- *WhoAmL 92*
**Jones**, Susan Sutton *WhoBlA 92*
**Jones**, Suzan Ellis 1953- *WhoAmP 91*
**Jones**, Suzanne Marie 1955- *WhoAmL 92*
**Jones**, Sylvester 1942-1983 *WhoBlA 92N*
**Jones**, T Benjamin 1912- *AmMWSc 92*
**Jones**, T. Dale 1965- *WhoRel 92*
**Jones**, T Lawrence *WhoIns 92*
**Jones**, Tappey Hughes 1948- *AmMWSc 92*
**Jones**, Terence Graham Parry 1942- *ConAu 35NR*
**Jones**, Terence Leavesley 1926- *Who 92*
**Jones**, Terence Valentine 1939- *Who 92*
**Jones**, Terrence Dale 1948- *WhoEnt 92*
**Jones**, Terry *ConAu 35NR*
**Jones**, Terry 1942- *IntMPA 92, SmATA 67 [port], Who 92*
**Jones**, Terry Lee 1945- *AmMWSc 92*
**Jones**, Thad 1923-1986 *NewAmDM*
**Jones**, Theodore *WhoAmP 91*
**Jones**, Theodore d1991 *NewYTBS 91*
**Jones**, Theodore 1923- *WhoBlA 92*
**Jones**, Theodore A. *WhoBlA 92*
**Jones**, Theodore Charles 1939- *AmMWSc 92*
**Jones**, Theodore Cornelius 1941- *WhoBlA 92*
**Jones**, Theodore Harold Douglas 1938- *AmMWSc 92, WhoWest 92*
**Jones**, Theodore Lawrence 1920- *WhoAmL 92, WhoFI 92*
**Jones**, Theodore Sidney 1911- *AmMWSc 92*
**Jones**, Theresa Diane 1953- *WhoBlA 92*
**Jones**, Theresa Mitchell 1917- *WhoBlA 92*
**Jones**, Thomas d1797 *DcNCBi 3*
**Jones**, Thomas A 1945- *WhoAmP 91*
**Jones**, Thomas Branch, Jr. 1930- *WhoFI 92*
**Jones**, Thomas Brooks *WhoAmL 92*
**Jones**, Thomas C. *WhoFI 92*
**Jones**, Thomas C 1946- *WhoIns 92*
**Jones**, Thomas Carlyle 1912- *AmMWSc 92*
**Jones**, Thomas E. *Who 92*
**Jones**, Thomas Evan 1944- *AmMWSc 92, WhoFI 92*
**Jones**, Thomas F. 1953- *WhoAmL 92*
**Jones**, Thomas Franklin, Jr. 1955- *WhoRel 92*
**Jones**, Thomas Frederick 1936- *WhoRel 92*
**Jones**, Thomas Glanville 1931- *Who 92*
**Jones**, Thomas H. *WhoMW 92*
**Jones**, Thomas Hubbard 1936- *AmMWSc 92*
**Jones**, Thomas Hughie 1927- *Who 92*
**Jones**, Thomas John, Jr. 1955- *WhoAmL 92*
**Jones**, Thomas L. 1941- *WhoBlA 92*
**Jones**, Thomas Laurens 1819-1887 *DcNCBi 3*
**Jones**, Thomas Lawton 1947- *WhoRel 92*
**Jones**, Thomas Leroy 1918- *WhoAmP 91*
**Jones**, Thomas M 1947- *WhoAmP 91*
**Jones**, Thomas McKissick 1816-1892 *DcNCBi 3*
**Jones**, Thomas Oswell 1908- *AmMWSc 92*
**Jones**, Thomas P 1774-1848 *BiInAmS*
**Jones**, Thomas Philip 1931- *IntWW 91, Who 92*
**Jones**, Thomas Robert 1950- *WhoWest 92*
**Jones**, Thomas Russell 1913- *WhoBlA 92*
**Jones**, Thomas S 1929- *AmMWSc 92*
**Jones**, Thomas S., Jr. 1882-1932 *BenetAL 91*
**Jones**, Thomas V 1920- *AmMWSc 92*
**Jones**, Thomas Victor 1920- *IntWW 91, WhoWest 92*
**Jones**, Thomas W 1949- *WhoIns 92*
**Jones**, Thomas Walter 1945- *AmMWSc 92*
**Jones**, Thomas Watson 1951- *WhoFI 92*
**Jones**, Thomas William 1955- *WhoRel 92, WhoWest 92*
**Jones**, Thornton Keith 1923- *WhoWest 92*
**Jones**, Tim *TwCPaSc*
**Jones**, Timothy Arthur *AmMWSc 92*
**Jones**, Timothy Earl 1948- *WhoBlA 92*
**Jones**, Timothy Emlyn 1948- *TwCPaSc*
**Jones**, Tom *DrAPF 91*
**Jones**, Tom 1940- *IntWW 91, WhoEnt 92*
**Jones**, Tom D. 1939- *WhoWest 92*
**Jones**, Tom L. 1954- *WhoRel 92*
**Jones**, Tommy Lee 1946- *IntMPA 92, WhoEnt 92*
**Jones**, Too Tall 1951- *WhoBlA 92*
**Jones**, Tracey Kirk, Jr. 1917- *WhoRel 92*
**Jones**, Trevor *Who 92*
**Jones**, Trevor 1945- *TwCPaSc*
**Jones**, Trevor David K. *Who 92*
**Jones**, Trevor O *AmMWSc 92*
**Jones**, Tristan 1924- *WrDr 92*
**Jones**, Ulysses, Jr 1951- *WhoAmP 91*
**Jones**, Ulysses Simpson, Jr 1918- *AmMWSc 92*
**Jones**, Vann Kinckle 1940- *WhoBlA 92*
**Jones**, Vaughan Frederick Randal 1952- *Who 92*
**Jones**, Velma Lois *WhoBlA 92*
**Jones**, Vera June *Who 92*
**Jones**, Vernon A., Jr. 1924- *WhoBlA 92*
**Jones**, Vernon Douglas 1937- *AmMWSc 92*
**Jones**, Vernon Quentin 1930- *WhoWest 92*
**Jones**, Victor Alan 1930- *AmMWSc 92*
**Jones**, Victoria Gene 1948- *WhoBlA 92*
**Jones**, Viola 1933- *WhoBlA 92*
**Jones**, Virgil *WhoAmP 91*
**Jones**, Virginia Lacy 1912- *WhoBlA 92*
**Jones**, Virginia Lacy 1912-1984 *HanAmWH, NotBlAW 92 [port]*
**Jones**, Vivian 1930- *WhoRel 92*
**Jones**, Walter *WhoRel 92*
**Jones**, Walter B. 1913- *AlmAP 92 [port]*
**Jones**, Walter B, Jr *WhoAmP 91*
**Jones**, Walter Beaman, Sr 1913- *WhoAmP 91*
**Jones**, Walter Dean 1938- *WhoMW 92*
**Jones**, Walter H 1922- *AmMWSc 92*
**Jones**, Walter Heath *Who 92*
**Jones**, Walter L. 1928- *WhoBlA 92*
**Jones**, Walter Leon 1955- *WhoFI 92*
**Jones**, Walter Raymond 1936- *WhoWest 92*
**Jones**, Wayne M 1954- *WhoAmP 91*
**Jones**, Welton H., Jr. 1936- *WhoEnt 92*
**Jones**, Wendell Oren 1941- *WhoWest 92*
**Jones**, Wesley Morris 1919- *AmMWSc 92*
**Jones**, Wilber Clark 1941- *AmMWSc 92*
**Jones**, Wilbur Devereux 1916- *WrDr 92*
**Jones**, Wilbur Douglas, Jr 1927- *AmMWSc 92*
**Jones**, Wilbur L. *WhoRel 92*
**Jones**, Wilfred 1926- *Who 92*
**Jones**, Wilfred Denton 1922- *WhoAmP 91*
**Jones**, William 1746-1794 *DcLB 109 [port]*
**Jones**, William 1871-1909 *BiInAmS*
**Jones**, William 1923- *TwCPaSc*
**Jones**, William 1934- *WhoBlA 92*
**Jones**, William A., Jr. 1934- *WhoBlA 92*
**Jones**, William Allen 1941- *WhoAmL 92, WhoBlA 92, WhoEnt 92*
**Jones**, William Armand Thomas Tristan G. *Who 92*
**Jones**, William Augustus, Jr. 1927- *WhoMW 92, WhoRel 92*
**Jones**, William B 1931- *AmMWSc 92*
**Jones**, William B 1937- *AmMWSc 92*
**Jones**, William B, Jr 1924- *AmMWSc 92*
**Jones**, William Barclay 1919- *AmMWSc 92*
**Jones**, William Bowdoin 1928- *WhoAmP 91, WhoBlA 92*
**Jones**, William Branch 1890-1943 *DcNCBi 3*
**Jones**, William C. 1933- *WhoBlA 92*
**Jones**, William Catron 1926- *WhoAmL 92*
**Jones**, William Charles 1937- *WhoWest 92*
**Jones**, William Davidson 1953- *AmMWSc 92*
**Jones**, William Denver 1935- *AmMWSc 92*
**Jones**, William Donnell 1955- *WhoBlA 92*
**Jones**, William Edward 1930- *WhoBlA 92*
**Jones**, William Emrys 1915- *Who 92*
**Jones**, William Ernest 1936- *AmMWSc 92*
**Jones**, William F 1927- *AmMWSc 92*
**Jones**, William George Tilston 1942- *Who 92*
**Jones**, William H 1932- *WhoAmP 91*
**Jones**, William Harold 1952- *WhoAmP 91*
**Jones**, William Hawood 1927- *WhoWest 92*
**Jones**, William Henry 1883-1963 *DcNCBi 3*
**Jones**, William Henry, Jr 1904- *AmMWSc 92*
**Jones**, William Henry, Jr. 1916- *WhoBlA 92*
**Jones**, William Houston 1932- *WhoFI 92*
**Jones**, William Howry 1920- *AmMWSc 92*
**Jones**, William J 1915- *AmMWSc 92, WhoBlA 92*
**Jones**, William James, Jr 1870-1917 *BiInAmS*
**Jones**, William Jenipher 1912- *WhoBlA 92, WhoRel 92*
**Jones**, William John 1926- *WhoEnt 92*
**Jones**, William Jonas, Jr 1941- *AmMWSc 92*
**Jones**, William Kenneth 1930- *WhoAmL 92*
**Jones**, William Lawless 1914- *WhoBlA 92*
**Jones**, William Leon 1949- *WhoAmP 91*
**Jones**, William Louis 1827-1914 *BiInAmS*
**Jones**, William Maurice 1930- *AmMWSc 92*
**Jones**, William Moses 1898- *WhoBlA 92N*
**Jones**, William O. *WhoBlA 92*
**Jones**, William Pearce A. *Who 92*
**Jones**, William Philip 1942- *AmMWSc 92, WhoMW 92*
**Jones**, William Ralph 1883-1915 *BiInAmS*
**Jones**, William Rex 1922- *WhoAmL 92*
**Jones**, William Ronald 1933- *WhoBlA 92*
**Jones**, William Sutton 1959- *WhoFI 92*
**Jones**, William Vernon 1935- *AmMWSc 92*
**Jones**, William W. 1928- *WhoBlA 92*
**Jones**, Willie 1741-1801 *DcNCBi 3*
**Jones**, Willie 1932- *WhoBlA 92*
**Jones**, Willie C. 1941- *WhoBlA 92*
**Jones**, Willis Knapp 1895- *ScFEYrs*
**Jones**, Winston William 1910- *AmMWSc 92*
**Jones**, Winton D, Jr 1941- *AmMWSc 92*
**Jones**, Winton Dennis, Jr. 1941- *WhoBlA 92*

**Jones**, Woodrow Harold 1913- *WhoBlA 92*
**Jones**, Wyn *Who 92*
**Jones**, Wynn 1939- *TwCPaSc*
**Jones**, Wynn Normington H. *Who 92*
**Jones**, Yvonne De Marr *WhoBlA 92*
**Jones**, Yvonne Harris *WhoBlA 92*
**Jones**, Yvonne Vivian 1946- *WhoBlA 92*
**Jones**, Zoia L. 1926- *WhoBlA 92*
**Jones-Evans**, Eric 1898- *IntAu&W 91*
**Jones-Gordon**, Cheryl Anne 1944- *WhoFI 92*
**Jones-Grimes**, Mable Christine 1943- *WhoBlA 92*
**Jones Hammond**, Katherine Ann 1953- *WhoMW 92*
**Jones Parry**, Emyr 1947- *Who 92*
**Jones-Parry**, Ernest 1908- *Who 92*
**Jones-Schenk**, Janea 1952- *WhoWest 92*
**Jones-Smith**, Jacqueline 1952- *WhoAmP 91, WhoFI 92*
**Jones-Trent**, Bernice R. 1946- *WhoBlA 92*
**Jones-Williams**, Dafydd Wyn 1916- *Who 92*
**Jong**, Erica *DrAPF 91*
**Jong**, Erica 1942- *BenetAL 91, ConNov 91, ConPo 91, FacFETw, HanAmWH, WrDr 92*
**Jong**, Erica Mann 1942- *IntAu&W 91, IntWW 91, WhoEnt 92*
**Jong**, Ing-Chang 1938- *AmMWSc 92*
**Jong**, Petrus J. S. de 1915- *IntWW 91*
**Jong**, Shung-Chang 1936- *AmMWSc 92*
**Jongen**, Joseph 1873-1953 *NewAmDM*
**Jongewaard**, David Lawrence 1946- *WhoRel 92*
**Jongeward**, George Ronald 1934- *WhoWest 92*
**Jongkind**, Johann Barthold 1819-1891 *ThHEIm*
**Joni**, Saj-nicole A *AmMWSc 92*
**Jonik**, John 1942- *WhoEnt 92*
**Jonker**, Nate *WhoAmP 91*
**Jonker**, Peter Emile 1948- *WhoWest 92*
**Jonkers**, Martinus Karel Petrus 1924- *WhoFI 92*
**Jonkiert**, Casimir S 1928- *WhoAmP 91*
**Jonkman**, Hans 1925- *Who 92*
**Jonleigh**, Leonie d1974 *TwCPaSc*
**Jonnard**, Aimison 1916- *AmMWSc 92*
**Jonnes**, Michael 1950- *WhoEnt 92*
**Jonquil** *ScFEYrs*
**Jons**, Hal *TwCWW 91*
**Jonsen**, Albert R 1931- *AmMWSc 92, IntWW 91*
**Jonson**, Ben 1572?-1637 *CnDBLB 1 [port], RfGEnL 91*
**Jonson**, Dan L 1943- *WhoIns 92*
**Jonsson**, Bjarni 1920- *AmMWSc 92*
**Jonsson**, Elias Snaeland 1943- *IntAu&W 91*
**Jonsson**, Eysteinn 1906- *IntWW 91*
**Jonsson**, Gisli 1929- *WhoFI 92*
**Jonsson**, Gregory Nisi 1950- *WhoAmL 92*
**Jonsson**, Haldor Turner, Jr 1929- *AmMWSc 92*
**Jonsson**, John Erik 1901- *AmMWSc 92*
**Jonsson**, John Norman 1925- *WhoRel 92*
**Jonsson**, Richard Eugene 1935- *WhoWest 92*
**Jonsson**, Scott Anthony 1951- *WhoAmL 92*
**Jonsson**, Stefan 1923- *IntAu&W 91*
**Jonsson**, Wilbur Jacob 1936- *AmMWSc 92*
**Jonte**, John Haworth 1918- *AmMWSc 92, WhoMW 92*
**Jontz**, Greggory Robert 1956- *WhoMW 92*
**Jontz**, James 1951- *AlmAP 92 [port], WhoAmP 91*
**Jontz**, James Prather 1951- *WhoMW 92*
**Jonzen**, Basil 1914- *TwCPaSc*
**Jonzen**, Karin 1914- *TwCPaSc, Who 92*
**Jonzon**, Anders 1948- *AmMWSc 92*
**Joor**, Joseph F 1848-1892 *BiInAmS*
**Joos**, Barbara 1957- *AmMWSc 92*
**Joos**, Bela 1953- *AmMWSc 92*
**Joos**, Howard Arthur 1922- *AmMWSc 92*
**Joos**, Josef 1878-1965 *EncTR 91*
**Joos**, Richard W 1934- *AmMWSc 92*
**Joose**, Barbara M. 1949- *WrDr 92*
**Jooss**, Kurt 1901-1979 *FacFETw*
**Joost-Gaugier**, Christiane Louise *WhoWest 92*
**Jooste**, Gerhardus Petrus d1990 *Who 92N*
**Joostens**, M. *WhoRel 92*
**Jope**, Edward Martyn 1915- *IntWW 91, Who 92*
**Joplin**, Albert Frederick 1919- *WhoFI 92, WhoWest 92*
**Joplin**, Graham Frank 1927- *IntWW 91*
**Joplin**, Janis 1943-1970 *NewAmDM*
**Joplin**, Janis 1945-1970 *FacFETw*
**Joplin**, Scott 1868-1917 *FacFETw, NewAmDM*
**Jopling**, Alan Victor 1924- *AmMWSc 92*
**Jopling**, Michael 1930- *IntWW 91, Who 92*
**Jopp**, Harold Dowling, Jr. 1946- *WhoRel 92*
**Joppa**, Leonard Robert 1930- *AmMWSc 92*
**Joppa**, Richard M 1929- *AmMWSc 92*
**Jopson**, Harry Gorgas Michener 1911- *AmMWSc 92*
**Joralemon**, Barbara Gail 1951- *WhoRel 92*
**Jorandby**, Richard Leroy 1938- *WhoAmL 92*
**Joray**, Paul Albert 1942- *WhoMW 92*
**Jorberg**, Lennart 1927- *IntWW 91*
**Jorch**, Harald Heinrich 1951- *AmMWSc 92*
**Jordahl**, Donald Clarence 1929- *WhoMW 92*
**Jordahl**, Mark Steven 1960- *WhoFI 92*
**Jordahl**, Ronald Ivan 1936- *WhoRel 92*
**Jordan**, A G 1930- *AmMWSc 92*
**Jordan**, Abbie H. *WhoBlA 92*
**Jordan**, Albert Gustav 1941- *AmMWSc 92*
**Jordan**, Albert Raymond 1906- *AmMWSc 92*
**Jordan**, Alexander Joseph, Jr. 1938- *WhoAmL 92*
**Jordan**, Alexander Walker, III 1945- *AmMWSc 92*
**Jordan**, Alma Theodora 1929- *WrDr 92*
**Jordan**, Andrew G 1939- *AmMWSc 92*
**Jordan**, Andrew Stephen 1936- *AmMWSc 92*
**Jordan**, Angel G 1930- *AmMWSc 92*
**Jordan**, Anne Devereaux 1943- *ConAu 135*
**Jordan**, Anne Knight *WhoBlA 92*
**Jordan**, Anne Saunders *DrAPF 91*
**Jordan**, Arthur Kent 1932- *AmMWSc 92*
**Jordan**, Barbara *DrAPF 91*
**Jordan**, Barbara 1936- *HanAmWH, NotBlAW 92 [port]*
**Jordan**, Barbara Charline 1936- *AmPolLe, WhoBlA 92*
**Jordan**, Barbara Leslie 1915- *IntAu&W 91*
**Jordan**, Benjamin Everett 1896-1974 *DcNCBi 3*
**Jordan**, Bettye Davis 1946- *WhoBlA 92*
**Jordan**, Brigitte *AmMWSc 92*
**Jordan**, Bryn *TwCWW 91*
**Jordan**, Byron Dale 1947- *AmMWSc 92*
**Jordan**, Carl Edward 1935- *WhoRel 92*
**Jordan**, Carl Frederick 1935- *AmMWSc 92*
**Jordan**, Carl Rankin 1924- *WhoBlA 92*
**Jordan**, Carole 1941- *Who 92*
**Jordan**, Carolyn D. 1941- *WhoBlA 92*
**Jordan**, Carolyne Lamar *WhoBlA 92*
**Jordan**, Casper LeRoy 1924- *WhoBlA 92*
**Jordan**, Cecile Blank 1937- *WhoRel 92*
**Jordan**, Charles Edward 1901-1974 *DcNCBi 3*
**Jordan**, Charles Edwin 1927- *AmMWSc 92*
**Jordan**, Charles F, Jr 1943- *WhoAmP 91*
**Jordan**, Charles Lee 1941- *WhoWest 92*
**Jordan**, Charles Lemuel 1922- *AmMWSc 92*
**Jordan**, Charles Milton 1949- *WhoAmL 92*
**Jordan**, Charles Morrell 1927- *WhoFI 92*
**Jordan**, Charles R. 1937- *WhoBlA 92*
**Jordan**, Charles Wesley 1933- *WhoBlA 92, WhoRel 92*
**Jordan**, Chris Sullivan 1924- *AmMWSc 92*
**Jordan**, Clarence 1912-1969 *RelLAm 91*
**Jordan**, Constance Brine 1919- *AmMWSc 92*
**Jordan**, Dan 1959- *WhoAmP 91*
**Jordan**, Dan W. 1946- *WhoRel 92*
**Jordan**, Daniel William 1810-1883 *DcNCBi 3*
**Jordan**, Danny Joseph 1948- *WhoWest 92*
**Jordan**, Darrell E. 1938- *WhoAmL 92*
**Jordan**, David Carlyle 1926- *AmMWSc 92*
**Jordan**, David Crichton *WhoAmP 91*
**Jordan**, David Francis, Jr. 1928- *WhoAmL 92*
**Jordan**, David Harold 1924- *Who 92*
**Jordan**, David Lee 1933- *WhoBlA 92*
**Jordan**, David M 1937- *AmMWSc 92*
**Jordan**, David M. 1960- *WhoRel 92*
**Jordan**, David Starr 1851-1931 *AmPeW*
**Jordan**, Don D. 1932- *WhoFI 92*
**Jordan**, Donald J 1916- *AmMWSc 92*
**Jordan**, Donna L. 1949- *WhoFI 92*
**Jordan**, Douglas Arthur 1918- *Who 92*
**Jordan**, Duane Paul 1935- *AmMWSc 92*
**Jordan**, Eddie Jack, Sr. 1927- *WhoBlA 92*
**Jordan**, Edmond Rhodes 1955- *WhoAmP 91*
**Jordan**, Edward C 1910- *AmMWSc 92*
**Jordan**, Edward Daniel 1931- *AmMWSc 92*
**Jordan**, Elizabeth 1867-1947 *BenetAL 91*
**Jordan**, Elke 1937- *AmMWSc 92*
**Jordan**, Ellen Kaye 1948- *WhoEnt 92*
**Jordan**, Ellen Rausen 1943- *WhoAmL 92*
**Jordan**, Emma Coleman 1946- *WhoAmL 92, WhoBlA 92*
**Jordan**, F. Gene 1932- *WhoFI 92*
**Jordan**, Francis Leo 1930- *Who 92*
**Jordan**, Frank 1941- *AmMWSc 92*
**Jordan**, Freddie L 1954- *AmMWSc 92*
**Jordan**, Frederick Douglass 1901- *WhoBlA 92*
**Jordan**, Frederick E. 1937- *WhoBlA 92*
**Jordan**, Gary Blake 1939- *AmMWSc 92*
**Jordan**, George Lee 1935- *WhoBlA 92*
**Jordan**, George Lyman, Jr 1921- *AmMWSc 92*
**Jordan**, George R, Jr 1920- *WhoIns 92*
**Jordan**, George Samuel 1944- *AmMWSc 92*
**Jordan**, George Washington, Jr. 1938- *WhoBlA 92*
**Jordan**, Gerald Ray 1896-1964 *DcNCBi 3*
**Jordan**, Gerard Michael 1929- *Who 92*
**Jordan**, Gilbert LeRoy 1924- *AmMWSc 92*
**Jordan**, Glenn 1936- *ConTFT 9, IntMPA 92, WhoEnt 92*
**Jordan**, Gregory Doty 1951- *WhoRel 92*
**Jordan**, Hamilton *IntWW 91*
**Jordan**, Harold Vernon 1924- *AmMWSc 92*
**Jordan**, Harold Willoughby 1937- *WhoBlA 92*
**Jordan**, Harry Frederick 1940- *AmMWSc 92*
**Jordan**, Helen Elaine 1926- *AmMWSc 92*
**Jordan**, Henrietta *IntMPA 92*
**Jordan**, Henry 1919- *Who 92*
**Jordan**, Henry Hellmut, Jr. 1921- *WhoFI 92*
**Jordan**, Henry Hunter, Jr 1943- *WhoAmP 91*
**Jordan**, Howard Emerson 1926- *AmMWSc 92*
**Jordan**, I. King 1943- *CurBio 91 [port]*
**Jordan**, J. St. Girard 1944- *WhoBlA 92*
**Jordan**, Jack Terrell *WhoWest 92*
**Jordan**, James A, Jr 1936- *AmMWSc 92*
**Jordan**, James Dempsey 1934- *WhoAmL 92*
**Jordan**, James Elgie 1949- *WhoRel 92*
**Jordan**, James Henry 1931- *AmMWSc 92*
**Jordan**, James Herbert 1946- *WhoWest 92*
**Jordan**, James Monroe, III 1957- *WhoAmL 92*
**Jordan**, James N 1925- *AmMWSc 92*
**Jordan**, James Peter 1948- *WhoFI 92*
**Jordan**, Janice Marie 1947- *WhoBlA 92*
**Jordan**, Jeffrey Guy 1950- *WhoWest 92*
**Jordan**, Joan Amelia 1948- *WhoEnt 92*
**Jordan**, John Allen, Jr. 1935- *WhoFI 92*
**Jordan**, John E. 1919- *WrDr 92*
**Jordan**, John Edward 1930- *WhoBlA 92*
**Jordan**, John M 1936- *WhoAmP 91*
**Jordan**, John Patrick 1934- *AmMWSc 92*
**Jordan**, John R., Jr. 1939- *WhoFI 92*
**Jordan**, John Richard, Jr 1921- *WhoAmP 91*
**Jordan**, John Storm 1952- *WhoFI 92*
**Jordan**, John W. *WhoRel 92*
**Jordan**, John Wesley 1941- *WhoBlA 92*
**Jordan**, John William 1912- *AmMWSc 92*
**Jordan**, Joseph 1919- *AmMWSc 92*
**Jordan**, Josephine E.C. 1935- *WhoBlA 92*
**Jordan**, Julie *WhoEnt 92*
**Jordan**, June *DrAPF 91*
**Jordan**, June 1936- *AfrAmW, BenetAL 91, ConPo 91, IntAu&W 91, NotBlAW 92, WrDr 92*
**Jordan**, June M. 1936- *WhoBlA 92*
**Jordan**, Kathleen Marie 1951- *WhoAmP 91*
**Jordan**, Keith *WhoAmP 91*
**Jordan**, Kelly Don 1961- *WhoFI 92*
**Jordan**, Kenneth A 1930- *AmMWSc 92*
**Jordan**, Kenneth David 1948- *AmMWSc 92*
**Jordan**, Kenneth Gary 1935- *AmMWSc 92*
**Jordan**, Kenneth L, Jr 1933- *AmMWSc 92*
**Jordan**, Kenneth Ulys 1944- *WhoBlA 92*
**Jordan**, Larry Clinton 1943- *WhoFI 92*
**Jordan**, Larry M *WhoAmP 91*
**Jordan**, Laura *WrDr 92*
**Jordan**, Lawrence Edward 1958- *WhoFI 92*
**Jordan**, Lee *ConAu 34NR, SmATA 66*
**Jordan**, Leonard R., Jr. 1950- *WhoAmL 92*
**Jordan**, Leroy A. 1941- *WhoBlA 92*
**Jordan**, Lillian *WhoAmP 91*
**Jordan**, Lois Heywood 1913- *WhoWest 92*
**Jordan**, Louis 1908-1975 *NewAmDM*
**Jordan**, Lowell Stephen 1930- *AmMWSc 92*
**Jordan**, Mabel B. 1912- *WhoBlA 92*
**Jordan**, Margaret Hayes 1943- *WhoBlA 92*
**Jordan**, Margaret Ilene 1950- *WhoMW 92*
**Jordan**, Marilyn E. 1944- *WhoBlA 92*
**Jordan**, Marjorie W. 1924- *WhoBlA 92*
**Jordan**, Mark H 1915- *AmMWSc 92*
**Jordan**, Marvin Evans, Jr. 1944- *WhoEnt 92*
**Jordan**, Mary Ann 1940- *AmMWSc 92*
**Jordan**, Mary H 1944- *WhoAmP 91*
**Jordan**, Matt *TwCWW 91*
**Jordan**, Michael 1963- *WhoBlA 92*
**Jordan**, Michael Adrian, II 1947- *WhoEnt 92*
**Jordan**, Michael Anthony 1931- *Who 92*
**Jordan**, Michael Douglas 1949- *WhoEnt 92*
**Jordan**, Michael Hugh 1936- *WhoFI 92*
**Jordan**, Michael Jeffery 1963- *BlkOlyM, IntWW 91, WhoMW 92*
**Jordan**, Michael Jeffrey 1963- *FacFETw*
**Jordan**, Michael Lewis 1945- *WhoEnt 92*
**Jordan**, Michelle Denise 1954- *WhoBlA 92*
**Jordan**, Mildred *ConAu 133*
**Jordan**, Milton C. *WhoBlA 92*
**Jordan**, Morris Lee 1939- *WhoRel 92*
**Jordan**, Murray Brandis 1936- *WhoEnt 92*
**Jordan**, Nancy Scattergood *WhoEnt 92*
**Jordan**, Neal F 1932- *AmMWSc 92*
**Jordan**, Neil 1950- *ConNov 91, IntDcF 2-2 [port], IntMPA 92, IntWW 91, WrDr 92*
**Jordan**, Neil Patrick 1950- *IntAu&W 91, WhoEnt 92*
**Jordan**, Nerius Fred, Jr. 1945- *WhoRel 92*
**Jordan**, Nicholas Theodore 1940- *WhoAmL 92*
**Jordan**, Nick M. 1949- *WhoMW 92*
**Jordan**, Octavio Manuel 1912- *WhoHisp 92*
**Jordan**, Orchid I. 1910- *WhoBlA 92*
**Jordan**, Orchid Irene 1910- *WhoAmP 91*
**Jordan**, Pamela Carole 1949- *WhoEnt 92*
**Jordan**, Pascual 1902-1980 *EncTR 91 [port]*
**Jordan**, Patricia Carter 1946- *WhoBlA 92*
**Jordan**, Patricia Robinson 1947- *WhoEnt 92*
**Jordan**, Patrick Joseph 1957- *WhoAmL 92*
**Jordan**, Paul H, Jr 1919- *AmMWSc 92*
**Jordan**, Peggy *WhoHisp 92*
**Jordan**, Peter Albion 1930- *AmMWSc 92*
**Jordan**, Peter C H 1936- *AmMWSc 92*
**Jordan**, Philip Dean 1940- *WhoRel 92*
**Jordan**, Philip Harding, Jr. 1931- *WhoMW 92*
**Jordan**, Pleasant 1812-1863 *DcNCBi 3*
**Jordan**, Preston LeRoy, Jr. 1954- *WhoRel 92*
**Jordan**, R. D. 1930- *WhoBlA 92*
**Jordan**, Ralph 1926- *WhoBlA 92*
**Jordan**, Randall Bryant 1951- *WhoRel 92*
**Jordan**, Randy Wayne 1952- *WhoRel 92*
**Jordan**, Raymond A, Jr 1943- *WhoAmP 91*
**Jordan**, Raymond Alan 1942- *WhoWest 92*
**Jordan**, Raymond Bruce 1912- *WhoWest 92*
**Jordan**, Richard 1938- *IntMPA 92*
**Jordan**, Richard A 1946- *WhoIns 92*
**Jordan**, Richard Alan 1953- *WhoRel 92*
**Jordan**, Richard Bowen 1902- *Who 92*
**Jordan**, Richard Buckner 1930- *WhoFI 92*
**Jordan**, Richard Charles 1909- *AmMWSc 92*
**Jordan**, Richard Thomas 1948- *WhoEnt 92, WhoFI 92*
**Jordan**, Richard Winslow 1958- *WhoRel 92*
**Jordan**, Robert *WhoBlA 92*
**Jordan**, Robert 1940- *WhoEnt 92*
**Jordan**, Robert, Jr 1920- *AmMWSc 92*
**Jordan**, Robert A. 1932- *WhoBlA 92*
**Jordan**, Robert B, III 1932- *WhoAmP 91*
**Jordan**, Robert H 1926- *WhoIns 92*
**Jordan**, Robert Howard, Jr. 1943- *WhoBlA 92*
**Jordan**, Robert Kenneth 1925- *AmMWSc 92*
**Jordan**, Robert L. 1906- *WhoBlA 92*
**Jordan**, Robert Lawrence 1941- *AmMWSc 92*
**Jordan**, Robert Leon 1928- *WhoAmL 92, WhoWest 92*
**Jordan**, Robert Leon 1934- *WhoAmL 92*
**Jordan**, Robert Manseau 1920- *AmMWSc 92*
**Jordan**, Robert R 1937- *AmMWSc 92*
**Jordan**, Robert Smith 1929- *WrDr 92*
**Jordan**, Robert Thomas 1937- *WhoFI 92, WhoMW 92*
**Jordan**, Roy Wilcox 1911- *WhoMW 92*
**Jordan**, Rudolf 1902- *BiDExR, EncTR 91 [port]*
**Jordan**, Russell Thomas *AmMWSc 92*
**Jordan**, Ruth *WrDr 92*
**Jordan**, Sally *WhoAmP 91*
**Jordan**, Sandra Dickerson 1951- *WhoAmL 92*
**Jordan**, Scott Wilson 1934- *AmMWSc 92*
**Jordan**, Sharon Lee 1952- *WhoAmP 91*
**Jordan**, Stanley 1959- *WhoBlA 92*
**Jordan**, Stanley Clark 1947- *AmMWSc 92*
**Jordan**, Steve Russell 1961- *WhoBlA 92*
**Jordan**, Steven Edward 1946- *WhoEnt 92*
**Jordan**, Steven Lee 1943- *AmMWSc 92*
**Jordan**, Stroud 1885-1947 *DcNCBi 3*
**Jordan**, Stuart Davis 1936- *AmMWSc 92*
**Jordan**, Susan *DrAPF 91*
**Jordan**, Terry L 1948- *WhoAmP 91*
**Jordan**, Thomas Fredrick 1936- *AmMWSc 92*

**Jordan**, Thomas Hillman 1948- *AmMWSc 92*
**Jordan**, Thomas L 1943- *AmMWSc 92*
**Jordan**, Thurman 1936- *WhoBlA 92*
**Jordan**, Truman H 1937- *AmMWSc 92*
**Jordan**, Vernon E., Jr. 1935- *WhoBlA 92*
**Jordan**, Vincent Andre 1965- *WhoBlA 92*
**Jordan**, W. Carl 1949- *WhoAmL 92*
**Jordan**, Wade H, Jr 1932- *AmMWSc 92*
**Jordan**, Walter Fant 1938- *WhoRel 92*
**Jordan**, Wayne Robert 1940- *AmMWSc 92*
**Jordan**, Wesley Lee 1941- *WhoBlA 92*
**Jordan**, Wilbert Cornelious 1944- *WhoBlA 92*
**Jordan**, Will *WhoEnt 92*
**Jordan**, Willard Clayton 1922- *AmMWSc 92*
**Jordan**, William Alan 1960- *WhoAmL 92*
**Jordan**, William Alfred, III 1934- *WhoBlA 92*
**Jordan**, William Brian 1936- *Who 92*
**Jordan**, William D 1922- *AmMWSc 92*
**Jordan**, William Hamilton 1944- *IntWW 91*
**Jordan**, William Kirby 1923- *AmMWSc 92*
**Jordan**, William Lee 1931- *WhoMW 92*
**Jordan**, William Malcolm 1936- *AmMWSc 92*
**Jordan**, William R, III 1944- *AmMWSc 92*
**Jordan**, William Reyneir, Jr. 1951- *WhoWest 92*
**Jordan**, William Stone, Jr 1917- *AmMWSc 92*
**Jordan**, Willis Pope, Jr 1918- *AmMWSc 92*
**Jordan-Dillon**, Araceli 1954- *WhoHisp 92*
**Jordan-Harris**, Katherine 1927- *WhoBlA 92*
**Jordan-Molero**, Jaime E 1941- *AmMWSc 92*
**Jordan-Moss**, Norman 1920- *Who 92*
**Jordana**, Jonn M. 1950- *WhoMW 92*
**Jordania**, Vakhtang 1942- *WhoEnt 92*
**Jorde**, Thomas 1947- *WhoAmL 92*
**Jorden**, Crystal Wood 1942- *WhoWest 92*
**Jorden**, James Roy 1934- *AmMWSc 92*
**Jorden**, Roger M 1935- *AmMWSc 92*
**Jordens**, Joseph Teresa Florent 1925- *IntWW 91*
**Jordin**, Marcus Wayne 1927- *AmMWSc 92*
**Jordon**, Deborah Elizabeth 1951- *WhoAmL 92, WhoFI 92*
**Jordon**, James T 1925- *WhoAmP 91*
**Jordon**, Lynn V. 1940- *WhoWest 92*
**Jordon**, Robert Earl 1938- *AmMWSc 92*
**Jordon**, Robert Mark 1950- *WhoRel 92*
**Jordy**, George Y 1932- *AmMWSc 92*
**Jordy**, William H. 1917- *WrDr 92*
**Jorg** *DrAPF 91*
**Jorge**, Antonio *WhoHisp 92*
**Jorge**, Edwin Santos 1940- *WhoHisp 92*
**Jorge**, Nuno Maria Roque 1947- *WhoFI 92*
**Jorge**, Silvia 1945- *WhoHisp 92*
**Jorgensen**, Anker 1922- *IntWW 91*
**Jorgensen**, Bo Barker 1946- *IntWW 91*
**Jorgensen**, Brian Kent 1958- *WhoAmL 92*
**Jorgensen**, Christine 1926-1989 *FacFETw*
**Jorgensen**, Clive D 1931- *AmMWSc 92*
**Jorgensen**, Darrell *WhoAmP 91*
**Jorgensen**, Donald Allen 1952- *WhoWest 92*
**Jorgensen**, Edvard 1950- *WhoFI 92*
**Jorgensen**, Erik 1921- *AmMWSc 92*
**Jorgensen**, Erik Holger 1916- *WhoAmL 92, WhoWest 92*
**Jorgensen**, Frank Nils 1951- *WhoFI 92*
**Jorgensen**, George Norman 1936- *AmMWSc 92*
**Jorgensen**, Gerald Thomas 1947- *WhoRel 92*
**Jorgensen**, Gordon D 1932- *WhoIns 92*
**Jorgensen**, Gordon David 1921- *WhoFI 92, WhoWest 92*
**Jorgensen**, Helmuth Erik Milo 1927- *AmMWSc 92*
**Jorgensen**, Ivar *TwCSFW 91, WrDr 92*
**Jorgensen**, James D 1948- *AmMWSc 92*
**Jorgensen**, Jens Erik 1936- *AmMWSc 92, WhoWest 92*
**Jorgensen**, Judith Ann *WhoWest 92*
**Jorgensen**, Judy Hesler 1939- *WhoMW 92*
**Jorgensen**, Kay Susan 1951- *WhoAmP 91*
**Jorgensen**, Lars 1837-1927 *RelLAm 91*
**Jorgensen**, Lennart Andrew 1947- *WhoFI 92, WhoWest 92*
**Jorgensen**, Lou Ann Birkbeck 1931- *WhoWest 92*
**Jorgensen**, Mark Christopher 1951- *WhoWest 92*
**Jorgensen**, Neal A 1935- *AmMWSc 92*
**Jorgensen**, Palle E T 1947- *AmMWSc 92*
**Jorgensen**, Paul A. 1916- *WrDr 92*
**Jorgensen**, Paul J 1930- *AmMWSc 92, WhoFI 92*
**Jorgensen**, Paul Victor 1952- *WhoAmL 92*
**Jorgensen**, Ralph Gubler 1937- *WhoAmL 92*
**Jorgensen**, Richard E. *DrAPF 91*
**Jorgensen**, Sven-Aage 1929- *IntWW 91*
**Jorgensen**, T. Dennis 1945- *WhoWest 92*
**Jorgensen**, William L 1949- *AmMWSc 92*
**Jorgenson**, Allen *ConAu 133*
**Jorgenson**, Dale W. 1933- *IntWW 91*
**Jorgenson**, Dale Weldeau 1933- *WhoFI 92*
**Jorgenson**, Edsel Carpenter 1926- *AmMWSc 92*
**Jorgenson**, Everett Thomas 1952- *WhoFI 92, WhoMW 92*
**Jorgenson**, Gordon Victor 1933- *AmMWSc 92*
**Jorgenson**, Ivar *ConAu 36NR, TwCSFW 91*
**Jorgenson**, James Richard 1926- *WhoEnt 92*
**Jorgenson**, James Wallace 1952- *AmMWSc 92*
**Jorgenson**, Wallace James 1923- *WhoEnt 92*
**Jorgenson**, Wayne James 1943- *WhoRel 92*
**Jorio**, Lorenzo 1927- *WhoEnt 92*
**Jorisch**, Gary Neal 1950- *WhoFI 92*
**Jorizzo**, Joseph L 1951- *AmMWSc 92*
**Jornales**, Robert Arnaldo 1945- *WhoWest 92*
**Jorndt**, Louis Daniel 1941- *WhoMW 92*
**Jorne**, Jacob 1941- *AmMWSc 92*
**Jorns**, Marilyn Schuman 1943- *AmMWSc 92*
**Joron**, Andrew *DrAPF 91*
**Jorre De St Jorre**, Danielle Marie-M. 1941- *Who 92*
**Jorstad**, John Leonard 1935- *AmMWSc 92*
**Jortner**, Joshua 1933- *IntWW 91*
**Jory**, Edward John 1936- *IntWW 91*
**Jory**, Farnham Stewart 1926- *AmMWSc 92*
**Jory**, Howard Roberts 1931- *AmMWSc 92*
**Joscelyn**, Archie 1899- *TwCWW 91*
**Joscelyn**, Kent Buckley 1936- *WhoAmL 92, WhoFI 92, WhoMW 92*
**Joscelyn**, William Wilkie 1926- *WhoAmP 91*
**Joscelyne**, Richard Patrick 1934- *Who 92*
**Jose I** 1714-1777 *BlkwCEP*
**Jose**, Donald Edwin 1947- *WhoAmL 92*
**Jose**, Felix 1965- *WhoHisp 92*
**Jose**, Jorge V 1949- *AmMWSc 92, WhoHisp 92*
**Jose**, Nicholas 1952- *IntAu&W 91*
**Jose**, Pedro A 1942- *AmMWSc 92*
**Jose**, Phyllis Ann 1949- *WhoMW 92*
**Jose-Kampfner**, Christina 1950- *WhoHisp 92*
**Josefchuk**, Gregory Joseph 1961- *WhoFI 92*
**Joseff**, Joan Castle 1922- *WhoFI 92*
**Josefowitz**, Natasha *DrAPF 91*
**Joselow**, Beth Baruch *DrAPF 91*
**Joselow**, Beth Baruch 1948- *ConAu 36NR*
**Joselyn**, Jo Ann Cram 1943- *AmMWSc 92*
**Josenhans**, James Gross 1932- *AmMWSc 92*
**Josenhans**, Paul J. *WhoAmL 92*
**Josenhans**, William T 1922- *AmMWSc 92*
**Joseph** *Who 92*
**Joseph** 1840?-1904 *RComAH*
**Joseph I** 1714-1777 *BlkwCEP*
**Joseph II** 1741-1790 *BlkwCEP*
**Joseph**, Baron 1918- *IntWW 91, Who 92*
**Joseph**, Chief 1840?-1904 *BenetAL 91*
**Joseph**, Metropolitan Bishop 1942- *WhoRel 92*
**Joseph**, Alfred S 1932- *AmMWSc 92*
**Joseph**, Allan Jay 1938- *WhoAmL 92*
**Joseph**, Anita Marie *WhoEnt 92*
**Joseph**, Antoine L. 1923- *WhoBlA 92*
**Joseph**, Bernard William 1929- *AmMWSc 92*
**Joseph**, Burton Norris, III 1951- *WhoMW 92*
**Joseph**, Cedric Luckie 1933- *IntWW 91*
**Joseph**, Daniel D 1929- *AmMWSc 92*
**Joseph**, Daniel Mordecai 1941- *WhoAmL 92*
**Joseph**, David *DrAPF 91*
**Joseph**, David J., Jr. 1916- *WhoFI 92*
**Joseph**, David Winram 1930- *AmMWSc 92*
**Joseph**, Diana J. 1958- *WhoAmL 92*
**Joseph**, Donald J 1922- *AmMWSc 92*
**Joseph**, Donald Louis 1942- *WhoFI 92*
**Joseph**, Earl Clark 1926- *WhoMW 92*
**Joseph**, Earl Clark, II 1956- *AmMWSc 92*
**Joseph**, Edward d1991 *NewYTBS 91*
**Joseph**, Edward David 1919- *AmMWSc 92*
**Joseph**, Erik 1959- *WhoEnt 92*
**Joseph**, Ezekiel 1938- *WhoWest 92*
**Joseph**, Frank Douglas 1937- *WhoBlA 92*
**Joseph**, George Manley 1930- *WhoAmL 92, WhoWest 92*
**Joseph**, Geraldine M 1923- *WhoAmP 91*
**Joseph**, Gregory Paul 1951- *WhoAmL 92*
**Joseph**, Herbert Leslie 1908- *Who 92*
**Joseph**, J Mehsen 1928- *AmMWSc 92*
**Joseph**, J Walter, Jr 1928- *AmMWSc 92*
**Joseph**, James 1930- *AmMWSc 92*
**Joseph**, James Alfred 1935- *WhoBlA 92*
**Joseph**, Jane 1942- *TwCPaSc*
**Joseph**, Jenny 1932- *ConPo 91, IntAu&W 91*
**Joseph**, Jeymohan 1953- *AmMWSc 92*
**Joseph**, John Mundancheril 1947- *AmMWSc 92*
**Joseph**, Joseph Paul 1935- *WhoAmP 91*
**Joseph**, Kenneth 1922- *IntMPA 92*
**Joseph**, Kenneth Robert 1928- *WhoRel 92*
**Joseph**, Larry Dennis 1952- *WhoEnt 92*
**Joseph**, Lawrence *DrAPF 91*
**Joseph**, Leslie *Who 92*
**Joseph**, Leslie 1925- *Who 92*
**Joseph**, Lily Delissa 1863-1940 *TwCPaSc*
**Joseph**, Lloyd Leroi 1934- *WhoBlA 92*
**Joseph**, M K 1914-1981 *TwCSFW 91*
**Joseph**, Marjory L 1917- *AmMWSc 92*
**Joseph**, Maurice Franklin 1905- *WhoAmP 91*
**Joseph**, Michael 1897-1958 *DcLB 112 [port]*
**Joseph**, Michael Anthony 1944- *WhoFI 92*
**Joseph**, Michael Thomas 1927- *WhoEnt 92*
**Joseph**, Mimi Silbert 1937- *WhoFI 92*
**Joseph**, Monica Anna Bilcheck 1926- *WhoEnt 92*
**Joseph**, Myron Lawrence 1936- *WhoAmL 92, WhoMW 92*
**Joseph**, Paul 1944- *WhoRel 92*
**Joseph**, Paul Abraham 1953- *WhoMW 92*
**Joseph**, Paul R 1951- *WhoAmL 92*
**Joseph**, Peter 1929- *TwCPaSc*
**Joseph**, Peter D 1936- *AmMWSc 92*
**Joseph**, Peter Maron 1939- *AmMWSc 92*
**Joseph**, Poet *DrAPF 91*
**Joseph**, Ramon R 1930- *AmMWSc 92*
**Joseph**, Raymond Alcide 1931- *WhoBlA 92*
**Joseph**, Richard Isaac 1936- *AmMWSc 92*
**Joseph**, Robert George 1948- *WhoAmL 92*
**Joseph**, Robert Thomas 1946- *WhoAmL 92*
**Joseph**, Ronald Evans 1936- *WhoRel 92*
**Joseph**, Rosaline Resnick 1929- *AmMWSc 92*
**Joseph**, Roy D 1937- *AmMWSc 92*
**Joseph**, Ruth *WhoAmP 91*
**Joseph**, Sammy William 1934- *AmMWSc 92*
**Joseph**, Samuel Kenneth 1949- *WhoRel 92*
**Joseph**, Solomon 1910- *AmMWSc 92*
**Joseph**, Stanley Robert 1930- *AmMWSc 92*
**Joseph**, Stephanie R. 1946- *WhoAmL 92*
**Joseph**, Stephen C *AmMWSc 92*
**Joseph**, Stephen M. *DrAPF 91*
**Joseph**, Stephen M 1938- *IntAu&W 91, WrDr 92*
**Joseph**, Susan B. 1958- *WhoAmL 92*
**Joseph**, Tam 1947- *TwCPaSc*
**Joseph**, Yves Bazin Jean 1948- *WhoEnt 92*
**Joseph-McIntyre**, Mary 1942- *WhoBlA 92*
**Joseph-Renaud**, Jean 1874- *ScFEYrs*
**Josephs**, Babette 1940- *WhoAmP 91*
**Josephs**, Jess J 1917- *AmMWSc 92*
**Josephs**, Larry d1991 *NewYTBS 91*
**Josephs**, Laurence *DrAPF 91*
**Josephs**, Melvin Jay 1926- *AmMWSc 92*
**Josephs**, Ray 1912- *WrDr 92*
**Josephs**, Robert 1937- *AmMWSc 92*
**Josephs**, Stephanie J. 1965- *WhoMW 92*
**Josephs**, Steven F 1950- *AmMWSc 92*
**Josephs**, Wilfred 1927- *ConCom 92, IntWW 91, Who 92*
**Josephsen**, Carl Thomas, Jr. 1947- *WhoWest 92*
**Josephson**, Alan S 1930- *AmMWSc 92*
**Josephson**, Brian David 1940- *AmMWSc 92, FacFETw, IntWW 91, Who 92, WhoNob 90*
**Josephson**, David Lane 1956- *WhoWest 92*
**Josephson**, Diana Hayward 1936- *WhoWest 92*
**Josephson**, Edward Samuel 1915- *AmMWSc 92*
**Josephson**, Erland 1923- *IntMPA 92, IntWW 91*
**Josephson**, Harold Allan 1944- *WhoWest 92*
**Josephson**, Joe P 1933- *WhoAmP 91*
**Josephson**, Leonard Melvin 1913- *AmMWSc 92*
**Josephson**, Marvin *LesBEnT 92*
**Josephson**, Marvin 1927- *IntMPA 92, WhoFI 92*
**Josephson**, Marvin 1935- *IntMPA 92*
**Josephson**, Matthew 1899-1978 *BenetAL 91*
**Josephson**, Robert Karl 1934- *AmMWSc 92*
**Josephson**, Ronald Victor 1942- *AmMWSc 92*
**Josephson**, William Howard 1934- *WhoAmL 92*
**Josephus** 35?-100 *EncEarC*
**Josephy**, Alvin M, Jr 1915- *IntAu&W 91, WrDr 92*
**Josey**, E. J. 1924- *WhoBlA 92*
**Josey**, Leronia Arnetta *WhoBlA 92*
**Josh** *ConAu 135*
**Joshi**, Aravind Krishna 1929- *AmMWSc 92*
**Joshi**, Bhairav Datt 1939- *AmMWSc 92*
**Joshi**, Damayanti 1932- *IntWW 91*
**Joshi**, Harideo 1921- *IntWW 91*
**Joshi**, Jayant Gopal 1932- *AmMWSc 92*
**Joshi**, Madhusudan Shankarrao 1928- *AmMWSc 92*
**Joshi**, Mukund Shankar 1947- *AmMWSc 92*
**Joshi**, Ramesh Chandra 1932- *AmMWSc 92*
**Joshi**, Sadanand D 1950- *AmMWSc 92*
**Joshi**, Sewa Ram 1933- *AmMWSc 92*
**Joshi**, Sharad Gopal *AmMWSc 92*
**Joshi**, Suresh Meghashyam *AmMWSc 92*
**Joshi**, Umashankar 1911- *IntAu&W 91*
**Joshi**, Vasudev Chhotalal 1938- *AmMWSc 92*
**Joshua**, Aaron 1957- *WhoWest 92*
**Joshua**, Henry 1934- *AmMWSc 92*
**Josi**, Tim 1950- *WhoAmP 91*
**Josiah Allen's Wife** *BenetAL 91*
**Josiah**, Walter J., Jr. 1933- *IntMPA 92*
**Josias**, Conrad S 1930- *AmMWSc 92*
**Josiassen**, Richard Carlton 1947- *AmMWSc 92*
**Josipovici**, Gabriel 1940- *ConNov 91, WrDr 92*
**Josipovici**, Gabriel David 1940- *IntAu&W 91*
**Joslin**, Alfred Hahn 1914- *WhoAmP 91*
**Joslin**, Benjamin Franklin 1796-1861 *BiInAmS*
**Joslin**, David Bruce 1936- *WhoRel 92*
**Joslin**, Gary James 1943- *WhoAmL 92*
**Joslin**, James E. 1932- *WhoRel 92*
**Joslin**, Norman E 1925- *WhoAmP 91*
**Joslin**, Norman Earl 1925- *WhoAmL 92*
**Joslin**, Peter David 1933- *Who 92*
**Joslin**, Richard Walter 1931- *WhoMW 92*
**Joslin**, Robert Scott 1929- *AmMWSc 92*
**Joslin**, Roger 1936- *WhoIns 92*
**Joslin**, Sesyle 1929- *IntAu&W 91, WrDr 92*
**Josling**, John Francis 1910- *IntAu&W 91, Who 92*
**Joslyn**, Dennis Joseph 1947- *AmMWSc 92*
**Joslyn**, John Alan 1945- *WhoEnt 92*
**Joslyn**, Kristine B 1948- *WhoAmP 91*
**Joslyn**, Wallace Danforth 1939- *WhoMW 92*
**Joson**, Nilo Floresta 1945- *WhoMW 92*
**Jospin**, Lionel Robert 1937- *IntWW 91*
**Josquin des Pres** 1440?-1521 *NewAmDM*
**Joss**, Frederick Augustus 1932- *WhoFI 92*
**Joss**, Judy Harue 1953- *WhoAmL 92*
**Joss**, Paul Christopher 1945- *AmMWSc 92*
**Joss**, William Hay 1927- *Who 92*
**Josselson**, Frank 1944- *WhoAmL 92*
**Josselyn**, John 1608?-1675 *BiInAmS*
**Josselyn**, John 1638-1675 *BenetAL 91*
**Jossem**, Edmund Leonard 1919- *AmMWSc 92*
**Jossem**, Jared H 1942- *WhoAmP 91*
**Josserand**, Robert Warren 1896- *WhoAmP 91*
**Josset**, Lawrence 1910- *Who 92*
**Jossi**, Jack William 1937- *AmMWSc 92*
**Jossi**, Steven Michael 1957- *WhoRel 92*
**Jost**, Dana Nelson 1925- *AmMWSc 92*
**Jost**, Donald E 1936- *AmMWSc 92*
**Jost**, Ernest 1928- *AmMWSc 92*
**Jost**, H. Peter 1921- *Who 92*
**Jost**, Hans Peter 1921- *AmMWSc 92*
**Jost**, Jean-Pierre 1937- *AmMWSc 92*
**Jost**, Lee Fred 1928- *WhoMW 92*
**Jost**, Patricia Cowan *AmMWSc 92*
**Jost**, Peter 1955- *WhoMW 92*
**Jost**, Peter Hafner 1949- *WhoAmL 92*
**Jost**, Richard Frederic, III 1947- *WhoAmL 92*
**Josten**, Roy Joseph 1940- *WhoAmL 92*
**Josten**, Werner 1885-1963 *NewAmDM*
**Jostlein**, Hans 1940- *AmMWSc 92*
**Jotcham**, Thomas Denis 1918- *WhoFI 92*
**Jotischky**, Andrew 1965- *ConAu 133*
**Joubert**, John 1927- *ConCom 92, NewAmDM*
**Joubin**, Franc Renault 1911- *AmMWSc 92*
**Joudi**, Tony Salim *WhoMW 92*
**Joughin**, G. Louis d1991 *NewYTBS 91*
**Joughin**, Michael 1926- *Who 92*
**Jouhaux**, Leon 1879-1954 *WhoNob 90*
**Joukhdar**, Mohammed Saleh 1932- *IntWW 91*
**Joullie**, Madeleine M 1927- *AmMWSc 92*
**Joung**, John Jongin 1941- *AmMWSc 92*

**Jourdain**, Francois 1876-1958 *DcTwDes, FacFETw*
**Jourdain**, Fritz 1847-1937 *DcTwDes*
**Jourdan**, Albert M, Jr *WhoAmP 91*
**Jourdan**, Louis 1921- *IntMPA 92, WhoEnt 92*
**Jourdian**, George William 1929- *AmMWSc 92*
**Jourdon**, Glenn Ritchey 1940- *WhoFI 92*
**Jourdren**, Marc Henri 1960- *WhoFI 92*
**Journeay**, Glen Eugene 1925- *AmMWSc 92*
**Journey**, Drexel Dahlke 1926- *WhoAmL 92, WhoFI 92*
**Journey**, Lula Mae 1934- *WhoBlA 92*
**Joutel**, Henri 1645?-1723? *BenetAL 91*
**Jouve**, Nicole Jeanne *WhoEnt 92*
**Jouven**, Pierre Jean Antoine 1908- *IntWW 91*
**Jouvet**, Louis 1887-1951 *FacFETw*
**Jouy**, Pierre Louis 1856-1894 *BiInAmS*
**Jova**, Joseph John 1916- *IntWW 91, WhoAmP 91, WhoHisp 92*
**Jovancicevic**, Vladimir 1947- *AmMWSc 92*
**Jovanov**, Branislav 1949- *WhoMW 92*
**Jovanovic**, M K 1913- *AmMWSc 92*
**Jovanovic**, Miroslav N. 1957- *WhoFI 92*
**Jovanovic**, Robert Paul 1935- *WhoRel 92*
**Jovanovich**, Jovan Vojislav 1928- *AmMWSc 92*
**Jovanovich**, Peter William 1949- *WhoFI 92*
**Jovanovich**, William *DrAPF 91*
**Jovanovich**, William 1920- *WrDr 92*
**Jovanovich**, William Iliya 1920- *IntWW 91*
**jovel**, jinn *DrAPF 91*
**Jovellanos**, Gaspar Melchor de 1744-1811 *BlkwCEP*
**Jovian** 331?-364 *EncEarC*
**Jovinian** d406? *EncEarC*
**Jowaiszas**, Susan Gail 1958- *WhoWest 92*
**Jowanowitsch**, Sophie *EncAmaz 91*
**Jowell**, Jeffrey Lionel 1938- *Who 92*
**Jowett**, Alfred 1914- *Who 92*
**Jowett**, David 1934- *AmMWSc 92*
**Jowett**, Percy Hague 1882-1955 *TwCPaSc*
**Jowitt**, Edwin 1929- *Who 92*
**Jowitt**, Juliet Diana Margaret 1940- *Who 92*
**Joxe**, Louis d1991 *NewYTBS 91 [port]*
**Joxe**, Louis 1901-1991 *CurBio 91N, IntWW 91, -91N*
**Joxe**, Pierre Daniel 1934- *IntWW 91*
**Joy**, Carla Marie 1945- *WhoWest 92*
**Joy**, Charles Arad 1823-1891 *BiInAmS*
**Joy**, Daniel Webster 1931- *WhoBlA 92*
**Joy**, David 1932- *Who 92*
**Joy**, David 1942- *IntAu&W 91, WrDr 92*
**Joy**, David Charles 1943- *AmMWSc 92*
**Joy**, David Michael 1952- *WhoFI 92*
**Joy**, Donald Marvin 1928- *WrDr 92*
**Joy**, Edward Bennett 1941- *AmMWSc 92*
**Joy**, George Cecil, III 1948- *AmMWSc 92*
**Joy**, James Bernard, Jr. 1937- *WhoBlA 92*
**Joy**, Joseph Wayne 1930- *AmMWSc 92*
**Joy**, Kenneth Wilfred 1935- *AmMWSc 92*
**Joy**, Michael Gerard Laurie 1916- *Who 92*
**Joy**, Michael Lawrence Grahame 1940- *AmMWSc 92*
**Joy**, P K 1940- *IntAu&W 91*
**Joy**, Peter 1926- *Who 92*
**Joy**, Robert 1951- *IntMPA 92*
**Joy**, Robert John Thomas 1929- *AmMWSc 92*
**Joy**, Robert McKernon 1941- *AmMWSc 92*
**Joy**, Robert Paul 1949- *WhoAmL 92*
**Joy**, Steve 1952- *TwCPaSc*
**Joy**, Thomas Alfred 1904- *Who 92, WrDr 92*
**Joy**, Timothy John 1956- *WhoWest 92*
**Joy**, Vincent Anthony 1920- *AmMWSc 92*
**Joyant**, Maurice 1864-1930 *ThHEIm*
**Joyce**, Blaine R 1925- *AmMWSc 92*
**Joyce**, David Paul 1960- *WhoFI 92*
**Joyce**, Donald Franklin 1938- *WhoBlA 92*
**Joyce**, Edwin A, Jr 1937- *AmMWSc 92*
**Joyce**, Eileen d1991 *IntWW 91, -91N*
**Joyce**, Eileen Alannah d1991 *Who 92N*
**Joyce**, Elaine 1947- *WhoEnt 92*
**Joyce**, Glenn Russell 1939- *AmMWSc 92*
**Joyce**, James 1882-1941 *CnDBLB 6 [port], FacFETw [port], LiExTwC, RfGEnL 91*
**Joyce**, James Daniel 1921- *WhoRel 92*
**Joyce**, James Edward 1926- *WhoIns 92*
**Joyce**, James Joseph, Jr. 1947- *WhoAmL 92*
**Joyce**, James Martin 1942- *AmMWSc 92*
**Joyce**, Jane Wilson *DrAPF 91*
**Joyce**, Jeremiah E 1943- *WhoAmP 91*
**Joyce**, Jerome J 1939- *WhoAmP 91*
**Joyce**, Joseph James 1943- *WhoAmL 92*
**Joyce**, Joseph M. *WhoAmL 92*
**Joyce**, Joseph Patrick 1951- *WhoFI 92*
**Joyce**, Michael G. 1950- *WhoEnt 92*
**Joyce**, Michael Patrick 1960- *WhoAmL 92*
**Joyce**, Michael Scott 1957- *WhoIns 92*
**Joyce**, Patricia Marie 1953- *WhoAmP 91*
**Joyce**, Raymond M H *WhoAmP 91*
**Joyce**, Richard Ross 1944- *AmMWSc 92*
**Joyce**, Robert Hyland 1928- *WhoAmL 92*
**Joyce**, Robert John H. *Who 92*
**Joyce**, Robert Joseph 1948- *WhoFI 92*
**Joyce**, Robert Michael 1915- *AmMWSc 92*
**Joyce**, Robin Hank 1960- *WhoWest 92*
**Joyce**, Roger 1943- *WhoEnt 92*
**Joyce**, Rose Marie *WhoHisp 92*
**Joyce**, Stephen Michael 1945- *WhoAmL 92*
**Joyce**, Susan M 1951- *WhoAmP 91*
**Joyce**, Tim 1958- *WhoAmP 91*
**Joyce**, Walter Joseph 1930- *WhoFI 92*
**Joyce**, William *DrAPF 91*
**Joyce**, William 1906-1946 *EncTR 91 [port]*
**Joyce**, William 1957- *ChILR 26 [port]*
**Joyce**, William B 1932- *AmMWSc 92*
**Joyce**, William Brooke 1906-1946 *BiDExR*
**Joyce**, William R., Jr. 1921- *Who 92*
**Joyce**, William Robert 1936- *WhoFI 92*
**Joye**, Afrie Songco 1942- *WhoRel 92*
**Joyet**, Alain Rene 1946- *WhoFI 92*
**Joyner**, Albert Lewis, Jr. 1946- *WhoRel 92*
**Joyner**, Alfrederick 1960- *BlkOlyM [port]*
**Joyner**, Andrew 1786-1856 *DcNCBi 3*
**Joyner**, Arthenia Lee 1943- *WhoBlA 92*
**Joyner**, Billy Norris 1932- *WhoIns 92*
**Joyner**, Claude C. 1950- *WhoBlA 92*
**Joyner**, Claude Reuben 1925- *AmMWSc 92*
**Joyner**, Conrad Francis 1931- *WhoAmP 91*
**Joyner**, Darla Jean 1947- *WhoWest 92*
**Joyner**, Dee Ann 1947- *WhoFI 92*
**Joyner**, Edmund Noah 1847-1939 *DcNCBi 3*
**Joyner**, Florence Griffith 1959- *FacFETw, WhoBlA 92*
**Joyner**, Gary Kelton 1957- *WhoAmL 92*
**Joyner**, Gordon L 1950- *WhoAmP 91, WhoBlA 92*
**Joyner**, Howard Sajon 1939- *AmMWSc 92*
**Joyner**, Irving L. 1944- *WhoBlA 92*
**Joyner**, James Yadkin 1862-1954 *DcNCBi 3*
**Joyner**, John Erwin 1935- *WhoBlA 92*
**Joyner**, John T, III 1928- *AmMWSc 92*
**Joyner**, Lemuel Martin 1928- *WhoBlA 92*
**Joyner**, Marjorie Stewart *WhoBlA 92*
**Joyner**, Powell Austin 1925- *AmMWSc 92*
**Joyner**, Ralph Delmer 1928- *AmMWSc 92*
**Joyner**, Ronald Wayne 1947- *AmMWSc 92*
**Joyner**, Rubin E. 1949- *WhoBlA 92*
**Joyner**, Seth 1964- *WhoBlA 92*
**Joyner**, Weyland Thomas 1929- *WhoFI 92*
**Joyner**, Weyland Thomas, Jr 1929- *AmMWSc 92*
**Joyner**, William A. 1933- *WhoBlA 92*
**Joyner**, William B 1929- *AmMWSc 92*
**Joyner**, William Henry, Jr 1946- *AmMWSc 92*
**Joyner**, William Lyman 1939- *AmMWSc 92*
**Joyner-Kersee**, Jackie 1962- *FacFETw, WhoBlA 92*
**Joyner-Kersee**, Jacqueline 1962- *BlkOlyM [port]*
**Joynes**, Stanley Knight, III 1954- *WhoAmL 92*
**Joynson**, Reuben Edwin, Jr 1926- *AmMWSc 92*
**Joynson-Hicks** *Who 92*
**Joynt**, Evelyn Gertrude 1919- *Who 92*
**Joynt**, Jack 1942- *WhoWest 92*
**Joynt**, Michael Charles S. *Who 92*
**Joynt**, Robert James 1925- *AmMWSc 92*
**Joys**, Terence Michael 1935- *AmMWSc 92*
**Jozoff**, Malcolm 1939- *WhoFI 92*
**Jozsa**, Frank Paul, Jr. 1941- *WhoFI 92*
**Jozsa**, Margaret Ann 1952- *WhoWest 92*
**Jozsef**, Attila 1905-1937 *FacFETw*
**Ju**, Frederick D 1929- *AmMWSc 92*
**Ju**, Jin Soon 1921- *AmMWSc 92*
**Juan Carlos I** 1938- *FacFETw, IntWW 91*
**Juan**, Prince 1913- *IntWW 91*
**Juana Ines de la Cruz** 1648?-1695 *SpAmWW*
**Juana la Betraneja** 1462-1530 *EncAmaz 91*
**Juanarena**, Douglas B. *WhoHisp 92*
**Juang**, Jer-Nan 1945- *AmMWSc 92*
**Juang**, Ling Ling 1949- *AmMWSc 92*
**Juanpere**, Nieves A. 1955- *WhoHisp 92*
**Juantorena**, Danger Alberto 1951- *BlkOlyM*
**Juarez**, Belia 1960- *WhoHisp 92*
**Juarez**, Benito 1806-1872 *BenetAL 91*
**Juarez**, David Hernandez 1946- *WhoHisp 92*
**Juarez**, Jacinto P. 1944- *WhoHisp 92*
**Juarez**, Jesus R. 1952- *WhoHisp 92*
**Juarez**, Jose 1955- *WhoHisp 92*
**Juarez**, Joseph M. 1956- *WhoHisp 92*
**Juarez**, Leo J. 1939- *WhoHisp 92*
**Juarez**, Maretta Liya Calimpong 1958- *WhoWest 92*
**Juarez**, Martin 1946- *WhoHisp 92, WhoMW 92, WhoRel 92*
**Juarez**, Nicandro *WhoHisp 92*
**Juarez**, Oscar F 1940- *WhoAmP 91*
**Juarez**, Robert Carrillo 1935- *WhoHisp 92*
**Juarez**, Rolando 1964- *WhoHisp 92*
**Juarez Robles**, Jennifer Jean 1957- *WhoHisp 92*
**Juarez-West**, Debra Ann 1958- *WhoHisp 92*
**Juarros**, Domingo 1752-1820 *HisDSpE*
**Juarroz**, Roberto 1925- *ConSpAP*
**Jubany Arnau**, Narcisco 1913- *WhoRel 92*
**Jubany Arnau**, Narciso 1916- *IntWW 91*
**Jubb**, Gerald Lombard, Jr 1943- *AmMWSc 92*
**Jubelirer**, Robert Carl 1937- *WhoAmP 91*
**Juberg**, Richard Caldwell 1930- *AmMWSc 92*
**Juberg**, Richard Kent 1929- *AmMWSc 92, WhoWest 92*
**Jubilee Singers** *NewAmDM*
**Jubran**, Raja Jubran 1957- *WhoFI 92*
**Juby**, Peter Frederick 1935- *AmMWSc 92*
**Juceam**, Robert E. 1940- *WhoAmL 92*
**Juchacz**, Maria 1879-1956 *EncTR 91*
**Juchau**, Mont Rawlings 1934- *AmMWSc 92*
**Jucker**, Hans 1927- *IntWW 91*
**Juckett**, Richard Ross 1956- *WhoAmP 91*
**Jud**, Henry G 1934- *AmMWSc 92*
**Jud**, William F. 1938- *WhoMW 92*
**Juda**, Annely 1914- *IntWW 91*
**Judah**, Aaron 1923- *WrDr 92*
**Judah**, Jay Stillson 1911- *WhoRel 92*
**Judah**, Samuel B. H. 1799?-1876 *BenetAL 91*
**Judas Iscariot** *EncEarC*
**Juday**, Dan *WhoRel 92*
**Juday**, Glenn Patrick 1950- *AmMWSc 92*
**Juday**, Richard Evans 1918- *AmMWSc 92*
**Judd** *Who 92*
**Judd**, Baron 1935- *Who 92*
**Judd**, Alan 1946- *WrDr 92*
**Judd**, Barry Gene 1946- *WhoWest 92*
**Judd**, Brian Raymond 1931- *AmMWSc 92*
**Judd**, Burke Haycock 1927- *AmMWSc 92*
**Judd**, Claud 1918- *WhoAmP 91*
**Judd**, Clifford Harold Alfred 1927- *Who 92*
**Judd**, Cyril *TwCSFW 91, WrDr 92*
**Judd**, David Lockhart 1923- *AmMWSc 92*
**Judd**, Denis 1938- *IntAu&W 91, WrDr 92*
**Judd**, Dennis L. 1954- *WhoAmL 92*
**Judd**, Donald 1928- *DcTwDes*
**Judd**, Donald Clarence 1928- *IntWW 91*
**Judd**, Dorothy Heiple 1922- *WhoMW 92*
**Judd**, Edward 1934- *IntMPA 92*
**Judd**, Eric Campbell 1918- *Who 92*
**Judd**, Floyd L 1934- *AmMWSc 92*
**Judd**, Frances K. *ConAu 134, SmATA 65*
**Judd**, Frank 1935- *WrDr 92*
**Judd**, Frank Wayne 1939- *AmMWSc 92*
**Judd**, Gary 1942- *AmMWSc 92*
**Judd**, Gary Stoddard 1940- *WhoFI 92*
**Judd**, Harlan Ekin, Jr 1943- *WhoAmP 91*
**Judd**, Harrison *WrDr 92*
**Judd**, James Thurston 1938- *WhoWest 92*
**Judd**, Jane Harter 1925- *AmMWSc 92*
**Judd**, Jerry Gorden 1946- *WhoRel 92*
**Judd**, June E *WhoAmP 91*
**Judd**, Laurie Maureen 1952- *WhoAmL 92*
**Judd**, Leonard R. 1939- *WhoWest 92*
**Judd**, Lewis Lund 1930- *AmMWSc 92*
**Judd**, Nadine *Who 92*
**Judd**, Naomi *WhoEnt 92*
**Judd**, O'Dean P 1937- *AmMWSc 92, WhoWest 92*
**Judd**, Orange 1822-1892 *BiInAmS*
**Judd**, R. Allen 1943- *WhoFI 92*
**Judd**, Ralph Waverly 1930- *IntAu&W 91*
**Judd**, Raymond Earl, Jr. 1934- *WhoRel 92*
**Judd**, Richard Donald 1940- *WhoWest 92*
**Judd**, Ross Leonard 1936- *AmMWSc 92*
**Judd**, Stanley H 1928- *AmMWSc 92*
**Judd**, Sylvester 1813-1853 *AmPeW*
**Judd**, Sylvester, III 1813-1853 *BenetAL 91*
**Judd**, Sylvester Dwight 1871-1905 *BiInAmS*
**Judd**, Thomas Eli 1927- *WhoWest 92*
**Judd**, Walter Henry 1898- *WhoAmP 91*
**Judd**, Walter Stephen 1951- *AmMWSc 92*
**Judd**, William Henry 1930- *WhoFI 92*
**Judd**, William Robert 1917- *AmMWSc 92, WhoMW 92*
**Judd**, William Wallace 1915- *AmMWSc 92*
**Judd**, Wynonna 1964- *WhoEnt 92*
**Jude** *EncEarC*
**Jude**, Thaddeus Victor 1951- *WhoAmP 91*
**Judell**, Harold Benn 1915- *WhoAmL 92*
**Judge**, Darrell L 1934- *AmMWSc 92*
**Judge**, Edward Thomas 1908- *Who 92*
**Judge**, Frank *DrAPF 91*
**Judge**, Frank D *AmMWSc 92*
**Judge**, George Garrett 1925- *WhoWest 92*
**Judge**, Harry George 1928- *Who 92, WrDr 92*
**Judge**, Igor 1941- *Who 92*
**Judge**, Jean Frances 1922- *WhoFI 92*
**Judge**, John Emmet 1912- *WhoFI 92, WhoMW 92*
**Judge**, Joseph Malachi 1930- *AmMWSc 92*
**Judge**, Leo Francis, Jr 1927- *AmMWSc 92*
**Judge**, Margaret Amoroso 1957- *WhoAmL 92*
**Judge**, Max David 1932- *AmMWSc 92*
**Judge**, Paul Frederick 1966- *WhoFI 92*
**Judge**, Roger John Richard 1938- *AmMWSc 92*
**Judge**, Steve 1953- *WhoFI 92*
**Judge**, Thomas Joseph 1927- *WhoFI 92, WhoMW 92*
**Judge**, Thomas Lee 1934- *IntWW 91, WhoAmP 91*
**Judge**, William Quan 1851-1896 *RelLAm 91*
**Judis**, Joseph 1929- *AmMWSc 92*
**Judish**, John Paul 1926- *AmMWSc 92*
**Judith** *EncAmaz 91*
**Judkins**, Joseph Faulcon, Jr 1938- *AmMWSc 92*
**Judkins**, Roddie Reagan 1941- *AmMWSc 92*
**Judson**, Arthur d1975 *LesBEnT 92*
**Judson**, Arthur 1881-1975 *FacFETw*
**Judson**, Betty Dorsey *WhoRel 92*
**Judson**, Burton Frederick 1928- *AmMWSc 92*
**Judson**, Charles B 1951- *WhoAmP 91*
**Judson**, Charles LeRoy 1926- *AmMWSc 92*
**Judson**, Charles Morrill 1919- *AmMWSc 92*
**Judson**, E. Z. C. 1823-1886 *BenetAL 91*
**Judson**, Edward 1844-1914 *RelLAm 91*
**Judson**, Horace Augustus 1941- *AmMWSc 92, WhoBlA 92, WhoWest 92*
**Judson**, John *DrAPF 91*
**Judson**, John 1930- *IntAu&W 91, WrDr 92*
**Judson**, Margaret Atwood d1991 *NewYTBS 91*
**Judson**, Margaret Atwood 1899-1991 *ConAu 134*
**Judson**, Philip Livingston 1941- *WhoAmL 92*
**Judson**, Ray W. 1926- *WhoWest 92*
**Judson**, Robert Edward 1946- *WhoWest 92*
**Judson**, Sheldon, Jr 1918- *AmMWSc 92*
**Judson**, Sylvia Shaw 1897-1978 *ConAu 133*
**Judson**, Walter Emery 1916- *AmMWSc 92*
**Judson**, William Lee 1842-1928 *DcTwDes*
**Judson**, William Thadius 1959- *WhoBlA 92*
**Judt**, Tony R. 1948- *WrDr 92*
**Judy**, Nancy Elizabeth 1931- *WhoAmP 91*
**Judy**, Richard Jay 1959- *WhoMW 92*
**Juech**, Stephen Paul 1952- *WhoAmL 92*
**Juel**, Donald H. 1942- *ConAu 35NR*
**Juenge**, Eric Carl 1927- *AmMWSc 92*
**Juergens**, George Ivar 1932- *WhoMW 92*
**Juergens**, John Louis 1925- *AmMWSc 92*
**Juergens**, Stephen J. 1947- *WhoAmL 92*
**Juergensen**, Hans 1919- *IntAu&W 91, WrDr 92*
**Juergensmeyer**, Elizabeth B 1940- *AmMWSc 92*
**Juergensmeyer**, Julian Conrad 1938- *WhoAmL 92*
**Juffa**, Michael Richard 1952- *WhoMW 92*
**Jugel**, Richard Dennis 1942- *WhoMW 92*
**Jugenheimer**, Robert William 1904- *AmMWSc 92*
**Jugnauth**, Aneerood 1930- *IntWW 91, Who 92*
**Juhasz**, Anne McCreary 1922- *WrDr 92*
**Juhasz**, Stephen 1913- *AmMWSc 92*
**Juhasz**, Stephen Eugene 1923- *AmMWSc 92*
**Juhasz**, Suzanne *DrAPF 91*
**Juhl**, Daniel Leo 1935- *WhoFI 92, WhoMW 92*
**Juhl**, Finn 1912- *DcTwDes*
**Juhl**, William G 1924- *AmMWSc 92*
**Juhn**, Gloria 1926- *WhoEnt 92*
**Juhola**, Carl 1920- *AmMWSc 92*
**Jukes**, Betty C. 1932- *WhoEnt 92*
**Jukes**, Geoffrey 1928- *WrDr 92*
**Jukes**, John 1923- *Who 92*
**Jukes**, John Andrew 1917- *Who 92*
**Jukes**, Thomas Hughes 1906- *AmMWSc 92*
**Jukkola**, George Duane 1945- *WhoWest 92*
**Julander**, Paula Foil 1939- *WhoAmP 91*
**Jules**, Leonard Herbert 1922- *AmMWSc 92*
**Julesz**, Bela 1928- *AmMWSc 92, IntWW 91*
**Julia**, Maria C. *WhoHisp 92*
**Julia**, Raul 1940- *IntMPA 92, WhoHisp 92*
**Julia**, Raul 1944- *WhoEnt 92*
**Julian** 331?-363 *EncEarC*

**Julian of Eclanum** 380?-455 *EncEarC*
**Julian of Halicarnassus** d527? *EncEarC*
**Julian of Norwich** *RfGEnL 91*
**Julian Pomerius** *EncEarC*
**Julian**, Anna Johnson *NotBlAW 92, WhoBlA 92*
**Julian**, Brian Kenneth 1954- *WhoAmL 92*
**Julian**, Charles William 1954- *WhoRel 92*
**Julian**, Dennis Wayne 1952- *WhoRel 92*
**Julian**, Desmond Gareth 1926- *Who 92*
**Julian**, Donald Benjamin 1922- *AmMWSc 92*
**Julian**, Edward A 1926- *AmMWSc 92*
**Julian**, Glenn Marcenia 1939- *AmMWSc 92*
**Julian**, Gordon Ray 1928- *AmMWSc 92*
**Julian**, Jim Lee 1954- *WhoAmL 92*
**Julian**, John Tyrone 1947- *WhoBlA 92*
**Julian**, Joseph Robert 1961- *WhoFI 92*
**Julian**, Kerry Edward 1962- *WhoFI 92, WhoMW 92*
**Julian**, Maureen M 1939- *AmMWSc 92*
**Julian**, Norman *DrAPF 91*
**Julian**, Percy L., Jr. 1940- *WhoBlA 92*
**Julian**, Raymond Charles 1952- *WhoFI 92*
**Julian**, Robert Richard 1931- *WhoEnt 92*
**Julian**, Timothy Ray 1956- *WhoRel 92*
**Julian**, William H 1939- *AmMWSc 92*
**Juliana** 1658-1733 *EncAmaz 91*
**Juliana Louise Emma Marie Wilhelmina** 1909- *IntWW 91*
**Julianelle**, Robert Lewis 1940- *WhoAmP 91*
**Julianna of Breteuil** *EncAmaz 91*
**Juliano**, Rudolph Lawrence 1941- *AmMWSc 92*
**Juliar**, Marvin Dale 1934- *WhoMW 92*
**Julich**, Wilhelm 1839?-1893 *BiInAmS*
**Julien**, A. M. 1903- *IntWW 91*
**Julien**, Alexis Anastay 1840-1919 *BiInAmS*
**Julien**, Claude Norbert 1925- *IntWW 91*
**Julien**, Denis Alan 1945- *WhoFI 92*
**Julien**, Hiram Paul 1929- *AmMWSc 92*
**Julien**, Howard L 1942- *AmMWSc 92*
**Julien**, Jean-Paul 1918- *AmMWSc 92*
**Julien**, Larry Marlin 1937- *AmMWSc 92*
**Julien**, Michael Frederick 1938- *Who 92*
**Julien**, Robert M 1942- *AmMWSc 92*
**Julien**, Robert Michael 1942- *WhoWest 92*
**Julienne du Guesdin** *EncAmaz 91*
**Julienne**, Paul Sebastian 1944- *AmMWSc 92*
**Julin**, Joseph Richard 1926- *WhoAmL 92, WhoFI 92*
**Julinao**, Peter C 1941- *AmMWSc 92*
**Juliot**, Virgil F. 1925- *WhoRel 92*
**Julis**, Karel 1929- *IntWW 91*
**Julius I** *EncEarC*
**Julius The Veteran** *EncEarC*
**Julius**, Edward Howard 1952- *WhoFI 92*
**Julius**, John Michael, III 1958- *WhoAmL 92*
**Julius**, Rich *DrAPF 91*
**Julius**, Stevo 1929- *AmMWSc 92*
**Julius Africanus**, Sextus 160?-240? *EncEarC*
**Juliussen**, J Egil 1943- *AmMWSc 92*
**Juliusson**, Marguerite 1956- *WhoEnt 92*
**Jull**, Anthony John Timothy 1951- *AmMWSc 92*
**Jull**, Edward Vincent 1934- *AmMWSc 92*
**Jull**, George W 1929- *AmMWSc 92*
**Julle**, Keith Leroy 1939- *WhoWest 92*
**Jullien**, Graham Arnold 1943- *AmMWSc 92*
**Jullien**, Jacques 1929- *IntWW 91*
**Jullien**, Louis Antoine 1812-1860 *NewAmDM*
**July**, Serge 1942- *IntWW 91*
**Julyan**, Frederick John 1927- *AmMWSc 92*
**Juma**, Sa'ad *Who 92N*
**Jumao-as**, Alex Baronda 1961- *WhoWest 92*
**Jumarie**, Guy Michael 1939- *AmMWSc 92*
**Jumars**, Peter Alfred 1948- *AmMWSc 92*
**Jumbe**, Aboud 1920- *IntWW 91*
**Jumbe**, Philbert Alexander 1946- *IntWW 91*
**Jumikis**, Alfreds Richards 1907- *AmMWSc 92*
**Juminer**, Bertene Gaetan 1927- *IntWW 91*
**Jumonville**, John Enoul, Jr 1942- *WhoAmP 91*
**Jump**, Bernard, Jr. 1938- *WhoFI 92*
**Jump**, Chester Jackson, Jr. 1918- *WhoRel 92*
**Jump**, Donald Wayne 1954- *WhoRel 92*
**Jump**, Gordon *WhoEnt 92*
**Jump**, Harry V 1914- *WhoAmP 91*
**Jump**, J Robert 1937- *AmMWSc 92*
**Jump**, John Austin 1913- *AmMWSc 92*
**Jump**, Linda Gail 1949- *WhoMW 92*
**Jump**, Lorin Keith 1928- *AmMWSc 92*
**Jumper**, Andrew Albert 1927- *WhoRel 92*
**Jumper**, Charles Frederick 1934- *AmMWSc 92*
**Jumper**, Eric J 1946- *AmMWSc 92*
**Jumper**, Eric John 1946- *WhoMW 92*
**Jumper**, Lynda Flanagin 1947- *WhoAmP 91*
**Jumper**, Sidney Roberts 1930- *AmMWSc 92*
**Jumsai**, Sumet 1939- *IntAu&W 91*
**Jun**, Xi Juan 1962- *TwCPaSc*
**Junak**, Steven Alan 1949- *WhoWest 92*
**Junaluska** 1779?-1858 *DcNCBi 3*
**Junchen**, David Lawrence 1946- *WhoFI 92*
**Juncosa**, Mario Leon 1921- *AmMWSc 92*
**Jundt**, Kevin John 1961- *WhoWest 92*
**June**, Roy Ethiel 1922- *WhoWest 92*
**June**, Vi 1932- *WhoAmP 91*
**Juneau**, Pierre 1922- *IntWW 91, WhoEnt 92, WhoFI 92*
**Junejo**, Muhammad Khan 1932- *IntWW 91*
**Junell**, Robert 1947- *WhoAmP 91*
**Junewicz**, James J. 1950- *WhoAmL 92*
**Jung**, Alvin Ray 1952- *WhoFI 92*
**Jung**, C G 1875-1961 *FacFETw [port]*
**Jung**, Cathy *WhoEnt 92*
**Jung**, Chan Yong 1928- *AmMWSc 92*
**Jung**, Dennis William *AmMWSc 92*
**Jung**, Donald T. 1953- *WhoWest 92*
**Jung**, Doris 1924- *WhoEnt 92*
**Jung**, Edgar 1894-1934 *EncTR 91 [port]*
**Jung**, Fred W., Jr. 1918- *WhoAmL 92*
**Jung**, Frederic Theodore *AmMWSc 92*
**Jung**, Fredo 1949- *WhoEnt 92*
**Jung**, Gerald Alvin 1930- *AmMWSc 92*
**Jung**, Glenn Harold 1924- *AmMWSc 92*
**Jung**, Hans-Gernot 1930- *IntWW 91*
**Jung**, Henry Hung 1957- *WhoWest 92*
**Jung**, Hilda Ziifle 1922- *AmMWSc 92*
**Jung**, James Moser 1928- *AmMWSc 92*
**Jung**, Jay Joseph 1950- *WhoRel 92*
**Jung**, John Andrew, Jr 1938- *AmMWSc 92*
**Jung**, Lawrence Kwok Leung 1950- *AmMWSc 92*
**Jung**, Loyle Shannon 1943- *WhoRel 92*
**Jung**, Michael Ernest 1947- *AmMWSc 92*
**Jung**, Nawab Mir Nawaz 1904- *IntWW 91*
**Jung**, Patricia Beattie 1949- *WhoRel 92*
**Jung**, Reinhard Paul 1946- *WhoFI 92*
**Jung**, Rodney Clifton 1920- *AmMWSc 92*
**Jung**, Rudolf 1882-1945 *BiDExR*
**Jung**, Samson Pang 1963- *WhoWest 92*
**Jung**, Timothy Tae Kun 1943- *WhoWest 92*
**Junga**, Frank Arthur 1934- *AmMWSc 92*
**Jungalwala**, Firoze Bamanshaw 1936- *AmMWSc 92*
**Jungalwalla**, Nowshir K. 1912- *IntWW 91*
**Jungas**, Robert Leando 1934- *AmMWSc 92*
**Jungbauer**, J. Steven 1959- *WhoMW 92*
**Jungbauer**, Mary Ann 1934- *AmMWSc 92*
**Jungbluth**, Connie Carlson 1955- *WhoFI 92, WhoWest 92*
**Jungbluth**, Kirk E. 1949- *WhoFI 92, WhoWest 92*
**Jungck**, Gerald Frederick 1929- *AmMWSc 92*
**Jungck**, John Richard 1944- *AmMWSc 92*
**Jungclaus**, Gregory Alan 1947- *AmMWSc 92*
**Junge**, Douglas 1938- *AmMWSc 92*
**Jungel**, Eberhard 1934- *WhoRel 92*
**Jungels**, Eleanor E 1922- *WhoAmP 91*
**Jungels**, Pierre Jean Marie Henri 1944- *Who 92*
**Junger**, Ernst 1895- *BiDExR, EncTR 91 [port], IntAu&W 91, IntWW 91*
**Junger**, Friedrich Georg 1898-1977 *EncTR 91*
**Junger**, Miguel C 1923- *AmMWSc 92*
**Jungerius**, Pieter Dirk 1933- *IntWW 91*
**Jungerman**, John 1921- *AmMWSc 92*
**Jungermann**, Eric 1923- *AmMWSc 92*
**Jungers**, Francis 1926- *IntWW 91*
**Jungius**, James 1923- *Who 92*
**Jungkind**, Donald Lee 1943- *AmMWSc 92*
**Jungkind**, Walter 1923- *WhoEnt 92*
**Jungman**, Robert Peter 1937- *WhoAmL 92*
**Jungmann**, Richard A 1928- *AmMWSc 92*
**Juni**, Elliot 1921- *AmMWSc 92*
**Junia**, Edward Xavier 1948- *WhoAmL 92*
**Junid**, Seri Sanusi bin 1943- *IntWW 91*
**Juniel**, Eunice Kimbrough 1931- *WhoRel 92*
**Junior**, E. J., III 1959- *WhoBlA 92*
**Junior**, Ester James, Jr. 1932- *WhoBlA 92*
**Junior**, Gary R 1940- *WhoAmP 91*
**Junior**, Samella E. 1931- *WhoBlA 92*
**Junipero**, Serra *BenetAL 91*
**Junk**, Paul Edwin 1929- *WhoFI 92, WhoMW 92*
**Junk**, Sam John 1939- *WhoAmP 91*
**Junk**, William A, Jr 1924- *AmMWSc 92*
**Junker**, Bobby Ray 1943- *AmMWSc 92*
**Junker**, Christine Rosetta 1953- *WhoMW 92*
**Junker**, Jeffrey Stephen 1962- *WhoEnt 92*
**Junkers**, Hugo 1859-1935 *EncTR 91 [port]*
**Junkhan**, George H 1929- *AmMWSc 92*
**Junkin**, John R, II *WhoAmP 91*
**Junkin**, Peter Joseph 1947- *WhoAmL 92*
**Junkin**, Raymond 1918- *IntMPA 92*
**Junkin**, Trey Kirk 1961- *WhoBlA 92*
**Junkin**, Zella Edith 1934- *WhoMW 92*
**Junkins**, Billy Eugene 1925- *WhoRel 92*
**Junkins**, Bobby Mac 1946- *WhoAmP 91*
**Junkins**, Donald *DrAPF 91*
**Junkins**, Donald 1931- *IntAu&W 91, WrDr 92*
**Junkins**, Jerry R *AmMWSc 92*
**Junkins**, Jerry Ray 1937- *WhoFI 92*
**Junkins**, John Lee 1943- *AmMWSc 92*
**Junkins**, Lowell Lee 1944- *WhoAmP 91*
**Junlowjiraya**, Viroj 1955- *WhoMW 92*
**Junor**, John 1919- *Who 92*
**Junor**, John Donald Brown 1919- *IntAu&W 91, IntWW 91*
**Junquera**, Mercedes 1930- *WhoHisp 92*
**Juntereal**, F A, Jr 1934- *WhoIns 92*
**Junz**, Helen B. *IntWW 91, WhoFI 92*
**Juo**, Pei-Show 1930- *AmMWSc 92*
**Juola**, Robert C 1940- *AmMWSc 92*
**Juorio**, Augusto Victor 1934- *AmMWSc 92*
**Jupe**, George Percival 1930- *Who 92*
**Jupin**, A. Alexandra 1944- *WhoEnt 92*
**Jupin**, J. Michael *WhoRel 92*
**Jupin**, Lawrence Earl 1939- *WhoWest 92*
**Jupiter**, Clyde Peter 1928- *WhoBlA 92*
**Jupnik**, Helen 1915- *AmMWSc 92*
**Jupp**, Kenneth Graham 1917- *Who 92*
**Juppe**, Alain Marie 1945- *IntWW 91*
**Jur**, Barbara A. 1945- *WhoMW 92*
**Jura**, Michael Alan 1947- *AmMWSc 92*
**Jurado**, Annmarie 1957- *WhoEnt 92*
**Jurado**, Katy 1927- *IntMPA 92*
**Jurado**, Patrick R. 1941- *WhoHisp 92*
**Jurado**, Rosendo B. 1913- *WhoHisp 92*
**Juran**, Joseph M 1904- *AmMWSc 92*
**Jurand**, Jerry George 1923- *AmMWSc 92*
**Juras**, JuliAnn Berg *WhoEnt 92*
**Jurasek**, Lubomir 1931- *AmMWSc 92*
**Juraska**, Janice Marie 1949- *AmMWSc 92*
**Jurch**, George Richard, Jr 1934- *AmMWSc 92*
**Jurcyk**, John Joseph, Jr. 1930- *WhoAmL 92*
**Jurd**, Leonard 1925- *AmMWSc 92*
**Jure**, Jorge Alcides 1953- *WhoEnt 92*
**Jurecki**, Casimer John Joseph 1952- *WhoWest 92*
**Juredine**, David Graydon 1937- *WhoFI 92*
**Juretschke**, Hellmut Joseph 1924- *AmMWSc 92*
**Jurf**, Amin N 1932- *AmMWSc 92*
**Jurgelski**, William, Jr 1931- *AmMWSc 92*
**Jurgemeyer**, Donald William 1920- *WhoAmL 92*
**Jurgens**, Conrad R 1947- *WhoIns 92*
**Jurgens**, Jurgen 1925- *NewAmDM*
**Jurgens**, Leonard John 1933- *WhoWest 92*
**Jurgens**, Marshall Herman 1941- *AmMWSc 92*
**Jurgens**, Paul Eugene 1927- *WhoAmP 91*
**Jurgensen**, Barbara 1928- *WhoMW 92, WhoRel 92*
**Jurgensen**, David Alan 1957- *WhoMW 92*
**Jurgensen**, Delbert F, Jr 1909- *AmMWSc 92*
**Jurgensen**, Manfred 1940- *IntAu&W 91*
**Jurgiel**, John Anthony 1937- *WhoMW 92*
**Juri**, Nilo 1949- *WhoAmP 91*
**Jurica**, Gerald Michael 1941- *AmMWSc 92*
**Jurich**, Anthony Peter 1947- *WhoMW 92*
**Juricic**, Davor 1928- *AmMWSc 92*
**Jurieu**, Pierre 1637-1713 *BlkwCEP*
**Jurin**, James 1684-1750 *BlkwCEP*
**Jurinac**, Sena 1921- *IntWW 91, NewAmDM, Who 92*
**Jurinak**, Jerome Joseph 1927- *AmMWSc 92*
**Jurinski**, Neil B 1938- *AmMWSc 92*
**Juris**, Marc Allan 1956- *WhoEnt 92*
**Jurist**, Ed 1916- *WhoEnt 92*
**Jurist**, John Michael 1943- *AmMWSc 92*
**Jurista**, Diana Mae 1940- *WhoRel 92*
**Jurjescu**, Octavian 1939- *WhoWest 92*
**Jurkat**, Martin Peter 1935- *AmMWSc 92*
**Jurkat**, Wolfgang Bernhard 1929- *AmMWSc 92*
**Jurkiewicz**, Maurice J 1924- *AmMWSc 92*
**Jurkowski**, John *DrAPF 91*
**Jurkus**, Algirdas Petras 1935- *AmMWSc 92*
**Jurmain**, Robert Douglas 1948- *AmMWSc 92*
**Jurmain**, Suzanne 1945- *ConAu 133*
**Jurock**, Oswald Erich 1944- *WhoFI 92*
**Jurow**, Martin 1911- *IntMPA 92*
**Jurs**, Peter Christian 1943- *AmMWSc 92*
**Jurschak**, Jay Aloysius 1952- *WhoWest 92*
**Jursinic**, Paul Andrew 1946- *AmMWSc 92*
**Jurtshuk**, Peter, Jr 1929- *AmMWSc 92*
**Jurukov**, Carla Tonka 1966- *WhoWest 92*
**Jury**, Archibald George 1907- *Who 92*
**Jury**, Eliahu I 1923- *AmMWSc 92*
**Jury**, Floyd Derwood 1934- *WhoMW 92*
**Jury**, William Austin 1946- *AmMWSc 92*
**Jusinski**, Leonard Edward 1955- *AmMWSc 92, WhoWest 92*
**Juskalian**, Lee Jon 1947- *WhoAmP 91*
**Jusko**, William Joseph 1942- *AmMWSc 92*
**Jussawalla**, Adil 1940- *ConPo 91*
**Jusserand**, Jean Jules 1855-1932 *BenetAL 91*
**Jussieu**, Antoine-Laurent de 1748-1836 *BlkwCEP*
**Just**, David Glen 1944- *WhoMW 92*
**Just**, George 1929- *AmMWSc 92*
**Just**, Gunther 1892-1950 *EncTR 91*
**Just**, Jennifer Ramsay 1958- *WhoEnt 92*
**Just**, John Josef 1938- *AmMWSc 92*
**Just**, Kurt W 1927- *AmMWSc 92*
**Just**, Richard 1948- *AmMWSc 92*
**Just**, Richard Eugene 1948- *WhoFI 92*
**Just**, Ward 1935- *BenetAL 91*
**Justen**, Lewis Leo 1951- *AmMWSc 92*
**Juster**, Allan 1922- *AmMWSc 92*
**Juster**, Daniel Calvin 1947- *WhoRel 92*
**Juster**, Mark Louis 1950- *WhoAmL 92*
**Juster**, Norman Joel 1924- *AmMWSc 92*
**Juster**, Norton 1929- *IntAu&W 91, WrDr 92*
**Justesen**, Don Robert 1930- *AmMWSc 92*
**Justham**, David Gwyn 1923- *Who 92*
**Justham**, Stephen Alton 1937- *AmMWSc 92*
**Justice**, Amos Isaac 1851-1945 *DcNCBi 3*
**Justice**, Bob Joe 1946- *WhoFI 92*
**Justice**, Brady Richmond, Jr. 1930- *WhoMW 92*
**Justice**, C. Graham 1968- *WhoEnt 92*
**Justice**, David Christopher 1966- *WhoBlA 92*
**Justice**, Donald *DrAPF 91*
**Justice**, Donald 1925- *BenetAL 91, ConPo 91, WrDr 92*
**Justice**, Donald Rodney 1925- *IntAu&W 91*
**Justice**, Edwin Judson 1867-1917 *DcNCBi 3*
**Justice**, Eunice McGhee 1922- *WhoRel 92*
**Justice**, Gregory Walter 1956- *WhoEnt 92*
**Justice**, Jack Burton 1931- *WhoAmL 92*
**Justice**, Jack R. *DrAPF 91*
**Justice**, James E 1933- *WhoIns 92*
**Justice**, James Horace 1941- *AmMWSc 92*
**Justice**, Jay David 1952- *WhoMW 92*
**Justice**, Keith Evans 1930- *AmMWSc 92*
**Justice**, Michael Hoke 1844-1919 *DcNCBi 3*
**Justice**, Norman E 1925- *WhoAmP 91, WhoBlA 92*
**Justice**, Ora Lynn 1942- *WhoRel 92*
**Justice**, Phillip Howard 1948- *WhoMW 92*
**Justice**, Raymond 1924- *AmMWSc 92*
**Justice**, Samuel James 1913- *WhoFI 92*
**Justice**, William F *WhoAmP 91*
**Justice**, William Wayne 1920- *WhoAmL 92*
**Justin** *EncEarC*
**Justin Martyr** d165? *EncEarC*
**Justin**, George *IntMPA 92*
**Justin**, James Robert 1933- *AmMWSc 92*
**Justin**, John, Jr. 1917- *News 92-2*
**Justin**, Joseph Eugene 1945- *WhoWest 92*
**Justin**, Lembit Peter 1928- *WhoFI 92*
**Justin**, Mark Allen 1962- *WhoEnt 92*
**Justinian I** 482-565 *EncEarC [port]*
**Justus of Urgel** d546? *EncEarC*
**Justus**, Carl Gerald 1939- *AmMWSc 92*
**Justus**, David Eldon 1936- *AmMWSc 92*
**Justus**, Jack Glenn 1931- *WhoFI 92*
**Justus**, Jerry T 1932- *AmMWSc 92*
**Justus**, Jerry Thomas *WhoWest 92*
**Justus**, Larry T 1932- *WhoAmP 91*
**Justus**, Norman Edward 1926- *AmMWSc 92*
**Justus**, Philip Stanley 1941- *AmMWSc 92*
**Justus**, Thomas Clyde 1964- *WhoRel 92*
**Justynowicz**, Bogdan Czeslaw 1939- *IntAu&W 91*
**Jusuf**, Andi Mohamad 1929- *IntWW 91*
**Jutikkala**, Eino Kaarlo Ilmari 1907- *IntWW 91*
**Jutila**, John W 1931- *AmMWSc 92*
**Jutkowitz**, Joel M 1942- *WhoAmP 91*
**Jutra**, Claude 1930-1986 *IntDcF 2-2*
**Jutras**, Michel Wilfrid 1936- *AmMWSc 92*
**Juvenal** 55?-127? *ClMLC 8 [port]*
**Juvencus** *EncEarC*
**Juves**, Jose A. 1944- *WhoHisp 92*
**Juvet**, Richard Spalding, Jr 1930- *AmMWSc 92, WhoWest 92*
**Juviler**, Amy Herz 1937- *WhoAmL 92*
**Juvinall**, Robert C 1917- *AmMWSc 92*
**Juxon**, John *WrDr 92*
**Juzeliunas**, Julius 1916- *SovUnBD*
**Jwo**, Chin-Hung 1956- *AmMWSc 92*
**Jyoti**, Swami Amar 1928- *RelLAm 91*
**Jyotir Maya Nanda**, Swami 1931- *RelLAm 91*
**Jyranki**, Antero 1933- *IntWW 91*
**Jyung**, Woon Heng 1934- *AmMWSc 92*

# K

**K.M.** *ConAu 134*
**K-Turkel,** Judi 1934- *WhoFI 92*
**Kaae,** James Lewis 1936- *AmMWSc 92*
**Kaae,** Kenneth W. 1953- *WhoWest 92*
**Kaahumanu** *EncAmaz 91*
**Kaar,** Jason Frederick 1960- *WhoAmL 92*
**Kaarsberg,** Ernest Andersen 1918- *AmMWSc 92*
**Kaarsted,** Tage 1928- *IntWW 91*
**Kaas,** Jon Howard 1937- *AmMWSc 92*
**Kaas,** Ludwig 1881-1952 *EncTR 91 [port]*
**Kaatz,** Leon Michael 1942- *WhoAmL 92*
**Kaatz,** Martin Richard 1924- *AmMWSc 92*
**Kaba,** Moises, III 1963- *WhoAmL 92*
**Kabachnik,** Martin Izrailevich 1908- *IntWW 91*
**Kaback,** David Brian 1950- *AmMWSc 92*
**Kaback,** Howard Ronald 1936- *AmMWSc 92*
**Kaback,** Stuart Mark 1934- *AmMWSc 92*
**Kabadi,** Balachandra N 1933- *AmMWSc 92*
**Kabak,** Douglas Thomas 1957- *WhoAmL 92*
**Kabak,** Irwin William 1936- *AmMWSc 92, WhoFI 92*
**Kabaker,** Richard Zohn 1935- *WhoAmL 92*
**Kabala,** Edward John 1942- *WhoAmL 92*
**Kabalevsky,** Dimitri Borisovich 1904-1987 *FacFETw*
**Kabalevsky,** Dmitri Borisovich 1904-1987 *NewAmDM*
**Kabalevsky,** Dmitriy Borisovich 1904-1987 *SovUnBD*
**Kabalka,** George Walter 1943- *AmMWSc 92*
**Kabalkin,** Barry E. 1955- *WhoAmL 92*
**Kabanda,** Celestin 1936- *IntWW 91*
**Kabara,** Jon Joseph 1926- *AmMWSc 92*
**Kabasin,** Gennadiy Sergeyevich 1937- *IntWW 91*
**Kabat,** David 1940- *AmMWSc 92*
**Kabat,** Elvin Abraham 1914- *AmMWSc 92, IntWW 91, WrDr 92*
**Kabat,** Hugh F 1932- *AmMWSc 92*
**Kabat,** Linda Georgette 1951- *WhoMW 92*
**Kabayama,** Michiomi Abraham 1926- *AmMWSc 92*
**Kabe,** Dattatraya G 1926- *AmMWSc 92*
**Kabel,** Richard Harvey 1932- *AmMWSc 92*
**Kabel,** Robert L 1932- *AmMWSc 92*
**Kaberle,** William Joseph 1951- *WhoRel 92*
**Kaberry,** Christopher Donald 1943- *Who 92*
**Kaberry of Adel,** Baron d1991 *Who 92N*
**Kabeya Wa Mukeba** 1935- *IntWW 91*
**Kabir,** Prabahan Kemal 1933- *AmMWSc 92*
**Kabisch,** William Thomas 1919- *AmMWSc 92*
**Kabkov,** Yakov Ivanovich 1908- *SovUnBD*
**Kablaoui,** Mahmoud Shafiq 1938- *AmMWSc 92*
**Kable,** Lawrence Philip 1926- *WhoFI 92, WhoIns 92*
**Kabler,** J D 1926- *AmMWSc 92*
**Kabler,** Milton Norris 1932- *AmMWSc 92*
**Kaboudan,** Mahmoud Ahmed 1949- *WhoFI 92*
**Kabra,** Pokar Mal 1942- *AmMWSc 92*
**Kacew,** Sam 1946- *AmMWSc 92*
**Kach,** Albert Wade 1947- *WhoAmP 91*
**Kachalov,** Vasiliy Ivanovich 1875-1948 *SovUnBD*
**Kachalovsky,** Yevgeniy Viktorovich 1926- *IntWW 91*
**Kachanov,** Mark L 1946- *AmMWSc 92*
**Kachhal,** Swatantra Kumar 1947- *AmMWSc 92*
**Kachikian,** Rouben 1926- *AmMWSc 92*
**Kachin,** Dmitri Ivanovich 1929- *IntWW 91*
**Kachinsky,** Robert Joseph 1937- *AmMWSc 92*
**Kachmar,** Jessie *DrAPF 91*
**Kachmar,** John Frederick 1916- *AmMWSc 92*
**Kachornprasart,** Sanan 1944- *IntWW 91*
**Kachouei,** Mahmoud H. *WhoWest 92*
**Kachru,** Yamuna 1933- *WhoMW 92*
**Kachur,** Barbara Anne *WhoMW 92*
**Kachura,** Boris Vasilievich 1930- *IntWW 91*
**Kachyna,** Karel 1924- *IntDcF 2-2*
**Kacir,** Barbara Brattin 1941- *WhoAmL 92, WhoEnt 92*
**Kacker,** Raghu N 1951- *AmMWSc 92*
**Kackley,** James R. *WhoMW 92*
**Kaclik,** Debi Louise 1953- *WhoFI 92*
**Kacmarcik,** Thomas 1925- *WhoFI 92*
**Kacser,** Claude 1934- *AmMWSc 92*
**Kacurovs'kyj,** Ihor 1918- *LiExTwC*
**Kaczmarczyk,** Alexander 1932- *AmMWSc 92*
**Kaczmarczyk,** Jan Andrzej 1949- *IntAu&W 91*
**Kaczmarczyk,** Walter J 1939- *AmMWSc 92*
**Kaczmarek,** Jan 1920- *IntWW 91*
**Kaczmarek,** Jane *WhoEnt 92*
**Kaczmarek,** Zdzislaw 1928- *IntWW 91*
**Kaczorowski,** Gregory John 1949- *AmMWSc 92*
**Kaczorowski,** Robert John 1938- *WhoAmL 92*
**Kaczynski,** David A 1939- *WhoAmP 91*
**Kaczynski,** Lech Aleksander 1949- *IntWW 91*
**Kaczynski,** William F. 1959- *WhoFI 92*
**Kadaba,** Pankaja Kooveli 1928- *AmMWSc 92*
**Kadaba,** Prasad Krishna 1924- *AmMWSc 92*
**Kadaba,** Prasanna V 1931- *AmMWSc 92*
**Kadan,** Ranjit Singh 1935- *AmMWSc 92*
**Kadan,** Savitri Singh 1934- *AmMWSc 92*
**Kadane,** David K. d1991 *NewYTBS 91*
**Kadane,** Joseph B. 1941- *WhoFI 92*
**Kadane,** Joseph Born 1941- *AmMWSc 92*
**Kadanka,** Zdenek Karel 1933- *AmMWSc 92*
**Kadanoff,** Leo P 1937- *AmMWSc 92*
**Kadanoff,** Leo Philip 1937- *IntWW 91*
**Kadar,** Dezso 1933- *AmMWSc 92*
**Kadar,** Jan 1918-1979 *IntDcF 2-2*
**Kadar,** Janos 1912-1989 *FacFETw*
**Kadare,** Ismail *IntWW 91*
**Kadas,** Mike 1956- *WhoAmP 91*
**Kaddori,** Fakhri Yassin 1932- *IntWW 91*
**Kade,** Charles Frederick, Jr 1914- *AmMWSc 92*
**Kadekaro,** Massako 1939- *AmMWSc 92*
**Kaden,** Ellen Oran *WhoAmL 92*
**Kaden,** Lewis B. 1942- *WhoAmL 92*
**Kader,** Adel Abdel 1941- *AmMWSc 92*
**Kader,** Nancy Stowe 1945- *WhoAmP 91*
**Kader,** Omar 1943- *WhoAmP 91*
**Kaderavek,** Karen *WhoEnt 92*
**Kaderlan,** Alice 1947- *WhoEnt 92*
**Kadesch,** Robert R 1922- *AmMWSc 92*
**Kadey,** Frederic L, Jr 1918- *AmMWSc 92*
**Kadhafi,** Col. *IntWW 91*
**Kadievitch,** Natalie D. 1964- *WhoAmL 92*
**Kadijevic,** Veljko *IntWW 91*
**Kadin,** Harold 1922- *AmMWSc 92*
**Kadin,** Paul J. 1951- *WhoFI 92*
**Kading,** Delores Ruth 1944- *WhoRel 92*
**Kading,** Kevin Henry 1957- *WhoFI 92*
**Kading,** Stanley Donald 1951- *WhoAmP 91*
**Kadis,** Barney Morris 1927- *AmMWSc 92*
**Kadis,** Solomon 1923- *AmMWSc 92*
**Kadis,** Vincent William 1922- *AmMWSc 92*
**Kadish,** Joshua David 1951- *WhoAmL 92*
**Kadish,** Karl Mitchell 1945- *AmMWSc 92*
**Kadish,** Sanford Harold 1921- *WhoAmL 92*
**Kadish,** Scott P. 1960- *WhoAmL 92*
**Kadison,** Richard Vincent 1925- *AmMWSc 92*
**Kadkade,** Prakash Gopal 1941- *AmMWSc 92*
**Kadlec,** John A 1931- *AmMWSc 92*
**Kadlec,** Robert Henry 1938- *AmMWSc 92*
**Kadlubar,** Fred F 1946- *AmMWSc 92*
**Kadner,** Carl George 1911- *AmMWSc 92, WhoWest 92*
**Kadner,** Robert Joseph 1942- *AmMWSc 92*
**Kado,** Clarence Isao 1936- *AmMWSc 92*
**Kadomtsev,** Boris Borisovich 1928- *IntWW 91*
**Kadonaga,** James Takuro 1958- *WhoFI 92*
**Kadoorie** *Who 92*
**Kadoorie,** Baron 1899- *IntWW 91, Who 92*
**Kadoorie,** Horace 1902- *IntWW 91, Who 92*
**Kador,** Peter Fritz 1949- *AmMWSc 92*
**Kadosa,** Pal 1903-1983 *NewAmDM*
**Kadota,** T Theodore 1930- *AmMWSc 92*
**Kadoum,** Ahmed Mohamed 1937- *AmMWSc 92*
**Kadra,** Nourredine 1943- *IntWW 91*
**Kadri,** Sibghat Ullah 1937- *Who 92*
**Kaduk,** Frank J 1916- *WhoAmP 91*
**Kaduma,** Ibrahim Mohamed 1937- *IntWW 91*
**Kadushin,** Alfred 1916- *WrDr 92*
**Kadyk,** John Amos 1929- *AmMWSc 92*
**Kadyrov,** Gairat Khamidullaevich 1939- *IntWW 91*
**Kadyrov,** Gayrat Khamidullaevich 1939- *SovUnBD*
**Kaebitzsch,** Reinhold Johannes *DrAPF 91*
**Kaech,** Andreas Christian 1958- *WhoEnt 92*
**Kaeding,** Warren William 1921- *AmMWSc 92*
**Kaegel,** Ray Martin 1925- *WhoFI 92*
**Kael,** Pauline *NewYTBS 91*
**Kael,** Pauline 1919- *BenetAL 91, IntAu&W 91, IntWW 91, WhoEnt 92, WrDr 92*
**Kaelber,** William Walbridge 1923- *AmMWSc 92*
**Kaelble,** David Hardie 1928- *AmMWSc 92*
**Kaelble,** Emmett Frank 1931- *AmMWSc 92*
**Kaelbling,** Margot 1936- *AmMWSc 92*
**Kaelin,** Jeannette Jill 1956- *WhoEnt 92*
**Kaellis,** Joseph 1925- *AmMWSc 92*
**Kaemmerer,** Glen Edward, Jr. 1960- *WhoMW 92*
**Kaemmerlen,** Cathy June 1949- *WhoEnt 92*
**Kaempf,** Robert Francis 1953- *WhoFI 92*
**Kaempffer,** Frederick Augustus 1920- *AmMWSc 92*
**Kaempffert,** Waldemar 1877-1956 *ScFEYrs*
**Kaep,** Louis J. 1903-1991 *NewYTBS 91*
**Kaericher,** John Conrad 1936- *WhoMW 92*
**Kaesberg,** Paul Joseph 1923- *AmMWSc 92*
**Kaeseberg,** Norman Allen 1947- *WhoEnt 92*
**Kaeser,** Clifford Richard 1936- *WhoAmL 92, WhoFI 92*
**Kaesler,** Roger LeRoy 1937- *AmMWSc 92*
**Kaestle,** Carl F. 1940- *IntWW 91*
**Kaesz,** Herbert David 1933- *AmMWSc 92*
**Kaetzel,** Marcia Aldyth *AmMWSc 92*
**Kafadar,** Karen 1953- *AmMWSc 92*
**Kafalas,** Peter 1925- *AmMWSc 92*
**Kafando,** Michel 1942- *IntWW 91*
**Kafaoglu,** Adnan Baser 1926- *IntWW 91*
**Kafatos,** Fotis C 1940- *AmMWSc 92*
**Kafatos,** Minas 1945- *AmMWSc 92*
**Kafengauz,** Lev Borisovich d1930? *SovUnBD*
**Kafer,** Enid Rosemary 1937- *AmMWSc 92*
**Kafer,** Etta 1925- *AmMWSc 92*
**Kafer,** Joyce Hettrich 1958- *WhoMW 92*
**Kafesjian,** R 1934- *AmMWSc 92*
**Kaff,** Albert Ernest 1920- *IntAu&W 91*
**Kaffer,** Roger Louis 1927- *WhoMW 92, WhoRel 92*
**Kaffezakis,** John George 1929- *AmMWSc 92*
**Kafin,** Robert Joseph 1942- *WhoAmL 92*
**Kafity,** Samir *WhoRel 92*
**Kafity,** Samir 1933- *Who 92*
**Kafka,** Alexandre 1917- *IntWW 91, WhoFI 92*
**Kafka,** Franz 1883-1924 *FacFETw [port], LiExTwC, TwCSFW 91A*
**Kafka,** Gerald Andrew 1951- *WhoAmL 92*
**Kafka,** Louis L *WhoAmP 91*
**Kafka,** Marian Stern 1927- *AmMWSc 92*
**Kafka,** Robert W 1937- *AmMWSc 92*
**Kafka,** Tomas 1936- *AmMWSc 92*
**Kafoglis,** Nicholas 1930- *WhoAmP 91*
**Kafoury,** Stephen 1941- *WhoAmP 91*
**Kafrawy,** Adel 1943- *AmMWSc 92*
**Kafrawy,** Hasaballah El- 1930- *IntWW 91*
**Kafri,** Oded 1944- *AmMWSc 92*
**Kagami,** Hideo 1923- *IntWW 91*
**Kagan** *Who 92*
**Kagan,** Baron 1915- *Who 92*
**Kagan,** Benjamin 1921- *AmMWSc 92*
**Kagan,** Benjamin M 1913- *AmMWSc 92*
**Kagan,** Daniel 1953- *WhoAmL 92*
**Kagan,** Daniel Griff 1960- *WhoEnt 92*
**Kagan,** David Dennis 1949- *WhoRel 92*
**Kagan,** Donald 1932- *WrDr 92*
**Kagan,** Fred 1920- *AmMWSc 92*

**Kagan**, George Irwin 1939- *WhoMW 92*
**Kagan**, Harvey Alexander 1937- *AmMWSc 92*
**Kagan**, Henry Enoch 1906-1969 *RelLAm 91*
**Kagan**, Herbert Marcus 1932- *AmMWSc 92*
**Kagan**, Irving 1936- *WhoAmL 92*
**Kagan**, Irving George 1919- *AmMWSc 92*
**Kagan**, Jacques 1933- *AmMWSc 92*
**Kagan**, Jeremy 1945- *IntMPA 92*
**Kagan**, Jerome 1929- *AmMWSc 92, WrDr 92*
**Kagan**, Joel 1943- *AmMWSc 92*
**Kagan**, Martin I. 1946- *WhoEnt 92*
**Kagan**, Patricia Amanda 1949- *WhoEnt 92*
**Kagan**, Richard Clark 1938- *WhoMW 92*
**Kagan**, Robert Alexander 1924- *WhoAmL 92*
**Kagan**, Robert Michael 1943- *WhoAmL 92*
**Kagan**, Stephen Bruce 1944- *WhoFI 92*
**Kagann**, Robert Howard 1946- *AmMWSc 92*
**Kaganov**, Alan Lawrence 1938- *AmMWSc 92*
**Kaganovich**, Lazar 1893-1961? *EncTR 91*
**Kaganovich**, Lazar M. 1893-1991 *CurBio 91N*
**Kaganovich**, Lazar Moisevich 1893- *SovUnBD*
**Kaganovich**, Lazar Moyseyevich d1991 *NewYTBS 91 [port]*
**Kaganovich**, Lazar Moyseyevich 1893- *FacFETw*
**Kagarise**, Ronald Eugene 1926- *AmMWSc 92*
**Kagarlitsky**, Boris 1958- *ConAu 134*
**Kagawa**, Kathleen Hatsuyo 1952- *WhoFI 92, WhoWest 92*
**Kagawa**, Toyohiko 1888-1960 *DcEcMov*
**Kagawa**, Yukio 1935- *AmMWSc 92*
**Kage**, Wilhelm 1889-1960 *DcTwDes*
**Kagedan**, Tom Elliot 1960- *WhoRel 92*
**Kagel**, Allen David 1945- *WhoAmP 91*
**Kagel**, John 1940- *WhoWest 92*
**Kagel**, Mauricio 1931- *ConCom 92, NewAmDM, WhoEnt 92*
**Kagel**, Ronald Oliver 1936- *AmMWSc 92*
**Kagemann**, Lawrence Edward, Sr. 1942- *WhoMW 92*
**Kagemoto**, Haro 1952- *WhoWest 92*
**Kagen**, Herbert Paul 1929- *AmMWSc 92, WhoMW 92*
**Kagetsu**, T J 1931- *AmMWSc 92*
**Kagey-Sobotka**, Anne 1940- *AmMWSc 92*
**Kageyama**, David Kenji 1948- *WhoWest 92*
**Kaghan**, Walter S 1919- *AmMWSc 92*
**Kagiwada**, Harriet Hatsune 1937- *AmMWSc 92*
**Kagiwada**, Reynold Shigeru 1938- *AmMWSc 92, WhoWest 92*
**Kah-ge-ga-gah-bowh**, Chief 1818-1863 *BenetAL 91*
**Kahalas**, Harvey 1941- *WhoFI 92*
**Kahale**, Nicolas Jean 1954- *WhoFI 92*
**Kahan**, Aaron d1991 *NewYTBS 91*
**Kahan**, Arcadius 1920-1982 *ConAu 135*
**Kahan**, Archie M 1917- *AmMWSc 92*
**Kahan**, Barry D 1939- *AmMWSc 92*
**Kahan**, George 1931- *Who 92*
**Kahan**, I Howard 1923- *AmMWSc 92*
**Kahan**, Jonathan Seth 1948- *WhoAmL 92*
**Kahan**, Lawrence 1944- *AmMWSc 92*
**Kahan**, Linda Beryl 1941- *AmMWSc 92*
**Kahan**, Mitchell Douglas 1951- *WhoMW 92*
**Kahan**, Norman 1922- *WhoRel 92*
**Kahan**, Samuel D. 1947- *WhoFI 92*
**Kahan**, Sheldon Jeremiah 1948- *WhoEnt 92, WhoWest 92*
**Kahan**, Sidney 1915- *AmMWSc 92*
**Kahan**, William M 1933- *AmMWSc 92, WhoWest 92*
**Kahana**, Kalman d1991 *NewYTBS 91*
**Kahana**, Sidney H 1933- *AmMWSc 92*
**Kahane**, Dennis Spencer 1947- *WhoAmL 92*
**Kahane**, Meir 1932- *BiDExR*
**Kahane**, Meir 1932-1990 *AnObit 1990, ConAu 133, CurBio 91N, News 91, RelLAm 91*
**Kahaner**, David Kenneth 1941- *AmMWSc 92*
**Kahaner**, Ellen *DrAPF 91*
**Kahanovsky**, Luis 1934- *WhoMW 92*
**Kahl**, J Wayne 1963- *WhoAmP 91*
**Kahle**, Anne Bettine 1934- *AmMWSc 92*
**Kahle**, Charles F 1930- *AmMWSc 92*
**Kahle**, M. Jackson 1955- *WhoWest 92*
**Kahle**, Melvin W, Jr 1935- *WhoAmP 91*
**Kahlenbeck**, Howard, Jr. 1929- *WhoAmL 92, WhoFI 92*
**Kahler**, Albert Comstock, III 1951- *AmMWSc 92*
**Kahler**, Alex L 1939- *AmMWSc 92*
**Kahler**, Erich Ernst 1906- *IntWW 91*
**Kahler**, Herbert Frederick 1936- *WhoFI 92*
**Kahler**, Hugh M. 1883-1969 *BenetAL 91*
**Kahler**, James Frederick 1943- *WhoWest 92*
**Kahler**, Richard Lee 1933- *AmMWSc 92*
**Kahles**, John Frank 1914- *AmMWSc 92*
**Kahlo**, Frida 1907-1954 *News 91 [port], -91-3 [port]*
**Kahlon**, Prem Singh 1936- *AmMWSc 92*
**Kahlor**, Robert A. *WhoMW 92*
**Kahn**, A Clark 1937- *AmMWSc 92*
**Kahn**, Alan Bruce 1940- *WhoFI 92*
**Kahn**, Alan Edwin 1929- *WhoAmL 92*
**Kahn**, Alan Richard 1932- *AmMWSc 92*
**Kahn**, Albert 1869-1942 *DcTwDes, FacFETw*
**Kahn**, Albert 1931- *AmMWSc 92*
**Kahn**, Alfred E. 1917- *IntWW 91*
**Kahn**, Alfred Edward 1917- *WhoAmP 91*
**Kahn**, Andre Santamaria 1949- *WhoEnt 92*
**Kahn**, Arnold Herbert 1928- *AmMWSc 92*
**Kahn**, Arthur B 1931- *AmMWSc 92*
**Kahn**, Arthur H. 1931- *WhoAmL 92*
**Kahn**, Arthur Jole 1921- *AmMWSc 92*
**Kahn**, Bernd 1928- *AmMWSc 92*
**Kahn**, Brian Stanley 1964- *WhoEnt 92*
**Kahn**, Burt Mitchell 1948- *WhoAmL 92*
**Kahn**, Carl Ronald 1944- *AmMWSc 92*
**Kahn**, Charles Howard 1926- *AmMWSc 92*
**Kahn**, Daniel Stephen 1935- *AmMWSc 92*
**Kahn**, David 1926- *AmMWSc 92*
**Kahn**, David 1930- *WrDr 92*
**Kahn**, David 1933- *AmMWSc 92*
**Kahn**, David E. 1932- *WhoEnt 92*
**Kahn**, David Miller 1925- *WhoAmL 92*
**Kahn**, David Victor 1930- *WhoAmL 92, WhoEnt 92*
**Kahn**, Donald Jay 1930- *AmMWSc 92*
**Kahn**, Donald R 1929- *AmMWSc 92*
**Kahn**, Donald W 1935- *AmMWSc 92*
**Kahn**, Douglas Allen 1934- *WhoAmL 92*
**Kahn**, Earl Lester 1919- *WhoWest 92*
**Kahn**, Edwin Leonard 1918- *WhoAmL 92*
**Kahn**, Ellen 1952- *WhoEnt 92*
**Kahn**, Elliott H 1926- *AmMWSc 92*
**Kahn**, Ellis Irvin 1936- *WhoAmL 92*
**Kahn**, Erich F.W. 1904-1980 *TwCPaSc*
**Kahn**, Felicia S 1926- *WhoAmP 91*
**Kahn**, Florence Prag 1866-1948 *HanAmWH*
**Kahn**, Frederic Jay 1941- *AmMWSc 92*
**Kahn**, Frida 1905- *WhoEnt 92*
**Kahn**, Harold A 1920- *AmMWSc 92*
**Kahn**, Herbert Charles 1938- *WhoAmL 92*
**Kahn**, Herman 1922-1983 *FacFETw*
**Kahn**, Irving B. *LesBEnT 92*
**Kahn**, Irwin William 1923- *WhoWest 92*
**Kahn**, Jack Henry 1923- *AmMWSc 92*
**Kahn**, James 1947- *IntAu&W 91, TwCSFW 91, WrDr 92*
**Kahn**, James Allan 1960- *WhoFI 92*
**Kahn**, James Robert 1953- *WhoAmL 92*
**Kahn**, James Steven 1931- *WhoMW 92*
**Kahn**, Jan Edward 1948- *WhoFI 92, WhoMW 92*
**Kahn**, Jeffrey Hay 1939- *WhoFI 92*
**Kahn**, John 1950- *ConAu 135*
**Kahn**, Joseph Stephan 1929- *AmMWSc 92*
**Kahn**, Judith *IntMPA 92*
**Kahn**, Laurence Michael 1947- *WhoAmL 92*
**Kahn**, Lawrence F 1945- *AmMWSc 92*
**Kahn**, Leo David *AmMWSc 92*
**Kahn**, Leonard B 1937- *AmMWSc 92*
**Kahn**, Leslie Ruth 1947- *WhoFI 92*
**Kahn**, Linda McClure *WhoWest 92*
**Kahn**, Lisa 1957- *WhoAmL 92*
**Kahn**, Louis I. 1901-1974 *DcTwDes, FacFETw*
**Kahn**, Madeline 1942- *IntMPA 92*
**Kahn**, Madeline Gail *WhoEnt 92*
**Kahn**, Manfred 1926- *AmMWSc 92*
**Kahn**, Marina Mayen 1951- *WhoHisp 92*
**Kahn**, Mark Leo 1921- *WhoAmL 92, WhoFI 92, WhoMW 92*
**Kahn**, Marvin William 1926- *AmMWSc 92*
**Kahn**, Michael *WhoEnt 92*
**Kahn**, Michael Alexander 1949- *WhoWest 92*
**Kahn**, Milton 1918- *AmMWSc 92*
**Kahn**, Milton 1934- *IntMPA 92*
**Kahn**, Miriam 1948- *WhoWest 92*
**Kahn**, Nancy Louise 1952- *WhoAmL 92*
**Kahn**, Norman 1932- *AmMWSc 92*
**Kahn**, Paul *DrAPF 91*
**Kahn**, Paul Markham 1935- *WhoFI 92, WhoIns 92, WhoWest 92*
**Kahn**, Paula 1940- *Who 92*
**Kahn**, Peter B 1935- *AmMWSc 92*
**Kahn**, Peter Jack 1939- *AmMWSc 92*
**Kahn**, Phyllis 1937- *WhoAmP 91*
**Kahn**, Raymond Henry 1926- *AmMWSc 92*
**Kahn**, Richard 1929- *IntMPA 92*
**Kahn**, Richard Dreyfus 1931- *WhoAmL 92*
**Kahn**, Richard Ferdinand 1905-1989 *FacFETw*
**Kahn**, Robert Elliot 1938- *AmMWSc 92*
**Kahn**, Robert Irving 1918- *WhoFI 92*
**Kahn**, Robert Phillip 1924- *AmMWSc 92*
**Kahn**, Roger 1927- *WrDr 92*
**Kahn**, Ronnetta Bisman *DrAPF 91*
**Kahn**, Samuel George 1929- *AmMWSc 92*
**Kahn**, Sandra S. 1942- *WhoMW 92*
**Kahn**, Sheldon F. 1940- *WhoEnt 92*
**Kahn**, Stanley David 1915- *WhoEnt 92*
**Kahn**, Steven Michael 1954- *WhoWest 92*
**Kahn**, Sy M. *DrAPF 91*
**Kahn**, Sy M. 1924- *WrDr 92*
**Kahn**, Sylvia Judy 1960- *WhoEnt 92*
**Kahn**, Ted Stewart 1933- *WhoWest 92*
**Kahn**, Walter K 1929- *AmMWSc 92*
**Kahn-Ackermann**, Georg 1918- *IntWW 91, Who 92*
**Kahne**, Stephen James 1937- *AmMWSc 92*
**Kahng**, Dawon 1931- *AmMWSc 92*
**Kahng**, Seun Kwon 1936- *AmMWSc 92*
**Kahng**, Sun Myong 1926- *WhoMW 92*
**Kahnk**, Donald Lee 1937- *WhoMW 92*
**Kahnke**, Jerome Hubert 1955- *WhoAmL 92*
**Kahnweiler**, Daniel-Henry 1884-1979 *FacFETw*
**Kahoe**, Michael Edward 1950- *WhoAmP 91*
**Kahr**, Gustav, Ritter von 1862-1934 *EncTR 91 [port]*
**Kahrilas**, Peter James 1953- *WhoMW 92*
**Kahrizi**, Mojtaba 1949- *AmMWSc 92*
**Kahrl**, Robert Conley 1946- *WhoAmL 92*
**Kahrs**, Margaret Elizabeth 1926- *WhoAmP 91*
**Kahrs**, Robert F 1930- *AmMWSc 92*
**Kahurananga**, Musa 1921- *Who 92*
**Kaider**, Michael Thomas 1962- *WhoMW 92*
**Kaier**, Edward John 1945- *WhoAmL 92*
**Kaifu**, Toshiki 1932- *IntWW 91*
**Kaigh**, David Lorin 1953- *WhoAmL 92*
**Kaighn**, James McElroy 1927- *WhoWest 92*
**Kaighn**, Morris Edward 1922- *AmMWSc 92*
**Kaigler**, Marie 1945- *WhoBlA 92*
**Kaigler-Reese**, Marie Madeleine 1945- *WhoBlA 92*
**Kaihoi**, Gregory P. 1957- *WhoAmL 92*
**Kaiko**, Takeshi 1930- *IntAu&W 91*
**Kail**, Brian Thomas 1952- *WhoMW 92*
**Kail**, Elizabeth Ann 1935- *WhoAmL 92*
**Kail**, Joseph Gerard 1946- *WhoWest 92*
**Kailath**, Thomas 1935- *AmMWSc 92*
**Kaim-Caudle**, Peter 1916- *WrDr 92*
**Kaim-Caudle**, Peter Robert 1916- *IntAu&W 91*
**Kaimal**, Jagadish Chandran 1930- *AmMWSc 92*
**Kain**, Eugene Charles, Jr. 1949- *WhoMW 92*
**Kain**, John F. 1935- *WrDr 92*
**Kain**, John Forrest 1935- *WhoFI 92*
**Kain**, Karen 1951- *IntWW 91*
**Kain**, Karen Alexandria 1951- *WhoEnt 92*
**Kain**, Richard Yerkes 1936- *AmMWSc 92, WhoMW 92*
**Kain**, Roger James Peter 1944- *Who 92*
**Kain**, Saul *ConAu 36NR*
**Kaindl**, Jean Margaret 1925- *WhoMW 92*
**Kaine**, Brian Paul *AmMWSc 92*
**Kainen**, Anna *DrAPF 91*
**Kainen**, Burton 1942- *WhoAmL 92*
**Kains**, Josephine *WrDr 92*
**Kainski**, Mercedes H 1923- *AmMWSc 92*
**Kainz**, Howard Paul 1933- *ConAu 35NR*
**Kaipainen**, Aune Helina 1933- *IntAu&W 91*
**Kaipainen**, Jouni 1956- *ConCom 92*
**Kaipkire** *EncAmaz 91*
**Kairoff**, Joshua David 1964- *WhoEnt 92*
**Kaisel**, S F 1922- *AmMWSc 92*
**Kaiser**, Armin Dale 1927- *AmMWSc 92*
**Kaiser**, Bo Paul 1917- *WhoFI 92*
**Kaiser**, Bydus Francis 1931- *WhoRel 92*
**Kaiser**, C William 1939- *AmMWSc 92*
**Kaiser**, Carl 1929- *AmMWSc 92*
**Kaiser**, Charles Benjamin, III 1957- *WhoAmL 92*
**Kaiser**, Charles Frederick 1942- *AmMWSc 92*
**Kaiser**, Christopher B 1941- *AmMWSc 92*
**Kaiser**, David Gilbert 1928- *AmMWSc 92*
**Kaiser**, David Lee 1944- *WhoMW 92*
**Kaiser**, David Randall 1963- *WhoFI 92*
**Kaiser**, Duane L *WhoAmP 91*
**Kaiser**, Edward William, Jr 1942- *AmMWSc 92, WhoMW 92*
**Kaiser**, Edwin Michael 1938- *AmMWSc 92*
**Kaiser**, Ernest Daniel 1915- *WhoBlA 92*
**Kaiser**, Georg 1875-1945 *FacFETw*
**Kaiser**, Georg 1878-1945 *LiExTwC*
**Kaiser**, George C 1928- *AmMWSc 92*
**Kaiser**, Gerard Alan 1932- *AmMWSc 92*
**Kaiser**, Henry J. 1882-1967 *DcTwDes*
**Kaiser**, Henry John 1882-1967 *FacFETw*
**Kaiser**, Hermann 1885-1945 *EncTR 91*
**Kaiser**, Inez Yeargan 1918- *WhoBlA 92*
**Kaiser**, Irwin Herbert 1918- *AmMWSc 92*
**Kaiser**, Ivan Irvin 1938- *AmMWSc 92*
**Kaiser**, Jack Allen Charles 1935- *AmMWSc 92*
**Kaiser**, Jakob 1888-1961 *EncTR 91*
**Kaiser**, James F 1929- *AmMWSc 92*
**Kaiser**, James Gordon 1943- *WhoBlA 92*
**Kaiser**, Jerome Frederich 1945- *WhoMW 92*
**Kaiser**, Joseph Anthony 1926- *AmMWSc 92*
**Kaiser**, Klaus L E 1941- *AmMWSc 92*
**Kaiser**, Lloyd Eugene 1927- *WhoEnt 92*
**Kaiser**, Mary Agnes 1948- *AmMWSc 92*
**Kaiser**, Michael Leroy 1941- *AmMWSc 92*
**Kaiser**, Peter 1938- *AmMWSc 92*
**Kaiser**, Philip M. 1913- *IntWW 91, Who 92*
**Kaiser**, Philip Mayer 1913- *WhoAmP 91*
**Kaiser**, Quentin C 1921- *AmMWSc 92*
**Kaiser**, Ralph Edmund 1950- *WhoAmP 91*
**Kaiser**, Reinhold 1927- *AmMWSc 92*
**Kaiser**, Reuben Charles 1927- *WhoAmP 91*
**Kaiser**, Richard Allen 1954- *WhoRel 92*
**Kaiser**, Richard Edward 1936- *AmMWSc 92*
**Kaiser**, Richard George *WhoMW 92*
**Kaiser**, Robert 1934- *AmMWSc 92*
**Kaiser**, Robert L 1931- *AmMWSc 92*
**Kaiser**, Steven Craig 1953- *WhoAmL 92*
**Kaiser**, Suzanne Billo 1948- *WhoFI 92*
**Kaiser**, Thomas Burton 1940- *AmMWSc 92*
**Kaiser**, Thomas G *WhoIns 92*
**Kaiser**, Thurman William 1927- *WhoFI 92*
**Kaiser**, Walter 1931- *ConAu 36NR*
**Kaiser**, Walter Christian, Jr. 1933- *WhoRel 92*
**Kaiser**, Ward L. 1923- *WrDr 92*
**Kaiser**, William Richard 1937- *AmMWSc 92*
**Kaiser**, Wolfgang A 1923- *AmMWSc 92*
**Kaiser-Kupfer**, Muriel I 1936- *AmMWSc 92*
**Kaiserman**, Howard Bruce 1957- *AmMWSc 92*
**Kaiserman-Abramof**, Ita Rebeca 1933- *AmMWSc 92*
**Kaistha**, Krishan K 1926- *AmMWSc 92*
**Kaita**, Robert 1952- *AmMWSc 92*
**Kaitschuk**, John Paul 1937- *WhoRel 92*
**Kaitz**, Haskell Abbott 1922- *WhoFI 92*
**Kaiuea**, Paul Eusebius Mea *WhoRel 92*
**Kaiyalethe**, John Kuruvilla 1936- *WhoMW 92, WhoRel 92*
**Kaizer**, Herbert 1930- *AmMWSc 92*
**Kajantie**, Keijo Olavi 1940- *IntWW 91*
**Kajanus**, Robert 1856-1933 *NewAmDM*
**Kajfez**, Darko 1928- *AmMWSc 92*
**Kaji**, Akira 1930- *AmMWSc 92*
**Kaji**, Hideko 1932- *AmMWSc 92*
**Kajiki**, Matazo 1919- *IntWW 91*
**Kajiyama**, Seiroku 1926- *IntWW 91*
**Kajor**, Michael Steven 1950- *WhoFI 92*
**Kak**, Avinash Carl 1944- *AmMWSc 92*
**Kak**, Subhash Chandra 1947- *AmMWSc 92*
**Kakac**, Carroll Conrad 1929- *WhoRel 92*
**Kakalec**, Joseph Michael 1930- *WhoRel 92*
**Kakar**, Anand Swaroop 1937- *AmMWSc 92*
**Kakar**, Rajesh Kumar 1950- *AmMWSc 92*
**Kakefuda**, Tsusyoshi 1929- *AmMWSc 92*
**Kakesako**, Lorna Buk Bong 1928- *WhoAmP 91*
**Kakhidze**, Dzhansug Ivanovich 1936- *IntWW 91*
**Kakinuki**, John C. 1956- *WhoAmL 92*
**Kakis**, Frederic Jacob 1930- *AmMWSc 92*
**Kakkar**, Vijay Vir 1937- *Who 92*
**Kaklamanos**, James 1956- *WhoAmP 91*
**Kaklaminis**, Apostolos 1936- *IntWW 91*
**Kako**, Kyohei Joe 1928- *AmMWSc 92*
**Kakos**, Peter John 1946- *WhoRel 92*
**Kakouris**, Constantine 1919- *IntWW 91*
**Kaku**, Michio 1947- *AmMWSc 92*
**Kakutani**, Shizuo 1911- *AmMWSc 92*
**Kalab**, Bruno Marie 1929- *AmMWSc 92*
**Kalab**, Miloslav 1929- *AmMWSc 92*
**Kalabis**, Viktor *ConCom 92*
**Kalaf**, Walter Nadeem 1925- *WhoRel 92*
**Kalafus**, Rudolph M 1937- *AmMWSc 92*
**Kalafut**, George Wendell 1934- *WhoFI 92*
**Kalahar**, Patricia Ann 1956- *WhoMW 92*
**Kalaher**, Richard Alan 1940- *WhoAmL 92*
**Kalai**, Ehud 1942- *AmMWSc 92*
**Kalainov**, Sam Charles 1930- *WhoIns 92*
**Kalakos**, John Emmanuel 1943- *WhoFI 92*
**Kalal**, Jim *WhoAmP 91*
**Kalam**, Tonu 1948- *WhoEnt 92*
**Kalanik**, Charles Thomas 1966- *WhoEnt 92*
**Kalant**, Harold 1923- *AmMWSc 92*
**Kalant**, Norman *AmMWSc 92*
**Kalantar**, Alfred Husayn 1934- *AmMWSc 92*

**Kalashnikoff**, Nicholas S. 1888-1961 *BenetAL 91*
**Kalashnikov**, Anatoliy Ivanovich 1930- *IntWW 91, SovUnBD*
**Kalashnikov**, Mikhail Timofeevich 1919- *SovUnBD*
**Kalashnikov**, Vladimir Ilich 1929- *IntWW 91*
**Kalasinsky**, Victor Frank 1949- *AmMWSc 92*
**Kalat**, Peter Anthony 1939- *WhoAmL 92*
**Kalat**, Virginia Lowry 1921- *WhoAmP 91*
**Kalathil**, James Sakaria 1935- *AmMWSc 92*
**Kalatozov**, Mikhail Konstantinovich 1903-1973 *SovUnBD*
**Kalb**, Benjamin Stuart 1948- *WhoEnt 92, WhoWest 92*
**Kalb**, Bernard *LesBEnT 92*
**Kalb**, G William 1943- *AmMWSc 92*
**Kalb**, Johann 1721-1780 *BlkwEAR*
**Kalb**, John W 1918- *AmMWSc 92*
**Kalb**, Jonathan 1959- *ConAu 135*
**Kalb**, Marty Joel 1941- *WhoMW 92*
**Kalb**, Marvin *IntMPA 92, LesBEnT 92*
**Kalb**, Richard Oskar 1960- *WhoFI 92*
**Kalba**, Kas 1945- *WhoEnt 92*
**Kalbach**, Constance 1944- *AmMWSc 92*
**Kalbach**, John Frederick 1914- *AmMWSc 92*
**Kalbach**, Paul Douglas 1947- *WhoEnt 92*
**Kalber**, David Michael 1948- *WhoEnt 92*
**Kalberer**, Augustine Anthony 1917- *WhoRel 92*
**Kalberer**, John Theodore, Jr 1936- *AmMWSc 92*
**Kalberlahn**, Hans Martin 1722-1759 *DcNCBi 3*
**Kalbfeld**, Brad Marshall 1954- *WhoEnt 92, WhoFI 92*
**Kalbfleisch**, George Randolph 1931- *AmMWSc 92*
**Kalbfleisch**, James G 1940- *AmMWSc 92*
**Kalbfleisch**, Martin 1804-1873 *BiInAmS*
**Kalcevic**, Timothy Francis 1950- *WhoFI 92, WhoMW 92*
**Kalcheim**, Lee 1938- *WrDr 92*
**Kalck**, Craig W 1948- *WhoIns 92*
**Kalckar**, Herman Moritz 1908- *AmMWSc 92, IntWW 91*
**Kaldjian**, Movses J 1925- *AmMWSc 92*
**Kaldor**, Andrew 1944- *AmMWSc 92*
**Kaldor**, George 1926- *AmMWSc 92*
**Kaldor**, Lee *WhoAmP 91*
**Kaldor**, Nicholas 1908-1986 *ConAu 134*
**Kale**, Anthony Michael 1970- *WhoEnt 92*
**Kale**, Herbert William, II 1931- *AmMWSc 92*
**Kalechofsky**, Roberta *DrAPF 91*
**Kalechofsky**, Roberta 1931- *IntAu&W 91*
**Kaledin**, Alexei Maksimovich 1861-1918 *FacFETw*
**Kalelkar**, Mohan Satish 1948- *AmMWSc 92*
**Kalemli**, Mustafa 1943- *IntWW 91*
**Kalen**, Thomas Harry 1938- *WhoFI 92*
**Kalenda**, Norman Wayne 1928- *AmMWSc 92*
**Kalenscher**, Alan Jay 1926- *WhoWest 92*
**Kalensher**, Bernard Earl 1927- *AmMWSc 92*
**Kaler**, Eric William 1956- *AmMWSc 92*
**Kaler**, James Bailey 1938- *AmMWSc 92, WhoEnt 92*
**Kaler**, James Otis 1848-1912 *BenetAL 91*
**Kaler**, Robert Joseph 1956- *WhoAmL 92*
**Kaley**, Gabor 1926- *AmMWSc 92*
**Kaley**, J R 1918- *WhoAmP 91*
**Kaley**, Robert George, II 1945- *AmMWSc 92*
**Kalf**, George Frederick 1930- *AmMWSc 92*
**Kalfayan**, Bernard *AmMWSc 92*
**Kalfayan**, Laura Jean 1953- *AmMWSc 92*
**Kalfayan**, Sarkis Hagop 1916- *AmMWSc 92*
**Kalff**, Jacob 1935- *AmMWSc 92*
**Kalfoglou**, George 1939- *AmMWSc 92*
**Kalfon**, Frederick Geoffrey 1941- *WhoFI 92*
**Kalfus**, Melvin 1931- *ConAu 134*
**Kalia**, Madhu P 1940- *AmMWSc 92*
**Kalia**, Ravindra Nath 1940- *WhoMW 92*
**Kaliakin**, Victor Nicholas 1956- *AmMWSc 92*
**Kalib**, David Leonard 1940- *WhoIns 92*
**Kaliba**, Layding *DrAPF 91*
**Kalichstein**, Joseph 1946- *IntWW 91, WhoEnt 92*
**Kaliher**, Michael Dennis 1947- *WhoWest 92*
**Kalik**, Barbara Faith 1936- *WhoAmP 91*
**Kalika**, Dale Michele 1948- *WhoFI 92*
**Kalikstein**, Kalman 1929- *AmMWSc 92*
**Kalil**, Ford 1925- *AmMWSc 92*
**Kalil**, James, Sr. 1919- *WhoFI 92*
**Kalil**, Margaret d1991 *NewYTBS 91*
**Kalil**, Michael d1991 *NewYTBS 91 [port]*
**Kalill**, Paul Michael 1943- *WhoAmL 92*
**Kalilombe**, Patrick-Augustine 1933- *IntWW 91*
**Kalimi**, Mohammed Yahya *AmMWSc 92*
**Kalin**, Ivan Petrovich *IntWW 91*
**Kalin**, Ivan Petrovich 1935- *SovUnBD*
**Kalin**, Leslie Rae 1948- *WhoAmL 92*
**Kalin**, Robert 1921- *AmMWSc 92*
**Kalina**, Robert E 1936- *AmMWSc 92*
**Kalina**, Steven Paul 1955- *WhoWest 92*
**Kaline**, Al 1934- *FacFETw*
**Kalinin**, Mikhail 1875-1946 *EncTR 91*
**Kalinin**, Mikhail Ivanovich 1875-1946 *FacFETw, SovUnBD*
**Kalinka**, Edward Michael 1954- *WhoAmL 92*
**Kalinowski**, Mathew Lawrence 1915- *AmMWSc 92*
**Kalinowski**, Raymond J. 1929- *WhoFI 92*
**Kalinowsky**, Lothar Bruno 1899- *IntWW 91*
**Kalinske**, A A 1911- *AmMWSc 92*
**Kalinsky**, Robert George 1945- *AmMWSc 92*
**Kalis**, Henry J 1937- *WhoAmP 91*
**Kalisch**, Gerhard Karl 1914- *AmMWSc 92*
**Kalischer**, Peter d1991 *NewYTBS 91*
**Kalish**, Arthur 1930- *WhoAmL 92*
**Kalish**, David 1939- *AmMWSc 92*
**Kalish**, Eddie *IntMPA 92*
**Kalish**, Herbert S 1922- *AmMWSc 92*
**Kalish**, Katherine McAulay 1945- *WhoAmL 92*
**Kalish**, Myron 1919- *WhoFI 92*
**Kalish**, Paddy 1955- *WhoMW 92*
**Kalish**, Ronald 1942- *WhoEnt 92*
**Kalisher**, Michael David Lionel 1941- *Who 92*
**Kaliski**, Alan Edward 1947- *WhoIns 92*
**Kaliski**, Martin Edward 1945- *AmMWSc 92*
**Kaliss**, Nathan 1907- *AmMWSc 92*
**Kalistratova**, Sofiya Vasil'evna 1907- *SovUnBD*
**Kaliszewski**, Charles Stanley 1950- *WhoRel 92*
**Kalivoda**, Frank E, Jr 1930- *AmMWSc 92*
**Kalka**, Morris 1949- *AmMWSc 92*
**Kalkbrenner**, Edward Joseph, Jr. 1942- *WhoWest 92*
**Kalkbrenner**, Frederic 1785-1849 *NewAmDM*
**Kalkhoff**, Ronald Kenneth 1933- *AmMWSc 92*
**Kalkin**, Gary 1950- *WhoEnt 92, WhoWest 92*
**Kalkofen**, Wolfgang 1931- *AmMWSc 92*
**Kalkstein**, Laurence Saul 1948- *AmMWSc 92*
**Kalkwarf**, Donald Riley 1924- *AmMWSc 92*
**Kalkwarf**, Kenneth Lee 1946- *AmMWSc 92*
**Kalkwarf**, Leonard V. 1928- *WhoRel 92*
**Kalla**, Susan Barbara 1955- *WhoFI 92*
**Kallaher**, Michael Joseph 1940- *AmMWSc 92*
**Kallai**, Gyula 1910- *IntWW 91*
**Kallai-Sanfacon**, Mary-Ann 1949- *AmMWSc 92*
**Kallal**, R J 1921- *AmMWSc 92*
**Kalland**, Gene Arnold 1936- *AmMWSc 92*
**Kalland**, Lloyd Austin 1914- *WhoRel 92*
**Kallander**, John William 1927- *AmMWSc 92*
**Kallas**, Aino 1878-1956 *LiExTwC*
**Kallas**, James Gus, Jr. 1928- *WhoRel 92*
**Kallay**, Michael Frank, II 1944- *WhoWest 92*
**Kallelis**, Theodore S 1912- *AmMWSc 92*
**Kallen**, Frank Clements 1928- *AmMWSc 92*
**Kallen**, H. M. 1882-1974 *BenetAL 91*
**Kallen**, Horace M 1882- *DcAmImH*
**Kallen**, Lucille *WrDr 92*
**Kallen**, Lucille Eve *IntAu&W 91*
**Kallen**, Roland Gilbert 1935- *AmMWSc 92*
**Kallen**, Thomas William 1938- *AmMWSc 92*
**Kallenbach**, Ernst Adolf Theodor 1926- *AmMWSc 92*
**Kallenbach**, Neville R 1938- *AmMWSc 92*
**Kallenberg**, John Kenneth 1942- *WhoWest 92*
**Kallenberger**, Larry Brian 1948- *WhoAmP 91*
**Kaller**, Cecil Louis 1930- *AmMWSc 92*
**Kallet**, Marilyn *DrAPF 91*
**Kalley**, Gordon S 1953- *AmMWSc 92*
**Kallfelz**, Francis A 1938- *AmMWSc 92*
**Kallfelz**, John Michael 1934- *AmMWSc 92*
**Kallgren**, Edward Eugene 1928- *WhoAmL 92*
**Kallgren-Miller**, Janine Ann 1962- *WhoEnt 92*
**Kallhoff**, Katherine *WhoRel 92*
**Kallianos**, Andrew George 1930- *AmMWSc 92*
**Kallianpur**, Gopinath 1925- *AmMWSc 92*
**Kallibjian**, Ara Edmon 1962- *WhoMW 92*
**Kallich**, Martin *WrDr 92*
**Kallick**, David A. 1945- *WhoAmL 92*
**Kallick**, Deborah Anne 1951- *WhoMW 92*
**Kallick**, Sonia Belle 1933- *WhoMW 92*
**Kallikak Family**, The *DcAmImH*
**Kallio**, Heikki Olavi 1937- *IntWW 91*
**Kallio**, Reino Emil 1919- *AmMWSc 92*
**Kalliokoski**, Jorma Osmo Kalervo 1923- *AmMWSc 92*
**Kallipateira** *EncAmaz 91*
**Kallipetis**, Michel Louis 1941- *Who 92*
**Kalliwoda**, Johann Wenzel 1801-1866 *NewAmDM*
**Kallman**, Burton Jay 1927- *AmMWSc 92*
**Kallman**, Klaus D 1928- *AmMWSc 92*
**Kallman**, Mary Jeanne 1948- *AmMWSc 92*
**Kallman**, Ralph Arthur 1934- *AmMWSc 92*
**Kallman**, Robert Friend 1922- *AmMWSc 92, WhoWest 92*
**Kallman**, William Michael 1947- *AmMWSc 92*
**Kallmann**, Silve 1915- *AmMWSc 92*
**Kallmann**, Stanley Walter 1943- *WhoAmL 92*
**Kallmyer**, Jerry Doane 1955- *WhoRel 92*
**Kallner**, Norman Gust 1950- *WhoMW 92*
**Kallo**, Robert Max 1923- *AmMWSc 92*
**Kallok**, Michael John 1948- *AmMWSc 92*
**Kallos**, George J 1936- *AmMWSc 92*
**Kallsen**, Henry Alvin 1926- *AmMWSc 92*
**Kallsen**, T.J. *DrAPF 91*
**Kallstrom**, Charles Clark 1943- *WhoMW 92*
**Kallus**, Frank Theodore 1936- *AmMWSc 92*
**Kalm**, Arne 1936- *WhoFI 92*
**Kalm**, Max John 1928- *AmMWSc 92*
**Kalm**, Pehr 1716-1779 *BlkwCEP*
**Kalm**, Peter 1716-1779 *BenetAL 91*
**Kalm**, William Dean 1951- *WhoWest 92*
**Kalma**, Arne Haerter 1941- *AmMWSc 92*
**Kalman**, Calvin Shea 1944- *AmMWSc 92*
**Kalman**, Gabor J 1929- *AmMWSc 92*
**Kalman**, Imre 1882-1953 *NewAmDM*
**Kalman**, Rudolf Emil 1930- *AmMWSc 92*
**Kalman**, Sumner Myron 1918- *AmMWSc 92*
**Kalman**, Thomas Ivan 1936- *AmMWSc 92*
**Kalmanir**, Karen Ann 1958- *WhoAmL 92*
**Kalmanoff**, Martin 1920- *WhoEnt 92*
**Kalmanovich**, Moisey Iosifich 1888-1937 *SovUnBD*
**Kalmanowicz**, Max 1948- *WhoEnt 92*
**Kalmanson**, Kenneth 1943- *AmMWSc 92*
**Kalmbach**, Sydney Hobart 1913- *AmMWSc 92*
**Kalme**, John S 1938- *AmMWSc 92*
**Kalms**, Stanley 1931- *Who 92*
**Kalmus**, Edwin F. 1893- *NewAmDM*
**Kalmus**, George Ernest 1935- *Who 92*
**Kalmus**, Gerhard Wolfgang 1942- *AmMWSc 92*
**Kalmus**, Henry P 1906- *AmMWSc 92*
**Kalmus**, Morris A. *DrAPF 91*
**Kalmus**, Natalie 1892-1965 *ReelWom*
**Kalnay**, Eugenia 1942- *AmMWSc 92, WhoHisp 92*
**Kalnbernzins**, Janis 1893-1986 *SovUnBD*
**Kalnberzin**, Yan Eduardovich 1893-1986 *SovUnBD*
**Kalnin**, Ilmar L 1926- *AmMWSc 92*
**Kalnins**, Arturs 1931- *AmMWSc 92*
**Kalnitsky**, George 1917- *AmMWSc 92*
**Kalo**, Kwamala 1929- *Who 92*
**Kalodner**, Howard Isaiah 1933- *WhoAmL 92*
**Kalodner**, John David 1949- *WhoEnt 92, WhoFI 92, WhoWest 92*
**Kalogeropoulos**, Theodore E 1931- *AmMWSc 92*
**Kalogjera**, Dalma Marija 1954- *WhoMW 92*
**Kalogredis**, Vasilios J. 1949- *WhoAmL 92*
**Kalonji**, Gretchen *AmMWSc 92*
**Kaloostian**, George H 1912- *AmMWSc 92*
**Kalos**, Malvin Howard 1928- *AmMWSc 92*
**Kalota**, Dennis Jerome 1945- *AmMWSc 92*
**Kalow**, Werner 1917- *AmMWSc 92*
**Kalpakian**, Laura *DrAPF 91*
**Kalpakjian**, Serope 1928- *AmMWSc 92*
**Kalra**, Jawahar 1949- *AmMWSc 92*
**Kalra**, S N 1927- *AmMWSc 92*
**Kalra**, Satya Paul 1939- *AmMWSc 92*
**Kalra**, Vijay Kumar 1942- *AmMWSc 92*
**Kalsbeck**, John Edward 1927- *AmMWSc 92*
**Kalser**, Konstantin 1920- *IntMPA 92*
**Kalser**, Martin 1923- *AmMWSc 92*
**Kalser**, Sarah Chinn 1929- *AmMWSc 92*
**Kalshoven**, Thomas N. *WhoRel 92*
**Kalsner**, Stanley 1936- *AmMWSc 92*
**Kalsow**, Carolyn Marie 1943- *AmMWSc 92*
**Kalt**, Howard Michael 1943- *WhoFI 92*
**Kalt**, Marvin Robert 1945- *AmMWSc 92*
**Kaltenbach**, Carl Colin 1939- *AmMWSc 92*
**Kaltenbach**, Hubert Leonard 1922- *WhoWest 92*
**Kaltenbach**, John Paul 1920- *AmMWSc 92, WhoMW 92*
**Kaltenbaugh**, Peter Charles, Jr. 1948- *WhoRel 92*
**Kaltenborn**, H V 1878-1965 *FacFETw*
**Kaltenborn**, Howard Scholl 1907- *AmMWSc 92*
**Kaltenbronn**, James S 1934- *AmMWSc 92*
**Kaltenbronn**, James Stanley 1934- *WhoMW 92*
**Kaltenbrunner**, Ernst 1903-1946 *BiDExR, EncTR 91 [port]*
**Kalter**, Bella Briansky *DrAPF 91*
**Kalter**, Harold 1924- *AmMWSc 92*
**Kalter**, Seymour Sanford 1918- *AmMWSc 92*
**Kalter**, Thomas Raymond 1947- *WhoWest 92*
**Kalthoff**, Frederick Robert 1931- *WhoEnt 92*
**Kalthoff**, James W. 1938- *WhoRel 92*
**Kalthoff**, Klaus Otto 1941- *AmMWSc 92*
**Kaltofen**, Erich L 1955- *AmMWSc 92*
**Kalton**, Robert Rankin 1920- *AmMWSc 92*
**Kaltreider**, D Frank 1912- *AmMWSc 92*
**Kaltsikes**, Pantouses John 1938- *AmMWSc 92*
**Kalu**, Dike Ndukwe 1938- *AmMWSc 92*
**Kalu Rinpoche**, Khyyab Je 1905-1989 *RelLAm 91*
**Kalule**, Ayub 1953- *IntWW 91*
**Kaluzienski**, Louis Joseph 1948- *AmMWSc 92*
**Kaluzsa**, Karen Louise 1958- *WhoMW 92*
**Kalvaria**, Leon 1958- *WhoFI 92*
**Kalvelage**, Franka Anna Maria 1958- *TwCPaSc*
**Kalver**, Gail Ellen 1948- *WhoEnt 92, WhoMW 92*
**Kalvinskas**, John J 1927- *AmMWSc 92*
**Kalvinskas**, John Joseph 1927- *WhoWest 92*
**Kalyan-Raman**, Krishna 1935- *AmMWSc 92*
**Kam**, Gar Lai 1936- *AmMWSc 92*
**Kam**, Gregg Robert 1963- *WhoFI 92*
**Kam**, James Ting 1945- *WhoFI 92*
**Kam**, James Ting-Kong 1945- *AmMWSc 92*
**Kam**, Lydia B 1952- *WhoIns 92*
**Kam**, Moshe 1955- *AmMWSc 92*
**Kam**, Ralph Thomas 1957- *WhoFI 92*
**Kamack**, H J 1918- *AmMWSc 92*
**Kamal**, Abdul Naim 1935- *AmMWSc 92*
**Kamal**, Aleph 1935- *IntAu&W 91*
**Kamal**, Aleph 1950- *ConAu 134*
**Kamal**, Mounir Mark 1936- *AmMWSc 92*
**Kamal**, Musa Rasim 1934- *AmMWSc 92*
**Kamaleson**, Samuel Theodore 1930- *WhoRel 92*
**Kamali**, Norma *IntWW 91*
**Kamali**, Norma 1945- *DcTwDes*
**Kamalidenov**, Sakash 1938- *IntWW 91*
**Kamalii**, Kinau Boyd 1930- *WhoAmP 91*
**Kaman**, Charles Henry 1943- *AmMWSc 92*
**Kaman**, Charles Huron 1919- *AmMWSc 92, WhoFI 92*
**Kaman**, Robert Lawrence 1941- *AmMWSc 92*
**Kamana**, Dunstan Weston 1937- *IntWW 91*
**Kamanda Wa Kamanda** 1940- *IntWW 91*
**Kamanga**, Reuben Chitandika 1929- *IntWW 91*
**Kamarck**, Andrew Martin 1914- *IntWW 91*
**Kamas**, Lewis Melvin 1921- *WhoAmP 91*
**Kamat**, Prashant V 1953- *AmMWSc 92*
**Kamata**, Fumio 1950- *WhoFI 92*
**Kamath**, Krishna 1920- *AmMWSc 92*
**Kamath**, Savitri Krishna 1930- *AmMWSc 92*
**Kamath**, Vasanth Rathnakar 1944- *AmMWSc 92*
**Kamath**, Yashavanth Katapady 1938- *AmMWSc 92*
**Kamatoy**, Lourdes Aguas 1945- *WhoMW 92*
**Kamau**, John Cauri 1923- *IntWW 91*
**Kamau**, Mosi 1955- *WhoBlA 92*
**Kamb**, Walter Barclay 1931- *AmMWSc 92*
**Kamba**, Walter Joseph 1931- *IntWW 91, Who 92*
**Kambara**, George Kiyoshi 1916- *AmMWSc 92*
**Kambayashi**, Tatsuji 1933- *AmMWSc 92*
**Kamber**, Bernard M. *IntMPA 92*
**Kamber**, Victor Samuel 1944- *WhoFI 92*
**Kambour**, Roger Peabody 1932- *AmMWSc 92*
**Kamboureli**, Smaro 1955- *IntAu&W 91*
**Kambysellis**, Michael Panagiotis 1935- *AmMWSc 92*

**Kamdar,** Madhusudan H 1930- AmMWSc 92
**Kamegai,** Minao 1932- AmMWSc 92
**Kamego,** Albert Amil 1941- AmMWSc 92
**Kamehameha I** DcAmImH
**Kamehameha IV** DcAmImH
**Kamei,** Masao 1916- IntWW 91
**Kamel,** Hyman 1919- AmMWSc 92
**Kamel,** Ted 1960- WhoAmP 91
**Kamel Ahmed,** Kamal El-Din 1927- IntWW 91
**Kamemoto,** Fred Isamu 1928- AmMWSc 92
**Kamemoto,** Haruyuki 1922- AmMWSc 92
**Kamen,** D. Jonathan 1953- WhoEnt 92
**Kamen,** Edward Walter 1945- AmMWSc 92
**Kamen,** Gary P AmMWSc 92
**Kamen,** Gloria 1923- ConAu 35NR
**Kamen,** Harry Paul 1933- WhoAmL 92, WhoFI 92
**Kamen,** Henry 1936- WrDr 92
**Kamen,** Martin D. 1913- IntWW 91
**Kamen,** Martin David 1913- AmMWSc 92
**Kamen-Kaye,** Maurice 1905- AmMWSc 92
**Kamenetz,** Herman Leo 1907- AmMWSc 92
**Kamenetz,** Rodger DrAPF 91
**Kamenev,** Lev Borisovich 1883-1936 FacFETw, SovUnBD
**Kamenka,** Eugene 1928- IntAu&W 91, IntWW 91, WrDr 92
**Kamens,** Harold 1917- WhoAmL 92
**Kamenszain,** Tamara 1947- ConSpAP
**Kamentsev,** Vladimir Mikhailovich 1928- IntWW 91
**Kamentsev,** Vladimir Mikhaylovich 1928- SovUnBD
**Kamentsky,** Louis A 1930- AmMWSc 92
**Kamerick,** Eileen Ann 1958- WhoAmL 92
**Kamerlingh Onnes,** Heike 1853-1926 WhoNob 90
**Kamerman,** Ken 1931- WhoAmP 91
**Kamerman,** Kenneth M. 1931- WhoWest 92
**Kamerow,** Norman Warren 1927- WhoFI 92
**Kamerschen,** Robert Jerome 1936- WhoFI 92
**Kames,** Henry Home 1696-1782 BlkwCEP
**Kames,** Kenneth F. 1935- WhoFI 92
**Kamey,** Paul 1912- IntMPA 92
**Kamhi,** Samuel Vitali 1922- WhoFI 92
**Kamien,** C Zelman 1927- AmMWSc 92
**Kamien,** Ethel N 1930- AmMWSc 92
**Kamil,** Abdullah 1919- IntWW 91
**Kamil,** Alan C. 1941- ConAu 134
**Kamil,** Alan Curtis 1941- AmMWSc 92
**Kamil,** Geoffrey Harvey 1942- Who 92
**Kamilli,** Diana Chapman 1941- AmMWSc 92
**Kamilli,** Robert Joseph 1947- AmMWSc 92, WhoWest 92
**Kamin,** Benjamin Alon 1953- WhoRel 92
**Kamin,** Blair Douglass 1957- WhoMW 92
**Kamin,** C Richard 1944- WhoAmP 91
**Kamin,** Franz DrAPF 91
**Kamin,** Henry 1920- AmMWSc 92
**Kamin,** Kay Hodes 1940- WhoMW 92
**Kamine,** Bernard Samuel 1943- WhoAmL 92, WhoWest 92
**Kaminer,** Benjamin 1924- AmMWSc 92
**Kaminetzky,** Harold Alexander 1923- AmMWSc 92
**Kaminker,** Jerome Alvin 1941- AmMWSc 92
**Kaminow,** Ivan Paul 1930- AmMWSc 92
**Kamins,** Barry Michael 1943- WhoAmL 92
**Kamins,** Bernard J. 1942- WhoAmL 92
**Kamins,** John Mark 1947- WhoAmL 92
**Kamins,** Philip E. 1936- WhoWest 92
**Kamins,** Theodore I 1941- AmMWSc 92
**Kaminskas,** Edvardas 1935- AmMWSc 92
**Kaminski,** Bronislaw 1940- IntWW 91
**Kaminski,** Charles Anthony WhoFI 92
**Kaminski,** Debora Rose 1963- WhoMW 92
**Kaminski,** Donald Leon 1940- AmMWSc 92
**Kaminski,** Edward Jozef 1926- AmMWSc 92
**Kaminski,** Ireneusz Gwidon 1925- IntAu&W 91
**Kaminski,** James Joseph 1947- AmMWSc 92
**Kaminski,** Janusz Zygmuni 1959- WhoEnt 92
**Kaminski,** Joan Mary 1947- AmMWSc 92
**Kaminski,** John WhoEnt 92
**Kaminski,** Joseph C 1943- WhoIns 92
**Kaminski,** Jozef 1919- IntWW 91
**Kaminski,** Stephanie 1943- WhoEnt 92
**Kaminski,** Zigmund Charles 1929- AmMWSc 92
**Kaminsky,** Alice R. WrDr 92
**Kaminsky,** Daniel DrAPF 91
**Kaminsky,** Grigoriy Naumovich 1895-1938 SovUnBD
**Kaminsky,** Horst 1927- IntWW 91
**Kaminsky,** Jack 1922- WrDr 92
**Kaminsky,** Larry Michael 1952- WhoAmL 92
**Kaminsky,** Laura 1956- WhoEnt 92
**Kaminsky,** Laurence Samuel 1940- AmMWSc 92
**Kaminsky,** Manfred Stephan 1929- AmMWSc 92
**Kaminsky,** Marc DrAPF 91
**Kaminsky,** Max 1908- NewAmDM
**Kaminsky,** Richard Alan 1951- WhoAmL 92
**Kaminsky,** Stuart 1934- IntAu&W 91, WrDr 92
**Kamisar,** Gordon Aaron 1960- WhoAmL 92
**Kamisar,** Yale 1929- WhoAmL 92
**Kamiyama,** Mikio 1936- AmMWSc 92
**Kamlang-Ek,** Arthit IntWW 91
**Kamlani,** Deirdre Shay 1959- WhoFI 92
**Kamlot,** Robert 1926- WhoEnt 92
**Kamm,** Donald E 1929- AmMWSc 92
**Kamm,** Dorinda 1952- IntAu&W 91, WrDr 92
**Kamm,** Gilbert G 1925- AmMWSc 92
**Kamm,** Jacob Oswald 1918- WhoFI 92, WhoMW 92, WrDr 92
**Kamm,** James A AmMWSc 92
**Kamm,** Jerome J 1933- AmMWSc 92
**Kamm,** Laurence Richard 1939- WhoEnt 92
**Kamm,** Marilyn Jane 1950- WhoAmL 92
**Kamm,** Roger Dale 1950- AmMWSc 92
**Kamman,** Alan Bertram 1931- WhoFI 92
**Kamman,** Harold William 1924- WhoRel 92
**Kammann,** Karl Philip, Jr 1936- AmMWSc 92
**Kammash,** Terry 1927- AmMWSc 92
**Kammen,** Harold Oscar 1927- AmMWSc 92
**Kammen,** Michael 1936- WrDr 92
**Kammen,** Michael G 1936- ConAu 34NR
**Kammer,** Ann Emma 1935- AmMWSc 92
**Kammer,** Kerry 1948- WhoAmP 91
**Kammer,** Paul A AmMWSc 92
**Kammeraad,** Adrian 1912- AmMWSc 92
**Kammerer,** Andrew Harmon 1956- WhoWest 92
**Kammerer,** Hans 1922- IntWW 91
**Kammerer,** Marvin Julius 1937- WhoAmP 91
**Kammerer,** William John 1931- AmMWSc 92
**Kammerman,** Arthur Charles Cyril 1915- WhoFI 92
**Kammerman,** Marcy Helene 1960- WhoAmL 92
**Kammermeier,** Martin A 1931- AmMWSc 92
**Kammermeyer,** Karl 1904- AmMWSc 92
**Kammerud,** Ronald Claire 1942- AmMWSc 92
**Kammholz,** Theophil Carl 1909- WhoAmL 92
**Kammler,** David W AmMWSc 92
**Kammula,** Raju G 1935- AmMWSc 92
**Kamo,** Roy 1921- WhoMW 92
**Kamoche,** Jidlaph Gitau 1942- WhoBlA 92
**Kamon,** Eliezer 1930- AmMWSc 92
**Kamougue,** Wadal Abdelkader IntWW 91
**Kamoun,** Malek AmMWSc 92
**Kamowitz,** Herbert M 1931- AmMWSc 92
**Kamowitz,** Sharon Shapiro 1958- WhoAmL 92
**Kamp,** Arthur Joseph, Jr. 1945- WhoAmL 92
**Kamp,** David Allen 1947- AmMWSc 92
**Kamp,** Norbert 1927- IntWW 91
**Kamp,** Ronald Carl 1934- WhoWest 92
**Kamp,** William Paul 1949- WhoMW 92
**Kampa Vilina,** Kathleen Ann 1959- WhoEnt 92
**Kampas,** Frank James 1946- AmMWSc 92
**Kampe,** Dennis James 1945- AmMWSc 92
**Kampelman,** Max M. 1920- IntWW 91, WhoAmL 92, WhoAmP 91
**Kampen,** Emerson 1928- WhoFI 92, WhoMW 92
**Kamper,** Robert Andrew 1933- AmMWSc 92
**Kamperschroer,** George R. 1949- WhoAmL 92
**Kampf,** William Ira 1943- WhoAmL 92
**Kamphoefner,** Fred J 1921- AmMWSc 92
**Kamphuis,** J William 1938- AmMWSc 92
**Kampley,** Linda DrAPF 91
**Kampmeier,** Christopher Martin 1951- WhoEnt 92
**Kampmeier,** Curtis Neil 1941- WhoMW 92
**Kampmeier,** Jack A 1935- AmMWSc 92
**Kampouris,** Emmanuel Andrew 1934- IntWW 91, WhoFI 92
**Kamprath,** Eugene John 1926- AmMWSc 92
**Kampschmidt,** Ralph Fred 1923- AmMWSc 92
**Kamra,** Om Perkash 1935- AmMWSc 92
**Kamran,** Mervyn Arthur 1938- AmMWSc 92
**Kamrass,** Lewis Howard 1959- WhoRel 92
**Kamrass,** Murray 1921- AmMWSc 92
**Kamrin,** Michael Arnold 1940- AmMWSc 92, WhoMW 92
**Kamshalov,** Aleksandr Ivanovich 1932- IntWW 91
**Kamsler,** Harold Milton 1911- WhoRel 92
**Kamuyu,** Jacqueline LeVerne 1947- WhoRel 92
**Kamykowski,** Daniel 1945- AmMWSc 92
**Kamyszew,** Christopher D. 1958- WhoMW 92
**Kan Yuet-Keung** 1913- Who 92
**Kan,** Henry 1921- WhoFI 92
**Kan,** Joseph Ruce 1938- AmMWSc 92
**Kan,** Kenny Wai 1966- WhoWest 92
**Kan,** Kon Cheong 1954- WhoFI 92
**Kan,** Lou Sing 1943- AmMWSc 92
**Kan,** Paul Man-Lok 1947- WhoFI 92
**Kan,** Peter Tai Yuen 1927- AmMWSc 92
**Kan,** Yuet Wai 1936- AmMWSc 92, IntWW 91, Who 92
**Kan-Mitchell,** June 1949- AmMWSc 92
**Kana,** Daniel D 1934- AmMWSc 92
**Kana'an,** Adli Sadeq 1931- AmMWSc 92
**Kanaan,** Taher Hamdi 1935- IntWW 91
**Kanabrocki,** Eugene Ladislaus 1922- AmMWSc 92
**Kanabus,** Henry DrAPF 91
**Kanagaratnam,** Kandiah 1922- IntWW 91
**Kanagy,** Steven Albert 1956- WhoFI 92
**Kanakamedala,** Raghaviah Veera 1927- WhoWest 92
**Kanakaratne,** Neville 1923- IntWW 91
**Kanakkanatt,** Antony 1935- AmMWSc 92
**Kanakkanatt,** Sebastian Varghese 1929- AmMWSc 92
**Kanal,** Laveen Nanik 1931- AmMWSc 92
**Kanaly,** Steven Francis 1946- WhoEnt 92
**Kanamori,** Hiroo 1936- AmMWSc 92
**Kanamori,** Masao 1911- IntWW 91
**Kanamueller,** Joseph M 1938- AmMWSc 92
**Kanan,** B D WhoAmP 91
**Kananack,** Arthur IntMPA 92
**Kananin,** Roman Grigorevich 1935- IntWW 91
**Kanao,** Minoru 1914- IntWW 91
**Kanarek,** Carol Mock 1953- WhoAmL 92
**Kanarek,** Robin Beth 1946- AmMWSc 92
**Kanarik,** Rosella 1909- AmMWSc 92
**Kanarkowski,** Edward Joseph 1947- WhoFI 92
**Kanarowski,** S M 1912- AmMWSc 92
**Kanarowski,** Stanley Martin 1912- WhoFI 92
**Kanas,** James Constantine 1956- WhoEnt 92
**Kanasewich,** Ernest Raymond 1931- AmMWSc 92
**Kanatzar,** Charles Leplie 1914- AmMWSc 92
**Kanatzidis,** Mercouri G 1957- AmMWSc 92
**Kanava,** Zoe 1933- IntAu&W 91
**Kanawa,** Kiri Te NewAmDM
**Kanazawa,** Shuzo 1910- IntWW 91
**Kancheli,** Giya 1935- ConCom 92
**Kanciruk,** Paul 1947- AmMWSc 92
**Kanczak,** Norbert M 1931- AmMWSc 92
**Kanda,** Motohisa 1943- AmMWSc 92
**Kandaras,** Homer Michael 1929- WhoAmP 91
**Kandel,** Abraham 1941- AmMWSc 92
**Kandel,** Eric Richard 1929- AmMWSc 92
**Kandel,** Lenore ConPo 91, WrDr 92
**Kandel,** Lynn Edward 1937- WhoMW 92
**Kandel,** Peter Thomas WhoFI 92
**Kandel,** Richard Joshua 1924- AmMWSc 92
**Kandel,** Stephen 1927- WhoEnt 92
**Kandel,** William Lloyd 1939- WhoAmL 92
**Kandell,** Alice S 1938- IntAu&W 91
**Kandell,** Marshall Jay 1937- WhoWest 92
**Kander,** John 1927- NewAmDM
**Kander,** John Harold 1927- WhoEnt 92
**Kandhal,** Prithvi Singh 1935- AmMWSc 92
**Kandil,** Abdel Hadi 1935- IntWW 91
**Kandiner,** Harold J 1917- AmMWSc 92
**Kandinsky,** Vasiliy Vasil'evich 1866-1944 SovUnBD
**Kandinsky,** Wassily 1866-1944 DcTwDes, FacFETw, ModArCr 2 [port]
**Kandoian,** A G 1911- AmMWSc 92
**Kandola,** Nerinder 1959- WhoWest 92
**Kandravy,** John 1935- WhoAmL 92
**Kandt,** Ronald Kirk 1954- WhoFI 92
**Kandutsch,** Andrew August 1926- AmMWSc 92
**Kane,** Agnes Brezak 1946- AmMWSc 92
**Kane,** Alice Theresa 1948- WhoAmL 92, WhoFI 92
**Kane,** Andrew William 1944- WhoMW 92
**Kane,** Anthony Thomas 1945- WhoAmL 92
**Kane,** Bartholomew Aloysius 1945- WhoWest 92
**Kane,** Bernard James 1932- AmMWSc 92
**Kane,** Betty Ann 1941- WhoAmP 91
**Kane,** Big Daddy 1968- ConMus 7 [port]
**Kane,** Bob 1916- Au&Arts 8 [port]
**Kane,** Brian 1948- DcTwDes
**Kane,** Carol 1952- IntMPA 92, WhoEnt 92
**Kane,** Cecelia D 1915- WhoAmP 91
**Kane,** Cheik Hamidou 1928- LiExTwC
**Kane,** Cynthia Marie WhoMW 92
**Kane,** Daniel E 1923- AmMWSc 92
**Kane,** David N 1945- WhoIns 92
**Kane,** David Sheridan 1940- WhoFI 92
**Kane,** Dennis LesBEnT 92
**Kane,** Donald Michael 1944- WhoIns 92
**Kane,** E D 1917- AmMWSc 92
**Kane,** Edward J 1951- WhoAmP 91
**Kane,** Edward James 1935- WhoFI 92
**Kane,** Edward L. 1938- WhoWest 92
**Kane,** Edward R 1918- AmMWSc 92, IntWW 91
**Kane,** Elisha Kent 1820-1857 BenetAL 91, BiInAmS
**Kane,** Elizabeth Ann 1937- WhoWest 92
**Kane,** Elleen Ann 1966- WhoMW 92
**Kane,** Falilou 1938- IntWW 91
**Kane,** Francis Joseph, Jr 1929- AmMWSc 92
**Kane,** George 1916- Who 92
**Kane,** George E 1925- AmMWSc 92
**Kane,** Gerard Thomas Matthew 1946- ConAu 133
**Kane,** Gordon Leon 1937- AmMWSc 92
**Kane,** Gordon Philo 1926- AmMWSc 92
**Kane,** Hal 1918- WhoEnt 92
**Kane,** Harnett Thomas 1910-1984 BenetAL 91
**Kane,** Harrison 1925- AmMWSc 92
**Kane,** Henry Edward 1917- AmMWSc 92
**Kane,** Howard L 1911- AmMWSc 92
**Kane,** Jack 1911- Who 92
**Kane,** Jack Allison 1921- WhoFI 92
**Kane,** Jacqueline Anne 1946- WhoBlA 92
**Kane,** James F 1942- AmMWSc 92
**Kane,** James Joseph 1929- AmMWSc 92
**Kane,** James Patrick 1946- WhoWest 92
**Kane,** James Robert 1959- WhoFI 92
**Kane,** Jeffrey Lee 1962- WhoMW 92
**Kane,** Jim TwCWW 91
**Kane,** John IntMPA 92
**Kane,** John Charles 1956- WhoFI 92
**Kane,** John J 1924- WhoAmP 91
**Kane,** John Joseph 1915- AmMWSc 92
**Kane,** John Power 1932- AmMWSc 92
**Kane,** John Robert 1936- AmMWSc 92
**Kane,** John Vincent, Jr 1928- AmMWSc 92
**Kane,** Joseph Charles 1935- WhoFI 92
**Kane,** Joseph James, Jr. 1948- WhoEnt 92
**Kane,** Joseph Thomas 1934- WhoFI 92
**Kane,** Josh LesBEnT 92
**Kane,** Julie DrAPF 91
**Kane,** Karen Marie 1947- WhoWest 92
**Kane,** Katherine DrAPF 91
**Kane,** Katherine D. 1950- WhoWest 92
**Kane,** Larry d1991 NewYTBS 91
**Kane,** Marilyn Elizabeth 1968- WhoEnt 92
**Kane,** Martin 1958- TwCPaSc
**Kane,** Martin Francis 1928- AmMWSc 92
**Kane,** Matthew Aloysius, Jr. 1958- WhoAmL 92
**Kane,** Michael Joseph 1922- WhoEnt 92
**Kane,** Patrick E. 1942- WhoEnt 92
**Kane,** Patrick F WhoAmP 91
**Kane,** Paul DrAPF 91
**Kane,** Racquel E. 1932- WhoFI 92
**Kane,** Richard James 1950- WhoRel 92
**Kane,** Richard Miles 1954- WhoFI 92
**Kane,** Robert B 1928- AmMWSc 92, WhoMW 92
**Kane,** Robert Edward 1931- AmMWSc 92
**Kane,** Robert F. 1951- WhoAmL 92
**Kane,** Robert Francis 1926- WhoAmP 91
**Kane,** Robert M 1942- WhoAmP 91
**Kane,** Rod ConAu 133
**Kane,** Ronald S 1944- AmMWSc 92
**Kane,** Sam 1919- WhoFI 92
**Kane,** Shannan May 1961- WhoAmL 92
**Kane,** Siegrun Dinklage 1938- WhoAmL 92
**Kane,** Stanley Bruce 1920- WhoFI 92
**Kane,** Stanley D. 1907- IntMPA 92
**Kane,** Stephen Roger 1951- WhoAmL 92
**Kane,** Stephen Shimmon 1917- AmMWSc 92
**Kane,** Stratton J 1938- WhoIns 92
**Kane,** Thomas R 1924- AmMWSc 92
**Kane,** Timothy Joseph 1946- WhoFI 92
**Kane,** Timothy Patrick 1962- WhoAmL 92
**Kane,** Tommy Henry 1964- WhoBlA 92
**Kane,** Walter Reilly 1926- AmMWSc 92
**Kane,** William J 1933- AmMWSc 92
**Kane,** William Theodore 1932- AmMWSc 92
**Kane,** Wilson IntAu&W 91X
**Kane-jo** EncAmaz 91
**Kane-Maguire,** Noel Andrew Patrick 1942- AmMWSc 92
**Kane-Vanni,** Patricia Ruth 1954- WhoAmL 92, WhoFI 92
**Kaneda,** Toshi 1925- AmMWSc 92

**Kanefsky**, Victor 1931- *WhoEnt 92*
**Kanegis**, Arthur L.D. 1947- *WhoWest 92*
**Kanehiro**, Kenneth Kenji 1934- *WhoWest 92*
**Kanehiro**, Yoshinori 1919- *AmMWSc 92*
**Kaneko**, Iwazo 1907- *IntWW 91*
**Kaneko**, Jiro Jerry 1924- *AmMWSc 92*
**Kaneko**, Lonny *DrAPF 91*
**Kaneko**, Mitsuru *WhoEnt 92*
**Kaneko**, Thomas Motomi 1914- *AmMWSc 92*
**Kanelidis**, Nick B. 1954- *WhoAmL 92*
**Kanellopoulos**, Panayotis 1902-1986 *FacFETw*
**Kanellos**, Nicolas 1945- *WhoHisp 92*
**Kanemaru**, Shin 1915- *IntWW 91*
**Kanemasu**, Edward Tsukasa 1940- *AmMWSc 92*
**Kanenaka**, Rebecca Yae 1958- *WhoWest 92*
**Kaner**, Harvey Sheldon 1930- *WhoAmL 92, WhoFI 92*
**Kanerva**, Ilkka Armas Mikael 1948- *IntWW 91*
**Kanes**, William H 1934- *AmMWSc 92*
**Kaneshige**, Harry Masato 1929- *AmMWSc 92, WhoMW 92*
**Kaneshige**, Melvin Yoshio 1948- *WhoAmL 92*
**Kaneshiro**, Edna Sayomi 1937- *AmMWSc 92*
**Kaneshiro**, Kenneth Yoshimitsu 1943- *AmMWSc 92*
**Kaneshiro**, Tsuneo 1930- *AmMWSc 92*
**Kanet**, Roger Edward 1936- *WhoMW 92*
**Kanew**, Jeff *IntMPA 92*
**Kaney**, Anthony Rolland 1940- *AmMWSc 92*
**Kanfer**, Julian Norman 1930- *AmMWSc 92*
**Kang Ke-ching** 1912- *EncAmaz 91*
**Kang Keqing** 1911- *IntWW 91*
**K'ang K'o-ch'ing** 1912- *EncAmaz 91*
**Kang Kyung-Shik** 1936- *IntWW 91*
**Kang Shi'en** 1915- *IntWW 91*
**Kang Sukhi** 1934- *ConCom 92*
**Kang Yonghe** 1915- *IntWW 91*
**Kang**, Benjamin Toyeong 1931- *WhoRel 92*
**Kang**, C Yong 1940- *AmMWSc 92*
**Kang**, Chang-Yuil 1954- *AmMWSc 92*
**Kang**, Chia-Chen Chu 1923- *AmMWSc 92*
**Kang**, Chin Huat 1953- *WhoRel 92*
**Kang**, David Soosang 1931- *AmMWSc 92*
**Kang**, Hyo *WhoEnt 92*
**Kang**, Ik-Ju 1928- *AmMWSc 92*
**Kang**, Joohee *AmMWSc 92*
**Kang**, Juan 1935- *WhoMW 92*
**Kang**, Jung Il 1942- *WhoFI 92*
**Kang**, Jung Wong 1933- *AmMWSc 92*
**Kang**, Kenneth S 1933- *AmMWSc 92*
**Kang**, Kewon 1934- *AmMWSc 92*
**Kang**, Kyungsik 1936- *AmMWSc 92*
**Kang**, Sung-Mo 1945- *WhoMW 92*
**Kang**, Sung-Mo Steve 1945- *AmMWSc 92*
**Kang**, Sungzong 1937- *AmMWSc 92*
**Kang**, Tae Wha *AmMWSc 92*
**Kang**, Uan Gen 1938- *AmMWSc 92*
**Kang**, Wi Jo 1930- *WhoRel 92*
**Kang**, Young Hoon 1922- *IntWW 91, Who 92*
**Kang**, Younghill 1903-1972 *BenetAL 91*
**Kang**, Yuan-Hsu *AmMWSc 92*
**Kanga**, Bahman Kersasp 1925- *WhoFI 92*
**Kangas**, Carlton Warren 1952- *WhoRel 92*
**Kangas**, Donald Arne 1929- *AmMWSc 92*
**Kangas**, Robert Jacob 1951- *WhoEnt 92*
**Kangro**, Bernard 1910- *LiExTwC*
**Kani**, John *IntWW 91*
**Kania**, Alan James 1949- *WhoFI 92, WhoWest 92*
**Kania**, Stasia *TwCPaSc*
**Kanick**, Virginia 1925- *AmMWSc 92*
**Kanidinc**, Salahattin 1927- *WhoEnt 92*
**Kaniecki**, Michael Joseph 1935- *WhoRel 92, WhoWest 92*
**Kaniecki**, Thaddeus John 1931- *AmMWSc 92*
**Kanig**, Joseph Louis 1921- *AmMWSc 92*
**Kanig**, Lavinia Ludlow 1916- *WhoAmP 91*
**Kanin**, Fay *IntMPA 92, ReelWom, WhoEnt 92*
**Kanin**, Garson 1912- *BenetAL 91, FacFETw [port], IntAu&W 91, IntMPA 92, IntWW 91, WhoEnt 92, WrDr 92*
**Kanin**, Michael 1910- *ConTFT 9, IntMPA 92, WhoEnt 92*
**Kaniuk**, Yoram 1930- *ConAu 134*
**Kanizay**, Stephen Peter 1924- *AmMWSc 92*
**Kanjorski**, Paul E. 1937- *AlmAP 92 [port]*
**Kanjorski**, Paul Edmund 1937- *WhoAmP 91*
**Kankaanpaa**, Matti 1927- *IntWW 91*
**Kankel**, Douglas Ray 1944- *AmMWSc 92*
**Kann**, Maria 1906- *IntAu&W 91*
**Kann**, Mark Eliot 1947- *WhoWest 92*
**Kann**, Peter Robert 1942- *WhoFI 92*
**Kannady**, Donald Joe 1949- *WhoRel 92*
**Kannappan**, Palaniappan 1934- *AmMWSc 92*
**Kanne**, Michael S *WhoAmP 91*
**Kanne**, Michael Stephen 1938- *WhoAmL 92, WhoMW 92*
**Kannel**, William B 1923- *AmMWSc 92*
**Kannenberg**, John L 1919- *WhoAmP 91*
**Kannenberg**, Lloyd C 1939- *AmMWSc 92*
**Kannenberg**, Lyndon William 1931- *AmMWSc 92*
**Kannengiesser**, Charles A. 1926- *WhoRel 92*
**Kanner**, Allan 1955- *WhoAmL 92*
**Kanner**, Helena Levine 1953- *WhoIns 92*
**Kannes**, Deno Ernest 1932- *WhoEnt 92*
**Kannewurf**, Carl Raeside 1931- *AmMWSc 92*
**Kanninen**, Melvin Fred 1935- *AmMWSc 92*
**Kanno**, Brian M. 1961- *WhoWest 92*
**Kannowski**, Paul Bruno 1927- *AmMWSc 92*
**Kannry**, Sybil 1931- *WhoFI 92*
**Kano**, Adeline Kyoko 1927- *AmMWSc 92*
**Kano**, Michihiko *IntWW 91*
**Kano-Sueoka**, Tamiko 1932- *AmMWSc 92*
**Kanode**, Roy Edgar 1960- *WhoRel 92*
**Kanofsky**, Alvin Sheldon 1939- *AmMWSc 92*
**Kanoho**, Ezra R 1927- *WhoAmP 91*
**Kanojia**, Ramesh Maganlal 1933- *AmMWSc 92*
**Kanopoulos**, Nick 1956- *AmMWSc 92*
**Kanouse**, Keith J. 1948- *WhoAmL 92*
**Kansfield**, Norman J. 1940- *WhoRel 92*
**Kansteiner**, Beau Kent 1934- *WhoMW 92*
**Kant**, Fred H 1930- *AmMWSc 92*
**Kant**, Harold Sanford 1931- *WhoEnt 92*
**Kant**, Immanuel 1724-1804 *BlkwCEP*
**Kant**, Kenneth James 1935- *AmMWSc 92*
**Kantack**, Benjamin H 1927- *AmMWSc 92*
**Kantak**, Kathleen Mary 1951- *AmMWSc 92*
**Kantar**, Ned Dolf 1946- *WhoEnt 92*
**Kantarat**, Panieng 1921- *IntWW 91*
**Kantaris**, Sylvia 1936- *ConPo 91, WrDr 92*
**Kante**, Mamadou Boubacar 1926- *IntWW 91*
**Kanten**, Lee Robert 1947- *WhoEnt 92*
**Kanter**, Burton Wallace 1930- *WhoAmL 92*
**Kanter**, Carl Irwin 1932- *WhoAmL 92*
**Kanter**, Gerald Sidney 1925- *AmMWSc 92*
**Kanter**, Hal *LesBEnT 92*
**Kanter**, Hal 1918- *IntMPA 92, WhoEnt 92*
**Kanter**, Helmut 1928- *AmMWSc 92*
**Kanter**, Ira E 1931- *AmMWSc 92*
**Kanter**, Irving 1924- *AmMWSc 92*
**Kanter**, Jay 1926- *IntMPA 92*
**Kanter**, Jay Ira 1926- *WhoEnt 92, WhoWest 92*
**Kanter**, Jerome Jacob 1957- *WhoMW 92*
**Kanter**, Manuel Allen 1924- *AmMWSc 92*
**Kanter**, Michael Howard 1956- *WhoWest 92*
**Kanter**, Robert D. 1952- *WhoEnt 92*
**Kanter**, Rosabeth Moss 1943- *IntWW 91*
**Kanter**, Shamai 1930- *WhoRel 92*
**Kanter**, Stephen 1946- *WhoAmL 92*
**Kanterman**, Stanley Alan 1958- *WhoFI 92*
**Kanth**, Rajani K. 1949- *WhoFI 92*
**Kantha**, Lakshmi *AmMWSc 92*
**Kantner**, Helen Johnson 1936- *WhoRel 92*
**Kantner**, Paul 1941- *WhoEnt 92*
**Kantner**, Robert Oburn 1934- *WhoRel 92*
**Kanto**, Peter *WrDr 92*
**Kantonen**, T. A. 1900- *WrDr 92*
**Kantonen**, Taito Almar 1900- *IntAu&W 91*
**Kantor**, Fred Stuart 1931- *AmMWSc 92*
**Kantor**, George Joseph 1937- *AmMWSc 92*
**Kantor**, Gideon 1925- *AmMWSc 92*
**Kantor**, Harvey Sherwin 1938- *AmMWSc 92*
**Kantor**, Igo 1930- *IntMPA 92, WhoWest 92*
**Kantor**, MacKinlay 1904-1977 *BenetAL 91, TwCWW 91*
**Kantor**, Mark Alan 1955- *WhoAmL 92*
**Kantor**, Nathan 1942- *WhoFI 92*
**Kantor**, Pamela 1957- *WhoEnt 92*
**Kantor**, Paul 1938- *WhoEnt 92*
**Kantor**, Paul B 1938- *AmMWSc 92*
**Kantor**, Sidney 1924- *AmMWSc 92*
**Kantor**, Simon William 1925- *AmMWSc 92*
**Kantor**, Tadeusz d1990 *IntWW 91N*
**Kantor**, Tadeusz 1915-1990 *AnObit 1990*
**Kantor-Berg**, Friedrich 1908-1979 *ConAu 133*
**Kantorovich**, Leonid Vital'evich 1912-1986 *SovUnBD, WhoNob 90*
**Kantorovitz**, Shmuel 1935- *AmMWSc 92*
**Kantorowich**, Roy Herman 1916- *Who 92*
**Kantounis**, Lizabeth Ann 1959- *WhoEnt 92*
**Kantowski**, Ronald 1939- *AmMWSc 92*
**Kantrowitz**, Adrian 1918- *AmMWSc 92, IntWW 91*
**Kantrowitz**, Arthur 1913- *AmMWSc 92*
**Kantrowitz**, Arthur Robert 1913- *IntWW 91*
**Kantrowitz**, Irwin H 1937- *AmMWSc 92*
**Kantrowitz**, Jean Rosensaft 1922- *WhoMW 92*
**Kantrowitz**, Susan Lee 1955- *WhoAmL 92*
**Kantz**, Paul Thomas 1941- *WhoWest 92*
**Kantz**, Paul Thomas, Jr 1941- *AmMWSc 92*
**Kantzer**, Kenneth Sealer 1917- *WhoMW 92, WhoRel 92*
**Kantzes**, James 1924- *AmMWSc 92*
**Kanuck**, George J, Jr *WhoAmP 91*
**Kanuk**, Leslie Lazar *WhoAmP 91*
**Kanungo**, R.N. 1935- *ConAu 135*
**Kanwal**, Ram Prakash 1924- *AmMWSc 92*
**Kany**, Judy C *WhoAmP 91*
**Kanyer**, Laurie Ann 1959- *WhoWest 92*
**Kanzeg**, David George 1948- *WhoMW 92*
**Kanzelmeyer**, James Herbert 1926- *AmMWSc 92*
**Kanzler**, Rudolf 1873-1956 *BiDExR*
**Kanzler**, Walter Wilhelm 1938- *AmMWSc 92*
**Kao**, Charles K 1933- *AmMWSc 92*
**Kao**, Cheng Chi 1941- *WhoWest 92*
**Kao**, Chien Yuan 1927- *AmMWSc 92*
**Kao**, Cliff Chihhaw 1956- *WhoFI 92*
**Kao**, David Teh-Yu 1936- *AmMWSc 92*
**Kao**, Fa-Ten 1934- *AmMWSc 92*
**Kao**, Frederick 1919- *AmMWSc 92*
**Kao**, Henry Yu-shu 1913- *IntWW 91*
**Kao**, John Y 1948- *AmMWSc 92*
**Kao**, Kung-Ying Tang 1917- *AmMWSc 92*
**Kao**, Kwan Chi 1926- *AmMWSc 92*
**Kao**, Ming-hsiung 1944- *AmMWSc 92*
**Kao**, Philip Min-Shien 1963- *WhoWest 92*
**Kao**, Race Li-Chan 1943- *AmMWSc 92*
**Kao**, Samuel Chung-Siung 1941- *AmMWSc 92*
**Kao**, Tai-Wu 1935- *AmMWSc 92*
**Kao**, Timothy Wu 1937- *AmMWSc 92*
**Kao**, Wen-Hong 1954- *AmMWSc 92, WhoMW 92*
**Kao**, William Chishon 1952- *WhoMW 92*
**Kao**, Yi-Han 1931- *AmMWSc 92*
**Kao**, Yuen-Koh 1941- *AmMWSc 92*
**Kaough**, Thomas Lee 1938- *WhoEnt 92*
**Kapacinskas**, Diane 1955- *WhoRel 92*
**Kapadia**, Abhaysingh J 1929- *AmMWSc 92*
**Kapadia**, Harivadan K. 1935- *WhoFI 92*
**Kapadia**, Vinodchandra Shivdas 1936- *WhoFI 92*
**Kapalin**, Jerman *WhoRel 92*
**Kapania**, Rakesh Kumar 1956- *AmMWSc 92*
**Kapany**, Narinder Singh 1927- *AmMWSc 92*
**Kapasouris**, Petros 1960- *WhoFI 92*
**Kapatkin**, Fred 1927- *WhoFI 92*
**Kapche**, Ronald Anthony 1941- *WhoFI 92*
**Kapecki**, Jon Alfred 1942- *AmMWSc 92*
**Kapek**, Antonin d1990 *IntWW 91N*
**Kapek**, Antonin 1922-1990 *FacFETw*
**Kapelner**, Alan *DrAPF 91*
**Kapelrud**, Arvid Schou 1912- *WrDr 92*
**Kaper**, Hans G 1936- *AmMWSc 92*
**Kaper**, Jacobus M 1931- *AmMWSc 92*
**Kaper**, James Bennett 1952- *AmMWSc 92*
**Kapetanakos**, Christos Anastasios 1936- *AmMWSc 92*
**Kapetanovic**, Izet Michael *AmMWSc 92*
**Kapfer**, A W *ScFEYrs*
**Kaphan**, Robert Charles 1944- *WhoFI 92*
**Kapi**, Mari 1950- *Who 92*
**Kapikian**, Albert Zaven 1930- *AmMWSc 92*
**Kapila**, Ashwani Kumar 1946- *AmMWSc 92*
**Kapilian**, Danny Ira 1956- *WhoEnt 92*
**Kapioltas**, John 1927- *WhoFI 92*
**Kapista**, Mikhail Sergeevich 1921- *SovUnBD*
**Kapitanets**, Ivan Matveyivich 1928- *IntWW 91*
**Kapitonov**, Ivan Vasil'evich 1915- *SovUnBD*
**Kapitsa**, Mikhail Stepanovich 1921- *IntWW 91*
**Kapitsa**, Petr Leonidovich 1894-1984 *SovUnBD*
**Kapitsa**, Pyotr Leonidovich 1894-1984 *FacFETw, WhoNob 90*
**Kapke**, Barry 1955- *WhoEnt 92*
**Kaplan**, Abner 1923- *AmMWSc 92*
**Kaplan**, Abraham 1931- *NewAmDM*
**Kaplan**, Alan Marc 1940- *AmMWSc 92*
**Kaplan**, Albert Sydney 1917- *AmMWSc 92*
**Kaplan**, Alex 1910- *AmMWSc 92*
**Kaplan**, Alexander E 1938- *AmMWSc 92*
**Kaplan**, Alexander Maxwell 1957- *WhoWest 92*
**Kaplan**, Allan *DrAPF 91*
**Kaplan**, Allen P 1940- *AmMWSc 92*
**Kaplan**, Allen Stanford 1939- *WhoRel 92*
**Kaplan**, Anatoliy L'vovich 1902-1980 *SovUnBD*
**Kaplan**, Andrew Gary 1941- *IntAu&W 91*
**Kaplan**, Andrew Pawling 1956- *WhoWest 92*
**Kaplan**, Andrew S. 1960- *WhoAmL 92*
**Kaplan**, Ann Esther 1926- *AmMWSc 92*
**Kaplan**, Arnold 1939- *AmMWSc 92*
**Kaplan**, Arthur Lewis 1933- *AmMWSc 92*
**Kaplan**, Barbara Joan 1941- *WhoWest 92*
**Kaplan**, Barry Hubert 1938- *AmMWSc 92*
**Kaplan**, Ben Augustus 1952- *WhoFI 92*
**Kaplan**, Bernard *DrAPF 91*
**Kaplan**, Bernard 1921- *AmMWSc 92*
**Kaplan**, Berton Harris 1930- *AmMWSc 92*
**Kaplan**, Betsy Byrns 1923- *WhoAmP 91*
**Kaplan**, Betty Lynn 1949- *WhoEnt 92*
**Kaplan**, Boris 1897- *IntMPA 92*
**Kaplan**, Bradley S. 1960- *WhoFI 92*
**Kaplan**, Brent J. 1958- *WhoAmL 92*
**Kaplan**, Carl Eliot 1939- *WhoAmL 92*
**Kaplan**, Charles Paul 1942- *WhoFI 92*
**Kaplan**, Daniel Eliot 1932- *AmMWSc 92*
**Kaplan**, Daniel I. 1943- *WhoFI 92*
**Kaplan**, Daniel Lee 1934- *WhoRel 92*
**Kaplan**, Daniel Moshe 1953- *AmMWSc 92*
**Kaplan**, David Gilbert 1944- *AmMWSc 92*
**Kaplan**, David Jeremy 1934- *AmMWSc 92*
**Kaplan**, David L 1918- *AmMWSc 92*
**Kaplan**, David Lee 1953- *AmMWSc 92*
**Kaplan**, David Michael *DrAPF 91*
**Kaplan**, Diane S. 1949- *WhoAmL 92*
**Kaplan**, Diane Susan 1957- *WhoEnt 92*
**Kaplan**, Donald Robert 1938- *AmMWSc 92*
**Kaplan**, Donald Sheldon 1938- *WhoWest 92*
**Kaplan**, Edward *DrAPF 91*
**Kaplan**, Edward Lynn 1920- *AmMWSc 92*
**Kaplan**, Edward Mitchell 1939- *WhoAmL 92*
**Kaplan**, Ehud 1942- *AmMWSc 92*
**Kaplan**, Emanuel 1910- *AmMWSc 92*
**Kaplan**, Ephraim Henry 1918- *AmMWSc 92*
**Kaplan**, Erica Lynn 1955- *WhoEnt 92*
**Kaplan**, Ervin 1918- *AmMWSc 92*
**Kaplan**, Eugene Herbert 1932- *AmMWSc 92*
**Kaplan**, Fred 1934- *AmMWSc 92*
**Kaplan**, Fred 1937- *DcLB 111 [port]*
**Kaplan**, Gabriel 1945- *IntMPA 92, WhoEnt 92*
**Kaplan**, Gary 1939- *WhoFI 92, WhoWest 92*
**Kaplan**, George Harry 1948- *AmMWSc 92*
**Kaplan**, Gerald 1939- *AmMWSc 92*
**Kaplan**, Gerald Frank 1942- *WhoAmL 92*
**Kaplan**, Gilbert B. 1951- *WhoAmL 92*
**Kaplan**, Harley Lance 1961- *WhoFI 92*
**Kaplan**, Harold 1916- *IntAu&W 91*
**Kaplan**, Harold Irwin 1927- *AmMWSc 92*
**Kaplan**, Harold M 1908- *AmMWSc 92*
**Kaplan**, Harry Arthur 1911- *AmMWSc 92*
**Kaplan**, Harvey 1924- *AmMWSc 92*
**Kaplan**, Harvey 1940- *AmMWSc 92*
**Kaplan**, Harvey Robert 1941- *AmMWSc 92*
**Kaplan**, Helen Singer 1929- *AmMWSc 92*
**Kaplan**, Henry 1918-1984 *FacFETw*
**Kaplan**, Henry J 1942- *AmMWSc 92*
**Kaplan**, Herman 1928- *AmMWSc 92*
**Kaplan**, Howard *DrAPF 91*
**Kaplan**, Howard Gordon 1941- *WhoAmL 92, WhoMW 92*
**Kaplan**, Howard Irvin 1945- *WhoWest 92*
**Kaplan**, Ian Theodore 1946- *WhoAmP 91*
**Kaplan**, Irving 1912- *AmMWSc 92*
**Kaplan**, Irving Eugene 1926- *WhoWest 92*
**Kaplan**, Isaac R 1929- *AmMWSc 92*
**Kaplan**, Jacob 1895- *IntWW 91*
**Kaplan**, Jacob Gordin 1922- *AmMWSc 92*
**Kaplan**, James 1951- *ConAu 135*
**Kaplan**, James Andrew 1951- *WhoAmL 92*
**Kaplan**, James Miller 1953- *WhoAmL 92*
**Kaplan**, Janet Gordon 1938- *WhoEnt 92*
**Kaplan**, Jared 1938- *WhoAmL 92, WhoFI 92, WhoMW 92*
**Kaplan**, Jerome 1926- *WhoAmP 91, WhoFI 92*
**Kaplan**, Jerome I 1926- *AmMWSc 92, WhoMW 92*
**Kaplan**, Jerry *AmMWSc 92*
**Kaplan**, Joel 1956- *ConAu 134*
**Kaplan**, Joel Howard 1938- *AmMWSc 92*
**Kaplan**, Joel Howard 1941- *AmMWSc 92*
**Kaplan**, Joel Stuart 1937- *WhoAmL 92*
**Kaplan**, Johanna *DrAPF 91*
**Kaplan**, Johanna 1942- *ConNov 91*
**Kaplan**, John Ervin 1950- *AmMWSc 92*
**Kaplan**, Jonathan 1947- *IntMPA 92*
**Kaplan**, Jonathan Harris 1957- *WhoFI 92*
**Kaplan**, Joseph 1902- *AmMWSc 92, Who 92*
**Kaplan**, Joseph 1902-1991 *CurBio 91N, NewYTBS 91 [port]*
**Kaplan**, Joseph 1941- *AmMWSc 92*
**Kaplan**, Joseph Henry Herbst 1937- *WhoAmL 92*

**Kaplan,** Joseph Herbert 1959- *WhoAmP 91*
**Kaplan,** Joseph Solte 1935- *WhoAmL 92*
**Kaplan,** Judith Helene 1938- *WhoFI 92*
**Kaplan,** Julius David 1941- *WhoWest 92*
**Kaplan,** Justin 1925- *BenetAL 91, DcLB 111 [port], WrDr 92*
**Kaplan,** Kenneth Franklin 1945- *WhoFI 92*
**Kaplan,** Laurence M. 1953- *WhoEnt 92*
**Kaplan,** Lawrence 1926- *AmMWSc 92*
**Kaplan,** Lawrence Jay 1943- *AmMWSc 92*
**Kaplan,** Lee Landa 1952- *WhoAmL 92*
**Kaplan,** Leonard 1939- *AmMWSc 92*
**Kaplan,** Leonard Eugene 1940- *WhoFI 92*
**Kaplan,** Leonard Louis 1928- *AmMWSc 92*
**Kaplan,** Lewis David 1917- *AmMWSc 92*
**Kaplan,** Lewis Kenneth 1933- *WhoEnt 92*
**Kaplan,** Louis Allen 1942- *WhoWest 92*
**Kaplan,** Madeline 1944- *WhoFI 92*
**Kaplan,** Manuel E 1928- *AmMWSc 92*
**Kaplan,** Mark Alan 1946- *WhoAmP 91*
**Kaplan,** Mark Norman 1930- *WhoAmL 92*
**Kaplan,** Mark Steven 1947- *AmMWSc 92*
**Kaplan,** Marshall Harvey 1939- *AmMWSc 92*
**Kaplan,** Martin Charles 1953- *AmMWSc 92*
**Kaplan,** Martin Francis 1940- *WhoMW 92*
**Kaplan,** Martin L 1923- *AmMWSc 92*
**Kaplan,** Martin L 1935- *AmMWSc 92*
**Kaplan,** Martin Mark 1915- *AmMWSc 92*
**Kaplan,** Maurice 1907- *AmMWSc 92*
**Kaplan,** Melvin 1927- *AmMWSc 92*
**Kaplan,** Melvin Hyman 1920- *AmMWSc 92*
**Kaplan,** Michael 1937- *AmMWSc 92*
**Kaplan,** Michael David 1948- *WhoAmL 92*
**Kaplan,** Mike 1943- *WhoEnt 92, WhoWest 92*
**Kaplan,** Milton *DrAPF 91*
**Kaplan,** Milton Emanuel 1914- *WhoWest 92*
**Kaplan,** Mordecai M. *DcAmImH*
**Kaplan,** Mordecai Menahem 1881-1983 *RelLAm 91*
**Kaplan,** Morton 1933- *AmMWSc 92*
**Kaplan,** Morton A 1921- *IntAu&W 91, WrDr 92*
**Kaplan,** Murray Lee 1941- *AmMWSc 92*
**Kaplan,** Neil Trevor 1942- *Who 92*
**Kaplan,** Noel H. 1946- *WhoAmL 92*
**Kaplan,** Norman M 1931- *AmMWSc 92*
**Kaplan,** Paul 1929- *AmMWSc 92*
**Kaplan,** Paul Alan d1991 *NewYTBS 91*
**Kaplan,** Paul Elias 1940- *WhoMW 92*
**Kaplan,** Philip 1918- *WhoRel 92*
**Kaplan,** Philip Charles 1961- *WhoAmL 92*
**Kaplan,** Phyllis Deen 1931- *AmMWSc 92*
**Kaplan,** Ralph Benjamin 1920- *AmMWSc 92*
**Kaplan,** Randy Kaye 1954- *WhoMW 92*
**Kaplan,** Raphael 1936- *AmMWSc 92*
**Kaplan,** Raymond 1929- *AmMWSc 92*
**Kaplan,** Richard *LesBEnT 92*
**Kaplan,** Richard E 1938- *AmMWSc 92*
**Kaplan,** Richard Emannuel 1938- *WhoWest 92*
**Kaplan,** Richard James 1925- *WhoEnt 92*
**Kaplan,** Richard Stephen 1945- *AmMWSc 92*
**Kaplan,** Robert *DrAPF 91*
**Kaplan,** Robert B. 1929- *WrDr 92*
**Kaplan,** Robert Barnett 1924- *WhoEnt 92*
**Kaplan,** Robert David 1939- *WhoAmL 92*
**Kaplan,** Robert Edward 1958- *WhoEnt 92*
**Kaplan,** Robert Joel 1947- *AmMWSc 92*
**Kaplan,** Robert Lewis 1928- *AmMWSc 92*
**Kaplan,** Robert Marshall 1936- *WhoFI 92, WhoWest 92*
**Kaplan,** Robert S 1940- *AmMWSc 92*
**Kaplan,** Ronald M 1946- *AmMWSc 92*
**Kaplan,** Ronald Paul 1948- *WhoAmL 92*
**Kaplan,** Ronald S 1957- *AmMWSc 92*
**Kaplan,** Ronald V. 1930- *WhoFI 92*
**Kaplan,** Sam H 1915- *AmMWSc 92*
**Kaplan,** Samuel 1916- *AmMWSc 92*
**Kaplan,** Samuel 1922- *AmMWSc 92*
**Kaplan,** Sandra Solon 1934- *AmMWSc 92*
**Kaplan,** Sanford Sandy 1950- *AmMWSc 92, WhoMW 92*
**Kaplan,** Selig N 1932- *AmMWSc 92*
**Kaplan,** Selna L 1927- *AmMWSc 92*
**Kaplan,** Shelby Jean 1947- *WhoWest 92*
**Kaplan,** Sheldon 1915- *WhoAmL 92, WhoMW 92*
**Kaplan,** Sheldon Zachary 1911- *WhoAmL 92*
**Kaplan,** Solomon Alexander 1924- *AmMWSc 92*
**Kaplan,** Stanley 1936- *AmMWSc 92, WhoMW 92*
**Kaplan,** Stanley A. d1991 *NewYTBS 91*
**Kaplan,** Stanley A 1938- *AmMWSc 92*
**Kaplan,** Stanley Baruch 1931- *AmMWSc 92*
**Kaplan,** Stanley Meisel 1922- *AmMWSc 92*
**Kaplan,** Stephen Robert 1937- *AmMWSc 92*
**Kaplan,** Steven 1953- *WhoAmL 92*
**Kaplan,** Steven B. 1953- *ConAu 135*
**Kaplan,** Steven F. 1956- *WhoFI 92*
**Kaplan,** Sumner Zalman 1920- *WhoAmL 92*
**Kaplan,** Susan Robin 1954- *WhoAmL 92*
**Kaplan,** Ted 1946- *WhoAmP 91*
**Kaplan,** Terry 1956- *WhoFI 92*
**Kaplan,** Theodore Norman 1935- *WhoFI 92*
**Kaplan,** Thomas Abraham 1926- *AmMWSc 92, WhoMW 92*
**Kaplan,** Wilfred 1915- *AmMWSc 92*
**Kaplan,** William 1922- *AmMWSc 92*
**Kaplan,** William 1938- *WhoMW 92*
**Kaplan,** William David 1914- *AmMWSc 92*
**Kaplansky,** Irving 1917- *AmMWSc 92, IntWW 91, WrDr 92*
**Kapleau,** Philip 1909- *RelLAm 91*
**Kapler,** Aleksei Y 1904-1979 *FacFETw*
**Kapler,** Hermann 1867-1941 *EncTR 91*
**Kapler,** Joseph Edward 1924- *AmMWSc 92*
**Kaplij,** Victor 1946- *WhoEnt 92*
**Kaplin,** William Albert 1942- *WhoAmL 92*
**Kaplon,** Morton Fischel 1921- *AmMWSc 92*
**Kaplow,** Herbert Elias 1927- *WhoEnt 92*
**Kaplow,** Leonard Samuel 1920- *AmMWSc 92*
**Kaplow,** Louis 1956- *WhoAmL 92, WhoFI 92*
**Kaplow,** Robert David 1947- *WhoAmL 92*
**Kaplowitz,** Bernard 1937- *WhoAmL 92*
**Kaplowitz,** Karen Jill 1946- *WhoAmL 92*
**Kaplowitz,** Richard Allen 1940- *WhoWest 92*
**Kapnek,** Abraham Bruce 1947- *WhoRel 92*
**Kapner,** Robert S 1927- *AmMWSc 92*
**Kapnick,** Harvey Edward, Jr. 1925- *IntWW 91*
**Kapnick,** Richard Bradshaw 1955- *WhoAmL 92, WhoFI 92*
**Kapnick,** Stewart 1956- *WhoFI 92*
**Kapocius,** Juozas *DcAmImH*
**Kapoor,** Amrit Lal 1931- *AmMWSc 92*
**Kapoor,** Anish 1954- *IntWW 91, TwCPaSc*
**Kapoor,** Brij M 1936- *AmMWSc 92*
**Kapoor,** Inder Prakash 1937- *AmMWSc 92*
**Kapoor,** Narinder N 1937- *AmMWSc 92*
**Kapoor,** Raj 1942-1988 *IntDcF 2-2 [port]*
**Kapoor,** S F 1934- *AmMWSc 92*
**Kapoor,** Shashi 1938- *IntMPA 92, IntWW 91*
**Kapoor,** Shiv Gopal 1948- *WhoMW 92*
**Kapor,** Mitchell David 1950- *WhoFI 92*
**Kapos,** Ervin 1931- *AmMWSc 92*
**Kapoulas,** George James 1953- *WhoEnt 92*
**Kapp,** Artur Iosepovich 1878-1952 *SovUnBD*
**Kapp,** Colin 1928?- *TwCSFW 91, WrDr 92*
**Kapp,** Edmond Xavier 1890-1978 *TwCPaSc*
**Kapp,** John Jacob 1729-1807 *DcNCBi 3*
**Kapp,** M Keith 1953- *WhoAmP 91*
**Kapp,** Michael Keith 1953- *WhoAmL 92*
**Kapp,** Ray 1925- *WhoRel 92*
**Kapp,** Robert Wesley, Jr *AmMWSc 92*
**Kapp,** Roger W. 1936- *WhoAmL 92*
**Kapp,** Villem Khansovich 1913-1964 *SovUnBD*
**Kapp,** Wolfgang 1858-1922 *BiDExR, EncTR 91 [port]*
**Kapp-Pierce,** Judith A *AmMWSc 92*
**Kappagoda,** C Tissa *AmMWSc 92*
**Kappas,** Attallah 1926- *AmMWSc 92*
**Kappe,** David Syme 1935- *AmMWSc 92*
**Kappel,** Ellen Sue 1959- *AmMWSc 92*
**Kappel,** Frederick R. 1902- *IntWW 91, Who 92*
**Kappel,** Henry Lawrence 1945- *WhoMW 92*
**Kappel,** Mark M. 1952- *WhoEnt 92*
**Kappenman,** Russell Francis 1938- *AmMWSc 92*
**Kappers,** Lawrence Allen 1941- *AmMWSc 92*
**Kappes,** Philip Spangler 1925- *WhoAmL 92, WhoMW 92*
**Kappler,** Herbert *EncTR 91*
**Kappler,** John W *AmMWSc 92*
**Kappner,** Augusta Souza 1944- *WhoBlA 92*
**Kappus,** Karl Daniel 1938- *AmMWSc 92*
**Kapral,** Frank Albert 1928- *AmMWSc 92, WhoMW 92*
**Kapral,** Hilarion 1948- *WhoRel 92*
**Kapral,** Raymond Edward 1942- *AmMWSc 92*
**Kapraun,** Donald Frederick 1945- *AmMWSc 92*
**Kaprelian,** Edward Karnig 1913- *AmMWSc 92*
**Kaprio,** Leo 1918- *IntWW 91*
**Kapron,** Felix Paul 1940- *AmMWSc 92*
**Kaprow,** Allan 1927- *FacFETw*
**Kapsales,** Peter Paul 1954- *WhoFI 92*
**Kapsalis,** John *DrAPF 91*
**Kapsalis,** John George 1927- *AmMWSc 92*
**Kapshandy,** Timothy Edward 1956- *WhoAmL 92*
**Kapstein,** Sherwin J *WhoAmP 91*
**Kaptain,** Eudokia 1945- *WhoIns 92*
**Kapteyn,** Paul Joan George 1928- *IntWW 91*
**Kapto,** Aleksandr Semenovich 1933- *IntWW 91, SovUnBD*
**Kaptur,** Marcia Carolyn 1946- *WhoMW 92*
**Kaptur,** Marcy 1946- *AlmAP 92 [port]*
**Kaptur,** Marcy C 1946- *WhoAmP 91*
**Kapture,** Mitzi *WhoEnt 92*
**Kapur,** Bhushan M 1938- *AmMWSc 92*
**Kapur,** Harish 1929- *ConAu 34NR*
**Kapur,** Kailash C 1941- *AmMWSc 92*
**Kapur,** Krishan Kishore 1930- *AmMWSc 92*
**Kapur,** Shakti Prakash 1932- *AmMWSc 92*
**Kapuscinski,** Jan 1936- *AmMWSc 92*
**Kapuscinski,** Ryszard 1932- *IntAu&W 91, IntWW 91*
**Kapusinski,** Albert Thomas 1937- *WhoFI 92*
**Kapust,** Lawrence Alan 1955- *WhoEnt 92*
**Kapusta,** George 1932- *AmMWSc 92*
**Kapustka,** Lawrence A 1948- *AmMWSc 92*
**Kapyrin,** Dmitri 1960- *ConCom 92*
**Karaban,** Roslyn Ann 1953- *WhoRel 92*
**Karabasov,** Yuriy Sergeyevich 1939- *IntWW 91*
**Karabasz,** Felix Francois 1939- *WhoMW 92*
**Karabatsos,** Elizabeth Ann 1932- *WhoWest 92*
**Karabatsos,** Gerasimos J 1932- *AmMWSc 92*
**Karabel,** Jerome Bernard 1950- *WhoWest 92*
**Karabell,** David Isiah 1939- *WhoAmL 92*
**Karabtchevsky,** Isaac 1934- *WhoEnt 92*
**Karacan,** Ismet 1927- *AmMWSc 92*
**Karachi,** Archbishop of 1918- *Who 92*
**Karadbil,** Leon Nathan 1920- *AmMWSc 92*
**Karadi,** Gabor 1924- *AmMWSc 92*
**Karadjordjevic,** Aleksandar *NewYTBS 91 [port]*
**Karady,** George Gyorgy 1930- *AmMWSc 92*
**Karady,** Sandor 1933- *AmMWSc 92*
**Karaevli,** Ahmet 1949- *IntWW 91*
**Karafin,** Lester 1926- *AmMWSc 92*
**Karageorge,** Michael *ConAu 34NR*
**Karageorghis,** Vassos 1929- *IntWW 91*
**Karagianes,** Manuel Tom 1932- *AmMWSc 92*
**Karajan,** Herbert von 1908-1989 *EncTR 91, FacFETw [port], NewAmDM*
**Karakas,** Rita S. *WhoRel 92*
**Karakash,** John J 1914- *AmMWSc 92*
**Karakashian,** Aram Simon 1939- *AmMWSc 92*
**Karakawa,** Walter Wataru *AmMWSc 92*
**Karakey,** Sherry JoAnne 1942- *WhoWest 92*
**Karal,** Frank Charles, Jr 1926- *AmMWSc 92*
**Karalis,** John Peter 1938- *WhoAmL 92*
**Karalunas,** Deborah Anne Haller 1956- *WhoAmL 92*
**Karam,** J. David 1958- *WhoMW 92*
**Karam,** Jim Daniel *AmMWSc 92*
**Karam,** John Harvey 1929- *AmMWSc 92*
**Karam,** Ratib A 1934- *AmMWSc 92*
**Karamanlis,** Constantine *FacFETw*
**Karamanlis,** Konstantinos G. 1907- *IntWW 91*
**Karamanos,** Teresa S 1956- *WhoAmP 91*
**Karamcheti,** K 1923- *AmMWSc 92*
**Karami,** Omar *IntWW 91*
**Karampelas,** Napoleon Demetrios 1904- *WhoRel 92*
**Karan,** David 1948- *WhoAmL 92*
**Karan,** Donna 1948- *IntWW 91*
**Karan,** Paul Richard 1936- *WhoAmL 92*
**Karan,** Pradyumna P 1930- *ConAu 35NR*
**Karanik,** John Alexander 1944- *WhoIns 92*
**Karanikas,** Alexander 1916- *IntAu&W 91, WrDr 92*
**Karanja,** Josphat Njuguna 1931- *IntWW 91, Who 92*
**Karantokis,** Nicolas Georgiou 1917- *WhoFI 92*
**Karaosmanoglu,** Attila 1932- *IntWW 91*
**Karaosmanoglu,** Ozgur 1962- *WhoFI 92*
**Karapostoles,** Demetrios Aristides 1936- *WhoFI 92*
**Karara,** H M 1928- *AmMWSc 92*
**Karas,** James Glynn 1933- *AmMWSc 92*
**Karas,** John Athan 1922- *AmMWSc 92*
**Karas,** Shawky Faltaous 1928- *WhoAmL 92*
**Karasaki,** Shuichi 1931- *AmMWSc 92*
**Karasawa,** Shunjiro 1930- *IntWW 91*
**Karasek,** Francis Warren 1919- *AmMWSc 92*
**Karasek,** Marvin A 1931- *AmMWSc 92*
**Karasick,** Carol 1941- *WhoFI 92*
**Karasiewicz,** Walter Richard 1942- *WhoFI 92*
**Karasik,** Gita 1953- *WhoEnt 92*
**Karassik,** Irwin R. 1929- *WhoAmL 92*
**Karasz,** Arthur 1907- *IntWW 91, WrDr 92*
**Karasz,** Frank Erwin 1933- *AmMWSc 92*
**Karatsu,** Osamu 1947- *WhoFI 92*
**Karatz,** Bruce E. 1945- *WhoFI 92, WhoWest 92*
**Karatzas,** Ioannis 1951- *AmMWSc 92*
**Karavdic,** Zlatan 1936- *IntWW 91*
**Karavia,** Lia Hadzopoulou 1932- *IntAu&W 91*
**Karavolas,** Harry J 1936- *AmMWSc 92*
**Karayannis,** Nicholas M 1931- *AmMWSc 92*
**Karayev,** Faraj 1943- *ConCom 92*
**Karayn,** James, Jr. 1933- *WhoEnt 92*
**Karban,** Richard 1954- *WhoWest 92*
**Karbo,** Karen *DrAPF 91*
**Karch,** Robert E. 1933- *WhoFI 92*
**Karcher,** Alan J 1943- *WhoAmP 91*
**Karcher,** John Drake 1939- *WhoFI 92*
**Karcher,** Susan Jean 1951- *WhoMW 92*
**Karchin,** Louis Samuel 1951- *WhoEnt 92*
**Karchmer,** Jean Herschel 1914- *AmMWSc 92*
**Karczmar,** Alexander George 1918- *AmMWSc 92*
**Karczmar,** Mieczyslaw 1923- *WhoFI 92*
**Kardelj,** Edvard 1910-1979 *FacFETw*
**Kardia,** Caroline 1951- *TwCPaSc*
**Kardiner,** Abram 1891-1981 *FacFETw*
**Kardish,** Laurence 1945- *IntMPA 92*
**Kardonsky,** Stanley 1941- *AmMWSc 92*
**Kardos,** Geza 1926- *AmMWSc 92*
**Kardos,** John Louis 1939- *AmMWSc 92*
**Kardos,** Mark S. 1951- *WhoAmL 92*
**Kardos,** Mel D. 1947- *WhoAmL 92*
**Kardos,** Otto 1907- *AmMWSc 92*
**Kardulias,** Paul Nick 1952- *WhoMW 92*
**Kare,** Graciela Salinas 1957- *WhoHisp 92*
**Kare,** Morley Richard 1922- *AmMWSc 92*
**Kareem,** Ahsan 1947- *AmMWSc 92*
**Karefa-Smart,** John Musselman 1915- *IntWW 91*
**Kareh,** Jorge 1960- *WhoHisp 92*
**Kareiva,** Peter Michael 1951- *AmMWSc 92*
**Karekin,** II *WhoRel 92*
**Karel,** Karin Johnson 1950- *AmMWSc 92*
**Karel,** Leonard 1912- *AmMWSc 92*
**Karel,** Marcus 1928- *AmMWSc 92*
**Karel,** Martin Lewis 1944- *AmMWSc 92*
**Karel,** Nola 1931- *WhoWest 92*
**Karelskaya,** Rimma Klavdiyevna 1927- *IntWW 91*
**Karem,** David Kevin 1943- *WhoAmP 91*
**Karem,** Michael G 1946- *WhoAmP 91*
**Kares,** Kaarlo Olavi 1903- *WhoRel 92*
**Karetnikov,** Nikolai 1930- *ConCom 92*
**Karetnikov,** Nikolai Nikolayevich 1930- *IntWW 91*
**Karetsky,** David A. d1991 *NewYTBS 91*
**Karfakis,** Mario George 1950- *AmMWSc 92*
**Karff,** Samuel Egal 1931- *WhoRel 92*
**Karg,** Gerhart 1936- *AmMWSc 92*
**Karg-Elert,** Sigfrid 1877-1933 *NewAmDM*
**Kargbo,** Tom Obakeh 1945- *IntWW 91*
**Karger,** Barry Lloyd 1939- *AmMWSc 92*
**Karger,** Delmar William 1913- *WrDr 92*
**Karger,** Patti 1918- *WhoAmL 92*
**Kargl,** Thomas E 1932- *AmMWSc 92*
**Karhilo,** Aarno 1927- *IntWW 91*
**Karickhoff,** Samuel Woodford 1943- *AmMWSc 92*
**Kariel,** Henry S. 1924- *WrDr 92*
**Karieva,** Bernara Rakhimovna 1936- *IntWW 91*
**Karig,** Daniel Edmund 1937- *AmMWSc 92*
**Karig,** Walter 1898?-1956 *BenetAL 91*
**Kariger,** Robert Lee 1931- *WhoWest 92*
**Karika,** Mark 1952- *WhoRel 92*
**Karikari,** John Agyei 1955- *WhoFI 92*
**Karim,** Aziz 1939- *AmMWSc 92*
**Karim,** Ghazi A 1934- *AmMWSc 92*
**Karim,** Khondkar Rezaul 1950- *AmMWSc 92*
**Karim,** Muhammad Bazlul 1949- *WhoMW 92*
**Karim,** Mustai 1919- *IntWW 91*
**Karim,** Wali J. 1951- *WhoBlA 92*
**Karim-Lamrani,** Mohammed 1919- *IntWW 91*
**Kariman,** Khalil 1944- *AmMWSc 92*
**Karimjee,** Tayabali Hassanali Alibhoy d1987 *Who 92N*
**Karimov,** Islam Abduganievich 1938- *SovUnBD*
**Karimov,** Islam Abduganiyevich 1938- *IntWW 91*
**Karin,** Sidney 1943- *AmMWSc 92*

**Karina**, Anna 1940- *IntMPA 92, IntWW 91*
**Karinattu**, Joseph J 1938- *AmMWSc 92*
**Karinen**, Arthur Eli 1919- *AmMWSc 92*
**Karinthy**, Ferenc 1921- *IntAu&W 91, IntWW 91*
**Karinthy**, Frigyes 1887-1938 *ScFEYrs*
**Karipides**, Anastas 1937- *AmMWSc 92*
**Karis**, William G. 1948- *WhoFI 92*
**Kariuki**, Julius 1961- *BlkOlyM [port]*
**Kariv-Miller**, Essie *AmMWSc 92*
**Karivalis**, Damianos George 1923- *WhoRel 92*
**Kariya**, Takashi 1925- *AmMWSc 92*
**Karjalainen**, Ahti d1990 *IntWW 91N*
**Karjalainen**, Ahti 1923-1990 *FacFETw*
**Karjanis**, Charles R 1954- *WhoAmP 91*
**Karjian**, Hovhannes *WhoRel 92*
**Kark**, Arthur Leslie 1910- *Who 92*
**Kark**, Austen Steven 1926- *IntWW 91, Who 92*
**Kark**, Evelyn Florence 1928- *Who 92*
**Kark**, Joanne Barbara 1953- *WhoMW 92*
**Kark**, Leslie *Who 92*
**Kark**, Nina Mary *Who 92*
**Kark**, Robert Adriaan Pieter 1940- *AmMWSc 92*
**Karkalits**, Olin Carroll, Jr 1916- *AmMWSc 92*
**Karkheck**, John Peter 1945- *AmMWSc 92*
**Karklins**, Olgerts Longins 1924- *AmMWSc 92*
**Karkoff**, Maurice 1927- *ConCom 92*
**Karkut**, Richard Theodore 1948- *WhoMW 92*
**Karkutt**, Marilyn N 1938- *WhoAmP 91*
**Karl**, Allan F. 1959- *WhoEnt 92*
**Karl**, Barry Dean 1927- *WhoMW 92*
**Karl**, Curtis Lee 1940- *AmMWSc 92*
**Karl**, David Joseph 1934- *AmMWSc 92*
**Karl**, Dennis 1954- *ConAu 134*
**Karl**, Elfriede 1933- *IntWW 91*
**Karl**, Frederick 1927- *WrDr 92*
**Karl**, Frederick Robert 1927- *IntAu&W 91*
**Karl**, Gabriel 1937- *AmMWSc 92*
**Karl**, Gregory Paul 1950- *WhoFI 92*
**Karl**, Herman Adolf 1947- *AmMWSc 92*
**Karl**, Michael M 1915- *AmMWSc 92*
**Karl**, Richard C 1920- *AmMWSc 92*
**Karl**, Robert Raymond, Jr 1945- *AmMWSc 92*
**Karl**, Stuart d1991 *LesBEnT 92 [port]*
**Karl**, Susan Margaret 1951- *AmMWSc 92*
**Karl**, Thomas Richard 1951- *AmMWSc 92*
**Karlan**, Marc Simeon 1942- *WhoMW 92*
**Karlander**, Edward P 1931- *AmMWSc 92*
**Karle**, Harry P 1927- *AmMWSc 92*
**Karle**, Isabella 1921- *IntWW 91*
**Karle**, Isabella Lugoski 1921- *AmMWSc 92*
**Karle**, Jean Marianne 1950- *AmMWSc 92*
**Karle**, Jerome 1918- *AmMWSc 92, IntWW 91, Who 92, WhoNob 90*
**Karlekar**, Bhalchandra Vasudeo 1939- *AmMWSc 92*
**Karlen**, Arno *DrAPF 91*
**Karlen**, Douglas Lawrence 1951- *AmMWSc 92*
**Karlen**, John 1933- *ConTFT 9*
**Karlen**, John Adam 1933- *WhoEnt 92*
**Karlen**, Merrill, Jr 1956- *WhoAmP 91*
**Karlen**, Peter Hurd 1949- *WhoAmL 92*
**Karler**, Ralph 1928- *AmMWSc 92*
**Karleskint**, Barry Michael 1941- *WhoWest 92*
**Karlfeldt**, Erik Axel 1864-1931 *FacFETw, WhoNob 90*
**Karlin**, Alvan A 1950- *AmMWSc 92*
**Karlin**, Arthur 1936- *AmMWSc 92*
**Karlin**, Bernie 1927- *SmATA 68 [port]*
**Karlin**, Fred 1936- *ConTFT 9, IntMPA 92*
**Karlin**, Gary Lee 1934- *WhoMW 92*
**Karlin**, Kenneth Daniel 1948- *AmMWSc 92*
**Karlin**, Michael Jonathan Abraham 1952- *WhoAmL 92*
**Karlin**, Myron D. 1918- *IntMPA 92, WhoEnt 92*
**Karlin**, Robert E 1916- *WhoAmP 91*
**Karlin**, Samuel 1924- *AmMWSc 92, IntWW 91, WhoWest 92*
**Karlin**, Teri Lea 1963- *WhoMW 92*
**Karlin**, Wayne 1945- *ConAu 133*
**Karliner**, Jerrold 1940- *AmMWSc 92*
**Karlinger**, Angela C 1903- *WhoAmP 91*
**Karlins**, M. William 1932- *NewAmDM*
**Karlins**, Mark *DrAPF 91*
**Karlins**, Martin William 1932- *WhoEnt 92*
**Karll**, Jo Ann 1948- *WhoAmP 91*
**Karll**, Robert E 1924- *AmMWSc 92*
**Karlof**, John Knox 1946- *AmMWSc 92*
**Karloff**, Boris 1887-1969 *FacFETw*
**Karlos**, Anthony Christ 1912- *WhoEnt 92*
**Karlov**, Vladimir Alekseevich 1914- *SovUnBD*
**Karlovitz**, Bela 1904- *AmMWSc 92*
**Karlow**, Edwin Anthony 1942- *AmMWSc 92*
**Karlowska**, Stanislawa de 1876-1952 *TwCPaSc*
**Karls**, John Spencer 1942- *WhoAmL 92*
**Karlson**, Alfred Gustav 1910- *AmMWSc 92*
**Karlson**, Ben Emil 1934- *WhoFI 92, WhoMW 92*
**Karlson**, Eskil Leannart 1920- *AmMWSc 92*
**Karlson**, Karl Eugene 1920- *AmMWSc 92*
**Karlson**, Ronald Henry 1947- *AmMWSc 92*
**Karlson**, Stephen Hopkins 1954- *WhoFI 92, WhoMW 92*
**Karlsson**, Erik Lennart 1918- *IntWW 91*
**Karlsson**, Sture Karl Fredrik 1925- *AmMWSc 92*
**Karlsson**, Ulf Lennart 1935- *AmMWSc 92*
**Karlstrom**, Ernest Leonard 1928- *AmMWSc 92*
**Karlstrom**, Thor Nels Vincent 1920- *AmMWSc 92*
**Karlton**, Lawrence K. 1935- *WhoAmL 92, WhoWest 92*
**Karmal**, Babrak 1929- *IntWW 91*
**Karmali**, Rashida A *AmMWSc 92*
**Karman**, Arthur Bennett 1936- *WhoMW 92*
**Karman**, James William 1947- *WhoWest 92*
**Karman**, Kenneth Allen 1943- *WhoFI 92*
**Karman**, Theodore von 1881-1963 *FacFETw*
**Karmas**, Endel *AmMWSc 92*
**Karmas**, George 1920- *AmMWSc 92*
**Karmazyn**, Morris 1950- *AmMWSc 92*
**Karmel**, Alex *DrAPF 91*
**Karmel**, Alexander D. 1904- *Who 92*
**Karmel**, Peter Henry 1922- *IntWW 91, Who 92, WrDr 92*
**Karmel**, Roberta S. 1937- *WhoAmL 92, WhoAmP 91*
**Karmen**, Arthur 1930- *AmMWSc 92*
**Karmis**, Michael E 1948- *AmMWSc 92*
**Karmonocky**, Lorraine Margaret 1941- *WhoRel 92*
**Karn**, James Frederick 1939- *AmMWSc 92*
**Karn**, Robert Cameron 1945- *AmMWSc 92*
**Karn**, Valerie Ann 1939- *Who 92*
**Karnad**, Girish 1938- *IntWW 91*
**Karnaky**, Karl John, Jr 1943- *AmMWSc 92*
**Karnath**, Joan Edna 1947- *WhoMW 92*
**Karnaugh**, Maurice 1924- *AmMWSc 92*
**Karnavati**, Rani *EncAmaz 91*
**Karner**, Frank Richard 1934- *AmMWSc 92*
**Karnes**, David K 1948- *WhoAmP 91*
**Karnes**, Evan Burton, II *WhoMW 92*
**Karney**, Charles Fielding Finch 1951- *AmMWSc 92*
**Karney**, Mark Steven 1948- *WhoEnt 92*
**Karni**, Edi 1944- *WhoFI 92*
**Karni**, Shlomo 1932- *AmMWSc 92*
**Karnik**, Avinash Ramkrishna 1940- *WhoWest 92*
**Karnofsky**, Brian Lee 1954- *WhoFI 92*
**Karnofsky**, Mollyne *DrAPF 91*
**Karnopp**, Bruce Harvey 1938- *AmMWSc 92*
**Karnopp**, Dean Charles 1934- *AmMWSc 92*
**Karnopp**, Dennis Charles 1942- *WhoAmL 92*
**Karnosky**, David Frank 1949- *AmMWSc 92*
**Karnovsky**, Manfred L 1918- *AmMWSc 92*
**Karnovsky**, Morris John 1926- *AmMWSc 92*
**Karnow**, Stanley 1925- *IntAu&W 91, WrDr 92*
**Karns**, Charles Franklin 1921- *WhoMW 92*
**Karns**, Charles W 1920- *AmMWSc 92*
**Karo**, Arnold Mitchell 1928- *AmMWSc 92*
**Karo**, Douglas Paul 1947- *AmMWSc 92*
**Karo**, Wolf 1924- *AmMWSc 92*
**Karol**, Alexander *IntAu&W 91X, WrDr 92*
**Karol**, Frederick J 1933- *AmMWSc 92*
**Karol**, John Jacob, Jr. 1935- *WhoEnt 92*
**Karol**, Lawrence Paul 1954- *WhoRel 92*
**Karol**, Mark J 1959- *AmMWSc 92*
**Karol**, Meryl Helene *AmMWSc 92*
**Karol**, Paul J 1941- *AmMWSc 92*
**Karol**, Robert Leon 1952- *WhoMW 92*
**Karol**, Robin A 1951- *AmMWSc 92*
**Karol**, Stephen John 1948- *WhoAmP 91*
**Karolak**, Dale Walter 1959- *WhoFI 92*
**Karoli**, Hermann 1906- *IntWW 91*
**Karoly**, Gabriel 1930- *AmMWSc 92*
**Karolyi**, Mihaly 1875-1955 *FacFETw*
**Karon**, John Marshall 1941- *AmMWSc 92*
**Karon**, Robert Allen 1949- *WhoEnt 92*
**Karoniaktatie** *DrAPF 91*
**Karoui**, Hamed 1927- *IntWW 91*
**Karow**, Armand Monfort, Jr 1941- *AmMWSc 92*
**Karp**, Aaron S. 1947- *WhoWest 92*
**Karp**, Abraham E 1915- *AmMWSc 92*
**Karp**, Abraham J. 1921- *WrDr 92*
**Karp**, Abraham Joseph 1921- *WhoRel 92*
**Karp**, Alan H 1946- *AmMWSc 92*
**Karp**, Arthur 1928- *AmMWSc 92*
**Karp**, Bennett C 1954- *AmMWSc 92*
**Karp**, David 1922- *IntAu&W 91, IntWW 91, Who 92, WhoEnt 92, WrDr 92*
**Karp**, David Ira 1954- *WhoAmL 92*
**Karp**, Gene 1936- *WhoAmL 92, WhoAmP 91*
**Karp**, Herbert Rubin 1921- *AmMWSc 92*
**Karp**, Howard 1926- *AmMWSc 92*
**Karp**, Jeffrey Randall 1951- *WhoAmL 92*
**Karp**, Laurence Edward 1939- *AmMWSc 92*
**Karp**, Marvin Louis 1934- *WhoAmL 92*
**Karp**, Nathan 1915- *WhoAmP 91*
**Karp**, Peter Simon 1935- *WhoFI 92*
**Karp**, Richard Dale 1943- *AmMWSc 92*
**Karp**, Richard M. 1929- *WhoFI 92*
**Karp**, Richard M 1935- *AmMWSc 92*
**Karp**, Samuel Noah 1924- *AmMWSc 92*
**Karp**, Sander Neil 1943- *WhoAmL 92*
**Karp**, Stewart 1932- *AmMWSc 92*
**Karp**, Warren B 1944- *AmMWSc 92*
**Karpan**, Kathleen Marie 1942- *WhoAmP 91, WhoWest 92*
**Karpat**, Kemal H. 1925- *WrDr 92*
**Karpati**, George *AmMWSc 92*
**Karpatkin**, Simon 1933- *AmMWSc 92*
**Karpechenko**, Georgiy Dmitrievich 1899-1942 *SovUnBD*
**Karpeh**, Enid Juah Hildegard 1957- *WhoBlA 92*
**Karpel**, Richard Leslie 1944- *AmMWSc 92*
**Karpeles**, Maud 1885-1976 *NewAmDM*
**Karpen**, James LaVern 1950- *WhoMW 92*
**Karpen**, Marian Joan 1944- *WhoFI 92*
**Karpen**, Michael Alan 1956- *WhoAmL 92*
**Karpenko**, Victor Nicholas 1922- *WhoWest 92*
**Karpetsky**, Timothy Paul *AmMWSc 92*
**Karpf**, Anne 1950- *IntAu&W 91*
**Karpf**, Dennis Del 1951- *WhoAmL 92*
**Karpf**, Juanita 1951- *WhoEnt 92*
**Karpf**, Steven Alan 1948- *WhoFI 92*
**Karpiak**, Stephen Edward 1947- *AmMWSc 92*
**Karpicke**, Gregory James 1955- *WhoMW 92*
**Karpiel**, Doris Catherine 1935- *WhoAmP 91*
**Karpienia**, Joseph Francis 1949- *WhoEnt 92*
**Karpilow**, Craig 1947- *WhoWest 92*
**Karpinski**, Helen Bernice *WhoAmP 91*
**Karpinski**, Jacek 1927- *WhoFI 92*
**Karpinsky**, Len Vyacheslavovich 1929- *SovUnBD*
**Karpinsky**, Vyacheslav Alekseevich 1880-1965 *SovUnBD*
**Karpiscak**, John, III 1957- *WhoMW 92*
**Karplus**, Martin 1930- *AmMWSc 92, IntWW 91*
**Karplus**, Robert 1927- *AmMWSc 92*
**Karplus**, Walter J 1927- *AmMWSc 92, WrDr 92*
**Karpoff**, Jonathan Mark 1957- *WhoFI 92*
**Karpov**, Anatoliy 1951- *SovUnBD*
**Karpov**, Anatoliy Yevgenievich 1951- *IntWW 91*
**Karpov**, Anatoly 1951- *FacFETw*
**Karpov**, Viktor 1928- *IntWW 91*
**Karpov**, Vladimir Vasil'evich 1922- *SovUnBD*
**Karpov**, Vladimir Vasilyevich 1922- *IntWW 91*
**Karpova**, Yevdokiya Fedorovna 1923- *SovUnBD*
**Karpowicz**, Ray Anthony 1925- *WhoEnt 92*
**Karpur**, Prasanna 1956- *WhoMW 92*
**Karr**, Alan Francis 1947- *AmMWSc 92*
**Karr**, Cheryl Lofgreen 1954- *WhoEnt 92, WhoWest 92*
**Karr**, Clarence, Jr 1923- *AmMWSc 92*
**Karr**, Daryl Kelly Paul James 1954- *WhoEnt 92*
**Karr**, David Dean 1953- *WhoAmL 92*
**Karr**, Douglas Brian 1953- *WhoMW 92*
**Karr**, Gary 1941- *NewAmDM*
**Karr**, Gerald Lee 1936- *WhoAmP 91, WhoMW 92*
**Karr**, James Barry 1945- *WhoFI 92*
**Karr**, James Presby 1941- *AmMWSc 92*
**Karr**, James Richard 1943- *AmMWSc 92*
**Karr**, Jo *WhoAmP 91*
**Karr**, Joseph Peter 1925- *WhoMW 92*
**Karr**, Mary *DrAPF 91*
**Karr**, Paul Michael James 1950- *WhoEnt 92*
**Karr**, Paul Spencer 1925- *WhoEnt 92*
**Karr**, Reynold Michael, Jr 1942- *AmMWSc 92*
**Karr**, Sharon Kay 1938- *WhoMW 92*
**Karr**, Thomas Michael 1959- *WhoAmL 92*
**Karr**, Timothy Ray 1952- *WhoMW 92*
**Karraker**, Robert Harreld 1931- *AmMWSc 92*
**Karran**, Graham 1939- *Who 92*
**Karras**, Alex 1935- *IntMPA 92, WhoEnt 92*
**Karras**, Donald George 1953- *WhoWest 92*
**Karras**, John M 1944- *WhoAmP 91*
**Karras**, Nolan E 1944- *WhoAmP 91*
**Karras**, Thomas William 1936- *AmMWSc 92*
**Karreman**, George 1920- *AmMWSc 92*
**Karreman**, Herman Felix 1913- *AmMWSc 92*
**Karren**, Kenneth W 1932- *AmMWSc 92*
**Karrer**, Kathleen Marie 1949- *AmMWSc 92*
**Karrer**, Paul 1889-1971 *WhoNob 90*
**Karrer**, Rathe Stevens 1930- *WhoMW 92*
**Karres**, F. Paul 1939- *WhoWest 92*
**Karrh**, Bruce Wakefield 1936- *WhoFI 92*
**Karriem**, Jaleelah *DrAPF 91*
**Karrow**, Paul Frederick 1930- *AmMWSc 92*
**Karryev**, Chary Soyunovich 1932- *IntWW 91*
**Karsan**, Nooruddin 1957- *WhoFI 92*
**Karsavin**, Lev Platonovich 1882-1952 *FacFETw*
**Karsavina**, Jean *DrAPF 91*
**Karsavina**, Tamara Platonovna 1885-1978 *FacFETw*
**Karsch**, Fred Joseph 1942- *AmMWSc 92*
**Karsen**, Sonja Petra 1919- *IntAu&W 91*
**Karsh**, Yousuf 1908- *FacFETw, IntWW 91, Who 92*
**Karski**, William Robert 1946- *WhoWest 92*
**Karson**, Allen Ronald 1947- *WhoFI 92*
**Karson**, Barry M. 1942- *WhoAmL 92*
**Karson**, Jeffrey Alan 1949- *AmMWSc 92*
**Karson**, Stanley *WhoHisp 92*
**Karst**, Kenneth Leslie 1929- *WhoAmL 92*
**Karsten**, Ian George Francis 1944- *Who 92*
**Karsten**, Kenneth Stephen 1913- *AmMWSc 92*
**Karsten**, Siegfried Guenther 1932- *WhoFI 92*
**Karstens**, Andres Ingver 1911- *AmMWSc 92*
**Karstensen**, Elmer Leland 1934- *WhoRel 92*
**Karta**, Nat *IntAu&W 91X*
**Kartak**, Mary Ellen 1949- *WhoMW 92*
**Kartalia**, Mitchell P. 1913- *WhoMW 92*
**Kartashov**, Nikolay Semenovich 1928- *IntWW 91*
**Karten**, Harvey J 1935- *AmMWSc 92*
**Karten**, Howard Aque 1940- *WhoAmL 92*
**Karten**, Marvin J 1931- *AmMWSc 92*
**Karter**, Jerome 1937- *WhoIns 92*
**Kartha**, Kutty Krishnan 1941- *AmMWSc 92*
**Kartha**, Mukund K 1936- *AmMWSc 92*
**Kartha**, Sreeharan 1948- *AmMWSc 92*
**Kartiganer**, Esther 1938- *WhoEnt 92*
**Kartiganer**, Joseph 1935- *WhoAmL 92*
**Kartje**, Jean Van Landuyt 1953- *WhoMW 92*
**Kartomi**, Margaret Joy 1940- *IntWW 91*
**Kartozian**, William F. 1938- *IntMPA 92*
**Kartte**, Wolfgang 1927- *IntWW 91*
**Kartvelishvili**, Dmitriy Levanovich 1927- *IntWW 91*
**Karty**, Chester James 1956- *WhoMW 92*
**Kartzev**, Vladimir Petrovich 1938- *IntWW 91*
**Kartzmark**, Elinor Mary 1926- *AmMWSc 92*
**Karu**, Gilda M. 1951- *WhoMW 92*
**Karukstis**, Kerry Kathleen 1955- *AmMWSc 92*
**Karulkar**, Pramod C 1950- *AmMWSc 92*
**Karunakaran**, Shri K. 1918- *IntWW 91*
**Karunamoorthy**, Swaminathan 1951- *WhoMW 92*
**Karunandhi**, Muthuvel 1924- *IntWW 91*
**Karunaratne**, Nuwarapaksa Hewayalage A M 1918- *IntWW 91*
**Karunasiri**, Gamani 1956- *AmMWSc 92*
**Karush**, Fred 1914- *AmMWSc 92*
**Karush**, William 1917- *AmMWSc 92*
**Karuza**, Sarunas Kazys 1940- *AmMWSc 92*
**Karve**, Mohan Dattatreya 1939- *AmMWSc 92*
**Karwan**, Mark Henry 1951- *AmMWSc 92*
**Karweik**, Dale Herbert 1948- *AmMWSc 92*
**Karwelis**, Donald Charles 1934- *WhoWest 92*
**Karwisch**, George August, Jr. 1936- *WhoMW 92*
**Karwoski**, John P 1940- *WhoAmP 91*
**Karzen**, Judith Hanelin 1940- *WhoEnt 92*
**Karzon**, David T 1920- *AmMWSc 92*
**Kas**, Arnold 1940- *AmMWSc 92*
**Kasahara**, Akira 1926- *AmMWSc 92*
**Kasahara**, Yukio 1925- *IntWW 91*
**Kasai**, Paul Haruo 1932- *AmMWSc 92*
**Kasama**, Hideto Peter 1946- *WhoWest 92*

**Kasamatsu**, Harumi AmMWSc 92
**Kasameyer**, Paul William 1943- AmMWSc 92
**Kasanof**, Robert 1929-1991 NewYTBS 91 [port]
**Kasanoff**, Lawrence 1959- WhoEnt 92
**Kasapligil**, Baki 1918- AmMWSc 92
**Kasaravalli**, Girish 1950- IntWW 91
**Kasarda**, Donald David 1933- AmMWSc 92
**Kasari**, Leonard Samuel 1924- WhoWest 92
**Kasarskis**, Edward Joseph 1946- AmMWSc 92
**Kasatkina**, Natal'ya Dmitrievna 1934- SovUnBD
**Kasatkina**, Natalya Dmitriyevna 1934- IntWW 91
**Kasavubu**, Joseph 1910-1969 FacFETw
**Kasbeer**, Stephen Frederick 1925- WhoMW 92
**Kasbekar**, Dinkar Kashinath 1932- AmMWSc 92
**Kascha** EncAmaz 91
**Kaschak**, Lillian Anne WhoFI 92
**Kascic**, Michael Joseph, Jr 1941- AmMWSc 92
**Kascsak**, Richard John 1947- AmMWSc 92
**Kasdan**, Lawrence 1948- FacFETw
**Kasdan**, Lawrence 1949- IntDcF 2-2, IntMPA 92
**Kasdan**, Lawrence Edward 1949- IntWW 91
**Kase**, Kenneth Raymond 1938- AmMWSc 92
**Kase**, Kingdon 1957- WhoAmL 92
**Kase**, Robert Warren 1951- WhoEnt 92
**Kasebier**, Gertrude Stanton 1852-1934 HanAmWH
**Kasee**, Thomas Wayne 1945- WhoMW 92
**Kaseff**, Gary WhoWest 92
**Kasel**, Julius Albert 1923- AmMWSc 92
**Kasemets**, Udo 1919- NewAmDM
**Kasemeyer**, Edward Johns 1945- WhoAmP 91
**Kaser**, Helmut Alfred 1912- IntWW 91
**Kaser**, J D 1929- AmMWSc 92
**Kaser**, Michael Charles 1926- IntWW 91, Who 92, WrDr 92
**Kaserow**, John Marion 1938- WhoRel 92
**Kaseta**, Francis William 1933- AmMWSc 92
**Kasevich**, Lawrence Stanley 1952- WhoFI 92
**Kasey**, Gary Leonard 1955- WhoRel 92
**Kash**, Don E. 1934- WrDr 92
**Kash**, Kathleen 1953- AmMWSc 92
**Kash**, Marsha Elaine DrAPF 91
**Kasha**, Al 1937- WhoEnt 92
**Kasha**, Henry AmMWSc 92
**Kasha**, Kenneth John 1933- AmMWSc 92
**Kasha**, Kevin 1961- WhoEnt 92
**Kasha**, Michael 1920- AmMWSc 92
**Kashani**, Hamid Reza 1955- WhoAmL 92
**Kashanian**, Shahriar 1960- WhoAmL 92
**Kashar**, Lawrence Joseph 1933- AmMWSc 92
**Kashatus**, William C 1929- AmMWSc 92
**Kashdan**, David Stuart 1950- AmMWSc 92
**Kashdan**, John 1917- TwCPaSc
**Kashef**, A I 1919- AmMWSc 92
**Kashfian**, Maurice A. 1964- WhoAmL 92
**Kashgarian**, Michael 1933- AmMWSc 92
**Kashi**, Joseph Leon 1950- WhoAmL 92
**Kashif**, Ghayth Nur 1933- WhoBlA 92
**Kashif**, Lonnie 1933- WhoBlA 92
**Kashin**, Philip 1930- AmMWSc 92
**Kashiwa**, Bryan Andrew 1952- AmMWSc 92
**Kashiwa**, Herbert Koro 1928- AmMWSc 92
**Kashiwagi**, Hiroshi DrAPF 91
**Kashiwagi**, Yusuke 1917- IntWW 91
**Kashkari**, Chaman Nath 1933- AmMWSc 92
**Kashket**, Eva Ruth 1936- AmMWSc 92
**Kashket**, Shelby 1931- AmMWSc 92
**Kashkoush**, Ismail I 1958- AmMWSc 92
**Kashlev**, Yuriy Borisovich 1934- IntWW 91
**Kashner**, Samuel DrAPF 91
**Kashnow**, Richard Allen 1942- AmMWSc 92
**Kashubeck**, Susan 1962- WhoMW 92
**Kashuck**, Claire WhoRel 92
**Kashulines**, Juanita E WhoAmP 91
**Kashy**, Edwin 1934- AmMWSc 92
**Kashyap**, Bhola Prasad 1948- WhoMW 92
**Kashyap**, Moti Lal 1939- AmMWSc 92
**Kashyap**, Rangasami Laksminarayana 1938- AmMWSc 92
**Kashyap**, Tapeshwar S 1929- AmMWSc 92
**Kasi**, Leela Peshkar 1939- AmMWSc 92
**Kasich**, John R. 1952- AlmAP 92 [port], WhoAmP 91, WhoMW 92
**Kasik**, John Edward 1927- AmMWSc 92
**Kasimos**, John Nicholas 1955- WhoMW 92
**Kasinsky**, Harold Edward 1941- AmMWSc 92
**Kasior**, Serjit Kaur 1949- WhoMW 92
**Kask**, John Laurence 1906- AmMWSc 92
**Kask**, Uno 1922- AmMWSc 92
**Kaska**, Harold Victor 1926- AmMWSc 92
**Kaska**, William Charles 1935- AmMWSc 92
**Kaskas**, James 1939- AmMWSc 92
**Kaske**, Karlheinz 1928- IntWW 91
**Kaskel**, Neal T. 1943- WhoWest 92
**Kaskinen Riesberg**, Barbara Kay 1952- WhoEnt 92
**Kasler**, Franz Johann 1930- AmMWSc 92
**Kasler**, Jeffery Edwin 1960- WhoWest 92
**Kaslick**, Ralph Sidney 1935- AmMWSc 92
**Kasloff**, Steve 1952- IntMPA 92
**Kaslow**, Christian Edward 1903- AmMWSc 92
**Kaslow**, David Edward 1942- AmMWSc 92
**Kaslow**, David Martin 1943- WhoEnt 92
**Kaslow**, John Francis 1932- WhoFI 92
**Kaslow**, Richard Alan 1943- AmMWSc 92
**Kasmin**, John 1934- IntWW 91, Who 92
**Kasmir**, Gail Alice 1958- WhoFI 92
**Kasner**, Fred E 1926- AmMWSc 92
**Kasner**, William Henry 1929- AmMWSc 92
**Kasoff**, Ira Ethan 1951- WhoWest 92
**Kasoff**, Lawrence Elliot 1949- WhoEnt 92
**Kasowitz**, Marc Elliot 1952- WhoAmL 92
**Kasowski**, Robert V 1944- AmMWSc 92
**Kasparek**, Stanley Vaclav 1929- AmMWSc 92
**Kasparov**, Garri Kimovich 1963- IntWW 91
**Kasparov**, Gary 1963- FacFETw [port], SovUnBD
**Kasparov**, Yuri 1955- ConCom 92
**Kasper**, Andrew E, Jr 1942- AmMWSc 92
**Kasper**, Charles Boyer 1935- AmMWSc 92
**Kasper**, Christine Eleana 1953- WhoWest 92
**Kasper**, Daniel M 1945- WhoAmP 91
**Kasper**, Dennis Lee AmMWSc 92
**Kasper**, Gerhard 1949- AmMWSc 92
**Kasper**, Hirschel 1935- WhoAmL 92, WhoMW 92
**Kasper**, Horst Manfred 1939- WhoAmL 92, WhoFI 92
**Kasper**, John Simon 1915- AmMWSc 92
**Kasper**, Joseph Emil 1920- AmMWSc 92
**Kasper**, Joseph F, Jr 1943- AmMWSc 92
**Kasper**, Michael Anthony 1946- WhoMW 92
**Kasper**, Steven Philip 1949- WhoEnt 92
**Kasper**, Walter Josef 1933- IntWW 91
**Kasperbauer**, Michael J 1929- AmMWSc 92
**Kasperczyk**, Jurgen 1941- WhoFI 92
**Kasperek**, George James 1944- AmMWSc 92
**Kasperko**, Jean Margaret 1949- WhoFI 92
**Kasperson**, Roger E. 1938- WrDr 92
**Kasprick**, Lyle Clinton 1932- WhoFI 92
**Kasprow**, Barbara Ann 1936- AmMWSc 92
**Kasprowicz**, Betty M 1941- WhoIns 92
**Kasprzak**, Lucian A 1943- AmMWSc 92
**Kasputis**, Edward 1961- WhoAmP 91
**Kasputys**, Joseph Edward 1936- WhoFI 92
**Kasrashvili**, Makvala 1946- IntWW 91
**Kasriel**, Robert H 1918- AmMWSc 92
**Kass**, Arthur 1931- WhoAmP 91
**Kass**, Benny Lee 1936- WhoFI 92
**Kass**, David Richard 1931- WhoMW 92
**Kass**, Edward Harold 1917- AmMWSc 92
**Kass**, Gus Sigmund 1915- WhoMW 92
**Kass**, Guss Sigmund 1915- AmMWSc 92
**Kass**, Jerome Allan 1937- WhoEnt 92
**Kass**, Leon Richard 1939- AmMWSc 92
**Kass**, Robert S 1946- AmMWSc 92
**Kass**, Seymour 1926- AmMWSc 92
**Kass**, William Edward 1950- WhoAmL 92
**Kassab**, Charles Shaw 1928- WhoMW 92
**Kassaby**, Chahira 1947- WhoFI 92
**Kassakhian**, Garabet Haroutioun 1944- AmMWSc 92
**Kassakian**, John Gabriel 1943- AmMWSc 92
**Kassal**, Robert James 1936- AmMWSc 92
**Kassam**, Saleem Abdulali 1949- AmMWSc 92
**Kassan**, Stuart S. 1946- WhoWest 92
**Kassander**, Arno Richard, Jr 1920- AmMWSc 92
**Kassander**, Peter John Paul 1948- WhoWest 92
**Kassar**, Mario IntMPA 92
**Kasschau**, Margaret Ramsey 1942- AmMWSc 92
**Kassebaum**, John Philip 1932- WhoAmL 92
**Kassebaum**, Nancy 1932- News 91 [port]
**Kassebaum**, Nancy Landon 1932- AlmAP 92 [port], AmPolLe, IntWW 91, WhoAmP 91, WhoMW 92
**Kassel**, James E 1930- WhoIns 92
**Kassem**, Abdul Karim 1914-1963 FacFETw
**Kassem**, Abdul-Rauf al- 1932- IntWW 91
**Kassim bin Mohammed Hussein** 1928- Who 92
**Kassirer**, Jerome Paul 1932- AmMWSc 92
**Kassis**, Mose 1926- WhoAmP 91
**Kassis**, Noura I. 1943- WhoWest 92
**Kassler**, Haskell A. 1936- WhoAmL 92
**Kassler**, J.C. ConAu 135
**Kassler**, Jamie C. 1938- ConAu 135
**Kassmeier**, Frances C 1929- WhoAmP 91
**Kassner**, Herbert Seymore 1931- WhoAmL 92
**Kassner**, James Lyle, Jr 1931- AmMWSc 92
**Kassner**, Michael Ernest 1950- WhoWest 92
**Kassner**, Richard J 1939- AmMWSc 92
**Kassof**, Allen H. 1930- WhoFI 92
**Kassouf**, John Fred 1954- WhoRel 92
**Kassover**, Jeffrey Abraham 1947- WhoRel 92
**Kassoy**, David Paul 1935- WhoAmL 92
**Kassoy**, David R 1938- AmMWSc 92
**Kast**, Jay Vance 1948- WhoWest 92
**Kast**, Jeff Allen 1958- WhoMW 92
**Kast**, Maggie 1938- WhoEnt 92
**Kastantin**, Joseph Thomas 1947- WhoMW 92
**Kastel**, Howard L. 1932- WhoAmL 92
**Kastel**, Kasriel B. 1943- WhoRel 92
**Kastel**, Warren ConAu 36NR
**Kastell**, Julie Pauline 1958- WhoFI 92
**Kastella**, Kenneth George 1933- AmMWSc 92
**Kasten**, Betty Lou 1938- WhoAmP 91
**Kasten**, David Wayne 1962- WhoEnt 92
**Kasten**, Frederick H 1927- AmMWSc 92
**Kasten**, Mary Alice C 1928- WhoAmP 91
**Kasten**, Neil Michael 1944- WhoMW 92
**Kasten**, Paul R 1923- AmMWSc 92
**Kasten**, Robert W., Jr. 1942- AlmAP 92 [port], IntWW 91, WhoAmP 91, WhoMW 92
**Kasten**, William Arthur 1956- WhoAmP 91
**Kastenbaum**, Marvin Aaron 1926- AmMWSc 92
**Kastenberg**, William Edward 1939- AmMWSc 92
**Kastenholz**, Claude E 1936- AmMWSc 92
**Kastenmeier**, Robert William 1924- WhoAmP 91
**Kastens**, Kim Anne 1954- AmMWSc 92
**Kastens**, Robert William 1942- WhoRel 92
**Kastin**, Abba J 1934- AmMWSc 92
**Kasting**, James Fraser 1953- AmMWSc 92
**Kastl**, Dian Evans 1953- WhoAmL 92, WhoFI 92
**Kastl**, Jorg 1922- IntWW 91
**Kastl**, Peter Robert 1949- AmMWSc 92
**Kastle**, Joseph Hoeing 1864-1916 BiInAmS
**Kastler**, Alfred 1902-1984 WhoNob 90
**Kastner**, Curtis Lynn 1944- AmMWSc 92
**Kastner**, Elliott 1933- IntMPA 92, IntWW 91
**Kastner**, Erich 1899-1974 EncTR 91 [port]
**Kastner**, Joseph 1907- WrDr 92
**Kastner**, Leslie James 1911- Who 92
**Kastner**, Marc Aaron 1945- AmMWSc 92
**Kastner**, Miriam AmMWSc 92
**Kastner**, Rick 1955- WhoEnt 92
**Kastner**, Shay Davidson 1944- WhoFI 92
**Kastner**, Sidney Oscar 1926- AmMWSc 92
**Kastrup**, Gladys Emma 1942- WhoMW 92
**Kasuba**, Romualdas AmMWSc 92
**Kasube**, Herbert Emil 1949- AmMWSc 92
**Kasulis**, Thomas Patrick 1948- WhoMW 92
**Kasunic**, Richard A 1947- WhoAmP 91
**Kasupski**, George Joseph 1946- AmMWSc 92
**Kasuya**, Shigeru 1926- IntWW 91
**Kasvinsky**, Peter John 1942- AmMWSc 92
**Kasy**, Melpakkam Duraiswamy 1932- WhoFI 92
**Kaszniak**, Alfred Wayne 1949- WhoWest 92
**Kataev**, Valentin Petrovich 1897-1986 SovUnBD
**Katahn**, Enid Miller 1932- WhoEnt 92
**Katahn**, T. L. 1955- WhoEnt 92
**Katai**, Andrew Andras 1937- WhoFI 92, WhoMW 92
**Kataria**, Yash P 1936- AmMWSc 92
**Katavolos**, William 1924- DcTwDes
**Katayama**, Arthur Shoji 1927- WhoAmL 92
**Katayama**, Daniel Hideo 1939- AmMWSc 92
**Katayama**, Tamio 1928- WhoWest 92
**Katchalski-Katzir**, Ephraim Who 92
**Katchen**, Bernard 1928- AmMWSc 92
**Katchen**, Julius 1926-1969 NewAmDM
**Katchen**, Marc Steven 1951- WhoMW 92
**Katcher**, David Abraham 1915- AmMWSc 92
**Katcher**, Leo d1991 NewYTBS 91
**Katcher**, Richard 1918- WhoAmL 92
**Katchman**, Arthur 1924- AmMWSc 92
**Katchman**, Don Evan 1954- WhoFI 92
**Katchmer**, George Andrew 1916- WrDr 92
**Katcoff**, Seymour 1918- AmMWSc 92
**Katekaru**, James 1935- AmMWSc 92
**Katell**, Sidney 1915- AmMWSc 92
**Katen**, Paul C 1943- AmMWSc 92
**Katenga-Kaunda**, Reid Willie 1929- Who 92
**Kater**, Stanley B 1943- AmMWSc 92
**Kater**, Victor Ricardo 1944- WhoMW 92
**Kates**, Henry E. 1939- WhoFI 92
**Kates**, J. DrAPF 91
**Kates**, Josef 1921- AmMWSc 92
**Kates**, Morris 1923- AmMWSc 92
**Kates**, Robert 1929- AmMWSc 92
**Kates**, Robert William 1929- IntWW 91
**Kateyev**, Valentin Petrovich 1897-1986 FacFETw
**Kath**, Robert Scott 1955- WhoAmL 92
**Kath**, William Lawrence 1957- AmMWSc 92
**Kathan**, Ralph Herman 1929- AmMWSc 92
**Kather**, Gerhard 1939- WhoWest 92
**Kathka**, David Arlin WhoWest 92
**Kathman**, R Deedee 1948- AmMWSc 92
**Kathol**, Anthony Louis 1964- WhoWest 92
**Katholi**, Charles Robinson 1941- AmMWSc 92
**Kathrein**, Michael Lee 1953- WhoMW 92
**Kathren**, Ronald Laurence 1937- AmMWSc 92
**Kathwari**, M. Farooq 1944- WhoFI 92
**Katic**, Peter 1954- WhoAmP 91
**Katiliskis**, Marius 1915-1980 LiExTwC
**Katims**, Milton 1909- NewAmDM
**Katin**, Peter 1930- IntWW 91
**Katin**, Peter Roy 1930- Who 92
**Katko**, John Michael 1962- WhoAmL 92
**Katkov**, Harold, Jr. 1957- WhoEnt 92
**Katleman**, Harris L. WhoEnt 92
**Katleman**, Harris L. 1928- IntMPA 92
**Kato**, Eileen A. 1950- WhoAmL 92
**Kato**, Frederick 1866-1909 BiInAmS
**Kato**, Ichiro 1922- IntWW 91
**Kato**, Ikunoshin AmMWSc 92
**Kato**, Koichi 1939- IntWW 91
**Kato**, Masanobu 1946- WhoAmL 92
**Kato**, Mutsuki 1926- IntWW 91
**Kato**, Shuichi 1919- IntAu&W 91, IntWW 91, WrDr 92
**Kato**, Susumu 1928- IntWW 91
**Kato**, Tadao 1916- IntWW 91, Who 92
**Kato**, Tosio 1917- AmMWSc 92
**Kato**, Walter Yoneo 1924- AmMWSc 92
**Katocs**, Andrew Stephen, Jr 1944- AmMWSc 92
**Katofsky**, Jeff Call 1963- WhoAmL 92
**Katoh**, Arthur 1933- AmMWSc 92
**Katon**, John Edward 1929- AmMWSc 92, WhoMW 92
**Katona**, George 1901-1981 FacFETw
**Katona**, Peter Geza 1937- AmMWSc 92
**Katopes**, Peter DrAPF 91
**Katopodis**, Gregory John 1947- WhoAmP 91
**Katosic**, George Richard 1944- WhoAmL 92
**Katovic**, Vladimir 1935- AmMWSc 92
**Katovich**, Michael J 1948- AmMWSc 92
**Katritzky**, Alan R 1928- AmMWSc 92
**Katritzky**, Alan Roy 1928- IntWW 91, Who 92
**Kats**, James Stephan 1948- WhoAmL 92
**Katsakiores**, George Nicholas 1924- WhoAmP 91
**Katsakiores**, Phyllis Hemeon 1934- WhoAmP 91
**Katsambas**, Christakis Joannou 1925- IntWW 91
**Katsampes**, Chris Peter 1910- AmMWSc 92
**Katsanis**, D J 1926- AmMWSc 92
**Katsanis**, Eleftherios P 1944- AmMWSc 92
**Katsaros**, Kristina B 1938- AmMWSc 92
**Katsav**, Moshe 1945- IntWW 91
**Katselas**, Milton George 1933- IntMPA 92, WhoEnt 92
**Katsenes**, John T. 1930- WhoWest 92
**Katsh**, M. Ethan 1945- ConAu 133, WhoAmL 92
**Katsh**, Salem Michael 1948- WhoAmL 92, WhoEnt 92
**Katsh**, Seymour 1918- AmMWSc 92
**Katsianis**, John Nick 1960- WhoMW 92
**Katsifaras**, Georgios 1935- IntWW 91
**Katsikis**, Miriam Polli DrAPF 91
**Katskee**, Jerry W. 1950- WhoAmL 92
**Katsman**, Yevgeniy Aleksandrovich 1890-1976 SovUnBD
**Katsnelson**, Inessa 1939- WhoMW 92

**Katsoris,** Constantine Nicholas 1932- *WhoAmL 92*
**Katsoyannis,** Panayotis G 1924- *AmMWSc 92*
**Katsumoto,** Kiyoshi 1936- *AmMWSc 92*
**Katt,** William 1955- *IntMPA 92*
**Kattakuzhy,** George Chacko 1944- *AmMWSc 92*
**Kattamis,** Theodoulos Zenon 1935- *AmMWSc 92*
**Kattan,** Ahmed A 1925- *AmMWSc 92*
**Kattan,** Naim 1928- *IntWW 91*
**Kattawar,** George W 1937- *AmMWSc 92*
**Katten,** Richard L 1946- *WhoIns 92*
**Kattenburg,** P. Clark 1946- *WhoAmL 92*
**Katterman,** Frank Reinald Hugh 1929- *AmMWSc 92*
**Katti,** Shriniwas Keshav 1936- *AmMWSc 92*
**Kattus,** J Robert 1922- *AmMWSc 92*
**Katushev,** Konstantin Fedorovich 1927- *SovUnBD*
**Katushev,** Konstantin Fyodorovich 1927- *IntWW 91*
**Katz,** Abraham 1926- *IntWW 91*
**Katz,** Adrian I 1932- *AmMWSc 92*
**Katz,** Adrian Izhack 1932- *WhoMW 92*
**Katz,** Alan Jeffrey 1947- *AmMWSc 92*
**Katz,** Andy 1961- *WhoAmP 91*
**Katz,** Arnold Martin 1932- *AmMWSc 92*
**Katz,** Arnold Martin 1940- *WhoFI 92*
**Katz,** Bennett David 1918- *WhoAmP 91*
**Katz,** Bernard 1911- *AmMWSc 92, IntWW 91, Who 92, WhoNob 90*
**Katz,** Bernard Saul 1932- *WhoFI 92*
**Katz,** Bobbi 1933- *IntAu&W 91, WrDr 92*
**Katz,** David Arthur 1953- *WhoRel 92*
**Katz,** David Harvey 1943- *AmMWSc 92*
**Katz,** David Robert 1947- *WhoEnt 92*
**Katz,** David Stephen 1936- *WhoEnt 92*
**Katz,** Donald L 1907- *AmMWSc 92*
**Katz,** Edward 1923- *AmMWSc 92*
**Katz,** Eli Joel 1937- *AmMWSc 92*
**Katz,** Eliot *DrAPF 91*
**Katz,** Ephraim 1932- *WrDr 92*
**Katz,** Ernst 1913- *AmMWSc 92*
**Katz,** Eugene Richard 1942- *AmMWSc 92*
**Katz,** Frances R 1937- *AmMWSc 92*
**Katz,** Frank Fred 1927- *AmMWSc 92*
**Katz,** Fred H 1930- *AmMWSc 92*
**Katz,** Friedrich 1927- *ConAu 134*
**Katz,** Gary M. 1941- *WhoAmL 92*
**Katz,** Gary Victor 1943- *AmMWSc 92*
**Katz,** George Maxim 1922- *AmMWSc 92*
**Katz,** Gerald *AmMWSc 92*
**Katz,** Gloria *IntMPA 92*
**Katz,** Gregory 1950- *WhoAmL 92*
**Katz,** Hadrian Ronald 1949- *WhoAmL 92*
**Katz,** Harold 1944- *WhoFI 92*
**Katz,** Harold A 1921- *WhoAmP 91*
**Katz,** Harold W 1923- *AmMWSc 92*
**Katz,** Henry 1937- *WhoIns 92*
**Katz,** Henry 1938- *WhoFI 92*
**Katz,** Herbert M 1926- *AmMWSc 92*
**Katz,** Hilda 1909- *IntAu&W 91, WhoFI 92*
**Katz,** Howard Evan 1954- *WhoAmL 92*
**Katz,** Ira 1933- *AmMWSc 92*
**Katz,** Irving 1933- *AmMWSc 92*
**Katz,** Irwin 1942- *WhoFI 92*
**Katz,** Irwin Alan 1940- *AmMWSc 92*
**Katz,** Israel 1917- *AmMWSc 92*
**Katz,** Israel Norman 1932- *AmMWSc 92*
**Katz,** J Lawrence 1927- *AmMWSc 92*
**Katz,** Jack 1934- *AmMWSc 92*
**Katz,** Janyce C. 1959- *WhoAmL 92*
**Katz,** Jay 1922- *AmMWSc 92, WhoAmL 92*
**Katz,** Jeffrey Harvey 1947- *WhoAmL 92*
**Katz,** Jerome Charles 1950- *WhoAmL 92*
**Katz,** Jerrold Pinya 1939- *WhoFI 92*
**Katz,** Jerry Benjamin 1947- *WhoFI 92*
**Katz,** Jerry Paul 1944- *WhoWest 92*
**Katz,** Joel Abraham 1944- *WhoEnt 92*
**Katz,** Joel David 1952- *WhoEnt 92*
**Katz,** John W. 1943- *WhoAmL 92, WhoWest 92*
**Katz,** Jonathan *DrAPF 91*
**Katz,** Jonathan Isaac 1951- *AmMWSc 92, WhoMW 92*
**Katz,** Joseph *AmMWSc 92*
**Katz,** Joseph J 1912- *AmMWSc 92*
**Katz,** Joseph L 1938- *AmMWSc 92*
**Katz,** Kent Roger 1955- *WhoMW 92*
**Katz,** Larry 1948- *WhoEnt 92*
**Katz,** Laura L. 1948- *WhoAmL 92*
**Katz,** Laurence Barry 1954- *AmMWSc 92*
**Katz,** Laurence M. 1940- *WhoAmL 92*
**Katz,** Leandro *DrAPF 91*
**Katz,** Leon 1909- *AmMWSc 92*
**Katz,** Leon 1919- *WhoEnt 92*
**Katz,** Leon 1921- *AmMWSc 92, WhoFI 92*
**Katz,** Leslie Rachel 1961- *WhoAmL 92*
**Katz,** Lewis 1923- *AmMWSc 92*
**Katz,** Lewis E 1940- *AmMWSc 92*
**Katz,** Lewis Robert 1938- *WhoAmL 92*
**Katz,** Louis 1932- *AmMWSc 92*
**Katz,** M. *WhoRel 92*
**Katz,** Manfred 1929- *AmMWSc 92*
**Katz,** Marc Alexander 1952- *WhoEnt 92*
**Katz,** Marc Jay 1963- *WhoEnt 92*
**Katz,** Mark David 1949- *WhoAmL 92*
**Katz,** Martin 1927- *AmMWSc 92*
**Katz,** Martin 1929- *WrDr 92*
**Katz,** Martin Howard 1931- *WhoAmP 91*
**Katz,** Marty 1947- *IntMPA 92, WhoEnt 92*
**Katz,** Marvin 1930- *WhoAmL 92*
**Katz,** Marvin L 1935- *AmMWSc 92*
**Katz,** Maurice Joseph 1937- *AmMWSc 92*
**Katz,** Max 1919- *AmMWSc 92*
**Katz,** Melvin Seymour 1915- *WhoAmL 92*
**Katz,** Menke *DrAPF 91*
**Katz,** Menke d1991 *NewYTBS 91*
**Katz,** Menke 1906- *IntAu&W 91, WrDr 92*
**Katz,** Menke 1906-1991 *ConAu 134*
**Katz,** Michael 1928- *AmMWSc 92, IntWW 91*
**Katz,** Michael Albert 1942- *WhoAmL 92*
**Katz,** Michael Bruce 1949- *WhoAmL 92*
**Katz,** Michael J. *DrAPF 91*
**Katz,** Michael Jeffery 1950- *WhoAmL 92*
**Katz,** Michael Ray 1944- *WrDr 92*
**Katz,** Michael S. 1947- *WhoEnt 92*
**Katz,** Milton 1907- *IntWW 91, Who 92*
**Katz,** Miriam Lesser 1942- *WhoMW 92*
**Katz,** Mitchell Jay 1964- *WhoFI 92*
**Katz,** Morris 1932- *WhoEnt 92*
**Katz,** Morris Howard 1920- *AmMWSc 92, WhoMW 92*
**Katz,** Morton 1934- *AmMWSc 92*
**Katz,** Morton Howard 1945- *WhoAmL 92*
**Katz,** Murray Alan 1941- *AmMWSc 92*
**Katz,** Murray L. 1932- *WhoFI 92*
**Katz,** Myer *WhoMW 92*
**Katz,** Norman 1925- *WhoFI 92*
**Katz,** Norman B. 1919- *IntMPA 92*
**Katz,** Norman L *AmMWSc 92*
**Katz,** Owen M 1932- *AmMWSc 92*
**Katz,** Pamela 1958- *WhoEnt 92*
**Katz,** Paul K *AmMWSc 92*
**Katz,** Perry Marc 1951- *WhoEnt 92, WhoWest 92*
**Katz,** Ralph Verne 1944- *AmMWSc 92*
**Katz,** Richard 1948- *WhoMW 92*
**Katz,** Richard 1950- *WhoAmP 91*
**Katz,** Richard Whitmore 1948- *AmMWSc 92*
**Katz,** Richard William 1954- *WhoAmL 92*
**Katz,** Robert 1917- *AmMWSc 92*
**Katz,** Robert 1928- *AmMWSc 92*
**Katz,** Robert Francis 1941- *WhoEnt 92, WhoFI 92*
**Katz,** Robert Herman 1925- *WhoIns 92*
**Katz,** Robert Nathan 1931- *WhoAmL 92*
**Katz,** Robert S 1936- *WhoAmP 91*
**Katz,** Robert Stephen 1944- *WhoMW 92*
**Katz,** Roger Martin 1945- *WhoFI 92*
**Katz,** Ronald Alan 1936- *WhoEnt 92*
**Katz,** Ronald Lewis 1932- *AmMWSc 92*
**Katz,** Ronald M. 1958- *WhoAmL 92*
**Katz,** Ronald Stanley 1945- *WhoAmL 92*
**Katz,** Samuel 1923- *AmMWSc 92*
**Katz,** Samuel Irving 1916- *WhoFI 92*
**Katz,** Samuel Lawrence 1927- *AmMWSc 92, IntWW 91*
**Katz,** Sanford N. 1933- *WrDr 92*
**Katz,** Sharon F. 1955- *WhoEnt 92*
**Katz,** Sheldon Lane 1948- *AmMWSc 92*
**Katz,** Sherman E. 1943- *WhoAmL 92*
**Katz,** Sidney 1909- *AmMWSc 92*
**Katz,** Sidney 1916- *AmMWSc 92*
**Katz,** Sidney 1924- *AmMWSc 92*
**Katz,** Sidney 1930- *AmMWSc 92*
**Katz,** Sidney A 1935- *AmMWSc 92*
**Katz,** Sol 1913- *AmMWSc 92*
**Katz,** Solomon H 1939- *AmMWSc 92*
**Katz,** Solomon Hertz 1939- *WhoRel 92*
**Katz,** Stanley Nider 1934- *WhoAmL 92*
**Katz,** Stephen Gary 1949- *WhoAmL 92*
**Katz,** Stephen I *AmMWSc 92*
**Katz,** Stephen J. 1947- *WhoAmL 92*
**Katz,** Stephen M. *WhoEnt 92*
**Katz,** Steve *DrAPF 91*
**Katz,** Steve 1935- *ConAu 14AS [port], ConNov 91, WrDr 92*
**Katz,** Steven Martin 1941- *WhoAmL 92*
**Katz,** Steven Theodore 1944- *WhoRel 92*
**Katz,** Susan A. *DrAPF 91*
**Katz,** Susan A 1939- *IntAu&W 91*
**Katz,** Susan Audrey 1956- *WhoEnt 92*
**Katz,** Susan Stanton 1951- *WhoAmL 92*
**Katz,** Thomas Joseph 1936- *AmMWSc 92*
**Katz,** Vera 1933- *WhoAmP 91*
**Katz,** Victor Joseph 1942- *AmMWSc 92*
**Katz,** Vincent *DrAPF 91*
**Katz,** Welwyn 1948- *WrDr 92*
**Katz,** William 1953- *AmMWSc 92*
**Katz,** William J 1925- *AmMWSc 92*
**Katz,** William Loren 1927- *WrDr 92*
**Katz,** William Michael 1940- *WhoEnt 92*
**Katz,** Yale H 1920- *AmMWSc 92*
**Katz-Levine,** Judy *DrAPF 91*
**Katz-Oz,** Avraham 1934- *IntWW 91*
**Katzav,** Moshe 1945- *IntWW 91*
**Katzbeck,** Karen Lynn 1951- *WhoWest 92*
**Katzberg,** Allan Alfred 1913- *AmMWSc 92*
**Katze,** Jon R 1939- *AmMWSc 92*
**Katzel,** Jeanine Alma 1948- *WhoMW 92*
**Katzen,** Daniel *WhoEnt 92*
**Katzen,** Howard M 1929- *AmMWSc 92*
**Katzen,** Jack d1991 *NewYTBS 91*
**Katzen,** Raphael 1915- *AmMWSc 92*
**Katzen,** Sally 1942- *WhoAmL 92*
**Katzen-Guthrie,** Joy Elaine 1958- *WhoEnt 92*
**Katzenbach,** Nicholas deBelleville *NewYTBS 91 [port]*
**Katzenbach,** Nicholas DeBelleville 1922- *IntWW 91*
**Katzenbach,** Shirley Steinman d1991 *NewYTBS 91*
**Katzenberg,** Jeffrey *LesBEnT 92*
**Katzenberg,** Jeffrey 1950- *IntMPA 92, WhoEnt 92, WhoWest 92*
**Katzenellenbogen,** Benita Schulman 1945- *AmMWSc 92*
**Katzenellenbogen,** John Albert 1944- *AmMWSc 92*
**Katzer,** Hans 1919- *IntWW 91*
**Katzin,** Gerald Howard 1932- *AmMWSc 92*
**Katzin,** Leonard Isaac 1915- *AmMWSc 92*
**Katzir,** Ephraim 1916- *IntWW 91, Who 92*
**Katzka,** Gabriel 1931-1990 *ConTFT 9*
**Katzman,** Allen *DrAPF 91*
**Katzman,** Arthur J 1904- *WhoAmP 91*
**Katzman,** Marshall David 1948- *WhoEnt 92*
**Katzman,** Philip Aaron 1906- *AmMWSc 92*
**Katzman,** Robert 1925- *AmMWSc 92*
**Katzmann,** Fred L 1929- *AmMWSc 92*
**Katzmann,** Gary Stephen 1953- *WhoAmL 92*
**Katzmann,** Robert Allen 1953- *WhoAmL 92*
**Katzner,** Donald Wahl 1938- *WhoFI 92*
**Katzoff,** Samuel 1909- *AmMWSc 92*
**Katzung,** Bertram George 1932- *AmMWSc 92, WhoWest 92*
**Kauber,** Christine Ann 1946- *WhoMW 92*
**Kaucher,** Eric George 1955- *WhoEnt 92*
**Kaucher,** James William 1958- *WhoAmL 92*
**Kauder,** Otto Samuel 1926- *AmMWSc 92*
**Kauer,** James Charles 1927- *AmMWSc 92*
**Kauer,** John Stuart 1943- *AmMWSc 92*
**Kauf,** David K 1933- *WhoIns 92*
**Kaufelt,** David A. *DrAPF 91*
**Kaufelt,** David A. 1939- *WrDr 92*
**Kaufelt,** Stanley Philip 1920- *WhoFI 92*
**Kaufert,** Dean R *WhoAmP 91*
**Kaufert,** Frank Henry 1905- *AmMWSc 92*
**Kaufert,** Joseph Mossman 1943- *AmMWSc 92*
**Kauff,** Peter L. 1941- *WhoEnt 92*
**Kauffeld,** Norbert M 1923- *AmMWSc 92*
**Kauffer,** E. McKnight 1890-1954 *TwCPaSc*
**Kauffer,** Edward McKnight 1890-1954 *DcTwDes, FacFETw*
**Kauffman,** Alan Charles 1939- *WhoAmL 92*
**Kauffman,** Bary Eugene 1948- *WhoFI 92*
**Kauffman,** Bruce William 1934- *WhoAmL 92*
**Kauffman,** Carol A 1943- *AmMWSc 92*
**Kauffman,** Daniel 1865-1944 *AmPeW, RelLAm 91*
**Kauffman,** Daun Howard 1957- *WhoFI 92*
**Kauffman,** Donald Goodwin 1918- *WhoWest 92*
**Kauffman,** Ellwood 1928- *AmMWSc 92*
**Kauffman,** Erle Galen 1933- *AmMWSc 92, WhoWest 92*
**Kauffman,** Frederick C 1936- *AmMWSc 92*
**Kauffman,** George Bernard 1930- *AmMWSc 92*
**Kauffman,** Glenn Monroe 1938- *AmMWSc 92*
**Kauffman,** Gregory Renis 1952- *WhoAmL 92*
**Kauffman,** Harold 1939- *AmMWSc 92*
**Kauffman,** James Frank 1937- *AmMWSc 92*
**Kauffman,** Janet *DrAPF 91*
**Kauffman,** Janet 1945- *BenetAL 91, WrDr 92*
**Kauffman,** Jeffrey Layne, Sr. 1961- *WhoRel 92, WhoWest 92*
**Kauffman,** Joel Mervin 1937- *AmMWSc 92*
**Kauffman,** John *WhoAmP 91*
**Kauffman,** John W 1925- *AmMWSc 92*
**Kauffman,** Kathleen Clubb 1954- *WhoAmL 92*
**Kauffman,** Kenneth Lee 1943- *WhoAmL 92*
**Kauffman,** Kreg Arlen 1950- *WhoAmL 92*
**Kauffman,** Leon A 1934- *AmMWSc 92*
**Kauffman,** Louis Hirsch 1945- *WhoMW 92*
**Kauffman,** Luke Edward 1941- *WhoRel 92*
**Kauffman,** Marvin Earl 1933- *AmMWSc 92*
**Kauffman,** Mitchell Elliott 1953- *WhoFI 92*
**Kauffman,** Neil Bennett 1947- *WhoFI 92*
**Kauffman,** Ralph Ezra *AmMWSc 92*
**Kauffman,** Raymond F 1952- *AmMWSc 92*
**Kauffman,** Reginald Wright 1877-1959 *BenetAL 91*
**Kauffman,** Robert Giller 1932- *AmMWSc 92*
**Kauffman,** Scott Lawrence 1956- *WhoEnt 92*
**Kauffman,** Shirley Louise 1924- *AmMWSc 92*
**Kauffman,** Steven Alan 1948- *WhoEnt 92*
**Kauffman,** Stuart Alan 1939- *AmMWSc 92*
**Kauffman,** William John 1945- *WhoEnt 92*
**Kauffman,** William Ray 1947- *WhoAmL 92*
**Kauffmann,** Angelica Catherina Maria Anna 1741-1807 *BlkwCEP*
**Kauffmann,** C. Michael 1931- *Who 92*
**Kauffmann,** Deborah Lynn 1954- *WhoRel 92*
**Kauffmann,** Nancy Lee 1948- *WhoRel 92*
**Kauffmann,** Sam Hay 1950- *WhoEnt 92*
**Kauffmann,** Stanley 1916- *WrDr 92*
**Kauffmann,** Stanley Jules 1916- *WhoEnt 92*
**Kaufman,** Alan Gilbert 1956- *WhoAmL 92*
**Kaufman,** Albert I. 1936- *WhoAmL 92*
**Kaufman,** Albert Irving 1938- *AmMWSc 92*
**Kaufman,** Allan N 1927- *AmMWSc 92*
**Kaufman,** Alvin B 1917- *AmMWSc 92*
**Kaufman,** Amy Rebecca 1951- *IntAu&W 91*
**Kaufman,** Andrew *DrAPF 91*
**Kaufman,** Andrew Lee 1931- *WhoAmL 92*
**Kaufman,** Andrew Michael 1949- *WhoAmL 92*
**Kaufman,** Andrew S. 1953- *WhoAmL 92*
**Kaufman,** Arnold 1928- *AmMWSc 92*
**Kaufman,** Arthur Stephen 1946- *WhoAmL 92*
**Kaufman,** Bel *DrAPF 91, IntAu&W 91, WrDr 92*
**Kaufman,** Bernard 1932- *AmMWSc 92*
**Kaufman,** Bernard Tobias 1927- *AmMWSc 92*
**Kaufman,** Boris 1926- *AmMWSc 92*
**Kaufman,** Brett 1954- *WhoFI 92*
**Kaufman,** Brian Alexander 1939- *WhoEnt 92*
**Kaufman,** Bruce A. 1960- *WhoFI 92*
**Kaufman,** C W 1911- *AmMWSc 92*
**Kaufman,** Carol 1954- *WhoAmL 92, WhoFI 92*
**Kaufman,** Charles 1937- *AmMWSc 92*
**Kaufman,** Charlotte Rothberg 1929- *WhoEnt 92*
**Kaufman,** Clemens Marcus 1909- *AmMWSc 92*
**Kaufman,** Daniel 1920- *AmMWSc 92*
**Kaufman,** Daniel Joseph, Jr. 1945- *WhoFI 92*
**Kaufman,** David A 1949- *WhoAmP 91*
**Kaufman,** David Allen 1967- *WhoEnt 92*
**Kaufman,** David Gordon 1943- *AmMWSc 92*
**Kaufman,** David Graham 1937- *WhoFI 92*
**Kaufman,** David Joseph 1931- *WhoAmL 92*
**Kaufman,** Don Allen 1940- *AmMWSc 92*
**Kaufman,** Donald Barry 1937- *AmMWSc 92*
**Kaufman,** Donald DeVere 1933- *AmMWSc 92*
**Kaufman,** Donald Wayne 1943- *AmMWSc 92*
**Kaufman,** Edward E 1939- *WhoAmP 91*
**Kaufman,** Edward Godfrey 1919- *AmMWSc 92*
**Kaufman,** Elaine Elkins 1923- *AmMWSc 92*
**Kaufman,** Ernest D 1931- *AmMWSc 92*
**Kaufman,** Frank Albert 1916- *WhoAmL 92*
**Kaufman,** Frank B 1943- *AmMWSc 92*
**Kaufman,** George G. 1933- *WhoFI 92*
**Kaufman,** George S. 1889-1961 *BenetAL 91, FacFETw [port]*
**Kaufman,** Gerald 1930- *Who 92, WrDr 92*
**Kaufman,** Gerald Bernard 1930- *IntWW 91*
**Kaufman,** Gerald Julius 1935- *WhoRel 92*
**Kaufman,** Glennis Ann 1947- *AmMWSc 92*
**Kaufman,** Gordon Dester 1925- *WhoRel 92*
**Kaufman,** Hal 1924- *IntMPA 92*
**Kaufman,** Hank 1918- *WhoEnt 92*
**Kaufman,** Harold Alexander 1933- *AmMWSc 92*
**Kaufman,** Harold Richard 1926- *AmMWSc 92*
**Kaufman,** Harry Morton 1939- *WhoMW 92*
**Kaufman,** Harvey 1931- *WhoFI 92*
**Kaufman,** Harvey Isidore 1937- *WhoMW 92*
**Kaufman,** Henry 1927- *IntWW 91*
**Kaufman,** Herbert Edward 1931- *AmMWSc 92*

**Kaufman**, Herbert Mark 1946- *WhoFI 92, WhoWest 92*
**Kaufman**, Herbert S 1935- *AmMWSc 92*
**Kaufman**, Herman S 1922- *AmMWSc 92*
**Kaufman**, Howard Norman 1926- *AmMWSc 92*
**Kaufman**, Hyman 1920- *AmMWSc 92*
**Kaufman**, Ira Gladstone 1909- *WhoAmL 92, WhoMW 92*
**Kaufman**, Irving 1925- *AmMWSc 92, WhoWest 92*
**Kaufman**, Irving Robert 1910- *WhoAmL 92*
**Kaufman**, J.L. *IntMPA 92*
**Kaufman**, Janice Norton 1923- *AmMWSc 92*
**Kaufman**, Jeffrey Allen 1952- *WhoFI 92, WhoMW 92*
**Kaufman**, Jerome Benzion 1934- *WhoMW 92*
**Kaufman**, John Gilbert, Jr 1931- *AmMWSc 92*
**Kaufman**, Jonathan Allan 1943- *WhoWest 92*
**Kaufman**, Joseph David 1957- *WhoAmL 92*
**Kaufman**, Joseph J 1921- *AmMWSc 92*
**Kaufman**, Joshua Jacob 1950- *WhoEnt 92*
**Kaufman**, Joyce J 1929- *AmMWSc 92*
**Kaufman**, Judith Lasker 1942- *WhoMW 92*
**Kaufman**, Julian Mortimer 1918- *WhoEnt 92*
**Kaufman**, Karl Lincoln 1911- *AmMWSc 92*
**Kaufman**, Kevin Scott 1959- *WhoAmL 92*
**Kaufman**, Larry 1931- *AmMWSc 92*
**Kaufman**, Leo 1930- *AmMWSc 92*
**Kaufman**, Leonard B. 1927- *IntMPA 92*
**Kaufman**, Leonard Lee 1939- *WhoAmL 92*
**Kaufman**, Lester Robert 1946- *WhoRel 92*
**Kaufman**, Linda 1947- *AmMWSc 92*
**Kaufman**, Lloyd 1945- *WhoEnt 92*
**Kaufman**, Lonny Fredrick 1948- *WhoWest 92*
**Kaufman**, Marc P *AmMWSc 92*
**Kaufman**, Marcus Maurice 1929- *WhoWest 92*
**Kaufman**, Mark David 1949- *WhoAmL 92*
**Kaufman**, Marshall F., III 1953- *WhoAmL 92*
**Kaufman**, Martin 1940- *AmMWSc 92*
**Kaufman**, Matthew Howard 1942- *Who 92*
**Kaufman**, Mavis Anderson 1919- *AmMWSc 92*
**Kaufman**, Mel 1958- *WhoBlA 92*
**Kaufman**, Michelle Stark 1954- *WhoMW 92*
**Kaufman**, Michelle Suzanne 1964- *WhoFI 92*
**Kaufman**, Mikhail Abramovich 1897-1980 *SovUnBD*
**Kaufman**, Miron 1950- *AmMWSc 92*
**Kaufman**, Myron Jay 1937- *AmMWSc 92*
**Kaufman**, Nathan 1915- *AmMWSc 92*
**Kaufman**, Paul Leon 1943- *AmMWSc 92, WhoMW 92*
**Kaufman**, Paul Michael 1949- *WhoAmL 92*
**Kaufman**, Peter Bishop 1928- *AmMWSc 92, WhoMW 92*
**Kaufman**, Philip 1936- *IntMPA 92, IntWW 91, WhoEnt 92*
**Kaufman**, Phyllis Cynthia 1945- *WhoAmL 92, WhoFI 92*
**Kaufman**, Priscilla C 1930- *AmMWSc 92*
**Kaufman**, Raymond 1917- *AmMWSc 92*
**Kaufman**, Raymond H 1925- *AmMWSc 92*
**Kaufman**, Richard C. 1951- *WhoAmL 92*
**Kaufman**, Robert d1991 *NewYTBS 91*
**Kaufman**, Robert 1931- *WhoEnt 92*
**Kaufman**, Robert Charles 1953- *WhoAmL 92*
**Kaufman**, Robert Max 1929- *WhoAmL 92*
**Kaufman**, Robert Scott 1961- *WhoFI 92*
**Kaufman**, Samuel 1913- *AmMWSc 92*
**Kaufman**, Scott Wayne 1949- *WhoFI 92*
**Kaufman**, Seymour 1924- *AmMWSc 92*
**Kaufman**, Sheldon Bernard 1929- *AmMWSc 92*
**Kaufman**, Shelley S. 1953- *WhoWest 92*
**Kaufman**, Shirley *DrAPF 91*
**Kaufman**, Sidney 1908- *AmMWSc 92*
**Kaufman**, Sol 1928- *AmMWSc 92*
**Kaufman**, Stanley 1941- *AmMWSc 92*
**Kaufman**, Stephen B 1944- *WhoAmP 91*
**Kaufman**, Stephen J 1943- *AmMWSc 92*
**Kaufman**, Stephen P. 1941- *WhoFI 92*
**Kaufman**, Stuart *DrAPF 91*
**Kaufman**, Sumner 1934- *WhoFI 92*
**Kaufman**, Susan Gail 1943- *WhoFI 92*
**Kaufman**, Thomas Charles 1944- *AmMWSc 92*
**Kaufman**, Thomas Frederick 1949- *WhoAmL 92*
**Kaufman**, Tod J 1952- *WhoAmP 91*
**Kaufman**, Victor 1925- *AmMWSc 92*
**Kaufman**, Victor 1943- *IntMPA 92*
**Kaufman**, Wallace V 1939- *WhoAmP 91*
**Kaufman**, William 1910- *AmMWSc 92*
**Kaufman**, William 1931- *AmMWSc 92*
**Kaufman**, William Carl, Jr 1923- *AmMWSc 92*
**Kaufman**, William Elliot 1938- *WhoRel 92*
**Kaufman**, William George 1949- *WhoAmP 91*
**Kaufman**, William Morris 1931- *AmMWSc 92*
**Kaufmann**, Alvern Walter 1924- *AmMWSc 92*
**Kaufmann**, Ann Marie 1949- *WhoMW 92*
**Kaufmann**, Anthony J 1936- *AmMWSc 92*
**Kaufmann**, Arnold Francis 1936- *AmMWSc 92*
**Kaufmann**, Arthur 1923- *IntWW 91*
**Kaufmann**, Christine 1945- *IntMPA 92*
**Kaufmann**, Edgar, Jr 1910-1989 *DcTwDes*
**Kaufmann**, Elton Neil 1943- *AmMWSc 92*
**Kaufmann**, Felix 1918- *WhoFI 92*
**Kaufmann**, Fritz d1991 *NewYTBS 91*
**Kaufmann**, Gerald Wayne 1940- *AmMWSc 92*
**Kaufmann**, Hans 1923- *WhoIns 92*
**Kaufmann**, Heidi Patrice Marie 1957- *WhoFI 92*
**Kaufmann**, Henry Mark 1929- *WhoFI 92*
**Kaufmann**, Jack 1942- *WhoAmL 92*
**Kaufmann**, Johan 1918- *IntWW 91*
**Kaufmann**, John Henry 1934- *AmMWSc 92*
**Kaufmann**, John Simpson 1931- *AmMWSc 92*
**Kaufmann**, Juliet Yli-Mattila *DrAPF 91*
**Kaufmann**, Karl 1900-1969 *BiDExR, EncTR 91 [port]*
**Kaufmann**, Kenneth James 1947- *AmMWSc 92*
**Kaufmann**, Kris Alfred 1962- *WhoEnt 92*
**Kaufmann**, Mark Steiner 1932- *WhoFI 92*
**Kaufmann**, Maurice John 1929- *AmMWSc 92*
**Kaufmann**, Merrill R 1941- *AmMWSc 92*
**Kaufmann**, Myron 1921- *WrDr 92*
**Kaufmann**, Myron S 1921- *IntAu&W 91*
**Kaufmann**, Peter John 1935- *AmMWSc 92*
**Kaufmann**, Richard L 1935- *AmMWSc 92*
**Kaufmann**, Robert Frank 1940- *AmMWSc 92*
**Kaufmann**, Sandra 1951- *WhoAmL 92*
**Kaufmann**, Thomas David 1922- *WhoWest 92*
**Kaufmann**, Thomas G 1938- *AmMWSc 92*
**Kaufmann**, William B 1936- *AmMWSc 92*
**Kaufmann**, William J 1942- *IntAu&W 91, WrDr 92*
**Kaufmann**, William Karl 1951- *AmMWSc 92*
**Kauger**, Yvonne 1937- *WhoAmL 92, WhoAmP 91*
**Kaugerts**, Juris E 1940- *AmMWSc 92*
**Kauker**, Michael Lajos 1935- *AmMWSc 92*
**Kaul**, Maharaj Krishen 1940- *AmMWSc 92*
**Kaul**, Mahendra Nath 1922- *Who 92*
**Kaul**, Mani 1942- *IntDcF 2-2*
**Kaul**, Pratap Kishen 1929- *IntWW 91*
**Kaul**, Prince Mohan 1906- *IntWW 91*
**Kaul**, Pushkar N *AmMWSc 92*
**Kaul**, Pushkar Nath 1933- *AmMWSc 92*
**Kaul**, Rakesh Kumar 1951- *WhoFI 92*
**Kaul**, Robert Bruce 1935- *AmMWSc 92*
**Kaul**, S K 1936- *AmMWSc 92*
**Kaul**, Sanjiv 1951- *AmMWSc 92*
**Kaul**, Saroop K. 1936- *WhoWest 92*
**Kaul**, Triloki Nath 1913- *IntWW 91*
**Kaul**, Vinita 1953- *IntAu&W 91*
**Kaula**, Prithvi Nath 1924- *IntWW 91*
**Kaula**, William Mason 1926- *AmMWSc 92*
**Kaulback**, Ronald John Henry 1909- *Who 92*
**Kaulius**, Steven Thomas 1958- *WhoFI 92*
**Kauls**, Albert Ernestovich 1938- *IntWW 91, SovUnBD*
**Kauluma**, James Humapanda *WhoRel 92*
**Kaumeyer**, Dorothy 1914- *ConAu 134*
**Kaunda**, David Kenneth 1924- *Who 92*
**Kaunda**, K. D. *ConAu 133*
**Kaunda**, Kenneth *ConAu 133*
**Kaunda**, Kenneth 1924- *ConBlB 2 [port], FacFETw [port]*
**Kaunda**, Kenneth D. *ConAu 133*
**Kaunda**, Kenneth David 1924- *ConAu 133, IntWW 91*
**Kaunda**, Reid Willie K. *Who 92*
**Kaune**, James Edward 1927- *WhoWest 92*
**Kaune**, William Tyler 1940- *AmMWSc 92*
**Kaunitz**, Hans 1905- *AmMWSc 92*
**Kaunitz**, Karen Rose Koppel 1951- *WhoAmL 92, WhoFI 92*
**Kaunitz**, Rita Davidson 1922- *WhoRel 92*
**Kaunitz**, Wenzel Anton, Furst von 1711-1794 *BlkwCEP*
**Kauntze**, Ralph 1911- *Who 92*
**Kaup**, David James 1939- *AmMWSc 92*
**Kaup**, Edgar George 1927- *AmMWSc 92*
**Kauper**, Thomas Eugene 1935- *WhoAmL 92*
**Kaupins**, Gundars Egons 1956- *WhoWest 92*
**Kaupp**, Verne H 1940- *AmMWSc 92*
**Kauppila**, Raymond William 1929- *AmMWSc 92*
**Kauppila**, Walter Eric 1942- *AmMWSc 92*
**Kaur**, Prabhjot *IntWW 91*
**Kaur**, Swaraj 1955- *WhoWest 92*
**Kaus**, Peter Edward 1924- *AmMWSc 92*
**Kaushal**, Jagan Nath *IntWW 91*
**Kaushik**, Azad Kumar 1955- *AmMWSc 92*
**Kaushik**, Narinder Kumar *AmMWSc 92*
**Kaushik**, Purushottam Lal 1930- *IntWW 91*
**Kaushik**, Surendra Kumar 1944- *WhoFI 92*
**Kautner**, Helmut 1908-1980 *EncTR 91 [port], IntDcF 2-2 [port]*
**Kautsky**, Karl Johann 1854-1938 *FacFETw*
**Kautt**, Glenn Gregory 1948- *WhoFI 92*
**Kautter**, David John 1948- *WhoAmL 92, WhoFI 92*
**Kautz**, Allan Douglas 1946- *WhoMW 92*
**Kautz**, Deborah E. 1963- *WhoFI 92*
**Kautz**, Frederick Alton, II 1950- *AmMWSc 92*
**Kautz**, Judith Ann 1943- *WhoWest 92*
**Kautz**, Mary E 1928- *WhoAmP 91*
**Kautz**, Richard Carl 1916- *WhoMW 92*
**Kautz**, Robert Frederick, Jr. 1958- *WhoFI 92, WhoWest 92*
**Kautzman**, Eric Thomas 1962- *WhoAmP 91*
**Kautzmann**, Dwight Clarence Harry 1945- *WhoAmL 92*
**Kauzlaric**, Stephen 1965- *WhoFI 92*
**Kauzlarich**, James J 1927- *AmMWSc 92*
**Kauzlarich**, Susan Mary 1958- *WhoWest 92*
**Kauzmann**, Walter 1916- *AmMWSc 92*
**Kauzmann**, Walter Joseph 1916- *IntWW 91*
**Kavaler**, Frederic 1926- *AmMWSc 92*
**Kavaler**, Lucy Estrin 1930- *IntAu&W 91*
**Kavaler**, Rebecca *DrAPF 91*
**Kavaler**, Rebecca 1933- *WrDr 92*
**Kavaljian**, Lee Gregory 1926- *AmMWSc 92*
**Kavalovski**, Charles 1936- *WhoEnt 92*
**Kavan**, Anna 1901-1968 *RfGEnL 91, TwCSFW 91*
**Kavan**, Joseph Orin 1957- *WhoAmL 92*
**Kavanagh**, Aidan Joseph 1929- *WhoRel 92*
**Kavanagh**, Cheryl Elizabeth 1949- *WhoFI 92*
**Kavanagh**, Dan *IntAu&W 91X, WrDr 92*
**Kavanagh**, Declan M. 1956- *IntMPA 92*
**Kavanagh**, Declan Mary 1956- *WhoRel 92*
**Kavanagh**, P. J. 1931- *ConPo 91, IntAu&W 91, Who 92, WrDr 92*
**Kavanagh**, Patrick 1904-1967 *RfGEnL 91*
**Kavanagh**, Patrick Bernard 1923- *Who 92*
**Kavanagh**, Paul *WrDr 92*
**Kavanagh**, Ralph William 1924- *AmMWSc 92*
**Kavanagh**, Robert John 1931- *AmMWSc 92*
**Kavanau**, Julian Lee 1922- *AmMWSc 92*
**Kavanaugh**, Cynthia *IntAu&W 91X, WrDr 92*
**Kavanaugh**, David Henry 1945- *AmMWSc 92*
**Kavanaugh**, Frank James 1934- *WhoEnt 92*
**Kavanaugh**, Ian *WrDr 92*
**Kavanaugh**, James 1932- *WrDr 92*
**Kavanaugh**, James Francis, Jr. 1949- *WhoAmL 92*
**Kavanaugh**, John Michael 1952- *WhoEnt 92*
**Kavanaugh**, Marilyn Leslie Sheeley 1945- *WhoAmL 92*
**Kavanaugh**, Patrick T. 1954- *WhoRel 92*
**Kavanaugh**, Paul Fred 1959- *WhoAmL 92*
**Kavanaugh**, Walter J 1933- *WhoAmP 91*
**Kavarnos**, George James *AmMWSc 92*
**Kavass**, Igor Ivar 1932- *WhoAmL 92*
**Kavassalis**, Tom A 1958- *AmMWSc 92*
**Kavathas**, Paula 1950- *AmMWSc 92*
**Kaveh**, Mostafa 1947- *AmMWSc 92*
**Kavenoff**, Ruth 1944- *AmMWSc 92*
**Kavensky**, Jodie Shagrin 1957- *WhoMW 92*
**Kaverin**, Venyamin Aleksandrovich 1902-1989 *SovUnBD*
**Kavesh**, Sheldon 1933- *AmMWSc 92*
**Kavic**, Lorne John 1936- *WrDr 92*
**Kavin**, Rebecca Jean 1946- *WhoFI 92, WhoWest 92*
**Kaviraj** *DrAPF 91*
**Kavner**, Julie 1951- *IntMPA 92, WhoEnt 92*
**Kavulich**, John Steven, II 1961- *WhoFI 92*
**Kawabata**, Yasunari 1899-1972 *FacFETw, WhoNob 90*
**Kawachi**, Michael Tateo 1955- *WhoAmL 92*
**Kawachika**, James Akio 1947- *WhoAmL 92*
**Kawaguchi**, Meredith Ferguson 1940- *WhoAmL 92*
**Kawahara**, Fred Katsumi 1921- *AmMWSc 92*
**Kawai**, Masataka 1943- *AmMWSc 92*
**Kawai**, Ryoichi 1917- *IntWW 91*
**Kawai**, Sharon K. 1947- *WhoWest 92*
**Kawaichi**, Ken Martin 1941- *WhoAmL 92*
**Kawakami**, Bertha C 1931- *WhoAmP 91*
**Kawakami**, Hiroshi 1942- *IntWW 91*
**Kawakubo**, Rei 1943- *IntWW 91*
**Kawalec**, Julian 1916- *IntAu&W 91*
**Kawalek**, Joseph Casimir, Jr 1945- *AmMWSc 92*
**Kawalerowicz**, Jerzy 1922- *IntDcF 2-2*
**Kawalerski**, Susan Mary 1952- *WhoEnt 92*
**Kawamoto**, Nobuhiko 1917- *IntWW 91*
**Kawamura**, Hiroshi 1927- *AmMWSc 92*
**Kawamura**, Kazuhiko 1939- *AmMWSc 92*
**Kawamura**, Robert Duane 1960- *WhoAmL 92*
**Kawamura**, Susumu 1929- *WhoWest 92*
**Kawamura**, Yukio 1951- *WhoFI 92*
**Kawanishi**, Hidenori *AmMWSc 92*
**Kawano**, Arnold Hubert 1948- *WhoAmL 92*
**Kawano**, James Conrad *WhoFI 92*
**Kawano**, Randall Toshio 1959- *WhoFI 92*
**Kawara**, Tsutomu 1937- *IntWW 91*
**Kawari**, Hamad Abdelaziz al- 1948- *IntWW 91*
**Kawasak**, Masao *WhoEnt 92*
**Kawasaki**, Edwin Pope 1926- *AmMWSc 92*
**Kawasaki**, Seiichi 1922- *IntWW 91*
**Kawasaki**, Teruo 1918- *IntWW 91*
**Kawase**, Makoto 1926- *AmMWSc 92*
**Kawashima**, Dale Scott 1956- *WhoEnt 92*
**Kawata**, Kazuyoshi 1924- *AmMWSc 92*
**Kawaters**, Woody H 1951- *AmMWSc 92*
**Kawatra**, Mahendra P 1935- *AmMWSc 92*
**Kawawa**, Rashidi Mfaume 1929- *IntWW 91*
**Kawecki**, John Anthony Boleslaw 1959- *WhoEnt 92*
**Kawharu**, Hugh 1927- *Who 92*
**Kawin**, Bruce F. *DrAPF 91*
**Kawin**, Bruce F. 1945- *WrDr 92*
**Kawin**, Bruce Frederick 1945- *IntAu&W 91, WhoEnt 92*
**Kawinski**, Wojciech 1939- *IntAu&W 91*
**Kawooya**, John Kasajja 1952- *AmMWSc 92*
**Kawula**, John Michael 1947- *WhoFI 92*
**Kawusu Conteh**, Sheku Bockari 1928- *IntWW 91*
**Kay**, Alan Cooke *WhoAmL 92, WhoWest 92*
**Kay**, Albert Joseph 1920- *WhoMW 92*
**Kay**, Alvin John 1938- *AmMWSc 92*
**Kay**, Andrew Watt 1916- *Who 92*
**Kay**, Bernard Hubert Gerard 1925- *Who 92*
**Kay**, Bonnie Jean 1941- *AmMWSc 92*
**Kay**, Brian Wilfrid 1921- *Who 92*
**Kay**, Carl J. 1956- *WhoFI 92*
**Kay**, Connie 1927- *NewAmDM*
**Kay**, Cyril Eyton 1902- *Who 92*
**Kay**, Cyril Max 1931- *AmMWSc 92*
**Kay**, David A. 1940- *NewYTBS 91 [port]*
**Kay**, David Clifford 1933- *AmMWSc 92*
**Kay**, David Cyril 1932- *AmMWSc 92*
**Kay**, Douglas *WhoEnt 92*
**Kay**, Edward Joseph 1952- *WhoFI 92*
**Kay**, Edward Leo 1924- *AmMWSc 92*
**Kay**, Elizabeth Alison 1928- *AmMWSc 92*
**Kay**, Ellen *WrDr 92*
**Kay**, Ellis Igor 1961- *WhoEnt 92*
**Kay**, Eric 1926- *AmMWSc 92*
**Kay**, Ernest 1915- *Who 92*
**Kay**, Fenton Ray 1942- *AmMWSc 92*
**Kay**, Geoffrey 1938- *WrDr 92*
**Kay**, George 1936- *WrDr 92*
**Kay**, Gilbert Lee *IntMPA 92*
**Kay**, Gordon 1916- *IntMPA 92*
**Kay**, Guy Gavriel *TwCSFW 91*
**Kay**, Guy Gavriel 1954- *ConAu 134*
**Kay**, H David 1943- *AmMWSc 92*
**Kay**, Harry 1919- *Who 92*
**Kay**, Herma Hill 1934- *WhoAmL 92*
**Kay**, Hershy 1919-1981 *FacFETw, NewAmDM*
**Kay**, Humphrey Edward Melville 1923- *Who 92*
**Kay**, Irvin 1924- *AmMWSc 92*
**Kay**, Jack Garvin 1930- *AmMWSc 92*
**Kay**, James Franklin 1948- *WhoRel 92*
**Kay**, James Robert 1952- *WhoAmL 92*
**Kay**, Janet L. 1957- *WhoEnt 92*
**Kay**, Jeffrey H. 1945- *WhoAmL 92*
**Kay**, Jill 1959- *TwCPaSc*
**Kay**, John *DrAPF 91*
**Kay**, John Anderson 1948- *IntWW 91*
**Kay**, John Chester 1937- *WhoWest 92*
**Kay**, John Menzies 1920- *Who 92*

**Kay**, John William 1943- Who 92
**Kay**, Jolyon Christopher 1930- Who 92
**Kay**, Judith 1952- WhoEnt 92
**Kay**, Judith Webb 1951- WhoRel 92
**Kay**, Kathleen 1958- WhoAmL 92
**Kay**, Kathleen A 1934- WhoAmP 91
**Kay**, Kelly W. 1954- WhoAmL 92
**Kay**, Kenneth George 1943- AmMWSc 92
**Kay**, Laurence D. 1937- WhoAmL 92
**Kay**, Mara IntAu&W 91
**Kay**, Marguerite M B 1947- AmMWSc 92
**Kay**, Maurice Ralph 1942- Who 92
**Kay**, Michael Aaron 1943- AmMWSc 92
**Kay**, Mortimer Isaia 1930- AmMWSc 92
**Kay**, Neil Vincent 1936- Who 92
**Kay**, Patrick Richard 1921- Who 92
**Kay**, Peter 1924- WhoAmP 91
**Kay**, Peter Steven 1937- AmMWSc 92
**Kay**, Robert Eugene 1925- AmMWSc 92
**Kay**, Robert Leo 1924- AmMWSc 92
**Kay**, Robert O 1922- WhoAmP 91
**Kay**, Robert Woodbury 1943- AmMWSc 92
**Kay**, Robin Langford 1919- WrDr 92
**Kay**, Saul 1914- AmMWSc 92
**Kay**, Stanley B. 1941- WhoAmL 92
**Kay**, Suzanne Mahlburg 1947- AmMWSc 92
**Kay**, Tom 1946- WhoEnt 92
**Kay**, Ulysses 1917- NewAmDM, WhoBlA 92, WhoEnt 92
**Kay**, Webster Bice 1900- AmMWSc 92
**Kay-Shuttleworth** Who 92
**Kaya**, Azmi 1933- AmMWSc 92
**Kaya**, Harry Kazuyoshi 1940- AmMWSc 92
**Kaya**, Robert Masayoshi 1914- WhoWest 92
**Kayaalp**, Orhan 1943- WhoFI 92
**Kayalar**, Lutfullah 1952- IntWW 91
**Kayani**, Joseph Thomas 1945- AmMWSc 92
**Kayar**, Susan Rennie 1953- AmMWSc 92
**Kayata**, Sahar Katib 1957- WhoMW 92
**Kayden**, Herbert J 1920- AmMWSc 92
**Kayden**, Mildred WhoEnt 92
**Kaye**, Albert L 1909- AmMWSc 92
**Kaye**, Albert Louis 1909- WhoMW 92
**Kaye**, Alvin Maurice 1930- AmMWSc 92
**Kaye**, Andrew W 1948- WhoIns 92
**Kaye**, Barrington 1924- WrDr 92
**Kaye**, Brian H 1932- AmMWSc 92
**Kaye**, Caren WhoEnt 92
**Kaye**, Christopher J 1957- AmMWSc 92
**Kaye**, Danny d1987 LesBEnT 92
**Kaye**, Danny 1913-1987 FacFETw, NewAmDM
**Kaye**, David Alexander Gordon 1919- Who 92
**Kaye**, Deborah J. 1960- WhoFI 92
**Kaye**, Deena Cheryl 1950- WhoEnt 92
**Kaye**, Donald 1931- AmMWSc 92
**Kaye**, Douglas Robert Beaumont 1909- Who 92
**Kaye**, Elaine Hilda 1930- Who 92
**Kaye**, Elizabeth Ann 1951- WhoMW 92
**Kaye**, Emmanuel 1914- Who 92
**Kaye**, Gene Warren 1950- WhoEnt 92
**Kaye**, Geoffrey John 1935- Who 92
**Kaye**, George Thomas 1944- AmMWSc 92
**Kaye**, George Wycherly ScFEYrs
**Kaye**, Geraldine 1925- IntAu&W 91, WrDr 92
**Kaye**, Gordon I 1935- AmMWSc 92
**Kaye**, Harvey Jordan 1949- IntWW 91, WhoMW 92
**Kaye**, Howard 1938- AmMWSc 92
**Kaye**, Ira B. 1937- WhoFI 92
**Kaye**, Jack Alan 1954- AmMWSc 92
**Kaye**, James Herbert 1937- AmMWSc 92
**Kaye**, Jerome Sidney 1930- AmMWSc 92
**Kaye**, John Phillip Lister L. Who 92
**Kaye**, Judith S 1938- WhoAmP 91
**Kaye**, Judy 1948- ConTFT 9, WhoEnt 92
**Kaye**, Kathleen A. 1948- WhoWest 92
**Kaye**, Kenneth Peter 1946- WhoMW 92
**Kaye**, Leslie 1952- WhoEnt 92, WhoWest 92
**Kaye**, Lori WhoFI 92
**Kaye**, M. M. 1908- WrDr 92
**Kaye**, M M 1911- IntAu&W 91
**Kaye**, Marc Mendell 1959- WhoAmL 92
**Kaye**, Marvin DrAPF 91
**Kaye**, Marvin 1938- WrDr 92
**Kaye**, Marvin Nathan 1938- IntAu&W 91, WhoEnt 92
**Kaye**, Mary Margaret Who 92
**Kaye**, Michael 1925- Who 92, WhoEnt 92
**Kaye**, Michael Peter 1935- AmMWSc 92
**Kaye**, Nancy Weber 1929- AmMWSc 92
**Kaye**, Nora 1920-1987 FacFETw
**Kaye**, Norman Joseph 1923- AmMWSc 92
**Kaye**, Richard Leon 1925- WhoEnt 92
**Kaye**, Richard Michael 1945- WhoFI 92, WhoMW 92
**Kaye**, Richard William 1939- WhoMW 92
**Kaye**, Robert 1917- AmMWSc 92
**Kaye**, Roger Godfrey 1946- Who 92
**Kaye**, Rosalind Anne Who 92
**Kaye**, Sammy 1910-1987 FacFETw
**Kaye**, Samuel 1917- AmMWSc 92
**Kaye**, Saul 1920- AmMWSc 92
**Kaye**, Sidney 1912- AmMWSc 92
**Kaye**, Stephen Rackow 1931- WhoAmL 92
**Kaye**, Stephen Vincent 1935- AmMWSc 92
**Kaye**, Steven E. 1956- WhoRel 92
**Kaye**, Stewart IntAu&W 91X
**Kaye**, Stuart Martin 1946- WhoAmL 92
**Kaye**, Sylvia Fine d1991 NewYTBS 91 [port]
**Kaye**, Tom WrDr 92
**Kaye**, Wilbur 1922- AmMWSc 92
**Kaye**, William Samuel 1953- WhoFI 92
**Kaye/Kantrowitz**, Melanie DrAPF 91
**Kaye Kesler**, Leslie 1956- WhoWest 92
**Kayes**, Stephen Geoffrey 1946- AmMWSc 92
**Kayfetz**, Victor Joel 1945- WhoWest 92
**Kayhart**, Marion 1926- AmMWSc 92
**Kayhart**, Roger V 1922- WhoAmP 91
**Kayla**, Ziya 1912- IntWW 91
**Kaylan**, Howard Lawrence 1947- WhoEnt 92, WhoWest 92
**Kayll**, Albert James 1935- AmMWSc 92
**Kayll**, Joseph Robert 1914- Who 92
**Kaylor**, Hoyt McCoy 1923- AmMWSc 92
**Kaylor**, Robert IntMPA 92
**Kaylor**, Robert David 1933- WhoRel 92
**Kayn**, Roland 1933- ConCom 92
**Kayne**, Fredrick Jay 1941- AmMWSc 92
**Kayne**, Herbert Lawrence 1934- AmMWSc 92
**Kayne**, Jon Barry 1943- WhoMW 92
**Kayne**, Marlene Steinmetz 1941- AmMWSc 92
**Kays**, M Allan 1934- AmMWSc 92
**Kays**, Stanley J 1945- AmMWSc 92
**Kays**, William Morrow 1920- AmMWSc 92
**Kaysen**, Carl 1920- IntWW 91, Who 92
**Kayser**, Boris Jules 1938- AmMWSc 92
**Kayser**, Francis X 1927- AmMWSc 92
**Kayser**, Kenneth Wayne 1947- WhoAmL 92
**Kayser**, Martha ScFEYrs
**Kayser**, Richard Francis 1925- AmMWSc 92
**Kayser**, Robert Helmut 1948- AmMWSc 92
**Kayson**, David 1921- WhoAmL 92
**Kayson**, Mary Beth WhoEnt 92
**Kaysone Phomvihane** 1925- FacFETw
**Kayton**, Howard H 1936- WhoIns 92
**Kayton**, Myron 1934- AmMWSc 92, WhoWest 92
**Kayyal**, Alawi Darwish 1936- IntWW 91
**Kaza**, Andrew Lee 1959- WhoEnt 92
**Kazahaya**, Masahiro Matt 1932- AmMWSc 92
**Kazakevich**, Emmanuil Genrikhovich 1913-1962 SovUnBD
**Kazakia**, Jacob Yakovos 1945- AmMWSc 92
**Kazakov**, Vasiliy Aleksandrovich 1916- IntWW 91, -91N
**Kazakov**, Vasiliy Ivanovich 1927- IntWW 91
**Kazakov**, Yuri Pavlovich 1927- ConAu 36NR
**Kazakov**, Yuriy Pavlovich 1927- IntWW 91
**Kazakov**, Yuriy Pavlovich 1927-1982 SovUnBD
**Kazakova**, Rimma Fedorovna 1932- SovUnBD
**Kazaks**, Peter Alexander 1940- AmMWSc 92
**Kazal**, Louis Anthony 1912- AmMWSc 92
**Kazan**, Basil Gibran 1914- WhoEnt 92
**Kazan**, Benjamin 1917- AmMWSc 92, WhoWest 92
**Kazan**, Chris d1991 NewYTBS 91
**Kazan**, Elia 1909- BenetAL 91, FacFETw, IntAu&W 91, IntDcF 2-2 [port], IntMPA 92, IntWW 91, Who 92, WhoEnt 92, WrDr 92
**Kazan**, Fredric 1933- WhoRel 92
**Kazan**, Lainie 1942- IntMPA 92, WhoEnt 92
**Kazan**, Robert Peter 1947- WhoMW 92
**Kazanjian**, Armen Roupen 1928- AmMWSc 92
**Kazanjian**, Howard G. 1943- IntMPA 92
**Kazanjian**, John Harold 1949- WhoAmL 92
**Kazanjoglous**, Elia 1909- IntWW 91
**Kazankina**, Tatyana 1951- IntWW 91, SovUnBD
**Kazanoff**, Theodore Leon 1922- WhoEnt 92
**Kazantzakis**, Nikos 1883-1957 FacFETw, LiExTwC
**Kazantzis**, Judith 1940- ConPo 91, WrDr 92
**Kazantzis**, Kentia Ann 1962- WhoWest 92
**Kazarezov**, Vladimir Vasilevich 1937- IntWW 91
**Kazarian**, Leon Edward AmMWSc 92
**Kazarinoff**, Michael N 1949- AmMWSc 92
**Kazarinoff**, Nicholas D 1929- AmMWSc 92
**Kazavtchinsky**, Ellis Igor 1961- WhoEnt 92
**Kazda**, Louis F 1916- AmMWSc 92
**Kazdan**, Jerry Lawrence 1937- AmMWSc 92
**Kazel**, Mitchell Steven 1959- WhoEnt 92
**Kazem**, Sayyed M 1938- AmMWSc 92
**Kazemi**, Homayoun 1934- AmMWSc 92
**Kazemi**, Hossein 1938- AmMWSc 92
**Kazemzadeh**, Firuz 1924- WhoRel 92, WrDr 92
**Kazen**, George Philip 1940- WhoAmL 92
**Kazerounian**, Kazem 1956- AmMWSc 92
**Kazes**, Emil 1926- AmMWSc 92
**Kazhdan**, David AmMWSc 92
**Kazi**, Abdul Halim 1935- AmMWSc 92
**Kazi**, Hyder Ali 1934- IntWW 91
**Kazi-Ferrouillet**, Kuumba 1951- WhoBlA 92
**Kazim**, Parvez IntWW 91
**Kazimi**, Mujid S 1947- AmMWSc 92
**Kazimierczuk**, Marian Kazimierz 1948- WhoMW 92
**Kazimirov**, Vladimir Nikolayevich IntWW 91
**Kazin**, Alfred 1915- BenetAL 91, FacFETw, IntWW 91, WrDr 92
**Kazinczy**, Ferenc 1759-1831 BlkwCEP
**Kazlauskas**, Edward John 1942- WhoWest 92
**Kazle**, Elynmarie 1958- WhoEnt 92, WhoWest 92
**Kazmaier**, Harold Eugene 1924- AmMWSc 92
**Kazmaier**, Peter Michael 1951- AmMWSc 92
**Kazmann**, Raphael Gabriel 1916- AmMWSc 92
**Kazmarek**, Linda Adams 1945- WhoRel 92
**Kazmerski**, Lawrence L 1945- AmMWSc 92
**Kaznoff**, Alexis I 1933- AmMWSc 92
**Kazura**, James 1946- AmMWSc 92
**Kazurinsky**, Tim 1950- IntMPA 92
**Ke Hua** 1915- IntWW 91
**Ke**, Paul Jenn 1934- AmMWSc 92
**Kea**, Perry Vernon 1953- WhoRel 92
**Keable-Elliott**, Anthony 1924- Who 92
**Keach**, James P. 1950- WhoEnt 92
**Keach**, John A, Jr 1938- WhoAmP 91
**Keach**, Margaret Sally 1903- WhoMW 92
**Keach**, Stacy 1942- IntMPA 92
**Keach**, Stacy, Jr. 1941- WhoEnt 92
**Keach**, Stacy, Sr. 1914- IntMPA 92, WhoEnt 92
**Keady**, George Cregan, Jr. 1924- WhoAmL 92
**Keagy**, Pamela M AmMWSc 92
**Keagy**, Robert Lloyd 1933- WhoWest 92
**Keahey**, Kenneth Karl 1923- AmMWSc 92
**Keairns**, Dale Lee 1940- AmMWSc 92
**Keal**, Edwin Ernest Frederick 1921- Who 92
**Kealey**, Edward J 1936- IntAu&W 91, WrDr 92
**Kealiinohomoku**, Joann Wheeler 1930- WhoWest 92
**Kealy**, Robin Andrew 1944- Who 92
**Keammerer**, Warren Roy 1946- AmMWSc 92
**Kean**, Arnold Wilfred Geoffrey 1914- Who 92
**Kean**, Benjamin Harrison 1912- AmMWSc 92
**Kean**, Charles Thomas 1941- WhoFI 92
**Kean**, Chester Eugene 1925- AmMWSc 92
**Kean**, Edward Louis 1925- AmMWSc 92
**Kean**, John Vaughan 1917- WhoAmL 92, WhoFI 92
**Kean**, Mary Stewart DrAPF 91
**Kean**, Thomas H. 1935- IntWW 91, WhoAmP 91
**Keana**, John F W 1939- AmMWSc 92
**Keane**, Cornelius J 1921- WhoAmP 91
**Keane**, Desmond St John 1941- Who 92
**Keane**, Edward Webb 1930- WhoAmL 92
**Keane**, Francis Joseph 1936- Who 92
**Keane**, Horace James Basil 1926- WhoBlA 92
**Keane**, J R 1937- AmMWSc 92
**Keane**, James 1952- WhoEnt 92
**Keane**, James Francis 1934- WhoAmP 91
**Keane**, James Ignatius 1944- WhoAmL 92
**Keane**, James Patrick 1946- WhoAmP 91
**Keane**, John 1954- TwCPaSc
**Keane**, John B 1928- IntAu&W 91, WrDr 92
**Keane**, John Brendan 1928- IntWW 91
**Keane**, John Francis, Jr 1922- AmMWSc 92
**Keane**, John Joseph 1839-1918 RelLAm 91
**Keane**, John Michael 1954- WhoAmP 91
**Keane**, Joyce 1938- WhoFI 92
**Keane**, Kenneth William 1921- AmMWSc 92
**Keane**, Kevin G. 1951- WhoAmL 92
**Keane**, Mary Nesta 1905- Who 92
**Keane**, Michael Patrick 1961- WhoFI 92, WhoMW 92
**Keane**, Molly 1904- ConNov 91
**Keane**, Noel 1938- ConAu 133
**Keane**, Peter Gerald 1943- WhoAmL 92
**Keane**, Richard 1909- Who 92
**Keane**, Richard J 1933- WhoAmP 91
**Keane**, Robert W AmMWSc 92
**Keaney**, William Regis 1937- WhoMW 92
**Keanini**, Russell Guy 1959- WhoWest 92
**Keans**, Sandra B 1942- WhoAmP 91
**Keany**, Francis J 1866?-1916 BiInAmS
**Keany**, John William 1923- IntWW 91
**Kear**, Bernard Henry 1931- AmMWSc 92
**Kear**, David 1923- IntWW 91
**Kear**, Edward B, Jr 1932- AmMWSc 92
**Kear**, Graham Francis 1928- Who 92
**Kear**, Maria Martha Ruscitella 1954- WhoAmL 92
**Kear**, Michael R. 1960- WhoRel 92
**Kearby**, Paul Doyle 1955- WhoRel 92
**Kearfott**, William Dunham 1864-1917 BiInAmS
**Kearl**, Willis Gordon 1927- AmMWSc 92
**Kearley** Who 92
**Kearley**, F. Furman 1932- WhoRel 92
**Kearley**, Francis Joseph, Jr 1921- AmMWSc 92
**Kearley**, Richard Irven, III 1953- WhoFI 92
**Kearley**, Timothy G. 1949- WhoAmL 92
**Kearney**, Brian 1935- Who 92
**Kearney**, Dickinson Roberts 1926- WhoWest 92
**Kearney**, Douglas Charles 1945- WhoAmL 92
**Kearney**, Hugh 1924- WrDr 92
**Kearney**, James Arthur 1956- WhoAmL 92
**Kearney**, Jeffrey Allen 1948- WhoAmL 92
**Kearney**, Jesse L. 1950- WhoBlA 92
**Kearney**, John Bernard 1951- WhoAmL 92
**Kearney**, John F 1945- AmMWSc 92
**Kearney**, Joseph 1939- TwCPaSc
**Kearney**, Joseph Matthew, Jr 1956- WhoAmP 91
**Kearney**, Joseph W 1922- AmMWSc 92
**Kearney**, Lawrence DrAPF 91
**Kearney**, Mary Patricia 1920- WhoAmP 91
**Kearney**, Michael John 1940- WhoFI 92
**Kearney**, Michael Joseph, Jr. 1949- WhoAmL 92
**Kearney**, Michael Sean 1947- AmMWSc 92
**Kearney**, Michelle LesBEnT 92
**Kearney**, Patrick Francis 1956- WhoMW 92
**Kearney**, Patrick Jude 1955- WhoWest 92
**Kearney**, Patrick O. 1958- WhoMW 92
**Kearney**, Philip C 1932- AmMWSc 92
**Kearney**, Philip Daniel 1933- AmMWSc 92
**Kearney**, Ramsey 1933- WhoEnt 92
**Kearney**, Richard D. 1914- IntWW 91
**Kearney**, Richard James 1927- WhoFI 92
**Kearney**, Robert Edward 1947- AmMWSc 92
**Kearney**, Robert James 1935- AmMWSc 92
**Kearney**, Robert P. DrAPF 91
**Kearney**, Sheila Jane 1961- WhoAmL 92
**Kearney**, Thomas B 1956- WhoIns 92
**Kearney**, Timothy Francis 1958- WhoFI 92
**Kearney**, William 1935- Who 92
**Kearney-Cooke**, Ann M. 1956- WhoMW 92
**Kearns**, Albert Osborn 1920- WhoRel 92
**Kearns**, David R 1935- AmMWSc 92
**Kearns**, David Todd 1930- IntWW 91, Who 92, WhoFI 92
**Kearns**, Donald Allen 1923- AmMWSc 92
**Kearns**, Francis Emner 1905- WhoRel 92
**Kearns**, Francis Xavier 1943- WhoWest 92
**Kearns**, Jacques Merlin 1930- WhoRel 92
**Kearns**, James Cannon 1944- WhoAmL 92
**Kearns**, James T 1938- WhoIns 92
**Kearns**, John Francis, III 1957- WhoAmL 92
**Kearns**, John J., III 1951- WhoAmL 92
**Kearns**, Lance Edward 1949- AmMWSc 92
**Kearns**, Lionel 1937- WrDr 92
**Kearns**, Merle Grace WhoAmP 91
**Kearns**, R Jerome 1936- WhoAmP 91
**Kearns**, Richard P WhoAmP 91
**Kearns**, Robert J 1946- AmMWSc 92
**Kearns**, Robert William 1927- AmMWSc 92
**Kearns**, Susan Regina 1957- WhoEnt 92
**Kearns**, Thomas J 1940- AmMWSc 92
**Kearns**, Thomas P 1922- AmMWSc 92
**Kearns**, William Edward 1934- Who 92
**Kearns**, William Michael, Jr. 1935- WhoFI 92
**Kearse**, Amalya 1937- WhoAmP 91
**Kearse**, Amalya Lyle 1937- WhoAmL 92, WhoBlA 92
**Kearse**, Barbara Stone 1936- WhoBlA 92
**Kearse**, David Grier 1937- WhoWest 92

**Kearse,** Gregory Sashi 1949- *WhoBlA 92*
**Kearsley,** Elliot Armstrong 1927- *AmMWSc 92*
**Kearton** *Who 92*
**Kearton,** Baron 1911- *IntWW 91, Who 92*
**Keasling,** Hugh Hilary 1922- *AmMWSc 92*
**Keasor,** Lloyd Weldon 1950- *BlkOlyM*
**Keast,** David N 1931- *AmMWSc 92*
**Keast,** Peter John 1961- *WhoMW 92*
**Keaster,** Armon Joseph 1933- *AmMWSc 92*
**Keat,** Paul Powell 1923- *AmMWSc 92*
**Keates,** Frederick L *ScFEYrs*
**Keates,** John 1915- *TwCPaSc*
**Keathley,** Naymond Haskins 1940- *WhoRel 92*
**Keating,** Barbara Helen 1950- *AmMWSc 92*
**Keating,** Bern 1915- *IntAu&W 91, WrDr 92*
**Keating,** Cornelius Francis 1925- *WhoEnt 92, WhoFI 92*
**Keating,** Donald Norman 1924- *Who 92*
**Keating,** Edward Thomas 1961- *WhoMW 92*
**Keating,** Eugene Kneeland 1928- *AmMWSc 92*
**Keating,** Francis Anthony, II 1944- *WhoAmL 92, WhoAmP 91*
**Keating,** Frank 1937- *IntAu&W 91, Who 92*
**Keating,** Gladys Brown 1923- *WhoAmP 91*
**Keating,** H R F 1926- *ConAu 34NR, WrDr 92*
**Keating,** Henry Reymond Fitzwalter 1926- *IntAu&W 91, IntWW 91, Who 92*
**Keating,** James T 1941- *AmMWSc 92*
**Keating,** John Joseph 1938- *AmMWSc 92*
**Keating,** John Richard 1934- *WhoRel 92*
**Keating,** Joy Marie 1944- *WhoWest 92*
**Keating,** Justin 1931- *IntWW 91*
**Keating,** Kathleen Irwin 1938- *AmMWSc 92*
**Keating,** Kay Rosamond Blundell 1943- *Who 92*
**Keating,** Kenneth L 1923- *AmMWSc 92*
**Keating,** L. Clark 1907- *WrDr 92*
**Keating,** Larry Grant 1944- *WhoWest 92*
**Keating,** Michael Francis 1947- *WhoMW 92*
**Keating,** Michael J 1944- *WhoAmP 91*
**Keating,** Michael Patrick 1958- *WhoFI 92*
**Keating,** Patrick Norman 1939- *AmMWSc 92*
**Keating,** Paul Blake, Jr. 1958- *WhoAmL 92*
**Keating,** Paul John 1944- *IntWW 91, Who 92*
**Keating,** Peter J. 1939- *WrDr 92*
**Keating,** Richard Clark 1937- *AmMWSc 92*
**Keating,** Richard P 1935- *WhoIns 92*
**Keating,** Robert B 1924- *WhoAmP 91*
**Keating,** Robert Clark 1915- *WhoAmL 92*
**Keating,** Robert Harold 1924- *WhoFI 92*
**Keating,** Robert Joseph 1944- *AmMWSc 92*
**Keating,** Stephen Flaherty 1918- *IntWW 91*
**Keating,** Terry Michael 1958- *WhoFI 92*
**Keating,** Thomas E *WhoIns 92*
**Keating,** Thomas F 1928- *WhoAmP 91*
**Keating,** Thomas Patrick 1949- *WhoFI 92*
**Keating,** Tristan Jack 1917- *WhoMW 92*
**Keating,** William Hypolitus 1799-1840 *BiInAmS*
**Keating,** William John 1927- *WhoMW 92*
**Keating,** William Patrick 1963- *WhoEnt 92*
**Keating,** William R *WhoAmP 91*
**Keating,** William Warren, III 1966- *WhoFI 92*
**Keatinge,** Cornelia Wyma 1952- *WhoAmL 92*
**Keatinge,** Edgar 1905- *Who 92*
**Keatinge,** Richard 1954- *WhoEnt 92*
**Keatinge,** Richard Harte 1919- *WhoAmL 92, WhoFI 92*
**Keatinge,** William Richard 1931- *IntWW 91, Who 92*
**Keaton,** Buster 1895-1966 *BenetAL 91, FacFETw [port], IntDcF 2-2 [port]*
**Keaton,** Clark M 1910- *AmMWSc 92*
**Keaton,** Diane *IntWW 91*
**Keaton,** Diane 1946- *IntMPA 92, WhoEnt 92*
**Keaton,** Kenneth Dillard 1953- *WhoEnt 92*
**Keaton,** Lawrence Cluer 1924- *WhoWest 92*
**Keaton,** Michael 1951- *IntMPA 92, WhoEnt 92*
**Keaton,** Michael John 1945- *AmMWSc 92*
**Keaton,** Paul W, Jr 1935- *AmMWSc 92*
**Keaton,** Theodore *WhoRel 92*
**Keaton,** William T. *WhoBlA 92*
**Keator,** Margaret Whitley 1945- *WhoAmP 91*
**Keats,** Arthur Stanley 1923- *AmMWSc 92*
**Keats,** Donald 1929- *NewAmDM*
**Keats,** Donald Howard 1929- *WhoEnt 92, WhoWest 92*
**Keats,** Eleanor *DrAPF 91*
**Keats,** Emma 1899?-1979? *ConAu 135, SmATA 68*
**Keats,** Frank Joseph 1950- *WhoWest 92*
**Keats,** Helen 1947- *TwCPaSc*
**Keats,** John 1795-1821 *CnDBLB 3 [port], DcLB 110 [port], RfGEnL 91*
**Keats,** John Bert 1936- *AmMWSc 92*
**Keats,** Roger A 1948- *WhoAmP 91*
**Keats,** Sheila 1929- *WhoEnt 92*
**Keats,** Theodore Eliot 1924- *AmMWSc 92*
**Keaty,** Robert Burke 1949- *WhoFI 92*
**Keaveney,** Raymond 1948- *IntWW 91*
**Keaveney,** William Patrick 1936- *AmMWSc 92*
**Keay,** John 1941- *IntAu&W 91, WrDr 92*
**Keay,** Leonard 1932- *AmMWSc 92*
**Keay,** Lou Carter 1927- *WhoWest 92*
**Keay,** Ronald William John 1920- *Who 92*
**Kebabian,** John Willis 1946- *AmMWSc 92*
**Kebarle,** Paul 1926- *AmMWSc 92*
**Kebbe,** Charles Maynard 1913- *WhoEnt 92*
**Kebin,** Ivan Gustavovich 1905- *SovUnBD*
**Keblawi,** Feisal Said 1935- *AmMWSc 92*
**Keble,** John 1792-1866 *RfGEnL 91*
**Kebler,** Richard William 1920- *AmMWSc 92*
**Kececioglu,** D B 1922- *AmMWSc 92*
**Kechkaylo,** William Valadmir 1927- *WhoMW 92*
**Keck,** Aaron Carter 1967- *WhoEnt 92*
**Keck,** Albert Philip 1934- *WhoFI 92*
**Keck,** Barbara Anne 1946- *WhoWest 92*
**Keck,** David Rhodes 1938- *WhoRel 92*
**Keck,** Donald Bruce 1941- *AmMWSc 92*
**Keck,** Durwin Julius 1953- *WhoRel 92*
**Keck,** George Fred 1895-1980 *DcTwDes, FacFETw*
**Keck,** James Collyer 1924- *AmMWSc 92*
**Keck,** Konrad 1928- *AmMWSc 92*
**Keck,** Leander Earl 1928- *WhoRel 92*
**Keck,** Max Hans 1919- *AmMWSc 92*
**Keck,** Max Johann 1939- *AmMWSc 92*
**Keck,** Michael Lee 1954- *WhoMW 92*
**Keck,** Philip Walter 1947- *WhoFI 92*
**Keck,** Richard Joseph 1963- *WhoFI 92, WhoMW 92*
**Keck,** Robert Clifton 1914- *WhoAmL 92, WhoFI 92, WhoMW 92*
**Keck,** Robert William 1941- *AmMWSc 92*
**Keck,** Winfield 1917- *AmMWSc 92*
**Keckel,** Peter J. 1942- *WhoFI 92*
**Keckley,** E. Weldon 1921- *WhoRel 92*
**Keckley,** Elizabeth 1824?-1907 *NotBlAW 92 [port]*
**Kedah,** The Sultan of 1927- *IntWW 91*
**Keddafi,** Mu'ammar al- *IntWW 91*
**Keddie,** Clifford Melville, Sr. 1925- *WhoWest 92*
**Keddy,** James Richard 1936- *AmMWSc 92*
**Keddy,** Paul Anthony 1953- *AmMWSc 92*
**Keder,** Wilbert Eugene 1928- *AmMWSc 92*
**Kedes,** Laurence H 1937- *AmMWSc 92, WhoWest 92*
**Keding,** Ann Clyrene 1944- *WhoFI 92, WhoWest 92*
**Kedir,** Mohammed 1953- *BlkOlyM*
**Kedourie,** Elie 1926- *IntWW 91, Who 92, WrDr 92*
**Kedrov,** Mikhail Nikolaevich 1893-1972 *SovUnBD*
**Kedrowski,** David Ray 1942- *WhoAmP 91*
**Kedzie,** Daniel P 1930- *WhoIns 92*
**Kedzie,** Daniel Peter 1930- *WhoMW 92*
**Kedzie,** Donald P *AmMWSc 92*
**Kedzie,** Robert Clark 1823-1902 *BiInAmS*
**Kedzie,** Robert Walter 1932- *AmMWSc 92*
**Kedzierska,** Anna 1932- *IntWW 91*
**Kedzierski,** Marek 1951- *LiExTwC*
**Kee,** Berthinia 1940- *WhoRel 92*
**Kee,** David Thomas 1929- *AmMWSc 92*
**Kee,** Howard Clark 1920- *WhoRel 92*
**Kee,** Marsha Goodwin 1942- *WhoBlA 92*
**Kee,** Norman Dean 1931- *WhoAmP 91*
**Kee,** Robert 1919- *IntAu&W 91, IntWW 91, Who 92, WrDr 92*
**Kee,** Sharon Phillips 1950- *WhoAmL 92*
**Kee,** Terry Michael 1953- *WhoAmL 92*
**Kee,** Virginia Moshang 1932- *WhoAmP 91*
**Kee,** William 1921- *Who 92*
**Keeble,** Curtis 1922- *IntWW 91, Who 92*
**Keeble,** John *DrAPF 91*
**Keeble,** John Robert 1944- *WhoWest 92*
**Keeble,** Marshall 1878-1968 *RelLAm 91*
**Keeble,** Neil H. 1944- *ConAu 135*
**Keeble,** Robert 1911- *Who 92*
**Keeble,** Thomas Whitfield 1918- *Who 92*
**Keedy,** Curtis Russell 1938- *AmMWSc 92*
**Keedy,** Hugh F 1926- *AmMWSc 92*
**Keedy,** Mervin Laverne 1920- *AmMWSc 92*
**Keedy,** Michael H 1943- *WhoAmP 91*
**Keefauver,** Timothy Gary 1958- *WhoWest 92*
**Keefe,** Deborah Lynn 1950- *AmMWSc 92*
**Keefe,** Denis 1930- *AmMWSc 92*
**Keefe,** Donald Joseph 1924- *WhoRel 92*
**Keefe,** Edmund M 1908- *WhoAmP 91*
**Keefe,** Harry Victor, Jr. 1922- *WhoFI 92*
**Keefe,** Jeffrey Francis 1926- *WhoRel 92*
**Keefe,** John B 1928- *WhoAmP 91*
**Keefe,** John Richard 1935- *AmMWSc 92*
**Keefe,** Robert Joseph 1934- *WhoAmP 91*
**Keefe,** Roger Manton 1919- *WhoFI 92*
**Keefe,** Thomas J 1937- *AmMWSc 92*
**Keefe,** Thomas Leeven 1937- *AmMWSc 92*
**Keefe,** William Edward 1923- *AmMWSc 92*
**Keefe,** William Joseph 1925- *WhoAmP 91*
**Keefer,** Carol Lyndon 1953- *AmMWSc 92*
**Keefer,** Dennis Ralph 1938- *AmMWSc 92*
**Keefer,** Don H. 1916- *WhoEnt 92*
**Keefer,** Donald Walker 1931- *AmMWSc 92*
**Keefer,** Larry Kay 1939- *AmMWSc 92*
**Keefer,** Raymond Marsh 1913- *AmMWSc 92*
**Keefer,** Robert Alan 1956- *WhoRel 92*
**Keefer,** Robert Dale 1937- *WhoMW 92*
**Keefer,** Robert Faris 1930- *AmMWSc 92*
**Keefer,** Scott King 1927- *WhoAmP 91*
**Keefer,** William Richard 1924- *AmMWSc 92*
**Keefer,** Yvonne June Kelsoe 1935- *WhoRel 92*
**Keeffe,** Barrie 1945- *IntAu&W 91, WrDr 92*
**Keeffe,** Barrie Colin 1945- *Who 92*
**Keeffe,** Bernard 1925- *IntWW 91*
**Keeffe,** James Richard 1937- *AmMWSc 92*
**Keeffe,** John Arthur 1930- *WhoAmL 92*
**Keeffe,** Mary Ann 1944- *WhoAmP 91*
**Keeffe,** Michael Sean 1953- *WhoEnt 92*
**Keefover,** Marvin Dale 1944- *WhoMW 92*
**Keegan,** Achsah D *AmMWSc 92*
**Keegan,** Denis Michael 1924- *Who 92*
**Keegan,** James Francis 1960- *WhoFI 92*
**Keegan,** Jane Ann 1950- *WhoFI 92*
**Keegan,** John *WhoAmP 91*
**Keegan,** John 1934- *IntWW 91, WrDr 92*
**Keegan,** John Desmond Patrick 1934- *IntAu&W 91*
**Keegan,** Kathleen Ann 1949- *WhoFI 92*
**Keegan,** Kevin 1951- *Who 92*
**Keegan,** Kevin Gerard 1962- *WhoFI 92*
**Keegan,** Mary 1914- *IntAu&W 91*
**Keegan,** Michael Richard 1952- *WhoFI 92*
**Keegan,** Peter William 1944- *WhoFI 92*
**Keegan,** Phil 1942- *WhoAmP 91*
**Keegan,** Susan Lynn 1960- *WhoMW 92*
**Keegan,** Thomas G 1939- *WhoAmP 91*
**Keegan,** William James 1938- *IntAu&W 91*
**Keegan,** William James Gregory 1938- *Who 92*
**Keegan-Hutchinson,** Karen 1946- *WhoAmP 91*
**Keegstra,** Kenneth G 1945- *AmMWSc 92*
**Keehn,** Philip Moses 1943- *AmMWSc 92*
**Keehn,** Silas 1930- *WhoFI 92, WhoMW 92*
**Keehner,** Michael Arthur Miller 1943- *WhoFI 92*
**Keel,** Alton G., Jr. 1943- *IntWW 91, WhoAmP 91*
**Keel,** Howard 1917- *WhoEnt 92*
**Keel,** Howard 1919- *IntMPA 92*
**Keel-Williams,** Mildred *DrAPF 91*
**Keelan,** Kevin Robert 1921- *WhoRel 92*
**Keele,** Doman Kent 1923- *AmMWSc 92*
**Keele,** Karen Frances 1961- *WhoMW 92*
**Keele,** Lyndon Alan 1928- *WhoFI 92*
**Keeler,** Clinton *DrAPF 91*
**Keeler,** Clyde Edgar 1900- *AmMWSc 92*
**Keeler,** Emmett Brown 1941- *AmMWSc 92*
**Keeler,** Harry Stephen 1890-1967 *ScFEYrs*
**Keeler,** James Edward 1857-1900 *BiInAmS*
**Keeler,** James Leonard 1935- *WhoFI 92*
**Keeler,** JoEllyn 1932- *WhoMW 92*
**Keeler,** John S 1929- *AmMWSc 92*
**Keeler,** John S 1949- *WhoAmP 91*
**Keeler,** Martin Harvey 1927- *AmMWSc 92*
**Keeler,** Ralph 1930- *AmMWSc 92*
**Keeler,** Randall Scott 1958- *WhoRel 92*
**Keeler,** Richard Fairbanks 1930- *AmMWSc 92*
**Keeler,** Robert Adolph 1920- *AmMWSc 92*
**Keeler,** Roger Norris 1930- *AmMWSc 92*
**Keeler,** Ross Vincent 1948- *WhoFI 92*
**Keeler,** Ruby 1909- *NewAmDM*
**Keeler,** Steven Robert 1954- *WhoEnt 92*
**Keeler,** Stuart P 1934- *AmMWSc 92*
**Keeler,** Vernes *WhoBlA 92*
**Keeler,** Virginia Lee 1930- *WhoAmP 91*
**Keeler,** William Henry 1931- *WhoRel 92*
**Keeley,** Dean Francis 1926- *AmMWSc 92*
**Keeley,** Edmund *DrAPF 91*
**Keeley,** Edmund LeRoy 1928- *WrDr 92*
**Keeley,** Fred W 1944- *AmMWSc 92*
**Keeley,** John L 1904- *AmMWSc 92*
**Keeley,** Jon E 1949- *AmMWSc 92*
**Keeley,** Larry Lee 1939- *AmMWSc 92*
**Keeley,** Richard Charles 1951- *WhoRel 92*
**Keeley,** Robert T, Jr *WhoAmP 91*
**Keeley,** Robert V 1929- *WhoAmP 91*
**Keeley,** Robert Vossler 1929- *IntWW 91*
**Keeley,** Sterling Carter 1948- *AmMWSc 92*
**Keeley,** Wayne Joseph 1956- *WhoEnt 92*
**Keeling,** Bobbie Lee 1931- *AmMWSc 92*
**Keeling,** Charles David 1928- *AmMWSc 92*
**Keeling,** Geraldine Ann 1946- *WhoEnt 92*
**Keeling,** Joe Keith 1936- *WhoMW 92*
**Keeling,** John 1921- *Who 92*
**Keeling,** John Michael 1947- *WhoAmP 91*
**Keeling,** Laura C. 1949- *WhoBlA 92*
**Keeling,** Lytle Bryant 1934- *WhoMW 92*
**Keeling,** Richard Paire 1931- *AmMWSc 92*
**Keeling,** Robert William Maynard 1917- *Who 92*
**Keeling,** Rolland Otis, Jr 1925- *AmMWSc 92*
**Keels,** James Dewey 1930- *WhoBlA 92*
**Keels,** Paul C. *WhoBlA 92*
**Keelung,** Hong *AmMWSc 92*
**Keely,** George Clayton 1926- *WhoAmL 92*
**Keely,** John Ernst Worrell 1827-1898 *BiInAmS*
**Keely,** Kenneth Lee, Jr. 1960- *WhoRel 92*
**Keely,** William Martin 1924- *AmMWSc 92*
**Keem,** John Edward 1948- *AmMWSc 92*
**Keemer,** Edgar B. 1913- *WhoBlA 92*
**Keemer,** Peter John Charles 1932- *Who 92*
**Keen,** Brenda Denniston 1949- *WhoAmL 92*
**Keen,** Carl L *AmMWSc 92*
**Keen,** Charles L 1922- *WhoAmP 91*
**Keen,** Charlotte Elizabeth 1943- *AmMWSc 92*
**Keen,** Constantine 1925- *WhoFI 92*
**Keen,** Dorothy Jean 1922- *AmMWSc 92*
**Keen,** Elizabeth *WhoEnt 92*
**Keen,** Ernest 1937- *WrDr 92*
**Keen,** James H 1948- *AmMWSc 92*
**Keen,** Kenneth Roger 1946- *Who 92*
**Keen,** Lawrence David 1963- *WhoMW 92*
**Keen,** Linda 1940- *AmMWSc 92*
**Keen,** Maria Elizabeth 1918- *WhoMW 92*
**Keen,** Maurice Hugh 1933- *Who 92*
**Keen,** Michael J 1935- *AmMWSc 92*
**Keen,** Noel Thomas 1940- *AmMWSc 92*
**Keen,** Ray Albert 1915- *AmMWSc 92*
**Keen,** Robert Eric 1944- *AmMWSc 92*
**Keen,** Sam *DrAPF 91*
**Keen,** Thomas William 1823-1886 *DcNCBi 3*
**Keen,** Veryl F 1923- *AmMWSc 92*
**Keen,** William Hubert 1944- *AmMWSc 92*
**Keenan,** Barbara 1941- *WhoWest 92*
**Keenan,** C. Robert, III 1954- *WhoAmL 92*
**Keenan,** Charles Borromeo 1940- *WhoAmL 92*
**Keenan,** Charles William 1922- *AmMWSc 92*
**Keenan,** Deborah *DrAPF 91*
**Keenan,** Dennis *WhoRel 92*
**Keenan,** Edward James 1948- *AmMWSc 92*
**Keenan,** Edward Joseph 1932- *WhoWest 92*
**Keenan,** Francis Joyce 1924- *WhoAmP 91*
**Keenan,** Henry Francis 1850-1928 *BenetAL 91*
**Keenan,** James George 1944- *WhoMW 92*
**Keenan,** James Ignatius, Jr 1932- *WhoIns 92*
**Keenan,** James Joseph 1931- *WhoFI 92*
**Keenan,** James Lee 1937- *WhoMW 92*
**Keenan,** John Douglas 1944- *AmMWSc 92*
**Keenan,** John Fontaine 1929- *WhoAmL 92*
**Keenan,** Joseph Aloysius 1938- *AmMWSc 92*
**Keenan,** Judy Ann 1958- *WhoAmL 92*
**Keenan,** Kathleen *WhoAmP 91*
**Keenan,** Kathleen Margaret 1934- *AmMWSc 92*
**Keenan,** Kevin Patrick 1951- *WhoAmL 92*
**Keenan,** Michael George 1948- *WhoAmL 92*
**Keenan,** Mike *WhoMW 92*
**Keenan,** Nancy A. *WhoWest 92*
**Keenan,** Nancy A 1952- *WhoAmP 91*
**Keenan,** Patrick John 1932- *IntWW 91*
**Keenan,** Paul John 1921- *WhoAmP 91*
**Keenan,** Peter Francis, Jr. 1949- *WhoAmL 92*
**Keenan,** Philip Childs 1908- *AmMWSc 92*
**Keenan,** Robert 1950- *WhoWest 92*
**Keenan,** Robert Gregory 1915- *AmMWSc 92*
**Keenan,** Robert Kenneth 1938- *AmMWSc 92*
**Keenan,** Robert Montgomery, Jr. 1936- *WhoAmL 92*
**Keenan,** Roy W *AmMWSc 92*
**Keenan,** Terrance *DrAPF 91*
**Keenan,** Thomas Aquinas 1927- *AmMWSc 92*
**Keenan,** Thomas K 1924- *AmMWSc 92*
**Keenan,** Thomas William 1942- *AmMWSc 92*
**Keenan,** William Jerome 1939- *AmMWSc 92*

**Keenan,** William John 1934- *WhoEnt 92*
**Keene,** Lt. *TwCWW 91*
**Keene,** Annabelle Mary 1948- *WhoMW 92*
**Keene,** Arthur 1930- *TwCPaSc*
**Keene,** Barry 1938- *WhoAmP 91*
**Keene,** Carolyn *ConAu 134, SmATA 65*
**Keene,** Christopher 1946- *IntWW 91, NewAmDM, WhoEnt 92*
**Keene,** Clifford H 1910- *AmMWSc 92*
**Keene,** David Wolfe 1941- *Who 92*
**Keene,** Derek John 1942- *Who 92*
**Keene,** Donald 1922- *IntAu&W 91, WrDr 92*
**Keene,** Floyd Stanley 1949- *WhoAmL 92*
**Keene,** Gloria 1939- *WhoHisp 92*
**Keene,** Harris J 1931- *AmMWSc 92*
**Keene,** Jack Donald 1947- *AmMWSc 92*
**Keene,** James *TwCWW 91*
**Keene,** James H 1930- *AmMWSc 92*
**Keene,** John Clark 1931- *WhoAmL 92*
**Keene,** John Robert R. *Who 92*
**Keene,** Michael Andrew 1956- *WhoMW 92*
**Keene,** Owen David 1934- *AmMWSc 92*
**Keene,** Sharon C. 1948- *WhoBlA 92*
**Keene,** Stephen Winslow 1938- *WhoIns 92*
**Keene,** Thomas Howard 1948- *WhoAmL 92*
**Keene,** Wayne Hartung 1937- *AmMWSc 92*
**Keene,** Willis Riggs 1932- *AmMWSc 92*
**Keenen,** Howard Gregory 1960- *WhoRel 92*
**Keener,** Carl Samuel 1931- *AmMWSc 92*
**Keener,** Charles Richard 1939- *WhoFI 92*
**Keener,** E L 1922- *AmMWSc 92*
**Keener,** Harold Marion 1943- *AmMWSc 92*
**Keener,** Harry Allan 1913- *AmMWSc 92*
**Keener,** Jay Dee 1945- *WhoFI 92*
**Keener,** Joyce *DrAPF 91*
**Keener,** Larry Hubert 1944- *WhoAmL 92*
**Keener,** Marvin Stanford 1943- *AmMWSc 92*
**Keener,** Robert W. 1931- *WhoWest 92*
**Keener,** Walter Ney 1880-1931 *DcNCBi 3*
**Keeney,** Arthur Hail 1920- *AmMWSc 92*
**Keeney,** Clifford Emerson 1921- *AmMWSc 92*
**Keeney,** Dennis Raymond 1937- *AmMWSc 92*
**Keeney,** Gary R. 1957- *WhoMW 92*
**Keeney,** James Donald 1943- *WhoAmL 92*
**Keeney,** Marisa Gesina 1927- *WhoMW 92*
**Keeney,** Mark 1921- *AmMWSc 92*
**Keeney,** Norwood Henry, Jr 1924- *AmMWSc 92*
**Keeney,** Philip G 1925- *AmMWSc 92*
**Keeney,** Ralph Lyons 1944- *AmMWSc 92*
**Keeney,** Ronald Meredith 1954- *WhoFI 92*
**Keeney,** Thomas Critchfield 1946- *WhoAmL 92*
**Keenleyside,** Hugh L. 1898- *WrDr 92*
**Keenleyside,** Hugh Llewellyn 1898- *IntWW 91, Who 92*
**Keenleyside,** Miles Hugh Alston 1929- *AmMWSc 92*
**Keenlyne,** Kent Douglas 1941- *AmMWSc 92*
**Keenmon,** Kendall Andrews 1920- *AmMWSc 92*
**Keenon,** Una H. R. 1933- *WhoAmL 92*
**Keens,** Thomas George 1946- *AmMWSc 92*
**Keens,** William *DrAPF 91*
**Keeny,** Jeffrey Paul 1960- *WhoMW 92*
**Keeny,** Jerry King 1943- *WhoFI 92*
**Keeny,** Spurgeon Milton, Jr 1924- *AmMWSc 92, WhoAmP 91*
**Keep,** Charles Reuben 1932- *Who 92*
**Keep,** Josiah 1849-1911 *BiInAmS*
**Keep,** Judith N. 1944- *WhoAmL 92*
**Keep,** William John 1842-1918 *BiInAmS*
**Keepers,** William L. 1938- *WhoWest 92*
**Keepin,** George Robert, Jr 1923- *AmMWSc 92*
**Keeping,** Charles 1924- *IntAu&W 91*
**Keepler,** Manuel 1944- *AmMWSc 92*
**Keeports,** David 1951- *AmMWSc 92*
**Keer,** Leon M 1934- *AmMWSc 92*
**Keeran,** James Fredrick 1941- *WhoEnt 92*
**Keeran,** Keith Peter 1943- *WhoRel 92*
**Kees,** Beverly 1941- *WhoWest 92*
**Kees,** Kenneth Lewis 1950- *AmMWSc 92*
**Kees,** Weldon 1914-1955 *BenetAL 91, FacFETw*
**Keese,** Charles Richard 1944- *AmMWSc 92*
**Keese,** John Stanley 1952- *WhoWest 92*
**Keesee,** John William 1913- *AmMWSc 92*
**Keesee,** Robert George 1953- *AmMWSc 92*
**Keesey,** Douglas Brooks 1964- *WhoEnt 92*
**Keesey,** Richard E 1934- *AmMWSc 92*
**Keeshan,** Bob *LesBEnT 92*
**Keeshan,** Bob 1927- *IntMPA 92, WhoEnt 92, WrDr 92*
**Keeshan,** Robert Edward 1950- *WhoAmL 92*
**Keesing,** Nancy 1923- *WrDr 92*
**Keesing,** Nancy Florence 1923- *IntAu&W 91*
**Keesing,** Roger M. 1935- *WrDr 92*
**Keesley,** William P 1953- *WhoAmP 91*
**Keesling,** James Edgar 1942- *AmMWSc 92*
**Keesom,** Pieter Hendrik 1917- *AmMWSc 92*
**Keet,** Jim 1949- *WhoAmP 91*
**Keeton,** John T, Jr *WhoAmP 91*
**Keeton,** Kathy *NewYTBS 91 [port]*
**Keeton,** Kent T *AmMWSc 92*
**Keeton,** Morris Teuton 1917- *WrDr 92*
**Keeton,** Paul C *WhoAmP 91*
**Keeton,** Raedene J.A. 1958- *WhoWest 92*
**Keeton,** Robert Ernest 1919- *WhoAmL 92*
**Keeton,** William R. 1951- *WhoEnt 92*
**Keets,** John David, Jr. 1948- *WhoMW 92*
**Keever,** Carolyn Anne 1948- *AmMWSc 92*
**Keevil,** Norman Bell 1910- *AmMWSc 92*
**Keevil,** Norman Bell 1938- *WhoFI 92, WhoWest 92*
**Keevil,** Thomas Alan 1947- *AmMWSc 92*
**Keezer,** Dexter M. 1895-1991 *NewYTBS 91 [port]*
**Kefalides,** Nicholas Alexander 1927- *AmMWSc 92*
**Kefauver,** Carey Estes 1903-1963 *AmPolLe, FacFETw*
**Keffala,** Ann Lazopoulos 1923- *WhoAmP 91*
**Keffalas,** John Spero 1950- *WhoFI 92*
**Keffer,** Charles Joseph 1941- *AmMWSc 92*
**Keffer,** Frederic 1919- *AmMWSc 92*
**Keffer,** James F 1933- *AmMWSc 92*
**Kefford,** Noel Price 1927- *AmMWSc 92*
**Kegel,** Gerhard Theodor Otto 1912- *IntWW 91*
**Kegel,** Gunter Heinrich Reinhard 1929- *AmMWSc 92*
**Kegel,** William George 1922- *WhoFI 92*
**Kegeles,** Gerson 1917- *AmMWSc 92*
**Kegeles,** Lawrence Steven 1947- *AmMWSc 92*
**Kegelman,** Matthew Roland 1928- *AmMWSc 92*
**Kegerreis,** Robert James 1921- *WhoMW 92*
**Keglar,** Shelvy Haywood 1947- *WhoBlA 92*
**Kegley,** Charles W., Jr. 1944- *ConAu 36NR*
**Kegley,** Jacquelyn Ann 1938- *WhoRel 92*
**Kegley,** Kathleen Quinlan 1964- *WhoFI 92*
**Kehaya,** Barbara M 1921- *WhoAmP 91*
**Kehew,** Alan Everett 1947- *AmMWSc 92*
**Kehl,** Jeffrey Anthony 1950- *WhoEnt 92*
**Kehl,** Randall Herman 1954- *WhoAmL 92*
**Kehl,** Shelley Sanders 1949- *WhoAmL 92*
**Kehl,** Theodore H 1933- *AmMWSc 92*
**Kehl,** William Brunner 1919- *AmMWSc 92*
**Kehle,** Robert Gordon 1951- *WhoEnt 92*
**Kehlenbeck,** Manfred Max 1937- *AmMWSc 92*
**Kehler,** Dorothea Faith 1936- *WhoWest 92*
**Kehler,** Philip Leroy 1936- *AmMWSc 92*
**Kehlmann,** Robert 1942- *WhoWest 92*
**Kehoe,** Alice Beck 1934- *WhoMW 92*
**Kehoe,** Brandt 1933- *AmMWSc 92*
**Kehoe,** Geoffrey Scott 1956- *WhoMW 92*
**Kehoe,** James W. 1925- *WhoAmL 92*
**Kehoe,** James Woodworth 1920- *WhoFI 92*
**Kehoe,** John Thomas 1930- *WhoWest 92*
**Kehoe,** L Paul 1938- *WhoAmP 91*
**Kehoe,** Lawrence Joseph 1940- *AmMWSc 92*
**Kehoe,** Marie-Louise 1928- *WhoAmP 91*
**Kehoe,** Richard J. *WhoRel 92*
**Kehoe,** Thomas J 1919- *AmMWSc 92*
**Kehoe,** Vincent Jeffre-Roux 1921- *WhoEnt 92, WhoWest 92*
**Kehr,** Clifton Leroy 1926- *AmMWSc 92*
**Kehr,** Josef 1904- *EncTR 91*
**Kehrel,** John D. 1954- *WhoFI 92*
**Kehrer,** James Paul 1951- *AmMWSc 92*
**Kehres,** Donald Wayne 1951- *WhoRel 92*
**Kehres,** Paul W 1922- *AmMWSc 92*
**Kehres,** Paul William 1922- *WhoMW 92*
**Kehres,** Robert William 1948- *WhoAmL 92*
**Kehrl,** Howard H 1923- *AmMWSc 92*
**Kehrli,** Randy Ray 1952- *WhoAmL 92*
**Kehrli,** Ronald Louis 1932- *WhoFI 92*
**Kehrwald,** Edward Paul 1952- *WhoMW 92*
**Kehrwald,** Leif Joseph 1957- *WhoRel 92*
**Keicher,** William Eugene 1947- *AmMWSc 92*
**Keidel,** Frederick Andrew 1926- *AmMWSc 92*
**Keiderling,** Kyle R 1942- *WhoAmP 91*
**Keiderling,** Timothy Allen 1947- *AmMWSc 92*
**Keier,** Richard Frederick 1939- *WhoAmP 91*
**Keifer,** Joseph Warren 1836-1932 *AmPolLe*
**Keifer,** Kenneth Jay 1953- *WhoEnt 92*
**Keiffer,** David Goforth 1931- *AmMWSc 92*
**Keiffer,** Edwin Gene 1929- *WhoFI 92*
**Keigher,** William Francis 1945- *AmMWSc 92*
**Keighin,** Charles William 1932- *AmMWSc 92*
**Keighley,** Michael Robert Burch 1943- *Who 92*
**Keighly-Peach,** Charles Lindsey 1902- *Who 92*
**Keightley,** Moy *TwCPaSc*
**Keightley,** Richard Charles 1933- *Who 92*
**Keigler,** John Edward 1929- *AmMWSc 92*
**Keihn,** Frederick George 1923- *AmMWSc 92*
**Keil,** Alfred Adolf Heinrich 1913- *AmMWSc 92*
**Keil,** Charles Kornhauser 1933- *WhoAmL 92*
**Keil,** David John 1946- *AmMWSc 92*
**Keil,** Jeffrey C. 1943- *WhoFI 92*
**Keil,** Julian E 1926- *AmMWSc 92*
**Keil,** Klaus 1934- *AmMWSc 92*
**Keil,** Lanny Charles 1936- *AmMWSc 92*
**Keil,** Norma Fern 1906- *WhoAmP 91*
**Keil,** Ode Richard 1942- *WhoMW 92*
**Keil,** Robert Gerald 1941- *AmMWSc 92*
**Keil,** Robert Matthes 1926- *WhoFI 92*
**Keil,** Stephen Lesley 1947- *AmMWSc 92*
**Keil,** Thomas H 1939- *AmMWSc 92*
**Keilbar,** Mona Hubbard *WhoAmP 91*
**Keilberth,** Joseph 1908-1968 *NewAmDM*
**Keilholtz,** William Leroy 1950- *WhoFI 92*
**Keilin,** Bertram 1922- *AmMWSc 92*
**Keilis-Borok,** Vladimir Isaakovich 1921- *IntWW 91*
**Keill,** John 1671-1721 *BlkwCEP*
**Keiller,** James Bruce 1938- *WhoRel 92*
**Keillor,** Garrison *ConAu 36NR, DrAPF 91*
**Keillor,** Garrison 1942- *BenetAL 91, IntAu&W 91, WrDr 92*
**Keillor,** Garrison Edward 1942- *IntWW 91, WhoEnt 92*
**Keillor,** Gary 1942- *ConAu 36NR*
**Keilman,** David 1951- *WhoMW 92*
**Keilp,** Joe 1944- *WhoAmL 92*
**Keils,** Lucinda Anne 1951- *WhoAmL 92*
**Keilson,** Julian 1924- *AmMWSc 92*
**Keily,** Hubert Joseph 1921- *AmMWSc 92*
**Keim,** Barbara Howell 1946- *AmMWSc 92*
**Keim,** Christopher Peter 1906- *AmMWSc 92*
**Keim,** Gerald Inman 1910- *AmMWSc 92*
**Keim,** John Eugene 1941- *AmMWSc 92*
**Keim,** Lon William 1943- *AmMWSc 92*
**Keim,** Michael Lee 1960- *WhoMW 92*
**Keim,** Michael Ray 1951- *WhoWest 92*
**Keim,** Robert Thomas 1949- *WhoWest 92*
**Keim,** Wayne Franklin 1923- *AmMWSc 92*
**Keimach,** Brad M. 1953- *WhoEnt 92*
**Keimer,** Samuel 1688-1739? *BenetAL 91*
**Keinath,** Gerald E 1924- *AmMWSc 92*
**Keinath,** Steven Ernest 1954- *AmMWSc 92*
**Keinath,** Thomas M 1941- *AmMWSc 92*
**Keiner,** Jeffrey Douglas 1946- *WhoAmL 92*
**Keiner,** Robert Bruce, Jr. 1942- *WhoAmL 92*
**Keino,** Kipchoge 1940- *BlkOlyM*
**Keip,** Fred Frank 1930- *WhoRel 92*
**Keip,** Margaret Ada 1938- *WhoRel 92*
**Keiper,** Ronald R 1941- *AmMWSc 92*
**Keir,** Gerald Janes 1943- *WhoWest 92*
**Keir,** James Dewar 1921- *Who 92*
**Keirans,** James Edward 1935- *AmMWSc 92*
**Keirn,** Richard Duane 1944- *WhoWest 92*
**Keirns,** James Jeffery 1947- *AmMWSc 92*
**Keirns,** Mary Hull 1947- *AmMWSc 92*
**Keirs,** Russell John 1915- *AmMWSc 92*
**Keisch,** Bernard 1932- *AmMWSc 92*
**Keiser,** Bernhard E 1928- *AmMWSc 92*
**Keiser,** Edmund Davis, Jr 1934- *AmMWSc 92*
**Keiser,** George McCurrach 1947- *AmMWSc 92*
**Keiser,** Harold D *AmMWSc 92*
**Keiser,** Harry R 1933- *AmMWSc 92*
**Keiser,** Henry Bruce 1927- *WhoAmL 92, WhoEnt 92, WhoFI 92*
**Keiser,** Jeffrey E 1941- *AmMWSc 92*
**Keiser,** John Howard 1936- *WhoWest 92*
**Keiser,** Stephen Charles 1955- *WhoFI 92*
**Keisler,** Howard Jerome 1936- *AmMWSc 92*
**Keisler,** James Edwin 1929- *AmMWSc 92*
**Keisling,** Phil *WhoAmP 91*
**Keisling,** Phillip A. 1955- *WhoWest 92*
**Keiss,** Isabelle 1931- *WhoRel 92*
**Keist,** Richard Theodore 1936- *WhoMW 92*
**Keister,** David C. 1940- *WhoEnt 92*
**Keister,** Donald Lee 1933- *AmMWSc 92*
**Keister,** James E 1914- *AmMWSc 92*
**Keister,** Jamieson Charles 1938- *AmMWSc 92*
**Keister,** Jean Clare 1931- *WhoWest 92*
**Keister,** Jerome Baird 1953- *AmMWSc 92*
**Keister,** Thomas C., Jr. 1939- *WhoFI 92*
**Keistler,** Betty Lou 1935- *WhoFI 92*
**Keitel,** Glenn H 1930- *AmMWSc 92*
**Keitel,** Harvey 1939- *IntMPA 92*
**Keitel,** Harvey 1947- *WhoEnt 92*
**Keitel,** Wilhelm 1882-1946 *EncTR 91 [port], FacFETw*
**Keiter,** Ellen Ann *AmMWSc 92*
**Keiter,** Richard Lee 1939- *AmMWSc 92*
**Keith** *Who 92*
**Keith,** A M *WhoAmP 91*
**Keith,** Agnes Newton 1901- *BenetAL 91*
**Keith,** Alexander MacDonald 1928- *WhoAmL 92, WhoMW 92*
**Keith,** Anne *EncAmaz 91*
**Keith,** Bill *WhoAmP 91*
**Keith,** Brahmachari 1947- *WhoEnt 92*
**Keith,** Brenda Elaine 1956- *WhoAmP 91*
**Keith,** Brian 1921- *ConTFT 9, IntMPA 92*
**Keith,** Brian Michael 1921- *WhoEnt 92*
**Keith,** Brian Richard 1944- *Who 92*
**Keith,** Bruce Edgar 1918- *WhoWest 92*
**Keith,** Carlton *ConAu 135, WrDr 92*
**Keith,** Charles Herbert 1926- *AmMWSc 92*
**Keith,** D. Judith 1947- *WhoAmL 92*
**Keith,** Dale Martin 1940- *WhoMW 92*
**Keith,** Damon J *WhoAmP 91*
**Keith,** Damon Jerome 1922- *WhoAmL 92, WhoBlA 92, WhoMW 92*
**Keith,** David *DrAPF 91, IntAu&W 91X, Who 92, WrDr 92*
**Keith,** David 1930- *WhoEnt 92*
**Keith,** David 1954- *IntMPA 92*
**Keith,** David Alexander 1944- *AmMWSc 92*
**Keith,** David Lee 1940- *AmMWSc 92*
**Keith,** David Lemuel 1954- *WhoEnt 92*
**Keith,** Debra L. 1956- *WhoAmL 92*
**Keith,** Dennis Dalton 1943- *AmMWSc 92*
**Keith,** Donald Edwards 1938- *AmMWSc 92*
**Keith,** Donald Merle 1928- *WhoAmP 91*
**Keith,** Doris T. 1924- *WhoBlA 92*
**Keith,** Ernest Alexander 1951- *AmMWSc 92*
**Keith,** Everett Earnest 1906- *WhoMW 92*
**Keith,** Frederick W, Jr 1921- *AmMWSc 92*
**Keith,** Garnett Lee, Jr. 1935- *WhoFI 92*
**Keith,** George 1638?-1716 *BenetAL 91*
**Keith,** Gordon 1908- *WhoWest 92*
**Keith,** H Douglas 1927- *AmMWSc 92*
**Keith,** Harold 1903- *IntAu&W 91, WrDr 92*
**Keith,** Harvey Douglas 1927- *AmMWSc 92*
**Keith,** James David 1940- *WhoMW 92*
**Keith,** James Melvin 1943- *WhoRel 92*
**Keith,** James Oliver 1932- *AmMWSc 92*
**Keith,** Jennie 1942- *AmMWSc 92*
**Keith,** Jerry M 1940- *AmMWSc 92*
**Keith,** John Ray 1948- *WhoAmP 91*
**Keith,** Karen C. 1957- *WhoBlA 92*
**Keith,** Kenneth 1937- *Who 92*
**Keith,** Kent Marsteller 1948- *WhoWest 92*
**Keith,** Lawrence H 1938- *AmMWSc 92*
**Keith,** Leroy 1939- *WhoBlA 92*
**Keith,** Lloyd Burrows 1931- *AmMWSc 92*
**Keith,** MacKenzie Lawrence 1912- *AmMWSc 92*
**Keith,** Margaret *EncAmaz 91*
**Keith,** Mary Addis 1928- *WhoMW 92*
**Keith,** Noel L. 1903-1981 *ConAu 133*
**Keith,** Norman Thomas 1936- *WhoWest 92*
**Keith,** Paul 1944- *WhoEnt 92*
**Keith,** Paula Myers 1950- *AmMWSc 92*
**Keith,** Pauline Mary 1924- *WhoWest 92*
**Keith,** Penelope 1939- *IntMPA 92*
**Keith,** Penelope Anne Constance *Who 92*
**Keith,** Penelope Anne Constance 1940- *IntWW 91*
**Keith,** Raymond J. 1942- *WhoRel 92*
**Keith,** Robert *DcNCBi 3*
**Keith,** Robert Allen 1924- *AmMWSc 92, WhoWest 92*
**Keith,** Robert Murray 1730-1795 *BlkwCEP*
**Keith,** Robert William 1926- *WhoFI 92*
**Keith,** Sean Paul 1961- *WhoRel 92*
**Keith,** Stephen C 1942- *WhoAmP 91*
**Keith,** Susan Elizabeth 1959- *WhoEnt 92*
**Keith,** Terry Eugene Clark 1940- *AmMWSc 92*
**Keith,** Theo Gordon, Jr 1939- *AmMWSc 92, WhoMW 92*
**Keith,** Thomas Joseph 1941- *WhoAmP 91*
**Keith,** Thomas Warren, Jr 1951- *WhoMW 92*
**Keith,** Warren Gray 1908- *AmMWSc 92*
**Keith,** William Raymond 1929- *WhoAmP 91*
**Keith-Jones,** Richard 1913- *Who 92*
**Keith-Lucas,** Bryan 1912- *Who 92, WrDr 92*
**Keith-Lucas,** David 1911- *Who 92*
**Keith Of Castleacre,** Baron 1916- *IntWW 91, Who 92*
**Keith of Kinkel,** Baron 1922- *Who 92*

**Keithley**, Bradford Gene 1951- *WhoAmL 92*
**Keithley**, George *DrAPF 91*
**Keithley**, Nancy Fitzgerald 1946- *WhoMW 92*
**Keithley**, Thomas William 1958- *WhoRel 92*
**Keithly**, Janet Sue 1941- *AmMWSc 92*
**Keitt**, George Wannamaker, Jr 1928- *AmMWSc 92*
**Keitt**, L. 1938- *WhoBlA 92*
**Keizer**, Clifford Richard 1918- *AmMWSc 92*
**Keizer**, Eugene O 1918- *AmMWSc 92*
**Keizer**, Joel Edward 1942- *AmMWSc 92*
**Kekedo**, Mary 1919- *Who 92*
**Kekkonen**, Urho K 1900-1986 *FacFETw*
**Kekoolani**, Dean Pua 1961- *WhoEnt 92*
**Kekwick**, Ralph Ambrose 1908- *IntWW 91, Who 92*
**Kelahan**, John Anthony, Jr. 1952- *WhoFI 92*
**Kelaher**, James Peirce 1951- *WhoAmL 92*
**Kelaiditis**, Anestis 1948- *WhoFI 92*
**Kelani**, Haissam 1926- *IntWW 91*
**Kelbas**, Kenneth 1957- *WhoEnt 92*
**Kelber**, Jeffry Alan 1952- *AmMWSc 92*
**Kelber**, Werner Heinz 1935- *WhoRel 92*
**Kelberer**, John Jacob 1926- *IntWW 91*
**Kelberer**, John Jacob 1926-1991 *NewYTBS 91 [port]*
**Kelbie**, David 1945- *Who 92*
**Kelble**, William Francis 1953- *WhoFI 92*
**Kelbley**, Stephen Paul 1942- *WhoFI 92*
**Kelburn**, Viscount of 1978- *Who 92*
**Kelch**, Benjamin Paul 1957- *WhoMW 92*
**Kelch**, Walter L 1948- *AmMWSc 92*
**Kelchner**, Burton L 1921- *AmMWSc 92*
**Kelchner**, Diane Lynn 1956- *WhoEnt 92*
**Keldysh**, Mstislav Vsevolodovich 1911-1978 *FacFETw*
**Kele**, Roger Alan 1943- *AmMWSc 92*
**Kelehan**, Kevin James 1951- *WhoAmL 92*
**Keleher**, J J 1926- *AmMWSc 92*
**Keleher**, James P. 1931- *WhoRel 92*
**Keleher**, Paul Donald 1931- *WhoFI 92*
**Keleinikov**, Andrei 1924- *SmATA 65 [port]*
**Kelemen**, Charles F 1943- *AmMWSc 92*
**Kelemen**, Denis George 1925- *AmMWSc 92*
**Kelemen**, Franklin Alexander 1950- *WhoMW 92*
**Kelemen**, Milko 1924- *ConCom 92, NewAmDM*
**Kelen**, Joyce Arlene 1949- *WhoWest 92*
**Kelen**, Stephen 1912- *IntAu&W 91, WrDr 92*
**Keler**, Hans von 1925- *IntWW 91*
**Keler**, Marianne Martha 1954- *WhoAmL 92*
**Kelesis**, Angela Michele 1960- *WhoWest 92*
**Keligian**, David Leo 1956- *WhoFI 92*
**Keliher**, Thomas Francis 1909- *AmMWSc 92*
**Kelin**, Debra Ann 1951- *WhoWest 92*
**Kelisky**, Richard Paul 1929- *AmMWSc 92*
**Kelkar**, Ram Vishnu 1958- *WhoFI 92*
**Kelker**, Douglas 1940- *AmMWSc 92*
**Kelker**, Sally Lorraine 1942- *WhoAmP 91*
**Kell**, Ernest Eugene, Jr. 1928- *WhoWest 92*
**Kell**, Ernie *WhoAmP 91*
**Kell**, George C. 1922- *WhoEnt 92*
**Kell**, Joseph *Who 92, WrDr 92*
**Kell**, Reginald 1906-1981 *NewAmDM*
**Kell**, Richard 1927- *ConPo 91, IntAu&W 91, WrDr 92*
**Kell**, Robert M 1922- *AmMWSc 92*
**Kell**, Vette Eugene 1915- *WhoFI 92*
**Kellaigh**, Kathleen 1955- *WhoEnt 92*
**Kellam**, Jeffrey Stanton 1944- *WhoEnt 92*
**Kellam**, Robert T 1922- *WhoAmP 91*
**Kelland**, Clarence Budington 1881-1964 *BenetAL 91*
**Kelland**, David Ross 1935- *AmMWSc 92*
**Kelland**, Gilbert James 1924- *Who 92*
**Kelland**, John William 1929- *Who 92*
**Kellar**, Arthur H. 1921-1990 *WhoBlA 92N*
**Kellar**, Gerald Dean 1916- *WhoRel 92*
**Kellar**, Kenneth Jon 1945- *AmMWSc 92*
**Kellar**, Marshal McGee 1932- *WhoFI 92*
**Kellar**, Paul Timothy 1950- *WhoAmL 92*
**Kellar**, Philip R *ScFEYrs*
**Kellar**, Raymond George 1957- *WhoWest 92*
**Kellas**, Arthur Roy Handasyde 1915- *IntWW 91, Who 92*
**Kellaway**, Peter 1920- *AmMWSc 92*
**Kellaway**, William 1926- *Who 92*
**Kellberg**, Love 1922- *IntWW 91*
**Kelleher**, Christopher Gerard 1954- *WhoEnt 92*
**Kelleher**, Daniel William 1931- *WhoFI 92*
**Kelleher**, Dennis L *AmMWSc 92*
**Kelleher**, Herbert David 1931- *WhoFI 92*
**Kelleher**, James Francis 1930- *IntWW 91*
**Kelleher**, James Joseph 1938- *AmMWSc 92*
**Kelleher**, James Joseph 1958- *WhoAmL 92*
**Kelleher**, Joan 1915- *Who 92*
**Kelleher**, John M. 1936- *WhoAmL 92*
**Kelleher**, Kathleen 1951- *WhoFI 92*
**Kelleher**, Mary Annunciata 1926- *WhoRel 92*
**Kelleher**, Matthew D 1939- *AmMWSc 92*
**Kelleher**, Matthew Dennis 1939- *WhoWest 92*
**Kelleher**, Michael Francis 1949- *WhoAmL 92*
**Kelleher**, Neil William 1923- *WhoAmP 91*
**Kelleher**, Philip Conboy 1928- *AmMWSc 92*
**Kelleher**, Raymond Joseph, Jr 1939- *AmMWSc 92*
**Kelleher**, Richard Cornelius 1949- *WhoFI 92, WhoWest 92*
**Kelleher**, Robert Joseph 1913- *WhoAmL 92, WhoWest 92*
**Kelleher**, Robert Neal 1943- *WhoWest 92*
**Kelleher**, Roger Thomson 1926- *AmMWSc 92*
**Kelleher**, Thomas F. 1923- *WhoAmL 92, WhoAmP 91*
**Kelleher**, Tony James 1933- *WhoEnt 92*
**Kelleher**, Victor 1939- *ConNov 91, IntAu&W 91, WrDr 92*
**Kelleher**, William Eugene, Jr. 1953- *WhoAmL 92*
**Kelleher**, William Joseph 1929- *AmMWSc 92*
**Kellems**, Rodney E *AmMWSc 92*
**Kellen**, Michael L 1948- *WhoIns 92*
**Kellen**, Stephen Max 1914- *WhoFI 92*
**Kellenbenz**, Hermann 1913- *IntWW 91*
**Kellenberg**, John Vincent 1962- *WhoFI 92*
**Kellenberger**, Randy Vern 1951- *WhoMW 92*
**Keller**, Alex Stephen 1928- *WhoAmL 92*
**Keller**, Andrew 1925- *IntWW 91, Who 92*
**Keller**, Arthur Charles 1901- *AmMWSc 92*
**Keller**, Arthur Michael 1957- *WhoWest 92*
**Keller**, Barry Lee 1937- *AmMWSc 92*
**Keller**, Bernard Gerard, Jr 1936- *AmMWSc 92*
**Keller**, Boris Aleksandrovich 1874-1945 *SovUnBD*
**Keller**, C. Graden, Jr. 1949- *WhoFI 92*
**Keller**, Carl Albert 1920- *WhoRel 92*
**Keller**, Carlos 1898- *BiDExR*
**Keller**, Charles A 1919- *AmMWSc 92*
**Keller**, Charles Ernest 1916-1990 *FacFETw*
**Keller**, Christoph, Jr. 1915- *WhoRel 92*
**Keller**, D Steven 1958- *AmMWSc 92*
**Keller**, Daniel Whittemore 1947- *WhoEnt 92*
**Keller**, David *DrAPF 91*
**Keller**, David Edward 1952- *WhoEnt 92*
**Keller**, David H 1880-1966 *ScFEYrs, TwCSFW 91*
**Keller**, David King 1948- *WhoWest 92*
**Keller**, David Lester 1919- *WhoAmP 91*
**Keller**, Dennis James 1941- *WhoMW 92*
**Keller**, Diane Cecelia 1955- *WhoRel 92*
**Keller**, Dolores Elaine 1926- *AmMWSc 92*
**Keller**, Donald V 1930- *AmMWSc 92*
**Keller**, Douglas Vern, Jr 1928- *AmMWSc 92*
**Keller**, E W 1936- *WhoAmP 91*
**Keller**, Edmond Joseph 1942- *WhoBlA 92*
**Keller**, Edward Anthony 1942- *AmMWSc 92*
**Keller**, Edward Clarence, Jr 1932- *AmMWSc 92*
**Keller**, Edward Lee 1941- *AmMWSc 92*
**Keller**, Edward Lowell 1939- *AmMWSc 92*
**Keller**, Eldon Lewis 1934- *AmMWSc 92*
**Keller**, Eliot Aaron 1947- *WhoEnt 92*
**Keller**, Elizabeth Beach 1917- *AmMWSc 92*
**Keller**, Emily *DrAPF 91*
**Keller**, F. Annette 1951- *WhoRel 92*
**Keller**, Frank Steven 1948- *WhoEnt 92*
**Keller**, Frederick Albert, Jr *AmMWSc 92*
**Keller**, Frederick Jacob 1934- *AmMWSc 92*
**Keller**, Gary D. 1943- *WhoHisp 92*
**Keller**, Gary William 1948- *WhoFI 92*
**Keller**, Geoffrey 1918- *AmMWSc 92*
**Keller**, George Anthony 1956- *WhoMW 92*
**Keller**, George E, II 1933- *AmMWSc 92*
**Keller**, George Earl 1940- *AmMWSc 92*
**Keller**, George H 1931- *AmMWSc 92*
**Keller**, George M. 1923- *IntWW 91*
**Keller**, George Matthew 1923- *WhoWest 92*
**Keller**, George R 1951- *WhoIns 92*
**Keller**, George Randy, Jr 1946- *AmMWSc 92*
**Keller**, Hans Gustav 1902- *IntWW 91*
**Keller**, Harold Willard 1937- *AmMWSc 92*
**Keller**, Harold William 1922- *WhoMW 92*
**Keller**, Helen 1880-1968 *BenetAL 91, RComAH, ReelWom*
**Keller**, Helen Adams 1880-1968 *AmPeW, FacFETw*
**Keller**, Herbert Bishop 1925- *AmMWSc 92*
**Keller**, Jack 1928- *AmMWSc 92*
**Keller**, Jack Arthur, Jr. 1952- *WhoRel 92*
**Keller**, Jaime 1936- *AmMWSc 92*
**Keller**, James Lloyd 1918- *AmMWSc 92*
**Keller**, James Robert 1954- *WhoAmL 92*
**Keller**, James Wesley 1958- *WhoFI 92, WhoWest 92*
**Keller**, Jeffrey Thomas 1946- *AmMWSc 92*
**Keller**, Jimmy Ray 1952- *WhoFI 92*
**Keller**, John Milton 1922- *WhoMW 92*
**Keller**, John Randall 1925- *AmMWSc 92*
**Keller**, John Walter 1937- *WhoMW 92*
**Keller**, Joseph *WhoAmP 91*
**Keller**, Joseph Bishop 1923- *AmMWSc 92, IntWW 91*
**Keller**, Joseph Edward, Jr 1936- *AmMWSc 92*
**Keller**, Joseph Herbert 1946- *AmMWSc 92*
**Keller**, Karen Anne 1953- *WhoEnt 92*
**Keller**, Kenneth Christen 1939- *WhoMW 92*
**Keller**, Kenneth F 1921- *AmMWSc 92*
**Keller**, Kenneth H 1934- *AmMWSc 92*
**Keller**, Kent Eugene 1941- *WhoWest 92*
**Keller**, Laura R *AmMWSc 92*
**Keller**, Laurie Joan 1958- *WhoMW 92*
**Keller**, Leland Edward 1923- *AmMWSc 92*
**Keller**, Lester Lee 1952- *WhoWest 92*
**Keller**, Madeleine *DrAPF 91*
**Keller**, Margaret Anne 1947- *AmMWSc 92*
**Keller**, Marion Wiles 1905- *AmMWSc 92*
**Keller**, Mark 1907- *IntAu&W 91*
**Keller**, Marthe 1945- *WhoEnt 92*
**Keller**, Marthe 1946- *IntMPA 92*
**Keller**, Martin David 1923- *AmMWSc 92*
**Keller**, Mary Barnett 1938- *WhoBlA 92*
**Keller**, Michael Crosley 1949- *WhoWest 92*
**Keller**, Millett Frederick 1915- *WhoAmP 91*
**Keller**, Myron Eugene 1923- *WhoAmP 91*
**Keller**, Oswald Lewin 1930- *AmMWSc 92*
**Keller**, Patricia J 1923- *AmMWSc 92*
**Keller**, Philip Charles 1939- *AmMWSc 92*
**Keller**, Philip Joseph 1941- *AmMWSc 92*
**Keller**, Raymond E 1945- *AmMWSc 92*
**Keller**, Reed Theodore 1938- *AmMWSc 92*
**Keller**, Rene Jacques 1914- *Who 92*
**Keller**, Richard Alan 1934- *AmMWSc 92*
**Keller**, Robert Alexander, III 1930- *WhoAmL 92*
**Keller**, Robert B 1924- *AmMWSc 92*
**Keller**, Robert Ellis 1923- *AmMWSc 92*
**Keller**, Robert H *AmMWSc 92*
**Keller**, Robert Lee 1945- *WhoWest 92*
**Keller**, Robert M. *WhoRel 92*
**Keller**, Robert Scott 1945- *WhoWest 92*
**Keller**, Ron L. 1936- *WhoRel 92*
**Keller**, Ronald E 1936- *WhoIns 92*
**Keller**, Ronald L 1937- *WhoAmP 91*
**Keller**, Roy Alan 1928- *AmMWSc 92*
**Keller**, Roy Fred 1927- *AmMWSc 92*
**Keller**, Rudolf 1933- *AmMWSc 92*
**Keller**, Rudolf Ernst 1920- *Who 92*
**Keller**, Seymour Paul 1922- *AmMWSc 92*
**Keller**, Shirley Irene 1938- *WhoAmP 91*
**Keller**, Stanley E 1921- *AmMWSc 92*
**Keller**, Stephen Jay 1940- *AmMWSc 92*
**Keller**, Susan Agnes 1952- *WhoFI 92, WhoWest 92*
**Keller**, Teddy Monroe 1944- *AmMWSc 92*
**Keller**, Thomas C S 1950- *AmMWSc 92*
**Keller**, Thomas Clements 1938- *WhoAmL 92*
**Keller**, Thomas Franklin 1931- *WhoFI 92*
**Keller**, Thomas Michael 1950- *WhoFI 92*
**Keller**, Thomas W 1949- *AmMWSc 92*
**Keller**, Vernon V 1926- *WhoAmP 91*
**Keller**, Waldo Frank 1929- *AmMWSc 92*
**Keller**, Walter Arthur 1954- *WhoRel 92*
**Keller**, Walter David 1900- *AmMWSc 92*
**Keller**, Walter Eric 1929- *WhoMW 92, WhoRel 92*
**Keller**, Wayne Allen 1964- *WhoAmL 92*
**Keller**, William D. 1934- *WhoAmL 92*
**Keller**, William Edward 1925- *AmMWSc 92*
**Keller**, William John 1920- *AmMWSc 92, WhoMW 92*
**Keller-Brinson**, Charlotte Jarvis 1913- *WhoBlA 92*
**Keller-Cohen**, Deborah 1948- *WhoMW 92*
**Kellerhals**, Glen E 1945- *AmMWSc 92*
**Kellerhouse**, Muriel Arline 1927- *WhoEnt 92*
**Kellerman**, Bert Joseph 1940- *WhoMW 92*
**Kellerman**, Edwin 1932- *WhoAmL 92*
**Kellerman**, Faye 1952- *WrDr 92*
**Kellerman**, Faye Marder 1952- *WhoWest 92*
**Kellerman**, Jonathan 1949- *IntAu&W 91, WrDr 92*
**Kellerman**, Karl F 1908- *AmMWSc 92*
**Kellerman**, Martin 1932- *AmMWSc 92*
**Kellerman**, Sally 1936- *IntMPA 92*
**Kellerman**, Sally Claire 1937- *WhoEnt 92*
**Kellerman**, William Ashbrook 1850-1908 *BiInAmS*
**Kellermann**, Bernhard 1879-1951 *ScFEYrs, TwCSFW 91A*
**Kellermann**, Kenneth Irwin 1937- *AmMWSc 92*
**Kellers**, Charles Frederick 1930- *AmMWSc 92*
**Kellerstrass**, Ernst Junior 1933- *AmMWSc 92*
**Kellert**, Carolyn Louise 1954- *WhoEnt 92, WhoMW 92*
**Kellett**, Alfred Henry 1904- *Who 92*
**Kellett**, Arnold 1926- *WrDr 92*
**Kellett**, Brian 1922- *Who 92*
**Kellett**, Brian Smith 1922- *IntWW 91*
**Kellett**, Claud Marvin 1928- *AmMWSc 92*
**Kellett**, E E 1864-1950 *ScFEYrs*
**Kellett**, Michelle 1950- *WhoWest 92*
**Kellett**, Stanley Charles 1940- *Who 92*
**Kellett-Bowman**, Edward Thomas 1931- *Who 92*
**Kellett-Bowman**, Elaine 1924- *Who 92*
**Kelley**, Albert J 1924- *AmMWSc 92*
**Kelley**, Albert Joseph 1924- *WhoFI 92*
**Kelley**, Alec Ervin 1923- *AmMWSc 92*
**Kelley**, Allen Frederick, Jr 1933- *AmMWSc 92*
**Kelley**, Arleon Leigh 1935- *WhoRel 92*
**Kelley**, Bruce Gunn 1954- *WhoIns 92*
**Kelley**, Carolyn Agnes 1958- *WhoRel 92*
**Kelley**, Catherine Bishop 1853-1944 *RelLAm 91*
**Kelley**, Charles Joseph 1943- *AmMWSc 92*
**Kelley**, Charles Thomas, Jr 1940- *AmMWSc 92*
**Kelley**, Charlotte Anne 1959- *WhoAmL 92*
**Kelley**, Chauncey Vernon 1913- *WhoEnt 92*
**Kelley**, Christine Ruth 1951- *WhoMW 92*
**Kelley**, Clarence M. 1911- *IntWW 91*
**Kelley**, Craig Douglas 1953- *WhoMW 92*
**Kelley**, Dale Russell 1939- *WhoAmP 91*
**Kelley**, Dana F 1920- *WhoAmP 91*
**Kelley**, Daniel, Jr. 1922- *WhoBlA 92*
**Kelley**, Darshan Singh 1947- *AmMWSc 92, WhoWest 92*
**Kelley**, David Charles 1957- *WhoEnt 92*
**Kelley**, David G 1928- *WhoAmP 91*
**Kelley**, David L 1949- *WhoAmP 91*
**Kelley**, Dean Maurice 1926- *WhoRel 92*
**Kelley**, DeForest 1920- *IntMPA 92*
**Kelley**, Delores G 1936- *WhoAmP 91, WhoBlA 92*
**Kelley**, Diana Lynn 1958- *WhoRel 92*
**Kelley**, Donald Clifford 1913- *AmMWSc 92*
**Kelley**, Donald E 1908- *WhoAmP 91*
**Kelley**, Donald Edmond 1943- *WhoFI 92*
**Kelley**, Donald Edmund, Jr. 1948- *WhoAmL 92*
**Kelley**, Douglas Eaton 1960- *WhoMW 92*
**Kelley**, Edgar Alan 1940- *WhoMW 92*
**Kelley**, Edgar Stillman 1857-1944 *NewAmDM*
**Kelley**, Edith Summers 1894-1956 *BenetAL 91*
**Kelley**, Edward Allen 1927- *WhoRel 92*
**Kelley**, Edward Watson, Jr. 1932- *WhoFI 92*
**Kelley**, Fenton Crosland 1926- *AmMWSc 92*
**Kelley**, Florence 1859-1932 *DcAmImH, HanAmWH, RComAH, WomSoc*
**Kelley**, Francis H. 1941- *WhoRel 92*
**Kelley**, Frank J 1924- *WhoAmP 91*
**Kelley**, Frank Joseph 1924- *WhoAmL 92, WhoMW 92*
**Kelley**, Frank Nicholas 1935- *AmMWSc 92*
**Kelley**, George G 1920- *AmMWSc 92*
**Kelley**, George Greene 1918- *AmMWSc 92*
**Kelley**, George W, Jr 1921- *AmMWSc 92*
**Kelley**, Glenn E *WhoAmP 91*
**Kelley**, Gordon Edward 1934- *WhoMW 92*
**Kelley**, Gregory M 1933- *AmMWSc 92*
**Kelley**, H. C. Ted 1931- *WhoRel 92*
**Kelley**, H. Lloyd, III 1940- *WhoMW 92*
**Kelley**, Harold H. 1921- *IntWW 91*
**Kelley**, Henry J 1926- *AmMWSc 92*
**Kelley**, Hoyt Frank 1923- *WhoAmP 91*
**Kelley**, Hubert 1899-1959 *ScFEYrs*
**Kelley**, Hubert & Barton, Fred T *ScFEYrs*
**Kelley**, Jack Albert 1920- *WhoBlA 92*
**Kelley**, Jack H 1932- *WhoIns 92*
**Kelley**, Jackson DeForest 1920- *WhoEnt 92*
**Kelley**, Jacquelyn Larson 1945- *WhoWest 92*
**Kelley**, Jacquie A *WhoAmP 91*
**Kelley**, James Charles 1940- *AmMWSc 92*
**Kelley**, James Durrett 1929- *AmMWSc 92*
**Kelley**, James Francis 1941- *WhoAmL 92*
**Kelley**, James Herald 1939- *WhoFI 92*
**Kelley**, James Kevin 1961- *WhoRel 92*
**Kelley**, James Leroy 1943- *AmMWSc 92*
**Kelley**, James Reeves *WhoAmP 91*

**Kelley,** James Russell 1948- *WhoAmL 92*
**Kelley,** Jason 1943- *AmMWSc 92*
**Kelley,** Jay Hilary 1920- *AmMWSc 92*
**Kelley,** Jim Lee 1947- *AmMWSc 92*
**Kelley,** Joan 1926- *Who 92*
**Kelley,** Joanna Elizabeth 1910- *Who 92*
**Kelley,** John Charles 1937- *WhoMW 92*
**Kelley,** John Daniel 1937- *AmMWSc 92, WhoFI 92*
**Kelley,** John Ernest 1919- *AmMWSc 92*
**Kelley,** John Francis, Jr 1920- *AmMWSc 92*
**Kelley,** John Fredric 1931- *AmMWSc 92*
**Kelley,** John Joseph, II 1933- *AmMWSc 92*
**Kelley,** John Le Roy 1916- *AmMWSc 92*
**Kelley,** John M 1926- *WhoAmP 91*
**Kelley,** John Michael 1948- *AmMWSc 92*
**Kelley,** John Patrick 1937- *WhoAmL 92*
**Kelley,** Joseph Douglas *WhoFI 92*
**Kelley,** Joseph Frank 1927- *WhoMW 92*
**Kelley,** Joseph Matthew 1929- *AmMWSc 92*
**Kelley,** Keith Wayne 1947- *AmMWSc 92*
**Kelley,** Kenneth William 1962- *WhoFI 92*
**Kelley,** Kevin Patrick 1954- *WhoWest 92*
**Kelley,** Larry Dean 1954- *WhoRel 92*
**Kelley,** Lee 1944- *WhoEnt 92*
**Kelley,** Leo P 1928- *IntAu&W 91, TwCSFW 91, TwCWW 91, WrDr 92*
**Kelley,** Leon A 1923- *AmMWSc 92*
**Kelley,** Leona A 1919- *WhoAmP 91*
**Kelley,** Lisa Stone 1947- *WhoWest 92*
**Kelley,** Louanna Elaine 1920- *WhoWest 92*
**Kelley,** Lyle Ardell 1944- *WhoFI 92*
**Kelley,** Mardene Sue Horst 1952- *WhoMW 92*
**Kelley,** Margaret Irene Williams 1954- *WhoWest 92*
**Kelley,** Mark Alan 1951- *WhoWest 92*
**Kelley,** Maurice Joseph 1916- *AmMWSc 92*
**Kelley,** Maurice Leslie, Jr 1924- *AmMWSc 92*
**Kelley,** Melodie Lynn 1956- *WhoMW 92*
**Kelley,** Michael C 1943- *AmMWSc 92*
**Kelley,** Michael J *AmMWSc 92*
**Kelley,** Michael James 1955- *WhoFI 92*
**Kelley,** Michael John 1942- *WhoMW 92*
**Kelley,** Myron Truman 1912- *AmMWSc 92*
**Kelley,** Neil Davis 1942- *AmMWSc 92*
**Kelley,** Niles Elmer 1916- *WhoWest 92*
**Kelley,** Pat 1967- *NewYTBS 91 [port]*
**Kelley,** Patricia Colleen 1953- *WhoFI 92*
**Kelley,** Patricia Hagelin 1953- *AmMWSc 92*
**Kelley,** Patrick *IntMPA 92*
**Kelley,** Patrick Michael 1948- *WhoAmP 91*
**Kelley,** Patrick Theodore 1958- *WhoEnt 92*
**Kelley,** Paul Leon 1934- *AmMWSc 92*
**Kelley,** Peck 1898-1980 *NewAmDM*
**Kelley,** Phillip Barry 1947- *WhoAmP 91*
**Kelley,** Ralph Byron 1934- *WhoAmL 92*
**Kelley,** Ralph Edward 1930- *AmMWSc 92*
**Kelley,** Randy Ervin 1952- *WhoMW 92*
**Kelley,** Ray *TwCWW 91*
**Kelley,** Raymond H 1922- *AmMWSc 92*
**Kelley,** Raymond John 1938- *WhoEnt 92*
**Kelley,** Richard *Who 92N*
**Kelley,** Richard Everett 1927- *WhoFI 92*
**Kelley,** Richard Roy 1933- *WhoWest 92*
**Kelley,** Robb Beardsley 1917- *WhoIns 92*
**Kelley,** Robert 1925- *WrDr 92*
**Kelley,** Robert Franklin 1961- *WhoFI 92, WhoWest 92*
**Kelley,** Robert Lee 1937- *AmMWSc 92*
**Kelley,** Robert N 1921- *WhoAmP 91*
**Kelley,** Robert Otis 1944- *AmMWSc 92, WhoWest 92*
**Kelley,** Robert Paul, Jr. 1942- *WhoWest 92*
**Kelley,** Robert W. *WhoRel 92*
**Kelley,** Robert W. 1940- *WhoBlA 92*
**Kelley,** Robert William 1913- *WhoBlA 92*
**Kelley,** Russell Victor 1934- *AmMWSc 92*
**Kelley,** Stanley Robert 1951- *WhoMW 92*
**Kelley,** Sylvia Johnson 1929- *WhoFI 92*
**Kelley,** Terry Wayne 1952- *WhoWest 92*
**Kelley,** Theresa Ann 1954- *WhoMW 92*
**Kelley,** Thomas F 1932- *AmMWSc 92*
**Kelley,** Thomas Joseph 1936- *WhoAmL 92*
**Kelley,** Thomas Neil 1929- *AmMWSc 92*
**Kelley,** Thomas Paul 1919- *WhoAmP 91*
**Kelley,** Timothy M 1947- *WhoAmP 91*
**Kelley,** Troy Xavier 1964- *WhoFI 92*
**Kelley,** Vicki E *AmMWSc 92*
**Kelley,** Vincent Charles 1916- *AmMWSc 92*
**Kelley,** Vincent Cooper 1904- *AmMWSc 92*
**Kelley,** Wallace Ryan 1950- *WhoEnt 92*
**Kelley,** Wilbourne Anderson, III *WhoBlA 92*
**Kelley,** William Douglas 1958- *WhoWest 92*
**Kelley,** William George 1959- *WhoRel 92*
**Kelley,** William Melvin *DrAPF 91*
**Kelley,** William Melvin 1937- *BenetAL 91, ConNov 91, WhoBlA 92, WrDr 92*
**Kelley,** William Nimmons 1939- *AmMWSc 92*
**Kelley,** William Robert 1956- *WhoMW 92*
**Kelley,** William Russell 1914- *AmMWSc 92*
**Kelley,** William S 1941- *AmMWSc 92*
**Kellgren,** Johan Henrik 1751-1795 *BlkwCEP*
**Kellgren,** John 1940- *AmMWSc 92*
**Kellgren,** Jonas Henrik 1911- *Who 92*
**Kellicott,** David Simons 1842-1898 *BiInAmS*
**Kellicott,** William Erskine 1878-1919 *BiInAmS*
**Kellie,** Gillian Lynne 1956- *WhoEnt 92*
**Kellie,** Luna Elizabeth Sanford 1857-1940 *HanAmWH*
**Kelliher,** Gerald James 1942- *AmMWSc 92*
**Kelliher,** Henry 1896- *Who 92*
**Kelling,** Bruce Dana 1957- *WhoWest 92*
**Kelling,** Clayton Lynn 1946- *AmMWSc 92*
**Kelling,** David Henry 1953- *WhoFI 92*
**Kelling,** Hans-Wilhelm 1932- *WrDr 92*
**Kellis,** Eugene F 1937- *WhoAmP 91*
**Kellis,** Michael John 1958- *WhoMW 92*
**Kellis,** Randal Anthony 1960- *WhoMW 92*
**Kellison,** Donna Louise George 1950- *WhoMW 92*
**Kellison,** Robert Clay 1931- *AmMWSc 92*
**Kellman,** Barnet Kramer 1947- *WhoEnt 92*
**Kellman,** Brian 1945- *WhoEnt 92*
**Kellman,** Denis Elliott 1948- *WhoBlA 92*
**Kellman,** Joseph 1920- *WhoMW 92*
**Kellman,** Mark Alec 1953- *WhoAmL 92*
**Kellman,** Raymond 1942- *AmMWSc 92*
**Kellman,** Simon 1934- *AmMWSc 92*
**Kellman,** Steven G 1947- *IntAu&W 91*
**Kellman,** Tony 1958- *IntAu&W 91*
**Kelln,** Elmer 1926- *AmMWSc 92*
**Kellner,** Aaron 1914- *AmMWSc 92*
**Kellner,** Bruce 1930- *WrDr 92*
**Kellner,** Carol Joan 1929- *WhoEnt 92*
**Kellner,** David Lee 1943- *WhoWest 92*
**Kellner,** Henry L 1905- *AmMWSc 92*
**Kellner,** Irwin L. 1938- *WhoFI 92*
**Kellner,** Jamie *WhoEnt 92*
**Kellner,** Jordan David 1938- *AmMWSc 92*
**Kellner,** Julie Smith 1961- *WhoEnt 92*
**Kellner,** Peter Lawrence 1943- *WhoFI 92*
**Kellner,** Robert Allen 1948- *WhoWest 92*
**Kellner,** Stephan Maria Eduard 1933- *AmMWSc 92*
**Kellock,** Andrew John 1958- *WhoWest 92*
**Kellock,** Jane Ursula 1925- *Who 92*
**Kellock,** Thomas Oslaf 1923- *Who 92*
**Kellogg,** Albert 1813-1887 *BiInAmS*
**Kellogg,** Brent Nelson 1951- *WhoWest 92*
**Kellogg,** C. Burton, II 1934- *WhoFI 92*
**Kellogg,** Charles Nathaniel 1938- *AmMWSc 92*
**Kellogg,** Charles Pezavia, Sr. 1927- *WhoRel 92*
**Kellogg,** Clara 1842-1916 *NewAmDM*
**Kellogg,** Clark 1961- *WhoBlA 92*
**Kellogg,** Craig Kent 1937- *AmMWSc 92*
**Kellogg,** David Larke 1958- *WhoWest 92*
**Kellogg,** David M. 1961- *WhoFI 92*
**Kellogg,** David Moulton, IV 1943- *WhoFI 92*
**Kellogg,** David Wayne 1941- *AmMWSc 92*
**Kellogg,** Dorothy M 1920- *WhoAmP 91*
**Kellogg,** Douglas Sheldon, Jr 1926- *AmMWSc 92*
**Kellogg,** Edward Samuel, III 1933- *WhoRel 92*
**Kellogg,** Edwin M 1939- *AmMWSc 92*
**Kellogg,** Elijah 1813-1901 *BenetAL 91*
**Kellogg,** Frank Billings 1856-1937 *AmPeW, AmPolLe [port], FacFETw, WhoNob 90*
**Kellogg,** Frederick 1929- *WhoWest 92*
**Kellogg,** Herbert H 1920- *AmMWSc 92*
**Kellogg,** Hilde *WhoAmP 91*
**Kellogg,** Jack Lorenzo 1933- *WhoFI 92*
**Kellogg,** James Crane 1939- *WhoAmL 92*
**Kellogg,** James Payson, Jr. 1953- *WhoWest 92*
**Kellogg,** Lillian Marie 1939- *AmMWSc 92*
**Kellogg,** Mark E. 1960- *WhoAmL 92*
**Kellogg,** Paul Jesse 1927- *AmMWSc 92*
**Kellogg,** Paul U 1879- *DcAmImH*
**Kellogg,** Paul Underwood 1879-1958 *AmPeW*
**Kellogg,** Peter R. 1942- *WhoFI 92*
**Kellogg,** Philip M. 1912- *IntMPA 92*
**Kellogg,** Ralph Henderson 1920- *AmMWSc 92*
**Kellogg,** Reginald J. 1933- *WhoBlA 92*
**Kellogg,** Richard Morrison 1939- *AmMWSc 92*
**Kellogg,** Robert LeRoy 1952- *WhoMW 92*
**Kellogg,** Royal Bruce 1930- *AmMWSc 92*
**Kellogg,** Spencer, II 1913- *AmMWSc 92*
**Kellogg,** Steven 1941- *IntAu&W 91, WrDr 92*
**Kellogg,** Thomas B 1942- *AmMWSc 92*
**Kellogg,** Thomas Floyd 1934- *AmMWSc 92*
**Kellogg,** Thomas L 1936- *WhoIns 92*
**Kellogg,** Tom N 1936- *WhoIns 92*
**Kellogg,** Will Keith 1860-1951 *FacFETw*
**Kellogg,** William Welch 1917- *AmMWSc 92*
**Kellor,** Frances A. 1873-1952 *WomSoc*
**Kellor,** Frances Alice 1873-1947 *DcAmImH*
**Kellor,** Frances Alice 1873-1952 *AmPeW*
**Kellou,** Mohamed 1931- *IntWW 91*
**Kellough,** Douglas Robert 1951- *WhoRel 92*
**Kellow,** Kathleen *IntAu&W 91X, Who 92, WrDr 92*
**Kellow,** Maurice Keith, Jr. 1946- *WhoFI 92*
**Kells,** Lyman Francis 1917- *AmMWSc 92*
**Kells,** Milton Carlisle 1920- *AmMWSc 92*
**Kells,** Phyllis Elaine 1932- *WhoMW 92*
**Kells,** Robert T *WhoAmP 91*
**Kellum,** Carmen Kaye 1952- *WhoFI 92*
**Kellum,** James Earl 1936- *WhoAmP 91*
**Kellum,** Norman Bryant, Jr. 1937- *WhoAmL 92*
**Kelly,** Alan *AmMWSc 92*
**Kelly,** Aloysius Oliver Joseph 1870-1911 *BiInAmS*
**Kelly,** Amy Schick 1940- *AmMWSc 92*
**Kelly,** Anne Catherine 1916- *WhoAmP 91*
**Kelly,** Anthony *Who 92*
**Kelly,** Anthony 1929- *IntWW 91*
**Kelly,** Arthur Lloyd 1937- *WhoFI 92, WhoMW 92*
**Kelly,** Asa, Jr 1922- *WhoAmP 91*
**Kelly,** B Wayne 1918- *AmMWSc 92*
**Kelly,** Barbara 1951- *TwCPaSc*
**Kelly,** Barbara Mary 1940- *Who 92*
**Kelly,** Basil *Who 92*
**Kelly,** Bernard V 1917- *WhoAmP 91*
**Kelly,** Billie Marion, Jr. 1959- *WhoRel 92*
**Kelly,** Brendan John 1962- *WhoMW 92*
**Kelly,** Brian *Who 92*
**Kelly,** Brian Andrew 1956- *WhoWest 92*
**Kelly,** Brian Matthew 1956- *WhoWest 92*
**Kelly,** Brian Roy 1964- *WhoMW 92*
**Kelly,** Brigit Pegeen *DrAPF 91*
**Kelly,** Cecilia Mary 1922- *WhoEnt 92*
**Kelly,** Charles Arthur 1932- *WhoAmL 92*
**Kelly,** Charles E 1920-1985 *FacFETw*
**Kelly,** Charles Eugene, II 1958- *WhoWest 92*
**Kelly,** Charles Henry 1930- *Who 92*
**Kelly,** Chris 1946- *WhoAmP 91*
**Kelly,** Christopher William 1946- *Who 92*
**Kelly,** Chuck H. 1930- *WhoEnt 92*
**Kelly,** Clark Andrew 1925- *AmMWSc 92*
**Kelly,** Conrad Michael 1944- *AmMWSc 92*
**Kelly,** Cynthia Anne 1954- *WhoAmP 91*
**Kelly,** Dan *WhoAmP 91*
**Kelly,** Dan, III 1938- *WhoAmP 91*
**Kelly,** Daniel Gordon 1964- *WhoMW 92*
**Kelly,** Daniel Grady, Jr. 1951- *WhoAmL 92*
**Kelly,** Daniel John 1940- *WhoMW 92*
**Kelly,** Dave *DrAPF 91*
**Kelly,** David A. 1938- *WhoBlA 92*
**Kelly,** David Francis 1940- *WhoRel 92*
**Kelly,** David Richard 1940- *WhoWest 92*
**Kelly,** David Stuart 1949- *WhoAmL 92*
**Kelly,** Deborah Anne 1962- *WhoAmL 92*
**Kelly,** DeeDee Helen 1941- *WhoAmP 91*
**Kelly,** Dennis D 1938- *AmMWSc 92*
**Kelly,** Dennis Joseph 1941- *WhoFI 92*
**Kelly,** Dennis Ray 1948- *WhoWest 92*
**Kelly,** Diana Helen 1955- *WhoAmL 92*
**Kelly,** Donald 1941- *WhoAmP 91*
**Kelly,** Donald C 1933- *AmMWSc 92*
**Kelly,** Donald Horton 1923- *AmMWSc 92*
**Kelly,** Donald P. 1922- *IntWW 91*
**Kelly,** Donald Philip 1922- *WhoFI 92, WhoMW 92*
**Kelly,** Donna C 1943- *WhoAmP 91*
**Kelly,** Dorothy Ann 1929- *WhoRel 92*
**Kelly,** Dorothy Helen 1944- *AmMWSc 92*
**Kelly,** Douglas *DcTwDes*
**Kelly,** Douglas Alexander 1952- *WhoFI 92*
**Kelly,** Douglas Elliott 1932- *AmMWSc 92*
**Kelly,** Dwight Michael 1953- *WhoEnt 92*
**Kelly,** E. J. 1947- *WhoAmL 92*
**Kelly,** Earl Lee 1956- *WhoBlA 92*
**Kelly,** Earl M *WhoAmP 91*
**Kelly,** Edgar Preston, Jr 1933- *AmMWSc 92*
**Kelly,** Edmund Joseph 1937- *WhoAmL 92*
**Kelly,** Edna Flannery 1906- *WhoAmP 91*
**Kelly,** Edward Joseph 1934- *AmMWSc 92*
**Kelly,** Edward Ronald 1928- *Who 92*
**Kelly,** Edward W 1935- *WhoAmP 91*
**Kelly,** Edwin Frost 1946- *WhoAmL 92*
**Kelly,** Edwin T. 1956- *WhoEnt 92*
**Kelly,** Eileen Patricia 1955- *WhoFI 92*
**Kelly,** Elizabeth Ann 1932- *WhoFI 92*
**Kelly,** Ellsworth 1923- *FacFETw, IntWW 91, News 92-1 [port]*
**Kelly,** Emmett 1898-1979 *FacFETw*
**Kelly,** Eric Damian 1947- *WhoAmL 92, WhoMW 92, WhoWest 92*
**Kelly,** Eric P. 1884-1960 *BenetAL 91*
**Kelly,** Ernest George, Jr. 1940- *WhoFI 92*
**Kelly,** Ernest L 1950- *AmMWSc 92*
**Kelly,** Eugene 1961- *WhoMW 92*
**Kelly,** Eugene Joseph 1949- *WhoEnt 92*
**Kelly,** Eugene Kevin 1943- *WhoMW 92*
**Kelly,** Everett A 1926- *WhoAmP 91*
**Kelly,** Felix 1917- *TwCPaSc*
**Kelly,** Florence Ann 1948- *WhoWest 92*
**Kelly,** Florida L. 1920- *WhoBlA 92*
**Kelly,** Floyd W, Jr 1941- *AmMWSc 92*
**Kelly,** Francis 1927- *TwCPaSc*
**Kelly,** Francis Joseph 1940- *AmMWSc 92*
**Kelly,** Francis Patrick 1950- *Who 92*
**Kelly,** Frank King 1914- *WhoWest 92*
**Kelly,** Frank Xavier, Jr. 1948- *WhoAmL 92*
**Kelly,** Gabrielle *IntMPA 92*
**Kelly,** Gail P. 1940-1991 *ConAu 133*
**Kelly,** Gail Paradise *IntWW 91*
**Kelly,** Gene 1912- *FacFETw, IntMPA 92, NewAmDM*
**Kelly,** Gene Curran 1912- *IntWW 91, WhoEnt 92*
**Kelly,** George 1887-1974 *BenetAL 91*
**Kelly,** George Anthony 1916- *WhoRel 92*
**Kelly,** George Eugene 1944- *AmMWSc 92*
**Kelly,** George Thomas 1941- *WhoWest 92*
**Kelly,** Gerald 1879-1972 *TwCPaSc*
**Kelly,** Gerald Oliver 1941- *WhoWest 92*
**Kelly,** Gerald Wayne 1944- *WhoFI 92*
**Kelly,** Grace *FacFETw*
**Kelly,** Graham *Who 92*
**Kelly,** Gregory 1954- *AmMWSc 92, WhoWest 92*
**Kelly,** Gregory M *AmMWSc 92*
**Kelly,** Gregory Maxwell 1930- *IntWW 91*
**Kelly,** Gretchen Lengel 1954- *WhoAmL 92*
**Kelly,** H. Andrew 1956- *WhoRel 92*
**Kelly,** Hannah 1937- *IntAu&W 91*
**Kelly,** Harley Lawrence 1937- *WhoFI 92*
**Kelly,** Harry Harbaugh 1947- *WhoFI 92*
**Kelly,** Henry Alexander 1946- *WhoAmL 92*
**Kelly,** Henry Charles 1945- *AmMWSc 92*
**Kelly,** Henry Curtis 1930- *AmMWSc 92*
**Kelly,** Herbert Brian 1921- *Who 92*
**Kelly,** Herman 1951- *WhoEnt 92*
**Kelly,** Hugh 1739-1777 *RfGEnL 91*
**Kelly,** Hugh P 1931- *AmMWSc 92*
**Kelly,** Hugh Rice 1942- *WhoAmL 92, WhoFI 92*
**Kelly,** Ida B. 1925- *WhoBlA 92*
**Kelly,** J. M. 1931-1991 *ConAu 133*
**Kelly,** J. Robert 1916- *WhoEnt 92*
**Kelly,** Jack 1927- *WhoAmP 91*
**Kelly,** Jack Arthur 1916- *WhoBlA 92*
**Kelly,** Jack Robert 1952- *WhoFI 92*
**Kelly,** James Anthony, Jr 1926- *WhoAmP 91*
**Kelly,** James Burton 1931- *WhoIns 92*
**Kelly,** James Clement 1928- *WhoBlA 92*
**Kelly,** James Johnson 1928- *WhoBlA 92*
**Kelly,** James L 1932- *AmMWSc 92*
**Kelly,** James McGirr *WhoAmL 92*
**Kelly,** James Michael 1947- *WhoAmL 92*
**Kelly,** James P. 1942- *WhoWest 92*
**Kelly,** James Patrick 1946- *WhoAmL 92*
**Kelly,** James Patrick 1951- *ConAu 135, TwCSFW 91*
**Kelly,** James Plunkett 1920- *IntAu&W 91*
**Kelly,** Janet Kimball 1964- *WhoRel 92*
**Kelly,** Jay Thomas 1950- *WhoMW 92*
**Kelly,** Jeff *SmATA 65*
**Kelly,** Jeffrey 1946- *SmATA 65*
**Kelly,** Jeffrey John 1942- *AmMWSc 92*
**Kelly,** Jeffrey Thomas 1960- *WhoMW 92*
**Kelly,** Jerome Bernard 1954- *WhoWest 92*
**Kelly,** Jerry Bob 1942- *WhoMW 92*
**Kelly,** Jim *IntMPA 92*
**Kelly,** Jim 1960- *News 91 [port]*
**Kelly,** John Barnes 1925- *WhoAmP 91*
**Kelly,** John Beckwith 1921- *AmMWSc 92*
**Kelly,** John C., Jr. 1936- *WhoMW 92*
**Kelly,** John F 1938- *WhoIns 92*
**Kelly,** John F 1939- *WhoAmP 91*
**Kelly,** John Francis 1931- *AmMWSc 92*
**Kelly,** John Francis 1949- *WhoAmL 92, WhoAmP 91, WhoMW 92*
**Kelly,** John G 1927- *WhoIns 92*
**Kelly,** John Henry 1952- *AmMWSc 92*
**Kelly,** John Howard 1948- *WhoWest 92*
**Kelly,** John Hubert 1939- *IntWW 91*
**Kelly,** John Joseph 1918- *WhoAmL 92*
**Kelly,** John Love 1924- *WhoFI 92*
**Kelly,** John Norman Davidson 1909- *IntWW 91, Who 92*
**Kelly,** John Patrick 1933- *WhoAmL 92*
**Kelly,** John Patrick 1952- *WhoAmL 92*
**Kelly,** John Paul, Jr. 1941- *WhoBlA 92*
**Kelly,** John Russell 1947- *WhoBlA 92*
**Kelly,** John Russell 1952- *AmMWSc 92*
**Kelly,** John Thomas 1925- *WhoAmL 92*
**Kelly,** John V 1926- *AmMWSc 92*
**Kelly,** John Vincent 1926- *WhoAmP 91*
**Kelly,** John William Basil 1920- *Who 92*
**Kelly,** Jonathan Falconbridge 1817-1855? *BenetAL 91*
**Kelly,** Jonie Lou 1930- *WhoEnt 92*

**Kelly,** Joseph Francis 1945- *WhoRel 92*
**Kelly,** Joseph J. *DrAPF 91*
**Kelly,** Joseph R. 1943- *WhoRel 92*
**Kelly,** Joseph Winston 1964- *WhoBlA 92*
**Kelly,** Josephine Kaye 1944- *WhoMW 92*
**Kelly,** Kathleen J. 1958- *WhoWest 92*
**Kelly,** Kenneth C 1928- *AmMWSc 92*
**Kelly,** Kenneth Harold 1953- *WhoFI 92*
**Kelly,** Kenneth William *AmMWSc 92*
**Kelly,** Kenneth William 1953- *WhoRel 92*
**Kelly,** Kevin 1953- *WhoAmP 91*
**Kelly,** Kevin Anthony 1945- *AmMWSc 92*
**Kelly,** Kevin James 1957- *WhoMW 92*
**Kelly,** Kevin John 1967- *WhoEnt 92*
**Kelly,** Kevin Richard 1949- *WhoWest 92*
**Kelly,** Kevin Thomas 1960- *WhoEnt 92*
**Kelly,** Laurence Charles Kevin 1933- *Who 92*
**Kelly,** Lawrence James, Sr 1935- *WhoAmP 91*
**Kelly,** Leontine 1920- *NotBlAW 92 [port]*
**Kelly,** Leontine T. C. *WhoBlA 92, WhoRel 92, WhoWest 92*
**Kelly,** Leroy Milton 1914- *AmMWSc 92*
**Kelly,** Linda 1936- *WrDr 92*
**Kelly,** Louis Gerard 1935- *WrDr 92*
**Kelly,** M T *IntAu&W 91*
**Kelly,** Mahlon George, Jr 1939- *AmMWSc 92*
**Kelly,** Margaret Blake 1935- *WhoAmP 91*
**Kelly,** Margaret Boyer 1929- *WhoAmP 91*
**Kelly,** Marie-Noele 1907- *WrDr 92*
**Kelly,** Marion Greenup 1947- *WhoBlA 92*
**Kelly,** Martin Joseph 1924- *AmMWSc 92*
**Kelly,** Mary 1927- *WrDr 92*
**Kelly,** Mary 1941- *TwCPaSc*
**Kelly,** Mary Elin 1949- *WhoWest 92*
**Kelly,** Mathew S. 1959- *WhoWest 92*
**Kelly,** Maureen Ann 1965- *WhoFI 92, WhoWest 92*
**Kelly,** Maureen H. *WhoEnt 92*
**Kelly,** Maurice 1919- *WrDr 92*
**Kelly,** Michael 1762-1826 *NewAmDM*
**Kelly,** Michael 1940- *Who 92*
**Kelly,** Michael 1948- *WhoAmP 91*
**Kelly,** Michael Alan 1943- *WhoWest 92*
**Kelly,** Michael David 1938- *AmMWSc 92*
**Kelly,** Michael Frederick 1951- *WhoAmL 92*
**Kelly,** Michael John 1937- *WhoAmL 92*
**Kelly,** Michael Kevin 1950- *WhoEnt 92*
**Kelly,** Michael P. 1951- *WhoMW 92*
**Kelly,** Michael Thomas 1943- *AmMWSc 92*
**Kelly,** Mick 1949- *TwCPaSc*
**Kelly,** Milton Leo 1935- *WhoBlA 92*
**Kelly,** Minton J 1921- *AmMWSc 92*
**Kelly,** Myra 1876-1910 *DcAmImH*
**Kelly,** Myra 1887-1910 *BenetAL 91*
**Kelly,** Nancy 1921- *IntMPA 92*
**Kelly,** Nelson Allen 1951- *AmMWSc 92*
**Kelly,** Nora Hickson 1910- *WrDr 92*
**Kelly,** Norman 1920- *WhoEnt 92*
**Kelly,** Orris Eugene 1926- *WhoRel 92*
**Kelly,** Owen 1932- *Who 92*
**Kelly,** Pat 1967- *NewYTBS 91 [port]*
**Kelly,** Patricia 1932- *WhoAmP 91*
**Kelly,** Patricia Jean 1946- *WhoEnt 92*
**Kelly,** Patrick *ConAu 34NR*
**Kelly,** Patrick 1949?-1990 *AnObit 1990*
**Kelly,** Patrick 1954-1990 *WhoBlA 92N*
**Kelly,** Patrick A. *Who 92*
**Kelly,** Patrick Altham 1938- *IntWW 91*
**Kelly,** Patrick Daniel 1952- *WhoAmL 92*
**Kelly,** Patrick F. 1929- *WhoAmL 92*
**Kelly,** Patrick Joseph 1926- *AmMWSc 92*
**Kelly,** Paul Alan 1943- *AmMWSc 92*
**Kelly,** Paul Hamilton 1937- *WhoWest 92*
**Kelly,** Paul J 1916- *AmMWSc 92*
**Kelly,** Paul James 1934- *AmMWSc 92*
**Kelly,** Paul Joseph, Jr. 1940- *WhoAmL 92*
**Kelly,** Paul Knox 1940- *WhoFI 92*
**Kelly,** Paul S 1939- *WhoAmP 91*
**Kelly,** Paul Sherwood 1927- *AmMWSc 92*
**Kelly,** Paul Thomas 1936- *WhoFI 92*
**Kelly,** Peter 1922- *Who 92*
**Kelly,** Peter Dillon 1948- *WhoAmP 91*
**Kelly,** Peter Galbraith 1937- *WhoAmP 91*
**Kelly,** Peter Michael 1922- *AmMWSc 92*
**Kelly,** Petra K 1947- *IntAu&W 91*
**Kelly,** Petra Karin 1947- *IntWW 91*
**Kelly,** Philip Charles 1948- *Who 92*
**Kelly,** Philip John 1946- *Who 92*
**Kelly,** Phyllis Matheis 1921- *WhoAmP 91*
**Kelly,** Randy C 1950- *WhoAmP 91*
**Kelly,** Raymond Case 1942- *WhoMW 92*
**Kelly,** Raymond Crain 1945- *AmMWSc 92*
**Kelly,** Raymond John, Jr. 1920- *WhoFI 92*
**Kelly,** Raymond Leroy 1921- *AmMWSc 92*
**Kelly,** Raymond M 1939- *WhoIns 92*
**Kelly,** Rebecca Noel 1959- *WhoFI 92*
**Kelly,** Regina Fogel 1943- *WhoAmL 92*
**Kelly,** Regis Baker 1940- *AmMWSc 92*
**Kelly,** Richard *DrAPF 91*
**Kelly,** Richard 1937- *ConAu 34NR, WrDr 92*
**Kelly,** Richard Delmer 1935- *AmMWSc 92*
**Kelly,** Richard F, Jr 1936- *WhoAmP 91*
**Kelly,** Richard Leo 1938- *WhoIns 92*
**Kelly,** Richard Smith 1925- *WhoAmL 92*
**Kelly,** Richard W 1935- *AmMWSc 92*
**Kelly,** Rita Kay 1951- *WhoEnt 92*
**Kelly,** Robert *DrAPF 91*
**Kelly,** Robert 1935- *ConPo 91, IntAu&W 91, WrDr 92*
**Kelly,** Robert Charles 1939- *AmMWSc 92*
**Kelly,** Robert Edward 1934- *AmMWSc 92*
**Kelly,** Robert Emmett 1929- *AmMWSc 92*
**Kelly,** Robert F. 1935- *WhoAmL 92*
**Kelly,** Robert Frank 1919- *AmMWSc 92*
**Kelly,** Robert Henry Graham 1945- *Who 92*
**Kelly,** Robert James 1923- *AmMWSc 92*
**Kelly,** Robert Lynn 1939- *WhoFI 92*
**Kelly,** Robert P 1938- *AmMWSc 92*
**Kelly,** Robert Snowden 1932- *WhoMW 92, WhoRel 92*
**Kelly,** Robert Talbot 1861-1935 *TwCPaSc*
**Kelly,** Robert Vincent, III 1962- *WhoFI 92*
**Kelly,** Robert Vincent, Jr. 1938- *WhoFI 92, WhoMW 92*
**Kelly,** Robert Withers 1926- *AmMWSc 92*
**Kelly,** Roberto Conrado 1964- *WhoBlA 92, WhoHisp 92*
**Kelly,** Ronald Burger 1920- *AmMWSc 92*
**Kelly,** Ronald David 1943- *WhoRel 92*
**Kelly,** Ros 1948- *IntWW 91*
**Kelly,** Rosaline 1922- *Who 92*
**Kelly,** Ruben David 1927- *WhoWest 92*
**Kelly,** Sally Marie *AmMWSc 92*
**Kelly,** Sam, Jr 1926- *WhoAmP 91*
**Kelly,** Sharon Marie 1950- *WhoAmL 92*
**Kelly,** Shaun P *WhoAmP 91*
**Kelly,** Stephanie Anita 1961- *WhoEnt 92*
**Kelly,** Susan Jean 1947- *AmMWSc 92*
**Kelly,** Sylvia *DrAPF 91*
**Kelly,** Thaddeus Elliott 1937- *AmMWSc 92*
**Kelly,** Theo 1907- *IntWW 91, Who 92*
**Kelly,** Thomas 1909- *WrDr 92*
**Kelly,** Thomas, Jr. 1951- *WhoBlA 92*
**Kelly,** Thomas Alan 1953- *WhoMW 92*
**Kelly,** Thomas Brooke 1943- *WhoFI 92*
**Kelly,** Thomas Cajetan 1931- *WhoRel 92*
**Kelly,** Thomas H 1942- *WhoIns 92*
**Kelly,** Thomas J 1941- *AmMWSc 92*
**Kelly,** Thomas Joseph 1929- *AmMWSc 92*
**Kelly,** Thomas Joseph 1956- *WhoFI 92*
**Kelly,** Thomas Lloyd, II 1958- *WhoFI 92*
**Kelly,** Thomas Maurice, III 1950- *WhoBlA 92*
**Kelly,** Thomas Michael 1941- *AmMWSc 92*
**Kelly,** Thomas Michael 1958- *WhoFI 92*
**Kelly,** Thomas Paine, Jr. 1912- *WhoAmL 92*
**Kelly,** Thomas Philip, Jr. 1936- *WhoAmL 92*
**Kelly,** Thomas Raymond 1893-1941 *RelLAm 91*
**Kelly,** Thomas Ross 1942- *AmMWSc 92*
**Kelly,** Tim 1937- *IntAu&W 91, WhoEnt 92, WrDr 92*
**Kelly,** Tim 1944- *WhoAmP 91*
**Kelly,** Timothy Michael 1947- *ConAu 133*
**Kelly,** Tish *WhoAmP 91*
**Kelly,** Tom 1950- *WhoMW 92*
**Kelly,** Verna Margaret 1940- *WhoAmP 91*
**Kelly,** Viana Eileen 1953- *WhoMW 92*
**Kelly,** Walt 1913-1973 *BenetAL 91*
**Kelly,** Walter James 1941- *AmMWSc 92*
**Kelly,** Wanda Sue 1948- *WhoAmL 92*
**Kelly,** William Albert 1927- *AmMWSc 92*
**Kelly,** William Alva 1937- *AmMWSc 92*
**Kelly,** William Bret 1922- *WhoWest 92*
**Kelly,** William Cary 1919- *AmMWSc 92*
**Kelly,** William Charles, Jr. 1946- *WhoAmL 92*
**Kelly,** William Clark 1922- *AmMWSc 92*
**Kelly,** William Cody 1922- *WhoFI 92*
**Kelly,** William Crowley 1929- *AmMWSc 92*
**Kelly,** William Daniel 1922- *AmMWSc 92*
**Kelly,** William Franklin, Jr. 1938- *WhoAmL 92*
**Kelly,** William Garrett 1947- *WhoAmL 92*
**Kelly,** William H 1926- *AmMWSc 92*
**Kelly,** William John, Sr. 1942- *WhoFI 92*
**Kelly,** William Robert 1944- *AmMWSc 92*
**Kelly,** William Theodore *Who 92*
**Kelly,** William Thomas 1919- *WhoAmP 91*
**Kelly,** Winfield M, Jr 1935- *WhoAmP 91*
**Kelly,** Wynton 1931-1971 *NewAmDM*
**Kelly-Fry,** Elizabeth *AmMWSc 92*
**Kelm,** Bonnie G. 1947- *WhoMW 92*
**Kelm,** Linda 1944- *WhoEnt 92*
**Kelm,** Thomas Arthur 1930- *WhoAmP 91*
**Kelman,** Arthur 1918- *AmMWSc 92, IntWW 91*
**Kelman,** Bruce Jerry 1947- *AmMWSc 92, WhoWest 92*
**Kelman,** Bryan Nivison 1925- *IntWW 91*
**Kelman,** Charles 1930- *IntWW 91*
**Kelman,** Donald Brian 1942- *WhoMW 92*
**Kelman,** Edward Michael 1943- *WhoEnt 92*
**Kelman,** Herbert Chanoch 1927- *WrDr 92*
**Kelman,** James 1946- *ConNov 91*
**Kelman,** L R 1919- *AmMWSc 92*
**Kelman,** Mark Gregory 1951- *WhoAmL 92*
**Kelman,** Robert Bernard 1930- *AmMWSc 92*
**Kelman,** Stuart Laurance 1942- *WhoRel 92*
**Kelman,** Wolfe 1923-1990 *AnObit 1990*
**Kelmar,** Steven B 1953- *WhoAmP 91*
**Kelmenson,** Leo-Arthur 1927- *WhoFI 92*
**Kelmers,** Andrew Donald 1929- *AmMWSc 92*
**Kelner,** Albert 1912- *AmMWSc 92*
**Kelnhofer,** William Joseph 1930- *AmMWSc 92*
**Kelpe,** Paul Robert 1948- *WhoMW 92*
**Kelpius,** Johannes 1673-1708 *NewAmDM*
**Kelsall,** William 1914- *Who 92*
**Kelsay,** June Lavelle 1925- *AmMWSc 92*
**Kelsch,** RaeAnn *WhoAmP 91*
**Kelsen,** Hans 1881-1973 *AmPeW, EncTR 91*
**Kelsen,** Keith Franklin 1958- *WhoEnt 92*
**Kelsey,** Charles Andrew 1935- *AmMWSc 92*
**Kelsey,** Edith Jeanine 1937- *WhoWest 92*
**Kelsey,** Edward Joseph 1948- *AmMWSc 92*
**Kelsey,** Eugene Lloyd 1932- *AmMWSc 92*
**Kelsey,** Frances Oldham 1914- *AmMWSc 92*
**Kelsey,** Gary Matthew 1954- *WhoBlA 92*
**Kelsey,** George Dennis Sale 1910- *WhoBlA 92*
**Kelsey,** Jennifer Louise 1942- *AmMWSc 92*
**Kelsey,** John 1920- *Who 92*
**Kelsey,** John Edward 1942- *AmMWSc 92*
**Kelsey,** John T 1921- *WhoAmP 91*
**Kelsey,** John Walter 1910- *WhoAmL 92*
**Kelsey,** Julian George 1922- *Who 92*
**Kelsey,** Lewis Preston 1914- *AmMWSc 92*
**Kelsey,** Linda 1946- *IntMPA 92*
**Kelsey,** Morris Irwin 1939- *AmMWSc 92*
**Kelsey,** Morton T. 1917- *WrDr 92*
**Kelsey,** Morton Trippe 1917- *IntAu&W 91*
**Kelsey,** Rick Guy 1948- *AmMWSc 92*
**Kelsey,** Ronald A 1923- *AmMWSc 92*
**Kelsey,** Ruben Clifford 1923- *AmMWSc 92*
**Kelsey,** Samuel 1906- *RelLAm 91*
**Kelsey,** Stephen Jorgensen 1940- *AmMWSc 92*
**Kelsh,** Dennis J 1936- *AmMWSc 92*
**Kelsh,** Jerome G 1940- *WhoAmP 91*
**Kelshaw,** Terence 1936- *WhoWest 92*
**Kelsick,** Osmund Randolph 1922- *Who 92*
**Kelso** 1957-1983 *FacFETw*
**Kelso,** Albert Frederick 1917- *AmMWSc 92*
**Kelso,** Alec John 1930- *AmMWSc 92*
**Kelso,** Becky 1948- *WhoAmP 91*
**Kelso,** Chuck *TwCWW 91*
**Kelso,** Donald Preston 1940- *AmMWSc 92*
**Kelso,** Edward Albert 1914- *AmMWSc 92*
**Kelso,** Gwendolyn Lee 1935- *WhoFI 92*
**Kelso,** John Clark 1959- *WhoAmL 92*
**Kelso,** John Morris 1922- *AmMWSc 92*
**Kelso,** John Richard Murray 1945- *AmMWSc 92*
**Kelso,** Louis O. 1913-1991 *ConAu 133*
**Kelso,** Louis Orth 1913-1991 *NewYTBS 91*
**Kelso,** Richard Miles 1937- *AmMWSc 92*
**Kelso,** Terry Alan 1948- *WhoMW 92*
**Kelson,** Irwin S 1932- *WhoIns 92*
**Kelston,** David Leo 1944- *WhoAmL 92*
**Keltch,** Peter Michael 1947- *WhoAmP 91*
**Kelterborn,** Rudolf 1931- *ConCom 92, NewAmDM*
**Keltie,** Richard Francis 1951- *AmMWSc 92*
**Kelting,** Ralph Walter 1918- *AmMWSc 92*
**Keltner,** Gary Grayson 1936- *WhoAmL 92*
**Keltner,** Ken d1991 *NewYTBS 91 [port]*
**Kelton,** Arthur Marvin, Jr. 1939- *WhoWest 92*
**Kelton,** Diane Elizabeth 1924- *AmMWSc 92*
**Kelton,** Elmer 1926- *ConAu 36NR, TwCWW 91, WrDr 92*
**Kelton,** Elmer Stephen 1926- *IntAu&W 91*
**Kelton,** Frank Caleb 1915- *AmMWSc 92*
**Kelton,** William A 1939- *WhoIns 92*
**Kelts,** Larry Jim 1937- *AmMWSc 92*
**Kelty,** Miriam C 1938- *AmMWSc 92*
**Kelvington,** Wilbur Lee 1929- *WhoMW 92*
**Kelway,** George Trevor d1990 *Who 92N*
**Kemal,** Yashar 1923- *IntAu&W 91, IntWW 91*
**Kemball,** Charles 1923- *IntWW 91, Who 92*
**Kemball,** Humphrey Gurdon 1919- *Who 92*
**Kemball,** John 1939- *Who 92*
**Kemball-Cook,** Brian Hartley 1912- *Who 92*
**Kember,** Anthony Joseph 1931- *Who 92*
**Kember,** Harry, Jr 1934- *WhoAmP 91*
**Kember,** William Percy 1932- *Who 92*
**Kemble,** Edward Windsor 1861-1933 *BenetAL 91*
**Kemble,** Ernest Dell 1935- *WhoMW 92*
**Kemble,** Fanny 1809-1893 *BenetAL 91, HanAmWH*
**Kemelhor,** Robert Elias 1919- *AmMWSc 92*
**Kemelman,** Harry 1908- *IntAu&W 91, WrDr 92*
**Kemeny,** Gabor 1933- *AmMWSc 92*
**Kemeny,** John *IntMPA 92*
**Kemeny,** John G. 1926- *IntWW 91, WrDr 92*
**Kemeny,** Lorant 1913- *AmMWSc 92*
**Kemeny,** Nancy E 1945- *AmMWSc 92*
**Kemic,** Stephen Bruce 1946- *AmMWSc 92*
**Kemler,** Katherine Penelope 1951- *WhoEnt 92*
**Kemmer,** Nicholas 1911- *IntWW 91, Who 92*
**Kemmerer,** Arthur Russell *AmMWSc 92*
**Kemmerer,** Peter Ream 1942- *WhoFI 92*
**Kemmerly,** Jack E 1924- *AmMWSc 92*
**Kemmeter,** Mark C. 1949- *WhoRel 92*
**Kemmett,** William *DrAPF 91*
**Kemmler,** Bradford Monte 1949- *WhoEnt 92*
**Kemnitz,** Joseph William 1947- *AmMWSc 92*
**Kemnitz,** Ralph Allen 1942- *WhoAmP 91*
**Kemoularia,** Claude de 1922- *IntWW 91*
**Kemp** *Who 92*
**Kemp,** Alson Remington, Jr. 1941- *WhoAmL 92*
**Kemp,** Arne K 1918- *AmMWSc 92*
**Kemp,** Arnold 1939- *Who 92*
**Kemp,** Arthur Derek 1959- *WhoMW 92*
**Kemp,** Athole Stephen Horsford 1917- *Who 92*
**Kemp,** Barrett George 1932- *WhoAmL 92*
**Kemp,** Barry *LesBEnT 92*
**Kemp,** Barry Michael 1949- *WhoEnt 92*
**Kemp,** Betty 1916- *WrDr 92*
**Kemp,** C. Robert 1934- *WhoBlA 92*
**Kemp,** Cuthbert Francis 1913- *Who 92*
**Kemp,** Daniel Schaeffer 1936- *AmMWSc 92*
**Kemp,** David 1945- *TwCPaSc*
**Kemp,** David Ashton McIntyre 1921- *Who 92*
**Kemp,** David Westley 1958- *WhoWest 92*
**Kemp,** Diane Legge 1949- *WhoMW 92*
**Kemp,** Edward Peter 1934- *Who 92*
**Kemp,** Emmerlyne Jane 1935- *WhoBlA 92*
**Kemp,** Emory Leland 1931- *AmMWSc 92*
**Kemp,** Eric Waldram *Who 92*
**Kemp,** Eric Waldram 1915- *IntWW 91*
**Kemp,** Gene 1926- *IntAu&W 91, WrDr 92*
**Kemp,** George John 1921- *Who 92*
**Kemp,** Gordon Arthur 1932- *AmMWSc 92*
**Kemp,** Graham Elmore 1927- *AmMWSc 92*
**Kemp,** Harold Steen 1917- *AmMWSc 92*
**Kemp,** Harry 1883-1960 *BenetAL 91*
**Kemp,** Harry Vincent 1911- *IntAu&W 91*
**Kemp,** Hubert Bond Stafford 1925- *Who 92*
**Kemp,** Ira Howard 1955- *WhoEnt 92*
**Kemp,** Jack F. 1935- *IntWW 91, WhoAmP 91*
**Kemp,** Jack French 1935- *AmPolLe*
**Kemp,** James Chalmers 1927- *AmMWSc 92*
**Kemp,** James Dillon 1923- *AmMWSc 92*
**Kemp,** James Hal 1904-1940 *DcNCBi 3*
**Kemp,** James Walker 1955- *WhoRel 92*
**Kemp,** Jeanne Frances 1942- *WhoWest 92*
**Kemp,** Jeremy 1935- *IntMPA 92*
**Kemp,** John 1763-1812 *BiInAmS*
**Kemp,** John Daniel 1940- *AmMWSc 92*
**Kemp,** John Wilmer 1920- *AmMWSc 92*
**Kemp,** Kathleen Nagy 1949- *WhoAmL 92*
**Kemp,** Kenneth Courtney 1925- *AmMWSc 92*
**Kemp,** Kenneth E 1941- *AmMWSc 92*
**Kemp,** Kenneth Oliver 1926- *Who 92*
**Kemp,** Kenneth Reginald 1921- *Who 92*
**Kemp,** L C, Jr 1907- *AmMWSc 92*
**Kemp,** Leslie Charles 1920- *Who 92*
**Kemp,** Louis Franklin, Jr 1940- *AmMWSc 92*
**Kemp,** Martin 1942- *WrDr 92*
**Kemp,** Martin John 1942- *IntAu&W 91, IntWW 91, Who 92*
**Kemp,** Marwin K 1942- *AmMWSc 92*
**Kemp,** Nancy Pribanich 1949- *WhoWest 92*
**Kemp,** Nelson Harvey 1927- *AmMWSc 92*
**Kemp,** Norman Everett 1916- *AmMWSc 92, WhoMW 92*
**Kemp,** Oliver 1916- *Who 92*
**Kemp,** Patricia Ann 1932- *WhoMW 92*
**Kemp,** Patrick Samuel 1932- *WhoWest 92*
**Kemp,** Paul James 1942- *AmMWSc 92, WhoWest 92*
**Kemp,** Paul Raymond 1949- *AmMWSc 92*
**Kemp,** Penny 1944- *WrDr 92*
**Kemp,** Peter *Who 92*
**Kemp,** Peter 1942- *WrDr 92*

**Kemp,** Peter Kemp 1904- *Who 92*
**Kemp,** Peter Warren 1948- *WhoEnt 92*
**Kemp,** Ralph Gene, Jr. 1944- *WhoFI 92*
**Kemp,** Ramey Floyd, Sr 1919- *WhoAmP 91*
**Kemp,** Robert Grant 1937- *AmMWSc 92*
**Kemp,** Robert Thayer 1928- *Who 92*
**Kemp,** Sally Rush 1933- *WhoEnt 92*
**Kemp,** Shawn T. 1969- *WhoBlA 92*
**Kemp,** Stephen James 1962- *WhoRel 92*
**Kemp,** Thomas Arthur 1915- *Who 92*
**Kemp,** Thomas Dupre, Jr. 1903- *WhoEnt 92*
**Kemp,** Walter Michael 1944- *AmMWSc 92*
**Kemp,** William Michael 1947- *AmMWSc 92*
**Kemp-Welch,** Joan 1906- *IntMPA 92*
**Kemp-Welch,** John 1936- *Who 92*
**Kemp-Welch,** Lucy 1869-1958 *TwCPaSc*
**Kemp-Williams,** Margaret Estelean 1948- *WhoAmL 92*
**Kempe,** John William Rolfe 1917- *Who 92*
**Kempe,** Kathleen G 1953- *WhoAmP 91*
**Kempe,** Lloyd L 1911- *AmMWSc 92*
**Kempe,** Ludwig George 1915- *AmMWSc 92*
**Kempe,** Margery *RfGEnL 91*
**Kempe,** Robert Aron 1922- *WhoFI 92*
**Kempe,** Rudolf 1910-1976 *FacFETw, NewAmDM*
**Kempen,** Rene Richard 1928- *AmMWSc 92*
**Kemper,** Casey Randolph 1947- *WhoFI 92*
**Kemper,** David Scott 1956- *WhoRel 92*
**Kemper,** David Woods, II 1950- *WhoFI 92*
**Kemper,** Gene Allen 1933- *AmMWSc 92*
**Kemper,** James Dee 1947- *WhoAmL 92*
**Kemper,** James Madison, Jr. 1921- *WhoFI 92*
**Kemper,** John D 1924- *AmMWSc 92*
**Kemper,** Kathleen Ann 1966- *AmMWSc 92*
**Kemper,** Kirby Wayne 1940- *AmMWSc 92*
**Kemper,** Lee H 1921- *WhoIns 92*
**Kemper,** Robert Schooley, Jr 1927- *AmMWSc 92*
**Kemper,** Troxey *DrAPF 91*
**Kemper,** Troxey 1915- *IntAu&W 91*
**Kemper,** Victor J. 1927- *IntMPA 92*
**Kemper,** Victor Jay 1927- *WhoEnt 92*
**Kemper,** William Alexander 1911- *AmMWSc 92*
**Kemperman,** Johannes Henricus Bernardus 1924- *AmMWSc 92*
**Kempf,** Donald G., Jr. 1937- *WhoAmL 92, WhoMW 92*
**Kempf,** Jane Elmira 1927- *WhoMW 92*
**Kempf,** Martine 1958- *WhoFI 92, WhoWest 92*
**Kempff,** Wilhelm 1895- *NewAmDM*
**Kempff,** Wilhelm 1895-1991 *NewYTBS 91*
**Kempff,** Wilhelm Walter Friedrich d1991 *Who 92N*
**Kemph,** John Patterson 1919- *AmMWSc 92*
**Kemphues,** Kenneth J 1950- *AmMWSc 92*
**Kempiners,** William Lee 1942- *WhoAmP 91*
**Kempinski,** Tom 1938- *WrDr 92*
**Kemple,** Marvin David 1942- *AmMWSc 92*
**Kempler,** Walter 1923- *AmMWSc 92*
**Kempley,** Rita A. 1945- *WhoEnt 92*
**Kempner,** David H *AmMWSc 92*
**Kempner,** Ellis Stanley 1932- *AmMWSc 92*
**Kempner,** Isaac Herbert, III 1932- *WhoFI 92*
**Kempner,** James Carroll 1939- *WhoFI 92*
**Kempner,** Joseph 1923- *AmMWSc 92*
**Kempner,** Maximilian Walter 1929- *WhoAmL 92*
**Kempner,** Robert M.W. 1899- *EncTR 91 [port]*
**Kempner,** Robert Max Wasilii 1899- *WhoAmL 92*
**Kempner,** Thomas 1930- *Who 92*
**Kempner,** Walter 1903- *AmMWSc 92*
**Kempny,** Josef 1920- *IntWW 91*
**Kempsell,** Jake 1940- *TwCPaSc*
**Kempski,** Ralph Aloisius 1934- *WhoRel 92*
**Kempson,** Rachel 1910- *Who 92*
**Kempson,** Ruth Margaret 1944- *Who 92*
**Kempson,** Stephen Allan 1948- *AmMWSc 92*
**Kempster,** Michael Edmund Ivor 1923- *Who 92*
**Kempter,** Charles Prentiss 1925- *AmMWSc 92*
**Kempthorne,** Dirk 1951- *WhoAmP 91*
**Kempthorne,** Dirk Arthur 1951- *WhoWest 92*
**Kempthorne,** Oscar 1919- *AmMWSc 92, WhoMW 92*
**Kempton,** Greta d1991 *NewYTBS 91*
**Kempton,** Jim D *WhoAmP 91*
**Kempton,** John P 1932- *AmMWSc 92*
**Kempton,** Todd Daniel 1968- *WhoRel 92*
**Kemsley,** Viscount 1909- *Who 92*
**Kemsley,** Alfred Newcombe d1987 *Who 92N*
**Kenaga,** Clare Burton 1927- *AmMWSc 92*
**Kenaga,** Duane Leroy 1920- *AmMWSc 92*
**Kenagy,** George James 1945- *AmMWSc 92*
**Kenagy,** John Warner 1945- *WhoWest 92*
**Kenagy,** Robert Coffman 1931- *WhoFI 92*
**Kenan,** Daniel Love 1780-1840 *DcNCBi 3*
**Kenan,** Felix d1785 *DcNCBi 3*
**Kenan,** James 1740-1810 *DcNCBi 3*
**Kenan,** Owen Hill 1872-1963 *DcNCBi 3*
**Kenan,** Owen Rand 1804-1887 *DcNCBi 3*
**Kenan,** Randall G. 1963- *WhoBlA 92*
**Kenan,** Richard P 1931- *AmMWSc 92*
**Kenan,** Sarah Graham 1876-1968 *DcNCBi 3*
**Kenan,** Thomas 1771-1843 *DcNCBi 3*
**Kenan,** Thomas Stephen 1838-1911 *DcNCBi 3*
**Kenan,** William Rand 1885-1903 *DcNCBi 3*
**Kenan,** William Rand, Jr. 1872-1965 *DcNCBi 3*
**Kenat,** Thomas Arthur 1942- *AmMWSc 92, WhoMW 92*
**Kenawell,** John Franklin 1943- *WhoFI 92, WhoMW 92*
**Kendal,** Felicity *Who 92*
**Kendal,** Felicity 1946- *IntWW 91*
**Kendall,** Amos 1789-1869 *AmPolLe*
**Kendall,** Aubyn 1919- *WrDr 92*
**Kendall,** Bruce Reginald Francis 1934- *AmMWSc 92*
**Kendall,** Burton Nathaniel 1940- *AmMWSc 92*
**Kendall,** Carol 1917- *IntAu&W 91, WrDr 92*
**Kendall,** Charles Terry 1949- *WhoRel 92*
**Kendall,** Christopher 1949- *WhoEnt 92*
**Kendall,** Cynthia Diane 1953- *WhoAmP 91*
**Kendall,** David George 1918- *IntWW 91, Who 92*
**Kendall,** David Nelson 1916- *AmMWSc 92*
**Kendall,** David Walter 1954- *WhoRel 92*
**Kendall,** David William 1935- *IntWW 91, Who 92*
**Kendall,** Denis *Who 92*
**Kendall,** Donald M. 1921- *IntWW 91*
**Kendall,** Donald McIntosh 1921- *WhoFI 92*
**Kendall,** Edward Calvin 1886-1972 *FacFETw, WhoNob 90*
**Kendall,** Ezra Otis 1818-1899 *BiInAmS*
**Kendall,** Francis M *AmMWSc 92*
**Kendall,** Frank 1940- *Who 92*
**Kendall,** G. W. 1809-1867 *BenetAL 91*
**Kendall,** George Charles, Jr. 1938- *WhoFI 92*
**Kendall,** Gordon *TwCSFW 91*
**Kendall,** Graham 1943- *Who 92*
**Kendall,** H B 1923- *AmMWSc 92*
**Kendall,** Halcombe Augustus 1934- *WhoFI 92*
**Kendall,** Harry White 1924- *AmMWSc 92*
**Kendall,** Henry 1839-1882 *RfGEnL 91*
**Kendall,** Henry Eli, Jr. 1905-1981 *DcNCBi 3*
**Kendall,** Henry Walter George 1916- *Who 92*
**Kendall,** Henry Way 1926- *AmMWSc 92, WhoNob 90*
**Kendall,** Henry Wiseman 1897-1968 *DcNCBi 3*
**Kendall,** James Tyldesley 1916- *AmMWSc 92*
**Kendall,** John Hugh 1942- *AmMWSc 92*
**Kendall,** John Seedoff 1928- *WhoMW 92*
**Kendall,** John Walker, Jr 1929- *AmMWSc 92*
**Kendall,** Kay Lynn 1950- *WhoMW 92*
**Kendall,** Kenyon Sumner, Jr. 1950- *WhoMW 92*
**Kendall,** Leon T 1928- *WhoIns 92*
**Kendall,** Lettie M. 1930- *WhoBlA 92*
**Kendall,** Mark Acton Robertson 1938- *WhoBlA 92*
**Kendall,** Michael Welt 1943- *AmMWSc 92*
**Kendall,** Ned 1808-1861 *NewAmDM*
**Kendall,** Norman 1912- *AmMWSc 92*
**Kendall,** Perry E 1921- *AmMWSc 92*
**Kendall,** Peter Landis 1936- *WhoEnt 92*
**Kendall,** Philip C *AmMWSc 92*
**Kendall,** Phillip Alan 1942- *WhoWest 92*
**Kendall,** Raymond Edward 1933- *Who 92*
**Kendall,** Richard 1946- *TwCPaSc*
**Kendall,** Richard B. 1952- *WhoAmL 92*
**Kendall,** Robert *DrAPF 91*
**Kendall,** Robert, Jr. 1947- *WhoBlA 92*
**Kendall,** Robert McCutcheon 1931- *AmMWSc 92*
**Kendall,** Robert Stanton 1921- *WhoMW 92*
**Kendall,** Shirley I. 1954- *WhoBlA 92*
**Kendall,** Thomas, Jr 1786?-1831 *BiInAmS*
**Kendall,** William Anderson 1924- *AmMWSc 92*
**Kendall,** William Denis 1903- *Who 92*
**Kendall,** William Leslie 1923- *Who 92*
**Kendall,** William T 1921- *WhoAmP 91*
**Kendall-Carpenter,** John 1925-1990 *AnObit 1990*
**Kende,** Andrew S 1932- *AmMWSc 92*
**Kende,** Hans Janos 1937- *AmMWSc 92*
**Kende,** Stephen James 1947- *WhoFI 92*
**Kendell,** Robert Evan 1935- *IntWW 91, Who 92*
**Kender,** Donald Nicholas 1948- *AmMWSc 92*
**Kender,** Walter John 1935- *AmMWSc 92*
**Kendig,** A Edward 1925- *WhoAmP 91*
**Kendig,** Diane *DrAPF 91*
**Kendig,** Edwin Lawrence, Jr 1911- *AmMWSc 92*
**Kendig,** Joan Johnston 1939- *AmMWSc 92, WhoWest 92*
**Kendig,** Martin William 1945- *AmMWSc 92*
**Kendle,** Nick Warren 1950- *WhoWest 92*
**Kendler,** Howard Harvard 1919- *WhoWest 92*
**Kendrew,** John 1917- *Who 92, WrDr 92*
**Kendrew,** John Cowdery 1917- *IntWW 91, WhoNob 90*
**Kendrick,** Aaron Baker 1905- *AmMWSc 92*
**Kendrick,** Alexander d1991 *NewYTBS 91*
**Kendrick,** Angela Lorene 1966- *WhoMW 92*
**Kendrick,** Artis G. 1914- *WhoBlA 92*
**Kendrick,** Baynard 1894-1977 *BenetAL 91*
**Kendrick,** Benjamin Burks 1884-1946 *DcNCBi 3*
**Kendrick,** Bonnie Karst 1965- *WhoFI 92*
**Kendrick,** Bryce 1933- *AmMWSc 92*
**Kendrick,** Carol Yvonne 1952- *WhoAmL 92*
**Kendrick,** Clinton Jansen 1943- *WhoFI 92*
**Kendrick,** Curtis 1921- *WhoBlA 92*
**Kendrick,** Curtis L. 1958- *WhoBlA 92*
**Kendrick,** Darryl D. 1956- *WhoAmL 92*
**Kendrick,** David Andrew 1937- *WhoFI 92*
**Kendrick,** Dolores *DrAPF 91*
**Kendrick,** Francis Joseph 1926- *AmMWSc 92*
**Kendrick,** Griff William 1927- *WhoBlA 92*
**Kendrick,** Hugh 1940- *AmMWSc 92*
**Kendrick,** James Blair, Jr 1920- *AmMWSc 92*
**Kendrick,** James Earl 1940- *WhoFI 92*
**Kendrick,** James Ervin 1948- *WhoRel 92*
**Kendrick,** James Kent 1959- *WhoFI 92*
**Kendrick,** James Michael 1952- *WhoEnt 92*
**Kendrick,** John Bebbington Bernard 1905- *Who 92*
**Kendrick,** John Edsel 1928- *AmMWSc 92*
**Kendrick,** Mark C. 1957- *WhoFI 92*
**Kendrick,** Pearl L 1890-1980 *FacFETw*
**Kendrick,** Peter Murray 1936- *WhoEnt 92*
**Kendrick,** Rae Hansen 1933- *WhoEnt 92*
**Kendrick,** Tommy L. 1923- *WhoBlA 92*
**Kendrick,** William Marvin *WhoWest 92*
**Kendrick,** William Monroe 1941- *WhoMW 92*
**Kendrix,** Moss H., Sr. 1917- *WhoBlA 92N*
**Kendry,** Alistair Carl 1957- *TwCPaSc*
**Kendzior,** Robert Joseph 1952- *WhoMW 92*
**Kendziorski,** Francis Richard 1931- *AmMWSc 92*
**Keneally,** Thomas 1935- *ConNov 91, LiExTwC, RfGEnL 91, WrDr 92*
**Keneally,** Thomas Michael 1935- *IntAu&W 91, IntWW 91, Who 92*
**Kenealy,** Michael Douglas 1947- *AmMWSc 92*
**Kenealy,** Patrick Francis 1939- *AmMWSc 92*
**Kenefick,** Robert Arthur 1937- *AmMWSc 92*
**Kenefick,** Tyler Ray 1962- *WhoMW 92*
**Kenelly,** John Willis, Jr 1935- *AmMWSc 92*
**Kenemore,** Lawrence D., Jr. 1944- *WhoWest 92*
**Kenen,** Peter Bain 1932- *WhoFI 92*
**Keneshea,** Francis Joseph 1921- *AmMWSc 92*
**Kenett,** Ron 1950- *AmMWSc 92*
**Kenfield,** Bret Daniel 1960- *WhoWest 92*
**Keng,** Peter C 1946- *AmMWSc 92*
**Kengo Wa Dondo** 1935- *IntWW 91*
**Kenig,** Marvin Jerry 1936- *AmMWSc 92*
**Kenilorea,** Peter 1943- *IntWW 91, Who 92*
**Kenilworth,** Baron 1954- *Who 92*
**Kenimer,** James G *AmMWSc 92*
**Kenins,** Talivaldis 1919- *NewAmDM*
**Kenison,** Howard 1946- *WhoAmL 92*
**Kenison,** Linda B 1943- *WhoAmP 91*
**Kenison,** Lynn T. 1943- *WhoWest 92*
**Kenison,** Raymond Robert 1932- *WhoMW 92*
**Kenison,** Robert John 1948- *WhoWest 92*
**Kenitzer,** Richard Edward 1958- *WhoEnt 92*
**Kenk,** Roman 1898- *AmMWSc 92*
**Kenk,** Vida Carmen 1939- *AmMWSc 92*
**Kenkare,** Divaker B 1936- *AmMWSc 92*
**Kenkel,** James Lawrence 1944- *WhoFI 92*
**Kenkel,** Joel Nicklas 1941- *WhoIns 92*
**Kenkel,** John V 1948- *AmMWSc 92*
**Kenkel,** William 1925- *WrDr 92*
**Kenknight,** Glenn 1910- *AmMWSc 92*
**Kenkre,** Vasudev Mangesh 1946- *AmMWSc 92*
**Kenley,** Elizabeth Sue 1945- *WhoFI 92*
**Kenley,** Richard Alan 1947- *AmMWSc 92*
**Kenlis,** Lord 1989- *Who 92*
**Kenly,** Granger Farwell 1919- *WhoFI 92*
**Kenna,** Bernard Thomas 1935- *AmMWSc 92*
**Kenna,** Diane Elizabeth Goodrich 1951- *WhoEnt 92*
**Kenna,** Edgar Douglas 1924- *WhoFI 92*
**Kenna,** John Thomas 1919- *WhoRel 92*
**Kenna,** Peter 1930- *IntAu&W 91, WrDr 92*
**Kennaby,** Noel Martin 1905- *Who 92*
**Kennaley,** Michael Thomas 1950- *WhoWest 92*
**Kennamer,** James Earl 1942- *AmMWSc 92*
**Kennamer,** Stephen Money 1954- *WhoAmP 91*
**Kennan,** Christopher James 1949- *WhoFI 92*
**Kennan,** George 1845-1924 *BenetAL 91*
**Kennan,** George 1904- *IntAu&W 91, RComAH, WrDr 92*
**Kennan,** George F. 1904- *BenetAL 91, FacFETw*
**Kennan,** George Frost 1904- *AmPeW, AmPolLe, IntWW 91, Who 92*
**Kennan,** Kent 1913- *ConCom 92*
**Kennan,** Kent Wheeler 1913- *NewAmDM, WhoEnt 92, WrDr 92*
**Kennan,** Wayne Alan 1951- *WhoEnt 92*
**Kennard,** Ann Margaret 1935- *WhoEnt 92*
**Kennard,** Donald Ray 1937- *WhoAmP 91*
**Kennard,** Elizabeth 1947- *WhoRel 92*
**Kennard,** George 1915- *ConAu 134*
**Kennard,** George Arnold Ford 1915- *Who 92*
**Kennard,** Joyce *WhoAmL 92, WhoWest 92*
**Kennard,** Joyce L *WhoAmP 91*
**Kennard,** Kenneth Clayton 1926- *AmMWSc 92*
**Kennard,** Olga 1924- *IntWW 91, Who 92*
**Kennard,** Patricia A. 1949- *WhoBlA 92*
**Kennard,** Peter Laurence 1945- *WhoFI 92*
**Kennard,** Raeburn Gleason 1946- *WhoAmL 92*
**Kennard,** Robert Alexander 1920- *WhoBlA 92*
**Kennard,** William Crawford 1921- *AmMWSc 92*
**Kennaway,** Alexander 1923- *Who 92*
**Kennaway,** John 1933- *Who 92*
**Kenneally,** Dennis Michael 1946- *WhoAmP 91*
**Kenneally,** Michael 1945- *ConAu 133*
**Kennedy** *Who 92*
**Kennedy,** Adrienne 1931- *BenetAL 91, BlkLC, ConLC 66 [port], IntAu&W 91, WrDr 92*
**Kennedy,** Adrienne Lita 1931- *WhoBlA 92, WhoEnt 92*
**Kennedy,** Aida Marie 1954- *WhoAmL 92*
**Kennedy,** Albert *Who 92*
**Kennedy,** Albert Joseph 1943- *AmMWSc 92*
**Kennedy,** Alex 1933- *WhoIns 92*
**Kennedy,** Alfred Doby 1939- *WhoEnt 92*
**Kennedy,** Alfred James 1921- *Who 92*
**Kennedy,** Alfred L 1818-1896 *BiInAmS*
**Kennedy,** Alistair 1957- *TwCPaSc*
**Kennedy,** Alton Edward 1926- *WhoAmP 91*
**Kennedy,** Andrew John 1935- *AmMWSc 92*
**Kennedy,** Ann Randtke 1946- *AmMWSc 92*
**Kennedy,** Anne Gamble 1920- *WhoBlA 92*
**Kennedy,** Annie Brown *WhoAmP 91*
**Kennedy,** Anthony John 1932- *AmMWSc 92*
**Kennedy,** Anthony M 1936- *FacFETw, IntWW 91*
**Kennedy,** Anthony McLeod 1936- *Who 92, WhoAmL 92, WhoAmP 91*
**Kennedy,** Arthur 1914- *IntMPA 92*
**Kennedy,** Arthur 1914-1990 *AnObit 1990*
**Kennedy,** Arthur Colville 1922- *Who 92*
**Kennedy,** Arthur Leo 1942- *WhoRel 92*
**Kennedy,** Arthur Ralph 1935- *WhoAmP 91*
**Kennedy,** Barbara Mae 1911- *AmMWSc 92*
**Kennedy,** Bernard Joseph 1931- *WhoFI 92*
**Kennedy,** Bernard Peter Mel 1952- *WhoRel 92*
**Kennedy,** Beth Blumenreich 1950- *WhoFI 92, WhoWest 92*
**Kennedy,** Beverly Kleban Burris 1943- *WhoFI 92*
**Kennedy,** Bill Wade 1929- *AmMWSc 92*

**Kennedy,** Brian Patrick 1961- *WhoAmP 91*
**Kennedy,** Brian T 1934- *WhoAmP 91*
**Kennedy,** Brooke 1955- *WhoEnt 92*
**Kennedy,** Burt 1922- *IntMPA 92*
**Kennedy,** Burt Raphael 1922- *WhoEnt 92*
**Kennedy,** Burton Mack 1949- *AmMWSc 92*
**Kennedy,** Byrl James 1921- *AmMWSc 92*
**Kennedy,** Cain James 1937- *WhoAmL 92, WhoAmP 91, WhoBlA 92*
**Kennedy,** Callas Faye 1954- *WhoBlA 92*
**Kennedy,** Calvin Fredrick 1933- *WhoRel 92*
**Kennedy,** Cedric 1898-1968 *TwCPaSc*
**Kennedy,** Charlene Farrington 1947- *WhoWest 92*
**Kennedy,** Charles 1920- *AmMWSc 92*
**Kennedy,** Charles Allen 1940- *WhoAmL 92, WhoMW 92*
**Kennedy,** Charles G. 1954- *WhoFI 92*
**Kennedy,** Charles Peter 1959- *Who 92*
**Kennedy,** Charles Rann 1871-1950 *BenetAL 91*
**Kennedy,** Cheryl Lynn 1946- *WhoMW 92*
**Kennedy,** Christopher Robbins 1959- *WhoWest 92*
**Kennedy,** Clyde 1912- *Who 92*
**Kennedy,** Cody *TwCWW 91*
**Kennedy,** Cornelia G *WhoAmP 91*
**Kennedy,** Cornelia Groefsema 1923- *WhoAmL 92, WhoMW 92*
**Kennedy,** Cornelius Bryant 1921- *WhoAmL 92*
**Kennedy,** Cortez 1968- *WhoBlA 92*
**Kennedy,** Corya Jean 1948- *WhoEnt 92*
**Kennedy,** Craig Allen 1951- *WhoAmP 91*
**Kennedy,** David 1768-1837 *DcNCBi 3*
**Kennedy,** David Boyd 1933- *WhoAmP 91*
**Kennedy,** David Laurence 1936- *WhoRel 92*
**Kennedy,** David Matthew 1905- *IntWW 91, Who 92*
**Kennedy,** David Michael 1941- *IntAu&W 91, WrDr 92*
**Kennedy,** David P 1923- *AmMWSc 92*
**Kennedy,** David Patrick 1954- *WhoAmP 91*
**Kennedy,** David Tinsley 1919- *WhoAmL 92*
**Kennedy,** David W. 1954- *WhoAmL 92*
**Kennedy,** Debra Joyce 1955- *WhoWest 92*
**Kennedy,** Diane Elmore 1947- *WhoAmP 91*
**Kennedy,** Donald *NewYTBS 91 [port]*
**Kennedy,** Donald 1931- *AmMWSc 92, IntWW 91, WhoAmP 91, WhoWest 92*
**Kennedy,** Donald Parker 1918- *WhoWest 92*
**Kennedy,** Duncan Tilly 1930- *AmMWSc 92*
**Kennedy,** Eamon 1921- *IntWW 91, Who 92*
**Kennedy,** Earl William 1932- *WhoMW 92, WhoRel 92*
**Kennedy,** Edward 1932- *WrDr 92*
**Kennedy,** Edward Arthur Gilbert 1920- *Who 92*
**Kennedy,** Edward Earl 1925- *AmMWSc 92*
**Kennedy,** Edward Francis 1932- *AmMWSc 92*
**Kennedy,** Edward James 1951- *WhoAmP 91*
**Kennedy,** Edward M. 1932- *AlmAP 92 [port]*
**Kennedy,** Edward Moore 1932- *AmPolLe, IntWW 91, Who 92, WhoAmP 91*
**Kennedy,** Edwin Lust 1904- *WhoFI 92*
**Kennedy,** Edwin Russell 1911- *AmMWSc 92*
**Kennedy,** Eldredge Johnson 1935- *AmMWSc 92*
**Kennedy,** Elhart James 1923- *AmMWSc 92*
**Kennedy,** Elizabeth Mae 1949- *WhoEnt 92*
**Kennedy,** Eugene Cullen 1928- *WhoMW 92*
**Kennedy,** Eugene P 1919- *AmMWSc 92*
**Kennedy,** Eugene Patrick 1919- *IntWW 91*
**Kennedy,** Eugene Richard 1919- *AmMWSc 92*
**Kennedy,** Evelyn Siefert 1927- *WhoFI 92*
**Kennedy,** F. Frederick, Jr. 1943- *WhoEnt 92*
**Kennedy,** Florynce 1916- *NotBlAW 92, WhoBlA 92*
**Kennedy,** Floyd C. 1925- *WhoBlA 92*
**Kennedy,** Flynt 1931- *AmMWSc 92*
**Kennedy,** Francis 1926- *Who 92*
**Kennedy,** Francis Barrett 1915- *WhoRel 92*
**Kennedy,** Frank Metler 1916- *AmMWSc 92*
**Kennedy,** Frank Robert 1914- *WhoAmL 92*
**Kennedy,** Frank Scott 1944- *AmMWSc 92*
**Kennedy,** Frederick A. 1925- *WhoBlA 92*
**Kennedy,** Frederick James 1937- *AmMWSc 92*
**Kennedy,** Gavin 1940- *WrDr 92*
**Kennedy,** Gene Allen 1928- *WhoAmP 91*
**Kennedy,** George 1925- *IntMPA 92*
**Kennedy,** George 1926- *WhoEnt 92*
**Kennedy,** George Arlie 1940- *AmMWSc 92*
**Kennedy,** George Danner 1926- *IntWW 91*
**Kennedy,** George Grady 1948- *AmMWSc 92*
**Kennedy,** George Hunt 1936- *AmMWSc 92*
**Kennedy,** George Michael 1926- *Who 92*
**Kennedy,** Gerald Hamilton 1907-1980 *RelLAm 91*
**Kennedy,** Goldie L 1905- *WhoAmP 91*
**Kennedy,** Harold Edward 1927- *WhoAmL 92, WhoFI 92*
**Kennedy,** Harold Laverne 1962- *WhoWest 92*
**Kennedy,** Harvey Edward 1928- *AmMWSc 92*
**Kennedy,** Hays 1893- *WhoBlA 92*
**Kennedy,** Helena Ann 1950- *Who 92*
**Kennedy,** Henry Harold, Jr. 1948- *WhoBlA 92*
**Kennedy,** Horas Tristram 1917- *Who 92*
**Kennedy,** Howard E. 1941- *WhoBlA 92*
**Kennedy,** Howard L 1928- *WhoAmP 91*
**Kennedy,** Ian 1930- *Who 92*
**Kennedy,** Ian Manning 1952- *AmMWSc 92*
**Kennedy,** Ian McColl 1941- *Who 92*
**Kennedy,** J C 1909- *WhoAmP 91*
**Kennedy,** J R 1925- *AmMWSc 92*
**Kennedy,** Jack, Jr 1956- *WhoAmP 91*
**Kennedy,** Jack Edward 1945- *WhoAmL 92*
**Kennedy,** Jack Leland 1924- *WhoAmL 92*
**Kennedy,** Jacqueline 1929- *FacFETw [port]*
**Kennedy,** Jacqueline Lee Bouvier *IntWW 91*
**Kennedy,** James *Who 92*
**Kennedy,** James A 1935- *AmMWSc 92*
**Kennedy,** James Andrew 1937- *WhoFI 92*
**Kennedy,** James Cecil 1935- *AmMWSc 92*
**Kennedy,** James Cox 1947- *WhoEnt 92, WhoFI 92*
**Kennedy,** James E. 1933- *WhoBlA 92*
**Kennedy,** James E. 1938- *WhoBlA 92*
**Kennedy,** James Harrington 1924- *WhoFI 92*
**Kennedy,** James Lynn 1950- *WhoEnt 92*
**Kennedy,** James M 1928- *AmMWSc 92*
**Kennedy,** James Vern 1934- *AmMWSc 92*
**Kennedy,** James William, Jr. 1940- *WhoWest 92*
**Kennedy,** Jay Richard d1991 *NewYTBS 91*
**Kennedy,** Jay Richard 1911- *WhoEnt 92*
**Kennedy,** Jayne 1951- *WhoBlA 92*
**Kennedy,** Jerry Dean 1934- *AmMWSc 92*
**Kennedy,** Jerry Wayne 1947- *WhoAmL 92*
**Kennedy,** Jimmie Vernon 1925- *WhoBlA 92*
**Kennedy,** Joanna Alicia Gore 1950- *Who 92*
**Kennedy,** John 1930- *Who 92*
**Kennedy,** John 1938- *WhoAmP 91*
**Kennedy,** John, Jr 1939- *WhoAmP 91*
**Kennedy,** John B 1932- *AmMWSc 92*
**Kennedy,** John B. 1951- *WhoMW 92*
**Kennedy,** John Bryan 1845-1915 *DcNCBi 3*
**Kennedy,** John Dale 1945- *WhoEnt 92*
**Kennedy,** John Edward 1916- *AmMWSc 92*
**Kennedy,** John Edward 1947- *WhoAmL 92*
**Kennedy,** John Elmo, Jr 1932- *AmMWSc 92*
**Kennedy,** John F 1917-1963 *RComAH*
**Kennedy,** John Fisher 1933- *AmMWSc 92*
**Kennedy,** John Fitzgerald 1917-1963 *AmPolLe [port], BenetAL 91, FacFETw [port]*
**Kennedy,** John Fitzgerald 1961- *WhoAmP 91*
**Kennedy,** John Foran 1924- *WhoMW 92*
**Kennedy,** John H, Jr 1954- *WhoAmP 91*
**Kennedy,** John Harvey 1933- *AmMWSc 92, WhoWest 92*
**Kennedy,** John Hines 1925- *AmMWSc 92*
**Kennedy,** John Joseph 1948- *WhoFI 92*
**Kennedy,** John Maxwell 1934- *Who 92*
**Kennedy,** John Patrick 1943- *WhoAmL 92*
**Kennedy,** John Paul 1941- *WhoAmP 91*
**Kennedy,** John Pendleton 1795-1870 *BenetAL 91*
**Kennedy,** John Robert 1925- *WhoMW 92*
**Kennedy,** John Robert 1937- *AmMWSc 92*
**Kennedy,** John Robert 1948- *WhoWest 92*
**Kennedy,** John Robert 1961- *WhoMW 92*
**Kennedy,** John Stodart 1912- *IntWW 91, Who 92*
**Kennedy,** John Thomas 1824-1913 *DcNCBi 3*
**Kennedy,** John William 1956- *WhoFI 92*
**Kennedy,** Jon 1950- *WhoWest 92*
**Kennedy,** Joseph 1888-1969 *AmPolLe*
**Kennedy,** Joseph 1923- *WrDr 92*
**Kennedy,** Joseph 1929- *IntAu&W 91*
**Kennedy,** Joseph Camp Griffith 1813-1887 *BiInAmS*
**Kennedy,** Joseph Everett 1930- *WhoAmP 91*
**Kennedy,** Joseph J., Jr. 1923- *WhoBlA 92*
**Kennedy,** Joseph P., II 1952- *AlmAP 92 [port], WhoAmP 91*
**Kennedy,** Joseph Patrick 1888-1969 *FacFETw*
**Kennedy,** Joseph Patrick 1932- *AmMWSc 92*
**Kennedy,** Joseph Paul 1928- *AmMWSc 92, WhoMW 92*
**Kennedy,** Joseph Winston 1932- *WhoAmL 92*
**Kennedy,** Joyce S. 1943- *WhoBlA 92*
**Kennedy,** Kael Behan 1941- *WhoFI 92*
**Kennedy,** Karel R. 1946- *WhoBlA 92*
**Kennedy,** Katherine Ash 1950- *AmMWSc 92*
**Kennedy,** Kathleen *IntMPA 92, WhoEnt 92*
**Kennedy,** Keith Furnival 1925- *WhoFI 92*
**Kennedy,** Keith Sanford 1945- *WhoFI 92, WhoMW 92*
**Kennedy,** Ken 1945- *AmMWSc 92*
**Kennedy,** Kenneth Adrian Raine 1930- *AmMWSc 92*
**Kennedy,** Kevin 1937- *Who 92*
**Kennedy,** Kieran A. 1935- *WrDr 92*
**Kennedy,** Kirby Kenneth 1958- *WhoRel 92*
**Kennedy,** L. Neal 1947- *WhoAmL 92*
**Kennedy,** L. Thomas 1934- *WhoWest 92*
**Kennedy,** Lawrence A 1937- *AmMWSc 92*
**Kennedy,** Leigh 1951- *TwCSFW 91, WrDr 92*
**Kennedy,** Lewis Ellery 1942- *WhoMW 92*
**Kennedy,** Ludovic 1919- *WrDr 92*
**Kennedy,** Ludovic Henry Coverley 1919- *IntAu&W 91, IntWW 91, Who 92*
**Kennedy,** M Keith 1947- *AmMWSc 92*
**Kennedy,** Marc J. 1945- *WhoAmL 92, WhoFI 92*
**Kennedy,** Margaret Wiener 1929- *AmMWSc 92*
**Kennedy,** Marigold Ann 1952- *WhoEnt 92*
**Kennedy,** Mark 1952- *WhoAmL 92, WhoAmP 91*
**Kennedy,** Mark Raymond 1957- *WhoFI 92*
**Kennedy,** Mark Thomas 1953- *WhoEnt 92*
**Kennedy,** Martin P 1931- *WhoAmP 91*
**Kennedy,** Marvin James 1931- *WhoBlA 92*
**Kennedy,** Mary *DrAPF 91*
**Kennedy,** Mary Bernadette 1947- *AmMWSc 92*
**Kennedy,** Mary Elizabeth 1926- *WhoRel 92*
**Kennedy,** Mary Madeline 1937- *WhoAmP 91*
**Kennedy,** Matthew W. 1921- *WhoBlA 92*
**Kennedy,** Matthew Washington 1921- *WhoEnt 92*
**Kennedy,** Maurice Venson 1925- *AmMWSc 92*
**Kennedy,** Michael *Who 92*
**Kennedy,** Michael 1926- *IntAu&W 91, IntWW 91, WrDr 92*
**Kennedy,** Michael Craig 1946- *AmMWSc 92*
**Kennedy,** Michael Denis 1937- *Who 92*
**Kennedy,** Michael Edward 1956- *Who 92*
**Kennedy,** Michael John 1937- *WhoAmL 92*
**Kennedy,** Michael John 1940- *AmMWSc 92*
**Kennedy,** Michael Lynn 1942- *AmMWSc 92*
**Kennedy,** Moira *Who 92*
**Kennedy,** Moorhead 1930- *WrDr 92*
**Kennedy,** Nathelyne Archie 1938- *WhoBlA 92*
**Kennedy,** Nigel 1956- *IntWW 91*
**Kennedy,** Nigel Paul 1956- *Who 92*
**Kennedy,** Ola B. 1932- *WhoBlA 92*
**Kennedy,** Orin 1939- *WhoEnt 92, WhoWest 92*
**Kennedy,** Patricia Ann Sullivan 1936- *WhoEnt 92*
**Kennedy,** Patrick J *WhoAmP 91*
**Kennedy,** Patrick James 1945- *AmMWSc 92*
**Kennedy,** Paul 1935- *Who 92*
**Kennedy,** Paul 1945- *IntAu&W 91*
**Kennedy,** Paul Michael 1945- *IntWW 91, WrDr 92*
**Kennedy,** Peter 1943- *WrDr 92*
**Kennedy,** Peter Carleton 1923- *AmMWSc 92*
**Kennedy,** Peter William 1956- *WhoFI 92*
**Kennedy,** Phillip J. *WhoMW 92*
**Kennedy,** Quentin J., Sr. 1933- *WhoFI 92*
**Kennedy,** Randall L. 1954- *WhoAmL 92*
**Kennedy,** Raymond *DrAPF 91*
**Kennedy,** Raymond McCormick, Jr. 1930- *WhoWest 92*
**Kennedy,** Richard 1932- *WrDr 92*
**Kennedy,** Richard L 1933- *WhoAmP 91*
**Kennedy,** Richard Paul 1949- *Who 92*
**Kennedy,** Richard Robert 1947- *WhoAmP 91*
**Kennedy,** Richard S. 1920- *DcLB 111 [port]*
**Kennedy,** Richard Terrance 1953- *WhoWest 92*
**Kennedy,** Richard Thomas 1919- *WhoAmP 91*
**Kennedy,** Rita M. 1948- *WhoHisp 92*
**Kennedy,** Robert *WhoAmP 91*
**Kennedy,** Robert A 1946- *AmMWSc 92*
**Kennedy,** Robert Alan 1946- *AmMWSc 92*
**Kennedy,** Robert B *WhoAmP 91*
**Kennedy,** Robert Delmont 1932- *WhoFI 92*
**Kennedy,** Robert E 1939- *AmMWSc 92*
**Kennedy,** Robert Emmet, Jr. 1941- *WrDr 92*
**Kennedy,** Robert Eugene 1942- *WhoFI 92*
**Kennedy,** Robert F 1925-1968 *FacFETw, RComAH*
**Kennedy,** Robert Francis 1925-1968 *AmPolLe [port]*
**Kennedy,** Robert Joseph 1962- *WhoMW 92*
**Kennedy,** Robert Lanny 1938- *WhoAmP 91*
**Kennedy,** Robert M. *WhoAmL 92*
**Kennedy,** Robert P 1939- *AmMWSc 92*
**Kennedy,** Robert Spayde 1933- *AmMWSc 92*
**Kennedy,** Robert William 1931- *AmMWSc 92*
**Kennedy,** Robert William 1961- *WhoMW 92*
**Kennedy,** Robert Wilson 1927- *AmMWSc 92*
**Kennedy,** Ronald J. 1938- *WhoMW 92*
**Kennedy,** Rosario 1945- *WhoHisp 92*
**Kennedy,** Russell Jordan 1917- *AmMWSc 92*
**Kennedy,** Rusty Lane 1964- *WhoRel 92*
**Kennedy,** Sam Delk 1926- *WhoFI 92*
**Kennedy,** Sandra Denise 1957- *WhoAmP 91, WhoBlA 92*
**Kennedy,** Sandra Gail 1943- *WhoRel 92*
**Kennedy,** Sheila Grace 1949- *WhoWest 92*
**Kennedy,** Stephen William 1949- *WhoAmP 91*
**Kennedy,** Susan P *WhoAmP 91*
**Kennedy,** T Richard 1935- *WhoIns 92*
**Kennedy,** Terry *DrAPF 91*
**Kennedy,** Thelma Temy 1925- *AmMWSc 92*
**Kennedy,** Theodore Reginald 1936- *WhoBlA 92*
**Kennedy,** Thomas *WhoEnt 92*
**Kennedy,** Thomas Alexander 1920- *Who 92*
**Kennedy,** Thomas Crawford 1932- *WhoWest 92*
**Kennedy,** Thomas E. *DrAPF 91*
**Kennedy,** Thomas Edgar 1958- *WhoFI 92*
**Kennedy,** Thomas Eugene 1944- *IntAu&W 91*
**Kennedy,** Thomas James, Jr 1920- *AmMWSc 92*
**Kennedy,** Thomas Lawrie 1928- *Who 92*
**Kennedy,** Thomas Maynard 1912- *WhoAmL 92*
**Kennedy,** Thomas Patrick 1932- *WhoEnt 92, WhoFI 92*
**Kennedy,** Thomas Patrick 1951- *WhoAmP 91*
**Kennedy,** Thomas William 1938- *AmMWSc 92*
**Kennedy,** Todd Harris 1959- *WhoEnt 92*
**Kennedy,** V. Wayne 1938- *WhoWest 92*
**Kennedy,** Vance Clifford 1923- *AmMWSc 92*
**Kennedy,** W Keith, Jr 1943- *AmMWSc 92*
**Kennedy,** Walter Jeff, Jr. 1928- *WhoMW 92*
**Kennedy,** Walter Lawrence 1920- *WhoAmP 91*
**Kennedy,** Walter P *WhoAmP 91*
**Kennedy,** Warren Walter 1922- *WhoFI 92*
**Kennedy,** Wilbert Keith 1919- *AmMWSc 92*
**Kennedy,** William *DrAPF 91*
**Kennedy,** William 1768-1834 *DcNCBi 3*
**Kennedy,** William 1928- *BenetAL 91, ConNov 91, WrDr 92*
**Kennedy,** William Alexander 1915- *AmMWSc 92*
**Kennedy,** William Andrew 1948- *Who 92*
**Kennedy,** William Bean 1926- *WhoRel 92*
**Kennedy,** William Francis 1918- *WhoAmL 92*
**Kennedy,** William J., III 1922- *WhoBlA 92*
**Kennedy,** William Joseph 1928- *IntAu&W 91, IntWW 91, WhoEnt 92*
**Kennedy,** William Robert 1927- *AmMWSc 92*
**Kennedy,** William Thomas 1952- *WhoWest 92*
**Kennedy,** William Thomas, Jr. 1928- *WhoBlA 92*
**Kennedy,** William Wayne 1937- *WhoFI 92*
**Kennedy,** Willie B 1923- *WhoAmP 91, WhoBlA 92*

**Kennedy**, X.J. *DrAPF 91*
**Kennedy**, X. J. 1929- *ConPo 91, WrDr 92*
**Kennedy**, Yvonne 1945- *WhoAmP 91, WhoBlA 92*
**Kennedy Franklin**, Linda Cheryl 1950- *WhoBlA 92*
**Kennedy-Good**, John 1915- *Who 92*
**Kennedy-Martin**, Troy 1932- *IntAu&W 91, Who 92*
**Kennedy-Minott**, Rodney *WhoWest 92*
**Kennedy-Overton**, Jayne 1951- *WhoBlA 92*
**Kennel**, Charles Frederick 1939- *AmMWSc 92, WhoWest 92*
**Kennel**, John Maurice 1927- *AmMWSc 92*
**Kennel**, Stephen John 1945- *AmMWSc 92*
**Kennel**, William E 1917- *AmMWSc 92*
**Kennell**, David Epperson 1932- *AmMWSc 92*
**Kennell**, John Hawks 1922- *AmMWSc 92*
**Kennell**, Richard Wayne 1952- *WhoEnt 92*
**Kennelley**, James A 1928- *AmMWSc 92*
**Kennelley**, Kevin James 1958- *AmMWSc 92*
**Kennelly**, Barbara B. 1936- *AlmAP 92 [port]*
**Kennelly**, Barbara Bailey 1936- *WhoAmP 91*
**Kennelly**, Brendan 1936- *ConPo 91, IntAu&W 91, WrDr 92*
**Kennelly**, Jayne Ellen 1946- *WhoMW 92*
**Kennelly**, John Jerome 1918- *WhoAmL 92, WhoMW 92*
**Kennelly**, Karen Margaret 1933- *WhoRel 92*
**Kennelly**, Laura Ballard *DrAPF 91*
**Kennelly**, Mary Marina 1919- *AmMWSc 92*
**Kennelly**, Tamara *DrAPF 91*
**Kennelly**, William J 1948- *AmMWSc 92*
**Kennemer**, William *WhoAmP 91*
**Kennemore**, Tim 1957- *WrDr 92*
**Kenner**, Charles Thomas 1910- *AmMWSc 92*
**Kenner**, David Vaupel 1958- *WhoAmL 92*
**Kenner**, Hugh 1923- *WrDr 92*
**Kenner**, Morton Roy 1925- *AmMWSc 92*
**Kenner**, Nancy Elizabeth 1959- *WhoAmL 92*
**Kenner**, Patricia E *WhoAmP 91*
**Kennerknecht**, Richard Eugene 1961- *WhoWest 92*
**Kennerley**, Anthony 1933- *Who 92*
**Kennerley**, George 1908- *TwCPaSc*
**Kennerly**, David Hume 1947- *WhoEnt 92*
**Kennerly**, George Warren 1922- *AmMWSc 92*
**Kennerly**, Roland Francis 1934- *WhoAmP 91*
**Kennet**, Baron 1923- *IntWW 91, Who 92*
**Kennet**, David Mark 1957- *WhoFI 92*
**Kennet**, Haim 1935- *AmMWSc 92*
**Kennet of the Dene**, Wayland Young 1923- *IntAu&W 91*
**Kenneth**, Rosalene 1939- *WhoEnt 92*
**Kennethson**, George 1910- *TwCPaSc*
**Kennett**, Colette Ann 1951- *WhoRel 92*
**Kennett**, James Peter 1940- *AmMWSc 92*
**Kennett**, Jiyu 1924- *RelLAm 91*
**Kennett**, Kathleen 1878-1947 *TwCPaSc*
**Kennett**, Roger H 1940- *AmMWSc 92*
**Kennett**, Ronald John 1935- *Who 92*
**Kennett**, Terence James 1927- *AmMWSc 92*
**Kennett Brown**, David 1938- *Who 92*
**Kennevick**, Jack C *WhoAmP 91*
**Kenneway**, Ernest Keating, Jr. 1938- *WhoFI 92*
**Kenney**, Anthony 1942- *Who 92*
**Kenney**, Brad Thomas 1956- *WhoRel 92*
**Kenney**, Catherine 1948- *ConAu 135*
**Kenney**, Charles 1950- *ConAu 135*
**Kenney**, Deborah Christine 1956- *WhoRel 92*
**Kenney**, Donald J 1925- *AmMWSc 92*
**Kenney**, Donald James 1947- *WhoMW 92*
**Kenney**, Edward Beckham 1929- *WhoAmP 91*
**Kenney**, Edward John 1924- *IntWW 91, Who 92*
**Kenney**, Erica G *WhoAmP 91*
**Kenney**, F. Donald 1918- *WhoFI 92*
**Kenney**, Francis T 1928- *AmMWSc 92*
**Kenney**, Frank Deming 1921- *WhoAmL 92*
**Kenney**, George T, Jr 1957- *WhoAmP 91*
**Kenney**, Gerald 1934- *AmMWSc 92*
**Kenney**, Gerald Raymond 1956- *WhoEnt 92*
**Kenney**, H. Wesley 1926- *IntMPA 92*
**Kenney**, Harry Wesley, III 1955- *WhoEnt 92*
**Kenney**, Harry Wesley, Jr. 1926- *WhoEnt 92*
**Kenney**, James Edward 1953- *WhoWest 92*
**Kenney**, James Francis 1926- *AmMWSc 92*
**Kenney**, James Franklin 1934- *AmMWSc 92*
**Kenney**, John Arthur 1948- *WhoAmL 92*
**Kenney**, John Joseph 1943- *WhoAmL 92*
**Kenney**, John William, III 1950- *WhoWest 92*
**Kenney**, Jon 1947- *WhoMW 92*
**Kenney**, Lawrence James 1930- *WhoRel 92*
**Kenney**, Malcolm Edward 1928- *AmMWSc 92*
**Kenney**, Margaret June 1935- *AmMWSc 92*
**Kenney**, Marianne 1933- *WhoWest 92*
**Kenney**, Mary Alice 1938- *AmMWSc 92*
**Kenney**, Nancy Jane *AmMWSc 92*
**Kenney**, Raymond Joseph, Jr. 1932- *WhoAmL 92*
**Kenney**, Richard 1948- *ConAu 134*
**Kenney**, Richard Alec 1924- *AmMWSc 92*
**Kenney**, Richard L. *DrAPF 91*
**Kenney**, Robert Warner 1922- *AmMWSc 92*
**Kenney**, Scott Robert 1956- *WhoFI 92*
**Kenney**, T Cameron 1931- *AmMWSc 92*
**Kenney**, Thomas Frederick 1941- *WhoEnt 92*
**Kenney**, Vincent Paul 1927- *AmMWSc 92*
**Kenney**, Virgil Cooper 1926- *WhoBlA 92*
**Kenney**, Walter T. 1930- *WhoBlA 92*
**Kenney**, Walter Thomas 1930- *WhoAmP 91*
**Kenney**, William Clark 1940- *AmMWSc 92*
**Kenney**, William Fitzgerald 1935- *WhoFI 92, WhoWest 92*
**Kenney**, William John 1904- *Who 92*
**Kenney-Wallace**, Geraldine Anne 1943- *AmMWSc 92*
**Kennick**, Walter Herbert 1920- *AmMWSc 92*
**Kennickell**, Ralph E., Jr. d1991 *NewYTBS 91*
**Kennicott**, Harrison 1937- *WhoFI 92*
**Kennicott**, James W. 1945- *WhoAmL 92*
**Kennicott**, Robert 1835-1866 *BiInAmS*
**Kennington**, Eric 1888-1960 *TwCPaSc*
**Kennington**, Garth Stanford 1915- *AmMWSc 92*
**Kennington**, Mack Humpherys 1923- *AmMWSc 92, WhoWest 92*
**Kennington**, Mary Ann 1954- *WhoWest 92*
**Kennington**, Thomas Benjamin 1856-1916 *TwCPaSc*
**Kennish**, John M 1945- *AmMWSc 92*
**Kennison**, John Frederick 1938- *AmMWSc 92*
**Kennison**, Wayne A 1925- *WhoAmP 91*
**Kennon**, Daniel, Jr. 1910- *WhoBlA 92*
**Kennon**, James Edward Campbell d1991 *Who 92N*
**Kennon**, John David 1917- *WhoIns 92*
**Kennon**, Patrick Joseph 1956- *WhoFI 92*
**Kennon**, Rozmond H. 1935- *WhoBlA 92*
**Kenny**, Adele *DrAPF 91*
**Kenny**, Adele 1948- *IntAu&W 91*
**Kenny**, Alexander Donovan 1925- *AmMWSc 92*
**Kenny**, Alfreida B. 1950- *WhoBlA 92*
**Kenny**, Andrew Augustine 1934- *AmMWSc 92*
**Kenny**, Anthony 1931- *IntAu&W 91, WrDr 92*
**Kenny**, Anthony John Patrick 1931- *IntWW 91, Who 92*
**Kenny**, Anthony Marriott 1939- *Who 92*
**Kenny**, Arthur William 1918- *Who 92*
**Kenny**, Bernard F, Jr 1946- *WhoAmP 91*
**Kenny**, Brian 1934- *Who 92*
**Kenny**, Brian Leslie Graham 1934- *IntWW 91*
**Kenny**, David Herman 1927- *AmMWSc 92*
**Kenny**, David John 1940- *Who 92*
**Kenny**, Douglas T. 1923- *IntWW 91*
**Kenny**, Douglas Timothy 1923- *Who 92*
**Kenny**, George Edward 1930- *AmMWSc 92*
**Kenny**, George James 1935- *WhoAmL 92*
**Kenny**, James Joseph *AmMWSc 92*
**Kenny**, John Edward 1945- *WhoFI 92*
**Kenny**, John Logan 1938- *WhoIns 92*
**Kenny**, Mary 1936- *IntAu&W 91*
**Kenny**, Maurice *DrAPF 91*
**Kenny**, Michael 1941- *IntWW 91, TwCPaSc, Who 92*
**Kenny**, Michael H. 1937- *WhoRel 92, WhoWest 92*
**Kenny**, Michael Thomas 1938- *AmMWSc 92*
**Kenny**, Roger Michael 1938- *WhoFI 92*
**Kenoe**, Henry Wolf 1907- *WhoAmL 92*
**Kenoff**, Jay Stewart 1946- *WhoWest 92*
**Kenrich**, John Lewis 1929- *WhoAmL 92, WhoFI 92*
**Kenrick**, Tony 1935- *IntAu&W 91, WrDr 92*
**Kensek**, Ronald P 1958- *AmMWSc 92*
**Kensey**, Calvin D. *WhoRel 92*
**Kensey**, John Howard 1947- *WhoMW 92*
**Kenshalo**, Daniel Ralph 1922- *AmMWSc 92*
**Kensinger**, George *WrDr 92*
**Kensington**, Area Bishop of 1935- *Who 92*
**Kensington**, Baron 1933- *Who 92*
**Kensington**, Holland 1945- *WhoWest 92*
**Kensit**, Patsy 1968- *ConTFT 9, IntMPA 92*
**Kensky**, Allan David 1946- *WhoRel 92*
**Kensler**, Charles Joseph 1915- *AmMWSc 92*
**Kenson**, Robert Earl 1939- *AmMWSc 92*
**Kenswood**, Baron 1930- *Who 92*
**Kent**, Duke of 1935 *Who 92R*
**Kent**, The Duke of 1935- *IntWW 91*
**Kent**, Alan Heywood 1946- *WhoAmL 92*
**Kent**, Alexander *WrDr 92*
**Kent**, Allen 1921- *AmMWSc 92*
**Kent**, Arthur *LesBEnT 92*
**Kent**, Arthur 1925- *IntAu&W 91, WrDr 92*
**Kent**, Arthur 1953- *News 91 [port]*
**Kent**, Arthur William 1913- *Who 92*
**Kent**, Barbara 1940- *AmMWSc 92*
**Kent**, Bill *WhoEnt 92*
**Kent**, Bion H 1925- *AmMWSc 92*
**Kent**, Bruce 1929- *IntWW 91, Who 92*
**Kent**, Bruce Eric 1932- *IntWW 91*
**Kent**, Claudia 1945- *AmMWSc 92*
**Kent**, Clement F 1927- *AmMWSc 92*
**Kent**, Clifford Eugene 1920- *AmMWSc 92, WhoRel 92*
**Kent**, Cynthia Stevens 1954- *WhoAmL 92*
**Kent**, Dale Vivienne 1942- *WrDr 92*
**Kent**, David W *WhoAmP 91*
**Kent**, Debra Susan 1960- *WhoEnt 92*
**Kent**, Dennis V 1946- *AmMWSc 92*
**Kent**, Donald Alan 1949- *WhoEnt 92*
**Kent**, Donald Martin 1933- *AmMWSc 92*
**Kent**, Donald Wetherald, Jr 1926- *AmMWSc 92*
**Kent**, Douglas Charles 1939- *AmMWSc 92*
**Kent**, Earle Lewis 1910- *AmMWSc 92*
**Kent**, Edgar Robert, Jr. 1941- *WhoFI 92*
**Kent**, Ernest 1955- *WhoBlA 92*
**Kent**, Evan Michael 1955- *WhoAmL 92*
**Kent**, Francis William 1942- *IntWW 91*
**Kent**, Frederick Heber 1905- *WhoAmL 92*
**Kent**, Gary Warner 1933- *WhoEnt 92*
**Kent**, Geoffrey 1914- *AmMWSc 92*
**Kent**, Geoffrey Charles 1922- *IntWW 91, Who 92*
**Kent**, George Cantine, Jr 1914- *AmMWSc 92*
**Kent**, Gordon *TwCSFW 91*
**Kent**, Gordon 1920- *AmMWSc 92*
**Kent**, Grady R. 1909-1964 *RelLAm 91*
**Kent**, Harold Simcox 1903- *Who 92*
**Kent**, Harry Christison 1930- *AmMWSc 92*
**Kent**, Harry Ross 1921- *WhoRel 92*
**Kent**, Helen *WrDr 92*
**Kent**, Henry Peter 1915- *AmMWSc 92*
**Kent**, Homer Austin, Jr. 1926- *WrDr 92*
**Kent**, James 1763-1847 *BenetAL 91*
**Kent**, James Donald, Jr. 1946- *WhoMW 92*
**Kent**, James Gardner 1952- *WhoMW 92*
**Kent**, James Guy 1952- *WhoWest 92*
**Kent**, James Ronald Fraser 1912- *AmMWSc 92*
**Kent**, Jean 1921- *IntMPA 92*
**Kent**, Joe 1938- *WhoAmP 91*
**Kent**, John B. 1939- *IntMPA 92*
**Kent**, John Franklin 1921- *AmMWSc 92*
**Kent**, John Philip Cozens 1928- *IntWW 91, Who 92*
**Kent**, Joseph C 1922- *AmMWSc 92*
**Kent**, Joseph Francis 1944- *AmMWSc 92*
**Kent**, Julie Ann 1969- *WhoEnt 92*
**Kent**, Kelvin *TwCSFW 91*
**Kent**, Larry *WhoWest 92*
**Kent**, Leslie Errol 1915- *IntWW 91*
**Kent**, Linda Gail 1946- *WhoEnt 92*
**Kent**, Lois Schoonover 1912- *AmMWSc 92, WhoMW 92*
**Kent**, Louise Andrews 1886-1969 *BenetAL 91*
**Kent**, M. Elizabeth 1943- *WhoAmL 92*
**Kent**, Mallory *TwCSFW 91*
**Kent**, Mark Earl 1956- *WhoFI 92*
**Kent**, Melvin Floyd 1953- *WhoBlA 92*
**Kent**, Michael Alan 1960- *WhoAmL 92*
**Kent**, Morton J. *LesBEnT 92*
**Kent**, Nicholas Roger 1950- *WhoMW 92*
**Kent**, Oda Allen 1945- *WhoRel 92*
**Kent**, Pamela *WrDr 92*
**Kent**, Paul J. 1955- *WhoRel 92*
**Kent**, Paul Welberry 1923- *Who 92*
**Kent**, Pendarell Hugh 1937- *Who 92*
**Kent**, Pete *TwCWW 91*
**Kent**, Philip *IntAu&W 91X, TwCSFW 91*
**Kent**, Raymond D 1942- *AmMWSc 92*
**Kent**, Robert Brydon 1921- *WhoAmL 92*
**Kent**, Robert Warren 1935- *WhoAmL 92, WhoFI 92*
**Kent**, Rockwell 1882-1971 *BenetAL 91*
**Kent**, Rolly *DrAPF 91*
**Kent**, Ronald Allan 1935- *AmMWSc 92*
**Kent**, Ronald Clive 1916- *Who 92*
**Kent**, Sidney Harcourt 1915- *Who 92*
**Kent**, Stephen Brian Henry 1945- *AmMWSc 92*
**Kent**, Stephen Matthew 1952- *AmMWSc 92*
**Kent**, Stephen Maurice 1942- *WhoMW 92*
**Kent**, Theodore Charles *WhoWest 92*
**Kent**, Thomas George 1925- *Who 92*
**Kent**, Thomas Hugh 1934- *AmMWSc 92*
**Kent**, Thomas Worrall 1922- *IntAu&W 91, IntWW 91*
**Kent**, Walter Henry 1851-1907 *BiInAmS*
**Kent**, William 1684-1748 *BlkwCEP*
**Kent**, William 1851-1918 *BiInAmS*
**Kent**, William Wallace, Jr. 1941- *WhoAmL 92*
**Kent Donahue**, Laura L *WhoAmP 91*
**Kent-Jones**, Trevor David 1940- *Who 92*
**Kentfield**, Graham Edward Alfred 1940- *Who 92*
**Kentfield**, John Alan Charles 1930- *AmMWSc 92*
**Kenton**, Glenn C 1943- *WhoAmP 91*
**Kenton**, Joseph S 1921- *WhoAmP 91*
**Kenton**, Maxwell *WrDr 92*
**Kenton**, Simon 1755-1836 *BenetAL 91*
**Kenton**, Stan 1911-1979 *FacFETw*
**Kenton**, Stan 1912-1979 *NewAmDM*
**Kenton**, Warren 1933- *WrDr 92*
**Kentridge**, Sydney 1922- *IntWW 91, Who 92*
**Kentris**, George Lawrence 1949- *WhoAmL 92*
**Kentros**, Arthur George 1956- *WhoAmL 92*
**Kentzer**, Czeslaw P 1925- *AmMWSc 92*
**Kenward**, Jean 1920- *IntAu&W 91, WrDr 92*
**Kenward**, Michael Ronald John 1945- *Who 92*
**Kenworthy** *Who 92*
**Kenworthy**, Alvin Lawrence 1915- *AmMWSc 92*
**Kenworthy**, Brian J. 1920- *WrDr 92*
**Kenworthy**, Cecil 1918- *Who 92*
**Kenworthy**, Frederick John 1943- *Who 92*
**Kenworthy**, Harry William 1947- *WhoFI 92*
**Kenworthy**, Joan Margaret 1933- *Who 92*
**Kenworthy**, Mary Kay 1957- *WhoAmP 91*
**Kenworthy-Browne**, Peter 1930- *Who 92*
**Kenworthy-Reynolds**, Linda Lou 1952- *WhoEnt 92*
**Keny**, Sharad Vasant 1946- *WhoWest 92*
**Kenya**, Archbishop of 1929- *Who 92*
**Kenyatta**, Jomo 1895?-1978 *FacFETw [port]*
**Kenyatta**, Mary 1944- *WhoBlA 92*
**Kenyatta**, Muhammad Isaiah 1944- *WhoBlA 92*
**Kenyon** *Who 92*
**Kenyon**, Baron 1917- *Who 92*
**Kenyon**, Alan J 1929- *AmMWSc 92*
**Kenyon**, Allen Stewart 1916- *AmMWSc 92*
**Kenyon**, Bruce Davis 1943- *WhoFI 92*
**Kenyon**, Bruce Guy 1929- *IntAu&W 91*
**Kenyon**, Clifford 1896- *Who 92*
**Kenyon**, Curtis *IntMPA 92*
**Kenyon**, David V. 1930- *WhoAmL 92*
**Kenyon**, Essek William 1867-1948 *RelLAm 91*
**Kenyon**, George 1912- *Who 92*
**Kenyon**, George Lommel 1939- *AmMWSc 92*
**Kenyon**, Hewitt 1920- *AmMWSc 92*
**Kenyon**, Ian Roy 1939- *Who 92*
**Kenyon**, Jack Scott 1922- *WhoAmP 91*
**Kenyon**, Jane *DrAPF 91*
**Kenyon**, John 1927- *IntAu&W 91, WrDr 92*
**Kenyon**, John Philipps 1927- *IntWW 91, Who 92*
**Kenyon**, Karen *DrAPF 91*
**Kenyon**, Kenneth James 1930- *WhoWest 92*
**Kenyon**, Kern Ellsworth 1938- *AmMWSc 92*
**Kenyon**, Leslie Harrison 1922- *WhoMW 92*
**Kenyon**, Michael 1931- *IntAu&W 91, WrDr 92*
**Kenyon**, Michael Lee 1943- *WhoFI 92*
**Kenyon**, Nicholas Roger 1951- *Who 92*
**Kenyon**, Richard A 1933- *AmMWSc 92*
**Kenyon**, Richard H 1942- *AmMWSc 92*
**Kenyon**, Richard R 1928- *AmMWSc 92*
**Kenyon**, Stephen C 1948- *AmMWSc 92*
**Kenyon**, Susan *DrAPF 91*
**Kenyon**, Terry Frazier 1955- *WhoAmL 92*
**Kenyon**, Wayne George 1933- *WhoAmP 91*
**Kenzie**, Ross Bruce 1931- *WhoFI 92*
**Kenzig**, Stephen Russell 1952- *WhoMW 92*
**Kenzo** 1940- *DcTwDes, IntWW 91*
**Kenzy**, John Quinton 1941- *WhoRel 92*
**Keogh**, Dermot Francis 1945- *IntAu&W 91*
**Keogh**, Heidi Helen Dake 1950- *WhoWest 92*
**Keogh**, James 1916- *IntAu&W 91, IntWW 91*

**Keogh**, Kevin 1935- WhoFI 92
**Keogh**, Michael John 1937- AmMWSc 92
**Keogh**, Richard John 1932- WhoWest 92
**Keogh**, Richard Neil 1940- AmMWSc 92
**Keohane**, Desmond John 1928- Who 92
**Keohane**, Kevin William 1923- Who 92
**Keohane**, Thomas Francis, Jr. 1934- WhoWest 92
**Keokuk** BenetAL 91
**Keon**, Barbara D 1956- WhoAmP 91
**Keon**, Wilbert Joseph 1935- AmMWSc 92
**Keonjian**, Edward 1909- AmMWSc 92
**Keough**, Allen Henry 1929- AmMWSc 92
**Keough**, Donald Raymond 1926- IntWW 91, WhoFI 92
**Keough**, James Gillman, Jr. 1947- WhoMW 92, WhoRel 92
**Keough**, Kevin Michael William 1943- AmMWSc 92
**Keown**, Donald G 1932- WhoIns 92
**Keown**, Ernest Ray 1921- AmMWSc 92
**Keown**, Kenneth K 1917- AmMWSc 92
**Keown**, Lauriston Livingston, Jr. 1942- WhoWest 92
**Keown**, Robert William 1929- AmMWSc 92
**Keown**, William Arvel 1920- WhoRel 92
**Kepa**, Sailosi Wai 1938- Who 92
**Kepecs**, Joseph Goodman 1912- AmMWSc 92
**Kepes**, Gyorgy 1906- DcTwDes, FacFETw
**Kepes**, John J 1928- AmMWSc 92
**Kepes**, Joseph John 1931- AmMWSc 92
**Kephart**, Horace Sowers 1862-1931 DcNCBi 3
**Kephart**, James William 1955- WhoAmL 92
**Kephart**, Richard N 1938- WhoAmP 91
**Kephart**, Robert David 1949- AmMWSc 92
**Kephart**, William M. 1921- WrDr 92
**Kepke**, Allen Neal 1935- WhoMW 92
**Kepler**, Carol R 1937- AmMWSc 92
**Kepler**, Harold B 1922- AmMWSc 92
**Kepler**, Johannes 1571-1630 ScFEYrs
**Kepler**, Raymond Glen 1928- AmMWSc 92
**Keplinger**, Bruce 1952- WhoAmL 92
**Keplinger**, Moreno Lavon 1929- AmMWSc 92
**Keplinger**, Orin Clawson 1918- AmMWSc 92
**Kepner**, Richard Edwin 1916- AmMWSc 92
**Kepner**, Rita Marie 1944- WhoWest 92
**Keppard**, Freddie 1889-1933 NewAmDM
**Keppel** Who 92
**Keppel**, Charlotte WrDr 92
**Keppel**, Francis 1916-1990 FacFETw
**Keppel**, Herbert Govert 1866-1918 BiInAmS
**Keppel**, William James 1941- WhoAmL 92
**Keppel-Jones**, Arthur 1909- IntAu&W 91, WrDr 92
**Kepper**, John C 1932- AmMWSc 92
**Kepper**, Robert Edgar 1935- AmMWSc 92
**Keppie**, John D 1942- AmMWSc 92
**Kepple**, Paul C 1936- AmMWSc 92
**Keppler**, Carl F ScFEYrs
**Keppler**, Ernest C 1918- WhoAmP 91
**Keppler**, Joan Erdey 1930- WhoAmL 92
**Keppler**, Joseph 1838-1894 BenetAL 91
**Keppler**, Wilhelm 1882-1960 EncTR 91 [port]
**Keppler**, William Edmund 1922- WhoFI 92
**Keppler**, William J 1937- AmMWSc 92
**Kepron**, Wayne 1942- AmMWSc 92
**Ker** Who 92
**Ker**, Angela 1933- TwCPaSc
**Ker**, David 1758-1805 DcNCBi 3
**Ker**, David 1842-1914 ScFEYrs
**Ker**, Dorian 1948- TwCPaSc
**Ker**, John William 1915- AmMWSc 92
**Keramidas**, Vassilis George 1938- AmMWSc 92
**Kerans**, Grattan 1941- WhoAmP 91
**Kerans**, Sally P WhoAmP 91
**Kerasotes**, George G. IntMPA 92
**Kerbecek**, Arthur J, Jr 1926- AmMWSc 92
**Kerbel'**, Lev Yefimovich 1917- SovUnBD
**Kerbel**, Robert Stephen 1945- AmMWSc 92
**Kerber**, Erich Rudolph 1926- AmMWSc 92
**Kerber**, Richard E 1939- AmMWSc 92
**Kerber**, Robert Charles 1938- AmMWSc 92
**Kerber**, Ronald Lee 1943- AmMWSc 92
**Kerber**, Walter Josef 1926- WhoRel 92
**Kerbey**, McFall, III 1951- WhoEnt 92
**Kerbis**, Gertrude Lempp WhoMW 92
**Kerbs**, Glenn Ivan 1953- WhoMW 92
**Kerby**, Bill 1937- WhoEnt 92
**Kerby**, Cleve Loy 1953- WhoRel 92
**Kerby**, Hoyle Ray 1932- AmMWSc 92
**Kerby**, John Vyvyan 1942- Who 92
**Kerce**, Robert H 1925- AmMWSc 92
**Kercher**, Conrad J 1926- AmMWSc 92
**Kercheval**, James William 1906- AmMWSc 92
**Kercheval**, Ken 1935- WhoEnt 92
**Kerchner**, Charles Taylor 1940- WhoWest 92
**Kerchner**, Harold Richard 1946- AmMWSc 92
**Kerchner**, Robert Matthew 1964- WhoEnt 92
**Kercho**, Randy Scott 1956- WhoFI 92
**Kerdel-Vegas**, Francisco 1928- IntWW 91, Who 92
**Kerdesky**, Francis A J 1953- AmMWSc 92
**Kereiakes**, James Gus 1924- AmMWSc 92
**Kerekes**, Joseph John 1949- WhoRel 92
**Kerekes**, Richard Joseph 1940- AmMWSc 92
**Kerekou**, Ahmed 1933- ConBlB 1 [port]
**Kerekou**, Mathieu 1933- IntWW 91
**Keren**, Joseph 1930- AmMWSc 92
**Kerensky**, Alexander Fedorovich 1881-1970 FacFETw [port]
**Kerensky**, Oleg 1930- WrDr 92
**Keres**, Karen Lynne 1945- WhoMW 92
**Kerester**, Charles John 1927- WhoAmL 92
**Keresztes**, K. Sandor 1944- IntWW 91
**Keresztury**, Dezso 1904- IntAu&W 91, IntWW 91
**Kereszty**, Roch A. 1933- WrDr 92
**Kerew**, Diana 1942- WhoEnt 92
**Kerfoot**, Branch Price 1925- AmMWSc 92, WhoWest 92
**Kerfoot**, Bruce T. 1938- WhoMW 92
**Kerfoot**, Wilson Charles 1944- AmMWSc 92
**Kerger**, Richard Marvin 1945- WhoAmL 92
**Kerich**, James Patrick 1938- WhoMW 92
**Kerin**, John Charles 1937- IntWW 91
**Kerins**, David 1948- WhoAmP 91
**Kerins**, Thomas Edward 1945- WhoFI 92
**Kerjaschki**, Dontscho 1947- AmMWSc 92
**Kerka**, William 1921- AmMWSc 92
**Kerkar**, Awdhoot Vasant 1963- AmMWSc 92
**Kerkay**, Julius 1934- AmMWSc 92
**Kerker**, Cynthia Maki 1957- WhoFI 92
**Kerker**, Gustave Adolph 1857-1923 NewAmDM
**Kerker**, Michael Alexander 1947- WhoEnt 92
**Kerker**, Milton 1920- AmMWSc 92
**Kerkman**, Daniel Joseph 1951- AmMWSc 92
**Kerkman**, Russel John 1948- AmMWSc 92
**Kerkorian**, Kirk 1917- IntMPA 92, WhoEnt 92, WhoWest 92
**Kerlan**, Joel Thomas 1940- AmMWSc 92
**Kerle**, Jacobus de 1532?-1591 NewAmDM
**Kerle**, Ronald Clive 1915- Who 92
**Kerlee**, Donald D 1926- AmMWSc 92
**Kerley**, Gary DrAPF 91
**Kerley**, Gerald Irwin 1941- AmMWSc 92
**Kerley**, Janice Johnson 1938- WhoFI 92
**Kerley**, Michael A 1941- AmMWSc 92
**Kerley**, Ottie Ray, II 1949- WhoRel 92
**Kerley**, Troy Lamar 1929- AmMWSc 92
**Kerlick**, George David 1949- AmMWSc 92
**Kerlikowske**, Elizabeth DrAPF 91
**Kerlin**, Merrill W 1921- WhoAmP 91
**Kerlin**, Michon Munson 1961- WhoFI 92
**Kerlin**, Thomas W 1936- AmMWSc 92
**Kerll**, Johann Kaspar 1627-1693 NewAmDM
**Kerma**, Ingrid 1942- TwCPaSc
**Kermack**, Stuart Ogilvy 1934- Who 92
**Kerman**, Arthur Kent 1929- AmMWSc 92
**Kerman**, Barry Martin 1945- WhoWest 92
**Kerman**, Joseph 1924- WrDr 92
**Kerman**, Joseph Wilfred 1924- Who 92, WhoEnt 92
**Kerman**, Judith DrAPF 91
**Kerman**, R A 1943- AmMWSc 92
**Kerman**, Sheppard 1928- WhoEnt 92
**Kerman**, Thea 1949- WhoAmL 92
**Kermani-Arab**, Vali 1939- AmMWSc 92
**Kermicle**, Jerry Lee 1936- AmMWSc 92
**Kermisch**, Dorian 1931- AmMWSc 92
**Kermode**, Frank 1919- IntWW 91, Who 92, WrDr 92
**Kermode**, Gwen 1950- WhoFI 92
**Kermode**, John Frank 1919- IntAu&W 91
**Kermode**, Ronald 1919- Who 92
**Kermott**, Marjorie Louise 1913- WhoAmP 91
**Kern**, Barkley August 1963- WhoEnt 92
**Kern**, Bernard Donald 1919- AmMWSc 92
**Kern**, Bliem DrAPF 91
**Kern**, Charles William 1935- AmMWSc 92
**Kern**, Clifford Dalton 1928- AmMWSc 92
**Kern**, Clifford H, III 1948- AmMWSc 92
**Kern**, Donald Michael 1951- WhoWest 92
**Kern**, Douglas Raymond 1961- WhoFI 92
**Kern**, Earl R 1940- AmMWSc 92
**Kern**, Edna Ruth 1945- WhoFI 92
**Kern**, Erich 1906- BiDExR
**Kern**, Eugene Francis 1919- WhoFI 92
**Kern**, Frank Edgar 1929- WhoMW 92
**Kern**, Fred, Jr 1918- AmMWSc 92
**Kern**, Gary L. 1937- WhoMW 92
**Kern**, George Calvin, Jr. 1926- WhoAmL 92
**Kern**, Gilbert Richard 1932- WhoMW 92
**Kern**, Gregory IntAu&W 91X, TwCSFW 91, WrDr 92
**Kern**, Howard Jeffrey 1960- WhoAmL 92
**Kern**, Jerome 1885-1945 BenetAL 91, FacFETw, NewAmDM
**Kern**, Jerome 1927- AmMWSc 92
**Kern**, John Philip 1939- AmMWSc 92
**Kern**, John W 1930- AmMWSc 92
**Kern**, John Worth, III 1928- WhoAmL 92
**Kern**, Josephine Ann 1938- WhoAmP 91
**Kern**, Karl-Heinz 1930- IntWW 91, Who 92
**Kern**, Kathleen Annette Grimes 1951- WhoMW 92
**Kern**, Kevin Walsh 1958- WhoAmL 92
**Kern**, Leila Rochelle 1942- WhoAmL 92
**Kern**, Michael Don 1938- AmMWSc 92
**Kern**, Patricia Joan 1933- WhoMW 92
**Kern**, Paul Alfred 1958- WhoWest 92
**Kern**, Paul Bentley 1882-1953 DcNCBi 3
**Kern**, Ralph Donald, Jr 1935- AmMWSc 92
**Kern**, Richard Bradley 1965- WhoMW 92
**Kern**, Robert Laurence 1936- WhoAmL 92
**Kern**, Roland James 1925- AmMWSc 92
**Kern**, Roy Fredrick 1918- AmMWSc 92
**Kern**, Russell Stephen 1952- WhoEnt 92
**Kern**, Ruth Angelina 1958- WhoMW 92
**Kern**, Stephen Douglas 1946- WhoRel 92
**Kern**, Thomas Raymond 1958- WhoWest 92
**Kern**, Tina Joy 1969- WhoRel 92
**Kern**, Vincent James 1951- WhoFI 92
**Kern**, Walter M D, Jr 1937- WhoAmP 91
**Kern**, Werner 1925- AmMWSc 92
**Kern**, William H 1927- AmMWSc 92
**Kern**, William Henry 1927- WhoWest 92
**Kern**, Wolfhard 1927- AmMWSc 92
**Kern-Foxworth**, Marilyn L. 1954- WhoBlA 92
**Kernaghan**, Eileen Shirley 1939- IntAu&W 91
**Kernaghan**, Roy Peter 1933- AmMWSc 92
**Kernan**, Anne 1933- AmMWSc 92
**Kernan**, Joseph E WhoAmP 91
**Kernan**, Richard M, Jr 1940- WhoIns 92
**Kernan**, Roderick Patrick 1928- IntWW 91
**Kernan**, Stephen Michael, Sr. 1947- WhoAmL 92
**Kernan**, Timothy Charles 1955- WhoAmP 91
**Kernan**, William J, Jr 1933- AmMWSc 92
**Kernberg**, Otto F 1928- AmMWSc 92
**Kernell**, Michael Lynn 1951- WhoAmP 91
**Kernell**, Robert Lee 1929- AmMWSc 92
**Kerner**, David 1936- WhoFI 92
**Kerner**, David Vincent 1936- WhoWest 92
**Kerner**, Edward Haskell 1924- AmMWSc 92
**Kerner**, Fred 1921- WhoFI 92, WrDr 92
**Kerner**, Howard Alex 1951- WhoEnt 92
**Kerner**, Joseph Frank, Jr. 1938- WhoMW 92
**Kerner**, Todd Michael 1963- WhoAmL 92
**Kerney**, Peter Joseph 1940- AmMWSc 92
**Kernick**, Phyllis T WhoAmP 91
**Kernis**, Aaron Jay 1960- ConCom 92
**Kernis**, Marten Murray 1941- AmMWSc 92
**Kernisant**, Lesly 1949- WhoBlA 92
**Kernish**, Edward Samuel 1946- WhoMW 92
**Kernish**, Susan Margaret 1949- WhoEnt 92
**Kernkamp**, Milton F 1911- AmMWSc 92
**Kernmayer**, Erich 1906- BiDExR
**Kernochan**, John Marshall 1919- WhoAmL 92
**Kernochan**, Sarah DrAPF 91
**Kernodle**, Obra Servesta, III 1947- WhoBlA 92
**Kernodle**, Rigdon Wayne 1919- WrDr 92
**Kernodle**, Una Mae 1947- WhoWest 92
**Kernohan**, Thomas Hugh 1922- Who 92
**Kernon**, Neil Anthony 1953- WhoEnt 92
**Kerns**, Barry Kevin 1954- WhoWest 92
**Kerns**, Bob Lee 1930- WhoAmP 91
**Kerns**, Christianne Finch 1958- WhoAmL 92
**Kerns**, David Marlow 1913- AmMWSc 92
**Kerns**, David Vincent 1917- WhoAmL 92
**Kerns**, Gertrude Yvonne 1931- WhoMW 92
**Kerns**, Hubie Jay, Jr. 1949- WhoEnt 92
**Kerns**, Janet Martha 1954- WhoRel 92
**Kerns**, Joanna de Varona 1953- WhoEnt 92
**Kerns**, Peggy 1941- WhoAmP 91
**Kerouac**, Jack 1922-1969 BenetAL 91, FacFETw, RComAH
**Kerper**, Matthew J 1922- AmMWSc 92
**Kerr** Who 92
**Kerr**, Alan Grainger 1935- Who 92
**Kerr**, Alexander Duncan, Jr. 1943- WhoAmL 92
**Kerr**, Alexander McBride 1921- WrDr 92
**Kerr**, Alfred 1867-1948 EncTR 91
**Kerr**, Allen 1926- Who 92
**Kerr**, Andrew, Jr 1914- AmMWSc 92
**Kerr**, Andrew Mark 1940- Who 92
**Kerr**, Andrew Stevenson 1918- Who 92
**Kerr**, Anthony Robert 1941- AmMWSc 92
**Kerr**, Arnold D 1928- AmMWSc 92
**Kerr**, Artemus P ScFEYrs
**Kerr**, Barry Jack 1949- WhoRel 92
**Kerr**, Breene Mitchell, Jr. 1952- WhoEnt 92
**Kerr**, Brian Francis 1948- Who 92
**Kerr**, Carl E 1926- AmMWSc 92
**Kerr**, Carole IntAu&W 91X, WrDr 92
**Kerr**, Carolyn Elizabeth 1955- WhoEnt 92
**Kerr**, Chester Brooks 1913- IntWW 91
**Kerr**, Clark 1911- IntWW 91, Who 92, WhoFI 92, WrDr 92
**Kerr**, Daniel Wilson 1796-1850 DcNCBi 3
**Kerr**, Dave 1945- WhoAmP 91
**Kerr**, David Leigh 1923- Who 92
**Kerr**, David Mills 1945- WhoMW 92
**Kerr**, David Nicol Sharp 1927- Who 92
**Kerr**, David Wylie 1943- IntWW 91, WhoFI 92
**Kerr**, Deborah 1921- FacFETw, IntMPA 92
**Kerr**, Deborah Jane 1921- IntWW 91, Who 92, WhoEnt 92
**Kerr**, Desmond Moore 1930- Who 92
**Kerr**, Donald Craig 1915- WhoRel 92
**Kerr**, Donald Frederick 1915- Who 92
**Kerr**, Donald L 1943- AmMWSc 92
**Kerr**, Donald M, Jr 1939- AmMWSc 92
**Kerr**, Donald MacLean, Jr. 1939- WhoFI 92
**Kerr**, Donald Philip 1938- AmMWSc 92
**Kerr**, Donald R 1938- AmMWSc 92
**Kerr**, Douglas S 1940- AmMWSc 92
**Kerr**, Edmund Hugh 1924- WhoAmL 92, WhoFI 92
**Kerr**, Edwin 1926- Who 92
**Kerr**, Elizabeth M. 1905- WrDr 92
**Kerr**, Eric Donald 1930- AmMWSc 92
**Kerr**, Ernest Andrew 1917- AmMWSc 92
**Kerr**, Ewing Thomas 1900- WhoWest 92
**Kerr**, Frances Mills 1919- WhoBlA 92
**Kerr**, Francis Robert Newsam 1916- Who 92
**Kerr**, Frank John 1918- AmMWSc 92
**Kerr**, Fraser 1931- IntMPA 92
**Kerr**, Fred A WhoAmP 91
**Kerr**, Frederick WrDr 92
**Kerr**, George E 1937- BlkOlyM
**Kerr**, George J 1954- WhoAmP 91
**Kerr**, George R 1930- AmMWSc 92
**Kerr**, George Thomson 1923- AmMWSc 92
**Kerr**, Gib 1927- WhoFI 92, WhoWest 92
**Kerr**, Gordon Charles 1945- WhoAmP 91
**Kerr**, Graham 1934- WrDr 92
**Kerr**, Gregory Alan 1950- WhoWest 92
**Kerr**, Guy Hardie 1953- WhoAmL 92
**Kerr**, Harold Delbert 1933- AmMWSc 92
**Kerr**, Harrison 1897-1978 NewAmDM
**Kerr**, Hortense R. 1926- WhoBlA 92
**Kerr**, Hugh Barkley 1922- AmMWSc 92
**Kerr**, Hugh Thomson 1909- WhoRel 92
**Kerr**, I Lawrence 1917- AmMWSc 92
**Kerr**, James 1928- Who 92
**Kerr**, James R. WhoRel 92
**Kerr**, James S S 1926- AmMWSc 92
**Kerr**, James W. 1914- WhoWest 92
**Kerr**, James Wilfrid 1897- WhoWest 92
**Kerr**, Janet Kay Kroell 1942- WhoAmL 92
**Kerr**, Janet Spence AmMWSc 92
**Kerr**, Jean 1922- WrDr 92
**Kerr**, Jean 1923- BenetAL 91, IntAu&W 91, IntWW 91
**Kerr**, Jimmie Barry 1934- WhoWest 92
**Kerr**, John 1782-1842 DcNCBi 3
**Kerr**, John 1931- IntMPA 92
**Kerr**, John 1937- Who 92
**Kerr**, John 1942- Who 92
**Kerr**, John, Jr. 1811-1879 DcNCBi 3
**Kerr**, John F. DrAPF 91
**Kerr**, John H, III 1936- WhoAmP 91
**Kerr**, John Hosea 1873-1958 DcNCBi 3
**Kerr**, John Hosea, Jr. 1900-1968 DcNCBi 3
**Kerr**, John M 1934- AmMWSc 92
**Kerr**, John Polk 1931- AmMWSc 92
**Kerr**, John Robert d1991 Who 92N
**Kerr**, John Robert 1914-1991 IntWW 91, -91N
**Kerr**, Judith 1923- IntAu&W 91, WrDr 92
**Kerr**, K. Austin WrDr 92
**Kerr**, Kathryn DrAPF 91
**Kerr**, Keron WhoAmP 91
**Kerr**, Kirklyn M 1936- AmMWSc 92
**Kerr**, Kleon Harding 1911- WhoWest 92
**Kerr**, Laura Beth 1969- WhoEnt 92
**Kerr**, Louise A. 1938- WhoHisp 92
**Kerr**, M. E. 1927- WrDr 92
**Kerr**, M E 1932- IntAu&W 91
**Kerr**, Marilyn Sue AmMWSc 92
**Kerr**, Mark Brickell 1860-1917 BiInAmS
**Kerr**, Mark Robert 1963- WhoWest 92
**Kerr**, Michael IntAu&W 91X, WrDr 92

**Kerr**, Michael 1921- Who 92
**Kerr**, Michael Crawford 1827-1876 AmPolLe
**Kerr**, Nancy Karolyn 1934- WhoRel 92
**Kerr**, Norman Story 1933- AmMWSc 92, WhoMW 92
**Kerr**, Orpheus C. BenetAL 91
**Kerr**, Philip 1956- WrDr 92
**Kerr**, Ralph Oliver 1926- AmMWSc 92
**Kerr**, Robert Benjamin 1943- WhoFI 92
**Kerr**, Robert Lowell 1936- AmMWSc 92
**Kerr**, Robert Mark 1932- WhoAmP 91
**Kerr**, Robert McDougall 1954- AmMWSc 92
**Kerr**, Robert Reid 1914- Who 92
**Kerr**, Robert Samuel, III 1950- WhoAmP 91
**Kerr**, Rose 1953- Who 92
**Kerr**, Sandria Neidus 1940- AmMWSc 92
**Kerr**, Stanley B. 1928- WhoFI 92
**Kerr**, Stratton H 1924- AmMWSc 92
**Kerr**, Sylvia Jean 1941- AmMWSc 92
**Kerr**, Sylvia Joann 1941- AmMWSc 92
**Kerr**, Theodore William, Jr 1912- AmMWSc 92
**Kerr**, Thomas Henry 1924- Who 92
**Kerr**, Thomas James 1927- AmMWSc 92
**Kerr**, Thomas Robert 1950- WhoAmP 91
**Kerr**, Vernon Norman 1928- WhoAmP 91
**Kerr**, Walter 1913- BenetAL 91, FacFETw, IntWW 91, WrDr 92
**Kerr**, Walter Craig 1858-1910 BiInAmS
**Kerr**, Walter F. 1913- WhoEnt 92
**Kerr**, Walter L. 1928- WhoBlA 92
**Kerr**, Warwick Estevam 1922- AmMWSc 92
**Kerr**, Washington Caruthers 1827-1885 BiInAmS, DcNCBi 3
**Kerr**, Wendle Louis 1917- AmMWSc 92
**Kerr**, William 1919- AmMWSc 92
**Kerr**, William Alexander B. Who 92
**Kerr**, William Andrew 1934- WhoAmL 92
**Kerr**, William Clayton 1940- AmMWSc 92
**Kerr**, William Francis Kennedy 1923- Who 92
**Kerr**, William G 1945- WhoAmP 91
**Kerr**, William Thomas 1941- WhoAmL 92
**Kerr y Baca**, Stephen P. 1944- WhoHisp 92
**Kerrebrock**, Jack Leo 1928- AmMWSc 92
**Kerrey**, Bob 1943- CurBio 91 [port], IntWW 91, NewYTBS 91 [port], News 91 [port], -91-3 [port], WhoMW 92
**Kerrey**, Joseph Robert 1943- WhoAmP 91
**Kerrey**, Robert 1943- AlmAP 92 [port]
**Kerri**, Kenneth D 1934- AmMWSc 92
**Kerrick**, David E 1951- WhoAmP 91
**Kerrick**, David Ellsworth 1951- WhoAmL 92
**Kerrick**, Derrill M 1940- AmMWSc 92
**Kerrick**, Wallace Glenn Lee AmMWSc 92
**Kerridge**, Kenneth A 1928- AmMWSc 92
**Kerrigan**, Anthony d1991 NewYTBS 91
**Kerrigan**, Anthony 1918- LiExTwC
**Kerrigan**, Edward J 1931- WhoAmP 91
**Kerrigan**, T.S. DrAPF 91
**Kerrigan**, Timothy George 1954- WhoAmL 92
**Kerrigan**, Walter W., II 1953- WhoFI 92, WhoMW 92
**Kerrigan**, William Paul 1953- WhoEnt 92
**Kerrl**, Hanns 1887-1941 EncTR 91 [port]
**Kerros**, Edward Paul 1954- WhoEnt 92
**Kerruish**, Charles 1917- IntWW 91, Who 92
**Kerry**, Knight of Who 92
**Kerry**, Erica 1943- WhoEnt 92
**Kerry**, John F. 1943- AlmAP 92 [port]
**Kerry**, John Forbes 1943- IntWW 91, NewYTBS 91 [port], WhoAmP 91
**Kerry**, John M WhoAmP 91
**Kerry**, Lois ConAu 36NR
**Kerry**, Michael 1923- Who 92
**Kerry**, Reta Christina 1923- WhoAmP 91
**Kersbergen**, Robert J D 1951- WhoIns 92
**Kerschen**, Edward John 1951- WhoWest 92
**Kerschner**, Jean 1922- AmMWSc 92
**Kerse**, Christopher Stephen 1946- Who 92
**Kersee**, Bobby WhoBlA 92
**Kersey**, B. Franklin, IV 1942- WhoBlA 92
**Kersey**, Bertha Brinnett 1956- WhoBlA 92
**Kersey**, Elizabeth T. 1956- WhoBlA 92
**Kersey**, Jerome 1962- WhoBlA 92
**Kersey**, John BlkwCEP
**Kersey**, John H 1938- AmMWSc 92
**Kersey**, Robert Lee, Jr 1922- AmMWSc 92
**Kersey**, Sharyn R 1951- WhoAmP 91
**Kersey**, Terry Lee 1947- WhoWest 92
**Kersh**, Cyril 1925- IntAu&W 91, Who 92, WrDr 92
**Kersh**, DeWitte Talmadge, Jr. 1930- WhoAmL 92
**Kershaw** Who 92
**Kershaw**, Baron 1936- Who 92
**Kershaw**, Anthony Who 92
**Kershaw**, David Stanley 1943- AmMWSc 92
**Kershaw**, Henry Aidan 1927- Who 92
**Kershaw**, Ian 1943- Who 92
**Kershaw**, John Anthony 1915- Who 92
**Kershaw**, John William 1943- WhoRel 92
**Kershaw**, Joseph Anthony 1935- Who 92
**Kershaw**, Kenneth Andrew 1930- AmMWSc 92
**Kershaw**, Michael Who 92
**Kershaw**, Newton Henry, Jr. 1946- WhoAmL 92
**Kershaw**, Peter IntAu&W 91X, WrDr 92
**Kershaw**, Philip Michael 1941- Who 92
**Kershaw**, Robert Alan 1947- WhoFI 92
**Kershaw**, Robert Barnsley 1952- WhoAmL 92
**Kershaw**, Thomas Abbott 1938- WhoFI 92
**Kershaw**, W. J. S., Mrs. Who 92
**Kershaw**, William Edgar Who 92
**Kershenbaum**, Aaron 1948- AmMWSc 92
**Kershenstein**, John Charles 1941- AmMWSc 92
**Kershner**, Carl John 1934- AmMWSc 92
**Kershner**, Irvin 1923- IntMPA 92
**Kershner**, Larry Dwane 1942- WhoMW 92
**Kershner**, William Franklin 1939- WhoAmL 92
**Kerss**, William 1931- Who 92
**Kerst**, A Fred 1940- AmMWSc 92
**Kerst**, Donald William 1911- AmMWSc 92, IntWW 91
**Kerstein**, Gary Richard 1960- WhoMW 92
**Kerstein**, Morris D 1938- AmMWSc 92
**Kersten**, Felix 1899-1960 FacFETw
**Kersten**, James Burke 1960- WhoAmP 91
**Kersten**, Miles S 1913- AmMWSc 92
**Kersten**, Miles Stokes 1913- WhoMW 92
**Kersten**, Robert D 1927- AmMWSc 92
**Kersten**, Timothy Wayne 1944- WhoFI 92, WhoWest 92
**Kerstetter**, Michael James 1936- WhoFI 92
**Kerstetter**, Rex E 1938- AmMWSc 92
**Kerstetter**, Theodore Harvey 1930- AmMWSc 92
**Kerstetter**, William E. 1946- WhoEnt 92
**Kersting**, Edwin Joseph 1919- AmMWSc 92
**Kersting**, Lisa Gayle WhoMW 92
**Kerstitch**, Alex 1945- WhoWest 92
**Kert**, Larry 1930-1991 NewYTBS 91 [port]
**Kertamus**, Norbert John 1932- AmMWSc 92
**Kertelge**, Karl 1926- WhoRel 92
**Kertesz**, Andrew 1938- AmMWSc 92
**Kertesz**, Istvan 1929-1973 NewAmDM
**Kertesz**, Jean Constance 1943- AmMWSc 92
**Kertesz**, Miklos 1948- AmMWSc 92
**Kerth**, Leroy Thomas 1928- AmMWSc 92
**Kertscher**, Richard H WhoAmP 91
**Kertscher**, Thomas Patrick 1961- WhoMW 92
**Kerttula**, Jalmar M WhoAmP 91
**Kerttula**, Jalmar M. 1928- WhoWest 92
**Kertz**, Alois Francis 1945- AmMWSc 92
**Kertz**, George J 1933- AmMWSc 92
**Kerwar**, Suresh 1937- AmMWSc 92
**Kerwin**, Brian 1949- IntMPA 92
**Kerwin**, Carolyn Ann 1950- WhoMW 92
**Kerwin**, Edward Michael, Jr 1927- AmMWSc 92
**Kerwin**, James Francis, Jr. 1956- WhoMW 92
**Kerwin**, John Larkin 1924- AmMWSc 92
**Kerwin**, Kenneth Hills, II 1939- WhoWest 92
**Kerwin**, Larkin 1924- IntWW 91, Who 92
**Kerwin**, Mary Ann Collins 1931- WhoAmL 92
**Kerwin**, Richard Martin 1922- AmMWSc 92
**Kerwin**, Thomas Hugh 1930- WhoFI 92
**Kerwin**, William J 1922- AmMWSc 92
**Keryczynskyj**, Leo Ihor 1948- WhoAmL 92
**Kerze**, Michael Anthony 1948- WhoRel 92
**Kerzman**, James A WhoAmP 91
**Kerzman**, Norberto Luis Maria 1943- AmMWSc 92
**Kerzner**, Jay Joel 1944- WhoWest 92
**Kerzner**, Robert Allen 1952- WhoFI 92
**Kerzner**, Robyn Patricia 1964- WhoRel 92
**Kesarwani**, Roop Narain 1932- AmMWSc 92
**Kesey**, Ken DrAPF 91
**Kesey**, Ken 1935- BenetAL 91, ConNov 91, FacFETw, SmATA 66 [port], WrDr 92
**Keshavadas**, Sant 1934- RelLAm 91
**Keshavan**, H R 1949- AmMWSc 92
**Keshavan**, Krishnaswamiengar 1929- AmMWSc 92
**Keshaviah**, Prakash Ramnathpur 1945- AmMWSc 92
**Keshian**, Richard 1934- WhoAmL 92
**Keshian**, Richard James 1957- WhoAmL 92
**Keshishev**, Konstantin Odisseyevich 1945- IntWW 91
**Keshock**, Edward G 1935- AmMWSc 92
**Kesik**, Andrzej B 1930- AmMWSc 92
**Kesisoglu**, Garbis 1936- WhoFI 92
**Keska**, Jerry Kazimierz 1945- WhoMW 92
**Keskkula**, Henno 1926- AmMWSc 92
**Kesler**, Benjamin Elias 1861-1952 RelLAm 91
**Kesler**, Clyde E 1922- AmMWSc 92
**Kesler**, Darrel J 1949- AmMWSc 92
**Kesler**, Earl Marshall 1920- AmMWSc 92
**Kesler**, G H 1920- AmMWSc 92
**Kesler**, Jay 1935- SmATA 65 [port]
**Kesler**, Jay Lewis 1935- WhoRel 92
**Kesler**, John A. 1923- WhoAmL 92
**Kesler**, Michael Glen 1955- WhoWest 92
**Kesler**, Morton Allen 1935- WhoAmL 92
**Kesler**, Oren Byrl 1939- AmMWSc 92
**Kesler**, Ruth Evalyn 1925- WhoAmP 91
**Kesler**, Stephen Edward 1940- AmMWSc 92
**Kesler**, Thomas L 1908- AmMWSc 92
**Keslering**, Timothy Scott 1957- IntAu&W 91
**Kesling**, Annette Elizabeth 1931- WhoMW 92
**Kesling**, Keith Kenton 1923- WhoMW 92
**Kesling**, Robert Vernon 1917- AmMWSc 92
**Kesling**, Willard Ray, Jr. 1948- WhoEnt 92
**Kesmodel**, Charles Myohl, Jr. 1931- WhoMW 92
**Kesmodel**, Larry Lee 1947- AmMWSc 92
**Kesner**, Gary M. 1961- WhoRel 92
**Kesner**, Leo 1931- AmMWSc 92
**Kesner**, Michael H 1945- AmMWSc 92
**Kesner**, Raymond Pierre 1940- AmMWSc 92
**Kesper**, Jeffrey Alan 1947- WhoEnt 92
**Kespohl**, Elke 1961- WhoFI 92
**Kess**, Sidney 1926- WhoFI 92
**Kessel**, Barney 1923- NewAmDM
**Kessel**, Brina 1925- AmMWSc 92, WhoWest 92
**Kessel**, David Harry 1931- AmMWSc 92, WhoMW 92
**Kessel**, Harlan Robert 1928- WhoWest 92
**Kessel**, John 1950- TwCSFW 91
**Kessel**, John Howard 1928- WrDr 92
**Kessel**, Mark 1941- WhoAmL 92
**Kessel**, Mary 1910- TwCPaSc
**Kessel**, Nancy 1947- WhoAmP 91
**Kessel**, Quentin Cattell 1938- AmMWSc 92
**Kessel**, Richard Glen 1931- AmMWSc 92
**Kessel**, Rosslyn William Ian 1929- AmMWSc 92
**Kessel**, William Ivor Neil 1925- Who 92
**Kesselhaut**, Arthur M 1935- WhoIns 92
**Kesselhaut**, Arthur Melvyn 1935- WhoWest 92
**Kessell**, Stephen Robert 1949- AmMWSc 92
**Kesselly**, Edward Binyah IntWW 91
**Kesselman**, Warren Arthur 1927- AmMWSc 92
**Kesselman**, Wendy IntAu&W 91, WrDr 92
**Kesselring**, Albert 1885-1960 EncTR 91 [port], FacFETw
**Kesselring**, Gloria Jean 1950- WhoRel 92
**Kesselring**, John Paul 1940- AmMWSc 92
**Kesselring**, Joseph BenetAL 91
**Kesselring**, Leo John 1933- WhoAmP 91
**Kessen**, William 1925- IntAu&W 91, WrDr 92
**Kessin**, Janet Anderson 1950- WhoEnt 92
**Kessin**, Richard Harry 1944- AmMWSc 92
**Kessinger**, Margaret Anne 1941- AmMWSc 92, WhoMW 92
**Kessinger**, Walter Paul, Jr 1930- AmMWSc 92
**Kessler**, A. D. 1923- WhoFI 92, WhoWest 92
**Kessler**, Alan Craig 1950- WhoAmL 92
**Kessler**, Alexander 1931- AmMWSc 92
**Kessler**, Andrew J. 1958- WhoFI 92
**Kessler**, Bernard Milton 1927- WhoFI 92
**Kessler**, Bernard V 1928- AmMWSc 92
**Kessler**, Dan 1924- AmMWSc 92
**Kessler**, David AmMWSc 92
**Kessler**, David 1951- News 92-1 [port], WhoAmP 91
**Kessler**, David A. NewYTBS 91 [port]
**Kessler**, David A. 1951- CurBio 91 [port]
**Kessler**, David Phillip 1934- AmMWSc 92, WhoMW 92
**Kessler**, Diane Cooksey 1947- WhoRel 92
**Kessler**, Dietrich 1936- AmMWSc 92
**Kessler**, Doris Henrietta 1935- WhoMW 92
**Kessler**, Edward J. 1943- WhoAmL 92
**Kessler**, Edwin, III 1928- AmMWSc 92
**Kessler**, Ellen Widen 1941- WhoAmL 92
**Kessler**, Ernest George, Jr 1940- AmMWSc 92
**Kessler**, Frederick Melvyn 1932- AmMWSc 92
**Kessler**, Fredric Lee 1952- WhoEnt 92
**Kessler**, George Aaron 1928- WhoRel 92
**Kessler**, George Morton 1917- AmMWSc 92
**Kessler**, Gerald 1930- AmMWSc 92
**Kessler**, Harold D 1921- AmMWSc 92
**Kessler**, Harry 1868-1937 EncTR 91 [port]
**Kessler**, Herbert Roland 1930- WhoAmL 92
**Kessler**, Howard David 1959- WhoEnt 92
**Kessler**, Irving Isar 1931- AmMWSc 92
**Kessler**, Irving Jack 1940- AmMWSc 92
**Kessler**, James Lee 1945- WhoRel 92
**Kessler**, Jascha DrAPF 91
**Kessler**, Jascha 1929- IntAu&W 91, WrDr 92
**Kessler**, Jeffrey L. 1954- WhoAmL 92
**Kessler**, Jerome 1942- WhoEnt 92
**Kessler**, Joan F. 1943- WhoAmL 92
**Kessler**, John Otto 1928- AmMWSc 92
**Kessler**, John Paul, Jr. 1946- WhoFI 92
**Kessler**, Judd Lewis 1938- WhoAmL 92
**Kessler**, Judd Stuart 1952- WhoFI 92
**Kessler**, Karl Gunther 1919- AmMWSc 92
**Kessler**, Karl Heinz 1960- WhoEnt 92
**Kessler**, Kenneth J, Jr 1933- AmMWSc 92
**Kessler**, Lauren Jeanne 1950- WhoWest 92
**Kessler**, Lawrence Bert 1946- WhoAmL 92, WhoEnt 92
**Kessler**, Lawrence W 1942- AmMWSc 92
**Kessler**, Leon M 1927- WhoFI 92
**Kessler**, Marie Elizabeth 1952- WhoAmL 92
**Kessler**, Mary Carolyn 1947- WhoAmP 91
**Kessler**, Michael Edward 1959- WhoEnt 92
**Kessler**, Michael K. 1956- WhoFI 92
**Kessler**, Miles B. 1951- WhoEnt 92
**Kessler**, Milton DrAPF 91
**Kessler**, Milton 1917- WhoFI 92
**Kessler**, Milton 1930- ConPo 91, WrDr 92
**Kessler**, Minuetta Shumiatcher 1914- WhoEnt 92
**Kessler**, Miriam DrAPF 91
**Kessler**, Nathan 1923- AmMWSc 92
**Kessler**, Philip Joel 1947- WhoAmL 92
**Kessler**, Ralph Kenneth 1943- WhoFI 92
**Kessler**, Richard Howard 1923- AmMWSc 92
**Kessler**, Robert Allen 1940- WhoWest 92
**Kessler**, Rod DrAPF 91
**Kessler**, Seymour 1928- AmMWSc 92
**Kessler**, Sharon DrAPF 91
**Kessler**, Silas George 1911- WhoRel 92
**Kessler**, Steven Fisher 1951- WhoAmL 92
**Kessler**, Stuart 1929- WhoFI 92
**Kessler**, Thomas J 1938- AmMWSc 92
**Kessler**, Walter Arnold 1953- WhoWest 92
**Kessler**, Wayne Vincent 1933- AmMWSc 92
**Kessler**, William Eugene 1944- WhoMW 92
**Kessler**, William J 1917- AmMWSc 92
**Kessler-Hodgson**, Lee Gwendolyn 1947- WhoEnt 92, WhoFI 92
**Kesslering**, Ralph Nicholas 1938- WhoRel 92
**Kessner**, Daniel Aaron 1946- WhoEnt 92
**Kessner**, David Morton 1932- AmMWSc 92
**Kessner**, Thomas 1946- WrDr 92
**Kestelman**, Morris 1905- TwCPaSc
**Kesten**, Arthur S 1934- AmMWSc 92
**Kesten**, Harry AmMWSc 92
**Kesten**, Heather Anne 1946- WhoFI 92
**Kesten**, Hermann 1900- IntAu&W 91, IntWW 91, LiExTwC
**Kesten**, Leonard Henry 1949- WhoAmL 92
**Kesten**, Paul W. d1956 LesBEnT 92
**Kestenbaum**, Harold Lee 1949- WhoAmL 92
**Kestenbaum**, Jerome 1919- WhoRel 92
**Kestenbaum**, Richard Charles 1931- AmMWSc 92
**Kestenbaum**, Richard Steven 1942- AmMWSc 92
**Kestenbaum**, Toni Trobe 1941- WhoFI 92
**Kestenberg**, Milton d1991 NewYTBS 91
**Kester**, Andrew Stephen 1932- AmMWSc 92
**Kester**, Dale Emmert 1922- AmMWSc 92
**Kester**, Dana R 1943 AmMWSc 92
**Kester**, Dennis Earl 1947- AmMWSc 92
**Kester**, Howard Anderson 1904-1977 DcNCBi 3
**Kester**, James Raymond 1941- WhoWest 92
**Kester**, John Barton 1924- WhoAmP 91
**Kester**, John Gordon 1938- WhoAmL 92
**Kester**, Marcia Gale DrAPF 91
**Kester**, Paul 1870-1933 BenetAL 91
**Kester**, Sheryl Marie 1961- WhoRel 92
**Kester**, Vaughan 1869-1911 BenetAL 91
**Kesterson**, Kelley James 1953- WhoMW 92
**Kesteven**, Michael 1940- AmMWSc 92
**Kestin**, J 1913- AmMWSc 92
**Kesting**, Robert E 1933- AmMWSc 92
**Kestler**, Frances Roe 1929- ConAu 135
**Kestler**, Maximiliano 1919- WhoFI 92
**Kestnbaum**, Albert S. 1939- WhoEnt 92
**Kestner**, Charles Phillip 1949- WhoRel 92
**Kestner**, Mark Otto 1947- AmMWSc 92

**Kestner,** Melvin Michael 1945- *AmMWSc 92*
**Kestner,** Neil R 1937- *AmMWSc 92*
**Kestner,** Robert Steven, Jr. 1954- *WhoAmL 92*
**Keston,** Albert S *AmMWSc 92*
**Keswick,** Henry Neville Lindley 1938- *IntWW 91, Who 92*
**Keswick,** John Chippendale Lindley 1940- *Who 92*
**Keswick,** Simon Lindley 1942- *IntWW 91, Who 92*
**Keswick,** William 1903-1990 *AnObit 1990*
**Ketcha,** Daniel Michael 1956- *AmMWSc 92*
**Ketcham,** Alfred Schutt 1924- *AmMWSc 92*
**Ketcham,** Bruce V 1918- *AmMWSc 92*
**Ketcham,** Chester Sawyer 1927- *WhoAmP 91*
**Ketcham,** Gregory F. 1963- *WhoEnt 92*
**Ketcham,** Orman Weston 1918- *WhoAmL 92*
**Ketcham,** Ralph Louis 1927- *WrDr 92*
**Ketcham,** Richard Scott 1948- *WhoAmL 92*
**Ketcham,** Robert Thomas 1889-1978 *RelLAm 91*
**Ketcham,** Roger 1926- *AmMWSc 92*
**Ketchel,** Melvin M 1922- *AmMWSc 92*
**Ketchell,** Joseph Gray 1862-1947 *ScFEYrs*
**Ketchen,** Eugene Earl 1921- *AmMWSc 92*
**Ketchen,** Mark B 1948- *AmMWSc 92*
**Ketchersid,** Wayne Lester, Jr. 1946- *WhoFI 92, WhoWest 92*
**Ketcherside,** James L 1935- *WhoIns 92*
**Ketcherside,** William Joseph 1931- *WhoMW 92*
**Ketchie,** Delmer O 1932- *AmMWSc 92*
**Ketchie,** Gary Joseph 1945- *WhoMW 92*
**Ketchledge,** Raymond Waibel 1919- *AmMWSc 92*
**Ketchman,** Jeffrey 1942- *AmMWSc 92*
**Ketchum,** Cliff *TwCWW 91*
**Ketchum,** Dorsey *WhoAmP 91*
**Ketchum,** Frank *TwCWW 91*
**Ketchum,** Gardner M 1919- *AmMWSc 92*
**Ketchum,** Gerald W 1949- *WhoAmP 91*
**Ketchum,** Jack *TwCWW 91*
**Ketchum,** Milo S 1910- *AmMWSc 92*
**Ketchum,** Milo Smith 1910- *WhoWest 92*
**Ketchum,** Paul Abbott 1942- *AmMWSc 92*
**Ketchum,** Philip 1902-1969 *TwCWW 91*
**Ketchum,** Richard M. 1922- *WrDr 92*
**Ketchum,** Robert George 1951- *WhoWest 92*
**Ketchum,** William C. 1931- *WrDr 92*
**Ketelaar,** Jan Arnold Albert 1908- *IntWW 91*
**Ketelbey,** Albert W. 1875-1959 *NewAmDM*
**Ketellapper,** Hendrik Jan 1925- *AmMWSc 92*
**Ketelsen,** James Lee 1930- *IntWW 91*
**Kethley,** John Bryan 1942- *AmMWSc 92, WhoMW 92*
**Kethley,** Thomas William 1913- *AmMWSc 92*
**Ketley,** Arthur Donald 1930- *AmMWSc 92*
**Ketley,** Jeanne Nelson 1938- *AmMWSc 92*
**Ketner,** Joseph Dale 1955- *WhoMW 92*
**Ketner,** Keith B 1921- *AmMWSc 92*
**Ketner,** Ralph Wright 1920- *WhoFI 92*
**Ketola,** H George *AmMWSc 92*
**Ketover,** Harriet Arlene *WhoAmP 91*
**Ketring,** Darold L 1930- *AmMWSc 92*
**Ketring,** James W 1940- *WhoIns 92*
**Ketsdever,** Matthew John 1960- *WhoWest 92*
**Ketsenberg,** Julius T. 1949- *WhoRel 92*
**Kettani,** M. Ali 1941- *ConAu 133*
**Kettel,** Edward Joseph 1925- *WhoWest 92*
**Kettel,** Louis John 1929- *AmMWSc 92*
**Kettelhack,** Guy 1951- *ConAu 134*
**Kettelkamp,** Donald B 1930- *AmMWSc 92*
**Kettelkamp,** Donald Benjamin 1930- *WhoMW 92*
**Kettelkamp,** Larry Dale 1933- *IntAu&W 91, WrDr 92*
**Kettell,** Samuel 1800-1855 *BenetAL 91*
**Kettemborough,** Clifford Russell 1953- *WhoWest 92*
**Kettenhofen,** Robert Frank 1923- *WhoWest 92*
**Ketter,** David E. 1945- *WhoAmL 92, WhoWest 92*
**Ketter,** James Patrick 1956- *WhoMW 92*
**Ketter,** Paul Stephen 1932- *WhoEnt 92*
**Ketter,** Robert L 1928- *AmMWSc 92*
**Ketterer,** Andrew 1949- *WhoAmP 91*
**Ketterer,** John Joseph 1921- *AmMWSc 92*
**Ketterer,** Paul Anthony 1941- *AmMWSc 92*
**Ketterer,** Thomas Robert 1961- *WhoEnt 92*
**Kettering,** Eunice Lea 1906- *WhoEnt 92*
**Kettering,** James David 1942- *AmMWSc 92, WhoWest 92*
**Ketteringham,** John M 1940- *AmMWSc 92*
**Ketterl,** Werner 1925- *IntWW 91*
**Ketterman,** Robert Charles 1957- *WhoEnt 92*
**Ketterson,** John Boyd 1934- *AmMWSc 92*
**Ketting,** Otto 1935- *ConCom 92*
**Kettinger,** Burton Edward, Jr. 1944- *WhoRel 92*
**Kettinger,** LeRoy William 1942- *WhoRel 92*
**Kettl,** Donald F. 1952- *ConAu 34NR*
**Kettle,** Alan Stafford Howard 1925- *Who 92*
**Kettle,** John Robert, III 1951- *WhoAmL 92, WhoEnt 92*
**Kettle,** Roy Henry Richard 1924- *Who 92*
**Kettler,** Robert Ronald 1940- *WhoMW 92*
**Kettleson,** David Noel 1938- *WhoMW 92*
**Kettlewell,** Marion M. 1914- *Who 92*
**Kettlewell,** Richard Wildman 1910- *Who 92*
**Kettman,** John Rutherford, Jr 1939- *AmMWSc 92*
**Kettner,** Charles Adrian 1946- *AmMWSc 92*
**Kettunen,** George 1930- *WhoAmP 91*
**Kety,** Seymour S 1915- *AmMWSc 92, IntWW 91*
**Ketzer,** John *DrAPF 91*
**Keucher,** William Frederick 1918- *WhoRel 92*
**Keudell,** Kenneth Carson 1941- *AmMWSc 92*
**Keudell,** Walter von 1884-1973 *EncTR 91*
**Keulegan,** Garbis 1890- *AmMWSc 92*
**Keulks,** George William 1938- *AmMWSc 92*
**Keuning,** Patricia Dubrava *DrAPF 91*
**Keuper,** Jerome Penn 1921- *AmMWSc 92*
**Keuris,** Tristan 1946- *ConCom 92*
**Keusch,** Gerald Tilden 1938- *AmMWSc 92*
**Keutcha,** Jean 1923- *IntWW 91*
**Kevan,** Douglas Keith McEwan 1920- *AmMWSc 92*
**Kevan,** Larry 1938- *AmMWSc 92*
**Kevan,** Peter Graham 1944- *AmMWSc 92*
**Kevane,** Clement Joseph 1922- *AmMWSc 92*
**Keve,** Paul W. 1913- *WrDr 92*
**Keverian,** George 1931- *WhoAmP 91*
**Kevern,** Niles Russell 1931- *AmMWSc 92*
**Keves,** Gyorgy 1935- *IntWW 91*
**Kevill,** Dennis Neil 1935- *AmMWSc 92, WhoMW 92*
**Kevill-Davies,** Christopher Evelyn 1913- *Who 92*
**Keville,** Errington 1901- *Who 92*
**Kevins,** David Vincent 1954- *WhoWest 92*
**Kevles,** Bettyann Holtzmann 1938- *WrDr 92*
**Kevles,** Daniel J. 1939- *WrDr 92*
**Kevles,** Daniel Jerome 1939- *AmMWSc 92*
**Kevlin,** Mary Louise 1948- *WhoAmL 92*
**Kevorkian,** Aram K 1942- *AmMWSc 92*
**Kevorkian,** Jack 1928?- *News 91 [port], -91-3 [port]*
**Kevorkian,** Jirair 1933- *AmMWSc 92*
**Kewish,** Ralph Wallace 1910- *AmMWSc 92*
**Key,** Addie J. 1933- *WhoBlA 92*
**Key,** Alexander 1904-1979 *TwCSFW 91*
**Key,** Anthony W 1939- *AmMWSc 92*
**Key,** Brian Michael 1947- *Who 92*
**Key,** Charles Daniel 1954- *WhoAmP 91*
**Key,** Charles R 1934- *AmMWSc 92*
**Key,** Clement Denis 1915- *Who 92*
**Key,** Clinton *WhoAmP 91*
**Key,** Dennis Russell 1941- *WhoWest 92*
**Key,** Frances Marie 1928- *WhoEnt 92*
**Key,** Francis Scott 1779-1843 *BenetAL 91, RComAH*
**Key,** Geoffrey 1941- *TwCPaSc*
**Key,** Jack Dayton 1934- *WhoMW 92*
**Key,** Joe Lynn 1933- *AmMWSc 92*
**Key,** John Leonard, II 1955- *WhoEnt 92*
**Key,** Juan Alfred 1951- *WhoBlA 92*
**Key,** June Roe 1917- *WhoBlA 92*
**Key,** Marcella Ann 1947- *WhoMW 92*
**Key,** Martin L. 1943- *WhoMW 92*
**Key,** Morris Dale 1939- *AmMWSc 92*
**Key,** Phyllis May 1942- *WhoWest 92*
**Key,** Robert 1945- *Who 92*
**Key,** Rodney J. 1958- *WhoAmL 92*
**Key,** Stephen Lewis 1943- *WhoFI 92*
**Key,** Ted 1912- *WhoEnt 92*
**Key,** Thomas Donnell Sporer 1928- *WhoRel 92*
**Key,** Zadie Bowling 1921- *WhoAmP 91*
**Keydel,** Frederick Reid 1928- *WhoAmL 92*
**Keye,** William Richard, Jr. 1943- *WhoWest 92*
**Keyes** *Who 92*
**Keyes,** Baron 1919- *Who 92*
**Keyes,** Alan L. 1950- *WhoBlA 92*
**Keyes,** Alfred Lee 1937- *WhoBlA 92*
**Keyes,** Andrew Jonathan, Sr. 1918- *WhoBlA 92*
**Keyes,** Charles Fenton 1937- *WhoRel 92*
**Keyes,** Claire *DrAPF 91*
**Keyes,** Daniel *DrAPF 91*
**Keyes,** Daniel 1927- *BenetAL 91, IntAu&W 91, TwCSFW 91, WhoMW 92, WrDr 92*
**Keyes,** Darlynn Ladd 1948- *WhoFI 92*
**Keyes,** David Elliot 1956- *AmMWSc 92*
**Keyes,** Evelyn 1919- *IntMPA 92*
**Keyes,** Everett A 1903- *AmMWSc 92*
**Keyes,** Holly Renfro 1952- *WhoEnt 92*
**Keyes,** Irwin 1952- *WhoEnt 92*
**Keyes,** Jack Lynn 1941- *AmMWSc 92*
**Keyes,** James Bondurant 1927- *WhoWest 92*
**Keyes,** James Dale 1958- *WhoWest 92*
**Keyes,** James Henry 1940- *WhoFI 92*
**Keyes,** James Lyman, Jr. 1928- *WhoMW 92*
**Keyes,** James Richard 1949- *WhoFI 92*
**Keyes,** Marion Alvah, IV 1938- *AmMWSc 92*
**Keyes,** Orval Andrew 1913- *WhoAmP 91*
**Keyes,** Paul Holt 1943- *AmMWSc 92*
**Keyes,** Paul Landis 1938- *AmMWSc 92, WhoMW 92*
**Keyes,** Paul W. *LesBEnT 92*
**Keyes,** Robert Lord *DrAPF 91*
**Keyes,** Robert William 1921- *AmMWSc 92*
**Keyes,** Sidney 1922-1943 *FacFETw, RfGEnL 91*
**Keyes,** Terence Charles 1957- *WhoEnt 92*
**Keyes,** Thomas Francis 1945- *AmMWSc 92*
**Keyfitz,** Nathan 1913- *IntWW 91, WrDr 92*
**Keyhoe,** Donald Edward 1897-1988 *ScFEYrs*
**Keyishian,** M. Deiter *DrAPF 91*
**Keyko,** George John 1924- *WhoFI 92*
**Keylock,** Leslie Robert 1933- *WhoRel 92*
**Keyloun,** Mark 1960- *IntMPA 92*
**Keynes,** Harvey Bayard 1940- *AmMWSc 92*
**Keynes,** John Maynard 1883-1946 *FacFETw*
**Keynes,** Richard Darwin 1919- *IntWW 91, Who 92*
**Keynes,** Stephen John 1927- *Who 92*
**Keys,** Alexander George William 1923- *Who 92*
**Keys,** Ancel 1904- *AmMWSc 92*
**Keys,** Bill 1923-1990 *AnObit 1990*
**Keys,** Brady, Jr. 1937- *WhoBlA 92*
**Keys,** Charles Everel 1921- *AmMWSc 92*
**Keys,** Christopher Banfield 1919- *Who 92*
**Keys,** Christopher Bennett 1946- *WhoMW 92*
**Keys,** Donald Fraser 1924- *WhoWest 92*
**Keys,** Doris Turner 1930- *WhoBlA 92*
**Keys,** John David 1922- *AmMWSc 92*
**Keys,** Kerry Shawn *DrAPF 91*
**Keys,** L Ken 1939- *AmMWSc 92*
**Keys,** Martha Elizabeth 1930- *WhoAmP 91*
**Keys,** Michael Brian 1948- *WhoAmP 91*
**Keys,** Randolph 1966- *WhoBlA 92*
**Keys,** Richard Taylor 1931- *AmMWSc 92*
**Keys,** Steven Franklin 1958- *WhoMW 92*
**Keys,** Thomas Edward 1908- *AmMWSc 92, WrDr 92*
**Keys,** William *Who 92*
**Keys,** William Wayland 1957- *WhoEnt 92*
**Keyser,** Christine Lynn 1956- *WhoMW 92*
**Keyser,** David Richard 1941- *AmMWSc 92*
**Keyser,** F Ray, Jr 1927- *WhoAmP 91*
**Keyser,** George F. 1932- *WhoBlA 92*
**Keyser,** John Alden, Jr. 1943- *WhoFI 92*
**Keyser,** Kerry R *WhoAmP 91*
**Keyser,** Les 1943- *WhoEnt 92*
**Keyser,** Martha Florence 1943- *WhoFI 92*
**Keyser,** N H 1918- *AmMWSc 92*
**Keyser,** Peter D 1945- *AmMWSc 92*
**Keyser,** Peter Dirck 1835-1897 *BiInAmS*
**Keyserling,** Harriet Selma 1922- *WhoAmP 91*
**Keyserling,** Hermann 1880-1946 *EncTR 91*
**Keyserling,** Leon H 1908-1987 *FacFETw*
**Keyston,** Stephani Ann 1955- *WhoWest 92*
**Keyt,** Alonzo Thrasher 1827-1885 *BiInAmS*
**Keyt,** Donald E 1927- *AmMWSc 92*
**Keyworth,** Donald Arthur 1930- *AmMWSc 92*
**Keyworth,** George A, II 1939- *AmMWSc 92, WhoAmP 91*
**Keyworth,** George Albert, II 1939- *IntWW 91, WhoFI 92*
**Keyzer,** Hendrik 1931- *AmMWSc 92*
**Kezdi,** Paul 1914- *AmMWSc 92*
**Kezdy,** Ferenc J 1929- *AmMWSc 92*
**Kezer,** Claude Dean 1933- *WhoEnt 92*
**Kezer,** Pauline Ryder 1942- *WhoAmP 91*
**Kezios,** Stothe Peter 1921- *AmMWSc 92*
**Kezlan,** Thomas Phillip 1935- *AmMWSc 92*
**Kgositsile,** Keorapetse 1938- *LiExTwC*
**Kgositsile,** Keorapetse William *DrAPF 91*
**Kgositsile,** Kkeorapetse 1938- *IntAu&W 91*
**Khabbaz,** Samir Anton 1932- *AmMWSc 92*
**Khachadurian,** Avedis K 1926- *AmMWSc 92*
**Khachatourians,** George G 1940- *AmMWSc 92*
**Khachaturian,** Aram Ilyich 1903-1978 *FacFETw*
**Khachaturian,** Narbey 1924- *AmMWSc 92*
**Khachaturian,** Zaven Setrak 1937- *AmMWSc 92*
**Khachaturov,** Tigran Sergeevich 1906-1989 *SovUnBD*
**Khaddam,** Abdel Halim *IntWW 91*
**Khadduri,** Majid 1908- *IntAu&W 91, IntWW 91*
**Khadduri,** Majid 1909- *WrDr 92*
**Khadzhinov,** Mikhail Ivanovich 1899-1980 *SovUnBD*
**Khail,** Muhammad Ali Aba al- 1935- *IntWW 91*
**Khain,** Viktor Yefimovich 1914- *IntWW 91*
**Khair,** Abdul Wahab 1941- *AmMWSc 92*
**Khair-Ud-Din,** Rt.Rev. *Who 92*
**Khairallah,** Edward A 1936- *AmMWSc 92*
**Khairallah,** Philip Asad 1928- *AmMWSc 92*
**Khaitan,** Krishan 1939- *IntWW 91*
**Khaketla,** Benett Makalo 1914- *IntWW 91*
**Khakoo,** Murtadha A 1953- *AmMWSc 92*
**Khalaf,** Kamel T 1922- *AmMWSc 92*
**Khalafalla,** Sanaa E 1924- *AmMWSc 92*
**Khaldeyev,** Mikhail Ivanovich 1921- *IntWW 91*
**Khaled,** Mohammad Abu 1942- *AmMWSc 92*
**Khalid,** Mansour 1931- *IntWW 91*
**Khalifa Bin Hamad Al-Thani** *IntWW 91*
**Khalifa,** Hamed bin Isa al- 1950- *IntWW 91*
**Khalifa,** Isa bin Sulman al- 1933- *IntWW 91*
**Khalifa,** Khalifa bin Sulman al- 1935- *IntWW 91*
**Khalifa,** Ramzi A 1940- *AmMWSc 92*
**Khalifah,** Raja Gabriel 1942- *AmMWSc 92*
**Khalikyar,** Fazle Haq 1934- *IntWW 91*
**Khalil Bey** 1831-1879 *ThHEIm*
**Khalil,** Elias Lafi 1957- *WhoMW 92*
**Khalil,** Fakhruddin 1933- *WhoFI 92*
**Khalil,** M Aslam Khan 1950- *AmMWSc 92*
**Khalil,** Michel 1935- *AmMWSc 92*
**Khalil,** Mohamed Thanaa 1933- *AmMWSc 92*
**Khalil,** Mustafa 1920- *IntWW 91*
**Khalil,** Shoukry Khalil Wahba 1930- *AmMWSc 92*
**Khalili,** Ali A 1932- *AmMWSc 92*
**Khalilov,** Kurban Ali 1906- *IntWW 91*
**Khalimsky,** Efim 1938- *WhoMW 92*
**Khalimsky,** Efim D 1938- *AmMWSc 92*
**Khalsa,** Sat Tara Singh 1953- *WhoWest 92*
**Khalsa,** Shakti Parwha Kaur 1929- *WhoWest 92*
**Khamenei,** Hojatoleslam Ali 1940- *IntWW 91*
**Khamenei,** Sayyed Ali 1940- *Who 92*
**Khamis,** Harry Joseph 1951- *AmMWSc 92*
**Khamis,** Mar Aprim *WhoRel 92*
**Khamisa,** Azim Noordin 1949- *WhoFI 92*
**Khamsy,** Saly 1931- *IntWW 91*
**Khan,** Abdul Azim 1950- *WhoWest 92*
**Khan,** Abdul Jamil 1940- *AmMWSc 92*
**Khan,** Abdul Waheed 1928- *AmMWSc 92*
**Khan,** Abraham *WhoHisp 92*
**Khan,** Abrahim Habibulla 1943- *WhoRel 92*
**Khan,** Ahmed M. 1955- *WhoWest 92*
**Khan,** Akbar 1940- *WhoBlA 92*
**Khan,** Akhtar Salamat 1944- *AmMWSc 92*
**Khan,** Ali Akbar 1922- *IntWW 91*
**Khan,** Amanullah Rashid 1927- *AmMWSc 92*
**Khan,** Amjad Ali 1945- *IntWW 91*
**Khan,** Anwar Ahmad 1934- *AmMWSc 92*
**Khan,** Ata M 1941- *AmMWSc 92*
**Khan,** Chaka 1953- *NewAmDM, WhoEnt 92*
**Khan,** Chaka 1954- *WhoBlA 92*
**Khan,** Faiz Mohammad 1938- *AmMWSc 92*
**Khan,** Ghulam Ishaq 1915- *IntWW 91, Who 92*
**Khan,** Hazrat Inayat 1882-1927 *RelLAm 91*
**Khan,** Humayun 1932- *IntWW 91, Who 92*
**Khan,** Imran *IntWW 91*
**Khan,** Inamullah 1914- *IntWW 91*
**Khan,** Iqbal M 1950- *AmMWSc 92*
**Khan,** Ismith 1925- *WrDr 92*
**Khan,** Jamil Akber 1952- *AmMWSc 92*
**Khan,** Mahbub R 1949- *AmMWSc 92*

**Khan**, Mahmood Ahmed 1945- *AmMWSc 92*
**Khan**, Masud Husain 1919- *IntAu&W 91*
**Khan**, Mehboob *IntDcF 2-2*
**Khan**, Mohamed Shaheed 1933- *AmMWSc 92*
**Khan**, Mohammad 1919- *IntWW 91*
**Khan**, Mohammad Asad *AmMWSc 92*
**Khan**, Mohammad Iqbal 1950- *AmMWSc 92*
**Khan**, Mohammed Abdul Quddus 1939- *AmMWSc 92*
**Khan**, Mohammed Nasrullah 1933- *AmMWSc 92*
**Khan**, Moin Haque 1955- *WhoMW 92*
**Khan**, Muhammad Ishtiaq 1934- *IntWW 91*
**Khan**, Mushtaq Ahmad 1939- *AmMWSc 92*
**Khan**, Muzaffar Ali 1938- *WhoFI 92*
**Khan**, Nasim A 1938- *AmMWSc 92*
**Khan**, Niazi Imran 1952- *IntWW 91*
**Khan**, Paul 1923- *AmMWSc 92*
**Khan**, Raana Liaquat Ali 1905-1990 *AnObit 1990*
**Khan**, Rasul Azim 1934- *AmMWSc 92*
**Khan**, Saad Akhtar 1958- *AmMWSc 92*
**Khan**, Sahabzada Yaqub 1920- *IntWW 91*
**Khan**, Sarbuland Bill 1951- *WhoWest 92*
**Khan**, Sardar Feroze 1941- *WhoRel 92*
**Khan**, Sekender Ali 1933- *AmMWSc 92*
**Khan**, Shabbir Ahmed 1945- *AmMWSc 92*
**Khan**, Shahamat Ullah 1937- *AmMWSc 92*
**Khan**, Shakil Ahmad *AmMWSc 92*
**Khan**, Sirajul Hossain 1926- *IntWW 91*
**Khan**, Steve Harris 1947- *WhoEnt 92*
**Khan**, Steven Shahid 1956- *WhoWest 92*
**Khan**, Sultana 1947- *AmMWSc 92*
**Khan**, Vilayat Inayat 1916- *RelLAm 91*
**Khan**, Winston 1934- *AmMWSc 92*
**Khan**, Zulfiqar Ali 1930- *IntWW 91*
**Khan Niazi**, Imran Ahmad *Who 92*
**Khandelwal**, Ramji Lal 1944- *AmMWSc 92*
**Khandker** *IntWW 91*
**Khandwala**, Atul S *AmMWSc 92*
**Khane**, Abd-El Rahman 1931- *IntWW 91*
**Khaner**, Jeffrey 1958- *WhoEnt 92*
**Khang**, Soon-Jai 1944- *AmMWSc 92*
**Khanh**, Emanuelle 1937- *IntWW 91*
**Khani**, Abdallah Fikri El- 1925- *IntWW 91*
**Khanjian**, John 1932- *WhoRel 92*
**Khanna**, Faqir Chand 1935- *AmMWSc 92*
**Khanna**, Hari Narayan 1944- *WhoWest 92*
**Khanna**, Harish 1955- *WhoFI 92*
**Khanna**, Jatinder Mohan 1936- *AmMWSc 92*
**Khanna**, Kailash Chand 1938- *WhoFI 92*
**Khanna**, Krishan L 1933- *AmMWSc 92*
**Khanna**, Pyare Lal 1945- *AmMWSc 92*
**Khanna**, Ravi 1944- *AmMWSc 92*
**Khanna**, Sardari Lal 1937- *AmMWSc 92*
**Khanna**, Shyam Mohan 1932- *AmMWSc 92*
**Khansari**, David Nemat 1944- *AmMWSc 92*
**Khanzadian**, Vahan 1939- *WhoEnt 92*
**Kharaka**, Yousif Khoshu 1941- *AmMWSc 92*
**Kharasch**, Evan David 1957- *WhoWest 92*
**Kharasch**, Norman 1914- *AmMWSc 92*
**Kharchev**, Konstantin Mikhailovich 1934- *IntWW 91*
**Khare**, Ashok Kumar 1948- *AmMWSc 92*
**Khare**, Bishun Narain 1933- *AmMWSc 92*
**Khare**, Mohan 1942- *AmMWSc 92, WhoFI 92*
**Khare**, R. S. *WrDr 92*
**Khargonekar**, Pramod P 1956- *AmMWSc 92*
**Kharlamov**, Aleksandr Pavlovich 1929- *IntWW 91*
**Kharlamov**, Mikhail Averkyevich 1913- *IntWW 91*
**Kharms**, Daniil Ivanovich 1905-1942 *SovUnBD*
**Kharrat**, Edward al- 1926- *IntWW 91*
**Khasat**, Namita 1960- *WhoFI 92*
**Khasat**, Vijay P. 1941- *WhoMW 92*
**Khashoggi**, Adnan M. 1935- *IntWW 91*
**Khasnabis**, Snehamay 1939- *AmMWSc 92*
**Khatami**, Mahin 1943- *AmMWSc 92*
**Khatchadourian**, Haig 1925- *IntAu&W 91*
**Khatchaturian**, Aram Il'yich 1903-1978 *NewAmDM*
**Khatena**, Joe 1925- *IntAu&W 91*
**Khatib**, Ahmed al- 1933- *IntWW 91*
**Khatib**, Hisham M 1936- *AmMWSc 92*
**Khatib**, Mohammad al- 1930- *IntWW 91*
**Khatib**, Mohammed Fathalla El- 1927- *IntWW 91*
**Khatib**, Syed Malik 1940- *WhoBlA 92*
**Khatib-Rahbar**, Mohsen 1954- *AmMWSc 92*
**Khatra**, Balwant Singh 1945- *AmMWSc 92*
**Khatri**, Hiralal C 1936- *AmMWSc 92*
**Khattab**, Ghazi M A 1930- *AmMWSc 92*
**Khattak**, Chandra Prakash 1944- *AmMWSc 92*
**Khattar**, Mukesh Kumar 1951- *WhoWest 92*
**Khavin**, Vladimir Vosifovich 1931- *IntWW 91*
**Khavkin**, Theodor 1919- *AmMWSc 92*
**Khaw**, Ban-An 1947- *AmMWSc 92*
**Khaw**, Kay-Tee 1950- *Who 92*
**Khaw**, Noeline 1944- *WhoWest 92*
**Khawaja**, Ikram Ullah 1942- *AmMWSc 92*
**Khawlah Bint al-Azwar al-Kindiyyah** *EncAmaz 91*
**Khayat**, Ali 1938- *AmMWSc 92*
**Khayata**, Abdul Wahab Ismail 1924- *IntWW 91*
**Khayeyev**, Izatullo Khayeyevich 1936- *IntWW 91*
**Khaykin**, Boris Emmanuelovich 1904-1978 *SovUnBD*
**Khazaee**, Malek Khosrow 1948- *WhoWest 92*
**Khazahnov**, Boris 1928- *LiExTwC*
**Khazan**, Naim 1921- *AmMWSc 92*
**Khediri**, El-Hadi 1934- *IntWW 91*
**Kheifits**, Iosif Yefimovich 1905- *SovUnBD*
**Kheiralla**, Ibrahim George 1849-1929 *RelLAm 91*
**Khelil**, Ismail 1932- *IntWW 91*
**Khera**, Ashok Kumar 1944- *WhoWest 92*
**Khera**, Kundan Singh 1922- *AmMWSc 92*
**Kherdian**, David *DrAPF 91*
**Kherdian**, David 1931- *ChlLR 24 [port], IntAu&W 91, WrDr 92*
**Khiem**, Tran Thien *IntWW 91*
**Khieu**, Samphan 1932- *IntWW 91*
**Khitrov**, Stepan Dmitriyevich 1910- *IntWW 91*
**Khitrun**, Leonid Ivanovich 1930- *IntWW 91*
**Khlebnikov**, Velemir 1885-1922 *SovUnBD*
**Khlebnikov**, Velemir Vladimirovich 1885-1922 *FacFETw*
**Khlefawi**, Abdel Rahman 1927- *IntWW 91*
**Khmara**, Edward Ilia 1947- *WhoEnt 92*
**Khmara**, Sergei 1905- *IntAu&W 91*
**Kho**, Boen Tong 1919- *AmMWSc 92*
**Kho**, Eusebio 1933- *WhoMW 92*
**Khoarai**, Paul *WhoRel 92*
**Khodadad**, Jena Khadem *AmMWSc 92*
**Khodasevich**, Vladislav Felitsyanovich 1886-1939 *SovUnBD*
**Khodasevich**, Vladislav Relitsianovich 1886-1939 *LiExTwC*
**Khodyrev**, Vladimir Yakovlevich 1930- *IntWW 91*
**Khoe**, Giok-djan 1946- *WhoFI 92*
**Khokhlov**, Boris Ivanovich 1932- *IntWW 91*
**Khokhlov**, Konstantin Pavlovich 1885-1956 *SovUnBD*
**Khokhlov**, Vitaly Sergeyevich 1938- *IntWW 91*
**Khokhlova**, Aleksandra Sergeevna 1897-1985 *SovUnBD*
**Kholodny**, Nikolay Grigor'evich 1882-1953 *SovUnBD*
**Khomeini**, Ruhollah 1900?-1989 *FacFETw [port]*
**Khomyakov**, Aleksandr Aleksandrovich 1932- *IntWW 91*
**Khoo**, Francis Kah Siang 1947- *Who 92*
**Khoo**, Teng Lek 1943- *AmMWSc 92*
**Khoobyarian**, Newton 1924- *AmMWSc 92*
**Khoraiche**, Antoine Pierre 1907- *IntWW 91, WhoRel 92*
**Khorana**, Brij Mohan 1939- *AmMWSc 92*
**Khorana**, Har Gobind 1922- *AmMWSc 92, IntWW 91, Who 92, WhoNob 90*
**Khorey**, David Eugene 1959- *WhoAmL 92*
**Khosah**, Robinson Panganai 1954- *AmMWSc 92*
**Khosh**, Mary Sivert 1942- *WhoFI 92, WhoMW 92*
**Khoshnevisan**, Mohsen Monte *AmMWSc 92*
**Khosla**, Gopal Das 1901- *IntAu&W 91, WrDr 92*
**Khosla**, Mahesh C 1925- *AmMWSc 92*
**Khosla**, Rajinder Paul 1933- *AmMWSc 92*
**Khosla**, Sheelkumar Lalchand 1934- *IntWW 91*
**Khosla**, Ved Mitter 1926- *WhoWest 92*
**Khouini**, Hamadi 1943- *Who 92*
**Khouri**, Fred John 1916- *WrDr 92*
**Khouri**, Issam 1934- *IntWW 91*
**Khouri**, Pierre 1929- *IntWW 91*
**Khoury**, Elia *WhoRel 92*
**Khoury**, George 1943- *AmMWSc 92*
**Khoury**, George Gilbert 1923- *WhoMW 92*
**Khoury**, Riad Philip 1935- *WhoFI 92*
**Khoury**, Rollin 1935- *WhoAmP 91*
**Khouzam**, Nelly N. 1958- *WhoAmL 92*
**Khovrin**, Nikolai Ivanovich 1922- *IntWW 91*
**Khrennikov**, Tikhon 1913- *NewAmDM*
**Khrennikov**, Tikhon Nikolaevich 1913- *SovUnBD*
**Khrennikov**, Tikhon Nikolayevich 1913- *FacFETw, IntWW 91*
**Khristoradnov**, Yuriy Nikolayevich 1929- *IntWW 91*
**Khrunichev**, Mikhail Vasil'evich 1901-1961 *SovUnBD*
**Khrushchev**, Nikita Sergeevich 1894-1971 *SovUnBD*
**Khrushchev**, Nikita Sergeyevich 1894-1971 *FacFETw [port]*
**Khrzhanovsky**, Andrei Yurevich 1939- *IntWW 91*
**Khrzhanovsky**, Andrey Yur'evich 1939- *SovUnBD*
**Khudaiberdyev**, Narmankhonmadi D. 1928- *IntWW 91*
**Khumalo**, S. A. *WhoRel 92*
**Khurana**, Krishan Kumar 1955- *AmMWSc 92*
**Khurana**, Shri Sundar Lal 1919- *IntWW 91*
**Khurana**, Surjit Singh 1931- *AmMWSc 92*
**Khuri**, Nicola Najib 1933- *AmMWSc 92*
**Khush**, Gurdev S 1935- *AmMWSc 92*
**Khush**, Gurdev Singh 1935- *IntWW 91*
**Khussaiby**, Salim Bin Mohammed Bin S. al- 1939- *IntWW 91*
**Khuweiter**, Abdul Aziz Abdallah al- 1927- *IntWW 91*
**Khwaja**, Tasneem Afzal 1936- *AmMWSc 92*
**Khwaja**, Waqas Ahmad 1952- *IntAu&W 91*
**Ki**, Kaze *DrAPF 91*
**Kiah**, Ruth Josephine 1927- *WhoBlA 92*
**Kiam**, Victor K., III 1959- *WhoFI 92*
**Kiang**, Assumpta 1939- *WhoWest 92*
**Kiang**, Chia Szu 1941- *AmMWSc 92*
**Kiang**, David Teh-Ming 1935- *AmMWSc 92*
**Kiang**, Heng-Pin 1949- *WhoAmL 92*
**Kiang**, Nelson Yuan-Sheng 1929- *AmMWSc 92*
**Kiang**, Robert L 1939- *AmMWSc 92*
**Kiang**, Ying Chao *AmMWSc 92*
**Kiang**, Yun-Tzu 1932- *AmMWSc 92*
**Kiano**, Julius Gikonyo 1926- *IntWW 91*
**Kiarsis**, Victor, Jr. 1951- *WhoFI 92*
**Kibaki**, Mwai 1931- *IntWW 91*
**Kibal'nikov**, Aleksandr Pavlovich 1912- *SovUnBD*
**Kibanda**, Simon-Pierre 1927- *IntWW 91*
**Kibbe**, James William 1926- *WhoFI 92*
**Kibbee**, Roland d1984 *LesBEnT 92*
**Kibbel**, William H, Jr 1923- *AmMWSc 92*
**Kibbey**, Donald Eugene 1912- *AmMWSc 92*
**Kibbey**, Maura Christine 1962- *AmMWSc 92*
**Kibbey**, Sidney Basil 1916- *Who 92*
**Kibbie**, John Patrick 1929- *WhoAmP 91*
**Kibble**, Edward Bruce 1940- *WhoWest 92*
**Kibble**, Thomas Walter Bannerman 1932- *IntWW 91, Who 92*
**Kibby**, Charles Leonard 1938- *AmMWSc 92*
**Kibby**, Robert Randel 1962- *WhoAmL 92*
**Kibe**, Yoshiaki 1926- *IntWW 91*
**Kibedi**, Wanume 1941- *IntWW 91*
**Kibedi Varga**, Aron 1930- *IntWW 91*
**Kibens**, Valdis 1936- *AmMWSc 92, WhoMW 92*
**Kibler**, Kenneth G 1940- *AmMWSc 92*
**Kibler**, Minifred Elizabeth Burrow 1911- *WhoAmP 91*
**Kibler**, Ray Franklin, III 1951- *WhoRel 92*
**Kibler**, Rhoda Smith 1947- *WhoAmL 92*
**Kibler**, Ruthann 1942- *AmMWSc 92*
**Kibria**, A. M. S. 1931- *IntWW 91*
**Kibrick**, Anne 1919- *IntWW 91*
**Kibrick**, Anne K 1919- *AmMWSc 92*
**Kibrick**, Sidney 1916- *AmMWSc 92*
**Kibrik**, Yevegeniy Adol'fovich 1906-1978 *SovUnBD*
**Kice**, John Lord 1930- *AmMWSc 92*
**Kicher**, Thomas Patrick 1937- *AmMWSc 92*
**Kick**, Francis Raymond, Jr. 1965- *WhoEnt 92*
**Kickbush**, Bill E. 1950- *WhoEnt 92, WhoWest 92*
**Kickel**, James Robert 1949- *WhoFI 92*
**Kickham**, Brian John 1957- *WhoFI 92*
**Kickler**, James A *WhoIns 92*
**Kickler**, Thomas Steven 1947- *AmMWSc 92*
**Kicklighter**, Claude Milton 1933- *WhoWest 92*
**Kicknosway**, Faye *DrAPF 91*
**Kicliter**, Ernest Earl, Jr 1945- *AmMWSc 92*
**Kicska**, Paul A 1932- *AmMWSc 92*
**Kidawa**, Anthony Stanley 1942- *AmMWSc 92*
**Kidd**, Bernard Sean Langford 1931- *AmMWSc 92*
**Kidd**, Cecil 1933- *Who 92*
**Kidd**, Charles 1952- *ConAu 134*
**Kidd**, Charles William 1952- *IntAu&W 91, Who 92*
**Kidd**, David Eugene 1930- *AmMWSc 92*
**Kidd**, David Thomas 1934- *WhoAmL 92*
**Kidd**, Debra Jean 1956- *WhoFI 92, WhoMW 92*
**Kidd**, Edwards Culver 1914- *WhoAmP 91*
**Kidd**, Foster 1924- *WhoBlA 92*
**Kidd**, Frank Alan 1952- *AmMWSc 92*
**Kidd**, Frank Forrest 1938- *Who 92*
**Kidd**, George, Jr. 1938- *WhoMW 92*
**Kidd**, George Joseph, Jr 1934- *AmMWSc 92*
**Kidd**, Harold J 1924- *AmMWSc 92*
**Kidd**, Herbert, Jr. *WhoBlA 92*
**Kidd**, James Lambert 1933- *WhoRel 92*
**Kidd**, John Edward 1936- *WhoAmL 92*
**Kidd**, John S. *WhoRel 92*
**Kidd**, John William 1911- *WhoMW 92*
**Kidd**, Katherine Ashby 1941- *WhoRel 92*
**Kidd**, Kenneth Kay 1941- *AmMWSc 92*
**Kidd**, Mae Street *WhoAmP 91*
**Kidd**, Mae Taylor Street *NotBlAW 92*
**Kidd**, Marion June 1923- *WhoAmP 91*
**Kidd**, Melvin Don 1937- *WhoFI 92*
**Kidd**, Michael *WhoEnt 92*
**Kidd**, Reuben Proctor 1913- *WhoWest 92*
**Kidd**, Richard 1952- *TwCPaSc*
**Kidd**, Richard Wayne 1947- *AmMWSc 92*
**Kidd**, Robert 1918- *Who 92*
**Kidd**, Robert Garth 1936- *AmMWSc 92*
**Kidd**, Robert Hugh 1944- *WhoFI 92*
**Kidd**, Ronald Alexander 1926- *Who 92*
**Kidd**, Russ *TwCWW 91*
**Kidd**, Virginia 1921- *IntAu&W 91*
**Kidd**, William 1645?-1701 *BenetAL 91*
**Kidd**, William 1803-1867 *DcLB 106*
**Kidd**, William B. *WhoRel 92*
**Kidd**, William Spencer Francis 1947- *AmMWSc 92*
**Kidd**, Willie Mae 1921- *WhoBlA 92*
**Kidde**, John Edgar 1946- *WhoWest 92*
**Kidde**, John Lyon 1934- *WhoFI 92*
**Kidder**, David Lee 1957- *WhoMW 92*
**Kidder**, Ernest H 1912- *AmMWSc 92*
**Kidder**, Fred Dockstater 1922- *WhoAmL 92*
**Kidder**, George Wallace, III 1934- *AmMWSc 92*
**Kidder**, George Wallace, Jr 1902- *AmMWSc 92*
**Kidder**, Gerald 1940- *AmMWSc 92*
**Kidder**, Gerald Marshall 1944- *AmMWSc 92*
**Kidder**, Harold Edward 1922- *AmMWSc 92*
**Kidder**, Jerome Henry 1842-1889 *BiInAmS*
**Kidder**, John Newell 1932- *AmMWSc 92*
**Kidder**, Margot 1948- *IntMPA 92, WhoEnt 92*
**Kidder**, Ray Edward 1923- *AmMWSc 92*
**Kidder**, Rolland Elliot 1940- *WhoAmP 91*
**Kidder**, S. Joseph 1953- *WhoRel 92*
**Kidder**, Tracy *SourALJ*
**Kidder**, Tracy 1945- *WrDr 92*
**Kidder**, William F 1912- *WhoAmP 91*
**Kiddoo**, Jean Lynn 1953- *WhoAmL 92*
**Kiddoo**, Michael Arthur, Jr. 1959- *WhoMW 92*
**Kiddoo**, Richard Clyde 1927- *WhoFI 92*
**Kiddoo**, Robert James 1936- *WhoFI 92, WhoWest 92*
**Kideckel**, Arnold 1939- *WhoAmL 92, WhoIns 92*
**Kidgell**, John Earle 1943- *Who 92*
**Kidgell**, Susan Campbell 1949- *WhoMW 92*
**Kidman**, Thomas Walter 1915- *Who 92*
**Kidnay**, Arthur J 1934- *AmMWSc 92*
**Kidner**, Michael 1917- *TwCPaSc*
**Kidney**, Gary Wayne 1953- *WhoWest 92*
**Kidu**, Buri 1945- *IntWW 91, Who 92*
**Kidwai**, Mohsina 1932- *IntWW 91*
**Kidwell**, Albert Laws 1919- *AmMWSc 92*
**Kidwell**, Carol 1923- *WrDr 92*
**Kidwell**, David Stephen 1940- *WhoFI 92*
**Kidwell**, John Andrew 1945- *WhoAmL 92*
**Kidwell**, Margaret Gale 1933- *AmMWSc 92*
**Kidwell**, Raymond Incledon 1926- *Who 92*
**Kidwell**, Roger Lynn 1938- *AmMWSc 92*
**Kidwell**, William Robert 1936- *AmMWSc 92*
**Kiebala**, Susan Marie 1952- *WhoMW 92*
**Kieber**, Walter 1931- *IntWW 91*
**Kiebert**, Kermit V *WhoAmP 91*
**Kiebitz**, Ashley Marion 1934- *WhoEnt 92*
**Kiebler**, John W 1928- *AmMWSc 92*
**Kieburtz**, R Bruce 1931- *AmMWSc 92*
**Kieburtz**, Richard B 1933- *AmMWSc 92*
**Kiech**, Earl Lockett 1949- *AmMWSc 92*
**Kiechle**, Frederick Leonard 1946- *AmMWSc 92, WhoMW 92*
**Kiecker**, Greg 1951- *WhoAmP 91*
**Kieckhefer**, Richard 1946- *WhoRel 92*
**Kieckhefer**, Robert William 1933- *AmMWSc 92*
**Kieda**, David Basil 1960- *WhoWest 92*
**Kiefer**, Anselm 1945- *IntWW 91, WorArt 1980 [port]*

**Kiefer**, Barry Irwin 1933- *AmMWSc 92*
**Kiefer**, Charles Randolph 1947- *AmMWSc 92*
**Kiefer**, David John 1938- *AmMWSc 92*
**Kiefer**, Edgar Francis 1934- *AmMWSc 92*
**Kiefer**, Harold Milton 1933- *AmMWSc 92*
**Kiefer**, John David 1940- *AmMWSc 92*
**Kiefer**, John Harold 1932- *AmMWSc 92*
**Kiefer**, Kali Ann 1961- *WhoFI 92, WhoMW 92*
**Kiefer**, Kurt 1955- *WhoMW 92*
**Kiefer**, Middleton *IntAu&W 91X*
**Kiefer**, Nat Gerard 1939- *WhoAmP 91*
**Kiefer**, Peter Turn 1934- *WhoEnt 92*
**Kiefer**, Ralph W 1934- *AmMWSc 92*
**Kiefer**, Raymond H 1927- *WhoIns 92, WhoMW 92*
**Kiefer**, Richard L 1937- *AmMWSc 92*
**Kiefer**, Richard Wagner 1913- *WhoAmL 92*
**Kiefer**, Rita *DrAPF 91*
**Kiefer**, Robert John 1936- *WhoWest 92*
**Kiefer**, Warren 1930- *IntAu&W 91, WrDr 92*
**Kiefert**, Alice Stockwell 1929- *WhoFI 92, WhoMW 92*
**Kieff**, Elliott Dan 1943- *AmMWSc 92*
**Kieffer**, Hugh Hartman 1939- *AmMWSc 92*
**Kieffer**, Jarold A 1923- *WhoAmP 91*
**Kieffer**, Nat 1930- *AmMWSc 92*
**Kieffer**, R. W. 1937- *WhoWest 92*
**Kieffer**, Stephen A 1935- *AmMWSc 92*
**Kieffer**, Susan Werner 1942- *AmMWSc 92*
**Kieffer**, William Franklin 1915- *AmMWSc 92*
**Kieft**, Gerald Nelson 1946- *WhoMW 92*
**Kieft**, John A 1941- *AmMWSc 92*
**Kieft**, Lester 1912- *AmMWSc 92*
**Kieft**, Richard Leonard 1945- *AmMWSc 92*
**Kieft**, Willem 1597-1647 *BenetAL 91*
**Kiehart**, Lawrence Robert 1938- *WhoMW 92*
**Kiehl**, Erich Henry 1920- *WhoRel 92*
**Kiehl**, Jeffrey Theodore 1952- *AmMWSc 92*
**Kiehl**, Richard Arthur 1948- *AmMWSc 92*
**Kiehlmann**, Eberhard 1937- *AmMWSc 92*
**Kiehn**, Mogens Hans 1918- *WhoWest 92*
**Kiehn**, Robert Mitchell 1929- *AmMWSc 92*
**Kiehne**, Anna Marie 1947- *WhoWest 92*
**Kiehne**, Kalvin Zeno 1955- *WhoAmP 91*
**Kiel**, Johnathan Lloyd 1949- *AmMWSc 92*
**Kiel**, Ollie Mae 1931- *WhoAmP 91*
**Kiel**, Otis Gerald 1931- *AmMWSc 92*
**Kiel**, Richard 1939- *ConTFT 9, IntMPA 92*
**Kielarowski**, Henry Edward 1946- *WhoWest 92*
**Kielczewski**, Grzegorz 1946- *WhoWest 92*
**Kielhorn**, Richard Werner 1931- *WhoWest 92*
**Kielich**, Christina Marie 1951- *WhoAmP 91*
**Kielkopf**, John F 1945- *AmMWSc 92*
**Kielmansegg**, Johann Adolf, Graf von 1906- *IntWW 91*
**Kielsmeier**, Catherine Jane *WhoWest 92*
**Kiely**, Benedict 1919- *ConNov 91, IntAu&W 91, WrDr 92*
**Kiely**, Dan Ray 1944- *WhoFI 92*
**Kiely**, David George 1925- *Who 92*
**Kiely**, Donald Edward 1938- *AmMWSc 92*
**Kiely**, Jerome 1925- *WrDr 92*
**Kiely**, John Roche 1906- *AmMWSc 92*
**Kiely**, John Steven 1951- *AmMWSc 92*
**Kiely**, Joseph Andrew 1944- *WhoAmL 92*
**Kiely**, Lawrence J 1922- *AmMWSc 92*
**Kiely**, Michael Lawrence 1938- *AmMWSc 92, WhoMW 92*
**Kiely**, Patrick James 1951- *WhoAmP 91*
**Kien**, C Lawrence 1946- *AmMWSc 92*
**Kienbaum**, Karen Smith 1943- *WhoAmL 92*
**Kienel**, Frederick Edward 1938- *WhoFI 92*
**Kiener**, John Leslie 1940- *WhoAmL 92*
**Kiener**, Ronald Charles 1954- *WhoRel 92*
**Kienholz**, Eldon W 1928- *AmMWSc 92*
**Kienhuis**, Ronald Lucas Christian 1949- *WhoEnt 92*
**Kieniewicz**, Stefan 1907- *IntWW 91*
**Kientz**, Marvin L 1936- *AmMWSc 92*
**Kienzle**, William X 1928- *IntAu&W 91, WrDr 92*
**Kienzler**, Klaus 1944- *WhoRel 92*
**Kiep**, Otto Karl 1886-1944 *EncTR 91 [port]*
**Kiep**, Walther Leisler 1926- *IntWW 91*
**Kiepura**, Sally 1938- *WhoRel 92*
**Kier**, Ann B 1949- *AmMWSc 92*
**Kier**, Lemont Burwell 1930- *AmMWSc 92*
**Kier**, Raymond Edward 1942- *WhoWest 92*
**Kierans**, Eric William 1914- *IntWW 91*
**Kieras**, Fred J *AmMWSc 92*
**Kierbow**, Julie Van Note Parker 1925- *AmMWSc 92*
**Kieren**, Thomas Henry 1941- *WhoFI 92*
**Kierkegaard**, Peder 1928- *IntWW 91*
**Kierkegaard**, Soren 1813-1855 *NinCLC 34 [port]*
**Kierkut**, Alan 1935- *WhoFI 92*
**Kierland**, Joseph Scott 1932- *WhoEnt 92*
**Kiernan**, Brian 1937- *WrDr 92*
**Kiernan**, Christopher Charles 1936- *Who 92*
**Kiernan**, Joan Julich 1943- *WhoAmP 91*
**Kiernan**, John Alan 1942- *AmMWSc 92*
**Kiernan**, Nicholas Raymond 1951- *WhoEnt 92*
**Kiernan**, William Joseph, Jr. 1932- *WhoAmL 92*
**Kiernat**, Bruce E. 1941- *WhoAmL 92*
**Kiersch**, George Alfred 1918- *AmMWSc 92, WhoWest 92*
**Kierscht**, Marcia Selland *WhoMW 92*
**Kierstead**, Henry Andrew 1922- *AmMWSc 92*
**Kierstead**, Richard Wightman 1927- *AmMWSc 92*
**Kies**, Constance 1934- *AmMWSc 92*
**Kies**, David M. 1944- *WhoAmL 92*
**Kies**, Kenneth J. 1952- *WhoAmL 92*
**Kies**, Leonard Charles 1947- *WhoEnt 92*
**Kies**, Marian Wood 1915- *AmMWSc 92*
**Kies**, Peter Steininger 1965- *WhoFI 92*
**Kieschnick**, John Henry 1942- *WhoRel 92*
**Kieschnick**, Melvin Martin 1927- *WhoRel 92*
**Kieschnick**, W F 1923- *AmMWSc 92*
**Kieschnick**, William F. 1923- *IntWW 91*
**Kiesel**, Stanley *DrAPF 91*
**Kieselbach**, Joseph Leo 1931- *WhoRel 92*
**Kieser**, John Frederick 1937- *WhoFI 92*
**Kiesewetter**, Louis William 1914- *WhoFI 92*
**Kiesewetter**, Mark Walter 1955- *WhoAmL 92*
**Kiesewetter**, William Burns 1915- *AmMWSc 92*
**Kiesinger**, Kurt Georg 1904-1988 *FacFETw*
**Kiesler**, Frederick 1890-1965 *DcTwDes, FacFETw*
**Kiesling**, Ernst W 1934- *AmMWSc 92*
**Kiesling**, Gerald Kenneth 1933- *WhoIns 92*
**Kiesling**, Richard Lorin 1922- *AmMWSc 92*
**Kieslowski**, Krysztof 1941- *IntDcF 2-2 [port]*
**Kieso**, Robert Alfred 1943- *AmMWSc 92*
**Kiess**, Edward Marion 1933- *AmMWSc 92*
**Kiessling**, George Anthony 1920- *AmMWSc 92*
**Kiessling**, Karen Ann Harris 1941- *WhoWest 92*
**Kiessling**, Oscar Edward 1901- *AmMWSc 92*
**Kiessling**, Ronald Frederick 1934- *WhoMW 92*
**Kiest**, Alan Scott 1949- *WhoWest 92*
**Kieswetter**, James Kay 1942- *WhoWest 92*
**Kietzmann**, Glenn Ernest, Jr. 1958- *WhoMW 92*
**Kiev**, Ari 1933- *WrDr 92*
**Kiev**, Marshall 1968- *WhoFI 92*
**Kieve**, Loren 1948- *WhoAmL 92*
**Kiever**, Paul Kenneth 1946- *WhoAmL 92*
**Kievman**, Carson 1949- *WhoEnt 92*
**Kiewe**, Jerome Mark 1961- *WhoRel 92*
**Kiewiet de Jonge**, Joost H A 1919- *AmMWSc 92*
**Kiewit**, David Arnold 1940- *AmMWSc 92*
**Kifer**, Alan Craig 1952- *WhoFI 92*
**Kifer**, Edward W 1938- *AmMWSc 92*
**Kifer**, Paul Edgar 1924- *AmMWSc 92*
**Kiff**, Ken 1935- *TwCPaSc*
**Kiffmeyer**, James George 1957- *WhoRel 92*
**Kiffmeyer**, Ralph R *WhoAmP 91*
**Kiffney**, Gustin Thomas, Jr 1930- *AmMWSc 92*
**Kiger**, John Andrew, Jr 1941- *AmMWSc 92*
**Kiger**, Robert William 1940- *AmMWSc 92*
**Kiger**, Ronald Lee 1940- *WhoWest 92*
**Kiggins**, Edward M 1929- *AmMWSc 92*
**Kightlinger**, Ray Milton 1931- *WhoFI 92*
**Kigin**, Thomas John 1948- *WhoAmL 92*
**Kihano**, Daniel James 1933- *WhoAmP 91*
**Kihara**, Hayato 1922- *AmMWSc 92*
**Kihl**, Young Whan 1932- *WhoMW 92*
**Kihle**, Donald Arthur 1934- *WhoAmL 92*
**Kihn**, Albert d1974 *LesBEnT 92*
**Kihn**, Harry 1912- *AmMWSc 92*
**Kiilsgaard**, Thor H 1919- *AmMWSc 92*
**Kiilu**, Raphael Muli 1938- *IntWW 91*
**Kijek**, Nancy 1963- *WhoFI 92*
**Kijewski**, Louis Joseph 1936- *AmMWSc 92*
**Kijima**, Shin 1949- *WhoFI 92*
**Kijima**, Torazo 1901- *IntWW 91*
**Kik**, Frank Nicholas 1935- *WhoRel 92*
**Kikabidze**, Vakhtang Konstantinovich 1938- *IntWW 91*
**Kikawada**, Isaac Mitzuru 1937- *WhoRel 92, WhoWest 92*
**Kikel**, Rudy John *DrAPF 91*
**Kiker**, Billy Frazier 1936- *WhoFI 92*
**Kiker**, Douglas d1991 *LesBEnT 92, NewYTBS 91 [port]*
**Kiker**, Douglas 1930-1991 *ConAu 135*
**Kiker**, Henry Roger 1949- *WhoRel 92*
**Kikhia**, Mansur Rashid 1931- *IntWW 91*
**Kiki**, Albert Maori 1931- *IntWW 91*
**Kiki**, Maori 1931- *Who 92*
**Kikkawa**, Yutaka *AmMWSc 92*
**Kikta**, Edward Joseph, Jr 1948- *AmMWSc 92*
**Kikuchi**, Chihiro 1914- *AmMWSc 92*
**Kikuchi**, Kiyoaki 1922- *IntWW 91*
**Kikuchi**, Ryoichi 1919- *AmMWSc 92*
**Kikuchi**, Shinya 1943- *AmMWSc 92*
**Kikudome**, Gary Yoshinori 1925- *AmMWSc 92*
**Kikumoto**, Charles David 1949- *WhoFI 92*
**Kikutake**, Kiyonori 1928- *IntWW 91*
**Kilambi**, Raj Varad 1933- *AmMWSc 92*
**Kilambi**, Srinvasacharyulu *AmMWSc 92*
**Kilander**, Donald J *WhoAmP 91*
**Kilanowski**, Michael Charles, Jr. 1948- *WhoAmL 92*
**Kilb**, Ralph Wolfgang 1931- *AmMWSc 92*
**Kilbane**, Thomas Stanton 1941- *WhoAmL 92*
**Kilberg**, Michael Steven 1951- *AmMWSc 92*
**Kilberg**, Richard Lloyd 1948- *WhoEnt 92*
**Kilberg**, William Jeffrey 1946- *WhoAmL 92, WhoAmP 91*
**Kilborn**, Peter Thurston 1939- *WhoFI 92*
**Kilborne**, George Briggs 1930- *WhoFI 92*
**Kilbourn**, Barry T 1939- *AmMWSc 92*
**Kilbourn**, Bernard Mason 1924- *WhoAmP 91*
**Kilbourn**, Joan Priscilla Payne 1936- *AmMWSc 92*
**Kilbourn**, Lawrence Winford 1956- *WhoRel 92*
**Kilbourn**, Matt *TwCWW 91*
**Kilbourn**, Oliver 1904- *TwCPaSc*
**Kilbourn**, William 1926- *WrDr 92*
**Kilbourne**, Barbara Jean 1941- *WhoFI 92*
**Kilbourne**, Christopher N. 1956- *WhoAmL 92*
**Kilbourne**, Edwin Dennis 1920- *AmMWSc 92*
**Kilbourne**, Edwin Michael 1953- *AmMWSc 92*
**Kilbourne**, Lewis Buckner 1947- *WhoFI 92*
**Kilbracken**, Baron 1920- *Who 92*
**Kilbracken**, Lord 1920- *WrDr 92*
**Kilbracken**, John Godley 1920- *IntAu&W 91*
**Kilbride**, Dennis J 1921- *WhoAmP 91*
**Kilbride**, James J 1934- *WhoIns 92*
**Kilburn**, Edwin Allen 1933- *WhoFI 92*
**Kilburn**, Henry Thomas, Jr. 1931- *WhoFI 92*
**Kilburn**, Kaye Hatch 1931- *AmMWSc 92, WhoWest 92*
**Kilburn**, S. Collins *WhoRel 92*
**Kilburn**, Tom 1921- *IntWW 91, Who 92*
**Kilbury**, Charles Debriel 1919- *WhoAmP 91*
**Kilby**, Craig McCoy 1959- *WhoAmP 91, WhoMW 92*
**Kilby**, Jack St Clair 1923- *AmMWSc 92*
**Kilby**, Michael Leopold 1924- *Who 92*
**Kilby**, Ronn Leonard 1951- *WhoEnt 92*
**Kilby**, William Hamlin 1931- *WhoAmL 92*
**Kilcarr**, Andrew Joseph 1932- *WhoAmL 92*
**Kilcrease**, Irvin Hugh, Jr. 1931- *WhoBlA 92*
**Kilcur**, James Francis 1951- *WhoAmL 92*
**Kildal**, Helge 1942- *AmMWSc 92*
**Kildare**, Marquess of 1948- *Who 92*
**Kildare**, Maurice *TwCWW 91*
**Kildare**, Michel Walter Andre 1935- *WhoBlA 92*
**Kildare And Leighlin**, Bishop of 1931- *Who 92*
**Kilday**, Warren D 1929- *AmMWSc 92*
**Kildee**, Dale E. 1929- *AlmAP 92 [port], WhoAmP 91, WhoMW 92*
**Kildoo-Brown**, Florence Ella 1918- *WhoAmP 91*
**Kildsig**, Dane Olin 1935- *AmMWSc 92*
**Kile**, Joseph David 1961- *WhoFI 92*
**Kile**, Raymond Lawrence 1946- *WhoWest 92*
**Kilen**, Thomas Clarence 1933- *AmMWSc 92*
**Kilenyi**, Edward A. 1911- *Who 92*
**Kiley**, Charles Walter 1944- *AmMWSc 92*
**Kiley**, Daniel Corcoran 1959- *WhoFI 92*
**Kiley**, Duane Eugene 1954- *WhoMW 92*
**Kiley**, James P 1952- *AmMWSc 92*
**Kiley**, John Edmund 1920- *AmMWSc 92*
**Kiley**, Leo Austin 1918- *AmMWSc 92*
**Kiley**, Liz 1956- *WhoEnt 92*
**Kiley**, Richard 1922- *IntMPA 92*
**Kiley**, Richard B *WhoAmP 91*
**Kiley**, Richard Paul 1922- *WhoEnt 92*
**Kiley**, Robert Ralph 1948- *WhoWest 92*
**Kiley**, Scott Thomas John 1960- *WhoEnt 92*
**Kilfedder**, James Alexander 1928- *Who 92*
**Kilfoil**, Geoffrey Everard 1939- *Who 92*
**Kilfoyle**, Peter 1946- *Who 92*
**Kilgarin**, Karen 1957- *WhoAmP 91*
**Kilgarlin**, William Wayne 1932- *WhoAmP 91*
**Kilgo**, John Carlisle 1861-1922 *DcNCBi 3*
**Kilgo**, Robert Lawton, Jr. 1949- *WhoAmL 92*
**Kilgore**, Bruce Moody 1930- *AmMWSc 92*
**Kilgore**, Delbert Lyle, Jr 1942- *AmMWSc 92*
**Kilgore**, Glenn Kennedy 1946- *WhoAmP 91*
**Kilgore**, James C 1928- *IntAu&W 91*
**Kilgore**, James Stanley 1931- *WhoMW 92*
**Kilgore**, Jeffrey Harper 1948- *WhoAmL 92*
**Kilgore**, Joe Madison 1918- *WhoAmP 91*
**Kilgore**, Joe Moffatt 1916- *WhoMW 92*
**Kilgore**, John *TwCWW 91*
**Kilgore**, Kathryn *DrAPF 91*
**Kilgore**, Kevin Patrick 1951- *WhoMW 92*
**Kilgore**, Lee A 1905- *AmMWSc 92*
**Kilgore**, LeRoy Wilson 1917- *WhoRel 92*
**Kilgore**, Lois Taylor 1922- *AmMWSc 92*
**Kilgore**, Sidney Wallis 1958- *WhoAmL 92*
**Kilgore**, Thomas, Jr. 1913- *WhoBlA 92*
**Kilgore**, Thomas M 1935- *WhoAmP 91*
**Kilgore**, Twanna Debbie 1954- *WhoBlA 92*
**Kilgore**, Wendell Warren 1929- *AmMWSc 92*
**Kilgore**, Wilson Roy 1949- *WhoRel 92*
**Kilgour**, Gordon Leslie 1929- *AmMWSc 92*
**Kilgour**, John Lowell 1924- *Who 92*
**Kilgour**, Lennox *BlkOlyM*
**Kilham**, Peter 1943- *AmMWSc 92*
**Kilham**, Susan Soltau 1943- *AmMWSc 92*
**Kilian**, Crawford 1941- *TwCSFW 91, WhoWest 92, WrDr 92*
**Kilian**, John James, II 1952- *WhoEnt 92*
**Kilian**, Michael D. 1939- *WhoEnt 92*
**Kilian**, Walter Daniel 1935- *WhoAmP 91*
**Kilimanjaro**, John Marshall 1930- *WhoBlA 92*
**Kilimnick**, Shaya M. 1947- *WhoRel 92*
**Kilinc**, Attila Ishak 1936- *AmMWSc 92*
**Kilkeary**, John 1932- *WhoIns 92*
**Kilkelly**, Marjorie L 1954- *WhoAmP 91*
**Kilkenny**, James H. 1923- *WhoBlA 92*
**Kilkenny**, John F. 1901- *WhoAmL 92*
**Kilkenny**, John Jude 1950- *WhoAmL 92*
**Kilker**, Charles John 1946- *WhoMW 92*
**Kilker**, James Robert 1946- *WhoAmL 92*
**Kilkson**, Henn 1930- *AmMWSc 92*
**Kilkson**, Rein 1927- *AmMWSc 92*
**Killaloe**, Bishop of 1922- *Who 92*
**Killam**, Anne Loretta 1928- *WhoAmP 91*
**Killam**, Dwight Delavan 1926- *WhoEnt 92*
**Killam**, Eleanor 1933- *AmMWSc 92*
**Killam**, Eva King 1921- *AmMWSc 92*
**Killam**, Everett Herbert 1938- *AmMWSc 92*
**Killam**, Keith Fenton, Jr 1927- *AmMWSc 92*
**Killanin**, Baron 1914- *IntWW 91, Who 92*
**Killanin**, Lord 1914- *IntAu&W 91*
**Killbourn**, Matt *WrDr 92*
**Killea**, Lucy 1922- *WhoHisp 92*
**Killea**, Lucy Lytle 1922- *WhoAmP 91*
**Killearn**, Baron 1919- *Who 92*
**Killebrew**, Flavius Charles 1949- *AmMWSc 92*
**Killebrew**, Gwendolyn 1939- *NewAmDM*
**Killebrew**, Harmon 1936- *FacFETw*
**Killeen**, Bruce 1926- *TwCPaSc*
**Killeen**, Edward Joseph 1954- *WhoEnt 92*
**Killeen**, Henry Walter 1946- *WhoAmL 92*
**Killeen**, John 1925- *AmMWSc 92*
**Killefer**, Campbell 1950- *WhoAmL 92*
**Killelea**, Joseph R 1917- *AmMWSc 92*
**Killen**, Carroll Gorden 1919- *WhoFI 92*
**Killen**, James 1925- *Who 92*
**Killen**, John Young, Jr 1949- *AmMWSc 92*
**Killen**, Kevin Paul 1956- *WhoEnt 92*
**Killen**, Patricia O'Connell 1951- *WhoRel 92*
**Killen**, Rosemary Margaret *AmMWSc 92*
**Killens**, John Oliver 1916- *IntAu&W 91*
**Killens**, John Oliver 1916-1987 *BenetAL 91*
**Killey**, Frances Ada 1911- *WhoAmP 91*
**Killgoar**, Paul Charles, Jr 1946- *AmMWSc 92*
**Killgore**, Charles A 1934- *AmMWSc 92*
**Killgrove**, James Lee 1951- *WhoEnt 92*
**Killiam**, Paul 1916- *IntMPA 92*
**Killian**, Carl Stanley 1933- *AmMWSc 92*
**Killian**, Charles Field 1959- *WhoEnt 92*
**Killian**, David Allen 1940- *WhoRel 92*
**Killian**, Frederick Luther 1942- *AmMWSc 92*
**Killian**, Gary Joseph 1945- *AmMWSc 92*
**Killian**, George Ernest 1924- *WhoWest 92*
**Killian**, Iris Louise 1962- *WhoBlA 92*

**Killian,** James R., Jr d1988 *LesBEnT 92*
**Killian,** Mark W 1955- *WhoAmP 91*
**Killian,** Nathan Rayne 1935- *WhoRel 92*
**Killian,** Patricia Dee 1942- *WhoAmP 91*
**Killian,** Richard M. 1942- *WhoWest 92*
**Killian,** Robert Kenneth 1919- *WhoAmP 91*
**Killian,** Robert Kenneth, Jr. 1947- *WhoAmL 92, WhoEnt 92*
**Killian,** Timothy Wayne 1961- *WhoRel 92*
**Killick,** Anthony John 1934- *Who 92*
**Killick,** John 1919- *Who 92*
**Killick,** John Edward 1919- *IntWW 91*
**Killick,** Kathleen Ann 1942- *AmMWSc 92*
**Killick,** Paul Victor St John 1916- *Who 92*
**Killick,** Tony *Who 92*
**Killigrew,** Thomas 1612-1683 *RfGEnL 91*
**Killin,** Charles Carr, III 1936- *WhoAmL 92*
**Killin,** Charles Clark 1923- *WhoAmL 92*
**Killingbeck,** Molly 1959- *BlkOlyM*
**Killingbeck,** Stanley 1929- *AmMWSc 92*
**Killinger,** Dennis K 1945- *AmMWSc 92*
**Killinger,** Kerry K. 1949- *WhoWest 92*
**Killinger,** Manfred von 1886-1944 *EncTR 91*
**Killingsworth,** Frank Russell 1873-1976 *RelLAm 91*
**Killingsworth,** James Woodrow, Jr. 1945- *WhoFI 92*
**Killingsworth,** Lawrence Madison 1946- *AmMWSc 92*
**Killingsworth,** R W 1925- *AmMWSc 92*
**Killingsworth,** Thomas Ike 1948- *WhoAmP 91*
**Killingsworth,** William David 1959- *WhoFI 92*
**Killingsworth Finley,** Sandra Jean 1950- *WhoBlA 92*
**Killion,** Frederick William, Jr. 1934- *WhoAmL 92*
**Killion,** Jeffrey Alden 1946- *WhoWest 92*
**Killion,** Jerald Jay 1942- *AmMWSc 92*
**Killion,** Lawrence Eugene 1924- *AmMWSc 92*
**Killion,** Theo M. 1951- *WhoBlA 92*
**Killip,** Christopher David 1946- *IntWW 91*
**Killman,** Daniel Lee 1954- *WhoEnt 92*
**Killmer,** George Theodore 1950- *WhoEnt 92*
**Killmond,** Frank 1934- *WhoEnt 92*
**Killoran,** Margaret Maureen 1944- *WhoRel 92*
**Killorin,** Robert Ware 1959- *WhoAmL 92*
**Killough,** George Boyd 1946- *WhoMW 92*
**Killough,** J. Scott 1957- *WhoAmL 92*
**Killough,** Jack Christopher 1948- *WhoFI 92, WhoWest 92*
**Killough,** Lee 1942- *IntAu&W 91, TwCSFW 91, WrDr 92*
**Killough,** Reginald Allen 1945- *WhoRel 92*
**Killpack,** Mona *TwCPaSc*
**Killpatrick,** Joseph E 1933- *AmMWSc 92*
**Killus,** James Peter, Jr. 1950- *WhoWest 92*
**Killworth,** Richard Allen 1943- *WhoAmL 92*
**Killy,** Jean-Claude 1943- *FacFETw*
**Kilmaine,** Baron 1948- *Who 92*
**Kilman,** James William 1931- *AmMWSc 92*
**Kilmann,** Ralph Herman 1946- *WhoFI 92*
**Kilmarnock,** Baron 1927- *Who 92*
**Kilmartin,** Edward John 1923- *WhoRel 92*
**Kilmartin,** Joseph Francis, Jr. 1924- *WhoFI 92*
**Kilmartin,** Mary Elizabeth 1946- *WhoEnt 92*
**Kilmartin,** Peter F *WhoAmP 91*
**Kilmartin,** Terence Kevin d1991 *Who 92N*
**Kilmartin,** Terence Kevin 1922- *IntAu&W 91*
**Kilmarx,** Mary Neidlinger 1927- *WhoAmP 91*
**Kilmer,** Aline 1888-1941 *BenetAL 91*
**Kilmer,** James E 1940- *WhoIns 92*
**Kilmer,** Joyce 1886 1918 *BenetAL 91, FacFETw*
**Kilmer,** Maurice Douglas 1928- *WhoWest 92*
**Kilmer,** Patricia Marie 1959- *WhoWest 92*
**Kilmer,** Paul Forest 1953- *WhoAmL 92*
**Kilmer,** Val *News 91*
**Kilmer,** Val 1959- *IntMPA 92*
**Kilmister,** Anthony 1931- *Who 92*
**Kilmister,** Clive William 1924- *Who 92, WrDr 92*
**Kilmore,** Bishop of 1926- *Who 92*
**Kilmore Elphin And Ardagh,** Bishop of 1918- *Who 92*
**Kilmorey,** Earl of *Who 92*
**Kilmuir,** Countess of *Who 92*
**Kilner Brown,** Ralph *Who 92*
**Kilonsky,** Anton F. 1929- *WhoMW 92*
**Kilp,** Gerald R 1931- *AmMWSc 92*
**Kilp,** Toomas 1948- *AmMWSc 92*
**Kilpack,** Bennett Boone 1930- *WhoWest 92*
**Kilpack,** Ruth Geibel *AmPeW*
**Kilpatrick,** Carolyn Cheeks 1945- *WhoAmP 91, WhoBlA 92*
**Kilpatrick,** Charles William 1944- *AmMWSc 92*
**Kilpatrick,** Daniel Lee 1951- *AmMWSc 92*
**Kilpatrick,** Don 1939- *WhoAmP 91*
**Kilpatrick,** Earl Buddy 1920- *AmMWSc 92*
**Kilpatrick,** George Roosevelt 1938- *WhoBlA 92*
**Kilpatrick,** George Stewart 1925- *Who 92*
**Kilpatrick,** James Jackson 1920- *WrDr 92*
**Kilpatrick,** Jeremy 1935- *AmMWSc 92*
**Kilpatrick,** John Michael 1953- *AmMWSc 92*
**Kilpatrick,** Judson *BenetAL 91*
**Kilpatrick,** Kerry Edwards 1939- *AmMWSc 92*
**Kilpatrick,** Robert 1924- *IntWW 91*
**Kilpatrick,** Robert 1926- *Who 92*
**Kilpatrick,** Robert Edward 1952- *WhoRel 92, WhoWest 92*
**Kilpatrick,** S James, Jr 1931- *AmMWSc 92*
**Kilpatrick,** Stephen Paul 1959- *WhoRel 92*
**Kilpatrick,** Stewart *Who 92*
**Kilpatrick,** Thomas E 1931- *WhoAmP 91*
**Kilpatrick,** Thomas Leonard 1937- *WhoMW 92*
**Kilpinen,** Michael Elder 1945- *WhoMW 92*
**Kilpper,** Robert William 1938- *AmMWSc 92*
**Kilroy,** Alix *Who 92*
**Kilroy,** James F. 1935- *ConAu 133*
**Kilroy,** Thomas 1934- *IntAu&W 91, WrDr 92*
**Kilroy-Silk,** Robert 1942- *Who 92*
**Kilsey,** George 1921- *WhoAmP 91*
**Kilsheimer,** John Robert 1923- *AmMWSc 92*
**Kilsheimer,** Sidney Arthur 1930- *AmMWSc 92*
**Kilson,** Marion D. de B. 1936- *WrDr 92*
**Kilson,** Martin Luther, Jr. 1931- *WhoBlA 92*
**Kilty,** Jerome Timothy 1922- *WhoEnt 92*
**Kiltz,** Sharon Saltzman 1937- *WhoAmP 91*
**Kilvert,** Francis 1840-1879 *RfGEnL 91*
**Kilvington,** Frank Ian 1924- *Who 92*
**Kilwardby,** Robert 1215?-1279 *DcLB 115*
**Kilworth,** Garry 1941- *IntAu&W 91, TwCSFW 91, WrDr 92*
**Kim** *ConAu 35NR*
**Kim Dae Jung** 1924- *IntWW 91*
**Kim Dong-Jo** 1918- *IntWW 91*
**Kim Il** 1910-1984 *FacFETw*
**Kim Il-sung** 1912- *FacFETw [port], IntWW 91*
**Kim Jong Il** 1942- *IntWW 91*
**Kim Jong Pil** 1926- *IntWW 91*
**Kim Joon-Sung** *IntWW 91*
**Kim Mahn-Je** 1934- *IntWW 91*
**Kim Sang-Hyup** 1920- *IntWW 91*
**Kim Woun-Gie** 1924- *IntWW 91*
**Kim Yong Shik** 1913- *IntWW 91*
**Kim Young Dong** 1951- *ConCom 92*
**Kim Young Sam** 1927- *IntWW 91*
**Kim,** Agnes Kyung-Hee 1937- *AmMWSc 92*
**Kim,** Benjamin Jin Chun 1949- *WhoMW 92*
**Kim,** Benjamin K 1933- *AmMWSc 92*
**Kim,** Boris Fincannon 1938- *AmMWSc 92*
**Kim,** Byung C 1934- *AmMWSc 92*
**Kim,** Byung Cho 1934- *WhoMW 92*
**Kim,** Byung Suk 1942- *AmMWSc 92*
**Kim,** Carl Stephen 1943- *AmMWSc 92*
**Kim,** Chang-Sik 1939- *AmMWSc 92*
**Kim,** Changhyun 1961- *AmMWSc 92*
**Kim,** Charles Chul 1945- *WhoWest 92*
**Kim,** Charles Wesley 1926- *AmMWSc 92*
**Kim,** Choon-Woo 1961- *WhoMW 92*
**Kim,** Chung Sul 1932- *AmMWSc 92*
**Kim,** Chung W 1934- *AmMWSc 92*
**Kim,** Dae Mann 1938- *AmMWSc 92*
**Kim,** David Sang Chul 1915- *WhoRel 92*
**Kim,** Donald Dongsuk 1945- *WhoEnt 92*
**Kim,** Dong-In 1948- *WhoAmL 92*
**Kim,** Dong Yun 1929- *AmMWSc 92*
**Kim,** Donna A 1952- *WhoAmP 91*
**Kim,** Earl 1920- *ConCom 92, NewAmDM, WhoEnt 92*
**Kim,** Edward Sung-Man 1930- *WhoRel 92*
**Kim,** Edward William 1949- *WhoWest 92*
**Kim,** Giho 1937- *AmMWSc 92*
**Kim,** Ha-Kyung Cho 1938- *WhoRel 92*
**Kim,** Han Joong 1937- *AmMWSc 92*
**Kim,** Han-Seob 1934- *AmMWSc 92*
**Kim,** Harry Hi-Soo 1922- *AmMWSc 92*
**Kim,** Hee-Jin 1927- *WhoRel 92*
**Kim,** Hee Joong 1934- *AmMWSc 92*
**Kim,** Ho-il 1958- *WhoAmL 92*
**Kim,** Hyeong Lak 1933- *AmMWSc 92*
**Kim,** Hyong Kap 1930- *AmMWSc 92*
**Kim,** Hyun Dju 1937- *AmMWSc 92*
**Kim,** Irving Ilwoong 1940- *WhoWest 92*
**Kim,** Jae Ho 1935- *AmMWSc 92*
**Kim,** Jae Hoon 1952- *AmMWSc 92*
**Kim,** Jai Bin 1934- *AmMWSc 92*
**Kim,** Jai Soo 1925- *AmMWSc 92*
**Kim,** Jay S. 1958- *WhoFI 92*
**Kim,** Jean Bartholomew 1940- *AmMWSc 92*
**Kim,** Jean Me 1962- *WhoAmL 92*
**Kim,** Jin Bai 1921- *AmMWSc 92*
**Kim,** Jinchoon 1943- *AmMWSc 92*
**Kim,** John K 1937- *AmMWSc 92*
**Kim,** Jonathan Jang-Ho 1932- *AmMWSc 92*
**Kim,** Joochul 1948- *WhoWest 92*
**Kim,** Juhee 1935- *AmMWSc 92*
**Kim,** Jung Won 1948- *IntWW 91*
**Kim,** Ke Chung 1934- *AmMWSc 92*
**Kim,** Kenneth 1931- *AmMWSc 92*
**Kim,** Keun Young 1928- *AmMWSc 92*
**Kim,** Ki-Han 1932- *AmMWSc 92*
**Kim,** Ki Hang 1936- *AmMWSc 92*
**Kim,** Ki Hong *AmMWSc 92*
**Kim,** Ki Hwan 1946- *AmMWSc 92, WhoMW 92*
**Kim,** Ki-Hyon 1933- *AmMWSc 92*
**Kim,** Ki-Soo 1942- *AmMWSc 92*
**Kim,** Kil Chol 1919- *AmMWSc 92*
**Kim,** Kwan Suk 1936- *WhoFI 92*
**Kim,** Kwang Shin 1937- *AmMWSc 92*
**Kim,** Kyekyoon K 1941- *AmMWSc 92*
**Kim,** Kyoo Hong 1948- *WhoFI 92*
**Kim,** Kyung Jae 1942- *LiExTwC*
**Kim,** Kyung Soo *AmMWSc 92*
**Kim,** Mi Ja *AmMWSc 92*
**Kim,** Michael Charles 1950- *WhoAmL 92*
**Kim,** Millie 1960- *WhoAmL 92*
**Kim,** Min Gyun 1964- *WhoWest 92*
**Kim,** Moon W *AmMWSc 92*
**Kim,** Myunghwan 1932- *AmMWSc 92*
**Kim,** Nelli 1957- *IntWW 91*
**Kim,** Paik Kee 1944- *AmMWSc 92*
**Kim,** Paul Chulhie 1963- *WhoFI 92*
**Kim,** Rhyn H 1936- *AmMWSc 92*
**Kim,** Richard 1932- *BenetAL 91*
**Kim,** Richard E. *DrAPF 91*
**Kim,** Richard E. 1932- *LiExTwC, WrDr 92*
**Kim,** Ryung-Soon 1938- *AmMWSc 92*
**Kim,** Sang Hyung 1942- *AmMWSc 92*
**Kim,** Sangduk 1930- *AmMWSc 92*
**Kim,** Seung U 1936- *AmMWSc 92*
**Kim,** Shoon Kyung 1920- *AmMWSc 92*
**Kim,** Soo Myung 1936- *AmMWSc 92*
**Kim,** Sooja K *AmMWSc 92*
**Kim,** Soon-Kyu 1932- *AmMWSc 92*
**Kim,** Stephan Sou-Hwan 1922- *WhoRel 92*
**Kim,** Stephen S. 1943- *WhoRel 92*
**Kim,** Stephen Sou-hwan 1922- *IntWW 91*
**Kim,** Sukyoung 1954- *AmMWSc 92*
**Kim,** Sun-Kee 1937- *AmMWSc 92*
**Kim,** Sung-Hou 1937- *AmMWSc 92*
**Kim,** Sung Kyu 1939- *AmMWSc 92, WhoMW 92*
**Kim,** Sung Wan 1940- *AmMWSc 92*
**Kim,** Sunwoong 1954- *WhoMW 92*
**Kim,** Tai Kyung 1927- *AmMWSc 92*
**Kim,** Thomas Joon-Mock 1936- *AmMWSc 92*
**Kim,** Tschangho John 1943- *WhoFI 92*
**Kim,** Uing W 1941- *AmMWSc 92*
**Kim,** Unsong William 1924- *IntAu&W 91*
**Kim,** Untae 1926- *AmMWSc 92*
**Kim,** Willa *ConTFT 9, WhoEnt 92*
**Kim,** Won 1948- *AmMWSc 92*
**Kim,** Woo Jong 1937- *AmMWSc 92*
**Kim,** Yee Sik 1928- *AmMWSc 92*
**Kim,** Yeong Ell *AmMWSc 92*
**Kim,** Yeong Wook 1925- *AmMWSc 92*
**Kim,** Yong Il 1945- *AmMWSc 92*
**Kim,** Yong-Ki 1932- *AmMWSc 92*
**Kim,** Yong Wook 1938- *AmMWSc 92*
**Kim,** Yoon Berm 1929- *AmMWSc 92*
**Kim,** Youn-Suk Ernest 1934- *WhoFI 92*
**Kim,** Young 1920- *WrDr 92*
**Kim,** Young Bae 1922- *AmMWSc 92*
**Kim,** Young C 1936- *AmMWSc 92*
**Kim,** Young Choo 1923- *Who 92*
**Kim,** Young Duc 1932- *AmMWSc 92*
**Kim,** Young Joo 1960- *AmMWSc 92*
**Kim,** Young Nok 1921- *AmMWSc 92*
**Kim,** Young Shik 1933- *AmMWSc 92*
**Kim,** Young Soo 1940- *WhoFI 92*
**Kim,** Young Tai 1930- *AmMWSc 92*
**Kim,** Yung Dai 1936- *AmMWSc 92*
**Kim,** Yungki 1935- *AmMWSc 92*
**Kim,** Zaezeung 1929- *AmMWSc 92*
**Kimack,** Michael Allen 1942- *WhoAmP 91*
**Kimatian,** Stephen H. 1941- *WhoEnt 92*
**Kimball** *Who 92*
**Kimball,** Baron 1928- *Who 92*
**Kimball,** Allyn Winthrop 1921- *AmMWSc 92*
**Kimball,** Alonzo Smith 1843-1897 *BiInAmS*
**Kimball,** Andrew Eyring 1949- *WhoFI 92*
**Kimball,** Aubrey Pierce 1926- *AmMWSc 92*
**Kimball,** Bruce Arnold 1941- *AmMWSc 92*
**Kimball,** Charles Alvah, III 1962- *WhoRel 92*
**Kimball,** Charles Newton 1911- *AmMWSc 92*
**Kimball,** Chase 1954- *WhoAmL 92*
**Kimball,** Chase Patterson 1932- *AmMWSc 92*
**Kimball,** Christian Edward 1955- *WhoAmL 92*
**Kimball,** Christopher John 1965- *WhoEnt 92*
**Kimball,** Clyde Walker 1942- *WhoAmP 91*
**Kimball,** Clyde William 1928- *AmMWSc 92, WhoMW 92*
**Kimball,** David Patten, III 1950- *WhoAmL 92*
**Kimball,** Dick 1937- *WhoEnt 92*
**Kimball,** Donald Robert 1938- *WhoMW 92*
**Kimball,** Donald W. 1947- *WhoWest 92*
**Kimball,** Edwin A 1834?-1898 *BiInAmS*
**Kimball,** Elden Allen 1931- *WhoFI 92*
**Kimball,** Frances Adrienne 1939- *AmMWSc 92*
**Kimball,** Frank *TwCWW 91*
**Kimball,** James N. 1934- *WhoFI 92*
**Kimball,** James Putnam 1836-1913 *BiInAmS*
**Kimball,** Jeffrey L. 1943- *WhoEnt 92*
**Kimball,** Jesse Dudley Baldwin 1947- *WhoAmL 92*
**Kimball,** John 1931- *WrDr 92*
**Kimball,** John Ward 1931- *AmMWSc 92*
**Kimball,** Kerry E *WhoAmP 91*
**Kimball,** Les Lewis 1941- *WhoRel 92*
**Kimball,** Miles Spencer 1960- *WhoFI 92*
**Kimball,** Paul Clark 1946- *AmMWSc 92*
**Kimball,** Paul Clark, Jr. 1943- *WhoAmL 92*
**Kimball,** Penn Townsend 1915- *IntAu&W 91*
**Kimball,** Ralph *TwCWW 91*
**Kimball,** Raymond Joel 1948- *WhoAmL 92*
**Kimball,** Richard 1948- *WhoAmP 91*
**Kimball,** Richard Allen, Jr 1943- *WhoAmP 91*
**Kimball,** Richard Fuller 1915- *AmMWSc 92*
**Kimball,** Richard Nephi 1936- *WhoWest 92*
**Kimball,** Robert Davern 1956- *WhoAmL 92*
**Kimball,** Rodney G d1900 *BiInAmS*
**Kimball,** Roger Stanley 1935- *WhoWest 92*
**Kimball,** Spencer Wooley 1895-1985 *RelLAm 91*
**Kimball,** Warren Forbes 1935- *IntWW 91*
**Kimball,** William Fisher 1959- *WhoEnt 92*
**Kimbel,** Philip 1925- *AmMWSc 92*
**Kimbell,** Alan Rea 1931- *WhoFI 92*
**Kimbell,** Jon Edward 1943- *WhoEnt 92*
**Kimbell,** Marion Joel 1923- *WhoWest 92*
**Kimbell,** Michael Alexander 1946- *WhoEnt 92*
**Kimber,** Brian Lee 1952- *WhoAmL 92*
**Kimber,** Charles Dixon 1912- *Who 92*
**Kimber,** Clarissa Therese 1929- *AmMWSc 92*
**Kimber,** Derek Barton 1917- *IntWW 91, Who 92*
**Kimber,** Gordon 1932- *AmMWSc 92*
**Kimber,** Herbert Frederick Sidney 1917- *Who 92*
**Kimber,** Lee *TwCWW 91*
**Kimber,** Lesly H. 1934- *WhoBlA 92*
**Kimberley,** Earl of 1924- *Who 92*
**Kimberley,** Berv 1929- *WhoAmP 91*
**Kimberling,** Charles Ronald 1950- *WhoAmP 91*
**Kimberling,** Clark Hershall 1942- *WhoMW 92*
**Kimberling,** John Farrell 1926- *WhoAmL 92*
**Kimberling,** William J 1940- *AmMWSc 92*
**Kimberly,** John 1817-1882 *DcNCBi 3*
**Kimberly,** Robert Parker *AmMWSc 92*
**Kimberly,** William Essick 1933- *WhoFI 92*
**Kimble,** Bettye Dorris 1936- *WhoBlA 92*
**Kimble,** Bo 1966- *WhoBlA 92*
**Kimble,** David 1921- *Who 92*
**Kimble,** Fred R 1949- *WhoAmP 91*
**Kimble,** George 1908- *Who 92, WrDr 92*
**Kimble,** Gerald Wayne 1928- *AmMWSc 92*
**Kimble,** Glenn Curry 1915- *AmMWSc 92*
**Kimble,** Harry Jeffrey 1949- *AmMWSc 92*
**Kimble,** James A. 1937- *WhoMW 92*
**Kimble,** Marcus Allen 1920- *WhoRel 92*
**Kimble,** Mark Stephen 1952- *WhoWest 92*
**Kimbler,** Delbert Lee 1945- *AmMWSc 92*
**Kimbler,** Larry Bernard 1938- *WhoFI 92*
**Kimbley,** Dennis *IntMPA 92*
**Kimblin,** Clive William 1938- *AmMWSc 92*
**Kimbrell,** Fuller Asbury *WhoAmP 91*
**Kimbrell,** Grady Ned 1933- *WhoWest 92*
**Kimbrell,** Jack T 1921- *AmMWSc 92*
**Kimbrell,** Jeffrey Andrew Drane 1956- *WhoMW 92*
**Kimbrew,** Joseph D. 1929- *WhoBlA 92*
**Kimbro,** Jean *WrDr 92*
**Kimbro,** John M. 1929- *WrDr 92*
**Kimbrough,** Charles *WhoEnt 92*
**Kimbrough,** Charles Austin 1941- *WhoAmL 92*

**Kimbrough**, Charles Edward 1927- *WhoBlA 92*
**Kimbrough**, Clarence B. 1922- *WhoBlA 92*
**Kimbrough**, Emily 1899- *IntAu&W 91*
**Kimbrough**, Emily 1899-1989 *BenetAL 91*
**Kimbrough**, Fred H. 1931- *WhoBlA 92*
**Kimbrough**, James W 1934- *AmMWSc 92*
**Kimbrough**, Kathryn *WrDr 92*
**Kimbrough**, Ralph Bradley, Jr. 1954- *WhoFI 92*
**Kimbrough**, Robert 1929- *IntAu&W 91, WrDr 92*
**Kimbrough**, Robert Averyt 1933- *WhoAmL 92*
**Kimbrough**, Robert L. 1922- *WhoBlA 92, WhoMW 92*
**Kimbrough**, Roosevelt 1932- *WhoBlA 92*
**Kimbrough**, Ted *WhoMW 92*
**Kimbrough**, Ted D. *WhoBlA 92*
**Kimbrough**, Theo Daniel, Jr 1933- *AmMWSc 92*
**Kimbrough**, Thomas J. 1934- *WhoBlA 92*
**Kimbrough**, William Walter, III 1928- *WhoMW 92*
**Kimbrough-Johnson**, Donna L. 1948- *WhoBlA 92*
**Kime**, Bradley Jay 1960- *WhoMW 92*
**Kime**, John William 1934- *WhoAmP 91*
**Kime**, Joseph Martin 1917- *AmMWSc 92*
**Kime**, Max Dean, Jr. 1949- *WhoFI 92*
**Kimel**, Jacob Daniel, Jr 1937- *AmMWSc 92*
**Kimel**, William R 1922- *AmMWSc 92*
**Kimelberg**, Harold Keith 1941- *AmMWSc 92*
**Kimeldorf**, George S 1940- *AmMWSc 92*
**Kimeli**, Kipkemboi *BlkOlyM*
**Kimelman**, Steven 1946- *WhoAmL 92*
**Kimenye**, Barbara *IntAu&W 91, WrDr 92*
**Kimerer**, Michael Daniel 1940- *WhoAmL 92*
**Kimerling**, Lionel Cooper 1943- *AmMWSc 92*
**Kimes**, Beverly Rae 1939- *IntAu&W 91*
**Kimes**, Brian Williams 1943- *AmMWSc 92*
**Kimes**, Thomas Fredric 1928- *AmMWSc 92*
**Kimes**, William Harold 1936- *WhoMW 92*
**Kimihira**, Ryozo 1938- *WhoFI 92*
**Kimler**, Bruce Franklin 1948- *AmMWSc 92*
**Kimlin**, Mary Jayne 1924- *AmMWSc 92*
**Kimm**, Peter Melia 1929- *WhoFI 92*
**Kimmance**, Peter Frederick 1922- *Who 92*
**Kimme**, Ernest Godfrey 1929- *AmMWSc 92, WhoWest 92*
**Kimmel**, Angela Mary 1957- *WhoAmL 92*
**Kimmel**, Bernard 1926- *WhoAmP 91*
**Kimmel**, Bruce Lee 1945- *AmMWSc 92*
**Kimmel**, Carole Anne 1944- *AmMWSc 92*
**Kimmel**, Charles Brown 1940- *AmMWSc 92*
**Kimmel**, Donald Loraine, Jr 1935- *AmMWSc 92*
**Kimmel**, Elias 1924- *AmMWSc 92*
**Kimmel**, Eric A. 1946- *WrDr 92*
**Kimmel**, Eugene Mark 1940- *WhoAmP 91*
**Kimmel**, Gary Lewis 1945- *AmMWSc 92*
**Kimmel**, Howard S 1938- *AmMWSc 92*
**Kimmel**, Joe Robert 1922- *AmMWSc 92*
**Kimmel**, Mark 1940- *WhoFI 92*
**Kimmel**, Michael George 1958- *WhoEnt 92*
**Kimmel**, Morton Richard 1940- *WhoAmL 92*
**Kimmel**, Robert Louis 1933- *WhoEnt 92*
**Kimmel**, Robert Michael 1943- *AmMWSc 92*
**Kimmel**, Robert O. 1928- *WhoFI 92, WhoWest 92*
**Kimmel**, Roger Lee 1943- *WhoMW 92*
**Kimmel**, William Griffiths 1945- *AmMWSc 92*
**Kimmel**, William Joseph 1947- *WhoFI 92*
**Kimmell**, Curtis Vollmer 1915- *WhoAmP 91*
**Kimmell**, Kenneth Luke 1960- *WhoAmL 92*
**Kimmell**, Lee H. 1950- *WhoFI 92*
**Kimmelman**, Burt *DrAPF 91*
**Kimmelman**, Gregory M. 1947- *WhoEnt 92*
**Kimmelman**, Seth 1951-1991 *NewYTBS 91*
**Kimmerle**, Frank 1940- *AmMWSc 92*
**Kimmey**, James William 1907- *AmMWSc 92*
**Kimmey**, Michael Bryant 1953- *WhoWest 92*
**Kimmich**, George Arthur 1941- *AmMWSc 92*
**Kimmins**, James Peter 1942- *AmMWSc 92*
**Kimmins**, Simon Edward Anthony 1930- *Who 92*
**Kimmins**, Warwick Charles 1941- *AmMWSc 92*
**Kimmitt**, Robert Michael 1947- *NewYTBS 91 [port]*
**Kimmons**, Carl Eugene 1920- *WhoBlA 92*
**Kimmons**, George H *AmMWSc 92*
**Kimmons**, Robert Lee 1926- *WhoFI 92*
**Kimmons**, Willie James 1944- *WhoBlA 92*
**Kimoto**, Masao 1947- *AmMWSc 92*
**Kimoto**, Walter Iwao 1932- *AmMWSc 92*
**Kimpel**, Benjamin Franklin 1905- *IntAu&W 91, WrDr 92*
**Kimpel**, James Froome 1942- *AmMWSc 92*
**Kimple**, John David 1967- *WhoEnt 92*
**Kimple**, Scott Carlisle 1966- *WhoFI 92*
**Kimport**, David Lloyd 1945- *WhoAmL 92*
**Kimpton**, John 1961- *TwCPaSc*
**Kimsey**, Lynn Siri 1953- *AmMWSc 92*
**Kimsey**, Marty E 1958- *WhoAmP 91*
**Kimsey**, Pierre Philippe 1953- *WhoEnt 92*
**Kimsey**, Rustin Ray 1935- *WhoRel 92, WhoWest 92*
**Kimsey**, Shirley I 1930- *WhoAmP 91*
**Kimsey**, Tim Peter 1942- *WhoMW 92*
**Kimura**, Arthur K 1948- *AmMWSc 92*
**Kimura**, Audy 1953- *WhoEnt 92*
**Kimura**, Eugene Tatsuru 1922- *AmMWSc 92*
**Kimura**, Hidenori 1941- *AmMWSc 92*
**Kimura**, Hiroshi 1927- *WhoWest 92*
**Kimura**, James Hiroshi 1944- *AmMWSc 92*
**Kimura**, Kazuo Kay 1920- *AmMWSc 92*
**Kimura**, Ken-ichi 1933- *AmMWSc 92*
**Kimura**, Mineo 1946- *AmMWSc 92*
**Kimura**, Motoo 1924- *IntWW 91*
**Kimura**, Naoki 1922- *AmMWSc 92*
**Kimura**, Tokuji 1925- *AmMWSc 92*
**Kimura**, Tsuto 1933- *WhoFI 92*
**Kinahan**, Charles Henry Grierson 1915- *Who 92*
**Kinahan**, Oliver John 1923- *Who 92*
**Kinahan**, Robert 1916- *Who 92*
**Kinard**, Frank Efird 1924- *AmMWSc 92*
**Kinard**, Fredrick William 1906- *AmMWSc 92*
**Kinard**, Helen Madison Marie Pawne *WhoBlA 92*
**Kinard**, James E, Jr *WhoAmP 91*
**Kinard**, Mike 1939- *WhoAmP 91*
**Kinard**, W Frank 1942- *AmMWSc 92*
**Kinariwala**, Bharat K 1926- *AmMWSc 92*
**Kinas**, Ernest Nicholas 1930- *WhoFI 92*
**Kinasewitz**, Gary Theodore 1946- *AmMWSc 92*
**Kinashi**, Doreen Ann 1957- *WhoWest 92*
**Kinbacher**, Edward John 1927- *AmMWSc 92*
**Kinberg**, Judy 1948- *WhoEnt 92*
**Kincade**, James 1925- *Who 92*
**Kincade**, John Patrick 1960- *WhoAmL 92*
**Kincade**, Michael Craig 1960- *WhoWest 92*
**Kincade**, Paul W 1944- *AmMWSc 92*
**Kincade**, Robert Tyrus 1941- *AmMWSc 92*
**Kincaid**, Dennis Campbell 1944- *AmMWSc 92*
**Kincaid**, Donald R 1936- *WhoAmP 91*
**Kincaid**, Eugene D., III 1941- *WhoAmL 92*
**Kincaid**, J.D. 1936- *TwCWW 91, WrDr 92*
**Kincaid**, Jamaica *DrAPF 91*
**Kincaid**, Jamaica 1949?- *BenetAL 91, BlkLC [port], ConLC 68 [port], ConNov 91, CurBio 91 [port], IntAu&W 91, LiExTwC, NotBlAW 92, WhoBlA 92, WrDr 92*
**Kincaid**, James Robert 1945- *AmMWSc 92*
**Kincaid**, Joan Payne *DrAPF 91*
**Kincaid**, Joe Kaylor 1948- *WhoWest 92*
**Kincaid**, Lloyd H 1925- *WhoAmP 91*
**Kincaid**, Marilyn Coburn 1947- *WhoMW 92*
**Kincaid**, Mark Lyndon 1959- *WhoAmL 92*
**Kincaid**, Paul Kent 1952- *WhoMW 92*
**Kincaid**, Randall L *AmMWSc 92*
**Kincaid**, Ronald Lee 1950- *AmMWSc 92*
**Kincaid**, Steven Alan 1943- *AmMWSc 92*
**Kincaid**, Thomas Gardiner 1937- *AmMWSc 92*
**Kincaid**, Wilfred Macdonald 1918- *AmMWSc 92, WhoMW 92*
**Kincaid**, William 1895-1967 *NewAmDM*
**Kincaid**, William K 1911- *WhoAmP 91*
**Kincannon**, Donny Frank 1933- *AmMWSc 92*
**Kincart**, Robert Owen 1949- *WhoFI 92*
**Kincey**, Wendell D. 1951- *WhoBlA 92*
**Kinch**, Anthony Alec 1926- *Who 92*
**Kinch**, Donald M 1913- *AmMWSc 92*
**Kinch**, E L Lee 1939- *WhoAmP 91*
**Kinch**, Henry S *WhoAmP 91*
**Kincheloe**, Lawrence Ray 1941- *WhoWest 92*
**Kinchen**, David G 1953- *AmMWSc 92*
**Kinchen**, John 1745?-1794 *DcNCBi 3*
**Kinchin Smith**, Michael 1921- *Who 92*
**Kincl**, Frantisek 1941- *IntWW 91*
**Kincl**, Fred Allan 1922- *AmMWSc 92*
**Kincl**, Rich Louis 1953- *WhoRel 92*
**Kincraig**, Lord 1918- *Who 92*
**Kind**, Charles Albert 1917- *AmMWSc 92*
**Kind**, Dieter Hans 1929- *IntWW 91*
**Kind**, Kenneth Wayne 1948- *WhoAmL 92, WhoWest 92*
**Kind**, Leon Saul 1922- *AmMWSc 92*
**Kind**, Phyllis Dawn 1933- *AmMWSc 92*
**Kindall**, Luther Martin 1942- *WhoBlA 92*
**Kindel**, H. Stephanie 1944- *WhoEnt 92*
**Kindel**, Joseph Martin 1943- *AmMWSc 92, WhoWest 92*
**Kindel**, Paul Kurt 1934- *AmMWSc 92*
**Kinder**, Eric 1927- *Who 92*
**Kinder**, Ira 1942- *WhoEnt 92*
**Kinder**, Ira George 1912- *WhoMW 92*
**Kinder**, Mickey Crawford, Jr. 1959- *WhoMW 92*
**Kinder**, Randolph Samuel, Jr. 1944- *WhoBlA 92*
**Kinder**, Terry Lynn 1958- *WhoFI 92*
**Kinder**, Thomas Hartley 1943- *AmMWSc 92*
**Kinderlehrer**, David 1941- *AmMWSc 92*
**Kinderman**, Edwin Max 1916- *AmMWSc 92*
**Kindermann**, Heinz 1894-1985 *EncTR 91*
**Kinders**, Robert James 1948- *AmMWSc 92*
**Kindersley** *Who 92*
**Kindersley**, Baron 1929- *Who 92*
**Kindersley**, Claude Richard Henry 1911- *Who 92*
**Kindersley**, David Guy 1915- *Who 92*
**Kindig**, Neal B 1928- *AmMWSc 92*
**Kindleberger**, Charles P., II 1910- *ConAu 36NR, WhoFI 92*
**Kindler**, Sharon Dean 1930- *AmMWSc 92*
**Kindler**, Walter 1940- *WhoEnt 92*
**Kindley**, Jeffrey Bowman 1945- *WhoEnt 92*
**Kindlund**, Newton C. 1940- *WhoFI 92*
**Kindness**, Thomas Norman 1929- *WhoAmP 91*
**Kindred**, Wendy 1937- *WrDr 92*
**Kindregan**, Charles 1964- *WhoAmL 92*
**Kindrick**, Robert LeRoy 1942- *WhoMW 92*
**Kinds**, Herbert Eugene 1933- *WhoMW 92*
**Kindschy**, Errol Roy 1938- *WhoAmP 91*
**Kindt**, Glenn W 1930- *AmMWSc 92*
**Kindt**, John Warren, Sr. 1950- *WhoAmL 92*
**Kindt**, Lois Jeannette 1927- *WhoAmP 91*
**Kindt**, Thomas James 1939- *AmMWSc 92*
**Kindwald**, Donald James 1961- *WhoAmL 92*
**Kineman**, Lanis Eugene 1926- *WhoRel 92*
**Kinen**, Philip John 1960- *WhoEnt 92*
**Kiner**, Ralph 1922- *FacFETw*
**Kiner**, Susan Louise 1954- *WhoMW 92*
**Kiner**, William Allen 1945- *WhoAmP 91*
**Kinersly**, Thorn 1923- *AmMWSc 92*
**King** *Who 92*
**King Crimson** *NewAmDM*
**King Curtis** 1934-1971 *NewAmDM*
**King Hu** 1931- *IntDcF 2-2*
**King Philip** *RComAH*
**King Philip** d1676 *BenetAL 91*
**King**, A Douglas, Jr 1933- *AmMWSc 92*
**King**, Alan 1927- *IntMPA 92, WhoEnt 92*
**King**, Alan E. 1938- *WhoMW 92*
**King**, Alan Jonathan 1954- *AmMWSc 92*
**King**, Albert 1905- *Who 92*
**King**, Albert 1924- *TwCWW 91*
**King**, Albert 1959- *WhoBlA 92*
**King**, Albert Freeman Africanus 1841-1914 *BiInAmS*
**King**, Albert Ignatius 1934- *AmMWSc 92*
**King**, Albert Leslie 1911- *Who 92*
**King**, Alexander 1900-1965 *BenetAL 91*
**King**, Alexander 1909- *Who 92*
**King**, Alexander Harvey 1954- *AmMWSc 92*
**King**, Alexander Hyatt 1911- *Who 92*
**King**, Alexander Vernon 1956- *WhoEnt 92*
**King**, Alfred Douglas, Jr 1933- *AmMWSc 92*
**King**, Alfred Meehan 1933- *WhoFI 92*
**King**, Alfred T 1813-1858? *BiInAmS*
**King**, Alison *Who 92*
**King**, Allen Lewis 1910- *AmMWSc 92*
**King**, Alvin M 1935- *WhoAmP 91*
**King**, Ames *TwCWW 91*
**King**, Amy C 1947- *WhoAmP 91*
**King**, Amy P 1928- *AmMWSc 92*
**King**, Andre Richardson 1931- *WhoEnt 92*
**King**, Andrea 1915- *IntMPA 92*
**King**, Anita 1931- *WhoBlA 92*
**King**, Ann Christie *AmMWSc 92*
**King**, Ann Ottoson 1946- *WhoAmL 92*
**King**, Anthony 1934- *WrDr 92*
**King**, Anthony Stephen 1934- *Who 92*
**King**, Arnold Kimsey, Jr. 1931- *WhoRel 92*
**King**, Arthur Francis 1937- *AmMWSc 92*
**King**, Arthur Thomas 1938- *WhoBlA 92, WhoFI 92*
**King**, Audrey 1942- *WhoAmL 92*
**King**, B. B. 1925- *IntWW 91, NewAmDM, WhoBlA 92, WhoEnt 92*
**King**, B G 1922- *AmMWSc 92*
**King**, Barbara De Anne 1941- *WhoRel 92, WhoWest 92*
**King**, Barbara Lewis 1930- *WhoBlA 92, WhoRel 92*
**King**, Barrington 1930- *WhoAmP 91*
**King**, Barry Frederick 1942- *AmMWSc 92*
**King**, Basil 1859-1928 *BenetAL 91*
**King**, Ben E. 1938- *ConMus 7 [port]*
**King**, Benjamin 1857-1894 *BenetAL 91*
**King**, Benton Davis 1919- *AmMWSc 92*
**King**, Bernard 1956- *WhoBlA 92*
**King**, Bernard David 1949- *WhoFI 92*
**King**, Betty 1919- *WrDr 92*
**King**, Betty 1932- *WhoAmP 91*
**King**, Betty Alice 1919- *IntAu&W 91*
**King**, Betty Blake 1957- *WhoFI 92*
**King**, Betty Louise 1943- *AmMWSc 92*
**King**, Betty Marie 1937- *WhoAmP 91*
**King**, Billie Jean 1943- *FacFETw, HanAmWH, IntWW 91, RComAH, Who 92, WrDr 92*
**King**, Blake 1921- *AmMWSc 92*
**King**, Brian Edmund 1928- *Who 92*
**King**, Bruce *WhoAmP 91*
**King**, Bruce 1924- *AlmAP 92 [port], WhoWest 92*
**King**, Bruce 1925- *WhoEnt 92*
**King**, Bruce 1933- *IntAu&W 91, WrDr 92*
**King**, C Judson, III 1934- *AmMWSc 92*
**King**, Calvin E. 1928- *WhoBlA 92*
**King**, Calvin Elijah 1928- *AmMWSc 92*
**King**, Carl Edward 1940- *WhoFI 92*
**King**, Carl Howie 1898-1967 *DcNCBi 3*
**King**, Carl Leander 1924- *WhoAmP 91*
**King**, Carole 1942- *ConMus 6 [port], FacFETw, NewAmDM, WhoEnt 92*
**King**, Caroline *TwCPaSc*
**King**, Carolyn Dineen *WhoAmP 91*
**King**, Carolyn Dineen 1938- *WhoAmL 92*
**King**, Cecilia D. 1950- *WhoBlA 92*
**King**, Celes, III 1923- *WhoBlA 92*
**King**, Ceola 1927- *WhoBlA 92*
**King**, Charles 1844-1933 *TwCWW 91*
**King**, Charles Abraham 1924- *WhoBlA 92*
**King**, Charles Andrew Buchanan 1915- *Who 92*
**King**, Charles Benjamin 1942- *WhoRel 92*
**King**, Charles C 1933- *AmMWSc 92*
**King**, Charles E. 1911- *WhoBlA 92*
**King**, Charles E. 1920- *WhoBlA 92*
**King**, Charles Everett 1934- *AmMWSc 92*
**King**, Charles Glen 1896-1988 *FacFETw*
**King**, Charles H. d1991 *NewYTBS 91*
**King**, Charles Homer 1938- *WhoMW 92*
**King**, Charles Larry 1950- *WhoRel 92*
**King**, Charles Martin M. *Who 92*
**King**, Charles Miller 1932- *AmMWSc 92*
**King**, Charles O 1916- *AmMWSc 92*
**King**, Charles Ross 1925- *WhoMW 92*
**King**, Charolette Elaine 1945- *WhoWest 92*
**King**, Cheryl E 1954- *AmMWSc 92*
**King**, Chi-Yu 1934- *AmMWSc 92*
**King**, Clarence 1842-1901 *BenetAL 91*
**King**, Clarence Maurice, Jr. 1934- *WhoBlA 92*
**King**, Clarence Rivers 1842-1901 *BiInAmS*
**King**, Claudia Louan 1940- *WhoEnt 92*
**King**, Clive 1924- *IntAu&W 91, WrDr 92*
**King**, Colbert I. 1939- *WhoBlA 92*
**King**, Colin Sainthill W. *Who 92*
**King**, Coretta Scott 1927- *HanAmWH, IntWW 91, NotBlAW 92 [port], RelLAm 91, WhoBlA 92*
**King**, Craig S. *WhoAmL 92*
**King**, Creston Alexander, Jr 1935- *AmMWSc 92*
**King**, Cynthia *DrAPF 91*
**King**, Cynthia 1925- *ConAu 36NR, WrDr 92*
**King**, Cynthia Anne 1960- *WhoMW 92*
**King**, Cyrus Arthur, II 1936- *WhoAmL 92*
**King**, Dan Gaither 1945- *WhoAmL 92*
**King**, Daniel Patrick 1942- *WhoFI 92*
**King**, Daniel Richard 1940- *WhoWest 92*
**King**, Darrell Lee 1937- *AmMWSc 92*
**King**, Dave 1946- *TwCPaSc*
**King**, David 1946- *WhoAmP 91*
**King**, David Alan 1957- *WhoFI 92*
**King**, David Anthony 1939- *Who 92*
**King**, David Beeman 1937- *AmMWSc 92*
**King**, David Burnett 1930- *WhoWest 92*
**King**, David George *AmMWSc 92*
**King**, David John 1955- *IntAu&W 91*
**King**, David Michael 1960- *WhoRel 92*
**King**, David Milton 1943- *WhoAmP 91*
**King**, David O 1938- *WhoAmP 91*
**King**, David Roy 1950- *WhoAmL 92*
**King**, David S 1949- *AmMWSc 92*
**King**, David Samuel *WhoEnt 92*
**King**, David Solomon 1936- *AmMWSc 92*
**King**, David Thane 1923- *AmMWSc 92*
**King**, David W. 1946- *WhoWest 92*
**King**, Debra Rowlett 1954- *WhoAmL 92*
**King**, Delbert Leo 1934- *AmMWSc 92*
**King**, Delmar K. 1947- *WhoFI 92*
**King**, Delutha Harold 1924- *WhoBlA 92*
**King**, Dennis 1897-1971 *NewAmDM*
**King**, Dennis Ray 1947- *WhoMW 92*
**King**, Denys Michael 1929- *Who 92*
**King**, Derek Barber 1915- *WhoBlA 92*
**King**, Diane Walker 1941- *WhoRel 92*
**King**, Dominic Benson 1928- *WhoAmL 92, WhoFI 92*

King, Dominique Desiree 1956- *WhoAmP 91*
King, Don 1931- *WhoBlA 92*
King, Donald Bruce 1931- *WhoAmL 92*
King, Donald E. 1934- *WhoBlA 92*
King, Donald Edward 1951- *WhoAmL 92*
King, Donald M 1935- *AmMWSc 92*
King, Donald Neal 1925- *WhoMW 92*
King, Donald West, Jr 1927- *AmMWSc 92*
King, Dorothy *TwCPaSc*
King, Dorothy E. *DrAPF 91*
King, Dorothy L. 1940- *WhoFI 92*
King, Dorothy Wei 1914- *AmMWSc 92*
King, Douglas James Edward 1919- *Who 92*
King, Edgar Lee *WhoBlA 92*
King, Edgar Pearce 1922- *AmMWSc 92*
King, Edmund James 1914- *Who 92*
King, Edward Dunham 1929- *WhoMW 92*
King, Edward Frazier 1935- *AmMWSc 92*
King, Edward J 1925- *WhoAmP 91*
King, Edward Laurie 1920- *Who 92*
King, Edward Louis 1920- *AmMWSc 92*
King, Edward P 1905- *AmMWSc 92*
King, Edward Smith 1848-1896 *BenetAL 91*
King, Edwin Wallace 1918- *AmMWSc 92*
King, Eileen Brenneman 1924- *AmMWSc 92*
King, Elbert Aubrey, Jr 1935- *AmMWSc 92*
King, Eleanor d1991 *NewYTBS 91 [port]*
King, Elizabeth *WhoAmP 91*
King, Elizabeth Norfleet 1925- *AmMWSc 92*
King, Elizabeth Raymond 1923- *AmMWSc 92*
King, Emery C. 1948- *WhoBlA 92*
King, Emmett Alonzo, III 1942- *WhoFI 92*
King, Ernest 1878-1956 *FacFETw, RComAH*
King, Estelle Holloway 1927- *WhoBlA 92*
King, Evelyn Mansfield 1907- *Who 92*
King, Felton *WhoRel 92*
King, Francis 1923- *ConNov 91, WrDr 92*
King, Francis Edward 1931- *WhoRel 92*
King, Francis Henry 1923- *IntAu&W 91, IntWW 91, Who 92*
King, Francis P. 1922- *WrDr 92*
King, Frank *WhoWest 92*
King, Frank 1919- *Who 92*
King, Frank Douglas 1919- *IntWW 91*
King, Frank P 1921- *WhoAmP 91*
King, Frank William 1922- *WhoWest 92*
King, Franklin G, Jr 1939- *AmMWSc 92*
King, Franklin Hiram 1848-1911 *BiInAmS*
King, Franklin Weaver 1942- *WhoAmL 92*
King, Fred Carlton, Jr. 1946- *WhoAmL 92*
King, Frederic 1937- *WhoWest 92*
King, Frederick Alexander 1925- *AmMWSc 92*
King, Frederick Ernest *Who 92*
King, Frederick J, Jr 1945- *WhoAmP 91*
King, Frederick Jessop 1928- *AmMWSc 92*
King, Garr Michael 1936- *WhoAmL 92*
King, Gary *WhoAmP 91*
King, Gayle Nathaniel 1948- *AmMWSc 92*
King, General Tye 1920- *AmMWSc 92*
King, George, III 1946- *AmMWSc 92*
King, George B 1848-1911 *BiInAmS*
King, George Raleigh 1931- *WhoFI 92, WhoMW 92*
King, Gerald Simon 1948- *WhoIns 92*
King, Gerald Wilfrid 1928- *AmMWSc 92*
King, Glen 1935- *WhoEnt 92*
King, Glynda Bowman 1946- *WhoAmP 91*
King, Gordon James 1932- *AmMWSc 92*
King, Grace Elizabeth 1851-1931 *BenetAL 91*
King, Gundar Julian 1926- *WhoWest 92*
King, Gwendolyn Stewart *WhoBlA 92*
King, Gwendolyn Stewart 1940- *WhoAmP 91*
King, H E 1922- *AmMWSc 92*
King, Harley *DrAPF 91*
King, Harold *WhoEnt 92*
King, Harold 1922- *AmMWSc 92, WhoMW 92*
King, Harold Lloyd 1926- *WhoAmP 91*
King, Harriss Thornton 1947- *AmMWSc 92*
King, Harry J 1934- *AmMWSc 92*
King, Hartley H 1936- *AmMWSc 92*
King, Henry 1592-1669 *RfGEnL 91*
King, Henry 1888-1982 *IntDcF 2-2*
King, Henry Churchill 1858-1934 *RelLAm 91*
King, Henry Lawrence 1928- *WhoAmL 92*
King, Henry Lee 1921- *AmMWSc 92*
King, Herbert Maxon 1864-1917 *BiInAmS*
King, Herman *IntMPA 92*
King, Herman 1915- *AmMWSc 92*
King, Hilary William 1919- *Who 92*
King, Hodge 1914- *WhoBlA 92*
King, Howard 1913- *WhoEnt 92*
King, Howard A. T. 1922-1988 *WhoBlA 92N*
King, Howard E 1924- *AmMWSc 92*
King, Howard O. 1925- *WhoBlA 92*
King, Howard Pickett 1939- *WhoAmL 92*
King, Hubert Wylam 1930- *AmMWSc 92*
King, Hulas H. 1946- *WhoBlA 92*
King, Indle Gifford 1934- *WhoEnt 92*
King, Isobel Wilson *Who 92*
King, Ivan R. 1927- *IntWW 91*
King, Ivan Robert 1927- *AmMWSc 92, WhoWest 92*
King, J. B. *WhoAmL 92*
King, J Earl 1946- *WhoIns 92*
King, Jack A. 1936- *WhoAmL 92, WhoIns 92*
King, James 1925- *NewAmDM*
King, James 1943- *BlkOlyM*
King, James, Jr 1933- *AmMWSc 92, WhoBlA 92*
King, James A., Jr. *WhoAmL 92*
King, James Allen 1940- *WhoMW 92*
King, James Armand 1962- *WhoAmL 92*
King, James B., Jr. 1914- *WhoBlA 92*
King, James Barton 1935- *WhoAmP 91*
King, James C 1932- *AmMWSc 92*
King, James Calvin 1945- *WhoEnt 92*
King, James Claude 1924- *AmMWSc 92*
King, James Clement 1904- *AmMWSc 92*
King, James Douglas 1934- *AmMWSc 92*
King, James E, Jr 1939- *WhoAmP 91*
King, James Edward 1940- *AmMWSc 92*
King, James Edward 1954- *WhoAmL 92*
King, James Frederick 1934- *AmMWSc 92*
King, James Joseph 1946- *WhoFI 92*
King, James Lawrence 1922- *Who 92*
King, James Lawrence 1927- *WhoAmL 92*
King, James Lawrence, Jr. 1935- *WhoWest 92*
King, James Lee 1953- *WhoMW 92*
King, James P *WhoAmP 91*
King, James P 1933- *AmMWSc 92*
King, James Roger 1927- *AmMWSc 92*
King, James S 1938- *AmMWSc 92*
King, Jane Cudlip Coblentz 1922- *WhoWest 92*
King, Janet Carlson 1941- *AmMWSc 92*
King, Jean Ledwith 1924- *WhoAmP 91*
King, Jeanne Faith 1934- *WhoBlA 92*
King, Jeffrey Lee 1955- *WhoEnt 92*
King, Jeffrey William Hitchen 1906- *Who 92*
King, Jerry Daniel 1945- *WhoAmP 91*
King, Jerry Porter 1935- *AmMWSc 92*
King, Jerry Wayne 1942- *WhoMW 92*
King, Jessie M. 1875-1949 *TwCPaSc*
King, Jessie Marion 1876-1949 *DcTwDes*
King, Jock *Who 92*
King, Joe Mack 1944- *AmMWSc 92*
King, John 1937- *WhoAmP 91*
King, John 1938- *AmMWSc 92*
King, John 1947- *WrDr 92*
King, John A *WhoAmP 91*
King, John A 1916- *AmMWSc 92*
King, John Allison 1935- *WhoFI 92*
King, John Arthur 1921- *AmMWSc 92*
King, John Arthur Charles 1933- *Who 92*
King, John B. 1908- *WhoBlA 92*
King, John Christopher 1933- *Who 92*
King, John Douglas 1934- *WhoFI 92*
King, John Edward 1922- *Who 92*
King, John Edward 1939- *AmMWSc 92*
King, John George Maydon 1908- *Who 92*
King, John Gordon 1925- *AmMWSc 92*
King, John Joseph 1924- *WhoFI 92, WhoMW 92*
King, John Kenneth 1958- *WhoRel 92*
King, John L. 1952- *WhoBlA 92*
King, John Mathews 1939- *AmMWSc 92*
King, John McKain 1927- *AmMWSc 92*
King, John Oliver 1914- *Who 92*
King, John Paul 1938- *AmMWSc 92*
King, John Q. Taylor, Sr. 1921- *WhoBlA 92*
King, John Smith, Jr. 1908- *WhoFI 92*
King, John Stuart 1927- *AmMWSc 92*
King, John Swinton 1920- *AmMWSc 92*
King, John Thomas 1935- *WhoBlA 92*
King, John W 1918- *WhoAmP 91*
King, John William 1938- *AmMWSc 92*
King, John William Beaufoy 1927- *Who 92*
King, Johnny *WhoRel 92*
King, Jonathan 1941- *AmMWSc 92*
King, Jonathan Stanton 1922- *AmMWSc 92*
King, Joseph 1914- *Who 92*
King, Joseph Berkshire 1944- *WhoFI 92*
King, Joseph Clement 1922- *WhoWest 92*
King, Joseph E 1941- *WhoIns 92*
King, Joseph E 1945- *WhoAmP 91*
King, Joseph Herbert 1939- *AmMWSc 92*
King, Joseph Hillery 1869-1946 *RelLAm 91*
King, Joseph Jerone 1910- *WhoFI 92, WhoWest 92*
King, Joseph Paul 1941- *WhoEnt 92*
King, Joseph Prather 1927- *WhoBlA 92*
King, Julian F. 1931- *WhoBlA 92*
King, Julius Wade 1922- *WhoAmP 91*
King, Katherine Chung-Ho 1937- *AmMWSc 92*
King, Katherine May 1952- *WhoMW 92*
King, Kendall Willard 1926- *AmMWSc 92*
King, Kenneth *DrAPF 91*
King, Kenneth, Jr 1930- *AmMWSc 92*
King, Kenneth Calloway 1942- *WhoFI 92*
King, Kenneth Edward 1925- *WhoMW 92*
King, Kenneth R *WhoAmP 91*
King, Kernan Francis 1944- *WhoAmL 92, WhoFI 92*
King, Kirby Leon 1938- *WhoEnt 92*
King, Kurleigh Dennis 1933- *IntWW 91*
King, L D Percival 1906- *AmMWSc 92*
King, L Ellis 1939- *AmMWSc 92*
King, Lafayette Carroll 1914- *AmMWSc 92*
King, Larry *LesBEnT 92 [port]*
King, Larry 1933- *NewYTBS 91 [port]*
King, Larry Dean 1939- *AmMWSc 92*
King, Larry Gene 1936- *AmMWSc 92*
King, Larry L 1929- *IntAu&W 91, SmATA 66, WhoEnt 92, WrDr 92*
King, Larry Michael 1942- *AmMWSc 92*
King, Lauren Alfred 1904- *WhoMW 92*
King, Lawrence C. *WhoBlA 92*
King, Lawrence Edward 1948- *WhoAmL 92*
King, Lawrence P. 1940- *WhoBlA 92*
King, Lawrence Philip 1929- *WhoAmL 92*
King, Leamon 1936- *BlkOlyM*
King, Lee Ann 1953- *WhoEnt 92*
King, Lee Curtis 1954- *AmMWSc 92*
King, Leonard 1950- *WhoWest 92*
King, Leonard James 1925- *IntWW 91, Who 92*
King, Leonard Tony 1926- *WhoFI 92*
King, LeRoy J. 1920- *WhoBlA 92*
King, Leslie Darnell 1949- *WhoAmP 91*
King, Leslie Rae, Jr. 1944- *WhoRel 92*
King, Lester Snow 1908- *AmMWSc 92*
King, Lewis H 1924- *AmMWSc 92*
King, Lewis Henry *WhoBlA 92*
King, Lewis M. 1942- *WhoBlA 92*
King, Linda Christine 1963- *WhoWest 92*
King, Llewellyn Joseph, Jr. *WhoFI 92*
King, Lloyd 1936- *WhoBlA 92*
King, Lloyd Elijah, Jr 1939- *AmMWSc 92*
King, Louis Blair 1925- *WhoRel 92*
King, Lowell Alvin 1932- *AmMWSc 92*
King, Lowell Restell 1932- *AmMWSc 92*
King, Lucy Jane 1932- *AmMWSc 92*
King, Lunsford Richardson 1937- *AmMWSc 92*
King, Mabel *ConTFT 9*
King, Malcolm Montgomery 1954- *WhoRel 92*
King, Marcellus, Jr. 1943- *WhoBlA 92*
King, Marcia 1940- *WhoWest 92*
King, Margaret Ann 1936- *WhoMW 92*
King, Marjorie Pitter 1921- *WhoAmP 91*
King, Mark Alexander, Jr. 1960- *WhoAmL 92*
King, Mark Edward 1958- *WhoAmL 92, WhoEnt 92*
King, Mark Edward 1959- *WhoRel 92*
King, Martha *DrAPF 91*
King, Martin Luther, Jr. 1929-1968 *AmPeW, BenetAL 91, BlkLC [port], ConBlB 1 [port], DcAmImH, DcEcMov, FacFETw [port], RComAH, RelLAm 91, WhoNob 90*
King, Martin Luther, Sr. 1899-1984 *RelLAm 91*
King, Marvin 1940- *AmMWSc 92*
King, Mary Booker 1937- *WhoBlA 92*
King, Mary-Claire 1946- *AmMWSc 92*
King, Mary Elizabeth 1940- *WhoAmP 91*
King, Mary Elizabeth Eskridge 1901-1973 *DcNCBi 3*
King, Mary Evelyn Marks 1954- *WhoRel 92*
King, Mary Margaret 1946- *AmMWSc 92*
King, Maryon Frederick 1953- *WhoMW 92*
King, Mattie M. 1919- *WhoBlA 92*
King, Maurice Athelstan 1936- *IntWW 91*
King, Merrill Kenneth 1938- *AmMWSc 92*
King, Mervyn Allister 1948- *IntWW 91, Who 92*
King, Michael *ConAu 133, LesBEnT 92 [port], Who 92*
King, Michael 1934- *Who 92*
King, Michael 1945- *IntAu&W 91*
King, Michael Dumont 1949- *AmMWSc 92*
King, Michael Gardner 1920- *Who 92*
King, Michael Howard 1943- *WhoAmL 92*
King, Michael Johnson 1957- *WhoWest 92*
King, Michael M 1944- *AmMWSc 92*
King, Michael Stuart 1931- *AmMWSc 92*
King, Morgana 1930- *WhoEnt 92*
King, Morris Kenton 1924- *AmMWSc 92*
King, Nancy Carol 1952- *WhoEnt 92*
King, Nettie 1891- *WhoBlA 92*
King, Nicholas S P 1940- *AmMWSc 92*
King, Noel Q. 1922- *WhoRel 92*
King, Norman 1933- *Who 92*
King, Norval William, Jr 1938- *AmMWSc 92*
King, Oliver *Who 92*
King, Patricia A *AmMWSc 92*
King, Patricia Ann 1942- *WhoAmL 92, WhoBlA 92*
King, Patricia E. 1943- *WhoBlA 92*
King, Patrick *WhoFI 92*
King, Paul *WrDr 92*
King, Paul H *WhoAmP 91*
King, Paul Harvey 1941- *AmMWSc 92*
King, Paul Louis 1934- *WhoIns 92*
King, Pee Wee 1914- *NewAmDM*
King, Pendleton 1844-1913 *DcNCBi 3*
King, Perry 1938- *DcTwDes*
King, Perry 1948- *ConTFT 9, IntMPA 92, WhoEnt 92*
King, Perry, Jr 1928- *AmMWSc 92*
King, Peter 1928- *IntMPA 92*
King, Peter Foster 1929- *AmMWSc 92, WhoMW 92*
King, Peter Francis 1922- *Who 92*
King, Peter Joseph 1938- *WhoAmL 92*
King, Peter Ramsay 1943- *AmMWSc 92*
King, Philip David 1935- *Who 92*
King, Phillip 1934- *IntWW 91, TwCPaSc, Who 92*
King, Philo Rockwell, III 1923- *WhoEnt 92*
King, Priscilla 1950- *WhoRel 92*
King, Rachel Hadley 1904- *WhoRel 92*
King, Ralph Malcolm MacDonald 1911- *Who 92*
King, Ray *TwCSFW 91*
King, Ray J 1933- *AmMWSc 92*
King, Ray John 1933- *WhoWest 92*
King, Raymond Dennis 1950- *WhoMW 92*
King, Raymond Lamprey 1929- *WhoAmP 91*
King, Raymond Leroy 1922- *AmMWSc 92*
King, Reatha Clark 1938- *AmMWSc 92, WhoBlA 92*
King, Reginald F. 1935- *WhoBlA 92*
King, Richard 1920- *Who 92*
King, Richard Allen 1939- *AmMWSc 92*
King, Richard Arthur 1934- *WhoAmP 91*
King, Richard Austin 1929- *AmMWSc 92*
King, Richard Devoid 1946- *WhoBlA 92*
King, Richard H. 1960- *WhoEnt 92*
King, Richard Joe 1937- *AmMWSc 92*
King, Richard S. 1925- *WhoWest 92*
King, Richard Warren 1925- *AmMWSc 92*
King, Riley B 1925- *FacFETw*
King, Robbins Sydney 1922- *AmMWSc 92*
King, Robert 1922- *AmMWSc 92*
King, Robert B 1950- *WhoIns 92*
King, Robert Bruce 1938- *AmMWSc 92*
King, Robert C. 1928- *WrDr 92*
King, Robert Charles 1928- *AmMWSc 92*
King, Robert Edward 1923- *AmMWSc 92*
King, Robert George Cecil 1927- *Who 92*
King, Robert Henry 1922- *WhoRel 92*
King, Robert James, Jr. 1953- *WhoAmL 92*
King, Robert L 1946- *WhoAmP 91*
King, Robert Lee 1946- *WhoAmL 92*
King, Robert Lee 1947- *WhoMW 92*
King, Robert Leonard 1938- *WhoFI 92*
King, Robert Lewis 1950- *WhoAmP 91*
King, Robert Lucien 1936- *WhoAmL 92*
King, Robert R. 1942- *WrDr 92*
King, Robert Samuel 1921- *WhoBlA 92*
King, Robert Shirley 1920- *Who 92*
King, Robert Timothy 1950- *WhoMW 92*
King, Robert W. *DrAPF 91*
King, Robert William 1929- *AmMWSc 92*
King, Robert Willis 1961- *AmMWSc 92*
King, Robert Wilson 1926- *WhoAmL 92*
King, Robert Wilson, Jr 1947- *AmMWSc 92*
King, Roger C 1919- *WhoAmP 91*
King, Roger Douglas 1943- *Who 92*
King, Roger Hatton 1941- *AmMWSc 92*
King, Roger M. *LesBEnT 92 [port]*
King, Ron *DrAPF 91*
King, Ronald 1914- *IntAu&W 91, WrDr 92*
King, Ronald Bruce 1942- *WhoFI 92*
King, Ronald Roy 1944- *WhoWest 92*
King, Ronold 1905- *AmMWSc 92*
King, Rosalie Rosso 1938- *WhoEnt 92*
King, Rosalyn Cain 1938- *WhoBlA 92*
King, Rosalyn Mercita 1948- *WhoFI 92*
King, Roy D. *WhoRel 92*
King, Roy Warbrick 1933- *AmMWSc 92*
King, Ruby E. 1931- *WhoBlA 92*
King, Ruby Ryan 1934- *WhoBlA 92*
King, Rufus 1755-1827 *AmPolLe, BlkwEAR*
King, Rufus 1893-1966 *ScFEYrs*
King, Rufus P. 1843-1923 *DcNCBi 3*
King, Ruth *Who 92*
King, Ruth Allen 1910- *WhoBlA 92, WhoFI 92*
King, Ruth G. 1933- *WhoBlA 92*
King, Ruth J. 1923- *WhoBlA 92*
King, S MacCallum 1926- *AmMWSc 92*
King, Sallie Behn 1952- *WhoRel 92*
King, Samuel 1948- *WhoFI 92*
King, Sanford MacCallum 1926- *WhoFI 92, WhoMW 92*
King, Sheldon Selig 1931- *AmMWSc 92, WhoWest 92*

**King**, Sheryl Jayne 1945- *WhoMW 92*
**King**, Stacey 1967- *WhoBlA 92*
**King**, Stanley Shih-Tung 1934- *AmMWSc 92, WhoMW 92*
**King**, Stephen 1947- *BenetAL 91, FacFETw, IntMPA 92, WrDr 92*
**King**, Stephen B 1941- *WhoAmP 91*
**King**, Stephen Edwin 1947- *IntAu&W 91, IntWW 91*
**King**, Stephen Murray *AmMWSc 92*
**King**, Stephen Robert 1942- *WhoMW 92*
**King**, Stephen Scott 1937- *WhoAmL 92*
**King**, Steve Mason 1951- *WhoAmL 92*
**King**, Steven Bruce 1949- *WhoFI 92*
**King**, Stoddard 1889-1933 *BenetAL 91*
**King**, Susan Bennett 1940- *WhoAmP 91*
**King**, Susan Marie 1956- *WhoRel 92*
**King**, Sydney 1916- *Who 92*
**King**, Talmadge Everett, Jr. 1948- *WhoBlA 92*
**King**, Te Piao 1930- *AmMWSc 92*
**King**, Teri 1940- *WrDr 92*
**King**, Terry Bower 1947- *WhoEnt 92*
**King**, Terry Lee 1945- *AmMWSc 92, WhoMW 92*
**King**, Thea 1925- *IntWW 91, Who 92*
**King**, Theodore Matthew 1931- *AmMWSc 92*
**King**, Theodore Oscar 1922- *AmMWSc 92*
**King**, Thomas Braxton 1954- *WhoWest 92*
**King**, Thomas Creighton 1928- *AmMWSc 92*
**King**, Thomas Edwin 1945- *WhoFI 92*
**King**, Thomas James 1950- *WhoFI 92*
**King**, Thomas Jeremy 1933- *IntWW 91, Who 92*
**King**, Thomas K C 1934- *AmMWSc 92*
**King**, Thomas Lawrence 1953- *WhoBlA 92*
**King**, Thomas Morgan 1940- *AmMWSc 92*
**King**, Thomas Starr 1824-1864 *BenetAL 91*
**King**, Timothy L 1952- *WhoAmP 91*
**King**, Tom Cobb, Jr 1915- *WhoAmP 91*
**King**, Tsoo E 1923- *AmMWSc 92*
**King**, Verna S 1916- *WhoAmP 91*
**King**, Vernon d1918 *BiInAmS*
**King**, Vincent 1935- *IntAu&W 91, TwCSFW 91, WrDr 92*
**King**, Virgie M 1940- *WhoAmP 91*
**King**, Vivian Kay 1946- *WhoWest 92*
**King**, W. James 1945- *WhoBlA 92*
**King**, Walter Bernard 1900- *AmMWSc 92*
**King**, Walter Maclan 1910- *Who 92*
**King**, Warren Earl 1947- *WhoBlA 92*
**King**, Wayne, II 1936- *WhoWest 92*
**King**, Wayne Alexander 1962- *Who 92*
**King**, Wayne Douglas 1955- *WhoAmP 91*
**King**, Weldon 1911- *WhoMW 92*
**King**, Wendell L 1940- *AmMWSc 92*
**King**, Wesley A. 1923- *WhoBlA 92*
**King**, William 1650-1729 *BlkwCEP*
**King**, William 1662-1712 *RfGEnL 91*
**King**, William Carl 1930- *WhoBlA 92*
**King**, William Charles 1957- *WhoRel 92*
**King**, William Connor 1927- *AmMWSc 92*
**King**, William Curtis 1933- *WhoWest 92*
**King**, William David 1953- *AmMWSc 92*
**King**, William Emmett, Jr 1943- *AmMWSc 92*
**King**, William Frank 1938- *WhoBlA 92*
**King**, William J. 1921- *WhoBlA 92*
**King**, William L. 1933- *WhoBlA 92*
**King**, William Lyon Mackenzie 1874-1950 *FacFETw [port]*
**King**, William Mattern 1930- *AmMWSc 92*
**King**, William McGuire 1947- *WhoRel 92*
**King**, William Moses 1927- *WhoBlA 92*
**King**, William Richard 1938- *WrDr 92*
**King**, William Robert, Jr 1924- *AmMWSc 92*
**King**, William Rufus de Vane 1786-1853 *AmPolLe*
**King**, William Rufus Devane 1786-1853 *DcNCBi 3*
**King**, William Stanely 1935- *AmMWSc 92*
**King**, William Stewart, II 1954- *WhoMW 92*
**King**, Willie James 1940- *WhoAmP 91*
**King**, Willis Jefferson 1886- *RelLAm 91*
**King**, Willis Kwongtsu 1936- *AmMWSc 92*
**King**, Wilton W 1937- *AmMWSc 92*
**King**, Winston Lee 1907- *WhoRel 92*
**King**, Woodie, Jr. 1937- *WhoBlA 92, WhoEnt 92*
**King**, Yolanda D. *WhoBlA 92*
**King**, Zalman 1941- *IntMPA 92*
**King-Hamilton**, Alan 1904- *Who 92*
**King-Hammond**, Leslie 1944- *WhoBlA 92*
**King-Hele**, Desmond 1927- *WrDr 92*
**King-Hele**, Desmond George 1927- *IntAu&W 91, IntWW 91, Who 92*
**King-Martin**, John Douglas 1915- *Who 92*
**King Murray**, Ronald *Who 92*
**King of Wartnaby**, Baron *Who 92*
**King Of Wartnaby**, Baron 1918 *IntWW 91*
**King-Reynolds**, Guy Edwin 1923- *Who 92*
**King-Smith**, Dick 1922- *IntAu&W 91, WrDr 92*
**King-Smith**, Ronald Gordon 1922- *IntAu&W 91*
**King-Tenison** *Who 92*
**Kingcade**, Alvin 1950- *WhoFI 92*
**Kingdom**, Roger 1962- *BlkOlyM*
**Kingdon**, Dwight Douglas 1960- *WhoFI 92*
**Kingdon**, Henry Shannon 1934- *AmMWSc 92*
**Kingdon**, John W. 1940- *WrDr 92*
**Kingdon**, Robert McCune 1927- *IntAu&W 91, WrDr 92*
**Kingdon**, Roger Taylor 1930- *Who 92*
**Kingery**, Bernard Troy 1920- *AmMWSc 92*
**Kingery**, Lionel Bruce *DrAPF 91*
**Kingery**, Margaret *DrAPF 91*
**Kingery**, W D 1926- *AmMWSc 92*
**Kingham**, James Frederick 1925- *Who 92*
**Kingham**, Richard Frank 1946- *WhoAmL 92*
**Kinghorn**, Alan Douglas 1947- *AmMWSc 92*
**Kinghorn**, Ernest 1907- *Who 92*
**Kinghorn**, William Oliver 1913- *Who 92*
**Kingi**, Henry Masao 1943- *WhoBlA 92, WhoEnt 92*
**Kingma**, Daphne Rose *DrAPF 91*
**Kingma**, P. *WhoRel 92*
**Kingman**, Dong 1911- *IntMPA 92*
**Kingman**, Elizabeth Yelm 1911- *WhoWest 92*
**Kingman**, Harry Ellis, Jr 1911- *AmMWSc 92*
**Kingman**, J. F. C. 1939- *WrDr 92*
**Kingman**, John 1939- *Who 92*
**Kingman**, John Frank Charles 1939- *IntWW 91*
**Kingman**, Lee 1919- *IntAu&W 91, SmATA 67 [port], WrDr 92*
**Kingman**, Robert Earl 1938- *AmMWSc 92*
**Kingon**, Alfred H 1935- *WhoAmP 91*
**Kingon**, Alfred Hugh 1931- *IntWW 91*
**Kingrea**, C L 1923- *AmMWSc 92*
**Kingrea**, James I 1928- *AmMWSc 92*
**Kingrey**, Jean Anne 1949- *WhoAmL 92*
**King's X** *ConMus 7 [port]*
**Kings Norton**, Baron 1902- *IntWW 91, Who 92*
**Kingsale**, Baron 1941- *Who 92*
**Kingsborough**, Viscount 1969- *Who 92*
**Kingsbury**, Alan 1960- *TwCPaSc*
**Kingsbury**, Carolyn Ann 1938- *WhoWest 92*
**Kingsbury**, Charles Alvin 1935- *AmMWSc 92*
**Kingsbury**, David Thomas 1940- *AmMWSc 92, WhoAmP 91*
**Kingsbury**, David Wilson 1933- *AmMWSc 92*
**Kingsbury**, Derek John 1926- *Who 92*
**Kingsbury**, Donald 1929- *TwCSFW 91, WrDr 92*
**Kingsbury**, Donald MacDonald 1929- *IntAu&W 91*
**Kingsbury**, Elizabeth W 1925- *AmMWSc 92*
**Kingsbury**, H Thayer 1921- *WhoAmP 91*
**Kingsbury**, Harley Ralph 1913- *WhoAmP 91*
**Kingsbury**, Herbert B 1934- *AmMWSc 92*
**Kingsbury**, John Francis 1947- *WhoAmP 91*
**Kingsbury**, John William 1952- *WhoEnt 92*
**Kingsbury**, Kenneth Earl, Jr. 1945- *WhoEnt 92*
**Kingsbury**, Robert Freeman 1912- *AmMWSc 92*
**Kingsbury**, Steven Harold 1948- *WhoEnt 92*
**Kingsbury**, Susan 1870-1949 *WomSoc*
**Kingsbury**, Suzanne Nelson 1956- *WhoAmL 92*
**Kingsbury**, Theodore Bryant 1828-1913 *DcNCBi 3*
**Kingsbury**, William Dennis 1941- *AmMWSc 92*
**Kingsbury-Smith**, Joseph 1908- *ConAu 133, IntAu&W 91, IntWW 91*
**Kingsdale**, James 1943- *WhoEnt 92*
**Kingsford**, Charles 1907- *WhoEnt 92*
**Kingsford**, Leonard O 1918- *WhoAmP 91*
**Kingshott**, Albert Leonard 1930- *Who 92*
**Kingshott**, Kenneth 1924- *Who 92*
**Kingshott**, Leonard *Who 92*
**Kingslake**, Rudolf 1903- *AmMWSc 92*
**Kingsland**, Graydon Chapman 1928- *AmMWSc 92*
**Kingsland**, Richard 1916- *Who 92*
**Kingsley**, Ben 1943- *IntMPA 92, IntWW 91, Who 92, WhoEnt 92*
**Kingsley**, Charles 1819-1875 *RfGEnL 91*
**Kingsley**, David John 1929- *Who 92*
**Kingsley**, Dorothy 1909- *IntMPA 92*
**Kingsley**, Emily Perl 1940- *WhoEnt 92*
**Kingsley**, Henry 1830-1876 *RfGEnL 91*
**Kingsley**, Henry A 1921- *AmMWSc 92*
**Kingsley**, Jack Dean 1934- *AmMWSc 92*
**Kingsley**, James Gordon 1933- *WhoMW 92*
**Kingsley**, John Piersall 1938- *WhoAmL 92*
**Kingsley**, Leonard E. 1929- *WhoWest 92*
**Kingsley**, Michael Charles Stephen 1941- *AmMWSc 92*
**Kingsley**, Patricia 1932- *WhoEnt 92*
**Kingsley**, Patrick 1908- *Who 92*
**Kingsley**, Roger James 1922- *Who 92*
**Kingsley**, Sidney 1906- *BenetAL 91, WhoEnt 92, WrDr 92*
**Kingsley**, Walter 1923- *IntMPA 92*
**Kingsley**, Walter Ingalls 1923- *WhoEnt 92*
**Kingsley**, Wayne Burtt 1942- *WhoFI 92*
**Kingsley**, William E 1934- *WhoIns 92*
**Kingsmill**, Hugh 1889-1949 *ScFEYrs*
**Kingsolver**, Barbara *DrAPF 91*
**Kingsolver**, Barbara 1955- *ConAu 134*
**Kingsolver**, Charles H 1914- *AmMWSc 92*
**Kingsolver**, John Mark 1925- *AmMWSc 92*
**Kingston**, Archbishop of 1926- *Who 92*
**Kingston**, Earl of 1943- *Who 92*
**Kingston Trio** *NewAmDM*
**Kingston**, Andrew Brownell 1958- *WhoAmL 92*
**Kingston**, Arthur Edward 1936- *IntWW 91*
**Kingston**, Charles Richard 1931- *AmMWSc 92*
**Kingston**, David George Ian 1938- *AmMWSc 92*
**Kingston**, David Lyman 1930- *AmMWSc 92*
**Kingston**, Frederick Temple 1925- *WrDr 92*
**Kingston**, George *WhoWest 92*
**Kingston**, George C *AmMWSc 92*
**Kingston**, Jack *WhoAmP 91*
**Kingston**, John Maurice 1914- *AmMWSc 92*
**Kingston**, Leo 1950- *WhoAmP 91*
**Kingston**, Maxine Hong 1940- *Au&Arts 8 [port], BenetAL 91, HanAmWH, IntAu&W 91, IntWW 91, ModAWWr, TwCWW 91, WrDr 92*
**Kingston**, Newton 1925- *AmMWSc 92*
**Kingston**, Paul L 1932- *AmMWSc 92*
**Kingston**, Robert Hildreth 1928- *AmMWSc 92*
**Kingston**, Syd *IntAu&W 91X, TwCWW 91*
**Kingston-Upon-Thames**, Bishop of 1941- *Who 92*
**Kington**, Miles 1941- *WrDr 92*
**Kington**, Miles Beresford 1941- *IntAu&W 91, Who 92*
**Kinhan**, James F *WhoAmP 91*
**Kinkade**, Edgar D. 1950- *WhoFI 92*
**Kinkade**, Kate 1951- *WhoWest 92*
**Kinkaid**, Matt *IntAu&W 91X, TwCWW 91*
**Kinkaid**, Robert William, Jr. 1959- *WhoAmL 92*
**Kinkead**, Verda Christine 1931- *WhoMW 92*
**Kinkead-Weekes**, Mark 1931- *IntAu&W 91, WrDr 92*
**Kinkel**, Anthony G 1960- *WhoAmP 91*
**Kinkel**, Arlyn Walter 1929- *AmMWSc 92*
**Kinkel**, Gary Steven 1956- *WhoRel 92*
**Kinkel**, Robert Steller, Jr. 1957- *WhoEnt 92*
**Kinlaw**, Dennis Franklin 1922- *WhoRel 92*
**Kinley**, George Raymond 1937- *WhoAmP 91*
**Kinley**, Peter 1926-1988 *TwCPaSc*
**Kinloch**, Bohun Baker, Jr 1934- *AmMWSc 92*
**Kinloch**, David 1951- *Who 92*
**Kinloch**, Donald Edmonds 1941- *WhoRel 92*
**Kinloch**, Gregory James 1946- *WhoRel 92*
**Kinloch**, Henry 1937- *Who 92*
**Kinloch**, Jerome 1943- *WhoBlA 92*
**Kinloch**, John 1907- *Who 92*
**Kinloch**, Robert Armstrong 1939- *AmMWSc 92*
**Kinloss**, Lady 1922- *Who 92*
**Kinloss**, Master of 1953- *Who 92*
**Kinlough-Rathbone**, Lorne R 1938- *AmMWSc 92*
**Kinman**, Riley Nelson 1936- *AmMWSc 92*
**Kinman**, Thomas David 1928- *AmMWSc 92*
**Kinn**, Donald Norman *AmMWSc 92*
**Kinn**, Gene Richard 1937- *WhoMW 92*
**Kinnaird** *Who 92*
**Kinnaird**, Lord 1912- *Who 92*
**Kinnaird**, John 1939- *TwCPaSc*
**Kinnaird**, Michael Leon 1945- *WhoBlA 92*
**Kinnaird**, Richard Farrell 1912- *AmMWSc 92*
**Kinnaman**, Theodore Dwight 1928- *WhoAmP 91*
**Kinnamon**, Donald Herbert 1937- *WhoAmP 91*
**Kinnamon**, Gregory Harold 1958- *WhoAmL 92*
**Kinnamon**, Keneth 1932- *WrDr 92*
**Kinnamon**, Kenneth Ellis 1934- *AmMWSc 92*
**Kinnamon**, Michael Kurt 1949- *WhoRel 92*
**Kinnan**, Joen Pritchard *WhoMW 92*
**Kinnan**, Roy Doug 1951- *WhoIns 92*
**Kinnard**, Matthew Anderson 1936- *AmMWSc 92*
**Kinnard**, William J, Jr 1932- *AmMWSc 92*
**Kinnavy**, M G 1921- *AmMWSc 92*
**Kinnear**, Ian Albert Clark 1924- *Who 92*
**Kinnear**, James Wesley, III 1928- *IntWW 91, WhoFI 92*
**Kinnear**, Leslie Gordon 1901-1976 *TwCPaSc*
**Kinnear**, Mary d1991 *NewYTBS 91*
**Kinnear**, Michael Steward Read 1937- *WrDr 92*
**Kinnear**, Nigel Alexander 1907- *Who 92*
**Kinneary**, Joseph Peter 1905- *WhoMW 92*
**Kinnebrew**, Jackson Metcalfe 1941- *WhoAmL 92*
**Kinnebrew**, Larry D. 1960- *WhoBlA 92*
**Kinnee**, Sandy 1947- *WhoWest 92*
**Kinnel**, Robin Bryan 1937- *AmMWSc 92*
**Kinnell**, Galway *DrAPF 91*
**Kinnell**, Galway 1927- *BenetAL 91, ConAu 34NR, ConPo 91, IntAu&W 91, IntWW 91, WrDr 92*
**Kinnell**, Ian 1943- *Who 92*
**Kinnen**, Edwin 1925- *AmMWSc 92*
**Kinnersley**, Ebenezer 1711-1778 *BiInAmS*
**Kinnersley**, William Morris 1944- *AmMWSc 92*
**Kinney**, Abbot 1850-1920 *BiInAmS*
**Kinney**, Abbott Ford 1909- *WhoFI 92*
**Kinney**, Aldon Monroe, Jr. 1921- *WhoAmL 92*
**Kinney**, Anthony John 1958- *AmMWSc 92*
**Kinney**, Arthur F. 1933- *WrDr 92*
**Kinney**, Arthur Frederick 1933- *IntAu&W 91*
**Kinney**, D. Claire 1960- *WhoWest 92*
**Kinney**, Douglas Merrill 1917- *AmMWSc 92*
**Kinney**, Edna M. 1905- *WhoBlA 92*
**Kinney**, Edward Coyle, Jr 1917- *AmMWSc 92*
**Kinney**, George Patrick 1959- *WhoEnt 92*
**Kinney**, Gilbert Ford 1907- *AmMWSc 92*
**Kinney**, Gregg Alan 1948- *WhoWest 92*
**Kinney**, Gregory Hoppes 1947- *WhoAmL 92*
**Kinney**, Harry Edwin 1924- *WhoAmP 91*
**Kinney**, Jan G 1954- *WhoAmP 91*
**Kinney**, John Francis 1937- *WhoRel 92*
**Kinney**, John James 1932- *AmMWSc 92, WhoMW 92*
**Kinney**, John Martin 1921- *AmMWSc 92*
**Kinney**, Kurt Nicholas 1948- *WhoFI 92*
**Kinney**, Larry Lee 1941- *AmMWSc 92*
**Kinney**, Lee Ann 1933- *WhoMW 92*
**Kinney**, Lisa 1951- *WhoAmP 91*
**Kinney**, Lisa Frances 1951- *WhoAmL 92, WhoWest 92*
**Kinney**, Lowell Duayne 1936- *WhoMW 92*
**Kinney**, Martha Jane 1936- *WhoAmP 91*
**Kinney**, Michael J 1937- *AmMWSc 92*
**Kinney**, Paula J 1929- *WhoAmP 91*
**Kinney**, Raleigh Earl 1938- *WhoWest 92*
**Kinney**, Ralph A 1930- *AmMWSc 92*
**Kinney**, Robert Bruce 1937- *AmMWSc 92*
**Kinney**, Robert E. 1935- *WhoFI 92*
**Kinney**, Stephen Hoyt, Jr. 1948- *WhoAmL 92*
**Kinney**, Terry B, Jr 1925- *AmMWSc 92*
**Kinney**, William Lee 1955- *WhoRel 92*
**Kinnict**, Kinni *DrAPF 91*
**Kinnicutt**, Francis Parker 1846-1913 *BiInAmS*
**Kinnicutt**, Leonard Parker 1854-1911 *BiInAmS*
**Kinnie**, Irvin Gray 1932- *AmMWSc 92*
**Kinnie**, Kenneth Ivan 1923- *WhoAmP 91*
**Kinniebrew**, Robert Lee 1942- *WhoBlA 92*
**Kinnison**, Gerald Lee 1931- *AmMWSc 92*
**Kinnison**, Harry Austin 1935- *WhoWest 92*
**Kinnison**, Robert Ray 1934- *AmMWSc 92*
**Kinnison**, Robert Wheelock 1914- *WhoWest 92*
**Kinnison**, Tom 1947- *WhoAmP 91*
**Kinnison**, William Andrew 1932- *WhoMW 92*
**Kinnmark**, Ingemar Per Erland 1953- *AmMWSc 92*
**Kinnock**, Neil 1942- *FacFETw [port]*
**Kinnock**, Neil Gordon 1942- *IntWW 91, Who 92*
**Kinnoin**, Meyer D *WhoAmP 91*
**Kinnoull**, Earl of 1935- *Who 92*
**Kino**, Eusebio Francisco 1644-1711 *BenetAL 91*
**Kino**, Eusebio Francisco 1645?-1711 *BiInAmS, HisDSpE*
**Kino**, Gordon Stanley 1928- *AmMWSc 92*
**Kinon**, Marion Hardy 1929- *WhoAmP 91*
**Kinoshita**, Florence Keiko 1941- *AmMWSc 92*
**Kinoshita**, Jin Harold 1922- *AmMWSc 92*
**Kinoshita**, Kay 1954- *AmMWSc 92*

**Kinoshita**, Keisuke 1912- *IntDcF 2-2 [port], IntMPA 92, IntWW 91*
**Kinoshita**, Kimio 1942- *AmMWSc 92*
**Kinoshita**, Shin'ichi 1925- *AmMWSc 92*
**Kinoshita**, Toichiro 1925- *AmMWSc 92*
**Kinoy**, Ernest *IntMPA 92, LesBEnT 92*
**Kinoy**, Sarah Jane d1991 *NewYTBS 91*
**Kinra**, Vikram Kumar 1946- *AmMWSc 92*
**Kinross**, Baron 1949- *Who 92*
**Kinross**, Albert 1870-1929 *ScFEYrs*
**Kinsbourne**, Marcel 1931- *AmMWSc 92*
**Kinsel**, J. Frank, Jr. 1949- *WhoAmL 92*
**Kinsel**, Norma Ann 1929- *AmMWSc 92*
**Kinsell**, Jeffrey Clift 1951- *WhoWest 92*
**Kinsella**, James 1959- *ConAu 134*
**Kinsella**, John Edward 1938- *AmMWSc 92*
**Kinsella**, John J 1926- *AmMWSc 92*
**Kinsella**, Ralph A, Jr 1919- *AmMWSc 92*
**Kinsella**, Thomas *DrAPF 91*
**Kinsella**, Thomas 1928- *ConPo 91, IntAu&W 91, IntWW 91, RfGEnL 91, Who 92, WrDr 92*
**Kinsella**, W.P. *DrAPF 91*
**Kinsella**, W. P. 1932- *BenetAL 91*
**Kinsella**, W.P. 1935- *Au&Arts 7 [port], ConAu 35NR, ConNov 91, WrDr 92*
**Kinsella**, William Patrick 1935- *IntWW 91, WhoWest 92*
**Kinser**, Dianne Lee 1944- *WhoFI 92*
**Kinser**, Donald LeRoy 1941- *AmMWSc 92*
**Kinser**, Douglas M 1947- *WhoAmP 91*
**Kinser**, Henry E. 1946- *WhoAmL 92*
**Kinser**, Katherine Anne 1954- *WhoAmL 92*
**Kinser**, Richard Edward 1936- *WhoFI 92*
**Kinsey**, Alfred Charles 1894-1956 *BenetAL 91*
**Kinsey**, Barbara Cutshall 1947- *WhoWest 92*
**Kinsey**, Bernard *WhoBlA 92*
**Kinsey**, Bernard Bruno 1910- *AmMWSc 92*
**Kinsey**, Carlos M. 1943- *WhoHisp 92*
**Kinsey**, David Webster 1939- *AmMWSc 92*
**Kinsey**, Elisabeth *WrDr 92*
**Kinsey**, Elizabeth *IntAu&W 91X*
**Kinsey**, James Humphreys 1932- *AmMWSc 92*
**Kinsey**, James Lloyd 1934- *AmMWSc 92*
**Kinsey**, John Aaron, Jr 1939- *AmMWSc 92*
**Kinsey**, Kenneth F 1933- *AmMWSc 92*
**Kinsey**, Kimberly Dawn 1966- *WhoRel 92*
**Kinsey**, Philip A 1931- *AmMWSc 92*
**Kinsey**, Philip Franck 1949- *WhoFI 92*
**Kinsey**, Robert Everett 1927- *WhoAmP 91*
**Kinsey**, Robert Keith 1957- *WhoFI 92*
**Kinsey**, Robert Wayne 1943- *WhoAmP 91*
**Kinsey**, Thomas Richard Moseley 1929- *Who 92*
**Kinsey**, William Henderson *AmMWSc 92*
**Kinsey-Jones**, Brian *IntAu&W 91X*
**Kinsinger**, Jack Burl 1925- *AmMWSc 92*
**Kinsinger**, James A 1944- *AmMWSc 92*
**Kinsinger**, Richard Estyn 1942- *AmMWSc 92*
**Kinski**, Klaus 1926- *IntWW 91, WhoEnt 92*
**Kinski**, Klaus 1926-1991 *NewYTBS 91 [port], News 92-2*
**Kinski**, Klaus 1928- *IntMPA 92*
**Kinski**, Nastassja *WhoEnt 92*
**Kinski**, Nastassja 1960- *IntMPA 92*
**Kinski**, Nastassja 1961- *IntWW 91*
**Kinsky**, Stephen Charles 1932- *AmMWSc 92*
**Kinsland**, Gary Lynn 1947- *AmMWSc 92*
**Kinsler**, Bruce Whitney 1947- *WhoWest 92*
**Kinsley**, Homan Benjamin, Jr 1940- *AmMWSc 92*
**Kinsley**, Michael E 1951- *WhoAmP 91*
**Kinslow**, Henry Cargile 1954- *WhoAmP 91*
**Kinsman**, Donald Markham 1923- *AmMWSc 92*
**Kinsman**, Donald Vincent 1943- *AmMWSc 92*
**Kinsman**, Francis Michael 1925- *Who 92*
**Kinsman**, Lawrence *DrAPF 91*
**Kinsman**, Lawrence Charles 1953- *IntAu&W 91*
**Kinsman**, Robert Preston 1949- *WhoFI 92, WhoWest 92*
**Kinsolving**, Augustus Blagden 1940- *WhoAmL 92*
**Kinsolving**, C Richard *AmMWSc 92*
**Kinsolving**, Charles McIlvaine, Jr 1927- *WhoAmP 91*
**Kinsolving**, Monique B. 1949- *WhoFI 92*
**Kinsolving**, Susan Baumann *DrAPF 91*
**Kinsolving**, Sylvia Crockett 1931- *WhoEnt 92*
**Kinson**, Gordon A 1935- *AmMWSc 92*
**Kinstle**, James Francis 1938- *AmMWSc 92*
**Kinstle**, Thomas Herbert 1936- *AmMWSc 92*
**Kintanar**, Agustin 1958- *AmMWSc 92*
**Kintanar**, Roman 1929- *IntWW 91*
**Kinter**, Lewis Boardman 1950- *AmMWSc 92*
**Kintigh**, Bob 1922- *WhoAmP 91*
**Kintner**, Earl Wilson 1912- *WhoAmL 92*
**Kintner**, Edwin E *AmMWSc 92*
**Kintner**, Janet Ide 1944- *WhoAmL 92*
**Kintner**, Robert E. d1980 *LesBEnT 92*
**Kintner**, Robert Roy 1928- *AmMWSc 92, WhoMW 92*
**Kintner**, William R. 1915- *IntWW 91*
**Kintore**, Earl of 1939- *Who 92*
**Kintz**, Ronald Joseph 1956- *WhoFI 92*
**Kintzele**, John Alfred 1936- *WhoAmL 92*
**Kintzer**, Sam 1951- *WhoEnt 92*
**Kintzer Shorey**, Evie Lynn 1958- *WhoEnt 92*
**Kintzi**, Greg James 1958- *WhoRel 92*
**Kintzing**, Donald C 1929- *WhoIns 92, WhoMW 92*
**Kinugasa**, Teinosuke 1896- *IntDcF 2-2 [port]*
**Kinyon**, Bill Oliver 1956- *WhoRel 92*
**Kinyon**, Brice W 1911- *AmMWSc 92*
**Kinyoun**, Joseph James 1860-1919 *BiInAmS*
**Kinzel**, Gary Lee 1944- *AmMWSc 92*
**Kinzel**, Jerry J 1952- *AmMWSc 92*
**Kinzelberg**, Harvey 1945- *WhoMW 92*
**Kinzer**, Earl T, Jr 1931- *AmMWSc 92*
**Kinzer**, H Grant 1937- *AmMWSc 92*
**Kinzer**, James Raymond 1928- *WhoAmL 92*
**Kinzer**, Robert Lee 1941- *AmMWSc 92*
**Kinzey**, Bertram Y, Jr 1921- *AmMWSc 92*
**Kinzey**, Warren Glenford 1935- *AmMWSc 92*
**Kinzie**, Jan Jordan 1959- *WhoAmL 92*
**Kinzie**, Jeannie Jones 1940- *AmMWSc 92*
**Kinzie**, Lauren Elizabeth 1959- *WhoAmL 92*
**Kinzie**, Mark Alan 1964- *WhoAmL 92*
**Kinzie**, Mary 1944- *ConAu 133, IntAu&W 91*
**Kinzie**, Raymond Wyant 1930- *WhoFI 92*
**Kinzie**, Robert Allen, III 1941- *AmMWSc 92*
**Kinzler**, Thomas Benjamin 1950- *WhoAmL 92*
**Kinzly**, Robert Edward 1939- *AmMWSc 92*
**Kio**, Stephen Hre 1937- *WhoRel 92*
**Kionka**, Edward James 1939- *WhoAmL 92*
**Kioski**, Thomas J. 1951- *WhoEnt 92*
**Kiousis**, Jane Anne 1949- *WhoMW 92*
**Kip**, Katherine *ScFEYrs*
**Kip**, Leonard 1826-1906 *ScFEYrs*
**Kiparsky**, Valentin Julius Alexander *Who 92N*
**Kipfer**, Barbara Ann 1954- *ConAu 134*
**Kiphart**, Kerry 1949- *AmMWSc 92*
**Kipiani**, David 1951- *SovUnBD*
**Kipkulei**, Benjamin Kipkech 1946- *Who 92*
**Kipling**, Arlin Lloyd 1936- *AmMWSc 92*
**Kipling**, Arthur Wellesley *ScFEYrs*
**Kipling**, Joseph Rudyard 1865-1936 *WhoNob 90*
**Kipling**, Rudyard 1865-1936 *CnDBLB 5 [port], FacFETw [port], PoeCrit 3 [port], RfGEnL 91, ScFEYrs, TwCSFW 91*
**Kiplinger**, Glenn Francis 1930- *AmMWSc 92*
**Kipnis**, Alexander 1891-1978 *FacFETw, NewAmDM*
**Kipnis**, David Morris 1927- *AmMWSc 92*
**Kipnis**, Igor 1930- *FacFETw, NewAmDM, WhoEnt 92*
**Kipnis**, Judith Robison 1931- *WhoRel 92*
**Kipp**, Egbert Mason 1914- *AmMWSc 92*
**Kipp**, Harold Lyman 1903- *AmMWSc 92*
**Kipp**, James Edwin 1953- *AmMWSc 92*
**Kipp**, June Carol 1932- *WhoWest 92*
**Kipp**, Raymond J 1922- *AmMWSc 92*
**Kippax**, Donald 1930- *AmMWSc 92*
**Kippax**, John 1915-1974 *TwCSFW 91*
**Kippax**, Lynn, Jr. 1948- *WhoEnt 92*
**Kippenberger**, Donald Justin 1947- *AmMWSc 92*
**Kippenhahn**, Rudolf 1926- *IntWW 91*
**Kippenhan**, C J 1919- *AmMWSc 92*
**Kipper**, Barbara Levy 1942- *WhoMW 92*
**Kipperman**, Lawrence I. 1941- *WhoAmL 92*
**Kippert**, Robert John, Jr. 1952- *WhoMW 92*
**Kipphardt**, Heinar 1922-1982 *LiExTwC*
**Kipping**, Vernon Louis 1921- *WhoEnt 92, WhoFI 92, WhoWest 92*
**Kippis**, Andrew 1725-1795 *BlkwCEP*
**Kipps**, Thomas Charles 1923- *AmMWSc 92*
**Kiprov**, Dobri D 1949- *AmMWSc 92*
**Kiprugut Chuma**, Wilson 1938- *BlkOlyM*
**Kir-Stimon**, William *DrAPF 91*
**Kiracofe**, John Harmon 1921- *WhoMW 92*
**Kiral**, Andrew John 1935- *WhoEnt 92*
**Kiralfy**, Albert Kenneth Roland 1915- *Who 92*
**Kirban**, Lloyd 1931- *WhoFI 92*
**Kirber**, Maria Wiener 1917- *AmMWSc 92*
**Kirbo**, Helen Virginia 1953- *WhoAmL 92*
**Kirby**, Ada M. *WhoHisp 92*
**Kirby**, Albert Charles 1941- *AmMWSc 92*
**Kirby**, Andrew Fuller 1955- *AmMWSc 92*
**Kirby**, Anthony John 1935- *IntWW 91, Who 92*
**Kirby**, Bruce John 1928- *AmMWSc 92*
**Kirby**, Bruno 1949- *IntMPA 92*
**Kirby**, Charles William, Jr. 1926- *WhoEnt 92*
**Kirby**, Charlotte Ives Cobb Godbe 1836-1908 *HanAmWH*
**Kirby**, Christopher *WhoEnt 92*
**Kirby**, Conrad Joseph, Jr 1941- *AmMWSc 92*
**Kirby**, Dan Laird 1946- *WhoFI 92, WhoMW 92*
**Kirby**, David *DrAPF 91*
**Kirby**, David Donald 1933- *Who 92*
**Kirby**, David Kurt 1957- *WhoWest 92*
**Kirby**, David Peter 1936- *WrDr 92*
**Kirby**, Dennis 1923- *Who 92*
**Kirby**, Dorothy Manville 1917- *WhoMW 92*
**Kirby**, Edward Paul 1928- *WhoAmP 91*
**Kirby**, Edward Paul 1941- *AmMWSc 92*
**Kirby**, Edwin Schneider 1938- *WhoMW 92*
**Kirby**, Frank Eugene 1928- *WhoMW 92*
**Kirby**, Franklin Hugh 1939- *WhoRel 92*
**Kirby**, Fred Morgan, II 1919- *WhoFI 92*
**Kirby**, George Albert, III 1944- *WhoAmP 91*
**Kirby**, Gilbert Walter 1914- *WrDr 92*
**Kirby**, Gordon William 1934- *Who 92*
**Kirby**, Gwendolen Maud 1911- *Who 92*
**Kirby**, Harmon E 1934- *WhoAmP 91*
**Kirby**, Harry Scott 1938- *WhoRel 92*
**Kirby**, Hilliard Walker 1949- *AmMWSc 92*
**Kirby**, Jacqueline 1946- *WhoBlA 92*
**Kirby**, James Edmund, Jr. 1933- *WhoRel 92*
**Kirby**, James M 1901- *AmMWSc 92*
**Kirby**, James Michael 1948- *WhoWest 92*
**Kirby**, James Ray 1933- *AmMWSc 92*
**Kirby**, James W 1947- *WhoAmP 91*
**Kirby**, Joe Patrick 1953- *WhoIns 92*
**Kirby**, John 1949- *TwCPaSc*
**Kirby**, John Joseph, Jr. 1939- *WhoAmL 92*
**Kirby**, Jon Allan 1948- *AmMWSc 92*
**Kirby**, Kate Page 1945- *AmMWSc 92*
**Kirby**, Kevin Arthur 1957- *WhoWest 92*
**Kirby**, Le Grand Carney, III 1941- *WhoAmL 92*
**Kirby**, Louis 1928- *Who 92*
**Kirby**, Louis Albert Francis 1928- *IntAu&W 91, IntWW 91*
**Kirby**, Margaret Loewy 1946- *AmMWSc 92*
**Kirby**, Maurice J 1916- *AmMWSc 92*
**Kirby**, Michael Donald 1939- *IntWW 91, Who 92*
**Kirby**, Money Alian 1914- *WhoBlA 92*
**Kirby**, Montanges 1953- *WhoBlA 92*
**Kirby**, Nancy J. 1940- *WhoBlA 92*
**Kirby**, Norman George 1926- *Who 92*
**Kirby**, Paul Edward 1949- *AmMWSc 92*
**Kirby**, Ralph C 1925- *AmMWSc 92*
**Kirby**, Richard 1904- *Who 92*
**Kirby**, Richard C 1922- *AmMWSc 92*
**Kirby**, Richard Melvin 1946- *WhoAmL 92*
**Kirby**, Rita Maye Knowles 1941- *WhoFI 92*
**Kirby**, Robert Edward, Jr. 1954- *WhoAmL 92*
**Kirby**, Robert Emmet 1921- *AmMWSc 92*
**Kirby**, Robion C 1938- *AmMWSc 92*
**Kirby**, Rodney Niel 1953- *WhoRel 92*
**Kirby**, Roger D 1942- *AmMWSc 92*
**Kirby**, Ronald Eugene 1947- *WhoMW 92*
**Kirby**, Steven Evans 1945- *WhoAmL 92*
**Kirby**, Thomas James 1951- *WhoMW 92*
**Kirby**, William 1817-1906 *BenetAL 91*
**Kirbye**, George d1634 *NewAmDM*
**Kirca**, Ali Coskun 1927- *IntWW 91*
**Kirch**, Lawrence S 1932- *AmMWSc 92*
**Kirch**, Leo *LesBEnT 92*
**Kirch**, Murray R 1940- *AmMWSc 92*
**Kirch**, Patrick Vinton 1950- *AmMWSc 92, WhoWest 92*
**Kirchberger**, Madeleine *AmMWSc 92*
**Kirchenbauer**, Diane *WhoAmP 91*
**Kircher**, Henry Winfried 1925- *AmMWSc 92*
**Kircher**, John Frederick 1929- *AmMWSc 92*
**Kircher**, John Joseph 1938- *WhoAmL 92, WhoMW 92*
**Kircher**, Marvin Larry 1950- *WhoWest 92*
**Kircher**, Morton S 1917- *AmMWSc 92*
**Kirchgessner**, Joseph L 1932- *AmMWSc 92*
**Kirchheimer**, Gloria L. *DrAPF 91*
**Kirchheimer**, Manfred Alexander 1931- *WhoEnt 92*
**Kirchheimer**, Waldemar Franz 1913- *AmMWSc 92*
**Kirchhofer**, Wilma Ardine Lyghtner 1940- *WhoBlA 92*
**Kirchhoff**, Charles William Henry 1853-1916 *BiInAmS*
**Kirchhoff**, Michael Kent 1963- *WhoMW 92*
**Kirchhoff**, William Hayes 1936- *AmMWSc 92*
**Kirchman**, Charles Vincent 1935- *WhoAmL 92*
**Kirchmayer**, Leon K 1924- *AmMWSc 92*
**Kirchner**, Alan Willard 1959- *WhoFI 92*
**Kirchner**, Emil J. 1942- *WrDr 92*
**Kirchner**, Ernst Karl 1937- *AmMWSc 92, WhoWest 92*
**Kirchner**, Ernst Ludwig 1880-1938 *FacFETw*
**Kirchner**, Frederick Karl 1911- *AmMWSc 92*
**Kirchner**, H P 1923- *AmMWSc 92*
**Kirchner**, James Gary 1938- *AmMWSc 92*
**Kirchner**, Johanna 1889-1944 *EncTR 91*
**Kirchner**, John Albert 1915- *AmMWSc 92*
**Kirchner**, John Howard 1933- *WhoMW 92*
**Kirchner**, Leon 1919- *ConCom 92, NewAmDM*
**Kirchner**, Peter James 1920- *Who 92*
**Kirchner**, Richard Jay 1930- *WhoMW 92*
**Kirchner**, Richard Martin 1941- *AmMWSc 92*
**Kirchner**, Robert P 1939- *AmMWSc 92*
**Kirchner**, William G *WhoAmP 91*
**Kirchner**, William Joseph 1923- *WhoMW 92*
**Kirchoff**, William F 1929- *AmMWSc 92*
**Kirchschlager**, Rudolf 1915- *IntWW 91*
**Kirchwey**, Freda 1893-1976 *AmPeW*
**Kirchwey**, George Washington 1855-1942 *AmPeW*
**Kirczenow**, George *AmMWSc 92*
**Kirdani**, Rashad Y 1929- *AmMWSc 92*
**Kirdar**, Nemir Amin 1936- *WhoFI 92*
**Kirdorf**, Emil 1847-1938 *BiDExR, EncTR 91 [port]*
**Kireef**, Ivan Nickolaievich 1902-1991 *NewYTBS 91*
**Kireeff**, Ivan Nickolaievich 1902-1991 *NewYTBS 91*
**Kireilis**, Ramon J. 1940- *WhoEnt 92, WhoWest 92*
**Kiremidjian**, Anne Setian 1949- *AmMWSc 92*
**Kirgo**, George 1926- *WhoEnt 92*
**Kiriazis**, James W. 1928- *WhoMW 92*
**Kirichenko**, Aleksey Illarionovich 1908-1975 *SovUnBD*
**Kirichenko**, Vadim Nikitich 1931- *IntWW 91*
**Kirichenko**, Yuriy Alekseyevich 1936- *IntWW 91*
**Kirila**, Carol Elizabeth 1952- *WhoMW 92*
**Kirilenko**, Andrei Pavlovich 1906-1990 *FacFETw*
**Kirilenko**, Andrey Pavlovich 1906-1990 *SovUnBD*
**Kirillin**, Vladimir Alekseyevich 1913- *FacFETw*
**Kirillov**, Vladimir Timofeevich 1889-1943 *SovUnBD*
**Kirinda**, Margaret B. 1946- *WhoRel 92*
**Kirk**, Alan Goodrich 1888-1963 *FacFETw*
**Kirk**, Alexander David 1934- *AmMWSc 92*
**Kirk**, Andy 1898- *NewAmDM*
**Kirk**, Barry 1933- *TwCPaSc*
**Kirk**, Ben Truett 1942- *AmMWSc 92*
**Kirk**, Betty Virginia 1923- *WhoAmP 91*
**Kirk**, Billy Edward 1927- *AmMWSc 92*
**Kirk**, Carl L 1901- *WhoIns 92*
**Kirk**, Carmen Zetler 1941- *WhoFI 92, WhoWest 92*
**Kirk**, Cassius Lamb, Jr. 1929- *WhoFI 92, WhoWest 92*
**Kirk**, Dale E 1918- *AmMWSc 92*
**Kirk**, Daniel Eddins 1924- *AmMWSc 92*
**Kirk**, David Arneil 1948- *WhoRel 92*
**Kirk**, David Blackburn 1921- *AmMWSc 92*
**Kirk**, David Clark 1924- *AmMWSc 92*
**Kirk**, David Livingstone 1934- *AmMWSc 92*
**Kirk**, Dennis Dean 1950- *WhoAmL 92*
**Kirk**, Donald 1938- *IntAu&W 91, WrDr 92*
**Kirk**, Donald Evan 1937- *AmMWSc 92*
**Kirk**, Donald James 1932- *WhoFI 92*
**Kirk**, Donald Wayne 1934- *AmMWSc 92*
**Kirk**, Edgar Lee 1923- *WhoEnt 92*
**Kirk**, Edgar S. *WhoRel 92*
**Kirk**, Eve 1900-1969 *TwCPaSc*
**Kirk**, Geoffrey Stephen 1921- *IntAu&W 91, IntWW 91, Who 92, WrDr 92*
**Kirk**, George W. 1837-1905 *DcNCBi 3*
**Kirk**, Grayson 1903- *IntWW 91*
**Kirk**, Grayson Louis 1903- *Who 92*
**Kirk**, Henry Port 1935- *WhoWest 92*

**Kirk**, Herbert Victor 1912- *Who 92*
**Kirk**, Hugh Adam 1916- *WhoMW 92*
**Kirk**, Irina *DrAPF 91*
**Kirk**, Ivan Wayne 1937- *AmMWSc 92*
**Kirk**, James Albert 1929- *WhoRel 92, WhoWest 92*
**Kirk**, James Curtis 1921- *AmMWSc 92*
**Kirk**, James Graham 1937- *WhoRel 92*
**Kirk**, Joanna 1963- *TwCPaSc*
**Kirk**, Joe Eckley, Jr 1939- *AmMWSc 92*
**Kirk**, John Gallatin 1938- *AmMWSc 92*
**Kirk**, John Henry 1907- *Who 92*
**Kirk**, John MacGregor 1938- *WhoAmL 92*
**Kirk**, John Robert, Jr. 1935- *WhoAmL 92*
**Kirk**, Jon 1961- *WhoEnt 92*
**Kirk**, Judd 1945- *WhoWest 92*
**Kirk**, Kent Sand 1948- *IntWW 91*
**Kirk**, Kent T 1940- *AmMWSc 92*
**Kirk**, Kevin Lee 1950- *WhoRel 92*
**Kirk**, Leroy W. 1924- *WhoBlA 92*
**Kirk**, Lucy Ruth *Who 92*
**Kirk**, Marilyn M 1927- *AmMWSc 92*
**Kirk**, Marshall 1957- *ConAu 135*
**Kirk**, Matthew *TwCWW 91*
**Kirk**, Maurice Blake 1921- *WhoAmL 92*
**Kirk**, Michael *IntAu&W 91X*
**Kirk**, Michael William 1963- *WhoAmL 92*
**Kirk**, Norman Andrew *DrAPF 91*
**Kirk**, Orville 1936- *WhoBlA 92*
**Kirk**, Patrick James 1965- *WhoFI 92*
**Kirk**, Patrick Laine 1948- *WhoAmL 92*
**Kirk**, Paul G. Jr 1938- *WhoAmP 91*
**Kirk**, Paul Grattan, Jr. 1938- *IntWW 91, WhoFI 92*
**Kirk**, Paul Wheeler, Jr 1931- *AmMWSc 92*
**Kirk**, Phillip James, Jr 1944- *WhoAmP 91*
**Kirk**, Phyllis 1930- *IntMPA 92*
**Kirk**, Phyllis O. 1943- *WhoBlA 92*
**Kirk**, R S 1922- *AmMWSc 92*
**Kirk**, Rahsaan Roland 1936-1977 *ConMus 6 [port], NewAmDM*
**Kirk**, Raymond Maurice 1923- *Who 92*
**Kirk**, Rea Helene 1944- *WhoWest 92*
**Kirk**, Richard Augustus 1930- *WhoFI 92, WhoWest 92*
**Kirk**, Robert Leonard 1929- *WhoFI 92*
**Kirk**, Robert Warren 1922- *AmMWSc 92*
**Kirk**, Roger 1930- *WhoAmP 91*
**Kirk**, Roger E 1930- *AmMWSc 92*
**Kirk**, Russell 1918- *FacFETw, IntAu&W 91, WrDr 92*
**Kirk**, Ruth *Who 92*
**Kirk**, Ruth M 1930- *WhoAmP 91*
**Kirk**, Sarah Virgo 1934- *WhoBlA 92*
**Kirk**, Stanley Reese 1938- *WhoAmL 92*
**Kirk**, Stephen Dean 1965- *WhoMW 92*
**Kirk**, Thomas Bernard Walter 1940- *AmMWSc 92*
**Kirk**, Wilber Wolfe 1932- *AmMWSc 92*
**Kirk**, Wiley Price 1942- *AmMWSc 92*
**Kirk**, William Arthur 1936- *AmMWSc 92, WhoMW 92*
**Kirk**, William Leroy 1930- *AmMWSc 92*
**Kirk**, Wyatt D. 1935- *WhoBlA 92*
**Kirk-Duggan**, Cheryl Ann 1951- *WhoBlA 92*
**Kirk-Greene**, Anthony *IntAu&W 91, WrDr 92*
**Kirk-Greene**, Christopher 1926- *WrDr 92*
**Kirkaldy**, George Willis 1873-1910 *BiInAmS*
**Kirkaldy**, J S 1926- *AmMWSc 92*
**Kirkbride**, Chalmer Gatlin 1906- *AmMWSc 92*
**Kirkbride**, Clyde Arnold 1924- *AmMWSc 92*
**Kirkbride**, Joseph Edward 1947- *WhoMW 92*
**Kirkbride**, Joseph Harold, Jr 1943- *AmMWSc 92*
**Kirkbride**, L D 1932- *AmMWSc 92*
**Kirkby**, Emma 1949- *IntWW 91, Who 92*
**Kirke**, David Walter 1915- *Who 92*
**Kirke**, Gerald Michael 1943- *WhoAmP 91*
**Kirkeby**, Oliver Murle 1930- *WhoRel 92*
**Kirkegaard**, Knud E. 1942- *IntWW 91*
**Kirkemo**, Harold 1915- *AmMWSc 92*
**Kirkendall**, Ernest Oliver 1914- *AmMWSc 92*
**Kirkendall**, Jeffrey Lawrence 1954- *WhoWest 92*
**Kirkendall**, John Neal 1938- *WhoAmL 92*
**Kirkendall**, Lester A. 1903- *WrDr 92*
**Kirkendall**, Lester Allen 1903- *IntAu&W 91*
**Kirkendall**, Thomas Dodge 1937- *AmMWSc 92*
**Kirkendall**, Walter Murray 1917- *AmMWSc 92*
**Kirkendoll**, Chester Arthur, II 1914- *WhoBlA 92*
**Kirkenslager**, Larry Keith 1944- *WhoAmP 91*
**Kirker**, Jack M. *WhoWest 92*
**Kirkham**, Dan Romanie 1932- *WhoWest 92*
**Kirkham**, Don 1908 *AmMWSc 92*
**Kirkham**, Donald Herbert 1936- *Who 92*
**Kirkham**, E. Bruce 1938- *WrDr 92*
**Kirkham**, Francis Robison 1904- *WhoAmL 92*
**Kirkham**, Ira Lloyd 1942- *WhoAmP 91*
**Kirkham**, James Alvin 1935- *WhoMW 92*
**Kirkham**, John Dudley Galtrey *Who 92*
**Kirkham**, John Spencer 1944- *WhoAmL 92, WhoWest 92*
**Kirkham**, Keith Edwin 1929- *Who 92*
**Kirkham**, M B *AmMWSc 92, WhoMW 92*
**Kirkham**, Wayne Wolpert 1918- *AmMWSc 92*
**Kirkham**, William R 1925- *AmMWSc 92*
**Kirkhill**, Baron 1930- *Who 92*
**Kirkhope**, Timothy John Robert 1945- *Who 92*
**Kirkien-Rzeszotarski**, Alicja M *AmMWSc 92*
**Kirkinen**, Heikki 1927- *IntWW 91*
**Kirking**, Clayton Carroll 1949- *WhoWest 92*
**Kirkland**, Alfred Younges 1917- *WhoAmL 92, WhoMW 92*
**Kirkland**, Alfred Younges, Jr. 1944- *WhoAmL 92*
**Kirkland**, Bertha Theresa *WhoFI 92*
**Kirkland**, Bertha Theresa 1916- *WhoWest 92*
**Kirkland**, Bryant Mays 1914- *WhoRel 92*
**Kirkland**, Caroline 1801-1864 *BenetAL 91*
**Kirkland**, Cornell R. *WhoBlA 92*
**Kirkland**, Gail Alicia 1960- *WhoBlA 92*
**Kirkland**, Gelsey 1953- *IntWW 91, WhoEnt 92, WrDr 92*
**Kirkland**, Gerry Paul 1943- *WhoMW 92*
**Kirkland**, Gordon Laidlaw, Jr 1943- *AmMWSc 92*
**Kirkland**, J. David, Jr. 1958- *WhoAmL 92*
**Kirkland**, Jack A. 1931- *WhoBlA 92*
**Kirkland**, James Ian 1954- *WhoWest 92*
**Kirkland**, James M 1947- *WhoAmP 91*
**Kirkland**, James T 1943- *AmMWSc 92*
**Kirkland**, Jerry J 1936- *AmMWSc 92*
**Kirkland**, John Clarence 1963- *WhoAmL 92*
**Kirkland**, John David 1933- *WhoAmL 92*
**Kirkland**, Joseph 1830-1894 *BenetAL 91*
**Kirkland**, Joseph Jack 1925- *AmMWSc 92*
**Kirkland**, Joseph Lane 1922- *Who 92, WhoAmP 91*
**Kirkland**, Lane 1922- *IntWW 91*
**Kirkland**, Leroy, Sr 1932- *WhoAmP 91*
**Kirkland**, Randall Lee 1952- *WhoFI 92*
**Kirkland**, Ray 1941- *WhoEnt 92*
**Kirkland**, Reo, Jr 1947- *WhoAmP 91*
**Kirkland**, Sally 1944- *IntMPA 92*
**Kirkland**, Theodore 1934- *WhoBlA 92*
**Kirkland**, William Alexander 1836-1898 *DcNCBi 3*
**Kirkland**, William Dennis 1961- *WhoRel 92*
**Kirkland**, William Wheedbee 1833-1915 *DcNCBi 3*
**Kirkland**, Willis L 1944- *AmMWSc 92*
**Kirkland**, Winifred Margaretta 1872-1943 *DcNCBi 3*
**Kirkland-Holmes**, Gloria 1952- *WhoBlA 92*
**Kirklin**, George Lincoln 1937- *WhoAmL 92*
**Kirklin**, John W 1917- *AmMWSc 92*
**Kirklin**, Perry William 1935- *AmMWSc 92, WhoBlA 92*
**Kirkman** *NewAmDM*
**Kirkman**, Henry Neil, Jr 1927- *AmMWSc 92*
**Kirkman**, Jacob 1710-1792 *NewAmDM*
**Kirkman**, James Watson 1910- *WhoMW 92*
**Kirkman**, Jay Urban, III 1954- *WhoAmP 91*
**Kirkman**, Michael Eugene 1954- *WhoRel 92*
**Kirkman**, Roger Norman 1949- *WhoEnt 92*
**Kirkman**, William Patrick 1932- *Who 92, WrDr 92*
**Kirkness**, Donald James 1919- *Who 92*
**Kirkorian**, Donald George 1938- *WhoWest 92*
**Kirkpatrick**, Anne Saunders 1938- *WhoMW 92*
**Kirkpatrick**, Charles Harvey 1931- *AmMWSc 92*
**Kirkpatrick**, Charles Milton 1915- *AmMWSc 92*
**Kirkpatrick**, Clayton 1915- *IntAu&W 91, IntWW 91*
**Kirkpatrick**, David *IntMPA 92*
**Kirkpatrick**, Diana M 1944- *AmMWSc 92*
**Kirkpatrick**, Diane 1933- *WhoMW 92*
**Kirkpatrick**, E T 1925- *AmMWSc 92*
**Kirkpatrick**, Edward Scott 1941- *AmMWSc 92*
**Kirkpatrick**, Eliel Frank 1919- *WhoMW 92*
**Kirkpatrick**, Foote *WhoEnt 92*
**Kirkpatrick**, Francis Hubbard 1943- *AmMWSc 92*
**Kirkpatrick**, Frank Gloyd 1942- *WhoRel 92*
**Kirkpatrick**, Garland Penn 1932- *WhoBlA 92*
**Kirkpatrick**, George Grier, Jr 1938- *WhoAmP 91*
**Kirkpatrick**, Howard Delane 1935- *WhoAmP 91*
**Kirkpatrick**, Ivone Elliott 1942- *Who 92*
**Kirkpatrick**, James W 1936- *AmMWSc 92*
**Kirkpatrick**, Jay Franklin 1940- *AmMWSc 92*
**Kirkpatrick**, Jeane 1926- *WhoAmP 91, WrDr 92*
**Kirkpatrick**, Jeane Duane Jordan 1926- *AmPolLe, IntWW 91*
**Kirkpatrick**, Jeanne 1926- *FacFETw*
**Kirkpatrick**, Jeffery Roger 1963- *WhoAmP 91*
**Kirkpatrick**, Joel Brian 1936- *AmMWSc 92*
**Kirkpatrick**, Joel Lee 1936- *AmMWSc 92*
**Kirkpatrick**, John d1991 *NewYTBS 91 [port]*
**Kirkpatrick**, John 1819-1869 *BiInAmS*
**Kirkpatrick**, John 1905- *NewAmDM*
**Kirkpatrick**, John Everett 1929- *WhoAmL 92*
**Kirkpatrick**, John Lister 1927- *Who 92*
**Kirkpatrick**, Larry Dale 1941- *AmMWSc 92*
**Kirkpatrick**, Mark Adams 1956- *AmMWSc 92*
**Kirkpatrick**, R James 1946- *AmMWSc 92*
**Kirkpatrick**, Ralph 1911-1984 *NewAmDM*
**Kirkpatrick**, Ralph Donald 1930- *AmMWSc 92, WhoMW 92*
**Kirkpatrick**, Richard Alan 1947- *WhoWest 92*
**Kirkpatrick**, Robert Hugh 1954- *WhoMW 92*
**Kirkpatrick**, Robert James 1946- *AmMWSc 92*
**Kirkpatrick**, Roy Lee 1940- *AmMWSc 92*
**Kirkpatrick**, Sidney Dale 1955- *WhoEnt 92*
**Kirkpatrick**, Smith *DrAPF 91*
**Kirkpatrick**, Susan 1942- *WhoWest 92*
**Kirkpatrick**, Susan Elizabeth *WhoAmP 91*
**Kirkpatrick**, Susan Elizabeth D. 1950- *WhoWest 92*
**Kirkpatrick**, Theodore Ross 1953- *AmMWSc 92*
**Kirkpatrick**, Thomas Anthony 1957- *WhoFI 92*
**Kirkpatrick**, Vicki Karen 1952- *WhoWest 92*
**Kirkpatrick**, William 1960- *WhoEnt 92*
**Kirkpatrick**, William Brown 1934- *Who 92*
**Kirkpatrick**, Willie D., III 1965- *WhoFI 92*
**Kirksey**, Avanelle 1926- *AmMWSc 92*
**Kirksey**, Donny Frank 1948- *AmMWSc 92*
**Kirksey**, Henry J *WhoAmP 91*
**Kirksey**, Howard Graden, Jr 1940- *AmMWSc 92*
**Kirksey**, Jack Edwin 1928- *WhoAmP 91*
**Kirksey**, Peter J. 1904- *WhoBlA 92*
**Kirksey**, Robert Frederick 1959- *WhoMW 92*
**Kirkup**, James 1918- *IntAu&W 91, IntWW 91*
**Kirkup**, James 1923- *ConPo 91, Who 92, WrDr 92*
**Kirkwood** *Who 92*
**Kirkwood**, Baron 1931- *Who 92*
**Kirkwood**, Lord 1932- *Who 92*
**Kirkwood**, Andrew Tristram Hammett 1944- *Who 92*
**Kirkwood**, Archy 1946- *Who 92*
**Kirkwood**, Charles Edward, Jr 1913- *AmMWSc 92*
**Kirkwood**, Daniel 1814-1895 *BiInAmS*
**Kirkwood**, Gene *IntMPA 92*
**Kirkwood**, Ian Candlish *Who 92*
**Kirkwood**, James *TwCSFW 91*
**Kirkwood**, James 1930- *IntAu&W 91*
**Kirkwood**, James Benjamine 1924- *AmMWSc 92*
**Kirkwood**, John 1947- *TwCPaSc*
**Kirkwood**, Kenneth 1919- *Who 92*
**Kirkwood**, Lawrence Robert 1941- *WhoAmP 91*
**Kirkwood**, Robert Carter 1939- *WhoAmP 91*
**Kirkwood**, Samuel 1920- *AmMWSc 92*
**Kirlin**, Judith Ann 1940- *WhoMW 92*
**Kirlin-Hackett**, Susan Kaye 1949- *WhoRel 92*
**Kirloskar**, Shantanu Laxman 1903- *IntWW 91*
**Kirmse**, Anne-Marie Rose 1941- *WhoRel 92*
**Kirmse**, Dale William 1938- *AmMWSc 92*
**Kirmser**, P G 1919- *AmMWSc 92*
**Kirmser**, Philip George 1919- *WhoMW 92*
**Kirnan**, Coleen Lorena 1962- *WhoWest 92*
**Kirnberger**, Johann Philipp 1721?-1783 *BlkwCEP, NewAmDM*
**Kiron**, Ravi 1959- *AmMWSc 92*
**Kirov**, Sergei Mironovich 1886-1934 *FacFETw*
**Kirov**, Sergey Mironovich 1886-1934 *SovUnBD*
**Kirpal**, Prem Nath 1909- *IntWW 91*
**Kirsanov**, Semen Isaakovich 1906-1972 *SovUnBD*
**Kirsch**, Charles Dee 1928- *WhoRel 92*
**Kirsch**, Donald R 1950- *AmMWSc 92*
**Kirsch**, Edwin Joseph 1924- *AmMWSc 92*
**Kirsch**, Elmer Edwin 1927- *WhoMW 92, WhoRel 92*
**Kirsch**, Francis William 1925- *AmMWSc 92*
**Kirsch**, Jack Frederick 1934- *AmMWSc 92*
**Kirsch**, Jeffrey Scott 1947- *WhoMW 92*
**Kirsch**, Joseph Lawrence, Jr 1942- *AmMWSc 92*
**Kirsch**, Laurence Stephen 1957- *WhoAmL 92*
**Kirsch**, Lawrence Edward 1938- *AmMWSc 92*
**Kirsch**, Milton 1923- *AmMWSc 92*
**Kirsch**, Philip H d1900? *BiInAmS*
**Kirsch**, Sarah 1935- *LiExTwC*
**Kirsch**, Wolff M 1931- *AmMWSc 92*
**Kirschbaum**, H S 1920- *AmMWSc 92*
**Kirschbaum**, James Louis 1940- *WhoFI 92*
**Kirschbaum**, Joel Bruce 1945- *AmMWSc 92*
**Kirschbaum**, Joel Jerome 1935- *AmMWSc 92*
**Kirschbaum**, Myron 1949- *WhoAmL 92*
**Kirschbaum**, Thomas H 1929- *AmMWSc 92*
**Kirschbraun**, Keith Donald 1957- *WhoAmL 92*
**Kirsche**, Edward George 1949- *WhoRel 92*
**Kirschenbaum**, Donald 1927- *AmMWSc 92*
**Kirschenbaum**, Kenneth 1948- *WhoAmL 92*
**Kirschenbaum**, Louis Jean 1943- *AmMWSc 92*
**Kirschenbaum**, Paulenne Roeske 1936- *WhoFI 92*
**Kirschenbaum**, Seth David 1949- *WhoAmL 92*
**Kirschenbaum**, Susan S 1943- *AmMWSc 92*
**Kirschenbaum**, William 1944- *WhoFI 92*
**Kirschke**, Gerald Joseph 1946- *WhoMW 92*
**Kirschner**, Anthony 1910- *WhoRel 92*
**Kirschner**, David *WhoEnt 92*
**Kirschner**, Kerry G 1946- *WhoAmP 91*
**Kirschner**, Leonard Burton 1923- *AmMWSc 92*
**Kirschner**, Marc S. 1942- *WhoAmL 92*
**Kirschner**, Marc Wallace 1945- *AmMWSc 92*
**Kirschner**, Marvin Abraham 1935- *AmMWSc 92*
**Kirschner**, Melvin Henry 1926- *WhoWest 92*
**Kirschner**, Richard Michael 1949- *WhoWest 92*
**Kirschner**, Robert H 1940- *AmMWSc 92*
**Kirschner**, Ronald Allen 1942- *AmMWSc 92*
**Kirschner**, Stanley 1927- *AmMWSc 92*
**Kirschstein**, Ruth L. 1926- *IntWW 91*
**Kirschstein**, Ruth Lillian 1926- *AmMWSc 92*
**Kirscht**, Robert Leon 1942- *WhoAmP 91*
**Kirschten**, Barbara Louise 1950- *WhoAmL 92*
**Kirsh**, Bernard 1946- *WhoEnt 92*
**Kirsh**, Herbert *WhoAmP 91*
**Kirsh**, Michael Alan 1952- *WhoFI 92*
**Kirshbaum**, Howard M *WhoAmP 91*
**Kirshbaum**, Howard M. 1938- *WhoAmL 92, WhoWest 92*
**Kirshbaum**, Jack D. 1902- *WhoWest 92*
**Kirshenbaum**, Abraham David 1919- *AmMWSc 92*
**Kirshenbaum**, Binnie *DrAPF 91*
**Kirshenbaum**, Gerald Steven 1944- *AmMWSc 92*
**Kirshenbaum**, Isidor 1917- *AmMWSc 92*
**Kirshenbaum**, Jerry 1938- *WhoEnt 92*
**Kirshenbaum**, Susan Mae 1939- *WhoEnt 92*
**Kirshner**, Alan I 1935- *WhoIns 92*
**Kirshner**, Don *LesBEnT 92*
**Kirshner**, Edward 1940- *WhoWest 92*
**Kirshner**, Howard Stephen 1946- *AmMWSc 92*
**Kirshner**, Norman 1923- *AmMWSc 92*
**Kirshner**, Robert Paul 1949- *AmMWSc 92*
**Kirshner**, Virginia K. 1921- *WhoEnt 92*
**Kirshon**, Vladimir Mikhaylovich 1902-1938 *SovUnBD*
**Kirsner**, Joseph Barnett 1909- *AmMWSc 92*
**Kirsner**, Stuart Bernard 1946- *WhoFI 92*
**Kirson**, Susan D. 1948- *WhoEnt 92*

**Kirsop,** Arthur Michael Benjamin 1931- *IntWW 91, Who 92*
**Kirst,** Hans Hellmut 1914- *IntAu&W 91*
**Kirst,** Hans Helmut 1914-1989 *FacFETw*
**Kirst,** Herbert Andrew 1944- *AmMWSc 92, WhoMW 92*
**Kirst,** Michael 1939- *IntWW 91*
**Kirst,** William James, Jr. 1923- *WhoWest 92*
**Kirstein,** John Audelbert 1925- *WhoRel 92*
**Kirstein,** John Herman 1925- *WhoEnt 92*
**Kirstein,** Lincoln 1907- *FacFETw, IntAu&W 91, IntWW 91, WrDr 92*
**Kirstein,** Lincoln Edward 1907- *Who 92*
**Kirstein,** Natalie *DrAPF 91*
**Kirstein,** Roger D. 1962- *WhoAmL 92*
**Kirsten,** Dorothy 1915- *WhoEnt 92*
**Kirsten,** Dorothy 1917- *NewAmDM*
**Kirsten,** Edward Bruce 1942- *AmMWSc 92*
**Kirsten,** Werner H 1925- *AmMWSc 92*
**Kirszenstein-Szewinska,** Irena 1946- *IntWW 91*
**Kirtland,** G B *IntAu&W 91X, WrDr 92*
**Kirtland,** Jared Potter 1793-1877 *BiInAmS*
**Kirtley,** Jane Elizabeth 1953- *WhoAmL 92*
**Kirtley,** John Robert 1949- *AmMWSc 92*
**Kirtley,** Mary Elizabeth 1935- *AmMWSc 92*
**Kirtley,** Robert Bassett 1949- *WhoWest 92*
**Kirtley,** Thomas L 1918- *AmMWSc 92*
**Kirtley,** William Raymond 1914- *AmMWSc 92*
**Kirtman,** Bernard 1935- *AmMWSc 92*
**Kirton,** Edwin Eggleston 1907-1986 *WhoBlA 92N*
**Kirton,** Hugh 1910- *Who 92*
**Kirton,** James *WrDr 92*
**Kirven,** Joe W. 1932- *WhoBlA 92*
**Kirven,** Mythe Yuvette 1956- *WhoBlA 92*
**Kirven,** Timothy J *WhoAmP 91*
**Kirven,** William James, III 1944- *WhoAmL 92*
**Kirwan,** Albert Dennis, Jr 1933- *AmMWSc 92*
**Kirwan,** Allan August 1945- *WhoAmL 92*
**Kirwan,** Archibald Laurence 1907- *Who 92*
**Kirwan,** Donald Frazier 1937- *AmMWSc 92*
**Kirwan,** Kent Aiken 1932- *WhoMW 92*
**Kirwan,** Laurence *Who 92*
**Kirwan,** Laurence Joseph 1941- *WhoAmP 91*
**Kirwan,** Ralph DeWitt 1942- *WhoAmL 92*
**Kirwan,** Roberta Claire *WhoBlA 92*
**Kirwan,** William E. 1938- *IntWW 91*
**Kirwan,** William English 1938- *AmMWSc 92*
**Kirwan-Taylor,** Peter Robin 1930- *WhoFI 92*
**Kirwin,** Gerald James 1929- *AmMWSc 92*
**Kiryak,** Nellia Pavlovna 1935- *IntWW 91*
**Kirz,** Janos 1937- *AmMWSc 92*
**Kis,** Danilo 1935-1989 *LiExTwC*
**Kis,** Miroslav Mirko 1942- *WhoRel 92*
**Kisabeth,** Tim Charles 1957- *WhoMW 92*
**Kisber,** Matthew Harris 1960- *WhoAmP 91*
**Kisch,** Alastair Royalton 1919- *Who 92*
**Kisch,** John Marcus 1916- *Who 92*
**Kisch,** Joseph Jay 1963- *WhoMW 92*
**Kisch,** Raymond R *WhoIns 92*
**Kisch,** Royalton *Who 92*
**Kischer,** Clayton Ward 1930- *AmMWSc 92, WhoWest 92*
**Kisekka,** Samson *IntWW 91*
**Kiselev,** Gennadiy Nikolayevich *IntWW 91*
**Kiselik,** Paul Howard 1937- *WhoFI 92*
**Kiser,** Donald Lee 1933- *AmMWSc 92*
**Kiser,** Howard Wayne 1939- *WhoRel 92*
**Kiser,** Jackson L. 1929- *WhoAmL 92*
**Kiser,** James Webb 1934- *WhoAmL 92, WhoFI 92*
**Kiser,** Kenneth M 1929- *AmMWSc 92*
**Kiser,** Lola Frances 1930- *AmMWSc 92*
**Kiser,** Nagiko Sato 1923- *WhoWest 92*
**Kiser,** Philip James 1947- *WhoMW 92*
**Kiser,** Raymond Douglas 1951- *WhoRel 92*
**Kiser,** Robert Wayne 1932- *AmMWSc 92*
**Kiser,** Roberta Katherine 1938- *WhoWest 92*
**Kiser,** Samuel Curtis 1944- *WhoAmP 91*
**Kiser,** Thelma Kay 1944- *WhoMW 92*
**Kish,** Carla Elene *WhoAmP 91*
**Kish,** Kenneth Alan 1947- *WhoMW 92*
**Kish,** Laszlo George 1922- *WhoFI 92*
**Kish,** Leslie 1910- *IntAu&W 91, WrDr 92*
**Kish,** Valerie Mayo 1944- *AmMWSc 92*
**ishel,** Chester Joseph 1915- *AmMWSc 92*
**ishi,** Glen Yo 1958- *WhoWest 92*
**ishi,** Keiji 1930- *AmMWSc 92*
**ishi,** Nobosuke 1896-1987 *FacFETw*
**ishi,** Yoshito 1937- *AmMWSc 92*
**ishimoto,** Yasunobu 1919- *IntWW 91*
**ishimoto,** Yasuo 1925- *AmMWSc 92*
**ishimoto,** Yuji 1938- *WhoFI 92*
**ishk,** Ahmed A 1954- *AmMWSc 92*
**ishkovsky,** Leonid *WhoRel 92*

**Kishon,** Ephraim 1924- *LiExTwC*
**Kishore,** Ganesh M 1953- *AmMWSc 92*
**Kishore,** Ganesh Murthy 1953- *WhoMW 92*
**Kishore,** Gollamudi Sitaram 1945- *AmMWSc 92*
**Kishpaugh,** Allan Richard 1937- *WhoFI 92*
**Kishtmand,** Ali 1935- *IntWW 91*
**Kisilev,** Tikhon Yakovlevich 1917-1983 *SovUnBD*
**Kisilevsky,** Robert 1937- *AmMWSc 92*
**Kisim,** Marwan al- 1938- *IntWW 91*
**Kiskaddon,** William V 1929- *WhoAmP 91*
**Kiskis,** Joseph Edward, Jr 1947- *AmMWSc 92*
**Kislik,** Richard William 1927- *WhoFI 92*
**Kisling,** Jacob Walter, Jr. 1937- *WhoMW 92*
**Kisliuk,** Paul 1922- *AmMWSc 92*
**Kisliuk,** Roy Louis 1928- *AmMWSc 92*
**Kisman,** Kenneth Edwin 1946- *AmMWSc 92*
**Kisner,** Ignatius 1925- *WhoAmP 91*
**Kisner,** James 1947- *ConAu 35NR*
**Kisner,** James Martin 1947- *IntAu&W 91*
**Kisner,** Robert Garland 1940- *WhoBlA 92*
**Kisor,** Henry Du Bois 1940- *WhoMW 92*
**Kispert,** Dorothy Lee 1928- *WhoBlA 92*
**Kispert,** Lowell Donald 1940- *AmMWSc 92*
**Kiss** *NewAmDM*
**Kiss,** Janos 1920- *WhoEnt 92, WhoMW 92*
**Kiss,** Klara 1930- *AmMWSc 92*
**Kiss,** Robert S. 1951- *WhoEnt 92*
**Kiss,** Robert S 1957- *WhoAmP 91*
**Kissa,** Erik 1923- *AmMWSc 92*
**Kissam,** Ed *DrAPF 91*
**Kissam,** William A 1927- *WhoAmP 91*
**Kissane,** Jean Charlotte 1946- *WhoAmL 92*
**Kissane,** John M 1928- *AmMWSc 92*
**Kissane,** Thomas 1927- *WhoAmL 92*
**Kissel,** Charles Louis 1947- *AmMWSc 92*
**Kissel,** David E 1943- *AmMWSc 92*
**Kissel,** John Walter 1925- *AmMWSc 92*
**Kissel,** Michael Case *WhoEnt 92*
**Kissel,** Peter Charles 1947- *WhoAmL 92*
**Kissel,** Thomas Robert 1947- *AmMWSc 92*
**Kissel,** William John 1941- *AmMWSc 92*
**Kissell,** Kenneth Eugene 1928- *AmMWSc 92*
**Kissen,** Abbott Theodore 1922- *AmMWSc 92*
**Kissick,** Gary *DrAPF 91*
**Kissin** *Who 92*
**Kissin,** Baron 1912- *IntWW 91, Who 92*
**Kissin,** Benjamin 1917- *AmMWSc 92*
**Kissin,** Evgeny 1971- *ConMus 6 [port]*
**Kissin,** G H 1914- *AmMWSc 92*
**Kissin,** Stephen Alexander 1942- *AmMWSc 92*
**Kissinger,** David George 1933- *AmMWSc 92*
**Kissinger,** H. P. *WhoRel 92*
**Kissinger,** Henry 1923- *FacFETw [port], WrDr 92*
**Kissinger,** Henry A 1923- *RComAH*
**Kissinger,** Henry Alfred 1923- *AmPolLe, IntAu&W 91, IntWW 91, Who 92, WhoAmP 91, WhoNob 90*
**Kissinger,** Homer Everett 1923- *AmMWSc 92*
**Kissinger,** John Calvin 1925- *AmMWSc 92*
**Kissinger,** Paul Bertram 1930- *AmMWSc 92*
**Kissinger,** Peter Thomas 1944- *AmMWSc 92*
**Kissinger,** Scott Ver Bryck 1958- *WhoAmL 92*
**Kissinger,** Warren Stauffer 1922- *WhoRel 92*
**Kissling,** Don Lester 1934- *AmMWSc 92*
**Kisslinger,** Carl 1926- *AmMWSc 92*
**Kisslinger,** Fred 1919- *AmMWSc 92*
**Kisslinger,** Lawrence E 1944- *WhoAmP 91*
**Kisslinger,** Leonard Sol 1930- *AmMWSc 92*
**Kissman,** Henry Marcel 1922- *AmMWSc 92*
**Kissmeyer-Nielsen,** Erik 1922- *AmMWSc 92*
**Kissner,** Mary Jean 1957- *WhoFI 92*
**Kissos,** Mary Saroukos 1933- *WhoMW 92*
**Kist,** Joseph Edmund 1929- *AmMWSc 92*
**Kister,** James Milton 1930- *AmMWSc 92, WhoMW 92*
**Kistiakowski,** George Bogdan 1900-1982 *FacFETw*
**Kistiakowsky,** Vera 1928- *AmMWSc 92*
**Kistler,** Alan L 1928- *AmMWSc 92*
**Kistler,** Darci 1964- *CurBio 91 [port]*
**Kistler,** Malathi K 1944- *AmMWSc 92*
**Kistler,** Richard Edwin 1931- *WhoWest 92*
**Kistler,** Robert L 1925- *WhoAmP 91*
**Kistler,** Ronald Wayne 1931- *AmMWSc 92*
**Kistler,** Vera *DrAPF 91*

**Kistler,** William *DrAPF 91*
**Kistler,** Wilson Stephen, Jr 1942- *AmMWSc 92*
**Kistner,** C. Richard 1936- *WhoMW 92*
**Kistner,** Clifford Richard 1936- *AmMWSc 92*
**Kistner,** David Harold 1931- *AmMWSc 92*
**Kistner,** Diane *DrAPF 91*
**Kistner,** Melvin Carl 1947- *WhoAmP 91*
**Kistner,** Ottmar Casper 1930- *AmMWSc 92*
**Kistner,** Robert William 1917- *WrDr 92*
**Kisvarsanyi,** Eva Bognar *AmMWSc 92*
**Kisvarsanyi,** Geza 1926- *AmMWSc 92*
**Kiszczak,** Czeslaw 1925- *IntWW 91*
**Kiszenick,** Walter 1918- *AmMWSc 92*
**Kit,** Gordon 1954- *WhoAmL 92*
**Kit,** Saul 1920- *AmMWSc 92*
**Kita Terujiro** 1883-1937 *BiDExR*
**Kita,** Ikki 1883-1937 *BiDExR*
**Kitabchi,** Abbas E 1933- *AmMWSc 92*
**Kitada,** Shinichi 1948- *WhoWest 92*
**Kitaenko,** Dmitriy Georgievich 1940- *SovUnBD*
**Kitagawa,** Ishimatsu *IntWW 91*
**Kitagawa,** Joseph Mitsuo 1915- *WhoRel 92*
**Kitagawa,** Takeshi 1916- *IntWW 91*
**Kitahata,** Luke Masahiko 1925- *AmMWSc 92*
**Kitahata-Sporn,** Amy 1957- *WhoEnt 92*
**Kitai,** Reuven 1924- *AmMWSc 92*
**Kitaigorodskii,** Sergei Alexander 1934- *AmMWSc 92*
**Kitaj,** R. B. 1932- *IntWW 91, TwCPaSc, Who 92*
**Kitajima,** Fred Takanori 1955- *WhoWest 92*
**Kitamura,** Hiroshi 1920- *Who 92*
**Kitano,** Harry H. L. 1926- *WrDr 92*
**Kitay,** Julian I 1927- *AmMWSc 92*
**Kitayama,** Takao 1941- *WhoFI 92*
**Kitayenko,** Dimitri Georgievitch 1940- *WhoEnt 92*
**Kitayenko,** Dmitriy Georgievich 1940- *IntWW 91*
**Kitayev,** Vladimir Sergeyevich 1931- *IntWW 91*
**Kitazawa,** George 1917- *AmMWSc 92*
**Kitbunchu,** Michael Michai 1929- *IntWW 91, WhoRel 92*
**Kitcatt,** Peter Julian 1927- *Who 92*
**Kitch,** Edmund Wells 1939- *WhoAmL 92, WhoFI 92*
**Kitchel,** Christine 1950- *WhoAmL 92*
**Kitchell,** James Frederick 1942- *AmMWSc 92*
**Kitchell,** Jennifer Ann 1945- *AmMWSc 92*
**Kitchell,** Ralph Lloyd 1919- *AmMWSc 92*
**Kitchell,** Samuel Farrand 1921- *WhoWest 92*
**Kitchelt,** Florence Ledyard Cross 1874-1961 *AmPeW*
**Kitchen,** Charles William 1926- *WhoAmL 92*
**Kitchen,** Frederick Bruford 1912- *Who 92*
**Kitchen,** Hyram 1932- *AmMWSc 92*
**Kitchen,** John Martin 1936- *WhoWest 92*
**Kitchen,** Jonathan Saville 1948- *WhoAmL 92*
**Kitchen,** Judith *DrAPF 91*
**Kitchen,** Lawrence Oscar 1923- *IntWW 91, WhoFI 92, WhoWest 92*
**Kitchen,** Martin 1936- *IntAu&W 91, WrDr 92*
**Kitchen,** Michael 1948- *Who 92*
**Kitchen,** Paddy 1934- *IntAu&W 91, WrDr 92*
**Kitchen,** Robert Maurice, Jr. 1963- *WhoEnt 92*
**Kitchen,** Stanley 1913- *Who 92*
**Kitchen,** Stephen Earl 1951- *WhoFI 92*
**Kitchen,** Sumner Wendell 1921- *AmMWSc 92*
**Kitchen,** Wayne Leroy 1948- *WhoBlA 92*
**Kitchener,** Ruth Mae 1907- *WhoAmP 91*
**Kitchener of Khartoum,** Earl 1919- *Who 92*
**Kitchens,** Ashton C. 1902- *WhoBlA 92*
**Kitchens,** Clarence Wesley, Jr 1943- *AmMWSc 92*
**Kitchens,** Frederick Lynton 1940- *WhoIns 92*
**Kitchens,** Frederick Lynton, Jr. 1940- *WhoFI 92*
**Kitchens,** Sherri Carp 1954- *WhoEnt 92*
**Kitchens,** Thomas Adren 1935- *AmMWSc 92*
**Kitchens,** Wiley M 1944- *AmMWSc 92*
**Kitchin,** Alvin Paul 1908-1983 *DcNCBi 3*
**Kitchin,** Claude 1869-1923 *DcNCBi 3*
**Kitchin,** John Francis 1953- *AmMWSc 92*
**Kitchin,** John Joseph 1933- *WhoEnt 92, WhoMW 92*
**Kitchin,** Laurence Tyson 1913- *Who 92*
**Kitchin,** Roy 1926- *TwCPaSc*
**Kitchin,** Thurman Delna 1885-1955 *DcNCBi 3*
**Kitchin,** William Hodge 1837-1901 *DcNCBi 3*

**Kitchin,** William Morlan, Jr. 1946- *WhoEnt 92*
**Kitchin,** William Walton 1866-1924 *DcNCBi 3*
**Kitching,** Arthur 1912- *TwCPaSc*
**Kitching,** George 1910- *Who 92*
**Kitching,** John Alwyne 1908- *IntWW 91, Who 92*
**Kitchings,** Atley Asher, Jr. 1925- *WhoAmL 92*
**Kite,** Francis Ervin 1918- *AmMWSc 92*
**Kite,** Joseph Hiram, Jr 1926- *AmMWSc 92*
**Kite,** L. Patricia 1940- *IntAu&W 91*
**Kite,** Pat *DrAPF 91*
**Kite,** Roger 1947- *TwCPaSc*
**Kite,** William McDougall 1923- *WhoAmL 92*
**Kithcart,** Larry E. 1939- *WhoBlA 92*
**Kithier,** Karel 1930- *AmMWSc 92*
**Kitman,** Jamie Lincoln 1957- *WhoEnt 92*
**Kitman,** Marvin *LesBEnT 92*
**Kito,** Teruo 1932- *WhoFI 92*
**Kitos,** Paul Alan 1927- *AmMWSc 92*
**Kitson** *Who 92*
**Kitson,** Alexander Harper 1921- *Who 92*
**Kitson,** Frank 1926- *Who 92*
**Kitson,** George McCullough 1922- *Who 92*
**Kitson,** John Aidan 1927- *AmMWSc 92*
**Kitson,** Linda 1945- *TwCPaSc*
**Kitson,** Linda Frances 1945- *IntWW 91*
**Kitson,** Michael William Lely 1926- *Who 92*
**Kitson,** Robert Edward 1918- *AmMWSc 92*
**Kitson,** Timothy 1931- *Who 92*
**Kitson,** William Kay 1941- *WhoMW 92*
**Kitt,** Eartha 1928- *FacFETw, IntMPA 92, NewAmDM, NotBlAW 92*
**Kitt,** Eartha Mae 1928- *IntWW 91, WhoBlA 92, WhoEnt 92*
**Kitt,** Tamara *IntAu&W 91X, SmATA 68, WrDr 92*
**Kitt,** Walter 1925- *WhoMW 92*
**Kitta,** John Noah 1951- *WhoAmL 92*
**Kittaka,** Robert Shinnosuke 1934- *AmMWSc 92*
**Kittani,** Ismat 1930- *IntWW 91*
**Kittel,** Charles 1916- *AmMWSc 92, IntWW 91*
**Kittel,** J Howard 1919- *AmMWSc 92*
**Kittel,** Peter 1945- *AmMWSc 92*
**Kittelberger,** John Stephen 1939- *AmMWSc 92*
**Kittell,** Ernest L 1927- *WhoAmP 91*
**Kittelson,** David Burnelle 1942- *AmMWSc 92*
**Kittelson,** Jerry Martin 1940- *WhoEnt 92*
**Kittelson,** John Edwards 1936- *WhoFI 92, WhoMW 92*
**Kitti,** Paul Andrew 1952- *WhoFI 92*
**Kittikachorn,** Thanom 1911- *IntWW 91*
**Kittila,** Richard Sulo 1917- *AmMWSc 92*
**Kitting,** Christopher Lee 1953- *AmMWSc 92*
**Kittinger,** George William 1921- *AmMWSc 92*
**Kittle,** Charles Frederick 1921- *AmMWSc 92*
**Kittle,** Paul Edwin 1948- *WhoWest 92*
**Kittleman,** Robert H 1926- *WhoAmP 91*
**Kittleson,** Henry Marshall 1929- *WhoAmL 92, WhoFI 92*
**Kittlitz,** Rudolf Gottlieb, Jr 1935- *AmMWSc 92*
**Kittner,** Edwin Henry 1925- *WhoFI 92*
**Kitto,** Frank 1903- *Who 92*
**Kitto,** Franklin Curtis 1954- *WhoWest 92*
**Kitto,** George Barrie 1937- *AmMWSc 92*
**Kitto,** John Buck, Jr. 1952- *WhoMW 92*
**Kittredge,** Clifford Proctor 1906- *AmMWSc 92*
**Kittredge,** George Lyman 1860-1941 *BenetAL 91*
**Kittredge,** John Bassett 1927- *WhoMW 92*
**Kittredge,** Mabel H 1867-1943 *DcAmImH*
**Kittredge,** William *DrAPF 91*
**Kittredge,** William 1932- *TwCWW 91, WrDr 92*
**Kittrell,** Benjamin Upchurch 1937- *AmMWSc 92*
**Kittrell,** Flemmie 1904-1980 *NotBlAW 92*
**Kittrell,** James Raymond 1940- *AmMWSc 92*
**Kittrell,** Pleasant Williams 1805-1867 *DcNCBi 3*
**Kittrell,** Steven Dan 1953- *WhoAmL 92*
**Kittrels,** Alonzo William 1939- *WhoBlA 92*
**Kittrick,** James Allen 1929- *AmMWSc 92*
**Kittross,** John Michael 1929- *WhoEnt 92*
**Kitts,** David Burlingame 1923- *AmMWSc 92*
**Kitts,** Elbert Walker 1939- *WhoRel 92*
**Kittsley,** Scott Loren 1921- *AmMWSc 92*
**Kituomba** *SmATA 67*
**Kitz,** Richard J 1929- *AmMWSc 92*
**Kitzelmann,** Michael 1916-1942 *EncTR 91*
**Kitzes,** Arnold S 1917- *AmMWSc 92*
**Kitzes,** George 1919- *AmMWSc 92*

**Kitzes**, Leonard Martin 1941- *AmMWSc 92*
**Kitzes**, William Fredric 1950- *WhoAmL 92*
**Kitzhaber**, John Albert 1947- *WhoAmP 91, WhoWest 92*
**Kitzinger**, Paul Ray 1942- *WhoFI 92*
**Kitzinger**, Sheila 1929- *WrDr 92*
**Kitzinger**, Sheila Helena Elizabeth 1929- *IntAu&W 91, IntWW 91, Who 92*
**Kitzinger**, Uwe 1928- *IntWW 91, Who 92, WrDr 92*
**Kitzke**, Eugene David 1923- *AmMWSc 92, WhoMW 92*
**Kitzmiller**, James Blaine 1918- *AmMWSc 92*
**Kitzmiller**, Karen B 1947- *WhoAmP 91*
**Kitzmiller**, Karl William 1931- *WhoMW 92*
**Kiuchi**, Takashi Tachi 1935- *WhoWest 92*
**Kiusalaas**, Jaan 1931- *AmMWSc 92*
**Kiuttu**, Ronald Neil 1957- *WhoHisp 92*
**Kivel**, Bennett 1928- *AmMWSc 92*
**Kivelson**, Daniel 1929- *AmMWSc 92*
**Kivelson**, Margaret Galland 1928- *AmMWSc 92, WhoWest 92*
**Kivengere**, Festo 1920- *IntWW 91*
**Kivenson**, Gilbert 1920- *AmMWSc 92*
**Kiver**, Eugene P 1937- *AmMWSc 92*
**Kiver**, Eugene Paul 1937- *WhoWest 92*
**Kiviat**, Abel 1892-1991 *NewYTBS 91 [port]*
**Kiviat**, Erik 1947- *AmMWSc 92*
**Kiviat**, Fred E 1940- *AmMWSc 92*
**Kivilaan**, Aleksander 1906- *AmMWSc 92*
**Kivinski**, Thomas Richard 1948- *WhoFI 92*
**Kivioja**, Lassi A 1927- *AmMWSc 92*
**Kivisild**, H R 1922- *AmMWSc 92*
**Kivlighn**, Herbert Daniel, Jr 1931- *AmMWSc 92*
**Kivlighn**, Salah Dean 1957- *AmMWSc 92*
**Kivnick**, Arnold 1923- *AmMWSc 92*
**Kiwiet**, John Johannes 1925- *WhoRel 92*
**Kiwitt**, Sidney 1928- *WhoEnt 92*
**Kiyabu**, Ken S 1937- *WhoAmP 91*
**Kiyasu**, John Yutaka 1927- *AmMWSc 92*
**Kizer**, Carolyn *DrAPF 91*
**Kizer**, Carolyn 1925- *BenetAL 91, ConPo 91, WrDr 92*
**Kizer**, Charles Andrew 1949- *WhoRel 92*
**Kizer**, Donald Earl 1921- *AmMWSc 92*
**Kizer**, Gary Allan *DrAPF 91*
**Kizer**, John Stephen 1945- *AmMWSc 92*
**Kizer**, Ramona K. 1936- *WhoMW 92*
**Kizer**, William M 1925- *WhoIns 92*
**Kizilbash**, Asad Hasan 1952- *WhoFI 92*
**Kjaer**, Sonja Kathleen 1935- *WhoWest 92*
**Kjaerholm**, Poul 1929-1980 *DcTwDes*
**Kjar**, Raymond Arthur 1938- *AmMWSc 92*
**Kjar**, Rolland William 1932- *WhoAmP 91*
**Kjeldaas**, Terje, Jr 1924- *AmMWSc 92*
**Kjeldgaard**, Edwin Andreas 1939- *AmMWSc 92*
**Kjeldsen**, Chris Kelvin 1939- *AmMWSc 92*
**Kjelgaard**, William L 1920- *AmMWSc 92*
**Kjellen**, Bo 1933- *IntWW 91*
**Kjellen**, Rudolf 1864-1922 *BiDExR*
**Kjellerson**, Mark Sheldon 1957- *WhoMW 92*
**Kjellerup**, Douglas L. 1941- *WhoFI 92*
**Kjellgren**, Bengt Hugo 1931- *WhoFI 92*
**Kjellmark**, Eric William, Jr. 1928- *WhoEnt 92*
**Kjellstrom**, Elving Joel 1922- *WhoFI 92*
**Kjelsberg**, Marcus Olaf 1932- *AmMWSc 92*
**Kjetsaa**, Geir 1937- *IntWW 91*
**Kjoller**, John Kai 1936- *WhoRel 92*
**Kjonaas**, Richard A 1949- *AmMWSc 92*
**Kjonaas**, Richard Allen 1949- *WhoMW 92*
**Kjonstad**, Asbjorn 1943- *IntWW 91*
**Kjos**, Victoria Ann 1953- *WhoAmL 92*
**Klaar**, Richard 1941- *WhoWest 92*
**Klaas**, Erwin Eugene 1935- *AmMWSc 92*
**Klaas**, Nicholas Paul 1925- *AmMWSc 92*
**Klaas**, Paul Barry 1952- *WhoAmL 92*
**Klaas**, Richard Lee 1945- *WhoFI 92*
**Klaasen**, Gene Allen 1941- *AmMWSc 92*
**Klaasen**, Mary Green 1942- *WhoRel 92*
**Klaassen**, Curtis Dean 1942- *AmMWSc 92*
**Klaassen**, Dwight Homer 1936- *AmMWSc 92*
**Klaassen**, Harold Eugene 1935- *AmMWSc 92*
**Klaaste**, Aggrey Zola 1940- *IntWW 91*
**Klabund** 1890-1928 *TwCLC 44 [port]*
**Klabunde**, Kenneth John 1943- *AmMWSc 92*
**Klabunde**, Michael Paul 1954- *WhoMW 92*
**Klabunde**, Richard Edwin 1948- *AmMWSc 92*
**Klacsmann**, John Anthony 1921- *AmMWSc 92*
**Kladias**, Nikolaos Antonios 1964- *WhoRel 92*
**Kladney**, David 1948- *WhoAmL 92*
**Klaehn**, Gary Robert 1950- *WhoMW 92*
**Klaerner**, Curtis Maurice 1920- *WhoFI 92*
**Klaes**, William Marvin 1959- *WhoEnt 92*
**Klafehn**, Richard Karl 1957- *WhoRel 92*
**Klaff**, Joseph Samuel 1965- *WhoEnt 92*
**Klafkowski**, Alfons 1912- *IntWW 91*
**Klafter**, Cary Ira 1948- *WhoAmL 92*
**Klafter**, Richard D 1936- *AmMWSc 92*
**Klager**, Karl 1908- *AmMWSc 92*
**Klages**, Gary William 1957- *WhoAmL 92*
**Klages**, Ludwig 1872-1956 *EncTR 91 [port]*
**Klagges**, Dietrich 1891-1971 *EncTR 91 [port]*
**Klagsbrun**, Samuel C. 1932- *WhoFI 92*
**Klagsbrunn**, Hans Alexander 1909- *WhoFI 92*
**Klahr**, Carl Nathan 1927- *AmMWSc 92*
**Klahr**, Gary Peter 1942- *WhoAmL 92*
**Klahr**, Myra *DrAPF 91*
**Klahr**, Philip 1946- *AmMWSc 92*
**Klahr**, Saulo 1935- *AmMWSc 92*
**Klaiber**, Fred Wayne 1940- *AmMWSc 92*
**Klaiber**, George Stanley 1916- *AmMWSc 92*
**Klaiman**, Miriam Holly 1953- *WhoRel 92*
**Klain**, George John *AmMWSc 92*
**Klain**, Jane *IntMPA 92, WhoEnt 92*
**Klain**, Ronald Alan 1961- *WhoAmL 92*
**Klain**, Stephen *IntMPA 92*
**Klainer**, Albert S 1935- *AmMWSc 92*
**Klainer**, Stanley M 1930- *AmMWSc 92*
**Klaits**, Joseph Aaron 1942- *IntAu&W 91*
**Klaja**, Laurencia *WhoEnt 92*
**Klakeg**, Clayton Harold 1920- *WhoWest 92*
**Klamkin**, Marian 1926- *WrDr 92*
**Klamkin**, Murray S 1921- *AmMWSc 92*
**Klammer**, Franz 1953- *FacFETw*
**Klammer**, Joseph Francis 1925- *WhoFI 92, WhoWest 92*
**Klammer**, Lynn Marie-Ittner 1963- *WhoMW 92*
**Klamon**, Lawrence Paine 1937- *WhoFI 92*
**Klamroth**, Bernhard 1910-1944 *EncTR 91*
**Klancnik**, James Michael 1942- *WhoAmL 92*
**Kland**, Mathilde June 1916- *AmMWSc 92*
**Klanderman**, Bruce Holmes 1938- *AmMWSc 92*
**Klanderman**, Joel Dean 1947- *WhoMW 92*
**Klanfer**, Karl 1904- *AmMWSc 92*
**Klaniczay**, Tibor 1923- *IntWW 91*
**Klaper**, Martin Jay 1947- *WhoAmL 92*
**Klaperman**, Gilbert 1921- *WhoRel 92*
**Klapisch-Zuber**, Christiane 1936- *IntWW 91*
**Klapman**, Jarvis Randolph 1916- *WhoAmP 91*
**Klapman**, Solomon Joel 1912- *AmMWSc 92*
**Klapp**, Enrique H. *WhoHisp 92*
**Klapper**, Byron D. 1938- *WhoFI 92*
**Klapper**, Clarence Edward 1908- *AmMWSc 92*
**Klapper**, David G 1944- *AmMWSc 92*
**Klapper**, Gail Heitler 1943- *WhoAmL 92*
**Klapper**, Gilbert 1934- *AmMWSc 92*
**Klapper**, Jacob 1930- *AmMWSc 92*
**Klapper**, Michael H 1937- *AmMWSc 92*
**Klappert**, Peter *DrAPF 91*
**Klappert**, Peter 1942- *IntAu&W 91, WrDr 92*
**Klapproth**, Paul J., III 1946- *WhoMW 92*
**Klapproth**, William Jacob, Jr 1920- *AmMWSc 92*
**Klaproth**, William Anthony 1963- *WhoEnt 92*
**Klar**, Arthur d1991 *NewYTBS 91*
**Klare**, George Roger 1922- *WrDr 92*
**Klare**, Hugh J. 1916- *WrDr 92*
**Klare**, Hugh John 1916- *Who 92*
**Klarenbeck**, Justin *WhoEnt 92*
**Klarenbeek**, Henrietta 1955- *WhoRel 92*
**Klarer**, Andrew Scott 1952- *WhoEnt 92*
**Klarer**, Fredrick 1948- *WhoAmL 92*
**Klarfeld**, Joseph 1935- *AmMWSc 92*
**Klarich**, David J 1963- *WhoAmP 91*
**Klarich**, Janet Carlson 1931- *WhoAmP 91*
**Klaristenfeld**, Harry I 1950- *WhoIns 92*
**Klaritch**, Thomas Michael, Sr. 1957- *WhoWest 92*
**Klarman**, Herbert E 1916- *AmMWSc 92*
**Klarman**, Karl J 1922- *AmMWSc 92*
**Klarman**, William L 1935- *AmMWSc 92*
**Klarmann**, Joseph 1928- *AmMWSc 92*
**Klas**, John Hall 1917- *WhoAmP 91*
**Klas**, Mary Louise 1930- *WhoAmL 92*
**Klase**, Irving Earl 1909- *WhoEnt 92*
**Klasen**, Karl d1991 *NewYTBS 91 [port]*
**Klasen**, Karl Ferdinand 1909-1991 *IntWW 91, -91N*
**Klasic**, Donald Frank 1944- *WhoAmL 92*
**Klasinc**, Leo 1937- *AmMWSc 92*
**Klasko**, Herbert Ronald 1949- *WhoAmL 92*
**Klasner**, John Samuel 1935- *AmMWSc 92, WhoMW 92*
**Klasnic**, John Charles 1939- *WhoFI 92*
**Klass**, Alan Arnold 1907- *AmMWSc 92*
**Klass**, Bernard Myron 1938- *WhoWest 92*
**Klass**, Donald Leroy 1926- *AmMWSc 92, WhoFI 92, WhoMW 92*
**Klass**, Michael R 1949- *AmMWSc 92*
**Klass**, Perri 1958- *WrDr 92*
**Klass**, Perri Elizabeth 1958- *IntAu&W 91*
**Klass**, Rosanne Traxler *WhoFI 92*
**Klass**, Sheila Solomon *DrAPF 91*
**Klass**, Sheila Solomon 1927- *WrDr 92*
**Klassen**, Albert D. 1931- *ConAu 133*
**Klassen**, Alvin Henry 1949- *WhoWest 92*
**Klassen**, David Morris 1939- *AmMWSc 92*
**Klassen**, Elmer Glen 1929- *WhoRel 92*
**Klassen**, J 1928- *AmMWSc 92*
**Klassen**, Jacob M. 1929- *WhoRel 92*
**Klassen**, Lynell W 1947- *AmMWSc 92*
**Klassen**, Norman Victor 1933- *AmMWSc 92*
**Klassen**, Rudolph Waldemar 1928- *AmMWSc 92*
**Klassen**, Waldemar 1935- *AmMWSc 92*
**Klatell**, Robert Edward 1945- *WhoAmL 92*
**Klatka**, Stanley Casimir 1962- *WhoMW 92*
**Klatskin**, Gerald 1910- *AmMWSc 92*
**Klatt**, Arthur Raymond 1943- *AmMWSc 92*
**Klatt**, Gary Brandt 1939- *AmMWSc 92*
**Klatt**, Gordon Roy 1942- *WhoWest 92*
**Klatt**, Leon Nicholas 1940- *AmMWSc 92*
**Klatte**, Eugene 1928- *AmMWSc 92*
**Klatzo**, Igor *AmMWSc 92*
**Klatzow**, Peter 1945- *ConCom 92*
**Klauber**, Edward d1954 *LesBEnT 92*
**Klauber**, Martin Innis 1956 *WhoRel 92*
**Klauber**, Melville Roberts 1933- *AmMWSc 92*
**Klauber**, William Allan *WhoFI 92*
**Klauberg**, William Joseph 1926- *WhoFI 92*
**Klaubert**, Dieter Heinz 1944- *AmMWSc 92*
**Klauck**, Daniel L. *DrAPF 91*
**Klauder**, John Rider 1932- *AmMWSc 92*
**Klaunig**, James E 1951- *AmMWSc 92*
**Klaus**, Charles 1935- *WhoAmL 92*
**Klaus**, E Erwin 1921- *AmMWSc 92*
**Klaus**, Ewald Fred, Jr 1928- *AmMWSc 92*
**Klaus**, Francois *WhoEnt 92*
**Klaus**, Jeffrey Benjamin 1957- *WhoAmL 92*
**Klaus**, Josef 1910- *IntWW 91*
**Klaus**, Kenneth Sheldon 1952- *WhoRel 92*
**Klaus**, Ronald Louis 1940- *AmMWSc 92*
**Klaus**, Suzanne Lynne 1956- *WhoMW 92*
**Klausen**, Raymond 1939- *WhoEnt 92*
**Klausener**, Erich 1885-1934 *EncTR 91 [port]*
**Klausing**, Friedrich Karl 1920-1944 *EncTR 91*
**Klausmeier**, Robert Edward 1926- *AmMWSc 92*
**Klausmeyer**, David Michael 1934- *WhoFI 92*
**Klausmeyer**, Peter Ballard 1942- *WhoMW 92*
**Klausner**, Hubert 1892-1939 *BiDExR*
**Klausner**, Jack Daniel 1945- *WhoAmL 92*
**Klausner**, Morley 1948- *WhoEnt 92, WhoFI 92*
**Klausner**, Willette Murphy 1939- *WhoBlA 92*
**Klauson**, Valter Ivanovich 1914- *IntWW 91*
**Klaustermeyer**, William Berner 1939- *AmMWSc 92*
**Klavano**, Paul Arthur 1919- *AmMWSc 92*
**Klaven**, Louisa Anne 1953- *WhoRel 92*
**Klaverkamp**, John Frederick 1941- *AmMWSc 92*
**Klavins**, Janis Vilberts 1921- *AmMWSc 92*
**Klaviter**, Helen Lothrop 1944- *WhoMW 92*
**Klaviter**, Jane *WhoEnt 92*
**Klawans**, Harold L. 1937- *WrDr 92*
**Klawe**, Maria Margaret 1951- *WhoWest 92*
**Klawe**, Witold L 1923- *AmMWSc 92*
**Klawiter**, Donald Casimir 1950- *WhoAmL 92*
**Klawonn**, William Edward 1954- *WhoAmL 92*
**Klay**, Robert Frank 1930- *AmMWSc 92*
**Klayman**, Daniel Leslie 1929- *AmMWSc 92*
**Klayman**, Raphael 1952- *WhoEnt 92*
**Klearman**, Margie 1933- *WhoAmP 91*
**Klearman**, Steven J. 1962- *WhoAmL 92*
**Kleb**, John Steven 1953- *WhoFI 92*
**Kleban**, Cheryl Christine 1955- *WhoFI 92*
**Kleban**, Morton H 1931- *AmMWSc 92*
**Kleban Mills**, Barbara *IntAu&W 91*
**Klebaner**, Benjamin Joseph 1926- *WhoFI 92*
**Klebanoff**, Howard Michael 1937- *WhoAmP 91*
**Klebanoff**, P S 1918- *AmMWSc 92*
**Klebanoff**, Seymour J 1927- *AmMWSc 92*
**Klebanoff**, Seymour Joseph 1927- *WhoWest 92*
**Klebanoff**, Stanley Milton 1926- *WhoAmL 92*
**Klebanov**, Igor Romanovich 1962- *AmMWSc 92*
**Klebba**, James Marshall 1942- *WhoAmL 92*
**Klebba**, Phillip E 1951- *AmMWSc 92*
**Klebba**, Raymond Allen 1934- *WhoMW 92*
**Klebe**, Giselher 1925- *IntWW 91*
**Klebe**, Robert John 1943- *AmMWSc 92*
**Kleber**, Eugene Victor 1920- *AmMWSc 92*
**Kleber**, Herbert David 1934- *AmMWSc 92*
**Kleber**, John William 1923- *AmMWSc 92*
**Klecka**, Miroslav Ezidor 1921- *AmMWSc 92*
**Kleckner**, Albert Louis 1909- *AmMWSc 92*
**Kleckner**, Betty Ann 1922- *WhoAmP 91*
**Kleckner**, Robert George, Jr. 1932- *WhoAmL 92*
**Kleckner**, Roger Eugene 1947- *WhoAmP 91*
**Kleczka**, Gerald D. 1943- *AlmAP 92 [port], WhoMW 92*
**Kleczka**, Gerald Daniel 1943- *WhoAmP 91*
**Kleczkowska**, Krystyna Felicja 1932- *IntAu&W 91*
**Klee**, Claude Blenc *AmMWSc 92*
**Klee**, Gerald D'Arcy 1927- *AmMWSc 92*
**Klee**, John P. 1941- *WhoAmL 92*
**Klee**, Karl Heinz *WhoFI 92*
**Klee**, Kenneth Nathan 1949- *WhoFI 92*
**Klee**, Lucille Holljes 1924- *AmMWSc 92*
**Klee**, Marc Howard 1955- *WhoFI 92*
**Klee**, Paul 1879-1940 *DcTwDes, EncTR 91 [port], FacFETw*
**Klee**, Victor La Rue 1925- *WhoWest 92*
**Klee**, Victor La Rue, Jr 1925- *AmMWSc 92*
**Kleeberg**, Irene Cumming 1932- *ConAu 35NR, SmATA 65*
**Kleefeld**, James William 1949- *WhoMW 92*
**Kleeman**, Charles Richard 1923- *AmMWSc 92*
**Kleeman**, Harry 1928- *Who 92*
**Kleen**, Harold J 1911- *AmMWSc 92*
**Kleene**, Stephen Cole 1909- *AmMWSc 92, IntWW 91*
**Klees**, Robert E. 1927- *IntMPA 92*
**Kleese**, William Carl 1940- *WhoWest 92*
**Klegon**, Kenneth Louis 1951- *WhoFI 92*
**Klehr**, Edwin Henry 1932- *AmMWSc 92*
**Klehr**, Harvey 1945- *WrDr 92*
**Klehs**, Henry John Wilhelm 1910- *WhoWest 92*
**Klehs**, Johan 1952- *WhoAmP 91*
**Klei**, Herbert Edward, Jr 1935- *AmMWSc 92*
**Klei**, Thomas Ray 1942- *AmMWSc 92*
**Kleiber**, Carlos 1930- *CurBio 91 [port], FacFETw, IntWW 91, NewAmDM*
**Kleiber**, Douglas Harold 1955- *WhoWest 92*
**Kleiber**, Erich 1890-1956 *FacFETw, NewAmDM*
**Kleidon**, Dennis A. 1942- *WhoMW 92*
**Kleier**, Daniel Anthony 1945- *AmMWSc 92*
**Kleier**, James Patrick 1956- *WhoAmL 92*
**Kleiman**, Bernard 1928- *WhoAmL 92, WhoFI 92, WhoMW 92*
**Kleiman**, Carey David 1950- *WhoEnt 92*
**Kleiman**, Devra Gail 1942- *AmMWSc 92*
**Kleiman**, Ed 1932- *ConAu 135*
**Kleiman**, Gary Howard 1952- *WhoEnt 92, WhoFI 92*
**Kleiman**, Harlan Philip 1940- *WhoWest 92*
**Kleiman**, Herbert 1933- *AmMWSc 92*
**Kleiman**, Howard 1929- *AmMWSc 92*
**Kleiman**, Mark Ira *WhoAmL 92*
**Kleiman**, Morton 1916- *AmMWSc 92*
**Klein**, A. M. 1909-1972 *BenetAL 91, RfGEnL 91*
**Klein**, Abel 1945- *AmMWSc 92*
**Klein**, Abraham 1927- *AmMWSc 92*
**Klein**, Alan Howard 1957- *WhoAmL 92*
**Klein**, Alan Victor 1962- *WhoAmL 92*
**Klein**, Albert Jonathan 1944- *AmMWSc 92*
**Klein**, Alexander 1923- *IntAu&W 91, WrDr 92*
**Klein**, Allan Winston 1945- *WhoAmP 91*
**Klein**, Allen 1931- *IntMPA 92*
**Klein**, Alvin *WhoEnt 92*
**Klein**, Andreas 1949- *WhoEnt 92*
**Klein**, Andrew John 1951- *AmMWSc 92*
**Klein**, Andrew Joseph 1957- *WhoAmL 92*
**Klein**, Andrew Manning 1941- *WhoAmL 92*
**Klein**, Anne Carolyn 1947- *WhoRel 92*
**Klein**, Anne Sceia 1942- *WhoFI 92*
**Klein**, Anthony Jay 1938- *WhoAmL 92*
**Klein**, Arnold William 1945- *WhoWest 92*
**Klein**, Arthur Luce 1916- *WhoEnt 92*
**Klein**, Attila Otto 1930- *AmMWSc 92*
**Klein**, August S 1924- *AmMWSc 92*

**Klein,** Barbara P 1936- *AmMWSc 92*
**Klein,** Barry Phillip 1956- *WhoRel 92*
**Klein,** Benjamin Garrett 1942- *AmMWSc 92*
**Klein,** Bernard 1914- *AmMWSc 92*
**Klein,** Bernard 1921- *WhoFI 92*
**Klein,** Bernat 1922- *Who 92*
**Klein,** Binnie *DrAPF 91*
**Klein,** Bob Moses 1949- *WhoEnt 92*
**Klein,** Calvin 1942- *DcTwDes, FacFETw*
**Klein,** Calvin Richard 1942- *IntWW 91*
**Klein,** Carol *DrAPF 91*
**Klein,** Cerry M 1955- *AmMWSc 92*
**Klein,** Charles 1867-1915 *BenetAL 91*
**Klein,** Charles Henle 1908- *WhoFI 92, WhoMW 92*
**Klein,** Christopher Carnahan 1953- *WhoFI 92*
**Klein,** Christopher Francis 1943- *AmMWSc 92*
**Klein,** Christopher James 1963- *WhoFI 92*
**Klein,** Claude A 1925- *AmMWSc 92*
**Klein,** Clayton C, Jr 1949- *WhoAmP 91*
**Klein,** Cornelis 1937- *AmMWSc 92*
**Klein,** Dale Edward 1947- *AmMWSc 92*
**Klein,** Dani Madlyn 1963- *WhoEnt 92*
**Klein,** David 1919- *IntWW 91*
**Klein,** David C 1940- *AmMWSc 92*
**Klein,** David Henry 1933- *AmMWSc 92*
**Klein,** David Joseph 1922- *AmMWSc 92*
**Klein,** David M 1946- *WhoIns 92*
**Klein,** David Robert 1927- *AmMWSc 92*
**Klein,** David Robert 1965- *WhoMW 92*
**Klein,** David Xavier 1908- *AmMWSc 92*
**Klein,** Deana Tarson 1925- *AmMWSc 92*
**Klein,** Dennis Franklin 1951- *WhoFI 92*
**Klein,** Diane M 1948- *AmMWSc 92*
**Klein,** Dixie E. 1950- *WhoRel 92*
**Klein,** Dolph 1928- *AmMWSc 92*
**Klein,** Donald Albert 1935- *AmMWSc 92*
**Klein,** Donald Franklin 1928- *AmMWSc 92*
**Klein,** Donald Lee 1930- *AmMWSc 92*
**Klein,** Douglas J 1942- *AmMWSc 92*
**Klein,** Dyann Leslie 1951- *WhoEnt 92*
**Klein,** Edith Miller 1915- *WhoAmP 91, WhoWest 92*
**Klein,** Edmund 1921- *AmMWSc 92*
**Klein,** Edward Lawrence 1936- *AmMWSc 92*
**Klein,** Eleanor 1919- *WhoWest 92*
**Klein,** Elena Buimovici 1930- *AmMWSc 92*
**Klein,** Elias 1924- *AmMWSc 92*
**Klein,** Elinore Barbara 1937- *WhoAmL 92*
**Klein,** Elizabeth *DrAPF 91*
**Klein,** Elizabeth Archer 1963- *WhoRel 92*
**Klein,** Francis Michael 1941- *AmMWSc 92*
**Klein,** Gary Gordon 1952- *WhoFI 92*
**Klein,** George 1925- *IntWW 91*
**Klein,** George Charles 1946- *WhoMW 92*
**Klein,** George deVries 1933- *AmMWSc 92*
**Klein,** Gerald I 1928- *AmMWSc 92*
**Klein,** Gerald Wayne 1939- *AmMWSc 92*
**Klein,** Gerard 1937- *TwCSFW 91A*
**Klein,** Gordon Leslie 1946- *AmMWSc 92*
**Klein,** Hans 1931- *IntWW 91*
**Klein,** Harold George 1929- *AmMWSc 92*
**Klein,** Harold J *IntMPA 92*
**Klein,** Harold Paul 1921- *AmMWSc 92*
**Klein,** Harold Sherman 1921- *WhoEnt 92*
**Klein,** Harriet Farber 1948- *WhoAmL 92*
**Klein,** Harry 1921- *WhoAmL 92*
**Klein,** Harvey Gerald 1930- *AmMWSc 92*
**Klein,** Helmut 1930- *IntWW 91*
**Klein,** Herbert A 1936- *AmMWSc 92*
**Klein,** Herbert G. *LesBEnT 92*
**Klein,** Herbert George 1918- *IntWW 91, WhoWest 92*
**Klein,** Howard Bruce 1950- *WhoAmL 92*
**Klein,** Howard Joseph 1941- *AmMWSc 92, WhoMW 92*
**Klein,** Imrich 1928- *AmMWSc 92*
**Klein,** Jacqueline K *WhoAmP 91*
**Klein,** James Edwin 1951- *WhoRel 92*
**Klein,** James H 1920- *AmMWSc 92*
**Klein,** James Mikel 1953- *WhoEnt 92, WhoWest 92*
**Klein,** Jan 1936- *AmMWSc 92*
**Klein,** Jeanne Marie 1952- *WhoMW 92*
**Klein,** Jeffrey Michael 1964- *WhoFI 92*
**Klein,** Jeffrey Steven 1953- *WhoAmP 91*
**Klein,** Jerry Alan 1945- *AmMWSc 92*
**Klein,** Jerry Lee 1947- *WhoRel 92*
**Klein,** Joanne Ruth 1949- *WhoEnt 92*
**Klein,** Joel Tibor 1923- *WhoRel 92*
**Klein,** John Irwin 1931- *WhoMW 92*
**Klein,** John Jacob 1929- *WhoFI 92*
**Klein,** John Nicholas, III 1946- *WhoAmP 91*
**Klein,** John Peter 1950- *AmMWSc 92*
**Klein,** John Sharpless 1922- *AmMWSc 92*
**Klein,** John Thomas 1958- *WhoMW 92*
**Klein,** Joseph 1936- *WhoAmL 92*
**Klein,** Joseph, Jr. 1931- *WhoFI 92*
**Klein,** Joseph Alan 1946- *WhoAmL 92*
**Klein,** Joseph Frederic 1849-1918 *BiInAmS*
**Klein,** Joseph Michelman 1936- *WhoEnt 92*
**Klein,** Josephine 1926- *WrDr 92*
**Klein,** Judah B. 1923- *WhoAmL 92*
**Klein,** June Robbins 1948- *WhoFI 92*
**Klein,** Katharine Sommer 1953- *WhoFI 92*
**Klein,** Kathleen Louise *WhoEnt 92*
**Klein,** Kip 1950- *WhoAmP 91*
**Klein,** Larry L 1953- *AmMWSc 92*
**Klein,** Lawrence R. 1920- *WrDr 92*
**Klein,** Lawrence Robert 1920- *IntWW 91, Who 92, WhoFI 92, WhoNob 90*
**Klein,** LeRoy 1926- *AmMWSc 92*
**Klein,** Lewis S 1932- *AmMWSc 92*
**Klein,** Linda Ann 1959- *WhoAmL 92*
**Klein,** Lonnie 1959- *WhoEnt 92*
**Klein,** Lorraine Margaret 1955- *WhoRel 92*
**Klein,** Lothar 1932- *NewAmDM*
**Klein,** Louis Edward 1920- *WhoFI 92*
**Klein,** Luella 1924- *AmMWSc 92*
**Klein,** Lynn E. 1950- *WhoWest 92*
**Klein,** Malcolm C. 1927- *IntMPA 92*
**Klein,** Manny 1908- *NewAmDM*
**Klein,** Marcus 1928- *WrDr 92*
**Klein,** Margaret Gordon 1936- *WhoAmL 92*
**Klein,** Martin Adalbert, III 1951- *WhoFI 92*
**Klein,** Martin I. 1947- *WhoAmL 92*
**Klein,** Martin Israel 1952- *WhoFI 92*
**Klein,** Martin J 1924- *AmMWSc 92*
**Klein,** Mary Kay *WhoRel 92*
**Klein,** Max 1925- *AmMWSc 92*
**Klein,** Melvin M 1913- *WhoAmP 91*
**Klein,** Melvin Phillip 1921- *AmMWSc 92*
**Klein,** Melvyn Norman 1941- *WhoEnt 92*
**Klein,** Michael *DrAPF 91*
**Klein,** Michael 1946- *AmMWSc 92*
**Klein,** Michael John 1940- *AmMWSc 92*
**Klein,** Michael Lawrence 1940- *AmMWSc 92*
**Klein,** Michael Roger 1942- *WhoAmL 92*
**Klein,** Michael Tully 1955- *AmMWSc 92*
**Klein,** Michael W 1931- *AmMWSc 92*
**Klein,** Miles Vincent 1933- *AmMWSc 92*
**Klein,** Milton M 1917- *AmMWSc 92*
**Klein,** Mina C. 1906-1979 *ConAu 133*
**Klein,** Mitchell Sardou 1947- *WhoEnt 92*
**Klein,** Morton 1914- *AmMWSc 92*
**Klein,** Morton 1925- *AmMWSc 92*
**Klein,** Morton Joseph 1928- *AmMWSc 92*
**Klein,** Nancy Kirkland 1954- *WhoEnt 92*
**Klein,** Nathan 1931- *AmMWSc 92*
**Klein,** Nelson Harold 1942- *AmMWSc 92*
**Klein,** Norma 1938- *IntAu&W 91*
**Klein,** Norman Stuart 1935- *WhoAmL 92*
**Klein,** Norman W 1931- *AmMWSc 92*
**Klein,** Paul Alvin 1941- *AmMWSc 92*
**Klein,** Paul E. 1934- *WhoAmL 92*
**Klein,** Paul James 1958- *WhoEnt 92*
**Klein,** Paul L. *LesBEnT 92*
**Klein,** Paul L. 1925- *WhoAmL 92*
**Klein,** Paul L. 1928- *IntMPA 92*
**Klein,** Paula Schwartz 1941- *WhoMW 92*
**Klein,** Peter 1945- *WhoEnt 92*
**Klein,** Peter Douglas 1927- *AmMWSc 92*
**Klein,** Peter John 1949- *WhoFI 92*
**Klein,** Peter William 1955- *WhoAmL 92, WhoFI 92*
**Klein,** Peter Wolfgang 1931- *IntWW 91*
**Klein,** Philip 1947- *WhoEnt 92*
**Klein,** Philip Alexander 1927- *WhoFI 92, WrDr 92*
**Klein,** Philipp Hillel 1926- *AmMWSc 92*
**Klein,** Ralph 1918- *AmMWSc 92*
**Klein,** Raymond Maurice 1938- *WhoAmL 92*
**Klein,** Richard A. 1946- *WhoMW 92*
**Klein,** Richard Daniel 1943- *WhoAmL 92*
**Klein,** Richard Dean 1932- *WhoFI 92*
**Klein,** Richard Joseph 1926- *AmMWSc 92*
**Klein,** Richard Lester 1929- *AmMWSc 92*
**Klein,** Richard Lewis 1945- *WhoWest 92*
**Klein,** Richard M 1923- *AmMWSc 92*
**Klein,** Richard M 1937- *AmMWSc 92*
**Klein,** Richard Morris 1942- *AmMWSc 92*
**Klein,** Richard Temple, Jr. 1956- *WhoMW 92*
**Klein,** Robert 1942- *IntMPA 92, WhoEnt 92*
**Klein,** Robert Allan 1947- *WhoFI 92*
**Klein,** Robert Arnold 1928- *WhoEnt 92*
**Klein,** Robert Charles 1927- *WhoFI 92*
**Klein,** Robert Edward 1926- *WhoFI 92*
**Klein,** Robert Herbert 1932- *AmMWSc 92*
**Klein,** Robert Joseph 1917- *WhoFI 92*
**Klein,** Robert Majer 1940- *WhoFI 92*
**Klein,** Robert Marshall 1957- *WhoAmL 92*
**Klein,** Robert Melvin 1949- *AmMWSc 92*
**Klein,** Robin 1936- *WrDr 92*
**Klein,** Ronald 1943- *AmMWSc 92*
**Klein,** Ronald Gary 1948- *WhoAmL 92*
**Klein,** Rudolf Ewald 1930- *Who 92*
**Klein,** Samuel Edwin 1946- *WhoAmL 92*
**Klein,** Scott Richard 1959- *WhoEnt 92*
**Klein,** Sheffield 1918- *WhoEnt 92*
**Klein,** Sherwin Jared 1919- *AmMWSc 92*
**Klein,** Sigrid Marta 1932- *AmMWSc 92*
**Klein,** Snira Lubovsky *WhoWest 92*
**Klein,** Stephen M. 1953- *WhoMW 92*
**Klein,** Stephen Thomas 1947- *WhoEnt 92*
**Klein,** Steven Paul 1959- *WhoMW 92*
**Klein,** Stuart M. 1932- *ConAu 134*
**Klein,** Theodore Eibon Donald 1947- *IntAu&W 91*
**Klein,** Thomas Michael 1959- *WhoAmL 92*
**Klein,** V A 1918- *AmMWSc 92*
**Klein,** Viola 1908-1973 *WomSoc*
**Klein,** Vladislav 1929- *AmMWSc 92*
**Klein,** Wallis Cherniack Weil 1941- *WhoMW 92*
**Klein,** Walter Charles 1918- *WhoFI 92*
**Klein,** Warren 1951- *WhoFI 92*
**Klein,** William 1943- *AmMWSc 92*
**Klein,** William A. 1931- *WhoAmL 92*
**Klein,** William Arthur 1929- *AmMWSc 92*
**Klein,** William H. *DrAPF 91*
**Klein,** William Richard 1937- *AmMWSc 92*
**Klein,** William Wade 1946- *WhoRel 92*
**Klein,** Yehuda Levi 1949- *WhoFI 92*
**Klein,** Zachary 1948- *ConAu 135*
**Kleinbart,** David Alan 1947- *WhoEnt 92*
**Kleinbaum,** Richard Nathan 1943- *WhoAmP 91*
**Kleinberg,** Diana Louise 1946- *WhoWest 92*
**Kleinberg,** Israel 1930- *AmMWSc 92*
**Kleinberg,** Jacob 1914- *AmMWSc 92*
**Kleinberg,** Lawrence 1943- *WhoFI 92*
**Kleinberg,** Marvin H. 1927- *WhoAmL 92*
**Kleinberg,** Norman Charles 1946- *WhoAmL 92*
**Kleinberg,** Robert Irwin 1937- *WhoFI 92*
**Kleinberg,** Robert Leonard 1949- *AmMWSc 92*
**Kleinberg,** Steven Eric 1961- *WhoEnt 92*
**Kleinberg,** William 1911- *AmMWSc 92*
**Kleindienst,** Richard Gordon 1923- *IntWW 91, Who 92, WhoAmP 91*
**Kleine-Ahlbrandt,** William Laird 1932- *WrDr 92*
**Kleiner,** Alexander F, Jr 1942- *AmMWSc 92*
**Kleiner,** Arnold Joel 1943- *WhoEnt 92*
**Kleiner,** Harry 1916- *IntMPA 92*
**Kleiner,** Kathleen Allen 1958- *WhoMW 92*
**Kleiner,** Sid 1931- *WhoEnt 92*
**Kleiner,** Susan Mala 1957- *AmMWSc 92*
**Kleiner,** Walter Bernhard 1918- *AmMWSc 92*
**Kleinerman,** Isaac *LesBEnT 92*
**Kleinerman,** Jerome 1924- *AmMWSc 92*
**Kleinert,** Edward Lewis 1949- *WhoFI 92*
**Kleinert,** Henry Bernhard 1917- *WhoRel 92*
**Kleinfeld,** A M 1941- *AmMWSc 92*
**Kleinfeld,** Andrew Jay 1945- *WhoAmL 92, WhoWest 92*
**Kleinfeld,** Erwin 1927- *AmMWSc 92*
**Kleinfeld,** Harold Alvin 1928- *WhoAmL 92*
**Kleinfeld,** Ira H 1947- *AmMWSc 92*
**Kleinfeld,** Margaret Humm 1938- *AmMWSc 92*
**Kleinfeld,** Ruth Grafman 1928- *AmMWSc 92*
**Kleingartner,** Archie 1936- *WhoEnt 92, WhoFI 92*
**Kleinglass,** Steven Peter 1947- *WhoMW 92*
**Kleinhaus,** Frank B 1869?-1908 *BiInAmS*
**Kleinhenz,** Christopher 1941- *WhoMW 92*
**Kleinhenz,** William A 1921- *AmMWSc 92*
**Kleinhofs,** Andris 1937- *AmMWSc 92*
**Kleinholz,** Lewis Hermann 1910- *AmMWSc 92*
**Kleinkopf,** Gale Eugene 1940- *AmMWSc 92*
**Kleinkopf,** Merlin Dean 1926- *AmMWSc 92*
**Kleinlein,** Kathy Lynn 1950- *WhoFI 92*
**Kleinman,** Arthur 1941- *IntWW 91*
**Kleinman,** Arthur Michael 1941- *AmMWSc 92*
**Kleinman,** Burton Howard 1923- *WhoMW 92*
**Kleinman,** Chemia Jacob 1932- *AmMWSc 92*
**Kleinman,** George 1951- *WhoFI 92*
**Kleinman,** Hynda Karen 1947- *AmMWSc 92*
**Kleinman,** Jack G 1944- *AmMWSc 92*
**Kleinman,** Kenneth Martin 1941- *AmMWSc 92*
**Kleinman,** Leonard 1933- *AmMWSc 92*
**Kleinman,** Leonard I 1935- *AmMWSc 92*
**Kleinman,** Michael Thomas 1942- *AmMWSc 92*
**Kleinman,** Ralph Ellis 1929- *AmMWSc 92*
**Kleinman,** Randall 1952- *WhoAmL 92, WhoIns 92*
**Kleinman,** Robert L P 1951- *AmMWSc 92*
**Kleinman,** Roberta Wilma 1942- *AmMWSc 92*
**Kleinman,** Sheila LaVon 1959- *WhoMW 92*
**Kleinman,** Susan Phyllis 1947- *WhoMW 92*
**Kleinmann,** Douglas Erwin 1942- *AmMWSc 92*
**Kleinpeter,** Edie Wagner 1931- *WhoEnt 92*
**Kleinpoppen,** Hans Johann Willi 1928- *Who 92*
**Kleinrock,** Leonard 1934- *AmMWSc 92, WhoWest 92*
**Kleinrock,** Martin Charles 1958- *AmMWSc 92*
**Kleinsasser,** Leland P *WhoAmP 91*
**Kleinschmidt,** Albert Willoughby 1913- *AmMWSc 92*
**Kleinschmidt,** Edward *DrAPF 91*
**Kleinschmidt,** Eric Walker 1955- *AmMWSc 92*
**Kleinschmidt,** R Stevens 1925- *AmMWSc 92*
**Kleinschmidt,** Roger Frederick 1919- *AmMWSc 92*
**Kleinschmidt,** Walter John 1918- *AmMWSc 92*
**Kleinschuster,** Jacob John 1943- *AmMWSc 92*
**Kleinschuster,** Stephen J, III 1939- *AmMWSc 92*
**Kleinsmith,** Gene 1942- *WhoWest 92*
**Kleinsmith,** Lewis Joel 1942- *AmMWSc 92*
**Kleinspehn,** George Gehret 1924- *AmMWSc 92*
**Kleinsteuber,** Tilmann Christoph Werner 1934- *AmMWSc 92*
**Kleinwort,** Kenneth 1935- *Who 92*
**Kleinzahler,** August *DrAPF 91*
**Kleinzeller,** Arnost 1914- *AmMWSc 92*
**Kleis,** John Dieffenbach 1912- *AmMWSc 92*
**Kleis,** Robert W 1925- *AmMWSc 92*
**Kleis,** William Delong 1924- *AmMWSc 92*
**Kleiser,** Randal 1946- *IntMPA 92*
**Kleist,** Ewald von 1881-1954 *EncTR 91 [port]*
**Kleist-Schmenzin,** Ewald von 1890-1945 *EncTR 91*
**Kleitman,** Daniel J 1934- *AmMWSc 92*
**Kleitman,** David 1931- *AmMWSc 92*
**Kleitsch,** William Philip 1912- *AmMWSc 92*
**Klejmont,** Rick Joseph 1954- *WhoEnt 92*
**Klekowski,** Edward Joseph, Jr 1940- *AmMWSc 92*
**Klem,** Alan 1949- *WhoEnt 92*
**Klem,** Herbert Viele 1937- *WhoMW 92, WhoRel 92*
**Klem,** Steven Michael 1959- *WhoRel 92*
**Klema,** Ernest Donald 1920- *AmMWSc 92*
**Klemann,** Lawrence Paul 1943- *AmMWSc 92*
**Klemarczyk,** Thaddeus E 1920- *WhoAmP 91*
**Klemas,** Victor V 1934- *AmMWSc 92*
**Klemchuk,** Peter Paul 1928- *AmMWSc 92*
**Klemens,** Paul Gustav 1925- *AmMWSc 92*
**Klement,** Frank L. 1908- *WrDr 92*
**Klement,** Vaclav 1935- *AmMWSc 92*
**Klement,** William, Jr 1937- *AmMWSc 92*
**Klemer,** Andrew Robert 1942- *AmMWSc 92*
**Klemic,** George Gerard 1949- *WhoFI 92*
**Klemin,** Diana *SmATA 65*
**Klemke,** Elmer Daniel 1926- *WhoMW 92*
**Klemm,** Arthur P, Jr 1948- *WhoAmP 91*
**Klemm,** David Eugene 1947- *WhoRel 92*
**Klemm,** Donald J 1938- *AmMWSc 92*
**Klemm,** H. Alexander 1960- *WhoFI 92*
**Klemm,** James L 1939- *AmMWSc 92*
**Klemm,** Laurence Justin 1938- *WhoMW 92*
**Klemm,** LeRoy Henry 1919- *AmMWSc 92, WhoWest 92*
**Klemm,** Lowell Erwin 1940- *WhoRel 92*
**Klemm,** Rebecca Jane 1950- *AmMWSc 92*
**Klemm,** Richard Andrew 1948- *AmMWSc 92*
**Klemm,** Richard O 1932- *WhoAmP 91*
**Klemm,** Robert David 1929- *AmMWSc 92*
**Klemm,** Waldemar Arthur, Jr 1934- *AmMWSc 92*
**Klemm,** William Robert 1934- *AmMWSc 92*
**Klemme,** Brent A. 1957- *WhoMW 92*
**Klemme,** Carl William 1928- *WhoFI 92*
**Klemme,** Hugh Douglas 1921- *AmMWSc 92*
**Klemmedson,** James Otto 1927- *AmMWSc 92*
**Klemmer,** Howard Wesley 1922- *AmMWSc 92*
**Klemmer,** John 1946- *WhoEnt 92*
**Klemola,** Arnold R 1931- *AmMWSc 92*
**Klemola,** Tapio 1934- *AmMWSc 92*
**Klemow,** Sheree F. 1956- *WhoEnt 92*
**Klemperer,** Friedrich W *AmMWSc 92*
**Klemperer,** Martin R 1931- *AmMWSc 92*
**Klemperer,** Otto 1885-1973 *EncTR 91 [port], FacFETw, NewAmDM*
**Klemperer,** W. David 1937- *WhoFI 92*

**Klemperer**, Walter George 1947- *AmMWSc 92*
**Klemperer**, William 1927- *AmMWSc 92, IntWW 91*
**Klempnauer**, Craig Stephen 1956- *WhoRel 92*
**Klempner**, Daniel 1943- *AmMWSc 92*
**Klempner**, Mark Steven 1949- *AmMWSc 92*
**Klems**, George J 1936- *AmMWSc 92*
**Klems**, Joseph Henry 1942- *AmMWSc 92*
**Klen**, Jurij 1891-1947 *LiExTwC*
**Klenau**, Paul von 1883-1946 *NewAmDM*
**Klenicki**, Leon 1930- *WhoRel 92*
**Klenin**, Marjorie A *AmMWSc 92*
**Klenk**, Ann Shirley 1951- *WhoEnt 92*
**Klenke**, Edward Frederick, Jr 1916- *AmMWSc 92*
**Klenknecht**, Kenneth S 1919- *AmMWSc 92*
**Klens**, Paul Frank 1918- *AmMWSc 92*
**Klensin**, John 1945- *AmMWSc 92*
**Klepal**, Dwayne Michael 1959- *WhoRel 92*
**Klepczynski**, William J 1939- *AmMWSc 92*
**Klepfisz**, Irena *DrAPF 91*
**Klepinger**, Brian Wiley 1937- *WhoWest 92*
**Klepinger**, John William 1945- *WhoWest 92*
**Klepinger**, Linda Lehman 1941- *AmMWSc 92*
**Kleppa**, Ole Jakob 1920- *AmMWSc 92*
**Kleppe**, Johan 1928- *IntWW 91*
**Kleppe**, Per 1923- *IntWW 91*
**Kleppe**, Thomas S. 1919- *IntWW 91*
**Klepper**, Cheryl Ann 1953- *WhoAmL 92*
**Klepper**, David Lloyd 1932- *AmMWSc 92*
**Klepper**, Elizabeth Lee 1936- *AmMWSc 92*
**Klepper**, Jochen 1903-1942 *EncTR 91 [port]*
**Klepper**, John Richard 1947- *AmMWSc 92*
**Klepper**, Martin 1947- *WhoAmL 92*
**Klepper**, Otto 1888-1957 *EncTR 91*
**Klepper**, Robert Samuel 1965- *WhoFI 92, WhoWest 92*
**Klepperich**, Thomas Joseph 1960- *WhoAmL 92*
**Kleppinger**, David Morris 1955- *WhoAmL 92*
**Kleppner**, Adam 1931- *AmMWSc 92*
**Kleppner**, Daniel 1932- *AmMWSc 92*
**Klepser**, Harry John 1908- *AmMWSc 92*
**Klerer**, Julius 1928- *AmMWSc 92*
**Klerer**, Melvin 1926- *AmMWSc 92*
**Klerlein**, Joseph Ballard 1948- *AmMWSc 92*
**Klerman**, Gerald L 1928- *AmMWSc 92*
**Klerman**, Lorraine Vogel 1929- *AmMWSc 92*
**Klesius**, Phillip Harry 1938- *AmMWSc 92*
**Klessig**, Daniel Frederick 1949- *AmMWSc 92*
**Klestadt**, Bernard 1925- *AmMWSc 92*
**Klestil**, Thomas 1932- *IntWW 91*
**Kletsky**, Earl J 1930- *AmMWSc 92*
**Klett**, Dennis R. 1952- *WhoRel 92*
**Klett**, Edwin Lee 1935- *WhoAmL 92*
**Klett**, James Elmer 1947- *AmMWSc 92*
**Kletzien**, Rolf Frederick 1946- *AmMWSc 92*
**Kletzsch**, Charles Frederick 1926- *WhoEnt 92*
**Klevan**, Rodney Conrad 1940- *Who 92*
**Klevana**, Leighton Quentin Joseph 1934- *WhoAmL 92, WhoFI 92*
**Klevans**, Edward Harris 1935- *AmMWSc 92*
**Klevatt**, Steve *WhoEnt 92*
**Klevay**, Leslie Michael *AmMWSc 92*
**Klevecz**, Robert Raymond 1939- *AmMWSc 92*
**Kleven**, Stanley H 1940- *AmMWSc 92*
**Kleven**, Thomas 1942- *WhoBlA 92*
**Klevens**, Joel Norton 1944- *WhoAmL 92*
**Klevit**, Alan Barre 1935- *WhoWest 92*
**Klevorick**, Alvin K. 1943- *WhoAmL 92*
**Klewans**, Samuel N. 1941- *WhoAmL 92*
**Klewin**, Thomas William 1921- *WhoRel 92*
**Kleyn**, Dick Henry 1929- *AmMWSc 92*
**Kliafa**, Maroula 1937- *IntAu&W 91*
**Kliban**, B. 1935-1990 *AnObit 1990, FacFETw, SmATA 66*
**Klibanov**, Aleksandr Il'ich *SovUnBD*
**Klibanov**, Alexander M 1949- *AmMWSc 92*
**Klibansky**, Raymond 1905- *Who 92*
**Klibi**, Chedli 1925- *IntWW 91*
**Klick**, Clifford C 1918- *AmMWSc 92*
**Klicka**, John Kenneth 1933- *AmMWSc 92*
**Kliebenstein**, Don 1936- *WhoFI 92*
**Kliebenstein**, James Bernard 1947- *AmMWSc 92*
**Kliebhan**, Mary Camille 1923- *WhoRel 92*
**Klieforth**, Harold Ernest 1927- *AmMWSc 92*
**Klieger**, Paul 1916- *AmMWSc 92*
**Kliejunas**, John Thomas 1943- *AmMWSc 92*
**Kliem**, Peter O 1938- *AmMWSc 92*
**Kliem**, Peter Otto 1938- *WhoFI 92*
**Klien**, Walter d1991 *NewYTBS 91, Who 92N*
**Klien**, Walter 1928- *IntWW 91, NewAmDM*
**Klien**, Wolfgang Josef 1942- *WhoWest 92*
**Klier**, Kamil 1932- *AmMWSc 92*
**Kliesen**, Janet Marie 1939- *WhoMW 92*
**Klietz**, Sheldon Henry 1935- *WhoRel 92*
**Kliever**, Lonnie Dean 1931- *WhoRel 92*
**Kliewer**, John Wallace 1924- *AmMWSc 92*
**Kliewer**, Kenneth L 1935- *AmMWSc 92*
**Kliewer**, Kenneth Lee 1935- *WhoMW 92*
**Kliewer**, Walter Mark 1933- *AmMWSc 92*
**Kliewer**, Warren *DrAPF 91*
**Kliger**, David Saul 1943- *AmMWSc 92*
**Kligman**, Albert Montgomery 1916- *AmMWSc 92*
**Kligman**, Ronald Lee 1940- *AmMWSc 92*
**Klijanowicz**, James Edward 1944- *AmMWSc 92*
**Klima**, Ivan 1931- *IntAu&W 91*
**Klima**, Martha Scanlan 1938- *WhoAmP 91*
**Kliman**, Allan 1933- *AmMWSc 92*
**Kliman**, Andrew Jeffrey 1955- *WhoFI 92*
**Kliman**, Gerald Burt 1931- *AmMWSc 92*
**Kliman**, Harvey Louis 1942- *AmMWSc 92*
**Kliman**, Sylvia May Stern 1934- *WhoEnt 92*
**Klimash**, Victor Andrew 1943- *WhoEnt 92*
**Klimaski**, James Robert 1946- *WhoAmL 92*
**Klimaszewski**, Mieczyslaw 1908- *IntWW 91*
**Klimback**, Elizabeth Marton 1949- *WhoEnt 92, WhoFI 92*
**Klimczak**, Walter John 1916- *AmMWSc 92*
**Klimek**, Joseph John 1946- *AmMWSc 92*
**Klimesz**, Henry Roman 1926- *WhoFI 92*
**Klimisch**, Richard L 1938- *AmMWSc 92*
**Klimke**, Darrell Earl 1939- *WhoMW 92*
**Klimko**, Eugene M 1939- *AmMWSc 92*
**Klimko**, Ronald James 1936- *WhoWest 92*
**Klimkowski**, Ann Francis 1931- *WhoMW 92, WhoRel 92*
**Klimkowski**, Charles Ronald 1935- *WhoMW 92*
**Klimm**, John C *WhoAmP 91*
**Klimo**, Jon *DrAPF 91*
**Klimov**, Elem 1933- *IntDcF 2-2, SovUnBD*
**Klimov**, Elem 1935- *IntWW 91*
**Klimov**, Valeriy Aleksandrovich 1931- *SovUnBD*
**Klimowski**, Andrzej 1949- *TwCPaSc*
**Klimpel**, Gary R *AmMWSc 92*
**Klimpel**, Richard Robert 1939- *AmMWSc 92*
**Klimsch**, Fritz 1870-1960 *EncTR 91*
**Klimstra**, Paul D 1933- *AmMWSc 92*
**Klimstra**, Willard David 1919- *AmMWSc 92*
**Klimt**, Gustav 1862-1918 *FacFETw*
**Klincewicz**, John Gregory 1954- *WhoRel 92*
**Klinck**, Cynthia Anne 1948- *WhoMW 92*
**Klinck**, Harold Rutherford 1922- *AmMWSc 92*
**Klinck**, Mary Ellen 1934- *WhoAmP 91*
**Klinck**, Ross Edward 1938- *AmMWSc 92*
**Klindworth**, Karl 1830-1916 *NewAmDM*
**Kline**, Alan Harrison 1961- *WhoEnt 92*
**Kline**, Allen Haber, Jr. 1954- *WhoAmL 92*
**Kline**, Arthur Jonathan 1928- *WhoWest 92*
**Kline**, Berry James 1941- *AmMWSc 92*
**Kline**, Bruce Clayton 1937- *AmMWSc 92*
**Kline**, Bruce Edward 1944- *WhoMW 92*
**Kline**, Charles C. 1946- *WhoAmL 92*
**Kline**, Charles Howard 1918- *AmMWSc 92*
**Kline**, Claire Benton, Jr. 1925- *WhoRel 92*
**Kline**, Daniel Louis 1917- *AmMWSc 92*
**Kline**, David Adam 1923- *WhoAmL 92*
**Kline**, David G 1934- *AmMWSc 92*
**Kline**, Donald 1933- *WhoEnt 92*
**Kline**, Donald Edgar 1928- *AmMWSc 92*
**Kline**, Eddie 1917- *WhoBlA 92*
**Kline**, Edward Samuel 1924- *AmMWSc 92*
**Kline**, Edwin A 1918- *AmMWSc 92*
**Kline**, Eric Stephan 1948- *WhoEnt 92*
**Kline**, Ernest Paul 1929- *WhoAmP 91*
**Kline**, Eugene Monroe 1914- *WhoAmL 92*
**Kline**, Faith Elizabeth 1937- *WhoAmP 91*
**Kline**, Frank Menefee 1928- *AmMWSc 92*
**Kline**, Franz 1910-1962 *FacFETw*
**Kline**, Fred W. 1918- *IntMPA 92*
**Kline**, Fred Walter 1918- *WhoWest 92*
**Kline**, Gary H. 1939- *WhoAmL 92*
**Kline**, George William, II 1949- *WhoEnt 92, WhoFI 92*
**Kline**, Gordon Mabey 1903- *AmMWSc 92*
**Kline**, H. Charles 1929- *WhoEnt 92*
**Kline**, Herbert 1909- *WhoEnt 92*
**Kline**, Ira 1924- *AmMWSc 92*
**Kline**, Irwin Kaven 1931- *AmMWSc 92*
**Kline**, J Edward 1947- *WhoAmP 91*
**Kline**, Jacob 1917- *AmMWSc 92*
**Kline**, James 1932- *WhoEnt 92*
**Kline**, James Edward 1941- *WhoAmL 92*
**Kline**, Jennie Katherine 1950- *AmMWSc 92*
**Kline**, Jerry Robert 1932- *AmMWSc 92*
**Kline**, John 1797-1864 *AmPeW*
**Kline**, John Anthony 1938- *WhoAmL 92*
**Kline**, Julie Ann 1965- *WhoFI 92*
**Kline**, Kenneth A 1939- *AmMWSc 92*
**Kline**, Kenneth Alan 1939- *WhoMW 92*
**Kline**, Kevin 1947- *IntMPA 92*
**Kline**, Kevin Delaney 1947- *IntWW 91, WhoEnt 92*
**Kline**, Larry Keith 1939- *AmMWSc 92*
**Kline**, Louise Letha 1944- *WhoMW 92*
**Kline**, Mable Cornelia Page 1928- *WhoMW 92*
**Kline**, Morris 1908- *AmMWSc 92, WrDr 92*
**Kline**, Nancy *DrAPF 91*
**Kline**, Nathan S. 1916-1983 *ConAu 36NR*
**Kline**, Otis Adelbert 1891-1946 *ScFEYrs, TwCSFW 91*
**Kline**, Pamela Iris 1958- *WhoWest 92*
**Kline**, Peter 1936- *WrDr 92*
**Kline**, Phil *WhoAmP 91*
**Kline**, Ralph Willard 1917- *AmMWSc 92*
**Kline**, Raymond Milton 1929- *AmMWSc 92*
**Kline**, Richard Stephen 1948- *WhoWest 92*
**Kline**, Richard William 1942- *AmMWSc 92*
**Kline**, Robert Andrew 1944- *WhoEnt 92*
**Kline**, Robert Joseph 1921- *AmMWSc 92*
**Kline**, Robert Mark 1955- *WhoWest 92*
**Kline**, Robert Reeves 1918- *WhoRel 92*
**Kline**, Ronald Alan 1952- *AmMWSc 92*
**Kline**, Stephen Jay 1922- *AmMWSc 92*
**Kline**, Steven Paul 1965- *WhoEnt 92*
**Kline**, Suzy 1943- *SmATA 67 [port]*
**Kline**, Suzy Weaver 1943- *IntAu&W 91*
**Kline**, Timothy Deal 1949- *WhoAmL 92*
**Kline**, Timothy George 1955- *WhoAmL 92*
**Kline**, Toni Beth 1950- *AmMWSc 92*
**Kline**, Virginia March 1926- *AmMWSc 92*
**Kline**, Walter d1991 *IntWW 91N*
**Kline**, William M. 1933- *WhoBlA 92*
**Klinedinst**, John David 1950- *WhoAmL 92*
**Klinedinst**, Keith Allen 1944- *AmMWSc 92*
**Klinedinst**, Paul Edward, Jr 1933- *AmMWSc 92*
**Klinedinst**, Thomas John, Jr. 1942- *WhoFI 92*
**Klinefelter**, Harry Fitch 1912- *AmMWSc 92*
**Klinefelter**, James Louis 1925- *WhoAmL 92, WhoAmP 91*
**Klinefelter**, Sarah Stephens 1938- *WhoEnt 92*
**Klinefelter**, Stanard T. 1947- *WhoAmL 92*
**Klinenberg**, James Robert 1934- *AmMWSc 92*
**Klinenberg**, Susan Beth 1961- *WhoEnt 92*
**Kling**, Gerald Fairchild 1941- *AmMWSc 92*
**Kling**, Jarrett Burt 1943- *WhoFI 92*
**Kling**, Lou Anne Beito 1939- *WhoAmP 91*
**Kling**, Ozro Ray 1942- *AmMWSc 92*
**Kling**, Paul 1929- *WhoEnt 92*
**Kling**, Richard W 1940- *WhoIns 92*
**Kling**, S Lee 1928- *WhoIns 92*
**Kling**, William, Jr 1954- *WhoAmP 91*
**Kling**, William Hugh 1942- *WhoMW 92*
**Klingaman**, David Charles 1934- *WhoFI 92, WhoMW 92*
**Klingaman**, William K, Sr *WhoAmP 91*
**Klingbeil**, Werner Walter 1932- *AmMWSc 92*
**Klingberg**, Douglas John 1941- *WhoMW 92*
**Klingberg**, William Gene 1916- *AmMWSc 92*
**Klinge**, Albert Frederick 1923- *AmMWSc 92*
**Klinge**, Carl George 1952- *WhoWest 92*
**Klinge**, J Kenneth 1938- *WhoAmP 91*
**Klingebiel**, Albert Arnold 1910- *AmMWSc 92*
**Klingele**, Harold Otto 1937- *AmMWSc 92*
**Klingeman**, Peter C 1934- *AmMWSc 92*
**Klingen**, Theodore James 1931- *AmMWSc 92*
**Klingenberg**, Joseph John 1919- *AmMWSc 92*
**Klingenberg**, Wilhelm 1924- *IntWW 91*
**Klingener**, David John 1937- *AmMWSc 92*
**Klingensmith**, Arthur Paul 1949- *WhoWest 92*
**Klingensmith**, George Bruce 1934- *AmMWSc 92*
**Klingensmith**, Mark Wayne 1961- *WhoEnt 92*
**Klingensmith**, Merle Joseph 1932- *AmMWSc 92*
**Klingensmith**, Raymond W 1931- *AmMWSc 92*
**Klingensmith**, Ritchel George 1942- *WhoFI 92*
**Klinger**, Allen 1937- *AmMWSc 92*
**Klinger**, Douglas Evan 1964- *WhoFI 92*
**Klinger**, Edward Franklin 1945- *WhoAmP 91*
**Klinger**, Eric 1933- *WrDr 92*
**Klinger**, Friedrich Maximilian von 1752-1831 *BlkwCEP*
**Klinger**, Harold P 1929- *AmMWSc 92*
**Klinger**, Harry Ernest 1956- *WhoWest 92*
**Klinger**, Lawrence Edward 1929- *AmMWSc 92*
**Klinger**, Leslie Stuart 1946- *WhoAmL 92*
**Klinger**, Thomas Scott 1955- *AmMWSc 92*
**Klinger**, Tony 1950- *IntMPA 92*
**Klinger**, William Russell 1939- *AmMWSc 92*
**Klingerman**, Robert Harvey 1939- *WhoFI 92*
**Klinges**, David Henry 1928- *WhoFI 92*
**Klinghammer**, Erich 1930- *AmMWSc 92*
**Klinghofer**, Clara 1900-1970 *TwCPaSc*
**Klinghoffer**, June F 1921- *AmMWSc 92*
**Klingle**, Philip Anthony 1950- *WhoAmL 92*
**Klingler**, Eugene H 1932- *AmMWSc 92*
**Klingman**, Alicia Lynn 1954- *WhoAmL 92*
**Klingman**, Darwin Dee 1944- *AmMWSc 92*
**Klingman**, Dayton L 1913- *AmMWSc 92*
**Klingman**, Gerda Isolde 1924- *AmMWSc 92*
**Klingman**, Jack Dennis 1927- *AmMWSc 92*
**Klingsberg**, Cyrus 1924- *AmMWSc 92*
**Klingsberg**, David 1934- *WhoAmL 92*
**Klingsberg**, Erwin 1921- *AmMWSc 92*
**Klingsmith**, Phil C 1949- *WhoAmP 91*
**Klingsporn**, Gary Wayne 1951- *WhoRel 92*
**Klinhormhual**, Everlida Llamas 1950- *WhoWest 92*
**Klink**, Brian Jeffery 1957- *WhoMW 92*
**Klink**, Fredric J. 1933- *WhoAmL 92*
**Klink**, Joel Richard 1935- *AmMWSc 92*
**Klink**, Marianne Barber 1949- *WhoAmP 91*
**Klink**, Paul Leo 1965- *WhoWest 92*
**Klink**, William H 1937- *AmMWSc 92*
**Klink**, William Richard 1933- *WhoRel 92*
**Klinke**, David J 1932- *AmMWSc 92*
**Klinker**, Sheila A *WhoAmP 91*
**Klinkhardt**, John T. 1952- *WhoMW 92*
**Klinkowitz**, Jerome 1943- *IntAu&W 91*
**Klinkowitz**, Jerome Francis 1943- *WhoMW 92*
**Klinksick**, Charles Theodore 1916- *WhoRel 92*
**Klinman**, Judith Pollock 1941- *AmMWSc 92*
**Klinman**, Norman Ralph 1937- *AmMWSc 92*
**Klinner**, Alvin Richard 1930- *WhoWest 92*
**Klint**, Kaare 1888-1954 *DcTwDes, FacFETw*
**Klint**, Kenneth 1936- *WhoWest 92*
**Klintworth**, Gordon K 1932- *AmMWSc 92*
**Klinzing**, George Engelbert 1938- *AmMWSc 92*
**Klinzman**, Frank W 1928- *WhoIns 92*
**Klionsky**, Bernard Leon 1925- *AmMWSc 92*
**Klionsky**, M. Matthew 1953- *WhoMW 92*
**Kliore**, Arvydas J 1935- *AmMWSc 92*
**Klioze**, Oscar 1919- *AmMWSc 92*
**Klip**, Dorothea A 1921- *AmMWSc 92*
**Klip**, Willem 1917- *AmMWSc 92*
**Klipa**, Jacqualine Lee 1950- *WhoMW 92*
**Klipfel**, Stephen Ralph 1948- *WhoFI 92*
**Kliphardt**, Raymond A 1917- *AmMWSc 92*
**Klippart**, John Hancock 1823-1878 *BiInAmS*
**Klippel**, John Howard 1944- *AmMWSc 92*
**Klipper**, Daniel Stephen 1953- *WhoFI 92*
**Klippert**, Richard Hobdell, Jr. 1940- *WhoWest 92*
**Klipple**, Edmund Chester 1906- *AmMWSc 92*
**Klipstein**, David Hampton 1930- *AmMWSc 92*
**Klipstein**, Frederick August 1928- *AmMWSc 92*
**Klipstein**, Kenneth H. d1991 *NewYTBS 91*
**Klipstein**, Robert Alan 1936- *WhoAmL 92*
**Klir**, George Jiri 1932- *AmMWSc 92*
**Klise**, Thomas S. 1928-1978 *ConAu 134*
**Klisiewicz**, Jeanne Marie 1947- *WhoRel 92*
**Klitgaard**, Howard Maynard 1924- *AmMWSc 92*
**Klitgaard**, Mogen 1906-1945 *LiExTwC*
**Klitzke**, Ramon Arthur, II 1955- *WhoAmL 92*
**Klitzky**, Bruce R. *WhoRel 92*
**Klitzman**, Bruce 1951- *AmMWSc 92*
**Klitzman**, Robert 1958- *ConAu 135*
**Klivington**, Kenneth Albert 1940- *AmMWSc 92*

**Kliwer**, James Karl 1928- *AmMWSc 92*
**Klobasa**, John Anthony 1951- *WhoAmL 92*
**Klobe**, Tom 1940- *WhoWest 92*
**Klobuchar**, Richard Louis 1948- *AmMWSc 92*
**Klobucher**, John Marcellus 1932- *WhoWest 92*
**Klobukowski**, Mariusz Andrzej 1948- *AmMWSc 92*
**Klock**, Benny LeRoy 1934- *AmMWSc 92*
**Klock**, Glen Orval 1937- *AmMWSc 92*
**Klock**, Harold F 1929- *AmMWSc 92*
**Klock**, John W 1928- *AmMWSc 92*
**Klock**, Steven Wayne 1954- *WhoMW 92*
**Klocke**, Francis J *AmMWSc 92*
**Klocke**, Robert Albert 1936- *AmMWSc 92*
**Klodowski**, Harry Francis, Jr. 1954- *WhoAmL 92*
**Klodt**, Gerald Joseph 1949- *WhoMW 92*
**Klodzinski**, Joseph Anthony 1942- *WhoFI 92, WhoMW 92*
**Kloefkorn**, William *DrAPF 91*
**Kloehn**, Ralph Anthony 1932- *WhoMW 92*
**Kloepfer**, Henry Warner 1913- *AmMWSc 92*
**Kloepfer**, John Warner 1947- *WhoRel 92*
**Kloepper**, David Alan 1945- *WhoFI 92*
**Kloesel**, Christian Johannes Wilhelm *WhoMW 92*
**Kloet**, Willem M *AmMWSc 92*
**Kloetzel**, John Arthur 1941- *AmMWSc 92*
**Kloetzel**, Milton Carl 1913- *AmMWSc 92*
**Klohs**, Murle William 1920- *WhoWest 92*
**Klohs**, Wayne D *AmMWSc 92*
**Klokholm**, Erik 1922- *AmMWSc 92*
**Klokker**, Jay *DrAPF 91*
**Kloman**, H. Felix 1933- *WhoFI 92*
**Klombers**, Norman 1923- *AmMWSc 92*
**Klomp**, Edward 1930- *AmMWSc 92*
**Klomparens**, Karen L 1950- *AmMWSc 92*
**Klompus**, Steven Jerome 1946- *WhoWest 92*
**Kloner**, Robert A. 1949- *WhoWest 92*
**Klonoff**, Robert Howard 1955- *WhoAmL 92*
**Klontz**, Everett Earl 1921- *AmMWSc 92*
**Kloos**, Edward John Michael, Jr. 1951- *WhoRel 92*
**Klootwijk**, Jaap 1932- *Who 92*
**Klopatek**, Jeffrey Matthew 1944- *AmMWSc 92*
**Klopf**, Donald W 1923- *ConAu 34NR*
**Klopf**, Frank P. 1939- *WhoEnt 92*
**Klopfenstein**, Charles E 1940- *AmMWSc 92*
**Klopfenstein**, Gary Carlton 1961- *WhoFI 92*
**Klopfenstein**, Kenneth F 1940- *AmMWSc 92*
**Klopfenstein**, Timothy J 1956- *WhoIns 92*
**Klopfenstein**, William Elmer 1935- *AmMWSc 92*
**Klopfer**, Peter Hubert 1930- *AmMWSc 92*
**Klopman**, Gilles 1933- *AmMWSc 92*
**Klopotek**, David L 1942- *AmMWSc 92*
**Klopp**, Calvin Trexler 1912- *AmMWSc 92*
**Klopp**, John C. 1971- *WhoEnt 92*
**Klopp**, Kenneth Hap 1942- *WhoWest 92*
**Kloppel**, Thomas Mathew 1950- *AmMWSc 92*
**Klopsteg**, Paul E. 1889-1991 *CurBio 91N, NewYTBS 91*
**Klopstock**, Friedrich Gottlieb 1724-1803 *BlkwCEP*
**Klores**, Jeffrey David 1958- *WhoFI 92*
**Klos**, Edward John 1925- *AmMWSc 92*
**Klos**, William Anton 1936- *AmMWSc 92*
**Klosak**, J Henry *WhoAmP 91*
**Klose**, John 1942- *WhoAmP 91*
**Klose**, Jules Zeiser 1927- *AmMWSc 92*
**Klose**, Thomas Richard 1946- *AmMWSc 92*
**Klose**, Wolfgang Dietrich E. A. 1930- *IntWW 91*
**Klosek**, Richard C 1933- *AmMWSc 92*
**Kloska**, Ronald Frank 1933- *WhoMW 92*
**Kloskowska**, Antonina 1919- *IntWW 91*
**Klosner**, Jerome M 1928- *AmMWSc 92*
**Kloss**, Heinz 1904-1987 *DcAmImH*
**Kloss**, Sharon Lynn 1956- *WhoAmL 92*
**Klossowski de Rola**, Balthasar 1908- *IntWW 91*
**Kloster**, Burton John, Jr. 1931- *WhoFI 92*
**Kloster**, Einar 1937- *IntWW 91*
**Klostermaier**, Klaus Konrad 1933- *WhoRel 92*
**Klosterman**, Albert Leonard 1942- *AmMWSc 92, WhoFI 92*
**Klosterman**, Harold J 1924- *AmMWSc 92*
**Klostermeyer**, Edward Charles 1919- *AmMWSc 92*
**Klostermeyer**, Lyle Edward 1944- *AmMWSc 92*
**Kloth**, Timothy Tom 1954- *WhoEnt 92, WhoMW 92*
**Klotman**, Paul *AmMWSc 92*
**Klotman**, Robert Howard 1918- *WhoEnt 92*
**Klots**, Cornelius E 1933- *AmMWSc 92*
**Klotsche**, John Chester 1942- *WhoAmL 92*
**Klott**, David Lee 1941- *WhoAmL 92, WhoFI 92*
**Klotter**, Ronald Lawrence 1960- *WhoFI 92*
**Klotz**, Arthur Paul 1913- *AmMWSc 92*
**Klotz**, Eugene Arthur 1935- *AmMWSc 92*
**Klotz**, Gregory Leonard 1957- *WhoEnt 92*
**Klotz**, Howard J 1934- *WhoIns 92*
**Klotz**, Irving Myron 1916- *AmMWSc 92, IntWW 91*
**Klotz**, James Allen 1922- *AmMWSc 92*
**Klotz**, Jerome Hamilton 1934- *AmMWSc 92*
**Klotz**, John William 1918- *AmMWSc 92, WhoRel 92*
**Klotz**, Louis Herman 1928- *AmMWSc 92*
**Klotz**, Lynn Charles 1940- *AmMWSc 92*
**Klotz**, Radford Werner 1955- *WhoFI 92*
**Klotz**, Richard Lawrence 1950- *AmMWSc 92*
**Klotz**, Stephen Paul 1947- *WhoWest 92*
**Klotzbach**, Gunter 1912- *IntWW 91*
**Klotzbach**, Robert J 1922- *AmMWSc 92*
**Klotzer**, Charles Lothar 1925- *WhoMW 92*
**Kloubec**, Richard W 1931- *WhoAmP 91*
**Kloucek**, Frank John 1956- *WhoAmP 91*
**Klouda**, Mary Ann Aberle 1937- *AmMWSc 92*
**Klowden**, Marc Jeffery 1948- *WhoWest 92*
**Klowden**, Marc Jeffrey 1948- *AmMWSc 92*
**Klowden**, Michael Louis 1945- *WhoAmL 92*
**Kluba**, Richard Michael 1947- *AmMWSc 92*
**Klubek**, Brian Paul 1948- *AmMWSc 92*
**Kluber**, Bernice Herrig 1923- *WhoWest 92*
**Klubes**, Philip 1935- *AmMWSc 92*
**Klucas**, Robert Vernon 1940- *AmMWSc 92*
**Kluck**, Clarence Joseph 1929- *WhoWest 92*
**Kluck**, John J. *WhoWest 92*
**Kluckhohn**, Clyde K. M. 1905-1960 *BenetAL 91*
**Klueh**, Ronald Lloyd 1936- *AmMWSc 92*
**Kluender**, Harold Clinton 1944- *AmMWSc 92*
**Kluepfel**, Dieter 1930- *AmMWSc 92*
**Kluesner**, Marian *WhoRel 92*
**Kluessendorf**, Joanne 1949- *AmMWSc 92*
**Kluetz**, Michael David 1948- *AmMWSc 92*
**Klug**, Aaron 1926- *AmMWSc 92, IntWW 91, Who 92, WhoNob 90*
**Klug**, David Jon 1964- *WhoMW 92*
**Klug**, Dennis Dwayne 1942- *AmMWSc 92*
**Klug**, John Edward 1950- *WhoMW 92*
**Klug**, John Joseph 1948- *WhoWest 92*
**Klug**, Michael J 1941- *AmMWSc 92*
**Klug**, Richard Daniel 1951- *WhoEnt 92*
**Klug**, Scott 1953- *AlmAP 92 [port]*
**Klug**, Scott Leo 1953- *WhoAmP 91, WhoMW 92*
**Klug**, William Stephen 1941- *AmMWSc 92*
**Kluge**, Alexander 1932- *IntDcF 2-2*
**Kluge**, Arnold Girard 1935- *AmMWSc 92*
**Kluge**, Hans Gunther von 1882-1944 *EncTR 91 [port]*
**Kluge**, John *LesBEnT 92*
**Kluge**, John 1914- *News 91 [port]*
**Kluge**, John Paul 1937- *AmMWSc 92*
**Kluge**, John Werner 1914- *IntWW 91*
**Kluge**, Kurt 1886-1940 *EncTR 91 [port]*
**Kluge**, Len H. 1945- *WhoEnt 92, WhoMW 92*
**Kluge**, Pamela Hollie 1948- *WhoBlA 92*
**Kluge**, Ralph William 1926- *WhoRel 92*
**Kluge**, William Frederick 1950- *WhoMW 92*
**Kluger**, Matthew Jay 1946- *AmMWSc 92*
**Kluger**, Ronald H 1943- *AmMWSc 92*
**Klugh**, Earl 1953- *WhoEnt 92*
**Klugheit**, Mark A. 1948- *WhoAmL 92*
**Klugherz**, Peter D 1942- *AmMWSc 92*
**Klugman**, Arnold Jay 1948- *WhoFI 92*
**Klugman**, Jack 1922- *IntMPA 92, WhoEnt 92*
**Klugman**, Stephan Craig 1945- *WhoMW 92*
**Klugt**, Cornelius J. van der 1925- *IntWW 91*
**Kluiber**, Rudolph W 1930- *AmMWSc 92*
**Kluksdahl**, Harris Eudell 1933- *AmMWSc 92*
**Klumb**, David L 1929- *WhoAmP 91*
**Klumpar**, David Michael 1943- *AmMWSc 92*
**Klumpp**, Stephen Paul 1952- *WhoMW 92*
**Klumpp**, Theodore George 1903- *AmMWSc 92*
**Klun**, Jerome Anthony 1939- *AmMWSc 92*
**Klundt**, Irwin Lee 1936- *AmMWSc 92*
**Klundt**, Larry A *WhoAmP 91*
**Klunzinger**, Thomas Edward 1944- *WhoAmP 91, WhoMW 92*
**Klurfeld**, David Michael 1951- *AmMWSc 92*
**Klus**, John P 1935- *AmMWSc 92*
**Kluse**, Michael 1951- *WhoMW 92*
**Klusendorf**, Roy Earl 1939- *WhoWest 92*
**Kluskens**, Larry F *AmMWSc 92*
**Klusman**, Judith 1956- *WhoAmP 91*
**Klusman**, Ronald William 1941- *AmMWSc 92*
**Klusmire**, Jon Dalton 1956- *WhoWest 92*
**Kluss**, Byron Curtis 1928- *AmMWSc 92*
**Klutchko**, Sylvester 1933- *AmMWSc 92*
**Klute**, Arnold 1921- *AmMWSc 92*
**Klutke**, Olaf 1961- *WhoMW 92*
**Klutsis**, Gustav Gustavovich 1895-1944 *SovUnBD*
**Kluttig**, Christian 1943- *WhoEnt 92*
**Klutts**, Robert Cliff 1940- *WhoMW 92*
**Kluttz**, Theodore Franklin 1848-1918 *DcNCBi 3*
**Klutznick**, Philip M. 1907- *WhoFI 92*
**Kluver**, Billy *ConAu 133*
**Kluver**, J W 1927- *AmMWSc 92*
**Kluver**, J. Wilhelm 1927- *ConAu 133*
**Kluxen**, Wolfgang 1922- *IntWW 91*
**Klyber**, Charles Arthur 1937- *WhoMW 92*
**Klyberg**, Charles John *Who 92*
**Klyce**, Stephen Downing 1942- *AmMWSc 92*
**Klychev**, Izzat 1923- *SovUnBD*
**Klyman**, Fred Irwin 1946- *WhoFI 92*
**Klymkowsky**, Michael W *AmMWSc 92*
**Klyne**, Barbara Evelyn *Who 92*
**Klyszewski**, Waclaw 1910- *IntWW 91*
**Klyuev**, Nikolay Alekseevich 1884-1937 *SovUnBD*
**Klyun**, Ivan 1870-1942 *FacFETw*
**Klyuyev**, Vladimir Grigorovich 1924- *IntWW 91*
**Kmak**, Walter S 1928- *AmMWSc 92*
**Kmet**, Joseph Paul 1942- *WhoWest 92*
**Kmet**, Rebecca Eugenia 1948- *WhoWest 92*
**Kmetec**, Emil Philip 1927- *AmMWSc 92*
**Kmetec**, Emil Phillip 1927- *WhoMW 92*
**Kmetz**, John Michael 1943- *AmMWSc 92*
**Kmiec**, Edward Urban 1936- *WhoRel 92*
**Kmiec**, Theodore Bernard, III 1962- *WhoAmL 92*
**Kmiecik**, James Edward 1936- *AmMWSc 92*
**Kmiotek**, Jacqueline J. 1959- *WhoAmL 92*
**Knaack**, Susan Francis 1942- *WhoEnt 92*
**Knaak**, Frederic W. 1953- *WhoMW 92*
**Knaak**, Fritz 1953- *WhoAmP 91*
**Knaak**, James Bruce 1932- *AmMWSc 92*
**Knaapen**, David Raymond 1958- *WhoAmL 92*
**Knab**, Frederick 1865-1918 *BiInAmS*
**Knabe**, George W, Jr 1924- *AmMWSc 92*
**Knabe**, Keith J. 1958- *WhoFI 92*
**Knabe**, Susan Anne 1961- *WhoMW 92*
**Knabe**, William 1803-1864 *NewAmDM*
**Knabenshue**, Edwin Mark 1954- *WhoRel 92*
**Knable**, Bobbie Margaret Brown 1936- *WhoBlA 92*
**Knacke**, Roger Fritz 1941- *AmMWSc 92*
**Knackstedt**, Gunter Wilhelm Karl 1929- *IntWW 91*
**Knaebel**, Kent Schofield 1951- *AmMWSc 92*
**Knaff**, David Barry 1941- *AmMWSc 92*
**Knaggs**, Edward Andrew 1922- *AmMWSc 92*
**Knaggs**, Kenneth James 1920- *Who 92*
**Knaifel**, Alexander 1943- *ConCom 92*
**Knaive**, Henry Louis 1902- *WhoBlA 92*
**Knake**, Barry Edward 1946- *WhoWest 92*
**Knake**, Ellery Louis 1927- *AmMWSc 92*
**Knap**, James E 1926- *AmMWSc 92*
**Knapczyk**, Jerome Walter 1938- *AmMWSc 92*
**Knaphus**, George 1924- *AmMWSc 92, WhoMW 92*
**Knapik**, Michael R *WhoAmP 91*
**Knapik**, Thomas Michael 1954- *WhoWest 92*
**Knapka**, Joseph J 1935- *AmMWSc 92*
**Knapman**, Paul Anthony 1944- *Who 92*
**Knapman**, Roger Maurice 1944- *Who 92*
**Knapp**, Adeline 1860-1909 *ScFEYrs*
**Knapp**, Anthony William 1941- *AmMWSc 92*
**Knapp**, Charles 1946- *IntWW 91*
**Knapp**, Charles Francis 1940- *AmMWSc 92*
**Knapp**, Charles H 1931- *AmMWSc 92*
**Knapp**, Cleon Talboys 1937- *WhoWest 92*
**Knapp**, Daniel Roger 1943- *AmMWSc 92*
**Knapp**, David *Who 92*
**Knapp**, David Allan 1938- *AmMWSc 92*
**Knapp**, David Arthur 1960- *WhoFI 92*
**Knapp**, David Edwin 1932- *AmMWSc 92*
**Knapp**, Dennis L. 1945- *WhoFI 92*
**Knapp**, Dennis Raymond 1912- *WhoAmL 92*
**Knapp**, Don 1932- *WhoAmP 91*
**Knapp**, Eber Guy 1916- *WhoWest 92*
**Knapp**, Edward *ConAu 134, SmATA 67*
**Knapp**, Edward Alan 1932- *AmMWSc 92*
**Knapp**, Edward Ronald 1919- *Who 92*
**Knapp**, Francis Marion 1924- *AmMWSc 92*
**Knapp**, Fred William 1928- *AmMWSc 92*
**Knapp**, Frederick Whiton 1915- *AmMWSc 92*
**Knapp**, Gary Alan 1951- *WhoRel 92*
**Knapp**, Gayle 1949- *AmMWSc 92, WhoWest 92*
**Knapp**, George G P 1923- *WhoIns 92*
**Knapp**, George L 1872- *ScFEYrs*
**Knapp**, George Werner 1916- *WhoRel 92*
**Knapp**, Gillian Revill 1944- *AmMWSc 92*
**Knapp**, Gordon Grayson 1930- *AmMWSc 92*
**Knapp**, Harold Anthony, Jr 1924- *AmMWSc 92*
**Knapp**, Harold Swayze, III 1966- *WhoEnt 92*
**Knapp**, Hermann 1832-1911 *BiInAmS*
**Knapp**, J. Burke 1913- *IntWW 91*
**Knapp**, James 1940- *Who 92*
**Knapp**, James Ian Keith 1943- *WhoAmP 91*
**Knapp**, Jeffrey *DrAPF 91*
**Knapp**, John David 1926- *Who 92*
**Knapp**, John J 1934- *WhoAmP 91*
**Knapp**, John Merrill 1914- *WhoEnt 92*
**Knapp**, John Victor 1940- *WhoMW 92*
**Knapp**, John Williams 1932- *AmMWSc 92*
**Knapp**, Joseph Leonce, Jr 1937- *AmMWSc 92*
**Knapp**, Joseph Palmer 1864-1951 *DcNCBi 3*
**Knapp**, Kenneth R. 1937- *WhoRel 92*
**Knapp**, Kenneth T 1930- *AmMWSc 92*
**Knapp**, Leslie W 1929- *AmMWSc 92*
**Knapp**, Malcolm Hammond 1939- *AmMWSc 92*
**Knapp**, Martin Wells 1853-1901 *RelLAm 91*
**Knapp**, Paul Joseph 1929- *WhoAmL 92*
**Knapp**, Peter Hobart 1916- *AmMWSc 92*
**Knapp**, Philip d1991 *NewYTBS 91*
**Knapp**, Philip Coombs 1858-1920 *BiInAmS*
**Knapp**, Richard Frederick 1939- *WhoEnt 92*
**Knapp**, Robert Hazard, Jr 1944- *AmMWSc 92*
**Knapp**, Robert Lester 1921- *AmMWSc 92*
**Knapp**, Robert Stanley 1940- *WhoWest 92*
**Knapp**, Roger 1943- *WhoAmP 91*
**Knapp**, Roger Dale 1943- *AmMWSc 92*
**Knapp**, Ronald R 1925- *WhoAmP 91*
**Knapp**, Roy M 1940- *AmMWSc 92*
**Knapp**, Samuel Lorenzo 1783-1838 *BenetAL 91*
**Knapp**, Stefan 1921- *IntWW 91*
**Knapp**, Terence Richard 1932- *WhoEnt 92*
**Knapp**, Theodore Martin 1947- *AmMWSc 92*
**Knapp**, Thomas Edwin 1925- *WhoWest 92*
**Knapp**, Thomas Joseph 1952- *WhoAmL 92*
**Knapp**, Trevor Frederick William B 1937- *Who 92*
**Knapp**, Whitman 1909- *WhoAmL 92*
**Knapp**, William Arnold, Jr 1925- *AmMWSc 92*
**Knapp**, William John 1916- *AmMWSc 92*
**Knapp**, William Melvin 1961- *WhoFI 92*
**Knapp**, Yoric Todd 1959- *WhoMW 92*
**Knapp-Fisher**, Edward George 1915- *Who 92, WrDr 92*
**Knappe**, Laverne F 1922- *AmMWSc 92*
**Knappenberger**, Herbert Allan 1932- *AmMWSc 92*
**Knappenberger**, John Joseph, III 1946- *WhoMW 92*
**Knappenberger**, Paul Henry, Jr 1942- *AmMWSc 92*
**Knappertsbusch**, Hans 1888-1965 *NewAmDM*
**Knapple**, Kevin Frederick 1954- *WhoAmP 91*
**Knapstein**, John William 1937- *WhoMW 92, WhoRel 92*
**Knaresborough**, Bishop Suffragan of 1932- *Who 92*
**Knarr**, Willard A 1947- *WhoIns 92*
**Knaster**, Tatyana 1933- *AmMWSc 92*
**Knatchbull** *Who 92*
**Knatterud**, Genell Lavonne *AmMWSc 92*
**Knaub**, Georgie Ann 1955- *WhoWest 92*
**Knauer**, Bruce Richard 1942- *AmMWSc 92*
**Knauer**, David Walter 1945- *WhoAmL 92*
**Knauer**, Thomas E *AmMWSc 92*
**Knauer**, Virginia Harrington 1915- *WhoAmP 91*
**Knauf**, Erich 1895-1944 *EncTR 91*
**Knauff**, Raymond Eugene 1925- *AmMWSc 92*
**Knauft**, David A 1951- *AmMWSc 92*
**Knauft**, Milford Roy, Jr 1918- *WhoAmP 91*
**Knaus**, Edward Elmer 1943- *AmMWSc 92*
**Knaus**, Kenneth Rheinold 1944- *WhoMW 92*

**Knaus**, Ronald Mallen 1937- AmMWSc 92
**Knaus**, William Lyle 1935- WhoMW 92
**Knausenberger**, Wulf H 1943- AmMWSc 92
**Knauss**, Jeffery Paul 1953- WhoMW 92
**Knauss**, John Atkinson 1925- AmMWSc 92, WhoFI 92
**Knauss**, K.A. 1948- WhoFI 92
**Knauss**, Robert Lynn 1931- WhoAmL 92
**Knauth**, Christopher Rutgers 1929- WhoAmL 92
**Knauth**, Stephen DrAPF 91
**Knavel**, Christopher Charles 1958- WhoRel 92
**Knavel**, Dean Edgar 1924- AmMWSc 92
**Knazek**, Richard Allan 1942- AmMWSc 92
**Kneale**, Bryan 1930- IntWW 91, TwCPaSc, Who 92
**Kneale**, Nigel 1922- ConTFT 9, TwCSFW 91, WrDr 92
**Kneale**, Samuel George 1921- AmMWSc 92
**Kneale**, William Calvert d1990 IntWW 91N
**Knebel**, Donald Earl 1946- WhoAmL 92, WhoFI 92
**Knebel**, Fletcher DrAPF 91
**Knebel**, Fletcher 1911- ConAu 36NR, ConNov 91, IntAu&W 91, WrDr 92
**Knebel**, Harley John 1941- AmMWSc 92
**Knebel**, Jack Gillen 1939- WhoWest 92
**Knebel**, John Albert 1936- WhoAmP 91
**Knebworth**, Viscount 1989- Who 92
**Knecht**, Ben Harrold 1938- WhoWest 92
**Knecht**, Charles Daniel 1932- AmMWSc 92
**Knecht**, David Jordan 1930- AmMWSc 92
**Knecht**, Laurance A 1932- AmMWSc 92
**Knecht**, Raymond Lawrence 1948- WhoWest 92
**Knecht**, Robert Jean 1926- IntAu&W 91, WrDr 92
**Knecht**, Walter Ludwig 1909- AmMWSc 92
**Knecht**, William L. 1946- WhoAmL 92
**Knechtli**, Ronald 1927- AmMWSc 92
**Knee**, David Isaac 1934- AmMWSc 92
**Knee**, Jonathan Arye 1961- WhoAmL 92
**Knee**, Stephen H. 1940- WhoAmL 92
**Knee**, Terence Edward Creasey 1932- AmMWSc 92
**Kneebone**, Alice Jeannette 1956- WhoWest 92
**Kneebone**, Leon Russell 1920- AmMWSc 92, WhoRel 92
**Kneebone**, Peter 1923-1990 AnObit 1990
**Kneebone**, William Robert 1922- AmMWSc 92
**Kneece**, Daniel Rufus, III 1956- WhoEnt 92, WhoWest 92
**Kneece**, Roland Royce, Jr 1939- AmMWSc 92
**Kneeland**, George Royal 1918- WhoAmP 91
**Kneeland**, Samuel 1821-1888 BiInAmS
**Kneevers**, Paul Joseph 1960- WhoEnt 92
**Knef**, Hildegard 1925- IntAu&W 91, IntWW 91
**Knefel**, Don Robert 1948- WhoMW 92
**Knehans**, Wendell Alan 1963- WhoMW 92
**Kneib**, Joseph A. 1948- WhoMW 92
**Kneib**, Ronald Thomas 1951- AmMWSc 92
**Kneip**, G D, Jr 1925- AmMWSc 92
**Kneip**, Stephen James 1949- WhoMW 92
**Kneip**, Theodore Joseph 1926- AmMWSc 92
**Kneipp**, George 1922- Who 92
**Kneisel**, Edmund M. 1946- WhoAmL 92
**Kneiser**, Richard John 1938- WhoFI 92, WhoMW 92
**Knell**, Catalaine WhoEnt 92
**Knell**, Charles Denne 1950- WhoAmL 92
**Knell**, Gary G 1950- WhoAmP 91
**Knell**, William Henry 1927- WhoAmP 91
**Kneller**, Alister Arthur 1927- Who 92
**Kneller**, Eckart Friedrich 1928- IntWW 91
**Kneller**, William Arthur 1929- AmMWSc 92
**Knepp**, Lee Emerson 1952- WhoAmP 91
**Knepp**, Stanley Gerald 1948- WhoFI 92
**Knepper**, Barry Michael 1950- WhoEnt 92
**Knepper**, Eugene Arthur 1926- WhoFI 92, WhoMW 92
**Knepper**, James Minter 1927- WhoEnt 92
**Knepper**, Jimmy 1927- NewAmDM
**Knepper**, Randolph Leroy 1950- WhoAmP 91
**Knepper**, William E 1909- WhoIns 92
**Knepper**, William Edgar 1929- WhoFI 92
**Kneppler**, Pamela Janice 1964- WhoFI 92
**Knerly**, Mary Johnson 1925- WhoFI 92, WhoMW 92
**Knerly**, Stephen John, Jr. 1949- WhoAmL 92
**Knerr**, Reinhard H 1939- AmMWSc 92
**Kness**, Richard Maynard 1937- WhoEnt 92
**Knestrick**, Martin Earl 1944- WhoFI 92
**Knevel**, Adelbert Michael 1922- AmMWSc 92
**Knevitt**, Charles Philip Paul 1952- IntAu&W 91
**Knezevic**, Stojan 1923- IntWW 91
**Kniazuk**, Michael 1914- AmMWSc 92
**Kniazzeh**, Alfredo G F 1938- AmMWSc 92
**Knibb**, Michael Anthony 1938- Who 92
**Knibbs**, H H 1874-1945 ScFEYrs, TwCWW 91
**Knicely**, Howard V. 1936- WhoFI 92
**Knick**, Steven Thomas 1954- WhoWest 92
**Knickerbocker**, Gerald 1943- WhoAmP 91
**Knickerbocker**, Robert Platt, Jr. 1944- WhoAmL 92
**Knickle**, Harold Norman 1936- AmMWSc 92
**Knickrehm**, Glenn Allen 1948- WhoFI 92
**Kniebes**, Duane Van 1926- AmMWSc 92
**Knief**, Ronald Allen 1944- AmMWSc 92
**Kniep**, Susan G 1943- WhoAmP 91
**Knierim**, Ann Wilson 1921- WhoAmP 91
**Knierim**, Kim Phillip 1945- WhoAmL 92, WhoWest 92
**Knierim**, Paul J 1965- WhoAmP 91
**Knierim**, Robert Valentine 1916- WhoWest 92
**Knieskern**, Peter D 1798-1871 BiInAmS
**Kniesler**, Frederick Cornelius 1930- WhoAmP 91
**Knievel**, Daniel Paul 1943- AmMWSc 92
**Kniffen**, Donald Avery 1933- AmMWSc 92
**Kniffen**, Jan Rogers 1948- WhoFI 92
**Knigge**, Karl Max 1926- AmMWSc 92
**Knigh**, Billy Earl, I 1939- WhoBlA 92
**Knight of Naples**, The EncAmaz 91
**Knight**, Al J WhoAmP 91
**Knight**, Alan Campbell 1922- AmMWSc 92
**Knight**, Alan Sydney 1946- Who 92
**Knight**, Alanna IntAu&W 91, WrDr 92
**Knight**, Alexander Francis 1939- Who 92
**Knight**, Alice Tirrell 1903- WhoAmP 91
**Knight**, Allan Runyon 1912- WhoRel 92
**Knight**, Allan Walton 1910- Who 92
**Knight**, Allen Warner 1932- AmMWSc 92
**Knight**, Andrew Stephen Bower 1939- IntAu&W 91, IntWW 91, Who 92
**Knight**, Anne Bradley 1942- AmMWSc 92
**Knight**, Arthur 1916-1991 ConAu 135
**Knight**, Arthur 1917- Who 92
**Knight**, Arthur Robert 1938- AmMWSc 92
**Knight**, Arthur Winfield DrAPF 91
**Knight**, Arumainayagam John 1927- WhoRel 92
**Knight**, Athelia Wilhelmenia 1950- WhoBlA 92
**Knight**, Bernard 1931- IntAu&W 91, WrDr 92
**Knight**, Bob WhoAmP 91
**Knight**, Bob 1944- WhoEnt 92
**Knight**, Brian Joseph 1941- Who 92
**Knight**, Bruce L 1942- AmMWSc 92
**Knight**, Bruce Winton 1930- AmMWSc 92
**Knight**, Bubba WhoBlA 92
**Knight**, Burton Wilder, II 1955- WhoAmP 91
**Knight**, Charles 1791-1873 DcLB 106 [port]
**Knight**, Charles 1901-1990 TwCPaSc
**Knight**, Charles Alfred 1936- AmMWSc 92
**Knight**, Charles Field 1936- WhoFI 92, WhoMW 92
**Knight**, Clifford Burnham 1926- AmMWSc 92
**Knight**, Cranston Sedrick 1950- IntAu&W 91
**Knight**, Cynthis Lee 1961- WhoEnt 92
**Knight**, D. M. WrDr 92
**Knight**, Damon 1922- ConAu 36NR, ScFEYrs, TwCSFW 91
**Knight**, David IntAu&W 91X, WrDr 92
**Knight**, David Bates 1939- AmMWSc 92
**Knight**, David Marcus 1936- IntAu&W 91
**Knight**, David Webster 1943- WhoAmL 92
**Knight**, David William 1954- WhoAmL 92
**Knight**, Dennis Hal 1937- AmMWSc 92
**Knight**, Dewey W., Jr. 1930- WhoBlA 92
**Knight**, Donald Branch ScFEYrs
**Knight**, Douglas Allan 1943- WhoRel 92
**Knight**, Douglas Maitland 1921- AmMWSc 92, IntWW 91, WhoFI 92
**Knight**, Douglas Reid 1941- WhoWest 92
**Knight**, Douglas Wayne 1938- AmMWSc 92
**Knight**, Edgar Wallace 1886-1953 DcNCBi 3
**Knight**, Edmund Alan 1919- Who 92
**Knight**, Elizabeth 1870-1933 BiDBrF 2
**Knight**, Eric 1897-1943 BenetAL 91, LiExTwC
**Knight**, Eric Lee 1959- WhoMW 92
**Knight**, Etheridge DrAPF 91
**Knight**, Etheridge d1991 NewYTBS 91
**Knight**, Etheridge 1931- ConPo 91, IntAu&W 91
**Knight**, Etheridge 1931-1991 BlkLC [port], ConAu 133, WhoBlA 92N
**Knight**, Floyd, Jr. 1959- WhoRel 92
**Knight**, Francis Grogan 1914- WhoAmP 91
**Knight**, Frank 1905- IntAu&W 91, WrDr 92
**Knight**, Frank B 1933- AmMWSc 92
**Knight**, Frank W., Jr. 1923- WhoBlA 92
**Knight**, Franklin W. 1942- WhoBlA 92
**Knight**, Fred Barrows 1925- AmMWSc 92
**Knight**, Fred G 1920- AmMWSc 92
**Knight**, Gareth WrDr 92
**Knight**, Geoffrey Cureton 1906- Who 92
**Knight**, Geoffrey Egerton 1921- Who 92
**Knight**, Geoffrey Wilfred 1920- Who 92
**Knight**, George A. F. 1909- WrDr 92
**Knight**, George Litch 1925- WhoRel 92
**Knight**, George R. 1941- WhoRel 92
**Knight**, Gladys 1944- NewAmDM, WhoEnt 92
**Knight**, Gladys Maria 1944- WhoBlA 92
**Knight**, Glenn B AmMWSc 92
**Knight**, Gregory 1949- Who 92
**Knight**, Hardwicke 1911- WrDr 92
**Knight**, Harold 1874-1961 TwCPaSc
**Knight**, Harold 1919- Who 92
**Knight**, Harold Edwin Holm, Jr. 1930- WhoFI 92
**Knight**, Harold Murray 1919- IntWW 91
**Knight**, Harry W. 1909- WhoFI 92
**Knight**, Heather Ann 1944- WhoEnt 92
**Knight**, Henry Cogswell 1789-1835 BenetAL 91
**Knight**, Henry Floyd 1948- WhoRel 92
**Knight**, Herbert Borwell 1928- WhoFI 92
**Knight**, Homer Talcott 1923- AmMWSc 92
**Knight**, J.Z. 1946- RelLAm 91
**Knight**, James Albert, Jr 1920- AmMWSc 92
**Knight**, James Allen 1918- AmMWSc 92, IntAu&W 91, WrDr 92
**Knight**, James Atwood 1954- WhoFI 92
**Knight**, James L. d1991 NewYTBS 91 [port]
**Knight**, James Milton 1933- AmMWSc 92
**Knight**, James William 1948- AmMWSc 92
**Knight**, Jeffrey Lin 1959- WhoAmL 92
**Knight**, Jeffrey Richard 1962- WhoWest 92
**Knight**, Jeffrey Russell 1936- Who 92
**Knight**, Jere Donald 1916- AmMWSc 92
**Knight**, Joan Christabel Jill Who 92
**Knight**, John C 1926- AmMWSc 92
**Knight**, John F., Jr. 1945- WhoBlA 92
**Knight**, John Lowden, Jr. 1915- WhoRel 92
**Knight**, John Paul 1963- WhoWest 92
**Knight**, John S 1895-1981 FacFETw
**Knight**, Jonathan Goodnow 1957- WhoEnt 92
**Knight**, Karl Frederick 1930- WrDr 92
**Knight**, Katherine Lathrop 1941- AmMWSc 92
**Knight**, Kenneth Earl 1964- WhoMW 92
**Knight**, Kenneth Vincent 1944- WhoFI 92
**Knight**, Kit DrAPF 91
**Knight**, Larry V 1935- AmMWSc 92
**Knight**, Laura 1877-1970 TwCPaSc
**Knight**, Leavitt Ashley ScFEYrs
**Knight**, Lee H, Jr 1928- AmMWSc 92
**Knight**, Linda Jean 1942- WhoRel 92
**Knight**, Linda Kay 1948- WhoAmL 92
**Knight**, Lon Bishop, Jr 1944- AmMWSc 92
**Knight**, Luther Augustus, Jr 1930- AmMWSc 92
**Knight**, Lyman Coleman 1915- AmMWSc 92
**Knight**, Lynnon Jacob 1920- WhoBlA 92
**Knight**, M L Mickey 1946- WhoAmP 91
**Knight**, Margery Harlow 1943- WhoAmP 91
**Knight**, Margot Haliday 1953- WhoEnt 92
**Knight**, Martha Irene 1939- WhoEnt 92
**Knight**, Mary Jean Maxson 1944- WhoEnt 92
**Knight**, Merrill D, III 1930- WhoIns 92
**Knight**, Michael 1932- Who 92
**Knight**, Muriel Bernice 1922- WhoBlA 92
**Knight**, Norman 1924- WhoEnt 92
**Knight**, Norman L. 1895-1972 TwCSFW 91
**Knight**, Norman LeRoy 1934- WhoRel 92
**Knight**, Ora Willis 1874-1913 BiInAmS
**Knight**, Patricia Marie 1952- AmMWSc 92
**Knight**, Paul Ford 1960- WhoRel 92
**Knight**, Paul R 1947- AmMWSc 92
**Knight**, Peggy Steed 1929- WhoAmP 91
**Knight**, Perry Vertrum 1928-1987 WhoBlA 92N
**Knight**, Peter Clayton 1947- Who 92
**Knight**, Philip Hampson 1938- WhoFI 92, WhoWest 92
**Knight**, Reo Lindsay 1931- IntWW 91
**Knight**, Richard, Jr. 1945- WhoBlA 92
**Knight**, Richard Carl 1929- WhoFI 92
**Knight**, Richard James 1915- Who 92
**Knight**, Richard Payne 1750-1824 BlkwCEP
**Knight**, Robert 1921- TwCPaSc
**Knight**, Robert Edward 1941- WhoFI 92, WhoMW 92
**Knight**, Robert Huntington 1919- WhoAmL 92
**Knight**, Robert Joseph 1945- WhoEnt 92
**Knight**, Robert Milton 1940- WhoMW 92
**Knight**, Robert Montgomery 1940- WhoMW 92
**Knight**, Robert S. 1929- WhoBlA 92
**Knight**, Robert Vernon 1935- WhoMW 92
**Knight**, Roger John Beckett 1944- Who 92
**Knight**, Sam Lanear 1936- WhoFI 92
**Knight**, Samuel Bradley 1913- AmMWSc 92
**Knight**, Sarah Kemble 1666-1727 BenetAL 91
**Knight**, Shirley 1936- IntMPA 92
**Knight**, Stephen 1938- AmMWSc 92
**Knight**, Stephen 1951-1985 ConAu 34NR
**Knight**, Stillman Depauw, Jr. 1947- WhoFI 92
**Knight**, Thomas A 1933- WhoAmP 91
**Knight**, Thomas J., Jr. 1955- WhoWest 92
**Knight**, Thomas Joseph 1937- WhoWest 92
**Knight**, Tobias d1719 DcNCBi 3
**Knight**, Vernon 1917- AmMWSc 92
**Knight**, Vick, Jr. 1928- WhoWest 92
**Knight**, W. H., Jr. 1954- WhoBlA 92
**Knight**, W. Wilder, II 1955- WhoAmL 92
**Knight**, Wallace E. DrAPF 91
**Knight**, Walter David 1919- AmMWSc 92
**Knight**, Walter R. 1933- WhoBlA 92
**Knight**, Walter Rea 1932- AmMWSc 92
**Knight**, Warburton Richard 1932- Who 92
**Knight**, Wilbur Clinton 1858-1903 BiInAmS
**Knight**, Wilbur Hall 1921- AmMWSc 92, WhoFI 92
**Knight**, William Allen, Jr 1914- AmMWSc 92
**Knight**, William Arnold 1915- Who 92
**Knight**, William Collins, Jr. 1938- WhoAmL 92
**Knight**, William Eric 1920- AmMWSc 92
**Knight**, William Kender 1924- WhoAmP 91
**Knight**, William Nicholas 1939- IntAu&W 91
**Knight**, William Rogers 1945- WhoBlA 92
**Knight**, William Thomas 1937- WhoAmL 92
**Knight**, Wilson Blaine 1955- AmMWSc 92
**Knight-Adkin**, F J ScFEYrs
**Knight-Pulliam**, Keshia 1979- WhoBlA 92
**Knighten**, James Leo 1943- AmMWSc 92
**Knighten**, James M 1938- WhoIns 92
**Knighten**, Robert Lee 1940- AmMWSc 92
**Knightley** Who 92
**Knightley**, Phillip 1929- WrDr 92
**Knightley**, Phillip George 1929- IntAu&W 91
**Knighton**, Jeffrey Holmes 1952- WhoRel 92
**Knighton**, Robert Syron 1914- WhoWest 92
**Knighton**, Wayne DuVont 1948- WhoEnt 92
**Knighton**, William Myles 1931- Who 92
**Knights** Who 92
**Knights**, Baron 1920- Who 92
**Knights**, John Christopher 1947- AmMWSc 92
**Knights**, L. C. 1906- WrDr 92
**Knights**, Lionel Charles 1906- IntAu&W 91, Who 92
**Knights**, Rosemary Margaret 1945- Who 92
**Knights**, Winifred 1899-1947 TwCPaSc
**Knijff**, Henri W. de 1931- WhoRel 92
**Kniker**, Charles Robert 1936- WhoMW 92
**Kniker**, William Theodore 1929- AmMWSc 92
**Knilans**, James Carter 1939- WhoMW 92
**Knilans**, Michael Jerome 1927- WhoFI 92
**Knill**, John Kenelm Stuart 1913- Who 92
**Knill**, John Lawrence 1934- IntWW 91, Who 92
**Knill**, Ronald John 1935- AmMWSc 92
**Knipe**, David Maclay 1932- WhoRel 92
**Knipe**, David Mahan 1950- AmMWSc 92
**Knipe**, Leslie Francis 1913- Who 92
**Knipe**, Richard Hubert 1927- AmMWSc 92
**Knipe**, W. Stan 1935- WhoFI 92
**Knipfel**, Jerry Earl 1941- AmMWSc 92
**Knipling**, Edward Fred 1909- AmMWSc 92, IntWW 91
**Knipmeyer**, Hubert Elmer 1929- AmMWSc 92
**Knipp**, Ernest A 1929- AmMWSc 92
**Knippa**, Gregory Duane 1954- WhoAmP 91
**Knipper**, Lev 1898-1974 NewAmDM

**Knipper-Chekhova,** Ol'ga Leonardovna 1868-1959 *SovUnBD*
**Knipper-Chekhova,** Olga Leonardovna 1870-1959 *FacFETw*
**Knippers,** Ottis Jewell, Jr 1944- *WhoAmP 91*
**Knipping Victoria,** Eladio 1933- *IntWW 91*
**Knipple,** Warren Russell 1934- *AmMWSc 92*
**Knipstein,** Wilbur Martin 1933- *WhoMW 92*
**Knirk,** Frederick George 1935- *WhoWest 92*
**Knirsch,** Hans 1877-1944 *EncTR 91*
**Kniseley,** Richard Newman 1930- *AmMWSc 92*
**Knisely,** Jay Wallace 1947- *WhoFI 92, WhoWest 92*
**Knisely,** William Hagerman 1922- *AmMWSc 92*
**Kniskern,** Joseph Warren 1951- *WhoAmL 92*
**Kniskern,** Verne Burton 1921- *AmMWSc 92*
**Knispel,** Scott Alan 1955- *WhoMW 92*
**Knister,** James A. 1937- *WhoFI 92*
**Knister,** Raymond 1899-1932 *BenetAL 91, RfGEnL 91*
**Knittel,** Marlon George 1952- *WhoMW 92*
**Knittel,** Martin Dean 1932- *AmMWSc 92*
**Knitter,** Paul Francis 1939- *WhoRel 92*
**Knittle,** Peter Joseph 1953- *WhoAmP 91*
**Knittle,** William Joseph, Jr. 1945- *WhoWest 92*
**Knizak,** Milan 1940- *IntWW 91*
**Knize,** Randall James 1953- *AmMWSc 92, WhoWest 92*
**Knobel,** LeRoy Lyle 1945- *AmMWSc 92*
**Knobel,** Ralph J 1933- *WhoAmP 91*
**Knobeloch,** F X Calvin 1925- *AmMWSc 92*
**Knobil,** Ernst 1926- *AmMWSc 92*
**Knoblauch,** David Leslie 1952- *WhoMW 92*
**Knobler,** Carolyn Berk 1934- *AmMWSc 92*
**Knobler,** Charles Martin 1934- *AmMWSc 92*
**Knobler,** Robert Leonard 1948- *AmMWSc 92*
**Knobloch,** Edgar 1953- *AmMWSc 92*
**Knobloch,** Hilda 1915- *AmMWSc 92*
**Knobloch,** Irving William 1907- *AmMWSc 92*
**Knobloch,** James Otis 1920- *AmMWSc 92*
**Knoblock,** Edward 1874-1945 *ScFEYrs*
**Knoblock,** Edward C 1920- *AmMWSc 92*
**Knoch,** Adolph Ernst 1874-1965 *RelLAm 91*
**Knoche,** Herman William 1934- *AmMWSc 92*
**Knochen,** Helmut 1910- *EncTR 91*
**Knock,** Gary Howard 1936- *WhoMW 92*
**Knockemus,** Ward Wilbur 1934- *AmMWSc 92*
**Knodel,** Elinor Livingston *AmMWSc 92*
**Knodel,** Raymond Willard 1932- *AmMWSc 92*
**Knodell,** Clayton William 1927- *WhoFI 92*
**Knodell,** Robert James 1932- *WhoMW 92*
**Knoderer,** Gabrielle Marie 1961- *WhoFI 92*
**Knodt,** Cloy Bernard 1917- *AmMWSc 92*
**Knoebel,** Leon Kenneth 1927- *AmMWSc 92*
**Knoebel,** Suzanne Buckner 1926- *AmMWSc 92*
**Knoechel,** Edwin Lewis 1931- *AmMWSc 92*
**Knoedler,** Elmer L 1912- *AmMWSc 92*
**Knoefel,** Peter Klerner 1906- *AmMWSc 92*
**Knoepfle,** John *DrAPF 91*
**Knoepfle,** John 1923- *ConPo 91, SmATA 66 [port], WrDr 92*
**Knoepfler,** Nestor B 1918- *AmMWSc 92*
**Knoepfler,** Peter Tamas 1929- *WhoWest 92*
**Knoernschild,** Eric Martin 1948- *WhoAmL 92*
**Knoerr,** Kenneth Richard 1927- *AmMWSc 92*
**Knoke,** James Dean 1941- *AmMWSc 92*
**Knoke,** John Keith 1930- *AmMWSc 92*
**Knoll,** Alan Howard 1951- *AmMWSc 92*
**Knoll,** Andrew Herbert 1951- *AmMWSc 92*
**Knoll,** Catherine Baker *WhoAmP 91*
**Knoll,** Erwin 1931- *IntAu&W 91*
**Knoll,** Florence Schust 1917- *DcTwDes*
**Knoll,** Franklin Jude 1940- *WhoAmP 91*
**Knoll,** Glenn F 1935- *AmMWSc 92*
**Knoll,** Glenn Frederick 1935- *WhoMW 92*
**Knoll,** Hans 1914-1955 *DcTwDes*
**Knoll,** Henry Albert 1922- *AmMWSc 92*
**Knoll,** Jack 1924- *AmMWSc 92*
**Knoll,** Jacob Egmont 1919- *IntWW 91*
**Knoll,** Jozsef 1925- *IntWW 91*
**Knoll,** Kenneth Mark 1941- *AmMWSc 92*
**Knoll,** Kristine Marie 1947- *WhoMW 92*
**Knoll,** Michael Steven 1957- *WhoFI 92*
**Knoll,** Milena Seborova 1916- *WhoEnt 92*
**Knollenberg,** Robert George 1939- *AmMWSc 92*
**Knollman,** Gilbert Carl 1928- *AmMWSc 92*
**Knollmeyer,** Michael J. 1962- *WhoAmL 92*
**Knollmueller,** Karl Otto 1931- *AmMWSc 92*
**Knollys** *Who 92*
**Knollys,** Viscount 1931- *Who 92*
**Knollys,** Eardley 1902- *TwCPaSc*
**Knop,** Charles M 1931- *AmMWSc 92*
**Knop,** Charles Philip 1927- *AmMWSc 92*
**Knop,** Edward Charles 1940- *WhoWest 92*
**Knop,** Harry William, Jr 1920- *AmMWSc 92*
**Knop,** Osvald 1922- *AmMWSc 92*
**Knopf,** Alfred, Jr. 1918- *IntWW 91*
**Knopf,** Alfred A. 1892-1984 *BenetAL 91, FacFETw*
**Knopf,** Barry Abraham 1946- *WhoAmL 92*
**Knopf,** Daniel Peter 1916- *AmMWSc 92*
**Knopf,** Fritz L 1945- *AmMWSc 92*
**Knopf,** Paul M 1936- *AmMWSc 92*
**Knopf,** Ralph Fred 1926- *AmMWSc 92*
**Knopf,** Robert John 1932- *AmMWSc 92*
**Knopf,** Terry Ann *WrDr 92*
**Knopfler,** Mark 1949- *WhoEnt 92*
**Knopick,** Paul E. 1948- *WhoMW 92*
**Knopka,** W N 1938- *AmMWSc 92*
**Knopoff,** Leon 1925- *AmMWSc 92, IntWW 91*
**Knopow,** Gary Alan 1947- *WhoFI 92*
**Knopp,** Alex Andrew 1947- *WhoAmP 91*
**Knopp,** James A 1940- *AmMWSc 92*
**Knopp,** Joe *WhoAmP 91*
**Knopp,** Marvin Isadore 1933- *AmMWSc 92*
**Knopp,** Robert H *AmMWSc 92*
**Knopp,** Walter 1922- *AmMWSc 92*
**Knoppers,** Antonie Theodoor 1915- *AmMWSc 92*
**Knorek,** Lee J 1921- *WhoAmP 91*
**Knorpel,** Henry 1924- *Who 92*
**Knorr,** Dietrich W 1944- *AmMWSc 92*
**Knorr,** Donald 1922- *DcTwDes*
**Knorr,** George E 1929- *AmMWSc 92*
**Knorr,** John Christian 1921- *WhoEnt 92, WhoMW 92*
**Knorr,** K. E. *ConAu 134*
**Knorr,** Klaus *ConAu 134*
**Knorr,** Klaus 1911- *WrDr 92*
**Knorr,** Klaus E. 1911-1990 *ConAu 134*
**Knorr,** Philip Noel 1916- *AmMWSc 92*
**Knorr,** Thomas George 1932- *AmMWSc 92*
**Knorre,** Dmitri Georgievich 1926- *IntWW 91*
**Knorst,** Judith Irene *WhoMW 92*
**Knospe,** William H 1929- *AmMWSc 92*
**Knot,** Alvan Paul 1949- *WhoAmL 92*
**Knotek,** Ivan 1936- *IntWW 91*
**Knotek,** Michael Louis 1943- *AmMWSc 92*
**Knoth,** Walter Henry, Jr 1930- *AmMWSc 92*
**Knott,** Albert Paul, Jr. 1935- *WhoBlA 92*
**Knott,** Bill *IntAu&W 91X, TwCWW 91, WrDr 92*
**Knott,** Bill 1940- *ConPo 91, IntAu&W 91, WrDr 92*
**Knott,** Carol Rede 1930- *WhoMW 92*
**Knott,** Donald Macmillan 1919- *AmMWSc 92*
**Knott,** Douglas Ronald 1927- *AmMWSc 92*
**Knott,** Elizabeth B. 1927- *WhoRel 92*
**Knott,** Esther Ramharacksingh 1959- *WhoRel 92*
**Knott,** Frank C. 1942- *WhoWest 92*
**Knott,** Fred Nelson 1933- *AmMWSc 92*
**Knott,** George 1893-1969 *TwCPaSc*
**Knott,** Herbert Frederick John Charles 1942- *WhoFI 92*
**Knott,** James Harry, III 1955- *WhoEnt 92*
**Knott,** John Frederick 1938- *Who 92*
**Knott,** John Laurence 1910- *Who 92*
**Knott,** John Ray, Jr. 1937- *WhoMW 92*
**Knott,** John Russell 1911- *AmMWSc 92*
**Knott,** Joseph F. d1991 *NewYTBS 91*
**Knott,** Mable Marguerite *WhoBlA 92*
**Knott,** Robert Edgar, Jr. 1947- *WhoMW 92*
**Knott,** Ronald George 1917- *Who 92*
**Knott,** Wiley Eugene 1938- *WhoFI 92, WhoWest 92*
**Knott,** Will C *IntAu&W 91X*
**Knott,** Will C. 1927- *TwCWW 91*
**Knott,** William Alan 1942- *WhoWest 92*
**Knott,** William C. 1927- *WrDr 92*
**Knott,** William Cecil, Jr 1927- *IntAu&W 91*
**Knotts,** Don 1924- *IntMPA 92, WhoEnt 92*
**Knous,** Ted R 1949- *AmMWSc 92*
**Knouse,** Charles Allison 1921- *WhoMW 92*
**Knouse,** Richard Edmund 1948- *WhoFI 92*
**Knowdell,** Richard Leon 1934- *WhoWest 92*
**Knowelden,** John 1919- *Who 92*
**Knowland,** Denis 1918-1985 *TwCPaSc*
**Knowland,** Raymond Reginald 1930- *Who 92*
**Knowler,** Lloyd A 1908- *AmMWSc 92*
**Knowles,** Aileen Foung 1942- *AmMWSc 92*
**Knowles,** Alison *DrAPF 91*
**Knowles,** Ann *Who 92*
**Knowles,** Barbara B 1937- *AmMWSc 92*
**Knowles,** Carrie J. *DrAPF 91*
**Knowles,** Cecil Martin 1918- *AmMWSc 92*
**Knowles,** Charles 1951- *Who 92*
**Knowles,** Charles Ernest 1937- *AmMWSc 92*
**Knowles,** Charles Otis 1938- *AmMWSc 92*
**Knowles,** Charles Timothy 1949- *WhoAmP 91*
**Knowles,** Christopher G 1943- *WhoIns 92*
**Knowles,** Colin George 1939- *Who 92*
**Knowles,** David *WhoAmP 91*
**Knowles,** David L. *WhoWest 92*
**Knowles,** David M 1927- *AmMWSc 92*
**Knowles,** Dorothy 1906- *WrDr 92*
**Knowles,** Eddie 1946- *WhoBlA 92*
**Knowles,** Em Claire 1952- *WhoBlA 92*
**Knowles,** Emmitt Clifton 1951- *WhoAmL 92*
**Knowles,** Francis Charles 1941- *AmMWSc 92*
**Knowles,** George Peter 1919- *Who 92*
**Knowles,** Harold Loraine 1905- *AmMWSc 92*
**Knowles,** Harrold B 1925- *AmMWSc 92*
**Knowles,** James Kenyon 1931- *AmMWSc 92, WhoWest 92*
**Knowles,** James Sheridan 1784-1862 *RfGEnL 91*
**Knowles,** Jeremy Randall 1935- *AmMWSc 92, IntWW 91, Who 92*
**Knowles,** John *DrAPF 91*
**Knowles,** John 1926- *BenetAL 91, ConNov 91, WrDr 92*
**Knowles,** John Appleton, III 1935- *AmMWSc 92*
**Knowles,** John Warwick 1920- *AmMWSc 92*
**Knowles,** Justin 1935- *TwCPaSc*
**Knowles,** Kevin G *WhoAmP 91*
**Knowles,** Lawrence John 1953- *WhoEnt 92*
**Knowles,** Leonard Joseph 1916- *Who 92*
**Knowles,** Malachi 1941- *WhoBlA 92*
**Knowles,** Michael 1942- *Who 92*
**Knowles,** Michael Ernest 1942- *Who 92*
**Knowles,** Patric 1911- *IntMPA 92*
**Knowles,** Patricia Ann 1944- *Who 92*
**Knowles,** Paulden Ford 1916- *AmMWSc 92*
**Knowles,** Peter Francis Arnold 1949- *Who 92*
**Knowles,** Richard 1917- *Who 92*
**Knowles,** Richard James Robert 1943- *AmMWSc 92*
**Knowles,** Richard N 1935- *AmMWSc 92*
**Knowles,** Richard T 1916- *WhoAmP 91*
**Knowles,** Robert Levis 1925- *WhoEnt 92*
**Knowles,** Roger 1929- *AmMWSc 92*
**Knowles,** Stanley Howard 1908- *IntWW 91*
**Knowles,** Stephen H 1940- *AmMWSc 92*
**Knowles,** Susanne 1911- *WrDr 92*
**Knowles,** Timothy 1938- *Who 92*
**Knowles,** Tony 1943- *WhoAmP 91*
**Knowles,** Warren P 1908- *WhoAmP 91*
**Knowles,** William E 1927- *WhoIns 92*
**Knowles,** William Leroy 1935- *WhoEnt 92*
**Knowles,** William W. 1941- *WhoBlA 92*
**Knowles,** Wyn 1923- *Who 92*
**Knowlton,** Carroll Babbidge, Jr 1926- *AmMWSc 92*
**Knowlton,** Clark S. 1919- *WhoWest 92*
**Knowlton,** David A 1938- *AmMWSc 92*
**Knowlton,** Derrick 1921- *IntAu&W 91, WrDr 92*
**Knowlton,** E Ute 1933- *WhoAmP 91*
**Knowlton,** Edgar Colby, Jr 1921- *IntAu&W 91*
**Knowlton,** Floyd M 1918- *AmMWSc 92*
**Knowlton,** Franklin W 1922- *WhoAmP 91*
**Knowlton,** Frederick Frank 1934- *AmMWSc 92*
**Knowlton,** George Franklin 1901- *AmMWSc 92*
**Knowlton,** Gregory Dean 1946- *AmMWSc 92*
**Knowlton,** Marie 1936- *WhoMW 92*
**Knowlton,** Nancy 1949- *AmMWSc 92*
**Knowlton,** Richard James 1928- *Who 92*
**Knowlton,** Richard L. 1932- *IntWW 91*
**Knowlton,** Robert Charles 1929- *AmMWSc 92*
**Knowlton,** Robert Earle 1939- *AmMWSc 92*
**Knox** *Who 92*
**Knox,** Alexander 1907- *IntMPA 92*
**Knox,** Alexander David 1925- *Who 92*
**Knox,** Alison Douglas 1933- *WhoAmL 92*
**Knox,** Andrew 1733?-1776 *DcNCBi 3*
**Knox,** Andrew Gibson 1923- *WhoAmP 91*
**Knox,** Angela Flynn 1940- *WhoEnt 92*
**Knox,** Ann B. *DrAPF 91*
**Knox,** Ann Louise 1935- *WhoRel 92*
**Knox,** Annie Bell 1894- *WhoBlA 92*
**Knox,** Arthur Lloyd 1932- *WhoAmP 91, WhoMW 92*
**Knox,** Arthur Stewart 1903- *AmMWSc 92*
**Knox,** Bernard MacGregor Walker 1914- *WrDr 92*
**Knox,** Bill *IntAu&W 91X, WrDr 92*
**Knox,** Bruce E 1931- *AmMWSc 92*
**Knox,** Bryce 1916- *Who 92*
**Knox,** Bryce Harry 1929- *Who 92*
**Knox,** Burnal Ray 1931- *AmMWSc 92*
**Knox,** Calvin *WrDr 92*
**Knox,** Calvin M. *ConAu 36NR, TwCSFW 91*
**Knox,** Carl Bradford, Jr. 1931- *WhoWest 92*
**Knox,** Carol Ruth 1938- *WhoRel 92*
**Knox,** Caroline *DrAPF 91*
**Knox,** Charles Kenneth 1938- *AmMWSc 92*
**Knox,** Charles Robert 1932- *WhoWest 92*
**Knox,** David *Who 92*
**Knox,** David Broughton 1916- *WrDr 92*
**Knox,** David Laidlaw 1933- *Who 92*
**Knox,** David Lalonde 1930- *AmMWSc 92*
**Knox,** Dick 1936- *WhoAmP 91*
**Knox,** Elizabeth 1959- *ConNov 91*
**Knox,** Ellis Gilbert 1928- *AmMWSc 92*
**Knox,** Francis Stratton, III 1941- *AmMWSc 92*
**Knox,** Franklin G 1937- *AmMWSc 92*
**Knox,** Gaylord Shearer 1923- *AmMWSc 92*
**Knox,** George F. 1943- *WhoBlA 92*
**Knox,** George L., III 1943- *WhoBlA 92*
**Knox,** George Levi, III 1943- *WhoFI 92*
**Knox,** George William 1853-1912 *RelLAm 91*
**Knox,** Gordon *IntMPA 92, WhoEnt 92*
**Knox,** Gordon, Jr 1943- *WhoAmP 91*
**Knox,** Henry 1750-1806 *AmPolLe [port], BlkwEAR*
**Knox,** Henry Macdonald 1916- *Who 92, WrDr 92*
**Knox,** Jack Rowles 1929- *AmMWSc 92*
**Knox,** James *DrAPF 91*
**Knox,** James Clarence 1941- *AmMWSc 92*
**Knox,** James Edwin 1937- *WhoAmL 92, WhoMW 92*
**Knox,** James L 1919- *AmMWSc 92*
**Knox,** James Lloyd 1929- *WhoRel 92*
**Knox,** James Marshall 1944- *WhoMW 92*
**Knox,** James Russell, Jr 1941- *AmMWSc 92*
**Knox,** Jean M. *Who 92*
**Knox,** John 1913- *Who 92*
**Knox,** John 1936- *Who 92*
**Knox,** John Andrew 1937- *Who 92*
**Knox,** John Henderson 1927- *Who 92*
**Knox,** John Leonard 1925- *Who 92*
**Knox,** John MacMurray 1946- *AmMWSc 92*
**Knox,** Jon Bruce 1939- *WhoMW 92*
**Knox,** Kenneth L 1920- *AmMWSc 92*
**Knox,** Kerro 1924- *AmMWSc 92*
**Knox,** Kerro, III 1957- *WhoEnt 92*
**Knox,** Kevin Bradford 1957- *WhoWest 92*
**Knox,** Kirvin L 1936- *AmMWSc 92*
**Knox,** Larry William 1942- *AmMWSc 92*
**Knox,** Laura Leigh 1961- *WhoAmL 92*
**Knox,** Linda Marie 1959- *WhoMW 92*
**Knox,** Philander Chase 1853-1921 *AmPolLe*
**Knox,** Randall Shaw 1949- *WhoAmP 91*
**Knox,** Ray 1926- *IntAu&W 91*
**Knox,** Richard Evert 1917- *WhoRel 92*
**Knox,** Robert 1904- *Who 92*
**Knox,** Robert Arthur 1943- *AmMWSc 92*
**Knox,** Robert Buick 1918- *WrDr 92*
**Knox,** Robert Burns 1917- *WhoRel 92*
**Knox,** Robert Gaylord 1956- *AmMWSc 92*
**Knox,** Robert Seiple 1931- *AmMWSc 92*
**Knox,** Ronald Arbuthnott 1888-1957 *ScFEYrs*
**Knox,** Samuel 1756-1832 *BenetAL 91*
**Knox,** Stanley 1940- *WhoBlA 92*
**Knox,** Susan Marie 1941- *WhoMW 92*
**Knox,** Thomas W. 1835-1896 *BenetAL 91*
**Knox,** Vincent Lawrence 1962- *WhoMW 92*
**Knox,** Walter Robert 1926- *AmMWSc 92*
**Knox,** Wayne D. P. 1947- *WhoBlA 92*
**Knox,** Wayne N 1927- *WhoAmP 91*
**Knox,** Wilbur Benjamin 1912- *WhoBlA 92*
**Knox,** William 1732-1810 *BlkwEAR*
**Knox,** William 1928- *IntAu&W 91, WrDr 92*
**Knox,** William Alexander 1907- *WhoEnt 92*
**Knox,** William Edward 1927- *Who 92*
**Knox,** William Franklin 1874-1944 *AmPolLe*
**Knox,** William Jordan 1921- *AmMWSc 92*
**Knox,** William Robert 1951- *WhoBlA 92*
**Knox-Benton,** Shirley 1937- *WhoBlA 92*
**Knox-Johnston,** Robin 1939- *IntAu&W 91, Who 92, WrDr 92*
**Knox-Lecky,** Samuel 1926- *Who 92*

**Knox-Mawer,** June Ellis 1930- *IntAu&W 91*
**Knox-Mawer,** Ronald 1925- *IntAu&W 91, Who 92*
**Knubel,** Frederick Herman 1870-1945 *RelLAm 91*
**Knuckles,** Joseph Lewis 1924- *AmMWSc 92*
**Knuckles,** Kenneth J. *WhoBlA 92*
**Knudsen,** Betty Ann 1926- *WhoAmP 91*
**Knudsen,** Conrad Calvert 1923- *IntWW 91, WhoFI 92*
**Knudsen,** Dennis Ralph 1943- *AmMWSc 92*
**Knudsen,** Eric Ingvald 1949- *AmMWSc 92, WhoWest 92*
**Knudsen,** Estelle Christine Hagen 1924- *WhoMW 92*
**Knudsen,** Harold Knud 1936- *AmMWSc 92*
**Knudsen,** J G 1920- *AmMWSc 92*
**Knudsen,** John R 1916- *AmMWSc 92*
**Knudsen,** Karen Ann 1943- *AmMWSc 92*
**Knudsen,** Kerry Lynde 1952- *WhoMW 92*
**Knudsen,** Margrethe June 1934- *WrDr 92*
**Knudsen,** Raymond Barnett 1919- *WhoRel 92*
**Knudsen,** Raymond Barnett, II 1941- *WhoRel 92*
**Knudsen,** Richard Carl *AmMWSc 92*
**Knudsen,** Semon Emil 1912- *IntWW 91, Who 92*
**Knudsen,** William Claire 1925- *AmMWSc 92*
**Knudsen,** William Signius 1879-1948 *AmPolLe*
**Knudslien,** Dewey Victor 1929- *IntAu&W 91*
**Knudson,** Albert Cornelius 1873-1953 *RelLAm 91*
**Knudson,** Alfred George, Jr 1922- *AmMWSc 92*
**Knudson,** Alvin Richard 1934- *AmMWSc 92*
**Knudson,** Danny Alan 1940- *WrDr 92*
**Knudson,** David Stewart 1941- *WhoAmP 91*
**Knudson,** Douglas Marvin 1936- *AmMWSc 92*
**Knudson,** Gregory Blair 1946- *AmMWSc 92, WhoWest 92*
**Knudson,** Kenneth 1927- *WhoAmP 91*
**Knudson,** Knute, Jr 1949- *WhoAmP 91*
**Knudson,** Melvin Robert 1917- *WhoWest 92*
**Knudson,** R.R. *ConAu 35NR*
**Knudson,** R R 1932- *IntAu&W 91, WrDr 92*
**Knudson,** Ronald Joel 1932- *AmMWSc 92*
**Knudson,** Rozanne 1932- *ConAu 35NR*
**Knudson,** Vernie Anton 1932- *AmMWSc 92*
**Knudson,** Warren 1953- *WhoMW 92*
**Knudtson,** John Thomas 1945- *AmMWSc 92*
**Knue,** Paul Frederick 1947- *WhoMW 92*
**Knuepfer,** Robert Claude, Jr. 1952- *WhoAmL 92*
**Knull,** Erhard 1929- *WhoMW 92, WhoRel 92*
**Knull,** Harvey Robert 1941- *AmMWSc 92*
**Knull,** Susan Beth 1962- *WhoMW 92*
**Knunyants,** Ivan Lyudvigovich 1906- *SovUnBD*
**Knup,** Stephen Charles 1942- *WhoFI 92*
**Knupp,** Larry Sheldon 1940- *WhoAmL 92*
**Knupp,** Patrick Michael 1953- *WhoWest 92*
**Knuppel,** William Harold 1939- *WhoAmP 91*
**Knussen,** Oliver 1952- *ConCom 92, IntWW 91, NewAmDM, Who 92*
**Knussmann,** Willard Theodore 1942- *WhoWest 92*
**Knust,** Chris R. 1962- *WhoMW 92*
**Knuteson,** Harold Douglas 1953- *WhoWest 92*
**Knuteson,** Miles Gene 1952- *WhoEnt 92, WhoMW 92*
**Knuth,** Adrian Terrence 1950- *WhoAmL 92*
**Knuth,** Daniel J *WhoAmP 91*
**Knuth,** Donald Ervin 1938- *AmMWSc 92, IntWW 91*
**Knuth,** Eldon L 1925- *AmMWSc 92*
**Knuth-Winterfeldt,** Kield Gustav 1908- *IntWW 91*
**Knuths,** Shalmerdean Ann 1938- *WhoMW 92*
**Knuths,** William Ronald 1955- *WhoFI 92*
**Knuti,** Paul August 1941- *WhoMW 92*
**Knutsford,** Viscount 1926- *Who 92*
**Knutson,** Byron *WhoAmP 91*
**Knutson,** Carroll Field 1924- *AmMWSc 92*
**Knutson,** Charles Dwaine 1934- *AmMWSc 92*
**Knutson,** Clarence Arthur, Jr 1937- *AmMWSc 92*
**Knutson,** David Harry 1934- *WhoAmL 92*
**Knutson,** David Lee 1959- *WhoAmL 92*
**Knutson,** David W 1941- *AmMWSc 92*
**Knutson,** Gerhard I. *WhoRel 92*
**Knutson,** Howard Arthur 1929- *WhoAmP 91, WhoMW 92*
**Knutson,** James Lawrence 1952- *WhoMW 92*
**Knutson,** John A 1940- *WhoIns 92*
**Knutson,** Kenneth Wayne 1932- *AmMWSc 92*
**Knutson,** Knute B 1909- *WhoAmP 91*
**Knutson,** Lanny Dean 1943- *WhoRel 92*
**Knutson,** Lloyd Vernon 1934- *AmMWSc 92*
**Knutson,** Lynn D 1946- *AmMWSc 92*
**Knutson,** Nancy Roxbury *DrAPF 91*
**Knutson,** Orville Kenneth 1922- *WhoAmP 91*
**Knutson,** Roger M 1933- *AmMWSc 92*
**Knutson,** Ronald Dale 1940- *WhoAmP 91*
**Knutson,** Ronald Gene 1934- *WhoMW 92*
**Knutson,** Sidney R 1915- *WhoAmP 91*
**Knutson,** Victoria P *AmMWSc 92*
**Knuttgen,** Howard G 1931- *AmMWSc 92*
**Knutton,** Harry 1921- *Who 92*
**Knutzen,** Raymond Edward 1941- *WhoAmL 92*
**Knyazyuk,** Mikhail Aleksandrovich *IntWW 91*
**Knych,** Edward Thomas 1942- *AmMWSc 92*
**Knycha,** Josef 1953- *WhoWest 92*
**Knye,** Cassandra *ConAu 36NR, IntAu&W 91X, WrDr 92*
**Knystautas,** Emile J *AmMWSc 92*
**Ko,** Allen Hiu-Ching 1953- *WhoWest 92*
**Ko,** Che Ming 1943- *AmMWSc 92*
**Ko,** Chien-Ping 1948- *AmMWSc 92*
**Ko,** Edmond Inq-Ming 1952- *AmMWSc 92*
**Ko,** Frank K 1947- *AmMWSc 92*
**Ko,** H C 1928- *AmMWSc 92*
**Ko,** Hon-Chung 1937- *AmMWSc 92*
**Ko,** Hon-Yim 1940- *AmMWSc 92*
**Ko,** Li-wen 1949- *AmMWSc 92*
**Ko,** Moses 1948- *WhoMW 92*
**Ko,** Pak Lim 1937- *AmMWSc 92*
**Ko,** Seung Kyun 1936- *WhoWest 92*
**Ko,** Wen Hsiung 1923- *AmMWSc 92, WhoMW 92*
**Ko,** Wen-hsiung 1939- *AmMWSc 92*
**Ko,** Winston Tai-Kan 1943- *AmMWSc 92*
**Ko,** Won *DrAPF 91*
**Kobak,** Alfred Julian, Jr. 1935- *WhoMW 92*
**Kobak,** James Benedict, Jr. 1944- *WhoAmL 92*
**Kobak,** Sharon Torreano 1943- *WhoMW 92*
**Kobal,** John d1991 *NewYTBS 91*
**Kobal,** John 1943?-1991 *ConAu 135*
**Kobal,** Ty S. 1955- *WhoWest 92*
**Koballa,** Thomas Raymond, Jr 1954- *AmMWSc 92*
**Kobata,** Akira 1933- *AmMWSc 92*
**Kobayashi,** Albert S 1924- *AmMWSc 92*
**Kobayashi,** Ann 1937- *WhoAmP 91*
**Kobayashi,** Atsumoto 1934- *WhoFI 92*
**Kobayashi,** Bertrand 1944- *WhoAmP 91*
**Kobayashi,** Chris *DrAPF 91*
**Kobayashi,** F M 1925- *AmMWSc 92*
**Kobayashi,** George S 1927- *AmMWSc 92*
**Kobayashi,** Hisashi 1938- *AmMWSc 92*
**Kobayashi,** Kazumi 1952- *AmMWSc 92*
**Kobayashi,** Koji 1907- *ConAu 133*
**Kobayashi,** Masaki 1916- *IntDcF 2-2, IntMPA 92*
**Kobayashi,** Nobuhisa 1950- *AmMWSc 92*
**Kobayashi,** Riki 1924- *AmMWSc 92*
**Kobayashi,** Roger Hideo 1947- *AmMWSc 92*
**Kobayashi,** Shiro 1924- *AmMWSc 92*
**Kobayashi,** Shoshichi 1932- *AmMWSc 92*
**Kobayashi,** Susumu 1939- *WhoFI 92*
**Kobayashi,** Taiyu 1912- *IntWW 91*
**Kobayashi,** Tom Toru *WhoEnt 92*
**Kobayashi,** Yutaka 1924- *AmMWSc 92*
**Kobben,** Andre J. F. 1925- *IntWW 91*
**Kobe,** Donald Holm 1934- *AmMWSc 92*
**Kober,** Albert Richard 1938- *WhoIns 92*
**Kober,** Arletta Refshauge 1919- *WhoMW 92*
**Kober,** Arthur 1900-1975 *BenetAL 91*
**Kober,** C L 1913- *AmMWSc 92*
**Kober,** Dieter 1920- *WhoMW 92*
**Kober,** Philip Mason 1952- *WhoMW 92*
**Kobernick,** Sidney D 1919- *AmMWSc 92*
**Koberstein,** Jeffrey Thomas 1952- *AmMWSc 92*
**Kobert,** Norman 1929- *WhoFI 92*
**Kobilinsky,** Lawrence 1946- *AmMWSc 92*
**Kobiske,** Ronald Albert 1938- *AmMWSc 92*
**Koblasa,** Georg Jan 1933- *WhoEnt 92*
**Koblentz,** Richard Steven 1950- *WhoAmL 92*
**Koblenz,** Michael Robert 1948- *WhoAmL 92, WhoFI 92*
**Kobler,** Frank Joseph 1915- *WhoMW 92*
**Kobler,** Linda *WhoEnt 92*
**Koblick,** Daniel Cecil 1922- *AmMWSc 92*
**Koblick,** Ian 1939- *AmMWSc 92*
**Koblin,** Donald Daryl 1949- *WhoWest 92*
**Koblin,** Ronald Lee 1946- *WhoWest 92*
**Koblinsky,** Chester John 1948- *AmMWSc 92*
**Koblitz,** Michael Jay 1949- *WhoFI 92*
**Kobluk,** David Ronald 1949- *AmMWSc 92*
**Kobrin,** Robert Jay 1937- *AmMWSc 92*
**Kobrin,** Tannis Claire 1953- *WhoEnt 92*
**Kobrine,** Arthur 1943- *AmMWSc 92*
**Kobritz,** Richard 1941- *WhoWest 92*
**Kobs,** Jeffrey Huffman 1959- *WhoAmL 92*
**Kobsa,** Henry 1929- *AmMWSc 92*
**Koburger,** John Alfred 1931- *AmMWSc 92*
**Kobus,** Richard Lawrence 1952- *WhoFI 92*
**Kobylarczyk,** Marguerite 1940- *WhoAmP 91*
**Kobylarz,** Brian Fred 1956- *WhoEnt 92*
**Kobylnyk,** Ronald William 1942- *AmMWSc 92*
**Kobza,** Dennis Jerome 1933- *WhoWest 92*
**Kobzarev,** Yuriy Borisovich 1905- *IntWW 91*
**Koc,** Vehbi 1901- *IntWW 91*
**Koca,** Lyle Edward 1964- *WhoMW 92*
**Kocaoglu,** Dundar F 1939- *AmMWSc 92, WhoFI 92, WhoWest 92*
**Kocatas,** Babur M 1927- *AmMWSc 92*
**Kocen,** JoAnn 1938- *WhoFI 92*
**Kocer,** Albert J 1930- *WhoAmP 91*
**Koch,** Alan R 1930- *AmMWSc 92*
**Koch,** Albert Acheson 1942- *WhoFI 92, WhoMW 92*
**Koch,** Arnold Theodore, Jr 1930- *WhoAmP 91, WhoFI 92*
**Koch,** Arthur Louis 1925- *AmMWSc 92*
**Koch,** Bruno Alfons 1929- *WhoEnt 92*
**Koch,** C. J. 1932- *ConNov 91, WrDr 92*
**Koch,** Carl Conrad 1937- *AmMWSc 92*
**Koch,** Carl Fred 1932- *AmMWSc 92*
**Koch,** Carl G. 1931- *WhoFI 92*
**Koch,** Carl Mark 1944- *AmMWSc 92*
**Koch,** Carole Jackson 1951- *WhoMW 92*
**Koch,** Charles de Ganahl 1935- *WhoFI 92, WhoMW 92*
**Koch,** Charles Frederick 1932- *AmMWSc 92*
**Koch,** Charles Rudolph Edward 1844-1916 *BiInAmS*
**Koch,** Christian Burdick 1922- *AmMWSc 92*
**Koch,** Christopher John 1932- *IntAu&W 91*
**Koch,** Claude *DrAPF 91*
**Koch,** David Alan 1961- *WhoEnt 92*
**Koch,** David Gilbert 1945- *AmMWSc 92*
**Koch,** David William 1942- *AmMWSc 92*
**Koch,** Diane Ruth 1956- *WhoMW 92*
**Koch,** Dietrich-Alex Gerhard 1942- *WhoRel 92*
**Koch,** Donald Leroy 1937- *AmMWSc 92*
**Koch,** Edna Mae 1951- *WhoAmL 92*
**Koch,** Edward I. 1924- *IntWW 91, WrDr 92*
**Koch,** Edward Irving 1924- *Who 92, WhoAmP 91*
**Koch,** Edward Richard 1953- *WhoAmL 92, WhoFI 92*
**Koch,** Elizabeth Anne 1936- *AmMWSc 92*
**Koch,** Elizabeth Carolyn 1961- *WhoAmL 92*
**Koch,** Erich 1896- *EncTR 91 [port]*
**Koch,** Erich 1896-1986 *BiDExR*
**Koch,** Frederick Bayard 1935- *AmMWSc 92*
**Koch,** Frederick Henry 1877-1944 *DcNCBi 3, FacFETw*
**Koch,** Gary Marlin 1941- *AmMWSc 92*
**Koch,** George Schneider, Jr 1926- *AmMWSc 92*
**Koch,** Gerald D 1924- *WhoAmP 91*
**Koch,** Gerald Douglas 1943- *WhoWest 92*
**Koch,** Gerald Lynn 1940- *WhoWest 92*
**Koch,** Glen Jay 1957- *WhoAmL 92*
**Koch,** Glenn A. 1929- *WhoRel 92*
**Koch,** Glenn Alan 1932- *WhoRel 92*
**Koch,** Harold D *WhoAmP 91*
**Koch,** Heinrich Hermann Robert 1843-1910 *WhoNob 90*
**Koch,** Heinz Frank 1932- *AmMWSc 92*
**Koch,** Helen Alice 1916- *WhoEnt 92*
**Koch,** Helmut 1908-1975 *NewAmDM*
**Koch,** Henry George 1948- *AmMWSc 92*
**Koch,** Herman William 1920- *AmMWSc 92*
**Koch,** Howard 1902- *IntMPA 92*
**Koch,** Howard A 1922- *AmMWSc 92*
**Koch,** Howard W. 1916- *IntMPA 92*
**Koch,** Howard W., Jr. 1945- *IntMPA 92, WhoEnt 92A*
**Koch,** Howard Winchel 1916- *WhoEnt 92*
**Koch,** Ilse 1906-1967 *EncTR 91 [port]*
**Koch,** Imelda 1927- *WhoRel 92*
**Koch,** J Frederick 1937- *AmMWSc 92*
**Koch,** James Verch 1942- *WhoWest 92*
**Koch,** Joanne 1929- *IntMPA 92, WhoEnt 92*
**Koch,** Joanne Barbara 1941- *IntAu&W 91*
**Koch,** Karl William 1933- *WhoRel 92*
**Koch,** Kathleen Day 1948- *WhoAmL 92*
**Koch,** Kay Frances 1936- *AmMWSc 92*
**Koch,** Kenneth *DrAPF 91*
**Koch,** Kenneth 1925- *BenetAL 91, ConAu 36NR, ConPo 91, IntAu&W 91, SmATA 65 [port], WrDr 92*
**Koch,** Kenneth Hobson 1955- *WhoFI 92*
**Koch,** Kevin A. 1958- *WhoRel 92, WhoWest 92*
**Koch,** Leonard John 1920- *AmMWSc 92*
**Koch,** Melvin Vernon 1940- *AmMWSc 92*
**Koch,** Mogens 1898- *DcTwDes*
**Koch,** Norman Edward 1934- *WhoWest 92*
**Koch,** Peter 1920- *AmMWSc 92*
**Koch,** Peter M 1945- *AmMWSc 92*
**Koch,** Pietro 1918-1945 *BiDExR*
**Koch,** Ralph 1957- *WhoFI 92*
**Koch,** Richard 1921- *AmMWSc 92*
**Koch,** Richard Carl 1930- *AmMWSc 92*
**Koch,** Richard Moncrief 1939- *AmMWSc 92*
**Koch,** Robert B 1923- *AmMWSc 92*
**Koch,** Robert F. 1956- *WhoRel 92*
**Koch,** Robert Harry 1929- *AmMWSc 92*
**Koch,** Robert Jacob 1926- *AmMWSc 92*
**Koch,** Robert Lawrence 1930- *WhoFI 92*
**Koch,** Robert Lewis 1949- *WhoFI 92*
**Koch,** Robert Milton 1924- *AmMWSc 92*
**Koch,** Ronald H 1949- *WhoIns 92*
**Koch,** Ronald Joseph 1939- *AmMWSc 92*
**Koch,** Ronald N 1941- *AmMWSc 92*
**Koch,** Rudy G 1939- *AmMWSc 92*
**Koch,** Russell Gordon 1954- *WhoWest 92*
**Koch,** Sidney 1935- *WhoFI 92*
**Koch,** Stanley D 1924- *AmMWSc 92*
**Koch,** Stephen *DrAPF 91*
**Koch,** Stephen Andrew 1948- *AmMWSc 92*
**Koch,** Stephen Douglas 1940- *AmMWSc 92*
**Koch,** Steven 1956- *WhoFI 92*
**Koch,** Steven A. 1952- *WhoFI 92*
**Koch,** Tad H 1943- *AmMWSc 92*
**Koch,** Theodore Augur 1925- *AmMWSc 92*
**Koch,** Therese 1924- *WhoRel 92*
**Koch,** Thomas F 1942- *WhoAmP 91*
**Koch,** Thomas L 1955- *AmMWSc 92*
**Koch,** Thomas Richard 1944- *AmMWSc 92*
**Koch,** Waldemar 1875-1912 *BiInAmS*
**Koch,** Walter Theodore 1923- *AmMWSc 92*
**Koch,** Werner 1926- *IntWW 91*
**Koch,** William Edward 1933- *AmMWSc 92*
**Koch,** William Frederick 1950- *AmMWSc 92*
**Koch,** William George 1924- *AmMWSc 92*
**Koch,** William Joseph 1949- *WhoMW 92*
**Koch,** William Julian 1924- *AmMWSc 92*
**Koch-Weser,** Dieter 1916- *AmMWSc 92*
**Koch-Weser,** Erich 1875-1944 *EncTR 91*
**Koch-Weser,** Jan 1930- *AmMWSc 92*
**Kochakian,** Charles Daniel 1908- *AmMWSc 92*
**Kochakian,** Garabed Daniel 1945- *WhoMW 92, WhoRel 92*
**Kochan,** Ivan 1923- *AmMWSc 92*
**Kochan,** Miriam 1929- *WrDr 92*
**Kochan,** Miriam Louise 1929- *IntAu&W 91*
**Kochan,** Robert George 1949- *AmMWSc 92*
**Kochan,** Walter J 1922- *AmMWSc 92*
**Kochanowski,** Barbara Ann 1957- *AmMWSc 92*
**Kochar,** Harvinder K 1953- *AmMWSc 92*
**Kochar,** Mahendr Singh 1943- *WhoMW 92*
**Kochel,** Ludwig von 1800-1877 *NewAmDM*
**Kochel,** Timothy Frank 1933- *WhoEnt 92*
**Kochemasov,** Vyacheslav Ivanovich 1918- *IntWW 91*
**Kochems,** Robert Gregory 1951- *WhoAmL 92*
**Kochen,** Manfred 1928- *AmMWSc 92*
**Kochen,** Simon Bernard 1934- *AmMWSc 92*
**Kocher,** Bryan S 1948- *AmMWSc 92*
**Kocher,** Carl A 1942- *AmMWSc 92*
**Kocher,** Charles William 1932- *AmMWSc 92*
**Kocher,** David Charles 1941- *AmMWSc 92*
**Kocher,** Emil Theodor 1841-1917 *WhoNob 90*
**Kocher,** Haribhajan S 1934- *AmMWSc 92*
**Kocher,** John Arthur 1945- *WhoAmP 91*
**Kocher,** Juanita Fay 1933- *WhoFI 92, WhoMW 92*
**Kocher,** Ronald Paul 1952- *WhoRel 92*
**Kocher,** Walter William 1934- *WhoAmL 92*

**Kocherga**, Anatoly Ivanovich 1947- *IntWW 91*
**Kochergin**, Edvard Stepanovich 1937- *IntWW 91*
**Kocherlakota**, Kathleen 1938- *AmMWSc 92*
**Kocherlakota**, Subrahmaniam 1935- *AmMWSc 92*
**Kochert**, Gary Dean 1939- *AmMWSc 92*
**Kochetkov**, Nikolay Konstantinovich 1915- *IntWW 91*
**Kochetkov**, Yuriy Petrovich 1932- *IntWW 91*
**Kochetov**, Vsevolod Anisimovich 1912-1973 *SovUnBD*
**Kochhar**, Devendra M 1938- *AmMWSc 92*
**Kochhar**, Man Mohan 1932- *AmMWSc 92*
**Kochhar**, Rajindar Kumar 1922- *AmMWSc 92*
**Kochhar**, Sunir 1958- *WhoFI 92*
**Kochheiser**, George W, Jr 1925- *WhoIns 92*
**Kochi**, Jay K. 1927- *IntWW 91*
**Kochi**, Jay Kazuo 1927- *AmMWSc 92*
**Kochman**, Philip Joel *WhoAmL 92*
**Kochman**, Ronald Lawrence 1946- *AmMWSc 92*
**Kochman**, Stanley Oscar 1946- *AmMWSc 92*
**Kochsmeier**, Bruce Stanley 1954- *WhoRel 92*
**Kochtitzky**, Lynne Dawson 1941- *WhoRel 92*
**Kochunny**, Chandra Mohan 1959- *WhoMW 92*
**Kochwa**, Shaul 1915- *AmMWSc 92*
**Koci**, Henry James 1952- *WhoFI 92*
**Koci**, Ludvik Frank 1936- *WhoMW 92*
**Kocian**, Joseph Vince 1949- *WhoMW 92*
**Kociba**, Richard Joseph 1939- *AmMWSc 92*
**Kocina**, Sharon 1962- *WhoWest 92*
**Kociolko**, John S 1949- *WhoAmP 91*
**Kocisko**, Stephen John 1915- *WhoRel 92*
**Kock**, Nils G. 1924- *IntWW 91*
**Kock**, Robert Marshall 1942- *WhoFI 92*
**Kock**, Virginia Stewart 1960- *WhoFI 92*
**Kock-Petersen**, Elsebeth 1949- *IntWW 91*
**Kocka**, Juergen 1941- *ConAu 133*
**Kocka**, Jurgen *ConAu 133*
**Kocks**, U Fred 1929- *AmMWSc 92*
**Kocman**, Ali 1943- *IntWW 91*
**Kocol**, Henry 1937- *AmMWSc 92*
**Kocon**, Richard William 1942- *AmMWSc 92*
**Kocoras**, Charles Petros 1938- *WhoAmL 92, WhoMW 92*
**Kocsis**, James Joseph 1920- *AmMWSc 92*
**Kocsis**, John 1948- *WhoAmP 91*
**Kocsis**, Zoltan 1952- *IntWW 91*
**Kocurek**, Michael Joseph 1943- *AmMWSc 92*
**Kocurko**, Michael John 1945- *AmMWSc 92*
**Koczak**, Michael Julius 1944- *AmMWSc 92*
**Koczera**, Robert Michael 1953- *WhoAmP 91*
**Koczian**, Heidi Marie 1966- *WhoMW 92*
**Koczwara**, Frantisek *NewAmDM*
**Koda**, Robert T 1933- *AmMWSc 92*
**Koda-Callan**, Elizabeth 1944- *SmATA 67*
**Kodaira**, Eimei 1944- *WhoWest 92*
**Kodaka**, Kunio 1932- *WhoFI 92*
**Kodaly**, Zoltan 1882-1967 *FacFETw, NewAmDM*
**Kodama**, Arthur Masayoshi 1931- *AmMWSc 92*
**Kodama**, Goji 1927- *AmMWSc 92*
**Kodama**, Hideomi 1931- *AmMWSc 92*
**Kodama**, Jiro Kenneth 1924- *AmMWSc 92*
**Kodama**, Robert Makoto 1932- *AmMWSc 92*
**Kodama**, Yoshio 1911-1984 *FacFETw*
**Kodamanoglu**, Nuri 1923- *IntWW 91*
**Kodavanti**, Prasada Rao S 1954- *AmMWSc 92*
**Kodes**, Jan 1946- *IntWW 91*
**Kodis**, Mary Caroline 1927- *WhoFI 92, WhoWest 92*
**Koditschek**, Leah K 1917- *AmMWSc 92*
**Kodjo**, Edem 1938- *IntWW 91*
**Kodner**, Martin 1934- *WhoMW 92*
**Kodres**, Uno Robert 1931- *AmMWSc 92*
**Kodrich**, William Ralph 1933- *AmMWSc 92*
**Koe**, B Kenneth 1925- *AmMWSc 92*
**Koebl**, James Joseph 1948- *WhoMW 92*
**Koech**, Peter 1958- *BlkOlyM*
**Koechlin**, Charles 1867-1950 *NewAmDM*
**Koechlin**, Samuel 1925- *IntWW 91*
**Koechlin-Smythe**, Patricia Rosemary 1928- *Who 92*
**Koechlin Von Stein**, Jorge Javier 1950- *WhoHisp 92*
**Koedel**, Robert Craig 1927- *WhoRel 92*
**Koeder**, Tamera Kathleen 1961- *WhoAmL 92*
**Koederitz**, Leonard Frederick 1946- *AmMWSc 92*
**Koegel**, William Fisher 1923- *WhoAmL 92*
**Koegle**, John S 1926- *AmMWSc 92*
**Koehl**, Camille Joan 1943- *WhoFI 92, WhoMW 92*
**Koehl**, Michael Peter 1962- *WhoFI 92*
**Koehl**, William John, Jr 1935- *AmMWSc 92*
**Koehler**, Andreas Martin 1930- *AmMWSc 92*
**Koehler**, Carlton Smith 1932- *AmMWSc 92*
**Koehler**, Carol McSteen 1938- *WhoMW 92*
**Koehler**, Dale Roland 1932- *AmMWSc 92*
**Koehler**, Don Edward 1942- *AmMWSc 92*
**Koehler**, Donald Otto 1937- *AmMWSc 92*
**Koehler**, Frank *TwCWW 91*
**Koehler**, Fred Eugene 1923- *AmMWSc 92*
**Koehler**, George Applegate 1921- *WhoEnt 92*
**Koehler**, Georges J.F. 1946- *WhoNob 90*
**Koehler**, Helmut A 1933- *AmMWSc 92*
**Koehler**, Henry M. 1931- *WhoMW 92*
**Koehler**, Henry Max 1931- *AmMWSc 92*
**Koehler**, Isabel Winifred 1903- *IntAu&W 91*
**Koehler**, James K 1933- *AmMWSc 92*
**Koehler**, James Stark 1914- *AmMWSc 92*
**Koehler**, John Edget 1941- *WhoFI 92*
**Koehler**, Judy 1926- *WhoAmP 91*
**Koehler**, Lawrence D 1932- *AmMWSc 92*
**Koehler**, Lawrence Dale 1932- *WhoMW 92*
**Koehler**, Mark E 1949- *AmMWSc 92*
**Koehler**, P Ruben 1931- *AmMWSc 92*
**Koehler**, Philip Edward 1943- *AmMWSc 92*
**Koehler**, Philip Gene 1947- *AmMWSc 92*
**Koehler**, Raymond Charles *AmMWSc 92*
**Koehler**, Richard Frederick, Jr 1945- *AmMWSc 92*
**Koehler**, Stanley *DrAPF 91*
**Koehler**, Thomas Richard 1932- *AmMWSc 92*
**Koehler**, Truman L, Jr 1931- *AmMWSc 92*
**Koehler**, Wilbert Frederick 1913- *AmMWSc 92*
**Koehler**, William Henry 1939- *AmMWSc 92*
**Koehler-Sapp**, Janice Mancinelli 1948- *WhoRel 92*
**Koehmstedt**, Paul Leon 1923- *AmMWSc 92*
**Koehn**, Charles William *WhoEnt 92*
**Koehn**, Emil Alvin 1916- *WhoAmP 91*
**Koehn**, Enno 1936- *AmMWSc 92*
**Koehn**, Ilse *ConAu 35NR*
**Koehn**, Ilse d1991 *NewYTBS 91*
**Koehn**, Ilse Charlotte 1929- *IntAu&W 91*
**Koehn**, Paul V 1931- *AmMWSc 92*
**Koehn**, Richard Karl 1940- *AmMWSc 92*
**Koehn**, William James 1936- *WhoAmL 92, WhoMW 92*
**Koehnke**, Francis 1918- *WhoAmP 91*
**Koehnlein**, John Martin, Sr. 1951- *WhoRel 92*
**Koekkoek**, Arnold Louis 1932- *WhoMW 92*
**Koekkoek**, John Wallace 1935- *WhoRel 92*
**Koelemay**, Ann W. 1930- *WhoMW 92*
**Koelemay**, Ralph Lawrence 1926- *WhoMW 92, WhoRel 92*
**Koella**, Carl O, Jr 1933- *WhoAmP 91*
**Koella**, Werner Paul 1917- *AmMWSc 92*
**Koelle**, George Brampton 1918- *AmMWSc 92, IntWW 91*
**Koelle**, Winifred Angenent 1926- *AmMWSc 92*
**Koeller**, Charles Timothy 1949- *WhoFI 92*
**Koeller**, Ralph Carl 1933- *AmMWSc 92*
**Koeller**, Robert Marion 1940- *WhoAmL 92, WhoMW 92*
**Koelling**, Dale Dean 1941- *AmMWSc 92*
**Koelling**, Melvin R 1937- *AmMWSc 92*
**Koelling**, Woodrow William 1918- *WhoFI 92, WhoMW 92*
**Koelmel**, Lorna Lee 1936- *WhoFI 92, WhoWest 92*
**Koelsch**, M. Oliver 1912- *WhoAmL 92*
**Koelsch**, Theodore Allen 1951- *WhoWest 92*
**Koelsche**, Charles L 1906- *AmMWSc 92*
**Koelsche**, Giles Alexander 1908- *AmMWSc 92*
**Koeltl**, John George 1945- *WhoAmL 92*
**Koeltzow**, Donald Earl 1944- *AmMWSc 92*
**Koelzer**, Victor A 1914- *AmMWSc 92*
**Koen**, Billy Vaughn 1938- *AmMWSc 92*
**Koen**, Vincent Rodolphe 1960- *WhoFI 92*
**Koenegstein**, Mildred Lorraine 1919- *WhoAmP 91*
**Koenekamp**, Fred J. 1922- *IntMPA 92*
**Koeng**, Fred R 1941- *AmMWSc 92*
**Koenig**, Aaron Joseph 1953- *WhoMW 92*
**Koenig**, Allen Edward 1939- *WhoWest 92*
**Koenig**, Carolyn DeWitt 1938- *WhoFI 92*
**Koenig**, Charles Jacob 1911- *AmMWSc 92*
**Koenig**, Charles Louis 1911- *AmMWSc 92*
**Koenig**, Daniel Rene 1936- *AmMWSc 92*
**Koenig**, Edward 1928- *AmMWSc 92*
**Koenig**, Eldo C 1919- *AmMWSc 92*
**Koenig**, Franz 1905- *WhoRel 92*
**Koenig**, Gary John 1947- *WhoMW 92*
**Koenig**, George Augustus 1844-1913 *BiInAmS*
**Koenig**, Ghisha 1921- *TwCPaSc*
**Koenig**, Gottfried Michael 1926- *ConCom 92*
**Koenig**, Harold 1921- *AmMWSc 92*
**Koenig**, Herman E 1924- *AmMWSc 92*
**Koenig**, Howard D. *DrAPF 91*
**Koenig**, Jack L 1933- *AmMWSc 92*
**Koenig**, James Bennett 1932- *AmMWSc 92*
**Koenig**, James J 1918- *AmMWSc 92*
**Koenig**, Jane Quinn 1935- *AmMWSc 92*
**Koenig**, Joan Foster 1930- *WhoAmP 91*
**Koenig**, John Henry 1909- *AmMWSc 92*
**Koenig**, John L. 1938- *WhoFI 92*
**Koenig**, John M. 1950- *WhoEnt 92*
**Koenig**, John Waldo 1920- *AmMWSc 92*
**Koenig**, Karl E 1947- *AmMWSc 92*
**Koenig**, Karl Joseph 1920- *AmMWSc 92*
**Koenig**, Katherine Steiner 1957- *WhoFI 92*
**Koenig**, Lloyd Randall 1929- *AmMWSc 92*
**Koenig**, Marie Harriet King 1919- *WhoWest 92*
**Koenig**, Mary Gonzalez 1936- *WhoHisp 92*
**Koenig**, Michael Edward Davison 1941- *AmMWSc 92, WhoMW 92*
**Koenig**, Milton G 1927- *AmMWSc 92*
**Koenig**, Nathan Hart 1915- *AmMWSc 92*
**Koenig**, Paul Edward 1929- *AmMWSc 92*
**Koenig**, Peter Frederick 1959- *WhoWest 92*
**Koenig**, Ralph E. 1933- *WhoAmL 92*
**Koenig**, Robert August 1933- *WhoMW 92, WhoRel 92*
**Koenig**, Rodney Curtis 1940- *WhoAmL 92*
**Koenig**, Seymour Hillel 1927- *AmMWSc 92*
**Koenig**, Stephen Edward 1945- *WhoRel 92*
**Koenig**, Thomas W 1938- *AmMWSc 92*
**Koenig**, Virgil Leroy 1913- *AmMWSc 92*
**Koenig**, Walter *IntMPA 92*
**Koenig**, Walter M. 1936- *WhoEnt 92*
**Koenigs**, Deo 1935- *WhoAmP 91*
**Koenigs**, Rita Scales 1952- *WhoAmL 92*
**Koenigsberg**, Ernest 1923- *AmMWSc 92*
**Koenigsberg**, Marvin Lee 1918- *WhoAmL 92*
**Koenigsberg**, Sol 1924- *WhoMW 92, WhoRel 92*
**Koenigsberger**, Helmut Georg 1918- *Who 92, WrDr 92*
**Koenigsberger**, Lynne Marie 1947- *WhoMW 92*
**Koenigsdorf**, Keith Bernard 1955- *WhoAmL 92*
**Koenigsmark**, Josef 1916- *IntAu&W 91*
**Koening**, Richard Paul 1921- *WhoMW 92*
**Koenke**, Robert J. 1947- *WhoMW 92*
**Koep**, Mary A 1932- *WhoAmP 91*
**Koepcke**, K. Bruce 1941- *WhoFI 92*
**Koepf**, Ernest Henry 1912- *AmMWSc 92*
**Koepf**, Michael *DrAPF 91*
**Koepf**, Werner Karl 1942- *WhoFI 92*
**Koepfer**, Donald Julius 1936- *WhoFI 92*
**Koepfinger**, J L 1925- *AmMWSc 92*
**Koepfle**, Michael Ignaz 1962- *WhoEnt 92*
**Koepfli**, Joseph B 1904- *AmMWSc 92*
**Koepke**, Barry George 1937- *AmMWSc 92, WhoMW 92*
**Koepke**, Don Lorenz 1938- *WhoFI 92*
**Koepke**, Donald Herbert 1923- *WhoMW 92*
**Koepke**, George Henry 1916- *AmMWSc 92*
**Koepke**, Jack Edward 1942- *WhoIns 92*
**Koepke**, John Arthur 1929- *AmMWSc 92*
**Koepnick**, Richard Borland 1944- *AmMWSc 92*
**Koepp**, Leila H 1945- *AmMWSc 92*
**Koepp**, Stephen John 1946- *AmMWSc 92*
**Koeppe**, David Edward 1939- *AmMWSc 92*
**Koeppe**, John K 1944- *AmMWSc 92*
**Koeppe**, Mary Kolean 1955- *AmMWSc 92*
**Koeppe**, Owen John 1926- *AmMWSc 92*
**Koeppe**, Roger E, II 1949- *AmMWSc 92*
**Koeppe**, Roger Erdman 1922- *AmMWSc 92*
**Koeppel**, Gary Merle 1938- *WhoWest 92*
**Koeppel**, William Edward 1951- *WhoAmP 91*
**Koeppen**, Bruce Michael 1951- *AmMWSc 92*
**Koeppen**, Raymond Bradley 1954- *WhoAmL 92, WhoMW 92*
**Koeppl**, Gerald Walter 1942- *AmMWSc 92*
**Koepsel**, Wellington Wesley 1921- *AmMWSc 92*
**Koepsell**, Paul L 1930- *AmMWSc 92*
**Koerber**, George G 1924- *AmMWSc 92*
**Koerber**, Walter Ludwig 1912- *AmMWSc 92*
**Koering**, Marilyn Jean 1938- *AmMWSc 92*
**Koerker**, Frederick William 1913- *AmMWSc 92*
**Koerker**, Robert Leland 1943- *AmMWSc 92*
**Koerner**, Ben Charles 1962- *WhoWest 92*
**Koerner**, E L 1931- *AmMWSc 92*
**Koerner**, Edward Wayne 1953- *WhoMW 92*
**Koerner**, Frank 1955- *WhoAmL 92*
**Koerner**, Henry d1991 *NewYTBS 91*
**Koerner**, James D. 1923- *WrDr 92*
**Koerner**, James Frederick 1929- *AmMWSc 92*
**Koerner**, Jane Goetze 1950- *WhoWest 92*
**Koerner**, Jerry Lynn 1950- *WhoWest 92*
**Koerner**, Jo Ellen 1946- *WhoMW 92*
**Koerner**, Philip Donald 1946- *WhoIns 92*
**Koerner**, Robert M 1933- *AmMWSc 92*
**Koerner**, T J 1954- *AmMWSc 92*
**Koerner**, Theodore Alfred William, Jr 1947- *AmMWSc 92*
**Koerner**, William Elmer 1923- *AmMWSc 92*
**Koerper**, Richard Arthur 1951- *WhoMW 92*
**Koertge**, Noretta 1935- *WhoMW 92*
**Koertge**, Ronald *DrAPF 91*
**Koerting**, Lola Elisabeth 1924- *AmMWSc 92*
**Koesem** *EncAmaz 91*
**Koestenbaum**, Phyllis *DrAPF 91*
**Koestenbaum**, Wayne *DrAPF 91*
**Koestenbaum**, Wayne 1958- *ConAu 134*
**Koester**, Berthold Karl 1931- *WhoWest 92*
**Koester**, Charles John 1929- *AmMWSc 92*
**Koester**, Charles R. 1915- *WhoRel 92*
**Koester**, Charles William 1910- *WhoMW 92*
**Koester**, Craig Richard 1953- *WhoRel 92*
**Koester**, Helmut Heinrich 1926- *WhoRel 92*
**Koester**, John D *AmMWSc 92*
**Koester**, Louis Julius, Jr 1925- *AmMWSc 92*
**Koester**, Robert Gregg 1932- *WhoEnt 92*
**Koester**, Rudolf 1936- *WhoWest 92*
**Koesterer**, Martin George 1933- *AmMWSc 92*
**Koestler**, Arthur 1905-1983 *CnDBLB 7 [port], FacFETw, LiExTwC, RfGEnL 91*
**Koestler**, Robert Charles 1932- *AmMWSc 92*
**Koestner**, Adalbert 1920- *AmMWSc 92*
**Koethe**, John *DrAPF 91*
**Koethe**, Susan M 1945- *AmMWSc 92*
**Koethke**, Charles Richard 1945- *WhoWest 92*
**Koetitz**, Jonathan Brynn 1956- *WhoEnt 92*
**Koetke**, Donald D 1937- *AmMWSc 92*
**Koetsch**, Philip 1935- *AmMWSc 92*
**Koetser**, David 1906- *WhoWest 92*
**Koetting**, Robert A. 1925- *WhoMW 92*
**Koetzle**, Thomas F 1943- *AmMWSc 92*
**Koevenig**, James L 1931- *AmMWSc 92*
**Koff**, Bernard Louis 1927- *AmMWSc 92*
**Koff**, Howard Michael 1941- *WhoAmL 92*
**Koff**, Raymond Steven 1939- *AmMWSc 92*
**Koff**, Richard M. 1926- *WrDr 92*
**Koff**, Robert *WhoEnt 92*
**Koff**, Robert Louis 1943- *WhoWest 92*
**Koffka**, Kurt 1886-1941 *FacFETw*
**Koffler**, David 1934- *AmMWSc 92*
**Koffler**, Henry 1922- *AmMWSc 92, WhoWest 92*
**Koffler**, Stephen Alexander 1942- *WhoFI 92*
**Koffler**, Warren William 1938- *WhoAmL 92*
**Koffman**, Elliot B 1942- *AmMWSc 92*
**Koffman**, Moe 1928- *NewAmDM*
**Kofford**, Cree-L 1933- *WhoAmL 92*
**Koffsky**, Peter Langer 1946- *WhoFI 92*
**Koffyberg**, Francois Pierre 1934- *AmMWSc 92*
**Kofink**, Wayne Alan 1949- *WhoRel 92*
**Kofler**, Richard Robert 1935- *AmMWSc 92*
**Kofod-Svendsen**, Flemming 1944- *IntWW 91*
**Kofoed**, Bart *WhoBlA 92*
**Kofoed**, J C 1893-1979 *ScFEYrs*
**Kofoed**, Niels Anker 1929- *IntWW 91*
**Kofoed-Hansen**, Otto Mogens 1921- *IntWW 91*
**Kofoid**, Melvin J 1910- *AmMWSc 92*
**Koford**, James Shingle 1938- *AmMWSc 92*
**Koford**, Kenneth John 1948- *WhoFI 92*
**Koford**, Stuart Keith 1953- *WhoMW 92*
**Kofranek**, Anton Miles 1921- *AmMWSc 92*
**Kofron**, James Thomas, Jr 1928- *AmMWSc 92*
**Kofron**, William G 1934- *AmMWSc 92*
**Kofsky**, Frank J. 1935- *WhoWest 92*
**Kofsky**, Irving Louis 1925- *AmMWSc 92*
**Kofstad**, Per Kristen 1929- *IntWW 91*

**Koft,** Bernard Waldemar 1921- *AmMWSc 92*
**Koga,** Rokutaro 1942- *AmMWSc 92, WhoWest 92*
**Koga,** Toyoki 1912- *AmMWSc 92*
**Kogali,** El Tayeb El *IntWW 91*
**Kogan,** Alma Estelle 1924- *WhoWest 92*
**Kogan,** Enrique A. *WhoHisp 92*
**Kogan,** Gerald 1933- *WhoAmL 92, WhoAmP 91*
**Kogan,** Leonid 1924-1982 *FacFETw, NewAmDM*
**Kogan,** Leonid Borisovich 1924-1982 *SovUnBD*
**Kogan,** Marcos 1933- *AmMWSc 92*
**Kogan,** Maurice 1930- *Who 92*
**Kogan,** Michael Sanford 1955- *WhoAmL 92*
**Kogan,** Nathan 1906- *WhoEnt 92*
**Kogan,** Norman 1919- *IntAu&W 91, WrDr 92*
**Kogan,** Richard Jay 1941- *WhoFI 92*
**Kogawa,** Joy 1935- *BenetAL 91, IntAu&W 91*
**Kogawa,** Joy Nozomi 1935- *WrDr 92*
**Kogel,** Marcus David 1903- *AmMWSc 92*
**Kogelnik,** H W 1932- *AmMWSc 92*
**Kogen,** Arnold Howard 1937- *WhoEnt 92*
**Koger,** Alfred Dennis, Jr. 1946- *WhoRel 92*
**Koger,** Frank Williams 1930- *WhoMW 92*
**Koger,** John W 1940- *AmMWSc 92*
**Koger,** Linwood Graves, III 1951- *WhoBlA 92*
**Koger,** Lisa 1953- *ConAu 133*
**Koger,** Marvin *AmMWSc 92*
**Koger,** Michael Pigott, Sr. 1953- *WhoBlA 92*
**Koglin,** Norman Alfred 1928- *WhoMW 92*
**Kogo,** Benjamin 1946- *BlkOlyM*
**Kogon,** Irving Charles 1923- *AmMWSc 92*
**Kogos,** L 1929- *AmMWSc 92*
**Kogovsek,** Daniel Charles 1951- *WhoAmL 92*
**Kogovsek,** John J 1946- *WhoAmP 91*
**Kogovsek,** Ray P 1941- *WhoAmP 91*
**Kogure,** Gohei 1924- *IntWW 91*
**Kogut,** John Benjamin 1945- *AmMWSc 92*
**Kogut,** Maurice D 1930- *AmMWSc 92*
**Koh,** Eunsook Tak 1936- *AmMWSc 92*
**Koh,** Eusebio Legarda 1931- *AmMWSc 92, WhoWest 92*
**Koh,** Kwangil 1931- *AmMWSc 92*
**Koh,** P K 1914- *AmMWSc 92*
**Koh,** Pun Kien 1914- *WhoFI 92*
**Koh,** Robert Cy 1938- *AmMWSc 92*
**Koh,** Severino Legarda 1927- *AmMWSc 92*
**Koh,** Tommy Thong Bee 1937- *IntWW 91*
**Kohan,** Davood 1946- *WhoWest 92*
**Kohan,** Dennis Lynn 1945- *WhoWest 92*
**Kohan,** Melvin Ira 1921- *AmMWSc 92*
**Kohane,** Theodore 1923- *AmMWSc 92*
**Kohel,** Russell James 1934- *AmMWSc 92*
**Kohin,** Barbara Castle 1932- *AmMWSc 92*
**Kohin,** Roger Patrick 1931- *AmMWSc 92*
**Kohl,** A L 1919- *AmMWSc 92*
**Kohl,** Baruch Frydman 1951- *WhoRel 92*
**Kohl,** Daniel Howard 1928- *AmMWSc 92*
**Kohl,** Deborah Gail 1954- *WhoAmL 92*
**Kohl,** Donald Lee 1954- *WhoAmL 92*
**Kohl,** Fred John 1942- *AmMWSc 92*
**Kohl,** Glen Arlen 1956- *WhoAmL 92*
**Kohl,** Harold 1923- *WhoRel 92*
**Kohl,** Harry Charles, Jr 1919- *AmMWSc 92*
**Kohl,** Helmut 1930- *FacFETw [port], IntWW 91, Who 92*
**Kohl,** Herb 1935- *AlmAP 92 [port]*
**Kohl,** Herbert 1935- *WhoAmP 91, WhoMW 92*
**Kohl,** Jerome 1918- *AmMWSc 92*
**Kohl,** John C 1908- *AmMWSc 92*
**Kohl,** John Leslie 1941- *AmMWSc 92*
**Kohl,** John Preston 1942- *WhoWest 92*
**Kohl,** Paul Albert 1952- *AmMWSc 92*
**Kohl,** Robert A 1936- *AmMWSc 92*
**Kohl,** Robert L. 1944- *WhoAmL 92*
**Kohl,** Schuyler G 1913- *AmMWSc 92*
**Kohl,** Steven Clark 1956- *WhoAmL 92*
**Kohl,** Stewart Allen 1955- *WhoMW 92*
**Kohl,** Walter H 1905- *AmMWSc 92*
**Kohland,** William Francis 1925- *AmMWSc 92*
**Kohlberg,** Jerome, Jr. 1925- *WhoFI 92*
**Kohlbrenner,** Philip John 1931- *AmMWSc 92*
**Kohlenberg,** Stanley 1932- *WhoFI 92*
**Kohler,** Bryan Earl 1940- *AmMWSc 92*
**Kohler,** Carl 1930- *AmMWSc 92*
**Kohler,** Constance Anne 1943- *AmMWSc 92*
**Kohler,** Dolores Marie 1928- *WhoWest 92*
**Kohler,** Donald Alvin 1928- *AmMWSc 92*
**Kohler,** Elaine Eloise Humphreys 1939- *AmMWSc 92*
**Kohler,** Eric Dave 1943- *WhoWest 92*
**Kohler,** Erwin Miller 1930- *AmMWSc 92*
**Kohler,** Foy 1908 1990 *AnObit 1990*
**Kohler,** Foy D. d1990 *IntWW 91N*
**Kohler,** Foy D. 1908-1990 *ConAu 133, CurBio 91N*
**Kohler,** Foy David d1990 *Who 92N*
**Kohler,** Foy David 1908- *Who 92*
**Kohler,** Fred Christopher 1946- *WhoFI 92*
**Kohler,** Gary John 1952- *WhoMW 92*
**Kohler,** George Oscar 1913- *AmMWSc 92*
**Kohler,** Harrison W. 1942- *WhoAmL 92*
**Kohler,** Heinz 1939- *AmMWSc 92*
**Kohler,** Irene *Who 92*
**Kohler,** Jeffrey Martin 1956- *WhoFI 92*
**Kohler,** John Dennis 1947- *WhoAmL 92*
**Kohler,** Kaufmann 1843-1926 *RelLAm 91*
**Kohler,** Louis 1820-1886 *NewAmDM*
**Kohler,** Mary Conway 1903-1986 *ConAu 135*
**Kohler,** Max A 1915- *AmMWSc 92*
**Kohler,** Peter 1938- *AmMWSc 92*
**Kohler,** Peter Francis 1935- *AmMWSc 92*
**Kohler,** Peter Ogden 1938- *WhoWest 92*
**Kohler,** R Ramon 1931- *AmMWSc 92*
**Kohler,** Robert Henry 1933- *AmMWSc 92*
**Kohler,** Russell Edward 1943- *WhoFI 92, WhoRel 92*
**Kohler,** Ruth DeYoung 1941- *WhoMW 92*
**Kohler,** Sandra *DrAPF 91*
**Kohler,** Sigurd H 1928- *AmMWSc 92*
**Kohler,** Steven Alan 1951- *WhoMW 92*
**Kohler,** Walter Charles 1929- *WhoWest 92*
**Kohler,** Wolfgang 1887-1967 *FacFETw*
**Kohlhaw,** Gunter B 1931- *AmMWSc 92*
**Kohlhepp,** Edward John 1943- *WhoFI 92*
**Kohlhepp,** Sue Joanne 1939- *AmMWSc 92*
**Kohlhof,** L L 1929- *WhoIns 92*
**Kohlhoff,** Hans-Peter 1948- *WhoAmP 91*
**Kohli,** Dilip 1947- *AmMWSc 92*
**Kohli,** Jai Dev 1918- *AmMWSc 92, WhoMW 92*
**Kohli,** Kawad *WhoRel 92*
**Kohlman,** David L 1937- *AmMWSc 92*
**Kohlman,** Val Marie *WhoMW 92*
**Kohlmayr,** Gerhard Franz 1930- *AmMWSc 92*
**Kohlmeier,** Ronald Harold 1936- *AmMWSc 92*
**Kohlmey,** Gunther 1913- *IntWW 91*
**Kohlmeyer,** Jan Justus 1928- *AmMWSc 92*
**Kohls,** Carl William 1931- *AmMWSc 92*
**Kohls,** Donald W 1934- *AmMWSc 92*
**Kohls,** Leon Hugo 1933- *WhoFI 92*
**Kohls,** Robert E 1931- *AmMWSc 92*
**Kohlstaedt,** Kenneth George 1908- *AmMWSc 92, WhoWest 92*
**Kohlstedt,** Sally Gregory 1943- *AmMWSc 92*
**Kohlwey,** Jane Ellen 1957- *WhoAmL 92*
**Kohman,** Truman Paul 1916- *AmMWSc 92*
**Kohmescher,** James Francis 1949- *WhoMW 92*
**Kohn,** Alan J. 1931- *WhoWest 92*
**Kohn,** Alan Jacobs 1931- *AmMWSc 92*
**Kohn,** Arnold J. 1940- *WhoAmL 92*
**Kohn,** Barry Allan 1950- *WhoMW 92*
**Kohn,** Barry Clarke 1955- *WhoFI 92*
**Kohn,** Ernest 1924- *WhoFI 92*
**Kohn,** Erwin 1923- *AmMWSc 92*
**Kohn,** Frank S 1942- *AmMWSc 92*
**Kohn,** Fred R *AmMWSc 92*
**Kohn,** Gerhard 1921- *WhoWest 92*
**Kohn,** Gustave K 1910- *AmMWSc 92*
**Kohn,** Guy Lindsay 1956- *WhoFI 92*
**Kohn,** Harold Elias 1914- *WhoAmL 92, WhoFI 92*
**Kohn,** Harold William 1920- *AmMWSc 92*
**Kohn,** Henry Irving 1909- *AmMWSc 92*
**Kohn,** Herbert Myron 1935- *AmMWSc 92*
**Kohn,** Howard Edward, II *IntMPA 92*
**Kohn,** Jack Arnold 1925- *AmMWSc 92*
**Kohn,** James P 1924- *AmMWSc 92*
**Kohn,** Janet Ann 1931- *WhoAmP 91*
**Kohn,** Joseph Carl 1957- *WhoAmL 92*
**Kohn,** Joseph John 1932- *AmMWSc 92*
**Kohn,** Karen Josephine 1951- *WhoEnt 92, WhoMW 92*
**Kohn,** Karl George 1926- *WhoEnt 92*
**Kohn,** Kurt William 1930- *AmMWSc 92*
**Kohn,** Larry Michael 1953- *WhoMW 92*
**Kohn,** Leonard David 1935- *AmMWSc 92*
**Kohn,** Lisa Salkovitz 1951- *WhoAmL 92*
**Kohn,** Mary Louise Beatrice 1920- *WhoMW 92*
**Kohn,** Michael 1934- *AmMWSc 92*
**Kohn,** Michael Bundy 1958- *WhoWest 92*
**Kohn,** Michael Charles 1941- *AmMWSc 92*
**Kohn,** Randolph Lawrence 1947- *WhoFI 92*
**Kohn,** Robert Alfred 1944- *WhoAmP 91*
**Kohn,** Robert Errant 1927- *WhoMW 92*
**Kohn,** Robert Samuel, Jr. 1949- *WhoFI 92, WhoWest 92*
**Kohn,** Ronald R. 1950- *WhoEnt 92*
**Kohn,** Shalom L. 1949- *WhoAmL 92*
**Kohn,** Stephen Martin 1956- *WhoAmL 92*
**Kohn,** Walter 1923- *AmMWSc 92, IntWW 91*
**Kohn,** Wanda Joy 1959- *WhoRel 92*
**Kohn,** William Henry 1915- *WhoRel 92*
**Kohn,** William Irwin 1951- *WhoAmL 92*
**Kohnen,** Michael Phillip 1942- *WhoFI 92*
**Kohnen,** Ralph William 1961- *WhoAmL 92*
**Kohner,** Pancho 1939- *IntMPA 92, WhoEnt 92*
**Kohner,** Peter 1948- *WhoFI 92*
**Kohner,** Susan 1936- *IntMPA 92*
**Kohnhorst,** Earl Eugene 1947- *AmMWSc 92*
**Kohnke,** Helmut 1901- *AmMWSc 92*
**Kohnop,** Louis Manuel 1920- *WhoEnt 92*
**Kohnstam,** George 1920- *Who 92*
**Kohnstamm,** Max 1914- *Who 92*
**Kohoban-Wickreme,** Alfred Silva 1914- *Who 92*
**Kohonen,** Teuvo Kalevi 1934- *IntWW 91*
**Kohout,** Frederick Charles, III 1940- *AmMWSc 92*
**Kohout,** Pavel 1928- *LiExTwC*
**Kohr,** Roland Ellsworth 1931- *WhoMW 92*
**Kohring,** Dagmar Luzia 1951- *WhoFI 92*
**Kohrman,** Arthur Fisher 1934- *AmMWSc 92*
**Kohrt,** Carl Fredrick 1943- *AmMWSc 92*
**Koht,** Paul 1913- *Who 92*
**Kohut,** Alexander 1842-1894 *RelLAm 91*
**Kohut,** John Walter 1946- *WhoFI 92*
**Kohut,** Robert John 1943- *AmMWSc 92*
**Koide,** Frank T 1935- *AmMWSc 92*
**Koide,** Roger Tai 1957- *AmMWSc 92*
**Koide,** Samuel Saburo 1923- *AmMWSc 92*
**Koike,** Hideo 1921- *AmMWSc 92*
**Koike,** Thomas Isao 1927- *AmMWSc 92*
**Koirala,** Matrika Prasad 1912- *IntWW 91*
**Koirtyohann,** Samuel Roy 1930- *AmMWSc 92, WhoMW 92*
**Koistinen,** Donald Peter 1927- *AmMWSc 92*
**Koiter,** Warner Tjardus 1914- *IntWW 91*
**Koivisto,** Don *WhoAmP 91*
**Koivisto,** Mauno Henrik 1923- *IntWW 91*
**Koivistoinen,** Eino Hannes 1907- *IntAu&W 91*
**Koivo,** Antti J 1932- *AmMWSc 92*
**Koivulehto,** Jorma Juhani 1934- *IntWW 91*
**Koizumi,** Carl Jan 1943- *AmMWSc 92, WhoWest 92*
**Koizumi,** Kiyomi 1924- *AmMWSc 92*
**Kojian,** Varujan Haig 1935- *WhoEnt 92, WhoWest 92*
**Kojima,** Haruo 1945- *AmMWSc 92*
**Kojima,** Kiyoshi 1920- *IntWW 91*
**Kojoian,** Gabriel 1927- *AmMWSc 92*
**Kojro,** Chester Anthony 1954- *WhoMW 92*
**Kok,** Frans Johan 1943- *WhoFI 92*
**Kok,** Loke-Tuck 1939- *AmMWSc 92*
**Kok,** Peter 1919- *WhoAmP 91*
**Kok,** Wim 1938- *IntWW 91*
**Kokal,** Kathleen Joan 1961- *WhoMW 92*
**Kokalis,** Soter George 1936- *AmMWSc 92*
**Kokame,** Glenn Megumi 1926- *AmMWSc 92*
**Kokas,** Eszter B *AmMWSc 92*
**Kokatnur,** Mohan Gundo 1930- *AmMWSc 92*
**Kokenge,** Bernard Russell 1939- *AmMWSc 92*
**Kokes,** Alois Harold 1955- *WhoAmL 92*
**Kokesh,** Fritz Carl 1943- *AmMWSc 92*
**Koki,** Stan 1946- *WhoAmP 91*
**Kokjer,** Kenneth Jordan 1941- *AmMWSc 92*
**Kokkinaki,** Vladimir 1904-1985 *FacFETw*
**Kokkinakis,** Demetrius Michael 1950- *AmMWSc 92*
**Kokko,** Juha Pekka *AmMWSc 92*
**Kokkonen,** Joonas 1921- *ConCom 92*
**Koknat,** Friedrich Wilhelm 1938- *AmMWSc 92*
**Kokoschka,** Oskar 1886-1980 *EncTR 91, FacFETw, LiExTwC, TwCPaSc*
**Kokoski,** Charles Joseph 1927- *AmMWSc 92*
**Kokoszka,** Gerald Francis 1938- *AmMWSc 92*
**Kokotailo,** George T 1919- *AmMWSc 92*
**Kokovtseva,** Olga *EncAmaz 91*
**Kokovtsov,** Vladimir Nikolayevich 1853-1942 *FacFETw*
**Koksanov,** Igor *IntWW 91*
**Kokta,** Bohuslav Vaclav 1940- *AmMWSc 92*
**Kokta,** Milan Rastislav 1941- *AmMWSc 92*
**Kokulis,** Paul Nicholas 1924- *WhoAmL 92*
**Kolaian,** Jack H 1929- *AmMWSc 92*
**Kolaja,** Jiri 1919- *IntWW 91*
**Kolakowski,** Donald Louis 1944- *AmMWSc 92*
**Kolakowski,** Leszek 1927- *IntWW 91, Who 92*
**Kolakowski,** Victoria Susan 1961- *WhoAmL 92*
**Koland,** David Jerome 1942- *WhoAmP 91*
**Kolane,** John Teboho 1926- *Who 92*
**Kolanoski,** Thomas Edwin 1937- *WhoFI 92, WhoWest 92*
**Kolar,** Edward Louis 1909- *WhoAmP 91*
**Kolar,** Jiri 1914- *IntWW 91*
**Kolar,** John Joseph 1922- *AmMWSc 92*
**Kolar,** Joseph George 1946- *WhoMW 92*
**Kolar,** Joseph Robert, Jr 1938- *AmMWSc 92*
**Kolar,** Milton Anton 1916- *WhoAmL 92*
**Kolar,** Oscar Clinton 1928- *AmMWSc 92*
**Kolasa,** Kathryn Marianne 1949- *AmMWSc 92*
**Kolaski,** Clinton Joseph 1938- *WhoMW 92*
**Kolat,** Robert S 1931- *AmMWSc 92*
**Kolata,** Dennis Robert 1942- *AmMWSc 92*
**Kolata,** James John 1942- *AmMWSc 92, WhoMW 92*
**Kolatkar,** Arun 1932- *ConPo 91, WrDr 92*
**Kolattukudy,** P E *AmMWSc 92*
**Kolb,** Alan Charles 1928- *AmMWSc 92*
**Kolb,** Annette 1870-1967 *LiExTwC*
**Kolb,** Barbara 1939- *ConCom 92, NewAmDM*
**Kolb,** Bryan Edward 1947- *AmMWSc 92*
**Kolb,** Charles Eugene, Jr 1945- *AmMWSc 92*
**Kolb,** Doris Kasey 1927- *AmMWSc 92*
**Kolb,** Edward William 1951- *AmMWSc 92*
**Kolb,** Erwin John 1924- *WhoRel 92*
**Kolb,** Felix Oscar 1921- *AmMWSc 92*
**Kolb,** Frances Arick d1991 *NewYTBS 91*
**Kolb,** Frank J., Jr. 1947- *WhoAmL 92*
**Kolb,** Frederick J, Jr 1917- *AmMWSc 92*
**Kolb,** Hans Werner 1920- *IntWW 91*
**Kolb,** Henry George 1950- *WhoAmL 92*
**Kolb,** James Joseph 1944- *WhoEnt 92*
**Kolb,** Jeffrey Barnes 1951- *WhoAmL 92*
**Kolb,** Jerry Wilbert 1935- *WhoFI 92*
**Kolb,** John Carl 1943- *WhoRel 92*
**Kolb,** Ken *DrAPF 91*
**Kolb,** Ken Lloyd 1926- *WhoEnt 92*
**Kolb,** Kenneth Emil 1928- *AmMWSc 92*
**Kolb,** Kenneth James 1956- *WhoEnt 92*
**Kolb,** Lawrence Coleman 1911- *AmMWSc 92*
**Kolb,** Leonard H 1913- *AmMWSc 92*
**Kolb,** R Frank, II 1946- *WhoAmP 91*
**Kolb,** Richard Eugene 1931- *WhoFI 92*
**Kolb,** Robert Allan 1941- *WhoRel 92*
**Kolb,** Vera 1948- *AmMWSc 92*
**Kolb,** Wade S., Jr. 1949- *WhoAmL 92*
**Kolb,** William Thomas 1956- *WhoMW 92*
**Kolbe,** Georg 1877-1947 *EncTR 91, FacFETw*
**Kolbe,** James Thomas 1942- *WhoAmP 91, WhoWest 92*
**Kolbe,** Jane Boegler 1944- *WhoMW 92*
**Kolbe,** Jim 1942- *AlmAP 92 [port]*
**Kolbe,** Karl William, Jr. 1926- *WhoAmL 92*
**Kolbe,** Maksymilian Maria 1894-1941 *FacFETw*
**Kolbe,** Maximilian 1894-1941 *EncTR 91 [port]*
**Kolbeck,** Andrew Gerard 1949- *WhoMW 92*
**Kolbeck,** John Francis 1952- *WhoFI 92*
**Kolbeck,** Ralph Carl 1944- *AmMWSc 92*
**Kolbenheyer,** Erwin Guido 1878-1962 *BiDExR, EncTR 91 [port]*
**Kolbenschlag,** Michael *WhoWest 92*
**Kolber,** Daniel Hackner 1953- *WhoAmL 92*
**Kolber,** Harry John 1918- *AmMWSc 92*
**Kolbert,** Colin Francis 1936- *Who 92*
**Kolbezen,** Martin 1914- *AmMWSc 92*
**Kolbin,** Genadiy Vasilevich 1927- *IntWW 91*
**Kolbin,** Gennadiy Vasil'evich 1927- *SovUnBD*
**Kolbjornsen,** Kenneth Edward 1944- *WhoWest 92*
**Kolbo,** Kevin P *WhoAmP 91*
**Kolbye,** Albert Christian, Jr 1935- *AmMWSc 92*
**Kolch,** Victor Frederick 1951- *WhoRel 92*
**Kolchak,** Alexander Vasilyevich 1873-1920 *FacFETw*
**Kolchin,** Ellis R. d1991 *NewYTBS 91*
**Kolchin,** Ellis Robert 1916- *AmMWSc 92*
**Kolchina,** Ol'ga Pavlovna 1918- *SovUnBD*
**Kolcsey,** Ferenc 1790-1838 *BlkwCEP*
**Kolda,** Thomas Joseph 1939- *WhoMW 92*
**Kolde,** Richard Arthur 1944- *WhoFI 92*
**Kolde,** Sandra Lee 1940- *WhoFI 92*
**Kolder,** Hansjoerg E 1926- *AmMWSc 92*
**Koldewyn,** William A 1942- *AmMWSc 92*
**Koldovsky,** Otakar 1930- *AmMWSc 92, WhoWest 92*
**Koldunov,** Aleksandr Ivanovich 1923- *IntWW 91, SovUnBD*
**Koldyke,** Mike *WhoMW 92*
**Koldys,** Mark Edward 1946- *WhoAmP 91*
**Kole,** James David 1960- *WhoAmL 92*
**Kole,** Janet Stephanie 1946- *WhoAmL 92*
**Kole-Harf,** Patricia Jean 1937- *WhoMW 92*
**Kolehmainen,** Jan Waldroy 1940- *WhoMW 92*
**Kolek,** Robert Louis 1936- *AmMWSc 92*

**Kolenbrander,** Harold Mark 1938- *AmMWSc 92*
**Koler,** Robert Donald 1924- *AmMWSc 92*
**Kolesar,** Edward S 1950- *AmMWSc 92*
**Kolesar,** Peter John 1936- *AmMWSc 92*
**Kolesar,** Peter Thomas 1942- *AmMWSc 92*
**Kolesari,** Gary Lee 1948- *AmMWSc 92*
**Koleske,** Carolyn Ann 1955- *WhoMW 92*
**Koleske,** Joseph Victor 1930- *AmMWSc 92*
**Kolesnikov,** Vladislav Grigoryevich 1925- *IntWW 91*
**Koleson,** Donald Ralph 1935- *WhoMW 92*
**Kolf,** James 1948- *WhoFI 92*
**Kolff,** Willem Johan 1911- *AmMWSc 92, IntWW 91*
**Kolhoff,** M J 1915- *AmMWSc 92*
**Koli,** Andrew Kaitan 1925- *AmMWSc 92*
**Kolibash,** William Anthony 1944- *WhoAmL 92*
**Kolin,** Alexander 1910- *AmMWSc 92, WhoWest 92*
**Kolinek,** Robert Brett 1954- *WhoFI 92, WhoMW 92*
**Koliner,** Ralph 1917- *AmMWSc 92*
**Kolingba,** Andre *IntWW 91*
**Kolins,** Wayne Alan 1944- *WhoFI 92*
**Kolinski,** Steven Scott 1960- *WhoMW 92*
**Kolinsky,** Martin 1936- *WrDr 92*
**Kolis,** Stanley Joseph *AmMWSc 92*
**Kolisch,** Rudolf 1896-1978 *NewAmDM*
**Kolisevski,** Lazar 1914- *IntWW 91*
**Koliwad,** Krishna M 1938- *AmMWSc 92*
**Kolka,** Margaret A 1952- *AmMWSc 92*
**Kolker,** Richard Lee 1939- *WhoAmP 91*
**Kolkey,** Daniel Miles 1952- *WhoAmL 92, WhoWest 92*
**Kolkman,** Paul F 1946- *WhoIns 92*
**Kolkmeyer,** Alexandra 1953- *WhoWest 92*
**Kollar,** Edward James 1934- *AmMWSc 92*
**Kollar,** Nathan R. *WhoRel 92*
**Kollar,** Sybil *DrAPF 91*
**Kollat,** David Truman 1938- *WhoFI 92*
**Kollataj,** Hugo 1750-1812 *BlkwCEP*
**Kolle Grondahl,** Kirsti 1943- *IntWW 91*
**Kollek,** Teddy 1911- *FacFETw*
**Kollek,** Theodore 1911- *IntWW 91*
**Kollen,** Wendell James 1935- *AmMWSc 92*
**Koller,** Arnold 1933- *IntWW 91*
**Koller,** Charles Richard 1920- *AmMWSc 92*
**Koller,** Don 1942- *WhoAmP 91*
**Koller,** Earl Leonard 1931- *AmMWSc 92*
**Koller,** Fred G. 1950- *WhoEnt 92*
**Koller,** Glenn R 1951- *AmMWSc 92*
**Koller,** Herbert Josef 1911- *IntWW 91*
**Koller,** James *DrAPF 91*
**Koller,** James 1936- *ConPo 91, WrDr 92*
**Koller,** Karen Kathryn 1949- *WhoMW 92*
**Koller,** Loren D 1940- *AmMWSc 92*
**Koller,** Marita A. 1955- *WhoMW 92*
**Koller,** Marvin Robert 1919- *WrDr 92*
**Koller,** Noemie 1933- *AmMWSc 92*
**Koller,** Robert Dene 1945- *AmMWSc 92*
**Koller,** Timothy Michael 1958- *WhoFI 92*
**Kollhoff,** Gerald Mark 1938- *WhoMW 92*
**Kollias,** Konstantinos V. 1901- *IntWW 91*
**Kollig,** Heinz Philipp 1928- *AmMWSc 92*
**Kollin,** Gary 1953- *WhoFI 92*
**Kollin,** Jonathan E. 1950- *WhoRel 92*
**Kolling,** Charles Joseph 1950- *WhoAmP 91*
**Kollins,** Michael Jerome 1912- *WhoMW 92*
**Kollios,** Paul *WhoAmP 91*
**Kollman,** Peter Andrew 1944- *AmMWSc 92*
**Kollmann,** Alvin Victor 1929- *WhoRel 92*
**Kollmann,** Victor John 1954- *WhoRel 92*
**Kollmeyer,** Justin Paul 1950- *WhoRel 92*
**Kollmorgen,** G Mark 1932- *AmMWSc 92*
**Kollo,** Rene 1937- *IntWW 91, NewAmDM*
**Kolloff,** Margaret Penelope Britton 1942- *WhoMW 92*
**Kollontai,** Aleksandra Mikhaylovna 1872-1952 *SovUnBD*
**Kollontai,** Alexandra 1872-1952 *WomSoc*
**Kollontay,** Alexandra Mikhailovna 1872-1952 *FacFETw*
**Kollros,** Jerry John 1917- *AmMWSc 92*
**Kollsman,** Paul 1900-1982 *FacFETw*
**Kollwitz,** Kathe 1867-1945 *EncTR 91 [port], FacFETw*
**Kolm,** Henry Herbert 1924- *AmMWSc 92*
**Kolm,** Ron *DrAPF 91*
**Kolman,** Bernard 1932- *AmMWSc 92*
**Kolman,** Marya Cody 1954- *WhoAmL 92*
**Kolmen,** Samuel Norman 1930- *AmMWSc 92*
**Kolmerten,** Carol A. 1946- *ConAu 135*
**Kolmes,** Steven Albert 1954- *AmMWSc 92*
**Kolmogorov,** Andrei Nikolayevich 1903- *FacFETw*
**Kolmogorov,** Andrey Nikolaevich 1903-1987 *SovUnBD*
**Kolmogorov,** Georgiy Dmitriyevich 1929- *IntWW 91*
**Kolo,** Sule 1926- *Who 92*
**Kolobielski,** Marjan 1915- *AmMWSc 92*
**Kolodkin,** Anatoliy Lazarevich 1928- *IntWW 91, SovUnBD*
**Kolodner,** Bernard Bruce 1945- *WhoAmL 92*
**Kolodner,** Harvey D. 1951- *WhoFI 92*
**Kolodner,** Ignace Izaak 1920- *AmMWSc 92*
**Kolodner,** Paul R 1953- *AmMWSc 92*
**Kolodner,** Richard David 1951- *AmMWSc 92*
**Kolodny,** Annette 1941- *BenetAL 91*
**Kolodny,** Gerald Mordecai 1937- *AmMWSc 92*
**Kolodny,** Nancy Harrison 1944- *AmMWSc 92*
**Kolodny,** Nathan 1938- *WhoEnt 92*
**Kolodny,** Stephen Arthur 1940- *WhoAmL 92, WhoWest 92*
**Kolodziej,** Bruno J 1934- *AmMWSc 92*
**Kolodziej,** Gloria *WhoAmP 91*
**Kolodziej,** Ryan Henry 1957- *WhoAmP 91*
**Kolodziejczyk,** Piotr 1939- *IntWW 91*
**Kolodziejski,** Charles W 1927- *WhoAmP 91*
**Kolodziejski,** Jerzy 1933- *IntWW 91*
**Kolodziejski,** Leslie Ann 1958- *AmMWSc 92*
**Kolodzy,** Paul John 1959- *AmMWSc 92*
**Kolomiets,** Yuriy Afanasiyevich 1925- *IntWW 91*
**Koloms,** Leonard 1940- *WhoFI 92*
**Kolopajlo,** Lawrence Hugh 1950- *AmMWSc 92*
**Kolor,** Michael Garrett 1934- *WhoFI 92*
**Kolotyrkin,** Yakov Mikhailovich 1910- *IntWW 91*
**Kolowa,** Sebastian *WhoRel 92*
**Kolozsi,** Dawn Marie Sirks 1969- *WhoMW 92*
**Kolozsvari Grandpierre,** Emil 1907- *IntAu&W 91, IntWW 91*
**Kolozvary,** Jon Joseph 1945- *WhoMW 92*
**Kolp,** Alan Lee 1944- *WhoRel 92*
**Kolp,** Bernard J 1928- *AmMWSc 92*
**Kolpakov,** Serafim Vasilyevich 1933- *IntWW 91*
**Kolpakova,** Irina *WhoEnt 92*
**Kolpakova,** Irina Aleksandrovna 1933- *IntWW 91, SovUnBD*
**Kolpas,** Laurie Puhn 1949- *WhoWest 92*
**Kolpas,** Sidney J. 1947- *WhoFI 92*
**Kolpitcke,** John Harry 1934- *WhoEnt 92, WhoMW 92*
**Kolsen,** Helmut Max 1926- *WrDr 92*
**Kolski,** Thaddeus L 1928- *AmMWSc 92*
**Kolsky,** Allan 1932- *WhoFI 92*
**Kolsky,** Barry 1957- *WhoEnt 92*
**Kolsky,** Harwood George 1921- *AmMWSc 92*
**Kolsky,** Herbert 1916- *AmMWSc 92*
**Kolsky,** Thomas A. 1942- *ConAu 135*
**Kolsrud,** Daniel Paul 1948- *WhoEnt 92*
**Kolsrud,** Gretchen Schabtach 1939- *AmMWSc 92*
**Kolsrud,** Henry Gerald 1923- *WhoWest 92*
**Kolstad,** Allen C 1931- *WhoAmP 91, WhoWest 92*
**Kolstad,** Eva 1918- *IntWW 91*
**Kolstad,** George Andrew 1919- *AmMWSc 92*
**Kolstad,** James L *WhoAmP 91*
**Kolstad,** John R. *WhoEnt 92*
**Kolstoe,** Gary Martin 1946- *WhoFI 92, WhoWest 92*
**Kolt,** Robert Paul 1953- *WhoEnt 92*
**Koltai,** Ralph 1924- *IntWW 91, Who 92*
**Koltai,** Stephen Miklos 1922- *WhoFI 92, WhoWest 92*
**Koltay,** Gabor 1950- *WhoEnt 92*
**Kolter,** Joe P. 1926- *AlmAP 92 [port]*
**Kolter,** Joseph Paul 1926- *WhoAmP 91*
**Kolterjahn,** Paul Henry 1924- *WhoFI 92*
**Kolthoff,** Izaak Maurits 1894- *AmMWSc 92*
**Koltinsky,** Terry Don 1954- *WhoMW 92*
**Kolts,** Harvey Seeley 1927- *WhoFI 92*
**Kol'tsov,** Nikolay Konstantinovich 1872-1940 *SovUnBD*
**Koltun,** Daniel S 1933- *AmMWSc 92*
**Koltun,** Stanley Phelps 1925- *AmMWSc 92*
**Koltun,** Walter Lang 1928- *AmMWSc 92*
**Koltveit,** James Mitchell 1941- *WhoFI 92, WhoMW 92*
**Koltzoff,** Nikolay Konstantinovich 1872-1940 *SovUnBD*
**Kolumban,** Nicholas *DrAPF 91*
**Kolvenbach,** Peter-Hans 1928- *IntWW 91, WhoRel 92*
**Kolvenbach,** Walter 1922- *IntWW 91*
**Kolvoord,** Philip Amadon 1932- *WhoAmL 92*
**Kolyer,** John M 1933- *AmMWSc 92*
**Kolzany,** Marja *EncAmaz 91*
**Komack,** James *LesBEnT 92*
**Komai,** Hirochika *AmMWSc 92*
**Komai,** Ray 1918- *DcTwDes*
**Komaiko,** Libby 1949- *WhoEnt 92*
**Koman** *EncAmaz 91*
**Komar,** Arthur Baraway 1931- *AmMWSc 92*
**Komar,** Keith William 1957- *WhoWest 92*
**Komar,** Paul D 1939- *AmMWSc 92*
**Komar,** Vitaliy 1943- *IntWW 91*
**Komarkova,** Vera 1942- *AmMWSc 92*
**Komarmy,** Julius Michael 1926- *AmMWSc 92*
**Komarneni,** Sridhar 1944- *AmMWSc 92*
**Komaroff,** Stanley 1935- *WhoAmL 92*
**Komarov,** Igor Sergeyevich 1917- *IntWW 91*
**Komarov,** Sergey Petrovich 1891-1957 *SovUnBD*
**Komarov,** Vladimir Leont'evich 1869-1945 *SovUnBD*
**Komarov,** Vladimir M 1927-1967 *FacFETw*
**Komarovsky,** Mirra 1905- *WomSoc*
**Komatsu,** Koh 1921- *IntWW 91*
**Komatsu,** S. Richard 1916- *WhoWest 92*
**Komatsu,** Sakyo 1931- *TwCSFW 91A*
**Komdat,** John Raymond 1943- *WhoFI 92, WhoWest 92*
**Komejan,** Delwyn Duane 1935- *WhoMW 92*
**Komen,** Leonard 1943- *WhoMW 92*
**Komenda,** Erwin 1904-1966 *DcTwDes, FacFETw*
**Komenda,** Frank Joseph 1934- *WhoAmP 91*
**Komensky,** Alan 1949- *WhoAmL 92*
**Komer,** Robert William 1922- *IntWW 91*
**Komet,** Leslie Gay 1963- *WhoEnt 92*
**Kometani,** Foumiko 1930- *ConAu 135*
**Komiak,** James Joseph 1953- *AmMWSc 92*
**Komin,** Robert Patrick, Jr. 1962- *WhoWest 92*
**Kominek,** Leo Aloysius 1937- *AmMWSc 92*
**Kominsky,** Neil Edward 1944- *WhoRel 92*
**Kominz,** David Richard 1924- *AmMWSc 92*
**Komisar,** Jerome Bertram 1937- *WhoWest 92*
**Komisar,** Robert Sigmund 1949- *WhoEnt 92*
**Komisaruk,** Barry Richard 1941- *AmMWSc 92*
**Komiskey,** Harold Louis *AmMWSc 92*
**Komito,** David Ross 1946- *WhoRel 92, WhoWest 92*
**Komiyama,** Jushiro 1928- *IntWW 91*
**Komkov,** Vadim 1919- *AmMWSc 92*
**Komleva,** Gabriela Trofimovna 1938- *IntWW 91*
**Komline,** Russell Marlow 1948- *WhoFI 92*
**Komlos,** Peter 1935- *IntWW 91*
**Komm,** Horace 1916- *AmMWSc 92*
**Kommandeur,** Jan 1929- *IntWW 91*
**Kommedahl,** Thor 1920- *AmMWSc 92, WhoMW 92*
**Kommerell,** Max 1902-1944 *EncTR 91*
**Komodikis,** Maria D. *LesBEnT 92*
**Komorek,** Michael Joesph, Jr 1952- *AmMWSc 92*
**Komoriya,** Akira *AmMWSc 92*
**Komornicki,** Andrew 1948- *AmMWSc 92*
**Komoroske,** John Herman 1949- *WhoAmP 91*
**Komoroski,** Richard Andrew 1947- *AmMWSc 92*
**Komorsky,** Linda Ann 1944- *WhoEnt 92*
**Komosa,** Marilyn Rozmarek 1931- *WhoAmL 92*
**Komoto,** Toshio 1911- *IntWW 91*
**Komov,** Oleg Konstantinovich 1922- *SovUnBD*
**Komp,** Barbara Ann 1954- *WhoMW 92*
**Komp,** Diane Marilyn 1940- *WhoRel 92*
**Kompala,** Dhinakar S 1958- *AmMWSc 92*
**Kompala,** Dhinakar Sathyanathan 1958- *WhoWest 92*
**Kompas,** John George 1946- *WhoEnt 92*
**Komplektov,** Viktor Georgiyevich 1932- *IntWW 91*
**Komroff,** Manuel 1890-1974 *BenetAL 91*
**Komson,** Linda Davidson 1942- *WhoAmP 91*
**Komunyakaa,** Yusef *DrAPF 91*
**Kon,** Mark A *AmMWSc 92*
**Kon,** Richard Henry 1952- *WhoFI 92*
**Konadu,** Samuel Asare 1932- *IntAu&W 91*
**Konarev,** Nikolai Semyonovich 1927- *IntWW 91*
**Konashevich,** Vladimir Mikhaylovich 1888-1963 *SovUnBD*
**Konat,** Gregory W 1947- *AmMWSc 92*
**Koncelik,** Susan 1946- *WhoWest 92*
**Konchalovsky,** Andrei *IntDcF 2-2*
**Konchalovsky,** Andrei 1937- *IntMPA 92*
**Konchalovsky,** Peter 1876-1956 *FacFETw*
**Konchalovsky,** Petr Petrovich 1876-1956 *SovUnBD*
**Konchar,** Jon Robert 1962- *WhoFI 92*
**Kondakov,** Mikhail Ivanovich 1920- *IntWW 91*
**Kondapavulur,** Venkateswara Rao Tirumala 1962- *WhoWest 92*
**Kondas,** Nicholas Frank 1929- *WhoFI 92*
**Konde,** Anthony Joseph 1912- *AmMWSc 92*
**Kondek,** Patricia Lee 1939- *WhoEnt 92*
**Kondelik,** Evelyn Marguerite 1937- *WhoAmP 91*
**Kondo,** Christine Satomi 1961- *WhoWest 92*
**Kondo,** Edward Shinichi 1939- *AmMWSc 92*
**Kondo,** Jo 1947- *ConCom 92*
**Kondo,** Norman Shigeru 1941- *AmMWSc 92*
**Kondo,** Tetsuo 1929- *IntWW 91*
**Kondo,** Yoji 1933- *AmMWSc 92*
**Kondo,** Yoshio 1910- *AmMWSc 92*
**Kondoleon,** Harry 1955- *IntAu&W 91, WrDr 92*
**Kondor,** Lu Ann 1963- *WhoEnt 92*
**Kondra,** Peter Alexander 1911- *AmMWSc 92*
**Kondracki,** Edward John 1932- *WhoAmL 92*
**Kondracki,** Henry 1953- *TwCPaSc*
**Kondrashin,** Kiril 1914-1981 *FacFETw*
**Kondrashin,** Kirill 1914-1981 *NewAmDM*
**Kondrashin,** Kirill Petrovich 1914-1981 *SovUnBD*
**Kondrasuk,** Jack John N. 1942- *WhoWest 92*
**Kondratenko,** Roman Isidorovich 1857-1904 *FacFETw*
**Kondrat'ev,** Nikolay Dmitrievich 1892-1938 *SovUnBD*
**Kondratieff,** Nikolay Dmitrievich 1892-1938 *SovUnBD*
**Kondratiyeva,** Maria Viktorovna 1934- *IntWW 91*
**Kondrich,** Ted V *WhoAmP 91*
**Kondwani,** Kofi Anum 1955- *WhoBlA 92*
**Konecci,** Eugene B 1925- *AmMWSc 92*
**Koneck,** John M. 1953- *WhoAmL 92*
**Konecky,** Edith *DrAPF 91*
**Konecky,** Milton Stuart 1922- *AmMWSc 92*
**Konen,** Harry P 1940- *AmMWSc 92*
**Konenkov,** Sergey Timofeevich 1874-1971 *SovUnBD*
**Koner,** Pauline 1912- *WhoEnt 92*
**Kones,** Richard 1948- *WhoFI 92*
**Konetzka,** Walter Anthony 1923- *AmMWSc 92*
**Konev,** Ivan Stepanovich 1897-1973 *SovUnBD*
**Konezny,** Lorette M. Sobol 1948- *WhoFI 92*
**Kong Fei** 1911- *IntWW 91*
**Kong Shiquan** 1909- *IntWW 91*
**Kong,** Chhon Phan 1952- *WhoRel 92*
**Kong,** Chuang Fong 1962- *WhoWest 92*
**Kong,** David 1950- *WhoFI 92*
**Kong,** Eric Siu-Wai 1953- *AmMWSc 92*
**Kong,** Jin Au 1942- *AmMWSc 92*
**Kong,** Luis John 1956- *WhoHisp 92*
**Kong,** Yi-Chi Mei 1934- *AmMWSc 92*
**Konhauser,** Joseph Daniel Edward 1924- *AmMWSc 92*
**Konheim,** Alan G 1934- *AmMWSc 92*
**Konheim,** John Stewart 1943- *WhoMW 92*
**Konicki,** William Charles 1952- *WhoRel 92*
**Konie,** Gwendoline C. 1938- *IntWW 91*
**Konieczny,** Sharon Louise 1952- *WhoMW 92*
**Konieczny,** Stephen Francis *AmMWSc 92*
**Konig,** Barbara 1925- *IntWW 91*
**Konig,** Franz 1905- *IntWW 91*
**Konig,** Herbert 1925- *IntWW 91*
**Konig,** Rene 1906- *IntWW 91*
**Konig,** Ronald H 1932- *AmMWSc 92*
**Konigsbacher,** Kurt S 1923- *AmMWSc 92*
**Konigsberg,** Alvin Stuart 1943- *AmMWSc 92*
**Konigsberg,** Charles Steven *WhoAmL 92*
**Konigsberg,** Conrad Isidore 1916-1976 *ConAu 134*
**Konigsberg,** Frank *LesBEnT 92*
**Konigsberg,** Frank 1933- *IntMPA 92*
**Konigsberg,** Ira 1935- *WhoEnt 92*
**Konigsberg,** Irwin R 1923- *AmMWSc 92*
**Konigsberg,** Moses 1912- *AmMWSc 92*
**Konigsberg,** William Henry 1930- *AmMWSc 92*
**Konigsburg,** E. L. 1930- *WrDr 92*
**Konijn,** Hendrik Salomon 1918- *AmMWSc 92*
**Konikoff,** John Jacob 1921- *AmMWSc 92*
**Konikoff,** Paula Karen 1947- *WhoFI 92*
**Konikow,** Leonard Franklin 1946- *AmMWSc 92*
**Koning,** Hans *DrAPF 91*
**Koning,** Hans 1921- *LiExTwC*
**Koning,** Hans 1924- *IntAu&W 91, WrDr 92*
**Koning,** Ross E 1953- *AmMWSc 92*
**Koningsberger,** Hans *DrAPF 91, WrDr 92*

**Koningstein**, Johannes A 1933- *AmMWSc 92*
**Konisek**, Colby James 1956- *WhoWest 92*
**Konishi**, Frank 1928- *AmMWSc 92*
**Konishi**, Masakazu 1933- *AmMWSc 92*
**Konisky**, Jordan 1941- *AmMWSc 92*
**Konitz**, Lee 1927- *NewAmDM*
**Konizer**, George Burr 1942- *AmMWSc 92*
**Konkel**, David Anthony 1948- *AmMWSc 92*
**Konkel**, Paul Edward 1933- *WhoWest 92*
**Konkel**, Philip M 1912- *AmMWSc 92*
**Konkle**, Janet Everest 1917- *WrDr 92*
**Konkle**, Thomas A. 1966- *WhoEnt 92*
**Konnak**, John William 1937- *WhoMW 92*
**Konner**, Benn Aron 1966- *WhoFI 92*
**Konner**, Joan *LesBEnT 92*
**Konner**, Kenneth Lloyd 1945- *WhoAmL 92*
**Konner**, Melvin 1946- *WrDr 92*
**Konnerth**, Karl Louis 1932- *AmMWSc 92*
**Konnick**, Ronald John 1943- *WhoWest 92*
**Konnyu**, Ernest L 1937- *WhoAmP 91*
**Konnyu**, Ernest Leslie 1937- *WhoWest 92*
**Kono**, Tetsuro 1925- *AmMWSc 92*
**Kono**, Toshihiko 1930- *IntAu&W 91*, *WhoEnt 92*
**Konold**, George Edward 1956- *WhoEnt 92*
**Konophaghos**, Constantine 1912- *IntWW 91*
**Konopinski**, Lech Kazimierz 1931- *IntAu&W 91*
**Konopinski**, Virgil J 1935- *AmMWSc 92*
**Konopisos**, Konstantine Andrew 1919- *WhoAmL 92*
**Konopka**, Allan Eugene 1950- *AmMWSc 92*
**Konopka**, Arthur Frederick 1940- *WhoAmL 92*
**Konopka**, Ronald J 1947- *AmMWSc 92*
**Konopuicki**, William Stanley 1945- *WhoWest 92*
**Konort**, Mark D 1918- *AmMWSc 92*
**Konotop**, Vasiliy Ivanovich 1916- *SovUnBD*
**Konovalov**, Vasiliy Nikolayevich *IntWW 91*
**Konowalow**, Daniel Dimitri 1929- *AmMWSc 92*, *WhoWest 92*
**Konowitz**, Herbert Henry 1937- *WhoAmP 91*, *WhoFI 92*
**Konrad**, Dusan 1935- *AmMWSc 92*
**Konrad**, Gerhard T 1935- *AmMWSc 92*
**Konrad**, Gyorgy 1933- *IntWW 91*
**Konradi**, Andrei 1931- *AmMWSc 92*
**Konsalik**, Heinz G. 1921- *IntWW 91*
**Konselman**, Douglas Derek 1958- *WhoAmL 92*
**Konshina**, Elena 1950- *ConCom 92*
**Konsis**, Kenneth Frank 1952- *WhoMW 92*
**Konsler**, Thomas Rhinehart 1925- *AmMWSc 92*
**Konstam**, Aaron Harry 1936- *AmMWSc 92*
**Konstant**, David Every *Who 92*
**Konstantinov**, Anatoliy Ustinovich 1923- *IntWW 91*
**Konstantinov**, Tzvetan Krumov *WhoEnt 92*
**Kontarsky**, Alfons 1932- *NewAmDM*
**Kontarsky**, Aloys 1931- *NewAmDM*
**Kontis**, Kris John 1954- *WhoWest 92*
**Kontny**, Vincent Lawrence 1937- *WhoFI 92*, *WhoWest 92*
**Kontogeorgis**, Georgios 1912- *IntWW 91*
**Kontogiorgis**, Michael Theodore 1948- *WhoRel 92*
**Kontorovich**, Vladimir 1951- *WhoFI 92*
**Kontos**, C William 1922- *WhoAmP 91*
**Kontos**, Carol A 1946- *WhoAmP 91*
**Kontos**, Constantine William 1922- *IntWW 91*
**Kontos**, Hermes A 1933- *AmMWSc 92*
**Kontos**, Spero L. 1922- *IntMPA 92*
**Kontosh**, Larry G. 1945- *WhoMW 92*
**Kontou**, Nana 1925- *IntAu&W 91*
**Kontras**, Stella B 1928- *AmMWSc 92*
**Kontz**, Robert James 1952- *WhoFI 92*
**Konuk**, Nejat 1928- *IntWW 91*
**Konvitz**, Jeffrey 1944- *IntAu&W 91*, *WrDr 92*
**Konvitz**, Jeffrey Steven 1944- *WhoEnt 92*
**Konvitz**, Milton R. 1908- *WrDr 92*
**Konwicki**, Tadeusz 1926- *IntWW 91*
**Konwin**, Thor Warner 1943- *WhoFI 92*
**Konya**, Calvin Joseph 1943- *AmMWSc 92*
**Konyegwackie**, Peter *BlkOlyM*
**Konyndyk**, Kenneth John, Jr. 1942- *WhoMW 92*
**Konz**, Stephan A 1933- *AmMWSc 92*
**Konzak**, Calvin Francis 1924- *AmMWSc 92*
**Konzelman**, Leroy Michael 1936- *AmMWSc 92*
**Konzen**, Lynn Marie 1960- *WhoMW 92*
**Konzett**, Heribert 1912- *IntWW 91*
**Konzo**, Seichi 1905- *AmMWSc 92*
**Koo**, Anthony Ying Chang 1918- *WhoFI 92*
**Koo**, Benjamin 1920- *AmMWSc 92*
**Koo**, David Chih-yuen 1951- *AmMWSc 92*
**Koo**, Delia Wei 1921- *AmMWSc 92*
**Koo**, George Ping Shan 1938- *WhoFI 92*
**Koo**, Kee P 1949- *AmMWSc 92*
**Koo**, Peter H *AmMWSc 92*
**Koo**, Robert Chung Jen 1921- *AmMWSc 92*
**Koo**, Sung Il *AmMWSc 92*
**Koo**, Ted Swei-Yen 1910- *AmMWSc 92*
**Koo**, V K Wellington 1887-1985 *FacFETw*
**Koob**, Charles Edward 1944- *WhoAmL 92*
**Koob**, Kenneth Leroy 1945- *WhoAmP 91*
**Koob**, Robert Duane 1941- *AmMWSc 92*, *WhoWest 92*
**Koob**, Robert Philip 1922- *AmMWSc 92*
**Koobs**, Dick Herman 1928- *AmMWSc 92*
**Koocher**, Glenn Stephen 1949- *WhoEnt 92*
**Koogler**, Russell Lewis 1938- *WhoWest 92*
**Kooh**, Sang Whay 1930- *AmMWSc 92*
**Kooi**, Benjamin Vander, Jr 1953- *WhoAmP 91*
**Kooij**, Theo 1933- *AmMWSc 92*
**Kooiker**, Leonie *ConAu 34NR*
**Kooistra**, Paul David 1942- *WhoMW 92*, *WhoRel 92*
**Kooistra**, William Henry 1936- *WhoMW 92*
**Kooken**, John Frederick 1931- *WhoFI 92*
**Kool**, Cornelius Orville 1927- *WhoRel 92*
**Koolish**, Lynda *DrAPF 91*
**Koomen**, Martin J 1917- *AmMWSc 92*
**Koon**, Charles E 1921- *WhoIns 92*
**Koon**, Delores K. *WhoRel 92*
**Koon**, Frank David 1958- *WhoRel 92*
**Koon**, Larry Labruce 1944- *WhoAmP 91*
**Koon**, Ray Harold 1934- *WhoWest 92*
**Koon**, Robin Charles 1953- *WhoWest 92*
**Koonce**, Andrea Lavender 1951- *AmMWSc 92*
**Koonce**, Derek Sean 1963- *WhoWest 92*
**Koonce**, John Peter 1932- *WhoFI 92*
**Koonce**, Kenneth Lowell 1939- *AmMWSc 92*
**Koonce**, Samuel David 1915- *AmMWSc 92*
**Koonen**, Alisa Georg'evna 1889-1974 *SovUnBD*
**Koong**, Ling-Jung *AmMWSc 92*
**Koonin**, Steven Elliot 1951- *AmMWSc 92*
**Koons**, Benjamin Franklin 1848-1903 *BiInAmS*
**Koons**, Charles Bruce 1929- *AmMWSc 92*
**Koons**, David Swarner 1930- *AmMWSc 92*
**Koons**, Donaldson 1917- *AmMWSc 92*
**Koons**, James L 1915- *WhoAmP 91*
**Koons**, Jeff 1955?- *News 91*, *WorArt 1980 [port]*
**Koons**, Michael Marion 1945- *WhoAmP 91*
**Koons**, Robert Arthur, Jr. 1949- *WhoAmL 92*
**Koonts**, J. Calvin *DrAPF 91*
**Koonts**, J Calvin 1924- *IntAu&W 91*
**Koonts**, Robert Henry 1927- *WhoAmL 92*
**Koontz**, Alfred Joseph, Jr. 1942- *WhoFI 92*, *WhoWest 92*
**Koontz**, Ann Teresa 1961- *WhoFI 92*
**Koontz**, Carl Lennis, II 1942- *WhoFI 92*
**Koontz**, Christian 1930- *WhoRel 92*
**Koontz**, Dean R. 1945- *ConAu 36NR*, *IntAu&W 91*, *TwCSFW 91*, *WrDr 92*
**Koontz**, Elizabeth Duncan 1919-1989 *NotBlAW 92 [port]*
**Koontz**, Eva Isabelle 1935- *WhoMW 92*
**Koontz**, Frank P 1932- *AmMWSc 92*
**Koontz**, Kenneth Starke 1959- *WhoFI 92*
**Koontz**, Margaret Ann 1947- *WhoWest 92*
**Koontz**, Philip G *AmMWSc 92*
**Koontz**, Tom *DrAPF 91*
**Koontz**, Warren Woodson, Jr 1932- *AmMWSc 92*
**Koonz**, Claudia *IntAu&W 91*
**Koop**, C. Everett 1916- *IntWW 91*
**Koop**, Charles Everett 1916- *AmMWSc 92*
**Koop**, Dennis Ray *AmMWSc 92*
**Koop**, John C 1919- *AmMWSc 92*
**Koop**, Theodore F. *LesBEnT 92*
**Kooper**, Sybil Hart d1991 *NewYTBS 91 [port]*
**Koopersmith**, Adrienne Sioux 1952- *WhoEnt 92*
**Koopersmith**, Jeffrey MacArthur 1948- *WhoFI 92*
**Koopersmith**, Kim 1959- *WhoAmL 92*
**Koopman**, Antonius Gerhardus Michael 1944- *IntWW 91*
**Koopman**, Augustus 1869-1941 *DcNCBi 3*
**Koopman**, Jacques d1991 *NewYTBS 91*
**Koopman**, Karl Friedrich 1920- *AmMWSc 92*
**Koopman**, Richard J W 1905- *AmMWSc 92*
**Koopman**, Ton 1944- *WhoEnt 92*
**Koopmann Parrish**, Reta Collene 1944- *WhoFI 92*
**Koopmans**, Henry Sjoerd 1944- *AmMWSc 92*
**Koopmans**, Lambert Herman 1930- *AmMWSc 92*
**Koopmans**, Tjalling Charles 1910-1985 *WhoNob 90*
**Koopowitz**, Harold 1940- *AmMWSc 92*
**Koops**, Mary Claire *Who 92*
**Koor**, Robert Stuart 1938- *WhoAmL 92*
**Koornhof**, Pieter Gerhardus Jacobus 1925- *IntWW 91*
**Koory**, Franklin George 1941- *WhoAmL 92*
**Koosed**, Margery Malkin 1948- *WhoAmL 92*
**Kooser**, Robert Galen 1941- *AmMWSc 92*
**Kooser**, Ted *DrAPF 91*
**Kooser**, Ted 1939- *ConPo 91*, *WrDr 92*
**Kooser**, Theodore John 1939- *IntAu&W 91*
**Kooshian**, Percy Victor 1933- *WhoRel 92*
**Koosis**, Paul 1929- *AmMWSc 92*
**Koostra**, Walter L 1934- *AmMWSc 92*
**Koot**, Hank M *WhoIns 92*
**Kootenay**, Bishop of 1937- *Who 92*
**Kootsey**, Joseph Mailen 1939- *AmMWSc 92*
**Kooyker-Romijn**, Johanna Maria 1927- *ConAu 34NR*
**Kooyman**, Gerald Lee 1934- *AmMWSc 92*
**Koozekanai**, Said H 1933- *AmMWSc 92*
**Kopal**, Zdenek 1914- *AmMWSc 92*, *Who 92*, *WrDr 92*
**Kopald**, Larry S. 1954- *WhoFI 92*
**Kopanski**, Joseph J 1960- *AmMWSc 92*
**Kopas**, George Thomas 1950- *WhoFI 92*
**Kopchick**, John J 1950- *AmMWSc 92*
**Kopchik**, Richard Michael 1941- *AmMWSc 92*
**Kopcke**, Karl-Heinz d1991 *NewYTBS 91*
**Kopczak**, Eugene Edward 1934- *WhoAmP 91*
**Kope**, Robert Glenn 1953- *AmMWSc 92*
**Kopecek**, Jindrich 1940- *AmMWSc 92*
**Kopech**, David Albert 1952- *WhoAmL 92*
**Kopecky**, Jan 1919- *IntWW 91*
**Kopecky**, Jane Marie 1962- *WhoMW 92*
**Kopecky**, Karl Rudolph 1932- *AmMWSc 92*
**Kopecky**, Kenneth John 1943- *WhoFI 92*
**Kopeczi**, Bela 1921- *IntWW 91*
**Kopel**, Dolores Blanke 1931- *WhoAmL 92*
**Kopel**, Gerald 1928- *WhoAmP 91*
**Kopel**, Joel Gerson 1953- *WhoFI 92*
**Kopel**, Robert Frank 1954- *WhoWest 92*
**Kopelent**, Marek 1932- *ConCom 92*
**Kopelev**, Lev 1907- *LiExTwC*
**Kopelev**, Lev Zinov'evich 1912- *SovUnBD*
**Kopelev**, Lev Zinovyevich 1912- *FacFETw*
**Kopell**, Bernard Morton 1933- *WhoEnt 92*
**Kopelman**, Jay B 1939- *AmMWSc 92*
**Kopelman**, Larry Gordon 1949- *WhoAmL 92*
**Kopelman**, Leonard 1940- *WhoFI 92*
**Kopelman**, Raoul 1933- *AmMWSc 92*
**Kopelowitz**, Lionel 1926- *Who 92*
**Kopelson**, Arnold 1935- *IntMPA 92*
**Kopenhaver**, Josephine Young 1908- *WhoWest 92*
**Koper**, Alex 1917- *WhoWest 92*
**Koper**, Francis Bernard 1944- *WhoMW 92*, *WhoRel 92*
**Koperwas**, Sam *DrAPF 91*
**Kopesky**, John Paul 1954- *WhoAmL 92*
**Kopetski**, Michael Joseph 1949- *WhoAmP 91*
**Kopetski**, Mike 1949- *AlmAP 92 [port]*, *WhoWest 92*
**Kopf**, Alfred Walter 1926- *AmMWSc 92*
**Kopf**, David 1930- *WhoMW 92*
**Kopf**, David Heath 1932- *WhoFI 92*
**Kopf**, Peter W 1944- *AmMWSc 92*
**Kopf**, Rudolph William 1922- *AmMWSc 92*
**Kopfler**, Frederick Charles 1938- *AmMWSc 92*
**Kopin**, Irwin J 1929- *AmMWSc 92*
**Kopis**, F. Jan 1942- *WhoMW 92*
**Kopis**, William Floyd 1943- *WhoAmL 92*
**Kopit**, Arthur 1937- *IntAu&W 91*, *WhoEnt 92*, *WrDr 92*
**Kopit**, Arthur L. 1937- *BenetAL 91*
**Kopito**, Ron Rieger 1954- *AmMWSc 92*
**Kopkin**, Aleksandr Gavrilovich 1927- *IntWW 91*
**Koplik**, Joel 1948- *AmMWSc 92*
**Koplin**, Donald Leroy 1932- *WhoWest 92*
**Koplitz**, Ronald Gene 1943- *WhoRel 92*
**Koplovitz**, Kay *LesBEnT 92 [port]*
**Koplow**, David Alexander 1951- *WhoAmL 92*
**Koplow**, Jane 1948- *AmMWSc 92*
**Koplowitz**, Jack 1944- *AmMWSc 92*
**Koplyay**, Janos Bernath 1924- *AmMWSc 92*
**Kopman**, Charles Edmund 1936- *WhoAmL 92*
**Kopmar**, Jerome Benjamin 1936- *WhoRel 92*
**Kopmeyer**, David Louis 1950- *WhoMW 92*
**Koponen**, Niilo E *WhoAmP 91*
**Kopp**, Bradford B. 1951- *WhoFI 92*
**Kopp**, Clarence Adam, Jr. 1927- *WhoRel 92*
**Kopp**, David Andrew 1949- *WhoRel 92*
**Kopp**, David Eugene 1951- *WhoWest 92*
**Kopp**, David James 1943- *WhoWest 92*
**Kopp**, Donald Lee 1935- *WhoAmP 91*
**Kopp**, Eugene H 1929- *AmMWSc 92*
**Kopp**, George Philip, Jr. 1927- *WhoRel 92*
**Kopp**, Jay Patrick 1938- *AmMWSc 92*
**Kopp**, Karl *DrAPF 91*
**Kopp**, Manfred Kurt 1932- *AmMWSc 92*
**Kopp**, Nancy Kornblith 1943- *WhoAmP 91*
**Kopp**, Oswald W 1918- *WhoMW 92*
**Kopp**, Otto Charles 1929- *AmMWSc 92*
**Kopp**, Quentin Lewis 1928- *WhoAmP 91*
**Kopp**, Richard E 1931- *AmMWSc 92*
**Kopp**, Richard L 1934- *IntAu&W 91*, *WrDr 92*
**Kopp**, Robert Walter 1935- *WhoAmL 92*
**Kopp**, Roger Alan 1940- *AmMWSc 92*
**Kopp**, Steven Eugene 1953- *WhoAmP 91*
**Kopp**, W. Brewster *WhoFI 92*
**Koppa**, Patricia Ann 1960- *WhoAmL 92*
**Koppa**, Rodger J 1936- *AmMWSc 92*
**Koppel**, Donald Theodore 1925- *WhoAmP 91*
**Koppel**, Gary Allen 1943- *AmMWSc 92*
**Koppel**, Henning 1918-1981 *DcTwDes*
**Koppel**, Lowell B 1935- *AmMWSc 92*
**Koppel**, Ted *IntWW 91*, *LesBEnT 92 [port]*
**Koppel**, Thomas Paul 1943- *WhoWest 92*
**Koppell**, Bonnie Jane 1956- *WhoRel 92*
**Koppell**, G Oliver 1940- *WhoAmP 91*
**Koppelman**, Charles *WhoEnt 92*
**Koppelman**, Elaine 1937- *AmMWSc 92*
**Koppelman**, Julius 1916- *WhoFI 92*
**Koppelman**, Kim Arden 1956- *WhoMW 92*
**Koppelman**, Lee Edward 1927- *AmMWSc 92*
**Koppelman**, Murray 1931- *WhoFI 92*
**Koppelman**, Ray 1922- *AmMWSc 92*, *WhoMW 92*
**Koppen**, Jerry Lynn 1945- *WhoIns 92*
**Koppen**, Marvin Charles 1952- *WhoAmP 91*
**Koppenaal**, Theodore J 1931- *AmMWSc 92*
**Koppendrayer**, LeRoy J 1941- *WhoAmP 91*
**Koppenheffer**, Thomas Lynn 1942- *AmMWSc 92*
**Koppenhoefer**, Robert Mack 1909- *WhoFI 92*
**Kopper**, Hilmar 1935- *IntWW 91*
**Kopperl**, Sheldon Jerome 1943- *AmMWSc 92*
**Kopperman**, Ralph David 1942- *AmMWSc 92*
**Koppes**, Gerald Joseph 1945- *WhoMW 92*
**Koppes**, Rebecca Ann 1952- *WhoAmL 92*
**Koppinger**, Thomas J 1941- *WhoIns 92*
**Kopple**, Kenneth D 1930- *AmMWSc 92*
**Kopplin**, J O 1925- *AmMWSc 92*
**Kopprasch**, Robert William 1947- *WhoFI 92*
**Koppus**, Betty Jane 1922- *WhoFI 92*
**Koprivica**, Dorothy Mary 1921- *WhoMW 92*
**Koprowska**, Irena 1917- *AmMWSc 92*
**Koprowski**, Hilary *AmMWSc 92*
**Koprowski**, Kenneth M. *DrAPF 91*
**Kops**, Adam 1956- *TwCPaSc*
**Kops**, Bernard 1926- *ConNov 91*, *ConPo 91*, *WrDr 92*
**Koptak**, Paul Edward 1955- *WhoRel 92*
**Koptyug**, Valentin Afanasiyevich 1931- *IntWW 91*
**Korach**, Kenneth Steven 1946- *AmMWSc 92*
**Korach**, Malcolm 1922- *AmMWSc 92*
**Korach**, William Mark 1945- *WhoFI 92*
**Korajczyk**, Robert Alan 1954- *WhoMW 92*
**Koral**, Randall 1959- *WhoEnt 92*
**Koralek**, Paul George 1933- *Who 92*
**Koran**, Dennis *DrAPF 91*
**Koran**, Lorrin Michael 1940- *AmMWSc 92*
**Koran**, Zoltan 1934- *AmMWSc 92*
**Koranda**, David Edward 1947- *WhoFI 92*
**Koranda**, J. Timothy 1950- *IntAu&W 91*
**Korangteng**, Daniel Agyei 1927- *WhoRel 92*
**Korant**, Bruce David 1943- *AmMWSc 92*
**Koranteng-Pipim**, Samuel 1957- *WhoRel 92*
**Koranyi**, Adam 1932- *AmMWSc 92*
**Korb**, Donald Lee 1948- *WhoAmL 92*
**Korb**, Kenneth Allan 1932- *WhoAmL 92*, *WhoFI 92*
**Korb**, Lawrence John 1930- *WhoWest 92*
**Korban**, Bernard 1923- *IntMPA 92*
**Korbar**, Marcia M 1955- *IntAu&W 91*
**Korbel**, Linda Anne 1949- *WhoMW 92*
**Korbin**, Thaddeus Michael 1951- *WhoWest 92*

**Korbitz**, Bernard Carl 1935- *WhoMW 92*
**Korbman**, Meyer Hyman 1925- *WhoRel 92*
**Korbuly**, Laszlo John 1935- *WhoMW 92*
**Korbut**, Olga Valentinovna 1955- *SovUnBD*
**Korbut**, Olga Valentinovna 1956- *FacFETw*
**Korc**, Murray 1947- *AmMWSc 92*, *WhoWest 92*
**Korcak**, Josef 1921- *IntWW 91*
**Korcek**, Stefan 1934- *AmMWSc 92*
**Korchak**, Ernest I 1934- *AmMWSc 92*
**Korchak**, Helen Marie *AmMWSc 92*
**Korchin**, Leo 1914- *AmMWSc 92*
**Korchnoi**, Victor 1931- *FacFETw*
**Korchynsky**, M 1918- *AmMWSc 92*
**Korcoulis**, Chris 1908- *WhoAmP 91*
**Korczak**, Edward Stanley 1945- *WhoMW 92*
**Korczak**, Janusz *ConAu 133*
**Korczak**, Janusz 1878-1942 *EncTR 91*, *SmATA 65*
**Korda**, Alexander 1893-1956 *FacFETw*, *IntDcF 2-2 [port]*
**Korda**, Edward J 1918- *AmMWSc 92*
**Korda**, Henry 1957- *TwCPaSc*
**Korda**, Marion Amelia 1922- *WhoEnt 92*
**Korda**, Michael 1933- *WrDr 92*
**Korda**, Michael Vincent 1933- *IntAu&W 91*, *IntWW 91*
**Korda**, Peter E 1931- *AmMWSc 92*
**Kordahl**, Eugene B. 1936- *WhoFI 92*
**Kordan**, Herbert Allen 1926- *AmMWSc 92*
**Kordenbrock**, Douglas William 1964- *WhoMW 92*
**Kordesch**, Karl Victor 1922- *AmMWSc 92*
**Kordestani**, Ben Khazael 1954- *WhoFI 92*
**Kordons**, Uldis 1941- *WhoAmL 92*
**Kordoski**, Edward William 1954- *AmMWSc 92*
**Kordova**, Nonna *AmMWSc 92*
**Korducki**, Barbara Joan 1956- *WhoWest 92*
**Kordyban**, Eugene S 1928- *AmMWSc 92*
**Korec**, Jan Chryzostom 1924- *WhoRel 92*
**Korecky**, Borivoj 1929- *AmMWSc 92*
**Korein**, Julius 1928- *AmMWSc 92*
**Koren**, Edward Franz 1946- *WhoAmL 92*
**Koren**, Henry J 1912- *ConAu 35NR*, *IntAu&W 91*
**Koren**, Henry Joseph 1912- *WrDr 92*
**Koren**, Petter Morch 1910- *IntWW 91*
**Koren**, Philip Francis 1945- *WhoAmL 92*
**Koren**, Samuel M 1941- *WhoIns 92*
**Koren'**, Sergey Gavrilovich 1907-1969 *SovUnBD*
**Koren**, Ulrik Vilhelm 1826-1910 *RelLAm 91*
**Korenbrot**, Juan Igal 1947- *AmMWSc 92*
**Korenman**, Stanley G 1933- *AmMWSc 92*
**Korenman**, Victor 1937- *AmMWSc 92*
**Korenstein**, Ralph 1951- *AmMWSc 92*
**Koretsky**, Vladimir Mikhaylovich 1890-1983 *SovUnBD*
**Koretz**, E. Barbara Pearlman 1952- *WhoWest 92*
**Koretz**, Jane Faith 1947- *AmMWSc 92*
**Korevaar**, Jacob 1923- *AmMWSc 92*
**Korf**, Anthony 1951- *WhoEnt 92*
**Korf**, Richard E 1956- *AmMWSc 92*
**Korf**, Richard Earl 1956- *WhoWest 92*
**Korf**, Richard Paul 1925- *AmMWSc 92*
**Korf**, Willy Wilhelm 1929- *IntWW 91*
**Korff**, Ira A. 1949- *IntMPA 92*, *WhoEnt 92*, *WhoFI 92*
**Korfhage**, Robert R 1930- *AmMWSc 92*
**Korfker**, Dena 1908- *WrDr 92*
**Korfmacher**, Walter Averill 1951- *AmMWSc 92*
**Korg**, Jacob 1922- *IntAu&W 91*, *WrDr 92*
**Korgen**, Benjamin Jeffry 1931- *AmMWSc 92*
**Korges**, Emerson 1911- *AmMWSc 92*
**Korhola**, Marja Anita 1954- *WhoEnt 92*
**Korhonen**, Gunnar Aleksander 1918- *IntWW 91*
**Korhonen**, Keijo Tero 1934- *IntWW 91*
**Korhonen**, Otto *DcTwDes*
**Korican**, Donald Richard 1957- *WhoMW 92*
**Korin**, Amos 1944- *AmMWSc 92*
**Korin**, Basil Peter 1932- *AmMWSc 92*
**Korin**, Pavel Dmitrievich 1892-1967 *SovUnBD*
**Korinek**, George Jiri 1927- *AmMWSc 92*
**Korinkova**, Kvetoslava 1940- *IntWW 91*
**Korinow**, Ira Lee 1951- *WhoRel 92*
**Korins**, Leopold *WhoFI 92*
**Korir**, Julius 1960- *BlkOlyM*
**Koritala**, Sanbasivaroa 1932- *AmMWSc 92*
**Koritan**, Van Lee 1948- *WhoEnt 92*
**Koritansky**, Gregory Emil 1949- *WhoRel 92*
**Koritnik**, Donald Raymond 1946- *AmMWSc 92*
**Koritz**, Gary Duane 1944- *AmMWSc 92*
**Koritz**, Seymour Benjamin 1921- *AmMWSc 92*
**Korkegi**, Robert Hani 1925- *AmMWSc 92*
**Korkin**, Aleksandr Gavriilovich 1927- *IntWW 91*
**Korle**, Sinan A. 1914- *IntWW 91*
**Korlen**, Gustav 1915- *IntWW 91*
**Korman**, A. Gerd 1928- *ConAu 35NR*
**Korman**, David Milton 1953- *WhoAmL 92*
**Korman**, Edward R. 1942- *WhoAmL 92*
**Korman**, Gordon 1963- *ChlLR 25 [port]*, *ConAu 34NR*
**Korman**, Gordon Richard 1963- *IntAu&W 91*
**Korman**, Harvey 1927- *IntMPA 92*
**Korman**, Harvey Herschel 1927- *WhoEnt 92*
**Korman**, James William 1943- *WhoAmL 92*
**Korman**, Jeffrey R *WhoAmP 91*
**Korman**, Lewis J. 1945- *IntMPA 92*, *WhoEnt 92*, *WhoFI 92*
**Korman**, N I 1916- *AmMWSc 92*
**Kormelink**, Helen Jean *WhoRel 92*
**Kormendi**, Roger Charles 1949- *WhoFI 92*
**Kormendy**, John 1948- *AmMWSc 92*
**Kormes**, John Winston 1935- *WhoAmL 92*, *WhoFI 92*
**Kormondy**, Edward J 1926- *IntAu&W 91*, *WrDr 92*
**Kormondy**, Edward John 1926- *WhoWest 92*
**Korn**, Alfons L 1906-1986 *ConAu 34NR*
**Korn**, Alfred 1930- *AmMWSc 92*
**Korn**, Allan Michael 1944- *WhoMW 92*
**Korn**, Barry Paul 1944- *WhoFI 92*
**Korn**, David 1933- *AmMWSc 92*
**Korn**, David 1934- *WhoAmP 91*
**Korn**, Edward David 1928- *AmMWSc 92*
**Korn**, Granino A 1922- *AmMWSc 92*
**Korn**, Halina 1902-1978 *TwCPaSc*
**Korn**, Harold Leon 1929- *WhoAmL 92*
**Korn**, Henry *DrAPF 91*
**Korn**, Hyman 1902-1991 *NewYTBS 91*
**Korn**, Joseph Howard 1947- *AmMWSc 92*
**Korn**, Lester Bernard 1936- *WhoFI 92*
**Korn**, Michael d1991 *NewYTBS 91*
**Korn**, Roy Joseph 1920- *AmMWSc 92*
**Korn**, Steven W. *WhoAmL 92*
**Korn**, Walter 1908- *WhoWest 92*
**Kornachuk**, John David 1959- *WhoWest 92*
**Kornacker**, Karl 1937- *AmMWSc 92*
**Kornai**, J 1928- *ConAu 35NR*
**Kornai**, Janos 1928- *IntWW 91*
**Kornberg**, Alan William 1952- *WhoAmL 92*
**Kornberg**, Arthur 1918- *AmMWSc 92*, *IntWW 91*, *News 92-1 [port]*, *Who 92*, *WhoNob 90*, *WhoWest 92*
**Kornberg**, Felice 1928- *WhoEnt 92*
**Kornberg**, Fred 1936- *AmMWSc 92*
**Kornberg**, Hans 1928- *IntWW 91*, *Who 92*
**Kornberg**, Joel Barry 1953- *WhoAmL 92*
**Kornberg**, Roger David 1947- *AmMWSc 92*
**Kornberg**, Thomas B 1948- *AmMWSc 92*
**Kornblatt**, Marshall Irving 1947- *WhoFI 92*
**Kornblith**, Carol Lee 1945- *AmMWSc 92*
**Kornblith**, Lester 1917- *AmMWSc 92*
**Kornbluh**, Edward Calvin 1926- *WhoAmP 91*
**Kornbluh**, Mark Lawrence 1955- *WhoMW 92*
**Kornblum**, Allan *DrAPF 91*
**Kornblum**, Cinda *DrAPF 91*
**Kornblum**, Nathan 1914- *AmMWSc 92*
**Kornblum**, Ronald Norman 1933- *AmMWSc 92*
**Kornblum**, Saul S 1934- *AmMWSc 92*
**Kornbluth**, C M 1923-1958 *TwCSFW 91*
**Kornbluth**, Richard Syd 1948- *AmMWSc 92*
**Kornbluth**, Sandra Joan 1951- *WhoFI 92*
**Korndorf**, Nikolai 1947- *ConCom 92*
**Kornegay**, Ervin Thaddeus 1931- *AmMWSc 92*
**Kornegay**, Francis A. 1913- *WhoBlA 92*
**Kornegay**, Hobert 1923- *WhoAmP 91*, *WhoBlA 92*
**Kornegay**, Horace Robinson 1924- *WhoAmP 91*
**Kornegay**, Roy Aubry, Jr. 1937- *WhoRel 92*
**Kornegay**, Wade Hampton 1865-1939 *DcNCBi 3*
**Kornegay**, Wade M. 1934- *WhoBlA 92*
**Kornegay**, Wilburt 1941- *WhoAmP 91*
**Kornegay**, William F. 1933- *WhoBlA 92*
**Kornel**, Ludwig 1923- *AmMWSc 92*
**Kornelly**, Irene Louise 1945- *WhoAmP 91*
**Korner**, Alexis 1928-1984 *NewAmDM*
**Korner**, Carol Ann 1960- *WhoMW 92*
**Korner**, Heinrich 1892-1945 *EncTR 91*
**Korner**, Jules Gilmer, III 1922- *WhoAmL 92*
**Korner**, Paul 1893-1957 *EncTR 91 [port]*
**Korner**, Stephan 1913- *IntWW 91*, *Who 92*, *WrDr 92*
**Kornet**, Milton Joseph 1935- *AmMWSc 92*
**Kornetsky**, Conan 1926- *AmMWSc 92*
**Kornfeil**, Fred 1924- *AmMWSc 92*
**Kornfeind**, Donald William 1955- *WhoEnt 92*
**Kornfeld**, Edmund Carl 1919- *AmMWSc 92*
**Kornfeld**, Lottie 1925- *AmMWSc 92*
**Kornfeld**, Mario O 1927- *AmMWSc 92*
**Kornfeld**, Robert Jonathan 1919- *IntAu&W 91*
**Kornfeld**, Rosalind Hauk 1935- *AmMWSc 92*
**Kornfeld**, Stuart Arthur 1936- *AmMWSc 92*
**Kornfield**, A T 1918- *AmMWSc 92*
**Kornfield**, Gary Carl 1953- *WhoAmL 92*
**Kornfield**, Irving Leslie 1945- *AmMWSc 92*
**Kornfield**, Jack I *AmMWSc 92*
**Korngold**, Alvin Leonard 1924- *WhoEnt 92*
**Korngold**, Erich Wolfgang 1897-1957 *FacFETw*, *NewAmDM*
**Korngold**, Robert *AmMWSc 92*
**Kornguth**, Herbert 1936- *WhoWest 92*
**Kornguth**, Steven E 1935- *AmMWSc 92*
**Kornhauser**, Alain Lucien 1944- *AmMWSc 92*
**Kornhauser**, Andrija 1930- *AmMWSc 92*
**Kornhauser**, Edward T 1925- *AmMWSc 92*
**Kornhauser**, Kenneth Richard 1947- *WhoFI 92*
**Kornhauser**, Lewis 1950- *WhoAmL 92*
**Kornhauser**, William 1925- *WrDr 92*
**Kornick**, Nicholas 1912- *WhoAmP 91*
**Kornicker**, Louis Sampson 1919- *AmMWSc 92*
**Kornicker**, William Alan 1956- *AmMWSc 92*
**Kornienko**, Anatoliy *IntWW 91*
**Kornienko**, Georgiy Markovich 1925- *IntWW 91*
**Kornilov**, Boris Petrovich 1907-1938 *SovUnBD*
**Kornilov**, Lavr Georgevich 1870-1918 *FacFETw*
**Kornilov**, Ludmilla *EncAmaz 91*
**Kornilov**, Vladimir Nikolaevich 1928- *IntWW 91*
**Kornilov**, Volkensteii *EncAmaz 91*
**Kornis**, Frederick Vance, Jr. 1950- *WhoRel 92*
**Kornman**, Brent D 1956- *AmMWSc 92*
**Kornowicz**, Edmund Edwin 1914- *WhoAmP 91*
**Kornreich**, Helen Kass 1931- *AmMWSc 92*
**Kornreich**, James David 1952- *WhoAmP 91*
**Kornreich**, Philipp G 1931- *AmMWSc 92*
**Korns**, Leota *DrAPF 91*
**Kornstein**, Edward 1929- *AmMWSc 92*
**Kornylak**, Andrew T 1917- *AmMWSc 92*
**Korobkin**, Irving 1925- *AmMWSc 92*
**Korody**, Anthony Vincent 1951- *WhoWest 92*
**Korol**, Bernard 1929- *AmMWSc 92*
**Korolev**, Boris Danilovich 1884-1963 *SovUnBD*
**Korolev**, Mikhail Antonovich 1931- *IntWW 91*
**Korolev**, Sergey Pavlovich 1907-1966 *SovUnBD*
**Korolev**, Yuri Konstantinovich 1929- *IntWW 91*
**Korolev**, Yuriy Konstantinovich 1929- *SovUnBD*
**Korologos**, Tom Chris 1933- *WhoFI 92*
**Korolow**, John Mark 1959- *WhoEnt 92*
**Koroly**, Mary Jo 1943- *AmMWSc 92*
**Koroma**, Abdul G. *IntWW 91*
**Koroma**, Sorie Ibrahim 1930- *IntWW 91*
**Koromilas**, Alec J 1964- *WhoAmP 91*
**Koronkowski**, Michael James 1964- *WhoMW 92*
**Koros**, Aurelia M Carissimo 1934- *AmMWSc 92*
**Koros**, Peter J 1932- *AmMWSc 92*
**Koros**, William John 1947- *AmMWSc 92*
**Korostoff**, Edward 1921- *AmMWSc 92*
**Korotchenko**, Demyan Sergeevich 1894-1969 *SovUnBD*
**Korotev**, Randall Lee 1949- *AmMWSc 92*
**Korotich**, Vitaliy Alekseevich 1936- *SovUnBD*
**Korotych**, Vitaliy Alekseyevich 1936- *IntWW 91*
**Korovin**, Konstant 1861-1939 *FacFETw*
**Korovin**, Konstantin 1860-1939 *LiExTwC*
**Korovin**, Yevgeniy Aleksandrovich 1892-1964 *SovUnBD*
**Korpel**, Adrianus 1932- *AmMWSc 92*
**Korper**, Samuel *AmMWSc 92*
**Korpinen**, Matti Ilmari 1938- *WhoFI 92*
**Korpman**, Ralph Andrew 1952- *AmMWSc 92*, *WhoFI 92*
**Korr**, Charles Paul 1939- *WhoMW 92*
**Korr**, Irvin Morris 1909- *AmMWSc 92*
**Korrick**, Ed Lawrence 1925- *WhoAmP 91*
**Korringa**, Jan 1915- *AmMWSc 92*
**Korry**, Edward M. 1922- *IntWW 91*
**Kors**, Michael 1959- *IntWW 91*
**Korsbaek**, Vagn Aage 1923- *IntWW 91*
**Korsch**, Barbara M 1921- *AmMWSc 92*
**Korsch**, Dietrich G 1937- *AmMWSc 92*
**Korschot**, Benjamin Calvin 1921- *WhoMW 92*
**Korsh**, James F 1938- *AmMWSc 92*
**Korshak**, Vasily Vladimirovich 1909- *IntWW 91*
**Korshoj**, Frank 1932- *WhoAmP 91*
**Korshoj**, Franklin Delano 1932- *WhoMW 92*
**Korslund**, Mary Katherine *AmMWSc 92*
**Korsmeyer**, Mary Drake 1937- *WhoAmL 92*
**Korsmeyer**, Stanley Joel *AmMWSc 92*
**Korsmo**, John Thomas 1950- *WhoAmP 91*
**Korson**, Roy 1922- *AmMWSc 92*
**Korsrud**, Gary Olaf 1942- *AmMWSc 92*
**Korst**, Donald Richardson 1924- *AmMWSc 92*
**Korst**, Helmut Hans 1916- *AmMWSc 92*
**Korst**, James Joseph 1931- *AmMWSc 92*
**Korst**, William Lawrence 1922- *AmMWSc 92*
**Korstad**, John Edward 1949- *AmMWSc 92*
**Korstjens**, Keith Allen 1929- *WhoRel 92*
**Korszen**, Dorothy Lynn *WhoAmL 92*
**Kort**, Margaret Alexander 1928- *AmMWSc 92*
**Kort**, Wesley A 1935- *ConAu 34NR*, *WrDr 92*
**Kort**, Wesley Albert 1935- *IntAu&W 91*
**Kort**, William B. 1931- *WhoMW 92*
**Kortanek**, Kenneth O 1936- *AmMWSc 92*
**Korte**, David Charles Jude 1955- *WhoAmL 92*
**Korte**, Karl Richard 1928- *WhoEnt 92*
**Korte**, William David 1937- *AmMWSc 92*
**Kortebein**, Stuart Rowland 1930- *WhoMW 92*
**Kortelainen**, Karl Efremovich *IntWW 91*
**Korteling**, Ralph Garret 1937- *AmMWSc 92*
**Korten**, David C 1937- *ConAu 34NR*
**Kortenhof**, Joseph Michael 1927- *WhoMW 92*
**Korth**, Fred 1909- *IntWW 91*
**Korth**, Gary E 1938- *AmMWSc 92*
**Korth**, James Scott 1963- *WhoRel 92*
**Korth**, Penne Percy 1942- *WhoAmP 91*
**Korth**, Philip Alan 1936- *WhoMW 92*
**Korthals**, Hendrik Albertus 1911- *IntWW 91*
**Korthals**, Robert W. 1933- *IntWW 91*
**Korthase**, Susan Stults 1951- *WhoMW 92*
**Korthuis**, Robert Cecil 1934- *WhoRel 92*
**Kortlandt**, Frederik H. H. 1946- *IntWW 91*
**Kortner**, Fritz 1892-1970 *EncTR 91*
**Kortner**, Peter 1924-1991 *ConAu 133*
**Kortright**, Frederic Lawrence 1867-1914 *BiInAmS*
**Kortright**, James McDougall 1927- *AmMWSc 92*
**Kortum**, Daniel James 1949- *WhoAmL 92*
**Korty**, John 1936- *IntMPA 92*
**Korty**, John Van Cleave 1936- *WhoEnt 92*
**Kortz**, Edwin Wunderly 1910- *WhoRel 92*
**Korvald**, Lars 1916- *IntWW 91*
**Korver**, Gerry Rozeboom 1952- *WhoMW 92*
**Korvick**, Maria Marinello 1946- *WhoHisp 92*
**Korwek**, Alexander Donald 1932- *AmMWSc 92*
**Korwin**, Yala H. *DrAPF 91*
**Korwin-Pawlowski**, Michael Lech 1941- *AmMWSc 92*
**Kory**, Mitchell 1914- *AmMWSc 92*
**Kory**, Ross Conklin 1918- *AmMWSc 92*
**Koryagin**, Anatoliy Ivanovich 1938- *IntWW 91*, *SovUnBD*
**Koryakin**, Yuriy Ivanovich 1935- *IntWW 91*
**Korytnyk**, Walter 1929- *AmMWSc 92*
**Korzelius**, Linda Diane 1955- *WhoRel 92*
**Korzeniewski**, Bohdan 1905- *IntWW 91*
**Korzenik**, Diana 1941- *ConAu 133*
**Korzeniowski**, Thomas Michael 1937- *WhoEnt 92*
**Korzenny**, Felipe 1947- *WhoHisp 92*
**Korzhavin**, Naum 1925- *IntWW 91*
**Korzhavin**, Naum 1939- *LiExTwC*
**Korzhavin**, Naum Moiseevich 1925- *SovUnBD*
**Korzhev**, Geliy Mikhaylovich 1925- *SovUnBD*
**Korzhev-Chuvelev**, Geliy Mikhaylovich 1925- *SovUnBD*
**Korzhev-Chuvelyov**, Gely Mikhailovich 1925- *IntWW 91*
**Kos**, Clair Michael 1911- *AmMWSc 92*
**Kos**, Edmund Peter 1958- *WhoAmL 92*
**Kos**, Edward Stanley 1928- *AmMWSc 92*

Kos, Joseph Frank AmMWSc 92
Kos, Ronald Joseph 1941- WhoEnt 92
Kos, Rudolph Edward 1945- WhoRel 92
Kosa, John 1914-1972 ConAu 34NR
Kosack, Rexford C 1953- WhoAmP 91
Kosai, Kenneth 1944- AmMWSc 92
Kosak, Alvin Ira 1924- AmMWSc 92
Kosak, Anthony James 1934- WhoMW 92
Kosak, John R 1930- AmMWSc 92
Kosaka, Tokusaburo 1916- IntWW 91
Kosakow, James Matthew 1954- WhoAmL 92
Kosanke, Robert Max 1917- AmMWSc 92
Kosanovich, Robert Joseph 1938- AmMWSc 92
Kosar, Bernie, Jr. 1963- WhoMW 92
Kosaraju, S Rao 1943- AmMWSc 92
Kosaric, Naim 1928- AmMWSc 92
Kosarin, Jonathan Henry 1951- WhoAmL 92
Kosasky, Harold Jack 1927- AmMWSc 92
Kosbab, Frederic Paul Gustav 1922- AmMWSc 92, IntAu&W 91
Koschier, Francis Joseph 1950- AmMWSc 92
Koschitzky, Mira WhoRel 92
Koschmieder, Ernst Lothar 1929- AmMWSc 92
Koschnick, Hans Karl-Heinrich 1929- IntWW 91
Koscielniak, Bruce 1947- ConAu 134, SmATA 67 [port]
Koscina, Sylva 1933- IntMPA 92
Kosciusko-Morizet, Jacques 1913- IntWW 91
Kosciuszko, Thaddeus DcAmImH
Kosciuszko, Thaddeus 1746-1817 BlkwEAR
Kosco, John C 1932- AmMWSc 92, WhoAmP 91
Kosco, Louis F 1932- WhoAmP 91
Kosecoff, Jacqueline Barbara 1949- WhoWest 92
Kosel, George Eugene 1923- AmMWSc 92
Kosel, Peter Bohdan 1946- AmMWSc 92, WhoMW 92
Kosersky, Donald Saadia 1932- AmMWSc 92
Kosh, Joseph William 1940- AmMWSc 92
Koshak, John Anthony 1938- WhoEnt 92
Koshel, Richard Donald 1936- AmMWSc 92
Kosher, Robert Andrew 1945- AmMWSc 92
Koshi, James H 1919- AmMWSc 92
Koshick, John Charles 1955- WhoEnt 92
Koshiro, Matsumoto, IX 1942- IntWW 91
Koshkin, Lev Nikolaevich 1912- IntWW 91
Koshkin, Mikhail Il'ich 1898-1940 SovUnBD
Koshland, Daniel E., Jr. 1920- IntWW 91
Koshland, Daniel Edward, Jr 1920- AmMWSc 92, WhoWest 92
Koshland, Marian Elliott 1921- AmMWSc 92, WhoWest 92
Koshoev, Tamirbeka Khudaybergenovich 1931- IntWW 91
Koshy, K Thomas 1924- AmMWSc 92
Kosiba, Walter Louis 1921- AmMWSc 92
Kosich, George J. 1934- WhoFI 92
Kosier, Frank J 1934- AmMWSc 92
Kosiewicz, Stanley Timothy 1944- AmMWSc 92
Kosik, Edwin Michael 1925- WhoAmL 92
Kosikowski, Frank Vincent 1916- AmMWSc 92
Kosiniak-Kamysz, Andrzej 1947- IntWW 91
Kosinski, Antoni A 1930- AmMWSc 92
Kosinski, Gerard A 1954- WhoAmP 91
Kosinski, James N 1940- WhoAmP 91
Kosinski, Jerzy DrAPF 91
Kosinski, Jerzy 1933- LiExTwC
Kosinski, Jerzy 1933-1991 BenetAL 91, ConAu 134, CurBio 91N, FacFETw, NewYTBS 91, News 91
Kosinski, Jerzy Nikodem d1991 Who 92N
Kosinski, Jerzy Nikodem 1933- IntAu&W 91
Kosinski, Richard John 1965- WhoWest 92
Kosinski, Robert Joseph 1949- AmMWSc 92
Kosinsky, Barbara Timm 1942- WhoMW 92
Kosior, Stanislav Vikent'evich 1889-1939 SovUnBD
Koskan, John M 1955- WhoAmP 91
Koski, Ann Louise 1951- WhoMW 92
Koski, Raymond Allen 1951- AmMWSc 92
Koski, Roger Allan 1954- WhoAmP 91
Koski, Walter S 1913- AmMWSc 92
Koskinas, Silas 1919- WhoRel 92
Koskinas, Stephan Aristotle 1946- WhoFI 92
Koskinen, Donald Steward 1928- WhoMW 92
Kosko, Eryk 1904- AmMWSc 92
Koskoff, Michael P. 1942- WhoAmL 92
Kosky, Philip George AmMWSc 92
Kosler, Zdenek 1928- IntWW 91
Koslow, Ira Lawrence 1945- WhoWest 92
Koslow, Julian Anthony 1947- AmMWSc 92
Koslow, Stephen Hugh 1940- AmMWSc 92
Koslowitz, Karen WhoAmP 91
Koslowski, Shirley Mae 1938- WhoAmP 91
Koslowsky, Vernon Theodore 1953- AmMWSc 92
Kosmahl, Henry G 1919- AmMWSc 92
Kosman, Daniel Jacob 1941- AmMWSc 92
Kosman, Joseph John 1957- WhoAmL 92
Kosman, Mary Ellen 1926- AmMWSc 92
Kosman, Warren Melvin 1946- AmMWSc 92
Kosmatka, John Benedict 1956- AmMWSc 92
Kosmetatos, Niki 1948- WhoMW 92
Kosmicki, Greg DrAPF 91
Kosof, Anna 1945- ConAu 35NR
Kosola, Vihtori Iisakki 1884-1936 BiDExR
Kosolapov, Richard Ivanovich 1930- IntWW 91
Kosovsky, Joel Mark 1957- WhoFI 92
Kosow, David Phillip 1936- AmMWSc 92
Kosow, Mimi 1934- WhoEnt 92
Kosower, Edward Malcolm 1929- AmMWSc 92
Kosowicz, Francis John 1946- WhoEnt 92
Kosowsky, David I 1930- AmMWSc 92
Koss, Donald A AmMWSc 92
Koss, Helen Levine 1922- WhoAmP 91
Koss, Leopold George 1920- AmMWSc 92
Koss, Mary Lyndon Pease 1948- WhoWest 92
Koss, Michael Campbell 1940- AmMWSc 92
Koss, Richard Allen, Jr. 1954- WhoFI 92
Koss, Valery Alexander 1941- AmMWSc 92
Kossack, Georg 1923- IntWW 91
Kossak-Szezucka, Zofia 1890-1968 LiExTwC
Kosse, Krisztina Maria 1943- WhoWest 92
Kossel, Karl Martin Leonhard Albrecht 1853-1927 WhoNob 90
Kossev, Atanas Nedialkov 1934- WhoEnt 92
Kossiakoff, Alexander 1914- AmMWSc 92
Kossler, William John 1937- AmMWSc 92
Kossmann, Charles Edward 1909- AmMWSc 92
Kossmann, Ernst Heinrich 1922- IntWW 91
Kossoff, David 1919- ConAu 35NR, IntAu&W 91, Who 92, WrDr 92
Kossoff, Leon 1926- TwCPaSc, WorArt 1980
Kossover, Herb Allan 1948- WhoEnt 92
Kossow, Sophia 1910- WhoEnt 92
Kossoy, Aaron David 1936- AmMWSc 92
Kossuth, Louis DcAmImH
Kossuth, Susan 1946- AmMWSc 92
Kost, Arthur Daniel 1943- WhoRel 92
Kost, Gerald Joseph 1945- WhoWest 92
Kost, Richard Stephen 1947- WhoAmP 91
Kost, Richard Stephen, Sr. 1947- WhoWest 92
Kost, William Elvidge 1941- WhoFI 92
Kosta, Louise Anne 1949- WhoFI 92
Kostandov, Leonid Arkad'evich 1915-1984 SovUnBD
Kostant, Bertram 1928- AmMWSc 92
Kostelanetz, Andre 1901-1980 NewAmDM
Kostelanetz, Boris 1911- WhoAmL 92
Kostelanetz, Richard DrAPF 91
Kostelanetz, Richard 1940- ConNov 91, ConPo 91, WrDr 92
Kostelic, Thomas Patrick 1954- WhoMW 92
Kostellow, Alexander J. 1897-1954 DcTwDes
Kostellow, Rowena Reed DcTwDes
Kostelnicek, Richard J 1942- AmMWSc 92
Kostelny, Albert Joseph, Jr. 1951- WhoAmL 92
Kostelnyk, Gavryl 1866-1948 SovUnBD
Kosten, Jeffrey Thomas 1960- WhoAmL 92
Kostenbader, Kenneth David, Jr 1941- AmMWSc 92
Kostenbauder, Harry Barr 1929- AmMWSc 92
Kostenbauer, John Harry 1946- WhoWest 92
Kostepen, Mehmet Hakan 1961- WhoMW 92
Koster, David F 1936- AmMWSc 92
Koster, Donald Nelson 1910- WrDr 92
Koster, Eugene S 1942- WhoIns 92
Koster, George Fred 1927- AmMWSc 92
Koster, Henri Johan de 1914- IntWW 91
Koster, Robert Allen 1941- AmMWSc 92
Koster, Rudolf AmMWSc 92
Koster, Simon 1900- IntAu&W 91
Koster, W P 1929- AmMWSc 92
Koster, William Henry 1944- AmMWSc 92
Koster, William Pfeiffer 1929- WhoFI 92
Koster Van Groos, August Ferdinand 1938- AmMWSc 92
Kostere, Kim Martin 1954- WhoMW 92
Kosterlitz, Hans Walter 1903- IntWW 91, Who 92
Kostetzky, Eaghor 1913-1983 LiExTwC
Kosteva, Jim 1952- WhoAmP 91
Kostic, Nenad M 1952- AmMWSc 92
Kostiner, Edward S 1940- AmMWSc 92
Kostiner, Eileen DrAPF 91
Kostishack, Daniel F 1940- AmMWSc 92
Kostiuk, Theodor 1944- AmMWSc 92
Kostizen, Erwin 1938- WhoRel 92
Kostka, Donald Paul, Jr. 1953- WhoFI 92
Kostka, William James, Jr. 1934- WhoWest 92
Kostkowski, Henry John 1926- AmMWSc 92
Kostmayer, Peter H. 1946- AlmAP 92 [port]
Kostmayer, Peter Houston 1946- WhoAmP 91
Kostner, Jaclyn Patti 1945- WhoWest 92
Kostner, William Charles 1952- WhoMW 92
Kostof, Spiro d1991 NewYTBS 91
Kostoff, Morris R 1933- AmMWSc 92
Kostohryz, Richard Joseph 1930- WhoAmP 91
Kostopoulos, George 1939- AmMWSc 92
Kostoulas, Ioannis Georgiou 1936- WhoFI 92, WhoWest 92
Kostov, Dimitar Tzvetkov 1932- IntWW 91
Kostreva, David Robert 1945- AmMWSc 92
Kostreva, Michael Martin 1948- AmMWSc 92
Kostrewski, Gary Steven 1954- WhoFI 92
Kostrichkin, Andrey Aleksandrovich 1901-1973 SovUnBD
Kostroun, Vaclav O 1938- AmMWSc 92
Kostrzewa, Richard Michael 1943- AmMWSc 92
Kostrzewski, Jan Karol 1915- IntWW 91
Kosturakis, Irene 1952- WhoAmL 92
Kostyniak, Paul J 1947- AmMWSc 92
Kostyo, Jack Lawrence 1931- AmMWSc 92
Kostyo, John Francis 1955- WhoAmL 92
Kostyrko, George Jurij 1937- AmMWSc 92
Kostyu, Donna D 1947- AmMWSc 92
Kosub, James Albert 1948- WhoAmL 92
Kosuri, Narayana Rao 1936- WhoMW 92
Kosut, Kenneth Paul 1949- WhoAmL 92
Kosuth, Joseph 1945- WorArt 1980 [port]
Kosygin, Aleksey Nikolaevich 1904-1980 SovUnBD
Kosygin, Alexei 1904-1980 FacFETw
Kosygin, Yuriy Aleksandrovich 1911- IntWW 91
Koszalka, Thomas R 1927- AmMWSc 92
Koszarowski, Tadeusz Tomasz 1915- IntWW 91
Koszarski, Richard 1947- WhoEnt 92
Koszewski, Bohdan Julius 1918- WhoMW 92
Kosztarab, Michael 1927- AmMWSc 92
Kot, Jozef 1936- IntAu&W 91
Kot, Peter Aloysius 1932- AmMWSc 92
Kot, Richard Anthony 1941- AmMWSc 92
Kotaite, Assad 1924- IntWW 91
Kotansky, D R 1939- AmMWSc 92
Kotb, Malak Y 1953- AmMWSc 92
Kotch, Alex 1926- AmMWSc 92, WhoMW 92
Kotch, Laurie Who 92
Kotcheff, Ted 1931- IntWW 91
Kotcheff, William Theodore 1931- IntMPA 92
Kotcher, Emil 1913- AmMWSc 92
Kotcher, Shirley J. W. 1924- WhoAmL 92, WhoFI 92
Kotchoubey, Andrew 1938- AmMWSc 92
Kotelnikov, Vladimir Aleksandrovich 1908- IntWW 91
Koten, John A. 1929- WhoFI 92
Kotey, Neil 1968- WhoEnt 92
Kothari, Bijay Singh 1928- WhoFI 92
Kothari, Rajni 1928- ConAu 35NR
Kothmann, Glenn Harold 1928- WhoAmP 91
Kothmann, Merwyn Mortimer 1940- AmMWSc 92
Kothny, Cecilia Astrid 1961- WhoFI 92
Kothny, Evaldo Luis 1925- AmMWSc 92
Koths, Jay Sanford 1926- AmMWSc 92
Koths, Kirston Edward 1948- AmMWSc 92
Kotiah, Thoddi C. 1941- WhoFI 92
Kotick, Michael Paul 1940- AmMWSc 92
Kotik, Petr 1942- ConCom 92
Kotila, Paul Myron 1950- AmMWSc 92
Kotin, Leon 1924- AmMWSc 92
Kotin, Leonard 1932- AmMWSc 92
Kotin, Paul 1916- AmMWSc 92
Kotin, Zhozef Yakovlevich 1908-1979 SovUnBD
Kotker, Mary Zane DrAPF 91
Kotker, Norman DrAPF 91
Kotker, Norman 1931- ConAu 35NR
Kotker, Norman R. 1931- WrDr 92
Kotker, Zane DrAPF 91
Kotker, Zane H. 1934- WrDr 92
Kotkin, David 1956- WhoEnt 92
Kotlarski, Ignacy Icchak 1923- AmMWSc 92
Kotlarz, Joseph S 1956- WhoAmP 91
Kotler, Donald P 1947- AmMWSc 92
Kotler, Martin Alan 1950- WhoAmL 92
Kotler, Pamela Lee 1946- WhoWest 92
Kotler, Philip 1931- IntAu&W 91, WrDr 92
Kotler, Richard Lee 1952- WhoAmL 92
Kotler, Steven 1947- WhoFI 92
Kotliar, Abraham Morris 1926- AmMWSc 92
Kotlowitz, Dan 1957- WhoEnt 92
Kotlowitz, Robert DrAPF 91, LesBEnT 92
Kotlowitz, Robert 1924- ConAu 36NR
Kotlyar, Nikolay Isaakovich 1935- IntWW 91
Kotnik, Louis John 1925- AmMWSc 92
Kotok, Laurence Allan 1946- WhoRel 92
Kotonski, Wlodzimierz 1925- IntWW 91, NewAmDM
Kotora, Michael Lynn 1951- WhoMW 92
Kotovych, George 1941- AmMWSc 92
Kotow, Piotr 1919- IntAu&W 91
Kotschmar, Hermann 1829-1909 NewAmDM
Kotschnig, John 1931- WhoEnt 92
Kotsmith, Suzanne Lee 1966- WhoMW 92
Kotsokoane, Joseph Riffat Larry 1922- IntWW 91, Who 92
Kotsonis, Ieronymos d1988 IntWW 91N
Kott, Edward 1939- AmMWSc 92
Kott, Jan 1914- IntWW 91, LiExTwC
Kottas, Harry 1910- AmMWSc 92
Kottcamp, Edward H, Jr 1934- AmMWSc 92
Kotter, F Ralph 1915- AmMWSc 92
Kottick, Edward Leon 1930- WhoEnt 92
Kottis, John Gregory 1925- WhoAmP 91
Kottkamp, Jeffrey Dean 1960- WhoAmL 92
Kottke, Bruce Allen 1929- AmMWSc 92
Kottke, Frederic James 1917- AmMWSc 92
Kottke, Frederick Edward 1926- WhoFI 92, WhoWest 92
Kottke, Marshall William 1964- WhoMW 92
Kottlowski, Frank Edward 1921- AmMWSc 92, WhoWest 92
Kottman, Clifford Alfons 1942- AmMWSc 92
Kottman, Roy Milton 1916- AmMWSc 92
Kottmeier, Peter Klaus 1928- AmMWSc 92
Kotto, Yaphet 1937- IntMPA 92
Kotto, Yaphet Fredrick 1944- IntWW 91, WhoBlA 92, WhoEnt 92
Kotula, Anthony W 1929- AmMWSc 92
Kotula, Karl Robert 1955- WhoMW 92
Kotulski, Rick 1945- WhoAmP 91
Kotval, Pesho Sohrab 1942- AmMWSc 92
Kotyk, Michael 1929- AmMWSc 92
Kotz, Arthur Rudolph 1933- AmMWSc 92
Kotz, John Carl 1937- AmMWSc 92
Kotz, Nathan K 1932- IntAu&W 91
Kotz, Samuel 1930- AmMWSc 92, ConAu 34NR
Kotze, Gert Jeremias 1928- IntWW 91
Kotzebue, Kenneth Lee 1933- AmMWSc 92
Kotzee, Flores Petrus 1926- IntWW 91
Kotzian, David Allen 1959- WhoAmL 92
Kotzig, Anton 1919- AmMWSc 92
Kotzwara, Franz 1730-1791 NewAmDM
Kotzwinkle, William 1938- IntAu&W 91, TwCSFW 91, WrDr 92
Kouandete, Maurice 1939- IntWW 91
Kouassi, Kwam IntWW 91
Kouba, Delore Loren 1919- AmMWSc 92
Kouba, Lisa Marco 1957- WhoAmL 92
Kouba, Richard WhoAmP 91
Kouba, Tony 1930- WhoAmP 91
Koubek, Edward 1937- AmMWSc 92
Koubek, Kristina M. 1965- WhoEnt 92
Koucky, Frank Louis 1927- WhoMW 92
Koucky, Frank Louis, Jr 1927- AmMWSc 92
Kouf, M. James, Jr. 1951- WhoEnt 92
Koufax, Sandy 1935- FacFETw [port]
Kougl, Patricia Anne 1919- WhoAmP 91
Kouhi, Elizabeth 1917- IntAu&W 91
Koul, Hira Lal 1943- AmMWSc 92
Koul, Maharaj Kishen 1941- AmMWSc 92
Koul, Omanand 1947- AmMWSc 92
Kouloumbis, Evangelos 1929- IntWW 91
Koulourianos, Dimitri 1930- IntWW 91
Koulourides, Theodore I 1925- AmMWSc 92

**Koumjian**, Vaughn DrAPF 91
**Koumoulides**, John 1938- ConAu 34NR
**Kounellis**, Jannis 1936- WorArt 1980
**Kounosu**, Shigeru 1928- AmMWSc 92
**Kouns**, Alan Terry 1941- IntAu&W 91
**Kountz**, Charles Edward, Jr 1946- WhoAmP 91
**Kountze**, Mabray 1910- WhoBlA 92
**Kountze**, Vallery J. WhoBlA 92
**Koupal**, Carl Mathias, Jr 1953- WhoAmP 91, WhoMW 92
**Koupernik**, Cyrille 1917- ConAu 35NR
**Koupf**, Gary I 1950- WhoIns 92
**Kourany**, Miguel 1924- AmMWSc 92
**Kourganoff**, Vladimir 1912- IntWW 91
**Kouri**, Donald Jack 1938- AmMWSc 92
**Kouris**, Peter Constantine 1928- WhoEnt 92
**Kouros**, Andreas Kyriakou 1918- IntWW 91
**Koury**, Aleah George 1925- WhoRel 92
**Koury**, Connie Woolpert 1952- WhoMW 92
**Koury**, Leo J d1991 NewYTBS 91
**Kouse**, Philip Charles 1952- WhoRel 92
**Koushanpour**, Esmail 1934- AmMWSc 92, WhoMW 92
**Kouskolekas**, Costas Alexander 1927- AmMWSc 92
**Kousky**, Vernon E 1943- AmMWSc 92
**Kousser**, Joseph Morgan 1943- WhoWest 92
**Koussevitzky**, Serge 1874-1951 FacFETw, NewAmDM
**Kout**, David Louis 1957- WhoAmL 92
**Koutros**, Stephen Anthony 1955- WhoFI 92
**Kouts**, Herbert John Cecil 1919- AmMWSc 92
**Koutsky**, James A 1939- AmMWSc 92
**Koutsogeorgas**, Agamemnon d1991 NewYTBS 91
**Koutsogiane**, Phillip Charles 1944- WhoAmL 92
**Koutsogiorgas**, Agamemnon d1991 IntWW 91, -91N
**Koutsoheras**, Ioannis IntWW 91
**Koutsohilis**, Kostas Kiriakos 1916- WhoMW 92
**Koutstaal**, Cornelis W. 1935- WhoWest 92
**Koutzen**, Nadia 1930- WhoEnt 92
**Kouvel**, James Spyros 1926- AmMWSc 92
**Kouymjian**, Dickran 1934- WhoWest 92
**Kouyoumjian**, Charles H. 1940- WhoFI 92
**Kouyoumzelis**, Theodore 1906- IntWW 91
**Kouzel**, Bernard 1920- AmMWSc 92
**Kouzes**, Richard Thomas 1947- AmMWSc 92
**Kovac**, Jeffrey Dean 1948- AmMWSc 92
**Kovac**, Richard DrAPF 91
**Kovac**, Steven 1954- WhoAmP 91
**Kovacevich**, Christopher 1928- WhoRel 92
**Kovacevich**, Janko Peter 1927- WhoMW 92
**Kovacevich**, Richard M. WhoMW 92
**Kovacevich**, Stephen B. Who 92
**Kovach**, Andrew Louis 1948- WhoFI 92
**Kovach**, Eugene George 1922- AmMWSc 92
**Kovach**, Francis J. 1918- ConAu 35NR
**Kovach**, George Daniel 1951- WhoEnt 92
**Kovach**, Jack 1940- AmMWSc 92, WhoMW 92
**Kovach**, Joseph William 1946- WhoFI 92, WhoMW 92
**Kovach**, Ladis Daniel 1914- AmMWSc 92
**Kovach**, Robert Louis 1934- WhoWest 92
**Kovach**, Robert Vincent 1944- WhoMW 92
**Kovach**, William David 1952- WhoFI 92
**Kovachevich**, Elizabeth Anne 1936- WhoAmL 92
**Kovachich**, Gyula Bertalan 1936- AmMWSc 92
**Kovacic**, Joseph Edward 1930- AmMWSc 92
**Kovacic**, Peter 1921- AmMWSc 92
**Kovacic**, William Evan 1952- WhoAmL 92
**Kovacik**, Karen DrAPF 91
**Kovacik**, Neal Stephen 1952- WhoFI 92, WhoMW 92
**Kovacs**, Andras 1925- IntDcF 2-2 [port], IntWW 91
**Kovacs**, Bela A 1921- AmMWSc 92
**Kovacs**, Bela Victor 1930- AmMWSc 92, WhoMW 92
**Kovacs**, Charles J 1941- AmMWSc 92
**Kovacs**, Charles Joseph Leslie 1945- WhoFI 92
**Kovacs**, Denes 1930- IntWW 91
**Kovacs**, Dianne Rohrer 1958- WhoRel 92
**Kovacs**, Ernie d1962 LesBEnT 92 [port]
**Kovacs**, Ernie 1919-1962 FacFETw
**Kovacs**, Eve Maria 1925- AmMWSc 92
**Kovacs**, Eve Veronika 1954- AmMWSc 92
**Kovacs**, Hanna 1919- AmMWSc 92
**Kovacs**, Imre 1913-1980 ConAu 34NR
**Kovacs**, Julius Stephen 1928- AmMWSc 92
**Kovacs**, Kalman T 1926- AmMWSc 92
**Kovacs**, Kit M 1956- AmMWSc 92
**Kovacs**, Laszlo 1933- IntMPA 92, WhoEnt 92A
**Kovacs**, Miklos I P 1936- AmMWSc 92
**Kovacs**, Sandor J, Jr 1947- AmMWSc 92
**Koval**, Carl Anthony 1952- AmMWSc 92
**Koval**, Charles Francis 1938- AmMWSc 92, WhoMW 92
**Koval**, Charles Terrance 1933- WhoFI 92
**Koval**, Daniel 1922- AmMWSc 92
**Koval**, George Carl 1936- WhoIns 92
**Koval**, Leslie R 1933- AmMWSc 92
**Koval**, Thomas Michael 1950- AmMWSc 92
**Koval'-Samborsky**, Ivan Ivanovich 1893-1962 SovUnBD
**Kovalak**, William Paul 1946- AmMWSc 92
**Kovalchuk**, Feodor Sawa 1924- WhoRel 92
**Kovalenko**, Ludmyla 1898-1969 LiExTwC
**Kovalev**, Anatoliy Gavrilovich 1923- IntWW 91
**Kovalev**, Mikhail Vasilevich 1925- IntWW 91
**Kovalevsky**, Jean 1929- IntWW 91
**Kovalsky**, Al 1933- WhoFI 92
**Kovaly**, John J 1928- AmMWSc 92
**Kovanda**, Janet Louise 1946- WhoFI 92
**Kovanov**, Vladimir Vasiliyevich 1909- IntWW 91
**Kovar**, Frederick Richard 1933- AmMWSc 92
**Kovar**, John Alvis 1932- AmMWSc 92
**Kovar**, Margaret W 1933- WhoAmP 91
**Kovarik**, Wenzel J WhoAmP 91
**Kovatch**, George 1934- AmMWSc 92
**Kovats**, Andre 1897- AmMWSc 92
**Kovats**, Michael DcAmImH
**Kove**, Martin WhoEnt 92
**Kovel**, Joel 1936- IntAu&W 91, WrDr 92
**Kovel**, Lee Ralph 1951- WhoEnt 92, WhoFI 92, WhoWest 92
**Kovel**, Ralph IntAu&W 91
**Kovel**, Ralph Mallory WrDr 92
**Kovel**, Terry Horvitz 1928- WrDr 92
**Koveleski**, Kathryn Delane 1925- WhoMW 92
**Koven**, Reginald de NewAmDM
**Kovesi-Domokos**, Susan 1939- AmMWSc 92
**Kovich**, Robert d1991 NewYTBS 91
**Kovich**, William Michael 1948- WhoMW 92
**Kovitz**, Arthur A 1928- AmMWSc 92
**Kovler**, Allen DrAPF 91
**Kovner**, Jacob L 1912- AmMWSc 92
**Kovolenko**, Samuel 1957- WhoAmP 91
**Kovrigina**, Mariya 1910- SovUnBD
**Kovtynovich**, Dan 1952- WhoWest 92
**Kow**, Lee-Ming AmMWSc 92
**Kowal**, Charles Thomas 1940- AmMWSc 92
**Kowal**, Daniel Henry 1956- WhoFI 92
**Kowal**, George M 1938- AmMWSc 92
**Kowal**, George Michael 1952- WhoEnt 92
**Kowal**, Jerome 1931- AmMWSc 92
**Kowal**, Norman Edward 1937- AmMWSc 92
**Kowal**, Robert Allen 1965- WhoEnt 92
**Kowal**, Robert Raymond 1939- AmMWSc 92
**Kowalak**, Albert Douglas 1936- AmMWSc 92
**Kowalcik**, Sherry Marketta 1954- WhoWest 92
**Kowalczewski**, Doreen Mary Thurlow 1926- WhoMW 92
**Kowalczyk**, Ellen Marie 1955- WhoAmP 91
**Kowalczyk**, Jeanne Stuart 1942- AmMWSc 92
**Kowalczyk**, Leon S 1908- AmMWSc 92
**Kowalenko**, Charles Grant 1946- AmMWSc 92
**Kowalewich**, Betty Jean 1930- WhoAmP 91
**Kowalewski**, Edward Joseph 1920- AmMWSc 92
**Kowalewski**, Francis Philip, Jr. 1922- WhoRel 92
**Kowalik**, Janusz Szczesny 1934- AmMWSc 92
**Kowalik**, Virgil C 1932- AmMWSc 92
**Kowalke**, Kim H 1948- IntAu&W 91, WhoEnt 92
**Kowall**, James Lionel 1926- WhoMW 92
**Kowalski**, Bruce Richard 1942- AmMWSc 92
**Kowalski**, Charles Joseph 1938- AmMWSc 92
**Kowalski**, Conrad John 1947- AmMWSc 92
**Kowalski**, David Francis 1947- AmMWSc 92
**Kowalski**, Donald T 1938- AmMWSc 92
**Kowalski**, Gregor 1949- Who 92
**Kowalski**, Kathiann Meissner 1955- WhoAmL 92
**Kowalski**, Kazimierz Maria 1926- IntAu&W 91
**Kowalski**, Kenneth L 1932- AmMWSc 92
**Kowalski**, Kenneth R. 1945- WhoWest 92
**Kowalski**, Leann 1955- WhoEnt 92
**Kowalski**, Ludwik 1931- AmMWSc 92
**Kowalski**, Marian 1936- IntAu&W 91
**Kowalski**, Michael Jerome 1947- WhoEnt 92
**Kowalski**, Neal Anthony 1945- WhoFI 92
**Kowalski**, Paul Randolph 1934- WhoRel 92
**Kowalski**, Richard 1940- AmMWSc 92
**Kowalski**, Richard S. 1944- WhoMW 92
**Kowalski**, Stanley Benedict 1935- AmMWSc 92
**Kowalski**, Stephen Wesley 1931- AmMWSc 92
**Kowalski**, Tadeusz 1922- AmMWSc 92
**Kowalski**, William Leonard 1955- WhoMW 92
**Kowalsky**, Arthur 1923- AmMWSc 92
**Kowalsky**, Elaine 1948- TwCPaSc
**Kowalsky**, William Allen 1946- WhoFI 92
**Kowalyshyn**, Russell 1918- WhoAmP 91
**Kowanko**, Nicholas 1934- AmMWSc 92
**Kowarski**, A Avinoam 1927- AmMWSc 92
**Kowarski**, Chana Rose 1929- AmMWSc 92
**Kowel**, Stephen Thomas 1942- AmMWSc 92
**Kowert**, Bruce Arthur 1942- AmMWSc 92
**Kowet**, Don 1937- ConAu 35NR
**Kowit**, Steve DrAPF 91
**Kowitz**, Aletha Amanda 1925- WhoFI 92, WhoMW 92
**Kowitz**, Claudia Theodora 1943- WhoWest 92
**Kowkabany**, George Norman 1923- AmMWSc 92
**Kowles**, Richard Vincent 1932- AmMWSc 92
**Kowlessar**, O Dhodanand AmMWSc 92
**Kownacki**, Mary Lou 1941- WhoRel 92
**Kownslar**, Allan O 1935- ConAu 35NR
**Kowolenko**, Michael D 1955- AmMWSc 92
**Koyama**, Kosuke 1929- ConAu 35NR, WhoRel 92
**Koyama**, Tetsuo 1935- AmMWSc 92
**Koyamba**, Alphonse IntWW 91
**Koyano**, Keiichirou 1953- WhoFI 92
**Kozak**, Antal 1936- AmMWSc 92
**Kozak**, Blanche Gurka 1920- WhoEnt 92
**Kozak**, David M. 1951- WhoAmL 92
**Kozak**, Ellen M 1944- WhoAmP 91
**Kozak**, Gary S 1938- AmMWSc 92
**Kozak**, Harley Jane IntMPA 92
**Kozak**, Harley Jane 1957- WhoEnt 92
**Kozak**, Henryk Jozef 1945- IntAu&W 91
**Kozak**, Jan 1921- IntWW 91
**Kozak**, John Joseph 1940- AmMWSc 92
**Kozak**, John W. 1943- WhoAmL 92, WhoMW 92
**Kozak**, Leslie P 1940- AmMWSc 92
**Kozak**, Marilyn Sue AmMWSc 92
**Kozak**, Marlene Galante 1952- WhoMW 92
**Kozak**, Roger Lee 1945- WhoMW 92
**Kozak**, Samuel J 1931- AmMWSc 92
**Kozak**, Wlodzimierz M 1927- AmMWSc 92
**Kozaki**, Mark Stephen 1958- WhoEnt 92
**Kozam**, George 1924- AmMWSc 92
**Kozar**, Martha Cecile 1963- WhoMW 92
**Kozarich**, John Warren 1949- AmMWSc 92
**Kozawa**, Akiya 1928- AmMWSc 92
**Kozberg**, Donna Walters DrAPF 91
**Kozberg**, Donna Walters 1952- WhoFI 92
**Kozberg**, Steven Freed 1953- WhoMW 92
**Kozbial**, Richard James 1933- WhoMW 92
**Kozee-Sands**, Debra 1955- WhoEnt 92
**Kozek**, Wieslaw Joseph 1939- AmMWSc 92
**Kozel**, Thomas Randall 1946- AmMWSc 92
**Kozelka**, Edward William 1912- WhoMW 92
**Kozelka**, Robert M 1926- AmMWSc 92
**Kozenko**, Theodore Frank 1941- WhoMW 92
**Kozer**, Jose DrAPF 91
**Kozer**, Jose 1940- ConAu 34NR, ConSpAP, WhoHisp 92
**Kozer**, Stephen Louis 1951- WhoMW 92
**Kozhedub**, Ivan N. d1991? NewYTBS 91
**Kozhuharov**, Christophor 1946- WhoFI 92
**Kozhuharov**, Ivan Hristov 1950- WhoEnt 92
**Koziar**, Joseph Cleveland 1946- AmMWSc 92
**Koziar**, Stephen Francis, Jr. 1944- WhoAmL 92
**Kozicki**, Daniel Raymond 1951- WhoMW 92
**Kozicki**, Henry 1924- WhoMW 92
**Kozicki**, William 1931- AmMWSc 92
**Kozicky**, Edward Louis 1918- AmMWSc 92
**Koziel**, Joyce Ann 1963- WhoMW 92
**Kozik**, Eugene 1924- AmMWSc 92
**Kozik**, Mark Alan 1955- WhoAmL 92
**Kozikowski**, Alan Paul 1948- AmMWSc 92
**Kozikowski**, Barbara Ann 1954- AmMWSc 92
**Kozikowski Perry**, Meta Jane 1964- WhoEnt 92
**Kozina**, Thomas Joseph 1930- WhoMW 92
**Kozinski**, Alex WhoAmP 91
**Kozinski**, Alex 1950- WhoAmL 92
**Kozinski**, Andrzei 1925- AmMWSc 92
**Kozintsev**, Grigori 1905-1973 IntDcF 2-2 [port]
**Kozintsev**, Grigoriy Mikhaylovich 1905-1973 SovUnBD
**Kozintsev**, Grigory Mikhailovich 1905-1973 FacFETw
**Koziol**, Brian Joseph 1951- AmMWSc 92
**Koziol**, Christopher Stephen 1959- WhoAmL 92
**Koziol**, Jozef 1939- IntWW 91
**Koziura**, Joseph F 1946- WhoAmP 91
**Kozlak**, Rita Burke 1919- WhoAmP 91
**Kozlik**, Michael David 1953- WhoAmL 92
**Kozlik**, Roland A 1921- AmMWSc 92
**Kozloff**, Eugene Nicholas 1920- AmMWSc 92
**Kozloff**, Lloyd M 1923- AmMWSc 92
**Kozlov**, Frol Romanovich 1908-1965 SovUnBD
**Kozlov**, Nikolay Timofeyevich 1925- IntWW 91
**Kozlov**, Petr Kuz'mich 1863-1935 SovUnBD
**Kozlovsky**, Ivan Semenovich 1900- SovUnBD
**Kozlovsky**, Sergey Vasil'evich 1885-1962 SovUnBD
**Kozlovsky**, Yevgeniy Aleksandrovich 1929- IntWW 91
**Kozlow**, Mark TwCWW 91
**Kozlowski**, Adrienne G. 1950- WhoEnt 92
**Kozlowski**, Adrienne Wickenden 1941- AmMWSc 92
**Kozlowski**, Betty Ann 1943- AmMWSc 92
**Kozlowski**, Don Robert 1937- AmMWSc 92
**Kozlowski**, Gerald P 1942- AmMWSc 92
**Kozlowski**, Janiece Rae 1959- WhoFI 92
**Kozlowski**, Lester Joseph 1953- AmMWSc 92
**Kozlowski**, Linda 1956- IntMPA 92
**Kozlowski**, Robert H 1928- AmMWSc 92
**Kozlowski**, Stanley Walter 1952- WhoMW 92
**Kozlowski**, Theodore R 1937- AmMWSc 92
**Kozlowski**, Theodore Thomas 1917- AmMWSc 92
**Kozlowski**, Walter G. 1934- WhoAmL 92
**Kozma**, Adam 1928- AmMWSc 92
**Kozma**, Lynn DrAPF 91
**Kozmon**, Laszlo 1957- WhoFI 92
**Kozniewska**, Halina 1920- IntWW 91
**Kozol**, Jonathan 1936- IntAu&W 91, IntWW 91, News 92-1 [port], WrDr 92
**Kozolchyk**, Boris 1934- WhoHisp 92, WhoWest 92
**Kozub**, Raymond Lee 1940- AmMWSc 92
**Kozubal**, Daniel James 1951- WhoMW 92
**Kozubek**, Stanely Michael 1947- WhoAmL 92
**Kozubowski**, Walter S 1939- WhoAmP 91
**Kozuch**, James Jeffrey 1950- WhoAmL 92
**Kozulin**, Alex 1949- IntAu&W 91
**Kozumplik**, Richalene May 1952- WhoMW 92
**Kra**, Irwin 1937- AmMWSc 92
**Kraabel**, Alf Thomas 1934- WhoRel 92
**Kraabel**, John Stanford AmMWSc 92
**Kraai**, Gerald Mark 1942- WhoAmL 92
**Kraakevik**, James Henry 1928- AmMWSc 92
**Kraakman**, Reinier H. 1949- WhoAmL 92
**Kraatz**, Charles Parry AmMWSc 92
**Kraatz**, Gloria H. 1943- WhoMW 92
**Kraay**, Gerrit Jacob 1935- AmMWSc 92
**Kraay**, Pauline TwCPaSc
**Krabacher**, Bernard 1925- AmMWSc 92
**Krabacher**, Bernard Joseph 1953- WhoAmL 92
**Krabbe**, Alan Robert 1945- WhoRel 92
**Krabbe**, Donald Louis 1934- WhoRel 92
**Krabbe**, Gregers Louis 1920- AmMWSc 92
**Krabbe**, Jeroen 1944- IntMPA 92, IntWW 91
**Krabbe**, Jeroen Aart 1944- WhoEnt 92
**Krabbenhoft**, Herman Otto 1945- AmMWSc 92
**Krabbenhoft**, Kenneth Louis 1931- AmMWSc 92
**Krabill**, Anthony Lynn 1967- WhoRel 92
**Krabill**, Robert Elmer 1934- WhoMW 92
**Krach**, Mitchell Peter 1924- WhoFI 92
**Kracher**, Alfred 1945- AmMWSc 92
**Kracke**, Robert Russell 1938- WhoAmL 92

**Krackov**, Lawrence Martin 1943- *WhoEnt 92, WhoFI 92*
**Krackov**, Mark Harry 1932- *AmMWSc 92*
**Krackow**, Jurgen 1923- *IntWW 91*
**Kracoff**, Ellen Karen 1950- *WhoAmL 92*
**Kraditor**, Aileen S. 1928- *ConAu 35NR*
**Kraeger-Rovey**, Catherine Eileen 1948- *WhoFI 92*
**Kraehe**, Enno E 1921- *ConAu 35NR*
**Kraehe**, Enno Edward 1921- *WrDr 92*
**Kraehmer**, Martha Florine 1958- *WhoMW 92*
**Kraeling**, Robert Russell 1942- *AmMWSc 92*
**Kraemer**, Duane Carl 1933- *AmMWSc 92*
**Kraemer**, Helena Chmura 1937- *AmMWSc 92*
**Kraemer**, Hendrik 1888-1965 *DcEcMov [port]*
**Kraemer**, J Hugo 1909- *AmMWSc 92*
**Kraemer**, James S 1919- *WhoAmP 91*
**Kraemer**, Jay Roy 1948- *WhoAmL 92*
**Kraemer**, John Francis 1941- *AmMWSc 92*
**Kraemer**, Karen Debra 1958- *WhoAmL 92*
**Kraemer**, Kenneth H 1943- *AmMWSc 92*
**Kraemer**, Kenneth L 1936- *ConAu 35NR*
**Kraemer**, Lillian Elizabeth 1940- *WhoAmL 92*
**Kraemer**, Louise Margaret 1910- *AmMWSc 92*
**Kraemer**, Louise Russert 1923- *AmMWSc 92*
**Kraemer**, Nicholas 1945- *Who 92*
**Kraemer**, Paul Michael 1930- *AmMWSc 92*
**Kraemer**, Philipp 1931- *WhoFI 92*
**Kraemer**, Richard H 1920- *ConAu 35NR*
**Kraemer**, Richard Thomas 1947- *WhoMW 92*
**Kraemer**, Robert Walter 1935- *AmMWSc 92*
**Kraemer**, William Francis 1934- *WhoEnt 92*
**Kraeuter**, John Norman 1942- *AmMWSc 92*
**Kraf**, Elaine *DrAPF 91*
**Krafft**, Geoffrey Arthur 1958- *AmMWSc 92*
**Krafft**, Joseph Martin 1923- *AmMWSc 92*
**Krafft**, Marie Elizabeth 1956- *AmMWSc 92*
**Krafft**, Maurice 1946-1991 *ConAu 134*
**Krafsur**, Elliot Scoville *AmMWSc 92*
**Krafsur**, Elliot Scoville 1939- *WhoMW 92*
**Kraft**, Alan M 1925- *AmMWSc 92*
**Kraft**, Allen Abraham 1923- *AmMWSc 92*
**Kraft**, Arthur 1944- *WhoFI 92*
**Kraft**, Benjamin F. 1948- *WhoBlA 92*
**Kraft**, C. William, III 1943- *WhoWest 92*
**Kraft**, C. William, Jr. 1903- *WhoAmL 92*
**Kraft**, Carol Joyce 1935- *WhoRel 92*
**Kraft**, Christopher C., Jr. 1924- *FacFETw*
**Kraft**, Christopher Columbus, Jr 1924- *AmMWSc 92, IntWW 91*
**Kraft**, David Charles 1957- *WhoEnt 92*
**Kraft**, David Werner 1933- *AmMWSc 92*
**Kraft**, Donald Harris 1943- *AmMWSc 92*
**Kraft**, Donald J 1936- *AmMWSc 92*
**Kraft**, Edward Michael 1944- *AmMWSc 92*
**Kraft**, George Howard 1936- *WhoWest 92*
**Kraft**, Gerald F 1928- *AmMWSc 92*
**Kraft**, Henry R. 1946- *WhoAmL 92*
**Kraft**, Hy 1899-1975 *ConAu 36NR*
**Kraft**, Irvin Alan 1921- *AmMWSc 92*
**Kraft**, Joan Creech 1943- *AmMWSc 92*
**Kraft**, John Christian 1929- *AmMWSc 92*
**Kraft**, John M 1938- *AmMWSc 92*
**Kraft**, Joseph *IntAu&W 91*
**Kraft**, Joseph 1924-1986 *ConAu 34NR*
**Kraft**, Kenneth Houston, Jr. 1934- *WhoFI 92*
**Kraft**, Kenneth J 1930- *AmMWSc 92*
**Kraft**, Leo 1922- *NewAmDM*
**Kraft**, Leo Abraham 1922- *WhoEnt 92*
**Kraft**, Lisbeth Martha 1920- *AmMWSc 92*
**Kraft**, Patricia Lynn *AmMWSc 92*
**Kraft**, Paul Donald 1957- *WhoMW 92*
**Kraft**, R Wayne 1925- *AmMWSc 92*
**Kraft**, Richard Austin *Who 92*
**Kraft**, Richard Lee 1958- *WhoAmL 92*
**Kraft**, Robert A. 1934- *WrDr 92*
**Kraft**, Robert Alan 1934- *WhoRel 92*
**Kraft**, Robert Paul 1927- *AmMWSc 92, IntWW 91*
**Kraft**, Sumner Charles 1928- *AmMWSc 92*
**Kraft**, Tanya Aline 1957- *WhoWest 92*
**Kraft**, Walter H 1938- *AmMWSc 92*
**Kraft**, William 1923- *NewAmDM*
**Kraft**, William Armstrong 1926- *WhoRel 92, WhoWest 92*
**Kraft**, William F. 1938- *WrDr 92*
**Kraft**, William Gerald 1944- *AmMWSc 92*
**Kraftson**, Raymond H. 1940- *WhoFI 92*
**Krafve**, Allen Horton 1937- *WhoFI 92, WhoMW 92*
**Krag**, Jens Otto 1914-1978 *FacFETw*
**Krag**, Olga 1937- *WhoWest 92*
**Kragerud**, Alv 1932- *IntWW 91*
**Kraggerud**, Egil 1939- *IntWW 91*
**Kraglund**, John 1922- *WhoEnt 92*
**Krah**, David Lee 1956- *AmMWSc 92*
**Krahel**, Thomas Stephen 1947- *WhoFI 92*
**Krahenbuhl**, James Lee 1942- *AmMWSc 92*
**Krahl**, Maurice Edward 1908- *AmMWSc 92*
**Krahl**, Nat W 1921- *AmMWSc 92*
**Krahling**, John *WhoAmP 91*
**Krahmer**, Donald L., Jr. 1957- *WhoAmL 92, WhoWest 92*
**Krahmer**, John Edward 1942- *WhoAmL 92*
**Krahmer**, Robert Lee 1932- *AmMWSc 92*
**Krahn**, James Arden 1963- *WhoMW 92*
**Krahn**, Robert Carl 1941- *AmMWSc 92*
**Krahn**, Thomas Richard 1943- *AmMWSc 92*
**Krahnke**, Harold C 1907- *AmMWSc 92*
**Krahula**, Joseph L 1923- *AmMWSc 92*
**Krahulik**, Jon D *WhoAmP 91*
**Kraicer**, Jacob 1931- *AmMWSc 92*
**Kraicer**, Peretz Freeman 1932- *AmMWSc 92*
**Kraichnan**, Robert Harry 1928- *AmMWSc 92*
**Kraig**, Ellen 1953- *AmMWSc 92*
**Kraigher**, Sergej 1914- *IntWW 91*
**Kraihanzel**, Charles S 1935- *AmMWSc 92*
**Kraijenhoff**, Gualtherus 1922- *IntWW 91*
**Kraiman**, Eugene Alfred 1929- *AmMWSc 92*
**Kraines**, David Paul 1941- *AmMWSc 92*
**Krainess**, Donald Philip 1929- *WhoAmL 92*
**Krainik**, Ardis 1929- *CurBio 91 [port], NewAmDM, WhoEnt 92, WhoMW 92*
**Krainin**, Julian Arthur 1941- *WhoEnt 92*
**Kraintz**, Leon 1924- *AmMWSc 92*
**Kraitchman**, Jerome 1926- *AmMWSc 92*
**Kraivichien**, Thanin 1927- *IntWW 91*
**Kraiza**, Edward Anthony 1947- *WhoFI 92*
**Krajca**, Kenneth Edward 1944- *AmMWSc 92*
**Krajcovic**, Stephen Vojtech 1914- *WhoFI 92*
**Krajewski**, John J 1931- *AmMWSc 92*
**Krajewski**, Lee Jerome 1942- *WhoMW 92*
**Krajina**, Borislav 1930- *IntWW 91*
**Krajina**, Vladimir Joseph 1905- *AmMWSc 92*
**Krajniak**, Edwin Anthony 1924- *WhoIns 92*
**Krakauer**, Albert Alexander 1937- *WhoFI 92*
**Krakauer**, Daniel *DrAPF 91*
**Krakauer**, Henry 1939- *AmMWSc 92*
**Krakauer**, Teresa *AmMWSc 92*
**Krake**, Keith Lawrence 1966- *WhoWest 92*
**Krakoff**, Irwin Harold 1923- *AmMWSc 92*
**Krakow**, Amy Ginzig 1950- *WhoFI 92*
**Krakow**, Burton 1928- *AmMWSc 92*
**Krakow**, Joseph S 1929- *AmMWSc 92*
**Krakower**, Bernard Hyman 1935- *WhoFI 92*
**Krakower**, Gerald W 1929- *AmMWSc 92*
**Krakowiak**, Edward T. 1928- *WhoMW 92*
**Krakowski**, Fred 1927- *AmMWSc 92*
**Krakowski**, Richard John 1946- *WhoAmL 92, WhoMW 92*
**Krakusin**, Roger K. 1942- *WhoAmL 92*
**Kral**, Robert 1926- *AmMWSc 92*
**Krall**, Albert Raymond 1922- *AmMWSc 92*
**Krall**, Allan M 1936- *AmMWSc 92*
**Krall**, Harry Levern 1907- *AmMWSc 92*
**Krall**, John Morton 1938- *AmMWSc 92*
**Krall**, Nicholas Anthony 1932- *AmMWSc 92*
**Kram**, Guenther Reinhard 1957- *WhoMW 92*
**Kram**, Shirley Wohl 1922- *WhoAmL 92*
**Kraman**, Cynthia *DrAPF 91*
**Kraman**, Steve Seth 1944- *AmMWSc 92*
**Kramarsky**, Lola Popper d1991 *NewYTBS 91*
**Krambeck**, Robert Harold 1943- *WhoFI 92*
**Kramberg**, Ross 1955- *WhoEnt 92*
**Kramer**, Aaron *DrAPF 91*
**Kramer**, Aaron 1921- *IntAu&W 91, WrDr 92*
**Kramer**, Aaron R 1932- *AmMWSc 92*
**Kramer**, Albert H 1940- *WhoAmP 91*
**Kramer**, Alex 1947- *WhoFI 92*
**Kramer**, Alex-Ann 1957- *WhoEnt 92*
**Kramer**, Alex John 1939- *WhoMW 92*
**Kramer**, Alfred William, Jr 1930- *AmMWSc 92*
**Kramer**, Andrew Michael 1944- *WhoAmL 92*
**Kramer**, Anne Pearce 1926- *WhoEnt 92, WhoWest 92*
**Kramer**, Barnett Sheldon 1948- *AmMWSc 92*
**Kramer**, Barry Alan 1948- *WhoWest 92*
**Kramer**, Bernard 1922- *AmMWSc 92*
**Kramer**, Bradley Alan 1958- *AmMWSc 92*
**Kramer**, Brian Dale 1942- *AmMWSc 92*
**Kramer**, Bruce Carlton 1953- *WhoFI 92*
**Kramer**, Bruce Michael 1949- *AmMWSc 92*
**Kramer**, Burton 1932- *WhoEnt 92*
**Kramer**, Carol Gertrude 1939- *WhoMW 92*
**Kramer**, Carolyn Margaret 1953- *AmMWSc 92*
**Kramer**, Charles Edwin 1947- *AmMWSc 92*
**Kramer**, Charles Lawrence 1928- *AmMWSc 92*
**Kramer**, Clyde Young 1925- *AmMWSc 92*
**Kramer**, Dale 1936- *IntAu&W 91, WrDr 92*
**Kramer**, David Buckley 1927- *AmMWSc 92*
**Kramer**, David William 1938- *WhoMW 92*
**Kramer**, Donald Thomas 1936- *WhoAmL 92*
**Kramer**, Earl Sidney 1940- *AmMWSc 92*
**Kramer**, Edward George 1950- *WhoAmL 92, WhoMW 92*
**Kramer**, Edward J 1939- *AmMWSc 92*
**Kramer**, Edwin J 1934- *WhoAmP 91*
**Kramer**, Elizabeth 1918- *AmMWSc 92*
**Kramer**, Elizabeth Maria 1954- *WhoMW 92*
**Kramer**, Elmer E 1914- *AmMWSc 92*
**Kramer**, Eugene L. 1939- *WhoAmL 92*
**Kramer**, Frank Richard 1926- *WhoAmL 92*
**Kramer**, Franklin 1923- *AmMWSc 92*
**Kramer**, Fred Russell 1942- *AmMWSc 92*
**Kramer**, George Mortimer 1929- *AmMWSc 92*
**Kramer**, George P. 1927- *WhoAmL 92*
**Kramer**, Gerald M 1922- *AmMWSc 92*
**Kramer**, Gisela A 1936- *AmMWSc 92*
**Kramer**, Gordon 1937- *WhoWest 92*
**Kramer**, Gordon Edward 1946- *WhoWest 92*
**Kramer**, Henry Herman 1930- *AmMWSc 92*
**Kramer**, Hilton 1928- *WrDr 92*
**Kramer**, Hugh E. 1929- *WhoFI 92, WhoWest 92*
**Kramer**, Irvin Raymond 1912- *AmMWSc 92*
**Kramer**, Irwin Raphael 1963- *WhoAmL 92*
**Kramer**, Ivor Robert Horton 1923- *Who 92*
**Kramer**, J. Daniel 1943- *WhoMW 92*
**Kramer**, J David R, Jr 1935- *AmMWSc 92*
**Kramer**, Jack 1921- *FacFETw*
**Kramer**, Jacob 1892-1962 *TwCPaSc*
**Kramer**, James G. 1954- *WhoEnt 92*
**Kramer**, James Joseph 1927- *WhoWest 92*
**Kramer**, James M *AmMWSc 92*
**Kramer**, James Richard 1931- *AmMWSc 92*
**Kramer**, Jane *SourALJ*
**Kramer**, Jane 1938- *IntAu&W 91, WrDr 92*
**Kramer**, Janice Kay 1944- *WhoMW 92*
**Kramer**, Jerome 1945- *IntMPA 92*
**Kramer**, Jerry Martin 1942- *AmMWSc 92*
**Kramer**, Joel Roy 1948- *WhoMW 92*
**Kramer**, John J 1931- *AmMWSc 92*
**Kramer**, John Karl Gerhard 1939- *AmMWSc 92*
**Kramer**, John Michael 1941- *AmMWSc 92*
**Kramer**, John Paul 1928- *AmMWSc 92*
**Kramer**, John William 1935- *AmMWSc 92*
**Kramer**, Jonathan Donald 1942- *WhoEnt 92*
**Kramer**, Josef 1906-1945 *EncTR 91*
**Kramer**, Joseph 1924- *WhoFI 92*
**Kramer**, Joshua N. 1956- *WhoEnt 92*
**Kramer**, Karen Lee 1950- *WhoMW 92*
**Kramer**, Karl Joseph 1942- *AmMWSc 92*
**Kramer**, Ken 1942- *WhoAmP 91*
**Kramer**, Kenneth Scott 1957- *WhoAmL 92*
**Kramer**, Kenneth Stephen 1941- *WhoAmL 92*
**Kramer**, Larry *DrAPF 91*
**Kramer**, Larry 1935- *IntAu&W 91, IntMPA 92, News 91 [port]*
**Kramer**, Laurie Maloff 1948- *WhoRel 92*
**Kramer**, Lawrence Stephen 1950- *WhoWest 92*
**Kramer**, Leonie 1924- *Who 92, WrDr 92*
**Kramer**, Leonie Judith 1924- *IntAu&W 91, IntWW 91*
**Kramer**, Lotte 1923- *ConPo 91, WrDr 92*
**Kramer**, Mark Kenneth 1957- *WhoAmL 92*
**Kramer**, Martin A 1941- *AmMWSc 92*
**Kramer**, Marvin Lewis 1931- *WhoWest 92*
**Kramer**, Mary E 1935- *WhoAmP 91*
**Kramer**, Mary Vincent 1957- *WhoFI 92*
**Kramer**, Matthew Stuart 1949- *WhoWest 92*
**Kramer**, Melinda Joyce 1960- *WhoFI 92*
**Kramer**, Michael Paul, Sr. 1945- *WhoFI 92*
**Kramer**, Milton 1928- *WhoEnt 92*
**Kramer**, Milton 1929- *AmMWSc 92*
**Kramer**, Mitchell Alvin 1933- *WhoAmL 92*
**Kramer**, Morton 1914- *AmMWSc 92*
**Kramer**, Noah Herbert 1924- *AmMWSc 92*
**Kramer**, Norman Clifford 1928- *AmMWSc 92*
**Kramer**, Paul Alan 1942- *AmMWSc 92*
**Kramer**, Paul J. 1904- *WrDr 92*
**Kramer**, Paul Jackson 1904- *AmMWSc 92, IntWW 91*
**Kramer**, Paul R. 1936- *WhoAmL 92*
**Kramer**, Paul Robert 1935- *AmMWSc 92*
**Kramer**, Philip 1915- *AmMWSc 92*
**Kramer**, Philip Joseph 1936- *WhoAmL 92*
**Kramer**, Raymond Arthur 1929- *AmMWSc 92*
**Kramer**, Raymond Edward 1919- *AmMWSc 92*
**Kramer**, Remi Thomas 1935- *WhoEnt 92*
**Kramer**, Richard A. 1938- *WhoEnt 92*
**Kramer**, Richard Allen *AmMWSc 92*
**Kramer**, Richard Eugene 1946- *WhoEnt 92*
**Kramer**, Richard Melvyn 1935- *AmMWSc 92*
**Kramer**, Robert *DrAPF 91*
**Kramer**, Robert 1927- *AmMWSc 92*
**Kramer**, Robert G *WhoAmP 91*
**Kramer**, Ronald Howard 1944- *WhoEnt 92*
**Kramer**, Ruth 1925- *WhoFI 92*
**Kramer**, Samuel Noah 1897-1990 *ConAu 133*
**Kramer**, Sandra 1943- *WhoEnt 92, WhoFI 92, WhoMW 92*
**Kramer**, Sheldon J 1938- *AmMWSc 92*
**Kramer**, Sherman Francis 1928- *AmMWSc 92*
**Kramer**, Sidney *IntMPA 92*
**Kramer**, Stanley 1913- *FacFETw, IntDcF 2-2 [port], IntWW 91*
**Kramer**, Stanley E. 1913- *IntMPA 92, WhoEnt 92*
**Kramer**, Stanley Phillip 1923- *AmMWSc 92*
**Kramer**, Stanley Zachary 1921- *AmMWSc 92*
**Kramer**, Stephen Henry 1950- *WhoFI 92*
**Kramer**, Stephen Leonard 1943- *AmMWSc 92*
**Kramer**, Steven David 1948- *AmMWSc 92*
**Kramer**, Theodore Tivadar 1928- *AmMWSc 92*
**Kramer**, Tim R 1943- *AmMWSc 92*
**Kramer**, Victor Mark 1927- *WhoFI 92*
**Kramer**, Walter Howard 1966- *WhoEnt 92*
**Kramer**, Werner 1917- *IntWW 91*
**Kramer**, Willard George, Jr. 1929- *WhoFI 92*
**Kramer**, William David 1944- *WhoAmL 92*
**Kramer**, William Geoffrey 1948- *AmMWSc 92*
**Kramer**, William J 1919- *AmMWSc 92*
**Kramer**, William S 1922- *AmMWSc 92*
**Kramer**, William Wayne 1943- *WhoEnt 92*
**Kramer-Badoni**, Rudolf 1913- *IntAu&W 91*
**Kramerich**, George L 1929- *AmMWSc 92*
**Kramish**, Arnold 1923- *AmMWSc 92*
**Kramlich**, John Charles 1951- *WhoWest 92*
**Kramm**, Deborah Ann 1949- *WhoFI 92*
**Kramm**, Deborah Lucille *WhoAmL 92, WhoFI 92*
**Kramme**, Joel Irwin 1941- *WhoMW 92*
**Kramme**, Michael Howard 1946- *WhoEnt 92*
**Kramon**, James Marshall 1944- *WhoAmL 92*
**Kramp**, Robert Charles 1942- *AmMWSc 92*
**Krampf**, John Edward 1947- *WhoAmL 92*
**Krampf**, Thomas *DrAPF 91*
**Krampitz**, Lester Orville 1909- *AmMWSc 92*
**Kramrisch**, Stella *Who 92*
**Kramsch**, Samuel Gottlieb 1756-1824 *DcNCBi 3*
**Kranbuehl**, David Edwin 1943- *AmMWSc 92*
**Kranc**, George M 1920- *AmMWSc 92*
**Kranc**, Stanley Charles 1942- *AmMWSc 92*
**Krane**, Dale Anthony 1943- *WhoMW 92*
**Krane**, Jonathan 1952- *IntMPA 92*
**Krane**, Kenneth Saul 1944- *AmMWSc 92*
**Krane**, Scott Harrison 1960- *WhoWest 92*
**Krane**, Stanley Garson 1937- *AmMWSc 92*
**Krane**, Stephen Martin 1927- *AmMWSc 92*
**Krane**, Steven Charles 1957- *WhoAmL 92*
**Kranenburg**, Hendrik Johannes 1955- *WhoFI 92*
**Kranendonk**, Carl John 1930- *WhoFI 92*
**Kranes**, David *DrAPF 91*
**Kranias**, Evangelia Galani *AmMWSc 92*
**Kranich**, Wilmer Leroy 1919- *AmMWSc 92*
**Kranidas**, Kathleen Collins *DrAPF 91*

**Kranidiotis**, Nicos 1911- IntWW 91
**Kranis**, Michael David 1955- WhoAmL 92
**Kranitz**, Hugh David WhoAmL 92
**Kranitz**, Morton Kiel 1926- WhoWest 92
**Kranjc**, Marko 1952- WhoMW 92
**Krannhals**, Paul 1883-1934 EncTR 91
**Krannich**, Larry Kent 1942- AmMWSc 92
**Kranowitz**, Alan Michael 1941- WhoAmP 91
**Kransberg-Talvi**, Marjorie 1959- WhoWest 92
**Kranseler**, Lawrence Michael 1958- WhoAmL 92
**Krantz**, Allen 1940- AmMWSc 92
**Krantz**, David S 1949- AmMWSc 92
**Krantz**, Douglas Edward 1948- WhoRel 92
**Krantz**, Douglas Stanley 1952- WhoEnt 92
**Krantz**, Gerald William 1928- AmMWSc 92
**Krantz**, Hazel 1920- WrDr 92
**Krantz**, Hazel Newman 1920- IntAu&W 91
**Krantz**, Judith IntAu&W 91, WrDr 92
**Krantz**, Judith 1927- BenetAL 91
**Krantz**, Judith 1928- IntWW 91
**Krantz**, Karl Walter 1918- AmMWSc 92
**Krantz**, Kermit Edward 1923- AmMWSc 92
**Krantz**, Reinhold John 1915- AmMWSc 92
**Krantz**, Sanford B 1934- AmMWSc 92
**Krantz**, Sheldon 1938- WhoAmL 92
**Krantz**, Stephen Falk 1923- WhoEnt 92
**Krantz**, Steve 1923- IntMPA 92
**Krantz**, Steven George 1951- AmMWSc 92, WhoMW 92
**Krantz**, William Bernard 1939- AmMWSc 92, WhoWest 92
**Kranwinkle**, Conrad Douglas 1940- WhoAmL 92, WhoWest 92
**Kranz**, Eugene Francis 1933- AmMWSc 92
**Kranz**, Kenneth Louis, Jr. 1946- WhoMW 92
**Kranz**, Mary Rosaria 1914- WhoMW 92
**Kranz**, Nancy Weston 1947- WhoFI 92
**Kranz**, Philip Neil 1943- WhoRel 92
**Kranzberg**, Melvin 1917- WrDr 92
**Kranze**, Clair Lorraine 1925- WhoAmP 91
**Kranzer**, Herbert C 1932- AmMWSc 92
**Kranzler**, Albert William 1916- AmMWSc 92
**Krapcho**, Andrew Paul 1932- AmMWSc 92
**Krapf**, George 1922- AmMWSc 92
**Krapf**, Norbert DrAPF 91
**Krapf**, Norbert 1943- IntAu&W 91
**Krapp**, Robert Martin IntAu&W 91X
**Krapu**, Gary Lee 1944- AmMWSc 92
**Kraras**, Gust C. 1921- WhoFI 92
**Krasavage**, Walter Joseph 1933- AmMWSc 92
**Krasean**, Thomas Karl 1940- WhoMW 92
**Krash**, Abe 1927- WhoAmL 92
**Krashes**, David 1925- AmMWSc 92
**Krashin**, Bernard R 1918- AmMWSc 92
**Krasicki**, Ignacy 1735-1801 BlkwCEP
**Krasilnikov**, Olga EncAmaz 91
**Krasilovsky**, Alexis Rafael 1950- WhoEnt 92, WhoWest 92
**Krasilovsky**, M. William 1926- WhoEnt 92
**Krasilovsky**, Phyllis 1926- IntAu&W 91, WrDr 92
**Krasin**, Leonid Borisovich 1870-1926 FacFETw, SovUnBD
**Krasin**, Yuriy Andreevich 1929- IntWW 91, SovUnBD
**Krasker**, Elaine S 1927- WhoAmP 91
**Kraskin**, Kenneth Stanford 1929- AmMWSc 92
**Krasko**, Michael John 1943- WhoFI 92
**Krasna**, Alvin Isaac 1929- AmMWSc 92
**Krasna**, Gary Marc 1960- WhoAmL 92
**Krasne**, Betty SmATA 66
**Krasner**, Daniel Walter 1941- WhoFI 92
**Krasner**, Gary 1953- WhoEnt 92
**Krasner**, Jerome L 1940- AmMWSc 92
**Krasner**, Joseph 1926- AmMWSc 92
**Krasner**, Lee 1908-1984 FacFETw
**Krasner**, Louis 1903- NewAmDM, WhoEnt 92
**Krasner**, Oscar Jay 1922- WhoWest 92
**Krasner**, Robert Irving 1929- AmMWSc 92
**Krasner**, Sol H 1923- AmMWSc 92
**Krasner**, William 1917- ConAu 35NR, IntAu&W 91, WrDr 92
**Krasney**, John Andrew 1940- AmMWSc 92
**Krasney**, Samuel Albert 1922- WhoFI 92
**Krasney**, Samuel Joseph 1925- WhoFI 92
**Krasno**, Louis Richard 1914- AmMWSc 92
**Krasnow**, Arthur Zev 1954- WhoMW 92
**Krasnow**, Frances 1894- AmMWSc 92
**Krasnow**, Jordan Philip 1944- WhoAmL 92
**Krasnow**, Marc Joseph 1961- WhoEnt 92
**Krasnow**, Marvin Ellman 1924- AmMWSc 92
**Krasny**, Harvey Charles 1945- AmMWSc 92
**Krasnyansky**, Anatole Lvovich 1930- WhoWest 92
**Krason**, Jan 1931- WhoFI 92
**Krason**, Stephen Marion 1954- WhoMW 92
**Krasovec**, Joze 1944- WhoRel 92
**Krasovskaya**, Vera Mikhailovna 1915- IntWW 91
**Krasovskaya**, Vera Mikhaylovna 1915- SovUnBD
**Krasovskiy**, Nikolay Nikolayevich 1924- IntWW 91
**Krass**, Allan S 1935- AmMWSc 92
**Krassner**, Brad Lee 1951- WhoEnt 92
**Krassner**, Jerry 1953- AmMWSc 92
**Krassner**, Stuart M 1935- AmMWSc 92
**Krasucki**, Henri 1924- IntWW 91
**Kraszewski**, Andrea Helena 1962- WhoFI 92
**Kratchenko**, Pavel Nikitovich 1926- WhoEnt 92
**Krathen**, David Howard 1946- WhoAmL 92
**Kratochvil**, Byron 1932- AmMWSc 92
**Kratochvil**, Clyde Harding 1923- AmMWSc 92
**Kratochvil**, Jiri 1944- AmMWSc 92
**Kratochvil**, Milos Vaclav d1988 IntWW 91N
**Kratochvil**, Susan Marie 1958- WhoMW 92
**Kratochvilova**, Jarmila 1951- IntWW 91
**Kratochwil**, Marian 1906- TwCPaSc
**Kratohvil**, Josip 1928- AmMWSc 92
**Kratovil**, Edward DeWolf 1944- WhoAmP 91
**Kratt**, Mary DrAPF 91
**Krattiger**, John Trubert 1916- AmMWSc 92
**Kratz**, Deborah Elizabeth 1953- WhoMW 92
**Kratz**, E. Lyn 1948- WhoEnt 92
**Kratz**, Howard Russel 1916- AmMWSc 92
**Kratz**, Russell Joseph 1946- WhoRel 92
**Kratz**, Timothy Harold 1965- WhoAmL 92
**Kratzel**, Robert Jeffrey 1949- AmMWSc 92
**Kratzenberg**, Damian 1878-1946 BiDExR
**Kratzer**, D Dal 1937- AmMWSc 92
**Kratzer**, Frank Howard 1918- AmMWSc 92
**Kratzer**, Guy Miller 1941- WhoAmP 91
**Kratzer**, Reinhold 1928- AmMWSc 92
**Kratzert**, Arthur William 1925- WhoAmP 91
**Kratzke**, Thomas Martin 1953- AmMWSc 92
**Krauch**, Carl Heinrich 1931- IntWW 91
**Krauel**, David Paul 1944- AmMWSc 92
**Kraul**, Edward Garcia 1930- WhoHisp 92
**Kraupp**, Otto 1920- IntWW 91
**Kraus**, Alan Edward 1953- WhoAmL 92
**Kraus**, Albert Andrew, Jr. 1948- WhoFI 92, WhoMW 92
**Kraus**, Alfred Andrew, Jr 1925- AmMWSc 92
**Kraus**, Alfred Paul 1916- AmMWSc 92
**Kraus**, Alfredo 1924- WhoEnt 92
**Kraus**, Alfredo 1927- NewAmDM
**Kraus**, Andreas 1922- IntWW 91
**Kraus**, Arthur Samuel 1925- AmMWSc 92
**Kraus**, Brenda Dene 1953- WhoMW 92
**Kraus**, C Raymond AmMWSc 92
**Kraus**, Carla 1940- IntAu&W 91
**Kraus**, Christine DrAPF 91
**Kraus**, David 1930- WhoRel 92
**Kraus**, Eric Bradshaw 1912- AmMWSc 92
**Kraus**, G. Thomas 1945- WhoWest 92
**Kraus**, Gary Paul 1953- WhoAmL 92
**Kraus**, George Andrew 1950- AmMWSc 92
**Kraus**, Hans-Joachim 1918- WhoRel 92
**Kraus**, Henry 1923- WhoMW 92
**Kraus**, Henry Emery 1914- WhoRel 92
**Kraus**, Herbert Myron 1921- WhoFI 92, WhoMW 92
**Kraus**, Hubert Adolph 1907- AmMWSc 92
**Kraus**, Jack Charles 1947- WhoMW 92
**Kraus**, James Ellsworth 1909- AmMWSc 92
**Kraus**, Jean Elizabeth Grau 1932- WhoFI 92
**Kraus**, Jeffrey Miles 1953- WhoWest 92
**Kraus**, Jeffrey T. 1956- WhoAmL 92
**Kraus**, Jess F 1936- AmMWSc 92
**Kraus**, Jim DrAPF 91
**Kraus**, Joanna Halpert 1937- WhoEnt 92, WrDr 92
**Kraus**, Joanna Maris Halpert WhoEnt 92
**Kraus**, John Daniel 1910- AmMWSc 92
**Kraus**, John Franklyn 1929- AmMWSc 92
**Kraus**, John Walter 1918- WhoWest 92
**Kraus**, Jon Eric 1951- AmMWSc 92
**Kraus**, Karl 1874-1936 EncTR 91 [port]
**Kraus**, Kenneth Emanuel 1956- WhoAmL 92
**Kraus**, Kenneth Wayne 1935- AmMWSc 92
**Kraus**, Lili 1905-1986 FacFETw, NewAmDM
**Kraus**, Lorraine Marquardt 1922- AmMWSc 92
**Kraus**, Michael WhoRel 92
**Kraus**, Norma Jean 1931- WhoFI 92
**Kraus**, Olen 1924- AmMWSc 92
**Kraus**, Oskar 1872-1942 EncTR 91
**Kraus**, Pansy Daegling 1916- WhoFI 92, WhoWest 92
**Kraus**, Philip A. 1950- WhoEnt 92
**Kraus**, Rae 1950- WhoEnt 92
**Kraus**, Richard Arnold 1937- WhoAmP 91
**Kraus**, Richard Charles 1953- WhoAmL 92
**Kraus**, Richard Stuart 1934- WhoFI 92
**Kraus**, Robert WhoAmP 91
**Kraus**, Robert 1925- IntAu&W 91, SmATA 65, WrDr 92
**Kraus**, Samuel 1925- AmMWSc 92
**Kraus**, Shirley Ruth 1919- AmMWSc 92
**Kraus**, Steven Gary 1954- WhoAmL 92
**Kraus**, Ted Richard 1945- WhoFI 92
**Kraus**, William Henry 1953- WhoRel 92
**Kraus**, William Ludwig 1922- AmMWSc 92
**Kraus-Friedmann**, Naomi 1933- AmMWSc 92
**Kraus Trujillo**, Alfredo 1924- WhoEnt 92
**Krausche**, Dolores Smoleny 1942- AmMWSc 92
**Krause**, Bernard Leo 1938- WhoEnt 92
**Krause**, Charles William 1952- WhoFI 92
**Krause**, Chester Lee 1923- WhoMW 92
**Krause**, Dale Curtiss 1929- AmMWSc 92
**Krause**, Daniel, Jr 1945- AmMWSc 92
**Krause**, Daphne Hylda 1927- WhoMW 92
**Krause**, David 1950- AmMWSc 92
**Krause**, David Wilfred 1950- AmMWSc 92
**Krause**, Douglas Paul 1956- WhoAmL 92
**Krause**, Eliot 1938- AmMWSc 92
**Krause**, Ernst Henry 1913- AmMWSc 92
**Krause**, Eugene Franklin 1937- AmMWSc 92
**Krause**, Gloria Rose 1922- WhoEnt 92
**Krause**, Gunther 1953- IntWW 91
**Krause**, Harold Allen 1940- WhoAmP 91
**Krause**, Harry Arthur 1951- WhoRel 92
**Krause**, Harry Dieter 1932- WhoAmL 92, WhoMW 92
**Krause**, Helen F 1919- WhoAmP 91
**Krause**, Helmut G L 1911- AmMWSc 92
**Krause**, Herbert 1905-1976 BenetAL 91, TwCWW 91
**Krause**, Herbert Francis 1942- AmMWSc 92
**Krause**, Horatio Henry 1918- AmMWSc 92
**Krause**, Irvin 1932- AmMWSc 92
**Krause**, Jerry 1939- WhoMW 92
**Krause**, Josef Gerald 1942- AmMWSc 92
**Krause**, Jyl Frowein 1955- WhoMW 92
**Krause**, Lawrence Berle 1929- WhoFI 92
**Krause**, Leonard Anthony 1925- AmMWSc 92
**Krause**, Lloyd O 1918- AmMWSc 92
**Krause**, Lucjan 1928- AmMWSc 92
**Krause**, Manfred Otto 1931- AmMWSc 92
**Krause**, Margarida Oliveira 1931- AmMWSc 92
**Krause**, Mark Stanley 1945- WhoEnt 92
**Krause**, Michael D 1952- WhoIns 92
**Krause**, Monte Aaron 1953- WhoEnt 92
**Krause**, Paul Carl, Jr 1932- AmMWSc 92
**Krause**, Paul Edward 1956- WhoRel 92
**Krause**, Paul Frederick 1945- AmMWSc 92
**Krause**, Peter James 1945- AmMWSc 92
**Krause**, Philip Allen 1939- WhoRel 92
**Krause**, Philip Crosland 1920- WhoFI 92
**Krause**, Ralph A 1909- AmMWSc 92
**Krause**, Ralph M 1931- AmMWSc 92
**Krause**, Reginald Frederick 1912- AmMWSc 92
**Krause**, Richard Lyle 1946- WhoAmL 92
**Krause**, Richard Michael 1925- AmMWSc 92
**Krause**, Robert Mortimer 1908- WhoMW 92
**Krause**, Ronald Alfred 1931- AmMWSc 92
**Krause**, Scott Francis 1930- WhoMW 92
**Krause**, Sonja 1933- AmMWSc 92
**Krause**, Thomas Otto 1944- AmMWSc 92
**Krause**, Tom 1934- NewAmDM
**Krause**, Victor Carter 1935- WhoAmP 91
**Krause**, Werner William 1937- WhoMW 92
**Krause**, William John 1942- AmMWSc 92
**Krausen**, Anthony Sharnik 1944- WhoMW 92
**Kraushaar**, Jack Jourdan 1923- AmMWSc 92
**Kraushaar**, William L. 1920- IntWW 91
**Kraushaar**, William Lester 1920- AmMWSc 92
**Kraushar**, Peter Maximilian 1934- WrDr 92
**Krauska**, Bernard Joseph 1961- WhoMW 92
**Krauskopf**, John 1928- AmMWSc 92
**Krauskopf**, Konrad 1910- WrDr 92
**Krauskopf**, Konrad Bates 1910- AmMWSc 92, IntWW 91
**Krausman**, Paul Richard 1946- AmMWSc 92
**Krausman**, Susan Kay 1949- WhoMW 92
**Krauss**, Alan Robert 1943- AmMWSc 92
**Krauss**, Beatrice Hilmer 1903- AmMWSc 92
**Krauss**, Bruno IntAu&W 91X
**Krauss**, Clemens 1893-1954 NewAmDM
**Krauss**, George 1933- AmMWSc 92
**Krauss**, Harry Edward 1945- WhoRel 92
**Krauss**, Herbert Harris 1940- AmMWSc 92
**Krauss**, Herbert Max 1915- WhoRel 92
**Krauss**, Janet DrAPF 91
**Krauss**, Jonathan Seth 1945- AmMWSc 92
**Krauss**, Lawrence Maxwell 1954- AmMWSc 92
**Krauss**, Marlene 1945- WhoFI 92
**Krauss**, Matt 1950- WhoAmP 91
**Krauss**, Robert Wallfar 1921- AmMWSc 92
**Krauss**, Ronald 1943- AmMWSc 92
**Krauss**, Ruth DrAPF 91
**Krauss**, Ruth 1911- IntAu&W 91, WrDr 92
**Krauss**, Sue Elizabeth 1951- WhoWest 92
**Krauss**, Werner 1884-1959 EncTR 91 [port]
**Krauss**, William Christopher 1863-1909 BiInAmS
**Krauss**, William Edward 1928- WhoMW 92
**Krausz**, Alexander Stephen 1924- AmMWSc 92
**Krausz**, Ernest 1931- WrDr 92
**Krausz**, Stephen 1950- AmMWSc 92
**Krausz**, Susan Beate WhoEnt 92
**Kraut**, Edgar A 1934- AmMWSc 92
**Kraut**, Gerald Anthony 1951- WhoFI 92
**Kraut**, Joseph 1926- AmMWSc 92
**Kraut**, Nate G. 1959- WhoAmL 92
**Kraut**, Richard Stephen 1941- WhoAmL 92
**Kraut**, Rochelle DrAPF 91
**Krautblatt**, Charles John 1950- WhoWest 92
**Krauter**, Adam WhoAmP 91
**Krauter**, Allan Irving 1941- AmMWSc 92
**Krauter**, Louis d1910 BiInAmS
**Krauth**, Charles Porterfield 1823-1883 RelLAm 91
**Krauthamer**, George Michael 1926- AmMWSc 92
**Krauthamer**, Nina 1951- WhoAmL 92
**Krauthammer**, Charles 1950- IntWW 91
**Krautheim**, Joel Charles 1962- WhoFI 92
**Krautkramer**, Raymond George 1908- WhoAmP 91
**Krautkremer**, James J 1934- WhoAmP 91
**Krautmann**, Anthony Charles 1956- WhoFI 92
**Krautschun**, Harvey C WhoAmP 91
**Krautter**, Elisa 1912?-1990 SmATA 65
**Krautter**, Frank 1953- WhoMW 92
**Krautz**, Fred Gerhard AmMWSc 92
**Krauzer**, Steven M. DrAPF 91
**Krauzer**, Steven M. 1948- TwCWW 91
**Kraval'**, Ivan Adamovich 1897-1938 SovUnBD
**Kravchuk**, Leonid Makarovich 1934- NewYTBS 91
**Kravchuk**, Robert Sacha 1955- WhoFI 92
**Kravets**, Vladimir A. 1930- IntWW 91
**Kravetz**, Dennis J. 1950- WhoMW 92
**Kravitch**, Phyllis A WhoAmP 91
**Kravitch**, Phyllis A. 1920- WhoAmL 92
**Kravitt**, Jason Harris Paperno 1948- WhoAmL 92
**Kravitz**, Edward Arthur 1932- AmMWSc 92
**Kravitz**, Ellen King 1929- WhoWest 92
**Kravitz**, Henry 1918- AmMWSc 92
**Kravitz**, Hilard Leonard 1917- WhoWest 92
**Kravitz**, Joseph Henry 1935- AmMWSc 92
**Kravitz**, Joyce 1950- WhoEnt 92
**Kravitz**, Lawrence C 1932- AmMWSc 92
**Kravitz**, Lenny WhoEnt 92
**Kravitz**, Lenny 1964?- News 91 [port]
**Kravitz**, Mark Richard 1950- WhoAmL 92
**Kravitz**, Rhonda A. Rios WhoHisp 92
**Kravitz**, Roberta 1944- TwCPaSc
**Kravitz**, William N. 1946- WhoAmL 92
**Kravitz**, Yaacov Jeffrey 1950- WhoRel 92
**Kravjansky**, Mikulas 1928- WhoWest 92
**Kravtsov**, Boris Vasilevich 1922- IntWW 91, SovUnBD
**Kraw**, George Martin 1949- WhoAmL 92, WhoFI 92, WhoWest 92
**Krawczak**, Arthur Henry 1913- WhoRel 92
**Krawczuk**, Aleksander 1922- IntWW 91
**Krawczuk**, John Edward 1938- WhoFI 92
**Krawczyk**, Monica 1887-1954 HanAmWH

**Krawetz**, Arthur Altshuler 1932- AmMWSc 92
**Krawetz**, Stephen Andrew 1955- AmMWSc 92
**Krawiec**, Richard DrAPF 91
**Krawiec**, Stanley J WhoAmP 91
**Krawiec**, Steven Stack 1941- AmMWSc 92
**Krawiecki**, Edward Charles, Jr 1952- WhoAmP 91
**Krawitz**, Herman Everett 1925- WhoEnt 92
**Kray**, Louis Robert 1938- AmMWSc 92
**Kraybill**, Edward K 1917- AmMWSc 92
**Kraybill**, Henry Lawrence 1918- AmMWSc 92
**Kraybill**, Herman Fink 1914- AmMWSc 92
**Kraybill**, Paul Nissley 1925- WhoRel 92
**Kraybill**, Richard R 1920- AmMWSc 92
**Kraychy**, Stephen 1928- AmMWSc 92
**Kraynak**, Matthew Edward 1927- AmMWSc 92
**Kraysler**, Stephen F 1942- WhoIns 92
**Krbechek**, Leroy O 1934- AmMWSc 92
**Krc**, Eugene Jaroslav 1958- WhoWest 92
**Krc**, John, Jr 1920- AmMWSc 92
**Krchma**, Stephen Peter 1947- WhoAmL 92
**Kreager**, Eileen Davis 1924- WhoFI 92, WhoMW 92
**Kream**, Barbara Elizabeth 1948- AmMWSc 92
**Kream**, Jacob 1919- AmMWSc 92
**Kreamer**, Barbara Osborn 1948- WhoAmP 91
**Krear**, Harry Robert 1922- AmMWSc 92
**Krebill**, Richard G 1936- AmMWSc 92
**Krebs**, Arno William, Jr. 1942- WhoAmL 92
**Krebs**, Carol Marie 1958- WhoMW 92
**Krebs**, David Alan 1958- WhoMW 92
**Krebs**, Edward H 1944- WhoAmP 91
**Krebs**, Edwin Gerhard 1918- AmMWSc 92
**Krebs**, Hans 1898-1945 EncTR 91
**Krebs**, Hans Adolf 1900-1981 FacFETw, WhoNob 90
**Krebs**, James John 1932- AmMWSc 92
**Krebs**, James N 1924- AmMWSc 92
**Krebs**, Johann Ludwig 1713-1780 NewAmDM
**Krebs**, John Hans 1926- WhoAmP 91
**Krebs**, John Richard 1945- IntWW 91, Who 92
**Krebs**, Julia Elizabeth 1943- AmMWSc 92
**Krebs**, Richard Allen 1947- WhoFI 92
**Krebs**, Robert Dixon 1931- AmMWSc 92
**Krebs**, Robert Duncan 1942- IntWW 91, WhoFI 92, WhoMW 92
**Krebs**, Robert Preston 1948- WhoAmP 91
**Krebs**, Roger Donavon 1949- WhoWest 92
**Krebs**, Stephen Jeffrey 1950- WhoWest 92
**Krebs**, Thomas Gary 1948- WhoAmL 92
**Krebs**, William A. W. d1991 NewYTBS 91
**Krebs**, William H 1938- AmMWSc 92
**Krebs**, William Hoyt 1938- WhoMW 92
**Krebsbach**, Karen K WhoAmP 91
**Krebsbach**, Scott Lee 1968- WhoAmP 91
**Kreckal**, Darlene Marie 1956- WhoEnt 92
**Kreckman**, James Andrew 1957- WhoFI 92
**Kredel**, Elmar Maria 1922- IntWW 91
**Kredi**, Olga Amary 1960- WhoHisp 92
**Kredich**, Nicholas M 1935- AmMWSc 92
**Kreegar**, Phillip Keith 1937- WhoMW 92
**Kreeger**, Julian Hillel 1940- WhoEnt 92
**Kreeger**, Russell Lowell 1946- AmMWSc 92
**Kreeger**, Saundra Sue 1939- WhoEnt 92
**Kreek**, Louis Francis, Jr. 1928- WhoAmL 92
**Kreep**, Gary George 1950- WhoWest 92
**Kreer**, Irene Overman 1926- WhoFI 92, WhoMW 92
**Kreer**, John B 1927- AmMWSc 92
**Kreevoy**, Maurice M 1928- AmMWSc 92
**Krefetz**, Gerald Saul 1932- WrDr 92
**Kreft**, Anthony Frank, III 1948- AmMWSc 92
**Kregal**, Ann DrAPF 91
**Kregel**, J. A. 1944- WrDr 92
**Kreger**, Elwyn Lorain 1924- WhoMW 92
**Kreger**, Jeffrey Paul 1967- WhoEnt 92
**Kreger**, Melvin Joseph 1937- WhoWest 92
**Kreglewski**, Alexander 1927- AmMWSc 92
**Kreh**, Donald Willard 1937- AmMWSc 92
**Kreh**, E J, Jr 1915- AmMWSc 92
**Kreh**, Richard Edward 1941- AmMWSc 92
**Krehbiel**, Frederick August 1941- WhoFI 92
**Krehbiel**, Frederick August, II 1941- WhoMW 92
**Krehbiel**, Robert WhoAmP 91
**Krehl**, Robert Paul 1960- WhoMW 92
**Kreibich**, Gert 1939- AmMWSc 92
**Kreibich**, Roland 1922- AmMWSc 92
**Kreider**, Carl 1914- WhoMW 92
**Kreider**, Donald Lester 1931- AmMWSc 92
**Kreider**, Eunice S 1941- AmMWSc 92
**Kreider**, Glenn Richard 1956- WhoRel 92
**Kreider**, Henry Royer 1911- AmMWSc 92
**Kreider**, Jack Leon 1941- AmMWSc 92
**Kreider**, John Wesley 1937- AmMWSc 92
**Kreider**, Kenneth Gruber 1937- AmMWSc 92
**Kreider**, Leonard Cale 1910- AmMWSc 92
**Kreider**, Leonard Emil 1938- WhoFI 92, WhoMW 92
**Kreidl**, Norbert J 1904- AmMWSc 92
**Kreidl**, Tobias Joachim 1954- AmMWSc 92
**Kreidle**, Kevin Zahl 1959- WhoAmL 92
**Kreidler**, Eric Russell 1939- AmMWSc 92
**Kreidler**, Myron Bradford 1943- WhoAmP 91
**Kreier**, Julius Peter 1926- AmMWSc 92
**Kreifeldt**, John Gene 1934- AmMWSc 92
**Kreifels**, Frank Anthony 1951- WhoAmL 92
**Kreiger**, Arthur Paul 1956- WhoAmL 92
**Kreighbaum**, William Eugene 1934- AmMWSc 92
**Kreil**, Curtis Lee 1955- WhoWest 92
**Kreilick**, Robert W 1938- AmMWSc 92
**Kreiling**, Daryl 1936- AmMWSc 92
**Kreiling**, William H 1923- AmMWSc 92
**Kreiman**, Robert T. 1924- IntMPA 92
**Kreimer**, Herbert Frederick, Jr 1936- AmMWSc 92
**Kreimes**, Paul Allen 1945- WhoMW 92, WhoRel 92
**Krein**, James Scott 1961- WhoAmL 92
**Krein**, Philip Theodore 1956- AmMWSc 92
**Krein**, Theodore James 1929- WhoMW 92
**Kreindler**, Robert Stanton 1927- WhoAmL 92
**Kreinin**, Mordechai 1930- WrDr 92
**Kreinin**, Mordechai Eliahu 1930- WhoFI 92, WhoMW 92
**Kreipke**, Merrill Vincent 1916- AmMWSc 92
**Kreis**, John Paul 1948- WhoAmL 92
**Kreis**, Ronald W 1942- AmMWSc 92
**Kreis**, Wilhelm 1873-1955 EncTR 91
**Kreis**, Willi 1924- AmMWSc 92
**Kreisberg**, Neil Ivan 1945- WhoFI 92
**Kreisel**, Georg 1923- IntWW 91, Who 92
**Kreisel**, Henry 1922- IntAu&W 91, WrDr 92
**Kreiser**, Frank David 1930- WhoMW 92
**Kreiser**, Ralph Rank 1941- AmMWSc 92
**Kreiser**, Thomas H 1935- AmMWSc 92
**Kreishman**, George Paul 1946- AmMWSc 92
**Kreisky**, Bruno d1990 IntWW 91N
**Kreisky**, Bruno 1911-1990 AnObit 1990, FacFETw
**Kreisle**, Leonardt F 1922- AmMWSc 92
**Kreisler**, Barry Benjamin 1945- WhoMW 92
**Kreisler**, Fritz 1875-1962 FacFETw [port], NewAmDM
**Kreisler**, Michael Norman 1940- AmMWSc 92
**Kreisman**, Jane Schexnayder 1948- WhoEnt 92
**Kreisman**, Norman Richard 1943- AmMWSc 92
**Kreiss**, Robert Allen 1942- WhoAmL 92
**Kreissl**, J. Scott 1946- WhoFI 92
**Kreiter**, Michael David 1947- WhoMW 92
**Kreiter**, Samuel David 1963- WhoMW 92
**Kreiter-Kurylo**, Carolyn DrAPF 91
**Kreith**, Frank 1922- AmMWSc 92
**Kreith**, Kurt 1932- AmMWSc 92
**Kreitler**, Robert Philip 1941- WhoFI 92
**Kreitman**, Benjamin Zvi 1920- WhoRel 92
**Kreitzberg**, Carl William 1937- AmMWSc 92
**Kreitzberg**, Fred Charles 1934- WhoWest 92
**Kreitzer**, David Martin 1942- WhoWest 92
**Kreitzer**, Jack DrAPF 91
**Kreitzer**, Jerry 1949- WhoAmP 91
**Kreitzer**, Michael Harvey 1942- WhoMW 92
**Kreitzman**, Ralph J. 1945- WhoAmL 92
**Kreitzman**, Stephen Neil 1939- AmMWSc 92
**Kreizinger**, Jean Dolloff 1931- AmMWSc 92
**Krejca**, Otomar 1921- IntWW 91
**Krejci**, Jaroslav 1916- WrDr 92
**Krejci**, John Joseph 1923- WhoMW 92
**Krejci**, Robert Henry 1943- AmMWSc 92, WhoWest 92
**Krejcsi**, Cynthia Ann 1948- WhoMW 92
**Krejsa**, Richard Joseph 1933- AmMWSc 92
**Krekeler**, Carl Herman 1920- AmMWSc 92
**Krekeler**, Heinz L. 1906- IntWW 91
**Krekorian**, Charles O'Neil 1941- AmMWSc 92
**Krekorian**, Michael H. DrAPF 91
**Krekorian**, Robert C 1962- WhoAmP 91
**Krekus**, Steven John 1937- WhoMW 92
**Krell**, George Frederick 1938- WhoWest 92
**Krell**, Robert Donald 1943- AmMWSc 92
**Krell**, Steven Paul 1946- WhoFI 92
**Krell**, Susan Karen 1941- WhoAmL 92
**Krell**, William 1873-1933 NewAmDM
**Krelle**, Wilhelm Ernst 1916- IntWW 91
**Kreloff**, Michael Allen 1946- WhoAmL 92
**Krelstein**, Ronald Douglas 1942- WhoAmL 92
**Krembs**, G M 1934- AmMWSc 92
**Kremen**, Pete 1951- WhoAmP 91
**Kremenak**, Charles Robert 1931- AmMWSc 92
**Krementz**, Edward Thomas 1917- AmMWSc 92
**Kremer**, Abi 1955- TwCPaSc
**Kremer**, Arthur Jerome 1935- WhoAmP 91
**Kremer**, Eugene R. 1938- WhoMW 92
**Kremer**, Gidon 1947- IntWW 91
**Kremer**, Gidon Markovich 1947- SovUnBD
**Kremer**, Honor Frances 1939- WhoFI 92
**Kremer**, James Nevin 1945- AmMWSc 92
**Kremer**, Joseph M 1921- WhoAmP 91
**Kremer**, Maurice A 1907- WhoAmP 91
**Kremer**, Patricia McCarthy 1947- AmMWSc 92
**Kremer**, Russell Eugene 1954- AmMWSc 92
**Kremers**, Howard Earl 1917- AmMWSc 92
**Kremers**, William Russell 1954- WhoMW 92
**Kremkau**, Frederick William 1940- AmMWSc 92
**Kremkoski**, Joe E 1949- WhoAmP 91
**Kreml**, Barbara Bloom 1933- WhoMW 92
**Kreml**, William Parker 1941- WhoFI 92
**Kremnev**, Roald Savvovich 1929- IntWW 91
**Kremp**, Gerhard Otto Wilhelm 1913- AmMWSc 92
**Kremp**, Herbert 1928- IntAu&W 91, IntWW 91
**Krempel**, Ralf Hugo Bernhard 1935- WhoWest 92
**Krempel**, Roger Ernest 1926- WhoWest 92
**Krempin**, Frederick Louis 1943- WhoFI 92
**Krempl**, Erhard 1934- AmMWSc 92
**Kremser**, Thurman Rodney 1932- AmMWSc 92
**Kremzner**, Leon T 1924- AmMWSc 92
**Kren**, George Michael 1926- WhoMW 92
**Kren**, Margo WhoMW 92
**Krendel**, Ezra Simon 1925- AmMWSc 92
**Krendl**, Cathy Stricklin 1945- WhoAmL 92
**Krenek**, Ernst d1991 NewYTBS 91 [port]
**Krenek**, Ernst 1900- ConCom 92, IntWW 91, NewAmDM, WhoEnt 92
**Krener**, Arthur James 1942- AmMWSc 92
**Krenitsky**, Thomas Anthony 1938- AmMWSc 92
**Krenkel**, Peter Ashton 1930- AmMWSc 92
**Krenos**, John Robert 1945- AmMWSc 92
**Krentler**, Kathleen Alice 1954- WhoWest 92
**Krentz**, Edgar Martin 1928- WrDr 92
**Krentz**, Jayne Ann 1948- WrDr 92
**Krenz**, Egon 1937- FacFETw, IntWW 91
**Krenz**, Jan 1926- IntWW 91
**Krenz**, Jerrold H 1934- AmMWSc 92
**Krenzelok**, Edward Paul 1947- AmMWSc 92
**Krenzer**, Sandi WhoAmP 91
**Krenzke**, Bette June 1944- WhoMW 92
**Krenzler**, Alvin Irving 1921- WhoAmL 92
**Krepakevich**, Jerry David 1946- WhoEnt 92
**Krepinsky**, Jiri J 1934- AmMWSc 92
**Krepps**, Ethel Constance 1937- WhoAmL 92
**Kreps**, David Marc 1950- WhoFI 92, WhoWest 92
**Kreps**, David Paul 1943- AmMWSc 92
**Kreps**, Juanita Morris 1921- HanAmWH, IntWW 91
**Krepshaw**, John David 1959- WhoMW 92
**Kresa**, Kent 1938- IntWW 91, WhoFI 92, WhoWest 92
**Kresch**, Alan J 1931- AmMWSc 92
**Krese**, Michael Joseph 1956- WhoMW 92
**Kreseski**, Mary Lee 1959- WhoFI 92
**Kresge**, Alexander Jerry 1926- AmMWSc 92
**Kresge**, Edward Nathan 1935- AmMWSc 92
**Kresh**, David DrAPF 91
**Kresh**, J Yasha 1948- AmMWSc 92
**Kresh**, Paul 1919- IntAu&W 91, WhoEnt 92, WrDr 92
**Kresheck**, Gordon C 1933- AmMWSc 92
**Kreshover**, Seymour J 1912- AmMWSc 92
**Kresina**, Thomas Francis 1954- AmMWSc 92
**Kreski**, Edward James 1952- WhoAmL 92
**Kreskin** 1935- WhoEnt 92
**Kresl**, Miles L., Jr. 1939- WhoMW 92
**Krespan**, Carl George 1926- AmMWSc 92
**Kress**, Bernard Hiram 1917- AmMWSc 92
**Kress**, Donnie Duane 1942- AmMWSc 92
**Kress**, Gloria W 1921- WhoAmP 91
**Kress**, Harold F. 1913- IntMPA 92
**Kress**, Kathleen Ann 1958- WhoAmL 92
**Kress**, Lance Whitaker 1945- AmMWSc 92
**Kress**, Lawrence Francis 1936- AmMWSc 92
**Kress**, Leonard DrAPF 91
**Kress**, Nancy DrAPF 91
**Kress**, Nancy 1948- IntAu&W 91
**Kress**, Ricky Allen 1959- WhoRel 92
**Kress**, Robert WhoRel 92
**Kress**, Thomas Joseph 1940- AmMWSc 92
**Kress**, Thomas Sylvester 1933- AmMWSc 92
**Kresse**, Jerome Thomas 1931- AmMWSc 92
**Kresse**, William Joseph 1958- WhoAmL 92
**Kressel**, Henry 1934- AmMWSc 92
**Kressel**, Herbert Yehude 1947- AmMWSc 92
**Kresta**, Jiri Erik 1934- AmMWSc 92
**Krestensen**, Elroy R 1921- AmMWSc 92
**Krestin**, David d1991 Who 92N
**Krestinsky**, Nikolay Nikolaevich 1883-1938 SovUnBD
**Kresy-Poree**, R. Jean 1931- WhoBlA 92
**Kretchik**, Walter Edward 1954- WhoMW 92
**Kretchmer**, Norman 1923- AmMWSc 92
**Kretchmer**, Richard Allan 1940- AmMWSc 92, WhoAmL 92, WhoMW 92
**Kretsch**, Mary Josephine AmMWSc 92
**Kretschmar**, William Edward 1933- WhoAmL 92, WhoAmP 91, WhoMW 92
**Kretschmer**, Albert Emil, Jr 1925- AmMWSc 92
**Kretsinger**, Robert 1937- AmMWSc 92
**Kretz**, Ralph AmMWSc 92
**Kretzenbacher**, Leopold 1912- IntWW 91
**Kretzinger**, Rik J. 1953- WhoWest 92
**Kretzmann**, Adalbert Raphael Alexander 1903- WhoRel 92
**Kretzmann**, Justus Paul 1913- WhoRel 92
**Kretzmer**, Ernest R 1924- AmMWSc 92
**Kretzmer**, Herbert 1925- IntAu&W 91, Who 92
**Kretzmer**, Peter Eugene 1957- WhoFI 92
**Kretzschmar**, John Richard 1933- WhoFI 92
**Kretzschmar**, Robert James 1943- WhoRel 92
**Kreuger**, Christopher WhoEnt 92
**Kreuger**, Kurt 1917- IntMPA 92
**Kreuger**, Kurt 1919- WhoEnt 92
**Kreul**, Lee Malcolm 1939- WhoMW 92
**Kreul**, Richard Theodore 1924- WhoAmP 91
**Kreutel**, Randall William, Jr 1934- AmMWSc 92
**Kreutner**, William 1941- AmMWSc 92
**Kreutz**, Edward C. 1926- WhoFI 92
**Kreutz**, James Kirk 1940- WhoAmP 91
**Kreutz-Delgado**, Kenneth Keith AmMWSc 92
**Kreutzberg**, Harald 1902-1968 EncTR 91
**Kreutzer**, Franklin David 1940- WhoAmL 92, WhoRel 92
**Kreutzer**, Richard D 1936- AmMWSc 92
**Kreutzer**, Rodolphe 1766-1831 NewAmDM
**Kreutzer**, William Alexander 1908- AmMWSc 92
**Kreutzer-Baraglia**, Lynne WhoMW 92
**Kreuz**, John Anthony 1933- AmMWSc 92
**Kreuzer**, Han Jurgen 1942- AmMWSc 92
**Kreuzer**, James Leon 1930- AmMWSc 92
**Kreuzer**, June April 1944- WhoAmP 91
**Kreuzer**, Lloyd Barton 1940- AmMWSc 92
**Kreuzer**, Terese Loeb 1943- WhoEnt 92
**Krevans**, Julius Richard 1924- AmMWSc 92, WhoWest 92
**Krevsky**, Seymour 1920- AmMWSc 92
**Krewer**, Semyon E 1915- AmMWSc 92
**Krewson**, Lyle Reid 1943- WhoAmP 91
**Krey**, Andrew Emil Victor 1948- WhoRel 92
**Krey**, Lewis Charles 1944- AmMWSc 92
**Krey**, Philip W 1927- AmMWSc 92
**Krey**, Phoebe Regina AmMWSc 92
**Kreyche**, Robert J. 1920-1974 ConAu 133
**Kreykes**, William 1937- WhoMW 92
**Kreyling**, Jule 1960- WhoAmL 92
**Kreymborg**, Alfred 1883-1966 BenetAL 91
**Kreysa**, Frank Joseph 1919- AmMWSc 92
**Krezanoski**, Joseph Z 1927- AmMWSc 92
**Krezdorn**, Roy R 1910- AmMWSc 92
**Krezoski**, John R 1947- AmMWSc 92
**Kriangsak Chomanan** 1917- IntWW 91
**Kribel**, Robert Edward 1937- AmMWSc 92
**Kricher**, John C 1944- AmMWSc 92
**Krichevsky**, Micah I 1931- AmMWSc 92
**Krick**, Irving Parkhurst 1906- AmMWSc 92

**Krick**, Merlyn Stewart 1938- *AmMWSc 92*
**Krick**, Patrick Joseph 1953- *WhoFI 92*
**Krickovich**, Joanne Marie 1958- *WhoMW 92*
**Kricorian**, Nancy *DrAPF 91*
**Krida**, Jeffrey David 1946- *WhoFI 92*
**Kridel**, Donald Joseph 1916- *AmMWSc 92*
**Kridelbaugh**, Stephen Joseph 1938- *WhoWest 92*
**Krider**, Edmund Philip 1940- *AmMWSc 92*
**Krider**, Jacob 1788-1874 *DcNCBi 3*
**Krider**, Jake Luther 1913- *AmMWSc 92*
**Krider**, Jaunita Faye 1933- *WhoAmP 91*
**Kriebel**, Howard Burtt 1921- *AmMWSc 92*
**Kriebel**, Mahlon E 1936- *AmMWSc 92*
**Kriebel**, Richard Marvin 1947- *AmMWSc 92*
**Krieble**, James G 1920- *AmMWSc 92*
**Krieck**, Ernst 1882-1947 *EncTR 91 [port]*
**Krieg**, Adrian Henry 1938- *WhoFI 92*
**Krieg**, Arthur F 1930- *AmMWSc 92*
**Krieg**, Daniel R 1943- *AmMWSc 92*
**Krieg**, David Charles 1936- *AmMWSc 92*
**Krieg**, Dorothy Linden 1919- *WhoEnt 92, WhoMW 92*
**Krieg**, Noel Roger 1934- *AmMWSc 92*
**Krieg**, Richard Edward, Jr 1942- *AmMWSc 92*
**Krieg**, Robert Anthony 1946- *WhoRel 92*
**Krieg**, Wendell Jordan 1906- *AmMWSc 92*
**Krieg**, William Lloyd 1946- *WhoFI 92*
**Kriegbaum**, Ray Phillip 1948- *WhoFI 92*
**Kriegbaum**, Richard Arnold 1941- *WhoRel 92, WhoWest 92*
**Kriege**, Owen Hobbs 1929- *AmMWSc 92*
**Kriegel**, Jay L. 1940- *WhoEnt 92, WhoFI 92*
**Kriegel**, Jerrold Donald 1938- *WhoFI 92*
**Kriegel**, Leonard *DrAPF 91*
**Kriegel**, Leonard 1933- *IntAu&W 91, WrDr 92*
**Kriegel**, Monroe W 1912- *AmMWSc 92*
**Krieger**, Allen Stephen 1941- *AmMWSc 92*
**Krieger**, Barbara Brockett 1947- *AmMWSc 92*
**Krieger**, Barry Israel 1956- *WhoRel 92*
**Krieger**, Bernard 1929- *WhoFI 92*
**Krieger**, Carl Henry 1911- *AmMWSc 92*
**Krieger**, Gary Lawrence 1948- *AmMWSc 92*
**Krieger**, Gary Robert 1951- *WhoWest 92*
**Krieger**, George Thomas 1942- *WhoFI 92*
**Krieger**, Henry Alan 1936- *AmMWSc 92*
**Krieger**, Howard Paul 1918- *AmMWSc 92*
**Krieger**, Ian *DrAPF 91*
**Krieger**, Irvin Mitchell 1923- *AmMWSc 92, WhoMW 92*
**Krieger**, Jeanne Kann 1944- *AmMWSc 92*
**Krieger**, Johann 1652-1735 *NewAmDM*
**Krieger**, Johann Philipp 1649-1725 *NewAmDM*
**Krieger**, John Newton 1948- *AmMWSc 92*
**Krieger**, Joseph Bernard 1937- *AmMWSc 92*
**Krieger**, Leslie Herbert 1938- *WhoFI 92*
**Krieger**, Murray 1923- *IntAu&W 91, WrDr 92*
**Krieger**, Paul Edward 1942- *WhoAmL 92, WhoFI 92*
**Krieger**, Roger B 1941- *AmMWSc 92*
**Krieger**, Roy Walter 1954- *WhoAmL 92*
**Krieger**, Sanford 1943- *WhoAmL 92*
**Krieger**, Sharron N. 1939- *WhoMW 92*
**Krieger**, Stephan Jacques 1937- *AmMWSc 92*
**Krieger**, Stu 1952- *WhoEnt 92*
**Krieger**, Ted *DrAPF 91*
**Krieger**, Tillie *WhoWest 92*
**Krieger**, William Carl 1946- *WhoWest 92*
**Kriegh**, James Douglas 1928- *AmMWSc 92*
**Krieghbaum**, Hillier 1902- *IntAu&W 91, WrDr 92*
**Kriegsman**, Edward Michael 1965- *WhoAmL 92*
**Kriegsman**, Helen 1924- *AmMWSc 92*
**Kriegsmann**, Gregory A 1946- *AmMWSc 92*
**Kriele**, Martin 1931- *IntWW 91*
**Kriendler**, Jeannette E. d1991 *NewYTBS 91*
**Krienke**, Carol Belle Manikowske 1917- *WhoFI 92, WhoWest 92*
**Krienke**, Ora Karl, Jr 1931- *AmMWSc 92*
**Kriens**, Richard Duane 1932- *AmMWSc 92*
**Krieps**, Robert 1922- *IntWW 91*
**Krier**, Carol Alnoth 1928- *AmMWSc 92*
**Krier**, Curtis Gene 1948- *WhoFI 92*
**Krier**, Cynthia Taylor 1950- *WhoAmP 91*
**Krier**, James Edward 1939- *WhoAmL 92*
**Krier**, John N. *IntMPA 92*
**Krier**, Joseph Roland 1946- *WhoFI 92*
**Krier**, Leon 1946- *IntWW 91*
**Kriesberg**, Jeffrey Ira 1949- *AmMWSc 92*
**Kriesberg**, Louis 1926- *WrDr 92*
**Kriesberg**, Simeon M. 1951- *WhoAmL 92*
**Kriesel**, Douglas Clare 1937- *AmMWSc 92*
**Kriess**, Fred Lewis, Jr. 1953- *WhoWest 92*
**Krigbaum**, Charles 1929- *WhoEnt 92*
**Krigbaum**, William Richard 1922- *AmMWSc 92*
**Krige**, Alice 1954- *IntMPA 92*
**Krigger**, Marilyn Francis 1940- *WhoBlA 92*
**Krigsvold**, Dale Thomas 1937- *AmMWSc 92*
**Krikhaar**, Anthony 1940- *TwCPaSc*
**Krikler**, Dennis Michael 1928- *Who 92*
**Krikler**, Leonard Gideon 1929- *Who 92*
**Krikorian**, Abraham D 1937- *AmMWSc 92*
**Krikorian**, Betty Linn 1943- *WhoAmL 92*
**Krikorian**, Esther *AmMWSc 92*
**Krikorian**, Gregory 1913- *Who 92*
**Krikorian**, John Sarkis, Jr 1941- *AmMWSc 92*
**Krikorian**, Oscar Harold 1930- *AmMWSc 92*
**Krikorian**, Thomas Michael 1951- *WhoEnt 92*
**Krikos**, George Alexander 1922- *AmMWSc 92*
**Krill**, Arthur Melvin 1921- *AmMWSc 92*
**Krill**, Mary Alice 1924- *WhoWest 92*
**Krill**, Paul Joseph 1960- *WhoWest 92*
**Krim**, Arthur B. 1910- *IntMPA 92, WhoWest 92*
**Krim**, Mathilde 1926- *AmMWSc 92*
**Krim Al-Khattabi**, Mohammad Abd El 1882-1963 *HisDSpE*
**Krimigis**, Stamatios Mike 1938- *AmMWSc 92*
**Krimm**, David Robert 1953- *WhoWest 92*
**Krimm**, Samuel 1925- *AmMWSc 92*
**Krimmel**, C Peter 1917- *AmMWSc 92*
**Krimmer**, Edward Charles 1933- *AmMWSc 92*
**Krin**, Sylvie *WrDr 92*
**Kriner**, William Arthur 1931- *AmMWSc 92*
**Kring**, James Burton 1921- *AmMWSc 92*
**Kring**, Stephen *WhoRel 92*
**Kring**, Walter Donald 1916- *WhoRel 92*
**Kringel**, Jerome Howard 1940- *WhoAmL 92*
**Krings**, Hermann 1913- *IntWW 91*
**Krings**, Vicki Lynn 1967- *WhoEnt 92*
**Krinitzsky**, E L 1924- *AmMWSc 92*
**Krinkle**, Philip B 1950- *WhoAmP 91*
**Krinsky**, Andrew Neal 1951- *WhoAmL 92*
**Krinsky**, Harris 1959- *WhoAmL 92*
**Krinsky**, Herman Y 1924- *AmMWSc 92*
**Krinsky**, Michael 1945- *WhoEnt 92*
**Krinsky**, Norman Irving 1928- *AmMWSc 92*
**Krinsky**, Philip Andrew 1959- *WhoFI 92*
**Krinsky**, Robert Daniel 1937- *WhoFI 92*
**Krinsky**, Samuel 1945- *AmMWSc 92*
**Krinsky**, William Lewis 1947- *AmMWSc 92*
**Krinsley**, Daniel B 1923- *AmMWSc 92*
**Krinsley**, David 1927- *AmMWSc 92*
**Krinsly**, Stuart Z. 1917- *WhoAmL 92, WhoFI 92*
**Kripalani**, Jiwatram Bhagwandas 1888-1982 *FacFETw*
**Kripalani**, Kishin J 1937- *AmMWSc 92*
**Kripke**, Bernard Robert 1939- *AmMWSc 92*
**Kripke**, Daniel Frederick 1941- *AmMWSc 92*
**Kripke**, Homer 1912- *WhoAmL 92*
**Kripke**, Margaret Louise 1943- *AmMWSc 92*
**Kripke**, Myer Samuel 1914- *WhoRel 92*
**Kripke**, Saul 1940- *WrDr 92*
**Kripke**, Saul Aaron 1940- *IntWW 91*
**Krippaehne**, William W 1917- *AmMWSc 92*
**Krippner**, Stanley Curtis 1932- *AmMWSc 92, WhoWest 92*
**Krips**, Josef 1902-1974 *FacFETw, NewAmDM*
**Krisano**, Maria Susana *WhoHisp 92*
**Krisch**, Alan David 1939- *AmMWSc 92*
**Krisch**, Henry 1931- *ConAu 134*
**Krisch**, Jean Peck 1939- *AmMWSc 92*
**Krisch**, Robert Earle 1937- *AmMWSc 92*
**Krische**, Vincent Edward 1938- *WhoRel 92*
**Krisciunas**, Kevin L 1953- *AmMWSc 92*
**Krise**, George Martin 1919- *AmMWSc 92*
**Krise**, Patricia Love 1959- *WhoWest 92*
**Krisel**, Gary *IntMPA 92*
**Krisel**, Maurice Arthur 1952- *WhoFI 92*
**Krish**, Tanya *Who 92*
**Krishan**, Awtar 1937- *AmMWSc 92*
**Krishen**, Anoop 1927- *AmMWSc 92*
**Krishen**, Kumar 1939- *AmMWSc 92*
**Krisher**, Albert Sherman 1929- *WhoMW 92*
**Krisher**, Lawrence Charles 1933- *AmMWSc 92*
**Krishna**, C R 1939- *AmMWSc 92*
**Krishna**, Gollapudi Gopal 1952- *AmMWSc 92*
**Krishna**, Gopi 1903-1984 *RelLAm 91*
**Krishna**, J Hari 1948- *AmMWSc 92*
**Krishna**, Kumar 1930- *AmMWSc 92*
**Krishna**, N Rama *AmMWSc 92*
**Krishna Rao**, Kotikalapudi Venkata 1923- *IntWW 91*
**Krishnaiah**, Paruchuri Rama 1932- *AmMWSc 92*
**Krishnamoorthi**, Sundaram 1947- *WhoMW 92*
**Krishnamoorthy**, Govindarajalu 1931- *AmMWSc 92*
**Krishnamurthy**, Lakshminarayanan 1941- *AmMWSc 92*
**Krishnamurthy**, Ramanathapur Gundachar 1931- *AmMWSc 92*
**Krishnamurthy**, Sundaram 1944- *AmMWSc 92*
**Krishnamurti**, Bhadriraju 1928- *IntWW 91*
**Krishnamurti**, Cuddalore Rajagopal 1929- *AmMWSc 92*
**Krishnamurti**, Jiddu 1895-1986 *FacFETw, RelLAm 91*
**Krishnamurti**, Pullabhotla V 1923- *AmMWSc 92*
**Krishnamurti**, Ruby Ebisuzaki 1934- *AmMWSc 92*
**Krishnamurti**, Tiruvalam N 1932- *AmMWSc 92*
**Krishnan**, Engil Kolaj 1942- *AmMWSc 92*
**Krishnan**, Gopal 1935- *AmMWSc 92*
**Krishnan**, K Ranga Rama 1956- *AmMWSc 92*
**Krishnan**, Kamala Sivasubramaniam 1937- *AmMWSc 92*
**Krishnan**, Natarajan 1928- *IntWW 91*
**Krishnan**, Rama 1931- *WhoMW 92*
**Krishnan**, Rappal Sangameswara 1911- *IntWW 91*
**Krishnan**, S. Ganesh 1955- *WhoMW 92*
**Krishnan**, Venkatanama 1929- *AmMWSc 92*
**Krishnappa**, Govindappa 1936- *AmMWSc 92*
**Krishnappan**, Bommanna Gounder 1943- *AmMWSc 92*
**Krishnaprasad**, Perinkulam S 1949- *AmMWSc 92*
**Krishnaswamy**, K. S. 1920- *IntWW 91*
**Krishnaswamy**, S V 1940- *AmMWSc 92*
**Krishtalka**, Leonard 1946- *AmMWSc 92*
**Krislov**, Samuel 1929- *WrDr 92*
**Kriss**, Joseph James 1942- *WhoFI 92*
**Kriss**, Joseph P 1919- *AmMWSc 92*
**Kriss**, Mary Elise 1947- *WhoRel 92*
**Kriss**, Michael Allen 1940- *AmMWSc 92*
**Krisst**, Raymond John 1937- *AmMWSc 92*
**Krist**, Gary *DrAPF 91*
**Krista**, Laverne Mathew 1931- *AmMWSc 92*
**Kristal**, Mark Bennett 1944- *AmMWSc 92*
**Kristensen**, Douglas Allan 1955- *WhoAmP 91*
**Kristensen**, Finn 1936- *IntWW 91*
**Kristensen**, Steven Arthur 1958- *WhoFI 92*
**Kristensen**, Sven Moller 1909- *IntWW 91*
**Kristeva**, Julia 1941- *FrenWW*
**Kristian**, Jerome 1934- *AmMWSc 92*
**Kristiansen**, Erling 1912- *IntWW 91, Who 92*
**Kristiansen**, Georg 1917- *IntWW 91*
**Kristiansen**, Magne 1932- *AmMWSc 92*
**Kristl**, Timothy O. 1943- *WhoAmL 92*
**Kristmanson**, Daniel D 1929- *AmMWSc 92*
**Kristof**, Agota *LiExTwC*
**Kristof**, Dennis Robert 1943- *WhoFI 92*
**Kristof**, Frank S. d1991 *NewYTBS 91 [port]*
**Kristoff**, James *WhoEnt 92*
**Kristoff**, Steven Randall 1955- *WhoMW 92*
**Kristoffersen**, Thorvald 1919- *AmMWSc 92*
**Kristofferson**, Kris 1936- *IntMPA 92, IntWW 91, WhoEnt 92*
**Kristol**, Daniel Marvin 1936- *WhoAmL 92*
**Kristol**, David Sol 1938- *AmMWSc 92*
**Kristol**, Irving 1920- *WrDr 92*
**Kristy**, James E. 1929- *WhoFI 92*
**Kristy**, Shawn 1963- *WhoEnt 92*
**Krisvoy**, James S. 1945- *WhoEnt 92*
**Krit**, Robert Lee 1920- *WhoFI 92, WhoMW 92*
**Kritchevsky**, David 1920- *AmMWSc 92*
**Krites**, Vance Richard 1942- *WhoAmP 91*
**Kritikos**, Haralambos N 1933- *AmMWSc 92*
**Kritselis**, William Nicholas 1931- *WhoAmL 92, WhoMW 92*
**Kritsky**, Gene Ralph 1953- *AmMWSc 92*
**Kritz**, Arnold H 1935- *AmMWSc 92*
**Kritz**, J 1918- *AmMWSc 92*
**Kritz-Silverstein**, Donna 1957- *AmMWSc 92*
**Kritzer**, Paul Eric 1942- *WhoAmL 92*
**Kritzman**, Ellen Baird 1936- *WhoWest 92*
**Kritzman**, Julius 1924- *AmMWSc 92*
**Krivak**, Thomas Gerald 1940- *AmMWSc 92*
**Krivanek**, Neil Douglas 1944- *AmMWSc 92*
**Krivanek**, Ondrej Ladislav 1950- *AmMWSc 92*
**Krivda**, George Edward, Jr 1956- *WhoAmP 91*
**Krivi**, Gwen Grabowski 1950- *AmMWSc 92*
**Krivine**, Alain 1941- *IntWW 91*
**Krivis**, Alan Frederick 1931- *AmMWSc 92*
**Krivit**, William 1925- *AmMWSc 92*
**Krivitzky**, Jerrold Steven 1957- *WhoAmL 92*
**Krivo**, David Alan 1950- *WhoFI 92*
**Krivosha**, Norman 1934- *WhoAmP 91*
**Krivosha**, Norman M 1934- *WhoIns 92*
**Krivoshia**, Eli, Jr. 1935- *WhoAmL 92*
**Krivoy**, William Aaron 1928- *AmMWSc 92*
**Kriyananda** 1926- *WhoEnt 92*
**Kriz**, George James 1936- *AmMWSc 92*
**Kriz**, George Stanley 1939- *AmMWSc 92*
**Kriz**, Rhoda Whitacre 1936- *WhoAmP 91*
**Krizan**, John Ernest 1934- *AmMWSc 92*
**Krizan**, Kelly Joe 1951- *WhoWest 92*
**Krizanic**, Juraj *DcAmImH*
**Krizay**, John 1926- *WhoWest 92*
**Krizek**, Donald Thomas 1935- *AmMWSc 92*
**Krizek**, Raymond John 1932- *AmMWSc 92*
**Krizek**, Thomas Joseph 1932- *AmMWSc 92*
**Krizsa**, Thomas Frederick 1948- *WhoFI 92*
**Krneta**, Michael L 1940- *WhoIns 92*
**Krnjevic**, Kresimir 1927- *AmMWSc 92*
**Kroc**, Ray 1902-1984 *RComAH*
**Kroc**, Ray A 1902-1984 *FacFETw*
**Kroc**, Robert Louis 1907- *AmMWSc 92*
**Krochmal**, Arnold 1919- *AmMWSc 92*
**Krochmal**, Jerome J 1930- *AmMWSc 92*
**Krochta**, William G 1930- *AmMWSc 92*
**Krock**, Hans-Jurgen 1942- *AmMWSc 92, WhoWest 92*
**Krock**, Larry Paul *AmMWSc 92*
**Kroeber**, Joe *WhoAmP 91*
**Kroeber**, Louis 1876-1960 *FacFETw*
**Kroeber**, Theodora 1897-1979 *FacFETw*
**Kroeger**, Berry d1991 *NewYTBS 91 [port]*
**Kroeger**, Donald Charles 1925- *AmMWSc 92*
**Kroeger**, Grace Lee 1928- *WhoAmP 91*
**Kroeger**, James Alan 1949- *WhoMW 92*
**Kroeger**, Peter G 1930- *AmMWSc 92*
**Kroeger**, Richard Alan 1955- *AmMWSc 92*
**Kroehler**, Armin Herbert 1922- *WhoRel 92*
**Kroeker**, Richard Mark 1952- *AmMWSc 92*
**Kroemer**, Adam Thomas 1966- *WhoEnt 92*
**Kroemer**, Herbert 1928- *AmMWSc 92*
**Kroenberg**, Berndt 1936- *AmMWSc 92*
**Kroener**, William Frederick, III 1945- *WhoAmL 92, WhoFI 92*
**Kroenert**, John Theodore 1921- *AmMWSc 92*
**Kroening**, Carl W 1928- *WhoAmP 91*
**Kroening**, John Leo 1934- *AmMWSc 92*
**Kroenke**, Loren William 1938- *AmMWSc 92*
**Kroenke**, William Joseph 1934- *AmMWSc 92*
**Kroes**, David Paul 1950- *WhoMW 92*
**Kroes**, Roger L 1935- *AmMWSc 92*
**Kroesen**, Jill *DrAPF 91*
**Kroetsch**, Robert 1927- *BenetAL 91, ConNov 91, IntAu&W 91, WrDr 92*
**Krofft**, Marty *LesBEnT 92*
**Krofft**, Sid *LesBEnT 92*
**Krog**, Carl Edward 1936- *WhoMW 92*
**Krog**, Eustace Walter 1917- *WrDr 92*
**Krogdahl**, Wasley Sven 1919- *AmMWSc 92*
**Kroger**, Althea 1946- *WhoAmP 91*
**Kroger**, F A 1915- *AmMWSc 92*
**Kroger**, Hanns H 1926- *AmMWSc 92*
**Kroger**, Harry 1936- *AmMWSc 92*
**Kroger**, Helmut Karl 1949- *AmMWSc 92*
**Kroger**, Larry A 1943- *AmMWSc 92*
**Kroger**, Manfred 1933- *AmMWSc 92*
**Krogh**, Desmond Charles 1931- *IntWW 91*
**Krogh**, Gordon Daniel 1952- *WhoMW 92*
**Krogh**, Lester Christensen 1925- *AmMWSc 92, WhoFI 92, WhoMW 92*
**Krogh**, Peter Sundehl, III 1953- *WhoWest 92*
**Krogh**, Richard Alan 1949- *WhoAmL 92*
**Krogh**, Schack August Steenberg 1874-1949 *WhoNob 90*
**Krogh**, Thomas Edvard 1936- *AmMWSc 92*
**Krogius**, Tristan Ernst Gunnar 1933- *WhoFI 92*
**Krogman**, Dean M *WhoAmP 91*
**Krogmann**, David William 1932- *AmMWSc 92*
**Krogmeier**, Charles J 1949- *WhoAmP 91*

**Krogmeier**, Kevin George 1951- *WhoMW 92*
**Krogsgaard-Larsen**, Povl 1941- *IntWW 91*
**Krogstad**, Blanchard Orlando 1921- *AmMWSc 92*
**Krogstad**, Donald John 1943- *AmMWSc 92*
**Kroh**, Glenn Clinton 1941- *AmMWSc 92*
**Krohmer**, Jack Stewart 1921- *AmMWSc 92*
**Krohn**, Albertine 1924- *AmMWSc 92*
**Krohn**, Barbara Rapchak 1954- *WhoMW 92*
**Krohn**, Burton Jay 1941- *AmMWSc 92*
**Krohn**, Daniel Alan 1949- *WhoAmL 92*
**Krohn**, Eugene 1932- *WhoFI 92*
**Krohn**, Herbert *DrAPF 91*
**Krohn**, John Leslie 1958- *AmMWSc 92*
**Krohn**, Kenneth Albert 1945- *AmMWSc 92, WhoWest 92*
**Krohn**, Kenneth Austin 1937- *WhoMW 92*
**Krohn**, Kenneth Robert 1946- *WhoEnt 92*
**Krohn**, Larry Dale 1948- *WhoRel 92*
**Krohn**, Peter Leslie 1916- *IntWW 91, Who 92*
**Krok**, Peter *DrAPF 91*
**Krokenberger**, Linda Rose 1954- *WhoWest 92*
**Krokoff**, Lowell Jay 1952- *WhoMW 92*
**Krol**, Arthur J 1925- *AmMWSc 92*
**Krol**, George J 1936- *AmMWSc 92*
**Krol**, John 1910- *WhoRel 92*
**Krol**, John Joseph 1910- *IntWW 91, RelLAm 91*
**Krol**, Joseph 1911- *AmMWSc 92, WhoFI 92*
**Krolczyk**, M. Daniel 1959- *WhoFI 92*
**Krolik**, Julian H 1950- *AmMWSc 92*
**Krolikowski**, Werner 1928- *IntWW 91*
**Kroll**, Alexander S. 1937- *IntWW 91*
**Kroll**, Bernard Hilton 1922- *AmMWSc 92*
**Kroll**, Boris d1991 *NewYTBS 91*
**Kroll**, Boris 1913- *DcTwDes*
**Kroll**, Burt *TwCWW 91*
**Kroll**, Charles Douglas 1949- *WhoRel 92*
**Kroll**, Charles L 1923- *AmMWSc 92*
**Kroll**, Emanuel 1919- *AmMWSc 92*
**Kroll**, Harry 1914- *AmMWSc 92*
**Kroll**, Harry Harrison 1888- *BenetAL 91*
**Kroll**, Jeri *DrAPF 91*
**Kroll**, John Ernest 1940- *AmMWSc 92*
**Kroll**, Judith *DrAPF 91*
**Kroll**, Lucien 1927- *IntWW 91*
**Kroll**, Martin Harris 1952- *AmMWSc 92*
**Kroll**, Martin N. 1937- *WhoAmL 92*
**Kroll**, Natasha 1914- *Who 92*
**Kroll**, Nathan 1911- *WhoEnt 92*
**Kroll**, Norman Myles 1922- *AmMWSc 92*
**Kroll**, Robert J 1928- *AmMWSc 92*
**Kroll**, Sol 1918- *WhoAmL 92*
**Kroll**, Steven 1941- *ConAu 35NR, SmATA 66 [port]*
**Kroll**, Steven Alexander 1947- *WhoFI 92*
**Kroll**, Una 1925- *Who 92*
**Kroll**, William 1901-1980 *NewAmDM*
**Kroll**, Woodrow Michael 1944- *WhoMW 92, WhoRel 92*
**Krolow**, Karl 1915- *IntWW 91*
**Krom**, Melven R 1931- *AmMWSc 92*
**Kroman**, Ronald Avron 1927- *AmMWSc 92*
**Kromann**, Paul Roger 1929- *AmMWSc 92*
**Kromann**, Rodney P 1931- *AmMWSc 92*
**Krombein**, Karl Von Vorse 1912- *AmMWSc 92*
**Kromer**, Helen *ConAu 34NR*
**Kromer**, Lawrence Frederick 1950- *AmMWSc 92*
**Kromhout**, Robert Andrew 1923- *AmMWSc 92*
**Krominga**, Lynn 1950- *WhoAmL 92*
**Kromko**, John 1940- *WhoAmP 91*
**Kromkowski**, Thomas 1942- *WhoAmP 91*
**Krommenhoek**, Hans Herman 1931- *WhoMW 92*
**Kromminga**, Albion Jerome 1933- *AmMWSc 92*
**Kron**, Gerald Edward 1913- *AmMWSc 92*
**Kronacker**, Paul Georges 1897- *IntWW 91*
**Kronauer**, Richard Ernest 1925- *AmMWSc 92*
**Kronberg**, Philipp Paul 1939- *AmMWSc 92*
**Kronberger**, Karlheinz 1940- *AmMWSc 92*
**Krone**, Gerald Sidney 1933- *WhoEnt 92*
**Krone**, Irene 1940- *WhoFI 92*
**Krone**, Julieanne Louise *NewYTBS 91 [port]*
**Krone**, Lawrence James 1940- *AmMWSc 92*
**Krone**, Lester H, Jr 1931- *AmMWSc 92*
**Krone**, Ralph Werner 1919- *AmMWSc 92*
**Krone**, Ray B 1922- *AmMWSc 92*
**Kronegger**, Maria Elizabeth 1932- *WrDr 92*
**Kronen**, Larry B. 1955- *WhoEnt 92*
**Kronenberg**, Mindy *DrAPF 91*
**Kronenberg**, Richard Samuel 1938- *AmMWSc 92*
**Kronenberg**, Stanley 1927- *AmMWSc 92*
**Kronenberg**, Susan *DrAPF 91*
**Kronenberger**, Louis 1904-1980 *BenetAL 91*
**Kronenfeld**, Judy *DrAPF 91*
**Kronenthal**, Richard Leonard 1928- *AmMWSc 92*
**Kronenwett**, Frederick Rudolph 1923- *AmMWSc 92*
**Kroner**, Arnold Friedrich 1939- *WhoFI 92*
**Kroner**, Klaus E 1926- *AmMWSc 92*
**Kronfeld**, David Schultz 1928- *AmMWSc 92*
**Kronfeld**, Leopold James 1941- *WhoAmP 91*
**Krongelb**, Sol 1932- *AmMWSc 92*
**Kronick**, David C 1932- *WhoAmP 91*
**Kronick**, Stephen Allen 1950- *WhoAmP 91*
**Kronick**, William *IntMPA 92*
**Kronin**, Charles 1954- *WhoAmL 92*
**Kronisch**, Myron Warren 1926- *WhoAmL 92*
**Kronk**, Bernard J. 1933- *WhoWest 92*
**Kronk**, Hudson V 1938- *AmMWSc 92*
**Kronmal**, Richard Aaron 1939- *AmMWSc 92*
**Kronman**, Anthony Townsend 1945- *WhoAmL 92*
**Kronman**, Carol Jane 1944- *WhoAmL 92*
**Kronman**, Joseph Henry 1931- *AmMWSc 92*
**Kronman**, Martin Jesse 1927- *AmMWSc 92*
**Kronmann**, Roger Bates 1937- *WhoRel 92*
**Kronmark**, Eric Allan 1931- *IntWW 91*
**Kronmiller**, C W *AmMWSc 92*
**Kronour**, Randall Jay 1952- *WhoFI 92*
**Kronschnabel**, Alan James 1923- *WhoEnt 92*
**Kronstad**, Warren Ervind 1932- *AmMWSc 92*
**Kronstein**, Karl Martin 1928- *AmMWSc 92*
**Kronstein**, Max 1895- *AmMWSc 92*
**Kronstein**, Werner J 1930- *WhoAmL 92*
**Krontiris-Litowitz**, Johanna Kaye 1952- *AmMWSc 92*
**Kronzon**, Itzhak 1939- *AmMWSc 92*
**Kroo**, Gyorgy 1926- *IntWW 91*
**Kroodsma**, Donald Eugene 1946- *AmMWSc 92*
**Kroodsma**, Roger Lee 1944- *AmMWSc 92*
**Krook**, Dorothea 1920- *IntWW 91, -91N*
**Krook**, Lennart Per 1924- *AmMWSc 92*
**Kroon**, Ciro Dominico 1916- *IntWW 91*
**Kroon**, James Lee 1926- *AmMWSc 92*
**Kroon**, Paulus Arie 1945- *AmMWSc 92*
**Kroon**, R P 1907- *AmMWSc 92*
**Kroon**, Richard Wayne 1964- *WhoWest 92*
**Kroon**, Rineke 1945- *TwCPaSc*
**Kroon**, Thomas Jay 1949- *WhoRel 92*
**Kroontje**, Wybe 1922- *AmMWSc 92*
**Krop**, Stephen 1911- *AmMWSc 92*
**Kropf**, Allen 1929- *AmMWSc 92*
**Kropf**, Donald Harris 1931- *AmMWSc 92*
**Kropotkin**, Piotr Alekseyevitch *ScFEYrs B*
**Kropotoff**, George Alex 1921- *WhoWest 92*
**Kropp**, James Edward 1939- *AmMWSc 92*
**Kropp**, John Leo 1934- *AmMWSc 92*
**Kropp**, Lloyd *IntAu&W 91, WrDr 92*
**Kropp**, Paul Joseph 1935- *AmMWSc 92*
**Kropp**, Richard P 1940- *WhoIns 92*
**Kropp**, William Rudolph, Jr 1936- *AmMWSc 92*
**Kroschewsky**, Julius Richard 1924- *AmMWSc 92*
**Krosnick**, Aaron Burton 1937- *WhoEnt 92*
**Krosnick**, Jon Alexander 1959- *WhoMW 92*
**Kross**, Jaan 1920- *IntAu&W 91*
**Kross**, Robert David 1931- *AmMWSc 92*
**Krost**, Barry *IntMPA 92*
**Kroszner**, Randall Scott 1962- *WhoMW 92*
**Krotee**, March Lee 1943- *WhoMW 92*
**Krothe**, Noel C 1938- *AmMWSc 92*
**Krotinger**, Myron Nathan 1914- *WhoAmL 92*
**Krotki**, Karol Jozef 1922- *WhoWest 92*
**Krotkov**, Robert Vladimir 1929- *AmMWSc 92*
**Kroto**, Harold Walter 1939- *Who 92*
**Krotov**, Viktor Vasil'evich *IntWW 91*
**Krotz**, Edward William 1925- *WhoMW 92*
**Krouk**, Nora 1920- *IntAu&W 91*
**Krouse**, George Raymond, Jr. 1945- *WhoAmL 92*
**Krouse**, Howard Roy 1935- *AmMWSc 92*
**Krouse**, Rodger Russell 1961- *WhoFI 92*
**Krouse**, Stan Samuel 1947- *WhoRel 92*
**Krouskop**, Thomas Alan 1945- *AmMWSc 92*
**Krovopuskov**, Viktor Leonidovich 1948- *IntWW 91, SovUnBD*
**Krow**, Grant Reese 1941- *AmMWSc 92*
**Krowas**, Rainer Heinz Adolph 1942- *WhoMW 92*
**Krowe**, Allen Julian 1932- *WhoFI 92*
**Krown**, Seymour Richard 1931- *WhoEnt 92*
**Krown**, Susan E 1946- *AmMWSc 92*
**Kroyer**, Haraldur 1921- *IntWW 91*
**Krska**, Robert T *WhoAmP 91*
**Krsul**, John Aloysius, Jr. 1938- *WhoAmL 92*
**Krubiner**, Alan Martin 1941- *AmMWSc 92*
**Kruchek**, Thomas Francis 1922- *WhoWest 92*
**Kruchenykh**, Aleksey Eliseevich 1886-1968 *SovUnBD*
**Kruchenykh**, Alexei Yeliseyevich 1886-1970 *FacFETw*
**Kruchina**, Nikolai Yefimovich 1928- *IntWW 91*
**Kruchina**, Nikolay Yefimovich 1928- *SovUnBD*
**Kruchkow**, Diane *DrAPF 91*
**Kruchten**, Marcia H. *DrAPF 91*
**Kruck**, Evelyn D. 1935- *WhoFI 92*
**Kruckeberg**, Arthur Rice 1920- *AmMWSc 92*
**Kruckemeyer**, Robert Joseph 1959- *WhoAmL 92*
**Kruckenberg**, Homer Andrew 1935- *WhoAmP 91*
**Kruckenberg**, Joyce LaVon 1938- *WhoAmP 91*
**Krucks**, William 1918- *WhoFI 92*
**Krucky**, Anton Chalmers 1952- *WhoWest 92*
**Kruczynski**, William Leonard 1943- *AmMWSc 92*
**Krudener**, Juliane Von 1764-1824 *FrenWW*
**Kruegel**, Alice Virginia 1939- *AmMWSc 92*
**Krueger**, Alan Douglas 1937- *WhoFI 92, WhoMW 92*
**Krueger**, Anne O. *WhoFI 92*
**Krueger**, Anne O. 1934- *IntWW 91*
**Krueger**, Arlin James 1933- *AmMWSc 92*
**Krueger**, Artur W. G. 1940- *WhoFI 92*
**Krueger**, Betty Jane 1923- *WhoFI 92, WhoMW 92*
**Krueger**, Bonnie Lee 1950- *WhoMW 92*
**Krueger**, Brady Kim 1952- *WhoMW 92*
**Krueger**, Charles Robert 1938- *AmMWSc 92*
**Krueger**, Cheryl Ann 1962- *WhoMW 92*
**Krueger**, Darrell William 1943- *WhoMW 92*
**Krueger**, David Allen 1939- *AmMWSc 92*
**Krueger**, David Keith 1936- *WhoRel 92*
**Krueger**, David Matthew 1955- *WhoRel 92*
**Krueger**, Donald Marc 1952- *WhoFI 92*
**Krueger**, Eugene Rex 1935- *AmMWSc 92*
**Krueger**, Everett Heath 1950- *WhoAmL 92*
**Krueger**, Frederick William 1943- *WhoWest 92*
**Krueger**, George Corwin 1922- *AmMWSc 92*
**Krueger**, Gerhard R F 1936- *AmMWSc 92*
**Krueger**, Jack N 1922- *AmMWSc 92*
**Krueger**, James 1938- *WhoAmL 92*
**Krueger**, James A. 1943- *WhoAmL 92*
**Krueger**, James Elwood 1926- *AmMWSc 92, WhoFI 92*
**Krueger**, James Harry 1936- *AmMWSc 92*
**Krueger**, James Herbert, Sr. 1943- *WhoFI 92*
**Krueger**, Jill Marie 1959- *WhoMW 92*
**Krueger**, John Charles 1951- *WhoFI 92*
**Krueger**, Jon Fredric 1957- *WhoEnt 92*
**Krueger**, Keatha Kathrine 1921- *AmMWSc 92*
**Krueger**, Keith Roger 1957- *WhoAmP 91*
**Krueger**, Kurt August 1962- *WhoEnt 92*
**Krueger**, Kurt Donn 1952- *WhoAmL 92, WhoAmP 91*
**Krueger**, Kurt Edward 1952- *WhoWest 92*
**Krueger**, Larry Eugene 1944- *WhoAmL 92, WhoWest 92*
**Krueger**, Lyle Dwight 1952- *WhoMW 92*
**Krueger**, Michelle Mary 1963- *WhoMW 92*
**Krueger**, Paul A 1906- *AmMWSc 92*
**Krueger**, Paul Carlton 1936- *AmMWSc 92*
**Krueger**, Paul Eric 1948- *WhoWest 92*
**Krueger**, Peter George 1940- *AmMWSc 92*
**Krueger**, Peter J 1934- *AmMWSc 92*
**Krueger**, Richard Arnold 1949- *WhoAmP 91*
**Krueger**, Richard H 1933- *WhoAmP 91*
**Krueger**, Robert A 1935- *AmMWSc 92*
**Krueger**, Robert Blair 1928- *WhoFI 92*
**Krueger**, Robert Carl 1920- *AmMWSc 92*
**Krueger**, Robert George 1938- *AmMWSc 92*
**Krueger**, Robert Harold 1926- *AmMWSc 92*
**Krueger**, Robert John 1948- *AmMWSc 92*
**Krueger**, Robert William 1916- *AmMWSc 92, WhoAmP 91*
**Krueger**, Roland Frederick 1918- *AmMWSc 92*
**Krueger**, Ronald L. 1930- *WhoEnt 92*
**Krueger**, Ronald P. 1940- *IntMPA 92*
**Krueger**, Tom *WhoAmP 91*
**Krueger**, William Arthur 1941- *AmMWSc 92*
**Krueger**, William Clement 1942- *AmMWSc 92*
**Krueger**, William E 1940- *AmMWSc 92*
**Krueger**, Willie Frederick 1921- *AmMWSc 92*
**Kruelle**, Carl Henry, Jr. 1938- *WhoRel 92*
**Kruener**, Harry Howard 1915- *WhoRel 92*
**Kruer**, William Leo 1942- *AmMWSc 92*
**Kruesi**, William R 1921- *AmMWSc 92*
**Krug**, Edward Charles 1947- *AmMWSc 92*
**Krug**, Edwin Herbert 1938- *WhoMW 92*
**Krug**, Fred Roy 1929- *WhoEnt 92*
**Krug**, John Christian 1938- *AmMWSc 92*
**Krug**, Judith Fingeret 1940- *WhoMW 92*
**Krug**, Robert Joseph 1935- *WhoFI 92*
**Krug**, Samuel Edward 1943- *AmMWSc 92*
**Krug**, Shirley 1958- *WhoAmP 91*
**Kruger**, Augusta *EncAmaz 91*
**Kruger**, Barbara 1945- *WorArt 1980 [port]*
**Kruger**, Bruce 1940- *WhoAmL 92*
**Kruger**, Charles Herman, Jr 1934- *AmMWSc 92, WhoWest 92*
**Kruger**, Fred W 1921- *AmMWSc 92*
**Kruger**, Fredrick Christian 1912- *AmMWSc 92*
**Kruger**, Gerhard 1908- *BiDExR, EncTR 91*
**Kruger**, Hardy 1928- *IntMPA 92, IntWW 91*
**Kruger**, Horst 1919- *IntWW 91*
**Kruger**, James Edward 1938- *AmMWSc 92*
**Kruger**, Jeffrey S. 1931- *IntMPA 92*
**Kruger**, John David 1952- *WhoWest 92*
**Kruger**, Lawrence 1929- *AmMWSc 92*
**Kruger**, Manfred Paul 1938- *IntWW 91*
**Kruger**, Owen L 1932- *AmMWSc 92*
**Kruger**, Paul 1925- *AmMWSc 92, WhoWest 92*
**Kruger**, Paul Robert 1957- *WhoWest 92*
**Kruger**, Prudence Margaret *Who 92*
**Kruger**, Richard Paul 1944- *AmMWSc 92*
**Kruger**, William Arnold 1937- *WhoMW 92*
**Kruger**, Wolf *WrDr 92*
**Kruger-Lutz**, Julie M. 1958- *WhoWest 92*
**Kruggel**, Kevin Gregory 1959- *WhoFI 92*
**Krugh**, Thomas Richard 1943- *AmMWSc 92*
**Kruglak**, Haym 1909- *AmMWSc 92*
**Krugler**, Arnold Frank 1933- *WhoRel 92*
**Krugler**, Richard Adolph 1925- *WhoRel 92*
**Kruglick**, Burton S 1925- *WhoAmP 91*
**Kruglick**, Lewis *DrAPF 91*
**Kruglova**, Zinaida Mikhaylovna 1923- *SovUnBD*
**Krugman**, Lou 1914- *WhoEnt 92*
**Krugman**, Saul 1911- *AmMWSc 92*
**Krugman**, Stanley Lee 1925- *WhoWest 92*
**Krugman**, Stanley Liebert 1932- *AmMWSc 92*
**Kruguer**, Ignacio 1939- *WhoFI 92*
**Kruh**, Daniel 1934- *AmMWSc 92*
**Kruh**, Robert Frank 1925- *AmMWSc 92*
**Kruidenier**, David 1921- *WhoFI 92*
**Kruidenier**, Francis Jeremiah 1913- *AmMWSc 92*
**Kruijtbosch**, Egbert Diederik Jan 1925- *IntWW 91*
**Kruisbeek**, Ada M 1938- *AmMWSc 92*
**Kruizenga**, Richard John 1930- *WhoFI 92*
**Kruk**, Tadeusz 1922- *IntAu&W 91*
**Krukowski**, Jan, Mrs. *WhoEnt 92*
**Krukowski**, Marilyn 1932- *AmMWSc 92*
**Krulitz**, Leo Morrion 1938- *WhoAmP 91*
**Krull**, Douglas A. 1958- *WhoAmL 92*
**Krull**, Edward Alexander 1929- *WhoMW 92*
**Krull**, Ira Stanley 1940- *AmMWSc 92*
**Krull**, John Norman 1939- *AmMWSc 92*
**Krulwich**, Terry Ann 1943- *AmMWSc 92*
**Krulwich**, Theodore Joseph 1953- *WhoAmP 91*
**Krum**, Alvin A 1928- *AmMWSc 92*
**Krum**, Jack Kern 1922- *AmMWSc 92*
**Krum**, Nelson Charles, Jr. 1953- *WhoWest 92*
**Kruman**, Mark Steven 1953- *WhoFI 92*
**Krumbein**, Aaron Davis 1921- *AmMWSc 92*
**Krumbein**, Charles Harvey 1944- *WhoAmL 92, WhoFI 92*
**Krumbein**, Simeon Joseph *AmMWSc 92*
**Krumbhaar**, George Douglas, Jr 1936- *WhoAmP 91*
**Krumboltz**, David Robert 1936- *WhoWest 92*
**Krumdieck**, Carlos L 1932- *AmMWSc 92*
**Krumhansl**, James Arthur 1919- *AmMWSc 92*
**Krumins**, Anita Ilze 1946- *IntAu&W 91*
**Krumm**, Charles Ferdinand 1941- *AmMWSc 92*
**Krumm**, Daniel J. 1926- *IntWW 91*
**Krumm**, Gene William 1942- *WhoMW 92*
**Krumm**, John McGill 1913- *WhoRel 92, WhoWest 92*

**Krumm**, William Thomas 1938- *WhoRel 92*
**Krummacher**, Hans-Henrik 1931- *IntWW 91*
**Krumme**, George William 1922- *WhoAmP 91*
**Krummel**, Donald William 1929- *WhoMW 92*
**Krummel**, William Marion 1928- *AmMWSc 92*
**Krummen**, William Jerome 1954- *WhoFI 92*
**Krummenacher**, Daniel 1925- *AmMWSc 92*
**Krump**, Jacqueline *WhoMW 92*
**Krump**, Jeffrey R. 1952- *WhoEnt 92*
**Krumpholtz**, Jean-Baptiste 1742-1790 *NewAmDM*
**Krumrei**, W C 1924- *AmMWSc 92*
**Krumreich**, Ted Alan 1956- *WhoAmL 92*
**Krupa**, Allen D 1946- *WhoIns 92*
**Krupa**, Allen Dennis 1946- *WhoFI 92*
**Krupa**, Gene 1909-1973 *FacFETw [port]*, *NewAmDM*
**Krupa**, Sagar 1940- *AmMWSc 92*
**Krupansky**, Robert B *WhoAmP 91*
**Krupansky**, Robert Bazil 1921- *WhoAmL 92*
**Krupinski**, Jerry W *WhoAmP 91*
**Krupinski**, Loretta 1940- *SmATA 67*
**Krupka**, Lawrence Ronald 1933- *AmMWSc 92*
**Krupka**, Milton Clifford 1924- *AmMWSc 92*
**Krupka**, Richard M 1932- *AmMWSc 92*
**Krupka**, Robert George 1949- *WhoFI 92*
**Krupke**, William F 1937- *AmMWSc 92*
**Krupman**, William Allan 1936- *WhoAmL 92*
**Krupnik**, Vee M. *WhoFI 92*
**Krupocki**, Robert Joseph 1932- *WhoIns 92*
**Krupp**, David Alan 1953- *AmMWSc 92*
**Krupp**, Edwin Charles 1944- *AmMWSc 92*, *WhoWest 92*
**Krupp**, Georg 1936- *IntWW 91*
**Krupp**, Iris M 1928- *AmMWSc 92*
**Krupp**, Marcus Abraham 1913- *AmMWSc 92*
**Krupp**, Margo *WhoMW 92*
**Krupp**, Neil B. 1941- *WhoMW 92*
**Krupp**, Patricia Powers *AmMWSc 92*
**Krupp**, Robert Allen 1951- *WhoRel 92*, *WhoWest 92*
**Krupp**, Robin Rector 1946- *ConAu 135*
**Krupp von Bohlen und Halbach**, Alfried 1907-1967 *EncTR 91 [port]*
**Krupp von Bohlen und Halbach**, Gustav 1870-1950 *EncTR 91 [port]*
**Krupsak**, Mary Anne 1932- *WhoAmP 91*
**Krupska**, Danya 1921- *WhoEnt 92*
**Krupskaya**, Nadezhda Konstantinova 1869-1939 *SovUnBD*
**Krupskaya**, Nadezhda Konstantinovna 1869-1939 *FacFETw*
**Krusberg**, Lorin Ronald 1932- *AmMWSc 92*
**Kruschwitz**, Walter Hillis 1920- *AmMWSc 92*
**Kruse**, Arthur Herman 1928- *AmMWSc 92*
**Kruse**, Carl William 1927- *AmMWSc 92*
**Kruse**, Conrad Edward 1923- *AmMWSc 92*
**Kruse**, Dennis K 1946- *WhoAmP 91*
**Kruse**, Douglas Charles 1951- *WhoFI 92*
**Kruse**, F. Michael *WhoAmL 92*
**Kruse**, Ferdinand Hobert 1925- *AmMWSc 92*
**Kruse**, Jeffrey Richard 1958- *WhoFI 92*
**Kruse**, John 1919- *ConAu 35NR*
**Kruse**, John Alphonse 1926- *WhoAmL 92*
**Kruse**, Jurgen M 1927- *AmMWSc 92*
**Kruse**, Kipp Colby 1949- *AmMWSc 92*, *WhoMW 92*
**Kruse**, Lawrence Ivan 1958- *AmMWSc 92*
**Kruse**, Lise Fiaux 1947- *WhoFI 92*
**Kruse**, Martin 1929- *IntWW 91*, *WhoRel 92*
**Kruse**, Max Lee 1961- *WhoMW 92*
**Kruse**, Olan Ernest 1921- *AmMWSc 92*
**Kruse**, Pamela Jean 1950- *WhoAmL 92*
**Kruse**, Paul Walters, Jr 1927- *AmMWSc 92*, *WhoMW 92*
**Kruse**, Robert Leroy 1941- *AmMWSc 92*
**Kruse**, Robert Louis 1938- *AmMWSc 92*
**Kruse**, Scott August 1947- *WhoAmL 92*
**Kruse**, Ulrich Ernst 1929- *AmMWSc 92*
**Kruse**, Walter M 1928- *AmMWSc 92*
**Kruse**, Wilbur Ferdinand 1922- *WhoMW 92*
**Krusen**, Edward Montgomery 1920- *AmMWSc 92*
**Krushensky**, Richard D 1932- *AmMWSc 92*
**Krusic**, Paul Joseph 1934- *AmMWSc 92*
**Krusick**, Margaret Ann 1956- *WhoAmP 91*
**Krusin**, Stanley 1908- *Who 92*
**Kruskal**, Joseph Bernard 1928- *AmMWSc 92*
**Kruskal**, Martin David 1925- *AmMWSc 92*
**Kruskal**, William Henry 1919- *AmMWSc 92*
**Krusoe**, James *DrAPF 91*
**Kruszewski**, Kenneth E 1945- *WhoAmP 91*
**Kruszewski**, Krzysztof 1939- *IntWW 91*
**Kruszewski**, Z. Anthony 1928- *ConAu 134*
**Krut**, Ansel 1959- *TwCPaSc*
**Krutak**, James John, Sr 1942- *AmMWSc 92*
**Krutch**, Joseph Wood 1893-1970 *BenetAL 91*, *FacFETw*
**Krutchen**, Charles M 1934- *AmMWSc 92*
**Krutchkoff**, David James 1938- *AmMWSc 92*
**Krutchkoff**, Richard Gerald 1933- *AmMWSc 92*
**Kruteck**, Laurence R. 1941- *WhoAmL 92*, *WhoFI 92*
**Krutilek**, Daniel Ray 1942- *WhoIns 92*
**Krutter**, Forrest Nathan 1954- *WhoAmL 92*, *WhoMW 92*
**Krutter**, Harry 1911- *AmMWSc 92*
**Krutzsch**, Henry C 1942- *AmMWSc 92*
**Krutzsch**, Philip Henry 1919- *AmMWSc 92*
**Kruus**, Jaan 1936- *AmMWSc 92*
**Kruus**, Peeter 1939- *AmMWSc 92*
**Kruuv**, Jack 1938- *AmMWSc 92*
**Kruvant**, M. Charito 1945- *WhoHisp 92*
**Kruzan**, Mark R 1960- *WhoAmP 91*
**Kruzan**, Timothy Ray *WhoRel 92*
**Kryczko**, Thaddeus Walter 1954- *WhoEnt 92*
**Kryder**, Mark Howard 1943- *AmMWSc 92*
**Kryger**, Roy George 1936- *AmMWSc 92*
**Krylenko**, Nikolay Vasil'evich 1885-1938 *SovUnBD*
**Krylov**, Sergey Borisovich 1888-1958 *SovUnBD*
**Krylova**, Vera *EncAmaz 91*
**Kryn**, Randall Lee 1949- *WhoFI 92*, *WhoMW 92*
**Krynitsky**, John Alexander 1918- *AmMWSc 92*
**Krys**, Alejandro J. 1967- *WhoHisp 92*
**Krys**, Sheldon J 1934- *WhoAmP 91*
**Krysan**, James Louis 1934- *AmMWSc 92*
**Kryshak**, Thomas E 1935- *WhoIns 92*
**Kryshtalowych**, Helen Zwenyslawa 1945- *WhoAmL 92*
**Krysiak**, Carolyn *WhoAmP 91*
**Krysiak**, Joseph Edward 1937- *AmMWSc 92*
**Krysiak**, Joseph Francis 1915- *WhoFI 92*
**Krysty**, Kaycee Wohleb 1951- *WhoFI 92*
**Krystyniak**, William F 1952- *WhoAmP 91*
**Kryter**, Karl David 1914- *AmMWSc 92*
**Kryuchkov**, Vasiliy Dmitrevich 1928- *IntWW 91*
**Kryuchkov**, Vladimir 1924- *IntWW 91*
**Kryuchkov**, Vladimir Aleksandrovich 1924- *SovUnBD*
**Krywolap**, George Nicholas 1936- *AmMWSc 92*
**Kryza**, Elmer Gregory 1922- *WhoAmP 91*
**Krzak**, Marian 1931- *IntWW 91*
**Krzanowski**, Joseph John, Jr 1940- *AmMWSc 92*
**Krzeminski**, Stephen F 1943- *AmMWSc 92*
**Krzesinski**, Thomas Steven 1947- *WhoFI 92*
**Krzhizhanovsky**, Gleb Maksimilyanovich 1872-1959 *SovUnBD*
**Krzyzagorski**, Klemens 1930- *IntAu&W 91*, *IntWW 91*
**Krzyzanowska**, Olga 1929- *IntWW 91*
**Krzyzanowski**, Eve 1951- *WhoEnt 92*
**Krzyzanowski**, Paul 1964- *AmMWSc 92*
**Krzyzanowski**, Richard Lucien 1932- *WhoAmL 92*
**Ksansnak**, James E. 1940- *WhoFI 92*
**Kshirsagar**, Anant Madhav 1931- *AmMWSc 92*
**Kshirsagar**, Girish Sharad 1960- *WhoMW 92*
**Ksienski**, A 1924- *AmMWSc 92*
**Ksir**, Charles Joseph 1945- *AmMWSc 92*
**Ksycki**, Mary Joecile 1913- *AmMWSc 92*
**Ktchen**, Mark Scott 1953- *WhoWest 92*
**Ku**, Albert B 1933- *AmMWSc 92*
**Ku**, Audrey Yeh *AmMWSc 92*
**Ku**, Bernard Siu-Man *AmMWSc 92*
**Ku**, Chia-Soon 1946- *AmMWSc 92*
**Ku**, David Nelson 1956- *AmMWSc 92*
**Ku**, Edmond Chiu-Choon 1932- *AmMWSc 92*
**Ku**, Han San 1935- *AmMWSc 92*
**Ku**, Harry Hsien Hsiang 1918- *AmMWSc 92*
**Ku**, Hsu-Tung 1933- *AmMWSc 92*
**Ku**, Ken Leong 1964- *WhoFI 92*
**Ku**, Mei-Chin Hsiao 1937- *AmMWSc 92*
**Ku**, Peh Sun 1922- *AmMWSc 92*
**Ku**, Robert Tien-Hung 1947- *AmMWSc 92*
**Ku**, Teh-Lung 1937- *AmMWSc 92*, *WhoWest 92*
**Ku**, Timothy Tao 1926- *AmMWSc 92*
**Ku**, Victor Chia-Tai 1942- *AmMWSc 92*
**Ku**, Victoria Feng 1930- *AmMWSc 92*
**Ku**, Y H 1902- *AmMWSc 92*
**Kuan**, Shia Shiong 1933- *AmMWSc 92*
**Kuan**, Teh S *AmMWSc 92*
**Kuan**, Tung-Sheng 1947- *AmMWSc 92*
**Kuang Ankun** *IntWW 91*
**Kuang Yaming** 1906- *IntWW 91*
**Kuang**, Yang 1965- *WhoWest 92*
**Kuba**, Edward Rudolph, Sr. 1911- *WhoMW 92*
**Kuba**, John Albert 1940- *WhoMW 92*
**Kubach**, David *DrAPF 91*
**Kubadinski**, Pencho 1918- *IntWW 91*
**Kubala**, Joseph Stephen 1955- *WhoEnt 92*
**Kubale**, Bernard Stephen 1928- *WhoAmL 92*
**Kubar**, Abd al-Majid *IntWW 91*
**Kubas**, Gregory Joseph 1945- *AmMWSc 92*
**Kubasch**, Keith Michael 1947- *WhoMW 92*
**Kubat**, David Alan 1946- *WhoAmL 92*
**Kubat**, Milan 1927- *IntWW 91*
**Kube**, Harold Deming 1910- *WhoFI 92*
**Kube**, Wilhelm 1887-1943 *BiDExR*, *EncTR 91 [port]*
**Kube-McDowell**, Michael P 1954- *TwCSFW 91*
**Kube-McDowell**, Michael Paul 1954- *IntAu&W 91*, *WhoEnt 92*
**Kubel**, Alfred 1909- *IntWW 91*
**Kubelik**, Jan 1880-1940 *FacFETw*
**Kubelik**, Rafael 1914- *FacFETw*, *IntWW 91*, *NewAmDM*, *Who 92*
**Kubena**, Leon Franklin 1940- *AmMWSc 92*
**Kubersky**, Edward Sidney 1947- *AmMWSc 92*
**Kubes**, George Jiri 1934- *AmMWSc 92*
**Kubesh**, Nell 1924- *WhoAmP 91*
**Kubetz**, Richard Paul, II 1954- *WhoMW 92*
**Kubiak**, Anthony James 1951- *WhoEnt 92*
**Kubiak**, Dan 1938- *WhoAmP 91*
**Kubiak**, Hieronim 1934- *IntWW 91*
**Kubiak**, Jon Stanley 1935- *WhoFI 92*
**Kubiak**, L B 1945- *WhoAmP 91*
**Kubic**, Charles Richard 1950- *WhoWest 92*
**Kubic**, Joseph Craig 1956- *WhoRel 92*
**Kubica**, George P 1929- *AmMWSc 92*
**Kubicek**, J.L. *DrAPF 91*
**Kubicek**, John D 1943- *AmMWSc 92*
**Kubicek**, Robert Vincent 1935- *WhoWest 92*
**Kubida**, William Joseph 1949- *WhoAmL 92*, *WhoFI 92*, *WhoWest 92*
**Kubik**, Gail 1914-1984 *NewAmDM*
**Kubik**, Jack L 1955- *WhoAmP 91*
**Kubik**, Peter W 1949- *AmMWSc 92*
**Kubik**, Robert N 1931- *AmMWSc 92*
**Kubilius**, Jonas 1921- *IntWW 91*
**Kubilus**, John Vito 1947- *WhoFI 92*
**Kubilus**, Norbert John 1948- *WhoFI 92*
**Kubin**, Rosa 1906- *AmMWSc 92*
**Kubina**, Gene 1948- *WhoAmP 91*
**Kubinski**, Henry A 1933- *AmMWSc 92*
**Kubis**, Joseph J 1938- *AmMWSc 92*
**Kubisen**, Steven Joseph, Jr 1952- *AmMWSc 92*
**Kubistal**, Patricia Bernice 1938- *WhoMW 92*
**Kubitschek**, Herbert Ernest 1920- *AmMWSc 92*
**Kubitz**, William John 1938- *AmMWSc 92*, *WhoMW 92*
**Kubler**, Donald Gene 1923- *AmMWSc 92*
**Kubler**, Friedrich Karl 1932- *WhoAmL 92*
**Kubler**, Hans 1922- *AmMWSc 92*, *WhoMW 92*
**Kubler-Ross**, Elisabeth 1926- *BenetAL 91*, *WrDr 92*
**Kubly**, Herbert *DrAPF 91*
**Kubly**, Herbert 1915- *WrDr 92*
**Kubly**, Herbert Oswald *IntAu&W 91*
**Kubo**, Gary Michael 1952- *WhoMW 92*
**Kubo**, Ralph Teruo 1942- *AmMWSc 92*
**Kubo**, Ryogo 1920- *IntWW 91*
**Kubota**, Mitsuru 1932- *AmMWSc 92*, *WhoWest 92*
**Kubota**, Toshi 1926- *AmMWSc 92*
**Kubrick**, Christine 1932- *TwCPaSc*
**Kubrick**, Stanley 1928- *FacFETw*, *IntAu&W 91*, *IntDcF 2-2 [port]*, *IntMPA 92*, *IntWW 91*, *Who 92*, *WhoEnt 92*, *WrDr 92*
**Kubsch**, Kim Karen 1956- *WhoWest 92*
**Kubu**, Edward Thomas 1926- *AmMWSc 92*
**Kuby**, Barbara Eleanor 1944- *WhoMW 92*
**Kuby**, Edward R 1938- *WhoIns 92*
**Kuby**, Edward Raymond 1938- *WhoFI 92*
**Kuby**, Lolette Beth *DrAPF 91*
**Kuby**, Stephen A 1925- *AmMWSc 92*
**Kubyak**, Nikolay Afanas'evich 1881-1937 *SovUnBD*
**Kubynski**, Jadwiga 1948- *AmMWSc 92*
**Kuc**, Joseph 1929- *AmMWSc 92*
**Kucan**, Milan 1941- *IntWW 91*
**Kucera**, Bohuslav 1923- *IntWW 91*
**Kucera**, Clare H 1925- *AmMWSc 92*
**Kucera**, Daniel William 1923- *WhoMW 92*, *WhoRel 92*
**Kucera**, Keith Edward 1960- *WhoMW 92*
**Kucera**, Louis Stephen 1935- *AmMWSc 92*
**Kucera**, Thomas J 1925- *AmMWSc 92*
**Kuceski**, Vincent Paul 1920- *AmMWSc 92*
**Kuchar**, Norman Russell 1939- *AmMWSc 92*
**Kucharek**, Thomas Albert 1939- *AmMWSc 92*
**Kucharek**, Wilma Samuella 1954- *WhoRel 92*
**Kuchars**, Daniel Joseph 1942- *WhoWest 92*
**Kucharski**, Marek 1947- *IntWW 91*
**Kucharsky**, David Eugene 1931- *WhoRel 92*
**Kucharz**, Lawrence *DrAPF 91*
**Kuchel**, Gaylon Lyle 1924- *WhoMW 92*
**Kuchel**, Otto George 1924- *AmMWSc 92*
**Kuchel**, Thomas Henry 1910- *WhoAmP 91*
**Kucheman**, Clark Arthur 1931- *WhoRel 92*, *WhoWest 92*
**Kuchenmeister**, Dennis Donald 1966- *WhoMW 92*
**Kucher**, Lawrence John 1954- *WhoEnt 92*
**Kuchera**, Michael Louis 1955- *WhoMW 92*
**Kuchera**, Thomas John 1929- *WhoAmP 91*
**Kucherlapati**, Raju Suryanarayana 1943- *AmMWSc 92*
**Kuchinskas**, Edward Joseph 1927- *AmMWSc 92*
**Kuchinski**, Steve 1928- *WhoAmP 91*
**Kuchler**, Christine Jean 1949- *WhoMW 92*
**Kuchler**, Kenneth Grant 1922- *WhoEnt 92*
**Kuchler**, Robert Joseph 1928- *AmMWSc 92*
**Kuchler**, Sandra Rose 1948- *WhoWest 92*
**Kuchment**, Peter A. 1949- *WhoMW 92*
**Kuchnir**, Franca Tabliabue 1935- *AmMWSc 92*
**Kuchnir**, Moyses 1936- *AmMWSc 92*
**Kuchta**, John Albert 1955- *WhoMW 92*
**Kuchta**, Thomas Walter 1942- *WhoMW 92*
**Kucic**, Joseph 1964- *WhoFI 92*
**Kucij**, Timothy Michael 1954- *WhoWest 92*
**Kucinski**, Leo 1904- *WhoEnt 92*
**Kuck**, Charles H. 1962- *WhoAmL 92*
**Kuck**, David Jerome 1937- *AmMWSc 92*
**Kuck**, James Chester 1912- *AmMWSc 92*
**Kuck**, John Frederick Read, Jr 1918- *AmMWSc 92*
**Kuck**, Julius Anson 1907- *AmMWSc 92*
**Kuckhoff**, Adam 1887-1943 *EncTR 91*
**Kucserik**, Mary Anne 1958- *WhoMW 92*
**Kuczenski**, Ronald Thomas 1944- *AmMWSc 92*
**Kuczkowski**, Joseph Edward 1939- *AmMWSc 92*
**Kuczkowski**, Robert Louis 1938- *AmMWSc 92*
**Kuczmarski**, Edward R 1949- *AmMWSc 92*
**Kuczmarski**, Susan Smith 1951- *WhoMW 92*
**Kuczora**, Paul Gerard 1954- *WhoMW 92*
**Kuczun**, Ann-Marie 1935- *WhoWest 92*
**Kuczwara**, Thomas Paul 1951- *WhoAmL 92*
**Kuczynski**, George Czeslaw 1914- *AmMWSc 92*
**Kuczynski**, Pedro Pablo *IntWW 91*
**Kuczynski**, Pedro-Pablo 1938- *WhoFI 92*
**Kudaka**, Geraldine *DrAPF 91*
**Kudan**, Harold Lewis 1932- *WhoRel 92*
**Kudelka**, James *WhoEnt 92*
**Kudenholdt**, Sharon Sue 1942- *WhoMW 92*
**Kudenov**, Jerry David 1946- *AmMWSc 92*
**Kuder**, Alice Ann 1957- *WhoRel 92*
**Kuder**, James Edgar 1939- *AmMWSc 92*
**Kuder**, Robert Clarence 1918- *AmMWSc 92*
**Kudian**, Mischa *IntAu&W 91*, *WrDr 92*
**Kudlich**, Robert A 1926- *AmMWSc 92*
**Kudlow**, Lawrence A. 1947- *IntWW 91*
**Kudlow**, Lawrence Alan 1947- *WhoAmP 91*, *WhoFI 92*
**Kudman**, Irwin 1936- *AmMWSc 92*
**Kudo**, Akira 1939- *AmMWSc 92*
**Kudo**, Albert Masakiyo 1937- *AmMWSc 92*
**Kudo**, Emiko Iwashita 1923- *WhoWest 92*
**Kudo**, Franklin Ty 1950- *WhoFI 92*, *WhoWest 92*
**Kudo**, Kenneth Masaaki 1943- *WhoRel 92*
**Kudravetz**, David Waller 1948- *WhoAmL 92*
**Kudrick**, Catherine Alice 1928- *WhoAmP 91*
**Kudrle**, Judy Sandberg 1951- *WhoAmP 91*

**Kudryashov**, Oleg 1932- *IntWW 91*
**Kudryavtsev**, Vladimir Nikolaevich 1923- *IntWW 91, SovUnBD*
**Kudsi**, Nazem el 1906- *IntWW 91*
**Kudzin**, Stanley Francis 1926- *AmMWSc 92*
**Kuebler**, David Wayne 1947- *WhoFI 92*
**Kuebler**, Harold W *ScFEYrs*
**Kuebler**, John Ralph, Jr 1924- *AmMWSc 92*
**Kuebler**, Richard Arthur 1947- *WhoEnt 92, WhoWest 92*
**Kuebler**, Roy Raymond, Jr 1911- *AmMWSc 92*
**Kuebler**, William Frank, Jr 1916- *AmMWSc 92*
**Kuebrich**, David 1943- *ConAu 134*
**Kuechenmeister**, Frederick William 1926- *WhoAmL 92, WhoFI 92*
**Kuechenmeister**, Karl Thomas 1946- *WhoEnt 92*
**Kuechle**, Richard Theodore 1930- *WhoWest 92*
**Kuecker**, John Frank 1932- *AmMWSc 92*
**Kuehl**, Guenter Hinrich 1928- *AmMWSc 92*
**Kuehl**, Hans H 1933- *AmMWSc 92*
**Kuehl**, Kevin Thomas 1958- *WhoMW 92*
**Kuehl**, LeRoy Robert 1931- *AmMWSc 92*
**Kuehl**, Nancy Louise 1947- *WhoFI 92*
**Kuehl**, Sheila James 1941- *WhoEnt 92*
**Kuehler**, Jack D *AmMWSc 92*
**Kuehler**, Jack Dwyer 1932- *WhoFI 92*
**Kuehn**, David Laurance 1940- *WhoEnt 92*
**Kuehn**, Glenn Dean 1942- *AmMWSc 92, WhoWest 92*
**Kuehn**, Harold Herman 1927 *AmMWSc 92*
**Kuehn**, Jerome H 1920- *AmMWSc 92*
**Kuehn**, Klaus Karl Albert 1938- *WhoWest 92*
**Kuehn**, Lorne Allan 1943- *AmMWSc 92*
**Kuehn**, Patricia Susan 1945- *WhoAmP 91*
**Kuehn**, Richard Arthur 1939- *WhoFI 92, WhoMW 92*
**Kuehn**, Ronald L., Jr. 1935- *WhoFI 92*
**Kuehne**, Benedict P. 1954- *WhoAmL 92*
**Kuehne**, Donald Leroy 1952- *AmMWSc 92*
**Kuehne**, Martin Eric 1931- *AmMWSc 92*
**Kuehne**, Robert Andrew 1927- *AmMWSc 92*
**Kuehnelt-Leddihn**, Erik 1909- *WrDr 92*
**Kuehner**, Bart Thomas 1968- *WhoFI 92*
**Kuehner**, Calvin Charles 1922- *AmMWSc 92*
**Kuehner**, John Alan 1931- *AmMWSc 92*
**Kuehner**, Marvin Ernest 1934- *WhoMW 92*
**Kuehnert**, Charles Carroll 1930- *AmMWSc 92*
**Kuehnert**, Deborah Anne 1949- *WhoFI 92*
**Kuehnert**, Fred Thomas 1943- *WhoEnt 92*
**Kuehnert**, Robert Gerhardt 1916- *WhoWest 92*
**Kuehnle**, Christopher Charles 1944- *WhoFI 92*
**Kuehnle**, Kenton Lee 1945- *WhoAmL 92, WhoMW 92*
**Kueker**, David William 1943- *AmMWSc 92*
**Kuell**, Charles L. 1933- *WhoWest 92*
**Kuellmer**, Frederick John 1924- *AmMWSc 92*
**Kuemmel**, Donald Francis 1927- *AmMWSc 92*
**Kuemmerle**, Nancy Benton Stevens 1948- *AmMWSc 92*
**Kuempel**, Edmund 1942- *WhoAmP 91*
**Kuenheim**, Eberhard von 1928- *IntWW 91*
**Kuenhold**, Kenneth Alan *AmMWSc 92*
**Kuenne**, Robert Eugene 1924- *IntAu&W 91, WrDr 92*
**Kuenneth**, John Robert 1932- *WhoRel 92*
**Kuenssberg**, Ekkehard von 1913- *Who 92*
**Kuenssberg**, Nicholas Christopher Dwelly 1942- *Who 92*
**Kuenstler**, Douglas Wayne 1964- *WhoFI 92*
**Kuenstler**, Frank *DrAPF 91*
**Kuentz**, Fred Stanton 1954- *WhoEnt 92*
**Kuenzel**, Robert Varde 1949- *WhoAmL 92*
**Kuenzel**, Wayne John 1942- *AmMWSc 92*
**Kuenzi**, Norbert James 1935- *AmMWSc 92*
**Kuenzi**, W David 1937- *AmMWSc 92*
**Kuenzler**, Edward Julian 1929- *AmMWSc 92*
**Kuenzli**, Gwen Lee 1936- *WhoMW 92*
**Kueper**, Theodore Vincent 1941- *AmMWSc 92*
**Kuerti**, Anton 1938- *NewAmDM*
**Kuerti**, Anton Emil 1938- *WhoEnt 92*
**Kuesel**, Thomas Robert 1926- *AmMWSc 92*
**Kuest**, Robert Dean 1944- *WhoRel 92*
**Kuester**, Dennis J. 1942- *WhoMW 92*
**Kuetemeyer**, Gregg Alan 1965- *WhoMW 92*
**Kuether**, Carl Albert 1915- *AmMWSc 92*
**Kuether**, John Frederick 1943- *WhoAmL 92*
**Kuettner**, Klaus E 1933- *AmMWSc 92*
**Kufeldt**, George 1923- *WhoRel 92*
**Kuff**, Edward Louis 1924- *AmMWSc 92*
**Kuffner**, Roy Joseph 1922- *AmMWSc 92*
**Kufrovich**, Frank J. *WhoFI 92*
**Kuftaro**, Ahmad *WhoRel 92*
**Kuftinec**, Mladen M 1943- *AmMWSc 92*
**Kugar**, Mark Curt 1959- *WhoFI 92*
**Kugblenu**, George Ofoe *WhoBlA 92*
**Kugel**, Henry W 1940- *AmMWSc 92*
**Kugel**, Jeffrey Auriel 1945- *WhoMW 92*
**Kugel**, Robert Benjamin 1923- *AmMWSc 92*
**Kugell**, Karen 1941- *WhoAmL 92*
**Kugelman**, Irwin Jay 1937- *AmMWSc 92*
**Kugle**, J. Alan 1937- *WhoAmL 92*
**Kugler**, George Charles 1941- *AmMWSc 92*
**Kugler**, Lawrence Dean 1941- *AmMWSc 92*
**Kuh**, Edwin 1925-1986 *ConAu 36NR*
**Kuh**, Ernest Shiu-Jen 1928- *AmMWSc 92*
**Kuh**, Peter Greenebaum 1921- *WhoAmL 92*
**Kuh**, Richard H. 1921- *WrDr 92*
**Kuh**, Richard Henry 1921- *WhoAmL 92*
**Kuhajek**, Eugene James 1934- *AmMWSc 92*
**Kuhar**, June Carolynn 1935- *WhoFI 92*
**Kuhar**, Michael Joseph 1944- *AmMWSc 92*
**Kuharic**, Franjo 1919- *IntWW 91, WhoRel 92*
**Kuharsky**, Andrew Sergius 1957- *WhoEnt 92*
**Kuhel**, James Joseph 1934- *WhoMW 92*
**Kuhfeld**, Peter 1952- *TwCPaSc*
**Kuhi**, Leonard Vello 1936- *AmMWSc 92*
**Kuhl**, David Edmund 1929- *AmMWSc 92, WhoMW 92*
**Kuhl**, Ernest Peter 1881-1981 *ConAu 133*
**Kuhl**, Frank Peter, Jr 1935- *AmMWSc 92*
**Kuhl**, Henry Young 1930- *WhoAmP 91*
**Kuhl**, John R, Jr 1943- *WhoAmP 91*
**Kuhl**, Ronald Webster 1938- *WhoWest 92*
**Kuhl**, Wayne Elliott 1947- *WhoWest 92*
**Kuhlau**, Friedrich 1786-1832 *NewAmDM*
**Kuhler**, Deborah Gail 1952- *WhoAmP 91, WhoMW 92*
**Kuhlers**, Daryl Lynn 1945- *AmMWSc 92*
**Kuhlik**, Bruce Neil 1956- *WhoAmL 92*
**Kuhlken**, Ken *DrAPF 91*
**Kuhlman**, Elmer George 1934- *AmMWSc 92*
**Kuhlman**, John Michael 1948- *AmMWSc 92*
**Kuhlman**, Kathryn 1907-1976 *RelLAm 91*
**Kuhlman**, Kimberly Ann 1954- *WhoMW 92*
**Kuhlman**, Thomas Ashford 1939- *WhoMW 92*
**Kuhlmann**, Fred Mark 1948- *WhoMW 92*
**Kuhlmann**, George Edward 1942- *AmMWSc 92*
**Kuhlmann**, Karl Frederick 1937- *AmMWSc 92*
**Kuhlmann**, Kathleen Mary 1950- *IntWW 91*
**Kuhlmann**, Marvin Earl 1931- *WhoRel 92*
**Kuhlmann-Wilsdorf**, Doris 1922- *AmMWSc 92*
**Kuhlthau**, A R 1921- *AmMWSc 92*
**Kuhlthau**, John Suydam 1937- *WhoAmL 92*
**Kuhn**, Adam 1741-1817 *BiInAmS*
**Kuhn**, Arthur Kline 1876-1954 *AmPeW*
**Kuhn**, Betsey Ann 1948- *WhoFI 92*
**Kuhn**, Cedric W 1930- *AmMWSc 92*
**Kuhn**, Charles 1919- *WhoFI 92*
**Kuhn**, Charles, III 1933- *AmMWSc 92*
**Kuhn**, Daisy Angelika 1930- *AmMWSc 92*
**Kuhn**, David Michael 1951- *WhoWest 92*
**Kuhn**, David Truman 1940- *AmMWSc 92*
**Kuhn**, Dennis Raymond 1949- *WhoFI 92*
**Kuhn**, Donald Marshall 1922- *WhoWest 92*
**Kuhn**, Donna Sue *DrAPF 91*
**Kuhn**, Eleanor Adele 1922- *WhoFI 92*
**Kuhn**, Ferdinand 1905-1978 *ConAu 36NR*
**Kuhn**, Frederick 1949- *WhoAmL 92*
**Kuhn**, Fritz 1896-1951 *BiDExR*
**Kuhn**, Gustav 1946- *IntWW 91*
**Kuhn**, Hans Heinrich 1924- *AmMWSc 92*
**Kuhn**, Harold William 1925- *AmMWSc 92*
**Kuhn**, Heinrich Gerhard 1904- *IntWW 91, Who 92*
**Kuhn**, Heinz 1912- *IntWW 91*
**Kuhn**, Howard A 1940- *AmMWSc 92*
**Kuhn**, James Paul 1937- *WhoFI 92*
**Kuhn**, Janice Oseth 1940- *AmMWSc 92*
**Kuhn**, John Stephen 1952- *WhoEnt 92*
**Kuhn**, Joseph Merritt 1954- *WhoMW 92*
**Kuhn**, Josephine M. Keller 1937- *WhoMW 92*
**Kuhn**, Karl Heinz 1919- *Who 92*
**Kuhn**, Klaus 1927- *AmMWSc 92*
**Kuhn**, Lesley *DrAPF 91*
**Kuhn**, Leslie A 1924- *AmMWSc 92*
**Kuhn**, Martin Clifford 1940- *AmMWSc 92*
**Kuhn**, Mary Croughan 1914- *WhoWest 92*
**Kuhn**, Matthew 1936- *AmMWSc 92*
**Kuhn**, Nicholas J 1955- *AmMWSc 92*
**Kuhn**, Paul 1935- *WhoRel 92*
**Kuhn**, Paul Hubert, Jr. 1943- *WhoFI 92*
**Kuhn**, Peter Mouat 1920- *AmMWSc 92*
**Kuhn**, Raymond Eugene 1942- *AmMWSc 92*
**Kuhn**, Reinhard 1930-1980 *ConAu 34NR*
**Kuhn**, Richard 1900-1967 *WhoNob 90*
**Kuhn**, Robert Edward 1949- *WhoAmP 91*
**Kuhn**, Robert Herman 1946- *WhoMW 92*
**Kuhn**, Robert Lawrence 1944- *WhoFI 92*
**Kuhn**, Ryan Anthony 1947- *WhoFI 92, WhoMW 92*
**Kuhn**, Thomas G. 1935- *IntMPA 92*
**Kuhn**, Thomas S 1922- *AmMWSc 92, IntAu&W 91, IntWW 91, WrDr 92*
**Kuhn**, Truman Howard 1908- *AmMWSc 92*
**Kuhn**, William E 1922- *AmMWSc 92*
**Kuhn**, William Frederick 1930- *AmMWSc 92*
**Kuhn**, William Lloyd 1925- *AmMWSc 92*
**Kuhn**, William R 1938- *AmMWSc 92*
**Kuhnau**, Johann 1660-1722 *NewAmDM*
**Kuhne**, Eric Robert 1951- *WhoFI 92*
**Kuhne**, Gunther Albert Hermann 1939- *IntWW 91*
**Kuhnen**, Michael d1991 *NewYTBS 91*
**Kuhnen**, Sybil Marie 1917- *AmMWSc 92*
**Kuhner**, Herbert *DrAPF 91*
**Kuhner**, Herbert 1935- *LiExTwC*
**Kuhnert**, Betty R 1944- *AmMWSc 92*
**Kuhnle**, Tom Christie 1955- *WhoFI 92*
**Kuhnlein**, Harriet V 1939- *AmMWSc 92*
**Kuhnlein**, John David 1956- *WhoMW 92*
**Kuhnley**, Lyle Carlton 1925- *AmMWSc 92*
**Kuhns**, Edward Douglas 1923- *WhoFI 92*
**Kuhns**, Ellen Swomley 1919- *AmMWSc 92*
**Kuhns**, John Farrell 1947- *AmMWSc 92, WhoMW 92*
**Kuhns**, Nancy Evelyn 1947- *WhoRel 92*
**Kuhns**, Richard 1924- *ConAu 36NR*
**Kuhns**, Sally Nelson 1952- *WhoEnt 92*
**Kuhns**, William *DrAPF 91*
**Kuhns**, William Joseph 1918- *AmMWSc 92*
**Kuhr**, James R *WhoIns 92*
**Kuhr**, Ronald John 1939- *AmMWSc 92*
**Kuhrau**, Edward W. 1935- *WhoAmL 92, WhoWest 92*
**Kuhrt**, Gordon Wilfred 1941- *Who 92*
**Kuhrt**, Wesley A 1917- *AmMWSc 92*
**Kuichling**, Emil 1848-1914 *BiInAmS*
**Kuida**, Hiroshi 1925- *AmMWSc 92*
**Kuijken**, Barthold 1949- *NewAmDM*
**Kuijken**, Sigiswald 1944- *NewAmDM*
**Kuijken**, Wieland 1938- *NewAmDM*
**Kuijt**, Job 1930- *AmMWSc 92*
**Kuiken**, Kenneth 1918- *AmMWSc 92*
**Kuiper**, Douglas Scott 1960- *WhoFI 92*
**Kuiper**, Gerard 1905-1973 *FacFETw*
**Kuiper**, Logan Keith 1940- *AmMWSc 92*
**Kuiper**, Thomas Bernardus Henricus 1945- *AmMWSc 92*
**Kuiper-Goodman**, Tine 1937- *AmMWSc 92*
**Kuipers**, Benjamin Jack 1949- *AmMWSc 92*
**Kuipers**, Carl Jacob 1905- *WhoAmP 91*
**Kuipers**, J. D. 1918- *IntWW 91*
**Kuipers**, Jack 1921- *AmMWSc 92*
**Kuipers**, John Melles 1918- *Who 92*
**Kuipers**, Paul Joseph 1951- *WhoMW 92*
**Kuitert**, John Herman 1908- *WhoAmP 91*
**Kuitert**, Louis Cornelius 1912- *AmMWSc 92*
**Kuivila**, Henry Gabriel 1917- *AmMWSc 92*
**Kujala**, Walfrid Eugene 1925- *WhoEnt 92*
**Kujath**, Marek Ryszard 1950- *AmMWSc 92*
**Kujawa**, Clifford James 1930- *WhoRel 92*
**Kujawa**, Raymond William 1961- *WhoEnt 92*
**Kujiraoka**, Hyosuke 1915- *IntWW 91*
**Kuk**, Robert Louis 1943- *WhoFI 92*
**Kuka**, King D. *DrAPF 91*
**Kukal**, Gerald Courtney 1943- *AmMWSc 92*
**Kukalis**, Sal M. 1954- *WhoWest 92*
**Kukes**, Simon G *AmMWSc 92*
**Kuki**, Atsuo *AmMWSc 92*
**Kukin**, Ira 1924- *AmMWSc 92*
**Kukkapuro**, Yrjo 1933- *DcTwDes*
**Kukkonen**, Carl Allan 1945- *AmMWSc 92, WhoWest 92*
**Kukla**, Cynthia Mary 1951- *WhoMW 92*
**Kukla**, Michael Joseph 1947- *AmMWSc 92*
**Kukla**, Walter Joseph 1933- *WhoFI 92*
**Kuklenski**, Richard Joseph 1949- *WhoMW 92*
**Kuklin**, Anthony Bennett 1929- *WhoAmL 92*
**Kuklin**, Jeffrey Peter 1935- *WhoAmL 92, WhoWest 92*
**Kukolich**, Stephen George 1940- *AmMWSc 92*
**Kukor**, Kathleen Ann 1959- *WhoMW 92*
**Kukovich**, Allen G 1947- *WhoAmP 91*
**Kukryniksy** *SovUnBD*
**Kuksis**, Arnis 1927- *AmMWSc 92*
**Kukulka**, Jozef 1929- *IntWW 91*
**Kukura**, Rita Anne 1947- *WhoFI 92*
**Kula**, Eric Bertil 1929- *AmMWSc 92*
**Kulacki**, Francis Alfred 1942- *AmMWSc 92*
**Kulaga**, Eugeniusz d1990 *IntWW 91N*
**Kulah**, Arthur F. *WhoRel 92*
**Kulak**, Geoffrey Luther 1936- *AmMWSc 92*
**Kulakov**, Fedor Davydovich 1918-1978 *SovUnBD*
**Kulakov**, Fyodor D 1918-1978 *FacFETw*
**Kulakova**, Galina Alekseevna 1942- *SovUnBD*
**Kulakowski**, Elliott C 1951- *AmMWSc 92*
**Kulakowski**, Lois Linder 1939- *WhoWest 92*
**Kulander**, Byron Rodney 1937- *AmMWSc 92*
**Kulander**, Kenneth Charles 1943- *AmMWSc 92*
**Kularatnam**, Karthigesapillai 1911- *IntWW 91*
**Kulas**, Myron J 1942- *WhoAmP 91*
**Kulat**, Terry L. 1949- *WhoRel 92*
**Kulawiz**, JoAnne Kiely 1935- *WhoAmL 92*
**Kulbin**, Vello 1937- *WhoFI 92*
**Kulcinski**, Gerald La Vern 1939- *AmMWSc 92*
**Kulcsar**, Kalman 1928- *IntWW 91*
**Kulczycki**, Anthony, Jr 1944- *AmMWSc 92*
**Kulczycki**, Lucas Luke 1911- *AmMWSc 92*
**Kulesh**, William Adam 1929- *WhoFI 92*
**Kulesha**, Kevin John 1956- *WhoFI 92*
**Kuleshov**, Lev 1899-1970 *IntDcF 2-2*
**Kuleshov**, Lev Vladimirovich 1899-1970 *FacFETw, SovUnBD*
**Kulesus**, Jeffrey Victor 1949- *WhoFI 92, WhoMW 92*
**Kulevsky**, Norman 1935- *AmMWSc 92*
**Kulfinski**, Frank Benjamin 1930- *AmMWSc 92*
**Kulgein**, Norman Gerald 1934- *AmMWSc 92*
**Kulhavy**, Raymond William 1940- *WhoWest 92*
**Kulhawy**, Fred Howard 1943- *AmMWSc 92*
**Kuli**, Vickie Sue 1958- *WhoRel 92*
**Kulich**, Roman Theodore 1953- *WhoMW 92*
**Kulick**, Barbara *TwCPaSc*
**Kulick**, Florence Olivia Post 1923- *WhoRel 92*
**Kulicki**, Krzysztof Bogdan 1938- *IntAu&W 91*
**Kulidzhanov**, Lev Aleksandrovich 1924- *IntWW 91, SovUnBD*
**Kulier**, Charles Peter 1935- *AmMWSc 92, WhoMW 92*
**Kulik**, Buzz *LesBEnT 92*
**Kulik**, Grigoriy Ivanovich 1890-1950? *SovUnBD*
**Kulik**, Joseph Michael 1957- *WhoAmL 92*
**Kulik**, Martin Michael 1932- *AmMWSc 92*
**Kulik**, Peter John 1964- *WhoMW 92*
**Kulik**, Seymour 1923- *IntMPA 92*
**Kulikov**, Viktor Georg'evich 1921- *SovUnBD*
**Kulikov**, Viktor Georgiyevich 1921- *IntWW 91*
**Kulikov**, Viktor Georgyevich 1921- *FacFETw*
**Kulikowski**, Casimir A 1944- *AmMWSc 92*
**Kulikowski**, M. Karl *DrAPF 91*
**Kulin**, Keith David 1948- *WhoEnt 92*
**Kulisheck**, Robert 1943- *WhoMW 92*
**Kulju**, Kenneth Raymond 1958- *WhoFI 92*
**Kulka**, Johannes Peter 1921- *AmMWSc 92*
**Kulka**, Konstanty Andrzej 1947- *IntWW 91*
**Kulkarni**, Anand K 1946- *AmMWSc 92*
**Kulkarni**, Anant Sadashiv 1934- *AmMWSc 92*
**Kulkarni**, Bidy 1930- *AmMWSc 92*
**Kulkarni**, Kishore Ganesh 1953- *WhoFI 92*
**Kulkarni**, Padmakar Venkatrao 1942- *AmMWSc 92*
**Kulkarni**, Prasad Shrikrishna 1943- *AmMWSc 92*
**Kulkarni**, Vaman Gunderao 1955- *WhoMW 92*
**Kulkarny**, Vijay Anand 1947- *AmMWSc 92*
**Kulke**, Bernhard 1932- *AmMWSc 92*
**Kulkosky**, Paul Joseph 1949- *AmMWSc 92, WhoWest 92*
**Kull**, Dove Montgomery *WhoWest 92*

**Kull**, Frederick Charles, Sr 1919- AmMWSc 92
**Kull**, Fredrick J 1935- AmMWSc 92
**Kull**, Lorenz A. 1937- WhoWest 92
**Kull**, Lorenz Anthony 1937- AmMWSc 92
**Kull**, William Franklin 1956- WhoWest 92
**Kulla**, Jean B 1949- AmMWSc 92
**Kullak**, Theodor 1818-1882 NewAmDM
**Kullback**, Joseph Henry 1933- AmMWSc 92
**Kullback**, Solomon 1907- AmMWSc 92
**Kullberg**, Rolf 1930- IntWW 91
**Kullberg**, Russell Gordon 1922- AmMWSc 92
**Kuller**, Jonathan Mark 1951- WhoAmL 92
**Kuller**, Robert G 1926- AmMWSc 92
**Kullerud**, Gunnar 1921- AmMWSc 92
**Kullgren**, Thomas Edward 1941- AmMWSc 92
**Kullman**, David Elmer 1940- AmMWSc 92
**Kullman**, William Francis, Jr. 1958- WhoMW 92, WhoRel 92
**Kullnig**, Rudolph K 1918- AmMWSc 92
**Kulm**, LaVerne Duane 1936- AmMWSc 92
**Kulmala**, Elmer Pete 1951- WhoAmL 92
**Kulman**, Herbert Marvin 1929- AmMWSc 92
**Kulok**, William Allan 1940- WhoFI 92
**Kulongoski**, Theodore Ralph 1940- WhoAmP 91
**Kulp**, Bernard Andrew 1923- AmMWSc 92
**Kulp**, Eileen S. WhoFI 92
**Kulp**, J. Robert 1935- WhoFI 92
**Kulp**, James Ellsworth 1933- WhoAmL 92
**Kulp**, Nancy d1991 NewYTBS 91 [port]
**Kulp**, Nancy 1921-1991 News 91, -91-3
**Kulp**, Stuart S 1925- AmMWSc 92
**Kulper**, Perry Dean 1953- WhoWest 92
**Kulski**, Julian Eugeniusz 1929- WhoFI 92
**Kulsrud**, Russell Marion 1928- AmMWSc 92
**Kulstad**, Guy Charles 1930- WhoWest 92
**Kultermann**, Udo 1927- IntAu&W 91, WrDr 92
**Kulukundis**, Eddie 1932- Who 92
**Kulwich**, Roman 1925- AmMWSc 92
**Kulwicki**, Bernard Michael 1935- AmMWSc 92
**Kulz**, Wilhelm 1875-1948 EncTR 91
**Kulzick**, Kenneth Edmund 1927- WhoEnt 92
**Kumagai**, Denice Jean 1956- WhoEnt 92
**Kumagai**, James 1934- WhoAmP 91
**Kumagai**, Lindy Fumio 1927- AmMWSc 92
**Kumagai**, Takenobu 1937- WhoFI 92
**Kumagai**, Yoshifumi 1915- IntWW 91
**Kumai**, Motoi 1920- AmMWSc 92
**Kumamoto**, Junji 1924- AmMWSc 92
**Kumanyika**, Shiriki K. 1945- WhoBlA 92
**Kumar**, Ajit 1940- AmMWSc 92
**Kumar**, Alok 1951- AmMWSc 92
**Kumar**, Cidambi Krishna 1937- AmMWSc 92
**Kumar**, Devendra 1944- AmMWSc 92
**Kumar**, Ganesh N 1948- AmMWSc 92
**Kumar**, K S P AmMWSc 92
**Kumar**, K Sharvan 1956- AmMWSc 92
**Kumar**, Kaplesh 1947- AmMWSc 92, WhoFI 92
**Kumar**, Krishan 1942- WrDr 92
**Kumar**, Krishan 1944- WhoFI 92
**Kumar**, Madhurendu B 1942- AmMWSc 92
**Kumar**, Mahesh C 1935- AmMWSc 92
**Kumar**, Nirmal 1941- WhoWest 92
**Kumar**, Pamela Eileen 1944- WhoFI 92
**Kumar**, Panganamala Ramana 1952- AmMWSc 92, WhoMW 92
**Kumar**, Pradeep 1949- AmMWSc 92
**Kumar**, Rajendra 1948- WhoWest 92
**Kumar**, Romesh 1944- AmMWSc 92
**Kumar**, S 1959- AmMWSc 92
**Kumar**, S Anand 1936- AmMWSc 92
**Kumar**, Satish 1933- IntAu&W 91
**Kumar**, Shiv K. 1921- ConPo 91, IntAu&W 91, WrDr 92
**Kumar**, Shiv Sharan 1939- AmMWSc 92
**Kumar**, Shrawan 1939- AmMWSc 92
**Kumar**, Soma 1924- AmMWSc 92
**Kumar**, Subodh 1953- WhoFI 92
**Kumar**, Sudhir 1933- AmMWSc 92
**Kumar**, Sudhir 1942- AmMWSc 92, WhoMW 92
**Kumar**, Suriender 1938- AmMWSc 92
**Kumar**, Sushil 1939- WhoMW 92
**Kumar**, Vijay 1945- AmMWSc 92
**Kumar**, Vinay 1944- AmMWSc 92
**Kumar**, Vipin 1956- AmMWSc 92
**Kumaran**, A Krishna 1932- AmMWSc 92
**Kumaran**, Alapati Krishna 1932- WhoMW 92
**Kumaran**, Mavinkal K 1946- AmMWSc 92
**Kumari**, Durga 1951- AmMWSc 92
**Kumaroo**, Kuziyilethu Krishnan 1931- AmMWSc 92
**Kumbar**, Mahadevappa M 1939- AmMWSc 92
**Kumbaraci-Jones**, Nuran Melek 1944- AmMWSc 92
**Kumbula**, Tendayi Sengerwe 1947- WhoBlA 92
**Kumcu**, Erdogan 1950- WhoFI 92
**Kume**, Tadashi 1932- IntWW 91
**Kume**, Yutaka 1921- IntWW 91, Who 92
**Kumin**, Maxine 1925- BenetAL 91, ConPo 91, WrDr 92
**Kumin**, Maxine W. DrAPF 91
**Kumin**, Maxine Winokur 1925- IntAu&W 91
**Kumins**, Charles Arthur 1915- AmMWSc 92
**Kumkumian**, Charles Simon 1920- AmMWSc 92
**Kumler**, Keith Allen 1939- WhoMW 92
**Kumler**, Marion Lawrence 1914- AmMWSc 92
**Kumler**, Marvin Lee 1940- WhoMW 92
**Kumler**, Philip L 1941- AmMWSc 92
**Kumler**, Rose Marie 1935- WhoWest 92
**Kumli**, Karl F 1927- AmMWSc 92
**Kumlien**, Ludwig 1853-1902 BiInAmS
**Kumlien**, Thure Ludwig Theodor 1819-1888 BiInAmS
**Kumm**, Doris 1929- WhoAmP 91
**Kumm**, Henry W. d1991 NewYTBS 91
**Kumm**, Henry W. 1901-1991 CurBio 91N
**Kumm**, William Howard 1931- WhoFI 92
**Kummell**, Charles Hugo 1836-1897 BiInAmS
**Kummer**, Glenn F. 1933- WhoWest 92
**Kummer**, Joseph T 1919- AmMWSc 92
**Kummer**, Lawrence Nathan 1955- WhoFI 92
**Kummer**, Martin 1936- AmMWSc 92
**Kummer**, Richard Edward, Jr. 1948- WhoAmL 92
**Kummer**, Ruth Mary Ann 1930- WhoRel 92
**Kummer**, W H 1925- AmMWSc 92
**Kummer**, Wolfgang 1935- IntWW 91
**Kummerle**, Herman Frederick 1936- WhoMW 92
**Kummerow**, Fred August 1914- AmMWSc 92
**Kummings**, Donald D. DrAPF 91
**Kummler**, Ralph H 1940- AmMWSc 92
**Kumorowski**, Victoria McKay 1947- WhoAmL 92
**Kumosinski**, Thomas Francis 1941- AmMWSc 92
**Kump**, Ernest Joseph 1911- IntWW 91
**Kump**, Lee Robert 1959- AmMWSc 92
**Kumpe**, William Edgar 1955- WhoAmL 92
**Kumpel**, Paul Gremminger 1935- AmMWSc 92
**Kun**, Bela 1886-1938 EncTR 91
**Kun**, Joyce Anne 1946- WhoMW 92
**Kun**, Kenneth Allan 1930- AmMWSc 92
**Kuna**, Samuel 1912- AmMWSc 92
**Kunaev**, Dinmukhamed Akhmedovich 1912- SovUnBD
**Kunasek**, Carl J WhoAmP 91
**Kunasz**, Ihor Andrew 1939- AmMWSc 92
**Kunath**, Anne Robinson 1932- WhoRel 92
**Kunath**, Robert Walter 1942- WhoFI 92
**Kunau**, Robert, Jr AmMWSc 92
**Kunayev**, Dinmukhamed Akhmedovich 1912- FacFETw
**Kunce**, Henry Warren 1925- AmMWSc 92
**Kuncel**, Ruth Boutin 1945- WhoMW 92
**Kuncewicz**, Eileen Who 92
**Kuncewiczowa**, Maria 1899- IntAu&W 91
**Kundahl**, George Gustavus 1940- WhoAmP 91, WhoFI 92
**Kundel**, Harold Louis 1933- AmMWSc 92
**Kundera**, Milan 1929- ConLC 68 [port], FacFETw, IntAu&W 91, IntWW 91, LiExTwC
**Kundert**, Alice E 1920- WhoAmP 91
**Kundert**, David J. 1942- WhoMW 92
**Kundert**, Esayas G 1918- AmMWSc 92
**Kundert**, Gust 1913- WhoAmP 91
**Kundig**, Fredericka Dodyk 1924- AmMWSc 92
**Kundig**, Werner AmMWSc 92
**Kundratitz**, Klemens 1962- WhoEnt 92
**Kundsin**, Ruth Blumfeld 1916- AmMWSc 92
**Kundt**, Ernst 1897-1947 EncTR 91
**Kundt**, John Fred 1926- AmMWSc 92
**Kundtz**, Jill Ellen 1953- WhoMW 92
**Kundtz**, John Andrew 1933- WhoAmL 92
**Kundu**, Mukul Ranjan 1930- AmMWSc 92
**Kundu**, Samar K AmMWSc 92
**Kundur**, Prabha Shankar 1939- AmMWSc 92
**Kunelius**, Heikki Tapani 1940- AmMWSc 92
**Kunene**, Daniel 1929- LiExTwC
**Kunene**, Mazisi 1930- LiExTwC
**Kuner**, Charles Michael 1951- WhoRel 92
**Kuneralp**, Zeki 1914- IntWW 91, Who 92
**Kunert**, Gunter 1929- IntWW 91, LiExTwC
**Kunes**, Ken R. 1932- WhoBlA 92
**Kunes**, Steven Mark 1956- WhoEnt 92
**Kunesh**, Charles Joseph 1948- AmMWSc 92
**Kunesh**, Jerry Paul 1938- AmMWSc 92
**Kung**, Ching 1939- AmMWSc 92
**Kung**, Ernest Chen-Tsun 1931- AmMWSc 92
**Kung**, Hans 1928- DcEcMov, FacFETw, IntWW 91, Who 92, WhoRel 92
**Kung**, Harold Hing Chuen 1949- AmMWSc 92
**Kung**, Hsiang-Fu 1942- AmMWSc 92
**Kung**, Hsiang-Tsung 1945- AmMWSc 92
**Kung**, Patrick C AmMWSc 92
**Kung**, Shain-Dow 1935- AmMWSc 92
**Kung Gong Pin-Mei**, Ignatius 1901- WhoRel 92
**Kunhardt**, Edith 1937- ConAu 134, SmATA 67 [port]
**Kunhardt**, Erich Enrique 1949- AmMWSc 92
**Kunich**, John Charles 1953- WhoAmL 92
**Kunicki**, Walter J 1958- WhoAmP 91
**Kunimura**, Tony T 1923- WhoAmP 91
**Kunin**, Arthur Saul 1925- AmMWSc 92
**Kunin**, Brett Keith 1948- WhoAmL 92
**Kunin**, Calvin Murry 1929- AmMWSc 92
**Kunin**, Devra L. DrAPF 91
**Kunin**, Madeleine May 1933- IntWW 91, WhoAmP 91
**Kunin**, Robert 1918- AmMWSc 92
**Kunis**, Abraham Maxwell 1914- WhoIns 92
**Kunisch**, Robert Dietrich 1941- WhoFI 92
**Kunishi**, Harry Mikio 1932- AmMWSc 92
**Kunisi**, Venkatasubban S AmMWSc 92
**Kunitz**, Stanley DrAPF 91
**Kunitz**, Stanley 1905- BenetAL 91, ConPo 91, IntAu&W 91, WrDr 92
**Kunitz**, Stanley J. 1905- IntWW 91
**Kunitzsch**, Paul Horst Robert 1930- IntWW 91
**Kuniyoshi**, Yasuo 1893-1953 FacFETw
**Kunjufu**, Jawanza 1953- WhoBlA 92
**Kunjukunju**, Pappy 1939- WhoFI 92
**Kunka**, Robert Leonard 1947- AmMWSc 92
**Kunkee**, Ralph Edward 1927- AmMWSc 92, WhoWest 92
**Kunkel**, David Nelson 1943- WhoAmL 92
**Kunkel**, David Scott 1943- WhoEnt 92
**Kunkel**, Harriott Orren 1922- AmMWSc 92
**Kunkel**, Joseph George 1942- AmMWSc 92
**Kunkel**, Larry Alan 1951- WhoWest 92
**Kunkel**, Louis M 1949- AmMWSc 92
**Kunkel**, Richard WhoAmP 91
**Kunkel**, Robert Scott, Jr. 1934- WhoMW 92
**Kunkel**, Russell Jeffrey 1942- WhoFI 92
**Kunkel**, Scott William 1945- WhoWest 92
**Kunkel**, William Eckart 1936- AmMWSc 92
**Kunkel**, Wulf Bernard 1923- AmMWSc 92
**Kunkemueller**, Henry 1935- WhoIns 92
**Kunkle**, Donald Edward 1928- AmMWSc 92
**Kunkle**, George Robert 1934- AmMWSc 92
**Kunkle**, William Joseph, Jr. 1941- WhoAmL 92
**Kuno**, Motoji IntMPA 92
**Kunos**, George 1942- AmMWSc 92
**Kunov**, Hans 1938- AmMWSc 92
**Kuns**, Brett Roger 1960- WhoMW 92
**Kunselman**, A Raymond 1942- AmMWSc 92
**Kunsman**, David Marvin 1949- WhoWest 92
**Kunstler**, William M 1919- IntAu&W 91, WrDr 92
**Kuntima**, Diangienda WhoRel 92
**Kuntz**, Daniel S. 1953- WhoAmL 92
**Kuntz**, Garland Parke Paul AmMWSc 92
**Kuntz**, Hal Goggan 1937- WhoFI 92
**Kuntz**, Irving 1925- AmMWSc 92
**Kuntz**, Irwin Douglas, Jr 1939- AmMWSc 92
**Kuntz**, James Thomas 1938- WhoFI 92
**Kuntz**, Joel Dubois 1946- WhoAmL 92
**Kuntz**, John Kenneth 1934- WhoMW 92, WhoRel 92, WrDr 92
**Kuntz**, John Marvin 1938- WhoMW 92
**Kuntz**, Lee Allan 1943- WhoAmL 92
**Kuntz**, Mary M. Kohls 1928- WhoMW 92
**Kuntz**, Mel Anton 1939- AmMWSc 92
**Kuntz**, Noella Mae 1950- WhoWest 92
**Kuntz**, Richard A 1939- AmMWSc 92
**Kuntz**, Robert Elroy 1916- AmMWSc 92
**Kuntz**, Robert Roy 1937- AmMWSc 92
**Kuntz**, William Henry 1954- WhoAmL 92
**Kuntzman**, Edward Lee 1955- WhoEnt 92
**Kuntzman**, Ronald Grover 1933- AmMWSc 92
**Kunyaev**, Stanislav Yur'evich 1932- SovUnBD
**Kunz**, Albert Barry 1940- AmMWSc 92
**Kunz**, Albert L 1933- AmMWSc 92
**Kunz**, April Brimmer 1954- WhoAmP 91
**Kunz**, Bernard Alexander 1952- AmMWSc 92
**Kunz**, Daniel James 1952- WhoWest 92
**Kunz**, Erich 1909- IntWW 91
**Kunz**, Harold Russell 1931- AmMWSc 92
**Kunz**, Heinz W 1938- AmMWSc 92
**Kunz**, John Melvin 1946- WhoRel 92
**Kunz**, Kaiser Schoen 1915- AmMWSc 92
**Kunz**, Kimberly Ann 1959- WhoAmL 92
**Kunz**, Lawrence Joseph WhoFI 92
**Kunz**, Peter DrAPF 91
**Kunz**, Rhonda Sue 1961- WhoMW 92
**Kunz**, Sidney Edmund 1935- AmMWSc 92
**Kunz**, Thomas Henry 1938- AmMWSc 92
**Kunz**, Walter Ernest 1918- AmMWSc 92
**Kunze**, Adolf Wilhelm Gerhard 1936- AmMWSc 92
**Kunze**, Diana Lee 1939- AmMWSc 92
**Kunze**, George William 1922- AmMWSc 92
**Kunze**, Horst 1909- IntWW 91
**Kunze**, Jay Frederick 1933- AmMWSc 92
**Kunze**, Neil Lee 1940- WhoAmP 91
**Kunze**, Otto Robert 1925- AmMWSc 92
**Kunze**, Ralph Carl 1925- WhoMW 92
**Kunze**, Ray A 1928- AmMWSc 92
**Kunze**, Raymond J 1928- AmMWSc 92
**Kunze**, Reiner 1933- IntWW 91, LiExTwC
**Kunze**, Reiner Alexander 1933- IntAu&W 91
**Kunze**, Richard Ernest 1838-1919 BiInAmS
**Kunzel**, Erich 1935- NewAmDM
**Kunzel**, Erich, Jr. 1935- WhoEnt 92
**Kunzle**, David Mark 1936- ConAu 36NR
**Kunzle**, Hans Peter 1940- AmMWSc 92
**Kunzler**, John Eugene 1923- AmMWSc 92
**Kunzman**, Wallace William, Jr. 1949- WhoAmL 92
**Kuo Wei-Fan** 1937- IntWW 91
**Kuo**, Albert Yi-Shuong 1939- AmMWSc 92
**Kuo**, Alex DrAPF 91
**Kuo**, Benjamin Chung-I 1930- AmMWSc 92
**Kuo**, Chan-Hwa 1931- AmMWSc 92
**Kuo**, Chao-Ying 1940- AmMWSc 92
**Kuo**, Charles C Y AmMWSc 92
**Kuo**, Cheng-Yih 1942- AmMWSc 92
**Kuo**, Chiang-Hai 1936- AmMWSc 92
**Kuo**, Ching-Ming 1935- AmMWSc 92
**Kuo**, Cho-Chou 1934- AmMWSc 92
**Kuo**, Chung-Ming 1935- AmMWSc 92
**Kuo**, Eric Yung-Huei 1934- AmMWSc 92
**Kuo**, Franklin F 1934- AmMWSc 92
**Kuo**, Gloria Liang-Hui 1926- IntAu&W 91
**Kuo**, Harng-Shen 1935- AmMWSc 92
**Kuo**, Hsiao-Lan 1915- AmMWSc 92
**Kuo**, Hui-Hsiung 1941- AmMWSc 92
**Kuo**, John Tsung-fen 1922- AmMWSc 92
**Kuo**, Jyh-Fa 1933- AmMWSc 92
**Kuo**, Lawrence C AmMWSc 92
**Kuo**, Mingshang 1949- AmMWSc 92
**Kuo**, Pao-Kuang 1935- AmMWSc 92
**Kuo**, Peter Te 1916- AmMWSc 92
**Kuo**, Ping-chia 1908- WhoWest 92
**Kuo**, Scot Charles 1961- AmMWSc 92
**Kuo**, Shan Sun 1922- AmMWSc 92
**Kuo**, Shiou 1943- AmMWSc 92
**Kuo**, Thomas Tzu Szu 1932- AmMWSc 92
**Kuo**, Tzee-Ke 1937- AmMWSc 92
**Kuo**, Yen-Long 1936- AmMWSc 92
**Kuo**, Ying L 1958- AmMWSc 92
**Kupa**, Mihaly 1941- IntWW 91
**Kupchak**, Kenneth Roy 1942- WhoAmL 92
**Kupchella**, Charles E 1942- AmMWSc 92
**Kupchick**, Alan Charles 1942- WhoFI 92
**Kupchik**, Eugene John 1929- AmMWSc 92
**Kupchik**, George Michael 1954- WhoMW 92
**Kupchik**, Herbert Z 1940- AmMWSc 92
**Kupcinet**, Essee Solomon WhoEnt 92
**Kupcinet**, Irv 1912- WhoMW 92
**Kupec**, Nancy Louise 1957- WhoAmP 91
**Kupel**, Richard E 1920- AmMWSc 92
**Kuper**, Adam 1941- WrDr 92
**Kuper**, George Henry 1940- WhoMW 92
**Kuper**, Hilda Beermer 1911- IntAu&W 91
**Kuper**, J B Horner 1909- AmMWSc 92
**Kuper**, Leo 1908- ConAu 35NR, IntAu&W 91, WrDr 92
**Kuperman**, Albert Sanford 1931- AmMWSc 92
**Kupersmith**, Leonard R. 1968- WhoFI 92
**Kupfer**, Benneth James 1952- WhoEnt 92
**Kupfer**, Carl 1928- AmMWSc 92
**Kupfer**, David 1928- AmMWSc 92
**Kupfer**, David J AmMWSc 92
**Kupfer**, Donald Harry 1918- AmMWSc 92
**Kupfer**, Fern 1946- ConAu 36NR
**Kupfer**, George Allan 1933- WhoMW 92
**Kupfer**, John Carlton 1955- AmMWSc 92
**Kupfer**, Sherman 1926- AmMWSc 92
**Kupferberg**, Harvey J 1933- AmMWSc 92
**Kupferberg**, Herbert 1918- IntAu&W 91, WrDr 92
**Kupferberg**, Lenn C 1951- AmMWSc 92
**Kupferberg**, Tuli DrAPF 91

**Kupferman**, Allan 1935- AmMWSc 92
**Kupferman**, Laurie A. 1966- WhoRel 92
**Kupferman**, Meyer 1926- NewAmDM, WhoEnt 92
**Kupferman**, Stuart L 1937- AmMWSc 92
**Kupferman**, Theodore R. 1920- WhoAmL 92, WhoAmP 91
**Kupfermann**, Irving 1938- AmMWSc 92
**Kupiecki**, Floyd Peter 1926- AmMWSc 92
**Kupik**, John Michael 1949- WhoFI 92
**Kupiszewski**, Henryk 1927- IntWW 91
**Kupjack**, Eugene J. d1991 NewYTBS 91 [port]
**Kupke**, Donald Walter 1922- AmMWSc 92
**Kupkovic**, Ladislav 1936- ConCom 92
**Kuppe**, Michael Stuart 1960- WhoMW 92
**Kuppenheimer**, John D, Jr 1941- AmMWSc 92
**Kupper**, Philip Lloyd 1940- WhoMW 92
**Kupperian**, James Edward, Jr 1925- AmMWSc 92
**Kupperman**, Henry John 1957- WhoAmL 92
**Kupperman**, Herbert Spencer 1915- AmMWSc 92
**Kupperman**, Joel J. 1936- ConAu 36NR
**Kupperman**, Louis Brandeis 1946- WhoAmL 92
**Kupperman**, Morton 1918- AmMWSc 92
**Kupperman**, Robert Harris 1935- AmMWSc 92
**Kupperman**, Stephen Henry 1953- WhoAmL 92
**Kuppermann**, Aron 1926- AmMWSc 92
**Kuppers**, James Richard 1920- AmMWSc 92
**Kupperstein**, Edward Raymond 1933- WhoEnt 92
**Kuppler**, Karl Brian 1956- WhoFI 92
**Kuppler**, Karl John 1955- WhoMW 92
**Kuppner**, Frank 1951- ConPo 91
**Kuppord**, Skelton ScFEYrs
**Kupreyanov**, Nikolay Nikolaevich 1894-1933 SovUnBD
**Kuprin**, Alexander Ivanovich 1870-1939 FacFETw
**Kupsch**, Walter Oscar 1919- AmMWSc 92
**Kupsco**, Thomas Richard 1956- WhoMW 92
**Kupst**, Mary Jo 1945- WhoMW 92
**Kupstas**, Edward Eugene 1921- AmMWSc 92
**Kuptsov**, Valentin Aleksandrovich 1937- IntWW 91
**Kura**, Miroslav 1924- WhoEnt 92
**Kurachi**, Kotoku 1941- AmMWSc 92
**Kuraishi**, Akari Luke 1959- WhoWest 92
**Kurajian**, George Masrob 1926- AmMWSc 92
**Kuralt**, Charles LesBEnT 92 [port]
**Kuralt**, Charles 1934- IntMPA 92
**Kuralt**, Charles Bishop 1934- WhoEnt 92A
**Kuramata**, Shiro 1934- DcTwDes
**Kuramitsu**, Howard Kikuo 1936- AmMWSc 92
**Kuranari**, Tadashi 1918- IntWW 91
**Kuranz**, Kyle Alan 1940- WhoMW 92
**Kuras**, Jeffrey Steven 1955- WhoMW 92
**Kurashige**, Brett Mitsuaki 1959- WhoWest 92
**Kurashige**, Wayne Itsuo 1955- WhoRel 92
**Kurashvili**, Boris Pavlovich 1925- IntWW 91, SovUnBD
**Kurata**, F 1914- AmMWSc 92
**Kurata**, Mamoru 1936- AmMWSc 92
**Kurath**, Dieter 1921- AmMWSc 92
**Kurath**, Paul 1924- AmMWSc 92
**Kurath**, Sheldon Frank 1928- AmMWSc 92
**Kuratowska**, Zofia 1931- IntWW 91
**Kurchacova**, Elva S 1921- AmMWSc 92
**Kurchatov**, Igor' Vasil'evich 1903-1960 SovUnBD
**Kurczewski**, Frank E 1936- AmMWSc 92
**Kurczynski**, Thaddeus Walter 1940- AmMWSc 92
**Kurdi**, Abdulrahman Abdulkadir 1941- ConAu 133
**Kureishi**, Hanif 1954- IntAu&W 91, IntWW 91, Who 92, WrDr 92
**Kureishi**, Hanif 1956- IntMPA 92
**Kurek**, Dolores Bodnar 1935- WhoMW 92
**Kurey**, Kristine Marie 1954- WhoWest 92
**Kurey**, Thomas John 1937- AmMWSc 92
**Kurfees**, Marshall Thomas 1957- WhoRel 92
**Kurfehs**, Harold Charles 1939- WhoFI 92
**Kurfess**, James Daniel 1940- AmMWSc 92
**Kuri**, Emile 1907- IntMPA 92
**Kuri**, John A. 1945- IntMPA 92
**Kuria**, Manasses Who 92, WhoRel 92
**Kuria**, Manasses 1929- IntWW 91
**Kuriakose**, Areekattuthazhayil 1933- AmMWSc 92
**Kurian**, George 1928- SmATA 65
**Kuriansky**, Judy 1947- WhoEnt 92
**Kurien**, Christopher 1931- WrDr 92
**Kurien**, Verghese 1921- IntWW 91
**Kuriger**, William Louis 1933- AmMWSc 92
**Kurihara**, Norman Hiromu 1938- AmMWSc 92
**Kurihara**, Yoshio 1930- AmMWSc 92
**Kurihara**, Yuko 1921- IntWW 91
**Kuris**, Armand Michael 1942- AmMWSc 92
**Kuritz**, Paul Thomas 1948- WhoEnt 92
**Kuritzkes**, Alexander Mark 1924- AmMWSc 92
**Kuriyama**, Kinya 1932- AmMWSc 92
**Kuriyama**, Masao 1931- AmMWSc 92
**Kurk**, Neal M WhoAmP 91
**Kurka**, Robert 1921-1957 NewAmDM
**Kurkjian**, Charles R 1929- AmMWSc 92
**Kurko**, Georgia Anne 1962- WhoRel 92
**Kurkotkin**, Semen Konstantinovich 1917- SovUnBD
**Kurkotkin**, Semyon Konstantinovich 1917- IntWW 91
**Kurkov**, Victor Peter 1936- AmMWSc 92
**Kurland**, Albert A 1914- AmMWSc 92
**Kurland**, Amy Elizabeth 1955- WhoEnt 92
**Kurland**, Harold Arthur 1952- WhoAmL 92
**Kurland**, Jeffrey Arnold 1943- AmMWSc 92
**Kurland**, Jonathan Joshua 1939- AmMWSc 92
**Kurland**, Leon Irwin 1941- WhoAmL 92
**Kurland**, Leonard T 1921- AmMWSc 92
**Kurland**, Lewis Stewart 1951- WhoAmL 92
**Kurland**, Michael 1938- IntAu&W 91, TwCSFW 91, WrDr 92
**Kurland**, Philip B. 1921- WhoAmL 92
**Kurland**, Robert John 1930- AmMWSc 92
**Kurland**, Sheldon 1928- WhoEnt 92
**Kurlander**, Carl Litman 1959- WhoEnt 92
**Kurlander**, Neale 1924- WhoFI 92
**Kurlantzick**, Sandra Maida 1955- WhoAmP 91
**Kurlinski**, John Parker 1948- WhoWest 92
**Kurlowicz**, Theodore Thomas 1953- WhoAmL 92
**Kurmes**, Ernest A 1931- AmMWSc 92
**Kurniawan**, Dewanto 1942- WhoFI 92
**Kurnick**, Allen Abraham 1921- AmMWSc 92
**Kurnick**, John Edmund 1942- AmMWSc 92
**Kurnick**, Nathaniel Bertrand 1917- AmMWSc 92
**Kurnow**, Ernest 1912- AmMWSc 92
**Kurobane**, Itsuo 1944- AmMWSc 92
**Kuroda**, Joseph Toshiyuki 1927- WhoAmP 91
**Kuroda**, Makoto 1932- IntWW 91
**Kuroda**, Mizuo 1919- IntWW 91
**Kuroda**, Paul Kazuo 1917- AmMWSc 92
**Kuroda**, Toyoji 1920- IntMPA 92
**Kuroda**, Yasumasa 1931- ConAu 35NR
**Kuroda**, Yutaka 1950- WhoWest 92
**Kuroedov**, Vladimir Alekseevich 1906- SovUnBD
**Kuroghlian**, Ellen Green 1945- WhoEnt 92
**Kurohara**, Samuel S 1931- AmMWSc 92
**Kurokawa**, Akemi 1943- WhoWest 92
**Kurokawa**, Kaneyuki 1928- AmMWSc 92
**Kurokawa**, Kisho 1934- IntWW 91
**Kurokawa**, Takeshi 1928- IntWW 91
**Kuroki**, Gary W AmMWSc 92
**Kuron**, Jacek 1934- IntWW 91
**Kurongku**, Peter Who 92, WhoRel 92
**Kuropatkin**, Alexei Nikolayevich 1848-1925 FacFETw
**Kurosaka**, Mitsuru 1935- AmMWSc 92
**Kurosawa**, Akira 1910- CurBio 91 [port], FacFETw [port], IntDcF 2-2 [port], IntMPA 92, IntWW 91, News 91 [port], Who 92, WhoEnt 92
**Kurose**, George 1924- AmMWSc 92
**Kuroski-De Bold**, Mercedes Lina 1942- AmMWSc 92
**Kurosky**, Alexander 1938- AmMWSc 92
**Kurowski**, Charles Edward 1952- WhoAmL 92
**Kurowski**, Gary John 1931- AmMWSc 92
**Kuroyanagi**, Noriyoshi 1930- AmMWSc 92
**Kuroyedov**, Vladimir Alexeyevich 1906- IntWW 91
**Kurrelmeyer**, Louis Hayner 1928- WhoAmL 92
**Kurri**, Jari 1960- WhoWest 92
**Kurrus**, Thomas William 1947- WhoAmL 92
**Kursanov**, Andrey Lvovich 1902- IntWW 91
**Kursell**, Otto von 1884-1967 EncTR 91 [port]
**Kursewicz**, Lee Z. 1916- WhoFI 92, WhoWest 92
**Kurshan**, Jerome 1919- AmMWSc 92
**Kurss**, Herbert 1924- AmMWSc 92
**Kurstedt**, Harold Albert, Jr 1939- AmMWSc 92
**Kursunoglu**, Behram N 1922- AmMWSc 92
**Kurt**, Carl Edward 1943- AmMWSc 92
**Kurt**, Fahrettin 1946- IntWW 91
**Kurta**, Allen 1952- AmMWSc 92
**Kurtag**, Gyorgy 1926- ConCom 92, IntWW 91
**Kurtenbach**, Aelred J 1934- AmMWSc 92
**Kurth**, Carol Lynn 1948- WhoFI 92
**Kurth**, Juliette Elizabeth 1960- WhoEnt 92
**Kurth**, Karen Kay 1941- WhoRel 92
**Kurth**, Patsy Ann 1941- WhoAmP 91
**Kurth**, Peter 1953- WrDr 92
**Kurth**, Robert Allen 1949- WhoRel 92
**Kurth**, Tammie Elaine 1960- WhoAmL 92
**Kurth**, Woodrow Walter 1914- WhoRel 92
**Kurti**, Nicholas 1908- IntWW 91, Who 92
**Kurtis**, Bill ConAu 133
**Kurtis**, Bill 1940- IntMPA 92
**Kurtis**, Stanley Allan 1950- WhoEnt 92
**Kurtis**, William Horton 1940- ConAu 133
**Kurtti**, Timothy John 1942- AmMWSc 92
**Kurtz**, A Peter 1942- AmMWSc 92
**Kurtz**, Anthony David 1929- AmMWSc 92
**Kurtz**, Arthur Digby 1929- WhoEnt 92
**Kurtz**, Bruce 1943- WhoWest 92
**Kurtz**, Charles Jewett, III 1940- WhoAmL 92
**Kurtz**, Clark N 1937- AmMWSc 92
**Kurtz**, David Allan 1932- AmMWSc 92
**Kurtz**, David Williams 1942- AmMWSc 92
**Kurtz**, Don DrAPF 91
**Kurtz**, Edwin Bernard, Jr 1926- AmMWSc 92
**Kurtz**, Efrem 1900- IntWW 91, NewAmDM
**Kurtz**, Eric M. 1960- WhoAmL 92
**Kurtz**, Gary 1940- IntMPA 92
**Kurtz**, George Wilbur 1928- AmMWSc 92
**Kurtz**, Harold John 1931- AmMWSc 92
**Kurtz**, Harvey A. 1950- WhoAmL 92
**Kurtz**, Henry 1796-1874 AmPeW
**Kurtz**, Jane Peterson 1927- WhoAmP 91
**Kurtz**, Jerome 1931- WhoAmL 92, WhoAmP 91
**Kurtz**, Joel Barry 1944- WhoFI 92
**Kurtz**, John F. 1942- WhoFI 92
**Kurtz**, Karen Barbara 1948- WhoMW 92
**Kurtz**, Katherine 1944- TwCSFW 91, WrDr 92
**Kurtz**, Katherine Irene 1944- IntAu&W 91
**Kurtz**, Lawrence Alfred 1940- AmMWSc 92
**Kurtz**, Lester Touby 1914- AmMWSc 92
**Kurtz**, Lloyd Sherer, Jr. 1934- WhoAmL 92
**Kurtz**, Marcia Lynn 1956- WhoAmL 92
**Kurtz**, Margot 1941- AmMWSc 92
**Kurtz**, Mark Edward 1946- AmMWSc 92
**Kurtz**, Michael L. 1941- ConAu 36NR
**Kurtz**, Myra Berman 1945- AmMWSc 92
**Kurtz**, Patti J 1957- IntAu&W 91
**Kurtz**, Paul Michael 1946- WhoAmL 92
**Kurtz**, Peter, Jr 1927- AmMWSc 92
**Kurtz**, Richard Leigh 1956- AmMWSc 92
**Kurtz**, Richard Robert 1945- AmMWSc 92
**Kurtz**, Robert Arthur 1943- WhoFI 92
**Kurtz**, Robert Roger 1941- WhoMW 92
**Kurtz**, Sandra Koss 1940- WhoAmL 92
**Kurtz**, Sheldon Francis 1943- WhoAmL 92
**Kurtz**, Stanley Morton 1926- AmMWSc 92
**Kurtz**, Steven Ross 1953- AmMWSc 92
**Kurtz**, Stewart K 1931- AmMWSc 92
**Kurtz**, Stuart Alan 1956- WhoMW 92
**Kurtz**, Swoosie WhoEnt 92
**Kurtz**, Swoosie 1944- IntMPA 92
**Kurtz**, Thomas Eugene 1928- AmMWSc 92
**Kurtz**, Thomas Gordon 1941- AmMWSc 92
**Kurtz**, Vernon Howard 1951- WhoRel 92
**Kurtz**, Vincent E 1926- AmMWSc 92
**Kurtz**, William Boyce 1941- AmMWSc 92
**Kurtze**, Douglas Alan 1954- AmMWSc 92
**Kurtzig**, Sandra L. 1946- WhoWest 92
**Kurtzke**, John F 1926- AmMWSc 92
**Kurtzman**, Allan Roger 1933- WhoFI 92
**Kurtzman**, Cletus Paul 1938- AmMWSc 92, WhoMW 92
**Kurtzman**, Ralph Harold, Jr 1933- AmMWSc 92
**Kurucz**, Robert Louis 1944- AmMWSc 92
**Kurup**, O N V 1931- IntAu&W 91
**Kurup**, Viswanath Parameswar 1936- AmMWSc 92
**Kurutz**, Kathern Darrah 1953- WhoWest 92
**Kury**, Franklin Leo 1936- WhoAmP 91
**Kuryk**, David Neal 1947- WhoAmL 92
**Kuryla**, William C 1934- AmMWSc 92
**Kurylo**, Michael John, III 1945- AmMWSc 92
**Kuryluk**, Ewa 1946- ConAu 135
**Kuryokhin**, Sergei 1955- IntWW 91
**Kurys**, Diane IntMPA 92, ReelWom
**Kurz**, David Wayne 1952- WhoMW 92
**Kurz**, Edward Philip 1921- WhoAmL 92
**Kurz**, Elsie Bowman DrAPF 91
**Kurz**, Gerhard Eugen 1939- WhoFI 92
**Kurz**, James Eckhardt 1934- AmMWSc 92
**Kurz**, Jerry Bruce 1949- WhoAmL 92
**Kurz**, Joan Clair 1932- WhoAmP 91
**Kurz**, Joseph Louis 1933- AmMWSc 92
**Kurz**, Judith Naomi WhoEnt 92
**Kurz**, Michael E 1941- AmMWSc 92
**Kurz**, Michael J 1952- WhoIns 92
**Kurz**, Mordecai 1934- WhoFI 92
**Kurz**, Richard J 1935- AmMWSc 92
**Kurz**, Richard Karl 1936- AmMWSc 92
**Kurz**, Richard Michael 1942- WhoIns 92
**Kurz**, Ron DrAPF 91
**Kurz**, Ron 1940- WrDr 92
**Kurz**, Selma 1874-1933 NewAmDM
**Kurz**, Thomas Patrick 1951- WhoAmL 92
**Kurz**, Wolfgang Gebhard Walter 1933- AmMWSc 92
**Kurzawska**, Ewa 1954- WhoMW 92
**Kurze**, Theodore 1922- AmMWSc 92
**Kurzel**, Richard Bernard 1944- WhoWest 92
**Kurzer**, Martin Joel 1938- WhoAmL 92
**Kurzhals**, Peter R 1937- AmMWSc 92
**Kurzman**, Dan 1929- IntAu&W 91, WrDr 92
**Kurzman**, Robert Graham 1932- WhoAmL 92
**Kurzman**, Stephen 1932- WhoAmP 91
**Kurzrock**, Razelle 1954- AmMWSc 92
**Kurzweg**, Frank Turner 1917- AmMWSc 92
**Kurzweg**, Ulrich H 1936- AmMWSc 92
**Kurzweil**, Erich Zvi 1911- WrDr 92
**Kurzweil**, Harvey 1945- WhoAmL 92
**Kurzweil**, Raymond 1948- ConAu 134
**Kurzweil**, Zvi Erich 1911- ConAu 36NR
**Kurzynowski**, David Joseph 1933- WhoMW 92
**Kus**, Christina Phyllis 1951- WhoMW 92
**Kusakabe**, Etsuji 1923- IntWW 91
**Kusalik**, Peter Gerard 1959- AmMWSc 92
**Kusano**, Kiyoshi 1933- AmMWSc 92
**Kusch**, Polycarp 1911- WhoNob 90
**Kusch**, Polykarp 1911- AmMWSc 92, IntWW 91, Who 92
**Kusche**, Lothar 1929- IntAu&W 91
**Kuschner**, Marvin 1919- AmMWSc 92
**Kuse**, James Russell 1930- WhoFI 92
**Kusek**, Karolina 1940- IntAu&W 91
**Kuser**, James Kerney, II 1960- WhoAmL 92
**Kuserk**, Frank Thomas 1951- AmMWSc 92
**Kushen**, Allan Stanford 1929- WhoFI 92
**Kushi**, Michio 1926- RelLAm 91
**Kushick**, Joseph N 1948- AmMWSc 92
**Kushida**, Toshimoto 1920- AmMWSc 92
**Kushin**, Kirk William 1967- WhoEnt 92
**Kushinsky**, Stanley 1930- AmMWSc 92
**Kushmeider**, Rose Marie 1956- WhoFI 92
**Kushmerick**, Martin Joseph 1937- AmMWSc 92
**Kushnaryov**, Vladimir Michael 1931- AmMWSc 92
**Kushner**, Aleksandr Semyonovich 1936- IntWW 91
**Kushner**, Andrew Barry 1951- WhoAmL 92
**Kushner**, Arthur S 1940- AmMWSc 92
**Kushner**, Bill DrAPF 91
**Kushner**, Brian Edward 1961- WhoEnt 92
**Kushner**, Carol 1950- ConAu 133
**Kushner**, Carol Scarvalone DrAPF 91
**Kushner**, David Edward 1958- WhoFI 92
**Kushner**, David Zakeri 1935- WhoEnt 92
**Kushner**, Donn 1927- ConAu 35NR, WrDr 92
**Kushner**, Donn Jean 1927- AmMWSc 92
**Kushner**, Geri Lynn 1959- WhoEnt 92
**Kushner**, Harold J 1933- AmMWSc 92
**Kushner**, Harold S. 1935- ConAu 36NR, IntAu&W 91, WrDr 92
**Kushner**, Harold Samuel 1935- WhoRel 92
**Kushner**, Harvey 1950- AmMWSc 92
**Kushner**, Harvey D 1930- AmMWSc 92
**Kushner**, Irving 1929- AmMWSc 92
**Kushner**, James Alan 1945- WhoAmL 92
**Kushner**, Jeffrey L. 1948- WhoFI 92
**Kushner**, Lawrence Maurice 1924- AmMWSc 92
**Kushner**, Leonard H. WhoWest 92
**Kushner**, Linda J 1939- WhoAmP 91
**Kushner**, Malcolm 1952- ConAu 134
**Kushner**, Michael Stephen 1957- WhoEnt 92
**Kushner**, Rose 1929-1990 AnObit 1990, FacFETw
**Kushner**, Samuel 1915- AmMWSc 92
**Kushner**, Sidney Ralph 1943- AmMWSc 92
**Kushner**, Thomas Nicholas 1964- WhoFI 92
**Kushner-Locke** LesBEnT 92
**Kushnick**, Theodore 1925- AmMWSc 92
**Kushwaha**, Rampratap S 1943- AmMWSc 92
**Kusiak**, Andrew 1949- AmMWSc 92

**Kusic**, George Larry, Jr 1935- *AmMWSc 92*
**Kusik**, Charles Lembit 1934- *AmMWSc 92*
**Kusin**, Vladimir V. 1929- *WrDr 92*
**Kusisto**, Raymond N. 1958- *WhoFI 92*
**Kuska**, Henry 1937- *AmMWSc 92*
**Kuskin**, Karla 1932- *IntAu&W 91, SmATA 68 [port], WrDr 92*
**Kusko**, Alexander 1921- *AmMWSc 92*
**Kuskova**, Ekaterina Dmitryevna 1869-1959 *FacFETw*
**Kuslan**, Louis Isaac 1922- *AmMWSc 92*
**Kusler**, James O'Dell 1947- *WhoMW 92*
**Kusler**, Jim 1947- *WhoAmP 91*
**Kusma**, Kyllikki 1943- *WhoAmL 92*
**Kusmer**, Toby Harold 1944- *WhoAmL 92*
**Kusnetz**, Howard L 1929- *AmMWSc 92*
**Kusnetz**, Hyman 1939- *WhoFI 92*
**Kusniewicz**, Andrzej 1904- *IntWW 91*
**Kusnitz**, Adele L *WhoAmP 91*
**Kuspira**, J 1928- *AmMWSc 92*
**Kuss**, Mark Davis 1956- *WhoAmL 92*
**Kuss**, Rene 1913- *IntWW 91*
**Kusse**, Bruce Raymond 1938- *AmMWSc 92*
**Kussel**, William Ferdinand, Jr. 1957- *WhoAmL 92*
**Kusserow**, Richard Phillip 1940- *WhoAmP 91*
**Kussman**, David Alan 1952- *WhoEnt 92*
**Kussmaul**, Keith 1939- *AmMWSc 92*
**Kust**, Roger Nayland 1935- *AmMWSc 92*
**Kuster**, Robert Kenneth 1932- *WhoWest 92*
**Kuster**, Theodore R 1943- *WhoAmP 91*
**Kustin**, Kenneth 1934- *AmMWSc 92*
**Kustom**, Robert L 1934- *AmMWSc 92*
**Kustow**, Michael 1929- *IntAu&W 91, WrDr 92*
**Kustow**, Michael David 1939- *Who 92*
**Kustra**, Bob 1943- *WhoAmP 91, WhoMW 92*
**Kustu**, Sydney Govons 1943- *AmMWSc 92*
**Kusuda**, Tamami 1925- *AmMWSc 92*
**Kusumaatmadja**, Mochtar 1929- *IntWW 91*
**Kusumoto**, Susan Yaeko 1963- *WhoWest 92*
**Kuswa**, Glenn Wesley 1940- *AmMWSc 92*
**Kusy**, Robert Peter 1947- *AmMWSc 92*
**Kuszak**, Jerome R 1951- *AmMWSc 92*
**Kuszak**, Jerome Raymond 1951- *WhoMW 92*
**Kutakhov**, Pavel Stepanovich 1914-1984 *SovUnBD*
**Kutakov**, Leonid Nikolayevich 1919- *IntWW 91*
**Kutal**, Charles Ronald 1944- *AmMWSc 92*
**Kutas**, Marta 1949- *AmMWSc 92*
**Kutasi**, Katalin Erzsebet 1956- *WhoFI 92*
**Kutasi**, Leslie, Jr 1959- *WhoAmP 91*
**Kutchai**, Howard C 1942- *AmMWSc 92*
**Kutcher**, Frank Edward, Jr. 1927- *WhoFI 92*
**Kutcher**, Stanley Paul 1951- *AmMWSc 92*
**Kutches**, Alexander Joseph 1941- *AmMWSc 92*
**Kutchins**, Allen Ira 1948- *WhoFI 92*
**Kuti**, Fela 1938- *ConMus 7 [port]*
**Kuti**, Fela Anikulapo 1938- *IntWW 91*
**Kutik**, Leon 1927- *AmMWSc 92*
**Kutilek**, Michael Joseph 1943- *AmMWSc 92*
**Kutkuhn**, Joseph Henry 1927- *AmMWSc 92*
**Kutler**, Benton 1920- *AmMWSc 92*
**Kutler**, Stanley I. 1934- *ConAu 36NR*
**Kutner**, Abraham 1919- *AmMWSc 92*
**Kutner**, Leon Jay 1928- *AmMWSc 92*
**Kutner**, Martin *IntMPA 92*
**Kutner**, Michael Henry 1937- *AmMWSc 92*
**Kutner**, Peter B. 1948- *WhoAmL 92*
**Kutney**, James Peter 1932- *AmMWSc 92*
**Kutrzeba**, Joseph Stanislaw 1927- *WhoEnt 92*
**Kuts**, Vladimir Petrovich 1927 1975 *SovUnBD*
**Kutscha**, Norman Paul 1937- *AmMWSc 92*
**Kutsche**, Paul 1927- *WhoWest 92*
**Kutscher**, Hans 1911- *IntWW 91, Who 92*
**Kutscher**, Ronald Earl 1932- *WhoFI 92*
**Kutschinski**, Dorothy Irene 1922- *WhoMW 92*
**Kutsher**, George Samuel 1921- *AmMWSc 92*
**Kutsky**, Roman Joseph 1922- *AmMWSc 92*
**Kuttab**, Simon Hanna 1946- *AmMWSc 92*
**Kutteh**, William Hanna 1954- *AmMWSc 92*
**Kutter**, Elizabeth Martin 1939- *AmMWSc 92*
**Kuttler**, Carl Martin, Jr. 1940- *WhoAmL 92*
**Kuttler**, James Robert 1941- *AmMWSc 92*
**Kuttner**, Henry 1915-1958 *TwCSFW 91*
**Kuttner**, Paul *DrAPF 91*
**Kuttner**, Stephan George 1907- *IntWW 91*
**Kuttner**, Stephan George 1909- *WhoWest 92*
**Kutun**, Barry 1941- *WhoAmP 91*
**Kutyna**, Donald Joseph 1933- *WhoWest 92*
**Kutz**, David 1951- *WhoEnt 92*
**Kutz**, Frederick Winfield 1939- *AmMWSc 92*
**Kutzen**, Jerome Jefferies 1923- *WhoFI 92*
**Kutzko**, Nicholas, Jr. 1934- *WhoFI 92*
**Kutzko**, Philip C 1946- *AmMWSc 92*
**Kutzman**, Raymond Stanley 1949- *AmMWSc 92*
**Kutzscher**, Edgar Walter 1906- *AmMWSc 92*
**Kuusinen**, Otto Vil'gel'movich 1881-1964 *SovUnBD*
**Kuuskoski-Vikatmaa**, Eeva Maija Kaarina 1946- *IntWW 91*
**Kuvin**, Joshua Saxe 1963- *WhoEnt 92*
**Kuwabara**, Dennis Matsuichi 1945- *WhoWest 92*
**Kuwabara**, Takeo 1904- *IntWW 91*
**Kuwahara**, Mitsunori 1936- *WhoFI 92*
**Kuwahara**, Steven Sadao 1940- *AmMWSc 92*
**Kuwait**, The Ruler of *IntWW 91*
**Kuwaiz**, Abdullah Ibrahim el 1939- *IntWW 91*
**Kuwana**, Theodore 1931- *AmMWSc 92*
**Kuwayama**, George 1925- *WhoWest 92*
**Kux**, Dennis 1931- *WhoAmP 91*
**Kuyatt**, Chris E 1930- *AmMWSc 92*
**Kuybyshev**, Valeryan Vladimirovich 1888-1935 *SovUnBD*
**Kuyk**, Dirk 1934- *ConAu 135*
**Kuykendall**, Crystal Arlene 1949- *WhoAmL 92, WhoBlA 92*
**Kuyper**, Lee Frederick 1949- *AmMWSc 92*
**Kuz**, Jarema *EncAmaz 91*
**Kuzel**, Norbert R 1923- *AmMWSc 92*
**Kuzell**, Christopher Frank 1927- *WhoEnt 92*
**Kuzell**, William Charles 1914- *WhoWest 92*
**Kuziak**, Douglas Peter 1942- *WhoWest 92*
**Kuzina**, Jan Celeste 1956- *WhoFI 92*
**Kuzinski**, Stanislaw 1923- *IntWW 91*
**Kuzma**, Greg *DrAPF 91*
**Kuzma**, Jan Waldemar 1936- *AmMWSc 92*
**Kuzma**, Joseph Francis 1915- *AmMWSc 92*
**Kuzma**, Lesia Chrysta 1956- *WhoAmL 92*
**Kuzma**, Paul Daniel 1965- *WhoRel 92*
**Kuzmak**, Joseph Milton 1922- *AmMWSc 92*
**Kuzmanovic**, B O 1914- *AmMWSc 92*
**Kuzmin**, Iosif Iosifovich 1910- *IntWW 91*
**Kuzmin**, Leonid Nikolaevich 1930- *IntWW 91*
**Kuzmin**, Michael Alekseyevich 1875-1936 *FacFETw*
**Kuz'min**, Mikhail Alekseevich 1872-1936 *SovUnBD*
**Kuz'min**, Nikolay Vasil'evich 1890- *SovUnBD*
**Kuz'mina**, Yelena Aleksandrovna 1909-1979 *SovUnBD*
**Kuznesof**, Paul Martin 1941- *AmMWSc 92*
**Kuznets**, Simon 1901-1985 *FacFETw*
**Kuznets**, Simon Smith 1901-1985 *WhoNob 90*
**Kuznetsov**, Anatoli 1929- *LiExTwC*
**Kuznetsov**, Nikolay Gerasimovich 1902-1974 *SovUnBD*
**Kuznetsov**, Pavel Varfolomeevich 1878-1968 *SovUnBD*
**Kuznetsov**, Vasiliy 1901-1990 *AnObit 1990*
**Kuznetsov**, Vasiliy Vasil'evich 1901- *SovUnBD*
**Kuznetsov**, Vasily V 1901-1991 *FacFETw*
**Kuznetsov**, Vladimir Nikolayevich 1916- *IntWW 91*
**Kuznetsov**, Yuriy Ivanovich *IntWW 91*
**Kuznik**, Mary Elizabeth *WhoEnt 92*
**Kuznik**, Susan Marie 1956- *WhoMW 92*
**Kuzwayo**, Ellen 1914- *ConAu 134*
**Kvaas**, T Arthur 1919- *AmMWSc 92*
**Kvalheim**, Kenneth Cecil 1957- *WhoAmP 91*
**Kvalnes-Krick**, Kalla L 1960- *AmMWSc 92*
**Kvalseth**, Tarald Oddvar 1938- *AmMWSc 92*
**Kvam**, Adolph L *WhoAmP 91*
**Kvam**, Donald Clarence 1932- *AmMWSc 92*
**Kvam**, Wayne *DrAPF 91*
**Kvandal**, Johan 1919- *ConCom 92*
**Kvapil**, Radoslav 1934- *IntWW 91*
**Kvasov**, Oleg Konstantinovich 1928- *IntWW 91*
**Kvech**, Otomar 1950- *ConCom 92*
**Kveglis**, Albert Andrew 1934- *AmMWSc 92*
**Kvenvolden**, Keith Arthur 1930- *AmMWSc 92, WhoWest 92*
**Kverndal**, Roald 1921- *WhoRel 92, WhoWest 92*
**Kvidal**, Mary 1943- *IntWW 91*
**Kviring**, Emmanuil Ionovich 1888-1937 *SovUnBD*
**Kvist**, Tage Nielsen 1942- *AmMWSc 92*
**Kvitsinsky**, Youli Aleksandrovich 1936- *IntWW 91*
**Kvitsinsky**, Yuliy Aleksandrovich 1936- *SovUnBD*
**Kwaan**, Hau Cheong 1931- *AmMWSc 92*
**Kwak**, Jan C T 1942- *AmMWSc 92*
**Kwak**, No Kyoon 1932- *WhoFI 92, WhoMW 92*
**Kwak**, Nowhan 1928- *AmMWSc 92*
**Kwak**, Yun Sik 1937- *AmMWSc 92*
**Kwakye**, Emmanuel Bamfo 1933- *Who 92*
**Kwall**, Jeffrey Louis 1955- *WhoAmL 92*
**Kwall**, Roberta Rosenthal 1955- *WhoAmL 92*
**Kwan**, Eddy 1959- *WhoWest 92*
**Kwan**, John Ying-Kuen 1947- *AmMWSc 92*
**Kwan**, King Chiu 1936- *AmMWSc 92*
**Kwan**, Paul Wing-Ling 1942- *AmMWSc 92*
**Kwan-Gett**, Clifford Stanley 1934- *AmMWSc 92*
**Kwapong**, Alex A. 1927- *IntWW 91*
**Kwapong**, Alexander Adum 1927- *Who 92*
**Kwart**, Harold 1916- *AmMWSc 92*
**Kwartler**, Charles Edward 1911- *AmMWSc 92*
**Kwasniewski**, Aleksander 1954- *IntWW 91*
**Kwatek**, Irwin *WhoAmL 92*
**Kwatny**, Eugene Michael 1943- *AmMWSc 92*
**Kwatra**, Subhash Chander 1941- *AmMWSc 92*
**Kwei**, Ti-Kang 1929- *AmMWSc 92*
**Kweller**, Goldie B. d1991 *NewYTBS 91*
**Kwentus**, Gerald K 1937- *AmMWSc 92*
**Kwiatek**, Jack 1924- *AmMWSc 92*
**Kwiatek**, Jamie Zveitel 1957- *WhoAmL 92*
**Kwiatkowski**, Anne Susan 1955- *WhoAmL 92*
**Kwiatkowski**, Edward Louis 1950- *WhoFI 92*
**Kwiatkowski**, Richard Michael 1958- *WhoFI 92*
**Kwicien**, John Martin 1950- *WhoIns 92*
**Kwiram**, Alvin L 1937- *AmMWSc 92*
**Kwit**, Nathaniel Troy, Jr. 1941- *IntMPA 92, WhoEnt 92*
**Kwiterovich**, Peter O, Jr 1940- *AmMWSc 92*
**Kwitowski**, Paul Thomas 1939- *AmMWSc 92*
**Kwitter**, Karen Beth 1951- *AmMWSc 92*
**Kwock**, Lester 1942- *AmMWSc 92*
**Kwok**, Clyde Chi Kai 1937- *AmMWSc 92*
**Kwok**, Hoi S 1951- *AmMWSc 92*
**Kwok**, Munson Arthur 1941- *AmMWSc 92*
**Kwok**, Stephen Pit-Fung 1952- *WhoRel 92*
**Kwok**, Sun 1949- *AmMWSc 92*
**Kwok**, Thomas Yu-Kiu *AmMWSc 92*
**Kwok**, Wo Kong 1936- *AmMWSc 92*
**Kwolek**, Stephanie Louise 1923- *AmMWSc 92*
**Kwon**, Dae-Bong 1952- *WhoMW 92*
**Kwon**, Paul Hakjoo 1937- *WhoMW 92*
**Kwon**, Peter Hisang 1921- *WhoRel 92*
**Kwon**, Tai Hyung 1932- *AmMWSc 92*
**Kwon-Chung**, Kyung Joo 1933- *AmMWSc 92*
**Kwong**, James Kin-Ping 1954- *WhoWest 92*
**Kwong**, Joseph N S 1916- *AmMWSc 92*
**Kwong**, Man Kam 1947- *AmMWSc 92*
**Kwong**, Peter Kong Kit 1936- *WhoRel 92*
**Kwong**, Raymond 1954- *WhoRel 92*
**Kwong**, Yui-Hoi Harris 1957- *AmMWSc 92*
**Kwouk**, Burt 1930- *WhoEnt 92*
**Kwun**, Kyung Whan 1929- *AmMWSc 92*
**Ky**, Nguyen Cao *IntWW 91*
**Ky**, Nguyen Cao 1930- *FacFETw [port]*
**Kyame**, George John 1910- *AmMWSc 92*
**Kyame**, Joseph John 1924- *AmMWSc 92*
**Kyanka**, George Harry 1941- *AmMWSc 92*
**Kyba**, Evan Peter 1940- *AmMWSc 92*
**Kybett**, Brian David 1938- *AmMWSc 92*
**Kyburg**, Henry 1928- *AmMWSc 92*
**Kyburg**, Henry E., Jr. 1928- *ConAu 36NR*
**Kycia**, Thaddeus F 1933- *AmMWSc 92*
**Kyd**, Thomas 1558?-1594 *RfGEnL 91*
**Kydd**, David Mitchell 1903- *AmMWSc 92*
**Kydd**, George Herman 1920- *AmMWSc 92*
**Kydd**, Paul Harriman 1930- *AmMWSc 92*
**Kydes**, Andy Steve 1945- *AmMWSc 92*
**Kydoniefs**, Anastasios D 1928- *AmMWSc 92*
**Kyer**, Ben Lewis 1956- *WhoFI 92*
**Kyger**, Joanne *DrAPF 91*
**Kyger**, Joanne 1934- *ConPo 91, IntAu&W 91, WrDr 92*
**Kyhl**, Robert Louis 1917- *AmMWSc 92*
**Kyhos**, Donald William 1929- *AmMWSc 92*
**Kyhos**, Thomas Flynn 1947- *WhoAmL 92*
**Kyker**, Charles Clinton 1962- *WhoRel 92*
**Kyker**, Granvil Charles, Jr. 1938- *WhoMW 92*
**Kyl**, Jon 1942- *AlmAP 92 [port]*
**Kyl**, Jon Llewellyn 1942- *WhoAmP 91, WhoWest 92*
**Kyle**, Alastair Boyd 1931- *WhoFI 92*
**Kyle**, Barry Albert 1947- *Who 92*
**Kyle**, Benjamin G 1927- *AmMWSc 92*
**Kyle**, Billy 1914-1966 *NewAmDM*
**Kyle**, Corinne Silverman 1930- *WhoFI 92*
**Kyle**, Duncan *IntAu&W 91, WrDr 92*
**Kyle**, Gene Magerl 1919- *WhoMW 92*
**Kyle**, Genghis 1923- *WhoBlA 92*
**Kyle**, Gerald Albert 1961- *WhoMW 92*
**Kyle**, Henry C, III 1951- *WhoIns 92*
**Kyle**, Henry Carper 1909- *WhoFI 92*
**Kyle**, Herbert Lee 1930- *AmMWSc 92*
**Kyle**, James 1925- *Who 92*
**Kyle**, James F 1950- *WhoAmP 91*
**Kyle**, John Dean 1935- *WhoFI 92*
**Kyle**, John Emery 1926- *WhoRel 92*
**Kyle**, Marcia Anchors 1959- *WhoAmL 92*
**Kyle**, Marcus Aurelius 1923- *WhoAmP 91*
**Kyle**, Martin Lawrence 1935- *AmMWSc 92*
**Kyle**, Mary J. *WhoBlA 92*
**Kyle**, Odes J., Jr. 1931- *WhoBlA 92*
**Kyle**, Philip R 1947- *AmMWSc 92*
**Kyle**, Richard Granville 1938- *WhoMW 92*
**Kyle**, Robert Arthur 1928- *AmMWSc 92*
**Kyle**, Robert Campbell, II 1935- *WhoFI 92, WhoMW 92*
**Kyle**, Robert Tourville 1910- *WhoWest 92*
**Kyle**, Thomas Gail 1936- *AmMWSc 92*
**Kyle**, Wendell H 1920- *AmMWSc 92*
**Kyler**, William Alexander 1938- *WhoAmL 92*
**Kyles**, Dwain Johann 1954- *WhoBlA 92*
**Kyles**, Josephine H. 1900- *WhoBlA 92*
**Kyles**, Sharron Faye 1950- *WhoBlA 92*
**Kylian**, Jiri 1947- *WhoEnt 92*
**Kyllo**, David Ole 1952- *WhoRel 92*
**Kylstra**, Johannes Arnold 1925- *AmMWSc 92*
**Kyman**, Alexander Leon 1929- *WhoFI 92*
**Kyme**, Brian Robert 1935- *Who 92*
**Kynaston**, Nicolas 1941- *IntWW 91, Who 92*
**Kyncl**, J Jaroslav 1936- *AmMWSc 92*
**Kyne**, Peter B. 1880-1957 *BenetAL 91, TwCWW 91*
**Kyner**, Joseph Latshaw 1934- *WhoMW 92*
**Kyo**, Machiko 1924- *IntMPA 92, IntWW 91*
**Kyprianou**, Demetrios 1931- *IntWW 91*
**Kyprianou**, Spyros 1932- *IntWW 91, Who 92*
**Kyrala**, Ali 1921- *AmMWSc 92*
**Kyrala**, George Amine 1946- *AmMWSc 92*
**Kyriakis**, John M *AmMWSc 92*
**Kyriakopoulos**, Nicholas 1937- *AmMWSc 92*
**Kyriazides**, Nikos Panayis 1927- *Who 92*
**Kyriazidis**, Nicolas 1927- *IntWW 91*
**Kyriazis**, Andreas P 1932- *AmMWSc 92*
**Kyriazis**, Arthur John 1958- *WhoAmL 92, WhoFI 92*
**Kyrill of Pittsburgh**, Bishop *WhoRel 92*
**Kyrillos**, Joseph M, Jr 1960- *WhoAmP 91*
**Kyrle Pope**, Michael Donald 1916- *Who 92*
**Kyrus**, Nicholas C. 1943- *WhoFI 92*
**Kysar**, Raymond L, Jr *WhoAmP 91*
**Kyser**, David Sheldon 1936- *AmMWSc 92*
**Kyser**, James Kern 1906-1985 *DcNCBi 3*
**Kyska**, Miroslav Jan 1928- *WhoRel 92*
**Kyte**, Jack Ernst 1947- *AmMWSc 92*
**Kyte**, Lydiane 1919- *WhoWest 92*
**Kythe**, Prem Kishore 1930- *AmMWSc 92*
**Kytle**, Ray *DrAPF 91*
**Kyung**, Jai Ho 1947- *AmMWSc 92*
**Kyung-Wha Chung** *IntWW 91*
**Kyvig**, David E. 1944- *ConAu 36NR*
**Kyvig**, David Edward 1944- *WhoMW 92*

# L

**L.U.K.E.** *AmPeW*
**La Lupe** d1992 *WhoHisp 92N*
**La,** Sung Yun 1936- *AmMWSc 92*
**La,** Vincent Vinh 1965- *WhoFI 92*
**Laage,** Gerhart 1925- *IntWW 91*
**Laakso,** John William 1915- *AmMWSc 92*
**Laale,** Hans W 1935- *AmMWSc 92*
**Laali,** Khosrow 1951- *AmMWSc 92*
**Laaly,** Heshmat Ollah 1927- *WhoWest 92*
**Laane,** Jaan 1942- *AmMWSc 92*
**Laarman,** Edward John 1949- *WhoRel 92*
**Laasonen,** Pentti 1928- *WhoRel 92*
**Laaspere,** Thomas 1927- *AmMWSc 92*
**Laatsch,** James Fred 1940- *WhoAmP 91*
**Laatsch,** Richard G 1931- *AmMWSc 92*
**Laba,** David Charles 1963- *WhoEnt 92*
**Laba,** Marvin 1928- *WhoFI 92*
**Labadie,** Bruce Alan 1950- *WhoEnt 92*
**LaBahn,** William Stefan 1948- *WhoAmL 92*
**Labala,** Jefferson Seiziegbuoh 1950- *WhoRel 92*
**Laban,** Rudolf von 1879-1958 *EncTR 91*
**Labana,** Santokh Singh 1936- *AmMWSc 92*
**Labanauskas,** Charles K 1923- *AmMWSc 92*
**Labandeira,** Conrad Christopher 1950- *WhoMW 92*
**Labanick,** George Michael 1950- *AmMWSc 92*
**LaBar,** Martin 1938- *AmMWSc 92*
**LaBar,** Tom *DrAPF 91*
**La Barbara,** Joan 1947- *ConCom 92, NewAmDM*
**Labarca,** Angela 1942- *WhoHisp 92*
**Labardakis,** Augoustinos 1938- *IntWW 91*
**La Bare,** M. *DrAPF 91*
**Labaree,** Robert *WhoEnt 92*
**Labarga,** Jorge 1952- *WhoAmL 92*
**LaBarge,** Joseph Albert 1937- *WhoRel 92*
**LaBarge,** Richard Allen 1934- *WhoFI 92*
**LaBarge,** Robert Gordon 1940- *AmMWSc 92*
**Labarre,** Anthony E, Jr 1922- *AmMWSc 92*
**LaBarre,** Mary Connelly 1945- *WhoRel 92*
**La Barre,** Michel de 1675?-1744? *NewAmDM*
**LaBarre,** Weston 1911- *WrDr 92*
**Labarrere-Paule,** Andre 1928- *IntWW 91*
**Labarthe,** Darwin Raymond 1939- *AmMWSc 92*
**Labarthe Correa,** Javier 1924- *IntWW 91*
**Labas,** Aleksandr Arkad'evich 1901-1983 *SovUnBD*
**Labat,** Jean Baptiste 1663-1738 *BenetAL 91*
**Labate,** Frank Richard 1959- *WhoRel 92*
**Labate,** Samuel 1918- *AmMWSc 92*
**Labavitch,** John Marcus 1943- *AmMWSc 92*
**Labay,** Eugene Benedict 1938- *WhoAmL 92*
**Labbadia,** Pasquale, III 1956- *WhoAmL 92*
**Labbe',** Armand Joseph 1944- *WhoWest 92*
**Labbe,** Robert Ferdinand 1922- *AmMWSc 92*
**Labbe,** Ronald Gilbert 1946- *AmMWSc 92*
**Labbett,** John Edgar 1950- *WhoFI 92*
**Labe,** Louise 1520?-1566 *FrenWW*
**Labe,** Louise 1526-1566 *EncAmaz 91*
**LaBeach,** Lloyd 1923- *BlkOlyM*
**LaBeau,** David Allen 1943- *WhoMW 92*
**La Beaumelle,** Laurent Angliviel de 1726-1773 *BlkwCEP*
**Labedz,** Bernice 1919- *WhoAmP 91*
**La Beet,** Octave M. d1991 *NewYTBS 91*
**LaBella,** Frank Sebastian 1931- *AmMWSc 92*
**LaBelle,** Edward Francis 1948- *AmMWSc 92*
**La Belle,** Mary Elizabeth 1950- *WhoMW 92*
**LaBelle,** Patti 1944- *WhoBlA 92, WhoEnt 92*
**La Belle,** Richard Donald, III 1961- *WhoAmL 92*
**Laben,** Robert Cochrane 1920- *AmMWSc 92*
**Labenske,** Victor Kris 1963- *WhoWest 92*
**Laber,** Larry Jackson 1937- *AmMWSc 92*
**LaBerge,** Gene L 1932- *AmMWSc 92*
**LaBerge,** Wallace E 1927- *AmMWSc 92*
**LaBerge,** Walter B 1924- *AmMWSc 92*
**Labes,** Mortimer Milton 1929- *AmMWSc 92*
**Labianca,** Dominick A 1943- *AmMWSc 92*
**Labianca,** Frank Michael 1939- *AmMWSc 92*
**LaBianca,** Oystein Sakala 1949- *WhoRel 92*
**Labib,** Abdel Rahman 1924- *IntWW 91*
**Labiche,** Eugene 1815-1888 *GuFrLit 1*
**Labidi,** Abdelwahab 1929- *IntWW 91*
**Labiner,** Paul Steven 1954- *WhoFI 92*
**Labinger,** Jay Alan 1947- *AmMWSc 92*
**Labinov,** Mark Semion 1956- *WhoMW 92*
**Labis,** Attilio 1936- *IntWW 91*
**Labisky,** Ronald Frank 1934- *AmMWSc 92*
**Lablache,** Luigi 1794-1858 *NewAmDM*
**La Blanc,** Charles Wesley, Jr. 1925- *WhoFI 92*
**La Blanc,** Robert Edmund 1934- *WhoFI 92*
**Laboda,** Henry M 1950- *AmMWSc 92*
**La Bombard,** Joan *DrAPF 91*
**LaBombard,** Joan Herman 1920- *IntAu&W 91*
**La Bombarda,** Michael *DrAPF 91*
**Labombarde,** Philip deGaspe 1921- *WhoAmP 91*
**Labonte,** Anthony Leo 1959- *WhoEnt 92*
**La Bonte,** Anton Edward 1935- *AmMWSc 92*
**La Bonte,** Clarence Joseph 1939- *WhoFI 92*
**Labonte,** Jovite 1933- *WhoIns 92*
**LaBoon,** Lawrence Joseph 1938- *WhoFI 92*
**LaBoon,** Robert Bruce 1941- *WhoFI 92*
**Laborde,** Alice L 1947- *AmMWSc 92*
**Laborde,** Ana Maria 1956- *WhoHisp 92*
**LaBorde,** Benjamin Franklin 1910- *WhoAmP 91*
**Laborde,** Raymond J 1927- *WhoAmP 91*
**LaBorde,** Ronald Anthony 1956- *WhoFI 92*
**Labosky,** John Joseph 1948- *WhoMW 92*
**Labosky,** Peter, Jr 1937- *AmMWSc 92*
**Labouchere,** George 1905- *Who 92*
**Labouisse,** H. R., Mrs. *Who 92*
**Labouisse,** Henry R 1904-1987 *FacFETw*
**Laboulaye,** Francois Rene de 1917- *IntWW 91*
**LaBounty,** James Francis, Sr 1942- *AmMWSc 92*
**Labour,** Magdeleine Eugenie 1908- *IntAu&W 91*
**Labov,** Jay Brian 1950- *AmMWSc 92*
**Labovitch,** Neville *Who 92*
**Labows,** John Norbert, Jr 1941- *AmMWSc 92*
**Laboy,** Eduardo 1957- *WhoHisp 92*
**Laboy,** Elizabeth 1940- *WhoHisp 92*
**LaBoy,** Jose Antonio 1949- *WhoHisp 92*
**Labrador Ruiz,** Enrique 1902-1991 *WhoHisp 92N*
**LaBranche,** Gary Alfred 1958- *WhoMW 92*
**LaBreche,** Anthony Wayne 1936- *WhoFI 92*
**LaBreche,** Lisbeth Marie 1965- *WhoMW 92*
**Labrecque,** Denis Cyrille 1955- *WhoEnt 92*
**LaBrecque,** Douglas R *AmMWSc 92*
**Labrecque,** Richard Joseph 1938- *WhoFI 92*
**Labrecque,** Thomas G. 1938- *WhoFI 92*
**LaBree,** Theodore Robert 1931- *AmMWSc 92*
**LaBrie,** David Andre 1937- *AmMWSc 92*
**Labrie,** Fernand 1937- *AmMWSc 92*
**Labrie,** Harrington 1909- *WhoBlA 92*
**Labrie,** Jean-Paul 1922- *WhoRel 92*
**LaBrie,** Peter, Jr. 1940- *WhoBlA 92*
**Labrie,** Vida Yvonne 1946- *WhoBlA 92*
**Labriola,** Anthony Joseph 1950- *WhoEnt 92*
**LaBroad,** Michael Edward 1957- *WhoMW 92*
**Labrosse,** G. *WhoRel 92*
**La Bruno,** Carmen Michael *DrAPF 91*
**La Bruyere,** Jean de 1645-1696 *LitC 17 [port]*
**Labry,** Robbie Shirley 1957- *WhoEnt 92*
**Labs,** Richard John 1956- *WhoFI 92*
**Labsvirs,** Janis 1907- *WhoFI 92, WhoMW 92*
**LaBua,** Paul J. 1941- *WhoFI 92*
**Labuda,** Gerard 1916- *IntWW 91*
**LaBudde,** Robert Arthur 1947- *AmMWSc 92*
**LaBudde,** Roy Christian 1921- *WhoAmL 92, WhoFI 92, WhoMW 92*
**Labute,** John Paul 1938- *AmMWSc 92*
**Labuz,** Ronald Matthew 1953- *IntAu&W 91*
**Labuza,** Theodore Peter 1940- *AmMWSc 92*
**Labys,** Walter C 1937- *ConAu 34NR*
**Lac,** Ming Q. 1948- *WhoFI 92*
**LaCaille,** Rupert Andrew 1917- *WhoBlA 92*
**Lacalle,** Luis Alberto 1941- *IntWW 91*
**Lacan,** Jacques 1901-1981 *FacFETw*
**Lacant,** Jacques 1915- *IntWW 91*
**Lacanych,** Igor Vasyl'ovich 1935- *WhoEnt 92*
**LaCasce,** Elroy Osborne, Jr 1923- *AmMWSc 92*
**LaCasse,** James Phillip 1948- *WhoAmL 92, WhoFI 92*
**Lacatena,** Victor Anthony 1924- *WhoAmP 91*
**La Cava,** Donald Leon 1928- *WhoEnt 92, WhoFI 92*
**La Cava,** Gregory 1892-1952 *IntDcF 2-2*
**LaCava,** John Robert 1947- *WhoAmL 92*
**Lacayo,** Carl Anthony 1962- *WhoFI 92*
**Lacayo,** Carmela G. 1943- *WhoHisp 92*
**Lacayo,** Henry L 1931- *WhoAmP 91*
**Lacaze,** Jeannou 1924- *IntWW 91*
**Lacefield,** Garry Dale 1945- *AmMWSc 92*
**LaCelle,** Paul 1929- *AmMWSc 92*
**Lacer,** Alfred Antonio 1952- *WhoAmL 92*
**Lacer,** Kathryn Lorene 1930- *WhoFI 92*
**Lacerra,** Ronald J 1939- *WhoIns 92*
**Lacewell,** Ronald Dale 1940- *AmMWSc 92*
**Lacey,** A. R. 1926- *WrDr 92*
**Lacey,** Beatrice Cates 1919- *AmMWSc 92, WhoMW 92*
**Lacey,** Bruce 1927- *TwCPaSc*
**Lacey,** Cassandra Overfelt 1943- *WhoEnt 92*
**Lacey,** Clifford George 1921- *Who 92*
**Lacey,** Daniel Damian 1950- *WhoMW 92*
**Lacey,** David Morgan 1950- *WhoAmL 92*
**Lacey,** Diane E. *WhoBlA 92*
**Lacey,** Douglas R. 1913-1973 *ConAu 134*
**Lacey,** Elizabeth Patterson *AmMWSc 92*
**Lacey,** Frank 1919- *Who 92*
**Lacey,** Frederick Bernard 1920- *WhoAmL 92*
**Lacey,** George William Brian 1926- *Who 92*
**Lacey,** Howard Elton 1937- *AmMWSc 92*
**Lacey,** Howard Raymond 1919- *WhoMW 92*
**Lacey,** Jack *WhoAmP 91*
**Lacey,** James Harry 1917-1989 *FacFETw*
**Lacey,** Janet 1903-1988 *DcEcMov*
**Lacey,** John Fairbank 1951- *WhoFI 92*
**Lacey,** John I 1915- *AmMWSc 92*
**Lacey,** Marc Steven 1965- *WhoBlA 92*
**Lacey,** Martha Jane 1931- *WhoRel 92*
**Lacey,** Nicola 1958- *WrDr 92*
**Lacey,** Richard Frederick 1931- *AmMWSc 92*
**Lacey,** Richard Westgarth 1940- *IntWW 91, Who 92*
**Lacey,** Robert 1944- *IntAu&W 91, WrDr 92*
**Lacey,** Wilbert, Jr. 1936- *WhoBlA 92*
**Lacey-Baker,** Creighton 1937- *WhoFI 92*
**Lach,** Alma Elizabeth *WhoMW 92*
**Lach,** John Louis 1927- *AmMWSc 92*
**Lach,** Joseph T 1934- *AmMWSc 92*
**Lach-Szyrma,** W S 1841-1915 *ScFEYrs*
**Lachaine,** Andre Raymond Joseph 1945- *AmMWSc 92*
**Lachaise,** Gaston 1882-1935 *FacFETw*
**Lachance,** Denis 1939- *AmMWSc 92*
**LaChance,** Donna Louise 1963- *WhoMW 92*
**Lachance,** Douglas A 1965- *WhoAmP 91*
**La Chance,** Leo Emery 1931- *AmMWSc 92*
**LaChance,** Murdock Henry 1920- *AmMWSc 92, WhoWest 92*
**Lachance,** Paul Albert 1933- *AmMWSc 92, WhoFI 92*
**Lachance,** Sherry *DrAPF 91*
**La Chapelle,** Mary *DrAPF 91*
**Lachapelle,** Rene Charles 1930- *AmMWSc 92*
**Lacharriere,** Guy Ladreit de 1919- *IntWW 91*

**LaChat**, Michael Ray 1948- *WhoRel 92*
**Lachenbruch**, Arthur Herold 1925- *AmMWSc 92*
**Lachenbruch**, Peter Anthony 1937- *AmMWSc 92*
**Lachenicht-Berkeley**, Angela Marie 1955- *WhoMW 92*
**Lachenmann**, Helmut 1935- *ConCom 92*
**Lacher**, Egon Leonhardt 1950- *WhoFI 92*
**Lacher**, Hans 1912- *IntWW 91*
**Lacher**, Lawrence Arthur 1958- *WhoRel 92*
**Lacher**, Robert Christopher 1940- *AmMWSc 92*
**Lacher**, Thomas Edward, Jr 1949- *AmMWSc 92*
**Lachin**, John Marion, III 1942- *AmMWSc 92*
**Lachman**, Alan B. 1935- *WhoWest 92*
**Lachman**, Branton George 1952- *WhoWest 92*
**Lachman**, Ed 1948- *IntMPA 92*
**Lachman**, Edward 1946- *WhoEnt 92*
**Lachman**, Irwin Morris 1930- *AmMWSc 92*
**Lachman**, Lawrence B 1947- *AmMWSc 92*
**Lachman**, Leon 1929- *AmMWSc 92*
**Lachman**, Marguerite Leanne 1943- *WhoFI 92*
**Lachman**, Mort *LesBEnT 92*
**Lachman**, Morton 1918- *WhoEnt 92*
**Lachman**, Ralph Steven 1935- *WhoBlA 92*
**Lachman**, Wade Randall 1954- *WhoRel 92*
**Lachmann**, Peter Julius 1931- *IntWW 91, Who 92*
**Lachmann**, Rainer 1940- *WhoRel 92*
**Lachner**, Ernest Albert 1915- *AmMWSc 92*
**Lachs**, Gerard 1934- *AmMWSc 92*
**Lachs**, Henry Lazarus 1927- *Who 92*
**Lachs**, John 1934- *WrDr 92*
**Lachs**, Manfred 1914- *IntWW 91, Who 92*
**Lachut**, Ervin R 1924- *WhoAmP 91*
**Lacina**, Ferdinand 1942- *IntWW 91*
**Laciura**, Ann Rauma 1952- *WhoMW 92*
**Lacivita**, Michael John 1924- *WhoMW 92*
**Lack**, Andrew *LesBEnT 92*
**Lack**, Henry Martyn 1909- *TwCPaSc*
**Lack**, James J 1944- *WhoAmP 91*
**Lack**, Larry Henry 1952- *WhoWest 92*
**Lack**, Leon 1922- *AmMWSc 92*
**Lackey**, Bernice Catherine 1917- *WhoAmP 91*
**Lackey**, Carolyn Jean 1948- *AmMWSc 92*
**Lackey**, Daniel Grady 1958- *WhoRel 92*
**Lackey**, E. K. *WhoRel 92*
**Lackey**, Edgar F. 1930- *WhoBlA 92*
**Lackey**, Edwin Keith *Who 92*
**Lackey**, Henry Grider 1947- *WhoAmP 91*
**Lackey**, Homer Baird 1920- *AmMWSc 92*
**Lackey**, James Alden 1938- *AmMWSc 92*
**Lackey**, Larry Alton, Sr. 1940- *WhoFI 92*
**Lackey**, Laurence *AmMWSc 92*
**Lackey**, Mary Josephine 1925- *Who 92*
**Lackey**, Mercedes R 1950- *IntAu&W 91*
**Lackey**, Robert T 1944- *AmMWSc 92*
**Lackey**, Robert Thomas 1944- *WhoWest 92*
**Lackey**, S. Allen *WhoAmL 92*
**Lackey**, Walter Jackson 1940- *AmMWSc 92*
**Lackland**, John 1939- *WhoAmL 92*
**Lackman**, Conway Lee 1938- *WhoFI 92*
**Lackman**, David Buell 1911- *AmMWSc 92*
**Lackner**, Henriette 1922- *AmMWSc 92*
**Lacko**, Andras Gyorgy 1936- *AmMWSc 92*
**Lacks**, Sanford 1934- *AmMWSc 92*
**Lacksonen**, James W 1936- *AmMWSc 92*
**LaClair**, Craig Lawrence 1945- *WhoAmL 92*
**La Claire**, John Willard, II 1951- *AmMWSc 92*
**Laclette**, Fernando Javier 1942- *WhoHisp 92*
**Laclos**, Pierre-Antoine-Francois C. de 1741-1803 *BlkwCEP*
**LaCluyse**, Stephan Lee 1950- *WhoMW 92*
**Laco**, Karol 1921- *IntWW 91*
**Lacoe**, R D d1901 *BiInAmS*
**Lacomba**, Justo *WhoHisp 92*
**Lacombe**, Henri 1913- *IntWW 91*
**Lacombe**, Rita Jeanne 1947- *WhoWest 92*
**Lacombe**, Rose 1768- *EncAmaz 91*
**Lacome**, Myer 1927- *Who 92*
**Lacon**, Edmund 1936- *Who 92*
**Laconte**, Pierre 1934- *IntWW 91*
**La Core**, Walter C. 1930- *WhoRel 92*
**La Corte**, Brian William 1963- *WhoAmL 92*
**LaCorte**, John N. d1991 *NewYTBS 91*
**Lacoss**, Richard Thaddee 1937- *AmMWSc 92*
**Lacoste**, Paul 1923- *IntWW 91, Who 92*
**Lacoste**, Rene John 1927- *AmMWSc 92*
**Lacoste**, Robert 1898-1989 *FacFETw*
**LaCount**, Robert Bruce 1935- *AmMWSc 92*
**LaCour**, Barry Louis 1954- *WhoAmL 92*
**La Cour**, Louis Bernard 1926- *WhoAmL 92, WhoBlA 92, WhoMW 92*
**LaCour**, Nathaniel Hawthorne 1938- *WhoBlA 92*
**Lacour**, Vanue B. 1915- *WhoBlA 92*
**Lacouture**, Peter George 1951- *AmMWSc 92*
**Lacovara**, Philip Allen 1943- *WhoAmL 92, WhoFI 92*
**Lacretelle**, Jacques de 1888-1985 *GuFrLit 1*
**Lacroix**, Christian Marie Marc 1951- *IntWW 91, Who 92*
**Lacroix**, Fernand 1919- *WhoRel 92*
**Lacroix**, Guy 1930- *AmMWSc 92*
**LaCroix**, Joseph Donald 1925- *AmMWSc 92*
**LaCroix**, Lucien Joseph 1929- *AmMWSc 92*
**Lacroix**, Norbert Hector Joseph 1940- *AmMWSc 92*
**Lacroix**, Raymond Joseph 1935- *WhoFI 92*
**La Croix**, Sumner Jonathan 1954- *WhoFI 92*
**Lactantius** 250?-325? *EncEarC*
**La Curne de Sainte-Palaye**, Jean-B. de 1697-1781 *BlkwCEP*
**Lacy**, Allen Wayne 1938- *WhoFI 92*
**Lacy**, Ann Matthews 1932- *AmMWSc 92*
**Lacy**, Benjamin Rice 1854-1929 *DcNCBi 4*
**Lacy**, Benjamin Rice, Jr. 1886-1981 *DcNCBi 4*
**Lacy**, Creighton Boutelle 1919- *IntAu&W 91, WhoRel 92, WrDr 92*
**Lacy**, Drury, Jr. 1802-1884 *DcNCBi 4*
**Lacy**, Edward J. 1922- *WhoBlA 92*
**Lacy**, Edwin Vemont 1937- *WhoMW 92*
**Lacy**, Elizabeth B *WhoAmP 91*
**Lacy**, Ernest 1863-1916 *BenetAL 91*
**Lacy**, Fern 1920- *WhoAmP 91*
**Lacy**, George Holcombe 1943- *AmMWSc 92*
**Lacy**, Herman Edgar 1935- *WhoMW 92*
**Lacy**, Hugh Maurice Pierce 1943- *Who 92*
**Lacy**, James Hargan 1951- *WhoRel 92*
**Lacy**, James Vincent 1952- *WhoAmP 91*
**Lacy**, John Ford 1944- *WhoAmL 92*
**Lacy**, John Trend 1928- *Who 92*
**Lacy**, Julia Caroline 1946- *AmMWSc 92*
**Lacy**, Karen Bevins 1946- *WhoRel 92*
**Lacy**, Lee Marva Lou 1942- *WhoWest 92*
**Lacy**, Leslie Alexander 1937- *WhoBlA 92*
**Lacy**, Lewis L 1941- *AmMWSc 92*
**Lacy**, Lucile C. 1945- *WhoEnt 92*
**Lacy**, Margaret Rose 1922- *WhoMW 92*
**Lacy**, Margriet Bruyn 1943- *WhoMW 92*
**Lacy**, Melvyn Leroy 1931- *AmMWSc 92*
**Lacy**, Michael Stephen 1944- *WhoAmL 92*
**Lacy**, Paul Eston 1924- *AmMWSc 92*
**Lacy**, Peter D 1920- *AmMWSc 92*
**Lacy**, Phillips 1945- *WhoRel 92*
**Lacy**, Ralph E 1915- *WhoAmP 91*
**Lacy**, Robert Kimbrough 1957- *WhoAmL 92*
**Lacy**, Robinson Burrell 1952- *WhoAmL 92*
**Lacy**, Russell Gwinn 1938- *WhoRel 92*
**Lacy**, Steve 1934- *NewAmDM, WhoEnt 92*
**Lacy**, Suzanne L. 1947- *WhoWest 92*
**Lacy**, Versia Lindsay 1929- *WhoBlA 92*
**Lacy**, W C 1916- *AmMWSc 92*
**Lacy**, W J 1928- *AmMWSc 92*
**Lacy**, William Frank 1945- *WhoEnt 92*
**Lacy**, William Sterling 1842-1899 *DcNCBi 4*
**Lacy**, William White 1923- *AmMWSc 92*
**Lacz**, Walter, Jr. 1947- *WhoFI 92*
**Laczko**, Brian John 1952- *WhoEnt 92*
**Lad**, Pramod Madhusudan 1948- *AmMWSc 92*
**Lad**, Robert Augustin 1919- *AmMWSc 92*
**Lada**, Arnold 1926- *AmMWSc 92*
**Lada**, Charles Joseph 1949- *AmMWSc 92*
**Ladage**, Kenneth Charles 1944- *WhoEnt 92*
**Ladanyi**, Branka Maria 1947- *AmMWSc 92*
**Ladanyi**, Branko 1922- *AmMWSc 92*
**Ladar**, Jerrold Morton 1933- *WhoAmL 92*
**Ladas**, Alice K 1921- *IntAu&W 91*
**Ladas**, Diana Margaret 1913- *Who 92*
**Ladas**, Gerasimos 1937- *AmMWSc 92*
**Ladas**, Ioannis 1920- *IntWW 91*
**Laday**, Kerney 1942- *WhoBlA 92*
**Ladd**, Alan, Jr. 1937- *IntMPA 92*
**Ladd**, Alan Walbridge, Jr. 1937- *WhoEnt 92, WhoFI 92, WhoWest 92*
**Ladd**, Carolyn Sue 1954- *WhoMW 92*
**Ladd**, Charles Barton 1957- *WhoAmP 91*
**Ladd**, Charles Cushing, III 1932- *AmMWSc 92*
**Ladd**, Cheryl 1951- *IntMPA 92, WhoEnt 92*
**Ladd**, Conrad Mervyn 1926- *AmMWSc 92*
**Ladd**, David Alan 1947- *IntMPA 92*
**Ladd**, Diane 1939- *IntMPA 92, WhoEnt 92*
**Ladd**, Donald McKinley, Jr. 1923- *WhoWest 92*
**Ladd**, Florence Cawthorne 1932- *WhoBlA 92*
**Ladd**, Jeffrey Raymond 1941- *WhoMW 92*
**Ladd**, John Curran 1945- *WhoAmL 92*
**Ladd**, John Herbert 1918- *AmMWSc 92*
**Ladd**, Joseph Brown 1764-1786 *BenetAL 91*
**Ladd**, Joseph C 1927- *WhoIns 92*
**Ladd**, Kaye Victoria 1941- *AmMWSc 92*
**Ladd**, Kenneth Paul 1938- *WhoRel 92*
**Ladd**, Sheldon Lane 1941- *AmMWSc 92*
**Ladd**, Steven K. 1960- *WhoFI 92*
**Ladd**, Thyril Leone, Jr 1931- *AmMWSc 92*
**Ladd**, William 1778-1841 *AmPeW, BenetAL 91*
**Ladd**, Woody 1951- *WhoFI 92*
**Ladd-Franklin**, Christine 1847-1930 *WomPsyc*
**Ladda**, Roger Louis 1936- *AmMWSc 92*
**Laddaga**, Lawrence Alexander 1957- *WhoAmL 92*
**Ladde**, Gangaram Shivlingappa 1940- *AmMWSc 92*
**Laddie**, Hugh Ian Lang 1946- *Who 92*
**Laddin**, Michael Phillip 1959- *WhoMW 92*
**Laddu**, Atul R 1940- *AmMWSc 92*
**Lade**, Robert Walter 1935- *AmMWSc 92*
**Ladehoff**, Robert Louis 1932- *WhoRel 92, WhoWest 92*
**La Delfe**, Peter Carl 1943- *AmMWSc 92*
**La Dell**, Edwin 1919-1970 *TwCPaSc*
**Laden**, Cynthia 1960- *WhoWest 92*
**Laden**, Karl 1932- *AmMWSc 92*
**Ladenheim**, Harry 1932- *AmMWSc 92*
**Ladenheim**, Kala *DrAPF 91*
**Ladenson**, Jack Herman 1942- *AmMWSc 92, WhoMW 92*
**Lader**, Malcolm Harold 1936- *IntWW 91*
**Laderach**, Paul A 1933- *WhoIns 92*
**Laderman**, A J 1930- *AmMWSc 92*
**Laderman**, Ezra 1924- *ConCom 92, NewAmDM, WhoEnt 92*
**Laderman**, Julian David 1948- *AmMWSc 92*
**Laderman**, Louis Nathan 1951- *WhoAmL 92*
**Laderoute**, Charles David 1948- *WhoFI 92*
**Ladgham**, Bahi 1913- *IntWW 91*
**Ladin**, Eugene 1927- *WhoFI 92*
**Ladinsky**, Gary 1947- *WhoEnt 92*
**Ladinsky**, Herbert 1935- *AmMWSc 92*
**Ladinsky**, Judith L 1938- *AmMWSc 92*
**Ladisch**, Michael R 1950- *AmMWSc 92, WhoMW 92*
**Ladisch**, Stephan 1947- *AmMWSc 92*
**Ladish**, Joseph Stanley 1943- *AmMWSc 92*
**Ladjevardi**, Hamid 1948- *WhoFI 92*
**Ladley**, Ronald Dean 1938- *WhoMW 92*
**Ladman**, Aaron J 1925- *AmMWSc 92*
**Ladner**, David William 1947- *AmMWSc 92*
**Ladner**, Heber Austin 1902- *WhoAmP 91*
**Ladner**, Jennifer Ann 1957- *WhoEnt 92*
**Ladner**, Kurt *WrDr 92*
**Ladner**, Mark P. 1953- *WhoAmL 92*
**Ladner**, Sidney Jules 1936- *AmMWSc 92*
**Lado**, Fred 1938- *AmMWSc 92*
**Lado**, Robert Anthony 1944- *WhoMW 92*
**La Douceur**, Dale Armand 1953- *WhoFI 92*
**Ladouceur**, David Jerome 1960- *WhoWest 92*
**Ladouceur**, Patricia Allaire 1955- *WhoWest 92*
**Ladovsky**, Nikolay Aleksandrovich 1881-1941 *SovUnBD*
**LaDow**, C. Stuart 1925- *WhoFI 92*
**Ladra**, Michael Ralph 1946- *WhoRel 92*
**Ladreit De Lacharriere**, Marc 1940- *IntWW 91*
**LaDriere**, Raymond Edward 1956- *WhoAmL 92*
**Ladson**, Louis Fitzgerald 1951- *WhoBlA 92*
**Ladson**, Thomas Alvin 1917- *AmMWSc 92*
**Ladt**, Carroll Hall 1948- *WhoAmP 91*
**La Du**, Bert Nichols, Jr 1920- *AmMWSc 92*
**LaDue**, Eddy Lorain 1939- *WhoFI 92*
**Ladue**, Peter Whiting 1950- *WhoEnt 92*
**LaDuke**, John Carl 1950- *AmMWSc 92*
**Ladwig**, E James 1938- *WhoAmP 91*
**Ladwig**, Harold Allen 1922- *AmMWSc 92*
**Lady Day** *NewAmDM*
**Lae**, William Mark 1962- *WhoEnt 92*
**Laegreid**, Ivar 1958- *WhoFI 92*
**Laemle**, Lois K 1941- *AmMWSc 92*
**Laemmle**, Carl 1867-1939 *FacFETw*
**Laemmle**, Joseph Thomas 1941- *AmMWSc 92*
**Laemmlen**, Franklin 1938- *AmMWSc 92*
**Laena** *EncAmaz 91*
**Laenen**, Remie 1926- *WhoMW 92*
**Laerm**, Joshua 1942- *AmMWSc 92*
**Laessig**, Ronald Harold 1940- *AmMWSc 92*
**Laessoe**, Jorgen 1924- *IntWW 91*
**Laet**, Johann De *BenetAL 91*
**Laetsch**, Theodore Willis 1940- *AmMWSc 92*
**Laetsch**, Watson McMillan 1933- *AmMWSc 92*
**Laeuchli**, Samuel 1924- *WhoRel 92*
**Laevastu**, Taivo 1923- *AmMWSc 92*
**Laeyendecker**, Leonardus 1930- *IntWW 91*
**Lafair**, Theodore 1927- *WhoFI 92*
**LaFalce**, John J. 1939- *AlmAP 92 [port], WhoAmP 91*
**La Farge**, Christopher 1897-1956 *BenetAL 91*
**LaFarge**, Christopher Grant F. 1954- *WhoFI 92*
**La Farge**, John 1835-1910 *BenetAL 91, DcTwDes*
**La Farge**, Oliver 1901-1963 *BenetAL 91, FacFETw, TwCWW 91*
**LaFarge**, Rupert Lealan 1943- *WhoFI 92*
**LaFargue**, Craig Joseph 1950- *WhoFI 92*
**LaFaro**, Scott 1936-1961 *NewAmDM*
**Lafata**, Salvatore 1945- *WhoMW 92*
**Lafaurie**, Jean 1914- *IntWW 91*
**LaFave**, Steven John 1953- *WhoMW 92*
**La Fayette** *BlkwEAR*
**Lafayette**, comtesse de 1634-1693 *FrenWW*
**Lafayette**, Marquis de 1757-1834 *BenetAL 91*
**Lafayette**, Bernard, Jr. 1940- *WhoBlA 92*
**Lafayette**, Ivan C *WhoAmP 91*
**LaFayette**, Kate Bulls 1935- *WhoBlA 92*
**Lafayette**, Rene M 1961- *WhoAmP 91*
**LaFeber**, Walter Frederick 1933- *WrDr 92*
**Lafee**, Alfredo 1921- *IntWW 91*
**La Fehr**, Thomas Robert 1934- *AmMWSc 92*
**Lafenestre**, Georges 1837-1919 *ThHEIm*
**Lafer**, Fred Seymour 1929- *WhoFI 92*
**Laferriere**, Arthur L 1933- *AmMWSc 92*
**Laferty**, Samuel B. 1956- *WhoMW 92*
**Lafever**, Howard N 1938- *AmMWSc 92*
**LaFever**, Robert Lyle 1946- *WhoRel 92*
**Laffan**, Kevin 1922- *WrDr 92*
**Laffer**, Arthur *IntWW 91*
**Lafferty**, James Francis 1927- *AmMWSc 92*
**Lafferty**, James M 1916- *AmMWSc 92*
**Lafferty**, Lawrence Elliott 1957- *WhoAmL 92*
**Lafferty**, Perry *LesBEnT 92*
**Lafferty**, Perry 1920- *IntMPA 92*
**Lafferty**, R A 1914- *IntAu&W 91, TwCSFW 91, WrDr 92*
**Lafferty**, Walter J 1934- *AmMWSc 92*
**Laffey**, Alice Leila 1944- *WhoRel 92*
**Laffin**, John 1922- *IntAu&W 91, WrDr 92*
**Laffin**, Robert James 1927- *AmMWSc 92*
**Laffite**, Jean 1780?-1826? *BenetAL 91*
**Laffitte**, Hector M. 1934- *WhoAmL 92*
**Laffitte**, Pierre Paul 1925- *IntWW 91*
**Laffler**, Thomas G 1946- *AmMWSc 92*
**Laffont**, Robert Raoul 1916- *IntWW 91*
**Laffoon**, David Leon 1939- *WhoFI 92*
**Laffoon**, John 1955- *AmMWSc 92*
**Laffoon**, Laura Elizabeth 1962- *WhoRel 92*
**Lafitte**, Francois 1913- *Who 92*
**Lafitte**, Gene Walpole 1930- *WhoAmL 92*
**Lafitte**, Jean 1780?-1826? *BenetAL 91*
**LaFlame**, Thomas Raymond 1928- *WhoEnt 92*
**Laflamme**, Gaston 1945- *AmMWSc 92*
**Lafler**, Kirk Paul 1956- *WhoWest 92*
**La Flesche**, Francis 1860-1932 *BenetAL 91*
**La Flesche**, Suzette 1854-1923 *BenetAL 91*
**La Fleur**, James Kemble 1930- *AmMWSc 92*
**LaFleur**, Kermit Stillman 1915- *AmMWSc 92*
**LaFleur**, Lawrence Eugene 1951- *WhoWest 92*
**Lafleur**, Louis Dwynn 1940- *AmMWSc 92*
**LaFleur**, Robert George 1929- *AmMWSc 92*
**Laflin**, Byron 1829-1901 *DcNCBi 4*
**Lafoe**, Lorin George 1930- *WhoMW 92*
**Lafolette**, James Richard 1954- *WhoRel 92*
**La Follette**, Bronson Cutting 1936- *WhoAmP 91*
**La Follette**, Douglas J 1940- *WhoAmP 91, WhoMW 92*
**LaFollette**, Ernest Carlton 1934- *WhoAmL 92*
**LaFollette**, Joan Christina 1959- *WhoRel 92*
**La Follette**, Marian W 1926- *WhoAmP 91*
**La Follette**, Robert M. 1855-1925 *BenetAL 91, RComAH*
**La Follette**, Robert Marion 1855-1925 *AmPolLe [port], FacFETw [port]*
**La Follette**, Robert Marion, Sr. 1855-1925 *AmPeW*
**La Follette**, Suzanne 1893-1983 *FacFETw*
**Lafon**, Earl Edward 1940- *AmMWSc 92*
**Lafon**, Guy Michel 1943- *AmMWSc 92*
**LaFon**, Stephen Woodrow 1953- *AmMWSc 92*
**Lafond**, Andre 1920- *AmMWSc 92*

**La Fond**, Eugene Cecil 1909- *AmMWSc 92*
**LaFond**, Stephen Dennis 1947- *WhoAmL 92*
**LaFond**, Thomas Joseph 1941- *WhoAmL 92, WhoMW 92*
**Lafont**, Bernadette *IntMPA 92*
**LaFontaine**, Edward 1952- *AmMWSc 92*
**La Fontaine**, Henri Marie 1854-1943 *WhoNob 90*
**Lafontaine**, Hernan 1934- *WhoHisp 92*
**Lafontaine**, Jean-Gabriel 1928- *AmMWSc 92*
**Lafontaine**, Oskar 1943- *IntWW 91*
**Lafontant**, Jewel 1922- *WhoAmP 91*
**Lafontant**, Jewel Stradford 1928- *NotBlAW 92*
**Lafontant**, Julien J. *WhoBlA 92*
**Lafontant-Mankarious**, Jewel 1922- *WhoBlA 92*
**Lafontsee**, Dane 1946- *WhoEnt 92, WhoMW 92*
**La Force**, James Clayburn, Jr. 1928- *WhoFI 92*
**LaFore**, E. T. *WhoHisp 92*
**LaForest**, Gerard V. 1926- *WrDr 92*
**La Forge**, Frank 1879-1953 *NewAmDM*
**LaForge**, Julie Ann 1961- *WhoAmL 92*
**Laforgue**, Jules 1860-1887 *GuFrLit 1, ThHElm*
**Lafornara**, Joseph Philip 1942- *AmMWSc 92*
**Laforte**, Conrad 1921- *IntWW 91*
**La Fortune**, Knolly Stephen 1920- *WrDr 92*
**La Fosse**, Robert *WhoEnt 92*
**LaFountain**, James Robert, Jr 1944- *AmMWSc 92*
**LaFountain**, Lester James, Jr 1942- *AmMWSc 92*
**Laframboise**, James Gerald 1938- *AmMWSc 92*
**Laframboise**, Marc Alexander 1915- *AmMWSc 92*
**La Framboise**, Terry Michael 1955- *WhoRel 92*
**LaFrance**, Jeanne Winant 1954- *WhoFI 92*
**Lafranchi**, Edward Alvin 1928- *AmMWSc 92*
**Lafratta**, Charles Anthony 1925- *WhoIns 92*
**La Frenais**, Ian 1937- *IntAu&W 91, Who 92*
**LaFreniere**, Nancy Lu 1956- *WhoMW 92*
**Lafrenz**, David E 1947- *AmMWSc 92*
**Lafuse**, Harry G 1930- *AmMWSc 92*
**LaFuze**, Joan Esterline *AmMWSc 92*
**LaFuze**, Pauliena B. 1905- *WhoWest 92*
**Lafving**, Brian Douglas 1953- *WhoAmL 92*
**Lag**, Jul 1915- *IntWW 91*
**Lagace**, Bernard 1930- *NewAmDM*
**Lagacos**, Eustace P. 1921- *Who 92*
**Lagakos**, Stephen William 1946- *AmMWSc 92*
**Lagally**, Max Gunter 1942- *AmMWSc 92*
**LaGambina**, Gerald Frank 1962- *WhoMW 92*
**LaGanga**, Donna Brandeis 1950- *WhoFI 92*
**La Ganga**, Thomas S 1927- *AmMWSc 92*
**Laganis**, Deno 1919- *AmMWSc 92*
**Laganis**, Evan Dean 1953- *AmMWSc 92*
**LaGarde**, Frederick H. 1928- *WhoBlA 92*
**Lagarde**, Paul 1934- *IntWW 91*
**Lagarde**, Paul de 1827-1891 *EncTR 91 [port]*
**Lagardelle**, Jean-Baptiste Joseph Hubert 1874-1958 *BiDExR*
**Lagardere**, Jean-Luc 1928- *IntWW 91*
**Lagareva**, Alexandra Ephimowna *EncAmaz 91*
**Lagarias**, Jeffrey Clark 1949- *AmMWSc 92*
**Lagarias**, John S 1921- *AmMWSc 92*
**Lagasse**, Bruce Kenneth 1940- *WhoWest 92*
**Lagasse**, Raphael 1927- *IntWW 91*
**La Gassey**, Homer C., Jr. 1924- *DcTwDes*
**Lagattolla**, Robert S 1931- *WhoIns 92*
**LaGattuta**, Margo *DrAPF 91*
**Lage**, Gary Lee 1941- *AmMWSc 92*
**Lage**, Janice M 1951- *AmMWSc 92*
**Lagen**, Themis T. 1967- *WhoMW 92*
**Lagendries**, Raymond 1943- *IntWW 91*
**La Geniere**, Renaud de 1925-1990 *IntWW 91, -91N*
**Lagerberg**, Jill M. Allen 1959- *WhoEnt 92*
**Lagercrantz**, Olof 1911- *IntWW 91*
**Lagerfeld**, Karl 1938- *IntWW 91*
**Lagerfield**, Karl 1938- *DcTwDes*
**Lagergren**, Carl Robert 1922- *AmMWSc 92*
**Lagergren**, Gunnar Karl Andreas 1912- *IntWW 91*
**Lagerkvist**, Par 1891-1951 *FacFETw*
**Lagerkvist**, Par Fabian 1891-1974 *WhoNob 90*
**Lagerlof**, Ronald Stephen 1956- *WhoWest 92*
**Lagerlof**, Selma 1858-1940 *FacFETw*
**Lagerlof**, Selma Ottilian Lovisa 1858-1940 *WhoNob 90*
**Lagerquist**, Lydia DeAne 1955- *WhoRel 92*
**Lagerstedt**, Harry Bert 1925- *AmMWSc 92*
**Lagerstrom**, John E 1922- *AmMWSc 92*
**Lages**, John David 1936- *WhoMW 92*
**Lageschulte**, Ray 1922- *WhoAmP 91*
**Lagesen**, Philip 1923- *Who 92*
**Laghari**, Javaid Rosoolbux 1950- *AmMWSc 92*
**Laghi**, Pio 1922- *WhoRel 92*
**Laghzaoui**, Mohammed 1906- *Who 92*
**Lagier**, Jennifer *DrAPF 91*
**Lagin**, Neil 1942- *WhoFI 92*
**Lagina**, James Joseph 1958- *WhoAmP 91*
**Lagle**, John Franklin 1938- *WhoAmL 92*
**Lagler**, Karl Frank 1912- *AmMWSc 92*
**Lago**, Armando M. 1939- *WhoHisp 92*
**Lago**, James 1921- *AmMWSc 92*
**Lago**, Paul Keith 1947- *AmMWSc 92*
**Lago**, Rafael A. *WhoHisp 92*
**Lagomarsino**, Carlos 1964- *WhoHisp 92*
**Lagomarsino**, Nancy *DrAPF 91*
**Lagomarsino**, Robert J. 1926- *AlmAP 92 [port]*
**Lagomarsino**, Robert John 1926- *WhoAmP 91, WhoWest 92*
**LaGore**, Carol Elaine 1950- *WhoMW 92*
**Lagorio**, Irene Rose 1921- *WhoWest 92*
**Lagos**, Archbishop of 1936- *Who 92*
**Lagos**, Bishop of *Who 92*
**Lagos**, Dickens M. 1936- *WhoHisp 92*
**Lagos**, James Harry 1951- *WhoAmL 92*
**Lagos**, Ramona C. 1942- *WhoHisp 92*
**Lagos**, Rene Guzman 1942- *WhoHisp 92*
**Lagoski**, Charles William 1949- *WhoMW 92*
**Lagowski**, Jeanne Mund 1929- *AmMWSc 92*
**Lagowski**, Joseph John 1930- *AmMWSc 92*
**LaGraff**, John Erwin 1940- *AmMWSc 92*
**LaGrand**, Louis E. 1935- *WrDr 92*
**LaGrange**, William Somers 1931- *AmMWSc 92*
**LaGreca**, John S. 1941- *WhoFI 92*
**LaGreca**, T.R. *DrAPF 91*
**LaGreen**, Alan Lennart 1951- *WhoWest 92*
**LaGrega**, Michael Denny 1944- *AmMWSc 92*
**LaGrone**, Mark M. 1959- *WhoRel 92*
**Lagrotta**, Frank 1958- *WhoAmP 91*
**Lagu**, Joseph 1931- *IntWW 91*
**LaGuardia**, Fiorello 1882-1947 *FacFETw [port], RComAH*
**La Guardia**, Fiorello Henry 1882-1947 *AmPolLe, DcAmImH*
**Laguardia**, Louis Manuel 1948- *WhoHisp 92*
**LaGuerre**, Eduardo 1948- *WhoHisp 92*
**La Guerre**, Irma-Estel *WhoHisp 92*
**Laguerre**, Michel S. 1943- *WhoBlA 92*
**Lagueruela**, Earline 1952- *WhoHisp 92*
**Lagueux**, Ronald Rene 1931- *WhoAmL 92*
**La Guma**, Alex 1925-1985 *LiExTwC*
**Laguna**, Asela Rodriguez 1946- *WhoHisp 92*
**Laguna**, Frederica de 1906- *IntWW 91*
**Laguna**, Miguel A., Jr. 1935- *WhoHisp 92*
**Laguna**, Richard B. 1940- *WhoHisp 92*
**Lagunoff**, David 1932- *AmMWSc 92*
**Lagunowich**, Laura Andrews 1960- *AmMWSc 92*
**Laguros**, Joakim George 1924- *AmMWSc 92*
**Lagutin**, Boris Nikolaevich 1938- *SovUnBD*
**Laha**, Radha Govinda 1930- *AmMWSc 92, WhoMW 92*
**Laha**, Robert Randall, Jr. 1951- *WhoRel 92*
**LaHaie**, Ivan Joseph 1954- *AmMWSc 92*
**Laham**, Quentin Nadime 1927- *AmMWSc 92*
**Laham**, Souheil 1926- *AmMWSc 92*
**Lahana**, James Robert 1951- *WhoAmL 92*
**La Harpe**, Frederic-Cesar de 1754-1838 *BlkwCEP*
**LaHay**, David George Michael 1949- *WhoEnt 92*
**Lahey**, Christine *DrAPF 91*
**Lahey**, Edward Vincent, Jr. 1939- *WhoAmL 92, WhoFI 92*
**Lahey**, M Eugene 1917- *AmMWSc 92*
**Lahey**, Regis Henry 1948- *WhoFI 92*
**Lahey**, Richard Thomas, Jr 1939- *AmMWSc 92*
**Lahey**, Thomas Joseph, Jr. 1940- *WhoWest 92*
**Lahey**, Thomas Patrick 1919- *WhoMW 92*
**Lahiri**, Kajal 1947- *WhoFI 92*
**Lahiri**, Sukhamay 1933- *AmMWSc 92*
**Lahiri**, Syamal Kumar 1940- *AmMWSc 92*
**Lahita**, Robert George 1945- *AmMWSc 92*
**Lahm**, Diane Chesley 1942- *WhoAmL 92*
**Lahman**, Larry D 1943- *WhoAmP 91*
**Lahmers**, David Earl, Sr. 1950- *WhoMW 92*
**Lahn**, Jacquelyn Jo 1952- *WhoAmP 91*
**Lahners**, Ronald Dean 1933- *WhoAmL 92*
**Lahnstein**, Manfred 1937- *IntWW 91, Who 92*
**Lahontan**, Louis-Armand D'Arce, Baron de 1666-1713? *BenetAL 91*
**Lahontan**, Louis-Armand de Lom, baron de 1666-1715 *BlkwCEP*
**Lahood**, Marvin J 1933- *IntAu&W 91, WrDr 92*
**LaHood**, Ray H 1945- *WhoAmP 91*
**Lahoti**, Goverdhan Das 1948- *AmMWSc 92*
**Lahr**, Charles Dwight 1945- *AmMWSc 92, WhoBlA 92*
**Lahr**, Gilbert M 1922- *AmMWSc 92*
**Lahr**, Jack Leroy 1934- *WhoAmL 92*
**Lahr**, John *DrAPF 91*
**Lahr**, John 1941- *WrDr 92*
**Lahr**, John William 1950- *WhoMW 92*
**Lahr**, Michael Lincoln 1955- *WhoFI 92*
**Lahr**, Todd Harold 1960- *WhoAmL 92*
**Lahti**, Christine 1950- *IntMPA 92, WhoEnt 92*
**Lahti**, Leslie Erwin 1932- *AmMWSc 92*
**Lahti**, Richard 1943- *WhoAmP 91*
**Lahti**, Robert A *AmMWSc 92*
**Lahtinen**, Anni 1914- *IntAu&W 91*
**LaHurd**, Carol Joan 1946- *WhoRel 92*
**Lai Choi San** *EncAmaz 91*
**Lai Shaoqi** 1915- *IntWW 91*
**Lai**, Chii-Ming 1935- *AmMWSc 92*
**Lai**, Ching-San 1946- *AmMWSc 92*
**Lai**, Chintu 1930- *AmMWSc 92*
**Lai**, Chun-Yen *AmMWSc 92*
**Lai**, David Chin 1931- *AmMWSc 92*
**Lai**, David Ying-lun 1947- *AmMWSc 92*
**Lai**, Elaine Y 1949- *AmMWSc 92*
**Lai**, Fong M 1942- *AmMWSc 92*
**Lai**, Francis 1932- *IntMPA 92*
**Lai**, Jai-Lue 1940- *AmMWSc 92*
**Lai**, John Christopher 1953- *WhoRel 92*
**Lai**, Juey Hong 1936- *AmMWSc 92, WhoMW 92*
**Lai**, Kai Sun *AmMWSc 92*
**Lai**, Kuo-Yann 1946- *AmMWSc 92*
**Lai**, Michael Ming-Chiao 1942- *AmMWSc 92*
**Lai**, Patrick Kinglun 1944- *AmMWSc 92*
**Lai**, Por-Hsiung *AmMWSc 92*
**Lai**, Ralph Wei-Meen 1936- *AmMWSc 92*
**Lai**, San-Cheng 1940- *AmMWSc 92*
**Lai**, Shin-Tse Jason 1951- *WhoFI 92, WhoWest 92*
**Lai**, Shu Tim 1938- *AmMWSc 92*
**Lai**, Tze Leung 1945- *AmMWSc 92*
**Lai**, W Michael 1931- *AmMWSc 92*
**Lai**, Waihang 1939- *WhoWest 92*
**Lai**, Whalen Wai-Lun 1944- *WhoRel 92*
**Lai**, Ying-San 1937- *AmMWSc 92*
**Lai**, Yu-Chin 1949- *AmMWSc 92*
**Lai**, Yuan-Zong 1941- *AmMWSc 92*
**Lai-Fook**, Joan Elsa I-Ling 1937- *AmMWSc 92*
**Lai-Fook**, Stephen J 1940- *AmMWSc 92*
**Laible**, Jon Morse 1937- *AmMWSc 92, WhoMW 92*
**Laible**, Roy C 1924- *AmMWSc 92*
**Laibowitz**, Robert 1937- *AmMWSc 92*
**Laibson**, Peter R 1933- *AmMWSc 92*
**Laidi**, Ahmed 1934- *Who 92*
**Laidig**, Eldon Lindley 1932- *WhoWest 92*
**Laidig**, Gary Wayne 1948- *WhoAmP 91*
**Laidig**, William Rupert 1927- *IntWW 91*
**Laidlaw**, Brett *DrAPF 91*
**Laidlaw**, Christophor 1922- *Who 92*
**Laidlaw**, Christophor Charles Fraser 1922- *IntWW 91*
**Laidlaw**, Colleen L. 1948- *WhoRel 92*
**Laidlaw**, David Hales 1961- *WhoWest 92*
**Laidlaw**, Harriet Davenport Wright Burton 1873-1949 *AmPeW*
**Laidlaw**, Harry Hyde, Jr 1907- *AmMWSc 92, WhoWest 92*
**Laidlaw**, John Coleman 1921- *AmMWSc 92*
**Laidlaw**, Renton 1939- *Who 92*
**Laidlaw**, Robert Stewart 1936 *WhoFI 92*
**Laidlaw**, William George 1936- *AmMWSc 92*
**Laidlaw**, William Samuel Hugh 1956- *WhoFI 92*
**Laidler**, Keith James 1916- *AmMWSc 92, WrDr 92*
**Laight**, Barry Pemberton *Who 92*
**Laika** *FacFETw*
**Laiken**, Nora Dawn 1946- *AmMWSc 92*
**Lail**, Doris Leonhardt 1937- *WhoAmP 91*
**Laiman**, Leah 1946- *WhoEnt 92*
**Laimbeer**, William 1934- *WhoMW 92*
**Laine**, Burton Oscar 1954- *WhoMW 92*
**Laine**, Cleo 1927- *IntWW 91, NewAmDM, Who 92, WhoBlA 92, WhoEnt 92*
**Laine**, Frankie 1913- *NewAmDM*
**Laine**, James Alan 1947- *WhoRel 92*
**Laine**, Jermu Tapani 1931- *IntWW 91*
**Laine**, Maurice Dee, Jr. 1924- *WhoWest 92*
**Laine**, Pekka Ilmari 1937- *IntWW 91*
**Laine**, Richard Mason 1947- *AmMWSc 92*
**Laine**, Roger Allan 1941- *AmMWSc 92*
**Laing** *Who 92*
**Laing**, Alastair Stuart 1920- *Who 92*
**Laing**, Alexander 1903-1976 *BenetAL 91*
**Laing**, Austen 1923- *Who 92*
**Laing**, Charles Corbett 1925- *AmMWSc 92*
**Laing**, Dean Patrick 1956- *WhoAmL 92*
**Laing**, Edward A. 1942- *WhoBlA 92*
**Laing**, Fred, II 1951- *WhoFI 92*
**Laing**, Frederick M 1919- *AmMWSc 92*
**Laing**, Gerald O. *Who 92*
**Laing**, Gerald Ogilvie- 1936- *IntWW 91*
**Laing**, James Findlay 1933- *Who 92*
**Laing**, Jennifer 1947- *IntWW 91*
**Laing**, John Archibald 1919- *Who 92*
**Laing**, John E 1939- *AmMWSc 92*
**Laing**, John Martin 1942- *Who 92*
**Laing**, John Maurice 1918- *Who 92*
**Laing**, Kirby *Who 92*
**Laing**, Leslie 1925- *BlkOlyM*
**Laing**, Martin *Who 92*
**Laing**, Maurice *Who 92*
**Laing**, Maurice 1918- *IntWW 91*
**Laing**, Patrick Gowans 1923- *AmMWSc 92*
**Laing**, Peter Anthony Neville Pennethorne 1922- *Who 92*
**Laing**, R D 1927-1989 *ConAu 34NR, FacFETw*
**Laing**, R. Stanley 1918- *IntWW 91*
**Laing**, Ronald Albert 1933- *AmMWSc 92*
**Laing**, Scott 1914- *Who 92*
**Laing**, Stanley *IntWW 91*
**Laing**, William Kirby 1916- *Who 92*
**Laing Of Dunphail**, Baron 1923- *IntWW 91, Who 92*
**Lainson**, Ralph 1927- *IntWW 91, Who 92*
**Laiosa**, Mark 1952- *WhoEnt 92*
**Laipis**, Philip James 1944- *AmMWSc 92*
**Lair**, Alan Van 1948- *AmMWSc 92*
**Lair**, Helen Humphrey 1918- *IntAu&W 91*
**Lair**, Helen May 1918- *WhoMW 92*
**Lair**, Robert Ed, Jr. 1939- *WhoRel 92*
**Lair**, Robert Leland 1932- *WhoMW 92*
**Laird**, Campbell 1936- *AmMWSc 92*
**Laird**, Charles David 1939- *AmMWSc 92*
**Laird**, Charles F 1941- *WhoAmP 91*
**Laird**, Christopher Eli 1942- *AmMWSc 92*
**Laird**, Cleve Watrous 1938- *AmMWSc 92*
**Laird**, Donald Ray 1950- *WhoRel 92*
**Laird**, Donald T 1926- *AmMWSc 92*
**Laird**, Doris Anne Marley 1931- *WhoEnt 92*
**Laird**, Edgar Ord 1915- *Who 92*
**Laird**, Edward DeHart, Jr. 1952- *WhoAmL 92*
**Laird**, Endell Johnston *Who 92*
**Laird**, Evalyn Walsh 1902- *WhoAmL 92*
**Laird**, Frank N. 1952- *WhoWest 92*
**Laird**, Gavin Harry 1933- *IntWW 91, Who 92*
**Laird**, Hugh Edward, II 1939- *AmMWSc 92*
**Laird**, Jack *LesBEnT 92*
**Laird**, James Charles 1937- *WhoMW 92*
**Laird**, Jere Don 1933- *WhoWest 92*
**Laird**, John Robert 1909- *Who 92*
**Laird**, John Robert 1942- *WhoFI 92*
**Laird**, Margaret Heather 1933- *Who 92*
**Laird**, Mary *WhoFI 92, WhoWest 92*
**Laird**, Melvin R. 1922- *Who 92*
**Laird**, Melvin Robert 1922- *IntWW 91, WhoAmP 91*
**Laird**, Michael *Who 92*
**Laird**, Naomi Affholder *WhoAmP 91*
**Laird**, Pamela Sue 1955- *WhoWest 92*
**Laird**, Paul Craig 1923- *WhoAmP 91*
**Laird**, Richard Joel 1939- *WhoAmP 91*
**Laird**, Robin *Who 92*
**Laird**, Rolon Kent 1948- *WhoWest 92*
**Laird**, Wilson Morrow 1915- *AmMWSc 92*
**Laires**, Fernando 1925- *WhoEnt 92*
**Lairet**, Dolores Person 1935- *WhoBlA 92*
**Laise**, Carol d1991 *NewYTBS 91 [port]*
**Laister**, Peter 1929- *IntWW 91, Who 92, WhoEnt 92*
**Laisure**, Sharon Emily Goode 1954- *WhoBlA 92*
**Lait**, Hayden David 1947- *WhoAmL 92*
**Lait**, Leonard Hugh Cecil 1930- *Who 92*
**Lait**, Robert 1921- *IntAu&W 91, WrDr 92*
**Laithwaite**, Eric Roberts 1921- *IntWW 91, Who 92, WrDr 92*
**Laithwaite**, John 1920- *Who 92*
**Laitin**, Howard 1931- *AmMWSc 92, WhoWest 92*
**Laitin**, Joseph 1914- *WhoAmP 91*
**Laitinen**, Herbert August 1915- *AmMWSc 92*
**Laitner**, John Alan 1947- *WhoWest 92*
**Laity**, David Sanford 1926- *AmMWSc 92*
**Laity**, John Lawrence 1942- *AmMWSc 92*
**Laity**, Richard Warren 1928- *AmMWSc 92*
**Laiuppa**, Mark Anthony 1957- *WhoWest 92*
**Lajara**, Cecilio Nicolas 1942- *WhoRel 92*
**Lajeunesse**, Michael A 1944- *WhoAmP 91*

**Lajoie,** Keith Bernard 1952- *WhoFI 92*
**Lajoinie,** Andre 1929- *IntWW 91*
**Lajous Martinez,** Adrian 1920- *IntWW 91*
**Lajtai,** Emery Zoltan 1934- *AmMWSc 92*
**Lajtha,** Abel 1922- *AmMWSc 92*
**Lajtha,** Laszlo George 1920- *Who 92*
**Lakas Bahas,** Ing. Demetrio Basilio 1925- *IntWW 91*
**Lakatos,** Andras Imre 1937- *AmMWSc 92*
**Lakatos,** Susan Carol 1960- *WhoFI 92*
**Lakatta,** Edward G 1944- *AmMWSc 92*
**Lake,** Alfreeda Elizabeth 1923- *WhoBlA 92*
**Lake,** Ann W. *WhoAmL 92*
**Lake,** Carnell Augustino 1967- *WhoBlA 92*
**Lake,** Charles Aka Keljikian 1928- *WhoEnt 92*
**Lake,** Charles Raymond 1943- *AmMWSc 92*
**Lake,** Charles William, Jr. 1918- *WhoFI 92, WhoMW 92*
**Lake,** David 1929- *TwCSFW 91, WrDr 92*
**Lake,** David John 1929- *IntAu&W 91*
**Lake,** David S. 1938- *WhoFI 92*
**Lake,** Edward 1934- *WhoFI 92*
**Lake,** Edwin S *WhoAmP 91*
**Lake,** Finley Edward 1934- *WhoWest 92*
**Lake,** George Russell 1953- *AmMWSc 92*
**Lake,** Graham 1923- *Who 92*
**Lake,** Isaac Beverly, Jr 1934- *WhoAmP 91*
**Lake,** James Albert *AmMWSc 92*
**Lake,** James Howard 1937- *WhoAmP 91*
**Lake,** John Graham 1870-1935 *RelLAm 91*
**Lake,** Joseph Edward 1941- *WhoAmP 91*
**Lake,** Kevin Bruce 1937- *WhoWest 92*
**Lake,** Lorraine Frances 1918- *AmMWSc 92*
**Lake,** Oliver *DrAPF 91*
**Lake,** Paul *DrAPF 91*
**Lake,** Paul Martin 1939- *WhoAmL 92*
**Lake,** Randall 1947- *WhoWest 92*
**Lake,** Randall Todd 1953- *WhoMW 92*
**Lake,** Ricki 1968- *IntMPA 92*
**Lake,** Ricki 1969?- *ConTFT 9*
**Lake,** Robert D 1930- *AmMWSc 92*
**Lake,** Robin Benjamin 1938- *AmMWSc 92*
**Lake,** Simeon Timothy, III 1944- *WhoAmL 92*
**Lake,** Stanley James 1926- *WhoWest 92*
**Lake,** Suzanne Philena 1929- *WhoEnt 92*
**Lake,** Walter L 1921- *WhoAmP 91*
**Lake,** William 1936- *WhoFI 92*
**Lake,** William Eastman 1953- *WhoMW 92*
**Lakein,** Richard Bruce 1941- *AmMWSc 92*
**Lakeman,** Enid 1903- *IntAu&W 91, Who 92, WrDr 92*
**Laken,** B. *WrDr 92*
**Laker,** Benjamin d1701 *DcNCBi 4*
**Laker,** Edwin Francis 1910-1980 *FacFETw*
**Laker,** Freddie 1922- *Who 92*
**Laker,** Frederick Alfred 1922- *IntWW 91*
**Laker,** Rosalind *WrDr 92*
**Lakers,** Anna Marie 1961- *WhoRel 92*
**Lakes,** Gordon Harry 1928- *Who 92*
**Lakes,** Roderic Stephen 1948- *AmMWSc 92*
**Lakey,** John Richard Angwin 1929- *Who 92*
**Lakey,** Othal H. *WhoRel 92*
**Lakey,** William Hall 1927- *AmMWSc 92*
**Lakhdhir,** Linda Bradshaw 1959- *WhoAmL 92*
**Lakhtakia,** Akhlesh 1957- *AmMWSc 92*
**Lakin,** James D *AmMWSc 92*
**Lakin,** Michael 1934- *Who 92*
**Lakin,** R.D. *DrAPF 91*
**Lakin,** Robert French 1936- *WhoWest 92*
**Laking,** George 1912- *IntWW 91, Who 92*
**Lakkaraju,** H S 1946- *AmMWSc 92*
**Lako,** Charles Michael, Jr. 1947- *WhoAmL 92*
**Lakoff,** Evelyn 1932- *WhoWest 92*
**Lakoski,** Joan Marie 1953- *AmMWSc 92*
**Lakowicz,** Joseph Raymond 1948- *AmMWSc 92*
**Lakritz,** Isaac 1952- *WhoRel 92*
**Lakritz,** Julian 1930- *AmMWSc 92*
**Laks,** David Bejnesh 1962- *AmMWSc 92*
**Laks,** Peter Edward 1953- *AmMWSc 92*
**Lakshin,** Vladimir Yakovlevich 1933- *SovUnBD*
**Lakshman,** M Raj 1938- *AmMWSc 92*
**Lakshmanan,** P R 1939- *AmMWSc 92*
**Lakshmanan,** Vaikuntam Iyer 1940- *AmMWSc 92*
**Lakshmi Bai,** the Rani of Jhansi *EncAmaz 91*
**Lakshmi-Ratan,** Ramnath Ayyan 1953- *WhoFI 92*
**Lakshmikantham,** Vangipuram 1926- *AmMWSc 92*
**Lakshminarayan,** S 1943- *AmMWSc 92*
**Lakshminarayana,** B 1935- *AmMWSc 92*
**Lakshminarayana,** J S S 1931- *AmMWSc 92*
**Lakshminarayanan,** Krishnaiyer 1924- *AmMWSc 92*
**Lakso,** Alan Neil 1948- *AmMWSc 92*
**Laktionov,** Aleksandr Ivanovich 1910-1972 *SovUnBD*
**Lakwena,** Alice *EncAmaz 91*
**Lal,** Bansi 1927- *IntWW 91*
**Lal,** Bipen Behari 1917- *IntWW 91*
**Lal,** Devendra 1929- *AmMWSc 92, IntWW 91, Who 92*
**Lal,** Devi 1914- *IntWW 91*
**Lal,** Harbans *AmMWSc 92*
**Lal,** Joginder 1923- *AmMWSc 92*
**Lal,** Kasturi 1956- *WhoMW 92*
**Lal,** Manohar 1934- *AmMWSc 92*
**Lal,** Mohan 1932- *AmMWSc 92*
**Lal,** P 1929- *IntAu&W 91*
**Lal,** Rattan 1944- *AmMWSc 92*
**Lal,** Ravindra Behari 1935- *AmMWSc 92*
**Lal,** Samarthji 1938- *AmMWSc 92*
**Lala,** Peeyush Kanti 1934- *AmMWSc 92*
**Lala,** Tapan Kanti *WhoWest 92*
**Lalancette,** Jean-Marc 1934- *AmMWSc 92*
**Lalancette,** Roger A 1939- *AmMWSc 92*
**Lalande,** Joseph-Jerome Lefrancais de 1732-1807 *BlkwCEP*
**Lalande,** Michel-Richard de 1657-1726 *NewAmDM*
**Lalandi-Emery,** Lina *Who 92*
**Lalandi-Emery,** Lina Madeleine *WhoEnt 92*
**Lalanne,** Bernard Michel L. *Who 92*
**LaLanne,** Jack *LesBEnT 92*
**Lalas,** Demetrius P 1942- *AmMWSc 92*
**Lalbhai,** Arvind N. 1918- *IntWW 91*
**Lalchandani,** Atam Prakash 1943- *AmMWSc 92*
**LaLeune,** Michael 1957- *WhoEnt 92*
**Lalezari,** Parviz 1931- *AmMWSc 92*
**La Liberte,** Ann Gillis 1942- *WhoEnt 92*
**Laliberte,** Garland E 1936- *AmMWSc 92*
**Laliberte,** Laurent Hector 1943- *AmMWSc 92*
**Lalich,** Joseph John 1909- *AmMWSc 92*
**Laliker,** Richard Henry 1945- *WhoFI 92*
**Lalique,** Rene 1860-1945 *DcTwDes, FacFETw*
**Lalive d'Epinay,** Jean-Flavien 1915- *IntWW 91*
**Lalive d'Epinay,** Pierre 1923- *IntWW 91*
**Lalka,** Judith Candelor 1947- *WhoAmL 92*
**Lall,** Abner Bishamber 1933- *AmMWSc 92*
**Lall,** Arthur Samuel 1911- *IntWW 91*
**Lall,** B Kent 1939- *AmMWSc 92*
**Lall,** Prithvi C 1931- *AmMWSc 92*
**Lall,** Santosh Prakash 1944- *AmMWSc 92*
**Lalla Aicha,** Princess *IntWW 91*
**Lallance,** Leroy Odom 1954- *WhoRel 92*
**Lallement,** Jacques Georges Paulin 1922- *IntWW 91*
**Lalley,** Peter Michael 1940- *AmMWSc 92*
**Lalli,** Carol Marie 1938- *AmMWSc 92*
**Lalli,** Michael Anthony 1955- *WhoAmL 92*
**Lallier,** Erna L. 1946- *WhoFI 92*
**Lallo,** M.J. *DrAPF 91*
**Lally,** Ann Marie 1914- *WhoMW 92*
**Lally,** Daniel Joseph 1963- *WhoMW 92*
**Lally,** Donald J, Jr *WhoAmP 91*
**Lally,** Douglas Robert 1962- *WhoFI 92*
**Lally,** Margaret *DrAPF 91*
**Lally,** Michael *DrAPF 91*
**Lally,** Michael David 1942- *WhoEnt 92*
**Lally,** Philip M 1925- *AmMWSc 92*
**Lally,** Thomas James 1964- *WhoFI 92*
**Lally,** Vincent Edward 1922- *AmMWSc 92*
**Lally,** William Joseph 1937- *WhoFI 92*
**Lally-Green,** Maureen Ellen 1949- *WhoAmL 92*
**Lalo,** Edouard 1823-1892 *NewAmDM*
**Lalo,** Pierre 1866-1943 *NewAmDM*
**Lalonde,** Brice *IntWW 91*
**Lalonde,** John Stephen, Sr. 1948- *WhoFI 92, WhoMW 92*
**LaLonde,** Leo Francis 1942- *WhoAmP 91*
**Lalonde,** Leo R *WhoAmP 91*
**Lalonde,** Marc 1929- *IntWW 91, Who 92*
**Lalonde,** Raymond 1940- *WhoAmP 91*
**LaLonde,** Robert Frederick 1922- *WhoAmP 91*
**LaLonde,** Robert Thomas 1931- *AmMWSc 92*
**Lalor,** Owen Patrick 1952- *WhoAmL 92*
**Lalor,** Patrick Joseph 1926- *IntWW 91*
**Lalor,** William Francis 1935- *AmMWSc 92*
**Lalouette,** Marie Joseph Gerard 1912- *Who 92*
**Laloy,** Jean Leonard 1912- *IntWW 91*
**La Lumia,** Frank Munzueto 1948- *WhoWest 92*
**Lalumiere,** Catherine 1935- *Who 92*
**Lalumiere,** Catherine 1936- *IntWW 91*
**La Luz,** Jose A. 1950- *WhoHisp 92*
**Lam,** Bernard Mingwai 1955- *WhoAmL 92*
**Lam,** Billy 1960- *WhoFI 92*
**Lam,** Chan F 1943- *AmMWSc 92*
**Lam,** Chow Shing 1947- *WhoMW 92*
**Lam,** Daniel J 1930- *AmMWSc 92*
**Lam,** Donald Paul 1952- *WhoFI 92*
**Lam,** Fuk Luen 1937- *AmMWSc 92*
**Lam,** Gabriel Kit Ying 1947- *AmMWSc 92*
**Lam,** Gerald N.Y.C. 1951- *WhoWest 92*
**Lam,** Gilbert Nim-Car 1951- *AmMWSc 92*
**Lam,** Harry Chi-Sing 1936- *AmMWSc 92*
**Lam,** John Ling-Yee 1940- *AmMWSc 92*
**Lam,** Judy 1965- *WhoWest 92*
**Lam,** Kai Shue 1949- *AmMWSc 92*
**Lam,** Kin Leung *AmMWSc 92*
**Lam,** Kui Chuen 1943- *AmMWSc 92*
**Lam,** Kwok-Wai 1935- *AmMWSc 92*
**Lam,** Leo Kongsui 1946- *AmMWSc 92*
**Lam,** Lui 1944- *WhoWest 92*
**Lam,** Martin Philip 1920- *Who 92*
**Lam,** Nghi Quoc 1945- *AmMWSc 92*
**Lam,** Nora 1932- *WhoRel 92*
**Lam,** Sau-Hai 1930- *AmMWSc 92*
**Lam,** Sheung Tsing 1934- *AmMWSc 92*
**Lam,** Stanley K *AmMWSc 92*
**Lam,** Tenny N 1940- *AmMWSc 92*
**Lam,** Truong Buu 1933- *IntAu&W 91, WrDr 92*
**Lam,** Tsit-Yuen 1942- *AmMWSc 92*
**Lam,** Vinh-Te 1939- *AmMWSc 92*
**Lam,** Yiu-Kuen Tony 1947- *AmMWSc 92*
**Lama,** Luciano 1921- *IntWW 91*
**LaMacchia,** John Thomas 1941- *WhoFI 92*
**Lamachia,** Joseph James 1946- *WhoEnt 92*
**Lamadrid,** Enrique R. 1948- *WhoHisp 92*
**Lamagra,** Anthony James 1935- *WhoEnt 92*
**La Maina,** Francis C. *WhoEnt 92*
**LaMalfa,** Joachim Jack 1915- *WhoMW 92*
**Lamalie,** Robert Eugene 1931- *WhoFI 92*
**Lamancusa,** Frank Guy 1963- *WhoAmL 92*
**LaMancuso,** John Lory 1954- *WhoAmL 92*
**LaManna,** Joseph Charles 1949- *AmMWSc 92*
**LaManna,** Ross James 1955- *WhoEnt 92*
**La Mantia,** Charles R 1939- *AmMWSc 92*
**LaMantia,** Charles Robert 1939- *WhoFI 92*
**Lamantia,** Philip 1927- *ConPo 91, IntAu&W 91, WrDr 92*
**Lamar,** Charles Wilbur, III 1948- *WhoAmL 92*
**Lamar,** Cleveland James 1924- *WhoBlA 92*
**LaMar,** David M 1918- *WhoAmP 91*
**Lamar,** Donald Frederick 1949- *WhoMW 92*
**La Mar,** Gerd Neustadter 1937- *AmMWSc 92*
**Lamar,** Howard Roberts 1923- *WrDr 92*
**Lamar,** Joseph R 1857-1916 *FacFETw*
**Lamar,** Mario Anselmo 1946- *WhoHisp 92*
**Lamar,** Mirabeau Buonaparte 1798-1859 *BenetAL 91*
**Lamar,** Ralph David 1936- *WhoAmL 92*
**Lamar,** Thomas Allen, Jr. 1936- *WhoAmL 92*
**Lamar,** William, Jr. 1952- *WhoBlA 92*
**Lamar,** William Fred 1934- *WhoRel 92*
**Lamar y Cortazar,** Jose Benigno de 1776-1830 *HisDSpE*
**LaMarca,** Anthony 1944- *WhoMW 92*
**La Marca,** Donald J. P. 1939- *WhoFI 92*
**LaMarca,** George Anthony 1945- *WhoAmL 92*
**LaMarca,** Michael James 1931- *AmMWSc 92*
**LaMarca,** Priscilla Frances 1941- *WhoEnt 92*
**Lamarche,** Francois 1960- *AmMWSc 92*
**Lamarche,** J L Gilles 1927- *AmMWSc 92*
**LaMarche,** Paul H 1929- *AmMWSc 92*
**LaMarche,** Paul Henry, Jr 1953- *AmMWSc 92*
**Lamarck,** Jean-Baptiste-Pierre-Antoine de 1744-1829 *BlkwCEP*
**LaMarr,** Catherine Elizabeth 1960- *WhoBlA 92*
**Lamarr,** Hedy 1915- *IntMPA 92*
**LaMarsh,** Jeanenne Marie 1943- *WhoMW 92*
**LaMarsh,** Pamela Sue 1946- *WhoMW 92*
**Lamartine,** Alphonse de Prat de 1790-1869 *GuFrLit 1*
**Lamas,** Jose Francisco 1940- *WhoHisp 92*
**Lamas,** Lorenzo 1958- *IntMPA 92, WhoEnt 92, WhoHisp 92*
**LaMaster,** Franklin Thomas 1955- *WhoRel 92*
**LaMaster,** Slater 1890- *ScFEYrs*
**LaMastro,** Robert Anthony 1956- *AmMWSc 92*
**LaMattina,** John Lawrence 1950- *AmMWSc 92*
**Lamaute,** Denise 1952- *WhoBlA 92*
**LaMay,** Joseph Charles 1947- *WhoEnt 92*
**LaMay,** Roger C. 1953- *WhoEnt 92*
**Lamaze,** George Paul 1945- *AmMWSc 92*
**Lamb** *Who 92*
**Lamb,** Albert *Who 92*
**Lamb,** Albert Thomas 1921- *Who 92*
**Lamb,** Angela K 1944- *WhoAmP 91*
**Lamb,** Archie C., Jr. 1955- *WhoAmL 92*
**Lamb,** Berton Lee, II 1945- *WhoWest 92*
**Lamb,** Charles 1775-1834 *CnDBLB 3 [port], DcLB 107 [port], RfGEnL 91*
**Lamb,** Charles F. 1934- *WhoRel 92*
**Lamb,** Charlotte *WrDr 92*
**Lamb,** Dana S. 1900-1986 *ConAu 134*
**Lamb,** Darlis Carol *WhoWest 92*
**Lamb,** David E 1932- *AmMWSc 92*
**Lamb,** Denis 1937- *IntWW 91*
**Lamb,** Dennis 1941- *AmMWSc 92*
**Lamb,** Donald E *WhoAmP 91*
**Lamb,** Donald Joseph 1931- *AmMWSc 92*
**Lamb,** Donald Quincy, Jr 1945- *AmMWSc 92*
**Lamb,** Donald R 1923- *AmMWSc 92*
**Lamb,** Edward 1902- *WhoAmP 91*
**Lamb,** Elizabeth Searle *DrAPF 91*
**Lamb,** Elizabeth Searle 1917- *IntAu&W 91, WrDr 92*
**Lamb,** F. Bruce 1913- *WrDr 92*
**Lamb,** Frank Bruce 1913- *WhoWest 92*
**Lamb,** Frederick Keithley 1945- *AmMWSc 92*
**Lamb,** Geoffrey Frederick *IntAu&W 91, WrDr 92*
**Lamb,** George Alexander 1934- *AmMWSc 92*
**Lamb,** George Colin 1923- *Who 92*
**Lamb,** George Lawrence, Jr 1931- *AmMWSc 92*
**Lamb,** George Marion 1928- *AmMWSc 92*
**Lamb,** George Robert 1922- *WhoFI 92*
**Lamb,** Gideon 1741-1781 *DcNCBi 4*
**Lamb,** Gordon Howard 1934- *WhoMW 92*
**Lamb,** H Richard 1929- *AmMWSc 92*
**Lamb,** Harold 1892-1962 *BenetAL 91*
**Lamb,** Harold Norman 1922- *Who 92*
**Lamb,** Harry Lee, Jr. 1947- *WhoAmL 92*
**Lamb,** Henry 1883-1960 *TwCPaSc*
**Lamb,** Howard Allen 1924- *WhoAmP 91*
**Lamb,** Hubert Horace 1913- *IntAu&W 91, WrDr 92*
**Lamb,** Isabelle Smith 1922- *WhoFI 92*
**Lamb,** J. Kevin 1956- *WhoEnt 92*
**Lamb,** J Parker, Jr 1933- *AmMWSc 92*
**Lamb,** James Allen 1941- *WhoWest 92*
**Lamb,** James B. 1919- *ConAu 133*
**Lamb,** James Bernard, Jr. 1943- *WhoWest 92*
**Lamb,** James C, III 1924- *AmMWSc 92*
**Lamb,** James Francis 1937- *AmMWSc 92*
**Lamb,** James L 1924- *WhoAmP 91*
**Lamb,** James L 1925- *AmMWSc 92*
**Lamb,** Joan Eugenia 1939- *WhoAmP 91*
**Lamb,** John 1922- *Who 92*
**Lamb,** John Calhoun 1836-1864 *DcNCBi 4*
**Lamb,** Joseph F. 1877-1960 *NewAmDM*
**Lamb,** Joseph Fairweather 1928- *Who 92*
**Lamb,** Karl A. 1933- *WrDr 92*
**Lamb,** Kenneth Henry Lowry 1923- *Who 92*
**Lamb,** Kenton Leroy 1941- *WhoMW 92*
**Lamb,** Kevin Thomas 1956- *WhoAmL 92*
**Lamb,** Larry 1929- *IntAu&W 91, Who 92*
**Lamb,** Lester Lewis 1932- *WhoFI 92*
**Lamb,** Lionel 1900- *Who 92*
**Lamb,** Lynton 1907-1977 *TwCPaSc*
**Lamb,** Michael Edward 1963- *WhoAmP 91*
**Lamb,** Michael K. 1958- *WhoRel 92*
**Lamb,** Mildred Shimonishi 1913- *WhoWest 92*
**Lamb,** Mina Marie Wolf 1910- *AmMWSc 92*
**Lamb,** Neven P 1932- *AmMWSc 92*
**Lamb,** Norman 1935- *WhoAmP 91*
**Lamb,** Patricia Clare *DrAPF 91*
**Lamb,** Patricia Frazer 1931- *IntAu&W 91*
**Lamb,** Patrick John 1938- *WhoFI 92*
**Lamb,** Patrick John 1957- *WhoAmL 92*
**Lamb,** Peter Winston 1946- *WhoEnt 92*
**Lamb,** Richard C 1933- *AmMWSc 92*
**Lamb,** Robert 1941- *ConAu 35NR*
**Lamb,** Robert Andrew 1950- *AmMWSc 92*
**Lamb,** Robert Cardon 1933- *AmMWSc 92*
**Lamb,** Robert Charles 1928- *AmMWSc 92*
**Lamb,** Robert Consay 1919- *AmMWSc 92*
**Lamb,** Robert E 1936- *WhoAmP 91*
**Lamb,** Robert Edward 1945- *AmMWSc 92*
**Lamb,** Robert Lee 1930- *WhoRel 92*
**Lamb,** Robert Michael 1952- *WhoAmL 92*
**Lamb,** Sandra Ina 1931- *AmMWSc 92*
**Lamb,** Tera A. 1943- *WhoRel 92, WhoWest 92*
**Lamb,** Thomas A 1927- *WhoAmP 91*
**Lamb,** Thomas B. 1897-1988 *DcTwDes*
**Lamb,** Walter Robert 1922- *AmMWSc 92*
**Lamb,** William 1835-1909 *DcNCBi 4*
**Lamb,** William Bolitho 1937- *AmMWSc 92*
**Lamb,** William John 1906- *Who 92*
**Lamb,** William Joseph 1929- *WhoEnt 92*
**Lamb,** Willis E., Jr. 1913- *Who 92*

**Lamb**, Willis Eugene, Jr 1913- *AmMWSc 92, IntWW 91, WhoNob 90, WhoWest 92*
**Lamb**, Wilson Gray, Jr. 1842-1922 *DcNCBi 4*
**Lamb-Brassington**, Kathryn Evelyn 1935- *WhoWest 92*
**Lamb-Hart**, Pamela Nyle 1961- *WhoRel 92*
**Lamba**, Ram Sarup 1941- *AmMWSc 92*
**Lamba**, Surendar Singh 1934- *AmMWSc 92*
**Lambach**, Walther 1885-1943 *EncTR 91*
**Lambart** *Who 92*
**Lambarth**, David Arnold 1940- *WhoFI 92*
**Lambdin**, Paris Lee 1941- *AmMWSc 92*
**Lambe**, Edward Dixon 1924- *AmMWSc 92*
**Lambe**, John Joseph 1926- *AmMWSc 92*
**Lambe**, Robert Carl 1927- *AmMWSc 92*
**Lambe**, T William 1920- *AmMWSc 92*
**Lambe**, Thomas Anthony 1930- *AmMWSc 92*
**Lambeck**, Kurt 1941- *IntWW 91*
**Lambek**, Joachim 1922- *AmMWSc 92*
**Lamberg**, Stanley Lawrence 1933- *AmMWSc 92*
**Lamberson**, C. Allen 1932- *WhoMW 92*
**Lamberson**, Harold Vincent, Jr 1945- *AmMWSc 92*
**Lamberson**, John Roger 1933- *WhoFI 92*
**Lamberson**, Leonard Roy 1937- *AmMWSc 92*
**Lambert** *Who 92*
**Lambert**, Viscount 1912- *Who 92*
**Lambert**, Alan L 1943- *AmMWSc 92*
**Lambert**, Alison 1957- *TwCPaSc*
**Lambert**, Anthony 1911- *Who 92*
**Lambert**, Benjamin Franklin 1933- *WhoBlA 92*
**Lambert**, Benjamin J., III 1937- *WhoBlA 92*
**Lambert**, Benjamin Joseph, III 1937- *WhoAmP 91*
**Lambert**, Bertus Loren 1937- *WhoWest 92*
**Lambert**, Brian Kerry 1941- *AmMWSc 92*
**Lambert**, Bruce Alan 1953- *WhoMW 92*
**Lambert**, Catholina 1834-1923 *DcAmImH*
**Lambert**, Charles Calvin 1935- *AmMWSc 92*
**Lambert**, Charles H. 1948- *WhoBlA 92*
**Lambert**, Charles Thomas 1946- *WhoMW 92*
**Lambert**, Christopher 1958- *IntMPA 92*
**Lambert**, Constant 1905-1951 *NewAmDM*
**Lambert**, Dale John 1946- *WhoAmP 91*
**Lambert**, Darwin 1916- *WrDr 92*
**Lambert**, David A 1954- *WhoAmP 91*
**Lambert**, David Alan 1954- *WhoMW 92*
**Lambert**, David Arthur Charles 1933- *Who 92*
**Lambert**, David Martin 1956- *WhoFI 92*
**Lambert**, Dennis Edson 1941- *WhoAmP 91*
**Lambert**, Derek 1929- *IntAu&W 91, WrDr 92*
**Lambert**, Diane *AmMWSc 92*
**Lambert**, Donald Avery 1932- *WhoMW 92*
**Lambert**, Edward 1901- *Who 92*
**Lambert**, Edward Howard 1915- *AmMWSc 92*
**Lambert**, Edward M, Jr 1958- *WhoAmP 91*
**Lambert**, Elisabeth *ConAu 35NR*
**Lambert**, Eric Thomas Drummond 1909- *Who 92*
**Lambert**, Eugene Isaak 1935- *WhoAmL 92*
**Lambert**, Francis Lincoln 1923- *AmMWSc 92*
**Lambert**, Frank Lewis 1918- *AmMWSc 92*
**Lambert**, Gavin 1924- *IntAu&W 91, WrDr 92*
**Lambert**, George 1923- *AmMWSc 92*
**Lambert**, George Robert 1933- *WhoAmL 92*
**Lambert**, Glenn Frederick 1918- *AmMWSc 92*
**Lambert**, Harold George 1910- *Who 92*
**Lambert**, Helen Haynes 1939- *AmMWSc 92*
**Lambert**, Henry Uvedale Antrobus 1925- *IntWW 91, Who 92*
**Lambert**, Herbert Ted 1938- *WhoAmP 91*
**Lambert**, Howard W 1937- *AmMWSc 92*
**Lambert**, Jack Leeper 1918- *AmMWSc 92*
**Lambert**, James LeBeau 1934- *AmMWSc 92*
**Lambert**, James Morrison 1928- *AmMWSc 92*
**Lambert**, Jane E. 1950- *WhoEnt 92*
**Lambert**, Janet Snyder 1894-1973 *BenetAL 91*
**Lambert**, Jean Denise 1950- *Who 92*
**Lambert**, Jean William 1914- *AmMWSc 92*
**Lambert**, Jeanette H. 1949- *WhoBlA 92*
**Lambert**, Jeremiah Daniel 1934- *WhoFI 92*
**Lambert**, Jerline 1938- *WhoMW 92*
**Lambert**, Jerry D. *WhoRel 92*
**Lambert**, Jerry Roy 1936- *AmMWSc 92*
**Lambert**, Joan 1946- *WhoAmP 91*
**Lambert**, Johann Heinrich 1728-1777 *BlkwCEP*
**Lambert**, John 1921- *Who 92*
**Lambert**, John B 1929- *AmMWSc 92*
**Lambert**, John Boyd 1929- *WhoMW 92*
**Lambert**, John Paul 1906- *WhoRel 92*
**Lambert**, John Paul 1964- *WhoWest 92*
**Lambert**, John Sinclair 1948- *Who 92*
**Lambert**, John T, Jr 1955- *WhoAmP 91*
**Lambert**, Joseph B 1940- *AmMWSc 92*
**Lambert**, Joseph Buckley 1940- *WhoMW 92*
**Lambert**, Joseph C. 1936- *WhoBlA 92*
**Lambert**, Joseph E 1948- *WhoAmP 91*
**Lambert**, Joseph Earl 1948- *WhoAmL 92*
**Lambert**, Joseph Michael 1942- *AmMWSc 92*
**Lambert**, Joseph Parker 1921- *AmMWSc 92*
**Lambert**, Judith A. Ungar 1943- *WhoAmL 92*
**Lambert**, Keith Harwood 1914- *WhoAmP 91*
**Lambert**, L. Gary 1937- *WhoWest 92*
**Lambert**, Lawrence Arthur 1921- *WhoAmP 91*
**Lambert**, LeClair Grier *WhoBlA 92, WhoMW 92*
**Lambert**, Leonard W. 1938- *WhoBlA 92*
**Lambert**, Lisa Gaye 1955- *WhoWest 92*
**Lambert**, Lloyd Laverne 1925- *WhoRel 92*
**Lambert**, Lloyd Milton, Jr 1929- *AmMWSc 92*
**Lambert**, Lloyd Tupper 1901- *WhoFI 92*
**Lambert**, Lorene Cook 1950- *WhoEnt 92*
**Lambert**, Lyn Dee 1954- *WhoAmL 92*
**Lambert**, Margaret 1906- *Who 92*
**Lambert**, Margaret Kidd 1940- *WhoAmP 91*
**Lambert**, Martha Lowery 1937- *WhoAmP 91*
**Lambert**, Mary *IntMPA 92*
**Lambert**, Mary Pulliam 1944- *AmMWSc 92*
**Lambert**, Maurice 1901-1964 *TwCPaSc*
**Lambert**, Maurice C 1918- *AmMWSc 92*
**Lambert**, Olaf Francis 1925- *Who 92*
**Lambert**, Pamela Susann 1945- *WhoMW 92*
**Lambert**, Patricia 1926- *Who 92*
**Lambert**, Paul C 1928- *WhoAmP 91*
**Lambert**, Paul Richard 1952- *WhoAmP 91*
**Lambert**, Paul Wayne 1937- *AmMWSc 92*
**Lambert**, Peter John Biddulph 1952- *Who 92*
**Lambert**, Phillip J. 1940- *WhoRel 92*
**Lambert**, Randall L. 1948- *WhoFI 92*
**Lambert**, Raymond Edward 1945- *WhoAmP 91*
**Lambert**, Reginald Max 1926- *AmMWSc 92*
**Lambert**, Richard Bowles, Jr 1939- *AmMWSc 92*
**Lambert**, Richard Peter 1944- *Who 92*
**Lambert**, Richard St John 1928- *AmMWSc 92*
**Lambert**, Richard William 1928- *WhoWest 92*
**Lambert**, Robert Daniel 1952- *WhoRel 92*
**Lambert**, Robert F 1924- *AmMWSc 92*
**Lambert**, Robert Gilbert 1930- *WhoFI 92*
**Lambert**, Robert Henry 1930- *AmMWSc 92*
**Lambert**, Robert J 1921- *AmMWSc 92*
**Lambert**, Robert John 1927- *AmMWSc 92*
**Lambert**, Roger Gayle 1930- *AmMWSc 92*
**Lambert**, Rogers Franklin 1929- *AmMWSc 92*
**Lambert**, Rollins Edward 1922- *WhoBlA 92*
**Lambert**, Ronald 1939- *AmMWSc 92*
**Lambert**, Royce Leone 1933- *AmMWSc 92*
**Lambert**, Samuel Fredrick 1928- *WhoBlA 92*
**Lambert**, Samuel M. d1991 *NewYTBS 91 [port]*
**Lambert**, Shirley Joan 1934- *WhoMW 92*
**Lambert**, Steven Charles 1947- *WhoAmL 92*
**Lambert**, T.J. 1951- *WhoWest 92*
**Lambert**, Thomas Howard 1926- *Who 92*
**Lambert**, Verity *IntMPA 92*
**Lambert**, Verity Ann *Who 92*
**Lambert**, Victor Roy 1955- *WhoMW 92*
**Lambert**, Walter Paul 1944- *AmMWSc 92*
**Lambert**, Wilfred Lee 1926- *WhoBlA 92*
**Lambert**, William M, Jr 1936- *AmMWSc 92*
**Lambert**, Yves Maurice 1936- *IntWW 91*
**Lamberth**, Royce C. 1943- *WhoAmL 92*
**Lamberti**, Joseph W 1929- *AmMWSc 92*
**Lamberti**, Michael Joseph 1958- *WhoWest 92*
**Lamberti**, Ralph James 1934- *WhoAmP 91*
**Lamberti**, Rose 1944- *WhoMW 92*
**Lamberton**, Donald McLean 1927- *WrDr 92*
**Lamberton**, William John 1948- *WhoAmP 91*
**Lamberts**, Austin E 1914- *AmMWSc 92*
**Lamberts**, Burton Lee 1919- *AmMWSc 92*
**Lamberts**, Robert L 1926- *AmMWSc 92*
**Lambertsen**, Christian James 1917- *AmMWSc 92*
**Lambertsen**, Eleanor C *AmMWSc 92*
**Lambertsen**, Richard H 1953- *AmMWSc 92*
**Lambertson**, Glen Royal 1926- *AmMWSc 92*
**Lambertson**, Milton David 1940- *WhoRel 92*
**Lamberty**, Patricia Ann 1942- *WhoAmP 91*
**Lambeth**, Archdeacon of *Who 92*
**Lambeth**, David N 1947- *AmMWSc 92*
**Lambeth**, David Odus 1941- *AmMWSc 92*
**Lambeth**, James Erwin 1916- *WhoAmP 91*
**Lambeth**, John Walter, Jr. 1896-1961 *DcNCBi 4*
**Lambeth**, John Walter, Sr. 1868-1934 *DcNCBi 4*
**Lambeth**, Thomas Willis 1935- *WhoAmP 91*
**Lambeth**, Victor Neal 1920- *AmMWSc 92*
**Lambie**, David 1925- *Who 92*
**Lambie-Nairn**, Martin John 1945- *Who 92*
**Lambin**, Henry Joseph 1921- *WhoMW 92*
**Lambing**, Peggy Ann 1953- *WhoMW 92*
**Lambird**, Perry Albert 1939- *AmMWSc 92, WhoAmP 91*
**Lambo**, Adeoye 1923- *IntWW 91*
**Lambo**, Thomas Adeoye 1923- *Who 92*
**Lamboll**, Alan Seymour 1923- *Who 92*
**Lambooy**, John Peter 1914- *AmMWSc 92*
**Lamborn**, Bjorn N A 1937- *AmMWSc 92*
**Lamborn**, LeRoy Leslie 1937- *WhoAmL 92, WhoMW 92*
**Lambot**, Isobel Mary 1926- *IntAu&W 91, WrDr 92*
**Lambourn**, George 1900-1977 *TwCPaSc*
**Lambrakis**, Christos 1934- *IntWW 91*
**Lambrakis**, Konstantine Christos 1936- *AmMWSc 92*
**Lambrecht**, Carol Ann 1958- *WhoMW 92*
**Lambrecht**, John William 1944- *WhoMW 92*
**Lambrecht**, Richard Merle 1943- *AmMWSc 92*
**Lambremont**, Edward Nelson 1928- *AmMWSc 92*
**Lambrinos**, Jorge J. 1944- *WhoHisp 92*
**Lambro**, Edward *WhoRel 92*
**Lambro**, Phillip 1935- *WhoEnt 92*
**Lambropoulos**, Peter Poulos 1935- *AmMWSc 92*
**Lambros**, Thomas Demetrios 1930- *WhoAmL 92*
**Lambrun**, Margaret *EncAmaz 91*
**Lambsdorff**, Otto Friedrich Wilhelm 1926- *IntWW 91*
**Lambson**, Roger O 1939- *AmMWSc 92*
**Lambton** *Who 92*
**Lambton**, Viscount 1922- *Who 92*
**Lambton**, Ann Katharine Swynford 1912- *Who 92*
**Lambton**, Anne *DrAPF 91*
**Lambton**, Antony 1922- *WrDr 92*
**Lamburn**, Patricia *Who 92*
**Lambuth**, Alan Letcher 1923- *AmMWSc 92*
**Lamby**, Werner 1924- *IntWW 91*
**Lamden**, Merton Philip 1919- *AmMWSc 92*
**Lamdin**, Ezra 1923- *AmMWSc 92*
**Lame**, Edwin Lever 1904- *AmMWSc 92*
**Lameier**, Jack 1942- *WhoEnt 92*
**Lameiro**, Gerard Francis 1949- *AmMWSc 92, WhoFI 92, WhoWest 92*
**Lamel**, Linda H 1943- *WhoIns 92*
**Lamelas**, Francisco Javier 1959- *AmMWSc 92*
**LaMell**, Philip Alan 1946- *WhoWest 92*
**Lamennais**, Hugues-Felicite Robert de 1782-1854 *GuFrLit 1*
**Lamensdorf**, David 1937- *AmMWSc 92*
**Lamer**, Antonio 1933- *Who 92*
**Lamere**, Denis Clifford 1949- *WhoWest 92*
**La Mers**, Thomas Herbert 1945- *AmMWSc 92*
**Lamerton**, Leonard Frederick 1915- *Who 92*
**La Mettrie**, Julien Offray de 1709-1751 *BlkwCEP*
**Lamey**, Howard Arthur 1929- *AmMWSc 92*
**Lamey**, Steven Charles 1944- *AmMWSc 92*
**Lamford**, Gerald 1928- *Who 92*
**Lamia**, Thomas Roger 1938- *WhoAmL 92*
**Lamie**, Edward Louis 1941- *AmMWSc 92*
**Laming**, Herbert 1936- *Who 92*
**Lamirande**, Emilien 1926- *WrDr 92*
**Lamizana**, Aboubakar Sangoule 1916- *IntWW 91*
**Lamjav**, Banzraghiin 1920- *IntWW 91*
**Lamkin**, Martha Dampf 1942- *WhoAmL 92*
**Lamkin**, Michael Deane 1945- *WhoEnt 92*
**Lamm**, A Uno 1904- *AmMWSc 92*
**Lamm**, Carolyn Beth 1948- *WhoAmL 92*
**Lamm**, Donald Stephen 1931- *IntWW 91*
**Lamm**, Foster Philip 1950- *AmMWSc 92*
**Lamm**, Michael Emanuel 1934- *AmMWSc 92*
**Lamm**, Norman 1927- *WhoRel 92*
**Lamm**, Richard D. 1935- *IntWW 91, WhoAmP 91*
**Lamm**, Richard Douglas 1935- *WhoWest 92*
**Lamm**, Warren Dennis 1947- *AmMWSc 92, WhoWest 92*
**Lamme**, Dennis Wayne 1955- *WhoWest 92*
**Lammers**, Ann Conrad 1945- *WhoRel 92, WhoWest 92*
**Lammers**, Duane A. 1961- *WhoEnt 92*
**Lammers**, Hans-Heinrich 1879-1962 *BiDExR, EncTR 91 [port]*
**Lammers**, Jerome Bryce 1937- *WhoAmP 91*
**Lammers**, Lennis Larry 1937- *WhoFI 92*
**Lammers**, Mark Edward 1931- *WhoEnt 92*
**Lammers**, Wim 1947- *AmMWSc 92*
**Lammert**, Thomas Edward 1947- *WhoAmL 92*
**Lammi-Keefe**, Carol J 1947- *AmMWSc 92*
**Lammie**, Patrick J *AmMWSc 92*
**Lammiman**, David Askey 1932- *Who 92*
**Lamming**, George *DrAPF 91*
**Lamming**, George 1927- *BenetAL 91, BlkLC [port], ConLC 66 [port], ConNov 91, LiExTwC, RfGEnL 91, WrDr 92*
**Lamneck**, David Arthur 1952- *WhoIns 92*
**Lamo deEspinosa Y Michels deChampourcin** 1941- *IntWW 91*
**LaMois**, Loyd *WhoRel 92*
**Lamola**, Angelo Anthony 1940- *AmMWSc 92*
**LaMon**, April Yvonnie 1961- *WhoHisp 92*
**Lamon**, Duncan d1798? *DcNCBi 4*
**Lamon**, Eddie William 1939- *AmMWSc 92*
**Lamon**, Harry Vincent, Jr. 1932- *WhoAmL 92, WhoFI 92*
**Lamon**, Jeanne 1949- *WhoEnt 92*
**Lamon**, Ward Hill 1828-1893 *BenetAL 91*
**Lamona**, Thomas Adrian 1925- *WhoFI 92*
**LaMonaca**, Joseph Salvador 1918- *WhoAmP 91*
**Lamond**, James Alexander 1928- *Who 92*
**Lamonde**, Andre M 1936- *AmMWSc 92*
**LaMondia**, James A 1957- *AmMWSc 92*
**Lamonica**, John 1954- *WhoWest 92*
**Lamonica**, Paul Raymond 1944- *WhoAmL 92*
**Lamonica**, Roberto De 1933- *IntWW 91*
**LaMonica**, William Joseph 1939- *WhoFI 92*
**LaMont**, Andre 1957- *WhoEnt 92*
**Lamont**, Archibald *ScFEYrs*
**Lamont**, Barbara 1939- *WhoBlA 92, WhoEnt 92*
**Lamont**, Corliss 1902- *RelLAm 91, WrDr 92*
**Lamont**, Deni d1991 *NewYTBS 91*
**Lamont**, Donal 1911- *IntWW 91*
**Lamont**, Donald Alexander 1947- *Who 92*
**Lamont**, Frances Stiles 1914- *WhoAmP 91*
**Lamont**, Gary Byron 1939- *AmMWSc 92*
**Lamont**, Gene 1946- *WhoMW 92*
**Lamont**, Jack T. 1957- *WhoRel 92*
**Lamont**, John Thomas 1938- *AmMWSc 92*
**Lamont**, John W 1942- *AmMWSc 92*
**Lamont**, Norman Stewart Hughson 1942- *IntWW 91, Who 92*
**Lamont**, Owen Austin 1966- *WhoFI 92*
**Lamont**, Patrick 1936- *AmMWSc 92*
**Lamont**, Patrick J. C. 1936- *WhoMW 92*
**LaMont**, Samuel 1936- *WhoMW 92*
**Lamont**, Susan Joy 1953- *AmMWSc 92*
**La Mont**, Tawana Faye 1948- *WhoFI 92*
**Lamont**, Thomas William 1870-1948 *AmPeW*
**Lamont-Brown**, Raymond 1939- *IntAu&W 91, WrDr 92*
**Lamontagne**, Gilles 1919- *Who 92*
**La Montagne**, John Ring 1943- *AmMWSc 92*
**La Montaine**, John 1920- *NewAmDM*
**LaMora**, Judy Lynne 1939- *WhoAmP 91*
**LaMore**, George Edward, Jr. 1930- *WhoRel 92*
**LaMoreaux**, David Albert 1924- *WhoMW 92*
**Lamoreaux**, Joyce 1938- *WhoWest 92*
**LaMoreaux**, Philip Elmer 1920- *AmMWSc 92*
**Lamorena**, Alberto Cristobal, III 1949- *WhoAmP 91*
**Lamorte**, Michael Francis 1926- *AmMWSc 92*
**Lamos**, Mark 1946- *ConTFT 9*
**Lamothe**, Irene Elise 1949- *WhoEnt 92*

**Lamothe,** Isidore J., Jr. 1924- *WhoBlA 92*
**Lamothe,** William E. 1926- *IntWW 91*
**LaMothe,** William Edward 1926- *WhoFI 92, WhoMW 92*
**LaMott,** Paul I 1917- *WhoAmP 91*
**LaMotte,** Carole Choate 1947- *AmMWSc 92*
**LaMotte,** Clifford Elton 1930- *AmMWSc 92*
**La Motte,** Ellen Newbold 1873-1961 *AmPeW*
**LaMotte,** Jean Moore 1938- *WhoBlA 92*
**LaMotte,** Lawrence Alan 1949- *WhoAmP 91*
**LaMotte,** Louis Cossitt, Jr 1928- *AmMWSc 92*
**Lamotte,** Robert Hill 1940- *AmMWSc 92*
**LaMotte,** William Mitchell 1938- *WhoFI 92, WhoMW 92*
**LaMountain,** Joseph R 1941- *WhoAmP 91*
**Lamour,** Dorothy *ConAu 134*
**Lamour,** Dorothy 1914- *IntMPA 92*
**L'Amour,** Louis 1908-1988 *BenetAL 91, FacFETw, TwCWW 91*
**Lamour,** Philippe 1903- *IntWW 91*
**Lamoureux,** Charles 1834-1899 *NewAmDM*
**Lamoureux,** Charles Harrington 1933- *AmMWSc 92*
**Lamoureux,** Gerald Lee 1939- *AmMWSc 92*
**Lamoureux,** Gilles 1934- *AmMWSc 92*
**Lamoureux,** Kimberly Ann 1963- *WhoMW 92*
**Lamoureux,** Paul Emile 1946- *WhoAmL 92*
**Lamoyi,** Edmundo 1952- *AmMWSc 92*
**Lamp,** George Emmett, Jr 1933- *AmMWSc 92*
**Lamp,** Herbert F 1919- *AmMWSc 92*
**Lamp,** John Ernest 1943- *WhoAmL 92*
**Lamp,** William Owen 1951- *AmMWSc 92*
**Lampard,** Martin Robert 1926- *Who 92*
**Lampart,** Abe 1953- *WhoFI 92*
**Lampart,** Hans Helmut 1957- *WhoWest 92*
**Lampathakis,** James Dean 1961- *WhoAmL 92*
**Lampe,** Agnes Laura 1899- *WhoEnt 92*
**Lampe,** Frederick Walter 1927- *AmMWSc 92*
**Lampe,** Henry Oscar 1927- *WhoAmP 91, WhoFI 92*
**Lampe,** Kenneth Francis 1928- *AmMWSc 92*
**Lampe,** Martin 1942- *AmMWSc 92*
**Lampedo** *EncAmaz 91*
**Lampedusa,** Giuseppi Tomasi Di 1896-1957 *FacFETw*
**Lampel,** Ronald B. 1943- *WhoFI 92*
**Lampell,** Millard 1919- *BenetAL 91, WhoEnt 92*
**Lampen,** J Oliver 1918- *AmMWSc 92*
**Lampen,** Richard Jay 1953- *WhoAmL 92*
**Lamper,** Mark Eliot 1950- *WhoEnt 92*
**Lampert,** Carl 1894-1944 *EncTR 91*
**Lampert,** Carl Matthew 1952- *AmMWSc 92*
**Lampert,** Catherine Emily 1946- *Who 92*
**Lampert,** Eleanor Verna *WhoFI 92*
**Lampert,** James B. 1938- *WhoAmL 92*
**Lampert,** Joseph A 1941- *WhoIns 92*
**Lampert,** Leonard Franklin 1919- *WhoMW 92*
**Lampert,** Michael A. 1951- *WhoAmL 92*
**Lampert,** Michael Allen 1958- *WhoAmL 92*
**Lampert,** Richard Harvey 1947- *WhoFI 92*
**Lampert,** Seymour 1920- *AmMWSc 92*
**Lampert,** Zohra 1937- *WhoEnt 92*
**Lamperti,** Albert A 1947- *AmMWSc 92*
**Lamperti,** John Williams 1932- *AmMWSc 92*
**Lampi,** Rauno Andrew 1929- *AmMWSc 92*
**Lamping,** William Jay 1954- *WhoAmL 92*
**Lampkin,** Al 1938- *WhoEnt 92*
**Lampkin,** Cheryl Lyvette 1961- *WhoBlA 92*
**Lampkin,** Daisy 1888-1965 *NotBlAW 92 [port]*
**Lampkin,** Ralph, Jr. 1957- *WhoEnt 92*
**Lampky,** James Robert 1927- *AmMWSc 92*
**Lampl,** Frank 1926- *Who 92*
**Lampley,** Calvin D. *WhoBlA 92*
**Lampley,** Edward Charles 1931- *WhoBlA 92*
**Lampley,** Handy Ellis 1949- *WhoBlA 92*
**Lampley,** Norma Mosley *WhoWest 92*
**Lampley,** Paul Clarence 1945- *WhoBlA 92*
**Lamplugh,** Lois 1921- *WrDr 92*
**Lamplugh,** Lois Violet 1921- *IntAu&W 91*
**Lampman,** Archibald 1861-1899 *BenetAL 91, RfGEnL 91*
**Lampman,** Gary Marshall 1937- *AmMWSc 92*
**Lamport,** Bernard d1991 *NewYTBS 91 [port]*
**Lamport,** Derek Thomas Anthony 1933- *AmMWSc 92*
**Lamport,** Leslie B 1941- *AmMWSc 92*
**Lamppa,** Gayle K *AmMWSc 92*
**Lamppa,** William R 1928- *IntAu&W 91, WrDr 92*
**Lampreia,** Jose d1991 *NewYTBS 91*
**Lamprey,** George S *WhoAmP 91*
**Lamprey,** Louise 1869-1951 *BenetAL 91*
**Lampson** *Who 92*
**Lampson,** Butler Wright 1943- *AmMWSc 92*
**Lampson,** Francis Keith 1924- *AmMWSc 92, WhoWest 92*
**Lampson,** George Peter 1919- *AmMWSc 92*
**Lampson,** Lois Alterman *AmMWSc 92*
**Lamptey,** Jonathan Charles 1950- *WhoMW 92*
**Lampton,** Christopher *SmATA 67*
**Lampton,** Michael Logan 1941- *AmMWSc 92*
**Lampton,** Nancy 1942- *WhoIns 92*
**Lamrani,** Mohammed Karim *IntWW 91*
**Lamsa,** George Mamishisho 1890-1975 *RelLAm 91*
**Lamson,** David Hinkley 1939- *WhoAmL 92*
**Lamson,** Evonne Viola 1946- *WhoFI 92*
**Lamster,** Hal B 1941- *AmMWSc 92*
**Lamster,** Ira Barry 1950- *AmMWSc 92*
**Lamun,** JoAnne 1939- *WhoEnt 92*
**LaMuth,** Henry Lewis 1942- *AmMWSc 92*
**Lamy,** Daryl John 1957- *WhoFI 92*
**Lamy,** Peter Paul 1925- *AmMWSc 92*
**Lamy,** Pierre 1855-1919 *ThHEIm*
**Lan,** Chuan-Tau Edward 1935- *AmMWSc 92*
**Lan,** David 1952- *WrDr 92*
**Lan,** David Mark 1952- *IntAu&W 91*
**Lan,** Donald Paul 1930- *WhoAmP 91*
**Lan,** Jyh-Yee 1956- *WhoMW 92*
**Lan,** Ming-Jye 1953- *AmMWSc 92*
**Lan,** Ming-Shong 1953- *WhoWest 92*
**Lan,** Shih-Jung 1938- *AmMWSc 92*
**Lana,** Edward Peter 1914- *AmMWSc 92*
**Lanam,** Linda L 1948- *WhoIns 92*
**Lanam,** Linda Lee 1948- *WhoAmL 92*
**Lanam,** Richard Delbert, Jr 1943- *AmMWSc 92*
**Lanc,** Erwin 1930- *IntWW 91*
**Lancaster,** Archdeacon of *Who 92*
**Lancaster,** Bishop of 1929- *Who 92*
**Lancaster,** Bishop Suffragan of 1943- *Who 92*
**Lancaster,** Barbara Anne 1947- *WhoEnt 92*
**Lancaster,** Barbara Mae 1930- *WhoFI 92*
**Lancaster,** Bill 1931- *WhoAmP 91*
**Lancaster,** Billy Douglas 1933- *WhoAmP 91*
**Lancaster,** Bruce 1896-1963 *BenetAL 91*
**Lancaster,** Burt 1913- *FacFETw, IntMPA 92*
**Lancaster,** Burt Stephen 1913- *IntWW 91*
**Lancaster,** Burton 1913- *WhoEnt 92*
**Lancaster,** Charles Doerr, Jr 1943- *WhoAmP 91*
**Lancaster,** Cleo 1948- *AmMWSc 92*
**Lancaster,** George Maurice 1934- *AmMWSc 92*
**Lancaster,** H. Martin 1943- *AlmAP 92 [port], WhoAmP 91*
**Lancaster,** Henry Oliver 1913- *IntWW 91, WrDr 92*
**Lancaster,** Herman Burtram 1942- *WhoBlA 92*
**Lancaster,** Jack R, Jr 1948- *AmMWSc 92*
**Lancaster,** James D 1919- *AmMWSc 92*
**Lancaster,** James Wayne, Jr. 1959- *WhoRel 92*
**Lancaster,** Jean 1909- *Who 92*
**Lancaster,** Jessie Leonard, Jr 1923- *AmMWSc 92*
**Lancaster,** Joan Cadogan *Who 92*
**Lancaster,** John 1903- *Who 92*
**Lancaster,** John 1937- *AmMWSc 92*
**Lancaster,** John Graham 1918- *WhoBlA 92*
**Lancaster,** Kathryn McLeod 1962- *WhoAmL 92*
**Lancaster,** Kelvin John 1924- *WhoFI 92*
**Lancaster,** Linda Rae 1949- *WhoFI 92*
**Lancaster,** Malcolm 1931- *AmMWSc 92*
**Lancaster,** Mark 1938- *IntWW 91, TwCPaSc*
**Lancaster,** Mark Alan 1953- *WhoRel 92*
**Lancaster,** Otis Ewing 1909- *AmMWSc 92*
**Lancaster,** Patricia Margaret 1929- *Who 92*
**Lancaster,** Ralph Ivan, Jr. 1930- *WhoAmL 92*
**Lancaster,** Rita Funderburk 1943- *WhoAmP 91*
**Lancaster,** Robert Samuel 1909- *WhoAmL 92*
**Lancaster,** Sheila *WrDr 92*
**Lancaster-Brown,** Peter 1927- *IntAu&W 91, WrDr 92*
**Lancaster Lewis,** Joan Cadogan 1918- *Who 92*
**Lance,** Alan G 1949- *WhoAmP 91*
**Lance,** Alan George 1949- *WhoAmL 92*
**Lance,** Betty Rita Gomez *DrAPF 91*
**Lance,** Eugene Mitchell 1933- *AmMWSc 92*
**Lance,** George M 1928- *AmMWSc 92*
**Lance,** James Waldo 1926- *IntWW 91, WrDr 92*
**Lance,** Jeanne *DrAPF 91*
**Lance,** John Du Boulay d1991 *Who 92N*
**Lance,** John Franklin 1916- *AmMWSc 92*
**Lance,** Larry K 1941- *WhoIns 92*
**Lance,** Leonard *WhoAmP 91*
**Lance,** Leslie *ConAu 34NR*
**Lance,** R H 1931- *AmMWSc 92*
**Lance,** Thomas Bertram 1931- *WhoAmP 91*
**Lance,** Valentine A 1940- *AmMWSc 92*
**Lance,** Wesley L 1908- *WhoAmP 91*
**Lancellotta,** John J 1953- *WhoAmP 91*
**Lancelot,** James Bennett 1952- *Who 92*
**Lanceray,** Yevgeniy Yevgen'evich 1878-1946 *SovUnBD*
**Lancet,** Michael Savage 1944- *AmMWSc 92*
**Lanchantin,** Gerard Francis 1929- *AmMWSc 92*
**Lanchbery,** John Arthur 1923- *IntWW 91, Who 92*
**Lanchester,** Edith 1871-1966 *BiDBrF 2*
**Lanchester,** Elsa 1902-1986 *ConAu 134, FacFETw*
**Lanchin,** Gerald 1922- *Who 92*
**Lancia,** Frederick Nicholas, II 1960- *WhoMW 92*
**Lanciani,** Carmine Andrew 1941- *AmMWSc 92*
**Lancione,** A G 1907- *WhoAmP 91*
**Lancione,** Bernard Gabe 1939- *WhoAmL 92, WhoAmP 91, WhoMW 92*
**Lancione,** Nelson 1921- *WhoAmP 91*
**Lancit,** Laurence Alan 1947- *WhoEnt 92*
**Lanckton,** Arthur Van Cleve 1942- *WhoAmL 92*
**Lancman,** Henry 1932- *AmMWSc 92*
**Lanctot,** Thomas Edward 1954- *WhoAmL 92*
**Land** *ConAu 134*
**Land,** Allan H. 1922- *WhoFI 92*
**Land,** Cecil E 1926- *AmMWSc 92*
**Land,** Charles Even 1937- *AmMWSc 92*
**Land,** Chester LaSalle 1938- *WhoBlA 92*
**Land,** David J 1939- *AmMWSc 92*
**Land,** Edward Wolff 1956- *WhoEnt 92*
**Land,** Edwin H. 1901-1991 *CurBio 91N*
**Land,** Edwin H 1909-1991 *FacFETw, NewYTBS 91 [port], News 91, -91-3*
**Land,** Edwin Herbert d1991 *IntWW 91N, Who 92N*
**Land,** Edwin Herbert 1909- *AmMWSc 92*
**Land,** Geoffrey Allison 1942- *AmMWSc 92*
**Land,** Georgianna Anderson 1940- *WhoBlA 92*
**Land,** Gillian *Who 92*
**Land,** Jane *WrDr 92*
**Land,** John Calhoun, III 1941- *WhoAmP 91*
**Land,** Judith Broten 1951- *WhoFI 92*
**Land,** Kenneth Dean 1931- *WhoWest 92*
**Land,** Lynton S 1940- *AmMWSc 92*
**Land,** Michael Francis 1942- *IntWW 91, Who 92*
**Land,** Ming Huey 1940- *AmMWSc 92*
**Land,** Peter Ashburner 1936- *WhoFI 92*
**Land,** Peter L 1929- *AmMWSc 92*
**Land,** Richard Dale 1946- *WhoRel 92*
**Land,** Richard Robert 1949- *WhoFI 92*
**Land,** Robert H 1924- *AmMWSc 92*
**Land,** Steven Jack 1946- *WhoRel 92*
**Land,** Stuart Jay 1930- *WhoAmL 92*
**Land,** Susan *DrAPF 91*
**Land,** Ted J 1936- *WhoAmP 91*
**Land,** Thornton Reddoch 1941- *WhoIns 92*
**Land,** Victoria Louise 1960- *WhoMW 92*
**Land,** William Everett 1908- *AmMWSc 92*
**Landa,** Abram 1902- *Who 92*
**Landa,** Alfonso Beaumont, II 1961- *WhoFI 92*
**Landa,** Diego de 1524-1579 *HisDSpE*
**Landa,** Lynda *Who 92*
**Landahl,** Herbert Daniel 1913- *AmMWSc 92*
**Landais,** Hubert Leon 1921- *IntWW 91*
**Landale,** Nancy Crosta 1962- *WhoAmL 92*
**Landar,** Herbert Jay 1927- *WhoWest 92*
**Landas Berghes,** Rudolph Francis E. de 1873-1920 *RelLAm 91*
**Landau,** Annette Henkin *DrAPF 91*
**Landau,** Barbara Ruth 1923- *AmMWSc 92*
**Landau,** Bernard Robert 1926- *AmMWSc 92*
**Landau,** Burton Joseph 1933- *AmMWSc 92*
**Landau,** David Paul 1941- *AmMWSc 92*
**Landau,** Dennis 1927- *Who 92*
**Landau,** Edward Frederick 1916- *AmMWSc 92*
**Landau,** Edythe *WhoEnt 92*
**Landau,** Ely *LesBEnT 92*
**Landau,** Ely 1920- *WhoEnt 92*
**Landau,** Ely A. 1920- *IntMPA 92*
**Landau,** Emanuel 1919- *AmMWSc 92*
**Landau,** Felix 1947- *WhoAmL 92*
**Landau,** George W 1920- *WhoAmP 91*
**Landau,** Jean-Pierre 1946- *IntWW 91*
**Landau,** Joseph Victor 1928- *AmMWSc 92*
**Landau,** Joseph White 1930- *AmMWSc 92*
**Landau,** Kenneth Wayne 1954- *WhoWest 92*
**Landau,** Lauri Beth 1952- *WhoFI 92*
**Landau,** Lev Davidovich 1908-1968 *WhoNob 90*
**Landau,** Martin 1931- *IntMPA 92*
**Landau,** Martin 1934- *WhoEnt 92*
**Landau,** Mason Stephen 1948- *WhoMW 92*
**Landau,** Matthew Paul 1949- *AmMWSc 92*
**Landau,** Michael Bruce 1953- *WhoAmL 92, WhoEnt 92*
**Landau,** Michael Roy 1946- *WhoFI 92*
**Landau,** Moshe 1912- *IntWW 91*
**Landau,** Peter 1935- *IntWW 91*
**Landau,** Peter Edward 1933- *WhoFI 92*
**Landau,** Ralph 1916- *AmMWSc 92*
**Landau,** Richard H. 1914- *IntMPA 92*
**Landau,** Richard Louis 1916- *AmMWSc 92*
**Landau,** Russ Mitchell 1954- *WhoEnt 92*
**Landau,** Saul 1936- *WhoEnt 92*
**Landau,** Shelly 1956- *WhoEnt 92*
**Landau,** Siegfried 1921- *WhoEnt 92*
**Landau,** Walter Loeber 1931- *WhoAmL 92*
**Landau,** William 1927- *AmMWSc 92*
**Landau,** William M 1924- *AmMWSc 92*
**Landauer,** Michael Robert 1946- *AmMWSc 92*
**Landauer,** Rolf William 1927- *AmMWSc 92*
**Landauro,** Sergio Antonio 1953- *WhoHisp 92*
**Landavazo,** George *WhoHisp 92*
**Landaw,** Stephen Arthur 1936- *AmMWSc 92*
**Landay,** Alan Lee 1955- *AmMWSc 92*
**Landay,** Andrew Herbert 1920- *WhoAmL 92*
**Landazuri Ricketts,** Juan 1913- *IntWW 91, WhoRel 92*
**Landberg,** Gail Louise 1945- *WhoMW 92*
**Landblom,** James Rodney 1945- *WhoMW 92*
**Landborg,** Richard John 1933- *AmMWSc 92*
**Lande,** Alexander 1936- *AmMWSc 92*
**Lande,** C Charles 1940- *WhoAmP 91*
**Lande,** David S 1944- *WhoAmP 91*
**Lande,** Gail Ruth 1962- *WhoAmL 92*
**Lande,** Kenneth 1932- *AmMWSc 92*
**Lande,** Lawrence Montague 1906- *WrDr 92*
**Lande,** Russell Scott 1951- *AmMWSc 92*
**Lande,** Saul 1930- *AmMWSc 92*
**Lande,** Sheldon Sidney 1941- *AmMWSc 92*
**Landecker,** David John 1951- *WhoWest 92*
**Landecker,** Peter Bruce 1942- *AmMWSc 92*
**Landefeld,** Charles Willis 1923- *WhoAmL 92*
**Landefeld,** Edward Kent 1933- *WhoIns 92*
**Landefeld,** Thomas Dale 1947- *AmMWSc 92, WhoMW 92*
**Landegger,** Carl Clement 1930- *WhoFI 92*
**Landeira,** Ricardo 1944- *WhoHisp 92*
**Landel,** Robert Franklin 1925- *AmMWSc 92*
**Landels,** William 1928- *Who 92*
**Landen,** Dinsdale 1932- *Who 92*
**Landen,** William Ross 1956- *WhoWest 92*
**Lander,** Arthur Douglas 1958- *AmMWSc 92*
**Lander,** Cresswoth Caleb 1925- *WhoBlA 92*
**Lander,** Ernest McPherson, Jr. 1915- *WrDr 92*
**Lander,** Horace N 1923- *AmMWSc 92*
**Lander,** Howard 1950- *WhoEnt 92*
**Lander,** Jack Robert 1921- *WrDr 92*
**Lander,** James French 1931- *AmMWSc 92*
**Lander,** Philip Howard 1941- *AmMWSc 92*
**Lander,** Richard Leon 1928- *AmMWSc 92*
**Lander,** Samuel 1833-1904 *DcNCBi 4*
**Lander,** William 1817-1868 *DcNCBi 4*
**Landerl,** Harold Paul 1922- *AmMWSc 92*
**Landeros,** Robert 1951- *WhoHisp 92*
**Landers,** Ann 1918- *WhoMW 92*
**Landers,** Audrey *WhoEnt 92*
**Landers,** Charles Thomas 1927- *WhoEnt 92*
**Landers,** David Scott 1962- *WhoAmL 92*

**Landers,** Derrick 1963- *WhoFI 92*
**Landers,** Earl James 1921- *AmMWSc 92*
**Landers,** H Lacy 1927- *WhoAmP 91*
**Landers,** Hal 1928- *IntMPA 92*
**Landers,** Harry 1921- *ConTFT 9*
**Landers,** James Walter 1927- *AmMWSc 92*
**Landers,** John Herbert, Jr 1921- *AmMWSc 92*
**Landers,** Kenneth Earl 1933- *AmMWSc 92*
**Landers,** Milton Harold 1950- *WhoMW 92*
**Landers,** Naaman Garnett 1938- *WhoBlA 92*
**Landers,** Patrick F, III 1959- *WhoAmP 91*
**Landers,** Renee Marie 1955- *WhoAmL 92*
**Landers,** Roger Q, Jr 1932- *AmMWSc 92*
**Landers,** Vernette Trosper 1912- *WhoWest 92*
**Landers,** William Lytle 1926- *WhoAmP 91*
**Landersman,** Stuart David 1930- *WhoWest 92*
**Landert,** Walter 1929- *IntAu&W 91*
**Landes,** Alan Hall 1951- *WhoRel 92*
**Landes,** Barbara Levy *WhoEnt 92*
**Landes,** Chester Grey 1903- *AmMWSc 92*
**Landes,** David S. 1924- *IntWW 91*
**Landes,** George Miller 1928- *WhoRel 92*
**Landes,** Hugh S 1924- *AmMWSc 92*
**Landes,** John D 1942- *AmMWSc 92*
**Landes,** Leo Julius 1924- *WhoRel 92*
**Landes,** Michael 1939- *IntMPA 92*
**Landes,** Morris Alex 1917- *WhoRel 92*
**Landes,** Robert Nathan 1930- *WhoAmL 92*
**Landes,** Ruth d1991 *NewYTBS 91*
**Landes,** Ruth 1908-1991 *ConAu 133*
**Landes,** William-Alan 1945- *WhoEnt 92*
**Landes,** William M. 1939- *WhoAmL 92, WhoFI 92*
**Landes-Fuss,** Marie-Gisele 1936- *IntAu&W 91*
**Landesberg,** Joseph Marvin 1939- *AmMWSc 92*
**Landesberg,** Steve *WhoEnt 92*
**Landesman,** Edward Milton 1938- *AmMWSc 92*
**Landesman,** Heidi *ConTFT 9*
**Landesman,** Herbert 1927- *AmMWSc 92*
**Landesman,** Jay 1919- *IntAu&W 91*
**Landesman,** Richard 1940- *AmMWSc 92*
**Landesman,** Toby Ann 1949- *WhoMW 92*
**Landfield,** Richard 1941- *WhoAmL 92*
**Landgarten,** Helen Barbara 1921- *WhoWest 92*
**Landgraf,** John Ralph 1937- *WhoRel 92*
**Landgraf,** Ronald William 1939- *AmMWSc 92*
**Landgraf,** Susan *DrAPF 91*
**Landgraf,** Vernon H 1924- *WhoAmP 91*
**Landgraf,** William Charles 1928- *AmMWSc 92*
**Landgrebe,** Albert R 1933- *AmMWSc 92*
**Landgrebe,** David Allen 1934- *AmMWSc 92*
**Landgrebe,** John A 1937- *AmMWSc 92*
**Landgren,** Craig Randall 1947- *AmMWSc 92*
**Landgren,** John Jeffrey 1947- *AmMWSc 92*
**Landholm,** Wallace Marven 1933- *WhoWest 92*
**Landi,** Stefano 1586-1639 *NewAmDM*
**Landin,** David Craig 1946- *WhoAmL 92*
**Landin,** Felix, Jr. 1941- *WhoHisp 92*
**Landing,** Benjamin Harrison 1920- *AmMWSc 92, WhoWest 92*
**Landini,** Francesco 1325?-1397 *NewAmDM*
**Landini,** Richard George 1929- *WhoMW 92*
**Landis,** Abraham L 1928- *AmMWSc 92*
**Landis,** Arthur Melvin 1944- *AmMWSc 92*
**Landis,** Brent William 1947- *WhoMW 92*
**Landis,** Bruce Chapman 1945- *WhoMW 92*
**Landis,** David M 1948- *WhoAmP 91*
**Landis,** David Morrison 1948- *WhoMW 92*
**Landis,** Dennis Michael Doyle 1945- *AmMWSc 92*
**Landis,** E K 1930- *AmMWSc 92*
**Landis,** Edgar David 1932- *WhoFI 92*
**Landis,** Edward Everett 1907- *AmMWSc 92*
**Landis,** Ellen Jamie 1941- *WhoWest 92*
**Landis,** Fred 1923- *AmMWSc 92*
**Landis,** Fred Simon 1943- *WhoWest 92*
**Landis,** George Harvey 1918- *WhoMW 92*
**Landis,** Harvey B 1953- *WhoAmP 91*
**Landis,** Homer Warren 1924- *WhoRel 92*
**Landis,** J. D. 1942- *WrDr 92*
**Landis,** James David 1942- *IntAu&W 91, WhoRel 92*
**Landis,** James Noble 1899- *AmMWSc 92*
**Landis,** John 1950- *IntDcF 2-2, IntMPA 92*
**Landis,** John David 1950- *WhoEnt 92*
**Landis,** John W 1917- *AmMWSc 92*
**Landis,** Kenesaw Mountain 1866-1944 *FacFETw*
**Landis,** Kenneth K *WhoAmP 91*
**Landis,** M. Scott 1955- *WhoRel 92*
**Landis,** Paul Groff 1932- *WhoRel 92*
**Landis,** Phillip Sherwood 1922- *AmMWSc 92*
**Landis,** Phyllis 1937- *WhoEnt 92*
**Landis,** Richard Gordon 1920- *WhoWest 92*
**Landis,** Robert Kumler, III 1953- *WhoFI 92*
**Landis,** Simon Mohler *ScFEYrs*
**Landis,** Story Cleland 1945- *AmMWSc 92*
**Landis,** Tomi Bednar 1959- *WhoEnt 92*
**Landis,** Vincent J 1928- *AmMWSc 92*
**Landis,** Wayne G 1952- *AmMWSc 92*
**Landiss,** Daniel Jay 1943- *AmMWSc 92*
**Landivar,** Rafael 1731-1793 *HisDSpE*
**Landle,** Jeff Charles 1957- *WhoFI 92*
**Landman,** Alfred 1933- *AmMWSc 92*
**Landman,** Donald Alan 1938- *AmMWSc 92*
**Landman,** Margaret 1953- *WhoFI 92*
**Landman,** Otto Ernest 1925- *AmMWSc 92*
**Landman,** Sylvia Ann 1938- *WhoWest 92*
**Landmann,** Wendell August 1919- *AmMWSc 92*
**Landmesser,** Harold Leon 1917- *WhoMW 92*
**Landmesser,** Lynn Therese 1943- *AmMWSc 92*
**Lando,** Barbara Ann 1940- *AmMWSc 92*
**Lando,** Jerome B 1932- *AmMWSc 92*
**Landolfi,** Nicholas F 1955- *AmMWSc 92*
**Landolfi,** Nicholas Francis 1955- *WhoWest 92*
**Landoll,** Leo Michael 1950- *AmMWSc 92*
**Landolph,** Joseph Richard, II 1948- *AmMWSc 92*
**Landolt,** Arlo Udell 1935- *AmMWSc 92*
**Landolt,** Jack Peter 1934- *AmMWSc 92*
**Landolt,** Marsha LaMerle 1948- *AmMWSc 92*
**Landolt,** Paul Albert 1912- *AmMWSc 92, WhoMW 92*
**Landolt,** Robert George 1939- *AmMWSc 92*
**Landolt,** Robert Raymond 1937- *AmMWSc 92*
**Landon,** Alf 1887-1987 *FacFETw [port]*
**Landon,** Alfred Mossman 1887-1987 *AmPolLe*
**Landon,** David H 1953- *WhoAmP 91*
**Landon,** David Neil 1936- *Who 92*
**Landon,** Erwin Jacob 1925- *AmMWSc 92*
**Landon,** H C Robbins 1926- *ConAu 34NR, IntAu&W 91, WrDr 92*
**Landon,** Herman A 1882-1960 *ScFEYrs*
**Landon,** Howard Chandler Robbins 1926- *IntWW 91, Who 92*
**Landon,** James Henry 1945- *WhoAmL 92*
**Landon,** John Campbell 1937- *AmMWSc 92, WhoFI 92*
**Landon,** John William 1937- *WhoRel 92*
**Landon,** Lucinda 1950- *WrDr 92*
**Landon,** Marshall Scott 1951- *WhoAmP 91*
**Landon,** Melville De Lancy 1839-1910 *BenetAL 91*
**Landon,** Michael d1991 *LesBEnT 92 [port]*
**Landon,** Michael 1936-1991 *CurBio 91N, NewYTBS 91 [port], News 92-1*
**Landon,** Robert Donald Wike, II 1940- *WhoAmL 92*
**Landon,** Robert E 1905- *AmMWSc 92*
**Landon,** Robert Gray 1928- *WhoMW 92*
**Landon,** Robert Kirkwood 1929- *WhoFI 92, WhoIns 92*
**Landon,** Sharon Rose 1965- *WhoMW 92*
**Landon,** Shayne J 1954- *AmMWSc 92*
**Landone,** Brown 1847-1945 *RelLAm 91*
**Landor,** John Henry 1927- *AmMWSc 92*
**Landor,** Walter Savage 1775-1864 *DcLB 107 [port], RfGEnL 91*
**Landovsky,** John 1935- *WhoEnt 92, WhoWest 92*
**Landovsky,** Rosemary Reid 1933- *WhoMW 92*
**Landow,** Nathan *WhoAmP 91*
**Landowne,** David 1942- *AmMWSc 92*
**Landowne,** Milton 1912- *AmMWSc 92*
**Landowska,** Wanda 1877-1959 *FacFETw*
**Landowska,** Wanda 1879-1959 *NewAmDM*
**Landowski,** Marcel 1915- *ConCom 92*
**Landowski,** Marcel Francois Paul 1915- *IntWW 91*
**Landphair,** Douglas Alan 1952- *WhoEnt 92, WhoMW 92*
**Landrau,** Marge 1939- *WhoHisp 92*
**Landre,** Debra Ann 1955- *WhoWest 92*
**Landreaux,** Kenneth Francis 1954- *WhoBlA 92*
**Landres,** Paul 1912- *IntMPA 92*
**Landreth,** Derek 1920- *Who 92*
**Landreth,** John Lewis 1917- *WhoEnt 92*
**Landreth,** Kenneth S 1947- *AmMWSc 92*
**Landreth,** Libbie 1952- *WhoWest 92*
**Landreth,** Lloyd Warren 1959- *WhoAmL 92*
**Landreth,** Ronald Ray 1949- *AmMWSc 92, WhoMW 92*
**Landriault,** Jacques Emile 1921- *WhoRel 92*
**Landrieu,** Mary 1955- *WhoAmP 91*
**Landrieu,** Mitch 1960- *WhoAmP 91*
**Landrieu,** Moon 1930- *IntWW 91*
**Landrigan,** Penelope Savage 1939- *WhoMW 92*
**Landrigan,** Philip J 1942- *AmMWSc 92*
**Landrock,** Arthur Harold 1919- *AmMWSc 92*
**Landron,** Michel John 1946- *WhoAmL 92, WhoEnt 92*
**Landru,** Trygve 1928- *WhoRel 92*
**Landrum,** Billy Frank 1920- *AmMWSc 92*
**Landrum,** John F. 1958- *WhoAmL 92*
**Landrum,** Joseph Emrich 1959- *WhoAmL 92*
**Landrum,** Larry James 1943- *WhoFI 92, WhoWest 92*
**Landrum,** Leslie Roger 1946- *AmMWSc 92*
**Landrum,** Michael Anthony 1958- *WhoRel 92*
**Landrum,** Phil M. 1907-1990 *CurBio 91N*
**Landrum,** Ralph Avery, Jr 1926- *AmMWSc 92*
**Landrum,** Tito Lee 1954- *WhoBlA 92*
**Landrum-Brummund,** Frances Ann 1918- *WhoEnt 92*
**Landry,** Caliste John, Jr. 1941- *WhoWest 92*
**Landry,** Dolores Branche 1928- *WhoBlA 92*
**Landry,** Donald Paul 1940- *WhoAmP 91*
**Landry,** Fernand 1930- *AmMWSc 92*
**Landry,** Gary Stephen 1946- *WhoRel 92*
**Landry,** L. Bartholomew 1936- *WhoBlA 92*
**Landry,** Larry David 1948- *WhoWest 92*
**Landry,** Lawrence Aloysius 1935- *WhoBlA 92*
**Landry,** Maggie 1951- *WhoEnt 92*
**Landry,** Mark Edward 1950- *WhoMW 92*
**Landry,** Mary Louise 1911- *WhoRel 92*
**Landry,** Michael Raymond 1948- *AmMWSc 92*
**Landry,** Monique 1937- *IntWW 91*
**Landry,** Richard Georges 1942- *AmMWSc 92*
**Landry,** Robert J *WhoAmP 91*
**Landry,** Robert John 1903-1991 *ConAu 134*
**Landry,** Robert Michael 1954- *WhoMW 92, WhoRel 92*
**Landry,** Robert Watson 1922- *WhoAmL 92*
**Landry,** Ron 1943- *WhoAmP 91*
**Landry,** Stuart Omer, Jr 1924- *AmMWSc 92*
**Landry,** Walter J 1931- *WhoAmP 91*
**Lands,** William Edward Mitchell 1930- *AmMWSc 92*
**Landsbaum,** Ellis M 1925- *AmMWSc 92*
**Landsberg,** Arne 1933- *AmMWSc 92*
**Landsberg,** Johanna D 1940- *AmMWSc 92*
**Landsberg,** Lewis 1938- *AmMWSc 92*
**Landsberg,** Otto 1869-1957 *EncTR 91*
**Landsberg,** Richard David 1956- *WhoFI 92*
**Landsberger,** Frank Robbert 1943- *AmMWSc 92*
**Landsbergis,** Algirdas 1924- *LiExTwC*
**Landsbergis,** Vitautas Vitautovich 1932- *SovUnBD*
**Landsbergis,** Vytautas 1932- *IntWW 91, News 91 [port], -91-3 [port]*
**Landsborough,** Ron James 1955- *WhoWest 92*
**Landsburg,** Alan *LesBEnT 92*
**Landsburg,** Alan 1933- *IntMPA 92*
**Landsburg,** Alexander Charles 1942- *AmMWSc 92*
**Landsburg,** Steven Elliot 1954- *WhoWest 92*
**Landshoff,** Rolf 1911- *AmMWSc 92*
**Landske,** Dorothy Suzanne 1937- *WhoAmP 91, WhoMW 92*
**Landsman,** David 1953- *AmMWSc 92*
**Landsman,** Douglas Anderson 1929- *AmMWSc 92*
**Landsman,** Michael Udell 1949- *WhoRel 92*
**Landsman,** Ron M. 1949- *WhoAmL 92*
**Landsman,** Sandy *DrAPF 91*
**Landsmark,** Theodore Carlisle 1946- *WhoBlA 92*
**Landsteiner,** Karl 1868-1943 *WhoNob 90*
**Landstreet,** John Darlington 1940- *AmMWSc 92*
**Landstrom,** D Karl 1937- *AmMWSc 92*
**Landstrom,** Donald Karl 1937- *WhoMW 92*
**Landt,** James Frederick 1926- *AmMWSc 92*
**Landucci,** Lawrence L 1939- *AmMWSc 92*
**Landureth,** Lewis James 1943- *WhoEnt 92*
**Landweber,** Lawrence H 1942- *AmMWSc 92*
**Landweber,** Louis 1912- *AmMWSc 92*
**Landweber,** Peter Steven 1940- *AmMWSc 92*
**Landwehr,** Arthur John 1934- *WhoMW 92, WhoRel 92*
**Landwehr,** James M 1945- *AmMWSc 92*
**Landwehr,** William Charles 1941- *WhoMW 92*
**Landy,** Arthur 1939- *AmMWSc 92*
**Landy,** Burton Aaron 1929- *WhoAmL 92*
**Landy,** James E. 1928- *WhoEnt 92*
**Landy,** Maurice *AmMWSc 92*
**Landy,** Richard Allen 1931- *WhoMW 92*
**Landzberg,** Abraham H 1929- *AmMWSc 92*
**Lane** *Who 92*
**Lane,** Baron 1918- *IntWW 91, Who 92*
**Lane,** Al *WhoAmP 91*
**Lane,** Alexander Z 1929- *AmMWSc 92*
**Lane,** Alfred Glen 1932- *AmMWSc 92*
**Lane,** Allan C. 1948- *WhoBlA 92*
**Lane,** Anthony John 1926- *Who 92*
**Lane,** Anthony John 1939- *Who 92*
**Lane,** Anthony Milner 1928- *IntWW 91, Who 92*
**Lane,** Anthony Thomas 1930- *WhoAmL 92*
**Lane,** Ardelle Catherine 1922- *AmMWSc 92*
**Lane,** Arthur Alan 1945- *WhoAmL 92*
**Lane,** Barry Michael 1932- *Who 92*
**Lane,** Belden Curnow 1943- *WhoRel 92*
**Lane,** Benjamin Clay 1952- *AmMWSc 92*
**Lane,** Bennie Ray 1935- *AmMWSc 92*
**Lane,** Bernard Owen 1925- *AmMWSc 92*
**Lane,** Bernard Paul 1938- *AmMWSc 92*
**Lane,** Brian M. 1951- *WhoMW 92*
**Lane,** Bruce Stuart 1932- *WhoAmL 92*
**Lane,** Burton 1912- *NewAmDM, WhoEnt 92*
**Lane,** Byron George 1933- *AmMWSc 92*
**Lane,** Carl Leaton 1928- *AmMWSc 92*
**Lane,** Carolyn 1926- *WrDr 92*
**Lane,** Cecelia Rose 1942- *WhoBlA 92*
**Lane,** Charles *NewYTBS 91*
**Lane,** Charles 1905- *ConTFT 9*
**Lane,** Charles 1953- *WhoEnt 92*
**Lane,** Charles A 1932- *AmMWSc 92*
**Lane,** Charles Edward 1909- *AmMWSc 92*
**Lane,** Charles Stuart 1924- *WhoFI 92*
**Lane,** Charlotte R 1948- *WhoAmP 91*
**Lane,** Chester Tevis, Jr. 1947- *WhoEnt 92*
**Lane,** Christopher M *WhoAmP 91*
**Lane,** Christopher Thomas 1941- *WhoFI 92*
**Lane,** Clarence D 1922- *WhoAmP 91*
**Lane,** David Earle 1943- *WhoRel 92*
**Lane,** David Goodwin 1945- *Who 92*
**Lane,** David John 1935- *Who 92*
**Lane,** David Judson 1927- *WhoAmP 91*
**Lane,** David Neil 1928- *Who 92*
**Lane,** David Pulaski, Sr. 1912- *WhoBlA 92*
**Lane,** David Stuart 1933- *IntAu&W 91, Who 92*
**Lane,** David William Stennis Stuart 1922- *Who 92*
**Lane,** Dennis Del 1950- *WhoMW 92*
**Lane,** Dewey Hobson, Jr 1934- *WhoAmP 91*
**Lane,** Diane 1963- *WhoEnt 92*
**Lane,** Diane 1965- *IntMPA 92*
**Lane,** Dick *WhoAmP 91*
**Lane,** Dina Hunter 1945- *WhoHisp 92*
**Lane,** Donald Clinton 1936- *WhoAmL 92*
**Lane,** Donald Steven 1956- *WhoAmP 91, WhoWest 92*
**Lane,** Donald Wilson 1934- *AmMWSc 92*
**Lane,** Douglas Calder 1945- *WhoFI 92*
**Lane,** Eddie Burgyone 1939- *WhoBlA 92*
**Lane,** Edward *IntAu&W 91X*
**Lane,** Edward Alphonso Richard 1953- *WhoFI 92*
**Lane,** Edwin David 1934- *AmMWSc 92*
**Lane,** Eleanor Tyson 1938- *WhoBlA 92*
**Lane,** Eric Trent 1938- *AmMWSc 92*
**Lane,** Ernest Paul 1933- *AmMWSc 92*
**Lane,** Forrest Eugene 1934- *AmMWSc 92*
**Lane,** Frank 1923- *AmMWSc 92*
**Lane,** Frank Joseph, Jr. 1934- *WhoAmL 92*
**Lane,** Frank Laurence 1912- *Who 92*
**Lane,** Frank W 1908- *IntAu&W 91*
**Lane,** Frederick Carpenter 1949- *WhoFI 92*
**Lane,** Gary 1941- *AmMWSc 92*
**Lane,** Gary 1943- *IntAu&W 91, WrDr 92*
**Lane,** George Ashel 1930- *AmMWSc 92, WhoMW 92*
**Lane,** George H 1924- *AmMWSc 92*
**Lane,** George Henry 1902- *WhoBlA 92*
**Lane,** George Lindsay 1921- *WhoRel 92*
**Lane,** George M 1928- *WhoAmP 91*
**Lane,** George S., Jr. 1932- *WhoBlA 92*
**Lane,** Gertrude 1914- *WhoEnt 92*
**Lane,** Gloria Julian 1932- *WhoWest 92*
**Lane,** Gordon Clifford 1952- *WhoAmL 92*

Lane, H Clifford 1950- AmMWSc 92
Lane, Harlan 1936- WrDr 92
Lane, Harold Elbert 1929- WhoRel 92
Lane, Harold Richard 1942- AmMWSc 92
Lane, Helen WrDr 92
Lane, Helen W AmMWSc 92
Lane, Hugh Percy 1875-1915 FacFETw, ThHEIm [port]
Lane, Isaac 1834-1937 RelLAm 91
Lane, James Dale 1937- AmMWSc 92
Lane, James F. 1953- WhoWest 92
Lane, James Henry 1833-1907 DcNCBi 4
Lane, James McConkey 1929- WhoFI 92
Lane, James Weldon 1926- WhoEnt 92
Lane, Janis Olene WhoBlA 92
Lane, Jeffrey Marvin 1960- WhoRel 92
Lane, Jerome 1966- WhoBlA 92
Lane, Joan Lorine 1938- WhoAmP 91
Lane, Joel 1740?-1795 DcNCBi 4
Lane, John DrAPF 91
Lane, John 1924- Who 92
Lane, John D AmMWSc 92
Lane, John Floyd 1940- WhoWest 92
Lane, John Gary 1942- WhoWest 92
Lane, John Henry 1924- WhoBlA 92
Lane, John Randolph 1835-1908 DcNCBi 4
Lane, John Rodger 1944- WhoWest 92
Lane, John S 1935- WhoIns 92
Lane, Jonathan Homer 1819-1880 BiInAmS
Lane, Joseph 1801-1881 DcNCBi 4
Lane, Joseph Robert 1917- AmMWSc 92
Lane, Jules V WhoIns 92
Lane, Julia A. 1927- WhoRel 92
Lane, Julius Forbes 1918- WhoBlA 92
Lane, June Ruth 1952- WhoWest 92
Lane, Kay Virjean 1943- WhoMW 92
Lane, Keith 1945- WhoIns 92
Lane, Keith Aldrich 1921- AmMWSc 92
Lane, Kendall W WhoAmP 91
Lane, Kenneth Edward, III 1958- WhoRel 92
Lane, Kenneth Frederick 1928- Who 92
Lane, Kenneth Robert 1942- WhoEnt 92
Lane, L W, Jr WhoAmP 91
Lane, Larry Scott WhoWest 92
Lane, Laurence William, Jr. 1919- WhoWest 92
Lane, Leo WhoAmP 91
Lane, Leonard James 1945- AmMWSc 92
Lane, Leslie Carl 1942- AmMWSc 92
Lane, Lois Kay AmMWSc 92
Lane, Louis 1923- NewAmDM, WhoEnt 92
Lane, Lunsford 1803-1863? DcNCBi 4
Lane, M Travis 1934- IntAu&W 91
Lane, Malcolm Daniel 1930- AmMWSc 92
Lane, Marcia DrAPF 91
Lane, Margaret 1907- IntAu&W 91, SmATA 65, Who 92
Lane, Mary DrAPF 91
Lane, Mary D. WrDr 92
Lane, Matthew Jay 1955- WhoAmL 92
Lane, Meredith Anne 1951- AmMWSc 92, WhoMW 92
Lane, Mervin DrAPF 91
Lane, Miriam Who 92
Lane, Montague 1929- AmMWSc 92
Lane, Nancy Jane 1936- AmMWSc 92
Lane, Nancy L. 1938- WhoBlA 92
Lane, Neal F 1938- AmMWSc 92
Lane, Nora Ruth 1936- WhoAmP 91
Lane, Norman Gary 1930- AmMWSc 92
Lane, Orris John, Jr 1932- AmMWSc 92
Lane, Pat 1939- BenetAL 91
Lane, Patrick 1939- ConPo 91, IntAu&W 91, WrDr 92
Lane, Paul Andrew 1961- WhoRel 92
Lane, Pinkie Gordon DrAPF 91
Lane, Pinkie Gordon 1923- NotBlAW 92, WhoBlA 92
Lane, Ralph 1530?-1603 DcNCBi 4
Lane, Ralph Norman Angell 1874-1967 WhoNob 90
Lane, Raymond Oscar 1924- AmMWSc 92
Lane, Richard 1926- WrDr 92
Lane, Richard 1928- WhoBlA 92
Lane, Richard Durelle 1953- AmMWSc 92
Lane, Richard L 1935- AmMWSc 92
Lane, Richard Merle 1944- WhoMW 92
Lane, Richard Neil 1944- AmMWSc 92
Lane, Robert WhoAmP 91
Lane, Robert Casey 1932- WhoAmL 92
Lane, Robert Gerhart 1931- WhoAmL 92
Lane, Robert Harold 1944- AmMWSc 92
Lane, Robert Kenneth 1937- AmMWSc 92
Lane, Robert Sidney 1944- AmMWSc 92
Lane, Roger Allan 1962- WhoAmL 92
Lane, Roger Lee 1945- AmMWSc 92
Lane, Ronald 1931- WrDr 92
Lane, Ronald Alan 1950- WhoAmL 92
Lane, Ronald Anthony Stuart 1917- IntWW 91, Who 92
Lane, Ronald Epey 1897- Who 92
Lane, Rose Wilder 1886-1968 TwCWW 91
Lane, Roumelia 1927- IntAu&W 91
Lane, Sarah Marie 1946- WhoMW 92
Lane, Stephen Mark 1948- AmMWSc 92
Lane, Theodore 1934- WhoFI 92
Lane, Thomas Knapp 1956- WhoFI 92
Lane, Tim Dennis 1954- WhoWest 92
Lane, Wallace 1911- AmMWSc 92
Lane, Wendy Evrard 1951- WhoFI 92
Lane, Wilfred Roger 1954- WhoMW 92
Lane, William Arthur 1958- WhoAmL 92, WhoFI 92
Lane, William Clay 1922- WhoBlA 92
Lane, William James 1925- AmMWSc 92
Lane, William Kenneth 1922- WhoWest 92
Lane, William L. 1931- WrDr 92
Lane, William Lister 1931- WhoRel 92
Lane, William M. WhoFI 92
Lane Fox, Robin James 1946- Who 92
Lane of Horsell, Baron 1925- Who 92
Lane-Oreiro, Laverne Teresa 1951- WhoWest 92
Lane-Reticker, Edward 1926- WhoAmL 92, WhoFI 92
Laneau, Richard Erwin 1930- WhoEnt 92
Lanegran, David Andrew 1941- WhoMW 92
Lanes, T. A. WhoRel 92
Lanesborough, Earl of 1918- Who 92
Lanewala, Mohammed A AmMWSc 92
Laney, Billie Eugene 1935- AmMWSc 92
Laney, Gary N. 1953- WhoEnt 92
Laney, Howard Elimuel 1925- WhoRel 92
Laney, J Carl 1948- ConAu 35NR
Laney, James E 1943- WhoAmP 91
Laney, James Thomas 1927- WhoRel 92
Laney, Leroy Olan 1943- WhoFI 92
Laney, Lucy 1854-1933 NotBlAW 92 [port]
Laney, Robert Louis, Jr. 1956- WhoBlA 92
Lanferman, David Paul WhoAmL 92
Lanford, Oscar E, III 1940- AmMWSc 92
Lanford, Robert Eldon 1951- AmMWSc 92
Lanford, Stephen P 1950- WhoAmP 91
Lanford, William Armistead 1944- AmMWSc 92
Lanford, William H 1935- WhoIns 92
Lang Dazhong 1933- IntWW 91
Lang, Andrew 1844-1912 RfGEnL 91, ScFEYrs
Lang, Andrew Charles 1966- WhoBlA 92
Lang, Andrew Richard 1924- IntWW 91, Who 92
Lang, Anton 1913- AmMWSc 92, IntWW 91
Lang, B. J. 1837-1909 NewAmDM
Lang, Berel 1933- ConAu 34NR
Lang, Bernhard 1946- WhoRel 92
Lang, Brian Andrew 1945- Who 92
Lang, Bruce Z 1937- AmMWSc 92
Lang, C Martin 1907- WhoAmP 91
Lang, C Max 1937- AmMWSc 92
Lang, Calvin Allen 1925- AmMWSc 92
Lang, Carroll Dennis 1943- WhoRel 92
Lang, Catherine Brown 1933- WhoAmL 92
Lang, Charles 1902- ConTFT 9, IntMPA 92
Lang, Charles, Jr. ConTFT 9
Lang, Charles B. ConTFT 9
Lang, Charles B., Jr. ConTFT 9
Lang, Charles H 1954- AmMWSc 92
Lang, Charles J. WhoBlA 92
Lang, Conrad Marvin 1939- AmMWSc 92
Lang, David 1913- IntMPA 92
Lang, David 1943- AmMWSc 92
Lang, David Marshall d1991 Who 92N
Lang, David Marshall 1924- IntAu&W 91, WrDr 92
Lang, David Marshall 1924-1991 ConAu 134
Lang, David Wayne 1954- WhoAmL 92
Lang, Derek 1913- Who 92, WrDr 92
Lang, Dimitrij Adolf 1926- AmMWSc 92
Lang, Donald F 1930- WhoIns 92
Lang, Eddie 1902-1933 NewAmDM
Lang, Enid Asher 1944- AmMWSc 92
Lang, Erich Karl 1929- AmMWSc 92
Lang, Everett Francis, Jr. 1942- WhoFI 92
Lang, Francis Harover 1907- WhoAmL 92, WhoFI 92
Lang, Frank Alexander 1937- AmMWSc 92
Lang, Frank Theodore 1938- AmMWSc 92
Lang, Fritz 1890-1976 FacFETw, IntDcF 2-2 [port]
Lang, Gene Eric 1962- WhoBlA 92
Lang, Gene Leo 1947- WhoAmP 91
Lang, George E, Jr 1942- AmMWSc 92
Lang, George Frank 1937- WhoWest 92
Lang, Gerald Edward 1945- AmMWSc 92
Lang, Gerhard Herbert 1927- AmMWSc 92
Lang, Gerhard Paul 1917- AmMWSc 92
Lang, Gladys Engel WrDr 92
Lang, Grace IntAu&W 91X
Lang, Harry George 1947- AmMWSc 92
Lang, Helga M 1928- AmMWSc 92
Lang, Henry George 1919- Who 92
Lang, Herrmann ScFEYrs
Lang, Hugh Montgomerie 1932- Who 92
Lang, Ian 1940- Who 92
Lang, Jack 1939- IntWW 91
Lang, James Frederick 1931- AmMWSc 92
Lang, James Richard 1945- WhoFI 92
Lang, Jennings 1915- IntMPA 92
Lang, John Albert, Jr. 1910-1974 DcNCBi 4
Lang, John Calvin, Jr 1942- AmMWSc 92
Lang, John Francis 1915- WhoAmL 92
Lang, John Harley 1927- Who 92
Lang, John Jacob 1952- WhoEnt 92
Lang, John Russell 1902- Who 92
Lang, Joseph Edward 1942- AmMWSc 92
Lang, Josephine 1815-1880 NewAmDM
Lang, Jovian Peter 1919- WhoRel 92
Lang, K. D. 1961- WhoEnt 92
Lang, Karl William 1953- WhoAmP 91
Lang, Kenneth Lyle 1936- AmMWSc 92
Lang, King IntAu&W 91X, TwCSFW 91, WrDr 92
Lang, Kurt 1924- WrDr 92
Lang, Lawrence George 1931- AmMWSc 92
Lang, Louis I 1949- WhoAmP 91
Lang, Marcus Titus 1920- WhoRel 92
Lang, Margaret Ruthven 1867-1972 NewAmDM
Lang, Margo Terzian WhoWest 92
Lang, Martin AmMWSc 92
Lang, Martin Andrew 1930- WhoRel 92
Lang, Martin T 1936- AmMWSc 92
Lang, Marvel 1949- WhoBlA 92
Lang, Maxwell George 1954- WhoWest 92
Lang, Neil Charles 1948- AmMWSc 92
Lang, Nevalon B. 1933- WhoWest 92
Lang, Norma Jean 1931- AmMWSc 92
Lang, Norma M 1939- AmMWSc 92
Lang, Norton David 1940- AmMWSc 92
Lang, Otto IntMPA 92
Lang, Otto Emil 1932- IntWW 91
Lang, Paul Henry 1901-1991 ConAu 135, NewYTBS 91
Lang, Pearl 1922- WhoEnt 92
Lang, Peter Michael 1930- AmMWSc 92
Lang, Philip Charles 1934- AmMWSc 92
Lang, Philip David 1929- WhoAmP 91
Lang, Raymond W 1930- AmMWSc 92
Lang, Richard Lewis 1951- WhoMW 92
Lang, Richard Warren 1949- WhoFI 92
Lang, Robert Arnold 1942- WhoFI 92
Lang, Robert Lee 1913- AmMWSc 92
Lang, Robert Phillip 1932- AmMWSc 92
Lang, Robert Todd 1924- WhoAmL 92
Lang, Roger H 1940- AmMWSc 92
Lang, Scott Wesley 1950- WhoAmP 91
Lang, Scott William 1959- WhoFI 92
Lang, Serge 1927- AmMWSc 92
Lang, Stanley Albert, Jr 1944- AmMWSc 92
Lang, Stephen 1952- IntMPA 92, WhoEnt 92
Lang, Susan S. 1950- SmATA 68 [port]
Lang, Terry Lee 1959- WhoMW 92
Lang, Theodore A WhoAmP 91
Lang, Theresa 1952- WhoFI 92
Lang, Thomas Frederick 1944- WhoAmL 92
Lang, Thomas G 1928- AmMWSc 92
Lang, Thompson Hughes 1946- WhoWest 92
Lang, Victoria Winifred 1955- WhoEnt 92
Lang, W. Richard 1936- WhoRel 92
Lang, William Adams 1932- WhoAmL 92
Lang, William Duncan 1925- Who 92
Lang, William Edward 1952- WhoWest 92
Lang, William Harry 1918- AmMWSc 92
Lang, William John 1955- WhoEnt 92
Lang, William Rawson 1909- WrDr 92
Lang, William Warner 1926- AmMWSc 92
Lang, Winston E. 1929- WhoBlA 92
Lang-Albright, Kathy 1949- WhoMW 92
Lang-Jeter, Lula L. WhoBlA 92
Langacker, Paul George 1946- AmMWSc 92
Langager, Bruce Allen 1942- AmMWSc 92
Langan, Glenn d1991 NewYTBS 91
Langan, Jim Mathew 1957- WhoEnt 92
Langan, Kevin J. 1955- WhoEnt 92
Langan, Peter St John Hevey 1942- Who 92
Langan, Thomas Augustine 1930- AmMWSc 92
Langan, William Bernard 1913- AmMWSc 92
Langart, T TwCSFW 91
Langbacka, Ralf Runar 1932- IntWW 91
Langbaum, Robert 1924- WrDr 92
Langbehn, August Julius 1851-1907 BiDExR
Langbehn, Julius 1851-1907 EncTR 91 [port]
Langbein, John Harriss 1941- WhoAmL 92, WrDr 92
Langberg, Barry Benson 1942- WhoAmL 92
Langbo, Arnold Gordon 1937- WhoMW 92
Langdale, Simon John Bartholomew 1937- Who 92
Langdale, Timothy James 1940- Who 92
Langdell, Robert Dana 1924- AmMWSc 92
Langdon, Allan Bruce 1941- AmMWSc 92
Langdon, Anthony James 1935- Who 92
Langdon, Augustus John 1913- Who 92
Langdon, Catherine Anne 1960- WhoFI 92
Langdon, David 1914- Who 92
Langdon, Edward Allen 1922- AmMWSc 92
Langdon, Glen George, Jr 1936- AmMWSc 92
Langdon, Harry 1884-1944 FacFETw
Langdon, Harry Norman 1929- WhoRel 92
Langdon, Herbert Lincoln 1935- AmMWSc 92
Langdon, James DrAPF 91
Langdon, John Who 92
Langdon, John Edmund 1944- WhoFI 92
Langdon, Jonathan Bertram Robert Louis 1939- Who 92
Langdon, Kenneth R 1928- AmMWSc 92
Langdon, Michael d1991 Who 92N
Langdon, Michael 1920- NewAmDM
Langdon, Michael 1920-1991 IntWW 91, -91N
Langdon, Philip 1947- WrDr 92
Langdon, Richard Garrett 1936- WhoMW 92
Langdon, Richard Norman Darbey 1919- Who 92
Langdon, Robert Adrian 1924- WrDr 92
Langdon, Robert Godwin 1923- AmMWSc 92
Langdon, Verne Loring 1941- WhoEnt 92, WhoWest 92
Langdon, Vicki N. 1960- WhoEnt 92
Langdon, William Jeff 1953- WhoMW 92
Langdon, William Keith 1916- AmMWSc 92
Langdon, William Mondeng 1914- AmMWSc 92
Langdon-Down, Antony Turnbull 1922- Who 92
Langdon-Down, Barbara Who 92
Lange, Art DrAPF 91
Lange, Barry Clifford 1952- AmMWSc 92
Lange, Billie Carola WhoEnt 92
Lange, Bruce Ainsworth 1948- AmMWSc 92
Lange, Bruce Michael 1952- WhoAmP 91
Lange, Charles Ford 1929- AmMWSc 92, WhoMW 92
Lange, Charles Gene 1942- AmMWSc 92
Lange, Charlotte 1931- WhoRel 92
Lange, Christian Lous 1869-1938 WhoNob 90
Lange, Christopher Stephen 1940- AmMWSc 92
Lange, David 1938- WhoAmL 92
Lange, David 1942- FacFETw
Lange, David Russell 1942- IntWW 91, Who 92
Lange, Dietz Christian 1933- WhoRel 92
Lange, Dorothea 1895-1965 FacFETw, RComAH
Lange, Eugene Albert 1923- AmMWSc 92
Lange, Frederick Edward, Jr. 1946- WhoMW 92
Lange, Frederick Emil 1908- WhoMW 92
Lange, Friedrich 1852-1917 BiDExR
Lange, Gail Laura 1946- AmMWSc 92
Lange, Gary David 1936- WhoMW 92
Lange, Gerald DrAPF 91
Lange, Gerald F WhoAmP 91
Lange, Geraldine Bernice 1925- WhoBlA 92
Lange, Gillian Northway 1936- WhoWest 92
Lange, Gordon David 1936- AmMWSc 92
Lange, Gordon Lloyd 1937- AmMWSc 92
Lange, Hartmut 1937- IntWW 91
Lange, Herbert 1909-1945 EncTR 91
Lange, Hermann 1922- IntWW 91
Lange, Hope 1931- IntMPA 92
Lange, Hope 1938- WhoEnt 92
Lange, Ian M 1940- AmMWSc 92
Lange, James Neil, Jr 1938- AmMWSc 92
Lange, Jessica 1949- IntMPA 92, IntWW 91, WhoEnt 92
Lange, John IntAu&W 91X, TwCSFW 91, WrDr 92
Lange, John Beucler 1928- WhoFI 92
Lange, Katherine JoAnn 1957- WhoMW 92
Lange, Kenneth L 1946- AmMWSc 92
Lange, Klaus Robert 1930- AmMWSc 92
Lange, Kurt 1906- AmMWSc 92
Lange, Leo Jerome 1928- AmMWSc 92
Lange, Lester Henry 1924- AmMWSc 92
Lange, Martha Lund 1902- WhoAmP 91
Lange, Marvin Robert 1948- WhoAmL 92
Lange, Oliver 1927- IntAu&W 91
Lange, Otto Ludwig 1927- IntWW 91
Lange, Paul E. 1960- WhoMW 92
Lange, Per 1901- IntWW 91
Lange, Robert Carl 1935- AmMWSc 92
Lange, Robert Dale 1920- AmMWSc 92
Lange, Robert Echlin, Jr AmMWSc 92

**Lange**, Rolf 1932- AmMWSc 92
**Lange**, Scott Leslie 1946- WhoMW 92
**Lange**, Ted WhoEnt 92
**Lange**, Ted W., III WhoBlA 92
**Lange**, Victor 1908- IntAu&W 91, WrDr 92
**Lange**, William E 1946- WhoAmL 92
**Lange**, William James 1930- AmMWSc 92
**Lange**, Winthrop Everett 1925- AmMWSc 92
**Lange**, Yvonne 1941- AmMWSc 92
**Langebartel**, Ray Gartner 1921- AmMWSc 92
**Langel**, DeeAnn 1958- WhoFI 92
**Langel**, Robert Allan 1937- AmMWSc 92
**Langeland**, Arne Lodvar 1928- IntWW 91
**Langeland**, Kaare 1916- AmMWSc 92
**Langella**, Frank 1940- ConTFT 9, IntMPA 92, WhoEnt 92
**Langemeijer**, Gerard Eduard 1903- IntWW 91
**Langen**, David Raymond 1943- WhoWest 92
**Langenau**, Edward E, Jr 1946- AmMWSc 92
**Langenberg**, Donald Newton 1932- AmMWSc 92
**Langenberg**, F C 1927- AmMWSc 92
**Langenberg**, Frederick Charles 1927- WhoFI 92, WhoMW 92
**Langenberg**, Patricia Warrington 1931- AmMWSc 92
**Langenberg**, Willem G 1928- AmMWSc 92
**Langendoen**, D. Terence 1939- WrDr 92
**Langenheim**, Jean Harmon 1925- AmMWSc 92, WhoWest 92
**Langenheim**, Ralph Louis, Jr 1922- AmMWSc 92
**Langenheim**, Roger Allen 1935- WhoAmL 92, WhoFI 92
**Langenthal**, Shari Joy 1955- WhoAmL 92
**Langenthal**, Stephen R. 1934- WhoEnt 92
**Langenwalter**, Gary Allan 1946- WhoFI 92
**Langer**, Andrew J. WhoFI 92
**Langer**, Arthur M 1936- AmMWSc 92
**Langer**, Bruce Alden 1953- WhoAmL 92
**Langer**, Carlton Earl 1954- WhoAmL 92
**Langer**, David 1927- WhoFI 92
**Langer**, Dennis Henry 1951- WhoMW 92
**Langer**, Dietrich Wilhelm 1930- AmMWSc 92
**Langer**, Eliezer 1946- WhoRel 92
**Langer**, Elizabeth 1946- WhoAmL 92
**Langer**, Eva Marie 1958- WhoWest 92
**Langer**, Frederick William 1951- WhoFI 92
**Langer**, Glenn A 1928- AmMWSc 92
**Langer**, Horst Gunter 1927- AmMWSc 92
**Langer**, James Stephen 1934- AmMWSc 92, WhoWest 92
**Langer**, Jindrich Henry 1946- WhoAmL 92
**Langer**, Lawrence Marvin 1913- AmMWSc 92
**Langer**, R M 1899- AmMWSc 92
**Langer**, Robert Samuel 1948- AmMWSc 92
**Langer**, Sidney 1925- AmMWSc 92, WhoWest 92
**Langer**, Steven 1926- WhoFI 92
**Langer**, Susanne K. 1895-1985 BenetAL 91, ConAu 34NR
**Langer**, Suzanne K 1895-1985 FacFETw
**Langer**, William David 1942- AmMWSc 92
**Langerak**, Edward Anthony 1944- WhoMW 92
**Langereis-Baca**, Maria 1930- WhoWest 92
**Langerman**, Duane L. 1943- WhoWest 92
**Langerman**, Neal Richard 1943- AmMWSc 92
**Langermann**, John Walther Rutledge-Gordon 1943- WhoFI 92
**Langevin**, James R WhoAmP 91
**Langevin**, Louis-de-Gonzague 1921- WhoRel 92
**L'Angevine** EncAmaz 91
**Langevoort**, Donald Carl 1951- WhoAmL 92
**Langfelder**, Leonard Jay 1933- AmMWSc 92
**Langfelder**, Ossie 1926- WhoAmP 91
**Langfitt**, John Nelson 1942- WhoRel 92
**Langfitt**, Thomas William 1927- AmMWSc 92
**Langford**, Baron 1912- Who 92
**Langford**, Anna Riggs WhoBlA 92
**Langford**, Anna Riggs 1917- WhoAmP 91
**Langford**, Anthony John 1936- Who 92
**Langford**, Arthur WhoAmP 91
**Langford**, Arthur, Jr. 1949- WhoBlA 92
**Langford**, Arthur Nicol 1910- AmMWSc 92
**Langford**, Athlyn Batten 1924- WhoAmP 91
**Langford**, Capri Lynn 1956- WhoWest 92
**Langford**, Charles D. 1922- WhoBlA 92
**Langford**, Charles Douglas 1922- WhoAmP 91
**Langford**, Charles Wesley 1938- WhoMW 92
**Langford**, Cooper Harold, III 1934- AmMWSc 92
**Langford**, David 1934- AmMWSc 92
**Langford**, David 1953- ConAu 135, TwCSFW 91, WrDr 92
**Langford**, Dean Ted 1939- WhoFI 92
**Langford**, Edgar Verden 1921- AmMWSc 92
**Langford**, Eric Siddon 1938- AmMWSc 92
**Langford**, Florence 1912- AmMWSc 92
**Langford**, Frances 1913- IntMPA 92
**Langford**, Fred F 1929- AmMWSc 92
**Langford**, Gary 1947- IntAu&W 91
**Langford**, Gary R. 1947- WrDr 92
**Langford**, George 1936- AmMWSc 92
**Langford**, George Malcolm 1944- AmMWSc 92
**Langford**, Gerald 1911- WrDr 92
**Langford**, Gerald Talmadge 1935- WhoFI 92
**Langford**, Herbert Gaines 1922- AmMWSc 92
**Langford**, James Beverly 1922- WhoAmP 91
**Langford**, James R. Jerome 1937- WrDr 92
**Langford**, John W. 1914- WhoBlA 92
**Langford**, John William 1932- WhoFI 92
**Langford**, Lorraine 1923- WhoAmP 91
**Langford**, Nathaniel Pitt 1832-1911 BilnAmS
**Langford**, Paul Brooks 1930- AmMWSc 92
**Langford**, Robert Bruce 1919- AmMWSc 92, WhoWest 92
**Langford**, Robert D. 1936- WhoFI 92
**Langford**, Roland Evans, Jr. 1936- WhoRel 92
**Langford**, Russell Hal 1925- AmMWSc 92
**Langford**, Sidney 1912- WhoRel 92
**Langford**, Thomas A. 1930- WhoRel 92
**Langford**, Thomas Anderson 1929- WhoRel 92
**Langford**, Victor C., III 1939- WhoBlA 92
**Langford**, William Finlay 1943- AmMWSc 92
**Langford-Holt**, John 1916- Who 92
**Langguth**, A.J. DrAPF 91
**Langhaar**, Henry Louis 1909- AmMWSc 92
**Langham**, Barbara D. DrAPF 91
**Langham**, James 1932- Who 92
**Langham**, John M. WhoBlA 92
**Langham**, Robert Fred 1912- AmMWSc 92
**Langhans**, Robert W 1929- AmMWSc 92
**Langhart**, Janet Floyd 1941- WhoBlA 92
**Langhauser**, Leon Henry 1937- WhoMW 92
**Langheinrich**, Armin P 1926- AmMWSc 92
**Langhinrichs**, Richard Alan 1921- WhoMW 92, WhoRel 92
**Langhoff**, Charles Anderson 1947- AmMWSc 92
**Langhoff**, Peter Wolfgang 1937- AmMWSc 92
**Langholm**, Neil IntAu&W 91X
**Langholz**, Armin Paul 1929- WhoMW 92
**Langhorne**, John 1735-1779 DcLB 109 [port], RfGEnL 91
**Langhorne**, Richard Tristan Bailey 1940- Who 92
**Langhorst**, Gary Arlen 1928- WhoWest 92
**Langhout**, Ernst Karel Otto 1930- WhoFI 92
**Langille**, Alan Ralph 1938- AmMWSc 92
**Langille**, Brian Lowell 1947- AmMWSc 92
**Langille**, Carole Glasser DrAPF 91
**Langille**, Robert C 1915- AmMWSc 92
**Langkilde**, Fagafaga D 1957- WhoAmP 91
**Langlais**, Jean 1907-1991 ConCom 92, NewAmDM, NewYTBS 91
**Langlais**, Jean-Francois-Hyacinthe 1907- IntWW 91
**Langland**, Joseph DrAPF 91
**Langland**, Joseph 1917- ConPo 91, WrDr 92
**Langland**, Neil Eugene 1951- WhoFI 92
**Langland**, Olaf Elmer 1925- AmMWSc 92
**Langland**, William 1332?-1390? RfGEnL 91
**Langlands**, Robert P 1936- AmMWSc 92
**Langlands**, Robert Phelan 1936- IntWW 91, Who 92
**Langleben**, Manuel Phillip 1924- AmMWSc 92
**Langley**, Albert E 1943- AmMWSc 92
**Langley**, Bob 1938- WrDr 92
**Langley**, Byron J WhoAmP 91
**Langley**, Dennis Mark 1952- WhoAmP 91
**Langley**, Desmond 1930- IntWW 91
**Langley**, G R 1931- AmMWSc 92
**Langley**, George A, III WhoAmP 91
**Langley**, Gill 1952- ConAu 133
**Langley**, Gordon Julian Hugh 1943- Who 92
**Langley**, Henry Desmond 1930- Who 92
**Langley**, Jimmy Don 1952- WhoAmL 92
**Langley**, John TwCWW 91
**Langley**, John Williams 1841-1918 BilnAmS
**Langley**, Katherine Emeline Gudger 1888-1948 DcNCBi 4
**Langley**, Keith A. 1959- WhoAmL 92
**Langley**, Kenneth Hall 1935- AmMWSc 92
**Langley**, Lawrence DeSales 1905- WhoAmP 91
**Langley**, Lester D. 1940- WrDr 92
**Langley**, Mark A. 1946- WhoRel 92
**Langley**, Maurice N 1913- AmMWSc 92
**Langley**, Neal Roger 1939- AmMWSc 92
**Langley**, Richard H 1937- WhoAmP 91
**Langley**, Richard Hanson WhoMW 92
**Langley**, Robert Archie 1937- AmMWSc 92
**Langley**, Robert Charles 1925- AmMWSc 92
**Langley**, Samuel Pierpont 1834-1906 BilnAmS, FacFETw
**Langley**, Stephen Gould 1938- WhoEnt 92
**Langley**, Teddy Lee 1943- WhoMW 92
**Langley**, Timothy Michael 1954- WhoRel 92
**Langley**, William Henry, Jr 1947- WhoAmP 91
**Langlois**, Bruce Edward 1937- AmMWSc 92
**Langlois**, Donald Harold 1940- WhoRel 92
**Langlois**, Geri WhoAmP 91
**Langlois**, Gordon Ellerby 1918- AmMWSc 92
**Langlois**, John Fraering 1963- WhoFI 92
**Langlois**, Michael Arthur 1956- WhoFI 92
**Langlois**, William Edwin 1933- AmMWSc 92
**Langlykke**, Asger Funder 1909- AmMWSc 92
**Langmade**, Calvin Jay 1954- WhoMW 92
**Langmuir**, Alexander D 1910- AmMWSc 92
**Langmuir**, David Bulkeley 1908- AmMWSc 92
**Langmuir**, Donald 1934- AmMWSc 92
**Langmuir**, Irving 1881-1957 WhoNob 90
**Langmuir**, Margaret Elizabeth Lang 1935- AmMWSc 92
**Langmuir**, Robert Vose 1912- AmMWSc 92, WhoFI 92, WhoWest 92
**Langner**, Gerald Conrad 1944- AmMWSc 92
**Langner**, Lawrence 1890-1962 BenetAL 91
**Langner**, Philip 1926- IntMPA 92
**Langner**, Ralph Rolland 1925- AmMWSc 92
**Langner**, Ronald O 1940- AmMWSc 92
**Lango**, Allithea Evelyn 1948- WhoAmL 92
**Langone**, John Joseph 1944- AmMWSc 92
**Langoni**, Carlos G. 1944- IntWW 91
**Langoni**, Richard Allen 1945- WhoWest 92
**Langoth**, Franz 1877-1953 BiDExR
**Langrana**, Noshir A 1946- AmMWSc 92
**Langreth**, David Chapman 1937- AmMWSc 92
**Langridge**, Philip Gordon 1939- Who 92
**Langridge**, Richard James 1932- Who 92
**Langridge**, Robert 1933- AmMWSc 92, WhoWest 92
**Langridge**, Ruth WhoEnt 92
**Langridge**, William Henry Russell 1938- AmMWSc 92
**Langrishe**, Hercules 1927- Who 92
**Langs**, Linda 1953- WhoEnt 92, WhoMW 92
**Langsam**, Ida Susan 1951- WhoEnt 92
**Langsam**, Michael 1938- AmMWSc 92
**Langsdorf**, Alexander, Jr 1912- AmMWSc 92
**Langsdorf**, Jesse Guthrie 1911- WhoAmL 92
**Langsdorf**, William Philip 1919- AmMWSc 92
**Langseth**, Keith L 1938- WhoAmP 91
**Langseth**, Marcus G 1932- AmMWSc 92
**Langseth**, Rollin Edward 1940- AmMWSc 92
**Langshaw**, George Henry 1939- Who 92
**Langsjoen**, Arne Nels 1919- AmMWSc 92
**Langsjoen**, Per Harald 1921- AmMWSc 92
**Langslet**, Lars Roar 1936- IntWW 91
**Langsley**, Donald Gene 1925- AmMWSc 92, WhoMW 92
**Langslow**, Derek Robert 1945- Who 92
**Langstaff**, Alan McGregor 1935- WhoRel 92
**Langstaff**, Gary Lee 1948- WhoFI 92
**Langstaff**, John Meredith 1920- SmATA 68 [port], WhoEnt 92
**Langstaff**, Launcelot BenetAL 91
**Langstaff**, Marguerite Terrell 1935- WhoAmL 92
**Langster**, Rodger Dale 1946- WhoAmP 91
**Langston**, Andrew A. 1929- WhoBlA 92
**Langston**, Charles Adam 1949- AmMWSc 92
**Langston**, Clarence Walter 1924- AmMWSc 92
**Langston**, Dave Thomas 1945- AmMWSc 92
**Langston**, Don 1937- WhoAmL 92
**Langston**, Edward Lee 1944- WhoAmP 91
**Langston**, Esther R. 1939- WhoBlA 92
**Langston**, Glen Irvin 1956- AmMWSc 92
**Langston**, Hiram Thomas 1912- AmMWSc 92
**Langston**, James Horace 1917- AmMWSc 92
**Langston**, Jane 1922- SmATA 68 [port]
**Langston**, Jimmy Byrd 1927- AmMWSc 92
**Langston**, John Antony S. Who 92
**Langston**, John Dallas 1881-1963 DcNCBi 4
**Langston**, Josephine Davidnell 1948- WhoBlA 92
**Langston**, Timothy Michael 1953- WhoWest 92
**Langston**, Wann, Jr 1921- AmMWSc 92
**Langston**, Wilmetta Ann Smith 1935- WhoBlA 92
**Langstone**, John Arthur William 1913- Who 92
**Langstroth**, George Forbes Otty 1936- AmMWSc 92
**Langton** Who 92
**Langton**, Basil Cedric 1912- WhoEnt 92
**Langton**, Bryan David 1936- Who 92
**Langton**, Daniel J. DrAPF 91
**Langton**, Daniel Webster 1864-1909 BilnAmS
**Langton**, Henry Algernon Who 92
**Langton**, Jane 1922- IntAu&W 91, WrDr 92
**Langton**, John 1932- TwCPaSc
**Langton**, Michael Edward 1949- WhoAmP 91
**Langton**, Roger W. DrAPF 91
**Langtry**, Alice S WhoAmP 91
**Langtry**, Ian Who 92
**Langtry**, James Ian 1939- Who 92
**Languetin**, Pierre 1923- IntWW 91
**Langum**, W. Sue 1934- WhoMW 92
**Langvardt**, Patrick William 1950- AmMWSc 92
**Langway**, Chester Charles, Jr 1929- AmMWSc 92
**Langweiler**, Marc 1952- AmMWSc 92
**Langwig**, John Edward 1924- AmMWSc 92
**Langwiser**, Nancy Carol 1957- WhoFI 92
**Langworthy**, Audrey 1938- WhoAmP 91
**Langworthy**, Audrey Hansen 1938- WhoMW 92
**Langworthy**, Harold Frederick 1940- AmMWSc 92
**Langworthy**, James Brian 1934- AmMWSc 92
**Langworthy**, Thomas Allan 1943- AmMWSc 92
**Langworthy**, William Clayton 1936- AmMWSc 92
**Lanham**, Arthur Abrel 1953- WhoEnt 92
**Lanham**, Charles Truman 1902-1978 FacFETw
**Lanham**, Honey Sue 1946- WhoAmP 91
**Lanham**, Howard Mitchell 1934- WhoIns 92
**Lanham**, Richard Alan 1936- WrDr 92
**Lanham**, Richard Henry, Jr AmMWSc 92
**Lanham**, Urless Norton 1918- AmMWSc 92
**Lanham**, William W ScFEYrs
**La Niece**, Peter George 1920- Who 92
**Lanier**, Anita Suzanne 1946- WhoEnt 92
**Lanier**, Anthony Wayne 1957- WhoBlA 92
**Lanier**, Bob 1948- WhoBlA 92
**Lanier**, Clifford Anderson 1844-1908 BenetAL 91
**Lanier**, David William 1934- WhoAmP 91
**Lanier**, Dorothy Copeland 1922- WhoBlA 92
**Lanier**, Edwin Sidney 1901-1983 DcNCBi 4
**Lanier**, Fran 1947- WhoBlA 92
**Lanier**, Gerald Norman 1937- AmMWSc 92
**Lanier**, Henry W. 1873-1958 BenetAL 91
**Lanier**, Horatio Axel 1955- WhoBlA 92
**Lanier**, James Franklin Doughty 1800-1881 DcNCBi 4
**Lanier**, James Olanda 1931- WhoAmL 92, WhoAmP 91, WhoFI 92
**Lanier**, Jon Robert 1963- WhoRel 92
**Lanier**, Joseph Lamar, Jr. 1932- WhoFI 92
**Lanier**, Karl Frederick, Jr. 1941- WhoFI 92
**Lanier**, Lewis L 1953- AmMWSc 92
**Lanier**, Marshall L. 1920- WhoBlA 92
**Lanier**, Nicholas 1588-1666 NewAmDM
**Lanier**, Richard Blackburn 1958- WhoFI 92
**Lanier**, Robert George 1940- AmMWSc 92
**Lanier**, Shelby, Jr. 1936- WhoBlA 92

**Lanier,** Sidney 1842-1881 *BenetAL 91*
**Lanier,** Sidney Arthur 1945- *WhoWest 92*
**Lanier,** Sidney Clopton 1842-1881 *DcNCBi 4*
**Lanier,** Sterling E 1927- *IntAu&W 91, TwCSFW 91, WrDr 92*
**Lanier,** Thomas 1923- *WhoFI 92*
**Lanier,** Timothy Hoyle 1954- *WhoFI 92*
**Lanier,** Willie 1945- *WhoBlA 92*
**Lanigan,** George Thomas 1845-1886 *BenetAL 91*
**Lanigan,** Karen Marie 1948- *WhoRel 92*
**Lanigan,** Robert J. 1928- *WhoFI 92, WhoMW 92*
**Lanin,** Howard d1991 *NewYTBS 91*
**La Nina** *EncAmaz 91*
**Laning,** J Halcombe 1920- *AmMWSc 92*
**Laning,** Stephen Henry 1918- *AmMWSc 92*
**Lanker,** Brian T. 1947- *ConAu 134*
**Lankering,** Thomas Robert 1956- *WhoWest 92*
**Lankester,** Richard Shermer 1922- *Who 92*
**Lankester,** Timothy Patrick *Who 92*
**Lankester,** Timothy Patrick 1942- *IntWW 91*
**Lankford,** Charles Ely 1912- *AmMWSc 92*
**Lankford,** Don Que 1937- *WhoAmP 91*
**Lankford,** J L 1920- *AmMWSc 92*
**Lankford,** Jefferson Lewis 1951- *WhoAmL 92*
**Lankford,** Linda Marie 1947- *WhoWest 92*
**Lankford,** S. A. *WhoRel 92*
**Lankford,** Thomas J 1926- *WhoAmP 91*
**Lankford,** Vernon Thomas, Jr. 1949- *WhoAmL 92*
**Lankford,** William Fleet 1938- *AmMWSc 92*
**Lanks,** Karl William 1942- *AmMWSc 92*
**Lanktree,** Cheryl Blanche 1953- *WhoWest 92*
**Lanman,** Charles 1819-1895 *BenetAL 91*
**Lanman,** Robert Charles 1930- *AmMWSc 92*
**Lann,** Joseph Sidney 1917- *AmMWSc 92*
**Lannaman,** Sonia M 1956- *BlkOlyM*
**Lannamann,** Richard Stuart 1947- *WhoFI 92*
**Lanneau,** Sophie Stevens 1881-1963 *DcNCBi 4*
**Lannefors,** Hans Ove 1951- *WhoMW 92*
**Lanner,** Ronald Martin 1930- *AmMWSc 92, WhoWest 92*
**Lanners,** H Norbert 1943- *AmMWSc 92*
**Lannert,** Kent Philip 1944- *AmMWSc 92*
**Lannert,** Robert Cornelius 1940- *WhoFI 92, WhoMW 92*
**Lannes,** William Joseph, III 1937- *WhoFI 92*
**Lanni,** Frederick *AmMWSc 92*
**Lannin,** Jeffrey S 1940- *AmMWSc 92*
**Lanning,** Bill Lester 1944- *WhoRel 92*
**Lanning,** David D 1928- *AmMWSc 92*
**Lanning,** Francis Chowing 1908- *AmMWSc 92*
**Lanning,** George *DrAPF 91*
**Lanning,** John Tate 1902-1976 *DcNCBi 4*
**Lanning,** Judith Ann 1936- *WhoEnt 92*
**Lanning,** William Clarence 1913- *AmMWSc 92*
**Lannon,** John Joseph 1937- *WhoFI 92, WhoMW 92*
**Lannon,** Peter Kenneth, Jr. 1955- *WhoAmL 92*
**Lannon,** William Edward 1940- *WhoAmP 91*
**L'Annunziata,** Michael Frank 1943- *AmMWSc 92*
**Lannutti,** Joseph Edward 1926- *AmMWSc 92*
**Lanois,** Daniel 1951- *News 91 [port]*
**Lanou,** Robert Eugene, Jr 1928- *AmMWSc 92*
**LaNoue,** John Long 1934- *WhoRel 92*
**La Noue,** Kathryn F 1934- *AmMWSc 92*
**Lanouette,** William 1940- *IntAu&W 91*
**Lanoux,** Sigred Boyd 1931- *AmMWSc 92*
**Lanovoy,** Vasiliy Semenovich 1934- *IntWW 91*
**Lanphear,** Charles Edward 1947- *WhoIns 92*
**Lanpher,** Bill Weston 1933- *WhoRel 92*
**Lanpher,** David Geoffrey 1959- *WhoRel 92*
**Lanphere,** Marvin Alder 1933- *AmMWSc 92*
**Lanphier,** Edward Howell 1922- *AmMWSc 92*
**Lanphier,** Thomas G, Jr 1890-1987 *FacFETw*
**Lans,** Allan *NewYTBS 91 [port]*
**Lans,** Asher Bob 1918- *WhoAmL 92*
**Lans,** Carl Gustav 1907- *WhoWest 92*
**Lansaw,** Charles Ray 1927- *WhoMW 92*
**Lansbury,** Angela 1925- *IntMPA 92, IntWW 91*
**Lansbury,** Angela Brigid 1925- *Who 92, WhoEnt 92*
**Lansbury,** Bruce 1930- *IntMPA 92*
**Lansbury,** Coral *WrDr 92*
**Lansbury,** Coral 1929-1991 *NewYTBS 91 [port]*
**Lansbury,** Edgar 1930- *IntMPA 92*
**Lansbury,** Edgar George 1930- *WhoEnt 92*
**Lansbury,** George 1859-1940 *FacFETw*
**Lansbury,** Peter Thomas 1933- *AmMWSc 92*
**Lansdale,** Joe R 1951- *TwCSFW 91, TwCWW 91, WrDr 92*
**Lansdell,** Herbert Charles 1922- *AmMWSc 92*
**Lansden,** Willie F. 1953- *WhoBlA 92*
**Lansdown,** A M 1939- *AmMWSc 92*
**Lansdown,** Gillian Elizabeth *Who 92*
**Lansdowne,** Marquess of 1912- *IntWW 91, Who 92*
**Lansdowne,** Karen Myrtle 1926- *WhoWest 92*
**Lanser,** Kathy Ann 1961- *WhoEnt 92*
**Lanser,** Leslie John 1935- *WhoRel 92*
**Lansere,** Yevgeniy Yevgen'evich 1878-1946 *SovUnBD*
**Lansey,** E. Gaines *WhoBlA 92*
**Lansey,** Yvonne F. 1946- *WhoBlA 92*
**Lansford,** Edwin Myers, Jr 1923- *AmMWSc 92*
**Lansford,** Henry Hollis 1929- *WhoWest 92*
**Lansford,** Theron George 1931- *WhoRel 92*
**Lansing,** Allan M 1929- *AmMWSc 92*
**Lansing,** John *WrDr 92*
**Lansing,** Marjorie 1916- *WhoAmP 91*
**Lansing,** Neal F, Jr 1916- *AmMWSc 92*
**Lansing,** Odell E 1867?-1918 *BiInAmS*
**Lansing,** Robert 1864-1928 *AmPeW, AmPolLe, FacFETw*
**Lansing,** Robert Howell 1928- *WhoEnt 92*
**Lansing,** Sherry *ReelWom*
**Lansing,** Sherry 1944- *IntMPA 92, IntWW 91*
**Lansing,** Trainor *ScFEYrs*
**Lansinger,** John Marcus 1932- *AmMWSc 92*
**Lanski,** Charles Philip 1943- *AmMWSc 92*
**Lansky,** Meyer 1902-1983 *FacFETw*
**Lansky,** Paul 1944- *ConCom 92, NewAmDM*
**Lansley,** Andrew David 1956- *Who 92*
**Lansner,** David Jeffrey 1947- *WhoAmL 92*
**Lanson,** Herman Jay 1913- *AmMWSc 92*
**Lant,** Harvey *TwCWW 91*
**Lanter,** Robert Jackson 1914- *AmMWSc 92*
**Lanter,** Sean Keith 1953- *WhoWest 92*
**Lanterman,** Elma 1917- *AmMWSc 92*
**Lantero,** Oreste John, Jr 1942- *AmMWSc 92*
**Lanthier,** Andre 1928- *AmMWSc 92*
**Lanthier,** Jonh Spencer 1940- *WhoFI 92*
**Lantos,** P R 1924- *AmMWSc 92*
**Lantos,** Robert *LesBEnT 92*
**Lantos,** Thomas Peter 1928- *WhoWest 92*
**Lantos,** Tom 1928- *AlmAP 92 [port], WhoAmP 91*
**Lantry,** Marilyn Martha 1932- *WhoAmP 91*
**Lantry,** Mike *IntAu&W 91X, WrDr 92*
**Lantz,** Barbara Louise 1938- *WhoMW 92*
**Lantz,** Cynthia Avis 1949- *WhoMW 92*
**Lantz,** David Carson 1946- *WhoMW 92*
**Lantz,** David Ernest 1855-1918 *BiInAmS*
**Lantz,** George Benjamin, Jr. 1936- *WhoRel 92*
**Lantz,** George Everett 1951- *WhoWest 92*
**Lantz,** Joanne Baldwin 1932- *WhoMW 92*
**Lantz,** John Edward 1911- *IntAu&W 91*
**Lantz,** Norman Foster 1937- *WhoWest 92*
**Lantz,** Thelma *DrAPF 91*
**Lantz,** Thomas Lee 1936- *AmMWSc 92*
**Lantz,** W. Franklin 1930- *WhoRel 92*
**Lantz,** Walter 1900- *IntMPA 92, WhoEnt 92*
**Lantz,** William Charles 1946- *WhoAmL 92*
**Lanusse,** Alejandro Agustin 1918- *IntWW 91*
**Lanvin,** Jeanne 1867-1946 *DcTwDes*
**Lanvin,** Yves Pierre d1989 *IntWW 91N*
**Lanyer,** Charles 1942- *WhoEnt 92*
**Lanyi,** Janos K 1937- *AmMWSc 92*
**Lanyon,** Hubert Peter David 1936- *AmMWSc 92*
**Lanyon,** Lance Edward 1944- *Who 92*
**Lanyon,** Peter 1918-1964 *TwCPaSc*
**Lanyon,** Wesley Edwin 1926- *AmMWSc 92*
**Lanz,** Adolf Josef 1874-1955 *BiDExR*
**Lanz,** David Howard *WhoEnt 92*
**Lanz,** John R 1927- *WhoIns 92*
**Lanz,** Josef 1874-1954 *EncTR 91 [port]*
**Lanza,** Giovanni 1926- *AmMWSc 92*
**Lanza,** Guy Robert 1939- *AmMWSc 92*
**Lanza,** Mario 1921-1959 *NewAmDM*
**Lanza,** Richard Charles 1939- *AmMWSc 92*
**Lanza-Jacoby,** Susan *AmMWSc 92*
**Lanzalone,** Charles James 1952- *WhoFI 92*
**Lanzano,** Bernadine Clare 1933- *AmMWSc 92*
**Lanzano,** Paolo 1923- *AmMWSc 92*
**Lanzano,** Ralph Eugene 1926- *WhoFI 92*
**Lanzara,** Ronald F *WhoAmP 91*
**Lanzen,** Greggory Einar 1951- *WhoRel 92*
**Lanzerotti,** Louis John 1938- *AmMWSc 92*
**Lanzerotti,** Mary Yvonne DeWolf 1938- *AmMWSc 92*
**Lanzieri,** Charles Frederick 1952- *WhoMW 92*
**Lanzillo,** Agostino 1886-1952 *BiDExR*
**Lanzkowsky,** Philip 1932- *AmMWSc 92*
**Lanzkron,** R W 1929- *AmMWSc 92*
**Lanzkron,** Rolf Wolfgang 1929- *WhoFI 92*
**Lanzl,** Lawrence Herman 1921- *AmMWSc 92, WhoMW 92*
**Lanzone,** Deborah von Hoffman 1952- *WhoA.nP 91*
**Lanzoni,** Vincent 1928- *AmMWSc 92*
**Lao Chongpin** 1936- *IntWW 91*
**Lao Tzu** *ClMLC 7 [port]*
**Lao,** Binneg Yanbing 1945- *AmMWSc 92*
**Lao,** Chang Sheng 1935- *AmMWSc 92*
**Lao,** Yan-Jeong 1936- *AmMWSc 92*
**Laodice I** *EncAmaz 91*
**Laos,** Roy *WhoHisp 92*
**La Padura,** Jason M. 1954- *WhoEnt 92*
**LaPage,** Ronald Neal 1946- *WhoMW 92*
**La Paille,** Gary Joseph 1954- *WhoAmP 91*
**LaPalma,** Marina deBellagente *DrAPF 91*
**LaPalme,** Donald William 1937- *AmMWSc 92*
**La Pasionaria** *FacFETw*
**Lapatin,** Philip Stuart 1949- *WhoAmL 92*
**Lapchak,** Paul Andrew 1960- *WhoWest 92*
**Lapciuc,** Israel *WhoHisp 92*
**Lape,** Michael John 1943- *WhoEnt 92*
**LaPerriere,** Jacqueline Doyle 1942- *AmMWSc 92*
**Laperruque,** Paul Michael 1948- *WhoWest 92*
**Lapesa Melgar,** Rafael 1908- *IntWW 91*
**Lapetina,** Eduardo G *AmMWSc 92*
**Lapeyre,** Gerald J 1934- *AmMWSc 92*
**Lapeyre,** Jean-Numa 1945- *AmMWSc 92*
**Lapeyrolerie,** Frank M. 1929- *WhoBlA 92*
**Lapeyrolerie,** Myra Evans 1959- *WhoBlA 92*
**Lapham,** Increase Allen 1811-1875 *BiInAmS*
**Lapham,** Lowell Winship 1922- *AmMWSc 92*
**Lapicki,** Andrzej 1924- *IntWW 91*
**Lapicki,** Gregory *AmMWSc 92*
**Lapides,** Jack 1914- *AmMWSc 92*
**Lapides,** Julian Lee 1931- *WhoAmP 91*
**Lapidge,** Michael 1942- *Who 92*
**Lapidus,** Arnold 1933- *AmMWSc 92*
**Lapidus,** Herbert 1931- *AmMWSc 92*
**Lapidus,** Jacqueline *DrAPF 91*
**La Pidus,** Jules Benjamin 1931- *AmMWSc 92*
**Lapidus,** Leonard 1929- *WhoFI 92*
**Lapidus,** Michel Laurent 1956- *AmMWSc 92*
**Lapidus,** Milton 1922- *AmMWSc 92*
**Lapidus,** Norman Israel 1930- *WhoFI 92*
**Lapidus,** Ted 1929- *IntWW 91*
**LaPier,** Terrence Walter 1954- *WhoFI 92*
**LaPierre,** Albert Wilson 1951- *WhoAmP 91*
**Lapierre,** Dominique 1931- *IntWW 91*
**LaPierre,** John 1681-1755? *DcNCBi 4*
**LaPierre,** Walter A 1910- *AmMWSc 92*
**Lapierre,** Yvon Denis 1936- *AmMWSc 92*
**LaPietra,** Joseph Richard 1932- *AmMWSc 92*
**Lapin,** A I E 1938- *AmMWSc 92*
**Lapin,** Abraham 1923- *AmMWSc 92*
**Lapin,** David Marvin 1939- *AmMWSc 92*
**Lapin,** Evelyn P 1933- *AmMWSc 92*
**Lapin,** Harvey I. 1937- *WhoAmL 92*
**Lapin,** Jonathan B. 1952- *WhoAmL 92*
**Lapin,** Sergey Georgievich 1912-1988 *SovUnBD*
**Lapin,** Stanley Phillip 1926- *WhoEnt 92*
**Lapine,** James 1949- *WrDr 92*
**Lapine,** James Elliot 1949- *WhoEnt 92*
**Lapins,** David Alan 1958- *WhoAmL 92*
**Lapinski,** Richard Allen 1953- *WhoFI 92*
**Lapinski,** Susan 1948- *IntAu&W 91*
**Lapis,** Karoly 1926- *IntWW 91*
**LaPitz,** Douglas William 1951- *WhoEnt 92*
**Lapke,** John Harrison 1960- *WhoAmL 92*
**Lapkin,** Milton 1929- *AmMWSc 92*
**Laplace,** Pierre Simon, marquis de 1749-1827 *BlkwCEP*
**LaPlanche,** Laurine A 1938- *AmMWSc 92*
**Laplante,** Andrew P. 1964- *WhoFI 92*
**LaPlante,** J P Normand *WhoAmP 91*
**LaPlante,** Roland H *WhoAmP 91*
**La Plante,** William Albert 1930- *WhoMW 92*
**La Plata,** George 1924- *WhoAmL 92, WhoHisp 92*
**Laplaza,** Miguel Luis 1938- *AmMWSc 92*
**Lapman,** Mark Charles 1950- *WhoFI 92*
**LaPoint,** William Joseph, Jr. 1962- *WhoFI 92*
**Lapointe,** Francis Charles 1939- *WhoAmP 91*
**Lapointe,** Jacques 1942- *AmMWSc 92*
**Lapointe,** Jo Anne D *WhoAmP 91*
**La Pointe,** Joseph L 1934- *AmMWSc 92*
**LaPointe,** Leonard Lyell 1939- *AmMWSc 92*
**LaPointe,** Neal Gerard 1960- *WhoMW 92*
**Lapointe,** Paul Andre 1934- *Who 92*
**LaPointe,** Paul-Marie 1929- *BenetAL 91*
**Lapointe,** Roger Lucien 1929- *WhoRel 92*
**LaPointe-Crump,** Janice Deane 1942- *WhoEnt 92*
**Lapolla,** Garibaldi M 1888-1954 *DcAmImH*
**LaPolla,** Louis D 1945- *WhoAmP 91*
**Laponce,** Jean Antoine 1925- *WrDr 92*
**Laponsky,** Alfred Baer 1921- *AmMWSc 92*
**Laporta,** Robert John 1942- *WhoFI 92*
**Laporte,** Cloyd, Jr. 1925- *WhoAmL 92*
**LaPorte,** Daniel Giles 1935- *WhoAmL 92*
**Laporte,** Gerald Joseph Sylvestre 1946- *WhoAmL 92*
**LaPorte,** James Edward 1949- *WhoFI 92*
**Laporte,** Jean-Marc 1937- *WhoRel 92*
**Laporte,** Leo Frederic 1933- *AmMWSc 92*
**LaPorte,** Ronald E 1949- *AmMWSc 92*
**Laporte,** William F. 1913- *IntWW 91*
**Laporte,** Yves Michel Frederic 1920- *IntWW 91*
**Laposa,** Joseph David 1938- *AmMWSc 92*
**Laposata,** Michael 1952- *AmMWSc 92*
**Lapostolle,** Pierre Marcel 1922- *AmMWSc 92*
**Lapotaire,** Jane 1944- *Who 92*
**Lapp,** H M 1922- *AmMWSc 92*
**Lapp,** Harry 1947- *WhoEnt 92*
**Lapp,** James Merrill 1937- *WhoRel 92*
**Lapp,** John Allen 1933- *WhoRel 92*
**Lapp,** Joseph L. 1942- *WhoRel 92*
**Lapp,** M 1932- *AmMWSc 92*
**Lapp,** Martin Stanley *AmMWSc 92*
**Lapp,** N LeRoy *AmMWSc 92*
**Lapp,** Neil Arden 1942- *AmMWSc 92*
**Lapp,** P A 1928- *AmMWSc 92*
**Lapp,** Thomas William 1937- *AmMWSc 92*
**Lapp,** Wayne Stanley 1936- *AmMWSc 92*
**Lappas,** Alfons 1929- *IntWW 91*
**Lappas,** Lewis Christopher 1921- *AmMWSc 92*
**Lappas,** Spero Thomas 1952- *WhoAmL 92, WhoFI 92*
**Lappe,** Donnie Gene 1955- *WhoAmL 92*
**Lappe,** Frances Moore 1944- *IntAu&W 91, WrDr 92*
**Lappe,** Rodney Wilson 1954- *AmMWSc 92*
**Lapper,** John 1921- *Who 92*
**Lapperre,** John Huber 1911- *WhoFI 92*
**Lappert,** Michael F. 1928- *IntWW 91*
**Lappert,** Michael Franz 1928- *Who 92*
**Lappin,** Brooke 1940- *WhoEnt 92*
**Lappin,** Gerald R 1919- *AmMWSc 92*
**Lappin,** John Walter 1940- *WhoFI 92*
**Lappin,** Lawrence Bradford 1960- *WhoFI 92*
**Lappin,** Robert Sidney 1928- *WhoAmL 92*
**Lapping,** Anne Shirley Lucas 1941- *Who 92*
**Lapping,** Brian 1937- *IntAu&W 91, WrDr 92*
**Lapping,** Peter Herbert 1941- *Who 92*
**Lapple,** Charles E 1916- *AmMWSc 92*
**Lapple,** Walter C 1921- *AmMWSc 92*
**Lapporte,** Seymour Jerome 1930- *AmMWSc 92*
**Laprade,** Mary Hodge 1929- *AmMWSc 92*
**Laprade,** William Thomas 1883-1975 *DcNCBi 4*
**Lapsley,** Alwyn Cowles 1920- *AmMWSc 92*
**Lapsley,** James Norvell, Jr. 1930- *WhoRel 92*
**Lapsley,** John 1916- *Who 92*
**Lapsley,** William W. 1910- *IntWW 91*
**Laptev,** Ivan Dmitrievich 1934- *SovUnBD*
**Laptev,** Ivan Dmitrievich 1936- *IntWW 91*
**Laptev,** Pavel Pavlovich 1928- *IntWW 91*
**Laptev,** Vladimir Viktorovich 1924- *IntWW 91, SovUnBD*
**Lapuck,** Jack Lester 1924- *AmMWSc 92*
**La Puma,** Salvatore *DrAPF 91*
**Lapun,** Paul 1923- *Who 92*
**Laquatra,** Idamarie *AmMWSc 92*
**Laquer,** Henry L 1919- *AmMWSc 92*
**Laqueur,** Peter 1941- *WhoFI 92*
**Laqueur,** Walter 1921- *IntAu&W 91, IntWW 91, Who 92, WrDr 92*
**Laquinta,** Fred John 1949- *WhoFI 92*
**Lara,** Adam R. 1959- *WhoHisp 92*
**Lara,** Agustin 1900-1970 *NewAmDM*
**Lara,** Edison R., Sr. *WhoBlA 92*
**Lara,** Henry 1960- *WhoFI 92, WhoHisp 92, WhoMW 92*
**Lara,** Jan *ConAu 34NR*
**Lara,** Jim S. 1944- *WhoHisp 92*
**Lara,** Juan Francisco 1943- *WhoHisp 92*
**Lara,** Linda O. 1939- *WhoHisp 92*

**Lara**, Marc 1944- *WhoHisp 92*
**Lara**, Myrella Gonzalez *WhoHisp 92*
**Lara**, Ricardo E. 1955- *WhoAmL 92*
**Lara-Braud**, Carolyn Weathersbee 1940- *AmMWSc 92*
**Lara Bustamante**, Fernando 1911- *IntWW 91*
**Lara y Aguilar**, Domingo Antonio 1783-1844 *HisDSpE*
**Larabell**, Carolyn A 1947- *AmMWSc 92*
**Larach**, Simon 1922- *AmMWSc 92*
**Laragh**, John Henry 1924- *AmMWSc 92*
**Laraia**, Carol 1935- *WhoEnt 92*
**Laraki**, Azeddine 1929- *IntWW 91*
**Laraki**, Moulay Ahmed 1931- *IntWW 91*
**Laramey**, Thomas Avriett, Jr. 1945- *WhoAmL 92*
**Laramore**, George Ernest 1943- *AmMWSc 92*
**Larance**, Charles Larry 1938- *WhoIns 92*
**Larason**, Linda H 1947- *WhoAmP 91*
**Larason**, Timothy Manuel 1939- *WhoAmL 92*
**La Raus**, Roger Alan 1939- *WhoMW 92*
**Laraway**, Steven Allan 1954- *WhoFI 92*
**Larbaud**, Valery 1881-1957 *GuFrLit 1*
**L'Archeveque**, Real Viateur *AmMWSc 92*
**Larco Cox**, Guillermo 1932- *IntWW 91*
**Larcom**, Christopher 1926- *Who 92*
**Larcom**, Lucy 1824-1893 *BenetAL 91, HanAmWH*
**Larcom**, Lyndon Lyle 1940- *AmMWSc 92*
**Lard**, Edwin Webster 1921- *AmMWSc 92*
**Lard**, Moses 1818-1880 *RelLAm 91*
**Lard**, Moses E. 1818-1880 *AmPeW*
**Lardas**, Konstantinos *DrAPF 91*
**Larde**, Enrique Roberto 1934- *WhoIns 92*
**Lardieri**, Olive Elizabeth 1955- *WhoAmL 92, WhoEnt 92*
**Lardner**, Henry Petersen 1932- *WhoFI 92, WhoMW 92*
**Lardner**, James F 1924- *AmMWSc 92*
**Lardner**, John 1912-1960 *BenetAL 91*
**Lardner**, Peter 1932- *WhoIns 92*
**Lardner**, Rex Lynford, Jr. 1944- *WhoEnt 92*
**Lardner**, Ring *DrAPF 91, SourALJ*
**Lardner**, Ring 1885-1933 *BenetAL 91, FacFETw*
**Lardner**, Ring, Jr 1915- *FacFETw*
**Lardner**, Ring W., Jr 1915- *IntAu&W 91, IntMPA 92*
**Lardner**, Ring Wilmer, Jr. 1915- *WhoEnt 92*
**Lardner**, Robin Willmott 1938- *AmMWSc 92*
**Lardner**, Thomas Joseph 1938- *AmMWSc 92*
**Lardy**, Henry Arnold 1917- *AmMWSc 92, IntWW 91*
**Lardy**, Lawrence James 1934- *AmMWSc 92*
**Lardy**, Nicholas Richard 1946- *WhoFI 92, WhoWest 92*
**Lardy**, Susan Marie 1937- *WhoMW 92, WhoRel 92*
**Lardy**, William J *WhoAmP 91*
**Laredo**, Betty *ConAu 34NR*
**Laredo**, David Cary 1950- *WhoWest 92*
**Laredo**, Jaime 1941- *NewAmDM*
**Laredo**, Julio Richard 1952- *WhoHisp 92*
**Larenz**, Karl 1903- *EncTR 91, IntWW 91*
**Lares**, Linda *WhoHisp 92*
**Larew**, H Gordon 1922- *AmMWSc 92*
**Large**, Alfred McKee 1912- *AmMWSc 92*
**Large**, David Clay 1945- *IntWW 91, WrDr 92*
**Large**, Donald 1937- *WhoAmP 91*
**Large**, E C d1976 *TwCSFW 91*
**Large**, Edward W. 1930- *WhoAmL 92, WhoFI 92*
**Large**, G. Gordon M. 1940- *WhoFI 92, WhoMW 92*
**Large**, Jerry D. 1954- *WhoBlA 92*
**Large**, John Barry 1930- *Who 92*
**Large**, Peter 1931- *Who 92*
**Large**, Richard L 1940- *AmMWSc 92*
**Large**, Stanley Eyre d1991 *Who 92N*
**Large**, Timothy Wallace 1942- *WhoFI 92, WhoRel 92*
**Largen**, Fredrick James 1937- *WhoRel 92*
**Largent**, David Lee 1937- *AmMWSc 92*
**Largent**, Max Dale 1923- *AmMWSc 92*
**Largis**, Elwood Eugene *AmMWSc 92*
**Largman**, Corey *AmMWSc 92*
**Largman**, Theodore 1923- *AmMWSc 92*
**Lari**, Robert Joseph 1931- *AmMWSc 92*
**Laria**, Maria 1959- *WhoHisp 92*
**Larimer**, David G. 1944- *WhoAmL 92*
**Larimer**, Frank William 1948- *AmMWSc 92*
**Larimer**, James Lynn 1932- *AmMWSc 92*
**Larimer**, Janet McMaster 1942- *WhoAmP 91*
**Larimer**, John William 1939- *AmMWSc 92*
**Larimore**, Richard Weldon 1923- *AmMWSc 92*
**Larin**, Alfredo 1925- *WhoHisp 92*
**Larin**, Yuriy 1882-1932 *SovUnBD*
**Larionov**, Mikhail Fyodorovich 1881-1964 *FacFETw*
**Laris**, Philip Charles 1931- *AmMWSc 92*
**La Riviere**, Jan Willem Maurits 1923- *IntWW 91*
**Larizabal**, Alfred C *WhoAmP 91*
**Larizadeh**, Mohammed Reza 1947- *WhoWest 92*
**Larizza**, Anthony Joseph 1965- *WhoFI 92*
**Lark**, Cynthia Ann 1928- *AmMWSc 92*
**Lark**, David Lee 1947- *WhoWest 92*
**Lark**, Ed 1930- *WhoEnt 92*
**Lark**, Karl Gordon 1930- *AmMWSc 92*
**Lark**, Neil LaVern 1934- *AmMWSc 92*
**Lark**, Nyya Fellecia 1952- *WhoEnt 92*
**Lark**, Raymond 1939- *WhoBlA 92*
**Larke**, R P Bryce 1936- *AmMWSc 92*
**Larken**, Anthea 1938- *Who 92*
**Larken**, Jeremy 1939- *Who 92*
**Larkin**, Alile Sharon *ReelWom*
**Larkin**, Amy *SmATA 65*
**Larkin**, Barry 1964- *WhoMW 92*
**Larkin**, Barry Louis 1964- *WhoBlA 92*
**Larkin**, Bruce F *WhoAmP 91*
**Larkin**, David 1941- *AmMWSc 92*
**Larkin**, David Charles 1948- *WhoAmL 92*
**Larkin**, Edward Charles 1937- *AmMWSc 92*
**Larkin**, Edward Colby 1951- *WhoFI 92*
**Larkin**, Edward P 1920- *AmMWSc 92*
**Larkin**, Felix E. 1909-1991 *NewYTBS 91 [port]*
**Larkin**, Felix Edward 1909- *IntWW 91*
**Larkin**, James J. 1925- *IntMPA 92, WhoEnt 92*
**Larkin**, Jeanne Holden 1931- *AmMWSc 92*
**Larkin**, Joan *DrAPF 91*
**Larkin**, Joan Kupersmith 1953- *WhoAmL 92*
**Larkin**, John Cuthbert 1906- *Who 92*
**Larkin**, John Michael 1937- *AmMWSc 92*
**Larkin**, John Montague 1936- *AmMWSc 92*
**Larkin**, K T 1920- *AmMWSc 92*
**Larkin**, Lawrence A 1937- *AmMWSc 92*
**Larkin**, Leo Andrew 1946- *WhoMW 92*
**Larkin**, Leo Paul, Jr. 1925- *WhoAmL 92*
**Larkin**, Lynn Haydock 1934- *AmMWSc 92*
**Larkin**, Mary Ann *DrAPF 91*
**Larkin**, Maurice 1932- *WrDr 92*
**Larkin**, Michael Carter 1953- *WhoWest 92*
**Larkin**, Michael Joseph 1941- *WhoFI 92*
**Larkin**, Nelle Jean 1925- *WhoWest 92*
**Larkin**, Patrick Tierman Gerard 1960- *WhoFI 92*
**Larkin**, Peter Anthony 1924- *AmMWSc 92*
**Larkin**, Peter J *WhoAmP 91*
**Larkin**, Philip 1922-1985 *CnDBLB 8 [port], FacFETw, RfGEnL 91*
**Larkin**, Robert Hayden 1946- *AmMWSc 92*
**Larkin**, Rochelle 1935- *IntAu&W 91, WrDr 92*
**Larkin**, Terence Alphonsus 1924- *IntWW 91*
**Larkin**, Thomas Oliver 1802-1858 *DcNCBi 4*
**Larkin**, Thomas Peter 1948- *WhoAmL 92*
**Larkin**, Wendy Davis 1944- *WhoWest 92*
**Larkin**, William 1918- *AmMWSc 92*
**Larkin**, William Albert 1926- *AmMWSc 92*
**Larkin**, William J, Jr 1928- *WhoAmP 91*
**Larkin**, William Thomas 1923- *WhoRel 92*
**Larkins**, Brian Allen 1946- *AmMWSc 92*
**Larkins**, E. Pat *WhoBlA 92*
**Larkins**, Ellis Lane 1923- *NewAmDM*
**Larkins**, Howard Lee 1941- *WhoMW 92*
**Larkins**, John Davis, Jr. 1909-1990 *DcNCBi 4*
**Larkins**, John Rodman 1913- *WhoBlA 92*
**Larkins**, John Rodman 1913-1980 *DcNCBi 4*
**Larkins**, Thomas Hassell, Jr 1939- *AmMWSc 92*
**Larkins**, William Conyers 1934- *WhoBlA 92*
**Larky**, Arthur I 1931- *AmMWSc 92*
**Larman**, Shyla June 1945- *WhoWest 92*
**Larmer**, Oscar Vance 1924- *WhoMW 92*
**Larmie**, Walter Esmond 1920- *AmMWSc 92*
**Larminie**, Geoffrey 1929- *Who 92*
**Larmore**, Lawrence Louis 1941- *AmMWSc 92*
**Larmore**, Lewis 1915- *AmMWSc 92*
**Larmour**, Edward Noel 1916- *Who 92*
**Larner**, Jeremy *DrAPF 91*
**Larner**, Joseph 1921- *AmMWSc 92*
**Larner**, Kenneth Lee 1938- *AmMWSc 92*
**Larner**, Stevan DeFreest 1930- *WhoEnt 92*
**Larney**, Violet Hachmeister 1920- *AmMWSc 92*
**Larntz**, Kinley 1945- *AmMWSc 92, WhoMW 92*
**Laro**, David 1942- *WhoAmL 92, WhoAmP 91, WhoMW 92*
**LaRocca**, Anthony Joseph 1923- *AmMWSc 92*
**La Rocca**, Joseph Paul 1920- *AmMWSc 92*
**LaRocca**, Joseph Thomas 1965- *WhoWest 92*
**LaRocca**, Patricia Darlene McAleer 1951- *WhoMW 92*
**La Rocca**, Renato V. 1957- *WhoFI 92*
**LaRocco**, Joseph Donald, Jr. 1948- *WhoEnt 92*
**LaRocco**, Larry 1946- *AlmAP 92 [port], WhoAmP 91, WhoWest 92*
**LaRoche**, David Lewis 1931- *WhoWest 92*
**Laroche**, Emmanuel Pierre 1914- *IntWW 91*
**Laroche**, Gerard A. 1927- *WhoBlA 92*
**Laroche**, Guy 1923- *DcTwDes*
**LaRoche**, Karl, Jr. 1927- *WhoEnt 92*
**La Roche**, Marie-Elaine 1949- *WhoFI 92*
**Larochelle**, Jacques 1946- *AmMWSc 92*
**La Rochelle**, John Hart 1924- *AmMWSc 92*
**Larochelle**, Roger B 1924- *WhoAmP 91*
**Larock**, Bruce E 1940- *AmMWSc 92*
**Larock**, Richard Craig 1944- *AmMWSc 92*
**La Rocque**, Eugene Philippe 1927- *WhoRel 92*
**La Rocque**, Joseph Alfred Aurele 1909- *AmMWSc 92*
**La Rocque**, Marilyn Ross Onderdonk 1934- *WhoWest 92*
**La Rocque De Severac**, Francois, Comte de 1885-1946 *BiDExR*
**Laronge**, Thomas Miller 1943- *WhoWest 92*
**LaRoque**, Dale Charles 1937- *WhoAmP 91*
**Laros**, Gerald Snyder, II 1930- *AmMWSc 92*
**La Rosa**, Fernando 1943- *WhoHisp 92*
**LaRosa**, Julius *LesBEnT 92*
**LaRosa**, Paul A *WhoAmP 91*
**Larose**, Lawrence Alfred 1958- *WhoAmL 92, WhoFI 92*
**LaRose**, Susan Trummel 1954- *WhoEnt 92*
**Larosiere de Champfeu**, Jacques Martin De *Who 92*
**Larosiere De Champfeu**, Jacques Martin de 1929- *IntWW 91*
**LaRossa**, Robert Alan 1951- *AmMWSc 92*
**Larouche**, Lyndon Hermyle 1922- *BiDExR*
**LaRow**, Edward J 1937- *AmMWSc 92*
**LaRowe**, Myron Edward 1939- *WhoAmL 92*
**Larpenteur**, Charles 1807-1872 *BenetAL 91*
**Larquie**, Andre Olivier 1938- *IntWW 91*
**Larrabee**, Allan Roger 1935- *AmMWSc 92*
**Larrabee**, Eric 1922-1990 *ConAu 133*
**Larrabee**, Martin Glover 1910- *AmMWSc 92, IntWW 91*
**Larrabee**, R D 1931- *AmMWSc 92*
**Larrabee**, Richard Brian 1940- *AmMWSc 92*
**Larrabee**, Scott Richard 1955- *WhoMW 92*
**Larragoite**, Patricio C. 1950- *WhoHisp 92*
**Larramendi Blakely**, Lara *WhoHisp 92*
**Larraz**, Carlos M. 1952- *WhoEnt 92*
**Larre**, Rene J. 1915- *IntWW 91*
**Larrea**, Milton Fernandez 1955- *WhoHisp 92*
**Larreta**, Enrique Rodriguez 1875-1961 *BenetAL 91*
**Larrick**, James William 1950- *AmMWSc 92*
**Larrick**, Nancy 1910- *IntAu&W 91, WrDr 92*
**Larrie**, Reginald Reese 1928- *WhoBlA 92*
**Larrison**, Peggy Jeanne 1957- *WhoRel 92*
**Larrison**, Roger A. 1947- *WhoRel 92*
**Larrivee**, Anne M 1943- *WhoAmP 91*
**Larroca**, Raymond G. 1930- *WhoAmL 92*
**Larrocha**, Alicia De 1923- *IntWW 91, NewAmDM*
**Larrocha y de la Calle**, Alicia de 1923- *NewAmDM*
**Larroquette**, John 1947- *IntMPA 92*
**Larrowe**, Boyd T 1923- *AmMWSc 92*
**Larrowe**, Vernon L 1921- *AmMWSc 92*
**Larry**, Charles Edward 1944- *WhoBlA 92*
**Larry**, David Heath 1941- *WhoAmL 92*
**Larry**, Jerald Henry 1944- *WhoAmP 91, WhoBlA 92*
**Larry**, John Robert 1939- *AmMWSc 92*
**Larry**, R. Heath 1914- *IntWW 91*
**Lars**, Claudia 1899-1974 *SpAmWW*
**Larsen**, Alan Scott *WhoAmL 92*
**Larsen**, Allan F 1919- *WhoAmP 91*
**Larsen**, Arnold Lewis 1927- *AmMWSc 92*
**Larsen**, Aubrey Arnold 1919- *AmMWSc 92*
**Larsen**, Austin Ellis 1923- *AmMWSc 92*
**Larsen**, Barbara Seliger 1956- *AmMWSc 92*
**Larsen**, Bobbi Jo 1964- *WhoMW 92*
**Larsen**, Charles Martin 1948- *WhoWest 92*
**Larsen**, Charles McLoud 1924- *AmMWSc 92*
**Larsen**, Charles Warren 1945- *WhoEnt 92*
**Larsen**, Clark Spencer 1952- *WhoMW 92*
**Larsen**, Cyril Anthony 1919- *Who 92*
**Larsen**, D. Sabin 1961- *WhoWest 92*
**Larsen**, David Carl 1948- *WhoAmP 91*
**Larsen**, David M 1936- *AmMWSc 92*
**Larsen**, David W 1936- *AmMWSc 92*
**Larsen**, Dean Le Roy 1927- *WhoRel 92, WhoWest 92*
**Larsen**, Don Hyrum 1917- *AmMWSc 92*
**Larsen**, Donna Kay *WhoWest 92*
**Larsen**, Edgar M. 1940- *WhoFI 92*
**Larsen**, Edgar Robert, Jr. 1950- *WhoMW 92*
**Larsen**, Edward William 1944- *AmMWSc 92*
**Larsen**, Edwin Merritt 1915- *AmMWSc 92*
**Larsen**, Egon 1904- *IntAu&W 91*
**Larsen**, Ellen Wynne 1942- *AmMWSc 92*
**Larsen**, Eric Russell 1928- *AmMWSc 92*
**Larsen**, Ernest Albert 1932- *WhoAmP 91*
**Larsen**, Fenton E 1934- *AmMWSc 92*
**Larsen**, Frederick Duane 1930- *AmMWSc 92*
**Larsen**, Harlan Wendell 1928- *WhoRel 92*
**Larsen**, Harold Cecil 1918- *AmMWSc 92*
**Larsen**, Harry Stites 1927- *AmMWSc 92*
**Larsen**, Helge 1915- *IntWW 91*
**Larsen**, Howard James 1925- *AmMWSc 92*
**Larsen**, Howland Aikens 1928- *AmMWSc 92*
**Larsen**, Jack Lenor 1927- *DcTwDes*
**Larsen**, Jack Lucas 1924- *WhoAmP 91*
**Larsen**, James Arthur 1921- *AmMWSc 92*
**Larsen**, James Bouton 1941- *AmMWSc 92*
**Larsen**, James Richard 1947- *WhoRel 92*
**Larsen**, James Victor 1942- *AmMWSc 92*
**Larsen**, Jeanne *DrAPF 91*
**Larsen**, Jeanne 1950- *ConAu 134*
**Larsen**, John B. 1946- *WhoFI 92*
**Larsen**, John Herbert, Jr 1929- *AmMWSc 92*
**Larsen**, John W 1940- *AmMWSc 92*
**Larsen**, Joseph Reuben 1927- *AmMWSc 92*
**Larsen**, Kai 1926- *IntWW 91*
**Larsen**, Kenneth Anton 1939- *WhoFI 92*
**Larsen**, Kenneth David 1947- *WhoWest 92*
**Larsen**, Kenneth Martin 1927- *AmMWSc 92*
**Larsen**, Kent Sheldon 1935- *WhoAmP 91*
**Larsen**, Knud Sonderhede 1938- *WhoWest 92*
**Larsen**, Lawrence Harold 1939- *AmMWSc 92*
**Larsen**, Leif Andreas 1906-1990 *FacFETw*
**Larsen**, Leland Malvern 1915- *AmMWSc 92*
**Larsen**, Libby 1950- *ConCom 92, NewAmDM*
**Larsen**, Lloyd Ashley 1936- *WhoRel 92*
**Larsen**, Lloyd Don 1944- *AmMWSc 92*
**Larsen**, Lowell George 1942- *WhoWest 92*
**Larsen**, Lynn Alvin 1943- *AmMWSc 92*
**Larsen**, M. Ramona 1930- *WhoEnt 92*
**Larsen**, Marilyn Ankeney 1940- *AmMWSc 92*
**Larsen**, Mark Arvid 1948- *WhoAmL 92*
**Larsen**, Mark Leif 1956- *WhoMW 92*
**Larsen**, Marlin Lee 1942- *AmMWSc 92*
**Larsen**, Mary Ann Indovina 1929- *WhoMW 92*
**Larsen**, Max Dean 1941- *AmMWSc 92*
**Larsen**, Michael John 1938- *AmMWSc 92, WhoMW 92*
**Larsen**, Miguel Folkmar 1953- *AmMWSc 92*
**Larsen**, Milton Page Milt 1931- *WhoWest 92*
**Larsen**, Nella 1891-1964 *AfrAmW, BlkLC [port], NotBlAW 92 [port]*
**Larsen**, Nella 1893-1964 *BenetAL 91*
**Larsen**, Oscar N, Jr 1929- *WhoAmP 91*
**Larsen**, Patricia Jane 1933- *WhoWest 92*
**Larsen**, Paul Emanuel 1933- *WhoRel 92*
**Larsen**, Paul M *AmMWSc 92*
**Larsen**, Peder Olesen 1934- *IntWW 91*
**Larsen**, Peter Foster *AmMWSc 92*
**Larsen**, Philip O 1940- *AmMWSc 92*
**Larsen**, Ralph Irving 1928- *AmMWSc 92*
**Larsen**, Ralph Stanley 1938- *IntWW 91*
**Larsen**, Richard George 1946- *WhoAmL 92*
**Larsen**, Richard Lee 1934- *WhoWest 92*
**Larsen**, Robert Dhu 1922- *WhoAmL 92*
**Larsen**, Robert LeRoy 1934- *WhoEnt 92*
**Larsen**, Robert Merritt 1948- *WhoAmL 92*
**Larsen**, Robert Paul 1926- *AmMWSc 92*
**Larsen**, Robert Peter 1921- *AmMWSc 92*
**Larsen**, Rolf 1934- *WhoAmL 92, WhoAmP 91*
**Larsen**, Ronald John 1937- *AmMWSc 92*
**Larsen**, Russell D 1936- *AmMWSc 92*
**Larsen**, Sigurd Yves 1933- *AmMWSc 92*

Larsen, Steven H 1944- AmMWSc 92, WhoMW 92
Larsen, Ted LeRoy 1935- AmMWSc 92
Larsen, Tracy Thomas 1959- WhoAmL 92
Larsen, Tulinda Deegan 1954- WhoFI 92
Larsen, Wendy Wilder DrAPF 91
Larsen, Wendy Wilder 1940- IntAu&W 91
Larsen, William L 1926- AmMWSc 92
Larsen-Basse, Jorn 1934- AmMWSc 92
Larsh, Howard William 1914- AmMWSc 92
Larson, Alan P WhoAmP 91
Larson, Allan Bennett 1943- AmMWSc 92
Larson, Allan Louis 1932- WhoMW 92, WhoRel 92
Larson, Alvin Junior 1928- WhoFI 92
Larson, Andrew Hessler 1931- AmMWSc 92
Larson, Arthur 1910- IntWW 91
Larson, Arthur Calvin 1938- WhoRel 92
Larson, Arvid Gunnar 1937- AmMWSc 92
Larson, Bennett Charles 1941- AmMWSc 92
Larson, Bob IntMPA 92
Larson, Bob Emil 1944- WhoEnt 92
Larson, Brent T. 1942- WhoEnt 92
Larson, Brian Loren 1950- WhoRel 92
Larson, Bruce Alan 1951- WhoEnt 92
Larson, Bruce LeRoy 1956- WhoMW 92
Larson, Bruce Linder 1927- AmMWSc 92
Larson, Bruce Robert 1955- WhoAmL 92
Larson, C. Erik 1962- WhoFI 92
Larson, Cal 1930- WhoAmP 91
Larson, Carl Shipley 1934- WhoMW 92
Larson, Charles 1922- IntAu&W 91, WrDr 92
Larson, Charles Barry 1932- WhoFI 92
Larson, Charles Conrad 1914- AmMWSc 92
Larson, Charles Fred 1936- AmMWSc 92, WhoFI 92
Larson, Charles Lester 1922- WhoEnt 92, WhoWest 92
Larson, Charles R. DrAPF 91
Larson, Clarence Edward 1909- AmMWSc 92, WhoAmP 91
Larson, Clem TwCWW 91
Larson, Curtis L 1920- AmMWSc 92
Larson, D Wayne 1938- AmMWSc 92
Larson, Dale Irving 1937- WhoAmL 92
Larson, Daniel John 1944- AmMWSc 92
Larson, Daniel Norris 1954- WhoWest 92
Larson, David Allen 1954- WhoAmL 92
Larson, Delray Lyle 1947- WhoAmP 91
Larson, Diane Kay 1949- WhoAmP 91
Larson, Don 1946- WhoAmP 91
Larson, Don Calder 1952- WhoWest 92
Larson, Donald Alfred 1930- AmMWSc 92
Larson, Donald Clayton 1934- AmMWSc 92
Larson, Donald Dumford 1951- WhoIns 92
Larson, Donald Harold 1959- WhoMW 92
Larson, Donald W 1940- AmMWSc 92
Larson, Doyle Eugene 1930- WhoMW 92
Larson, Earl Richard 1911- WhoAmL 92, WhoMW 92
Larson, Edward William, Jr 1923- AmMWSc 92
Larson, Edwin E 1931- AmMWSc 92
Larson, Elaine Lucille 1943- AmMWSc 92
Larson, Emilie Gustava 1919- WhoMW 92
Larson, Eric George 1957- AmMWSc 92
Larson, Eric Victor 1957- WhoWest 92
Larson, Esther Elisabeth 1908-1978 ConAu 134
Larson, Everett Gerald 1935- AmMWSc 92
Larson, Frank Clark 1920- AmMWSc 92
Larson, Franklin Artemus, Jr. 1936- WhoMW 92
Larson, Frederic Roger 1942- AmMWSc 92
Larson, Frederick Anthony 1953- WhoAmL 92
Larson, Frederick H. 1913- Who 92
Larson, Gary 1950- CurBio 91 [port], WrDr 92
Larson, Gary Eugene 1936- AmMWSc 92
Larson, Gaylen Nevoy 1940- WhoFI 92
Larson, George H 1915- AmMWSc 92
Larson, Gerald James 1938- WhoRel 92
Larson, Gerald Louis 1942- AmMWSc 92
Larson, Glen A. LesBEnT 92
Larson, Gustav Olof 1926- AmMWSc 92
Larson, Harold Joseph 1934- AmMWSc 92
Larson, Harold Olaf 1921- AmMWSc 92
Larson, Harold Phillip 1938- AmMWSc 92
Larson, Harry Thomas 1921- AmMWSc 92
Larson, Harvey Casper 1922- WhoAmP 91
Larson, Hugo R 1925- AmMWSc 92
Larson, Ingemar W 1928- AmMWSc 92
Larson, Jack 1933- ConTFT 9
Larson, James D 1935- AmMWSc 92
Larson, James Lee 1931- WhoWest 92
Larson, Jay Reinhold 1932- AmMWSc 92
Larson, Jean McLaughlin 1925- WhoAmP 91
Larson, Jeff S. 1958- WhoMW 92
Larson, Jerry King 1941- AmMWSc 92
Larson, Jerry L. 1936- WhoAmL 92, WhoAmP 91, WhoMW 92
Larson, Jill Davis 1947- WhoEnt 92
Larson, John B 1948- WhoAmP 91
Larson, John David 1941- WhoIns 92
Larson, John Grant 1933- AmMWSc 92
Larson, John Hyde 1930- WhoFI 92
Larson, John William 1935- WhoAmL 92
Larson, Joseph Stanley 1933- AmMWSc 92
Larson, Julia Louise Fink 1950- WhoFI 92
Larson, Karen Elaine 1947- WhoMW 92
Larson, Kenneth Allen 1935- AmMWSc 92
Larson, Kenneth Blaine 1930- AmMWSc 92
Larson, Kenneth Curtis 1940- AmMWSc 92
Larson, Kris DrAPF 91
Larson, Larry Lee 1939- AmMWSc 92
Larson, Laurence Arthur 1930- AmMWSc 92
Larson, Lawrence John 1904- WhoFI 92
Larson, Lawrence Raymond 1930- WhoRel 92
Larson, Lawrence T 1930- AmMWSc 92
Larson, Lee Edward 1937- AmMWSc 92
Larson, LeRoy Wilbur 1939- WhoEnt 92
Larson, Lester Leroy 1923- AmMWSc 92
Larson, Lester Mikkel 1918- AmMWSc 92
Larson, M B 1927- AmMWSc 92
Larson, Marian Gertrude 1927- WhoMW 92
Larson, Mark Edward, Jr. 1947- WhoAmL 92, WhoFI 92
Larson, Mark Jefferson 1959- WhoAmL 92
Larson, Mark Stuart 1951- WhoMW 92
Larson, Mark Vincent 1954- WhoAmL 92
Larson, Maureen Inez 1955- WhoWest 92
Larson, Maurice A 1927- AmMWSc 92
Larson, Merlyn Milfred 1928- AmMWSc 92
Larson, Michael Len 1944- WhoFI 92
Larson, Mitchell Euray 1957- WhoEnt 92
Larson, Muriel Koller IntAu&W 91
Larson, Muriel Koller 1924- WrDr 92
Larson, Nancy Celeste 1951- WhoMW 92
Larson, Nancy Marie 1946- AmMWSc 92
Larson, Nils H 1934- WhoAmP 91
Larson, Omer R 1931- AmMWSc 92
Larson, Omer Richard 1931- WhoMW 92
Larson, Patricia Bryan 1954- WhoAmP 91
Larson, Paul David 1966- WhoMW 92
Larson, Paul Martin 1949- WhoAmL 92
Larson, Paul Stanley 1907- AmMWSc 92
Larson, Philip Rodney 1923- AmMWSc 92
Larson, R.A. DrAPF 91
Larson, Rachel Harris 1913- AmMWSc 92
Larson, Raymond Everett 1954- WhoRel 92
Larson, Reginald Einar 1934- AmMWSc 92
Larson, Richard 1928- WhoAmP 91
Larson, Richard Albert 1930- WhoFI 92
Larson, Richard Allen 1941- AmMWSc 92
Larson, Richard Bondo 1941- AmMWSc 92
Larson, Richard Carl 1942- WhoWest 92
Larson, Richard Gustavus 1940- AmMWSc 92
Larson, Richard I 1937- AmMWSc 92
Larson, Richard James 1954- WhoMW 92
Larson, Richard Jeffrey 1935- WhoAmP 91
Larson, Robert Allan 1958- WhoAmL 92
Larson, Robert Craig 1934- WhoFI 92
Larson, Robert Edward, Jr. 1939- WhoRel 92
Larson, Robert Elof 1932- AmMWSc 92
Larson, Robert Frederick 1930- WhoEnt 92, WhoMW 92
Larson, Robert J 1932- WhoAmP 91
Larson, Robert Walter 1927- WhoWest 92
Larson, Robert Wayne 1957- WhoEnt 92, WhoFI 92, WhoWest 92
Larson, Rocky Lee 1946- WhoFI 92
Larson, Rodney Allen 1952- WhoAmP 91
Larson, Roger 1943- AmMWSc 92
Larson, Roger James 1946- WhoMW 92
Larson, Roger Joseph 1933- WhoMW 92
Larson, Roland Edwin 1941- AmMWSc 92
Larson, Ron Lynn 1957- WhoRel 92
Larson, Ronald L WhoAmP 91
Larson, Roy Axel 1931- AmMWSc 92
Larson, Ruby Ila 1914- AmMWSc 92
Larson, Russell Edward 1917- AmMWSc 92
Larson, Russell L 1928- AmMWSc 92
Larson, Sanford J 1929- AmMWSc 92
Larson, Taft Alfred 1910- WhoAmP 91
Larson, Thomas D WhoAmP 91
Larson, Thomas D 1928- AmMWSc 92
Larson, Thomas E 1926- AmMWSc 92
Larson, Vaughn Leroy 1931- AmMWSc 92
Larson, Vernon C 1923- AmMWSc 92
Larson, Vernon LeRoy 1948- WhoAmP 91
Larson, Vicki Lord 1944- WhoMW 92
Larson, Victor E. 1898-1981 ConAu 134
Larson, Vincent H 1917- AmMWSc 92
Larson, Vivian M 1931- AmMWSc 92
Larson, Wilbur John 1921- AmMWSc 92
Larson, Wilbur S 1923- AmMWSc 92
Larson, William Earl 1921- AmMWSc 92
Larsson, John 1938- Who 92
Larsson, Lars-Erik 1908- IntWW 91
Larsson, Lars-Erik 1908-1986 NewAmDM
Larter, Edward Nathan 1923- AmMWSc 92
Larter, Raima 1955- AmMWSc 92
Lartigue, Donald Joseph 1934- AmMWSc 92
Lartigue, Jacques-Henri 1896-1986 FacFETw
Lartigue, Louis C. Who 92
La Rue, Carl Forman 1929- WhoAmL 92
LaRue, James Arthur 1923- AmMWSc 92
LaRue, Janice NaDine 1936- WhoEnt 92
La Rue, Jerrold A 1923- AmMWSc 92
LaRue, Karl McLaine 1940-1988 WhoBlA 92N
LaRue, L.H. 1938- ConAu 135
LaRue, Paul Hubert 1922- WhoAmL 92
La Rue, Pierre de 1460?-1518 NewAmDM
LaRue, Robert D 1922- AmMWSc 92
LaRue, Thomas A 1935- AmMWSc 92
LaRussa, Anthony, Jr. 1944- WhoWest 92
La Russa, Joseph Anthony 1925- AmMWSc 92
LaRusso, Anthony Carl 1949- WhoFI 92
La Russo, Nicholas F AmMWSc 92
Larusso-Reis, Michael 1956- WhoHisp 92
Larusson, Jodi Laureen 1963- WhoEnt 92
Larwa, David John 1948- WhoMW 92
Lary, Banning Kent 1949- WhoFI 92
Laryea, Seth Abang 1948- WhoRel 92, WhoWest 92
Larzelere, Harry J 1941- WhoIns 92
Larzelere, Robert Earl 1945- WhoMW 92
Lasaga, Antonio C 1949- AmMWSc 92
Lasaga, Manuel 1952- WhoHisp 92
Lasagna, Louis 1923- AmMWSc 92
LaSala, Edward Francis 1928- AmMWSc 92
La Salle, John Randall WhoHisp 92
LaSalle, Jon George 1948- WhoAmP 91
La Salle, Peter 1947- WrDr 92
La Salle, Rene Robert Cavelier, Sieur de 1643-1687 BenetAL 91
La Salle, Roch 1929- IntWW 91
La Salle, Victor TwCSFW 91, WrDr 92
Lasana, Oronde DrAPF 91
LaSane, Joanna Emma 1935- WhoBlA 92
Lasarow, William Julius 1922- WhoWest 92
Lasater, David B. 1948- WhoRel 92
Lasater, Donald E. 1925- WhoFI 92
Lasater, Donna Kathleen 1948- WhoAmP 91
Lasater, Herbert Alan 1931- AmMWSc 92
Lasca, Norman P, Jr 1934- AmMWSc 92
Las Casas, Bartolome de 1474-1566 BenetAL 91
Las Casas, Bartolome de 1484-1566 HisDSpE
Lascelles Who 92
Lascelles, Viscount 1950- Who 92
Lascelles, Henry Anthony 1912- Who 92
Lascelles, June 1924- AmMWSc 92
Lascelles, Mary Madge 1900- Who 92
Lasch, Christopher 1932- WrDr 92
Lasch, James Richard 1925- WhoMW 92
Lasch, Moira K. 1951- NewYTBS 91 [port]
Lascher, Alan Alfred 1941- WhoAmL 92
Lascher, Edward Leonard 1928- WhoAmL 92
Laschever, Norman Lewis 1918- AmMWSc 92
Laschi, Luisa 1760?-1790? NewAmDM
Lasday, Albert Henry 1920- AmMWSc 92
Lasdun, Denys 1914- Who 92
Lasdun, Denys Louis 1914- IntWW 91
Lasecki, Robert Richard 1943- WhoFI 92, WhoMW 92
Lasee, Alan J 1937- WhoAmP 91
Lasek, Raymond J 1940- AmMWSc 92
La Selva, Vincent 1929- WhoEnt 92
Lasenby, Jack 1931- SmATA 65 [port]
La Serna, Jose de 1770-1831 HisDSpE
Laserson, Gregory 1923- AmMWSc 92
La Seur, Noel Edwin 1922- AmMWSc 92
Lasfargues, Etienne Yves 1916- AmMWSc 92
Lash, Adele Margaret 1949- WhoMW 92
Lash, Donald R 1912- WhoAmP 91
Lash, Israel George 1810-1878 DcNCBi 4
Lash, Jacob 1760-1821 DcNCBi 4
Lash, James W 1929- AmMWSc 92
Lash, Jennifer 1938- WrDr 92
Lash, N. L. A. 1934- WrDr 92
Lash, Nicholas Langrishe Alleyne 1934- Who 92
Lash, Richard Anthony 1961- WhoAmL 92
Lash, Thomas Allen 1956- WhoWest 92
Lasheen, Aly M 1919- AmMWSc 92
LaShelle, Charles Stanton 1947- WhoFI 92
Lashen, Edward S 1934- AmMWSc 92
Lasher, Donald R 1929- WhoIns 92
Lasher, Donald Rex 1929- WhoFI 92
Lasher, Earl Parsons, III 1941- WhoAmL 92
Lasher, Esther Lu 1923- WhoRel 92
Lasher, Gordon 1926- AmMWSc 92
Lasher, Howard Louis 1944- WhoAmP 91
Lasher, Steven Howe 1944- WhoFI 92
Lasher, Sue WhoWest 92
Las Heras, Juan Gregorio de 1780-1866 HisDSpE
Lashewycz-Rubycz, Romana A 1952- AmMWSc 92
Lashinger, Joseph A, Jr 1953- WhoAmP 91
Lashinsky, Philip 1940- WhoEnt 92
Lashinsky, Sue WhoWest 92
Lashkarashvili, Tamara Vasiliyevna 1916- IntWW 91
Lashkowitz, Herschel WhoAmP 91
Lashlee, Frank P 1937- WhoAmP 91
Lashley, Barbara Ann 1942- WhoBlA 92
Lashley, Curtis Dale 1956- WhoAmL 92, WhoMW 92
Lashley, Gerald Ernest 1935- AmMWSc 92
Lashley, Karl 1890-1958 FacFETw
Lashley, Virginia Stephenson Hughes 1924- WhoWest 92
Lashman, Shelley Bortin 1917- WhoAmL 92
Lashmar, Paul Christopher 1954- IntAu&W 91
Lashmet, Peter K 1929- AmMWSc 92
Lashmore, David S 1946- AmMWSc 92
Lashner, Bret Auerbach 1954- AmMWSc 92, WhoMW 92
Lashof, Joyce Cohen 1926- AmMWSc 92
Lashof, Richard Kenneth 1922- AmMWSc 92
Lashof, Theodore William 1918- AmMWSc 92
Lashomb, James Harold 1942- AmMWSc 92
Lashuay, Kenneth Edward 1955- WhoAmP 91
Lashutka, Gregory S. 1944- WhoMW 92
Lashway, Joseph William 1927- WhoAmP 91
Lasiecka, Irena 1948- AmMWSc 92
Lasinski, Barbara Forman 1941- AmMWSc 92
Lasiter, Jack Brinkley 1930- WhoFI 92
Laska, Eugene 1938- AmMWSc 92
Laska, John Larry 1941- WhoFI 92
Laska, Vera 1928- IntAu&W 91
Laskar, Amulya Lal 1931- AmMWSc 92
Laskar, Renu Chakravarti 1932- AmMWSc 92
Laskaris, Constantine 1918- IntWW 91
Laskaris, Trifon Evangelos 1944- AmMWSc 92
Lasker, Barry Michael 1939- AmMWSc 92
Lasker, David Raymond 1950- IntAu&W 91
Lasker, Gabriel 1912- AmMWSc 92
Lasker, George Eric AmMWSc 92
Lasker, Howard Robert 1952- AmMWSc 92
Lasker, Reuben 1929- AmMWSc 92
Lasker, Sigmund E 1923- AmMWSc 92
Lasker-Schuler, Else 1869-1945 LiExTwC
Laskey, D. Robert 1943- WhoWest 92
Laskey, Ronald Alfred 1945- Who 92
Laskey, Thomas Penrose 1931- WhoAmP 91
Laski, Bernard 1915- AmMWSc 92
Laski, Frida 1885- BiDBrF 2
Laski, Harold 1893-1950 FacFETw
Laski, James J, Jr WhoAmP 91
Laski, Marghanita 1915-1988 FacFETw
Laskin, Allen I 1928- AmMWSc 92
Laskin, Barbara Virginia 1939- WhoWest 92
Laskin, Bora 1912-1984 FacFETw
Laskin, Daniel M 1924- AmMWSc 92
Laskin, Emily Jane 1953- WhoEnt 92
Laskin, Lee B 1936- WhoAmP 91
Laskin, Pam DrAPF 91
Lasko, Allen Howard 1941- WhoWest 92
Lasko, Carol Ann 1954- WhoMW 92
Lasko, Peter Erik 1924- IntWW 91, Who 92
Laskoff, Robert Alan 1945- WhoAmL 92
Laskowski, Edward L 1943- AmMWSc 92
Laskowski, Leonard Francis, Jr 1919- AmMWSc 92
Laskowski, Linda Jean 1950- WhoWest 92
Laskowski, Michael, Jr 1930- AmMWSc 92
Laskowski, Michael Bernard 1943- AmMWSc 92
Laskus, Jacek Wojciech 1951- WhoEnt 92

**Lasky**, Frank Michael 1940- *WhoEnt 92*
**Lasky**, George Arthur 1940- *WhoFI 92*
**Lasky**, Jack Samuel 1930- *AmMWSc 92, WhoFI 92*
**Lasky**, Jesse Louis, Jr 1910- *IntAu&W 91*
**Lasky**, Melvin Jonah 1920- *Who 92*
**Lasky**, Suzanne Terry *WhoEnt 92*
**Lasky**, Victor 1918- *IntAu&W 91*
**Lasky**, Victor 1918-1990 *AnObit 1990, FacFETw*
**Laslavic**, Thomas Joseph 1954- *WhoFI 92*
**Laslett**, Lawrence Jackson 1913- *AmMWSc 92*
**Laslett**, Peter 1915- *IntWW 91, Who 92*
**Lasley**, Betty Jean 1927- *AmMWSc 92*
**Lasley**, Bill Lee 1941- *AmMWSc 92*
**Lasley**, Harold F 1948- *WhoAmP 91*
**Lasley**, John Foster 1913- *AmMWSc 92, WhoMW 92*
**Lasley**, Phelbert Quincy, III 1940- *WhoBlA 92*
**Lasley**, Stephen Michael 1950- *AmMWSc 92*
**Lasley**, Thomas J. 1947- *WhoMW 92*
**Laslie**, Berry 1947- *WhoAmP 91*
**Lasmanis**, Raymond 1938- *WhoWest 92*
**Las Munecas**, Ildefonso de d1816 *HisDSpE*
**Lasnier**, Forest Wilfred 1927-1991 *WhoRel 92*
**Lasoff**, Mark *WhoEnt 92*
**Lasok**, Dominik 1921- *Who 92*
**Lason**, Alexander 1951- *ConCom 92*
**LaSor**, William Sanford 1911-1991 *ConAu 133*
**Lasorda**, Tom Charles 1927- *WhoWest 92*
**La Sorsa**, William George 1945- *WhoAmL 92*
**La Spina**, Greye 1880-1969 *ScFEYrs*
**Lass**, Norman J 1943- *AmMWSc 92*
**Lassalle**, Harriet 1958- *TwCPaSc*
**Lassalle**, Jacques Louis Bernard 1936- *IntWW 91*
**Lassally**, Walter 1926- *IntMPA 92*
**Lassen**, John Kai 1942- *WhoAmL 92*
**Lassen**, Laurence E 1932- *AmMWSc 92*
**Lassen**, Sandra Lake *DrAPF 91*
**Lassen**, Ulrik V 1930- *IntWW 91*
**Lassen-Willems**, James Rutherford 1944- *WhoRel 92*
**Lasser**, Elliott Charles 1922- *AmMWSc 92*
**Lasser**, Howard Gilbert 1926- *AmMWSc 92*
**Lasser**, Joseph Robert 1923- *WhoFI 92*
**Lasser**, Louise *WhoEnt 92*
**Lasser**, Louise 1941- *IntMPA 92*
**Lasser**, Robert Paul 1948- *WhoFI 92*
**Lasserre**, Bruno Marie Andre 1954- *IntWW 91*
**Lassers**, Willard J. 1919- *WhoAmL 92*
**Lasseter**, Edward Lynn, Jr. 1946- *WhoAmL 92*
**Lasseter**, Kenneth Carlyle 1942- *AmMWSc 92*
**Lassettre**, Edwin Nichols 1911- *AmMWSc 92*
**Lassettre**, Edwin Richie 1934- *WhoWest 92*
**Lassie** *FacFETw*
**Lassila**, Jaakko Sakari 1928- *IntWW 91*
**Lassila**, Kenneth Eino 1934- *AmMWSc 92*
**Lassiter**, Charles Albert 1927- *AmMWSc 92*
**Lassiter**, Charles Keeling *DrAPF 91*
**Lassiter**, James Edward, Jr. 1934- *WhoBlA 92*
**Lassiter**, James Hugh 1945- *WhoAmP 91*
**Lassiter**, James Morris, Jr. 1941- *WhoFI 92*
**Lassiter**, John 1937- *WhoBlA 92*
**Lassiter**, John 1941- *WhoAmP 91*
**Lassiter**, Ray Roberts 1937- *AmMWSc 92*
**Lassiter**, Rena Bingham 1886-1960 *DcNCBi 4*
**Lassiter**, Valentino *WhoRel 92*
**Lassiter**, William Edmund 1927- *AmMWSc 92*
**Lassiter**, William Stone 1939- *AmMWSc 92*
**Lassiter**, Wright Lowenstein, Jr. 1934- *WhoBlA 92*
**Lasslo**, Andrew 1922- *AmMWSc 92*
**Lassman**, Howard B *AmMWSc 92*
**Lasso**, Orlando di 1532-1594 *NewAmDM*
**Lasson**, Kenneth 1943- *WhoAmL 92, WrDr 92*
**Lassus**, Roland de *NewAmDM*
**Lasswell**, Marcia 1927- *WrDr 92*
**Lasswell**, Mary 1905- *WhoEnt 92*
**Lasswitz**, Kurd 1848-1910 *ScFEYrs, TwCSFW 91A*
**Last**, Arthur W 1918- *AmMWSc 92*
**Last**, Christopher Neville 1935- *Who 92*
**Last**, Jerold Alan 1940- *AmMWSc 92, WhoWest 92*
**Last**, Joan 1908- *WrDr 92*
**Last**, John Murray 1926- *AmMWSc 92*
**Last**, John William 1940- *Who 92*
**Last**, Marie Walker *TwCPaSc*
**Last**, Raymond Jack 1903- *Who 92*
**Last**, Robert L 1958- *AmMWSc 92*
**Last**, Sondra Carole 1932- *IntAu&W 91*
**Laster**, Alma Ingram 1939- *WhoMW 92*
**Laster**, Atlas, Jr. 1948- *WhoMW 92*
**Laster**, Danny Bruce 1942- *AmMWSc 92*
**Laster**, Leonard 1928- *AmMWSc 92*
**Laster**, Owen 1938- *WhoEnt 92*
**Laster**, Richard 1923- *AmMWSc 92, WhoFI 92*
**Laster**, William Russell, Jr 1926- *AmMWSc 92*
**Lastowka**, James Anthony 1951- *WhoAmP 91*
**Lastra**, Cesar R. 1939- *WhoHisp 92*
**Lastra**, Pedro M. *DrAPF 91*
**Lastra**, William A. 1956- *WhoWest 92*
**Lastrapes**, William Dud *WhoAmP 91*
**Lasuen**, Leanna 1955- *WhoAmP 91*
**Lasure**, Linda Lee 1946- *AmMWSc 92*
**LaSusa**, Barbara E. 1961- *WhoAmL 92*
**La Susa**, Lawrence R. 1960- *WhoAmL 92*
**Laswell**, Bette Dowdell 1937- *WhoFI 92*
**Laswell**, Troy James 1920- *AmMWSc 92*
**Laszewski**, Ronald M 1947- *AmMWSc 92*
**Laszlo**, Andor 1914- *IntWW 91*
**Laszlo**, Andrew 1926- *IntMPA 92*
**Laszlo**, Charles Andrew 1935- *AmMWSc 92*
**Laszlo**, Ervin 1932- *WrDr 92*
**Laszlo**, Paul 1900- *DcTwDes*
**Laszlo**, Tibor S 1912- *AmMWSc 92*
**Lata**, Gene Frederick 1922- *AmMWSc 92, WhoMW 92*
**Lataif**, Lawrence P. 1943- *WhoAmL 92*
**Latanision**, Ronald Michael 1942- *AmMWSc 92*
**Latarjet**, Raymond 1911- *IntWW 91*
**Latch**, Dana May 1943- *AmMWSc 92*
**Latcholia**, Kenneth Edward 1922- *WhoBlA 92*
**Latchum**, James Levin 1918- *WhoAmL 92*
**Latecoere**, Pierre M. 1964- *WhoFI 92*
**Lateef**, Abdul Bari 1939- *AmMWSc 92*
**Lateef**, Ahmed 1930- *WhoEnt 92*
**Lateef**, Yusef 1920- *WhoBlA 92, WhoEnt 92*
**Lateef**, Yusef 1921- *NewAmDM*
**Latef**, Javed Anver 1943- *WhoFI 92*
**Lateiner**, Donald 1944- *ConAu 135*
**Lateiner**, Jacob 1928- *NewAmDM*
**Lateiner**, Roger Martin 1945- *WhoEnt 92*
**Latella**, Robert Natale 1942- *WhoAmL 92*
**Latella**, Salvatore Philip 1919- *WhoEnt 92*
**Laterza**, Franco B. 1961- *WhoAmL 92*
**Laterza**, Vito 1926- *IntWW 91*
**Latey**, John 1914- *Who 92*
**Lath**, Pradeep Kailash Chandra 1959- *WhoFI 92*
**Latham** *Who 92*
**Latham**, Baron 1954- *Who 92*
**Latham**, Allen, Jr 1908- *AmMWSc 92, WhoFI 92*
**Latham**, Archie J 1926- *AmMWSc 92*
**Latham**, Arthur Charles 1930- *Who 92*
**Latham**, Bernice Grant 1945- *WhoBlA 92*
**Latham**, Cecil Thomas 1924- *Who 92*
**Latham**, Christopher George Arnot 1933- *Who 92*
**Latham**, Daniel Henry 1952- *WhoEnt 92*
**Latham**, David Nicholas Ramsay 1942- *Who 92*
**Latham**, David Winslow 1940- *AmMWSc 92*
**Latham**, DeWitt Robert 1928- *AmMWSc 92*
**Latham**, Don Jay 1938- *AmMWSc 92, WhoWest 92*
**Latham**, Eugenia Marie 1922- *WhoFI 92*
**Latham**, Harold S. 1887-1964 *BenetAL 91*
**Latham**, Jean Lee 1902- *IntAu&W 91, SmATA 68 [port], WrDr 92*
**Latham**, John 1921- *TwCPaSc*
**Latham**, Lenn Learner 1901-197-? *ConAu 135*
**Latham**, Louis Charles 1840-1895 *DcNCBi 4*
**Latham**, Lyndon Clint 1943- *WhoRel 92*
**Latham**, Mark Daniel 1962- *WhoAmL 92*
**Latham**, Mary Elizabeth *WhoRel 92*
**Latham**, Maude Moore 1871-1951 *DcNCBi 4*
**Latham**, Mavis *WrDr 92*
**Latham**, Michael Anthony 1942- *Who 92*
**Latham**, Michael Charles 1928- *AmMWSc 92*
**Latham**, Patricia Horan 1941- *WhoAmL 92*
**Latham**, Patricia Suzanne 1946- *AmMWSc 92*
**Latham**, Peter Anthony 1925- *Who 92*
**Latham**, Philip 1902-1981 *TwCSFW 91*
**Latham**, R James 1942- *WhoAmP 91*
**Latham**, Raymond R., Jr. 1945- *WhoFI 92*
**Latham**, Richard 1920- *DcTwDes*
**Latham**, Richard Brunton 1947- *Who 92*
**Latham**, Richard Thomas Paul 1934- *Who 92*
**Latham**, Robert Clifford 1912- *Who 92*
**Latham**, Ross, Jr 1932- *AmMWSc 92*
**Latham**, Weldon Hurd 1947- *WhoBlA 92*
**Latham**, Wilbur Joseph, Jr. 1940- *WhoAmL 92*
**Latham**, William 1961- *TwCPaSc*
**Latham**, William Peters 1917- *WhoEnt 92*
**Latham**, William Roberts, III 1944- *WhoFI 92*
**Lathan**, Mark Joseph 1961- *WhoMW 92*
**La Thangue**, Henry Herbert 1859-1929 *TwCPaSc*
**Lathe**, Grant Henry 1913- *Who 92*
**Lathem**, Ray Warren, Jr. 1952- *WhoRel 92*
**Lathem**, Willoughby 1923- *AmMWSc 92*
**Lathen**, Calvin Wesley 1940- *WhoWest 92*
**Lathen**, Emma *IntAu&W 91, WrDr 92*
**Lathen**, John William 1916- *WhoBlA 92*
**Latherow**, Clifford Brandon 1915- *WhoAmP 91*
**Latherow**, Jerry Allen 1951- *WhoAmL 92*
**Lathers**, Claire M *AmMWSc 92*
**Lathi**, Bhagawandas Pannalal 1933- *WhoWest 92*
**Lathiere**, Bernard 1929- *IntWW 91*
**Lathon**, Lamar Lavantha 1967- *WhoBlA 92*
**Lathrop**, Arthur LaVern 1918- *AmMWSc 92*
**Lathrop**, Earl Wesley 1924- *AmMWSc 92*
**Lathrop**, George Parsons 1851-1898 *BenetAL 91, ScFEYrs*
**Lathrop**, Gordon Wendel 1939- *WhoRel 92*
**Lathrop**, Irvin Tunis 1927- *WhoWest 92*
**Lathrop**, James Cameron 1946- *WhoWest 92*
**Lathrop**, James Rodney 1929- *WhoWest 92*
**Lathrop**, Jay Wallace 1927- *AmMWSc 92*
**Lathrop**, John 1740-1816 *BiInAmS*
**Lathrop**, Julia Clifford 1858-1932 *DcAmImH, HanAmWH*
**Lathrop**, Katherine Austin 1915- *AmMWSc 92*
**Lathrop**, Kaye Don 1932- *AmMWSc 92*
**Lathrop**, Lawrence Erwin, Jr. 1942- *WhoWest 92*
**Lathrop**, Mitchell Lee 1937- *WhoAmL 92, WhoWest 92*
**Lathrop**, Philip 1916- *IntMPA 92*
**Lathrop**, Richard C 1924- *AmMWSc 92*
**Lathrop**, Rose Hawthorne 1851-1926 *BenetAL 91*
**Lathrop**, Virginia Terrell 1902-1974 *DcNCBi 4*
**Lathwell**, Douglas J 1922- *AmMWSc 92*
**Laties**, Alan M 1931- *AmMWSc 92*
**Laties**, George Glushanok 1920- *AmMWSc 92*
**Laties**, Victor Gregory 1926- *AmMWSc 92*
**Latifah**, Queen *NewYTBS 91 [port]*
**Latimer**, Allie B. *WhoBlA 92*
**Latimer**, Bruce Millikin 1953- *AmMWSc 92*
**Latimer**, Catherine A. 1895?-1948 *NotBlAW 92*
**Latimer**, Clinton Narath 1924- *AmMWSc 92*
**Latimer**, Clive 1915- *DcTwDes*
**Latimer**, Courtenay Robert 1911- *Who 92*
**Latimer**, Frank Edward 1947- *WhoBlA 92*
**Latimer**, George 1935- *WhoAmL 92, WhoAmP 91, WhoMW 92*
**Latimer**, Graham 1926- *Who 92*
**Latimer**, Howard Leroy 1929- *AmMWSc 92*
**Latimer**, Ina Pearl 1934- *WhoBlA 92*
**Latimer**, James Harold 1934- *WhoEnt 92, WhoMW 92*
**Latimer**, Jennifer Ann 1953- *WhoBlA 92*
**Latimer**, John H 1941- *WhoAmP 91*
**Latimer**, John Stratford, Jr. 1956- *WhoEnt 92*
**Latimer**, Kenneth Alan 1943- *WhoAmL 92*
**Latimer**, Paul Henry 1925- *AmMWSc 92*
**Latimer**, Radcliffe Robertson 1933- *IntWW 91*
**Latimer**, Robert *Who 92*
**Latimer**, Steve B. 1927- *WhoBlA 92*
**Latimer**, Thomas Hugh 1932- *WhoMW 92*
**Latin**, Donald Edward 1930- *WhoFI 92*
**Latini**, Henry Peter *WhoWest 92*
**Latner**, Albert Louis 1912- *Who 92*
**Latney**, Harvey, Jr. 1944- *WhoBlA 92*
**Latno**, Arthur Clement, Jr. 1929- *WhoFI 92*
**Latore**, Daniel J 1939- *WhoIns 92*
**Latorella**, A Henry 1940- *AmMWSc 92*
**Latoria**, Michael Frank 1943- *WhoEnt 92*
**LaTorre**, Donald Rutledge 1938- *AmMWSc 92*
**LaTorre**, L. Donald 1937- *WhoFI 92*
**LaTorre**, Louis 1953- *WhoFI 92*
**Latorre**, Robert G. 1949- *WhoHisp 92*
**Latorre**, Robert George 1949- *AmMWSc 92*
**LaTorre**, Ruben *WhoHisp 92*
**Latorre**, V R 1931- *AmMWSc 92*
**Latorre**, Victor Robert 1931- *WhoWest 92*
**Latouche**, Louis 1823-1897 *ThHEIm*
**La Touf**, Larry 1939- *WhoFI 92*
**LaTour**, Kathleen Mary McBride 1946- *WhoMW 92*
**Latour**, Maurice Quentin de 1704-1788 *BlkwCEP*
**Latour**, Patrice Contamine De *ScFEYrs*
**Latour**, Pierre Richard 1940- *AmMWSc 92*
**Latour-Adrien**, Maurice 1915- *IntWW 91, Who 92*
**Latourette**, Harold Kenneth 1924- *AmMWSc 92*
**Latourette**, Howard Bennett 1918- *AmMWSc 92*
**La Tourette**, Jacqueline 1926- *IntAu&W 91*
**La Tourette**, John Ernest 1932- *IntWW 91, WhoFI 92, WhoMW 92*
**Latourette**, Kenneth Scott 1884-1968 *EncEarC, RelLAm 91*
**La Tourrette**, Jacqueline 1926- *ConAu 34NR, WrDr 92*
**La Tourrette**, James Thomas 1931- *AmMWSc 92*
**Latovick**, Paula Rae 1954- *WhoAmL 92*
**Latow**, Roberta 1931- *IntAu&W 91*
**Latrobe**, Benjamin Henry 1764-1820 *BenetAL 91, BiInAmS*
**Latrobe**, John H. B. 1803-1891 *BenetAL 91*
**La Trobe-Bateman**, Richard George S 1938- *Who 92*
**Latronico**, Philip Francis Anthony 1954- *WhoRel 92*
**Latschar**, Carl Ernest 1919- *AmMWSc 92*
**Latshaw**, David Rodney 1939- *AmMWSc 92*
**Latshaw**, J David *AmMWSc 92*
**Latshaw**, Sandra Jo 1954- *WhoMW 92*
**Latsis**, Otto Rudolfovich 1934- *IntWW 91, SovUnBD*
**Latsis**, Peter C. 1919- *IntMPA 92*
**Latt**, David Michael 1966- *WhoEnt 92*
**Latta**, Allen Jay 1961- *WhoAmL 92*
**Latta**, Bruce McKee 1940- *AmMWSc 92*
**Latta**, Bryan Michael 1946- *AmMWSc 92*
**Latta**, Delbert L 1920- *WhoAmP 91*
**Latta**, Edward Dilworth 1851-1925 *DcNCBi 4*
**Latta**, Gordon 1923- *AmMWSc 92*
**Latta**, Gregory Edwin 1952- *WhoBlA 92*
**Latta**, Harrison 1918- *AmMWSc 92*
**Latta**, Jean Carolyn 1943- *WhoFI 92*
**Latta**, John *DrAPF 91*
**Latta**, John Neal 1944- *AmMWSc 92*
**Latta**, Richard J. 1946- *WrDr 92*
**Latta**, Robert William 1934- *WhoFI 92*
**Latta**, William Braden, Jr. 1949- *WhoAmL 92*
**Latta**, William Carl 1925- *AmMWSc 92*
**Latta**, William Charlton 1902- *WhoRel 92*
**Lattanzi**, Matt *IntMPA 92*
**Lattanzio**, Stephen Paul 1949- *WhoWest 92*
**Lattanzio**, Vito 1926- *IntWW 91*
**Lattauzio**, John *WhoAmP 91*
**Latter**, Albert L 1920- *AmMWSc 92*
**Latter**, Leslie William 1921- *Who 92*
**Latter**, Richard 1923- *AmMWSc 92*
**Latterell**, Joseph J 1932- *AmMWSc 92*
**Latterell**, Joseph James 1932- *WhoMW 92*
**Latterell**, Patrick Francis 1958- *WhoFI 92*
**Latterell**, Richard L 1928- *AmMWSc 92*
**Lattes**, Jean-Claude J. 1941- *WhoFI 92*
**Lattes**, Raffaele 1910- *AmMWSc 92*
**Lattes**, Robert 1927- *IntWW 91*
**Latteur**, Jean Pierre 1936- *IntWW 91*
**Lattime**, Edmund Charles 1951- *AmMWSc 92*
**Lattimer**, Agnes Dolores 1928- *WhoBlA 92*
**Lattimer**, James Michael 1950- *AmMWSc 92*
**Lattimer**, Robert Phillips 1945- *AmMWSc 92*
**Lattimore**, Caroline Louise 1945- *WhoBlA 92*
**Lattimore**, Everett Carrigan 1927-1991 *WhoBlA 92N*
**Lattimore**, Michael Howard 1938- *WhoEnt 92*
**Lattimore**, Oliver Louis, Sr. 1893-1987 *WhoBlA 92N*
**Lattimore**, Owen 1900- *BenetAL 91*
**Lattimore**, Owen 1900-1989 *FacFETw*
**Lattimore**, Richard *FacFETw*
**Lattimore**, Richmond 1906-1984 *BenetAL 91*
**Lattimore**, Samuel Allen 1828-1913 *BiInAmS*
**Lattimore**, Vergel Lyronne 1953- *WhoRel 92*
**Lattin**, Danny Lee 1942- *AmMWSc 92*
**Lattin**, John D 1927- *AmMWSc 92*
**Lattin**, Vernon E. 1938- *WhoHisp 92*
**Lattman**, Eaton Edward 1940- *AmMWSc 92*
**Lattman**, Laurence Harold 1923- *AmMWSc 92*
**Latto**, Douglas 1913- *Who 92*

**Latto,** Lawrence Jay 1920- *WhoAmL 92*
**Latto,** Lewis M., Jr. 1940- *WhoEnt 92*
**Lattocha,** Michael Anthony 1963- *WhoFI 92*
**Lattre,** Andre Marie Joseph De 1923- *IntWW 91*
**Lattre de Tassigny,** Jean de 1889-1952 *FacFETw*
**Lattuada,** Alberto 1914- *IntDcF 2-2 [port], IntMPA 92*
**Lattuada,** Charles P 1933- *AmMWSc 92*
**Lattuca,** Joseph J. 1947- *WhoMW 92*
**Latus,** Timothy Dexter 1946- *WhoRel 92*
**Latymer,** Baron 1926- *Who 92*
**Latynina,** Larisa Semenovna 1934- *SovUnBD*
**Latz,** Arje 1927- *AmMWSc 92*
**Latz,** Howard W 1933- *AmMWSc 92*
**Latz,** William John 1943- *WhoFI 92*
**Latzer,** Richard N 1937- *WhoIns 92*
**Lau,** Alan Chong *DrAPF 91*
**Lau,** B. Peck 1932- *WhoWest 92*
**Lau,** Brad W C 1950- *AmMWSc 92*
**Lau,** Catherine Y 1951- *AmMWSc 92*
**Lau,** Cheryl *WhoWest 92*
**Lau,** Cheryl Ann 1944- *WhoAmP 91*
**Lau,** Cheuk Kun 1951- *AmMWSc 92*
**Lau,** Daniel B T 1919- *WhoIns 92*
**Lau,** Eugene Wing Iu 1931- *WhoAmL 92*
**Lau,** Francis You King 1924- *AmMWSc 92*
**Lau,** Jark Chong 1935- *AmMWSc 92*
**Lau,** Jeffrey Daniel 1948- *WhoAmL 92*
**Lau,** John H 1946- *AmMWSc 92*
**Lau,** John Herbert 1926- *WhoMW 92*
**Lau,** John Tze 1948- *WhoFI 92*
**Lau,** Joseph T Y 1953- *AmMWSc 92*
**Lau,** Judith Wisdom 1942- *WhoFI 92*
**Lau,** Kenneth W 1941- *AmMWSc 92*
**Lau,** L Stephen 1929- *AmMWSc 92*
**Lau,** Maureen Treacy 1946- *WhoEnt 92*
**Lau,** Michele Denise 1960- *WhoFI 92, WhoMW 92*
**Lau,** Ngar-Cheung 1953- *AmMWSc 92*
**Lau,** Philip T S 1935- *AmMWSc 92*
**Lau,** Roland 1943- *AmMWSc 92*
**Lau,** S S 1941- *AmMWSc 92*
**Lau,** Theodor Ludwig 1670-1740 *BlkwCEP*
**Lau,** Thomas Shun-Kwong 1950- *WhoWest 92*
**Lau,** Yiu-Wa August 1948- *AmMWSc 92*
**Lau-Cam,** Cesar A 1940- *AmMWSc 92*
**Laub,** Alan John 1948- *AmMWSc 92*
**Laub,** Leslie Ann 1961- *WhoFI 92*
**Laub,** Richard J 1945- *AmMWSc 92*
**Laub,** Richard Steven 1945- *AmMWSc 92*
**Laub,** William Murray 1924- *WhoAmP 91*
**Laubach,** Charles 1836-1904 *BiInAmS*
**Laubach,** Frank Charles 1884-1970 *DcEcMov*
**Laubach,** Gerald D 1926- *AmMWSc 92, IntWW 91*
**Laubach,** Gerald David 1926- *WhoFI 92*
**Laubacher,** Denise Reynolds *DrAPF 91*
**Laubaugh,** Frederick 1926- *WhoFI 92*
**Laube,** Roger Gustav 1921- *WhoFI 92, WhoWest 92*
**Laubenthal,** Allan R. *WhoRel 92*
**Lauber,** Daniel M. 1949- *WhoAmL 92*
**Lauber,** Jean Kautz 1926- *AmMWSc 92*
**Lauber,** John K 1942- *WhoAmP 91*
**Lauber,** Lynn 1952- *ConAu 133*
**Lauber,** Mignon Diane *WhoFI 92, WhoWest 92*
**Lauber,** Nancy Lee Avery 1932- *WhoRel 92*
**Lauber,** Patricia Mary 1943- *WhoAmP 91*
**Lauber,** Peg Carlson *DrAPF 91*
**Lauber,** Thornton Stuart 1924- *AmMWSc 92*
**Laubert,** Helen Rossbach 1927- *WhoFI 92*
**Lauchengco,** Jose Yujuico, Jr. 1936- *WhoAmL 92, WhoWest 92*
**Lauchlan,** Douglas Martyn 1931- *WhoEnt 92*
**Lauchle,** Gerald Clyde 1945- *AmMWSc 92*
**Lauchner,** Aden Jesse 1932- *WhoMW 92*
**Lauck,** Anthony Joseph 1908- *WhoMW 92*
**Lauck,** David R 1930- *AmMWSc 92*
**Lauck,** Francis W 1918- *AmMWSc 92*
**Laucke,** Condor 1914- *Who 92*
**Laucke,** Condor Louis 1914- *IntWW 91*
**Laud,** Purushottam Waman 1948- *AmMWSc 92*
**Lauda,** Andreas-Nikolaus 1949- *IntWW 91*
**Laudadio,** Marilyn Grace 1951- *WhoEnt 92*
**Laude,** Horton Meyer 1915- *AmMWSc 92*
**Laudeman,** Scott King 1958- *WhoWest 92*
**Laudenslager,** James Bishop 1945- *AmMWSc 92*
**Laudenslager,** Mark LeRoy 1947- *AmMWSc 92*
**Lauder,** Estee *IntWW 91, WhoFI 92*
**Lauder,** Estee 1908?- *News 92-2 [port]*
**Lauder,** Harry 1870-1950 *FacFETw, NewAmDM*
**Lauder,** Jean Miles 1945- *AmMWSc 92*
**Lauder,** Leonard Alan 1933- *WhoFI 92*
**Lauder,** Piers Robert Dick- *Who 92*
**Lauder,** Robert E. 1934- *ConAu 134*
**Lauder,** Ronald S 1944- *WhoAmP 91*
**Lauder,** Ronald Stephen 1944- *IntWW 91*
**Lauderbach,** William Charles 1942- *WhoFI 92, WhoMW 92*
**Lauderback,** David Ryan 1938- *WhoMW 92*
**Lauderdale,** Earl of 1911- *Who 92*
**Lauderdale,** Master of *Who 92*
**Lauderdale,** Clint Arlen 1932- *WhoAmP 91*
**Lauderdale,** James W, Jr 1937- *AmMWSc 92*
**Lauderdale,** Katherine Sue 1954- *WhoAmL 92, WhoEnt 92*
**Lauderdale,** Robert A, Jr 1922- *AmMWSc 92*
**Laudicina,** Paul A. 1949- *WhoFI 92*
**Laudise,** Robert Alfred 1930- *AmMWSc 92*
**Laudon,** Thomas S 1932- *AmMWSc 92*
**Laudonniere,** Rene Goulaine de *BenetAL 91*
**Laudor,** Richard Saul 1957- *WhoAmL 92*
**Laudy,** Louis Hyacinth 1842?-1905 *BiInAmS*
**Laue,** Max Theodor Felix von 1879-1960 *WhoNob 90*
**Laue,** Max von 1879-1960 *EncTR 91 [port]*
**Lauenroth,** William Karl 1945- *AmMWSc 92*
**Lauenstein,** Ann Gail 1949- *WhoMW 92*
**Lauenstein,** Milton Charles 1926- *WhoFI 92*
**Lauer,** B E 1907- *AmMWSc 92*
**Lauer,** Barbara Estelle *WhoRel 92*
**Lauer,** Clinton Dillman 1926- *WhoFI 92*
**Lauer,** David Allan 1944- *AmMWSc 92*
**Lauer,** Eliot 1949- *WhoAmL 92*
**Lauer,** Elizabeth 1932- *WhoEnt 92*
**Lauer,** Eugene John 1920- *AmMWSc 92*
**Lauer,** Florian Isidore 1928- *AmMWSc 92*
**Lauer,** George 1936- *AmMWSc 92, WhoWest 92*
**Lauer,** Gerald J 1934- *AmMWSc 92*
**Lauer,** James Lothar 1920- *AmMWSc 92*
**Lauer,** John David 1945- *WhoEnt 92*
**Lauer,** Reinhard 1935- *IntWW 91*
**Lauer,** Robert B 1942- *AmMWSc 92*
**Lauer,** Robert Harold 1933- *WhoWest 92*
**Lauerman,** Lloyd Herman, Jr 1933- *AmMWSc 92*
**Lauersen,** Floyd E. 1933- *WhoWest 92*
**Lauf,** Peter Kurt 1933- *AmMWSc 92*
**Laufenburger,** Roger Allyn 1921- *WhoAmP 91*
**Laufer,** Allan Henry 1936- *AmMWSc 92*
**Laufer,** Beatrice *WhoEnt 92*
**Laufer,** Daniel A 1938- *AmMWSc 92*
**Laufer,** Hans 1929- *AmMWSc 92*
**Laufer,** Igor 1944- *AmMWSc 92*
**Laufer,** Jacob 1949- *WhoAmL 92*
**Laufer,** Leonard Justin 1965- *WhoFI 92*
**Laufer,** Robert J 1932- *AmMWSc 92*
**Laufer,** William *DrAPF 91*
**Laufersweiler,** Joseph Daniel 1930- *AmMWSc 92*
**Lauff,** George Howard 1927- *AmMWSc 92*
**Lauffenburger,** Douglas Alan 1953- *AmMWSc 92*
**Lauffenburger,** James C 1938- *AmMWSc 92*
**Lauffer,** Donald Eugene 1940- *AmMWSc 92*
**Lauffer,** Max Augustus, Jr 1914- *AmMWSc 92*
**Laufman,** Harold 1912- *AmMWSc 92*
**Laufman,** Harrington Butler 1947- *WhoMW 92*
**Laug,** George Milton 1923- *AmMWSc 92*
**Laugerud Garcia,** Kjell Eugenio 1930- *IntWW 91*
**Laugharne,** Albert 1931- *Who 92*
**Laughbaum,** Edward David 1944- *WhoMW 92*
**Laughead,** W.B. *BenetAL 91*
**Laughery,** Ronald D. 1940- *WhoRel 92*
**Laughinghouse,** Charles O'Hagan 1871-1930 *DcNCBi 4*
**Laughland,** Bruce 1931- *Who 92*
**Laughlin,** Alexander William 1936- *AmMWSc 92*
**Laughlin,** Alice 1918- *AmMWSc 92*
**Laughlin,** Allen Bradley 1946- *WhoFI 92*
**Laughlin,** Bruce James 1930- *WhoAmP 91*
**Laughlin,** Christine Nelson 1942- *WhoFI 92*
**Laughlin,** David Eugene 1947- *AmMWSc 92*
**Laughlin,** Edward Noel 1943- *WhoMW 92*
**Laughlin,** Ethelreda R 1922- *AmMWSc 92*
**Laughlin,** Florence 1910- *WrDr 92*
**Laughlin,** Greg 1942- *AlmAP 92 [port], WhoAmP 91*
**Laughlin,** Harry H 1880-1953 *DcAmImH*
**Laughlin,** Hugh Collins 1938- *WhoRel 92*
**Laughlin,** J Francis 1928- *WhoAmP 91*
**Laughlin,** James 1914- *ConPo 91, IntAu&W 91, WrDr 92*
**Laughlin,** James, IV 1914- *BenetAL 91*
**Laughlin,** James Harold, Jr. 1941- *WhoAmL 92*
**Laughlin,** James Patrick 1951- *WhoAmL 92*
**Laughlin,** James Stanley 1936- *AmMWSc 92*
**Laughlin,** John Charles Hugh 1942- *WhoRel 92*
**Laughlin,** John Paul 1950- *WhoAmL 92*
**Laughlin,** John Seth 1918- *AmMWSc 92*
**Laughlin,** Keith Eugene 1951- *WhoAmP 91*
**Laughlin,** Kevin Michael 1956- *WhoWest 92*
**Laughlin,** Louis Gene 1937- *WhoFI 92*
**Laughlin,** R G W 1942- *AmMWSc 92*
**Laughlin,** Robert Arthur 1939- *WhoFI 92*
**Laughlin,** Robert Gene 1930- *AmMWSc 92*
**Laughlin,** Ruth Evelyn 1916- *WhoFI 92*
**Laughlin,** Susan 1932- *WhoAmP 91*
**Laughlin,** Terry Xavier 1936- *WhoFI 92*
**Laughlin,** Thomas Bernard 1925- *WhoRel 92*
**Laughlin,** Timothy Robert 1947- *WhoFI 92*
**Laughlin,** Tom 1938- *IntMPA 92, WhoEnt 92*
**Laughlin,** William Sceva 1919- *AmMWSc 92*
**Laughlin,** Winston Means 1917- *AmMWSc 92*
**Laughnan,** John Raphael 1919- *AmMWSc 92*
**Laughner,** William James, Jr 1943- *AmMWSc 92*
**Laughon,** Robert Bush 1934- *AmMWSc 92*
**Laughter,** Arline H *AmMWSc 92*
**Laughter,** Ron D. 1948- *WhoAmL 92*
**Laughter,** Sylvia M. 1959- *WhoWest 92*
**Laughton,** Anthony Seymour 1927- *IntWW 91, Who 92*
**Laughton,** Bruce 1928- *ConAu 133*
**Laughton,** Charles 1899-1962 *FacFETw*
**Laughton,** James R., Jr. 1959- *WhoFI 92*
**Laughton,** John Dudley 1948- *WhoAmL 92*
**Laughton,** Paul MacDonell 1923- *AmMWSc 92*
**Lauhoff,** Herman E 1933- *WhoAmP 91*
**Laukes,** Helen Hamen 1923- *WhoMW 92*
**Laukhuf,** Walden Louis Shelburne 1943- *AmMWSc 92*
**Laukonis,** Joseph Vainys 1925- *AmMWSc 92*
**Laul,** Jagdish Chander 1939- *AmMWSc 92*
**Laulainen,** Nels Stephen 1941- *AmMWSc 92*
**Laulicht,** Murray Jack 1940- *WhoAmL 92*
**Laumann,** Curt William 1963- *WhoWest 92*
**Laumann,** Edward Otto 1938- *WhoMW 92*
**Laumer,** Keith 1925- *IntAu&W 91, TwCSFW 91, WrDr 92*
**Laumoli,** Tuia T 1948- *WhoAmP 91*
**Launcelot Langstaff** *BenetAL 91*
**Launder,** Frank 1906- *IntDcF 2-2 [port]*
**Launder,** Frank, and Sidney Gilliat *IntDcF 2-2 [port]*
**Launderville,** Dale *WhoRel 92*
**Laundre,** John William 1949- *AmMWSc 92*
**Launer,** Dale Mark 1952- *WhoEnt 92*
**Launer,** Philip Jules 1922- *AmMWSc 92*
**Launer,** Richard Merrill 1954- *WhoMW 92*
**Launey,** George Volney, III 1942- *WhoFI 92*
**Launius,** Charles Edwin 1948- *WhoEnt 92*
**Laupus,** William E 1921- *AmMWSc 92*
**Laura,** Ernesto Guido 1932- *IntWW 91*
**Laura,** Patricio Adolfo Antonio 1935- *AmMWSc 92*
**Laurain,** Jean 1921- *IntWW 91*
**Laurance,** Leonard Clark 1932- *WhoWest 92*
**Laurance,** Neal L 1932- *AmMWSc 92*
**Laure,** Maurice 1917- *IntWW 91*
**Laure,** Phillip John 1949- *WhoWest 92*
**Laureano-Vega,** Manuel 1956- *WhoHisp 92*
**Laurel and Hardy** *FacFETw [port]*
**Laurel,** Oscar, Jr. *WhoHisp 92*
**Laurel,** Oscar, Sr. *WhoHisp 92*
**Laurel,** Salvador Hidalgo 1928- *IntWW 91*
**Laurel,** Stan 1890-1965 *FacFETw [port]*
**Lauren,** Ralph 1939- *DcTwDes, FacFETw, IntWW 91, WhoFI 92*
**Laurence,** Alfred Edward 1910- *AmMWSc 92*
**Laurence,** Christopher *Who 92*
**Laurence,** Dan H. 1920- *WrDr 92*
**Laurence,** Dan Hyman 1920- *Who 92*
**Laurence,** Geoffrey Cameron 1943- *AmMWSc 92*
**Laurence,** George Frederick 1947- *Who 92*
**Laurence,** John A 1945- *AmMWSc 92*
**Laurence,** John Harvard Christopher 1929- *Who 92*
**Laurence,** Kenneth Allen 1928- *AmMWSc 92*
**Laurence,** Margaret 1926- *BenetAL 91*
**Laurence,** Margaret 1926-1987 *RfGEnL 91, TwCWW 91*
**Laurence,** Peter 1923- *Who 92*
**Laurence,** Robert L 1936- *AmMWSc 92*
**Laurencot,** Henry Jules 1929- *AmMWSc 92*
**Laurendeau,** Normand Maurice 1944- *AmMWSc 92, WhoMW 92*
**Laurene,** Arne Thomas 1951- *WhoFI 92*
**Laurens,** Andre 1934- *Who 92*
**Laurens,** Andre Antoine 1934- *IntWW 91*
**Laurens,** Henry 1724-1792 *BenetAL 91, BlkwEAR*
**Laurenson,** Charles Raymond 1956- *WhoWest 92*
**Laurenson,** James Tait 1941- *Who 92*
**Laurenson,** Robert Mark 1938- *AmMWSc 92*
**Laurent,** Jacques 1919- *IntAu&W 91, IntWW 91*
**Laurent,** Jerome King 1940- *WhoFI 92, WhoMW 92*
**Laurent,** John 1931- *WhoAmP 91*
**Laurent,** John Frank 1946- *WhoAmP 91*
**Laurent,** Mery 1849-1900 *ThHEIm*
**Laurent,** Pierre 1925- *AmMWSc 92*
**Laurent,** Robert Denis 1939- *WhoFI 92, WhoMW 92*
**Laurent,** Robert Louis, Jr. 1955- *WhoFI 92*
**Laurent,** Roger 1938- *AmMWSc 92*
**Laurent,** Sebastian Marc 1926- *AmMWSc 92*
**Laurent,** Stephan 1948- *WhoEnt 92*
**Laurent,** Torvard Claude 1930- *IntWW 91*
**Laurenti,** Jeffrey 1950- *WhoAmP 91*
**Laurents,** Arthur 1918- *BenetAL 91, ConTFT 9, IntAu&W 91, IntMPA 92, IntWW 91, WhoEnt 92, WrDr 92*
**Laurents,** Luanne Parker 1950- *WhoMW 92*
**Laurenzano,** Robert Salvatore 1946- *WhoFI 92*
**Laurenzi,** Bernard John 1938- *AmMWSc 92*
**Laurenzi,** Gustave 1926- *AmMWSc 92*
**Laurenzo,** Frederick C. *WhoHisp 92*
**Laurenzo,** Ninfa R. 1924- *WhoHisp 92*
**Laurenzo,** Roland D. *WhoHisp 92*
**Laurenzo,** Vincent D 1939- *IntWW 91*
**Laurenzo,** Vincent Dennis 1939- *WhoFI 92*
**Laures,** Robert Anthony 1942- *WhoMW 92*
**Lauret,** Curtis Bernard, Jr. 1945- *WhoFI 92, WhoIns 92*
**Lauri-Volpi,** Giacomo 1892-1979 *NewAmDM*
**Lauria,** Dan 1947- *WhoEnt 92*
**Lauria,** Lawrence Frederick 1951- *WhoEnt 92*
**Laurice** *WhoEnt 92*
**Lauricella,** Frances Hank 1930- *WhoAmP 91*
**Laurie,** Andre 1845-1909 *ScFEYrs*
**Laurie,** Edward James 1925- *WrDr 92*
**Laurie,** Gordon William 1953- *AmMWSc 92*
**Laurie,** John Sewall 1925- *AmMWSc 92*
**Laurie,** Marilyn *WhoFI 92*
**Laurie,** Piper 1932- *IntMPA 92, WhoEnt 92*
**Laurie,** Robert Bayley 1931- *Who 92*
**Laurie,** Robert Peter 1925- *Who 92*
**Laurie,** Robert Stephen 1936- *IntWW 91*
**Laurie,** Robin 1938- *Who 92*
**Laurie,** Rona *WrDr 92*
**Laurie,** Rona 1916- *IntAu&W 91*
**Laurie,** Victor William 1935- *AmMWSc 92*
**Lauriente,** Mike 1922- *AmMWSc 92*
**Laurier,** Wilfrid 1841-1919 *FacFETw*
**Laurimore,** Ann 1943- *WhoMW 92*
**Laurin,** Andre Frederic 1929- *AmMWSc 92*
**Laurin,** Pierre 1939- *WhoFI 92*
**Laurin,** Pushpamala *AmMWSc 92*
**Laurino,** Anthony C 1910- *WhoAmP 91*
**Laurino,** Robert Dennis 1951- *WhoAmL 92*
**Laurino,** William J 1941- *WhoAmP 91*
**Laurion,** Ronald R 1961- *WhoAmP 91*
**Lauristin,** Marju 1942- *IntWW 91*
**Lauristin,** Mar'yu Iokhannesovna 1942- *SovUnBD*
**Lauriston,** Alexander Clifford 1927- *Who 92*
**Lauriston,** Richard Basil 1917- *Who 92*
**Lauritzen,** Erik Middleton 1953- *WhoWest 92*
**Lauritzen,** Peter O 1935- *AmMWSc 92*
**Laurmann,** John Alfred 1926- *AmMWSc 92*
**Lauro,** Salvatore Anthony 1945- *WhoFI 92*

**Lauro**, Shirley Mezvinsky 1933- *IntAu&W 91, WhoEnt 92*
**Laurs**, Robert Michael 1939- *AmMWSc 92*
**Laursen**, E M 1919- *AmMWSc 92*
**Laursen**, Elmer 1916- *WhoRel 92*
**Laursen**, Gary A 1942- *AmMWSc 92*
**Laursen**, Gladys Marie 1914- *WhoMW 92*
**Laursen**, Paul Herbert 1929- *AmMWSc 92*
**Laursen**, Richard Allan 1938- *AmMWSc 92*
**Laursen**, Soren N S 1935- *WhoIns 92*
**Laursen**, Steven Brent 1951- *WhoMW 92*
**Laurus**, Archbishop 1928- *WhoRel 92*
**Lausberg**, Heinrich 1912- *IntWW 91*
**Lausch**, Robert Nagle 1938- *AmMWSc 92*
**Lauscher**, Hermann 1877-1962 *WhoNob 90*
**Lause**, Timothy Wayne 1952- *WhoMW 92*
**Laush**, George 1921- *AmMWSc 92*
**Laushey**, Louis M 1917- *AmMWSc 92*
**Laushman**, Roger H 1950- *AmMWSc 92*
**Laushway**, Francis Aaron 1952- *WhoRel 92*
**Lauson**, Henry Dumke 1912- *AmMWSc 92*
**Laustsen**, Agnete 1935- *IntWW 91*
**Laut**, Agnes C. 1871-1936 *BenetAL 91*
**Laut**, Harold William 1933- *WhoIns 92*
**Laut**, Philip Blaise 1960- *WhoMW 92*
**Lautaro** 1535?-1557 *HisDSpE*
**Lautenbach**, Terry 1938- *WhoBlA 92*
**Lautenberg**, Frank R. 1924- *AlmAP 92 [port], CurBio 91 [port], IntWW 91, WhoAmP 91*
**Lautenberger**, William J 1943- *AmMWSc 92*
**Lautens**, Mark 1959- *AmMWSc 92*
**Lautenschlaeger**, Friedrich Karl 1934- *AmMWSc 92*
**Lautenschlager**, Eugene Paul 1937- *AmMWSc 92*
**Lautenschlager**, Hans Werner 1927- *IntWW 91*
**Lautenschlager**, Peggy A 1955- *WhoAmP 91*
**Lautenschlager**, Thomas J *WhoAmP 91*
**Lauter**, Ed 1940- *IntMPA 92*
**Lauter**, James Donald 1931- *WhoFI 92*
**Lauter**, Ken *DrAPF 91*
**Lauterbach**, Ann *DrAPF 91*
**Lauterbach**, George Ervin 1927- *AmMWSc 92*
**Lauterbach**, John Harvey 1944- *AmMWSc 92*
**Lauterbach**, Karen Elaine 1950- *WhoMW 92*
**Lauterbach**, Richard Thomas 1946- *AmMWSc 92*
**Lauterbur**, Paul Christian 1929- *AmMWSc 92*
**Lauterpacht**, Elihu 1928- *Who 92*
**Lauterstein**, Ingeborg 1933- *WrDr 92*
**Lauth**, Gayle Ellen 1941- *WhoMW 92*
**Lauth**, Harold Vincent 1933- *WhoWest 92*
**Lauth**, Robert Edward 1927- *WhoFI 92, WhoWest 92*
**Lauti**, Toaripi 1928- *IntWW 91, Who 92*
**Lautieri**, Antoinette Sylvia 1955- *WhoFI 92*
**Lautman**, Don A. d1991 *NewYTBS 91*
**Lautmann**, Rudiger 1935- *IntWW 91*
**Lautreamont**, Comte de 1846-1870 *GuFrLit 1*
**Lautt**, Wilfred Wayne 1946- *AmMWSc 92*
**Lauture**, Denize *DrAPF 91*
**Lautz**, Lindsay Allan 1947- *WhoEnt 92*
**Lautzenheiser**, Barbara J 1938- *WhoIns 92*
**Lautzenheiser**, Clarence Eric 1921- *AmMWSc 92*
**Lautzenhiser**, Niann Kay 1945- *WhoMW 92*
**Lautzenhiser**, Roger Eugene, Jr. 1954- *WhoMW 92*
**Lauver**, Dean C 1920- *AmMWSc 92*
**Lauver**, Milton Renick 1920- *AmMWSc 92*
**Lauver**, Richard William 1943- *AmMWSc 92*
**Lauver**, Robert A. 1943- *WhoRel 92*
**Laux**, David Charles 1945- *AmMWSc 92*
**Laux**, Dorianne *DrAPF 91*
**Laux**, Russell Frederick 1918- *WhoAmL 92, WhoFI 92*
**Lauzanne**, Bernard 1916- *IntWW 91*
**Lauzier**, Raymond B 1948- *AmMWSc 92*
**Lauzon**, Robert Maurice 1948- *WhoRel 92*
**Lauzon**, Rodrigue Vincent 1937- *AmMWSc 92*
**Lavagnino**, Edward Ralph 1930- *AmMWSc 92*
**LaVail**, Jennifer Hart 1943- *AmMWSc 92*
**LaVail**, Matthew Maurice 1943- *AmMWSc 92*
**Laval**, Claire de *EncAmaz 91*
**Laval**, Gabrielle de *EncAmaz 91*
**Laval**, Pierre 1883-1945 *EncTR 91 [port], FacFETw [port]*
**Laval**, William Norris 1922- *AmMWSc 92*
**LaValle**, Gerald J 1932- *WhoAmP 91*
**LaValle**, Irving Howard 1939- *WhoFI 92*
**LaValle**, Kenneth P 1939- *WhoAmP 91*
**LaValle**, Placido Dominick 1937- *AmMWSc 92*
**Lavallee**, Andre 1936- *AmMWSc 92*
**Lavallee**, Calixa 1842-1891 *NewAmDM*
**Lavallee**, Charles Phillip 1928- *WhoEnt 92*
**Lavallee**, David Kenneth 1945- *AmMWSc 92*
**Lavallee**, Lorraine Doris 1931- *AmMWSc 92*
**LaVallee**, Roderick Leo 1936- *WhoFI 92*
**Lavalleja**, Juan Antonio 1784-1853 *HisDSpE*
**Lavan**, Alton 1946- *WhoBlA 92*
**Lavan**, John Martin 1911- *Who 92*
**Lavan**, Spencer *WhoRel 92*
**Lavanchy**, Andre C 1922- *AmMWSc 92*
**Lavanish**, Jerome Michael 1940- *AmMWSc 92*
**La Vaque**, Theodore Joseph 1940- *WhoMW 92*
**Lavarden**, Manuel Jose de 1754-1809 *HisDSpE*
**Lavater**, Johann Kaspar 1741-1801 *BlkwCEP*
**LaVay**, Richard Alan 1953- *WhoAmP 91*
**Lavdas**, Leonidas G. 1947- *WhoRel 92*
**Lave**, Charles Arthur 1938- *WhoFI 92*
**Lave**, Lester B. 1939- *IntWW 91*
**Lave**, Lester Bernard 1939- *WhoFI 92*
**Lave**, Roy E, Jr 1935- *AmMWSc 92*
**LaVean**, Michael Gilbert 1954- *WhoMW 92*
**LaVeist**, Thomas Alexis 1961- *WhoBlA 92*
**Lavell**, Alan Joseph 1946- *WhoWest 92*
**Lavelle**, Arthur 1921- *AmMWSc 92*
**LaVelle**, Betty Sullivan Dougherty 1941- *WhoAmL 92*
**Lavelle**, Brian Francis David 1941- *WhoAmL 92, WhoFI 92*
**Lavelle**, Charles Joseph 1950- *WhoAmL 92*
**Lavelle**, Donald Eugene 1933- *WhoMW 92, WhoRel 92*
**LaVelle**, Faith Wilson 1921- *AmMWSc 92*
**Lavelle**, George Cartwright 1937- *WhoMW 92*
**Lavelle**, James W 1930- *AmMWSc 92*
**Lavelle**, John William 1943- *AmMWSc 92*
**Lavelle**, Michael Joseph 1934- *WhoMW 92*
**Lavelle**, Rita Marie 1947- *WhoWest 92*
**Lavelle**, Robert R. 1915- *WhoBlA 92*
**Lavelle**, Roger Garnett 1932- *IntWW 91, Who 92*
**LaVelle-Nichols**, Robin Ann 1959- *WhoFI 92*
**Lavelli**, Evelyn Elaine 1955- *WhoRel 92*
**Laven**, Arnold *IntMPA 92*
**Lavenant**, Rene Paul, Jr. 1925- *WhoAmL 92*
**Lavendel**, Henry W 1919- *AmMWSc 92*
**Lavender**, Aaron Edward 1951- *WhoRel 92*
**Lavender**, Denis Peter 1926- *AmMWSc 92*
**Lavender**, DeWitt Earl 1938- *AmMWSc 92*
**Lavender**, Gerard 1943- *Who 92*
**Lavender**, John Francis 1929- *AmMWSc 92*
**Lavender**, Robert Eugene 1926- *WhoAmL 92, WhoAmP 91*
**Lavenstein**, Cyril 1891- *TwCPaSc*
**Laventhol**, David 1933- *IntWW 91*
**Laventhol**, David Abram 1933- *WhoFI 92, WhoWest 92*
**Laver**, Christian Eby 1957- *WhoMW 92*
**Laver**, Frederick John Murray 1915- *Who 92*
**Laver**, John David Michael Henry 1938- *Who 92*
**Laver**, Murray Lane 1932- *AmMWSc 92*
**Laver**, Patrick Martin 1932- *Who 92*
**Laver**, Robert Carl 1957- *WhoRel 92*
**Laver**, Rod 1938- *FacFETw*
**Laver**, Rod George 1938- *IntWW 91*
**Laver**, Steven K *WhoIns 92*
**Laver**, William Graeme 1929- *Who 92*
**Laveran**, Charles Louis Alphonse 1845-1922 *WhoNob 90*
**Laverdi**, Edna B. *WhoHisp 92*
**Laverdiere**, Marc Richard 1946- *AmMWSc 92*
**Laverdure**, Rodman James 1942- *WhoWest 92*
**LaVerendrye**, Pierre deVarennes, Sieur de 1685-1749 *BenetAL 91*
**Laverge**, Hendrik Johannes 1941- *WhoFI 92*
**LaVergne**, Colin Robert 1949- *WhoRel 92*
**Lavergne**, Lee 1932- *WhoEnt 92*
**La Vergne**, Marie-Madeleine Pioche de 1634-1693 *FrenWW*
**Lavergneau**, Rene L. 1933- *WhoBlA 92*
**Laverick**, Elizabeth 1925- *Who 92*
**Lavering**, Fred Bernard 1933- *WhoFI 92*
**Laverman**, Bruce Glen 1940- *WhoRel 92*
**Laverne**, Erwine 1909- *DcTwDes*
**Laverne**, Estelle 1915- *DcTwDes*
**Lavernia**, Enrique Jose 1960- *AmMWSc 92, WhoWest 92*
**Lavernia**, Milton 1935- *WhoHisp 92*
**Laverock**, George Charles 1944- *WhoEnt 92*
**Lavers**, Norman *DrAPF 91*
**Lavers**, Norman 1935- *IntAu&W 91*
**Lavers**, Patricia Mae 1919- *Who 92*
**Lavers**, Richard Marshall 1947- *WhoMW 92*
**Laverty**, Donald *ConAu 36NR, SmATA 66*
**Laverty**, John Joseph 1938- *AmMWSc 92*
**Laverty**, Roger Montgomery, III 1947- *WhoFI 92*
**Lavery**, Bryony 1947- *WrDr 92*
**Lavery**, Emmet 1902-1986 *BenetAL 91*
**Lavery**, J. Patrick 1942- *WhoMW 92*
**Lavery**, John 1856-1941 *TwCPaSc*
**Lavery**, Vincent Joseph 1936- *WhoWest 92*
**Laves**, Benjamin Samuel 1946- *WhoAmL 92*
**Lavett**, Diane Kathryn Juricek 1944- *AmMWSc 92*
**LaVey**, Anton 1930- *RelLAm 91*
**Lavey**, Kevin J. *DrAPF 91*
**Lavi**, Abrahim 1934- *AmMWSc 92*
**Lavia**, Lynn Alan 1948- *AmMWSc 92*
**La Via**, Mariano Francis 1926- *AmMWSc 92*
**Lavid**, Jean Stern 1943- *WhoMW 92*
**Lavidge**, Robert James 1921- *WhoFI 92*
**Lavier**, Bertrand 1949- *IntWW 91*
**Laviera**, Tato 1951- *WhoHisp 92*
**Lavigne**, Andre Andre 1932- *AmMWSc 92*
**Lavigne**, David M 1946- *AmMWSc 92*
**Lavigne**, Denise Marie 1956- *WhoMW 92*
**Lavigne**, Eileen Marie 1963- *WhoAmL 92*
**Lavigne**, Lawrence Neil 1957- *WhoAmL 92*
**Lavigne**, Maurice J 1918- *AmMWSc 92*
**Lavigne**, Robert James 1930- *AmMWSc 92, WhoWest 92*
**Lavigne**, Thomas Mathew James 1962- *WhoAmL 92*
**Lavik**, Paul Sophus 1915- *AmMWSc 92*
**LaVilla**, Robert E 1926- *AmMWSc 92*
**Lavilla Alsina**, Landelino 1927- *IntWW 91*
**LaVilla-Havelin**, James S. *DrAPF 91*
**Lavin**, Bernice E. 1925- *WhoFI 92*
**Lavin**, Christine 1952?- *ConMus 6 [port]*
**Lavin**, Deborah Margaret 1939- *Who 92*
**Lavin**, Edward 1916- *AmMWSc 92*
**Lavin**, J Gerard 1932- *AmMWSc 92*
**Lavin**, Jenna Rae 1968- *WhoEnt 92*
**Lavin**, Karen M. 1957- *WhoAmL 92*
**Lavin**, Laurence Michael 1940- *WhoWest 92*
**Lavin**, Linda 1937- *IntMPA 92, WhoEnt 92*
**Lavin**, Mary 1912- *ConNov 91, FacFETw, IntAu&W 91, IntWW 91, RfGEnL 91, Who 92, WrDr 92*
**Lavin**, Paul Edward 1944- *WhoRel 92*
**Lavin**, Peter Masland 1935- *AmMWSc 92*
**Lavin**, Philip Todd 1946- *AmMWSc 92*
**Lavin**, Rafael *WhoHisp 92*
**Lavin**, S.R. *DrAPF 91*
**Lavin**, William Kane 1944- *WhoFI 92*
**Lavine**, Adrienne Gail 1958- *AmMWSc 92*
**Lavine**, Charles David 1947- *WhoAmL 92*
**Lavine**, David 1929- *WhoAmP 91*
**Lavine**, Gary J. *WhoAmL 92*
**Lavine**, Henry Wolfe 1936- *WhoAmL 92*
**Lavine**, James Philip 1944- *AmMWSc 92*
**Lavine**, Lawrence Neal 1951- *WhoFI 92*
**Lavine**, Leroy S 1918- *AmMWSc 92*
**Lavine**, Richard Bengt 1938- *AmMWSc 92*
**Lavine**, Robert Alan 1941- *AmMWSc 92*
**La Vine**, Ronald Scott 1957- *WhoWest 92*
**Lavine**, Sigmund Arnold 1908- *WrDr 92*
**Lavine**, Thelma Zeno *WhoRel 92*
**Lavington**, Cyril Michael d1990 *Who 92N*
**Lavington**, Michael Richard 1943- *WhoFI 92*
**Lavinsky**, Larry Monroe 1929- *WhoAmL 92*
**Laviolette**, Francis A 1919- *AmMWSc 92*
**La Violette**, Paul Estronza 1930- *AmMWSc 92*
**Lavish**, Edward Charles 1937- *WhoEnt 92*
**Lavit**, Theodore Howard 1939- *WhoAmP 91*
**La Vita**, Roberto 1950- *WhoFI 92*
**Lavkulich**, Leslie Michael 1939- *AmMWSc 92*
**Lavochkin**, Semen Alekseevich 1900-1960 *SovUnBD*
**Lavoie**, Alvin Charles 1956- *AmMWSc 92*
**LaVoie**, Edmond J 1950- *AmMWSc 92*
**Lavoie**, Marcel Elphege 1917- *AmMWSc 92*
**Lavoie**, Ronald Leonard 1933- *AmMWSc 92*
**Lavoie**, Russell Matthew 1960- *WhoFI 92*
**Lavoie**, Serge 1963- *WhoEnt 92*
**LaVoie**, Steven Paul *DrAPF 91*
**Lavoisier**, Antoine-Laurent 1743-1794 *BlkwCEP*
**Lavond**, Paul Dennis *TwCSFW 91*
**Lavorando**, Joseph, Jr 1953- *WhoAmP 91*
**Lavorato**, Charles Samuel 1949- *WhoAmL 92*
**Lavorato**, Louis A 1934- *WhoAmP 91*
**Lavrent'ev**, Mikhail Alekseevich 1900-1980 *SovUnBD*
**Lavrentiev**, Alexander 1954- *ConAu 135*
**Lavrenyov**, Boris Andreyevich 1894-1952 *FacFETw*
**Lavrov**, Vladimir Sergeyevich 1919- *IntWW 91*
**Lavrovsky**, Leonid Mikhaylovich 1905-1967 *SovUnBD*
**Lavrushin**, Vladimir 1912- *IntWW 91*
**Lavy**, Terry Lee 1936- *AmMWSc 92*
**Law** *Who 92*
**Law**, Alan Greenwell 1936- *AmMWSc 92*
**Law**, Albert G 1931- *AmMWSc 92*
**Law**, Amy Stauber 1938- *AmMWSc 92*
**Law**, Andrew 1749-1821 *NewAmDM*
**Law**, Andrew Bonar 1858-1923 *FacFETw*
**Law**, Annie E 1840?-1889 *BiInAmS*
**Law**, Bernard F. 1931- *IntWW 91*
**Law**, Bernard Francis 1931- *RelLAm 91, WhoRel 92*
**Law**, Bob 1934- *IntWW 91, TwCPaSc*
**Law**, Bruce Malcolm 1956- *AmMWSc 92*
**Law**, Cecil E 1922- *AmMWSc 92*
**Law**, Clarene 1933- *WhoAmP 91*
**Law**, Dale Allen 1948- *WhoMW 92*
**Law**, David H 1927- *AmMWSc 92*
**Law**, David Martin *AmMWSc 92*
**Law**, Dennis Lee 1944- *WhoMW 92*
**Law**, Duncan K., Jr. 1955- *WhoFI 92*
**Law**, Ellen Marie 1960- *WhoAmL 92*
**Law**, Ellen T. 1918- *WhoBlA 92*
**Law**, Eric W 1949- *AmMWSc 92*
**Law**, Francis C P 1941- *AmMWSc 92*
**Law**, Francis Stephen 1916- *Who 92*
**Law**, George Llewellyn 1929- *Who 92*
**Law**, George Robert John 1928- *AmMWSc 92*
**Law**, Gerald H 1944- *WhoAmP 91*
**Law**, Horace 1911- *Who 92*
**Law**, Horace Rochfort 1911- *IntWW 91*
**Law**, Hsiang-Yi David 1949- *AmMWSc 92*
**Law**, Hung-Fai Stephen 1950- *WhoWest 92*
**Law**, James 1926- *Who 92*
**Law**, James Calvin 1959- *WhoMW 92*
**Law**, James George 1944- *WhoWest 92*
**Law**, James L 1926- *WhoAmP 91*
**Law**, Jimmy 1942- *AmMWSc 92*
**Law**, John 1671-1729 *BenetAL 91, BlkwCEP*
**Law**, John 1930- *AmMWSc 92*
**Law**, John 1941- *TwCPaSc*
**Law**, John Harold 1931- *AmMWSc 92*
**Law**, John Manning 1927- *WhoAmL 92*
**Law**, John Philip 1937- *IntMPA 92*
**Law**, John Phillip 1937- *WhoEnt 92*
**Law**, Jon Andrew 1956- *WhoFI 92*
**Law**, Katharine 1935- *WhoAmL 92*
**Law**, Lindsay *IntMPA 92*
**Law**, Lloyd William 1910- *AmMWSc 92*
**Law**, M Eprevel 1943- *WhoAmP 91, WhoBlA 92*
**Law**, Margaret Elizabeth 1934- *AmMWSc 92*
**Law**, Michael R. 1947- *WhoAmL 92*
**Law**, Paul Arthur 1934- *AmMWSc 92*
**Law**, Peter Koi 1946- *AmMWSc 92*
**Law**, Phillip Garth 1912- *IntWW 91, Who 92*
**Law**, Rhea Fogarty 1949- *WhoAmL 92*
**Law**, Roger Alan 1933- *WhoAmL 92*
**Law**, Rudy Karl 1956- *WhoBlA 92*
**Law**, Sallie Chapman Gordon 1805-1894 *DcNCBi 4*
**Law**, Stephen J *WhoAmP 91*
**Law**, Sylvia 1931- *Who 92*
**Law**, Sylvia A. 1942- *WhoAmL 92*
**Law**, Thomas Melvin 1926- *WhoBlA 92*
**Law**, Veldon Lee 1952- *WhoMW 92*
**Law**, William 1686-1761 *BlkwCEP*
**Law**, William Brough 1932- *AmMWSc 92*
**Law**, William Charles, Jr. 1947- *WhoMW 92*
**Law-Smith**, David John 1940- *WhoFI 92*
**Law-Smith**, Robert 1914- *IntWW 91, Who 92*
**Lawaetz**, Bent 1939- *WhoAmP 91*
**Lawaetz**, Frits 1907- *WhoAmP 91*
**LaWare**, John Patrick 1928- *WhoFI 92*
**Lawatsch**, Frank Emil, Jr. 1944- *WhoAmL 92*
**Lawden**, Derek Frank 1919- *IntWW 91, WrDr 92*
**Lawder**, Donald *DrAPF 91*
**Lawes**, Henry 1596-1662 *NewAmDM*
**Lawes**, Verna 1927- *WhoBlA 92*
**Lawes**, William 1602-1645 *NewAmDM*
**Lawford**, George Ross 1941- *AmMWSc 92*
**Lawford**, Valentine George Nicholas d1991 *NewYTBS 91*
**Lawhon**, John E., III 1934- *WhoAmL 92*

**Lawhorn,** John B. 1925- *WhoBlA 92*
**Lawhorn,** Robert Martin 1943- *WhoBlA 92*
**Lawhorne,** Thomas W, Sr 1924- *WhoAmP 91*
**Lawing,** Raymond Quinton 1910- *WhoBlA 92*
**Lawing,** William Dennis 1935- *AmMWSc 92*
**Lawlah,** Gloria Gary 1939- *WhoAmP 91, WhoBlA 92*
**Lawler,** Adrian Russell 1940- *AmMWSc 92*
**Lawler,** Anne DeVoe 1953- *WhoAmL 92*
**Lawler,** Cheney Paul 1961- *WhoRel 92*
**Lawler,** Edward James 1908- *WhoAmL 92*
**Lawler,** Eugene L 1933- *AmMWSc 92*
**Lawler,** Geoffrey John 1954- *Who 92*
**Lawler,** George Herbert 1923- *AmMWSc 92*
**Lawler,** Gregory Francis 1955- *AmMWSc 92*
**Lawler,** J. Richmond 1949- *WhoEnt 92*
**Lawler,** James E 1946- *AmMWSc 92*
**Lawler,** James Edward 1951- *AmMWSc 92*
**Lawler,** James Henry Lawrence 1936- *AmMWSc 92*
**Lawler,** James Michael 1954- *WhoWest 92*
**Lawler,** James Ronald 1929- *IntWW 91*
**Lawler,** Joab 1796-1838 *DcNCBi 4*
**Lawler,** John Patrick 1934- *AmMWSc 92*
**Lawler,** Kathy Anne 1958- *WhoAmL 92*
**Lawler,** Larry 1939- *WhoAmP 91*
**Lawler,** Lucille 1908- *WrDr 92*
**Lawler,** Martin Timothy 1937- *AmMWSc 92*
**Lawler,** Michael Gerard 1933- *WhoRel 92*
**Lawler,** Patrick *DrAPF 91*
**Lawler,** Peter 1921- *Who 92*
**Lawler,** Ray 1921- *RfGEnL 91, WrDr 92*
**Lawler,** Richard 1895-1982 *FacFETw*
**Lawler,** Ronald George 1938- *AmMWSc 92*
**Lawler,** Susan George 1940- *WhoMW 92*
**Lawless,** Carey 1957- *WhoEnt 92*
**Lawless,** Edward William 1931- *AmMWSc 92*
**Lawless,** Gary *DrAPF 91*
**Lawless,** Gregory Benedict 1940- *AmMWSc 92*
**Lawless,** James George 1942- *AmMWSc 92*
**Lawless,** John A 1957- *WhoAmP 91*
**Lawless,** John Craig 1958- *WhoFI 92*
**Lawless,** John Langie, Jr. 1955- *WhoWest 92*
**Lawless,** Joseph Francis, III 1945- *WhoAmP 91*
**Lawless,** Kenneth Robert 1922- *AmMWSc 92*
**Lawless,** Kirby Gordon, Jr 1924- *WhoAmP 91*
**Lawless,** Michael William 1948- *WhoWest 92*
**Lawless,** Philip Austin 1943- *AmMWSc 92*
**Lawless,** Robert C 1957- *WhoAmP 91*
**Lawless,** Robert William 1937- *WhoFI 92*
**Lawless,** Ronald 1960- *WhoMW 92*
**Lawless,** Ronald Edward 1924- *WhoFI 92*
**Lawless,** William Josselyn, Jr 1919- *WhoAmP 91*
**Lawless,** William N 1936- *AmMWSc 92*
**Lawley,** Alan 1933- *AmMWSc 92*
**Lawley,** Leonard Edward 1922- *Who 92*
**Lawley,** Susan 1946- *Who 92*
**Lawley,** Susan Marc 1951- *WhoFI 92*
**Lawley,** Thomas J *AmMWSc 92*
**Lawlor,** Andrew James 1939- *WhoFI 92*
**Lawlor,** Augustine 1956- *WhoFI 92*
**Lawlor,** Bonnie 1944- *WhoFI 92*
**Lawlor,** Bruce Michael 1948- *WhoAmP 91*
**Lawlor,** John James 1918- *Who 92, WrDr 92*
**Lawlor,** Michael P *WhoAmP 91*
**Lawlor,** Putrisha 1959- *TwCPaSc*
**Lawlor,** Richard Patrick 1946- *WhoAmP 91*
**Lawlor,** Richard W. 1946- *WhoAmL 92*
**Lawman,** Michael John Patrick 1949- *AmMWSc 92*
**Lawman,** Peter 1951- *TwCPaSc*
**Lawn,** Beverly *DrAPF 91*
**Lawn,** Connie Ellen 1944- *WhoEnt 92*
**Lawn,** John C *WhoAmP 91*
**Lawn,** Richard John 1949- *WhoEnt 92*
**Lawner,** Lynne *DrAPF 91*
**Lawniczak,** James Michael 1951- *WhoAmL 92, WhoMW 92*
**Lawrance,** David Paul 1952- *WhoMW 92*
**Lawrance,** John Ernest 1928- *Who 92*
**Lawrance,** June Cynthia 1933- *Who 92*
**Lawrance,** Keith Cantwell 1923- *Who 92*
**Lawrason,** F Douglas 1919- *AmMWSc 92*
**Lawrence** *BenetAL 91, Who 92*
**Lawrence** d258 *EncEarC [port]*
**Lawrence,** Baron 1937- *Who 92*
**Lawrence of Arabia** 1888-1935 *FacFETw [port]*
**Lawrence,** Addison Lee 1935- *AmMWSc 92*
**Lawrence,** Alan 1928- *WhoEnt 92*
**Lawrence,** Albert 1961- *BlkOlyM*
**Lawrence,** Albert Weaver 1928- *WhoFI 92, WhoIns 92*
**Lawrence,** Alexander Leonard 1948- *WhoAmL 92*
**Lawrence,** Alonzo William 1937- *AmMWSc 92*
**Lawrence,** Andrea Mead 1932- *WhoWest 92*
**Lawrence,** Annie L. 1926- *WhoBlA 92*
**Lawrence,** Arabella Susan 1871-1947 *BiDBrF 2*
**Lawrence,** Arnold Walter d1991 *Who 92N*
**Lawrence,** Arnold Walter 1900-1990 *IntWW 91N*
**Lawrence,** Arnold Walter 1900-1991 *IntWW 91*
**Lawrence,** Ashley 1934-1990 *AnObit 1990*
**Lawrence,** Azar Malcolm 1952- *WhoBlA 92*
**Lawrence,** Barbara *WhoAmP 91*
**Lawrence,** Barbara 1930- *IntMPA 92*
**Lawrence,** Barbara 1944- *WhoFI 92*
**Lawrence,** Barbara Corell 1927- *WhoFI 92*
**Lawrence,** Berta *IntAu&W 91, WrDr 92*
**Lawrence,** Bill d1972 *LesBEnT 92*
**Lawrence,** Brian Michael 1961- *WhoMW 92*
**Lawrence,** Caleb James *Who 92*
**Lawrence,** Caleb James 1941- *WhoMW 92, WhoRel 92*
**Lawrence,** Carl Eugene 1954- *WhoEnt 92*
**Lawrence,** Carmen Mary 1948- *Who 92*
**Lawrence,** Carol 1935- *WhoEnt 92*
**Lawrence,** Charles B. 1920- *WhoBlA 92*
**Lawrence,** Charles Joseph 1959- *WhoMW 92*
**Lawrence,** Charles R. 1943- *WhoAmL 92*
**Lawrence,** Christopher Nigel 1936- *Who 92*
**Lawrence,** Christopher William 1934- *AmMWSc 92*
**Lawrence,** Claudette Antoinette 1963- *WhoFI 92*
**Lawrence,** Clifford Hugh 1921- *Who 92*
**Lawrence,** D. H. 1885-1930 *BenetAL 91, CnDBLB 6 [port], FacFETw [port], LiExTwC, RfGEnL 91*
**Lawrence,** Dale Nolan 1944- *AmMWSc 92*
**Lawrence,** Dana Jeffrey 1953- *WhoMW 92*
**Lawrence,** David 1929- *Who 92*
**Lawrence,** David A 1945- *AmMWSc 92*
**Lawrence,** David Herbert 1885-1930 *TwCPaSc*
**Lawrence,** David Joseph 1951- *AmMWSc 92*
**Lawrence,** David Norman 1941- *WhoRel 92*
**Lawrence,** David Reed 1939- *AmMWSc 92*
**Lawrence,** Dean Grayson 1901- *WhoWest 92*
**Lawrence,** Denis 1940- *WhoAmP 91*
**Lawrence,** Dennis George Charles 1918- *Who 92*
**Lawrence,** Donald Buermann 1911- *AmMWSc 92*
**Lawrence,** Donald Gilbert 1932- *AmMWSc 92*
**Lawrence,** Edward 1935- *WhoBlA 92*
**Lawrence,** Edward Charles 1952- *WhoFI 92*
**Lawrence,** Eileen 1946- *TwCPaSc*
**Lawrence,** Eileen B. 1919- *WhoBlA 92*
**Lawrence,** Eleanor Baker 1936- *WhoEnt 92*
**Lawrence,** Erma Jean 1926- *WhoBlA 92*
**Lawrence,** Ernest 1901-1958 *RComAH*
**Lawrence,** Ernest Orlando 1901-1958 *FacFETw, WhoNob 90*
**Lawrence,** Eva M 1930- *WhoAmP 91*
**Lawrence,** Frances Elizabeth 1925- *WhoWest 92*
**Lawrence,** Francis Joseph 1925- *AmMWSc 92*
**Lawrence,** Frank Gilbert 1962- *WhoWest 92*
**Lawrence,** Franklin Isaac Latimer 1905- *AmMWSc 92*
**Lawrence,** Frederick Van Buren, Jr 1938- *AmMWSc 92*
**Lawrence,** Gary Dale 1947- *WhoFI 92*
**Lawrence,** Gene Grant 1942- *WhoRel 92*
**Lawrence,** Geoffrey 1880-1971 *CurBio 91N*
**Lawrence,** Geoffrey Charles 1915- *Who 92*
**Lawrence,** George Calvin 1918- *WhoBlA 92*
**Lawrence,** George Edwin 1920- *AmMWSc 92*
**Lawrence,** George Melvin 1937- *AmMWSc 92*
**Lawrence,** George Newbold 1806-1895 *BiInAmS*
**Lawrence,** Gerald Graham 1947- *WhoFI 92*
**Lawrence,** Gertrude 1898-1952 *FacFETw, NewAmDM*
**Lawrence,** Gloria Edith *WhoAmP 91*
**Lawrence,** Guy Kempton 1914- *Who 92*
**Lawrence,** Happy James 1944- *WhoWest 92*
**Lawrence,** Henry 1951- *WhoBlA 92*
**Lawrence,** Henry Richard 1946- *Who 92*
**Lawrence,** Henry Sherwood 1916- *AmMWSc 92, IntWW 91*
**Lawrence,** Irvin E, Jr 1926- *AmMWSc 92*
**Lawrence,** Ivan John 1936- *Who 92*
**Lawrence,** J. Rodney 1945- *WhoAmL 92*
**Lawrence,** Jacob 1917- *FacFETw, RComAH, WhoWest 92*
**Lawrence,** Jacob A. 1917- *WhoBlA 92*
**Lawrence,** James Albert 1910- *WhoWest 92*
**Lawrence,** James Bland 1947- *WhoFI 92*
**Lawrence,** James Franklin 1949- *WhoBlA 92*
**Lawrence,** James Franklin 1950- *AmMWSc 92*
**Lawrence,** James Harold, Jr 1932- *AmMWSc 92*
**Lawrence,** James Kaufman Lebensburger 1940- *WhoAmL 92*
**Lawrence,** James Neville Peed 1929- *AmMWSc 92*
**Lawrence,** James T. 1921- *WhoBlA 92*
**Lawrence,** James Vantine 1918- *AmMWSc 92*
**Lawrence,** Janice 1962- *BlkOlyM*
**Lawrence,** Jay 1908- *WhoEnt 92*
**Lawrence,** Jeanne Bentley 1951- *AmMWSc 92*
**Lawrence,** Jerome 1915- *IntAu&W 91, SmATA 65 [port], WhoEnt 92, WhoWest 92, WrDr 92*
**Lawrence,** Joan McEwen Bills 1932- *WhoEnt 92*
**Lawrence,** Joan W *WhoAmP 91*
**Lawrence,** Joanne Lee 1953- *WhoEnt 92*
**Lawrence,** John 1933- *Who 92*
**Lawrence,** John 1934- *TwCPaSc*
**Lawrence,** John 1943- *AmMWSc 92*
**Lawrence,** John Alan 1949- *WhoAmP 91*
**Lawrence,** John Benjamin 1871-1968 *RelLAm 91*
**Lawrence,** John E. 1941- *WhoBlA 92*
**Lawrence,** John H d1991 *NewYTBS 91 [port]*
**Lawrence,** John Hundale 1904- *AmMWSc 92*
**Lawrence,** John Keeler 1940- *AmMWSc 92*
**Lawrence,** John Kidder 1949- *WhoAmL 92, WhoFI 92, WhoMW 92*
**Lawrence,** John M 1937- *AmMWSc 92*
**Lawrence,** John Malcolm, Jr. 1934- *WhoAmL 92*
**Lawrence,** John McCune 1916- *AmMWSc 92*
**Lawrence,** John Medlock 1919- *AmMWSc 92*
**Lawrence,** John Patrick 1928- *Who 92*
**Lawrence,** John Perrin 1951- *WhoFI 92*
**Lawrence,** John Thornett 1920- *Who 92*
**Lawrence,** John Waldemar 1907- *Who 92*
**Lawrence,** John Warren 1928- *WhoEnt 92, WhoMW 92*
**Lawrence,** John Wilfred 1933- *Who 92*
**Lawrence,** Joseph D, Jr 1924- *AmMWSc 92*
**Lawrence,** Joseph Ivers *ScFEYrs*
**Lawrence,** Joseph Joshua 1836-1909 *DcNCBi 4*
**Lawrence,** Josephine 1890-1978 *BenetAL 91*
**Lawrence,** Joshua 1778-1843 *DcNCBi 4*
**Lawrence,** Joy Elizabeth 1926- *WhoEnt 92*
**Lawrence,** Karen 1949- *IntAu&W 91*
**Lawrence,** Karen Ann 1951- *IntAu&W 91*
**Lawrence,** Kathleen Ann 1946- *WhoAmP 91*
**Lawrence,** Kathleen Rockwell *DrAPF 91*
**Lawrence,** Kathleen Wilson 1940- *WhoAmP 91*
**Lawrence,** Kenneth Bridge 1918- *AmMWSc 92*
**Lawrence,** Kent L 1937- *AmMWSc 92*
**Lawrence,** Kurt C 1962- *AmMWSc 92*
**Lawrence,** Leonard E. 1937- *WhoBlA 92*
**Lawrence,** Lesley *WrDr 92*
**Lawrence,** Lonnie R. 1946- *WhoBlA 92*
**Lawrence,** Louise 1943- *IntAu&W 91, WrDr 92*
**Lawrence,** Marc 1910- *ConTFT 9*
**Lawrence,** Marc 1913- *WhoEnt 92*
**Lawrence,** Marc 1914- *IntMPA 92*
**Lawrence,** Margaret Morgan 1914- *NotBlAW 92, WhoBlA 92*
**Lawrence,** Margery Hulings 1934- *WhoFI 92*
**Lawrence,** Mark d1991 *NewYTBS 91*
**Lawrence,** Mark W 1958- *WhoAmP 91*
**Lawrence,** Mary *ConAu 135, TwCPaSc*
**Lawrence,** Mary d1991 *NewYTBS 91*
**Lawrence,** Mary 1918- *IntAu&W 91*
**Lawrence,** Matthew Kimbrell 1956- *WhoFI 92*
**Lawrence,** Merle 1915- *AmMWSc 92*
**Lawrence,** Merlisa Evelyn 1965- *WhoBlA 92*
**Lawrence,** Michael Edward 1955- *WhoRel 92*
**Lawrence,** Michael Hugh 1920- *Who 92*
**Lawrence,** Michelle 1948- *WhoAmP 91*
**Lawrence,** Montague Schiele 1923- *WhoBlA 92*
**Lawrence,** Murray *Who 92*
**Lawrence,** Norman B 1928- *WhoAmP 91*
**Lawrence,** P *IntAu&W 91X, WrDr 92*
**Lawrence,** Patrick *Who 92*
**Lawrence,** Paul Frederic *WhoBlA 92*
**Lawrence,** Paul J 1940- *AmMWSc 92*
**Lawrence,** Paula Denise 1959- *WhoWest 92*
**Lawrence,** Pauline Olive 1945- *AmMWSc 92*
**Lawrence,** Pelham Bissell 1945- *WhoFI 92*
**Lawrence,** Peter Anthony 1941- *IntWW 91, Who 92*
**Lawrence,** Phenis Joseph 1926- *WhoEnt 92*
**Lawrence,** Phil Dean 1957- *WhoRel 92*
**Lawrence,** Philip Linwood 1923- *AmMWSc 92*
**Lawrence,** Philip Martin 1950- *WhoBlA 92*
**Lawrence,** Ralph Alan 1931- *WhoRel 92*
**Lawrence,** Ralph Waldo 1941- *WhoMW 92*
**Lawrence,** Rawlin Victor 1946- *WhoEnt 92*
**Lawrence,** Raymond Eugene 1921- *WhoRel 92*
**Lawrence,** Raymond Jeffery 1939- *AmMWSc 92*
**Lawrence,** Richard *Who 92*
**Lawrence,** Richard Aubrey 1947- *AmMWSc 92*
**Lawrence,** Richard Dean 1944- *WhoAmL 92*
**Lawrence,** Richard Sellers 1934- *WhoEnt 92*
**Lawrence,** Robert 1912-1981 *NewAmDM*
**Lawrence,** Robert Cutting, III 1938- *WhoAmL 92*
**Lawrence,** Robert D 1943- *AmMWSc 92*
**Lawrence,** Robert Don 1941- *WhoWest 92*
**Lawrence,** Robert G 1921- *AmMWSc 92*
**Lawrence,** Robert G 1932- *WhoIns 92*
**Lawrence,** Robert Hoe 1861-1897 *BiInAmS*
**Lawrence,** Robert L. 1919- *IntMPA 92*
**Lawrence,** Robert Marshall 1923- *AmMWSc 92*
**Lawrence,** Robert Swan 1938- *AmMWSc 92, IntWW 91*
**Lawrence,** Rodell 1946- *WhoBlA 92*
**Lawrence,** Sanford Hull 1919- *WhoWest 92*
**Lawrence,** Sigmund J 1918- *AmMWSc 92*
**Lawrence,** Stanton Townley, III 1945- *WhoAmL 92*
**Lawrence,** Steve 1935- *IntMPA 92, WhoEnt 92*
**Lawrence,** Steven B. 1960- *WhoEnt 92*
**Lawrence,** Steven C 1924- *IntAu&W 91, TwCWW 91, WrDr 92*
**Lawrence,** T E 1888-1935 *FacFETw [port], LiExTwC*
**Lawrence,** Theresa A. B. 1953- *WhoBlA 92*
**Lawrence,** Thomas Albert 1895- *Who 92*
**Lawrence,** Thomas Edwin, Jr 1941- *WhoAmP 91*
**Lawrence,** Thomas Patterson 1946- *WhoFI 92*
**Lawrence,** Thomas R., Jr. 1929- *WhoBlA 92*
**Lawrence,** Timothy 1942- *Who 92*
**Lawrence,** Vinnedge Moore 1940- *AmMWSc 92*
**Lawrence,** Viola 1895-1973 *ReelWom [port]*
**Lawrence,** Viola Poe 1926- *WhoBlA 92*
**Lawrence,** W H C *ScFEYrs*
**Lawrence,** Walter, Jr 1925- *AmMWSc 92*
**Lawrence,** Walter Edward 1942- *AmMWSc 92*
**Lawrence,** Walter Nicholas Murray 1935- *IntWW 91, Who 92*
**Lawrence,** Willard Earl 1917- *AmMWSc 92*
**Lawrence,** William 1850-1941 *BenetAL 91*
**Lawrence,** William 1954- *Who 92*
**Lawrence,** William Chase 1934- *AmMWSc 92*
**Lawrence,** William F *WhoAmP 91*
**Lawrence,** William Homer 1928- *AmMWSc 92*
**Lawrence,** William Mason 1918- *AmMWSc 92*
**Lawrence,** William Robert 1942- *Who 92*
**Lawrence,** William Wesley 1939- *WhoBlA 92*
**Lawrence-Evans,** Sandra 1938- *WhoBlA 92*

**Lawrence-Jones,** Christopher 1940- *Who 92*
**Lawrence-Schultz,** Vicki 1949- *IntMPA 92*
**Lawrenson,** Peter John 1933- *IntWW 91, Who 92*
**Lawrenz,** Donald R 1923- *WhoIns 92*
**Lawrenz,** Frances Patricia 1947- *AmMWSc 92*
**Lawrey,** James Donald 1949- *AmMWSc 92*
**Lawrey,** Keith 1940- *Who 92*
**Lawrie,** Duncan H 1943- *AmMWSc 92*
**Lawrie,** Peter 1945- *WhoIns 92*
**Lawrimore,** Eugene Salmon Napier 1947- *WhoAmL 92, WhoAmP 91*
**Lawroski,** Harry 1928- *AmMWSc 92*
**Lawroski,** Stephen 1914- *AmMWSc 92*
**Laws,** Clarence A. 1911- *WhoBlA 92*
**Laws,** Courtney Alexander 1934- *Who 92*
**Laws,** Curtis Lee 1868-1946 *RelLAm 91*
**Laws,** David Garrard 1930- *WhoMW 92*
**Laws,** Edward Allen 1945- *AmMWSc 92*
**Laws,** Edward Ernest, III 1945- *WhoWest 92*
**Laws,** Edward Raymond, Jr 1938- *AmMWSc 92*
**Laws,** Frederick Geoffrey 1928- *Who 92*
**Laws,** John Grant McKenzie 1945- *Who 92*
**Laws,** John William 1921- *Who 92*
**Laws,** Kenneth L. 1935- *WhoEnt 92*
**Laws,** Kenneth Lee 1935- *AmMWSc 92*
**Laws,** Leonard Stewart 1917- *AmMWSc 92*
**Laws,** Priscilla Watson 1940- *AmMWSc 92*
**Laws,** Richard Maitland 1926- *IntWW 91, Who 92*
**Laws,** Robert E 1926- *WhoIns 92*
**Laws,** Romulus Don 1868-1951 *DcNCBi 4*
**Laws,** Ruth M. 1912- *WhoBlA 92*
**Laws,** Stephen Charles 1950- *Who 92*
**Laws-Brown,** Diane Elaine 1946- *WhoRel 92*
**Laws-Clay,** Velma 1940- *WhoMW 92*
**Laws-Coats,** Laurie Ann 1954- *WhoAmL 92*
**Lawson** *Who 92*
**Lawson,** Al 1948- *WhoAmP 91*
**Lawson,** Alfred E 1929- *WhoAmP 91*
**Lawson,** Alfred James 1950- *WhoFI 92*
**Lawson,** Alfred William 1869-1954 *RelLAm 91, ScFEYrs*
**Lawson,** Andrew Cowper, II 1946- *AmMWSc 92*
**Lawson,** Anton Eric 1945- *AmMWSc 92*
**Lawson,** Barbara Ellen 1963- *WhoFI 92*
**Lawson,** Ben Frank 1939- *WhoAmL 92*
**Lawson,** Benjamin F 1931- *AmMWSc 92*
**Lawson,** Bert Allen 1947- *WhoWest 92*
**Lawson,** Betty Noyes 1928- *WhoAmP 91, WhoMW 92*
**Lawson,** Bruce Alan 1947- *WhoFI 92*
**Lawson,** Bruce B. 1948- *WhoBlA 92*
**Lawson,** Carole Jean 1944- *WhoRel 92*
**Lawson,** Cassell Avon 1937- *WhoBlA 92*
**Lawson,** Charles Alden 1951- *AmMWSc 92*
**Lawson,** Charles H., III 1931- *WhoBlA 92*
**Lawson,** Charles L 1931- *AmMWSc 92*
**Lawson,** Chet *IntAu&W 91X, WrDr 92*
**Lawson,** Christopher 1922- *Who 92*
**Lawson,** Dana Alex 1958- *WhoAmP 91*
**Lawson,** Daniel David 1929- *AmMWSc 92, WhoWest 92*
**Lawson,** Danny *WhoBlA 92*
**Lawson,** David Edward 1939- *AmMWSc 92*
**Lawson,** David Francis 1945- *AmMWSc 92*
**Lawson,** David Hamilton 1939- *Who 92*
**Lawson,** David Jerald 1930- *WhoRel 92*
**Lawson,** David Michael 1943- *AmMWSc 92*
**Lawson,** Denis 1947- *ConTFT 9*
**Lawson,** Dewey Tull 1944- *AmMWSc 92*
**Lawson,** Dominic 1956- *IntWW 91*
**Lawson,** Dominic Ralph Campden 1956- *Who 92*
**Lawson,** Donald Douglas 1924- *Who 92*
**Lawson,** E Elim 1926- *WhoAmP 91*
**Lawson,** E. Thomas 1931- *WhoMW 92, WhoRel 92*
**Lawson,** Edmund James 1948- *Who 92*
**Lawson,** Edward Earle 1946- *AmMWSc 92*
**Lawson,** Elizabeth Ann 1947- *Who 92*
**Lawson,** Elizabeth Harris *WhoBlA 92*
**Lawson,** Eugene Kistler 1939- *WhoAmP 91*
**Lawson,** Everett Leroy 1938- *WhoRel 92, WhoWest 92*
**Lawson,** F. D. *WhoRel 92*
**Lawson,** Fred 1888-1963 *TwCPaSc*
**Lawson,** Fred Avery 1919- *AmMWSc 92*
**Lawson,** Fred Raulston 1936- *WhoFI 92*
**Lawson,** Frederick Charles William 1917- *Who 92*
**Lawson,** Gary B. 1945- *WhoAmL 92*
**Lawson,** Gerald Hartley 1933- *Who 92*
**Lawson,** Helen *DrAPF 91*
**Lawson,** Henry 1867-1922 *RfGEnL 91*
**Lawson,** Herbert Blaine, Jr 1942- *AmMWSc 92*
**Lawson,** Herbert Horace 1926- *WhoMW 92*
**Lawson,** Herman A. 1920- *WhoBlA 92*
**Lawson,** Hugh 1697?-1772 *DcNCBi 4*
**Lawson,** Hugh McDowall 1912- *Who 92*
**Lawson,** Ian Douglas Napier 1917- *Who 92*
**Lawson,** J. Jenice Evelyn 1952- *WhoMW 92*
**Lawson,** J. Ranaldo 1943- *WhoBlA 92*
**Lawson,** James 1798-1880 *BenetAL 91*
**Lawson,** James 1938- *IntAu&W 91, WrDr 92*
**Lawson,** James Everett 1933- *AmMWSc 92*
**Lawson,** James Gregory 1943- *WhoMW 92*
**Lawson,** James Lee 1949- *WhoWest 92*
**Lawson,** James Llewellyn 1915- *AmMWSc 92*
**Lawson,** James M., Jr. 1928- *WhoBlA 92*
**Lawson,** James Raymond 1919- *WhoEnt 92*
**Lawson,** James Robert 1939- *Who 92*
**Lawson,** James Robert 1945- *AmMWSc 92*
**Lawson,** James W *AmMWSc 92*
**Lawson,** James William Corcoran 1931- *WhoAmL 92*
**Lawson,** Jean Kerr 1941- *WhoFI 92*
**Lawson,** Jennifer *LesBEnT 92*
**Lawson,** Jennifer 1946- *ConBlB 1 [port], WhoBlA 92, WhoEnt 92*
**Lawson,** Jimmie Brown 1934- *AmMWSc 92*
**Lawson,** Jimmie Don 1942- *AmMWSc 92*
**Lawson,** Joel S 1924- *AmMWSc 92*
**Lawson,** John d1711 *BenetAL 91, BiInAmS*
**Lawson,** John 1674-1711 *DcNCBi 4*
**Lawson,** John Alexander Reid 1920- *Who 92*
**Lawson,** John Charles Arthur Digby 1912- *Who 92*
**Lawson,** John D 1949- *AmMWSc 92*
**Lawson,** John David 1923- *IntWW 91, Who 92*
**Lawson,** John Douglas 1937- *AmMWSc 92*
**Lawson,** John Edward 1931- *AmMWSc 92*
**Lawson,** John Edwin 1933- *AmMWSc 92*
**Lawson,** John Howard 1894-1977 *LiExTwC*
**Lawson,** John Howard 1895-1977 *BenetAL 91*
**Lawson,** Juan 1939- *AmMWSc 92*
**Lawson,** Kenneth Dare 1934- *AmMWSc 92*
**Lawson,** Kent DeLance 1921- *AmMWSc 92*
**Lawson,** Larry Dale 1946- *AmMWSc 92*
**Lawson,** Lawyer 1941- *WhoBlA 92*
**Lawson,** Leigh 1943- *ConTFT 9*
**Lawson,** Lesley *Who 92*
**Lawson,** Lesley 1949- *IntWW 91*
**Lawson,** Lynn George 1949- *WhoAmP 91*
**Lawson,** Marguerite Payne 1935- *WhoWest 92*
**Lawson,** Marjorie McKenzie 1912- *NotBlAW 92, WhoBlA 92*
**Lawson,** Mark McCarroll 1961- *WhoAmL 92*
**Lawson,** Martin Deyo 1951- *WhoFI 92*
**Lawson,** Matthew S. 1946- *WhoMW 92*
**Lawson,** Merlin Paul 1941- *AmMWSc 92*
**Lawson,** Michael *WrDr 92*
**Lawson,** Mildred Wiker 1922- *AmMWSc 92*
**Lawson,** Neal D 1916- *AmMWSc 92*
**Lawson,** Neil 1908- *Who 92*
**Lawson,** Nigel 1932- *IntWW 91, Who 92*
**Lawson,** Norman C 1929- *AmMWSc 92*
**Lawson,** Peter G 1928- *WhoAmP 91*
**Lawson,** Quentin Roosevelt 1933- *WhoBlA 92*
**Lawson,** Randall Clayton, II 1948- *WhoFI 92*
**Lawson,** Richard *ConTFT 9*
**Lawson,** Richard 1927- *Who 92*
**Lawson,** Richard George 1927- *IntWW 91*
**Lawson,** Richard Henry 1932- *Who 92*
**Lawson,** Richard Laverne 1929- *IntWW 91*
**Lawson,** Robert Barrett 1911- *AmMWSc 92*
**Lawson,** Robert Bernard 1940- *AmMWSc 92*
**Lawson,** Robert Clarence 1883-1961 *RelLAm 91*
**Lawson,** Robert Davis 1926- *AmMWSc 92*
**Lawson,** Robert L. 1950- *WhoBlA 92*
**Lawson,** Robert William, Jr. 1908- *WhoAmL 92*
**Lawson,** Robert William, Jr 1942- *WhoAmP 91*
**Lawson,** Robin Alastair 1939- *WhoWest 92*
**Lawson,** Rodger S 1943- *WhoIns 92*
**Lawson,** Rosanne Tauber 1946- *WhoWest 92*
**Lawson,** Sarah 1928- *IntMPA 92*
**Lawson,** Sonia 1934- *TwCPaSc, Who 92*
**Lawson,** Stephen 1942- *TwCPaSc*
**Lawson,** Thomas Cheney 1955- *WhoFI 92, WhoWest 92*
**Lawson,** Thomas Seay, Jr. 1935- *WhoAmL 92*
**Lawson,** Thomas Towles 1938- *WhoAmL 92*
**Lawson,** Todd S. *DrAPF 91*
**Lawson,** Tony 1961- *WhoEnt 92*
**Lawson,** W.B. *BenetAL 91*
**Lawson,** Walter I., Jr. 1950- *WhoBlA 92*
**Lawson,** Walter William 1940- *WhoWest 92*
**Lawson,** William 1934- *AmMWSc 92*
**Lawson,** William Burrows 1929- *AmMWSc 92*
**Lawson,** William Burton 1930- *WhoRel 92*
**Lawson,** William Daniel 1948- *WhoBlA 92*
**Lawson,** William David, III 1924- *WhoFI 92*
**Lawson,** William Emmett 1922- *WhoBlA 92*
**Lawson,** William Howard, Jr. 1946- *WhoAmL 92*
**Lawson,** William R. 1943- *WhoBlA 92*
**Lawson,** William Vinton, Jr 1931- *WhoAmP 91*
**Lawson Johnston** *Who 92*
**Lawson Johnston,** Hugh de Beauchamp 1914- *Who 92*
**Lawson-Tancred,** Henry 1924- *Who 92*
**Lawson-Thomas,** Althean Shannon 1953- *WhoBlA 92*
**Lawston,** Marjorie Gray 1928- *WhoBlA 92*
**Lawter,** J Mike 1947- *WhoAmP 91*
**Lawther,** Patrick Joseph 1921- *Who 92*
**Lawther,** Robert M 1927- *WhoAmP 91*
**Lawton,** Alexander R, III 1938- *AmMWSc 92*
**Lawton,** Alfred Henry 1916- *AmMWSc 92*
**Lawton,** Alistair *Who 92*
**Lawton,** Barbara Perry 1930- *WhoMW 92*
**Lawton,** Bettina Mary 1954- *WhoAmL 92*
**Lawton,** Charles *TwCWW 91, WrDr 92*
**Lawton,** Denis 1931- *Who 92*
**Lawton,** Emil Abraham 1922- *AmMWSc 92*
**Lawton,** Eric 1947- *WhoAmL 92*
**Lawton,** Frank 1915- *Who 92*
**Lawton,** Franklin Joseph 1943- *WhoFI 92*
**Lawton,** Frederick 1911- *Who 92*
**Lawton,** George K 1873-1901 *BiInAmS*
**Lawton,** Gregory Moss 1958- *WhoFI 92*
**Lawton,** Harold Walter 1899- *Who 92*
**Lawton,** Jacqueline Agnes 1933- *WhoFI 92*
**Lawton,** John Alistair 1929- *Who 92*
**Lawton,** John Arthur 1913- *Who 92*
**Lawton,** John G 1923- *AmMWSc 92*
**Lawton,** John Hartley 1943- *Who 92*
**Lawton,** Kim Audrey 1963- *WhoRel 92*
**Lawton,** Leon Redford 1924- *WhoRel 92*
**Lawton,** Lorilee Ann 1947- *WhoFI 92*
**Lawton,** Louis David 1936- *Who 92*
**Lawton,** Mark Edward 1949- *WhoAmP 91*
**Lawton,** Mary Cecilia 1935- *WhoAmL 92*
**Lawton,** Michael James 1953- *WhoWest 92*
**Lawton,** Philip Charles Fenner 1912- *Who 92*
**Lawton,** Richard G 1934- *AmMWSc 92*
**Lawton,** Richard L 1918- *AmMWSc 92*
**Lawton,** Richard Woodruff 1920- *AmMWSc 92*
**Lawton,** Robert Arthur 1932- *AmMWSc 92*
**Lawton,** Stephen Latham 1939- *AmMWSc 92*
**Lawton,** William Harvey 1937- *AmMWSc 92*
**Lawvere,** Francis William 1937- *AmMWSc 92*
**Lawwill,** Stanley Joseph 1916- *AmMWSc 92*
**Lawyer,** Arthur L *AmMWSc 92*
**Lawyer,** Cyrus J., III 1943- *WhoBlA 92*
**Lawyer,** Verne 1923- *WhoAmL 92*
**Lawyer,** Vivian 1946- *WhoBlA 92*
**Lawyer,** Vivian Jury 1932- *WhoAmL 92, WhoMW 92*
**Lawzi,** Ahmed Abdel Kareem al- 1925- *IntWW 91*
**Lax,** Anneli 1922- *AmMWSc 92*
**Lax,** Benjamin 1915- *AmMWSc 92*
**Lax,** Edward 1931- *AmMWSc 92*
**Lax,** Eric 1944- *WrDr 92*
**Lax,** Louis Carl 1930- *AmMWSc 92*
**Lax,** Melvin 1922- *AmMWSc 92, IntWW 91*
**Lax,** Melvin David 1947- *AmMWSc 92*
**Lax,** Michael 1929- *DcTwDes*
**Lax,** Michael H. 1949- *WhoAmL 92*
**Lax,** Peter D. 1926- *IntWW 91*
**Lax,** Peter David 1926- *AmMWSc 92*
**Lax,** Robert 1915- *IntAu&W 91*
**Laxalt,** Paul 1922- *IntWW 91, WhoAmP 91*
**Laxer,** Cary 1955- *AmMWSc 92*
**Laxness,** Halldor 1902- *FacFETw, IntAu&W 91, IntWW 91*
**Laxness,** Halldor Kiljan 1902- *Who 92, WhoNob 90*
**Laxpati,** Sharad R 1938- *AmMWSc 92*
**Laxton,** Donald Kenneth 1956- *WhoFI 92*
**Lay,** Christopher David 1946- *WhoAmP 91*
**Lay,** David Clark 1941- *AmMWSc 92*
**Lay,** Donald P *WhoAmP 91*
**Lay,** Donald Pomeroy 1926- *WhoAmL 92, WhoMW 92*
**Lay,** Douglas M 1936- *AmMWSc 92*
**Lay,** George William 1860-1932 *DcNCBi 4*
**Lay,** Graeme 1944- *IntAu&W 91*
**Lay,** John Charles 1948- *AmMWSc 92*
**Lay,** Kenneth W 1939- *AmMWSc 92*
**Lay,** Patti Jane 1955- *WhoAmL 92*
**Lay,** Richard Neville 1938- *Who 92*
**Lay,** Skipper 1940- *WhoAmL 92*
**Lay,** Steven R 1944- *AmMWSc 92*
**Lay,** Terry Lynn 1947- *WhoFI 92*
**Lay,** Thorne 1956- *AmMWSc 92*
**Laya,** Jaime C. 1939- *IntWW 91*
**Layard,** Michael Henry Gordon 1936- *Who 92*
**Layard,** Peter Richard Grenville 1934- *IntWW 91*
**Layard,** Richard 1934- *Who 92*
**Laybe,** Sue *WhoAmP 91*
**Laybourn,** Hale 1923- *WhoFI 92, WhoMW 92*
**Laybourne,** George Thomas 1929- *WhoFI 92*
**Laybourne,** Geraldine *LesBEnT 92 [port]*
**Laybourne,** Paul C 1919- *AmMWSc 92*
**Laychock,** Suzanne Gale 1949- *AmMWSc 92*
**Laycock,** Harold Douglas 1948- *WhoRel 92*
**Laycock,** Maurice Vivian 1938- *AmMWSc 92*
**Laycock,** William Anthony 1930- *AmMWSc 92*
**Laycraft,** James Herbert 1924- *Who 92, WhoWest 92*
**Layden,** Anthony Michael 1946- *Who 92*
**Layden,** Charles Max 1941- *WhoAmL 92*
**Layden,** Donald William, Jr. 1957- *WhoMW 92*
**Layden,** Francis Patrick 1932- *WhoWest 92*
**Layden,** George Kavanaugh 1929- *AmMWSc 92*
**Layden,** John 1926- *Who 92*
**Layden,** John E., III 1940- *WhoMW 92*
**Layden,** Patrick John 1949- *Who 92*
**Laye,** Camara 1928-1980 *BlkLC [port], LiExTwC*
**Laye,** Evelyn 1900- *Who 92*
**Laye,** John Edward 1933- *WhoWest 92*
**Laye,** Ronald Curtis 1945- *AmMWSc 92*
**Layer,** Meredith Mitchum 1946- *WhoFI 92*
**Layer,** Robert Wesley 1928- *AmMWSc 92*
**Layfield,** Arthur Wayne 1960- *WhoFI 92*
**Layfield,** Frank 1921- *Who 92*
**Layloff,** Thomas 1937- *AmMWSc 92*
**Layman,** Christopher Hope 1938- *Who 92*
**Layman,** David Michael 1955- *WhoAmL 92*
**Layman,** Don Lee 1938- *AmMWSc 92*
**Layman,** Donald Keith 1950- *AmMWSc 92*
**Layman,** Earl Robert 1932- *WhoAmP 91*
**Layman,** Fred Dale 1931- *WhoRel 92*
**Layman,** Richard 1947- *ConAu 35NR*
**Layman,** Ronald Ray 1944- *WhoAmP 91*
**Layman,** Wilbur A 1929- *AmMWSc 92*
**Layman,** William Arthur 1929- *AmMWSc 92*
**Laymon,** Heather R. 1948- *WhoBlA 92*
**Laymon,** John W. 1945- *WhoBlA 92*
**Layne,** Clyde Browning 1947- *AmMWSc 92*
**Layne,** Donald Jay 1929- *WhoMW 92*
**Layne,** Donald Sainteval 1931- *AmMWSc 92*
**Layne,** James Nathaniel 1926- *AmMWSc 92*
**Layne,** Porter Preston 1945- *AmMWSc 92*
**Layne,** Richard C 1936- *AmMWSc 92*
**Layng,** Edwin Tower 1909- *AmMWSc 92*
**Layson,** Allen Webster 1931- *WhoAmP 91*
**Layson,** William M 1934- *AmMWSc 92*
**Laytin,** Jeffrey Lawrence 1945- *WhoAmL 92*
**Layton** *Who 92*
**Layton,** Baron 1947- *Who 92*
**Layton,** Bentley *WrDr 92*
**Layton,** Billy Jim 1924- *NewAmDM*
**Layton,** Christopher Walter 1929- *Who 92*
**Layton,** David Warren 1948- *AmMWSc 92*
**Layton,** Donald Harvey 1950- *WhoFI 92*
**Layton,** E Miller, Jr 1931- *AmMWSc 92*

**Layton,** Edwin Thomas, Jr 1928- *AmMWSc 92*
**Layton,** Garland Mason 1925- *WhoAmL 92, WhoFI 92*
**Layton,** Geoffrey 1884-1964 *CurBio 91N*
**Layton,** George L 1921- *WhoAmP 91*
**Layton,** Harry Christopher 1938- *WhoFI 92*
**Layton,** Irving 1912- *BenetAL 91, ConPo 91, IntAu&W 91, RfGEnL 91, WrDr 92*
**Layton,** Jack Malcolm 1917- *AmMWSc 92*
**Layton,** Les 1947- *WhoMW 92*
**Layton,** Mark E. 1951- *WhoFI 92*
**Layton,** Richard Gary 1935- *AmMWSc 92*
**Layton,** Robert G. 1923- *IntWW 91*
**Layton,** Thomas William 1927- *AmMWSc 92*
**Layton,** W. I. 1913- *WrDr 92*
**Layton,** William George 1931- *WhoFI 92*
**Layton,** William Isaac 1913- *AmMWSc 92*
**Layton,** William W. 1915- *WhoBlA 92*
**Layzer,** Arthur James 1927- *AmMWSc 92*
**Layzer,** David 1925- *AmMWSc 92*
**Lazamon** 1200?- *RfGEnL 91*
**Lazar,** Aaron Jack 1956- *WhoMW 92*
**Lazar,** Benjamin Edward 1930- *AmMWSc 92*
**Lazar,** Dale Steven 1952- *WhoAmL 92*
**Lazar,** Irving Paul 1907- *WhoEnt 92*
**Lazar,** J. Brett 1937- *WhoWest 92*
**Lazar,** Jeffrey Bennett 1944- *WhoRel 92*
**Lazar,** Lon David 1960- *WhoAmL 92*
**Lazar,** Nancy R. 1957- *WhoFI 92*
**Lazar,** Norman Henry 1929- *AmMWSc 92*
**Lazar,** Philippe 1936- *IntWW 91*
**Lazar,** Raymond Michael 1939- *WhoAmL 92*
**Lazar,** Sandra Jean 1939- *WhoMW 92*
**Lazar-Wesley,** Eliane M 1953- *AmMWSc 92*
**Lazarchick,** John 1942- *AmMWSc 92*
**Lazard,** Naomi *DrAPF 91*
**LaZare,** Howard Ted 1936- *WhoEnt 92*
**Lazareth,** Otto William, Jr 1938- *AmMWSc 92*
**Lazareth,** William Henry 1928- *WhoRel 92*
**Lazarev,** Petr Petrovich 1878-1942 *SovUnBD*
**Lazaridis,** Anastas 1940- *AmMWSc 92*
**Lazaridis,** Christina Nicholson 1942- *AmMWSc 92*
**Lazaridis,** Nassos A 1943- *AmMWSc 92*
**Lazaridis,** Nassos Athanasios 1943- *WhoMW 92*
**Lazaro,** Eric Joseph 1921- *AmMWSc 92*
**Lazarof,** Henri 1932- *NewAmDM*
**Lazaroff,** Norman 1927- *AmMWSc 92*
**Lazarou Walsh,** Celeste 1958- *WhoEnt 92*
**Lazarow,** Paul B 1945- *AmMWSc 92*
**Lazarre,** Jane *DrAPF 91*
**Lazarski,** Joanne Louise 1946- *WhoMW 92*
**Lazarte,** Jaime Esteban 1943- *AmMWSc 92*
**Lazarus,** A.L. *DrAPF 91*
**Lazarus,** A. L. 1914- *WrDr 92*
**Lazarus,** Allan Kenneth 1931- *AmMWSc 92*
**Lazarus,** Arnold Leslie 1914- *IntAu&W 91*
**Lazarus,** Arthur, Jr. 1926- *WhoAmL 92*
**Lazarus,** Bruce I. 1954- *WhoAmL 92*
**Lazarus,** David 1921- *AmMWSc 92*
**Lazarus,** Emma 1849-1884 *DcAmImH*
**Lazarus,** Emma 1849-1887 *BenetAL 91, HanAmWH*
**Lazarus,** Gerald Sylvan 1939- *AmMWSc 92*
**Lazarus,** Ian Rodney 1959- *WhoWest 92*
**Lazarus,** Jonathan Doniel 1951- *WhoFI 92*
**Lazarus,** Lawrence H *AmMWSc 92*
**Lazarus,** Marc Samuel 1946- *AmMWSc 92*
**Lazarus,** Margaret Louise 1949- *WhoEnt 92*
**Lazarus,** Mary Ann 1951- *WhoMW 92*
**Lazarus,** Paul N. 1913- *IntMPA 92*
**Lazarus,** Paul N, III 1938- *IntMPA 92*
**Lazarus,** Peter 1926- *Who 92*
**Lazarus,** Rachel Mordecai 1788-1838 *DcNCBi 4*
**Lazarus,** Richard S. 1922- *WrDr 92*
**Lazarus,** Richard Stanley 1922- *WhoWest 92*
**Lazarus,** Robert Stephen d1991 *Who 92N*
**Lazarus,** Rochelle Braff 1947- *WhoFI 92*
**Lazarus,** Roger Ben 1925- *AmMWSc 92*
**Lazarus,** Sara Louise 1948- *WhoEnt 92*
**Lazarus,** Simon, III 1941- *WhoAmP 91*
**Lazarus,** Theodore R. 1919- *IntMPA 92*
**Lazay,** Paul Duane 1939- *AmMWSc 92, WhoFI 92*
**Lazda,** Velta Abuls 1939- *AmMWSc 92*
**Lazear,** Jesse William 1866-1900 *BiInAmS*
**Lazechko,** Molly 1926- *WhoAmP 91*
**Lazell,** James Draper 1939- *AmMWSc 92*
**Lazenby,** Alec 1927- *IntWW 91, Who 92*
**Lazenby,** Fred Wiehl 1932- *WhoIns 92*
**Lazenby,** Nat *TwCWW 91*
**Lazenby,** Norman 1914- *TwCWW 91, WrDr 92*
**Lazenby,** Robert Alfred 1941- *WhoAmL 92*
**Lazenby,** William Rane 1850-1916 *BiInAmS*
**Lazenski,** David Paul 1952- *WhoAmL 92*
**Lazer,** Hank *DrAPF 91*
**Lazer,** William 1924- *WrDr 92*
**Lazerow,** Herbert Irvin 1939- *WhoAmL 92*
**Lazerson,** Earl Edwin 1930- *AmMWSc 92, WhoMW 92*
**Lazo,** Jacqui Fiske 1951- *WhoAmL 92*
**Lazo,** John Stephen 1948- *AmMWSc 92*
**Lazo,** Nelson 1957- *WhoHisp 92*
**Lazo-Wasem,** Edgar A 1926- *AmMWSc 92*
**Lazok,** Claudia Ann Dufek 1948- *WhoWest 92*
**Lazor,** Theodosius 1933- *WhoRel 92*
**Lazorchak,** Joseph Michael 1957- *WhoFI 92*
**Lazos,** James Nicholas 1954- *WhoFI 92*
**Lazovsky,** Louis Aryeh 1956- *WhoRel 92*
**Lazowska,** Edward Delano 1950- *AmMWSc 92, WhoWest 92*
**Lazzara,** Bernadette 1948- *WhoEnt 92*
**Lazzara,** Craig Joseph 1953- *WhoFI 92*
**Lazzara,** Dennis Joseph 1948- *WhoMW 92*
**Lazzara,** Ralph 1934- *AmMWSc 92*
**Lazzari,** Eugene Paul 1931- *AmMWSc 92*
**Lazzarini,** Albert John 1952- *AmMWSc 92*
**Lazzarini,** Richard Lynn 1960- *WhoWest 92*
**Lazzarini,** Robert A 1931- *AmMWSc 92*
**Lazzaro,** Clifford Emanuel 1959- *WhoAmL 92*
**Le Duc Tho** d1990 *IntWW 91N*
**Le Duc Tho** 1911- *WhoNob 90*
**Le Duc Tho** 1911-1990 *AnObit 1990, CurBio 91N, FacFETw, News 91*
**Le Van Luong** 1910- *IntWW 91*
**Le,** Chap Than 1948- *AmMWSc 92*
**Le,** Francois Phuc 1953- *WhoFI 92*
**Le,** Heng-Chun *AmMWSc 92*
**Le,** Khanh Tuong 1936- *WhoWest 92*
**Le,** Quang Dinh 1950- *WhoWest 92*
**Le,** Tom Savage 1948- *WhoMW 92*
**Lea,** Arden Otterbein 1926- *AmMWSc 92*
**Lea,** Christopher Gerald 1917- *Who 92*
**Lea,** David Edward 1937- *Who 92*
**Lea,** Eleanor Lucille 1916- *WhoMW 92*
**Lea,** George Harris d1990 *Who 92N*
**Lea,** Henry Charles 1825-1909 *BenetAL 91, BiInAmS, RelLAm 91*
**Lea,** Homer 1876-1912 *BenetAL 91*
**Lea,** Isaac 1792-1886 *BiInAmS*
**Lea,** James Alton 1950- *WhoRel 92*
**Lea,** James Dighton 1933- *AmMWSc 92*
**Lea,** James Wesley, Jr 1941- *AmMWSc 92*
**Lea,** Jeanne Evans 1931- *WhoBlA 92*
**Lea,** John 1923- *Who 92*
**Lea,** Julian d1990 *Who 92N*
**Lea,** Lorenzo Bates 1925- *WhoFI 92*
**Lea,** Luke 1879-1945 *DcNCBi 4*
**Lea,** Mathew Carey 1823-1897 *BiInAmS*
**Lea,** Michael Anthony 1939- *AmMWSc 92*
**Lea,** Pat 1928- *WhoAmP 91*
**Lea,** Robert Martin 1931- *AmMWSc 92*
**Lea,** Robert Norman 1939- *WhoWest 92*
**Lea,** Solomon 1807-1897 *DcNCBi 4*
**Lea,** Susan Maureen 1948- *AmMWSc 92*
**Lea,** Sydney *DrAPF 91*
**Lea,** Thomas 1973- *Who 92*
**Lea,** Tom 1907- *BenetAL 91, IntAu&W 91, TwCWW 91, WhoEnt 92, WrDr 92*
**Lea,** Wallace Bruce 1947- *WhoFI 92*
**Lea,** Wayne Adair 1940- *AmMWSc 92*
**Lea,** Wendy Smith 1954- *WhoFI 92*
**Leab,** Daniel Josef 1936- *WrDr 92*
**Leabhart,** Thomas Glenn 1944- *WhoEnt 92, WhoWest 92*
**Leabo,** Dick Albert 1921- *AmMWSc 92*
**Leace,** Donal Richard 1939- *WhoBlA 92*
**Leach,** Alan Ross 1952- *WhoFI 92*
**Leach,** Albert Ernest 1864-1910 *BiInAmS*
**Leach,** Allan William 1931- *Who 92*
**Leach,** Barbara Mary 1945- *WhoAmP 91*
**Leach,** Barbara Wills 1925- *WhoBlA 92*
**Leach,** Barrie William 1945- *AmMWSc 92*
**Leach,** Bernard 1887-1979 *DcTwDes, FacFETw*
**Leach,** Berton Joe 1932- *AmMWSc 92*
**Leach,** Britt 1938- *WhoEnt 92*
**Leach,** Charles Guy Rodney 1934- *Who 92*
**Leach,** Charles Morley 1924- *AmMWSc 92*
**Leach,** Claude *WhoAmP 91*
**Leach,** Clive William 1934- *Who 92*
**Leach,** David Andrew 1911- *Who 92*
**Leach,** Donald Paul 1945- *WhoFI 92*
**Leach,** Douglas Edward 1920- *WrDr 92*
**Leach,** Edward Tad Arthur 1946- *WhoMW 92*
**Leach,** Ernest Bronson 1924- *AmMWSc 92*
**Leach,** Eugene 1955- *WhoEnt 92*
**Leach,** Franklin Rollin 1933- *AmMWSc 92*
**Leach,** Harold Hunter, Jr. 1954- *WhoAmL 92*
**Leach,** Henry 1923- *IntWW 91, Who 92*
**Leach,** Henry Goddard 1880-1970 *AmPeW*
**Leach,** James Albert Smith 1942- *WhoMW 92*
**Leach,** James Francis 1953- *WhoFI 92*
**Leach,** James Hess 1959- *WhoFI 92*
**Leach,** James L 1918- *AmMWSc 92*
**Leach,** James Madison Brown 1815-1891 *DcNCBi 4*
**Leach,** James Moore 1924- *AmMWSc 92*
**Leach,** James Thomas 1805-1883 *DcNCBi 4*
**Leach,** Jeffrey Dale 1954- *WhoMW 92*
**Leach,** Jim 1942- *AlmAP 92 [port], WhoAmP 91*
**Leach,** John Kline 1922- *AmMWSc 92*
**Leach,** John W. 1948- *WhoAmL 92*
**Leach,** Karen Lynn *AmMWSc 92*
**Leach,** Leonard Joseph 1924- *AmMWSc 92*
**Leach,** Mark E. 1961- *WhoFI 92*
**Leach,** Norman 1912- *Who 92*
**Leach,** Norman Edward 1940- *WhoRel 92*
**Leach,** Paul Arthur 1915- *Who 92*
**Leach,** Penelope 1937- *IntAu&W 91, WrDr 92*
**Leach,** Richard Maxwell, Jr. 1934- *WhoFI 92, WhoWest 92*
**Leach,** Robert Ellis 1931- *AmMWSc 92*
**Leach,** Robin 1939- *WhoAmP 91*
**Leach,** Robin 1941- *WhoEnt 92*
**Leach,** Rodney *Who 92*
**Leach,** Rodney 1932- *Who 92*
**Leach,** Roland Melville, Jr 1932- *AmMWSc 92*
**Leach,** Ronald 1907- *Who 92*
**Leach,** Ronald George 1907- *IntWW 91*
**Leach,** Ronald W 1944- *WhoIns 92*
**Leach,** Ronold 1944- *AmMWSc 92*
**Leach,** Russell 1922- *WhoAmL 92, WhoAmP 91*
**Leach,** Terry Ray 1949- *WhoAmL 92*
**Leach,** William Matthew 1933- *AmMWSc 92*
**Leach,** William Pinkney, III 1956- *WhoAmL 92*
**Leach-Huntoon,** Carolyn S 1940- *AmMWSc 92*
**Leachman,** Cloris *LesBEnT 92*
**Leachman,** Cloris 1930- *IntMPA 92, WhoEnt 92*
**Leacock,** Ferdinand S. 1934- *WhoBlA 92*
**Leacock,** John *BenetAL 91*
**Leacock,** Richard 1921- *IntDcF 2-2*
**Leacock,** Robert A 1935- *AmMWSc 92*
**Leacock,** Robert Arthur 1935- *WhoMW 92*
**Leacock,** Robert Jay 1939- *AmMWSc 92*
**Leacock,** Stephen 1869-1944 *BenetAL 91, FacFETw, RfGEnL 91, ScFEYrs*
**Leacock,** Stephen Jerome 1943- *WhoAmL 92, WhoBlA 92*
**Leadabrand,** Ray Laurence 1927- *AmMWSc 92*
**Leadbeater,** Charles Webster 1854-1934 *RelLAm 91*
**Leadbeater,** Howell 1919- *Who 92*
**Leadbelly** 1885?-1949 *ConMus 6 [port], NewAmDM*
**Leadbetter,** Alan James 1934- *Who 92*
**Leadbetter,** David Hulse 1908- *Who 92*
**Leadbetter,** Edward Renton 1934- *AmMWSc 92*
**Leadbitter,** Edward 1919- *Who 92*
**Leader,** Alan H. 1938- *WhoFI 92*
**Leader,** Chari Ann 1954- *WhoMW 92*
**Leader,** Gordon Robert 1916- *AmMWSc 92*
**Leader,** Jeffery James 1963- *WhoWest 92*
**Leader,** John Carl 1938- *AmMWSc 92, WhoMW 92*
**Leader,** Lois Anne 1953- *WhoRel 92*
**Leader,** Michael Kirby 1948- *WhoEnt 92*
**Leader,** Morton 1928- *WhoFI 92*
**Leader,** Robert John 1933- *WhoAmL 92*
**Leader,** Robert Wardell 1919- *AmMWSc 92*
**Leader,** Solomon 1925- *AmMWSc 92*
**Leaders,** Floyd Edwin, Jr 1931- *AmMWSc 92*
**Leadon,** Bernard M 1917- *AmMWSc 92*
**Leadon,** Denise Lynn 1959- *WhoWest 92*
**Leaf,** Alexander 1920- *AmMWSc 92, IntWW 91*
**Leaf,** Boris 1919- *AmMWSc 92*
**Leaf,** Douglass, Jr. 1927- *WhoFI 92*
**Leaf,** Glenn *WhoRel 92*
**Leaf,** Munro 1905-1976 *BenetAL 91, ChILR 25 [port]*
**Leaf,** Robert Stephen 1931- *WhoFI 92*
**Leafe,** Joseph A *WhoAmP 91*
**Leafgren,** Frederick Alden 1931- *WhoMW 92*
**Leagre,** Richard Morris 1937- *WhoAmL 92*
**League,** Cheryl Perry 1945- *WhoBlA 92*
**League,** David *WhoAmL 92*
**Leahey,** Miles Cary 1952- *WhoFI 92*
**Leahey,** Patrick Leonard 1961- *WhoWest 92*
**Leahy,** Arthur Stephen 1951- *WhoFI 92*
**Leahy,** Bernard Ryder 1938- *WhoMW 92*
**Leahy,** Denis Alan 1952- *AmMWSc 92*
**Leahy,** Elizabeth Clare 1911- *WhoAmP 91*
**Leahy,** J. Michael 1946- *WhoWest 92*
**Leahy,** Jeannette 1927- *WhoEnt 92*
**Leahy,** John 1928- *Who 92*
**Leahy,** John Austin 1931- *WhoRel 92*
**Leahy,** John H. G. 1928- *IntWW 91*
**Leahy,** John Martin 1886- *ScFEYrs*
**Leahy,** John Paul 1936- *WhoFI 92*
**Leahy,** Lourdes C. 1962- *WhoHisp 92*
**Leahy,** Mary Gerald 1917- *AmMWSc 92*
**Leahy,** Patrick *DrAPF 91*
**Leahy,** Patrick J. 1940- *AlmAP 92 [port], WhoAmP 91*
**Leahy,** Patrick Joseph 1940- *IntWW 91*
**Leahy,** Richard Edgar 1953- *WhoMW 92*
**Leahy,** Richard Gordon 1929- *AmMWSc 92*
**Leahy,** T. Liam 1952- *WhoWest 92*
**Leahy,** Thomas F. *LesBEnT 92*
**Leahy,** Thomas Francis 1937- *WhoEnt 92, WhoFI 92*
**Leahy,** William *DrAPF 91*
**Leaist,** Derek Gordon 1955- *AmMWSc 92*
**Leak,** John Clay, Jr 1928- *AmMWSc 92*
**Leak,** Lee Virn 1932- *AmMWSc 92, WhoBlA 92*
**Leake,** Bernard Elgey 1932- *Who 92*
**Leake,** David *Who 92*
**Leake,** Donald L 1931- *AmMWSc 92*
**Leake,** Donald Lewis 1931- *WhoEnt 92*
**Leake,** Donelson Martin 1938- *WhoAmL 92*
**Leake,** Kerry Alexander 1966- *WhoRel 92*
**Leake,** Larry B 1950- *WhoAmP 91*
**Leake,** Lowell 1928- *WhoMW 92*
**Leake,** Lowell, Jr 1928- *AmMWSc 92*
**Leake,** Mildred Breland 1916- *WhoAmP 91*
**Leake,** Penny Yvonne 1947- *WhoMW 92*
**Leake,** Philip Gregory 1958- *WhoWest 92*
**Leake,** Preston Hildebrand 1929- *AmMWSc 92*
**Leake,** Sam D 1945- *WhoAmP 91*
**Leake,** Velmalene Stevens 1930- *WhoAmP 91*
**Leake,** Walter Francis 1799-1879 *DcNCBi 4*
**Leake,** Warren Thomas, Jr. 1954- *WhoAmL 92*
**Leake,** William Stuart, Jr. 1942- *WhoWest 92*
**Leake,** William Walter 1926- *AmMWSc 92*
**Leake,** Willie Mae James 1932- *WhoBlA 92*
**Leakey,** Arundell Rea 1915- *Who 92*
**Leakey,** David Martin 1932- *Who 92*
**Leakey,** Felix William 1922- *Who 92*
**Leakey,** Jonathan *FacFETw*
**Leakey,** Julian Edwin Arundell 1951- *AmMWSc 92*
**Leakey,** Louis S B 1903-1972 *FacFETw*
**Leakey,** Mary *FacFETw*
**Leakey,** Mary 1913- *WrDr 92*
**Leakey,** Mary Douglas 1913- *IntWW 91, Who 92*
**Leakey,** Richard *FacFETw*
**Leakey,** Richard 1944- *WrDr 92*
**Leakey,** Richard Erskine Frere 1944- *IntWW 91, Who 92*
**Leaks,** Sylvester 1927- *WhoBlA 92*
**Leal,** Alfred G. *WhoHisp 92*
**Leal,** Antonio, Jr. 1946- *WhoHisp 92, WhoMW 92*
**Leal,** Carol Ann 1941- *WhoBlA 92*
**Leal,** Gloria 1954- *WhoAmL 92*
**Leal,** H. Allan 1917- *IntWW 91*
**Leal,** J. Gilbert 1946- *WhoHisp 92*
**Leal,** Joseph Rogers 1918- *AmMWSc 92*
**Leal,** Julian 1959- *WhoEnt 92*
**Leal,** L Gary 1943- *AmMWSc 92*
**Leal,** Luis 1907- *WhoHisp 92*
**Leal,** Manuel D. *WhoHisp 92*
**Leal,** Martin Gary 1962- *WhoHisp 92*
**Leal,** Orlando Jimenez 1941- *WhoEnt 92*
**Leal,** Raymond Robert 1946- *WhoHisp 92*
**Leal,** Robert L. 1945- *WhoHisp 92*
**Leal,** Rosie B. 1933- *WhoHisp 92*
**Leal,** Steve *WhoHisp 92*
**Leal,** Widad 1959- *WhoHisp 92*
**Leale,** B C 1930- *IntAu&W 91*
**Leale,** Olivia Mason 1944- *WhoWest 92*
**Lealman,** Brenda 1939- *WhoRel 92*
**Lealofi IV,** Tupua Tamasese 1922- *IntWW 91*
**Leaman,** J. Richard, Jr. 1934- *WhoFI 92*
**Leaman,** Jack Ervin 1932- *WhoWest 92*
**Leaman,** Paul Calvin 1929- *WhoRel 92*
**Leaman,** Stephen James 1947- *WhoIns 92, WhoMW 92*
**Leamer,** Edward Emery 1944- *WhoFI 92*
**Leamer,** Laurence Allen 1941- *ConAu 35NR*
**Leaming,** Edward 1861-1916 *BiInAmS*

**Leaming**, Marj Patricia *WhoWest 92*
**Leamon**, Tom B 1940- *AmMWSc 92*
**Leamy**, Cameron J D 1932- *WhoIns 92*
**Leamy**, Harry John 1940- *AmMWSc 92*
**Leamy**, Larry Jackson 1940- *AmMWSc 92*
**Lean**, David d1991 *Who 92N*
**Lean**, David 1908-1991 *ConAu 134, CurBio 91N, FacFETw, IntDcF 2-2 [port], IntWW 91, -91N, NewYTBS 91*
**Lean**, David Robert Samuel 1937- *AmMWSc 92*
**Lean**, Eric Gung-Hwa 1938- *AmMWSc 92*
**Lean**, Geoffrey 1947- *IntAu&W 91*
**Leander of Seville** 540?-600? *EncEarC*
**Leander**, Daniel Vance 1925- *WhoRel 92*
**Leander**, John David 1944- *AmMWSc 92*
**Leander**, Zarah 1907-1981 *EncTR 91 [port]*
**Leandro**, Francis Gerard 1963- *WhoWest 92*
**Leaney**, Alfred Robert Clare 1909- *WrDr 92*
**Leaning**, David *Who 92*
**Leaning**, William Henry Dickens 1934- *AmMWSc 92*
**Leanza**, Frank 1923- *WhoEnt 92*
**Leap**, Darrell Ivan 1937- *AmMWSc 92*
**Leaper**, Robert Anthony Bernard 1921- *Who 92*
**Leaphart**, Eldridge 1927- *WhoBlA 92*
**Leapman**, Edwina 1934- *TwCPaSc*
**Leapman**, Michael Henry 1938- *IntAu&W 91*
**Leapor**, Mary 1722-1746 *BlkwCEP, DcLB 109*
**Lear**, Bert 1917- *AmMWSc 92*
**Lear**, Cyril James 1911- *IntAu&W 91*
**Lear**, Edward 1812-1888 *RfGEnL 91*
**Lear**, Evelyn *IntWW 91*
**Lear**, Evelyn 1928- *NewAmDM*
**Lear**, Floyd Raymond, III 1942- *WhoFI 92*
**Lear**, Frances 1923- *CurBio 91 [port]*
**Lear**, Frances Loeb 1923- *WhoFI 92*
**Lear**, Gerard Robert 1939- *WhoAmL 92*
**Lear**, Joe Kent 1960- *WhoMW 92*
**Lear**, John 1909- *WrDr 92*
**Lear**, Jonathan *WrDr 92*
**Lear**, Joyce *Who 92*
**Lear**, Martha Weinman 1932- *IntAu&W 91*
**Lear**, Norman *LesBEnT 92*
**Lear**, Norman 1922- *FacFETw, IntMPA 92*
**Lear**, Norman Milton 1922- *WhoEnt 92, WhoWest 92*
**Lear**, Peter *IntAu&W 91X, WrDr 92*
**Lear**, William Dennis 1960- *WhoEnt 92*
**Lear**, William M, Jr 1950- *WhoAmP 91*
**Lear**, William Powell 1902-1978 *FacFETw*
**Learmont**, John 1934- *Who 92*
**Learmonth**, Andrew 1916- *WrDr 92*
**Learmonth**, Arthur B., Jr. 1946- *WhoFI 92, WhoMW 92*
**Learn**, Arthur Jay 1933- *AmMWSc 92*
**Learn**, Doris Lynn 1949- *WhoFI 92*
**Learned Blacksmith**, The *BenetAL 91*
**Learned**, James Roy 1920- *WhoAmL 92*
**Learned**, John Gregory 1940- *AmMWSc 92*
**Learned**, Michael 1939- *IntMPA 92, WhoEnt 92*
**Learned**, Robert Eugene 1928- *AmMWSc 92*
**Learoyd**, Roderick Alastair Brook 1913- *Who 92*
**Learson**, Robert Joseph 1938- *AmMWSc 92*
**Leary**, Arthur Pearson 1949- *WhoAmL 92*
**Leary**, Arthur William 1956- *WhoFI 92*
**Leary**, Brian Leonard 1929- *Who 92*
**Leary**, Charles Randolph 1930- *WhoRel 92*
**Leary**, Edward A. 1913- *WrDr 92*
**Leary**, Francis Christian 1949- *AmMWSc 92*
**Leary**, Gari Lovaas 1938- *WhoEnt 92*
**Leary**, Harvey Lee, Jr *AmMWSc 92*
**Leary**, James E. 1935- *WhoBlA 92*
**Leary**, James Francis 1948- *AmMWSc 92*
**Leary**, John Dennis 1934- *AmMWSc 92*
**Leary**, John Kelly 1956- *WhoFI 92*
**Leary**, John Vincent 1937- *AmMWSc 92*
**Leary**, Lewis 1906-1990 *BenetAL 91*
**Leary**, Michael Robert 1952- *WhoEnt 92*
**Leary**, Nancy Jane 1952- *WhoFI 92*
**Leary**, Nancy May 1955- *WhoAmL 92*
**Leary**, Norma Jean Ehrhart 1926- *WhoRel 92*
**Leary**, Ralph John 1929- *AmMWSc 92*
**Leary**, Robin Janell 1954- *WhoMW 92*
**Leary**, Rolfe Albert 1938- *AmMWSc 92*
**Leary**, Shelby Jean 1936- *WhoAmP 91*
**Leary**, Thomas Barrett 1931- *WhoAmL 92*
**Leary**, Timothy 1920- *FacFETw*
**Leary**, Vincent Joseph 1943- *WhoEnt 92*
**Leas**, J W 1916- *AmMWSc 92*
**Lease**, Gary Lloyd 1940- *WhoRel 92*
**Lease**, Jane Etta 1924- *WhoWest 92*
**Lease**, Joseph *DrAPF 91*
**Lease**, M Harry, Jr 1927- *WhoAmP 91*
**Lease**, Mary Elizabeth Clyens 1850-1933 *HanAmWH*
**Lease**, Richard Jay 1914- *WhoWest 92*
**Leask**, Henry 1913- *Who 92*
**Leask**, John Edward, Jr. 1957- *WhoMW 92*
**Leask**, R A 1919- *AmMWSc 92*
**Leason**, Robert W. 1930- *WhoFI 92*
**Leasor**, James 1923- *IntAu&W 91, Who 92, WrDr 92*
**Leasor**, Jane 1922- *WhoRel 92*
**Leates**, Margaret *Who 92*
**Leath**, Kenneth T 1931- *AmMWSc 92*
**Leath**, Marvin 1931- *WhoAmP 91*
**Leath**, Paul Larry 1941- *AmMWSc 92*
**Leatham**, Aubrey 1920- *Who 92*
**Leatham**, Mary Ellen Jeppesen 1928- *WhoAmP 91*
**Leathart**, James Anthony 1915- *Who 92*
**Leathem**, William Dolars 1931- *AmMWSc 92*
**Leather**, Edwin 1919- *Who 92*
**Leather**, Edwin Hartley Cameron 1919- *IntWW 91*
**Leather**, George *WrDr 92*
**Leather**, Gerald Roger 1937- *AmMWSc 92*
**Leather**, Ted *Who 92*
**Leatherland**, Baron 1898- *Who 92*
**Leatherland**, John F 1943- *AmMWSc 92*
**Leatherman**, Allen H 1935- *WhoIns 92*
**Leatherman**, Anna D 1909- *AmMWSc 92*
**Leatherman**, Hugh Kenneth, Sr 1931- *WhoAmP 91*
**Leatherman**, Nelson E 1939- *AmMWSc 92*
**Leatherman**, Omar S., Jr. *WhoBlA 92*
**Leatherman**, Stephen Parker 1947- *AmMWSc 92*
**Leathers** *Who 92*
**Leathers**, Viscount 1908- *IntWW 91, Who 92*
**Leathers**, Chester Ray 1929- *AmMWSc 92*
**Leatherwood**, Barbara Jean 1939- *WhoRel 92*
**Leatherwood**, James M 1930- *AmMWSc 92*
**Leatherwood**, Larry Lee 1939- *WhoBlA 92*
**Leatherwood**, Lillie 1964- *BlkOlyM*
**Leatherwood**, Paul Randolph Scott, Jr. 1932- *WhoMW 92*
**Leatherwood**, Robert P. 1920- *WhoBlA 92*
**Leatherwood**, Thomas Lee, Jr. 1929- *WhoRel 92*
**Leathrum**, James Frederick 1937- *AmMWSc 92*
**Leathwood**, Barry 1941- *Who 92*
**Leaton**, Anne *DrAPF 91*
**Leaton**, Edward K. 1928- *WhoFI 92*
**Leatto**, Renne 1952- *WhoEnt 92*
**Leaud**, Jean-Pierre 1944- *IntMPA 92*
**Leautaud**, Paul 1872-1956 *GuFrLit 1*
**Leav**, Irwin 1937- *AmMWSc 92*
**Leavel**, Willard Hayden 1927- *WhoAmP 91*
**Leavell**, Allen 1957- *WhoBlA 92*
**Leavell**, Dorothy R. 1944- *WhoBlA 92*
**Leavell**, Landrum Pinson, II 1926- *WhoRel 92*
**Leavell**, Thomas Wayne 1943- *WhoFI 92*
**Leavell**, Walter F. 1934- *WhoBlA 92*
**Leavens**, Peter Backus 1939- *AmMWSc 92*
**Leavens**, William Barry, III 1946- *WhoFI 92*
**Leavenworth**, Frances Wilson 1934- *WhoAmP 91*
**Leavenworth**, Howard W, Jr 1928- *AmMWSc 92*
**Leavenworth**, Melines Conklin 1796-1862 *BiInAmS*
**Leavenworth**, Richard S 1930- *AmMWSc 92*
**Leaver**, Christopher 1937- *IntWW 91, Who 92*
**Leaver**, Christopher John 1942- *IntWW 91, Who 92*
**Leaver**, Peter Lawrence Oppenheim 1944- *Who 92*
**Leaver**, Ruth *IntAu&W 91X, WrDr 92*
**Leaver**, Vincent Wayne 1947- *WhoRel 92*
**Leavett**, Alan 1924- *Who 92*
**Leavey**, John Anthony 1915- *Who 92*
**Leavey**, Norma *WhoFI 92*
**Leavey**, Terrance Charles 1947- *WhoWest 92*
**Leavis**, F R 1895-1978 *FacFETw, RfGEnL 91*
**Leavis**, Paul Clifton 1944- *AmMWSc 92*
**Leavitt**, Brent E. 1947- *WhoAmL 92*
**Leavitt**, Caroline *DrAPF 91*
**Leavitt**, Christopher Pratt 1927- *AmMWSc 92*
**Leavitt**, Dana Gibson 1925- *WhoFI 92*
**Leavitt**, David 1961- *WrDr 92*
**Leavitt**, Dixie L 1929- *WhoAmP 91*
**Leavitt**, Dudley 1772-1851 *BenetAL 91, BiInAmS*
**Leavitt**, Erasmus Darwin 1836-1916 *BiInAmS*
**Leavitt**, Fred I. 1940- *WhoWest 92*
**Leavitt**, Fred W 1928- *AmMWSc 92*
**Leavitt**, Jack Duane 1948- *WhoEnt 92*
**Leavitt**, Jeffrey Stuart 1946- *WhoAmL 92, WhoMW 92*
**Leavitt**, John Adams 1932- *AmMWSc 92*
**Leavitt**, John Logan 1956- *WhoMW 92*
**Leavitt**, Joshua 1794-1873 *AmPeW*
**Leavitt**, Julian *WhoFI 92*
**Leavitt**, Julian Jacob 1918- *AmMWSc 92*
**Leavitt**, Lois Hutcheon 1920- *WhoWest 92*
**Leavitt**, Marc Laurence 1947- *AmMWSc 92*
**Leavitt**, Martin Jack 1940- *WhoAmL 92, WhoMW 92*
**Leavitt**, Neal Scott 1955- *WhoWest 92*
**Leavitt**, Ned 1942- *WhoEnt 92*
**Leavitt**, Robert F. *WhoRel 92*
**Leavitt**, Sturgis Elleno 1888-1976 *DcNCBi 4*
**Leavitt**, Terry Van 1950- *WhoAmL 92*
**Leavitt**, Todd Page 1951- *WhoEnt 92*
**Leavitt**, Wendell William 1938- *AmMWSc 92*
**Leavitt**, William Grenfell 1916- *AmMWSc 92, WhoMW 92*
**Leavy**, Edward *WhoAmP 91*
**Leavy**, Edward 1929- *WhoAmL 92*
**Leavy**, Linda C. 1947- *WhoFI 92*
**Leavy**, Paul Matthew 1923- *AmMWSc 92*
**Leax**, John *DrAPF 91*
**Leazar**, Augustus 1843-1905 *DcNCBi 4*
**Leazer**, Gary Herbert 1944- *WhoRel 92*
**Leback**, Warren G. 1924- *WhoFI 92*
**Lebacqz**, Karen Aneda 1945- *WhoRel 92*
**Le Bailly**, Louis 1915- *Who 92*
**Lebamoff**, Ivan A 1932- *WhoAmP 91*
**Lebamoff**, Ivan Argire 1932- *WhoMW 92*
**LeBaron**, Anne 1953- *ConCom 92*
**LeBaron**, Anthony *TwCSFW 91*
**LeBaron**, Charles Frederick, Jr. 1949- *WhoAmL 92*
**LeBaron**, Donald Ralph 1926- *WhoAmP 91*
**LeBaron**, Edward Wayne, Jr. 1930- *WhoAmL 92*
**LeBaron**, Ervil Morrell 1925-1981 *RelLAm 91*
**LeBaron**, Francis Newton 1922- *AmMWSc 92*
**LeBaron**, Homer McKay 1926- *AmMWSc 92*
**LeBaron**, Joel Franklin 1923-1972 *RelLAm 91*
**LeBaron**, William 1814-1876 *BiInAmS*
**Le Bas**, Edward 1904-1966 *TwCPaSc*
**Le Bas**, Philip 1925- *TwCPaSc*
**LeBaudour**, Diane Elizabeth *WhoWest 92*
**LeBeau**, Christopher John 1959- *WhoWest 92*
**LeBeau**, Gary D *WhoAmP 91*
**Le Beau**, Luise Adolpha 1850-1927 *NewAmDM*
**Le Beau**, Stephen Edward 1954- *AmMWSc 92*
**LeBeau**, Teri Schwartz 1949- *WhoMW 92*
**LeBeauf**, Sabrina *WhoEnt 92*
**Lebeck**, Steven Wade 1953- *WhoMW 92*
**Lebed**, Hartzel Zangwill 1928- *WhoFI 92*
**Lebedev**, Peter Nikolayevich 1866-1912 *FacFETw*
**Lebedev**, Vladimir Vasil'evich 1891-1967 *SovUnBD*
**Lebedev**, Yevgeniy Alekseyevich 1917- *IntWW 91*
**Lebedeva**, Sarra Dmitrievna 1892-1967 *SovUnBD*
**Lebedoff**, David Michael 1938- *WhoAmP 91*
**Lebegern**, Howard Fisher, Jr 1927- *WhoAmP 91*
**Lebegue**, Daniel Simon Georges 1943- *IntWW 91*
**Lebegue**, Nicolas-Antoine 1631?-1702 *NewAmDM*
**Lebel**, Irenee Remi 1926- *WhoAmP 91*
**Lebel**, Jack Lucien 1933- *AmMWSc 92*
**LeBel**, Jean Eugene 1922- *AmMWSc 92*
**LeBel**, Norman Albert 1931- *AmMWSc 92*
**Lebel**, Robert 1924- *WhoRel 92*
**LeBel**, Roland Guy 1932- *AmMWSc 92*
**Lebel**, Susan 1959- *AmMWSc 92*
**LeBell**, June 1944- *WhoEnt 92*
**LeBelle**, Doug Scott 1957- *WhoEnt 92*
**Leben**, Curt 1917- *AmMWSc 92*
**Leben**, Jeffrey Michael 1948- *WhoAmL 92*
**Lebenbaum**, Matthew T 1917- *AmMWSc 92*
**Lebensohn**, Zigmond Meyer 1910- *AmMWSc 92*
**Lebenstein**, Jan 1930- *IntWW 91*
**Lebenthal**, Emanuel 1936- *AmMWSc 92*
**Lebentritt**, Julia *DrAPF 91*
**Leber**, Georg 1920- *IntWW 91*
**Leber**, Julius 1891-1945 *EncTR 91 [port]*
**Leber**, Mariann C. 1921- *WhoBlA 92*
**Leber**, Phyllis Ann 1949- *AmMWSc 92*
**Leber**, Sam 1925- *AmMWSc 92*
**Leber**, Steven E. 1941- *WhoEnt 92*
**Leberman**, Paul R 1904- *AmMWSc 92*
**Lebermann**, Kenneth Wayne *AmMWSc 92*
**Lebeter**, Fred 1903- *Who 92*
**Lebhar**, Bertram *ScFEYrs*
**Lebherz**, Christopher Grant 1963- *WhoAmL 92*
**Lebherz**, Herbert G 1941- *AmMWSc 92*
**Lebiedzik**, Jozef 1940- *AmMWSc 92*
**LeBien**, Tucker W 1948- *AmMWSc 92*
**Lebioda**, Dariusz Thomas 1958- *IntAu&W 91*
**LeBlanc**, Adrian David 1940- *AmMWSc 92*
**LeBlanc**, Annette M. 1965- *SmATA 68 [port]*
**LeBlanc**, Arthur Edgar 1923- *AmMWSc 92*
**Le Blanc**, Bart *IntWW 91*
**Leblanc**, Camille Andre 1898- *Who 92*
**LeBlanc**, Carl James 1942- *WhoFI 92*
**LeBlanc**, Donald Joseph 1942- *AmMWSc 92*
**LeBlanc**, Francis Ernest 1935- *AmMWSc 92*
**Leblanc**, Gabriel 1927- *AmMWSc 92*
**Leblanc**, Jacques Arthur 1921- *AmMWSc 92*
**LeBlanc**, James E. 1942- *WhoMW 92*
**Leblanc**, Jean-Bernard 1707-1781 *BlkwCEP*
**LeBlanc**, Jeffrey Irwin 1951- *WhoFI 92*
**LeBlanc**, Jerald Thomas 1943- *AmMWSc 92*
**LeBlanc**, Jerry 1956- *WhoAmP 91*
**LeBlanc**, John Keith 1945- *WhoMW 92*
**LeBlanc**, Larry Joseph 1947- *AmMWSc 92*
**Leblanc**, Leonard Joseph 1937- *AmMWSc 92*
**Le Blanc**, Marcel A R 1929- *AmMWSc 92*
**Leblanc**, Maurice 1864-1941 *ScFEYrs*
**LeBlanc**, Michael Stephen 1952- *WhoMW 92*
**LeBlanc**, Norman Francis 1926- *AmMWSc 92*
**LeBlanc**, Oliver Harris, Jr 1931- *AmMWSc 92*
**LeBlanc**, Richard Philip 1946- *WhoAmL 92*
**LeBlanc**, Richard Robert 1943- *WhoMW 92*
**LeBlanc**, Robert Bruce 1925- *AmMWSc 92*
**Leblanc**, Roger M 1942- *AmMWSc 92*
**Leblanc**, Romeo A. 1927- *IntWW 91*
**Leblanc**, Rufus Joseph 1917- *AmMWSc 92*
**LeBlanc**, Sam A, III 1938- *WhoAmP 91*
**Le Blanc**, Shirley Maurie 1939- *WhoWest 92*
**LeBlanc**, Tina *WhoEnt 92*
**LeBlanc**, Whitney Joseph 1933- *WhoEnt 92*
**LeBlang**, Skip Alan 1953- *WhoAmL 92*
**LeBlang**, Theodore Raymond 1949- *WhoAmL 92*
**LeBleu**, Conway 1918- *WhoAmP 91*
**Leblon**, Jean Marcel 1928- *WhoWest 92*
**Leblond**, C. P. 1910- *Who 92*
**Leblond**, Charles Philippe 1910- *AmMWSc 92, IntWW 91*
**LeBlond**, Michael Harry 1950- *WhoFI 92*
**LeBlond**, Paul Henri 1938- *AmMWSc 92*
**LeBlond**, Richard Emmett, Jr. 1924- *WhoEnt 92*
**LeBlond**, Richard Knight, II 1920- *IntWW 91*
**Lebo**, George Robert 1937- *AmMWSc 92*
**Lebo**, Kevin Joseph 1961- *WhoFI 92*
**Lebo**, William C., Jr. *WhoAmL 92*
**LeBoeuf**, Michael 1942- *WrDr 92*
**Lebofsky**, Larry Allen 1947- *AmMWSc 92*
**LeBold**, William Kerns 1923- *WhoMW 92*
**Lebotsa**, Mohamane Masimole 1927- *IntWW 91*
**Lebouder**, Jean-Pierre 1944- *IntWW 91*
**Lebourg**, Albert-Charles 1849-1928 *ThHEIm*
**LeBoutillier**, John 1953- *WhoAmP 91*
**LeBouton**, Albert V 1937- *AmMWSc 92*
**Lebovits**, Moses 1951- *WhoAmL 92*
**Lebovitz**, Herman Abbie 1923- *WhoMW 92*
**Lebovitz**, Norman Ronald 1935- *AmMWSc 92*
**Lebovitz**, Phil Stanley 1940- *WhoMW 92*
**Lebovitz**, Robert Mark 1937- *AmMWSc 92*
**Lebow**, Edward Michael 1948- *WhoAmL 92*
**Lebow**, Irwin L 1926- *AmMWSc 92*
**Lebow**, Jeanne 1951- *ConAu 135*
**Lebow**, Leonard Stanley 1929- *WhoEnt 92*
**Lebow**, Mark Denis 1940- *WhoAmL 92*
**LeBow**, Michael David 1941- *AmMWSc 92*
**Lebow**, Victor 1902-1980 *ConAu 133*
**Lebowitz**, Albert 1922- *WrDr 92*
**Lebowitz**, Catharine Koch 1915- *WhoAmP 91*
**Lebowitz**, Elliot 1941- *AmMWSc 92*
**Lebowitz**, J. Leon 1921- *WhoAmL 92*
**Lebowitz**, Jacob 1935- *AmMWSc 92*

**Lebowitz**, Jacob Mordecai 1936- *AmMWSc 92*
**Lebowitz**, Joel L. 1930- *IntWW 91*
**Lebowitz**, Joel Louis 1930- *AmMWSc 92*
**Lebowitz**, Michael David 1939- *AmMWSc 92*
**Leboy**, Phoebe Starfield 1936- *AmMWSc 92*
**Lebra**, Takie Sugiyama 1930- *WhoWest 92*
**Le Breton**, David Francis Battye 1931- *IntWW 91, Who 92*
**Le Breton**, Guy C 1946- *AmMWSc 92*
**LeBreton**, Pierre Robert 1942- *AmMWSc 92*
**Lebrija**, Francis 1950- *WhoHisp 92*
**Lebro**, Theodore Peter 1910- *WhoFI 92*
**Le Brocquy**, Louis 1916- *FacFETw, IntWW 91, TwCPaSc, Who 92*
**Lebron**, Michael A., III 1954- *WhoHisp 92*
**LeBron**, Victor 1950- *WhoHisp 92*
**Lebrun**, Albert 1871-1950 *EncTR 91*
**Lebrun**, Christopher 1951- *TwCPaSc*
**Le Brun**, Christopher Mark 1951- *IntWW 91*
**Lebrun**, Claude 1929- *SmATA 66 [port]*
**Lebrun**, Francois *WhoEnt 92*
**Le Brun**, Jacques 1931- *WhoRel 92*
**Le Brun**, Michael David 1956- *WhoAmL 92*
**LeBrun**, Roger Arthur 1946- *AmMWSc 92*
**Lebrun Moratinos**, Jose Ali 1919- *IntWW 91, WhoRel 92*
**Lebsock**, Kenneth L 1921- *AmMWSc 92*
**Leburton**, Edmond Jules Isidore 1915- *IntWW 91*
**Le Cain**, Errol 1941-1989 *SmATA 68 [port]*
**Le Cam**, Lucien Marie 1924- *AmMWSc 92*
**Le Camus**, Antoine 1722-1772 *BlkwCEP*
**Lecanuet**, Jean Adrien Francois 1920- *IntWW 91*
**Lecar**, Harold 1935- *AmMWSc 92*
**Lecar**, Myron 1930- *AmMWSc 92*
**Le Carre**, John *IntAu&W 91X, IntWW 91, Who 92*
**le Carre**, John 1931- *CnDBLB 8 [port], ConNov 91, FacFETw [port], RfGEnL 91, WrDr 92*
**Lecat**, Jean-Philippe 1935- *IntWW 91*
**Lecca**, Pedro J. *WhoHisp 92*
**Lecce**, James Giacomo 1926- *AmMWSc 92*
**Lecerf**, Olivier Marie Maurice 1929- *IntWW 91*
**LeCesne**, Terrel M. 1939- *WhoBlA 92*
**Lech**, John James 1940- *AmMWSc 92*
**Lechebo**, Semie 1935- *WhoBlA 92*
**Lecheler**, Robert Joseph 1955- *WhoRel 92*
**Le Cheminant**, Peter 1920- *Who 92*
**Le Cheminant**, Peter 1926- *Who 92*
**Lechevalier**, Hubert Arthur 1926- *AmMWSc 92*
**Lechevalier**, Mary P 1928- *AmMWSc 92*
**Lechin Oquendo**, Juan 1915- *IntWW 91*
**Lechin Suarez**, Juan 1921- *IntWW 91, Who 92*
**Lechleider**, J W 1933- *AmMWSc 92*
**Lechler**, George Price, III 1955- *WhoWest 92*
**Lechmere**, Berwick 1917- *Who 92*
**Lechner**, Alfred James, Jr. 1948- *WhoAmL 92*
**Lechner**, Bernard J 1932- *AmMWSc 92*
**Lechner**, Carol 1929- *WhoEnt 92*
**Lechner**, George William 1931- *WhoMW 92*
**Lechner**, Ira Mark 1934- *WhoAmP 91*
**Lechner**, James Albert 1933- *AmMWSc 92*
**Lechner**, John Fred 1942- *AmMWSc 92*
**Lechner**, Joseph H 1951- *AmMWSc 92*
**Lechner**, Robert 1918- *WrDr 92*
**Lechner**, Robert Joseph 1931- *AmMWSc 92*
**Lechon**, J. Daniel 1929- *WhoHisp 92*
**Lechowich**, Richard V 1933- *AmMWSc 92*
**Lechowicz**, Lisa Marie 1954- *WhoFI 92*
**Lechowicz**, Martin John 1947- *AmMWSc 92*
**Lechowicz**, Thaddeus Stanley 1938- *WhoAmP 91*
**Lecht**, Leonard A. 1920- *WrDr 92*
**Lechtenberg**, Victor L 1945- *AmMWSc 92*
**Lechtman**, Max D 1935- *AmMWSc 92*
**Leck**, Charles Frederick 1944- *AmMWSc 92*
**Leck**, Glorianne Mae 1941- *WhoMW 92*
**Leckar**, Stephen Craig 1948- *WhoAmL 92*
**Leckerling**, Jon P. 1948- *WhoAmL 92*
**Leckey**, Andrew A. 1949- *WhoMW 92*
**Leckie**, Frederick Alexander 1929- *AmMWSc 92*
**Leckie**, John 1911- *Who 92*
**Leckie**, Robin B 1931- *WhoIns 92*
**Lecklitner**, Myron Lynn 1942- *AmMWSc 92*
**Leckner**, Carole H 1946- *IntAu&W 91*
**Leckonby**, Roy Alan 1949- *AmMWSc 92*
**Leckrone**, David Stanley 1942- *AmMWSc 92*
**Lecky**, Arthur Terence 1919- *Who 92*
**Lecky**, Renee Jeanne 1927- *WhoFI 92*
**Lecky**, Samuel K. *Who 92*
**Le Clair**, Douglas Marvin 1955- *WhoAmL 92, WhoWest 92*
**LeClair**, Gary David 1955- *WhoAmL 92*
**LeClair**, J. Maurice 1927- *IntWW 91*
**Leclair**, Jean-Marie 1697-1764 *NewAmDM*
**LeClaire**, Claire Dean 1910- *AmMWSc 92*
**LeClaire**, Cynthia *DrAPF 91*
**Le Claire**, Mark 1957- *TwCPaSc*
**LeClaire**, Robert William 1956- *WhoIns 92*
**Leclant**, Jean 1920- *IntWW 91*
**Leclerc**, Charles J 1912- *WhoAmP 91*
**Leclerc**, Edouard 1926- *IntWW 91*
**Leclerc**, Ivor 1915- *WrDr 92*
**Leclerc**, Jean 1657-1736 *BlkwCEP*
**Leclercq**, Henri 1869-1945 *EncEarC*
**Leclercq**, Jenniene Ann *WhoEnt 92*
**LeClere**, David Anthony 1954- *WhoAmL 92*
**Le Clezio**, Jean 1940- *GuFrLit 1*
**Le Clezio**, Jean Marie Gustave 1940- *IntWW 91*
**Lecocq**, Charles 1832-1918 *NewAmDM*
**Le Coeur**, Jacques 1832-1882 *ThHEIm*
**LeCompte**, Edward Hank, Jr. 1958- *WhoWest 92*
**Le Compte**, Jane *DrAPF 91*
**LeCompte**, Jane 1948- *ConAu 133*
**LeCompte**, Peggy Lewis 1938- *WhoBlA 92*
**Lecomte**, Eugene Lucien 1929- *WhoIns 92*
**Leconfield**, Baron *Who 92*
**LeConte**, John 1818-1891 *BiInAmS*
**LeConte**, John Eatton, Jr 1784-1860 *BiInAmS*
**LeConte**, John Lawrence 1825-1883 *BiInAmS*
**LeConte**, Joseph 1823-1901 *BenetAL 91, BiInAmS*
**LeConte**, Louis 1782-1838 *BiInAmS*
**Leconte de Lisle**, Charles 1818-1894 *GuFrLit 1*
**Lecoq de Boisbaudran**, Horace 1802-1897 *ThHEIm*
**Le Corbusier** 1887-1965 *DcTwDes, FacFETw*
**LeCornec**, Michael Thomas 1954- *WhoFI 92*
**LeCount**, Llewellyn 1878?-1900 *BiInAmS*
**LeCount**, Lori Jean 1958- *WhoMW 92*
**Lecours**, Magda M. 1935- *WhoHisp 92*
**Lecours**, Michel 1940- *AmMWSc 92*
**Lecours**, Philip Ruben 1935- *WhoHisp 92*
**Lecourt**, Robert 1908- *IntWW 91, Who 92*
**Le Couteur**, Kenneth James 1920- *IntWW 91*
**LeCron**, Mary Frazer 1914- *WhoWest 92*
**Lecroy**, Hoyt Franklin 1941- *WhoEnt 92*
**L'Ecuyer**, Jacques 1937- *AmMWSc 92*
**L'Ecuyer**, Mel R 1936- *AmMWSc 92*
**Leczynski**, Barbara Ann 1954- *AmMWSc 92*
**Led Zeppelin** *FacFETw, NewAmDM*
**LeDay**, John Austin 1931- *WhoBlA 92*
**Ledbetter**, Beverly Elizabeth *WhoAmL 92*
**Ledbetter**, Calvin Reville, Jr 1929- *WhoAmP 91*
**Ledbetter**, Carl Scotius 1910- *WhoWest 92*
**Ledbetter**, Dale 1942- *WhoFI 92*
**Ledbetter**, Harvey Don 1926- *AmMWSc 92*
**Ledbetter**, Huddie *NewAmDM*
**Ledbetter**, Huddie 1888-1949 *FacFETw*
**Ledbetter**, J. Lee 1931- *WhoFI 92*
**Ledbetter**, Jack T. *DrAPF 91*
**Ledbetter**, James Fendig 1961- *WhoAmL 92*
**Ledbetter**, Jeffrey A *AmMWSc 92*
**Ledbetter**, Joe O 1927- *AmMWSc 92*
**Ledbetter**, Joel Yowell 1911- *WhoAmP 91*
**Ledbetter**, Marie Ensley 1923- *WhoAmP 91*
**Ledbetter**, Mary Lee Stewart 1944- *AmMWSc 92*
**Ledbetter**, Myron C 1923- *AmMWSc 92*
**Ledbetter**, Robert L. 1934-1983 *WhoBlA 92N*
**Ledbetter**, Ruth Pope *WhoBlA 92*
**Ledbetter**, Sandra Shumard 1948- *WhoAmP 91*
**Ledbetter**, Steven R *AmMWSc 92*
**Ledbetter**, W B 1934- *AmMWSc 92*
**Ledbetter-Straight**, Nora Kathleen 1934- *WhoFI 92*
**Ledder**, Diane Alison 1952- *WhoWest 92*
**Leddick**, Alice Susan 1948- *WhoFI 92*
**Leddicotte**, George Comer 1947- *WhoFI 92*
**Leddy**, James Jerome 1929- *AmMWSc 92*
**Leddy**, John Francis 1911- *IntWW 91*
**Leddy**, John Henry 1929- *WhoAmL 92*
**Leddy**, John M 1914- *WhoAmP 91*
**Leddy**, John Plunkett 1931- *AmMWSc 92*
**Leddy**, Robert Carten 1960- *WhoAmL 92*
**Leddy**, Susan 1939- *AmMWSc 92*
**Lede**, Naomi W. 1934- *WhoBlA 92*
**Ledebur**, Linas Vockroth, Jr. 1925- *WhoAmL 92*
**Ledee**, Robert 1927- *WhoBlA 92*
**Ledeen**, Lydia Hailparn 1938- *WhoEnt 92*
**Ledeen**, Robert 1928- *AmMWSc 92*
**Ledenyov**, Roman 1930- *ConCom 92*
**Leder**, Arie Cornelis 1946- *WhoRel 92*
**Leder**, Frederic 1939- *AmMWSc 92*
**Leder**, Herbert Jay 1922- *IntMPA 92*
**Leder**, Irwin Gordon 1920- *AmMWSc 92*
**Leder**, Lawrence H. 1927- *WrDr 92*
**Leder**, Lewis Beebe 1920- *AmMWSc 92*
**Leder**, Philip 1934- *AmMWSc 92*
**Lederberg**, Esther Miriam 1922- *AmMWSc 92*
**Lederberg**, Joshua 1925- *AmMWSc 92, IntWW 91, Who 92, WhoNob 90*
**Lederberg**, Seymour 1928- *AmMWSc 92*
**Lederberg**, Victoria 1937- *WhoAmP 91*
**Lederer**, C Michael 1938- *AmMWSc 92*
**Lederer**, Jerome F 1902- *AmMWSc 92*
**Lederer**, Johann *DcNCBi 4*
**Lederer**, John *BenetAL 91*
**Lederer**, John Martin 1930- *WhoWest 92*
**Lederer**, Leslie T. *WhoAmL 92*
**Lederer**, Lillian Day d1991 *NewYTBS 91*
**Lederer**, Marie A 1927- *WhoAmP 91*
**Lederer**, Marion Irvine 1920- *WhoWest 92*
**Lederer**, Max Donald, Jr. 1960- *WhoAmL 92*
**Lederer**, Peter David 1930- *WhoAmL 92*
**Lederer**, Richard 1916- *IntMPA 92*
**Lederer**, Walther 1908- *WhoFI 92*
**Lederer**, William Jonathan *AmMWSc 92*
**Lederis**, Karolis 1920- *AmMWSc 92*
**Lederleitner**, Joseph Benedict 1922- *WhoAmL 92*
**Lederman**, Bruce H. 1960- *WhoAmL 92*
**Lederman**, Bruce R. 1942- *WhoAmL 92*
**Lederman**, David 1942- *Who 92*
**Lederman**, David Mordechai 1944- *AmMWSc 92*
**Lederman**, Frank L 1949- *AmMWSc 92*
**Lederman**, Ira Seth 1953- *WhoAmL 92*
**Lederman**, Jess 1955- *WhoFI 92*
**Lederman**, Leon M. 1922- *IntWW 91*
**Lederman**, Leon Max 1922- *AmMWSc 92, Who 92, WhoMW 92, WhoNob 90*
**Lederman**, Peter B 1931- *AmMWSc 92*
**Ledermann**, Erich 1908- *WrDr 92*
**Ledesma**, Carmen Alicia 1956- *WhoHisp 92*
**Le Desma**, Hector Escobar 1924- *WhoHisp 92*
**Ledesma**, Jaime Emilio 1952- *WhoHisp 92*
**Ledesma**, James Vela 1941- *WhoHisp 92*
**Ledesma**, Jane Leal 1946- *WhoHisp 92*
**Ledesma**, Mary Louise 1933- *WhoAmP 91*
**Ledesma**, Rosa 1954- *WhoHisp 92*
**Ledesma**, Victor Cervantes 1930- *WhoHisp 92*
**Ledesma Bartret**, Fernando 1939- *IntWW 91*
**Ledesma Ramos**, Ramiro 1905-1936 *BiDExR*
**Ledford**, Barry Edward 1942- *AmMWSc 92*
**Ledford**, Gary Alan 1946- *WhoWest 92*
**Ledford**, Richard Allison 1931- *AmMWSc 92*
**Ledford**, Thomas Howard 1942- *AmMWSc 92*
**Ledford**, Toni Dandridge 1942- *WhoFI 92*
**Ledger**, Frank 1899- *Who 92*
**Ledger**, Frank 1929- *Who 92*
**Ledger**, Janet *TwCPaSc*
**Ledger**, Joseph Francis *Who 92*
**Ledger**, Philip 1937- *Who 92*
**Ledger**, Philip Stevens 1937- *IntWW 91*
**Ledger**, Ronald Joseph 1920- *Who 92*
**Ledgerwood**, Thomas L. 1952- *WhoAmL 92*
**Lediaev**, John P 1940- *AmMWSc 92*
**Ledig**, F Thomas 1938- *AmMWSc 92*
**Ledig-Rowohlt**, Heinrich Maria 1908- *IntWW 91*
**Ledin**, George, Jr 1946- *AmMWSc 92*
**Ledin**, James Alan 1961- *WhoWest 92*
**Ledingham**, John Gerard Garvin 1929- *Who 92*
**Ledingham**, John Marshall 1916- *Who 92*
**Ledinh**, Tony 1941- *WhoFI 92*
**Le-Dinh-Phuoc** 1941- *WhoWest 92*
**Ledinko**, Nada 1925- *AmMWSc 92*
**Ledley**, Brian G 1928- *AmMWSc 92*
**Ledley**, Fred David 1954- *AmMWSc 92*
**Ledley**, Robert Steven 1926- *AmMWSc 92*
**Ledley**, Tamara Shapiro 1954- *AmMWSc 92*
**Ledlie**, John Kenneth 1942- *Who 92*
**Ledlow**, Robert Louis 1934- *WhoRel 92*
**Ledney**, George David 1937- *AmMWSc 92*
**Lednicer**, Daniel 1929- *AmMWSc 92*
**Lednicky**, H. Maurice *WhoRel 92*
**Ledon**, Ann M. 1957- *WhoHisp 92*
**Le Donne**, Carmella Elizabeth 1926- *WhoRel 92*
**LeDonne**, Robert J. 1929- *WhoEnt 92*
**Le Douarin**, Nicole Marthe 1930- *IntWW 91*
**LeDoux**, Chris Lee 1948- *WhoEnt 92*
**Ledoux**, Claude-Nicolas 1736-1806 *BlkwCEP*
**Ledoux**, Denis *DrAPF 91*
**Le Doux**, Harold A. *WhoHisp 92*
**Ledoux**, Jack 1928- *WhoFI 92*
**Ledoux**, James W 1960- *WhoAmP 91*
**LeDoux**, Jerome G. 1930- *WhoBlA 92*
**Ledoux**, Louis V. 1880-1948 *BenetAL 91*
**Ledoux**, Paul Martin 1949- *IntAu&W 91*
**Ledoux**, Pierre 1914- *IntWW 91*
**Ledoux**, Robert Louis 1933- *AmMWSc 92*
**Ledsome**, John R 1932- *AmMWSc 92*
**Ledsome**, Neville Frank 1929- *Who 92*
**Leduc**, Alphonse 1804-1868 *NewAmDM*
**Leduc**, Elizabeth 1921- *AmMWSc 92*
**Leduc**, Gerard 1934- *AmMWSc 92*
**Le Duc**, J-Adrien Maher 1924- *AmMWSc 92*
**Le Duc**, Jack 1942- *WhoEnt 92*
**Le Duc**, James Wayne 1945- *AmMWSc 92*
**Leduc**, Paul 1942- *IntDcF 2-2*
**Leduc**, Sharon Kay 1943- *AmMWSc 92*
**Leduc**, Violette 1907-1972 *FrenWW, GuFrLit 1*
**LeDuff**, Stephanie Carmel 1953- *WhoBlA 92*
**Leduy**, Anh 1946- *AmMWSc 92*
**Ledward**, Gilbert 1888-1960 *TwCPaSc*
**Ledwell**, Thomas Austin 1938- *AmMWSc 92*
**Ledwidge**, Bernard 1915- *Who 92*
**Ledwidge**, Patrick Joseph 1928- *WhoAmL 92*
**Ledwidge**, William Bernard John 1915- *IntWW 91*
**Ledwig**, Donald Eugene 1937- *WhoEnt 92, WhoFI 92*
**Ledwin**, William F 1937- *WhoIns 92*
**Ledwith**, Anthony 1933- *Who 92*
**Ledwith**, Frank 1907- *WrDr 92*
**Ledwitz-Rigby**, Florence Ina 1946- *AmMWSc 92*
**Ledworowski**, Dariusz 1949- *IntWW 91*
**Ledyard**, John 1751-1789 *BenetAL 91*
**Ledzewicz-Kowalewska**, Urszula Agnieszka 1955- *WhoMW 92*
**Ledzinski**, Stanley Paul 1959- *WhoFI 92*
**Lee Hsien Loong** 1952- *IntWW 91*
**Lee Huan** 1917- *IntWW 91*
**Lee Kim Sai** 1937- *IntWW 91*
**Lee Kuan Yew** 1923- *FacFETw, IntWW 91, Who 92*
**Lee San Choon** 1935- *IntWW 91*
**Lee Sang** 1910-1937 *LiExTwC*
**Lee Sang-Ok** *IntWW 91*
**Lee Ta-Hai** 1919- *IntWW 91*
**Lee Teng-hui** 1923- *FacFETw, IntWW 91*
**Lee Tsung-Dao** 1926- *IntWW 91*
**Lee Won Kyung** 1922- *IntWW 91*
**Lee Yock Suan** 1946- *IntWW 91*
**Lee Yong Leng** 1930- *IntWW 91, Who 92*
**Lee**, Aaron 1948- *WhoBlA 92*
**Lee**, Addison Earl 1914- *AmMWSc 92*
**Lee**, Adrian Gordon 1929- *WhoAmP 91*
**Lee**, Afton M., Sr. 1898- *WhoBlA 92*
**Lee**, Al *DrAPF 91*
**Lee**, Aldora G. *WhoWest 92*
**Lee**, Alfred Harrison, III 1932- *WhoRel 92*
**Lee**, Alfred M 1951- *AmMWSc 92*
**Lee**, Alfred McClung 1906- *IntAu&W 91, WrDr 92*
**Lee**, Alfred Tze-Hau 1939- *AmMWSc 92*
**Lee**, Allan Wren 1924- *WhoRel 92*
**Lee**, Allen *Who 92*
**Lee**, Allen Francis, Jr. 1943- *WhoBlA 92*
**Lee**, Amy Jo 1956- *WhoEnt 92*
**Lee**, Amy Shiu 1947- *AmMWSc 92*
**Lee**, Ana Rubi 1960- *WhoHisp 92*
**Lee**, Andre L. 1943- *WhoBlA 92*
**Lee**, Andrea 1953- *BlkLC [port], WhoBlA 92*
**Lee**, Andrew *IntAu&W 91X, WrDr 92*
**Lee**, Andrew Hung-To 1957- *WhoWest 92*
**Lee**, Ann 1736-1784 *BlkwEAR, HanAmWH, RComAH*
**Lee**, Anna *IntMPA 92*
**Lee**, Anna 1913- *WhoEnt 92*
**Lee**, Anthony 1941- *AmMWSc 92*
**Lee**, Anthony Asa 1947- *WhoRel 92*
**Lee**, Anthony L 1934- *AmMWSc 92*
**Lee**, Arlon Wayne 1948- *WhoRel 92*
**Lee**, Arthur 1740-1792 *BenetAL 91, BlkwEAR*
**Lee**, Arthur 1912- *Who 92*
**Lee**, Arthur Carl 1886-1974 *DcNCBi 4*
**Lee**, Arthur Clair 1923- *AmMWSc 92*
**Lee**, Arthur James 1920- *Who 92*
**Lee**, Aubrey W. 1934- *WhoBlA 92*
**Lee**, Audrey *DrAPF 91*
**Lee**, Barbara Lee Pickeral 1943- *WhoAmP 91*
**Lee**, Barbara Tutt 1946- *WhoAmP 91*
**Lee**, Benedict Huk Kun 1940- *AmMWSc 92*
**Lee**, Bernard d1991 *NewYTBS 91*
**Lee**, Bernard S 1934- *AmMWSc 92*

Lee, Bernard Scott 1935-1991 WhoBlA 92N
Lee, Bernard Tunghao 1944- WhoWest 92
Lee, Bertram M. 1939- WhoBlA 92
Lee, Bertram M., Sr. WhoFI 92, WhoWest 92
Lee, Biing-Lin 1943- WhoMW 92
Lee, Bill Walker 1954- WhoEnt 92
Lee, Bonni IntMPA 92
Lee, Brenda 1944- NewAmDM
Lee, Brian Edward 1952- WhoAmL 92
Lee, Brian Keith 1961- WhoWest 92
Lee, Bruce Ambrose 1934- WhoAmP 91
Lee, Burnell 1955- AmMWSc 92
Lee, Burtrand Insung 1952- AmMWSc 92
Lee, Byungkook 1941- AmMWSc 92
Lee, C H 1919- AmMWSc 92
Lee, Candie Ching Wah 1950- WhoWest 92
Lee, Carl, III 1961- WhoBlA 92
Lee, Carlton Koon Mung 1947- WhoFI 92
Lee, Carol Frances 1955- WhoAmL 92
Lee, Chandler Bancroft WhoBlA 92
Lee, Charles 1731-1782 BenetAL 91, BlkwEAR
Lee, Charles Alexander 1922- AmMWSc 92
Lee, Charles Alfred 1801-1872 BiInAmS
Lee, Charles Cochrane 1834-1862 DcNCBi 4
Lee, Charles Douglas 1945- WhoWest 92
Lee, Charles Edward 1927- WhoRel 92
Lee, Charles Gary, Sr. 1948- WhoBlA 92
Lee, Charles Lowry 1950- WhoMW 92
Lee, Charles McDowell 1925- WhoAmP 91
Lee, Charles Northam 1925- AmMWSc 92
Lee, Charles Richard 1942- AmMWSc 92
Lee, Charles Richard 1949- WhoFI 92
Lee, Charlie WhoBlA 92
Lee, Charlotte O. 1930- WhoBlA 92
Lee, Che-Hung R AmMWSc 92
Lee, Chen Hui 1929- AmMWSc 92
Lee, Cheng-Chun 1922- AmMWSc 92
Lee, Cheng-few 1939- WhoFI 92
Lee, Cheng-Sheng AmMWSc 92
Lee, Cheuk Man 1929- AmMWSc 92
Lee, Chi-Hang 1939- AmMWSc 92
Lee, Chi-Ho 1941- AmMWSc 92
Lee, Chi-Jen 1936- AmMWSc 92
Lee, Chi Myeung 1957- WhoFI 92
Lee, Chi-Yu Gregory 1945- AmMWSc 92
Lee, Chin-Chiu 1934- AmMWSc 92
Lee, Chin Ok 1939- AmMWSc 92
Lee, Ching-Li 1942- AmMWSc 92
Lee, Ching-Tse 1940- AmMWSc 92
Lee, Ching Tsung 1937- AmMWSc 92
Lee, Ching-Wen 1921- AmMWSc 92
Lee, Chong Sung 1939- AmMWSc 92
Lee, Choong Woong 1935- AmMWSc 92
Lee, Choung Mook 1935- AmMWSc 92
Lee, Christopher 1922- IntMPA 92
Lee, Christopher Frank Carandini 1922- IntWW 91, Who 92, WhoEnt 92
Lee, Christopher Heinz 1965- WhoWest 92
Lee, Chuan-Pu 1931- AmMWSc 92
Lee, Chung 1936- AmMWSc 92
Lee, Chung Ha 1939- WhoMW 92
Lee, Chung N 1931- AmMWSc 92
Lee, Clara Marshall 1946- WhoBlA 92
Lee, Clarence Edgar 1931- AmMWSc 92
Lee, Clement William Khan 1938- WhoRel 92
Lee, Clifford G 1925- WhoAmP 91
Lee, Clifton Valjean 1929- WhoBlA 92
Lee, Cody M. 1910- WhoBlA 92
Lee, Consella Almetter WhoBlA 92
Lee, Craig Chun-Kuo 1954- AmMWSc 92
Lee, Cynthia 1953- WhoAmL 92
Lee, Cynthia Shou-Pin 1954- WhoWest 92
Lee, D William 1927- AmMWSc 92
Lee, Daeyong 1933- AmMWSc 92
Lee, Dah-Yinn 1934- AmMWSc 92
Lee, Dai-Keong 1915- WhoEnt 92
Lee, Daisy Si 1934- AmMWSc 92
Lee, Dale George 1937- WhoBlA 92
Lee, Dan M. 1926- WhoAmL 92
Lee, Daniel 1918- WhoBlA 92
Lee, Daniel David 1941- WhoWest 92
Lee, Daniel Dixon, Jr 1935- AmMWSc 92
Lee, Daniel Kuhn 1946- WhoFI 92
Lee, Daniel McKinnon 1926- WhoAmP 91
Lee, Daniel Richard 1956- WhoFI 92
Lee, Darryl Auburn 1959- WhoRel 92
Lee, Darryl J. WhoAmL 92
Lee, David DrAPF 91
Lee, David Allan 1937- AmMWSc 92
Lee, David Anson 1956- WhoWest 92
Lee, David Bracken 1949- WhoAmP 91
Lee, David Chang 1940- WhoMW 92
Lee, David Charles 1950- AmMWSc 92
Lee, David John 1930- Who 92
Lee, David John Pryer 1912- Who 92
Lee, David K H AmMWSc 92
Lee, David Louis 1948- AmMWSc 92
Lee, David Mallin 1944- AmMWSc 92
Lee, David Morris 1931- AmMWSc 92
Lee, David Oi 1940- AmMWSc 92
Lee, David Robert 1945- AmMWSc 92
Lee, David Webster 1942- AmMWSc 92
Lee, Dayle 1961- WhoEnt 92
Lee, Debra Louise 1954- WhoBlA 92
Lee, Dennis 1939- BenetAL 91, ConPo 91, WrDr 92
Lee, Dennis Beynon 1939- IntAu&W 91
Lee, Dennis Patrick 1955- WhoAmL 92
Lee, Der-Tsai 1949- AmMWSc 92
Lee, Desmond Who 92
Lee, Desmond 1908- WrDr 92
Lee, Detroit 1916- WhoBlA 92
Lee, Diana Mang AmMWSc 92
Lee, Dick 1923- TwCPaSc
Lee, Dik Lun 1956- WhoFI 92
Lee, Do Ik 1937- AmMWSc 92
Lee, Do-Jae 1928- AmMWSc 92
Lee, Doh-Yeel AmMWSc 92
Lee, Don DrAPF 91
Lee, Don L. 1942- ConPo 91, IntAu&W 91, WhoBlA 92, WrDr 92
Lee, Donald 1931- WrDr 92
Lee, Donald Garry 1935- AmMWSc 92
Lee, Donald J. 1927- WhoAmL 92
Lee, Donald Jack 1932- AmMWSc 92
Lee, Donald William 1947- AmMWSc 92
Lee, Dong Chan 1922- IntWW 91
Lee, Dong Hoon 1938- AmMWSc 92
Lee, Donna Lynn 1956- WhoWest 92
Lee, Dorothea 1930- WhoBlA 92
Lee, Douglas Harry Kedgwin 1905- AmMWSc 92
Lee, E Bruce 1932- AmMWSc 92, WhoMW 92
Lee, E Stanley 1930- AmMWSc 92
Lee, Edgar Rogers 1936- WhoMW 92
Lee, Edward 1914- Who 92
Lee, Edward B. 1962- WhoWest 92
Lee, Edward Brooke, Jr. 1917- WhoFI 92
Lee, Edward Graham 1931- IntWW 91
Lee, Edward Hsien-Chi 1935- AmMWSc 92
Lee, Edward Ming 1959- WhoRel 92
Lee, Edward Prentiss 1942- AmMWSc 92
Lee, Edward S. 1935- WhoBlA 92
Lee, Edward Stanley 1907- Who 92
Lee, Edwin Archibald 1914- WhoBlA 92
Lee, El Franco 1949- WhoAmP 91
Lee, Eleanor 1931- WhoAmP 91
Lee, Eliza Buckminster 1788?-1864 BenetAL 91
Lee, Elizabeth Anne 1952- WhoMW 92
Lee, Elizabeth Briant 1908- WomSoc
Lee, Ellen Szeto AmMWSc 92
Lee, Elsie 1912- IntAu&W 91
Lee, Emerson Howard 1921- AmMWSc 92
Lee, Erastus Henry 1916- AmMWSc 92
Lee, Eric H M 1944- WhoAmP 91
Lee, Eric Kin-Lam 1948- AmMWSc 92
Lee, Ernest Y AmMWSc 92
Lee, Ethel Delaney 1926- WhoAmP 91
Lee, Eun Sul 1934- AmMWSc 92
Lee, Ezell 1933- WhoAmP 91
Lee, Fang-Jen Scott 1957- AmMWSc 92
Lee, Felicia R. 1956- WhoBlA 92
Lee, Floyd Denman 1938- AmMWSc 92
Lee, Forrest A., Sr. 1937- WhoBlA 92
Lee, Fran 1910- WhoEnt 92
Lee, Fred 1955- WhoRel 92
Lee, Fred C AmMWSc 92
Lee, Fred D., Jr. 1947- WhoBlA 92
Lee, Frederick Cushing 1950- WhoFI 92
Lee, Frederick Strube 1927- AmMWSc 92
Lee, Gabriel S., Jr. 1922- WhoBlA 92
Lee, Garrett 1946- AmMWSc 92
Lee, Garth Loraine 1920- AmMWSc 92
Lee, Gary A 1933- WhoAmP 91
Lee, Gary Albert 1941- AmMWSc 92
Lee, George C 1932- AmMWSc 92
Lee, George Douglas 1951- WhoEnt 92
Lee, George H, II 1939- AmMWSc 92
Lee, George Hsien-Yi 1963- WhoFI 92
Lee, George Ranson 1925- Who 92
Lee, George Russell 1912- Who 92
Lee, George Washington 1894-1976 BlkLC [port]
Lee, Gerald E. 1958- WhoBlA 92
Lee, Gilbert Brooks 1913- WhoMW 92
Lee, Gilbert Henry Clifton d1991 Who 92N
Lee, Glen K. 1950- WhoWest 92
Lee, Glenn Richard 1932- AmMWSc 92
Lee, Gloria AmMWSc 92
Lee, Gloria 1912- WhoEnt 92
Lee, Gloria 1926-1962 RelLAm 91
Lee, Gloria A. 1940- WhoBlA 92
Lee, Gordon C. 1916-1972 ConAu 135
Lee, Gordon M 1917- AmMWSc 92
Lee, Grace Tze 1953- WhoWest 92
Lee, Greta Marlene AmMWSc 92
Lee, Griff C 1926- AmMWSc 92
Lee, Guy Milicon, Jr. 1928- WhoBlA 92
Lee, Gwendolin Kuei 1932- WhoEnt 92, WhoMW 92
Lee, H C 1933- AmMWSc 92
Lee, H. Rex LesBEnT 92
Lee, Hamilton 1921- IntAu&W 91
Lee, Hanchow 1935- WhoWest 92
Lee, Hannah Farnham 1780-1865 BenetAL 91
Lee, Harley Clyde 1901- AmMWSc 92
Lee, Harold Bingham 1899-1973 RelLAm 91
Lee, Harold Hon-Kwong 1934- AmMWSc 92
Lee, Harold Philip 1944- WhoFI 92
Lee, Harper DrAPF 91
Lee, Harper 1926- BenetAL 91
Lee, Harvey S 1949- AmMWSc 92
Lee, Harvie Ho 1937- AmMWSc 92
Lee, Haynes A 1932- AmMWSc 92
Lee, Helen Jackson 1908- WhoBlA 92
Lee, Henry Who 92
Lee, Henry 1756-1818 BenetAL 91
Lee, Henry 1952- WhoAmL 92
Lee, Henry, II 1787-1837 BenetAL 91
Lee, Henry C 1938- AmMWSc 92
Lee, Henry Desmond 1908- Who 92
Lee, Henry Desmond Pritchard 1908- IntWW 91
Lee, Henry Joung 1941- AmMWSc 92
Lee, Hermione IntAu&W 91
Lee, Hermione 1948- IntWW 91
Lee, Honkon 1920- IntWW 91
Lee, Hoong-Chien 1941- AmMWSc 92
Lee, Howard WrDr 92
Lee, Howard N. 1934- WhoBlA 92
Lee, Howard Nathaniel 1934- WhoAmP 91
Lee, Hsi-Nan 1946- AmMWSc 92
Lee, Hsin-Yi AmMWSc 92
Lee, Hu 1959- WhoWest 92
Lee, Hua 1952- AmMWSc 92
Lee, Hua-Tsun 1937- AmMWSc 92
Lee, Hulbert Austin 1923- AmMWSc 92
Lee, Hyung Mo 1926- AmMWSc 92
Lee, I P 1935- AmMWSc 92
Lee, I-Yang 1946- AmMWSc 92
Lee, Insup 1955- AmMWSc 92
Lee, Intak 1936- WhoAmL 92
Lee, Irvin H. 1932-1980 ConAu 133
Lee, Isaac 1945- WhoRel 92
Lee, Ivy, Jr. 1909- WhoWest 92
Lee, J. Daniel, Jr. 1938- WhoFI 92, WhoIns 92
Lee, J. E. WhoRel 92
Lee, J. Kenneth WhoBlA 92
Lee, J Tyler 1951- WhoIns 92
Lee, Ja H 1925- AmMWSc 92
Lee, Jack 1929- WhoEnt 92
Lee, Jack Edwin, II 1950- WhoAmP 91
Lee, Jae Yoon 1938- WhoMW 92
Lee, James A 1925- AmMWSc 92
Lee, James B 1930- AmMWSc 92
Lee, James C 1941- AmMWSc 92
Lee, James Douglas 1954- WhoAmL 92
Lee, James E. 1921- IntWW 91
Lee, James E. 1940- WhoBlA 92
Lee, James Edward, Jr. 1939- WhoMW 92
Lee, James Giles 1942- Who 92
Lee, James King 1940- WhoFI 92, WhoWest 92
Lee, James Mahngill 1942- WhoWest 92
Lee, James Matthew 1937- IntWW 91, Who 92
Lee, James Norman 1956- AmMWSc 92
Lee, James Stuart 1934- Who 92
Lee, James Victor 1939- WhoFI 92
Lee, Janet Lynne 1966- WhoMW 92
Lee, Jang Y AmMWSc 92
Lee, Janice Eva 1961- WhoEnt 92
Lee, Janis K 1945- WhoAmP 91
Lee, Jarena 1783- NotBlAW 92
Lee, Jason Davis 1949- WhoFI 92
Lee, Jean Chor-Yin Wong 1941- AmMWSc 92
Lee, Jeanne DrAPF 91
Lee, Jeffrey Stephen 1944- AmMWSc 92
Lee, Jen-Shih 1940- AmMWSc 92
Lee, Jennie 1904-1988 FacFETw
Lee, Jerome G. 1924- WhoAmL 92
Lee, Jerome Odell 1955- WhoRel 92
Lee, Jesse 1758-1816 DcNCBi 4
Lee, Jim 1940- WhoAmP 91
Lee, Joe WhoAmL 92
Lee, Joe 1939- AmMWSc 92
Lee, Joe R. 1940- WhoFI 92, WhoMW 92
Lee, John 1931- IntAu&W 91, WrDr 92
Lee, John 1948- WhoEnt 92
Lee, John A. 1891-1982 RfGEnL 91
Lee, John A N 1934- AmMWSc 92
Lee, John Alexander Hugh 1925- AmMWSc 92
Lee, John C AmMWSc 92
Lee, John C., III WhoBlA 92
Lee, John Chaeseung 1941- AmMWSc 92
Lee, John Cheung Han 1945- AmMWSc 92
Lee, John Chonghoon, Sr. 1928- WhoAmL 92, WhoFI 92
Lee, John Chung 1937- AmMWSc 92
Lee, John D 1924- AmMWSc 92
Lee, John Denis 1929- AmMWSc 92
Lee, John Edward, Jr 1933- WhoAmP 91
Lee, John Edwin 1928- WhoAmP 91
Lee, John Hak Shan 1938- AmMWSc 92
Lee, John Jin 1948- WhoWest 92
Lee, John Joseph 1933- AmMWSc 92
Lee, John Joseph 1942- IntWW 91
Lee, John K AmMWSc 92
Lee, John Marshall 1950- WhoWest 92
Lee, John Michael Hubert 1927- Who 92
Lee, John Norman 1944- AmMWSc 92
Lee, John Robert E. 1935- WhoBlA 92
Lee, John Robert Louis 1942- Who 92
Lee, John Thomas Cyril 1927- Who 92
Lee, John W. 1942- WhoAmL 92
Lee, John William 1935- AmMWSc 92
Lee, John Woodrow, Jr. 1952- WhoFI 92
Lee, John Yuchu 1948- AmMWSc 92
Lee, Johnny 1946- WhoEnt 92
Lee, Johnson Y. 1955- WhoFI 92
Lee, Joie 1962?- ConBlB 1 [port]
Lee, Jon H 1934- AmMWSc 92
Lee, Jonathan K P 1937- AmMWSc 92
Lee, Jonathan Owen 1951- WhoFI 92
Lee, Jong Hyuk 1941- WhoWest 92
Lee, Jong Sun 1932- AmMWSc 92
Lee, Jordan Grey 1914- AmMWSc 92
Lee, Joseph Bracken 1899- WhoAmP 91
Lee, Joseph Chuen Kwun 1938- AmMWSc 92
Lee, Joseph Shing 1939- WhoFI 92
Lee, Joshua Alexander 1924- AmMWSc 92
Lee, Joyce Isabel 1913- IntAu&W 91
Lee, Judith Ann 1932- WhoAmP 91
Lee, Jui Shuan 1913- AmMWSc 92
Lee, Julian IntAu&W 91X, SmATA 68, WrDr 92
Lee, Julie 1961- WhoWest 92
Lee, June B 1933- WhoAmP 91
Lee, June Key 1943- AmMWSc 92
Lee, Kah-Hock 1941- AmMWSc 92
Lee, Kai-Fong AmMWSc 92
Lee, Kai-Fong 1939- WhoMW 92
Lee, Kai-Lin 1935- AmMWSc 92
Lee, Kai Nien 1945- AmMWSc 92
Lee, Kang In 1946- AmMWSc 92
Lee, Karen S. DrAPF 91
Lee, Kate Leary 1946- WhoFI 92, WhoWest 92
Lee, Katherine I. 1942- WhoBlA 92
Lee, Kathryn Adele Bunding AmMWSc 92
Lee, Kathryn Adele Bunding 1949- WhoMW 92
Lee, Keenan 1936- AmMWSc 92
Lee, Ken 1953- AmMWSc 92
Lee, Kenneth 1937- AmMWSc 92
Lee, Kenneth E 1961- WhoAmP 91
Lee, Kermit J., Jr. 1934- WhoBlA 92
Lee, Kermit L. 1938- WhoBlA 92
Lee, Keun Myung 1945- AmMWSc 92
Lee, Keun Sok 1954- WhoFI 92
Lee, King C AmMWSc 92
Lee, Kiuck 1922- AmMWSc 92
Lee, Kok-Meng 1952- AmMWSc 92
Lee, Kotik Kai 1941- AmMWSc 92
Lee, Kuei-shien 1937- IntAu&W 91
Lee, Kun Il 1944- WhoMW 92
Lee, Kuo-Hsiung 1940- AmMWSc 92
Lee, Kurk WhoBlA 92
Lee, Kwang 1942- AmMWSc 92
Lee, Kwang Soo 1918- AmMWSc 92
Lee, Kwang-Yuan 1919- AmMWSc 92
Lee, Kyo Seon 1935- WhoFI 92
Lee, Kyu Taik 1921- AmMWSc 92
Lee, Kyung No AmMWSc 92
Lee, L H N 1923- AmMWSc 92
Lee, Ladonna Y 1950- WhoAmP 91
Lee, Lance 1942- IntAu&W 91
Lee, Lansing Burrows, Jr. 1919- WhoAmL 92
Lee, Lanton Lawrence 1965- WhoMW 92
Lee, Laura Eileen 1950- WhoFI 92
Lee, Laurie Who 92
Lee, Laurie 1914- ConPo 91, IntAu&W 91, IntWW 91, RfGEnL 91, WrDr 92
Lee, LaVerne C. 1933- WhoBlA 92
Lee, Lawrence Cho 1953- WhoFI 92
Lee, Lawrence Hwa Ni 1923- WhoMW 92
Lee, Lawrence Michael 1949- WhoAmL 92
Lee, Lawrence Winston 1938- WhoFI 92
Lee, Lawrence Wood 1947- WhoWest 92
Lee, Lela A 1950- AmMWSc 92
Lee, Lena King 1911- WhoAmP 91
Lee, Lena S. King WhoBlA 92
Lee, Leonard Henry 1914- Who 92
Lee, Leron 1948- WhoBlA 92
Lee, Leslie Alexander 1852-1908 BiInAmS
Lee, Leslie Warren 1949- WhoFI 92
Lee, Li-Young DrAPF 91
Lee, Lieng-Huang 1924- AmMWSc 92
Lee, Lih-Syng 1945- AmMWSc 92
Lee, Lila J. 1923- WhoWest 92
Lee, Linwood Lawrence, Jr 1928- AmMWSc 92
Lee, Lloyd Lieh-Shen 1942- AmMWSc 92
Lee, Lois 1950- WhoWest 92
Lee, Long Chi 1940- AmMWSc 92, WhoWest 92
Lee, Lora Jane 1954- WhoEnt 92
Lee, Lorraine 1959- WhoHisp 92
Lee, Lou-Chuang 1947- AmMWSc 92
Lee, Lou S. 1943- WhoWest 92
Lee, Lu-Yuan AmMWSc 92
Lee, Luaine WhoEnt 92
Lee, Lyndon Edmund, Jr 1912- AmMWSc 92
Lee, M Howard 1937- AmMWSc 92
Lee, M. Owen 1930- WrDr 92

**Lee,** M. Russell *WhoRel 92*
**Lee,** Mabel 1886-1985 *ConAu 134*
**Lee,** Malcolm Kenneth 1943- *Who 92*
**Lee,** Manfred B. *BenetAL 91*
**Lee,** Manny 1965- *WhoHisp 92*
**Lee,** Margaret Anne 1930- *WhoWest 92*
**Lee,** Margaret Carol 1955- *WhoBlA 92*
**Lee,** Margaret Kendig 1942- *WhoEnt 92*
**Lee,** Margaret Norma 1928- *WhoMW 92*
**Lee,** Margaret S. 1936- *WhoBlA 92*
**Lee,** Maria Berl *DrAPF 91*
**Lee,** Marietta Y W T 1943- *AmMWSc 92*
**Lee,** Mark Anthony 1958- *WhoBlA 92*
**Lee,** Martha 1946- *WhoWest 92*
**Lee,** Martha Eugenia 1952- *WhoWest 92*
**Lee,** Martin Alan 1945- *AmMWSc 92*
**Lee,** Martin J G 1942- *AmMWSc 92*
**Lee,** Martin Jerome 1943- *AmMWSc 92*
**Lee,** Martin Joe *AmMWSc 92*
**Lee,** Marva Jean 1938- *WhoMW 92*
**Lee,** Mary Elizabeth 1935- *WhoAmP 91*
**Lee,** Mary Gene 1939- *WhoRel 92*
**Lee,** Mary S *WhoAmP 91*
**Lee,** Maryat *IntAu&W 91*
**Lee,** Mathew Hung Mun 1931- *AmMWSc 92*
**Lee,** Matt *TwCSFW 91*
**Lee,** Max 1931- *WhoRel 92*
**Lee,** May D-Ming 1949- *AmMWSc 92*
**Lee,** Melvin 1926- *AmMWSc 92*
**Lee,** Melvin Joseph 1929- *WhoRel 92*
**Lee,** Men Hui 1933- *AmMWSc 92*
**Lee,** Merlin Raymond 1928- *AmMWSc 92*
**Lee,** Michael Charles M. *Who 92*
**Lee,** Michael David 1950- *WhoEnt 92*
**Lee,** Michael Eric 1945- *WhoFI 92*
**Lee,** Michael G. W. 1947- *WhoAmL 92*
**Lee,** Michael Insley 1951- *WhoMW 92*
**Lee,** Michael Waring 1953- *WhoBlA 92*
**Lee,** Michele 1942- *IntMPA 92, WhoEnt 92*
**Lee,** Mildred 1908- *IntAu&W 91*
**Lee,** Mildred Kimble 1919- *WhoBlA 92*
**Lee,** Mimi 1964- *WhoWest 92*
**Lee,** Min-Shiu 1940- *AmMWSc 92*
**Lee,** Ming Cho 1930- *WhoEnt 92*
**Lee,** Ming-Liang 1936- *AmMWSc 92*
**Lee,** Ming T 1940- *AmMWSc 92*
**Lee,** Ming Tzer 1940- *WhoMW 92*
**Lee,** Minyoung 1938- *AmMWSc 92*
**Lee,** Mitchell David 1961- *WhoWest 92*
**Lee,** Momi Minn 1920- *WhoAmP 91*
**Lee,** Mordecai 1948- *WhoAmP 91, WhoMW 92, WhoRel 92*
**Lee,** Murlin E. 1957- *WhoWest 92*
**Lee,** Nancy L *AmMWSc 92*
**Lee,** Nancy M *AmMWSc 92*
**Lee,** Nancy Zee-Nee Ma 1940- *AmMWSc 92*
**Lee,** Nathaniel 1645?-1692? *RfGEnL 91*
**Lee,** Nelda S. 1941- *WhoFI 92*
**Lee,** Nelson Eugene 1941- *WhoRel 92*
**Lee,** Nelson John 1950- *WhoAmL 92*
**Lee,** Noel 1924- *ConCom 92*
**Lee,** Norman K 1934- *AmMWSc 92*
**Lee,** Norman Randall 1929- *WhoWest 92*
**Lee,** Norvel L. R. 1924- *WhoBlA 92*
**Lee,** Norvel La Follette Ray 1924- *BlkOlyM*
**Lee,** Oliver B. 1926- *WhoBlA 92*
**Lee,** Oscar 1953- *WhoMW 92*
**Lee,** Pali Jae 1929- *WhoWest 92*
**Lee,** Pamela Anne 1960- *WhoFI 92, WhoWest 92*
**Lee,** Parkin 1953- *WhoAmL 92*
**Lee,** Patricia I 1937- *WhoAmP 91*
**Lee,** Patricia Taylor 1936- *WhoEnt 92*
**Lee,** Patrick *TwCWW 91, WrDr 92*
**Lee,** Patrick A 1946- *AmMWSc 92*
**Lee,** Patrick Herbert 1929- *Who 92*
**Lee,** Paul Chun Hwan 1922- *Who 92*
**Lee,** Paul D 1940- *AmMWSc 92*
**Lee,** Paul Hamilton 1960- *WhoFI 92*
**Lee,** Paul King-lung 1942- *WhoFI 92*
**Lee,** Paul L 1944- *AmMWSc 92*
**Lee,** Paul P. 1960- *WhoAmL 92*
**Lee,** Pauline W. 1933- *WhoBlA 92*
**Lee,** Peggy 1920- *IntMPA 92, NewAmDM, WhoEnt 92*
**Lee,** Peter Chung-Yi 1934- *AmMWSc 92*
**Lee,** Peter E 1930- *AmMWSc 92*
**Lee,** Peter Gavin 1934- *Who 92*
**Lee,** Peter H. 1929- *WrDr 92*
**Lee,** Peter H Y 1939- *AmMWSc 92*
**Lee,** Peter James 1938- *WhoRel 92*
**Lee,** Peter Redvers 1960- *WhoEnt 92*
**Lee,** Peter Van Arsdale 1923- *AmMWSc 92*
**Lee,** Peter Wankyoon 1939- *AmMWSc 92*
**Lee,** Peter Y. 1959- *WhoWest 92*
**Lee,** Philip Randolph 1924- *AmMWSc 92*
**Lee,** Ping 1950- *AmMWSc 92*
**Lee,** Ping-Cheung 1939- *AmMWSc 92*
**Lee,** Pinky *LesBEnT 92*
**Lee,** Pui Kum 1916- *AmMWSc 92*
**Lee,** Qwihee Park 1941- *WhoWest 92*
**Lee,** R. H. 1932- *WhoRel 92*
**Lee,** Ralph Barrett, Jr. 1945- *WhoRel 92*
**Lee,** Ralph Edward 1921- *AmMWSc 92*
**Lee,** Ralph Kelly 1951- *WhoWest 92*
**Lee,** Randy J. 1950- *WhoMW 92*
**Lee,** Ranger *TwCWW 91*
**Lee,** Ray H 1918- *AmMWSc 92*
**Lee,** Raymond Curtis 1929- *AmMWSc 92*
**Lee,** Raymond William, Jr. 1930- *WhoFI 92*
**Lee,** Rena *DrAPF 91*
**Lee,** Rex E 1935- *WhoAmP 91*
**Lee,** Richard Fayao 1941- *AmMWSc 92*
**Lee,** Richard Francis James 1967- *WhoRel 92, WhoWest 92*
**Lee,** Richard Harlo 1947- *WhoAmL 92*
**Lee,** Richard Henry 1732-1794 *AmPolLe, BenetAL 91, BlkwEAR [port]*
**Lee,** Richard Henry 1954- *WhoWest 92*
**Lee,** Richard J 1944- *AmMWSc 92*
**Lee,** Richard James 1947- *WhoAmL 92*
**Lee,** Richard K C 1909- *AmMWSc 92*
**Lee,** Richard Norman 1939- *AmMWSc 92*
**Lee,** Richard Shao-Lin 1929- *AmMWSc 92*
**Lee,** Richard Thomas 1944- *WhoBlA 92*
**Lee,** Ritten Edward, III, Mrs. *WhoEnt 92*
**Lee,** Robert 1929- *WhoRel 92*
**Lee,** Robert Andrew 1923- *WhoWest 92*
**Lee,** Robert Bumjung 1937- *AmMWSc 92*
**Lee,** Robert E. *LesBEnT 92*
**Lee,** Robert E. 1807-1870 *BenetAL 91, RComAH*
**Lee,** Robert E. 1918- *BenetAL 91, IntAu&W 91, SmATA 65, WrDr 92*
**Lee,** Robert E. 1924- *WhoBlA 92*
**Lee,** Robert E 1932- *AmMWSc 92*
**Lee,** Robert E. 1950- *WhoEnt 92*
**Lee,** Robert E, Jr 1936- *AmMWSc 92*
**Lee,** Robert Edward, Jr. 1941- *WhoAmL 92*
**Lee,** Robert Edwin 1918- *WhoEnt 92*
**Lee,** Robert Emile 1948- *WhoBlA 92*
**Lee,** Robert Erich 1955- *WhoFI 92*
**Lee,** Robert Greene 1886- *RelLAm 91*
**Lee,** Robert H. C. 1897- *WhoBlA 92*
**Lee,** Robert Hugh 1950- *WhoFI 92*
**Lee,** Robert Jerome 1914- *AmMWSc 92*
**Lee,** Robert John 1929- *AmMWSc 92*
**Lee,** Robert W 1931- *AmMWSc 92*
**Lee,** Roberto 1937- *AmMWSc 92*
**Lee,** Roger Edwin Mark 1940- *WhoWest 92*
**Lee,** Roger Ruojia 1958- *WhoWest 92*
**Lee,** Roland Robert 1954- *AmMWSc 92*
**Lee,** Ronald B. 1932- *WhoBlA 92*
**Lee,** Ronald Norman 1935- *AmMWSc 92*
**Lee,** Ronald S 1938- *AmMWSc 92*
**Lee,** Ronnie 1942- *AmMWSc 92*
**Lee,** Rose Hum 1904-1964 *WomSoc*
**Lee,** Rosie 1935- *TwCPaSc*
**Lee,** Rotan 1906- *WhoBlA 92*
**Lee,** Rowland Thomas Lovell 1920- *Who 92*
**Lee,** Roy Noble 1915- *WhoAmL 92, WhoAmP 91*
**Lee,** Ruben 1955- *WhoHisp 92*
**Lee,** Russell Curtis 1932- *WhoRel 92*
**Lee,** S. *DrAPF 91*
**Lee,** Sally 1943- *ConAu 134, SmATA 67 [port]*
**Lee,** Sammy, I 1920- *WhoWest 92*
**Lee,** Samuel C 1937- *AmMWSc 92*
**Lee,** Samuel S H 1930- *WhoAmP 91*
**Lee,** Sara Nell 1934- *WhoRel 92*
**Lee,** Sarah 1961- *TwCPaSc*
**Lee,** Shaw-Guang Lin 1944- *AmMWSc 92*
**Lee,** Sheila Jackson 1950- *WhoBlA 92*
**Lee,** Sherman Emery 1918- *WrDr 92*
**Lee,** Shih-Shun 1936- *AmMWSc 92*
**Lee,** Shih-Ying 1918- *AmMWSc 92*
**Lee,** Shirley Freeman 1928- *WhoBlA 92*
**Lee,** Shirley Williams 1924- *WhoAmP 91*
**Lee,** Shui Lung 1938- *AmMWSc 92*
**Lee,** Shuishih Sage 1948- *AmMWSc 92, WhoMW 92*
**Lee,** Shung-Yan Luke 1938- *AmMWSc 92*
**Lee,** Shyh-Yuan 1943- *AmMWSc 92*
**Lee,** Si Duk 1932- *AmMWSc 92*
**Lee,** Sidney Phillip 1920- *WhoAmP 91*
**Lee,** Silas, III 1954- *WhoBlA 92*
**Lee,** Sin Hang 1932- *AmMWSc 92*
**Lee,** Siu-Lam 1941- *AmMWSc 92*
**Lee,** Soo K. 1940- *WhoMW 92*
**Lee,** Sook 1929- *AmMWSc 92*
**Lee,** Sophia 1750-1824 *BlkwCEP*
**Lee,** Spike *NewYTBS 91*
**Lee,** Spike 1957- *IntDcF 2-2 [port], IntMPA 92, IntWW 91, WhoBlA 92, WhoEnt 92, WrDr 92*
**Lee,** Stanley *Who 92*
**Lee,** Stanley L 1919- *AmMWSc 92*
**Lee,** Stephen 1801-1879 *DcNCBi 4*
**Lee,** Stephen E. 1938- *WhoAmL 92*
**Lee,** Stephen Sheng-hao 1945- *WhoMW 92*
**Lee,** Steve S 1948- *AmMWSc 92*
**Lee,** Steven Michael 1954- *WhoAmL 92*
**Lee,** Steven Wayne 1951- *WhoMW 92*
**Lee,** Stratton Creighton 1920- *WhoBlA 92*
**Lee,** Stuart M 1920- *AmMWSc 92*
**Lee,** Sue Ying 1940- *AmMWSc 92*
**Lee,** Suk Young 1940- *AmMWSc 92*
**Lee,** Sun 1920- *AmMWSc 92*
**Lee,** Sun-Ock 1943- *WhoEnt 92*
**Lee,** Sung J 1942- *AmMWSc 92*
**Lee,** Sung Mook 1933- *AmMWSc 92*
**Lee,** Sunggyu 1952- *AmMWSc 92, WhoMW 92*
**Lee,** Susan *ConAu 135*
**Lee,** Sydney 1866-1949 *TwCPaSc*
**Lee,** T Jerry 1937- *WhoIns 92*
**Lee,** T P 1933- *AmMWSc 92*
**Lee,** T S 1931- *AmMWSc 92*
**Lee,** Tanith 1947- *IntAu&W 91, TwCSFW 91, WrDr 92*
**Lee,** Ted C K 1940- *AmMWSc 92*
**Lee,** Teh-Hsuang 1936- *AmMWSc 92*
**Lee,** Teh Hsun 1917- *AmMWSc 92*
**Lee,** Ten Ching *AmMWSc 92*
**Lee,** Terry 1935- *TwCPaSc*
**Lee,** Theodore Robert 1923- *WhoAmP 91*
**Lee,** Theodosia L. Crawford 1919-1983 *WhoBlA 92N*
**Lee,** Theresa *AmMWSc 92*
**Lee,** Thomas *ScFEYrs*
**Lee,** Thomas 1943- *WhoAmP 91*
**Lee,** Thomas Bailey 1873-1948 *DcNCBi 4*
**Lee,** Thomas Dongho 1940- *WhoAmL 92*
**Lee,** Thomas F. 1925- *WhoBlA 92*
**Lee,** Thomas Gayle Lycongthuan 1939- *WhoRel 92*
**Lee,** Thomas Henry 1923- *AmMWSc 92*
**Lee,** Thomas Joseph, Jr. 1921- *WhoFI 92*
**Lee,** Thomas Stirling 1857-1916 *TwCPaSc*
**Lee,** Thomas W 1937- *AmMWSc 92*
**Lee,** Tien-Chang 1943- *AmMWSc 92*
**Lee,** Timothy Earl 1947- *WhoMW 92*
**Lee,** Ting David, Jr. 1933- *WhoWest 92*
**Lee,** Tom Stewart 1941- *WhoAmL 92*
**Lee,** Tong-Nyong 1927- *AmMWSc 92*
**Lee,** Tonia Renee 1963- *WhoWest 92*
**Lee,** Tony Jer-Fu 1942- *AmMWSc 92*
**Lee,** Tsung Dao 1926- *AmMWSc 92, Who 92, WhoNob 90*
**Lee,** Tsung-Shung Harry 1943- *AmMWSc 92*
**Lee,** Tsung Ting 1923- *AmMWSc 92*
**Lee,** Tung-Ching 1941- *AmMWSc 92*
**Lee,** Tyre Douglas, Jr 1946- *WhoAmP 91*
**Lee,** Tyrone Yiu-Huen 1944- *AmMWSc 92*
**Lee,** Tyronne T. 1949- *WhoBlA 92*
**Lee,** Tzoong-Chyh 1936- *AmMWSc 92*
**Lee,** Van Spencer 1942- *WhoBlA 92*
**Lee,** Victor Ho 1960- *WhoAmL 92*
**Lee,** Victor Lewis 1956- *WhoFI 92*
**Lee,** Vin-Jang 1937- *AmMWSc 92*
**Lee,** Vin Jang Thomas 1937- *WhoWest 92*
**Lee,** Ving Jick 1951- *AmMWSc 92*
**Lee,** Virginia Ann 1922- *AmMWSc 92*
**Lee,** Virginia Ann 1930- *WhoAmP 91*
**Lee,** Virginia Diane 1939- *WhoRel 92*
**Lee,** Vivian Booker 1938- *WhoBlA 92*
**Lee,** W. David 1944- *WhoWest 92*
**Lee,** W. Storrs, III 1906- *WrDr 92*
**Lee,** Wai-Hon 1942- *AmMWSc 92*
**Lee,** Walter William, Jr. 1931- *WhoEnt 92*
**Lee,** Warren Ford 1941- *AmMWSc 92*
**Lee,** Wayne C 1917- *IntAu&W 91, TwCWW 91, WrDr 92*
**Lee,** Wei-Kuo 1943- *AmMWSc 92*
**Lee,** Wei-Li S 1945- *AmMWSc 92*
**Lee,** Wei-Ming 1936- *AmMWSc 92*
**Lee,** William *BenetAL 91, IntAu&W 91X, WrDr 92*
**Lee,** William 1907- *Who 92*
**Lee,** William Carey 1895-1948 *DcNCBi 4*
**Lee,** William Charles 1938- *WhoAmL 92*
**Lee,** William Chien-Yeh 1932- *AmMWSc 92*
**Lee,** William Franklin, III 1929- *WhoEnt 92*
**Lee,** William H. 1936- *WhoBlA 92*
**Lee,** William Henry 1946- *WhoEnt 92*
**Lee,** William Hung Kan 1940- *AmMWSc 92*
**Lee,** William J 1925- *WhoAmP 91*
**Lee,** William J. 1936- *WhoBlA 92*
**Lee,** William James 1922- *WhoRel 92*
**Lee,** William John 1936- *AmMWSc 92*
**Lee,** William Johnson 1924- *WhoAmL 92*
**Lee,** William Marshall 1922- *WhoAmL 92, WhoMW 92*
**Lee,** William Marshall, Jr. 1948- *WhoAmL 92*
**Lee,** William Morris, Jr. 1943- *WhoWest 92*
**Lee,** William Orvid 1927- *AmMWSc 92*
**Lee,** William Osborne, Jr. 1934- *WhoAmL 92*
**Lee,** William Richard 1953- *WhoAmP 91*
**Lee,** William Roscoe 1930- *AmMWSc 92*
**Lee,** William Rowland *WrDr 92*
**Lee,** William States 1929- *AmMWSc 92, WhoFI 92*
**Lee,** William Storrs, III 1906- *IntAu&W 91*
**Lee,** William Swain 1935- *WhoAmP 91*
**Lee,** William Thomas 1942- *WhoBlA 92*
**Lee,** William Thomas 1958- *AmMWSc 92*
**Lee,** William Wai-Lim 1948- *AmMWSc 92*
**Lee,** William Wei 1923- *AmMWSc 92*
**Lee,** Wilma 1921- *NewAmDM*
**Lee,** Wilson 1962- *WhoWest 92*
**Lee,** Won-Kyoo 1940- *WhoMW 92*
**Lee,** Wonyong 1930- *AmMWSc 92*
**Lee,** Woong Man 1938- *AmMWSc 92*
**Lee,** Wooyoung 1938- *AmMWSc 92*
**Lee,** Y C 1948- *AmMWSc 92*
**Lee,** Yat-Shir *AmMWSc 92*
**Lee,** Yien-Hwei 1937- *AmMWSc 92*
**Lee,** Yim Tin 1950- *AmMWSc 92*
**Lee,** Ying Kao 1932- *AmMWSc 92*
**Lee,** Yong Yung 1936- *AmMWSc 92*
**Lee,** Young Hie 1946- *AmMWSc 92*
**Lee,** Young-Hoon 1935- *AmMWSc 92*
**Lee,** Young Jack 1942- *AmMWSc 92*
**Lee,** Young-Jin 1946- *AmMWSc 92*
**Lee,** Young Woo 1941- *WhoFI 92*
**Lee,** Yuan Chuan 1932- *AmMWSc 92*
**Lee,** Yuan Tseh 1936- *AmMWSc 92, IntWW 91, Who 92, WhoNob 90, WhoWest 92*
**Lee,** Yue-Wei 1946- *AmMWSc 92*
**Lee,** Yuen San 1939- *AmMWSc 92*
**Lee,** Yung 1932- *AmMWSc 92*
**Lee,** Yung-Chang 1935- *AmMWSc 92*
**Lee,** Yung-Cheng 1956- *AmMWSc 92*
**Lee,** Yung-Keun 1929- *AmMWSc 92*
**Lee-Barber,** John 1905- *Who 92*
**Lee Chu-Ming,** Martin 1938- *Who 92*
**Lee-Franzini,** Juliet 1933- *AmMWSc 92*
**Lee-Gulley,** Patricia Amy 1953- *WhoWest 92*
**Lee-Ham,** Doo Young 1932- *AmMWSc 92*
**Lee-Hankey,** William 1869-1952 *TwCPaSc*
**Lee-Huang,** Sylvia 1930- *AmMWSc 92*
**Lee-Miller,** Stephanie 1950- *WhoBlA 92*
**Lee Peng-Fei,** Allen 1940- *Who 92*
**Lee-Potter,** Jeremy Patrick 1934- *Who 92*
**Lee-Ruff,** Edward 1944- *AmMWSc 92*
**Lee-Smith,** Hughie 1915- *WhoBlA 92*
**Lee-Steere,** Ernest 1912- *Who 92*
**Lee-Whiting,** Graham Edward 1926- *AmMWSc 92*
**Leean,** Joseph 1942- *WhoAmP 91, WhoMW 92*
**Leeb,** Charles Samuel 1945- *WhoWest 92*
**Leeb,** Jonathan M. 1960- *WhoFI 92*
**Leeb,** Wilhelm, Ritter von 1876-1956 *EncTR 91 [port]*
**Leebron,** David Wayne 1955- *WhoAmL 92*
**Leech,** David Bruce 1934- *Who 92*
**Leech,** Geoffrey Bosdin 1918- *AmMWSc 92*
**Leech,** Geoffrey Neil 1936- *IntAu&W 91, Who 92, WrDr 92*
**Leech,** H William 1940- *AmMWSc 92*
**Leech,** James William 1947- *WhoFI 92*
**Leech,** John 1925- *Who 92*
**Leech,** John George E. *ScFEYrs*
**Leech,** Joseph 1720-1803 *DcNCBi 4*
**Leech,** Kenneth 1939- *Who 92, WrDr 92*
**Leech,** Margaret 1893-1974 *BenetAL 91*
**Leech,** Robert Leland 1938- *AmMWSc 92*
**Leech,** Robert Milton 1921- *WhoEnt 92*
**Leech,** Robert Radcliffe 1919- *Who 92*
**Leech,** Stephen H 1942- *AmMWSc 92*
**Leech,** William Charles d1990 *Who 92N*
**Leecing,** Walden Albert 1932- *WhoWest 92*
**Leed,** Jacob *DrAPF 91*
**Leed,** Jacob 1924- *WrDr 92*
**Leed,** Michael William 1952- *WhoFI 92*
**Leed,** Russell Ernest 1915- *AmMWSc 92*
**Leedale,** Harry Heath d1991 *Who 92N*
**Leeder,** Joseph Gorden 1916- *AmMWSc 92*
**Leedham,** Clive D 1928- *AmMWSc 92*
**Leedom,** E. Paul 1925- *WhoFI 92*
**Leedom,** Edwin Conover 1805- *BiInAmS*
**Leedom,** John Milton 1933- *AmMWSc 92*
**Leedom,** John Nesbett *WhoAmP 91*
**Leedom,** Richard R. 1955- *WhoEnt 92*
**Leedom-Ackerman,** Joanne *DrAPF 91*
**Leeds,** Archdeacon of *Who 92*
**Leeds,** Bishop of 1930- *Who 92*
**Leeds,** Albert Ripley 1843-1902 *BiInAmS*
**Leeds,** Barry H. 1940- *WrDr 92*
**Leeds,** Christopher 1935- *Who 92, WrDr 92*
**Leeds,** Daniel 1652-1720 *BenetAL 91, BiInAmS*
**Leeds,** David Emerson 1958- *WhoAmP 91*
**Leeds,** J Venn, Jr 1932- *AmMWSc 92*
**Leeds,** John 1705-1790 *BiInAmS*
**Leeds,** Josiah W. 1841-1908 *AmPeW*
**Leeds,** Martin N. 1916- *IntMPA 92*
**Leeds,** Morton Harold 1921- *WrDr 92*
**Leeds,** Morton W 1916- *AmMWSc 92*
**Leeds,** Phil *ConTFT 9*
**Leeds,** Steven David 1950- *WhoEnt 92*
**Leeds-Horwitz,** Susan Beth 1950- *WhoWest 92*
**Leedy,** Clark D 1933- *AmMWSc 92*
**Leedy,** Daniel Loney 1912- *AmMWSc 92*
**Leedy,** Paul D. 1908- *WrDr 92*
**Leef,** Audrey V 1922- *AmMWSc 92*
**Leef,** George Charles 1951- *WhoMW 92*

**Leef**, James Lewis 1937- *AmMWSc 92*
**Leeg**, Kenton J 1911- *AmMWSc 92*
**Leehey**, Patrick 1921- *AmMWSc 92*
**Leek**, Everett Paul 1929- *WhoBlA 92*
**Leek**, Jay Wilbur 1928- *WhoFI 92*
**Leek**, Sandra D. 1954- *WhoBlA 92*
**Leeke**, John F. 1939- *WhoBlA 92*
**Leekley**, John Robert 1943- *WhoAmL 92, WhoFI 92*
**Leekley**, Robert Mitchell 1911- *AmMWSc 92*
**Leekpai**, Chuan 1938- *IntWW 91*
**Leela**, Srinivasa *AmMWSc 92*
**Leeland**, Steven Brian 1951- *WhoWest 92*
**Leeling**, Jerry L 1936- *AmMWSc 92*
**Leeman**, Bary Alan 1943- *WhoMW 92*
**Leeman**, Cliff 1913-1986 *NewAmDM*
**Leeman**, James Edwin 1928- *WhoFI 92*
**Leeman**, Susan Epstein 1930- *AmMWSc 92*
**Leemann**, Christoph Willy 1939- *AmMWSc 92*
**Leemans**, Victor Louis 1901-1971 *BiDExR*
**Leemhuis**, John Peter, Sr. 1930- *WhoAmL 92*
**Leeming**, David John 1939- *AmMWSc 92*
**Leeming**, Geraldine Margaret *Who 92*
**Leeming**, Ian 1948- *Who 92*
**Leeming**, John Coates 1927- *Who 92*
**Leemputte**, Patrick John 1957- *WhoFI 92*
**Leen**, Todd Kevin 1955- *WhoWest 92*
**Leene**, Hendrik 1937- *WhoRel 92*
**Leenhardt**, Roger 1903-1985 *IntDcF 2-2*
**Leenheer**, Mary Janeth 1954- *AmMWSc 92*
**Leenhoff**, Leon 1852-1925 *ThHElm [port]*
**Leenhouts**, Lewis Grant *IntMPA 92*
**Leep**, Herman Ross 1940- *AmMWSc 92*
**Leeper**, Dennis Burton 1941- *AmMWSc 92*
**Leeper**, Harold Harris 1916- *WhoAmL 92*
**Leeper**, Harold Murray 1920- *AmMWSc 92*
**Leeper**, Herbert Andrew, Jr 1942- *AmMWSc 92*
**Leeper**, John Robert 1947- *AmMWSc 92*
**Leeper**, Kathie Alice 1944- *WhoMW 92*
**Leeper**, Lemuel Cleveland 1927- *WhoBlA 92*
**Leeper**, Lucius Walter 1922- *WhoBlA 92*
**Leeper**, Ramon Joe 1948- *AmMWSc 92, WhoFI 92*
**Leeper**, Robert Dwight 1924- *AmMWSc 92*
**Leeper**, Robert J 1958- *WhoAmP 91*
**Leeper**, Robert Walz 1915- *AmMWSc 92*
**Leeper**, Ronald J 1944- *WhoAmP 91*
**Leeper**, Ronald James 1944- *WhoBlA 92*
**Leer**, Mary Kelley 1950- *WhoEnt 92*
**Leerar**, Philip Eric 1967- *WhoMW 92*
**Leerburger**, Benedict A. 1932- *WrDr 92*
**Leerburger**, Benedict Alan 1932- *AmMWSc 92*
**Leers**, Johann von 1902-1965 *BiDExR, EncTR 91*
**Leertouwer**, Lammert 1932- *WhoRel 92*
**Lees**, Alistair John 1955- *AmMWSc 92*
**Lees**, Anthony David 1917- *IntWW 91, Who 92*
**Lees**, Anthony Philip 1930- *WhoFI 92*
**Lees**, Antony *Who 92*
**Lees**, Benjamin 1924- *ConCom 92, NewAmDM, WhoEnt 92*
**Lees**, Brian P 1953- *WhoAmP 91*
**Lees**, C. Norman 1929- *Who 92*
**Lees**, David 1936- *Who 92*
**Lees**, David Bryan 1936- *IntWW 91*
**Lees**, David Eric Berman 1950- *AmMWSc 92*
**Lees**, Dennis Samuel 1924- *Who 92*
**Lees**, Derwent 1885-1931 *TwCPaSc*
**Lees**, Francis Anthony 1931- *WhoFI 92*
**Lees**, Geoffrey William 1920- *Who 92*
**Lees**, George Edward 1948- *AmMWSc 92*
**Lees**, Marjorie Berman 1923- *AmMWSc 92*
**Lees**, Martin H 1929- *AmMWSc 92*
**Lees**, Nicholas Ernest Samuel 1939- *Who 92*
**Lees**, Norman *Who 92*
**Lees**, Norman Douglas 1945- *AmMWSc 92*
**Lees**, Ray 1931- *WrDr 92*
**Lees**, Robert S 1934- *AmMWSc 92*
**Lees**, Robin Lowther 1931- *Who 92*
**Lees**, Ronald Beresford d1991 *Who 92N*
**Lees**, Ronald Edward 1935- *AmMWSc 92*
**Lees**, Ronald Milne 1939- *AmMWSc 92*
**Lees**, Sidney 1917- *AmMWSc 92*
**Lees**, Thomas 1925- *Who 92*
**Lees**, Thomas Harcourt Ivor 1941- *Who 92*
**Lees**, Thomas Masson 1917- *AmMWSc 92*
**Lees**, Wayne Lowry 1914- *AmMWSc 92*
**Lees**, William 1924- *Who 92*
**Lees**, William Antony Clare 1935- *Who 92*
**Lees**, William Glenwood 1916- *WhoFI 92*
**Lees-Milne**, James 1908- *IntAu&W 91, IntWW 91, Who 92, WrDr 92*
**Lees-Spalding**, Ian Jaffery 1920- *Who 92*
**Leese**, Arnold Spencer 1878-1956 *BiDExR*
**Leese**, John Albert 1932- *AmMWSc 92*
**Leese**, John Arthur 1930- *IntAu&W 91, IntWW 91, Who 92*
**Leese**, John Henry Vernon 1901- *Who 92*
**Leese**, Oliver 1894-1978 *CurBio 91N*
**Leeseberg**, Martin Walter 1915- *WhoRel 92*
**Leeser**, David O 1917- *AmMWSc 92*
**Leeser**, Isaac 1806-1868 *DcAmImH*
**Leeson**, Charles Roland 1926- *AmMWSc 92*
**Leeson**, Janet Caroline Tollefson 1933- *WhoMW 92*
**Leeson**, Lewis Joseph 1927- *AmMWSc 92*
**Leeson**, Robert 1928- *IntAu&W 91, WrDr 92*
**Leeson**, Thomas Sydney 1926- *AmMWSc 92*
**Leestma**, Jan E 1938- *AmMWSc 92*
**Leestma**, Jan Edward 1938- *WhoMW 92*
**Leet**, Gerald 1913- *TwCPaSc*
**Leet**, James Jay 1947- *WhoAmP 91*
**Leet**, Judith *DrAPF 91*
**Leet**, Richard Hale 1926- *WhoFI 92, WhoMW 92*
**Leetch**, James Frederick 1929- *AmMWSc 92*
**Leete**, Edward 1928- *AmMWSc 92*
**Leete**, Lawrence Francis 1944- *WhoMW 92*
**Leete**, Richard Callender 1939- *WhoWest 92*
**Leets**, Peter John 1946- *WhoFI 92*
**Leety**, William Ross 1945- *WhoRel 92*
**Leetz**, John Richard 1933- *WhoMW 92*
**Leeuw**, Gene R 1944- *WhoAmP 91*
**Leeuw**, Ton de 1926- *ConCom 92, NewAmDM*
**Leeuwenhoek**, Antony van 1632-1723 *BlkwCEP*
**Leevy**, Carroll M 1920- *AmMWSc 92, WhoBlA 92*
**Leewood**, Jack 1913- *IntMPA 92*
**LeFante**, Joseph A 1928- *WhoAmP 91*
**Le Fante**, Michael 1954- *WhoIns 92*
**LeFanu**, Elizabeth *Who 92*
**Le Fanu**, George Victor 1925- *Who 92*
**Le Fanu**, Mark 1946- *Who 92*
**LeFanu**, Nicola 1947- *ConCom 92*
**LeFanu**, Nicola Frances 1947- *Who 92*
**Le Fanu**, Sheridan 1814-1873 *RfGEnL 91*
**Le Fanu**, Victor *Who 92*
**Lefar**, Morton Saul 1937- *AmMWSc 92*
**Le Faure**, Georges 1856-1935 *ScFEYrs*
**Le Fave**, Gene Marion 1924- *WhoFI 92*
**Lefavour**, Edward B 1854-1889 *BiInAmS*
**Lefco**, Kathy Nan 1949- *WhoAmL 92*
**Lefco**, Stanley Morris 1947- *WhoAmL 92*
**Lefcoe**, Neville 1925- *AmMWSc 92*
**Lefcoe**, Vann H. 1943- *WhoAmL 92*
**Lefcourt**, Carol H. d1991 *NewYTBS 91*
**Lefcourt**, Carol Halper *WhoFI 92*
**Lefcowitz**, Barbara F. *DrAPF 91*
**Lefebure**, Leo Dennis 1952- *WhoRel 92*
**Lefebure**, Molly *IntAu&W 91, WrDr 92*
**Lefebvre**, Arthur Henry 1923- *Who 92*
**Lefebvre**, Claude 1931- *WhoEnt 92*
**Le Febvre**, Eugene Allen 1929- *AmMWSc 92*
**Lefebvre**, Gerald Alan 1950- *WhoAmL 92*
**Lefebvre**, James Kenneth 1943- *WhoMW 92, WhoWest 92*
**Lefebvre**, Jean-Pierre 1942- *IntDcF 2-2*
**Lefebvre**, Marcel 1905-1991 *CurBio 91N, IntWW 91, -91N, NewYTBS 91*
**Lefebvre**, Mario 1957- *AmMWSc 92*
**Lefebvre**, Paul Alvin 1950- *AmMWSc 92*
**Lefebvre**, Rene 1923- *AmMWSc 92*
**Lefebvre**, Richard Harold 1933- *AmMWSc 92*
**Lefebvre**, Roland J 1923- *WhoAmP 91*
**Lefebvre**, Yvon 1931- *AmMWSc 92*
**Lefer**, Allan Mark 1936- *AmMWSc 92*
**Lefer**, Diane *DrAPF 91*
**Lefever**, Kenneth Ernest 1915- *Who 92*
**Lefever**, Maxine Lane 1931- *WhoEnt 92*
**Lefever**, Robert Allen 1927- *AmMWSc 92*
**Lefevers**, Pearl Ray 1937- *WhoAmP 91*
**Lefevre**, Adam *DrAPF 91*
**LeFevre**, David E. 1944- *WhoAmL 92*
**Lefevre**, Donald Keith 1956- *WhoMW 92*
**Lefevre**, Edwin 1871-1943 *BenetAL 91*
**LeFevre**, Egbert 1858-1914 *BiInAmS*
**Lefevre**, George, Jr 1917- *AmMWSc 92*
**Lefevre**, Greg Louis 1947- *WhoWest 92*
**Lefevre**, Harlan W 1929- *AmMWSc 92*
**LeFevre**, Jean Adele 1930- *WhoRel 92*
**LeFevre**, Marian E Willis 1923- *AmMWSc 92*
**LeFevre**, Paul Green 1919- *AmMWSc 92*
**LeFevre**, Perry Deyo 1921- *WhoRel 92*
**LeFevre**, Roger Stanley 1960- *WhoFI 92, WhoWest 92*
**Leff**, Alan R 1945- *AmMWSc 92*
**Leff**, David 1933- *WhoAmL 92*
**Leff**, Gordon 1926- *Who 92, WrDr 92*
**Leff**, Harvey Sherwin 1937- *AmMWSc 92, WhoWest 92*
**Leff**, Judith 1935- *AmMWSc 92*
**Leff**, Marvin 1940- *WhoRel 92*
**Leff**, Randall S. 1951- *WhoAmL 92*
**Leff**, Robert S. 1947- *WhoWest 92*
**Leff**, Sanford Leonard 1918- *WhoFI 92*
**Leffak**, Ira Michael 1947- *AmMWSc 92*
**Leffall**, LaSalle Doheny, Jr 1930- *AmMWSc 92, WhoBlA 92*
**Leffek**, Kenneth Thomas 1934- *AmMWSc 92*
**Leffel**, Claude Spencer, Jr 1921- *AmMWSc 92*
**Leffel**, Robert Cecil 1925- *AmMWSc 92*
**Leffel**, Russell C 1948- *WhoAmP 91*
**Leffel**, Russell Calvin 1948- *WhoMW 92*
**Leffel**, Tim Scott 1964- *WhoEnt 92*
**Leffell**, Abraham Bernard 1926- *WhoRel 92*
**Leffell**, W O 1912- *AmMWSc 92*
**Lefferdink**, John S 1951- *WhoAmP 91*
**Leffert**, Charles Benjamin 1922- *AmMWSc 92*
**Leffert**, Hyam Lerner 1944- *AmMWSc 92*
**Lefferts**, Edward Allen 1933- *WhoWest 92*
**Lefferts**, George *IntMPA 92, WhoEnt 92*
**Leffew**, Kenneth W 1950- *AmMWSc 92*
**Leffingwell**, John C 1938- *AmMWSc 92*
**Leffingwell**, Thomas Pegg, Jr 1926- *AmMWSc 92*
**Leffland**, Ella 1931- *ConAu 35NR, SmATA 65 [port], WrDr 92*
**Leffler**, Amos J 1924- *AmMWSc 92*
**Leffler**, Charles William 1947- *AmMWSc 92*
**Leffler**, Esther Barbara 1925- *AmMWSc 92*
**Leffler**, Harry Rex 1942- *AmMWSc 92*
**Leffler**, James R 1946- *WhoIns 92*
**Leffler**, John Edward 1920- *AmMWSc 92*
**Leffler**, Marlin Templeton 1911- *AmMWSc 92*
**Leffler**, Sheldon S 1942- *WhoAmP 91*
**Lefford**, Maurice J 1930- *AmMWSc 92*
**Lefiti**, Fa'afetai *WhoAmP 91*
**Lefko**, Jeffrey Jay 1945- *WhoFI 92*
**Lefko**, Morris E. 1907- *IntMPA 92*
**Lefkoff**, Merle Schlesinger 1938- *WhoAmP 91*
**Lefkowith**, Edwin Frank 1931- *WhoFI 92*
**Lefkowitz**, Alan Zoel 1932- *WhoAmL 92*
**Lefkowitz**, David Ian 1964- *WhoEnt 92*
**Lefkowitz**, David Neil 1964- *WhoEnt 92*
**Lefkowitz**, Deborah Gail 1958- *WhoEnt 92*
**Lefkowitz**, Howard N. 1936- *WhoAmL 92*
**Lefkowitz**, Hugh Walter 1930- *WhoFI 92*
**Lefkowitz**, Irving 1921- *AmMWSc 92*
**Lefkowitz**, Issai 1926- *AmMWSc 92*
**Lefkowitz**, Ivan Martin 1952- *WhoAmL 92*
**Lefkowitz**, Jerome 1931- *WhoAmL 92*
**Lefkowitz**, Jerry 1945- *WhoFI 92*
**Lefkowitz**, Lewis Benjamin, Jr 1930- *AmMWSc 92*
**Lefkowitz**, Louis J 1904- *WhoAmP 91*
**Lefkowitz**, Mary 1935- *WrDr 92*
**Lefkowitz**, Robert Joseph 1943- *AmMWSc 92*
**Lefkowitz**, Ruth Lea 1949- *WhoEnt 92*
**Lefkowitz**, Ruth Samson 1910- *AmMWSc 92*
**Lefkowitz**, Stanley A 1943- *AmMWSc 92*
**Lefkowitz**, Stanley S 1933- *AmMWSc 92*
**Leflar**, Charles Joseph Finger 1953- *WhoMW 92*
**le Fleming**, Morris John 1932- *Who 92*
**Le Fleming**, Peter Henry John 1923- *Who 92*
**le Fleming**, Quentin 1949- *Who 92*
**Lefler**, Hugh Talmage 1901-1981 *DcNCBi 4*
**Lefler**, Lawrence Glenn 1926- *WhoAmP 91*
**Lefley**, Robert Herman 1927- *WhoMW 92*
**Le Floch-Prigent**, Loik 1943- *IntWW 91*
**LeFlore**, Larry 1949- *WhoBlA 92*
**LeFlore**, Obie Laurence, Jr. 1951- *WhoBlA 92*
**LeFlore**, Robert, Jr 1931- *WhoAmP 91*
**LeFlore**, William B. 1930- *WhoBlA 92*
**Leflores**, George O., Jr. 1921- *WhoBlA 92*
**Lefond**, Anne May 1917- *WhoWest 92*
**LeForge**, P.V. *DrAPF 91*
**Lefort**, Henry G 1928- *AmMWSc 92*
**Lefrak**, Edward Arthur 1943- *AmMWSc 92*
**LeFrak**, Francine 1950- *WhoEnt 92*
**LeFrak**, Samuel J. 1918- *WhoFI 92*
**Lefrancois**, Jacques 1929- *IntWW 91*
**Lefrancois**, Leo 1956- *AmMWSc 92*
**Lefstein**, Norman 1937- *WhoAmL 92, WhoMW 92*
**Leftin**, Harry Paul 1926- *AmMWSc 92*
**Lefton**, Lew Edward 1960- *AmMWSc 92*
**Lefton**, Norman Barry 1934- *WhoMW 92*
**Lefton**, Phyllis 1949- *AmMWSc 92*
**Leftridge**, William K. 1904- *WhoBlA 92*
**Leftwich**, Bill James 1923- *WhoAmP 91*
**Leftwich**, James Stephen 1956- *WhoWest 92*
**Leftwich**, Keith C 1954- *WhoAmP 91*
**Leftwich**, Norma Bogues 1948- *WhoBlA 92*
**Leftwich**, Willie L. 1937- *WhoBlA 92*
**Le Gac**, Jean 1936- *WorArt 1980*
**Legal**, Casimer Claudius, Jr 1915- *AmMWSc 92*
**LeGall**, Terrence George 1954- *WhoBlA 92*
**Le Gallienne**, Eva d1991 *Who 92N*
**Le Gallienne**, Eva 1899- *IntWW 91*
**Le Gallienne**, Eva 1899-1991 *BenetAL 91, ConAu 134, CurBio 91N, NewYTBS 91 [port], SmATA 68*
**Legan**, Kenneth Dale 1946- *WhoAmP 91*
**Legan**, Robert William 1936- *WhoFI 92*
**Legan**, Sandra Jean 1946- *AmMWSc 92*
**Legan**, Thomas L. 1933- *WhoFI 92*
**Legard**, Charles Thomas *Who 92*
**Legarda**, Benito Fernandez 1926- *WhoFI 92*
**Legare**, Henri Francis 1918- *WhoRel 92*
**Legare**, Hugh Swinton 1797-1843 *BenetAL 91*
**Legare**, James Matthewes 1823-1859 *BenetAL 91*
**Legare**, Richard J 1934- *AmMWSc 92*
**Legaspi**, Adrian 1952- *AmMWSc 92*
**Legat**, Michael 1923- *WrDr 92*
**Legat**, Michael Ronald 1923- *IntAu&W 91*
**Legates**, James Edward 1922- *AmMWSc 92*
**LeGates**, John Crews 1940- *WhoFI 92*
**Legatowicz**, Aleksander 1923- *IntWW 91*
**Legault**, Albert 1919- *AmMWSc 92*
**Legazpi**, Miguel Lopez de d1572 *HisDSpE*
**Legeckis**, Richard Vytautas 1941- *AmMWSc 92*
**Legendre**, Andre 1918- *IntWW 91*
**LeGendre**, Henri A. 1924- *WhoBlA 92*
**Legendre**, Louis 1945- *AmMWSc 92*
**Legendre**, Pierre 1946- *AmMWSc 92*
**Leger**, Fernand 1881-1955 *FacFETw*
**Leger**, Marie-Rene Auguste Alexis Saint-L 1887-1975 *WhoNob 90*
**Leger**, Paul Emile d1991 *NewYTBS 91 [port]*
**Leger**, Paul Emile 1904- *IntWW 91, RelLAm 91, Who 92*
**Leger**, Ray 1925- *WhoAmP 91*
**Leger**, Richard Roubine 1935- *WhoWest 92*
**Leger**, Robert M 1921- *AmMWSc 92*
**Leger**, Walter John, Jr. 1951- *WhoAmL 92*
**Leger**, Wendy Jo 1965- *WhoWest 92*
**Legere**, Werner 1912- *IntAu&W 91*
**Legerton**, Clarence W, Jr 1922- *AmMWSc 92*
**Legett**, John 1742-1812 *DcNCBi 4*
**Legg**, Allan Aubrey R. *Who 92*
**Legg**, Brian James 1945- *Who 92*
**Legg**, Cyrus Julian Edmund 1946- *Who 92*
**Legg**, David Alan 1947- *AmMWSc 92*
**Legg**, David E. 1955- *WhoWest 92*
**Legg**, Ivan 1937- *AmMWSc 92*
**Legg**, James C 1936- *AmMWSc 92, WhoMW 92*
**Legg**, John Wallis 1936- *AmMWSc 92*
**Legg**, Joseph Ogden 1920- *AmMWSc 92*
**Legg**, Keith 1924- *Who 92*
**Legg**, Kenneth Deardorff 1943- *AmMWSc 92*
**Legg**, Merle Alan 1926- *AmMWSc 92*
**Legg**, Reagan Houston 1924- *WhoAmL 92*
**Legg**, Ronald Otis 1945- *WhoMW 92*
**Legg**, Thomas Harry 1929- *AmMWSc 92*
**Legg**, Thomas Stuart 1935- *Who 92*
**Legg**, William Jefferson 1925- *WhoAmL 92*
**Leggat**, Lois Burnett 1917- *WhoAmP 91*
**Leggat**, Richard Durning 1927- *WhoAmL 92*
**Leggatt**, Alexander 1940- *WrDr 92*
**Leggatt**, Alexander Maxwell 1940- *IntAu&W 91*
**Leggatt**, Andrew 1930- *Who 92*
**Leggatt**, Hugh 1925- *Who 92*
**Legge** *Who 92*
**Legge**, Charles Alexander 1930- *WhoAmL 92*
**Legge**, James 1861-1940 *ScFEYrs*
**Legge**, John David 1921- *WrDr 92*
**Legge**, Michael 1944- *Who 92*
**Legge**, Norman Reginald 1919- *AmMWSc 92*
**Legge**, Ronald *ScFEYrs*
**Legge**, Russel Donald 1935- *WhoRel 92*
**Legge**, Thomas Nelson 1936- *AmMWSc 92*
**Legge**, William 1731-1801 *BlkwEAR*
**Legge**, William Gordon 1913- *Who 92*
**Legge-Schwarzkopf**, Elisabeth *Who 92*
**Leggett**, Anne Marie 1947- *WhoMW 92*
**Leggett**, Clarence 1911- *Who 92*
**Leggett**, Douglas Malcolm Aufrere 1912- *Who 92*
**Leggett**, James Everett 1926- *AmMWSc 92*

**Leggett**, John *DrAPF 91*
**Leggett**, Malcolm H 1937- *WhoIns 92*
**Leggett**, Mortimer 1821-1896 *ScFEYrs*
**Leggett**, Otis A 1919- *WhoAmP 91*
**Leggett**, Paul Arthur 1946- *WhoRel 92*
**Leggett**, Renee 1949- *WhoBlA 92*
**Leggett**, Robert Dean 1929- *AmMWSc 92*
**Leggett**, Stephen *DrAPF 91*
**Leggett**, Thomas Parrish 1945- *WhoAmL 92*
**Leggett**, Vincent Omar 1953- *WhoBlA 92*
**Leggett**, Walter Edward, Jr. 1952- *WhoAmL 92*
**Leggett**, William 1801-1839 *BenetAL 91*
**Leggett**, William C 1939- *AmMWSc 92*
**Leggett**, William Henry 1816-1882 *BiInAmS*
**Leggette**, Lemire 1949- *WhoBlA 92*
**Leggette**, Violet Olevia Brown *WhoAmP 91, WhoBlA 92*
**Leggon**, Herman W. 1930- *WhoBlA 92*
**Legh** *Who 92*
**Legh-Jones**, Piers Nicholas 1943- *Who 92*
**Leghorn**, Thomas Arthur 1956- *WhoAmL 92*
**Legiardi-Laura**, Roland *DrAPF 91*
**Legin**, Joel Lawrence 1952- *WhoAmL 92*
**Leginska**, Ethel 1886-1970 *NewAmDM*
**Legler**, Donald Wayne 1931- *AmMWSc 92*
**Legler**, John Marshall 1930- *AmMWSc 92*
**Legler**, Philip *DrAPF 91*
**Legler**, Warren Karl 1930- *AmMWSc 92*
**Legner**, E Fred 1932- *AmMWSc 92*
**Lego**, Paul Edward 1930- *IntWW 91, WhoFI 92*
**Le Goc**, Michel Jean-Louis 1921- *WhoFI 92*
**LeGoff**, Eugene 1934- *AmMWSc 92*
**Le Goff**, Jacques Louis 1924- *IntWW 91*
**Le Goff**, Rene Jean 1944- *WhoFI 92*
**Legorreta Vilchis**, Ricardo 1931- *IntWW 91*
**Legoshin**, Vladimir Grigor'evich 1904-1954 *SovUnBD*
**Le Goy**, Raymond Edgar Michel 1919- *IntWW 91, Who 92*
**Legrain**, Pierre Emile 1889-1929 *DcTwDes*
**LeGrand**, Bob 1943- *WhoBlA 92*
**LeGrand**, Donald George 1930- *AmMWSc 92*
**LeGrand**, Etienne Randall 1956- *WhoBlA 92*
**LeGrand**, Frank Edward 1926- *AmMWSc 92*
**LeGrand**, Harry E 1917- *AmMWSc 92*
**Legrand**, Michel 1932- *ConTFT 9, NewAmDM*
**Legrand**, Michel Jean 1932- *IntMPA 92, WhoEnt 92*
**Legrand**, Shawn Pierre 1960- *WhoWest 92*
**LeGrand**, Yvette Marie 1950- *WhoBlA 92*
**Le Grange**, Louis 1928- *IntWW 91*
**Legras**, Guy 1938- *IntWW 91*
**Legrenzi**, Giovanni 1626-1690 *NewAmDM*
**Le Grice**, F. Edwin 1911- *Who 92*
**Le Grice**, Jeremy 1936- *TwCPaSc*
**Le Grice**, Malcolm 1940- *IntDcF 2-2*
**Legrid**, Gloria Jean 1929- *WhoAmP 91*
**Legros**, Alphonse 1837-1911 *ThHEIm*
**LeGros**, John Edward 1923- *WhoFI 92*
**LeGrow**, Gary Edward 1938- *AmMWSc 92*
**Legters**, Llewellyn J 1932- *AmMWSc 92*
**LeGuerrier**, Jules 1915- *WhoRel 92*
**Leguey-Feilleux**, Jean-Robert 1928- *WhoMW 92*
**Le Guin**, Ursula K. *DrAPF 91*
**Le Guin**, Ursula K. 1929- *BenetAL 91, ConNov 91, FacFETw, IntAu&W 91, TwCSFW 91, WrDr 92*
**Le Guin**, Ursula Kroeber 1929- *IntWW 91*
**Leguizamo**, John *WhoHisp 92*
**Leguizamon**, Edgard 1945- *WhoHisp 92*
**Legum**, Colin 1919- *IntAu&W 91, WrDr 92*
**Legum**, Jeffrey Alfred 1941- *WhoFI 92*
**Legwaila**, Legwaila Joseph 1937- *IntWW 91*
**Leh**, Dennis Edward 1946- *WhoAmP 91*
**Lehan**, Frank W 1923- *AmMWSc 92*
**Lehan**, Jonathan Michael 1947- *WhoAmL 92*
**Lehan**, Robert Rogers 1933- *WhoEnt 92*
**Lehane**, Maureen *Who 92*
**Lehar**, Franz 1870-1948 *FacFETw, NewAmDM*
**Leheny**, Robert Francis 1938- *AmMWSc 92*
**LeHew**, Jeannette Elaine 1946- *WhoWest 92*
**Lehiste**, Ilse 1922- *AmMWSc 92*
**Lehman**, Alfred Baker 1931- *AmMWSc 92*
**Lehman**, Ambrose Edwin 1851-1917 *BiInAmS*
**Lehman**, August F 1924- *AmMWSc 92*
**Lehman**, Barry Alan 1948- *WhoRel 92*
**Lehman**, Christopher MacFarlane 1941- *WhoMW 92*
**Lehman**, Clifford R. 1951- *WhoMW 92*
**Lehman**, Curt *WhoRel 92*
**Lehman**, David *DrAPF 91*
**Lehman**, David Hershey *AmMWSc 92*
**Lehman**, David R 1940- *WhoIns 92*
**Lehman**, David Walter 1956- *WhoMW 92*
**Lehman**, Dennis Dale 1945- *AmMWSc 92*
**Lehman**, Denny 1952- *WhoFI 92*
**Lehman**, Donald Richard 1940- *AmMWSc 92*
**Lehman**, Duane Stanley 1932- *AmMWSc 92*
**Lehman**, Dwight Allen 1947- *WhoRel 92*
**Lehman**, Edgar R 1933- *WhoIns 92*
**Lehman**, Edwin *WhoRel 92*
**Lehman**, Emma Augusta 1841-1922 *DcNCBi 4*
**Lehman**, Ernest 1920- *IntMPA 92*
**Lehman**, Ernest Dale 1942- *AmMWSc 92*
**Lehman**, Eugene H 1913- *AmMWSc 92*
**Lehman**, Evelyn Jeanne 1930- *WhoAmL 92*
**Lehman**, Gary Douglas 1951- *WhoWest 92*
**Lehman**, Gladys *IntMPA 92*
**Lehman**, Grace Church 1941- *AmMWSc 92*
**Lehman**, Guy Walter 1923- *AmMWSc 92*
**Lehman**, Harry J 1935- *WhoAmP 91*
**Lehman**, Harry Jac 1935- *WhoAmL 92*
**Lehman**, Harvey Eugene *AmMWSc 92*
**Lehman**, Harvey J. 1905- *WhoBlA 92*
**Lehman**, Hugh Roberts 1921- *AmMWSc 92*
**Lehman**, Israel Robert 1924- *AmMWSc 92*
**Lehman**, James Daniel 1951- *WhoMW 92*
**Lehman**, James Orten 1932- *WhoRel 92*
**Lehman**, Jeffrey Mark 1947- *WhoFI 92*
**Lehman**, Joe Junior 1921- *AmMWSc 92*
**Lehman**, John Alan 1951- *WhoWest 92*
**Lehman**, John Michael 1942- *AmMWSc 92*
**Lehman**, John Theodore 1952- *AmMWSc 92*
**Lehman**, Kevin C *WhoIns 92*
**Lehman**, Leland Charles 1920- *WhoMW 92*
**Lehman**, Meir 1925- *Who 92*
**Lehman**, Meir M 1925- *AmMWSc 92*
**Lehman**, Michael A 1943- *WhoAmP 91*
**Lehman**, Palmer Smith 1948- *WhoAmL 92*
**Lehman**, Patty Steele 1951- *WhoAmP 91*
**Lehman**, Paul Evan *TwCWW 91*
**Lehman**, Paul R. 1931- *WhoEnt 92, WhoMW 92*
**Lehman**, Paul Robert 1941- *WhoBlA 92*
**Lehman**, Peter Robert 1944- *WhoEnt 92*
**Lehman**, R Sherman 1930- *AmMWSc 92*
**Lehman**, Richard H. 1948- *AlmAP 92 [port], WhoAmP 91*
**Lehman**, Richard Henry 1948- *WhoWest 92*
**Lehman**, Richard Lawrence 1929- *AmMWSc 92*
**Lehman**, Richard Leroy 1930- *WhoAmL 92*
**Lehman**, Robert Harold 1929- *AmMWSc 92*
**Lehman**, Roger H 1921- *AmMWSc 92*
**Lehman**, Ronald F, II 1946- *WhoAmP 91*
**Lehman**, Scott Nelson 1961- *WhoWest 92*
**Lehman**, Thomas Alan 1939- *AmMWSc 92*
**Lehman**, Warren Winfred 1930- *WhoMW 92*
**Lehman**, William 1913- *AlmAP 92 [port], WhoAmP 91*
**Lehman**, William Francis 1926- *AmMWSc 92*
**Lehman**, William Jeffrey 1945- *AmMWSc 92*
**Lehman**, Yvonne 1936- *IntAu&W 91, WrDr 92*
**Lehman Major**, Robin 1957- *WhoWest 92*
**Lehman-Meyer**, Katherine Josephine 1963- *WhoEnt 92*
**Lehmann**, A Spencer 1916- *AmMWSc 92*
**Lehmann**, Andrew George 1922- *Who 92*
**Lehmann**, Bruce Neal 1955- *WhoFI 92*
**Lehmann**, Elroy Paul 1928- *AmMWSc 92*
**Lehmann**, Erich Leo 1917- *AmMWSc 92, IntWW 91*
**Lehmann**, Geoffrey 1940- *ConPo 91, IntAu&W 91, WrDr 92*
**Lehmann**, Gilbert Mark 1933- *AmMWSc 92*
**Lehmann**, Gustav William 1844-1906 *BiInAmS*
**Lehmann**, Heinz E. 1911- *IntWW 91*
**Lehmann**, Heinz Edgar 1911- *AmMWSc 92*
**Lehmann**, Henry 1929- *WhoWest 92*
**Lehmann**, Hermann Peter 1937- *AmMWSc 92*
**Lehmann**, John 1907- *DcLB 112 [port]*
**Lehmann**, John Frederick 1907- *IntAu&W 91*
**Lehmann**, John R 1934- *AmMWSc 92*
**Lehmann**, Justus Franz 1921- *AmMWSc 92*
**Lehmann**, Lilli 1848-1929 *FacFETw, NewAmDM*
**Lehmann**, Liza 1862-1918 *NewAmDM*
**Lehmann**, Lotte 1888-1976 *FacFETw, NewAmDM*
**Lehmann**, Marie 1851-1931 *NewAmDM*
**Lehmann**, Michael S. 1957- *WhoEnt 92*
**Lehmann**, Nolan 1944- *WhoFI 92*
**Lehmann**, Olga *TwCPaSc*
**Lehmann**, Richard J. *WhoWest 92*
**Lehmann**, Richard William 1950- *WhoMW 92*
**Lehmann**, Rosamond 1901-1990 *AnObit 1990, RfGEnL 91*
**Lehmann**, Rosamund 1907- *IntAu&W 91*
**Lehmann**, Rudolf 1856-1929 *ScFEYrs*
**Lehmann**, Uwe E. G. 1950- *WhoEnt 92*
**Lehmann**, Wilma Helen 1929- *AmMWSc 92*
**Lehmann-Haupt**, Christopher 1934- *WrDr 92*
**Lehmberg**, Stanford Eugene 1931- *IntWW 91, WrDr 92*
**Lehmer**, Derrick Henry 1905- *AmMWSc 92*
**Lehmkuhl**, Dennis Merle 1942- *AmMWSc 92*
**Lehmkuhl**, L Don 1930- *AmMWSc 92*
**Lehmkuhl**, Lois D. 1925- *WhoMW 92*
**Lehn**, Jean-Marie 1939- *Who 92*
**Lehn**, Jean-Marie Pierre 1939- *IntWW 91, WhoNob 90*
**Lehn**, John Steven 1953- *WhoWest 92*
**Lehn**, Kenneth Matthew 1954- *WhoFI 92*
**Lehn**, William Lee 1932- *AmMWSc 92, WhoMW 92*
**Lehnardt**, Detlef Gunter 1941- *WhoAmL 92*
**Lehne**, Richard Karl 1920- *AmMWSc 92*
**Lehner**, Andreas Friedrich 1953- *AmMWSc 92*
**Lehner**, Christine *DrAPF 91*
**Lehner**, George Alexander, Jr. 1948- *WhoAmL 92*
**Lehner**, Guydo R 1928- *AmMWSc 92*
**Lehner**, Mark Allen 1951- *WhoAmP 91*
**Lehner**, Philip Nelson 1940- *AmMWSc 92*
**Lehner**, Richard Anthony 1946- *WhoEnt 92*
**Lehner**, Robert Joseph 1936- *WhoAmL 92*
**Lehnert**, James Patrick 1936- *AmMWSc 92*
**Lehnert**, Shirley Margaret 1934- *AmMWSc 92*
**Lehnhoff**, Terry Franklin 1939- *AmMWSc 92*
**Lehninger**, Ernst Francis 1917- *WhoMW 92, WhoRel 92*
**Lehoczky**, John Paul 1943- *AmMWSc 92*
**Lehoux**, Jean-Guy 1939- *AmMWSc 92*
**Lehovec**, Kurt 1918- *AmMWSc 92*
**Lehr**, Carlton G 1921- *AmMWSc 92*
**Lehr**, David 1910- *AmMWSc 92*
**Lehr**, Gary Fulton 1952- *AmMWSc 92*
**Lehr**, Gustav J 1929- *WhoIns 92*
**Lehr**, Hanns H 1908- *AmMWSc 92*
**Lehr**, James Jerome 1931- *WhoFI 92, WhoWest 92*
**Lehr**, Jay H 1936- *AmMWSc 92*
**Lehr**, John Frederick 1946- *WhoRel 92*
**Lehr**, Louis Anthony, Jr. 1928- *WhoAmL 92*
**Lehr**, Marvin Harold 1933- *AmMWSc 92*
**Lehr**, Milt 1924- *WhoAmP 91*
**Lehr**, Roland E 1942- *AmMWSc 92*
**Lehr**, Stanford Bud 1912- *WhoAmP 91*
**Lehr**, Ursula M. 1930- *IntWW 91*
**Lehrberger**, James Joseph 1943- *WhoRel 92*
**Lehrer**, Gerard Michael 1927- *AmMWSc 92*
**Lehrer**, Harold Z 1927- *AmMWSc 92*
**Lehrer**, Harris Irving 1939- *AmMWSc 92*
**Lehrer**, James 1934- *WrDr 92*
**Lehrer**, James C. *LesBEnT 92*
**Lehrer**, James Charles 1934- *WhoAmP 91*
**Lehrer**, Kenneth Eugene 1946- *WhoFI 92*
**Lehrer**, Paul Lindner 1928- *AmMWSc 92*
**Lehrer**, Paul Michael 1941- *AmMWSc 92*
**Lehrer**, Robert N 1922- *AmMWSc 92*
**Lehrer**, Samuel Bruce 1943- *AmMWSc 92*
**Lehrer**, Sherwin Samuel 1934- *AmMWSc 92*
**Lehrer**, Stanley 1929- *WrDr 92*
**Lehrer**, Thomas Andrew 1928- *Who 92, WhoEnt 92*
**Lehrer**, Tom 1928- *ConMus 7 [port], NewAmDM*
**Lehrer**, William Peter, Jr 1916- *AmMWSc 92, WhoWest 92*
**Lehring**, Betty J *WhoAmP 91*
**Lehrman**, George Philip 1926- *AmMWSc 92*
**Lehrman**, Irving 1911- *WhoRel 92*
**Lehrman**, Leonard Jordan 1949- *WhoEnt 92*
**Lehrman**, Margaret McBride 1944- *WhoEnt 92*
**Lehrman**, Paul David 1952- *WhoEnt 92*
**Lehrsch**, Gary Allen 1954- *AmMWSc 92*
**Lehtinen**, Seppo Ilmari 1937- *WhoFI 92*
**Lehto**, Arlene I 1939- *WhoAmP 91*
**Lehto**, Mark R 1956- *AmMWSc 92*
**Lehto**, Mark Reino 1956- *WhoMW 92*
**Lehto**, Olli Erkki 1925- *IntWW 91*
**Lehto**, Sakari Tapani 1923- *IntWW 91*
**Lei Jieqiong** 1905- *IntWW 91*
**Lei Renmin** 1909- *IntWW 91*
**Lei Yang** 1920- *IntWW 91*
**Lei**, David Kai Yui 1944- *AmMWSc 92*
**Lei**, Shau-Ping Laura 1953- *AmMWSc 92*
**Le'iato**, Filifaiesca A 1930- *WhoAmP 91*
**Leib**, Amos Patten 1917-1977 *ConAu 133*
**Leibach**, Fredrick Hartmut 1930- *AmMWSc 92*
**Leibacher**, John W 1941- *AmMWSc 92*
**Leibbrandt**, Vernon Dean 1944- *AmMWSc 92*
**Leibel**, Wayne Stephan 1951- *AmMWSc 92*
**Leibell**, Vincent L, III 1946- *WhoAmP 91*
**Leiber**, Fritz *DrAPF 91*
**Leiber**, Fritz 1910- *ConNov 91, TwCSFW 91, WrDr 92*
**Leiber**, Jay S. 1928- *WhoFI 92*
**Leibert**, Richard William 1948- *WhoWest 92*
**Leibfreid**, Ronald Arthur 1940- *WhoEnt 92*
**Leibhardt**, Edward 1919- *AmMWSc 92*
**Leibholz**, Stephen W 1932- *AmMWSc 92*
**Leibholz**, Stephen Wolfgang 1932- *WhoFI 92*
**Leibler**, Kenneth Robert 1949- *IntWW 91, WhoFI 92*
**Leibman**, Kenneth Charles 1923- *AmMWSc 92*
**Leibman**, Lawrence Fred 1947- *AmMWSc 92*
**Leibman**, Ron 1937- *IntMPA 92, WhoEnt 92*
**Leibniz**, Gottfried Wilhelm 1646-1716 *BlkwCEP*
**Leibo**, Stanley Paul 1937- *AmMWSc 92*
**Leibold**, Arthur William, Jr. 1931- *WhoAmL 92*
**Leibold**, Jay 1957- *WrDr 92*
**Leibold**, Werner 1936- *WhoWest 92*
**Leibovic**, K Nicholas 1921- *AmMWSc 92*
**Leibovich**, Sidney 1939- *AmMWSc 92*
**Leibovitz**, Annie 1949- *CurBio 91 [port]*
**Leibovitz**, Mitchell G. 1945- *WhoFI 92*
**Leibow**, Kenneth 1928- *WhoWest 92*
**Leibow**, Ronald Louis 1939- *WhoAmL 92*
**Leibow**, Scott Jon 1962- *WhoWest 92*
**Leibowitt**, Sol David 1912- *WhoAmL 92*
**Leibowitz**, Gerald Martin 1936- *AmMWSc 92*
**Leibowitz**, Howard A. 1941- *WhoFI 92*
**Leibowitz**, Jack Richard 1929- *AmMWSc 92*
**Leibowitz**, Judith d1990 *NewYTBS 91*
**Leibowitz**, Julian Lazar 1947- *AmMWSc 92*
**Leibowitz**, Leonard 1931- *AmMWSc 92, WhoMW 92*
**Leibowitz**, Lewis Phillip 1942- *AmMWSc 92*
**Leibowitz**, Martin Albert 1935- *AmMWSc 92*
**Leibowitz**, Marvin 1950- *WhoAmL 92*
**Leibowitz**, Michael Jonathan 1945- *AmMWSc 92*
**Leibowitz**, Norman 1947- *WhoFI 92*
**Leibowitz**, Rene 1913-1972 *NewAmDM*
**Leibowitz**, Sam 1913- *IntMPA 92*
**Leibowitz**, Sarah Fryer 1941- *AmMWSc 92*
**Leibrecht**, John Joseph 1930- *WhoMW 92, WhoRel 92*
**Leibson**, Charles M. 1929- *WhoAmL 92, WhoAmP 91*
**Leibson**, Irving 1926- *AmMWSc 92*
**Leibson**, Norman Howard 1945- *WhoWest 92*
**Leibson**, Paul Joseph 1952- *AmMWSc 92*
**Leibtag**, David Lewis 1949- *WhoMW 92*
**Leibu**, Henry J 1917- *AmMWSc 92*
**Leiby**, Clare C, Jr 1924- *AmMWSc 92*
**Leiby**, Larry Raymond 1947- *WhoAmL 92*
**Leiby**, Robert William 1949- *AmMWSc 92*
**Leicester**, Archdeacon of *Who 92*
**Leicester**, Bishop of 1940- *Who 92*
**Leicester**, Earl of 1909- *Who 92*
**Leicester**, Provost of *Who 92*
**Leich**, Douglas Albert 1947- *AmMWSc 92*
**Leichhardt**, Jerrine Kay 1931- *WhoMW 92*
**Leichman**, Kenneth William 1937- *WhoFI 92*
**Leichner**, Gene H 1929- *AmMWSc 92*
**Leichner**, Peter K 1939- *AmMWSc 92*
**Leichnetz**, George Robert 1942- *AmMWSc 92*
**Leicht**, Thomas E 1950- *WhoIns 92*
**Leichter**, Franz S 1930- *WhoAmP 91*
**Leichter**, Joseph 1932- *AmMWSc 92*
**Leid**, R Wes 1945- *AmMWSc 92*
**Leidel**, Donald Charles 1927- *WhoAmP 91*
**Leidel**, Edwin M., Jr. 1938- *WhoRel 92*

Leiden, Warren Robert 1949- WhoAmL 92
Leider, Emily Wortis DrAPF 91
Leider, Frida 1888-1975 NewAmDM
Leider, Gerald J. 1931- IntMPA 92
Leider, Herman R 1929- AmMWSc 92
Leider, Jerry 1931- ConTFT 9
Leiderman, P Herbert 1924- AmMWSc 92
Leidersdorf, Craig B 1950- AmMWSc 92
Leidheiser, Henry, Jr 1920- AmMWSc 92
Leidich, Robert John 1946- WhoAmL 92
Leidigh, Richard Keith 1953- WhoWest 92
Leiding, Rudolf Wilhelm Karl 1914- IntWW 91
Leidy, Blaine I 1923- AmMWSc 92
Leidy, Joseph 1823-1891 BiInAmS
Leidy, Ross Bennett 1939- AmMWSc 92
Leier, Carl V 1944- AmMWSc 92
Leies, Gerard M 1918- AmMWSc 92
Leies, John Gerard 1909- WhoRel 92
Leif, Robert Cary 1938- AmMWSc 92
Leifer, Alan Jay 1959- WhoFI 92
Leifer, Calvin 1929- AmMWSc 92
Leifer, Elihu Inselbuch 1940- WhoAmL 92
Leifer, Herbert Norman 1925- AmMWSc 92
Leifer, Larry J AmMWSc 92
Leifer, Leslie 1929- AmMWSc 92
Leifer, Steven Jon 1938- WhoFI 92
Leifer, Zer 1941- AmMWSc 92
Leiferman, Sylvia Weiner d1991 NewYTBS 91
Leifeste, Roger Rae 1954- WhoAmL 92
Leifield, Robert Francis 1928- AmMWSc 92
Leifland, Leif 1925- IntWW 91, Who 92
Leifman, Lev Jacob 1929- AmMWSc 92
Leiga, Algird George 1933- AmMWSc 92
Leigh Who 92
Leigh, Baron 1935- Who 92
Leigh, Amanda Kay Gregory 1954- WhoEnt 92
Leigh, Archibald Denis 1915- Who 92
Leigh, Byron Timothy 1949- WhoFI 92
Leigh, Charles Henry 1926- AmMWSc 92
Leigh, Christopher Humphrey de Verd 1943- Who 92
Leigh, Donald C 1929- AmMWSc 92
Leigh, Edward Julian Egerton 1950- Who 92
Leigh, Egbert G, Jr 1940- AmMWSc 92
Leigh, Geoffrey 1933- Who 92
Leigh, Hoyle 1942- WhoWest 92
Leigh, Jack P 1922- WhoAmP 91
Leigh, James W., Jr. 1927- WhoBlA 92
Leigh, Janet ConAu 134
Leigh, Janet 1927- IntMPA 92, WhoEnt 92
Leigh, Jennifer Jason 1958- IntMPA 92, WhoEnt 92
Leigh, John 1755?-1796 DcNCBi 4
Leigh, John 1909- Who 92
Leigh, Kathryn Suzanne 1946- WhoWest 92
Leigh, Leonard Herschel 1935- Who 92
Leigh, Mike 1943- IntAu&W 91, IntWW 91, Who 92, WrDr 92
Leigh, Mitch 1928- NewAmDM
Leigh, Neville 1922- Who 92
Leigh, Peter William John 1929- Who 92
Leigh, Richard Harris 1943- IntAu&W 91
Leigh, Richard Woodward 1942- AmMWSc 92
Leigh, Robert Edward 1931- WhoWest 92
Leigh, Roberta WrDr 92
Leigh, Roger 1925- TwCPaSc
Leigh, Stephen 1951- ConAu 135, TwCSFW 91, WrDr 92
Leigh, Suzanna 1945- IntMPA 92
Leigh, Thomas Francis 1923- AmMWSc 92
Leigh, Vivien 1913-1967 FacFETw
Leigh, William Alvin 1929- WhoBlA 92
Leigh Fermor, Patrick IntAu&W 91, WrDr 92
Leigh Fermor, Patrick 1915- ConAu 35NR
Leigh Guzman, Gustavo 1920- IntWW 91
Leigh-Pemberton, John 1911- Who 92
Leigh-Pemberton, Robert 1927- IntWW 91, Who 92
Leighly, Hollis Philip, Jr 1923- AmMWSc 92
Leighninger, David Scott 1920- WhoWest 92
Leight, Nathan David 1959- WhoFI 92
Leight, Walter Gilbert 1922- AmMWSc 92
Leighton, Albert C. 1919- WrDr 92
Leighton, Alexander 1908- WrDr 92
Leighton, Alexander Hamilton 1908- AmMWSc 92
Leighton, Alvah Theodore, Jr 1929- AmMWSc 92
Leighton, Charles Cutler 1938- AmMWSc 92
Leighton, Christopher Paul 1954- WhoRel 92
Leighton, David Struan Robertson 1928- WhoFI 92
Leighton, Dorothea Cross 1908- AmMWSc 92
Leighton, Edward WrDr 92
Leighton, Frederick Archibald 1948- AmMWSc 92
Leighton, Freeman Beach 1924- AmMWSc 92
Leighton, George Neves 1912- WhoBlA 92
Leighton, Henry Alexander 1929- WhoWest 92
Leighton, Henry George 1940- AmMWSc 92
Leighton, John 1822-1912 DcTwDes
Leighton, John Elliott 1959- WhoAmL 92
Leighton, Joseph 1921- AmMWSc 92
Leighton, Lee TwCWW 91, WrDr 92
Leighton, Len TwCWW 91
Leighton, Leonard Horace 1920- Who 92
Leighton, Loren Frederick 1926- WhoAmP 91
Leighton, Margaret 1922-1976 FacFETw
Leighton, Mark Stephen 1956- WhoEnt 92
Leighton, Michael 1935- Who 92
Leighton, Morris Wellman 1926- AmMWSc 92
Leighton, Porter D 1932- WhoAmP 91
Leighton, Robert Benjamin 1919- AmMWSc 92, IntWW 91
Leighton, Ronald 1930- Who 92
Leighton, Terrance J 1944- AmMWSc 92
Leighton, Walter 1907- AmMWSc 92
Leighton of St Mellons, Baron 1922- Who 92
Leighton Williams, John Who 92
Leija, Joseph G. 1957- WhoHisp 92
Leijon, Anna-Greta 1939- IntWW 91
Leijonhufvud, Axel Stig Bengt 1933- IntWW 91, WhoFI 92
Leik, Jean AmMWSc 92
Leiken, Earl Murray 1942- WhoAmL 92
Leikin, Jerrold Blair 1954- AmMWSc 92
Leiman, Eugene A. 1914- WhoAmL 92
Leiman, Sid Zalman 1941- WhoRel 92
Leimanis, Eugene 1905- AmMWSc 92, WhoWest 92
Leimbach, Marti 1963- ConLC 65 [port]
Leimback, Harry WhoAmP 91
Leimgruber, Richard M AmMWSc 92
Leimkiller, Floyd Nelson 1944- WhoRel 92
Leimkuhler, Ferdinand F 1928- AmMWSc 92
Lein, Allen 1913- AmMWSc 92, WhoWest 92
Lein, Barry Elliott 1947- WhoEnt 92
Lein, Don Curtis 1934- WhoFI 92, WhoMW 92
Leinbach, F Harold 1929- AmMWSc 92
Leinbach, Ralph C, Jr 1928- AmMWSc 92
Leinbach, Traugott 1796-1863 DcNCBi 4
Leinberger, Christopher Brown 1951- WhoWest 92
Leinen, Daniel Joseph 1958- WhoMW 92
Leinen, Margaret Sandra 1946- AmMWSc 92
Leinen, Robert John 1957- WhoAmL 92
Leinenweber, Harry Daniel 1937- WhoAmL 92, WhoAmP 91
Leiner, Carl Elton 1952- WhoRel 92
Leinhardt, Theodore Edward 1921- AmMWSc 92
Leinieks, Valdis 1932- WhoMW 92
Leininger, Harold Vernon 1925- AmMWSc 92
Leininger, Paul Miller 1911- AmMWSc 92
Leininger, Robert Irvin 1919- AmMWSc 92, WhoMW 92
Leininger, Scott Robert 1950- WhoMW 92
Leino, Deanna Rose 1937- WhoWest 92
Leinonen, Tatu Einari 1938- IntWW 91
Leinroth, Jean Paul, Jr 1920- AmMWSc 92
Leins, Mark Roger 1965- WhoEnt 92
Leinsdorf, Erich 1912- FacFETw, IntWW 91, NewAmDM, Who 92, WhoEnt 92
Leinster, Duke of 1914- Who 92
Leinster, Murray TwCWW 91
Leinster, Murray 1896-1975 ScFEYrs, TwCSFW 91
Leinung, John Martin 1954- WhoFI 92
Leinweber, Franz Josef 1931- AmMWSc 92
Leipart, Theodor 1867-1947 EncTR 91 [port]
Leiper, Esther M. DrAPF 91
Leiper, Henry Smith 1891-1975 AmPeW
Leipnik, Roy Bergh 1924- AmMWSc 92
Leipold, Martin H 1932- AmMWSc 92
Leipold, William Charles, Jr. 1949- WhoFI 92
Leipper, Dale F 1914- AmMWSc 92
Leipuner, Lawrence Bernard 1928- AmMWSc 92
Leipziger, Fredric Douglas 1929- AmMWSc 92
Leir, Richard Lee 1947- WhoMW 92
Leiris, Michel 1901-1990 GuFrLit 1
Leirner, Sheila 1948- IntWW 91
Leis, Brian Norman 1947- AmMWSc 92
Leis, Donald George 1919- AmMWSc 92
Leis, Jonathan Peter 1944- AmMWSc 92, WhoMW 92
Leise, Esther M 1953- AmMWSc 92
Leise, Fred 1949- WhoEnt 92
Leiseca, Sergio Alfredo, Jr. 1946- WhoHisp 92
Leisen, Mitchell 1898-1972 IntDcF 2-2 [port]
Leisen, Robert Thomas 1931- WhoFI 92
Leiser, Clara d1991 NewYTBS 91
Leiser, Eric J. 1960- WhoWest 92
Leiser, Ernest LesBEnT 92
Leiserson, Lee 1916- AmMWSc 92
Leishman, Frederick John 1919- Who 92
Leising, Jean 1949- WhoAmP 91
Leisler, Jacob 1640-1691 BenetAL 91
Leisman, Gilbert Arthur 1924- AmMWSc 92
Leisner, Anthony Baker 1941- WhoFI 92
Leisner, David 1953- WhoEnt 92
Leisner, Russell Mark 1956- WhoAmL 92
Leiss, Ernst L 1952- AmMWSc 92
Leiss, James Elroy 1924- AmMWSc 92
Leissa, A W 1931- AmMWSc 92
Leist, M C 1940- WhoAmP 91
Leist, Robert Campbell 1956- WhoAmL 92
Leisten, Arthur Gaynor 1941- WhoAmL 92, WhoFI 92
Leister, Harry M 1941- AmMWSc 92
Leister, Sandra Carter WhoMW 92
Leistner, Mary Edna 1929- WhoMW 92
Leisure, Peter Keeton 1929- WhoAmL 92
Leisure, Robert Glenn 1938- AmMWSc 92, WhoWest 92
Leisy, Douglas Jerald 1954- WhoWest 92
Leisy, James Franklin 1927- IntAu&W 91
Leitch, David Alexander 1931- Who 92
Leitch, David Bruce 1940- WrDr 92
Leitch, David R 1948- WhoAmP 91
Leitch, Donovan IntMPA 92
Leitch, Dougald Bruce 1956- WhoAmL 92
Leitch, George 1915- Who 92
Leitch, Gordon James AmMWSc 92
Leitch, Joel Steven 1952- WhoRel 92
Leitch, Leonard Christie 1914- AmMWSc 92
Leitch, Maurice IntAu&W 91, WrDr 92
Leitch, Monty S. DrAPF 91
Leitch, William Andrew 1915- Who 92
Leite, Antonio Dias, Jr. 1920- IntWW 91
Leite, Richard Joseph 1923- AmMWSc 92
Leitel, Ira 1944- WhoAmL 92
Leiter, Donald Eugene 1932- WhoRel 92
Leiter, Edward Henry 1942- AmMWSc 92
Leiter, Elliot 1933- AmMWSc 92
Leiter, Howard Allen 1918- AmMWSc 92
Leiter, John M. 1951- WhoAmL 92
Leiter, Jonathan DrAPF 91
Leiter, Joseph 1915- AmMWSc 92
Leiterman, Richard Mark 1935- WhoEnt 92
Leith Who 92
Leith, Andrew George F. Who 92
Leith, ArDean 1947- AmMWSc 92
Leith, Carlton James 1919- AmMWSc 92
Leith, Cecil Eldon, Jr 1923- AmMWSc 92
Leith, David W G S 1937- AmMWSc 92
Leith, Emmett Norman 1927- AmMWSc 92
Leith, John Douglas 1931- AmMWSc 92
Leith, John Haddon 1919- WhoRel 92
Leith, Prudence Margaret 1940- Who 92
Leith, Prue 1940- WrDr 92
Leith, Thomas Henry 1927- AmMWSc 92
Leith, William Cumming 1925- AmMWSc 92
Leith-Buchanan, Charles 1939- Who 92
Leithauser, Brad DrAPF 91
Leithauser, Brad 1953- BenetAL 91, ConPo 91, WrDr 92
Leithead, James Douglas 1911- Who 92
Leithead, R. James 1930- WhoAmL 92
Leithman, John Kenneth 1930- WhoAmP 91
Leitman, Marshall J 1941- AmMWSc 92
Leitmann, G 1925- AmMWSc 92
Leitmann, George 1925- WhoWest 92
Leitner, Alfred 1921- AmMWSc 92
Leitner, David Walker 1953- WhoEnt 92
Leitner, Elliot 1930- WhoIns 92
Leitner, Ferdinand 1912- NewAmDM
Leitner, Gregory Marc 1957- WhoAmL 92
Leitner, Kay Syms 1938- WhoAmP 91
Leitner, Mark Matthew 1958- WhoAmL 92
Leitner, Paul R. 1928- WhoAmL 92
Leitner, Philip 1936- AmMWSc 92
Leito, Ben M. 1923- IntWW 91
Leitten, Brian Joseph 1949- WhoMW 92
Leitz, Fred John, Jr 1921- AmMWSc 92
Leitz, Frederick Henry 1928- AmMWSc 92
Leitz, Robert C., III 1944- ConAu 133
Leitz, Victoria Mary AmMWSc 92
Leitzel, James Robert C 1936- AmMWSc 92
Leitzel, Joan Phillips 1936- AmMWSc 92
Leitzke, Jacque Herbert 1929- WhoFI 92, WhoMW 92
Leitzmann, Claus 1933- AmMWSc 92
Leiviska, Nancy Lynn 1948- WhoEnt 92
Leivo, Carl Eric 1950- WhoWest 92
Leivo, William John 1915- AmMWSc 92
Leiwig, Timothy Dean 1957- WhoMW 92
Leja, J 1918- AmMWSc 92
Leja, Stanislaw 1912- AmMWSc 92
LeJambre, Susan E 1942- WhoAmP 91
Lejeune, Anthony 1928- WrDr 92
Le Jeune, Claude 1528?-1600 NewAmDM
LeJeune, Dennis Edward 1942- WhoMW 92
Lejeune, Jerome Jean Louis Marie 1926- IntWW 91
LeJeune, Joseph Guillaume 1914- WhoFI 92
Lejeune, Michael L. 1918- IntWW 91
Lejeune, Michel 1907- IntWW 91
Lejeune-Jung, Paul 1882-1944 EncTR 91
Lejins, Voldemars Petrovich 1920- IntWW 91
Lejnieks, L. Arno 1928- WhoFI 92
Lekai, Louis J. 1916- WrDr 92
Lekan, Briana Marker 1955- WhoMW 92
Lekatz, Randall Paul 1962- WhoFI 92
Lekberg, Robert David 1920- WhoMW 92
Lekeux, Pierre Marie 1954- AmMWSc 92
Lekganyane, Barnabas WhoRel 92
Lekhanya, Justin IntWW 91
Leklem, James Erling 1941- AmMWSc 92
Lekota, Mosiuoa Patrick 1948- IntWW 91
LeLacheur, Edward A WhoAmP 91
LeLacheur, Robert Murray 1920- AmMWSc 92
Leland, Anne Gibbs 1941- WhoEnt 92
Leland, Burton 1948- WhoAmP 91
Leland, Charles Godfrey BenetAL 91
Leland, Charles Godfrey 1824-1903 ScFEYrs
Leland, Christopher Towne DrAPF 91
Leland, David 1947- IntMPA 92
Leland, Dawn Carolyn 1920- WhoAmP 91
Leland, Frances E 1932- AmMWSc 92
Leland, Harold R 1931- AmMWSc 92
Leland, Jeremy Francis David 1932- IntAu&W 91, WrDr 92
Leland, Joyce F. 1941- WhoBlA 92
Leland, Marc Ernest 1938- WhoAmP 91
Leland, Mickey 1944-1989 ConBlB 2 [port]
Leland, Paula Susan 1953- WhoMW 92
Leland, Richard G. 1949- WhoAmL 92
Leland, Stanley Edward, Jr 1926- AmMWSc 92, WhoMW 92
Leland, Thomas W, Jr 1924- AmMWSc 92
Leland, Wallace Thompson 1922- AmMWSc 92
Le Lannou, Maurice 1906- IntWW 91
Lelchuk, Alan DrAPF 91
Lelchuk, Alan 1938- ConNov 91, WrDr 92
Lele, Padmakar Pratap 1927- AmMWSc 92
Lele, Shreedhar G 1931- AmMWSc 92
Leleiko, Neal Simon 1946- AmMWSc 92
Le Levier, Robert Ernest 1923- AmMWSc 92
Leliaert, Richard Maurice 1940- WhoRel 92
Lellinger, David Bruce 1937- AmMWSc 92
Lello, Walter Barrington 1931- Who 92
Lellouche, Gerald S 1930- AmMWSc 92
Leloir, Luis Federico 1906-1987 WhoNob 90
Lelong, Michel Georges 1932- AmMWSc 92
Lelong, Pierre Alexandre 1931- IntWW 91
Lelong, Pierre Jacques 1912- IntWW 91
Lelouch, Claude 1937- IntDcF 2-2 [port], IntMPA 92, IntWW 91
Lelyveld, Arthur Joseph 1913- WhoRel 92
Lelyveld, Gail Annick 1948- WhoEnt 92
Lelyveld, Joseph 1937- IntAu&W 91
Lem, Kwok Wai 1952- AmMWSc 92
Lem, Nora Wan 1953- WhoWest 92
Lem, Richard Douglas 1933- WhoWest 92
Lem, Stanislaw 1921- FacFETw, IntAu&W 91, IntWW 91, TwCSFW 91A
Lema-Moya, Jose WhoAmP 91
Lemaev, Nikolay Vasilevich 1929- IntWW 91
LeMahieu, James Joseph 1936- WhoFI 92
Lemaire, Irma AmMWSc 92
Lemaire, Paul J 1953- AmMWSc 92
LeMaistre, Charles Aubrey 1924- AmMWSc 92
Le Maistre, Christopher William 1938- AmMWSc 92
Lemaitre, Georges Edouard 1894-1966 FacFETw
Lemal, David M 1934- AmMWSc 92
Lemaldi, Eleanora Yolanda Renna 1920- WhoAmP 91
Leman, Alexander B. 1926- IntWW 91
Leman, Allen Duane 1944- AmMWSc 92
Leman, Loren D 1950- WhoAmP 91
Leman, Martin 1934- TwCPaSc
Lemann, Jacob, Jr 1929- AmMWSc 92
Lemann, Thomas Berthelot 1926- WhoAmL 92

**Lemanski,** Kenneth Michael 1954- *WhoAmP 91*
**Lemanski,** Larry Frederick 1943- *AmMWSc 92*
**Lemanski,** Michael Francis 1946- *AmMWSc 92*
**LeMarbe,** Edward Stanley 1952- *WhoFI 92*
**Lemarchand,** Elizabeth 1906- *IntAu&W 91, WrDr 92*
**Le Marchant,** Francis 1939- *TwCPaSc, Who 92*
**Le Marechal,** Robert Norford 1939- *Who 92*
**LeMaster,** David 1949- *WhoAmP 91*
**LeMaster,** Edwin William 1940- *AmMWSc 92*
**Lemaster,** J.R. *DrAPF 91*
**LeMaster,** J. R. 1934- *WrDr 92*
**LeMaster,** James Gary 1946- *WhoAmP 91*
**Lemasters,** John J 1947- *AmMWSc 92*
**LeMasters,** Kim *IntMPA 92*
**Le Masurier,** Robert 1913- *Who 92*
**LeMasurier,** Wesley Ernest 1934- *AmMWSc 92*
**Le Mat,** Paul 1952- *IntMPA 92*
**LeMay,** Alan 1899- *BenetAL 91*
**LeMay,** Alan 1899-1964 *TwCWW 91*
**LeMay,** Charlotte Zihlman 1919- *AmMWSc 92*
**LeMay,** Curtis 1906-1990 *AnObit 1990*
**LeMay,** Curtis E. d1990 *IntWW 91N*
**LeMay,** Curtis Emerson 1906-1990 *FacFETw*
**Le May,** G. H. L. 1920- *WrDr 92*
**LeMay,** Harold E, Jr 1940- *AmMWSc 92*
**Lemay,** Jean-Paul 1923- *AmMWSc 92*
**LeMay,** Ronald T. *WhoMW 92*
**Lemay,** Thomas J. 1802-1863 *DcNCBi 4*
**Lembach,** Kenneth James 1939- *AmMWSc 92*
**Lembcke,** Cay 1885?-1965 *BiDExR*
**Lembeck,** William Jacobs 1928- *AmMWSc 92*
**Lemberg,** Aleksandr Yanovich 1921- *IntWW 91*
**Lemberg,** Howard Lee 1949- *AmMWSc 92*
**Lemberg,** Louis 1916- *AmMWSc 92*
**Lemberg,** Steven Floyd 1953- *WhoMW 92*
**Lemberg,** Thomas Michael 1946- *WhoAmL 92*
**Lemberger,** August Paul 1926- *AmMWSc 92*
**Lemberger,** Louis 1937- *AmMWSc 92*
**Lemberger,** Norma 1944- *WhoFI 92*
**Lembke,** Janet *DrAPF 91*
**Lembke,** Roger Roy 1940- *AmMWSc 92*
**Lembo,** Nicholas J 1929- *AmMWSc 92*
**Lembo,** Vincent Joseph 1950- *WhoAmL 92*
**Lemcke,** Dixie Lynn 1964- *WhoFI 92*
**Lemcoe,** M M *AmMWSc 92*
**Lemcool,** Herbert William, Jr. 1941- *WhoMW 92*
**Leme,** Hugo de Almeida 1917- *IntWW 91*
**Le Mee,** Jean M 1931- *AmMWSc 92*
**Lemeh,** Dorotha Hill *WhoBlA 92*
**Le Mehaute,** Bernard J 1927- *AmMWSc 92*
**Lemelin,** Roger 1919- *BenetAL 91, IntWW 91*
**Le Melle,** Gerald Anthony 1962- *WhoAmL 92*
**LeMelle,** Tilden J. 1929- *WhoBlA 92*
**LeMelle,** Wilbert John 1931- *WhoBlA 92*
**Lemen,** Robert Norton 1943- *WhoAmP 91*
**Le Menager,** Lois M. 1934- *WhoMW 92*
**Lemens,** William Vernon, Jr. 1935- *WhoFI 92*
**Lement,** Bernard S 1917- *AmMWSc 92*
**Lemer,** Andrew Charles 1944- *WhoFI 92*
**Lemer-Korney,** Ellen Terry 1943- *WhoWest 92*
**Lemerle,** Paul 1927- *IntWW 91*
**Lemery,** John David 1950- *WhoFI 92*
**Lemesh,** Nicholas Thomas 1946- *WhoEnt 92*
**Lemeshev,** Sergey Yakovlevich 1902-1977 *SovUnBD*
**Lemeshow,** Stanley Alan 1948- *AmMWSc 92*
**LeMessurier,** William James 1926- *AmMWSc 92*
**Lemieux,** Joseph 1902- *Who 92*
**Lemieux,** Joseph Henry 1931- *IntWW 91*
**LeMieux,** Linda Dailey 1953- *WhoWest 92*
**LeMieux,** Norman Taylor 1961- *WhoWest 92*
**Lemieux,** Raymond Urgel 1920- *AmMWSc 92, IntWW 91, Who 92*
**Leming,** Charles William 1943- *AmMWSc 92*
**Lemire,** Andre 1943- *WhoFI 92*
**Lemire,** David Stephen 1949- *WhoWest 92*
**Lemire,** George 1929- *WhoAmP 91*
**Lemire,** Robert James 1945- *AmMWSc 92*
**Lemire,** Roland A *WhoAmP 91*
**Lemire,** Ronald John 1933- *AmMWSc 92*
**Lemish,** John 1921- *AmMWSc 92*
**Lemkau,** Paul V 1909- *AmMWSc 92*
**Lemke,** Calvin A 1921- *AmMWSc 92*
**Lemke,** Carlton Edward 1920- *AmMWSc 92*
**Lemke,** Cheryl Lynn 1960- *WhoEnt 92*
**Lemke,** Cindy Ann 1963- *WhoMW 92*
**Lemke,** Corrine LaRue 1934- *WhoMW 92*
**Lemke,** Donald G 1932- *AmMWSc 92*
**Lemke,** George William 1943- *WhoMW 92*
**Lemke,** Helmut *IntWW 91N*
**Lemke,** James Underwood 1929- *AmMWSc 92*
**Lemke,** Judith A. 1952- *WhoAmL 92*
**Lemke,** LeRoy Walter 1935- *WhoAmP 91*
**Lemke,** Michael Robert 1958- *WhoRel 92*
**Lemke,** Paul Arenz 1937- *AmMWSc 92*
**Lemke,** Ronald Dennis 1941- *AmMWSc 92*
**Lemke,** Steve Warner 1951- *WhoRel 92*
**Lemke,** Thomas Franklin 1942- *AmMWSc 92*
**Lemke,** Thomas Lee 1940- *AmMWSc 92*
**Lemke,** William *WhoAmP 91*
**Lemke,** William Frederick 1878-1950 *AmPolLe*
**Lemkey,** Frankin David 1937- *AmMWSc 92*
**Lemkin,** James Anthony 1926- *Who 92*
**Lemle,** Robert Spencer 1953- *WhoAmL 92, WhoFI 92*
**Lemlein,** Neal C. *IntMPA 92*
**Lemley,** Jack Kenneth 1935- *Who 92*
**Lemley,** Robert Tyrone 1941- *WhoEnt 92*
**Lemlich,** Robert 1926- *AmMWSc 92*
**Lemly,** Samuel 1791-1848 *DcNCBi 4*
**Lemm,** Arthur Warren 1952- *AmMWSc 92*
**Lemmenes,** Mark Glen 1943- *WhoRel 92*
**Lemmerhirt,** Wayne Alan 1951- *WhoFI 92*
**Lemmerman,** Karl Edward 1923- *AmMWSc 92*
**Lemming,** John Frederick 1943- *AmMWSc 92*
**Lemmon,** Cyril Whitefield 1901- *Who 92*
**Lemmon,** David Hector 1931- *Who 92*
**Lemmon,** Donald H 1935- *AmMWSc 92*
**Lemmon,** George Colborne *Who 92*
**Lemmon,** George Colborne 1932- *WhoRel 92*
**Lemmon,** Harry T 1930- *WhoAmP 91*
**Lemmon,** Harry Thomas 1930- *WhoAmL 92*
**Lemmon,** Jack 1925- *FacFETw, IntMPA 92, IntWW 91, WhoEnt 92*
**Lemmon,** John Gill 1832-1908 *BiInAmS*
**Lemmon,** Marilyn Sue 1939- *WhoFI 92*
**Lemmon,** Richard Millington 1919- *AmMWSc 92*
**Lemmon,** Willard Lincoln 1924- *WhoAmP 91*
**Lemmond,** Charles D, Jr 1929- *WhoAmP 91*
**Lemmons,** Herbert Michael 1952- *WhoBlA 92*
**Lemmons,** Thom 1955- *ConAu 134*
**Lemnios,** A Z 1931- *AmMWSc 92*
**Lemnios,** William Zachary 1925- *AmMWSc 92*
**Lemnitzer,** Lyman L 1899-1988 *FacFETw*
**Le Moal,** Henri-Jean Alain 1912- *IntWW 91*
**Lemoine,** Albert N, Jr 1918- *AmMWSc 92*
**Lemoine,** Danny 1951- *WhoAmP 91*
**Lemoine,** Lawrence Louis 1951- *WhoFI 92*
**Lemon,** Bob 1920- *FacFETw*
**Lemon,** Chester Earl 1955- *WhoBlA 92*
**Lemon,** Dawnay 1912- *Who 92*
**Lemon,** Diana Jean 1951- *WhoWest 92*
**Lemon,** Don Mark *ScFEYrs*
**Lemon,** Edgar Rothwell 1921- *AmMWSc 92*
**Lemon,** Gary Dale 1948- *WhoMW 92*
**Lemon,** Jerry Wayne 1935- *WhoRel 92*
**Lemon,** Lee Thomas 1931- *IntAu&W 91, WrDr 92*
**Lemon,** Leslie Gene 1940- *WhoAmL 92, WhoFI 92*
**Lemon,** Leslie Roy 1947- *AmMWSc 92*
**Lemon,** Liz 1949- *TwCPaSc*
**Lemon,** Meadowlark 1932- *WhoBlA 92*
**Lemon,** Michael Wayne, Sr. 1953- *WhoBlA 92*
**Lemon,** Peter Willian Reginald 1951- *AmMWSc 92*
**Lemon,** Roy Richard Henry 1927- *AmMWSc 92*
**Lemon,** William Jacob 1932- *WhoAmL 92*
**LeMond,** Greg 1962- *FacFETw*
**Lemonde,** Andre 1921- *AmMWSc 92*
**LeMone,** David V 1932- *AmMWSc 92*
**Le Mone,** Evelyn Frances 1907- *WhoEnt 92*
**LeMone,** Margaret Anne 1946- *AmMWSc 92*
**Lemonick,** Aaron 1923- *AmMWSc 92*
**Lemonides,** Charles Spencer 1962- *WhoFI 92*
**Lemons,** Charles Fred 1926- *WhoAmP 91*
**Lemons,** Charles Thurman 1949- *WhoWest 92*
**Lemons,** Jack Eugene 1937- *AmMWSc 92*
**Lemons,** James Stanley 1938- *WrDr 92*
**Lemons,** Jimmie Wayne 1958- *WhoRel 92*
**Lemons,** Thomas M 1934- *AmMWSc 92*
**Lemont,** Francesca Mary 1965- *WhoEnt 92*
**Lemontt,** Jeffrey Fielding 1944- *AmMWSc 92*
**Lemos,** Anthony M 1930- *AmMWSc 92*
**Lemos,** David 1956- *WhoWest 92*
**Lemos,** Noah Marcelino 1956- *WhoHisp 92*
**Lemos,** Ramon Marcelino 1927- *WhoHisp 92, WrDr 92*
**Lemos Simmonds,** Carlos *IntWW 91*
**Lemp,** John, Jr. 1936- *WhoFI 92*
**Lemp,** John Frederick, Jr 1928- *AmMWSc 92*
**Lemper,** Anthony Louis 1939- *AmMWSc 92*
**Lemper,** Ute 1963- *IntWW 91*
**Lempert,** Edward T 1961- *WhoAmP 91*
**Lempert,** Joseph 1913- *AmMWSc 92*
**Lempert,** Lonnie David 1951- *WhoFI 92*
**Lempert,** Neil 1933- *AmMWSc 92*
**Lempert,** Richard Owen 1942- *WhoAmL 92*
**Lempicki,** Alexander 1922- *AmMWSc 92*
**Lempke,** Robert Everett 1924- *AmMWSc 92*
**Lempp,** Steffen 1959- *WhoMW 92*
**Lempres,** Martin Vincent 1962- *WhoMW 92*
**Lemus,** Fraterno 1948- *WhoHisp 92*
**Lemus,** Jose Maria 1911- *IntWW 91*
**Lemyre,** C 1934- *AmMWSc 92*
**Lena,** Adolph J 1925- *AmMWSc 92*
**Lena,** Dan 1955- *ConAu 134*
**Lena,** Marie *ConAu 134*
**Lena,** Marie H. 1956- *ConAu 134*
**Lenaert,** Henri 1915- *IntWW 91*
**Lenaerts,** Guido J. 1950- *WhoMW 92*
**Lenagh,** Tod C. 1959- *WhoFI 92*
**Lenaghan,** Brenda 1941- *TwCPaSc*
**Lenaghan,** Michael John 1943- *WhoMW 92*
**Lenahan,** Timothy George 1956- *WhoAmL 92*
**Lenard,** Andrew 1927- *AmMWSc 92*
**Lenard,** John 1937- *AmMWSc 92*
**Lenard,** Lloyd Edgar 1922- *WhoAmP 91, WhoFI 92*
**Lenard,** Mark 1927- *ConTFT 9*
**Lenard,** Michael Barry 1955- *WhoAmL 92, WhoFI 92, WhoWest 92*
**Lenard,** Philipp 1862-1947 *EncTR 91 [port]*
**Lenard,** Philipp Eduard Anton von 1862-1947 *WhoNob 90*
**Lenarz,** William Henry 1940- *AmMWSc 92*
**Lence,** Julio G. *WhoHisp 92*
**Lenchner,** Nathaniel Herbert 1923- *AmMWSc 92*
**Lendais,** Jean-Pierre 1937- *WhoAmL 92*
**Lendall,** Jim Everett 1947- *WhoAmP 91*
**Lendaris,** George G 1935- *AmMWSc 92*
**Lender,** Adam *AmMWSc 92*
**Lenders,** Jozef Gerard 1957- *WhoEnt 92*
**Lenders,** Patrick Madeleine 1947- *WhoWest 92*
**Lendio,** Darolyn Hatsuko 1958- *WhoAmL 92*
**Lendl,** Ivan 1960- *FacFETw, IntWW 91*
**Lendrum,** Alan Chalmers 1906- *Who 92*
**Lendt,** Harold Hanford 1922- *WhoMW 92*
**Lendvai,** Paul 1929- *WrDr 92*
**Lenel,** Fritz 1907- *AmMWSc 92*
**Lener,** Walter 1925- *AmMWSc 92*
**Lenert,** Louis Henry 1936- *WhoFI 92*
**Lenes,** Bruce Allan 1949- *AmMWSc 92*
**Leney,** Lawrence 1917- *AmMWSc 92*
**Lenfant,** Claude J M 1928- *AmMWSc 92*
**Lenfest,** Harold Fitz Gerald 1930- *WhoEnt 92*
**Leng,** Douglas E 1928- *AmMWSc 92*
**Leng,** Earl Reece 1921- *AmMWSc 92*
**Leng,** Marguerite Lambert 1926- *AmMWSc 92*
**Leng,** Peter 1925- *Who 92*
**Leng,** Virginia Helen Antoinette 1955- *Who 92*
**Lenga,** J. Thomas 1942- *WhoAmL 92*
**Lengefeld,** William Chris 1937- *WhoWest 92*
**Lengel,** Robert Charles 1957- *AmMWSc 92*
**Lengemann,** Frederick William 1925- *AmMWSc 92*
**Lengerich,** Dorothy Anne *WhoRel 92*
**L'Engle,** Madeleine 1918- *BenetAL 91, IntAu&W 91, TwCSFW 91, WrDr 92*
**Lengomin,** Juan Alberto 1953- *WhoHisp 92*
**Lengyel,** Bela Adalbert 1910- *AmMWSc 92*
**Lengyel,** Cornel 1915- *WrDr 92*
**Lengyel,** Cornel Adam *DrAPF 91*
**Lengyel,** G 1927- *AmMWSc 92*
**Lengyel,** Istvan 1931- *AmMWSc 92*
**Lengyel,** Judith Ann 1945- *AmMWSc 92*
**Lengyel,** Menyhert Melchior 1880-1974 *LiExTwC*
**Lengyel,** Peter 1929- *AmMWSc 92*
**Lenhard,** James M *AmMWSc 92*
**Lenhard,** Joseph Andrew 1929- *AmMWSc 92*
**Lenhardt,** Alfonso Emanuel 1943- *WhoBlA 92*
**Lenhardt,** Martin Louis 1944- *AmMWSc 92*
**Lenhart,** Ben B. 1934- *WhoMW 92*
**Lenhart,** Gary *DrAPF 91*
**Lenhart,** Jack G 1929- *AmMWSc 92*
**Lenherr,** Donald William 1940- *WhoIns 92*
**Lenhert,** Anne Gerhardt 1936- *AmMWSc 92*
**Lenhert,** Donald H 1934- *AmMWSc 92*
**Lenhert,** P Galen 1933- *AmMWSc 92*
**Lenhoff,** Howard Maer 1929- *AmMWSc 92*
**Leni,** Paul 1885-1929 *IntDcF 2-2 [port]*
**Leniado-Chira,** Joseph 1934- *WhoEnt 92*
**Leniart,** Daniel Stanley 1943- *AmMWSc 92*
**Lenica,** Jan 1928- *IntWW 91*
**Lenihan,** Brian Joseph 1930- *IntWW 91, Who 92*
**Lenihan,** J Michael *WhoAmP 91*
**Lenihan,** Kevin Michael 1952- *WhoFI 92*
**Lenihan,** Patrick Miner 1937- *WhoFI 92*
**Lenihan,** William Farringer 1930- *WhoAmL 92*
**Lenin** 1870-1924 *FacFETw [port]*
**Lenin,** Vladimir Il'ich 1870-1924 *SovUnBD*
**Lenington,** Jerry Eugene 1938- *WhoWest 92*
**Lenix-Hooker,** Catherine Jeanette 1947- *WhoBlA 92*
**Lenk,** Barbara Ann 1950- *WhoAmL 92*
**Lenk,** Christa C. 1950- *WhoAmL 92*
**Lenk,** Hans Albert Paul 1935- *IntWW 91*
**Lenk,** Thomas 1933- *IntWW 91*
**Lenke,** Gerd Michael 1927- *WhoMW 92*
**Lenke,** Hal *DrAPF 91*
**Lenke,** Roger Rand 1946- *AmMWSc 92*
**Lenker,** Floyd William 1933- *WhoMW 92*
**Lenker,** Susan Stamm 1945- *AmMWSc 92*
**Lenker,** William Fred 1923- *WhoAmP 91*
**Lenkoski,** L Douglas 1925- *AmMWSc 92*
**Lenling,** William James 1961- *AmMWSc 92*
**Lenn,** Nicholas Joseph 1938- *AmMWSc 92*
**Lennard,** Hugh Dacre B. *Who 92*
**Lennartz,** David Carl 1955- *WhoWest 92*
**Lennartz,** Michelle R *AmMWSc 92*
**Lennarz,** William J 1934- *AmMWSc 92*
**Lenneberg,** Hans 1924- *WhoEnt 92*
**Lennep,** Emile van 1915- *IntWW 91*
**Lennette,** Edwin Herman 1908- *AmMWSc 92, WhoWest 92*
**Lenney,** James F. 1918- *WhoWest 92*
**Lenney,** James Francis 1918- *AmMWSc 92*
**Lennick,** Robert Brent 1956- *WhoRel 92*
**Lennie,** Douglas 1910- *Who 92*
**Lenning,** James Eric 1947- *WhoFI 92*
**Lenning,** John Orlin 1933- *WhoEnt 92*
**Lennings,** Manfred 1934- *IntWW 91*
**Lennkh,** Georg 1939- *IntWW 91*
**Lennon,** Arthur Thomas 1923- *WhoAmP 91*
**Lennon,** Ciaran 1947- *TwCPaSc*
**Lennon,** Dennis d1991 *Who 92N*
**Lennon,** Edward Joseph 1927- *AmMWSc 92*
**Lennon,** Frank M. 1938- *WhoFI 92*
**Lennon,** Gordon 1911- *Who 92*
**Lennon,** John 1940-1980 *FacFETw [port], NewAmDM*
**Lennon,** John W 1917- *AmMWSc 92*
**Lennon,** Patrick James 1950- *AmMWSc 92*
**Lennon,** Peter Dean 1949- *WhoAmP 91*
**Lennon,** Thomas F. 1951- *WhoEnt 92*
**Lennon,** Vanda Alice 1943- *AmMWSc 92*
**Lennon,** William H 1838-1913 *BiInAmS*
**Lennox** *Who 92*
**Lennox,** Arlene Judith 1942- *AmMWSc 92*
**Lennox,** Charlotte 1729?-1804 *RfGEnL 91*
**Lennox,** Charlotte 1730?-1804 *BlkwCEP*
**Lennox,** Charlotte Ramsay 1720-1804 *BenetAL 91*
**Lennox,** David Preston 1952- *WhoRel 92*
**Lennox,** Donald Haughton 1924- *AmMWSc 92*
**Lennox,** Edward Newman 1925- *WhoFI 92*
**Lennox,** Gloria 1931- *WhoWest 92*
**Lennox,** Lionel Patrick Madill 1949- *Who 92*
**Lennox,** Robert Bruce 1957- *AmMWSc 92*
**Lennox,** Robert Smith 1909- *Who 92*
**Lennox,** William C 1937- *AmMWSc 92*
**Lennox-Boyd** *Who 92*
**Lennox-Boyd,** Mark Alexander 1943- *Who 92*

**Lennox-Boyd,** Simon Ronald Rupert *IntWW 91*
**Lennox-Smith,** Judith 1953- *ConAu 134*
**Leno,** Jay *LesBEnT 92*
**Leno,** Jay 1950- *IntMPA 92, WhoEnt 92*
**Leno,** M John 1944- *WhoAmP 91*
**Le Noble,** William Jacobus 1928- *AmMWSc 92*
**Lenoff,** Michele Malka 1961- *WhoAmL 92*
**Lenoir,** Gloria Cisneros 1951- *WhoFI 92*
**Lenoir,** Henry 1912- *WhoBlA 92*
**Lenoir,** Kip 1943- *WhoBlA 92*
**Lenoir,** Walter Waightstill 1823-1890 *DcNCBi 4*
**Lenoir,** William 1751-1839 *DcNCBi 4*
**Lenoir,** William Benjamin 1939- *AmMWSc 92*
**LeNoir,** William Cannon, Jr 1929- *AmMWSc 92*
**LeNoire,** Rosetta 1911- *WhoBlA 92*
**Lenon,** Herbert Lee 1939- *AmMWSc 92*
**Lenon,** Richard Allen 1920- *WhoFI 92*
**Lenowitz,** Harris *DrAPF 91*
**Lenox,** James 1800-1880 *BenetAL 91*
**Lenox,** Marjory Allen 1944- *WhoRel 92*
**Lenox,** Ronald Sheaffer 1948- *AmMWSc 92*
**Lenox,** Timothy Leonard, II 1956- *WhoMW 92*
**Lenpi,** Gertrud *DcAmImH*
**Lenroot,** Katharine F. 1891-1982 *CurBio 91N*
**Lenschow,** Donald Henry 1938- *AmMWSc 92*
**Lense,** Edward *DrAPF 91*
**Lensink,** Everett R *WhoAmP 91*
**Lenski,** Lois 1893-1974 *BenetAL 91, ChILR 26 [port]*
**Lensky,** Leib d1991 *NewYTBS 91*
**Lenstra,** Hendrik W 1949- *AmMWSc 92*
**Lent,** Berkeley 1921- *WhoAmP 91*
**Lent,** Blair 1930- *IntAu&W 91, WrDr 92*
**Lent,** John A. 1936- *WrDr 92*
**Lent,** Kent Robert 1939- *WhoWest 92*
**Lent,** Norman F. 1931- *AlmAP 92 [port], WhoAmP 91*
**Lente,** Frederick Divoux 1823-1883 *DcNCBi 4*
**Lentes,** David Eugene 1951- *WhoFI 92, WhoWest 92*
**Lentfoehr,** Mary Therese 1902-1981 *HanAmWH*
**Lentine,** John Anthony 1960- *WhoAmL 92*
**Lentini,** Eugene Anthony 1929- *AmMWSc 92*
**Lentino,** James V. 1961- *WhoFI 92*
**Lentol,** Joseph Roland 1943- *WhoAmP 91*
**Lenton,** Aylmer Ingram 1927- *IntWW 91*
**Lenton,** Ingram 1927- *Who 92*
**Lenton,** Philip A 1919- *AmMWSc 92*
**Lents,** Don Glaude 1949- *WhoMW 92*
**Lents,** Peggy Iglauer 1950- *WhoMW 92*
**Lentulov,** Aristarkh Vasil'evich 1882-1943 *SovUnBD*
**Lentz,** Barry R 1944- *AmMWSc 92*
**Lentz,** Bernard Frederic 1948- *WhoFI 92*
**Lentz,** Charles Wesley 1924- *AmMWSc 92, WhoMW 92*
**Lentz,** Claude Peter 1919- *AmMWSc 92*
**Lentz,** Daniel K. 1942- *NewAmDM*
**Lentz,** Gary Lynn 1943- *AmMWSc 92*
**Lentz,** Harold James 1947- *WhoAmL 92*
**Lentz,** Linda Kay 1936- *WhoMW 92*
**Lentz,** Mark Steven 1949- *AmMWSc 92*
**Lentz,** Paul Jackson, Jr 1944- *AmMWSc 92*
**Lentz,** Paul Lewis 1918- *AmMWSc 92*
**Lentz,** Richard David 1942- *WhoMW 92*
**Lentz,** Thomas Lawrence 1939- *AmMWSc 92*
**Lenya,** Lotte 1898-1981 *FacFETw, NewAmDM*
**Lenya,** Lotte 1900-1981 *EncTR 91 [port]*
**Lenz,** Alfred C 1929- *AmMWSc 92*
**Lenz,** Arno T 1906- *AmMWSc 92*
**Lenz,** Charles Eldon 1926- *AmMWSc 92*
**enz,** Edward Arnold 1942- *WhoAmL 92*
**enz,** Fritz 1887-1976 *EncTR 91*
**enz,** George H 1939- *AmMWSc 92*
**enz,** George Richard 1941- *AmMWSc 92*
**enz,** Henry Paul 1925- *WhoFI 92*
**enz,** Jacob Michael Reinhold 1751-1792 *BlkwCEP*
**enz,** Kay 1953- *IntMPA 92, WhoEnt 92*
**enz,** Kenneth Robert 1957- *WhoRel 92*
**enz,** Paul Heins 1938- *AmMWSc 92*
**enz,** Peter Gernard 1946- *WhoEnt 92*
**enz,** Philip Joseph 1940- *WhoWest 92*
**enz,** Robert William 1926- *AmMWSc 92*
**enz,** Siegfried 1926- *IntWW 91*
**enz,** Widukind 1919- *IntWW 91*
**enz,** William C. 1958- *WhoRel 92*
**enzen,** K H 1921- *AmMWSc 92*
**enzen,** Louis Christmas 1943- *WhoAmL 92*
**enzo,** Thomas John 1949- *WhoWest 92*
**eo I** 400?-474 *EncEarC*
**eo Africanus** 1485?- *HisDSpE*
**eo I,** The Great *EncEarC*
**Leo,** Albert Joseph 1925- *AmMWSc 92*
**Leo,** Gerhard William 1930- *AmMWSc 92*
**Leo,** Karen Ann 1945- *WhoWest 92*
**Leo,** Kathleen Ripley *DrAPF 91*
**Leo,** Leonardo 1694-1744 *NewAmDM*
**Leo,** Malcolm 1944- *WhoEnt 92*
**Leo,** Mary *Who 92*
**Leo,** Mary Gaye 1951- *WhoEnt 92, WhoWest 92*
**Leo,** Robert Joseph 1939- *WhoWest 92*
**Leomporra,** Dominique 1960- *WhoEnt 92*
**Leon,** Abilio *WhoHisp 92*
**Leon,** Arthur Sol 1931- *AmMWSc 92*
**Leon,** B J 1932- *AmMWSc 92*
**Leon,** Edward 1925- *WhoFI 92, WhoMW 92*
**Leon,** Fernando Luis 1916- *WhoHisp 92*
**Leon,** H I 1924- *AmMWSc 92*
**Leon,** Henry A 1928- *AmMWSc 92*
**Leon,** Heriberto 1956- *WhoHisp 92*
**Leon,** Jack Paul 1930- *WhoAmL 92*
**Leon,** John 1934- *Who 92*
**Leon,** Kenneth Allen 1937- *AmMWSc 92*
**Leon,** Luis Manuel, Jr. 1955- *WhoHisp 92*
**Leon,** Melvin 1936- *AmMWSc 92*
**Leon,** Michael Allan 1947- *AmMWSc 92*
**Leon,** Myron A 1926- *AmMWSc 92*
**Leon,** Pedro Cieza de *HisDSpE*
**Leon,** Ralph 1929- *WhoHisp 92*
**Leon,** Ramon V 1948- *AmMWSc 92*
**Leon,** Raymond J. 1949- *WhoHisp 92*
**Leon,** Reinaldo, Jr. 1957- *WhoHisp 92*
**Leon,** Robert Leonard 1925- *AmMWSc 92*
**Leon,** Robert S. 1947- *WhoHisp 92*
**Leon,** Rolando Luis 1952- *WhoAmL 92*
**Leon,** Shalom A 1935- *AmMWSc 92*
**Leon,** Sol 1913- *IntMPA 92*
**Leon,** Tania J. 1943- *WhoBlA 92, WhoHisp 92*
**Leon,** Tania Justina 1943- *WhoEnt 92*
**Leon,** Wilmer J., Jr. 1920- *WhoBlA 92*
**Leon Guerrero,** Juan Duenas 1935- *WhoHisp 92*
**Leon Guerrero,** Wilfred Pacelle 1942- *WhoWest 92*
**Leon Pinelo,** Antonio 1590?-1660 *HisDSpE*
**Leon Portilla,** Miguel 1926- *IntWW 91*
**Leonard,** A 1938- *AmMWSc 92*
**Leonard,** Alan Thomas 1917- *WhoMW 92*
**Leonard,** Arlene Athena 1917- *WhoAmP 91*
**Leonard,** Arnold S 1930- *AmMWSc 92*
**Leonard,** Arthur J. 1950- *WhoAmL 92*
**Leonard,** B F 1921- *AmMWSc 92*
**Leonard,** Bernard Michael 1947- *WhoFI 92*
**Leonard,** Bill *LesBEnT 92*
**Leonard,** Billie Charles 1934- *AmMWSc 92*
**Leonard,** Bob, Jr 1950- *WhoAmP 91*
**Leonard,** Bowen Raydo, Jr 1926- *AmMWSc 92*
**Leonard,** Brian E. 1936- *IntWW 91*
**Leonard,** Brian Kelly 1958- *WhoEnt 92*
**Leonard,** Brian Phillip 1936- *AmMWSc 92*
**Leonard,** Burleigh C. W. 1951- *WhoAmL 92*
**Leonard,** Byrdie A. Larkin *WhoBlA 92*
**Leonard,** Byron Peter 1925- *AmMWSc 92*
**Leonard,** Carl Kiser 1937- *WhoMW 92*
**Leonard,** Carol 1945- *WhoAmP 91*
**Leonard,** Carolyn Marie 1943- *WhoBlA 92*
**Leonard,** Catherine W. 1909- *WhoBlA 92*
**Leonard,** Charles Brown, Jr 1934- *AmMWSc 92*
**Leonard,** Charles Grant 1939- *AmMWSc 92*
**Leonard,** Charles Lester 1861-1913 *BiInAmS*
**Leonard,** Chester D 1907- *AmMWSc 92*
**Leonard,** Christiana Morison 1938- *AmMWSc 92*
**Leonard,** Clara Temple 1828-1904 *HanAmWH*
**Leonard,** Constance 1923- *IntAu&W 91, WrDr 92*
**Leonard,** Craig Eugene 1949- *WhoMW 92*
**Leonard,** Daniel 1740-1829 *BenetAL 91*
**Leonard,** David E 1934- *AmMWSc 92*
**Leonard,** David Henry 1933- *WhoEnt 92*
**Leonard,** David Morse 1949- *WhoAmL 92*
**Leonard,** Dick *Who 92*
**Leonard,** Dick 1930- *IntAu&W 91*
**Leonard,** Edward 1932- *AmMWSc 92*
**Leonard,** Edward Charles, Jr 1927- *AmMWSc 92*
**Leonard,** Edward H 1919- *AmMWSc 92*
**Leonard,** Edward Joseph 1926- *AmMWSc 92*
**Leonard,** Edwin Deane 1929- *WhoAmL 92*
**Leonard,** Elizabeth Adney 1917- *WhoWest 92*
**Leonard,** Ellen Marie 1944- *AmMWSc 92*
**Leonard,** Elmore 1925- *ConNov 91, IntAu&W 91, TwCWW 91, WrDr 92*
**Leonard,** Elmore John 1925- *IntWW 91*
**Leonard,** Emilio Manuel, Jr. 1945- *WhoHisp 92*
**Leonard,** George Edmund 1940- *WhoFI 92*
**Leonard,** George Jay 1946- *WhoEnt 92*
**Leonard,** Gerald E 1924- *WhoAmP 91*
**Leonard,** Gerald Thomas 1954- *WhoAmP 91*
**Leonard,** Gloria Jean 1947- *WhoBlA 92*
**Leonard,** Graham Douglas 1921- *IntWW 91, Who 92, WhoRel 92*
**Leonard,** H. Jeffrey 1954- *WhoFI 92*
**Leonard,** Hamilton John 1926- *Who 92*
**Leonard,** Henry Eugene 1956- *WhoMW 92*
**Leonard,** Henry Siggins, Jr 1930- *AmMWSc 92*
**Leonard,** Herbert B. *LesBEnT 92*
**Leonard,** Hugh 1926- *FacFETw, IntAu&W 91, IntWW 91, Who 92, WrDr 92*
**Leonard,** Jack E 1943- *AmMWSc 92*
**Leonard,** Jacques Walter 1936- *AmMWSc 92*
**Leonard,** James Charles Beresford Whyte 1905- *Who 92*
**Leonard,** James Joseph 1924- *AmMWSc 92*
**Leonard,** Janet Louise 1953- *AmMWSc 92*
**Leonard,** Jeff 1955- *WhoBlA 92*
**Leonard,** Jerris 1931- *WhoAmP 91*
**Leonard,** John *DrAPF 91, Who 92*
**Leonard,** John Alex 1937- *AmMWSc 92*
**Leonard,** John Dunbar, Jr. 1933- *WhoFI 92*
**Leonard,** John Edward 1918- *AmMWSc 92*
**Leonard,** John Erwyn 1947- *WhoFI 92*
**Leonard,** John Joseph 1949- *AmMWSc 92*
**Leonard,** John Lander 1935- *AmMWSc 92*
**Leonard,** John W *AmMWSc 92*
**Leonard,** Joseph Thomas 1932- *AmMWSc 92*
**Leonard,** Joseph William 1930- *AmMWSc 92*
**Leonard,** Juanita Louise Evans 1939- *WhoRel 92*
**Leonard,** June 1926- *WhoAmP 91*
**Leonard,** Kathleen Mary 1954- *AmMWSc 92*
**Leonard,** Keith 1921- *TwCPaSc*
**Leonard,** Kurt John 1939- *AmMWSc 92*
**Leonard,** Larry Dale 1948- *WhoAmL 92*
**Leonard,** Laurence 1932- *AmMWSc 92*
**Leonard,** Leon Lank, Sr. 1922- *WhoBlA 92*
**Leonard,** Margaret J *WhoAmP 91*
**Leonard,** Martha Frances 1916- *AmMWSc 92*
**Leonard,** Maurice 1939- *WrDr 92*
**Leonard,** Michael 1933- *TwCPaSc*
**Leonard,** Michael A. 1937- *WhoMW 92*
**Leonard,** Michael William 1916- *Who 92*
**Leonard,** Molly Ann 1932- *WhoAmP 91*
**Leonard,** Nelson Jordan 1916- *AmMWSc 92, IntWW 91*
**Leonard,** Paul Roger 1943- *WhoAmP 91*
**Leonard,** Peter 1952- *WhoEnt 92*
**Leonard,** Philip Dale 1948- *WhoEnt 92*
**Leonard,** Ralph Avery 1937- *AmMWSc 92*
**Leonard,** Ray Charles 1956- *IntWW 91*
**Leonard,** Raymond Wesley 1909- *WhoFI 92*
**Leonard,** Regina Mary 1926- *WhoRel 92*
**Leonard,** Reid Hayward 1918- *AmMWSc 92*
**Leonard,** Richard D, Jr *WhoIns 92*
**Leonard,** Richard Lawrence 1930- *Who 92*
**Leonard,** Robert Beverly 1922- *WhoFI 92*
**Leonard,** Robert Dougherty 1942- *WhoMW 92*
**Leonard,** Robert F 1934- *AmMWSc 92*
**Leonard,** Robert Gresham 1937- *AmMWSc 92*
**Leonard,** Robert Sean 1969- *IntMPA 92*
**Leonard,** Robert Stuart 1930- *AmMWSc 92*
**Leonard,** Robert Thomas 1943- *AmMWSc 92*
**Leonard,** Roy J 1929- *AmMWSc 92*
**Leonard,** Sheldon *LesBEnT 92*
**Leonard,** Sheldon 1907- *IntMPA 92, WhoEnt 92*
**Leonard,** Silvio 1955- *BlkOlyM*
**Leonard,** Stanley Lee 1926- *AmMWSc 92*
**Leonard,** Sugar Ray 1957- *WhoBlA 92*
**Leonard,** Sugar Ray Charles 1956- *BlkOlyM*
**Leonard,** Thomas A 1946- *WhoAmP 91*
**Leonard,** Thomas Aloysius 1946- *WhoAmL 92*
**Leonard,** Thomas Joseph 1937- *AmMWSc 92*
**Leonard,** Tim 1940- *WhoAmP 91*
**Leonard,** Timothy Dwight 1940- *WhoAmL 92*
**Leonard,** Tom 1944- *ConPo 91, IntAu&W 91, WrDr 92*
**Leonard,** Vincent Albert 1957- *WhoEnt 92*
**Leonard,** Walter Fenner 1907- *WhoBlA 92*
**Leonard,** Walter J. 1929- *WhoBlA 92*
**Leonard,** Walter Raymond 1923- *AmMWSc 92*
**Leonard,** Warren J 1952- *AmMWSc 92*
**Leonard,** Will Ernest, Jr. 1935- *WhoAmL 92*
**Leonard,** William Ellery 1876-1944 *BenetAL 91*
**Leonard,** William F. 1926- *WhoAmL 92*
**Leonard,** William F 1938- *AmMWSc 92*
**Leonard,** William George 1951- *WhoMW 92*
**Leonard,** William J, Jr 1936- *AmMWSc 92*
**Leonard,** William L. *WhoAmL 92*
**Leonard,** William R 1947- *WhoAmP 91*
**Leonard,** William Wilson 1934- *AmMWSc 92*
**Leonard,** Zenas 1809-1857 *BenetAL 91*
**Leonard-Williams,** Harold Guy 1911- *Who 92*
**Leonarda,** Isabella *NewAmDM*
**Leonardi,** Jeffrey Thomas 1961- *WhoEnt 92*
**Leonardich,** Agnes M. *WhoRel 92*
**Leonardo,** Louis Charles 1953- *WhoWest 92*
**Leonards,** G A 1921- *AmMWSc 92*
**Leonberger,** Frederick John 1947- *AmMWSc 92*
**Leoncavallo,** Ruggero 1857-1919 *NewAmDM*
**Leondopoulos,** Jordan *WhoEnt 92*
**Leone,** Bryan Anthony 1946- *WhoRel 92*
**Leone,** Charles Abner 1918- *AmMWSc 92*
**Leone,** Frank 1939- *WhoEnt 92*
**Leone,** Frank Harrison 1944- *WhoWest 92*
**Leone,** Fred Charles 1922- *AmMWSc 92*
**Leone,** Giovanni 1908- *IntWW 91*
**Leone,** Ida Alba 1922- *AmMWSc 92*
**Leone,** James A 1937- *AmMWSc 92*
**Leone,** James William 1944- *WhoMW 92*
**Leone,** John J 1946- *WhoAmP 91*
**Leone,** Joseph Lawrence, Jr. 1948- *WhoAmL 92*
**Leone,** L Ruthe 1924- *WhoAmP 91*
**Leone,** Lucile P 1902- *AmMWSc 92*
**Leone,** Lyn 1950- *WhoAmP 91*
**Leone,** Lynn *DrAPF 91*
**Leone,** Patrick John 1955- *WhoWest 92*
**Leone,** Ronald Edmund 1942- *AmMWSc 92*
**Leone,** Sergio 1921-1989 *FacFETw*
**Leone,** Sergio 1929-1989 *IntDcF 2-2 [port]*
**Leone,** Stephen Robert 1948- *AmMWSc 92*
**Leone,** William Charles 1924- *WhoFI 92, WhoWest 92*
**Leonesio-Mons,** Claudia Carruth 1952- *WhoEnt 92*
**Leonetti,** Matthew Frank *WhoEnt 92*
**Leonetti,** Michael Edward 1955- *WhoFI 92, WhoMW 92*
**Leonetti,** Philip *NewYTBS 91 [port]*
**Leoney,** Antoinette E. M. 1950- *WhoBlA 92*
**Leong,** Carol Jean 1942- *WhoFI 92, WhoWest 92*
**Leong,** G. Keong 1950- *WhoMW 92*
**Leong,** George H. *DrAPF 91*
**Leong,** Gor Yun *IntAu&W 91X*
**Leong,** Jo-Ann Ching 1942- *AmMWSc 92*
**Leong,** Joseph P 1915- *WhoAmP 91*
**Leong,** Kam Choy 1920- *AmMWSc 92*
**Leong,** Russell C. *DrAPF 91*
**Leonhard,** Kurt Albert Ernst 1910- *IntWW 91*
**Leonhard,** William E 1914- *AmMWSc 92*
**Leonhardt,** Clifton Andrew 1947- *WhoAmP 91*
**Leonhardt,** Earl A 1919- *AmMWSc 92*
**Leonhardt,** Ernst 1885-1945 *BiDExR*
**Leonhardt,** Frederick Wayne 1949- *WhoAmL 92*
**Leonhardt,** Gustav 1928- *NewAmDM*
**Leonhardt,** Rudolf Walter 1921- *IntWW 91*
**Leonhardt,** Thomas Wilburn 1943- *WhoWest 92*
**Leonhart,** William 1919- *IntWW 91*
**Leoni,** Raul 1905-1972 *FacFETw*
**Leoni,** Robert Joseph 1930- *WhoMW 92*
**Leonidov,** Ivan Il'ich 1902-1959 *SovUnBD*
**Leonidov,** Leonid Mironovich 1873-1943 *SovUnBD*
**Leonin** *NewAmDM*
**Leonora,** John 1928- *AmMWSc 92*
**Leonov,** Aleksey Arkhipovich 1934- *IntWW 91*
**Leonov,** Alexei 1934- *FacFETw*
**Leonov,** Leonid Maksimovich 1899- *FacFETw*
**Leonov,** Pavel Artemovich 1918- *SovUnBD*
**Leontie,** Roger Eugene 1937- *WhoWest 92*
**Leontief,** Estelle *DrAPF 91*
**Leontief,** Wassily 1906- *FacFETw, IntWW 91, Who 92, WhoFI 92, WrDr 92*
**Leontief,** Wassily W 1906- *WhoNob 90*
**Leontieff,** Alexandre 1948- *IntWW 91*
**Leontieva,** Valentina Mikhailovna 1923- *IntWW 91*
**Leontis,** T E 1917- *AmMWSc 92*

**Leontius of Byzantium** d543? *EncEarC*
**Leontsinis,** George John 1937- *WhoAmL 92*
**Leonty,** Metropolitan 1876-1965 *RelLAm 91*
**Leopold II** 1747-1792 *BlkwCEP*
**Leopold III** 1901-1983 *EncTR 91 [port], FacFETw*
**Leopold and Loeb** *FacFETw [port]*
**Leopold,** Aldo 1887-1948 *BenetAL 91, FacFETw*
**Leopold,** Aldo Carl 1919- *AmMWSc 92*
**Leopold,** Bengt 1922- *AmMWSc 92*
**Leopold,** Daniel J *AmMWSc 92*
**Leopold,** Donald Joseph 1956- *AmMWSc 92*
**Leopold,** Estella 1927- *AmMWSc 92*
**Leopold,** G. Vernon 1923- *WhoAmL 92*
**Leopold,** Irving Henry 1915- *WhoWest 92*
**Leopold,** Jay Robert 1964- *WhoFI 92*
**Leopold,** John Peter 1946- *WhoAmL 92*
**Leopold,** Josef 1889-1941 *BiDExR*
**Leopold,** Louis Emanuel 1922- *WhoAmP 91*
**Leopold,** Luna Bergere 1915- *AmMWSc 92, IntWW 91*
**Leopold,** M Edwin 1934- *WhoIns 92*
**Leopold,** Mark F. 1950- *WhoAmL 92*
**Leopold,** Reuven 1938- *AmMWSc 92*
**Leopold,** Robert L 1922- *AmMWSc 92*
**Leopold,** Robert Summers 1915- *AmMWSc 92*
**Leopold,** Roger Allen 1937- *AmMWSc 92*
**Leopold,** Stratton Peter 1943- *WhoEnt 92*
**Leopold,** Warren Edward 1953- *WhoIns 92*
**Leopold,** Wilbur Richard, III 1949- *AmMWSc 92*
**Leoro-Franco,** Galo *Who 92*
**Leoschke,** William Leroy 1927- *AmMWSc 92, WhoMW 92*
**Leotard,** Francois Gerard Marie 1942- *IntWW 91*
**Leovy,** Conway B 1933- *AmMWSc 92*
**Lepa,** Robert Arthur 1958- *WhoFI 92*
**LePage,** Gerald Alvin 1917- *WhoWest 92*
**LePage,** Raoul 1938- *AmMWSc 92*
**Le Page,** Wilbur R 1911- *AmMWSc 92*
**Le Page du Pratz,** Antoine Simon 1690?-1775 *BenetAL 91*
**Le Paige,** Louis-Adrien 1712-1802 *BlkwCEP*
**Lepak,** David John 1959- *WhoAmP 91*
**Lepak,** Richard Herman 1945- *WhoMW 92*
**Le Pan,** Douglas 1914- *BenetAL 91, ConPo 91, WrDr 92*
**Lepan,** Douglas Valentine 1914- *IntAu&W 91*
**Lepape,** Harry Leonard 1930- *WhoWest 92*
**Lepard,** David William 1937- *AmMWSc 92*
**LePard,** Leslie Susan Ford 1956- *WhoMW 92*
**Lepelstat,** Martin L. 1947- *WhoAmL 92*
**Le Pen,** Jean-Marie 1928- *BiDExR, IntWW 91*
**Le Pensec,** Louis 1937- *IntWW 91*
**Leper,** Thomas d1718? *DcNCBi 4*
**Lepera,** Leonard J. 1941- *WhoWest 92*
**Lepeschkin,** Eugene 1914- *AmMWSc 92*
**Lepeshinskaya,** Ol'ga Borisovna 1871-1963 *SovUnBD*
**Lepeshinskaya,** Olga Vasilyevna 1916- *FacFETw*
**Lepic,** Ludovic-Napoleon 1839-1889 *ThHEIm [port]*
**Le Pichon,** Xavier 1937- *IntWW 91*
**Lepie,** Albert Helmut 1923- *AmMWSc 92*
**L'Epine,** Margherita de 1683?-1746 *NewAmDM*
**Lepine,** Robert Neil 1956- *WhoRel 92*
**Leplae,** Luc A 1930- *AmMWSc 92*
**Lepley,** Arthur Ray 1933- *AmMWSc 92*
**LePley,** Patrick Huntington 1948- *WhoAmL 92*
**Lepman,** Martha 1957- *WhoMW 92*
**Lepock,** James Ronald 1948- *AmMWSc 92*
**Le Poer,** Baron 1987- *Who 92*
**Le Poer Trench** *Who 92*
**Le Poer Trench,** Brinsley *Who 92*
**Lepoff,** Jack H 1923- *AmMWSc 92*
**Lepore,** Amato V 1918- *WhoAmP 91*
**Lepore,** Dominick *DrAPF 91*
**Lepore,** Frank 1937- *WhoEnt 92*
**Lepore,** John A 1935- *AmMWSc 92*
**Lepore,** Joseph Vernon 1922- *AmMWSc 92*
**Leporiere,** Ralph Dennis 1932- *WhoWest 92*
**Le Pors,** Anicet 1931- *IntWW 91*
**Le Portz,** Yves 1920- *IntWW 91, Who 92*
**Leposky,** George C 1943- *IntAu&W 91*
**Leposky,** Rosalie E 1942- *IntAu&W 91*
**Lepoutre,** Pierre 1933- *AmMWSc 92*
**Lepovetsky,** Barney Charles 1926- *AmMWSc 92*
**Lepovitz,** Helena Waddy 1945- *ConAu 135*
**Lepow,** Leslie Hugh 1949- *WhoAmL 92*
**Lepow,** Martha Lipson 1927- *AmMWSc 92*
**Lepowsky,** James Ivan 1944- *AmMWSc 92*
**Lepp,** Cyrus Andrew 1946- *AmMWSc 92*
**Lepp,** Henry 1922- *AmMWSc 92*
**Lepp,** Tara Marie 1958- *WhoRel 92, WhoWest 92*
**Leppanen,** Urpo Olavi 1944- *IntWW 91*
**Leppard,** Gary Grant 1940- *AmMWSc 92*
**Leppard,** Keith Andre 1924- *Who 92*
**Leppard,** Raymond 1927- *NewAmDM*
**Leppard,** Raymond John 1927- *IntWW 91, Who 92, WhoEnt 92, WhoMW 92*
**Leppelmeier,** Gilbert Williston 1936- *AmMWSc 92*
**Lepper,** Bradley Thomas 1955- *WhoMW 92*
**Lepper,** Mark H 1917- *AmMWSc 92*
**Lepper,** Mark Roger 1944- *WhoWest 92*
**Lepper,** Thomas d1718? *DcNCBi 4*
**Leppert,** Charles, Jr 1932- *WhoAmP 91*
**Leppi,** Theodore John 1933- *AmMWSc 92*
**Leppich,** Guy Michael 1948- *WhoRel 92*
**Leppik,** Margaret White 1943- *WhoAmP 91*
**Leppin,** Dana Marie 1966- *WhoRel 92*
**Lepping,** George 1947- *Who 92*
**Leppla,** Stephen Howard 1941- *AmMWSc 92*
**Lepple,** Frederick Karl 1944- *AmMWSc 92*
**Leppoc,** Derfla *TwCSFW 91*
**Leprette,** Jacques 1920- *IntWW 91*
**Leprince,** Marie Beaumont de 1711-1780 *BlkwCEP*
**Leprince-Ringuet,** Louis 1901- *IntWW 91*
**Leps,** Ants Arvo 1936- *WhoEnt 92*
**Leps,** Thomas MacMaster 1914- *AmMWSc 92*
**Lepschy,** Giulio Ciro 1935- *Who 92*
**Lepse,** Paul Arnold 1937- *AmMWSc 92*
**Lepselter,** Martin P 1929- *AmMWSc 92*
**Lepsinger,** Debbie 1952- *WhoEnt 92*
**Lepson,** Benjamin 1924- *AmMWSc 92*
**Lepson,** Ruth *DrAPF 91*
**Leptich,** Pamela Sue 1947- *WhoMW 92*
**L'Epy,** Heliogenes De *ScFEYrs*
**Le Quesne,** Charles Martin 1917- *IntWW 91, Who 92*
**Le Quesne,** Godfray 1924- *IntWW 91, Who 92*
**LeQuesne,** James Richard 1957- *WhoWest 92*
**Le Quesne,** Leslie Philip 1919- *Who 92*
**Le Quesne,** Martin *IntWW 91, Who 92*
**Le Quesne,** Philip William 1939- *AmMWSc 92*
**Le Queux,** William 1864-1927 *ScFEYrs*
**Le Queux,** William & Wilson, H W *ScFEYrs*
**LeQuire,** Virgil Shields 1921- *AmMWSc 92*
**Leraaen,** Allen Keith 1951- *WhoFI 92, WhoWest 92*
**Leray,** Jean 1906- *IntWW 91*
**Lerbekmo,** John Franklin 1924- *AmMWSc 92*
**Lerch,** Irving A 1938- *AmMWSc 92*
**Lerch,** James Stanley 1942- *WhoFI 92*
**Lerch,** Robert Bond 1960- *WhoEnt 92*
**Lerch,** Sharon *DrAPF 91*
**Lerch,** Stanford Earl 1933- *WhoWest 92*
**Lerche,** Peter Fritz Franz 1928- *IntWW 91*
**Lercher,** Bruce L 1930- *AmMWSc 92*
**Lerdahl,** Robert G. 1962- *WhoMW 92*
**Lerer,** Seth 1955- *WrDr 92*
**Lerew,** Parker David 1948- *WhoAmP 91*
**Le Riche,** William Harding 1916- *AmMWSc 92, WrDr 92*
**Leritz,** Lawrence Robert 1952- *WhoEnt 92*
**Le Riverend,** Julio 1916- *IntWW 91*
**Le Riverend,** Pablo 1907- *WhoHisp 92*
**Lerman,** Abraham 1935- *AmMWSc 92*
**Lerman,** Allen H. 1943- *WhoFI 92*
**Lerman,** Beryl 1948- *TwCPaSc*
**Lerman,** Charles Lew 1948- *AmMWSc 92*
**Lerman,** Eileen R. 1947- *WhoWest 92*
**Lerman,** Eleanor *DrAPF 91*
**Lerman,** Gerald Steven 1951- *WhoFI 92*
**Lerman,** Kenneth Barry 1947- *WhoFI 92*
**Lerman,** Leonard Solomon 1925- *AmMWSc 92*
**Lerman,** Liz A. 1947- *WhoEnt 92*
**Lerman,** Manuel 1943- *AmMWSc 92*
**Lerman,** Michael Isaac 1932- *AmMWSc 92*
**Lerman,** Rhoda *DrAPF 91*
**Lerman,** Rhoda 1936- *WrDr 92*
**Lerman,** Robert Irving 1944- *WhoFI 92*
**Lerman,** Sidney 1927- *AmMWSc 92*
**Lerman,** Stephen Paul 1944- *AmMWSc 92*
**Lerman,** Steven I 1944- *AmMWSc 92*
**Lerman,** Zafra Margolin 1937- *WhoMW 92*
**Lermonde,** Vivian Claire 1949- *WhoFI 92, WhoMW 92*
**Lerner,** Aaron Bunsen 1920- *AmMWSc 92*
**Lerner,** Alan Burton 1930- *WhoFI 92*
**Lerner,** Alan Jay 1918-1986 *BenetAL 91, FacFETw [port]*
**Lerner,** Albert Martin 1929- *AmMWSc 92*
**Lerner,** Alexander Robert 1946- *WhoFI 92*
**Lerner,** Alfred 1933- *WhoMW 92*
**Lerner,** Andrea 1954- *ConAu 134*
**Lerner,** Andrew Mark 1955- *WhoEnt 92*
**Lerner,** Arnold Stanley 1930- *WhoEnt 92*
**Lerner,** Arthur *DrAPF 91*
**Lerner,** B J 1921- *AmMWSc 92*
**Lerner,** Charles 1944- *WhoFI 92*
**Lerner,** Daniel Merril 1932- *WhoEnt 92*
**Lerner,** David Evan 1944- *AmMWSc 92*
**Lerner,** David Roger 1950- *WhoEnt 92*
**Lerner,** Edward Clarence 1924- *AmMWSc 92*
**Lerner,** Franklin 1927- *WhoFI 92*
**Lerner,** Frederic Howard 1957- *WhoFI 92*
**Lerner,** Gerda 1920- *SmATA 65 [port]*
**Lerner,** Harry 1939- *WhoAmL 92*
**Lerner,** Herbert J. 1938- *WhoFI 92*
**Lerner,** Jeno 1894-1948 *NewAmDM*
**Lerner,** Joseph *IntMPA 92*
**Lerner,** Joseph 1942- *AmMWSc 92*
**Lerner,** Jules 1941- *AmMWSc 92*
**Lerner,** Larry 1949- *WhoEnt 92*
**Lerner,** Laurence 1925- *ConPo 91, LiExTwC, WrDr 92*
**Lerner,** Laurence David 1925- *IntAu&W 91*
**Lerner,** Lawrence Robert 1943- *AmMWSc 92*
**Lerner,** Lawrence S 1934- *AmMWSc 92*
**Lerner,** Leon Maurice 1938- *AmMWSc 92*
**Lerner,** Leonard Joseph 1922- *AmMWSc 92*
**Lerner,** Linda *DrAPF 91*
**Lerner,** Lionel John 1931- *WhoFI 92*
**Lerner,** Louis L 1915- *AmMWSc 92*
**Lerner,** Max 1902- *BenetAL 91, IntWW 91, Who 92, WrDr 92*
**Lerner,** Max Kasner 1916- *WhoAmL 92*
**Lerner,** Melvin 1917- *AmMWSc 92*
**Lerner,** Michael Paul 1941- *AmMWSc 92*
**Lerner,** Moisey 1931- *AmMWSc 92*
**Lerner,** Narcinda Reynolds 1933- *AmMWSc 92*
**Lerner,** Neil S. 1955- *WhoMW 92*
**Lerner,** Norman Conrad *AmMWSc 92*
**Lerner,** Pauline 1948- *AmMWSc 92*
**Lerner,** Peter M *WhoAmP 91*
**Lerner,** Richard Alan 1938- *AmMWSc 92*
**Lerner,** Richard Edward 1941- *WhoEnt 92*
**Lerner,** Rita Guggenheim 1929- *AmMWSc 92*
**Lerner,** Robert E. 1940- *WrDr 92*
**Lerner,** Robert Earl 1940- *IntAu&W 91*
**Lerner,** Robert Gibbs 1936- *AmMWSc 92*
**Lerner,** Samuel 1908- *AmMWSc 92*
**Lerner,** Sheldon 1939- *WhoWest 92*
**Lerner,** Sidney Isaac 1932- *AmMWSc 92*
**Lerner,** Stephen Alexander 1938- *WhoMW 92*
**Lerner,** Stuart L 1930- *WhoIns 92*
**Lernoux,** Penny 1940-1989 *LiExTwC*
**Le Roi,** David 1915- *IntAu&W 91*
**Leroi,** George Edgar 1936- *AmMWSc 92*
**LeRoith,** Derek 1945- *AmMWSc 92*
**Lerolle,** Henry 1852-1929 *ThHEIm*
**LeRoux,** David Bain 1951- *WhoIns 92*
**LeRoux,** Edgar Joseph 1922- *AmMWSc 92*
**LeRoux,** Edmund Frank 1925- *AmMWSc 92*
**Leroux,** Gaston 1868-1927 *ScFEYrs, SmATA 65 [port]*
**Le Roux,** Jean-Louis 1927- *WhoEnt 92, WhoWest 92*
**Leroux,** Pierre 1942- *AmMWSc 92*
**LeRoy,** Adrian 1520?-1598 *NewAmDM*
**LeRoy,** Andre Francois 1933- *AmMWSc 92*
**Le Roy,** Claude 1937- *IntAu&W 91*
**Leroy,** David Henry 1947- *WhoAmP 91, WhoWest 92*
**LeRoy,** Donald James 1913- *AmMWSc 92*
**LeRoy,** Edward Carwile 1933- *AmMWSc 92*
**LeRoy,** Gen *ConAu 134*
**Le Roy,** Laura *WhoEnt 92*
**Leroy,** Louis 1812-1885 *ThHEIm*
**LeRoy,** Mervyn 1900-1987 *IntDcF 2-2 [port]*
**Leroy,** Pascale Renee 1961- *WhoEnt 92*
**Leroy,** Robert Frederick 1950- *AmMWSc 92*
**LeRoy,** Robert James 1943- *AmMWSc 92*
**LeRoy,** Rodney Lash 1941- *AmMWSc 92*
**Le Roy Ladurie,** Emmanuel 1929- *IntWW 91*
**Le Roy Ladurie,** Emmanuel Bernard 1929- *Who 92*
**LeRoy-Lewis,** David Henry 1918- *Who 92*
**Lersch,** Heinrich 1889-1936 *EncTR 91 [port]*
**Lersch,** Philipp 1898-1972 *EncTR 91*
**Lersten,** Nels R 1932- *AmMWSc 92*
**LeRud,** David Glen 1955- *WhoRel 92*
**Lerude,** Warren Leslie 1937- *WhoWest 92*
**Lervik,** Ase Hiorth 1933- *IntWW 91*
**Lerway,** Philip Robert 1944- *WhoAmL 92*
**Les,** Edwin Paul 1923- *AmMWSc 92*
**Lesage,** Alain Rene 1668-1747 *BlkwCEP*
**LeSage,** Leo G 1935- *AmMWSc 92*
**Lesar,** Hiram Henry 1912- *WhoAmL 92*
**LeSatz,** Stephen, Jr. 1937- *WhoAmL 92*
**Lescano,** Javier A. 1935- *WhoHisp 92*
**Lescarboura,** Jaime Aquiles 1937- *AmMWSc 92*
**Lescaze,** William 1896-1969 *DcTwDes, FacFETw*
**Leschak,** Peter M 1951- *IntAu&W 91*
**Leschetizky,** Theodor 1830-1915 *NewAmDM*
**Lescoe,** David 1952- *WhoEnt 92*
**Lescoe,** John J *WhoAmP 91*
**Lescoulie,** Jack d1987 *LesBEnT 92*
**Lescovitz,** Victor John 1953- *WhoAmP 91*
**Lescrenier,** Charles 1935- *WhoFI 92*
**Lescroart,** John T. 1948- *WrDr 92*
**Lesechko,** Mikhail Avksent'evich 1909-1984 *SovUnBD*
**Leseman,** Robert G 1940- *WhoIns 92*
**Leseman,** Robert Graham 1940- *WhoFI 92*
**Leser,** Ernst George 1943- *AmMWSc 92*
**Leser,** Ralph Ulrich 1905- *AmMWSc 92*
**Lesh,** Angela Dawn 1947- *WhoFI 92*
**Lesh,** Philip Chapman 1940- *WhoEnt 92*
**Lesh,** Thomas Allan 1929- *AmMWSc 92*
**Lesh-Laurie,** Georgia Elizabeth 1938- *AmMWSc 92*
**LeShan,** Eda J. 1922- *WrDr 92*
**LeSher,** Dean Allen 1927- *AmMWSc 92*
**Lesher,** Frank Michael 1948- *WhoAmL 92*
**Lesher,** Gary Allen 1950- *AmMWSc 92*
**Lesher,** George Yohe 1926- *AmMWSc 92*
**Lesher,** John Lee, Jr. 1934- *WhoFI 92*
**Lesher,** Margaret Lisco 1932- *WhoWest 92*
**Lesher,** Richard Lee 1933- *WhoEnt 92, WhoFI 92*
**Lesher,** William Elton 1932- *WhoRel 92*
**Leshner,** Alan Irvin 1944- *AmMWSc 92*
**Leshner,** Stan 1942- *WhoEnt 92*
**Leshy,** John 1913- *WhoAmP 91*
**Lesiak,** Lucille Ann 1946- *WhoEnt 92*
**LeSieg,** Theo *ConAu 135, SmATA 67, WrDr 92*
**Lesikar,** Arnold Vincent 1937- *AmMWSc 92*
**Lesikar,** Raymond Vincent 1922- *WrDr 92*
**Lesinski,** John Silvester 1913- *AmMWSc 92*
**Lesjak,** Ron Francis 1943- *WhoRel 92*
**Lesk,** Ann Berger 1947- *WhoAmL 92*
**Leske,** Adrian Max 1936- *WhoRel 92*
**Leskien,** Hermann 1939- *IntWW 91*
**Lesko,** Kevin Thomas 1956- *AmMWSc 92*
**Lesko,** Patricia Marie 1947- *AmMWSc 92*
**Lesko,** Stephen Albert 1931- *AmMWSc 92*
**Leskovyansky,** John Joseph 1925- *WhoAmL 92*
**Leskowitz,** Sidney 1922- *AmMWSc 92*
**Lesley,** Frank David 1944- *AmMWSc 92*
**Lesley,** George D. 1944- *WhoWest 92*
**Lesley,** J Peter 1819-1903 *BiInAmS*
**Leslie** *Who 92*
**Leslie,** Lord 1958- *Who 92*
**Leslie,** Alan *Who 92*
**Leslie,** Aleen 1908- *IntMPA 92*
**Leslie,** Ann 1931- *WhoAmP 91*
**Leslie,** Ann Elizabeth Mary *Who 92*
**Leslie,** Charles Miller 1923- *AmMWSc 92*
**Leslie,** Colin Alan 1922- *Who 92*
**Leslie,** David Clement 1924- *Who 92*
**Leslie,** Desmond 1921- *IntAu&W 91, WrDr 92*
**Leslie,** Donald S., Jr. 1925- *IntWW 91*
**Leslie,** Douglas L. 1942- *WhoAmL 92*
**Leslie,** Eliza 1787-1858 *BenetAL 91*
**Leslie,** Ernest Kenneth 1911- *Who 92*
**Leslie,** Frank 1821-1880 *BenetAL 91, RComAH*
**Leslie,** Gerrie Allen 1941- *AmMWSc 92*
**Leslie,** Gilbert Frank 1909- *Who 92*
**Leslie,** Gordon A 1946- *WhoIns 92*
**Leslie,** Henry Arthur 1921- *WhoFI 92*
**Leslie,** James 1720?-1781 *DcNCBi 4*
**Leslie,** James 1934- *AmMWSc 92*
**Leslie,** James Bolton 1922- *Who 92*
**Leslie,** James C 1933- *AmMWSc 92*
**Leslie,** James D 1935- *AmMWSc 92*
**Leslie,** Jerome Russell 1939- *AmMWSc 92, WhoMW 92*
**Leslie,** Joan 1925- *IntMPA 92*
**Leslie,** John 1766-1832 *BlkwCEP*
**Leslie,** John 1916- *Who 92*
**Leslie,** John Edward, III 1960- *WhoFI 92*
**Leslie,** John Ethelbert 1910-1991 *NewYTBS 91*
**Leslie,** John Franklin 1953- *AmMWSc 92*
**Leslie,** John Wayland d1991 *Who 92N*
**Leslie,** John William 1923- *WhoFI 92*
**Leslie,** Kathleen Frances 1942- *WhoWest 92*
**Leslie,** Kenneth *Who 92*
**Leslie,** Larry L. 1938- *WhoWest 92*
**Leslie,** Larry M 1949- *WhoAmP 91*
**Leslie,** LeAnne Catherine 1963- *WhoEnt 92*
**Leslie,** Marcia Louise 1952- *WhoBlA 92*
**Leslie,** Marvin Earl 1938- *WhoRel 92*
**Leslie,** Michael J. 1960- *WhoFI 92*

**Leslie**, Michael Ross 1957- *WhoAmL 92*
**Leslie**, Miriam Florence Folline Squier 1836-1914 *BenetAL 91*
**Leslie**, O. H. *WrDr 92*
**Leslie**, Paul Willard 1948- *AmMWSc 92*
**Leslie**, Percy Theodore 1915- *Who 92*
**Leslie**, Peter 1931- *Who 92*
**Leslie**, Peter Evelyn 1931- *IntWW 91*
**Leslie**, Reo Napoleon, Jr. 1953- *WhoRel 92*
**Leslie**, Robert Anthony 1942- *IntWW 91*
**Leslie**, Robert B 1939- *WhoAmP 91*
**Leslie**, Robert Campbell 1917- *WhoRel 92*
**Leslie**, Robert Franklin 1911- *IntAu&W 91*
**Leslie**, Robert Lorne 1947- *WhoAmL 92, WhoWest 92*
**Leslie**, Rochelle *DrAPF 91*
**Leslie**, Ronald Allan 1948- *AmMWSc 92*
**Leslie**, Seymour Marvin 1922- *WhoEnt 92*
**Leslie**, Stephen Howard 1918- *AmMWSc 92*
**Leslie**, Steven Wayne 1946- *AmMWSc 92*
**Leslie**, Theodore *Who 92*
**Leslie**, Thomas M 1954- *AmMWSc 92*
**Leslie**, Tim 1942- *WhoAmP 91*
**Leslie**, Wallace Dean 1922- *AmMWSc 92*
**Leslie**, Ward S. *WrDr 92*
**Leslie**, William C 1920- *AmMWSc 92*
**Leslie**, William Houghton 1932- *WhoRel 92*
**Leslie Melville** *Who 92*
**Lesly**, Philip 1918- *WhoFI 92, WhoMW 92, WrDr 92*
**Lesman**, Michael Steven 1953- *WhoAmL 92, WhoFI 92*
**Lesmeister**, John Steven 1955- *WhoAmP 91*
**Lesmez**, Arthur Gerard 1959- *WhoAmL 92*
**Lesnaw**, Judith Alice 1940- *AmMWSc 92*
**Lesner**, Mark Allen 1954- *WhoMW 92*
**Lesner**, Sharon A 1951- *AmMWSc 92*
**Lesniak**, Linda 1948- *AmMWSc 92*
**Lesniak**, Raymond 1946- *WhoAmP 91*
**Lesniak**, Rose *DrAPF 91*
**Lesnick**, Howard 1931- *WhoAmL 92*
**Lesniewski**, Suzanne 1938- *WhoRel 92*
**Lesnik**, Steven Harris 1940- *WhoMW 92*
**Lesotho**, King of *IntWW 91*
**LeSourd**, Leonard 1919- *ConAu 135*
**LeSourd**, Leonard Earle 1919- *WhoRel 92*
**LeSourd**, Nancy Susan Oliver 1953- *WhoAmL 92*
**Lesourne**, Jacques Francois 1928- *Who 92*
**Lesperance**, Pierre J 1934- *AmMWSc 92*
**Lespinasse**, Julie de 1732-1776 *FrenWW*
**Lespinasse**, Julie-Jeanne Eleonor de 1732-1776 *BlkwCEP*
**Lesquereux**, Leo 1806-1889 *BiInAmS*
**Less**, David Arnold 1952- *WhoEnt 92*
**Lessac**, Frane 1954- *IntAu&W 91*
**Lessard**, Charles Stephen 1936- *WhoHisp 92*
**Lessard**, Claude 1949- *IntWW 91*
**Lessard**, Deborah Marie 1958- *WhoAmL 92*
**Lessard**, James Louis 1943- *AmMWSc 92*
**Lessard**, Jean 1936- *AmMWSc 92*
**Lessard**, John Ayres 1920- *WhoEnt 92*
**Lessard**, Raymond W. 1930- *WhoRel 92*
**Lessard**, Richard R 1943- *AmMWSc 92*
**Lessard**, Robert Bernard 1931- *WhoAmP 91*
**Lessard**, Roger Alain 1944- *AmMWSc 92*
**Lesse**, Henry 1926- *AmMWSc 92*
**Lessell**, Simmons 1933- *AmMWSc 92*
**Lessels**, Norman 1938- *IntWW 91, Who 92*
**Lessen**, Martin 1920- *AmMWSc 92*
**Lesseps**, Roland Joseph 1933- *AmMWSc 92*
**Lesser**, Craig Philip 1961- *WhoAmL 92*
**Lesser**, Eugene *DrAPF 91*
**Lesser**, Felice A. 1953- *WhoEnt 92*
**Lesser**, Frederick Alan 1934- *WhoWest 92*
**Lesser**, Harvey Lloyd 1951- *WhoWest 92*
**Lesser**, Henry 1947- *WhoAmL 92*
**Lesser**, Joel Steven 1966- *WhoEnt 92*
**Lesser**, Laurence 1938- *WhoEnt 92*
**Lesser**, Len 1922- *WhoEnt 92*
**Lesser**, Margo Rogers 1950- *WhoAmL 92*
**Lesser**, Milton *WrDr 92*
**Lesser**, Milton 1928- *IntAu&W 91, TwCSFW 91*
**Lesser**, Peter John 1957- *WhoEnt 92*
**Lesser**, Rika *DrAPF 91*
**Lesser**, Seymour Herman 1929- *WhoEnt 92*
**Lesser**, Sidney Lewis 1912- *Who 92*
**Lesser**, Sol 1890-1980 *FacFETw*
**Lesser**, William Melville 1927- *WhoAmL 92*
**Lesshafft**, Charles Thomas, Jr 1918- *AmMWSc 92*
**Lessick**, Mira L. 1949- *WhoMW 92*
**Lessie**, Thomas Guy 1936- *AmMWSc 92*
**Lessin**, Lawrence Stephen 1937- *AmMWSc 92*
**Lessing**, Charlotte *IntAu&W 91, Who 92*
**Lessing**, Doris *DrAPF 91*
**Lessing**, Doris 1919- *CnDBLB 8 [port], ConAu 14AS [port], ConNov 91, FacFETw, LiExTwC, RfGEnL 91, TwCSFW 91, Who 92, WhoEnt 92, WrDr 92*
**Lessing**, Doris May 1919- *IntAu&W 91, IntWW 91*
**Lessing**, Gotthold Ephraim 1729-1781 *BlkwCEP*
**Lessing**, Peter 1938- *AmMWSc 92*
**Lessios**, Harilaos Angelou 1951- *AmMWSc 92*
**Lessiter**, Mike 1969- *ConAu 135*
**Lessler**, Judith Thomasson 1943- *AmMWSc 92*
**Lessler**, Milton A 1915- *AmMWSc 92*
**Lessman**, Gary M 1938- *AmMWSc 92*
**Lessman**, Robert Edward 1947- *WhoAmL 92*
**Lessmann**, Richard Carl 1942- *AmMWSc 92*
**Lessmeier**, Michael L. 1954- *WhoAmL 92*
**Lessner**, Howard E 1927- *AmMWSc 92*
**Lessner**, Michael Marc 1956- *WhoEnt 92*
**Lesso**, William George 1931- *AmMWSc 92*
**Lessof**, Maurice Hart 1924- *Who 92*
**Lessoff**, Howard 1930- *AmMWSc 92*
**Lessoff**, Jeffrey Lewis 1956- *WhoAmL 92*
**Lessor**, Arthur Eugene, Jr 1925- *AmMWSc 92*
**Lessor**, Delbert Leroy 1941- *AmMWSc 92*
**Lessor**, Edith Schroeder 1930- *AmMWSc 92*
**Lessore**, Helen 1907- *TwCPaSc, Who 92*
**Lessore**, John 1939- *TwCPaSc*
**Lessy**, Roy Paul, Jr. 1944- *WhoAmL 92*
**Lester**, Andrew Douglas 1939- *WhoRel 92*
**Lester**, Anthony Paul 1936- *IntWW 91, Who 92*
**Lester**, Betty J. 1945- *WhoBlA 92*
**Lester**, Charles Edwards 1815-1890 *BenetAL 91*
**Lester**, Charles Emory 1933- *WhoMW 92*
**Lester**, Charles Turner 1911- *AmMWSc 92*
**Lester**, David 1916- *AmMWSc 92*
**Lester**, David 1942- *WrDr 92*
**Lester**, David Vincent 1945- *WhoEnt 92*
**Lester**, Donald 1944- *WhoBlA 92*
**Lester**, Donald Thomas 1934- *AmMWSc 92*
**Lester**, Elton J. 1944- *WhoBlA 92*
**Lester**, G. A. 1943- *WrDr 92*
**Lester**, Gene 1910- *WhoEnt 92*
**Lester**, George Ronald 1934- *AmMWSc 92*
**Lester**, Henry Allen 1945- *AmMWSc 92*
**Lester**, Jacqueline 1949- *WhoBlA 92*
**Lester**, James Luther 1932- *WhoAmP 91*
**Lester**, James P 1944- *ConAu 35NR*
**Lester**, James Theodore 1932- *Who 92*
**Lester**, Jerry *LesBEnT 92*
**Lester**, John Bernard 1945- *AmMWSc 92*
**Lester**, John Clayton 1940- *WhoWest 92*
**Lester**, John James Nathaniel, II 1952- *WhoWest 92*
**Lester**, Joseph Eugene 1942- *AmMWSc 92*
**Lester**, Julius 1939- *IntAu&W 91, WhoBlA 92, WrDr 92*
**Lester**, Larry James 1947- *AmMWSc 92*
**Lester**, Laurie Dell 1955- *WhoMW 92*
**Lester**, Mark 1958- *IntMPA 92*
**Lester**, Mark Leslie 1946- *IntMPA 92*
**Lester**, Nina Mack *WhoBlA 92*
**Lester**, Pamela Robin 1958- *WhoEnt 92*
**Lester**, R C 1922- *WhoAmP 91*
**Lester**, Richard 1932- *FacFETw, IntDcF 2-2 [port], IntMPA 92, IntWW 91, Who 92, WhoEnt 92*
**Lester**, Richard Allen 1908- *WhoFI 92*
**Lester**, Richard Garrison 1925- *AmMWSc 92*
**Lester**, Robert Carlton 1933- *WhoRel 92*
**Lester**, Robert Leonard 1929- *AmMWSc 92*
**Lester**, Roger 1929- *AmMWSc 92*
**Lester**, Scott D. 1956- *WhoAmL 92*
**Lester**, Sonny 1924- *WhoEnt 92*
**Lester**, Terry Leroy 1950- *WhoEnt 92, WhoWest 92*
**Lester**, Terry Thomas 1953- *WhoRel 92*
**Lester**, Theodore 1909-1989 *WhoBlA 92N*
**Lester**, Urban Alexander 1929- *WhoAmL 92*
**Lester**, William Alexander, Jr 1937- *AmMWSc 92, WhoBlA 92*
**Lester**, William Lewis 1932- *AmMWSc 92*
**Lester**, William Walter 1916- *WhoWest 92*
**Lester Smith**, Ernest *Who 92*
**Lestikow**, James M. 1948- *WhoAmL 92*
**Lestingi**, Joseph Francis 1935- *AmMWSc 92*
**Leston**, Gerd 1924- *AmMWSc 92*
**Lestor**, Joan *Who 92*
**LeStourgeon**, Wallace Meade 1943- *AmMWSc 92*
**Lestrade**, John Patrick 1949- *AmMWSc 92*
**L'Estrange**, Anna *IntAu&W 91X, WrDr 92*
**Lestrange**, Kenneth J 1933- *WhoIns 92*
**Lestz**, Earl *IntMPA 92*
**Lestz**, Sidney J *AmMWSc 92*
**Le Suer**, Meridel 1900- *WrDr 92*
**Lesueur**, Charles Alexandre 1778-1846 *BiInAmS*
**Le Sueur**, Meridel 1900- *BenetAL 91, TwCWW 91*
**LeSueur**, Stephen C. 1952- *ConAu 133*
**LeSueur**, Susan M 1952- *WhoAmP 91*
**Lesur**, Daniel *NewAmDM*
**Lesure**, Frank Gardner 1927- *AmMWSc 92*
**Le Surf**, Joseph Eric 1929- *AmMWSc 92*
**Leswing**, James Bartholomew 1948- *WhoRel 92*
**Leszczycki**, Stanislaw Marian 1907- *IntWW 91*
**Leszczynski**, Stanislaw 1677-1766 *BlkwCEP*
**Leszek**, Michael 1943- *WhoNob 90*
**L'Etang**, Hugh Joseph Charles James 1917- *Who 92*
**Letarte**, Jacques 1934- *AmMWSc 92*
**Letarte**, Michelle Vinlaine 1947- *AmMWSc 92*
**Letcher**, David Wayne 1941- *AmMWSc 92*
**Letcher**, John Henry, III 1936- *AmMWSc 92*
**Letcher**, Stephen Vaughan 1935- *AmMWSc 92*
**Letchford**, Stanley 1924- *WrDr 92*
**Letchworth**, William P 1823-1910 *DcAmImH*
**Letelier**, Orlando 1932-1976 *FacFETw*
**Letey**, John, Jr 1933- *AmMWSc 92*
**Letey**, John Joseph, Jr. 1933- *WhoWest 92*
**Lethaby**, William Richard 1857-1931 *DcTwDes*
**Lethbridge**, Robert 1947- *ConAu 135*
**Lethbridge**, Thomas 1950- *Who 92*
**Letizia**, Gabriel Joseph 1950- *AmMWSc 92*
**Letkeman**, Peter 1938- *AmMWSc 92*
**Letko**, Ken *DrAPF 91*
**Leto**, Salvatore 1937- *AmMWSc 92*
**Leto**, Sam S., Jr. *WhoHisp 92*
**Le Tocq**, Eric George 1918- *Who 92*
**LeTourneau**, Budd W 1932- *AmMWSc 92*
**LeTourneau**, Duane John 1926- *AmMWSc 92*
**Letourneau**, George E 1928- *WhoAmP 91*
**LeTourneau**, Mark Stephen 1955- *WhoWest 92*
**LeTourneux**, Jean 1935- *AmMWSc 92*
**Letowska**, Ewa Anna 1940- *IntWW 91*
**Letowsky**, Martin Elliot 1951- *WhoAmL 92*
**Letsie**, Joshua Sekhobe 1947- *IntWW 91*
**Letsie**, Thaabe 1940- *IntWW 91*
**Letsinger**, Robert Lewis 1921- *AmMWSc 92*
**Letsky**, Steven Craig 1950- *WhoMW 92*
**Letson**, David 1961- *WhoFI 92*
**Letson**, Harry Farnham Germaine 1896- *Who 92*
**Letson**, Johnny Lee 1949- *WhoFI 92*
**Letson**, S R 1940- *WhoAmP 91*
**Letsou**, Costas George 1927- *WhoAmL 92*
**Lett**, Gerald William 1926- *WhoBlA 92*
**Lett**, Gregory Scott 1958- *AmMWSc 92*
**Lett**, John Terence 1933- *AmMWSc 92*
**Lett**, Mack Edward 1929- *WhoAmP 91*
**Lett**, Philip W, Jr 1922- *AmMWSc 92*
**Lett**, Phillip David 1952- *WhoWest 92*
**Lett**, Raymond D 1934- *WhoAmP 91*
**Lett**, Thomas Patrick 1948- *WhoFI 92*
**Lett**, Winston Tatum 1947- *WhoAmL 92, WhoAmP 91*
**Lett-Haines**, Arthur 1894-1978 *TwCPaSc*
**Letter**, Louis N. 1937- *IntMPA 92*
**Letterhaus**, Bernhard 1894-1944 *EncTR 91 [port]*
**Letterman**, David *LesBEnT 92*
**Letterman**, David 1947- *IntMPA 92, WhoEnt 92*
**Letterman**, Gordon Sparks 1914- *AmMWSc 92*
**Letterman**, Herbert 1936- *AmMWSc 92*
**Letterman**, Ira Spencer 1915- *WhoAmP 91*
**Letterman**, Russell Paul 1933- *WhoAmP 91*
**Lettieri**, Richard Joseph 1947- *WhoAmL 92*
**Lettieri**, Thomas Robert 1952- *AmMWSc 92*
**Lettofsky**, Alan Bernard 1937- *WhoRel 92*
**Letton**, James Carey 1933- *AmMWSc 92*
**Lettow**, Charles Frederick 1941- *WhoAmL 92, WhoFI 92*
**Letts**, Anthony Ashworth 1935- *Who 92*
**Letts**, Charles Trevor 1905- *Who 92*
**Letts**, J. Spencer 1934- *WhoAmL 92*
**Letts**, Lindsay Gordon 1948- *AmMWSc 92*
**Lettvin**, Jerome Y 1920- *AmMWSc 92*
**Lettvin**, Theodore 1926- *WhoEnt 92*
**Letuli**, Olo Uluao Misilagi 1919- *WhoAmL 92*
**Letumu**, Talauega F *WhoAmP 91*
**Letwin**, Jeffrey William 1953- *WhoAmL 92*
**Letwin**, Leon 1929- *WhoAmL 92*
**Letwin**, William 1922- *Who 92*
**Leu**, Donald A, Jr 1951- *WhoAmP 91*
**Leu**, Ming C 1951- *AmMWSc 92*
**Leu**, Richard William 1935- *AmMWSc 92*
**Leuba**, Christopher 1929- *WhoEnt 92*
**Leube**, Kurt Rudolph 1943- *WhoWest 92*
**Leubert**, Alfred Otto Paul 1922- *WhoFI 92*
**Leubevere** *EncAmaz 91*
**Leubner**, Gerhard Walter 1921- *AmMWSc 92*
**Leubner**, Ingo Herwig 1938- *AmMWSc 92*
**Leubsdorf**, Carl Philipp 1938- *WhoFI 92*
**Leuchars**, Peter Raymond 1921- *Who 92*
**Leuchars**, William 1920- *Who 92*
**Leuchtag**, H Richard 1927- *AmMWSc 92*
**Leuchtman**, Stephen Nathan 1945- *WhoAmL 92*
**Leuck**, Claire M *WhoAmP 91*
**Leuck**, Frank P. 1940- *WhoFI 92*
**Leuckert**, Jean Elizabeth *Who 92*
**Leukart**, Richard Henry, II 1942- *WhoAmL 92*
**Leukel**, Francis Parker 1922- *WhoWest 92*
**Leung Tung** 1946- *LiExTwC*
**Leung**, Albert Yuk-Sing 1938- *AmMWSc 92*
**Leung**, Alexander Kwok-Chu 1948- *AmMWSc 92*
**Leung**, Benjamin Shuet-Kin 1938- *AmMWSc 92*
**Leung**, Charles Cheung-Wan 1946- *AmMWSc 92*
**Leung**, Christopher Chung-Kit 1939- *AmMWSc 92*
**Leung**, Chung Ngoc 1956- *AmMWSc 92*
**Leung**, David Wai-Hung 1951- *AmMWSc 92*
**Leung**, Donald Yap Man 1949- *AmMWSc 92*
**Leung**, Firman 1957- *WhoFI 92*
**Leung**, Frederick C 1952- *AmMWSc 92*
**Leung**, Irene Sheung-Ying 1934- *AmMWSc 92*
**Leung**, Joseph Yuk-Tong 1950- *AmMWSc 92, WhoFI 92*
**Leung**, Ka-Ngo *AmMWSc 92*
**Leung**, Kam-Ching 1935- *AmMWSc 92*
**Leung**, Lai-Wo Stan 1952- *AmMWSc 92*
**Leung**, Pak Sang 1935- *AmMWSc 92*
**Leung**, Peter 1955- *AmMWSc 92*
**Leung**, Philip Man Kit 1933- *AmMWSc 92*
**Leung**, Philip Min Bun 1932- *AmMWSc 92*
**Leung**, Raymond Tat-Ming 1954- *WhoFI 92*
**Leung**, So Wah 1918- *AmMWSc 92*
**Leung**, Wai Yan *AmMWSc 92*
**Leung**, Wing Hai 1937- *AmMWSc 92*
**Leung**, Woon F 1954- *AmMWSc 92*
**Leuninger**, Franz 1898-1945 *EncTR 91*
**Leupena**, Tupua 1922- *Who 92*
**Leupold**, George Fred, Jr. 1942- *WhoFI 92*
**Leupold**, Herbert August 1931- *AmMWSc 92*
**Leus McFarlen**, Patricia Cheryl 1954- *WhoWest 92*
**Leuschen**, M Patricia 1943- *AmMWSc 92*
**Leuschner**, Wilhelm 1890-1944 *EncTR 91 [port]*
**Leussing**, Daniel, Jr 1924- *AmMWSc 92*
**Leussink**, Hans 1912- *IntWW 91*
**Leutenegger**, Walter 1941- *AmMWSc 92*
**Leutermann**, John Gerard 1955- *WhoAmP 91*
**Leutert**, Werner Walter 1922- *AmMWSc 92*
**Leutgoeb**, Rosalia Aloisia 1901- *AmMWSc 92*
**Leutheuser**, Sylvia Mae 1924- *WhoAmP 91*
**Leutheusser**, H J 1927- *AmMWSc 92*
**Leuthner**, Robert Alfred 1960- *WhoFI 92*
**Leutwiler**, Fritz 1924- *IntWW 91, Who 92*
**Leuty**, Gerald Johnston 1919- *WhoWest 92*
**Leutze**, Willard Parker 1927- *AmMWSc 92*
**Leutzinger**, Rudolph L 1922- *AmMWSc 92*
**Leuver**, Robert Joseph 1927- *WhoWest 92*
**Leuze**, Rex Ernest 1922- *AmMWSc 92*
**Lev**, Donald *DrAPF 91*
**Lev**, Judith Wilkens 1944- *WhoFI 92*
**Lev**, Maurice 1908- *AmMWSc 92*
**Lev-Ran**, Arye 1930- *AmMWSc 92*
**Leva**, James Robert 1932- *WhoFI 92*
**Levada**, William Joseph 1936- *WhoRel 92, WhoWest 92*
**Leval**, Pierre Nelson 1936- *WhoAmL 92*
**Le Van**, Daniel Hayden 1924- *WhoFI 92*
**LeVan**, Marijo O'Connor 1936- *AmMWSc 92*
**LeVan**, Martin Douglas, Jr 1949- *AmMWSc 92*
**LeVan**, Molly Susan 1950- *WhoAmL 92*
**Levan**, Nhan 1936- *AmMWSc 92*

**Levand**, Gloria Diana 1912- WhoEnt 92
**Levand**, Oscar 1927- AmMWSc 92
**Levande**, Robert M. 1949- WhoFI 92
**LeVander**, Harold 1910- WhoAmP 91
**LeVander**, Harold Powrie, Jr. 1940- WhoAmL 92
**Levander**, Orville Arvid 1940- AmMWSc 92
**Levandowski**, Donald William 1927- AmMWSc 92
**Levandowsky**, Michael 1935- AmMWSc 92
**Levang**, Patsy Lee 1949- WhoRel 92
**Levanon**, Yosef 1941- WhoRel 92
**Levant**, Oscar d1972 LesBEnT 92
**Levant**, Oscar 1906-1972 NewAmDM
**Levar**, Patrick WhoAmP 91
**Levard**, Georges 1912- IntWW 91
**Levarie**, Siegmund 1914- WhoEnt 92
**Levary**, Reuven Robert 1944- WhoMW 92
**Levasseur**, Maurice Edgar 1953- AmMWSc 92
**Levathes**, Peter G. LesBEnT 92
**Levatino**, Adrienne Marie 1952- WhoAmL 92
**Le Vay**, David 1915- WrDr 92
**LeVay**, Simon 1943- News 92-2 [port]
**Levchuk**, John W 1942- AmMWSc 92
**Levdansky**, David K 1954- WhoAmP 91
**Leve**, Samuel 1910- WhoEnt 92
**LeVeau**, Barney Francis 1939- AmMWSc 92
**LeVee**, Jeffrey A. 1959- WhoAmL 92
**LeVeen**, Harry Henry 1916- AmMWSc 92
**Leveille**, Gilbert Antonio 1934- AmMWSc 92
**Leveille**, Walter Henry, Jr. 1945- WhoRel 92
**Levell**, Dorsey E. WhoRel 92
**Levell**, Edward, Jr. 1931- WhoBlA 92
**Levelt**, Willem J. M. 1938- ConAu 133, IntWW 91
**Levelton**, B Harding 1925- AmMWSc 92
**Leven**, Earl of 1924- Who 92
**Leven**, Charles Louis 1928- WhoFI 92, WhoMW 92
**Leven**, Richard Michael 1940- WhoFI 92
**Leven**, Robert Maynard 1955- AmMWSc 92
**Leven**, Stanley 1919- WhoAmL 92
**Levenberg**, Diane DrAPF 91
**Levenberg**, Milton Irwin 1937- AmMWSc 92
**Levenbook**, Leo 1919- AmMWSc 92
**Levendosky**, Charles DrAPF 91
**Levendosky**, Charles 1936- IntAu&W 91
**Levene**, Ben 1938- IntWW 91, TwCPaSc, Who 92
**Levene**, Cyril 1926- AmMWSc 92
**Levene**, Howard 1914- AmMWSc 92
**Levene**, John Reuben 1929- AmMWSc 92
**Levene**, Malcolm Irvin 1951- Who 92
**Levene**, Peter 1941- Who 92
**Levene**, Peter Keith 1941- IntWW 91
**Levene**, Ralph Zalman 1927- AmMWSc 92
**Levengood**, Paul Kugler 1942- WhoFI 92
**Levenson**, Alan Bradley 1935- WhoAmL 92, WhoFI 92
**Levenson**, Alan Ira 1935- AmMWSc 92, WhoWest 92
**Levenson**, Christopher 1934- ConPo 91, IntAu&W 91, WrDr 92
**Levenson**, Fred DrAPF 91
**Levenson**, Harold Samuel 1916- AmMWSc 92
**Levenson**, James B 1944- AmMWSc 92
**Levenson**, Jordan WhoEnt 92
**Levenson**, Laurie L. 1956- WhoAmL 92
**Levenson**, Leonard L 1928- AmMWSc 92
**Levenson**, Marc David 1945- AmMWSc 92
**Levenson**, Mark Steven 1957- WhoAmL 92
**Levenson**, Milton 1923- AmMWSc 92
**Levenson**, Morris E 1914- AmMWSc 92
**Levenson**, Robert AmMWSc 92
**Levenson**, Stanley Melvin 1916- AmMWSc 92
**Levenspiel**, Octave 1926- AmMWSc 92
**Levenstein**, Harold 1923- AmMWSc 92
**Levenstein**, Irving 1912- AmMWSc 92
**Levenstein**, Roslyn M. 1920- WhoWest 92
**Levental**, Valery Ya Korlerich 1942- IntWW 91
**Leventhal**, A. Linda 1943- WhoAmL 92
**Leventhal**, Aaron J. 1941- WhoMW 92
**Leventhal**, Ann Z. DrAPF 91
**Leventhal**, Bennett 1949- ConAu 135
**Leventhal**, Brigid Gray 1935- AmMWSc 92
**Leventhal**, Carl M 1933- AmMWSc 92
**Leventhal**, Colin David 1946- Who 92
**Leventhal**, Edwin Alfred 1934- AmMWSc 92
**Leventhal**, Ellen Iris 1949- WhoFI 92
**Leventhal**, Harold 1919- WhoEnt 92
**Leventhal**, Howard 1931- AmMWSc 92
**Leventhal**, Howard Ellis 1940- WhoWest 92
**Leventhal**, Jacob J 1937- AmMWSc 92
**Leventhal**, Leon 1922- AmMWSc 92
**Leventhal**, Marvin 1937- AmMWSc 92
**Leventhal**, Stephen Henry 1949- AmMWSc 92
**Leventhorpe**, Collett 1815-1889 DcNCBi 4
**Leventis**, Michael 1944- TwCPaSc
**Leventis**, Phil Peter 1945- WhoAmP 91
**Leveque**, Jean Andre Eugene 1929- IntWW 91
**Leveque**, Jean Maxime 1923- IntWW 91
**Le Veque**, Matthew Kurt 1958- WhoWest 92
**LeVeque**, William Judson 1923- AmMWSc 92
**Lever** Who 92
**Lever**, Alfred B P 1936- AmMWSc 92
**Lever**, Charles 1806-1872 RfGEnL 91
**Lever**, Christopher Who 92
**Lever**, Cyril, Jr 1929- AmMWSc 92
**Lever**, Jeremy Frederick 1933- IntWW 91, Who 92
**Lever**, John Michael 1928- Who 92
**Lever**, Julia Elizabeth 1945- AmMWSc 92
**Lever**, Lafayette 1960- WhoBlA 92
**Lever**, Paul 1944- Who 92
**Lever**, Reginald Frank 1930- AmMWSc 92
**Lever**, Tresham Christopher 1932- Who 92
**Lever**, Walter Frederick 1909- AmMWSc 92
**Lever Of Manchester**, Baron 1914- IntWW 91, Who 92
**Leverant**, Gerald Robert 1940- AmMWSc 92
**Levere**, Richard David 1931- AmMWSc 92
**Levere**, Trevor Harvey 1944- AmMWSc 92
**Leverence**, John 1946- WrDr 92
**Leverenz**, Humboldt Walter 1909- AmMWSc 92
**Leverenz**, Ted E 1941- WhoAmP 91
**Leverett**, Dennis Hugh 1931- AmMWSc 92
**Leverett**, M C 1910- AmMWSc 92
**Leverhulme**, Viscount 1915- IntWW 91, Who 92
**Leverich**, Kathleen DrAPF 91
**Leveridge**, Richard 1670?-1758 NewAmDM
**Levering**, Robert 1944- WhoFI 92
**Leverington**, James Patrick 1950- WhoRel 92
**Levermore**, Charles Herbert 1856-1927 AmPeW
**Levermore**, Claudette Madge 1939- WhoBlA 92
**Leversedge**, Leslie Frank 1904- Who 92
**Leverson**, Ada 1862-1933 RfGEnL 91
**LeVert**, Eddie WhoBlA 92
**LeVert**, Francis E 1939- AmMWSc 92
**LeVert**, Francis E. 1940- WhoBlA 92
**Leverton**, Colin Allen H. Who 92
**Leverton**, Walter Frederick 1922- AmMWSc 92
**Levertov**, Denise DrAPF 91
**Levertov**, Denise 1923- BenetAL 91, ConLC 66 [port], ConPo 91, CurBio 91 [port], IntAu&W 91, WrDr 92
**Leveson**, Lord 1959- Who 92
**Leveson**, Brian Henry 1949- Who 92
**Leveson Gower** Who 92
**Levesque**, Allen Henry 1936- AmMWSc 92
**Levesque**, Charles Louis 1913- AmMWSc 92
**Levesque**, Georges Henri 1903- IntWW 91, WhoRel 92
**Levesque**, J Michael 1953- WhoAmP 91
**Levesque**, Louis 1908- Who 92, WhoRel 92
**Levesque**, Mary E WhoAmP 91
**Levesque**, Maurice J 1925- WhoAmP 91
**Levesque**, Rene 1922-1987 FacFETw [port]
**Levesque**, Rene J A 1926- AmMWSc 92
**Levetan**, Liane 1936- WhoAmP 91
**Levetin Avery**, Estelle 1945- AmMWSc 92
**Levetown**, Robert Alexander 1935- WhoAmL 92
**Levey**, Allan C 1935- WhoAmP 91
**Levey**, Barry WhoAmP 91
**Levey**, Douglas J 1957- AmMWSc 92
**Levey**, Gerald Saul 1937- AmMWSc 92
**Levey**, Gerrit 1924- AmMWSc 92
**Levey**, Harold Abram 1924- AmMWSc 92
**Levey**, Jack Silver 1950- WhoAmL 92
**Levey**, Marc M. 1947- WhoAmL 92
**Levey**, Michael 1927- IntAu&W 91, IntWW 91, Who 92, WrDr 92
**Levey**, Sandra Collins 1944- WhoFI 92, WhoWest 92
**Levi Strauss** FacFETw
**Levi**, Anthony Frederic John 1959- AmMWSc 92
**Levi**, Anthony H. T. 1929- WrDr 92
**Levi**, Arrigo 1926- IntWW 91
**Levi**, Barbara Goss 1943- AmMWSc 92
**Levi**, Carlo 1902-1975 FacFETw, LiExTwC
**Levi**, Connie 1939- WhoAmP 91
**Levi**, David 1740-1799 BlkwCEP
**Levi**, David F. 1951- WhoAmL 92
**Levi**, David Winterton 1921- AmMWSc 92
**Levi**, Doro 1898- IntWW 91
**Levi**, Edward H. 1911- WrDr 92
**Levi**, Edward Hirsch 1911- IntWW 91, Who 92, WhoAmL 92, WhoAmP 91, WhoMW 92
**Levi**, Elliott J 1940- AmMWSc 92
**Levi**, Enrico 1918- AmMWSc 92
**Levi**, Herbert A. 1931- WhoWest 92
**Levi**, Herbert Walter 1921- AmMWSc 92
**Levi**, Hermann 1839-1900 NewAmDM
**Levi**, Irving 1914- AmMWSc 92
**Levi**, Jan Heller DrAPF 91
**Levi**, Michael Phillip 1941- AmMWSc 92
**Levi**, Nannette 1926- WhoEnt 92
**Levi**, Peter 1931- ConAu 34NR, ConPo 91, IntAu&W 91, WrDr 92
**Levi**, Peter Chad Tigar 1931- Who 92
**Levi**, Primo 1919- IntAu&W 91
**Levi**, Primo 1919-1987 FacFETw, LiExTwC
**Levi**, Renato 1926- Who 92
**Levi**, Robert Hofeller 1948- WhoEnt 92
**Levi**, Roberto 1934- AmMWSc 92
**Levi**, Steven Channing 1948- WhoWest 92
**Levi**, Toni Mergentime DrAPF 91
**Levi**, Y. Leo 1926- ConAu 36NR
**Levi**, Yoel 1950- WhoEnt 92
**Levi-Montalcini**, Rita 1909- AmMWSc 92, IntWW 91, Who 92, WhoNob 90
**Levi-Sandri**, Lionello 1910- IntWW 91
**Levi Setti**, Riccardo 1927- AmMWSc 92
**Levi-Strauss**, Claude 1908- FacFETw, GuFrLit 1, IntWW 91, Who 92
**Levialdi**, Stefano 1936- AmMWSc 92
**Leviant**, Curt DrAPF 91
**Levich**, Calman 1921- AmMWSc 92
**Levick**, George Michael 1953- WhoEnt 92
**Levick**, Richard Scott 1957- WhoAmL 92
**Levick**, William Russell 1931- IntWW 91, Who 92
**LeVie**, Donn, Jr. 1951- ConAu 134
**Levie**, Hallie R. 1939- WhoAmL 92
**Levie**, Harold Walter 1949- AmMWSc 92
**Levie**, Joseph Henry WhoAmL 92
**Levie**, Mark Robert 1951- WhoAmL 92
**Levie**, Simon Hijman 1925- IntWW 91
**Le Vien**, Jack 1918- IntMPA 92
**Levien**, Joy WhoAmL 92
**Levien**, Louise 1952- AmMWSc 92
**Levien**, Roger Eli 1935- AmMWSc 92
**Levien**, Sonya 1895-1960 ReelWom
**Leviev**, Milcho Isaacov 1937- WhoEnt 92
**Levin**, A Leo 1919- WhoAmP 91
**Levin**, Aaron R 1929- AmMWSc 92
**Levin**, Alan M. 1943- IntMPA 92
**Levin**, Alfred A 1928- AmMWSc 92
**Levin**, Alvin Irving 1921- WhoEnt 92, WhoWest 92
**Levin**, Andrew C 1946- WhoAmP 91
**Levin**, Andrew Eliot 1954- AmMWSc 92
**Levin**, Barbara Chernov 1939- AmMWSc 92
**Levin**, Barry Edward 1942- AmMWSc 92
**Levin**, Bernard 1928- IntAu&W 91, Who 92, WrDr 92
**Levin**, Betsy 1935- WhoAmL 92
**Levin**, Betty 1927- WrDr 92
**Levin**, Betty Lowenthal 1927- IntAu&W 91
**Levin**, Bob DrAPF 91
**Levin**, Bruce 1948- AmMWSc 92
**Levin**, Bruce Allen 1941- WhoAmL 92
**Levin**, Burton WhoAmP 91
**Levin**, Carl 1934- AlmAP 92 [port], IntWW 91, WhoMW 92
**Levin**, Charles Leonard 1926- WhoAmL 92, WhoAmP 91, WhoMW 92
**Levin**, Clifford Ellis 1947- WhoWest 92
**Levin**, David Harold 1928- WhoAmL 92
**Levin**, David Marshall 1954- WhoFI 92
**Levin**, David Peter WhoFI 92
**Levin**, Donald Robert 1947- WhoFI 92
**Levin**, Donna 1954- ConAu 134
**Levin**, Donna Susan 1958- WhoAmL 92
**Levin**, E Theodore 1944- WhoAmP 91
**Levin**, Edward M. 1934- WhoAmL 92
**Levin**, Edwin Roy 1927- AmMWSc 92
**Levin**, Elliott Dordeck 1941- WhoAmL 92
**Levin**, Ellis B 1945- WhoAmP 91
**Levin**, Eugene 1934- AmMWSc 92
**Levin**, Frank S 1933- AmMWSc 92
**Levin**, Franklyn Kussel 1922- AmMWSc 92
**Levin**, Geoffrey Arthur 1955- AmMWSc 92
**Levin**, Gerald LesBEnT 92
**Levin**, Gerald 1929- WrDr 92
**Levin**, Gerald Manuel 1939- WhoFI 92
**Levin**, Gerson 1939- AmMWSc 92
**Levin**, Gideon 1936- AmMWSc 92
**Levin**, Gilbert Victor 1924- AmMWSc 92
**Levin**, Harold Leonard 1929- AmMWSc 92
**Levin**, Harry 1912- IntAu&W 91, IntWW 91, WrDr 92
**Levin**, Harvey Steven 1946- AmMWSc 92
**Levin**, Henry Bernard 1928- IntWW 91
**Levin**, Hervey Phillip 1942- WhoAmL 92
**Levin**, Howard Jay 1945- WhoFI 92
**Levin**, Ira 1929- BenetAL 91, ConNov 91, ConTFT 9, CurBio 91 [port], SmATA 66 [port], TwCSFW 91, WrDr 92
**Levin**, Ira William 1935- AmMWSc 92
**Levin**, Irvin 1912- AmMWSc 92
**Levin**, Irving H 1915- WhoAmP 91
**Levin**, Irving H. 1921- IntMPA 92
**Levin**, Jack 1932- AmMWSc 92
**Levin**, Jack S. 1936- WhoAmL 92
**Levin**, Jacob Joseph 1926- AmMWSc 92
**Levin**, James Benesch 1940- WhoAmL 92
**Levin**, Jay B 1951- WhoAmP 91
**Levin**, Jerome Allen 1939- AmMWSc 92
**Levin**, Jerry Wayne 1944- WhoFI 92
**Levin**, John Abbott 1952- WhoAmL 92
**Levin**, Jonathan Vigdor 1927- WhoFI 92
**Levin**, Joseph David 1918- AmMWSc 92
**Levin**, Joseph W 1939- WhoIns 92
**Levin**, Judith Goldstein 1934- AmMWSc 92
**Levin**, Kathryn J 1944- AmMWSc 92
**Levin**, Kenneth Sherman 1937- WhoMW 92
**Levin**, Lawrence Adam 1953- WhoMW 92
**Levin**, Leonid A 1948- AmMWSc 92
**Levin**, Mario 1953- WhoWest 92
**Levin**, Mark Jay 1957- WhoEnt 92
**Levin**, Mark Milton 1946- WhoMW 92
**Levin**, Marshall Abbott 1920- WhoAmL 92
**Levin**, Martin Allen 1949- AmMWSc 92
**Levin**, Meyer 1905-1981 BenetAL 91
**Levin**, Michael WhoEnt 92
**Levin**, Michael 1958- ConAu 135
**Levin**, Michael David 1942- WhoAmL 92
**Levin**, Michael Elliott 1942- WhoFI 92
**Levin**, Michael H 1936- AmMWSc 92
**Levin**, Michael Moshe 1955- WhoWest 92
**Levin**, Morris A 1934- AmMWSc 92
**Levin**, Morton Loeb 1903- AmMWSc 92
**Levin**, Murray Laurence 1935- AmMWSc 92
**Levin**, Murray Simon 1943- WhoAmL 92
**Levin**, Myrtilla Fones 1938- WhoAmP 91
**Levin**, Nathan 1915- AmMWSc 92
**Levin**, Norman Lewis 1924- AmMWSc 92
**Levin**, Peter Jay 1942- WhoAmL 92
**Levin**, Phillis DrAPF 91
**Levin**, Richard 1910- Who 92
**Levin**, Richard Barry 1956- WhoAmL 92
**Levin**, Richard Charles 1947- WhoFI 92
**Levin**, Richard Lee 1947- WhoWest 92
**Levin**, Richard Louis 1922- IntAu&W 91, WrDr 92
**Levin**, Robert Aaron 1929- AmMWSc 92
**Levin**, Robert Alan 1957- WhoFI 92, WhoWest 92
**Levin**, Robert B. IntMPA 92
**Levin**, Robert Barry 1943- WhoEnt 92
**Levin**, Robert Daniel 1930- WhoAmL 92
**Levin**, Robert David 1947- WhoEnt 92
**Levin**, Robert E 1930- AmMWSc 92
**Levin**, Robert Edmond 1931- AmMWSc 92
**Levin**, Robert Harold 1915- AmMWSc 92
**Levin**, Robert Martin 1945- AmMWSc 92
**Levin**, Robert Neal 1954- WhoMW 92
**Levin**, Robert P. 1953- WhoAmL 92
**Levin**, Roger L 1936- AmMWSc 92
**Levin**, Roger Michael 1942- WhoAmL 92
**Levin**, Roger Phillip 1956- WhoFI 92
**Levin**, Ronald Harold 1945- AmMWSc 92
**Levin**, Roy 1948- AmMWSc 92
**Levin**, S Benedict 1910- AmMWSc 92
**Levin**, Samuel Joseph 1935- AmMWSc 92
**Levin**, Sander 1931- WhoMW 92
**Levin**, Sander M. 1931- AlmAP 92 [port], WhoAmP 91
**Levin**, Seymour A 1922- AmMWSc 92
**Levin**, Seymour R 1934- AmMWSc 92
**Levin**, Sidney Seamore 1929- AmMWSc 92
**Levin**, Simon 1942- WhoAmL 92
**Levin**, Simon Asher 1941- AmMWSc 92
**Levin**, Simon Eugene 1920- AmMWSc 92
**Levin**, Stanley d1991 NewYTBS 91
**Levin**, Stephen Howard 1955- WhoAmL 92
**Levin**, Steven Scott 1957- WhoFI 92
**Levin**, Stuart Franklin 1933- WhoEnt 92
**Levin**, Susan Bass 1952- WhoAmP 91
**Levin**, Tereska DrAPF 91
**Levin**, Toni Isola 1954- WhoRel 92
**Levin**, Victor Alan 1941- AmMWSc 92
**Levin**, Wayne 1940- AmMWSc 92
**Levin**, William Cohn 1917- AmMWSc 92
**Levin**, William Edward 1954- WhoWest 92
**Levin**, William Michael 1949- WhoWest 92
**Levin**, Zev 1940- AmMWSc 92

**Levin-Rice,** Patricia Oppenheim 1932- *WhoMW 92*
**Levinas,** Michael 1949- *ConCom 92*
**Levine,** Aaron M. 1947- *WhoFI 92*
**Levine,** Aaron William 1943- *AmMWSc 92*
**Levine,** Alan 1948- *WhoAmL 92*
**Levine,** Alan J. 1947- *WhoEnt 92, WhoFI 92*
**Levine,** Alan Stewart 1944- *AmMWSc 92*
**Levine,** Alfred Martin 1941- *AmMWSc 92*
**Levine,** Allan 1956- *ConAu 135*
**Levine,** Allen Stuart 1949- *AmMWSc 92*
**Levine,** Alvin Saul 1925- *AmMWSc 92*
**Levine,** Anne-Marie *DrAPF 91*
**Levine,** Arnold David 1925- *AmMWSc 92*
**Levine,** Arnold J 1939- *AmMWSc 92*
**Levine,** Arnold Milton 1916- *AmMWSc 92, WhoWest 92*
**Levine,** Arthur Samuel 1936- *AmMWSc 92*
**Levine,** Barry Franklin 1942- *AmMWSc 92*
**Levine,** Barry R. 1953- *WhoAmL 92*
**Levine,** Benjamin 1931- *WhoAmL 92, WhoFI 92*
**Levine,** Bernard *WhoMW 92*
**Levine,** Bernard Benjamin 1928- *AmMWSc 92*
**Levine,** Bernard L. 1934- *WhoMW 92*
**Levine,** Beryl J 1935- *WhoAmP 91*
**Levine,** Beryl Joyce 1935- *WhoAmL 92, WhoMW 92*
**Levine,** Betty K 1933- *SmATA 66*
**Levine,** Carl Morton 1931- *WhoEnt 92*
**Levine,** Charles 1922- *AmMWSc 92*
**Levine,** Charles A. 1897-1991 *NewYTBS 91 [port]*
**Levine,** Charles H 1939-1988 *ConAu 35NR*
**LeVine,** D J 1921- *AmMWSc 92*
**Levine,** Daniel 1920- *AmMWSc 92*
**Levine,** David 1926- *IntWW 91*
**Levine,** David Ethan 1955- *WhoAmL 92*
**Levine,** David Ian 1960- *WhoFI 92*
**Levine,** David Knudsen 1955- *WhoFI 92*
**Levine,** David M. *DrAPF 91*
**Levine,** David Morris 1939- *AmMWSc 92*
**Levine,** Donald Martin 1929- *AmMWSc 92*
**Levine,** Duane Gilbert 1933- *AmMWSc 92*
**Levine,** Edward Leslie 1927- *WhoFI 92*
**Levine,** Ellen *DrAPF 91*
**Levine,** Elliot Myron 1937- *AmMWSc 92*
**Levine,** Eric Michael 1952- *WhoRel 92*
**Levine,** Eugene 1925- *AmMWSc 92*
**Levine,** Gail Janice 1947- *WhoMW 92*
**Levine,** Gary Lauren 1961- *WhoMW 92*
**Levine,** Geoffrey 1942- *AmMWSc 92*
**Levine,** Gerald Richard 1936- *WhoFI 92*
**Levine,** Harold 1922- *AmMWSc 92*
**Levine,** Harold 1928- *AmMWSc 92*
**Levine,** Harold 1931- *WhoAmL 92, WhoFI 92*
**Levine,** Harvey Robert 1931- *AmMWSc 92*
**Levine,** Herbert d1991 *NewYTBS 91 [port]*
**Levine,** Herbert B. 1930- *WhoAmL 92*
**Levine,** Herbert Jerome 1928- *AmMWSc 92*
**Levine,** Herman Saul 1922- *AmMWSc 92*
**Levine,** Hillel 1946- *WhoRel 92*
**Levine,** Howard Allen 1942- *AmMWSc 92*
**Levine,** Howard Arnold 1932- *WhoAmP 91*
**Levine,** Howard Bernard 1928- *AmMWSc 92*
**Levine,** I. Robert 1932- *WhoFI 92*
**Levine,** Ira Noel 1937- *AmMWSc 92*
**Levine,** Irving 1921- *WhoFI 92*
**Levine,** Irving R. *LesBEnT 92*
**Levine,** Irving Raskin *WhoFI 92*
**Levine,** Israel E. 1923- *WrDr 92*
**Levine,** J S 1915- *AmMWSc 92*
**Levine,** Jack 1907- *AmMWSc 92*
**Levine,** Jack 1915- *IntWW 91*
**Levine,** James 1943- *FacFETw, IntWW 91, NewAmDM, WhoEnt 92*
**Levine,** Jay Joseph 1954- *WhoFI 92*
**Levine,** Jeffrey 1945- *AmMWSc 92*
**Levine,** Jerome Lester 1940- *WhoAmL 92*
**Levine,** Jerome Paul 1937- *AmMWSc 92*
**Levine,** Jerry David 1952- *AmMWSc 92*
**Levine,** Joel S 1942- *AmMWSc 92*
**Levine,** Joel Seth 1947- *WhoWest 92*
**Levine,** John David 1936- *WhoAmL 92*
**Levine,** Jon David 1945- *AmMWSc 92*
**Levine,** Jon Howard 1941- *AmMWSc 92*
**Levine,** Joseph 1912- *WhoEnt 92*
**Levine,** Joseph H 1926- *AmMWSc 92*
**Levine,** Jules David 1937- *AmMWSc 92*
**Levine,** Jules Ivan 1938- *AmMWSc 92*
**Levine,** Keith Farrel 1955- *WhoMW 92*
**Levine,** Lainie 1942- *WhoEnt 92*
**Levine,** Laura Sue 1943- *WhoEnt 92*
**Levine,** Laurence 1926- *AmMWSc 92*
**Levine,** Laurence E. 1941- *WhoFI 92*
**Levine,** Laurence Harvey 1946- *WhoAmL 92*
**Levine,** Lawrence 1924- *AmMWSc 92*
**Levine,** Lawrence Elliott 1941- *AmMWSc 92*
**Levine,** Lee 1954- *WhoAmL 92*
**Levine,** Leo Meyer 1922- *AmMWSc 92*
**Levine,** Leon 1934- *AmMWSc 92*
**Levine,** Leonard 1929- *AmMWSc 92*
**Levine,** Leonard P 1932- *AmMWSc 92*
**Levine,** Louis 1921- *AmMWSc 92*
**Levine,** Maita Faye 1930- *AmMWSc 92*
**Levine,** Marilyn Markovich 1930- *WhoAmL 92*
**Levine,** Mark David 1944- *AmMWSc 92*
**Levine,** Mark Lee 1943- *WhoFI 92*
**Levine,** Martin 1925- *AmMWSc 92*
**Levine,** Martin David 1938- *AmMWSc 92*
**Levine,** Mel 1943- *AlmAP 92 [port]*
**Levine,** Meldon E 1943- *WhoAmP 91*
**Levine,** Meldon Edises 1943- *WhoWest 92*
**Levine,** Melvin Charles 1930- *WhoAmL 92, WhoFI 92*
**Levine,** Melvin Mordecai 1925- *AmMWSc 92*
**Levine,** Michael 1939- *ConAu 133*
**Levine,** Michael 1954- *WhoWest 92*
**Levine,** Michael Elias 1941- *WhoFI 92*
**Levine,** Michael Joseph 1945- *WhoWest 92*
**Levine,** Michael Lawrence 1947- *WhoFI 92*
**Levine,** Michael S 1944- *AmMWSc 92*
**Levine,** Michael Steven 1955- *AmMWSc 92*
**Levine,** Michael W 1943- *AmMWSc 92*
**LeVine,** Micheal Joseph 1940- *AmMWSc 92*
**Levine,** Miriam *DrAPF 91*
**Levine,** Montague 1922- *Who 92*
**Levine,** Mortimer 1922- *WrDr 92*
**Levine,** Myron 1926- *AmMWSc 92, WhoMW 92*
**Levine,** Nat 1900-1989 *FacFETw*
**Le Vine,** Nathalie Christian 1929- *WhoEnt 92*
**Levine,** Nathan 1930- *AmMWSc 92*
**Levine,** Norman 1923- *BenetAL 91, ConNov 91, IntAu&W 91*
**Levine,** Norman 1924- *WrDr 92*
**Levine,** Norman Dion 1912- *AmMWSc 92, WhoMW 92*
**Levine,** Norman G *WhoIns 92*
**Levine,** O Robert *AmMWSc 92*
**Levine,** Oscar 1923- *AmMWSc 92*
**Levine,** Paul Hersh 1935- *AmMWSc 92*
**Levine,** Paul Howard 1937- *AmMWSc 92*
**Levine,** Peter David 1944- *WhoMW 92*
**Levine,** Philip *DrAPF 91*
**Levine,** Philip 1928- *BenetAL 91, ConPo 91, WrDr 92*
**Levine,** Phillip J 1934- *AmMWSc 92*
**Levine,** Rachmiel 1910- *AmMWSc 92, IntWW 91*
**Levine,** Randolph Herbert 1946- *AmMWSc 92*
**Levine,** Randy Lewis 1955- *WhoAmL 92*
**Levine,** Rhea Joy Cottler 1939- *AmMWSc 92*
**Levine,** Richard Arthur 1933- *WhoEnt 92*
**Levine,** Richard Frederick 1946- *WhoEnt 92*
**Levine,** Richard Joseph 1939- *AmMWSc 92*
**Levine,** Richard S 1947- *AmMWSc 92*
**Levine,** Robert 1919- *AmMWSc 92*
**Levine,** Robert 1926- *AmMWSc 92*
**Levine,** Robert Alan 1932- *AmMWSc 92*
**Levine,** Robert Jeffrey 1956- *WhoAmL 92*
**Levine,** Robert John 1934- *AmMWSc 92*
**LeVine,** Robert Murray 1956- *WhoWest 92*
**Levine,** Robert Paul 1926- *AmMWSc 92*
**Levine,** Robert S 1921- *AmMWSc 92*
**Levine,** Robert Sidney 1942- *WhoMW 92*
**Levine,** Ronald Jay 1953- *WhoAmL 92*
**Levine,** Russell Evan 1960- *WhoMW 92*
**Levine,** Ruth *WhoEnt 92*
**Levine,** Ruth R *AmMWSc 92*
**Levine,** Samuel 1921- *AmMWSc 92*
**Levine,** Samuel Bruce 1949- *WhoRel 92*
**Levine,** Samuel Gale 1928- *AmMWSc 92*
**Levine,** Samuel Harold 1925- *AmMWSc 92*
**Levine,** Samuel Milton 1929- *WhoAmL 92*
**Levine,** Samuel W 1916- *AmMWSc 92*
**Levine,** Sanford Harold 1938- *WhoAmL 92*
**Levine,** Saul 1938- *AmMWSc 92*
**Levine,** Scott 1956- *WhoEnt 92*
**Levine,** Seymour 1922- *AmMWSc 92*
**Levine,** Seymour 1924- *WhoAmL 92*
**Levine,** Seymour 1925- *AmMWSc 92, IntWW 91*
**Levine,** Sherrie 1947- *WorArt 1980 [port]*
**Levine,** Sol 1922- *IntWW 91*
**Levine,** Sol 1928- *WhoFI 92*
**Levine,** Solomon L. 1923- *WhoAmL 92*
**Levine,** Solomon Leon 1940- *AmMWSc 92*
**Levine,** Stanley Walter 1929- *WhoFI 92*
**Levine,** Stephen 1937- *ConAu 35NR*
**Levine,** Stephen Alan 1938- *AmMWSc 92*
**Levine,** Steven Alan 1951- *WhoFI 92, WhoMW 92*
**Levine,** Steven Donald 1956- *WhoAmL 92*
**Levine,** Steven Jon 1942- *WhoAmL 92*
**Levine,** Stuart 1932- *IntAu&W 91*
**Levine,** Stuart George 1932- *WrDr 92*
**Levine,** Sumner Norton 1923- *AmMWSc 92*
**Levine,** Sydney 1923- *Who 92*
**Levine,** Ted Morell 1927- *WhoFI 92*
**LeVine,** Terry Mark 1951- *WhoAmL 92*
**Levine,** Walter 1930- *AmMWSc 92*
**Levine,** William Michael 1952- *WhoAmL 92*
**Levine,** William Silver 1941- *AmMWSc 92*
**Levine-Freidus,** Gail *SmATA 65*
**Levine-Goffman,** Laura Amy 1959- *WhoFI 92*
**LeViness,** Peter Osmund 1958- *WhoRel 92*
**Leving,** Jeffery Mark 1951- *WhoAmL 92*
**Levinge,** Richard 1946- *Who 92*
**Levinger,** Bernard Werner 1928- *AmMWSc 92*
**Levinger,** Joseph S 1921- *AmMWSc 92*
**Levinger,** Moshe 1935- *News 92-1 [port]*
**Levings,** Charles Sandford, III 1930- *AmMWSc 92*
**Levings,** Colin David 1942- *AmMWSc 92*
**Levings,** Theresa Lawrence 1952- *WhoAmL 92*
**Levingston,** Clifford Eugene 1961- *WhoBlA 92*
**Levingston,** Ernest Lee 1921- *WhoFI 92*
**Levingston,** John Colville Bowring 1929- *WhoFI 92*
**Levingston,** Jon Stuart 1958- *WhoFI 92*
**Levingston,** Keith David 1957- *WhoFI 92*
**Levingston,** Roberto Marcelo 1920- *IntWW 91*
**Levins,** John Raymond 1944- *WhoFI 92*
**Levins,** Richard 1930- *AmMWSc 92*
**Levins-Morales,** Aurora *DrAPF 91*
**Levins Morales,** Ricardo Manuel 1956- *WhoHisp 92*
**Levinskas,** George Joseph 1924- *AmMWSc 92*
**Levinsky,** Frieda L. *DrAPF 91*
**Levinsky,** Norman George 1929- *AmMWSc 92*
**Levinsky,** Walter John 1920- *AmMWSc 92*
**Levinson,** Alfred Abraham 1927- *AmMWSc 92*
**Levinson,** Alfred Stanley 1932- *AmMWSc 92*
**Levinson,** Art *IntMPA 92*
**Levinson,** Arthur David 1950- *AmMWSc 92, WhoWest 92*
**Levinson,** Barry 1932- *IntMPA 92, WrDr 92*
**Levinson,** Barry 1942- *IntDcF 2-2*
**Levinson,** Barry L. 1932- *WhoEnt 92*
**Levinson,** Charles 1936- *AmMWSc 92*
**Levinson,** Charles Bernard 1912- *WhoMW 92*
**Levinson,** Daniel Ronald 1949- *WhoAmP 91*
**Levinson,** David N *WhoAmP 91*
**Levinson,** David W 1925- *AmMWSc 92*
**Levinson,** Deirdre *DrAPF 91*
**Levinson,** Deirdre 1931- *IntAu&W 91*
**Levinson,** Gilbert E 1928- *AmMWSc 92*
**Levinson,** Harry 1922- *IntAu&W 91, WhoFI 92, WrDr 92*
**Levinson,** Joel N. 1947- *WhoWest 92*
**Levinson,** John Z 1916- *AmMWSc 92*
**Levinson,** Kenneth Lee 1953- *WhoAmL 92, WhoFI 92, WhoWest 92*
**Levinson,** Kenneth S. 1947- *WhoAmL 92*
**Levinson,** Lawrence Edward 1930- *WhoFI 92*
**Levinson,** Leslie Harold 1929- *WhoAmL 92*
**Levinson,** Lionel Monty 1943- *AmMWSc 92*
**Levinson,** Mark 1929- *AmMWSc 92*
**Levinson,** Mark Lawrence 1940- *WhoEnt 92*
**Levinson,** Martin Harold 1929- *WhoEnt 92*
**Levinson,** Norm *IntMPA 92, WhoEnt 92*
**Levinson,** Olga May *WrDr 92*
**Levinson,** Paul Howard 1952- *WhoAmL 92*
**Levinson,** Peter Joseph 1943- *WhoAmL 92*
**Levinson,** Philip Joel 1947- *WhoFI 92*
**Levinson,** Riki Friedberg *IntAu&W 91*
**Levinson,** Salmon Oliver 1865-1941 *AmPeW*
**Levinson,** Sanford Victor 1941- *WhoAmL 92*
**Levinson,** Sidney Bernard 1911- *AmMWSc 92*
**Levinson,** Simon Rock 1946- *AmMWSc 92*
**Levinson,** Stanley S *AmMWSc 92*
**Levinson,** Stephen 1944- *AmMWSc 92*
**Levinson,** Stephen Curtis 1947- *Who 92*
**Levinson,** Steven R 1947- *AmMWSc 92*
**Levinson,** Stuart Alan 1920- *AmMWSc 92*
**Levinson,** Warren E 1933- *AmMWSc 92*
**Levinson,** Warren Edward 1933- *WhoWest 92*
**Levinson-Link** *LesBEnT 92*
**Levinstein,** Henry 1919- *AmMWSc 92*
**Levinstein,** Mark Steven 1958- *WhoAmL 92*
**Levinthal,** Charles F 1945- *AmMWSc 92*
**Levinthal,** Cyrus d1990 *IntWW 91N*
**Levinthal,** Cyrus 1922- *AmMWSc 92*
**Levinthal,** Elliott Charles 1922- *AmMWSc 92*
**Levinthal,** Mark 1941- *AmMWSc 92, WhoMW 92*
**Levinton,** Jeffrey Sheldon 1946- *AmMWSc 92*
**Levintow,** Leon 1921- *AmMWSc 92*
**Levion,** Leon L *WhoAmP 91*
**Levis,** Alexander Henry 1940- *AmMWSc 92*
**Levis,** C A 1926- *AmMWSc 92*
**Levis,** Derek George 1911- *Who 92*
**Levis,** Donald J 1936- *AmMWSc 92*
**Levis,** James J 1926- *WhoIns 92*
**Levis,** Larry *DrAPF 91*
**Levis,** Larry 1946- *ConPo 91, IntAu&W 91, WrDr 92*
**Levis,** William Walter, Jr 1918- *AmMWSc 92*
**Levison,** Barry 1932- *IntWW 91*
**Levison,** Charles *ConTFT 9*
**Levison,** Harold George 1947- *WhoAmL 92*
**Levison,** Mary Irene 1923- *Who 92*
**Levison,** Matthew Edmund 1937- *AmMWSc 92*
**Levison,** Sandra Peltz 1941- *AmMWSc 92*
**Levison,** Stanley 1912-1979 *FacFETw*
**Levison,** William H 1936- *AmMWSc 92*
**Levister,** Ernest Clayton, Jr. 1936- *WhoBlA 92*
**Levister,** Robert L. 1918- *WhoBlA 92*
**Levister,** Wendell P. 1928- *WhoBlA 92*
**Levit,** Edithe J 1926- *AmMWSc 92*
**Levit,** Ginger 1937- *WhoEnt 92*
**Levit,** Heloise B. 1937- *WhoEnt 92*
**Levit,** Jay Joseph 1934- *WhoAmL 92*
**Levit,** Lawrence Bruce 1942- *AmMWSc 92*
**Levit,** Milton 1924- *WhoFI 92*
**Levit,** Robert Jules 1916- *AmMWSc 92*
**Levit,** Solomon Grigor'evich 1894-1938 *SovUnBD*
**Levit,** Victor B 1930- *WhoIns 92*
**Levit,** Victor Bert 1930- *WhoAmL 92*
**Levit,** William Harold, Jr. 1938- *WhoAmL 92, WhoFI 92*
**Levitan,** Aida Tomas 1948- *WhoHisp 92*
**Levitan,** Alexander Allen 1939- *AmMWSc 92*
**Levitan,** Dan 1957- *WhoFI 92*
**Levitan,** David Maurice 1915- *WhoAmL 92*
**Levitan,** Donald 1928- *WhoFI 92*
**Levitan,** Herbert 1939- *AmMWSc 92*
**Levitan,** James A. 1925- *WhoAmL 92*
**Levitan,** Katherine D. 1933- *WhoAmL 92*
**Levitan,** Laurence 1933- *WhoAmP 91*
**Levitan,** Max 1921- *AmMWSc 92*
**Levitan,** Michael Leonard 1941- *AmMWSc 92*
**Levitan,** Mortimer *ScFEYrs*
**Levitan,** Paul d1976 *LesBEnT 92*
**Levitan,** Roger Stanley 1933- *WhoAmL 92, WhoWest 92*
**Levitan,** Ruven 1927- *AmMWSc 92*
**Levitan,** Stephen Richard 1956- *WhoFI 92*
**Levitas,** Alfred Dave 1920- *AmMWSc 92*
**Levitas,** Elliott Harris 1930- *WhoAmP 91*
**Levithan,** Jack 1947- *WhoFI 92*
**Leviticus,** Louis I 1931- *AmMWSc 92*
**Levitin,** Anatoliy Emmanuilovich 1915- *SovUnBD*
**Levitin,** Nancy B. 1960- *WhoAmL 92*
**Levitin,** Sonia 1934- *SmATA 68 [port], WrDr 92*
**Levitin-Krasnov,** Anotoly Emmanuilovich 1915- *LiExTwC*
**Leviton,** Alan 1938- *AmMWSc 92*
**Leviton,** Alan Edward 1930- *AmMWSc 92*
**Levitsky,** Aleksandr Andreevich 1885-1965 *SovUnBD*
**Levitsky,** Grigoriy Andreevich 1878-1942 *SovUnBD*
**Levitsky,** Lynne Lipton 1942- *AmMWSc 92*
**Levitsky,** Melvyn 1938- *WhoAmP 91*
**Levitsky,** Myron 1930- *AmMWSc 92*
**Levitsky,** Sidney 1936- *AmMWSc 92*
**Levitt,** Albert P 1924- *AmMWSc 92*
**Levitt,** Annabel Wood *DrAPF 91*
**Levitt,** Arthur, III 1957- *WhoEnt 92*
**Levitt,** Barrie 1935- *AmMWSc 92*
**Levitt,** Beverly Diane 1939- *WhoEnt 92*
**Levitt,** David George 1942- *AmMWSc 92*
**Levitt,** George 1925- *AmMWSc 92*
**Levitt,** Israel Monroe 1908- *AmMWSc 92*
**Levitt,** Jacob 1911- *AmMWSc 92*
**Levitt,** Jaren 1946- *WhoFI 92*
**Levitt,** Lawrence David 1944- *WhoFI 92, WhoWest 92*

**Levitt**, Leon *WhoMW 92*
**Levitt**, LeRoy P 1918- *AmMWSc 92*
**Levitt**, Marvin Frederick 1920- *AmMWSc 92*
**Levitt**, Melvin 1925- *AmMWSc 92*
**Levitt**, Michael D 1935- *AmMWSc 92*
**Levitt**, Morton *AmMWSc 92*
**Levitt**, Peter *DrAPF 91*
**Levitt**, Robert Elwood 1926- *WhoAmP 91*
**Levitt**, Rodney Charles 1929- *WhoEnt 92*
**Levitt**, Ronald Stephen 1944- *WhoAmL 92*
**Levitt**, Ruby Rebecca 1907- *IntMPA 92*
**Levitt**, Seymour H 1928- *AmMWSc 92*
**Levitt**, Sidney 1947- *SmATA 68 [port]*
**Levitt Topol**, Robin April *WhoAmL 92*
**LeVitus**, Jodie Ellen 1957- *WhoEnt 92*
**Levitz**, Hilbert 1931- *AmMWSc 92*
**Levitz**, Mortimer 1921- *AmMWSc 92*
**Levitzky**, Michael Gordon 1947- *AmMWSc 92*
**Levkov**, Jerome Stephen 1939- *AmMWSc 92*
**Levmore**, Saul 1953- *WhoAmL 92*
**Levovitz**, Pesach Zechariah 1922- *WhoRel 92*
**Levow**, Roy Bruce 1943- *AmMWSc 92*
**Levoy**, Myron 1930- *WrDr 92*
**Levshin**, Boris Venedictovich 1926- *IntWW 91*
**Levy**, Adolph J. 1936- *WhoAmL 92*
**Levy**, Alain 1946- *WhoEnt 92*
**Levy**, Alan 1932- *IntAu&W 91, WrDr 92*
**Levy**, Alan 1937- *AmMWSc 92*
**Levy**, Alan B 1945- *AmMWSc 92*
**Levy**, Alan C 1930- *AmMWSc 92*
**Levy**, Alan David 1938- *WhoWest 92*
**Levy**, Alan Joseph 1955- *AmMWSc 92*
**Levy**, Alan M. 1940- *WhoAmL 92*
**Levy**, Alan Richard 1957- *WhoEnt 92*
**Levy**, Allan Edward 1942- *Who 92*
**Levy**, Allan Henry 1929- *AmMWSc 92*
**Levy**, Ariel 1944- *WhoEnt 92*
**Levy**, Arnold Stuart 1941- *WhoFI 92, WhoMW 92*
**Levy**, Arthur 1921- *AmMWSc 92*
**Levy**, Arthur James 1947- *WhoEnt 92*
**Levy**, Arthur Louis 1917- *AmMWSc 92*
**Levy**, Arthur Maurice 1930- *AmMWSc 92*
**Levy**, Barbara Rifkin 1941- *WhoEnt 92*
**Levy**, Barnet M 1917- *AmMWSc 92*
**Levy**, Barry David 1951- *WhoAmL 92*
**Levy**, Bern 1929- *WhoEnt 92*
**Levy**, Bernard *IntMPA 92*
**Levy**, Bernard, Jr 1924- *AmMWSc 92*
**Levy**, Bernard-Henri 1948- *IntWW 91*
**Levy**, Boris 1927- *AmMWSc 92*
**Levy**, Bud 1928- *IntMPA 92*
**Levy**, Burton 1912- *WhoEnt 92*
**Levy**, Charles Kingsley 1924- *AmMWSc 92*
**Levy**, Charles M. 1939- *WhoAmL 92*
**Levy**, Coleman Bertram 1939- *WhoAmL 92*
**Levy**, Daniel 1940- *AmMWSc 92*
**Levy**, Daniel 1957- *WhoFI 92*
**Levy**, David *IntMPA 92, LesBEnT 92, WhoEnt 92, WhoWest 92*
**Levy**, David 1932- *WhoAmL 92, WhoWest 92*
**Levy**, David 1937- *WhoFI 92*
**Levy**, David 1938- *IntWW 91*
**Levy**, David 1949- *WhoAmL 92*
**Levy**, David Alfred 1930- *AmMWSc 92*
**Levy**, David Edward 1941- *AmMWSc 92*
**Levy**, David Franklin 1945- *WhoMW 92*
**Levy**, David Henry 1951- *WhoAmL 92*
**Levy**, David Steven 1955- *WhoWest 92*
**Levy**, Deborah Louise 1950- *AmMWSc 92*
**Levy**, Dennis Martyn 1936- *Who 92*
**Levy**, Donald Harris 1939- *AmMWSc 92, WhoMW 92*
**Levy**, Donald M 1935- *AmMWSc 92*
**Levy**, Edward 1929- *NewAmDM*
**Levy**, Edward Irving 1929- *WhoEnt 92*
**Levy**, Edward Kenneth *AmMWSc 92*
**Levy**, Edward Robert 1927- *AmMWSc 92*
**Levy**, Elinor Miller 1942- *AmMWSc 92*
**Levy**, Elizabeth 1942- *ConAu 34NR*
**Levy**, Emanuel 1918- *WhoIns 92*
**Levy**, Emmanuel 1900-1986 *TwCPaSc*
**Levy**, Ernst 1895-1981 *NewAmDM*
**Levy**, Eugene 1946- *IntMPA 92*
**Levy**, Eugene F. 1947- *WhoAmL 92*
**Levy**, Eugene Howard 1944- *AmMWSc 92, WhoWest 92*
**Levy**, Ewart Maurice 1897- *Who 92*
**Levy**, Fred, Jr. d1991 *NewYTBS 91*
**Levy**, Gabor Bela 1913- *AmMWSc 92*
**Levy**, George Charles 1944- *AmMWSc 92*
**Levy**, George Joseph 1927- *Who 92*
**Levy**, George Michael 1948- *WhoAmL 92*
**Levy**, Gerald Frank 1938- *AmMWSc 92*
**Levy**, Gerhard 1928- *AmMWSc 92*
**Levy**, Gloriann 1943- *WhoRel 92*
**Levy**, Hans Richard 1929- *AmMWSc 92*
**Levy**, Harris Benjamin 1928- *AmMWSc 92*
**Levy**, Harvey Louis 1935- *AmMWSc 92*
**Levy**, Harvey Merrill 1928- *AmMWSc 92*
**Levy**, Herbert Monte 1923- *WhoAmL 92*
**Levy**, Herman M. 1904- *IntMPA 92*
**Levy**, Hilton Bertram 1916- *AmMWSc 92*
**Levy**, Howard *DrAPF 91*
**Levy**, I. Richard 1959- *WhoAmL 92*
**Levy**, Irvin L. 1929- *WhoFI 92*
**Levy**, Isaac d1975 *LesBEnT 92*
**Levy**, J Langley *ScFEYrs*
**Levy**, Jack Benjamin 1941- *AmMWSc 92*
**Levy**, Jacob Newman 1938- *WhoFI 92*
**Levy**, Jacques Bernard 1937- *IntWW 91*
**Levy**, James Peter 1940- *WhoFI 92*
**Levy**, Jane 1945- *WhoWest 92*
**Levy**, Jerome Seymour 1942- *WhoAmL 92*
**Levy**, Jerre Marie 1938- *AmMWSc 92*
**Levy**, JoAnn 1941- *ConAu 134*
**Levy**, Joel Howard 1938- *WhoFI 92*
**Levy**, John *DrAPF 91*
**Levy**, John Court 1926- *Who 92*
**Levy**, John Edward 1954- *WhoEnt 92*
**Levy**, Jonathan Frederick 1935- *IntAu&W 91, WhoEnt 92*
**Levy**, Jordan 1943- *WhoAmP 91*
**Levy**, Joseph 1913- *AmMWSc 92*
**Levy**, Joseph Benjamin 1923- *AmMWSc 92*
**Levy**, Joseph Louis 1947- *WhoFI 92*
**Levy**, Joseph Victor 1928- *AmMWSc 92, WhoWest 92*
**Levy**, Jules V. 1923- *IntMPA 92*
**Levy**, Julia Gerwing 1934- *AmMWSc 92*
**Levy**, Kenneth 1927- *WhoEnt 92*
**Levy**, Lawrence S 1933- *AmMWSc 92*
**Levy**, Leland David 1934- *WhoAmP 91*
**Levy**, Leo 1928- *AmMWSc 92*
**Levy**, Leon d1978 *LesBEnT 92*
**Levy**, Leon Bruce 1937- *AmMWSc 92*
**Levy**, Leon Sholom 1930- *AmMWSc 92*
**Levy**, Leonard Alvin 1935- *AmMWSc 92, WhoMW 92*
**Levy**, Leonard W. 1923- *WrDr 92*
**Levy**, Louis 1923- *AmMWSc 92*
**Levy**, Louis A 1941- *AmMWSc 92*
**Levy**, Louis Edward 1846-1919 *BiInAmS*
**Levy**, Louis Edward 1932- *WhoFI 92*
**Levy**, Louis Michael 1931- *WhoWest 92*
**Levy**, M Frank 1925- *AmMWSc 92*
**Levy**, Marian Muller 1942- *WhoFI 92*
**Levy**, Marilyn 1922- *AmMWSc 92*
**Levy**, Marilyn 1937- *ConAu 135, SmATA 67 [port]*
**Levy**, Mark Allan 1939- *WhoAmL 92*
**Levy**, Mark Allan 1950- *WhoEnt 92*
**Levy**, Mark B 1951- *AmMWSc 92*
**Levy**, Mark Irving 1949- *WhoAmL 92*
**Levy**, Mark Ivan 1946- *WhoWest 92*
**Levy**, Martin J Linden 1925- *AmMWSc 92*
**Levy**, Marvin David 1932- *NewAmDM, WhoEnt 92*
**Levy**, Matthew Nathan 1922- *AmMWSc 92*
**Levy**, Maurice 1922- *IntWW 91*
**Levy**, Michael *IntMPA 92*
**Levy**, Michael 1946- *WhoFI 92*
**Levy**, Michael R 1935- *AmMWSc 92*
**Levy**, Moises 1930- *AmMWSc 92*
**Levy**, Morris 1944- *AmMWSc 92*
**Levy**, Morris Stephen 1962- *WhoFI 92*
**Levy**, Mortimer 1924- *AmMWSc 92*
**Levy**, Nelson Louis 1941- *AmMWSc 92*
**Levy**, Newton, Jr 1935- *AmMWSc 92*
**Levy**, Norman 1935- *IntMPA 92, WhoEnt 92*
**Levy**, Norman B 1931- *AmMWSc 92*
**Levy**, Norman J 1931- *WhoAmP 91*
**Levy**, Norman Stuart 1940- *AmMWSc 92*
**Levy**, Owen *DrAPF 91*
**Levy**, Paul 1941- *AmMWSc 92, Who 92*
**Levy**, Paul F 1934- *AmMWSc 92*
**Levy**, Paul W 1921- *AmMWSc 92*
**Levy**, Penelope Ann 1942- *WhoWest 92*
**Levy**, Peter Haskell 1960- *WhoAmL 92*
**Levy**, Peter Michael 1936- *AmMWSc 92*
**Levy**, Philip Marcus 1934- *Who 92*
**Levy**, Ralph *LesBEnT 92*
**Levy**, Ralph 1932- *AmMWSc 92*
**Levy**, Ram Leon 1933- *AmMWSc 92*
**Levy**, Raymond Haim 1927- *IntWW 91*
**Levy**, Rene Hanania 1942- *AmMWSc 92*
**Levy**, Ricardo Benjamin 1945- *AmMWSc 92*
**Levy**, Richard 1944- *AmMWSc 92*
**Levy**, Richard Allen *AmMWSc 92*
**Levy**, Richard C. 1947- *WhoEnt 92*
**Levy**, Robert 1938- *AmMWSc 92*
**Levy**, Robert Aaron 1926- *AmMWSc 92*
**Levy**, Robert Edward 1939- *AmMWSc 92, WhoFI 92*
**Levy**, Robert I 1937- *AmMWSc 92*
**Levy**, Robert Isaac 1924- *WhoWest 92*
**Levy**, Robert Isaac 1937- *IntWW 91*
**Levy**, Robert J. *DrAPF 91*
**Levy**, Robert S 1920- *AmMWSc 92*
**Levy**, Robert Sigmund 1921- *AmMWSc 92*
**Levy**, Roger 1950- *ConAu 134*
**Levy**, Ronald Fred 1944- *AmMWSc 92*
**Levy**, Salomon 1926- *AmMWSc 92*
**Levy**, Sam Malcolm 1901- *WhoMW 92*
**Levy**, Samuel C 1937- *AmMWSc 92*
**Levy**, Samuel Robert 1931- *WhoAmL 92*
**Levy**, Samuel Wolfe 1922- *AmMWSc 92*
**Levy**, Sander Alvin *AmMWSc 92*
**Levy**, Seth Allen 1959- *WhoAmL 92*
**Levy**, Shawn Anthony 1961- *WhoEnt 92*
**Levy**, Sheila Ellen 1941- *WhoWest 92*
**Levy**, Stephen *DrAPF 91*
**Levy**, Steven Mark 1963- *WhoAmL 92*
**Levy**, Stuart B 1938- *AmMWSc 92*
**Levy**, Susan M. 1942- *WhoMW 92*
**Levy**, Thomas David 1943- *WhoFI 92*
**Levy**, Valerie Lowe *WhoBIA 92*
**Levy**, Victor Miles, Jr. 1931- *WhoBIA 92*
**Levy**, Walter James 1911- *IntWW 91*
**Levy**, William N. 1941- *WhoAmL 92*
**Levy**, Yisrael 1926-1990 *FacFETw*
**Lew**, Chel Wing 1935- *AmMWSc 92*
**Lew**, Gloria Maria 1934- *AmMWSc 92*
**Lew**, Hin 1921- *AmMWSc 92*
**Lew**, John S 1934- *AmMWSc 92*
**Lew**, Richard C. 1960- *WhoWest 92*
**Lew**, Ronald S. W. 1941- *WhoAmL 92, WhoWest 92*
**Lew**, Salvador 1929- *WhoEnt 92, WhoHisp 92*
**Lewald**, Theodor 1860-1947 *EncTR 91*
**Lewallen**, Elinor Grace Kirby 1919- *WhoRel 92*
**Lewand**, Franklin Thomas 1946- *WhoAmL 92*
**Lewand**, Thomas *WhoAmP 91*
**Lewando**, Jan 1909- *Who 92*
**Lewando**, Jan Alfred 1909- *IntWW 91*
**Lewandos**, Glenn S *AmMWSc 92*
**Lewandowski**, Andrew Anthony 1946- *WhoFI 92*
**Lewandowski**, Bohdan 1926- *IntWW 91*
**Lewandowski**, Dennis Thomas 1945- *WhoMW 92*
**Lewandowski**, Jan 1933- *IntAu&W 91*
**Lewandowski**, Janusz 1952- *IntWW 91*
**Lewandowski**, John Joseph 1956- *AmMWSc 92, WhoMW 92*
**Lewandowski**, Melvin A 1930- *AmMWSc 92*
**Lewandowski**, Michalene Maria 1920- *WhoMW 92*
**Lewandowski**, Stanley Richard, Jr. 1937- *WhoWest 92*
**Lewandowski**, Stephen *DrAPF 91*
**Lewars**, Errol George *AmMWSc 92*
**Lewbart**, Marvin Louis 1929- *AmMWSc 92*
**Lewbel**, Arthur Harris 1956- *WhoFI 92*
**Lewellen**, A. Wayne 1944- *IntMPA 92*
**Lewellen**, Bill 1951- *WhoAmP 91*
**Lewellen**, Michael Elliott 1960- *WhoBIA 92*
**Lewellen**, Robert Thomas 1940- *AmMWSc 92*
**Lewellen**, Rollo Lee 1932- *WhoWest 92*
**Lewellen**, William Stephen 1933- *AmMWSc 92*
**Lewelling**, John 1715?-1794 *DcNCBi 4*
**Lewellyn**, Jess William, Jr. 1960- *WhoEnt 92*
**Lewen**, John Henry 1920- *Who 92*
**Lewent**, Judy C. 1949- *WhoFI 92*
**Lewenthal**, Raymond 1926- *NewAmDM*
**Lewenz**, George F 1920- *AmMWSc 92*
**Lewer**, Michael Edward 1933- *Who 92*
**Lewerenz**, Sarah 1956- *WhoAmP 91*
**Lewers**, Benjamin Hugh 1932- *Who 92*
**Lewert**, Robert Murdoch 1919- *AmMWSc 92*
**Lewes**, Suffragan Bishop of 1932- *Who 92*
**Lewes**, Charles *WrDr 92*
**Lewes**, John Hext 1903- *Who 92*
**Lewes And Hastings**, Archdeacon of *Who 92*
**Lewey**, Scot Michael 1958- *WhoMW 92*
**Lewick**, Halpern 1888-1962 *LiExTwC*
**Lewin** *Who 92*
**Lewin**, Baron 1920- *IntWW 91, Who 92*
**Lewin**, Alfred S 1951- *AmMWSc 92*
**Lewin**, Anita Hana 1935- *AmMWSc 92*
**Lewin**, Dennis 1944- *WhoEnt 92*
**Lewin**, Frank 1925- *WhoEnt 92*
**Lewin**, Jack Jacob 1932- *WhoFI 92*
**Lewin**, Joyce Chismore 1926- *AmMWSc 92*
**Lewin**, Lawrence M 1932- *AmMWSc 92*
**Lewin**, Leonard 1919- *AmMWSc 92*
**Lewin**, Leonard C. *DrAPF 91*
**Lewin**, Marsha Denice 1941- *WhoFI 92*
**Lewin**, Martin J. 1949- *WhoAmL 92*
**Lewin**, Michael 1956- *WhoEnt 92*
**Lewin**, Michael Z. 1942- *WrDr 92*
**Lewin**, Michael Zinn 1942- *IntAu&W 91*
**Lewin**, Moshe 1921- *WrDr 92*
**Lewin**, Ralph Arnold 1921- *AmMWSc 92, WhoWest 92*
**Lewin**, Rebecca *DrAPF 91*
**Lewin**, Rhoda G. 1929- *ConAu 135*
**Lewin**, Rhoda Greene 1929- *WhoMW 92*
**Lewin**, Ronald 1914-1984 *FacFETw*
**Lewin**, Seymour Z 1921- *AmMWSc 92*
**Lewin**, Travis H.D. 1933- *WhoAmL 92*
**Lewin**, Victor 1930- *AmMWSc 92*
**Lewin**, Walter H G 1936- *AmMWSc 92*
**Lewine**, Jeffrey George 1955- *WhoEnt 92*
**Lewine**, Richard 1910- *WhoEnt 92*
**Lewine**, Robert F. *LesBEnT 92*
**Lewine**, Robert F. 1913- *IntMPA 92, WhoEnt 92*
**Lewinsky**, Herbert Christian 1928- *IntWW 91*
**Lewinson**, Victor A 1918- *AmMWSc 92*
**Lewinton**, Christopher 1932- *Who 92*
**Lewis** *Who 92*
**Lewis**, Baron 1928- *IntWW 91*
**Lewis Family** *NewAmDM*
**Lewis**, A D M 1920- *AmMWSc 92*
**Lewis**, A. Duff, Jr. 1939- *WhoFI 92*
**Lewis**, Aaron 1945- *AmMWSc 92*
**Lewis**, Adam Anthony Murless *Who 92*
**Lewis**, Alan A. d1991 *NewYTBS 91*
**Lewis**, Alan Ervin 1936- *AmMWSc 92*
**Lewis**, Alan Graham 1934- *AmMWSc 92*
**Lewis**, Alan James *AmMWSc 92*
**Lewis**, Alan James 1943- *AmMWSc 92*
**Lewis**, Alan Laird *AmMWSc 92*
**Lewis**, Albert Dale Milton 1920- *WhoMW 92*
**Lewis**, Albert Gamaliel, III 1954- *WhoAmL 92*
**Lewis**, Albert L. *WhoRel 92*
**Lewis**, Albert Ray 1960- *WhoBIA 92*
**Lewis**, Alexander D 1912- *AmMWSc 92*
**Lewis**, Alexander Ingersoll, III 1946- *WhoAmL 92*
**Lewis**, Alexander L. 1910- *WhoBIA 92*
**Lewis**, Alfred Allan 1929- *WhoEnt 92*
**Lewis**, Alfred George 1920- *Who 92*
**Lewis**, Alfred Henry 1857-1914 *TwCWW 91*
**Lewis**, Alfred Henry 1858-1914 *BenetAL 91*
**Lewis**, Allan *WhoEnt 92*
**Lewis**, Allen 1909- *IntWW 91, Who 92, WhoRel 92*
**Lewis**, Allen Rogers 1947- *AmMWSc 92*
**Lewis**, Almera P. 1935- *WhoBIA 92*
**Lewis**, Alun 1915-1944 *FacFETw, RfGEnL 91*
**Lewis**, Alun Kynric 1928- *Who 92*
**Lewis**, Alvin 1935- *WhoBIA 92*
**Lewis**, Alvin Bower, Jr. 1932- *WhoAmL 92*
**Lewis**, Alvin Edward 1916- *AmMWSc 92, WhoWest 92*
**Lewis**, Alvin Thomas 1912- *WhoRel 92*
**Lewis**, Andre 1960- *WhoBIA 92*
**Lewis**, Andre Leon 1955- *WhoEnt 92*
**Lewis**, Andrew 1918- *Who 92*
**Lewis**, Andrew L, Jr 1931- *WhoAmP 91*
**Lewis**, Andrew Lindsay, Jr. 1931- *IntWW 91*
**Lewis**, Ann M *WhoAmP 91*
**Lewis**, Anne A. 1905- *WhoBIA 92*
**Lewis**, Anthea 1948- *TwCPaSc*
**Lewis**, Anthony *Who 92*
**Lewis**, Anthony 1927- *IntAu&W 91, WhoAmP 91*
**Lewis**, Anthony Harold, Jr. 1953- *WhoBIA 92*
**Lewis**, Anthony Meredith 1940- *Who 92*
**Lewis**, Anthony Robert 1938- *Who 92*
**Lewis**, Anthony Wetzel 1942- *AmMWSc 92*
**Lewis**, Arlene Jane Quiring 1934- *WhoEnt 92*
**Lewis**, Armand Francis 1932- *AmMWSc 92*
**Lewis**, Arnold D 1920- *AmMWSc 92*
**Lewis**, Arnold Leroy, II 1952- *AmMWSc 92*
**Lewis**, Arthur *IntWW 91*
**Lewis**, Arthur 1915- *WrDr 92*
**Lewis**, Arthur 1916- *IntMPA 92*
**Lewis**, Arthur 1935- *WhoEnt 92*
**Lewis**, Arthur A., Jr. 1925- *WhoBIA 92*
**Lewis**, Arthur B 1901- *AmMWSc 92*
**Lewis**, Arthur Edward 1929- *AmMWSc 92*
**Lewis**, Arthur O, Jr 1920- *ScFEYrs*
**Lewis**, Arthur W. 1926- *WhoBIA 92*
**Lewis**, Arthur William John 1917- *Who 92*
**Lewis**, Aubrey C. 1935- *WhoBIA 92*
**Lewis**, Austin James 1945- *AmMWSc 92*
**Lewis**, Avis Ida 1918- *WhoAmP 91*
**Lewis**, Barbara Cline 1948- *WhoWest 92*
**Lewis**, Barry 1929- *Who 92*
**Lewis**, Barry Kent 1949- *WhoMW 92*
**Lewis**, Benjamin Marzluff 1925- *AmMWSc 92*
**Lewis**, Bernard 1899- *AmMWSc 92*
**Lewis**, Bernard 1905- *Who 92*
**Lewis**, Bernard 1916- *IntWW 91, Who 92*
**Lewis**, Bertha Ann 1927- *AmMWSc 92*
**Lewis**, Bertie 1931- *Who 92*
**Lewis**, Billie 1929- *WhoBIA 92*
**Lewis**, Brent Renault 1958- *WhoWest 92*
**Lewis**, Brian 1954- *WhoEnt 92*
**Lewis**, Brian Keith 1962- *WhoFI 92*
**Lewis**, Brian Kreglow 1932- *AmMWSc 92*
**Lewis**, Brian Murray 1943- *AmMWSc 92*
**Lewis**, Brian William 1959- *WhoAmL 92*
**Lewis**, Bryan W 1959- *WhoAmP 91*
**Lewis**, Byron E. 1931- *WhoBIA 92*

**Lewis**, C. S. 1898-1963 *CnDBLB 7 [port], FacFETw, RfGEnL 91, TwCSFW 91*
**Lewis**, C S, Jr 1920- *AmMWSc 92*
**Lewis**, Cameron David 1920- *AmMWSc 92*
**Lewis**, Carl 1961- *FacFETw, IntWW 91, WhoBlA 92*
**Lewis**, Carmie Perrotta 1929- *AmMWSc 92*
**Lewis**, Cary B., Jr. 1921- *WhoBlA 92*
**Lewis**, Cecil Arthur 1898- *IntAu&W 91, Who 92*
**Lewis**, Cecil Day *RfGEnL 91*
**Lewis**, Cecil Dwain 1929- *WhoRel 92*
**Lewis**, Charles *IntAu&W 91X*
**Lewis**, Charles Arlen 1943- *WhoMW 92*
**Lewis**, Charles Bady 1913- *WhoBlA 92*
**Lewis**, Charles Bertrand 1842-1924 *BenetAL 91*
**Lewis**, Charles E 1928- *AmMWSc 92*
**Lewis**, Charles Edwin 1928- *IntWW 91*
**Lewis**, Charles Grant 1948- *WhoBlA 92*
**Lewis**, Charles H. 1923- *WhoBlA 92*
**Lewis**, Charles J 1924- *WhoAmP 91*
**Lewis**, Charles J 1927- *AmMWSc 92*
**Lewis**, Charles Joseph 1917- *AmMWSc 92*
**Lewis**, Charles McArthur 1949- *WhoBlA 92*
**Lewis**, Charles Michael 1949- *WhoBlA 92*
**Lewis**, Charles Robert 1960- *WhoEnt 92*
**Lewis**, Charles Spencer 1928- *WhoFI 92*
**Lewis**, Charles Thomas 1956- *WhoEnt 92*
**Lewis**, Charles William 1920- *AmMWSc 92*
**Lewis**, Charles William 1926- *WhoAmP 91*
**Lewis**, Charlotte 1955- *BlkOlyM*
**Lewis**, Christopher A *WhoAmP 91*
**Lewis**, Christopher Harvey 1944- *WhoWest 92*
**Lewis**, Claire E. 1952- *WhoAmL 92*
**Lewis**, Clark Houston 1929- *AmMWSc 92*
**Lewis**, Claude Irenius 1935- *AmMWSc 92*
**Lewis**, Claudia L 1907- *IntAu&W 91*
**Lewis**, Claudia Louise 1907- *WrDr 92*
**Lewis**, Clayton W. *DrAPF 91*
**Lewis**, Cleveland Arthur 1942- *WhoBlA 92*
**Lewis**, Clifford Jackson 1912- *AmMWSc 92*
**Lewis**, Colston A. 1914- *WhoBlA 92*
**Lewis**, Cornelius Crawford 1921- *AmMWSc 92*
**Lewis**, Craig 1956- *WhoEnt 92*
**Lewis**, Craig Graham David 1930- *WhoFI 92*
**Lewis**, Cynthia Lucille 1948- *AmMWSc 92*
**Lewis**, Dan 1910- *IntWW 91, Who 92*
**Lewis**, Daniel 1946- *WhoBlA 92*
**Lewis**, Daniel Edwin 1910- *WhoAmL 92*
**Lewis**, Daniel Frederick 1954- *WhoEnt 92*
**Lewis**, Daniel Joseph 1950- *WhoRel 92*
**Lewis**, Daniel M. 1944- *WhoAmL 92*
**Lewis**, Daniel Moore 1945- *AmMWSc 92*
**Lewis**, Daniel Ralph 1944- *AmMWSc 92*
**Lewis**, Danny Harve 1948- *AmMWSc 92*
**Lewis**, David 1953- *WhoMW 92*
**Lewis**, David 1955- *TwCPaSc*
**Lewis**, David Baker 1944- *WhoBlA 92*
**Lewis**, David Carl 1957- *WhoFI 92*
**Lewis**, David Courtenay M. *Who 92*
**Lewis**, David Edwin 1951- *AmMWSc 92*
**Lewis**, David Franklin 1948- *WhoWest 92*
**Lewis**, David Gareth 1931- *Who 92*
**Lewis**, David Harold 1925- *AmMWSc 92*
**Lewis**, David Henry L. *Who 92*
**Lewis**, David Howard 1959- *WhoWest 92*
**Lewis**, David Hughes 1950- *WhoWest 92*
**Lewis**, David John 1948- *WhoAmL 92*
**Lewis**, David Kellogg 1941- *IntWW 91*
**Lewis**, David Kenneth 1943- *AmMWSc 92*
**Lewis**, David Kent 1938- *AmMWSc 92*
**Lewis**, David Malcolm 1928- *Who 92*
**Lewis**, David Robert Andrew 1953- *WhoAmL 92*
**Lewis**, David S, Jr 1917- *AmMWSc 92*
**Lewis**, David Sloan, Jr. 1917- *IntWW 91*
**Lewis**, David Thomas 1909- *Who 92*
**Lewis**, David Thomas 1935- *AmMWSc 92*
**Lewis**, David W 1930- *AmMWSc 92*
**Lewis**, Dawnn *WhoEnt 92*
**Lewis**, De Witt *ScFEYrs*
**Lewis**, Delano Eugene 1938- *WhoBlA 92, WhoFI 92*
**Lewis**, Dennis Allen 1942- *AmMWSc 92*
**Lewis**, Dennis Aubrey 1928- *Who 92*
**Lewis**, Dennis Carroll 1940- *WhoWest 92*
**Lewis**, Derek 1946- *Who 92*
**Lewis**, Derek Lamont 1956- *WhoWest 92*
**Lewis**, Diane 1936- *WhoFI 92*
**Lewis**, Diane Claire 1945- *WhoBlA 92*
**Lewis**, Diane Patricia 1956- *WhoFI 92*
**Lewis**, Dick Edgar 1938- *WhoBlA 92*
**Lewis**, Donald Edward 1931- *AmMWSc 92*
**Lewis**, Donald Everett 1931- *AmMWSc 92*
**Lewis**, Donald Gordon 1926- *Who 92*
**Lewis**, Donald Howard 1936- *AmMWSc 92*
**Lewis**, Donald John 1926- *AmMWSc 92*
**Lewis**, Donald Richard 1920- *AmMWSc 92*
**Lewis**, Donna Ruth 1953- *WhoRel 92*
**Lewis**, Douglas 1938- *WhoRel 92*
**Lewis**, Douglas Grinslade 1938- *WhoFI 92*
**Lewis**, Douglas Scott 1951- *AmMWSc 92*
**Lewis**, Duane 1942- *WhoAmP 91*
**Lewis**, Dudley Barksdale, Jr 1942- *WhoAmP 91*
**Lewis**, E Grey *WhoAmP 91*
**Lewis**, E. Grey 1937- *WhoAmL 92*
**Lewis**, Edmonia 1843?-1911? *HanAmWH*
**Lewis**, Edmonia 1845?- *NotBlAW 92 [port]*
**Lewis**, Edward *IntMPA 92*
**Lewis**, Edward Alan 1946- *WhoRel 92*
**Lewis**, Edward B 1918- *AmMWSc 92, IntWW 91, WhoWest 92*
**Lewis**, Edward Lyn 1930- *AmMWSc 92*
**Lewis**, Edward Morland 1903-1943 *TwCPaSc*
**Lewis**, Edward R 1919- *AmMWSc 92*
**Lewis**, Edward Sheldon 1920- *AmMWSc 92*
**Lewis**, Edward T. 1940- *WhoBlA 92*
**Lewis**, Edwin 1881-1959 *RelLAm 91*
**Lewis**, Edwin Reynolds 1934- *AmMWSc 92, WhoWest 92*
**Lewis**, Elizabeth Ellen 1964- *WhoAmL 92*
**Lewis**, Elma 1921- *NotBlAW 92*
**Lewis**, Elma I. 1921- *WhoBlA 92*
**Lewis**, Elsie Makel 1914- *WhoBlA 92*
**Lewis**, Emanuel *WhoBlA 92*
**Lewis**, Emily Jane 1955- *WhoAmL 92*
**Lewis**, Emmanuel 1971- *IntMPA 92*
**Lewis**, Enoch 1776-1856 *AmPeW, BiInAmS*
**Lewis**, Ephron H. *WhoBlA 92*
**Lewis**, Erma 1926- *WhoBlA 92*
**Lewis**, Erma Jean 1943- *WhoBlA 92*
**Lewis**, Ernest Crosby 1934- *WhoAmP 91*
**Lewis**, Ernest Gordon 1918- *Who 92*
**Lewis**, Estelle *BenetAL 91*
**Lewis**, Esyr ap Gwilym 1926- *Who 92*
**Lewis**, Evelyn 1946- *WhoFI 92*
**Lewis**, Evelyn Hodges 1907- *WhoWest 92*
**Lewis**, Exum Percival 1863-1926 *DcNCBi 4*
**Lewis**, F.R. *DrAPF 91*
**Lewis**, Fawn Dianne 1963- *WhoWest 92*
**Lewis**, Faye 1896-1982 *ConAu 135*
**Lewis**, Felton Edwin 1923- *WhoBlA 92*
**Lewis**, Flora *WrDr 92*
**Lewis**, Floyd Edward 1938- *WhoBlA 92*
**Lewis**, Forbes Downer 1942- *AmMWSc 92*
**Lewis**, Francis Hotchkiss, Jr 1937- *AmMWSc 92*
**Lewis**, Francis James 1930- *WhoFI 92*
**Lewis**, Frank Harlan 1919- *AmMWSc 92*
**Lewis**, Frank Leroy 1949- *AmMWSc 92*
**Lewis**, Frank Ross 1931- *WhoBlA 92*
**Lewis**, Frederick Carlton 1961- *BlkOlyM [port], WhoBlA 92*
**Lewis**, Frederick D 1943- *AmMWSc 92*
**Lewis**, Frederick John 1944- *WhoAmL 92*
**Lewis**, Frederick Thomas 1941- *WhoWest 92*
**Lewis**, G. Douglass *WhoRel 92*
**Lewis**, Gail R. 1943- *WhoFI 92*
**Lewis**, Geoffrey David 1933- *IntWW 91*
**Lewis**, Geoffrey Lewis 1920- *Who 92*
**Lewis**, George 1900-1968 *NewAmDM*
**Lewis**, George 1931- *WhoFI 92*
**Lewis**, George 1952- *NewAmDM*
**Lewis**, George Campbell, Jr 1919- *AmMWSc 92*
**Lewis**, George Edward 1908- *AmMWSc 92*
**Lewis**, George Edwin 1933- *AmMWSc 92*
**Lewis**, George McCormick 1940- *AmMWSc 92, WhoWest 92*
**Lewis**, George Q. 1916-1979 *ConAu 135*
**Lewis**, George R 1924- *AmMWSc 92*
**Lewis**, George Ralph 1941- *WhoBlA 92, WhoFI 92*
**Lewis**, George Tolbert, III 1955- *WhoAmP 91*
**Lewis**, Gerald 1934- *WhoAmP 91*
**Lewis**, Gerald David 1922- *WhoEnt 92*
**Lewis**, Gerald Jorgensen 1933- *WhoWest 92*
**Lewis**, Gibson D 1936- *WhoAmP 91*
**Lewis**, Giles Floyd, Jr. 1927- *WhoRel 92*
**Lewis**, Gillian Marjorie 1945- *Who 92*
**Lewis**, Glenn C 1920- *AmMWSc 92*
**Lewis**, Glenn Joseph 1960- *WhoRel 92*
**Lewis**, Gloria Jane 1929- *WhoMW 92*
**Lewis**, Gordon 1933- *AmMWSc 92*
**Lewis**, Gordon Depew 1929- *AmMWSc 92*
**Lewis**, Gordon K. d1991 *NewYTBS 91*
**Lewis**, Graceanna 1821-1912 *BiInAmS*
**Lewis**, Graham Pritchard 1927- *Who 92*
**Lewis**, Grant Stephen 1942- *WhoAmL 92*
**Lewis**, Green Pryor, Jr. 1945- *WhoBlA 92*
**Lewis**, Gregory Allen 1961- *WhoWest 92*
**Lewis**, Gus Edward 1932- *WhoBlA 92*
**Lewis**, Gwynedd Margaret 1911- *Who 92*
**Lewis**, Gwynne David 1928- *AmMWSc 92*
**Lewis**, H Clay 1913- *AmMWSc 92*
**Lewis**, H Ralph 1931- *AmMWSc 92, WhoBlA 92*
**Lewis**, Hardie Dossie 1939- *WhoWest 92*
**Lewis**, Harold Allen 1945- *WhoFI 92*
**Lewis**, Harold Craig 1944- *WhoAmP 91*
**Lewis**, Harold G. 1938- *IntMPA 92*
**Lewis**, Harold Walter 1917- *AmMWSc 92*
**Lewis**, Harold Warren 1923- *AmMWSc 92*
**Lewis**, Harry *DrAPF 91*
**Lewis**, Harry Sinclair 1885-1951 *WhoNob 90*
**Lewis**, Harvey Dellmond, Jr. 1918- *WhoRel 92*
**Lewis**, Harvey Jay 1937- *WhoAmL 92*
**Lewis**, Harvey Spencer 1883-1939 *RelLAm 91*
**Lewis**, Harvye Fleming 1917- *AmMWSc 92*
**Lewis**, Helen Elizabeth 1951- *WhoEnt 92*
**Lewis**, Helen Middleton 1905- *WhoBlA 92*
**Lewis**, Helen Morris 1852-1933 *DcNCBi 4*
**Lewis**, Henry 1932- *NewAmDM, WhoBlA 92*
**Lewis**, Henry Carvill 1853-1888 *BiInAmS*
**Lewis**, Henry Ervin 1936- *WhoEnt 92*
**Lewis**, Henry Nathan 1926- *Who 92*
**Lewis**, Henry Rafalsky 1925- *AmMWSc 92, WhoFI 92*
**Lewis**, Henry S., Jr. 1935- *WhoBlA 92*
**Lewis**, Henry W. 1927- *WhoBlA 92*
**Lewis**, Henry Wilkins 1856-1936 *DcNCBi 4*
**Lewis**, Herbert J. Whitfield 1911- *Who 92*
**Lewis**, Herbert S. 1934- *WrDr 92*
**Lewis**, Herman William 1923- *AmMWSc 92*
**Lewis**, Hilda Present 1925- *WhoWest 92*
**Lewis**, Homer Dick 1926- *AmMWSc 92*
**Lewis**, Horacio Delano 1944- *WhoHisp 92*
**Lewis**, Houston A. 1920- *WhoBlA 92*
**Lewis**, Huey 1951- *WhoEnt 92*
**Lewis**, Hugh B. 1940- *WhoMW 92*
**Lewis**, Hurtle John *Who 92*
**Lewis**, Hylan Garnet 1911- *WhoBlA 92*
**Lewis**, Hywel David 1910- *Who 92, WrDr 92*
**Lewis**, Ian 1932- *IntMPA 92*
**Lewis**, Ian Talbot 1929- *Who 92*
**Lewis**, Ida Elizabeth 1935- *NotBlAW 92, WhoBlA 92*
**Lewis**, Ioan Myrddin 1930- *Who 92*
**Lewis**, Ira Wayne 1950- *AmMWSc 92*
**Lewis**, Irving James 1918- *AmMWSc 92*
**Lewis**, Irwin C *AmMWSc 92*
**Lewis**, J. B., Jr. 1929- *WhoBlA 92*
**Lewis**, J E 1941- *AmMWSc 92*
**Lewis**, J Gary, III 1946- *WhoAmP 91*
**Lewis**, J. Parry 1927- *WrDr 92*
**Lewis**, J R 1920- *AmMWSc 92*
**Lewis**, J. R. 1933- *WrDr 92*
**Lewis**, Jack A 1939- *AmMWSc 92*
**Lewis**, Jack P 1919- *ConAu 34NR, SmATA 65 [port]*
**Lewis**, Jack Pearl 1919- *WrDr 92*
**Lewis**, Jacqueline *WhoAmP 91*
**Lewis**, James *WhoAmP 91*
**Lewis**, James, Jr. 1930- *WhoBlA 92*
**Lewis**, James A 1930- *WhoAmP 91*
**Lewis**, James A 1933- *WhoAmP 91*
**Lewis**, James B. 1947- *WhoBlA 92*
**Lewis**, James Beliven 1947- *WhoAmP 91, WhoWest 92*
**Lewis**, James Berton 1911- *WhoAmL 92*
**Lewis**, James Chester 1936- *AmMWSc 92*
**Lewis**, James Clement 1915- *AmMWSc 92*
**Lewis**, James Earl 1931- *WhoBlA 92*
**Lewis**, James Earl 1939- *WhoFI 92*
**Lewis**, James Edward 1923- *WhoBlA 92*
**Lewis**, James Fredrick 1937- *WhoRel 92*
**Lewis**, James Kelley 1924- *AmMWSc 92*
**Lewis**, James Laban, III 1942- *AmMWSc 92*
**Lewis**, James Luther 1912- *WhoFI 92*
**Lewis**, James Pettis 1933- *AmMWSc 92*
**Lewis**, James R. 1938- *WhoBlA 92*
**Lewis**, James Vernon 1915- *AmMWSc 92*
**Lewis**, James W L 1938- *AmMWSc 92*
**Lewis**, James William 1937- *WhoWest 92*
**Lewis**, James Woodrow 1912- *WhoAmP 91*
**Lewis**, Jane Sanford 1918- *AmMWSc 92*
**Lewis**, Janet *DrAPF 91*
**Lewis**, Janet 1899- *BenetAL 91, ConNov 91, IntAu&W 91, TwCWW 91, WrDr 92*
**Lewis**, Janet 1937- *WhoMW 92*
**Lewis**, Janie Carol 1957- *WhoWest 92*
**Lewis**, Jason Alvert, Jr. 1941- *WhoFI 92, WhoWest 92*
**Lewis**, Jasper Phelps 1917- *AmMWSc 92*
**Lewis**, Jay Arlan 1962- *WhoRel 92*
**Lewis**, Jeanette 1941- *WhoRel 92*
**Lewis**, Jeffrey George 1956- *WhoWest 92*
**Lewis**, Jeffrey P. 1953- *WhoAmL 92*
**Lewis**, Jerome A. 1927- *WhoFI 92*
**Lewis**, Jerome Whitney 1951- *WhoRel 92*
**Lewis**, Jerrold 1928- *WhoEnt 92*
**Lewis**, Jerry *LesBEnT 92*
**Lewis**, Jerry 1926- *FacFETw, IntDcF 2-2 [port], IntMPA 92, IntWW 91, WhoEnt 92*
**Lewis**, Jerry 1934- *AlmAP 92 [port], WhoAmP 91, WhoWest 92*
**Lewis**, Jerry D. 1912- *WhoEnt 92*
**Lewis**, Jerry Lee 1935- *FacFETw, NewAmDM, WhoEnt 92*
**Lewis**, Jerry Michael 1953- *WhoEnt 92*
**Lewis**, Jerry Parker 1931- *AmMWSc 92*
**Lewis**, Jesse C 1929- *AmMWSc 92*
**Lewis**, Jesse Cornelius 1929- *WhoBlA 92*
**Lewis**, Jesse J. 1925- *WhoBlA 92*
**Lewis**, Jessica Helen 1917- *AmMWSc 92*
**Lewis**, Jim 1943- *WhoAmP 91*
**Lewis**, Joan *Who 92*
**Lewis**, Joan Elizabeth 1961- *WhoAmL 92*
**Lewis**, Joel *DrAPF 91*
**Lewis**, John 1916- *ConAu 133*
**Lewis**, John 1920- *NewAmDM*
**Lewis**, John 1940- *ConBlB 2 [port], WhoAmP 91*
**Lewis**, John Arthur 1934- *Who 92*
**Lewis**, John Bradley 1925- *AmMWSc 92*
**Lewis**, John Clark, Jr. 1935- *WhoWest 92*
**Lewis**, John E 1939- *AmMWSc 92*
**Lewis**, John Elliott 1942- *Who 92*
**Lewis**, John Elliott 1953- *WhoFI 92*
**Lewis**, John Francis 1932- *WhoAmL 92*
**Lewis**, John Furman 1934- *WhoAmL 92, WhoFI 92*
**Lewis**, John G 1920- *AmMWSc 92*
**Lewis**, John Hardy, Jr. 1936- *WhoAmL 92*
**Lewis**, John Henry 1938- *WhoEnt 92*
**Lewis**, John Hubbard 1929- *AmMWSc 92*
**Lewis**, John Hubert Richard 1943- *Who 92*
**Lewis**, John L 1880-1969 *FacFETw [port], RComAH*
**Lewis**, John L, Jr 1929- *AmMWSc 92*
**Lewis**, John Michael Hardwicke 1919- *Who 92*
**Lewis**, John Milton 1931- *WhoEnt 92*
**Lewis**, John Morgan 1920- *AmMWSc 92*
**Lewis**, John N. C. 1912- *WrDr 92*
**Lewis**, John Owen 1935- *WhoWest 92*
**Lewis**, John R. 1940- *AlmAP 92 [port]*
**Lewis**, John R 1954- *WhoAmP 91*
**Lewis**, John Raymond 1918- *AmMWSc 92*
**Lewis**, John Reed 1915- *AmMWSc 92*
**Lewis**, John Reilly 1944- *WhoEnt 92*
**Lewis**, John Robert 1940- *WhoBlA 92*
**Lewis**, John S., Jr. 1941- *WhoWest 92*
**Lewis**, John Simpson 1941- *AmMWSc 92*
**Lewis**, John Thomson Condell 1955- *WhoWest 92*
**Lewis**, John Vernon Radcliffe 1917- *IntWW 91*
**Lewis**, John Wiley, III 1945- *WhoFI 92*
**Lewis**, John William 1958- *WhoAmL 92*
**Lewis**, John Wilson 1930- *WhoWest 92*
**Lewis**, Johnnye Lynn 1948- *WhoWest 92*
**Lewis**, Jonathan Fiske 1953- *WhoMW 92*
**Lewis**, Jonathan Joseph 1958- *AmMWSc 92*
**Lewis**, Joseph 1889-1968 *RelLAm 91*
**Lewis**, Joseph Anthony 1927- *Who 92*
**Lewis**, Joseph H. 1907?- *IntDcF 2-2, IntMPA 92*
**Lewis**, Katherine *AmMWSc 92*
**Lewis**, Kathy Pearce *DrAPF 91*
**Lewis**, Keith Wayne 1956- *WhoFI 92*
**Lewis**, Keith William 1927- *Who 92*
**Lewis**, Kemp Plummer 1880-1952 *DcNCBi 4*
**Lewis**, Kenneth 1916- *Who 92*
**Lewis**, Kenneth 1934- *WhoFI 92, WhoWest 92*
**Lewis**, Kenneth D 1949- *AmMWSc 92*
**Lewis**, Kenneth Frank Mackay 1897- *Who 92*
**Lewis**, Kern Allen 1961- *WhoAmL 92*
**Lewis**, Kevin 1943- *WhoRel 92*
**Lewis**, Kit 1911- *TwCPaSc*
**Lewis**, Kynric *Who 92*
**Lewis**, L Gaunce, Jr 1949- *AmMWSc 92*
**Lewis**, Larry Gene, Sr. 1945- *WhoRel 92*
**Lewis**, Lauretta F. *WhoBlA 92*
**Lewis**, Lawrence Guy 1941- *AmMWSc 92*
**Lewis**, Lawrence Vernon Harcourt 1932- *IntWW 91*
**Lewis**, Lena Armstrong 1910- *AmMWSc 92*
**Lewis**, Lennox 1965- *BlkOlyM*
**Lewis**, Leo E., III 1956- *WhoBlA 92*
**Lewis**, Leon 1833-1920 *ScFEYrs*
**Lewis**, Leonard 1909- *Who 92*
**Lewis**, Leonard John 1909- *Who 92*
**Lewis**, Leonard Jonathan 1915- *WhoMW 92*
**Lewis**, Leroy C. 1917- *WhoBlA 92*
**Lewis**, Leroy Crawford 1940- *AmMWSc 92*
**Lewis**, Lesley 1909- *WrDr 92*
**Lewis**, Leslie Arthur 1940- *AmMWSc 92*
**Lewis**, Lillian J. 1926- *WhoBlA 92*
**Lewis**, Linda 1946- *ConAu 135, SmATA 67 [port]*
**Lewis**, Linda Christine 1949- *WhoFI 92*
**Lewis**, Lloyd 1891-1949 *BenetAL 91*

**Lewis,** Lloyd E., Jr. 1926- *WhoBlA 92*
**Lewis,** Lloyd Edward, Jr. 1926- *WhoFI 92*
**Lewis,** Louise Hope 1962- *WhoAmL 92*
**Lewis,** Lowell N 1931- *AmMWSc 92*
**Lewis,** Luana Kay 1955- *WhoFI 92*
**Lewis,** Lynn Loraine 1929- *AmMWSc 92*
**Lewis,** Malcolm 1946- *WhoWest 92*
**Lewis,** Marc Simon 1926- *AmMWSc 92*
**Lewis,** Marcia Ann 1944- *WhoWest 92*
**Lewis,** Margaret 1942- *ConAu 135*
**Lewis,** Margaret Nast 1911- *AmMWSc 92*
**Lewis,** Margaret S 1954- *WhoAmP 91*
**Lewis,** Margaret W. *WhoBlA 92*
**Lewis,** Margo 1937- *WhoEnt 92*
**Lewis,** Marian L Moore 1937- *AmMWSc 92*
**Lewis,** Marian V 1929- *WhoAmP 91*
**Lewis,** Marilyn W. 1944- *WhoFI 92*
**Lewis,** Marion Elizabeth 1920- *WhoWest 92*
**Lewis,** Marion Jean 1925- *AmMWSc 92*
**Lewis,** Marjorie Herrera 1957- *WhoHisp 92*
**Lewis,** Mark Douglas 1949- *WhoAmP 91*
**Lewis,** Mark Earldon 1951- *WhoWest 92*
**Lewis,** Mark Eugene 1962- *WhoRel 92*
**Lewis,** Mark Henry 1950- *AmMWSc 92*
**Lewis,** Mark Richard 1950- *WhoAmL 92*
**Lewis,** Mark Sanders 1949- *WhoWest 92*
**Lewis,** Martha S. 1924- *WhoBlA 92*
**Lewis,** Martin Edward 1958- *WhoFI 92, WhoMW 92*
**Lewis,** Martin Richard, Jr. 1938- *WhoBlA 92*
**Lewis,** Martyn John Dudley 1945- *Who 92*
**Lewis,** Marvin E. d1991 *NewYTBS 91*
**Lewis,** Mary Ann 1916- *WhoAmP 91*
**Lewis,** Mary Etta 1928- *WhoWest 92*
**Lewis,** Mary Mount 1921- *WhoWest 92*
**Lewis,** Maryann 1964- *WhoFI 92*
**Lewis,** Matthew, Jr. 1930- *WhoBlA 92*
**Lewis,** Matthew Gregory 1775-1818 *RfGEnL 91*
**Lewis,** Maureen Ann 1952- *WhoFI 92*
**Lewis,** Maurice 1943- *WhoBlA 92*
**Lewis,** Maynah 1919- *IntAu&W 91*
**Lewis,** McDaniel 1894-1978 *DcNCBi 4*
**Lewis,** Meade 1905-1964 *NewAmDM*
**Lewis,** Meharry Hubbard 1936- *WhoBlA 92*
**Lewis,** Mel 1929-1990 *AnObit 1990, NewAmDM*
**Lewis,** Melanie 1964- *WhoBlA 92*
**Lewis,** Meriwether 1774-1809 *BenetAL 91, BiInAmS*
**Lewis,** Merle Dean 1947- *WhoMW 92*
**Lewis,** Mervyn *IntAu&W 91X, WrDr 92*
**Lewis,** Michael 1937- *IntAu&W 91*
**Lewis,** Michael 1943- *TwCPaSc*
**Lewis,** Michael Anthony 1948- *AmMWSc 92*
**Lewis,** Michael ap Gwilym 1930- *Who 92*
**Lewis,** Michael Edward 1951- *AmMWSc 92*
**Lewis,** Michael Eugene 1958- *WhoRel 92*
**Lewis,** Michael J. 1939- *IntMPA 92*
**Lewis,** Michael Samuel 1937- *Who 92*
**Lewis,** Milton 1921- *AmMWSc 92*
**Lewis,** Milton F. 1913- *WhoFI 92*
**Lewis,** Monica 1925- *IntMPA 92*
**Lewis,** Morgan V. 1935- *WhoMW 92*
**Lewis,** Morris, Jr. 1911- *WhoFI 92*
**Lewis,** Mort R. 1908-1991 *ConAu 134*
**Lewis,** Morton 1936- *AmMWSc 92*
**Lewis,** Nancy Patricia 1956- *WhoWest 92*
**Lewis,** Naomi *Who 92*
**Lewis,** Nathan Saul 1955- *AmMWSc 92*
**Lewis,** Neeley Charles *WhoAmP 91*
**Lewis,** Neil Jeffrey 1945- *AmMWSc 92*
**Lewis,** Nell Battle 1893-1956 *DcNCBi 4*
**Lewis,** Neville Brice 1936- *IntWW 91*
**Lewis,** Nina Alissa 1954- *AmMWSc 92*
**Lewis,** Norman *Who 92*
**Lewis,** Norman 1912- *WhoWest 92, WrDr 92*
**Lewis,** Olen Hales, Jr 1937- *WhoAmP 91*
**Lewis,** Ora Lee 1930- *WhoBlA 92*
**Lewis,** Oscar 1914-1970 *BenetAL 91*
**Lewis,** Owen *DrAPF 91*
**Lewis,** Patric Robert 1947- *WhoWest 92*
**Lewis,** Patricia Gimbel 1945- *WhoAmL 92*
**Lewis,** Paul Herbert 1924- *AmMWSc 92*
**Lewis,** Paul Jay 1952- *WhoWest 92*
**Lewis,** Paul Kermith, Jr 1931- *AmMWSc 92*
**Lewis,** Paul Richard 1949- *WhoAmL 92*
**Lewis,** Paul Weldon 1943- *AmMWSc 92*
**Lewis,** Paul Wesley 1963- *WhoRel 92*
**Lewis,** Percy Lee 1937- *WhoBlA 92*
**Lewis,** Peter *ConAu 133, IntAu&W 91*
**Lewis,** Peter 1937- *Who 92, WrDr 92*
**Lewis,** Peter 1939- *TwCPaSc*
**Lewis,** Peter Adrian Walter 1932- *AmMWSc 92*
**Lewis,** Peter B 1933- *WhoIns 92*
**Lewis,** Peter Elvet 1937- *ConAu 133*
**Lewis,** Peter Ronald 1926- *Who 92*
**Lewis,** Peter Tyndale 1929- *Who 92*
**Lewis,** Philip Jonah 1962- *WhoRel 92*
**Lewis,** Philip M 1931- *AmMWSc 92*
**Lewis,** Polly Meriwether 1949- *WhoBlA 92*
**Lewis,** Prinic Herbert, Sr. 1930- *WhoBlA 92*
**Lewis,** R. W. B. 1917- *BenetAL 91, DcLB 111 [port]*
**Lewis,** Ralph Jay, III 1942- *WhoFI 92, WhoWest 92*
**Lewis,** Ralph M. 1904-1987 *RelLAm 91*
**Lewis,** Ralph William 1911- *AmMWSc 92*
**Lewis,** Ramsey 1935- *NewAmDM*
**Lewis,** Ramsey Emanuel, Jr. 1935- *WhoBlA 92, WhoEnt 92*
**Lewis,** Randolph Vance 1950- *AmMWSc 92*
**Lewis,** Raymond Gray 1910- *BlkOlyM*
**Lewis,** Reggie 1965- *WhoBlA 92*
**Lewis,** Reginald F. *NewYTBS 91 [port]*
**Lewis,** Reginald F. 1942- *WhoBlA 92, WhoFI 92*
**Lewis,** Reginald Ricardo 1958- *WhoMW 92*
**Lewis,** Richard *DrAPF 91, Who 92, WhoEnt 92*
**Lewis,** Richard d1990 *IntWW 91N, Who 92N*
**Lewis,** Richard 1700?-1734 *BenetAL 91*
**Lewis,** Richard 1914-1990 *AnObit 1990, FacFETw*
**Lewis,** Richard 1935- *Who 92*
**Lewis,** Richard 1948?- *News 92-1 [port]*
**Lewis,** Richard Elias 1924- *WhoEnt 92*
**Lewis,** Richard H 1937- *WhoAmP 91*
**Lewis,** Richard Hayes 1937- *WhoAmL 92*
**Lewis,** Richard Henry 1832-1917 *DcNCBi 4*
**Lewis,** Richard Henry 1850-1926 *DcNCBi 4*
**Lewis,** Richard Jay 1933- *WhoFI 92*
**Lewis,** Richard John 1935- *AmMWSc 92*
**Lewis,** Richard John, Sr. 1936- *WhoBlA 92*
**Lewis,** Richard Thomas 1943- *AmMWSc 92*
**Lewis,** Richard U. 1926- *WhoBlA 92*
**Lewis,** Rita Hoffman 1947- *WhoFI 92*
**Lewis,** Robert 1932- *WhoMW 92*
**Lewis,** Robert Allen 1943- *AmMWSc 92*
**Lewis,** Robert Allen 1945- *AmMWSc 92*
**Lewis,** Robert David 1944- *WhoAmL 92*
**Lewis,** Robert Donald 1897- *AmMWSc 92*
**Lewis,** Robert Earl 1929- *AmMWSc 92*
**Lewis,** Robert Edward 1903- *WhoBlA 92*
**Lewis,** Robert Edwin, Jr 1947- *AmMWSc 92*
**Lewis,** Robert Frank 1920- *AmMWSc 92*
**Lewis,** Robert Glenn 1937- *AmMWSc 92*
**Lewis,** Robert Hall 1926- *NewAmDM*
**Lewis,** Robert Henry 1921- *WhoRel 92*
**Lewis,** Robert Hugh Cecil 1925- *Who 92*
**Lewis,** Robert Lee 1949- *WhoMW 92*
**Lewis,** Robert Lee, III 1949- *WhoWest 92*
**Lewis,** Robert Louis 1936- *WhoBlA 92*
**Lewis,** Robert Miller 1937- *AmMWSc 92*
**Lewis,** Robert Minturn 1924- *AmMWSc 92*
**Lewis,** Robert Q. *LesBEnT 92*
**Lewis,** Robert Q. 1920-1991 *NewYTBS 91 [port]*
**Lewis,** Robert Richards, Jr 1927- *AmMWSc 92*
**Lewis,** Robert Taber 1932- *AmMWSc 92*
**Lewis,** Robert Turner 1923- *WhoWest 92*
**Lewis,** Robert Warren 1943- *AmMWSc 92*
**Lewis,** Robert Welborn 1953- *WhoFI 92*
**Lewis,** Robert William 1930- *IntAu&W 91, WhoMW 92*
**Lewis,** Roger Allen 1941- *AmMWSc 92, WhoWest 92*
**Lewis,** Roger Allen 1953- *WhoRel 92*
**Lewis,** Roger Charles 1944- *WhoAmP 91*
**Lewis,** Roger Curzon 1909- *Who 92*
**Lewis,** Roland Swaine 1908- *Who 92*
**Lewis,** Rollin Dale 1949- *WhoWest 92*
**Lewis,** Ron 1952- *WhoFI 92*
**Lewis,** Ron E 1953- *WhoAmP 91*
**Lewis,** Ronald Alexander 1968- *WhoBlA 92*
**Lewis,** Ronald C. 1934- *WhoBlA 92*
**Lewis,** Ronald Wayne 1943- *WhoAmL 92*
**Lewis,** Roscoe Warfield 1920- *AmMWSc 92*
**Lewis,** Roy *WrDr 92*
**Lewis,** Roy 1913- *WrDr 92*
**Lewis,** Roy Roosevelt 1935- *WhoWest 92*
**Lewis,** Roy Stephen 1944- *AmMWSc 92*
**Lewis,** Ruby Anne 1941- *WhoWest 92*
**Lewis,** Russell Cooper 1940- *WhoMW 92*
**Lewis,** Russell J 1929- *AmMWSc 92*
**Lewis,** Russell M 1930- *AmMWSc 92*
**Lewis,** Samella 1924- *WhoBlA 92*
**Lewis,** Samella Sanders 1924- *NotBlAW 92*
**Lewis,** Samuel, Jr. 1953- *WhoBlA 92*
**Lewis,** Samuel Leonard 1896-1971 *RelLAm 91*
**Lewis,** Samuel Winfield 1930- *IntWW 91, WhoAmP 91*
**Lewis,** Sarah Anna Blanche Robinson 1824-1880 *BenetAL 91*
**Lewis,** Sean D. *Who 92*
**Lewis,** Shannon *WrDr 92*
**Lewis,** Shari 1934- *WhoEnt 92*
**Lewis,** Sheldon Noah 1934- *AmMWSc 92, WhoFI 92*
**Lewis,** Sherman 1942- *WhoBlA 92*
**Lewis,** Sherman Richard, Jr. 1936- *WhoFI 92*
**Lewis,** Sherry M *AmMWSc 92*
**Lewis,** Shirley Jeane 1937- *WhoWest 92*
**Lewis,** Sidney Allison 1945- *WhoFI 92*
**Lewis,** Silas Davis 1930- *AmMWSc 92*
**Lewis,** Simon 1945- *TwCPaSc*
**Lewis,** Simon Andrew 1948- *AmMWSc 92*
**Lewis,** Sinclair 1884-1951 *FacFETw*
**Lewis,** Sinclair 1885-1951 *BenetAL 91, ConAu 133, RComAH*
**Lewis,** Standley Eugene 1940- *AmMWSc 92*
**Lewis,** Stephen 1937- *IntWW 91*
**Lewis,** Stephen 1959- *TwCPaSc*
**Lewis,** Stephen Albert 1942- *AmMWSc 92*
**Lewis,** Stephen B 1940- *AmMWSc 92*
**Lewis,** Stephen C 1943- *WhoAmP 91*
**Lewis,** Stephen Christopher 1950- *WhoBlA 92*
**Lewis,** Stephen H. 1948- *WhoAmL 92*
**Lewis,** Stephen Richmond, Jr. 1939- *WhoMW 92*
**Lewis,** Stephen Robert 1920- *AmMWSc 92*
**Lewis,** Sterling Thomas, Jr 1951- *WhoAmP 91*
**Lewis,** Steve 1969- *BlkOlyM*
**Lewis,** Steven Craig 1943- *AmMWSc 92*
**Lewis,** Steven M 1948- *AmMWSc 92*
**Lewis,** Stuart Charles 1940- *WhoFI 92*
**Lewis,** Stuart Miley 1945- *WhoAmL 92*
**Lewis,** Susanna Maxwell *AmMWSc 92*
**Lewis,** Sydney 1919- *WhoFI 92*
**Lewis,** Sylvia Austin 1921- *WhoBlA 92*
**Lewis,** T Skipwith 1936- *AmMWSc 92*
**Lewis,** Ted D 1949- *WhoAmP 91*
**Lewis,** Terence 1928- *Who 92*
**Lewis,** Terence 1935- *Who 92*
**Lewis,** Terence R. 1938- *WhoRel 92*
**Lewis,** Terry *WhoBlA 92*
**Lewis,** Theodore 1924- *AmMWSc 92*
**Lewis,** Theodore E 1926- *WhoIns 92*
**Lewis,** Therthenia W. 1947- *WhoBlA 92*
**Lewis,** Thomas Brinley 1938- *AmMWSc 92*
**Lewis,** Thomas E 1947- *WhoAmP 91*
**Lewis,** Thomas F 1924- *WhoAmP 91*
**Lewis,** Thomas L. T. 1918- *WrDr 92*
**Lewis,** Thomas Loftus Townshend 1918- *Who 92*
**Lewis,** Thomas P 1936- *IntAu&W 91, WhoBlA 92, WrDr 92*
**Lewis,** Thomas Tandy 1941- *WhoMW 92*
**Lewis,** Thomas Wayne 1961- *WhoRel 92*
**Lewis,** Thomas William 1949- *WhoWest 92*
**Lewis,** Timothy Edward 1956- *WhoWest 92*
**Lewis,** Timothy Miller 1959- *WhoRel 92*
**Lewis,** Todd Vernon 1949- *WhoWest 92*
**Lewis,** Tom 1924- *AlmAP 92 [port]*
**Lewis,** Tony *Who 92*
**Lewis,** Tony 1967- *WhoHisp 92*
**Lewis,** Trabue *WhoAmP 91*
**Lewis,** Tracy Royal 1947- *WhoFI 92, WhoWest 92*
**Lewis,** Trent R 1932- *AmMWSc 92*
**Lewis,** Trevor 1933- *Who 92*
**Lewis,** Trevor John 1940- *AmMWSc 92*
**Lewis,** Trevor Oswin 1935- *Who 92*
**Lewis,** Urban James 1923- *AmMWSc 92*
**Lewis,** Vance De Spain 1909- *AmMWSc 92*
**Lewis,** Vera Margaret *Who 92*
**Lewis,** Vincent V. 1938- *WhoBlA 92*
**Lewis,** Viola Gambrill 1939- *WhoBlA 92*
**Lewis,** Virginia Hill 1948- *WhoBlA 92*
**Lewis,** Virginia Lorraine 1960- *WhoMW 92*
**Lewis,** Vivian M. *WhoBlA 92*
**Lewis,** Voltaire *ConAu 35NR*
**Lewis,** W. Arthur 1915-1991 *ConAu 134*
**Lewis,** W. Arthur 1930- *WhoBlA 92*
**Lewis,** W David 1931- *AmMWSc 92, WrDr 92*
**Lewis,** Wallace Joe 1942- *AmMWSc 92*
**Lewis,** Walter 1893-1981 *WhoBlA 92N*
**Lewis,** Walter Hepworth 1930- *AmMWSc 92*
**Lewis,** Walter Laughn 1924- *WhoAmL 92*
**Lewis,** Walton A. 1910- *WhoBlA 92*
**Lewis,** Wendell J. 1949- *WhoBlA 92*
**Lewis,** Wilfrid Bennett 1908- *AmMWSc 92*
**Lewis,** Willard Deming 1915- *AmMWSc 92*
**Lewis,** William 1936- *WhoEnt 92*
**Lewis,** William A., Jr. 1946- *WhoBlA 92*
**Lewis,** William Arthur d1991 *Who 92N*
**Lewis,** William Arthur 1915- *IntWW 91, WhoBlA 92, WhoNob 90*
**Lewis,** William Arthur 1915-1991 *NewYTBS 91*
**Lewis,** William Arthur, Jr 1946- *WhoAmP 91*
**Lewis,** William E 1940- *AmMWSc 92*
**Lewis,** William Gaston 1835-1901 *DcNCBi 4*
**Lewis,** William Headley, Jr. 1934- *WhoFI 92*
**Lewis,** William Henry, Jr. 1942- *WhoAmL 92*
**Lewis,** William James 1945- *AmMWSc 92*
**Lewis,** William Madison 1922- *AmMWSc 92*
**Lewis,** William Mason 1929- *AmMWSc 92*
**Lewis,** William Perry 1929- *AmMWSc 92*
**Lewis,** William Russell 1926- *WrDr 92*
**Lewis,** William Scheer 1927- *WhoFI 92*
**Lewis,** William Sylvester 1952- *WhoBlA 92*
**Lewis,** William W *WhoAmP 91*
**Lewis,** William Walker 1942- *WhoFI 92*
**Lewis,** Willie Mae 1943- *WhoBlA 92*
**Lewis,** Woodrow *WhoAmP 91, WhoBlA 92*
**Lewis,** Wyndham 1882-1957 *RfGEnL 91*
**Lewis,** Wyndham 1884-1957 *FacFETw*
**Lewis-Bowen,** Thomas Edward Ifor 1933- *Who 92*
**Lewis-Jones,** Gwilym 1922- *Who 92*
**Lewis-Kolbus,** Melinda Anne 1958- *WhoFI 92*
**Lewis of Newnham,** Baron 1928- *Who 92*
**Lewis-Pierson,** Priscilla Mary 1958- *WhoAmL 92*
**Lewis-Smith,** Anne 1925- *WrDr 92*
**Lewisham,** Archdeacon of *Who 92*
**Lewisham,** Viscount 1949- *Who 92*
**Lewishon,** Ludwig 1882-1955 *DcAmImH*
**Lewisohn,** Anthony Clive Leopold 1925- *Who 92*
**Lewisohn,** James *DrAPF 91*
**Lewisohn,** Ludwig 1882-1955 *ScFEYrs*
**Lewisohn,** Ludwig 1883-1955 *BenetAL 91*
**Lewisohn,** Michael J.R. 1959- *TwCPaSc*
**Lewisohn,** Neville Joseph 1922- *Who 92*
**Lewison,** Kim Martin Jordan 1952- *Who 92*
**Lewison,** Peter George Hornby 1911- *Who 92*
**Lewiston,** Norman James 1938- *AmMWSc 92*
**Lewitsky,** Grigoriy Andreevich 1878-1942 *SovUnBD*
**Le Witt,** Jan d1991 *Who 92N*
**Le Witt,** Jan 1907- *IntWW 91*
**Lewitt,** Michael Eric 1957- *WhoFI 92*
**Lewitt,** Miles Martin 1952- *WhoFI 92, WhoWest 92*
**Lewitt,** Sol 1928- *IntWW 91*
**Lewitter,** Lucjan Ryszard 1922- *Who 92*
**Lewittes,** Mordecai Henry *ConAu 133*
**Lewittes,** Morton H. 1911-1990 *ConAu 133*
**Lewitzky,** Bella 1916- *WhoEnt 92, WhoWest 92*
**Lewnes,** Peter A. 1929- *WhoFI 92*
**Lewontin,** Richard Charles 1929- *AmMWSc 92*
**Leworthy,** Roger *TwCPaSc*
**Lewter,** Andy C., Sr. 1929- *WhoBlA 92*
**Lewthwaite,** Gordon Rowland 1925- *WhoWest 92*
**Lewthwaite,** Rainald Gilfrid 1913- *Who 92*
**Lewthwaite,** William Anthony 1912- *Who 92*
**Lewty,** Marjorie 1906- *IntAu&W 91, WrDr 92*
**Lewty,** Simon 1941- *TwCPaSc*
**Lewy,** Alfred James 1945- *AmMWSc 92*
**Lewy,** Casimir d1991 *IntWW 91N, Who 92N*
**Lewy,** Guenter 1923- *IntAu&W 91*
**Lewy,** Leonard Jack 1951- *WhoRel 92*
**Lewyn,** Michael Evan 1963- *WhoAmL 92*
**Lewyn,** Thomas Mark 1930- *WhoAmL 92*
**Lex,** R G, Jr 1924- *AmMWSc 92*
**Lexa,** Vladimir 1937- *IntWW 91*
**Lexau,** Henry 1928- *WhoRel 92*
**Lexau,** Joan M *IntAu&W 91, WrDr 92*
**Ley,** Alice Chetwynd 1913- *IntAu&W 91, WrDr 92*
**Ley,** Allyn Bryson 1918- *AmMWSc 92*
**Ley,** Andrew James 1945- *WhoAmL 92*
**Ley,** Arthur Harris 1903- *Who 92*
**Ley,** B James 1921- *AmMWSc 92*
**Ley,** Francis 1907- *Who 92*
**Ley,** Herbert L, Jr *AmMWSc 92*
**Ley,** Hermann Hubert 1911- *IntWW 91*
**Ley,** Robert 1890-1945 *BiDExR, EncTR 91 [port]*
**Ley,** Steven Victor 1945- *Who 92*
**Ley,** Willy 1906-1969 *BenetAL 91, FacFETw*
**Leybold,** Dennis 1954- *WhoAmL 92*
**Leybold,** Timothy Paul 1957- *WhoFI 92*
**Leybourn,** Carol 1933- *WhoEnt 92*
**Leybourne,** A E, III 1934- *AmMWSc 92*
**Leyda,** James Perkins 1935- *AmMWSc 92*
**Leyden,** Donald E 1938- *AmMWSc 92*

**Leyden**, Michael Joseph, II 1950- *WhoFI 92*
**Leyden**, Richard Noel 1948- *AmMWSc 92*
**Leydet**, Francois Guillaume 1927- *WhoWest 92*
**Leydig**, Gary William 1955- *WhoAmL 92*
**Leydon**, Joseph Patrick 1952- *WhoEnt 92*
**Leydorf**, Frederick Leroy 1930- *WhoAmL 92*
**Leydorf**, Glenn E 1914- *AmMWSc 92*
**Leyendecker**, Bede Lamar 1960- *WhoEnt 92*
**Leyendecker**, Philip Jordon 1914- *AmMWSc 92*
**Leygue**, Louis Georges 1905- *IntWW 91*
**Leyland**, Philip Vyvian N. *Who 92*
**Leyland**, Ronald Arthur 1940- *Who 92*
**Leyman**, John Raymond *WhoEnt 92*
**Leymaster**, Glen Ronald 1915- *AmMWSc 92*
**Leynaud**, George Gregory 1958- *WhoAmL 92*
**Leyon**, Robert Edward 1936- *AmMWSc 92*
**Leypoldt**, Charles Wesley 1947- *WhoRel 92*
**Leyrac**, Monique 1928- *NewAmDM*
**Leyse**, Carl F 1917- *AmMWSc 92*
**Leyser**, Karl 1920- *WrDr 92*
**Leyser**, Karl Joseph 1920- *IntWW 91, Who 92*
**Leysieffer**, Frederick Walter 1933- *AmMWSc 92*
**Leyson**, Dativo Borces 1930- *WhoFI 92*
**Leyson**, Jose Florante Justininane 1946- *AmMWSc 92*
**Leyton**, Israel 1927- *WhoHisp 92*
**Leyton**, Nevil d1987 *Who 92N*
**Leyton**, Sophie *IntAu&W 91X, WrDr 92*
**Leyva**, Jason Fernand 1953- *WhoMW 92*
**Leyva**, Nick Tom 1953- *WhoHisp 92*
**Lezama**, Jose Luis 1946- *WhoHisp 92*
**Lezama Lima**, Jose 1910-1976 *ConSpAP, DcLB 113 [port]*
**Lezama Lima**, Jose 1912-1976 *BenetAL 91*
**Lezcano**, Ismael, IV 1951- *WhoHisp 92*
**Leznoff**, Clifford Clark 1940- *AmMWSc 92*
**Lhamon**, William Taylor, Jr. 1945- *WhoEnt 92*
**L'Herbier**, Marcel 1888-1979 *IntDcF 2-2*
**Lhermitte**, Francois Augustin 1921- *IntWW 91*
**Lhermitte**, Leon 1844-1925 *ThHEIm*
**Lhermitte**, Roger M 1920- *AmMWSc 92*
**L'Heureux**, Jacques 1939- *AmMWSc 92*
**L'Heureux**, John *DrAPF 91*
**L'Heureux**, John 1934- *WrDr 92*
**L'Heureux**, Maurice Victor 1914- *AmMWSc 92*
**L'Heureux**, N. J., Jr. *WhoRel 92*
**L'Heureux**, Robert J 1940- *WhoAmP 91*
**Lhevinne**, Josef 1874-1944 *FacFETw, NewAmDM*
**Lhevinne**, Rosina 1880-1976 *FacFETw, NewAmDM*
**Lhila**, Ramesh Chand *AmMWSc 92*
**Lho Shin-Yong** 1930- *IntWW 91*
**Lhotka**, Floyd Leonard 1932- *WhoFI 92*
**Lhotka**, John Francis 1921- *AmMWSc 92*
**L'Hour**, Jean 1932- *WhoRel 92*
**L'Huillier**, Peter 1926- *WhoRel 92*
**Li Baohua** 1908- *IntWW 91*
**Li Chang** 1914- *IntWW 91*
**Li Chang'an** 1935- *IntWW 91*
**Li Changchun** 1944- *IntWW 91*
**Li Chen**, Major General *EncAmaz 91*
**Li Choh-Ming** 1912- *IntWW 91*
**Li Da** 1905- *IntWW 91*
**Li Daoyu** 1932- *IntWW 91*
**Li Delun** 1917- *IntWW 91*
**Li Dengying** 1914- *IntWW 91*
**Li Desheng** 1916- *IntWW 91*
**Li Ding** 1927- *IntWW 91*
**Li Dingzhong** 1930- *IntWW 91*
**Li Dongye** 1917- *IntWW 91*
**Li Fang** 1925- *IntWW 91*
**Li Feng** 1921- *IntWW 91*
**Li Fengping** *IntWW 91*
**Li Furong** 1942- *IntWW 91*
**Li Fushan** 1940- *IntWW 91*
**Li Gang** 1926- *IntWW 91*
**Li Genshen** 1931- *IntWW 91*
**Li Guixian** 1937- *IntWW 91*
**Li Guohao** 1913- *IntWW 91*
**Li Guowen** 1930- *IntWW 91*
**Li Hao** 1927- *IntWW 91*
**Li Heng** 1898- *IntWW 91*
**Li Hou** 1923- *IntWW 91*
**Li Huaji** 1931- *IntWW 91*
**Li Huamin** 1915- *IntWW 91*
**Li Huifen** 1941- *IntWW 91*
**Li Jianzhen** 1907- *IntWW 91*
**Li Jijun** *IntWW 91*
**Li Jiulong**, Lieut-Gen. 1929- *IntWW 91*
**Li Ka-Shing** 1928- *IntWW 91*
**Li Keyu** 1929- *IntWW 91*
**Li Kongzheng** 1959- *IntWW 91*
**Li Kwoh-Ting** 1910- *IntWW 91*
**Li Lanqing** 1932- *IntWW 91*
**Li Li'an** 1920- *IntWW 91*
**Li Ligong** 1925- *IntWW 91*
**Li Lin** 1923- *IntWW 91*
**Li Ling** 1913- *IntWW 91*
**Li Lingwei** 1964- *IntWW 91*
**Li Luye** 1925- *IntWW 91*
**Li Menghua** 1922- *IntWW 91*
**Li Ming** 1927- *IntWW 91*
**Li Ning** 1963- *IntWW 91*
**Li Peng** 1928- *FacFETw, IntWW 91*
**Li Qi** 1908- *IntWW 91*
**Li Qiang** 1905- *IntWW 91*
**Li Qiming** 1908- *IntWW 91*
**Li Qing** 1920- *IntWW 91*
**Li Qingkui** *IntWW 91*
**Li Qingwei** 1920- *IntWW 91*
**Li Qun** 1912- *IntWW 91*
**Li Renlin** 1918- *IntWW 91*
**Li Rui** *IntWW 91*
**Li Ruihuan** 1935- *IntWW 91*
**Li Ruishan** *IntWW 91*
**Li Senmao** 1930- *IntWW 91*
**Li Shoushan** *IntWW 91*
**Li Shuiqing** 1905- *IntWW 91*
**Li Shuzheng** *IntWW 91*
**Li Tieying** 1937- *IntWW 91*
**Li Tingdong** 1932- *IntWW 91*
**Li Tuo** 1939- *LiExTwC*
**Li Xianji** 1943- *IntWW 91*
**Li Xiannian** 1909- *IntWW 91*
**Li Ximing** 1936- *IntWW 91*
**Li Xinliang** 1936- *IntWW 91*
**Li Xipu** *IntWW 91*
**Li Xuanhua** 1922- *IntWW 91*
**Li Xu'e** 1929- *IntWW 91*
**Li Xuezhi** 1923- *IntWW 91*
**Li Yan** 1943- *IntWW 91*
**Li Yaowen** 1918- *IntWW 91*
**Li Yuanchao** 1950- *IntWW 91*
**Li Yuhang** *WhoRel 92*
**Li Yunchang** 1908- *IntWW 91*
**Li Yunchuan** 1919- *IntWW 91*
**Li Zemin** 1934- *IntWW 91*
**Li Zewang** *IntWW 91*
**Li Zhengwu** *IntWW 91*
**Li Zhengyou** 1936- *IntWW 91*
**Li Zhuang** *IntWW 91*
**Li Zhun** 1928- *IntWW 91*
**Li Ziqi** *IntWW 91*
**Li**, Bing Xi 1934- *WhoFI 92*
**Li**, C C 1932- *AmMWSc 92*
**Li**, Che-Yu 1934- *AmMWSc 92*
**Li**, Chi-Tang 1934- *AmMWSc 92*
**Li**, Chia-Chuan 1946- *AmMWSc 92*
**Li**, Chia-Yu 1941- *AmMWSc 92*
**Li**, Chin-Hsiu 1938- *AmMWSc 92, WhoMW 92*
**Li**, Ching Chun 1912- *AmMWSc 92*
**Li**, Cho-Ming d1991 *NewYTBS 91*
**Li**, Choh Hao 1913-1987 *FacFETw*
**Li**, Choh-Ming d1991 *Who 92N*
**Li**, Chou H 1923- *AmMWSc 92*
**Li**, Christian Francis 1963- *WhoFI 92*
**Li**, Chung-Hsiung 1939- *AmMWSc 92*
**Li**, Eldon Y. 1952- *WhoWest 92*
**Li**, Fook Kow 1922- *Who 92*
**Li**, Frederick P 1940- *AmMWSc 92*
**Li**, George Su-Hsiang 1943- *AmMWSc 92*
**Li**, Hong 1962- *AmMWSc 92*
**Li**, Hsin Lang 1930- *AmMWSc 92*
**Li**, Hsueh Ming 1939- *AmMWSc 92*
**Li**, Hung Chiang 1921- *AmMWSc 92*
**Li**, J C M 1925- *AmMWSc 92*
**Li**, James C C *AmMWSc 92*
**Li**, Jane C. 1939- *WhoMW 92*
**Li**, Jane Chiao 1939- *AmMWSc 92*
**Li**, Jane-Yu Ho 1946- *WhoFI 92*
**Li**, Jeanne B 1944- *AmMWSc 92*
**Li**, John C. P. 1925- *WhoRel 92*
**Li**, John Kong-Jiann 1950- *AmMWSc 92*
**Li**, Joseph Kwok-Kwong 1940- *WhoWest 92*
**Li**, Kam W 1934- *AmMWSc 92*
**Li**, Kelvin K 1934- *AmMWSc 92*
**Li**, Kuang-Pang 1938- *AmMWSc 92*
**Li**, Kun 1923- *AmMWSc 92*
**Li**, Li-Hsieng 1933- *AmMWSc 92*
**Li**, Ling-Fong 1944- *AmMWSc 92*
**Li**, Lu Ku 1936- *AmMWSc 92*
**Li**, Ming Chiang 1935- *AmMWSc 92*
**Li**, Norman Chung 1913- *AmMWSc 92*
**Li**, Norman N 1933- *AmMWSc 92, WhoMW 92*
**Li**, Paul Michael 1938- *WhoWest 92*
**Li**, Pei-Ching 1919- *AmMWSc 92*
**Li**, Pen H 1933- *AmMWSc 92*
**Li**, Peter Joseph 1938- *WhoRel 92*
**Li**, Peter Wai-Kwong 1952- *AmMWSc 92, WhoWest 92*
**Li**, Ping-kwong 1938- *WhoRel 92*
**Li**, Seung P 1932- *AmMWSc 92*
**Li**, Sheng-San 1938- *AmMWSc 92*
**Li**, Shin-Hwa 1958- *AmMWSc 92, WhoWest 92*
**Li**, Simon Fook Sean 1922- *Who 92*
**Li**, Steven Shoei-Lung 1938- *AmMWSc 92*
**Li**, Su-Chen 1935- *AmMWSc 92*
**Li**, Tao Ping 1920- *AmMWSc 92*
**Li**, Thomas M *AmMWSc 92*
**Li**, Tien-yi 1915- *IntAu&W 91, WrDr 92*
**Li**, Tien-Yien 1945- *AmMWSc 92*
**Li**, Ting Kai 1934- *AmMWSc 92*
**Li**, Tingye 1931- *AmMWSc 92*
**Li**, Weiping 1963- *WhoMW 92*
**Li**, Wen-Ch'ing Winnie 1948- *AmMWSc 92*
**Li**, Wen-Hsiung 1942- *AmMWSc 92*
**Li**, Wu-Shyong 1943- *AmMWSc 92*
**Li**, Yao Tzu 1914- *AmMWSc 92*
**Li**, Yaxin 1958- *WhoMW 92*
**Li**, Ying Sing 1938- *AmMWSc 92*
**Li**, Yu-Teh 1934- *AmMWSc 92*
**Li**, Yuan 1936- *AmMWSc 92*
**Li**, Zi-Cai 1939- *AmMWSc 92*
**Lia**, Gary Peter 1941- *WhoFI 92, WhoIns 92*
**Lia**, James Douglas 1939- *WhoAmL 92*
**Li'a**, Tufele *WhoAmP 91*
**Liaboe**, Gary Philip 1955- *WhoMW 92*
**Liacos**, Paul J 1929- *WhoAmP 91*
**Liacos**, Paul Julian 1929- *WhoAmL 92*
**Liadov** *NewAmDM*
**Lial**, Margaret Louise 1927- *WhoWest 92*
**Lian**, Eric Chun-Yet 1938- *AmMWSc 92*
**Lian**, Shawn 1958- *AmMWSc 92*
**Liang Buting** 1921- *IntWW 91*
**Liang Chengye** 1924- *IntWW 91*
**Liang Dong-Cai** 1932- *IntWW 91*
**Liang Lingguang** 1916- *IntWW 91*
**Liang Ning** 1952- *IntWW 91*
**Liang Shoupan** *IntWW 91*
**Liang Xiang** *IntWW 91*
**Liang Xiaosheng** 1949- *IntWW 91*
**Liang**, Chang-seng 1941- *AmMWSc 92*
**Liang**, Charles C 1934- *AmMWSc 92*
**Liang**, Charles Shih-Tung 1940- *AmMWSc 92*
**Liang**, Ching Yu 1916- *AmMWSc 92*
**Liang**, Edison Park-Tak 1947- *AmMWSc 92*
**Liang**, George H 1934- *AmMWSc 92*
**Liang**, Isabella Y S *AmMWSc 92*
**Liang**, Jason Chia 1935- *WhoWest 92*
**Liang**, Jeffrey Der-Shing 1915- *WhoWest 92*
**Liang**, Joseph Jen-Yin *AmMWSc 92*
**Liang**, Kai 1934- *AmMWSc 92*
**Liang**, Keng-San 1943- *AmMWSc 92*
**Liang**, Shou Chu 1920- *AmMWSc 92*
**Liang**, Shoudan 1961- *AmMWSc 92*
**Liang**, Shoudeng 1959- *AmMWSc 92*
**Liang**, Shu-Mei 1949- *AmMWSc 92*
**Liang**, Tehming 1945- *AmMWSc 92*
**Liang**, Tung 1932- *AmMWSc 92*
**Liang**, Wei Chuan 1936- *AmMWSc 92*
**Liang**, Yola Yueh-o 1947- *AmMWSc 92*
**Lianides**, Sylvia Panagos 1931- *AmMWSc 92*
**Lianis**, Georgios 1926- *IntWW 91*
**Liantonio**, Thomas Victor 1951- *WhoEnt 92, WhoMW 92*
**Liao Bingxiong** 1915- *IntWW 91*
**Liao Hansheng** 1911- *IntWW 91*
**Liao Hui** 1941- *IntWW 91*
**Liao Kaiming** 1940- *IntWW 91*
**Liao**, Eric Nan-Kang 1938- *WhoWest 92*
**Liao**, Hsueh-Liang 1941- *AmMWSc 92*
**Liao**, Martha 1948- *AmMWSc 92*
**Liao**, Mei-June *AmMWSc 92*
**Liao**, Paul Foo-Hung 1944- *AmMWSc 92*
**Liao**, Ping-huang 1946- *AmMWSc 92*
**Liao**, Shu-Chung 1939- *AmMWSc 92*
**Liao**, Shuen-Kuei 1940- *AmMWSc 92*
**Liao**, Shutsung 1931- *AmMWSc 92, WhoMW 92*
**Liao**, Sung Jui 1917- *AmMWSc 92*
**Liao**, Ta-Hsiu 1942- *AmMWSc 92*
**Liao**, Tsung-Kai 1923- *AmMWSc 92*
**Liao Poon-Huai**, Donald 1929- *Who 92*
**Liapakis**, Pamela Anagnos 1947- *WhoAmL 92*
**Liaquat**, Ali Khan 1896-1951 *FacFETw*
**Liaquat Ali Khan**, Raana d1990 *IntWW 91N*
**Liardet**, Guy Francis 1934- *Who 92*
**Liardet**, Henry Maughan 1906- *Who 92*
**Lias-Booker**, Ava Elaine 1961- *WhoAmL 92*
**Liaskos**, George *DrAPF 91*
**Liau**, Zong-Long 1950- *AmMWSc 92*
**Liautaud**, Loretta Torres 1942- *WhoHisp 92*
**Liauw**, Koei-Liang 1935- *AmMWSc 92*
**Liaw**, Hang Ming 1936- *WhoWest 92*
**Liaw**, Jye Ren 1946- *AmMWSc 92*
**Liba**, Peter Michael 1940- *WhoEnt 92*
**Libackyj**, Anfir 1926- *WhoRel 92*
**Libaek**, Sven Erik 1938- *WhoEnt 92*
**Liban**, Eric 1921- *AmMWSc 92*
**Libanio Christo**, Carlos Alberto 1944- *IntWW 91*
**Libassi**, F Peter 1930- *WhoIns 92*
**Libassi**, Frank Peter 1930- *WhoAmP 91, WhoFI 92*
**Libbey**, Laura Jean 1862-1924 *BenetAL 91*
**Libbey**, Leonard Morton 1930- *AmMWSc 92*
**Libbey**, Robert David 1962- *WhoEnt 92*
**Libbey**, William Jerry 1942- *AmMWSc 92*
**Libbin**, Anne Edna 1950- *WhoAmL 92*
**Libbin**, James David 1950- *WhoWest 92*
**Libby**, Carol Baker 1949- *AmMWSc 92*
**Libby**, David Alan 1959- *WhoMW 92*
**Libby**, Donald Gerald 1934- *Who 92*
**Libby**, Frederick Joseph 1874-1970 *AmPeW*
**Libby**, Gene R. 1951- *WhoAmL 92*
**Libby**, Jack L *WhoAmP 91*
**Libby**, John Kelway 1926- *WhoFI 92*
**Libby**, Paul A 1921- *AmMWSc 92*
**Libby**, Paul Robert 1934- *AmMWSc 92*
**Libby**, Peter 1947- *AmMWSc 92*
**Libby**, Richard Allan 1958- *WhoWest 92*
**Libby**, Robert Harold 1930- *WhoIns 92*
**Libby**, Ronald T. 1941- *ConAu 135*
**Libby**, Wallace L, Jr. 1931- *WhoIns 92*
**Libby**, Wayne G. 1938- *WhoRel 92*
**Libby**, Willard F 1908-1980 *FacFETw [port]*
**Libby**, Willard Frank 1908-1980 *WhoNob 90*
**Libby**, Willard Gurnea 1929- *AmMWSc 92*
**Libby**, William John 1932- *AmMWSc 92*
**Libedinsky**, Yuri Nikolayevich 1898- *FacFETw*
**Libedinsky**, Yuriy Nikolaevich 1898-1959 *SovUnBD*
**Libelo**, Louis Francis 1930- *AmMWSc 92*
**Liber**, John Douglas 1938- *WhoAmL 92*
**Libera**, Richard Joseph 1929- *AmMWSc 92*
**Libera**, Sharon *DrAPF 91*
**Liberace** d1987 *LesBEnT 92*
**Liberace** 1919-1987 *FacFETw, NewAmDM*
**Liberaki**, Margarita 1919- *IntWW 91*
**Liberatore**, Frederick Anthony 1944- *AmMWSc 92*
**Liberatus** *EncEarC*
**Liberia-Peters**, Maria *IntWW 91*
**Liberius** *EncEarC*
**Liberles**, Arno 1934- *AmMWSc 92*
**Liberman**, Alexander 1912- *IntWW 91*
**Liberman**, Allen Harvey 1943- *AmMWSc 92*
**Liberman**, Anatoly 1937- *WhoMW 92*
**Liberman**, Arthur David 1940- *AmMWSc 92*
**Liberman**, David Bruce 1943- *WhoMW 92*
**Liberman**, Frank P. 1917- *IntMPA 92*
**Liberman**, Irving 1937- *AmMWSc 92*
**Liberman**, Keith Gordon 1956- *WhoAmL 92*
**Liberman**, Lee Marvin 1921- *WhoFI 92, WhoMW 92*
**Liberman**, Martin Henry 1936- *AmMWSc 92*
**Liberman**, Robert Paul 1937- *AmMWSc 92*
**Liberman**, Serge Israel 1942- *IntAu&W 91*
**Liberman**, Tatiana du Plessix 1906-1991 *NewYTBS 91 [port]*
**Liberman**, Yevsey Grigorievich 1897-1983 *SovUnBD*
**Libert**, Donald Joseph 1928- *WhoAmL 92, WhoFI 92*
**Liberta**, Anthony E 1933- *AmMWSc 92*
**Liberti**, Frank Nunzio 1939- *AmMWSc 92*
**Liberti**, Joseph Pollara 1937- *AmMWSc 92*
**Liberti**, Paul A 1936- *AmMWSc 92*
**Liberti**, Ray 1946- *WhoAmP 91*
**Libertini**, Richard *IntMPA 92*
**Libertiny**, George Zoltan 1934- *AmMWSc 92*
**Liberty**, Arthur Lasenby 1843-1917 *DcTwDes*
**Liberty**, Marcus 1968- *WhoBlA 92*
**Liberty**, Maria *WhoEnt 92*
**Libet**, Benjamin 1916- *AmMWSc 92*
**Libgober**, Anatoly S. 1949- *WhoMW 92*
**Libin**, Jerome B. 1936- *WhoAmL 92*
**Libin**, Paul 1930- *WhoEnt 92*
**Libka**, Robert John 1951- *WhoMW 92*
**Libles**, Richard Harry 1945- *WhoMW 92*
**Libman**, Alan David 1943- *WhoWest 92*
**Libo**, Kenneth 1937- *ConAu 133*
**Liboff**, Abraham R 1927- *AmMWSc 92*
**Liboff**, Richard L 1931- *AmMWSc 92*
**Libonati**, Joseph Peter 1941- *AmMWSc 92*
**Libonati**, Michael Ernest 1944- *WhoAmL 92*
**Libous**, Alfred Joseph 1928- *WhoAmP 91*
**Libous**, Thomas W 1953- *WhoAmP 91*
**Libove**, Charles 1923- *AmMWSc 92*
**Libow**, Leslie S *AmMWSc 92*
**Libowitz**, George Gotthart 1923- *AmMWSc 92*
**Libowitz**, Richard Lawrence 1948- *WhoRel 92*
**Librande**, Leonard Theodore 1943- *WhoRel 92*
**LiBretto**, John Charles 1947- *WhoEnt 92*
**Librizzi**, Charles 1936- *WhoEnt 92*
**Libro**, Antoinette *DrAPF 91*
**Libsch**, Joseph F 1918- *AmMWSc 92*
**Liburdy**, Robert P 1947- *AmMWSc 92*
**Liburo**, Almando 1953- *WhoAmP 91*
**Libussa** *EncAmaz 91*

**Licari**, James John 1930- *AmMWSc 92*
**Licata**, Anne Elizabeth 1934- *WhoAmP 91*
**Licata**, Arthur Frank 1947- *WhoAmL 92*
**Liccar**, Michael James 1955- *WhoFI 92*
**Liccardi**, Vincent G. *IntMPA 92*
**Licea**, Carlos J. 1948- *WhoHisp 92*
**Licea**, Rafael V. 1943- *WhoHisp 92*
**Liceaga**, Carlos Arturo 1958- *AmMWSc 92*
**Li-Chan**, Eunice 1953- *AmMWSc 92*
**Lichfield**, Archdeacon of *Who 92*
**Lichfield**, Bishop of 1934- *Who 92*
**Lichfield**, Dean of *Who 92*
**Lichfield**, Earl of 1939- *IntWW 91, Who 92*
**Lichfield**, Nathaniel 1916- *Who 92*
**Lichine**, Alexis 1913-1989 *FacFETw*
**Lichine**, David, Mme *Who 92*
**Lichnerowicz**, Andre 1915- *IntWW 91*
**Lichota**, Edith Fischer 1928- *WhoFI 92*
**Lichstein**, Herman Carlton 1918- *AmMWSc 92*
**Licht**, Arthur Lewis 1934- *AmMWSc 92*
**Licht**, Paul 1938- *AmMWSc 92*
**Licht**, Richard A 1948- *WhoAmP 91*
**Licht**, Sheldon 1932- *WhoFI 92*
**Licht**, Stuart Lawrence 1954- *AmMWSc 92*
**Licht**, W. Jr 1915- *AmMWSc 92*
**Lichtblau**, Irwin Milton 1936- *AmMWSc 92*
**Lichtblau**, Myron I. 1925- *WrDr 92*
**Lichten**, Nancy Gay 1960- *WhoMW 92*
**Lichten**, Thomas Rogers 1946- *WhoAmL 92*
**Lichten**, William Lewis 1928- *AmMWSc 92*
**Lichtenbaum**, Stephen 1939- *AmMWSc 92*
**Lichtenberg**, Allan J *AmMWSc 92*
**Lichtenberg**, Bernhard 1875-1943 *EncTR 91 [port]*
**Lichtenberg**, Byron Kurt 1948- *AmMWSc 92*
**Lichtenberg**, Don Bernett 1928- *AmMWSc 92*
**Lichtenberg**, Georg Christoph 1742-1799 *BlkwCEP*
**Lichtenberg**, Jacqueline 1942- *IntAu&W 91, TwCSFW 91, WrDr 92*
**Lichtenberg**, Larry Ray 1938- *WhoWest 92*
**Lichtenberg**, Myles Louis 1960- *WhoAmL 92*
**Lichtenberg**, Paul 1911- *IntWW 91*
**Lichtenberg**, Philip 1926- *WrDr 92*
**Lichtenberger**, Arthur Carl 1900- *RelLAm 91*
**Lichtenberger**, Dennis Lee 1947- *AmMWSc 92*
**Lichtenberger**, Frank H. 1937- *WhoIns 92*
**Lichtenberger**, Gerald Burton 1945- *AmMWSc 92*
**Lichtenberger**, Harold V 1920- *AmMWSc 92*
**Lichtenberger**, Lee S 1952- *WhoAmP 91*
**Lichtenberger**, William Robert 1925- *WhoIns 92*
**Lichtendorf**, Arthur Eli 1936- *WhoFI 92*
**Lichtenfels**, James Ralph 1939- *AmMWSc 92*
**Lichtenstadter**, Ilse d1991 *NewYTBS 91*
**Lichtenstadter**, Ilse 1907-1991 *ConAu 134*
**Lichtenstein**, Aaron 1933- *WhoRel 92*
**Lichtenstein**, Chase Walter 1936- *WhoFI 92*
**Lichtenstein**, E Paul 1915- *AmMWSc 92*
**Lichtenstein**, Elissa Charlene 1954- *WhoAmL 92*
**Lichtenstein**, Gaston 1879-1954 *DcNCBi 4*
**Lichtenstein**, Harris Arnold 1941- *AmMWSc 92*
**Lichtenstein**, Harvey 1929- *WhoEnt 92*
**Lichtenstein**, Lawrence Jay 1929- *WhoAmL 92*
**Lichtenstein**, Lawrence M 1934- *AmMWSc 92*
**Lichtenstein**, Natalie G. 1953- *WhoAmL 92*
**Lichtenstein**, Robert Jay 1948- *WhoAmL 92*
**Lichtenstein**, Roy 1923- *IntWW 91, Who 92*
**Lichtenthaler**, G W d1893 *BiInAmS*
**Lichtenwalner**, Hart K 1923- *AmMWSc 92*
**Lichter**, Barry D 1931- *AmMWSc 92*
**Lichter**, Edward A 1928- *AmMWSc 92*
**Lichter**, Edward Arthur 1928- *WhoMW 92*
**Lichter**, James Joseph 1939- *AmMWSc 92*
**Lichter**, Robert 1941- *AmMWSc 92*
**Lichter-Heath**, Laurie Jean 1951- *WhoAmL 92*
**Lichterman**, Harvey S. 1940- *WhoAmL 92*
**Lichterman**, Ivor Yitzchak 1953- *WhoRel 92*
**Lichti**, Reuben Boyd 1923- *WhoAmP 91*
**Lichti**, Roger L 1945- *AmMWSc 92*
**Lichtig**, Leo Kenneth 1953- *AmMWSc 92*
**Lichtin**, J Leon 1924- *AmMWSc 92, WhoMW 92*
**Lichtin**, Norman Nahum 1922- *AmMWSc 92*
**Lichtman**, David 1927- *AmMWSc 92*
**Lichtman**, Herbert Charles 1921- *AmMWSc 92*
**Lichtman**, Irwin A 1920- *AmMWSc 92*
**Lichtman**, Marshall A 1934- *AmMWSc 92*
**Lichtner**, Francis Thomas, Jr 1953- *AmMWSc 92*
**Lichton**, Ira Jay 1928- *AmMWSc 92*
**Lichtwardt**, Robert William 1924- *AmMWSc 92*
**Lichty**, Richard Wynn 1943- *WhoFI 92*
**Lichty**, Robert Eldon, Jr. 1940- *WhoRel 92*
**Lichty**, Warren Dewey, Jr. 1930- *WhoFI 92*
**Licini**, Jerome Carl 1958- *AmMWSc 92*
**Licinian** *EncEarC*
**Licinius** 250?-324 *EncEarC*
**Licitra**, Salvatore M 1919- *WhoIns 92*
**Lick**, Dale W 1938- *AmMWSc 92*
**Lick**, Dale Wesley 1938- *IntWW 91*
**Lick**, Don R 1934- *AmMWSc 92*
**Lick**, Wilbert James 1933- *AmMWSc 92*
**Licke**, Wallace John 1945- *WhoFI 92*
**Lickhalter**, Merlin Eugene 1934- *WhoMW 92*
**Lickiss**, Michael Gillam 1934- *Who 92*
**Lickle**, Garrison duPont 1954- *WhoAmL 92*
**Lickle**, William Cauffiel 1929- *WhoFI 92*
**Lickley**, Robert 1912- *Who 92*
**Licklider**, J. C. R. d1990 *IntWW 91N*
**Licklider**, Joseph Carl Robnett 1915- *AmMWSc 92*
**Licklider**, Roy E. 1941- *WrDr 92*
**Licko**, Vojtech 1932- *AmMWSc 92*
**Lickorish**, Leonard John 1921 *Who 92*
**Lickteig**, Dan W 1907- *WhoAmP 91*
**Lickteig**, Theodore James 1958- *WhoAmL 92*
**Lidbury**, John 1912- *Who 92*
**Liddell** *Who 92*
**Liddell**, Alasdair Donald MacDuff 1949- *Who 92*
**Liddell**, Anna Forbes 1891-1979 *DcNCBi 4*
**Liddell**, Bobby, Jr. 1952- *WhoRel 92*
**Liddell**, Craig Mason 1958- *AmMWSc 92*
**Liddell**, Donald Woollven 1917- *Who 92*
**Liddell**, Helen Lawrie 1950- *Who 92*
**Liddell**, Jennifer *Who 92*
**Liddell**, John Robert 1908- *Who 92*
**Liddell**, Robert *Who 92*
**Liddell**, Robert 1908- *IntAu&W 91, LiExTwC, WrDr 92*
**Liddell**, Robert William, Jr 1913- *AmMWSc 92*
**Liddell**, William David 1951- *AmMWSc 92*
**Lidderdale**, David 1910- *Who 92*
**Liddiard**, Richard England 1917- *IntWW 91, Who 92*
**Liddiard**, Ronald 1932- *Who 92*
**Liddicoat**, Richard Thomas, Jr 1918- *AmMWSc 92, WhoWest 92*
**Liddicoet**, Thomas Herbert 1927- *AmMWSc 92*
**Liddie**, Edward 1959- *BlkOlyM*
**Liddington**, Jill 1946- *WrDr 92*
**Liddle**, Charles George 1936- *AmMWSc 92*
**Liddle**, Grant Winder 1921- *AmMWSc 92*
**Liddle**, Leonard Merritt 1885-1920 *BiInAmS*
**Liddle**, Peter 1934- *IntAu&W 91, WrDr 92*
**Liddy**, James 1934- *WrDr 92*
**Lide**, David Reynolds, Jr 1928- *AmMWSc 92*
**Lide**, Mary Ruth *IntAu&W 91*
**Lide**, Robert Wilson 1922- *AmMWSc 92*
**Lide**, William Ernest 1950- *WhoBlA 92*
**Lider**, Edward W. 1922- *IntMPA 92*
**Lidholm**, Ingvar 1921- *ConCom 92, NewAmDM*
**Lidiak**, Edward George 1934- *AmMWSc 92*
**Lidicker**, William Zander, Jr 1932- *AmMWSc 92*
**Lidin**, Bodil Inger Maria 1939- *AmMWSc 92*
**Lidin**, Vladimir Germanovich 1894-1979 *SovUnBD*
**Lidman**, Ralph Oscar 1922- *WhoAmP 91*
**Lidman**, Sara 1923- *IntWW 91*
**Lidman**, William G 1921- *AmMWSc 92*
**Lidofsky**, Leon Julian 1924- *AmMWSc 92*
**Lidov**, Arthur d1990 *NewYTBS 91*
**Lidow**, Eric 1912- *AmMWSc 92*
**Lidstone**, Christopher Drake 1955- *WhoWest 92*
**Lidstone**, Herrick Kenley, Jr. 1949- *WhoAmL 92*
**Lidstone**, John Barrie Joseph 1929- *IntAu&W 91*
**Lidtke**, Doris Keefe 1929- *AmMWSc 92*
**Lidz**, Theodore 1910- *AmMWSc 92, WrDr 92*
**Lie**, Jonas 1899-1945 *BiDExR*
**Lie**, Lars Gunnar 1938- *IntWW 91*
**Lie**, Trygve 1896-1968 *FacFETw [port]*
**Lie**, Wen-Rong 1957- *AmMWSc 92*
**Lieb**, Arthur Hilary 1920- *WhoAmL 92*
**Lieb**, Carl Sears 1949- *AmMWSc 92*
**Lieb**, Elliott Hershel 1932- *AmMWSc 92*
**Lieb**, Fred 1888-1980 *FacFETw*
**Lieb**, Margaret 1923- *AmMWSc 92*
**Lieb**, Selma Rose 1932- *WhoAmP 91*
**Lieb**, Wanda Moffett 1933- *WhoFI 92*
**Lieb**, William Robert 1940- *AmMWSc 92*
**Liebaert**, Michael Scott 1953- *WhoFI 92*
**Liebau**, Frederic Jack, Jr. 1963- *WhoWest 92*
**Liebe**, Donald Charles 1942- *AmMWSc 92*
**Liebe**, Richard Milton 1932- *AmMWSc 92*
**Liebehenschel**, Arthur 1901-1948 *EncTR 91*
**Liebeler**, Wesley J. 1931- *WhoAmL 92*
**Liebelt**, Annabel Glockler 1926- *AmMWSc 92*
**Liebelt**, Arthur H *WhoIns 92*
**Liebelt**, Robert Arthur 1927- *AmMWSc 92*
**Liebenauer**, Paul 1935- *AmMWSc 92*
**Liebenberg**, Donald Henry 1932- *AmMWSc 92*
**Liebenberg**, Stanley Phillip 1945- *AmMWSc 92*
**Liebeneiner**, Wolfgang 1905- *EncTR 91 [port]*
**Liebenfels**, Jorg Lanz von *EncTR 91*
**Liebenow**, J. Gus 1925- *WhoMW 92*
**Lieber**, Anna 1947- *WhoEnt 92*
**Lieber**, Charles Donald 1921- *WhoRel 92*
**Lieber**, Charles Saul 1931- *AmMWSc 92*
**Lieber**, David Leo 1925- *WhoRel 92, WhoWest 92*
**Lieber**, Edward Martin 1940- *WhoFI 92*
**Lieber**, Francis 1800-1872 *BenetAL 91*
**Lieber**, Gary L. 1949- *WhoAmL 92*
**Lieber**, Marvin Sidney 1934- *WhoAmL 92*
**Lieber**, Michael 1936- *AmMWSc 92*
**Lieber**, Oscar Montgomery 1830-1862 *BiInAmS*
**Lieber**, Richard L *AmMWSc 92*
**Lieber**, Robert J. 1941- *WrDr 92*
**Lieber**, Robert James 1941- *IntAu&W 91*
**Lieber**, Stephen Andrew 1925- *WhoFI 92*
**Lieber**, Todd *DrAPF 91*
**Lieberfarb**, Warren *IntMPA 92*
**Liebergen**, Patrick Michael 1949- *WhoMW 92*
**Lieberman**, Abraham N 1938- *AmMWSc 92*
**Lieberman**, Alvin 1921- *AmMWSc 92*
**Lieberman**, Anne Marie 1946- *WhoFI 92*
**Lieberman**, Arthur Stuart 1931- *AmMWSc 92*
**Lieberman**, Barbara Jean 1952- *WhoAmL 92*
**Lieberman**, Bruce A. 1954- *WhoFI 92*
**Lieberman**, Burton Barnet 1938- *AmMWSc 92*
**Lieberman**, Charles 1948- *WhoFI 92*
**Lieberman**, Daniel 1919- *AmMWSc 92*
**Lieberman**, David 1953- *WhoAmL 92*
**Lieberman**, David Armin 1964- *WhoMW 92*
**Lieberman**, Diana Dale 1949- *AmMWSc 92*
**Lieberman**, Douglas Mark 1960- *WhoAmL 92*
**Lieberman**, Edward Marvin 1938- *AmMWSc 92*
**Lieberman**, Edwin James 1934- *AmMWSc 92*
**Lieberman**, ElissaBeth 1964- *WhoRel 92*
**Lieberman**, Eugene 1918- *WhoAmL 92, WhoMW 92*
**Lieberman**, Fredric 1940- *WhoEnt 92, WhoWest 92*
**Lieberman**, Gail Forman 1943- *WhoFI 92*
**Lieberman**, Gary Mitchell 1952- *WhoMW 92*
**Lieberman**, Gerald J 1925- *AmMWSc 92*
**Lieberman**, Gerald Jacob 1948- *WhoMW 92*
**Lieberman**, Herbert *DrAPF 91*
**Lieberman**, Herbert 1933- *WrDr 92*
**Lieberman**, Herbert A 1920- *AmMWSc 92*
**Lieberman**, Hillel 1942- *AmMWSc 92*
**Lieberman**, Ilene s 1947- *WhoAmP 91*
**Lieberman**, Irving 1921- *AmMWSc 92*
**Lieberman**, Jack 1926- *AmMWSc 92*
**Lieberman**, James 1921- *AmMWSc 92*
**Lieberman**, James Lance 1952- *WhoWest 92*
**Lieberman**, John Joseph 1948- *WhoEnt 92*
**Lieberman**, Joseph I. 1942- *AlmAP 92 [port], IntWW 91, WhoAmP 91*
**Lieberman**, Laurence *DrAPF 91*
**Lieberman**, Laurence 1935- *ConAu 36NR, ConPo 91, WrDr 92*
**Lieberman**, Leslie Sue 1944- *AmMWSc 92*
**Lieberman**, Melvyn 1938- *AmMWSc 92*
**Lieberman**, Michael A 1950- *AmMWSc 92*
**Lieberman**, Michael Merril 1944- *AmMWSc 92*
**Lieberman**, Michael Williams 1941- *AmMWSc 92*
**Lieberman**, Milton Eugene 1934- *AmMWSc 92*
**Lieberman**, Morton Leonard 1937- *AmMWSc 92*
**Lieberman**, Robert *IntMPA 92*
**Lieberman**, Robert 1924- *AmMWSc 92*
**Lieberman**, Robert Howard 1941- *IntAu&W 91*
**Lieberman**, Rochelle Phyllis 1940- *WhoFI 92*
**Lieberman**, Rosemarie C. 1948- *WhoHisp 92*
**Lieberman**, Samuel 1911-1981 *ConAu 134*
**Lieberman**, Samuel Victor 1914- *AmMWSc 92*
**Lieberman**, Seymour 1916- *AmMWSc 92, IntWW 91*
**Lieberman**, Stuart Jay 1957- *WhoAmL 92*
**Liebermann**, Howard Horst 1949- *AmMWSc 92*
**Liebermann**, Leonard Norman 1915- *AmMWSc 92*
**Liebermann**, Max 1847-1935 *EncTR 91 [port]*
**Liebermann**, Robert C 1942- *AmMWSc 92*
**Liebermann**, Rolf 1910- *ConCom 92, IntWW 91, NewAmDM*
**Liebermann von Sonnenberg**, Max 1848-1911 *EncTR 91*
**Lieberson**, Sanford 1936- *IntMPA 92*
**Liebert**, James William 1946- *AmMWSc 92*
**Liebert**, Robert Allen 1952- *WhoEnt 92*
**Lieberthal**, Gary *LesBEnT 92*
**Liebes**, Dorothy 1899-1972 *DcTwDes, FacFETw*
**Liebes**, Raquel 1938- *WhoFI 92*
**Liebes**, Sidney, Jr 1929- *AmMWSc 92*
**Liebeskind**, Herbert 1921- *AmMWSc 92*
**Liebeskind**, Lanny Steven 1950- *AmMWSc 92*
**Liebetrau**, Richard Mark 1953- *WhoFI 92*
**Liebhardt**, William C 1936- *AmMWSc 92*
**Liebhart**, Vincent J. 1940- *WhoEnt 92*
**Liebig**, Nelda Faye 1930- *WhoRel 92*
**Liebig**, Phoebe Stone 1933- *WhoWest 92*
**Liebig**, William John 1923- *AmMWSc 92*
**Lieblein**, Seymour 1923- *AmMWSc 92*
**Liebler**, Edward Charles 1939- *WhoMW 92*
**Liebler**, M.L. *DrAPF 91*
**Liebling**, A. J. 1904-1963 *BenetAL 91*
**Liebling**, Barry Andrew 1949- *WhoFI 92*
**Liebling**, Estelle 1880-1970 *NewAmDM*
**Liebling**, Jerome Robert 1944- *WhoWest 92*
**Liebling**, Mordechai Eliahu 1948- *WhoRel 92*
**Liebling**, Norman Robert 1917- *WhoFI 92, WhoMW 92*
**Liebling**, Otto 1925- *WhoFI 92*
**Liebling**, Richard Stephen 1938- *AmMWSc 92*
**Liebling**, Tina 1953- *WhoAmL 92*
**Liebman**, Alan Joel 1943- *WhoFI 92*
**Liebman**, Arnold Alvin 1931- *AmMWSc 92*
**Liebman**, Arthur *ScFEYrs*
**Liebman**, Emmanuel 1925- *WhoFI 92*
**Liebman**, Frederick Melvin 1922- *AmMWSc 92*
**Liebman**, Herbert *DrAPF 91*
**Liebman**, Herbert 1935- *WhoEnt 92*
**Liebman**, Jeffrey Mark 1946- *AmMWSc 92*
**Liebman**, Jeffrey Mitchell 1969- *WhoEnt 92*
**Liebman**, Joel Fredric 1947- *AmMWSc 92*
**Liebman**, Jon C 1934- *AmMWSc 92*
**Liebman**, Joshua Loth 1907-1948 *RelLAm 91*
**Liebman**, Judith Stenzel 1936- *AmMWSc 92*
**Liebman**, Max d1981 *LesBEnT 92*
**Liebman**, Paul Arno 1933- *AmMWSc 92*
**Liebman**, Ronald Stanley 1943- *WhoAmL 92, WhoFI 92*
**Liebman**, Susan Weiss 1947- *AmMWSc 92*
**Liebmann**, Herman 1915- *WhoFI 92*
**Liebmann**, Irina 1943- *IntAu&W 91*
**Liebmann**, Seymour W. 1928- *WhoFI 92*
**Liebmann**, Vern Lloyd 1953- *WhoWest 92*
**Liebner**, Edwin J 1921- *AmMWSc 92*
**Liebnitz**, Paul W 1935- *AmMWSc 92*
**Liebowitz**, Harold 1924- *AmMWSc 92*
**Liebowitz**, Jonathan S. 1932- *WhoAmL 92*
**Liebowitz**, Judith Laurel 1960- *WhoEnt 92*
**Liebowitz**, Shelly B. 1946- *WhoFI 92*
**Liebowitz**, Stan J. 1950- *WhoFI 92*
**Liebowitz**, Stephen Marc *AmMWSc 92*
**Liebschutz**, Sanford Jay 1930- *WhoAmL 92*
**Liebson**, Sidney Harold 1920- *AmMWSc 92*
**Liechtenstein**, Prince of *IntWW 91*
**Liechty**, Clinton 1949- *WhoWest 92*
**Liechty**, Milton R. 1923- *WhoMW 92*
**Liechty**, Richard Dale 1925- *AmMWSc 92*

**Liechty**, Ronald Wayne 1933- *WhoRel 92*
**Lied**, Michael Robert 1953- *WhoAmL 92*
**Lieder**, Bernard L *WhoAmP 91*
**Liederbach**, Carole B. 1944- *WhoMW 92*
**Liedl**, Gerald L 1933- *AmMWSc 92*
**Liedtke**, Armin Adolf 1941- *WhoWest 92*
**Liedtke**, William C., Jr. d1991 *NewYTBS 91*
**Lief**, Harold Isaiah 1917- *AmMWSc 92*
**Liegey**, Francis William 1923- *AmMWSc 92*
**Liegl**, Joseph Leslie 1948- *WhoAmL 92*
**Liehr**, Daniel Bruce 1951- *WhoFI 92*
**Liehr**, Joachim G 1942- *AmMWSc 92*
**Lielmezs**, Janis 1926- *AmMWSc 92*
**Liem Sioe Liong** 1917- *IntWW 91*
**Liem**, Karel F 1935- *AmMWSc 92*
**Liem**, Khian Kioe 1942- *WhoMW 92*
**Liem**, Ronald Kian Hong 1946- *AmMWSc 92*
**Liemohn**, Harold Benjamin 1935- *AmMWSc 92*
**Lien Chan** 1936- *IntWW 91*
**Lien**, Bruce Hawkins 1927- *WhoMW 92*
**Lien**, Eric Jung-Chi 1937- *AmMWSc 92, WhoWest 92*
**Lien**, Eric Louis 1946- *AmMWSc 92*
**Lien**, Hwachii 1930- *AmMWSc 92*
**Lienau**, Bonnie Louise Roszak 1944- *WhoWest 92*
**Liendo**, Hector Javier 1950- *WhoHisp 92*
**Liendo**, Horacio Tomas 1924- *IntWW 91*
**Lienemann**, Delmar Arthur, Sr. 1920- *WhoMW 92*
**Lienenbrugger**, Herbert Gene 1942- *WhoFI 92*
**Liener**, Irvin Ernest 1919- *AmMWSc 92*
**Lienesch**, John Harry 1943- *WhoMW 92*
**Lienhard**, Gustav E 1938- *AmMWSc 92*
**Lienhard**, John H 1930- *AmMWSc 92*
**Lienhart**, James Lee 1935- *WhoEnt 92*
**Lienk**, Siegfried Eric 1916- *AmMWSc 92*
**Lientz**, Bennet Price 1942- *AmMWSc 92*
**Lieouchi** *EncAmaz 91*
**Liepa**, Andris *WhoEnt 92*
**Liepa**, Andris 1962- *IntWW 91*
**Liepa**, George Uldis 1946- *AmMWSc 92*
**Liephart**, Roger Arthur 1943- *WhoMW 92*
**Liepins**, Atis Aivars 1935- *AmMWSc 92*
**Liepins**, Raimond 1930- *AmMWSc 92*
**Liepman**, H P 1913- *AmMWSc 92*
**Liepmann**, H Wolfgang 1914- *AmMWSc 92*
**Liepmann**, Hans Wolfgang 1914- *IntWW 91*
**Lier**, Frank George 1913- *AmMWSc 92*
**Lier**, John 1924- *AmMWSc 92*
**Lier**, Nancy Jean 1942- *WhoMW 92*
**Lies**, Thomas Andrew 1929- *AmMWSc 92*
**Liesch**, Jerrold Michael 1949- *AmMWSc 92*
**Liese**, Homer C 1931- *AmMWSc 92*
**Lieske**, Henry Louis 1911- *WhoRel 92*
**Liesner**, Hans Hubertus 1929- *IntWW 91, Who 92*
**Liesse**, Richard William 1954- *WhoFI 92*
**Lietaer**, B. A. 1942- *WrDr 92*
**Lieteau**, Halvan Joseph 1931- *WhoBlA 92*
**Lieth**, Helmut Heinrich Friedrich 1925- *AmMWSc 92*
**Lietman**, Paul Stanley 1934- *AmMWSc 92*
**Lietz**, Gerard Paul 1937- *AmMWSc 92*
**Lietz**, Jeremy Jon 1933- *WhoMW 92*
**Lietz**, Robert *DrAPF 91*
**Lietzen**, John Hervy 1947- *WhoWest 92*
**Lietzke**, David Albert 1940- *AmMWSc 92*
**Lietzke**, Milton Henry 1920- *AmMWSc 92*
**Lieu**, Hou-Shun 1921- *WrDr 92*
**Lieu**, Tzeng-Shwu Sue 1953- *WhoFI 92*
**Lieux**, Meredith Hoag 1939- *AmMWSc 92*
**Lievertz**, Alfred Hubert 1943- *WhoFI 92*
**Liew**, Chong Kiew 1938- *WhoFI 92*
**Liew**, Choong-Chin 1937- *AmMWSc 92*
**Lifar**, Serge 1905-1986 *FacFETw*
**Lifchitz**, Max 1948- *WhoEnt 92, WhoHisp 92*
**Life**, Lawrence Leland 1943- *WhoEnt 92*
**Lifer**, Charles William 1938- *WhoMW 92*
**Lifford**, Viscount 1949- *Who 92*
**Lifka**, Bernard William 1931- *AmMWSc 92*
**Lifland**, John C. 1933- *WhoAmL 92*
**Lifoifoi**, Jose R 1936- *WhoAmP 91*
**Lifschitz**, Aliza *WhoHisp 92*
**Lifschitz**, Meyer David 1942- *AmMWSc 92*
**Lifschultz**, Phillip 1927- *WhoAmL 92, WhoFI 92*
**Lifshin**, Lyn *DrAPF 91*
**Lifshin**, Lyn 1942- *ConPo 91*
**Lifshin**, Lyn 1948- *WrDr 92*
**Lifshitz**, Howard Victor 1945- *WhoMW 92, WhoRel 92*
**Lifshitz**, Leatrice *DrAPF 91*
**Lifshutz**, Bernard Lee 1926- *WhoAmP 91*
**Lifson**, Nathan 1911- *AmMWSc 92*
**Lifson**, Shneior 1914- *IntWW 91*
**Lifson**, William E 1921- *AmMWSc 92*
**Lifton**, Betty Jean *IntAu&W 91*
**Lifton**, Betty Jean 1926- *WrDr 92*
**Lifton**, Robert Jay 1926- *ConLC 67 [port], SmATA 66 [port], WrDr 92*
**Lifton**, Robert Kenneth 1928- *WhoFI 92, WhoRel 92*
**Lifton**, Walter 1918- *WrDr 92*
**Ligachev**, Yegor Kuzmich 1920- *IntWW 91, SovUnBD*
**Lige**, Peter 1941- *WhoFI 92*
**Ligeti**, Gyorgy 1923- *ConCom 92, NewAmDM*
**Ligeti**, Gyorgy Sandor 1923- *IntWW 91, Who 92*
**Liggero**, John 1921- *WrDr 92*
**Liggero**, Samuel Henry 1942- *AmMWSc 92*
**Liggett**, Hunter *TwCWW 91*
**Liggett**, James Alexander 1934- *AmMWSc 92*
**Liggett**, James David 1946- *WhoRel 92*
**Liggett**, Lawrence Melvin 1917- *AmMWSc 92*
**Liggett**, Thomas 1918- *AmPeW, WrDr 92*
**Liggett**, Thomas Milton 1944- *AmMWSc 92, WhoWest 92*
**Liggett**, Twila Marie Christensen 1944- *WhoEnt 92*
**Liggett**, Walter Stewart, Jr 1940- *AmMWSc 92*
**Liggins**, Edmund 1909- *Who 92*
**Liggins**, Graham Collingwood *Who 92*
**Liggins**, Graham Collingwood 1926- *IntWW 91*
**Liggio**, Carl Donald 1943- *WhoAmL 92*
**Ligh**, Steve 1937- *AmMWSc 92*
**Light**, Albert 1927- *AmMWSc 92*
**Light**, Alfred Robert 1949- *WhoAmL 92*
**Light**, Amos Ellis 1910- *AmMWSc 92*
**Light**, Arthur Heath *WhoRel 92*
**Light**, Charles Randolph 1940- *WhoAmL 92*
**Light**, Christopher Upjohn 1937- *WhoMW 92*
**Light**, David 1919- *Who 92*
**Light**, Douglas B 1956- *AmMWSc 92*
**Light**, Irwin Joseph 1934- *AmMWSc 92*
**Light**, Jo Knight 1936- *WhoFI 92*
**Light**, John Caldwell 1934- *AmMWSc 92, WhoMW 92*
**Light**, John Henry 1924- *AmMWSc 92*
**Light**, John Ralph 1955- *WhoIns 92*
**Light**, John Robert 1941- *WhoAmL 92*
**Light**, Judith Ellen *WhoEnt 92*
**Light**, Ken 1951- *WhoWest 92*
**Light**, Kenneth B. 1932- *WhoFI 92*
**Light**, Kenneth Freeman 1922- *AmMWSc 92*
**Light**, Kim Edward 1951- *AmMWSc 92*
**Light**, Matthew David 1962- *WhoWest 92*
**Light**, Mitchell A 1921- *AmMWSc 92*
**Light**, Randy Scott 1956- *WhoFI 92*
**Light**, Robert S *WhoAmP 91*
**Light**, Robley Jasper 1935- *AmMWSc 92*
**Light**, Russell Jeffers 1949- *WhoAmL 92*
**Light**, Stephen Robert 1946- *WhoMW 92*
**Light**, Thomas Burwell 1928- *AmMWSc 92*
**Light**, Truman S 1922- *AmMWSc 92*
**Light**, Walter Frederick 1923- *IntWW 91*
**Light**, William Randall 1958- *WhoAmL 92*
**Lightbody**, Andy Ray 1953- *WhoWest 92*
**Lightbody**, Ian 1921- *Who 92*
**Lightbody**, James James 1939- *AmMWSc 92*
**Lightbody**, Roden S 1943- *WhoAmP 91*
**Lightbown**, David Lincoln 1932- *Who 92*
**Lightbown**, Ronald William 1932- *Who 92*
**Lightcap**, Jeanne Fichter 1961- *WhoFI 92*
**Lighter**, Eric Aaron 1950- *WhoFI 92, WhoWest 92*
**Lighter**, Lawrence 1935- *WhoAmL 92*
**Lighterman**, Mark S 1960- *AmMWSc 92*
**Lightfoot**, Christopher Kelly 1958- *WhoAmL 92*
**Lightfoot**, Claude M. 1910- *WhoBlA 92*
**Lightfoot**, Donald Richard 1940- *AmMWSc 92*
**Lightfoot**, E N, Jr 1925- *AmMWSc 92*
**Lightfoot**, George Michael 1936- *Who 92*
**Lightfoot**, Gordon 1938- *NewAmDM*
**Lightfoot**, Gordon Meredith 1938- *WhoEnt 92*
**Lightfoot**, Jean Drew *WhoBlA 92*
**Lightfoot**, Jean Harvey 1935- *WhoBlA 92*
**Lightfoot**, Jim *WhoMW 92*
**Lightfoot**, Jim Ross 1938- *AlmAP 92 [port], WhoAmP 91*
**Lightfoot**, Joe Dean 1961- *WhoMW 92*
**Lightfoot**, Joseph Barber 1828-1889 *EncEarC*
**Lightfoot**, Louis Norman 1948- *WhoWest 92*
**Lightfoot**, Maxwell Gordon 1886-1911 *TwCPaSc*
**Lightfoot**, Moses 1915-1989 *WhoBlA 92N*
**Lightfoot**, Ralph B 1913- *AmMWSc 92*
**Lightfoot**, Sara Lawrence *WhoBlA 92*
**Lightfoot**, Terry 1935- *NewAmDM*
**Lightfoot**, Warren Bricken 1938- *WhoAmL 92*
**Lightfoot**, William Carl 1938- *WhoEnt 92*
**Lightfoot**, William P. 1920- *WhoBlA 92*
**Lightfoot**, William P, Jr *WhoAmP 91*
**Lightfoote**, William Edward, II 1942- *WhoBlA 92*
**Lighthall**, Timothy Duane 1962- *WhoRel 92*
**Lighthall**, William Douw 1857-1954 *BenetAL 91*
**Lighthill**, James 1924- *IntWW 91, Who 92*
**Lightman**, Alan Paige 1948- *AmMWSc 92*
**Lightman**, Gavin Anthony 1939- *Who 92*
**Lightman**, Harold 1906- *Who 92*
**Lightman**, Ivor Harry 1928- *Who 92*
**Lightman**, Lionel 1928- *Who 92*
**Lightman**, M.A. 1915- *IntMPA 92*
**Lightner**, A. LeRoy, Jr. 1921- *WhoFI 92*
**Lightner**, Alice 1904-1988 *TwCSFW 91*
**Lightner**, Clarence *WhoAmP 91*
**Lightner**, Clarence E. 1921- *WhoBlA 92*
**Lightner**, David A 1939- *AmMWSc 92*
**Lightner**, Drew Warren 1948- *WhoMW 92*
**Lightner**, James Edward 1937- *AmMWSc 92*
**Lightner**, Robert Lee 1949- *WhoEnt 92*
**Lightner**, Ruth H. 1940- *WhoFI 92*
**Lighton**, Christopher Robert 1897- *Who 92*
**Lighton**, John R B 1952- *AmMWSc 92*
**Lights**, Rikki *DrAPF 91*
**Lightsey**, Deborah A *WhoAmP 91*
**Lightsey**, Paul Alden 1944- *AmMWSc 92*
**Lightsey**, Ralph 1918- *WhoRel 92*
**Lightsey**, Wallace Kay 1957- *WhoAmL 92*
**Lightstone**, Ronald 1938- *WhoAmL 92, WhoEnt 92, WhoFI 92*
**Lightwood**, Carol Wilson 1941- *WhoFI 92, WhoWest 92*
**Lighty**, JoAnn Slama 1960- *AmMWSc 92*
**Lighty**, Richard William 1933- *AmMWSc 92*
**Lighty**, William Curtis 1956- *WhoRel 92*
**Ligi**, Elio Emiliano *DrAPF 91*
**Ligler**, Frances Smith 1951- *AmMWSc 92*
**Ligman**, Dean V. 1931- *WhoMW 92*
**Ligman**, James Edmund 1950- *WhoAmL 92*
**Lignarolo**, Fini 1950- *WhoHisp 92*
**Ligne**, Charles-Joseph, prince de 1735-1811 *BlkwCEP*
**Lignell**, Kathleen *DrAPF 91*
**Lignelli**, Ronald Joseph 1958- *WhoEnt 92*
**Ligomenides**, Panos Aristides 1928- *AmMWSc 92*
**Ligon**, Bradford V 1922- *WhoAmP 91*
**Ligon**, Claude M. 1935- *WhoBlA 92*
**Ligon**, Doris Hillian 1936- *WhoBlA 92*
**Ligon**, James David 1939- *AmMWSc 92*
**Ligon**, James Guthrie, Jr. 1947- *WhoFI 92*
**Ligon**, James T 1936- *AmMWSc 92*
**Ligon**, Woodfin Vaughan, Jr 1944- *AmMWSc 92*
**Ligotti**, Thomas 1953- *IntAu&W 91*
**Liguori**, Frank E. 1917-1980 *ConAu 134*
**Liguori**, James A. *WhoRel 92*
**Liguori**, Vincent Robert 1928- *AmMWSc 92*
**Lih**, Marshall Min-Shing 1936- *AmMWSc 92*
**Lihn**, Enrique 1929- *BenetAL 91*
**Lihn**, Enrique 1929-1988 *ConSpAP*
**Liikanen**, Erkki Antero 1950- *IntWW 91*
**Liimatainen**, T M 1910- *AmMWSc 92*
**Liittschwager**, John M 1934- *AmMWSc 92*
**Lijewski**, Lawrence Edward 1948- *AmMWSc 92*
**Lijinsky**, William 1928- *AmMWSc 92*
**Lijn**, Liliane *DrAPF 91*
**Lijoi**, Peter Bruno 1953- *WhoAmL 92, WhoFI 92*
**Likaku**, Victor Timothy 1934- *Who 92*
**Like**, Arthur A *AmMWSc 92*
**Like**, Ronald Hoyt 1944- *WhoMW 92*
**Liken**, Paula Kay 1955- *WhoWest 92*
**Likens**, Gene E. 1935- *IntWW 91*
**Likens**, Gene Elden 1935- *AmMWSc 92*
**Likens**, James Dean 1937- *WhoFI 92*
**Likens**, Suzanne Alicia 1945- *WhoWest 92*
**Liker**, Jack 1926- *WhoFI 92*
**Likes**, Carl James 1916- *AmMWSc 92*
**Likhachev**, Dmitriy Sergeevich 1906- *SovUnBD*
**Likhachev**, Dmitriy Sergeyevich 1906- *IntWW 91*
**Likhachev**, Ivan Alekseevich 1896-1956 *SovUnBD*
**Likierman**, Andrew 1943- *Who 92*
**Likins**, Keith Lee 1946- *WhoMW 92*
**Likins**, Peter William 1936- *AmMWSc 92*
**Likness**, Lawrence Richard 1929- *WhoRel 92*
**Likoff**, William 1912- *AmMWSc 92*
**Likuski**, Robert Keith 1937- *AmMWSc 92*
**Lilburn**, Douglas 1915- *ConCom 92*
**Lile**, Bill 1946- *WhoAmP 91*
**Lile**, Laird Andrew 1960- *WhoAmL 92*
**Lilenfeld**, Harvey Victor 1945- *AmMWSc 92*
**Liles**, Bruce David 1945- *WhoMW 92*
**Liles**, Frances Rose 1943- *WhoFI 92*
**Liles**, James Neil 1930- *AmMWSc 92*
**Liles**, Malcolm Henry 1950- *WhoFI 92*
**Liles**, Mike James 1945- *WhoAmP 91*
**Liles**, Rutledge Richardson 1942- *WhoAmL 92*
**Liles**, Samuel Lee 1942- *AmMWSc 92*
**Liley**, Nicholas Robin 1936- *AmMWSc 92*
**Liley**, Peter Edward 1927- *AmMWSc 92, WhoMW 92*
**Lilford**, Baron 1931- *Who 92*
**Lilie**, Daniel R. 1942- *WhoMW 92*
**Lilieholm**, Robert John 1960- *WhoFI 92*
**Lilien**, Mark Ira 1953- *WhoFI 92*
**Lilien**, Otto Michael 1924- *AmMWSc 92*
**Lilienfield**, Lawrence Spencer 1927- *AmMWSc 92*
**Lilienthal**, Alfred M 1913- *IntAu&W 91*
**Lilienthal**, David Eli 1899-1981 *AmPolLe*
**Lilienthal**, Meta 1876-1947 *DcAmImH*
**Lili'uokalani** 1838-1917 *NewAmDM*
**Liliuokalani**, Queen *DcAmImH*
**Lilje**, Hanns 1899-1977 *DcEcMov, EncTR 91 [port]*
**Liljebeck**, Roy C. 1937- *WhoFI 92*
**Liljegren**, Dorothy *WhoAmP 91*
**Liljestrand**, Bengt Tson 1919- *IntWW 91*
**Lill**, Gordon Grigsby 1918- *AmMWSc 92*
**Lill**, John Richard 1944- *IntWW 91, Who 92*
**Lill**, Patsy Henry 1943- *AmMWSc 92*
**Lillard**, Dorris Alton 1936- *AmMWSc 92*
**Lillard**, John Franklin, III 1947- *WhoAmL 92*
**Lillard**, Leo, II 1939- *WhoBlA 92*
**Lillard**, Robert Emmitt 1907- *WhoBlA 92*
**Lillard**, W. Lovell 1936- *WhoBlA 92*
**Lillee**, Dennis K. 1949- *IntWW 91*
**Lillegraven**, Jason Arthur 1938- *AmMWSc 92*
**Lillehaug**, Duane A. 1950- *WhoAmL 92*
**Lillehoj**, Eivind B 1928- *AmMWSc 92*
**Lillehoj**, Hyun Soon 1949- *AmMWSc 92*
**Lilleland**, Omund 1899- *AmMWSc 92*
**Lilleleht**, L U 1930- *AmMWSc 92*
**Liller**, William 1927- *AmMWSc 92*
**Lillesand**, Thomas Martin 1946- *AmMWSc 92*
**Lillevik**, Hans Andreas 1916- *AmMWSc 92*
**Lilley**, Albert Frederick 1932- *WhoAmL 92*
**Lilley**, Arthur Edward 1928- *AmMWSc 92*
**Lilley**, Cheryl 1953- *WhoEnt 92*
**Lilley**, Daniel T 1920- *WhoAmP 91*
**Lilley**, David Grantham *AmMWSc 92*
**Lilley**, Geoffrey Michael 1919- *Who 92*
**Lilley**, George 1851?-1904 *BiInAmS*
**Lilley**, James Roderick 1928- *IntWW 91, WhoAmP 91*
**Lilley**, Jimmy Dan 1938- *WhoRel 92*
**Lilley**, John Richard 1934- *AmMWSc 92*
**Lilley**, Mili Della *WhoEnt 92, WhoFI 92*
**Lilley**, Peter Bruce 1943- *IntWW 91, Who 92*
**Lilley**, Sandra 1963- *WhoHisp 92*
**Lilley**, William Richard 1934- *WhoWest 92*
**Lilliard of Ancrum** *EncAmaz 91*
**Lillibridge**, Anny *EncAmaz 91*
**Lillich**, Richard B. 1933- *WhoAmL 92*
**Lillich**, Thomas Tyler 1943- *AmMWSc 92*
**Lillicrap**, Harry George 1913- *Who 92*
**Lillicropp**, Arthur Reginald, III 1947- *WhoRel 92*
**Lillie**, Beatrice 1894-1989 *NewAmDM*
**Lillie**, Beatrice Gladys 1898-1989 *FacFETw*
**Lillie**, Betty Jane 1926- *WhoMW 92, WhoRel 92*
**Lillie**, Charles Frederick 1936- *AmMWSc 92*
**Lillie**, Eleanor Heldstab 1929- *WhoWest 92*
**Lillie**, John Howard 1940- *AmMWSc 92*
**Lillie**, John Mitchell 1937- *WhoFI 92, WhoWest 92*
**Lillie**, Mildred Loree 1915- *WhoWest 92*
**Lillie**, Richard Horace 1918- *WhoFI 92, WhoMW 92*
**Lillie**, Robert Jones 1921- *AmMWSc 92*
**Lillie**, Vernell A. 1931- *WhoBlA 92*
**Lilliefors**, Hubert W 1928- *AmMWSc 92*
**Lillien**, Irving 1929- *AmMWSc 92*
**Lillingston**, George David I. I. *Who 92*
**Lillington**, Alexander 1643-1697 *DcNCBi 4*
**Lillington**, Glen Alan 1926- *AmMWSc 92*
**Lillington**, John Alexander 1720?-1786 *DcNCBi 4*
**Lillington**, Kenneth 1916- *IntAu&W 91, WrDr 92*
**Lillis**, Joan Frances 1936- *WhoAmP 91*
**Lillis**, William G. 1930- *WhoFI 92*
**Lillo**, George 1691-1739 *RfGEnL 91*
**Lillo**, George 1693-1739 *BlkwCEP*

**Lillwitz,** Larry Dale 1944- *WhoMW 92*
**Lillwitz,** Lawrence Dale 1944- *AmMWSc 92*
**Lilly,** Arnys Clifton, Jr 1934- *AmMWSc 92*
**Lilly,** David J 1931- *AmMWSc 92*
**Lilly,** Diane Palmer *WhoMW 92*
**Lilly,** Doris d1991 *NewYTBS 91 [port]*
**Lilly,** Doris 1926-1991 *ConAu 135*
**Lilly,** Douglas Keith 1929- *AmMWSc 92*
**Lilly,** Edward Guerrant, Jr. 1925- *WhoFI 92*
**Lilly,** Elizabeth 1933- *WhoEnt 92*
**Lilly,** Frank 1930- *AmMWSc 92, IntWW 91*
**Lilly,** Graham C. 1938- *WhoAmL 92*
**Lilly,** John Russell 1929- *AmMWSc 92*
**Lilly,** John Thomas 1960- *WhoAmL 92*
**Lilly,** Leland Lando *WhoEnt 92*
**Lilly,** Malcolm Douglas 1936- *Who 92*
**Lilly,** Michael Alexander 1946- *WhoWest 92*
**Lilly,** Percy Lane 1927- *AmMWSc 92*
**Lilly,** Shannon Jeanne 1966- *WhoEnt 92*
**Lilly,** Thomas Joseph 1931- *WhoAmL 92*
**Lilly,** Thomas More 1942- *WhoFI 92*
**Lillya,** Clifford Peter 1910- *WhoEnt 92*
**Lillya,** Clifford Peter 1937- *AmMWSc 92*
**Lillywhite,** Harvey B 1943- *AmMWSc 92*
**Lilov,** Alexander Vassilev 1933- *IntWW 91*
**Lily,** Susan Dean 1946- *WhoAmP 91*
**Lim Chong Eu** 1919- *IntWW 91*
**Lim Keng Yaik** 1939- *IntWW 91*
**Lim Kim San** 1916- *IntWW 91*
**Lim Pin** 1936- *IntWW 91, Who 92*
**Lim,** Alexander Te 1942- *AmMWSc 92*
**Lim,** Daniel V 1948- *AmMWSc 92*
**Lim,** David J 1935- *AmMWSc 92*
**Lim,** Edward C 1932- *AmMWSc 92*
**Lim,** Genny *DrAPF 91*
**Lim,** H C 1935- *AmMWSc 92*
**Lim,** Han-Hoe 1894- *Who 92*
**Lim,** Henry Chol 1935- *WhoWest 92*
**Lim,** Hong Seh 1958- *AmMWSc 92*
**Lim,** James Khai-Jin 1933- *AmMWSc 92*
**Lim,** Johng Ki 1930- *AmMWSc 92*
**Lim,** Kim 1936- *IntWW 91*
**Lim,** Kiok-Puan 1947- *AmMWSc 92*
**Lim,** Larry Kay 1948- *WhoWest 92*
**Lim,** Ramon 1933- *AmMWSc 92*
**Lim,** Shirley Geok-Lin 1944- *IntAu&W 91*
**Lim,** Shun Ping 1947- *WhoMW 92*
**Lim,** Sonia Yii 1924- *WhoRel 92*
**Lim,** Sung Man *AmMWSc 92*
**Lim,** Sung Man 1934- *WhoMW 92*
**Lim,** Teck-Kah 1942- *AmMWSc 92*
**Lim,** Teong Cheng 1939- *AmMWSc 92*
**Lim,** Young Woon 1935- *AmMWSc 92*
**Lim Fat,** Edouard *Who 92*
**Lima,** Anthony Karl 1946- *WhoFI 92*
**Lima,** Dan Dennis 1946- *WhoRel 92*
**Lima,** Donald Allan 1953- *WhoWest 92*
**Lima,** Frank *DrAPF 91*
**Lima,** Gail M 1957- *AmMWSc 92*
**Lima,** George Charles 1921- *WhoAmP 91*
**Lima,** George Silva 1919- *WhoAmP 91, WhoBlA 92*
**Lima,** Gustavo Raul *WhoHisp 92*
**Lima,** John J 1940- *AmMWSc 92*
**Lima,** Robert *DrAPF 91*
**Lima,** Robert 1935- *IntAu&W 91, WrDr 92*
**Lima,** Robert F., Jr. 1935- *WhoHisp 92*
**Liman,** Arthur L. 1932- *WhoAmL 92*
**LiMandri,** Charles Salvatore 1955- *WhoWest 92*
**Limann,** Hilla 1934- *IntWW 91, Who 92*
**Limardo,** Felix R. 1952- *WhoHisp 92*
**Limareva,** Maria *EncAmaz 91*
**Limarzi,** Louis Robert 1903- *AmMWSc 92*
**Limauro,** Stephen L *WhoIns 92*
**Limb,** Ben Quincy 1936- *WhoAmL 92*
**Limb,** John Ormond *AmMWSc 92*
**Limbacher,** James L. 1926- *WrDr 92*
**Limback,** Edna Rebecca 1945- *WhoMW 92*
**Limbaugh,** Marc Wayne 1953- *WhoRel 92*
**Limbaugh,** Ronald Hadley 1938- *WhoWest 92*
**Limbaugh,** Rush *News 91 [port], -91-3 [port]*
**Limbaugh,** Stephen Nathaniel 1927- *WhoAmL 92*
**Limbert,** David Edwin 1942- *AmMWSc 92*
**Limbert,** Douglas A 1948- *AmMWSc 92*
**Limbert,** Michael Victor 1969- *WhoEnt 92*
**Limbird,** Lee Eberhardt 1948- *AmMWSc 92*
**Limbu** *Who 92*
**Limburg,** James Wallace 1935- *WhoMW 92, WhoRel 92*
**Limburg,** Peter R 1929- *IntAu&W 91, WrDr 92*
**Limburg,** Val Evert 1938- *WhoEnt 92*
**Limburg,** William W 1935- *AmMWSc 92*
**Limehouse,** Thomas A 1958- *WhoAmP 91*
**Limerick,** Countess of 1935- *Who 92*
**Limerick,** Earl of 1930- *IntWW 91, Who 92*
**Limerick,** Jack McKenzie, Sr 1910- *AmMWSc 92*
**Limerick And Killaloe,** Bishop of 1933- *Who 92*
**Limhaisen,** Mohammed Abdulraham 1949- *WhoFI 92*
**Limkeman,** Darrell Roger 1950- *WhoAmP 91*
**Limkemann,** Margaret Alice 1941- *WhoEnt 92*
**Limmer,** Warren E *WhoAmP 91*
**Limoges,** Craig Steven 1953- *WhoFI 92*
**Limoges,** Richard Roland 1948- *WhoFI 92*
**Limon,** Donald William 1932- *Who 92*
**Limon,** Jose 1908-1972 *FacFETw*
**Limonov,** Eduard 1943- *ConLC 67 [port]*
**Limonov,** Eduard 1952- *IntAu&W 91, IntWW 91*
**Limp,** John David 1950- *WhoMW 92*
**Limpach,** Erich 1899-1965 *EncTR 91*
**Limpert,** Frederick Arthur 1921- *AmMWSc 92*
**Limpert,** Rudolf 1936- *AmMWSc 92*
**Lin Biao** 1908-1971 *FacFETw*
**Lin Chin-Sheng** 1916- *IntWW 91*
**Lin Ching-Hsia** 1955- *IntWW 91*
**Lin Fengmian** 1900- *IntWW 91*
**Lin Hanxiong** 1929- *IntWW 91*
**Lin Hujia** 1916- *IntWW 91*
**Lin Jianqing** 1921- *IntWW 91*
**Lin Lanying** 1917- *IntWW 91*
**Lin Lin** 1910- *IntWW 91*
**Lin Liyun** 1933- *IntWW 91*
**Lin Mohan** 1913- *IntWW 91*
**Lin Ping** 1920- *IntWW 91*
**Lin Ruo** 1924- *IntWW 91*
**Lin Yang-Kang** 1927- *IntWW 91*
**Lin Yincai** 1930- *IntWW 91*
**Lin Yutang** 1895-1976 *BenetAL 91*
**Lin Zhaohua** 1936- *IntWW 91*
**Lin Zhun** 1927- *IntWW 91*
**Lin,** Alice Lee Lan 1937- *AmMWSc 92, WhoFI 92*
**Lin,** Benjamin Ming-Ren *AmMWSc 92*
**Lin,** Bor-Luh 1935- *AmMWSc 92*
**Lin,** Chang Kwei 1941- *AmMWSc 92*
**Lin,** Charlie Yeongching 1956- *AmMWSc 92*
**Lin,** Che 1932- *WhoWest 92*
**Lin,** Che-Shung 1933- *AmMWSc 92*
**Lin,** Chi-Wei 1937- *AmMWSc 92*
**Lin,** Chia Chiao 1916- *AmMWSc 92, IntWW 91*
**Lin,** Chii-Dong *AmMWSc 92*
**Lin,** Chin-Chu 1935- *WhoMW 92*
**Lin,** Chin-Chung 1937- *AmMWSc 92*
**Lin,** Chin-Tarng 1938- *AmMWSc 92*
**Lin,** Ching Y 1940- *AmMWSc 92*
**Lin,** Chinlon 1945- *AmMWSc 92*
**Lin,** Chistopher Chuang-I 1941- *WhoFI 92*
**Lin,** Cho-Liang 1960- *IntWW 91*
**Lin,** Chun Chia 1930- *AmMWSc 92, WhoMW 92*
**Lin,** Denis Chung Kam 1944- *AmMWSc 92*
**Lin,** Diane Chang 1944- *AmMWSc 92*
**Lin,** Dong Liang 1947- *AmMWSc 92*
**Lin,** Duo-Liang 1930- *AmMWSc 92*
**Lin,** Edmund Chi Chien 1928- *AmMWSc 92*
**Lin,** Fu Hai 1928- *AmMWSc 92*
**Lin,** George Hung-Yin 1938- *AmMWSc 92*
**Lin,** Grace Woan-Jung *AmMWSc 92*
**Lin,** H 1919- *AmMWSc 92*
**Lin,** Hsiu-san 1935- *AmMWSc 92*
**Lin,** Hun-Chi 1953- *WhoWest 92*
**Lin,** Hung Chang 1919- *AmMWSc 92*
**Lin,** Jack Kuowei 1951- *WhoMW 92*
**Lin,** James C H 1932- *AmMWSc 92*
**Lin,** James Chih-I 1942- *AmMWSc 92*
**Lin,** James Peicheng 1949- *AmMWSc 92, WhoWest 92*
**Lin,** James W. 1954- *WhoFI 92*
**Lin,** Jason Zse-Cherng 1955- *WhoWest 92*
**Lin,** Jeong-Long 1935- *AmMWSc 92*
**Lin,** Jia Ding 1931- *AmMWSc 92*
**Lin,** Jia-Yuan Jason 1955- *WhoFI 92*
**Lin,** Jian *AmMWSc 92*
**Lin,** Jiann-Tsyh 1940- *AmMWSc 92*
**Lin,** Jiunn H 1943- *AmMWSc 92*
**Lin,** John Pung-Fu 1955- *WhoFI 92*
**Lin,** Josh Chia Hsin 1954- *WhoWest 92*
**Lin,** Kuang-Farn 1936- *AmMWSc 92*
**Lin,** Kuang-Ming 1932- *AmMWSc 92*
**Lin,** Kuang-Tzu Davis 1940- *AmMWSc 92*
**Lin,** Kwan-Chow *AmMWSc 92*
**Lin,** Larry Y H *AmMWSc 92*
**Lin,** Lawrence I-Kuei 1948- *AmMWSc 92*
**Lin,** Lawrence Shuh Liang 1938- *WhoWest 92*
**Lin,** Leewen *AmMWSc 92*
**Lin,** Lei 1944- *WhoWest 92*
**Lin,** Leu-Fen Hou *AmMWSc 92*
**Lin,** Mao-Shiu 1931- *AmMWSc 92*
**Lin,** Maya *NewYTBS 91 [port]*
**Lin,** Michael C 1938- *AmMWSc 92*
**Lin,** Ming Chang 1936- *AmMWSc 92*
**Lin,** Mow Shiah 1941- *AmMWSc 92*
**Lin,** Otto Chui Chau 1938- *AmMWSc 92*
**Lin,** P M 1928- *AmMWSc 92*
**Lin,** Paul C S *AmMWSc 92*
**Lin,** Paul Kuang-Hsien 1946- *AmMWSc 92*
**Lin,** Pi-Erh 1938- *AmMWSc 92*
**Lin,** Ping-Wha 1925- *AmMWSc 92*
**Lin,** Renee C *AmMWSc 92*
**Lin,** Reng-Lang 1937- *AmMWSc 92*
**Lin,** Robert I-San 1942- *AmMWSc 92*
**Lin,** Robert Peichung 1942- *AmMWSc 92*
**Lin,** See-Yan 1939- *IntWW 91*
**Lin,** Shao-Chi 1925- *AmMWSc 92*
**Lin,** Sheng Hsien 1937- *AmMWSc 92*
**Lin,** Shin 1945- *AmMWSc 92*
**Lin,** Shu 1936- *AmMWSc 92*
**Lin,** Shwu-Yeng Tzen 1934- *AmMWSc 92*
**Lin,** Shyi-Jang 1951- *WhoWest 92*
**Lin,** Sin-Shong 1933- *AmMWSc 92*
**Lin,** Sping 1918- *AmMWSc 92*
**Lin,** Stephen Fang-Maw 1937- *AmMWSc 92*
**Lin,** Stephen Y 1939- *AmMWSc 92*
**Lin,** Steven An-Yhi 1933- *WhoMW 92*
**Lin,** Sue Chin 1936- *AmMWSc 92*
**Lin,** Sui 1929- *AmMWSc 92*
**Lin,** Sung P 1937- *AmMWSc 92*
**Lin,** Tai-Shun 1938- *AmMWSc 92*
**Lin,** Tao 1958- *WhoWest 92*
**Lin,** Ted 1958- *WhoEnt 92*
**Lin,** Thomas Wen-shyoung 1944- *WhoWest 92*
**Lin,** Tian-Min 1935- *WhoRel 92*
**Lin,** Tien-Sung Tom 1938- *AmMWSc 92*
**Lin,** Tsau-Yen 1932- *AmMWSc 92*
**Lin,** Tsue-Ming 1935- *AmMWSc 92*
**Lin,** Tsung-Min 1916- *AmMWSc 92*
**Lin,** Tu 1941- *AmMWSc 92*
**Lin,** Tung Hua 1911- *AmMWSc 92*
**Lin,** Tung-Po 1926- *AmMWSc 92*
**Lin,** Tung Yen 1911- *AmMWSc 92*
**Lin,** Tz-Hong 1934- *AmMWSc 92*
**Lin,** Wallace *DrAPF 91*
**Lin,** Wei-Ching 1930- *AmMWSc 92*
**Lin,** Wen-C 1926- *AmMWSc 92*
**Lin,** Wen Chun 1926- *WhoWest 92*
**Lin,** Willy 1944- *AmMWSc 92*
**Lin,** Wunan 1942- *AmMWSc 92*
**Lin,** Wuu-Long 1939- *WhoFI 92*
**Lin,** Y K 1923- *AmMWSc 92*
**Lin,** Yeong-Jer 1936- *AmMWSc 92*
**Lin,** Yeoniching Charles 1956- *WhoWest 92*
**Lin,** Yi-Jong 1944- *AmMWSc 92*
**Lin,** Yong Yeng 1933- *AmMWSc 92*
**Lin,** You-Feng 1932- *AmMWSc 92*
**Lin,** Yu-Chong 1935- *AmMWSc 92, WhoWest 92*
**Lin,** Yue Jee 1945- *AmMWSc 92*
**Lin,** Yuh Meei 1941- *WhoMW 92*
**Lin-Chung,** Pay-June *AmMWSc 92*
**Lin-Vien,** Daimay *AmMWSc 92*
**Linacre,** Gordon 1920- *IntWW 91, Who 92*
**Linahan,** Shawn Brooke 1960- *WhoEnt 92*
**Linaker,** Lawrence Edward 1934- *IntWW 91, Who 92*
**Linaker,** Mike 1940- *TwCWW 91*
**Linam,** Jay H 1931- *AmMWSc 92*
**Linan,** Francisco S. 1948- *WhoHisp 92*
**Linane,** William Edward 1928- *WhoMW 92*
**Linarelli,** John 1958- *WhoAmL 92*
**Linares,** Guillermo 1950- *WhoHisp 92*
**Linares,** Henry Amaya 1941- *WhoHisp 92*
**Linares,** Nora Alice 1954- *WhoAmP 91*
**Linask,** Kersti Katrin 1945- *AmMWSc 92*
**Linaweaver,** Brad 1952- *TwCSFW 91*
**Linaweaver,** F. Pierce 1934- *WhoFI 92*
**Linaweaver,** Frank Pierce 1934- *AmMWSc 92*
**Linberg,** Ernest John 1947- *WhoWest 92*
**Lincecum,** Gideon 1793-1874 *BiInAmS*
**Linch,** Estrella Vinzon 1944- *WhoFI 92*
**Linch,** Mark David 1956- *WhoFI 92*
**Lincicome,** David Richard 1914- *AmMWSc 92*
**Lincicome,** David Van Cleave 1945- *WhoFI 92*
**Linck,** Albert John 1926- *AmMWSc 92*
**Linck,** Richard Wayne 1945- *AmMWSc 92*
**Linck,** Robert George 1938- *AmMWSc 92*
**Lincks,** Beth Arlene 1955- *WhoEnt 92*
**Linclau,** Denise Marie 1951- *WhoMW 92*
**Lincoln,** Archdeacon of *Who 92*
**Lincoln,** Bishop of 1936- *Who 92*
**Lincoln,** Dean of *Who 92*
**Lincoln,** Earl of 1913- *Who 92*
**Lincoln,** Abbey *WhoBlA 92, WhoEnt 92*
**Lincoln,** Abbey 1930- *NotBlAW 92*
**Lincoln,** Abraham 1809-1865 *AmPolLe [port], BenetAL 91, RComAH*
**Lincoln,** Alexander, III 1943- *WhoWest 92*
**Lincoln,** Anthony 1911- *Who 92*
**Lincoln,** Anthony Leslie Julian d1991 *Who 92N*
**Lincoln,** Bruce Kenneth 1948- *IntAu&W 91*
**Lincoln,** C. Eric 1924- *WhoBlA 92, WrDr 92*
**Lincoln,** Catherine Ruth 1941- *WhoAmP 91*
**Lincoln,** Charles Albert 1939- *AmMWSc 92*
**Lincoln,** Crawford 1928- *WhoFI 92*
**Lincoln,** David Erwin 1944- *AmMWSc 92*
**Lincoln,** Dennis William 1939- *Who 92*
**Lincoln,** Edmond Lynch 1949- *WhoFI 92*
**Lincoln,** Elizabeth *DrAPF 91*
**Lincoln,** Emma Ethel 1914- *WhoAmP 91*
**Lincoln,** Eugene 1923- *WhoRel 92*
**Lincoln,** F. Ashe *Who 92*
**Lincoln,** Franklin Benjamin, Jr. 1908- *WhoAmL 92*
**Lincoln,** Geoffrey *ConTFT 9, IntAu&W 91X, WrDr 92*
**Lincoln,** Georgianna *WhoAmP 91*
**Lincoln,** J William 1940- *WhoAmP 91*
**Lincoln,** Jeannette Virginia 1915- *AmMWSc 92*
**Lincoln,** Jeannine Marguerite 1935- *WhoAmP 91*
**Lincoln,** Joseph C. 1870-1944 *BenetAL 91*
**Lincoln,** Kenneth Arnold 1922- *AmMWSc 92*
**Lincoln,** Kenneth Robert 1943- *ConAu 36NR*
**Lincoln,** Les *ConAu 34NR*
**Lincoln,** Lewis Lauren 1926- *AmMWSc 92*
**Lincoln,** Lucian Abraham 1926- *WhoMW 92*
**Lincoln,** Mary Todd 1818-1882 *PorAmW [port]*
**Lincoln,** Maurice *ScFEYrs*
**Lincoln,** Nancy Hanks *DcNCBi 4*
**Lincoln,** Richard Criddle 1942- *AmMWSc 92*
**Lincoln,** Richard G 1923- *AmMWSc 92*
**Lincoln,** Sandra Eleanor 1939- *WhoWest 92*
**Lincoln,** Thomas L. 1929- *WhoWest 92*
**Lincoln,** Victor D 1941- *WhoIns 92*
**Lincoln,** Victoria 1904-1981 *BenetAL 91*
**Lind,** Alan 1959- *WhoWest 92*
**Lind,** Alexander R 1925- *AmMWSc 92*
**Lind,** Arthur Charles 1932- *AmMWSc 92*
**Lind,** Carol Johnson 1926- *AmMWSc 92*
**Lind,** Charles Douglas 1930- *AmMWSc 92*
**Lind,** David Arthur 1918- *AmMWSc 92*
**Lind,** Douglas A 1946- *AmMWSc 92*
**Lind,** Earl Frederic 1934- *WhoFI 92*
**Lind,** Jakov 1927- *LiExTwC*
**Lind,** Jenny 1820-1887 *NewAmDM*
**Lind,** Jim 1955- *WhoAmP 91*
**Lind,** Jon Robert 1935- *WhoAmL 92*
**Lind,** Jose 1964- *WhoHisp 92*
**Lind,** Karen *DrAPF 91*
**Lind,** Kendra Johnson 1947- *WhoWest 92*
**Lind,** Levi Robert 1906- *IntAu&W 91, WrDr 92*
**Lind,** Marilyn Marlene 1934- *WhoAmP 91*
**Lind,** Maurice David 1934- *AmMWSc 92, WhoWest 92*
**Lind,** Nathalie 1918- *IntWW 91*
**Lind,** Niels Christian 1930- *AmMWSc 92*
**Lind,** Owen Thomas 1934- *AmMWSc 92*
**Lind,** Per 1916- *Who 92*
**Lind,** Robert Clarence 1937- *WhoFI 92*
**Lind,** Robert Wayne 1939- *AmMWSc 92*
**Lind,** Terrie Lee 1948- *WhoWest 92*
**Lind,** Thomas A 1918- *WhoAmP 91*
**Lind,** Vance Gordon 1935- *AmMWSc 92*
**Lind,** Wilton H 1927- *AmMWSc 92*
**Linda,** Gerald 1946- *WhoFI 92*
**Lindaas,** Elroy *WhoAmP 91*
**Lindahl,** Carl J. 1946- *WhoWest 92*
**Lindahl,** Charles Blighe 1939- *AmMWSc 92*
**Lindahl,** Elder M. 1926- *WhoRel 92*
**Lindahl,** Josua 1844-1912 *BiInAmS*
**Lindahl,** Lasse Allan 1944- *AmMWSc 92*
**Lindahl,** Ronald 1948- *AmMWSc 92*
**Lindahl,** Ronald Gunnar 1948- *AmMWSc 92*
**Lindahl,** Roy Lawrence 1925- *AmMWSc 92*
**Lindahl,** Tomas Robert 1938- *Who 92*
**Lindal,** Gunnar F 1936- *AmMWSc 92*
**Lindamood,** John Benford 1929- *AmMWSc 92*
**Lindars,** Barnabas *WrDr 92*
**Lindars,** Barnabas 1923-1991 *ConAu 135*
**Lindars,** Frederick C. 1923- *WrDr 92*
**Lindars,** Frederick Chevallier 1923- *Who 92*
**Lindau,** David Steuer 1926- *WhoAmL 92*
**Lindau,** Evert Ingolf 1942- *AmMWSc 92*
**Lindau,** James H. 1933- *WhoFI 92, WhoMW 92*
**Lindau,** James Harold 1933- *WhoAmP 91*
**Lindau,** Joan *DrAPF 91*
**Lindauer,** Erik D. 1956- *WhoAmL 92*
**Lindauer,** George Conrad 1935- *AmMWSc 92*
**Lindauer,** Ivo Eugene 1931- *AmMWSc 92*
**Lindauer,** Lois Lyons 1933- *ConAu 35NR*
**Lindauer,** Martin 1918- *IntWW 91*

**Lindauer**, Maurice William 1924- *AmMWSc 92*
**Lindbeck**, Assar 1930- *WrDr 92*
**Lindbeck**, Wendell Arthur 1912- *AmMWSc 92*
**Lindberg**, Carter Harry 1937- *WhoRel 92*
**Lindberg**, Charles David 1928- *WhoAmL 92, WhoMW 92*
**Lindberg**, Craig Robert *AmMWSc 92*
**Lindberg**, David 1948- *WhoWest 92*
**Lindberg**, David Henderson 1937- *WhoRel 92*
**Lindberg**, David Robert 1948- *AmMWSc 92*
**Lindberg**, David Seaman, Sr 1929- *AmMWSc 92*
**Lindberg**, Dennis Anton 1945- *WhoRel 92*
**Lindberg**, Donald Allan Bror 1933- *AmMWSc 92*
**Lindberg**, Donna Jeanne 1944- *WhoRel 92*
**Lindberg**, Duane R. *WhoRel 92*
**Lindberg**, Edward E 1938- *AmMWSc 92*
**Lindberg**, Francis Laurence, Jr. 1948- *WhoMW 92*
**Lindberg**, George Donald 1925- *AmMWSc 92*
**Lindberg**, George W. 1932- *WhoAmL 92, WhoMW 92*
**Lindberg**, Helge 1926- *WhoFI 92*
**Lindberg**, James George 1940- *AmMWSc 92*
**Lindberg**, Jeffrey 1954- *WhoMW 92*
**Lindberg**, John Albert, Jr 1934- *AmMWSc 92*
**Lindberg**, Lois Helen 1932- *AmMWSc 92*
**Lindberg**, Magnus 1958- *ConCom 92*
**Lindberg**, R G 1924- *AmMWSc 92*
**Lindberg**, Russell Harry 1921- *WhoMW 92*
**Lindberg**, Steven Edward 1942- *AmMWSc 92*
**Lindberg**, Steven Eric 1947- *AmMWSc 92*
**Lindberg**, Thomas Harold 1952- *WhoRel 92*
**Lindberg**, Timothy J. 1955- *WhoEnt 92*
**Lindberg**, Vern Wilton 1949- *AmMWSc 92*
**Lindbergh**, Anne Morrow 1906- *BenetAL 91, IntAu&W 91, WrDr 92*
**Lindbergh**, Anne Spencer Morrow 1906- *Who 92*
**Lindbergh**, Charles A. 1902-1974 *BenetAL 91, RComAH*
**Lindbergh**, Charles Augustus 1902-1974 *FacFETw [port]*
**Lindblad**, William John 1954- *AmMWSc 92*
**Lindblade**, Eric N 1916- *WhoAmP 91*
**Lindblade**, Eric Norman, Jr. 1952- *WhoRel 92*
**Lindblom**, Gunnel 1931- *IntMPA 92*
**Lindblom**, Marjorie Press 1950- *WhoAmL 92*
**Lindblom**, Seppo Olavi 1935- *IntWW 91*
**Lindbloom**, Kenneth Dean 1946- *WhoFI 92*
**Lindborg**, Henry John 1944- *WhoMW 92*
**Lindburg**, Donald Gilson 1932- *AmMWSc 92*
**Lindburg**, Lela Almeta 1906- *WhoAmP 91*
**Linde**, Alan Trevor 1938- *AmMWSc 92*
**Linde**, Hans Arthur 1924- *WhoAmP 91, WhoWest 92*
**Linde**, Harry Wight 1926- *AmMWSc 92*
**Linde**, Leonard M 1928- *AmMWSc 92*
**Linde**, Lucille Mae Jacobson 1919- *WhoWest 92*
**Linde**, Nancy *DrAPF 91*
**Linde**, Peter Franz 1926- *AmMWSc 92*
**Linde**, Richard B. L. 1919- *WhoRel 92*
**Linde**, Ronald K 1940- *AmMWSc 92*
**Linde**, Ronald Keith 1940- *WhoMW 92*
**Linde**, Shirley *IntAu&W 91*
**Linde**, Shirley Motter *WrDr 92*
**Linde**, Terry Brian 1950- *WhoWest 92*
**Linde**, William Walker 1932- *WhoAmP 91*
**Lindeberg**, George Kline 1930- *AmMWSc 92*
**Lindeke**, Jonathan Michael 1948- *WhoAmL 92*
**Lindelien**, James Wallace 1957- *WhoEnt 92*
**Lindell**, Ismo Veikko 1939- *AmMWSc 92*
**Lindell**, Thomas Jay 1941- *AmMWSc 92*
**Lindelof**, J O 1852- *ScFEYrs*
**Lindeman**, Alfred 1940- *WhoAmL 92*
**Lindeman**, Anne *WhoAmP 91*
**Lindeman**, Fredrik Otto 1936- *IntWW 91*
**Lindeman**, Jack *DrAPF 91*
**Lindeman**, Robert D 1930- *AmMWSc 92*
**Lindemann**, Carl, Jr. d1985 *LesBEnT 92*
**Lindemann**, Charles Benard 1946- *AmMWSc 92*
**Lindemann**, Corinne Reif 1960- *WhoMW 92*
**Lindemann**, Stephen William 1939- *WhoAmL 92*
**Lindemann**, Wallace W 1925- *AmMWSc 92*
**Lindemann**, William Conrad 1948- *AmMWSc 92*
**Lindemer**, Arthur Kent 1963- *WhoEnt 92*
**Lindemer**, Terrence Bradford 1936- *AmMWSc 92*
**Lindemeyer**, Rochelle G 1952- *AmMWSc 92*
**Lindemulder**, Carol Ann 1936- *WhoWest 92*
**Linden**, Anya 1933- *Who 92*
**Linden**, Carol D 1949- *AmMWSc 92*
**Linden**, Charles 1832?-1888 *BiInAmS*
**Linden**, Dennis Robert 1942- *AmMWSc 92*
**Linden**, Duane B 1930- *AmMWSc 92*
**Linden**, Hal 1931- *IntMPA 92, WhoEnt 92*
**Linden**, Henry R 1922- *AmMWSc 92*
**Linden**, Henry Robert 1922- *WhoMW 92*
**Linden**, James Carl 1942- *AmMWSc 92*
**Linden**, Joel Morris 1952- *AmMWSc 92*
**Linden**, Kurt Joseph 1936- *AmMWSc 92*
**Linden**, Matthew McKinley 1970- *WhoRel 92*
**Linden**, Theodore Anthony 1938- *WhoWest 92*
**Linden**, Walther 1895-1943 *EncTR 91*
**Lindenau**, Judith Wood *DrAPF 91*
**Lindenauer**, S Martin 1932- *AmMWSc 92*
**Lindenbaum**, S J 1925- *AmMWSc 92*
**Lindenbaum**, Sandford Richard 1948- *WhoAmL 92*
**Lindenbaum**, Siegfried 1930- *AmMWSc 92, WhoMW 92*
**Lindenberg**, Benjamin Benno 1920- *WhoFI 92*
**Lindenberg**, Earl Gene 1934- *WhoMW 92*
**Lindenberg**, Katja 1941- *AmMWSc 92*
**Lindenberg**, Mary Jean 1952- *WhoAmL 92*
**Lindenberg**, Richard 1911- *AmMWSc 92*
**Lindenberger**, Herbert Samuel 1929- *WhoWest 92*
**Lindenblad**, Irving Werner 1929- *AmMWSc 92*
**Lindenfeld**, Peter 1925- *AmMWSc 92*
**Lindenkohl**, Adolph 1833-1904 *BiInAmS*
**Lindenlaub**, John Charles 1933- *AmMWSc 92*
**Lindenmayer**, Aristid 1925- *AmMWSc 92*
**Lindenmayer**, George Earl 1940- *AmMWSc 92*
**Lindenmeier**, Charles William 1930- *AmMWSc 92*
**Lindenmeyer**, Paul Henry 1921- *AmMWSc 92*
**Lindenstadt**, Glen Daniel 1960- *WhoFI 92*
**Lindenstrauss**, Joram 1936- *IntWW 91*
**Linder**, Allan David 1925- *AmMWSc 92*
**Linder**, Bruno 1924- *AmMWSc 92*
**Linder**, Clarence H 1903- *AmMWSc 92*
**Linder**, Don *DrAPF 91*
**Linder**, Donald Ernst 1938- *AmMWSc 92, WhoAmP 91*
**Linder**, Ernest G 1902- *AmMWSc 92*
**Linder**, Forrest Edward 1906- *AmMWSc 92*
**Linder**, Greg Vincent 1955- *WhoMW 92*
**Linder**, Harris Joseph 1928- *AmMWSc 92*
**Linder**, Harvey Ronald 1949- *WhoAmL 92*
**Linder**, Irvin Ray 1931- *WhoEnt 92*
**Linder**, James 1954- *AmMWSc 92*
**Linder**, Jeffrey Mark 1950- *WhoAmP 91*
**Linder**, John E 1942- *WhoAmP 91*
**Linder**, John Scott 1935- *AmMWSc 92*
**Linder**, Louis Jacob 1916- *AmMWSc 92*
**Linder**, Lowell Irl 1940- *IntAu&W 91*
**Linder**, Maria C *AmMWSc 92*
**Linder**, Regina 1945- *AmMWSc 92*
**Linder**, Robert D. 1934- *WrDr 92*
**Linder**, Robert Joe 1937- *WhoEnt 92*
**Linder**, Seymour Martin 1925- *AmMWSc 92*
**Linder**, Solomon Leon 1929- *AmMWSc 92*
**Linderberg**, Jan Erik 1934- *IntWW 91*
**Linderman**, Charles L *WhoAmP 91*
**Linderman**, Frank B. 1868-1938 *BenetAL 91*
**Linderman**, Jeanne Herron 1931- *WhoRel 92*
**Linderman**, Robert G 1939- *AmMWSc 92*
**Linderoth**, Karl-Axel 1927- *IntWW 91*
**Linders**, James Gus 1936- *AmMWSc 92*
**Lindert**, Michael Allen 1962- *WhoMW 92*
**Lindesay-Bethune** *Who 92*
**Lindesmith**, Larry Alan 1938- *WhoMW 92*
**Lindesmith**, Ruth Mildred 1914- *WhoAmP 91*
**Lindestrom**, Peter Martensson *BenetAL 91*
**Lindfors**, Karl Russell 1937- *AmMWSc 92*
**Lindfors**, Viveca *WhoEnt 92*
**Lindfors**, Viveca 1920- *IntMPA 92*
**Lindgren**, Alice Marilyn Lindell 1937- *AmMWSc 92*
**Lindgren**, Armas *DcTwDes*
**Lindgren**, Arne Sigfrid 1932- *WhoAmL 92*
**Lindgren**, Bernard William 1924- *AmMWSc 92*
**Lindgren**, Charlotte Holt 1924- *IntAu&W 91*
**Lindgren**, Clark Allen 1958- *AmMWSc 92*
**Lindgren**, David Leonard 1906- *AmMWSc 92*
**Lindgren**, Donald 1930- *WhoRel 92*
**Lindgren**, E Rune 1919- *AmMWSc 92*
**Lindgren**, Frank Tycko 1924- *AmMWSc 92*
**Lindgren**, Gordon Edward 1936- *AmMWSc 92*
**Lindgren**, Henry Clay 1914- *WrDr 92*
**Lindgren**, Jay Randolph 1961- *WhoAmP 91*
**Lindgren**, Jon 1938- *WhoAmP 91*
**Lindgren**, Richard Arthur 1940- *AmMWSc 92*
**Lindgren**, Robert Kemper 1939- *WhoFI 92, WhoWest 92*
**Lindgren**, Steven Obed 1949- *WhoAmP 91*
**Lindgren**, Theodore F 1923- *WhoAmP 91*
**Lindgren**, William Dale 1936- *WhoMW 92*
**Lindgren**, William Frederick 1942- *AmMWSc 92*
**Lindh**, Allan Goddard 1943- *AmMWSc 92*
**Lindh**, Patricia Sullivan 1928- *WhoAmP 91*
**Lindh**, Sten 1922- *IntWW 91*
**Lindh**, Ylva Anna Maria 1957- *IntWW 91*
**Lindhard**, Jens 1922- *IntWW 91*
**Lindhardt**, Poul Georg 1910- *IntWW 91*
**Lindheim**, James Bruce 1945- *WhoFI 92*
**Lindheim**, Richard David 1939- *WhoEnt 92, WhoFI 92*
**Lindheimer**, Ferdinand Jacob 1801-1879 *BiInAmS*
**Lindheimer**, Marshall D 1932- *AmMWSc 92*
**Lindholm**, Carl Edward 1929- *WhoFI 92*
**Lindholm**, Charles T. 1946- *ConAu 134*
**Lindholm**, Clifford F, II 1930- *WhoAmP 91*
**Lindholm**, Frances Marion 1918- *WhoAmP 91*
**Lindholm**, Fredrik Arthur 1936- *AmMWSc 92*
**Lindholm**, John C 1923- *AmMWSc 92*
**Lindholm**, Kelly Gail 1963- *WhoEnt 92*
**Lindholm**, Kenneth Edward 1951- *WhoFI 92*
**Lindholm**, Richard Theodore 1960- *WhoWest 92*
**Lindholm**, Richard W. 1913- *WrDr 92*
**Lindholm**, Robert D 1940- *AmMWSc 92*
**Lindholm**, Robert McClure 1935- *WhoMW 92*
**Lindholm**, Ronald Dale 1958- *WhoRel 92*
**Lindholm**, Roy Charles 1937- *AmMWSc 92*
**Lindholm**, Sven Olof 1903- *BiDExR*
**Lindholm**, Ulric S 1931- *AmMWSc 92*
**Lindholm**, William Charles 1932- *WhoRel 92*
**Lindhorst**, Taylor Erwin 1928- *AmMWSc 92*
**Lindig**, Bill M. 1936- *WhoFI 92*
**Lindine**, Jack Michael, Jr. 1949- *WhoEnt 92*
**Lindisfarne**, Archdeacon of *Who 92*
**Lindler**, Micah Clement 1958- *WhoEnt 92*
**Lindley**, Arnold 1902- *Who 92*
**Lindley**, Arnold Lewis George 1902- *IntWW 91*
**Lindley**, Barry Drew 1939- *AmMWSc 92, WhoMW 92*
**Lindley**, Bryan Charles 1932- *Who 92*
**Lindley**, Charles A 1924- *AmMWSc 92*
**Lindley**, Charles Allen 1950- *WhoRel 92*
**Lindley**, Charles Edward 1921- *AmMWSc 92*
**Lindley**, Dennis Victor 1923- *Who 92*
**Lindley**, Ernest K. 1899-1979 *CurBio 91N*
**Lindley**, James 1735-1779 *DcNCBi 4*
**Lindley**, John M, III 1945- *WhoAmP 91*
**Lindley**, John Van 1838-1918 *DcNCBi 4*
**Lindley**, John William 1920- *WhoAmP 91*
**Lindley**, Jonathan 1756-1828 *DcNCBi 4*
**Lindley**, Kenneth Eugene 1924- *AmMWSc 92*
**Lindley**, Norman Dale 1937- *WhoWest 92*
**Lindman**, Erick Leroy, Jr 1938- *AmMWSc 92*
**Lindman-Strafford**, Kerstin Margareta 1939- *IntAu&W 91*
**Lindmayer**, Joseph 1929- *AmMWSc 92*
**Lindner**, Carl *DrAPF 91*
**Lindner**, Carl H 1919- *WhoIns 92*
**Lindner**, Carl H, III 1953- *WhoIns 92*
**Lindner**, Carl Henry 1919- *IntWW 91, WhoFI 92, WhoMW 92*
**Lindner**, Dennis G. 1936- *WhoAmL 92*
**Lindner**, Duane Lee 1950- *AmMWSc 92*
**Lindner**, Elek 1924- *AmMWSc 92*
**Lindner**, Elizabeth M 1951- *WhoIns 92*
**Lindner**, Gerhard 1930- *IntWW 91, Who 92*
**Lindner**, James William 1954- *WhoEnt 92*
**Lindner**, Luther Edward 1942- *AmMWSc 92*
**Lindner**, Manfred 1919- *AmMWSc 92*
**Lindner**, Robert David 1920- *WhoIns 92*
**Lindner**, Terrell M. 1915- *IntMPA 92*
**Lindner**, Vicki *DrAPF 91*
**Lindo**, Edwin Thessalonians 1953- *WhoRel 92*
**Lindo**, J. Trevor 1925- *WhoBlA 92*
**Lindo-Fuentes**, Hector 1952- *WhoHisp 92*
**Lindon**, Jerome 1925- *IntWW 91*
**Lindon**, Timothy J. 1955- *WhoAmL 92*
**Lindop**, Norman 1921- *Who 92*
**Lindop**, Patricia Joyce 1930- *Who 92*
**Lindorff**, David Everett 1945- *AmMWSc 92*
**Lindorff**, Joyce Zankel 1950- *WhoEnt 92*
**Lindower**, John Oliver 1929- *AmMWSc 92*
**Lindquist**, Anders Gunnar 1942- *AmMWSc 92*
**Lindquist**, David Gregory 1946- *AmMWSc 92*
**Lindquist**, Everett Carlton 1912- *WhoMW 92*
**Lindquist**, Evert E 1935- *AmMWSc 92*
**Lindquist**, Larry Easton 1936- *WhoWest 92*
**Lindquist**, Leland Adrian 1947- *WhoMW 92*
**Lindquist**, Michael Lee 1953- *WhoWest 92*
**Lindquist**, Ray *DrAPF 91*
**Lindquist**, Raymond Irving 1907- *WhoRel 92*
**Lindquist**, Richard Kenneth 1942- *AmMWSc 92*
**Lindquist**, Richard Wallace 1933- *AmMWSc 92*
**Lindquist**, Robert Arvid 1929- *WhoAmP 91*
**Lindquist**, Robert Henry 1928- *AmMWSc 92*
**Lindquist**, Robert John 1948- *WhoFI 92*
**Lindquist**, Robert Marion 1923- *AmMWSc 92*
**Lindquist**, Robert Nels 1942- *AmMWSc 92*
**Lindquist**, Sheryl Ann 1939- *WhoWest 92*
**Lindquist**, Stanley Elmer 1917- *WhoWest 92*
**Lindquist**, Wallace Alfred, Jr. 1926- *WhoMW 92*
**Lindquist**, Wallace Lawrence, Jr 1934- *WhoAmP 91*
**Lindquist**, William Brent 1953- *AmMWSc 92*
**Lindqvist**, Bengt 1936- *IntWW 91*
**Lindqvist**, Gunnar Jan 1950- *WhoFI 92*
**Lindroos**, Arthur E 1922- *AmMWSc 92*
**Lindros**, Eric 1973- *News 92-1 [port]*
**Lindsay** *Who 92*
**Lindsay**, Earl of 1955- *Who 92*
**Lindsay**, Master of 1991- *Who 92*
**Lindsay**, Bertha 1897-1990 *AnObit 1990*
**Lindsay**, Beverly 1947- *WhoBlA 92*
**Lindsay**, Bruce George 1947- *AmMWSc 92*
**Lindsay**, Bryan Eugene *DrAPF 91*
**Lindsay**, Charles McCown 1932- *AmMWSc 92, WhoMW 92*
**Lindsay**, Colin 1744-1817 *DcNCBi 4*
**Lindsay**, Courtenay Traice David 1910- *Who 92*
**Lindsay**, Crawford B. 1905- *WhoBlA 92*
**Lindsay**, Crawford Callum Douglas 1939- *Who 92*
**Lindsay**, David 1490?-1555 *RfGEnL 91*
**Lindsay**, David 1876-1945 *TwCSFW 91*
**Lindsay**, David 1878-1945 *ScFEYrs*
**Lindsay**, David Taylor 1935- *AmMWSc 92*
**Lindsay**, Delbert W 1924- *AmMWSc 92*
**Lindsay**, Derek Michael 1944- *AmMWSc 92*
**Lindsay**, Donald Dunrod 1910- *Who 92*
**Lindsay**, Doris White 1937- *WhoEnt 92*
**Lindsay**, Dwight Marsee 1921- *AmMWSc 92*
**Lindsay**, Eddie H. S. 1931- *WhoBlA 92*
**Lindsay**, Emery 1951- *WhoRel 92*
**Lindsay**, Everett Harold, Jr 1931- *AmMWSc 92*
**Lindsay**, Fernand 1928- *WhoEnt 92*
**Lindsay**, Freda Theresa 1914- *WhoRel 92*
**Lindsay**, George Edmund 1916- *AmMWSc 92*
**Lindsay**, George Nelson 1919- *WhoAmL 92*
**Lindsay**, George Peter 1948- *WhoAmL 92*
**Lindsay**, Gilbert W. 1900-1990 *WhoBlA 92N*
**Lindsay**, Glenn Frank 1935- *AmMWSc 92*
**Lindsay**, Hague Leland, Jr 1929- *AmMWSc 92*
**Lindsay**, Harry Lee 1925- *AmMWSc 92*
**Lindsay**, Hilarie Elizabeth 1922- *IntAu&W 91*
**Lindsay**, Horace Augustin 1938- *WhoBlA 92*
**Lindsay**, Howard 1889-1968 *BenetAL 91*
**Lindsay**, Hugh *Who 92*
**Lindsay**, Hugh Alexander 1926- *AmMWSc 92*

**Lindsay**, Inabel Burns 1900-1983 *NotBlAW 92*
**Lindsay**, Jack 1900- *IntAu&W 91*
**Lindsay**, Jack 1900-1990 *AnObit 1990, RfGEnL 91*
**Lindsay**, James Edward, Jr 1928- *AmMWSc 92*
**Lindsay**, James Gordon, Jr 1941- *AmMWSc 92*
**Lindsay**, James Harvey Kincaid Stewart 1915- *Who 92*
**Lindsay**, James Louis 1906- *Who 92*
**Lindsay**, James Wiley 1934- *WhoFI 92, WhoMW 92*
**Lindsay**, John 1921- *WrDr 92*
**Lindsay**, John C 1959- *WhoAmP 91*
**Lindsay**, John Edmund Fredric 1935- *Who 92*
**Lindsay**, John Maurice 1918- *Who 92*
**Lindsay**, John Vliet 1921- *IntWW 91, Who 92, WhoAmP 91*
**Lindsay**, Kenneth Lawson 1925- *AmMWSc 92*
**Lindsay**, Kenneth Martin d1991 *Who 92N*
**Lindsay**, Loelia 1902- *ConAu 133*
**Lindsay**, Maurice *Who 92*
**Lindsay**, Maurice 1918- *ConPo 91, WrDr 92*
**Lindsay**, Michael Bruce 1947- *WhoFI 92*
**Lindsay**, Norman 1879-1969 *SmATA 67 [port]*
**Lindsay**, Norman Roy 1936- *WhoWest 92*
**Lindsay**, Orland Ugham *Who 92*
**Lindsay**, Rachel *WrDr 92*
**Lindsay**, Raymond H 1928- *AmMWSc 92*
**Lindsay**, Reginald C. 1945- *WhoBlA 92*
**Lindsay**, Richard H 1934- *AmMWSc 92*
**Lindsay**, Richard Paul 1945- *WhoWest 92*
**Lindsay**, Robert 1949- *IntMPA 92*
**Lindsay**, Robert Clarence 1936- *AmMWSc 92*
**Lindsay**, Robert Kendall 1934- *AmMWSc 92*
**Lindsay**, Robert V. 1926- *IntWW 91*
**Lindsay**, Shannon David 1962- *WhoWest 92*
**Lindsay**, Stan Andrew 1949- *WhoMW 92*
**Lindsay**, Stephen Prout 1944- *WhoAmL 92*
**Lindsay**, Stuart Martin 1951- *WhoWest 92*
**Lindsay**, Vachel 1879-1931 *BenetAL 91, ConAu 135, FacFETw*
**Lindsay**, W N 1913- *AmMWSc 92*
**Lindsay**, Willard Lyman 1926- *AmMWSc 92*
**Lindsay**, William Germer, Jr 1928- *AmMWSc 92*
**Lindsay**, William Neish, III 1947- *WhoWest 92*
**Lindsay**, William Tenney, Jr 1924- *AmMWSc 92*
**Lindsay-Hogg**, Edward William 1910- *Who 92*
**Lindsay of Birker**, Baron 1909- *Who 92*
**Lindsay of Dowhill**, Ronald Alexander 1933- *Who 92*
**Lindsay-Smith**, Iain-Mor 1934- *Who 92*
**Lindsell**, Harold 1913- *WhoRel 92*
**Lindsey**, Archdeacon of *Who 92*
**Lindsey**, Earl of 1931- *Who 92*
**Lindsey**, Alton Anthony 1907- *AmMWSc 92, WhoMW 92*
**Lindsey**, Ben B. 1869-1943 *BenetAL 91*
**Lindsey**, Brenda Lynn 1958- *WhoWest 92*
**Lindsey**, Bruce Gilbert 1949- *AmMWSc 92*
**Lindsey**, Byron Trent 1935- *WhoWest 92*
**Lindsey**, Casimir Charles 1923- *AmMWSc 92*
**Lindsey**, David *WrDr 92*
**Lindsey**, David 1944- *TwCWW 91*
**Lindsey**, David Allen 1942- *AmMWSc 92*
**Lindsey**, Donald L 1937- *AmMWSc 92*
**Lindsey**, Dortha Ruth 1926- *AmMWSc 92*
**Lindsey**, Edward Stormont 1930- *AmMWSc 92*
**Lindsey**, Gary Douglas 1948- *WhoEnt 92*
**Lindsey**, George Roy 1920- *AmMWSc 92*
**Lindsey**, George Thomas 1936- *WhoEnt 92*
**Lindsey**, Gerald Herbert 1934- *AmMWSc 92*
**Lindsey**, Gordon J. 1906-1973 *RelLAm 91*
**Lindsey**, Hal *WhoRel 92, WrDr 92*
**Lindsey**, James Russell 1933- *AmMWSc 92*
**Lindsey**, Jerome W. 1932- *WhoBlA 92*
**Lindsey**, Jim *DrAPF 91*
**Lindsey**, Johanna 1952- *WrDr 92*
**Lindsey**, John Cunningham 1953- *WhoWest 92*
**Lindsey**, John Hall, Jr. 1938- *WhoWest 92*
**Lindsey**, John Morton 1930- *WhoFI 92*
**Lindsey**, Julia Page 1948- *AmMWSc 92*
**Lindsey**, Karen *DrAPF 91*
**Lindsey**, Lawrence Benjamin 1954- *WhoFI 92*
**Lindsey**, Mark Kelly 1955- *WhoFI 92*
**Lindsey**, Mark Wayne 1960- *WhoWest 92*
**Lindsey**, Marvin Frederick *AmMWSc 92*
**Lindsey**, Melvin Wesley 1955- *WhoEnt 92*
**Lindsey**, Mort 1923- *WhoEnt 92*
**Lindsey**, Norma Jack 1929- *AmMWSc 92*
**Lindsey**, Ouida 1927- *WhoBlA 92*
**Lindsey**, Richard Edward 1952- *WhoEnt 92, WhoMW 92*
**Lindsey**, Richard J 1956- *WhoAmP 91*
**Lindsey**, Richard Lee 1948- *WhoRel 92*
**Lindsey**, Robert G, Jr 1921- *WhoAmP 91*
**Lindsey**, Robert Sours 1913- *WhoAmL 92*
**Lindsey**, Roland Gray 1927- *AmMWSc 92*
**Lindsey**, S. L. 1909- *WhoBlA 92*
**Lindsey**, Scott Earl 1960- *WhoMW 92*
**Lindsey**, Susan Paige 1951- *WhoMW 92*
**Lindsey**, Terry Lamar 1950- *WhoBlA 92*
**Lindsey**, Theophilus 1723-1808 *BlkwCEP*
**Lindsey**, Thomas Kenneth 1959- *WhoAmL 92*
**Lindsey**, W H *WhoAmP 91*
**Lindsey**, William B 1922- *AmMWSc 92*
**Lindsey**, William Dennis 1950- *WhoRel 92*
**Lindskog**, Gustaf Elmer 1903- *AmMWSc 92*
**Lindskog**, Norbert F. 1932- *WhoMW 92*
**Lindsley**, Dan Leslie, Jr 1925- *AmMWSc 92*
**Lindsley**, Dana Frederick 1949- *WhoRel 92*
**Lindsley**, David Ford 1936- *AmMWSc 92*
**Lindsley**, Donald B 1907- *AmMWSc 92*
**Lindsley**, Donald Benjamin 1907- *IntWW 91*
**Lindsley**, Donald Hale 1934- *AmMWSc 92*
**Lindsley**, Herbert Piper 1913- *WhoFI 92*
**Lindsley**, Jerry Charles 1956- *WhoAmP 91*
**Lindsley**, Michelle LaBrosse 1962- *WhoWest 92*
**Lindstedt**, P M 1917- *AmMWSc 92*
**Lindstedt-Siva**, K June 1941- *AmMWSc 92*
**Lindsten**, Jan Eric 1935- *IntWW 91*
**Lindstrom**, Barry Lee 1952- *WhoWest 92*
**Lindstrom**, Daniel Lee 1960- *WhoAmL 92*
**Lindstrom**, David John 1945- *AmMWSc 92*
**Lindstrom**, Donald Fredrick, Jr. 1943- *WhoRel 92*
**Lindstrom**, Duaine Gerald 1937- *AmMWSc 92*
**Lindstrom**, Eldon Roy 1944- *WhoMW 92*
**Lindstrom**, Eugene Shipman 1923- *AmMWSc 92*
**Lindstrom**, Frederick Burgess 1915- *WhoWest 92*
**Lindstrom**, Fredrick Thomas 1940- *AmMWSc 92*
**Lindstrom**, Gary J 1939- *AmMWSc 92*
**Lindstrom**, Ivar E, Jr 1929- *AmMWSc 92*
**Lindstrom**, Jon Martin 1945- *AmMWSc 92*
**Lindstrom**, Jon Robert 1957- *WhoEnt 92*
**Lindstrom**, Marilyn Martin 1946- *AmMWSc 92*
**Lindstrom**, Merlin Ray 1951- *AmMWSc 92*
**Lindstrom**, Nina Lucille 1940- *WhoFI 92, WhoWest 92*
**Lindstrom**, Richard Edward 1932- *AmMWSc 92*
**Lindstrom**, Richard Lyndon 1947- *WhoMW 92*
**Lindstrom**, Richard S 1927- *AmMWSc 92*
**Lindstrom**, Terry Donald 1951- *AmMWSc 92*
**Lindstrom**, Torsten L. 1921- *IntWW 91*
**Lindstrom**, Ulla 1909- *IntWW 91*
**Lindstrom**, Wendell Don 1927- *AmMWSc 92*
**Lindt**, Auguste Rudolph 1905- *IntWW 91, Who 92*
**Lindt**, Jan Thomas 1942- *AmMWSc 92*
**Lindvall**, F C 1903- *AmMWSc 92*
**Lindvall**, Michael Lloyd 1947- *WhoRel 92*
**Lindwall**, Raymond Russell 1921- *IntWW 91*
**Lindy**, Jeffrey Marc 1958- *WhoAmL 92*
**Lindzen**, Richard Siegmund 1940- *AmMWSc 92*
**Lindzey**, Gardner 1920- *WhoWest 92*
**Line**, David *WrDr 92*
**Line**, Frances Mary 1940- *Who 92*
**Line**, John Paul 1929- *AmMWSc 92*
**Line**, Maurice Bernard 1928- *Who 92, WrDr 92*
**Lineback**, Charles David 1948- *WhoIns 92*
**Lineback**, David R 1934- *AmMWSc 92*
**Lineback**, Jerry Alvin 1938- *AmMWSc 92*
**Linebarger**, Jim *DrAPF 91*
**Linebarger**, Libby 1947- *WhoAmP 91*
**Lineberger**, Larry Watson 1943- *WhoFI 92, WhoWest 92*
**Lineberger**, Robert Daniel 1948- *AmMWSc 92*
**Lineberger**, William Carl 1939- *AmMWSc 92*
**Lineberry**, Albert S, Sr 1918- *WhoAmP 91*
**Lineberry**, Gustavus Ernest 1870-1952 *DcNCBi 4*
**Linehan**, Anthony John 1931- *Who 92*
**Linehan**, John Andrew 1924- *WhoAmP 91*
**Linehan**, John Henry 1938- *AmMWSc 92*
**Linehan**, Urban Joseph 1911- *AmMWSc 92*
**Linehan**, William Marston 1947- *AmMWSc 92*
**Linell**, Martin Larsson 1849-1897 *BiInAmS*
**Linemeyer**, David L *AmMWSc 92*
**Linenthal**, Edward Tabor 1947- *WhoRel 92*
**Linenthal**, Mark *DrAPF 91*
**Liner**, Richard Mark 1953- *WhoWest 92*
**Lines**, Allan EuGene 1941- *WhoMW 92*
**Lines**, Malcolm Ellis 1936- *AmMWSc 92*
**Lines**, Moray 1922- *Who 92*
**Lines**, Vincent 1909-1968 *TwCPaSc*
**Linett**, Deena *DrAPF 91*
**Liney**, George, Jr. 1931- *WhoFI 92*
**Linfield**, James Clark Taylor 1955- *WhoWest 92*
**Linfield**, Warner Max 1918- *AmMWSc 92*
**Linfoot**, John Ardis 1931- *AmMWSc 92*
**Linford**, Alan C. *Who 92*
**Linford**, Dee d1971 *TwCWW 91*
**Linford**, Gary Joe 1940- *AmMWSc 92*
**Linford**, Golden C 1927- *WhoAmP 91*
**Linford**, Laurance Dee 1951- *WhoWest 92*
**Linford**, Lilli Ann 1960- *WhoEnt 92*
**Linford**, Rulon Kesler 1943- *AmMWSc 92*
**Ling Liong Sik** 1943- *IntWW 91*
**Ling Qing** 1923- *IntWW 91*
**Ling Yun** 1917- *IntWW 91*
**Ling**, Alan Campbell 1940- *AmMWSc 92*
**Ling**, Alfred Soy Chou 1928- *AmMWSc 92*
**Ling**, Amy *WhoMW 92*
**Ling**, Arthur George 1913- *Who 92*
**Ling**, Chung-Mei 1931- *AmMWSc 92*
**Ling**, Daniel 1926- *AmMWSc 92*
**Ling**, Daniel Seth, Jr 1924- *AmMWSc 92*
**Ling**, Edwin Rodger 1931- *IntAu&W 91*
**Ling**, F F 1927- *AmMWSc 92*
**Ling**, Fergus Alan Humphrey 1914- *Who 92*
**Ling**, George M 1923- *AmMWSc 92*
**Ling**, Gilbert Ning 1919- *AmMWSc 92*
**Ling**, Hao 1959- *AmMWSc 92*
**Ling**, Harry Wilson 1927- *AmMWSc 92*
**Ling**, Hsin Yi 1930- *AmMWSc 92*
**Ling**, Hubert 1942- *AmMWSc 92*
**Ling**, Huei 1934- *AmMWSc 92*
**Ling**, Hung Chi 1950- *AmMWSc 92*
**Ling**, James Gi-Ming 1930- *AmMWSc 92*
**Ling**, James J. 1922- *IntWW 91*
**Ling**, Jeffrey 1939- *Who 92*
**Ling**, John De Courcy *Who 92*
**Ling**, Joseph Tso-Ti 1919- *AmMWSc 92*
**Ling**, Nicholas Chi-Kwan 1940- *AmMWSc 92*
**Ling**, Peter J. 1956- *ConAu 135*
**Ling**, Robert Francis 1939- *AmMWSc 92*
**Ling**, Roger 1942- *WrDr 92*
**Ling**, Rung Tai 1943- *AmMWSc 92*
**Ling**, Samuel Chen-Ying 1929- *AmMWSc 92*
**Ling**, Suilin 1930- *WhoFI 92*
**Ling**, Ta-Yung 1943- *AmMWSc 92*
**Ling**, Ting H 1919- *AmMWSc 92*
**Ling**, William Norman 1937- *WhoFI 92*
**Lingafelter**, Edward Clay, Jr 1914- *AmMWSc 92*
**Lingane**, James Joseph 1909- *AmMWSc 92*
**Lingane**, Peter James 1940- *AmMWSc 92*
**Lingappa**, Banadakoppa Thimmappa 1927- *AmMWSc 92*
**Lingappa**, Jaisri Rao 1959- *AmMWSc 92*
**Lingappa**, Yamuna 1929- *AmMWSc 92*
**Lingard**, Anthony 1916- *Who 92*
**Lingard**, Joan *WrDr 92*
**Lingard**, Joan Amelia 1932- *IntAu&W 91*
**Lingard**, Robin Anthony 1941- *Who 92*
**Lingelbach**, Albert Lane 1940- *WhoAmL 92*
**Lingelbach**, D D 1925- *AmMWSc 92*
**Lingelbach**, Doris 1928- *WhoAmP 91*
**Lingelbach**, Robert Alexander 1953- *WhoEnt 92*
**Lingeman**, Richard 1931- *IntAu&W 91, WrDr 92*
**Lingenfelser**, Angelus Joseph 1909- *WhoRel 92*
**Lingenfelter**, Richard Emery 1934- *AmMWSc 92, WrDr 92*
**Lingerfelt**, B. Eugene, Jr. 1955- *WhoRel 92*
**Lingg**, Al J 1938- *AmMWSc 92*
**Lingle**, Kathleen McCall 1944- *WhoFI 92*
**Lingle**, Sarah Elizabeth 1955- *AmMWSc 92*
**Lingle**, Scott David 1953- *WhoMW 92*
**Lingle**, Walter Lee 1868-1956 *DcNCBi 4*
**Lingo**, Robert Samuel 1941- *WhoAmL 92*
**Lingrel**, Jerry B 1935- *AmMWSc 92*
**Lingren**, Wesley Earl 1930- *AmMWSc 92*
**Lings**, Martin 1909- *Who 92*
**Linguet**, Simon-Nicolas-Henri 1736-1794 *BlkwCEP*
**Lingwood**, Clifford Alan 1950- *AmMWSc 92*
**Linhardt**, Margarita Agcaoili 1947- *WhoWest 92*
**Linhardt**, Robert John 1953- *AmMWSc 92, WhoMW 92*
**Linhares**, Claudette Jeanne 1937- *WhoAmP 91*
**Linhart**, Rickey Wayne 1953- *WhoFI 92, WhoMW 92*
**Linhart**, Yan Bohumil 1939- *AmMWSc 92*
**Lini**, Walter Hadye 1942- *IntWW 91*
**Liniers y Bremond**, Santiago Antonio M de 1753-1810 *HisDSpE*
**Lining**, John 1708-1760 *BiInAmS*
**Lininger**, Lloyd Lesley 1939- *AmMWSc 92*
**Linington**, Elizabeth 1921- *IntAu&W 91*
**Linington**, Victor A 1908- *WhoAmP 91*
**Linis**, Viktors 1916- *AmMWSc 92*
**Link**, Antony Cole 1947- *WhoAmL 92*
**Link**, Arthur A 1914- *WhoAmP 91*
**Link**, Arthur S 1920- *IntAu&W 91, WrDr 92*
**Link**, Bernard Alvin 1941- *AmMWSc 92*
**Link**, Christoph 1933- *IntWW 91*
**Link**, Conrad Barnett 1912- *AmMWSc 92*
**Link**, E. G. 1952- *WhoMW 92*
**Link**, E. G. Jay 1952- *WhoFI 92*
**Link**, Edwin A 1904-1981 *FacFETw*
**Link**, Frank Albert 1930- *WhoMW 92*
**Link**, Fred M 1904- *AmMWSc 92*
**Link**, Frederick M. 1930- *WrDr 92*
**Link**, Garnett William, Jr 1945- *AmMWSc 92*
**Link**, George Hamilton 1939- *WhoAmL 92*
**Link**, Gordon Littlepage 1932- *AmMWSc 92*
**Link**, Harriet Mae 1934- *WhoAmP 91*
**Link**, John Clarence 1908- *AmMWSc 92*
**Link**, Mary Catherine Molly 1934- *WhoWest 92*
**Link**, Peter K 1930- *AmMWSc 92*
**Link**, Raymond Arthur 1954- *WhoFI 92*
**Link**, Robert Allen 1932- *WhoFI 92*
**Link**, Roger Paul 1910- *AmMWSc 92*
**Link**, William 1933- *IntMPA 92*
**Link**, William B 1928- *AmMWSc 92*
**Link**, William Edward 1921- *AmMWSc 92*
**Link**, William Richard 1943- *WhoFI 92*
**Link**, William Theodore 1933- *WhoEnt 92*
**Linke**, Gaile Marie 1938- *WhoMW 92*
**Linke**, Harald Arthur Bruno 1936- *AmMWSc 92*
**Linke**, Johannes 1900- *EncTR 91*
**Linke**, Richard Alan 1946- *AmMWSc 92*
**Linke**, Richard O. *LesBEnT 92*
**Linke**, Simon 1958- *TwCPaSc*
**Linke**, Simpson 1917- *AmMWSc 92*
**Linke**, William Finan 1924- *AmMWSc 92*
**Linke-Ellis**, Nanci Elizabeth 1949- *WhoEnt 92*
**Linkenheimer**, Wayne Henry 1928- *AmMWSc 92*
**Linker**, Alfred 1919- *AmMWSc 92*
**Linkie**, William Sinclair 1931- *Who 92*
**Linkins**, Arthur Edward 1945- *AmMWSc 92*
**Linkkila**, Leslie Elizabeth 1959- *WhoWest 92*
**Linklater**, Eric 1899-1974 *RfGEnL 91*
**Linklater**, Magnus Duncan 1942- *Who 92*
**Linklater**, Nelson Valdemar 1918- *Who 92*
**Linklater**, William Joseph 1942- *WhoAmL 92*
**Linkletter**, Art *LesBEnT 92 [port]*
**Linkletter**, Art 1912- *IntAu&W 91, IntMPA 92, WrDr 92*
**Linkletter**, Arthur Gordon 1912- *WhoEnt 92*
**Linkous**, T Cecil 1920- *WhoAmP 91*
**Linkow**, Leonard I 1926- *AmMWSc 92*
**Links**, Mary *Who 92*
**Linkus**, Joseph William 1945- *WhoMW 92*
**Linley**, Viscount 1961- *Who 92*
**Linley**, Marilyn Williams 1922- *WhoEnt 92*
**Linley**, Thomas 1733-1795 *NewAmDM*
**Linley**, Thomas 1756-1778 *NewAmDM*
**Linlithgow**, Marquess of 1946- *Who 92*
**Linman**, James William 1924- *AmMWSc 92*
**Linn**, Brian James 1947- *WhoAmL 92, WhoWest 92*
**Linn**, Bruce Oscar 1929- *AmMWSc 92*
**Linn**, Carl Barnes 1907- *AmMWSc 92*
**Linn**, Carole Anne 1945- *WhoWest 92*
**Linn**, DeVon Wayne 1929- *AmMWSc 92*
**Linn**, Donald Edward, Jr. 1954- *WhoMW 92*
**Linn**, Eldon R 1934- *WhoIns 92*
**Linn**, James Eldon, II 1943- *WhoFI 92, WhoMW 92*
**Linn**, James Herbert 1925- *WhoFI 92*
**Linn**, John Blair 1777-1804 *BenetAL 91*
**Linn**, John Charles *AmMWSc 92*
**Linn**, John J 1935- *WhoIns 92*
**Linn**, Leonard Jess 1917- *WhoAmP 91*
**Linn**, Manson Bruce 1908- *AmMWSc 92*

**Linn,** Raymond Sayre 1920- *WhoEnt 92*
**Linn,** Robert Bruce 1943- *WhoIns 92*
**Linn,** Stahle 1886-1959 *DcNCBi 4*
**Linn,** Stuart Michael 1940- *AmMWSc 92*
**Linn,** William Joseph 1927- *AmMWSc 92*
**Linn-Baker,** Mark 1954- *IntMPA 92*
**Linna,** Timo Juhani 1937- *AmMWSc 92*
**Linnabary,** Steven Ralph 1954- *WhoAmP 91*
**Linnaeus,** Carolus 1707-1778 *BlkwCEP*
**Linnane,** Anthony William 1930- *IntWW 91, Who 92*
**Linnartz,** Norwin Eugene 1926- *AmMWSc 92*
**Linne,** Carl von 1707-1778 *BlkwCEP*
**Linne,** Robert Steven 1943- *WhoAmL 92, WhoMW 92*
**Linnehan,** Joseph Arthur, Jr. 1953- *WhoAmL 92*
**Linnell,** Albert Paul 1922- *AmMWSc 92*
**Linnell,** David George Thomas 1930- *Who 92*
**Linnell,** Richard D 1920- *AmMWSc 92*
**Linnell,** Robert Hartley 1922- *AmMWSc 92*
**Linnemann,** Hans 1931- *IntWW 91*
**Linnemann,** Hans-Martin *WhoRel 92*
**Linnemann,** Roger E 1931- *AmMWSc 92*
**Linnenkugel,** Rita Catherine 1948- *WhoRel 92*
**Linner,** Anders Ingemar 1959- *WhoMW 92*
**Linner,** Carl Sture 1917- *IntWW 91*
**Linner,** John Gunnar 1943- *AmMWSc 92*
**Linnert,** George Edwin 1916- *AmMWSc 92*
**Linnert,** Terrence Gregory 1946- *WhoAmL 92*
**Linnerud,** Ardell Chester 1931- *AmMWSc 92*
**Linnett,** Michael Joseph 1926- *Who 92*
**Linney,** Romulus *DrAPF 91*
**Linney,** Romulus 1930- *WrDr 92*
**Linney,** Romulus Zachariah 1841-1910 *DcNCBi 4*
**Linnoila,** Markku *AmMWSc 92*
**Linnstaedter,** Jerry Leroy 1937- *AmMWSc 92*
**Linoff,** Alan Lee 1934- *WhoFI 92*
**Linowes,** David Francis 1917- *WhoFI 92, WhoMW 92, WrDr 92*
**Linowes,** Harry Michael 1928- *WhoFI 92*
**Linowes,** R. Robert 1922- *WhoAmL 92*
**Linowitz,** Sol Myron 1913- *IntWW 91, WhoAmP 91, WhoFI 92*
**Linowski,** John Walter 1945- *AmMWSc 92*
**Lins,** Thomas Wesley 1923- *AmMWSc 92*
**Lins do Rego,** Jose 1901-1957 *BenetAL 91*
**Linsay,** Ernest Charles 1942- *AmMWSc 92*
**Linscheid,** Harold Wilbert 1906- *AmMWSc 92*
**Linschitz,** Henry 1919- *AmMWSc 92*
**Linscott,** Dean L 1932- *AmMWSc 92*
**Linscott,** Jerry R. 1941- *WhoAmL 92*
**Linscott,** Scott 1963- *WhoRel 92*
**Linscott,** William Dean 1930- *AmMWSc 92*
**Linsenmeyer,** John Michael 1940- *WhoAmL 92*
**Linsey,** Nathaniel L. *WhoBlA 92*
**Linsey,** Nathaniel L. 1926- *WhoRel 92*
**Linskens,** Hansferdinand 1921- *IntWW 91*
**Linsky,** Cary Bruce 1942- *AmMWSc 92*
**Linsky,** David Paul 1957- *WhoAmL 92*
**Linsky,** Jeffrey L 1941- *AmMWSc 92*
**Linsky,** Leonard 1922- *ConAu 134*
**Linsley,** Earle Gorton 1910- *AmMWSc 92*
**Linsley,** James Harvey 1787-1843 *BilnAmS*
**Linsley,** John 1925- *AmMWSc 92*
**Linsley,** Joseph Hatch 1859-1901 *BilnAmS*
**Linsley,** Ray K, Jr 1917- *AmMWSc 92*
**Linsley,** Robert Martin 1930- *AmMWSc 92*
**Linsley,** Stephen Cutler 1960- *WhoEnt 92*
**Linsman,** William David 1945- *WhoEnt 92*
**Linson,** Art *IntMPA 92*
**Linson,** Robert Edward 1922- *WhoMW 92*
**Linss,** Wilhelm Camill 1926- *WhoRel 92*
**Linssen,** Robert Joseph 1940- *WhoWest 92*
**Linstead,** Stephen Guy 1941- *Who 92*
**Linstedt,** Kermit Daniel 1940- *AmMWSc 92*
**Linstedt,** Walter Griffiths 1933- *WhoAmL 92*
**Linstone,** Harold A 1924- *AmMWSc 92*
**Linstromberg,** Walter William 1912- *AmMWSc 92*
**Linstrum,** Derek 1925- *WrDr 92*
**Lint,** Jody Christine 1956- *WhoMW 92*
**Lintermans,** Gloria 1943- *WhoEnt 92*
**Lintermans,** Gloria 1947- *IntAu&W 91*
**Linthicum,** John *DrAPF 91*
**Lintner,** Carl John, Jr 1917- *AmMWSc 92*
**Lintner,** Joseph Albert 1822-1898 *BilnAmS*
**Linton,** Alan Henry Spencer 1919- *Who 92*
**Linton,** Arlene Mae 1949- *WhoWest 92*
**Linton,** Barbara J 1952- *WhoAmP 91*
**Linton,** Everett Percival 1906- *AmMWSc 92*
**Linton,** Fred E J 1938- *AmMWSc 92*
**Linton,** Gladys Morris 1930- *WhoAmP 91*
**Linton,** Gordon J 1948- *WhoAmP 91, WhoBlA 92*
**Linton,** Jack Arthur 1936- *WhoAmL 92*
**Linton,** John Leroy 1945- *WhoEnt 92*
**Linton,** Patrick Hugo 1925- *AmMWSc 92*
**Linton,** Richard William 1951- *AmMWSc 92*
**Linton,** Robert D 1954- *WhoIns 92*
**Linton,** Robert David 1954- *WhoFI 92*
**Linton,** Ron M 1929- *WhoAmP 91*
**Linton,** Ruth Coleman 1955- *WhoWest 92*
**Linton,** Samuel C 1923- *WhoAmP 91*
**Linton,** Sheila Lorraine 1950- *WhoBlA 92*
**Linton,** Thomas LaRue 1935- *AmMWSc 92*
**Linton,** Virginia *DrAPF 91*
**Linton,** William, Jr. 1942- *WhoMW 92*
**Linton,** William Carl 1929- *WhoAmP 91*
**Linton,** William Henry 1925- *WhoWest 92*
**Linton,** William James 1812-1897 *BenetAL 91*
**Lintott,** Henry 1908- *IntWW 91, Who 92*
**Lintott,** Robert Edward 1932- *Who 92*
**Lintvedt,** Richard Lowell 1937- *AmMWSc 92*
**Lintz,** Joseph, Jr 1921- *AmMWSc 92*
**Linus** d80? *EncEarC*
**Linvill,** John G 1919- *AmMWSc 92*
**Linville,** Jacob Hays 1825-1906 *BilnAmS*
**Linville,** Judith Ann 1943- *WhoMW 92*
**Linville,** Larry Lavon 1939- *WhoEnt 92*
**Linxwiler,** James David 1949- *WhoAmL 92, WhoFI 92*
**Linxwiler,** Louis Major, Jr. 1931- *WhoWest 92*
**Linyard,** Richard 1930- *WhoBlA 92*
**Linz,** Anthony James 1948- *WhoMW 92*
**Linz,** Arthur 1926- *AmMWSc 92*
**Linz,** Peter 1936- *AmMWSc 92*
**Linzer,** Melvin 1937- *AmMWSc 92*
**Linzer,** Peter 1939- *WhoAmL 92*
**Linzey,** Bobby Lee 1938- *WhoAmP 91*
**Linzner,** Charles 1948- *WhoAmL 92*
**Linzy,** William James, Jr. 1944- *WhoAmL 92*
**Lioi,** Anthony Pasquale 1949- *AmMWSc 92*
**Liolin,** Arthur E. *WhoRel 92*
**Lion,** Harold Holland 1923- *WhoEnt 92*
**Lion,** Jacques Kenneth 1922- *Who 92*
**Lion,** James Simon, Jr. 1961- *WhoFI 92*
**Lionaes,** Aase 1907- *IntWW 91*
**Lionakis,** George 1924- *WhoWest 92*
**Lionberger,** Erle Talbot Lund 1933- *WhoAmP 91*
**Lionel,** Robert *WrDr 92*
**Lionett,** David J 1943- *WhoAmP 91*
**Lionetti,** Fabian Joseph 1918- *AmMWSc 92*
**Lionetti,** Frank Carmine 1947- *WhoEnt 92*
**Lionni,** Leo 1910- *DcTwDes, IntAu&W 91, WrDr 92*
**Lions,** Jacques L. 1928- *IntWW 91*
**Lionti,** Vincent Joseph 1959- *WhoEnt 92*
**Lior,** Noam 1940- *AmMWSc 92*
**Liota,** Vincent Donald 1929- *WhoEnt 92*
**Liotta,** Lance *AmMWSc 92*
**Liotta,** P.H. *DrAPF 91*
**Liotta,** Ray 1955- *IntMPA 92*
**Liou,** Juhn G 1939- *AmMWSc 92*
**Liou,** Kuo-Nan 1943- *AmMWSc 92*
**Liou,** Sy-Hwang 1951- *WhoMW 92*
**Lioy,** Franco 1932- *AmMWSc 92*
**Lioy,** Paul James 1947- *AmMWSc 92*
**Lipari,** Nunzio Ottavio 1945- *AmMWSc 92*
**Lipatov,** Vil Vladimirovich 1927- *IntWW 91*
**Lipatti,** Dinu 1917-1950 *FacFETw, NewAmDM*
**Lipchik,** Harold 1928- *WhoWest 92*
**Lipchitz,** Jacques 1891-1973 *FacFETw*
**Lipcon,** Charles Roy 1946- *WhoAmL 92*
**Lipe,** John Arthur 1943- *AmMWSc 92*
**Lipe,** Linda Bon 1948- *WhoFI 92*
**Lipe,** Marlys Gascho 1957- *WhoMW 92*
**Lipe,** Michael Alexander 1944- *WhoRel 92*
**Lipeles,** Martin 1938- *AmMWSc 92*
**Lipeles,** Maxine Ina 1953- *WhoAmL 92*
**Lipely,** Kim Renee 1955- *WhoEnt 92*
**Lipetz,** Leo Elijah 1921- *AmMWSc 92*
**Lipford,** Rocque Edward 1938- *WhoAmL 92*
**Lipfriend,** Alan 1916- *Who 92*
**Lipicky,** Raymond John 1933- *AmMWSc 92*
**Lipin,** Alfred Jerome 1920- *WhoAmP 91*
**Lipin,** Bruce Reed 1947- *AmMWSc 92*
**Lipinski,** Boguslaw 1933- *AmMWSc 92*
**Lipinski,** Christopher Andrew 1944- *AmMWSc 92*
**Lipinski,** Daniel Michael 1948- *WhoMW 92*
**Lipinski,** Edward 1888-1986 *FacFETw*
**Lipinski,** Matthew Edmund 1952- *WhoAmL 92*
**Lipinski,** Walter C 1927- *AmMWSc 92*
**Lipinski,** William O. 1937- *AlmAP 92 [port], WhoAmP 91*
**Lipinski,** William Oliver 1937- *WhoMW 92*
**Lipinsky,** Edward Solomon 1929- *AmMWSc 92*
**Lipinsky de Orlov,** Lino S. 1958- *WhoAmL 92, WhoWest 92*
**Lipinsky de Orlov,** Lucian Christopher 1962- *WhoFI 92*
**Lipka,** Benjamin 1929- *AmMWSc 92*
**Lipka,** James J 1954- *AmMWSc 92*
**Lipke,** Dennis Charles 1946- *WhoRel 92*
**Lipke,** Peter Nathan 1950- *AmMWSc 92*
**Lipke,** William G 1936- *AmMWSc 92*
**Lipkin,** David 1913- *AmMWSc 92*
**Lipkin,** George 1930- *AmMWSc 92*
**Lipkin,** Harry Jeannot 1921- *AmMWSc 92*
**Lipkin,** Lewis Edward 1925- *AmMWSc 92*
**Lipkin,** Mack 1907- *AmMWSc 92*
**Lipkin,** Martin 1926- *AmMWSc 92*
**Lipkin,** Mary Castleman Davis 1907- *WhoWest 92*
**Lipkin,** Miles Henry J. *Who 92*
**Lipkin,** Semen Izrailevich 1911- *IntWW 91, SovUnBD*
**Lipkin,** Seymour 1927- *NewAmDM, WhoEnt 92*
**Lipkowitz,** Kenny Barry 1950- *AmMWSc 92*
**Lipkowski,** Jean-Noel de 1920- *IntWW 91*
**Lipman,** David 1931- *IntAu&W 91, WhoMW 92, WrDr 92*
**Lipman,** David J *AmMWSc 92*
**Lipman,** Elinor *DrAPF 91*
**Lipman,** Eugene Jay 1919- *WhoRel 92*
**Lipman,** Harvey Bennett 1952- *WhoMW 92*
**Lipman,** Joel *DrAPF 91*
**Lipman,** Joel Abelman 1942- *WhoMW 92*
**Lipman,** Joseph 1938- *AmMWSc 92*
**Lipman,** Marc Joseph 1950- *AmMWSc 92*
**Lipman,** Mark Andrew 1960- *WhoEnt 92*
**Lipman,** Matthew 1923- *WrDr 92*
**Lipman,** Maureen Diane 1946- *Who 92*
**Lipman,** Peter Waldman 1935- *AmMWSc 92*
**Lipman,** Richard Mark 1959- *WhoMW 92*
**Lipman,** Stanley 1929- *WhoFI 92*
**Lipman,** Sumner H 1941- *WhoAmP 91*
**Lipman,** William McCullem, Jr. 1954- *WhoRel 92*
**Lipman,** Wynona M *WhoAmP 91*
**Lipmann,** Fritz Albert 1899-1986 *WhoNob 90*
**Lipner,** Alan J. 1938- *WhoFI 92*
**Lipner,** Harry Joel 1922- *AmMWSc 92*
**Lipner,** Jay C. d1991 *NewYTBS 91 [port]*
**Lipner,** Julius Joseph 1946- *WhoRel 92*
**Lipner,** Lee David 1943- *WhoMW 92*
**Lipner,** Linda S. 1948- *WhoWest 92*
**Lipner,** Steven Barnett 1943- *AmMWSc 92*
**Lipnick,** Robert Louis 1941- *AmMWSc 92*
**Lipo,** Thomas Anthony 1938- *AmMWSc 92*
**Lipoff,** Norman Harold 1936- *WhoRel 92*
**Lipomi,** Michael Joseph 1953- *WhoWest 92*
**Lipovetsky,** Leonidas B. 1937- *WhoEnt 92*
**Lipovsek,** Marjana 1946- *IntWW 91*
**Lipovski,** Gerald John 1944- *AmMWSc 92*
**Lipowitz,** Jonathan 1937- *AmMWSc 92*
**Lipowski,** Stanley Arthur 1905- *AmMWSc 92*
**Lipowski,** Zbigniew J 1924- *AmMWSc 92*
**Lipp,** Brady Thomas 1958- *WhoFI 92*
**Lipp,** Carl Frederick 1924- *WhoWest 92*
**Lipp,** Jonathan Barry 1950- *WhoMW 92*
**Lipp,** Robert I. 1938- *IntWW 91*
**Lipp,** Steven Alan 1944- *AmMWSc 92*
**Lippa,** David Anthony 1948- *WhoFI 92*
**Lippa,** Erik Alexander 1945- *AmMWSc 92*
**Lippa,** Linda Susan Mottow 1951- *AmMWSc 92*
**Lippai,** Steven Edward *WhoIns 92*
**Lippard,** George 1822-1854 *BenetAL 91*
**Lippard,** Lucy R. *DrAPF 91*
**Lippard,** Stephen J 1940- *AmMWSc 92*
**Lippart,** Thomas E. 1937- *WhoRel 92*
**Lippe,** Jane *DrAPF 91*
**Lippe,** Philipp Maria 1929- *WhoWest 92*
**Lippe,** Robert Lloyd 1923- *AmMWSc 92*
**Lippel,** Kenneth 1929- *AmMWSc 92*
**Lipper,** David Alan 1961- *WhoRel 92*
**Lipperman,** Robert L 1954- *WhoIns 92*
**Lippert,** Albert 1925- *WhoFI 92*
**Lippert,** Anne *WhoAmP 91*
**Lippert,** Bruce J *AmMWSc 92*
**Lippert,** Byron E 1929- *AmMWSc 92*
**Lippert,** Christopher Nelson 1952- *WhoMW 92*
**Lippert,** Ernest Laverne, Jr. 1931- *WhoMW 92*
**Lippert,** Julius 1895-1956 *EncTR 91 [port]*
**Lippert,** Laverne Francis 1928- *AmMWSc 92*
**Lippert,** Robert J., Jr. 1928- *IntMPA 92*
**Lippert,** Ronald S 1949- *IntAu&W 91*
**Lippert,** Vernon Elroy 1954- *WhoMW 92*
**Lippes,** Gerald Sanford 1940- *WhoAmL 92, WhoFI 92*
**Lippes,** Jack 1924- *AmMWSc 92*
**Lippes,** Richard James 1944- *WhoAmL 92*
**Lippett,** Ronnie Leon 1960- *WhoBlA 92*
**Lippincott & Margulies** *DcTwDes*
**Lippincott,** Barbara Barnes 1934- *AmMWSc 92*
**Lippincott,** Ezra Parvin 1939- *AmMWSc 92*
**Lippincott,** J. Gordon 1909- *DcTwDes*
**Lippincott,** James Andrew 1930- *AmMWSc 92*
**Lippincott,** James Starr 1819-1885 *BilnAmS*
**Lippincott,** Jonathan Ramsay 1946- *WhoMW 92*
**Lippincott,** Marian Ball 1934- *WhoFI 92*
**Lippincott,** Philip Edward 1935- *WhoFI 92*
**Lippincott,** Robert, III 1947- *WhoIns 92*
**Lippincott,** Sara Jane 1823-1904 *BenetAL 91*
**Lippincott,** Sarah Lee 1920- *AmMWSc 92*
**Lippincott-Schwartz,** Jennifer 1952- *AmMWSc 92*
**Lippitt,** Elizabeth Charlotte *WhoWest 92*
**Lippitt,** Frederick 1916- *WhoAmP 91*
**Lippitt,** Louis 1924- *AmMWSc 92, WhoWest 92*
**Lippitz,** Charles Aronin 1926- *WhoEnt 92*
**Lippke,** Hagen 1936- *AmMWSc 92*
**Lippman,** Alfred, Jr 1908- *AmMWSc 92*
**Lippman,** Alfred Julian 1900- *WhoFI 92*
**Lippman,** Barry 1949- *WhoFI 92*
**Lippman,** Charles David 1944- *WhoRel 92*
**Lippman,** Frederick 1935- *WhoAmP 91*
**Lippman,** Gary Edwin *AmMWSc 92*
**Lippman,** Janis Joyce 1960- *WhoEnt 92*
**Lippman,** Lois H. 1925- *WhoBlA 92*
**Lippman,** Marc Estes 1945- *AmMWSc 92*
**Lippmann,** Bruce Allan 1950- *WhoFI 92*
**Lippmann,** David Zangwill 1925- *AmMWSc 92*
**Lippmann,** Gabriel Jonas 1845-1921 *WhoNob 90*
**Lippmann,** Heinz Israel 1908- *AmMWSc 92*
**Lippmann,** Irwin 1930- *AmMWSc 92*
**Lippmann,** Marcelo Julio 1939- *AmMWSc 92*
**Lippmann,** Morton 1932- *AmMWSc 92*
**Lippmann,** Seymour A 1919- *AmMWSc 92*
**Lippmann,** Walter 1889-1974 *AmPeW, BenetAL 91, FacFETw [port], RComAH*
**Lippmann,** Wilbur 1930- *AmMWSc 92*
**Lippold,** Jeffrey Howard 1954- *WhoFI 92*
**Lippold,** Richard 1915- *FacFETw, IntWW 91*
**Lippold,** Roland Will 1916- *WhoWest 92*
**Lippold,** Tim Theodore 1954- *WhoMW 92*
**Lipps,** Emma Lewis 1919- *AmMWSc 92*
**Lipps,** Frank B 1933- *AmMWSc 92*
**Lipps,** Frederick Wiessner 1929- *AmMWSc 92*
**Lipps,** Jere Henry 1939- *AmMWSc 92, WhoWest 92*
**Lipps,** Louis Adam 1962- *WhoBlA 92*
**Lipps,** Ros 1925- *WhoEnt 92*
**Lippson,** Robert Lloyd 1931- *AmMWSc 92*
**Lippy,** Charles Howard 1943- *WhoRel 92*
**Lips,** Evan Edwin 1918- *WhoAmP 91*
**Lips,** Hilaire John 1918- *AmMWSc 92*
**Lipschultz,** Frederick Phillip 1937- *AmMWSc 92*
**Lipschultz,** Geri *DrAPF 91*
**Lipschultz,** Howard Elliott 1947- *WhoFI 92*
**Lipschutz,** Michael Elazar 1937- *AmMWSc 92*
**Lipscomb,** Al 1925- *WhoAmP 91*
**Lipscomb,** Albert *WhoAmP 91*
**Lipscomb,** Anna Rose Feeny 1945- *WhoWest 92*
**Lipscomb,** Darryl L. 1953- *WhoBlA 92*
**Lipscomb,** David 1831-1917 *AmPeW, RelLAm 91*
**Lipscomb,** David M 1935- *AmMWSc 92*
**Lipscomb,** Dennis 1942- *ConTFT 9*
**Lipscomb,** Elizabeth Lois 1927- *AmMWSc 92*
**Lipscomb,** Emanuel A. 1926- *WhoBlA 92*
**Lipscomb,** Frederick Elvy 1902- *Who 92*
**Lipscomb,** James Louis 1947- *WhoAmL 92*
**Lipscomb,** John Bailey 1950- *WhoRel 92*
**Lipscomb,** John DeWald 1947- *AmMWSc 92*
**Lipscomb,** Mance 1895-1976 *NewAmDM*
**Lipscomb,** Nathan Thornton 1934- *AmMWSc 92*
**Lipscomb,** Oscar Hugh 1931- *WhoRel 92*
**Lipscomb,** Paul Rogers 1914- *AmMWSc 92*

**Lipscomb**, Richard Henry 1918- WhoEnt 92
**Lipscomb**, Robert DeWald 1917- AmMWSc 92
**Lipscomb**, Wanda Dean 1953- WhoBlA 92
**Lipscomb**, Wendell R. 1920- WhoBlA 92
**Lipscomb**, William Nunn 1919- Who 92, WhoNob 90, WrDr 92
**Lipscomb**, William Nunn, Jr 1919- AmMWSc 92, IntWW 91
**Lipscombe**, Margaret Ann 1939- WhoBlA 92
**Lipset**, Seymour M 1922- FacFETw
**Lipset**, Seymour Martin 1922- IntWW 91, WhoWest 92, WrDr 92
**Lipsett**, Frederick Roy 1925- AmMWSc 92
**Lipsey**, David Lawrence 1948- IntAu&W 91, Who 92
**Lipsey**, Freda Culwell 1926- WhoAmP 91
**Lipsey**, Joseph, Jr. 1934- WhoFI 92
**Lipsey**, Michael Ross 1959- WhoFI 92
**Lipsey**, Richard George 1928- Who 92
**Lipsey**, Robert Edward 1926- WhoFI 92
**Lipsey**, Sally Irene 1926- AmMWSc 92
**Lipsey**, Sandra Dee 1943- WhoFI 92
**Lipshitz**, Howard David 1955- AmMWSc 92, WhoWest 92
**Lipshitz**, Stanley Paul 1943- AmMWSc 92
**Lipshultz**, Larry I 1942- AmMWSc 92
**Lipshultz**, Stanley Lewis 1944- WhoAmL 92
**Lipshutz**, Nelson Richard 1942- AmMWSc 92
**Lipshutz**, Robert Jay 1955- WhoWest 92
**Lipshutz**, Robert Jerome 1921- WhoAmP 91
**Lipsich**, H David 1920- AmMWSc 92
**Lipsick**, Joseph Steven 1955- AmMWSc 92
**Lipsig**, Ethan 1948- WhoAmL 92
**Lipsig**, Joseph 1930- AmMWSc 92
**Lipsitt**, Don Richard 1927- AmMWSc 92
**Lipsitt**, Harry A 1931- AmMWSc 92
**Lipsitt**, Lewis Paeff 1929- AmMWSc 92
**Lipsitt**, Paul Daniel 1926- WhoAmL 92
**Lipsitz**, Lou DrAPF 91
**Lipsitz**, Lou 1938- WrDr 92
**Lipsitz**, Paul 1923- AmMWSc 92
**Lipsitz**, Philip Joseph 1928- AmMWSc 92
**Lipsitz**, Robert Joel 1949- WhoAmL 92
**Lipsius**, Justus 1547-1606 LitC 16 [port]
**Lipsius**, Stephen Lloyd 1947- AmMWSc 92
**Lipski**, Alexander 1919- WhoRel 92
**Lipski**, Jan Josef 1926-1991 NewYTBS 91 [port]
**Lipski**, Jan Jozef 1926- IntWW 91
**Lipski**, Witold 1925- IntWW 91
**Lipsky**, Burton G. 1937- WhoAmL 92
**Lipsky**, Ian David 1957- WhoWest 92
**Lipsky**, Joan 1919- WhoAmP 91
**Lipsky**, Joan Miller 1919- WhoAmL 92
**Lipsky**, Joseph Albin 1930- AmMWSc 92
**Lipsky**, Linda Ethel 1939- WhoFI 92
**Lipsky**, Oldrich d1986 IntWW 91N
**Lipsky**, Seymour Richard 1924- AmMWSc 92
**Lipsky**, Stephen E 1932- AmMWSc 92
**Lipsky**, Vladimir Ippolitovich 1863-1937 SovUnBD
**Lipsman**, Paulee 1947- WhoAmP 91
**Lipsman**, Richard Marc 1946- WhoAmL 92
**Lipsman**, William Stuart 1949- WhoAmL 92
**Lipson**, Ashley S. 1945- WhoAmL 92
**Lipson**, Barry J. 1938- WhoAmL 92
**Lipson**, Charles Barry 1946- WhoFI 92
**Lipson**, Edward David 1944- AmMWSc 92
**Lipson**, Glenn Scott 1957- WhoMW 92
**Lipson**, Henry 1910-1991 IntWW 91, -91N
**Lipson**, Henry Solomon d1991 Who 92N
**Lipson**, Herbert George 1925- AmMWSc 92
**Lipson**, Jack Louis 1932- WhoAmL 92
**Lipson**, Joseph Isaac 1927- AmMWSc 92
**Lipson**, Leon 1921- WhoAmL 92
**Lipson**, Melvin Alan 1936- AmMWSc 92
**Lipson**, Paul Charles 1950- WhoFI 92
**Lipson**, Richard L 1931- AmMWSc 92
**Lipson**, Samuel L 1913- AmMWSc 92
**Lipson**, Steven Mark 1945- AmMWSc 92
**Lipstate**, Eugene Jacob 1927- WhoFI 92
**Lipstein**, Kurt 1909- Who 92, WrDr 92
**Lipstone**, Howard H. 1928- IntMPA 92
**Lipstone**, Howard Harold 1928- WhoEnt 92, WhoWest 92
**Lipstone**, Jane N. 1931- WhoEnt 92
**Lipsyte**, Robert 1938- Au&Arts 7 [port], SmATA 68 [port], WrDr 92
**Liptak**, Gregory James 1940- WhoEnt 92
**Liptay**, Albert 1941- AmMWSc 92
**Liptock**, Edward Richard 1929- WhoRel 92
**Lipton**, Adam Shepherd 1964- WhoAmL 92
**Lipton**, Allan 1938- AmMWSc 92
**Lipton**, Benjamin d1991 NewYTBS 91
**Lipton**, Benjamin Bernard 1912- WhoAmL 92
**Lipton**, Charles 1928- WhoFI 92
**Lipton**, Charles Jules 1931- WhoFI 92
**Lipton**, David A. 1906- IntMPA 92
**Lipton**, Dean 1919- WrDr 92
**Lipton**, Jack Philip 1952- WhoWest 92
**Lipton**, James Bart 1962- WhoEnt 92
**Lipton**, James Matthew 1938- AmMWSc 92
**Lipton**, Jeffrey Marc 1942- WhoFI 92
**Lipton**, John M 1936- WhoAmP 91
**Lipton**, Laurie 1953- TwCPaSc
**Lipton**, Lenny 1940- WhoEnt 92, WrDr 92
**Lipton**, Lester 1936- WhoFI 92
**Lipton**, Martin 1931- WhoFI 92
**Lipton**, Michael Forrester 1950- AmMWSc 92
**Lipton**, Morris Abraham 1915- AmMWSc 92
**Lipton**, Peggy WhoEnt 92
**Lipton**, Peggy 1947?- ConTFT 9
**Lipton**, Robert Stephen 1942- WhoAmL 92
**Lipton**, Rochelle Leah 1943- WhoEnt 92
**Lipton**, Stuart Anthony 1942- Who 92
**Lipton**, Werner Jacob 1928- AmMWSc 92
**Liptzin**, Sol 1901- IntAu&W 91, WrDr 92
**Lipworth**, Maurice Sydney 1931- IntWW 91
**Lipworth**, Sydney 1931- Who 92
**Liquido**, Nicanor Javier 1953- WhoWest 92
**Lira**, Emil Patrick 1934- AmMWSc 92
**Lira**, Jose Arturo 1950- WhoHisp 92
**Lira**, Ricardo 1957- WhoHisp 92
**Lira**, Ted d1992 WhoHisp 92N
**Lira-Powell**, Julianne Hortensia 1945- WhoHisp 92
**Lirely**, Samuel Christopher 1941- WhoWest 92
**Lirely**, Stephen W. 1955- WhoRel 92
**Liriano**, Nelson Arturo 1964- WhoHisp 92
**Li Rosi**, Angelo C 1941- WhoIns 92
**Lis**, Adam W 1925- AmMWSc 92
**Lis**, Elaine Walker 1924- AmMWSc 92
**Lis**, John Thomas 1948- AmMWSc 92
**Lis**, Steven Andrew 1950- AmMWSc 92
**Lisa**, Donald Julius 1935- WhoAmL 92
**Lisa**, Joseph F 1937- WhoAmP 91
**Lisak**, Robert Philip 1941- AmMWSc 92
**Lisano**, Michael Edward 1942- AmMWSc 92
**Lisardi**, Andrew H. 1947- WhoHisp 92
**Lisburne**, Earl of 1918- Who 92
**Liscano**, Juan 1915- ConSpAP
**Lisch**, Howard 1950- WhoAmL 92
**Lischer**, Ludwig F 1915- AmMWSc 92
**Lischer**, Richard Alan 1943- WhoRel 92
**Lischka**, Kurt 1909- EncTR 91
**Li-Scholz**, Angela 1936- AmMWSc 92
**Liscum**, Laura 1954- AmMWSc 92
**Lisella**, Frank Scott 1936- AmMWSc 92
**Lisenbee**, Alvis Lee 1940- AmMWSc 92
**Lisette**, Gabriel 1919- IntWW 91
**Lish**, Gordon DrAPF 91
**Lish**, Mark Edward 1962- WhoAmL 92
**Lish**, Paul Merrill 1921- AmMWSc 92
**Lisher**, James Richard 1947- WhoAmL 92, WhoMW 92
**Lisher**, John Leonard 1950- WhoAmL 92, WhoMW 92
**Lishka**, Edward Joseph 1949- WhoMW 92
**Lishman**, William Alwyn 1931- Who 92
**Lishner**, Laurence H. 1947- WhoAmL 92
**Lisi**, Virna 1937- IntMPA 92
**Lisicky**, Paul Alexander DrAPF 91
**Lisio**, Donald John 1934- WhoMW 92
**Lisitsky**, Lazar' Markovich 1890-1941 SovUnBD
**Lisitsyan**, Pavel Gerasimovich 1911- SovUnBD
**Lisk**, Barbara WhoAmP 91
**Lisk**, Donald J 1930- AmMWSc 92
**Lisk**, Edward Stanley 1934- WhoEnt 92
**Lisk**, Jill 1938- WrDr 92
**Lisk**, Robert Douglas 1934- AmMWSc 92
**Liska**, Bernard Joseph 1931- AmMWSc 92
**Liska**, John J WhoAmP 91
**Liska**, Kenneth J 1929- AmMWSc 92
**Liskay**, Robert Michael 1948- AmMWSc 92
**Liskey**, Nathan Eugene 1937- AmMWSc 92
**Liskov**, Barbara H 1939- AmMWSc 92
**Liskov**, Richard G 1949- WhoIns 92
**Lisle** Who 92
**Lisle**, Baron 1903- Who 92
**Lisle**, Janet Taylor 1947- SmATA 14AS [port]
**Lisle**, Laurie 1942- ConAu 133
**Lisman**, Frederick Louis 1939- AmMWSc 92
**Lisman**, Henry 1913- AmMWSc 92
**Lisman**, Michael Ray 1952- WhoRel 92
**Lisman**, Perry Hall 1932- AmMWSc 92
**Lisnek**, Paul Michael 1958- WhoAmL 92
**Lisnik**, John 1946- WhoAmP 91
**Lisnyanskaya**, Inna L'vovna 1928- IntWW 91
**Lisonbee**, Lorenzo Kenneth 1914- AmMWSc 92
**Lisowski**, Anthony Francis 1952- WhoAmP 91
**Lisowski**, Joseph DrAPF 91
**Lispector**, Clarice 1917-1977 BenetAL 91
**Lispector**, Clarice 1925-1977 DcLB 113 [port], FacFETw
**Liss**, Alan 1947- AmMWSc 92
**Liss**, David Ben 1955- WhoEnt 92
**Liss**, Herbert Myron 1931- WhoFI 92, WhoMW 92
**Liss**, Ivan Barry 1938- AmMWSc 92
**Liss**, Leopold 1923- AmMWSc 92
**Liss**, Maurice 1926- AmMWSc 92
**Liss**, Norman 1932- WhoAmL 92
**Liss**, Norman Richard 1947- WhoFI 92
**Liss**, Robert H 1936- AmMWSc 92
**Liss**, Sheldon B. 1936- WrDr 92
**Liss**, William John 1947- AmMWSc 92
**Lissaman**, Peter Barry Stuart 1931- AmMWSc 92
**Lissant**, Ellen Kern 1922- AmMWSc 92
**Lissant**, Kenneth Jordan 1920- AmMWSc 92
**Lissauer**, David Arie 1945- AmMWSc 92
**Lissens**, Rene Felix 1912- IntAu&W 91
**Lissitzky**, El 1890-1941 DcTwDes, FacFETw, SovUnBD
**Lissmann**, Hans Werner 1909- IntWW 91, Who 92
**Lissner**, David 1931- AmMWSc 92
**Lissouba**, Pascal 1931- IntWW 91
**List**, Albert, Jr 1928- AmMWSc 92
**List**, Arthur David 1935- WhoAmL 92
**List**, Charles Edward 1941- WhoMW 92
**List**, Douglass William 1955- WhoFI 92
**List**, Eugene 1918-1985 FacFETw, NewAmDM
**List**, Garrett 1943- NewAmDM
**List**, Guido Karl Anton von 1848-1919 BiDExR
**List**, Harvey L 1924- AmMWSc 92
**List**, Henry Clay WhoAmP 91
**List**, James Carl 1926- AmMWSc 92
**List**, John DeWitt 1935- WhoFI 92
**List**, Raymond Edward 1944- WhoFI 92
**List**, Robert Frank 1936- IntWW 91, WhoAmL 92, WhoAmP 91, WhoFI 92
**List**, Roland 1929- AmMWSc 92, IntWW 91
**List**, Shelley DrAPF 91
**List**, Wilhelm 1880-1971 EncTR 91 [port]
**Listau**, Thor 1938- IntWW 91
**Lister** Who 92
**Lister**, Alton Lavelle 1958- WhoBlA 92
**Lister**, Charles 1938- WhoAmL 92
**Lister**, Charles Allan 1918- AmMWSc 92
**Lister**, Clive R B 1936- AmMWSc 92
**Lister**, David Alfred 1939- WhoBlA 92
**Lister**, Earl Edward 1934- AmMWSc 92
**Lister**, Frederick Monie 1923- AmMWSc 92
**Lister**, Geoffrey Richard 1937- Who 92
**Lister**, Harry Joseph 1936- WhoFI 92
**Lister**, Hugh Lawrence 1935- WhoWest 92
**Lister**, James 1923- Who 92
**Lister**, Joe U 1927- WhoAmP 91
**Lister**, John Field 1916- Who 92
**Lister**, Margot Ruth 1949- Who 92
**Lister**, Mark David 1953- AmMWSc 92
**Lister**, Maurice Wolfenden 1914- AmMWSc 92
**Lister**, Moira 1923- IntMPA 92
**Lister**, Patrick Who 92
**Lister**, R. P. 1914- WrDr 92
**Lister**, Raymond 1919- Who 92
**Lister**, Raymond George 1919- IntAu&W 91, WrDr 92
**Lister**, Richard Malcolm 1928- AmMWSc 92, WhoMW 92
**Lister**, Richard Percival 1914- IntAu&W 91
**Lister**, Robert Patrick 1922- Who 92
**Lister**, Ruth Who 92
**Lister**, Stephen Anthony 1942- WhoFI 92
**Lister**, Thomas Henry 1800-1842 ScFEYrs A
**Lister**, Thomas Mosie 1921- WhoEnt 92
**Lister**, Tom 1924- Who 92
**Lister**, Toney J WhoAmP 91
**Lister**, Unity 1913- Who 92
**Lister**, Willa M. 1940- WhoBlA 92
**Lister-Kaye**, John 1946- Who 92
**Listerman**, Thomas Walter 1938- AmMWSc 92
**Listerud**, Mark Boyd 1924- WhoWest 92
**Listgarten**, Max 1935- AmMWSc 92
**Listiak**, Richard Lance 1944- WhoMW 92
**Liston**, Albert Morris 1940- WhoWest 92
**Liston**, Hardy, Jr. WhoBlA 92
**Liston**, Hugh H. 1917- WhoBlA 92
**Liston**, James Malcolm 1909- Who 92
**Liston**, Melba Doretta 1926- NewAmDM
**Liston**, Robert N 1933- WhoIns 92
**Liston**, Ronald Argyle 1926- AmMWSc 92
**Listov**, Vladimir Vladimirovich 1931- IntWW 91, SovUnBD
**Listowel**, Earl of 1906- IntWW 91, Who 92
**Listowski**, Richard Francis 1941- WhoAmP 91
**Listowsky**, Irving 1935- AmMWSc 92
**Lisulo**, Daniel Muchiwa 1930- IntWW 91
**Lisy**, James Michael 1952- AmMWSc 92
**Liszka**, James J. 1950- WhoWest 92
**Liszka**, Walter Julian 1945- WhoAmL 92
**Liszt**, Franz 1811-1886 NewAmDM
**Liszt**, Harvey Steven 1945- AmMWSc 92
**Lit**, Alfred 1914- AmMWSc 92
**Lit**, John Wai-Yu 1937- AmMWSc 92
**Litan**, Robert Eli 1950- WhoFI 92
**Litchfield**, Carter 1932- AmMWSc 92
**Litchfield**, Jack Watson 1909- Who 92
**Litchfield**, Jean Anne 1942- WhoMW 92
**Litchfield**, John Hyland 1929- AmMWSc 92, WhoMW 92
**Litchfield**, John Shirley Sandys 1903- Who 92
**Litchfield**, Kent 1938- WhoRel 92
**Litchfield**, Landis Hugh 1940- WhoRel 92
**Litchfield**, Ruby 1912- Who 92
**Litchfield**, William John 1950- AmMWSc 92
**Litchford**, George B 1918- AmMWSc 92
**Litchy**, James Mark 1940- WhoMW 92
**Lites**, John Thomas 1937- WhoEnt 92
**Lites**, Larry Tommie 1947- WhoRel 92
**Litherland**, Albert Edward 1928- AmMWSc 92, IntWW 91, Who 92
**Litherland**, Robert Kenneth 1930- Who 92
**Lithgow**, John 1945- IntMPA 92
**Lithgow**, John Arthur 1945- WhoEnt 92
**Lithgow**, William 1934- Who 92
**Litke**, John David 1944- AmMWSc 92
**Litke**, Larry Lavoe 1949- AmMWSc 92
**Litman**, Bernard 1920- AmMWSc 92
**Litman**, Burton Joseph 1935- AmMWSc 92
**Litman**, Gary William 1945- AmMWSc 92
**Litman**, Irving Isaac 1925- AmMWSc 92
**Litman**, Nathan 1946- AmMWSc 92
**Litman**, Raymond Stephen 1936- WhoFI 92
**Litman**, Ruth Ann 1959- WhoWest 92
**Litolff**, Henry 1818-1891 NewAmDM
**Litosch**, Irene 1952- AmMWSc 92
**Litov**, Richard Emil AmMWSc 92
**Litovitz**, Theodore Aaron 1923- AmMWSc 92
**Litowinsky**, Olga DrAPF 91
**Litrownik**, Alan Jay 1945- WhoWest 92
**Litsch**, Daniel George 1947- WhoFI 92
**Litsey**, Linus R AmMWSc 92
**Litsey**, Roy Thomas WhoWest 92
**Litsey Ford**, Sarah 1901- IntAu&W 91
**Litsky**, Bertha Yanis 1920- AmMWSc 92
**Litsky**, Warren 1924- AmMWSc 92
**Litster**, James David 1938- AmMWSc 92
**Litt**, Iris DrAPF 91
**Litt**, Iris 1928- IntAu&W 91
**Litt**, Larry DrAPF 91
**Litt**, Michael 1933- AmMWSc 92
**Litt**, Mitchell 1932- AmMWSc 92
**Litt**, Mortimer 1925- AmMWSc 92
**Litt**, Morton Herbert 1926- AmMWSc 92
**Litt**, Theodor 1880-1969 EncTR 91
**Littauer**, Ernest Lucius 1936- AmMWSc 92
**Littauer**, Raphael Max 1925- AmMWSc 92
**Littel**, Laura Joan 1957- WhoMW 92
**Littell**, Arthur Simpson 1925- AmMWSc 92
**Littell**, Eliakim 1797-1870 BenetAL 91
**Littell**, Franklin H. 1917- ConAu 134
**Littell**, Franklin Hamlin 1917- WhoRel 92
**Littell**, Jessica Fuller 1958- WhoFI 92
**Littell**, Lawrence Michael 1949- WhoWest 92
**Littell**, Ramon Clarence 1942- AmMWSc 92
**Littell**, Robert 1935- IntAu&W 91, WrDr 92
**Littell**, Robert E 1936- WhoAmP 91
**Littell**, Robert Stuart 1937- WhoFI 92
**Littell**, Ross DcTwDes
**Littell**, William 1768-1824 BenetAL 91
**Litten**, Charlotte Elaine 1944- WhoMW 92
**Litten**, Jonathan Jay 1960- WhoAmL 92
**Litten**, Raye Z, III AmMWSc 92
**Litterer**, Joseph A 1926- ConAu 35NR
**Litterer**, Karen Sue 1962- WhoEnt 92
**Litteria**, Marilyn 1931- AmMWSc 92
**Litterst**, Charles Lawrence 1944- AmMWSc 92
**Littin**, Miguel 1942- IntDcF 2-2
**Littky**, Dennis S 1944- WhoAmP 91
**Little Anthony** 1940- NewAmDM
**Little Carpenter** DcNCBi 4
**Little Richard** 1932- WhoBlA 92, WhoEnt 92
**Little Richard** 1935?- NewAmDM
**Little Walter** 1930-1968 NewAmDM
**Little**, A Brian 1925- AmMWSc 92
**Little**, Alex G 1943- AmMWSc 92
**Little**, Alexandre 1945- WhoMW 92

**Little,** Angela C 1920- *AmMWSc 92*
**Little,** Barbara Charon 1931- *WhoAmP 91*
**Little,** Bill Frank 1932- *WhoMW 92*
**Little,** Brenda Joyce *AmMWSc 92*
**Little,** Brian Keith 1959- *WhoBlA 92*
**Little,** Brian Woods 1945- *AmMWSc 92*
**Little,** Bryan 1913- *WrDr 92*
**Little,** Bryan Desmond Greenway 1913- *IntAu&W 91*
**Little,** C *ScFEYrs*
**Little,** Carl *DrAPF 91*
**Little,** Carl Maurice 1924- *WhoEnt 92*
**Little,** Charles Curtis 1954- *WhoFI 92*
**Little,** Charles Dean 1944- *WhoAmL 92*
**Little,** Charles Durwood, Jr 1946- *AmMWSc 92*
**Little,** Charles E. 1931- *WrDr 92*
**Little,** Charles Edward 1926- *AmMWSc 92*
**Little,** Charles Gordon 1924- *AmMWSc 92*
**Little,** Charles Harrison Anthony 1939- *AmMWSc 92*
**Little,** Charles Oran 1935- *AmMWSc 92*
**Little,** Chester H. 1907- *WhoBlA 92*
**Little,** Christopher Hood 1949- *WhoAmL 92*
**Little,** Clarence E. *WhoBlA 92*
**Little,** Cleavon 1939- *IntMPA 92*
**Little,** Cleavon Jake 1939- *WhoBlA 92, WhoEnt 92*
**Little,** Craig Franklin 1958- *WhoEnt 92*
**Little,** Dennis Gage 1935- *WhoFI 92*
**Little,** Douglas Macfarlan d1990 *Who 92N*
**Little,** Duane Ewing 1937- *WhoAmP 91*
**Little,** E. Neal, Jr. 1927- *WhoAmL 92*
**Little,** Edward Herman 1881-1981 *DcNCBi 4*
**Little,** Edwin Demetrius 1926- *AmMWSc 92*
**Little,** Elbert Luther, Jr 1907- *AmMWSc 92*
**Little,** F. A., Jr. 1936- *WhoAmL 92*
**Little,** Francis H *ScFEYrs*
**Little,** General T. 1946- *WhoBlA 92*
**Little,** George 1731-1800 *DcNCBi 4*
**Little,** George Daniel 1929- *WhoRel 92*
**Little,** George E, Jr 1921- *WhoAmP 91*
**Little,** Gerald Bob 1939- *WhoRel 92*
**Little,** Geraldine C. *DrAPF 91*
**Little,** Geraldine Clinton 1925- *IntAu&W 91*
**Little,** Gwynne H 1941- *AmMWSc 92*
**Little,** Harold Franklin 1932- *AmMWSc 92*
**Little,** Henry Nelson 1920- *AmMWSc 92*
**Little,** Herman Kernel 1951- *WhoBlA 92*
**Little,** Ian 1918- *WrDr 92*
**Little,** Ian M D 1918- *ConAu 34NR*
**Little,** Ian Malcolm David 1918- *IntWW 91, Who 92*
**Little,** J Anderson 1945- *WhoAmP 91*
**Little,** Jack Edward 1938- *WhoFI 92*
**Little,** James Alexander 1922- *AmMWSc 92*
**Little,** James Kelly, Jr. 1925- *WhoBlA 92*
**Little,** James Noel 1940- *AmMWSc 92*
**Little,** Janet 1759-1813 *BlkwCEP*
**Little,** Jean 1932- *IntAu&W 91, SmATA 68 [port], WrDr 92*
**Little,** John Bertram 1929- *AmMWSc 92*
**Little,** John Clayton 1933- *AmMWSc 92*
**Little,** John Dutton Conant 1928- *AmMWSc 92*
**Little,** John Eric Russell 1913- *Who 92*
**Little,** John Llewellyn 1919- *AmMWSc 92*
**Little,** John Pat, III 1964- *WhoFI 92*
**Little,** John Philip Brooke B. *Who 92*
**Little,** John Russell, Jr 1930- *AmMWSc 92*
**Little,** John Russell, Jr. 1932- *WhoAmL 92*
**Little,** John Stanley 1931- *AmMWSc 92*
**Little,** John Troy 1964- *WhoRel 92*
**Little,** John Wesley 1935- *WhoFI 92*
**Little,** John Wesley 1941- *AmMWSc 92*
**Little,** Joseph Alexander 1918- *AmMWSc 92*
**Little,** Joyce Currie 1934- *AmMWSc 92*
**Little,** Julia Elizabeth 1932- *WhoWest 92*
**Little,** Kenneth *ConAu 36NR*
**Little,** Kenneth Arthur 1955- *WhoMW 92*
**Little,** Kenneth Lindsay d1991 *Who 92N*
**Little,** Leone Bryson 1924- *WhoBlA 92*
**Little,** Loren Everton 1941- *WhoEnt 92*
**Little,** Mark McKenna 1957- *WhoFI 92*
**Little,** Maurice Dale 1928- *AmMWSc 92*
**Little,** Michael Alan 1937- *AmMWSc 92*
**Little,** Mitchell Stuart 1960- *WhoFI 92*
**Little,** Monroe Henry 1950- *WhoBlA 92*
**Little,** N Clayton 1933- *WhoAmP 91*
**Little,** Nelson 1924- *WhoAmP 91*
**Little,** Patricia *WhoAmP 91*
**Little,** Patrick Joseph 1958- *AmMWSc 92*
**Little,** Perry L 1928- *AmMWSc 92*
**Little,** Randel Quincy, Jr 1927- *AmMWSc 92*
**Little,** Raymond Daniel 1947- *AmMWSc 92*
**Little,** Reuben R. 1933- *WhoBlA 92*
**Little,** Rich 1938- *IntMPA 92*
**Little,** Richard Allen 1939- *AmMWSc 92, WhoMW 92*
**Little,** Richard Caruthers 1938- *WhoEnt 92*
**Little,** Rick Ray 1955- *WhoMW 92*
**Little,** Robert 1939- *AmMWSc 92*
**Little,** Robert Benjamin 1955- *WhoBlA 92*
**Little,** Robert Clement 1925- *Who 92*
**Little,** Robert Colby 1920- *AmMWSc 92*
**Little,** Robert E 1933- *AmMWSc 92*
**Little,** Robert L. 1938- *ConBlB 2 [port]*
**Little,** Robert Lewis 1929- *AmMWSc 92*
**Little,** Robert Narvaez, Jr 1913- *AmMWSc 92*
**Little,** Ronald Eugene 1937- *WhoBlA 92*
**Little,** Royal 1896-1989 *FacFETw*
**Little,** Sarah Alden 1959- *AmMWSc 92*
**Little,** Stephen Abbot 1942- *WhoAmP 91*
**Little,** Stephen James 1939- *AmMWSc 92*
**Little,** Stuart West 1921- *WhoEnt 92*
**Little,** T D 1942- *WhoAmP 91*
**Little,** Thomas Alfred 1955- *WhoWest 92*
**Little,** Thomas Francis *Who 92*
**Little,** Thomas Mayer 1935- *WhoFI 92*
**Little,** Thomas Morton 1910- *AmMWSc 92*
**Little,** Timothy Alan 1963- *WhoRel 92*
**Little,** Timothy Harold 1940- *WhoMW 92*
**Little,** W Matthew 1922- *WhoAmP 91*
**Little,** William 1691?-1734 *DcNCBi 4*
**Little,** William 1775-1848 *DcNCBi 4*
**Little,** William Arthur 1930- *AmMWSc 92*
**Little,** William Asa 1931- *AmMWSc 92*
**Little,** William C 1950- *AmMWSc 92*
**Little,** William Frederick 1929- *AmMWSc 92*
**Little,** William Henry 1948- *WhoWest 92*
**Little,** William Person 1765-1829 *DcNCBi 4*
**Little,** Willie Howard 1949- *WhoBlA 92*
**Little,** Winston Woodard, Jr 1938- *AmMWSc 92*
**Little-Marenin,** Irene Renate 1941- *AmMWSc 92*
**Littlechild,** Stephen Charles 1943- *Who 92*
**Littledale,** Freya *WrDr 92*
**Littledale,** Freya Lota *IntAu&W 91*
**Littledike,** Ernest Travis 1935- *AmMWSc 92*
**Littlefield,** Donald Bruce 1946- *WhoWest 92*
**Littlefield,** John Walley 1925- *AmMWSc 92*
**Littlefield,** Larry James 1938- *AmMWSc 92*
**Littlefield,** Lawrence Crosby, Jr. 1938- *WhoFI 92*
**Littlefield,** Milton Smith 1830-1899 *DcNCBi 4*
**Littlefield,** Neil Adair 1935- *AmMWSc 92*
**Littlefield,** Nick *WhoAmL 92*
**Littlefield,** Rick M 1952- *WhoAmP 91*
**Littlefield,** Roy Everett, III 1952- *WhoAmL 92, WhoFI 92*
**Littlefield,** Warren *LesBEnT 92 [port], WhoEnt 92, WhoWest 92*
**Littleford,** William Donaldson 1914- *WhoEnt 92*
**Littlejohn,** Alan Morrison 1925- *Who 92*
**Littlejohn,** Bill C. 1944- *WhoBlA 92*
**Littlejohn,** Cameron Bruce 1913- *WhoAmP 91*
**Littlejohn,** Doris 1935- *Who 92*
**Littlejohn,** Edward J. 1935- *WhoBlA 92*
**Littlejohn,** John B., Jr. 1942- *WhoBlA 92*
**Littlejohn,** Joseph Phillip 1937- *WhoBlA 92*
**Littlejohn,** Lanny F 1942- *WhoAmP 91*
**Littlejohn,** Marvin Leroy 1923- *WhoAmP 91*
**Littlejohn,** Oliver Marsilius 1924- *AmMWSc 92*
**Littlejohn,** Samuel Gleason 1921- *WhoBlA 92*
**Littlejohn,** Walter L. 1932- *WhoBlA 92*
**Littlejohn,** William Hunter 1929- *Who 92*
**Littlejohn,** William Woolsey 1946- *WhoWest 92*
**Littlejohn Cook,** George Steveni 1919- *Who 92*
**Littlepage,** Jack Leroy 1935 *AmMWSc 92*
**Littler,** Geoffrey 1930- *Who 92*
**Littler,** Mark Masterton 1939- *AmMWSc 92*
**Littler,** Shirley 1932- *Who 92*
**Littler,** William Brian 1908- *Who 92*
**Littleton** *Who 92*
**Littleton,** Arthur C. 1942- *WhoBlA 92*
**Littleton,** Carol *ReelWom*
**Littleton,** Christine A. 1952- *WhoAmL 92*
**Littleton,** H T J 1921- *AmMWSc 92*
**Littleton,** Harvey 1922- *DcTwDes*
**Littleton,** John Edward 1943- *AmMWSc 92*
**Littleton,** Mark *BenetAL 91*
**Littleton,** Preston A, Jr *AmMWSc 92*
**Littleton,** Ralph Douglass 1908- *WhoBlA 92*
**Littleton,** Robert T 1916- *AmMWSc 92*
**Littleton,** Rupert, Jr. 1950- *WhoBlA 92*
**Littleton,** William Neuel 1939- *WhoEnt 92*
**Littlewit,** Humphrey *ConAu 133*
**Littlewood,** Lady 1909- *Who 92*
**Littlewood,** Barbara Shaffer 1941- *AmMWSc 92*
**Littlewood,** James 1922- *Who 92*
**Littlewood,** Joan *IntWW 91, Who 92*
**Littlewood,** Roland Kay 1942- *AmMWSc 92*
**Littleworth,** Dennis Kent 1942- *WhoMW 92*
**Littman,** Armand 1921- *AmMWSc 92*
**Littman,** Bruce H 1944- *AmMWSc 92*
**Littman,** Harold 1922- *WhoFI 92*
**Littman,** Howard 1927- *AmMWSc 92*
**Littman,** Irving 1940- *WhoFI 92*
**Littman,** Lynne *IntMPA 92*
**Littman,** Mark 1920- *IntWW 91, Who 92*
**Littman,** Michael I. 1960- *WhoAmL 92*
**Littman,** Walter 1929- *AmMWSc 92, WhoMW 92*
**Littmann,** Martin F 1919- *AmMWSc 92*
**Litto,** George *IntMPA 92*
**Litton,** Abram 1814-1901 *BiInAmS*
**Litton,** Andrew 1959- *IntWW 91*
**Litton,** George Washington 1910- *AmMWSc 92*
**Litton,** James Howard 1934- *WhoRel 92*
**Litton,** Peter Stafford 1921- *Who 92*
**Litton,** Terry Edmund 1941- *WhoRel 92*
**Litton,** Thomas Marc 1955- *WhoAmL 92*
**Littrell,** Barry Wayne 1956- *WhoAmL 92*
**Littrell,** David Lee 1948- *WhoEnt 92*
**Littrell,** George H, Jr 1934- *WhoAmP 91*
**Litts,** Stephen Douglas 1943- *WhoAmP 91*
**Lituchy,** Terri Robin 1964- *WhoFI 92*
**Litvack,** Sanford Martin 1936- *WhoAmL 92*
**Litvak,** Anatole 1902-1974 *IntDcF 2-2 [port]*
**Litvak,** Austin S 1933- *AmMWSc 92*
**Litvak,** Marvin Mark 1933- *AmMWSc 92*
**Litvak,** Ronald 1938- *WhoMW 92*
**Litvak King,** Jaime 1933- *IntWW 91*
**Litvan,** Gerard Gabriel 1927- *AmMWSc 92*
**Litvin,** Martin Jay 1928- *WhoMW 92*
**Litvinoff,** Emanuel 1915- *ConNov 91, IntAu&W 91, WrDr 92*
**Litvinoff,** Si 1929- *IntMPA 92*
**Litvinov,** Maksim Maksimovich 1876-1951 *EncTR 91 [port]*
**Litvinov,** Maxim Maximovich 1876-1951 *FacFETw*
**Litvinov,** Pavel Mikhailovich 1940- *IntWW 91*
**Litvinov,** Sergey K. 1938- *IntWW 91*
**Litwack,** Gerald 1929- *AmMWSc 92*
**Litwack,** Leon 1929- *WrDr 92*
**Litwak,** Leo *DrAPF 91*
**Litwak,** Robert Seymour 1924- *AmMWSc 92*
**Litwhiler,** Daniel W 1942- *AmMWSc 92*
**Litwin,** Alan Henry 1957- *WhoFI 92*
**Litwin,** Burton Lawrence 1931- *WhoAmL 92, WhoEnt 92*
**Litwin,** Harvey 1931- *WhoEnt 92*
**Litwin,** Lawrence Baine 1945- *WhoAmL 92*
**Litwin,** Lenore S. 1955- *WhoMW 92*
**Litwin,** Martin Stanley 1930- *AmMWSc 92*
**Litwin,** Michael Joseph 1947- *WhoFI 92*
**Litwin,** Paul Jeffrey 1955- *WhoEnt 92*
**Litwin,** Stephen David 1934- *AmMWSc 92*
**Litwiniszyn,** Jerzy 1914- *IntWW 91*
**Litwinowicz,** Manfred Siegmund 1950- *WhoEnt 92*
**Litwok,** Evelyn 1951- *WhoFI 92*
**Litwos** *ConAu 134*
**Litwos** 1846-1916 *WhoNob 90*
**Litynski,** Daniel Mitchell 1943- *AmMWSc 92*
**Litz,** Charles Joseph, Jr. 1928- *WhoWest 92*
**Litz,** Jo Ellen 1951- *WhoAmP 91*
**Litz,** Lawrence Marvin 1921- *AmMWSc 92*
**Litz,** Richard Earle 1944- *AmMWSc 92*
**Litzenberger,** Leonard Nelson 1945- *AmMWSc 92*
**Litzenberger,** Samuel Cameron 1914- *AmMWSc 92*
**Litzenboerger,** Wolfgang 1935- *WhoFI 92*
**Litzky,** Eric Neal 1961- *WhoFI 92*
**Litzmann,** Karl 1850-1936 *EncTR 91 [port]*
**Liu Anyuan** 1927- *IntWW 91*
**Liu Baiyu** 1916- *IntWW 91*
**Liu Bingyan** 1915- *IntWW 91*
**Liu Bocheng** 1892-1986 *FacFETw*
**Liu Chieh** d1991 *NewYTBS 91 [port]*
**Liu Chieh** 1906-1991 *IntWW 91, -91N*
**Liu Chin Ting** *EncAmaz 91*
**Liu Chun** 1918- *IntWW 91*
**Liu Da-ren** 1939- *LiExTwC*
**Liu Danian** 1915- *IntWW 91*
**Liu Danzhai** 1931- *IntWW 91*
**Liu Daosheng** 1915- *IntWW 91*
**Liu Fangren** 1936- *IntWW 91*
**Liu Fuzhi** 1917- *IntWW 91*
**Liu Guofan** 1929- *IntWW 91*
**Liu Guoguang** 1923- *IntWW 91*
**Liu Haiqing** 1914- *IntWW 91*
**Liu Haisu** 1896- *IntWW 91*
**Liu Hongru** 1930- *IntWW 91*
**Liu Huanzhang** 1930- *IntWW 91*
**Liu Huaqing** 1916- *IntWW 91*
**Liu Jianfeng** 1936- *IntWW 91*
**Liu Jianzhang** *IntWW 91*
**Liu Jie** *IntWW 91*
**Liu Jingsong** 1933- *IntWW 91*
**Liu Kaiqu** 1924- *IntWW 91*
**Liu Keming** 1919- *IntWW 91*
**Liu Lantao** 1910- *IntWW 91*
**Liu Lifeng** 1918- *IntWW 91*
**Liu Lin** 1918- *IntWW 91*
**Liu Minghui** 1914- *IntWW 91*
**Liu Nianqu** 1945- *IntWW 91*
**Liu Qingyou** *IntWW 91*
**Liu Shahe** 1931- *IntWW 91*
**Liu Shan** *IntWW 91*
**Liu Shaohui** 1940- *IntWW 91*
**Liu Shaoqi** 1898-1974 *FacFETw*
**Liu Shaotang** 1936- *IntWW 91*
**Liu Shuqing** *IntWW 91*
**Liu Shusheng** 1926- *IntWW 91*
**Liu Tianfu** 1926- *IntWW 91*
**Liu Wei** 1912- *IntWW 91*
**Liu Weiming** 1938- *IntWW 91*
**Liu Xian** 1915- *IntWW 91*
**Liu Xiang** *NewYTBS 91*
**Liu Xiaoqing** 1952- *IntWW 91*
**Liu Xinwu** 1942- *IntWW 91*
**Liu Xiyao** 1916- *IntWW 91*
**Liu Yi** 1930- *IntWW 91*
**Liu Youfa** 1922- *IntWW 91*
**Liu Youguang** 1914- *IntWW 91*
**Liu Yujie** *IntWW 91*
**Liu Zaifu** *LiExTwC*
**Liu Zhen** 1915- *IntWW 91*
**Liu Zheng** 1929- *IntWW 91*
**Liu Zhengwei** 1930- *IntWW 91*
**Liu Zhenhua** 1921- *IntWW 91*
**Liu Zhijian** 1912- *IntWW 91*
**Liu Zihou** 1911- *IntWW 91*
**Liu,** Alice Yee-Chang 1948- *AmMWSc 92*
**Liu,** Andrew T C 1929- *AmMWSc 92*
**Liu,** Bede 1934- *AmMWSc 92*
**Liu,** Benjamin Lyan 1950- *WhoWest 92*
**Liu,** Benjamin Y H 1934- *AmMWSc 92*
**Liu,** C K 1921- *AmMWSc 92*
**Liu,** Chain T *AmMWSc 92*
**Liu,** Chamond 1948- *AmMWSc 92*
**Liu,** Chao-Han 1939- *AmMWSc 92*
**Liu,** Chen-Ching 1954- *AmMWSc 92*
**Liu,** Chen Ya 1924- *AmMWSc 92*
**Liu,** Chi-Li 1952- *AmMWSc 92*
**Liu,** Chi-Sheng 1934- *AmMWSc 92*
**Liu,** Chien 1921- *AmMWSc 92*
**Liu,** Ching Shi 1935- *AmMWSc 92*
**Liu,** Ching-Tong 1931- *AmMWSc 92*
**Liu,** Chong Tan 1936- *AmMWSc 92*
**Liu,** Chuan Sheng 1939- *AmMWSc 92*
**Liu,** Chui Fan 1930- *AmMWSc 92*
**Liu,** Chui Hsun 1931- *AmMWSc 92*
**Liu,** Chung-Chiun 1936- *AmMWSc 92*
**Liu,** Chung Laung 1934- *AmMWSc 92*
**Liu,** Chung-Yen *AmMWSc 92*
**Liu,** Darrell T 1932- *AmMWSc 92*
**Liu,** David H 1928- *AmMWSc 92*
**Liu,** David Shiao-Kung 1940- *AmMWSc 92*
**Liu,** Dickson Lee Shen 1935- *AmMWSc 92*
**Liu,** Edwin H 1942- *AmMWSc 92*
**Liu,** Fengming 1957- *WhoAmL 92*
**Liu,** Fook Fah 1934- *AmMWSc 92*
**Liu,** Frank C 1926- *AmMWSc 92*
**Liu,** Fred Wei Jui 1926- *AmMWSc 92*
**Liu,** Frederick F 1919- *AmMWSc 92*
**Liu,** Fu-Wen *AmMWSc 92*
**Liu,** Gerald Hanmin 1944- *WhoWest 92*
**Liu,** Han-Shou 1930- *AmMWSc 92*
**Liu,** Hao-Wen 1926- *AmMWSc 92*
**Liu,** Henry 1936- *AmMWSc 92*
**Liu,** Houng-Zung 1931- *AmMWSc 92*
**Liu,** Hsing-Jang 1942- *AmMWSc 92*
**Liu,** Hua-Kuang 1939- *AmMWSc 92*
**Liu,** J T C 1934- *AmMWSc 92*
**Liu,** Jia ming 1953- *AmMWSc 92, WhoWest 92*
**Liu,** John *AmMWSc 92*
**Liu,** John K 1930- *AmMWSc 92*
**Liu,** Joseph Jeng-Fu 1940- *AmMWSc 92*
**Liu,** Katherine Chang *WhoWest 92*
**Liu,** Lee 1933- *WhoMW 92*
**Liu,** Leroy Fong 1949- *AmMWSc 92*
**Liu,** Liu 1930- *AmMWSc 92*
**Liu,** Lon-Chang *AmMWSc 92*
**Liu,** Matthew J P 1935- *AmMWSc 92*
**Liu,** Maw-Shung 1940- *AmMWSc 92*
**Liu,** Mian 1960- *AmMWSc 92*
**Liu,** Michael M 1953- *WhoAmP 91*
**Liu,** Michael T H 1939- *AmMWSc 92*
**Liu,** Ming-Biann 1942- *AmMWSc 92*
**Liu,** Ming-Tsan 1934- *AmMWSc 92*
**Liu,** Pan-Tai 1941- *AmMWSc 92*
**Liu,** Paul Chi 1935- *AmMWSc 92*
**Liu,** Paul Ishen *AmMWSc 92*
**Liu,** Philip L-F 1946- *AmMWSc 92*
**Liu,** Pinghui Victor 1924- *AmMWSc 92*

**Liu**, Qing-Huo 1963- *AmMWSc 92*
**Liu**, Ralph Yieh-Min 1958- *WhoFI 92*
**Liu**, Ray Ho 1942- *AmMWSc 92*
**Liu**, Robert Shing-Hei 1938- *AmMWSc 92*
**Liu**, Ruey-Wen 1930- *AmMWSc 92*
**Liu**, S G 1933- *AmMWSc 92*
**Liu**, Samuel Hsi-Peh 1934- *AmMWSc 92*
**Liu**, Shaotang 1936- *IntAu&W 91*
**Liu**, Shin-Tse 1932- *WhoWest 92*
**Liu**, Shing Kin Francis 1953- *WhoFI 92*
**Liu**, Si-Kwang 1925- *AmMWSc 92*
**Liu**, Siakisone *WhoAmP 91*
**Liu**, Stephen C Y 1927- *AmMWSc 92*
**Liu**, Stephen Shu Ning *DrAPF 91*
**Liu**, Stephen Shu-ning 1930- *WhoWest 92*
**Liu**, Ta-Jo 1951- *AmMWSc 92*
**Liu**, Tai-Ping 1945- *AmMWSc 92*
**Liu**, Teh-Yung 1932- *AmMWSc 92*
**Liu**, Ting-Ting Y 1949- *AmMWSc 92*
**Liu**, Tony Chen-Yeh 1943- *AmMWSc 92*
**Liu**, Ts'un-yan 1917- *IntWW 91*
**Liu**, Tsz-Ming 1931- *Who 92*
**Liu**, Tung 1926- *AmMWSc 92*
**Liu**, Vi-Cheng 1917- *AmMWSc 92*
**Liu**, Wei-Min 1945- *WhoMW 92*
**Liu**, Wen Chih 1921- *AmMWSc 92*
**Liu**, Wing Kam 1952- *AmMWSc 92, WhoMW 92*
**Liu**, Wing-Ki 1950- *AmMWSc 92*
**Liu**, Wingyuen Timothy 1946- *AmMWSc 92*
**Liu**, Wu-chi 1907- *IntAu&W 91, WrDr 92*
**Liu**, Yick Wah Edmund 1953- *WhoFI 92*
**Liu**, Young King 1934- *AmMWSc 92, WhoMW 92*
**Liu**, Yu *AmMWSc 92*
**Liu**, Yu-Ying 1944- *AmMWSc 92*
**Liu**, Yung-Pin *AmMWSc 92*
**Liu**, Yung Sheng 1944- *AmMWSc 92*
**Liu**, Yung Yuan 1950- *AmMWSc 92*
**Liu-Ger**, Tsu-Huei 1943- *AmMWSc 92*
**Liuima**, Francis Aloysius 1919- *AmMWSc 92*
**Liukkonen**, John Robie 1942- *AmMWSc 92*
**Liukkonen**, Karen Elaine 1958- *WhoFI 92*
**Liuzzi**, Robert C. 1944- *WhoFI 92, WhoMW 92*
**Liuzzo**, Joseph Anthony 1926- *AmMWSc 92*
**Livadary**, Paul John 1937- *WhoAmL 92*
**Livadas**, Dennis James 1914- *WhoAmP 91*
**Livak**, Lydia d1943 *EncAmaz 91*
**Livanos**, Peter E, Jr 1937- *WhoAmP 91*
**Livanov**, Boris Nikolaevich 1904-1972 *SovUnBD*
**Livant**, Peter David 1948- *AmMWSc 92*
**Livarchik**, George Ronald 1954- *WhoAmL 92*
**Livatino**, Melvin William 1940- *WhoMW 92*
**Livaudais**, Marcel, Jr. 1925- *WhoAmL 92*
**Livdahl**, Philip V 1923- *AmMWSc 92*
**Live**, David H 1946- *AmMWSc 92*
**Live**, Israel 1907- *AmMWSc 92*
**Lively**, David Harryman 1930- *AmMWSc 92*
**Lively**, Donald Earl 1947- *WhoAmL 92*
**Lively**, Ira J. 1926- *WhoBlA 92*
**Lively**, Penelope 1933- *ConNov 91, WrDr 92*
**Lively**, Penelope Margaret 1933- *IntAu&W 91, IntWW 91, Who 92*
**Lively**, Pierce 1921- *WhoAmL 92*
**Lively**, Roderick Lavern 1917- *WhoAmP 91*
**Livengood**, David Robert 1937- *AmMWSc 92*
**Livengood**, Henry *WhoAmP 91*
**Livengood**, John B 1947- *WhoAmP 91*
**Livengood**, Michael Gene 1953- *WhoRel 92*
**Livengood**, Samuel Miller 1917- *AmMWSc 92*
**Liverman**, James Leslie 1921- *AmMWSc 92*
**Liverman**, John Gordon 1920- *Who 92*
**Liverman**, Thomas Phillip George 1923- *AmMWSc 92*
**Livermon**, Carl Raby 1883-1968 *DcNCBi 4*
**Livermore**, David Andrew 1967- *WhoRel 92*
**Livermore**, Mary Ashton 1820-1905 *HanAmWH*
**Livermore**, Paul Webster 1944- *WhoRel 92*
**Livermore**, Putnam 1922- *WhoAmP 91*
**Livermore**, Rosalind Robb 1918- *WhoAmP 91*
**Liverpool**, Archbishop of 1920- *Who 92*
**Liverpool**, Archdeacon of *Who 92*
**Liverpool**, Auxiliary Bishops of *Who 92*
**Liverpool**, Bishop of 1929- *Who 92*
**Liverpool**, Dean of *Who 92*
**Liverpool**, Earl of 1944- *Who 92*
**Liverpool**, Charles Eric 1946- *WhoBlA 92*
**Liversage**, Richard Albert 1925- *AmMWSc 92*
**Liversidge**, Douglas 1913- *IntAu&W 91*
**Liversidge**, Henry Douglas 1913- *WrDr 92*
**Livesay**, Ann Louise 1951- *WhoAmP 91*
**Livesay**, Charles Jackson 1949- *WhoMW 92*
**Livesay**, Dorothy 1909- *BenetAL 91, ConAu 36NR, ConPo 91, RfGEnL 91, WrDr 92*
**Livesay**, George Roger 1924- *AmMWSc 92*
**Livesay**, Michael 1936- *Who 92*
**Livesay**, Thomas Andrew 1945- *WhoWest 92*
**Livesey**, Bernard Joseph Edward 1944- *Who 92*
**Livesey**, Robert Shaw 1947- *WhoMW 92*
**Livesey**, Ronald John Dearden 1935- *Who 92*
**Livett**, Bruce G 1943- *AmMWSc 92*
**Livigni**, Russell A 1934- *AmMWSc 92*
**Livigni**, Russell Anthony 1934- *AmMWSc 92*
**Living Colour** *ConMus 7 [port]*
**Livingood**, Clarence Swinehart 1911- *AmMWSc 92*
**Livingood**, James Weston 1910- *WrDr 92*
**Livingood**, John N B 1913- *AmMWSc 92*
**Livingood**, Marvin D 1918- *AmMWSc 92*
**Livings**, Henry 1929- *IntAu&W 91, Who 92, WrDr 92*
**Livingston**, Alan Wendell *WhoEnt 92*
**Livingston**, Albert Edward 1936- *AmMWSc 92*
**Livingston**, Ann Chambliss 1952- *WhoAmL 92*
**Livingston**, Bernard *DrAPF 91*
**Livingston**, Clark Holcomb 1920- *AmMWSc 92*
**Livingston**, Dana Alan 1957- *WhoWest 92*
**Livingston**, Daniel Isadore 1919- *AmMWSc 92*
**Livingston**, Daniel McKean 1957- *WhoAmL 92*
**Livingston**, David M 1941- *AmMWSc 92*
**Livingston**, Dennis Delmer, Jr. 1952- *WhoEnt 92*
**Livingston**, Donald Earl 1924- *WhoAmP 91*
**Livingston**, Edward 1764-1836 *AmPolLe*
**Livingston**, Edward Michael 1948- *WhoAmL 92*
**Livingston**, Frederick Cross 1946- *WhoEnt 92*
**Livingston**, G E 1927- *AmMWSc 92*
**Livingston**, George Herbert 1916- *WhoRel 92*
**Livingston**, Graham 1928- *Who 92*
**Livingston**, Harold 1924- *WhoEnt 92*
**Livingston**, Hugh Duncan 1940- *AmMWSc 92*
**Livingston**, James Barrett d1991 *Who 92N*
**Livingston**, James Craig 1930- *WhoRel 92*
**Livingston**, James Duane 1930- *AmMWSc 92*
**Livingston**, James Leo 1940- *WhoMW 92*
**Livingston**, Jay 1915- *IntMPA 92*
**Livingston**, Jay Harold 1915- *WhoEnt 92*
**Livingston**, Jeffrey Edward 1963- *WhoAmL 92*
**Livingston**, Jon Jerald 1935- *WhoWest 92*
**Livingston**, Joyce *WhoBlA 92*
**Livingston**, Knox W 1919- *AmMWSc 92*
**Livingston**, L. Benjamin 1931- *WhoBlA 92*
**Livingston**, Lee Franklin 1942- *WhoFI 92*
**Livingston**, Linda 1942- *AmMWSc 92*
**Livingston**, Marie Leigh 1955- *WhoWest 92*
**Livingston**, Marilyn Laurene 1940- *AmMWSc 92*
**Livingston**, Melanie McKenzie 1962- *WhoAmL 92*
**Livingston**, Myra Cohn *DrAPF 91*
**Livingston**, Myra Cohn 1926- *IntAu&W 91, SmATA 68 [port], WhoWest 92, WrDr 92*
**Livingston**, Nancy 1935- *ConAu 134, WrDr 92*
**Livingston**, Neal David 1951- *WhoWest 92*
**Livingston**, Patricia Ann 1954- *WhoWest 92*
**Livingston**, Patrick Malcolm 1963- *WhoMW 92*
**Livingston**, Penni Sue 1961- *WhoAmL 92*
**Livingston**, Ralph 1919- *AmMWSc 92*
**Livingston**, Randall Murch 1949- *WhoAmL 92*
**Livingston**, Richard Lee 1940- *WhoAmP 91*
**Livingston**, Robert Burr 1918- *AmMWSc 92*
**Livingston**, Robert Henry 1934- *ConAu 134*
**Livingston**, Robert L. 1943- *AlmAP 92 [port]*
**Livingston**, Robert L, Jr 1943- *WhoAmP 91*
**Livingston**, Robert R. 1746-1813 *AmPolLe, BlkwEAR*
**Livingston**, Robert Simpson 1914- *AmMWSc 92*
**Livingston**, Rudolph 1928- *WhoBlA 92*
**Livingston**, Stanley Bernard 1950- *WhoEnt 92*
**Livingston**, William 1723-1790 *BlkwEAR*
**Livingston**, William Charles 1927- *AmMWSc 92*
**Livingston Booth**, John Dick 1918- *Who 92*
**Livingston-White**, Deborah J. H. 1947- *WhoBlA 92*
**Livingston-White**, Deborah Joyce Halimah 1947- *IntAu&W 91*
**Livingstone**, Daniel Archibald 1927- *AmMWSc 92*
**Livingstone**, Douglas 1932- *ConPo 91, IntAu&W 91, WrDr 92*
**Livingstone**, Frank Brown 1928- *AmMWSc 92*
**Livingstone**, Harrison Edward *DrAPF 91*
**Livingstone**, James 1912- *Who 92*
**Livingstone**, Ken 1945- *Who 92*
**Livingstone**, Ken Robert 1945- *IntWW 91*
**Livingstone**, Michael Edwin 1953- *WhoWest 92*
**Livingstone**, Trudy Dorothy Zweig 1946- *WhoEnt 92*
**Livolsi**, Frank William, Jr. 1938- *WhoAmL 92*
**Livsey**, Richard Arthur Lloyd 1935- *Who 92*
**Livsey**, Robert Callister 1936- *WhoAmL 92*
**Livziey**, James Gerald 1927- *WhoWest 92*
**Liyong**, Taban lo 1938- *IntAu&W 91*
**Liyong**, Taban lo 1938- *WrDr 92*
**Liyong**, Taban lo 1939- *ConPo 91, LiExTwC*
**Lizalde**, Eduardo 1929- *ConSpAP*
**Lizardi**, Joseph 1941- *WhoHisp 92*
**Lizarraga**, David C. *WhoHisp 92*
**Lizarralde**, Nestor R. 1955- *WhoHisp 92*
**Lizichev**, Aleksey Dmitrievich 1928- *IntWW 91, SovUnBD*
**Ljotic**, Dimitriye V. 1891-1945 *BiDExR*
**Ljubicic**, Nikola 1916- *IntWW 91*
**Ljubicic Drozdowski**, Miladin Peter 1921- *WhoWest 92*
**Ljung**, Harvey Albert 1905- *AmMWSc 92*
**Ljungberg**, Betty Marion *WhoRel 92*
**Ljungdahl**, Lars Gerhard 1926- *AmMWSc 92*
**Ljunggren**, Olof 1933- *IntWW 91*
**Ljungqvist**, Bengt 1937- *IntWW 91*
**Llacuna**, Flora Magdalena *WhoMW 92*
**Llaguno**, Magaly 1940- *WhoHisp 92*
**Llama**, Manuel *WhoHisp 92*
**Llamas**, Vicente Jose 1944- *AmMWSc 92*
**Llandaff**, Bishop of 1934- *Who 92*
**Llandaff**, Dean of *Who 92*
**Llanos**, Luis Socorro, Sr. 1940- *WhoHisp 92*
**Llarena**, Elsa de 1921- *IntAu&W 91*
**Llaurado**, Josep G 1927- *AmMWSc 92*
**Llerandi**, Edward X. 1962- *WhoHisp 92*
**Llerandi**, Manuel *WhoHisp 92*
**Llerandi**, Richard Henry 1963- *WhoHisp 92*
**Lleras Camargo**, Alberto 1903-1990 *FacFETw*
**Lleras Camargo**, Alberto 1906-1990 *AnObit 1990*
**Lleras Restrepo**, Carlos 1908- *IntWW 91*
**Lleshi**, Haxhi 1913- *IntWW 91*
**Llewellin**, John Richard Allan *Who 92*
**Llewellyn**, Alun 1903- *IntAu&W 91, TwCSFW 91*
**Llewellyn**, Bryan Henry 1927- *Who 92*
**Llewellyn**, Charles Elroy, Jr 1922- *AmMWSc 92*
**Llewellyn**, David Thomas 1943- *Who 92*
**Llewellyn**, David Treharne 1916- *Who 92*
**Llewellyn**, David Walter 1930- *Who 92*
**Llewellyn**, Donald Rees 1919- *Who 92*
**Llewellyn**, Frederick Eaton 1917- *WhoFI 92, WhoWest 92*
**Llewellyn**, Gerald Cecil 1940- *AmMWSc 92*
**Llewellyn**, Henry Morton 1911- *Who 92*
**Llewellyn**, Hubert Sherman 1963- *WhoEnt 92*
**Llewellyn**, J Anthony 1933- *AmMWSc 92*
**Llewellyn**, Jack Rowbottom 1919- *Who 92*
**Llewellyn**, James Bruce 1927- *WhoBlA 92*
**Llewellyn**, John *DcNCBi 4*
**Llewellyn**, John 1933- *IntWW 91*
**Llewellyn**, John Desmond S. *Who 92*
**Llewellyn**, John Francis Morgan 1921- *Who 92*
**Llewellyn**, John Frederick 1947- *WhoWest 92*
**Llewellyn**, John Schofield, Jr. 1935- *WhoFI 92*
**Llewellyn**, Leonard Frank 1933- *WhoFI 92*
**Llewellyn**, Michael 1921- *Who 92*
**Llewellyn**, Ralph A 1933- *AmMWSc 92*
**Llewellyn**, Richard 1907-1983 *FacFETw*
**Llewellyn**, Richard Morgan 1937- *Who 92*
**Llewellyn**, Timothy David 1947- *Who 92*
**Llewellyn**, William H. Samuel 1858-1941 *TwCPaSc*
**Llewellyn**, William Somers 1907- *Who 92*
**Llewellyn-Jones**, Derek 1923- *ConAu 34NR, WrDr 92*
**Llewellyn-Jones**, Frank *Who 92*
**Llewellyn-Jones**, Frank 1907- *WrDr 92*
**Llewellyn Jones**, Ilston Percival 1916- *Who 92*
**Llewellyn Smith**, Christopher Hubert 1942- *IntWW 91, Who 92*
**Llewellyn-Smith**, Elizabeth 1934- *IntWW 91*
**Llewellyn-Smith**, Elizabeth Marion 1934- *Who 92*
**Llewellyn Smith**, Michael John 1939- *Who 92*
**Llewelyn**, John Michael D. V. *Who 92*
**Llewelyn-Davies** *Who 92*
**Llewelyn-Davies**, Richard 1912-1981 *FacFETw*
**Llewelyn-Davies of Hastoe**, Baroness 1915- *Who 92*
**Llewelyn-Owens**, Joan 1919- *ConAu 36NR, WrDr 92*
**Llinas**, Miguel 1938- *AmMWSc 92*
**Llinas**, Rodolfo 1934- *AmMWSc 92*
**Llinga** *EncAmaz 91*
**Llop**, Henry Chesnel 1950- *WhoFI 92*
**Lloreda Caicedo**, Rodrigo 1942- *IntWW 91*
**Llorens**, Hector Roberto 1947- *WhoHisp 92*
**Llorens**, Marcelo Gustavo 1957- *WhoHisp 92*
**Llorente**, Rigoberto Lino 1956- *WhoHisp 92*
**Llowarch**, Martin Edge 1935- *IntWW 91, Who 92*
**Lloyd** *Who 92*
**Lloyd**, A. C. 1916- *WrDr 92*
**Lloyd**, Albert Kingsley 1903- *Who 92*
**Lloyd**, Anthony 1929- *Who 92*
**Lloyd**, Anthony Joseph 1950- *Who 92*
**Lloyd**, Antony Charles 1916- *Who 92*
**Lloyd**, Barbara Ann 1943- *WhoBlA 92*
**Lloyd**, Bertram Thomas 1941- *WhoFI 92*
**Lloyd**, Bertram Trevor 1938- *Who 92*
**Lloyd**, Brian Beynon 1920- *Who 92*
**Lloyd**, Bruce Louis 1951- *WhoEnt 92*
**Lloyd**, Celeste Scalise 1959- *WhoAmL 92*
**Lloyd**, Charles Allen 1944- *WhoAmL 92*
**Lloyd**, Charles Wait 1914- *AmMWSc 92*
**Lloyd**, Charles William 1915- *Who 92*
**Lloyd**, Christine Marie Evert *IntWW 91*
**Lloyd**, Christopher 1921- *Who 92*
**Lloyd**, Christopher 1938- *IntMPA 92, WhoEnt 92*
**Lloyd**, Christopher Hamilton 1945- *Who 92*
**Lloyd**, Christopher Raymond 1951- *AmMWSc 92*
**Lloyd**, Clive 1944- *IntWW 91*
**Lloyd**, Clive Hubert 1944- *Who 92*
**Lloyd**, D.H. *DrAPF 91*
**Lloyd**, Darrell Clive Arthur 1928- *Who 92*
**Lloyd**, David *WhoBlA 92*
**Lloyd**, David 1920- *NewAmDM*
**Lloyd**, David Bernard 1938- *Who 92*
**Lloyd**, David Livingstone, Jr. 1952- *WhoAmL 92*
**Lloyd**, David Mark 1945- *Who 92*
**Lloyd**, David Richard 1939- *Who 92*
**Lloyd**, David Robert 1937- *IntWW 91*
**Lloyd**, David Tecwyn 1914- *IntAu&W 91*
**Lloyd**, Denis Thelwall 1924- *Who 92*
**Lloyd**, Dennis 1915- *WrDr 92*
**Lloyd**, Denys *Who 92*
**Lloyd**, Don 1932- *WhoAmP 91*
**Lloyd**, Douglas Roy 1948- *AmMWSc 92*
**Lloyd**, Douglas Seward 1939- *AmMWSc 92*
**Lloyd**, Edward 1815-1890 *DcLB 106 [port]*
**Lloyd**, Edward C 1915- *AmMWSc 92*
**Lloyd**, Edwin Phillips 1929- *AmMWSc 92*
**Lloyd**, Elizabeth Jane 1928- *TwCPaSc*
**Lloyd**, Elliott 1947- *WhoEnt 92*
**Lloyd**, Emily 1971- *IntMPA 92*
**Lloyd**, Euan 1923- *IntMPA 92*
**Lloyd**, Eve *Who 92*
**Lloyd**, Fran Celeste 1942- *WhoFI 92*
**Lloyd**, Frances Mary *Who 92*
**Lloyd**, Francis Leon, Jr. 1955- *WhoAmL 92*
**Lloyd**, Frederick Ebenezer John 1859-1933 *RelLAm 91*
**Lloyd**, Frederick John 1913- *Who 92*
**Lloyd**, Geoffrey Ernest Richard 1933- *IntAu&W 91, IntWW 91, Who 92, WrDr 92*
**Lloyd**, George 1913- *ConCom 92*
**Lloyd**, George Lussington 1931- *WhoBlA 92*
**Lloyd**, George Peter 1926- *Who 92*
**Lloyd**, George Walter Selwyn 1913- *IntWW 91, Who 92*
**Lloyd**, Georgia 1913- *WhoMW 92*
**Lloyd**, Glyn d1991 *Who 92N*
**Lloyd**, Harold 1894-1971 *FacFETw [port]*
**Lloyd**, Harris Horton 1937- *AmMWSc 92*
**Lloyd**, Henry Demarest 1847-1903 *BenetAL 91*

**Lloyd**, Henry Malcolm 1935- *WhoAmL 92*
**Lloyd**, Henry Morgan 1911- *Who 92*
**Lloyd**, Howell Arnold 1937- *WrDr 92*
**Lloyd**, Hugh *ConAu 133, SmATA 65*
**Lloyd**, Humphrey John 1939- *Who 92*
**Lloyd**, Ian 1921- *Who 92*
**Lloyd**, Illtyd Rhys 1929- *Who 92*
**Lloyd**, James *WrDr 92*
**Lloyd**, James 1906-1974 *TwCPaSc*
**Lloyd**, James 1932- *WhoBlA 92*
**Lloyd**, James Armon 1933- *AmMWSc 92*
**Lloyd**, James Edward 1933- *AmMWSc 92*
**Lloyd**, James Fredrick 1922- *WhoAmP 91*
**Lloyd**, James Melwood, II 1955- *WhoRel 92*
**Lloyd**, James Monteith 1911- *Who 92*
**Lloyd**, James Newell 1932- *AmMWSc 92*
**Lloyd**, James T. 1941- *WhoAmL 92*
**Lloyd**, James Woodman 1940- *WhoAmL 92*
**Lloyd**, Jimmie Mitchell 1948- *WhoRel 92*
**Lloyd**, John Edward 1940- *AmMWSc 92*
**Lloyd**, John Graham 1938- *Who 92*
**Lloyd**, John Nicol Fortune 1946- *IntAu&W 91, IntWW 91, Who 92*
**Lloyd**, John Peter 1915- *Who 92*
**Lloyd**, John Raymond *Who 92*
**Lloyd**, John Stoddard 1914- *WhoAmL 92*
**Lloyd**, John William 1944- *WhoFI 92*
**Lloyd**, John Willie, III 1943- *AmMWSc 92*
**Lloyd**, John Wilson 1940- *Who 92*
**Lloyd**, Jonathan 1948- *ConCom 92*
**Lloyd**, Joseph Ross *DcNCBi 4*
**Lloyd**, Joseph Wesley 1914- *WhoWest 92*
**Lloyd**, Joseph Wilsey 1940- *WhoRel 92*
**Lloyd**, June 1928- *Who 92*
**Lloyd**, Kenneth Oliver 1936- *AmMWSc 92*
**Lloyd**, Kingsley *Who 92*
**Lloyd**, L Keith 1941- *AmMWSc 92*
**Lloyd**, Larry Allen 1947- *WhoMW 92*
**Lloyd**, Laurance H 1915- *AmMWSc 92*
**Lloyd**, Leona Loretta 1949- *WhoAmL 92, WhoBlA 92*
**Lloyd**, Leonia Jannetta 1949- *WhoBlA 92*
**Lloyd**, Leslie 1924- *Who 92*
**Lloyd**, Levanah *IntAu&W 91X, WrDr 92*
**Lloyd**, Lewis Ewan 1924- *AmMWSc 92*
**Lloyd**, Lewis Kevin 1959- *WhoBlA 92*
**Lloyd**, Lola Maverick 1875-1944 *AmPeW*
**Lloyd**, Marilyn 1929- *AlmAP 92 [port], WhoAmP 91*
**Lloyd**, Mary Ellen 1947- *WhoAmP 91*
**Lloyd**, Michael Jeffrey 1948- *WhoEnt 92*
**Lloyd**, Michael Raymond 1927- *Who 92*
**Lloyd**, Milton Harold 1925- *AmMWSc 92*
**Lloyd**, Monte 1927- *AmMWSc 92*
**Lloyd**, Nelson Albert 1926- *AmMWSc 92*
**Lloyd**, Nicholas 1942- *Who 92*
**Lloyd**, Nicholas Markley 1942- *IntAu&W 91*
**Lloyd**, Norman 1914- *IntMPA 92, WhoEnt 92*
**Lloyd**, Norman Edward 1929- *AmMWSc 92*
**Lloyd**, Peter *Who 92*
**Lloyd**, Peter 1907- *Who 92*
**Lloyd**, Peter Cutt 1927- *WrDr 92*
**Lloyd**, Peter Frederick Victor 1932- *WhoMW 92*
**Lloyd**, Peter Gordon 1920- *Who 92*
**Lloyd**, Peter Robert Cable 1937- *Who 92*
**Lloyd**, Phil Andrew 1952- *WhoBlA 92*
**Lloyd**, Rachel 1839-1900 *BiInAmS*
**Lloyd**, Ray Dix 1930- *AmMWSc 92*
**Lloyd**, Raymond Anthony 1941- *WhoBlA 92*
**Lloyd**, Raymond Clare 1927- *AmMWSc 92*
**Lloyd**, Raymond Joseph 1942- *WhoFI 92*
**Lloyd**, Richard 1928- *Who 92*
**Lloyd**, Richard D. 1956- *WhoWest 92*
**Lloyd**, Richard Eyre d1991 *Who 92N*
**Lloyd**, Richard Hey 1933- *Who 92*
**Lloyd**, Robert *DrAPF 91*
**Lloyd**, Robert 1916- *AmMWSc 92*
**Lloyd**, Robert Andrew 1940- *IntWW 91, Who 92*
**Lloyd**, Robert Michael 1938- *AmMWSc 92*
**Lloyd**, Robert Tredway 1930- *WhoEnt 92*
**Lloyd**, Roseann *DrAPF 91*
**Lloyd**, Seton 1902- *IntWW 91*
**Lloyd**, Seton Howard Frederick 1902- *Who 92*
**Lloyd**, Steve 1952- *WhoAmP 91*
**Lloyd**, Susan Rebecca 1959- *WhoFI 92*
**Lloyd**, T. O. 1934- *WrDr 92*
**Lloyd**, Thomas d1770 *DcNCBi 4*
**Lloyd**, Thomas 1710?-1792 *DcNCBi 4*
**Lloyd**, Thomas Blair 1921- *AmMWSc 92*
**Lloyd**, Thomas Reese 1920- *WhoAmP 91*
**Lloyd**, Timothy Andrew Wigram 1946- *Who 92*
**Lloyd**, Trevor *Who 92*
**Lloyd**, Trevor Owen 1934- *IntAu&W 91*
**Lloyd**, Wallis A 1926- *AmMWSc 92*
**Lloyd**, Wanda 1949- *WhoBlA 92*
**Lloyd**, Weldon S 1939- *AmMWSc 92*
**Lloyd**, William Gilbert 1923- *AmMWSc 92*
**Lloyd**, William J., Sr. 1923- *WhoFI 92*
**Lloyd**, William Nelson 1920- *WhoAmP 91*
**Lloyd**, William Robert, Jr 1947- *WhoAmP 91*
**Lloyd**, Winston Dale 1929- *AmMWSc 92*
**Lloyd Davies**, John Robert *Who 92*
**Lloyd Davies**, Trevor Arthur 1909- *Who 92*
**Lloyd-Edwards**, Norman 1933- *Who 92*
**Lloyd-Eley**, John 1923- *Who 92*
**Lloyd George** *Who 92*
**Lloyd George**, David 1863-1945 *EncTR 91 [port], FacFETw [port]*
**Lloyd George of Dwyfor**, Earl 1924- *Who 92*
**Lloyd-Hughes**, Trevor Denby 1922- *Who 92*
**Lloyd-Jacob**, David Oliver 1938- *Who 92*
**Lloyd Jones**, Charles Beynon *Who 92*
**Lloyd Jones**, David Elwyn d1991 *Who 92N*
**Lloyd-Jones**, David Mathias 1934- *IntWW 91, Who 92*
**Lloyd-Jones**, David Trevor 1917- *Who 92*
**Lloyd-Jones**, Hugh 1922- *IntAu&W 91, IntWW 91, Who 92, WrDr 92*
**Lloyd-Jones**, Jean 1929- *WhoAmP 91*
**Lloyd Jones**, Richard 1933- *Who 92*
**Lloyd-Jones**, Robert 1931- *Who 92*
**Lloyd-Mostyn** *Who 92*
**Lloyd of Hampstead**, Baron 1915- *Who 92*
**Lloyd of Kilgerran**, Baron d1991 *Who 92N*
**Lloyd Owen**, David Lanyon 1917- *Who 92*
**Lloyd Webber**, Andrew 1948- *ConMus 6 [port], FacFETw, IntWW 91, NewAmDM, Who 92, WhoEnt 92*
**Lloyd Webber**, Julian 1951- *IntWW 91, Who 92*
**Llubien**, Jose H. *DrAPF 91*
**Lluch**, Jose Francisco 1954- *AmMWSc 92*
**Lluch**, Myrna 1950- *WhoHisp 92*
**Lluch Martin**, Ernest 1937- *IntWW 91*
**Llywelyn**, Morgan 1937- *IntAu&W 91, WrDr 92*
**Lnenicka**, Gregory Allen 1952- *AmMWSc 92*
**Lnenicka**, William J 1922- *AmMWSc 92*
**Lo Jui-Ching** 1906-1978 *FacFETw*
**Lo**, Adrian Hsiang-yun 1949- *WhoEnt 92*
**Lo**, Andrew W *AmMWSc 92*
**Lo**, Andrew W. 1960- *WhoFI 92*
**Lo**, Arthur W 1916- *AmMWSc 92*
**Lo**, Cheng Fan 1937- *AmMWSc 92*
**Lo**, Chu Shek *AmMWSc 92*
**Lo**, Clifford W 1951- *AmMWSc 92*
**Lo**, David S 1932- *AmMWSc 92*
**Lo**, Elizabeth Shen 1926- *AmMWSc 92*
**Lo**, George Albert 1934- *AmMWSc 92*
**Lo**, Grace S *AmMWSc 92*
**Lo**, Hilda K *AmMWSc 92*
**Lo**, Howard H 1937- *AmMWSc 92*
**Lo**, Kenneth Hsiao Chien 1913- *Who 92*
**Lo**, Kwok-Yung 1947- *AmMWSc 92, WhoMW 92*
**Lo**, Mike Mei-Kuo 1936- *AmMWSc 92*
**Lo**, Sansom Chi-Kwong 1965- *WhoWest 92*
**Lo**, Theodore Ching-Yang 1943- *AmMWSc 92*
**Lo**, Theresa Nong 1945- *AmMWSc 92*
**Lo**, W C 1924- *AmMWSc 92*
**Lo**, Waituck 1919- *WhoWest 92*
**Lo**, Wayne *AmMWSc 92*
**Lo**, Winston W. 1938- *ConAu 133*
**Lo**, Woo-Kuen 1945- *AmMWSc 92*
**Lo**, Y T 1920- *AmMWSc 92*
**Loach**, Ken 1937- *IntDcF 2-2 [port]*
**Loach**, Kenneth 1936- *IntWW 91, Who 92*
**Loach**, Kenneth William 1934- *AmMWSc 92*
**Loach**, Paul A 1934- *AmMWSc 92*
**Loader**, Clive Roland 1965- *AmMWSc 92*
**Loader**, Leslie 1923- *Who 92*
**Loades**, David Henry 1937- *Who 92*
**Loades**, David Michael 1934- *IntAu&W 91, WrDr 92*
**Loadholt**, Claude Boyd 1940- *AmMWSc 92*
**Loan**, Leonard Donald 1930- *AmMWSc 92*
**Loan**, Raymond Wallace 1931- *AmMWSc 92*
**Loane**, Marcus Lawrence 1911- *IntWW 91, Who 92*
**Loar**, James M 1944- *AmMWSc 92*
**Loarie**, Thomas Merritt 1946- *WhoWest 92*
**Loatman**, Robert Bruce 1945- *AmMWSc 92*
**Loats**, John Timothy 1954- *WhoAmL 92*
**Loaysa**, Juan Garcia Jofre de 148-?-1527 *HisDSpE*
**Lobanov**, Andrey Mikhaylovich 1900-1959 *SovUnBD*
**Lobanov**, Vassily 1947- *ConCom 92*
**Lobanov-Rostovsky**, Oleg 1934- *WhoEnt 92, WhoMW 92*
**Lobashev**, Vladimir Mikhailovich 1934- *IntWW 91*
**Lobato**, Francesca *WhoHisp 92*
**Lobato**, Toribio Q. 1954- *WhoHisp 92*
**Lobaugh**, Bruce 1953- *AmMWSc 92*
**LoBaugh**, Leslie E., Jr. *WhoAmL 92*
**Lobb**, Donald Edward 1940- *AmMWSc 92*
**Lobb**, Howard Leslie Vicars 1909- *Who 92*
**Lobb**, Jacob d1773 *DcNCBi 4*
**Lobb**, James Taylor 1958- *WhoAmL 92*
**Lobb**, R Kenneth 1925- *AmMWSc 92*
**Lobb**, William Atkinson 1951- *WhoFI 92*
**Lobbia**, John E. 1941- *WhoFI 92, WhoMW 92*
**Lobdell**, David Hill 1930- *AmMWSc 92*
**Lobdell**, Frank 1921- *WhoWest 92*
**Lobe**, Paul 1875-1967 *EncTR 91 [port]*
**Lobeck**, Charles Champlin 1926- *AmMWSc 92*
**Lobel**, Anita 1934- *IntAu&W 91, WrDr 92*
**Lobel**, Arnold 1933-1987 *BenetAL 91*
**Lobel**, Charles Irving 1921- *WhoWest 92*
**Lobel**, Irving 1917- *WhoFI 92*
**Lobel**, Martin 1941- *WhoAmL 92*
**Lobel**, Steven A 1952- *AmMWSc 92*
**Lobell**, Michael 1941- *IntMPA 92*
**Lobell**, William Joseph 1947- *WhoWest 92*
**Lo Bello**, Joseph David 1940- *WhoFI 92*
**Lobene**, Ralph Rufino 1924- *AmMWSc 92*
**Lobenfeld**, Eric Jay 1950- *WhoAmL 92*
**Lobenherz**, William Ernest 1949- *WhoAmL 92*
**Lobenstine**, Clark *WhoRel 92*
**Lober**, Lionel M. 1933- *WhoEnt 92*
**Lober**, Paul Hallam 1919- *AmMWSc 92*
**Loberg**, Peter Eric 1943- *WhoFI 92*
**LoBianco**, Robert d1991 *NewYTBS 91*
**Lo Bianco**, Tony 1936- *IntMPA 92, WhoEnt 92A*
**LoBiondo**, Frank A 1946- *WhoAmP 91*
**Lobitz**, W. Charles, III 1943- *WhoWest 92*
**Lobkowicz**, Frederick 1932- *AmMWSc 92*
**Lobkowicz**, Nicholas 1931- *IntWW 91*
**Lobl**, Herbert Max 1932- *WhoAmL 92*
**Lobl**, Thomas Jay 1944- *AmMWSc 92, WhoWest 92*
**Loble**, Lester H., II 1941- *WhoAmL 92*
**Lobmeyr**, Ludwig 1829-1917 *DcTwDes*
**Lobner**, Kneeland Harkness 1919- *WhoWest 92*
**Lobo**, Angelo Peter 1939- *AmMWSc 92*
**Lobo**, Cecil T 1934- *AmMWSc 92*
**Lobo**, Francis X 1925- *AmMWSc 92*
**Lobo**, Jennifer Helena 1954- *WhoFI 92*
**Lobo**, Jose Carlos 1942- *IntWW 91*
**Lobo**, Paul A 1928- *AmMWSc 92*
**Lobo**, Richard M. 1936- *WhoHisp 92*
**Lobo**, Rogerio Hyndman 1923- *Who 92*
**Lobo**, Walter E 1905- *AmMWSc 92*
**Lobov**, Oleg Ivanovich 1937- *IntWW 91, SovUnBD*
**Lobov**, Semen Semenovich 1888-1937 *SovUnBD*
**Lobov**, Vladimir Nikolayevich 1935- *IntWW 91*
**LoBriglio**, Tara A. 1961- *WhoFI 92*
**Lobron**, Richard John 1957- *WhoFI 92*
**Lobrutto**, Vincent Anthony 1950- *WhoEnt 92*
**Lobsenz**, Amelia *WhoFI 92*
**Lobsinger**, Thomas 1927- *WhoWest 92*
**Lobstein**, Otto Ervin 1922- *AmMWSc 92*
**LoBue**, Joseph 1934- *AmMWSc 92*
**Lobuglio**, Albert Francis 1938- *AmMWSc 92*
**Lo Buglio**, Rudecinda Ann 1934- *WhoHisp 92*
**Lobunez**, Walter 1920- *AmMWSc 92*
**Localio**, S Arthur 1911- *AmMWSc 92*
**LoCascio**, James Edward 1955- *WhoMW 92*
**Locascio**, Mark Alexander 1957- *WhoAmL 92*
**Locascio**, Salvadore J 1933- *AmMWSc 92*
**Locasio**, Ann Lee 1959- *WhoRel 92*
**Locatelli**, Joseph John 1934- *WhoEnt 92*
**Locatelli**, Pietro Antonio 1695-1764 *NewAmDM*
**Loch**, Baron d1991 *Who 92N*
**Loch**, Anita Ann 1948- *WhoMW 92*
**Loch**, John Robert 1940- *WhoMW 92*
**Loch**, Patricia Ann 1944- *WhoWest 92*
**Loche**, Lee Edward 1926- *WhoBlA 92*
**Lochen**, Einar 1918- *IntWW 91*
**Lochen**, Yngvar Formo 1931- *IntWW 91*
**Locher**, Duane 1947- *WhoMW 92*
**Locher**, Gottfried Wilhelm 1911- *WhoRel 92*
**Locher**, Ralph S 1915- *WhoAmP 91*
**Locher**, Richard Earl 1929- *WhoMW 92*
**Lochhaas**, Thomas John *DrAPF 91*
**Lochhead**, Douglas 1922- *BenetAL 91, WrDr 92*
**Lochhead**, Douglas Grant 1922- *IntAu&W 91*
**Lochhead**, John Hutchison 1909- *AmMWSc 92*
**Lochhead**, Kenneth Campbell 1926- *IntWW 91*
**Lochhead**, Liz 1947- *ConPo 91, IntAu&W 91, WrDr 92*
**Lochhead**, Robert Bruce 1952- *WhoAmL 92*
**LoChiano**, Stephen Anthony 1949- *WhoFI 92*
**Lochman**, Jan Milic 1922- *WrDr 92*
**Lochman-Balk**, Christina 1907- *AmMWSc 92*
**Lochmiller**, Kurtis L. 1952- *WhoWest 92*
**Lochmuller**, Charles Howard 1940- *AmMWSc 92*
**Lochner**, Janis Elizabeth 1954- *AmMWSc 92*
**Lochner**, Jim Warren 1940- *WhoWest 92*
**Lochner**, John Meldrum 1946- *WhoFI 92*
**Lochner**, Louis Paul 1887-1975 *AmPeW*
**Lochner**, Robert Herman 1939- *AmMWSc 92*
**Lochner**, Robin Paul 1962- *WhoFI 92*
**Lochstet**, William A 1936- *AmMWSc 92*
**Lochte**, Dick 1944- *WrDr 92*
**Lochte**, Richard Samuel 1946- *WhoEnt 92*
**Lochtenberg**, Bernard Hendrik 1931- *WhoFI 92*
**Lo Cicero**, Joe 1965- *WhoEnt 92*
**LoCicero**, Joseph Castelli 1914- *AmMWSc 92*
**Lock**, Albert Larry, Jr. 1947- *WhoFI 92, WhoMW 92*
**Lock**, Alexander *WhoWest 92*
**Lock**, Brian Edward 1944- *AmMWSc 92*
**Lock**, Colin James Lyne 1933- *AmMWSc 92*
**Lock**, Duncan *Who 92*
**Lock**, G S H 1935- *AmMWSc 92*
**Lock**, George David 1929- *Who 92*
**Lock**, Graham *Who 92*
**Lock**, James Albert 1948- *AmMWSc 92*
**Lock**, James Sidney 1927- *WhoRel 92*
**Lock**, John Arthur 1922- *Who 92*
**Lock**, John Duncan 1918- *Who 92*
**Lock**, John Richard 1941- *WhoAmL 92*
**Lock**, Keith Elliott 1959- *WhoEnt 92*
**Lock**, Kenneth 1932- *AmMWSc 92*
**Lock**, Robert Joseph 1955- *WhoMW 92*
**Lock**, Stephen Penford 1929- *Who 92*
**Lock**, Thomas Graham 1931- *IntWW 91, Who 92*
**Lock**, William Rowland 1932- *WhoEnt 92*
**Lockard**, Isabel 1915- *AmMWSc 92*
**Lockard**, J David 1929- *AmMWSc 92*
**Lockard**, Jon Onye 1932- *WhoBlA 92*
**Lockard**, Raymond G 1925- *AmMWSc 92*
**Lockart**, Barbetta 1947- *WhoWest 92*
**Lockart**, Royce Zeno, Jr 1928- *AmMWSc 92*
**Locke**, Alain 1886-1954 *BenetAL 91, TwCLC 43 [port]*
**Locke**, Arthur James 1915- *WhoAmP 91*
**Locke**, Ben Zion 1921- *AmMWSc 92*
**Locke**, Bernadette 1958- *WhoBlA 92*
**Locke**, Carl Edwin, Jr 1936- *AmMWSc 92*
**Locke**, Carla Renee 1967- *WhoEnt 92*
**Locke**, Charles O. 1896?-1977 *TwCWW 91*
**Locke**, Charles Stanley 1929- *WhoFI 92, WhoMW 92*
**Locke**, David Creighton 1939- *AmMWSc 92*
**Locke**, David Henry 1927- *WhoAmP 91*
**Locke**, David Ross *BenetAL 91*
**Locke**, Dick 1947- *WhoAmP 91*
**Locke**, Don C. 1943- *WhoBlA 92*
**Locke**, Duane *DrAPF 91*
**Locke**, Edith Raymond 1921- *WhoEnt 92*
**Locke**, Edward *DrAPF 91*
**Locke**, Edwin Allen, Jr. 1910- *IntWW 91*
**Locke**, Edwin C. 1960- *WhoEnt 92*
**Locke**, Elsie 1912- *WrDr 92*
**Locke**, Elsie Violet 1912- *IntAu&W 91*
**Locke**, Francis 1722-1796 *DcNCBi 4*
**Locke**, Gary F *WhoAmP 91*
**Locke**, George 1936- *ScFEYrs*
**Locke**, Harold Ogden 1931- *AmMWSc 92*
**Locke**, Henry Daniel, Jr. 1936- *WhoBlA 92*
**Locke**, Hubert G. 1934- *WhoBlA 92, WrDr 92*
**Locke**, Hubert Gaylord 1934- *IntAu&W 91, WhoWest 92*
**Locke**, Jack Lambourne 1921- *AmMWSc 92*
**Locke**, John 1632-1704 *BenetAL 91, BlkwCEP, BlkwEAR, RfGEnL 91*
**Locke**, John 1792-1856 *BiInAmS*
**Locke**, John Erwin 1939- *WhoFI 92*
**Locke**, John Gardner 1926- *WhoWest 92*
**Locke**, John Howard 1920- *WhoAmL 92*
**Locke**, John Howard 1923- *Who 92*
**Locke**, John Lauderdale 1940- *AmMWSc 92*
**Locke**, John Wesley 1938- *WhoFI 92*
**Locke**, Joseph J 1946- *WhoIns 92*
**Locke**, Kevin 1954- *WhoRel 92*
**Locke**, Krystyna Kopaczyk 1926- *AmMWSc 92*
**Locke**, Lewis Dwight, Jr. 1954- *WhoMW 92*
**Locke**, Louis Noah 1928- *AmMWSc 92*
**Locke**, Mamie Evelyn 1954- *WhoBlA 92*
**Locke**, Matthew 1621-1677 *NewAmDM*
**Locke**, Matthew 1730-1801 *DcNCBi 4*

Locke, Matthew J 1957- *WhoAmP 91*
Locke, Maury David 1940- *WhoAmL 92*
Locke, Michael 1929- *AmMWSc 92*
Locke, Peter Fredrick, Jr 1937- *WhoAmP 91*
Locke, Philip M 1937- *AmMWSc 92*
Locke, Ralph Christopher 1953- *WhoAmL 92*
Locke, Ralph P 1949- *IntAu&W 91, WhoEnt 92*
Locke, Randy Lee 1944- *WhoWest 92*
Locke, Raymond Kenneth 1940- *AmMWSc 92*
Locke, Richard Adams 1800-1871 *ScFEYrs*
Locke, Sondra 1947- *IntMPA 92*
Locke, Stanley 1934- *AmMWSc 92*
Locke, Steven Elliot 1945- *AmMWSc 92*
Locke, William 1916- *AmMWSc 92*
Locke, William Henry 1947- *WhoAmL 92*
Locke-Elliott, Sumner *ConAu 134*
Lockemy, James E 1949- *WhoAmP 91*
Locker, Dale Le Roy 1929- *WhoAmP 91*
Locker, John L 1930- *AmMWSc 92*
Locker-Lampson, Frederick 1821-1895 *RfGEnL 91*
Lockerbie, Andrew Norville 1961- *WhoRel 92*
Lockerbie, D Bruce 1935- *IntAu&W 91, WrDr 92*
Lockerby, Michael J. 1956- *WhoAmL 92*
Lockerman, Bradley 1955- *WhoEnt 92*
Lockerman, Geneva Lorene Reuben 1928- *WhoBlA 92*
Locket, Arnold, Jr. 1929- *WhoBlA 92*
Lockett, Bradford R. 1945- *WhoBlA 92*
Lockett, Callen Michael 1958- *WhoWest 92*
Lockett, Clodovia 1913- *AmMWSc 92*
Lockett, Harold James 1924- *WhoBlA 92, WhoMW 92*
Lockett, James D. *WhoBlA 92*
Lockett, James Donald 1945- *WhoMW 92*
Lockett, Peter Paul 1932- *WhoWest 92*
Lockett, Pierre *WhoEnt 92*
Lockett, Reginald 1933- *Who 92*
Lockett, Sandra Bokamba 1946- *WhoBlA 92*
Lockett, Tyler C 1932- *WhoAmP 91*
Lockett, Tyler Charles 1932- *WhoAmL 92, WhoMW 92*
Lockette, Agnes Louise 1927- *WhoBlA 92*
Lockette, Nicole Mercedes 1958- *WhoBlA 92*
Lockey, Richard Funk 1940- *AmMWSc 92*
Lockhart, Benham Edward 1945- *AmMWSc 92*
Lockhart, Brian Alexander 1942- *Who 92*
Lockhart, Brooks Javins 1920- *AmMWSc 92*
Lockhart, Caroline 1875-1962 *TwCWW 91*
Lockhart, Daniel Craig 1952- *WhoMW 92*
Lockhart, Eugene, Jr. 1961- *WhoBlA 92*
Lockhart, F J 1916- *AmMWSc 92*
Lockhart, Frank Roper 1931- *Who 92*
Lockhart, Gemma 1956- *WhoMW 92*
Lockhart, George Richard 1953- *WhoRel 92*
Lockhart, Haines Boots 1920- *AmMWSc 92*
Lockhart, Haines Boots, Jr 1946- *AmMWSc 92*
Lockhart, Harry Eugene 1949- *Who 92*
Lockhart, James 1930- *IntWW 91*
Lockhart, James Alexander 1850-1905 *DcNCBi 4*
Lockhart, James Arthur 1926- *AmMWSc 92*
Lockhart, James B. 1936- *WhoBlA 92*
Lockhart, James Blakely 1936- *WhoFI 92*
Lockhart, James Lawrence 1930- *Who 92*
Lockhart, James Marcus 1948- *AmMWSc 92*
Lockhart, John Gibson 1794-1854 *DcLB 110 [port]*
Lockhart, June 1925- *ConTFT 9, IntMPA 92*
Lockhart, Kenneth Burton 1916- *WhoWest 92*
Lockhart, Lillian Hoffman 1930- *AmMWSc 92*
Lockhart, Lillie Marie 1943- *WhoBlA 92*
Lockhart, Nell Henderson 1936- *WhoRel 92*
Lockhart, Richard Spence 1927- *WhoAmP 91*
Lockhart, Robert W. 1941- *WhoBlA 92*
Lockhart, Rosalie Pergantis 1938- *WhoEnt 92*
Lockhart, Simon John Edward Francis S. *Who 92*
Lockhart, Verdree 1924- *WhoBlA 92*
Lockhart, William Howard 1957- *WhoRel 92*
Lockhart, William Lafayette 1936- *AmMWSc 92*
Lockhart, William Raymond 1925- *AmMWSc 92*
Lockhart-Moss, Eunice Jean 1942- *WhoBlA 92*
Lockhart-Mummery, Christopher John 1947- *Who 92*
Lockington, William Neale 1842?-1902 *BiInAmS*
Locklair, Dan Steven 1949- *WhoEnt 92*
Locklear, Horace 1942- *WhoAmP 91*
Lockley, Andrew John Harold 1951- *Who 92*
Lockley, Clyde William 1938- *WhoBlA 92*
Lockley, Harold 1916- *Who 92*
Lockley, Ronald Mathias 1903- *IntAu&W 91, Who 92, WrDr 92*
Lockley, Stephen Randolph 1943- *Who 92*
Locklin, Gerald *DrAPF 91*
Locklin, Gerald Ivan 1941- *IntAu&W 91, WrDr 92*
Locklin, James R. 1958- *WhoBlA 92*
Locklin, Kenneth Robert 1949- *WhoFI 92*
Locklin, William Ray 1942- *WhoFI 92*
Lockman, Dianne L. 1944- *WhoMW 92*
Lockman, Norman Alton 1938- *WhoBlA 92*
Lockman-Brooks, Linda 1953- *WhoBlA 92*
Locko, Stephen Michael 1953- *WhoFI 92*
Lockrem, Lloyd Clifford, Jr 1934- *WhoAmP 91*
Lockridge, Ernest *DrAPF 91*
Lockridge, Frances d1963 *BenetAL 91*
Lockridge, Kenneth A. 1940- *ConAu 134*
Lockridge, Oksana Maslivec 1941- *AmMWSc 92*
Lockridge, Richard 1898-1982 *BenetAL 91*
Lockridge, Ross 1914-1948 *BenetAL 91*
Lockrow, Arthur Lynn 1945- *WhoEnt 92*
Lockshin, Michael Dan 1937- *AmMWSc 92*
Lockshin, Richard Ansel 1937- *AmMWSc 92*
Lockspeiser, Ben d1990 *Who 92N*
Lockspeiser, Ben 1891-1990 *AnObit 1990*
Lockton, Janet K *WhoAmP 91*
Lockwood, Baroness 1924- *Who 92*
Lockwood, Annea 1939- *ConCom 92*
Lockwood, Arthur H 1947- *AmMWSc 92*
Lockwood, Belva Ann Bennett 1830-1917 *AmPeW*
Lockwood, Belva Ann Bennett McNall 1830-1917 *HanAmWH*
Lockwood, Charles Henry, II 1943- *WhoAmL 92*
Lockwood, Daniel Ralph 1948- *WhoRel 92*
Lockwood, David 1929- *IntWW 91, Who 92, WrDr 92*
Lockwood, David John 1942- *AmMWSc 92*
Lockwood, Dean H 1937- *AmMWSc 92*
Lockwood, Dorothy 1903- *TwCPaSc*
Lockwood, Frances Ellen *AmMWSc 92*
Lockwood, Francis Cummins 1864-1948 *BenetAL 91*
Lockwood, Frank James 1931- *WhoFI 92, WhoMW 92*
Lockwood, Gary 1937- *IntMPA 92*
Lockwood, Gary Lee 1946- *WhoAmL 92*
Lockwood, George Shellington 1935- *WhoWest 92*
Lockwood, George Wesley 1941- *AmMWSc 92*
Lockwood, Grant John 1931- *AmMWSc 92*
Lockwood, Harold Raymond 1927- *WhoMW 92*
Lockwood, Ingersoll 1841-1918 *ScFEYrs*
Lockwood, James Clinton 1946- *WhoBlA 92*
Lockwood, Jeffrey Alan 1960- *AmMWSc 92*
Lockwood, John Alexander 1919- *AmMWSc 92*
Lockwood, John LeBaron 1924- *AmMWSc 92*
Lockwood, John Paul 1939- *AmMWSc 92*
Lockwood, Joseph Flawith d1991 *IntWW 91N, Who 92N*
Lockwood, Leigh Willard 1947- *WhoFI 92*
Lockwood, Linda Gail 1936- *AmMWSc 92*
Lockwood, Margaret 1916-1990 *AnObit 1990, FacFETw*
Lockwood, Molly Ann 1936- *WhoFI 92*
Lockwood, Peter Van Norden 1940- *WhoAmL 92*
Lockwood, Phyllis J 1932- *WhoAmP 91*
Lockwood, Ralph Gregory 1942- *WhoEnt 92*
Lockwood, Robert 1920- *Who 92*
Lockwood, Robert A 1932- *WhoAmP 91*
Lockwood, Robert Greening 1928- *AmMWSc 92*
Lockwood, Robert Philip 1949- *WhoRel 92*
Lockwood, Roger 1936- *IntMPA 92*
Lockwood, Samuel 1819-1894 *BiInAmS*
Lockwood, W. B. 1927- *WrDr 92*
Lockwood, William H. 1925- *WhoEnt 92*
Lockwood, William Rutledge 1929- *AmMWSc 92*
Lockyer, Austin 1929- *Who 92*
Lockyer, Bill 1941- *WhoAmP 91*
Lockyer, Roger Walter 1927- *IntAu&W 91, WrDr 92*
Locock, Robert A 1935- *AmMWSc 92*
Loconto, Frank Xavier 1931- *WhoEnt 92*
LoConto, Paul Francis 1947- *WhoAmL 92*
Locre, Peter E. *DrAPF 91*
Locy, David Keith 1948- *WhoFI 92*
Locy, Robert Donald 1947- *AmMWSc 92*
Loda, Richard Thomas 1948- *AmMWSc 92*
Lodahl, Michael Eugene 1955- *WhoRel 92*
Lodato, David Nicolas *WhoFI 92*
Lodato, Michael W 1932- *AmMWSc 92*
Lodder, Jerry Matthew 1959- *WhoWest 92*
Lodding, Mary Enid *WhoRel 92*
Lodeman, Ernest Gustavus 1867-1896 *BiInAmS*
Loden, Barbara 1932-1980 *ReelWom*
Loden, Barbara 1934-1980 *FacFETw*
Loden, Michael Simpson 1945- *AmMWSc 92*
Loden, Rachel *DrAPF 91*
Loder *Who 92*
Loder, Edwin Robert 1925- *AmMWSc 92*
Loder, Giles Rolls 1914- *Who 92*
Loder, Max A., Sr. 1940- *WhoMW 92*
Lodewijk, Eric 1940- *AmMWSc 92*
Lodge, Anton James Corduff 1944- *Who 92*
Lodge, Arthur Scott 1922- *AmMWSc 92*
Lodge, Chester Ray 1923- *AmMWSc 92*
Lodge, David 1935- *ConNov 91, WrDr 92*
Lodge, David John 1935- *FacFETw, IntAu&W 91, IntWW 91, Who 92*
Lodge, David Michael 1957- *AmMWSc 92*
Lodge, David William 1957- *WhoEnt 92*
Lodge, David Williams 1941- *WhoFI 92*
Lodge, Edward J. 1933- *WhoAmL 92*
Lodge, Geoffrey Arthur 1930- *IntWW 91, Who 92*
Lodge, George Cabot 1873-1909 *BenetAL 91*
Lodge, George Cabot 1927- *WhoAmP 91*
Lodge, Henry Cabot 1850-1924 *AmPeW, BenetAL 91, DcAmImH, FacFETw*
Lodge, Henry Cabot, II 1902-1985 *FacFETw [port]*
Lodge, Henry Cabot, Jr. 1902-1985 *AmPolLe*
Lodge, Herman 1928- *WhoBlA 92*
Lodge, James Piatt, Jr 1926- *AmMWSc 92*
Lodge, James Robert 1925- *AmMWSc 92*
Lodge, John Davis 1903-1985 *FacFETw*
Lodge, Malcolm A 1939- *AmMWSc 92*
Lodge, Michael L. 1957- *WhoFI 92*
Lodge, Oliver Raymond William Wynlayne 1922- *Who 92*
Lodge, Richard 1949- *WhoAmP 91*
Lodge, Sheila 1929- *WhoAmP 91*
Lodge, Thomas 1558-1625 *RfGEnL 91*
Lodge, Thomas 1909- *Who 92, WrDr 92*
Lodge, Thomas C. S. *Who 92*
Lodge, Timothy Patrick 1954- *AmMWSc 92*
Lodhi, Mohammad Arfin Khan 1933- *AmMWSc 92*
Lodish, Harvey Franklin 1941- *AmMWSc 92*
Lodmell, Donald Louis 1939- *AmMWSc 92*
Lodoen, Clayton A *WhoAmP 91*
Lodoen, Gary Arthur 1943- *AmMWSc 92*
Lodwick, Gwilym Savage 1917- *AmMWSc 92*
Lodwick, Seeley G 1920- *WhoAmP 91*
Loe, Daniel Robert 1956- *WhoRel 92*
Loe, Harald 1926- *AmMWSc 92*
Loe, Joseph Wayne 1938- *WhoWest 92*
Loe, Roland Weslay 1955- *WhoRel 92*
Loeb, Alex Lewis 1955- *AmMWSc 92*
Loeb, Arthur Lee 1923- *AmMWSc 92*
Loeb, Charles P., Jr. 1927- *WhoBlA 92*
Loeb, David 1939- *WhoEnt 92*
Loeb, DeAnn Jean 1960- *WhoMW 92*
Loeb, Gerald Eli 1948- *AmMWSc 92*
Loeb, Jennifer Susan 1958- *WhoEnt 92*
Loeb, Jerod M 1949- *AmMWSc 92*
Loeb, Jerome Thomas 1940- *WhoFI 92*
Loeb, John Hilder d1991 *NewYTBS 91*
Loeb, John Langeloth 1902- *WhoFI 92*
Loeb, John Langeloth, Jr. 1930- *IntWW 91, WhoAmP 91, WhoFI 92*
Loeb, John William 1937- *WhoMW 92*
Loeb, Joyce Lichtgarn 1936- *WhoWest 92*
Loeb, Karen *DrAPF 91*
Loeb, Lawrence Arthur 1936- *AmMWSc 92*
Loeb, Marcia Joan 1933- *AmMWSc 92*
Loeb, Marilyn Rosenthal 1930- *AmMWSc 92*
Loeb, Marshall Robert 1929- *WhoFI 92*
Loeb, Marvin Phillip 1926- *WhoWest 92*
Loeb, Morris 1863-1912 *BiInAmS*
Loeb, Peter Albert 1937- *AmMWSc 92*
Loeb, Peter Kenneth 1936- *WhoFI 92*
Loeb, Robert J. 1948- *WhoFI 92, WhoMW 92*
Loeb, Ronald Marvin 1932- *WhoAmL 92*
Loeb, Virgil, Jr 1921- *AmMWSc 92, WhoMW 92*
Loeb, Walter Ferdinand 1925- *WhoFI 92*
Loeb, William 1905-1981 *FacFETw*
Loebbaka, David S 1939- *AmMWSc 92*
Loebe, Albert Carl 1948- *WhoAmL 92*
Loebel, Kurt 1921- *WhoEnt 92*
Loebenstein, William Vaille 1914- *AmMWSc 92*
Loeber, Adolph Paul 1920- *AmMWSc 92*
Loeber, John Frederick 1942- *AmMWSc 92*
Loebig, Wilfred F. 1936- *WhoMW 92*
Loebl, Ernest Moshe 1923- *AmMWSc 92*
Loebl, James David 1927- *WhoWest 92*
Loebl, Richard Ira 1945- *AmMWSc 92*
Loeblich, Alfred Richard, III 1941- *AmMWSc 92*
Loeblich, Alfred Richard, Jr 1914- *AmMWSc 92*
Loeblich, Helen Nina 1917- *AmMWSc 92*
Loeblich, Karen Elizabeth 1944- *AmMWSc 92*
Loebner, Egon Ezriel 1924- *AmMWSc 92*
Loechelt, Cecil P 1935- *AmMWSc 92*
Loechinger, Carol Marie 1949- *WhoMW 92*
Loeckle, Raymond Craig 1945- *WhoWest 92*
Loeffel, Bruce 1943- *WhoFI 92*
Loeffler, Albert L, Jr 1927- *AmMWSc 92*
Loeffler, Charles Martin 1861-1935 *NewAmDM*
Loeffler, Donald Lee 1930- *WhoEnt 92*
Loeffler, Frank Joseph 1928- *AmMWSc 92*
Loeffler, Henry Kenneth 1938- *WhoRel 92*
Loeffler, Larry James 1932- *AmMWSc 92*
Loeffler, Robert Hugh 1943- *WhoAmL 92*
Loeffler, Robert J 1922- *AmMWSc 92*
Loeffler, Thomas G 1946- *WhoAmP 91*
Loeffler, William Robert 1949- *WhoFI 92*
Loegering, Daniel John 1943- *AmMWSc 92*
Loehle, Craig S 1952- *AmMWSc 92*
Loehlin, James Herbert 1934- *AmMWSc 92*
Loehman, Ronald Ernest 1943- *AmMWSc 92*
Loehnis, Anthony David 1936- *IntWW 91, Who 92*
Loehnis, Clive 1902- *Who 92*
Loehr, Dorthea Marylyn 1929- *WhoMW 92*
Loehr, Marla 1937- *WhoMW 92, WhoRel 92*
Loehr, Raymond Charles 1931- *AmMWSc 92*
Loehr, Thomas E 1949- *WhoAmP 91*
Loehr, Thomas Michael 1939- *AmMWSc 92*
Loehrke, Richard Irwin 1935- *AmMWSc 92*
Loehwing, Rudi Charles 1957- *WhoWest 92*
Loeillet, Jean-Baptiste 1680-1730 *NewAmDM*
Loeillet, Jean-Baptiste 1688-1720? *NewAmDM*
Loeks, Barrie Lawson 1953- *WhoEnt 92*
Loeliger, David A 1939- *AmMWSc 92*
Loen, Douglas Todd 1953- *WhoMW 92*
Loengard, John 1934- *ConAu 133*
Loening, Kurt L 1924- *AmMWSc 92*
Loening, Kurt Leopold 1924- *WhoMW 92*
Loening, Peter Bernd 1957- *WhoFI 92*
Loenning, Per 1928- *IntWW 91*
Loeper, F Joseph 1944- *WhoAmP 91*
Loeper, John J. 1929- *WrDr 92*
Loeper, Wilhelm 1883-1935 *EncTR 91 [port]*
Loeppert, Richard Henry 1914- *AmMWSc 92*
Loeppert, Richard Henry, Jr 1944- *AmMWSc 92*
Loeppky, Richard N 1937- *AmMWSc 92*
Loera, George *WhoHisp 92*
Loertscher, Thomas F 1944- *WhoAmP 91*
Loerzer, Bruno 1891-1960 *EncTR 91 [port]*
Loesch, David Wayne 1961- *WhoFI 92*
Loesch, Harold Carl 1926- *AmMWSc 92*
Loesch, Jacob *DcNCBi 4*
Loesch, Jacob 1722-1782 *DcNCBi 4*
Loesch, Joseph G 1930- *AmMWSc 92*
Loesch, Judith Ann 1946- *WhoMW 92*
Loesch, Katharine Taylor 1922- *WhoEnt 92, WhoMW 92*
Loesch, Robert Kendrick 1941- *WhoRel 92*
Loesch-Fries, Loretta Sue 1947- *AmMWSc 92*
Loesche, Walter J 1935- *AmMWSc 92*
Loescher, Wayne Harold 1942- *AmMWSc 92*
Loeser, Eugene William 1926- *AmMWSc 92*
Loeser, Frederic Gregg 1940- *WhoMW 92*
Loeser, John David 1935- *AmMWSc 92*
Loeser, Katinka *DrAPF 91*

**Loeser**, Katinka 1913-1991 ConAu 133, NewYTBS 91 [port]
**Loeslie**, Donavon Charles 1938- WhoAmP 91
**Loesser**, Arthur 1894-1969 NewAmDM
**Loesser**, Frank 1910-1969 FacFETw, NewAmDM
**Loessin**, Edgar Ray 1928- WhoEnt 92
**Loether**, Herman John 1930- WrDr 92
**Loetterle**, Gerald John 1906- AmMWSc 92
**Loev**, Bernard 1928- AmMWSc 92
**Loevendie**, Theo 1930- ConCom 92
**Loevi**, Francis Joseph, Jr. 1945- WhoFI 92
**Loevinger**, Lee LesBEnT 92
**Loevinger**, Lee 1913- WhoAmL 92, WhoAmP 91, WhoFI 92
**Loew**, Alan David 1937- WhoFI 92
**Loew**, David N. 1949- WhoWest 92
**Loew**, Ellis Roger 1947- AmMWSc 92
**Loew**, Franklin Martin 1939- AmMWSc 92
**Loew**, Gilda Harris AmMWSc 92
**Loew**, Leslie Max 1947- AmMWSc 92
**Loew**, Patricia Ann 1943- WhoFI 92, WhoMW 92
**Loew**, Ralph William 1907- WhoRel 92
**Loewe**, Carl 1796-1869 NewAmDM
**Loewe**, Frederick 1904-1988 BenetAL 91, FacFETw, NewAmDM
**Loewe**, Michael 1922- ConAu 133
**Loewe**, William Edward 1932- AmMWSc 92
**Loewen**, Erwin G 1921- AmMWSc 92
**Loewen**, Roland Phillip 1913- WhoFI 92
**Loewenberg**, Susan Albert WhoEnt 92
**Loewenfeld**, Irene Elizabeth 1921- AmMWSc 92
**Loewenguth**, Alfred 1911- NewAmDM
**Loewenson**, Ruth Brandenburger AmMWSc 92
**Loewenstein**, Alan Jonathan 1956- WhoFI 92
**Loewenstein**, Andrea Freud DrAPF 91
**Loewenstein**, Egon Israel 1912- WhoRel 92
**Loewenstein**, Ernest Victor 1931- AmMWSc 92
**Loewenstein**, Howard 1924- AmMWSc 92
**Loewenstein**, Joseph Edward 1937- AmMWSc 92
**Loewenstein**, Louis Klee 1927- WrDr 92
**Loewenstein**, Matthew Samuel 1941- AmMWSc 92
**Loewenstein**, Michael 1933- WhoMW 92
**Loewenstein**, Morrison 1915- AmMWSc 92
**Loewenstein**, Walter B 1926- AmMWSc 92
**Loewenstein**, Walter Bernard 1926- WhoWest 92
**Loewenstein**, Werner Randolph 1926- AmMWSc 92
**Loewenthal**, Lois Anne 1926- AmMWSc 92
**Loewi**, Otto 1873-1961 WhoNob 90
**Loewinger**, Kenneth Jeffery 1945- WhoAmL 92
**Loewinsohn**, Ron DrAPF 91
**Loewinsohn**, Ron 1937- IntAu&W 91, WrDr 92
**Loewinsohn**, Ronald William 1937- WhoWest 92
**Loewus**, Frank A 1919- AmMWSc 92
**Loewus**, Mary W 1923- AmMWSc 92
**Loewy**, Ariel Gideon 1925- AmMWSc 92
**Loewy**, Arthur D 1943- AmMWSc 92
**Loewy**, Benjamin Wilfred 1915- WhoEnt 92
**Loewy**, Erich Hans 1927- WhoMW 92
**Loewy**, Kathy 1948- WhoWest 92
**Loewy**, Raymond 1893-1986 DcTwDes
**Loewy**, Raymond Fernand 1893-1986 FacFETw
**Loewy**, Robert G 1926- AmMWSc 92
**Lof**, John L C 1915- AmMWSc 92
**Lofaro**, Thomas John 1948- WhoEnt 92
**Lofas**, Lars Ingvar, Jr. 1962- WhoEnt 92
**Lo Faso**, Fred Joseph 1932- WhoFI 92
**Loferski**, Joseph J 1925- AmMWSc 92
**Loff**, Betty Garland 1932- WhoRel 92, WhoWest 92
**Loffelman**, Frank Fred 1925- AmMWSc 92
**Loffredo**, Eugene Edward 1932- WhoRel 92
**Loffredo**, Vincent J WhoAmP 91
**Lofgreen**, Glen Pehr 1919- AmMWSc 92
**Lofgren**, Charles Augustin 1939- WhoWest 92
**Lofgren**, Clifford Swanson 1925- AmMWSc 92
**Lofgren**, Edward Joseph 1914- AmMWSc 92
**Lofgren**, Gary Ernest 1941- AmMWSc 92
**Lofgren**, James R 1931- AmMWSc 92
**Lofgren**, Karl Adolph 1915- AmMWSc 92
**Lofgren**, Philip Allen 1944- AmMWSc 92
**Lofink**, Vincent A WhoAmP 91
**Loflin**, Harold Clayton 1943- WhoAmP 91
**Lofquist**, George W 1930- AmMWSc 92
**Lofquist**, Marvin John 1943- AmMWSc 92
**Lofstad**, Knut 1927- IntWW 91
**Lofstrom**, Douglas Jerry 1949- WhoEnt 92
**Lofstrom**, John Gustave 1927- AmMWSc 92
**Loft**, Abram 1922- WhoEnt 92
**Loft**, John T 1932- AmMWSc 92
**Loftesness**, Scott James 1947- WhoFI 92
**Loftfield**, Robert Berner 1919- AmMWSc 92
**Lofthouse**, Geoffrey 1925- Who 92
**Lofthouse**, John Alfred 1917- Who 92
**Lofthouse**, Reginald George Alfred 1916- Who 92
**Lofthouse**, Russ Wilbert 1945- WhoWest 92
**Loftin**, Eloise DrAPF 91
**Loftin**, John Dalton 1955- WhoAmL 92
**Lofting**, Hugh 1886-1947 BenetAL 91
**Loftis**, Curtis Bryant 1952- WhoEnt 92
**Loftness**, Robert L 1922- AmMWSc 92
**Lofton**, Andrew James 1950- WhoBlA 92
**Lofton**, C.A. DrAPF 91
**Lofton**, Dorothy W. 1925- WhoBlA 92
**Lofton**, James 1956- WhoBlA 92
**Lofton**, James Shepherd 1943- WhoAmP 91
**Lofton**, James Thomas 1938- WhoRel 92
**Lofton**, Kevin Eugene 1954- WhoBlA 92
**Lofton**, Mellanese 1941- WhoBlA 92
**Lofton**, Ollie Rae 1926- WhoRel 92
**Lofton**, Thomas Milton 1929- WhoAmL 92
**Loftsgaarden**, Don Owen 1939- AmMWSc 92
**Loftsgard**, Nancy Lee C 1957- WhoAmP 91
**Loftus**, Viscount 1943- Who 92
**Loftus**, James Michael 1961- WhoEnt 92
**Loftus**, Jerome Charles 1936- WhoAmL 92
**Loftus**, Joseph P, Jr 1930- AmMWSc 92
**Loftus**, Robert A 1918- WhoAmP 91
**Loftus**, Robert Gordon 1930- WhoMW 92
**Loftus**, Thomas A 1945- WhoAmP 91
**Loftus**, Thomas Daniel 1930- WhoAmL 92, WhoFI 92, WhoWest 92
**Loftus**, William Michael 1944- WhoIns 92
**Logachev**, Nikolay Alekseyevich 1929- IntWW 91
**Logan**, Adella Hunt 1863-1915 NotBlAW 92
**Logan**, Alan 1937- AmMWSc 92
**Logan**, Alphonso 1908- WhoBlA 92
**Logan**, Alvin DeQuanta 1957- WhoWest 92
**Logan**, April Charise 1952- WhoAmL 92
**Logan**, Benjamin Henry, II 1943- WhoAmL 92, WhoBlA 92
**Logan**, Brian Anthony 1938- AmMWSc 92
**Logan**, Brian Matthew 1947- WhoFI 92
**Logan**, Carolyn Alice 1949- WhoBlA 92
**Logan**, Carolyn Elizabeth 1943- WhoFI 92
**Logan**, Charles Donald 1924- AmMWSc 92
**Logan**, Charles Ira 1942- WhoWest 92
**Logan**, Cheryl Ann 1945- AmMWSc 92
**Logan**, Cornelius Ambrosius 1806-1853 BenetAL 91
**Logan**, Cynthia Weeks 1950- WhoRel 92
**Logan**, David 1956- WhoBlA 92
**Logan**, David Alexander 1952- AmMWSc 92
**Logan**, David Brian Carleton 1943- Who 92
**Logan**, David Mackenzie 1937- AmMWSc 92
**Logan**, David Samuel 1918- WhoFI 92
**Logan**, David Walker 1948- WhoWest 92
**Logan**, Dayton Norris 1927- WhoRel 92
**Logan**, Donald 1917- Who 92
**Logan**, Douglas Who 92
**Logan**, Douglas George 1943- WhoEnt 92
**Logan**, Ford IntAu&W 91X, TwCWW 91, WrDr 92
**Logan**, Francis Dummer 1931- WhoAmL 92
**Logan**, Fred J, Jr 1952- WhoAmP 91
**Logan**, Frenise A. 1920- WhoBlA 92
**Logan**, George, III 1942- WhoBlA 92
**Logan**, George Bryan 1909- AmMWSc 92
**Logan**, George Washington 1815-1889 DcNCBi 4
**Logan**, H L 1896- AmMWSc 92
**Logan**, Harold James 1951- WhoBlA 92
**Logan**, Henry Vincent 1942- WhoFI 92
**Logan**, Hugh WhoAmP 91
**Logan**, Jake TwCWW 91, WrDr 92
**Logan**, James 1674-1751 BenetAL 91, BiInAmS
**Logan**, James 1725?-1780 BenetAL 91
**Logan**, James 1927- Who 92
**Logan**, James Columbus AmMWSc 92
**Logan**, James David 1940- WhoWest 92
**Logan**, James Edward 1920- AmMWSc 92
**Logan**, James K WhoAmP 91
**Logan**, James Kenneth 1929- WhoAmL 92, WhoMW 92
**Logan**, Jane Elizabeth 1921- WhoAmP 91
**Logan**, Jay WhoAmP 91
**Logan**, Jesse Alan 1944- AmMWSc 92
**Logan**, John 1923-1987 BenetAL 91
**Logan**, John Merle 1934- AmMWSc 92
**Logan**, Joseph Dandridge, III 1940- WhoAmL 92
**Logan**, Joseph Granville, Jr 1920- AmMWSc 92
**Logan**, Joseph Leroy 1922- WhoBlA 92
**Logan**, Joseph Murray 1935- WhoFI 92
**Logan**, Joseph Prescott 1921- WhoMW 92
**Logan**, Joseph Skinner 1932- AmMWSc 92
**Logan**, Joshua 1908-1988 BenetAL 91, FacFETw
**Logan**, Juan Leon 1946- WhoBlA 92
**Logan**, Kathryn Vance 1946- AmMWSc 92
**Logan**, Kenneth R. 1944- WhoAmL 92
**Logan**, Langston Duvall 1951- WhoRel 92
**Logan**, Lawrence Paul 1947- WhoAmL 92
**Logan**, Lee Robert 1932- WhoWest 92
**Logan**, Leonard Gilmore, Jr. 1937- WhoAmL 92
**Logan**, Linda Rae 1947- WhoMW 92
**Logan**, Lloyd 1932- WhoBlA 92
**Logan**, Lloyd Raymond, Jr 1921- WhoAmP 91
**Logan**, Lowell Alvin 1921- AmMWSc 92
**Logan**, Malcolm Ian 1931- IntWW 91, Who 92
**Logan**, Marjorie Behn 1924- WhoAmP 91
**Logan**, Mark IntAu&W 91X, WrDr 92
**Logan**, Mark Knowles 1959- WhoAmL 92
**Logan**, Martha Daniell 1704-1779 BiInAmS
**Logan**, Matt TwCWW 91
**Logan**, Olive 1839-1909 BenetAL 91
**Logan**, Polly E 1925- WhoAmP 91
**Logan**, R S 1918- AmMWSc 92
**Logan**, Ralph Andre 1926- AmMWSc 92
**Logan**, Raymond Douglas 1920- Who 92
**Logan**, Robert F. B. 1932- WhoWest 92
**Logan**, Robert Faid Bell 1932- Who 92
**Logan**, Robert Kalman 1939- AmMWSc 92
**Logan**, Robert M. WhoRel 92
**Logan**, Rowland Elizabeth 1923- AmMWSc 92
**Logan**, Sean D 1966- WhoAmP 91
**Logan**, Steve WhoAmP 91
**Logan**, Stewart Jay 1958- WhoRel 92
**Logan**, Ted Joe 1931- AmMWSc 92
**Logan**, Terry James 1943- AmMWSc 92
**Logan**, Thomas Muldrup 1808-1876 BiInAmS
**Logan**, Thomas W. S., Sr. 1912- WhoBlA 92
**Logan**, Thomas Wilson Stearly, Sr. 1912- WhoRel 92
**Logan**, Vincent Who 92
**Logan**, Wade Hampton, III 1944- WhoAmL 92
**Logan**, William DrAPF 91
**Logan**, William Alfred 1933- WhoWest 92
**Logan**, William Philip Dowie 1914- Who 92
**Logan**, William Stevenson 1920- WhoRel 92
**Logan**, Willie, Jr 1957- WhoAmP 91
**Logan**, Willis Hubert 1943- WhoBlA 92
**Logan-Tooson**, Linda Ann 1950- WhoBlA 92
**Logcher**, Robert Daniel 1935- AmMWSc 92
**Logeman**, David Malcolm 1955- WhoFI 92
**Logemann**, Jerilyn Ann 1942- AmMWSc 92
**LoGerfo**, John J 1918- AmMWSc 92
**Logghe**, Joan DrAPF 91
**Loggia**, Robert 1930- IntMPA 92, WhoEnt 92
**Loggins**, Donald Anthony 1951- AmMWSc 92
**Loggins**, Edward M. 1930- WhoFI 92
**Loggins**, Kenny 1947- WhoEnt 92
**Loggins**, Phillip Edwards 1921- AmMWSc 92
**Loggins**, Sarrah Young 1932- WhoAmP 91
**Logic**, Joseph Richard 1935- AmMWSc 92
**Logie**, Dennis Wayne 1940- WhoRel 92
**Login**, Robert Bernard 1942- AmMWSc 92
**Loginov**, Vadim Petrovich 1927- IntWW 91
**Loginov**, William Alex 1963- WhoAmL 92
**Logler**, Frank Joseph, Jr. 1948- WhoFI 92
**Logli**, Paul Albert 1949- WhoMW 92
**Logothetis**, Anestis 1921- ConCom 92, NewAmDM
**Logothetis**, Anestis Leonidas 1934- AmMWSc 92
**Logothetis**, Eleftherios Miltiadis AmMWSc 92
**Logothetopoulos**, J 1918- AmMWSc 92
**Lograsso**, Don 1951- WhoAmP 91
**Logsdail**, Nicholas 1945- Who 92
**Logsdon**, Charles Eldon 1921- AmMWSc 92
**Logsdon**, Donald Francis, Jr 1940- AmMWSc 92
**Logsdon**, John Mortimer, III 1937- AmMWSc 92
**Logsdon**, Samuel Wayne 1950- WhoMW 92
**Logue**, Christopher 1926- ConPo 91, IntAu&W 91, Who 92, WrDr 92
**Logue**, Frank 1924- WhoAmP 91
**Logue**, J C 1920- AmMWSc 92
**Logue**, James Nicholas 1946- AmMWSc 92
**Logue**, James Thomas 1925- WhoAmP 91
**Logue**, John 1933- IntAu&W 91
**Logue**, Marshall Woford 1942- AmMWSc 92
**Logue**, Peter Calvin 1958- WhoEnt 92
**Logue**, Richard J WhoAmP 91
**Logue-Kinder**, Joan 1943- WhoBlA 92
**Logullo**, Francis Mark 1939- AmMWSc 92
**Logunov**, Anatoly Alekseyevich 1926- IntWW 91
**Loh**, Arthur Tsung Yuan 1923- WhoFI 92
**Loh**, Edwin Din 1948- AmMWSc 92
**Loh**, Eugene C 1933- AmMWSc 92
**Loh**, Horace H 1936- AmMWSc 92
**Loh**, Philip Choo-Seng 1925- AmMWSc 92
**Loh**, Pichon P. Y. 1928- WrDr 92
**Loh**, Robert Daniel, Jr. 1951- WhoFI 92
**Loh**, Roland Ru-loong 1942- AmMWSc 92
**Lohafer**, Douglas Allen 1949- WhoFI 92, WhoWest 92
**Lohan**, Dirk 1938- WhoMW 92
**Loher**, Werner J 1929- AmMWSc 92
**Lohia**, Renagi Renagi 1945- IntWW 91
**Lohman**, Arthur G 1950- IntAu&W 91
**Lohman**, James Charles 1951- WhoAmL 92
**Lohman**, Kenneth Elmo 1897- AmMWSc 92
**Lohman**, Loretta Cecelia 1944- WhoWest 92
**Lohman**, Marion Beth Simpson Becker 1918- WhoWest 92
**Lohman**, Richard Verne 1951- WhoAmL 92
**Lohman**, Stanley William 1907- AmMWSc 92
**Lohman**, Timothy George 1940- AmMWSc 92
**Lohman**, Timothy Michael 1951- AmMWSc 92
**Lohman**, William Francis 1948- WhoFI 92
**Lohmann**, Donald Gene 1940- WhoFI 92
**Lohmann**, Jeanne DrAPF 91
**Lohmeyer**, James Arthur 1947- WhoRel 92
**Lohmuller**, Martin Nicholas 1919- WhoRel 92
**Lohmussaar**, Tonu 1935- WhoMW 92
**Lohn**, Alois Josef 1934- WhoFI 92
**Lohner**, Donald J 1939- AmMWSc 92
**Lohnes**, Robert Alan 1937- AmMWSc 92
**Lohoefener**, Mary Jo 1955- WhoAmP 91
**Lohouse**, Dennis Elmer 1953- WhoFI 92
**Lohr**, Alexander 1885-1947 EncTR 91 [port]
**Lohr**, Delmar Frederick, Jr 1934- AmMWSc 92
**Lohr**, Dennis Evan 1944- AmMWSc 92
**Lohr**, George 1931- WhoAmP 91
**Lohr**, George E. 1931- WhoAmL 92, WhoWest 92
**Lohr**, Harold Russell 1922- WhoMW 92, WhoRel 92
**Lohr**, Helmut H. W. 1931- IntWW 91
**Lohr**, John Michael 1944- AmMWSc 92
**Lohr**, Lawrence Luther, Jr 1937- AmMWSc 92
**Lohr**, Lenox Riley d1968 LesBEnT 92
**Lohr**, Vera M 1924- WhoAmP 91
**Lohr**, William James 1949- WhoIns 92
**Lohrasbi**, Jahanshah 1949- WhoFI 92, WhoWest 92
**Lohrding**, Ronald Keith 1941- AmMWSc 92
**Lohre**, John Owen 1932- WhoFI 92
**Lohrengel**, Carl Frederick, II 1939- AmMWSc 92
**Lohrer**, Richard Baker 1932- WhoFI 92
**Lohrman**, William Walter 1954- WhoFI 92
**Lohrmann**, Rolf 1930- AmMWSc 92
**Lohse**, Bernhard 1928- WhoRel 92
**Lohse**, Carleton Leslie 1936- AmMWSc 92
**Lohse**, David John 1952- AmMWSc 92
**Lohse**, Eduard 1924- IntWW 91
**Lohse**, Edward E. WhoRel 92
**Lohse**, Heinrich 1896-1964 BiDExR
**Lohse**, Hinrich 1896-1964 EncTR 91 [port]
**Lohtia**, Rajinder Paul 1938- AmMWSc 92
**Lohuis**, Delmont John 1914- AmMWSc 92
**Loichinger**, Daniel Fred 1957- WhoMW 92
**Loiello**, John Peter 1943- WhoAmP 91
**Loigman**, Harold 1930- AmMWSc 92
**Loire**, Norman Paul 1927- AmMWSc 92
**Lois**, George 1931- DcTwDes
**Loiselle**, Gilles 1929- Who 92
**Loizzi**, Robert Francis 1935- AmMWSc 92
**Loizzo**, Gary Alexander 1945- WhoEnt 92
**Loja**, Aleksandrs 1936- WhoAmP 91
**Lo-Johansson**, Ivar 1901-1990 AnObit 1990

**Lok,** Roger 1943- *AmMWSc 92*
**Lok,** Silmond Ray 1948- *WhoMW 92*
**Lokay,** Joseph Donald 1929- *AmMWSc 92*
**Loke,** Kit Choy 1945- *WhoAmL 92*
**Lokeman,** Joseph R. 1935- *WhoBlA 92*
**Loken,** Halvar Young 1944- *AmMWSc 92*
**Loken,** James B *WhoAmP 91*
**Loken,** Johan Christen 1944- *IntWW 91*
**Loken,** Keith I 1929- *AmMWSc 92*
**Loken,** Merle Kenneth 1924- *AmMWSc 92*
**Loken,** Stewart Christian 1943- *AmMWSc 92*
**Lokensgard,** Jerrold Paul 1940- *AmMWSc 92*
**Loker,** John 1938- *TwCPaSc*
**Lokhorst,** Jonathan Robert 1962- *WhoFI 92*
**Lokken,** Donald Arthur 1937- *AmMWSc 92*
**Lokken,** James Arnold 1933- *WhoRel 92*
**Lokken,** Lawrence 1939- *WhoAmL 92*
**Lokken,** Leslie Ferris 1926- *WhoAmP 91*
**Lokken,** Stanley Jerome 1931- *AmMWSc 92*
**Lokoloko,** Tore 1930- *IntWW 91, Who 92*
**Loll,** Robert Arnold 1958- *WhoAmL 92*
**Lolla,** John Joseph 1953- *WhoRel 92*
**Lollar,** Cecil Edward 1938- *WhoAmP 91*
**Lollar,** Robert Miller 1915- *AmMWSc 92, WhoFI 92, WhoMW 92*
**Lolley,** Richard Newton 1933- *AmMWSc 92*
**Lolley,** William Randall 1931- *WhoRel 92*
**Lolli,** Andrew Ralph 1917- *WhoFI 92*
**Lolli,** Ettore 1908- *IntWW 91*
**Lollobrigida,** Gina 1927- *IntMPA 92, IntWW 91*
**Loly,** Peter Douglas 1941- *AmMWSc 92*
**Lom,** Herbert 1917- *IntMPA 92, IntWW 91*
**Lomakin,** Viktor Pavlovich 1926- *IntWW 91*
**Lomako,** Petr Fadeevich 1904- *SovUnBD*
**Loman,** James Mark 1954- *AmMWSc 92*
**Loman,** M Laverne 1928- *AmMWSc 92*
**Lomanitz,** Ross 1921- *AmMWSc 92*
**Lomas,** Alfred 1928- *Who 92*
**Lomas,** Charles Gardner *AmMWSc 92*
**Lomas,** Peter 1923- *WrDr 92*
**Lomas,** Ronald Leroy 1942- *WhoBlA 92*
**LoMascolo,** Angelo Romualdo 1946- *WhoAmL 92*
**Lomask,** Milton 1909-1991 *ConAu 135*
**Lomason,** William Keithledge 1910- *WhoFI 92*
**Lomax,** Alan 1915- *BenetAL 91, IntWW 91, NewAmDM*
**Lomax,** Bliss *TwCWW 91*
**Lomax,** Dervey A. *WhoBlA 92*
**Lomax,** Eddie 1923- *AmMWSc 92*
**Lomax,** Frank, III 1937- *WhoBlA 92*
**Lomax,** Harvard 1922- *AmMWSc 92*
**Lomax,** Janis Rachel 1945- *Who 92*
**Lomax,** Joan Evelyn 1932- *WhoMW 92*
**Lomax,** John, III 1944- *WhoEnt 92*
**Lomax,** John A. 1867-1948 *BenetAL 91*
**Lomax,** John H. 1924- *WhoFI 92*
**Lomax,** Margaret Irene 1938- *AmMWSc 92*
**Lomax,** Marion 1953- *ConAu 133*
**Lomax,** Michael Wilkins *WhoBlA 92*
**Lomax,** Pearl Cleage 1948- *WhoBlA 92*
**Lomax,** Peter 1928- *AmMWSc 92*
**Lomax,** Rachel *Who 92*
**Lomax,** Ronald J 1934- *AmMWSc 92*
**Lomax,** Terri Lynn 1953- *WhoWest 92*
**Lomax,** Walter P. 1932- *WhoBlA 92*
**Lomb,** Henry 1828-1908 *BiInAmS*
**Lombana,** Hector Jesus 1952- *WhoAmL 92*
**Lombard,** Alain 1940- *NewAmDM*
**Lombard,** Alan Linn 1961- *WhoEnt 92*
**Lombard,** Arthur J. 1941- *WhoAmL 92*
**Lombard,** Carole 1908-1942 *FacFETw*
**Lombard,** Charles F. *Who 92*
**Lombard,** David Bishop 1930- *AmMWSc 92*
**Lombard,** David Norman 1949- *WhoAmL 92*
**Lombard,** Guy Davenport 1872?-1907 *BiInAmS*
**Lombard,** Jacques 1923- *IntWW 91*
**Lombard,** James M 1938- *WhoAmP 91*
**Lombard,** John Cutler 1918- *WhoWest 92*
**Lombard,** John James, Jr. 1934- *WhoAmL 92*
**Lombard,** Julian H 1947- *AmMWSc 92*
**Lombard,** Louise Scherger 1921- *AmMWSc 92*
**Lombard,** Porter Bronson 1930- *AmMWSc 92*
**Lombard,** Richard Eric 1943- *AmMWSc 92*
**Lombard,** Richard Spencer 1928- *WhoAmL 92*
**Lombardi,** Curtis Jay 1952- *WhoAmL 92*
**Lombardi,** David Ennis, Jr. 1940- *WhoAmL 92*
**Lombardi,** Eugene Patsy 1923- *WhoEnt 92*
**Lombardi,** Gabriel Gustavo 1954- *AmMWSc 92*
**Lombardi,** John Rocco 1941- *AmMWSc 92*
**Lombardi,** Joseph David 1948- *WhoFI 92*
**Lombardi,** Leon J *WhoAmP 91*
**Lombardi,** Louis, Jr 1946- *WhoIns 92*
**Lombardi,** Max H 1932- *AmMWSc 92*
**Lombardi,** Patrick Joseph 1948- *WhoWest 92*
**Lombardi,** Paul Schoenfeld 1940- *AmMWSc 92*
**Lombardi,** Salvatore Nick 1943- *WhoMW 92*
**Lombardi,** Tarky James, Jr 1929- *WhoAmP 91*
**Lombardi,** Vince 1913-1970 *FacFETw*
**Lombardini,** John Barry 1941- *AmMWSc 92*
**Lombardino,** Joseph George 1933- *AmMWSc 92*
**Lombardo,** Anthony 1939- *AmMWSc 92*
**Lombardo,** Bonnie Jane 1941- *WhoEnt 92*
**Lombardo,** David Albert 1947- *WhoMW 92*
**Lombardo,** Diana 1964- *WhoEnt 92*
**Lombardo,** Eugene Vincent 1938- *WhoFI 92*
**Lombardo,** Gaetano 1940- *WhoFI 92, WhoMW 92*
**Lombardo,** Gian S. *DrAPF 91*
**Lombardo,** Goffredo 1920- *IntMPA 92*
**Lombardo,** Guy 1902-1977 *FacFETw, NewAmDM*
**Lombardo,** John N 1942- *WhoIns 92*
**Lombardo,** Michael John 1927- *WhoAmL 92*
**Lombardo,** Nicholas John 1953- *WhoWest 92*
**Lombardo,** Philip Joseph 1935- *WhoEnt 92*
**Lombardo,** R J 1921- *AmMWSc 92*
**Lombardo,** Robert James 1941- *WhoEnt 92*
**Lombardo,** Victor Anthony 1911- *WhoEnt 92*
**Lombardo Trostorff,** Danielle Maria 1951- *WhoAmL 92*
**Lombe,** Edward Christopher E. *Who 92*
**Lombos,** Bela Anthony 1931- *AmMWSc 92*
**Lomedico,** Peter T *AmMWSc 92*
**Lomeli,** Alfred Paul 1925- *WhoHisp 92*
**Lomeli,** Francisco A. 1947- *WhoHisp 92*
**Lomeli,** Jesse 1943- *WhoWest 92*
**Lomeli,** Marta 1952- *WhoWest 92*
**Lomeli,** Refugio 1941- *WhoHisp 92, WhoWest 92*
**Lomen,** David Orlando 1937- *AmMWSc 92*
**Lomen,** Mary Elizabeth 1919- *WhoAmP 91*
**Lomer,** Dennis Roy 1923- *Who 92*
**Lomer,** Geoffrey John 1932- *Who 92*
**Lomer,** William Michael 1926- *Who 92*
**Lomeyko,** Vladimir Borisovich 1929- *IntWW 91*
**Lominadze,** Vissarion Vissarionovich 1897-1935 *SovUnBD*
**Lomita,** Solomon 1937- *IntMPA 92*
**Lommel,** J M 1932- *AmMWSc 92*
**Lomnicki,** John Joseph 1948- *WhoMW 92*
**Lomnicki,** Tadeusz 1927- *IntWW 91*
**Lomnitz,** Cinna 1925- *AmMWSc 92*
**Lomon,** Earle Leonard 1930- *AmMWSc 92*
**Lomon,** Ruth Margaret 1930- *WhoEnt 92*
**Lomonaco,** Alfonso d1932 *DcAmImH*
**Lomonaco,** Samuel James, Jr 1939- *AmMWSc 92*
**Lomonosoff,** James Marc 1951- *WhoFI 92*
**Lomonosov,** Mikhail Vasilyevich 1711-1765 *BlkwCEP*
**Lomonosov,** Vladimir Grigoryevich 1928- *IntWW 91*
**Lomont,** John S 1924- *AmMWSc 92*
**Lomotey,** Kofi 1950- *WhoBlA 92*
**Lomov,** Georgiy Ippolitovich 1888-1938 *SovUnBD*
**Lomperis,** Timothy John 1947- *IntAu&W 91*
**Lomrantz,** Merle Robin 1954- *WhoRel 92*
**Lomurro,** Donald Michael 1950- *WhoAmL 92*
**Lon Nol** 1913- *FacFETw*
**Lona Reyes,** Arturo 1925- *WhoRel 92*
**Lonabaugh,** Ellsworth Eugene 1923- *WhoAmL 92*
**Lonadier,** Frank Dalton 1932- *AmMWSc 92*
**Lonard,** Robert 1942- *AmMWSc 92*
**Lonberg-Holm,** Knud Karl 1931- *AmMWSc 92*
**Loncar,** Budimir *IntWW 91*
**Loncrini,** Donald Francis 1930- *AmMWSc 92*
**Lond,** Harley Weldon 1946- *WhoEnt 92*
**Londen,** Doris May 1930- *WhoAmP 91*
**Londen,** Jack Winston 1929- *WhoAmP 91*
**Londergan,** John Timothy 1943- *AmMWSc 92, WhoMW 92*
**Londesborough,** Baron 1959- *Who 92*
**London,** Archdeacon of *Who 92*
**London,** Bishop of 1940- *Who 92*
**London,** A L 1913- *AmMWSc 92*
**London,** Arthur Hill, Jr. 1903-1976 *DcNCBi 4*
**London,** Arthur Hill, Sr. 1874-1969 *DcNCBi 4*
**London,** Artur 1915-1986 *FacFETw*
**London,** Barry *IntMPA 92*
**London,** Barry Joseph 1946- *WhoAmL 92*
**London,** Charles Stuart 1946- *WhoEnt 92*
**London,** Clement B. G. 1928- *WhoBlA 92*
**London,** David 1953- *AmMWSc 92*
**London,** Eddie 1934- *WhoBlA 92*
**London,** Edward Charles 1944- *WhoBlA 92*
**London,** Edythe D 1948- *AmMWSc 92*
**London,** Frank Marsden 1876-1945 *DcNCBi 4*
**London,** Fritz Wolfgang 1900-1954 *DcNCBi 4*
**London,** George 1919-1985 *NewAmDM*
**London,** George 1920-1985 *FacFETw*
**London,** Gilbert J 1931- *AmMWSc 92*
**London,** Henry Adolphus 1808-1882 *DcNCBi 4*
**London,** Henry Armand 1846-1918 *DcNCBi 4*
**London,** Henry Mauger 1879-1939 *DcNCBi 4*
**London,** Herbert I 1939- *IntAu&W 91, WrDr 92*
**London,** Ira D. 1931- *WhoAmL 92*
**London,** Irving Myer 1918- *AmMWSc 92, IntWW 91*
**London,** J Kay *ScFEYrs*
**London,** Jack 1876-1916 *BenetAL 91, FacFETw, RComAH, ScFEYrs, TwCSFW 91, TwCWW 91*
**London,** Jack & Goddard, Charles William *ScFEYrs*
**London,** Jack E 1905- *BlkOlyM*
**London,** James Albert 1956- *WhoBlA 92*
**London,** James Harry 1949- *WhoAmL 92*
**London,** Jerry 1937- *IntMPA 92*
**London,** John 1747-1816 *DcNCBi 4*
**London,** Jonathan *DrAPF 91*
**London,** Julie 1926- *IntMPA 92*
**London,** Julius 1917- *AmMWSc 92*
**London,** Laura *IntAu&W 91, -91X, WrDr 92*
**London,** Mark David 1947- *AmMWSc 92*
**London,** Mark S. 1949- *WhoAmL 92*
**London,** Martin 1934- *WhoAmL 92*
**London,** Mel 1923- *WhoEnt 92*
**London,** Meyer 1871-1926 *AmPolLe, DcAmImH*
**London,** Milton H. 1916- *IntMPA 92*
**London,** Morris *AmMWSc 92*
**London,** Ray William 1943- *AmMWSc 92, WhoFI 92, WhoWest 92*
**London,** Robert Alan 1941- *WhoFI 92, WhoWest 92*
**London,** Robert Elliot 1946- *AmMWSc 92*
**London,** Roberta Levy *WhoBlA 92*
**London,** Roy Laird 1943- *WhoEnt 92*
**London,** Sheri Faith 1955- *WhoFI 92*
**London,** Terry 1940- *WhoAmP 91*
**London,** William Lord 1838-1916 *DcNCBi 4*
**London,** William Thomas 1932- *AmMWSc 92*
**London Central,** Bishop In *Who 92*
**London East,** Bishop In *Who 92*
**London North,** Bishop In *Who 92*
**London West,** Bishop In *Who 92*
**Londonderry,** Marchioness of *Who 92*
**Londonderry,** Marquess of 1937- *Who 92*
**Londono Paredes,** Julio 1938- *IntWW 91*
**Londre,** Felicia Mae Hardison 1941- *WhoEnt 92*
**Londrigan,** Paul James 1942- *WhoMW 92*
**Lone,** John 1952- *IntMPA 92*
**Lone,** M Aslam 1937- *AmMWSc 92*
**Lonegan,** Thomas Lee 1932- *WhoFI 92*
**Loneker,** Ronald Anthony, Jr. 1966- *WhoEnt 92*
**Loneman,** Richard Eugene 1953- *WhoMW 92*
**Lonergan,** Dennis Arthur 1949- *AmMWSc 92*
**Lonergan,** Joyce 1934- *WhoAmP 91*
**Lonergan,** Kevin 1954- *WhoAmL 92*
**Lonergan,** Thomas A *AmMWSc 92*
**Lonergan,** Thomas Francis, III 1941- *WhoWest 92*
**Lonergan,** Wallace Gunn 1928- *WhoWest 92*
**Loney,** Carolyn Patricia 1944- *WhoBlA 92*
**Loney,** Glenn Meredith 1928- *WhoEnt 92, WrDr 92*
**Loney,** Joanne Marie 1950- *WhoAmP 91*
**Loney,** Joy C 1938- *WhoAmP 91*
**Loney,** Martin 1944- *WrDr 92*
**Loney,** Paul Martin 1954- *WhoMW 92*
**Loney,** Robert Ahlberg 1922- *AmMWSc 92*
**Long** *Who 92*
**Long Meg** *EncAmaz 91*
**Long,** Viscount 1929- *Who 92*
**Long,** A A 1937- *IntAu&W 91, WrDr 92*
**Long,** Alan Jack 1944- *AmMWSc 92*
**Long,** Alan K 1950- *AmMWSc 92*
**Long,** Alexander B 1943- *AmMWSc 92*
**Long,** Alexis Boris 1944- *AmMWSc 92*
**Long,** Alfred B. 1909- *WhoFI 92*
**Long,** Alton Los, Jr 1932- *AmMWSc 92*
**Long,** Amelia Reynolds 1904-1978 *ScFEYrs*
**Long,** Andre Edwin 1957- *WhoAmL 92*
**Long,** Andrew Fleming, Jr 1938- *AmMWSc 92*
**Long,** Andrew Theodore 1866-1946 *DcNCBi 4*
**Long,** Andu Trisa 1958- *WhoBlA 92*
**Long,** Athelstan Charles Ethelwulf 1919- *Who 92*
**Long,** Austin 1936- *AmMWSc 92*
**Long,** Austin Richard 1949- *WhoWest 92*
**Long,** Barbara Collier 1943- *WhoBlA 92*
**Long,** Benjamin Franklin 1852-1925 *DcNCBi 4*
**Long,** Beth 1948- *WhoAmP 91*
**Long,** Billy Wayne 1948- *AmMWSc 92*
**Long,** Bobby *WhoAmP 91*
**Long,** Bruce J 1951- *WhoAmP 91*
**Long,** Burke O'Connor *WhoRel 92*
**Long,** Calvin H 1927- *AmMWSc 92*
**Long,** Calvin Lee 1928- *AmMWSc 92*
**Long,** Calvin Thomas 1927- *AmMWSc 92*
**Long,** Carl F 1928- *AmMWSc 92*
**Long,** Carole Ann 1944- *AmMWSc 92*
**Long,** Cathy 1924- *WhoAmP 91*
**Long,** Cedric William 1937- *AmMWSc 92*
**Long,** Charles Alan 1936- *AmMWSc 92, WhoMW 92*
**Long,** Charles Anthony 1945- *AmMWSc 92*
**Long,** Charles E. 1940- *WhoAmL 92*
**Long,** Charles H. 1926- *WhoBlA 92*
**Long,** Charles Henry, Jr. 1923- *WhoRel 92*
**Long,** Charles Houston 1926- *WhoRel 92*
**Long,** Charles Joseph 1935- *AmMWSc 92*
**Long,** Charles Thomas 1942- *WhoAmL 92*
**Long,** Charlie Renn 1936- *WhoAmP 91*
**Long,** Christopher Francis 1955- *WhoAmL 92*
**Long,** Christopher William 1938- *Who 92*
**Long,** Clarence Dickinson, III 1943- *WhoAmL 92*
**Long,** Clarence Dickinson, Jr *WhoAmP 91*
**Long,** Claudine Fern 1938- *AmMWSc 92*
**Long,** Clifford A 1931- *AmMWSc 92*
**Long,** Connie Sue 1954- *WhoRel 92*
**Long,** Crawford Williamson 1815-1878 *BiInAmS*
**Long,** Cynthia 1956- *IntAu&W 91*
**Long,** Dale Donald 1935- *AmMWSc 92*
**Long,** Daniel Albright 1844-1933 *DcNCBi 4*
**Long,** Daniel R 1938- *AmMWSc 92*
**Long,** Daniel Ray 1953- *WhoMW 92*
**Long,** Darrel Graham Francis 1947- *AmMWSc 92*
**Long,** Daryl Clyde 1939- *AmMWSc 92*
**Long,** David *DrAPF 91*
**Long,** David G *AmMWSc 92*
**Long,** David Gordon 1952- *WhoFI 92*
**Long,** David Michael 1929- *AmMWSc 92*
**Long,** Deborah Joyce 1953- *WhoAmL 92*
**Long,** Devona Anderson 1939- *WhoAmP 91*
**Long,** Doc *DrAPF 91*
**Long,** Donald Gregory 1937- *WhoFI 92*
**Long,** Donald Robert 1949- *WhoMW 92*
**Long,** Donlin Martin 1934- *AmMWSc 92*
**Long,** Doranne Louise 1959- *WhoWest 92*
**Long,** Doughtry *DrAPF 91*
**Long,** Douglas 1925-1990 *AnObit 1990*
**Long,** Douglas Charles 1950- *WhoMW 92*
**Long,** Earl Ellsworth 1919- *AmMWSc 92*
**Long,** Ed 1934- *WhoAmP 91*
**Long,** Edward, Jr. 1946- *WhoAmL 92*
**Long,** Edward B 1927- *AmMWSc 92*
**Long,** Edward Leroy, Jr. 1924- *WrDr 92*
**Long,** Edward R 1942- *AmMWSc 92*
**Long,** Edward Richardson, Jr 1941- *AmMWSc 92*
**Long,** Ellenmae Quan 1927- *WhoEnt 92*
**Long,** Elliot 1928- *TwCWW 91, WrDr 92*
**Long,** Emmett Thaddeus 1923- *WhoWest 92*
**Long,** Eric Charles 1962- *WhoWest 92*
**Long,** Eugene Thomas 1935- *WrDr 92*
**Long,** F M 1929- *AmMWSc 92*
**Long,** Frank Belknap 1903- *IntAu&W 91, ScFEYrs, TwCSFW 91*
**Long,** Franklin A 1910- *AmMWSc 92*
**Long,** G Thomas 1945- *WhoAmP 91*
**Long,** Garda Theresa 1925- *WhoRel 92*
**Long,** Gary John 1941- *AmMWSc 92*
**Long,** Gary Vincent 1939- *WhoMW 92*
**Long,** Gene Alan 1955- *WhoFI 92*
**Long,** George 1922- *AmMWSc 92*

**Long,** George Gilbert 1929- *AmMWSc 92*
**Long,** George Louis 1943- *AmMWSc 92*
**Long,** Gerald 1923- *IntAu&W 91, IntWW 91, Who 92*
**Long,** Grant Andrew 1966- *WhoBlA 92*
**Long,** Gregory Alan 1948- *WhoAmL 92*
**Long,** H M 1924- *AmMWSc 92*
**Long,** H. Owen 1921- *WhoFI 92*
**Long,** Helen Halter 1906- *IntAu&W 91*
**Long,** Henry Andrew 1910- *WhoBlA 92*
**Long,** Henry Arlington 1937- *WhoFI 92*
**Long,** Hilda Sheets 1903- *WhoAmP 91*
**Long,** Homer J. 1921- *WhoMW 92*
**Long,** Howard Charles 1918- *AmMWSc 92*
**Long,** Howard M. 1960- *WhoBlA 92*
**Long,** Hubert Arthur 1912- *Who 92*
**Long,** Huey 1893-1935 *BenetAL 91, RComAH*
**Long,** Huey Pierce 1893-1935 *AmPolLe [port], BiDExR, FacFETw [port]*
**Long,** Irene *WhoBlA 92*
**Long,** J C 1959- *WhoAmP 91*
**Long,** Jack A *WhoAmP 91*
**Long,** Jacob Alson 1846-1923 *DcNCBi 4*
**Long,** Jacob Elmer 1880-1955 *DcNCBi 4*
**Long,** James, Jr. 1931- *WhoBlA 92*
**Long,** James Alexander 1926- *WhoBlA 92*
**Long,** James Alvin 1917- *AmMWSc 92*
**Long,** James Delbert 1939- *AmMWSc 92*
**Long,** James DeWitt 1948- *WhoRel 92*
**Long,** James Duncan 1925- *AmMWSc 92*
**Long,** James E 1938- *WhoAmP 91*
**Long,** James Eugene *WhoAmP 91*
**Long,** James Frantz 1931- *AmMWSc 92*
**Long,** James Harvey, Jr. 1944- *WhoWest 92*
**Long,** James Jay 1959- *WhoAmL 92*
**Long,** James L. 1937- *WhoBlA 92*
**Long,** James S. 1936- *WhoBlA 92*
**Long,** James Stanley 1952- *WhoRel 92*
**Long,** James William 1943- *AmMWSc 92*
**Long,** Jan M 1952- *WhoAmP 91*
**Long,** Jan Michael 1952- *WhoMW 92*
**Long,** Jay Edwards 1938- *WhoRel 92*
**Long,** Jefferson Marion, Jr 1927- *WhoAmP 91*
**Long,** Jerome R 1935- *AmMWSc 92*
**Long,** Jill 1952- *AlmAP 92 [port], WhoAmP 91, WhoMW 92*
**Long,** Jim T 1923- *AmMWSc 92*
**Long,** Jimmy Dale 1931- *WhoAmP 91*
**Long,** Joan Dorothy *IntWW 91*
**Long,** John 1946- *WhoAmP 91*
**Long,** John, Jr. 1785-1857 *DcNCBi 4*
**Long,** John A 1927- *AmMWSc 92*
**Long,** John Arthur 1934- *AmMWSc 92*
**Long,** John Bennie 1923- *WhoBlA 92*
**Long,** John D, III 1930- *WhoAmP 91*
**Long,** John Davis 1838-1915 *AmPolLe*
**Long,** John Douglas 1920- *WhoIns 92*
**Long,** John Edward 1941- *WhoBlA 92*
**Long,** John Frederick 1924- *AmMWSc 92*
**Long,** John Harper 1856-1918 *BiInAmS*
**Long,** John Kelley 1921- *AmMWSc 92*
**Long,** John Luther 1861-1927 *BenetAL 91*
**Long,** John Michael 1953- *WhoAmP 91*
**Long,** John Paul 1926- *AmMWSc 92*
**Long,** John Reed 1922- *AmMWSc 92*
**Long,** John Richard 1931- *Who 92*
**Long,** John Sanderson 1913- *Who 92*
**Long,** John Vernon 1946- *WhoRel 92*
**Long,** John Vincent 1910- *AmMWSc 92*
**Long,** John Wesley 1859-1926 *DcNCBi 4*
**Long,** Joseph J, Sr 1921- *WhoAmP 91*
**Long,** Joseph Pote 1913- *AmMWSc 92*
**Long,** Josh Getzen 1923- *WhoRel 92*
**Long,** Juanita Outlaw *WhoBlA 92*
**Long,** Keith Royce 1922- *AmMWSc 92*
**Long,** Kenneth Maynard 1932- *AmMWSc 92*
**Long,** Kenneth Robert 1940- *WhoAmL 92*
**Long,** Kevin Jay 1961- *WhoMW 92*
**Long,** Kristina Marie 1957- *WhoMW 92*
**Long,** Larry L 1955- *AmMWSc 92*
**Long,** Lawrence William 1942- *AmMWSc 92*
**Long,** Leland Timothy 1940- *AmMWSc 92*
**Long,** Lem, Jr. *WhoRel 92*
**Long,** Leon Eugene 1933- *AmMWSc 92*
**Long,** Lewis, Jr 1936- *WhoAmP 91*
**Long,** Linda Ann 1952- *WhoAmL 92*
**Long,** Linda D 1954- *WhoAmP 91*
**Long,** Linda Kay Usrey 1944- *WhoWest 92*
**Long,** Lorna Erickson 1944- *WhoFI 92*
**Long,** Lyda Belknap *TwCSFW 91*
**Long,** Lydia D 1953- *WhoAmP 91*
**Long,** Lyle Norman 1954- *AmMWSc 92*
**Long,** Marceau 1926- *IntWW 91*
**Long,** Marguerite 1874-1966 *NewAmDM*
**Long,** Marjorie Jean 1950- *WhoAmL 92*
**Long,** Marshall 1936- *WhoAmP 91*
**Long,** Maurice W 1925- *AmMWSc 92*
**Long,** Maxine Master 1943- *WhoAmL 92*
**Long,** Michael Edgar 1946- *AmMWSc 92*
**Long,** Michael Harold 1951- *WhoAmL 92*
**Long,** Michael Scott 1953- *WhoAmP 91*
**Long,** Michael Thomas 1942- *WhoAmP 91*
**Long,** Nate 1930- *WhoBlA 92, WhoWest 92*
**Long,** Neal Basil 1936- *WhoFI 92*
**Long,** Newell Hillis 1905- *WhoEnt 92*
**Long,** Nicholas 1726?-1797 *DcNCBi 4*
**Long,** Nicholas Kinsey 1939- *WhoMW 92*
**Long,** Norris Franklin, Jr. 1958- *WhoRel 92*
**Long,** Olivier 1915- *IntWW 91, Who 92*
**Long,** Ophelia 1940- *WhoBlA 92*
**Long,** Pamela Marjorie 1930- *Who 92*
**Long,** Paul Eastwood, Jr 1942- *AmMWSc 92*
**Long,** Perrin H., Jr. *WhoMW 92*
**Long,** Philip Lowell, Sr. 1921- *WhoRel 92*
**Long,** R B 1923- *AmMWSc 92*
**Long,** R. Gregory 1960- *WhoMW 92*
**Long,** Randall Craig 1958- *WhoWest 92*
**Long,** Randy James 1956- *WhoAmL 92*
**Long,** Raymond Bruce 1946- *WhoAmP 91*
**Long,** Raymond Carl 1939- *AmMWSc 92*
**Long,** Richard 1945- *IntWW 91, TwCPaSc, WorArt 1980*
**Long,** Richard A. 1927- *WhoBlA 92*
**Long,** Richard Alan 1949- *WhoFI 92*
**Long,** Richard Allan 1940- *WhoWest 92*
**Long,** Richard Bradbury 1934- *WhoEnt 92*
**Long,** Richard Paul 1934- *AmMWSc 92*
**Long,** Robert *DrAPF 91*
**Long,** Robert A. 1931- *IntMPA 92*
**Long,** Robert Albert, Jr. 1934- *WhoFI 92*
**Long,** Robert Allen 1941- *AmMWSc 92*
**Long,** Robert Byron 1923- *AmMWSc 92*
**Long,** Robert C Biggy 1919- *WhoAmP 91*
**Long,** Robert Douglas *WhoFI 92*
**Long,** Robert Emmet *DrAPF 91*
**Long,** Robert Emmet 1934- *IntAu&W 91*
**Long,** Robert Hill *DrAPF 91*
**Long,** Robert Leroy 1936- *AmMWSc 92*
**Long,** Robert Livingston 1937- *WhoFI 92*
**Long,** Robert Merrill 1938- *WhoFI 92, WhoWest 92*
**Long,** Robert Nahum 1937- *WhoMW 92*
**Long,** Robert Radcliffe 1919- *AmMWSc 92*
**Long,** Ronald Alex 1948- *WhoFI 92*
**Long,** Ronald K 1932- *AmMWSc 92*
**Long,** Rufus Alexander 1923- *WhoFI 92*
**Long,** Russell B. 1918- *IntWW 91, WhoAmP 91*
**Long,** Russell Harrison 1956- *WhoWest 92*
**Long,** Sally Yates 1941- *AmMWSc 92*
**Long,** Sarah Ann 1943- *WhoMW 92*
**Long,** Sharon Rugel 1951- *AmMWSc 92, WhoWest 92*
**Long,** Shelley *WhoEnt 92*
**Long,** Shelley 1949- *IntMPA 92*
**Long,** Shirley D *IntAu&W 91*
**Long,** Speedy O 1928- *WhoAmP 91*
**Long,** Steffan 1929- *WhoBlA 92*
**Long,** Stephen Carrel Mike 1951- *WhoAmL 92*
**Long,** Stephen Harriman 1784-1864 *BiInAmS*
**Long,** Stephen Ingalls 1946- *WhoWest 92*
**Long,** Stephen Michael 1954- *WhoAmL 92*
**Long,** Sterling K 1927- *AmMWSc 92*
**Long,** Steven Alan 1959- *WhoRel 92*
**Long,** Stuart A 1945- *AmMWSc 92*
**Long,** Sylvester Clark *DcNCBi 4*
**Long,** Terrill Jewett 1932- *AmMWSc 92*
**Long,** Thad Gladden 1938- *WhoAmL 92*
**Long,** Thomas E 1944- *WhoIns 92*
**Long,** Thomas Lawrence 1953- *WhoRel 92*
**Long,** Thomas Michael 1943- *WhoFI 92*
**Long,** Thomas Ross 1929- *AmMWSc 92*
**Long,** Thomas Williams Mason 1886-1941 *DcNCBi 4*
**Long,** Verne Everett 1925- *WhoAmP 91*
**Long,** Walter K 1919- *AmMWSc 92*
**Long,** Walter Kyle, Jr 1944- *AmMWSc 92*
**Long,** Westray Battle 1901-1972 *DcNCBi 4*
**Long,** William Ellis 1930- *AmMWSc 92*
**Long,** William H., Jr. 1947- *WhoBlA 92*
**Long,** William Henry 1928- *AmMWSc 92*
**Long,** William Joseph 1922- *Who 92*
**Long,** William L 1927- *WhoAmP 91*
**Long,** William Lee 1938- *WhoMW 92*
**Long,** William Leslie 1958- *WhoRel 92*
**Long,** William Lunsford 1890-1964 *DcNCBi 4*
**Long,** William Samuel 1839-1924 *DcNCBi 4*
**Long,** Willis Franklin 1934- *AmMWSc 92*
**Long,** Wilmer Newton, Jr 1918- *AmMWSc 92*
**Long Lance,** Buffalo Child 1890-1932 *DcNCBi 4*
**Longabarba,** Bona *EncAmaz 91*
**Longacre,** John Russell, II 1953- *WhoFI 92*
**Longacre,** Richard Dawson 1921- *WhoFI 92*
**Longacre,** Ronald Shelley 1941- *AmMWSc 92*
**Longacre,** Susan Ann Burton 1941- *AmMWSc 92*
**Longair,** Malcolm 1941- *WrDr 92*
**Longair,** Malcolm Sim 1941- *Who 92*
**Longaker,** Richard Pancoast, II 1950- *WhoAmL 92*
**Longan,** George Baker, III 1934- *WhoMW 92*
**Longanbach,** James Robert 1942- *AmMWSc 92*
**Longardner,** Craig Theodor 1955- *WhoMW 92*
**Longbaugh,** Harry *IntAu&W 91X, WrDr 92*
**Longbottom,** Charles Brooke 1930- *Who 92*
**Longbrake,** William Arthur 1943- *WhoWest 92*
**Longchampt,** Michel 1934- *WhoFI 92*
**Longcope,** Christopher 1928- *AmMWSc 92*
**Longcroft,** James George Stoddart 1929- *Who 92*
**Longden,** Gilbert 1902- *Who 92*
**Longden,** Henry Alfred 1909- *Who 92*
**Longden,** Wilson 1936- *Who 92*
**Longdon,** George *TwCSFW 91*
**Longenecker,** Bryan Michael 1942- *AmMWSc 92*
**Longenecker,** Herbert Eugene 1912- *AmMWSc 92*
**Longenecker,** John Bender 1930- *AmMWSc 92*
**Longenecker,** William Hilton 1918- *AmMWSc 92*
**Longerbeam,** Richard Lee 1943- *WhoFI 92*
**Longerich,** Henry Perry 1940- *AmMWSc 92*
**Longest,** William Douglas 1929- *AmMWSc 92*
**Longfellow,** David G 1942- *AmMWSc 92*
**Longfellow,** Henry Wadsworth 1807-1882 *BenetAL 91, RComAH*
**Longfellow,** Samuel 1819-1892 *BenetAL 91*
**Longfield,** James Edgar 1925- *AmMWSc 92*
**Longfield,** Michael David 1928- *Who 92*
**Longfield,** William Herman 1938- *WhoFI 92*
**Longford,** Countess of 1906- *IntWW 91, Who 92*
**Longford,** Earl of 1905- *IntWW 91, Who 92, WrDr 92*
**Longford,** Elizabeth *Who 92*
**Longford,** Elizabeth 1906- *IntAu&W 91, WrDr 92*
**Longford,** Francis A Parkenham, Earl of 1905- *IntAu&W 91*
**Longhi,** John 1946- *AmMWSc 92*
**Longhi,** Raymond 1935- *AmMWSc 92*
**Longhofer,** Ronald Stephen 1946- *WhoAmL 92, WhoMW 92*
**Longhouse,** Alfred Delbert 1912- *AmMWSc 92*
**Longhurst,** Alan R 1925- *AmMWSc 92*
**Longhurst,** Andrew Henry 1939- *Who 92*
**Longhurst,** John Charles 1947- *AmMWSc 92*
**Longhurst,** John Thomas 1940- *WhoEnt 92*
**Longinaker,** Jay Woodrow 1953- *WhoAmL 92*
**Longini,** Ira Mann, Jr 1948- *AmMWSc 92*
**Longini,** Richard Leon 1913- *AmMWSc 92*
**Longinus** *EncEarC*
**Longland,** Cedric James d1991 *Who 92N*
**Longland,** Jack 1905- *Who 92*
**Longland,** John Laurence *Who 92*
**Longley,** Ann Rosamund 1942- *Who 92*
**Longley,** B Jack 1913- *AmMWSc 92*
**Longley,** Christopher Quentin Mori 1961- *WhoMW 92*
**Longley,** Glenn, Jr 1942- *AmMWSc 92*
**Longley,** H Jerry 1926- *AmMWSc 92*
**Longley,** James Baird 1920- *AmMWSc 92*
**Longley,** Lawrence Douglas 1939- *WhoAmP 91, WhoMW 92*
**Longley,** Michael 1939- *ConPo 91, IntAu&W 91, WrDr 92*
**Longley,** Norman 1900- *Who 92*
**Longley,** Robert W 1925- *AmMWSc 92*
**Longley,** W.B. *IntWW 91, WrDr 92*
**Longley,** W Warren 1909- *AmMWSc 92*
**Longley,** William Joseph 1938- *AmMWSc 92*
**Longley,** William Warren, Jr 1937- *AmMWSc 92*
**Longley-Cook,** Mark T 1943- *AmMWSc 92*
**Longman,** Peter Martin 1946- *Who 92*
**Longman,** Richard Winston 1943- *AmMWSc 92*
**Longmate,** Norman Richard 1925- *IntAu&W 91, WrDr 92*
**Longmire,** Dennis B 1944- *AmMWSc 92*
**Longmire,** George 1915- *WhoAmP 91*
**Longmire,** Martin Shelling 1931- *AmMWSc 92*
**Longmire,** William Polk, Jr. 1913- *IntWW 91*
**Longmore,** Andrew Centlivres 1944- *Who 92*
**Longmore,** William Joseph 1931- *AmMWSc 92*
**Longmuir,** Alan Gordon 1941- *AmMWSc 92*
**Longmuir,** Ian Stewart 1922- *AmMWSc 92*
**Longnecker,** Daniel Sidney 1931- *AmMWSc 92*
**Longnecker,** David Eugene 1939- *AmMWSc 92*
**Longo,** Alessandro 1864-1945 *NewAmDM*
**Longo,** Dan L 1949- *AmMWSc 92*
**Longo,** Daniel Robert 1952- *WhoMW 92*
**Longo,** Fran R. 1962- *WhoAmL 92*
**Longo,** Frank Joseph 1939- *AmMWSc 92*
**Longo,** Frederick R 1930- *AmMWSc 92*
**Longo,** John M 1939- *AmMWSc 92*
**Longo,** Joseph Thomas 1942- *AmMWSc 92*
**Longo,** Lawrence Daniel 1926- *AmMWSc 92*
**Longo,** Luigi 1900-1980 *FacFETw*
**Longo,** Michael Joseph 1935- *AmMWSc 92*
**Longo,** Michael Joseph 1937- *WhoEnt 92*
**Longo,** Pat Joseph 1929- *WhoEnt 92*
**Longo,** Pietro 1935- *IntWW 91*
**Longo,** Robert 1953- *WorArt 1980 [port]*
**Longo,** Ronald Anthony 1952- *WhoAmL 92*
**Longo,** Thomas J 1942- *WhoAmP 91*
**Longobardi,** AnitaRose Teresa 1961- *WhoFI 92*
**Longobardi,** Joseph J. *WhoAmL 92*
**Longobardi,** Nino 1953- *WorArt 1980*
**Longobardo,** Anna Kazanjian *AmMWSc 92*
**Longobardo,** Guy S 1928- *AmMWSc 92*
**Longone,** Daniel Thomas 1932- *AmMWSc 92*
**Longoria,** Frank A. 1935- *WhoHisp 92*
**Longoria,** John A. *WhoHisp 92*
**Longoria,** Jose Francisco, Jr. 1944- *WhoHisp 92*
**Longoria,** Jose L. 1947- *WhoHisp 92*
**Longoria,** Leovaldo Carol 1927- *WhoHisp 92*
**Longoria,** Raul L. *WhoHisp 92*
**Longoria,** Raul L 1921- *WhoAmP 91*
**Longoria,** Roberto 1963- *WhoHisp 92*
**Longoria,** Salvador Gonzalez, Jr. 1958- *WhoHisp 92*
**Longpre,** Edwin Keith 1933- *AmMWSc 92*
**Longrigg,** John Stephen 1923- *Who 92*
**Longrigg,** Roger 1929- *WrDr 92*
**Longrigg,** Roger Erskine 1929- *IntAu&W 91, Who 92*
**Longroy,** Allan Leroy 1936- *AmMWSc 92*
**Longshore,** Diane 1944- *WhoAmP 91*
**Longshore,** John David 1936- *AmMWSc 92*
**Longshore,** Thomas Ellwood 1812-1898 *AmPeW*
**Longstreet,** Augustus Baldwin 1790-1870 *BenetAL 91*
**Longstreet,** Harry Stephen 1940- *WhoEnt 92*
**Longstreet,** James 1821-1904 *BenetAL 91*
**Longstreet,** Stephen 1907- *BenetAL 91, IntAu&W 91, IntMPA 92, WhoEnt 92, WhoWest 92, WrDr 92*
**Longstreet,** Victor Mendell 1907- *WhoAmP 91*
**Longstreth,** David J 1948- *AmMWSc 92*
**Longstreth,** Miers Fisher 1819-1891 *BiInAmS*
**Longstreth,** Morris 1846-1914 *BiInAmS*
**Longstreth,** W. Thacher 1920- *ConAu 134*
**Longstreth Thompson,** Francis Michael *Who 92*
**Longsworth,** Paul Morgan 1962- *WhoAmP 91*
**Longtin,** Bruce 1913- *AmMWSc 92*
**Longtin,** James Gerard 1955- *WhoAmL 92*
**Longuet,** Gregory Arthur 1945- *WhoFI 92*
**Longuet-Higgins,** Hugh Christopher 1923- *IntWW 91, Who 92*
**Longuet-Higgins,** Michael Selwyn 1925- *IntWW 91, Who 92*
**Longus** *ClMLC 7*
**Longval,** Gloria 1931- *WhoHisp 92*
**Longwell,** John Ploeger 1918- *AmMWSc 92*
**Longwell,** P A 1919- *AmMWSc 92*
**Longworth,** Alice Roosevelt 1884-1980 *FacFETw, HanAmWH*
**Longworth,** Ian Heaps 1935- *Who 92*
**Longworth,** James W 1938- *AmMWSc 92*
**Longworth,** Nicholas *FacFETw*
**Longworth,** Nicholas 1869-1931 *AmPolLe*
**Longworth,** Philip 1933- *IntAu&W 91, WrDr 92*
**Longworth,** Ruskin 1927- *AmMWSc 92*
**Longworth,** Tom *WhoAmP 91*
**Longworth,** Wilfred Roy 1923- *Who 92*
**Longy,** Georges 1868-1930 *NewAmDM*
**Longyear,** Barry 1942- *IntAu&W 91, TwCSFW 91*
**Longyear,** Barry B. 1942- *WrDr 92*

**Longyear**, Judith Querida 1938- *AmMWSc 92, WhoMW 92*
**Longyear**, Rey Morgan 1930- *WhoEnt 92*
**Lonigro**, Andrew Joseph 1936- *AmMWSc 92*
**Lonky**, Martin Leonard 1944- *AmMWSc 92*
**Lonneke**, Michael Dean 1943- *WhoEnt 92*
**Lonnerdal**, Bo L 1948- *AmMWSc 92*
**Lonnes**, Jerome LeRoy 1938- *WhoAmL 92*
**Lonnes**, Perry Bert 1940- *AmMWSc 92*
**Lonngren**, Karl E 1938- *AmMWSc 92*
**Lonning**, Inge Johan 1938- *IntWW 91, WhoRel 92*
**Lonning**, Per 1928- *WhoRel 92*
**Lonnqvist**, Ulf 1936- *IntWW 91*
**Lonon**, Tana Jo 1951- *WhoEnt 92*
**Lonsdale**, Earl Of 1922- *Who 92*
**Lonsdale**, Edward Middlebrook 1915- *AmMWSc 92*
**Lonsdale**, Elston Holmes 1868-1898 *BiInAmS*
**Lonsdale**, Errol Henry Gerrard 1913- *Who 92*
**Lonsdale**, Frederick 1881-1954 *RfGEnL 91*
**Lonsdale**, Harold Kenneth 1932- *AmMWSc 92*
**Lonsdale**, Pamela *IntMPA 92*
**Lonsdale**, Robert Henry H. *Who 92*
**Lonsdale**, Roger Harrison 1934- *Who 92*
**Lonsdale**, Steven 1952- *ConAu 36NR*
**Lonsdale**, Timothy James 1949- *WhoEnt 92*
**Lonsdale-Eccles**, John David 1946- *AmMWSc 92*
**Lonsdorf**, Richard G. 1922- *WhoAmL 92*
**Lonski**, Joseph 1943- *AmMWSc 92*
**Lonsway**, Thomas Joseph 1944- *WhoAmP 91*
**Lont**, Wallace Eugene 1940- *WhoRel 92*
**Lontz**, Robert Jan 1936- *AmMWSc 92*
**Lonzetta**, Charles Michael 1950- *AmMWSc 92*
**Loo**, Billy Wei-Yu 1939- *AmMWSc 92*
**Loo**, Francis T C 1927- *AmMWSc 92*
**Loo**, Jeffrey *DrAPF 91*
**Loo**, Lester Baker 1937- *WhoFI 92*
**Loo**, Melanie Wai Sue 1948- *AmMWSc 92*
**Loo**, Thomas Ming 1957- *WhoFI 92*
**Loo**, Ti Li 1918- *AmMWSc 92*
**Loo**, Yen-Hoong 1914- *AmMWSc 92*
**Looby**, Joseph Lawrence 1917- *WhoAmP 91*
**Loofbourrow**, Alan G 1912- *AmMWSc 92*
**Looijen**, Anthony Ij. A. 1921- *IntWW 91*
**Look**, Bradley M. 1959- *WhoEnt 92*
**Look**, David C 1938- *AmMWSc 92*
**Look**, Dwight Chester, Jr 1938- *AmMWSc 92*
**Look**, Theone Priscilla Fish 1924- *WhoAmP 91*
**Look**, Vivian Ann *WhoWest 92*
**Looker**, Cecil Thomas *Who 92N*
**Looker**, James Howard 1922- *AmMWSc 92*
**Looker**, Jerome J 1935- *AmMWSc 92*
**Looker**, Patricia *DrAPF 91*
**Lookhart**, George LeRoy 1943- *AmMWSc 92*
**Looks**, Harry Andrew 1952- *WhoMW 92*
**Lookstein**, Haskel 1932- *WhoRel 92*
**Looman**, Gary John 1938- *WhoRel 92*
**Looman**, James R. 1952- *WhoAmL 92*
**Looman**, Jan 1919- *AmMWSc 92*
**Loomans**, Kathryn Elizabeth 1953- *WhoEnt 92*
**Loomans**, Maurice Edward 1933- *AmMWSc 92*
**Loomer**, Alfred J. 1962- *WhoFI 92*
**Loomes**, Brian 1938- *WrDr 92*
**Loomie**, Albert Joseph 1922- *IntAu&W 91, WrDr 92*
**Loomis**, Albert Geyer 1893- *AmMWSc 92*
**Loomis**, Alden Albert 1934- *AmMWSc 92*
**Loomis**, Christopher Knapp 1947- *WhoWest 92*
**Loomis**, Dawn Marie 1952- *WhoEnt 92, WhoWest 92*
**Loomis**, Earl Alfred, Jr 1921- *AmMWSc 92*
**Loomis**, Eben Jenks 1828-1912 *BiInAmS*
**Loomis**, Edward 1924- *WrDr 92*
**Loomis**, Elias 1811-1889 *BiInAmS*
**Loomis**, Frederick B 1915- *AmMWSc 92*
**Loomis**, Gary Lee 1943- *AmMWSc 92*
**Loomis**, Harold George 1925- *AmMWSc 92*
**Loomis**, Harvey Worthington 1865-1930 *NewAmDM*
**Loomis**, Henry *LesBEnT 92*
**Loomis**, Henry 1919- *IntWW 91, WhoEnt 92*
**Loomis**, Herschel Hare, Jr 1934- *AmMWSc 92*
**Loomis**, Howard Krey 1927- *WhoFI 92, WhoMW 92*
**Loomis**, James Phillip 1929- *WhoEnt 92*
**Loomis**, Jerry J. 1936- *WhoMW 92*
**Loomis**, John Howard, III 1950- *WhoMW 92*
**Loomis**, Lee Rodger 1951- *WhoFI 92*
**Loomis**, Mahlon 1826-1886 *BiInAmS*
**Loomis**, Mary Jeanette *WhoWest 92*
**Loomis**, Noel M 1905-1979 *TwCWW 91*
**Loomis**, Richard Biggar 1925- *AmMWSc 92*
**Loomis**, Robert Arthur 1936- *WhoMW 92*
**Loomis**, Robert Henry 1923- *AmMWSc 92*
**Loomis**, Robert Morgan 1922- *AmMWSc 92*
**Loomis**, Robert Simpson 1928- *AmMWSc 92*
**Loomis**, Sabra *DrAPF 91*
**Loomis**, Stephen Henry 1952- *AmMWSc 92*
**Loomis**, Ted Albert 1917- *AmMWSc 92*
**Loomis**, Timothy Patrick 1946- *AmMWSc 92*
**Loomis**, Walter David 1926- *AmMWSc 92*
**Loomis**, Wendell Sylvester 1926- *WhoAmL 92*
**Loomis**, William Farnsworth, Jr 1940- *AmMWSc 92*
**Loomis**, Worth 1923- *WhoFI 92*
**Loon**, Jimmy 1952- *WhoWest 92*
**Loone**, Eero 1935- *IntWW 91, SovUnBD*
**Looney**, Claudia Arlene 1946- *WhoFI 92, WhoWest 92*
**Looney**, Cullen Rogers 1946- *WhoAmP 91*
**Looney**, Dennis Joseph, Jr 1934- *WhoIns 92*
**Looney**, J.W. 1944- *WhoAmL 92*
**Looney**, Martin Michael 1948- *WhoAmP 91*
**Looney**, Norman 1942- *WhoFI 92*
**Looney**, Norman E 1938- *AmMWSc 92*
**Looney**, Patrick Steven 1950- *WhoAmL 92*
**Looney**, Ralph Edwin 1924- *WhoWest 92*
**Looney**, Ralph William 1931- *AmMWSc 92*
**Looney**, Richard Carl 1934- *WhoRel 92*
**Looney**, Robert Dudley 1919- *WhoAmL 92*
**Looney**, Stephen Warwick 1952- *AmMWSc 92*
**Looney**, William Boyd 1922- *AmMWSc 92*
**Looney**, William Francis, Jr. 1931- *WhoAmL 92*
**Loonin**, Larry 1941- *WhoEnt 92*
**Loonsk**, Susan Elizabeth 1957- *WhoMW 92*
**Loop**, Dwight Frederick 1952- *WhoEnt 92*
**Loop**, John Wickwire 1924- *AmMWSc 92*
**Loop**, Michael Stuart 1946- *AmMWSc 92*
**Loope**, Richard Nicholas 1949- *WhoFI 92*
**Looper**, Donald Ray 1952- *WhoAmL 92*
**Looper-Fago**, Annette Marie 1960- *WhoEnt 92*
**Loory**, Stuart Hugh 1932- *WhoEnt 92*
**Loos**, Adolf 1870-1933 *DcTwDes, FacFETw*
**Loos**, Anita 1893-1981 *BenetAL 91, FacFETw, ReelWom*
**Loos**, Charles Delbert 1925- *WhoAmP 91*
**Loos**, Charles Louis 1823-1912 *AmPeW*
**Loos**, Hendricus G 1925- *AmMWSc 92*
**Loos**, Hermann A 1876?-1900 *BiInAmS*
**Loos**, James Stavert 1940- *AmMWSc 92*
**Loos**, Karl Rudolf 1939- *AmMWSc 92*
**Loos**, Mary 1914- *IntMPA 92*
**Loos**, Robert Willis, III 1958- *WhoEnt 92*
**Loos**, William Christensen 1944- *WhoAmL 92, WhoWest 92*
**Loose**, Leland David 1940- *AmMWSc 92*
**Loose**, Mary Ellen 1954- *WhoEnt 92*
**Loosen**, Ann Marita 1923- *WhoRel 92*
**Looser**, Heidi 1942- *WhoMW 92*
**Loosley**, Brian 1948- *Who 92*
**Loosley**, Stanley George Henry d1991 *Who 92N*
**Loosley**, William Robert *ConAu 135*
**Loosli**, John Kasper 1909- *AmMWSc 92*
**Loosli**, S Lynn 1935- *WhoAmP 91*
**Loots**, Barbara *DrAPF 91*
**Loov**, Robert Edmund 1933- *AmMWSc 92*
**Looyenga**, Robert William 1939- *AmMWSc 92*
**Lopach**, James J. 1942- *ConAu 135*
**Lopach**, James Joseph 1942- *WhoWest 92*
**Lopacki**, Edward Joseph, Jr. 1947- *WhoAmL 92*
**Lopardo**, Vincent Joseph 1925- *AmMWSc 92*
**Lopata**, Helena Znaniecka 1925- *WomSoc*
**Lopata**, Martin Barry 1939- *WhoWest 92*
**Lopate**, Phillip *DrAPF 91*
**Lopatin**, Dennis Edward 1948- *AmMWSc 92*
**LoPatin**, Florence 1928- *WhoFI 92*
**Lopatin**, Judy *DrAPF 91*
**Lopatin**, William 1946- *AmMWSc 92*
**Lopatka**, Adam 1928- *IntWW 91*
**Lopatka**, Kenneth Thaddeus 1947- *WhoAmL 92*
**Lopatnikoff**, Nikolai 1903-1976 *NewAmDM*
**Lopdrup**, Kim Axel 1958- *WhoFI 92*
**Loper**, Carl R, Jr 1932- *AmMWSc 92*
**Loper**, David Eric 1940- *AmMWSc 92*
**Loper**, Gerald D 1937- *AmMWSc 92*
**Loper**, Gerald Milton 1936- *AmMWSc 92*
**Loper**, James L. *LesBEnT 92*
**Loper**, James Leaders 1931- *WhoEnt 92, WhoWest 92*
**Loper**, John C 1931- *AmMWSc 92*
**Loper**, Robert Bruce 1925- *WhoEnt 92*
**Loper**, Samuel Ward 1835-1910 *BiInAmS*
**Loper**, Warren Edward 1929- *WhoWest 92*
**Loper**, Willard H 1926- *AmMWSc 92*
**Loperena**, Ernesto 1942- *WhoHisp 92*
**Lopes** *Who 92*
**Lopes**, Antonio Simoes 1934- *IntWW 91*
**Lopes**, Davey 1945- *WhoBlA 92*
**Lopes**, Francisco Caetano, Jr. 1959- *WhoHisp 92*
**Lopes**, Henri 1937- *IntWW 91*
**Lopes**, Joseph Alonzo 1949- *WhoAmP 91*
**Lopes**, Maria J *WhoAmP 91*
**Lopes**, Michael *DrAPF 91*
**Lopes**, William H. 1946- *WhoBlA 92*
**Lopes-Graca**, Fernando 1906- *ConCom 92, IntWW 91*
**Lopez**, Aaron Galicia 1933- *WhoHisp 92*
**Lopez**, Abe *WhoHisp 92*
**Lopez**, Abel 1950- *WhoRel 92*
**Lopez**, Adalberto 1943- *WhoHisp 92*
**Lopez**, Aguilar Enrique 1955- *IntAu&W 91*
**Lopez**, Al 1908- *WhoHisp 92*
**Lopez**, Alberto Munoz 1960- *WhoHisp 92*
**Lopez**, Alfonso J. 1946- *WhoHisp 92*
**Lopez**, Amalia Rebecca 1963- *WhoHisp 92*
**Lopez**, Ana M. 1956- *WhoHisp 92*
**Lopez**, Angel Andres 1943- *WhoHisp 92*
**Lopez**, Ann Aurelia 1945- *WhoHisp 92*
**Lopez**, Anna B. 1962- *WhoHisp 92*
**Lopez**, Anthony 1919- *AmMWSc 92*
**Lopez**, Anthony Gene, Jr. 1953- *WhoHisp 92*
**Lopez**, Antonio 1934- *WhoHisp 92*
**Lopez**, Antonio Manuel, Jr. 1949- *WhoHisp 92*
**Lopez**, Antonio Vincent 1938- *AmMWSc 92*
**Lopez**, Armando X. 1958- *WhoHisp 92*
**Lopez**, Arthur Larry 1943- *WhoHisp 92*
**Lopez**, Augustin V. 1931- *WhoHisp 92*
**Lopez**, Aura A. 1933- *WhoHisp 92*
**Lopez**, Barry *DrAPF 91*
**Lopez**, Barry 1945- *SmATA 67 [port]*
**Lopez**, Barry Holstun 1945- *WhoWest 92*
**Lopez**, Carlos 1942- *AmMWSc 92*
**Lopez**, Carlos Jose 1949- *WhoHisp 92*
**Lopez**, Carlos Urrutia 1932- *WhoHisp 92*
**Lopez**, Carmen Luisa 1951- *WhoHisp 92*
**Lopez**, Carol Robertson 1951- *WhoAmP 91*
**Lopez**, Carolyn Catherine 1951- *WhoMW 92*
**Lopez**, Charles Joseph, Jr. 1948- *WhoRel 92*
**Lopez**, Daniel *WhoHisp 92*
**Lopez**, David 1942- *WhoAmL 92*
**Lopez**, David 1951- *WhoHisp 92*
**Lopez**, David Barwis 1938- *WhoHisp 92*
**Lopez**, David Ruben 1951- *WhoHisp 92*
**Lopez**, David Tiburcio 1939- *WhoAmL 92*
**Lopez**, Delia Olivia 1943- *WhoHisp 92*
**Lopez**, Diana Montes De Oca 1937- *AmMWSc 92*
**Lopez**, Eddie *WhoHisp 92*
**Lopez**, Eddie 1929- *WhoHisp 92*
**Lopez**, Edward A. 1943- *WhoHisp 92*
**Lopez**, Edward Alexander 1954- *WhoHisp 92*
**Lopez**, Edward J *WhoAmP 91*
**Lopez**, Elizabeth Marie 1955- *WhoHisp 92*
**Lopez**, Emiliano, Jr. 1959- *WhoEnt 92*
**Lopez**, Enrique Angel 1940- *WhoHisp 92*
**Lopez**, Eric *WhoHisp 92*
**Lopez**, Erika Anne 1957- *WhoEnt 92*
**Lopez**, Ernie Manuel 1951- *WhoHisp 92*
**Lopez**, Estanislao 1786-1838 *HisDSpE*
**Lopez**, Felix C. 1957- *WhoHisp 92*
**Lopez**, Felix Caridad *WhoHisp 92*
**Lopez**, Fidencio Leal, Jr. 1951- *WhoHisp 92*
**Lopez**, Francis P. *WhoHisp 92*
**Lopez**, Franklin A. 1942- *WhoHisp 92*
**Lopez**, Gabriel Reyes 1950- *WhoHisp 92*
**Lopez**, Gary William 1951- *WhoEnt 92*
**Lopez**, Genaro 1947- *AmMWSc 92, WhoHisp 92*
**Lopez**, Gerald P. 1948- *WhoAmL 92*
**Lopez**, Gerard F. *WhoHisp 92*
**Lopez**, Gloria Berta-Cruz 1937- *WhoHisp 92*
**Lopez**, Gloria E. 1951- *WhoHisp 92*
**Lopez**, Gloria Margarita 1948- *WhoHisp 92*
**Lopez**, Guillermo 1919- *WhoHisp 92*
**Lopez**, Hector 1947- *WhoHisp 92*
**Lopez**, Hugo Roberto 1930- *WhoHisp 92*
**Lopez**, Humberto S. *WhoHisp 92*
**Lopez**, Humberto Salazar 1944- *WhoHisp 92*
**Lopez**, Ignacio Javier 1956- *WhoHisp 92*
**Lopez**, Irene F. *WhoHisp 92*
**Lopez**, Isabel Lucia 1961- *WhoHisp 92*
**Lopez**, Isabel O. *WhoHisp 92*
**Lopez**, Israel 1922- *WhoHisp 92*
**Lopez**, Jack, Jr. 1953- *WhoFI 92*
**Lopez**, Jaime V. 1954- *WhoAmL 92*
**Lopez**, Javier *WhoHisp 92*
**Lopez**, Javier Ortiz 1967- *WhoHisp 92*
**Lopez**, Jesus Luis 1951- *WhoHisp 92*
**Lopez**, Joanne Carol 1952- *WhoHisp 92*
**Lopez**, Joe Eddie 1939- *WhoAmP 91*
**Lopez**, Joe Eddy 1939- *WhoHisp 92*
**Lopez**, John F. 1949- *WhoHisp 92*
**Lopez**, John J. 1947- *WhoHisp 92*
**Lopez**, John William 1957- *WhoHisp 92*
**Lopez**, Jorge Alberto 1955- *AmMWSc 92, WhoHisp 92*
**Lopez**, Jose Ignacio, Sr. 1932- *WhoHisp 92*
**Lopez**, Jose Luis 1955- *WhoHisp 92*
**Lopez**, Jose M. 1949- *WhoAmL 92*
**Lopez**, Jose M., Jr. 1949- *WhoHisp 92*
**Lopez**, Jose Manuel 1950- *AmMWSc 92*
**Lopez**, Jose R. 1940- *WhoHisp 92*
**Lopez**, Jose R. 1945- *WhoHisp 92*
**Lopez**, Jose Rafael 1957- *WhoHisp 92*
**Lopez**, Jose Tomas 1949- *WhoHisp 92*
**Lopez**, Josefina 1969- *WhoHisp 92*
**Lopez**, Joseph 1952- *WhoHisp 92*
**Lopez**, Joseph Andrew 1948- *WhoFI 92*
**Lopez**, Joseph Anthony 1951- *WhoHisp 92*
**Lopez**, Kamala M. 1964- *WhoHisp 92*
**Lopez**, Lawrence Anthony 1939- *WhoHisp 92*
**Lopez**, Leonard Anthony 1940- *AmMWSc 92*
**Lopez**, Leopold Rene 1955- *WhoEnt 92*
**Lopez**, Louis 1954- *WhoHisp 92*
**Lopez**, Louis Rey 1946- *WhoHisp 92*
**Lopez**, Lourdes 1958- *WhoHisp 92*
**Lopez**, Luz E. *WhoHisp 92*
**Lopez**, Manuel, Sr. 1950- *WhoHisp 92*
**Lopez**, Manuel Dennis d1991 *WhoHisp 92N*
**Lopez**, Marcelo 1951- *WhoWest 92*
**Lopez**, Marciano 1934- *WhoHisp 92*
**Lopez**, Marco Antonio 1957- *WhoHisp 92*
**Lopez**, Marcus 1934- *WhoHisp 92*
**Lopez**, Maria del Carmen 1954- *AmMWSc 92*
**Lopez**, Mario 1942- *WhoHisp 92*
**Lopez**, Marisela 1956- *WhoHisp 92*
**Lopez**, Martha Louise 1947- *WhoHisp 92*
**Lopez**, Marvin J. 1937- *WhoHisp 92*
**Lopez**, Mary Gardner 1920- *WhoBlA 92*
**Lopez**, Michael F. 1952- *WhoHisp 92*
**Lopez**, Michael John 1937- *WhoHisp 92*
**Lopez**, Miguel E. 1941- *WhoHisp 92*
**Lopez**, Miriam *WhoHisp 92*
**Lopez**, Nancy 1957- *WhoHisp 92*
**Lopez**, Narciso 1798- *HisDSpE*
**Lopez**, Norberto H. 1938- *WhoHisp 92*
**Lopez**, Omar S. 1955- *WhoHisp 92*
**Lopez**, Oscar *WhoHisp 92*
**Lopez**, Oscar D. 1954- *WhoHisp 92*
**Lopez**, Pablo Vincent 1964- *WhoHisp 92*
**Lopez**, Paul Galileo 1953- *WhoEnt 92*
**Lopez**, Pedro Ramon *WhoHisp 92*
**Lopez**, Priscilla 1948- *WhoEnt 92, WhoHisp 92*
**Lopez**, R C Gerald 1957- *AmMWSc 92*
**Lopez**, Rafael 1929- *AmMWSc 92, WhoHisp 92*
**Lopez**, Rafael C. 1931- *WhoHisp 92*
**Lopez**, Ramon Rossi 1950- *WhoAmL 92*
**Lopez**, Raul Jose 1959- *WhoHisp 92*
**Lopez**, Raymond Henry 1940- *WhoHisp 92*
**Lopez**, Ricardo *WhoHisp 92*
**Lopez**, Ricardo Rafael 1957- *WhoHisp 92*
**Lopez**, Richard 1943- *WhoHisp 92*
**Lopez**, Richard 1962- *WhoRel 92*
**Lopez**, Richard Clarence 1949- *WhoHisp 92*
**Lopez**, Richard E. 1945- *WhoHisp 92*
**Lopez**, Richard G. 1934- *WhoHisp 92*
**Lopez**, Rigoberto Adolfo 1957- *WhoHisp 92*
**Lopez**, Robert 1940- *WhoHisp 92*
**Lopez**, Roberto J. 1968- *WhoHisp 92*
**Lopez**, Roberto Monte Carlo 1932- *WhoHisp 92*
**Lopez**, Rose Mary 1938- *WhoAmP 91*
**Lopez**, Rosemary 1963- *WhoHisp 92*
**Lopez**, Roy Charles 1948- *WhoWest 92*
**Lopez**, Rubin R. 1947- *WhoHisp 92*
**Lopez**, Salvador P. 1911- *IntWW 91*
**Lopez**, Steven Regeser 1953- *WhoHisp 92*
**Lopez**, Steven Richard 1944- *WhoWest 92*
**Lopez**, Thomas *WhoHisp 92*
**Lopez**, Thomas Louis 1945- *WhoHisp 92*
**Lopez**, Thomas Marsh 1943- *WhoWest 92*
**Lopez**, Thomas R. *WhoHisp 92*
**Lopez**, Tina L. *WhoHisp 92*
**Lopez**, Tomas 1967- *WhoHisp 92*
**Lopez**, Tony *WhoHisp 92*
**Lopez**, Trini 1937- *WhoEnt 92, WhoHisp 92*
**Lopez**, Vicky E. 1952- *WhoHisp 92*
**Lopez**, Vincente *WhoHisp 92*

**Lopez**, Vito 1941- WhoAmP 91
**Lopez**, Vito J. 1941- WhoHisp 92
**Lopez**, Welquis Raimundo 1954- WhoHisp 92
**Lopez**, William, Sr. 1950- WhoHisp 92
**Lopez**, Yolanda Elva 1951- WhoHisp 92
**Lopez Adorno**, Pedro J. 1954- WhoHisp 92
**Lopez-Alves**, Fernando 1950- WhoHisp 92
**Lopez Arellano**, Oswaldo 1921- IntWW 91
**Lopez Avina**, Antonio 1915- WhoRel 92
**Lopez-Bayron**, Juan L. 1955- WhoHisp 92
**Lopez-Berestein**, Gabriel 1947- AmMWSc 92
**Lopez-Calderon**, Jose Luis 1948- WhoHisp 92
**Lopez-Cambil**, Rafael WhoHisp 92
**Lopez-Castro**, Amadeo, Jr. WhoHisp 92
**Lopez-Cepero**, Robert Michael 1943- WhoHisp 92
**Lopez-Cobos**, Jesus 1940- IntWW 91, WhoEnt 92, WhoMW 92
**Lopez Contreras**, Eleazar 1883-1973 FacFETw
**Lopez de Gamero**, Iliana Veronica 1963- WhoHisp 92
**Lopez de Gomara**, Francisco 1511-1566? HisDSpE
**Lopez de Lacarra**, Amalia 1956- WhoHisp 92
**Lopez de Legazpi**, Miguel HisDSpE
**Lopez DeLetona Y Nunez DelPino**, Jose M. 1922- IntWW 91
**Lopez de Mendoza**, Victor WhoHisp 92
**Lopez de Victoria**, Juan de Dios WhoRel 92
**Lopez-Elarba**, Eloisa 1963- WhoHisp 92
**Lopez-Enriquez**, Alberto T. 1954- WhoHisp 92
**Lopez-Escobar**, Edgar George Kenneth 1937- AmMWSc 92
**Lopez Galarza**, Hector 1940- WhoHisp 92
**Lopez Galarza**, Hector A 1940- WhoAmP 91
**Lopez-Garcia**, Antonio 1936- IntWW 91, WorArt 1980
**Lopez-Gonzalez**, Margarita Maria 1947- WhoHisp 92
**Lopez-Heredia**, Jose 1922- WhoHisp 92
**Lopez Hernandez**, Juan 1928- WhoAmP 91, WhoHisp 92
**Lopez-Ibor**, Juan Jose 1941- IntWW 91
**Lopez-Isa**, Jose WhoHisp 92
**Lopez-Jaena**, Graciano 1856-1896 HisDSpE
**Lopez-Lee**, David WhoHisp 92
**Lopez-Lopez**, Fernando Jose WhoHisp 92
**Lopez-Majano**, Vincent 1921- AmMWSc 92
**Lopez-Marron**, Jose M. 1947- WhoHisp 92
**Lopez-Mayhew**, Barbara D. 1959- WhoHisp 92
**Lopez-McKnight**, Gloria 1937- WhoHisp 92
**Lopez Michelsen**, Alfonso 1913- IntWW 91
**Lopez-Morillas**, Juan 1913- WhoHisp 92
**Lopez-Nieves**, Carlos Juan 1948- WhoAmP 91, WhoHisp 92
**Lopez-Otin**, Maria E. 1950- WhoHisp 92
**Lopez-Permouth**, Sergio Roberto 1957- WhoHisp 92
**Lopez-Portillo Y Pacheco**, Jose 1920- IntWW 91
**Lopez Rayon**, Ignacio 1773-1832 HisDSpE
**Lopez Rega**, Jose 1916?-1989 FacFETw
**Lopez Rodo**, Laureano 1920- IntWW 91
**Lopez Rodriguez**, Nicolas de Jesus 1936- WhoRel 92
**Lopez-Romo**, Daniel Francisco 1945- WhoAmL 92
**Lopez-Sanabria**, Sixto 1928- WhoHisp 92
**Lopez Sanchez**, Maria del Pilar 1949- WhoHisp 92
**Lopez-Santolino**, Alfredo 1931- AmMWSc 92
**Lopez-Sanz**, Mariano 1931- WhoHisp 92
**Lopez Trujillo**, Alfonso 1935- IntWW 91, WhoRel 92
**Lopez-Trujillo**, Virginia M. WhoHisp 92
**Lopez-Vasquez**, Alfonso 1950- WhoHisp 92
**Lopez Velarde**, Ramon 1888-1921 BenetAL 91
**Lopez-Videla G.**, Ana Doris 1934- WhoHisp 92
**Lopez-Woodward**, Dina 1956- WhoHisp 92
**Lopez y Fuentes**, Gregorio 1895-1966 BenetAL 91
**LoPiccolo**, Joseph 1943- WhoMW 92
**Lopina**, Robert F 1936- AmMWSc 92
**Lopina**, Robert Ferguson 1936- WhoWest 92
**Lo Pinto**, Richard William 1942- AmMWSc 92
**Lopo**, Alina C 1951- AmMWSc 92
**Lopokova**, Lydia 1892-1981 FacFETw
**Loppnow**, Harald AmMWSc 92
**Loppnow**, Milo Alvin 1914- WhoRel 92
**Lopreato**, Joseph 1928- WrDr 92
**Loprest**, Frank James 1929- AmMWSc 92
**LoPresti**, Michael, Jr 1947- WhoAmP 91
**Lopresti**, Philip V 1932- AmMWSc 92
**Lopresto**, John George 1940- WhoAmP 91
**Lopukhov**, Fedor Vasil'evich 1886-1973 SovUnBD
**Lopukhova**, Ludmila A. WhoEnt 92
**Lopushinsky**, Theodore 1937- AmMWSc 92
**Lopushinsky**, William 1930- AmMWSc 92
**Lopuszynski**, Ted 1938- WhoAmP 91
**Loquasto**, Klaus Wolfgang 1946- WhoMW 92
**Loquasto**, Santo WhoEnt 92A
**Loraine**, Philip WrDr 92
**Loram**, David 1924- Who 92
**Loran**, Martin IntAu&W 91X, TwCSFW 91
**Lorance**, Elmer Donald 1940- AmMWSc 92, WhoWest 92
**Lorand**, John Peter 1936- AmMWSc 92
**Lorand**, Laszlo 1923- AmMWSc 92
**Loranger**, William Farrand 1925- AmMWSc 92
**Lorant**, Stefan 1901- IntAu&W 91, IntWW 91, Who 92, WrDr 92
**Lorasch**, Keith John 1957- WhoEnt 92
**Lorbeer**, James W 1931- AmMWSc 92
**Lorber**, Herbert William 1929- AmMWSc 92
**Lorber**, Howard Mark 1948- WhoFI 92
**Lorber**, John Jude 1937- WhoAmL 92
**Lorber**, Mortimer 1926- AmMWSc 92
**Lorber**, Richard Jan 1946- WhoEnt 92
**Lorber**, Victor 1912- AmMWSc 92
**Lorca**, Federico Garcia FacFETw
**Lorch**, Edgar Raymond 1907- AmMWSc 92
**Lorch**, Ernest Henry 1932- WhoFI 92
**Lorch**, Joan 1923- AmMWSc 92
**Lorch**, Lee 1915- AmMWSc 92
**Lorch**, Steven Kalman 1944- AmMWSc 92
**Lord Crowther-Hunt** ConAu 133
**Lord Haw-Haw** EncTR 91
**Lord High Commissioner** ScFEYrs
**Lord Mountbatten** ConAu 133
**Lord Rayleigh** 1842-1919 WhoNob 90
**Lord**, Alan 1929- IntWW 91, Who 92
**Lord**, Albert Bates d1991 NewYTBS 91
**Lord**, Albert Bates 1912-1991 ConAu 135
**Lord**, Allison WrDr 92
**Lord**, Andrew 1950- TwCPaSc
**Lord**, Arthur E, Jr 1935- AmMWSc 92
**Lord**, Arthur N 1932- AmMWSc 92
**Lord**, Barbara Joanni 1939- WhoAmL 92
**Lord**, Beman 1924-1991 ConAu 135
**Lord**, Bette Bao 1938- IntAu&W 91
**Lord**, Betty Bao 1938- WrDr 92
**Lord**, Charles Edwin 1928- WhoAmP 91
**Lord**, Charles Robert 1920- WhoRel 92
**Lord**, Clyde Ormond 1937- WhoBlA 92
**Lord**, David Hill 1945- WhoWest 92
**Lord**, Dottie T. 1945- WhoFI 92
**Lord**, Edith M AmMWSc 92
**Lord**, Elizabeth Mary 1949- AmMWSc 92
**Lord**, Evelyn M WhoAmP 91
**Lord**, Geoffrey 1928- Who 92
**Lord**, Graham John 1943- IntAu&W 91, WrDr 92
**Lord**, Harold Wesley 1931- AmMWSc 92
**Lord**, Harold Wilbur 1905- AmMWSc 92, WhoWest 92
**Lord**, Harry Chester, III 1939- AmMWSc 92
**Lord**, Jack 1930- IntMPA 92, WhoEnt 92, WhoWest 92
**Lord**, Jacklynn Jean 1940- WhoWest 92
**Lord**, Jacqueline Ward 1936- WhoFI 92
**Lord**, James Gregory 1947- WhoMW 92
**Lord**, Jeffrey TwCSFW 91, WrDr 92
**Lord**, Jere Johns 1922- AmMWSc 92
**Lord**, Jere Williams, Jr 1910- AmMWSc 92
**Lord**, Jimmy WhoAmP 91
**Lord**, John Herent 1928- Who 92
**Lord**, John Vernon 1939- WrDr 92
**Lord**, John William 1938- WhoWest 92
**Lord**, Joseph S., III d1991 NewYTBS 91 [port]
**Lord**, Keith Edward 1958- WhoFI 92
**Lord**, Marjorie WhoEnt 92
**Lord**, Mia W. 1920- WhoWest 92
**Lord**, Michael Nicholson 1938- Who 92
**Lord**, Nancy DrAPF 91, WrDr 92
**Lord**, Nathaniel Wright 1854-1911 BiInAmS
**Lord**, Ottis Kermit, Jr. 1943- WhoFI 92
**Lord**, Peter Herent 1925- Who 92
**Lord**, Peter Reeves 1923- AmMWSc 92
**Lord**, Robert 1945- WrDr 92
**Lord**, Robert Needham 1945- IntAu&W 91
**Lord**, Samuel Smith, Jr 1927- AmMWSc 92
**Lord**, Walter 1917- IntAu&W 91, WrDr 92
**Lord**, Warren John 1948- WhoRel 92
**Lord**, Wesley Webb 1936- WhoAmP 91
**Lord**, William B 1929- AmMWSc 92
**Lord**, William Burton Housley 1919- Who 92
**Lord**, William Dennis 1952- WhoEnt 92
**Lord**, William E. LesBEnT 92
**Lord**, William John 1921- AmMWSc 92
**Lord**, William Rogers 1847-1916 BiInAmS
**Lord**, William Wilberforce 1819-1907 BenetAL 91
**Lord**, Willis A 1918- WhoAmP 91
**Lord**, Winston 1937- IntWW 91
**Lordahl**, Jo Ann DrAPF 91
**Lordan**, Beth DrAPF 91
**Lorde**, Audre DrAPF 91
**Lorde**, Audre 1934- AfrAmW, BenetAL 91, BlkLC [port], ConPo 91, HanAmWH, NotBlAW 92, WrDr 92
**Lorde**, Audre Geraldine 1934- WhoBlA 92
**Lordeman**, James Engelbert 1923- WhoFI 92
**Lordi**, Nicholas George 1930- AmMWSc 92
**Lords**, James Lafayette 1928- AmMWSc 92
**Lore**, John M, Jr 1921- AmMWSc 92
**Lore**, Victor Richard 1946- WhoWest 92
**Lorea**, Frank A. 1944- WhoHisp 92
**Loree**, Thomas Robert 1936- AmMWSc 92
**Lorell**, Jack 1916- WhoWest 92
**Lorelle** ScFEYrs
**Lorelli**, Michael Kevin 1950- WhoFI 92
**Loreman**, Ronald Lee 1932- WhoEnt 92, WhoMW 92
**Loren**, Sophia 1934- FacFETw, IntMPA 92, IntWW 91, Who 92, WhoEnt 92
**Lorence**, Matthew C AmMWSc 92
**Lorengar**, Pilar 1928- NewAmDM
**Lorensen**, Lyman Edward 1923- AmMWSc 92
**Lorente**, Steven Joseph 1950- WhoEnt 92
**Lorente De No**, Rafael 1902- AmMWSc 92
**Lorents**, Alden C 1937- AmMWSc 92
**Lorents**, Donald C 1929- AmMWSc 92
**Lorentson**, Holly Jean 1956- WhoWest 92
**Lorentz**, Francis 1942- IntWW 91
**Lorentz**, George G 1910- AmMWSc 92
**Lorentz**, Hendrik Antoon 1853-1928 WhoNob 90
**Lorentz**, Pare 1905- BenetAL 91, IntDcF 2-2
**Lorentz**, Stanislaw 1899- IntWW 91
**Lorentzen**, Annemarie Rostvik 1921- IntWW 91
**Lorentzen**, Bent 1935- ConCom 92
**Lorentzen**, Keith Eden 1921- AmMWSc 92
**Lorentzen**, Kenneth Neil 1951- WhoFI 92
**Lorentzen**, Robert Roy 1935- WhoFI 92
**Lorentzen**, Robert Roy, Jr. 1942- WhoEnt 92
**Lorenz**, Carl Edward 1933- AmMWSc 92
**Lorenz**, Donald H 1936- AmMWSc 92
**Lorenz**, Edward Norton 1917- AmMWSc 92
**Lorenz**, Felix Alfred, Jr. 1922- WhoRel 92
**Lorenz**, Gary Wayne 1949- WhoFI 92
**Lorenz**, James Michael 1965- WhoFI 92
**Lorenz**, John Douglas 1942- AmMWSc 92
**Lorenz**, Klaus J 1936- AmMWSc 92
**Lorenz**, Konrad 1903-1989 EncTR 91, FacFETw
**Lorenz**, Konrad Zacharias 1903- AmMWSc 92
**Lorenz**, Konrad Zacharias 1903-1989 ConAu 35NR, WhoNob 90
**Lorenz**, Max R 1930- AmMWSc 92
**Lorenz**, Oscar Anthony 1914- AmMWSc 92
**Lorenz**, Patricia Ann 1938- AmMWSc 92
**Lorenz**, Philip Boalt 1920- AmMWSc 92
**Lorenz**, Philip Jack, Jr 1924- AmMWSc 92
**Lorenz**, Ralph William 1907- AmMWSc 92
**Lorenz**, Richard Arnold 1942- AmMWSc 92
**Lorenz**, Richard Theodore, Jr. 1931- WhoAmL 92
**Lorenz**, Roman R 1935- AmMWSc 92
**Lorenz**, Ronald Theodore 1936- WhoMW 92
**Lorenz**, Sarah WrDr 92
**Lorenz**, Timothy Carl 1947- WhoWest 92
**Lorenz**, Werner 1891-1974 EncTR 91 [port]
**Lorenz**, Werner 1921- IntWW 91
**Lorenzen**, Carl Julius 1938- AmMWSc 92
**Lorenzen**, Gary Lee 1946- WhoMW 92
**Lorenzen**, Howard O 1912- AmMWSc 92
**Lorenzen**, Janice R 1950- AmMWSc 92
**Lorenzen**, Jerry Alan 1944- AmMWSc 92
**Lorenzen**, Paul Peter Wilhelm 1915- IntWW 91
**Lorenzen**, Robert Frederick 1924- WhoWest 92
**Lorenzetti**, Ole J 1936- AmMWSc 92
**Lorenzetti**, Regina Anne 1948- WhoWest 92
**Lorenzi**, Armandina 1947- WhoHisp 92
**Lorenzo**, Antonio V 1928- AmMWSc 92
**Lorenzo**, Ariel 1956- WhoWest 92
**Lorenzo**, F 1947- WhoIns 92
**Lorenzo**, Francisco A. 1940- IntWW 91, WhoFI 92
**Lorenzo**, Frank A. 1940- WhoHisp 92
**Lorenzo**, George Albert 1943- AmMWSc 92
**Lorenzo**, Laura 1957- WhoHisp 92
**Lorenzo**, Lynn Robin 1966- WhoHisp 92
**Lorenzo**, Nicholas Francis, Jr. 1942- WhoAmL 92
**Loret**, Jean-Marie 1918-1985 EncTR 91
**Loretta**, Countess of Sponheim EncAmaz 91
**Loretz**, Andrew 1762-1812 DcNCBi 4
**Loretz**, Christopher Alan 1951- AmMWSc 92
**Loretz**, Thomas J 1951- AmMWSc 92
**Lorey**, Frank William 1929- AmMWSc 92, WhoFI 92
**Lorey**, Michael Patrick 1965- WhoEnt 92
**Lorge**, Mary Jo WhoAmP 91
**Lorge**, Michael M. 1953- WhoAmL 92
**Lorge**, William D 1960- WhoAmP 91
**Lorgus**, Wayne Robert 1953- WhoFI 92
**Loria**, Edward Albert 1919- AmMWSc 92
**Loria**, Martin A. 1951- WhoAmL 92
**Loria**, Robert Claude 1962- WhoHisp 92
**Loria**, Roger Moshe 1940- AmMWSc 92
**Loriaux**, D Lynn 1940- AmMWSc 92
**Lorimer**, Desmond 1925- IntWW 91
**Lorimer**, Ernest McFaul 1952- WhoAmL 92
**Lorimer**, George Horace 1867-1937 BenetAL 91
**Lorimer**, George Huntly 1942- AmMWSc 92, IntWW 91, Who 92
**Lorimer**, Hew Martin 1907- Who 92
**Lorimer**, John William 1929- AmMWSc 92
**Lorimer**, Nancy L 1947- AmMWSc 92
**Lorimer**, Thomas Desmond 1925- Who 92
**Lorimer**, Thomas Harold 1955- WhoRel 92
**Lorin**, Amii WrDr 92
**Lorincz**, Allan Levente 1924- AmMWSc 92
**Lorincz**, Andrew Endre 1926- AmMWSc 92
**Lorincz-Nagy**, Janos 1931- Who 92
**Lorinczi**, George Gabriel 1929- WhoAmL 92
**Loring**, Arthur 1947- WhoFI 92
**Loring**, Arthur Paul 1936- AmMWSc 92
**Loring**, Blake M 1914- AmMWSc 92
**Loring**, David William 1956- AmMWSc 92
**Loring**, Douglas Howard 1934- AmMWSc 92
**Loring**, Emilie d1951 BenetAL 91
**Loring**, Gloria Jean 1946- WhoEnt 92
**Loring**, John Hayes 1926- WhoAmP 91
**Loring**, John Robbins 1939- IntWW 91
**Loring**, Lynn E. 1949- IntMPA 92
**Loring**, Richard Tuttle 1929- WhoRel 92
**Loring**, Roger Frederic 1958- AmMWSc 92
**Loring**, Stephen H 1946- AmMWSc 92
**Loring**, William Bacheller 1915- AmMWSc 92
**Loring**, William Ellsworth 1920- AmMWSc 92
**Loring**, William Wing 1818-1886 DcNCBi 4
**Lorinsky**, Larry 1944- WhoFI 92, WhoWest 92
**Lorio**, Peter Leonce, Jr 1927- AmMWSc 92
**Lorio**, Philip Donatien, III 1948- WhoAmL 92
**Loriod**, Yvonne 1924- IntWW 91, NewAmDM
**Loris**, Joseph James 1943-1987 WhoBlA 92N
**Lorman**, Barbara K 1932- WhoAmP 91
**Lorman**, Janis Susdorf 1944- WhoMW 92
**Lorman**, William Rudolph 1910- WhoWest 92
**Lorne**, Marquess of 1968- Who 92
**Lorne**, Simon Michael 1946- WhoFI 92
**Lorntz**, Joyce Hanscom 1945- WhoRel 92
**Lorona**, John H. WhoHisp 92
**Lorona**, Marie A. 1938- WhoHisp 92
**Lorr**, Kathy Auchincloss DrAPF 91
**Lorrain**, Paul 1916- AmMWSc 92
**Lorraine**, Kay 1946- WhoEnt 92
**Lorraine**, Paul TwCSFW 91
**Lorre**, Peter 1904-1964 FacFETw
**Lorrimer**, Claire IntAu&W 91X
**Lorrimer**, Claire 1921- WrDr 92
**Lorsch**, Harold G 1919- AmMWSc 92
**Lorscheider**, Aloisio 1924- IntWW 91, WhoRel 92
**Lorscheider**, Fritz Louis 1939- AmMWSc 92
**Lorthridge**, James E. WhoBlA 92
**Lortie**, Pierre 1947- WhoFI 92
**Lorton**, Steven Paul 1950- WhoMW 92
**Lorts**, Jack E. DrAPF 91
**Lortz**, David Michael 1945- WhoMW 92
**Lortzing**, Albert 1801-1851 NewAmDM

**Lorusso**, Anthony Michael 1940- *WhoAmL 92*
**Lorusso**, Edward N. S. 1949- *ConAu 133*
**Lorusso**, Tina Marie Elena 1957- *WhoEnt 92*
**Lorwin**, Lewis Levitzki 1883-1970 *AmPeW*
**Lory**, Dave Joseph 1959- *WhoEnt 92*
**Lory**, Earl C 1906- *WhoAmP 91*
**Lory**, Henry James 1936- *AmMWSc 92*
**Los**, Cornelis Albertus 1951- *WhoFI 92*
**Los**, Marinus 1933- *AmMWSc 92*
**Losaberidze**, Ketevan 1949- *SovUnBD*
**Losada**, Jorge *WhoHisp 92*
**Los Angeles**, Victoria de 1923- *NewAmDM*
**Loscalzo**, Anne Grace 1917- *AmMWSc 92*
**Loscalzo**, Anthony Joseph 1946- *WhoAmL 92*
**Loscalzo**, Joseph 1951- *AmMWSc 92*
**Loscavio**, Elizabeth *WhoEnt 92*
**Loscheider**, Paul Henry 1954- *WhoMW 92*
**Loscher**, Robert A 1930- *AmMWSc 92*
**Loschiavo**, Linda Ann 1947- *IntAu&W 91*
**Loschiavo**, Samuel Ralph 1924- *AmMWSc 92*
**Loschnak**, Franz 1940- *IntWW 91*
**LoSecco**, John M 1950- *AmMWSc 92*
**Losee**, David Lawrence 1939- *AmMWSc 92*
**Losee**, Ferril A 1928- *AmMWSc 92*
**Losee**, John Frederick, Jr. 1951- *WhoMW 92*
**Loseff**, Jeffrey Clark 1952- *WhoEnt 92*
**Losekamp**, Bernard Francis 1936- *AmMWSc 92*
**Loseke**, Scott Alan 1960- *WhoFI 92*
**Loser**, Randy Dennis 1955- *WhoAmL 92*
**Losev**, Sergey Andreyevich 1927- *IntWW 91*
**Losey**, George Spahr, Jr 1942- *AmMWSc 92*
**Losey**, Gerald Otis 1930- *AmMWSc 92*
**Losey**, Joseph 1909-1984 *FacFETw, IntDcF 2-2 [port]*
**Losey**, Ralph Colby 1951- *WhoAmL 92*
**Losh**, J. Michael 1946- *WhoFI 92*
**Loshuertos**, Robert Herman 1937- *WhoRel 92*
**Losi**, Maxim John 1939- *WhoFI 92*
**Losice**, Abraham Solomon 1960- *WhoFI 92*
**Losick**, Richard Marc 1943- *AmMWSc 92*
**Losin**, Edward Thomas 1923- *AmMWSc 92*
**Losinska**, Kathleen Mary 1924- *Who 92*
**Losowsky**, Monty Seymour 1931- *Who 92*
**Losoya**, Jack *WhoHisp 92*
**Losoya**, Raul C. *WhoHisp 92*
**Lospalluto**, Joseph John 1925- *AmMWSc 92*
**Loss**, Frank J 1936- *AmMWSc 92*
**Loss**, Ira Saul 1945- *WhoFI 92*
**Loss**, Joe 1909-1990 *AnObit 1990, FacFETw*
**Loss**, John C. 1931- *WhoFI 92*
**Loss**, Louis 1914- *WhoAmL 92, WrDr 92*
**Loss**, Margaret Ruth 1946- *WhoAmL 92*
**Lossau**, Carl Shipley 1931- *WhoMW 92*
**Losse**, John William, Jr. 1916- *WhoFI 92*
**Lossing**, Frederick Pettit 1915- *AmMWSc 92*
**Lossinsky**, Albert S 1946- *AmMWSc 92*
**Lossky**, Vladimir 1903-1958 *DcEcMov*
**Lossy**, Rella *DrAPF 91*
**Losten**, Basil Harry 1930- *WhoRel 92*
**Lostoski**, Paul Robert 1934- *WhoMW 92*
**Losty**, Howard Harold Walter 1926- *Who 92*
**LoSurdo**, Antonio 1943- *AmMWSc 92*
**Lota**, Gerd-Peter Emil 1944- *WhoFI 92*
**Lotan**, James 1931- *AmMWSc 92*
**Lotan**, Reuben 1946- *AmMWSc 92*
**LoTempio**, Julia Matild 1934- *WhoFI 92*
**Loten**, Alexander William 1925- *Who 92*
**Loth**, Eric 1961- *WhoMW 92*
**Loth**, John Lodewyk 1933- *AmMWSc 92*
**Loth**, Stanislaw Jerzy 1929- *WhoEnt 92*
**Lothe**, Jens 1931- *IntWW 91*
**Lothenbach**, Frank W 1956- *WhoIns 92*
**Lothian**, Marquess of 1922- *Who 92*
**Lothian**, Noel 1915- *WrDr 92*
**Lothman**, Carl D. 1955- *WhoAmL 92*
**Lothrop**, Amy *BenetAL 91*
**Lothrop**, Harriett Mulford Stone 1844-1924 *BenetAL 91*
**Lothrop**, Henry W 1844?-1904 *BiInAmS*
**Lothstein**, Leonard 1954- *AmMWSc 92*
**Loti**, Pierre 1850-1923 *GuFrLit 1*
**Lotito**, Nicholas Anthony 1949- *WhoAmL 92*
**Lotkin**, Ralph Louis 1946- *WhoAmL 92*
**Lotlikar**, Prabhakar Dattaram 1928- *AmMWSc 92*
**Lotman**, Yuriy Mikhailovich 1922- *IntWW 91*
**Lotman**, Yuriy Mikhaylovich 1922- *SovUnBD*
**Lotocky**, Innocent H. 1915- *WhoRel 92*
**Loton**, Brian Thorley 1929- *IntWW 91, Who 92*
**Lotrich**, Victor Arthur 1934- *AmMWSc 92*
**Lotruglio**, Anthony F. 1938- *WhoFI 92*
**Lotspeich**, Frederick Benjamin 1914- *AmMWSc 92*
**Lotspeich**, Frederick Jackson 1925- *AmMWSc 92*
**Lotspeich**, James Fulton 1922- *AmMWSc 92*
**Lotspiech**, John E. 1924- *WhoFI 92*
**Lotstein**, James I. 1944- *WhoAmL 92*
**Lott**, Arnold S. 1912- *WrDr 92*
**Lott**, Bernard Maurice 1922- *Who 92*
**Lott**, Brenda Louise 1955- *WhoFI 92*
**Lott**, Bret *DrAPF 91*
**Lott**, Bret 1958- *IntAu&W 91*
**Lott**, Carolyn Ann 1958- *WhoEnt 92*
**Lott**, David Stuart 1943- *WhoAmL 92*
**Lott**, Davis Newton 1913- *WhoWest 92*
**Lott**, Felicity Ann 1947- *IntWW 91*
**Lott**, Felicity Ann Emwhyla 1947- *Who 92*
**Lott**, Fred Wilbur, III 1943- *AmMWSc 92*
**Lott**, Fred Wilbur, Jr 1917- *AmMWSc 92*
**Lott**, Gay Lloyd 1937- *WhoBlA 92*
**Lott**, George d1991 *NewYTBS 91*
**Lott**, James *DrAPF 91*
**Lott**, James Robert 1924- *AmMWSc 92*
**Lott**, James Stewart 1920- *AmMWSc 92*
**Lott**, John Alfred 1936- *AmMWSc 92*
**Lott**, John Norman Arthur 1943- *AmMWSc 92*
**Lott**, Joyce Greenberg *DrAPF 91*
**Lott**, Layman Austin 1937- *AmMWSc 92*
**Lott**, Milton 1919- *TwCWW 91, WrDr 92*
**Lott**, Penelope 1957- *TwCPaSc*
**Lott**, Peter De Forest 1933- *WhoFI 92*
**Lott**, Peter F 1927- *AmMWSc 92*
**Lott**, Ronnie 1959- *WhoBlA 92*
**Lott**, Sam Houston, Jr 1936- *AmMWSc 92*
**Lott**, Trent 1941- *AlmAP 92 [port], IntWW 91, WhoAmP 91*
**Lott**, Yancey Davis, Jr 1939- *WhoAmP 91*
**Lotta**, Michael A. 1955- *WhoAmL 92*
**Lotter**, Charles R. 1937- *WhoAmL 92*
**Lottes**, John Douglas 1946- *WhoRel 92*
**Lottes**, P A 1926- *AmMWSc 92*
**Lotti**, Antonio 1667?-1740 *NewAmDM*
**Lotti**, Victor J 1938- *AmMWSc 92*
**Lottinville**, Mary-Margaret 1949- *WhoRel 92*
**Lottman**, Herbert 1927- *WrDr 92*
**Lottman**, Robert P 1933- *AmMWSc 92*
**Lotts**, Adolphus Lloyd 1934- *AmMWSc 92*
**Lotuaco**, Luisa Go 1938- *WhoMW 92*
**Lotufo**, Donald Arthur 1932- *WhoFI 92*
**Lotven**, Howard Lee 1959- *WhoAmL 92, WhoMW 92*
**Lotwin**, Stanford Gerald 1930- *WhoAmL 92*
**Lotz**, Arthur William 1927- *WhoFI 92*
**Lotz**, Denton 1939- *WhoRel 92*
**Lotz**, George Michael 1928- *WhoEnt 92*
**Lotz**, Jack Coldwell 1929- *WhoIns 92*
**Lotz**, Kurt 1912- *Who 92*
**Lotz**, R. James, Jr. 1932- *WhoFI 92*
**Lotz**, W Gregory *AmMWSc 92*
**Lotz**, Wolfgang 1912-1981 *ConAu 34NR, SmATA 65*
**Lotze**, Michael T 1952- *AmMWSc 92*
**Lotzenhiser**, George William 1923- *WhoEnt 92*
**Lotzova**, Eva *AmMWSc 92*
**Lou**, Alex Yih-Chung 1938- *AmMWSc 92*
**Lou**, David Yeong-Suei 1937- *AmMWSc 92*
**Lou**, Kingdon 1922- *AmMWSc 92*
**Lou**, Peter Louis 1945- *AmMWSc 92*
**Louard**, Agnes A. 1922- *WhoBlA 92*
**Louargand**, Marc Andrew 1945- *WhoFI 92*
**Loubere**, Lou A. 1923- *WrDr 92*
**Louch**, Alfred Richard 1927- *WhoWest 92*
**Louchheim**, Kathleen 1903-1991 *ConAu 133*
**Louchheim**, Katie *ConAu 133*
**Louchheim**, Katie 1903-1991 *CurBio 91N, NewYTBS 91 [port]*
**Louchheim**, Katie S. 1903-1991 *IntWW 91, -91N*
**Louchheim**, William Sandel, Jr. 1930- *WhoWest 92*
**Louck**, James Donald 1928- *AmMWSc 92*
**Loucks**, Daniel Peter 1932- *AmMWSc 92*
**Loucks**, John C. 1943- *WhoMW 92*
**Loucks**, Orie Lipton 1931- *AmMWSc 92, WhoMW 92*
**Loucks**, Ralph Bruce, Jr. 1924- *WhoFI 92*
**Loucks**, Richard Newcomb, III 1919- *WhoEnt 92*
**Loucks**, Steven D 1961- *WhoAmP 91*
**Loucks**, Vernon R., Jr. 1934- *IntWW 91, WhoFI 92, WhoMW 92*
**Loucky-Ramsey**, Joanna Ruth 1954- *WhoRel 92*
**Loud**, Alden Vickery 1925- *AmMWSc 92*
**Loud**, Oliver Schule 1911- *AmMWSc 92*
**Loud**, Patricia C *ConAu 135*
**Loud**, Stewart Nelson, Jr. 1940- *WhoWest 92*
**Loud**, Warren Simms 1921- *AmMWSc 92, WhoMW 92*
**Louda**, Svata Mary *AmMWSc 92*
**Louden**, Albert 1942- *TwCPaSc*
**Louden**, Henderson Nathaniel, Sr. 1928- *WhoBlA 92*
**Louden**, Janice Hunt 1957- *WhoWest 92*
**Louden**, L Richard 1933- *AmMWSc 92*
**Louden**, Willard Charles 1925- *WhoWest 92*
**Louderback**, Peter Darragh 1931- *WhoFI 92*
**Louderback**, Robert J 1929- *WhoAmP 91*
**Louderback**, Truman Eugene 1946- *WhoWest 92*
**Loudermilk**, Gary Wayne 1947- *WhoRel 92*
**Loudermilk**, Joey M. 1953- *WhoAmL 92*
**Loudner**, Gary Lee 1954- *WhoEnt 92*
**Loudon**, Aarnout Alexander 1936- *IntWW 91*
**Loudon**, Catherine 1958- *AmMWSc 92*
**Loudon**, Craig Michael 1950- *WhoEnt 92*
**Loudon**, David Lamond 1944- *WhoFI 92*
**Loudon**, Donald Hoover 1937- *WhoMW 92*
**Loudon**, Dorothy 1933- *IntMPA 92, WhoEnt 92*
**Loudon**, Douglas M. 1944- *WhoFI 92*
**Loudon**, George Ernest 1942- *Who 92*
**Loudon**, Gordon Marcus 1942- *AmMWSc 92*
**Loudon**, John Duncan Ott 1924- *Who 92*
**Loudon**, John Hugo 1905- *IntWW 91, Who 92*
**Loudon**, Robert G 1925- *AmMWSc 92*
**Loudon**, Rodney 1934- *IntWW 91, Who 92*
**Loudon**, Samuel 1727?-1813 *BenetAL 91*
**Loudoun** *BlkwEAR*
**Loudoun**, Countess of 1919- *Who 92*
**Loudoun**, Robert Beverley 1922- *Who 92*
**Loudova**, Ivana 1941- *ConCom 92*
**Louekoski**, Matti Kalevi 1941- *IntWW 91*
**Louet**, Philippe Marie Alexandre Gabriel 1933- *IntWW 91*
**Louganis**, Gregory 1960- *FacFETw*
**Lougeay**, Ray Leonard 1944- *AmMWSc 92*
**Lougee**, George S 1948- *WhoAmP 91*
**Lougee**, Richard William 1956- *WhoAmP 91*
**Lough**, Charles Allen 1946- *WhoIns 92*
**Lough**, John 1913- *IntWW 91, Who 92*
**Lough**, John William, Jr 1943- *AmMWSc 92*
**Lough**, Raymond Everett 1935- *WhoAmP 91*
**Loughary**, Thomas Michael 1959- *WhoMW 92*
**Loughborough**, Archdeacon Of *Who 92*
**Loughborough**, Lord 1986- *Who 92*
**Loughborough**, John Norton 1832-1924 *RelLAm 91*
**Lougheed**, Peter 1928- *IntWW 91, Who 92*
**Lougheed**, Thomas Robert 1941- *WhoFI 92*
**Loughheed**, Thomas Crossley 1929- *AmMWSc 92*
**Loughlin**, Bernard D 1917- *AmMWSc 92*
**Loughlin**, Charles William 1914- *Who 92*
**Loughlin**, James Francis 1894- *AmMWSc 92*
**Loughlin**, Mary Anne Elizabeth 1956- *WhoEnt 92*
**Loughlin**, Richard J. 1932- *WhoWest 92*
**Loughlin**, Richard L. *DrAPF 91*
**Loughlin**, Richard L & Popp, Lilian M *ScFEYrs*
**Loughlin**, Richard Lawrence 1907- *ScFEYrs*
**Loughlin**, Thomas Richard 1943- *AmMWSc 92*
**Loughlin**, Timothy Arthur 1942- *AmMWSc 92*
**Loughman**, Barbara Ellen Evers 1940- *AmMWSc 92*
**Loughmiller**, Brian Scott 1960- *WhoAmL 92*
**Loughran**, Edward Dan 1928- *AmMWSc 92*
**Loughran**, Eileen Agnes 1951- *WhoEnt 92*
**Loughran**, Gerard Andrew 1918- *WhoMW 92*
**Loughran**, Gerard Andrew, Sr 1918- *AmMWSc 92*
**Loughran**, James 1931- *IntWW 91, Who 92*
**Loughran**, James Newman 1940- *WhoRel 92, WhoWest 92*
**Loughrey**, F. Joseph 1949- *WhoMW 92*
**Loughrey**, Thomas James 1940- *WhoMW 92*
**Loughridge**, John Halsted, Jr. 1945- *WhoAmL 92*
**Loughridge**, Michael Samuel 1936- *AmMWSc 92*
**Loughridge**, Robert Foster, Jr. 1935- *WhoFI 92*
**Loughridge**, Robert Hills 1843-1917 *BiInAmS*
**Loughrin**, Jay Richardson 1943- *WhoEnt 92*
**Loughry**, Frank Glade 1910- *AmMWSc 92*
**Loughton**, Arthur 1931- *AmMWSc 92*
**Loui**, Michael Conrad 1955- *AmMWSc 92*
**Loui**, Patricia M. L. 1949- *WhoWest 92*
**Louie**, David Mark 1951- *WhoAmL 92*
**Louie**, David Wong *DrAPF 91*
**Louie**, Dexter Stephen *AmMWSc 92*
**Louie**, Ming 1948- *AmMWSc 92*
**Louie**, Raymond 1936- *AmMWSc 92*
**Louie**, Robert Eugene 1929- *AmMWSc 92*
**Louie**, Steven Gwon Sheng 1949- *AmMWSc 92*
**Louis XIV** 1638-1715 *BlkwCEP*
**Louis XV** 1710-1774 *BlkwCEP*
**Louis XVI** 1754-1793 *BlkwCEP*
**Louis**, Adrian C. *DrAPF 91*
**Louis**, Antoine 1723-1792 *BlkwCEP*
**Louis**, Conan Noel 1951- *WhoAmL 92*
**Louis**, David F *WhoAmP 91*
**Louis**, Dean Sherwood 1936- *WhoMW 92*
**Louis**, Jean 1907- *IntMPA 92*
**Louis**, Jean Francois 1932- *AmMWSc 92*
**Louis**, Joe 1914-1981 *FacFETw [port], RComAH*
**Louis**, John 1924- *AmMWSc 92*
**Louis**, John Jeffrey 1925- *WhoAmP 91*
**Louis**, John Jeffry, Jr. 1925- *IntWW 91, Who 92*
**Louis**, Joseph 1948- *WhoBlA 92*
**Louis**, Kenneth C 1938- *WhoIns 92*
**Louis**, Kwok Toy 1927- *AmMWSc 92*
**Louis**, Lawrence Hua-Hsien 1908- *AmMWSc 92*
**Louis**, Lester 1928- *WhoEnt 92*
**Louis**, Morris 1912-1962 *FacFETw*
**Louis**, Pat *IntAu&W 91X*
**Louis**, Pierre 1913- *IntWW 91*
**Louis**, Suchet Lesperance 1935- *WhoBlA 92*
**Louis**, Thomas Michael 1944- *AmMWSc 92*
**Louis**, Virgie Lee 1945- *WhoMW 92*
**Louis**, William Joseph 1928- *WhoEnt 92*
**Louis-Dreyfus**, Robert Louis Maurice 1946- *IntWW 91*
**Louis-Ferdinand**, Robert T *AmMWSc 92*
**Louise**, Queen of Prussia 1776-1810 *EncAmaz 91*
**Louise**, Ann *DrAPF 91*
**Louise**, Esther *DrAPF 91*
**Louise**, Tina *IntMPA 92*
**Louisoder**, Florian Ralph 1958- *WhoEnt 92*
**Louisos**, Tom 1943- *WhoAmP 91*
**Louistall-Monroe**, Victorine Augusta 1912- *WhoBlA 92*
**Louisy**, Allan *IntWW 91, Who 92*
**Louk**, Rose Agnes 1920- *WhoRel 92*
**Loullis**, Costas Christou 1950- *AmMWSc 92*
**Loulou**, Richard Jacques 1944- *AmMWSc 92*
**Louly**, Mohamed Mahmoud Ould Ahmed *IntWW 91*
**Lounasmaa**, Olli Viktor 1930- *IntWW 91*
**Lounibos**, Leon Philip 1947- *AmMWSc 92*
**Lounsberry**, Gary Richard 1944- *WhoMW 92*
**Lounsbury**, Charles B. 1942- *WhoMW 92*
**Lounsbury**, Franklin 1912- *AmMWSc 92*
**Lounsbury**, Gary David 1953- *WhoWest 92*
**Lounsbury**, John Baldwin 1936- *AmMWSc 92*
**Loup**, Francois Bernard 1940- *WhoEnt 92*
**Lourance**, Robert L. 1949- *WhoRel 92*
**Lourd**, Barry Blaine 1962- *WhoWest 92*
**Lourdusamy**, Simon 1924- *IntWW 91, WhoRel 92*
**Lourenco**, Ruy Valentim 1929- *AmMWSc 92, WhoMW 92*
**Lourey**, Becky J 1943- *WhoAmP 91*
**Louria**, Donald Bruce 1928- *AmMWSc 92*
**Lourie**, Alan D *WhoAmP 91*
**Lourie**, Alan David 1935- *AmMWSc 92, WhoAmL 92*
**Lourie**, Arthur Vincent 1892-1966 *NewAmDM*
**Lourie**, Charles Michael 1940- *WhoEnt 92*
**Lourie**, Dick *DrAPF 91*
**Lourie**, Eugene 1903-1991 *NewYTBS 91*
**Lourie**, Herbert 1929- *AmMWSc 92*
**Lourie**, Isadore E 1932- *WhoAmP 91*
**Lourie**, Iven *DrAPF 91*
**Lourie**, Sylvain 1928- *IntWW 91*
**Loury**, Glenn Cartman 1948- *WhoBlA 92*
**Lousada**, Anthony 1907- *Who 92*
**Lousberg**, Peter Herman 1931- *WhoAmL 92, WhoMW 92*
**Loustau-Lalanne**, Bernard Michel 1938- *IntWW 91, Who 92*
**Loustaunau**, Joaquin 1936- *AmMWSc 92*
**Loutfy**, Aly 1935- *IntWW 91*
**Loutfy**, Rafik Omar 1943- *AmMWSc 92*
**Louth**, Baron 1929- *Who 92*
**Louth**, Andrew 1944- *WhoRel 92*
**Louth**, Rexford L. 1962- *WhoRel 92*

**Louthan,** Robert *DrAPF 91*
**Loutit,** John Freeman 1910- *IntWW 91, Who 92*
**Loutrel,** Claude Yves 1930- *WhoFI 92*
**Louttit,** Richard Talcott 1932- *AmMWSc 92*
**Louttit,** Robert Irving 1929- *AmMWSc 92*
**Loutzenhiser,** Carolyn Ann 1942- *WhoMW 92*
**Louvau,** Gordon Ernest 1928- *WhoWest 92*
**Louvier,** Alain 1945- *IntWW 91*
**Louvin Brothers** *NewAmDM*
**Louw,** Eli van der Merwe 1927- *IntWW 91*
**Louw,** Eugene 1931- *IntWW 91*
**Louw,** Raymond 1926- *IntAu&W 91, IntWW 91*
**Loux,** Gordon Dale 1938- *WhoFI 92, WhoRel 92, WhoWest 92*
**Loux,** Joseph Anthony, Jr. 1945- *WhoRel 92*
**Loux,** Michael Joseph 1942- *WhoMW 92*
**Loux,** Richard Charles 1929- *WhoFI 92*
**Louys,** Pierre 1870-1925 *GuFrLit 1*
**Lovaglia,** Anthony Richard 1923- *AmMWSc 92*
**Lovald,** Roger Allen 1938- *AmMWSc 92*
**Lovallo,** Patricia Gaffney 1957- *WhoFI 92*
**Lovallo,** William Robert 1946- *AmMWSc 92*
**Lovas,** Francis John 1941- *AmMWSc 92*
**Lovass-Nagy,** Victor 1923- *AmMWSc 92*
**Lovat,** Baron 1911- *Who 92*
**Lovat,** Master of 1939- *Who 92*
**Lovat,** Leonard Scott 1926- *Who 92*
**Lovato,** Andrew Leo 1955- *WhoHisp 92*
**Lovato,** Eugene Daniel 1951- *WhoHisp 92*
**Lovato,** Johnny R. 1966- *WhoHisp 92*
**Lovato,** Michael 1965- *WhoHisp 92*
**Lovato,** Robert L. 1937- *WhoHisp 92*
**Lovatt,** Arthur Kingsbury, Jr. 1920- *WhoFI 92, WhoWest 92*
**Lovatt,** Carol Jean 1947- *AmMWSc 92*
**Lovdahl,** Bruce Martin 1946- *WhoAmP 91*
**Love,** Alfred Henry 1830-1913 *AmPeW*
**Love,** Allan Walter 1916- *AmMWSc 92*
**Love,** Andrew Henry Garmany 1934- *IntWW 91, Who 92*
**Love,** B.D. *DrAPF 91*
**Love,** Barbara 1946- *WhoBlA 92*
**Love,** Bruce Blackburn 1929- *WhoRel 92*
**Love,** Calvin Miles 1937- *AmMWSc 92*
**Love,** Carl G 1940- *AmMWSc 92*
**Love,** Clarence C. 1922- *WhoBlA 92*
**Love,** Clarence Chester 1922- *WhoAmP 91*
**Love,** Clinton Kenneth 1952- *WhoMW 92*
**Love,** David *IntAu&W 91X*
**Love,** David Vaughan 1919- *AmMWSc 92*
**Love,** David Waxham 1946- *AmMWSc 92*
**Love,** Douglas Allen *WhoEnt 92*
**Love,** Edith Holmes 1950- *WhoEnt 92*
**Love,** Edward M., Jr. 1952- *WhoBlA 92*
**Love,** Eleanor Young *WhoBlA 92*
**Love,** Ezekiel 1944- *WhoBlA 92*
**Love,** Frank, Jr 1927- *WhoAmP 91*
**Love,** George H. d1991 *NewYTBS 91 [port]*
**Love,** George H. 1900-1991 *CurBio 91N*
**Love,** George Hayward 1924- *WhoBlA 92*
**Love,** George M 1944- *AmMWSc 92*
**Love,** George Ranier 1949- *WhoAmL 92*
**Love,** Glen Scott 1958- *WhoAmL 92*
**Love,** Gordon Ross 1937- *AmMWSc 92*
**Love,** Harold M 1919- *WhoAmP 91*
**Love,** Harry Schroeder, Jr 1927- *AmMWSc 92*
**Love,** Harry Willard 1949- *WhoRel 92*
**Love,** Helene A. 1962- *WhoMW 92*
**Love,** Howard McClintic 1930- *IntWW 91*
**Love,** Hugh Morrison 1926- *AmMWSc 92*
**Love,** James Ralph 1937- *WhoBlA 92*
**Love,** James Spencer 1896-1962 *DcNCBi 4*
**Love,** Janice 1952- *WhoRel 92*
**Love,** Jerry Bert 1950- *WhoFI 92, WhoMW 92*
**Love,** Jim 1938- *AmMWSc 92*
**Love,** Jimmy Carson 1962- *WhoRel 92*
**Love,** Jimmy Dwane 1946- *AmMWSc 92*
**Love,** Joe W. 1937- *WhoBlA 92*
**Love,** John *DrAPF 91*
**Love,** John David 1913- *AmMWSc 92*
**Love,** John Scott 1945- *WhoFI 92*
**Love,** Joseph E, Jr 1920- *AmMWSc 92*
**Love,** Josephine Harreld 1914- *NotBlAW 92*
**Love,** L J Cline 1940- *AmMWSc 92*
**Love,** Laurie Miller 1960- *WhoWest 92*
**Love,** Leon 1923- *AmMWSc 92*
**Love,** Mabel R. 1908- *WhoBlA 92*
**Love,** Mac E 1921- *WhoAmP 91*
**Love,** Makere Rangiatea Ralph 1907- *Who 92*
**Love,** Margaret C. 1942- *WhoAmL 92*
**Love,** Mark Steven 1950- *WhoAmL 92*
**Love,** Mildred L. 1941- *WhoBlA 92*
**Love,** Miron Anderson 1920- *WhoAmL 92*
**Love,** Norman Duane 1939- *AmMWSc 92*
**Love,** Philip Noel 1939- *Who 92*
**Love,** Ralph *Who 92*
**Love,** Raymond Charles 1953- *AmMWSc 92*
**Love,** Richard Harrison 1939- *AmMWSc 92*
**Love,** Robert Calvin Grier 1840-1907 *DcNCBi 4*
**Love,** Robert Merton 1909- *AmMWSc 92*
**Love,** Rodney Marvin 1908- *WhoAmP 91*
**Love,** Roosevelt Sam 1933- *WhoBlA 92*
**Love,** Russell Jacques 1931- *AmMWSc 92*
**Love,** Ruth B. 1935- *NotBlAW 92, WhoBlA 92*
**Love,** Samuel A, Jr 1945- *WhoAmP 91*
**Love,** Sandra *DrAPF 91*
**Love,** Sandra Rae 1947- *WhoWest 92*
**Love,** Shirley 1940- *WhoEnt 92*
**Love,** Shirley Dean 1933- *WhoAmP 91*
**Love,** Sydney Francis 1923- *AmMWSc 92*
**Love,** Thomas Clifford 1947- *WhoBlA 92*
**Love,** Thomas Teel 1931- *WhoAmL 92*
**Love,** Tom *WhoAmP 91*
**Love,** Tom Jay, Jr 1923- *AmMWSc 92*
**Love,** Walter Bennett, Jr. 1921- *WhoAmL 92*
**Love,** Warner Edwards 1922- *AmMWSc 92*
**Love,** William Alfred 1932- *AmMWSc 92*
**Love,** William Carter 1784-1824 *DcNCBi 4*
**Love,** William F 1925- *AmMWSc 92*
**Love,** William Gary 1941- *AmMWSc 92*
**Lovecchio,** Frank Vito 1943- *AmMWSc 92*
**Lovecraft,** H. P. 1890-1937 *BenetAL 91, ConAu 133, FacFETw, ScFEYrs, TwCSFW 91*
**Loveday,** Alan 1928- *Who 92*
**Loveday,** Harold Maxwell 1923- *IntWW 91*
**Loveday,** John 1926- *ConPo 91, WrDr 92*
**Lovegrove,** Fred Hampton, Jr 1939- *WhoAmP 91*
**Lovegrove,** Geoffrey David 1919- *Who 92*
**Lovegrove,** Robert Emerson 1943- *WhoWest 92*
**Lovejoy,** Alan Kent 1939- *WhoWest 92*
**Lovejoy,** David Arnold 1943- *AmMWSc 92*
**Lovejoy,** Derek R 1928- *AmMWSc 92*
**Lovejoy,** Donald Walker 1931- *AmMWSc 92*
**Lovejoy,** Elijah P. 1802-1837 *BenetAL 91*
**Lovejoy,** George Montgomery, Jr. 1930- *WhoFI 92*
**Lovejoy,** Jack 1937- *ConAu 35NR*
**Lovejoy,** Jefferson Marshall 1814-1877 *DcNCBi 4*
**Lovejoy,** Lee Harold 1936- *WhoFI 92*
**Lovejoy,** Owen 1811-1864 *BenetAL 91*
**Lovejoy,** Owen 1943- *AmMWSc 92*
**Lovejoy,** Roland William 1931- *AmMWSc 92*
**Lovejoy,** Roya Lynn 1946- *WhoAmL 92*
**Lovejoy,** Thomas E 1941- *AmMWSc 92*
**Lovejoy,** Virginia K 1927- *WhoAmP 91*
**Lovejoy,** William Joseph 1940- *WhoFI 92, WhoMW 92*
**Lovekamp,** Carl Lorenz 1932- *WhoAmP 91*
**Lovelace,** Earl of 1951- *Who 92*
**Lovelace,** Alan Mathieson 1929- *AmMWSc 92*
**Lovelace,** C James 1934- *AmMWSc 92*
**Lovelace,** Claud William Venton 1934- *AmMWSc 92*
**Lovelace,** David Wayne 1948- *WhoRel 92*
**Lovelace,** Dean Alan 1946- *WhoBlA 92*
**Lovelace,** Earl 1935- *ConNov 91, IntAu&W 91, WrDr 92*
**Lovelace,** Gloria Elaine 1945- *WhoBlA 92*
**Lovelace,** John C. 1926- *WhoBlA 92*
**Lovelace,** Linda Diane 1948- *WhoMW 92*
**Lovelace,** Onzalo Robert 1940- *WhoBlA 92*
**Lovelace,** Richard 1618-1657? *RfGEnL 91*
**Lovelace,** Richard Van Evera 1941- *AmMWSc 92*
**Lovelace,** Susan Marie Fite 1952- *WhoRel 92*
**Lovelady,** Rueben Leon 1958- *WhoBlA 92*
**Loveland,** Don C 1916- *WhoAmP 91*
**Loveland,** Donald William 1934- *AmMWSc 92*
**Loveland,** Eugene Franklin 1920- *WhoFI 92*
**Loveland,** Holly Standish 1947- *WhoFI 92, WhoMW 92*
**Loveland,** Robert Edward 1938- *AmMWSc 92*
**Loveland,** Walter 1939- *AmMWSc 92*
**Lovelass,** Nancy Jean 1948- *WhoWest 92*
**Loveless,** Alton E. 1937- *WhoRel 92*
**Loveless,** Donald Steven 1957- *WhoWest 92*
**Loveless,** George Group 1940- *WhoAmL 92*
**Loveless,** Harry Richard 1919- *WhoMW 92*
**Loveless,** Howard Louis, Jr. 1953- *WhoFI 92*
**Loveless,** Mary Hewitt d1991 *NewYTBS 91*
**Loveless,** Ralph Peyton 1936- *WhoAmL 92*
**Loveless,** Scott E *AmMWSc 92*
**Loveless,** William Michael 1949- *WhoEnt 92*
**Lovelett-Distad,** Carolyn Thonette 1953- *WhoMW 92*
**Lovell,** A. Buffum *WhoAmL 92*
**Lovell,** Arnold Henry d1990 *Who 92N*
**Lovell,** Barry Wade 1960- *WhoFI 92*
**Lovell,** Bernard 1913- *FacFETw, IntAu&W 91, IntWW 91, Who 92, WrDr 92*
**Lovell,** Bernard Wentzel *AmMWSc 92*
**Lovell,** Carl Erwin, Jr. 1945- *WhoAmL 92*
**Lovell,** Charles C. 1929- *WhoAmL 92*
**Lovell,** Charles W, Jr 1922- *AmMWSc 92*
**Lovell,** Edward George 1939- *AmMWSc 92*
**Lovell,** Emily Kalled 1920- *WhoWest 92*
**Lovell,** Francis Joseph, III 1949- *WhoFI 92*
**Lovell,** Glenn Michael 1948- *WhoEnt 92*
**Lovell,** Harold Lemuel 1922- *AmMWSc 92*
**Lovell,** James 1928- *FacFETw*
**Lovell,** James Byron 1927- *AmMWSc 92*
**Lovell,** James C. 1926- *WhoFI 92*
**Lovell,** Jeffrey Dale 1952- *WhoFI 92, WhoWest 92*
**Lovell,** Kenneth Ernest Walter 1919- *Who 92*
**Lovell,** Malcolm R, Jr *WhoAmP 91*
**Lovell,** Marc *WrDr 92*
**Lovell,** Margaret 1939- *TwCPaSc*
**Lovell,** Mary Ann 1943- *WhoMW 92*
**Lovell,** Michael C. 1930- *WhoFI 92*
**Lovell,** Richard Arlington 1930- *AmMWSc 92*
**Lovell,** Richard Thomas 1934- *AmMWSc 92*
**Lovell,** Robert Edmund 1921- *AmMWSc 92*
**Lovell,** Robert Gibson 1920- *AmMWSc 92*
**Lovell,** Robert Marlow, Jr. 1930- *WhoFI 92, WhoIns 92*
**Lovell,** Robert R 1937- *AmMWSc 92*
**Lovell,** Stuart Estes 1928- *AmMWSc 92*
**Lovell,** Theodore 1928- *WhoFI 92*
**Lovell,** Tom 1909- *WhoWest 92*
**Lovell,** Walter Carl 1934- *WhoFI 92*
**Lovell-Davis** *Who 92*
**Lovell-Davis,** Baron 1924- *Who 92*
**Lovelock,** David *AmMWSc 92*
**Lovelock,** Douglas 1923- *IntWW 91, Who 92*
**Lovelock,** James Ephraim 1919- *IntWW 91, Who 92*
**Lovelock,** Yann Rufus 1939- *IntAu&W 91*
**Lovely,** Richard Herbert 1941- *AmMWSc 92*
**Lovely,** Thomas Dixon 1930- *WhoFI 92*
**Loveman,** E Barry 1942- *WhoAmP 91*
**Loveman,** Gail Jean 1949- *WhoFI 92*
**Loveman,** Stephen Charles Gardner 1943- *Who 92*
**Loven,** Charles John 1937- *WhoWest 92*
**Lovenberg,** Walter M. 1934- *WhoFI 92*
**Lovenberg,** Walter McKay 1934- *AmMWSc 92*
**Lovendusky,** James Vincent 1957- *WhoEnt 92*
**Lovenheim,** David A 1942- *WhoAmP 91*
**Loventhal,** Milton 1923- *WhoWest 92*
**Lover,** Samuel 1797-1868 *RfGEnL 91*
**Loverde,** James M. *DrAPF 91*
**Lo Verde,** Philip Thomas 1946- *AmMWSc 92*
**Loveridge,** John 1912- *Who 92*
**Loveridge,** John 1925- *Who 92*
**Lovering,** Edward Gilbert 1934- *AmMWSc 92*
**Lovering,** Eugene Harrison, Jr. 1952- *WhoRel 92*
**Lovering,** John Francis 1930- *Who 92*
**Lovering,** Joseph 1813-1892 *BiInAmS*
**Lovering,** Richard S. 1954- *WhoAmL 92*
**Lovering,** Thomas Seward 1896- *AmMWSc 92*
**Loverro-Sprick,** Andrea 1954- *WhoEnt 92*
**Lovesey,** Peter 1936- *IntAu&W 91, WrDr 92*
**Lovestedt,** Stanley Almer 1913- *AmMWSc 92*
**Lovestone,** Jay 1898-1990 *AnObit 1990, FacFETw*
**Lovetri,** Jeannette Louise 1949- *WhoEnt 92*
**Lovett,** Cummings Samuel 1917- *RelLAm 91*
**Lovett,** Edmund J, III *AmMWSc 92*
**Lovett,** Edward P. 1902- *WhoBlA 92*
**Lovett,** Eva G 1940- *AmMWSc 92*
**Lovett,** Gary Martin 1953- *AmMWSc 92*
**Lovett,** James Satterthwaite 1925- *AmMWSc 92*
**Lovett,** John Robert 1931- *AmMWSc 92, WhoFI 92*
**Lovett,** Joseph 1933- *AmMWSc 92*
**Lovett,** Leon *WhoEnt 92*
**Lovett,** Leonard 1939- *WhoBlA 92*
**Lovett,** Leroy Clifton, Jr. 1922- *WhoEnt 92*
**Lovett,** Lisa A. Richlich 1963- *WhoMW 92*
**Lovett,** Mack, Jr. 1931- *WhoBlA 92*
**Lovett,** Paul Scott 1940- *AmMWSc 92*
**Lovett,** Radford Dow 1933- *WhoFI 92*
**Lovett,** Robert Morss 1870-1956 *BenetAL 91*
**Lovett,** William Anthony 1934- *WhoAmL 92*
**Lovett,** Willie Clinton 1939- *WhoAmP 91*
**Lovette,** Lawrence Roger 1935- *WhoRel 92*
**Lovewell,** John 1691-1725 *BenetAL 91*
**Lovewell,** Joseph Taplin 1833-1918 *BiInAmS*
**Loveys,** Ralph A 1929- *WhoAmP 91*
**Lovich,** Jeffrey Edward *AmMWSc 92*
**Lovick,** Albert Ernest Fred 1912- *Who 92*
**Lovick,** John d1733 *DcNCBi 4*
**Lovick,** Robert Clyde 1921- *AmMWSc 92*
**Lovick,** Thomas 1680-1759 *DcNCBi 4*
**Lovig,** Lawrence, III 1942- *WhoFI 92*
**Lovill,** Edward Francis 1842-1925 *DcNCBi 4*
**Lovill,** John 1929- *Who 92*
**Lovin,** Hugh Taylor 1928- *WhoWest 92*
**Lovin,** Robin Warren 1946- *WhoRel 92*
**Loving,** Albert A., Jr. 1920- *WhoBlA 92*
**Loving,** Charles Roy 1957- *WhoWest 92*
**Loving,** James Leslie, Jr. 1944- *WhoBlA 92*
**Loving,** Jean Franklin 1925- *WhoWest 92*
**Loving,** Oyoko *DrAPF 91*
**Loving,** Pamela Yvonne 1943- *WhoBlA 92*
**Loving,** Rose 1927- *WhoBlA 92*
**Loving,** Susan B. *WhoAmL 92*
**Lovinger,** Andrew Joseph 1948- *AmMWSc 92*
**Lovinger,** Robert Jay 1932- *WhoMW 92*
**Lovingood,** Judson Allison 1936- *AmMWSc 92*
**Lovings,** L Edward 1932- *WhoAmP 91*
**Lovins,** Amory Bloch 1947- *WhoWest 92*
**Lovins,** Robert E 1935- *AmMWSc 92*
**Lovitt,** Craig Edward 1932- *WhoAmP 91*
**Lovitz,** Jon 1957- *IntMPA 92, WhoEnt 92*
**Lovoi,** Paul Anthony 1947- *WhoFI 92*
**Lovorn,** Thomas Eugene 1938- *WhoRel 92*
**Lovrien,** Rex Eugene 1928- *AmMWSc 92*
**Lovshin,** Leonard Louis, Jr 1942- *AmMWSc 92*
**Lovvik,** Daryl Vaughn 1941- *WhoWest 92*
**Lovy,** Andrew 1935- *WhoMW 92*
**Low** *Who 92*
**Low,** Alan 1916- *Who 92*
**Low,** Alfred D. 1913- *WrDr 92*
**Low,** Anthony 1935- *WrDr 92*
**Low,** Barbara Wharton 1920- *AmMWSc 92*
**Low,** Bobbi Stiers 1942- *AmMWSc 92*
**Low,** Boon-Chye 1946- *AmMWSc 92*
**Low,** Chow-Eng 1938- *AmMWSc 92*
**Low,** Daniel Tien Kee 1898- *WhoAmP 91*
**Low,** David *DrAPF 91*
**Low,** David Alan 1952- *WhoWest 92*
**Low,** Denise *DrAPF 91*
**Low,** Denise Lea 1949- *WhoMW 92*
**Low,** Donald Anthony 1927- *Who 92*
**Low,** Dorothy Mackie 1916- *IntAu&W 91, WrDr 92*
**Low,** Emmet Francis, Jr 1922- *AmMWSc 92*
**Low,** Ethelbert Holland 1930- *WhoEnt 92*
**Low,** Francis Eugene 1921- *AmMWSc 92, IntWW 91*
**Low,** Frank James 1933- *AmMWSc 92*
**Low,** Frank Norman 1911- *AmMWSc 92*
**Low,** G. David *NewYTBS 91 [port]*
**Low,** George M 1926-1984 *FacFETw*
**Low,** Graeme 1928- *Who 92*
**Low,** Hans 1921- *AmMWSc 92*
**Low,** James Alexander 1925- *AmMWSc 92*
**Low,** James Morrison- 1925- *Who 92*
**Low,** John Henry 1954- *WhoFI 92*
**Low,** John R, Jr 1909- *AmMWSc 92*
**Low,** Juliette 1860-1927 *HanAmWH*
**Low,** Kenneth Brooks, Jr 1936- *AmMWSc 92*
**Low,** Lawrence J 1921- *AmMWSc 92*
**Low,** Leone Yarborough 1935- *AmMWSc 92*
**Low,** Loh-Lee 1948- *AmMWSc 92*
**Low,** M David 1935- *AmMWSc 92*
**Low,** Manfred Josef Dominik 1928- *AmMWSc 92*
**Low,** Marc E 1935- *AmMWSc 92*
**Low,** Mary Alice 1949- *AmMWSc 92*
**Low,** Merry Cook 1925- *WhoWest 92*
**Low,** Morton David 1935- *AmMWSc 92*
**Low,** Niels Leo 1916- *AmMWSc 92*
**Low,** Norman C, Jr 1925- *WhoAmP 91*
**Low,** Patricia Enid Rose 1932- *WhoBlA 92*
**Low,** Paul R *AmMWSc 92*
**Low,** Peter W. 1937- *WhoAmL 92*
**Low,** Philip Funk 1921- *AmMWSc 92*
**Low,** Philip Stewart 1947- *AmMWSc 92*
**Low,** Rachael *IntAu&W 91*
**Low,** Richard H. 1927- *WhoEnt 92*
**Low,** Robert A 1919- *WhoAmP 91*

**Low**, Robert Burnham 1940- *AmMWSc 92*
**Low**, Sarah 1964- *TwCPaSc*
**Low**, Stephen 1927- *IntWW 91*, *WhoAmP 91*
**Low**, Suzanne Claire 1948- *WhoAmL 92*
**Low**, Teresa Lingchun Kao 1941- *AmMWSc 92*
**Low**, Walter Cheney 1950- *AmMWSc 92*
**Low**, William 1922- *AmMWSc 92*
**Low**, Wye Ming 1960- *WhoAmL 92*
**Lowam**, Ron *TwCSFW 91*
**Lowance**, Franklin Elta 1907- *AmMWSc 92*
**Lowbury**, Edward 1913- *ConPo 91*, *WrDr 92*
**Lowbury**, Edward Joseph Lister 1913- *IntAu&W 91*
**Lowden**, Desmond Scott 1937- *IntAu&W 91*, *WrDr 92*
**Lowden**, Gordon Stuart 1927- *Who 92*
**Lowden**, J Alexander 1933- *AmMWSc 92*
**Lowden**, Janice Marie Ely 1956- *WhoRel 92*
**Lowden**, Richard Max 1943- *AmMWSc 92*
**Lowder**, J Elbert 1940- *AmMWSc 92*
**Lowder**, James N 1950- *AmMWSc 92*
**Lowder**, Jerry E. 1932- *WhoEnt 92*
**Lowder**, Leah Denise 1965- *WhoAmL 92*
**Lowder**, Wayne Morris 1933- *AmMWSc 92*
**Lowdermilk**, Dale 1948- *WhoEnt 92*, *WhoWest 92*
**Lowdermilk**, Robert Elbert, III 1951- *WhoRel 92*
**Lowdermilk**, Walter Clay 1888-1974 *DcNCBi 4*
**Lowdin**, Per-Olov 1916- *AmMWSc 92*
**Lowe**, A L, Jr 1927- *AmMWSc 92*
**Lowe**, A Lynn *WhoAmP 91*
**Lowe**, Al 1946- *WhoWest 92*
**Lowe**, Alan Dennis 1953- *WhoRel 92*
**Lowe**, Aubrey F. 1940- *WhoBlA 92*
**Lowe**, Billy Troy 1949- *WhoRel 92*
**Lowe**, Carl Clifford 1919- *AmMWSc 92*
**Lowe**, Chad 1968- *IntMPA 92*
**Lowe**, Charles Herbert, Jr 1920- *AmMWSc 92*
**Lowe**, Charles Upton 1921- *AmMWSc 92*
**Lowe**, Clarence 1946- *WhoAmP 91*
**Lowe**, Cortnie A. *DrAPF 91*
**Lowe**, David d1965 *LesBEnT 92*
**Lowe**, David Alexander 1942- *Who 92*
**Lowe**, David Bruce Douglas 1935- *Who 92*
**Lowe**, David Ming-Li 1932- *WhoWest 92*
**Lowe**, David Nicoll 1909- *Who 92*
**Lowe**, Donald Ray 1942- *AmMWSc 92*
**Lowe**, Douglas 1922- *Who 92*
**Lowe**, Douglas Ackley 1942- *IntWW 91*, *Who 92*
**Lowe**, Duane Rayburne 1942- *WhoMW 92*
**Lowe**, Edgar 1905- *Who 92*
**Lowe**, Edwin Nobles 1912- *WhoAmL 92*
**Lowe**, Eugene Yerby, Jr. 1949- *WhoBlA 92*
**Lowe**, Eward Joseph 1935- *WhoMW 92*
**Lowe**, Forrest Gilbert 1927- *AmMWSc 92*
**Lowe**, Frank 1927- *WhoEnt 92*
**Lowe**, Frank Budge 1941- *IntWW 91*, *Who 92*
**Lowe**, Gary Allen 1951- *WhoRel 92*
**Lowe**, Geoffrey Colin 1920- *Who 92*
**Lowe**, Gordon 1933- *Who 92*
**Lowe**, Harry J 1919- *AmMWSc 92*
**Lowe**, Hazel Marie 1936- *WhoBlA 92*
**Lowe**, Irving J 1929- *AmMWSc 92*
**Lowe**, Jack Ira 1927- *AmMWSc 92*
**Lowe**, Jackie *WhoBlA 92*
**Lowe**, James Edward 1946- *AmMWSc 92*
**Lowe**, James Edward, Jr. 1950- *WhoBlA 92*
**Lowe**, James Harry, Jr 1931- *AmMWSc 92*
**Lowe**, James N 1936- *AmMWSc 92*
**Lowe**, James Urban, II 1921- *AmMWSc 92*
**Lowe**, James Willard 1963- *WhoAmL 92*
**Lowe**, Janet Marie 1924- *AmMWSc 92*
**Lowe**, Jeanne Catherine 1942- *WhoRel 92*
**Lowe**, Jeff 1952- *TwCPaSc*
**Lowe**, Joe Allen 1945- *WhoRel 92*
**Lowe**, John 1922- *Who 92*
**Lowe**, John, III 1916- *AmMWSc 92*
**Lowe**, John Edward 1935- *AmMWSc 92*
**Lowe**, John Eric Charles 1907- *Who 92*
**Lowe**, John Evelyn 1928- *Who 92*
**Lowe**, John Fletcher, Jr. 1932- *WhoRel 92*
**Lowe**, John Philip 1936- *AmMWSc 92*
**Lowe**, John Stanley 1941- *WhoAmL 92*
**Lowe**, Jonathan F. *DrAPF 91*
**Lowe**, Jonathan Wayne 1947- *WhoAmL 92*
**Lowe**, Josiah L 1905- *AmMWSc 92*
**Lowe**, Kenneth Gordon 1917- *Who 92*
**Lowe**, Kurt Emil 1905- *AmMWSc 92*
**Lowe**, Lawrence E 1933- *AmMWSc 92*
**Lowe**, Louis Robert, Jr. 1937- *WhoAmL 92*
**Lowe**, Mary Johnson 1924- *WhoAmL 92*
**Lowe**, Nick 1949- *ConMus 6 [port]*, *WhoEnt 92*
**Lowe**, Oariona 1948- *WhoWest 92*
**Lowe**, Peter 1938- *TwCPaSc*
**Lowe**, Philip L. 1917- *IntMPA 92*
**Lowe**, Philip M. 1944- *IntMPA 92*
**Lowe**, Philip Martin 1947- *Who 92*
**Lowe**, Ralph Edward 1931- *WhoAmL 92*
**Lowe**, Randall Brian 1948- *WhoAmL 92*
**Lowe**, Rex Loren 1943- *AmMWSc 92*
**Lowe**, Richard Bryant, III 1941- *WhoBlA 92*
**Lowe**, Richard Gerald, Jr. 1960- *WhoFI 92*, *WhoWest 92*
**Lowe**, Richie Howard 1935- *AmMWSc 92*
**Lowe**, Rob 1964- *IntMPA 92*, *WhoEnt 92*
**Lowe**, Robert B 1946- *WhoAmP 91*
**Lowe**, Robert Charles 1949- *WhoFI 92*
**Lowe**, Robert David 1930- *Who 92*
**Lowe**, Robert Franklin, Jr 1941- *AmMWSc 92*
**Lowe**, Robert Peter 1935- *AmMWSc 92*
**Lowe**, Robert Stanley 1923- *WhoAmL 92*
**Lowe**, Robson 1905- *IntAu&W 91*, *Who 92*
**Lowe**, Ronald Edsel 1935- *AmMWSc 92*
**Lowe**, Roy Goins 1926- *WhoMW 92*
**Lowe**, Samuel M. 1918- *WhoBlA 92*
**Lowe**, Scott Miller 1942- *WhoBlA 92*
**Lowe**, Stephen 1947- *WrDr 92*
**Lowe**, Stephen Richard 1944- *Who 92*
**Lowe**, Steve *DrAPF 91*
**Lowe**, Sue Esther 1954- *WhoWest 92*
**Lowe**, Sylvia Oneice 1946- *WhoBlA 92*
**Lowe**, Terrance Alexander 1951- *WhoMW 92*
**Lowe**, Terry Curtis 1955- *AmMWSc 92*
**Lowe**, Thaddeus Sobieski Coulincourt 1832-1913 *BiInAmS*
**Lowe**, Thomas 1963- *Who 92*
**Lowe**, Thomas G. 1815-1869 *DcNCBi 4*
**Lowe**, Todd Parker 1959- *WhoFI 92*
**Lowe**, Veronica Ann 1951- *Who 92*
**Lowe**, Warren 1922- *AmMWSc 92*
**Lowe**, William Douglas 1959- *WhoAmL 92*
**Lowe**, William Webb 1920- *AmMWSc 92*
**Lowe-Krentz**, Linda Jean 1953- *AmMWSc 92*
**Lowell**, A I 1925- *AmMWSc 92*
**Lowell**, Abbott Lawrence 1856-1943 *AmPeW*, *BenetAL 91*
**Lowell**, Alan I. 1939- *WhoFI 92*
**Lowell**, Amy 1874-1925 *BenetAL 91*, *FacFETw*, *ModAWWr*
**Lowell**, Elizabeth 1944- *WrDr 92*
**Lowell**, Francis Cabot 1775-1817 *BiInAmS*
**Lowell**, Frank 1960- *WhoEnt 92*
**Lowell**, Gary Richard 1942- *AmMWSc 92*
**Lowell**, H. Bret 1953- *WhoAmL 92*
**Lowell**, Jacqueline Peters *WhoFI 92*
**Lowell**, James Diller 1933- *AmMWSc 92*
**Lowell**, James Russell 1819-1891 *BenetAL 91*
**Lowell**, Josephine Shaw 1843-1905 *DcAmImH*
**Lowell**, Percival *ScFEYrs B*
**Lowell**, Percival 1855-1916 *BiInAmS*, *FacFETw*
**Lowell**, Philip S 1931- *AmMWSc 92*
**Lowell**, Richard Scott 1956- *WhoAmL 92*
**Lowell**, Robert 1917-1977 *BenetAL 91*, *FacFETw*, *PoeCrit 3 [port]*, *RComAH*
**Lowell**, Robert Paul 1943- *AmMWSc 92*
**Lowell**, Robert Traill Spence 1816-1891 *BenetAL 91*
**Lowell**, Sherman Cabot 1918- *AmMWSc 92*
**Lowell**, Susan Deborah 1950- *IntAu&W 91*
**Lowen**, Alexander 1910- *IntAu&W 91*, *WrDr 92*
**Lowen**, Allen Wayne 1946- *WhoRel 92*
**Lowen**, Gerard G 1921- *AmMWSc 92*
**Lowen**, Marilyn *DrAPF 91*
**Lowen**, W 1921- *AmMWSc 92*
**Lowenberg**, Michael 1943- *WhoAmL 92*
**Lowenfeld**, John 1931- *WhoMW 92*
**Lowenfels**, Lewis David 1935- *WhoAmL 92*
**Lowenfels**, Manna *DrAPF 91*
**Lowenfish**, Lee Elihu 1942- *WhoEnt 92*
**Lowengrub**, Morton 1935- *AmMWSc 92*
**Lowenhaupt**, Benjamin 1918- *AmMWSc 92*
**Lowenhaupt**, Charles Abraham 1947- *WhoAmL 92*
**Lowenkamp**, William Charles, Jr 1941- *IntAu&W 91*
**Lowensohn**, Howard Stanley 1931- *AmMWSc 92*
**Lowenstam**, Heinz Adolf 1912- *AmMWSc 92*
**Lowenstam**, Steven 1945- *WhoWest 92*
**Lowenstein**, Carl David 1934- *AmMWSc 92*
**Lowenstein**, Daniel Hays 1943- *WhoAmL 92*
**Lowenstein**, Derek Irving 1943- *AmMWSc 92*
**Lowenstein**, Edward 1934- *AmMWSc 92*
**Lowenstein**, Harold Louis 1939- *WhoAmP 91*
**Lowenstein**, Henry Ernest 1925- *WhoEnt 92*
**Lowenstein**, J G 1927- *AmMWSc 92*
**Lowenstein**, James Gordon 1927- *WhoAmP 91*
**Lowenstein**, Jerold Marvin 1926- *AmMWSc 92*
**Lowenstein**, John Hood 1941- *AmMWSc 92*
**Lowenstein**, John Martin 1926- *AmMWSc 92*
**Lowenstein**, Louis 1925- *WhoAmL 92*
**Lowenstein**, Michael Zimmer 1938- *AmMWSc 92*
**Lowenstein**, Otto Egon 1906- *Who 92*
**Lowenstein**, Peter David 1935- *WhoAmL 92*
**Lowenstein**, Tom *DrAPF 91*
**Lowenthal**, Andrew 1954- *WhoMW 92*
**Lowenthal**, Dennis David 1942- *AmMWSc 92*
**Lowenthal**, Douglas H 1948- *AmMWSc 92*
**Lowenthal**, Henry 1931- *WhoFI 92*
**Lowenthal**, Joseph Jacob, Jr. 1954- *WhoAmL 92*
**Lowenthal**, Leo 1900- *WrDr 92*
**Lowenthal**, Margaret 1929- *WhoAmP 91*
**Lowenthal**, Mitchell Alan 1956- *WhoAmL 92*
**Lowenthal**, Mort 1931- *WhoFI 92*
**Lowenthal**, Richard Mark 1942- *WhoWest 92*
**Lowenthal**, Werner 1930- *AmMWSc 92*
**Lowentrout**, Peter Murray 1948- *WhoRel 92*
**Lower**, Elmer W. *LesBEnT 92*
**Lower**, Ian Philip 1959- *WhoFI 92*
**Lower**, Louis Gordon, II 1945- *WhoMW 92*
**Lower**, Lynn Lee 1946- *WhoAmL 92*
**Lower**, Philip Edward 1949- *WhoAmL 92*
**Lower**, Robert D. 1936- *WhoWest 92*
**Lower**, Stephen K 1933- *AmMWSc 92*
**Lower**, William Russell 1930- *AmMWSc 92*
**Lowerre**, Susan 1962- *ConAu 134*
**Lowers**, Harry Dean 1960- *WhoRel 92*
**Lowery**, Bill 1947- *AlmAP 92 [port]*
**Lowery**, Birl 1950- *WhoBlA 92*
**Lowery**, Bruce *DrAPF 91*
**Lowery**, Carolyn T. 1940- *WhoBlA 92*
**Lowery**, Donald Elliott 1956- *WhoBlA 92*
**Lowery**, James Lincoln, Jr. 1932- *WhoRel 92*
**Lowery**, John Clayton, Jr. 1940- *WhoRel 92*
**Lowery**, Joseph E. *WhoRel 92*
**Lowery**, Joseph E. 1924- *ConBlB 2 [port]*, *WhoBlA 92*
**Lowery**, Joseph E. 1925- *RelLAm 91*
**Lowery**, Kem Gerald 1965- *WhoRel 92*
**Lowery**, Lee Leon, Jr 1938- *AmMWSc 92*
**Lowery**, Mark David 1955- *WhoRel 92*
**Lowery**, Mike *DrAPF 91*
**Lowery**, R L 1935- *AmMWSc 92*
**Lowery**, Robert 1924- *WhoFI 92*
**Lowery**, Robert O. 1916- *WhoBlA 92*
**Lowery**, Sarah 1925- *WhoAmP 91*
**Lowery**, Thomas J 1922- *AmMWSc 92*
**Lowery**, William D 1947- *WhoAmP 91*
**Lowery**, William David 1947- *WhoWest 92*
**Lowery**, William Herbert 1925- *WhoAmL 92*
**Lowery**, William Theophilus, Jr. 1957- *WhoRel 92*
**Lowes**, Albert Charles 1932- *WhoAmL 92*
**Lowes**, Brian Edward 1935- *AmMWSc 92*
**Lowes**, John Livingston 1867-1945 *BenetAL 91*
**Lowes**, Peter Donald 1926- *Who 92*
**Lowey**, Nita M. 1937- *AlmAP 92 [port]*, *WhoAmP 91*
**Lowey**, Susan 1933- *AmMWSc 92*
**Lowhagen**, Birger 1924- *IntWW 91*
**Lowi**, Alvin, Jr 1929- *AmMWSc 92*, *WhoWest 92*
**Lowie**, Robert H. 1883-1957 *BenetAL 91*
**Lowig**, Henry Francis Joseph 1904- *AmMWSc 92*, *WhoWest 92*
**Lowing**, Anne *IntAu&W 91X*, *WrDr 92*
**Lowinger**, Paul *AmMWSc 92*
**Lowinger**, Paul Ludwig 1923- *WhoWest 92*
**Lowitz**, David Aaron 1928- *AmMWSc 92*
**Lowman**, Bertha Pauline 1929- *AmMWSc 92*
**Lowman**, Isom 1946- *WhoBlA 92*
**Lowman**, Larry Loyd *WhoWest 92*
**Lowman**, Paul Daniel, Jr 1931- *AmMWSc 92*
**Lowman**, Robert Morris 1912- *AmMWSc 92*
**Lowman**, Zelvin Don 1921- *WhoAmP 91*
**Lown**, Bernard 1921- *AmMWSc 92*
**Lown**, Elizabeth D 1932- *WhoAmP 91*
**Lown**, James William 1934- *AmMWSc 92*
**Lowndes**, Allan 1921-1979 *TwCPaSc*
**Lowndes**, David Alan 1947- *WhoWest 92*
**Lowndes**, Douglas H, Jr 1940- *AmMWSc 92*
**Lowndes**, Herbert Edward 1943- *AmMWSc 92*
**Lowndes**, John Foy 1931- *WhoAmL 92*
**Lowndes**, Joseph M 1955- *AmMWSc 92*
**Lowndes**, Rawlins 1721?-1800 *BlkwEAR*
**Lowndes**, Robert A W 1916- *IntAu&W 91*, *TwCSFW 91*, *WrDr 92*
**Lowndes**, Robert P 1939- *AmMWSc 92*
**Lowney**, Edmund Dillahunty 1931- *AmMWSc 92*
**Lowney**, Jeremiah Ralph 1946- *AmMWSc 92*
**Lowney**, Paul Benjamin 1922- *IntAu&W 91*
**Lowney**, Stephen James 1958- *WhoAmL 92*
**Lownie**, H W, Jr 1918- *AmMWSc 92*
**Lownie**, Ralph Hamilton 1924- *Who 92*
**Lownsbery**, Benjamin Ferris 1920- *AmMWSc 92*
**Lowrance**, Edward Walton 1908- *AmMWSc 92*
**Lowrance**, William Wilson, Jr 1943- *AmMWSc 92*
**Lowrey**, Alice 1905- *Who 92*
**Lowrey**, Charles Boyce 1941- *AmMWSc 92*
**Lowrey**, E. James 1928- *WhoFI 92*
**Lowrey**, George Minter 1943- *WhoAmP 91*
**Lowrey**, Richard William 1938- *WhoFI 92*
**Lowrey**, Timothy Kemper 1953- *WhoWest 92*
**Lowrie**, Allen 1937- *AmMWSc 92*
**Lowrie**, Harman Smith 1926- *AmMWSc 92*
**Lowrie**, Ivor Morris *ScFEYrs*
**Lowrie**, William G. 1943- *WhoMW 92*
**Lowright**, Richard Henry 1940- *AmMWSc 92*
**Lowry** *Who 92*
**Lowry**, Baron 1919- *IntWW 91*, *Who 92*
**Lowry**, A. Leon, Sr. *WhoBlA 92*
**Lowry**, Barry Keith 1957- *WhoRel 92*
**Lowry**, Bates 1923- *IntWW 91*
**Lowry**, Betty *DrAPF 91*
**Lowry**, Beverly *DrAPF 91*
**Lowry**, Beverly 1938- *WrDr 92*
**Lowry**, Bierne C. 1959- *WhoEnt 92*
**Lowry**, Bright Anderson 1936- *AmMWSc 92*
**Lowry**, Bruce Roy 1952- *WhoAmL 92*
**Lowry**, Candace Elizabeth 1950- *WhoWest 92*
**Lowry**, Charles A 1931- *WhoAmP 91*
**Lowry**, Charles W. 1905- *WrDr 92*
**Lowry**, Charles Wesley 1905- *WhoRel 92*
**Lowry**, Dennis Martin 1953- *WhoMW 92*
**Lowry**, Dick *IntMPA 92*
**Lowry**, Dick M. *WhoEnt 92*
**Lowry**, Edith Elizabeth 1897-1970 *RelLAm 91*
**Lowry**, Edward Francis, Jr. 1930- *WhoAmL 92*
**Lowry**, Eric G 1916- *AmMWSc 92*
**Lowry**, Eugene Laverne 1933- *WhoRel 92*
**Lowry**, Frederick Sherwood 1935- *WhoRel 92*
**Lowry**, George Gordon 1929- *AmMWSc 92*
**Lowry**, Gerald Lafayette 1928- *AmMWSc 92*
**Lowry**, Henry Berry 1846?-1872? *DcNCBi 4*
**Lowry**, Houston Putnam 1955- *WhoAmL 92*
**Lowry**, Hunt 1954- *IntMPA 92*
**Lowry**, James E. 1942- *WhoBlA 92*
**Lowry**, James Hamilton 1939- *WhoBlA 92*, *WhoFI 92*
**Lowry**, James Lee 1931- *AmMWSc 92*
**Lowry**, James Rolf 1930- *WhoMW 92*
**Lowry**, James Saxon 1922- *WhoMW 92*
**Lowry**, Jean 1921- *AmMWSc 92*
**Lowry**, Jerald Frank 1939- *AmMWSc 92*
**Lowry**, Joan Marie Dondrea 1935- *WhoEnt 92*, *WhoMW 92*
**Lowry**, John Patrick 1920- *IntWW 91*, *Who 92*
**Lowry**, John Selmes, III 1943- *WhoMW 92*
**Lowry**, Larry Lorn 1947- *WhoWest 92*
**Lowry**, Laurence Stephen 1887-1976 *TwCPaSc*
**Lowry**, Lewis Roy, Jr 1928- *AmMWSc 92*
**Lowry**, Lois 1937- *WrDr 92*
**Lowry**, Malcolm 1909-1957 *BenetAL 91*, *CnDBLB 7 [port]*, *FacFETw*, *LiExTwC*, *RfGEnL 91*
**Lowry**, Michael Edward 1939- *WhoAmP 91*
**Lowry**, Mike 1939- *WhoWest 92*
**Lowry**, Mina Gertrude 1882-1986 *BenetAL 91*
**Lowry**, Nancy 1938- *AmMWSc 92*
**Lowry**, Noreen Margaret 1925- *Who 92*
**Lowry**, Oliver Howe 1910- *AmMWSc 92*, *IntWW 91*

**Lowry**, Pat Who 92
**Lowry**, Patricia Lynn Otto 1947- WhoAmL 92
**Lowry**, Philip Holt 1918- AmMWSc 92
**Lowry**, Ralph A 1926- AmMWSc 92
**Lowry**, Richard John 1924- Who 92
**Lowry**, Ritchie Peter 1926- WrDr 92
**Lowry**, Robert DrAPF 91
**Lowry**, Robert 1919- WrDr 92
**Lowry**, Robert James 1912- AmMWSc 92
**Lowry**, Robert James 1919- IntAu&W 91
**Lowry**, Robert Ronald 1932- WhoWest 92
**Lowry**, Stephen Frederick 1947- AmMWSc 92
**Lowry**, Terry Bryson 1951- WhoRel 92
**Lowry**, Thomas Hastings 1938- AmMWSc 92
**Lowry**, Wallace Dean 1917- AmMWSc 92
**Lowry**, Wayne Mitchell 1934- WhoRel 92
**Lowry**, William E., Jr. 1935- WhoBlA 92
**Lowry**, William K, Jr 1951- WhoIns 92
**Lowry**, William Ketchin, Jr. 1951- WhoFI 92
**Lowry**, William Thomas 1942- AmMWSc 92
**Lowry**, Wilson McNeil 1913- WhoEnt 92
**Lowry-Corry** Who 92
**Lowson**, Ian 1944- Who 92
**Lowther** Who 92
**Lowther**, Viscount 1949- Who 92
**Lowther**, Charles 1946- Who 92
**Lowther**, Frank Eugene 1929- AmMWSc 92, WhoFI 92
**Lowther**, Gerald Halbert 1924- WhoAmL 92, WhoMW 92
**Lowther**, James David 1939- AmMWSc 92
**Lowther**, James E WhoAmP 91
**Lowther**, John Lincoln 1943- AmMWSc 92
**Lowther**, John Luke 1923- Who 92
**Lowther**, John Stewart 1925- AmMWSc 92
**Lowthian**, Petrena 1931- WhoMW 92
**Lowum**, David Donald 1932- WhoFI 92
**Lowy**, Bernard 1916- AmMWSc 92
**Lowy**, Douglas R AmMWSc 92
**Lowy**, George Theodore 1931- WhoAmL 92
**Lowy**, Jay Stanton 1935- WhoEnt 92
**Lowy**, Martin Lee 1950- WhoAmL 92
**Lowy**, Peter Herman 1914- AmMWSc 92
**Lowy**, R Joel 1956- AmMWSc 92
**Lowy**, Stanley H 1922- AmMWSc 92
**Lowy**, Steven Robert 1951- WhoEnt 92
**Loxam**, John Gordon 1927- Who 92
**Loxley**, Thomas Edward 1940- AmMWSc 92
**Loxmith**, John IntAu&W 91X, WrDr 92
**Loxton**, David d1988 LesBEnT 92
**Loy**, Francis David Lindley 1927- Who 92
**Loy**, James Brent 1941- AmMWSc 92
**Loy**, John Wilson, Jr. 1938- WhoMW 92
**Loy**, Michael Ming-Tak 1945- AmMWSc 92
**Loy**, Mina 1882-1986 BenetAL 91
**Loy**, Myrna 1905- IntMPA 92, WhoEnt 92
**Loy**, Rebekah 1947- AmMWSc 92
**Loy**, Robert Graves 1924- AmMWSc 92
**Loy**, Samuel White 1949- WhoRel 92
**Loya**, Ofelia Olivares 1929- WhoHisp 92
**Loyalka**, Sudarshan Kumar 1943- AmMWSc 92
**Loyd**, Christopher Lewis 1923- Who 92
**Loyd**, David Heron 1941- AmMWSc 92
**Loyd**, Francis Alfred 1916- Who 92
**Loyd**, John Anthony Thomas 1933- Who 92
**Loyd**, Julian 1926- Who 92
**Loyd**, Marianne DrAPF 91
**Loyd**, Walter, Jr. 1951- WhoBlA 92
**Loyden**, Edward 1923- Who 92
**Loyless**, P. Edward, Jr. 1949- WhoFI 92
**Loyn**, Henry Royston 1922- IntWW 91, Who 92
**Loynachan**, Thomas Eugene 1945- AmMWSc 92
**Loynd**, Richard Birkett 1927- WhoFI 92, WhoMW 92
**Loynes**, John H 1933- WhoIns 92
**Loynes**, John Hamilton 1933- WhoFI 92
**Loza**, Enrique WhoHisp 92
**Lozada-Rossy**, Joyce 1952- WhoHisp 92
**Lozano**, Adrian 1921- WhoHisp 92
**Lozano**, Antonio, Jr. 1914- WhoHisp 92
**Lozano**, Conrad WhoHisp 92
**Lozano**, Denise M. 1951- WhoHisp 92
**Lozano**, Edgardo A 1924- AmMWSc 92
**Lozano**, Frank Philip 1924- WhoHisp 92
**Lozano**, Fred C. 1949- WhoHisp 92
**Lozano**, Ignacio Eugenio, Jr. 1927- WhoHisp 92
**Lozano**, John Manuel 1930- WhoHisp 92, WhoRel 92
**Lozano**, Jorge Anthony 1962- WhoHisp 92
**Lozano**, Jose Carlos 1958- WhoHisp 92
**Lozano**, Leonard J. 1935- WhoHisp 92
**Lozano**, Martha 1953- WhoWest 92
**Lozano**, Minerva D. WhoHisp 92
**Lozano**, Pedro 1697-1752 HisDSpE
**Lozano**, Robert 1918- WhoHisp 92
**Lozano**, Rudolf J. WhoHisp 92
**Lozano**, Rudy WhoHisp 92
**Lozano**, Rudy 1942- WhoAmL 92, WhoMW 92
**Lozano**, Wilfredo 1946- WhoHisp 92
**Lozano Centanino**, Monica Cecilia 1956- WhoHisp 92
**Lozeau**, Donnalee M 1960- WhoAmP 91
**Lozen** EncAmaz 91
**Lozeron**, Homer A 1934- AmMWSc 92
**Lozier**, Daniel William 1941- AmMWSc 92
**Lozier**, James Edward 1949- WhoAmL 92
**Lozinsky**, Mikhail Leonidovich 1886-1955 SovUnBD
**Lozowski**, James Michael 1946- WhoFI 92
**Lozoya-Solis**, Jesus 1910- IntWW 91
**Lozzio**, Carmen Bertucci 1931- AmMWSc 92
**Lu Dadong** IntWW 91
**Lu Dong** 1915- IntWW 91
**Lu Gongxun** 1935- IntWW 91
**Lu Ji** 1909- IntWW 91
**Lu Jiaxi** 1915- IntWW 91
**Lu Liangshu** 1924- IntWW 91
**Lu Maozeng** 1928- IntWW 91
**Lu Peijian** 1928- IntWW 91
**Lu Qihui** 1936- IntWW 91
**Lu Qikeng** 1927- IntWW 91
**Lu Qin'an** 1941- IntWW 91
**Lu Shengzhong** 1952- IntWW 91
**Lu Shuxiang** 1904- IntWW 91
**Lu Wenfu** 1928- IntWW 91
**Lu Yanshao** 1909- IntWW 91
**Lu Zhengcao** 1905- IntWW 91
**Lu Zhixian** IntWW 91
**Lu**, Adolph 1942- AmMWSc 92
**Lu**, Anthony Y H 1937- AmMWSc 92
**Lu**, Benjamin C Y 1926- AmMWSc 92
**Lu**, Benjamin Chi-Ko 1932- AmMWSc 92
**Lu**, Carlos T. 1959- WhoFI 92
**Lu**, Chih Yuan 1950- AmMWSc 92
**Lu**, Christopher D 1951- AmMWSc 92
**Lu**, Frank Chao 1915- AmMWSc 92
**Lu**, Frank Kerping 1954- AmMWSc 92
**Lu**, Grant 1956- AmMWSc 92
**Lu**, Guo-Wei 1932- AmMWSc 92
**Lu**, Gwei-Djen 1904- Who 92
**Lu**, Hsieng S 1947- AmMWSc 92
**Lu**, John Kuew-Hsiung 1937- AmMWSc 92
**Lu**, Kau U 1939- AmMWSc 92
**Lu**, Kuo Chin 1917- AmMWSc 92
**Lu**, Kuo Hwa 1923- AmMWSc 92
**Lu**, Le-Wu 1933- AmMWSc 92
**Lu**, Linyu Laura 1957- WhoFI 92
**Lu**, Mary Kwang-Ruey Chao 1935- AmMWSc 92
**Lu**, Matthias 1919- WhoRel 92
**Lu**, Matthias Chi-Hwa 1940- AmMWSc 92
**Lu**, Nancy Chao 1941- AmMWSc 92, WhoWest 92
**Lu**, Pau-Chang 1930- AmMWSc 92
**Lu**, Phillip Kehwa 1932- AmMWSc 92
**Lu**, Ponzy 1942- AmMWSc 92
**Lu**, Renne Chen 1944- AmMWSc 92
**Lu**, Shih-Lai 1946- AmMWSc 92
**Lu**, Simon Wenfeng 1968- WhoMW 92
**Lu**, Toh-Ming 1943- AmMWSc 92
**Lu**, Wei-Kao 1933- AmMWSc 92
**Lu**, Wei-yang 1950- AmMWSc 92
**Lu**, Wuan-Tsun 1939- WhoWest 92
**Lu**, Yeh-Pei AmMWSc 92
**Luallen**, Donna Jean 1964- WhoMW 92
**Luan Jujie** 1958- IntWW 91
**Luard**, Evan d1991 Who 92N
**Luard**, Nicholas 1937- IntAu&W 91, WrDr 92
**Lubac**, Henri Sonier de 1896- IntWW 91
**Lubachivsky**, Myroslav Ivan 1914- IntWW 91, WhoRel 92
**Lubalin**, Herb 1918-1982 DcTwDes
**Luban**, Marshall 1936- AmMWSc 92
**Luban**, Suzanne Adele 1959- WhoAmL 92
**Lubar**, Joel F 1938- AmMWSc 92, WrDr 92
**Lubaroff**, David Martin 1938- AmMWSc 92
**Lubatti**, Henry Joseph 1937- AmMWSc 92
**Lubawski**, James Lawrence 1946- WhoMW 92
**Lubawy**, William Charles 1944- AmMWSc 92
**Lubbe**, Marinus van der 1909-1934 EncTR 91 [port]
**Lubben**, Henry Claus 1938- WhoRel 92
**Lubbers**, Arend Donselaar 1931- WhoMW 92
**Lubbers**, Jeffrey Scott 1949- WhoAmL 92
**Lubbers**, Ruud Frans Marie 1939- IntWW 91
**Lubberts**, Gerrit 1935- AmMWSc 92
**Lubbock** Who 92
**Lubbock**, Christopher William Stuart 1920- Who 92
**Lubbock**, James Edward 1924- WhoFI 92, WhoMW 92
**Lubchansky**, David L. 1948- WhoFI 92
**Lubchenco**, Jane 1947- AmMWSc 92
**Lubcke**, Harry R. 1905- IntMPA 92
**Lubcke**, Harry Raymond 1905- AmMWSc 92
**Lubeck**, Marvin Jay 1929- WhoWest 92
**Lubeck**, Michael D AmMWSc 92
**Lubeck**, Vincent 1654-1740 NewAmDM
**Lubecker**, Carolyn Kent 1964- WhoEnt 92
**Lubega**, Seth Gasuza 1936- AmMWSc 92
**Lubell**, David 1932- AmMWSc 92
**Lubell**, David G. 1929- WhoEnt 92
**Lubell**, Jerry Ira 1943- AmMWSc 92
**Lubell**, Martin S 1932- AmMWSc 92
**Lubell**, Michael S 1943- AmMWSc 92
**Lubenow**, Josef Karl 1945- WhoMW 92
**Lubensky**, Tom C 1943- AmMWSc 92
**Luber**, Thomas Julian 1949- WhoAmL 92, WhoFI 92
**Luberda**, George Joseph 1930- WhoAmL 92
**Luberoff**, Benjamin Joseph 1925- AmMWSc 92
**Lubert**, Ira Mark 1950- WhoFI 92
**Lubet**, Ronald A 1946- AmMWSc 92
**Lubet**, Steven 1949- WhoAmL 92
**Lubetkin**, Berthold DcTwDes
**Lubetkin**, Berthold 1901-1990 AnObit 1990
**Lubetkin**, James Green 1942- WhoMW 92
**Lubetsky**, Elsen DrAPF 91
**Lubic**, Robert Bennett 1929- WhoEnt 92
**Lubic**, Ruth Watson 1927- AmMWSc 92
**Lubich Silvia**, Chiara 1920- IntWW 91
**Lubick**, Donald C 1926- WhoAmP 91
**Lubimir**, Anton A 1926- WhoIns 92
**Lubin**, Arthur IntMPA 92
**Lubin**, Arthur Richard 1947- AmMWSc 92
**Lubin**, Bernard 1923- AmMWSc 92, IntAu&W 91, WrDr 92
**Lubin**, Clarence Isaac 1900- AmMWSc 92
**Lubin**, Howard WhoEnt 92
**Lubin**, Isador 1896-1978 FacFETw
**Lubin**, Jonathan Darby 1936- AmMWSc 92
**Lubin**, Martin 1923- AmMWSc 92
**Lubin**, Peter Scott 1957- WhoAmL 92
**Lubin**, Stanley 1941- WhoAmL 92
**Lubin**, Steven 1942- IntWW 91, WhoEnt 92
**Lubinger**, Eva 1930- IntAu&W 91
**Lubiniecki**, Anthony Stanley 1946- AmMWSc 92
**Lubinski**, Arthur 1910- AmMWSc 92
**Lubis**, Mochtar 1922- IntWW 91
**Lubitsch**, Ernst 1892-1947 FacFETw, IntDcF 2-2 [port]
**Lubitz**, Cecil Robert 1925- AmMWSc 92
**Lubitz**, Lester Marc 1948- WhoMW 92
**Lubkeman**, Dale Lewis 1963- WhoAmP 91
**Lubker**, Robert A 1920- AmMWSc 92
**Lubkin**, Elihu 1933- AmMWSc 92
**Lubkin**, Gloria Becker 1933- AmMWSc 92
**Lubkin**, James Leigh 1925- AmMWSc 92
**Lublin**, Fred D 1946- AmMWSc 92
**Lublin**, Paul 1924- AmMWSc 92
**Lubliner**, J 1935- AmMWSc 92
**Lubman**, David 1934- AmMWSc 92, WhoWest 92
**Lubman**, David Mitchell 1954- AmMWSc 92
**Luboff**, Norman 1917-1987 NewAmDM
**Luborsky**, Fred Everett 1923- AmMWSc 92
**Luborsky**, Judith Lee AmMWSc 92
**Luborsky**, Samuel William 1931- AmMWSc 92
**Lubotsky**, Mark 1931- IntWW 91
**Lubovitch**, Lar WhoEnt 92
**Lubow**, Akiba 1949- WhoRel 92
**Lubow**, Nathan Myron 1929- WhoFI 92
**Lubowe**, Anthony G 1937- AmMWSc 92
**Lubowsky**, Jack 1940- AmMWSc 92
**Lubran**, Myer Michael 1915- AmMWSc 92
**Lubrano**, Mike 1961- WhoFI 92
**Luby**, Dallas W 1940- WhoIns 92
**Luby**, Elliot Donald 1924- AmMWSc 92
**Luby**, Jason 1929- WhoAmP 91
**Luby**, Patrick Joseph 1930- AmMWSc 92
**Luby**, Robert James 1928- AmMWSc 92
**Luby**, Thomas S WhoAmP 91
**Lucado**, Max Lee 1955- WhoRel 92
**Lucal**, Martha Jane 1938- WhoAmL 92
**Lucan**, Earl of 1934- Who 92
**Lucander**, Henry 1940- WhoFI 92
**Lucansky**, Patrick Alex 1936- WhoAmL 92
**Lucansky**, Terry Wayne 1942- AmMWSc 92
**Lucantoni**, David Michael 1954- AmMWSc 92
**Lucas** Who 92
**Lucas**, Alexander Ralph 1931- AmMWSc 92, WhoMW 92
**Lucas**, Anthony DcAmImH
**Lucas**, Arthur Monroe 1947- WhoMW 92, WhoRel 92
**Lucas**, Artie WhoAmP 91
**Lucas**, Barbara DrAPF 91
**Lucas**, Barbara 1911- WrDr 92
**Lucas**, Bert Albert 1933- WhoMW 92, WhoRel 92
**Lucas**, Brian Humphrey 1940- Who 92
**Lucas**, C. Payne 1933- WhoBlA 92
**Lucas**, Calvin Glenn 1929- WhoRel 92
**Lucas**, Carol N 1940- AmMWSc 92
**Lucas**, Catherine E. WhoWest 92
**Lucas**, Celia 1938- IntAu&W 91, WrDr 92
**Lucas**, Charles C. 1927- WhoBlA 92
**Lucas**, Charles Vivian 1914- Who 92
**Lucas**, Christopher Charles 1920- Who 92
**Lucas**, Christopher John 1940- WrDr 92
**Lucas**, Clarence 1866-1947 NewAmDM
**Lucas**, Colin Robert 1943- AmMWSc 92
**Lucas**, Craig 1951- CurBio 91 [port], IntWW 91, WhoEnt 92
**Lucas**, Cynthia WhoEnt 92
**Lucas**, Cyril 1909- IntWW 91, Who 92
**Lucas**, Dale Charles 1944- WhoMW 92
**Lucas**, David E 1950- WhoAmP 91
**Lucas**, David Eugene 1950- WhoBlA 92
**Lucas**, David Owen 1942- AmMWSc 92
**Lucas**, Deborah Jean 1958- WhoFI 92
**Lucas**, Donald Leo 1930- WhoWest 92
**Lucas**, Dorothy J. 1949- WhoBlA 92
**Lucas**, Douglas M 1929- AmMWSc 92
**Lucas**, Earl S. 1938- WhoBlA 92
**Lucas**, Edgar Arthur 1933- AmMWSc 92
**Lucas**, Edward C 1941- WhoAmP 91
**Lucas**, Frank D 1960- WhoAmP 91
**Lucas**, Fred Vance 1922- AmMWSc 92
**Lucas**, Frederick Vance, Jr 1949- AmMWSc 92
**Lucas**, Gene Allan 1928- AmMWSc 92
**Lucas**, George LesBEnT 92, TwCSFW 91
**Lucas**, George 1944- FacFETw, IntDcF 2-2 [port], IntMPA 92, IntWW 91, Who 92
**Lucas**, George 1945- BenetAL 91
**Lucas**, George Blanchard 1915- AmMWSc 92
**Lucas**, George Bond 1924- AmMWSc 92
**Lucas**, George W., Jr. 1944- WhoEnt 92, WhoWest 92
**Lucas**, Georges 1915- IntWW 91
**Lucas**, Gerald Robert 1942- WhoBlA 92
**Lucas**, Glenn E 1951- AmMWSc 92
**Lucas**, Glennard Ralph 1916- AmMWSc 92
**Lucas**, Gregory Dean 1951- WhoAmL 92
**Lucas**, Henry C, Jr 1944- AmMWSc 92
**Lucas**, Ian Albert McKenzie 1926- Who 92
**Lucas**, Ivor Thomas Mark 1927- Who 92
**Lucas**, J B 1929- AmMWSc 92
**Lucas**, J R 1929- ConAu 35NR
**Lucas**, James Evans 1933- WhoEnt 92
**Lucas**, James Howard 1927- WhoIns 92
**Lucas**, James Kenneth 1944- WhoEnt 92
**Lucas**, James L. 1923- WhoBlA 92
**Lucas**, James M 1941- AmMWSc 92
**Lucas**, James R 1922- WhoAmP 91
**Lucas**, James Raymond 1950- WhoFI 92
**Lucas**, James Robert 1947- AmMWSc 92
**Lucas**, Jay Harris 1942- WhoMW 92
**Lucas**, Jeffrey Wayne 1951- WhoMW 92
**Lucas**, Jo Desha 1921- WhoAmL 92
**Lucas**, Joe Nathan 1945- AmMWSc 92
**Lucas**, John 1937- WrDr 92
**Lucas**, John 1953- WhoBlA 92
**Lucas**, John Allen 1943- WhoAmL 92
**Lucas**, John Harding 1920- WhoBlA 92
**Lucas**, John J AmMWSc 92
**Lucas**, John Michael 1921- Who 92
**Lucas**, John Paul 1945- AmMWSc 92
**Lucas**, John Randolph 1926- IntAu&W 91
**Lucas**, John Randolph 1929- Who 92, WrDr 92
**Lucas**, John W 1923- AmMWSc 92
**Lucas**, Juanita F. WhoMW 92
**Lucas**, Julia Lanese 1953- WhoEnt 92
**Lucas**, June H WhoAmP 91
**Lucas**, Kathleen Marion 1945- WhoAmL 92
**Lucas**, Keith Stephen 1924- Who 92
**Lucas**, Kenneth Ross 1939- AmMWSc 92
**Lucas**, Larry WhoAmP 91
**Lucas**, Leo Alexander 1912- WhoBlA 92
**Lucas**, Leon Thomas 1942- AmMWSc 92
**Lucas**, Linda Gail 1947- WhoBlA 92
**Lucas**, Lola L. 1954- WhoMW 92
**Lucas**, Lynne M. 1954- WhoEnt 92
**Lucas**, Malcolm Millar 1927- WhoAmL 92, WhoAmP 91, WhoWest 92
**Lucas**, Maurice 1952- WhoBlA 92
**Lucas**, Maurice F. 1944- WhoBlA 92
**Lucas**, Myron Cran 1946- AmMWSc 92
**Lucas**, Oscar Nestor 1932- AmMWSc 92
**Lucas**, Percy Belgrave 1915- Who 92
**Lucas**, Peter Charles 1934- IntWW 91
**Lucas**, Peter George 1942- WhoFI 92
**Lucas**, Raleigh Barclay 1914- Who 92
**Lucas**, Rendella 1910- WhoBlA 92
**Lucas**, Robert Alan 1935- AmMWSc 92
**Lucas**, Robert Anthony 1939- WhoWest 92
**Lucas**, Robert Elmer 1916- AmMWSc 92
**Lucas**, Robert Frank 1935- WhoAmL 92
**Lucas**, Roy Edward, Jr. 1955- WhoRel 92
**Lucas**, Russell Vail, Jr 1928- AmMWSc 92

**Lucas**, Shirley Agnes Hoyt 1921- WhoMW 92
**Lucas**, Stephen Lee 1948- WhoRel 92
**Lucas**, Steven Mitchell 1948- WhoAmL 92
**Lucas**, Suzanne 1939- WhoWest 92
**Lucas**, Thomas 1930- Who 92
**Lucas**, Thomas J. 1951- WhoMW 92
**Lucas**, Thomas Ramsey 1939- AmMWSc 92
**Lucas**, Timothy Scott 1946- WhoFI 92
**Lucas**, Valerie Patricia 1951- WhoRel 92
**Lucas**, Victoria ConAu 34NR, WhoBlA 92
**Lucas**, Virgil Hilry 1907- WhoBlA 92
**Lucas**, Vivian Who 92
**Lucas**, W.F. DrAPF 91
**Lucas**, William 1928- WhoBlA 92
**Lucas**, William Franklin 1933- AmMWSc 92
**Lucas**, William Jasper 1926- WhoFI 92
**Lucas**, William John 1945- AmMWSc 92
**Lucas**, William R 1922- AmMWSc 92
**Lucas**, William Ray, Jr. 1955- WhoAmL 92
**Lucas**, William S. 1917- WhoBlA 92
**Lucas**, Willie Lee 1924- WhoBlA 92
**Lucas**, Wilmer Francis, Jr. 1927- WhoBlA 92
**Lucas-Edwards**, Florence V. 1915-1987 WhoBlA 92N
**Lucas Garcia**, Fernando Romeo IntWW 91
**Lucas-Lenard**, Jean Marian 1937- AmMWSc 92
**Lucas of Chilworth**, Baron 1926- Who 92
**Lucas of Crudwell**, Baroness 1919- Who 92
**Lucas-Tauchar**, Margaret Frances 1956- WhoMW 92
**Lucas-Tooth**, John 1932- Who 92
**Lucast**, Donald Hurrell 1946- AmMWSc 92
**Lucatorto**, Thomas B 1937- AmMWSc 92
**Lucca**, Carmen D. DrAPF 91
**Lucca**, David Alan 1957- WhoFI 92
**Lucca**, Frank Ralph 1952- WhoEnt 92
**Lucca**, John J 1921- AmMWSc 92
**Lucca**, Thomas George 1938- WhoFI 92
**Lucchesi**, Ann Marie 1962- WhoWest 92
**Lucchesi**, Benedict Robert AmMWSc 92
**Lucchesi**, Claude A 1929- AmMWSc 92
**Lucchesi**, Gary 1955- IntMPA 92
**Lucchesi**, John Charles 1934- AmMWSc 92
**Lucchesi**, Lionel Louis 1939- WhoMW 92
**Lucchesi**, Marianne Veglia 1952- WhoEnt 92, WhoWest 92
**Lucchesi**, Peter J 1926- AmMWSc 92
**Lucchi**, Leonard Louis 1958- WhoAmP 91
**Lucchino**, Frank Joseph 1939- WhoAmP 91
**Lucchitta**, Baerbel Koesters 1938- AmMWSc 92
**Lucchitta**, Ivo 1937- AmMWSc 92
**Lucci**, Robert Dominick 1950- AmMWSc 92
**Lucci**, Susan WhoEnt 92
**Luce**, Charles F. 1917- IntWW 91
**Luce**, Clare IntAu&W 91
**Luce**, Clare Boothe 1903-1987 AmPolLe [port], BenetAL 91, FacFETw
**Luce**, Dennis Charles 1962- WhoRel 92
**Luce**, Gay 1930- WrDr 92
**Luce**, Gregory DrAPF 91
**Luce**, Henry 1898-1967 RComAH
**Luce**, Henry, III 1925- IntWW 91
**Luce**, Henry R. 1898-1967 BenetAL 91, FacFETw
**Luce**, James Edward 1935- AmMWSc 92
**Luce**, James W 1947- WhoIns 92
**Luce**, Jean 1895-1964 DcTwDes
**Luce**, Margaret Mary 1946- WhoMW 92
**Luce**, Melissa Hambrick 1961- WhoAmL 92
**Luce**, Priscilla Mark 1947- WhoMW 92
**Luce**, R Duncan 1925- AmMWSc 92
**Luce**, Richard 1936- Who 92
**Luce**, Richard Napier 1936- IntWW 91
**Luce**, Robert Duncan 1925- IntWW 91, WhoWest 92
**Luce**, Robert James 1929- AmMWSc 92
**Luce**, Thomas Richard Harman 1939- Who 92
**Luce**, William WhoEnt 92
**Luce**, William Glenn 1936- AmMWSc 92
**Lucebert** 1924- IntWW 91
**Lucenko**, Anatol, Jr. 1963- WhoMW 92
**Lucenta**, Dominic A. 1953- WhoMW 92
**Lucente**, Rosemary Dolores 1935- WhoWest 92
**Lucero**, Alvin K. WhoHisp 92
**Lucero**, Amarante L., Jr. 1947- WhoHisp 92
**Lucero**, C. Steven 1967- WhoHisp 92
**Lucero**, Frank WhoAmP 91
**Lucero**, Helen R. 1943- WhoHisp 92
**Lucero**, Juan M. 1947- WhoHisp 92
**Lucero**, Leonor Jon 1966- WhoHisp 92
**Lucero**, Marcela DrAPF 91
**Lucero**, Michael L. 1953- WhoHisp 92
**Lucero**, Orlando 1958- WhoAmL 92
**Lucero**, Ricardo 1940- WhoHisp 92
**Lucero**, Richard L. WhoHisp 92
**Lucero**, Rosalba 1964- WhoHisp 92
**Lucero**, Rose M. 1954- WhoHisp 92
**Lucero**, Stephanie Denise 1957- WhoHisp 92
**Lucero**, Stephen Paul 1955- WhoHisp 92
**Lucero-Schayes**, Wendy 1964- WhoHisp 92
**Lucet**, Charles Ernest d1990 Who 92N
**Lucey**, Carol Ann 1943- AmMWSc 92
**Lucey**, Edgar C 1945- AmMWSc 92
**Lucey**, Jack 1929- WhoWest 92
**Lucey**, James D. 1923- WrDr 92
**Lucey**, Jerold Francis 1926- AmMWSc 92
**Lucey**, John Edward 1941- WhoAmP 91
**Lucey**, John William 1935- AmMWSc 92, WhoMW 92
**Lucey**, Juliana Margaret AmMWSc 92
**Lucey**, Lawrence Haydn 1947- WhoAmL 92
**Lucey**, Martin Noel 1920- Who 92
**Lucey**, Patrick Joseph 1918- IntWW 91, WhoAmP 91
**Lucey**, Robert Francis 1926- AmMWSc 92
**Luchaire**, Jean 1901-1946 BiDExR
**Lucher**, Lynne Annette 1954- AmMWSc 92
**Luchese**, Jack Joseph 1948- WhoFI 92
**Luchies**, John Elmer 1912- WhoRel 92
**Luchins**, Edith Hirsch 1921- AmMWSc 92
**Luchinsky**, Petr Kirillovich 1940- IntWW 91, SovUnBD
**Luchishkin**, Sergey Alekseevich 1902- SovUnBD
**Luchko**, Klara Stepanovna 1925- IntWW 91
**Luchs**, Fred Emil 1904- WhoRel 92
**Luchs**, James Kenneth 1933- WhoAmL 92
**Luchsinger**, Fred W. 1921- IntWW 91
**Luchsinger**, John Francis, Jr. 1944- WhoAmL 92
**Luchsinger**, Wayne Wesley 1924- AmMWSc 92
**Lucht**, Albert F 1919- WhoAmP 91
**Lucht**, Carroll L. 1942- WhoAmL 92
**Lucht**, John Charles 1933- WhoFI 92
**Lucht**, Sondra Moore 1942- WhoAmP 91
**Luchtel**, Daniel Lee 1942- AmMWSc 92
**Luchterhand**, Ralph Edward 1952- WhoFI 92, WhoWest 92
**Lucia**, Ellis 1922- WrDr 92
**Lucia**, Ellis Joel 1922- IntAu&W 91
**Lucia**, William C 1957- WhoIns 92
**Lucian** ScFEYrs
**Lucian of Antioch** d312 EncEarC
**Lucian of Samosata** 115?-200 EncEarC
**Lucian of Samosata** 125?-195? ScFEYrs
**Lucian**, Miriam Laura 1945- WhoWest 92
**Luciana**, Salvatore 1897-1962 FacFETw
**Luciano**, Charles 1897-1962 FacFETw
**Luciano**, Felipe DrAPF 91
**Luciano**, Mark Joseph 1959- WhoWest 92
**Lucid**, Michael Francis 1937- AmMWSc 92
**Lucid**, Shannon W. NewYTBS 91 [port]
**Lucido**, Frank A. 1945- WhoRel 92
**Lucido**, John Anthony 1952- WhoFI 92
**Lucie**, Doug 1953- WrDr 92
**Lucie-Smith**, Edward 1933- ConPo 91, Who 92, WrDr 92
**Lucie-Smith**, John Edward McKenzie 1933- IntAu&W 91
**Lucier**, Alvin 1931- ConCom 92, NewAmDM
**Lucier**, George W 1943- AmMWSc 92
**Lucier**, John J 1917- AmMWSc 92
**Lucier**, Ted 1947- WhoAmP 91
**Lucietta**, Jerry Ray 1938- WhoMW 92
**Lucifer of Cagliari** d370? EncEarC
**Lucilla** EncEarC
**Lucina**, Mary DrAPF 91
**Lucini**, Gian Pietro 1867-1914 DcLB 114
**Lucio**, Eduardo, Jr 1946- WhoAmP 91
**Lucio**, Eduardo A. 1946- WhoHisp 92
**Lucio Paredes**, Antonio Jose 1923- IntWW 91
**Lucis**, Ojars Janis 1924- AmMWSc 92
**Lucis**, Ruta 1925- AmMWSc 92
**Lucius I** EncEarC
**Lucius**, Wulf D. von 1938- IntWW 91
**Luck**, Clyde Alexander, Jr. 1929- WhoBlA 92
**Luck**, David Jonathan Lewis 1929- AmMWSc 92
**Luck**, Dennis Noel 1939- AmMWSc 92
**Luck**, Dwight Dean 1955- WhoMW 92
**Luck**, Etta Robena WhoBlA 92
**Luck**, John Virgil 1926- AmMWSc 92
**Luck**, Leon D 1921- AmMWSc 92
**Luck**, Richard Earle 1950- AmMWSc 92
**Luck**, Russell M 1926- AmMWSc 92
**Lucke**, Robert Lancaster 1945- AmMWSc 92
**Lucke**, Robert Vito 1930- WhoMW 92
**Lucke**, William E 1936- AmMWSc 92
**Lucke Summers**, Mary Clarinda 1958- WhoFI 92
**Lucken**, Karl Allen 1937- AmMWSc 92
**Luckenbaugh**, Carroll Charles 1935- WhoRel 92
**Luckenbill-Edds**, Louise 1936- AmMWSc 92
**Luckens**, Mark Manfred 1912- AmMWSc 92
**Lucker**, Raymond Alphonse 1927- WhoRel 92
**Luckert**, H J 1905- AmMWSc 92
**Luckett**, Byron Edward, Jr. 1951- WhoWest 92
**Luckett**, Richard 1943- WhoWest 92
**Luckett**, Winter Patrick 1937- AmMWSc 92
**Luckey**, Alwyn Hall 1960- WhoAmL 92
**Luckey**, Egbert Hugh 1920- AmMWSc 92
**Luckey**, Evelyn F. 1926- WhoBlA 92
**Luckey**, George William 1925- AmMWSc 92
**Luckey**, Irene 1949- WhoBlA 92
**Luckey**, Paul David, Jr 1928- AmMWSc 92
**Luckey**, T. D. 1919- WrDr 92
**Luckey**, Thomas Donnell 1919- AmMWSc 92
**Luckham**, David Comptom 1936- AmMWSc 92
**Luckhardt**, Charles Edward, Jr. 1932- WhoAmL 92
**Luckhardt**, Esther Doughty WhoAmP 91
**Luckhart**, Elton Wagner 1910- WhoAmP 91
**Luckhoo**, Edward Victor 1912- Who 92
**Luckhoo**, Joseph 1917- Who 92
**Luckhoo**, Lionel 1914- Who 92
**Luckhoo**, Lionel Alfred 1914- IntWW 91
**Lucki**, Salomon 1931- WhoAmL 92
**Luckinbill**, Lawrence 1934- IntMPA 92
**Lucking**, Peter Stephen 1945- WhoFI 92, WhoMW 92
**Luckless**, John IntAu&W 91X
**Luckman**, Chris 1945- WhoEnt 92
**Luckman**, Sharon Gersten 1945- WhoEnt 92
**Luckmann**, William Henry 1926- AmMWSc 92
**Luckner**, Herman Richard, III 1933- WhoMW 92
**Luckock**, Arlene Suzanne 1948- AmMWSc 92
**Luckring**, R M 1917- AmMWSc 92
**Lucktenberg**, Kathryn 1958- WhoEnt 92
**Lucky**, George W 1923- AmMWSc 92
**Lucky**, Robert W 1936- AmMWSc 92
**Lucovsky**, Gerald 1935- AmMWSc 92
**Lucraft**, Howard WhoEnt 92
**Lucus**, Emma Turner 1949- WhoBlA 92
**Lucy**, Edmund J. W. H. C. R. F. Who 92
**Lucy**, Nicholas Robert 1940- WhoAmP 91
**Lucy**, William 1933- WhoBlA 92
**Lucyk**, Edward J 1942- WhoAmP 91
**Luczak**, Alojzy Andrzej 1930- IntAu&W 91
**Ludbrook**, John 1929- WrDr 92
**Ludden**, Allen d1981 LesBEnT 92
**Ludden**, Gerald D 1937- AmMWSc 92
**Ludden**, John Franklin 1930- WhoFI 92
**Ludden**, LaVerne L. WhoMW 92
**Ludden**, Paul W 1950- AmMWSc 92
**Ludden**, Thomas Marcellus 1946- AmMWSc 92
**Luddendorf**, Erich Friedrich Wilhelm 1865-1937 BiDExR
**Luddington**, Donald 1920- Who 92
**Luddy**, Thomas Michael 1952- WhoFI 92
**Luddy**, Tom IntMPA 92
**Luddy**, William F 1910- WhoAmP 91
**Ludeke**, Carl Arthur 1914- AmMWSc 92
**Ludeke**, Rudolf 1937- AmMWSc 92
**Ludeks**, Modris Janis 1924- WhoAmP 91
**Ludel**, Jacqueline 1945- AmMWSc 92
**Ludema**, Kenneth C 1928- AmMWSc 92
**Ludeman**, Kate 1946- WhoWest 92
**Ludemann**, Carl Arnold 1934- AmMWSc 92
**Ludendorff**, Erich 1856-1937 EncTR 91 [port]
**Ludendorff**, Erich 1865-1937 FacFETw [port]
**Luder**, Owen 1928- IntWW 91, Who 92
**Luders**, Adam 1950- WhoEnt 92
**Luders**, Gustav 1865-1913 NewAmDM
**Luders**, Richard Christian 1934- AmMWSc 92
**Ludgin**, Chester Hall 1925- WhoEnt 92
**Ludin**, Fritz 1941- WhoEnt 92
**Ludin**, Roger Louis 1944- AmMWSc 92
**Ludington**, John Samuel 1928- WhoFI 92, WhoMW 92
**Ludington**, Martin A 1943- AmMWSc 92
**Ludington**, Martin Lammert 1934- WhoMW 92
**Ludington**, Sally Marie 1943- WhoMW 92
**Ludke**, Heinz 1949- WhoEnt 92
**Ludke**, James Larry 1942- AmMWSc 92
**Ludlam**, Lillian J 1918- WhoAmP 91
**Ludlam**, Valerie Pope 1932- WhoBlA 92
**Ludlam**, William Myrton 1931- AmMWSc 92
**Ludley**, Richard 1931- WhoBlA 92
**Ludlow**, Archdeacon of Who 92
**Ludlow**, Bishop Suffragan of 1928- Who 92
**Ludlow**, Anne WhoRel 92
**Ludlow**, Christy L 1944- AmMWSc 92
**Ludlow**, Douglas Kent 1957- WhoMW 92
**Ludlow**, Fitz Hugh 1836-1870 BenetAL 91
**Ludlow**, Geoffrey WrDr 92
**Ludlow**, Howard Thomas 1921- WrDr 92
**Ludlow**, Jacob Lott 1862-1930 DcNCBi 4
**Ludlow**, Mark Anthony 1957- WhoRel 92
**Ludlow**, Noah Miller 1795-1886 BenetAL 91
**Ludlow**, Robin 1931- Who 92
**Ludlum**, David Blodgett 1929- AmMWSc 92
**Ludlum**, George B ScFEYrs
**Ludlum**, John Charles 1913- AmMWSc 92
**Ludlum**, Kenneth Hills 1929- AmMWSc 92
**Ludlum**, Robert 1927- IntAu&W 91, IntWW 91, WrDr 92
**Ludman**, Allan 1943- AmMWSc 92
**Ludman**, Harold 1933- Who 92
**Ludman**, Jacques Ernest 1934- AmMWSc 92
**Ludmerer**, Kenneth Marc 1947- WhoMW 92
**Ludolf**, Marilyn Marie Keaton 1932- WhoRel 92
**Ludolph**, Robert Charles 1948- WhoAmL 92
**Ludovici**, Louis Nicholas 1940- WhoEnt 92
**Ludovici**, Peter Paul 1920- AmMWSc 92
**Ludowese**, Marcellinus Francis 1925- WhoAmP 91, WhoMW 92
**Ludsin**, Steven Alan 1948- WhoFI 92
**Ludtke**, Paul Jeffrey 1957- WhoFI 92
**Luduena**, Richard Froilan 1946- AmMWSc 92
**Ludvigsen**, Carl W, Jr AmMWSc 92
**Ludvigsen**, Richard E. 1950- WhoWest 92
**Ludvigson**, David Lee 1938- WhoFI 92
**Ludvigson**, Joan WhoAmP 91
**Ludvigson**, Susan DrAPF 91
**Ludwell**, Philip 1638?-1723? DcNCBi 4
**Ludwick**, Adriane Gurak 1941- AmMWSc 92
**Ludwick**, John Calvin, Jr 1922- AmMWSc 92
**Ludwick**, Larry Martin 1941- AmMWSc 92
**Ludwick**, Ruth Elizabeth 1951- WhoMW 92
**Ludwick**, Thomas Murrell 1915- AmMWSc 92
**Ludwiczak**, Dominik 1939- IntWW 91
**Ludwiczak**, Robert Joseph 1943- WhoAmP 91
**Ludwig**, Allen Clarence, Sr 1938- AmMWSc 92
**Ludwig**, Charles Heberle 1920- AmMWSc 92
**Ludwig**, Christa Who 92, WhoEnt 92
**Ludwig**, Christa 1928- IntWW 91, NewAmDM
**Ludwig**, Claus Berthold 1924- AmMWSc 92
**Ludwig**, Curt WhoAmP 91
**Ludwig**, Donald A 1933- AmMWSc 92
**Ludwig**, Edmund Vincent 1928- WhoAmL 92
**Ludwig**, Edward James 1937- AmMWSc 92
**Ludwig**, Emil 1881-1948 EncTR 91 [port], LiExTwC
**Ludwig**, Eugene Allan 1946- WhoAmL 92
**Ludwig**, Frank Arno 1931- AmMWSc 92
**Ludwig**, Frederic C 1924- AmMWSc 92
**Ludwig**, Frederick John, Sr 1928- AmMWSc 92
**Ludwig**, Garry 1940- AmMWSc 92
**Ludwig**, George H 1927- AmMWSc 92
**Ludwig**, Gerald W 1930- AmMWSc 92
**Ludwig**, Glenn Edward 1946- WhoRel 92
**Ludwig**, Harvey F 1916- AmMWSc 92
**Ludwig**, Hermann-Henry 1954- WhoMW 92
**Ludwig**, Howard C 1916- AmMWSc 92
**Ludwig**, Hubert Joseph 1934- AmMWSc 92, WhoMW 92
**Ludwig**, Irving H. IntMPA 92
**Ludwig**, Jack DrAPF 91
**Ludwig**, Jack 1922- ConNov 91, WrDr 92
**Ludwig**, James George 1940- WhoEnt 92
**Ludwig**, John, Jr. WhoRel 92
**Ludwig**, John Howard 1913- AmMWSc 92
**Ludwig**, John McKay 1935- WhoEnt 92A
**Ludwig**, Kristine Nicole 1969- WhoEnt 92
**Ludwig**, Margaret G WhoAmP 91
**Ludwig**, Martha Louise 1931- AmMWSc 92
**Ludwig**, Oliver George 1935- AmMWSc 92
**Ludwig**, Patric E. 1939- WhoMW 92
**Ludwig**, R. Scott 1944- WhoFI 92
**Ludwig**, Robert Carl 1944- WhoEnt 92
**Ludwig**, Rolf Martin 1924- WhoWest 92
**Ludwig**, Scott Edward 1958- WhoAmL 92

**Ludwig**, Theodore Frederick 1924- AmMWSc 92
**Ludwig**, Theodore Mark 1936- WhoRel 92
**Ludwig**, Vernell Patrick 1944- WhoFI 92
**Ludwig**, William John 1955- WhoFI 92
**Ludwin**, Isadore 1915- AmMWSc 92
**Ludwinski**, Stephen Craig 1951- WhoAmL 92
**Ludwiszewski**, Raymond Bernard 1958- WhoAmL 92
**Lue-Hing**, Cecil 1930- AmMWSc 92, WhoBlA 92
**Luebbe**, Ray Henry, Jr 1931- AmMWSc 92
**Luebbers**, Jerome F WhoAmP 91
**Luebbers**, Ralph H 1906- AmMWSc 92
**Luebbers**, Rita Mary 1956- WhoRel 92
**Luebbers**, Roy Bernard 1918- WhoAmP 91
**Luebbers**, Thomas Alphonse 1942- WhoAmL 92
**Luebering**, Carol 1935- WhoMW 92
**Luebke**, Emmeth August 1915- AmMWSc 92
**Luebke**, Frederick Carl 1927- IntAu&W 91, WrDr 92
**Luebke**, Martin Frederick 1917- WhoRel 92
**Luebke**, Mary Elizabeth 1961- WhoFI 92
**Luebke**, Paul WhoAmP 91
**Luebs**, Ralph Edward 1922- AmMWSc 92
**Lueck**, Charles Henry 1928- AmMWSc 92
**Lueck**, Dwayne Martin 1953- WhoRel 92
**Lueck**, Raymond Glen 1952- WhoMW 92
**Lueck**, Thomas H. WhoMW 92
**Luecke**, Donald H 1936- AmMWSc 92
**Luecke**, Glenn Richard 1944- AmMWSc 92
**Luecke**, Joseph E. 1927- WhoFI 92, WhoMW 92
**Luecke**, Richard H 1930- AmMWSc 92
**Luecke**, Richard William 1917- AmMWSc 92
**Luecke**, Walter Edward 1932- WhoMW 92
**Luedde**, Charles Edwin Howell 1944- WhoFI 92
**Luedde**, Christopher Shryock 1951- WhoRel 92
**Luedecke**, Lloyd O 1934- AmMWSc 92
**Luedeman**, John Keith 1941- AmMWSc 92
**Lueder**, Ernst H 1932- AmMWSc 92
**Luederitz**, Alexander 1932- IntWW 91
**Lueders**, Edward DrAPF 91
**Lueders**, Wayne Richard 1947- WhoAmL 92
**Luedi**, Mark 1919- WhoFI 92
**Luedtke**, Charles Henry 1941- WhoMW 92
**Luedtke**, Kurt 1938- IntMPA 92
**Luedtke**, Norman D 1928- WhoIns 92
**Luedtke**, Roland Alfred 1924- WhoAmP 91
**Lueg**, Russell E 1929- AmMWSc 92
**Lueger**, Karl 1844-1910 BiDExR, EncTR 91 [port]
**Lueger**, Susan Ann 1953- WhoMW 92
**Luegge**, Willard Arthur 1931- WhoWest 92
**Luehr**, Charles Poling 1930- AmMWSc 92
**Luehrman**, Kathleen Suzanne 1956- WhoRel 92
**Luehrmann**, Arthur Willett, Jr 1931- AmMWSc 92
**Luehrmann**, William John 1951- WhoFI 92
**Luehrs**, Dean C 1939- AmMWSc 92
**Lueken**, John Joseph 1964- WhoMW 92
**Lueking**, Donald Robert 1946- AmMWSc 92
**Lueking**, Frederick Dean 1928- WhoRel 92
**Luelf**, Stephen Walter 1942- WhoAmP 91
**Luellen**, Charles J. 1929- IntWW 91, WhoFI 92
**Luellen**, Valentina WrDr 92
**Luelling**, Henderson 1809-1878 DcNCBi 4
**Luenberger**, David Gilbert 1937- AmMWSc 92, WhoWest 92
**Luening**, Otto 1900- ConCom 92, NewAmDM, WhoEnt 92
**Luepker**, Wayne Robert 1949- WhoAmL 92
**Luer**, Carl A 1948- AmMWSc 92
**Luera**, Anita Favela 1955- WhoHisp 92
**Luers**, William H 1929- WhoAmP 91
**Luers**, William Henry 1929- IntWW 91
**Luerssen**, Frank W 1927- AmMWSc 92
**Luerssen**, Frank Wonson 1927- IntWW 91, WhoFI 92, WhoMW 92
**Lueschen**, William Everett 1942- AmMWSc 92
**Luessenhop**, Alfred John 1926- AmMWSc 92
**Luetchens**, Melvin Harvey 1939- WhoRel 92
**Luetke**, Charles Costello 1923- WhoAmL 92
**Luettgen**, Michael John 1960- WhoMW 92
**Luettgens**, Floyd Roy 1935- WhoIns 92
**Luetzelschwab**, John William 1940- AmMWSc 92
**Luevano**, Fred, Jr. 1943- WhoWest 92
**Luevano**, Rosalva 1959- WhoHisp 92
**Luff**, Alan Harold Frank 1928- Who 92
**Luff**, Geoffrey Shadrack 1933- Who 92
**Luff**, Paul Karl 1953- WhoMW 92
**Luff**, Richard William Peter 1927- Who 92
**Luffingham**, John Kingley 1928- Who 92
**Luffman**, Dale Edward 1947- WhoRel 92
**Luffy**, Robert H. 1947- WhoFI 92
**Lufkin**, Dan W. IntMPA 92
**Lufkin**, Daniel Harlow 1930- AmMWSc 92
**Lufkin**, Joseph Charles Francis 1955- WhoFI 92
**Luft**, Arthur Christian 1915- Who 92
**Luft**, Friedrich 1911- IntWW 91
**Luft**, Harold S. 1947- WhoFI 92
**Luft**, Harold Stephen 1947- AmMWSc 92
**Luft**, Herbert 1942- WhoWest 92
**Luft**, John Herman 1927- AmMWSc 92
**Luft**, Lorna 1952- ConTFT 9
**Luft**, Ludwig 1926- AmMWSc 92
**Luft**, Rene Wilfred 1943- WhoFI 92, WhoWest 92
**Luft**, Richard 1938- WhoAmP 91
**Luft**, Stanley Jeremie 1927- AmMWSc 92
**Luft**, Ulrich Cameron 1910- AmMWSc 92
**Luftglass**, Murray Arnold 1931- WhoFI 92
**Luftig**, Ronald Bernard 1939- AmMWSc 92
**Lugar**, Richard Charles AmMWSc 92
**Lugar**, Richard G. 1932- AlmAP 92 [port]
**Lugar**, Richard Green 1932- IntWW 91, WhoAmP 91, WhoMW 92
**Lugassy**, Armand Amram 1933- AmMWSc 92
**Lugay**, Joaquin Castro 1938- AmMWSc 92
**Luger**, George F 1940- AmMWSc 92
**Luger**, George Fletcher 1940- WhoWest 92
**Luger**, Michael Ian 1950- WhoFI 92
**Lugger**, Otto 1844-1901 BiInAmS
**Lughermo**, Joseph M. 1936- WhoFI 92
**Luginbuhl**, Geraldine Hobson 1944- AmMWSc 92
**Luginbuhl**, Vi Larimore 1932- WhoAmP 91
**Luginbuhl**, William Hossfeld 1929- AmMWSc 92
**Lugmair**, Guenter Wilhelm 1940- AmMWSc 92
**Lugo**, Adrian C. 1947- WhoHisp 92
**Lugo**, Ariel WhoHisp 92
**Lugo**, Elena 1938- WhoHisp 92
**Lugo**, Herminio Lugo 1918- AmMWSc 92
**Lugo**, Jesse S. 1953- WhoHisp 92
**Lugo**, Jose C 1926- WhoAmP 91
**Lugo**, Loni G. 1948- WhoHisp 92
**Lugo**, Luis E. 1951- WhoHisp 92
**Lugo**, Luis Robert 1946- WhoRel 92
**Lugo**, Robert M. 1933- WhoHisp 92
**Lugo**, Sean Reed 1967- WhoHisp 92
**Lugo**, Tracy Gross AmMWSc 92
**Lugo-Lopez**, Miguel Angel 1921- AmMWSc 92
**Lugones**, Leopoldo 1874-1938 BenetAL 91, BiDExR
**Lugosi**, Bela 1882-1956 FacFETw [port]
**Lugovina**, Francisco, III 1939- WhoHisp 92
**Lugovskoy**, Vladimir Aleksandrovich 1901-1957 SovUnBD
**Lugt**, Hans Josef 1930- AmMWSc 92
**Lugthart**, Garrit John, Jr 1923- AmMWSc 92
**Luh**, Bor Shiun 1916- AmMWSc 92
**Luh**, Jiang 1932- AmMWSc 92
**Luh**, Johnson Yang-Seng 1925- AmMWSc 92
**Luh**, Yuhshi 1949- AmMWSc 92
**Luhan**, Joseph Anton 1901- AmMWSc 92
**Luhan**, Mabel Dodge 1879-1962 BenetAL 91, HanAmWH
**Luhby**, Adrian Leonard 1916- AmMWSc 92
**Luhman**, Adelbert Alfred 1933- WhoMW 92
**Luhman**, William Simon 1934- WhoMW 92
**Luhmann**, Niklas 1927- IntWW 91
**Luhn**, Robert Daniel 1948- WhoRel 92
**Luhn**, William George 1946- WhoEnt 92
**Luhrmann**, Thomas DrAPF 91
**Luhrs**, Janet Anne 1942- WhoAmP 91, WhoEnt 92
**Lui**, David Harrison 1960- WhoAmL 92
**Lui**, Ming Wah 1938- WhoFI 92
**Lui**, Wilbert-Kho Tan 1960- WhoFI 92
**Lui**, Yiu-Kwan 1937- AmMWSc 92
**Luibrand**, Richard Thomas 1945- AmMWSc 92
**Luigs**, A. Melvin, Jr. 1953- WhoFI 92
**Luikart**, John Ford 1949- WhoWest 92
**Luine**, Victoria Nall 1945- AmMWSc 92
**Luis**, Don de Velasco DcNCBi 4
**Luis**, Juan 1940- WhoAmP 91
**Luis**, Juanita Bolland 1950- WhoIns 92
**Luis**, Olga Maria 1958- WhoHisp 92
**Luis**, William 1948- WhoBlA 92
**Luisada**, Aldo Augusto 1901- AmMWSc 92
**Luisi**, Sharon Kay 1957- WhoMW 92
**Luiso**, Anthony 1944- WhoMW 92
**Luithly**, Douglas Eric 1953- WhoRel 92
**Luizzi**, Ronald 1953- WhoWest 92
**Lujan**, Ben WhoAmP 91, WhoHisp 92
**Lujan**, Edward L WhoAmP 91
**Lujan**, Edward L. 1932- WhoHisp 92, WhoWest 92
**Lujan**, Eugene David 1940- WhoHisp 92
**Lujan**, Herman WhoHisp 92
**Lujan**, Joe Martinez 1932- WhoHisp 92
**Lujan**, John Porras 1942- WhoHisp 92
**Lujan**, Manuel, Jr. 1928- IntWW 91, WhoAmP 91, WhoHisp 92
**Lujan**, Paul Harold 1964- WhoRel 92
**Lujan**, Pilar C WhoAmP 91
**Lujan**, Richard Sanchez 1942- WhoHisp 92
**Lujan**, Robert R. 1938- WhoHisp 92
**Luk**, Gordon David 1950- AmMWSc 92
**Luk**, King Sing 1932- AmMWSc 92
**Luka**, Archbishop 1877-1961 SovUnBD
**Luka**, Janos 1948- WhoMW 92
**Lukach**, Arthur S., Jr. 1935- WhoFI 92
**Lukach**, Carl Andrew 1930- AmMWSc 92
**Lukacs**, Eugene 1906- AmMWSc 92
**Lukacs**, Gjorgy 1885-1971 FacFETw
**Lukacs**, Gyorgy 1885-1971 LiExTwC
**Lukacs**, John 1923- WrDr 92
**Lukacs**, Michael Edward 1946- WhoFI 92
**Lukacs**, Robin Alan 1961- WhoAmL 92
**Lukanov**, Andrei Karlov 1938- IntWW 91
**Lukas**, Gaze Elmer 1907- WhoFI 92
**Lukas**, George 1931- AmMWSc 92
**Lukas**, J Anthony 1933- IntAu&W 91, WrDr 92
**Lukas**, Joan Donaldson 1942- AmMWSc 92
**Lukas**, Richard Conrad 1937- IntAu&W 91, WrDr 92
**Lukas**, Ronald John 1949- AmMWSc 92
**Lukas**, Susan DrAPF 91
**Lukasewycz**, Omelan Alexander AmMWSc 92
**Lukashuk**, Igor' Ivanovich 1926- SovUnBD
**Lukasiewicz**, Julius 1919- AmMWSc 92
**Lukasik**, Stephen Joseph 1931- AmMWSc 92, WhoWest 92
**Lukaski**, Henry Charles 1947- AmMWSc 92
**Lukaszewski**, James Edmund 1942- WhoFI 92
**Luke** EncEarC
**Luke**, Baron 1905- IntWW 91, Who 92
**Luke**, Charles Stanley 1952- WhoRel 92
**Luke**, Clyde Elliot 1942- WhoWest 92
**Luke**, Eben Livesey 1930- IntWW 91
**Luke**, Eric Neville 1956- WhoEnt 92
**Luke**, Herbert Hodges 1923- AmMWSc 92
**Luke**, James Lindsay 1932- AmMWSc 92
**Luke**, John Anderson 1925- WhoFI 92
**Luke**, Jon Christian 1940- AmMWSc 92
**Luke**, Keye d1991 NewYTBS 91 [port]
**Luke**, Lance L. 1955- WhoFI 92, WhoWest 92
**Luke**, Patricia Ann 1934- WhoFI 92
**Luke**, Peter 1919- IntAu&W 91, IntMPA 92, Who 92, WrDr 92
**Luke**, Robert A 1938- AmMWSc 92, WhoWest 92
**Luke**, Sherrill David 1928- WhoBlA 92
**Luke**, Stanley D 1928- AmMWSc 92
**Luke**, Thomas IntAu&W 91X, WrDr 92
**Luke**, Warren K. K. 1944- WhoFI 92, WhoWest 92
**Luke**, Yudell Leo 1918- AmMWSc 92
**Lukehart**, Charles Martin 1946- AmMWSc 92
**Lukehart**, John Stephen 1944- WhoFI 92
**Luken**, Charles WhoAmP 91, WhoMW 92
**Luken**, Charles J. 1951- AlmAP 92 [port]
**Luken**, Thomas A 1925- WhoAmP 91
**Lukenbill**, Gregg WhoWest 92
**Lukens**, Alan W 1924- WhoAmP 91
**Lukens**, Donald E 1931- WhoAmP 91
**Lukens**, Fred Addison 1954- WhoMW 92
**Lukens**, Herbert Richard, Jr 1921- AmMWSc 92
**Lukens**, Isaiah 1779-1846 BiInAmS
**Lukens**, Laura Greever 1959- WhoWest 92
**Lukens**, Lewis Nelson 1927- AmMWSc 92
**Lukens**, Paul Bourne 1934- WhoFI 92
**Lukens**, Paul W, Jr 1928- AmMWSc 92
**Lukens**, Raymond 1947- WhoEnt 92
**Lukens**, Raymond James 1930- AmMWSc 92
**Luker**, George Malcolm 1955- WhoWest 92
**Luker**, Kristin 1946- WhoAmL 92, WrDr 92
**Luker**, Maurice Sylvester, Jr. 1934- WhoRel 92
**Luker**, Richard Allen 1939- WhoWest 92
**Luker**, William Dean 1920- AmMWSc 92
**Lukert**, Michael T 1937- AmMWSc 92
**Lukert**, Phil Dean 1931- AmMWSc 92
**Lukes**, Milan 1933- IntWW 91
**Lukes**, Robert Michael 1923- AmMWSc 92
**Lukes**, Steven M. 1941- WrDr 92
**Lukes**, Steven Michael 1941- Who 92
**Lukes**, Thomas Mark 1920- AmMWSc 92
**Lukey**, Joan A. 1949- WhoAmL 92
**Lukezic**, Bret Rush 1956- WhoEnt 92
**Lukezic**, Felix Lee 1933- AmMWSc 92
**Lukianenko**, Lev Hryhorovych 1927- IntWW 91, SovUnBD
**Lukic**, Jelena 1962- TwCPaSc
**Lukin**, L S 1925- AmMWSc 92
**Lukin**, Marvin 1928- AmMWSc 92
**Lukinov**, Ivan Illarionovich 1927- IntWW 91
**Lukman**, Rilwanu 1938- IntWW 91
**Lukoji**, Mulumba IntWW 91
**Lukonin**, Mihail Kuz'mich 1918-1976 SovUnBD
**Lukonin**, Nikolay Fedorovich 1928- IntWW 91
**Lukov**, Hristo Nikolov 1887-1943 BiDExR
**Lukow**, Odean Michelin AmMWSc 92
**Lukowiak**, Kenneth Daniel 1947- AmMWSc 92
**Lukyanienko**, Vladimir Matveyevich 1937- IntWW 91
**Lukyanov**, Anatoliy Ivanovich 1930- IntWW 91, SovUnBD
**Lula**, George 1948- WhoFI 92
**Lull**, David B 1923- AmMWSc 92
**Lull**, David John 1944- WhoRel 92
**Lull**, Susan TwCSFW 91
**Lull**, Timothy Frank 1943- WhoRel 92, WhoWest 92
**Lulla**, Jack D AmMWSc 92
**Lulla**, Kotusingh 1935- AmMWSc 92
**Lulloff**, Earl King 1946- WhoAmP 91
**Lully**, Jean-Baptiste 1632-1687 NewAmDM
**Lulua**, Abdul-Wahid 1931- IntAu&W 91
**Lum**, Bert Kwan Buck 1929- AmMWSc 92
**Lum**, Darrell H.Y. DrAPF 91
**Lum**, Herman 1926- WhoAmP 91
**Lum**, Herman Tsui Fai 1926- WhoAmL 92, WhoWest 92
**Lum**, Kin K 1940- AmMWSc 92
**Lum**, Kwong-Yen 1926- WhoWest 92
**Lum**, Lawrence AmMWSc 92
**Lum**, Michael 1959- WhoMW 92
**Lum**, Patrick Tung Moon 1928- AmMWSc 92
**Lum**, Vincent Yu-Sun 1933- AmMWSc 92
**Lum**, Wing Tek DrAPF 91
**Lumadue**, Donald Dean 1938- WhoFI 92
**Lumb**, Ethel Sue 1916- AmMWSc 92
**Lumb**, George Dennett 1917- AmMWSc 92
**Lumb**, Judith Rae H 1943- AmMWSc 92
**Lumb**, Ralph F 1921- AmMWSc 92
**Lumb**, Roger H 1940- AmMWSc 92
**Lumb**, William Valjean 1921- AmMWSc 92
**Lumbard**, Eliot Howland 1925- WhoAmL 92
**Lumbers**, Sydney Blake 1933- AmMWSc 92
**Lumchuan** 1928?-1985 EncAmaz 91
**Lumeng**, Lawrence 1939- AmMWSc 92
**Lumenta**, D. J. WhoRel 92
**Lumet**, Sidney LesBEnT 92
**Lumet**, Sidney 1924- FacFETw, IntDcF 2-2 [port], IntMPA 92, IntWW 91, Who 92, WhoEnt 92
**Lumiere brothers**, the FacFETw
**Lumiere**, Auguste 1862-1954 FacFETw
**Lumiere**, Louis 1864-1948 FacFETw, IntDcF 2-2
**Lumina**, Machila Joshua 1939- IntWW 91
**Lumingkewas**, Stefanus Buang 1937- WhoFI 92
**Lumley** Who 92
**Lumley**, Viscount 1973- Who 92
**Lumley**, Joanna IntAu&W 91
**Lumley**, Joanna 1946- IntWW 91
**Lumley**, John L 1930- AmMWSc 92
**Lumley-Jones**, Iain Christopher 1939- WhoWest 92
**Lumley-Savile** Who 92
**Lumm**, Randolph Stephen 1949- WhoHisp 92
**Lumma**, William Carl, Jr 1941- AmMWSc 92
**Lummis**, Cynthia M 1954- WhoAmP 91
**Lumpe**, Sheila 1935- WhoAmP 91
**Lumpkin**, Bruce Keyser 1944- WhoEnt 92
**Lumpkin**, Charles Henry, Jr 1943- WhoAmP 91
**Lumpkin**, Kirk DrAPF 91
**Lumpkin**, Lee Roy 1925- AmMWSc 92
**Lumpkin**, Michael Dirksen 1953- AmMWSc 92
**Lumpkin**, Royce Edgar 1942- WhoEnt 92
**Lumpp**, James William 1909- WhoMW 92
**Lumry**, Rufus Worth, II 1920- AmMWSc 92
**Lumsby**, George N. 1935- WhoBlA 92
**Lumsdaine**, David 1931- ConCom 92
**Lumsdaine**, Edward 1937- AmMWSc 92, WhoMW 92
**Lumsdaine**, Nicola Frances Who 92

**Lumsden,** Catherine Louise 1948- *WhoAmP 91*
**Lumsden,** Charles John 1949- *AmMWSc 92*
**Lumsden,** David 1928- *Who 92*
**Lumsden,** David James 1928- *IntWW 91*
**Lumsden,** David Norman 1935- *AmMWSc 92*
**Lumsden,** G Quincey, Jr *WhoAmP 91*
**Lumsden,** George Innes 1926- *Who 92*
**Lumsden,** James Alexander 1915- *IntWW 91, Who 92*
**Lumsden,** Keith Grant 1935- *Who 92*
**Lumsden,** Louisa Innes 1840-1935 *BiDBrF 2*
**Lumsden,** Richard 1938- *AmMWSc 92*
**Lumsden,** Robert Douglas 1938- *AmMWSc 92*
**Lumsden,** William Watt, Jr 1920- *AmMWSc 92*
**Lumumba,** Patrice 1925-1961 *FacFETw*
**Lun,** Seahawk 1956- *WhoRel 92*
**Luna,** Albert *WhoHisp 92*
**Luna,** Albert, III 1950- *WhoAmP 91*
**Luna,** Carmen E. 1959- *WhoHisp 92*
**Luna,** Carmen Encinas 1959- *WhoWest 92*
**Luna,** Casey 1931- *WhoAmP 91, WhoWest 92*
**Luna,** Casey E. 1931- *WhoHisp 92*
**Luna,** Chris *WhoHisp 92*
**Luna,** Dennis R. 1946- *WhoHisp 92, WhoWest 92*
**Luna,** Elizabeth J 1951- *AmMWSc 92*
**Luna,** Fred 1931- *WhoAmP 91, WhoHisp 92*
**Luna,** Gregory 1932- *WhoAmP 91, WhoHisp 92*
**Luna,** Humberto *WhoHisp 92*
**Luna,** Juan 1857-1899 *HisDSpE*
**Luna,** Mickie Solorio 1945- *WhoHisp 92*
**Luna,** Nidia Casilda R. 1926- *WhoHisp 92*
**Luna,** Patricia Adele 1956- *WhoFI 92*
**Luna,** Richard S. *WhoHisp 92*
**Luna,** Rodrigo F. 1940- *WhoHisp 92*
**Luna,** William 1936- *WhoHisp 92*
**Luna,** William Paul 1962- *WhoHisp 92*
**Luna,** Wilson 1951- *WhoHisp 92*
**Luna Solorzano,** Maria Isela 1964- *WhoHisp 92*
**Lunacharsky,** Anatoliy Vasil'evich 1875-1933 *SovUnBD*
**Lunacharsky,** Anatoly Vasilyevich 1875-1933 *FacFETw*
**Lunan,** Duncan 1945- *WrDr 92*
**Lunan,** Duncan Alasdair 1945- *IntAu&W 91*
**Lunardini,** Virgil J, Jr 1935- *AmMWSc 92*
**Lunceford,** Jimmie 1902-1947 *NewAmDM*
**Lunceford,** Joe Elbert 1937- *WhoRel 92*
**Lunch,** John 1919- *Who 92*
**Lunchick,** Curt 1953- *AmMWSc 92*
**Lund,** Anders Edward 1928- *AmMWSc 92*
**Lund,** Arthur Kermit 1933- *WhoFI 92, WhoWest 92*
**Lund,** Charles Edward 1946- *AmMWSc 92*
**Lund,** Daniel J. 1958- *WhoFI 92*
**Lund,** Daryl B 1941- *AmMWSc 92*
**Lund,** David Harrison 1927- *WhoAmL 92*
**Lund,** Donald S 1932- *AmMWSc 92*
**Lund,** Douglas 1940- *WhoMW 92*
**Lund,** Douglas E 1933- *AmMWSc 92*
**Lund,** Edwin Harrison 1954- *WhoFI 92*
**Lund,** Eric 1948- *WhoRel 92*
**Lund,** Frederick H 1929- *AmMWSc 92*
**Lund,** Gerald N. 1939- *WrDr 92*
**Lund,** Gerald Niels 1939- *IntAu&W 91*
**Lund,** Gregory Edward 1958- *WhoMW 92*
**Lund,** Gudrun 1930- *ConCom 92*
**Lund,** Hartvig Roald 1933- *AmMWSc 92*
**Lund,** Henning 1929- *IntWW 91*
**Lund,** J Kenneth 1933- *AmMWSc 92*
**Lund,** James Louis 1926- *WhoAmL 92*
**Lund,** John Edward 1939- *AmMWSc 92*
**Lund,** John Richard 1960- *WhoWest 92*
**Lund,** John Turner 1929- *AmMWSc 92*
**Lund,** John Walter Guerrier 1912- *IntWW 91, Who 92*
**Lund,** Jordan Keith 1957- *WhoEnt 92*
**Lund,** Lanny Jack 1943- *AmMWSc 92*
**Lund,** Lois Ann 1927- *WhoMW 92*
**Lund,** Louis Harold 1919- *AmMWSc 92*
**Lund,** Mark Wylie 1952- *AmMWSc 92*
**Lund,** Melvin Robert 1922- *AmMWSc 92*
**Lund,** Morris Duane 1930- *WhoWest 92*
**Lund,** Pauline Kay 1955- *AmMWSc 92*
**Lund,** Peter *LesBEnT 92*
**Lund,** Peter Anthony 1941- *WhoEnt 92*
**Lund,** Richard 1939- *AmMWSc 92*
**Lund,** Rodney Cookson 1936- *Who 92*
**Lund,** Roslyn Rosen *DrAPF 91*
**Lund,** Steve 1923- *AmMWSc 92*
**Lund,** Steven Jay 1953- *WhoAmL 92*
**Lund,** Timothy Joseph 1961- *WhoEnt 92, WhoMW 92*
**Lund,** Victor L. 1947- *WhoFI 92*
**Lund,** William Albert, Jr 1930- *AmMWSc 92*
**Lund,** Zoe Tamerlaine 1962- *WhoEnt 92*
**Lundahl,** Craig Raymond 1943- *WhoWest 92*
**Lundahl,** Steven Mark 1955- *WhoEnt 92*
**Lundberg,** Arne S. 1911- *IntWW 91*
**Lundberg,** Bo Klas Oskar 1907- *IntWW 91*
**Lundberg,** Donald E. 1916- *WrDr 92*
**Lundberg,** Douglas Taylor 1947- *WhoWest 92*
**Lundberg,** Eric Gwynn 1948- *WhoAmL 92*
**Lundberg,** George David 1933- *AmMWSc 92*
**Lundberg,** George David, II 1933- *WhoMW 92*
**Lundberg,** Gustave Harold 1901- *AmMWSc 92*
**Lundberg,** Henry 1931- *IntWW 91*
**Lundberg,** John Kessander 1934- *WhoFI 92*
**Lundberg,** John L 1924- *AmMWSc 92*
**Lundberg,** John Thomas 1956- *WhoEnt 92*
**Lundberg,** Jon Clark 1961- *WhoEnt 92*
**Lundberg,** Lance Brown 1956- *WhoFI 92*
**Lundberg,** Larry Thomas 1938- *WhoFI 92*
**Lundberg,** Robert Dean 1928- *AmMWSc 92*
**Lundblad,** Roger Lauren 1939- *AmMWSc 92*
**Lundbom,** Jack Russell 1939- *WhoRel 92*
**Lundby,** Julius Eric 1944- *WhoIns 92*
**Lundby,** Mary Adelaide 1948- *WhoAmP 91*
**Lunde,** Asbjorn Rudolph 1927- *WhoAmL 92*
**Lunde,** Barbara Kegerreis 1937- *AmMWSc 92*
**Lunde,** Brian Alan 1954- *WhoAmP 91*
**Lunde,** David *DrAPF 91*
**Lunde,** Diane *DrAPF 91*
**Lunde,** Dolores Benitez 1929- *WhoWest 92*
**Lunde,** Donald Theodore 1937- *WhoWest 92*
**Lunde,** Erik Sheldon 1940- *WhoMW 92*
**Lunde,** Gulbrand Oscar Johan 1901-1942 *BiDExR*
**Lunde,** Karen Tamm 1944- *WhoWest 92*
**Lunde,** Kenneth E 1918- *AmMWSc 92*
**Lunde,** Marvin Clarence, Jr. 1936- *WhoFI 92*
**Lunde,** Milford Norman 1924- *AmMWSc 92*
**Lunde,** Peter J 1931- *AmMWSc 92*
**Lundeberg,** Knut Olafson 1859-1942? *RelLAm 91*
**Lundeberg,** Philip 1923- *WrDr 92*
**Lundeen,** Allan Jay 1932- *AmMWSc 92*
**Lundeen,** Ardelle Anne 1929- *WhoMW 92*
**Lundeen,** Carl Victor, Jr 1943- *AmMWSc 92*
**Lundeen,** Daniel N. 1957- *WhoAmL 92*
**Lundeen,** Glen Alfred 1922- *AmMWSc 92*
**Lundeen,** John Anton 1952- *WhoFI 92*
**Lundeen,** Robert West 1921- *IntWW 91*
**Lundegard,** John Thomas 1931- *WhoFI 92*
**Lundegard,** Robert James 1927- *AmMWSc 92*
**Lundelius,** Ernest Luther, Jr 1927- *AmMWSc 92*
**Lundell,** Albert Thomas 1931- *AmMWSc 92*
**Lundell,** Barbara Mildred 1934- *WhoWest 92*
**Lundell,** Frederick Waldemar 1924- *AmMWSc 92*
**Lundell,** O Robert 1931- *AmMWSc 92*
**Lunden,** Allyn Oscar 1931- *AmMWSc 92*
**Lundergan,** Charles Donald 1923- *AmMWSc 92*
**Lundergan,** Jerry 1947- *WhoAmP 91*
**Lunderville,** Gerald Paul 1941- *WhoWest 92*
**Lunderville,** Howard P 1923- *WhoAmP 91*
**Lundfelt,** Fred *WhoAmP 91*
**Lundgreen-Nielsen,** Flemming Torkild J. 1937- *IntWW 91*
**Lundgren,** Carl Allin 1955- *WhoFI 92, WhoMW 92*
**Lundgren,** Claes Erik Gunnar 1931- *AmMWSc 92*
**Lundgren,** Clara Eloise 1951- *WhoFI 92*
**Lundgren,** Dale A 1932- *AmMWSc 92*
**Lundgren,** David L 1931- *AmMWSc 92*
**Lundgren,** David Russell 1955- *WhoWest 92*
**Lundgren,** Dolph 1959- *ConTFT 9, IntMPA 92*
**Lundgren,** Harry Richard 1928- *AmMWSc 92*
**Lundgren,** J Richard 1942- *AmMWSc 92*
**Lundgren,** Kenneth B 1948- *WhoIns 92*
**Lundgren,** Lawrence Elmer 1952- *WhoRel 92*
**Lundgren,** Lawrence William, Jr 1932- *AmMWSc 92*
**Lundgren,** Mark David 1958- *WhoRel 92*
**Lundgren,** Robert Allen 1957- *WhoRel 92*
**Lundgren,** Shirlie Marie *WhoAmP 91*
**Lundgren,** Susan Elaine 1949- *WhoWest 92*
**Lundgren-Weber,** Gail 1955- *WhoAmL 92*
**Lundholm,** J G, Jr 1925- *AmMWSc 92*
**Lundin,** Ann Frances 1941- *WhoWest 92*
**Lundin,** Bruce T 1919- *AmMWSc 92*
**Lundin,** Carl Axel Robert 1851-1915 *BiInAmS*
**Lundin,** Carl D 1934- *AmMWSc 92*
**Lundin,** David Erik 1949- *WhoAmL 92*
**Lundin,** Frank E, Jr 1928- *AmMWSc 92*
**Lundin,** Judith *DrAPF 91*
**Lundin,** Robert Enor 1927- *AmMWSc 92*
**Lundin,** Robert Folke 1936- *AmMWSc 92*
**Lundine,** Cindy Raye 1946- *WhoFI 92*
**Lundine,** Stanley N 1939- *WhoAmP 91*
**Lunding,** Christopher Hanna 1946- *WhoAmL 92*
**Lundkvist,** Artur d1991 *NewYTBS 91*
**Lundquist,** Burton Russell 1927- *AmMWSc 92*
**Lundquist,** Charles Arthur 1928- *AmMWSc 92*
**Lundquist,** Homer *WhoAmP 91*
**Lundquist,** Marjorie Ann 1938- *AmMWSc 92*
**Lundquist,** Pamela T. 1951- *WhoEnt 92*
**Lundquist,** Verne *LesBEnT 92*
**Lundquist,** Violet Elvira 1912- *WhoWest 92*
**Lundquist,** Wallace 1923- *WhoAmL 92*
**Lundsager,** C Bent 1925- *AmMWSc 92*
**Lundstedt,** Sven Bertil 1926- *WhoMW 92*
**Lundstrom,** Hans Olof 1927- *IntWW 91*
**Lundstrom,** Louis C 1915- *AmMWSc 92*
**Lundstrom,** Lowell *WhoRel 92*
**Lundstrom,** Mark Steven 1951- *AmMWSc 92*
**Lundstrom,** Mary Meyer 1948- *WhoWest 92*
**Lundstrom,** Marylin Rose 1954- *WhoFI 92*
**Lundstrom,** Ronald Charles 1952- *AmMWSc 92*
**Lundvall,** Richard 1920- *AmMWSc 92*
**Lundwall,** Sam J. 1941- *TwCSFW 91, WrDr 92*
**Lundy,** Benjamin 1789-1839 *BenetAL 91*
**Lundy,** John Kent 1946- *AmMWSc 92, WhoWest 92*
**Lundy,** Ray 1916- *WhoAmP 91*
**Lundy,** Richard Alan 1934- *AmMWSc 92*
**Lundy,** Sadie Allen 1918- *WhoFI 92, WhoMW 92*
**Lundy,** Ted Sadler 1933- *AmMWSc 92, WhoAmP 91*
**Lunenberg,** Engelbartus 1922- *IntWW 91*
**Lunenfeld,** Bruno 1927- *IntWW 91*
**Luner,** Philip 1925- *AmMWSc 92*
**Luner,** Stephen Jay 1940- *AmMWSc 92*
**Lunev,** Aleksandr 1965- *WhoEnt 92*
**Lung,** David Darling 1947- *WhoFI 92*
**Lunger,** Charles William 1927- *WhoFI 92*
**Lungren,** Daniel Edward 1946- *WhoAmL 92, WhoAmP 91, WhoWest 92*
**Lungren,** John Howard 1925- *WhoAmL 92, WhoMW 92*
**Lungren,** Maurice Carlson 1916- *WhoMW 92*
**Lungstrom,** Leon 1915- *AmMWSc 92*
**Lunin,** Martin 1917- *AmMWSc 92*
**Lunine,** Jonathan Irving 1959- *AmMWSc 92*
**Lunk,** William Allan 1919- *AmMWSc 92*
**Lunka,** Victor William, Jr. 1955- *WhoFI 92*
**Lunkov,** Nikolai Mitrofanovich 1919- *IntWW 91, Who 92*
**Lunn,** Anthony Crowther 1946- *AmMWSc 92*
**Lunn,** Carolyn 1960- *SmATA 67 [port]*
**Lunn,** David Ramsay *Who 92*
**Lunn,** Janet 1928- *SmATA 68 [port], WrDr 92*
**Lunn,** Janet Louise 1928- *IntAu&W 91*
**Lunn,** Jean *DrAPF 91*
**Lunn,** Michael Scott 1962- *WhoMW 92*
**Lunn,** Peter Northcote 1914- *Who 92*
**Lunn,** Robert David 1940- *WhoMW 92*
**Lunney,** David Clyde *AmMWSc 92*
**Lunney,** Joan K 1946- *AmMWSc 92*
**Lunny,** William Francis 1938- *Who 92*
**Luns,** Joseph Marie Antoine Hubert 1911- *IntWW 91, Who 92*
**Lunsford,** Bascom Lamar 1882-1973 *DcNCBi 4*
**Lunsford,** Carl Dalton 1927- *AmMWSc 92*
**Lunsford,** Donald Wayne 1938- *WhoRel 92*
**Lunsford,** Jack Horner 1936- *AmMWSc 92*
**Lunsford,** Jesse V 1923- *AmMWSc 92*
**Lunsford,** M. Rosser *DrAPF 91*
**Lunsford,** Ralph D 1934- *AmMWSc 92*
**Lunstrum,** Kathryn Joann 1960- *WhoMW 92*
**Lunt and Fontanne** *FacFETw*
**Lunt,** Alfred 1892-1977 *FacFETw*
**Lunt,** Elizabeth Anne 1951- *WhoAmL 92*
**Lunt,** George 1943- *WrDr 92*
**Lunt,** Harry Edward 1924- *AmMWSc 92*
**Lunt,** Horace G. 1918- *ConAu 134*
**Lunt,** James Doiran 1917- *Who 92, WrDr 92*
**Lunt,** Larry Vernon 1943- *WhoAmP 91*
**Lunt,** Owen Raynal 1921- *AmMWSc 92*
**Lunt,** Ronald Geoffrey 1913- *Who 92*
**Lunt,** Steele Ray 1935- *AmMWSc 92*
**Lunt,** Stephen Cammett 1945- *WhoAmL 92*
**Lunt,** Teresa Frances 1954- *WhoWest 92*
**Lunts,** Lazar Adolf'ovich 1892-1980 *SovUnBD*
**Lunts,** Lev Natanovich 1901-1924 *FacFETw, SovUnBD*
**Luntz,** Charles Eliot 1943- *WhoMW 92*
**Luntz,** Myron 1940- *AmMWSc 92*
**Lunz,** Elisabeth 1939- *WhoRel 92*
**Luo Bin Ji** 1917- *IntWW 91*
**Luo Gan** 1935- *IntWW 91*
**Luo Guibo** 1908- *IntWW 91*
**Luo Pingan** 1945- *IntWW 91*
**Luo Qingchang** 1920- *IntWW 91*
**Luo Shangcai** 1929- *IntWW 91*
**Luo Tian** *IntWW 91*
**Luo Yuanzheng** 1924- *IntWW 91*
**Luo,** Bin Ji 1917- *IntAu&W 91*
**Luo,** Peilin 1913- *AmMWSc 92*
**Luoma,** Ernie Victor 1932- *AmMWSc 92*
**Luoma,** John Robert Vincent 1938- *AmMWSc 92*
**Luongo,** Cesar Augusto 1954- *AmMWSc 92*
**Luongo,** John Patrick 1949- *WhoEnt 92*
**Luongo,** Lucille Francesca 1948- *WhoEnt 92*
**Luongo,** Stephen Earle 1947- *WhoAmL 92*
**Luonuansuu,** James Gregory 1966- *WhoRel 92*
**Lupacchino,** Donato G. 1960- *WhoFI 92*
**Lupack,** Alan *DrAPF 91*
**Lupan,** David Martin 1945- *AmMWSc 92*
**Lupash,** Lawrence O 1942- *AmMWSc 92*
**Luper,** Clara M. 1923- *WhoBlA 92*
**Luper,** Jerry Eulen 1941- *WhoWest 92*
**Lupert,** Leslie Allan 1946- *WhoAmL 92*
**Lupertz,** Markus 1941- *WorArt 1980*
**Lupinacci,** Julio Cesar 1929- *IntWW 91*
**Lupino,** Ida 1918- *HanAmWH, IntMPA 92, ReelWom [port], WhoEnt 92*
**Lupinski,** John Henry 1927- *AmMWSc 92*
**Luplow,** Wayne Charles 1940- *AmMWSc 92*
**Lupo,** Mary E. *NewYTBS 91 [port]*
**Lupo,** Robert Edward Smith 1953- *WhoFI 92*
**Lupo,** Samuel E *WhoAmP 91*
**Lupo,** Thomas A. 1948- *WhoFI 92*
**Lupoff,** Richard A 1935- *TwCSFW 91, WrDr 92*
**Lupoff,** Richard Allen 1935- *IntAu&W 91*
**Lupone,** Patti 1949- *IntMPA 92, WhoEnt 92*
**Lupovitz,** Sally 1930- *WhoAmP 91*
**Luppi,** Howard L *WhoAmP 91*
**Luppold,** Chris Allen 1950- *WhoFI 92*
**Lupro,** Charles *WhoAmP 91*
**Lupski,** James Richard 1957- *AmMWSc 92*
**Lupton,** Charles Hamilton, Jr 1919- *AmMWSc 92*
**Lupton,** John Edward 1944- *AmMWSc 92*
**Lupton,** John Mather, III 1947- *WhoAmP 91*
**Lupton,** Thomas 1918- *Who 92*
**Lupton,** William Hamilton 1930- *AmMWSc 92*
**Lupu,** Ira C. 1946- *WhoAmL 92*
**Lupu,** Radu 1945- *IntWW 91, Who 92, WhoEnt 92*
**Luqi** 1949- *AmMWSc 92*
**Lura,** Mick 1948- *WhoAmP 91*
**Lura,** Richard Dean 1945- *AmMWSc 92*
**Luraghi,** Giuseppe 1905- *IntWW 91*
**Lurain,** John Robert, III 1946- *AmMWSc 92*
**Luraschi,** Luigi G. 1906- *IntMPA 92*
**Lurcat,** Andre 1894-1970 *DcTwDes*
**Lurcat,** Jean 1892-1966 *DcTwDes, FacFETw*
**Lurch,** E Norman 1919- *AmMWSc 92*
**Lurey,** Alfred Saul 1942- *WhoAmL 92*
**Lurgan,** Baron d1991 *Who 92N*
**Lurgan,** Baron 1911- *Who 92*
**Luria,** Aleksandr R 1902- *FacFETw*
**Luria,** S. E. 1912-1991 *ConAu 133*
**Luria,** S M 1929- *AmMWSc 92*
**Luria,** Salvador 1912- *WrDr 92*
**Luria,** Salvador 1912-1991 *CurBio 91N*
**Luria,** Salvador E. 1912-1991 *NewYTBS 91 [port]*
**Luria,** Salvador Edward d1991 *IntWW 91N, Who 92N*
**Luria,** Salvador Edward 1912- *AmMWSc 92, WhoNob 90*
**Luria,** Salvador Edward 1912-1991 *FacFETw*
**Luria-Sukenick,** Lynn *DrAPF 91*
**Lurie,** Alan Gordon 1946- *AmMWSc 92*
**Lurie,** Alan Jeffrey 1942- *WhoFI 92*

**Lurie**, Alison *DrAPF 91, IntAu&W 91*
**Lurie**, Alison 1926- *BenetAL 91, ConNov 91, IntWW 91, Who 92, WrDr 92*
**Lurie**, Arnold Paul 1932- *AmMWSc 92*
**Lurie**, Fred Marcus 1930- *AmMWSc 92*
**Lurie**, Harold 1919- *AmMWSc 92*
**Lurie**, Henry Albert 1923- *WhoMW 92*
**Lurie**, Joan B 1941- *AmMWSc 92*
**Lurie**, Jonathan Adam 1956- *WhoMW 92*
**Lurie**, Morris 1938- *ConAu 133, ConNov 91, WrDr 92*
**Lurie**, Norman A 1940- *AmMWSc 92*
**Lurie**, Paul Michael 1941- *WhoAmL 92*
**Lurie**, Ranan Raymond 1932- *IntWW 91*
**Lurie**, Robert A. *WhoWest 92*
**Lurie**, Robert M 1931- *AmMWSc 92*
**Lurie**, Ron *WhoAmP 91*
**Lurie**, Susan Sheila Galitzer 1948- *WhoRel 92*
**Lurie**, Toby *DrAPF 91*
**Lurie**, William L. 1931- *WhoFI 92*
**Lurix**, Paul Leslie, Jr 1949- *AmMWSc 92, WhoFI 92*
**Lurkis**, Alexander 1908- *AmMWSc 92*
**Luro**, Horatio d1991 *NewYTBS 91 [port]*
**Lurton**, H. William 1929- *WhoFI 92, WhoMW 92*
**Lurton**, Horace H 1844-1914 *FacFETw*
**Lurvey**, Ira Harold 1935- *WhoAmL 92*
**Lurvey**, Mildred Edwina 1927- *WhoAmP 91*
**Luryi**, Serge 1947- *AmMWSc 92*
**Lusaka**, Paul John Firmino 1935- *IntWW 91*
**Lusas**, Edmund W 1931- *AmMWSc 92*
**Lusby**, John Martin 1943- *Who 92*
**Lusby**, William Robert 1940- *AmMWSc 92*
**Luschei**, Glenna *DrAPF 91*
**Luscher**, Ulrich 1932- *AmMWSc 92*
**Luschikov**, Anatoliy Pavlovich 1917- *IntWW 91*
**Luscombe**, David Edward 1938- *IntWW 91, Who 92*
**Luscombe**, Herbert Alfred 1916- *AmMWSc 92*
**Luscombe**, Lawrence Edward 1924- *Who 92*
**Luse**, Keith *WhoAmP 91*
**Luserke**, Martin 1880-1968 *EncTR 91*
**Lush**, Christopher Duncan 1928- *Who 92*
**Lush**, George 1912- *Who 92*
**Lush**, George Hermann 1912- *IntWW 91*
**Lushbaugh**, Clarence Chancelum 1916- *AmMWSc 92*
**Lushbough**, Channing Harden 1929- *AmMWSc 92*
**Lushev**, Petr Georgevich 1923- *IntWW 91, SovUnBD*
**Lushington**, John 1938- *Who 92*
**Lusignan**, Bruce Burr 1936- *AmMWSc 92*
**Lusignan**, Guy de 1929- *IntWW 91*
**Lusinchi**, Jaime 1924- *IntWW 91*
**Lusis**, Aldons Jekabs 1947- *AmMWSc 92*
**Lusis**, Janis Voldmarovich 1939- *SovUnBD*
**Lusk**, Charles Michael, III 1948- *WhoFI 92*
**Lusk**, Daniel *DrAPF 91*
**Lusk**, Georgia Lee 1893-1971 *HanAmWH*
**Lusk**, Joan Edith 1942- *AmMWSc 92*
**Lusk**, Lisa Marie 1957- *WhoAmL 92*
**Lusk**, William Thompson 1838-1897 *BiInAmS*
**Luska**, Sidney *BenetAL 91*
**Luskin**, Evan Ross 1946- *WhoEnt 92, WhoMW 92*
**Luskin**, Leo Samuel 1914- *AmMWSc 92*
**Luskin**, Mitchell B 1951- *AmMWSc 92*
**Luskin**, Mitchell Barry 1951- *WhoMW 92*
**Luskin**, Robert David 1950- *WhoAmL 92*
**Lusnar**, Mark Patrick 1965- *WhoFI 92*
**Luss**, Dan 1938- *AmMWSc 92*
**Luss**, Gerald *DcTwDes*
**Lusser**, Markus 1931- *IntWW 91*
**Lussier**, Andre 1933- *AmMWSc 92*
**Lussier**, Barbara M. 1956- *WhoFI 92*
**Lussier**, Gilles L 1934- *AmMWSc 92*
**Lussier**, Martin P 1920- *WhoAmP 91*
**Lussier**, Roger Jean 1943- *AmMWSc 92*
**Lusskin**, Robert Miller 1921- *AmMWSc 92*
**Lust**, Peter, Jr. 1960- *WhoWest 92*
**Lust**, Reimar 1923- *IntWW 91, Who 92*
**Lustbader**, Edward David 1946- *AmMWSc 92*
**Lustbader**, Eric 1946- *IntAu&W 91*
**Lustbader**, Eric Van *WrDr 92*
**Lustbader**, Philip Lawrence 1949- *WhoAmL 92*
**Luste**, Joseph Francis, Jr. 1940- *WhoFI 92*
**Lusted**, Lee Browning 1922- *AmMWSc 92*
**Lustenader**, Barbara Diane 1953- *WhoFI 92*
**Luster**, Deanna Mee Yee 1962- *WhoEnt 92*
**Luster**, Martin A *WhoAmP 91*
**Luster**, Michael I 1947- *AmMWSc 92*
**Lustgarten**, Celia S. *DrAPF 91*
**Lustgarten**, Ira Howard 1929- *WhoAmL 92*
**Lustgarten**, Ronald Krisses 1942- *AmMWSc 92*
**Lustgarten**, Steven Paul 1951- *WhoEnt 92*
**Lustgarten**, Stewart J. 1943- *WhoFI 92*
**Lustick**, Sheldon Irving 1934- *AmMWSc 92*
**Lustig**, Alvin 1915-1955 *DcTwDes*
**Lustig**, Arnost 1926- *IntAu&W 91, IntWW 91, LiExTwC*
**Lustig**, Bernard 1902- *AmMWSc 92*
**Lustig**, Harry 1925- *AmMWSc 92*
**Lustig**, Howard E 1925- *AmMWSc 92*
**Lustig**, Judith Joy 1943- *WhoWest 92*
**Lustig**, Matthew Joseph 1960- *WhoFI 92*
**Lustig**, Max 1932- *AmMWSc 92*
**Lustig**, Norman I. 1938- *WhoAmL 92*
**Lustig**, Richard Lawrence 1950- *WhoEnt 92*
**Lustig**, Stanley 1933- *AmMWSc 92, WhoMW 92*
**Lustig**, William 1955- *WhoEnt 92*
**Lustiger**, Jean-Marie 1926- *IntWW 91, Who 92, WhoRel 92*
**Lustman**, Benjamin 1914- *AmMWSc 92*
**Lusty**, Carol Jean 1936- *AmMWSc 92*
**Lusty**, Robert Frith d1991 *Who 92N*
**Lusztig**, George 1946- *AmMWSc 92, IntWW 91, Who 92*
**Lusztig**, Peter Alfred 1930- *WhoFI 92*
**Lutali**, A P 1919- *WhoAmP 91*
**Lutcher**, Nellie 1915- *WhoBlA 92*
**Lutchmeenaraidoo**, Seetanah 1944- *IntWW 91*
**Luten**, Thomas d1731? *DcNCBi 4*
**Luten**, Thomas Dee 1950- *WhoBlA 92*
**Lutenski**, Richard P *WhoIns 92*
**Luter**, Asa Boyd, Jr. 1949- *WhoRel 92*
**Luter**, John 1919- *WhoWest 92*
**Lutes**, Charlene McClanahan 1938- *AmMWSc 92*
**Lutes**, Dallas D 1925- *AmMWSc 92*
**Lutes**, Loren Daniel 1939- *AmMWSc 92*
**Lutes**, Olin S 1922- *AmMWSc 92*
**Luteyn**, James Leonard 1948- *AmMWSc 92*
**Lutfi**, Aly *IntWW 91*
**Lutgen**, Mike 1951- *WhoEnt 92*
**Luth**, James Curtis 1961- *WhoFI 92*
**Luth**, Kathleen Zinser 1950- *WhoMW 92*
**Luth**, Thomas Edward 1952- *WhoAmL 92*
**Luth**, William Clair 1934- *AmMWSc 92*
**Luther**, Arthur William 1919- *Who 92*
**Luther**, Dale Eugene 1932- *WhoRel 92*
**Luther**, Edward Turner 1928- *AmMWSc 92*
**Luther**, George Aubrey 1933- *WhoMW 92*
**Luther**, George William, III 1947- *AmMWSc 92*
**Luther**, Hans 1879-1962 *EncTR 91 [port]*
**Luther**, Herbert George 1914- *AmMWSc 92*
**Luther**, Holger Martin 1940- *AmMWSc 92*
**Luther**, James Borden 1960- *WhoMW 92, WhoRel 92*
**Luther**, Lester Charles 1931- *AmMWSc 92*
**Luther**, Lucius Calvin 1929- *WhoBlA 92*
**Luther**, M Ida *WhoAmP 91*
**Luther**, Martin *TwCSFW 91*
**Luther**, Martin 1895-1945 *EncTR 91*
**Luther**, Marvin L 1934- *AmMWSc 92*
**Luther**, Nancy J 1945- *WhoAmP 91*
**Luther**, Norman Y 1936- *AmMWSc 92*
**Luther**, Randall P., Jr. 1966- *WhoMW 92*
**Luther**, Richard Wayne 1945- *WhoAmP 91*
**Luther**, Seth *BenetAL 91*
**Luther**, Stephen G 1949- *WhoAmP 91*
**Luther**, Susan Militzer *DrAPF 91*
**Luther**, William Paul 1945- *WhoAmP 91*
**Luther-Ayres**, Jacquelyn Lee 1960- *WhoMW 92*
**Lutherer**, Lorenz O 1936- *AmMWSc 92*
**Luthey**, Graydon Dean, Jr. 1955- *WhoAmL 92*
**Luthey**, Joe Lee 1943- *AmMWSc 92*
**Luthra**, Harvinder Singh 1945- *AmMWSc 92*
**Luthra**, Krishan Lal 1949- *AmMWSc 92*
**Luthuli**, Albert John 1898-1967 *FacFETw, WhoNob 90*
**Luthy**, Chella *WhoHisp 92*
**Luthy**, David *WhoRel 92*
**Luthy**, Jakob Wilhelm 1919- *AmMWSc 92*
**Luthy**, Richard Godfrey 1945- *AmMWSc 92*
**Lutin**, David Louis 1919- *WhoWest 92*
**Lutjeharms**, Joseph Earl 1933- *WhoMW 92*
**Lutjens**, Gunther 1887-1941 *EncTR 91*
**Lutkie**, Wouter Leonardus 1887-1968 *BiDExR*
**Lutkowski**, Noel J 1944- *WhoIns 92*
**Lutomski**, Halina Jozefa 1932- *WhoEnt 92*
**Luton**, Edgar Frank 1921- *AmMWSc 92*
**Luton**, Jean-Marie 1942- *IntWW 91*
**Luton**, John D 1922- *WhoAmP 91*
**Luton**, Thomas d1731? *DcNCBi 4*
**Lutoslawski**, Witold 1913- *ConCom 92, CurBio 91 [port], FacFETw, IntWW 91, NewAmDM, Who 92*
**Lutrick**, Monroe Cornelius 1927- *AmMWSc 92*
**Lutsch**, Edward F 1930- *AmMWSc 92*
**Lutsk**, Bruce Martin 1942- *WhoAmL 92*
**Lutsko**, Dwight Edward 1947- *WhoFI 92*
**Lutsky**, Irving 1926- *AmMWSc 92*
**Lutsky**, Sheldon Jay 1943- *WhoFI 92*
**Lutt**, Carl J 1921- *AmMWSc 92*
**Lutten**, Thomas d1731? *DcNCBi 4*
**Lutter**, Charles William, Jr. 1944- *WhoAmL 92*
**Lutter**, Leonard C *AmMWSc 92*
**Lutter**, Marcus Michael 1930- *IntWW 91*
**Lutter**, Paul Allen 1946- *WhoAmL 92*
**Lutterloh**, Thomas S. 1816-1900 *DcNCBi 4*
**Luttges**, Marvin Wayne 1941- *AmMWSc 92*
**Luttinen**, Vilho Matti 1936- *IntWW 91*
**Luttinger**, Abigail *DrAPF 91*
**Luttinger**, Joaquin Mazdak 1923- *AmMWSc 92*
**Luttjohann**, John Robert 1956- *WhoAmL 92*
**Luttmann**, Frederick William 1940- *AmMWSc 92*
**Luttner**, Edward F. 1942- *WhoMW 92*
**Lutton**, Delos Nelson 1945- *WhoAmL 92*
**Lutton**, John D 1937- *AmMWSc 92*
**Lutton**, John Kazuo 1949- *AmMWSc 92*
**Lutton**, John V. 1939- *WhoRel 92*
**Luttrell**, Dan C. 1952- *WhoWest 92*
**Luttrell**, Eric Martin 1941- *AmMWSc 92*
**Luttrell**, Geoffrey Walter Fownes 1919- *Who 92*
**Luttrell**, George Howard 1941- *AmMWSc 92*
**Luttrell**, Ruth 1926- *WhoRel 92*
**Luttrull**, Shirley JoAnn 1937- *WhoMW 92*
**Lutts**, John A 1932- *AmMWSc 92*
**Luttwak**, Edward 1942- *IntAu&W 91, WrDr 92*
**Luttwak**, Edward Nicolae 1942- *IntWW 91*
**Lutu**, Fa'asuka S *WhoAmP 91*
**Lutvak**, Mark Allen 1939- *WhoFI 92*
**Lutwak**, Erwin 1946- *AmMWSc 92*
**Lutwak**, Leo 1928- *AmMWSc 92*
**Luty**, Fritz 1928- *AmMWSc 92*
**Lutyens**, Edwin Landseer 1869-1944 *DcTwDes, FacFETw*
**Lutyens**, Elisabeth 1906-1983 *NewAmDM*
**Lutyens**, Mary 1908- *IntAu&W 91, Who 92, WrDr 92*
**Lutz**, Albert William 1924- *AmMWSc 92*
**Lutz**, Anna Deppen 1929- *WhoRel 92*
**Lutz**, Arthur Leroy 1908- *AmMWSc 92*
**Lutz**, Barry Lafean 1944- *AmMWSc 92*
**Lutz**, Bruce Charles 1920- *AmMWSc 92*
**Lutz**, Carol Lombard 1931- *WhoAmL 92, WhoAmP 91*
**Lutz**, Donald Alexander 1940- *AmMWSc 92*
**Lutz**, Earlin Harold 1928- *WhoRel 92*
**Lutz**, Edith Ledford 1914- *WhoAmP 91*
**Lutz**, Elizabeth May 1928- *WhoAmL 92*
**Lutz**, George John 1933- *AmMWSc 92*
**Lutz**, Giles A. 1910-1982 *TwCWW 91*
**Lutz**, Harold John 1900- *AmMWSc 92*
**Lutz**, Harry Frank 1936- *AmMWSc 92*
**Lutz**, Iri Karist 1934- *WhoAmP 91*
**Lutz**, Jeffrey Christian 1959- *WhoWest 92*
**Lutz**, John 1939- *WrDr 92*
**Lutz**, John Shafroth 1943- *WhoAmL 92, WhoFI 92, WhoWest 92*
**Lutz**, John Thomas 1939- *IntAu&W 91*
**Lutz**, Joseph Philip 1951- *WhoFI 92*
**Lutz**, Julie Haynes 1944- *AmMWSc 92*
**Lutz**, Karl Evan 1949- *WhoAmL 92*
**Lutz**, Larry Edward 1938- *WhoAmP 91*
**Lutz**, Loma Lee 1946- *WhoRel 92*
**Lutz**, Marianne Christine 1922- *Who 92*
**Lutz**, Paul E 1934- *AmMWSc 92*
**Lutz**, Peter Louis 1939- *AmMWSc 92*
**Lutz**, Raymond 1935- *AmMWSc 92*
**Lutz**, Raymond Paul 1932- *AmMWSc 92*
**Lutz**, Richard Arthur 1949- *AmMWSc 92*
**Lutz**, Robert A. 1932- *IntWW 91*
**Lutz**, Robert Anthony 1932- *WhoMW 92*
**Lutz**, Robert William 1937- *AmMWSc 92*
**Lutz**, Thomas Edward 1940- *AmMWSc 92*
**Lutz**, William Andrew 1944- *WhoFI 92*
**Lutz**, William Lan 1944- *WhoAmL 92*
**Lutz**, Wilson Boyd 1927- *AmMWSc 92*
**Lutze**, Frederick Henry, Jr 1937- *AmMWSc 92*
**Lutze**, Viktor 1890-1943 *BiDExR, EncTR 91 [port]*
**Lutzenhiser**, Glenn Andrew 1933- *WhoEnt 92*
**Lutzer**, David John 1943- *AmMWSc 92*
**Lutzker**, Edythe d1991 *NewYTBS 91*
**Lutzker**, Edythe 1904- *AmMWSc 92*
**Lutzker**, Edythe 1904-1991 *ConAu 135*
**Lutzker**, Elliot Howard 1953- *WhoAmL 92*
**Luus**, George Aarne 1937- *WhoMW 92*
**Luus**, R 1939- *AmMWSc 92*
**Luvaas**, John Luther 1918- *WhoAmL 92*
**Luvaas**, William *DrAPF 91*
**LuValle**, James Ellis 1912- *AmMWSc 92, BlkOlyM*
**Luvisi**, Lee 1937- *WhoEnt 92*
**Luvisi**, Leslie Anne 1951- *WhoEnt 92*
**Luvsangombo**, Sonomyn 1924- *IntWW 91*
**Luvsanravdan**, Namsrayn 1923- *IntWW 91*
**Lux**, David Edward 1959- *WhoMW 92*
**Lux**, Gene 1926- *WhoAmP 91*
**Lux**, Guillermo 1938- *WhoHisp 92*
**Lux**, Jimmy *ConAu 135*
**Lux**, John H. 1918- *WhoFI 92*
**Lux**, Julie McDonnell 1951- *WhoEnt 92*
**Lux**, Samuel E, IV *AmMWSc 92*
**Lux**, Thomas *DrAPF 91*
**Lux**, Thomas 1946- *ConPo 91*
**Luxa**, Marcey *WhoRel 92*
**Luxeder**, Martin Robert 1959- *WhoMW 92*
**Luxembourg**, Grand Duke of *IntWW 91*
**Luxemburg**, Jack Alan 1949- *WhoRel 92*
**Luxemburg**, Rosa 1871-1919 *FacFETw*
**Luxemburg**, Wilhelmus Anthonius Josephus 1929- *AmMWSc 92*
**Luxenberg**, Arthur Martin 1959- *WhoAmL 92*
**Luxenberg**, Harold Richard 1921- *AmMWSc 92*
**Luxenberg**, Michael Don 1945- *WhoWest 92*
**Luxhoj**, James Thomas 1956- *AmMWSc 92*
**Luxmoore**, Christopher Charles 1926- *Who 92*
**Luxmoore**, Robert John 1940- *AmMWSc 92*
**Luxner**, Michael David 1950- *WhoEnt 92*
**Luxon**, Benjamin 1937- *NewAmDM*
**Luxon**, Benjamin Matthew 1937- *IntWW 91, Who 92*
**Luxon**, Bruce Arlie 1955- *AmMWSc 92*
**Luxon**, James Thomas 1934- *AmMWSc 92*
**Luxton**, William John 1909- *Who 92*
**Luyben**, William Landes 1933- *AmMWSc 92*
**Luyendyk**, Bruce Peter 1943- *AmMWSc 92*
**Luykx**, Peter 1937- *AmMWSc 92*
**Luyt**, Richard 1915- *Who 92*
**Luyt**, Richard Edmonds 1915- *IntWW 91*
**Luyten**, James Reindert 1941- *AmMWSc 92*
**Luyten**, Willem Jacob 1899- *AmMWSc 92, WhoMW 92*
**Luz**, Hans 1926- *IntWW 91*
**Luzadre**, John Hinkle 1921- *WhoMW 92*
**Luzbetak**, Louis J. 1918- *WrDr 92*
**Luzhak**, Christopher John 1966- *WhoEnt 92*
**Luzovich**, Steven Albert 1960- *WhoWest 92*
**Luzzaschi**, Luzzasco 1545?-1607 *NewAmDM*
**Luzzatto**, Edgar 1914- *WhoAmL 92*
**Luzzatto**, Lucio 1936- *Who 92*
**Luzzi**, Theodore E, Jr 1927- *AmMWSc 92*
**Luzzio**, Anthony Joseph 1924- *AmMWSc 92*
**Luzzio**, Frederick Anthony 1953- *AmMWSc 92*
**Lvov**, Alexey Fyodorovich 1798-1870 *NewAmDM*
**Lvov**, Arkady 1931- *LiExTwC*
**Lvov**, Georgi Yevgenevich 1861-1925 *FacFETw*
**Lwin**, U. 1912- *IntWW 91*
**Lwoff**, Andre Michael 1902- *WhoNob 90*
**Lwoff**, Andre Michel 1902- *IntWW 91, Who 92*
**Lwowski**, Walter Wilhelm Gustav 1928- *AmMWSc 92*
**Lyadov**, Anatoly 1855-1914 *NewAmDM*
**Lyakhov**, Vladimir Afanasevich 1941- *IntWW 91*
**Lyall**, Andrew Gardiner 1929- *Who 92*
**Lyall**, Gavin 1932- *WrDr 92*
**Lyall**, Gavin Tudor 1932- *IntAu&W 91, Who 92*
**Lyall**, Katharine Culbert 1941- *WhoFI 92*
**Lyall**, Katharine Elizabeth *Who 92*
**Lyall**, Michael Rodney 1945- *WhoFI 92*
**Lyall**, Tony Allen 1949- *WhoIns 92*
**Lyall**, William Chalmers 1921- *Who 92*
**Lyall Grant**, Ian Hallam 1915- *Who 92*
**Lyandres**, Yulian Semenovich 1931- *ConAu 35NR*
**Lyapunov**, Aleksey Andreevich 1911-1973 *SovUnBD*
**Lyatoshins'ky**, Boris Mykolayovich 1895-1968 *SovUnBD*
**Lyautey**, Louis Hubert 1854-1934 *FacFETw*
**Lybarger**, John Steven 1956- *WhoWest 92*
**Lybarger**, Marjorie Kathryn 1956- *WhoWest 92*
**Lybbert**, Daniel Boden 1944- *WhoWest 92*
**Lybbert**, Donald 1923- *NewAmDM*
**Lybbert**, Richard B. 1947- *WhoFI 92*

**Lybeck,** A H 1919- *AmMWSc 92*
**Lybeck,** Ray 1926- *WhoAmP 91*
**Lybecker,** Martin Earl 1945- *WhoAmL 92*
**Lybrand,** Terry Paul 1957- *AmMWSc 92*
**Lybyer,** Michael J 1947- *WhoAmP 91*
**Lycan,** Gilbert L. 1909- *WrDr 92*
**Lycette,** R 1926- *AmMWSc 92*
**Lyda,** Stuart D 1930- *AmMWSc 92*
**Lyda,** Wesley John 1914- *WhoBlA 92*
**Lyddon,** Derek 1925- *Who 92*
**Lyden,** Fremont James 1926- *WrDr 92*
**Lyden,** John C. 1959- *WhoRel 92*
**Lydgate,** John 1370?-1449 *RfGEnL 91*
**Lydiat,** Anne 1947- *TwCPaSc*
**Lydic,** Frank Aylsworth 1909- *WhoMW 92*
**Lydick,** Dennis Gene 1953- *WhoMW 92*
**Lydick,** Lawrence Tupper 1916- *WhoAmL 92, WhoWest 92*
**Lyding,** Arthur R 1925- *AmMWSc 92*
**Lydolph,** Donald Joseph 1945- *WhoRel 92*
**Lydolph,** Paul Edward 1924- *WrDr 92*
**Lydon,** James 1923- *IntMPA 92*
**Lydon,** Tommy 1955- *TwCPaSc*
**Lydy,** David Lee 1936- *AmMWSc 92*
**Lye,** Robert J 1955- *AmMWSc 92*
**Lye,** William Frank 1930- *WhoWest 92*
**Lyell** *Who 92*
**Lyell,** Baron 1939- *Who 92*
**Lyell,** Charles 1797-1875 *BenetAL 91*
**Lyell,** Eric Scott 1964- *WhoWest 92*
**Lyell,** Nicholas 1938- *Who 92*
**Lyells,** Ruby E. Stutts *WhoBlA 92*
**Lyerla,** Bradford Peter 1954- *WhoAmL 92*
**Lyerla,** Jo Ann Harding 1940- *AmMWSc 92*
**Lyerla,** Timothy Arden 1940- *AmMWSc 92*
**Lyerly,** Herbert Kim 1958- *AmMWSc 92*
**Lyerly,** Jacob Martin Luther 1862-1923 *DcNCBi 4*
**Lyford,** John H, Jr 1928- *AmMWSc 92*
**Lyford,** Sidney John, Jr 1937- *AmMWSc 92*
**Lyga,** Patricia Martin 1956- *WhoAmL 92*
**Lygo,** Raymond 1924- *Who 92*
**Lygo,** Raymond Derek 1924- *IntWW 91*
**Lygre,** David Gerald 1942- *AmMWSc 92*
**Lyjak,** Robert Fred *AmMWSc 92*
**Lyke,** Edward Bonsteel 1937- *AmMWSc 92*
**Lyke,** James P. 1939- *WhoBlA 92*
**Lyke,** James Patterson 1939- *WhoRel 92*
**Lykes,** Joseph T., III 1948- *WhoFI 92*
**Lykiard,** Alexis 1940- *IntAu&W 91, WrDr 92*
**Lykins,** Jay Arnold 1947- *WhoFI 92, WhoWest 92*
**Lykke,** Ivar 1873-1950 *WhoNob 90*
**Lykkebak,** Donald Alan 1946- *WhoAmL 92*
**Lykken,** David Thoreson 1928- *AmMWSc 92*
**Lykken,** David Thorson 1928- *WhoMW 92*
**Lykken,** Glenn Irven 1939- *AmMWSc 92*
**Lykos,** Peter George 1927- *AmMWSc 92*
**Lykoudis,** Paul S *AmMWSc 92*
**Lykova,** Lidiya Pavlovna 1913- *SovUnBD*
**Lyle,** Alexander Walter Barr 1958- *Who 92*
**Lyle,** Archibald Michael 1919- *Who 92*
**Lyle,** Benjamin Franklin 1933- *AmMWSc 92*
**Lyle,** Eugene P., Jr. 1873-1961 *ScFEYrs*
**Lyle,** Everett Samuel, Jr 1927- *AmMWSc 92*
**Lyle,** Freddrenna M. 1951- *WhoBlA 92*
**Lyle,** Gavin Archibald 1941- *Who 92*
**Lyle,** Gloria Gilbert 1923- *AmMWSc 92*
**Lyle,** James Albert 1916- *AmMWSc 92*
**Lyle,** John Brooke 1958- *WhoAmL 92*
**Lyle,** John William, Jr 1950- *WhoAmP 91*
**Lyle,** K. Curtis *DrAPF 91*
**Lyle,** Katie Letcher *DrAPF 91*
**Lyle,** Leon Richards 1941- *AmMWSc 92*
**Lyle,** Michael *Who 92*
**Lyle,** Percy H., Jr. 1937- *WhoBlA 92*
**Lyle,** Robert Edward, Jr 1926- *AmMWSc 92*
**Lyle,** Roberta Branche Blacke 1929- *WhoBlA 92*
**Lyle,** Ron 1943- *WhoBlA 92*
**Lyle,** Sandy *Who 92*
**Lyle,** W. W. *WhoRel 92*
**Lyle,** William Montgomery 1913- *AmMWSc 92*
**Lyle-Smyth,** Alan *WrDr 92*
**Lyles,** A.C. 1918- *IntMPA 92*
**Lyles,** Dewayne 1947- *WhoBlA 92*
**Lyles,** Gary Donald 1942- *WhoWest 92*
**Lyles,** Jean Elizabeth Caffey 1942- *WhoMW 92*
**Lyles,** Leon 1932- *AmMWSc 92*
**Lyles,** Leonard E. 1936- *WhoBlA 92*
**Lyles,** Lester Everett 1962- *WhoBlA 92*
**Lyles,** Madeline Lolita 1953- *WhoBlA 92*
**Lyles,** Marie Clark 1952- *WhoBlA 92*
**Lyles,** Ronny Carter 1950- *WhoRel 92*
**Lyles,** Roy E 1923- *WhoAmP 91*
**Lyles,** Sanders Truman 1907- *AmMWSc 92*
**Lyles,** William K. *WhoBlA 92*
**Lyly,** John 1554?-1606? *RfGEnL 91*
**Lyman,** Arthur Joseph 1953- *WhoMW 92*
**Lyman,** Benjamin Smith 1835-1920 *BiInAmS*
**Lyman,** Beverly Ann 1956- *AmMWSc 92*
**Lyman,** Charles Parker 1848?-1918 *BiInAmS*
**Lyman,** Charles Peirson 1912- *AmMWSc 92*
**Lyman,** Charles Robert 1948- *WhoAmL 92*
**Lyman,** Chester Smith 1814-1890 *BiInAmS*
**Lyman,** David 1936- *WhoFI 92*
**Lyman,** David Eliot 1935- *WhoEnt 92*
**Lyman,** David Hollis 1939- *WhoEnt 92*
**Lyman,** Donald Joseph 1926- *AmMWSc 92*
**Lyman,** Dorothy 1947- *ConTFT 9*
**Lyman,** Ernest McIntosh 1910- *AmMWSc 92*
**Lyman,** Francesca 1951- *ConAu 133*
**Lyman,** Frank Lewis 1921- *AmMWSc 92*
**Lyman,** Frederic A 1934- *AmMWSc 92*
**Lyman,** Gary Herbert 1946- *AmMWSc 92*
**Lyman,** Harvard 1931- *AmMWSc 92*
**Lyman,** John 1921- *AmMWSc 92*
**Lyman,** John L 1944- *AmMWSc 92*
**Lyman,** John Tompkins 1932- *AmMWSc 92*
**Lyman,** Kenneth Harper 1952- *WhoAmL 92*
**Lyman,** Mary Reddington Ely 1887-1975 *RelLAm 91*
**Lyman,** Nathan Marquis 1955- *WhoAmL 92*
**Lyman,** Ona Rufus 1930- *AmMWSc 92*
**Lyman,** Peggy 1950- *WhoEnt 92*
**Lyman,** Phillip Casey 1947- *WhoAmL 92*
**Lyman,** Princeton Nathan 1935- *WhoAmP 91*
**Lyman,** Richard Donald McKay 1956- *WhoFI 92*
**Lyman,** Richard Wall 1923- *WhoWest 92*
**Lyman,** Theodore 1833-1897 *BiInAmS*
**Lyman,** Theodore Benedict 1815-1893 *DcNCBi 4*
**Lyman,** W Stuart 1924- *AmMWSc 92*
**Lyman,** Webster S. 1922- *WhoBlA 92*
**Lyman,** William Ray 1920- *AmMWSc 92*
**Lymangrover,** John R 1944- *AmMWSc 92*
**Lymbery,** Robert Davison 1920- *Who 92*
**Lymington,** Viscount 1981- *Who 92*
**Lymington,** John 1911-1983 *TwCSFW 91*
**Lymn,** Richard Wesley 1944- *AmMWSc 92*
**Lympany,** Moura 1916- *IntWW 91, Who 92*
**Lynam,** Desmond Michael 1942- *Who 92*
**Lynch,** Allan William 1942- *WhoWest 92*
**Lynch,** Benjamin Leo 1923- *AmMWSc 92*
**Lynch,** Bohun 1884-1928 *ScFEYrs*
**Lynch,** Brian Maurice 1930- *AmMWSc 92*
**Lynch,** Carol Becker 1942- *AmMWSc 92*
**Lynch,** Carole Yard 1951- *WhoAmL 92*
**Lynch,** Charles Allen 1927- *WhoFI 92, WhoWest 92*
**Lynch,** Charles Andrew 1935- *AmMWSc 92*
**Lynch,** Charles H. *DrAPF 91*
**Lynch,** Charles Thomas 1918- *WhoEnt 92, WhoWest 92*
**Lynch,** Craig Taylor 1959- *WhoAmL 92*
**Lynch,** Dan K 1920- *AmMWSc 92*
**Lynch,** Daniel C 1929- *WhoAmP 91*
**Lynch,** Daniel Matthew 1921- *AmMWSc 92*
**Lynch,** Daniel Patrick 1949- *WhoAmL 92*
**Lynch,** Darrel Luvene 1921- *AmMWSc 92*
**Lynch,** David 1939- *Who 92*
**Lynch,** David 1946- *ConLC 66 [port], IntDcF 2-2 [port], IntMPA 92, IntWW 91*
**Lynch,** David Dexter 1934- *AmMWSc 92*
**Lynch,** David Dillon 1940- *WhoFI 92, WhoWest 92*
**Lynch,** David H 1950- *AmMWSc 92*
**Lynch,** David K. 1946- *WhoEnt 92*
**Lynch,** David William 1932- *AmMWSc 92, WhoMW 92*
**Lynch,** Denis Patrick 1951- *AmMWSc 92*
**Lynch,** Dermot Roborg 1940- *AmMWSc 92*
**Lynch,** Derrick Charles 1966- *WhoRel 92*
**Lynch,** Don Murl 1934- *AmMWSc 92*
**Lynch,** Donald MacLeod 1911- *Who 92*
**Lynch,** Edward 1941- *WhoAmP 91*
**Lynch,** Edward Conover 1933- *AmMWSc 92*
**Lynch,** Edward M. d1991 *NewYTBS 91*
**Lynch,** Eliza *EncAmaz 91*
**Lynch,** Eloise 1927- *WhoAmP 91*
**Lynch,** Eric *IntAu&W 91X, TwCWW 91*
**Lynch,** Eric Daniel 1966- *WhoWest 92*
**Lynch,** Eugene Darrel 1921- *AmMWSc 92*
**Lynch,** Eugene F. 1931- *WhoAmL 92*
**Lynch,** Eugene Patrick 1961- *WhoFI 92*
**Lynch,** Fran Jackie 1948- *WhoFI 92*
**Lynch,** Frances *IntAu&W 91X, WrDr 92*
**Lynch,** Francis Charles 1944- *WhoAmL 92*
**Lynch,** Francis J *WhoAmP 91*
**Lynch,** Francis Xavier 1918- *WhoRel 92*
**Lynch,** Frank W 1921- *AmMWSc 92*
**Lynch,** Frank William 1921- *IntWW 91, WhoFI 92*
**Lynch,** Frederick Henry 1867-1934 *AmPeW*
**Lynch,** George Edward 1917- *WhoRel 92*
**Lynch,** George K. 1913- *WhoBlA 92*
**Lynch,** George Michael 1943- *WhoFI 92*
**Lynch,** George Robert 1941- *AmMWSc 92*
**Lynch,** Gerard E. 1951- *WhoAmL 92*
**Lynch,** Gerard Francis 1945- *AmMWSc 92*
**Lynch,** Gregory P. 1949- *WhoAmL 92*
**Lynch,** Harry James 1929- *AmMWSc 92*
**Lynch,** Henry T 1928- *AmMWSc 92*
**Lynch,** Herbert Henry 1930- *WhoMW 92*
**Lynch,** Hollis R. 1935- *WhoBlA 92*
**Lynch,** Isabelle Clark 1924- *WhoAmP 91*
**Lynch,** J. Christopher 1961- *WhoAmL 92*
**Lynch,** Jack *WhoAmP 91*
**Lynch,** Jack 1930- *WhoEnt 92*
**Lynch,** James Alexander 1923- *WhoMW 92*
**Lynch,** James B, Jr 1933- *WhoIns 92*
**Lynch,** James Carlyle 1942- *AmMWSc 92*
**Lynch,** James Edward 1951- *WhoAmL 92*
**Lynch,** James Patrick 1952- *WhoFI 92*
**Lynch,** John 1917- *Who 92*
**Lynch,** John 1927- *IntAu&W 91, Who 92, WrDr 92*
**Lynch,** John A 1938- *WhoAmP 91*
**Lynch,** John August 1947- *AmMWSc 92*
**Lynch,** John Brown 1929- *AmMWSc 92*
**Lynch,** John Douglas 1942- *AmMWSc 92*
**Lynch,** John E. 1924- *WhoRel 92*
**Lynch,** John Edward 1923- *AmMWSc 92*
**Lynch,** John Edward, Jr. 1952- *WhoAmL 92*
**Lynch,** John Gregory, Jr. 1943- *WhoAmL 92*
**Lynch,** John J D 1947- *WhoAmP 91*
**Lynch,** John Mary 1917- *IntWW 91*
**Lynch,** John Patrick 1943- *WhoWest 92*
**Lynch,** John Peter 1942- *WhoAmL 92*
**Lynch,** John Thomas 1938- *AmMWSc 92*
**Lynch,** Joseph Howard 1943- *WhoMW 92*
**Lynch,** Joseph J, Jr 1956- *AmMWSc 92*
**Lynch,** Kathleen Marie 1949- *WhoAmL 92*
**Lynch,** Kelly 1959- *IntMPA 92*
**Lynch,** Lemuel 1808-1893 *DcNCBi 4*
**Lynch,** Leon 1935- *WhoBlA 92*
**Lynch,** Lillie Riddick *WhoBlA 92*
**Lynch,** Linda Zanetti 1933- *WhoFI 92*
**Lynch,** Lorenzo A., Sr. 1932- *WhoBlA 92*
**Lynch,** Luke D 1921- *WhoIns 92*
**Lynch,** Luke Daniel, Jr. 1945- *WhoAmL 92*
**Lynch,** M. Elizabeth 1947- *WhoBlA 92*
**Lynch,** Margaret A 1939- *WhoAmP 91*
**Lynch,** Marta 1925-1985 *SpAmWW*
**Lynch,** Martin Patrick James 1924- *Who 92*
**Lynch,** Marvin James 1950- *WhoMW 92*
**Lynch,** Mary Ann *DrAPF 91*
**Lynch,** Mary Ann Bruchac 1944- *WhoEnt 92*
**Lynch,** Mary Patricia 1932- *WhoFI 92*
**Lynch,** Maurice Patrick 1936- *AmMWSc 92*
**Lynch,** Michael James 1952- *WhoMW 92*
**Lynch,** Michael Joseph 1953- *WhoFI 92*
**Lynch,** Myra Clark 1938- *WhoAmL 92*
**Lynch,** Nathaniel Merriman 1942- *WhoEnt 92*
**Lynch,** Neil L 1930- *WhoAmP 91*
**Lynch,** Neil Lawrence 1930- *WhoAmL 92*
**Lynch,** Patrick 1917- *IntWW 91, Who 92*
**Lynch,** Patrick 1941- *WhoAmL 92*
**Lynch,** Paul M. *IntMPA 92*
**Lynch,** Peter George 1932- *WhoEnt 92*
**Lynch,** Peter John 1936- *AmMWSc 92*
**Lynch,** Peter Robin 1927- *AmMWSc 92*
**Lynch,** Raymond Terry 1942- *WhoWest 92*
**Lynch,** Richard 1936- *IntMPA 92*
**Lynch,** Richard Bristol 1951- *WhoMW 92*
**Lynch,** Richard G 1934- *AmMWSc 92*
**Lynch,** Richard Vance, III 1944- *AmMWSc 92*
**Lynch,** Richard Wallace 1939- *AmMWSc 92*
**Lynch,** Robert Berger 1931- *WhoAmL 92, WhoWest 92*
**Lynch,** Robert D. 1933- *WhoBlA 92*
**Lynch,** Robert Earl 1943- *AmMWSc 92*
**Lynch,** Robert Emmett 1932- *AmMWSc 92, WhoMW 92*
**Lynch,** Robert Michael 1944- *AmMWSc 92*
**Lynch,** Robert W 1937- *WhoAmP 91*
**Lynch,** Rose Peabody 1949- *WhoFI 92*
**Lynch,** Rufus Sylvester 1946- *WhoBlA 92*
**Lynch,** Sandra Lea 1946- *WhoAmL 92*
**Lynch,** Sonia 1938- *WhoFI 92*
**Lynch,** Steven Paul 1946- *AmMWSc 92*
**Lynch,** T E 1914- *AmMWSc 92*
**Lynch,** Teresa *WhoAmP 91*
**Lynch,** Thomas *DrAPF 91*
**Lynch,** Thomas A 1947- *WhoAmP 91*
**Lynch,** Thomas Edmund 1947- *WhoAmP 91*
**Lynch,** Thomas John 1941- *AmMWSc 92*
**Lynch,** Thomas Joseph 1960- *WhoFI 92*
**Lynch,** Thomas Joseph, Jr. 1952- *WhoFI 92*
**Lynch,** Thomas Wimp 1930- *WhoAmL 92*
**Lynch,** Timothy Bruce 1949- *WhoAmP 91*
**Lynch,** Timothy Jeremiah-Mahoney 1952- *WhoAmL 92*
**Lynch,** Timothy Joseph 1954- *WhoEnt 92*
**Lynch,** Vincent De Paul 1927- *AmMWSc 92*
**Lynch,** Vivian Elizabeth 1940- *WhoAmL 92, WhoFI 92*
**Lynch,** Wayne Keith 1948- *WhoFI 92*
**Lynch,** Wesley Clyde 1944- *AmMWSc 92*
**Lynch,** William C 1937- *AmMWSc 92*
**Lynch,** William E. 1930- *WrDr 92*
**Lynch,** William Ernest, Jr. 1938- *WhoMW 92*
**Lynch,** William M. 1962- *WhoWest 92*
**Lynch,** William Thomas, Jr. 1942- *WhoFI 92*
**Lynch-Blosse,** Richard Hely 1953- *Who 92*
**Lynch-Robinson,** Niall 1918- *Who 92*
**Lyncheski,** John E. 1945- *WhoAmL 92*
**Lyncheski,** Robert F 1934- *WhoIns 92*
**Lynd,** Grant Albert 1949- *WhoAmL 92, WhoWest 92*
**Lynd,** Helen Merrell 1896-1982 *BenetAL 91, WomSoc*
**Lynd,** Julian Quentin 1922- *AmMWSc 92*
**Lynd,** Langtry Emmett 1919- *AmMWSc 92*
**Lynd,** Robert S. 1892-1970 *BenetAL 91*
**Lynd,** Staughton 1929- *AmPeW, ConAu 133*
**Lynd,** Teresa Cruz 1952- *WhoHisp 92*
**Lyndaker,** Bruce Wayne 1952- *WhoRel 92*
**Lynde,** Francis 1856-1930 *ScFEYrs*
**Lynde,** Richard Arthur 1942- *AmMWSc 92*
**Lynden-Bell,** Donald 1935- *IntWW 91, Who 92*
**Lyndon,** Roger Conant 1917- *AmMWSc 92*
**Lyndon,** Victor *IntMPA 92*
**Lynds,** Beverly T 1929- *AmMWSc 92*
**Lynds,** Clarence Roger 1928- *AmMWSc 92*
**Lynds,** Dennis *DrAPF 91*
**Lynds,** Dennis 1924- *IntAu&W 91, WrDr 92*
**Lyndsay,** David *RfGEnL 91*
**Lyne,** Adrian *IntMPA 92, IntWW 91, WhoEnt 92*
**Lyne,** June D *WhoAmP 91*
**Lyne,** Leonard Murray, Sr 1919- *AmMWSc 92*
**Lyne,** Michael 1912-1989 *TwCPaSc*
**Lyne,** Michael Dillon 1919- *Who 92*
**Lyne,** Roderic Michael John 1948- *Who 92*
**Lyne,** Stephen R 1935- *WhoAmP 91*
**Lyne,** Timothy J. 1919- *WhoRel 92*
**Lynen,** Feodor Felix Konrad 1911-1979 *WhoNob 90*
**Lynes,** James William, Sr. 1928- *WhoMW 92*
**Lynes,** Russell 1910- *BenetAL 91, WrDr 92*
**Lynes,** Russell 1910-1991 *ConAu 135, CurBio 91N, NewYTBS 91*
**Lyness,** Donald Joseph 1940- *WhoMW 92*
**Lynette,** Eileen Linda 1952- *WhoWest 92*
**Lyng,** Richard Edmund 1918- *IntWW 91, WhoAmP 91*
**Lyngaas,** Michael E 1951- *WhoIns 92*
**Lynham,** John Marmaduke, Jr. 1952- *WhoAmL 92*
**Lynk,** Edgar Thomas 1941- *AmMWSc 92*
**Lynk,** Roy 1932- *Who 92*
**Lynley,** Carol 1942- *IntMPA 92*
**Lynley,** Carol Ann 1942- *WhoEnt 92*
**Lynn,** Archdeacon of *Who 92*
**Lynn,** Bishop Suffragan of 1935- *Who 92*
**Lynn,** Ann 1934- *IntMPA 92*
**Lynn,** Arthur Dellert, Jr. 1921- *WhoMW 92*
**Lynn,** Bruce Newton 1925- *WhoAmP 91*
**Lynn,** Charles Randal 1954- *WhoWest 92*
**Lynn,** David Clark 1948- *WhoWest 92*
**Lynn,** Denis Heward 1947- *AmMWSc 92*
**Lynn,** Edwin Charles 1935- *WhoRel 92*
**Lynn,** Elizabeth A 1946- *TwCSFW 91*
**Lynn,** Frank *IntAu&W 91X*
**Lynn,** Fred L 1924- *WhoAmP 91*
**Lynn,** Frederick Anson 1946- *WhoFI 92*
**Lynn,** George Gambrill 1946- *WhoAmL 92*
**Lynn,** Hugh Bailey 1914- *AmMWSc 92*
**Lynn,** James Elvis 1920- *WhoBlA 92*
**Lynn,** James T. 1927- *WhoFI 92*
**Lynn,** James Thomas 1927- *IntWW 91*
**Lynn,** Janet 1953- *WhoEnt 92*

**Lynn,** Jeffrey 1909- *IntMPA 92*
**Lynn,** Jeffrey Whidden 1947- *AmMWSc 92*
**Lynn,** John R 1930- *AmMWSc 92*
**Lynn,** John Wendell 1925- *AmMWSc 92*
**Lynn,** Jonathan 1943- *IntAu&W 91, WrDr 92*
**Lynn,** Jonathan Adam 1943- *Who 92, WhoEnt 92*
**Lynn,** Judanna 1942- *WhoEnt 92*
**Lynn,** Karyl V. 1922- *WhoFI 92*
**Lynn,** Katherine Lyn 1954- *WhoWest 92*
**Lynn,** Kelvin G 1948- *AmMWSc 92*
**Lynn,** Laurence Edwin, Jr. 1937- *WhoMW 92*
**Lynn,** Loretta 1935- *NewAmDM*
**Lynn,** Loretta Webb 1935- *WhoEnt 92*
**Lynn,** Louis B. 1949- *WhoBlA 92*
**Lynn,** Marcy Hedy 1962- *WhoEnt 92*
**Lynn,** Maurice Kenneth 1951- *Who 92*
**Lynn,** Merrill 1930- *AmMWSc 92*
**Lynn,** Michael Kenton 1953- *WhoEnt 92, WhoWest 92*
**Lynn,** Michael Robert 1957- *WhoMW 92*
**Lynn,** Naomi B. 1933- *WhoHisp 92*
**Lynn,** R Emerson 1920- *AmMWSc 92*
**Lynn,** Ralph Beverley 1921- *AmMWSc 92*
**Lynn,** Raymond J 1928- *AmMWSc 92*
**Lynn,** Richard 1930- *Who 92, WrDr 92*
**Lynn,** Richard Joseph 1953- *WhoEnt 92*
**Lynn,** Robert K 1947- *AmMWSc 92*
**Lynn,** Robert Thomas 1931- *AmMWSc 92*
**Lynn,** Robert William 1943- *WhoMW 92*
**Lynn,** Robert Wood 1925- *WhoRel 92*
**Lynn,** Roger Yen Shen 1941- *AmMWSc 92*
**Lynn,** Sandra *DrAPF 91*
**Lynn,** Scott 1928- *AmMWSc 92*
**Lynn,** Stephen Allen 1945- *WhoAmL 92*
**Lynn,** Terry 1961- *WhoAmL 92*
**Lynn,** Thomas Neil, Jr 1930- *AmMWSc 92*
**Lynn,** Vera 1917- *IntWW 91, Who 92*
**Lynn,** Walter R 1928- *AmMWSc 92*
**Lynn,** Warren Clark 1935- *AmMWSc 92*
**Lynn,** Wilfred 1905- *Who 92*
**Lynn,** William Dory 1922- *WhoRel 92*
**Lynn,** William Gardner 1905- *AmMWSc 92*
**Lynn,** William Max 1927- *WhoRel 92*
**Lynn,** William Sanford 1922- *AmMWSc 92*
**Lynn,** Yen-Mow 1935- *AmMWSc 92*
**Lynne,** Gary Dean 1944- *WhoFI 92*
**Lynne,** Gillian *Who 92*
**Lynne,** Gillian Barbara *WhoEnt 92*
**Lynne,** James Broom 1920- *IntAu&W 91, WrDr 92*
**Lynne,** Robert D. *WhoRel 92*
**Lynne,** Seybourn Harris 1907- *WhoAmL 92*
**Lynne-Davies,** Patricia 1933- *AmMWSc 92*
**Lynne-O'Brien,** Vincent 1935- *WhoEnt 92*
**Lynskey,** Edward C. *DrAPF 91*
**Lynskey,** Martin J 1951- *WhoIns 92*
**Lynton,** Ann *IntAu&W 91X*
**Lynton,** Ernest Albert 1926- *AmMWSc 92*
**Lynton,** Harold Stephen 1909- *WhoAmL 92*
**Lynton,** Norbert 1927- *WrDr 92*
**Lynton,** Norbert Casper 1927- *Who 92*
**Lynts,** George Willard 1936- *AmMWSc 92*
**Lynyrd Skynyrd** *NewAmDM*
**Lyo,** SungKwun Kenneth 1941- *AmMWSc 92*
**Lyon** *Who 92*
**Lyon,** Alexander Ward 1931- *Who 92*
**Lyon,** Arthur S, Jr 1951- *WhoIns 92*
**Lyon,** Bruce Arnold 1951- *WhoAmL 92*
**Lyon,** Bryce Dale 1920- *IntAu&W 91*
**Lyon,** Buck *TwCWW 91*
**Lyon,** Cameron Kirby 1923- *AmMWSc 92*
**Lyon,** Carl Francis, Jr. 1943- *WhoAmL 92*
**Lyon,** Charles Herbert Randolph 1943- *WhoFI 92*
**Lyon,** Christina Margaret 1952- *Who 92*
**Lyon,** Clare *Who 92*
**Lyon,** Colin Stewart 1926- *Who 92*
**Lyon,** David *DrAPF 91*
**Lyon,** David 1936- *Who 92*
**Lyon,** David Louis 1935- *AmMWSc 92*
**Lyon,** David N 1919- *AmMWSc 92*
**Lyon,** Donald Wilkinson 1916- *AmMWSc 92*
**Lyon,** Duane Edgar 1939- *AmMWSc 92*
**Lyon,** Earle 1923- *IntMPA 92*
**Lyon,** Edward Spafford 1926- *AmMWSc 92*
**Lyon,** Edwin Leon 1947- *WhoAmL 92*
**Lyon,** Elinor 1921- *WrDr 92*
**Lyon,** Elinor Bruce 1921- *IntAu&W 91*
**Lyon,** Francis D. 1905- *IntMPA 92*
**Lyon,** Francis Davis 1905- *WhoEnt 92*
**Lyon,** Francis Merton d1916 *ScFEYrs A*
**Lyon,** Francis Strother 1800-1882 *DcNCBi 4*
**Lyon,** George Ella *DrAPF 91*
**Lyon,** George Ella 1949- *SmATA 68 [port]*
**Lyon,** George Leonidas 1881-1916 *DcNCBi 4*
**Lyon,** Gordon Edward 1942- *AmMWSc 92*
**Lyon,** Gordon Frederick 1922- *AmMWSc 92*
**Lyon,** Harris Merton 1883-1916 *BenetAL 91*
**Lyon,** Harvey William 1920- *AmMWSc 92*
**Lyon,** Homer Legrand 1879-1956 *DcNCBi 4*
**Lyon,** Irving 1921- *AmMWSc 92, WhoWest 92*
**Lyon,** James 1735-1794 *BenetAL 91, NewAmDM*
**Lyon,** James Burroughs 1930- *WhoAmL 92, WhoFI 92*
**Lyon,** James Robert 1927- *WhoMW 92*
**Lyon,** Jeffrey 1943- *WhoMW 92*
**Lyon,** Jeffrey A *AmMWSc 92*
**Lyon,** John 1765?-1814 *DcNCBi 4*
**Lyon,** John B 1927- *AmMWSc 92*
**Lyon,** John Blakeslee, Jr 1925- *AmMWSc 92*
**Lyon,** John David Richard 1936- *IntWW 91*
**Lyon,** K C 1908- *AmMWSc 92*
**Lyon,** Lawrence Bruce 1947- *WhoEnt 92*
**Lyon,** Leonard Jack 1929- *AmMWSc 92*
**Lyon,** Lyman Max 1944- *WhoFI 92*
**Lyon,** Lyman R *IntAu&W 91X*
**Lyon,** Mark Andrew 1953- *WhoWest 92*
**Lyon,** Mary Frances 1925- *IntWW 91, Who 92*
**Lyon,** Michael William 1954- *WhoMW 92*
**Lyon,** Milton 1923- *WhoEnt 92*
**Lyon,** Nancy S 1951- *WhoAmP 91*
**Lyon,** Neil David 1956- *WhoFI 92*
**Lyon,** Norieta Marie 1958- *WhoEnt 92*
**Lyon,** Philip Kirkland 1944- *WhoAmL 92, WhoEnt 92, WhoFI 92*
**Lyon,** Randolph Matthew 1955- *WhoFI 92*
**Lyon,** Richard Hale 1920- *AmMWSc 92*
**Lyon,** Richard Jordan 1942- *WhoAmL 92*
**Lyon,** Richard Kenneth 1933- *AmMWSc 92*
**Lyon,** Richard Norton 1916- *AmMWSc 92*
**Lyon,** Rick *DrAPF 91*
**Lyon,** Risden Allen 1919- *WhoEnt 92*
**Lyon,** Robert 1923- *Who 92*
**Lyon,** Robert Lyndon 1927- *AmMWSc 92*
**Lyon,** Ronald James Pearson 1928- *AmMWSc 92*
**Lyon,** Scott James 1961- *WhoMW 92*
**Lyon,** Sidney Smith 1807-1872 *BilnAmS*
**Lyon,** Stanley Douglas 1917- *IntWW 91, Who 92*
**Lyon,** Sterling 1927- *Who 92*
**Lyon,** Sterling Rufus Webster 1927- *IntWW 91*
**Lyon,** Stewart *Who 92*
**Lyon,** Sue 1946- *IntMPA 92*
**Lyon,** Ted B, Jr 1948- *WhoAmP 91*
**Lyon,** Thomas D. 1959- *WhoFI 92*
**Lyon,** Waldo 1914- *AmMWSc 92*
**Lyon,** Wayne Barton 1932- *WhoFI 92, WhoMW 92*
**Lyon,** Wilford Charles, Jr 1935- *WhoIns 92*
**Lyon,** William 1923- *WhoWest 92*
**Lyon,** William Francis 1937- *AmMWSc 92*
**Lyon,** William Graham 1944- *AmMWSc 92*
**Lyon,** William Scrugham 1852-1916 *BilnAmS*
**Lyon,** William Southern, Jr 1922- *AmMWSc 92*
**Lyon,** Zachariah Inge 1815-1887 *DcNCBi 4*
**Lyon-Dalberg-Acton** *Who 92*
**Lyon-Rodman,** Sylvia 1946- *WhoEnt 92*
**Lyons,** A. Bates 1944- *WhoBlA 92*
**Lyons,** Allan Stuart 1929- *WhoFI 92*
**Lyons,** Arthur 1946- *ConAu 35NR, IntAu&W 91, WrDr 92*
**Lyons,** Arthur Edward 1931- *WhoWest 92*
**Lyons,** Bernard 1913- *IntWW 91, Who 92*
**Lyons,** Carl J 1924- *AmMWSc 92*
**Lyons,** Champ, Jr. 1940- *WhoAmL 92*
**Lyons,** Charles A., Jr. 1926- *WhoBlA 92*
**Lyons,** Charles Albert 1929- *Who 92*
**Lyons,** Charles David 1932- *WhoRel 92*
**Lyons,** Charles H. S., Jr. 1917- *WhoBlA 92*
**Lyons,** Charles Michael 1943- *WhoAmP 91*
**Lyons,** Charles R. 1933- *WhoEnt 92*
**Lyons,** Chopeta C. *DrAPF 91*
**Lyons,** David 1935- *WrDr 92*
**Lyons,** David Barry 1935- *IntAu&W 91, WhoAmL 92*
**Lyons,** Delphine C *TwCSFW 91, WrDr 92*
**Lyons,** Dennis Gerald 1931- *WhoAmL 92*
**Lyons,** Dennis John 1916- *Who 92*
**Lyons,** Donald Edwin 1932- *WhoMW 92*
**Lyons,** Donald Herbert 1929- *AmMWSc 92*
**Lyons,** Donald Wallace 1945- *WhoBlA 92*
**Lyons,** Dorothy Marawee 1907- *IntAu&W 91, WrDr 92*
**Lyons,** Dorothy Schill 1928- *WhoMW 92*
**Lyons,** Earle Vaughan, Jr. 1917- *WhoRel 92*
**Lyons,** Edward 1926- *Who 92*
**Lyons,** Edward Arthur 1943- *AmMWSc 92*
**Lyons,** Edward Houghton *Who 92*
**Lyons,** Edward P *WhoAmP 91*
**Lyons,** Elena *IntAu&W 91X, WrDr 92*
**Lyons,** Elizabeth *TwCPaSc*
**Lyons,** Eugene T 1931- *AmMWSc 92*
**Lyons,** Garry Fairfax 1956- *IntAu&W 91*
**Lyons,** Gene 1943- *IntAu&W 91*
**Lyons,** George 1947- *WhoRel 92*
**Lyons,** George D 1928- *AmMWSc 92*
**Lyons,** George Sage 1936- *WhoAmL 92*
**Lyons,** George W. C., Sr. 1923- *WhoBlA 92*
**Lyons,** Grant *DrAPF 91*
**Lyons,** Hamilton 1918- *Who 92*
**Lyons,** Harold 1919- *AmMWSc 92*
**Lyons,** Jack 1916- *Who 92*
**Lyons,** James 1910- *Who 92*
**Lyons,** James E., Sr. *WhoBlA 92*
**Lyons,** James Edward 1937- *AmMWSc 92*
**Lyons,** James Francis 1934- *WhoFI 92*
**Lyons,** James Martin 1929- *AmMWSc 92*
**Lyons,** James Robert, Jr. 1955- *WhoAmL 92*
**Lyons,** Jan H. 1951- *WhoFI 92*
**Lyons,** Jerry Lee 1939- *WhoFI 92*
**Lyons,** John 1926- *Who 92*
**Lyons,** John 1932- *IntWW 91, Who 92*
**Lyons,** John Albert 1934- *WhoMW 92*
**Lyons,** John Bartholomew 1916- *AmMWSc 92*
**Lyons,** John Edward *WhoFI 92*
**Lyons,** John Matthew 1948- *WhoEnt 92, WhoFI 92*
**Lyons,** John Rolland 1909- *WhoMW 92*
**Lyons,** John Winship 1930- *AmMWSc 92, WhoAmP 91*
**Lyons,** Joseph Aloysius 1879-1939 *FacFETw*
**Lyons,** Joseph F 1920- *AmMWSc 92*
**Lyons,** Joseph Paul 1947- *AmMWSc 92*
**Lyons,** Jude 1946- *WhoEnt 92*
**Lyons,** Kenneth Brent 1946- *AmMWSc 92*
**Lyons,** Kevin Joseph 1945- *WhoAmL 92*
**Lyons,** Kevin W. 1956- *WhoAmL 92*
**Lyons,** Lawrence Ernest 1922- *IntWW 91*
**Lyons,** Lloyd Carson 1942- *WhoBlA 92*
**Lyons,** Malcolm Cameron 1929- *Who 92*
**Lyons,** Marcus *SmATA 66*
**Lyons,** Michael 1943- *TwCPaSc*
**Lyons,** Michael J. 1930- *WhoMW 92*
**Lyons,** Michael Thomas 1949- *Who 92*
**Lyons,** Moira K *WhoAmP 91*
**Lyons,** Nance 1943- *WhoAmL 92*
**Lyons,** Nancy I 1946- *AmMWSc 92*
**Lyons,** Nick 1932- *WrDr 92*
**Lyons,** Patricia M 1947- *WhoAmP 91*
**Lyons,** Paul Christopher 1938- *AmMWSc 92*
**Lyons,** Paul Michael 1932- *WhoEnt 92*
**Lyons,** Paul Vincent 1939- *WhoAmL 92*
**Lyons,** Peter Bruce 1943- *AmMWSc 92*
**Lyons,** Peter Francis 1942- *AmMWSc 92*
**Lyons,** Philip Augustine 1916- *AmMWSc 92*
**Lyons,** Phillip Michael, Sr. 1941- *WhoFI 92*
**Lyons,** Polly Sue 1940- *WhoMW 92*
**Lyons,** Richard *DrAPF 91*
**Lyons,** Richard W. *WhoRel 92*
**Lyons,** Robert Hagen 1954- *WhoAmL 92*
**Lyons,** Robert P. 1912- *WhoBlA 92*
**Lyons,** Rudolph d1991 *Who 92N*
**Lyons,** Russell David 1957- *AmMWSc 92*
**Lyons,** Russette M 1953- *AmMWSc 92*
**Lyons,** Sara Marion 1932- *WhoAmP 91*
**Lyons,** Stuart 1928- *IntMPA 92*
**Lyons,** Stuart Randolph 1943- *Who 92*
**Lyons,** Terence Patrick 1919- *Who 92*
**Lyons,** Thomas G 1931- *WhoAmP 91*
**Lyons,** Thomas Patrick 1953- *WhoFI 92*
**Lyons,** Thomas Patrick 1954- *WhoAmL 92*
**Lyons,** Thomas Patrick 1957- *WhoFI 92*
**Lyons,** Thomas Tolman 1934- *IntAu&W 91, WrDr 92*
**Lyons,** Tommy Joe 1952- *WhoWest 92*
**Lyons,** Virginia 1932- *WhoAmP 91*
**Lyons,** W. T. 1919- *WrDr 92*
**Lyons,** William B. 1924-1984 *WhoBlA 92N*
**Lyons,** William Berry 1947- *AmMWSc 92*
**Lyons,** William Harry 1947- *WhoMW 92*
**Lyons,** William Kimbel 1953- *WhoMW 92*
**Lypkivsky,** Vasyl' 1864-1938? *SovUnBD*
**Lyra,** Synesio, Jr. 1938- *WhoRel 92*
**Lyras,** Dean Stephen 1950- *WhoEnt 92*
**Lyre,** Pinchbeck *ConAu 36NR*
**Lyrene,** Paul Magnus 1946- *AmMWSc 92*
**Lys,** Christian 1864-1922 *ScFEYrs*
**Lys,** Jeremy Eion Alleyne 1938- *AmMWSc 92*
**Lysaght** *Who 92*
**Lysak,** Patricia Requa 1947- *WhoFI 92*
**Lysak,** Robert Louis 1955- *AmMWSc 92*
**Lysaught,** Jerome P. 1930- *WrDr 92*
**Lyschik,** R.A. *DrAPF 91*
**Lysen,** John C 1931- *AmMWSc 92*
**Lysen,** King *WhoAmP 91*
**Lysenko,** Trofim Denisovich 1898-1976 *FacFETw, SovUnBD*
**Lyser,** Katherine May 1933- *AmMWSc 92*
**Lysiak,** Richard John 1928- *AmMWSc 92*
**Lysippe** *EncAmaz 91*
**Lysle,** Yolonda Shea 1959- *WhoRel 92*
**Lysmer,** John 1931- *AmMWSc 92*
**Lysne,** Peter C 1939- *AmMWSc 92*
**Lyson,** Valerie Marie 1962- *WhoRel 92*
**Lyssarides,** Vassos 1920- *IntWW 91*
**Lyst,** John Henry 1933- *WhoMW 92*
**Lyster,** Mark Allan 1953- *AmMWSc 92*
**Lyster,** Michael Dale 1943- *WhoMW 92*
**Lysycia,** Anthony 1959- *TwCPaSc*
**Lysyj,** Ihor 1929- *AmMWSc 92*
**Lysyk,** Kenneth Martin 1934- *IntWW 91*
**Lytch,** James 1814-1890 *DcNCBi 4*
**Lytel,** Elaine G 1923- *WhoAmP 91*
**Lythall,** Basil Wilfrid 1919- *Who 92*
**Lythcott,** George I 1918- *AmMWSc 92*
**Lythcott,** Janice Logue 1950- *WhoBlA 92*
**Lythgo,** Wilbur Reginald 1920- *Who 92*
**Lythgoe,** Basil 1913- *IntWW 91, Who 92*
**Lythgoe,** Clive 1937- *WhoEnt 92*
**Lythgoe,** Ian Gordon 1914- *Who 92*
**Lytle,** Alice A. *WhoBlA 92*
**Lytle,** Andrew *DrAPF 91*
**Lytle,** Andrew 1902- *BenetAL 91, ConNov 91, IntAu&W 91, WrDr 92*
**Lytle,** Archibald 1730-1790 *DcNCBi 4*
**Lytle,** Brian Dean 1958- *WhoAmL 92*
**Lytle,** Carl David 1941- *AmMWSc 92*
**Lytle,** Charles Franklin 1932- *AmMWSc 92*
**Lytle,** Dean Winton 1927- *AmMWSc 92*
**Lytle,** Farrel Wayne 1934- *AmMWSc 92*
**Lytle,** Fred Edward 1943- *AmMWSc 92*
**Lytle,** Loy Denham 1943- *AmMWSc 92*
**Lytle,** Lutie 1871?- *HanAmWH*
**Lytle,** Marilyn Mercedes 1948- *WhoBlA 92*
**Lytle,** Raymond Alfred 1919- *AmMWSc 92*
**Lytle,** William F 1932- *WhoAmP 91*
**Lytle,** William F. 1940- *WhoBlA 92*
**Lyttelton** *Who 92*
**Lyttelton,** George 1709-1773 *RfGEnL 91*
**Lyttelton,** George 1883-1962 *ConAu 134*
**Lyttelton,** Humphrey Richard Adeane 1921- *IntWW 91, Who 92*
**Lyttle,** Bradford Janes 1927- *AmPeW, WhoMW 92*
**Lyttle,** James Brian Chambers 1932- *Who 92*
**Lyttle,** John Gordon d1991 *Who 92N*
**Lyttle,** Ross Orville 1932- *WhoWest 92*
**Lyttleton,** Humphrey 1921- *NewAmDM*
**Lyttleton,** Raymond Arthur 1911- *IntWW 91, Who 92*
**Lytton** *Who 92*
**Lytton,** Earl of 1950- *Who 92*
**Lytton,** Bernard 1926- *AmMWSc 92*
**Lytton,** Henry 1867-1936 *NewAmDM*
**Lytton,** Jack L 1933- *AmMWSc 92*
**Lytton,** Robert Leonard 1937- *AmMWSc 92*
**Lytton Cobbold** *Who 92*
**Lytton of Knebworth,** Baron *RfGEnL 91*
**Lyubeznik,** Gennady 1957- *WhoMW 92*
**Lyubimenko,** Vladimir Nikolaevich 1873-1937 *SovUnBD*
**Lyubimov,** Yuriy Petrovich 1917- *IntWW 91, SovUnBD*
**Lyubshin,** Stanislav Andreyevich 1933- *IntWW 91*
**Lyubsky,** Sergey 1945- *AmMWSc 92*
**Lyulka,** Arkhip 1908-1984 *FacFETw*
**Lyveden,** Baron 1915- *Who 92*

# M

**M. Quad** *BenetAL 91*
**M. A.** 1841- *ScFEYrs*
**Ma Chi-Chuang** 1912- *IntWW 91*
**Ma Chung-Ch'en** *IntWW 91*
**Ma Dayou** 1915- *IntWW 91*
**Ma Feng** 1922- *IntWW 91*
**Ma Feng-i** *EncAmaz 91*
**Ma Guorui** *IntWW 91*
**Ma Hong** 1920- *IntWW 91*
**Ma Hui** 1915- *IntWW 91*
**Ma Jirong** 1914- *IntWW 91*
**Ma Lin** 1925- *Who 92*
**Ma Ming** 1937- *IntWW 91*
**Ma Shijun** 1915- *IntWW 91*
**Ma Shui-long** 1939- *ConCom 92*
**Ma Sizhong** 1931- *IntWW 91*
**Ma Szu-Chung** *IntWW 91*
**Ma Wenrui** 1909- *IntWW 91*
**Ma Xin** 1917- *IntWW 91*
**Ma Xingyuan** 1917- *IntWW 91*
**Ma Ying Taphan** *EncAmaz 91*
**Ma Yuan** 1930- *IntWW 91*
**Ma Yuhuai** 1917- *IntWW 91*
**Ma Zhongchen** 1936- *IntWW 91*
**Ma,** Benjamin Mingli 1924- *AmMWSc 92*
**Ma,** Cindy Waisze 1962- *WhoFI 92*
**Ma,** Cynthia Sanman 1940- *AmMWSc 92*
**Ma,** Er-Chieh 1922- *AmMWSc 92*
**Ma,** Fai 1954- *AmMWSc 92*
**Ma,** Fengchow C. 1919- *WhoWest 92*
**Ma,** Hiao-Tsiun 1911-1991 *NewYTBS 91*
**Ma,** Joseph T 1925- *AmMWSc 92*
**Ma,** Laurence Jun-chao 1937- *WhoMW 92*
**Ma,** Mark T 1933- *AmMWSc 92*
**Ma,** Maw-Suen 1947- *AmMWSc 92*
**Ma,** Nancy Shui-Fong *AmMWSc 92*
**Ma,** Te Hsiu 1924- *AmMWSc 92*
**Ma,** Terence P 1958- *AmMWSc 92*
**Ma,** Tso-Ping 1945- *AmMWSc 92*
**Ma,** Tsu Sheng 1911- *AmMWSc 92*
**Ma,** William Hsioh-Lien 1947- *AmMWSc 92*
**Ma,** Yi Hua 1936- *AmMWSc 92*
**Ma,** Yo Yo 1955- *IntWW 91, NewAmDM*
**Ma,** Yuan Yuan 1952- *WhoFI 92*
**Ma,** Z Ming 1942- *AmMWSc 92*
**Ma El-Anin,** Cheikh 1830-1910 *HisDSpE*
**Maa,** Jer-Shen 1944- *AmMWSc 92*
**Maack,** Christopher A 1949- *AmMWSc 92*
**Ma'afala,** Finagalouatasi S *WhoAmP 91*
**Maag,** Peter 1919- *IntWW 91, NewAmDM, WhoEnt 92*
**Maag,** Urs Richard 1938- *AmMWSc 92*
**Maahs,** Charles H. *WhoRel 92*
**Maahs,** Edward Ralph 1939- *WhoMW 92*
**Maahs,** Howard Gordon 1939- *AmMWSc 92*
**Maahs,** Kenneth Henry, Sr. 1940- *WhoRel 92*
**Maalouf,** Amin *LiExTwC*
**Maan,** Bashir Ahmed 1926- *Who 92*
**Maar,** James Richard 1943- *AmMWSc 92*
**Maar,** Joseph Henry *WhoEnt 92*
**Maarbjerg,** Mary Penzold 1943- *WhoFI 92*
**Maartmann-Moe,** Peter Sigval 1955- *WhoWest 92*
**Maas,** Eugene Vernon 1936- *AmMWSc 92*
**Maas,** James Weldon 1929- *AmMWSc 92*
**Maas,** Jane Brown *WhoFI 92*
**Maas,** John Lewis 1940- *AmMWSc 92*
**Maas,** Keith Allan 1936- *AmMWSc 92, WhoEnt 92*
**Maas,** Melanie Rose 1948- *WhoMW 92*
**Maas,** Peter 1929- *WrDr 92*
**Maas,** Peter 1939- *AmMWSc 92*
**Maas,** Stephen Joseph 1950- *AmMWSc 92*
**Maas,** Werner Karl 1921- *AmMWSc 92*
**Maasberg,** Albert Thomas 1915- *AmMWSc 92*
**Maasberg,** Michael William 1947- *WhoMW 92*
**Maass,** Alfred Roland 1918- *AmMWSc 92*
**Maass,** Edward Herbert 1957- *WhoFI 92*
**Maass,** Hermann 1897-1944 *EncTR 91*
**Maass,** Wolfgang Siegfried Gunther 1929- *AmMWSc 92*
**Maass-Moreno,** Roberto 1952- *AmMWSc 92*
**Maassab,** Hunein Fadlo 1928- *AmMWSc 92*
**Maatman,** Gerald L 1930- *WhoIns 92*
**Maatman,** Gerald Leonard 1930- *WhoFI 92*
**Maatman,** Russell Wayne 1923- *AmMWSc 92*
**Maazel,** Lorin 1930- *FacFETw, IntWW 91, NewAmDM, Who 92, WhoEnt 92*
**Mabbett,** Ian William 1939- *IntAu&W 91, WrDr 92*
**Mabbott,** Douglas C 1893?-1918 *BiInAmS*
**Mabbs,** Alfred Walter 1921- *Who 92*
**Mabbs,** Kenneth Arthur 1952- *WhoFI 92*
**Mabbutt,** Mary 1951- *TwCPaSc*
**Mabe,** Manabu 1924- *IntWW 91*
**Mabee,** Carleton 1914- *WrDr 92*
**Mabee,** Keith Vance 1947- *WhoIns 92*
**Mabee,** Sandra Ivonne 1955- *WhoWest 92*
**Maben,** Burton Freeman 1961- *WhoMW 92*
**Maben,** Hayward C., Jr. 1922- *WhoBlA 92*
**Mabey,** Joelle Lynn 1967- *WhoRel 92*
**Mabey,** Ralph Rampton 1944- *WhoAmL 92*
**Mabey,** Richard Thomas 1941- *IntAu&W 91, Who 92, WrDr 92*
**Mabey,** William Ray 1941- *AmMWSc 92*
**Mabie,** Curtis Parsons 1932- *AmMWSc 92*
**Mabie,** Hamilton Horth 1914- *AmMWSc 92*
**Mabie,** Hamilton Wright 1845-1916 *BenetAL 91*
**Mabie,** Ruth Marie *WhoWest 92*
**Mabillon,** Jean 1632-1707 *BlkwCEP*
**Mabin,** Joseph E. *WhoBlA 92*
**Mabini,** Apolinario 1864-1903 *HisDSpE*
**Mable,** Richard Wayne 1957- *WhoAmL 92*
**Mabley,** Jackie 1894-1975 *NotBlAW 92*
**Mabley,** Jackie 1898-1975 *DcNCBi 4*
**Mabli,** Charles E 1941- *WhoIns 92*
**Mably,** Gabriel Bonnot de 1709-1785 *BlkwCEP*
**Mabon,** Dickson 1925- *Who 92*
**Mabon,** Inez Camprubi d1992 *WhoHisp 92N*
**Mabrey,** Harold Leon 1933- *WhoBlA 92*
**Mabrey,** Marsha Eve 1949- *WhoBlA 92*
**Mabrie,** Herman James, III 1948- *WhoBlA 92*
**Mabrouk,** Ahmed Fahmy 1923- *AmMWSc 92*
**Mabrouk,** Ezzidin Ali 1932- *IntWW 91*
**Mabry,** Edward L. 1936- *WhoBlA 92*
**Mabry,** Frank Lyon 1948- *WhoAmL 92*
**Mabry,** Herbert H *WhoAmP 91*
**Mabry,** James C., IV 1957- *WhoFI 92*
**Mabry,** John William 1950- *AmMWSc 92*
**Mabry,** Malcolm H, Jr 1933- *WhoAmP 91*
**Mabry,** Paul Davis 1943- *AmMWSc 92, WhoMW 92*
**Mabry,** Sharon Cody 1945- *WhoEnt 92*
**Mabry,** Tom Joe 1932- *AmMWSc 92*
**Mabson,** Robert Langley 1931- *WhoRel 92*
**Mabuchi,** Katsuhide 1942- *AmMWSc 92*
**Mabus,** Ray *WhoAmP 91*
**Mabus,** Ray 1948- *AlmAP 92 [port]*
**Mabus,** Raymond Edwin, Jr. 1948- *IntWW 91*
**Maby,** Cedric 1915- *Who 92*
**Mac,** Michael John 1951- *AmMWSc 92*
**MacAdam,** David Lewis 1910- *AmMWSc 92*
**MacAdam,** Keith Bradford 1944- *AmMWSc 92*
**Macadam,** Peter 1921- *IntWW 91, Who 92*
**MacAdams,** Lewis 1944- *WrDr 92*
**MacAfee,** Norman *DrAPF 91*
**Macagno,** Eduardo *WhoHisp 92*
**Macaione,** Domenic Paul 1937- *AmMWSc 92*
**Macal,** Zdenek 1936- *NewAmDM, WhoEnt 92, WhoMW 92*
**Macalady,** Donald Lee 1941- *AmMWSc 92*
**MacAlister,** Robert Stuart 1924- *WhoWest 92*
**Macallan,** Andrew *Who 92, WrDr 92*
**MacAllister,** Jack Alfred 1927- *WhoFI 92, WhoWest 92*
**MacAlpine,** Gordon Madeira 1945- *AmMWSc 92*
**Macaluso,** Anthony, Sr 1939- *AmMWSc 92*
**Macaluso,** Frank Augustus 1931- *WhoFI 92*
**Macaluso,** Marc David 1957- *WhoFI 92*
**Macaluso,** Mary Christelle 1931- *AmMWSc 92*
**Macaluso,** Pat 1916- *AmMWSc 92*
**Macaluso,** Theodore F. *WhoEnt 92*
**Macan,** William Alexander, IV 1942- *WhoAmL 92*
**MacAndrew** *Who 92*
**MacAndrew,** Baron 1945- *Who 92*
**Macapagal,** Diosdado 1910- *IntWW 91*
**MacApp,** C C 1917?-1971 *TwCSFW 91*
**Macara,** Douglas *Who 92N*
**Macara,** Hugh Kenneth 1913- *Who 92*
**Macaranas,** Howard I 1955- *WhoAmP 91*
**Macarell,** John D 1933- *WhoIns 92*
**Macario,** Alberto J L 1935 *AmMWSc 92*
**Macarius Magnes** *EncEarC*
**Macarius The Great** 300?-390? *EncEarC*
**Macarron Jaime,** Ricardo 1926- *IntWW 91*
**Macarthur,** Arthur Leitch 1913- *Who 92*
**MacArthur,** Brian 1940- *Who 92*
**MacArthur,** Brian Henry 1949- *WhoFI 92*
**MacArthur,** Charles 1895-1956 *BenetAL 91*
**MacArthur,** Charles, Mrs. *Who 92*
**Macarthur,** Charles Ramsay *Who 92*
**MacArthur,** Diana Taylor 1933- *WhoFI 92*
**MacArthur,** Donald M 1931- *AmMWSc 92*
**MacArthur,** Douglas 1880-1964 *FacFETw [port], RComAH*
**MacArthur,** Douglas, II 1909- *IntWW 91*
**MacArthur,** Duncan W 1956- *AmMWSc 92*
**MacArthur,** Ian 1925- *Who 92*
**Mac Arthur,** James 1937- *IntMPA 92, WhoEnt 92*
**MacArthur,** John Duncan 1936- *AmMWSc 92*
**MacArthur,** John Wood 1922- *AmMWSc 92*
**Macartney,** Clarence Edward Noble 1879-1957 *RelLAm 91*
**Macartney,** John Barrington 1917- *Who 92*
**Macartney,** Lawson 1957- *AmMWSc 92*
**MacAskill,** Kenneth M 1928- *WhoAmP 91*
**Macaulay,** Alexander S 1942- *WhoAmP 91*
**Macaulay,** Allen F. 1949- *WhoEnt 92*
**Macaulay,** Andrew James 1937- *AmMWSc 92*
**Macaulay,** Catharine 1731-1791 *BlkwCEP*
**Macaulay,** Catherine Sawbridge 1731-1791 *BlkwEAR*
**Macaulay,** Colin Alexander 1931- *WhoFI 92*
**Macaulay,** David 1946- *ConAu 34NR, IntAu&W 91, WrDr 92*
**Macaulay,** Janet Stewart Alison 1909- *Who 92*
**Macaulay,** John Clinton 1943- *WhoFI 92*
**Macaulay,** Robert Erwin 1930- *WhoMW 92*
**Macaulay,** Rose 1881-1958 *RfGEnL 91, ScFEYrs, TwCLC 44 [port]*
**Macaulay,** Thomas 1800-1859 *CnDBLB 4 [port]*
**Macaulay,** Thomas Babington 1800-1859 *RfGEnL 91*
**Macaulay,** Tom 1951- *WhoAmP 91*
**Macaulay-Graham,** Catherine Sawbridge 1731-1791 *BlkwEAR*
**Macaulay of Bragar,** Baron *Who 92*
**Macauley,** Charles Cameron 1923- *WhoWest 92*
**MacAuley,** Philip Christopher 1957- *WhoEnt 92*
**Macauley,** Robie *DrAPF 91*
**Macauley,** Robie 1919- *BenetAL 91, ConNov 91, WrDr 92*
**Macauley,** William Francis 1943- *WhoAmL 92*
**MacAvoy,** R A 1949- *TwCSFW 91*
**Mac Avoy,** Roberta Ann 1949- *IntAu&W 91, WrDr 92*
**MacAvoy,** Thomas Coleman 1928- *AmMWSc 92*
**Macay,** Spruce 1755?-1808 *DcNCBi 4*
**Macbeath,** Alexander Murray 1923- *Who 92*
**Macbeath,** Innis 1928- *WrDr 92*
**MacBeth,** George 1932- *ConPo 91, IntAu&W 91, WrDr 92*
**MacBeth,** George Mann 1932- *Who 92*
**Macbeth,** Hugh James 1947- *WhoFI 92*
**Macbeth,** Robert 1934- *WhoBlA 92*
**Macbeth,** Robert Alexander 1920- *AmMWSc 92*
**MacBride,** John *FacFETw*
**MacBride,** Mary H *WhoAmP 91*
**MacBride,** Roger Lea 1929- *WhoAmP 91*
**MacBride,** Sean 1904-1988 *FacFETw, WhoNob 90*

**MacBride,** Thomas Jamison 1914- *WhoAmL 92, WhoWest 92*
**MacBride,** William Lane, Jr. 1951- *WhoFI 92*
**MacBryde,** Robert 1913-1966 *TwCPaSc*
**MacBurney,** Edward Harding 1927- *WhoMW 92, WhoRel 92*
**MacCabe,** Brian Farmer 1914- *Who 92*
**MacCabe,** Colin Myles Joseph 1949- *Who 92*
**MacCabe,** Gladys 1918- *TwCPaSc*
**MacCabe,** Jeffrey Allan 1943- *AmMWSc 92*
**MacCabe,** Max 1917- *TwCPaSc*
**Maccabee,** Bruce Sargent 1942- *AmMWSc 92*
**MacCaffrey,** Wallace T. 1920- *ConAu 134*
**MacCaig,** Norman 1910- *ConAu 34NR, RfGEnL 91, Who 92, WrDr 92*
**Maccaig,** Norman Alexander 1914- *IntAu&W 91*
**MacCallum,** Crawford John 1929- *AmMWSc 92*
**MacCallum,** Donald Kenneth 1939- *AmMWSc 92*
**MacCallum,** John Bruce 1876-1906 *BiInAmS*
**MacCallum,** Lorene 1928- *WhoWest 92*
**MacCamy,** Richard C 1925- *AmMWSc 92*
**Mac Cana,** Proinsias 1926- *Who 92*
**Maccanico,** Antonio 1924- *IntWW 91*
**MacCann,** Richard Dyer 1920- *WhoEnt 92*
**MacCannell,** Juliet Flower 1943- *IntAu&W 91*
**MacCannell,** Keith Leonard 1934- *AmMWSc 92*
**MacCanon,** Donald Moore 1924- *AmMWSc 92*
**MacCarley,** Carl Arthur 1954- *WhoWest 92*
**Maccarone,** Toni Lynn 1967- *WhoWest 92*
**MacCarthy,** Fiona 1940- *WrDr 92*
**MacCarthy,** Jean Juliet *AmMWSc 92*
**MacCarthy,** John Peters 1933- *WhoFI 92*
**MacCarthy,** Patrick 1946- *AmMWSc 92*
**MacCarthy,** Terence 1934- *WhoAmL 92*
**MacCarty,** Collin Stewart 1915- *AmMWSc 92*
**MacCauley,** Hugh Bournonville 1922- *WhoFI 92, WhoWest 92*
**MacChesney,** John Burnette 1929- *AmMWSc 92*
**Macchi,** I Alden 1922- *AmMWSc 92*
**Macchia,** Donald Dean 1948- *AmMWSc 92*
**Macchia,** Frank Domonick 1952- *WhoRel 92*
**Macchia,** Joseph D 1935- *WhoIns 92*
**Macchia,** Joseph Dominick 1935- *WhoFI 92*
**Macchia,** Stephen Anthony 1956- *WhoRel 92*
**Macchia,** Vincent Michael 1933- *WhoAmL 92*
**Macchio,** Ralph 1962- *IntMPA 92*
**Maccini,** John Andrew 1928- *AmMWSc 92*
**MacClane,** Edward James 1907- *WhoBlA 92*
**MacClaren,** Robert H 1913- *AmMWSc 92*
**MacClean,** Walter Lee 1935- *WhoMW 92*
**MacCleery,** Douglas Watson 1942- *WhoAmP 91*
**MacClennan,** Robert Walton 1940- *WhoEnt 92*
**Macclesfield,** Archdeacon of *Who 92*
**Macclesfield,** Earl of 1914- *Who 92*
**MacClinchie,** Robert Clanahan 1910- *WhoWest 92*
**MacClintock,** Copeland 1930- *AmMWSc 92*
**MacCluer,** Jean Walters 1937- *AmMWSc 92*
**Maccoby,** Eleanor Emmons 1917- *WomPsyc*
**Maccoby,** Michael 1933- *IntAu&W 91, WhoFI 92, WrDr 92*
**MacColl,** D.S. 1859-1948 *ThHEIm*
**MacColl,** Dugald Sutherland 1859-1948 *TwCPaSc*
**MacColl,** Ewan 1915-1989 *FacFETw*
**MacColl,** Hugh *ScFEYrs*
**MacColl,** Robert 1942- *AmMWSc 92*
**MacCollam,** Joel Allan 1946- *WhoRel 92*
**MacCollom,** George Butterick 1925- *AmMWSc 92*
**MacCombie,** Bruce Franklin 1943- *WhoEnt 92*
**MacConnell,** James H 1931- *WhoAmP 91*
**MacConnell,** John Griffith 1942- *AmMWSc 92*
**MacConnell,** William Preston 1918- *AmMWSc 92*
**MacConochie,** John Angus 1908- *Who 92*
**Mac Corkindale,** Simon 1952- *IntMPA 92*
**MacCorkle,** Emmett Wallace, III 1942- *WhoFI 92, WhoWest 92*
**MacCormac,** Richard Cornelius 1938- *IntWW 91, Who 92*
**Maccormac,** Vincent Peter 1936- *WhoIns 92*
**MacCormick,** Donald Neil 1941- *Who 92*
**MacCormick,** Iain Somerled MacDonald 1939- *Who 92*
**MacCormick,** Neil *Who 92*
**MacCormick,** Neil 1941- *IntWW 91, WrDr 92*
**MacCoss,** Malcolm 1947- *AmMWSc 92*
**MacCourt,** Donald *WhoEnt 92*
**MacCoy,** Clinton Viles 1905- *AmMWSc 92*
**Maccracken,** Mary 1926- *IntAu&W 91, WrDr 92*
**MacCracken,** Mary Jo 1943- *WhoMW 92*
**MacCracken,** Michael Calvin 1942- *AmMWSc 92*
**MacCraig,** Norman 1910- *ConPo 91*
**MacCrate,** Robert 1921- *WhoAmL 92*
**Mac Cready,** Paul Beattie 1925- *WhoWest 92*
**MacCready,** Paul Beattie, Jr 1925- *AmMWSc 92*
**MacCreigh,** James *IntAu&W 91X, TwCSFW 91*
**MacCrimmon,** Hugh Ross 1923- *AmMWSc 92*
**MacCrindle,** Robert Alexander 1928- *Who 92*
**MacCrone,** Robert K 1933- *AmMWSc 92*
**MacCulley,** Robert John 1918- *WhoRel 92*
**MacCulloch,** Campbell *ScFEYrs*
**MacCulloch,** Malcolm John 1936- *Who 92*
**MacCurdy,** John A. 1947- *WhoFI 92*
**MacDermot,** Brian 1914- *Who 92*
**Macdermot,** Niall 1916- *IntWW 91, Who 92*
**MacDermott,** Edmond Geoffrey *Who 92*
**MacDermott,** John Clarke 1927- *IntWW 91, Who 92*
**MacDermott,** Richard J, Jr *AmMWSc 92*
**MacDermott,** Thomas Jerome 1960- *WhoFI 92*
**MacDiarmid,** Alan Graham 1927- *AmMWSc 92*
**MacDiarmid,** Hugh 1892-1978 *CnDBLB 7 [port], FacFETw, RfGEnL 91*
**MacDiarmid,** William Donald 1926- *AmMWSc 92*
**MacDonagh,** Oliver Ormond Gerard 1924- *Who 92*
**Macdonald** *Who 92*
**Macdonald,** Baron 1947- *Who 92*
**Macdonald,** Alastair A 1920- *IntAu&W 91*
**Macdonald,** Alastair John Peter 1940- *Who 92*
**MacDonald,** Alex Bruce 1934- *AmMWSc 92*
**MacDonald,** Alexander, Jr 1936- *AmMWSc 92*
**MacDonald,** Alexander Daniel 1923- *AmMWSc 92*
**Macdonald,** Alistair d1991 *Who 92N*
**MacDonald,** Alistair Archibald 1927- *Who 92*
**Macdonald,** Alistair H. 1925- *Who 92*
**MacDonald,** Allan d1792? *DcNCBi 4*
**MacDonald,** Allan Hugh 1951- *AmMWSc 92*
**MacDonald,** Amy 1951- *ConAu 135*
**Macdonald,** Angus Cameron 1931- *Who 92*
**Macdonald,** Angus John 1940- *Who 92*
**Macdonald,** Angus Stewart 1935- *Who 92*
**MacDonald,** Arthur 1919- *Who 92*
**MacDonald,** Betty 1908-1958 *BenetAL 91*
**MacDonald,** Caleb Alan 1933- *WhoFI 92*
**Macdonald,** Calum Alasdair 1956- *Who 92*
**MacDonald,** Carol *WhoAmP 91*
**Macdonald,** Caroline 1948- *WrDr 92*
**MacDonald,** Carolyn Trott 1941- *AmMWSc 92*
**MacDonald,** Celsa M. 1941- *WhoMW 92*
**MacDonald,** Charles *WhoAmP 91*
**MacDonald,** Charles B. 1922-1990 *ConAu 133*
**MacDonald,** Charles Ray 1929- *WhoMW 92, WhoRel 92*
**MacDonald,** Claudia L. *WhoRel 92*
**MacDonald,** Clyde, Jr 1929- *WhoAmP 91*
**Macdonald,** Cynthia *DrAPF 91*
**Macdonald,** David Cameron 1936- *Who 92*
**MacDonald,** David Howard 1934- *AmMWSc 92*
**MacDonald,** David J 1932- *AmMWSc 92*
**MacDonald,** David Richard 1953- *WhoMW 92*
**Macdonald,** David Robert 1930- *WhoAmL 92*
**MacDonald,** David Roy 1940- *WhoRel 92*
**MacDonald,** Dennis Ronald 1946- *WhoRel 92*
**MacDonald,** Donald 1712-1784? *DcNCBi 4*
**Macdonald,** Donald Farquhar Macleod 1915- *Who 92*
**Macdonald,** Donald Hardman d1990 *Who 92N*
**Macdonald,** Donald Ian 1931- *WhoAmP 91*
**MacDonald,** Donald Laurie 1922- *AmMWSc 92*
**MacDonald,** Donald MacKenzie 1928- *AmMWSc 92*
**MacDonald,** Donald P. 1931- *WhoAmL 92*
**MacDonald,** Donald Paul 1931- *WhoAmP 91*
**Macdonald,** Donald Stovel 1932- *IntWW 91, Who 92*
**Macdonald,** Douglas Gordon 1939- *AmMWSc 92*
**Macdonald,** Dwight 1906-1982 *BenetAL 91, FacFETw*
**MacDonald,** Elizabeth Helen 1942- *WhoEnt 92*
**MacDonald,** Elmer *WhoAmP 91*
**MacDonald,** Eve Lapeyrouse 1929- *AmMWSc 92*
**Macdonald,** Fergus 1936- *IntWW 91*
**MacDonald,** Flora 1722-1790 *BlkwEAR, DcNCBi 4, EncAmaz 91*
**Macdonald,** Flora Isabel 1926- *IntWW 91, Who 92*
**MacDonald,** Frances 1873-1921 *TwCPaSc*
**MacDonald,** Frances 1874-1921 *DcTwDes*
**MacDonald,** Frances 1914- *TwCPaSc*
**MacDonald,** George 1824-1905 *RfGEnL 91, TwCSFW 91*
**Macdonald,** George Grant 1921- *Who 92*
**MacDonald,** Gerald Glenn 1959- *WhoAmL 92*
**MacDonald,** Gerald V. 1938- *WhoMW 92*
**Macdonald,** Gordon J 1934- *AmMWSc 92*
**MacDonald,** Gordon James Fraser 1929- *AmMWSc 92, IntWW 91*
**Macdonald,** Gus *Who 92*
**MacDonald,** Harold Carleton 1930- *AmMWSc 92*
**Macdonald,** Herbert 1902- *Who 92*
**MacDonald,** Hope 1928- *ConAu 135*
**Macdonald,** Howard *Who 92*
**MacDonald,** Hubert C, Jr 1941- *AmMWSc 92*
**Macdonald,** Hugh Ian 1929- *Who 92*
**Macdonald,** Hugh John 1940- *Who 92*
**Macdonald,** Iain Smith 1927- *Who 92*
**MacDonald,** Ian *Who 92*
**Macdonald,** Ian Alexander 1939- *Who 92*
**Macdonald,** Ian David 1932- *WrDr 92*
**Macdonald,** Ian Francis 1942- *AmMWSc 92*
**Macdonald,** Ian Grant 1928- *IntWW 91, Who 92*
**MacDonald,** Isabel Lillias *Who 92*
**MacDonald,** J E H 1873-1932 *FacFETw*
**Macdonald,** Jake M 1949- *IntAu&W 91*
**MacDonald,** James d1991 *NewYTBS 91*
**MacDonald,** James 1952- *AmMWSc 92*
**Macdonald,** James Alexander 1908- *Who 92*
**MacDonald,** James Cameron 1926- *AmMWSc 92*
**MacDonald,** James Douglas 1948- *AmMWSc 92*
**Macdonald,** James Ellis 1950- *WhoWest 92*
**Mac Donald,** James Hector 1925- *WhoRel 92*
**MacDonald,** James Ramsay 1866-1937 *EncTR 91 [port]*
**Macdonald,** James Reid 1918- *AmMWSc 92*
**Macdonald,** James Ross 1923- *AmMWSc 92, IntWW 91*
**MacDonald,** James Scott 1948- *AmMWSc 92*
**MacDonald,** Joel Brian 1946- *WhoRel 92*
**Macdonald,** John Alexander 1956- *WhoRel 92*
**Macdonald,** John B. 1918- *Who 92*
**Macdonald,** John Barfoot 1918- *AmMWSc 92*
**Macdonald,** John Charles 1910- *Who 92*
**MacDonald,** John Chisholm 1933- *AmMWSc 92*
**MacDonald,** John D. 1916-1986 *BenetAL 91, FacFETw, TwCSFW 91*
**MacDonald,** John Donald 1938- *Who 92*
**MacDonald,** John G. 1957- *WhoFI 92*
**MacDonald,** John Grant 1932- *Who 92*
**Macdonald,** John Howard 1928- *Who 92*
**MacDonald,** John James 1925- *AmMWSc 92*
**MacDonald,** John Lauchlin 1938- *AmMWSc 92*
**Macdonald,** John M. 1920- *WrDr 92*
**Macdonald,** John Marshall 1920- *AmMWSc 92*
**Macdonald,** John Reginald 1931- *Who 92*
**MacDonald,** John Robert 1954- *AmMWSc 92*
**MacDonald,** Joseph A 1910- *WhoAmP 91*
**Macdonald,** Joseph Albert Friel 1942- *WhoFI 92*
**MacDonald,** Joseph Faber 1932- *WhoRel 92*
**MacDonald,** Joseph Neil 1950- *WhoRel 92*
**Macdonald,** Kenneth 1930- *Who 92*
**Macdonald,** Kenneth Craig 1947- *AmMWSc 92*
**MacDonald,** Kenneth J 1926- *WhoAmP 91*
**Macdonald,** Kevin Angus 1960- *WhoFI 92*
**Macdonald,** Lenna Ruth 1962- *WhoAmL 92*
**MacDonald,** Lynn Merle 1942- *WhoAmP 91*
**Macdonald,** Malcolm *IntAu&W 91X, WrDr 92*
**MacDonald,** Margaret *Who 92*
**MacDonald,** Margaret 1865-1933 *DcTwDes, FacFETw*
**MacDonald,** Margo 1944- *Who 92*
**MacDonald,** Mark A 1942- *WhoAmP 91*
**MacDonald,** Marnie L *AmMWSc 92*
**Mac Donald,** Matthew Anita 1938- *WhoRel 92*
**MacDonald,** Maurice B 1931- *WhoAmP 91*
**MacDonald,** Michael J *AmMWSc 92*
**Macdonald,** Morag 1947- *Who 92*
**MacDonald,** Noel C 1940- *AmMWSc 92*
**MacDonald,** Norman Scott 1917- *AmMWSc 92*
**MacDonald,** Norval Woodrow 1913- *WhoWest 92*
**MacDonald,** Patricia Lillig 1941- *WhoMW 92*
**MacDonald,** Paul Cloren *AmMWSc 92*
**Macdonald,** Peter Moore 1953- *AmMWSc 92*
**Mac Donald,** Philip *IntMPA 92*
**MacDonald,** R. Fulton 1940- *WhoFI 92*
**MacDonald,** R Neil 1935- *AmMWSc 92*
**MacDonald,** Ralph 1944- *WhoBlA 92*
**MacDonald,** Ramsay 1866-1937 *FacFETw*
**MacDonald,** Richard Annis 1928- *AmMWSc 92*
**MacDonald,** Richard G 1953- *AmMWSc 92*
**MacDonald,** Robert DeForest 1945- *WhoWest 92*
**MacDonald,** Robert Neal 1916- *AmMWSc 92*
**MacDonald,** Robert W 1943- *WhoIns 92*
**Macdonald,** Roderick 1921- *Who 92*
**Macdonald,** Roderick, Jr 1926- *AmMWSc 92*
**Macdonald,** Roderick Francis 1951- *Who 92*
**MacDonald,** Roderick Patterson 1924- *AmMWSc 92*
**Macdonald,** Ronald Clarence 1911- *Who 92*
**Macdonald,** Ronald John 1919- *Who 92*
**MacDonald,** Ronald S. 1952- *WhoFI 92*
**MacDonald,** Rosemary A 1930- *AmMWSc 92*
**MacDonald,** Ross 1915-1983 *BenetAL 91, FacFETw*
**MacDonald,** Russell Earl 1928- *AmMWSc 92*
**MacDonald,** Ruth S *AmMWSc 92*
**MacDonald,** Sharon Ethel 1952- *WhoEnt 92*
**MacDonald,** Simon Gavin George 1923- *Who 92, WrDr 92*
**Macdonald,** Susan *DrAPF 91*
**MacDonald,** T.T. *DcLB 112*
**Macdonald,** Thomas Brian 1911- *Who 92*
**Macdonald,** Thomas Conchar 1909- *Who 92*
**MacDonald,** Thomas Cook, Jr. 1929- *WhoAmL 92*
**MacDonald,** Thomas Gerard 1956- *WhoAmL 92*
**MacDonald,** Thomas Joseph, Jr. 1940- *WhoFI 92*
**MacDonald,** Thomas Thornton 1951- *AmMWSc 92*
**Macdonald,** Timothy Lee 1948- *AmMWSc 92*
**Macdonald,** Torbert H. d1976 *LesBEnT 92*
**Macdonald,** Virginia B 1920- *WhoAmP 91*
**Macdonald,** Virginia Brooks 1918- *WhoWest 92*
**MacDonald,** Wayne Douglas 1954- *WhoAmP 91*
**MacDonald,** William 1927- *AmMWSc 92*
**MacDonald,** William Colt 1891- *TwCWW 91*
**MacDonald,** William David 1937- *AmMWSc 92*
**MacDonald,** William E, Jr 1916- *AmMWSc 92*
**MacDonald,** William L. 1921- *WrDr 92*
**MacDonald,** William L. 1949- *WhoFI 92, WhoWest 92*
**Macdonald,** William Weir 1927- *Who 92*
**MacDonald,** Willis Goss 1863-1910 *BiInAmS*
**MacDonald,** Wilson 1880-1967 *BenetAL 91*

**MacDonald-Glenn,** Linda S. 1955- *WhoAmL 92*
**Macdonald of Clanranald,** Ranald A 1934- *Who 92*
**Macdonald of Gwaenysgor,** Baron 1915- *Who 92*
**Macdonald of Sleat** *Who 92*
**MacDonald Scott,** Mary *Who 92*
**Macdonald-Smith,** Hugh 1923- *Who 92*
**Macdonald-Smith,** Sydney 1908- *Who 92*
**MacDonell of Glengarry,** Aeneas Ranald D 1913- *Who 92*
**Mac Doniels,** Joseph William 1941- *WhoMW 92*
**MacDonnell,** G.J. Stillson 1947- *WhoAmL 92*
**MacDonnell,** John Joseph 1927- *AmMWSc 92*
**MacDonnell,** Joseph Francis 1929- *AmMWSc 92*
**MacDonnell,** Robert Alan 1942- *WhoAmL 92*
**Macdonnell,** T M 1923- *WhoAmP 91*
**MacDonnell,** Wilfred Donald 1911- *AmMWSc 92*
**MacDonough,** Robert Howard 1941- *WhoWest 92*
**MacDoran,** Peter Frank 1941- *AmMWSc 92*
**Macdouall,** Robertson *IntAu&W 91X*
**MacDougal,** Gary Edward 1936- *WhoFI 92, WhoMW 92*
**MacDougal,** John *SmATA 66, TwCSFW 91*
**MacDougall,** David Mercer d1991 *Who 92N*
**MacDougall,** Donald 1912- *IntWW 91, Who 92*
**MacDougall,** Edward Bruce 1939- *AmMWSc 92*
**MacDougall,** Genevieve Rockwood 1914- *WhoMW 92*
**Macdougall,** Iver Cameron 1926- *WhoAmL 92*
**Macdougall,** John Douglas 1944- *AmMWSc 92*
**MacDougall,** Laura Margaret *Who 92*
**MacDougall,** Malcolm D. *WhoFI 92*
**MacDougall,** Malcolm Edward 1938- *WhoAmL 92*
**MacDougall,** Mary Katherine *WhoRel 92*
**Macdougall,** Neil 1932- *Who 92*
**Macdougall,** Patrick Lorn 1939- *IntWW 91, Who 92*
**MacDougall,** Priscilla Ruth 1944- *WhoAmL 92*
**MacDougall,** Robert Douglas 1922- *AmMWSc 92*
**MacDougall,** Ruth Doan *DrAPF 91*
**MacDougall,** William Roderick 1914- *WhoAmL 92*
**MacDowall,** David William 1930- *Who 92*
**Macdowall,** Ian d1991 *NewYTBS 91*
**MacDowell,** Andie *IntMPA 92, WhoEnt 92*
**MacDowell,** Andie 1958?- *ConTFT 9*
**MacDowell,** Denis W H 1924- *AmMWSc 92*
**Macdowell,** Douglas Maurice 1931- *IntAu&W 91, WrDr 92*
**MacDowell,** Edward d1908 *FacFETw*
**MacDowell,** Edward 1860-1908 *NewAmDM*
**MacDowell,** Edward A. 1861-1908 *BenetAL 91*
**MacDowell,** James William 1953- *WhoEnt 92*
**MacDowell,** John 1717-1763 *DcNCBi 4*
**MacDowell,** John Fraser 1932- *AmMWSc 92*
**MacDowell,** Katherine Sherwood 1849-1883 *BenetAL 91*
**MacDowell,** Michael Alan 1947- *WhoFI 92*
**MacDowell,** Robert W 1924- *AmMWSc 92*
**MacDowell,** Samuel Wallace 1929- *AmMWSc 92*
**Macduff,** Earl of 1961- *Who 92*
**MacDuff,** Andrew *TwCSFW 91*
**Mace,** Ada L *WhoAmP 91*
**Mace,** Alan Arthur 1946- *WhoRel 92*
**Mace,** Arnett C, Jr 1937- *AmMWSc 92*
**Mace,** Barbara Jean 1945- *WhoAmP 91*
**Mace,** Brian Anthony 1948- *Who 92*
**Mace,** David Robert 1907-1990 *ConAu 133*
**Mace,** Eugene William 1933- *WhoRel 92*
**Mace,** Helene G 1918- *WhoAmP 91*
**Mace,** John 1932- *Who 92*
**Mace,** John Weldon 1938- *AmMWSc 92*
**Mace,** Kenneth Dean 1926- *AmMWSc 92*
**Mace,** Matthew A. 1960- *WhoAmL 92*
**Mace,** Thomas 1612?-1706? *NewAmDM*
**MacEachen,** Allan J. 1921- *IntWW 91*
**MacEachen,** Allan Joseph 1921- *Who 92*
**MacEachern,** Diane 1952- *ConAu 133*
**Macebuh,** Sandy *IntAu&W 91*
**Maceda,** Jose 1917- *ConCom 92*
**Macedo,** Helder Malta 1935- *Who 92*
**Macedo,** Joelmir Campos de Araripe *IntWW 91*
**Macedo,** Richard Stanley 1941- *WhoFI 92*
**Macek,** Andrej 1926- *AmMWSc 92*
**Macek,** Anna Michaella 1950- *WhoWest 92*
**Macek,** Carl Frank, Jr. 1951- *WhoEnt 92*
**Macek,** Josef 1922- *IntWW 91*
**Macek,** Joseph 1937- *AmMWSc 92*
**Macek,** Robert James 1936- *AmMWSc 92*
**Macel,** Stanley Charles, III 1938- *WhoAmL 92*
**MacEllven,** Douglass Thornton 1945- *WhoAmL 92*
**MacEntee,** Sean 1889-1984 *FacFETw*
**Maceo y Grajales,** Antonio 1848-1896 *HisDSpE*
**MacEoin,** Denis 1949- *WrDr 92*
**MacEoin,** Gary 1909- *WrDr 92*
**Macer,** George Armen, Jr. 1948- *WhoWest 92*
**Macer,** Richard Charles Franklin 1928- *Who 92*
**Macer-Story,** Eugenia 1945- *IntAu&W 91*
**Maceri,** Marco Antonio 1954- *WhoEnt 92*
**Macero,** Daniel Joseph 1928- *AmMWSc 92*
**Macero,** Teo 1925- *NewAmDM, WhoEnt 92*
**Macesich,** George 1927- *WrDr 92*
**MacEvoy,** John Anthony 1947- *WhoAmL 92*
**Mac Ewan,** Deborah Ginsburg 1956- *WhoFI 92*
**MacEwan,** Douglas W 1924- *AmMWSc 92*
**MacEwan,** Gwendolyn 1941- *BenetAL 91*
**Macewan,** J W Grant 1902- *IntAu&W 91*
**MacEwan,** Nigel Savage 1933- *WhoFI 92*
**MacEwen,** Ann Maitland 1918- *Who 92*
**MacEwen,** Edward Carter 1938- *WhoFI 92*
**MacEwen,** George David *WhoFI 92*
**MacEwen,** James Douglas 1926- *AmMWSc 92*
**MacEwen,** Malcolm 1911- *Who 92*
**Macey,** Carn *TwCWW 91, WrDr 92*
**Macey,** David Edward 1929- *Who 92*
**Macey,** Eric Harold 1936- *Who 92*
**Macey,** Jonathan R. 1955- *WhoAmL 92*
**Macey,** Morris William 1922- *WhoAmL 92*
**Macey,** Robert Irwin 1926- *AmMWSc 92*
**Macey,** Wade Thomas 1936- *AmMWSc 92*
**Macfadden,** Bernarr 1868-1955 *BenetAL 91*
**MacFadden,** Donald Lee 1926- *AmMWSc 92*
**MacFadden,** Howard 1946- *WhoAmP 91*
**MacFadden,** James Edward 1967- *WhoEnt 92*
**MacFadden,** Kenneth Orville 1945- *AmMWSc 92*
**MacFadyen,** Alexander Hugh 1931- *WhoFI 92*
**Macfadyen,** Amyan 1920- *WrDr 92*
**Macfadyen,** Donald James Dobbie 1945- *Who 92*
**MacFadyen,** John Archibald, Jr 1922- *AmMWSc 92*
**Macfarlan,** Robert Murray 1940- *WhoAmL 92*
**Macfarland,** Charles Steadman 1866-1956 *RelLAm 91*
**MacFarland,** Charles Stedman 1866-1956 *AmPeW*
**MacFarland,** Craig George 1943- *AmMWSc 92, WhoWest 92*
**MacFarland,** George Arthur, III 1936- *WhoWest 92*
**Macfarlane** *Who 92*
**Macfarlane,** Alan Donald James 1941- *IntWW 91, Who 92*
**MacFarlane,** Alexander 1851-1913 *BiInAmS*
**MacFarlane,** Alistair George James 1931- *IntWW 91, Who 92*
**Macfarlane,** Alwyn James Cecil 1922- *Who 92*
**Macfarlane,** Anne Bridget 1930- *Who 92*
**Macfarlane,** David Gordon 1947- *WhoMW 92*
**Macfarlane,** David Neil 1936- *Who 92*
**MacFarlane,** Donald d1991 *Who 92N*
**MacFarlane,** Donald Robert 1930- *AmMWSc 92*
**MacFarlane,** Duncan Leo 1962- *AmMWSc 92*
**Macfarlane,** George 1916- *Who 92*
**Macfarlane,** George Gray 1916- *IntWW 91*
**MacFarlane,** Gordon Frederick 1925- *WhoWest 92*
**Macfarlane,** James 1819-1885 *BiInAmS*
**Macfarlane,** James Wright 1908- *Who 92*
**MacFarlane,** John 1948- *TwCPaSc*
**Macfarlane,** John Granger 1929- *WhoAmP 91*
**MacFarlane,** John O'Donnell 1920- *AmMWSc 92*
**MacFarlane,** John T 1923- *AmMWSc 92*
**Macfarlane,** Leslie John 1924- *IntAu&W 91, WrDr 92*
**Macfarlane,** M James 1921- *WhoAmP 91*
**MacFarlane,** Malcolm David 1940- *AmMWSc 92*
**Macfarlane,** Malcolm Harris 1933- *AmMWSc 92*
**Macfarlane,** Neil *Who 92*
**Macfarlane,** Norman Somerville *IntWW 91*
**MacFarlane,** Robert, Jr 1930- *AmMWSc 92*
**MacFarlane,** Robert Goudie 1917- *Who 92*
**Macfarlane,** Roger Morton 1938- *AmMWSc 92*
**Macfarlane,** Ronald Duncan 1933- *AmMWSc 92*
**Macfarlane,** Ross Andrew 1954- *WhoAmL 92*
**Macfarlane,** William Thomson 1925- *Who 92*
**Macfarlane of Bearsden,** Baron 1926- *Who 92*
**MacFarquhar,** Roderick Lemonde 1930- *Who 92*
**MacFarren,** George 1813-1887 *NewAmDM*
**MacGee,** Joseph 1925- *AmMWSc 92*
**MacGibbon,** Barbara Haig 1928- *Who 92*
**MacGibbon,** Jean 1913- *IntAu&W 91, WrDr 92*
**MacGill,** George Roy Buchanan 1905- *Who 92*
**MacGillivray,** Archibald Dean 1929- *AmMWSc 92*
**MacGillivray,** Barron Bruce 1927- *Who 92*
**MacGillivray,** Ian 1920- *Who 92*
**MacGillivray,** Jeffrey Charles 1952- *AmMWSc 92*
**MacGillivray,** Lois Ann 1937- *WhoRel 92*
**MacGillivray,** M Ellen 1925- *AmMWSc 92*
**MacGillivray,** Margaret Hilda 1930- *AmMWSc 92*
**Macgillivray,** O A *WhoIns 92*
**MacGinnis,** Francis Robert 1924- *Who 92*
**MacGlashan,** Donald W, Jr 1953- *AmMWSc 92*
**MacGlashan,** Maureen Elizabeth 1938- *Who 92*
**Macgougan,** John 1913- *Who 92*
**MacGowan,** Alice 1858- *ScFEYrs*
**MacGowan,** Christopher 1948- *ConAu 133*
**MacGowan,** Daniel Jerome 1815-1893 *BiInAmS*
**Macgowan,** Jonathan *ConAu 134*
**Macgowan,** Kenneth 1888-1963 *BenetAL 91*
**Mac Gowan,** Mary Eugenia 1928- *WhoAmL 92*
**MacGrath,** Harold 1871-1932 *BenetAL 91*
**Mac Graw,** Ali 1939- *IntMPA 92, WhoEnt 92*
**MacGreevy,** Thomas 1893-1967 *LiExTwC*
**MacGregor,** Alexander William 1938- *AmMWSc 92*
**MacGregor,** C W 1908- *AmMWSc 92*
**Macgregor,** David Roy 1925- *IntAu&W 91*
**MacGregor,** Donald Max 1949- *AmMWSc 92, WhoMW 92*
**MacGregor,** Dorathea M 1925- *WhoAmP 91*
**MacGregor,** Douglas 1925- *AmMWSc 92*
**Macgregor,** Edwin 1931- *Who 92*
**MacGregor,** Elizabeth Ann 1941- *AmMWSc 92*
**MacGregor,** Geddes *Who 92*
**Macgregor,** Geddes 1909- *IntAu&W 91, WhoRel 92, WrDr 92*
**MacGregor,** Ian Duncan 1935- *AmMWSc 92*
**MacGregor,** Ian Kinloch 1912- *IntWW 91, Who 92*
**Macgregor,** James Grierson 1905- *IntAu&W 91*
**MacGregor,** James Grierson 1934- *AmMWSc 92*
**MacGregor,** James Murdoch *TwCSFW 91*
**Macgregor,** James Murdoch 1925- *WrDr 92*
**MacGregor,** John Geddes 1909- *Who 92*
**MacGregor,** John M. 1941- *ConAu 133*
**Macgregor,** John Malcolm 1946- *Who 92*
**MacGregor,** John Roddick Russell 1937- *IntWW 91, Who 92*
**Macgregor,** John Roy 1913- *Who 92*
**Macgregor,** Kenneth Robert 1906- *WhoIns 92*
**Macgregor,** Loren J 1950- *IntAu&W 91*
**MacGregor,** Malcolm Douglas 1945- *WhoRel 92*
**MacGregor,** Malcolm Herbert 1926- *AmMWSc 92*
**MacGregor,** Neil *Who 92*
**MacGregor,** Robert Neil 1946- *IntWW 91, Who 92*
**MacGregor,** Ronal Roy 1939- *AmMWSc 92*
**MacGregor,** Ronald John 1938- *AmMWSc 92*
**MacGregor,** Stephen Mayo 1957- *WhoRel 92*
**MacGregor,** Susan Katriona 1941- *Who 92*
**MacGregor,** Thomas Harold 1933- *AmMWSc 92*
**MacGregor,** W.Y. 1855-1923 *TwCPaSc*
**Macgregor-Hastie,** Roy Alasdhair Niall 1929- *IntAu&W 91*
**MacGregor of MacGregor,** Gregor 1925- *Who 92*
**MacGugan,** Douglas Campbell 1950- *WhoWest 92*
**MacGuigan,** Mark R. 1931- *IntWW 91, WrDr 92*
**MacGuigan,** Mark Rudolph 1931- *Who 92*
**Mach,** Alexander 1902-1980 *BiDExR*
**Mach,** David 1956- *TwCPaSc*
**Mach,** Donald Eugene 1936- *WhoEnt 92*
**Mach,** Elyse 1942- *WhoEnt 92*
**Mach,** George Robert 1928- *AmMWSc 92*
**Mach,** Martin Henry 1940- *AmMWSc 92, WhoWest 92*
**Mach,** Stanislaw 1938- *IntWW 91*
**Mach,** William Howard 1945- *AmMWSc 92*
**Macha Moup Guadh** *EncAmaz 91*
**Macha,** Milo 1918- *AmMWSc 92*
**Machac,** Josef 1954- *AmMWSc 92*
**Machacek,** Marie Esther 1947- *AmMWSc 92*
**Machacek,** Milos 1932- *AmMWSc 92*
**Machacek,** Oldrich 1930- *AmMWSc 92*
**Machado,** Alfredo C. d1991 *NewYTBS 91*
**Machado,** Antonio 1875-1939 *DcLB 108 [port]*
**Machado,** Clarence P. 1930- *WhoHisp 92*
**Machado,** David 1938- *WhoEnt 92*
**Machado,** Donald Carl, Sr. 1928- *WhoAmL 92*
**Machado,** Emilio Alfredo 1927- *AmMWSc 92*
**Machado,** Gus *WhoHisp 92*
**Machado,** Hector Antonio 1960- *WhoHisp 92*
**Machado,** Joao Somane 1946- *WhoRel 92*
**Machado,** Jose Luis 1951- *WhoHisp 92*
**Machado,** Julio 1965- *WhoHisp 92*
**Machado,** Lois N. 1945- *WhoHisp 92*
**Machado,** Manuel 1874-1947 *DcLB 108 [port]*
**Machado,** Manuel Antonio, Jr. 1939- *WhoHisp 92*
**Machado,** Melinda 1961- *WhoHisp 92*
**Machado,** Mike M. *WhoHisp 92*
**Machado,** Rodolfo 1942- *WhoHisp 92*
**Machado de Assis,** Joachim Maria 1839-1908 *BenetAL 91*
**Machado de Assis,** Joaquim Maria 1839-1908 *BlkLC [port]*
**MacHale,** Joseph P. 1951- *WhoFI 92*
**Machalek,** Milton David 1941- *AmMWSc 92*
**Machalinski,** Richard 1955- *WhoIns 92*
**Machanic,** Scott Lawrence 1952- *WhoAmL 92*
**Machara,** Joseph Andrew 1954- *WhoAmL 92*
**MacHarg,** Kenneth David Riley 1942- *WhoRel 92*
**Macharski,** Franciszek 1927- *IntWW 91, WhoRel 92*
**MacHatton,** Joseph Edward 1940- *WhoFI 92*
**Machaut,** Guillaume de 1300?-1377 *NewAmDM*
**Machavariani,** Aleksey Davidovich 1913- *SovUnBD*
**Mache,** Francois-Bernard 1935- *ConCom 92, IntWW 91*
**Machell,** Greville 1929- *AmMWSc 92*
**Machemehl,** Jerry Lee 1938- *AmMWSc 92*
**Machemer,** Paul Ewers 1919- *AmMWSc 92*
**Machemer,** Robert 1933- *AmMWSc 92*
**Machen,** Arthur 1863-1947 *RfGEnL 91*
**Machen,** Arthur Webster, Jr. 1920- *WhoAmL 92*
**Machen,** John Gresham 1881-1937 *RelLAm 91*
**Macher,** Frank E. 1941- *WhoMW 92*
**Macheret,** Aleksandr Venyaminovich 1896-1979 *SovUnBD*
**Macherey,** Robert E 1918- *AmMWSc 92*
**Machette,** Michael N 1949- *AmMWSc 92*
**Machi,** Anthony 1948- *WhoEnt 92*
**Machida,** Gerald Kiyoyuku 1937- *WhoAmP 91*
**Machiele,** Delwyn Earl 1938- *AmMWSc 92*
**Machin,** Arnold 1911- *TwCPaSc, Who 92*
**Machin,** David 1934- *IntAu&W 91, Who 92*
**Machin,** Edward Anthony 1925- *Who 92*
**Machin,** J 1937- *AmMWSc 92*
**Machin,** Kenneth Arthur 1936- *Who 92*
**Machinis,** Peter Alexander 1912- *WhoMW 92*

**Machito** 1915-1984 *FacFETw*
**Machle,** Edward Johnstone 1918- *WhoRel 92*
**Machleder,** Warren Harvey 1943- *AmMWSc 92*
**Machler,** Erwin 1925- *WhoFI 92*
**Machlin,** E S 1920- *AmMWSc 92*
**Machlin,** Irving 1919- *AmMWSc 92*
**Machlin,** Lawrence Judah 1927- *AmMWSc 92*
**Machlis,** Joseph *WhoEnt 92*
**Machlowitz,** Roy Alan 1921- *AmMWSc 92*
**Machlup,** Stefan 1927- *AmMWSc 92*
**Machne,** Xenia 1921- *AmMWSc 92*
**Machol,** Robert E 1917- *AmMWSc 92*
**Machold,** Roland Morris 1936- *WhoFI 92*
**Machon,** Richard Daniel 1946- *WhoWest 92*
**Machover,** Maurice 1931- *AmMWSc 92*
**Machover,** Tod 1953- *ConCom 92*
**Machray,** Robert 1831-1904 *RelLAm 91*
**Machray,** Robert 1945- *WhoEnt 92*
**Macht,** Martin Benzyl 1918- *AmMWSc 92*
**Macht,** Paul Michael 1956- *WhoFI 92*
**Machta,** Jonathan Lee 1951- *AmMWSc 92*
**Machtinger,** Lawrence Arnold 1936- *AmMWSc 92*
**Machtinger,** Leonard S. 1941- *WhoAmL 92*
**Machtley,** Ronald K. 1948- *AlmAP 92 [port], WhoAmP 91*
**Machuca-Carriel,** Alejandro 1953- *WhoHisp 92*
**Machuga,** Edward Theodore 1925- *WhoFI 92*
**Machulak,** Edward Leon 1926- *WhoMW 92*
**Machung,** Anne 1947- *ConAu 133*
**Machusko,** Andrew Joseph, Jr 1937- *AmMWSc 92*
**Maciag,** Gregory A 1947- *WhoIns 92*
**Maciag,** Thomas Edward 1946- *AmMWSc 92*
**Maciag,** William John, Jr 1936- *AmMWSc 92*
**Macias,** Edward S 1944- *AmMWSc 92*
**Macias,** Fernando R *WhoAmP 91*
**Macias,** Fernando R. 1952- *WhoHisp 92*
**Macias,** Jesus Diego 1933- *WhoHisp 92*
**Macias,** Jose Miguel *WhoHisp 92*
**Macias,** Manuel Jato 1929- *WhoHisp 92*
**Macias,** Norma A. 1953- *WhoHisp 92*
**Macias,** Reynaldo Flores *WhoHisp 92*
**Macias N.,** Felipe E. *WhoHisp 92*
**Macias Nguema Biyogo Negue Ndong,** F. 1924-1979 *HisDSpE*
**Maciejko,** Roman 1946- *AmMWSc 92*
**Maciel,** Gary Emmet 1935- *AmMWSc 92*
**Maciel,** Rene 1958- *WhoHisp 92*
**MacIlraith,** William 1961- *TwCPaSc*
**MacIlroy,** John Whittington 1946- *WhoAmL 92*
**MacInnes,** Archibald 1919- *Who 92*
**MacInnes,** Colin 1914-1976 *RfGEnL 91*
**MacInnes,** David Fenton, Jr 1943- *AmMWSc 92*
**MacInnes,** Hamish 1930- *Who 92*
**MacInnes,** Helen 1907-1985 *BenetAL 91, FacFETw*
**MacInnes,** Keith Gordon 1935- *Who 92*
**MacInnes,** Mairi *DrAPF 91*
**MacInnes,** Tom 1867-1951 *BenetAL 91*
**MacInnis,** Austin J 1931- *AmMWSc 92*
**MacInnis,** Cameron 1926- *AmMWSc 92*
**Macinnis,** Joseph Beverley 1937- *IntWW 91*
**MacInnis,** Martin Benedict 1925- *AmMWSc 92*
**MacIntosh,** Alexander John 1921- *WhoFI 92*
**Macintosh,** Farquhar 1923- *Who 92*
**MacIntosh,** Frank Campbell 1909- *AmMWSc 92, IntWW 91, Who 92*
**Macintosh,** Joan 1919- *Who 92*
**Macintosh,** Joan 1924- *WrDr 92*
**Macintosh,** Kerry Lynn 1957- *WhoAmL 92*
**MacIntosh,** Michael Kirk 1944- *WhoRel 92, WhoWest 92*
**MacIntosh,** Susan Caryl 1953- *WhoWest 92*
**Macintyre,** Alasdair 1929- *WrDr 92*
**MacIntyre,** Alasdair Chalmers 1929- *Who 92*
**Macintyre,** Angus Donald 1935- *Who 92*
**Macintyre,** Bruce Alexander 1942- *AmMWSc 92*
**MacIntyre,** Duncan 1915- *IntWW 91, Who 92*
**MacIntyre,** Elisabeth 1916- *WrDr 92*
**MacIntyre,** Giles T 1926- *AmMWSc 92*
**MacIntyre,** Iain 1924- *IntWW 91, Who 92*
**MacIntyre,** John R 1908- *AmMWSc 92*
**Macintyre,** Malcolm Neil 1919- *AmMWSc 92*
**Macintyre,** Stephen S 1947- *AmMWSc 92*
**Macintyre,** William Ian 1943- *Who 92*
**MacIntyre,** William James 1920- *AmMWSc 92*

**Macioce,** Frank Michael, Jr. 1945- *WhoAmL 92*
**Macioci,** R. Nikolas *DrAPF 91*
**Maciolek,** John A 1928- *AmMWSc 92*
**Maciolek,** Ralph Bartholomew 1939- *AmMWSc 92*
**Macior,** Lazarus Walter 1926- *AmMWSc 92*
**MacIsaac,** Fred 1886-1940 *ScFEYrs*
**MacIver,** Dale 1923- *WhoAmP 91*
**MacIver,** Donald Stuart 1927- *AmMWSc 92*
**MacIver,** Linda B. 1946- *WhoFI 92*
**MacIver,** Loren 1909- *IntWW 91*
**MacIver,** Lorne Dale 1923- *WhoAmL 92*
**Mack,** Alan Osborne 1918- *Who 92*
**Mack,** Alan Wayne 1947- *WhoMW 92*
**Mack,** Alexander Ross 1927- *AmMWSc 92*
**Mack,** Alistair 1955- *TwCPaSc*
**Mack,** Ally Faye 1943- *WhoBlA 92*
**Mack,** Astrid Karona 1935- *WhoBlA 92*
**Mack,** Brenda Lee 1940- *WhoWest 92*
**Mack,** Brian John 1949- *Who 92*
**Mack,** Cedric Manuel 1960- *WhoBlA 92*
**Mack,** Charles Daniel, III 1942- *WhoWest 92*
**Mack,** Charles Edward, Jr 1912- *AmMWSc 92*
**Mack,** Charles J. d1976 *LesBEnT 92*
**Mack,** Charles Lawrence, Jr 1926- *AmMWSc 92*
**Mack,** Charles Richard 1942- *WhoBlA 92*
**Mack,** Cleveland J., Sr. 1912- *WhoBlA 92*
**Mack,** Connie 1862-1956 *FacFETw*
**Mack,** Connie 1940- *WhoAmP 91*
**Mack,** Connie, III 1940- *AlmAP 92 [port], IntWW 91*
**Mack,** Curtis Lee 1942- *WhoAmL 92*
**Mack,** Daniel J. *WhoBlA 92*
**Mack,** David Barry 1959- *WhoMW 92*
**Mack,** David L 1940- *WhoAmP 91*
**Mack,** Dennis Wayne 1943- *WhoFI 92*
**Mack,** Dick A 1921- *AmMWSc 92*
**Mack,** Donald J. 1937- *WhoBlA 92*
**Mack,** Donald R 1925- *AmMWSc 92*
**Mack,** Donna *DrAPF 91*
**Mack,** Doris Ann 1945- *WhoMW 92*
**Mack,** E. James 1952- *WhoMW 92*
**Mack,** Earle Irving 1939- *WhoFI 92*
**Mack,** Edgar J. 1909- *WhoMW 92*
**Mack,** Edward John 1916- *WhoFI 92*
**Mack,** Faite 1919- *WhoBlA 92*
**Mack,** Francis Marion 1949- *WhoAmL 92*
**Mack,** Frank J. 1922- *WhoRel 92*
**Mack,** Fred Clarence 1940- *WhoBlA 92*
**Mack,** Frederick K 1924- *AmMWSc 92*
**Mack,** Gary W 1954- *AmMWSc 92*
**Mack,** Gladys Walker 1934- *WhoBlA 92*
**Mack,** Gordon H. 1927- *WhoBlA 92*
**Mack,** Harry John 1926- *AmMWSc 92*
**Mack,** James Carl 1948- *WhoWest 92*
**Mack,** James E. 1941- *WhoBlA 92*
**Mack,** James Patrick 1939- *AmMWSc 92*
**Mack,** Jan Cook 1948- *WhoWest 92*
**Mack,** Jeffrey G 1952- *WhoAmP 91*
**Mack,** Joan 1943- *WhoBlA 92*
**Mack,** Joanne Schateen 1957- *WhoWest 92*
**Mack,** John Edward 1947- *WhoFI 92*
**Mack,** John Edward, III 1934- *WhoFI 92*
**Mack,** John L. 1942- *WhoBlA 92*
**Mack,** John W. 1937- *WhoBlA 92*
**Mack,** Joseph S 1919- *WhoAmP 91*
**Mack,** Joseph Stephen 1947- *WhoWest 92*
**Mack,** Judi Ann 1951- *WhoMW 92*
**Mack,** Julia Cooper *WhoBlA 92*
**Mack,** Julia Cooper 1920- *WhoAmL 92*
**Mack,** Julie Cooper 1920- *WhoAmP 91*
**Mack,** Julius L 1930- *AmMWSc 92*
**Mack,** Katherine Foy 1958- *WhoWest 92*
**Mack,** Keith Robert 1933- *Who 92*
**Mack,** Kevin 1962- *WhoBlA 92*
**Mack,** Lawrence Lloyd 1942- *AmMWSc 92*
**Mack,** Lawrence R 1932- *AmMWSc 92*
**Mack,** Leslie Eugene 1929- *AmMWSc 92*
**Mack,** Louie 1923- *WhoAmP 91*
**Mack,** Lurene Kirkland 1948- *WhoBlA 92*
**Mack,** Mark Philip 1950- *AmMWSc 92, WhoFI 92*
**Mack,** Maynard 1909- *DcLB 111 [port], IntAu&W 91, WrDr 92*
**Mack,** Michael E 1939- *AmMWSc 92*
**Mack,** Michael J 1925- *AmMWSc 92*
**Mack,** Michael LaVoy 1959- *WhoRel 92*
**Mack,** Miranda 1955- *WhoBlA 92*
**Mack,** Nate 1956- *WhoBlA 92*
**Mack,** Paul Beymer 1956- *WhoAmL 92*
**Mack,** Pearl Willie 1941- *WhoBlA 92*
**Mack,** Phyllis Green 1941- *WhoBlA 92*
**Mack,** Richard A. d1963 *LesBEnT 92*
**Mack,** Richard Bruce 1928- *AmMWSc 92*
**Mack,** Richard Norton 1945- *AmMWSc 92*
**Mack,** Robert Emmet 1924- *AmMWSc 92*
**Mack,** Roderick O'Neal 1955- *WhoBlA 92*
**Mack,** Rudy Eugene, Sr. 1941- *WhoBlA 92*
**Mack,** Russel Travis 1945- *AmMWSc 92*

**Mack,** Seymour 1922- *AmMWSc 92*
**Mack,** Stephen W. 1954- *WhoFI 92, WhoMW 92*
**Mack,** Steven Ray 1956- *WhoMW 92*
**Mack,** Sylvia Jenkins 1931- *WhoBlA 92*
**Mack,** Ted d1976 *LesBEnT 92*
**Mack,** Theodore 1936- *WhoAmL 92*
**Mack,** Thomas McCulloch 1936- *AmMWSc 92*
**Mack,** Thomas Russell 1955- *WhoRel 92*
**Mack,** Timothy Patrick 1953- *AmMWSc 92*
**Mack,** Voyce J. 1921- *WhoBlA 92*
**Mack,** Walter Noel *AmMWSc 92*
**Mack,** Walter S. 1895-1990 *AnObit 1990*
**Mack,** Walter Staunton 1895-1990 *FacFETw*
**Mack,** Wilbur Ollio 1919- *WhoBlA 92*
**Mack,** William Joseph 1943- *WhoMW 92*
**Mack,** Winfred Berdell 1871?-1918 *BiInAmS*
**Mack Bride,** Johnny 1926- *TwCWW 91, WrDr 92*
**Mack Smith,** Denis 1920- *IntWW 91, Who 92, WrDr 92*
**Mackail,** Dennis 1892- *ScFEYrs*
**Mackal,** Roy Paul 1925- *AmMWSc 92*
**Mackaness,** George Bellamy 1922- *AmMWSc 92, Who 92*
**Mackauer,** Manfred 1932- *AmMWSc 92*
**Mackauf,** Stephen Henry 1945- *WhoAmL 92*
**Mackay** *Who 92*
**Mackay,** Alan Lindsay 1926- *Who 92*
**Mackay,** Alastair 1911- *Who 92*
**Mackay,** Alexander Russell 1911- *WhoWest 92*
**MacKay,** Andrew Dougal 1946- *WhoFI 92*
**MacKay,** Andrew James 1949- *Who 92*
**Mackay,** Arthur Stewart 1909- *Who 92*
**MacKay,** Buddy 1933- *WhoAmP 91*
**Mackay,** Charles 1927- *Who 92*
**Mackay,** Claire 1930- *WrDr 92*
**Mackay,** Claire Lorraine 1930- *IntAu&W 91*
**Mackay,** Colin Crichton 1943- *Who 92*
**MacKay,** Colin Francis 1926- *AmMWSc 92*
**MacKay,** Donald 1937- *WrDr 92*
**Mackay,** Donald Alexander Morgan 1926- *AmMWSc 92*
**MacKay,** Donald Douglas 1908- *AmMWSc 92*
**Mackay,** Donald George 1929- *Who 92*
**MacKay,** Donald Iain 1937- *Who 92*
**Mackay,** Donald Sage 1946- *Who 92*
**Mackay,** Edward 1936- *WhoMW 92*
**Mackay,** Eileen Alison 1943- *Who 92*
**Mackay,** Elmer MacIntosh 1936- *IntWW 91*
**Mackay,** Eric Beattie 1922- *IntAu&W 91, Who 92*
**Mackay,** Eric MacLachlan 1921- *Who 92*
**MacKay,** Faye L. *WhoRel 92*
**MacKay,** Francis Patrick 1929- *AmMWSc 92*
**Mackay,** George Patrick Gordon 1914- *Who 92*
**Mackay,** Gordon *Who 92*
**Mackay,** James Alexander 1936- *IntAu&W 91, WrDr 92*
**MacKay,** James R 1930- *WhoAmP 91*
**Mackay,** John 1914- *Who 92*
**Mackay,** John Alexander 1889-1983 *DcEcMov, RelLAm 91*
**MacKay,** John Warwick 1923- *AmMWSc 92*
**Mackay,** Kenneth 1859-1935 *ScFEYrs*
**Mackay,** Kenneth 1917- *Who 92*
**MacKay,** Kenneth Donald 1942- *AmMWSc 92*
**MacKay,** Kenneth Pierce, Jr 1939- *AmMWSc 92*
**Mackay,** Lottie Elizabeth Bohm 1927- *AmMWSc 92*
**MacKay,** Malcolm 1940- *WhoFI 92*
**MacKay,** Norman 1936- *Who 92*
**Mackay,** Peter 1940- *Who 92*
**Mackay,** Ralph Stuart 1924- *AmMWSc 92*
**Mackay,** Raymond Arthur 1939- *AmMWSc 92*
**Mackay,** Rosemary Joan 1936- *AmMWSc 92*
**Mackay,** Simon *WrDr 92*
**MacKay,** Vivian Louise 1947- *AmMWSc 92*
**Mackay,** W B F 1914- *AmMWSc 92*
**Mackay,** William Calder d1990 *Who 92N*
**Mackay,** William Charles 1939- *AmMWSc 92*
**Mackay Lewis,** Kenneth Frank *Who 92*
**Mackay of Ardbrecknish,** Baron 1938- *Who 92*
**Mackay Of Clashfern,** Baron 1927- *IntWW 91, Who 92*
**Mackaye,** Harold Steele 1866-1928 *ScFEYrs*
**MacKaye,** Percy 1875-1956 *BenetAL 91*
**MacKaye,** Steele 1842-1894 *BenetAL 91*

**Macke,** August 1887-1914 *FacFETw*
**Macke,** Gerald Fred 1939- *AmMWSc 92*
**Macke,** H Jerry 1922- *AmMWSc 92*
**Macke,** Harry Jerry 1922- *WhoMW 92*
**Macke,** Kenneth A. 1938- *WhoFI 92, WhoMW 92*
**MacKeigan,** Ian Malcolm 1915- *Who 92*
**Mackel,** Audley Maurice 1904- *WhoBlA 92*
**Mackel,** Audley Maurice, III 1955- *WhoBlA 92*
**Mackel,** Marilyn Hortense 1945- *WhoWest 92*
**MacKellar,** Alan Douglas 1936- *AmMWSc 92*
**MacKellar,** James Marsh 1931- *WhoRel 92*
**MacKellar,** Michael John Randal 1938- *IntWW 91*
**MacKellar,** William John 1935- *AmMWSc 92*
**Mackelworth,** R W 1930- *IntAu&W 91, TwCSFW 91, WrDr 92*
**Mackendrick,** Alexander 1912- *IntDcF 2-2 [port]*
**MacKendrick,** Donald Anthony 1925- *WhoAmP 91*
**MacKenna,** Robert Ogilvie 1913- *Who 92*
**MacKenna,** Tracy 1963- *TwCPaSc*
**MacKennal,** Bertrum 1863-1931 *TwCPaSc*
**MacKenroth,** Joyce Ellen 1946- *WhoWest 92*
**Mackensen,** August von 1849-1945 *EncTR 91*
**Mackensie,** Alan P 1932- *AmMWSc 92*
**Mackenzie** *Who 92*
**MacKenzie,** Alexander 1764-1820 *BenetAL 91*
**Mackenzie,** Alexander 1847-1935 *NewAmDM*
**Mackenzie,** Alexander Alwyne H. C. B. M. *Who 92*
**Mackenzie,** Alexander George Anthony A 1913- *Who 92*
**Mackenzie,** Allan *Who 92*
**Mackenzie,** Andrew Carr 1911- *IntAu&W 91, WrDr 92*
**MacKenzie,** Andrew Ross 1934- *WhoFI 92*
**MacKenzie,** Angus Finley 1932- *AmMWSc 92*
**Mackenzie,** Anne 1949- *WhoAmP 91*
**Mackenzie,** Archibald Robert Kerr 1915- *Who 92*
**Mackenzie,** Charles E 1943- *WhoAmP 91*
**Mackenzie,** Charles Westlake, III 1946- *AmMWSc 92*
**Mackenzie,** Colin Dalzell 1919- *Who 92*
**Mackenzie,** Colin Scott 1938- *Who 92*
**Mackenzie,** Compton 1883-1972 *RfGEnL 91*
**Mackenzie,** Compton 1883-1973 *FacFETw*
**Mackenzie,** Cortlandt John Gordon 1920- *AmMWSc 92*
**Mackenzie,** Cosmo Glenn 1907- *AmMWSc 92*
**Mackenzie,** Dana Nance 1958- *WhoMW 92*
**Mackenzie,** David 1927- *IntAu&W 91, WrDr 92*
**MacKenzie,** David Brindley 1927- *AmMWSc 92*
**Mackenzie,** David James Masterton 1905- *Who 92*
**Mackenzie,** David John 1929- *Who 92*
**MacKenzie,** David Robert 1941- *AmMWSc 92*
**Mackenzie,** David Webb 1956- *WhoEnt 92*
**Mackenzie,** Donald 1918- *IntAu&W 91, WrDr 92*
**Mackenzie,** Donald Matthew, Jr. 1944- *WhoRel 92*
**MacKenzie,** Donald Robertson 1921- *AmMWSc 92*
**MacKenzie,** Esmie 1887-1965 *TwCPaSc*
**Mackenzie,** Frederick Theodore 1934- *AmMWSc 92*
**MacKenzie,** George Allan 1931- *WhoFI 92, WhoMW 92*
**Mackenzie,** George Henry 1940- *AmMWSc 92*
**MacKenzie,** Gillian Rachel *Who 92*
**MacKenzie,** Ginny *DrAPF 91*
**MacKenzie,** Gregor *Who 92*
**MacKenzie,** Hector Uisdean 1940- *Who 92*
**Mackenzie,** Henry 1745-1831 *RfGEnL 91*
**Mackenzie,** Hugh Stirling 1913- *Who 92*
**Mackenzie,** Ian *WhoHisp 92*
**Mackenzie,** Ian 1914- *IntWW 91*
**Mackenzie,** Ian Clayton 1909- *Who 92*
**MacKenzie,** Innes Keith 1922- *AmMWSc 92*
**Mackenzie,** James 1924- *Who 92*
**MacKenzie,** James Alexander Mackintosh 1928- *Who 92*
**Mac Kenzie,** James Donald 1924- *WhoRel 92*
**MacKenzie,** James Gregor 1927- *Who 92*

**MacKenzie,** James Sargent Porteous 1916- *Who 92*
**MacKenzie,** James W 1925- *AmMWSc 92*
**Mackenzie,** Jean West *DrAPF 91*
**Mackenzie,** Jeremy John George 1941- *Who 92*
**MacKenzie,** Jill Whittier 1947- *WhoMW 92*
**Mackenzie,** Joan Finnigan 1925- *IntAu&W 91*
**Mackenzie,** John 1919- *WhoFI 92*
**Mackenzie,** John Alexander 1915- *Who 92*
**Mackenzie,** John Anderson Ross 1927- *WhoRel 92*
**Mackenzie,** John D 1926- *AmMWSc 92*
**Mackenzie,** Keith Roderick Turing d1990 *Who 92N*
**Mackenzie,** Kelvin Calder 1946- *IntAu&W 91, Who 92*
**Mackenzie,** Kenneth 1913-1955 *RfGEnL 91*
**Mackenzie,** Kenneth Alexander James 1859-1920 *BiInAmS*
**Mackenzie,** Kenneth Donald 1937- *WhoMW 92*
**Mackenzie,** Kenneth Edward 1910- *Who 92*
**MacKenzie,** Kenneth John 1943- *Who 92*
**Mackenzie,** Kenneth Roderick d1991 *Who 92N*
**Mackenzie,** Kenneth Victor 1911- *AmMWSc 92*
**MacKenzie,** Kenneth William Stewart 1915- *Who 92*
**MacKenzie,** Malcolm Kerr 1926- *WhoAmL 92*
**MacKenzie,** Malcolm R 1935- *AmMWSc 92*
**Mackenzie,** Maxwell Weir 1907- *IntWW 91, Who 92*
**Mackenzie,** Michael Philip 1937- *Who 92*
**Mackenzie,** Norman H. 1915- *WrDr 92*
**Mackenzie,** Norman Hugh 1915- *IntAu&W 91*
**Mackenzie,** Peter Douglas 1949- *Who 92*
**MacKenzie,** Richard D 1943- *WhoIns 92*
**Mackenzie,** Richard Stanley 1933- *AmMWSc 92*
**MacKenzie,** Robert Douglas 1928- *AmMWSc 92*
**MacKenzie,** Robert Earl 1920- *AmMWSc 92*
**MacKenzie,** Robert Earl 1941- *AmMWSc 92*
**MacKenzie,** Robert Tail 1867-1938 *TwCPaSc*
**Mackenzie,** Roderick McQuhae 1942- *Who 92*
**MacKenzie,** Scott, Jr 1920- *AmMWSc 92*
**MacKenzie,** Thomas D 1945- *WhoIns 92*
**Mackenzie,** Wallace John 1921- *Who 92*
**Mackenzie,** William James Millar 1909- *Who 92*
**Mackenzie Crooks,** Lewis 1909- *Who 92*
**Mackenzie of Gairloch** *Who 92*
**Mackenzie of Mornish,** John Hugh Munro 1925- *Who 92*
**Mackenzie Smith,** Peter 1946- *Who 92*
**Mackenzie Stuart** *Who 92*
**Mackenzie-Stuart,** Baron 1924- *Who 92*
**Mackenzie-Stuart of Dean,** Lord 1924- *IntWW 91*
**Mackeown,** James 1961- *TwCPaSc*
**Mackeown,** Thomas Frederick William 1904- *Who 92*
**MacKerell,** Alexander Donald, Jr 1959- *AmMWSc 92*
**Mackerer,** Carl Robert 1940- *AmMWSc 92*
**Mackerras,** Charles 1925- *IntWW 91, NewAmDM, Who 92*
**Mackerras,** Charles Mac Laurin 1925- *WhoEnt 92*
**Mackerras,** Colin Patrick 1939- *WrDr 92*
**Mackerras,** Colin Patrick 1949- *IntAu&W 91*
**Mackeson,** Rupert 1941- *Who 92*
**Mackesy,** Piers Gerald 1924- *IntAu&W 91, Who 92, WrDr 92*
**Mackevett,** Edward M 1918- *AmMWSc 92*
**Mackey,** Andrew, Jr. 1939- *WhoBlA 92*
**Mackey,** Bruce Ernest 1939- *AmMWSc 92*
**Mackey,** Dallas L. 1920- *WhoFI 92*
**Mackey,** Elizabeth Jocelyn 1927- *WhoEnt 92*
**Mackey,** Ernan *ConAu 34NR*
**Mackey,** George W 1916- *AmMWSc 92*
**Mackey,** George Whitelaw 1916- *IntWW 91*
**Mackey,** Henry James 1935- *AmMWSc 92*
**Mackey,** James E 1940- *AmMWSc 92*
**Mackey,** James P 1930- *AmMWSc 92*
**Mackey,** James Patrick 1934- *IntWW 91, Who 92*
**Mackey,** Jeffrey Allen 1952- *WhoRel 92*
**Mackey,** John *Who 92*
**Mackey,** Joseph K 1951- *WhoAmP 91*
**Mackey,** Joseph R, Jr 1950- *WhoAmP 91*
**Mackey,** Mary *DrAPF 91*
**Mackey,** Mary Lou 1945- *WhoEnt 92*
**Mackey,** Michael Charles 1942- *AmMWSc 92*
**Mackey,** Richard *WhoEnt 92*
**Mackey,** Robert George 1920- *WhoAmL 92*
**Mackey,** Robert Joseph 1946- *WhoMW 92*
**Mackey,** Sally 1930- *WhoRel 92*
**Mackey,** Sean Charles 1963- *WhoWest 92*
**Mackey,** Sheldon Elias 1913- *WhoRel 92*
**Mackey,** Stanley D. *WhoRel 92*
**Mackey,** William Arthur d1990 *Who 92N*
**Mackey,** William Arthur Godfrey 1946- *WhoFI 92*
**Mackey,** William Gawen 1924- *Who 92*
**Macki,** Jack W 1939- *AmMWSc 92*
**MacKichan,** Barry Bruce 1944- *AmMWSc 92*
**MacKichan,** Janis Jean 1951- *AmMWSc 92*
**Mackie** *Who 92*
**Mackie,** Alastair 1925- *ConPo 91, IntAu&W 91, WrDr 92*
**Mackie,** Alastair Cavendish Lindsay 1922- *Who 92*
**Mackie,** Andrew George 1927- *Who 92*
**MacKie,** Charles U. 1862-1920 *TwCPaSc*
**Mackie,** Clive David Andrew 1929- *Who 92*
**Mackie,** Daniel Glenn 1956- *WhoMW 92*
**Mackie,** Eric Dermott 1924- *Who 92*
**MacKie,** George 1920- *TwCPaSc, Who 92*
**Mackie,** George Alexander 1945- *AmMWSc 92*
**Mackie,** George Owen 1929- *AmMWSc 92, Who 92*
**Mackie,** Jerry *WhoAmP 91*
**Mackie,** Lily Edna Minerva 1926- *Who 92*
**Mackie,** Maitland 1912- *Who 92*
**Mackie,** Margaret Davidson 1914- *WrDr 92*
**Mackie,** Philip 1918- *IntAu&W 91*
**Mackie,** Richard John 1933- *AmMWSc 92, WhoWest 92*
**Mackie,** Robert Gordon 1940- *IntWW 91, WhoEnt 92*
**Mackie,** Shirley M. 1929- *WhoEnt 92*
**Mackie-Mason,** Jeffrey King 1959- *WhoFI 92, WhoMW 92*
**Mackie of Benshie,** Baron 1919- *Who 92*
**Mackiewicz,** Aleksander 1944- *IntWW 91*
**Mackiewicz,** Edward Robert 1951- *WhoAmL 92*
**Mackiewicz,** John Stanley 1930- *AmMWSc 92*
**Mackilligin,** David Patrick Robert 1939- *Who 92*
**Mackin,** Catherine d1982 *LesBEnT 92*
**Mackin,** Don 1937- *WhoAmP 91*
**Mackin,** Dorothy Mae 1917- *WhoEnt 92*
**Mackin,** Edward *ConAu 34NR*
**Mackin,** Jeanne 1951- *ConAu 134*
**Mackin,** Robert Brian 1960- *AmMWSc 92*
**Mackin,** Robert James, Jr 1925- *AmMWSc 92, WhoWest 92*
**Mackin,** Shari Lee 1966- *WhoFI 92*
**Mackin,** Theodore James 1922- *WhoRel 92*
**Mackin,** William Michael *AmMWSc 92*
**MacKinlay,** Bruce 1912- *Who 92*
**Mackinlay,** Leila 1910- *WrDr 92*
**Mackinlay,** Leila Antoinette Sterling 1910- *IntAu&W 91*
**Mackinley,** Elizabeth 1965- *TwCPaSc*
**MacKinney,** Archie Allen, Jr 1929- *AmMWSc 92*
**MacKinney,** Arland Lee 1931- *AmMWSc 92*
**Mackinney,** Herbert William 1907- *AmMWSc 92*
**MacKinney,** Loren Carey 1891-1963 *DcNCBi 4*
**Mackinnon,** Anne *WhoAmP 91*
**MacKinnon,** Catharine A. *NewYTBS 91 [port]*
**MacKinnon,** Catherine A. 1947- *WrDr 92*
**MacKinnon,** Donald MacKenzie 1913- *Who 92*
**MacKinnon,** Edward Michael 1928 *WhoWest 92*
**MacKinnon,** George E. 1906- *WhoAmL 92*
**Mac Kinnon,** Gregory Aloysius 1925- *WhoRel 92*
**MacKinnon,** Nancy W 1925- *WhoAmP 91*
**Mackinnon,** Patricia *Who 92*
**MacKinnon,** Sine 1901- *TwCPaSc*
**MacKinnon,** Stephen Robert 1940- *ConAu 36NR*
**Mackinnon,** Una Patricia 1911- *Who 92*
**Mackintosh** *Who 92*
**Mackintosh,** Allan Roy 1936- *Who 92*
**Mackintosh,** Athole S. 1926-1977 *ConAu 134*
**Mackintosh,** Cameron 1946- *ConTFT 9, CurBio 91 [port], WhoEnt 92*
**Mackintosh,** Cameron Anthony 1946- *IntWW 91, Who 92*
**Mackintosh,** Charles Rennie 1868-1928 *DcTwDes, FacFETw, TwCPaSc*
**Mackintosh,** Duncan Robert d1991 *Who 92N*
**MacKintosh,** Frederick Roy 1943- *WhoWest 92*
**Mackintosh,** James Buckton 1856-1891 *BiInAmS*
**Mackintosh,** John Malcolm 1921- *Who 92*
**Mackintosh,** Malcolm *Who 92*
**Mackintosh,** Margaret *TwCPaSc*
**Mackintosh,** Nicholas John 1935- *IntWW 91, Who 92*
**Mackintosh of Halifax,** Viscount 1958- *Who 92*
**Mackintosh of Mackintosh,** Lachlan Ronald 1928- *Who 92*
**Mackiw,** Vladimir Nicolaus 1923- *AmMWSc 92*
**Macklem,** Peter Tiffany 1931- *AmMWSc 92*
**Macklen,** Victor Harry Burton 1919- *Who 92*
**Mackler,** Bruce 1920- *AmMWSc 92*
**Mackler,** Bruce F 1942- *AmMWSc 92*
**Mackler,** Saul Allen 1913- *AmMWSc 92*
**Mackles,** Leonard 1929- *AmMWSc 92*
**Mackley,** Ian Warren 1942- *Who 92*
**Macklin,** Anderson D. *WhoBlA 92*
**Macklin,** Bruce 1917- *Who 92*
**Macklin,** Charles 1699-1797 *RfGEnL 91*
**Macklin,** David Drury 1928- *Who 92*
**Macklin,** Elizabeth *DrAPF 91*
**Macklin,** F. Douglas *WhoRel 92*
**Macklin,** John Lee 1933- *WhoMW 92*
**Macklin,** John W. 1939- *WhoBlA 92*
**Macklin,** John Welton 1939- *AmMWSc 92*
**Macklin,** Larry D *WhoAmP 91*
**Macklin,** Martin 1934- *AmMWSc 92*
**Macklin,** Martin Rodbell 1934- *WhoMW 92*
**Macklin,** Philip Alan 1925- *AmMWSc 92, WhoMW 92*
**Macklin,** Richard Lawrence 1920- *AmMWSc 92*
**Macklin,** Ruth 1938- *AmMWSc 92*
**Macklin,** William Edward 1945- *WhoAmP 91*
**Mackman,** Nigel 1959- *AmMWSc 92*
**Mackmurdo,** Arthur Heygate 1851-1942 *DcTwDes*
**Macknight,** Anthony Dunstan Crawfurd 1938- *IntWW 91*
**Macknight,** Ella 1904- *Who 92*
**Mac Knight,** James *WhoRel 92*
**Macknight,** Thomas *DcNCBi 4*
**Mac Knight,** William John 1936- *AmMWSc 92*
**Macko,** Douglas John 1943- *AmMWSc 92*
**Macko,** Spencer Allan 1964- *WhoMW 92*
**Macko,** Stephen Alexander 1951- *AmMWSc 92*
**Mackoul,** Sabry Joseph 1940- *WhoFI 92*
**MacKow,** Erich Reuter 1956- *WhoWest 92*
**Mackowiak,** Elaine DeCusatis 1940- *AmMWSc 92*
**Mackowski,** William D 1916- *WhoAmP 91*
**Macksey,** Harry Michael 1947- *AmMWSc 92*
**Macksey,** K J 1923- *IntAu&W 91, WrDr 92*
**Macksey,** Kenneth John 1923- *Who 92*
**Mackson,** Chester John 1919- *AmMWSc 92*
**Mackulak,** Gerald Thomas 1952- *AmMWSc 92*
**Mackus,** Algimantas 1932-1964 *LiExTwC*
**Mackway-Girardi,** Ann Marie 1943- *AmMWSc 92*
**Mackworth,** Cecily *IntAu&W 91, WrDr 92*
**Mackworth,** David Arthur Geoffrey 1912- *Who 92*
**Mackworth-Young,** Robert Christopher 1920- *Who 92*
**Macky,** Peter Wallace 1937- *WhoRel 92*
**MacLachlan,** Alexander 1933- *WhoFI 92*
**Maclachlan,** Gordon Alistair 1930- *AmMWSc 92*
**MacLachlan,** James Angell 1938- *AmMWSc 92*
**MacLachlan,** James Crawford 1923- *AmMWSc 92*
**MacLachlan,** James M. d1991 *NewYTBS 91*
**MacLachlan,** Janet A. *WhoBlA 92*
**MacLachlan,** Janet Angel *WhoEnt 92*
**MacLachlan,** Kyle 1959?- *ConTFT 9*
**Mac Lachlan,** Kyle 1960- *IntMPA 92, WhoEnt 92*
**MacLachlan,** Patricia *WrDr 92*
**Maclagan,** Michael 1914- *Who 92, WrDr 92*
**Maclagan,** Philip D. 1901-1972 *TwCPaSc*
**Maclaine,** Allan H 1924- *IntAu&W 91, WrDr 92*
**Maclaine,** Archibald 1728-1790 *DcNCBi 4*
**Mac Laine,** Shirley 1934- *IntMPA 92, IntWW 91, RelLAm 91, WhoEnt 92, WrDr 92*
**MacLane,** Jack *WrDr 92*
**MacLane,** Saunders 1909- *AmMWSc 92, IntWW 91, WhoMW 92*
**MacLaren,** A. Allan 1938- *WrDr 92*
**Mac Laren,** David Sergeant 1931- *WhoFI 92*
**Mac Laren,** David Sergeant 1941- *WhoMW 92*
**Maclaren,** Donald 1886-1917 *TwCPaSc*
**MacLaren,** Hamish Duncan d1990 *Who 92N*
**Maclaren,** Ian *IntAu&W 91X*
**Maclaren,** James Henry 1864-1928 *AmPeW*
**MacLaren,** Malcolm Donald 1936- *AmMWSc 92*
**Maclaren,** Noel K 1939- *AmMWSc 92*
**Maclaren,** Peter 1964- *TwCPaSc*
**MacLaren,** Richard Oliver 1924- *AmMWSc 92*
**MacLaren,** Walter Rogers 1910- *WhoWest 92*
**MacLatchy,** Cyrus Shantz 1941- *AmMWSc 92*
**MacLauchlin,** Robert Kerwin 1931- *WhoEnt 92, WhoWest 92*
**MacLaughlin,** Douglas Earl 1938- *AmMWSc 92*
**MacLaughlin,** Harry Hunter 1927- *WhoAmL 92, WhoMW 92*
**Maclaurin,** Colin 1698-1746 *BlkwCEP*
**MacLaurin,** Ian 1937- *Who 92*
**MacLaurin,** Ian Charter 1937- *IntWW 91*
**Maclaurin,** Richard Cockburn 1870-1920 *BiInAmS*
**Maclaurin,** Robert 1961- *TwCPaSc*
**MacLaury,** Michael Risley 1943- *AmMWSc 92*
**MacLaury,** Richard Joyce 1918- *WhoAmL 92*
**MacLaverty,** Bernard 1942- *ConNov 91*
**Maclay** *Who 92*
**Maclay,** Baron 1942- *Who 92*
**Maclay,** Charles Wylie 1929- *AmMWSc 92*
**Maclay,** G Jordan 1942- *AmMWSc 92*
**Maclay,** James 1864-1919 *BiInAmS*
**Maclay,** William Nevin 1924- *AmMWSc 92*
**Maclean,** Lord 1916-1990 *AnObit 1990*
**MacLean,** Lord 1938- *Who 92*
**Maclean,** Alasdair 1926- *ConPo 91, WrDr 92*
**MacLean,** Alistair 1922-1987 *TwCWW 91*
**MacLean,** Angus Dhu 1877-1937 *DcNCBi 4*
**MacLean,** Annie Marion 1870?-1934 *WomSoc*
**MacLean,** Art *WrDr 92*
**Maclean,** Arthur *IntAu&W 91X, TwCSFW 91, WrDr 92*
**MacLean,** Babcock 1946- *WhoAmL 92*
**MacLean,** Barbara Barondess 1907- *WhoEnt 92*
**MacLean,** Barry L. 1938- *WhoMW 92*
**MacLean,** Bonnie Kuseske 1942- *AmMWSc 92*
**Mac Lean,** Charles Rex 1912- *WhoAmL 92*
**MacLean,** David Andrew 1952- *AmMWSc 92*
**MacLean,** David Bailey 1923- *AmMWSc 92*
**MacLean,** David Belmont 1941- *AmMWSc 92*
**MacLean,** David Cameron 1933- *AmMWSc 92*
**Maclean,** David John 1953- *Who 92*
**Maclean,** Donald 1930- *Who 92*
**Maclean,** Donald Isadore 1929- *AmMWSc 92*
**MacLean,** Donald Murdo d1991 *Who 92N*
**Maclean,** Eileen *WhoAmP 91*
**Maclean,** Euan 1929- *Who 92*
**Maclean,** Fitzroy 1911- *IntAu&W 91, WrDr 92*
**MacLean,** Gary Earl 1949- *WhoMW 92*
**Maclean,** Graeme Stanley 1950 *AmMWSc 92*
**MacLean,** Hector Charles Donald 1908- *Who 92*
**Maclean,** Hector Ronald 1931- *Who 92*
**Maclean,** Iain Stewart 1956- *WhoRel 92*
**MacLean,** J. Angus 1914- *IntWW 91*
**Maclean,** John 1771-1814 *BiInAmS*
**MacLean,** John Alexander 1903- *Who 92*
**MacLean,** John Angus 1914- *Who 92*
**MacLean,** John Duncan 1929- *WhoFI 92*
**Maclean,** Katherine 1925- *IntAu&W 91, TwCSFW 91, WrDr 92*
**Maclean,** Kenneth *DrAPF 91*
**MacLean,** Kenneth Smedley 1914- *Who 92*
**Maclean,** Lachlan Hector Charles 1942- *Who 92*
**MacLean,** Lloyd Douglas 1924- *AmMWSc 92*
**MacLean,** Murdo 1943- *Who 92*
**Maclean,** Norman 1902-1990 *TwCWW 91*

**MacLean,** Paul Donald 1913- *AmMWSc 92*
**MacLean,** Peter Duncan 1930- *WhoRel 92*
**MacLean,** Ranald Norman Munro *Who 92*
**Maclean,** Robert 1908- *Who 92*
**MacLean,** Sorley 1911- *ConPo 91, WrDr 92*
**MacLean,** Stephen Frederick, Jr 1943- *AmMWSc 92*
**MacLean,** Wallace H 1931- *AmMWSc 92*
**Maclean,** Walter M 1924- *AmMWSc 92*
**Maclean,** Will 1941- *TwCPaSc*
**Maclean,** William 1757-1828 *DcNCBi 4*
**MacLean,** William C, Jr 1940- *AmMWSc 92*
**MacLean,** William Plannette, III 1943- *AmMWSc 92*
**MacLean,** William Q, Jr 1934- *WhoAmP 91*
**Maclean of Dochgarroch,** Allan Murray 1950- *Who 92*
**Maclean of Dunconnel,** Fitzroy 1911- *IntWW 91*
**Maclean of Dunconnel,** Fitzroy Hew 1911- *Who 92*
**MacLeary,** Alistair Ronald 1940- *Who 92*
**MacLeary,** Donald Whyte 1937- *Who 92*
**Macleay,** John Henry James 1931- *Who 92*
**MacLeay,** Ronald E 1935- *AmMWSc 92*
**Maclehose** *Who 92*
**MacLehose of Beoch,** Baron 1917- *IntWW 91, Who 92*
**MacLeish,** Andrew 1923- *WhoMW 92*
**MacLeish,** Archibald 1892-1982 *BenetAL 91, ConLC 68 [port], FacFETw [port], LiExTwC*
**MacLeish,** Rod *LesBEnT 92*
**MacLellan,** Andrew Patrick 1925- *Who 92*
**MacLellan,** George Douglas Stephen 1922- *Who 92*
**MacLellan,** Patrick *Who 92*
**MacLellan,** Robin d1991 *Who 92N*
**MacLennan,** Alastair 1912- *Who 92*
**MacLennan,** Alastair 1943- *TwCPaSc*
**MacLennan,** Carol G 1938- *AmMWSc 92*
**MacLennan,** David Herman 1937- *AmMWSc 92*
**MacLennan,** David Ross 1945- *Who 92*
**MacLennan,** Donald Allan 1936- *AmMWSc 92*
**Maclennan,** Duncan 1949- *Who 92*
**MacLennan,** Graeme Andrew Yule 1942- *Who 92*
**MacLennan,** Hugh d1990 *IntWW 91N, Who 92N*
**MacLennan,** Hugh 1907- *BenetAL 91, IntAu&W 91*
**MacLennan,** Hugh 1907-1990 *AnObit 1990, CurBio 91N, FacFETw, RfGEnL 91*
**Maclennan,** Robert Adam Ross 1936- *IntWW 91, Who 92*
**Macleod** *Who 92*
**Macleod,** Alison 1920- *IntAu&W 91, WrDr 92*
**MacLeod,** Alistair 1936- *WrDr 92*
**MacLeod,** Angus d1991 *Who 92N*
**MacLeod,** Aubrey Seymour H. *Who 92*
**MacLeod,** Calum Alexander 1935- *Who 92*
**MacLeod,** Carol Louise *AmMWSc 92*
**MacLeod,** Charlotte 1922- *IntAu&W 91, WrDr 92*
**MacLeod,** Denis Frederick 1954- *WhoMW 92*
**Macleod,** Donald 1913- *WhoRel 92*
**MacLeod,** Donald Alexander 1938- *Who 92*
**MacLeod,** Donald Francis Graham 1917- *Who 92*
**MacLeod,** Donald Iain Archibald 1945- *AmMWSc 92*
**MacLeod,** Ellen Jane *WrDr 92*
**Macleod,** Ellen Jane 1918- *IntAu&W 91*
**MacLeod,** Ellis Gilmore 1928- *AmMWSc 92*
**Macleod,** Fiona *RfGEnL 91*
**Macleod,** Gavin 1931- *IntMPA 92, WhoEnt 92*
**MacLeod,** George F. d1991 *NewYTBS 91 [port]*
**Macleod,** Hugh Angus 1933- *AmMWSc 92*
**Macleod,** Hugh Angus McIntosh 1933- *WhoWest 92*
**MacLeod,** Hugh Roderick 1929- *Who 92*
**MacLeod,** Iain Alasdair 1939- *Who 92*
**Macleod,** Ian Buchanan 1933- *Who 92*
**MacLeod,** Jean S. 1908- *WrDr 92*
**Macleod,** Jean Sutherland 1908- *IntAu&W 91*
**MacLeod,** John Alexander 1945- *AmMWSc 92*
**Macleod,** John Amend 1942- *WhoFI 92*
**MacLeod,** John Daniel, Jr. 1922- *WhoRel 92*
**MacLeod,** John James Rickard 1876-1935 *WhoNob 90*
**MacLeod,** John Maxwell 1952- *Who 92*
**MacLeod,** John Munroe 1937- *AmMWSc 92*
**MacLeod,** Kathleen Bromley 1953- *WhoWest 92*
**MacLeod,** Lloyd Beck 1930- *AmMWSc 92*
**MacLeod,** Maxwell *Who 92*
**MacLeod,** Michael Christopher 1947- *AmMWSc 92*
**Macleod,** Nathaniel William Hamish 1940- *Who 92*
**Macleod,** Nigel Ronald Buchanan 1936- *Who 92*
**MacLeod,** Norman Cloud 1931- *WhoWest 92*
**MacLeod,** Norman Donald 1932- *Who 92*
**Macleod,** Robert *IntAu&W 91X, WrDr 92*
**Macleod,** Robert 1906- *IntAu&W 91, TwCWW 91*
**MacLeod,** Robert Angus 1921- *AmMWSc 92*
**Macleod,** Robert M *AmMWSc 92*
**MacLeod,** Robert Meredith 1929- *AmMWSc 92*
**MacLeod,** Roderick *Who 92*
**MacLeod,** Roderick 1892?-1984 *FacFETw*
**MacLeod,** Sheila 1939- *TwCSFW 91, WrDr 92*
**MacLeod,** Stuart Maxwell 1943- *AmMWSc 92*
**Macleod of Borve,** Baroness 1915- *Who 92*
**MacLeod of Fuinary,** Baron d1991 *Who 92N*
**MacLeod of MacLeod,** John 1935- *Who 92*
**Macleod-Smith,** Alastair Macleod 1916- *Who 92*
**MacLiammoir,** Micheal 1899-1978 *FacFETw*
**Maclin,** Ernest 1931- *AmMWSc 92*
**Maclin,** Harry Tracy, Jr. 1925- *WhoRel 92*
**Maclin,** Melvin M. 1929- *WhoBlA 92N*
**Macloskie,** George 1834-1920 *BiInAmS*
**Mac Low,** Jackson *DrAPF 91*
**Mac Low,** Jackson 1922- *ConPo 91, IntAu&W 91, WrDr 92*
**Maclure,** John 1934- *Who 92*
**Maclure,** Stuart 1926- *Who 92*
**Maclure,** William 1763-1840 *BiInAmS*
**MacMahan,** Horace Arthur, Jr 1928- *AmMWSc 92*
**MacMahon,** Aline d1991 *NewYTBS 91 [port]*
**Mac Mahon,** Aline 1899- *IntMPA 92*
**Macmahon,** Arthur W. 1890-1980 *ConAu 135*
**MacMahon,** Brian 1923- *AmMWSc 92, IntWW 91*
**Macmahon,** Bryan Michael 1909- *IntAu&W 91, WrDr 92*
**MacMahon,** Gerald John 1909- *Who 92*
**MacMahon,** Harold Edward 1901- *AmMWSc 92*
**MacMahon,** James A 1939- *AmMWSc 92*
**MacMahon,** Will *ScFEYrs*
**MacManamy,** Gary Allan 1946- *WhoRel 92*
**MacManus,** John Leslie Edward 1920- *Who 92*
**MacManus,** Susan Ann 1947- *WhoFI 92*
**MacMaster,** Douglas Joseph, Jr. 1930- *WhoFI 92*
**Macmaster,** Robert Ellsworth 1919- *WrDr 92*
**Macmiadhachain,** Padraig 1929- *TwCPaSc*
**Macmillan** *Who 92*
**Macmillan and Company** *DcLB 106*
**Macmillan,** Barclay and Macmillan *DcLB 106*
**Macmillan,** A d1896 *DcLB 106 [port]*
**Macmillan,** Alexander 1940- *WhoAmL 92*
**Macmillan,** Alexander McGregor Graham 1920- *Who 92*
**Macmillan,** Alexander Ross 1922- *Who 92*
**MacMillan,** Andrew 1928- *Who 92*
**Macmillan,** Chrystal 1872-1937 *BiDBrF 2*
**Macmillan,** D d1857 *DcLB 106 [port]*
**MacMillan,** David Paul 1943- *WhoFI 92*
**MacMillan,** Donald B. 1874-1970 *BenetAL 91*
**MacMillan,** Douglas Clark 1912- *AmMWSc 92*
**MacMillan,** Ernest 1893-1973 *NewAmDM*
**Macmillan,** Gilleasbuig Iain 1942- *Who 92*
**Macmillan,** Graham *Who 92*
**Macmillan,** Harold 1894-1986 *FacFETw [port]*
**Macmillan,** Iain Alexander 1923- *Who 92*
**MacMillan,** J H 1928- *AmMWSc 92*
**MacMillan,** Jake *Who 92*
**MacMillan,** Jake 1924- *IntWW 91*
**MacMillan,** James 1959- *ConCom 92*
**MacMillan,** James G 1942- *AmMWSc 92*
**MacMillan,** John 1924- *Who 92*
**MacMillan,** John Richard Alexander 1932- *Who 92*
**MacMillan,** Joseph Edward 1930- *AmMWSc 92*
**Macmillan,** Kenneth 1929- *FacFETw, IntWW 91, Who 92*
**MacMillan,** Kip Van Metre 1937- *WhoMW 92*
**Macmillan,** Matthew 1926- *Who 92*
**Macmillan,** Norman Hillas 1941- *AmMWSc 92*
**MacMillan,** Patti 1947- *WhoAmP 91*
**Macmillan,** Robert Hugh 1921- *Who 92*
**Macmillan,** Robert S 1924- *AmMWSc 92*
**Macmillan,** Robert Smith 1924- *WhoFI 92, WhoWest 92*
**Macmillan,** Wallace 1913- *Who 92*
**Macmillan,** William Boyd Robertson 1927- *Who 92*
**Macmillan,** William Hooper 1923- *AmMWSc 92*
**MacMillan,** William Wallace 1927- *WhoAmL 92*
**Macmillan of Ovenden,** Viscount 1974- *Who 92*
**MacMillen,** Richard Edward 1932- *AmMWSc 92*
**MacMillian,** Stuart A 1951- *AmMWSc 92*
**MacMinn,** Richard Dean 1946- *WhoFI 92*
**MacMullen,** Clinton William 1909- *AmMWSc 92*
**MacMullen,** Douglas Burgoyne 1919- *WhoWest 92*
**MacMullen,** Neil Harvard 1938- *WhoEnt 92*
**Mac Murray,** Fred 1908- *IntMPA 92*
**MacMurray,** Fred 1908-1991 *NewYTBS 91 [port], News 92-2*
**MacMurray,** Helen Marie 1960- *WhoAmL 92*
**MacMurray,** Mary Bell McMillan *Who 92*
**MacMurrough,** Eva *EncAmaz 91*
**Macnab,** Geoffrey 1899- *Who 92*
**MacNab,** Iain 1890-1967 *TwCPaSc*
**Macnab,** P. A. 1903- *WrDr 92*
**Macnab,** Robert Marshall 1940- *AmMWSc 92*
**Macnab,** Roy 1923- *ConPo 91, WrDr 92*
**Macnab,** Roy Martin 1923- *IntAu&W 91*
**Macnab of Macnab,** James Charles 1926- *Who 92*
**MacNabb,** Byron Gordon 1910- *IntWW 91*
**Macnaghten,** Patrick 1927- *Who 92*
**Macnaghten,** Robin Donnelly 1927- *Who 92*
**Macnair,** Maurice John Peter 1919- *Who 92*
**MacNair,** Ralph 1742-1784 *DcNCBi 4*
**Macnair,** Richard Nelson 1929- *AmMWSc 92*
**MacNamara,** Brinsley 1890-1963 *RfGEnL 91*
**MacNamara,** Laurie Jo 1963- *WhoRel 92*
**Macnamara,** Thomas E 1929- *AmMWSc 92*
**MacNamee,** James K 1916- *AmMWSc 92*
**Macnaughtan,** Don 1939- *WhoAmP 91*
**Macnaughtan,** Donald, Jr 1939- *AmMWSc 92*
**MacNaughton,** Angus Athole 1931- *IntWW 91, WhoFI 92, WhoWest 92*
**MacNaughton,** Donald Sinclair 1917- *IntWW 91, WhoFI 92*
**MacNaughton,** Earl Bruce 1919- *AmMWSc 92*
**Macnaughton,** Iris Carruthers *TwCPaSc*
**Macnaughton,** Malcolm 1925- *Who 92*
**Macnaughton,** Malcolm Campbell 1925- *IntWW 91*
**Mac Naughton,** Robert 1966- *IntMPA 92*
**MacNaughton Turner,** Ann Louise 1948- *WhoAmL 92*
**Macneacail,** Aonghas 1942- *IntAu&W 91*
**Macnee,** Alan B 1920- *AmMWSc 92*
**Macnee,** Alan Breck 1920- *WhoMW 92*
**Macnee,** Patrick 1922- *WhoEnt 92*
**Macneice,** Corinna *TwCPaSc*
**MacNeice,** Louis 1907-1963 *FacFETw, RfGEnL 91*
**MacNeil,** Cornell 1922- *NewAmDM*
**MacNeil,** Cornell Hill 1922- *IntWW 91*
**Macneil,** Duncan *IntAu&W 91X, WrDr 92*
**MacNeil,** Hugh S 1925- *WhoAmP 91*
**Macneil,** Ian Roderick 1929- *WhoAmL 92, WrDr 92*
**MacNeil,** Joseph H 1931- *AmMWSc 92*
**MacNeil,** Joseph Neil *Who 92*
**Mac Neil,** Joseph Neil 1924- *WhoRel 92*
**MacNeil,** Michael 1952- *AmMWSc 92*
**MacNeil,** Robert *LesBEnT 92 [port]*
**Macneil,** Robert 1931- *IntAu&W 91*
**Macneil of Barra,** Ian Roderick 1929- *Who 92*
**MacNeill,** Ben Dixon 1889-1960 *DcNCBi 4*
**MacNeill,** Ian B 1931- *AmMWSc 92*
**MacNeill,** Janet Smith 1720-1791 *DcNCBi 4*
**MacNeish,** Richard Stockton 1918- *IntWW 91*
**Mac Nelly,** Jeffrey Kenneth 1947- *WhoMW 92*
**MacNeven,** William James 1763-1841 *BiInAmS*
**MacNichol,** Edward Ford, Jr 1918- *AmMWSc 92*
**Mac Nicol,** Peter 1954- *IntMPA 92*
**MacNider,** George Mallett 1884-1917 *BiInAmS*
**MacNider,** William de Berniere 1881-1951 *DcNCBi 4*
**MacNintch,** John Edwin 1935- *AmMWSc 92*
**Macnish,** James Martin, Jr. 1935- *WhoAmL 92*
**MacNish,** Linda J. *WhoEnt 92*
**Maco,** Paul Stephen, Jr. 1952- *WhoAmL 92*
**Macom,** Arthur *ScFEYrs*
**Macomber,** Harold M *WhoAmP 91*
**Macomber,** Hilliard Kent 1933- *AmMWSc 92*
**Macomber,** John D. 1928- *WhoFI 92*
**Macomber,** Richard Wiltz 1932- *AmMWSc 92*
**Macomber,** Thomas Wesson 1912- *AmMWSc 92*
**Macon,** Irene Elizabeth 1935- *WhoFI 92, WhoMW 92*
**Macon,** Jane Haun 1946- *WhoAmL 92*
**Macon,** Nathaniel 1758-1837 *AmPolLe, DcNCBi 4*
**Macon,** Nathaniel 1926- *AmMWSc 92*
**Macon,** Norman *WhoBlA 92*
**Macon,** Richard Laurence 1944- *WhoAmL 92*
**Macon,** Uncle Dave 1870-1952 *NewAmDM*
**Macon,** William Hartwell 1923- *WhoAmP 91*
**Maconchy,** Elizabeth 1907- *ConCom 92, NewAmDM, Who 92*
**Maconi,** Richard Curtis 1922- *WhoFI 92*
**Macosko,** Christopher Ward 1944- *AmMWSc 92*
**Macouda** *EncAmaz 91*
**Macoun,** Michael John 1914- *Who 92*
**Macovescu,** George 1913- *IntWW 91*
**Macovski,** Albert 1929- *AmMWSc 92*
**Macoy,** Ian Wilson 1963- *WhoFI 92*
**MacPeek,** Donald Lester 1928- *AmMWSc 92*
**MacPhail,** Andy *WhoMW 92*
**MacPhail,** Bruce Dugald 1939- *Who 92*
**MacPhail,** Bruce Ian 1949- *WhoAmL 92*
**Macphail,** Iain Duncan 1938- *Who 92*
**Macphail,** Moray St John 1912- *AmMWSc 92*
**MacPhail,** Richard Allyn 1953- *AmMWSc 92*
**MacPhail,** Robert C 1945- *AmMWSc 92*
**Macphail,** Stuart 1947- *AmMWSc 92*
**MacPhail,** William C. *LesBEnT 92*
**MacPhee,** Charles William *WhoEnt 92*
**MacPhee,** Craig Robert 1944- *WhoFI 92, WhoMW 92*
**Macpherson** *Who 92*
**Macpherson,** Alexander Calderwood 1939- *Who 92*
**Macpherson,** Alistair Kenneth 1936- *AmMWSc 92*
**Macpherson,** Andrew Hall 1932- *AmMWSc 92*
**Macpherson,** Colin Robertson 1925- *AmMWSc 92*
**Macpherson,** Cullen H 1927- *AmMWSc 92*
**MacPherson,** David Allan 1960- *WhoFI 92*
**Macpherson,** George A. 1935- *TwCPaSc*
**MacPherson,** Greg 1949- *WhoEnt 92*
**MacPherson,** Herbert Grenfell 1911- *AmMWSc 92*
**Macpherson,** James 1736-1796 *BlkwCEP, DcLB 109 [port], RfGEnL 91*
**Macpherson,** Jay 1931- *IntAu&W 91, WrDr 92*
**Macpherson,** Jeanie 1897-1946 *ReelWom [port]*
**MacPherson,** Jennifer B. *DrAPF 91*
**Macpherson,** Keith 1920- *Who 92*
**MacPherson,** Keith Duncan 1920- *IntWW 91*
**MacPherson,** Margaret 1908- *WrDr 92*
**Macpherson,** Neil 1954- *TwCPaSc*
**MacPherson,** Robert Duncan 1944- *AmMWSc 92*
**Macpherson,** Roderick Ewen 1916- *Who 92*
**Macpherson,** Roderick Ian 1935- *AmMWSc 92*
**Macpherson,** Ronald Thomas Stewart 1920- *Who 92*
**Macpherson,** Sophie 1957- *TwCPaSc*
**MacPherson,** Stewart Myles 1908- *Who 92*
**Macpherson,** Tommy *Who 92*
**Macpherson of Cluny,** William 1926- *Who 92*
**Macpherson of Drumochter,** Baron 1924- *Who 92*
**Macphie,** Duncan Love 1930- *Who 92*

**MacQuade,** Robert *WhoRel 92*
**Macquaker,** Donald Francis 1932- *Who 92*
**MacQuarrie,** Ian Gregor 1933- *AmMWSc 92*
**Macquarrie,** John 1919- *IntWW 91, Who 92, WhoRel 92, WrDr 92*
**MacQuarrie,** Ronald Anthony 1943- *AmMWSc 92*
**Macque,** Giovanni de 1548?-1614 *NewAmDM*
**Macqueen,** Angus 1910- *Who 92*
**MacQueen,** Angus James 1912- *WhoRel 92*
**MacQueen,** John 1929- *ConAu 133, Who 92, WrDr 92*
**MacQueen,** Robert Mitchell 1939- *WhoMW 92*
**MacQueen,** Robert Moffat 1938- *AmMWSc 92, WhoWest 92*
**Macqueen,** Roger Webb 1935- *AmMWSc 92*
**MacQueen,** William Johnstone 1943- *WhoMW 92*
**MacQueen,** Winifred 1928- *ConAu 133*
**MacQuillan,** Anthony M 1928- *AmMWSc 92*
**MacQuitty,** James Lloyd 1912- *Who 92*
**MacQuown,** William Charles, Jr 1915- *AmMWSc 92*
**MacRae,** Alfred Urquhart 1932- *AmMWSc 92*
**MacRae,** Andrew Richard 1946- *AmMWSc 92*
**MacRae,** Bette Jayne 1920- *WhoAmP 91*
**MacRae,** Cameron Farquhar, III 1942- *WhoAmL 92*
**MacRae,** Christopher 1937- *Who 92*
**Macrae,** David 1837-1907 *BenetAL 91*
**MacRae,** Donald Alexander 1916- *AmMWSc 92, WhoMW 92*
**MacRae,** Donald Gunn 1921- *Who 92*
**MacRae,** Donald Richard 1934- *AmMWSc 92*
**MacRae,** Edith Krugelis 1919- *AmMWSc 92*
**MacRae,** Elizabeth Ann 1825-1907 *DcNCBi 4*
**MacRae,** Herbert F 1926- *AmMWSc 92*
**MacRae,** Hugh 1865-1951 *DcNCBi 4*
**MacRae,** James Cameron 1838-1909 *DcNCBi 4*
**MacRae,** John *DcNCBi 4*
**Macrae,** John Esmond Campbell 1932- *Who 92*
**MacRae,** Kenneth Charles 1944- *Who 92*
**MacRae,** Mary Jenkins 1954- *WhoFI 92*
**Macrae,** Mason 1894- *TwCWW 91*
**MacRae,** Neil D 1935- *AmMWSc 92*
**MacRae,** Patrick Daniel 1928- *AmMWSc 92*
**Macrae,** Robert 1915- *Who 92*
**MacRae,** Robert Alexander 1935- *AmMWSc 92*
**MacRae,** Robert E 1934- *AmMWSc 92*
**MacRae,** Thomas Henry 1948- *AmMWSc 92*
**MacRae,** William 1834-1882 *DcNCBi 4*
**Macrander,** Albert Tiemen 1950- *AmMWSc 92*
**Macreadie,** John Lindsay 1946- *Who 92*
**Macready,** Nevil 1921- *Who 92*
**Macready,** R G *ScFEYrs*
**Macreamoinn,** Sean 1921- *IntWW 91*
**Macri,** Frank John 1923- *AmMWSc 92*
**Macridis,** Roy C. d1991 *NewYTBS 91*
**Macrina The Younger** 327?-379? *EncEarC*
**Macris,** Nicholas T 1931- *AmMWSc 92*
**Macriss,** Robert A 1930- *AmMWSc 92*
**MacRobbie,** Enid Anne Campbell 1931- *Who 92*
**Macrone,** John 1809-1837 *DcLB 106*
**Macrory,** Patrick 1911- *Who 92*
**Macrory,** Patrick Francis John 1941- *WhoAmL 92*
**MacShane,** Frank 1927- *DcLB 111 [port], IntAu&W 91, WrDr 92*
**MacSharry,** Ray 1938- *IntWW 91*
**MacSharry,** Raymond 1938- *Who 92*
**MacSparran,** James 1693-1757 *BenetAL 91*
**MacSwan,** Iain Christie 1921- *AmMWSc 92*
**MacSween,** Joseph Michael 1933- *AmMWSc 92*
**MacSweeney,** Barry 1948- *ConPo 91, IntAu&W 91, WrDr 92*
**MacSwiney,** Mary Margarite 1872-1942 *BiDBrF 2*
**Mactaggart,** Fiona 1953- *Who 92*
**Mactaggart,** John 1951- *Who 92*
**MacTaggart,** William 1903-1981 *TwCPaSc*
**Mactaggart,** William Alexander 1906- *Who 92*
**MacTaggart,** William Keith 1929- *Who 92*
**Mactal,** Romeo A. 1938- *WhoFI 92*
**MacTavish,** John N 1939- *AmMWSc 92*
**MacThomais,** Ruaraidh *WrDr 92*
**MacThomas of Finegand,** Andrew Patrick C 1942- *Who 92*
**Macur,** George J 1933- *AmMWSc 92*
**Macur,** Patricia Alice *WhoFI 92*
**Macura,** Stanislav 1946- *WhoEnt 92*
**Macurda,** Donald Bradford, Jr 1936- *AmMWSc 92*
**Macurdy,** John 1929- *NewAmDM*
**Macurdy,** John Edward 1929- *WhoEnt 92*
**Macvean,** Jean *WrDr 92*
**Macvey,** John Wishart 1923- *IntAu&W 91*
**Macvicar,** Angus 1908- *IntAu&W 91, WrDr 92*
**MacVicar,** Kenneth 1921- *Who 92*
**MacVicar,** Margaret L.A. d1991 *NewYTBS 91 [port]*
**MacVicar,** Margaret Love Agnes 1943- *AmMWSc 92*
**Macvicar,** Neil 1920- *Who 92*
**MacVicar,** Robert William 1918- *AmMWSc 92*
**MacVicar-Whelan,** Patrick James *AmMWSc 92*
**MacVittie,** Thomas Joseph 1941- *AmMWSc 92*
**Mac Watters,** Virginia Elizabeth *WhoEnt 92*
**MacWhorter,** Alexander 1734-1807 *DcNCBi 4*
**MacWhorter,** Robert Bruce 1930- *WhoAmL 92*
**MacWilliam,** Alexander Gordon 1923- *Who 92*
**MacWilliams,** Dalton Carson 1928- *AmMWSc 92*
**Macy,** Bill 1922- *WhoEnt 92*
**Macy,** Bruce Wendell 1930- *WhoFI 92*
**Macy,** Homer Leven 1900- *WhoAmP 91*
**Macy,** Janet Kuska 1935- *WhoEnt 92*
**Macy,** John 1877-1932 *BenetAL 91*
**Macy,** John W., Jr. d1986 *LesBEnT 92*
**Macy,** Judith K *WhoAmP 91*
**Macy,** Michael Gaylord 1957- *WhoWest 92*
**Macy,** Patricia Ann 1955- *WhoEnt 92*
**Macy,** Ralph William 1905- *AmMWSc 92*
**Macy,** Richard J *WhoAmP 91*
**Macy,** Richard J. 1930- *WhoAmL 92, WhoWest 92*
**Macy,** Rocky Gene 1948- *WhoMW 92*
**Macy,** Ruth Carol 1952- *WhoEnt 92*
**Macy,** William Wray, Jr 1944- *AmMWSc 92*
**Maczees,** William John, Jr. 1936- *WhoFI 92*
**Maczulski,** Margaret Louise 1949- *WhoFI 92*
**MacZura,** George 1930- *AmMWSc 92*
**Madaio,** Michael P *AmMWSc 92*
**Madalena,** James Roger *WhoAmP 91*
**Madame Sans-Gene** *EncAmaz 91*
**Madan,** Bal Krishna 1911- *IntWW 91*
**Madan,** Mahendra Pratap 1926- *AmMWSc 92*
**Madan,** Rabinder Nath 1935- *AmMWSc 92*
**Madan,** Ram Chand 1939- *AmMWSc 92*
**Madan,** Stanley Krishen 1922- *AmMWSc 92*
**Madan,** Ved P 1942- *AmMWSc 92*
**Madani,** Sam Mohammad 1952- *WhoWest 92*
**Madansky,** Albert 1934- *AmMWSc 92*
**Madansky,** Leon 1923- *AmMWSc 92*
**Madaras,** Ronald John 1942- *AmMWSc 92*
**Madariaga,** Francisco 1927- *ConSpAP*
**Madariaga,** Isabel Margaret De 1919- *Who 92*
**Madariaga,** Salvador De 1886- *ScFEYrs*
**Madariaga,** Salvador de 1886-1978 *LiExTwC*
**Madariaga y Rojo,** Salvador de 1886-1978 *LiExTwC*
**Maday,** Clarence Joseph 1929- *AmMWSc 92*
**Maddack,** Donald James 1961- *WhoMW 92*
**Maddaiah,** Vaddanahally Thimmaiah 1929- *AmMWSc 92*
**Maddala,** Gangadharrao Soundaryarao 1933- *WhoFI 92*
**Maddela,** Orlando *WhoRel 92*
**Madden,** Albert Frederick 1917- *Who 92*
**Madden,** Anne 1932- *TwCPaSc*
**Madden,** Bartley Joseph 1943- *WhoMW 92*
**Madden,** Bernard Patrick 1947- *WhoAmP 91*
**Madden,** Bill 1915- *IntMPA 92*
**Madden,** Bill 1945- *ConAu 133*
**Madden,** Charles 1906- *TwCPaSc, Who 92*
**Madden,** Colin Duncan 1915- *Who 92*
**Madden,** David *DrAPF 91, IntMPA 92*
**Madden,** David 1933- *ConNov 91, WrDr 92*
**Madden,** David Larry 1932- *AmMWSc 92*
**Madden,** Deirdre 1960- *ConAu 133*
**Madden,** Diane Sloane 1945- *WhoWest 92*
**Madden,** Edward George, Jr. 1924- *WhoAmL 92*
**Madden,** Frances Brett 1918- *WhoWest 92*
**Madden,** Frederick *Who 92*
**Madden,** Frederick 1917- *IntWW 91*
**Madden,** Geoffrey Sean Patrick 1958- *WhoFI 92*
**Madden,** Gerald Patrick 1942- *WhoFI 92*
**Madden,** Hannibal Hamlin, Jr 1931- *AmMWSc 92*
**Madden,** James H 1924- *AmMWSc 92*
**Madden,** Jerome Anthony 1948- *WhoAmL 92*
**Madden,** Jerry 1923- *WhoEnt 92*
**Madden,** Jerry Agnew 1943- *WhoAmP 91*
**Madden,** John *LesBEnT 92 [port]*
**Madden,** John Dale 1957- *WhoAmL 92*
**Madden,** John Joseph 1943- *AmMWSc 92*
**Madden,** John Joseph 1946- *WhoAmL 92*
**Madden,** John Philip *WhoEnt 92*
**Madden,** John William, III 1937- *WhoAmL 92*
**Madden,** Keith Patrick 1953- *AmMWSc 92*
**Madden,** L V *AmMWSc 92*
**Madden,** Loretto Anne 1922- *WhoRel 92*
**Madden,** Martin Gerard 1949- *WhoAmP 91*
**Madden,** Max 1941- *Who 92*
**Madden,** Michael 1936- *Who 92*
**Madden,** Michael Preston 1948- *AmMWSc 92*
**Madden,** Nena 1948- *WhoWest 92*
**Madden,** Palmer Brown 1945- *WhoAmL 92*
**Madden,** Patrick John 1926- *WhoAmL 92*
**Madden,** Paul Daniel 1948- *WhoWest 92*
**Madden,** Paul Robert 1926- *WhoAmL 92, WhoWest 92*
**Madden,** Richard Blaine 1929- *WhoFI 92, WhoWest 92*
**Madden,** Richard Lewis 1951- *WhoFI 92*
**Madden,** Richard M 1928- *AmMWSc 92*
**Madden,** Robert E 1925- *AmMWSc 92*
**Madden,** Robert Phyfe 1928- *AmMWSc 92*
**Madden,** Sidney Clarence 1907- *AmMWSc 92*
**Madden,** Stephan DuPont 1954- *WhoAmL 92*
**Madden,** Stephen James, Jr 1936- *AmMWSc 92*
**Madden,** Tara Roth 1942- *IntAu&W 91*
**Madden,** Theodore Richard 1925- *AmMWSc 92*
**Madden,** Thomas Lee 1942- *AmMWSc 92*
**Madden-Work,** Betty I. 1915- *WrDr 92*
**Maddern,** Wayne James Anketell 1944- *WhoEnt 92*
**Maddex,** Phillip J 1917- *AmMWSc 92*
**Maddin,** Charles Milford 1927- *AmMWSc 92*
**Maddin,** Robert 1918- *AmMWSc 92*
**Maddison,** Angela Mary *WrDr 92*
**Maddison,** Angus 1926- *WrDr 92*
**Maddison,** Carol *WrDr 92*
**Maddison,** Vincent Albert 1915- *Who 92*
**Maddock,** Joseph 1722-1796 *DcNCBi 4*
**Maddock,** Marshall 1928- *AmMWSc 92*
**Maddock,** R B 1912- *IntAu&W 91, WrDr 92*
**Maddock,** Rosemary Schroer 1919- *WhoWest 92*
**Maddock,** Thomas, Jr 1907- *AmMWSc 92*
**Maddocks,** Arthur Frederick 1922- *IntWW 91, Who 92*
**Maddocks,** Bertram Catterall 1932- *Who 92*
**Maddocks,** Fiona Hamilton 1955- *Who 92*
**Maddocks,** Kenneth 1907- *Who 92*
**Maddocks,** Margaret 1906- *WrDr 92*
**Maddocks,** Margaret Kathleen Avern 1906- *IntAu&W 91*
**Maddocks,** Morris Henry St John 1928- *Who 92*
**Maddocks,** Rosalie Frances 1938- *AmMWSc 92*
**Maddocks,** William Henry 1921- *Who 92*
**Maddox,** Alva Hugh 1930- *WhoAmP 91*
**Maddox,** Barbara Jean 1947- *WhoAmP 91*
**Maddox,** Billy Hoyte 1932- *AmMWSc 92*
**Maddox,** Carl *IntAu&W 91X, TwCSFW 91, WrDr 92*
**Maddox,** Conroy 1912- *TwCPaSc*
**Maddox,** E Farrell 1931- *WhoAmP 91*
**Maddox,** Elton Preston, Jr. 1946- *WhoBlA 92*
**Maddox,** Esther Lee 1929- *WhoEnt 92*
**Maddox,** Garry Lee 1949- *WhoBlA 92*
**Maddox,** Greggory Roy 1957- *WhoRel 92*
**Maddox,** Jack H. 1927- *WhoBlA 92*
**Maddox,** James Franklin 1934- *WhoAmP 91*
**Maddox,** James Kelly, Jr. 1946- *WhoRel 92*
**Maddox,** Jim 1938- *WhoAmP 91*
**Maddox,** John 1925- *Who 92*
**Maddox,** John Earl 1935- *WhoRel 92*
**Maddox,** John Sheppard, Jr. 1927- *WhoEnt 92*
**Maddox,** Joseph Vernard 1938- *AmMWSc 92*
**Maddox,** Kempson d1990 *Who 92N*
**Maddox,** Larry A 1943- *AmMWSc 92*
**Maddox,** Luther Warren 1924- *WhoAmP 91*
**Maddox,** Margaret Johnnetta Simms 1952- *WhoBlA 92*
**Maddox,** Marjorie *DrAPF 91*
**Maddox,** Neva Wiley Pemberton 1919- *WhoAmP 91*
**Maddox,** Ode L 1912- *WhoAmP 91*
**Maddox,** Odinga Lawrence 1939- *WhoBlA 92, WhoRel 92*
**Maddox,** R N 1925- *AmMWSc 92*
**Maddox,** Randy Lynn 1953- *WhoRel 92*
**Maddox,** Richard Lee 1952- *WhoEnt 92*
**Maddox,** Robert A, Jr *WhoAmP 91*
**Maddox,** Robert James 1931- *WrDr 92*
**Maddox,** Robert Lytton 1924- *WhoAmL 92*
**Maddox,** Roger Wayne 1950- *WhoRel 92*
**Maddox,** Ronald 1930- *Who 92*
**Maddox,** Ronald C. *WhoRel 92*
**Maddox,** V Harold, Jr 1923- *AmMWSc 92*
**Maddox,** William Eugene 1937- *AmMWSc 92*
**Maddox,** Yvonne T *AmMWSc 92*
**Maddrell,** Beverly Jean 1943- *WhoAmP 91*
**Maddrell,** Geoffrey Keggen 1936- *Who 92*
**Maddrell,** Simon Hugh Piper 1937- *Who 92*
**Maddrey,** Elizabeth Huntley 1942- *WhoAmP 91*
**Maddry,** Charles Edward 1876-1962 *DcNCBi 4*
**Maddux,** Don Stewart 1940- *WhoAmP 91*
**Maddux,** Elmer L 1934- *WhoAmP 91*
**Maddux,** Parker Ahrens 1939- *WhoAmL 92*
**Maddy,** Joe 1891-1966 *NewAmDM*
**Maddy,** Keith Thomas 1923- *AmMWSc 92*
**Maddy,** Kenneth Hilton 1923- *AmMWSc 92*
**Maddy,** Kenneth Leon 1934- *WhoAmP 91, WhoWest 92*
**Maddy,** Y. A. 1936- *WrDr 92*
**Madeira,** Edward Walter, Jr. 1928- *WhoAmL 92*
**Madeira,** Francis King Carey 1917- *WhoEnt 92*
**Madel,** David 1938- *Who 92*
**Madeleine de Saint-Nectaire** *EncAmaz 91*
**Madeleva,** Mary *BenetAL 91*
**Madelin,** Alain 1946- *IntWW 91*
**Madelung,** Wilferd Willy Ferdinand 1930- *Who 92*
**Maden,** Margaret 1940- *Who 92*
**Mader,** Charles Lavern 1930- *AmMWSc 92, WhoWest 92*
**Mader,** Daniel Edward 1949- *WhoMW 92*
**Mader,** Daniel Ralph 1954- *WhoFI 92*
**Mader,** Donald Lewis 1926- *AmMWSc 92*
**Mader,** Friedrich W 1866- *ScFEYrs*
**Mader,** Ivan John 1923- *AmMWSc 92*
**Mader,** Kelly F 1952- *WhoAmP 91*
**Mader,** Kelly Forbes 1952- *WhoWest 92*
**Madera,** Joseph J. 1927- *WhoRel 92*
**Madera,** Maria S. 1953- *WhoHisp 92*
**Madera Fernandez,** Jose E. 1936- *WhoHisp 92*
**Madera-Orsini,** Frank 1916- *AmMWSc 92*
**Madera-Orsini,** Frank M. 1916- *WhoHisp 92*
**Maderna,** Bruno 1920-1973 *NewAmDM*
**Maderson,** Paul F A 1938- *AmMWSc 92*
**Maderspach,** Victor 1918- *AmMWSc 92*
**Madesani,** Grazia 1871-1936 *WhoNob 90*
**Madeson,** Marvin Louis 1925- *WhoAmP 91*
**Madey,** Richard 1922- *AmMWSc 92, WhoMW 92*
**Madey,** Robert W 1933- *AmMWSc 92*
**Madey,** Theodore Eugene 1937- *AmMWSc 92*
**Madge,** Charles 1912- *ConPo 91, WrDr 92*
**Madge,** Charles Henry 1912- *Who 92*
**Madge,** James Richard 1924- *Who 92*
**Madges,** William 1952- *WhoRel 92*
**Madgett,** Diana 1928- *TwCPaSc*
**Madgett,** Naomi Long *DrAPF 91*
**Madgett,** Naomi Long 1923- *BenetAL 91, IntAu&W 91, NotBlAW 92, WhoBlA 92, WrDr 92*
**Madgwick,** Clive 1934- *TwCPaSc*
**Madhav,** Ram 1938- *AmMWSc 92*
**Madhavan,** Ananthanarayanan 1933- *IntWW 91*
**Madhavan,** Kornath *AmMWSc 92*
**Madhavan,** Kunchithapatham 1945- *AmMWSc 92*
**Madhavpeddi,** Kalidas Venkat 1955- *WhoFI 92*
**Madhu,** Swaminathan 1931- *AmMWSc 92*

**Madhubuti**, Haki R. ConPo 91, DrAPF 91, WrDr 92
**Madhubuti**, Haki R. 1942- BlkLC [port], WhoBlA 92
**Madia**, Chunilal Kalidas 1922- IntAu&W 91, IntWW 91
**Madia**, Giorgio 1965- WhoEnt 92
**Madia**, William J AmMWSc 92
**Madias**, Nicolaos E 1944- AmMWSc 92
**Madich**, Bernadine Marie Hoff 1934- WhoMW 92
**Madigan**, Amy 1957- IntMPA 92
**Madigan**, Dennis Eugene 1952- WhoEnt 92
**Madigan**, Edward 1936- IntWW 91
**Madigan**, Edward R 1936- WhoAmP 91, WhoMW 92
**Madigan**, John William 1937- WhoFI 92, WhoMW 92
**Madigan**, Michael J 1942- WhoAmP 91
**Madigan**, Michael Joseph 1942- WhoMW 92
**Madigan**, Robert 1942- WhoAmP 91
**Madigan**, Roger A 1930- WhoAmP 91
**Madigan**, Russel 1920- Who 92
**Madigan**, Russel Tullie 1920- IntWW 91
**Madigosky**, Walter Myron 1933- AmMWSc 92
**Madin**, Stewart Harvey 1918- AmMWSc 92
**Madinger**, Charles Brent 1952- WhoRel 92
**Madison**, Alfreda Louise 1911- WhoBlA 92
**Madison**, Bernard L 1941- AmMWSc 92
**Madison**, Cleo 1883-1964 ReelWom [port]
**Madison**, Dale Martin 1942- AmMWSc 92
**Madison**, Dolley Payne Todd 1768-1849 DcNCBi 4
**Madison**, Dolly 1768-1849 BenetAL 91
**Madison**, Don Harvey 1945- AmMWSc 92
**Madison**, Eddie L., Jr. 1930- WhoBlA 92
**Madison**, Frank WrDr 92
**Madison**, George H 1939- WhoAmP 91
**Madison**, Guy 1922- IntMPA 92
**Madison**, Hank TwCWW 91
**Madison**, Holt TwCWW 91
**Madison**, Jacqueline Edwina 1951- WhoBlA 92
**Madison**, James 1749-1812 BiInAmS
**Madison**, James 1751-1836 AmPolLe [port], BenetAL 91, BlkwCEP, BlkwEAR [port], RComAH
**Madison**, James 1933- WhoAmP 91
**Madison**, James Allen 1928- AmMWSc 92
**Madison**, James Raymond 1931- WhoAmL 92
**Madison**, James Thomas 1933- AmMWSc 92
**Madison**, John Herbert, Jr 1918- AmMWSc 92
**Madison**, Joseph Edward 1949- WhoBlA 92
**Madison**, Leatrice Branch 1922- WhoBlA 92
**Madison**, Leonard Lincoln 1920- AmMWSc 92
**Madison**, Richard 1932- WhoBlA 92
**Madison**, Robert Lee 1867-1954 DcNCBi 4
**Madison**, Robert P. 1923- WhoBlA 92
**Madison**, Roberta Solomon 1932- AmMWSc 92
**Madison**, Ronald L. 1942- WhoBlA 92
**Madison**, Shannon L. 1927- WhoBlA 92
**Madison**, Stanley D. 1932- WhoBlA 92
**Madison**, T. Jerome 1940- WhoFI 92
**Madison**, Vincent Stewart 1943- AmMWSc 92
**Madison**, William L. 1933- WhoBlA 92
**Madissoo**, Harry 1924- AmMWSc 92
**Madix**, Robert James 1938- AmMWSc 92, WhoWest 92
**Madiyalakan**, Ragupathy 1952- AmMWSc 92
**Madl**, Ferenc 1931- IntWW 91
**Madl**, Ronald 1944- AmMWSc 92
**Madla**, Frank 1937- WhoAmP 91, WhoHisp 92
**Madlock**, Bill, Jr. 1951- WhoBlA 92
**Madni**, Asad Mohamed 1947- WhoWest 92
**Madoc** 1150?-1180? BenetAL 91
**Madoc-Jones**, Hywel 1938- AmMWSc 92
**Madoff**, Michelle WhoAmP 91
**Madoff**, Morton A 1927- AmMWSc 92
**Madog ab Owain Gwynedd** 1150?-1180? BenetAL 91
**Madole**, Donald Wilson 1932- WhoFI 92
**Madole**, Richard 1936- AmMWSc 92
**Madon**, Major Lynn 1953- WhoFI 92
**Madonia**, Lee 1960- WhoMW 92
**Madonia**, Valerie WhoEnt 92
**Madonna** 1958?- ConTFT 9, IntMPA 92, IntWW 91, WhoEnt 92
**Madonna**, Steven John, Sr. 1942- WhoAmL 92
**Mador**, Irving Lester 1921- AmMWSc 92
**Madore**, Bernadette 1918- AmMWSc 92, WhoRel 92
**Madore**, Monica Agnes 1955- AmMWSc 92
**Madory**, Richard Eugene 1931- WhoAmL 92
**Madow**, Leo 1915- AmMWSc 92
**Madras**, Bertha K 1942- AmMWSc 92
**Madrazo**, Alfonso A 1931- AmMWSc 92
**Madri**, Joseph Anthony AmMWSc 92
**Madrid**, Alyce Janine 1959- WhoHisp 92
**Madrid**, Arturo WhoHisp 92
**Madrid**, Carlos, Jr. WhoHisp 92
**Madrid**, Chilo L. 1945- WhoHisp 92
**Madrid**, Donna Kay 1937- WhoWest 92
**Madrid**, Joe Hernandez 1944- WhoHisp 92
**Madrid**, Jose Saul 1956- WhoHisp 92
**Madrid**, Lauren Lee 1958- WhoEnt 92
**Madrid**, Leasher Dennis 1949- WhoHisp 92, WhoWest 92
**Madrid Hurtado**, Miguel de la IntWW 91
**Madrid-Mendenhall**, Cassandra 1962- WhoHisp 92
**Madrid-Mirabal**, Henry Alexander 1943- WhoHisp 92
**Madrigal**, Ray 1944- WhoHisp 92
**Madril**, Lee Ann 1944- WhoWest 92
**Madritsch**, Robert Ernst 1948- WhoMW 92
**Madron**, Thomas Wm 1937- WhoAmP 91
**Madry**, Maude Holt 1949- WhoBlA 92
**Madrzyk**, John S 1939- WhoAmP 91
**Madsen**, Daniels Hayes 1962- WhoWest 92
**Madsen**, David Burton 1946- WhoMW 92, WhoRel 92
**Madsen**, David Christy 1943- AmMWSc 92
**Madsen**, David Warren 1953- WhoEnt 92
**Madsen**, Donald H 1922- AmMWSc 92
**Madsen**, Dorothy Louise WhoMW 92
**Madsen**, Francis Armstrong, Jr 1931- WhoAmP 91
**Madsen**, Fred Christian 1945- AmMWSc 92
**Madsen**, Henry Stephen 1924- WhoAmL 92
**Madsen**, Hunter 1955- ConAu 133
**Madsen**, Ib Henning 1942- IntWW 91
**Madsen**, James Henry, Jr 1932- AmMWSc 92
**Madsen**, Ken WhoAmP 91
**Madsen**, Kenneth Olaf 1926- AmMWSc 92
**Madsen**, Mette 1924- IntWW 91
**Madsen**, Natasha R 1938- WhoAmP 91
**Madsen**, Neil Bernard 1928- AmMWSc 92
**Madsen**, Ole Secher 1941- AmMWSc 92
**Madsen**, Paul O 1927- AmMWSc 92
**Madsen**, Richard Alfred 1933- AmMWSc 92
**Madsen**, Richard Wellington 1938- WhoAmL 92
**Madsen**, Robert Grady 1962- WhoWest 92
**Madsen**, Roger B 1947- WhoAmP 91
**Madsen**, Roger Bryan 1947- WhoWest 92
**Madsen**, Stephen Stewart 1951- WhoAmL 92
**Madsen**, Victor Arviel 1931- AmMWSc 92
**Madsen**, Virginia 1963- IntMPA 92
**Madson**, Arthur DrAPF 91
**Madson**, Gary Kent 1937- WhoAmP 91
**Madson**, John Andrew 1920- WhoMW 92
**Maduakor**, Obiajuru 1942- WhoRel 92
**Madubuike**, Ihechukwu 1943- ConAu 134
**Madubuike**, Ihechukwu 1944- IntWW 91
**Maduri**, Bruce Carl 1956- WhoRel 92
**Maduro**, John Lawrence 1921- WhoAmP 91
**Maduro**, Otto 1945- WhoRel 92
**Maeck**, John Van Sicklen 1914- AmMWSc 92
**Maecklberghe**, Margo 1932- TwCPaSc
**Maeda**, J. A. 1940- WhoFI 92, WhoWest 92
**Maeda**, Kazuo 1919- IntWW 91
**Maeder**, Gary William 1949- WhoAmL 92
**Maeder**, P F 1923- AmMWSc 92
**Maegaard**, Jan 1926- ConCom 92
**Maegaard**, Jan Carl Christian 1926- IntWW 91
**Maeght**, Aime 1906-1981 FacFETw
**Maehara**, Kenneth Takayuki 1942- WhoFI 92
**Maehl**, William Harvey 1915- WhoWest 92
**Maehler**, Herwig Gustav Theodor 1935- IntWW 91, Who 92
**Maehr**, Hubert 1935- AmMWSc 92
**Maeks**, Joel 1934- AmMWSc 92
**Mael**, Barry Sheldon 1958- WhoRel 92
**Maelzel**, Johann Nepomuk 1772-1838 NewAmDM
**Maenchen**, George 1928- AmMWSc 92
**Maender**, Otto William 1940- AmMWSc 92
**Maengwyn-Davies**, Gertrude Diane 1910- AmMWSc 92
**Maenza**, Ronald Morton 1936- AmMWSc 92
**Maerker**, Gerhard 1923- AmMWSc 92
**Maerker**, John Malcolm 1945- AmMWSc 92
**Maerker**, Richard Erwin 1928- AmMWSc 92
**Maerkle**, Doreen 1958- WhoAmL 92
**Maerov**, Shelly WhoRel 92
**Maerz**, Florence Szerlag DrAPF 91
**Maes**, James Alfredo 1947- WhoHisp 92
**Maes**, Jeanette C. DrAPF 91
**Maes**, John Leopold 1923- WhoRel 92
**Maes**, Petra Jimenez WhoAmL 92
**Maes**, Petra Jimenez 1947- WhoHisp 92
**Maes**, Roman M WhoAmP 91
**Maes**, Roman M. 1943- WhoHisp 92
**Maes-Jelinek**, Hena WrDr 92
**Maese**, Vivian Ann 1954- WhoAmL 92
**Maestas**, Billy D. 1951- WhoHisp 92
**Maestas**, Elizabeth 1935- WhoAmP 91
**Maestas**, Ronald W. 1946- WhoHisp 92
**Maestas**, Samuel J. 1953- WhoHisp 92
**Maestas**, Sigfredo WhoHisp 92
**Maestas-Flores**, Margarita 1948- WhoHisp 92
**Maestre**, Marcos Francisco 1932- AmMWSc 92
**Maestrello**, Lucio 1928- AmMWSc 92
**Maestro**, Giulio 1942- IntAu&W 91, WrDr 92
**Maestrone**, Gianpaolo 1930- AmMWSc 92
**Maeterlinck**, Maurice 1862-1949 GuFrLit 1, SmATA 66 [port]
**Maeterlinck**, Mauritius Polydorus Maria B 1862-1949 WhoNob 90
**Maewal**, Akhilesh 1949- AmMWSc 92
**Maez**, Albert R 1939- AmMWSc 92
**Maez**, Yvette Georgina 1965- WhoHisp 92
**Maeztu y Whitney**, Ramiro, Conde de 1875-1936 BiDExR
**Maezumi**, Hakuyu Taizan 1931- RelLAm 91
**Mafatlal**, Arvind N. 1923- IntWW 91
**Mafe**, Daniel 1957- TwCPaSc
**Mafee**, Mahmood Forootan 1941- AmMWSc 92
**Maffei**, Betty Jane 1928- WhoWest 92
**Maffei**, Dorothy J. 1951- WhoEnt 92
**Maffei**, Francesco Scipione, Marchese di 1675-1755 BlkwCEP
**Maffei**, Rocco John 1949- WhoAmL 92
**Maffei**, Stephen Roger 1939- WhoFI 92
**Maffei**, Thomas Francis 1947- WhoAmL 92
**Maffett**, Andrew L 1921- AmMWSc 92
**Maffey** Who 92
**Maffie**, Michael Otis 1948- WhoWest 92
**Maffitt**, John Newland 1819-1886 DcNCBi 4
**Maffly**, LeRoy Herrick 1927- AmMWSc 92
**Maffre**, Muriel 1966- WhoEnt 92
**Mafnas**, Jose P WhoAmP 91
**Maga**, Dominic Joseph 1946- WhoMW 92
**Maga**, Hubert Coutoucou 1916- IntWW 91
**Maga**, Joseph Andrew 1940- AmMWSc 92
**Magaard**, Lorenz Carl 1934- AmMWSc 92
**Magalhaes Pinto**, Jose de 1909- IntWW 91
**Magaloff**, Nikita 1912- IntWW 91
**Magalska**, James M 1942- WhoIns 92
**Magana**, Bertha WhoHisp 92
**Magana**, Manuel Rodelo 1931- WhoHisp 92
**Magana**, Raoul Daniel 1911- WhoHisp 92
**Magana Borja**, Alvaro 1926- IntWW 91
**Magana Garcia**, Sabas 1921- WhoRel 92
**Maganini**, Quinto 1897-1974 NewAmDM
**Magarey**, Rupert d1990 Who 92N
**Magargal**, Larry Elliot 1941- AmMWSc 92
**Magargal**, Wells Wrisley, II AmMWSc 92
**Magarian**, Charles Aram 1927- AmMWSc 92
**Magarian**, Edward O 1935- AmMWSc 92
**Magarian**, Elizabeth Ann 1940- AmMWSc 92
**Magarian**, Liberty 1958- WhoAmL 92
**Magarian**, Robert Armen 1930- AmMWSc 92
**Magarinos D.**, Victor 1924- IntWW 91
**Magarity**, Gregory T. 1947- WhoAmL 92
**Magary**, Dennis Robert 1951- WhoRel 92
**Magasanik**, Boris 1919- AmMWSc 92
**Magasi**, Laszlo P 1935- AmMWSc 92
**Magat**, Eugene Edward 1919- AmMWSc 92
**Magaw**, James Ellsworth 1932- WhoRel 92
**Magazine**, Michael Jay 1943- AmMWSc 92
**Magaziner**, Elliot Albert 1921- WhoEnt 92
**Magaziner**, Henry J. 1911- IntWW 91
**Magaziner**, Henry Jonas 1911- AmMWSc 92
**Magde**, Douglas 1942- AmMWSc 92
**Magder**, Jules 1934- AmMWSc 92
**Magdoff**, Frederick Robin 1942- AmMWSc 92
**Magdoff-Fairchild**, Beatrice AmMWSc 92
**Mage**, Michael Gordon 1934- AmMWSc 92
**Mage**, Rose G 1935- AmMWSc 92
**Mageau**, Mary 1934- ConCom 92
**Mageau**, Richard Paul 1941- AmMWSc 92
**Magee**, Aden Combs, III 1930- AmMWSc 92
**Magee**, Bill WhoAmP 91
**Magee**, Bruce Robert 1958- WhoRel 92
**Magee**, Bryan 1930- IntAu&W 91, Who 92, WrDr 92
**Magee**, Donal Francis 1924- AmMWSc 92
**Magee**, Douglas MacArthur 1942- WhoAmP 91
**Magee**, Forrest Craig 1943- WhoEnt 92
**Magee**, Frank L. 1896-1991 NewYTBS 91
**Magee**, Gordon Lloyd 1951- WhoRel 92
**Magee**, James Roland 1959- WhoEnt 92
**Magee**, John Francis 1926- AmMWSc 92, WhoFI 92
**Magee**, John Lafayette 1914- AmMWSc 92
**Magee**, John Robert 1916- AmMWSc 92
**Magee**, John Storey, Jr 1931- AmMWSc 92
**Magee**, Judy 1914- WhoEnt 92
**Magee**, Leslie Jae 1933- WhoRel 92
**Magee**, Lloyd E 1923- WhoAmP 91
**Magee**, Lyman Abbott 1926- AmMWSc 92
**Magee**, Michael Jack 1946- AmMWSc 92
**Magee**, Paul Terry 1937- AmMWSc 92
**Magee**, Reginald Arthur Edward d1989 IntWW 91N
**Magee**, Richard Stephen 1941- AmMWSc 92
**Magee**, Robert Walter 1951- WhoBlA 92
**Magee**, Sadie E. 1932- WhoBlA 92
**Magee**, Stephen Pat 1943- WhoFI 92
**Magee**, Thomas Alexander 1930- AmMWSc 92
**Magee**, Thomas Eston, Jr. 1947- WhoRel 92
**Magee**, Thomas P 1956- WhoAmP 91
**Magee**, Thomas Robert 1951- WhoEnt 92
**Magee**, Wayne Edward 1929- AmMWSc 92
**Magee**, Wes 1939- ConPo 91, IntAu&W 91, WrDr 92
**Magee**, William Lovel 1929- AmMWSc 92
**Magee**, William Thomas 1923- AmMWSc 92
**Magel**, Kenneth I 1950- AmMWSc 92
**Magel**, Mark Lawrence 1960- WhoEnt 92
**Magellan**, Ferdinand 1480?-1521 HisDSpE
**Magen**, David 1945- IntWW 91
**Magen**, Hughes WhoEnt 92
**Magen**, Jed Gary 1953- WhoMW 92
**Magen**, Myron S 1936- AmMWSc 92
**Magenta**, Muriel 1932- WhoWest 92
**Mager**, Artur 1919- AmMWSc 92
**Mager**, Don DrAPF 91
**Mager**, Mart 1935- IntAu&W 91
**Mager**, Milton 1920- AmMWSc 92
**Magerlein**, Barney John 1919- AmMWSc 92
**Magerlein**, James Michael 1950- AmMWSc 92
**Magerman**, Joel David 1960- WhoFI 92
**Magers**, Rose 1960- BlkOlyM
**Magg**, Rebecca Anne Tryon 1950- WhoMW 92
**Maggal**, Moshe Morris 1908- WhoRel 92, WhoWest 92, WrDr 92
**Maggard**, Jim 1946- WhoAmP 91
**Maggard**, Samuel P 1933- AmMWSc 92
**Maggard**, Woodrow Wilson, Jr. 1947- WhoFI 92
**Maggenti**, Armand Richard 1933- AmMWSc 92
**Maggin**, Bruce 1943- WhoEnt 92
**Maggio**, Bruno 1944- AmMWSc 92
**Maggio**, Edward Thomas 1947- AmMWSc 92
**Maggio**, Michael John 1951- WhoEnt 92, WhoMW 92
**Maggio**, Mike DrAPF 91
**Maggio**, Rosalie 1943- IntAu&W 91
**Maggiolo**, Allison Joseph 1943- WhoAmL 92
**Maggioni**, John Alexander 1965- WhoFI 92
**Maggiora**, Gerald M 1938- AmMWSc 92
**Maggiore**, Carl Jerome 1943- AmMWSc 92
**Maggs**, Colin Gordon 1932- WrDr 92
**Maggs**, Peter Blount 1936- WhoAmL 92
**Maggs**, William Jack 1914- Who 92
**Maghour**, Kamel Hassan 1935- IntWW 91
**Maghrabi**, Mahmoud Sulaiman 1935- IntWW 91
**Magid**, Andy Roy 1944- AmMWSc 92
**Magid**, Gail Avrum 1934- WhoWest 92
**Magid**, Ken SmATA 65
**Magid**, Lee 1926- WhoEnt 92
**Magid**, Linda Lee Jenny 1946- AmMWSc 92
**Magid**, Ronald 1938- AmMWSc 92
**Magida**, Arthur Jay 1945- WhoRel 92
**Magidoff**, Robert 1905- ScFEYrs

**Magidson**, Peggy Adrienne 1951- WhoHisp 92
**Magie**, Allan Rupert 1936- AmMWSc 92
**Magie**, Robert Ogden 1906- AmMWSc 92
**Magill**, Clint William 1941- AmMWSc 92
**Magill**, David Thomas 1935- AmMWSc 92
**Magill**, Elizabeth 1959- TwCPaSc
**Magill**, Frank J WhoAmP 91
**Magill**, Frank John 1927- WhoAmL 92, WhoMW 92
**Magill**, Graham Reese 1915- Who 92
**Magill**, Jane Mary 1940- AmMWSc 92
**Magill**, Joseph Henry 1928- AmMWSc 92
**Magill**, Kathleen A. DrAPF 91
**Magill**, Kenneth Derwood, Jr 1933- AmMWSc 92
**Magill**, Robert Earle 1947- AmMWSc 92
**Magill**, Thomas Pleines 1903- AmMWSc 92
**Magin**, Douglas Richard 1947- WhoRel 92
**Magin**, Ralph Walter 1937- AmMWSc 92
**Maginn**, William 1794-1842 DcLB 110 [port]
**Maginnes**, Edward Alexander 1933- AmMWSc 92
**Maginnis**, John Edward 1919- Who 92
**Maginnis**, Ken 1938- Who 92
**Maginnis**, Ninamary Buba 1956- WhoFI 92
**Maginnis**, Robert Joseph Patrick 1942- WhoWest 92
**Maginot**, Andre 1877-1932 EncTR 91, FacFETw
**Magis**, Thomas H WhoIns 92
**Magison**, Ernest Carroll 1926- AmMWSc 92
**Magisos**, Joel Hans 1929- WhoMW 92
**Magistretti**, Vico 1920- DcTwDes, IntWW 91
**Maglacas**, A Mangay AmMWSc 92
**Maglaras**, Arthur D WhoAmP 91
**Magleby**, Karl LeGrande AmMWSc 92
**Magley**, Theodore R 1927- WhoIns 92
**Maglich**, Bogdan 1928- AmMWSc 92
**Maglio**, Anthony E. d1991 NewYTBS 91
**Magliola-Zoch**, Doris AmMWSc 92
**Magliozzi**, Ray 1950?- News 91 [port]
**Magliozzi**, Tom 1938?- News 91 [port]
**Magliulo**, Anthony Rudolph 1931- AmMWSc 92
**Magliveras**, Spyros Simos 1938- AmMWSc 92
**Magloire**, Paul 1907- IntWW 91
**Magnani**, David P WhoAmP 91
**Magnani**, John Louis 1952- AmMWSc 92
**Magnani**, Nicholas J 1942- AmMWSc 92
**Magnano**, Salvatore Paul 1934- WhoFI 92
**Magnant**, Lawrence C, Jr 1949- WhoIns 92
**Magnant**, Suzanne Leonhard 1946- WhoAmL 92
**Magnanti**, Thomas L 1945- AmMWSc 92
**Magnarelli**, Louis Anthony 1945- AmMWSc 92
**Magneli**, Arne 1914- IntWW 91
**Magnell**, Kenneth Robert 1938- AmMWSc 92
**Magner**, Fredric Michael 1950- WhoFI 92
**Magner**, James, Jr. DrAPF 91
**Magner**, James E 1928- IntAu&W 91
**Magner**, James Edmund, Jr. 1928- WhoMW 92
**Magner**, Martin 1900- WhoEnt 92
**Magner**, Rachel Harris WhoFI 92
**Magnes**, Harry Alan 1948- WhoFI 92
**Magnes**, Judah L DcAmImH
**Magnes**, Judah Leon 1877-1948 AmPeW, RelLAm 91
**Magneson**, Roger Dean 1950- WhoWest 92
**Magness**, Bob John 1924- WhoWest 92
**Magness**, Michael Kenneth 1948- WhoAmL 92
**Magness**, Milton S. 1952- WhoRel 92
**Magness**, Rhonda Ann 1946- WhoWest 92
**Magness**, Sallie Stockard DcNCBi 4
**Magness**, T A 1927- AmMWSc 92
**Magniac**, Vernon St Clair Lane 1908- Who 92
**Magnien**, Ernest 1925- AmMWSc 92
**Magnin**, Etienne Nicolas 1922- AmMWSc 92
**Magno**, Michael Gregory 1942- AmMWSc 92
**Magno**, Richard 1944- AmMWSc 92
**Magnoli**, Albert IntMPA 92
**Magnon**, Alberto H., Jr. 1934- WhoFI 92
**Magnum**, Wyatt D. 1961- WhoEnt 92
**Magnus**, Arne 1922- AmMWSc 92
**Magnus**, Donald WhoAmP 91
**Magnus**, George 1930- AmMWSc 92
**Magnus**, Laurence 1955- Who 92
**Magnus**, Martin WhoRel 92
**Magnus**, Philip Douglas 1943- Who 92
**Magnus**, Ralph Arthur 1926- WhoMW 92
**Magnus**, Samuel Woolf 1910- Who 92, WrDr 92
**Magnusen**, Olga C. 1949- WhoHisp 92
**Magnuson**, Alan Douglas 1942- WhoWest 92
**Magnuson**, Ann 1956- IntMPA 92
**Magnuson**, David Allen 1939- WhoMW 92
**Magnuson**, Donald Richard 1951- WhoWest 92
**Magnuson**, Eugene Robert 1933- AmMWSc 92
**Magnuson**, Gerald Edward 1930- WhoAmL 92, WhoFI 92
**Magnuson**, Gustav Donald 1926- AmMWSc 92
**Magnuson**, Harold Joseph 1913- AmMWSc 92
**Magnuson**, James Andrew 1942- AmMWSc 92
**Magnuson**, Jerry Ross 1943- WhoIns 92
**Magnuson**, John Joseph 1934- AmMWSc 92
**Magnuson**, Nancy Susanne 1942- AmMWSc 92
**Magnuson**, Paul Arthur 1937- WhoAmL 92
**Magnuson**, Roger James 1945- WhoAmL 92
**Magnuson**, Vincent Richard 1942- AmMWSc 92
**Magnuson**, Warren Roger 1921- WhoRel 92
**Magnuson**, Winifred Lane 1935- AmMWSc 92
**Magnussen**, Einar 1931- IntWW 91
**Magnussen**, Erik 1940- DcTwDes
**Magnussen**, Max Gene 1927- WhoWest 92
**Magnusson**, Magnus 1929- IntAu&W 91, Who 92, WrDr 92
**Magnusson**, Philip C 1917- AmMWSc 92
**Magnusson**, Sigurdur A. 1928- IntAu&W 91
**Magnusson**, Thor Eyfeld 1937- IntWW 91
**Mago**, Gyula Antal 1938- AmMWSc 92
**Magolske**, Charles J. 1959- WhoFI 92
**Magometov**, Soltan Kekezevich IntWW 91
**Magonet**, Jonathan David 1942- Who 92
**Magoon**, Harold F 1916- WhoAmP 91
**Magoon**, Leslie Blake, III 1941- AmMWSc 92
**Magoon**, Patrick Michael 1953- WhoMW 92
**Magor**, Louis Roland 1945- WhoEnt 92
**Magor**, Walter 1911- Who 92
**Magorian**, James DrAPF 91
**Magorian**, James 1942- IntAu&W 91
**Magorian**, Michelle 1947- ConAu 135, SmATA 67 [port]
**Magorian**, Thomas R 1928- AmMWSc 92
**Magoss**, Imre V 1919- AmMWSc 92
**Magouirk**, Jeffrey Kevins 1961- WhoFI 92
**Magoulias**, Nicholas John 1931- WhoRel 92
**Magoun**, Horace Winchell 1907- AmMWSc 92
**Magovern**, George J AmMWSc 92
**Magowan**, Charles S d1907 BiInAmS
**Magowan**, Peter Alden 1942- IntWW 91, WhoFI 92, WhoWest 92
**Magowan**, Robin DrAPF 91
**Magram**, Saul H. WhoAmL 92
**Magrans**, Berta 1958- WhoFI 92
**Magrans**, Ralph 1947- WhoFI 92
**Magras**, Clement 1948- WhoAmP 91
**Magrath**, Ian 1944- AmMWSc 92
**Magre**, Steve Harvey 1948- WhoAmP 91
**Magri**, Charles George 1956- IntWW 91
**Magri**, Malcolm Joseph 1950- WhoMW 92
**Magrill**, Barry Jon 1951- WhoEnt 92
**Magrill**, Joe Richard, Jr. 1946- WhoRel 92
**Magris**, Claudio 1939- ConAu 133, IntWW 91
**Magritte**, Rene 1898-1967 FacFETw
**Magruder**, B. Lloyd 1933- WhoAmL 92
**Magruder**, Elizabeth 1956- WhoEnt 92
**Magruder**, Ernest P d1915 BiInAmS
**Magruder**, Robert A. 1958- WhoRel 92
**Magruder**, Thomas Malone 1930- WhoWest 92
**Magruder**, Willis Jackson 1935- AmMWSc 92
**Magrutsch**, Walter 1929- Who 92
**Maguder**, Theodore Leo, Jr 1939- AmMWSc 92
**Mague**, Joel Tabor 1940- AmMWSc 92
**Maguire**, Albert Michael 1922- Who 92
**Maguire**, Andrew 1939- WhoAmP 91
**Maguire**, Bassett 1904- AmMWSc 92
**Maguire**, Bassett, Jr 1927- AmMWSc 92
**Maguire**, Benjamin Waldo 1920- Who 92
**Maguire**, Cary McIlwaine 1928- WhoFI 92
**Maguire**, Catherine M. 1961- WhoEnt 92
**Maguire**, Don ScFEYrs
**Maguire**, Gerald Quentin, Jr 1955- AmMWSc 92
**Maguire**, Gregory 1954- WrDr 92
**Maguire**, Harold John 1912- Who 92
**Maguire**, Helen M AmMWSc 92
**Maguire**, Henry C, Jr 1928- AmMWSc 92
**Maguire**, Hugh 1926- Who 92
**Maguire**, James Dale 1930- AmMWSc 92
**Maguire**, James Henry 1944- WhoWest 92
**Maguire**, John David 1932- WhoWest 92
**Maguire**, Joseph F. 1919- WhoRel 92
**Maguire**, Kevin 1958- WhoEnt 92
**Maguire**, Mairead C. Who 92
**Maguire**, Margaret Louise 1944- WhoAmL 92
**Maguire**, Marjorie Paquette 1925- AmMWSc 92
**Maguire**, Max Raymond 1928- WhoRel 92
**Maguire**, Michael Who 92
**Maguire**, Michael 1945- IntAu&W 91, WrDr 92
**Maguire**, Mildred May 1933- AmMWSc 92
**Maguire**, Patrick Joseph 1953- WhoWest 92
**Maguire**, Robert Francis, III 1935- WhoFI 92
**Maguire**, Robert James 1946- AmMWSc 92
**Maguire**, Robert Kenneth 1923- Who 92
**Maguire**, Thomas A. 1949- WhoFI 92
**Maguire**, Thomas Eldon 1952- WhoWest 92
**Maguire**, Waldo Who 92
**Maguire**, Yu Ping 1947- AmMWSc 92
**Maguire-Krupp**, Marjorie Anne 1955- WhoFI 92
**Magwire**, Craig A 1922- AmMWSc 92
**Magyar**, Elaine Stedman 1946- AmMWSc 92
**Magyar**, Gabriel 1914- WhoEnt 92
**Magyar**, James Emery 1945- WhoFI 92
**Magyar**, James George 1947- AmMWSc 92
**Mah Soo-Lay** 1909- IntWW 91
**Mah**, John Jenien, Sr. 1934- WhoFI 92
**Mah**, Richard S H 1934- AmMWSc 92
**Mah**, Robert A 1932- AmMWSc 92
**Mahachi**, Moven Enock 1948- IntWW 91
**Mahadeva**, Madhu Narayan 1930- AmMWSc 92
**Mahadeva**, Manoranjan 1955- WhoFI 92
**Mahadeva**, Wijeyaraj Anandakumar 1952- WhoFI 92
**Mahadevan**, Parameswar 1926- AmMWSc 92
**Mahadevan**, Selvakumaran 1948- AmMWSc 92
**Mahadeviah**, Inally 1928- AmMWSc 92
**Mahadik**, Sahebarao P 1941- AmMWSc 92
**Mahady**, Catherine Mary 1936- WhoRel 92
**Mahaffey**, Kathryn Rose 1943- AmMWSc 92
**Mahaffey**, Marcia Jeanne Hixson WhoWest 92
**Mahaffey**, Mary Ann WhoAmP 91
**Mahaffey**, Merrill 1937- WorArt 1980 [port]
**Mahaffey**, Michael Wayne 1948- WhoAmP 91
**Mahaffey**, Vicki 1952- ConAu 133
**Mahaffy**, James Francis 1947- WhoMW 92
**Mahaffy**, John Harlan AmMWSc 92
**Mahajan**, Damodar K AmMWSc 92
**Mahajan**, Om Prakash 1936- AmMWSc 92
**Mahajan**, Roop Lal 1943- AmMWSc 92
**Mahajan**, Satish Chander 1935- AmMWSc 92
**Mahajan**, Subhash 1939- AmMWSc 92
**Mahajan**, Sudesh K 1948- AmMWSc 92
**Mahajan**, Swadesh Mitter 1944- AmMWSc 92
**Mahak**, Francine Timothy 1950- WhoWest 92
**Mahal**, Taj 1942- WhoEnt 92
**Mahalak**, Edward E 1921- WhoAmP 91
**Mahalingam**, Lalgudi Muthuswamy 1946- AmMWSc 92
**Mahalingam**, R AmMWSc 92
**Mahall**, Bruce Elliott 1946- AmMWSc 92
**Mahan**, Alfred T BenetAL 91
**Mahan**, Alfred Thayer 1840-1914 AmPeW, RComAH
**Mahan**, Dennis Hart 1802-1871 BiInAmS
**Mahan**, Donald C 1938- AmMWSc 92
**Mahan**, Dulany, Jr. 1914- WhoAmL 92
**Mahan**, Eugene Robert 1933- WhoAmP 91
**Mahan**, Frank Hoyt 1867-1905 DcNCBi 4
**Mahan**, Gene WhoAmP 91
**Mahan**, Gerald Dennis 1937- AmMWSc 92
**Mahan**, Jeanne F 1921- WhoAmP 91
**Mahan**, Kent Ira 1942- AmMWSc 92
**Mahan**, Michael Wilson 1951- WhoEnt 92
**Mahan**, Robert E. 1946- WhoAmL 92
**Mahan**, Suman Mulakhraj 1955- AmMWSc 92
**Mahan**, Susan Jennifer 1963- WhoAmL 92
**Mahan-Powell**, Lena 1951- WhoBlA 92
**Mahanaim**, Anna DrAPF 91
**Mahanes**, Michael Wayne 1956- WhoEnt 92
**Mahaney**, Calvin Merritt 1929- WhoIns 92
**Mahaney**, John Gage 1927- WhoWest 92
**Mahaney**, Stephen Ross 1948- WhoWest 92
**Mahanna**, Robert Dean 1925- WhoMW 92
**Mahanthappa**, Kalyana T 1934- AmMWSc 92
**Mahanti**, Subhendra Deb 1945- AmMWSc 92
**Mahany**, Carolyne T WhoAmP 91
**Mahapatra**, Jayanta 1928- ConPo 91
**Mahar**, John Henry 1934- WhoFI 92
**Mahar**, Patrick Larry 1963- WhoRel 92
**Mahar**, Thomas J 1949- AmMWSc 92
**Mahar**, William F, Jr 1919- WhoAmP 91
**Mahar**, William F, Jr 1947- WhoAmP 91
**Maharaj Ji**, Guru 1957- RelLAm 91
**Mahard**, Richard H 1915- AmMWSc 92
**Maharis**, George 1928- IntMPA 92
**Maharishi Mahesh Yogi** RelLAm 91
**Mahasandana**, Suli 1919- IntWW 91
**Mahathero**, Visuddhananda 1909- WhoRel 92
**Mahathir bin Mohamad** 1925- Who 92
**Mahathir Bin Mohamed** 1925- IntWW 91
**Mahathir bin Mohammad**, Seri 1925- FacFETw
**Mahavier**, William S 1930- AmMWSc 92
**Mahay**, Stephen Thomas 1947- WhoWest 92
**Mahboubi**, Ezzat 1929- AmMWSc 92
**Mahbubani**, Kishore 1948- IntWW 91
**Mahbubuzzaman**, Mohammad 1929- IntWW 91
**Mahdi**, Sadiq Al 1936- IntWW 91
**Mahdi Al Tajir**, Mohamed 1931- IntWW 91
**Mahdy**, Mohamed Sabet 1930- AmMWSc 92
**Mahe**, Henry Edward, Jr 1936- WhoAmP 91
**Mahendroo**, Prem P 1931- AmMWSc 92
**Maher**, Charles Stanley 1956- WhoMW 92
**Maher**, Daniel Carl 1954- WhoFI 92
**Maher**, David Willard 1934- WhoEnt 92, WhoMW 92
**Maher**, Dennis Patrick 1938- WhoWest 92
**Maher**, Edward Joseph 1939- WhoAmL 92
**Maher**, F J 1915- AmMWSc 92
**Maher**, Fran 1938- WhoFI 92
**Maher**, Frank Aloysius 1941- WhoMW 92
**Maher**, Galeb Hamid 1937- AmMWSc 92
**Maher**, Genevieve Arlington 1959- WhoMW 92
**Maher**, George Garrison 1919- AmMWSc 92
**Maher**, James Vincent 1942- AmMWSc 92
**Maher**, James William 1948- WhoMW 92
**Maher**, John Edward 1925- WhoFI 92
**Maher**, John Francis 1929- AmMWSc 92
**Maher**, John Francis 1938- WhoRel 92
**Maher**, John Francis 1943- WhoFI 92, WhoWest 92
**Maher**, John Philip 1942- AmMWSc 92
**Maher**, Joseph Anthony 1929- WhoRel 92
**Maher**, Laurence James 1926- WhoFI 92
**Maher**, Leo T. d1991 NewYTBS 91
**Maher**, Louis James, Jr 1933- AmMWSc 92
**Maher**, Mary Z. 1941- WhoEnt 92
**Maher**, Michael John 1928- AmMWSc 92
**Maher**, Norman Allen 1931- WhoWest 92
**Maher**, Patrick Joseph 1936- WhoFI 92
**Maher**, Paul Regis 1925- WhoRel 92
**Maher**, Philip Kenerick 1930- AmMWSc 92
**Maher**, Richard Joseph 1943- WhoMW 92
**Maher**, Stephen Trivett 1949- WhoAmL 92
**Maher**, Stuart Wilder 1918- AmMWSc 92
**Maher**, Terence 1941- Who 92
**Maher**, Terence Anthony 1935- IntWW 91, Who 92
**Maher**, Terry Marina 1955- WhoMW 92, WhoRel 92
**Maher**, Thomas Dunseath 1945- WhoAmL 92
**Maher**, Thomas George 1947- WhoEnt 92
**Maher**, Timothy John 1953- AmMWSc 92
**Maher**, Veronica Mary 1931- AmMWSc 92
**Maher**, William Alan 1929- WhoAmP 91
**Maher**, William Francis 1916- Who 92
**Maher**, William J 1927- AmMWSc 92
**Maher**, William James 1937- WhoFI 92
**Maher**, William Michael 1947- WhoEnt 92
**Mahern**, Louis J, Jr WhoAmP 91
**Mahesh Yogi**, Maharishi 1911?- News 91 [port], -91-3 [port]
**Mahesh**, Virendra B 1932- AmMWSc 92
**Maheshwari**, Kewal Krishnan AmMWSc 92
**Maheshwari**, Shriram 1931- IntAu&W 91, WrDr 92
**Maheswari**, Shyam P 1947- AmMWSc 92

**Mahey,** John Andrew 1932- WhoMW 92
**Mahfouz,** Naguib 1911- FacFETw, IntAu&W 91, Who 92, WhoNob 90
**Mahfuz,** Nagib 1911- IntWW 91
**Mahfuz,** Najib 1911?- WhoNob 90
**Mahgoub,** Mohammed Ahmed 1908- IntWW 91
**Mahig,** Joseph 1930- AmMWSc 92
**Mahilum,** Benjamin Comawas 1931- AmMWSc 92
**Mahin,** George E. 1914- WhoBlA 92
**Mahin,** James Richard 1948- WhoRel 92
**Mahindra,** Keshub 1923- IntWW 91
**Mahl,** Mearl Carl 1938- AmMWSc 92
**Mahla,** Frederick BiInAmS
**Mahlberg,** Paul Gordon 1928- AmMWSc 92
**Mahle,** Christoph E 1938- AmMWSc 92
**Mahle,** Nels H 1943- AmMWSc 92
**Mahle,** Patsy Beghtel 1942- WhoRel 92
**Mahler,** Bruce Paul 1948- WhoEnt 92
**Mahler,** Carol DrAPF 91
**Mahler,** David 1911- WhoWest 92
**Mahler,** David S 1946- AmMWSc 92
**Mahler,** Glenn Richard 1949- WhoWest 92
**Mahler,** Gustav 1860-1911 FacFETw [port], NewAmDM
**Mahler,** Halfdan 1923- AmMWSc 92, IntWW 91
**Mahler,** Halfdan Theodor 1923- Who 92
**Mahler,** Henry 1832-1895 DcNCBi 4
**Mahler,** Jerry 1957- WhoEnt 92
**Mahler,** Margaret S 1897-1985 FacFETw
**Mahler,** Richard Joseph 1934- AmMWSc 92
**Mahler,** Robert Frederick 1924- Who 92
**Mahler,** Robert John 1932- AmMWSc 92
**Mahler,** Scott A. 1964- WhoFI 92
**Mahler,** Stephanie Irene 1952- WhoFI 92
**Mahler,** Theodore Wesley 1942- WhoIns 92
**Mahler,** Walter 1929- AmMWSc 92
**Mahler,** William Fred 1930- AmMWSc 92
**Mahler-Sussman,** Leona DrAPF 91
**Mahlman,** Bert H 1922- AmMWSc 92
**Mahlman,** Harvey Arthur 1923- AmMWSc 92
**Mahlman,** Jerry David 1940- AmMWSc 92
**Mahlman,** Robert Otto 1934- WhoEnt 92
**Mahlo,** Edwin K 1923- AmMWSc 92
**Mahlstede,** John Peter 1923- AmMWSc 92
**Mahlum,** Dale Duane 1930- WhoWest 92
**Mahlum,** Daniel Dennis 1933- AmMWSc 92
**Mahmoodi,** Parviz 1931- AmMWSc 92
**Mahmoodi,** Suzanne Hoegh 1935- WhoMW 92
**Mahmoud,** Adel A F 1941- AmMWSc 92
**Mahmoud,** Aly Ahmed 1935- AmMWSc 92
**Mahmoud,** Ben 1935- WhoMW 92
**Mahmoud,** Hormoz Massoud 1918- AmMWSc 92
**Mahmoud,** Ibrahim Younis 1933- AmMWSc 92
**Mahmud,** Sultan IntWW 91
**Mahmud,** Anisul Islam 1947- IntWW 91
**Mahmud Husain,** Syed Abul Basher 1916- IntWW 91, Who 92
**Mahner,** Jerry Wayne 1964- WhoRel 92
**Mahnic,** Frank, Jr 1946- WhoAmP 91
**Mahnk,** Karen 1956- WhoAmL 92
**Mahnke,** Kurt Luther 1945- WhoMW 92
**Maho,** Tyrone Jay 1963- WhoAmL 92
**Mahofski,** Stephen Samuel 1961- WhoEnt 92
**Mahon,** Alice 1937- Who 92
**Mahon,** Arthur Joseph 1934- WhoAmL 92
**Mahon,** Charles Joseph 1939- Who 92
**Mahon,** Denis Who 92
**Mahon,** Denis 1910- IntWW 91
**Mahon,** Derek 1941- ConPo 91, FacFETw, IntAu&W 91, WrDr 92
**Mahon,** Gerald Thomas 1922- Who 92
**Mahon,** Harold P 1931- AmMWSc 92
**Mahon,** Jeanne DrAPF 91
**Mahon,** John Denis 1910- Who 92
**Mahon,** John K. 1912- WrDr 92
**Mahon,** Margaret Mary 1928- WhoFI 92
**Mahon,** Peter 1909- Who 92
**Mahon,** Rita 1949- AmMWSc 92
**Mahon,** William 1940- Who 92
**Mahon,** William A 1929- AmMWSc 92
**Mahone,** Barbara J. WhoBlA 92
**Mahone,** Colt TwCWW 91
**Mahoney,** Arthur W 1939- AmMWSc 92
**Mahoney,** Bernard Launcelot, Jr 1936- AmMWSc 92
**Mahoney,** Charles Cyril 1903-1968 TwCPaSc
**Mahoney,** Charles Lindbergh 1928- AmMWSc 92
**Mahoney,** Con 1927- WhoAmP 91
**Mahoney,** Dennis Leonard 1950- Who 92
**Mahoney,** Dennis Martin 1941- WhoFI 92
**Mahoney,** Francis James 1914- WhoAmP 91
**Mahoney,** Francis Joseph 1936- AmMWSc 92
**Mahoney,** Gerard M. d1991 NewYTBS 91
**Mahoney,** J Daniel WhoAmP 91
**Mahoney,** J. Daniel 1931- WhoAmL 92
**Mahoney,** James A, Jr 1935- WhoIns 92
**Mahoney,** James Edward 1952- WhoAmL 92
**Mahoney,** James F WhoAmP 91
**Mahoney,** James P. 1927- WhoRel 92
**Mahoney,** James Patrick 1925- WhoRel 92
**Mahoney,** Joan Munroe 1938- AmMWSc 92
**Mahoney,** John WhoAmP 91
**Mahoney,** John 1940- IntMPA 92
**Mahoney,** John Aloysius 1931- Who 92
**Mahoney,** John J. DcAmImH
**Mahoney,** Kathleen Mary 1954- WhoAmL 92
**Mahoney,** Keith Weston 1939- WhoBlA 92
**Mahoney,** Margaret E 1924- AmMWSc 92
**Mahoney,** Mary 1845-1926 NotBlAW 92
**Mahoney,** Mary L 1945- WhoAmP 91
**Mahoney,** Maureen E. 1954- WhoAmL 92
**Mahoney,** Michael James 1960- WhoFI 92, WhoWest 92
**Mahoney,** Michael John 1954- WhoMW 92
**Mahoney,** Michael S 1939- AmMWSc 92
**Mahoney,** Olivia 1952- ConAu 133
**Mahoney,** Patricia Aileen 1952- WhoAmL 92
**Mahoney,** Patrick B 1930- WhoIns 92
**Mahoney,** Patrick Morgan 1929- IntWW 91
**Mahoney,** Richard WhoAmP 91, WhoWest 92
**Mahoney,** Richard John 1934- IntWW 91, WhoFI 92, WhoMW 92
**Mahoney,** Robert Patrick 1934- AmMWSc 92
**Mahoney,** Robert William 1936- WhoFI 92, WhoMW 92
**Mahoney,** Rosemary 1961- ConAu 135
**Mahoney,** Thomas Arthur 1928- WrDr 92
**Mahoney,** Thomas Henry Donald 1913- WhoAmP 91
**Mahoney,** Walter C 1951- AmMWSc 92
**Mahoney,** William C 1927- AmMWSc 92
**Mahoney,** William Grattan 1925- WhoAmL 92
**Mahoney,** William Patrick, Jr 1916- WhoAmP 91
**Mahony,** David Edward AmMWSc 92
**Mahony,** Francis Joseph 1915- Who 92
**Mahony,** Harold Andrew 1933- WhoAmL 92
**Mahony,** Jodie Kirby, II 1939- WhoAmP 91
**Mahony,** John Daniel 1931- AmMWSc 92
**Mahony,** John Keefer d1990 Who 92N
**Mahony,** Phillip DrAPF 91
**Mahony,** Roger Michael 1926- RelLAm 91
**Mahony,** Roger Michael 1936- WhoRel 92, WhoWest 92
**Mahony,** Sheila LesBEnT 92
**Mahood,** Gail Ann 1951- AmMWSc 92
**Mahorn,** Rick Allen 1958- WhoBlA 92
**Mahorsky,** Jody DrAPF 91
**Mahowald,** Anthony Eugene 1946- WhoMW 92
**Mahowald,** Anthony P 1932- AmMWSc 92
**Mahowald,** Mark Edward 1931- AmMWSc 92
**Mahowald,** Theodore Augustus 1930- AmMWSc 92
**Mahowald,** Thomas Alan 1955- WhoMW 92
**Mahraun,** Arthur 1890-1950 BiDExR, EncTR 91
**Mahrer,** Neil Bert 1943- WhoEnt 92
**Mahrle,** Benjamin Carl 1942- WhoFI 92
**Mahrous,** Haroun 1921- AmMWSc 92
**Mahrt,** Jerome L 1937- AmMWSc 92
**Mahtab,** M Ashraf 1935- AmMWSc 92
**Mahtook,** Robert A., Jr. 1958- WhoAmL 92
**Mahuron,** D Jack 1935- WhoAmP 91
**Mahy,** Brian Wilfred John 1937- Who 92
**Mahy,** Margaret 1936- Au&Arts 8 [port], IntAu&W 91, WrDr 92
**Mahy,** Margaret May 1936- Who 92
**Mai Taie** EncAmaz 91
**Mai,** Gottfried Erhard Willy 1940- IntAu&W 91
**Mai,** Harold Leverne 1928- WhoWest 92
**Mai,** Henry Donghung 1930- WhoMW 92
**Mai,** Klaus L 1930- AmMWSc 92
**Mai,** William Frederick 1916- AmMWSc 92
**Maiale,** Nicholas Joseph 1951- WhoAmP 91
**Maibach,** Ben C., III 1946- WhoFI 92
**Maibach,** Howard I 1929- AmMWSc 92
**Maibaum,** Matthew 1946- IntAu&W 91
**Maibaum,** Richard d1991 NewYTBS 91 [port]
**Maibaum,** Richard 1909-1991 ConAu 133
**Maibenco,** Helen Craig 1917- AmMWSc 92
**Maickel,** Roger Philip 1933- AmMWSc 92
**Maicki,** Carol WhoAmP 91
**Maid of Saragossa,** The EncAmaz 91
**Maid,** The EncAmaz 91
**Maida,** Adam J. 1930- WhoRel 92
**Maida,** George Francis 1955- WhoEnt 92
**Maiden,** Colin James 1933- IntWW 91, Who 92
**Maiden,** Jennifer 1949- ConPo 91, WrDr 92
**Maiden,** Robert Mitchell 1933- Who 92
**Maidenberg,** Anthony 1947- WhoAmP 91
**Maidenberg,** David Harris 1949- WhoAmP 91
**Maidique,** Modesto A. 1940- WhoHisp 92
**Maidlow,** Dolores Mary 1934- WhoMW 92
**Maidman,** Bret Arron 1962- WhoAmL 92
**Maidman,** Richard Harvey Mortimer 1933- WhoFI 92
**Maidman,** Stephen Paul 1954- WhoAmL 92
**Maidment,** Francis Edward 1942- Who 92
**Maidment,** Kenneth 1910-1990 AnObit 1990
**Maidment,** Kenneth John d1990 Who 92N
**Maidment,** Ted Who 92
**Maidou,** Henri 1936- IntWW 91
**Maidstone,** Archdeacon of Who 92
**Maidstone,** Bishop Suffragan of 1935- Who 92
**Maidstone,** Viscount 1967- Who 92
**Maiello,** Anthony Joseph 1943- WhoEnt 92
**Maiello,** John Michael 1942- AmMWSc 92
**Maienschein,** Fred 1925- AmMWSc 92
**Maienschein,** Jane Ann 1950- AmMWSc 92
**Maier,** Charles Robert 1928- AmMWSc 92
**Maier,** Chris Thomas 1949- AmMWSc 92
**Maier,** Cornell C. 1925- WhoWest 92
**Maier,** Eugene Alfred 1929- AmMWSc 92
**Maier,** Eugene Edward J 1937- WhoAmP 91
**Maier,** Eugene Jacob Rudolph 1931- AmMWSc 92
**Maier,** Francis Xavier 1948- WhoRel 92
**Maier,** Frank d1990 NewYTBS 91
**Maier,** George D 1930- AmMWSc 92
**Maier,** Gerald James 1928- WhoFI 92
**Maier,** Harold Geistweit 1937- WhoAmL 92
**Maier,** Herbert Nathaniel 1943- AmMWSc 92
**Maier,** Johnnie A, Jr 1951- WhoAmP 91
**Maier,** Karl George 1937- WhoFI 92
**Maier,** Paul Luther 1930- IntAu&W 91, WhoRel 92, WrDr 92
**Maier,** Paul Victor 1947- WhoFI 92
**Maier,** Peter Klaus 1929- WhoAmL 92
**Maier,** Richard Franklin 1925- WhoAmP 91
**Maier,** Robert Andrew 1949- WhoFI 92
**Maier,** Robert Hawthorne 1927- AmMWSc 92, WhoFI 92
**Maier,** Robert J 1951- AmMWSc 92
**Maier,** Robert S 1957- AmMWSc 92
**Maier,** Siegfried 1930- AmMWSc 92
**Maier,** V P 1930- AmMWSc 92
**Maier,** Walter Arthur 1893-1950 RelLAm 91
**Maier,** William Bryan, II 1937- AmMWSc 92
**Maier,** William Christopher 1965- WhoFI 92
**Maierhofer,** Charles Richard 1911- AmMWSc 92
**Maierhofer,** Louis Joseph 1927- WhoEnt 92
**Maiese,** Dominic 1919- WhoAmP 91
**Maietta,** Julia L 1909- WhoAmP 91
**Maigret,** Maureen Elaine 1944- WhoAmP 91
**Maiguashca,** Mesias 1938- ConCom 92
**Maihack,** Samuel Paul 1955- WhoRel 92
**Maihofer,** Werner 1918- IntWW 91
**Maij-Weggen,** Hanja 1943- IntWW 91
**Maikish,** Charles John 1946- WhoAmL 92
**Maikowski,** Hans Eberhard 1908-1933 EncTR 91
**Maikowski,** Thomas Robert 1947- WhoRel 92
**Mail,** Audrey Maureen 1924- WrDr 92
**Mailen,** James Clifford 1937- AmMWSc 92
**Mailer,** Norman DrAPF 91, NewYTBS 91 [port], SourALJ
**Mailer,** Norman 1923- BenetAL 91, ConNov 91, FacFETw [port], RComAH, Who 92, WrDr 92
**Mailer,** Norman Kingsley 1923- IntAu&W 91, IntWW 91
**Maillard** EncAmaz 91
**Maillard,** Pierre 1916- IntWW 91
**Maillart,** Ella 1903- IntWW 91, Who 92
**Maillart,** Robert 1872-1940 DcTwDes, FacFETw
**Maillet,** Antonine 1929- BenetAL 91
**Maillet,** Benoit de 1656-1738 BlkwCEP
**Maillet,** Pierre Paul Georges 1923- IntWW 91
**Mailliard,** William Somers 1917- WhoAmP 91
**Maillie,** Hugh David 1932- AmMWSc 92
**Maillol,** Aristide 1861-1944 FacFETw
**Maillot,** Patrick Gilles 1958- AmMWSc 92, WhoWest 92
**Mailloux,** Gerard 1945- AmMWSc 92
**Mailloux,** Gordon Emery 1920- WhoAmP 91
**Mailloux,** Robert Joseph 1938- AmMWSc 92
**Mailman,** Beatrice Alice 1926- WhoAmP 91
**Mailman,** David Sherwin 1938- AmMWSc 92
**Mailman,** Richard Bernard 1945- AmMWSc 92
**Mails,** Thomas E. 1920?- ConAu 134
**Maiman,** George 1939- WhoFI 92
**Maiman,** Theodore Harold 1927- AmMWSc 92
**Maimane,** Arthur John 1932- IntAu&W 91
**Maimon,** Moshe ben 1138-1204 DcLB 115 [port]
**Maimoni,** Arturo 1927- AmMWSc 92
**Maimonides,** Moses 1138-1204 DcLB 115 [port]
**Main,** A. Donald WhoRel 92
**Main,** Alexander Russell 1925- AmMWSc 92
**Main,** Andrew James 1942- AmMWSc 92
**Main,** Barbara Alice 1922- WhoAmP 91
**Main,** Charles Edward 1933- AmMWSc 92
**Main,** Darrell Franklin 1943- WhoMW 92
**Main,** David 1929- IntMPA 92
**Main,** Douglas Martin 1959- WhoRel 92
**Main,** Frank Fiddes 1905- Who 92
**Main,** James Hamilton Prentice 1933- AmMWSc 92
**Main,** John AmPeW
**Main,** John Roy 1930- Who 92
**Main,** Laurie 1922- WhoEnt 92
**Main,** N. James 1929- WhoRel 92
**Main,** Peter 1925- Who 92
**Main,** Robert Andrew 1923- AmMWSc 92
**Main,** Robert Gail 1932- WhoEnt 92, WhoWest 92
**Main,** Robert Gordon, Jr. 1951- WhoAmL 92
**Main,** Robin-Lee 1964- WhoAmL 92
**Main,** Stephen Paul 1940- AmMWSc 92, WhoMW 92
**Main,** William 1844?-1918 BiInAmS
**Main,** William Francis 1921- AmMWSc 92
**Maina,** Charles Gatere 1931- IntWW 91
**Mainardi,** Cesare Roberto Giovanni 1962- WhoMW 92
**Mainardi,** James Albert 1939- WhoIns 92
**Maine,** Charles Eric 1921- TwCSFW 91
**Maine,** Connie G WhoAmP 91
**Maine,** John 1942- TwCPaSc
**Maine,** Thomas d1896 BiInAmS
**Mainelli,** Helen Kenik 1935- WhoRel 92
**Mainer,** James Emmitt 1898-1971 DcNCBi 4
**Maines,** C Bruce 1926- WhoIns 92
**Maines,** Clifford Bruce 1926- WhoFI 92, WhoWest 92
**Maines,** James Dennis 1937- Who 92
**Maines,** Mahin D 1941- AmMWSc 92
**Mainey,** Donald E WhoAmP 91
**Maingard de la Ville es Offrans,** Rene 1917- Who 92
**Maini,** Amar 1911- Who 92
**Mainier,** Robert 1925- AmMWSc 92
**Mainieri,** Mike 1938- WhoEnt 92
**Mainigi,** Kumar D AmMWSc 92
**Mainil,** Pierre 1925- IntWW 91
**Mainland,** Gordon Bruce 1945- AmMWSc 92, WhoMW 92
**Maino,** John Carlton, II 1953- WhoMW 92
**Maino,** Vernon Carter AmMWSc 92
**Mainone,** Robert Franklin 1929- WrDr 92
**Mainor,** Thomas Foy 1934- WhoRel 92
**Mains,** Gilbert Joseph 1929- AmMWSc 92
**Mains,** Richard E 1947- AmMWSc 92
**Mains,** Robert M 1918- AmMWSc 92
**Mainster,** Martin Aron 1942- AmMWSc 92
**Mainwaring,** Maurice K. C. Who 92
**Mainwaring,** William Lewis 1935- WhoFI 92
**Maio,** Domenic Anthony 1935- AmMWSc 92
**Maio,** Joseph James 1929- AmMWSc 92
**Maio,** Keith David 1957- WhoFI 92
**Maiocchi,** Christine 1949- WhoAmL 92
**Maiolo,** Joseph DrAPF 91
**Maione,** Theodore E 1956- AmMWSc 92
**Maiorana,** Virginia Catherine 1947- AmMWSc 92
**Maiorino,** Michael Joseph 1955- WhoFI 92

**Maiorov**, Boris Aleksandrovich 1938- *SovUnBD*
**Maiotti**, Dennis Paul 1950- *WhoMW 92*
**Mair**, Alexander *Who 92*
**Mair**, Alexander 1922- *Who 92*
**Mair**, Alexander Craig 1948- *IntAu&W 91*
**Mair**, Bruce Logan 1951- *WhoMW 92*
**Mair**, Charles 1838-1927 *BenetAL 91, RfGEnL 91*
**Mair**, Craig 1948- *WrDr 92*
**Mair**, Edward MacDonald 1951- *WhoFI 92*
**Mair**, H Allen *IntAu&W 91X*
**Mair**, John Magnus 1912- *Who 92*
**Mair**, Robert Dixon 1921- *AmMWSc 92*
**Mair**, William Austyn 1917- *Who 92*
**Maire o Ciaragain** *EncAmaz 91*
**Maire**, Edmond 1931- *IntWW 91*
**Mairhuber**, John Carl 1922- *AmMWSc 92*
**Mairie**, Simone 1939- *IntWW 91*
**Mairose**, Paul Timothy 1956- *WhoWest 92*
**Mairowitz**, David 1943- *WrDr 92*
**Mairs**, Candyce Wenborg 1958- *WhoMW 92*
**Mairs**, Nancy *DrAPF 91*
**Mairs**, Nancy 1943- *WrDr 92*
**Mais** *Who 92*
**Mais**, Baron 1911- *Who 92*
**Mais**, Dale E 1952- *AmMWSc 92*
**Mais**, Francis Thomas 1927- *Who 92*
**Mais**, Hugh 1907- *Who 92*
**Mais**, Roger 1905-1955 *RfGEnL 91*
**Mais Of Walbrook**, Baron 1911- *IntWW 91*
**Maisch**, Henry Charles Christian 1862-1901 *BiInAmS*
**Maisch**, John Michael 1831-1893 *BiInAmS*
**Maisch**, Weldon Frederick 1935- *AmMWSc 92*
**Maisch**, William George 1929- *AmMWSc 92*
**Maisel**, Allan Steven 1949- *WhoAmL 92*
**Maisel**, Carolyn *DrAPF 91*
**Maisel**, Darrell Keith 1947- *WhoFI 92, WhoMW 92*
**Maisel**, Herbert 1930- *AmMWSc 92*
**Maisel**, Melvin L 1924- *WhoIns 92*
**Maisel**, Michael 1947- *WhoFI 92*
**Maisel**, Sherman Joseph 1918- *IntWW 91*
**Maisey**, Michael Norman 1939- *Who 92*
**Maish**, Frank Anthony 1953- *WhoAmP 91*
**Maisky**, Mischa 1948- *IntWW 91*
**Maisner**, Aleksander 1921- *Who 92*
**Maison**, Donald J, Jr 1947- *WhoAmP 91*
**Maisonrouge**, Jacques G. 1924- *IntWW 91*
**Maisonrouge**, Jacques Gaston 1924- *Who 92*
**Maissel**, Leon I 1930- *AmMWSc 92*
**Maistre**, Joseph, Comte de 1753-1821 *GuFrLit 1*
**Maistre**, Roy de 1894- *TwCPaSc*
**Maitama-Sule**, Alhaji Yusuf 1929- *IntWW 91*
**Maith**, Sheila Francine 1961- *WhoBlA 92*
**Maitland** *Who 92*
**Maitland**, Master of 1965- *Who 92*
**Maitland**, Viscount 1937- *Who 92*
**Maitland**, Alastair George 1916- *Who 92*
**Maitland**, David Henry 1922- *Who 92*
**Maitland**, David Johnston 1922- *WhoRel 92*
**Maitland**, Donald 1922- *Who 92*
**Maitland**, Donald James Dundas 1922- *IntWW 91*
**Maitland**, Edward 1824-1897 *ScFEYrs*
**Maitland**, Guy Edison Clay 1942- *WhoAmL 92, WhoAmP 91*
**Maitland**, James Dean 1960- *WhoWest 92*
**Maitland**, John W, Jr 1936- *WhoAmP 91*
**Maitland**, Leo C. 1928- *WhoBlA 92*
**Maitland**, Margaret *ConAu 35NR*
**Maitland**, Paul 1863-1909 *TwCPaSc*
**Maitland**, Richard John 1952- *Who 92*
**Maitland Davies**, Keith Laurence 1938- *Who 92*
**Maitland-Makgill-Crichton** *Who 92*
**Maitland Smith**, Geoffrey 1933- *IntWW 91, Who 92*
**Maitlis**, Peter M. 1933- *IntWW 91*
**Maitlis**, Peter Michael 1933- *Who 92*
**Maitra**, Priyatosh 1930- *WrDr 92*
**Maitra**, Umadas *AmMWSc 92*
**Maitre**, Edmond 1840-1898 *ThHEIm [port]*
**Maitre**, Muriel L 1920- *WhoAmP 91*
**Maitzen**, Dolores Ann 1952- *WhoWest 92*
**Maiwurm**, James John 1948- *WhoAmL 92*
**Maixner**, R R 1945- *WhoAmP 91*
**Maiyegun**, Nojim *BlkOlyM*
**Maizeaux**, Pierre des 1673-1745 *BlkwCEP*
**Maizell**, Robert Edward 1924- *AmMWSc 92*
**Maja-Pearce**, Adewale 1953- *IntAu&W 91*
**Majak**, Walter 1942- *AmMWSc 92*
**Majali**, Abdel Salam 1925- *IntWW 91*
**Majarakis**, James Demetrios 1915- *AmMWSc 92*
**Majchier**, Vincent R *WhoAmP 91*
**Majchrowicz**, Edward 1920- *AmMWSc 92*
**Majchrowicz**, Paul Richard 1947- *WhoFI 92*
**Majdalani**, Nassim Mikail 1912- *IntWW 91*
**Majek**, Mark Wayne 1957- *WhoAmP 91*
**Majekodunmi**, Moses Adekoyejo 1916- *IntWW 91*
**Majernik**, Barbara Ellen 1942- *WhoRel 92*
**Majerus**, Philip W 1936- *AmMWSc 92*
**Majeske**, Daniel Lee 1947- *WhoRel 92*
**Majeski**, Hank d1991 *NewYTBS 91*
**Majete**, Clayton Aaron 1941- *WhoBlA 92*
**Majette**, L. Dean 1947- *WhoRel 92*
**Majewski**, Aleksander 1926- *IntAu&W 91*
**Majewski**, Frank Walter 1922- *WhoIns 92*
**Majewski**, Henryk *IntWW 91*
**Majewski**, Janusz 1931- *IntAu&W 91, IntWW 91*
**Majewski**, Robert Francis 1927- *AmMWSc 92*
**Majewski**, Theodore E 1925- *AmMWSc 92*
**Majhanovich**, Steve 1926- *WhoAmP 91*
**Majied-Muhammad**, Arthur 1921- *WhoRel 92*
**Majithia**, Jayanti 1938- *AmMWSc 92*
**Majithia**, Surendra Singh 1895- *Who 92*
**Majkrzak**, Charles Francis 1950- *AmMWSc 92*
**Majmudar**, Harit 1929- *AmMWSc 92*
**Majmundar**, Hasmukhrai Hiralal 1932- *AmMWSc 92*
**Majo**, Gian Francesco 1732-1770 *NewAmDM*
**Major** *Who 92*
**Major**, Alan S *WhoAmP 91*
**Major**, Andre Wilfrid 1942- *WhoEnt 92*
**Major**, Benjamin 1924- *WhoBlA 92*
**Major**, Beverly Bruhn 1935- *WhoAmP 91*
**Major**, Charles 1856-1913 *BenetAL 91*
**Major**, Charles Walter 1926- *AmMWSc 92*
**Major**, Clarence *DrAPF 91*
**Major**, Clarence 1936- *BenetAL 91, BlkLC [port], ConNov 91, ConPo 91, IntWW 91, WhoBlA 92, WrDr 92*
**major**, devorah *DrAPF 91*
**Major**, Fouad George 1929- *AmMWSc 92*
**Major**, Gerald Hilson, Jr. 1931- *WhoRel 92*
**Major**, Gerri 1894-1984 *NotBlAW 92*
**Major**, Henrymae M. 1935- *WhoBlA 92*
**Major**, J. Russell 1921- *WrDr 92*
**Major**, Jack 1917- *AmMWSc 92*
**Major**, Jean-Louis 1937- *IntWW 91*
**Major**, John 1943- *FacFETw [port], IntWW 91, News 91 [port], Who 92*
**Major**, John 1945- *Who 92*
**Major**, John Keene 1924- *AmMWSc 92, WhoEnt 92*
**Major**, Julie C. 1964- *TwCPaSc*
**Major**, Kathleen 1906- *IntWW 91, Who 92*
**Major**, Kevin 1949- *IntAu&W 91, WrDr 92*
**Major**, Marguerite Louise 1929- *WhoWest 92*
**Major**, Mary Jo 1955- *WhoEnt 92*
**Major**, Paul Charles 1947- *WhoBlA 92*
**Major**, Robert Wayne 1937- *AmMWSc 92*
**Major**, Schwab Samuel, Jr 1924- *AmMWSc 92*
**Majorelle**, Louis 1859-1926 *DcTwDes*
**Majorinus** d313? *EncEarC*
**Majors**, E. B. *WrDr 92*
**Majors**, Edith Sara 1920- *WhoBlA 92*
**Majors**, Lee 1939- *IntMPA 92*
**Majors**, Lee 1940- *WhoEnt 92*
**Majors**, Mary E. 1912- *WhoBlA 92*
**Majors**, Mattie Carolyn 1945- *WhoBlA 92*
**Majors**, Ronald E 1941- *AmMWSc 92*
**Majors**, Simon *TwCSFW 91*
**Majumdar**, Dalim K 1934- *AmMWSc 92*
**Majumdar**, Debaprasad 1941- *AmMWSc 92*
**Majumdar**, S K 1938- *AmMWSc 92*
**Majumdar**, Samir Ranjan 1936- *AmMWSc 92*
**Majumdar**, Shyamal K 1938- *AmMWSc 92*
**Majumdar**, Somendu Bikas 1943- *WhoFI 92*
**Majury**, James Herbert Samuel 1921- *Who 92*
**Mak**, Chi Fai 1960- *WhoWest 92*
**Mak**, Gilbert Kwok Kwong 1963- *WhoWest 92*
**Mak**, King Kuen 1946- *AmMWSc 92*
**Mak**, Linda Louise 1947- *AmMWSc 92*
**Mak**, Raymond Tong 1958- *WhoAmL 92*
**Mak**, Sioe Tho 1932- *AmMWSc 92*
**Mak**, Stanley 1933- *AmMWSc 92*
**Mak**, William Wai-Nam 1949- *AmMWSc 92*
**Makadok**, Stanley 1941- *WhoFI 92*
**Makalou**, Oumar 1934- *WhoFI 92*
**Makar**, Adeeb Bassili *AmMWSc 92*
**Makar**, Boshra Halim 1928- *AmMWSc 92*
**Makar**, Charles Stroud 1954- *WhoAmL 92*
**Makarem**, Anis H 1933- *AmMWSc 92*
**Makarenko**, Anton Semyonovich 1888-1939 *SovUnBD*
**Makarewicz**, Joseph Chester 1947- *AmMWSc 92*
**Makarewicz**, Peter James 1952- *AmMWSc 92*
**Makarezos**, Nikolaos 1919- *IntWW 91*
**Makari**, Victor Emmanuel 1941- *WhoRel 92*
**Makarios III** 1913-1977 *FacFETw*
**Makaroff**, Juanita Lou 1934- *WhoEnt 92*
**Makarov**, Askold Anatolevich 1925- *IntWW 91*
**Makarov**, Igor Mikhailovich 1927- *IntWW 91*
**Makarov**, Oleg 1933- *FacFETw*
**Makarov**, Stepan Osipovich 1848-1904 *FacFETw*
**Makarov**, Valeriy Leonidovich 1937- *IntWW 91, SovUnBD*
**Makarova**, Inna Vladimirovna 1926- *IntWW 91*
**Makarova**, Natalia 1940- *ConTFT 9, FacFETw, IntWW 91, Who 92*
**Makarova**, Nataliya 1940- *SovUnBD*
**Makarova**, Tamara Fedorovna 1907- *SovUnBD*
**Makarski**, Henryk 1946- *IntAu&W 91*
**Makasa**, Kapasa 1922- *IntWW 91*
**Makavejev**, Dusan 1932- *IntDcF 2-2*
**Makdah**, Imad Jad 1961- *WhoFI 92*
**Makdani**, Dhiren D *AmMWSc 92*
**Make**, Barry Jay 1947- *WhoWest 92*
**Make**, Isabel Rose 1947- *WhoWest 92*
**Makeba**, Miriam 1932- *ConBlB 2 [port]*
**Makeev**, Valentin Nikolaevich 1930- *SovUnBD*
**Makeka**, Thabo 1947- *IntWW 91*
**Makela**, Gregory Strickler 1958- *WhoFI 92*
**Makela**, Lloyd Edward 1936- *AmMWSc 92*
**Makemie**, Francis 1658?-1708 *BenetAL 91, DcAmImH*
**Makemson**, John Christopher 1942- *AmMWSc 92*
**Makenete**, Strong Thabo 1923- *IntWW 91*
**Makepeace**, Chris 1964- *IntMPA 92*
**Makepeace**, Christopher 1964- *WhoEnt 92*
**Makepeace**, Darryl Lee 1941- *WhoFI 92, WhoMW 92, WhoWest 92*
**Makepeace**, Gershom Reynolds 1919- *AmMWSc 92*
**Makepeace**, John 1939- *Who 92*
**Makepeace-Warne**, Antony 1937- *Who 92*
**Maker**, Paul Donne 1934- *AmMWSc 92*
**Makeyev**, Evgeny Nikolaevich 1928- *IntWW 91*
**Makeyev**, Valentin Nikolaevich 1930- *IntWW 91*
**Makgill** *Who 92*
**Makgill Crichton Maitland**, John David 1925- *Who 92*
**Makhija**, Suraj Parkash 1936- *AmMWSc 92*
**Makhkamov**, Kakhar Makhkamovich 1932- *IntWW 91, SovUnBD*
**Makhlouf**, Gabriel Michel 1929- *AmMWSc 92*
**Makhlouf**, Mansour Vincent 1954- *WhoMW 92*
**Makhoul**, John Ibrahim 1942- *AmMWSc 92*
**Makhulu**, Walter Paul Khotso *Who 92*
**Makhulu**, Walter Paul Khotso 1935- *IntWW 91, WhoRel 92*
**Maki**, Arthur George, Jr 1930- *AmMWSc 92*
**Maki**, August Harold 1930- *AmMWSc 92*
**Maki**, Fumihiko 1928- *IntWW 91*
**Maki**, Karen Clauson 1958- *WhoAmL 92*
**Maki**, Kazumi 1936- *AmMWSc 92*
**Maki**, Leroy Robert 1927- *AmMWSc 92*
**Makielski**, Sarah Kimball 1938- *AmMWSc 92*
**Makin**, Earle Clement, Jr 1917- *AmMWSc 92*
**Makinen**, Kauko K 1937- *AmMWSc 92*
**Makinen**, Marvin William 1939- *AmMWSc 92*
**Makinodan**, Takashi 1925- *AmMWSc 92*
**Makins** *Who 92*
**Makins**, Nora *Who 92*
**Makins**, Paul 1913- *Who 92*
**Makinson**, Randell L. 1932- *WrDr 92*
**Makinson**, William 1915- *Who 92*
**Makita**, Takashi 1935- *AmMWSc 92*
**Makk**, Karoly 1925- *IntWW 91*
**Makkawi**, Khalil 1930- *Who 92*
**Makker**, Sudesh Paul 1941- *AmMWSc 92*
**Makki**, Mohammed Hassan 1933- *IntWW 91*
**Maklakov**, Vasily Alexandrovich 1870-1957 *FacFETw*
**Makle**, Vivian B. *WhoBlA 92*
**Makley**, William Kerien 1954- *WhoWest 92*
**Maklouf**, Raphael David 1937- *Who 92*
**Makman**, Maynard Harlan 1933- *AmMWSc 92*
**Mako** 1933- *IntMPA 92*
**Mako**, William Lawrence 1958- *WhoMW 92*
**Makofske**, Mary *DrAPF 91*
**Makofske**, William Joseph 1943- *AmMWSc 92*
**Makofski**, Robert Anthony 1930- *AmMWSc 92*
**Makokha**, James A. N. 1951- *WhoBlA 92*
**Makomaski**, Andrzej Henryk 1932- *AmMWSc 92*
**Makoul**, Tom James 1949- *WhoEnt 92*
**Makous**, Walter L 1934- *AmMWSc 92*
**Makowiecki**, Andrzej 1938- *IntAu&W 91*
**Makowka**, Leonard 1953- *AmMWSc 92*
**Makowski**, Edgar Leonard 1927- *AmMWSc 92*
**Makowski**, Lee 1949- *AmMWSc 92*
**Makowski**, Mieczyslaw Paul 1922- *AmMWSc 92*
**Makowski**, Robert John 1926- *WhoFI 92, WhoMW 92*
**Makowski**, Roberte Marie Denise *AmMWSc 92*
**Makrauer**, George A. 1944- *WhoMW 92*
**Makrianes**, James Konstantin, Jr. 1925- *WhoFI 92*
**Makris**, Andreas 1930- *WhoEnt 92*
**Makris**, Jimmy 1962- *WhoFI 92*
**Makriyannis**, Alexandros 1939- *AmMWSc 92*
**Maksimov**, Leonid Aleksandrovich 1931- *IntWW 91*
**Maksimov**, Lev Iosifovich 1928- *IntWW 91*
**Maksimov**, Vladimir Emelyanovich 1932- *SovUnBD*
**Maksimov**, Vladimir Yemelyanovich 1932- *IntWW 91*
**Maksimov**, Yuriy Pavlovich 1924- *IntWW 91, SovUnBD*
**Maksimova**, Yekaterina Sergeevna 1939- *SovUnBD*
**Maksimova**, Yekaterina Sergeyevna 1939- *IntWW 91*
**Maksoudian**, Y Leon 1933- *AmMWSc 92*
**Maksud**, Michael George 1932- *AmMWSc 92*
**Maksymiuk**, Jerzy *WhoEnt 92*
**Maksymiuk**, Jerzy 1936- *IntWW 91*
**Maksymiuk**, Stephen Gerard 1961- *WhoFI 92*
**Maksymowicz**, John Robert 1956- *WhoWest 92*
**Maksymowych**, Roman 1924- *AmMWSc 92*
**Maktoum**, Hamdan bin Rashid al- 1945- *IntWW 91*
**Maktoum**, Maktoum bin Rashid al- 1943- *IntWW 91*
**Maktoum**, Muhammad bin Rashid al- 1946- *IntWW 91*
**Maktoum**, Rashid Bin Said al- d1990 *IntWW 91N*
**Makuen**, George Hudson 1855-1917 *BiInAmS*
**Makupson**, Amyre Porter 1947- *WhoEnt 92*
**Makupson**, Walter H. 1946- *WhoBlA 92*
**Makuta**, Friday Lewis 1936- *Who 92*
**Mal**, Ajit Kumar 1937- *AmMWSc 92*
**Mala**, Theodore Anthony 1946- *WhoWest 92*
**Malabo**, Cristino Seriche Bioke *IntWW 91*
**Malabre**, Alfred Leopold, Jr. 1931- *WhoFI 92*
**Malaby**, David William, Jr. 1956- *WhoAmL 92*
**Malacara**, Daniel 1937- *AmMWSc 92*
**Malach**, Herbert John 1922- *WhoAmL 92*
**Malachowski**, Mitchell Raymond 1955- *WhoWest 92*
**Malacinksi**, George M 1940- *AmMWSc 92*
**Malaczynski**, Gerard W 1942- *AmMWSc 92*
**Malagodi**, Giovanni Francesco d1991 *IntWW 91N*
**Malagodi**, Giovanni Francesco 1904- *IntWW 91*
**Malagon**, Frank Marino *WhoEnt 92*
**Malagrino**, Silvia Adriana 1950- *WhoHisp 92*
**Malah**, David 1943- *AmMWSc 92*
**Malahoff**, Alexander 1939- *AmMWSc 92*
**Malaiya**, Yashwant Kumar 1951- *AmMWSc 92, WhoFI 92*
**Malakouti**, Nezam 1947- *WhoMW 92*
**Malamed**, Sasha 1928- *AmMWSc 92*
**Malamud**, Bernard 1914-1986 *BenetAL 91, FacFETw [port]*
**Malamud**, Daniel F 1939- *AmMWSc 92*
**Malamud**, Ernest I 1932- *AmMWSc 92*
**Malamud**, Herbert 1925- *AmMWSc 92*
**Malamud**, Nathan 1903- *AmMWSc 92*
**Malamy**, Michael Howard 1938- *AmMWSc 92*
**Malan**, Daniel F 1874-1959 *FacFETw*

Malan, Magnus Andre de Merindol 1930- IntWW 91
Malan, Pedro 1943- IntWW 91
Malan, Rian 1954- ConAu 133, LiExTwC
Malan, Rodwick LaPur 1916- AmMWSc 92
Malan, Wynand Charl 1943- IntWW 91
Maland, Charles John 1949- WhoEnt 92
Maland, David 1929- IntAu&W 91, Who 92, WrDr 92
Malandra, Geri Hockfield 1949- WhoMW 92
Malanga, Carl Joseph 1939- AmMWSc 92
Malanga, Gerard DrAPF 91
Malangoni, Mark Alan 1949- WhoMW 92
Malanify, John Joseph 1934- AmMWSc 92
Malanjuk, Jevhen 1897-1968 LiExTwC
Malanowski, Tony Benedict 1957- WhoEnt 92
Malany, Le Grand Lynn 1941- WhoMW 92
Malaparte, Curzio 1898-1957 BiDExR
Malaret, Hiram, Jr. 1954- WhoHisp 92
Malarkey, Edward Cornelius 1936- AmMWSc 92
Malarkey, Martin Francis, Jr. 1918- WhoEnt 92
Malas, Marlena Kleinman WhoEnt 92
Malaschak, M Dolores 1923- IntAu&W 91
Malashevich, Bruce Peter 1952- WhoFI 92
Malashock, Edward Marvin 1923- AmMWSc 92
Malasky, Ilene Post 1938- WhoFI 92
Malaspina, Alex 1931- AmMWSc 92, WhoFI 92
Malat, Jiri 1953- WhoEnt 92
Malatesta EncAmaz 91
Malatesta, Edward Joseph, Jr. 1932- WhoRel 92
Malatesta, Lamberto 1912- IntWW 91
Malatesta, Mary Anne 1954- WhoAmL 92
Malatesta, Parisina EncAmaz 91
Malathi, Parameswara AmMWSc 92
Malaud, Philippe 1925- IntWW 91
Malaurie, Jean 1922- IntWW 91
Malave, Angel L. WhoHisp 92
Malave, Humberto 1957- WhoHisp 92
Malave, Lilliam M. 1958- WhoHisp 92
Malave-Colon, Eddie G. 1963- WhoHisp 92
Malaviya, Bimal K 1935- AmMWSc 92
Malavolta, Euripedes 1926- IntWW 91
Malawista, Stephen E 1934- AmMWSc 92
Malaysia, The Yang di Pertuan Agung of IntWW 91
Malbach, Howard I. 1929- WhoWest 92
Malbica, Joseph Orazio 1925- AmMWSc 92
Malbon, Craig Curtis 1950- AmMWSc 92
Malbon, Wendell Endicott 1918- AmMWSc 92
Malbrock, Jane C AmMWSc 92
Malbroue, Joseph, Jr. 1949- WhoBlA 92
Malchick, Sherwin Paul 1929- AmMWSc 92
Malchiodi, Cathy Ann 1953- WhoWest 92
Malchion EncEarC
Malchon, Jeanne K 1923- WhoAmP 91
Malchow, Bruce Virgil 1940- WhoRel 92
Malcohn, Elissa DrAPF 91
Malcolm X DcAmImH
Malcolm X 1925-1965 BenetAL 91, BlkLC [port], FacFETw, RComAH, RelLAm 91
Malcolm, A. Pat 1949- WhoMW 92
Malcolm, Alexander Russell 1936- AmMWSc 92
Malcolm, Dan ConAu 36NR
Malcolm, David Kingsley 1938- Who 92
Malcolm, David Peter Michael 1919- Who 92
Malcolm, David Robert 1926- AmMWSc 92
Malcolm, Derek Elliston Michael 1932- Who 92
Malcolm, Dugald 1917- IntWW 91, Who 92
Malcolm, Earl Walter 1937- AmMWSc 92
Malcolm, Ellen 1923- Who 92
Malcolm, George 1917- IntWW 91, NewAmDM, Who 92
Malcolm, Gerald Who 92
Malcolm, Howard 1799-1879 AmPeW
Malcolm, James Bradford 1943- WhoAmP 91
Malcolm, Janet May 1925- AmMWSc 92
Malcolm, John 1936- WrDr 92
Malcolm, John Laurence 1913- Who 92
Malcolm, John Lowrie 1920- AmMWSc 92
Malcolm, Kenneth W 1920- WhoAmP 91
Malcolm, Norman 1911-1990 AnObit 1990
Malcolm, Richard Ward 1933- WhoWest 92
Malcolm, River DrAPF 91
Malcolm, Robert Calvin 1928- WhoRel 92
Malcolm, Wilfred Gordon 1933- IntWW 91, Who 92
Malcolm, William Gerald 1916- Who 92
Malcolmson, Kenneth Forbes 1911- Who 92
Malcom, Harris Ray 1953- WhoRel 92
Malcom, Shirley Mahaley 1946- AmMWSc 92, WhoBlA 92
Malcuit, Robert Joseph 1936- AmMWSc 92
Malczewski, Patricia Elwell 1940- WhoWest 92
Maldacker, Thomas Anton 1946- AmMWSc 92
Malde, Gualtiero WrDr 92
Malde, Harold Edwin 1923- AmMWSc 92, WhoWest 92
Malden Who 92
Malden, Viscount 1944- Who 92
Malden, Karl 1914- IntMPA 92
Malden, Karl 1916- WhoEnt 92
Maldonado, Adal Alberto 1947- WhoHisp 92
Maldonado, Agustin Lopez 1943- WhoHisp 92
Maldonado, Alfonso Javier 1960- WhoHisp 92
Maldonado, Betti WhoHisp 92
Maldonado, C Daniel 1928- AmMWSc 92
Maldonado, Candy 1960- WhoHisp 92
Maldonado, Carl 1945- WhoAmP 91, WhoHisp 92
Maldonado, Carlos 1966- WhoHisp 92
Maldonado, Che 1954- WhoHisp 92
Maldonado, Clifford Daniel 1928- WhoHisp 92
Maldonado, Daniel Chris 1942- WhoAmP 91, WhoHisp 92
Maldonado, David, Jr. 1943- WhoHisp 92
Maldonado, Enrique S., Jr. 1949- WhoHisp 92
Maldonado, Gregory Matthew 1958- WhoEnt 92
Maldonado, Halda WhoHisp 92
Maldonado, Irma 1946- WhoHisp 92
Maldonado, Jesus Maria DrAPF 91
Maldonado, Jesus Maria 1944- WhoHisp 92
Maldonado, Jose 1904- WhoHisp 92
Maldonado, Juan WhoHisp 92
Maldonado, Juan Jose 1946- WhoAmP 91, WhoHisp 92
Maldonado, Juan R. 1938- WhoHisp 92
Maldonado, Juan Ramon 1938- AmMWSc 92
Maldonado, Macario Olivarez 1944- WhoHisp 92
Maldonado, Michael Mark 1952- WhoHisp 92
Maldonado, Ned Lucas 1943- WhoHisp 92
Maldonado, Norman I. 1935- WhoHisp 92
Maldonado, Reynaldo A. 1949- WhoHisp 92
Maldonado, Roberto 1951- WhoMW 92
Maldonado, Tomas 1922- DcTwDes
Maldonado, Virginia 1947- WhoHisp 92
Maldonado, Zoraida 1953- WhoHisp 92
Maldonado-Bear, Rita Marinita 1938- WhoFI 92, WhoHisp 92
Maldonado Velez, Roberto 1952- WhoHisp 92
Maldonado Velez, Roberto, Jr 1952- WhoAmP 91
Maldonado y Sotomayor, Pedro Vicente 1709-1748 HisDSpE
Male, David Ronald 1929- Who 92
Male, James William 1945- AmMWSc 92
Male, Peter John Ellison 1920- Who 92
Male, William 1927- WhoRel 92
Maleady, N R 1916- AmMWSc 92
Malebo, Vincent Moeketse 1931- IntWW 91
Malebranche, Nicolas 1638-1715 BlkwCEP
Malec, Emily Keller DrAPF 91
Malec, Ivo 1925- ConCom 92
Malec, William Frank 1940- WhoFI 92
Malecela, Cigwiyemisi John Samwel 1934- Who 92
Malecela, John William Samuel 1934- IntWW 91
Malech, Harry Lewis 1946- AmMWSc 92
Malecha, Spencer R 1943- AmMWSc 92
Malechek, John Charles 1942- AmMWSc 92
Maleckar, James R 1954- AmMWSc 92
Malecki, David Michael 1948- WhoMW 92
Malecki, Ignacy 1912- IntWW 91
Malecki, James Henry 1936- WhoAmL 92
Malee, Thomas Michael 1947- WhoAmL 92
Maleeny, Robert Timothy 1931- AmMWSc 92
Maleeny, Timothy Vincent WhoWest 92
Malefakis, Edward 1932- WrDr 92
Malek, Emile Abdel 1922- AmMWSc 92
Malek, Frederic Vincent 1936- WhoAmP 91, WhoFI 92, WhoMW 92
Malek, James S. 1941- WrDr 92
Malek, Jeffrey 1951- WhoFI 92
Malek, John DrAPF 91
Malek, Miroslaw 1947- AmMWSc 92
Malek, Rami Sami 1970- WhoEnt 92
Malek, Reda 1931- IntWW 91
Malek, Redha 1931- Who 92
Malek, Richard Barry 1936- AmMWSc 92
Malekebu, Daniel Sharp 1889- WhoBlA 92
Maleki, Reza Arabian 1955- WhoMW 92
Malekou, Paul 1938- IntWW 91
Malemud, Charles J 1945- AmMWSc 92
Malemud, Lee L. 1948- WhoMW 92
Malencik, Dean A AmMWSc 92
Malenfant, Arthur Lewis 1937- AmMWSc 92
Malenka, Bertram Julian 1923- AmMWSc 92
Malenkov, Georgi Maximillianovich 1902-1988 FacFETw
Malenkov, Georgiy Maksimilyanovich 1902-1988 SovUnBD
Maler, George J 1924- AmMWSc 92
Maler, Leopardo M. 1937- IntWW 91
Malerba, Luigi 1927- IntWW 91
Malerich, Charles 1944- AmMWSc 92
Malerich, Steven Floyd 1957- WhoIns 92
Males, Alba Rosa 1943- WhoHisp 92
Males, James Robert 1945- AmMWSc 92
Males, William James WhoEnt 92, WhoWest 92
Malesherbes, Christian-Guillaume de L de 1721-1794 BlkwCEP
Maleska, Martin Edmund 1944- WhoFI 92
Malet, Edward William St Lo d1990 Who 92N
Malet, Guy Seymour 1900-1973 TwCPaSc
Malet, Harry 1936- Who 92
Malet, Hugh 1928- WrDr 92
Maletsky, Evan M 1932- AmMWSc 92
Malette, William Graham 1922- AmMWSc 92
Maletz, Herbert Naaman 1913- WhoAmL 92
Malevich, Kasimir 1878-1935 DcTwDes
Malevich, Kazimir 1878-1935 FacFETw
Malevich, Kazimir Serverinovich 1878-1935 SovUnBD
Malewicz, Barbara Maria 1942- AmMWSc 92
Malewitz, Thomas Donald 1929- AmMWSc 92
Malewski, Edward 1943- WhoWest 92
Maley, Frank 1929- AmMWSc 92
Maley, Gladys Feldott 1926- AmMWSc 92
Maley, Martin Paul 1936- AmMWSc 92
Maley, S W 1928- AmMWSc 92
Maley, Wayne A 1927- AmMWSc 92
Malezi-Hollingsworth, Elizabeth Mary B. 1932- WhoEnt 92
Malfatti, Franco Maria 1927- IntWW 91
Malfatti Di Montetretto, Francesco 1920- IntWW 91
Malghan, Subhaschandra Gangappa 1947- AmMWSc 92
Malgoire, Jean-Claude 1940- NewAmDM
Malgonkar, Manohar 1913- ConNov 91, IntAu&W 91, WrDr 92
Malherbe, Abraham Johannes, VI 1930- WhoRel 92
Malherbe, Rene Cornelis 1942- IntWW 91
Malherbe, Roger F 1946- AmMWSc 92
Malhiot, Robert 1926- AmMWSc 92
Malhotra, Ashwani 1943- AmMWSc 92
Malhotra, Inder 1930- ConAu 135
Malhotra, Kanuj 1967- WhoFI 92
Malhotra, Om P AmMWSc 92
Malhotra, R. N. 1926- IntWW 91
Malhotra, Sudarshan Kumar 1933- AmMWSc 92
Malhotra, Vijay Kumar 1946- WhoWest 92
Malhoutra, Manmohan 1937- IntWW 91
Mali, Jane Lawrence 1937- ConAu 36NR
Malian, Ida Marguerite 1950- WhoWest 92
Malibran, Maria 1808-1836 NewAmDM
Malick, Jeffrey Bevan 1942- AmMWSc 92
Malick, Joan Bradner 1943- WhoRel 92
Malick, Terence 1943- IntMPA 92
Malick, Terrence 1943- IntDcF 2-2 [port]
Malicoat, Douglas Roy 1949- WhoWest 92
Malietoa Tanumafili II 1913- IntWW 91
Malik, Asrar B 1945- AmMWSc 92
Malik, Bidhubhusan 1895- Who 92
Malik, Brenda Gooden 1951- WhoEnt 92
Malik, Charles Habib 1906-1987 FacFETw
Malik, David Joseph 1945- AmMWSc 92
Malik, Fazley Bary 1934- AmMWSc 92
Malik, Gerald Irwin 1941- WhoMW 92
Malik, Gunwantsingh Jaswantsingh 1921- IntWW 91
Malik, Helen Theresa 1943- WhoFI 92
Malik, Jim Gorden 1928- AmMWSc 92
Malik, John S 1920- AmMWSc 92
Malik, Joseph Martin 1944- AmMWSc 92, WhoMW 92
Malik, Kathryn Jean 1960- WhoMW 92
Malik, Mazhar N 1940- AmMWSc 92
Malik, Norbert Richard 1936- AmMWSc 92
Malik, Om Parkash 1932- AmMWSc 92
Malik, Vedpal Singh 1942- AmMWSc 92
Malik, Yakov A 1906-1980 FacFETw
Malim, Nigel Hugh 1919- Who 92
Malin, Amir Jacob 1954- IntMPA 92
Malin, David Alan 1951- WhoRel 92
Malin, David Herbert 1944- AmMWSc 92
Malin, Edyth Theresa Lasky 1926- AmMWSc 92
Malin, Evangeline May 1928- WhoWest 92
Malin, Howard Gerald 1941- AmMWSc 92
Malin, Irving 1934- WrDr 92
Malin, John Michael 1942- AmMWSc 92
Malin, Michael Charles 1950- AmMWSc 92
Malin, Murray Edward 1927- AmMWSc 92
Malin, Peter WrDr 92
Malin, Robert Abernethy 1931- WhoFI 92
Malin, Shimon 1937- AmMWSc 92
Malin, Steven Robert 1951- WhoFI 92
Malin, Stuart Robert Charles 1936- Who 92
Malin, Suzi 1950- TwCPaSc
Malina, Frank J 1912-1981 FacFETw
Malina, Joseph F, Jr 1935- AmMWSc 92
Malina, Judith 1926- WhoEnt 92
Malina, Marshall Albert 1928- AmMWSc 92
Malina, Michael 1936- WhoAmL 92
Malina, Robert Marion 1937- AmMWSc 92
Malinak, Lawrence Clinton 1940- WhoWest 92
Malinauskas, Anthony Peter 1935- AmMWSc 92
Malinche HisDSpE
Malinda, James Anthony, III 1963- WhoWest 92
Malindzak, George S, Jr 1933- AmMWSc 92
Maling, Arthur 1923- IntAu&W 91, WrDr 92
Maling, George Croswell, Jr 1931- AmMWSc 92
Malinga, Norman Zombodze Magugu 1938- IntWW 91
Malinin, George I 1929- AmMWSc 92
Malinin, Theodore I 1933- AmMWSc 92
Malino, Jerome R. 1911- WhoRel 92
Malino, John Gray 1939- WhoFI 92
Malinovsky, Rodion Yakovlevich 1898-1967 FacFETw, SovUnBD
Malinow, Manuel R 1920- AmMWSc 92
Malinow, Manuel Rene 1920- WhoWest 92
Malinowitz, Michael DrAPF 91
Malinowski, Arthur Anthony 1929- WhoAmL 92
Malinowski, Bronislaw 1884-1942 FacFETw
Malinowski, Dennis Edmund 1948- WhoMW 92
Malinowski, Edmund R 1932- AmMWSc 92
Malins, Donald Clive 1931- AmMWSc 92
Malins, Humfrey Jonathan 1945- Who 92
Malins, Julian Henry 1950- Who 92
Malins, Penelope Who 92
Malinvaud, Edmond 1923- IntWW 91
Malipiero, Gian Francesco 1882-1973 NewAmDM
Malis, Leonard I 1919- AmMWSc 92
Maliszewski, Charles R 1954- AmMWSc 92
Maliszewski, Thaddeus Walenty 1922- WhoAmP 91
Malita, Mircea 1927- IntWW 91
Malitson, Harriet Hutzler 1926- AmMWSc 92
Malitz, Sidney 1923- AmMWSc 92
Malizia, Samuel Joe 1954- WhoAmL 92
Maljers, Floris 1933- IntWW 91
Maljers, Floris Anton 1933- Who 92
Malkames, Don Karl 1926- WhoEnt 92
Malkani, Mohan J 1933- AmMWSc 92
Malkasian, George D, Jr 1927- AmMWSc 92
Malkevitch, Joseph 1942- AmMWSc 92
Malkiel, Burton Gordon 1932- WhoFI 92
Malkiel, Saul 1912- AmMWSc 92
Malkiel, Theresa Serber 1874-1949 DcAmImH, HanAmWH
Malkiel, Yakov 1914- WrDr 92
Malkin, Aaron 1926- AmMWSc 92
Malkin, Cary Jay 1949- WhoAmL 92
Malkin, Harold Marshall 1923- AmMWSc 92
Malkin, Irving 1925- AmMWSc 92
Malkin, Judd D. 1937- WhoMW 92
Malkin, Lawrence 1930- IntAu&W 91
Malkin, Leonard Isadore 1936- AmMWSc 92
Malkin, Martin F 1937- AmMWSc 92
Malkin, Richard 1940- AmMWSc 92

**Malkin**, Stephen 1941- AmMWSc 92
**Malkinson**, Alvin Maynard 1941- AmMWSc 92
**Malkinson**, Frederick David 1924- AmMWSc 92
**Malko**, George DrAPF 91
**Malko**, Nikolay 1883-1961 NewAmDM
**Malkoff**, Alan Richard 1946- WhoFI 92
**Malkovich**, John 1953- IntMPA 92, IntWW 91, WhoEnt 92
**Malkovich**, Mark Paul, III 1930- WhoEnt 92
**Malkus**, David Starr 1945- AmMWSc 92
**Malkus**, Frederick C, Jr 1913- WhoAmP 91
**Malkus**, Willem Van Rensselaer 1923- AmMWSc 92
**Mall**, Franklin Paine 1862-1917 BiInAmS
**Mall**, Myron Merriell 1940- WhoFI 92
**Mall**, Shankar 1943- AmMWSc 92
**Mallaby**, Christopher 1936- Who 92
**Mallaby**, Christopher Leslie George 1936- IntWW 91
**Mallalieu**, Baroness 1945- Who 92
**Mallams**, Alan Keith 1940- AmMWSc 92
**Mallams**, John Thomas 1923- AmMWSc 92
**Mallan**, Francis Scott 1964- WhoFI 92
**Mallard**, Albert Knight 1937- WhoWest 92
**Mallard**, Thomas Irvin 1946- WhoWest 92
**Mallardi**, Michael Patrick 1934- WhoEnt 92, WhoFI 92
**Mallare**, Priscilla Erfe WhoMW 92
**Mallarme**, Stephane 1842-1898 GuFrLit 1, PoeCrit 4 [port], ThHEIm [port]
**Mallary**, Peter T 1953- WhoAmP 91
**Mallary**, Richard Walker 1929- WhoAmP 91
**Mallas**, Kenneth Murial 1932- WhoAmP 91
**Malle**, Louis 1932- FacFETw, IntDcF 2-2 [port], IntMPA 92, IntWW 91, Who 92, WhoEnt 92
**Mallea**, Eduardo 1903-1982? BenetAL 91
**Mallen**, Ronald Edward 1942- WhoAmL 92
**Maller**, Abraham H. 1907- WhoAmL 92
**Maller**, Allen Stephen 1938- WhoRel 92, WhoWest 92
**Maller**, James Leighton AmMWSc 92
**Mallers**, Anthony 1933- IntMPA 92
**Mallery**, Charles Henry 1943- AmMWSc 92
**Mallery**, Garrick 1831-1894 BiInAmS
**Mallery**, Gary Dean 1939- WhoFI 92
**Mallet**, David 1705?-1765 RfGEnL 91
**Mallet**, Ivo Who 92
**Mallet**, John Valentine Granville 1930- Who 92
**Mallet**, John William 1832-1912 BiInAmS
**Mallet**, Philip Louis Victor 1926- Who 92
**Mallet**, Robert Albert Marie Georges 1915- IntWW 91
**Mallet**, Robert Christopher 1959- WhoFI 92
**Mallet**, Roger 1912- Who 92
**Mallet**, Victorin Noel 1944- AmMWSc 92
**Mallet-Joris**, Francoise 1930- FrenWW, GuFrLit 1
**Mallet-Stevens**, Robert 1886-1945 DcTwDes, FacFETw
**Mallett**, Charles Beatty 1816-1872 DcNCBi 4
**Mallett**, Charles Peter 1792-1873 DcNCBi 4
**Mallett**, Conrad L. 1928- WhoBlA 92
**Mallett**, Conrad L., Jr. 1953- WhoBlA 92
**Mallett**, Conrad LeRoy, Jr. 1953- WhoMW 92
**Mallett**, Conrad Richard 1919- Who 92
**Mallett**, Daryl Furumi 1969- IntAu&W 91
**Mallett**, Edmund Stansfield 1923- Who 92
**Mallett**, Francis Anthony 1924- Who 92
**Mallett**, Gordon Edward 1927- AmMWSc 92
**Mallett**, Jane 1899-1984 FacFETw
**Mallett**, Peter 1925- Who 92
**Mallett**, Peter, Jr. 1744-1805 DcNCBi 4
**Mallett**, Russell Lloyd 1935- AmMWSc 92
**Mallett**, William Peter 1819-1889 DcNCBi 4
**Mallett**, William Robert 1932- AmMWSc 92, WhoWest 92
**Mallette**, Carol L. WhoBlA 92
**Mallette**, John M 1932- AmMWSc 92, WhoBlA 92
**Mallette**, Malcolm Carroll 1941- WhoAmL 92
**Malley**, Arthur 1931- AmMWSc 92
**Malley**, Howard G. 1945- WhoEnt 92
**Malley**, James Henry Michael 1940- WhoWest 92
**Malley**, Joseph Hanson 1956- WhoAmL 92
**Malley**, Linda Angevine 1955- AmMWSc 92
**Malli**, Gulzari Lal 1938- AmMWSc 92
**Mallia**, Anantha Krishna 1941- AmMWSc 92
**Malliarakis**, Jean-Gilles 1944- BiDExR
**Mallick**, Craig David 1952- WhoAmL 92
**Mallik**, Arup Kumar 1943- AmMWSc 92
**Mallik**, Provash WrDr 92
**Mallik**, Umesh 1916- WrDr 92
**Mallin**, Jay 1927- WhoEnt 92, WrDr 92
**Mallin**, Morton Lewis 1926- AmMWSc 92
**Mallin**, Stewart Adam Thomson 1924- Who 92
**Mallinckrodt**, Georg Wilhelm von Who 92
**Malling**, Gerald F 1938- AmMWSc 92
**Malling**, Heinrich Valdemar 1931- AmMWSc 92
**Mallinson**, Anthony William 1923- Who 92
**Mallinson**, Dennis Hainsworth 1921- Who 92
**Mallinson**, George Greisen 1917- AmMWSc 92, WhoMW 92
**Mallinson**, Jeremy WrDr 92
**Mallinson**, Jeremy John Crosby 1937- IntAu&W 91
**Mallinson**, John Charles 1932- WhoWest 92
**Mallinson**, John Russell 1943- Who 92
**Mallinson**, Vernon 1910- WrDr 92
**Mallinson**, William Arthur 1922- Who 92
**Mallinson**, William John 1942- Who 92
**Mallipudi**, Carmen D. C. 1950- WhoHisp 92
**Mallis**, Arnold 1910- AmMWSc 92
**Mallisham**, Joseph W. 1928- WhoBlA 92
**Mallison**, George Franklin 1928- AmMWSc 92
**Mallmann**, Alexander James 1937- AmMWSc 92
**Mallock**, William Hurrell 1849-1923 RfGEnL 91
**Mallon**, Edward John 1944- WhoIns 92
**Mallon**, Florencia Elizabeth 1951- WhoHisp 92
**Mallon**, Harry A. d1991 NewYTBS 91
**Mallon**, Joseph Laurence 1942- Who 92
**Mallon**, Mark Lee 1948- WhoFI 92
**Mallon**, Peter Charles 1936- WhoEnt 92
**Mallon**, Robert James 1948- WhoFI 92
**Mallon**, Seamus 1936- Who 92
**Mallon**, Thomas 1951- WrDr 92
**Mallonee**, James Edgar 1915- AmMWSc 92
**Mallorie**, Paul Richard 1923- Who 92
**Mallory**, Arenia C. 1904-1977 NotBlAW 92
**Mallory**, Charles King, III 1936- WhoAmL 92
**Mallory**, Charles Shannon WhoRel 92
**Mallory**, Charles William 1925- AmMWSc 92
**Mallory**, Clelia Wood 1938- AmMWSc 92
**Mallory**, Drew WrDr 92
**Mallory**, Frank Bryant 1933- AmMWSc 92
**Mallory**, Frank Fenson 1944- AmMWSc 92
**Mallory**, Herbert Dean 1923- AmMWSc 92
**Mallory**, J Albert ScFEYrs
**Mallory**, Janice Dianne Davis 1957- WhoAmL 92
**Mallory**, Kathleen Moore 1879-1954 RelLAm 91
**Mallory**, Lee DrAPF 91
**Mallory**, Marilyn May WhoRel 92
**Mallory**, Merrit Lee 1938- AmMWSc 92
**Mallory**, Robert 1941- WhoAmP 91
**Mallory**, Thomas E 1940- AmMWSc 92
**Mallory**, Troy L. 1923- WhoFI 92, WhoMW 92
**Mallory**, Virgil Standish 1919- AmMWSc 92
**Mallory**, Willam R AmMWSc 92
**Mallory**, William G d1918 BiInAmS
**Mallory**, William Henry 1919- WhoBlA 92
**Mallory**, William L WhoAmP 91, WhoBlA 92
**Mallory**, William Wyman 1917- AmMWSc 92
**Mallory-Young**, Shirley 1942- WhoRel 92
**Mallott**, Byron Ivar 1943- WhoWest 92
**Malloum**, Felix 1932- IntWW 91
**Mallov**, Samuel 1919- AmMWSc 92
**Mallow**, Jeffry Victor 1938- AmMWSc 92
**Mallows**, Colin Lingwood 1930- AmMWSc 92
**Mallows**, Harry Russell 1920- Who 92
**Malloy**, Alfred Marcus 1903- AmMWSc 92
**Malloy**, Donald Jon 1950- AmMWSc 92
**Malloy**, Edward Aloysius 1941- WhoMW 92, WhoRel 92
**Malloy**, H. Rembert 1913- WhoBlA 92
**Malloy**, Helen G. 1898- WhoBlA 92
**Malloy**, James Joseph 1941- WhoMW 92
**Malloy**, John, Jr 1959- WhoAmP 91
**Malloy**, John B 1928- AmMWSc 92
**Malloy**, Johnn Edward 1940- WhoEnt 92
**Malloy**, Kathleen Sharon 1948- WhoAmL 92, WhoFI 92, WhoIns 92, WhoMW 92
**Malloy**, Martin Gerard 1949- WhoAmL 92
**Malloy**, Michael H AmMWSc 92
**Malloy**, Michael Patrick 1951- WhoAmL 92
**Malloy**, Michele 1950- WhoAmL 92
**Malloy**, Paul Thomas 1943- WhoFI 92
**Malloy**, Sean Joseph 1954- WhoEnt 92
**Malloy**, Thomas Bernard, Jr 1941- AmMWSc 92
**Malloy**, Thomas Patrick 1941- AmMWSc 92
**Mallozzi**, Edward J 1945- WhoIns 92
**Mallozzi**, Philip James 1937- AmMWSc 92
**Malm**, Donald E G 1930- AmMWSc 92
**Malm**, Norman R 1931- AmMWSc 92
**Malm**, Rita P. 1932- WhoFI 92
**Malm**, Roger Charles 1949- WhoAmL 92
**Malman**, Laurie L. 1946- WhoAmL 92
**Malmberg**, Emil Antone 1956- WhoWest 92
**Malmberg**, John Holmes 1927- AmMWSc 92
**Malmberg**, Marjorie Schooley 1921- AmMWSc 92
**Malmberg**, Paul Rovelstad 1923- AmMWSc 92
**Malmberg**, Philip Ray 1920- AmMWSc 92
**Malme**, Charles I 1931- AmMWSc 92
**Malmer**, Reynold William 1929- WhoMW 92
**Malmesbury**, Bishop Suffragan of 1929- Who 92
**Malmesbury**, Earl of 1907- Who 92
**Malmgren**, Dallin 1949- ConAu 133, SmATA 65 [port]
**Malmgren**, Rene Louise 1938- WhoWest 92
**Malmgren**, Richard Axel 1921- AmMWSc 92
**Malmqvist**, Goran David 1924- IntWW 91
**Malmstadt**, Howard Vincent 1922- AmMWSc 92
**Malmstedt**, David Raymond 1955- WhoMW 92
**Malmsten**, Carl 1888-1972 DcTwDes
**Malmuth**, Bruce 1937- IntMPA 92, WhoEnt 92
**Malmuth**, Daniel Saul 1944- WhoEnt 92
**Malmuth**, Norman David 1931- AmMWSc 92, WhoWest 92
**Malnassy**, Louis Sturges 1952- WhoMW 92
**Malo**, Alvaro WhoHisp 92
**Malo**, Jacques 1950- AmMWSc 92
**Malocha**, Donald C 1950- AmMWSc 92
**Maloff**, Bruce L 1953- AmMWSc 92
**Maloff**, Elisa 1960- WhoAmL 92
**Maloff**, Saul DrAPF 91
**Malofsky**, Bernard Miles 1937- AmMWSc 92
**Malohn**, Donald A. 1928- WhoWest 92
**Malone**, Amanda Ella 1929- WhoBlA 92
**Malone**, Annie Turnbo 1868?-1957 HanAmWH
**Malone**, Annie Turnbo 1869-1957 NotBlAW 92 [port]
**Malone**, Bennett 1944- WhoAmP 91
**Malone**, Brenda Richardson 1954- WhoAmL 92
**Malone**, Charles A. WhoBlA 92
**Malone**, Claudine Berkeley WhoBlA 92
**Malone**, Cleo 1934- WhoBlA 92
**Malone**, Creighton Paul 1933- AmMWSc 92
**Malone**, Daniel Lee 1949- WhoFI 92, WhoMW 92
**Malone**, Daniel Patrick 1953- WhoAmL 92
**Malone**, David John 1954- WhoFI 92
**Malone**, David Roy 1943- WhoAmL 92, WhoAmP 91
**Malone**, Denis 1922- Who 92
**Malone**, Dennis P 1932- AmMWSc 92
**Malone**, Diana 1935- AmMWSc 92
**Malone**, Dorothy 1925- IntMPA 92
**Malone**, Dumas 1892-1986 BenetAL 91
**Malone**, E.T., Jr. DrAPF 91
**Malone**, Edwin Scott, III 1938- WhoEnt 92
**Malone**, Eugene William 1930- WhoBlA 92
**Malone**, Gerald 1950- Who 92
**Malone**, Gloria S. 1928- WhoBlA 92
**Malone**, Gregory Dale 1956- WhoMW 92
**Malone**, Hank DrAPF 91
**Malone**, J. Deotha 1932- WhoBlA 92
**Malone**, Jack Darroll 1953- WhoMW 92
**Malone**, James Hiram 1930- WhoBlA 92
**Malone**, James L 1931- WhoAmP 91
**Malone**, James Michael 1946- AmMWSc 92
**Malone**, James W 1925- AmMWSc 92
**Malone**, James William 1920- WhoMW 92, WhoRel 92
**Malone**, Jeff Nigel 1961- WhoBlA 92
**Malone**, Joe L. DrAPF 91
**Malone**, John C. LesBEnT 92
**Malone**, John C. 1941- WhoFI 92, WhoWest 92
**Malone**, John Irvin 1941- AmMWSc 92
**Malone**, John Raymond 1920- WhoMW 92
**Malone**, Joseph 1954- WhoAmP 91
**Malone**, Joseph James 1932- AmMWSc 92
**Malone**, Karl 1963- WhoBlA 92, WhoWest 92
**Malone**, Laurence Joseph 1957- WhoFI 92
**Malone**, Leo Jackson, Jr 1938- AmMWSc 92
**Malone**, Linda Ann 1954- WhoAmL 92
**Malone**, Lloyd Alvin, Jr. 1964- WhoEnt 92
**Malone**, M. Ray 1937- WhoMW 92
**Malone**, Mark A WhoAmP 91
**Malone**, Marvin DrAPF 91
**Malone**, Marvin Herbert 1930- AmMWSc 92, WhoWest 92
**Malone**, Michael DrAPF 91
**Malone**, Michael 1942- WrDr 92
**Malone**, Michael Dale 1955- WhoMW 92
**Malone**, Michael Gregory 1942- WhoBlA 92
**Malone**, Michael John 1948- WhoAmL 92
**Malone**, Michael Joseph 1930- AmMWSc 92
**Malone**, Michael Patrick DrAPF 91
**Malone**, Michael Patrick 1960- WhoEnt 92
**Malone**, Michael Peter 1940- WhoWest 92
**Malone**, Michael Stuart 1937- WhoFI 92
**Malone**, Mike 1932- WhoAmP 91, WhoWest 92
**Malone**, Moses Eugene 1955- WhoBlA 92
**Malone**, Pamela 1954- WhoMW 92
**Malone**, Pamela Altfeld DrAPF 91
**Malone**, Philip Garcin 1941- AmMWSc 92
**Malone**, Richard 1937- WhoRel 92
**Malone**, Richard Sankey 1909-1985 FacFETw
**Malone**, Richard Wayne 1951- WhoFI 92
**Malone**, Robert Charles 1945- AmMWSc 92
**Malone**, Robert J. 1945- WhoWest 92
**Malone**, Robert Winston, Jr. 1951- WhoRel 92
**Malone**, Sandra Dorsey WhoBlA 92
**Malone**, Stanley R. 1924- WhoBlA 92
**Malone**, Stephen D 1944- AmMWSc 92
**Malone**, Sue Anderson 1930- WhoMW 92
**Malone**, Thomas AmMWSc 92
**Malone**, Thomas C 1943- AmMWSc 92
**Malone**, Thomas E 1926- AmMWSc 92
**Malone**, Thomas Ellis 1926- WhoBlA 92
**Malone**, Thomas Francis 1917- AmMWSc 92, IntWW 91, WhoFI 92
**Malone**, Thomas William 1946- WhoAmL 92, WhoFI 92
**Malone**, Timothy Owen 1950- WhoEnt 92
**Malone**, Tom 1947- WhoEnt 92
**Malone**, Vincent 1931- Who 92
**Malone**, Vivian 1942- NotBlAW 92
**Malone**, Walter 1866-1915 ScFEYrs
**Malone**, William Grady 1915- WhoAmL 92
**Malone**, Winfred Francis 1935- AmMWSc 92
**Malone-Lee**, Michael Charles 1941- Who 92
**Maloney**, Andrew J. 1931- NewYTBS 91 [port]
**Maloney**, Carolyn Bosher 1948- WhoAmP 91
**Maloney**, Carolyn Scott 1950- WhoMW 92
**Maloney**, Charles Calvin 1930- WhoBlA 92
**Maloney**, Cheryl Ann 1949- WhoMW 92
**Maloney**, Clifford Joseph 1910- AmMWSc 92
**Maloney**, Daniel Edwin 1926- AmMWSc 92
**Maloney**, Daniel Leo 1941- WhoMW 92, WhoRel 92
**Maloney**, David Lynn 1954- WhoMW 92
**Maloney**, Dennis DrAPF 91
**Maloney**, George Thomas 1932- WhoFI 92
**Maloney**, Gerald P. 1933- WhoMW 92
**Maloney**, J O 1915- AmMWSc 92
**Maloney**, J. Patrick 1929- WhoRel 92
**Maloney**, James 1939- WhoAmP 91
**Maloney**, James Edward 1951- WhoAmL 92
**Maloney**, James Francis 1926- WhoIns 92
**Maloney**, James H WhoAmP 91
**Maloney**, James Vincent, Jr 1925- AmMWSc 92
**Maloney**, John DrAPF 91
**Maloney**, John F 1936- AmMWSc 92
**Maloney**, John P 1929- AmMWSc 92
**Maloney**, John Patrick 1929- WhoMW 92
**Maloney**, John Peter 1951- WhoEnt 92
**Maloney**, Joseph Anthony, Jr. 1942- WhoMW 92
**Maloney**, Joseph Francis 1930- WhoAmP 91
**Maloney**, Kenneth Long 1945- AmMWSc 92
**Maloney**, Kenneth Morgan 1941- AmMWSc 92
**Maloney**, Linda Mitchell 1939- WhoRel 92

**Maloney,** Mark A 1957- *WhoIns 92*
**Maloney,** Mary Agnes 1947- *WhoAmP 91*
**Maloney,** Mary Elizabeth 1962- *WhoAmL 92*
**Maloney,** Mary Patricia 1955- *WhoAmP 91*
**Maloney,** Marynell 1955- *WhoAmL 92*
**Maloney,** Michael Eamon 1940- *WhoMW 92*
**Maloney,** Michael John 1932- *Who 92*
**Maloney,** Michael Joseph, Jr 1929- *WhoAmP 91*
**Maloney,** Michael Patrick 1944- *WhoAmL 92*
**Maloney,** Michael Stephen 1947- *AmMWSc 92*
**Maloney,** Patrick Christopher 1949- *WhoEnt 92*
**Maloney,** Paul Joseph 1954- *WhoFI 92*
**Maloney,** Peter Charles 1941- *AmMWSc 92*
**Maloney,** Ray 1951- *ConAu 133*
**Maloney,** Robert B. 1933- *WhoAmL 92*
**Maloney,** Robert E., Jr. 1942- *WhoAmL 92*
**Maloney,** Simone 1936- *WhoFI 92*
**Maloney,** Stephen Ward 1953- *WhoMW 92*
**Maloney,** Susan Joyce 1966- *WhoMW 92*
**Maloney,** Therese A 1929- *WhoIns 92*
**Maloney,** Therese Adele 1929- *WhoFI 92*
**Maloney,** Thomas Edward 1923- *AmMWSc 92*
**Maloney,** Thomas J. 1922- *WhoWest 92*
**Maloney,** Thomas M 1931- *AmMWSc 92, WhoAmP 91*
**MaLoney,** Thomas Martin 1931- *WhoWest 92*
**Maloney,** Timothy Francis 1956- *WhoAmP 91*
**Maloney,** Timothy James 1949- *AmMWSc 92*
**Maloney,** William Thomas 1935- *AmMWSc 92*
**Malony,** Henry Newton, Jr. 1931- *WhoRel 92*
**Maloof,** Farahe 1921- *AmMWSc 92*
**Maloof,** Farahe Paul 1950- *WhoAmL 92*
**Maloof,** Giles Wilson 1932- *AmMWSc 92, WhoWest 92*
**Maloof,** James Aloysius 1919- *WhoAmP 91*
**Maloof,** Richard C. 1945- *WhoFI 92*
**Maloof,** Sam 1916- *DcTwDes*
**Malooley,** David Joseph 1951- *WhoFI 92, WhoMW 92*
**Maloon,** Jeffrey Lee 1958- *WhoAmL 92*
**Maloon,** Jerry L. 1938- *WhoMW 92*
**Malory,** Thomas *RfGEnL 91*
**Malory,** Thomas 1410?-1471 *CnDBLB 1*
**Malotky,** Lyle Oscar 1946- *AmMWSc 92*
**Malott,** Adele Renee 1935- *WhoWest 92*
**Malott,** Deane Waldo 1898- *IntWW 91, Who 92*
**Malott,** Dwight Ralph 1947- *WhoWest 92*
**Malott,** Harry C 1921- *WhoAmP 91*
**Malott,** Kia Doane 1943- *WhoMW 92*
**Malott,** Robert H. 1926- *IntWW 91*
**Malott,** Robert Harvey 1926- *WhoFI 92, WhoMW 92*
**Malotte,** Albert Hay 1895-1964 *NewAmDM*
**Malouf,** David 1934- *ConNov 91, ConPo 91, IntAu&W 91, WrDr 92*
**Malouf,** David George Joseph 1934- *IntWW 91*
**Malouf,** Emil Edward 1916- *AmMWSc 92*
**Malouf,** Frederick LeRoy 1954- *WhoWest 92*
**Malouf,** George M 1950- *AmMWSc 92*
**Malouf,** Robert Edward 1946- *AmMWSc 92*
**Malouf-Cundy,** Pamela Bonnie 1956- *WhoEnt 92*
**Malousek,** Richard A. 1952- *WhoMW 92*
**Malovany,** Gerald Martin 1940- *WhoFI 92*
**Malowany,** Alfred Stephen 1939- *AmMWSc 92*
**Maloy,** John Owen 1932- *AmMWSc 92*
**Maloy,** Joseph T 1939- *AmMWSc 92*
**Maloy,** Otis Cleo, Jr 1930- *AmMWSc 92*
**Maloy,** Robert 1935- *IntWW 91*
**Maloy,** W Lee 1940- *AmMWSc 92*
**Malozemoff,** Alexis P *AmMWSc 92*
**Malozemoff,** Plato 1909- *AmMWSc 92*
**Malpas,** James Spencer 1931- *Who 92*
**Malpas,** Robert 1927- *IntWW 91, Who 92, WhoFI 92*
**Malpass,** Brian William 1937- *Who 92*
**Malpass,** Dennis B *AmMWSc 92*
**Malpass,** Eric 1910- *WrDr 92*
**Malpass,** Eric Lawson 1910- *IntAu&W 91*
**Malphurs,** Roger Edward 1933- *WhoFI 92, WhoWest 92*
**Malpica-Padilla,** Rafael *WhoRel 92*
**Malpott,** Virgule *ConAu 34NR*
**Malqinhu** 1930- *IntWW 91*
**Malraux,** Andre 1901-1976 *ConAu 34NR, EncTR 91 [port], FacFETw, GuFrLit 1*
**Malry,** Lenton 1931- *WhoBlA 92*
**Malsberger,** Richard Griffith 1923- *AmMWSc 92*
**Malski,** James Joseph 1958- *WhoFI 92*
**Malsky,** Stanley Joseph 1925- *AmMWSc 92, WhoFI 92*
**Malsom,** Marilyn Faye 1934- *WhoAmP 91*
**Malson,** Charles Francis, Jr. 1951- *WhoRel 92*
**Malson,** Rex Richard 1931- *WhoFI 92, WhoWest 92*
**Malstrom,** Robert Arthur 1950- *AmMWSc 92*
**Malt,** Ronald A 1931- *AmMWSc 92*
**Malt,** Ronald Bradford 1954- *WhoAmL 92, WhoFI 92*
**Malta,** Archbishop of 1928- *Who 92*
**Malta,** Victor Guillermo 1928- *WhoHisp 92*
**Maltby,** Antony John 1928- *Who 92*
**Maltby,** Frederick L 1917- *AmMWSc 92*
**Maltby,** John Newcombe 1928- *IntWW 91, Who 92*
**Maltby,** Per Eugen 1933- *IntWW 91*
**Maltby,** Richard 1914-1991 *NewYTBS 91*
**Maltby,** Richard Eldridge, Jr. 1937- *WhoEnt 92*
**Maltby,** Sally 1943- *TwCPaSc*
**Maltenfort,** George Gunther 1913- *AmMWSc 92*
**Malter,** Arnold S. 1934- *IntWW 91*
**Maltese,** George J 1931- *AmMWSc 92*
**Maltese,** Serphin R 1932- *WhoAmP 91*
**Malthaner,** W A 1915- *AmMWSc 92*
**Malthouse,** Eric 1914- *TwCPaSc*
**Malthus,** Thomas *RfGEnL 91*
**Malthus,** Thomas Robert 1766-1834 *BlkwCEP, DcLB 107 [port]*
**Maltin,** Freda 1923- *WhoWest 92*
**Maltin,** Leonard 1950- *WhoEnt 92*
**Maltravers,** Lord *DcNCBi 4*
**Maltravers,** Lord 1987- *Who 92*
**Maltsberger,** David Charles 1960- *WhoRel 92*
**Maltsev,** Nikolay 1928- *IntWW 91*
**Maltsev,** Viktor Fyodorovich 1917- *IntWW 91*
**Maltz,** Albert 1908-1985 *BenetAL 91*
**Maltz,** Andrew Hal 1960- *WhoEnt 92, WhoWest 92*
**Maltz,** Dana Hollinger 1958- *WhoAmL 92*
**Maltz,** Kenneth Jay 1948- *WhoEnt 92*
**Maltz,** Martin Sidney 1941- *AmMWSc 92*
**Maltz,** Michael D 1938- *AmMWSc 92*
**Maltz,** Michael David 1938- *WhoMW 92*
**Maltz,** Milton Selwyn 1929- *WhoEnt 92*
**Maltz,** Robert 1935- *WhoMW 92*
**Maltzeff,** Eugene M 1912- *AmMWSc 92*
**Malucelli,** Kenneth Francis 1938- *WhoEnt 92*
**Malueg,** Kenneth Wilbur 1938- *AmMWSc 92*
**Maluga,** Thomas Michael 1937- *WhoRel 92*
**Malumphy,** Sharon Mary 1950- *WhoMW 92*
**Malushi,** Sheila *DrAPF 91*
**Malveaux,** Floyd *WhoBlA 92*
**Malveaux,** Floyd J 1940- *AmMWSc 92*
**Malven,** Paul Vernon 1938- *AmMWSc 92*
**Malvern,** Viscount 1949- *Who 92*
**Malvestiti,** Abel Orlando 1913- *WhoHisp 92*
**Malvick,** Allan J 1935- *AmMWSc 92*
**Malville,** John McKim 1934- *AmMWSc 92*
**Malvin,** Gary M 1954- *AmMWSc 92*
**Malvin,** Marc S. 1945- *WhoEnt 92*
**Malvin,** Nancy Ann 1950- *WhoMW 92*
**Malvin,** Reuben L. 1942- *WhoBlA 92*
**Malvin,** Richard L 1927- *AmMWSc 92*
**Malvin,** Richard Lester 1927- *WhoMW 92*
**Maly,** Edward J 1942- *AmMWSc 92*
**Maly,** George Joseph, Jr. 1933- *WhoAmL 92*
**Malyshev,** Vadim Mikhailovich 1932- *IntWW 91*
**Malyshev,** Vyacheslav Aleksandrovich 1902-1957 *SovUnBD*
**Malyshkin,** Alexander Georgyevich 1892-1938 *FacFETw*
**Malz,** Edward 1924- *WhoAmL 92*
**Malzahn,** Don Edwin 1945- *AmMWSc 92*
**Malzahn,** Ray Andrew 1929- *AmMWSc 92*
**Malzbender,** Thomas 1959- *WhoWest 92*
**Malzberg,** Barry 1939- *IntAu&W 91, WrDr 92*
**Malzberg,** Barry N. 1939- *TwCSFW 91*
**Malzer,** Gary Lee 1945- *AmMWSc 92*
**Mamaea** *EncAmaz 91*
**Mamaeva,** Nina Vasilevna 1923- *IntWW 91*
**Mamak,** Walter Julian 1950- *WhoMW 92*
**Mamalakis,** Markos John 1932- *WhoFI 92, WhoMW 92*
**Mamaloni,** Solomon 1943- *IntWW 91, Who 92*
**Mamandras,** Antonios H 1949- *AmMWSc 92*
**Mamantov,** Gleb 1931- *AmMWSc 92*
**Mamas and the Papas,** The *NewAmDM*
**Mamat,** Frank Trustick 1949- *WhoAmL 92, WhoFI 92, WhoMW 92*
**Mamba,** George Mbikwakhe 1932- *IntWW 91, Who 92*
**Mamelak,** Joseph Simon 1923- *AmMWSc 92*
**Mamert,** Jean Albert 1928- *IntWW 91*
**Mamet,** Bernard Leon 1937- *AmMWSc 92*
**Mamet,** David 1947- *BenetAL 91, FacFETw, IntMPA 92, WrDr 92*
**Mamet,** David Alan 1947- *IntWW 91, Who 92, WhoEnt 92*
**Mamiaka,** Raphael 1936- *IntWW 91*
**Mamie,** Pierre *WhoRel 92*
**Mamiya,** Richard T 1925- *AmMWSc 92*
**Mamleyev,** Yuri *DrAPF 91*
**Mamlin,** Gennadiy Semenovich 1925- *IntWW 91*
**Mamlok,** Ursula 1928- *NewAmDM*
**Mammel,** Russell Norman 1926- *WhoFI 92, WhoMW 92*
**Mammi,** Oscar 1926- *IntWW 91*
**Mamo,** Anthony 1909- *Who 92*
**Mamo,** Anthony Joseph 1909- *IntWW 91*
**Mamo,** George William 1955- *WhoFI 92, WhoRel 92*
**Mamola,** Karl Charles 1942- *AmMWSc 92*
**Mamonova,** Tatyana *IntAu&W 91*
**Mamoulian,** Rouben 1897-1987 *IntDcF 2-2 [port]*
**Mamoulian,** Rouben 1898-1987 *FacFETw*
**Mamrack,** Mark Donovan 1951- *AmMWSc 92*
**Mamrak,** Sandra Ann 1944- *AmMWSc 92*
**Mamula,** Branko 1921- *IntWW 91*
**Mamut,** Mary Catherine 1923- *WhoMW 92*
**Man,** Archdeacon of *Who 92*
**Man O'War** 1917-1947 *FacFETw*
**Man Ray** 1890-1976 *ModArCr 2 [port]*
**Man,** Chi-Sing 1947- *AmMWSc 92*
**Man,** Eugene H 1923- *AmMWSc 92*
**Man,** Evelyn Brower 1904- *AmMWSc 92*
**Man,** Maurice 1921- *TwCPaSc*
**Man,** Shu-Fan Paul 1945- *AmMWSc 92*
**Man-Kin,** Mak 1939- *AmMWSc 92*
**Man Ray,** Juliet d1991 *NewYTBS 91 [port]*
**Mana-Zucca** 1885-1981 *NewAmDM*
**Manabe,** Syukuro 1931- *AmMWSc 92*
**Manac'h,** Etienne Manoel 1910- *IntWW 91*
**Manaenkov,** Yuriy Alekseevich 1936- *SovUnBD*
**Manafort,** Paul John, Jr 1949- *WhoAmP 91*
**Manafort,** Paul John, Sr 1923- *WhoAmP 91*
**Managadze,** Nodar Shotayevich 1943- *IntWW 91*
**Manahan,** John Gregory 1947- *WhoMW 92*
**Manahan,** Larry W *WhoAmP 91*
**Manahan,** Matthew David 1964- *WhoAmL 92*
**Manak,** Rita C *AmMWSc 92*
**Manaker,** Arnold Martin 1947- *WhoFI 92*
**Manaker,** Robert Anthony 1918- *AmMWSc 92*
**Manakkil,** Thomas Joseph 1933- *AmMWSc 92*
**Manakos,** Froso 1931- *WhoAmP 91*
**Manalich,** Ramiro 1958- *WhoAmL 92*
**Manalis,** Melvyn S 1939- *AmMWSc 92*
**Manalo,** Pacita 1932- *AmMWSc 92*
**Manar,** Tom J 1937- *WhoAmP 91*
**Manara,** James Anthony 1945- *WhoWest 92*
**Manard,** Robert Lynn, III 1947- *WhoAmL 92*
**Manary,** Richard Deane 1944- *WhoFI 92, WhoWest 92*
**Manasek,** Francis John 1940- *AmMWSc 92*
**Manasrah,** Mustafa Moh'd 1940- *WhoFI 92*
**Manassah,** Jamal Tewfek 1945- *AmMWSc 92, WhoFI 92*
**Manasse,** Fred Kurt 1935- *AmMWSc 92*
**Manasse,** George 1938- *IntMPA 92*
**Manasse,** George H. 1938- *WhoEnt 92*
**Manasse,** Roger 1930- *AmMWSc 92, WhoWest 92*
**Manasseh,** Leonard Sulla 1916- *IntWW 91, Who 92*
**Manaster,** Alfred B 1938- *AmMWSc 92*
**Manatos,** Andrew E 1944- *WhoAmP 91*
**Manatt,** Charles Taylor 1936- *IntWW 91*
**Manatt,** Kathleen Gordon 1948- *WhoFI 92, WhoMW 92*
**Manatt,** Stanley L 1933- *AmMWSc 92*
**Manatt,** Stanley Lawrence 1933- *WhoWest 92*
**Manayenkov,** Yuriy Aleksandrovich 1936- *IntWW 91*
**Manbeck,** Harry Frederick, Jr. 1926- *WhoAmL 92, WhoAmP 91*
**Manber,** David *WhoEnt 92*
**Manby,** C.R. 1920- *IntMPA 92*
**Manby,** Mervyn Colet 1915- *Who 92*
**Mancall,** Elliott L 1927- *AmMWSc 92*
**Mance,** Andrew Mark 1952- *AmMWSc 92*
**Mance,** John J. 1926- *WhoBlA 92*
**Mance,** Jonathan Hugh 1943- *Who 92*
**Mance,** Junior 1928- *NewAmDM*
**Mance,** Mary Howarth *Who 92*
**Mancera Aguayo,** Miguel 1932- *IntWW 91*
**Mancha,** Guillermo 1943- *WhoHisp 92*
**Mancha,** Lupe *WhoHisp 92*
**Mancham,** James Richard Marie 1939- *IntWW 91, Who 92*
**Manche,** Emanuel Peter 1931- *AmMWSc 92*
**Manchee,** Eric Best 1918- *AmMWSc 92*
**Manchel,** Frank 1935- *IntAu&W 91, WhoEnt 92, WrDr 92*
**Mancheski,** Frederick J *AmMWSc 92*
**Mancheski,** Frederick John 1926- *WhoFI 92*
**Manchester,** Archdeacon of *Who 92*
**Manchester,** Bishop of 1924- *Who 92*
**Manchester,** Dean of *Who 92*
**Manchester,** Duke of 1938- *Who 92*
**Manchester,** James Eugene 1855-1913 *BiInAmS*
**Manchester,** Kenneth Edward 1925- *AmMWSc 92*
**Manchester,** Paul Brunson 1942- *WhoFI 92*
**Manchester,** R Henry 1915- *WhoAmP 91*
**Manchester,** William 1913- *Who 92*
**Manchester,** William 1922- *BenetAL 91, IntWW 91, SmATA 65 [port], Who 92, WhoEnt 92, WrDr 92*
**Manchester,** William 1925- *IntAu&W 91*
**Manchin,** A James 1927- *WhoAmP 91*
**Manchin,** Joe, III 1947- *WhoAmP 91*
**Manchin,** Mark Anthony 1952- *WhoAmP 91*
**Mancia,** Adrienne *IntMPA 92*
**Mancias,** Fernando G. *WhoHisp 92*
**Mancilla,** Joseph, Jr. 1947- *WhoAmL 92*
**Mancinelli,** Alberto L 1931- *AmMWSc 92*
**Mancinelli,** Luigi 1848-1921 *NewAmDM*
**Mancini,** Ernest Anthony 1947- *AmMWSc 92*
**Mancini,** Giuseppe Federico 1927- *IntWW 91*
**Mancini,** Henry 1924- *FacFETw, IntMPA 92, IntWW 91, NewAmDM, WhoEnt 92*
**Mancini,** Joseph A 1918- *WhoAmP 91*
**Mancini,** Louis Joseph 1950- *WhoWest 92*
**Mancini,** Robert Karl 1954- *WhoWest 92*
**Mancini,** Salvatore *WhoAmP 91*
**Mancini,** William F. 1959- *WhoWest 92*
**Mancino,** Douglas Michael 1949- *WhoAmL 92*
**Mancke,** Richard Bell 1943- *WhoFI 92*
**Manclark,** Charles Robert 1928- *AmMWSc 92*
**Manco Inca** 1516?-1545 *HisDSpE*
**Manco,** Hugo R. 1930- *WhoHisp 92*
**Mancroft** *Who 92*
**Mancroft,** Baron 1957- *Who 92*
**Mancuso,** Frank 1922- *WhoAmP 91*
**Mancuso,** Frank, Jr. 1958- *IntMPA 92*
**Mancuso,** Frank G. *IntWW 91*
**Mancuso,** Frank G. 1933- *IntMPA 92, WhoEnt 92*
**Mancuso,** Frank O 1918- *WhoAmP 91*
**Mancuso,** James Vincent 1916- *WhoFI 92*
**Mancuso,** Joseph Edward 1955- *WhoMW 92*
**Mancuso,** Joseph J 1933- *AmMWSc 92*
**Mancuso,** Richard Vincent 1938- *AmMWSc 92*
**Mancuso,** Robert James 1949- *WhoFI 92*
**Mand,** Martin G. 1936- *WhoFI 92*
**Mandal,** Anil Kumar 1935- *AmMWSc 92*
**Mandarino,** Joseph Anthony 1929- *AmMWSc 92*
**Mandat,** Eric Paul 1957- *WhoEnt 92*
**Mandava,** Naga Bhushan 1934- *AmMWSc 92*
**Mandel,** Alan Roger 1935- *WhoEnt 92*
**Mandel,** Andrea Sue 1951- *AmMWSc 92*
**Mandel,** Benjamin J 1912- *AmMWSc 92*
**Mandel,** Charlotte *DrAPF 91*
**Mandel,** David Alan 1963- *WhoAmL 92*
**Mandel,** Dominic Robert 1956- *WhoWest 92*
**Mandel,** Eli 1922- *BenetAL 91, ConPo 91, IntAu&W 91, WrDr 92*
**Mandel,** Ernest 1923- *IntAu&W 91, WrDr 92*
**Mandel,** Harold George 1924- *AmMWSc 92*
**Mandel,** Herbert Maurice 1924- *WhoFI 92*
**Mandel,** Hermann 1882-1946 *EncTR 91*
**Mandel,** Howard Clayton 1956- *WhoWest 92*
**Mandel,** Howie *WhoEnt 92*
**Mandel,** Howie 1955- *ConTFT 9*

Mandel, Irwin D 1922- AmMWSc 92
Mandel, Jack N. 1911- WhoFI 92
Mandel, James A 1934- AmMWSc 92
Mandel, Jeff 1952- WhoEnt 92, WhoWest 92
Mandel, John 1914- AmMWSc 92
Mandel, John Herbert 1925- AmMWSc 92
Mandel, Joseph David 1940- WhoAmL 92
Mandel, Karyl Lynn 1935- WhoFI 92, WhoMW 92
Mandel, Lazaro J 1940- AmMWSc 92
Mandel, Leonard 1927- AmMWSc 92
Mandel, Leslie Ann 1945- WhoFI 92
Mandel, Lewis Richard 1936- AmMWSc 92
Mandel, Loring LesBEnT 92
Mandel, Loring 1928- IntMPA 92, WhoEnt 92
Mandel, Manley 1923- AmMWSc 92
Mandel, Martin Louis 1944- WhoAmL 92
Mandel, Marvin 1920- IntWW 91
Mandel, Maurice, II WhoAmL 92
Mandel, Morton 1924- AmMWSc 92
Mandel, Morton Leon 1921- WhoFI 92
Mandel, Neil 1947- AmMWSc 92
Mandel, Newton W. 1926- WhoAmL 92
Mandel, Oscar DrAPF 91
Mandel, Oscar 1926- WhoWest 92, WrDr 92
Mandel, Richard Garfield 1950- WhoAmL 92
Mandel, Robert IntMPA 92
Mandel, Robert Livingstain 1957- WhoAmL 92
Mandel, Robert Michael WhoWest 92
Mandel, Ronnie Sue 1936- WhoEnt 92
Mandel, Siegfried 1922- IntAu&W 91, WhoWest 92
Mandel, Zoltan 1924- AmMWSc 92
Mandela, Nelson 1918- ConBlB 1 [port], FacFETw [port], WrDr 92
Mandela, Nelson Rolihlahia 1918- IntWW 91, Who 92
Mandela, Winnie FacFETw [port]
Mandela, Winnie 1934- ConBlB 2 [port], IntWW 91
Mandelbaum, Allen DrAPF 91
Mandelbaum, Bernard 1922- WhoRel 92
Mandelbaum, David Gideon 1959- WhoAmL 92
Mandelbaum, Frank 1934- WhoFI 92
Mandelbaum, Hugo 1901- AmMWSc 92
Mandelbaum, Isidore AmMWSc 92
Mandelbaum, Moshe Y. 1933- IntWW 91
Mandelberg, Hirsch I 1934- AmMWSc 92
Mandelberg, Martin 1946- AmMWSc 92
Mandelbrot, Benoit B 1924- AmMWSc 92, IntWW 91, WhoFI 92
Mandelcorn, Lyon 1926- AmMWSc 92
Mandelis, Andreas 1952- AmMWSc 92
Mandelkern, Leo 1922- AmMWSc 92
Mandelkern, Mark 1933- AmMWSc 92, WhoWest 92
Mandelkern, Mark Alan 1943- AmMWSc 92
Mandell, Abe 1922- IntMPA 92
Mandell, Alan 1926- AmMWSc 92
Mandell, Arnold J 1934- AmMWSc 92
Mandell, Ellen Sue 1952- WhoEnt 92
Mandell, Gary Lee 1957- WhoFI 92
Mandell, Joel 1939- WhoAmL 92
Mandell, Lawrence Howard 1946- WhoFI 92
Mandell, Leon 1927- AmMWSc 92
Mandell, Marvin DrAPF 91
Mandell, Mitchell Gregory 1960- WhoAmL 92
Mandell, Robert Burton 1933- AmMWSc 92
Mandell, Samuel W. W. 1943- WhoAmL 92
Mandell, William Mark 1960- WhoAmL 92
Mandels, Mary Hickox 1917- AmMWSc 92
Mandel'shtam, Nadezhda Yakovlevna 1899-1980 SovUnBD
Mandel'shtam, Osip Emil'evich 1891-1938 SovUnBD
Mandelshtam, Osip Emilievich 1891-1938 LiExTwC
Mandelson, Peter Benjamin 1953- Who 92
Mandelstam, Joel 1919- Who 92
Mandelstam, Osip 1891-1938 FacFETw
Mandelstam, Osip Emilievich 1891-1938 LiExTwC
Mandelstam, Paul 1925- AmMWSc 92
Mandelstam, Stanley Who 92
Mandelstam, Stanley 1928- AmMWSc 92, IntWW 91
Mandelstamm, Allan Beryle 1928- WhoFI 92
Mandelstamm, Jerome Robert 1932- WhoAmL 92
Mander, Charles 1921- Who 92
Mander, Jane 1877-1949 RfGEnL 91
Mander, Lewis Norman 1939- Who 92
Mander, Michael Harold 1936- Who 92
Mander, Noel Percy 1912- Who 92
Manders, Karl Lee 1927- AmMWSc 92, WhoMW 92
Manders, Peter William 1953- AmMWSc 92
Manderscheid, Lester Vincent 1930- AmMWSc 92, WhoMW 92
Mandeville, Viscount 1962- Who 92
Mandeville, Bernard 1670-1733 BlkwCEP
Mandeville, Charles Earle 1919- AmMWSc 92
Mandics, Peter Alexander 1937- AmMWSc 92
Mandil, Claude 1942- IntWW 91
Mandil, I Harry 1919- AmMWSc 92
Mandile, Anthony M WhoAmP 91
Mandilovitch, Miko WhoMW 92
Mandine, Salvador G. 1921- WhoFI 92
Manditsch, Milena EncAmaz 91
Mandl, Alexander Ernst 1938- AmMWSc 92
Mandl, Herbert Jay 1945- WhoRel 92
Mandl, Ines 1917- AmMWSc 92
Mandl, Paul 1917- AmMWSc 92
Mandl, Richard H 1934- AmMWSc 92
Mandle, Robert Joseph 1919- AmMWSc 92
Mandli, Jean WhoRel 92
Mandly, Charles Robert, Jr. 1957- WhoAmL 92
Mandoe, Kriesnadath 1935- IntWW 91
Mandos, Melissa 1963- WhoEnt 92
Mandra, York T 1922- AmMWSc 92
Mandrake, Mark Wayne 1954- WhoEnt 92
Mandrell, Barbara Ann 1948- WhoEnt 92
Mandrell, Gene Douglas 1944- WhoMW 92
Mandt, Patricia Trott 1958- WhoAmL 92
Manduca, John A. 1927- IntWW 91
Manduca, John Alfred 1927- Who 92
Manduca, Paul Victor Sant 1951- Who 92
Manduell, John 1928- Who 92
Mandula, Jeffrey Ellis 1941- AmMWSc 92
Manduley, Ilma Morell 1929- AmMWSc 92
Mandy, Ivan 1918- IntWW 91
Mandy, William John 1933- AmMWSc 92
Mane, Sateesh Ramchandra 1959- AmMWSc 92
Manea, Norman 1936- LiExTwC
Manea-Manoliu, Maria 1934- WhoWest 92
Maneatis, George A AmMWSc 92
Maneatis, George A. 1926- WhoFI 92, WhoWest 92
Manecke, Ruth Mary 1930- WhoEnt 92
Manegdeg, Jacob Magarro 1930- WhoAmP 91
Maneiro, Pedro A., Sr. 1939- WhoHisp 92
Maneke, Jean Ann 1954- WhoAmL 92
Maneker, Morton M. 1932- WhoAmL 92
Manekshaw, Sam Hormuzji Framji Jamshedji 1914- IntWW 91
Manela, Robert Alan 1959- WhoFI 92
Manelli, Donald Dean 1936- WhoEnt 92, WhoMW 92
Manen, Carol-Ann 1943- AmMWSc 92
Manenti, Thomas Joseph 1951- WhoFI 92
Maner, John William 1946- WhoFI 92
Maner, Martin 1946- ConAu 135
Maner, Martin Wallace 1946- WhoMW 92
Manera, Paul Allen 1930- AmMWSc 92
Maneri, Carl C 1933- AmMWSc 92
Maneri, Joseph Gabriel WhoEnt 92
Maners, Wendell R. 1955- WhoRel 92
Manes, Christopher 1957- ConAu 133
Manes, Ernest Gene 1943- AmMWSc 92
Manes, Fritz IntMPA 92
Manes, Fritz 1936- WhoWest 92
Manes, Kennneth Rene 1942- AmMWSc 92
Manes, Milton 1918- AmMWSc 92
Manes, Stephen DrAPF 91
Manes, Stephen Gabriel 1940- WhoEnt 92
Manescu, Corneliu 1916- IntWW 91
Maness, Donald B. 1939- WhoBlA 92
Maness, George Andrew WhoFI 92
Maness, Ina Mae 1921- WhoAmP 91
Manessier, Alfred 1911- IntWW 91
Manet, Edouard 1832-1883 ThHElm [port]
Manet, Julie ThHElm
Manewitz, Mark Lee 1946- WhoAmL 92
Maney, Thomas 1795?-1864 DcNCBi 4
Maney, William Jack 1949- WhoIns 92
Manford, Barbara Ann 1929- WhoEnt 92
Manfred, Carl Lawrence 1918- WhoRel 92
Manfred, Frederick 1912- ConNov 91, TwCWW 91, WrDr 92
Manfred, Frederick Feikema DrAPF 91
Manfred, Frederick Feikema 1912- BenetAL 91, IntAu&W 91
Manfred, Freya DrAPF 91
Manfredi, Arthur Frank, Jr 1944- AmMWSc 92
Manfredi, Joseph John 1952- WhoFI 92
Manfro, Patrick James 1947- WhoEnt 92, WhoMW 92
Mang, Douglas Arthur 1942- WhoAmL 92
Mangakis, Georgios Alexandros 1922- IntWW 91
Mangan, Celeste Bateman 1956- WhoBlA 92
Mangan, James Clarence 1803-1849 RfGEnL 91
Mangan, Jerrome 1934- AmMWSc 92
Mangan, Joseph F. 1943- WhoFI 92
Mangan, Kathy DrAPF 91
Mangan, Mona 1945- WhoEnt 92
Mangan, Patrick Harold 1921- WhoAmP 91
Mangan, Priscilla A 1926- WhoAmP 91
Mangan, Robert Lawrence 1945- AmMWSc 92
Mangan, Terence Joseph 1938- WhoWest 92
Manganaro, James Lawrence 1939- AmMWSc 92
Manganelli, Raymond M AmMWSc 92
Manganello, S J 1930- AmMWSc 92
Manganiello, Eugene J 1914- AmMWSc 92
Manganiello, Louis O J 1915- AmMWSc 92
Manganiello, Vincent Charles 1939- AmMWSc 92
Mangano, Anthony 1961- WhoEnt 92
Mangano, Antonio 1869-1951 DcAmImH
Mangasarian, Olvi Leon 1934- AmMWSc 92
Mangat, Baldev Singh 1935- AmMWSc 92
Mange, Arthur P 1931- AmMWSc 92
Mange, Franklin Edwin 1928- AmMWSc 92
Mange, Phillip Warren 1925- AmMWSc 92
Mangel, LeRoy Dwight 1945- WhoWest 92
Mangels, John Donald 1926- WhoFI 92, WhoWest 92
Mangelsdorf, Clark P 1928- AmMWSc 92
Mangelsdorf, Paul Christoph 1899- AmMWSc 92
Mangelsdorf, Paul Christoph, Jr 1925- AmMWSc 92
Mangelsdorff, Albert 1928- NewAmDM
Mangelson, Farrin Leon 1912- AmMWSc 92
Mangelson, Nolan Farrin 1936- AmMWSc 92
Mangen, Lawrence Raymond 1927- AmMWSc 92
Manger, Martin C 1937- AmMWSc 92
Manger, Walter Leroy 1944- AmMWSc 92
Manger, William Muir 1920- AmMWSc 92
Manges, James Horace 1927- WhoFI 92
Mangham, Jesse Roger 1922- AmMWSc 92
Mangham, William Desmond 1924- Who 92
Manghirmalani, Mona 1968- WhoFI 92, WhoWest 92
Manghirmalani, Ramesh 1953- WhoFI 92
Manghnani, Murli Hukumal 1936- AmMWSc 92
Mangia, Angelo James 1954- WhoAmL 92
Mangiamele, Suzanne C. 1958- WhoAmL 92
Mangiameli, John Vincent 1948- WhoMW 92
Mangiapane, Joseph Arthur 1926- WhoFI 92
Mangiardi, Maureen Grace 1946- WhoEnt 92
Mangiarelli, Richard Donald 1940- WhoWest 92
Mangiarotti, Angelo 1921- DcTwDes
Mangieri, Robert Paul 1941- WhoIns 92
Mangiero, Susan Marlena 1956- WhoFI 92
Mangin, Charles-Henri 1942- WhoFI 92
Mangino, Matthew Thomas 1962- WhoAmL 92
Mangino, Robert Matthew 1936- WhoIns 92
Mangione, Chuck 1940- WhoEnt 92
Mangione, Jerre DrAPF 91
Mangione, Jerre 1909- BenetAL 91, ConNov 91, WrDr 92
Mangione, Peter Lawrence 1943- WhoMW 92
Mangklaratna, Chamras 1921- IntWW 91
Mangla, P. B. 1936- IntWW 91
Manglapus, Raul S. 1918- IntWW 91
Manglitz, George Rudolph 1926- AmMWSc 92
Manglona, Benjamin T 1938- WhoAmP 91
Manglona, Herman M WhoAmP 91
Manglona, Paul Atalig WhoAmP 91
Mango, C. A. 1928- WrDr 92
Mango, Cyril Alexander 1928- Who 92
Mango, Frank Donald 1932- AmMWSc 92
Mango, Karin N. 1936- WrDr 92
Mangold, Donald J 1929- AmMWSc 92
Mangold, Robert Peter 1937- IntWW 91
Mangold, Thomas Cornelius 1934- Who 92
Mangope, Lucas Manyane 1923- IntWW 91
Mangrum, John Fuller 1922- WhoRel 92
Mangual, Theresa Y. 1958- WhoHisp 92
Mangulis, Visvaldis 1930- AmMWSc 92
Mangum, Adolphus Williamson 1834-1890 DcNCBi 4
Mangum, Billy Wilson 1931- AmMWSc 92
Mangum, Charles M. L. 1933- WhoBlA 92
Mangum, Charlotte P 1938- AmMWSc 92
Mangum, Fredrick Anthony 1938- AmMWSc 92
Mangum, Jeffrey Gary 1962- AmMWSc 92
Mangum, John Harvey 1933- AmMWSc 92
Mangum, Peter Gordon 1957- WhoRel 92
Mangum, Priestley Hinton, Jr. 1829-1907 DcNCBi 4
Mangum, Robert Ernest, Jr. 1940- WhoAmL 92
Mangum, Robert J. 1921- WhoBlA 92
Mangum, Ronald Scott 1944- WhoAmL 92
Mangum, William C, Jr 1934- WhoAmP 91
Mangum, William David 1953- WhoRel 92
Mangum, Willie Person 1792-1861 AmPolLe, DcNCBi 4
Mangum, Willie Person, Jr. 1827-1881 DcNCBi 4
Mangus, Marvin D 1924- AmMWSc 92
Mangus, Richard W 1930- WhoAmP 91
Mangwazu, Timon Sam 1933- IntWW 91, Who 92
Manhart, Joseph Heritage 1930- AmMWSc 92
Manhart, Robert 1925- AmMWSc 92
Manhas, Maghar Singh 1922- AmMWSc 92
Manhattan Transfer NewAmDM
Manheim, Chris James 1954- WhoAmP 91
Manheim, Frank T 1930- AmMWSc 92
Manheim, Jarol B. 1946- WrDr 92
Manheim, Michael Alan WhoEnt 92
Manheim, Werner 1915- IntAu&W 91
Manheimer, Jacob Allan 1957- WhoAmL 92
Manheimer, Wallace Milton 1942- AmMWSc 92
Manhire, Bill 1946- ConPo 91, IntAu&W 91, WrDr 92
Manhold, Earl Kenneth, III 1952- WhoMW 92
Manhold, John Henry, Jr 1919- AmMWSc 92
Manhood, Harold Alfred d1991 Who 92N
Mani EncEarC
Mani, Rama I 1927- AmMWSc 92
Maniacci, Michael Patrick 1961- WhoMW 92
Maniar, Atish Chandra 1926- AmMWSc 92
Maniatis, Thomas Peter 1943- AmMWSc 92
Manibog, G Monty 1930- WhoAmP 91
Manibusan, Joaquin WhoAmP 91
Manibusan, Joaquin V. E. WhoAmL 92
Manibusan, Marilyn 1948- WhoAmP 91
Manickam, Janardhan 1946- AmMWSc 92
Manigat, Leslie 1930- IntWW 91
Manigault, Walter William 1939- WhoBlA 92
Maniglia, Frank A. 1929- WhoEnt 92
Maniglia, Rosario 1918- AmMWSc 92
Manigo, George F., Jr. 1934- WhoBlA 92
Manikfan, Hussein 1936- IntWW 91
Maniktala, Ravinder Kumar 1947- WhoMW 92
Manildi, Marta Anne 1952- WhoAmL 92
Manilla, John Allan 1941- WhoFI 92
Maniloff, Jack 1938- AmMWSc 92
Manilow, Barry 1946- WhoEnt 92
Manilow, Barry 1949- IntWW 91
Maninger, Ralph Carroll 1918- AmMWSc 92
Manion, Daniel A 1942- WhoAmP 91
Manion, Daniel Anthony 1942- WhoAmL 92
Manion, James J 1922- AmMWSc 92
Manion, Jerald Monroe 1940- AmMWSc 92
Manion, Paul T 1940- WhoAmP 91
Manion, Synde 1956- WhoRel 92
Maniotis, James 1929- AmMWSc 92
Manire, George Philip 1919- AmMWSc 92
Manire, James McDonnell 1918- WhoAmL 92
Manis, Archie L 1939- AmMWSc 92
Manis, Merle E 1934- AmMWSc 92
Maniscalco, Ignatius Anthony 1944- AmMWSc 92
Maniscalco, James William 1953- WhoRel 92
Maniscalco, Joseph Stephen 1936- WhoIns 92
Maniusis, Iuozas IntWW 91
Manizer, Matvey Genrikhovich 1891-1966 SovUnBD

**Manjarrez,** Victor M 1933- *AmMWSc 92*
**Manji,** Kurbanali Mohamed 1950- *WhoMW 92*
**Manjoine,** Michael J 1914- *AmMWSc 92*
**Manjula,** Belur N 1943- *AmMWSc 92*
**Manjunath,** Puttaswamy 1952- *AmMWSc 92*
**Manjura,** Bonnie Doreen 1956- *WhoFI 92*
**Manka,** Charles K 1938- *AmMWSc 92*
**Manka,** Dan P 1914- *AmMWSc 92*
**Mankaba,** David d1991 *NewYTBS 91*
**Mankau,** Reinhold 1928- *AmMWSc 92*
**Mankau,** Sarojam Kurudamannil 1930- *AmMWSc 92*
**Manke,** Arthur Edward 1960- *WhoEnt 92*
**Manke,** Curtis Edwin 1933- *WhoAmP 91*
**Manke,** David Jacob 1938- *WhoMW 92*
**Manke,** Phillip Gordon 1929- *AmMWSc 92*
**Mankel,** Francis Xavier 1935- *WhoRel 92*
**Mankes,** Russell Francis 1949- *AmMWSc 92*
**Mankiewicz,** Don 1922- *WhoAmP 91*
**Mankiewicz,** Don M. 1922- *IntMPA 92*
**Mankiewicz,** Frank 1924- *IntWW 91*
**Mankiewicz,** Herman J 1897-1953 *FacFETw*
**Mankiewicz,** Joseph L. 1909- *BenetAL 91, FacFETw, IntDcF 2-2 [port], IntMPA 92*
**Mankiewicz,** Joseph Leo 1909- *IntAu&W 91, IntWW 91, Who 92, WhoEnt 92*
**Mankiewicz,** Tom 1942- *IntMPA 92*
**Mankin,** Charles John 1932- *AmMWSc 92*
**Mankin,** Dwight Dale 1961- *WhoFI 92*
**Mankin,** Jacqueline Lee 1958- *WhoMW 92*
**Mankin,** Richard Wendell 1948- *AmMWSc 92*
**Mankin,** Robert Stephen 1939- *WhoFI 92*
**Mankin,** Valentin Borisovich 1938- *SovUnBD*
**Mankin,** William Gray 1940- *AmMWSc 92*
**Mankiw,** Nicholas Gregory 1958- *WhoFI 92*
**Mankoff,** Albert William 1926- *WhoWest 92*
**Mankofsky,** Isidore 1931- *WhoEnt 92*
**Mankowitz,** Wolf 1924- *ConNov 91, IntAu&W 91, IntMPA 92, IntWW 91, Who 92, WrDr 92*
**Manktelow,** Michael Richard John *Who 92*
**Manley,** Albert 1908- *WhoBlA 92*
**Manley,** Albert Leslie 1945- *IntWW 91*
**Manley,** Audrey Forbes 1934- *AmMWSc 92, WhoBlA 92*
**Manley,** Bravitt Cola, Jr. 1955- *WhoFI 92*
**Manley,** Charles Howland 1943- *AmMWSc 92*
**Manley,** David Thomas 1938- *WhoFI 92, WhoMW 92*
**Manley,** Delariviere 1672?-1724 *RfGEnL 91*
**Manley,** Dexter 1959- *WhoBlA 92*
**Manley,** Donald Gene 1946- *AmMWSc 92*
**Manley,** Edna d1990 *TwCPaSc*
**Manley,** Emmett S 1936- *AmMWSc 92*
**Manley,** Frank *IntAu&W 91*
**Manley,** Frank 1930- *WrDr 92*
**Manley,** Harold J 1930- *AmMWSc 92*
**Manley,** Ivor Thomas 1931- *Who 92*
**Manley,** John Henry 1907- *AmMWSc 92*
**Manley,** John Ruffin 1925- *WhoBlA 92*
**Manley,** John Stevan 1949- *WhoRel 92*
**Manley,** Kathleen Elizabeth Baird 1940- *WhoWest 92*
**Manley,** Kim 1943- *AmMWSc 92*
**Manley,** Lance Filson 1945- *WhoFI 92*
**Manley,** Marshall 1940- *WhoFI 92, WhoIns 92*
**Manley,** Mary Delariviere 1663-1724 *BlkwCEP*
**Manley,** Michael 1925- *FacFETw [port]*
**Manley,** Michael Norman 1924- *IntWW 91, Who 92*
**Manley,** Nancy Jane 1951- *WhoFI 92*
**Manley,** Norman Gillette *WhoMW 92*
**Manley,** Norman Washington *FacFETw*
**Manley,** Richard Shannon 1932- *WhoAmP 91*
**Manley,** Richard Walter 1934- *WhoFI 92*
**Manley,** Robert Merrill, Jr. 1947- *WhoRel 92*
**Manley,** Rockliffe St John 1925- *AmMWSc 92*
**Manley,** Thomas Clinton 1911- *AmMWSc 92*
**Manley,** Thomas Roy 1918- *AmMWSc 92*
**Manley,** Will *WhoWest 92*
**Manlove,** Benson 1943- *WhoBlA 92*
**Manlove,** Colin 1942- *WrDr 92*
**Manly,** Alex *DcNCBi 4*
**Manly,** Basil 1798-1868 *DcNCBi 4*
**Manly,** Basil, Jr. 1825-1892 *RelLAm 91*
**Manly,** Charles 1795-1871 *DcNCBi 4*
**Manly,** Charles M, III 1950- *WhoAmP 91*
**Manly,** Donald G 1930- *AmMWSc 92*
**Manly,** Jethro Oates 1914- *AmMWSc 92*
**Manly,** Kenneth Fred 1941- *AmMWSc 92*
**Manly,** Marc Edward 1952- *WhoAmL 92*
**Manly,** Marline *TwCWW 91*
**Manly,** Matthias Evans 1801-1881 *DcNCBi 4*
**Manly,** Philip James 1944- *AmMWSc 92*
**Manly,** Samuel 1945- *WhoAmL 92*
**Manly,** Sarah G 1927- *WhoAmP 91*
**Manly,** William D 1923- *AmMWSc 92*
**Manmiller,** Joseph C 1925- *WhoAmP 91*
**Mann** *Who 92*
**Mann,** Abby *LesBEnT 92*
**Mann,** Abby 1927- *IntMPA 92*
**Mann,** Alan Eugene 1939- *AmMWSc 92*
**Mann,** Alexander 1853-1908 *TwCPaSc*
**Mann,** Alfred 1917- *WhoEnt 92*
**Mann,** Alfred Kenneth 1920- *AmMWSc 92*
**Mann,** Allan R. 1949- *TwCPaSc*
**Mann,** Andrew Hudson, Jr. 1947- *WhoRel 92*
**Mann,** Anthony 1907-1967 *IntDcF 2-2 [port]*
**Mann,** Benjamin Howard 1958- *WhoFI 92, WhoMW 92*
**Mann,** Benjamin Michael 1948- *AmMWSc 92*
**Mann,** Beth Madeline 1959- *WhoAmL 92*
**Mann,** Bruce Alan 1934- *WhoAmL 92*
**Mann,** Bruce H. 1950- *WhoAmL 92*
**Mann,** Cathleen 1896-1959 *TwCPaSc*
**Mann,** Charles *TwCWW 91*
**Mann,** Charles 1961- *WhoBlA 92*
**Mann,** Charles Edward *DrAPF 91*
**Mann,** Charles Kellogg 1934- *WhoFI 92*
**Mann,** Charles Kenneth 1928- *AmMWSc 92*
**Mann,** Charles Roy 1941- *AmMWSc 92*
**Mann,** Charles W 1935- *WhoAmP 91*
**Mann,** Chris 1948- *ConPo 91, WrDr 92*
**Mann,** Christian John 1931- *AmMWSc 92*
**Mann,** Christopher Michael Zithulele 1948- *IntAu&W 91*
**Mann,** Chuck *TwCWW 91*
**Mann,** Clarence Charles 1929- *WhoFI 92*
**Mann,** Colin Nicholas 1942- *Who 92*
**Mann,** Daniel d1991 *NewYTBS 91 [port]*
**Mann,** Daniel 1912- *IntMPA 92*
**Mann,** David Edwin, Jr 1922- *AmMWSc 92*
**Mann,** David Emerson 1924- *WhoAmP 91*
**Mann,** David R 1944- *AmMWSc 92*
**Mann,** David S *WhoAmP 91*
**Mann,** David Scott 1939- *WhoMW 92*
**Mann,** David William 1947- *WhoMW 92, WhoRel 92*
**Mann,** Delbert *LesBEnT 92*
**Mann,** Delbert 1920- *IntMPA 92, WhoEnt 92*
**Mann,** Donald Cameron 1949- *WhoFI 92*
**Mann,** Donald J. 1949- *WhoAmL 92*
**Mann,** Donald Robert 1930- *WhoWest 92*
**Mann,** E.B. 1902- *TwCWW 91*
**Mann,** Eddie 1951- *WhoEnt 92*
**Mann,** Edna 1928- *TwCPaSc*
**Mann,** Emily 1952- *WrDr 92*
**Mann,** Emily Betsy 1952- *WhoEnt 92*
**Mann,** Eric John 1921- *Who 92*
**Mann,** Erika 1905-1969 *BenetAL 91, EncTR 91, LiExTwC*
**Mann,** Ezra B 1914- *WhoAmP 91*
**Mann,** Felix Bernard 1931- *Who 92*
**Mann,** Francis Anthony 1914- *IntAu&W 91*
**Mann,** Francis George 1917- *Who 92*
**Mann,** Frank E 1920- *WhoAmP 91*
**Mann,** Franklin Balch 1941- *WhoAmP 91*
**Mann,** Fred Rychen 1937- *WhoRel 92*
**Mann,** Frederick Alexander d1991 *Who 92N*
**Mann,** Frederick Alexander 1907- *IntWW 91*
**Mann,** Frederick Michael 1948- *AmMWSc 92*
**Mann,** Frederick R 1903-1987 *FacFETw*
**Mann,** Gary Allen 1954- *WhoRel 92*
**Mann,** Genie Grant 1951- *WhoWest 92*
**Mann,** George *Who 92*
**Mann,** George Levier 1901- *WhoBlA 92*
**Mann,** George Stanley 1932- *WhoFI 92*
**Mann,** George Vernon 1917- *AmMWSc 92*
**Mann,** Golo 1909- *IntWW 91*
**Mann,** Gordon Hossley 1928- *WhoRel 92*
**Mann,** Gordon Lee, Jr. 1921- *WhoWest 92*
**Mann,** Grace Carrol 1928- *WhoEnt 92*
**Mann,** Harold 1931- *WhoAmP 91*
**Mann,** Harrington 1864-1937 *TwCPaSc*
**Mann,** Heinrich 1871-1950 *EncTR 91, LiExTwC*
**Mann,** Helen Louise 1943- *WhoAmP 91*
**Mann,** Henry Berthold 1905- *WhoWest 92*
**Mann,** Henry Dean 1943- *WhoFI 92*
**Mann,** Herbie 1930- *NewAmDM, WhoEnt 92*
**Mann,** Horace 1701-1786 *BlkwCEP*
**Mann,** Horace 1796-1859 *BenetAL 91, RComAH*
**Mann,** Horace 1844-1868 *BiInAmS*
**Mann,** James *WrDr 92*
**Mann,** James 1913- *AmMWSc 92*
**Mann,** James Edward, Jr 1936- *AmMWSc 92*
**Mann,** James Robert 1920- *WhoAmP 91*
**Mann,** James Scrimgeour 1883-1946 *TwCPaSc*
**Mann,** Jeff *WhoEnt 92*
**Mann,** Jessica *IntAu&W 91, WrDr 92*
**Mann,** Jill 1943- *Who 92*
**Mann,** John Allen 1921- *AmMWSc 92*
**Mann,** John Frederick 1930- *Who 92*
**Mann,** John Kevin 1956- *WhoWest 92*
**Mann,** John Martin 1946- *WhoRel 92*
**Mann,** John Roger 1956- *WhoAmL 92*
**Mann,** Joseph B. 1939- *WhoBlA 92*
**Mann,** Joseph Bird 1923- *AmMWSc 92*
**Mann,** Josephine *WrDr 92*
**Mann,** Kenneth Gerard 1941- *AmMWSc 92*
**Mann,** Kenneth H 1923- *AmMWSc 92*
**Mann,** Kenneth Walker 1914- *WhoRel 92*
**Mann,** Klaus 1906-1949 *BenetAL 91, EncTR 91 [port], LiExTwC*
**Mann,** Larry N 1934- *AmMWSc 92*
**Mann,** Laura J. 1957- *WhoMW 92*
**Mann,** Lawrence, Jr 1926- *AmMWSc 92*
**Mann,** Leslie Bernard 1919- *AmMWSc 92*
**Mann,** Lewis Theodore, Jr 1925- *AmMWSc 92*
**Mann,** Lloyd Godfrey 1922- *AmMWSc 92*
**Mann,** Louie Lynn 1940- *WhoRel 92*
**Mann,** Marion 1920- *AmMWSc 92, WhoBlA 92*
**Mann,** Martin Edward 1943- *Who 92*
**Mann,** Marvin L. 1933- *WhoFI 92*
**Mann,** Maurice 1929- *WhoFI 92*
**Mann,** Merton L, Jr *WhoAmP 91*
**Mann,** Michael *IntMPA 92*
**Mann,** Michael 1930- *Who 92*
**Mann,** Michael Ashley 1924- *Who 92*
**Mann,** Michael David 1944- *AmMWSc 92, WhoMW 92*
**Mann,** Michael K. *WhoEnt 92*
**Mann,** Michael K. 1943- *ConAu 134*
**Mann,** Michael Martin 1939- *WhoFI 92, WhoWest 92*
**Mann,** Murray G. *Who 92*
**Mann,** Nancy Robbins 1925- *AmMWSc 92*
**Mann,** Nathaniel Edward 1953- *WhoRel 92*
**Mann,** Nicholas *Who 92*
**Mann,** Pamela d1840 *EncAmaz 91*
**Mann,** Patricia Kathleen Randall 1937- *Who 92*
**Mann,** Paul 1917- *AmMWSc 92*
**Mann,** Paul Thomas 1875-1955 *WhoNob 90*
**Mann,** Pauline *Who 92*
**Mann,** Peggy *ConAu 35NR, DrAPF 91, IntAu&W 91, WrDr 92*
**Mann,** Perry E 1921- *WhoAmP 91*
**Mann,** Peter H 1926- *IntAu&W 91*
**Mann,** Peter Woodley 1924- *Who 92*
**Mann,** Philip Melvin 1940- *WhoBlA 92*
**Mann,** Philip Roy 1948- *WhoAmL 92*
**Mann,** Phillip 1942- *TwCSFW 91, WrDr 92*
**Mann,** Phillip Lynn 1944- *WhoMW 92*
**Mann,** Ralph Willard 1916- *AmMWSc 92*
**Mann,** Ranveer S 1924- *AmMWSc 92*
**Mann,** Richard *WhoBlA 92*
**Mann,** Richard A 1921- *AmMWSc 92*
**Mann,** Robert Bruce 1955- *AmMWSc 92*
**Mann,** Robert David 1941- *WhoAmL 92*
**Mann,** Robert Nathaniel 1920- *WhoEnt 92*
**Mann,** Robert Samuel 1936- *WhoWest 92*
**Mann,** Robert Steven 1952- *WhoAmL 92*
**Mann,** Robert W 1924- *AmMWSc 92*
**Mann,** Robert Wellesley 1924- *IntWW 91*
**Mann,** Ronald Francis 1931- *AmMWSc 92*
**Mann,** Rupert 1946- *Who 92*
**Mann,** Stanley Joseph 1932- *AmMWSc 92*
**Mann,** Stephen Ashby 1947- *WhoFI 92*
**Mann,** Steven Gerald 1944- *WhoFI 92*
**Mann,** Terry Lawrence 1948- *WhoAmP 91*
**Mann,** Thaddeus Robert Rudolph 1908- *IntWW 91, Who 92*
**Mann,** Thomas 1875-1955 *BenetAL 91, EncTR 91 [port], FacFETw [port], LiExTwC, TwCLC 44 [port]*
**Mann,** Thomas, Jr 1949- *WhoAmP 91*
**Mann,** Thomas J., Jr. 1949- *WhoBlA 92*
**Mann,** Thomas Nicholson 1797-1824 *DcNCBi 4*
**Mann,** Thomas William, Jr. 1949- *WhoWest 92*
**Mann,** Thurston 1920- *AmMWSc 92*
**Mann,** Timothy Chun-Chock 1961- *WhoRel 92*
**Mann,** Wallace Vernon, Jr 1930- *AmMWSc 92*
**Mann,** Wilfrid Basil 1908- *AmMWSc 92*
**Mann,** William Anthony 1943- *AmMWSc 92*
**Mann,** William Neville 1911- *Who 92*
**Mann,** William Robert 1920- *AmMWSc 92*
**Mann,** Yuri Vladimirovich 1929- *IntWW 91*
**Manna,** Zohar 1939- *AmMWSc 92*
**Manne,** Alan S *AmMWSc 92*
**Manne,** Alan S. 1925- *WhoWest 92*
**Manne,** Henry G. 1928- *WrDr 92*
**Manne,** S. Anthony 1940- *IntMPA 92*
**Manne,** Shelly 1920-1984 *NewAmDM*
**Manne,** Veeraswamy 1952- *AmMWSc 92*
**Manne,** William Stuart 1951- *WhoWest 92*
**Mannella,** Gene Gordon 1931- *AmMWSc 92*
**Manner,** Richard John 1920- *AmMWSc 92*
**Mannerheim,** Carl Gustav, Baron von 1867-1951 *EncTR 91 [port]*
**Mannerheim,** Carl Gustav Emil 1867-1951 *FacFETw*
**Mannering,** Gilbert James 1917- *AmMWSc 92*
**Mannering,** Jerry Vincent 1929- *AmMWSc 92*
**Manners** *Who 92*
**Manners,** Baron 1923- *Who 92*
**Manners,** Miss *WrDr 92*
**Manners,** David 1912- *IntAu&W 91*
**Manners,** Elizabeth Maude 1917- *Who 92*
**Manners,** Gerald 1932- *Who 92, WrDr 92*
**Manners,** J. Hartley 1870-1928 *BenetAL 91*
**Manners,** Nancy *WhoWest 92*
**Manners,** Robert Alan 1913- *WrDr 92*
**Manners,** Thomas 1929- *Who 92*
**Manners,** Tyler Paul 1960- *WhoWest 92*
**Mannes,** David 1866-1959 *NewAmDM*
**Mannes,** Elena Sabin 1943- *WhoEnt 92*
**Mannes,** Marya 1904-1990 *AnObit 1990*
**Manney,** Bridget *DrAPF 91*
**Manney,** Richard 1936- *WhoFI 92*
**Manney,** Russell Field, Jr. 1933- *WhoRel 92*
**Manney,** Thomas Richard 1933- *AmMWSc 92*
**Manney,** William A. 1931- *WhoBlA 92*
**Mannheim,** Carole I. 1949- *WhoMW 92*
**Manni,** Victor Macedonio 1940- *WhoHisp 92*
**Mannie,** William Edward 1931- *WhoBlA 92*
**Mannik,** Mart 1932- *AmMWSc 92*
**Manning,** Aubrey William George 1930- *Who 92*
**Manning,** Blanche M 1934- *WhoAmP 91*
**Manning,** Blanche Marie 1934- *WhoBlA 92*
**Manning,** Brenda Dale 1945- *AmMWSc 92*
**Manning,** Brent V. 1950- *WhoAmL 92*
**Manning,** Burt *WhoFI 92*
**Manning,** Charles Henry 1844-1919 *BiInAmS*
**Manning,** Charles Richard, Jr 1930- *AmMWSc 92*
**Manning,** Christopher Ashley 1945- *WhoFI 92*
**Manning,** Cleo Willard 1915- *AmMWSc 92*
**Manning,** Craig Edward 1959- *AmMWSc 92*
**Manning,** Curtis William 1952- *WhoFI 92*
**Manning,** Daniel Ricardo 1966- *WhoBlA 92*
**Manning,** Danny 1966- *BlkOlyM*
**Manning,** David *TwCWW 91*
**Manning,** David 1938- *WrDr 92*
**Manning,** David Edwin 1961- *WhoAmL 92*
**Manning,** David Treadway 1928- *AmMWSc 92*
**Manning,** Dean David 1940- *AmMWSc 92*
**Manning,** Dick d1991 *NewYTBS 91*
**Manning,** Donald J 1929- *WhoAmP 91*
**Manning,** Donald O. *WhoWest 92*
**Manning,** Douglas C. 1954- *WhoEnt 92*
**Manning,** Eddie James 1952- *WhoBlA 92*
**Manning,** Eilene M. 1930- *WhoEnt 92*
**Manning,** Ellis E 1933- *WhoIns 92*
**Manning,** Eric 1940- *WhoWest 92*
**Manning,** Eric G 1940- *AmMWSc 92*
**Manning,** Ernest Charles 1908- *IntWW 91*
**Manning,** Evelyn 1945- *WhoBlA 92*
**Manning,** Francis Joseph 1933- *WhoAmP 91*
**Manning,** Francis S 1933- *AmMWSc 92*
**Manning,** Frederick Allan 1904- *Who 92*
**Manning,** Frederick J 1947- *WhoIns 92*
**Manning,** Gary Lon 1947- *WhoRel 92*
**Manning,** Geoffrey 1929- *Who 92*
**Manning,** George Lincoln 1865-1914 *BiInAmS*
**Manning,** Gerald Stuart 1940- *AmMWSc 92*
**Manning,** Glenn M. 1935- *WhoBlA 92*
**Manning,** Gordon *LesBEnT 92*
**Manning,** Guy Vincent 1949- *WhoAmL 92*

**Manning,** Harold Edwin 1935- *AmMWSc 92*
**Manning,** Helen Harton 1921- *WhoEnt 92*
**Manning,** Henry Eugene 1935- *WhoMW 92*
**Manning,** Howard Kenneth 1953- *WhoFI 92*
**Manning,** Howard Nick, Jr. 1943- *WhoBlA 92*
**Manning,** Hubert Vernon 1918- *WhoBlA 92*
**Manning,** Irwin 1929- *AmMWSc 92*
**Manning,** Isaac Hall 1866-1946 *DcNCBi 4*
**Manning,** James Harvey 1940- *AmMWSc 92*
**Manning,** James Matthew 1939- *AmMWSc 92*
**Manning,** James Smith 1859-1938 *DcNCBi 4*
**Manning,** Jane 1938- *IntWW 91*
**Manning,** Jane A. 1947- *WhoBlA 92*
**Manning,** Jane Marian 1938- *Who 92*
**Manning,** JaRue Stanley 1934- *AmMWSc 92*
**Manning,** Jean Bell 1937- *WhoBlA 92*
**Manning,** Jerome Alan 1929- *WhoAmL 92*
**Manning,** Jerome Edward 1940- *AmMWSc 92*
**Manning,** Jerry Edsel 1944- *AmMWSc 92*
**Manning,** John 1803-1872 *DcNCBi 4*
**Manning,** John, Jr. 1830-1899 *DcNCBi 4*
**Manning,** John Craige 1920- *AmMWSc 92*
**Manning,** John Hall 1889-1963 *DcNCBi 4*
**Manning,** John Joseph 1930- *WhoFI 92*
**Manning,** John Randolph 1932- *AmMWSc 92*
**Manning,** John W 1930- *AmMWSc 92*
**Manning,** John Willard 1950- *WhoAmL 92*
**Manning,** Kenneth Alan 1951- *WhoAmL 92*
**Manning,** Laurence 1899-1972 *TwCSFW 91*
**Manning,** Laurence A 1923- *AmMWSc 92*
**Manning,** Leah 1886-1977 *BiDBrF 2*
**Manning,** Lynn *DrAPF 91*
**Manning,** M Joseph 1924- *WhoAmP 91*
**Manning,** M L 1900- *AmMWSc 92*
**Manning,** Marie *BenetAL 91*
**Manning,** Marsha *WrDr 92*
**Manning,** Mary 1947- *WhoWest 92*
**Manning,** Mary Jo 1942- *WhoEnt 92*
**Manning,** Matthew Nickerson 1962- *WhoFI 92*
**Manning,** Maurice 1937- *AmMWSc 92*
**Manning,** Monis Joseph 1931- *AmMWSc 92*
**Manning,** Olivia 1908-1980 *FacFETw, RfGEnL 91*
**Manning,** Patricia Kamaras 1953- *WhoWest 92*
**Manning,** Patrick Augustus Mervyn 1946- *IntWW 91*
**Manning,** Patrick James 1938- *AmMWSc 92*
**Manning,** Patrick Joseph 1944- *WhoMW 92*
**Manning,** Paul 1912- *IntAu&W 91*
**Manning,** Peter J *WhoAmP 91*
**Manning,** Peter K 1940- *ConAu 34NR*
**Manning,** Phil Richard 1921- *AmMWSc 92*
**Manning,** R Davis, Jr *AmMWSc 92*
**Manning,** R E 1927- *AmMWSc 92*
**Manning,** Ralph Kenneth, Jr. 1922- *WhoAmL 92*
**Manning,** Randolph H. 1947- *WhoBlA 92*
**Manning,** Raymond B 1934- *AmMWSc 92*
**Manning,** Reuben D. 1931- *WhoBlA 92*
**Manning,** Richard E 1926- *WhoAmP 91*
**Manning,** Richard Howard 1948- *WhoMW 92*
**Manning,** Richard L 1957- *WhoFI 92*
**Manning,** Robert Alan 1949- *WhoFI 92*
**Manning,** Robert Joseph 1919- *IntAu&W 91, IntWW 91*
**Manning,** Robert Joseph 1920- *AmMWSc 92*
**Manning,** Robert M 1956- *AmMWSc 92*
**Manning,** Robert Nickerson 1938- *WhoEnt 92*
**Manning,** Robert Thomas 1927- *AmMWSc 92*
**Manning,** Ronald Arthur 1931- *WhoMW 92*
**Manning,** Ronald Lee 1951- *WhoMW 92*
**Manning,** Rosemary 1911- *IntAu&W 91, WrDr 92*
**Manning,** Roy *TwCWW 91*
**Manning,** Sam P *WhoAmP 91*
**Manning,** Sherrell Dane *AmMWSc 92*
**Manning,** Stanley 1921- *IntAu&W 91*
**Manning,** Thomas Courtland 1825-1887 *DcNCBi 4*
**Manning,** Thomas Courtland 1952- *WhoAmL 92*
**Manning,** Thomas Henry 1911- *Who 92*
**Manning,** Thomas Joseph 1955- *WhoMW 92*
**Manning,** Timothy 1909-1989 *FacFETw, RelLAm 91*
**Manning,** V C *WhoAmP 91*
**Manning,** Vannoy Hartrog 1839-1892 *DcNCBi 4*
**Manning,** Victor Patrick, Jr. 1945- *WhoFI 92*
**Manning,** Walter Scott 1933- *WhoFI 92*
**Manning,** William C. 1945- *WhoRel 92*
**Manning,** William Dudley, Jr. 1934- *WhoFI 92*
**Manning,** William George 1923- *WhoFI 92*
**Manning,** William Henry 1951- *WhoAmL 92*
**Manning,** William Joseph 1926- *WhoAmL 92*
**Manning,** William Joseph 1941- *AmMWSc 92*
**Manning-Sanders,** Ruth 1895- *IntAu&W 91*
**Manningham-Buller** *Who 92*
**Mannino,** Calogero 1939- *IntWW 91*
**Mannino,** Edward Francis 1941- *WhoAmL 92*
**Mannino,** J. Davis 1949- *WhoWest 92*
**Mannino,** Joseph Robert 1941- *AmMWSc 92*
**Mannino,** Joseph Robert, Jr. 1941- *WhoMW 92*
**Mannino,** Raphael James 1947- *AmMWSc 92*
**Mannion,** James Michael 1945- *WhoAmP 91*
**Mannion,** John F X 1932- *WhoIns 92*
**Mannion,** John Francis Xavier 1932- *WhoFI 92*
**Mannis,** Estelle Claire 1936- *WhoAmL 92*
**Mannis,** Fred 1937- *AmMWSc 92*
**Mannis,** Valerie Sklar 1939- *WhoMW 92*
**Mannix,** David K. 1952- *IntMPA 92*
**Mannix,** Edward T *AmMWSc 92*
**Mannix,** Kevin Leese 1949- *WhoAmP 91*
**Manno,** Barbara Reynolds 1936- *AmMWSc 92*
**Manno,** Joseph Eugene 1942- *AmMWSc 92*
**Manno,** Theodore Paul *WhoAmL 92*
**Mannocci,** Lino 1945- *TwCPaSc*
**Mannshardt,** Steven Barry *WhoEnt 92*
**Mannweiler,** Gordon B 1916- *AmMWSc 92*
**Mannweiler,** Paul S. *WhoMW 92*
**Mannweiler,** Paul Steven 1949- *WhoAmP 91*
**Manny,** Bruce Andrew 1944- *AmMWSc 92, WhoMW 92*
**Mano,** D. Keith *DrAPF 91*
**Mano,** D Keith 1942- *IntAu&W 91*
**Mano,** Ronald Makoto 1942- *WhoFI 92*
**Manocha,** Manmohan Singh 1935- *AmMWSc 92*
**Manocha,** Sohan Lall 1936- *AmMWSc 92*
**Manoff,** Dinah 1958- *IntMPA 92*
**Manoff,** Dinah Beth *WhoEnt 92*
**Manoff,** Robert Karl 1944- *IntAu&W 91*
**Manogue,** William H 1926- *AmMWSc 92*
**Manohar,** Murli 1947- *AmMWSc 92*
**Manoilescu,** Mihail 1891-1950 *BiDExR*
**Manolson,** Morris Frank 1959- *AmMWSc 92*
**Manon,** Eduardo 1943- *WhoWest 92*
**Manooch,** Charles Samuel, III 1943- *AmMWSc 92*
**Manoogian,** Armen 1934- *AmMWSc 92*
**Manoogian,** Richard Alexander 1936- *WhoMW 92*
**Manoogian,** Sion d1991 *NewYTBS 91*
**Manookin,** David Reynolds 1944- *WhoEnt 92*
**Manor,** Jason *WrDr 92*
**Manor,** Robert Michael 1953- *WhoMW 92, WhoRel 92*
**Manor,** Vranna Lee 1946- *WhoRel 92*
**Manos,** Bruce John 1953- *WhoAmL 92*
**Manos,** Constantine T 1933- *AmMWSc 92*
**Manos,** John M. 1922- *WhoAmL 92, WhoMW 92*
**Manos,** Pete Lazaros 1936- *WhoFI 92*
**Manos,** Philip 1928- *AmMWSc 92*
**Manos,** William P 1919- *AmMWSc 92*
**Manosky,** Robert Stanley 1943- *WhoEnt 92*
**Manougian,** Edward 1929- *AmMWSc 92*
**Manougian,** Manoug N 1935- *AmMWSc 92*
**Manougian,** Nancy Johnson 1948- *WhoAmL 92*
**Manoukian,** Noel Edwin 1938- *WhoAmP 91*
**Manousakis,** Efstratios 1957- *AmMWSc 92*
**Manowitz,** Bernard 1922- *AmMWSc 92*
**Manowitz,** Paul 1940- *AmMWSc 92*
**Manqour,** Nasir Hamad al- 1927- *IntWW 91*
**Manring,** Edward Raymond 1921- *AmMWSc 92*
**Manrique,** Jaime *DrAPF 91*
**Manrique,** Jaime 1949- *WhoHisp 92*
**Manrique,** Julius C. 1932- *WhoHisp 92*
**Manriquez,** Rolando Paredes 1951- *AmMWSc 92*
**Manross,** Mary Ann 1949- *WhoWest 92*
**Manross,** Newton Spaulding 1828?-1862 *BiInAmS*
**Mans,** Keith Douglas Rowland 1946- *Who 92*
**Mans,** Rowland Spencer Noel 1921- *Who 92*
**Mans,** Rusty Jay 1930- *AmMWSc 92*
**Mans,** Walter A. 1942- *WhoWest 92*
**Mansager,** Felix Norman 1911- *IntWW 91, Who 92*
**Mansbach,** Charles M, II 1937- *AmMWSc 92*
**Mansberger,** Arlie Roland, Jr 1922- *AmMWSc 92*
**Mansbridge,** Francis 1943- *ConAu 133*
**Mansbridge,** Michael *WhoRel 92*
**Mansel,** James Seymour Denis 1907- *Who 92*
**Mansel,** Philip 1943- *Who 92*
**Mansel-Jones,** David 1926- *Who 92*
**Mansel Lewis,** David Courtenay 1927- *Who 92*
**Mansell,** Buford H. L. 1938- *WhoBlA 92*
**Mansell,** Darrel 1934- *WrDr 92*
**Mansell,** Gerard Evelyn Herbert 1921- *Who 92*
**Mansell,** Nigel 1954- *IntWW 91*
**Mansell,** Robert Shirley 1938- *AmMWSc 92*
**Mansell-Jones,** Richard 1940- *Who 92*
**Mansen,** Steven Robert 1955- *WhoFI 92*
**Manser,** George R. 1931- *WhoMW 92*
**Manser,** John *Who 92*
**Manser,** Martin Hugh 1952- *IntAu&W 91*
**Manser,** Michael John 1929- *IntWW 91, Who 92*
**Manser,** Peter John 1939- *Who 92*
**Mansergh,** Nicholas d1991 *IntWW 91N, Who 92N*
**Mansergh,** Nicholas 1910-1991 *ConAu 133*
**Manses,** Simon Louis 1953- *WhoEnt 92*
**Mansfeld,** Florian Berthold 1938- *AmMWSc 92*
**Mansfield** *Who 92*
**Mansfield,** Alfred William, III *WhoMW 92*
**Mansfield,** Andrew 1954- *TwCPaSc*
**Mansfield,** Andrew K. 1931- *WhoBlA 92*
**Mansfield,** Arthur Walter 1926- *AmMWSc 92*
**Mansfield,** Bruce Edgar 1926- *WrDr 92*
**Mansfield,** Carl Major 1928- *WhoBlA 92*
**Mansfield,** Charles M d1917 *BiInAmS*
**Mansfield,** Charles Robert 1938- *AmMWSc 92*
**Mansfield,** Christopher Charles 1950- *WhoAmL 92, WhoFI 92*
**Mansfield,** Claudine Trotter 1921- *WhoAmP 91*
**Mansfield,** Clifton Tyler 1936- *AmMWSc 92*
**Mansfield,** David Parks 1912- *Who 92*
**Mansfield,** Edward Gerard 1921- *Who 92*
**Mansfield,** Eric Alan 1951- *WhoEnt 92*
**Mansfield,** Eric Harold 1923- *IntWW 91, Who 92*
**Mansfield,** Gerard *Who 92*
**Mansfield,** Gregory James Edward 1957- *WhoRel 92*
**Mansfield,** Harry Edgar 1942- *WhoFI 92*
**Mansfield,** Irving *LesBEnT 92*
**Mansfield,** J. Kenneth 1921- *IntWW 91*
**Mansfield,** James Norman, III 1951- *WhoAmL 92*
**Mansfield,** Jan 1946- *WhoMW 92*
**Mansfield,** Jared 1759-1830 *BiInAmS*
**Mansfield,** Jerry Leonard 1947- *WhoAmP 91*
**Mansfield,** John E 1938- *AmMWSc 92*
**Mansfield,** John H. 1928- *WhoAmL 92*
**Mansfield,** John Michael 1945- *AmMWSc 92*
**Mansfield,** Joseph Victor 1907- *AmMWSc 92*
**Mansfield,** Karen Lee 1942- *WhoAmL 92, WhoMW 92*
**Mansfield,** Katherine *ConAu 134*
**Mansfield,** Katherine 1888-1923 *FacFETw, LiExTwC, RfGEnL 91, ShSCr 9 [port]*
**Mansfield,** Kevin Thomas 1940- *AmMWSc 92*
**Mansfield,** Larry Everett 1939- *AmMWSc 92*
**Mansfield,** Lawrence Frederick 1922- *WhoFI 92*
**Mansfield,** Lois E 1941- *AmMWSc 92*
**Mansfield,** Marc L 1955- *AmMWSc 92*
**Mansfield,** Maynard Joseph 1930- *AmMWSc 92, WhoMW 92*
**Mansfield,** Michael 1941- *Who 92*
**Mansfield,** Michael J 1903- *WhoAmP 91*
**Mansfield,** Michael Joseph 1903- *IntWW 91*
**Mansfield,** Michele R. 1961- *WhoFI 92*
**Mansfield,** Mike 1903- *FacFETw*
**Mansfield,** Peter 1933- *IntWW 91, Who 92*
**Mansfield,** Philip 1926- *Who 92*
**Mansfield,** Philip Robert Aked 1926- *IntWW 91*
**Mansfield,** Ralph 1912- *AmMWSc 92*
**Mansfield,** Rene *ScFEYrs, -A*
**Mansfield,** Richard 1854-1907 *BenetAL 91*
**Mansfield,** Richard Earl 1936- *WhoMW 92*
**Mansfield,** Roger Leo 1944- *AmMWSc 92, WhoWest 92*
**Mansfield,** Ruth Stiles 1917- *WhoAmP 91*
**Mansfield,** Terence Arthur 1937- *IntWW 91, Who 92*
**Mansfield,** Terence Gordon 1938- *Who 92*
**Mansfield,** Victor Neil 1941- *AmMWSc 92*
**Mansfield,** W. Ed 1937- *WhoBlA 92*
**Mansfield,** William Amos 1929- *WhoAmL 92*
**Mansfield And Mansfield,** Earl of 1930- *Who 92*
**Mansfield Cooper,** William 1903- *Who 92*
**Manshard,** Walther 1923- *IntWW 91*
**Manshardt,** Thomas Brewster 1927- *WhoEnt 92*
**Mansheim,** David John 1945- *WhoAmP 91*
**Manshio,** Calvin Katsumi 1947- *WhoMW 92*
**Manship,** Douglas 1918- *WhoEnt 92*
**Manship,** Paul 1885-1966 *FacFETw*
**Mansho,** Rene Michie 1949- *WhoWest 92*
**Mansholt,** Sicco Leendert 1908- *IntWW 91*
**Mansi,** Nicholas Anthony 1930- *WhoAmP 91*
**Mansinghka,** Surendra Kumar 1944- *WhoWest 92*
**Mansinha,** Lalatendu 1937- *AmMWSc 92*
**Mansk,** Sharon Sue 1948- *WhoEnt 92*
**Manske,** Brian Edward 1949- *WhoRel 92*
**Manske,** John Thomas 1952- *WhoAmP 91*
**Manske,** Wendell J 1924- *AmMWSc 92*
**Mansker,** Robert Thomas 1941- *WhoAmP 91*
**Manski,** Charles Frederick 1948- *WhoMW 92*
**Manski,** Wladyslaw J 1915- *AmMWSc 92*
**Mansmann,** Carol Los *WhoAmP 91*
**Mansmann,** Carol Los 1942- *WhoAmL 92*
**Mansmann,** Herbert Charles, Jr 1924- *AmMWSc 92*
**Manso de Velasco,** Jose Antonio 1688-1764 *HisDSpE*
**Manson,** Allison Ray 1939- *AmMWSc 92*
**Manson,** Anders Urban 1947- *WhoFI 92*
**Manson,** Arthur 1928- *IntMPA 92*
**Manson,** Bevan *WhoEnt 92*
**Manson,** Charles 1934- *FacFETw*
**Manson,** David Joseph 1952- *WhoEnt 92, WhoWest 92*
**Manson,** Donald Joseph 1930- *AmMWSc 92*
**Manson,** Eddy Lawrence *WhoEnt 92*
**Manson,** Ian Stuart 1929- *Who 92*
**Manson,** James Bolivar 1879-1945 *TwCPaSc*
**Manson,** Joseph Richard 1942- *AmMWSc 92*
**Manson,** Joyce Laverne *WhoRel 92*
**Manson,** Lionel Arnold 1923- *AmMWSc 92*
**Manson,** Marsden 1850-1931 *ScFEYrs*
**Manson,** Michael Asher 1931- *WhoRel 92*
**Manson,** Michael Irving 1951- *WhoWest 92*
**Manson,** Nancy Hurt *AmMWSc 92*
**Manson,** Otis Frederick 1822-1888 *DcNCBi 4*
**Manson,** S S 1919- *AmMWSc 92*
**Manson,** Samuel Stanford 1919- *WhoMW 92*
**Manson,** Simon V 1921- *AmMWSc 92*
**Manson,** Steven Trent 1940- *AmMWSc 92*
**Manson-Hing,** Lincoln Roy 1927- *AmMWSc 92*
**Mansoor,** Lutfi Gabrie, Jr. 1941- *WhoHisp 92*
**Mansoor,** Menahem 1911- *WrDr 92*
**Mansoori,** G Ali 1940- *AmMWSc 92*
**Mansour,** Mohamed 1928- *AmMWSc 92*
**Mansour,** Tag Eldin 1924- *AmMWSc 92*
**Mansouri,** Lotfollah 1929- *WhoEnt 92, WhoWest 92*
**Manspeizer,** Warren 1933- *AmMWSc 92*
**Mansperger,** Dale Elliott 1908- *WhoMW 92*
**Manstein,** Erich von 1887-1973 *EncTR 91 [port], FacFETw*
**Mansur,** Charles I 1918- *AmMWSc 92*
**Mansur,** Charles Isaiah 1918- *WhoMW 92*
**Mansur,** Louis Kenneth 1944- *AmMWSc 92*
**Mansur,** Mallikarjun 1910- *IntWW 91*

Mansur, Paul Max 1926- WhoEnt 92
Mansur, Susan Clark 1942- WhoEnt 92
Mansurian, Tigran 1939- ConCom 92
Mant, Arthur Keith 1919- IntWW 91, Who 92
Mant, Cecil George d1990 Who 92N
Mant, Keith Who 92
Mantai, Kenneth Edward 1942- AmMWSc 92
Mantatisi EncAmaz 91
Mantegna, Joe 1947- IntMPA 92, News 92-1 [port]
Mantegna, Joe Anthony 1947- WhoEnt 92
Mantei, Erwin Joseph 1938- AmMWSc 92
Mantei, Kenneth Alan 1940- AmMWSc 92
Manteiga, Roland Marcello 1920- WhoHisp 92
Mantel, Hilary 1952- ConNov 91, IntAu&W 91, WrDr 92
Mantel, Kenneth Haskell 1927- WhoFI 92
Mantel, Linda Habas 1939- AmMWSc 92
Mantel, Samuel J., Jr. 1921- WrDr 92
Mantelet, Jean d1991 IntWW 91N, NewYTBS 91
Mantell, Charles 1937- Who 92
Mantell, Charles L 1897- AmMWSc 92
Mantell, Gerald Jerome 1923- AmMWSc 92
Mantell, M I 1917- AmMWSc 92
Manteo DcNCBi 4
Mantes, Ernest George, Jr 1937- WhoAmP 91
Manteuffel, Thomas Albert 1948- AmMWSc 92
Mantey, Patrick E 1938- AmMWSc 92
Manthe, Cora De Munck 1928- WhoFI 92
Manthei, Richard Dale 1935- WhoFI 92
Manthei, Robin Dickey 1956- WhoMW 92
Manthey, Arthur Adolph 1935- AmMWSc 92
Manthey, John August 1925- AmMWSc 92
Manthorp, Brian Robert 1934- Who 92
Manthorpe, John Jeremy 1936- Who 92
Mantil, Joseph Chacko 1937- AmMWSc 92
Mantilla, Felix 1955- WhoHisp 92
Mantilla, Mercedes 1936- WhoHisp 92
Mantilla, Nectario Ruben 1940- WhoFI 92
Mantione, Sandra Marie WhoFI 92
Mantle, C Lee 1911- WhoAmP 91
Mantle, Charles Darrin 1964- WhoMW 92
Mantle, J B 1919- AmMWSc 92
Mantle, Jonathan IntAu&W 91
Mantle, Mickey 1931- FacFETw
Mantler, Michael, Mrs. 1938- WhoEnt 92
Manton, Baron 1924- Who 92
Manton, Edwin Alfred Grenville 1909- WhoIns 92
Manton, Karis Brewster 1903- WhoMW 92, WhoRel 92
Manton, Thomas J. 1932- AlmAP 92 [port], WhoAmP 91
Mantovani 1905-1980 NewAmDM
Mantsch, Henry H 1935- AmMWSc 92
Mantsch, Paul Matthew 1941- AmMWSc 92
Mantsev, Vasiliy Nikolaevich 1888-1939 SovUnBD
Mantz, Paul 1821-1895 ThHElm
Manuel, Dale WhoHisp 92
Manuel, Dale 1949- WhoAmP 91
Manuel, Dan Douglas 1947- WhoRel 92
Manuel, Dennis Lee 1945- WhoMW 92
Manuel, Edward 1949- WhoBlA 92
Manuel, John N. 1921- WhoBlA 92
Manuel, Keith Harley 1947- WhoRel 92
Manuel, Kenneth R. 1961- WhoRel 92
Manuel, Lionel, Jr. 1962- WhoBlA 92
Manuel, Louis Calvin 1937- WhoBlA 92
Manuel, Oliver K 1936- AmMWSc 92
Manuel, Orion Wendell 1939- WhoRel 92
Manuel, Ralph Nixon 1936- WhoMW 92
Manuel, Rex 1930- WhoAmP 91
Manuel, Robert 1916- IntWW 91
Manuel, Ron Ervil 1951- WhoRel 92
Manuel, Thomas Asbury 1936- AmMWSc 92
Manuelian, Haig Der 1926- WhoAmL 92
Manuelidis, Elias Emmanuel 1918- AmMWSc 92
Manulis, Martin LesBEnT 92
Manulis, Martin 1915- IntMPA 92, WhoEnt 92
Manus, Mark E 1923- WhoAmP 91
Manus, Willard 1930- WhoEnt 92
Manuszak, Janet Marie 1959- WhoFI 92
Manuwal, David Allen 1942- AmMWSc 92
Manvel, Bennet 1943- AmMWSc 92
Manville, John Fieve 1941- AmMWSc 92
Manville, Philip Brook 1950- WhoFI 92
Manwaring, Randle 1912- IntAu&W 91, Who 92
Manwiller, Floyd George 1934- AmMWSc 92
Many, Robert Todd 1958- WhoFI 92
Manyakin, Sergei Iosifovich 1923- IntWW 91
Manyan, David Richard 1936- AmMWSc 92
Manyik, Robert Michael 1928- AmMWSc 92
Manz, August Frederick 1929- AmMWSc 92
Manz, Wolfgang 1960- IntWW 91
Manzanares, Juan Manuel 1953- WhoHisp 92
Manzano, Eugene Gerard 1954- WhoWest 92
Manzano, Sonia WhoHisp 92
Manzella, Peter Franics 1962- WhoFI 92
Manzelli, Manlio Arthur 1917- AmMWSc 92
Manzer, Franklin Edward 1932- AmMWSc 92
Manzer, Isa-Belle ScFEYrs
Manzi, Anthony 1956- WhoFI 92
Manzi, Jacki 1929- WhoAmP 91
Manzi, Joseph Edward 1945- WhoMW 92
Manzi, Michel 1849-1915 ThHElm
Manziarly, Marcelle de 1899-1989 NewAmDM
Manzie, Gordon 1930- Who 92
Manzini, Raimondo 1913- Who 92
Manzo, Anthony Joseph 1928- WhoWest 92
Manzo, Edward David 1950- WhoAmL 92
Manzo, Rene Paul AmMWSc 92
Manzoni, Giacomo 1932- ConCom 92, IntWW 91
Manzu, Giacomo d1991 IntWW 91N, Who 92N
Manzu, Giacomo 1908- FacFETw
Manzu, Giacomo 1908-1991 CurBio 91N, NewYTBS 91 [port]
Mao Lirui 1905- IntWW 91
Mao Tse-tung 1893-1976 FacFETw [port]
Mao Zedong FacFETw
Mao Zhiyong 1929- IntWW 91
Mao, Chung-Ling 1936- AmMWSc 92
Mao, Ho-Kwang 1941- AmMWSc 92
Mao, Ivan Ling 1940- AmMWSc 92
Mao, James Chieh Hsia 1928- AmMWSc 92
Ma'o, Leo'o Va'a 1945- WhoAmP 91
Mao, Shing 1935- AmMWSc 92
Mao, Simon Jen-Tan 1946- AmMWSc 92
Maowad, Rene 1925-1989 FacFETw
Mapa, Placido 1932- IntWW 91
Mapanje, Jack ConPo 91, WrDr 92
Mapel, Patricia Jolene 1933- WhoMW 92
Mapelli, Roland Lawrence 1922- WhoFI 92, WhoWest 92
Mapes, Charles Victor 1836-1916 BiInAmS
Mapes, Gene Kathleen 1946- AmMWSc 92
Mapes, Glynn Dempsey 1939- WhoEnt 92
Mapes, Gordon Bidwell 1961- WhoRel 92
Mapes, James Jay 1806-1866 BiInAmS
Mapes, Mary A IntAu&W 91X, WrDr 92
Mapes, Pierson WhoEnt 92, WhoFI 92
Mapes, Richard Mather, Sr. 1925- WhoRel 92
Mapes, Royal Herbert 1942- AmMWSc 92, WhoMW 92
Mapes, William Edward 1934- WhoFI 92
Mapes, William Henry 1939- AmMWSc 92
Maple, Eric William 1915- IntAu&W 91, WrDr 92
Maple, Gilbert Roy 1945- WhoRel 92
Maple, Goldie M. 1937- WhoBlA 92
Maple, Gordon Extra 1932- IntAu&W 91
Maple, Graham John 1947- Who 92
Maple, M Brian 1939- AmMWSc 92
Maple, Mary Alice 1953- WhoAmL 92
Maple, Vetrelle 1915- WhoBlA 92
Maple, William Thomas 1942- AmMWSc 92
Maples, Donna Elaine 1953- WhoRel 92
Maples, Evelyn Lucille Palmer 1919- IntAu&W 91
Maples, Evelyn Palmer 1919- WrDr 92
Maples, Glennon 1932- AmMWSc 92
Maples, Jeffrey Stanley 1916- Who 92
Maples, Jimmie Kay 1940- WhoMW 92
Maples, John Cradock 1943- Who 92
Maples, Louis Charles 1918- AmMWSc 92
Maples, Percy L 1938- WhoAmP 91
Maples, R. Benton 1946- WhoFI 92
Maples, Ricky Eugene 1958- WhoFI 92
Maples, William Bruce, Jr. 1953- WhoRel 92
Maples, William Paul 1929- AmMWSc 92
Maples, William Ross 1937- AmMWSc 92
Maples Earle, E. E. Who 92
Maples-Pacheco, Elizabeth Mae 1941- WhoWest 92
Maponya, Richard John 1926- IntWW 91
Mapother, Dillon Edward 1921- AmMWSc 92
Mapother, William Reibert 1938- WhoAmL 92
Mapp, Alf Johnson, Jr 1925- IntAu&W 91, WrDr 92
Mapp, Calvin R. 1924- WhoBlA 92
Mapp, David Kenneth, Jr. 1951- WhoBlA 92
Mapp, Edward WrDr 92
Mapp, Edward C. WhoBlA 92
Mapp, Frederick Everett 1910- AmMWSc 92, WhoBlA 92
Mapp, John Robert 1950- WhoBlA 92
Mapp, Yolanda I. 1930- WhoBlA 92
Mapplethorpe, Robert 1946-1989 FacFETw
Mappus, Theodore Tobias, Jr 1926- WhoAmP 91
Mapula, Olga 1938- WhoHisp 92
Maqusi, Mohammad 1944- AmMWSc 92
Mar, Countess of 1940- Who 92
Mar, Earl of 1921- Who 92
Mar Markus 1927- WhoRel 92
Mar, Mistress of 1963- Who 92
Mar, Bernice L. 1957- WhoFI 92
Mar, Brian W 1933- AmMWSc 92
Mar, Eugene 1940- WhoAmL 92
Mar, James Wah 1920- AmMWSc 92
Mar, Laureen D. DrAPF 91
Mar, Maria WhoHisp 92
Mar, Raymond W 1942- AmMWSc 92
Mar Gregorios, Benedict 1916- IntWW 91
Mar Thoma, Alexander WhoRel 92
Mara, Adele 1923- IntMPA 92
Mara, Francis Gerard 1950- WhoAmP 91
Mara, Gertrud Elisabeth 1749-1833 NewAmDM
Mara, Kamisese Kapaiwai Tuimacilai 1920- IntWW 91, Who 92
Mara, Michael Kelly 1952- AmMWSc 92
Mara, Richard Thomas 1923- AmMWSc 92
Mara, Timothy Gerald 1949- WhoMW 92
Marable, Fate 1890-1947 NewAmDM
Marable, Herman, Jr. 1962- WhoMW 92
Marable, June Morehead 1924- WhoBlA 92
Marable, Nina Louise 1939- AmMWSc 92
Marable, Richard O 1949- WhoAmP 91
Maradona, Diego 1961?- News 91 [port], -91-3 [port]
Maradona, Diego Armando 1960- FacFETw, IntWW 91
Maradudin, Alexei 1931- AmMWSc 92
Marafino, Vincent Norman 1930- WhoFI 92
Maragos, Samuel C 1922- WhoAmP 91
Maragoudakis, Michael E 1932- AmMWSc 92
Marah, Bran Jerome 1966- WhoEnt 92
Marahrens, August 1875-1950 EncTR 91
Marai, Sandor 1900-1989 LiExTwC
Maraini, Dacia 1936- IntAu&W 91, IntWW 91
Maraini, Fosco 1912- IntWW 91
Marais, Jean 1913- IntMPA 92, IntWW 91
Marais, Marin 1656-1728 NewAmDM
Maraj, James Ajodhya 1930- Who 92
Marak, Joseph P., Jr. 1947- WhoAmL 92
Marakas, John Lambros 1926- WhoFI 92
Maraldo, Ushanna WhoWest 92
Maraman, William Joseph 1923- WhoWest 92
Maramarco, Anthony Martin 1949- WhoFI 92
Maramis, Johan Boudewijn Paul 1922- IntWW 91
Maramorosch, Karl 1915- AmMWSc 92
Maramzin, Vladimir Rafailovich 1934- IntWW 91
Maran, Janice Wengerd 1942- AmMWSc 92
Maran, Joe 1933- WhoAmL 92
Maran, Stephen Paul 1938- AmMWSc 92
Maranda, Pierre 1930- WrDr 92
Maranda, Pierre Jean 1930- IntWW 91
Marangos, Paul Jerome 1947- AmMWSc 92
Marano, Gerald Alfred 1944- AmMWSc 92
Marano, Richard Michael 1960- WhoAmL 92, WhoAmP 91
Marano, Russell DrAPF 91
Marans, J. Eugene 1940- WhoAmL 92
Marans, Mardi IntMPA 92
Marans, Nelson Samuel 1924- AmMWSc 92
Marans, Robert Warren 1934- WhoMW 92
Marantz, Laurence Boyd 1935- AmMWSc 92
Marantz, Philip F. 1934- WhoAmL 92
Maranville, Jerry Wesley 1940- AmMWSc 92
Maranville, Lawrence Frank 1919- AmMWSc 92
Maras, Karl IntAu&W 91X, TwCSFW 91
Marasch, Milton R. 1937- WhoWest 92
Marascia, Frank Joseph 1928- AmMWSc 92
Marash, Alan Scott 1965- WhoFI 92
Marash, Randy J 1955- WhoIns 92
Marash, Stanley Albert 1938- WhoFI 92
Marat, Jean-Paul 1744-1793 BlkwCEP
Marathay, Arwind Shankar 1933- AmMWSc 92
Maratita, Edward Ulloa WhoAmP 91
Maratita, Mameto Ulloa 1951- WhoAmP 91
Maravall Herrero, Jose Maria 1942- IntWW 91
Maravetz, Lester L 1937- AmMWSc 92
Maravich, Mary Louise 1951- WhoWest 92
Maravich, Pistol Pete 1948-1988 FacFETw
Maraviglia, Maurizio 1878-1955 BiDExR
Maravolo, Nicholas Charles 1940- AmMWSc 92
Maraynes, Allan Lawrence 1950- WhoEnt 92
Maraziti, Joseph J. d1991 NewYTBS 91 [port]
Marban, Eduardo 1954- AmMWSc 92
Marbeck NewAmDM
Marberry, Constance Sue 1960- WhoMW 92
Marberry, James E 1931- AmMWSc 92
Marble, Alexander 1902- AmMWSc 92
Marble, Alice 1913-1990 AnObit 1990, CurBio 91N, FacFETw
Marble, Dan 1810-1849 BenetAL 91
Marble, Donald Raymond 1938- WhoAmP 91
Marble, Frank E 1918- AmMWSc 92
Marble, Howard Bennett, Jr 1923- AmMWSc 92
Marbley, Harlan J 1943- BlkOlyM
Marbo, Camille 1883- ScFEYrs
Marboe, Charles Chostner AmMWSc 92
Marburg, Stephen 1933- AmMWSc 92
Marburg, Theodore 1862-1946 AmPeW
Marburg-Goodman, Jeffrey Emil 1957- WhoAmL 92
Marburger, Richard Eugene 1928- AmMWSc 92
Marbury, Carl Harris 1935- WhoBlA 92
Marbury, Donald Lee 1949- WhoBlA 92
Marbury, Howard W. 1924- WhoBlA 92
Marbury, Martha G. 1946- WhoBlA 92
Marbury, Virginia Lomax 1918- WhoFI 92
Marbury, William Ardis 1917- WhoFI 92
Marc, David 1951- WhoWest 92
Marc, Franz 1880-1916 FacFETw
Marc de Chazal, L E 1921- AmMWSc 92
Marcantonio, Vito 1902-1954 DcAmImH
Marcatili, Enrique A J 1925- AmMWSc 92
Marce, Roger Raymond, Sr. 1940- WhoAmL 92
Marceau, Felicien 1913- IntAu&W 91, IntWW 91
Marceau, Marcel 1923- FacFETw, IntWW 91, Who 92, WhoEnt 92
Marceau, Normand Luc 1942- AmMWSc 92
Marceau, Richard E. 1926- WhoMW 92
Marcee, Emerson 1918- WhoBlA 92
Marcel, Gabriel 1889-1973 FacFETw
Marceleno, Troy 1937- WhoHisp 92
Marcelin, George 1948- AmMWSc 92
Marcellas, Thomas Wilson 1937- WhoFI 92
Marcelli, Joseph F 1926- AmMWSc 92
Marcellin, Raymond 1914- IntWW 91
Marcellini, Dale Leroy 1937- AmMWSc 92
Marcellino, Fred 1939- SmATA 68 [port]
Marcellino, George Raymond 1949- AmMWSc 92
Marcellinus EncEarC
Marcello, Alessandro 1669-1747 NewAmDM
Marcello, Benedetto 1686-1739 NewAmDM
Marcello, Leo Luke DrAPF 91
Marcellus d298 EncEarC
Marcellus of Ancyra 280?-374 EncEarC
Marcellus, John Robert, III 1939- WhoEnt 92
Marcelo, Cynthia Luz 1945- AmMWSc 92
Marcelynas, Richard Chadwick 1937- WhoWest 92
Marcere, Norma Snipes 1908- WhoBlA 92
March, Aaron Gold 1960- WhoAmL 92
March, Alden 1795-1869 BiInAmS
March, Alex LesBEnT 92
March, Anthony 1951- WhoBlA 92
March, Beryl Elizabeth 1920- AmMWSc 92
March, Derek 1930- Who 92
March, Donald 1942- IntMPA 92
March, Edgar James 1946- WhoMW 92
March, Hilary WrDr 92
March, James Gardner 1928- WhoWest 92
March, Jerry 1929- AmMWSc 92
March, Joseph Moncure 1899-1977 BenetAL 91
March, Kathleen Patricia 1949- WhoAmL 92, WhoWest 92
March, Lionel John 1934- Who 92
March, N. H. 1927- WrDr 92
March, Norman Henry 1927- Who 92
March, Philip Kappes 1929- WhoRel 92
March, Ralph Burton 1919- AmMWSc 92

**March**, Raymond Evans 1934- *AmMWSc 92*
**March**, Richard Pell 1922- *AmMWSc 92*
**March**, Robert Henry 1937- *AmMWSc 92*
**March**, Robert Herbert 1934- *AmMWSc 92*
**March**, Ronald Edward 1943- *WhoMW 92*
**March**, Salvatore T 1950- *AmMWSc 92*
**March**, Valerie *Who 92*
**March**, Werner 1894-1976 *EncTR 91*
**March**, William 1893-1954 *BenetAL 91*
**March And Kinrara**, Earl of 1955- *Who 92*
**Marc'Hadour**, Germain Pierre 1921- *WhoRel 92*
**Marchais**, Georges 1920- *IntWW 91*
**Marchais**, Pierre Julien 1924- *IntWW 91*
**Marchal**, Andre 1894-1980 *NewAmDM*
**Marchal**, Jean 1905- *IntWW 91*
**Marchalonis**, John Jacob 1940- *AmMWSc 92*
**Marchamley**, Baron 1922- *Who 92*
**Marchand**, Alan Philip 1940- *AmMWSc 92*
**Marchand**, E Roger 1936- *AmMWSc 92*
**Marchand**, Erich Watkinson 1914- *AmMWSc 92*
**Marchand**, Jean-Paul 1933- *AmMWSc 92*
**Marchand**, Leslie A 1900- *IntAu&W 91, WrDr 92*
**Marchand**, Margaret O 1925- *AmMWSc 92*
**Marchand**, Melanie Annette 1962- *WhoBlA 92*
**Marchand**, Nancy 1928- *IntMPA 92, WhoEnt 92*
**Marchand**, Nathan 1916- *AmMWSc 92*
**Marchand**, Philippe 1939- *IntWW 91*
**Marchand**, Richard 1952- *AmMWSc 92*
**Marchandise-Franquet**, Jacques 1918- *IntWW 91*
**Marchant**, Barrie Kemp 1951- *WhoMW 92*
**Marchant**, Bradley Jay 1947- *WhoFI 92*
**Marchant**, Catherine *IntAu&W 91X, Who 92, WrDr 92*
**Marchant**, David Dennis 1943- *AmMWSc 92*
**Marchant**, David Isaac, Sr. 1947- *WhoRel 92*
**Marchant**, David J. 1939- *WhoAmL 92*
**Marchant**, Douglas J 1925- *AmMWSc 92*
**Marchant**, Edgar Vernon 1915- *Who 92*
**Marchant**, Frederick 1872?-1942 *DcNCBi 4*
**Marchant**, George John Charles 1916- *Who 92*
**Marchant**, Graham Leslie 1945- *Who 92*
**Marchant**, Guillaume Henri, Jr 1946- *AmMWSc 92*
**Marchant**, Ken 1951- *WhoAmP 91*
**Marchant**, Larry Conrad, Jr 1962- *WhoAmP 91*
**Marchant**, Leland Condo 1931- *AmMWSc 92*
**Marchant**, Omar *WhoHisp 92*
**Marchant**, T Eston 1921- *WhoAmP 91*
**Marchant**, Thomas Mood, III 1940- *WhoAmP 91*
**Marchant**, Tony 1959- *WrDr 92*
**Marchase**, Richard Banfield 1948- *AmMWSc 92*
**Marchaterre**, John Frederick 1932- *AmMWSc 92, WhoMW 92*
**Marchbanks**, Claude V 1923- *WhoAmP 91*
**Marchbanks**, Samuel *IntAu&W 91X*
**Marche**, Gary Eldon 1953- *WhoFI 92*
**Marchello**, Joseph M 1933- *AmMWSc 92*
**Marchenko**, Anatoliy Tikhonovich 1938-1986 *SovUnBD*
**Marchese**, Francis Thomas 1949- *AmMWSc 92*
**Marchese**, Lamar Vincent 1943- *WhoEnt 92, WhoWest 92*
**Marchesi**, Luigi 1755-1829 *NewAmDM*
**Marchesi**, Mathilde 1821-1913 *NewAmDM*
**Marchesi**, Vincent T 1935- *AmMWSc 92*
**Marchesi de Castrone**, Mathilde 1821-1913 *NewAmDM*
**Marchesini**, Maurice Robert 1964- *WhoFI 92*
**Marchessault**, Robert Henri 1928- *AmMWSc 92*
**Marchetta**, Frank Carmelo 1920- *AmMWSc 92*
**Marchette**, Nyven John 1928- *AmMWSc 92*
**Marchetti**, Alfred Paul 1940- *AmMWSc 92*
**Marchetti**, Marco Anthony 1936- *AmMWSc 92*
**Marchewka-Brown**, Nicole *DrAPF 91*
**Marchi**, John Joseph 1921- *WhoAmL 92, WhoAmP 91*
**Marchi**, Jon 1946- *WhoWest 92*
**Marchin**, George Leonard 1940- *AmMWSc 92, WhoMW 92*
**Marchini**, Italo 1953- *WhoEnt 92*
**Marchinton**, Robert Larry 1939- *AmMWSc 92*
**Marchione**, Michael Louis 1954- *WhoMW 92*
**Marchioro**, Karen Louise 1933- *WhoAmP 91*
**Marchioro**, Thomas Louis 1928- *AmMWSc 92*
**Marchiselli**, Vincent Andrew 1928- *WhoAmP 91*
**Marchman**, Fred A. *DrAPF 91*
**Marchman**, James F, III 1943- *AmMWSc 92*
**Marchman**, Robert Anthony 1958- *WhoBlA 92*
**Marchman**, Victor Yater 1927- *WhoRel 92*
**Marcho**, Robert Kent 1943- *WhoRel 92*
**Marchok**, Ann Catherine 1936- *AmMWSc 92*
**Marchuk**, Guri Ivanovich 1925- *IntWW 91*
**Marchwood**, Viscount 1936- *Who 92*
**Marcia** d193 *EncEarC*
**Marcial**, Edwin 1940- *WhoHisp 92*
**Marcial**, Minette 1963- *WhoRel 92*
**Marcian** 392?-457 *EncEarC*
**Marciano**, Anthony R 1942- *WhoAmP 91*
**Marciano**, Rocky 1923-1969 *FacFETw*
**Marciano**, William Joseph 1947- *AmMWSc 92*
**Marcianus** *EncEarC*
**Marcil**, Mary Karen 1938- *WhoRel 92*
**Marcil**, William Christ, Sr. 1936- *WhoMW 92*
**Marcillo**, Carlos E. 1939- *WhoHisp 92*
**Marcin**, Max 1879-1948 *BenetAL 91*
**Marciniak**, Ewa J *AmMWSc 92*
**Marciniak**, Thomas Joseph 1940- *WhoMW 92*
**Marcinkevicius**, Iustinas Moteiaus 1930- *IntWW 91*
**Marcinkoski**, Gerald Michael 1950- *WhoAmL 92*
**Marcinkowski**, M J 1931- *AmMWSc 92*
**Marcinkowsky**, Arthur Ernest 1931- *AmMWSc 92*
**Marcinkus**, Paul C. 1922- *WhoRel 92*
**Marcinkus**, Paul Casimir 1922- *IntWW 91*
**Marcion** d154? *EncEarC*
**Marcis**, Richard G. 1940- *WhoFI 92*
**Marcker**, Kjeld Adrian 1932- *IntWW 91*
**Marckoon**, Stuart Ellsworth 1958- *WhoEnt 92*
**Marckwardt**, Harold Thomas 1920- *WhoWest 92*
**Marco** *ConAu 133*
**Marco**, Anton Nicholas 1943- *WhoWest 92*
**Marco**, David Duane 1951- *WhoWest 92*
**Marco**, Gino Joseph 1924- *AmMWSc 92*
**Marcon**, Fred R 1937- *WhoIns 92*
**Marconi**, Dominic Anthony 1927- *WhoRel 92*
**Marconi**, Gary G 1944- *AmMWSc 92*
**Marconi**, Guglielmo 1874-1937 *FacFETw [port], WhoNob 90*
**Marcopoulos**, Christos 1925- *IntWW 91*
**Marcos**, Ferdinand 1917-1989 *FacFETw [port]*
**Marcos**, Imelda Romualdez 1930?- *IntWW 91*
**Marcos**, Luis Rojas 1943- *WhoHisp 92*
**Marcos**, M. A. *WhoRel 92*
**Marcotte**, Brian Michael 1949- *AmMWSc 92*
**Marcotte**, Gary Richard 1952- *WhoFI 92*
**Marcotte**, Ivan Allen 1961- *WhoFI 92*
**Marcotte**, Patrick Allen 1952- *AmMWSc 92*
**Marcotte**, Robert S. 1932- *WhoFI 92, WhoIns 92*
**Marcotte**, Ronald Edward 1939- *AmMWSc 92*
**Marcou**, Jules 1824-1898 *BiInAmS*
**Marcoux**, Elizabeth Louise 1952- *WhoWest 92*
**Marcoux**, Frank W 1952- *AmMWSc 92*
**Marcoux**, Jules E 1924- *AmMWSc 92*
**Marcoux**, William C 1956- *WhoAmP 91*
**Marcovicci**, Andrea 1948- *IntMPA 92*
**Marcovitz**, Alan Bernard 1936- *AmMWSc 92*
**Marcovitz**, Leonard Edward 1934- *WhoFI 92*
**Marcu**, Kenneth Brian 1950- *AmMWSc 92*
**Marcucci**, Nicholas John 1956- *WhoMW 92*
**Marcucci**, Robert Phillip 1930- *WhoEnt 92*
**Marcum**, James Benton 1938- *AmMWSc 92*
**Marcum**, Joseph L 1923- *WhoIns 92*
**Marcum**, Joseph LaRue 1923- *WhoFI 92, WhoMW 92*
**Marcum**, Michael Ray 1964- *WhoMW 92*
**Marcus** *EncEarC*
**Marcus Aurelius** 121-180 *EncEarC*
**Marcus**, Aaron Jacob 1925- *AmMWSc 92*
**Marcus**, Abraham 1930- *AmMWSc 92*
**Marcus**, Adele *WhoEnt 92*
**Marcus**, Adrianne *DrAPF 91*
**Marcus**, Allan H 1939- *AmMWSc 92*
**Marcus**, Ann *LesBEnT 92*
**Marcus**, Anthony Martin 1929- *AmMWSc 92*
**Marcus**, Barry Philip 1953- *WhoAmL 92*
**Marcus**, Bernard 1924- *WhoAmL 92*
**Marcus**, Bernard 1929- *WhoFI 92*
**Marcus**, Bruce David 1937- *AmMWSc 92*
**Marcus**, Bryan Harry 1949- *AmMWSc 92*
**Marcus**, Bunita 1952- *ConCom 92*
**Marcus**, Burton H. 1934- *WhoFI 92*
**Marcus**, Carol Joyce 1943- *AmMWSc 92*
**Marcus**, Carol Silber 1939- *AmMWSc 92*
**Marcus**, Claude 1924- *IntWW 91, WhoFI 92*
**Marcus**, Craig Brian 1939- *WhoAmL 92*
**Marcus**, David 1926- *ConAu 134*
**Marcus**, Donald 1946- *ConAu 134*
**Marcus**, Donald M 1930- *AmMWSc 92*
**Marcus**, Edward 1918- *WhoFI 92*
**Marcus**, Edward Leonard 1927- *WhoAmP 91*
**Marcus**, Egerton *BlkOlyM*
**Marcus**, Elliot M 1932- *AmMWSc 92*
**Marcus**, Frank 1928- *WrDr 92*
**Marcus**, Frank 1933- *AmMWSc 92*
**Marcus**, Frank I 1928- *AmMWSc 92*
**Marcus**, Frank Isadore 1928- *WhoWest 92*
**Marcus**, Frank Ulrich 1928- *IntAu&W 91, Who 92*
**Marcus**, Gail Halpern 1947- *AmMWSc 92*
**Marcus**, George Jacob 1933- *AmMWSc 92*
**Marcus**, Gladys d1991 *NewYTBS 91*
**Marcus**, Greil Gerstley 1945- *WhoEnt 92*
**Marcus**, Hal 1950- *WhoFI 92*
**Marcus**, Harold G. 1936- *WrDr 92*
**Marcus**, Harris L 1931- *AmMWSc 92*
**Marcus**, Jacob Rader 1896- *WhoMW 92*
**Marcus**, James Elbert 1949- *WhoFI 92*
**Marcus**, Jeffrey Howard 1950- *WhoWest 92*
**Marcus**, John 1941- *WhoFI 92*
**Marcus**, John Michael 1950- *WhoEnt 92*
**Marcus**, John Stanley *AmMWSc 92*
**Marcus**, Joseph 1928- *AmMWSc 92*
**Marcus**, Jules Alexander 1919- *AmMWSc 92*
**Marcus**, Julie Mara 1966- *WhoFI 92*
**Marcus**, Larry *ConAu 133*
**Marcus**, Larry David 1949- *WhoEnt 92*
**Marcus**, Laurence R. 1947- *ConAu 135*
**Marcus**, Lawrence B. 1925- *ConAu 133*
**Marcus**, Lee Evan 1953- *WhoFI 92*
**Marcus**, Leonard S. 1950- *ConAu 134*
**Marcus**, Leslie F 1930- *AmMWSc 92*
**Marcus**, Louis 1936- *IntMPA 92*
**Marcus**, Lynne 1945- *WhoFI 92*
**Marcus**, M Boyd, Jr 1952- *WhoAmP 91*
**Marcus**, Marie Eleanor 1914- *WhoEnt 92*
**Marcus**, Mark 1944- *AmMWSc 92*
**Marcus**, Mark Jay 1941- *WhoAmP 91*
**Marcus**, Marshall Matthew 1933- *WhoFI 92*
**Marcus**, Marvin 1927- *AmMWSc 92*
**Marcus**, Melvin Gerald 1929- *AmMWSc 92*
**Marcus**, Melvin Gerlad 1929- *WhoWest 92*
**Marcus**, Melvin L 1940- *AmMWSc 92*
**Marcus**, Michael Alan 1952- *AmMWSc 92*
**Marcus**, Michael Barry 1936- *AmMWSc 92*
**Marcus**, Michael Jay 1946- *AmMWSc 92*
**Marcus**, Mordecai *DrAPF 91*
**Marcus**, Morton *DrAPF 91*
**Marcus**, Nancy Helen 1950- *AmMWSc 92*
**Marcus**, Norman 1932- *WhoAmL 92*
**Marcus**, Norman Martin 1956- *WhoEnt 92*
**Marcus**, Owen 1953- *WhoWest 92*
**Marcus**, Paul Malcolm 1921- *AmMWSc 92*
**Marcus**, Philip Irving 1927- *AmMWSc 92*
**Marcus**, Philip Selmar 1936- *AmMWSc 92*
**Marcus**, Philip Stephen 1951- *AmMWSc 92*
**Marcus**, Phillip L. 1941- *ConAu 134*
**Marcus**, Richard 1946- *AmMWSc 92*
**Marcus**, Richard Cantrell 1938- *WhoFI 92*
**Marcus**, Robert 1925- *WhoWest 92*
**Marcus**, Robert Boris 1934- *AmMWSc 92*
**Marcus**, Robert Brown 1918- *AmMWSc 92*
**Marcus**, Robert Bruce 1942- *WhoAmL 92*
**Marcus**, Robert S 1947- *WhoAmP 91*
**Marcus**, Robert Troy 1949- *AmMWSc 92*
**Marcus**, Rudolph Arthur 1923- *AmMWSc 92, IntWW 91*
**Marcus**, Rudolph Julius 1926- *AmMWSc 92*
**Marcus**, Ruth Barcan 1921- *IntWW 91*
**Marcus**, Sanford M 1932- *AmMWSc 92*
**Marcus**, Stanley *DrAPF 91*
**Marcus**, Stanley 1905- *IntWW 91, WrDr 92*
**Marcus**, Stanley 1916- *AmMWSc 92*
**Marcus**, Stanley 1946- *WhoAmL 92*
**Marcus**, Stanley Raymond 1916- *AmMWSc 92*
**Marcus**, Stanton Craig 1956- *WhoWest 92*
**Marcus**, Stephen 1939- *AmMWSc 92*
**Marcus**, Stephen Cecil 1932- *WhoFI 92*
**Marcus**, Steven 1928- *IntAu&W 91*
**Marcus**, Steven Irl 1949- *AmMWSc 92*
**Marcus**, Walter F., Jr. 1927- *WhoAmL 92, WhoAmP 91*
**Marcusa**, Fred Haye 1946- *WhoAmL 92*
**Marcuse**, Dietrich 1929- *AmMWSc 92*
**Marcuse**, Frederick Lawrence 1916- *WrDr 92*
**Marcuse**, Herbert 1889-1979 *LiExTwC*
**Marcuse**, Herbert 1898-1979 *BenetAL 91, FacFETw*
**Marcuse**, Judith Rose 1947- *WhoEnt 92*
**Marcuse**, Richard Frederick 1944- *WhoEnt 92*
**Marcuse**, William 1924- *WhoFI 92*
**Marcuss**, Stanley Joseph 1942- *WhoAmL 92*
**Marcuvitz**, Nathan 1913- *AmMWSc 92*
**Marcy**, Joseph Edwin *AmMWSc 92*
**Marcy**, Mary Edna 1866-1922 *AmPeW*
**Marcy**, Oliver 1820-1899 *BiInAmS*
**Marcy**, Randolph Barnes 1812-1887 *BenetAL 91*
**Marcy**, Willard 1916- *AmMWSc 92*
**Marcy**, William Learned 1786-1857 *AmPolLe*
**Marczewski**, Jan d1990 *IntWW 91N*
**Marczynska**, Barbara Mary *AmMWSc 92*
**Marczynski**, Robert Alan 1956- *WhoAmL 92*
**Marczynski**, Thaddeus John 1920- *AmMWSc 92*
**Mardall**, Cyril Leonard 1909- *IntWW 91*
**Mardary**, Bishop 1889-1935 *RelLAm 91*
**Mardell**, Fred Robert 1934- *WhoMW 92*
**Mardell**, Peggy Joyce 1927- *Who 92*
**Mardellis**, Anthony 1920- *AmMWSc 92*
**Marden**, Brice 1938- *WorArt 1980 [port]*
**Marden**, Donald Harlow 1936- *WhoAmP 91*
**Marden**, John Iglehart 1951- *AmMWSc 92*
**Marden**, John Louis 1919- *Who 92*
**Marden**, Morris 1905- *AmMWSc 92*
**Mardenborough**, Leslie A. 1948- *WhoBlA 92*
**Marder**, A R 1940- *AmMWSc 92*
**Marder**, Bernard Arthur 1928- *Who 92*
**Marder**, Eve Esther 1948- *AmMWSc 92*
**Marder**, Harold K. 1949- *WhoFI 92*
**Marder**, Herman Lowell 1931- *AmMWSc 92*
**Marder**, Samuel 1930- *WhoEnt 92*
**Marder**, Stanley 1926- *AmMWSc 92*
**Marderosian**, Ardash 1930- *WhoEnt 92*
**Mardh**, Per-Anders 1941- *IntWW 91*
**Mardian**, Daniel 1917- *WhoFI 92*
**Mardian**, James K W 1946- *AmMWSc 92*
**Mardian**, Robert Charles, Jr. 1947- *WhoWest 92*
**Mardiney**, Annie E. Fairchild 1956- *WhoEnt 92*
**Mardiney**, Michael Ralph, Jr 1934- *AmMWSc 92*
**Mardirosian**, Tom 1947- *WhoEnt 92*
**Mardiross**, Edward 1947- *WhoFI 92*
**Mardis**, Richard Lyle 1963- *WhoEnt 92*
**Mardis**, Verdena Fox 1914- *WhoMW 92*
**Mardix**, Shmuel 1931- *AmMWSc 92*
**Mardon**, Kenric La Touche 1905- *Who 92*
**Mardzhanishvili**, Kote 1872-1933 *SovUnBD*
**Mardzhanov**, Konstantin Aleksandrovich 1872-1933 *SovUnBD*
**Mare**, Cornelius John 1934- *AmMWSc 92*
**Mare**, John 1739-1803 *DcNCBi 4*
**Mare**, William Harold 1918- *WhoRel 92*
**Maready**, William Frank 1932- *WhoAmL 92*
**Marechal**, Andre 1916- *IntWW 91*
**Marechal**, Joan 1943- *WhoEnt 92*
**Marechal**, Pierre-Sylvain 1750-1803 *BlkwCEP*
**Maree**, John B. 1924- *IntWW 91*
**Marei**, Ibrahim 1939- *WhoWest 92*
**Marei**, Sayed Ahmed 1913- *IntWW 91*
**Marek**, Ann Armstrong 1935- *WhoAmP 91*
**Marek**, Cecil John 1940- *AmMWSc 92*
**Marek**, Charles R 1940- *AmMWSc 92*
**Marek**, Daniel Richard 1949- *WhoEnt 92*
**Marek**, Edmund Anthony 1948- *AmMWSc 92*
**Marek**, John 1940- *Who 92*
**Marek**, Richard 1933- *IntAu&W 91*
**Marek**, Vladimir 1928- *WhoEnt 92*
**Marello**, Laura *DrAPF 91*
**Maren**, Thomas Hartley 1918- *AmMWSc 92*
**Marencic**, Richard J 1927- *WhoIns 92*
**Marenghi**, John Henry 1952- *WhoFI 92*
**Marengo**, Norman Payson 1913- *AmMWSc 92*
**Marengo**, Pier Carlo 1926- *IntWW 91*
**Marenstein**, Harold *IntMPA 92*

**Marenus,** Kenneth D *AmMWSc 92*
**Marenzio,** Luca 1553?-1599 *NewAmDM*
**Mares,** Bill 1940- *WhoAmP 91*
**Mares,** Donald J. *WhoHisp 92*
**Mares,** Donald J 1957- *WhoAmP 91*
**Mares,** Ernest Anthony *DrAPF 91*
**Mares,** Frank 1932- *AmMWSc 92*
**Mares,** Jan W *WhoAmP 91*
**Mares,** Michael Allen 1945- *AmMWSc 92, WhoHisp 92*
**Mares,** Pablo 1913- *WhoHisp 92*
**Maresca,** Rosalia Loretta 1923- *WhoEnt 92*
**Maresco,** Stephen Peter 1928- *WhoFI 92*
**Maresh,** Richard 1917- *WhoAmP 91*
**Maret,** S Melissa 1953- *AmMWSc 92*
**Maretskaya,** Vera Petrovna 1906-1973 *SovUnBD*
**Maretzki,** Andrew 1926- *AmMWSc 92*
**Marez,** Jesus M. 1963- *WhoHisp 92*
**Marezio,** Massimo 1930- *AmMWSc 92*
**Marfat,** Anthony 1951- *AmMWSc 92*
**Marfey,** Sviatopolk Peter 1925- *AmMWSc 92*
**Marg,** Elwin 1918- *AmMWSc 92*
**Margach,** Charles Boyd 1912- *AmMWSc 92*
**Margadale,** Baron 1906- *Who 92*
**Margain,** Hugo B. 1913- *Who 92*
**Margalef,** Ramon 1919- *IntWW 91*
**Margalit,** Shlomo 1914- *WhoRel 92*
**Margalith,** Ethan Harold 1955- *WhoWest 92*
**Margalus,** William T *WhoAmP 91*
**Marganian,** Vahe Mardiros 1938- *AmMWSc 92*
**Margaret Maultasch,** Countess of Tirol 1318-1369 *EncAmaz 91*
**Margaret of Anjou** 1430-1482 *EncAmaz 91*
**Margaret of Antioch** *EncAmaz 91*
**Margaret of Attenduli** 1375- *EncAmaz 91*
**Margaret of Denmark** 1353-1411 *EncAmaz 91*
**Margaret of Provence** *EncAmaz 91*
**Margaret of Valois** 1553-1615 *EncAmaz 91*
**Margaret,** Princess 1930 *Who 92R*
**Margaret Rose,** Princess 1930- *IntWW 91*
**Margaretten,** William 1929- *AmMWSc 92*
**Margarita,** Peter A. 1947- *WhoWest 92*
**Margaritoff,** Dimitri Andrej 1947- *WhoFI 92*
**Margaritondo,** Giorgio 1946- *AmMWSc 92*
**Margason,** Geoffrey 1933- *Who 92*
**Margaziotis,** Demetrius John 1938- *AmMWSc 92*
**Margen,** Sheldon 1919- *AmMWSc 92*
**Margenau,** Henry 1901- *IntAu&W 91*
**Margeot,** Jean 1916- *IntWW 91, WhoRel 92*
**Marger,** Edwin 1928- *WhoAmL 92*
**Margerie,** Emmanuel Jacquin de 1924- *IntWW 91*
**Margerison,** Richard Bennett 1932- *AmMWSc 92*
**Margerison,** Thomas Alan 1923- *Who 92*
**Margerit,** Robert 1910- *IntAu&W 91*
**Margerum,** Dale William 1929- *AmMWSc 92, WhoMW 92*
**Margerum,** Donald L 1926- *AmMWSc 92*
**Margerum,** John David 1929- *AmMWSc 92*
**Margerum,** Roger Williams 1930- *WhoBlA 92*
**Margerum,** Sonya L 1930- *WhoAmP 91*
**Margesson** *Who 92*
**Margesson,** Viscount 1922- *Who 92*
**Margeton,** Stephen George 1945- *WhoAmL 92*
**Margetson,** John 1927- *IntWW 91, Who 92*
**Margetts,** Edward Lambert 1920- *AmMWSc 92*
**Marggraff,** Lewis James 1958- *WhoWest 92*
**Margheritona** *EncAmaz 91*
**Margiotta,** Donna Louise 1952- *WhoMW 92*
**Margly,** Violet R. 1931- *WhoAmL 92*
**Margo,** Curtis Edward 1948- *AmMWSc 92*
**Margol,** Irving 1930- *WhoFI 92, WhoWest 92*
**Margoliash,** Emanuel 1920- *AmMWSc 92, IntWW 91*
**Margolies,** Jay Owen 1951- *WhoMW 92*
**Margolies,** Michael N 1938- *AmMWSc 92*
**Margolies,** Raymond 1920- *WhoMW 92*
**Margolin,** Barry Herbert 1943- *AmMWSc 92*
**Margolin,** Burt M 1950- *WhoAmP 91*
**Margolin,** Eric Mitchell 1953- *WhoAmL 92*
**Margolin,** Esar Gordon 1924- *AmMWSc 92*
**Margolin,** Harold 1922- *AmMWSc 92*
**Margolin,** Janet 1943- *IntMPA 92*
**Margolin,** Jerome 1927- *AmMWSc 92*
**Margolin,** Michael *DrAPF 91*
**Margolin,** Paul 1923- *AmMWSc 92*
**Margolin,** Solomon B 1920- *AmMWSc 92*
**Margolin,** Sydney Gerald 1909- *AmMWSc 92*
**Margolin,** Victor 1941- *WrDr 92*
**Margolis,** Andrew S. 1962- *WhoAmL 92*
**Margolis,** Asher J 1914- *AmMWSc 92*
**Margolis,** Asher Jacob 1914- *WhoMW 92*
**Margolis,** Bernard 1926- *AmMWSc 92*
**Margolis,** Bernard Allen 1948- *WhoWest 92*
**Margolis,** David Israel 1930- *WhoFI 92*
**Margolis,** Diane Rothbard 1933- *WhoAmP 91*
**Margolis,** Donald L. 1945- *WhoWest 92*
**Margolis,** Eugene 1935- *WhoAmL 92*
**Margolis,** Frank L 1938- *AmMWSc 92*
**Margolis,** Gary *DrAPF 91*
**Margolis,** Gerald Lawrence 1953- *WhoAmL 92*
**Margolis,** Gwen 1934- *WhoAmP 91*
**Margolis,** Harold Stephen 1946- *AmMWSc 92*
**Margolis,** Jack Selig 1932- *AmMWSc 92*
**Margolis,** James David 1955- *WhoAmP 91*
**Margolis,** Jeffrey Robert 1957- *WhoFI 92*
**Margolis,** John D. 1941- *ConAu 134*
**Margolis,** Joseph 1924- *WrDr 92*
**Margolis,** Lawrence Stanley 1935- *WhoAmL 92*
**Margolis,** Leo 1927- *AmMWSc 92*
**Margolis,** Marvin Allen 1934- *WhoAmL 92*
**Margolis,** Philip Marcus 1925- *AmMWSc 92*
**Margolis,** Renee Kleimann 1938- *AmMWSc 92*
**Margolis,** Richard J. 1929-1991 *ConAu 134, NewYTBS 91, SmATA 67*
**Margolis,** Richard Urdangen 1937- *AmMWSc 92*
**Margolis,** Robert Lewis 1946- *AmMWSc 92*
**Margolis,** Robert Si 1965- *WhoWest 92*
**Margolis,** Ronald Neil 1950- *AmMWSc 92*
**Margolis,** Sam Aaron 1933- *AmMWSc 92*
**Margolis,** Sidney O. 1925- *WhoFI 92*
**Margolis,** Simeon 1931- *AmMWSc 92*
**Margolis,** Stephen Barry 1950- *AmMWSc 92*
**Margolis,** Stephen G 1931- *AmMWSc 92*
**Margolis,** William J. *DrAPF 91*
**Margolius,** Harry Stephen 1938- *AmMWSc 92*
**Margolskee,** Robert F 1954- *AmMWSc 92*
**Margon,** Bruce Henry 1948- *AmMWSc 92*
**Margoshes,** Marvin 1925- *AmMWSc 92*
**Margossian,** Sarkis S 1940- *AmMWSc 92*
**Margotta,** Maurice Howard, Jr. *WhoFI 92*
**Margraf,** Douglas Owen 1962- *WhoFI 92*
**Margrave,** John 1924- *IntWW 91*
**Margrave,** John Lee 1924- *AmMWSc 92*
**Margrave,** Thomas Ewing, Jr 1938- *AmMWSc 92*
**Margrethe II** 1940- *IntWW 91*
**Margrie,** Victor Robert 1929- *Who 92*
**Margroff,** Robert E. 1930- *ConAu 134*
**Marguerite de Bressieux** *EncAmaz 91*
**Marguerite De Navarre** 1492-1549 *FrenWW*
**Marguerite de Provence,** Queen of France 1221-1295 *EncAmaz 91*
**Margueritte** *DrAPF 91*
**Margulies,** Beth Zeldes 1954- *WhoAmL 92*
**Margulies,** Burke William 1943- *WhoAmL 92*
**Margulies,** David Harvey 1949- *AmMWSc 92*
**Margulies,** Jimmy 1951- *ConAu 133*
**Margulies,** Martin B. 1940- *WhoAmL 92*
**Margulies,** Maurice 1931- *AmMWSc 92*
**Margulies,** Seymour 1933- *AmMWSc 92*
**Margulies,** Stan 1920- *IntMPA 92*
**Margulies,** Walter *DcTwDes*
**Margulies,** William George 1940- *AmMWSc 92*
**Margulis,** Alexander Rafailo 1921- *AmMWSc 92*
**Margulis,** Eleanor Weinberg 1934- *WhoMW 92*
**Margulis,** Howard Lee 1961- *WhoAmL 92*
**Margulis,** Lynn 1938- *AmMWSc 92, IntWW 91*
**Margulis,** Thomas N 1937- *AmMWSc 92*
**Margulois,** David 1912- *WhoEnt 92*
**Margus,** Paul E 1948- *WhoIns 92*
**Marguth,** Gilbert R, Jr 1934- *WhoAmP 91*
**Marhatta,** Hari Prasad 1945- *WhoFI 92*
**Mari,** Maria Del Carmen 1959- *WhoHisp 92*
**Maria** *EncAmaz 91*
**Maria de Molina,** Queen of Castile d1321 *EncAmaz 91*
**Maria Eleanora** d1655 *EncAmaz 91*
**Maria Theresa** 1717-1780 *BlkwCEP, EncAmaz 91*
**Maria,** Narendra Lal 1928- *AmMWSc 92*
**Mariacher,** Marcia K. 1952- *WhoFI 92*
**Mariah,** Paul *DrAPF 91*
**Mariah,** Paul 1937- *WrDr 92*
**Mariam,** Mengistu Haile 1937- *IntWW 91*
**Mariam,** Thomas Fred 1957- *WhoEnt 92*
**Marianelli,** Robert Silvio 1941- *AmMWSc 92*
**Mariani,** Carlo Maria 1935- *IntWW 91*
**Mariani,** Carlos 1957- *WhoAmP 91, WhoHisp 92*
**Mariani,** Henry A 1924- *AmMWSc 92*
**Mariani,** Linda Lisa 1952- *WhoAmL 92*
**Mariani,** Paul *DrAPF 91*
**Mariani,** Paul 1940- *DcLB 111 [port]*
**Mariani,** Toni Ninetta *AmMWSc 92*
**Mariani,** Vincent Michael 1962- *WhoEnt 92*
**Marianik,** Charles Gabor 1946- *WhoFI 92*
**Mariano,** Charlie 1923- *NewAmDM*
**Mariano,** Patrick S 1942- *AmMWSc 92*
**Mariano,** Robert Anthony 1938- *WhoFI 92*
**Marianowski,** Leonard George 1935- *AmMWSc 92*
**Marians,** Kenneth J *AmMWSc 92*
**Mariategui,** Jose Carlos 1895-1930 *BenetAL 91*
**Mariategui,** Sandro 1922- *IntWW 91*
**Marich,** Man Singh Shrestha 1942- *FacFETw*
**Marichal,** Juan 1938- *WhoHisp 92*
**Maricich,** Tom John 1938- *AmMWSc 92*
**Marick,** Michael Miron 1957- *WhoAmL 92*
**Maricle,** Gary Lee 1953- *WhoMW 92*
**Maricle,** Russell Cletus 1943- *WhoAmP 91*
**Maricondi,** Chris 1941- *AmMWSc 92*
**Maricq,** Hildegard Rand 1925- *AmMWSc 92*
**Maricq,** John 1922- *AmMWSc 92*
**Marie de Brabancon** *EncAmaz 91*
**Marie de France** *ClMLC 8 [port], FrenWW*
**Marie Fourre de Poix** *EncAmaz 91*
**Marie,** Aurelius John Baptiste Lamothe 1904- *IntWW 91*
**Marie-Christine,** Princess of Espinoy 1545-1582 *EncAmaz 91*
**Marie-Victoire,** Ollie *WhoAmL 92*
**Marieb,** Elaine Nicpon 1936- *AmMWSc 92*
**Mariella,** Raymond Peel 1919- *AmMWSc 92*
**Marien,** Daniel 1925- *AmMWSc 92*
**Marien,** Robert 1952- *WhoEnt 92*
**Marienau,** John C. 1948- *WhoMW 92*
**Marienchild,** Eva 1957- *WhoFI 92*
**Marienthal,** James Edward 1953- *WhoEnt 92*
**Marietta,** Beth 1950- *WhoAmP 91*
**Mariette,** Pierre-Jean 1694-1774 *BlkwCEP*
**Marik,** Jan 1920- *AmMWSc 92*
**Marikovsky,** Yehuda 1924- *AmMWSc 92*
**Marilao,** Rosella Querubin 1939- *WhoMW 92*
**Marill,** Alvin H. 1934- *IntMPA 92*
**Marilupe,** Sister 1950- *WhoRel 92*
**Marimont,** Rosalind Brownstone 1921- *AmMWSc 92*
**Marin,** Alfred *WrDr 92*
**Marin,** Charles Ray 1942- *WhoEnt 92*
**Marin,** Cheech 1946- *WhoHisp 92*
**Marin,** Connie Flores 1939- *WhoHisp 92*
**Marin,** Frank 1940- *WhoHisp 92*
**Marin,** Gerardo 1947- *WhoHisp 92*
**Marin,** Jaime G. 1961- *WhoHisp 92*
**Marin,** Jean 1909- *IntWW 91*
**Marin,** John 1870-1953 *FacFETw*
**Marin,** Luis Munoz *RComAH*
**Marin,** Manuel 1949- *Who 92*
**Marin,** Matthew Gruen *AmMWSc 92*
**Marin,** Miguel Angel 1938- *AmMWSc 92*
**Marin,** Myra 1964- *WhoHisp 92*
**Marin,** Orlando 1963- *WhoHisp 92*
**Marin,** Richard 1946- *IntMPA 92*
**Marin,** Richard Anthony 1946- *WhoEnt 92*
**Marin,** Rosaura 1952- *WhoHisp 92*
**Marin,** Salvador *WhoHisp 92*
**Marin,** Vasile 1904-1937 *BiDExR*
**Marin,** Vincent Arul 1959- *WhoMW 92*
**Marin Gonzalez,** Manuel 1949- *IntWW 91*
**Marin-Padilla,** Miguel 1930- *AmMWSc 92*
**Marin-Rosa,** Carlos 1944- *WhoHisp 92*
**Marina,** Dona *HisDSpE*
**Marina,** Gloria *WhoEnt 92*
**Marina,** Jeanne *DrAPF 91*
**Marinac,** William Martin 1940- *WhoMW 92*
**Marinaccio,** Charles L 1933- *WhoAmP 91*
**Marinaccio,** Charles Lindbergh 1933- *WhoAmL 92*
**Marinaccio,** Paul J 1937- *AmMWSc 92*
**Marinak,** Jeanne LeeAnn 1951- *WhoWest 92*
**Marinaro,** Edward Francis 1950- *WhoEnt 92*
**Marinaro,** Gary *WhoAmP 91*
**Marinchak,** Roger Alan 1952- *AmMWSc 92*
**Marindin,** Henry Louis Francois 1843-1904 *BiInAmS*
**Marine,** Clyde Lockwood 1936- *WhoFI 92, WhoMW 92*
**Marine,** Nick *ConAu 35NR*
**Marine,** William Murphy 1932- *AmMWSc 92*
**Marinelli,** Arthur Joseph, Jr. 1942- *WhoAmL 92*
**Marinelli,** Donald 1953- *WhoEnt 92*
**Marinelli,** Giovanni 1879-1944 *BiDExR*
**Marinelli,** Joseph John 1943- *WhoMW 92*
**Marinello,** Robert Maggio 1945- *WhoIns 92*
**Marinello,** Thomas J. 1955- *WhoRel 92*
**Marinenko,** George 1935- *AmMWSc 92*
**Mariner,** James Walter 1926- *WhoWest 92*
**Mariner,** William Martin 1949- *WhoWest 92*
**Marinescu,** Bogdan *IntWW 91*
**Marinetti,** Filippo T 1876-1944 *FacFETw*
**Marinetti,** Filippo Tommaso 1876-1944 *BiDExR, DcLB 114 [port]*
**Marinetti,** Guido V 1918- *AmMWSc 92*
**Marinez,** Guadalupe *WhoHisp 92*
**Marinez,** Juan 1946- *WhoHisp 92*
**Marinez Ruiz,** Jose 1873-1967 *FacFETw*
**Maring,** Norman H. 1914- *WhoRel 92*
**Marini,** Manuel Augusto 1939- *WhoHisp 92*
**Marini,** Marino 1901-1980 *FacFETw*
**Marini,** Mario A 1925- *AmMWSc 92*
**Marini,** Robert C *AmMWSc 92*
**Marini,** Robert Charles 1931- *WhoFI 92*
**Marini-Bettolo,** Giovanni Battista 1915- *IntWW 91*
**Marini-Roig,** Luis Enrique 1949- *WhoHisp 92*
**Marinik,** Steve J. 1924- *WhoMW 92*
**Marinis,** Thomas Paul, Jr. 1943- *WhoAmL 92*
**Marinko,** Monica Marie 1948- *WhoMW 92*
**Marino,** A A 1941- *AmMWSc 92*
**Marino,** Carlos 1947- *WhoMW 92*
**Marino,** Eugene A. 1934- *RelLAm 91*
**Marino,** Eugene Antonio 1934- *WhoBlA 92*
**Marino,** Frank Joseph *WhoMW 92*
**Marino,** Gary Orlando 1944- *WhoFI 92*
**Marino,** Gigi *DrAPF 91*
**Marino,** James F *WhoIns 92*
**Marino,** James Frank 1939- *WhoEnt 92*
**Marino,** Jan *DrAPF 91*
**Marino,** John *WhoAmP 91*
**Marino,** Joseph Paul 1942- *AmMWSc 92*
**Marino,** Josephine Diana 1945- *WhoAmP 91*
**Marino,** Michael Frank 1948- *WhoAmL 92*
**Marino,** Pamela A 1951- *AmMWSc 92*
**Marino,** Ralph John 1928- *WhoAmP 91*
**Marino,** Richard Matthew 1957- *AmMWSc 92*
**Marino,** Robert 1948- *WhoEnt 92*
**Marino,** Robert Anthony 1943- *AmMWSc 92*
**Marino,** Rose Linda 1950- *WhoHisp 92*
**Marino,** Ruth Elizabeth Reiff 1924- *WhoEnt 92*
**Marino,** Santiago 1788-1854 *HisDSpE*
**Marino,** Susan *WrDr 92*
**Marino,** William Francis 1948- *WhoFI 92*
**Marinoff,** Benjamin David 1953- *WhoEnt 92*
**Marinos,** Pete Nick 1935- *AmMWSc 92*
**Marinovic,** Nancy *WhoHisp 92*
**Marinstein,** Edward Ross 1960- *WhoAmL 92*
**Marinus** *EncEarC*
**Marinus** d260? *EncEarC*
**Marinus,** Martin Gerard 1944- *AmMWSc 92*
**Marinuzzi,** Gino 1882-1945 *NewAmDM*
**Mario,** Ernest 1938- *IntWW 91, Who 92, WhoFI 92*
**Mario,** Giovanni Matteo 1810-1883 *NewAmDM*
**Mario,** Queena 1896-1951 *NewAmDM*
**Marion,** Alexander Peter 1915- *AmMWSc 92*
**Marion,** Antoine Fortune 1846-1900 *ThHElm*
**Marion,** C P 1920- *AmMWSc 92*
**Marion,** Caryl *WhoAmP 91*
**Marion,** Christopher James, III 1953- *WhoEnt 92*
**Marion,** Claud Collier *WhoBlA 92*
**Marion,** David H. 1939- *WhoAmL 92*
**Marion,** Frances 1887-1973 *ReelWom [port]*
**Marion,** Francis 1732?-1795 *BenetAL 91, BlkwEAR*
**Marion,** Fred D. 1959- *WhoBlA 92*
**Marion,** Graciela Angel 1938- *WhoHisp 92*
**Marion,** James Edsel 1935- *AmMWSc 92*

**Marion**, Jerry Baskerville 1929- AmMWSc 92
**Marion**, John Louis 1933- WhoFI 92
**Marion**, Mildred Ruth 1904- WhoMW 92
**Marion**, Paul DrAPF 91
**Marion**, Paul Jules Andre 1899-1954 BiDExR
**Marion**, Robert Howard 1945- AmMWSc 92
**Marion**, Wayne Richard 1947- AmMWSc 92
**Marion**, William W 1930- AmMWSc 92
**Mariota**, Tuiasosopo, II WhoAmP 91
**Mariotti**, Gianfranco 1933- WhoEnt 92
**Mariotti**, Sylvia EncAmaz 91
**Mariottini**, Claude Francisco 1942- WhoRel 92
**Maris**, Charles Robert 1948- WhoMW 92
**Maris**, Humphrey John 1939- AmMWSc 92
**Maris**, Maria R. DrAPF 91
**Maris**, Nicholas Paul 1955- WhoWest 92
**Maris**, Roger 1934-1985 FacFETw
**Mariscal**, Richard North 1935- AmMWSc 92
**Marisi**, Dan Quirinus 1940- AmMWSc 92
**Mariska**, John Thomas 1950- AmMWSc 92
**Maritain**, Jacques 1882-1973 FacFETw
**Marius Mercator** EncEarC
**Marius**, Kenneth Anthony 1937- WhoBlA 92
**Marivaux**, Pierre Carlet de 1688-1763 BlkwCEP
**Mariwalla**, Gopal Chetanram 1944- WhoFI 92
**Marjanczyk**, Joseph Anicetus 1921- WhoRel 92
**Marjoribanks**, Edyth Leslia 1927- Who 92
**Marjoribanks**, James Alexander Milne 1911- IntWW 91, Who 92
**Marjoribanks**, Kevin McLeod 1940- Who 92
**Marjoribanks**, Leslia Who 92
**Mark** EncEarC
**Mark of Fort Lauderdale**, Bishop WhoRel 92
**Mark Twain** BenetAL 91
**Mark**, Alan Francis 1932- IntWW 91
**Mark**, Alan Samuel 1947- WhoAmL 92
**Mark**, Andrew Peery 1950- WhoEnt 92
**Mark**, Anthony Doran 1952- WhoEnt 92
**Mark**, Arthur 1948- WhoWest 92
**Mark**, Cheryl DeAnne 1957- WhoMW 92
**Mark**, David WhoEnt 92, WhoMW 92
**Mark**, David Fu-Chi 1950- AmMWSc 92
**Mark**, Denis Hugh 1951- WhoAmL 92
**Mark**, Dennis John 1953- WhoAmL 92
**Mark**, Earl Larry 1940- AmMWSc 92
**Mark**, Freemon A. 1948- WhoBlA 92
**Mark**, Hans 1929- WhoAmP 91
**Mark**, Hans Michael 1929- AmMWSc 92, IntWW 91
**Mark**, Harold Wayne 1949- AmMWSc 92
**Mark**, Harry Berst, Jr 1934- AmMWSc 92
**Mark**, Henry Allen 1909- WhoFI 92
**Mark**, Herbert 1921- AmMWSc 92
**Mark**, Herman F. 1895- IntWW 91
**Mark**, Herman Francis 1895- AmMWSc 92
**Mark**, J Carson 1913- AmMWSc 92
**Mark**, James 1914- Who 92
**Mark**, James Edward 1934- AmMWSc 92
**Mark**, James Wai-Kee 1943- AmMWSc 92
**Mark**, Jan 1943- IntAu&W 91, WrDr 92
**Mark**, Jon Wei AmMWSc 92
**Mark**, Laurence M. IntMPA 92
**Mark**, Laurence Maurice WhoEnt 92
**Mark**, Leonard S. 1951- WhoMW 92
**Mark**, Lester Charles 1918- AmMWSc 92
**Mark**, Lloyd K 1925- AmMWSc 92
**Mark**, Melvin 1922- AmMWSc 92
**Mark**, Norman Barry 1939- WhoEnt 92
**Mark**, Peter 1940- WhoEnt 92
**Mark**, Reuben 1939- IntWW 91
**Mark**, Richard Steve 1948- WhoAmL 92
**Mark**, Robert 1917- IntWW 91, Who 92
**Mark**, Robert 1930- AmMWSc 92
**Mark**, Robert Vincent 1942- AmMWSc 92
**Mark**, Roger G 1939- AmMWSc 92
**Mark**, Samuel 1951- WhoHisp 92
**Mark**, Shelley Muin 1922- WhoFI 92
**Mark**, Shew-Kuey 1936- AmMWSc 92
**Mark**, Stephen Leonard 1947- WhoAmL 92
**Mark**, Wendy DrAPF 91
**Markakis**, Pericles 1920- AmMWSc 92
**Markall**, Francis 1905- Who 92
**Markancek**, James Irvin 1953- WhoMW 92
**Markanda**, Raj Kumar 1940- WhoMW 92
**Markandaya**, Kamala IntAu&W 91
**Markandaya**, Kamala 1924- ConNov 91, LiExTwC, WrDr 92
**Markaryants**, Vladimir Surenovich 1934- IntWW 91, SovUnBD
**Markavitch**, Stanley G. 1943- WhoRel 92
**Marke**, Julius Jay 1913- WhoAmL 92
**Markee**, David James 1942- WhoWest 92
**Markee**, Katherine Madigan 1931- AmMWSc 92, WhoMW 92
**Markees**, Diether Gaudenz 1919- AmMWSc 92
**Markel**, Anthony Foster 1942- WhoIns 92
**Markel**, Gregory Arthur 1945- WhoAmL 92
**Markel**, Robert Thomas 1943- WhoAmP 91
**Markelius**, Sven 1889-1972 DcTwDes, FacFETw
**Markell**, David Lawrence 1953- WhoAmL 92
**Markell**, Edward Kingsmill 1918- AmMWSc 92
**Markell**, Robert LesBEnT 92
**Markellis**, Anthony Steven 1952- WhoEnt 92
**Markels**, Michael, Jr 1926- AmMWSc 92, WhoFI 92
**Marken**, Gideon Andrew, III 1940- WhoEnt 92, WhoWest 92
**Markenscoff**, Pauline 1952- AmMWSc 92
**Marker**, Chris 1921- IntDcF 2-2
**Marker**, David 1937- AmMWSc 92
**Marker**, Jamsheed K. A. 1922- IntWW 91
**Marker**, Judith WhoRel 92
**Marker**, Leon 1922- AmMWSc 92
**Marker**, Leonard K. 1913- WhoEnt 92
**Marker**, Marc Linthacum 1941- WhoAmL 92, WhoFI 92, WhoWest 92
**Marker**, Thomas F 1919- AmMWSc 92
**Marker**, Willi 1894-1940 EncTR 91
**Markert**, Claus O 1946- AmMWSc 92
**Markert**, Clement L. 1917- IntWW 91
**Markert**, Clement Lawrence 1917- AmMWSc 92
**Markert**, James MacDowell 1934- WhoFI 92
**Markert**, Joan Frances 1946- WhoEnt 92
**Markert**, Joy 1942- IntAu&W 91
**Markert**, Russell 1899-1990 FacFETw
**Markesbery**, William Ray 1932- AmMWSc 92
**Markesinis**, Basil Spyridonos 1944- Who 92
**Marketos**, George B. 1947- WhoMW 92
**Markette-Malone**, Sharon 1956- WhoBlA 92
**Markevich**, Darlene Julia 1949- AmMWSc 92
**Markevich**, Igor 1912-1983 NewAmDM
**Markey**, Beatrice 1913- WhoBlA 92
**Markey**, Brian Michael 1956- WhoAmL 92
**Markey**, Christian Edward, Jr. 1929- WhoAmL 92
**Markey**, David John 1940- WhoAmP 91
**Markey**, Edward J. 1946- AlmAP 92 [port], WhoAmP 91
**Markey**, Howard T WhoAmP 91
**Markey**, Howard Thomas 1920- WhoAmL 92
**Markey**, Paul Victor 1959- WhoEnt 92
**Markey**, Robert Guy 1939- WhoAmL 92
**Markey**, Sanford Philip 1942- AmMWSc 92
**Markey**, Winston Roscoe 1929- AmMWSc 92
**Markezinis**, Spyros 1909- IntWW 91
**Markfield**, Wallace DrAPF 91
**Markfield**, Wallace 1926- BenetAL 91, ConNov 91, IntAu&W 91, WrDr 92
**Markgraf**, Diane Marie 1968- WhoMW 92
**Markgraf**, J Hodge 1930- AmMWSc 92
**Markham**, Beryl 1902-1986 FacFETw
**Markham**, Charles 1924- Who 92
**Markham**, Charles Buchanan 1926- WhoAmL 92, WhoAmP 91
**Markham**, Charles Henry 1923- AmMWSc 92
**Markham**, Claire Agnes 1919- AmMWSc 92
**Markham**, Dean Paul 1948- WhoAmP 91
**Markham**, E. A. 1939- ConPo 91, WrDr 92
**Markham**, Edwin 1852-1940 BenetAL 91
**Markham**, Elizabeth Mary 1929- AmMWSc 92
**Markham**, George Douglas 1951- AmMWSc 92
**Markham**, Houston, Jr. 1942- WhoBlA 92
**Markham**, James J 1928- AmMWSc 92
**Markham**, Jerry Wayne 1948- WhoAmL 92
**Markham**, Jonne Pearson 1926- WhoAmP 91
**Markham**, Jordan Jeptha 1916- AmMWSc 92
**Markham**, Kenneth Ronald 1937- IntWW 91
**Markham**, Marcella d1991 NewYTBS 91
**Markham**, Marion M. DrAPF 91
**Markham**, Monte 1938- IntMPA 92, WhoEnt 92
**Markham**, Reed B. 1957- WhoFI 92, WhoWest 92
**Markham**, Robert IntAu&W 91X, WrDr 92
**Markham**, Robert Wilson, III 1943- WhoRel 92
**Markham**, Sarah 1909- IntAu&W 91
**Markham**, Thomas Lowell 1939- AmMWSc 92
**Markham**, William Edwin 1922- WhoAmP 91
**Markhart**, Albert H, Jr 1919- AmMWSc 92
**Markhart**, Albert Henry, III 1951- AmMWSc 92
**Markievicz**, Con 1868-1927 FacFETw
**Markievicz**, Constance 1876-1927 EncAmaz 91
**Markiewicz**, Alfred John 1928- WhoRel 92
**Markiewicz**, Betty P. 1935- WhoMW 92
**Markiewicz**, Robert Stephen 1947- AmMWSc 92
**Markiewicz**, Wladyslaw 1920- IntWW 91
**Markiewitz**, Kenneth Helmut 1927- AmMWSc 92
**Markim**, Alfred 1927- WhoEnt 92
**Markin**, Carole Beth WhoEnt 92
**Markin**, Rom J. 1932- WhoWest 92
**Markind**, Daniel Benson 1959- WhoAmL 92
**Marking**, Henry 1920- Who 92
**Marking**, Henry Ernest 1920- IntWW 91
**Marking**, Ralph H 1935- AmMWSc 92
**Marking**, Theodore Joseph, Jr. 1945- WhoMW 92
**Markinson**, Martin 1931- WhoEnt 92
**Markiw**, Roman Teodor 1923- AmMWSc 92
**Markland**, Francis Swaby, Jr 1936- AmMWSc 92
**Markland**, Jeffrey Thomas 1940- WhoAmP 91
**Markland**, William A 1920- WhoAmP 91
**Markland**, William R 1919- AmMWSc 92
**Markle**, Cheri Virginia Cummins 1936- WhoMW 92
**Markle**, Douglas Frank 1947- AmMWSc 92
**Markle**, Fletcher d1991 LesBEnT 92
**Markle**, Fletcher 1921-1991 DcLB Y91N [port], NewYTBS 91
**Markle**, George Michael 1939- AmMWSc 92
**Markle**, John, Jr. 1931- WhoAmL 92, WhoAmP 91
**Markle**, Peter IntMPA 92
**Markle**, Ronald A 1951- AmMWSc 92
**Markley**, Francis Landis 1939- AmMWSc 92
**Markley**, J Keith 1959- WhoAmP 91
**Markley**, John Lute 1941- AmMWSc 92
**Markley**, Joseph Cowles 1956- WhoAmP 91
**Markley**, Lowell Dean 1942- AmMWSc 92
**Markley**, Lynn McMaster 1938- WhoFI 92, WhoMW 92
**Markley**, Theresa Lynn 1958- WhoAmL 92
**Markley**, William A, Jr 1925- AmMWSc 92
**Markley**, William Ambrose 1932- WhoRel 92
**Marklund**, Richard Gustav 1945- WhoFI 92
**Markman**, Raymond Jerome 1927- WhoEnt 92
**Markman**, Robert P 1938- WhoAmP 91
**Markman**, Ronald 1931- WhoMW 92
**Markman**, Sherman 1920- WhoFI 92
**Markman**, Stephen J. 1949- WhoAmL 92
**Marko**, John Robert 1938- AmMWSc 92
**Marko**, Katherine D. 1913- WrDr 92
**Marko**, Katherine Dolores 1913- IntAu&W 91
**Marko**, Kenneth Andrew 1946- AmMWSc 92
**Markoe**, Francis Hartman 1856-1907 BiInAmS
**Markoe**, George F H d1896 BiInAmS
**Markoe**, M. Allen 1927- WhoWest 92
**Markoe**, Peter 1752?-1792 BenetAL 91
**Markoe**, Thomas Masters 1819-1901 BiInAmS
**Markoff**, Gary David 1956- WhoFI 92
**Markoff**, Sol DrAPF 91
**Markoosie** 1942- WrDr 92
**Markopoulos**, Andrew John 1931- WhoMW 92
**Markopoulos**, Gregory 1928- IntDcF 2-2
**Markos**, Chris 1926- WhoMW 92
**Markos**, Donald William 1933- WhoWest 92
**Markosek**, Joseph F 1950- WhoAmP 91
**Markoski**, Joseph Peter 1948- WhoAmL 92
**Markov**, Dmitriy Fyodorovich 1913- IntWW 91
**Markov**, Georgi I. 1920-1978 LiExTwC
**Markov**, Georgiy Mokeyevich 1911- IntWW 91
**Markov**, Leonid Vasilevich 1927- IntWW 91
**Markov**, Moisey Aleksandrovich 1908- IntWW 91
**Markov**, Nikolai Evgenevich 1866- BiDExR
**Markova**, Alicia 1910- FacFETw, IntWW 91, Who 92
**Markovetz**, Allen John 1933- AmMWSc 92
**Markovic**, Ante 1924- CurBio 91 [port], IntWW 91
**Markovic**, Vida E. 1916- WrDr 92
**Markovich**, Eric 1964- WhoRel 92
**Markovich-Treece**, Patricia Helen 1941- WhoFI 92, WhoWest 92
**Markovits**, Inga 1937- WhoAmL 92
**Markovits**, Richard Spencer 1942- WhoAmL 92
**Markovits**, Ronald D WhoIns 92
**Markovitz**, Alvin 1929- AmMWSc 92
**Markovitz**, Hershel 1921- AmMWSc 92
**Markovitz**, Mark 1938- AmMWSc 92
**Markowitz**, Abraham Sam 1921- AmMWSc 92
**Markowitz**, Allan Henry 1941- AmMWSc 92
**Markowitz**, David 1935- AmMWSc 92
**Markowitz**, Harold 1925- AmMWSc 92
**Markowitz**, Harry M. 1927- IntWW 91, Who 92, WhoFI 92, WhoNob 90, WrDr 92
**Markowitz**, Lewis Harrison 1933- WhoAmL 92
**Markowitz**, Martin 1945- WhoAmP 91
**Markowitz**, Milton 1918- AmMWSc 92
**Markowitz**, Robert 1935- IntMPA 92
**Markowitz**, Samuel Solomon 1931- AmMWSc 92, WhoWest 92
**Markowitz**, William 1907- AmMWSc 92
**Markowski**, Gregory Ray 1947- AmMWSc 92
**Markowski**, Henry Joseph 1929- AmMWSc 92, WhoMW 92
**Marks** Who 92
**Marks**, Alfred 1921- IntMPA 92
**Marks**, Alfred Finlay 1932- AmMWSc 92
**Marks**, Arthur 1927- IntMPA 92
**Marks**, Arthur Ronald 1927- WhoEnt 92
**Marks**, B Mayes, Jr 1959- WhoAmP 91
**Marks**, Bernard Herman 1921- AmMWSc 92
**Marks**, Bernard Montague 1923- Who 92
**Marks**, Bruce 1937- WhoEnt 92
**Marks**, Burton Stewart 1924- AmMWSc 92
**Marks**, Charles Frank 1938- AmMWSc 92
**Marks**, Charles Hardaway 1921- WhoAmP 91
**Marks**, Charles Herbert 1930- WhoRel 92
**Marks**, Charles L 1936- WhoIns 92
**Marks**, Claude d1991 NewYTBS 91
**Marks**, Claude 1915- WhoEnt 92
**Marks**, Claude 1915-1991 ConAu 134
**Marks**, Colin H 1933- AmMWSc 92
**Marks**, Craig AmMWSc 92
**Marks**, Dale 1948- WhoAmP 91
**Marks**, Darrell L 1936- AmMWSc 92
**Marks**, David Hunter 1939- AmMWSc 92
**Marks**, Dawn Beatty 1937- AmMWSc 92
**Marks**, Debra Lynn 1963- WhoEnt 92
**Marks**, Dennis William 1944- AmMWSc 92
**Marks**, Derek 1960- TwCPaSc
**Marks**, Diana Rochelle 1957- WhoEnt 92
**Marks**, Dorothy Lind 1900- WhoWest 92
**Marks**, E Matthew 1942- WhoIns 92
**Marks**, Edwin Potter 1925- AmMWSc 92
**Marks**, Eli S. 1911-1991 ConAu 133
**Marks**, Esther L. 1927- WhoMW 92
**Marks**, Frederick Howe 1942- WhoFI 92
**Marks**, Gerald A 1949- AmMWSc 92
**Marks**, Gerald Samuel 1930- AmMWSc 92
**Marks**, Harry T. d1991 NewYTBS 91
**Marks**, Henry L 1935- AmMWSc 92
**Marks**, Herbert Edward 1935- WhoAmL 92
**Marks**, Herman H WhoAmP 91
**Marks**, Ira Alan 1942- WhoWest 92
**Marks**, J ConAu 34NR, DrAPF 91
**Marks**, James Duncan 1961- WhoAmL 92
**Marks**, Janet DrAPF 91
**Marks**, Jay Stewart 1937- AmMWSc 92
**Marks**, Jean C 1934- WhoAmP 91
**Marks**, Jeannette 1875-1964 BenetAL 91
**Marks**, Jerome W. 1915- WhoAmL 92
**Marks**, John Boyd 1928- WhoAmP 91
**Marks**, John Emile Who 92
**Marks**, John Henry 1925- Who 92
**Marks**, Justin Davis, Jr. 1940- WhoRel 92
**Marks**, Kenneth Robert 1945- WhoFI 92
**Marks**, L Whit 1926- AmMWSc 92
**Marks**, Laurence D 1954- AmMWSc 92
**Marks**, Laurie J. 1957- ConAu 135, SmATA 68
**Marks**, Lawrence Edward 1941- AmMWSc 92
**Marks**, Lee Otis 1944- WhoBlA 92
**Marks**, Leon Joseph 1925- AmMWSc 92
**Marks**, Leonard Harold 1916- IntWW 91

**Marks,** Leonard M. 1942- WhoAmL 92
**Marks,** Lillian Alicia 1910- FacFETw
**Marks,** Louis Denton, Jr. 1949- WhoMW 92
**Marks,** Louis Sheppard 1917- AmMWSc 92
**Marks,** Marc Lincoln 1927- WhoAmP 91
**Marks,** Merle Byron 1925- WhoWest 92
**Marks,** Merton Eleazer 1932- WhoAmL 92
**Marks,** Meyer Benjamin 1907- AmMWSc 92
**Marks,** Michael Eugene 1951- WhoAmL 92
**Marks,** Michael George 1931- WhoAmL 92
**Marks,** Michael J. 1938- WhoAmL 92
**Marks,** Milton, Jr 1920- WhoAmP 91
**Marks,** Murry Aaron 1933- WhoAmL 92
**Marks,** Neville 1930- AmMWSc 92
**Marks,** Paul A 1926- AmMWSc 92
**Marks,** Paul Alan 1926- IntWW 91
**Marks,** Paula Mitchell 1951- ConAu 135
**Marks,** Percy 1891-1956 BenetAL 91
**Marks,** Peter Amasa 1948- WhoWest 92
**Marks,** Peter J AmMWSc 92
**Marks,** Raymond H. 1922- WhoFI 92
**Marks,** Richard Charles 1945- Who 92
**Marks,** Richard Dickinson 1942- WhoRel 92
**Marks,** Richard E. IntMPA 92
**Marks,** Richard Henry Lee 1943- AmMWSc 92
**Marks,** Robert 1955- WhoEnt 92
**Marks,** Robert Bosler 1953- WhoEnt 92
**Marks,** Robert Herman, Jr 1922- WhoAmP 91
**Marks,** Ronald Arthur 1942- WhoAmL 92
**Marks,** Ronald Lee 1934- AmMWSc 92
**Marks,** Rose M. 1938- WhoBlA 92
**Marks,** Ruth A 1940- WhoIns 92
**Marks,** Sallie Belle 1891-1968 DcNCBi 4
**Marks,** Sandy Cole, Jr 1937- AmMWSc 92
**Marks,** Sharon Lea 1942- WhoWest 92
**Marks,** Shula Eta 1936- Who 92
**Marks,** Solon 1827-1914 BiInAmS
**Marks,** Stan 1929- WrDr 92
**Marks,** Stanley IntAu&W 91
**Marks,** Theodore Lee 1935- WhoAmL 92
**Marks,** Thomas, Jr 1951- AmMWSc 92
**Marks,** Tobin Jay 1944- AmMWSc 92
**Marks,** Tom 1956- WhoAmL 92
**Marks,** William Dennis 1849-1914 BiInAmS
**Marks,** William J. 1944- WhoWest 92
**Marks of Broughton,** Baron 1920- Who 92
**Marksheffel,** Edward Everett 1949- WhoWest 92
**Markson,** David DrAPF 91
**Markson,** David 1927- ConLC 67 [port], ConNov 91
**Markson,** David M. 1927- WrDr 92
**Markson,** Hadassah Binder 1927- WhoEnt 92
**Markson,** Ralph Joseph 1931- AmMWSc 92
**Markstahler,** Joyce Bolster 1933- WhoEnt 92
**Markstein,** George Henry 1911- AmMWSc 92
**Markstein,** Stephen F. 1942- WhoAmL 92
**Markstrom,** Paul Ragnvald 1921- WhoRel 92
**Markstrom,** Wilbur Jack 1930- WhoAmL 92
**Markum,** Joseph Lee 1964- WhoRel 92
**Markum,** Richard Alan 1959- WhoRel 92
**Markun,** Frank O. 1947- WhoFI 92
**Markun,** Rachel 1957- WhoAmL 92
**Markunas,** Albert Lee 1947- WhoMW 92
**Markunas,** Peter Charles 1911- AmMWSc 92
**Markus,** Gabor 1922- AmMWSc 92
**Markus,** Joel Seth 1950- WhoMW 92
**Markus,** Julia DrAPF 91
**Markus,** Julia 1939- WrDr 92
**Markus,** Kenneth M. 1957- WhoEnt 92
**Markus,** Lawrence 1922- AmMWSc 92
**Markus,** Rika 1910- Who 92
**Markus,** Robert Austin 1924- Who 92
**Markus,** Robert M. 1930- WhoFI 92
**Markuszewski,** Richard 1941- AmMWSc 92
**Markuszka,** Nancy Ann 1951- WhoMW 92
**Markwald,** Roger R 1943- AmMWSc 92
**Markwell,** Dick Robert 1925- AmMWSc 92
**Markwick,** Edward ScFEYrs
**Markwood,** James S 1954- WhoAmP 91
**Markwood,** Lewis Ardra 1932- WhoRel 92
**Markwood,** Ronald Paul 1933- WhoMW 92
**Markworth,** Alan John 1937- AmMWSc 92, WhoMW 92
**Marky,** William Bernard 1938- WhoEnt 92
**Marland,** Alkis Joseph 1943- WhoFI 92
**Marland,** Gregg 1942- AmMWSc 92
**Marland,** Melissa Kaye 1955- WhoAmL 92
**Marland,** Michael 1934- Who 92, WrDr 92
**Marland,** Paul 1940- Who 92
**Marland,** Sidney P., Jr. 1914- IntWW 91
**Marlane,** Judith 1937- WhoEnt 92, WhoFI 92
**Marlantes,** Leo 1916- WhoWest 92
**Marlar,** Robin Geoffrey 1931- Who 92
**Marlas,** James Constantine 1937- WhoFI 92
**Marlatt,** Abby Lindsey 1916- AmMWSc 92
**Marlatt,** Daphne DrAPF 91
**Marlatt,** Daphne 1942- BenetAL 91, ConPo 91, WrDr 92
**Marlatt,** Daphne Shirley 1942- IntAu&W 91
**Marlatt,** William Edgar 1931- AmMWSc 92
**Marlborough,** Duke of 1926- Who 92
**Marlborough,** John Michael 1940- AmMWSc 92
**Marlenee,** Ron 1935- AlmAP 92 [port]
**Marlenee,** Ronald Charles 1935- WhoAmP 91, WhoWest 92
**Marler,** David Steele 1941- Who 92
**Marler,** Dennis Ralph Greville 1927- Who 92
**Marler,** Peter 1928- AmMWSc 92
**Marler,** Peter Robert 1928- IntWW 91
**Marlesford,** Baron 1931- Who 92
**Marlett,** De Otis Loring 1911- WhoFI 92
**Marlett,** Judith Ann WhoMW 92
**Marlett,** Judith Ann 1943- AmMWSc 92
**Marlette,** Ralph R 1920- AmMWSc 92
**Marley,** Bob 1945-1981 FacFETw [port]
**Marley,** Gerald C 1938- AmMWSc 92
**Marley,** Stephen J 1930- AmMWSc 92
**Marley,** Ziggy 1968- WhoEnt 92
**Marliave,** Jeffrey Burton 1949- AmMWSc 92
**Marlin,** James Wilson, Jr. 1934- WhoMW 92
**Marlin,** Joe Alton 1935- AmMWSc 92
**Marlin,** Robert Lewis 1937- AmMWSc 92
**Marling,** Charles 1951- Who 92
**Marling,** Jacob 1774-1833 DcNCBi 4
**Marlis,** Stefanie DrAPF 91
**Marliss,** Errol Basil 1941- AmMWSc 92
**Marlo,** Timothy Louis 1964- WhoFI 92
**Marlor,** Clark Strang 1922- WrDr 92
**Marlow,** Andrew Joseph 1944- WhoEnt 92
**Marlow,** Antony Rivers 1940- Who 92
**Marlow,** Bruce Wendell 1949- WhoIns 92
**Marlow,** David Ellis 1935- Who 92
**Marlow,** James Allen 1955- WhoAmL 92
**Marlow,** Joyce 1929- IntAu&W 91, WrDr 92
**Marlow,** Keith Winton 1928- AmMWSc 92
**Marlow,** Max WrDr 92
**Marlow,** Michael Louis 1953- WhoFI 92, WhoWest 92
**Marlow,** Nancy Jane 1946- WhoMW 92
**Marlow,** Orval Lee, II 1956- WhoAmL 92
**Marlow,** Ronald William 1949- AmMWSc 92
**Marlow,** William Henry 1924- AmMWSc 92
**Marlow,** William Henry 1944- AmMWSc 92
**Marlowe,** Amy Bell SmATA 67
**Marlowe,** Christopher 1564-1593 CnDBLB 1 [port], DramC 1 [port], RfGEnL 91
**Marlowe,** Derek 1938- IntAu&W 91, WrDr 92
**Marlowe,** Donald E 1916- AmMWSc 92
**Marlowe,** Edward 1935- AmMWSc 92
**Marlowe,** George Albert, Jr 1925- AmMWSc 92
**Marlowe,** Hugh IntAu&W 91X, Who 92, WrDr 92
**Marlowe,** James Irvin 1932- AmMWSc 92
**Marlowe,** Katherine WrDr 92
**Marlowe,** Stephen IntAu&W 91X
**Marlowe,** Stephen 1928- WrDr 92
**Marlowe,** Sylvia 1908-1981 NewAmDM
**Marlowe,** Thomas Johnson 1917- AmMWSc 92
**Marlowe,** Tommy Herold 1939- WhoRel 92
**Marmaduke,** Arthur Sandford 1926- WhoWest 92
**Marmann,** Sigrid 1938- WhoFI 92, WhoWest 92
**Marmar,** Earl Sheldon 1950- AmMWSc 92
**Marmarelis,** Vasilis Z 1949- AmMWSc 92
**Marmaud,** John Edmund 1961- WhoEnt 92
**Marmer,** Gary James 1938- AmMWSc 92
**Marmer,** Melvin E. 1933- WhoAmL 92
**Marmer,** William Nelson 1943- AmMWSc 92
**Marmet,** Gottlieb John 1946- WhoAmL 92
**Marmet,** Paul 1932- AmMWSc 92
**Marmillion,** Valsin Albert 1950- WhoAmP 91
**Marmion,** Barrie P. 1920- Who 92
**Marmion,** Frank J, Jr 1917- WhoAmP 91
**Marmion,** Shakerley 1603?-1639 RfGEnL 91
**Marmion,** William Henry 1907- WhoRel 92
**Marmolejo,** Adela Villa 1957- WhoHisp 92
**Marmon,** Dennis Carl 1949- WhoFI 92
**Marmontel,** Jean-Francois 1723-1799 BlkwCEP
**Marmor,** Michael F 1941- AmMWSc 92
**Marmor,** Robert Samuel 1943- AmMWSc 92
**Marmor,** Solomon 1926- AmMWSc 92
**Marmur,** Jacland 1901- BenetAL 91
**Marmur,** Julius 1926- AmMWSc 92
**Marnan,** John Fitzgerald d1990 Who 92N
**Marnell,** Anthony Austin, II 1949- WhoWest 92
**Marner,** Eugene 1936- WhoEnt 92
**Marner,** Wilbur Joseph 1937- AmMWSc 92
**Marnett,** Lawrence Joseph 1947- AmMWSc 92
**Marney,** Carlyle 1916-1978 ConAu 135
**Marnoch,** Lord 1938- Who 92
**Marohn,** Ann Elizabeth 1946- WhoMW 92
**Marois,** Harriet Sukoneck 1945- WhoWest 92
**Marois,** Robert Leo 1935- AmMWSc 92
**Maroko,** Simon Wolf 1923- WhoMW 92
**Maroldy,** Donald James 1925- WhoAmL 92
**Marom,** Emanuel 1934- AmMWSc 92
**Marom,** Eran 1962- WhoFI 92
**Maron,** Margaret WrDr 92
**Maron,** Melvin Earl 1924- AmMWSc 92
**Maron,** Michael 1948- WhoEnt 92
**Maron,** Michael Brent 1949- AmMWSc 92
**Maron,** Monika 1941- LiExTwC
**Maronde,** Robert Francis 1920- AmMWSc 92, WhoWest 92
**Maroney,** Arthur Ervey, Jr. 1940- WhoFI 92
**Maroney,** Jack Drennan 1924- WhoAmL 92
**Maroney,** James Francis, III 1951- WhoAmL 92
**Maroney,** Jane P 1923- WhoAmP 91
**Maroney,** Michael Jeffrey 1957- WhoEnt 92
**Maroney,** Samuel Patterson, Jr 1926- AmMWSc 92
**Marongiu,** Giovanni 1929- IntWW 91
**Maroni,** Donna F 1938- AmMWSc 92
**Maroni,** Gustavo Primo 1941- AmMWSc 92
**Maroni,** Victor August 1942- AmMWSc 92
**Maroscher,** Janice 1963- WhoMW 92
**Marotta,** Alphonse S WhoAmP 91
**Marotta,** Charles Anthony 1945- AmMWSc 92
**Marotta,** Charles Rocco 1925- AmMWSc 92
**Marotta,** George Raymond 1926- WhoWest 92
**Marotta,** Paul David 1957- WhoAmL 92
**Marotta,** Sabath Fred 1929- AmMWSc 92
**Marotti,** Joseph Andrew 1945- WhoMW 92
**Marotz,** James Edward 1960- WhoMW 92
**Marouf,** Taha Muhyiddin 1924- IntWW 91
**Maroulis,** Peter James 1951- AmMWSc 92
**Marousky,** Francis John 1935- AmMWSc 92
**Marov,** Gaspar J 1920- AmMWSc 92
**Marovich,** George M. 1931- WhoAmL 92, WhoMW 92
**Marovitch,** Antoine WhoRel 92
**Marovitz,** Abraham Lincoln 1905- WhoMW 92
**Marovitz,** James Lee 1939- WhoAmL 92
**Marovitz,** William A 1944- WhoAmP 91, WhoMW 92
**Marowitz,** Charles 1934- IntAu&W 91, Who 92, WrDr 92
**Marozsan,** Stephen Simon 1925- WhoMW 92
**Marpesia** EncAmaz 91
**Marple,** Dennis Neil 1945- AmMWSc 92
**Marple,** Dorothy Jane 1926- WhoRel 92
**Marple,** Dudley Tyng Fisher 1927- AmMWSc 92
**Marple,** Stanley, Jr 1920- AmMWSc 92
**Marple,** Stanley Lawrence, Jr 1947- AmMWSc 92
**Marple,** Virgil Alan 1939- AmMWSc 92
**Marples,** Brian John 1907- IntWW 91, Who 92
**Marpurg,** Friedrich Wilhelm 1718-1795 NewAmDM
**Marquand,** David 1934- Who 92
**Marquand,** J P 1893-1960 FacFETw
**Marquand,** John P. 1893-1960 BenetAL 91
**Marquand,** John P., Jr. DrAPF 91
**Marquard,** Henry Francis 1954- WhoAmL 92
**Marquard,** Paul Joseph 1958- WhoWest 92
**Marquard,** William A. 1920- IntWW 91
**Marquard,** William Albert 1920- WhoFI 92
**Marquardt,** Charles L 1936- AmMWSc 92
**Marquardt,** Christel Elisabeth 1935- WhoAmL 92
**Marquardt,** Diana 1954- AmMWSc 92
**Marquardt,** Donald Wesley 1929- AmMWSc 92
**Marquardt,** Hans Wilhelm Joe 1938- AmMWSc 92
**Marquardt,** James Leonard 1957- WhoEnt 92, WhoWest 92
**Marquardt,** Kathleen Patricia 1944- WhoFI 92
**Marquardt,** Klaus Max 1926- IntWW 91
**Marquardt,** Larry Dean 1950- WhoMW 92
**Marquardt,** Meril E 1926- WhoIns 92
**Marquardt,** Meril Eugene 1926- WhoWest 92
**Marquardt,** Richard G 1923- WhoAmP 91
**Marquardt,** Robert Richard 1943- WhoAmL 92
**Marquardt,** Roland Paul 1913- AmMWSc 92
**Marquardt,** Ronald Ralph 1935- AmMWSc 92
**Marquardt,** Warren William AmMWSc 92
**Marquardt,** William Charles 1924- AmMWSc 92
**Marquart,** John R 1933- AmMWSc 92
**Marquart,** John Robert 1933- WhoMW 92
**Marquart,** Ronald Gary 1938- AmMWSc 92
**Marques,** Joao Reis WhoRel 92
**Marques,** Rene 1919-1979 DcLB 113 [port]
**Marques,** Walter Waldemar Pego 1936- WhoFI 92
**Marquess,** Lawrence Wade 1950- WhoAmL 92, WhoWest 92
**Marquess,** William Hoge 1918- WhoIns 92
**Marquet,** Adrien Theodore Ernest 1884-1955 BiDExR
**Marquette,** Gayle Dean 1932- WhoRel 92
**Marquette,** I. Edward 1950- WhoAmL 92
**Marquette,** Jacques 1637-1675 BenetAL 91
**Marquez,** Alfred Martinez 1931- WhoWest 92
**Marquez,** Alfredo C. 1922- WhoAmL 92, WhoWest 92
**Marquez,** Alfredo Chavez 1922- WhoHisp 92
**Marquez,** Anthony Philip 1950- WhoWest 92
**Marquez,** Camilo Raoul 1942- WhoBlA 92
**Marquez,** Emilio Eustaquio 1938- WhoRel 92
**Marquez,** Enrique 1952- WhoHisp 92
**Marquez,** Felix S. 1942- WhoHisp 92
**Marquez,** Francisco Javier 1947- WhoHisp 92
**Marquez,** Gabriel Garcia IntWW 91, NewYTBS 91 [port]
**Marquez,** Gabriel Garcia 1928- IntAu&W 91, Who 92
**Marquez,** Harold B. 1935- WhoHisp 92
**Marquez,** Janet Sue 1955- WhoWest 92
**Marquez,** Joaquin Alfredo 1942- WhoAmL 92
**Marquez,** Jose D. L. WhoHisp 92
**Marquez,** Joseph A 1930- AmMWSc 92
**Marquez,** Leo 1932- WhoHisp 92
**Marquez,** Lorenzo Antonio, Jr. 1940- WhoHisp 92
**Marquez,** Maria D. 1931- WhoHisp 92
**Marquez,** Martina Zenaida 1935- WhoHisp 92, WhoWest 92
**Marquez,** Maxine F. 1940- WhoHisp 92
**Marquez,** Nancy WhoHisp 92
**Marquez,** Pascual Gregory 1937- WhoHisp 92
**Marquez,** Rosa Luisa 1947- WhoHisp 92
**Marquez,** Rosalinda C. WhoHisp 92
**Marquez,** Rosanna Alicia 1959- WhoHisp 92
**Marquez,** Tony Estevan, Jr. 1966- WhoHisp 92
**Marquez,** Victor Esteban 1943- AmMWSc 92
**Marquez De La Plata Irrarrazaval,** Alfonso 1933- IntWW 91
**Marquez Sterling,** Carlos d1991 NewYTBS 91
**Marquez Sterling,** Carlos 1898-1991 WhoHisp 92N
**Marquez-Villanueva,** Francisco 1931- WhoHisp 92
**Marquina,** Gerardo E. 1950- WhoHisp 92
**Marquis** Who 92
**Marquis,** David Alan 1934- AmMWSc 92
**Marquis,** Don 1878-1937 BenetAL 91
**Marquis,** Edward Thomas 1939- AmMWSc 92
**Marquis,** Gail Annette 1954- BlkOlyM
**Marquis,** James Douglas 1921- Who 92
**Marquis,** Judith Kathleen 1946- AmMWSc 92
**Marquis,** Marilyn A 1926- AmMWSc 92

**Marquis,** Norman Ronald 1936- AmMWSc 92
**Marquis,** Robert E 1934- AmMWSc 92
**Marquis,** William Oscar 1944- WhoAmL 92
**Marquit,** Erwin 1926- AmMWSc 92
**Marquit,** Marla Denise 1965- WhoWest 92
**Marqusee,** Jeffrey Alan 1954- AmMWSc 92
**Marr,** Allen Gerald 1929- AmMWSc 92
**Marr,** Carmel Carrington WhoAmP 91, WhoBlA 92
**Marr,** David Erskine 1939- WhoAmL 92
**Marr,** David G. 1937- WrDr 92
**Marr,** David Henry 1938- AmMWSc 92
**Marr,** David Marshall 1943- WhoWest 92
**Marr,** Geoffrey Vickers IntWW 91
**Marr,** Henry L. 1927- WhoEnt 92, WhoMW 92
**Marr,** J. Joseph WhoMW 92
**Marr,** James Joseph 1938- AmMWSc 92
**Marr,** John Maurice 1920- AmMWSc 92
**Marr,** Leslie 1922- TwCPaSc
**Marr,** Leslie Lynn 1922- Who 92
**Marr,** Luther Reese 1925- WhoEnt 92
**Marr,** Robert B 1932- AmMWSc 92
**Marr,** Thomas J. 1942- WhoMW 92
**Marr,** Warren, II 1916- WhoBlA 92
**Marr,** Wilhelm 1819-1904 EncTR 91
**Marr,** William W 1936- IntAu&W 91
**Marr,** William Wei-Yi 1936- AmMWSc 92, WhoMW 92
**Marr-Johnson,** Frederick James Maugham 1936- Who 92
**Marra,** Dorothea Catherine 1922- AmMWSc 92
**Marra,** Kathy Shields 1954- WhoMW 92
**Marra,** Michael Dominick 1922- AmMWSc 92
**Marra,** Peter Gerald 1940- WhoWest 92
**Marra,** Samuel Patrick 1927- WhoMW 92
**Marracci,** Thomas Kenneth 1965- WhoWest 92
**Marraccino,** Robert Louis 1960- WhoWest 92
**Marrack,** Philip Reginald 1922- Who 92
**Marrack,** Philippa Charlotte 1945- AmMWSc 92
**Marraffino,** Elizabeth DrAPF 91
**Marrapese,** Casto 1918- WhoRel 92
**Marrapese,** Edward V 1942- WhoAmP 91
**Marrapode,** Thomas Randall WhoMW 92
**Marras,** William Steven 1952- AmMWSc 92
**Marrazzi,** Mary Ann 1945- AmMWSc 92
**Marre,** Romola Mary 1920- Who 92
**Marreco,** Anne IntAu&W 91X, WrDr 92
**Marrello,** Vincent 1947- AmMWSc 92
**Marrero,** Charles A. 1942- WhoHisp 92
**Marrero,** Dilka E. 1961- WhoHisp 92
**Marrero,** Hector G 1955- AmMWSc 92
**Marrero,** Manuel WhoAmP 91
**Marrero,** Manuel 1954- WhoHisp 92
**Marrero,** Thomas R. 1936- WhoHisp 92
**Marrero,** Thomas Raphael 1936- AmMWSc 92
**Marrero-Favreau,** Gloria 1948- WhoHisp 92
**Marrero Hueca,** Manuel WhoHisp 92
**Marrero Perez,** Anibal WhoHisp 92
**Marrero Perez,** Annibal WhoAmP 91
**Marrese,** Richard John 1931- AmMWSc 92
**Marrett,** Cora B. 1942- WhoBlA 92
**Marriage,** Lowell Dean 1923- AmMWSc 92
**Marric,** J.J. ConAu 135
**Marrinan,** James P. LesBEnT 92
**Marriner,** David Richard 1934- WhoFI 92
**Marriner,** John P 1948- AmMWSc 92
**Marriner,** Neville 1924- ConMus 7 [port], IntWW 91, NewAmDM, Who 92
**Marriott,** Alan 1952- TwCPaSc
**Marriott,** B Gladys 1922- WhoAmP 91
**Marriott,** Bryant Hayes 1936- Who 92
**Marriott,** Crittenden 1867-1932 ScFEYrs
**Marriott,** David Daniel 1939- WhoAmP 91
**Marriott,** Frederick 1860-1941 TwCPaSc
**Marriott,** Henry Joseph Llewellyn 1917- AmMWSc 92
**Marriott,** Hugh Cavendish S. Who 92
**Marriott,** John Brook 1922- Who 92
**Marriott,** John Miles 1935- Who 92
**Marriott,** John W., Jr. 1932- WhoFI 92
**Marriott,** Lawrence Frederick 1913- AmMWSc 92
**Marriott,** Martin Marriott 1932- Who 92
**Marriott,** Richard 1929- AmMWSc 92
**Marriott,** Richard Edwin 1939- WhoFI 92
**Marriott,** Salima Siler 1940- WhoAmP 91, WhoBlA 92
**Marris,** James Hugh Spencer 1937- Who 92
**Marris,** Robin Lapthorn 1924- Who 92
**Marris,** Stephen Nicholson 1930- IntWW 91, Who 92
**Marrison,** Geoffrey Edward 1923- Who 92
**Marro,** Michael Carminie 1953- WhoWest 92
**Marrocco,** Richard Thomas 1943- AmMWSc 92
**Marron,** Darlene Lorraine 1946- WhoFI 92
**Marron,** Donald Baird 1934- WhoFI 92
**Marron,** Michael Thomas 1943- AmMWSc 92
**Marrone,** Daniel Scott 1950- WhoFI 92
**Marrone,** John Joseph 1946- WhoMW 92
**Marrone,** Michael Joseph 1937- AmMWSc 92
**Marrone,** Pamela Gail 1956- AmMWSc 92
**Marrone,** Paul Vincent 1932- AmMWSc 92
**Marroquin,** Francisco 1477- HisDSpE
**Marroquin,** Manuel A. 1947- WhoHisp 92
**Marroquin,** Mario 1955- WhoHisp 92
**Marroquin,** Mauricio 1945- WhoHisp 92
**Marroquin,** Patricia 1957- WhoHisp 92
**Marroquin,** Samuel Najar 1932- WhoHisp 92
**Marrow,** Christopher Charles 1947- WhoFI 92
**Marrow,** Marva Jan 1948- WhoWest 92
**Marrow,** Steven Paul 1961- WhoFI 92
**Marrow-Mooring,** Barbara A. 1945- WhoBlA 92
**Marrs,** Barry Lee 1942- AmMWSc 92
**Marrs,** John Baxter 1947- WhoMW 92
**Marrs,** Leo Richard, Jr. 1949- WhoWest 92
**Marrs,** Raphael Hildan 1966- WhoBlA 92
**Marrs,** Rick Roy 1952- WhoRel 92
**Marrs,** Roscoe Earl 1946- AmMWSc 92
**Marrs,** Stella 1932- WhoBlA 92
**Marrujo,** Ralph WhoHisp 92
**Marrus,** Eliot WhoRel 92
**Marrus,** Richard 1932- AmMWSc 92
**Marryat,** Frank BenetAL 91
**Marryat,** Frederick 1792-1838 ScFEYrs
**Marryat,** Frederick 1792-1848 BenetAL 91, RfGEnL 91
**Mars,** Alvin 1943- WhoRel 92
**Mars,** Forrest, Jr. WhoFI 92
**Mars,** Harvey WhoEnt 92
**Mars,** Kenneth 1936- IntMPA 92
**Mars,** Robert 1955- WhoWest 92
**Mars,** Robert Sumner, Jr. 1926- WhoFI 92
**Mars-Jones,** Adam 1954- ConNov 91, Who 92
**Mars-Jones,** William 1915- Who 92
**Marsalis,** Branford 1960- CurBio 91 [port], NewAmDM, WhoBlA 92, WhoEnt 92
**Marsalis,** Ellis WhoEnt 92A
**Marsalis,** Wynton 1961- ConMus 6 [port], FacFETw [port], IntWW 91, NewAmDM, WhoBlA 92, WhoEnt 92
**Marsano,** Francis C WhoAmP 91
**Marsch,** Carol Willa 1925- WhoMW 92
**Marsch,** Lucy-Leone 1912- IntAu&W 91
**Marsch,** Mitch 1953- WhoRel 92
**Marschall,** Albert Rhoades 1921- AmMWSc 92
**Marschall,** Charles Joseph 1939- WhoIns 92
**Marschall,** Charles W 1930- AmMWSc 92
**Marschall von Bieberstein,** Wilhelm 1890-1935 EncTR 91
**Marscher,** William Donnelly 1948- AmMWSc 92
**Marschner,** Edward Charles 1945- WhoAmL 92
**Marschner,** Heinrich August 1795-1861 NewAmDM
**Marschner,** Walter Arthur 1940- WhoAmP 91
**Marsden,** Arthur Whitcombe 1911- Who 92
**Marsden,** Brian Geoffrey 1937- AmMWSc 92
**Marsden,** Brian William Hugh 1932- WhoFI 92
**Marsden,** D J 1933- AmMWSc 92
**Marsden,** David 1938- Who 92
**Marsden,** David Bartlet 1948- WhoEnt 92
**Marsden,** Edmund Murray 1946- Who 92
**Marsden,** Frank 1923- Who 92
**Marsden,** Halsey M 1933- AmMWSc 92
**Marsden,** Herci Ivana 1937- WhoEnt 92
**Marsden,** Jerrold Eldon 1942- AmMWSc 92
**Marsden,** John 1950- ConAu 135, SmATA 66
**Marsden,** John Christopher 1937- Who 92
**Marsden,** K C WhoAmP 91
**Marsden,** Nigel 1940- Who 92
**Marsden,** Peter Nicholas 1932- Who 92
**Marsden,** Peter Richard Valentine 1940- IntAu&W 91, WrDr 92
**Marsden,** Ralph Walter 1911- AmMWSc 92
**Marsden,** Richard 1675?-1742 DcNCBi 4
**Marsden,** Richard Anton 1966- WhoEnt 92
**Marsden,** Rufus 1695-1750 DcNCBi 4
**Marsden,** Sullivan S, Jr 1922- AmMWSc 92
**Marsden,** Susan 1931- Who 92
**Marsden,** William 1940- Who 92
**Marsden-Smedley,** Philip 1961- ConAu 135
**Marse Henry** 1840-1921 BenetAL 91
**Marsee,** Susanne Irene 1941- WhoEnt 92
**Marseille,** Hans-Joachim 1919-1942 EncTR 91 [port]
**Marsella,** Anthony Samuel 1947- WhoAmP 91
**Marsh** Who 92
**Marsh,** Baron 1928- IntWW 91, Who 92
**Marsh,** Alice Garrett 1908- AmMWSc 92
**Marsh,** Alphonso Howard 1938- WhoBlA 92
**Marsh,** B J 1940- WhoAmP 91
**Marsh,** Bazil Roland 1921- Who 92
**Marsh,** Beaton 1914- WhoAmP 91
**Marsh,** Ben Franklin 1940- WhoBlA 92
**Marsh,** Benjamin Bruce 1926- AmMWSc 92
**Marsh,** Benjamin Franklin 1927- WhoAmP 91
**Marsh,** Benjamin V 1818- BiInAmS
**Marsh,** Bertrand Duane 1938- AmMWSc 92
**Marsh,** Brice Felix 1938- WhoAmP 91
**Marsh,** Bruce Burton 1934- AmMWSc 92
**Marsh,** Bruce David 1947- AmMWSc 92
**Marsh,** Cedric 1924- AmMWSc 92
**Marsh,** Chas 1938- WhoEnt 92
**Marsh,** Clare Teitgen 1934- WhoMW 92
**Marsh,** Clayton Edward 1942- WhoMW 92
**Marsh,** Daniel Aloysius, Jr. 1941- WhoAmL 92
**Marsh,** Daniel G 1937- WhoAmP 91
**Marsh,** Dave 1950- SmATA 66 [port]
**Marsh,** David George 1940- AmMWSc 92
**Marsh,** David Paul 1934- AmMWSc 92
**Marsh,** Derick Rupert Clement 1928- IntWW 91, WrDr 92
**Marsh,** Donald Charles Burr 1926- AmMWSc 92
**Marsh,** Donald Gene 1936- WhoBlA 92
**Marsh,** Donald Jay 1934- AmMWSc 92
**Marsh,** Doris Elaine 1931- WhoEnt 92
**Marsh,** Doug 1958- WhoBlA 92
**Marsh,** Edward Frank Who 92
**Marsh,** Frank I 1924- WhoAmP 91
**Marsh,** Frank Irving 1924- WhoMW 92
**Marsh,** Frank Lewis 1899- AmMWSc 92
**Marsh,** Frederick Leon 1935- AmMWSc 92
**Marsh,** Geoffrey Gordon Ward Who 92
**Marsh,** George Perkins 1801-1882 BenetAL 91, BiInAmS
**Marsh,** Gordon Victor 1929- Who 92
**Marsh,** Helen Unger 1925- WhoMW 92
**Marsh,** Henry Hooper 1898- Who 92
**Marsh,** Henry John 1913- Who 92
**Marsh,** Henry L., III 1933- WhoBlA 92
**Marsh,** Howard Stephen 1942- AmMWSc 92
**Marsh,** Hugh Leroy, Jr. 1929- WhoFI 92
**Marsh,** James 1794-1842 BenetAL 91
**Marsh,** James Alexander, Jr 1940- AmMWSc 92
**Marsh,** James Lawrence 1945- AmMWSc 92
**Marsh,** James Robert 1947- WhoWest 92
**Marsh,** Jayne Elizabeth 1954- WhoEnt 92
**Marsh,** Jean 1934- IntMPA 92
**Marsh,** Jean Lyndsey Torren 1934- Who 92, WhoEnt 92
**Marsh,** Joan Knight 1934- WhoEnt 92
**Marsh,** John Who 92
**Marsh,** John 1904- IntAu&W 91, Who 92, WrDr 92
**Marsh,** John F WhoAmP 91
**Marsh,** John L 1916- AmMWSc 92
**Marsh,** John O, Jr 1926- WhoAmP 91
**Marsh,** John Richard 1935- WhoIns 92
**Marsh,** Jon Kevin 1959- WhoMW 92
**Marsh,** Joseph Virgil 1952- WhoFI 92
**Marsh,** Julian Bunsick 1926 AmMWSc 92
**Marsh,** Kenneth Lee 1952- WhoWest 92
**Marsh,** Kenneth Neil 1939- AmMWSc 92
**Marsh,** Leland C 1928- AmMWSc 92
**Marsh,** Leonard George 1930- Who 92
**Marsh,** Malcolm F. 1928- WhoAmL 92, WhoWest 92
**Marsh,** Marcus M 1949- WhoAmP 91
**Marsh,** Max Martin 1923- AmMWSc 92, WhoMW 92
**Marsh,** McAfee 1939- WhoBlA 92
**Marsh,** Michael Raymond 1957- WhoFI 92
**Marsh,** Miles L. WhoFI 92
**Marsh,** Nevill Francis 1907- Who 92
**Marsh,** Ngaio 1895-1982 RfGEnL 91
**Marsh,** Ngaio 1899-1982 FacFETw
**Marsh,** Norman Stayner 1913- Who 92, WrDr 92
**Marsh,** Othniel Charles 1831-1899 BiInAmS
**Marsh,** Ozan James 1920- WhoEnt 92
**Marsh,** Paul Christopher 1955- WhoEnt 92
**Marsh,** Paul Malcolm 1936- AmMWSc 92
**Marsh,** Paul Rodney 1947- Who 92
**Marsh,** Pearl-Alice 1946- WhoBlA 92
**Marsh,** Peter T. 1935- WrDr 92
**Marsh,** R. Bruce 1929- WhoMW 92
**Marsh,** Richard Edward 1922- AmMWSc 92
**Marsh,** Richard Floyd 1939- AmMWSc 92
**Marsh,** Richard L 1946- AmMWSc 92
**Marsh,** Robert 1926-1979 ConAu 134
**Marsh,** Robert Cecil 1944- AmMWSc 92
**Marsh,** Robert Charles 1924- WhoMW 92
**Marsh,** Robert Henry 1837-1924 DcNCBi 4
**Marsh,** Robert Houston 1959- WhoAmP 91
**Marsh,** Robert James 1954- WhoMW 92
**Marsh,** Robert Mortimer 1931- WrDr 92
**Marsh,** Robert Thomas 1925- WhoFI 92, WhoWest 92
**Marsh,** Roger 1949- ConCom 92
**Marsh,** Shirley Mae 1925- WhoAmP 91
**Marsh,** Stephen Lawrence 1952- WhoAmL 92
**Marsh,** Stuart Emmet 1951- WhoWest 92
**Marsh,** Susan 1958- WhoFI 92
**Marsh,** Tamra Gwendolyn 1946- WhoBlA 92
**Marsh,** Terrence George 1941- AmMWSc 92
**Marsh,** Thomas Archie 1951- WhoWest 92
**Marsh,** William A., Jr. 1927- WhoBlA 92
**Marsh,** William Ernest 1939- AmMWSc 92
**Marsh,** William Laurence 1926- AmMWSc 92
**Marsh,** William Robert 1948- WhoMW 92
**Marsh-Lott,** Freddie Alexander 1949- WhoBlA 92
**Marshak,** Alan Howard 1938- AmMWSc 92
**Marshak,** Harvey 1927- AmMWSc 92
**Marshak,** Marvin Lloyd 1946- AmMWSc 92, WhoMW 92
**Marshak,** Robert E. 1916- IntWW 91
**Marshak,** Robert Eugene 1916- AmMWSc 92, WrDr 92
**Marshak,** Robert Reuben 1923- AmMWSc 92
**Marshak,** Samuil Yakovlevich 1887-1964 SovUnBD
**Marshak,** Stephen 1955- WhoMW 92
**Marshal,** Kit WhoWest 92
**Marshalek,** Eugene Richard 1936- AmMWSc 92, WhoMW 92
**Marshall** Who 92
**Marshall,** Alan 1938- IntMPA 92
**Marshall,** Alan George 1944- AmMWSc 92, WhoMW 92
**Marshall,** Alan R., Mrs. Who 92
**Marshall,** Alan Ralph Who 92
**Marshall,** Albert Prince 1914- WhoBlA 92
**Marshall,** Alexander Badenoch 1924- IntWW 91, Who 92
**Marshall,** Alton Garwood 1921- WhoFI 92
**Marshall,** Anita 1938- WhoBlA 92
**Marshall,** Ann Kelsey 1951- WhoAmP 91
**Marshall,** Anne Marie 1947- WhoAmL 92
**Marshall,** Archibald 1866-1934 ScFEYrs
**Marshall,** Armina d1991 NewYTBS 91
**Marshall,** Arthur, Jr. 1914- WhoRel 92
**Marshall,** Arthur C Who 92
**Marshall,** Arthur Elliott, Jr. 1960- WhoAmL 92
**Marshall,** Arthur Gregory George 1903- Who 92
**Marshall,** Arthur Hedley 1904- Who 92
**Marshall,** Arthur K. 1911- WhoAmL 92, WhoWest 92
**Marshall,** Arthur Stirling-Maxwell 1929- Who 92
**Marshall,** Betty J. 1950- WhoBlA 92
**Marshall,** Beulah Marian 1929- WhoEnt 92
**Marshall,** Bruce Thomas 1947- WhoRel 92
**Marshall,** Burke 1922- WhoAmL 92
**Marshall,** C. Travis 1926- WhoFI 92
**Marshall,** Cak 1943- WhoEnt 92
**Marshall,** Calvin Bromley, III 1932- WhoBlA 92
**Marshall,** Carl Leroy 1914- WhoBlA 92
**Marshall,** Carolyn Ann M. 1935- WhoRel 92
**Marshall,** Carolyn Ann McMurray 1935- WhoMW 92
**Marshall,** Carter Lee 1936- AmMWSc 92, WhoBlA 92
**Marshall,** Catherine 1880-1961 BiDBrF 2
**Marshall,** Cedric Russell 1936- IntWW 91, Who 92
**Marshall,** Charlene Jennings 1933- WhoBlA 92

**Marshall**, Charles Edmund 1903- AmMWSc 92
**Marshall**, Charles F 1943- AmMWSc 92
**Marshall**, Charles H. 1898-1983 WhoBlA 92N
**Marshall**, Charles Richard 1961- AmMWSc 92
**Marshall**, Charles Wheeler 1906- AmMWSc 92
**Marshall**, Christopher 1709-1797 BenetAL 91
**Marshall**, Christopher John 1964- WhoMW 92
**Marshall**, Clair Addison 1911- AmMWSc 92
**Marshall**, Cliff 1939- WhoAmP 91
**Marshall**, Clifford Wallace 1928- AmMWSc 92
**Marshall**, Cody WhoRel 92
**Marshall**, Colin 1933- IntWW 91, Who 92
**Marshall**, Colinette Gaillard 1945- WhoMW 92
**Marshall**, Consuelo B. 1936- WhoBlA 92
**Marshall**, Consuelo Bland 1936- WhoAmL 92
**Marshall**, Dale Earnest 1934- AmMWSc 92
**Marshall**, Dale Livingston 1944- WhoFI 92
**Marshall**, Daniel Alfred 1937- WhoAmP 91
**Marshall**, David 1941- Who 92
**Marshall**, David Lawrence 1939- WhoWest 92
**Marshall**, David Rollins 1959- WhoAmL 92
**Marshall**, David Saul 1908- IntWW 91
**Marshall**, David Scott 1942- TwCPaSc
**Marshall**, David Scott 1950- WhoAmP 91
**Marshall**, David Vance 1950- WhoAmL 92
**Marshall**, Delbert Allan 1937- AmMWSc 92, WhoMW 92
**Marshall**, Denis 1916- Who 92
**Marshall**, Don 1947- WhoAmL 92
**Marshall**, Don A., Sr. 1929- WhoBlA 92
**Marshall**, Donald D 1934- AmMWSc 92
**Marshall**, Donald E 1947- AmMWSc 92
**Marshall**, Donald Irving 1924- AmMWSc 92
**Marshall**, Donald James 1933- AmMWSc 92
**Marshall**, Donald James 1934- WhoBlA 92
**Marshall**, Donald Tompkins 1933- WhoFI 92
**Marshall**, Dorothy B. WhoWest 92
**Marshall**, E.G. 1910- IntMPA 92
**Marshall**, Edison 1894-1967 BenetAL 91
**Marshall**, Edison Tesla 1894-1967 ScFEYrs
**Marshall**, Edmund Ian 1940- Who 92
**Marshall**, Edward WrDr 92
**Marshall**, Edwin Cochran 1946- WhoBlA 92
**Marshall**, Elizabeth Margaret 1926- WrDr 92
**Marshall**, Ellen Ruth 1949- WhoAmL 92
**Marshall**, Eric 1955- WhoEnt 92
**Marshall**, Etta Marie-Imes 1932- WhoBlA 92
**Marshall**, Evelyn 1897- IntAu&W 91
**Marshall**, Finley Dee 1930- AmMWSc 92
**Marshall**, Francis J 1923- AmMWSc 92
**Marshall**, Frank IntMPA 92
**Marshall**, Frank Britt, III 1943- WhoBlA 92
**Marshall**, Frank Graham 1942- Who 92
**Marshall**, Frank W. WhoEnt 92
**Marshall**, Franklin Nick 1933- AmMWSc 92
**Marshall**, Fredda Who 92
**Marshall**, Frederic William 1721-1802 DcNCBi 4
**Marshall**, Frederick J 1920- AmMWSc 92
**Marshall**, Frederick James 1925- AmMWSc 92
**Marshall**, Gailen D, Jr 1950- AmMWSc 92
**Marshall**, Garland Ross 1940- AmMWSc 92
**Marshall**, Garry LesBEnT 92
**Marshall**, Garry 1934- IntMPA 92, WhoEnt 92
**Marshall**, Gary TwCWW 91
**Marshall**, Geoffrey 1929- IntWW 91, Who 92, WrDr 92
**Marshall**, George C 1880-1959 FacFETw [port], RComAH
**Marshall**, George Catlett 1880-1959 AmPolLe, WhoNob 90
**Marshall**, George Nichols 1920- WhoRel 92
**Marshall**, Gloria A. 1938- WhoBlA 92
**Marshall**, Grayson William, Jr 1943- AmMWSc 92, WhoWest 92
**Marshall**, Harold D. 1936- WhoFI 92
**Marshall**, Harold Gene 1928- AmMWSc 92
**Marshall**, Harold George 1929- AmMWSc 92
**Marshall**, Hazel Eleanor Who 92
**Marshall**, Heather 1949- AmMWSc 92
**Marshall**, Helen M WhoAmP 91
**Marshall**, Henry H. 1954- WhoBlA 92
**Marshall**, Henry Peter 1924- AmMWSc 92
**Marshall**, Herbert A. 1916- WhoBlA 92
**Marshall**, Herbert P.J. d1991 NewYTBS 91
**Marshall**, Herbert Percival James d1991 Who 92N
**Marshall**, Howard Lowen 1931- WhoEnt 92
**Marshall**, Howard Wright 1923- Who 92
**Marshall**, Hugh Phillips 1934- Who 92
**Marshall**, Humphry 1722-1801 BenetAL 91, BiInAmS
**Marshall**, I. N. 1931- ConAu 134
**Marshall**, J. Howard, II 1905- IntWW 91
**Marshall**, J Howard, III 1936- AmMWSc 92
**Marshall**, J P ScFEYrs
**Marshall**, Jack DrAPF 91
**Marshall**, Jack 1937- ConPo 91, IntAu&W 91, WrDr 92
**Marshall**, James 1941- Who 92
**Marshall**, James 1942- IntAu&W 91, WrDr 92
**Marshall**, James Arthur 1935- AmMWSc 92
**Marshall**, James E 1936- WhoIns 92
**Marshall**, James John 1943- AmMWSc 92
**Marshall**, James Kenneth 1952- WhoWest 92
**Marshall**, James Lawrence 1940- AmMWSc 92
**Marshall**, James Thomas 1941- WhoEnt 92
**Marshall**, James Tilden, Jr 1945- AmMWSc 92
**Marshall**, James Vance IntAu&W 91X, WrDr 92
**Marshall**, Janice 1946- WhoIns 92
**Marshall**, Jean McElroy 1922- AmMWSc 92
**Marshall**, Jeffrey Allan 1959- WhoRel 92
**Marshall**, Jeffrey David 1957- WhoAmL 92
**Marshall**, Jeremy Who 92
**Marshall**, John Who 92
**Marshall**, John 1755-1835 AmPolLe [port], RComAH
**Marshall**, John 1915- Who 92
**Marshall**, John 1922- Who 92, WrDr 92
**Marshall**, John Alexander 1922- Who 92
**Marshall**, John Aloysius 1928- WhoRel 92
**Marshall**, John Clifford 1935- AmMWSc 92
**Marshall**, John David 1940- WhoAmL 92
**Marshall**, John Dent 1946- WhoBlA 92
**Marshall**, John Donald 1921- WhoBlA 92
**Marshall**, John Foster 1948- AmMWSc 92
**Marshall**, John Jeremy 1938- Who 92
**Marshall**, John Leslie 1940- Who 92
**Marshall**, John McClellan 1943- WhoAmL 92
**Marshall**, John Patrick 1950- WhoAmL 92
**Marshall**, John Paul WhoEnt 92, WhoFI 92, WhoWest 92
**Marshall**, John Potter 1824?-1901 BiInAmS
**Marshall**, John Roger 1944- Who 92
**Marshall**, John Romney 1933- AmMWSc 92
**Marshall**, John Treutlen 1934- WhoAmL 92
**Marshall**, Jonnie Clanton 1932- WhoBlA 92
**Marshall**, Joseph Andrew 1937- AmMWSc 92
**Marshall**, Judy K. 1958- WhoRel 92
**Marshall**, Keith AmMWSc 92
**Marshall**, Keith MacDonald 1943- WhoMW 92
**Marshall**, Kenneth Aloe 1927- WhoMW 92
**Marshall**, Kenneth D 1941- AmMWSc 92
**Marshall**, Kneale Thomas 1936- AmMWSc 92
**Marshall**, Lawrence C. 1959- WhoAmL 92
**Marshall**, Lee D. 1956- WhoMW 92
**Marshall**, Lenore Guinzburg 1897-1971 AmPeW
**Marshall**, Leonard 1961- WhoBlA 92
**Marshall**, Leonel BlkOlyM
**Marshall**, Leslie Brusletten 1943- AmMWSc 92
**Marshall**, Lester Bell 1928- WhoWest 92
**Marshall**, Lewis West, Jr. 1958- WhoBlA 92
**Marshall**, Linda Rae 1940- WhoMW 92
**Marshall**, Lois 1925- NewAmDM
**Marshall**, Louis 1856-1929 DcAmImH
**Marshall**, Louise Hanson 1908- AmMWSc 92
**Marshall**, Margaret 1908- WrDr 92
**Marshall**, Margaret Anne 1949- IntWW 91, Who 92
**Marshall**, Marilyn Josephine 1945- WhoAmL 92
**Marshall**, Mark Anthony 1937- Who 92
**Marshall**, Martin John 1914- Who 92
**Marshall**, Mary Aydelotte 1921- WhoAmP 91
**Marshall**, Mary Jones WhoWest 92
**Marshall**, Maryan Lorraine 1940- AmMWSc 92
**Marshall**, Matthias Murray 1841-1912 DcNCBi 4
**Marshall**, Maurice K 1921- AmMWSc 92
**Marshall**, Meryl Corinblit 1949- WhoAmP 91, WhoEnt 92
**Marshall**, Michael Who 92
**Marshall**, Michael Eric 1936- Who 92
**Marshall**, Murray Mark, Jr. 1918- WhoRel 92
**Marshall**, Nelson 1914- AmMWSc 92
**Marshall**, Noel Hedley 1934- Who 92
**Marshall**, Norman Barry 1926- AmMWSc 92
**Marshall**, Norman Bertram 1915- Who 92
**Marshall**, Norton Little 1927- AmMWSc 92
**Marshall**, Oshley Roy 1920- Who 92
**Marshall**, Owen 1941- ConNov 91
**Marshall**, P. J. 1933- WrDr 92
**Marshall**, Patricia Mary 1930- WhoAmP 91
**Marshall**, Paul M. 1947- WhoBlA 92
**Marshall**, Paul Macklin 1923- WhoFI 92
**Marshall**, Paule DrAPF 91
**Marshall**, Paule 1929- AfrAmW, BenetAL 91, BlkLC [port], ConNov 91, IntAu&W 91, WrDr 92
**Marshall**, Paule Burke 1929- NotBlAW 92, WhoBlA 92
**Marshall**, Penny LesBEnT 92, ReelWom
**Marshall**, Penny 1942- IntMPA 92, News 91 [port], -91-3 [port]
**Marshall**, Penny 1943- WhoEnt 92
**Marshall**, Percy Edwin Alan J. Who 92
**Marshall**, Peter IntMPA 92
**Marshall**, Peter 1902-1949 RelLAm 91
**Marshall**, Peter 1924- IntWW 91, Who 92
**Marshall**, Peter 1930- Who 92
**Marshall**, Peter Izod 1927- Who 92
**Marshall**, Peter James 1933- Who 92
**Marshall**, Peter L. 1930- WhoEnt 92
**Marshall**, Peter W. 1947- WhoEnt 92
**Marshall**, Philippa Frances 1920- Who 92
**Marshall**, Pluria W., Sr. 1937- WhoBlA 92
**Marshall**, Pluria William, Jr. 1962- WhoBlA 92
**Marshall**, Prentice Henry 1926- WhoMW 92
**Marshall**, Ray 1928- IntWW 91
**Marshall**, Reese 1942- WhoBlA 92
**Marshall**, Rich James 1944- WhoRel 92
**Marshall**, Richard Allen 1935- AmMWSc 92
**Marshall**, Richard Blair 1928- AmMWSc 92
**Marshall**, Richard Douglass 1931- WhoBlA 92
**Marshall**, Richard Lee 1950- WhoWest 92
**Marshall**, Richard Oliver 1922- AmMWSc 92
**Marshall**, Richard Treeger 1925- WhoAmL 92
**Marshall**, Robert 1920- Who 92
**Marshall**, Robert Chapman 1955- WhoAmL 92
**Marshall**, Robert Charles 1931- WhoFI 92
**Marshall**, Robert Emmett 1947- WhoWest 92
**Marshall**, Robert Herman 1925- AmMWSc 92
**Marshall**, Robert I 1946- WhoAmP 91
**Marshall**, Robert James 1918- WhoRel 92
**Marshall**, Robert Leckie 1913- Who 92
**Marshall**, Robert Michael 1930- Who 92
**Marshall**, Robert P 1930- AmMWSc 92
**Marshall**, Robert T 1932- AmMWSc 92
**Marshall**, Roger Sydenham 1913- Who 92
**Marshall**, Rosalind Kay IntAu&W 91, WrDr 92
**Marshall**, Rosamund 1900- BenetAL 91
**Marshall**, Rosemarie 1943- AmMWSc 92
**Marshall**, Roy Who 92
**Marshall**, Roy 1920- WrDr 92
**Marshall**, Russell Who 92
**Marshall**, Russell Frank 1941- WhoFI 92
**Marshall**, Russell Leon 1905- WhoBlA 92
**Marshall**, Ruth 1961- IntAu&W 91
**Marshall**, Sally DrAPF 91
**Marshall**, Sally J 1949- AmMWSc 92
**Marshall**, Sally Jean 1949- WhoWest 92
**Marshall**, Samson A 1924- AmMWSc 92
**Marshall**, Samuel Wilson 1934- AmMWSc 92
**Marshall**, Sarah Catherine Wood 1914-1983 RelLAm 91
**Marshall**, Scott WhoWest 92
**Marshall**, Scott Mark 1958- WhoMW 92
**Marshall**, Sheila Hermes 1934- WhoAmL 92
**Marshall**, Sherrie Patrice 1953- WhoFI 92
**Marshall**, Sheryl 1949- WhoFI 92
**Marshall**, Stanley V 1927- AmMWSc 92
**Marshall**, Steve 1943- WhoEnt 92
**Marshall**, Steven Michael 1936- WhoEnt 92
**Marshall**, Tari Beth 1955- WhoMW 92
**Marshall**, Teresa Lynn 1964- IntAu&W 91
**Marshall**, Theodore 1927- AmMWSc 92
**Marshall**, Thomas C 1935- AmMWSc 92
**Marshall**, Thomas Daniel 1929- Who 92
**Marshall**, Thomas O 1920- WhoAmP 91
**Marshall**, Thomas Riley 1854-1925 AmPolLe
**Marshall**, Thomas W 1940- WhoAmP 91
**Marshall**, Thurgood NewYTBS 91 [port]
**Marshall**, Thurgood 1908- AmPolLe, ConBlB 1 [port], FacFETw [port], IntWW 91, RComAH, Who 92, WhoAmL 92, WhoAmP 91, WhoBlA 92
**Marshall**, Thurgood, Jr. 1956- WhoBlA 92
**Marshall**, Timothy H. 1949- WhoBlA 92
**Marshall**, Tom 1938- IntAu&W 91, WrDr 92
**Marshall**, Tom, Sr. 1927- WhoBlA 92
**Marshall**, Tom Stanley 1953- WhoWest 92
**Marshall**, Valerie Margaret 1945- Who 92
**Marshall**, Victor R 1947- WhoAmP 91
**Marshall**, Victor Riton 1947- WhoAmL 92
**Marshall**, Vincent dePaul 1943- AmMWSc 92
**Marshall**, Walter Lincoln 1925- AmMWSc 92
**Marshall**, Warren 1922- WhoBlA 92
**Marshall**, Wayne Edward 1944- AmMWSc 92
**Marshall**, Wilber Buddyhia 1962- WhoBlA 92
**Marshall**, Wilfred L. 1935- WhoBlA 92
**Marshall**, William ConAu 133
**Marshall**, William 1912- Who 92
**Marshall**, William 1944- WrDr 92
**Marshall**, William C WhoAmP 91
**Marshall**, William Emmett AmMWSc 92
**Marshall**, William G 1942- WhoAmP 91
**Marshall**, William Gilbert 1946- WhoMW 92
**Marshall**, William Hampton 1912- AmMWSc 92
**Marshall**, William Horace 1924- WhoBlA 92
**Marshall**, William Huston 1926- WhoAmP 91
**Marshall**, William Joseph 1929- AmMWSc 92
**Marshall**, William Leitch 1925- AmMWSc 92
**Marshall**, William Leonard 1944- ConAu 133
**Marshall**, William Porter 1950- WhoAmL 92, WhoMW 92
**Marshall**, William Smithson 1951- AmMWSc 92
**Marshall**, Winston Stanley 1937- AmMWSc 92
**Marshall**, Wolf 1949- WhoWest 92
**Marshall**, Zena 1926- IntMPA 92
**Marshall-Andrews**, Robert Graham 1944- Who 92
**Marshall Evans**, David Who 92
**Marshall Of Goring**, Baron 1932- IntWW 91, Who 92
**Marshall of Leeds**, Baron d1990 Who 92N
**Marshall-Walker**, Denise Elizabeth 1952- WhoBlA 92
**Marshall-Walker**, Robert William 1945- WhoWest 92
**Marsham** Who 92
**Marshburn**, Christopher Shawn 1961- WhoAmL 92
**Marshburn**, Everett Lee 1948- WhoBlA 92
**Marshburn**, Sandra DrAPF 91
**Marshek**, Kurt M 1943- AmMWSc 92
**Marshi**, Gabriel Nicholas 1957- WhoFI 92
**Marsho**, Thomas V 1940- AmMWSc 92
**Marsi**, Kenneth Larue 1928- AmMWSc 92
**Marsicano**, Nicholas d1991 NewYTBS 91
**Marsico**, Ronald S 1947- WhoAmP 91
**Marsiglio dei Mainardini** 1275?-1342? DcLB 115
**Marsilius of Padua** 1275?-1342? DcLB 115
**Marske**, John William 1963- WhoFI 92
**Marsland**, David B 1926- AmMWSc 92
**Marsland**, Edward Abson 1923- Who 92
**Marsland**, T Anthony 1937- AmMWSc 92
**Marsnik**, Bernard J 1934- WhoAmP 91
**Marsocci**, Velio Arthur 1928- AmMWSc 92
**Marsten**, Richard IntAu&W 91X, TwCSFW 91, WrDr 92
**Marsten**, Richard B 1925- AmMWSc 92
**Marsters**, Gerald F 1932- AmMWSc 92
**Marston**, Bertram WhoAmP 91
**Marston**, Charles H 1932- AmMWSc 92

**Marston,** Edgar Jean, III 1939- *WhoAmL 92, WhoFI 92*
**Marston,** George Andrews 1908- *AmMWSc 92*
**Marston,** Jeff *WhoAmP 91*
**Marston,** Jerrilyn Greene 1945- *WhoAmL 92*
**Marston,** John 1576?-1634 *RfGEnL 91*
**Marston,** John Westland 1819-1890 *RfGEnL 91*
**Marston,** Michael 1936- *WhoFI 92, WhoWest 92*
**Marston,** Philip Leslie 1948- *AmMWSc 92*
**Marston,** Robert Andrew 1937- *WhoFI 92*
**Marston,** Robert E 1922- *WhoAmP 91*
**Marston,** Robert Quarles 1923- *AmMWSc 92, IntWW 91*
**Marston,** Ronald Clyde 1942- *WhoFI 92*
**Marszalek,** John F. 1939- *WrDr 92*
**Marta,** Ferenc 1929- *IntWW 91*
**Marta,** Richard Dale 1941- *WhoFI 92*
**Martan,** Joseph Rudolf 1949- *WhoFI 92, WhoMW 92*
**Martarella,** Franc David *WhoEnt 92*
**Martel,** Eva Leona 1945- *WhoFI 92*
**Martel,** Gene 1916- *IntMPA 92*
**Martel,** Hardy C 1927- *AmMWSc 92*
**Martel,** Marty *WhoEnt 92*
**Martel,** William 1927- *AmMWSc 92*
**Martell,** Arthur Earl 1916- *AmMWSc 92*
**Martell,** Edward A 1918- *AmMWSc 92*
**Martell,** Edward Drewett d1989 *Who 92N*
**Martell,** Hugh 1912- *Who 92*
**Martell,** James *IntAu&W 91X, TwCWW 91*
**Martell,** Michael Joseph, Jr 1932- *AmMWSc 92*
**Martell,** Ralph G. *DrAPF 91*
**Martell,** Saundra Adkins 1946- *WhoAmL 92*
**Martellaro,** Joseph A 1924- *IntAu&W 91*
**Martellaro,** Joseph Alexander 1924- *WhoMW 92, WrDr 92*
**Martelli,** Claudio 1944- *IntWW 91*
**Martelli,** Diego 1838-1896 *ThHEIm [port]*
**Martelli,** George Ansley 1903- *WrDr 92*
**Martello,** Leo Louis 1931- *RelLAm 91*
**Martello,** Richard 1945- *WhoMW 92*
**Martellock,** Arthur Carl 1928- *AmMWSc 92*
**Marten,** David Franklin 1948- *AmMWSc 92*
**Marten,** Francis William 1916- *Who 92*
**Marten,** Gordon C 1935- *AmMWSc 92*
**Marten,** James Frederick 1931- *AmMWSc 92*
**Martens,** Alexander E 1923- *AmMWSc 92*
**Martens,** Betsy Van der Veer 1954- *WhoFI 92*
**Martens,** Christopher Sargent 1946- *AmMWSc 92*
**Martens,** David Charles 1933- *AmMWSc 92*
**Martens,** Donald Mathias 1925- *WhoMW 92*
**Martens,** Edward John 1938- *AmMWSc 92*
**Martens,** Harold Arthur 1941- *WhoWest 92*
**Martens,** Hinrich R 1934- *AmMWSc 92*
**Martens,** James Hart Curry 1901- *AmMWSc 92*
**Martens,** John Dale 1943- *WhoFI 92*
**Martens,** John George 1945- *WhoAmP 91*
**Martens,** John William 1934- *AmMWSc 92*
**Martens,** Larry D. *WhoRel 92*
**Martens,** Leslie Vernon 1938- *AmMWSc 92*
**Martens,** Lyle Charles 1935- *WhoMW 92*
**Martens,** Margaret Elizabeth *AmMWSc 92*
**Martens,** Ralph R. 1943- *IntMPA 92*
**Martens,** Roy Michael 1950- *WhoFI 92, WhoMW 92*
**Martens,** Vernon Edward 1912- *AmMWSc 92*
**Martens,** Waldo Gerald 1921- *WhoAmP 91*
**Martens,** Wilfried 1936- *IntWW 91*
**Martens,** William Stephen 1935- *AmMWSc 92*
**Martensen,** Hans Ludvig *WhoRel 92*
**Martensen,** Todd Martin 1943- *AmMWSc 92*
**Martenson,** David Louis 1934- *WhoAmP 91*
**Martenson,** Jan 1933- *IntWW 91*
**Martenson,** Russell Eric *AmMWSc 92*
**Martensson,** Arne 1951- *IntWW 91*
**Marth,** Edward C *WhoAmP 91*
**Marth,** Elmer Herman 1927- *AmMWSc 92*
**Marthers,** John James 1931- *WhoAmP 91*
**Marti,** Jose 1853-1895 *BenetAL 91*
**Marti,** Kurt 1936- *AmMWSc 92*
**Marti,** Mariano 1721-1792 *HisDSpE*
**Marti,** Ramon *WhoHisp 92*
**Marti de Cid,** Dolores 1916- *WhoHisp 92*
**Marti y Perez,** Jose 1853-1895 *HisDSpE*
**Martian,** Dan Leonard 1959- *WhoRel 92*
**Marticelli,** Joseph John 1921- *WhoAmL 92*
**Martignole,** Jacques 1939- *AmMWSc 92*
**Martignoni,** Mauro Emilio 1926- *AmMWSc 92*
**Martika** 1969- *WhoHisp 92*
**Martimucci,** Richard Anthony 1934- *WhoFI 92*
**Martin** *Who 92*
**Martin and Lewis** *LesBEnT 92*
**Martin of Braga** 520?-580? *EncEarC*
**Martin of Tours** 316?-397 *EncEarC [port]*
**Martin,** Pere 1810?-1880? *ThHEIm*
**Martin,** A. Damien d1991 *NewYTBS 91*
**Martin,** A W 1926- *WhoAmP 91*
**Martin,** Aaron J 1928- *AmMWSc 92*
**Martin,** Adam Andrew Ogilvie McCrae 1961- *WhoWest 92*
**Martin,** Agnes 1912- *IntWW 91*
**Martin,** Alan Joseph 1959- *WhoAmL 92*
**Martin,** Albert Edwin 1931- *AmMWSc 92*
**Martin,** Albert Joseph 1940- *WhoEnt 92*
**Martin,** Alexander 1738-1807 *DcNCBi 4*
**Martin,** Alexander Robert 1928- *AmMWSc 92*
**Martin,** Alfred 1919- *AmMWSc 92*
**Martin,** Alvin Charles 1933- *WhoAmL 92*
**Martin,** Amon Achilles, Jr. 1940- *WhoBlA 92*
**Martin,** Andrea 1947- *WhoEnt 92*
**Martin,** Andrew *Who 92*
**Martin,** Andrew Douglas 1960- *WhoFI 92*
**Martin,** Angela M. Coker 1953- *WhoBlA 92*
**Martin,** Angelique Marie 1954- *WhoRel 92*
**Martin,** Anne Henrietta 1875-1951 *AmPeW*
**Martin,** Annie B. 1925- *WhoBlA 92*
**Martin,** Anthony Franz 1956- *WhoMW 92*
**Martin,** Anthony G. 1945- *WhoHisp 92*
**Martin,** Anthony R., III 1945- *WhoAmL 92*
**Martin,** Archer John Porter 1910- *IntWW 91, Who 92, WhoNob 90*
**Martin,** Arlene Patricia 1926- *AmMWSc 92*
**Martin,** Arnold Lee, Jr. 1939- *WhoBlA 92*
**Martin,** Arnold R 1936- *AmMWSc 92*
**Martin,** Artemas 1835-1918 *BiInAmS*
**Martin,** Arthur Bryan 1928- *Who 92*
**Martin,** Arthur Francis 1918- *AmMWSc 92*
**Martin,** Arthur Joseph 1947- *WhoAmL 92*
**Martin,** Arthur Raymond 1949- *WhoMW 92*
**Martin,** Arthur Wesley 1910- *AmMWSc 92*
**Martin,** Arthur Wesley, III 1935- *AmMWSc 92*
**Martin,** Aubran Wayne d1991 *NewYTBS 91*
**Martin,** Augustus Christian 1944- *WhoAmL 92*
**Martin,** Barbara Bursa 1934- *AmMWSc 92*
**Martin,** Barbara Fern 1948- *WhoAmP 91*
**Martin,** Baron H. 1926- *WhoBlA 92*
**Martin,** Basil Douglas 1941- *WhoBlA 92*
**Martin,** Benjamin 1704-1782 *BlkwCEP*
**Martin,** Benny Morris 1957- *WhoAmL 92*
**Martin,** Bernard Loyal 1928- *AmMWSc 92*
**Martin,** Bertha M. 1928- *WhoBlA 92*
**Martin,** Beverly Ann 1951- *WhoEnt 92*
**Martin,** Bill, Jr. 1916- *SmATA 67*
**Martin,** Billy Joe 1933- *AmMWSc 92*
**Martin,** Billy Ray 1943- *AmMWSc 92*
**Martin,** Blair Alison 1965- *WhoEnt 92*
**Martin,** Blanche 1937- *WhoBlA 92*
**Martin,** Bobby L. 1948- *WhoFI 92*
**Martin,** Boston Faust 1927- *AmMWSc 92*
**Martin,** Boyce F, Jr 1935- *WhoAmP 91*
**Martin,** Boyce Ficklen, Jr. 1935- *WhoAmL 92*
**Martin,** Boyd A. 1911- *WrDr 92*
**Martin,** Boyd Archer 1911- *WhoWest 92*
**Martin,** Brian Kermit 1944- *WhoFI 92*
**Martin,** Bruce *TwCWW 91, Who 92*
**Martin,** Bruce Alan *WhoEnt 92*
**Martin,** Bruce Douglas 1934- *AmMWSc 92*
**Martin,** Burchard V. 1933- *WhoAmL 92*
**Martin,** Cam J. 1942- *WhoFI 92*
**Martin,** Carl E. 1931- *WhoBlA 92*
**Martin,** Carol 1948- *WhoBlA 92*
**Martin,** Carol Lahaman 1926- *WhoAmP 91*
**Martin,** Carolann Frances 1935- *WhoEnt 92*
**Martin,** Carolyn Ann 1943- *WhoBlA 92*
**Martin,** Carroll James *AmMWSc 92*
**Martin,** Catherine 1948- *WhoRel 92*
**Martin,** Catherine Carol 1920- *WhoAmP 91*
**Martin,** Celia Hare 1914- *WhoAmP 91*
**Martin,** Celia Lopez 1946- *WhoHisp 92*
**Martin,** Charles *DrAPF 91*
**Martin,** Charles Bee 1931- *WhoAmP 91*
**Martin,** Charles Edmund 1939- *Who 92*
**Martin,** Charles Edward, Sr. 1943- *WhoBlA 92*
**Martin,** Charles Emanuel 1891-1977 *AmPeW*
**Martin,** Charles Everett 1929- *AmMWSc 92*
**Martin,** Charles Everett 1944- *AmMWSc 92*
**Martin,** Charles Henry 1848-1931 *DcNCBi 4*
**Martin,** Charles J 1921- *AmMWSc 92*
**Martin,** Charles John 1935- *AmMWSc 92*
**Martin,** Charles Neil, Jr. 1942- *WhoFI 92*
**Martin,** Charles R 1953- *AmMWSc 92*
**Martin,** Charles Samuel 1936- *AmMWSc 92*
**Martin,** Charles Wade 1952- *WhoRel 92*
**Martin,** Charles Wayne 1932- *AmMWSc 92, WhoMW 92*
**Martin,** Charles Wellington, Jr 1933- *AmMWSc 92*
**Martin,** Charles William 1943- *AmMWSc 92*
**Martin,** Charlie *Who 92*
**Martin,** Cheri Christian 1956- *WhoMW 92*
**Martin,** Cheryl 1965- *WhoEnt 92*
**Martin,** Christopher 1942- *WhoEnt 92*
**Martin,** Christopher Bruce 1948- *WhoWest 92*
**Martin,** Christopher George 1938- *Who 92*
**Martin,** Christopher Michael 1928- *AmMWSc 92*
**Martin,** Christopher Sanford 1938- *Who 92*
**Martin,** Chrys Anne 1953- *WhoAmL 92*
**Martin,** Chuck 1891-1954 *TwCWW 91*
**Martin,** Clarence F *WhoAmP 91*
**Martin,** Clarence L. *WhoBlA 92*
**Martin,** Clay Nelson 1961- *WhoAmL 92*
**Martin,** Clyde Verne 1933- *WhoWest 92*
**Martin,** Connie Ruth 1955- *WhoAmL 92*
**Martin,** Constance R 1923- *AmMWSc 92*
**Martin,** Cornelius A. *WhoBlA 92*
**Martin,** Cortez Hezekiah *WhoBlA 92*
**Martin,** Curtis Jerome 1949- *WhoBlA 92*
**Martin,** Dale Ross 1935- *WhoRel 92*
**Martin,** Dan Merrill 1939- *WhoMW 92*
**Martin,** Dana 1946- *WhoAmP 91*
**Martin,** Daniel E. 1932- *WhoBlA 92*
**Martin,** Daniel E, Sr 1932- *WhoAmP 91*
**Martin,** Daniel Ezekiel, Jr. 1963- *WhoBlA 92*
**Martin,** Daniel William 1918- *AmMWSc 92*
**Martin,** Danny David 1946- *WhoRel 92*
**Martin,** Darnell *WhoMW 92*
**Martin,** Darryl James 1950- *WhoEnt 92*
**Martin,** Darryl Wayne 1948- *WhoFI 92*
**Martin,** David *DrAPF 91*
**Martin,** David 1915- *IntAu&W 91, WrDr 92*
**Martin,** David 1933-1990 *AnObit 1990*
**Martin,** David 1950- *WhoEnt 92*
**Martin,** David Alan 1948- *WhoAmL 92*
**Martin,** David Alfred 1929- *IntAu&W 91, Who 92, WrDr 92*
**Martin,** David Dale 1925- *WhoFI 92, WhoMW 92*
**Martin,** David Dalferes 1954- *WhoWest 92*
**Martin,** David E 1929- *AmMWSc 92*
**Martin,** David Edward 1939- *AmMWSc 92*
**Martin,** David Franklin 1952- *WhoMW 92*
**Martin,** David H 1947- *WhoIns 92*
**Martin,** David John Pattison 1945- *Who 92*
**Martin,** David Kevin 1960- *WhoEnt 92*
**Martin,** David L. 1938- *WhoFI 92*
**Martin,** David Lee 1941- *AmMWSc 92*
**Martin,** David Louis 1950- *WhoFI 92, WhoWest 92*
**Martin,** David Michael 1947- *WhoFI 92*
**Martin,** David O'B. 1944- *AlmAP 92 [port]*
**Martin,** David O'Brien 1944- *WhoAmP 91*
**Martin,** David Traeger 1964- *WhoEnt 92*
**Martin,** David Wayne 1953- *WhoEnt 92*
**Martin,** David Weir 1954- *Who 92*
**Martin,** David William 1942- *AmMWSc 92, WhoMW 92*
**Martin,** David William, Jr 1941- *AmMWSc 92*
**Martin,** David Willis 1927- *AmMWSc 92*
**Martin,** Davis Carney 1923- *WhoRel 92, WhoWest 92*
**Martin,** Dean *LesBEnT 92*
**Martin,** Dean 1917- *IntMPA 92, IntWW 91, NewAmDM, WhoEnt 92*
**Martin,** Dean Frederick 1933- *AmMWSc 92*
**Martin,** Dean Monroe 1942- *WhoRel 92*
**Martin,** Demas Bunyan 1934- *WhoRel 92*
**Martin,** Dennis Charles 1960- *WhoMW 92*
**Martin,** Dennis John 1947- *AmMWSc 92*
**Martin,** Dennis Michael 1952- *WhoRel 92*
**Martin,** Denny Ross 1952- *WhoAmL 92*
**Martin,** Derek H. 1929- *Who 92*
**Martin,** Deric Kriston 1959- *WhoFI 92*
**Martin,** DeWayne 1935- *AmMWSc 92*
**Martin,** Dewey 1923- *IntMPA 92*
**Martin,** Dom 1950- *WhoWest 92*
**Martin,** Don Eugene 1953- *WhoMW 92*
**Martin,** Don Stanley, Jr 1919- *AmMWSc 92*
**Martin,** Donald *WhoFI 92*
**Martin,** Donald Beckwith 1927- *AmMWSc 92*
**Martin,** Donald Creagh 1937- *WhoMW 92*
**Martin,** Donald Crowell 1929- *AmMWSc 92*
**Martin,** Donald E 1937- *WhoIns 92*
**Martin,** Donald Leon 1920- *WhoAmL 92*
**Martin,** Donald Ray 1915- *AmMWSc 92*
**Martin,** Donald Walter 1934- *WhoWest 92*
**Martin,** Doug 1957- *WhoBlA 92*
**Martin,** Douglas 1939- *ConAu 133*
**Martin,** Douglas 1955- *WhoRel 92*
**Martin,** Douglas K *WhoAmP 91*
**Martin,** Douglas Leonard 1930- *AmMWSc 92*
**Martin,** Douglas S d1914 *BiInAmS*
**Martin,** Drake Evans 1949- *WhoMW 92*
**Martin,** Duncan Willis 1931- *AmMWSc 92*
**Martin,** D'Urville 1939- *WhoBlA 92*
**Martin,** E. Gregory 1931- *WhoAmL 92*
**Martin,** Edmund Fible 1902- *IntWW 91*
**Martin,** Edward 1936- *WhoBlA 92*
**Martin,** Edward Anthony 1935- *WhoBlA 92*
**Martin,** Edward Fontaine 1942- *WhoAmL 92*
**Martin,** Edward J, Jr 1934- *WhoIns 92*
**Martin,** Edward Lee 1954- *WhoFI 92*
**Martin,** Edward Shaffer 1939- *AmMWSc 92*
**Martin,** Edward Williford 1929- *AmMWSc 92, WhoBlA 92*
**Martin,** Edwin Dennis 1920- *IntMPA 92*
**Martin,** Edwin J, Jr 1925- *AmMWSc 92*
**Martin,** Edwin McCammon 1908- *WhoAmP 91*
**Martin,** Edwin Webb d1991 *NewYTBS 91*
**Martin,** Elden William 1932- *AmMWSc 92*
**Martin,** Elisa S 1931- *WhoAmP 91*
**Martin,** Elizabeth Mason 1934- *WhoAmP 91*
**Martin,** Elliot Edwards 1924- *WhoEnt 92*
**Martin,** Elmer Dale 1934- *AmMWSc 92*
**Martin,** Elmer P. 1946- *WhoBlA 92*
**Martin,** Ernest D 1921- *WhoAmP 91*
**Martin,** Ernest Douglass 1928- *WhoBlA 92*
**Martin,** Ernest Franklin 1945- *WhoEnt 92*
**Martin,** Ernest George Buckley 1948- *WhoAmP 91*
**Martin,** Ernest Lee 1932- *WhoRel 92*
**Martin,** Ernest Walter *WrDr 92*
**Martin,** Estrella Martinez 1945- *WhoHisp 92*
**Martin,** Eugene Christopher 1925- *AmMWSc 92*
**Martin,** Eva M. 1939- *SmATA 65*
**Martin,** Evelyn B. 1908- *WhoBlA 92*
**Martin,** Evelyn Fairfax 1926- *Who 92*
**Martin,** F. David 1920- *WrDr 92*
**Martin,** F X 1922- *IntAu&W 91, WrDr 92*
**Martin,** Frances 1948- *WhoBlA 92*
**Martin,** Francis Troy K. *Who 92*
**Martin,** Francis W 1911- *AmMWSc 92*
**Martin,** Francois-Xavier 1762-1846 *DcNCBi 4*
**Martin,** Frank 1890-1974 *FacFETw, NewAmDM*
**Martin,** Frank Burke 1937- *AmMWSc 92*
**Martin,** Frank Elbert 1913- *AmMWSc 92*
**Martin,** Frank Garland 1932- *AmMWSc 92*
**Martin,** Frank Gene 1938- *AmMWSc 92*
**Martin,** Frank Vernon 1921- *Who 92*
**Martin,** Franklin Farnarwance 1950- *WhoBlA 92*
**Martin,** Franklin Wayne 1928- *AmMWSc 92*
**Martin,** Fred 1926- *WhoBlA 92*
**Martin,** Freddie Anthony 1945- *AmMWSc 92*
**Martin,** Frederic *IntAu&W 91X*
**Martin,** Frederick 1908- *WhoFI 92*
**Martin,** Frederick N 1931- *AmMWSc 92*
**Martin,** Frederick Royal 1919- *Who 92*
**Martin,** Frederick Wight 1936- *AmMWSc 92*
**Martin,** Fredric *ConAu 36NR, WrDr 92*
**Martin,** G William, Jr 1946- *AmMWSc 92*
**Martin,** Gail Roberta 1944- *AmMWSc 92*
**Martin,** Gary DeWayne 1954- *WhoRel 92, WhoWest 92*
**Martin,** Gary Edwin 1949- *AmMWSc 92*
**Martin,** Gary O. 1944- *WhoEnt 92*
**Martin,** Geoffrey *Who 92*
**Martin,** Geoffrey Haward 1928- *Who 92, WrDr 92*
**Martin,** Geoffrey John 1934- *WrDr 92*
**Martin,** George *AmMWSc 92*
**Martin,** George 1826-1886 *BiInAmS*

**Martin,** George 1926- *ConMus 6*
**Martin,** George 1940- *WhoWest 92*
**Martin,** George A 1831?-1904 *BiInAmS*
**Martin,** George Alexander, Jr. 1943- *WhoBlA 92*
**Martin,** George Burnie, III 1952- *WhoMW 92*
**Martin,** George C 1910- *AmMWSc 92*
**Martin,** George C 1933- *AmMWSc 92*
**Martin,** George Dominic 1946- *WhoFI 92*
**Martin,** George Dwight 1953- *WhoBlA 92*
**Martin,** George Edward 1932- *AmMWSc 92*
**Martin,** George Franklin, Jr 1937- *AmMWSc 92*
**Martin,** George Gilmore 1944- *WhoAmL 92*
**Martin,** George H 1917- *AmMWSc 92*
**Martin,** George Henry 1926- *Who 92*
**Martin,** George Joseph 1932- *WhoFI 92*
**Martin,** George Maybee 1906- *WhoAmL 92, WhoWest 92*
**Martin,** George Monroe 1927- *AmMWSc 92*
**Martin,** George R R 1948- *TwCSFW 91, WrDr 92*
**Martin,** George Reilly 1933- *AmMWSc 92*
**Martin,** George Steven 1943- *AmMWSc 92*
**Martin,** George Whitney 1926- *WrDr 92*
**Martin,** Gertrude S. *WhoBlA 92*
**Martin,** Gina 1957- *TwCPaSc*
**Martin,** Gladys Irene 1929- *WhoAmP 91*
**Martin,** Glenn 1886-1955 *FacFETw*
**Martin,** Gloria Alice 1940- *WhoWest 92*
**Martin,** Gordon Eugene 1925- *AmMWSc 92*
**Martin,** Gordon Mather 1915- *AmMWSc 92, WhoMW 92*
**Martin,** Grace B. *DrAPF 91*
**Martin,** Graham A 1912-1990 *FacFETw*
**Martin,** Greg D 1954- *WhoAmP 91*
**Martin,** Gregory Emmett *AmMWSc 92*
**Martin,** Gregory Keith 1956- *WhoAmL 92*
**Martin,** Gregory Kevin 1954- *WhoMW 92*
**Martin,** Guillermo Joaquin 1942- *WhoHisp 92*
**Martin,** Gwendolyn Rose 1926- *WhoAmP 91, WhoBlA 92*
**Martin,** Hans Carl 1937- *AmMWSc 92*
**Martin,** Harold 1918- *WhoAmP 91*
**Martin,** Harold B. 1928- *WhoBlA 92*
**Martin,** Harold Roland 1919- *AmMWSc 92*
**Martin,** Harry Corpening 1920- *WhoAmL 92, WhoAmP 91*
**Martin,** Harry Lee 1956- *AmMWSc 92*
**Martin,** Harry Stratton, III 1943- *WhoAmL 92*
**Martin,** Helen Dorothy *WhoBlA 92*
**Martin,** Helen Reimensnyder 1868-1939 *BenetAL 91*
**Martin,** Henri-Jean 1924- *IntWW 91*
**Martin,** Henry Alan 1949- *WhoAmL 92*
**Martin,** Henry James 1910- *Who 92*
**Martin,** Henry Newell 1848-1896 *BiInAmS*
**Martin,** Herbert Lloyd 1921- *AmMWSc 92*
**Martin,** Herbert Woodward *DrAPF 91*
**Martin,** Herman Henry, Jr. 1961- *WhoBlA 92*
**Martin,** Hilda C 1934- *WhoAmP 91*
**Martin,** Horace F 1931- *AmMWSc 92*
**Martin,** Hoyle Henry 1921- *WhoBlA 92*
**Martin,** Hugh Jack, Jr 1926- *AmMWSc 92*
**Martin,** I. Maximillian *WhoBlA 92*
**Martin,** Ian 1946- *Who 92, WhoFI 92*
**Martin,** Ian Alexander 1935- *Who 92, WhoFI 92, WhoMW 92*
**Martin,** Ignacio 1928- *WhoHisp 92*
**Martin,** Ionis Bracy 1936- *WhoBlA 92*
**Martin,** J. Landis 1945- *WhoFI 92*
**Martin,** J W *AmMWSc 92*
**Martin,** Jack 1927- *AmMWSc 92*
**Martin,** Jack E 1931- *AmMWSc 92*
**Martin,** Jack Elmo 1936- *WhoRel 92*
**Martin,** Jack Lee 1952- *WhoFI 92*
**Martin,** Jacques 1908- *IntWW 91, WhoRel 92*
**Martin,** James *DrAPF 91, WhoAmP 91*
**Martin,** James 1742-1834 *DcNCBi 4*
**Martin,** James 1933- *ConAu 134*
**Martin,** James Alfred, Jr. 1917- *WhoRel 92*
**Martin,** James Arthur 1903- *Who 92*
**Martin,** James Arthur 1944- *AmMWSc 92*
**Martin,** James Brown 1953- *Who 92*
**Martin,** James Bruce 1916- *WhoMW 92*
**Martin,** James C. 1938- *WhoBlA 92*
**Martin,** James Cullen 1928- *AmMWSc 92*
**Martin,** James Cuthbert 1927- *AmMWSc 92*
**Martin,** James D 1927- *WhoIns 92*
**Martin,** James Edward 1949- *AmMWSc 92, WhoMW 92*
**Martin,** James Ellis 1952- *AmMWSc 92*
**Martin,** James Eugene 1953- *WhoIns 92*
**Martin,** James Francis 1945- *WhoAmP 91*
**Martin,** James Franklin 1917- *AmMWSc 92*
**Martin,** James Frederick 1944- *WhoEnt 92*
**Martin,** James G. 1935- *AlmAP 92 [port]*
**Martin,** James Green 1819-1878 *DcNCBi 4*
**Martin,** James Grubbs 1935- *IntWW 91, WhoAmP 91*
**Martin,** James Hanley 1960- *WhoAmL 92*
**Martin,** James Harold 1931- *AmMWSc 92*
**Martin,** James Henry, III 1943- *AmMWSc 92*
**Martin,** James Larence 1940- *WhoBlA 92*
**Martin,** James Lee 1948- *WhoAmP 91, WhoWest 92*
**Martin,** James Lee 1953- *WhoAmL 92*
**Martin,** James Luther, Jr. 1917- *WhoRel 92*
**Martin,** James Milton 1914- *AmMWSc 92*
**Martin,** James Patrick 1946- *WhoWest 92*
**Martin,** James Paul 1929- *WhoAmP 91*
**Martin,** James Paxman 1914- *AmMWSc 92*
**Martin,** James Phillip 1952- *WhoRel 92*
**Martin,** James R. 1941- *WhoHisp 92*
**Martin,** James Richard 1949- *AmMWSc 92*
**Martin,** James Russell 1947- *WhoAmL 92*
**Martin,** James S 1936- *WhoIns 92*
**Martin,** James Tillison 1946- *AmMWSc 92*
**Martin,** James Turner, Jr. 1953- *WhoRel 92*
**Martin,** James Tyrone 1942- *WhoBlA 92*
**Martin,** James W. 1932- *WhoBlA 92*
**Martin,** James William 1949- *WhoAmL 92, WhoEnt 92*
**Martin,** Janet 1927- *Who 92*
**Martin,** Janet Mischelle 1948- *WhoWest 92*
**Martin,** Janette G. *DrAPF 91*
**Martin,** Janette Gould 1957- *IntAu&W 91*
**Martin,** Jay 1935- *DcLB 111 [port]*
**Martin,** Jay Ronald 1944- *AmMWSc 92*
**Martin,** Jean Frazier 1955- *WhoEnt 92*
**Martin,** Jeffery Allen 1967- *WhoBlA 92*
**Martin,** Jeffrey Alan 1953- *WhoFI 92*
**Martin,** Jeffrey Scott 1961- *WhoEnt 92*
**Martin,** Jeffrey W. 1961- *WhoEnt 92*
**Martin,** Jeffry Ray 1954- *WhoWest 92*
**Martin,** Jerald Lynn 1953- *WhoHisp 92*
**Martin,** Jerome 1902- *AmMWSc 92*
**Martin,** Jerry 1941- *WhoRel 92*
**Martin,** Jerry, Jr 1930- *AmMWSc 92*
**Martin,** Jerry D. 1935- *WhoMW 92, WhoRel 92*
**Martin,** Jim *DrAPF 91*
**Martin,** Jim Frank 1944- *AmMWSc 92*
**Martin,** Joan M. *DrAPF 91*
**Martin,** Joanne Mitchell 1947- *WhoBlA 92*
**Martin,** Joe 1948- *WhoAmP 91*
**Martin,** Joel Jerome 1939- *AmMWSc 92*
**Martin,** Joel William 1955- *AmMWSc 92*
**Martin,** John A 1935- *AmMWSc 92*
**Martin,** John Alfred 1921- *WhoAmP 91*
**Martin,** John Allen 1947- *WhoAmP 91*
**Martin,** John B 1922- *AmMWSc 92*
**Martin,** John Bruce 1922- *WhoMW 92*
**Martin,** John Campbell 1926- *AmMWSc 92*
**Martin,** John Charles 1943- *WhoAmL 92*
**Martin,** John Charles 1953- *WhoAmL 92*
**Martin,** John Christopher 1926- *Who 92*
**Martin,** John David 1939- *AmMWSc 92*
**Martin,** John David 1945- *WhoFI 92*
**Martin,** John Douglas K. *Who 92*
**Martin,** John E. 1945- *WhoWest 92*
**Martin,** John Edward 1916- *WhoWest 92*
**Martin,** John Edward 1930- *WhoRel 92*
**Martin,** John Edward Ludgate 1918- *Who 92*
**Martin,** John Emmett 1951- *WhoRel 92*
**Martin,** John Francis Ryde 1943- *Who 92*
**Martin,** John Gordon 1937- *WhoBlA 92*
**Martin,** John Governor 1929- *WhoRel 92*
**Martin,** John Gregory 1963- *WhoRel 92*
**Martin,** John Harvey 1932- *AmMWSc 92*
**Martin,** John Henderson 1951- *WhoWest 92*
**Martin,** John Holland 1935- *AmMWSc 92*
**Martin,** John Howard 1944- *WhoFI 92*
**Martin,** John J 1922- *AmMWSc 92*
**Martin,** John J. 1934- *WhoFI 92*
**Martin,** John J 1940- *WhoIns 92*
**Martin,** John James 1943- *WhoMW 92*
**Martin,** John Joseph 1922- *WhoAmP 91*
**Martin,** John Joseph 1931- *WhoAmL 92*
**Martin,** John Joseph Charles 1940- *IntWW 91*
**Martin,** John L 1941- *WhoAmP 91*
**Martin,** John Lee 1923- *AmMWSc 92*
**Martin,** John Leslie 1908- *IntWW 91, Who 92*
**Martin,** John Marshall, Jr 1918- *WhoAmP 91*
**Martin,** John Miller d1991 *Who 92N*
**Martin,** John Munson 1948- *AmMWSc 92*
**Martin,** John Perry, Jr *AmMWSc 92*
**Martin,** John Powell 1925- *Who 92*
**Martin,** John Robert 1923- *AmMWSc 92*
**Martin,** John S 1928- *WhoIns 92*
**Martin,** John Samuel 1948- *AmMWSc 92*
**Martin,** John Sanford 1886-1957 *DcNCBi 4*
**Martin,** John Scott 1934- *AmMWSc 92*
**Martin,** John Sinclair 1931- *Who 92*
**Martin,** John Thomas 1920- *WhoBlA 92*
**Martin,** John Thomas 1924- *WhoMW 92*
**Martin,** John Victor 1948- *WhoRel 92*
**Martin,** John W. 1924- *WhoBlA 92*
**Martin,** John Walter, Jr 1922- *AmMWSc 92*
**Martin,** John William 1946- *WhoMW 92*
**Martin,** John William, Jr. 1936- *WhoAmL 92, WhoFI 92*
**Martin,** John William Prior 1934- *Who 92*
**Martin,** Johnny Benjamin 1947- *WhoFI 92*
**Martin,** Jonathan Arthur 1942- *Who 92*
**Martin,** Jorge Luis 1953- *WhoHisp 92*
**Martin,** Joseph 1740-1808 *DcNCBi 4*
**Martin,** Joseph, Jr. 1915- *WhoAmL 92, WhoFI 92, WhoWest 92*
**Martin,** Joseph B 1938- *AmMWSc 92*
**Martin,** Joseph J 1916- *AmMWSc 92*
**Martin,** Joseph James 1966- *WhoWest 92*
**Martin,** Joseph John 1833-1900 *DcNCBi 4*
**Martin,** Joseph Patrick, Jr 1952- *AmMWSc 92*
**Martin,** Joseph Robert 1947- *WhoFI 92*
**Martin,** Joseph William, Jr. 1884-1968 *AmPolLe, FacFETw*
**Martin,** Joshua Wesley, III 1944- *WhoBlA 92*
**Martin,** Josiah 1737-1786 *DcNCBi 4*
**Martin,** Judith 1938- *WrDr 92*
**Martin,** Julia M. 1924- *WhoBlA 92*
**Martin,** Julia Mae 1924- *AmMWSc 92*
**Martin,** Julie 1938- *ConAu 133*
**Martin,** Julio Mario 1922- *AmMWSc 92*
**Martin,** Julius McMillan, Jr. 1952- *WhoMW 92*
**Martin,** June Johnson Caldwell *WhoWest 92*
**Martin,** Kathryn Helen 1940- *AmMWSc 92*
**Martin,** Kathryn Lee 1935- *WhoWest 92*
**Martin,** Kelly Joseph 1960- *WhoMW 92*
**Martin,** Kenneth 1905-1984 *TwCPaSc*
**Martin,** Kenneth David 1952- *WhoWest 92*
**Martin,** Kenneth Edward 1944- *AmMWSc 92*
**Martin,** Kenneth Frank 1948- *WhoFI 92*
**Martin,** Kenneth Peter, Mrs. *Who 92*
**Martin,** Kevin John 1948- *WhoMW 92*
**Martin,** Kiel d1990 *NewYTBS 91 [port]*
**Martin,** Kumiko Oizumi 1941- *AmMWSc 92*
**Martin,** L Morgan *WhoAmP 91*
**Martin,** L Robbin 1939- *AmMWSc 92*
**Martin,** Larry A 1957- *WhoAmP 91*
**Martin,** Larry Dean 1943- *AmMWSc 92, WhoMW 92*
**Martin,** Larry Lorenz Hillary, II 1949- *WhoWest 92*
**Martin,** Laura Ann 1953- *WhoRel 92*
**Martin,** Laura Belle 1915- *WhoMW 92*
**Martin,** Laurence 1928- *WrDr 92*
**Martin,** Laurence Woodward 1928- *IntAu&W 91, IntWW 91, Who 92*
**Martin,** Lawrence Leo 1942- *AmMWSc 92*
**Martin,** Lawrence Raymond 1935- *WhoBlA 92*
**Martin,** Lee *DrAPF 91*
**Martin,** Lee 1920- *WhoMW 92*
**Martin,** Lee 1938- *WhoBlA 92*
**Martin,** Lee Edwin 1948- *WhoMW 92*
**Martin,** Leonard Austin, II 1949- *WhoWest 92*
**Martin,** Lequita Jerelene Alexander 1933- *WhoAmP 91*
**Martin,** LeRoy 1929- *WhoBlA 92*
**Martin,** LeRoy Brown, Jr 1926- *AmMWSc 92*
**Martin,** Leslie *IntWW 91, Who 92*
**Martin,** Leslie Vaughan 1919- *Who 92*
**Martin,** Lester W 1923- *AmMWSc 92*
**Martin,** Linda Spencer 1946- *AmMWSc 92*
**Martin,** Lloyd W 1934- *AmMWSc 92*
**Martin,** Loren Dale 1940- *WhoAmL 92*
**Martin,** Loren Gene 1942- *AmMWSc 92*
**Martin,** Lori Anne 1958- *IntAu&W 91*
**Martin,** Louis 1936- *BlkOlyM*
**Martin,** Louis E. 1912- *WhoBlA 92*
**Martin,** Ludwig Markus 1909- *IntWW 91*
**Martin,** Luis 1927- *WhoHisp 92*
**Martin,** Luther 1748-1826 *BlkwEAR*
**Martin,** Luther Howard, Jr 1937- *IntAu&W 91*
**Martin,** Lynn *DrAPF 91*
**Martin,** Lynn 1939- *IntWW 91, News 91 [port]*
**Martin,** Lynn Gary 1936- *WhoRel 92*
**Martin,** Lynn Morley 1939- *WhoAmP 91*
**Martin,** Madeleine d1991 *NewYTBS 91*
**Martin,** Malcolm Alan *AmMWSc 92*
**Martin,** Malcolm Chester 1926- *WhoRel 92*
**Martin,** Malcolm Elliot 1935- *WhoAmL 92*
**Martin,** Malcolm Mencer 1920- *AmMWSc 92*
**Martin,** Manuel, Jr. 1934- *WhoHisp 92*
**Martin,** Margaret Eileen 1915- *AmMWSc 92*
**Martin,** Margaret F 1932- *WhoAmP 91*
**Martin,** Margaret Pearl 1915- *AmMWSc 92*
**Martin,** Mari Lacressa 1962- *WhoWest 92*
**Martin,** Maria 1796-1863 *BiInAmS*
**Martin,** Maria Sonia 1951- *WhoHisp 92*
**Martin,** Marjorie 1942- *IntAu&W 91, WrDr 92*
**Martin,** Mark Steven 1963- *WhoRel 92*
**Martin,** Mark Wayne 1930- *AmMWSc 92*
**Martin,** Mary d1990 *LesBEnT 92*
**Martin,** Mary 1907-1969 *TwCPaSc*
**Martin,** Mary 1913-1990 *AnObit 1990, FacFETw, NewAmDM, News 91*
**Martin,** Mary 1914-1990 *CurBio 91N*
**Martin,** Mary Agnes 1925- *WhoAmP 91*
**Martin,** Mary E. Howell 1941- *WhoBlA 92*
**Martin,** Mary Ellen *WhoAmP 91*
**Martin,** Maxine Smith 1944- *WhoBlA 92*
**Martin,** Maydean Kau'ionamoku Ling How T. 1960- *WhoWest 92*
**Martin,** McKinley C. 1936- *WhoBlA 92*
**Martin,** Michael 1943- *AmMWSc 92*
**Martin,** Michael Dale *WhoMW 92*
**Martin,** Michael David 1944- *WhoAmL 92*
**Martin,** Michael Dennis 1945- *WhoAmL 92*
**Martin,** Michael Eugene 1947- *WhoFI 92*
**Martin,** Michael John 1945- *Who 92*
**Martin,** Michael John 1950- *WhoRel 92*
**Martin,** Michael McCulloch 1935- *AmMWSc 92*
**Martin,** Michael Rex 1952- *WhoAmL 92*
**Martin,** Michael Todd 1962- *WhoEnt 92*
**Martin,** Michael Townsend 1941- *WhoFI 92*
**Martin,** Miguel D. 1949- *WhoHisp 92*
**Martin,** Miguel Lazaro 1952- *WhoHisp 92*
**Martin,** Mike 1960- *WhoAmP 91*
**Martin,** Millicent *WhoEnt 92*
**Martin,** Millicent 1934- *IntMPA 92*
**Martin,** Mitch Wayne 1957- *WhoRel 92*
**Martin,** Monroe Harnish 1907- *AmMWSc 92*
**Martin,** Montez Cornelius, Jr. 1940- *WhoBlA 92*
**Martin,** Nancy Caroline 1948- *AmMWSc 92*
**Martin,** Nancy L. 1931- *WhoWest 92*
**Martin,** Nathaniel Frizzel Grafton 1928- *AmMWSc 92*
**Martin,** Ned Harold 1945- *AmMWSc 92*
**Martin,** Noel 1922- *WhoEnt 92*
**Martin,** Norman K 1930- *WhoIns 92*
**Martin,** Norman Marshall 1924- *AmMWSc 92*
**Martin,** Oliver Samuel 1919- *Who 92*
**Martin,** Osmond Peter *WhoRel 92*
**Martin,** Paige Arlene 1951- *WhoAmL 92*
**Martin,** Pamela Sue 1953- *IntMPA 92*
**Martin,** Patricia *DrAPF 91*
**Martin,** Patricia Ann 1955- *WhoEnt 92*
**Martin,** Patricia Ann 1964- *WhoMW 92*
**Martin,** Patricia Elizabeth 1951- *WhoBlA 92*
**Martin,** Patrick Albert 1950- *WhoFI 92*
**Martin,** Patrick William 1916- *Who 92*
**Martin,** Paul *DrAPF 91, WhoRel 92*
**Martin,** Paul 1938- *WhoFI 92*
**Martin,** Paul Bain 1946- *AmMWSc 92*
**Martin,** Paul Cecil 1931- *AmMWSc 92*
**Martin,** Paul Edward 1928- *WhoAmL 92, WhoFI 92*
**Martin,** Paul Joseph 1936- *AmMWSc 92*
**Martin,** Paul Joseph James 1903- *IntWW 91, Who 92*
**Martin,** Paul Schultz 1928- *AmMWSc 92*
**Martin,** Paul W. 1940- *WhoBlA 92*
**Martin,** Peppy 1946- *WhoAmP 91*
**Martin,** Pete *WhoHisp 92*
**Martin,** Peter *Who 92*
**Martin,** Peter 1931- *WrDr 92*
**Martin,** Peter Anthony 1946- *Who 92*
**Martin,** Peter C 1928- *WhoAmP 91*
**Martin,** Peter Gordon 1947- *AmMWSc 92*
**Martin,** Peter Lawrence de Carteret 1920- *Who 92*
**Martin,** Peter Lewis 1918- *Who 92*
**Martin,** Peter William 1939- *WhoAmL 92*
**Martin,** Peter Wilson 1938- *AmMWSc 92*
**Martin,** Phil *WhoAmP 91*
**Martin,** Philip 1931- *IntAu&W 91*
**Martin,** Phillip 1927- *TwCPaSc*
**Martin,** Phillip Dwight 1943- *WhoMW 92*
**Martin,** Phillip Hammond 1940- *WhoAmL 92*
**Martin,** Preston 1923- *WhoFI 92, WhoWest 92*
**Martin,** Quinn d1987 *LesBEnT 92*

**Martin**, R Brad *WhoAmP 91*
**Martin**, R Russell 1936- *AmMWSc 92*
**Martin**, Radcliffe *ScFEYrs*
**Martin**, Ralph 1920- *WrDr 92*
**Martin**, Ralph Guy 1920- *IntAu&W 91*
**Martin**, Ralph H 1923- *AmMWSc 92*
**Martin**, Ray 1936- *WhoWest 92*
**Martin**, Ray Elwood 1942- *WhoRel 92*
**Martin**, Ray Ivan 1930- *WhoRel 92*
**Martin**, Rayfus 1930- *WhoBlA 92*
**Martin**, Raymond Albert 1925- *WhoRel 92*
**Martin**, Raymond Bruce 1934- *WhoMW 92*
**Martin**, Raymond Edward 1957- *WhoFI 92*
**Martin**, Raymond Leslie 1926- *Who 92*
**Martin**, Raymond Walter 1952- *WhoAmL 92*
**Martin**, Reddrick Linwood 1934- *WhoBlA 92*
**Martin**, Reginald 1956- *IntAu&W 91*
**Martin**, Renee Cohen 1928- *WhoFI 92*
**Martin**, Rex *IntAu&W 91X*
**Martin**, Rhona 1922- *IntAu&W 91, WrDr 92*
**Martin**, Richard Alan 1944- *AmMWSc 92*
**Martin**, Richard Blazo 1917- *AmMWSc 92*
**Martin**, Richard Cornish 1936- *WhoBlA 92*
**Martin**, Richard Graham 1932- *Who 92*
**Martin**, Richard Hadley, Jr 1924- *AmMWSc 92*
**Martin**, Richard Harvey 1932- *AmMWSc 92*
**Martin**, Richard Hugo 1936- *AmMWSc 92*
**Martin**, Richard J. *DrAPF 91*
**Martin**, Richard Lee 1950- *AmMWSc 92*
**Martin**, Richard McFadden 1942- *AmMWSc 92*
**Martin**, Richard McKelvy 1936- *AmMWSc 92*
**Martin**, Richard N. 1922- *WhoFI 92*
**Martin**, Richard William 1950- *WhoMW 92*
**Martin**, Rick J. 1946- *WhoFI 92*
**Martin**, Robert *IntAu&W 91X*
**Martin**, Robert, Jr. 1784-1848 *DcNCBi 4*
**Martin**, Robert Allen 1930- *IntAu&W 91*
**Martin**, Robert Allen 1944- *AmMWSc 92*
**Martin**, Robert Andrew 1914- *Who 92*
**Martin**, Robert Bernard 1918- *IntAu&W 91, WrDr 92*
**Martin**, Robert Bruce 1929- *AmMWSc 92*
**Martin**, Robert Bruce 1938- *Who 92*
**Martin**, Robert Burton 1935- *WhoWest 92*
**Martin**, Robert C 1926- *WhoIns 92*
**Martin**, Robert Donald 1943- *WhoMW 92*
**Martin**, Robert Edward 1928- *WhoMW 92*
**Martin**, Robert Edward 1948- *WhoBlA 92*
**Martin**, Robert Eugene 1930- *AmMWSc 92*
**Martin**, Robert Eugene, Jr. 1948- *WhoRel 92*
**Martin**, Robert Francois Churchill 1941- *AmMWSc 92*
**Martin**, Robert Frederick 1938- *AmMWSc 92*
**Martin**, Robert Frederick, Sr. 1942- *WhoMW 92*
**Martin**, Robert G 1935- *AmMWSc 92*
**Martin**, Robert Gregory 1959- *WhoWest 92*
**Martin**, Robert J 1947- *WhoAmP 91*
**Martin**, Robert Joseph 1956- *WhoMW 92*
**Martin**, Robert L 1912- *WhoAmP 91*
**Martin**, Robert Lawrence 1933- *AmMWSc 92*
**Martin**, Robert Leonard 1919- *AmMWSc 92*
**Martin**, Robert Lionel 1920- *WhoMW 92*
**Martin**, Robert Logan 1950- *Who 92*
**Martin**, Robert O 1931- *AmMWSc 92*
**Martin**, Robert Paul 1943- *AmMWSc 92*
**Martin**, Robert R *WhoAmP 91*
**Martin**, Robert William 1936- *WhoFI 92*
**Martin**, Robert William 1961- *WhoFI 92*
**Martin**, Robin Bradley *WhoEnt 92*
**Martin**, Robin Geoffrey 1921- *Who 92*
**Martin**, Robyn Denise 1954- *WhoEnt 92*
**Martin**, Rod 1954- *WhoBlA 92*
**Martin**, Roderick 1940- *WrDr 92*
**Martin**, Rodger C. *DrAPF 91*
**Martin**, Roger *WhoHisp 92*
**Martin**, Roger Allen 1934- *WhoAmP 91*
**Martin**, Roger Charles 1931- *AmMWSc 92*
**Martin**, Roger John 1951- *WhoRel 92*
**Martin**, Roger John Adam 1941- *Who 92*
**Martin**, Roger Leon Rene 1915- *IntWW 91*
**Martin**, Roland M 1949- *WhoAmP 91*
**Martin**, Ronald 1919- *Who 92*
**Martin**, Ronald Andrew 1946- *WhoMW 92*
**Martin**, Ronald Dewitt 1946- *WhoRel 92*
**Martin**, Ronald Keith 1956- *WhoRel 92*
**Martin**, Ronald Lavern 1922- *AmMWSc 92*
**Martin**, Ronald LeRoy 1932- *AmMWSc 92*
**Martin**, Rosetta P. 1930- *WhoBlA 92*
**Martin**, Roy A 1920- *AmMWSc 92*
**Martin**, Roy F 1932- *WhoIns 92*
**Martin**, Roy Joseph, Jr 1943- *AmMWSc 92*
**Martin**, Roy Peter 1931- *Who 92*
**Martin**, Ruby Julene Wheeler 1931- *WhoBlA 92*
**Martin**, Rudolph G. 1916- *WhoBlA 92*
**Martin**, Rufus Russell 1936- *AmMWSc 92*
**Martin**, Rupert Claude d1991 *Who 92N*
**Martin**, Russell 1958- *WhoRel 92*
**Martin**, Russell F. 1929- *WhoBlA 92*
**Martin**, Russell James 1939- *AmMWSc 92*
**Martin**, Ruth *IntAu&W 91X*
**Martin**, S W 1958- *AmMWSc 92*
**Martin**, Sallie 1895-1988 *WhoBlA 92N*
**Martin**, Sally 1936- *WhoAmP 91*
**Martin**, Samuel 1918- *WhoBlA 92*
**Martin**, Samuel Clark 1916- *AmMWSc 92*
**Martin**, Samuel Frederick Radcliffe 1918- *Who 92*
**Martin**, Samuel Preston, III 1916- *AmMWSc 92*
**Martin**, Sandy 1949- *WhoEnt 92*
**Martin**, Sara 1884-1955 *NotBlAW 92*
**Martin**, Scott *IntAu&W 91X*
**Martin**, Scott Elmore 1946- *AmMWSc 92*
**Martin**, Scott Graddy 1947- *WhoWest 92*
**Martin**, Scott McClung 1943- *AmMWSc 92*
**Martin**, Seelye 1940- *AmMWSc 92*
**Martin**, Shedrick M., Jr. 1927- *WhoBlA 92*
**Martin**, Shirley Marie 1944- *WhoFI 92*
**Martin**, Sidney 1918- *Who 92*
**Martin**, Sidney, Sr 1919- *WhoAmP 91*
**Martin**, Siva 1925- *WhoAmL 92*
**Martin**, Stanley Buel 1927- *AmMWSc 92*
**Martin**, Stanley Lawrence 1938- *WhoWest 92*
**Martin**, Stanley William Frederick 1934- *Who 92*
**Martin**, Steele Wade 1926- *WhoRel 92*
**Martin**, Stephen David 1947- *WhoMW 92*
**Martin**, Stephen Frederick 1943- *WhoFI 92*
**Martin**, Stephen Frederick 1946- *AmMWSc 92*
**Martin**, Stephen George 1941- *AmMWSc 92*
**Martin**, Stephen Gunther 1937- *WhoEnt 92*
**Martin**, Stephen Holiday 1956- *WhoAmP 91*
**Martin**, Stephen I 1926- *WhoIns 92*
**Martin**, Stephen Joseph 1922- *WhoEnt 92*
**Martin**, Stephen-Paul *DrAPF 91*
**Martin**, Steve *IntWW 91, LesBEnT 92, WhoEnt 92*
**Martin**, Steve 1945- *FacFETw [port], IntMPA 92, News 92-2 [port]*
**Martin**, Steven Abram 1965- *WhoEnt 92*
**Martin**, Steven E. 1956- *WhoAmL 92*
**Martin**, Stoddard H 1948- *IntAu&W 91*
**Martin**, Sunny 1913- *WhoWest 92*
**Martin**, Susan Fry 1952- *WhoAmL 92*
**Martin**, Susan Scott 1938- *AmMWSc 92*
**Martin**, Sylvia 1913-1981 *ConAu 135*
**Martin**, Sylvia Cooke 1938- *WhoBlA 92*
**Martin**, Talmage McKinley, Jr 1923- *WhoAmP 91*
**Martin**, Tara Kathleen 1956- *WhoRel 92*
**Martin**, Tellis Alexander 1919- *AmMWSc 92*
**Martin**, Terence Edwin 1941- *AmMWSc 92*
**Martin**, Terrence H 1936- *WhoAmP 91*
**Martin**, Terry Joe 1947- *AmMWSc 92*
**Martin**, Terry Zachry 1946- *AmMWSc 92*
**Martin**, Thomas A 1924- *AmMWSc 92*
**Martin**, Thomas Ballantyne 1901- *Who 92*
**Martin**, Thomas Fabian John 1946- *AmMWSc 92*
**Martin**, Thomas Geoffrey 1940- *Who 92*
**Martin**, Thomas George, III 1931- *AmMWSc 92*
**Martin**, Thomas L, Jr 1921- *AmMWSc 92*
**Martin**, Thomas MacDonald 1947- *WhoAmL 92*
**Martin**, Thomas Michael 1940- *WhoRel 92*
**Martin**, Thomas Rhodes 1953- *WhoEnt 92*
**Martin**, Thomas Waring 1925- *AmMWSc 92*
**Martin**, Thomas Wesley, III 1947- *WhoWest 92*
**Martin**, Timothy Patrick 1948- *WhoEnt 92*
**Martin**, Tom *TwCWW 91*
**Martin**, Tony 1913- *IntMPA 92*
**Martin**, Tony 1942- *WhoBlA 92*
**Martin**, Tracey Ellen 1959- *WhoMW 92*
**Martin**, Trevor Ian 1943- *AmMWSc 92*
**Martin**, Troy Wayne 1953- *WhoRel 92*
**Martin**, Truman Glen 1928- *AmMWSc 92*
**Martin**, Valerie 1948- *WrDr 92*
**Martin**, Valerie M. *DrAPF 91*
**Martin**, Vernon Emil 1929- *WhoEnt 92*
**Martin**, Vicki Lynn 1954- *WhoWest 92*
**Martin**, Victor Cecil 1915- *Who 92*
**Martin**, Victoria Carolyn 1945- *IntAu&W 91, WrDr 92*
**Martin**, Virginia Lorelle 1939- *AmMWSc 92*
**Martin**, W. Mike 1943- *WhoWest 92*
**Martin**, Wallace A *WhoAmP 91*
**Martin**, Walter 1912- *WhoAmL 92*
**Martin**, Walter L. 1951- *WhoBlA 92*
**Martin**, Walter Lee 1921- *WhoIns 92*
**Martin**, Warham Lance 1937- *WhoRel 92*
**Martin**, Warren Gregory 1948- *WhoRel 92*
**Martin**, Wayne *WhoRel 92*
**Martin**, Wayne 1965- *WhoBlA 92*
**Martin**, Wayne Dudley 1920- *AmMWSc 92*
**Martin**, Wayne Holderness 1931- *AmMWSc 92*
**Martin**, Wayne Mallott 1950- *WhoFI 92, WhoMW 92*
**Martin**, Wayne Willard 1943- *WhoRel 92*
**Martin**, Webber *ConAu 36NR*
**Martin**, Wendy *WrDr 92*
**Martin**, Wilfred Samuel 1910- *AmMWSc 92*
**Martin**, Willard John 1915- *AmMWSc 92*
**Martin**, William A 1932- *WhoIns 92*
**Martin**, William Alison 1878?-1936 *TwCPaSc*
**Martin**, William Aubert 1931- *WhoAmL 92*
**Martin**, William Butler, Jr 1923- *AmMWSc 92*
**Martin**, William Charles 1923- *WhoAmL 92*
**Martin**, William Clarence 1923- *AmMWSc 92*
**Martin**, William Clyde 1893- *RelLAm 91*
**Martin**, William Clyde 1929- *AmMWSc 92*
**Martin**, William Conway 1956- *WhoRel 92*
**Martin**, William David 1942- *AmMWSc 92*
**Martin**, William Eugene 1941- *AmMWSc 92*
**Martin**, William Franklin, Jr. 1919- *WhoWest 92*
**Martin**, William Gilbert 1931- *AmMWSc 92*
**Martin**, William H *WhoAmP 91*
**Martin**, William Haywood, III 1938- *AmMWSc 92*
**Martin**, William Joseph 1830-1896 *DcNCBi 4*
**Martin**, William Joseph 1953- *WhoAmP 91*
**Martin**, William Joseph, Jr. 1868-1943 *DcNCBi 4*
**Martin**, William L, Jr 1936- *AmMWSc 92*
**Martin**, William Louis, Jr. 1957- *WhoWest 92*
**Martin**, William Macphail 1919- *AmMWSc 92*
**Martin**, William McChesney, Jr. 1906- *Who 92*
**Martin**, William N 1945- *WhoAmP 91*
**Martin**, William Oliver 1919- *WhoIns 92*
**Martin**, William Paxman 1912- *AmMWSc 92*
**Martin**, William R. 1926- *WhoBlA 92*
**Martin**, William R. 1945- *WhoMW 92*
**Martin**, William Randolph 1922- *AmMWSc 92*
**Martin**, William Raymond 1939- *WhoFI 92*
**Martin**, William Robert 1921- *AmMWSc 92*
**Martin**, William Robert 1927- *WhoFI 92*
**Martin**, William Royall, Jr 1926- *AmMWSc 92*
**Martin**, William Travis, Sr. 1930- *WhoEnt 92*
**Martin**, William Truett 1924- *WhoAmP 91*
**Martin**, Yvonne Connolly 1936- *AmMWSc 92*
**Martin-Alonso**, Olga 1959- *WhoFI 92*
**Martin-Artajo**, Alberto 1904?-1979 *FacFETw*
**Martin-Bates**, James Patrick 1912- *Who 92*
**Martin-Bird**, Richard Dawnay 1910- *Who 92*
**Martin-Bowen**, Lindsey 1949- *WhoMW 92*
**Martin del Campo**, Diego Ramiro 1929- *WhoFI 92*
**Martin-Deleon**, Patricia Anastasia *AmMWSc 92*
**Martin du Gard**, Roger 1881-1958 *FacFETw, GuFrLit 1, WhoNob 90*
**Martin Fernandez**, Miguel 1943- *IntWW 91*
**Martin Garcia**, Fernando *WhoAmP 91*
**Martin-Hemphill** *Who 92*
**Martin-Jenkins**, Christopher Dennis A 1945- *IntAu&W 91, Who 92*
**Martin-Jenkins**, Dennis Frederick 1911- *Who 92*
**Martin Mateo**, Ramon 1928- *IntWW 91*
**Martin Villa**, Rodolfo 1934- *IntWW 91*
**Martin y Soler**, Vicente 1754-1806 *NewAmDM*
**Martina**, Dominico F. *IntWW 91*
**Martinazzoli**, Mino Fermo 1931- *IntWW 91*
**Martindale**, Alan Rawes 1930- *Who 92*
**Martindale**, Andrew 1932- *WrDr 92*
**Martindale**, Hilda 1875-1952 *BiDBrF 2*
**Martindale**, Isaac C 1842-1893 *BiInAmS*
**Martindale**, Larry Richard 1938- *WhoMW 92*
**Martindale**, Louisa 1839-1914 *BiDBrF 2*
**Martindale**, Louisa 1873-1966 *BiDBrF 2*
**Martindale**, Wallace S 1930- *AmMWSc 92*
**Martindale**, William Earl 1923- *AmMWSc 92*
**Martindell**, Ann Clark *WhoAmP 91*
**Martineau**, Charles Herman 1908- *Who 92*
**Martineau**, Gerard M 1958- *WhoAmP 91*
**Martineau**, Harriet 1802- *BenetAL 91*
**Martineau**, Harriet 1802-1876 *RfGEnL 91, WomSoc*
**Martineau**, Paul 1921- *IntWW 91*
**Martineau**, Reed Lynn 1932- *WhoAmL 92*
**Martineau**, Robert Arnold Schurhoff 1913- *Who 92*
**Martineau**, Ronald 1946- *AmMWSc 92*
**Martineau-Walker**, Roger Antony *Who 92*
**Martinec**, Emil Louis 1927- *AmMWSc 92*
**Martinek**, George William 1932- *AmMWSc 92*
**Martinek**, Robert George 1919- *AmMWSc 92*
**Martinelli**, Alfred Walter 1928- *WhoFI 92*
**Martinelli**, Angelo R 1927- *WhoAmP 91*
**Martinelli**, Eloy Eduardo 1954- *WhoMW 92*
**Martinelli**, Ernest A 1919- *AmMWSc 92*
**Martinelli**, Giovanni 1885-1969 *FacFETw*
**Martinelli**, Giovanni Innocenzo *WhoRel 92*
**Martinelli**, Kenneth Dean 1946- *WhoIns 92*
**Martinelli**, Mario, Jr 1922- *AmMWSc 92*
**Martinelli**, Michael John 1958- *WhoMW 92*
**Martinelli**, Ramon U 1938- *AmMWSc 92*
**Martinelli**, Rosemary 1957- *WhoFI 92*
**Martinello**, Giovanni 1885-1969 *NewAmDM*
**Martines**, Karen Louise 1952- *WhoWest 92*
**Martines**, Steven L. *WhoHisp 92*
**Martinet**, Gilles 1916- *IntAu&W 91, IntWW 91*
**Martinet**, Louis 1810-1894 *ThHEIm*
**Martinette**, Jan 1938- *WhoAmP 91*
**Martinetti**, Ronald Anthony 1945- *WhoWest 92*
**Martinez**, A *WhoHisp 92*
**Martinez**, A Julio *AmMWSc 92*
**Martinez**, Adele Virginia Hansen 1920- *WhoHisp 92*
**Martinez**, Al 1929- *WhoHisp 92*
**Martinez**, Albert 1941- *WhoHisp 92*
**Martinez**, Albert 1945- *WhoFI 92*
**Martinez**, Alejandro *WhoHisp 92*
**Martinez**, Alejandro Macias 1951- *WhoHisp 92*
**Martinez**, Alex G. *WhoHisp 92*
**Martinez**, Alex J. 1950- *WhoHisp 92*
**Martinez**, Alex J. 1951- *WhoHisp 92*
**Martinez**, Alfred P. 1939- *WhoHisp 92*
**Martinez**, Andrew Arthur 1941- *WhoHisp 92*
**Martinez**, Anna Louise 1952- *WhoHisp 92*
**Martinez**, Anthony Leonard 1961- *WhoRel 92*
**Martinez**, Anthony M. *WhoHisp 92*
**Martinez**, Antonio F. *WhoHisp 92*
**Martinez**, Aristides 1937- *WhoHisp 92*
**Martinez**, Armando 1938- *WhoHisp 92*
**Martinez**, Armando 1961- *BlkOlyM*
**Martinez**, Arthur *WhoHisp 92*
**Martinez**, Arthur D. *WhoHisp 92*
**Martinez**, Arturo David 1966- *WhoWest 92*
**Martinez**, Augusto Julio 1930- *WhoHisp 92*
**Martinez**, Avelino 1940- *WhoHisp 92*
**Martinez**, Azalia Veronica 1950- *WhoHisp 92*
**Martinez**, Ben *WhoAmP 91, WhoHisp 92*
**Martinez**, Blas M. 1935- *WhoHisp 92*
**Martinez**, Bob 1934- *News 92-1 [port], WhoHisp 92*
**Martinez**, Bobby R. *WhoHisp 92*
**Martinez**, Camilla Maria 1954- *WhoWest 92*
**Martinez**, Camilo Amado, Jr. 1935- *WhoHisp 92*
**Martinez**, Cari-Anne J. 1958- *WhoHisp 92*
**Martinez**, Carlos Alberto 1965- *WhoHisp 92*
**Martinez**, Carmelo 1960- *WhoHisp 92*

**Martinez**, Cecilia Gonzalez 1958- *WhoHisp 92*
**Martinez**, Celestino 1945- *WhoHisp 92*
**Martinez**, Cervando, Jr. 1941- *WhoHisp 92*
**Martinez**, Cesar Augusto 1944- *WhoHisp 92*
**Martinez**, Charles 1953- *WhoHisp 92*
**Martinez**, Charles A. 1938- *WhoHisp 92*
**Martinez**, Cleopatria 1948- *WhoHisp 92*
**Martinez**, D M 1918- *WhoAmP 91*
**Martinez**, Daniel Agustin 1954- *WhoHisp 92*
**Martinez**, Daniel Lee 1948- *WhoAmP 91*
**Martinez**, Danny 1948- *WhoHisp 92*
**Martinez**, Dave 1964- *WhoHisp 92*
**Martinez**, David *WhoAmP 91*
**Martinez**, David 1963- *WhoHisp 92*
**Martinez**, David G. *WhoHisp 92*
**Martinez**, David Herrera 1937- *WhoHisp 92*
**Martinez**, David Joseph 1950- *WhoWest 92*
**Martinez**, David Richard 1945- *WhoMW 92*
**Martinez**, Delia E 1948- *WhoAmP 91*
**Martinez**, Dennis 1955- *WhoHisp 92*
**Martinez**, Dennis 1965- *WhoHisp 92*
**Martinez**, Diego Gutierrez 1948- *WhoHisp 92*
**Martinez**, Dionisio D. 1956- *WhoHisp 92*
**Martinez**, Edgar 1963- *WhoHisp 92*
**Martinez**, Edgardo Ruben 1943- *WhoHisp 92*
**Martinez**, Edward Ernest 1954- *WhoHisp 92*
**Martinez**, Efren 1949- *WhoHisp 92*
**Martinez**, Elmer 1933- *WhoHisp 92*
**Martinez**, Eloise Fontanet 1931- *WhoHisp 92*
**Martinez**, Elsie Consuelo 1946- *WhoEnt 92*
**Martinez**, Eluid Levi 1944- *WhoHisp 92*
**Martinez**, Elvin L 1934- *WhoAmP 91, WhoHisp 92*
**Martinez**, Erminio E. 1943- *WhoHisp 92*
**Martinez**, Ernest Alcario, Jr. 1941- *WhoHisp 92*
**Martinez**, Ernesto *BlkOlyM*
**Martinez**, Ernesto, Jr. 1941- *WhoHisp 92*
**Martinez**, Esteban Conde 1932- *WhoHisp 92*
**Martinez**, Estela M. *WhoHisp 92*
**Martinez**, Evelyn Romero 1944- *WhoHisp 92*
**Martinez**, Florian 1927- *WhoHisp 92*
**Martinez**, Frank 1955- *WhoHisp 92*
**Martinez**, Gabriel Guerrero, Jr. 1951- *WhoHisp 92*
**Martinez**, George 1955- *WhoHisp 92*
**Martinez**, George R 1920- *WhoAmP 91*
**Martinez**, Gerald Lafayette 1939- *WhoHisp 92*
**Martinez**, Gina Amelia 1960- *WhoHisp 92*
**Martinez**, Guillermo *WhoHisp 92*
**Martinez**, Gustave *WhoEnt 92*
**Martinez**, Harold H. *WhoHisp 92*
**Martinez**, Harold Joseph 1959- *WhoHisp 92*
**Martinez**, Hector 1962- *WhoFI 92*
**Martinez**, Henry J. *WhoHisp 92*
**Martinez**, Humberto L. 1944- *WhoHisp 92*
**Martinez**, Ignacio E. 1931- *WhoHisp 92*
**Martinez**, Irene B. 1944- *WhoHisp 92*
**Martinez**, J Ricardo *AmMWSc 92*
**Martinez**, James Jose 1955- *WhoHisp 92*
**Martinez**, Jeordano 1946- *WhoEnt 92*
**Martinez**, Jeordano Severo *WhoHisp 92*
**Martinez**, Jesus M. *WhoHisp 92*
**Martinez**, Jo Ann 1950- *WhoEnt 92*
**Martinez**, Joe L. 1944- *WhoHisp 92*
**Martinez**, Joe L, Jr 1944- *AmMWSc 92*
**Martinez**, John L 1922- *AmMWSc 92*
**Martinez**, John Lee 1934- *WhoHisp 92*
**Martinez**, John Stanley 1930- *WhoHisp 92, WhoWest 92*
**Martinez**, John Z. 1946- *WhoHisp 92*
**Martinez**, Jorge 1940- *WhoHisp 92*
**Martinez**, Jorge 1945- *AmMWSc 92*
**Martinez**, Jose 1942- *WhoHisp 92*
**Martinez**, Jose 1950- *WhoHisp 92*
**Martinez**, Jose Angel 1946- *WhoHisp 92*
**Martinez**, Jose de Jesus d1991 *NewYTBS 91*
**Martinez**, Jose E 1922- *AmMWSc 92*
**Martinez**, Jose E 1943- *AmMWSc 92*
**Martinez**, Jose E. 1954- *WhoHisp 92*
**Martinez**, Jose M., Jr. 1933- *WhoHisp 92*
**Martinez**, Jose Martin 1954- *WhoHisp 92*
**Martinez**, Joseph 1941- *WhoHisp 92*
**Martinez**, Joseph Phillip 1948- *WhoHisp 92*
**Martinez**, Joseph V. *WhoHisp 92*
**Martinez**, Juan David 1962- *WhoHisp 92*
**Martinez**, Juan Manuel 1948- *WhoFI 92*
**Martinez**, Judith 1955- *WhoHisp 92*
**Martinez**, Julia Jaramillo 1926- *WhoHisp 92*
**Martinez**, Julio Enrique 1943- *WhoEnt 92*
**Martinez**, Julio Enrique, Jr. 1943- *WhoHisp 92*
**Martinez**, Julio J 1943- *WhoAmP 91, WhoHisp 92*
**Martinez**, Kenneth A. 1935- *WhoHisp 92*
**Martinez**, Kenneth John 1949- *WhoEnt 92*
**Martinez**, Laudelina *WhoHisp 92*
**Martinez**, Lee William 1953- *WhoHisp 92*
**Martinez**, Leodoro, Jr. 1949- *WhoHisp 92*
**Martinez**, Lilliam *WhoHisp 92*
**Martinez**, Lorenzo *BlkOlyM*
**Martinez**, Luis *BlkOlyM*
**Martinez**, Luis Osvaldo 1927- *AmMWSc 92*
**Martinez**, Lupe 1945- *WhoHisp 92*
**Martinez**, Luz Alvarez *WhoHisp 92*
**Martinez**, M. A. Laura 1960- *WhoHisp 92*
**Martinez**, M. Salome 1947- *WhoHisp 92*
**Martinez**, Manuel C. 1945- *WhoHisp 92*
**Martinez**, Manuel S. *WhoHisp 92*
**Martinez**, Marciano 1939- *WhoHisp 92*
**Martinez**, Marcos L. 1955- *WhoHisp 92*
**Martinez**, Maria J. 1951- *WhoHisp 92*
**Martinez**, Maria Montoya 1881?-1980 *HanAmWH*
**Martinez**, Mario G., Jr. 1924- *WhoHisp 92*
**Martinez**, Mario Guillermo, Jr 1924- *AmMWSc 92*
**Martinez**, Marlo R. 1957- *WhoHisp 92*
**Martinez**, Martin *WhoHisp 92*
**Martinez**, Mary Jane 1953- *WhoHisp 92*
**Martinez**, Matt C. *WhoHisp 92*
**Martinez**, Matt G., Sr. 1917- *WhoHisp 92*
**Martinez**, Matthew G. 1929- *AlmAP 92 [port], WhoAmP 91, WhoHisp 92*
**Martinez**, Matthew Gilbert 1929- *WhoWest 92*
**Martinez**, Melquiades R. 1946- *WhoAmL 92*
**Martinez**, Melvin H. *WhoHisp 92*
**Martinez**, Mercurio, Jr. 1937- *WhoHisp 92*
**Martinez**, Michael C. 1954- *WhoHisp 92, WhoWest 92*
**Martinez**, Michael E. *WhoHisp 92*
**Martinez**, Michael J. *WhoHisp 92*
**Martinez**, Michael N. *WhoAmL 92*
**Martinez**, Michael N 1949- *WhoAmP 91, WhoHisp 92*
**Martinez**, Miguel A. 1930- *WhoHisp 92*
**Martinez**, Miguel Agustin 1937- *WhoHisp 92*
**Martinez**, Miguel Angel 1930- *WhoMW 92*
**Martinez**, Nabar Enrique 1946- *WhoHisp 92*
**Martinez**, Narciso 1911- *WhoHisp 92*
**Martinez**, Octavio Nestor, Jr. 1961- *WhoHisp 92*
**Martinez**, Octavio Vincent 1947- *AmMWSc 92, WhoHisp 92*
**Martinez**, Orlando 1944- *BlkOlyM*
**Martinez**, Orlando 1957- *WhoHisp 92*
**Martinez**, Oscar J. 1943- *WhoHisp 92*
**Martinez**, Oscar Luis 1952- *WhoHisp 92*
**Martinez**, Osmundo Oscar, Jr. 1954- *WhoAmL 92*
**Martinez**, Pablo Patrick 1949- *WhoWest 92*
**Martinez**, Patricia Hincapie 1959- *WhoHisp 92*
**Martinez**, Paul Edward 1952- *WhoHisp 92*
**Martinez**, Pedro 1924- *WhoHisp 92*
**Martinez**, Pedro L. 1951- *WhoHisp 92*
**Martinez**, Pete *WhoHisp 92*
**Martinez**, Pete, Jr. 1943- *WhoHisp 92*
**Martinez**, Pete R. 1937- *WhoHisp 92*
**Martinez**, R. Diane 1955- *WhoHisp 92*
**Martinez**, Rafael Juan 1927- *AmMWSc 92*
**Martinez**, Ralph *WhoBlA 92*
**Martinez**, Ralph T., Jr. 1925- *WhoHisp 92*
**Martinez**, Ramon Jaime 1968- *WhoBlA 92, WhoHisp 92*
**Martinez**, Ramona Elizabeth 1943- *WhoHisp 92*
**Martinez**, Raul 1953- *WhoHisp 92*
**Martinez**, Raul Cisneros 1942- *WhoHisp 92*
**Martinez**, Raul L 1949- *WhoAmP 91*
**Martinez**, Raul O. *WhoHisp 92*
**Martinez**, Raymond 1953- *WhoHisp 92*
**Martinez**, Ricardo Pedro 1945- *WhoHisp 92*
**Martinez**, Ricardo Salazar 1951- *WhoHisp 92*
**Martinez**, Rich 1950- *WhoHisp 92*
**Martinez**, Richard *WhoHisp 92*
**Martinez**, Richard 1952- *WhoHisp 92*
**Martinez**, Richard 1955- *WhoHisp 92*
**Martinez**, Richard Anthony 1951- *WhoMW 92*
**Martinez**, Richard Isaac 1944- *AmMWSc 92, WhoHisp 92*
**Martinez**, Robert 1934- *IntWW 91, WhoAmP 91*
**Martinez**, Robert 1943- *WhoAmP 91, WhoHisp 92*
**Martinez**, Robert 1949- *WhoHisp 92*
**Martinez**, Robert A. *WhoHisp 92*
**Martinez**, Robert A 1943- *WhoAmP 91, WhoHisp 92*
**Martinez**, Robert Manuel 1943- *AmMWSc 92*
**Martinez**, Robert Orlando 1944- *WhoHisp 92*
**Martinez**, Roman, IV 1947- *WhoFI 92*
**Martinez**, Roman Octaviano 1958- *WhoAmP 91, WhoHisp 92*
**Martinez**, Rosa Borrero 1956- *WhoHisp 92*
**Martinez**, Ruben Martin 1948- *WhoWest 92*
**Martinez**, Ruben O. 1952- *WhoHisp 92*
**Martinez**, Ruben Orlando 1952- *WhoWest 92*
**Martinez**, Sally Verdugo 1934- *WhoHisp 92*
**Martinez**, Salutario 1935- *WhoHisp 92*
**Martinez**, Salvador Matiella 1926- *WhoWest 92*
**Martinez**, Seledon C., Sr. 1921- *WhoHisp 92*
**Martinez**, Serge Anthony 1942- *WhoHisp 92*
**Martinez**, Sergio E. 1919- *WhoHisp 92*
**Martinez**, Steven Frank 1956- *WhoMW 92*
**Martinez**, Sylvia Ann 1951- *WhoHisp 92*
**Martinez**, Timothy J. 1961- *WhoHisp 92*
**Martinez**, Tino 1967- *WhoHisp 92*
**Martinez**, Tomas Eloy 1935- *LiExTwC*
**Martinez**, Tomas Eugene 1949- *WhoHisp 92*
**Martinez**, Tony, Jr. *WhoHisp 92*
**Martinez**, Tony Ramon 1958- *WhoHisp 92*
**Martinez**, Victor Hipolito 1924- *IntWW 91*
**Martinez**, Vilma S. 1943- *WhoHisp 92*
**Martinez**, Virginia 1949- *WhoHisp 92*
**Martinez**, Walter 1951- *WhoAmP 91, WhoHisp 92*
**Martinez**, Walter Kenneth, Jr. 1959- *WhoHisp 92*
**Martinez**, William Eliu 1959- *WhoHisp 92*
**Martinez**, William G. 1938- *WhoHisp 92*
**Martinez**, Yvette 1954- *WhoHisp 92*
**Martinez**, Zarela 1947- *WhoHisp 92*
**Martinez**, Zilliam *WhoHisp 92*
**Martinez-Alvarez**, Francisco J. 1960- *WhoHisp 92*
**Martinez Benitez**, Candida 1923- *WhoAmP 91*
**Martinez-Bonati**, Felix *WhoHisp 92*
**Martinez-Borchard**, Richard *WhoHisp 92*
**Martinez-Brawley**, Emilia E. *WhoHisp 92*
**Martinez-Burgoyne**, Toni 1943- *WhoHisp 92*
**Martinez Campos**, Arsenio 1831-1900 *HisDSpE*
**Martinez-Carrion**, Marino 1936- *AmMWSc 92*
**Martinez-Chavez**, Diana 1955- *WhoHisp 92*
**Martinez Companon y Bujando**, Baltasar J 1737-1797 *HisDSpE*
**Martinez Cruz**, Americo 1938- *WhoAmP 91, WhoHisp 92*
**Martinez de Irala**, Domingo 1510?-1557 *HisDSpE*
**Martinez De Peron**, Maria Estela 1931- *IntWW 91*
**Martinez de Pinillos**, Joaquin Victor 1941- *AmMWSc 92, WhoHisp 92*
**Martinez de Rosas Correa**, Juan 1759-1813 *HisDSpE*
**Martinez Duarte**, Elena *WhoAmP 91*
**Martinez Esteruelas**, Cruz 1932- *IntWW 91*
**Martinez-Fonts**, Alberto, Jr. 1943- *WhoHisp 92*
**Martinez-Fonts**, Pedro A. 1945- *WhoHisp 92*
**Martinez Gandara**, Julio Antonio 1931- *WhoHisp 92*
**Martinez-Garduno**, Beatriz 1940- *WhoHisp 92*
**Martinez-Hernandez**, Antonio 1944- *AmMWSc 92*
**Martinez-Lopez**, Jorge Ignacio 1926- *AmMWSc 92, WhoHisp 92*
**Martinez-Lopez**, Norman P. *WhoHisp 92*
**Martinez-Lopez**, Norman Petronio 1943- *AmMWSc 92*
**Martinez-Maldonado**, Manuel 1937- *AmMWSc 92, WhoHisp 92*
**Martinez Marquez**, Guillermo d1992 *WhoHisp 92N*
**Martinez-Miranda**, Luz Josefina 1956- *WhoHisp 92*
**Martinez-Nazario**, Ronaldo 1958- *WhoHisp 92*
**Martinez Ordonez**, Jose Roberto 1922- *IntWW 91*
**Martinez-Paula**, Emilio *WhoHisp 92*
**Martinez-Poblanno**, Irene Elizabeth 1954- *WhoHisp 92*
**Martinez-Purson**, Rita 1955- *WhoHisp 92*
**Martinez-Ramirez**, Jose Roberto 1954- *WhoHisp 92*
**Martinez Rivas**, Carlos 1924- *ConSpAP*
**Martinez-Roach**, N. Patricia 1949- *WhoHisp 92*
**Martinez-Romero**, Sergio 1936- *WhoHisp 92*
**Martinez Smith**, Elizabeth *WhoWest 92*
**Martinez Somalo**, Eduardo 1927- *IntWW 91, WhoRel 92*
**Martinez Toro**, Vilma 1959- *WhoHisp 92*
**Martinez Zuviria**, Gustavo 1915- *Who 92*
**Marting**, Janet Samuelson *DrAPF 91*
**Marting**, Michael G. 1948- *WhoAmL 92, WhoMW 92*
**Martini**, Padre *NewAmDM*
**Martini**, Arthur Pete 1943- *WhoWest 92*
**Martini**, Carlo Maria 1927- *IntWW 91, Who 92, WhoRel 92*
**Martini**, Catherine Marie 1924- *AmMWSc 92*
**Martini**, Charles C 1940- *WhoIns 92*
**Martini**, David Joseph 1953- *WhoWest 92*
**Martini**, Emil P., Jr. 1928- *WhoFI 92, WhoWest 92*
**Martini**, Fritz 1909- *IntWW 91*
**Martini**, Galen *DrAPF 91*
**Martini**, Giovanni Battista 1706-1784 *NewAmDM*
**Martini**, Ireneo Peter 1935- *AmMWSc 92*
**Martini**, Johann Paul Aegidius 1741-1816 *NewAmDM*
**Martini**, Mario 1939- *AmMWSc 92*
**Martini**, Richard John 1955- *WhoEnt 92*
**Martini**, Richard K. 1952- *WhoEnt 92*
**Martini**, Robert E. 1932- *WhoFI 92, WhoWest 92*
**Martini**, Teri 1930- *IntAu&W 91, WrDr 92*
**Martini-Urdaneta**, Alberto 1930- *IntWW 91*
**Martinis**, John Anthony 1930- *WhoAmP 91*
**Martino**, Babette 1956- *WhoEnt 92*
**Martino**, David 1958- *WhoRel 92*
**Martino**, Donald 1931- *ConCom 92, NewAmDM*
**Martino**, Donald James 1931- *WhoEnt 92*
**Martino**, Eva Ellena 1926- *WhoEnt 92*
**Martino**, Joseph Paul 1931- *AmMWSc 92, WhoMW 92*
**Martino**, Nina Florence 1952- *WhoEnt 92*
**Martino**, Robert Salvatore 1931- *WhoMW 92*
**Martino**, Rocco Leonard 1929- *WhoFI 92*
**Martino**, Steve *WhoEnt 92*
**Martinon**, Jean 1910-1976 *NewAmDM*
**Martins**, Antonio Gentil da Silva 1930- *IntWW 91*
**Martins**, Donald Henry 1945- *AmMWSc 92*
**Martins**, Paul G. 1956- *WhoFI 92*
**Martins**, Peter 1946- *FacFETw, IntWW 91, WhoEnt 92*
**Martins**, Rudolf 1915- *IntWW 91*
**Martins-Green**, Manuela 1947- *WhoWest 92*
**Martins-Green**, Manuela M 1947- *AmMWSc 92*
**Martinsek**, Adam Thomas 1953- *AmMWSc 92*
**Martinsen**, Jon Nils 1936- *WhoMW 92*
**Martinson**, Candace 1949- *AmMWSc 92*
**Martinson**, Charlie Anton 1934- *AmMWSc 92, WhoMW 92*
**Martinson**, Constance Frye 1932- *WhoEnt 92, WhoWest 92*
**Martinson**, David *DrAPF 91*
**Martinson**, Dawn Rose 1965- *WhoMW 92*
**Martinson**, Edwin O 1910- *AmMWSc 92*
**Martinson**, Harold Gerhard 1943- *AmMWSc 92*
**Martinson**, Harry 1904-1978 *ConAu 34NR, FacFETw*
**Martinson**, Harry Edmund 1904-1978 *WhoNob 90*
**Martinson**, Ida Marie 1936- *AmMWSc 92, IntWW 91*
**Martinson**, John Robert 1935- *WhoWest 92*
**Martinson**, Julia Ellenor 1951- *WhoWest 92*
**Martinson**, Robert William 1946- *WhoAmP 91*
**Martinson**, Sergey Aleksandrovich 1899- *SovUnBD*
**Martinson**, William D. 1924-1979 *ConAu 135*
**Martinsons**, Aleksandrs 1912- *AmMWSc 92*
**Martinu**, Bohuslav 1890-1959 *FacFETw, NewAmDM*
**Martirano**, Salvatore 1927- *NewAmDM*
**Martire**, Daniel Edward 1937- *AmMWSc 92*
**Martis**, Robert A. 1963- *WhoEnt 92*
**Martland**, Carl Douglas 1946- *AmMWSc 92*
**Martland**, Steve 1959- *ConCom 92*

**Martlew,** Eric Anthony 1949- *Who 92*
**Martling,** W Kent 1924- *WhoAmP 91*
**Martner,** Samuel 1918- *AmMWSc 92*
**Marto,** Paul James 1938- *AmMWSc 92, WhoWest 92*
**Martocci,** Joseph Patrick, Jr. 1952- *WhoAmL 92*
**Martoglio,** Jeanne Marie 1961- *WhoAmL 92*
**Martoia,** Ronald Steven 1962- *WhoRel 92*
**Marton,** Andrew 1904- *IntMPA 92*
**Marton,** Emery 1922- *WhoAmL 92*
**Marton,** Eva 1943- *WhoEnt 92*
**Marton,** John P 1926- *WhoAmP 91*
**Marton,** Joseph 1919- *AmMWSc 92*
**Marton,** Laurence Jay 1944- *AmMWSc 92*
**Marton,** Michael 1942- *WhoEnt 92*
**Marton,** Renata 1910- *AmMWSc 92*
**Marton,** Victor William 1951- *WhoAmL 92*
**Martone,** Michael *DrAPF 91*
**Martone,** Michael 1955- *IntAu&W 91*
**Martone,** Patricia Ann 1947- *WhoAmL 92*
**Martone,** William Anthony 1949- *WhoFI 92*
**Martonmere,** Baron 1963- *Who 92*
**Martono** 1925- *IntWW 91*
**Martonosi,** Anthony 1928- *AmMWSc 92*
**Martorell,** Joseph Anthony 1939- *WhoHisp 92*
**Martori,** Joseph Peter 1941- *WhoAmL 92*
**Martre,** Jean Francois Henri 1928- *IntWW 91*
**Marts,** Albert Lee 1950- *WhoRel 92*
**Martschink,** Sherry Shealy 1949- *WhoAmP 91*
**Martsolf,** J David 1932- *AmMWSc 92*
**Martt,** Jack M 1922- *AmMWSc 92*
**Marttila,** James Konstantin 1948- *WhoMW 92*
**Marttinen,** Tauno 1912- *ConCom 92*
**Martucci,** John A 1932- *AmMWSc 92*
**Martucci,** Thomas F 1933- *WhoIns 92*
**Martucci,** William Christopher 1952- *WhoAmL 92*
**Marturet,** Eduardo 1953- *WhoEnt 92*
**Marty,** Francois 1904- *IntWW 91, Who 92, WhoRel 92*
**Marty,** John 1956- *WhoMW 92*
**Marty,** John J 1949- *WhoAmP 91*
**Marty,** Julio E. *WhoHisp 92*
**Marty,** Lawrence A 1926- *WhoAmP 91*
**Marty,** Martin E 1928- *IntAu&W 91, IntWW 91, WrDr 92*
**Marty,** Martin Emil 1928- *RelLAm 91, WhoRel 92*
**Marty,** Robert Joseph 1931- *AmMWSc 92*
**Marty,** Roger Henry 1942- *AmMWSc 92, WhoMW 92*
**Marty,** Sid 1944- *IntAu&W 91, WrDr 92*
**Marty,** Wayne George 1932- *AmMWSc 92*
**Martyn,** Charles Roger Nicholas 1925- *Who 92*
**Martyn,** David William 1949- *WhoFI 92, WhoMW 92*
**Martyn,** Edward 1859-1923 *RfGEnL 91*
**Martyn,** James Louis 1925- *WhoRel 92*
**Martyn,** Phillip *TwCSFW 91*
**Martynenko,** Vladimir Nikiforovich 1923- *IntWW 91*
**Martynov,** Leonid Nikolaevich 1905-1980 *SovUnBD*
**Martynov,** Nikolay Vasiliyevich 1910- *IntWW 91*
**Martynov,** Vladen Arkad'evich 1929- *SovUnBD*
**Martynov,** Vladilen Arkadevich 1929- *IntWW 91*
**Martyr,** Peter 1457-1526 *BenetAL 91*
**Martz,** Bill L 1922- *AmMWSc 92*
**Martz,** Carl Scott 1958- *WhoWest 92*
**Martz,** Dowell Edward 1923- *AmMWSc 92*
**Martz,** Eric 1940- *AmMWSc 92*
**Martz,** Fredric A 1935- *AmMWSc 92*
**Martz,** Harry Edward, Jr 1957- *AmMWSc 92*
**Martz,** Harry Franklin, Jr 1942- *AmMWSc 92*
**Martz,** Linda 1939- *ConAu 135*
**Martz,** Louis 1913- *IntAu&W 91, WrDr 92*
**Martz,** Lyle F 1922- *AmMWSc 92*
**Maruca,** Robert Eugene 1941- *AmMWSc 92*
**Marulla** *EncAmaz 91*
**Marullo,** Nicasio Philip 1930- *AmMWSc 92*
**Marumoto,** Barbara C 1939- *WhoAmP 91*
**Marumoto,** William Hideo 1934- *WhoFI 92*
**Marusich,** Wilbur Lewis *AmMWSc 92*
**Maruska,** Edward Joseph 1934- *WhoMW 92*
**Marusyk,** Raymond George 1942- *AmMWSc 92*
**Maruta,** Hiroshi 1942- *AmMWSc 92*
**Maruta,** Leszek 1930- *IntAu&W 91*
**Maruvada,** P Sarma 1938- *AmMWSc 92*
**Maruya,** Saiichi 1925- *ConAu 135*
**Maruyama,** Allen 1926- *WhoRel 92*
**Maruyama,** George Masao 1918- *AmMWSc 92*
**Maruyama,** Henry Hatsuo 1923- *WhoWest 92*
**Maruyama,** Koshi 1932- *AmMWSc 92*
**Maruyama,** Masao 1914- *IntWW 91*
**Maruyama,** Tani Kathleen 1956- *WhoMW 92*
**Maruyama,** Yosh 1930- *AmMWSc 92*
**Marvar,** Raymond James 1954- *WhoAmL 92*
**Marvasti,** Akbar Barzegar 1952- *WhoFI 92*
**Marve,** Eugene Raymond 1960- *WhoBlA 92*
**Marvel,** Andrew Scott 1961- *WhoEnt 92*
**Marvel,** Billy Bryan 1913- *WhoAmP 91*
**Marvel,** Ik *BenetAL 91*
**Marvel,** John Thomas 1938- *AmMWSc 92*
**Marvel,** John W 1926- *WhoAmP 91*
**Marvel,** Kenneth Robert 1952- *WhoAmL 92*
**Marvel,** Mason E 1921- *AmMWSc 92*
**Marvel,** William d1991 *NewYTBS 91*
**Marvel Jova,** Thomas S. 1935- *WhoHisp 92*
**Marvell,** Andrew 1621-1678 *CnDBLB 2 [port], RfGEnL 91*
**Marvil,** Patricia De L. *WhoHisp 92*
**Marvin,** Blanche 1926- *IntAu&W 91*
**Marvin,** Charles *DrAPF 91*
**Marvin,** Charles Arthur 1942- *WhoAmL 92*
**Marvin,** David Edward Shreve 1950- *WhoMW 92*
**Marvin,** Enoch Mather 1823-1877 *RelLAm 91*
**Marvin,** Frank Olin 1852-1915 *BiInAmS*
**Marvin,** Frederick 1923- *WhoEnt 92*
**Marvin,** Helen Rhyne 1917- *WhoAmP 91*
**Marvin,** Henry Howard, Jr 1923- *AmMWSc 92*
**Marvin,** Horace Newell 1915- *AmMWSc 92*
**Marvin,** James 1820-1901 *BiInAmS*
**Marvin,** John George 1912- *WhoRel 92*
**Marvin,** Julie *WrDr 92*
**Marvin,** Mel 1941- *WhoEnt 92*
**Marvin,** Mike 1945- *WhoEnt 92*
**Marvin,** Philip 1916- *WrDr 92*
**Marvin,** Philip Roger 1916- *AmMWSc 92*
**Marvin,** Richard F 1926- *AmMWSc 92*
**Marvin,** Ursula Bailey 1921- *AmMWSc 92*
**Marvin,** W.R. *TwCWW 91*
**Marvine,** Archibald R 1848-1876 *BiInAmS*
**Marwah,** Joe 1952- *AmMWSc 92*
**Marwick,** Alan David 1946- *AmMWSc 92*
**Marwick,** Arthur 1936- *IntAu&W 91, WrDr 92*
**Marwick,** Arthur John Brereton 1936- *Who 92*
**Marwick,** Brian 1908- *Who 92*
**Marwick,** Ewan 1952- *Who 92*
**Marwick,** Max Gay 1916- *WrDr 92*
**Marwil,** Jonathan L 1940- *ConAu 35NR*
**Marwil,** S J 1921- *AmMWSc 92*
**Marwin,** Richard Martin 1918- *AmMWSc 92*
**Marwitz,** John D 1937- *AmMWSc 92*
**Marwood,** William *ConAu 133*
**Marx Brothers** *FacFETw*
**Marx,** Angelina Buonamassa 1926- *WhoEnt 92*
**Marx,** Anne *DrAPF 91*
**Marx,** Arthur 1921- *IntAu&W 91, WrDr 92*
**Marx,** Chico 1887-1961 *FacFETw*
**Marx,** Claudia Jeanne 1953- *WhoEnt 92*
**Marx,** Donald Henry 1936- *AmMWSc 92*
**Marx,** Egon 1937- *AmMWSc 92*
**Marx,** Elizabeth Ellen 1945- *WhoEnt 92*
**Marx,** Enid 1902- *TwCPaSc*
**Marx,** Enid Crystal Dorothy 1902- *Who 92*
**Marx,** Gary T. 1938- *WrDr 92*
**Marx,** George 1838-1895 *BiInAmS*
**Marx,** George Donald 1936- *AmMWSc 92*
**Marx,** Gerald Vincent 1926- *WhoWest 92*
**Marx,** Gerhard Albert Manfred 1959- *WhoMW 92*
**Marx,** Gertie F 1912- *AmMWSc 92*
**Marx,** Groucho d1977 *LesBEnT 92*
**Marx,** Groucho 1890?-1977 *FacFETw*
**Marx,** Gummo 1893?-1977 *FacFETw*
**Marx,** Gyorgy 1927- *IntWW 91*
**Marx,** Harpo 1888-1964 *FacFETw*
**Marx,** Hymen 1925- *AmMWSc 92*
**Marx,** James A. 1958- *WhoAmL 92*
**Marx,** James John, Jr 1944- *AmMWSc 92*
**Marx,** Jay Neil 1945- *AmMWSc 92*
**Marx,** John Norbert 1937- *AmMWSc 92*
**Marx,** Joseph 1882-1964 *NewAmDM*
**Marx,** Joseph Vincent 1943- *AmMWSc 92*
**Marx,** Karl 1818-1883 *EncTR 91*
**Marx,** Kenneth Allan *AmMWSc 92*
**Marx,** Kenneth Donald 1940- *AmMWSc 92*
**Marx,** Marvin d1975 *LesBEnT 92*
**Marx,** Michael 1933- *AmMWSc 92*
**Marx,** Michael David 1946- *AmMWSc 92*
**Marx,** Owen Cox 1947- *WhoAmL 92*
**Marx,** Paul Christian 1929- *AmMWSc 92*
**Marx,** Robert 1936- *IntAu&W 91, WrDr 92*
**Marx,** Robert Joseph 1927- *WhoRel 92*
**Marx,** Robert Kirk 1950- *WhoEnt 92*
**Marx,** Samuel 1902- *IntMPA 92*
**Marx,** Stephen John 1942- *AmMWSc 92*
**Marx,** Sue Elaine *WhoEnt 92*
**Marx,** Suzanne *WhoWest 92*
**Marx,** Wilhelm 1863-1946 *EncTR 91 [port]*
**Marx,** Zeppo 1901-1979 *FacFETw*
**Marxhausen,** Victor Herschel 1926- *WhoRel 92*
**Marxheimer,** Rene B 1923- *AmMWSc 92*
**Marxman,** Gerald Albert 1933- *WhoWest 92*
**Marxsen,** Willi 1919- *WhoRel 92*
**Mary** *EncEarC [port]*
**Mary,** Countess of Falconberg 1636-1712 *EncAmaz 91*
**Mary,** Lady Bankes d1661 *EncAmaz 91*
**Mary Leo,** Sister *Who 92*
**Mary of Guelders,** Queen of Scotland 1433-1463 *EncAmaz 91*
**Mary of Hungary** 1505-1558 *EncAmaz 91*
**Mary,** Nouri Y 1929- *AmMWSc 92*
**Maryanoff,** Bruce Eliot 1947- *AmMWSc 92*
**Maryanoff,** Cynthia Anne Milewski 1949- *AmMWSc 92*
**Maryanski,** Fred J 1946- *AmMWSc 92*
**Marychurch,** Peter 1927- *Who 92*
**Marye,** Madison Ellis 1925- *WhoAmP 91*
**Maryland,** Mary Angela 1953- *WhoBlA 92*
**Maryon Davis,** Alan Roger 1943- *Who 92*
**Marzan,** Julio *DrAPF 91*
**Marzani,** Carl 1912- *WrDr 92*
**Marzano,** Angelo Mario 1929- *WhoFI 92*
**Marzella,** Louis 1948- *AmMWSc 92*
**Marzetti,** Lawrence Arthur 1917- *AmMWSc 92*
**Marzia** *EncAmaz 91*
**Marziano,** Fredric G. *WhoFI 92*
**Marzilli,** Jim *WhoAmP 91*
**Marzke,** Robert Franklin 1938- *AmMWSc 92*
**Marzluf,** George A 1935- *AmMWSc 92*
**Marzluff,** William Frank, Jr 1945- *AmMWSc 92*
**Marzolf,** George Richard 1935- *AmMWSc 92*
**Marzoni,** Pettersen *ScFEYrs*
**Marzulli,** Francis Nicholas 1917- *AmMWSc 92*
**Marzulli,** John Anthony 1923- *WhoAmL 92*
**Marzulli,** John Anthony, Jr. 1953- *WhoAmL 92*
**Marzzacco,** Charles Joseph 1942- *AmMWSc 92*
**Mas,** Luis Pablo 1924- *WhoHisp 92*
**Mas Canosa,** Jorge L. 1939- *WhoHisp 92*
**Masa,** George 1882?-1933 *DcNCBi 4*
**Masaitis,** Ceslovas 1912- *AmMWSc 92*
**Masak,** Ronald Alan 1936- *WhoEnt 92*
**Masaki Hojo** *EncAmaz 91*
**Masaki,** Steven M. 1955- *WhoWest 92*
**Masaliev,** Absamat Masalevich 1933- *IntWW 91*
**Masaliev,** Absamat Masalievich 1933- *SovUnBD*
**Masamune,** Satoru 1928- *AmMWSc 92*
**Masani,** Minoo 1905- *IntWW 91*
**Masani,** Pesi Rustom 1919- *AmMWSc 92*
**Masanoff,** Michael David 1951- *WhoAmL 92*
**Masao,** Maruyama 1914- *WrDr 92*
**Masaoka,** Michikazu 1937- *IntWW 91*
**Masaoka,** Mike M. d1991 *NewYTBS 91*
**Masaracchia,** Ruthann A 1942- *AmMWSc 92*
**Masarraza,** Rafael *WhoHisp 92*
**Masaryk,** Alice 1879-1966 *WomSoc*
**Masaryk,** Jan 1886-1948 *EncTR 91, FacFETw [port]*
**Masaryk,** Tomas Garrigue 1850-1937 *EncTR 91 [port], FacFETw [port]*
**Masat,** Robert James 1928- *AmMWSc 92*
**Mascagni,** Pietro 1863-1945 *NewAmDM*
**Mascall,** Eric Lionel 1905- *IntWW 91, Who 92, WrDr 92*
**Mascarenas,** Fred Loi, Jr. 1953- *WhoAmL 92*
**Mascarenas,** Mark Scott 1962- *WhoHisp 92*
**Mascarenhas,** Joseph Peter 1929- *AmMWSc 92*
**Mascari,** Charles Joseph 1948- *WhoAmL 92*
**Mascavage,** Joseph Peter 1956- *WhoFI 92*
**Mascheroni,** Eleanor Earle 1955- *WhoFI 92*
**Mascheroni,** P Leonardo 1935- *AmMWSc 92*
**Masching,** Frances Marie 1926- *WhoMW 92*
**Maschke,** Heinrich 1853-1908 *BiInAmS*
**Maschler,** Fay 1945- *Who 92*
**Maschler,** Thomas Michael 1933- *IntAu&W 91, IntWW 91, Who 92*
**Mascia,** Joseph Serafino 1939- *WhoFI 92*
**Masciandaro,** Ronald Francis 1962- *WhoEnt 92*
**Masciantonio,** Philip 1929- *AmMWSc 92*
**Mascioli,** Rocco Lawrence 1928- *AmMWSc 92*
**Masco,** Dorothy Beryl 1918- *WhoAmP 91*
**Mascoll,** Edward G. 1935- *WhoBlA 92*
**Mascotte,** John Pierre 1939- *WhoFI 92*
**Masden,** Glenn W 1933- *AmMWSc 92*
**Masdeu,** Frida C. 1953- *WhoHisp 92*
**Masdottir,** Valgerdur Thora 1935- *IntAu&W 91*
**Mase,** Darrel Jay 1905- *AmMWSc 92*
**Mase,** Raymond James 1951- *WhoEnt 92*
**Masefield,** Geoffrey 1911- *IntAu&W 91, WrDr 92*
**Masefield,** John 1878-1967 *CnDBLB 5 [port], RfGEnL 91*
**Masefield,** John Thorold 1939- *IntWW 91, Who 92*
**Masefield,** Joseph R. 1933- *IntMPA 92*
**Masefield,** Peter 1914- *Who 92*
**Masefield,** Peter Gordon 1914- *IntWW 91*
**Masek,** Barry Michael 1955- *WhoMW 92*
**Masek,** Bruce James 1950- *AmMWSc 92*
**Masek,** George Edward 1927- *AmMWSc 92*
**Masekela,** Hugh 1931- *ConMus 7 [port]*
**Masekela,** Hugh 1939- *ConBlB 1 [port], IntWW 91*
**Masel,** Richard Isaac 1951- *AmMWSc 92*
**Masella,** Joseph 1950- *WhoIns 92*
**Maselli,** Giorgio 1947- *WhoFI 92*
**Maselli,** James Michael 1935- *AmMWSc 92*
**Maselli,** John Anthony 1928- *AmMWSc 92*
**Maser,** Chris 1938- *AmMWSc 92*
**Maser,** Frederick Ernest 1908- *WhoRel 92*
**Maser,** Karl A 1937- *WhoIns 92*
**Maser,** Morton D 1934- *AmMWSc 92*
**Masera,** Rainer Stefano 1944- *IntWW 91*
**Maserati,** Ettore 1894-1990 *AnObit 1990*
**Maseri,** Attilio 1935- *IntWW 91, Who 92*
**Maserick,** Peter H 1933- *AmMWSc 92*
**Maserjian,** Joseph 1929- *AmMWSc 92*
**Masey,** Mary Lou d1991 *NewYTBS 91*
**Masey,** Mary Lou 1932-1991 *ConAu 134*
**Mash,** Eric Jay 1943- *AmMWSc 92*
**Mash,** Jerry L. 1937- *WhoAmL 92*
**Mashaly,** Magdi Mohamed 1944- *AmMWSc 92*
**Masham,** Damaris 1658-1708 *BlkwCEP*
**Masham of Ilton,** Baroness 1935- *Who 92*
**Mashat,** Muhammad Sadiq al- 1930- *IntWW 91*
**Mashaw,** Jerry L. 1941- *WhoAmL 92*
**Mashburn,** Guerry Leonard 1952- *WhoFI 92*
**Mashburn,** Louise Tull 1930- *AmMWSc 92*
**Mashburn,** Thompson Arthur, Jr 1936- *AmMWSc 92*
**Mashburn,** W K *ScFEYrs*
**Masheke,** Malimba *IntWW 91*
**Masherov,** Petr Mironovich 1918-1980 *SovUnBD*
**Mashhoon,** Bahram 1947- *AmMWSc 92*
**Mashhour,** Mashhour Ahmad 1918- *IntWW 91*
**Mashimo,** Paul Akira 1926- *AmMWSc 92*
**Mashitz,** Isaac 1952- *WhoIns 92*
**Mashkov,** Il'ya Ivanovich 1881-1944 *SovUnBD*
**Mashologu,** Mothusi Thamsanga 1939- *IntWW 91*
**Mashtots** 361?-440 *EncEarC*
**Masi,** Alfonse Thomas 1930- *AmMWSc 92*
**Masi,** Dennis 1942- *TwCPaSc*
**Masi,** J. Roger 1954- *WhoAmL 92*
**Masi,** James Vincent 1938- *AmMWSc 92*
**Masi,** Jane Virginia 1947- *WhoFI 92*
**Masi,** Thomas A. 1955- *WhoFI 92*
**Masica,** Mark Alexis 1955- *WhoAmL 92*
**Masiello,** Alberta *WhoEnt 92*
**Masiello,** Alberta d1990 *NewYTBS 91*
**Masiello,** Anthony M 1947- *WhoAmP 91*
**Masiello,** Thomas *DrAPF 91*
**Masiero,** Ronald J 1942- *WhoIns 92*
**Masik,** Konstantin Ivanovich 1936- *IntWW 91*
**Masin,** Michael Terry 1945- *WhoAmL 92*
**Masina,** Giulietta 1921- *IntMPA 92, IntWW 91*
**Masini,** Al *LesBEnT 92*
**Masini,** Donna *DrAPF 91*
**Masinter,** Edgar Martin 1931- *WhoAmL 92*
**Masire,** Quett Ketumile Joni 1925- *IntWW 91, Who 92*
**Mask,** Larry W. 1949- *WhoRel 92*
**Maskal,** John 1918- *AmMWSc 92*
**Maskalunas,** Ronald 1940- *WhoFI 92*

**Maskar,** Deborah Katharine 1958- *WhoEnt 92*
**Maskell,** Donald Andrew 1963- *WhoWest 92*
**Masken,** James Frederick 1927- *AmMWSc 92*
**Masker,** Warren Edward 1943- *AmMWSc 92*
**Masket,** Edward Seymour 1923- *WhoEnt 92*
**Maskin,** Eric S 1950- *AmMWSc 92*
**Maskit,** Bernard 1935- *AmMWSc 92*
**Maslach,** George James 1920- *AmMWSc 92*
**Maslak,** Przemyslaw Boleslaw 1954- *AmMWSc 92*
**Masland,** Charles Henry, IV 1955- *WhoFI 92*
**Masland,** Lynne S. 1940- *WhoWest 92*
**Masland,** Richard Harry 1942- *AmMWSc 92*
**Maslanik,** John Harold 1954- *WhoWest 92*
**Maslanka,** Daniel Chester 1955- *WhoEnt 92*
**Maslansky,** Paul 1933- *IntMPA 92*
**Maslen,** David Peter 1948- *WhoAmL 92*
**Maslen,** Stephen Harold 1926- *AmMWSc 92*
**Maslennikov,** Arkadiy Afrikanovich 1931- *IntWW 91, SovUnBD*
**Maslennikov,** Nikolay Ivanovich 1921- *IntWW 91*
**Maslin,** David Michael E. *Who 92*
**Maslin,** Harry 1948- *WhoEnt 92, WhoWest 92*
**Maslin,** Harvey Lawrence 1939- *WhoWest 92*
**Maslin,** Simeon Joseph 1931- *WhoRel 92*
**Maslo,** William Ralph 1946- *WhoFI 92*
**Masloff,** Sophie 1917- *WhoAmP 91*
**Maslov,** Viktor Pavlovich 1930- *IntWW 91*
**Maslow,** David E 1943- *AmMWSc 92*
**Maslow,** Jonathan E. 1948- *WrDr 92*
**Maslow,** Jonathan Evan 1948- *IntAu&W 91*
**Maslow,** Phyllis F. 1927- *WhoWest 92*
**Maslow,** Richard Emanuel 1929- *WhoWest 92*
**Maslow,** Walter 1928- *WhoEnt 92*
**Maslowski,** Mark Alan 1950- *WhoMW 92*
**Maslyk,** Cheri Ann 1949- *WhoFI 92*
**Maslyukov,** Yuriy Dmitrievich 1937- *IntWW 91, SovUnBD*
**Masnada,** Dante A. 1953- *WhoFI 92*
**Masnari,** Nino A 1935- *AmMWSc 92*
**Masner,** Lubomir 1934- *AmMWSc 92*
**Masnyk,** Ihor Jarema 1930- *AmMWSc 92*
**Maso,** Carole *DrAPF 91*
**Maso,** Henry Frank 1919- *AmMWSc 92*
**Masoero,** Arthur Roger 1935- *WhoWest 92*
**Masol,** Vitaliy Andreevich 1928- *SovUnBD*
**Masol,** Vitaliy Andreyevich 1928- *IntWW 91*
**Mason** *Who 92*
**Mason & Hamlin** *NewAmDM*
**Mason,** A.E.W. 1865-1948 *RfGEnL 91*
**Mason,** Alastair Michael Stuart 1944- *Who 92*
**Mason,** Allen Smith 1932- *AmMWSc 92*
**Mason,** Amos Lawrence 1842-1914 *BiInAmS*
**Mason,** Anthony 1925- *Who 92*
**Mason,** Anthony Frank 1925- *IntWW 91*
**Mason,** Anthony Halstead 1938- *WhoWest 92*
**Mason,** Arnold Henry 1885-1963 *TwCPaSc*
**Mason,** Arthur 1876- *BenetAL 91*
**Mason,** Arthur Allen 1925- *AmMWSc 92*
**Mason,** Arthur Malcolm 1915- *Who 92*
**Mason,** B. J. 1945- *WhoBlA 92*
**Mason,** Basil John 1923- *IntWW 91, Who 92*
**Mason,** Belinda d1991 *NewYTBS 91*
**Mason,** Beryl Troxell 1907- *AmMWSc 92*
**Mason,** Biddy 1818-1891 *NotBlAW 92 [port]*
**Mason,** Billy Josephine 1918- *WhoBlA 92*
**Mason,** Bobbie Ann *DrAPF 91*
**Mason,** Bobbie Ann 1940- *BenetAL 91, ConNov 91, IntAu&W 91, WrDr 92*
**Mason,** Brenda Diane 1947- *WhoBlA 92*
**Mason,** Brian Harold 1917- *AmMWSc 92*
**Mason,** Brian Wayne 1959- *WhoAmP 91*
**Mason,** Bruce 1921-1982 *RfGEnL 91*
**Mason,** Bruce 1939- *WhoFI 92, WhoMW 92*
**Mason,** Bruce Bonner 1923- *WhoAmP 91*
**Mason,** Carl *TwCWW 91*
**Mason,** Caroline Faith Vibert 1942- *AmMWSc 92*
**Mason,** Catherine Emily *Who 92*
**Mason,** Charles 1728?-1786 *BiInAmS*
**Mason,** Charles Eugene 1943- *AmMWSc 92*
**Mason,** Charles Harrison 1866-1961 *RelLAm 91*
**Mason,** Charles Morgan 1906- *AmMWSc 92*
**Mason,** Charles Perry 1932- *AmMWSc 92*
**Mason,** Charles R. 1945- *WhoMW 92*
**Mason,** Charles Thomas, III 1954- *WhoFI 92*
**Mason,** Charles Thomas, Jr 1918- *AmMWSc 92*
**Mason,** Cheryl Annette 1954- *WhoBlA 92*
**Mason,** Chuck *TwCWW 91*
**Mason,** Clifford L. 1932- *WhoBlA 92*
**Mason,** Conrad Jerome 1932- *AmMWSc 92*
**Mason,** Craig Watson 1954- *WhoFI 92*
**Mason,** Curtis Leonel 1919- *AmMWSc 92*
**Mason,** D M 1921- *AmMWSc 92*
**Mason,** D R 1920- *AmMWSc 92*
**Mason,** DaCosta V. 1916- *WhoBlA 92*
**Mason,** Daniel Gregory 1873-1953 *NewAmDM*
**Mason,** David Aaron 1940- *WhoFI 92, WhoMW 92*
**Mason,** David Arthur 1946- *Who 92*
**Mason,** David Dickenson 1917- *AmMWSc 92*
**Mason,** David Ernest 1928- *WhoFI 92*
**Mason,** David Kean 1928- *Who 92*
**Mason,** David Lamont 1934- *AmMWSc 92*
**Mason,** David Marion 1958- *WhoAmP 91*
**Mason,** David McArthur 1912- *AmMWSc 92*
**Mason,** David Raymond 1936- *WhoRel 92*
**Mason,** David Thomas 1937- *AmMWSc 92*
**Mason,** Dean Towle 1932- *AmMWSc 92, WhoWest 92*
**Mason,** Dennis Howard 1916- *Who 92*
**Mason,** Don Wales 1945- *WhoMW 92*
**Mason,** Donald F., Jr. 1954- *WhoAmL 92*
**Mason,** Donald Frank 1926- *AmMWSc 92*
**Mason,** Donald Joseph 1931- *AmMWSc 92*
**Mason,** Douglas R *TwCSFW 91*
**Mason,** Douglas Rankine 1918- *IntAu&W 91, WrDr 92*
**Mason,** Earl James 1923- *AmMWSc 92*
**Mason,** Earl James, Jr. 1923- *WhoMW 92*
**Mason,** Earl Sewell 1935- *AmMWSc 92*
**Mason,** Ebenezer Porter 1819-1840 *BiInAmS*
**Mason,** Edith 1893-1973 *NewAmDM*
**Mason,** Edmund 1911- *WrDr 92*
**Mason,** Edward Allen 1919- *WhoEnt 92*
**Mason,** Edward Allen 1926- *AmMWSc 92*
**Mason,** Edward Archibald 1924- *AmMWSc 92*
**Mason,** Edward Eaton 1920- *AmMWSc 92, WhoMW 92*
**Mason,** Edward James 1923- *WhoBlA 92*
**Mason,** Elliott Bernard 1943- *AmMWSc 92*
**Mason,** Ellsworth 1917- *IntAu&W 91*
**Mason,** F. Van Wyck 1901-1978 *BenetAL 91*
**Mason,** Frances Jane *Who 92*
**Mason,** Francis K 1928- *IntAu&W 91, WrDr 92*
**Mason,** Franklin Harrell 1929- *WhoEnt 92*
**Mason,** Franklin Rogers 1936- *WhoFI 92*
**Mason,** Frederick 1913- *Who 92*
**Mason,** Frederick Cecil 1913- *IntWW 91*
**Mason,** Gary Howard 1954- *WhoEnt 92*
**Mason,** Genevieve Ann 1936- *WhoMW 92*
**Mason,** George 1725-1792 *AmPolLe [port], BlkwEAR, RComAH*
**Mason,** George Frederick Peter 1921- *Who 92*
**Mason,** George Robert 1932- *AmMWSc 92, WhoMW 92*
**Mason,** Gilbert Rutledge 1928- *WhoBlA 92*
**Mason,** Grant William 1940- *AmMWSc 92*
**Mason,** Gregory Henry 1944- *WhoMW 92*
**Mason,** Grenville R 1934- *AmMWSc 92*
**Mason,** H. Carl 1926- *WhoWest 92*
**Mason,** Harold Frederick 1925- *AmMWSc 92*
**Mason,** Harold L 1901- *AmMWSc 92*
**Mason,** Harold Lee 1944- *WhoRel 92*
**Mason,** Harry Louis 1935- *AmMWSc 92*
**Mason,** Haydn Trevor 1929- *IntAu&W 91, WrDr 92*
**Mason,** Henry 1831-1890 *NewAmDM*
**Mason,** Henry Lowell, III 1941- *WhoAmL 92*
**Mason,** Herbert 1927- *IntAu&W 91, WrDr 92*
**Mason,** Herbert Warren, Jr. 1932- *WhoRel 92*
**Mason,** Herman, Jr. 1962- *WhoBlA 92*
**Mason,** Herman Charles 1910- *AmMWSc 92*
**Mason,** Hilda Howland M. *WhoBlA 92*
**Mason,** Hilda Howland Mae 1916- *WhoAmP 91*
**Mason,** Homer Livingston 1938- *WhoAmP 91*
**Mason,** Howard Francis 1910- *WhoAmP 91*
**Mason,** Howard Keith 1949- *WhoBlA 92*
**Mason,** Ida Renee 1964- *WhoMW 92*
**Mason,** J Philip Hanson, Jr 1930- *AmMWSc 92*
**Mason,** Jackie *IntMPA 92*
**Mason,** Jackie 1934- *WhoEnt 92*
**Mason,** James 1909-1984 *FacFETw*
**Mason,** James Albert 1929- *WhoWest 92*
**Mason,** James Donald 1937- *WhoRel 92*
**Mason,** James Eugene 1954- *WhoMW 92*
**Mason,** James Ian 1944- *AmMWSc 92*
**Mason,** James Lester 1923- *WhoRel 92*
**Mason,** James Michael 1943- *AmMWSc 92*
**Mason,** James Michael 1950- *WhoFI 92*
**Mason,** James Murray 1798-1871 *AmPolLe*
**Mason,** James O 1930- *AmMWSc 92*
**Mason,** James Osterman 1930- *WhoAmP 91*
**Mason,** James Russell 1954- *AmMWSc 92*
**Mason,** James Stephen 1935- *Who 92*
**Mason,** James Weir 1836-1905 *BiInAmS*
**Mason,** James Willard 1933- *AmMWSc 92*
**Mason,** Jeffrey Roger 1957- *WhoMW 92*
**Mason,** Jerry d1991 *NewYTBS 91*
**Mason,** Jesse David *AmMWSc 92*
**Mason,** Jesse W. 1912-1990 *WhoBlA 92N*
**Mason,** Joe Ben 1910- *WhoRel 92, WhoWest 92*
**Mason,** Joel B 1955- *AmMWSc 92*
**Mason,** John *IntWW 91, TwCSFW 91, Who 92*
**Mason,** John 1600-1672 *BenetAL 91*
**Mason,** John 1927- *IntWW 91, Who 92*
**Mason,** John Dudley 1949- *IntMPA 92, WhoFI 92*
**Mason,** John Frederick 1913- *AmMWSc 92*
**Mason,** John Grove 1929- *AmMWSc 92*
**Mason,** John Hugh 1929- *AmMWSc 92*
**Mason,** John Kenyon French 1919- *Who 92*
**Mason,** John L 1923- *AmMWSc 92*
**Mason,** John Milton 1938- *WhoAmL 92*
**Mason,** John Wayne 1924- *AmMWSc 92*
**Mason,** Kenneth 1949- *WhoBlA 92*
**Mason,** Kenneth Bruce 1928- *Who 92*
**Mason,** Kenneth M. 1917- *IntMPA 92*
**Mason,** Kenneth Staveley 1931- *Who 92*
**Mason,** Larry Gordon 1937- *AmMWSc 92*
**Mason,** Lee W. *WrDr 92*
**Mason,** Lena Doolin 1864- *NotBlAW 92*
**Mason,** Linda 1946- *WhoMW 92*
**Mason,** Lowell 1792-1872 *NewAmDM*
**Mason,** Luther Roscoe 1927- *WhoBlA 92*
**Mason,** Major Albert, III 1940- *WhoBlA 92*
**Mason,** Malcolm 1945- *AmMWSc 92*
**Mason,** Marilyn 1925- *NewAmDM*
**Mason,** Marilyn Gell 1944- *WhoMW 92*
**Mason,** Marion 1933- *AmMWSc 92*
**Mason,** Marsha *WhoEnt 92*
**Mason,** Marsha 1942- *IntMPA 92*
**Mason,** Marshall W. 1940- *WhoEnt 92*
**Mason,** Mary Ann Bryan 1802-1881 *DcNCBi 4*
**Mason,** Matthew DuPont, III 1947- *WhoFI 92*
**Mason,** Max Garrett 1944- *AmMWSc 92*
**Mason,** Merle 1920- *AmMWSc 92*
**Mason,** Michael Duane 1950- *WhoRel 92*
**Mason,** Monica 1941- *Who 92*
**Mason,** Morton Freeman 1902- *AmMWSc 92*
**Mason,** Nicholas 1938- *WrDr 92*
**Mason,** Nina Lea 1915- *IntAu&W 91*
**Mason,** Norbert 1930- *AmMWSc 92*
**Mason,** Norman Ronald 1929- *AmMWSc 92*
**Mason,** Olivia 1928- *WhoMW 92*
**Mason,** Orenthia Delois 1952- *WhoBlA 92*
**Mason,** Otis Tufton 1838-1908 *BiInAmS*
**Mason,** Pamela 1918- *IntMPA 92*
**Mason,** Pamela Georgina Walsh *Who 92*
**Mason,** Pamela Helen 1922- *WhoEnt 92*
**Mason,** Paul 1935- *WhoAmP 91*
**Mason,** Perry Shipley, Jr 1938- *AmMWSc 92*
**Mason,** Peter *Who 92*
**Mason,** Peter 1914- *ConAu 35NR*
**Mason,** Peter Geoffrey 1914- *Who 92*
**Mason,** Philip 1906- *IntAu&W 91, IntWW 91, Who 92, WrDr 92*
**Mason,** R.A.K. 1905-1971 *RfGEnL 91*
**Mason,** Raymond 1922- *TwCPaSc*
**Mason,** Richard 1919- *Who 92*
**Mason,** Richard Anthony 1932- *Who 92*
**Mason,** Richard Canfield 1923- *AmMWSc 92*
**Mason,** Richard Edward, Jr. 1949- *WhoFI 92*
**Mason,** Richard John 1929- *Who 92*
**Mason,** Richard Randolph 1930- *AmMWSc 92*
**Mason,** Richard Sharpe 1795-1874 *DcNCBi 4*
**Mason,** Richard Stewart 1921- *WhoEnt 92*
**Mason,** Robert 1946- *TwCPaSc*
**Mason,** Robert C 1920- *AmMWSc 92*
**Mason,** Robert C. 1942- *ConAu 134*
**Mason,** Robert Edward 1934- *AmMWSc 92*
**Mason,** Robert McSpadden 1941- *WhoMW 92*
**Mason,** Robert P, Jr 1918- *WhoAmP 91*
**Mason,** Robert Paige 1931- *AmMWSc 92*
**Mason,** Robert Thomas 1959- *AmMWSc 92*
**Mason,** Rodney Jackson 1939- *AmMWSc 92*
**Mason,** Ronald 1930- *IntWW 91, Who 92*
**Mason,** Ronald Charles 1912- *IntAu&W 91, WrDr 92*
**Mason,** Ronald Edward 1948- *WhoBlA 92*
**Mason,** Ronald George 1916- *AmMWSc 92*
**Mason,** Sonja Kay 1939- *WhoAmP 91*
**Mason,** Stanley 1917- *IntAu&W 91*
**Mason,** Stephen Carl 1949- *WhoMW 92*
**Mason,** Stephen Finney 1923- *IntWW 91, Who 92*
**Mason,** Stephen Olin 1952- *WhoMW 92*
**Mason,** Steven Charles 1936- *WhoFI 92, WhoMW 92*
**Mason,** Steven MacArthur 1950- *WhoAmL 92*
**Mason,** Sydney 1920- *IntWW 91, Who 92*
**Mason,** Thomas Albert 1936- *WhoAmL 92*
**Mason,** Thomas Alexander 1944- *WhoMW 92*
**Mason,** Thomas John 1944- *WhoMW 92*
**Mason,** Thomas Joseph 1942- *AmMWSc 92*
**Mason,** Thomas Oliver 1952- *AmMWSc 92*
**Mason,** Thomas William 1946- *WhoMW 92*
**Mason,** Thomas Williams 1839-1921 *DcNCBi 4*
**Mason,** Tim Robert 1930- *AmMWSc 92*
**Mason,** Timothy Ian Godson 1945- *Who 92*
**Mason,** Tom Lee 1944- *WhoAmP 91*
**Mason,** V Bradford 1942- *AmMWSc 92*
**Mason,** W Roy, III 1943- *AmMWSc 92*
**Mason,** Walter W. *Who 92*
**Mason,** William 1725-1797 *BlkwCEP, RfGEnL 91*
**Mason,** William 1906- *TwCPaSc*
**Mason,** William Alfred 1898- *WhoBlA 92*
**Mason,** William Arthur 1945- *WhoRel 92*
**Mason,** William C *AmMWSc 92*
**Mason,** William Charles 1955- *WhoFI 92*
**Mason,** William E. 1934- *WhoBlA 92*
**Mason,** William Ernest 1929- *Who 92*
**Mason,** William Hickmon 1936- *AmMWSc 92*
**Mason,** William Thomas, Jr. 1926- *WhoBlA 92*
**Mason,** William van Horn 1930- *AmMWSc 92*
**Mason,** Zack Dean 1957- *WhoAmL 92*
**Mason-Feilder,** Clive Lee 1940- *WhoWest 92*
**Mason Of Barnsley,** Baron 1924- *IntWW 91, Who 92*
**Masoom,** Abulkhair Muhammad 1954- *WhoMW 92*
**Masoro,** Edward Joseph 1924- *AmMWSc 92*
**Masouredis,** Serafeim Panagiotis 1922- *WhoWest 92*
**Masouredis,** Serafeim Panogiotis 1922- *AmMWSc 92*
**Masover,** Gerald K 1935- *AmMWSc 92*
**Masquelier,** Marc Lemoyne 1958- *WhoMW 92*
**Masri,** Ahmad Fathi Al- 1932- *IntWW 91*
**Masri,** Merle Sid 1927- *AmMWSc 92*
**Masri,** Sami F 1939- *AmMWSc 92*
**Masri,** Taher Nashat 1942- *IntWW 91, Who 92*
**Masry,** Salem El 1938- *AmMWSc 92*
**Mass,** Edna Elaine 1954- *WhoBlA 92*
**Mass,** Mike 1951- *WhoAmP 91*
**Mass,** William *IntAu&W 91X*
**Massa,** Dennis Jon 1945- *AmMWSc 92*
**Massa,** Edward Clement 1907- *WhoWest 92*
**Massa,** Frank 1906- *AmMWSc 92*
**Massa,** Heidi 1957- *WhoAmL 92*
**Massa,** Louis 1940- *AmMWSc 92*
**Massa,** Mary Elizabeth 1952- *WhoAmL 92*
**Massa,** Patrick Charles 1946- *WhoAmL 92*
**Massa,** Roland 1933- *WhoHisp 92*
**Massa,** Tobias 1950- *AmMWSc 92*
**Massachusettensis** *BenetAL 91*
**Massachusetts Queen,** The *EncAmaz 91*

Massad, L. Clark 1966- WhoMW 92
Massad, Stephen Albert 1950- WhoAmL 92
Massalitinova, Varvara Osipovna 1878-1945 SovUnBD
Massalski, T B 1926- AmMWSc 92
Massanari, Robert Michael 1940- WhoMW 92
Massanari, Ronald Lee 1941- WhoRel 92
Massaquoi, Hans J. 1926- WhoBlA 92
Massar, Michael Maurice 1949- WhoRel 92
Massari, Kerry Michael 1943- WhoAmL 92
Massari, V John 1945- AmMWSc 92
Massarik, Fred 1926- ConAu 35NR
Massaro, Donald John 1932- AmMWSc 92
Massaro, Edward Joseph 1933- AmMWSc 92
Massaro, Lorraine 1950- WhoAmL 92
Massaro, Sheryl DrAPF 91
Massarsky, Steven Jay 1948- WhoEnt 92
Massasoit d1661 BenetAL 91
Massaua, John Roger 1947- WhoFI 92
Massaux, Edouard 1920- IntWW 91
Masse, Arthur N 1928- AmMWSc 92
Masse, Donald D. 1934- WhoBlA 92
Masse', Donald Duane 1934- WhoMW 92
Masse, Marcel 1936- IntWW 91, Who 92
Masse, Marcel 1940- IntWW 91
Masse, Mark Henry 1952- WhoMW 92
Masse, Scott Leon 1963- WhoAmL 92
Masse, Yvon H. 1935- WhoFI 92
Massee, D. Michael 1937- WhoEnt 92
Massee, Jasper Cortenus 1871-1965 RelLAm 91
Massee, Truman Winfield 1930- AmMWSc 92
Massel, Elihu Saul 1940- WhoAmL 92
Massel, Gary Alan 1939- AmMWSc 92
Massell, Paul Barry 1948- AmMWSc 92
Massell, Theodore Benedict 1907- WhoWest 92
Massell, Wulf F 1943- AmMWSc 92
Masselos, William 1920- NewAmDM
Massen, Osa 1916- IntMPA 92
Massenburg, Tony Arnel 1967- WhoBlA 92
Massenet, Jules 1842-1912 NewAmDM
Massengale, Jimmy Edgar 1942- WhoIns 92
Massengale, M A 1933- AmMWSc 92
Massengale, Martin Andrew 1933- IntWW 91, WhoMW 92
Massengill, Dennis Alan 1946- WhoMW 92
Massengill, Raymond 1937- AmMWSc 92
Massereene, Viscount 1914- Who 92
Masserman, Jules Homan 1905- AmMWSc 92
Massevitch, Alla 1918- Who 92
Massevitch, Alla Genrikhovna 1918- IntWW 91
Massey, Albert P 1940- WhoAmP 91
Massey, Andrew J. 1946- WhoWest 92
Massey, Andrew John 1946- WhoEnt 92
Massey, Anna 1937- IntMPA 92, Who 92
Massey, Carrie Lee 1922- WhoBlA 92
Massey, Daniel 1933- IntMPA 92, Who 92
Massey, Deobrah Prescott 1956- WhoRel 92
Massey, Donald Wayne 1938- WhoFI 92
Massey, Doreen Elizabeth 1938- Who 92
Massey, Douglas Gordon 1926- AmMWSc 92, WhoWest 92
Massey, Eddie H 1939- AmMWSc 92
Massey, Frank Jones, Jr 1919- AmMWSc 92
Massey, Fredrick Alan 1938- AmMWSc 92
Massey, Gail Austin 1936- AmMWSc 92
Massey, Hamilton W. WhoBlA 92
Massey, Harold B. 1924- WhoWest 92
Massey, Herbert Fane, Jr 1926- AmMWSc 92
Massey, Jack T 1927- WhoIns 92
Massey, Jacquelene Sharp 1947- WhoBlA 92
Massey, James D. WhoMW 92
Massey, James Earl 1930- WhoBlA 92, WhoRel 92, WrDr 92
Massey, James L 1934- AmMWSc 92
Massey, James L. 1943- WhoFI 92
Massey, James T. 1947- WhoAmL 92
Massey, Jimmy R 1940- AmMWSc 92
Massey, Joan Leslie 1966- WhoRel 92
Massey, Joe Thomas 1917- AmMWSc 92
Massey, John Boyd 1950- AmMWSc 92
Massey, Karen B 1948- WhoIns 92
Massey, Karen Elaine 1960- WhoMW 92
Massey, L G 1918- AmMWSc 92
Massey, Linda Kathleen Locke 1945- AmMWSc 92
Massey, Marion Lawrence 1932- WhoAmL 92
Massey, Michael G 1946- WhoAmP 91
Massey, Michael John 1947- AmMWSc 92
Massey, Philip Louis 1952- AmMWSc 92
Massey, Raymond Lee 1948- WhoAmL 92
Massey, Reginald Harold 1946- WhoBlA 92
Massey, Richard Sargent 1936- WhoFI 92
Massey, Robert Unruh 1922- AmMWSc 92
Massey, Roy Cyril 1934- Who 92
Massey, Ruth Braselton 1919- WhoAmP 91
Massey, Steven James 1959- WhoMW 92
Massey, Stewart Richard 1957- WhoFI 92
Massey, Tom C 1931- WhoAmP 91
Massey, Vincent 1887-1967 FacFETw
Massey, Vincent 1926- AmMWSc 92, IntWW 91, Who 92
Massey, Walter Eugene 1938- AmMWSc 92, WhoBlA 92
Massey, Wilbur Fisk 1839-1923 DcNCBi 4
Massey, William Edmund Devereux 1901- Who 92
Massey, William Ferguson 1856-1925 FacFETw
Massey, William S 1920- AmMWSc 92
Massey, Wynetta Pauline 1964- WhoAmL 92
Massey, Zachary David 1864-1923 DcNCBi 4
Massiah, Thomas Frederick 1926- AmMWSc 92
Massialas, Byron G. 1929- WrDr 92
Massie, Allan 1938- ConNov 91, WrDr 92
Massie, Allan Johnstone 1938- Who 92
Massie, Barry Michael 1944- AmMWSc 92
Massie, Edward 1910- AmMWSc 92
Massie, Edward Lindsey, Jr. 1929- WhoFI 92
Massie, Erin Lynn 1963- WhoWest 92
Massie, Harold Raymond 1943- AmMWSc 92
Massie, Henry Murray, Jr. 1942- WhoAmL 92
Massie, Joseph Logan 1921- WrDr 92
Massie, Michael Earl 1947- WhoAmL 92
Massie, N A 1944- AmMWSc 92
Massie, Noel David 1949- WhoAmL 92
Massie, Robert Joseph 1949- WhoFI 92
Massie, Samuel Proctor 1919- AmMWSc 92, WhoBlA 92
Massier, Paul Ferdinand 1923- AmMWSc 92
Massik, Michael 1958- AmMWSc 92
Massine, Leonide 1895-1979 FacFETw
Massing, Hede 1899-1981 FacFETw
Massinger, Philip 1583?-1640? RfGEnL 91
Massingham, Gordon Lawrence 1940- WhoEnt 92
Massingham, Harold 1932- IntAu&W 91, WrDr 92
Massingham, John Dudley 1930- Who 92
Massingill, Gary Lee 1946- WhoWest 92
Massingill, John Lee, Jr 1941- AmMWSc 92
Massion, Walter Herbert 1923- AmMWSc 92
Massip, Roger 1904- IntAu&W 91
Massler, Howard Arnold 1946- WhoAmL 92, WhoEnt 92
Massler, Maury 1912- AmMWSc 92
Masso, Jon Dickinson 1941- AmMWSc 92
Massof, Robert W 1948- AmMWSc 92
Massoletti, Dexter James, Sr. 1941- WhoWest 92
Massom, Margaret M 1944- WhoAmP 91
Masson, Andre 1896-1987 FacFETw
Masson, D Bruce 1932- AmMWSc 92
Masson, David I 1915- TwCSFW 91, WrDr 92
Masson, Jacques 1924- IntWW 91
Masson, Jeffrey Moussaieff 1941- IntAu&W 91, WrDr 92
Masson, Paul Jean-Marie 1920- IntWW 91
Masson, Robert B. d1991 NewYTBS 91
Masson, Robin Abrahamson 1952- WhoAmL 92
Masson, Tom 1866-1934 ScFEYrs A
Masson, Yves Michel 1936- WhoWest 92
Massopust, Leo Carl, Jr 1920- AmMWSc 92
Massoth, Leon 1956- WhoWest 92
Massoud, Ahmed Shah 1953- IntWW 91
Massoud, Hisham Z 1949- AmMWSc 92
Massoud, Monir Fouad 1930- AmMWSc 92
Massover, William H 1941- AmMWSc 92
Massu, Jacques 1908- IntWW 91
Massura, Eileen Kathleen 1925- WhoMW 92
Massy Who 92
Massy, Baron 1921- Who 92
Massy-Greene, Brian 1916- IntWW 91, Who 92
Mast, Cecil B 1927- AmMWSc 92
Mast, Frank 1927- WhoAmL 92
Mast, Frederick William 1910- WhoFI 92
Mast, Gerald 1940- IntAu&W 91
Mast, Gregg Alan 1952- WhoRel 92
Mast, Kent E. 1943- WhoAmL 92
Mast, Mae Jerene 1922- WhoMW 92
Mast, Morris G 1940- AmMWSc 92
Mast, P Edward 1926- AmMWSc 92
Mast, Richard F 1931- AmMWSc 92
Mast, Robert Edward 1953- WhoFI 92
Mast, Robert F 1934- AmMWSc 92
Mast, Roy Clark 1924- AmMWSc 92
Mast, Terry S 1943- AmMWSc 92
Mastalerz, John W 1926- AmMWSc 92
Mastalir, Paul Francis 1955- WhoMW 92
Mastandrea, Frank J WhoAmP 91
Mastascusa, Edward John 1938- AmMWSc 92
Mastel, Royston John 1917- Who 92
Masteller, Edwin C 1934- AmMWSc 92
Masteller, Rand Alex 1951- WhoAmP 91
Masteller, Robert Michael 1950- WhoWest 92
Masten, Jeffrey Paul 1948- WhoAmL 92, WhoAmP 91
Masten, Michael K 1939- AmMWSc 92
Mastenbrook, S Martin, Jr 1946- AmMWSc 92
Master, Simon Harcourt 1944- IntWW 91, Who 92
Masterman, Patricia Dinan 1927- WhoRel 92
Masterman, Stillman 1831-1863 BiInAmS
Masterman, Walter S 1876- ScFEYrs
Masters and Johnson FacFETw
Masters, Barbara J. 1933- WhoAmL 92
Masters, Ben 1947- ConTFT 9, IntMPA 92
Masters, Bettie Sue Siler 1937- AmMWSc 92
Masters, Brian John Who 92
Masters, Brian William 1954- WhoEnt 92
Masters, Bruce Allen 1936- AmMWSc 92
Masters, Burton Joseph 1929- AmMWSc 92
Masters, Charles Day 1929- AmMWSc 92
Masters, Christopher 1947- Who 92
Masters, Christopher Fanstone 1942- AmMWSc 92, WhoMW 92
Masters, Dennis Lynn 1960- WhoFI 92, WhoMW 92
Masters, Edgar Lee 1868-1950 BenetAL 91, ConAu 133
Masters, Edgar Lee 1869-1950 FacFETw
Masters, Edward E. 1924- WhoFI 92
Masters, Edwin M 1931- AmMWSc 92
Masters, Frank Wynne 1920- AmMWSc 92
Masters, Gary WhoEnt 92
Masters, George William 1940- WhoFI 92
Masters, Greg DrAPF 91
Masters, Hilary DrAPF 91
Masters, Hilary 1928- BenetAL 91
Masters, Jack Gerald 1931- WhoMW 92
Masters, John Alan 1927- AmMWSc 92
Masters, John Edward 1913- AmMWSc 92
Masters, John Michael 1942- AmMWSc 92
Masters, Kenneth Halls 1943- WhoAmP 91
Masters, Larry William 1941- AmMWSc 92
Masters, Laurance E 1932- WhoIns 92
Masters, Olga 1919-1986 ConAu 135
Masters, Robert Donald 1929- WhoEnt 92
Masters, Robert Wayne 1914- AmMWSc 92
Masters, Roger D. 1933- WrDr 92
Masters, Roger Davis 1933- WhoAmL 92
Masters, Sheila Valerie Who 92
Masters, William H 1915- ConAu 34NR, WrDr 92
Masters, William Howell 1915- AmMWSc 92, FacFETw
Masterson, Carlin 1940- WhoEnt 92
Masterson, Dan DrAPF 91
Masterson, J. B. WrDr 92
Masterson, Joseph Bernard, Jr. 1947- WhoMW 92
Masterson, Kenneth Rhodes 1944- WhoAmL 92
Masterson, Kleber Sanlin, Jr 1932- AmMWSc 92
Masterson, Mary Stuart 1966- IntMPA 92
Masterson, Michael Jon 1946- WhoAmP 91
Masterson, Norton Edward 1902- WhoIns 92
Masterson, Peter 1934- IntMPA 92, WhoEnt 92
Masterson, Shannon Patricia 1961- WhoEnt 92
Masterson, Thomas Marshall 1959- WhoFI 92
Masterson, Valerie IntWW 91, Who 92
Masterson, Valerie 1937- NewAmDM
Masterson, Wendy Lynn 1963- WhoEnt 92
Masterson, Whit WrDr 92
Masterson, William Lloyd 1949- WhoMW 92
Masterton, Graham 1946- IntAu&W 91, WrDr 92
Masterton, Nancy N 1930- WhoAmP 91
Masterton, William Lewis 1927- AmMWSc 92
Mastin, Charles Wayne 1943- AmMWSc 92
Mastin, Gary Arthur 1954- WhoWest 92
Mastin, John 1865-1932 ScFEYrs
Mastny, Vojtech 1936- WrDr 92
Mastorakis, Nico 1941- IntMPA 92
Mastos, Louis T, Jr 1921- WhoIns 92
Mastrangelo, Evelino William 1923- WhoAmP 91
Mastrangelo, Michael Joseph 1938- AmMWSc 92
Mastrangelo, Richard Edward 1938- WhoAmP 91
Mastrangelo, Sebastian Vito Rocco 1925- AmMWSc 92
Mastrantonio, Mary Elizabeth 1958- IntMPA 92, WhoEnt 92A
Mastrantonis, George 1906-1988 RelLAm 91
Mastriana, Robert Alan 1949- WhoMW 92
Mastrini, Jane Reed 1948- WhoWest 92
Mastro, Andrea M 1944- AmMWSc 92
Mastro, Randy Michael 1956- WhoAmL 92
Mastroianni, Luigi, Jr 1925- AmMWSc 92
Mastroianni, Marcello 1923- FacFETw
Mastroianni, Marcello 1924- IntMPA 92, IntWW 91, WhoEnt 92
Mastrolia, Lilyan Spitzer 1934- IntAu&W 91
Mastromarco, Dan Ralph 1958- WhoAmL 92
Mastromarino, Anthony John 1940- AmMWSc 92
Mastronardi, Judith Anthony 1965- WhoEnt 92
Mastronardi, Richard 1947- AmMWSc 92
Mastropaolo, Joseph AmMWSc 92
Mastrosimone, William 1947- IntAu&W 91, WrDr 92
Mastrototaro, John Joseph 1960- AmMWSc 92
Masubuchi, Koichi 1924- AmMWSc 92
Masuelli, Frank John 1921- AmMWSc 92
Masui, Yoshio 1931- AmMWSc 92
Masuku, Lookout 1939-1986 FacFETw
Masuoka, Hiroyuki 1923- IntWW 91
Masur, Dorothea E 1923- WhoAmP 91
Masur, Harold Q 1909- IntAu&W 91, WrDr 92
Masur, Kurt NewYTBS 91 [port]
Masur, Kurt 1927- IntWW 91, NewAmDM, WhoEnt 92
Masur, Richard 1948- IntMPA 92
Masur, Sandra Kazahn 1938- AmMWSc 92
Masur, Wolodymyr Mark 1964- WhoAmL 92
Masurekar, Prakash Sharatchandra 1941- AmMWSc 92
Masurel, Jean-Louis Antoine Nicolas 1940- IntWW 91
Masurok, Yuri IntWW 91
Masursky, Harold d1990 IntWW 91N
Masursky, Harold 1922- FacFETw
Masursky, Harold 1923- AmMWSc 92
Masursky, Harold 1923-1990 AnObit 1990
Masut, Remo Antonio 1948- AmMWSc 92
Masys, Daniel R AmMWSc 92
Mata, Daya 1914- RelLAm 91
Mata Hari 1876-1917 FacFETw
Mata, Eduardo 1942- IntWW 91, NewAmDM, WhoEnt 92, WhoHisp 92
Mata, Edward WhoHisp 92
Mata, Guillermo Gonzalo 1949- WhoHisp 92
Mata, Leonardo J 1933- AmMWSc 92
Mata, Marina Martha 1966- WhoHisp 92
Mata, Pedro F. 1944- WhoHisp 92
Mata-Pistokache, Theresa 1959- WhoHisp 92
Mata-Toledo, Ramon A. 1949- WhoHisp 92
Mata-Toledo, Ramon Alberto 1949- AmMWSc 92
Matabane, Sebiletso Mokone 1945- WhoBlA 92
Mataca, Petero Who 92
Mataga, Peter Andrew 1959- AmMWSc 92
Mataga, Petero WhoRel 92
Matalon, David A. IntMPA 92
Matalon, Moshe 1949- AmMWSc 92
Matalon, Norma 1949- WhoFI 92
Matalon, Sadis 1948- AmMWSc 92
Matalon, Vivian 1929- WhoEnt 92
Matamoros, Lourdes M. 1963- WhoHisp 92
Matamoros, Mariano 1770-1814 HisDSpE
Matan, Lillian Kathleen 1937- WhoWest 92
Matane, Paulias 1932- Who 92
Matane, Paulias Nguna 1931- IntWW 91

**Matanky,** Robert William 1955- *WhoMW 92*
**Matano,** Robert Stanley 1925- *IntWW 91*
**Matanoski,** Genevieve M 1930- *AmMWSc 92*
**Matanzima,** Kaiser 1915- *IntWW 91*
**Matar,** Said E 1934- *AmMWSc 92*
**Matarazzo,** Joseph Dominic 1925- *AmMWSc 92, WhoWest 92*
**Matare,** Herbert Franz 1912- *AmMWSc 92*
**Matas,** Julio 1931- *WhoHisp 92*
**Matas,** Myra Dorothea 1938- *WhoWest 92*
**Matas,** Raquel M. 1956- *WhoHisp 92*
**Matasovic,** Marilyn Estelle 1946- *WhoFI 92*
**Mata'utia,** Tuiafono 1929- *WhoAmP 91*
**Matayoshi,** Herbert Tatsuo 1928- *WhoAmP 91*
**Matayoshi,** Ronald Fumio 1953- *WhoWest 92*
**Matcha,** Jack *DrAPF 91*
**Matcha,** Robert Louis 1938- *AmMWSc 92*
**Matches,** Arthur Gerald 1929- *AmMWSc 92*
**Matches,** Jack Ronald 1930- *AmMWSc 92*
**Matchett,** Andrew James 1950- *AmMWSc 92, WhoMW 92*
**Matchett,** Johnson, Jr. 1942- *WhoBlA 92*
**Matchett,** William H. *DrAPF 91*
**Matchett,** William H 1923- *IntAu&W 91, WrDr 92*
**Matchett,** William H 1932- *AmMWSc 92*
**Matchette,** Phyllis Lee 1921- *WhoMW 92*
**Matchie,** Thomas F 1933- *WhoAmP 91*
**Matcovich,** Thomas J 1929- *AmMWSc 92*
**Mate,** Martin *Who 92*
**Mate,** Martin 1929- *WhoRel 92*
**Mateas,** Kenneth Edward 1949- *WhoAmL 92*
**Mateer,** C. Fred 1948- *WhoMW 92*
**Mateer,** Charles Quentin 1922- *WhoAmP 91*
**Mateer,** Frank Marion 1921- *AmMWSc 92*
**Mateer,** Niall John 1950- *AmMWSc 92*
**Mateer,** Richard Austin 1940- *AmMWSc 92*
**Mateer,** Richard S 1923- *AmMWSc 92*
**Mateescu,** Gheorghe D 1928- *AmMWSc 92*
**Matei,** Paul Valentin 1948- *WhoWest 92*
**Mateja,** John Frederick 1950- *AmMWSc 92*
**Mateja,** Michael E. 1938- *WhoFI 92*
**Matejka,** Michael G. 1953- *WhoMW 92*
**Mateker,** Emil Joseph, Jr 1931- *AmMWSc 92*
**Mateles,** Richard I 1935- *AmMWSc 92*
**Mateo,** Fernando 1958- *WhoHisp 92*
**Mateo,** Juan A., Jr. 1956- *WhoHisp 92*
**Mateo,** Julio, Jr. 1959- *WhoAmL 92*
**Mater,** Dwight Albert, III 1958- *WhoMW 92*
**Mater,** Gene P. 1926- *WhoEnt 92*
**Matera,** Richard Ernest 1925- *WhoRel 92*
**Matern,** Hermann 1893-1971 *EncTR 91*
**Materne,** David 1956- *WhoMW 92*
**Maternowski,** John Anthony 1937- *WhoMW 92*
**Mates,** Lawrence A., II 1954- *WhoFI 92*
**Mates,** Michael John 1934- *Who 92*
**Mates,** Robert Edward 1935- *AmMWSc 92*
**Matese,** John J 1938- *AmMWSc 92*
**Matesich,** Mary Andrew 1939- *AmMWSc 92, WhoRel 92*
**Matey,** James Regis 1951- *AmMWSc 92*
**Mateyka,** Gregory Jonathan 1961- *WhoEnt 92*
**Math,** John *WhoBlA 92*
**Mathabane,** Mark 1960- *WrDr 92*
**Mathabane,** Mark Johannes 1960- *WhoBlA 92*
**Mathai,** Arak M 1935- *AmMWSc 92*
**Mathaudhu,** Sukhdev Singh 1946- *WhoWest 92*
**Mathe,** Georges 1922- *IntWW 91*
**Mathealira,** Morena Lechesa 1928- *IntWW 91*
**Matheney,** Matthew Pierce 1930- *WhoRel 92*
**Matheny,** Adam Pence, Jr 1932- *AmMWSc 92*
**Matheny,** Ellis Leroy, Jr 1939- *AmMWSc 92*
**Matheny,** James Donald 1925- *AmMWSc 92*
**Matheny,** James Lafayette 1943- *AmMWSc 92*
**Matheny,** Paul Edward, Jr. 1947- *WhoRel 92*
**Matheny,** Rebecca Jean 1949- *WhoWest 92*
**Matheny,** Rita M 1922- *WhoAmP 91*
**Matheny,** Robert Duane 1924- *WhoRel 92*
**Matheny,** Robert Lavesco 1933- *WhoWest 92*
**Matheny,** Ruth Ann 1918- *WhoRel 92*
**Matheny,** Timothy Earl 1952- *WhoRel 92*
**Matheny,** Tom Harrell *WhoAmL 92*
**Mather,** Anne *WrDr 92*
**Mather,** Berkely *IntAu&W 91, WrDr 92*
**Mather,** Betty Bang 1927- *WhoEnt 92*
**Mather,** Bruce 1939- *NewAmDM*
**Mather,** Bryant 1916- *AmMWSc 92*
**Mather,** Carol *Who 92*
**Mather,** Charles E, III 1934- *WhoIns 92*
**Mather,** Cotton 1662?-1727? *BiInAmS*
**Mather,** Cotton 1663-1728 *BenetAL 91, RComAH*
**Mather,** David Carol 1919- *Who 92*
**Mather,** E. Cotton 1918- *WhoWest 92*
**Mather,** Edward Chantry 1937- *AmMWSc 92*
**Mather,** Fred 1833-1900 *BiInAmS*
**Mather,** Graham Christopher Spencer 1954- *IntWW 91, Who 92*
**Mather,** Herbert 1934- *WhoRel 92*
**Mather,** Ian Heywood 1945- *AmMWSc 92*
**Mather,** Increase 1639-1723 *BenetAL 91, BiInAmS, RComAH*
**Mather,** Jane H 1922- *AmMWSc 92*
**Mather,** Jennie Powell *AmMWSc 92*
**Mather,** John Carl 1938- *WhoRel 92*
**Mather,** John Cromwell 1946- *AmMWSc 92*
**Mather,** John Douglas 1936- *Who 92*
**Mather,** John Norman 1942- *AmMWSc 92*
**Mather,** John Russell 1923- *AmMWSc 92*
**Mather,** Joseph Ray 1934- *WhoWest 92*
**Mather,** Katharine Kniskern 1916- *AmMWSc 92*
**Mather,** Keith Benson 1922- *AmMWSc 92*
**Mather,** Kirtley F 1888-1978 *ConAu 35NR, SmATA 65*
**Mather,** Leonard 1909- *WrDr 92*
**Mather,** Leonard Charles d1991 *Who 92N*
**Mather,** Leonard Charles 1909-1991 *IntWW 91, -91N*
**Mather,** Richard 1596-1669 *BenetAL 91*
**Mather,** Robert Eugene 1918- *AmMWSc 92*
**Mather,** Robert Laurance 1921- *AmMWSc 92*
**Mather,** Roger Frederick 1917- *AmMWSc 92, WhoEnt 92*
**Mather,** Samuel 1706-1785 *BenetAL 91*
**Mather,** Shirley Brown 1948- *WhoRel 92*
**Mather,** William 1913- *Who 92*
**Mather,** William Williams 1804-1859 *BiInAmS*
**Mather-Hempler,** Portia Ann 1949- *WhoRel 92*
**Mathern,** Dennis Charles 1951- *WhoFI 92*
**Mathern,** Tim 1950- *WhoAmP 91, WhoMW 92*
**Matheron,** Michael Earl 1947- *WhoWest 92*
**Mathers,** Alexander Pickens 1909- *AmMWSc 92*
**Mathers,** George Schrader 1887?-1918 *BiInAmS*
**Mathers,** Jerry 1948- *ConTFT 9*
**Mathers,** Peter 1931- *ConNov 91, IntAu&W 91, WrDr 92*
**Mathers,** Robert 1928- *Who 92*
**Mathers,** Samuel Liddell 1854-1918 *RelLAm 91*
**Mathes,** David Wayne 1933- *WhoEnt 92*
**Mathes,** James R. *WhoBlA 92*
**Mathes,** Kenneth Natt 1913- *AmMWSc 92*
**Mathes,** Martin Charles 1935- *AmMWSc 92*
**Mathes,** Stephen Jon 1945- *WhoAmL 92*
**Matheson,** Alan Adams 1932- *WhoAmL 92*
**Matheson,** Alastair Taylor 1929- *AmMWSc 92*
**Matheson,** Ann 1940- *ConAu 133*
**Matheson,** Arthur Ralph 1915- *AmMWSc 92*
**Matheson,** Dale Whitney 1937- *AmMWSc 92*
**Matheson,** David Stewart 1945- *AmMWSc 92*
**Matheson,** De Loss H 1908- *AmMWSc 92*
**Matheson,** Don 1948- *IntAu&W 91*
**Matheson,** Duncan *Who 92*
**Matheson,** Ivan M 1926- *WhoAmP 91*
**Matheson,** James Adam Louis 1912- *Who 92*
**Matheson,** James Gunn 1912- *Who 92*
**Matheson,** John Mackenzie 1912- *Who 92*
**Matheson,** Louis *Who 92*
**Matheson,** Louis 1912- *IntWW 91*
**Matheson,** Richard 1926- *IntAu&W 91, TwCSFW 91, WrDr 92*
**Matheson,** Richard Christian 1953- *WhoEnt 92*
**Matheson,** Samuel Pritchard 1852-1942 *RelLAm 91*
**Matheson,** Scott Milne, Jr. 1953- *WhoAmL 92*
**Matheson,** Stephen Charles Taylor 1939- *Who 92*
**Matheson,** Sylvia A. *WrDr 92*
**Matheson,** Tim 1947- *IntMPA 92, WhoEnt 92*
**Matheson,** William Angus, Jr. 1919- *WhoMW 92*
**Matheson of Matheson,** Torquhil 1925- *Who 92*
**Matheu,** Domingo 1765-1831 *HisDSpE*
**Matheu,** Federico M. *WhoHisp 92*
**Mathew,** Arnold Harris 1852-1919 *RelLAm 91*
**Mathew,** Chempolil Thomas 1933- *AmMWSc 92*
**Mathew,** John Charles 1927- *Who 92*
**Mathew,** Mathai *AmMWSc 92*
**Mathew,** Ray 1929- *WrDr 92*
**Mathew,** Theobald David 1942- *Who 92*
**Mathewes,** David A 1931- *AmMWSc 92*
**Mathewes,** Rolf Walter 1946- *AmMWSc 92*
**Mathewes,** Shannon Louise 1963- *WhoWest 92*
**Mathews,** A L 1940- *AmMWSc 92*
**Mathews,** Arthur Kenneth 1906- *Who 92*
**Mathews,** Barbara Lynn 1958- *WhoWest 92*
**Mathews,** Bruce Eugene 1929- *AmMWSc 92*
**Mathews,** C A *AmMWSc 92*
**Mathews,** Carmen Sylva 1918- *WhoEnt 92*
**Mathews,** Carole *IntMPA 92*
**Mathews,** Charles Robert 1925- *WhoFI 92*
**Mathews,** Christopher King 1937- *AmMWSc 92*
**Mathews,** Collis Weldon 1938- *AmMWSc 92*
**Mathews,** Cornelius 1817-1889 *BenetAL 91, ScFEYrs*
**Mathews,** David 1935- *IntWW 91*
**Mathews,** Denis 1913- *TwCPaSc*
**Mathews,** Derek Lynn 1951- *WhoWest 92*
**Mathews,** Donald R 1931- *AmMWSc 92*
**Mathews,** Edward Gilbert, Jr. 1915- *WhoFI 92*
**Mathews,** Elkin d1921 *DcLB 112 [port]*
**Mathews,** F Scott 1934- *AmMWSc 92*
**Mathews,** F.X. *DrAPF 91*
**Mathews,** Frances Amelia 1932- *WhoAmP 91*
**Mathews,** Fred Lawrence 1929- *WhoMW 92*
**Mathews,** Frederick John 1918- *AmMWSc 92*
**Mathews,** Gary Ray 1944- *WhoMW 92*
**Mathews,** George *WhoBlA 92*
**Mathews,** Harry *DrAPF 91*
**Mathews,** Harry 1930- *ConNov 91*
**Mathews,** Harry T 1931- *AmMWSc 92*
**Mathews,** Henry Mabbett 1940- *AmMWSc 92*
**Mathews,** Herbert Lester 1949- *AmMWSc 92*
**Mathews,** Ian Richard 1933- *IntWW 91*
**Mathews,** James Harold 1946- *WhoRel 92*
**Mathews,** Jean H 1941- *WhoAmP 91*
**Mathews,** Jeremy Fell 1941- *Who 92*
**Mathews,** Jerold Chase 1930- *AmMWSc 92*
**Mathews,** John *WhoRel 92*
**Mathews,** John David 1947- *AmMWSc 92*
**Mathews,** John Joseph 1894?-1979 *BenetAL 91*
**Mathews,** John Joseph 1895-1962 *TwCWW 91*
**Mathews,** Joseph F 1933- *AmMWSc 92*
**Mathews,** Kathleen Vogel 1951- *WhoEnt 92*
**Mathews,** Keith E. 1944- *WhoBlA 92*
**Mathews,** Kenneth Pine 1921- *AmMWSc 92, WhoWest 92*
**Mathews,** Larry Arthur 1936- *AmMWSc 92, WhoWest 92*
**Mathews,** Lawrence Talbert 1947- *WhoBlA 92*
**Mathews,** Louise Robison 1917- *WhoFI 92*
**Mathews,** M V 1926- *AmMWSc 92*
**Mathews,** Marina Sarah Dewe *Who 92*
**Mathews,** Martin Benjamin 1912- *AmMWSc 92*
**Mathews,** Michael Stone 1940- *WhoFI 92*
**Mathews,** Nancy Ellen 1958- *AmMWSc 92*
**Mathews,** Richard *DrAPF 91*
**Mathews,** Robert Daniel 1928- *WhoFI 92*
**Mathews,** Robert Thomas 1919- *AmMWSc 92*
**Mathews,** Russell Lloyd 1921- *WrDr 92*
**Mathews,** Shailer 1863-1941 *RelLAm 91*
**Mathews,** Sharon Walker 1947- *WhoEnt 92*
**Mathews,** W E 1921- *AmMWSc 92*
**Mathews,** Walter Kelly 1937- *AmMWSc 92*
**Mathews,** Warren W 1939- *WhoAmP 91*
**Mathews,** William Harry 1931- *WhoMW 92*
**Mathews,** William Henry 1919- *AmMWSc 92*
**Mathews,** William Phillip 1868-1918 *BiInAmS*
**Mathews,** Willis Woodrow 1917- *AmMWSc 92*
**Mathews-Roth,** Micheline Mary 1934- *AmMWSc 92*
**Mathewson,** Christopher 1880-1925 *FacFETw*
**Mathewson,** Christopher Colville 1941- *AmMWSc 92*
**Mathewson,** Francis Alexander Lavens 1905- *AmMWSc 92*
**Mathewson,** George Atterbury 1935- *WhoAmL 92*
**Mathewson,** George Ross 1940- *Who 92*
**Mathewson,** Hugh Spalding 1921- *WhoMW 92*
**Mathewson,** James H 1929- *AmMWSc 92*
**Mathewson,** James L 1938- *WhoAmP 91*
**Mathewson,** Peter Scott 1947- *WhoRel 92*
**Mathewson,** Rita Ann 1960- *WhoMW 92*
**Mathezer,** Gordon 1938- *WhoWest 92*
**Mathia,** Mary Loyola 1921- *WhoRel 92*
**Mathias,** Betty Jane 1923- *WhoWest 92*
**Mathias,** Charles McC 1922- *IntWW 91*
**Mathias,** Charles McC, Jr 1922- *WhoAmP 91*
**Mathias,** Charles McCurdy, Jr. 1922- *WhoAmL 92*
**Mathias,** Frank Paul 1952- *WhoMW 92*
**Mathias,** Frank Russell Bentley 1927- *Who 92*
**Mathias,** Harry Michael 1945- *WhoEnt 92, WhoWest 92*
**Mathias,** Joseph Marshall 1914- *WhoAmL 92*
**Mathias,** Joseph Simon 1925- *AmMWSc 92*
**Mathias,** Leslie Michael 1935- *WhoWest 92*
**Mathias,** Lionel Armine 1907- *Who 92*
**Mathias,** Lon Jay 1948- *AmMWSc 92*
**Mathias,** Margaret Grossman 1928- *WhoFI 92, WhoMW 92*
**Mathias,** Melvin Merle 1939- *AmMWSc 92*
**Mathias,** Mildred Esther 1906- *AmMWSc 92*
**Mathias,** Pauline Mary 1928- *Who 92*
**Mathias,** Peter 1928- *IntWW 91, Who 92, WrDr 92*
**Mathias,** Richard Hughes d1991 *Who 92N*
**Mathias,** Robert A 1927- *AmMWSc 92*
**Mathias,** Robert Bruce 1930- *FacFETw, WhoAmP 91*
**Mathias,** Roland 1915- *ConPo 91, WrDr 92*
**Mathias,** Roland Glyn 1915- *IntAu&W 91*
**Mathias,** Sean Gerard 1956- *WhoEnt 92*
**Mathias,** Susan Joy 1955- *WhoAmL 92*
**Mathias,** William 1934- *ConCom 92, IntWW 91, Who 92*
**Mathias,** Winifred Rachel d1988 *Who 92N*
**Mathiason,** Dennis R 1941- *AmMWSc 92*
**Mathie,** Gordon William 1924- *WhoEnt 92*
**Mathies,** Allen Wray, Jr 1930- *AmMWSc 92, WhoWest 92*
**Mathies,** James Crosby 1919- *AmMWSc 92*
**Mathies,** Margaret Jean 1935- *AmMWSc 92*
**Mathiesen,** Matthias 1931- *IntWW 91*
**Mathiesen,** Thomas J 1947- *ConAu 34NR*
**Mathieson,** Alfred Herman 1917- *AmMWSc 92*
**Mathieson,** Arthur C 1937- *AmMWSc 92*
**Mathieson,** Craig B. 1955- *WhoEnt 92*
**Mathieson,** Donald Lindsay 1936- *WrDr 92*
**Mathieson,** Garrett Alfred 1952- *WhoFI 92*
**Mathieson,** Janet Hilary *Who 92*
**Mathieson,** William Allan Cunningham 1916- *Who 92*
**Mathieu,** Bertrand *DrAPF 91*
**Mathieu,** Daniel Robert 1950- *WhoRel 92*
**Mathieu,** Georges 1921- *FacFETw*
**Mathieu,** Georges Victor Adolphe 1921- *IntWW 91*
**Mathieu,** Helen M 1940- *WhoAmP 91*
**Mathieu,** Leo Gilles 1932- *AmMWSc 92*
**Mathieu,** Richard D 1926- *AmMWSc 92*
**Mathieu,** Robert Edward 1941- *WhoRel 92*
**Mathieu,** Robert Ernest 1947- *WhoRel 92*
**Mathieu,** Robert Joseph 1935- *WhoFI 92*
**Mathieu,** Roger Maurice 1924- *AmMWSc 92*
**Mathieu,** Thomas C 1936- *WhoAmP 91*
**Mathile,** Clayton Lee 1941- *WhoMW 92*
**Mathioudakis,** Michael Robert 1963- *WhoMW 92*
**Mathiprakasam,** Balakrishnan 1942- *AmMWSc 92, WhoMW 92*
**Mathis,** Billy John 1932- *AmMWSc 92*
**Mathis,** Cleopatra *DrAPF 91*
**Mathis,** David 1947- *WhoBlA 92*
**Mathis,** David B. *WhoMW 92*
**Mathis,** Don Elliott 1950- *WhoMW 92*

**Mathis,** Earnest, Jr. 1959- WhoFI 92
**Mathis,** Edith 1938- IntWW 91, NewAmDM
**Mathis,** Elmertha Burton 1948- WhoBlA 92
**Mathis,** Frank 1937- WhoBlA 92
**Mathis,** George Russell 1926- WhoEnt 92
**Mathis,** Jack David 1931- WhoFI 92, WhoMW 92
**Mathis,** James Forrest 1925- AmMWSc 92, WhoFI 92
**Mathis,** James L 1925- AmMWSc 92
**Mathis,** John Prentiss 1944- WhoAmL 92
**Mathis,** John Samuel 1931- AmMWSc 92
**Mathis,** Johnny 1935- FacFETw, WhoBlA 92, WhoEnt 92
**Mathis,** June 1892-1927 ReelWom
**Mathis,** Marsha Debra 1953- WhoFI 92
**Mathis,** Nathan WhoAmP 91
**Mathis,** Patricia Norton 1943- WhoFI 92
**Mathis,** Philip Monroe 1942- AmMWSc 92
**Mathis,** Richard Weldon 1945- WhoEnt 92
**Mathis,** Robert Fletcher 1946- AmMWSc 92
**Mathis,** Robert Lee 1934- WhoBlA 92
**Mathis,** Robert Lloyd 1942- WhoRel 92
**Mathis,** Robert Rex 1947- WhoRel 92
**Mathis,** Ronald Floyd 1942- AmMWSc 92
**Mathis,** Sallye Brooks WhoBlA 92
**Mathis,** Sharon Bell DrAPF 91
**Mathis,** Sharon Bell 1937- WhoBlA 92, WrDr 92
**Mathis,** Thaddeus P. 1942- WhoBlA 92
**Mathis,** Walter Lee, Sr. 1940- WhoBlA 92
**Mathis,** Wayne Neilsen 1945- AmMWSc 92
**Mathis,** William Ervin 1931- WhoEnt 92
**Mathis,** William Henry, III 1963- WhoRel 92
**Mathis,** William Lawrence 1964- WhoBlA 92
**Mathis-Eddy,** Darlene DrAPF 91
**Mathis-Eddy,** Darlene 1937- IntAu&W 91, IntWW 91
**Mathisen,** Chris WhoAmP 91
**Mathisen,** Harold Clifford 1924- WhoFI 92
**Mathisen,** Irwin Wald, Jr. 1928- WhoFI 92
**Mathisen,** Ole Alfred 1919- AmMWSc 92
**Mathisen-Reid,** Rhoda Sharon 1942- WhoMW 92
**Mathison,** Gary W 1945- AmMWSc 92
**Mathison,** Ian William 1938- AmMWSc 92, WhoMW 92
**Mathison,** John Ed 1938- WhoRel 92
**Mathison,** Thomas Walter 1961- WhoFI 92
**Mathison,** Volney G ScFEYrs
**Mathison-Bowie,** Stephen Loch 1955- WhoRel 92
**Mathison-Bowie,** Tiare Louise 1953- WhoRel 92
**Mathna,** Woodrow Wilson 1913- WhoAmP 91
**Mathrani,** Arjun K. WhoFI 92
**Mathre,** Donald Eugene 1938- AmMWSc 92
**Mathre,** Lawrence Gerhard 1925- WhoRel 92
**Mathre,** Owen Bertwell 1929- AmMWSc 92
**Mathsen,** Don Verden 1948- AmMWSc 92
**Mathsen,** Ronald M 1938- AmMWSc 92
**Mathsson,** Karl Bruno 1907-1988 DcTwDes
**Mathur,** Ashok WhoWest 92
**Mathur,** Carolyn Frances 1947- AmMWSc 92
**Mathur,** Dilip 1941- AmMWSc 92
**Mathur,** Ike 1943- WhoFI 92, WhoMW 92
**Mathur,** Maya Swarup 1939- AmMWSc 92
**Mathur,** Murari Lal 1931- IntWW 91
**Mathur,** Pershottam Prasad 1938- AmMWSc 92
**Mathur,** R M 1936- AmMWSc 92
**Mathur,** Subbi AmMWSc 92
**Mathur,** Sukhdev Prashad 1934- AmMWSc 92
**Mathur,** Suresh Chandra 1930- AmMWSc 92
**Mathur,** Vijay K. 1939- WhoMW 92
**Mathur,** Virendra Kumar AmMWSc 92
**Mathur,** Vishnu Sahai 1934- AmMWSc 92
**Mathwich,** Dale F. 1934- WhoFI 92, WhoIns 92
**Mathy,** Pamela Ann 1952- WhoAmL 92
**Mathys,** Kenneth Larue 1949- WhoMW 92
**Mathys,** Peter 1950- AmMWSc 92
**Matia,** Paul Ramon 1937- WhoAmP 91
**Matias-Rivera,** Jenice C. 1952- WhoHisp 92
**Matick,** Richard Edward 1933- AmMWSc 92
**Matiella,** Ana Consuelo 1951- WhoHisp 92
**Matienzo,** Luis J 1944- AmMWSc 92
**Matienzo,** Peter WhoHisp 92
**Matienzo Cintron,** Rosendo 1855-1913 HisDSpE
**Matienzo y Peralta,** Juan de 1520?-1580? HisDSpE
**Matijevic,** Egon 1922- AmMWSc 92
**Matijevich,** John S 1927- WhoAmP 91
**Matilal,** B. K. 1935- WrDr 92
**Matilal,** Bimal Krishna d1991 Who 92N
**Matilal,** Bimal Krishna 1935-1991 ConAu 134
**Matilda Augustus of England** 1102-1167 EncAmaz 91
**Matilda of Boulogne** 1103?-1152 EncAmaz 91
**Matilda of Ramsbury** EncAmaz 91
**Matilda of Tuscany** 1046-1115 EncAmaz 91
**Matilla,** Alfredo 1937- WhoHisp 92
**Matilsky,** Terry Allen 1947- AmMWSc 92
**Matin,** Abdul 1932- IntWW 91
**Matin,** Abdul 1941- WhoWest 92
**Matin,** M. A. 1937- IntWW 91
**Matin,** Shaikh Badarul 1944- AmMWSc 92
**Matinki,** Raila Elisabeth 1963- WhoWest 92
**Matis,** James Henry 1941- AmMWSc 92
**Matise,** Salvatore Anthony 1945- WhoAmL 92
**Matisoff,** Gerald 1951- AmMWSc 92, WhoMW 92
**Matisse,** Henri 1869-1954 FacFETw
**Matisse,** Pierre 1900-1989 FacFETw
**Matjeka,** Edward Ray 1943- AmMWSc 92
**Matkin,** Oris Arthur 1917- AmMWSc 92
**Matkovich,** Vlado Ivan 1924- AmMWSc 92
**Matkowsky,** Bernard J 1939- AmMWSc 92
**Matkowsky,** Bernard Judah 1939- WhoMW 92
**Matlack,** Albert Shelton 1923- AmMWSc 92
**Matlack,** Ardena Lavonne 1930- WhoAmP 91
**Matlack,** Don 1929- WhoAmP 91
**Matlack,** George Miller 1921- AmMWSc 92
**Matlack,** Rex William 1957- WhoFI 92
**Matlaga,** Richard Allen. 1944- WhoFI 92
**Matlhabaphiri,** Gaotlhaetse Utlwang S 1949- Who 92
**Matlin,** Albert R 1955- AmMWSc 92
**Matlin,** David DrAPF 91
**Matlin,** Marlee 1965- ConTFT 9, IntMPA 92, News 92-2 [port], WhoEnt 92
**Matlin,** Robin Beth 1952- WhoAmL 92
**Matlins,** Stuart M. 1940- WhoFI 92
**Matlis,** Eben 1923- AmMWSc 92
**Matlock,** Daniel Budd 1947- AmMWSc 92
**Matlock,** Gibb B 1931- AmMWSc 92
**Matlock,** Hudson 1919- AmMWSc 92
**Matlock,** Jack F, Jr 1929- WhoAmP 91
**Matlock,** Jack Foust 1929- Who 92
**Matlock,** Jack Foust, Jr. 1929- IntWW 91
**Matlock,** John Hudson 1944- AmMWSc 92
**Matlock,** Kenneth Jerome 1928- WhoFI 92
**Matlock,** Kent WhoBlA 92
**Matlock,** Matty 1907-1978 NewAmDM
**Matlock,** Rex Leon 1934- AmMWSc 92
**Matlock,** Stephen J. 1949- WhoWest 92
**Matlock,** Terry Joe 1962- WhoAmP 91
**Matlon,** Chris J. WhoFI 92
**Matlow,** Sheldon Leo 1928- AmMWSc 92
**Matney,** Donald Ray 1946- WhoRel 92
**Matney,** Thomas Stull 1928- AmMWSc 92
**Matney,** William C., Jr. 1924- WhoBlA 92
**Mato,** William Michael 1942- WhoWest 92
**Matocha,** Charles K 1929- AmMWSc 92
**Matoff,** Michelle Lynn 1963- WhoWest 92
**Matoka,** Peter Wilfred 1930- IntWW 91, Who 92
**Matolengwe,** Patrick Monwabisi 1937- Who 92
**Matolka,** Scott Anthony 1958- WhoFI 92
**Matolyak,** John 1939- AmMWSc 92
**Matomaki,** Tauno 1937- IntWW 91
**Maton,** Paul Nicholas 1947- AmMWSc 92
**Matonak,** Ronald E. 1945- WhoEnt 92
**Matonovich,** John S 1959- WhoAmP 91
**Matorin,** Robert Martin 1946- WhoEnt 92
**Matory,** Deborah Love 1929- WhoBlA 92
**Matory,** William Earle, Jr. 1950- WhoBlA 92
**Matos,** German Esteban 1947- WhoHisp 92
**Matos,** Israel 1954- WhoHisp 92
**Matos,** Joseph Federico 1966- WhoRel 92
**Matos,** Maria M. 1950- WhoHisp 92
**Matos,** Philip Waite 1936- WhoFI 92
**Matos,** Rafael Enrique 1967- WhoHisp 92
**Matos,** Ramona Salgado WhoHisp 92
**Matos,** Wilfredo 1940- WhoHisp 92
**Matos Paoli,** Francisco 1915- WhoHisp 92
**Matossian,** Jesse N 1952- AmMWSc 92
**Matossian,** Jesse Nerses 1952- WhoWest 92
**Matour,** James Michael 1954- WhoAmL 92
**Matousek,** Rose C. 1922- WhoMW 92
**Matovcik,** Lisa M 1955- AmMWSc 92
**Matovich,** Mitchel Joseph, Jr. 1927- WhoEnt 92, WhoWest 92
**Matovinovic,** Josip 1914- AmMWSc 92
**Matranga,** Jack Francis 1926- WhoEnt 92
**Matray,** James I. 1948- ConAu 135
**Matsakis,** Demetrios Nicholas 1949- AmMWSc 92
**Matsanoff,** Yordan 1961- WhoMW 92
**Matsas,** Nestor 1935- IntAu&W 91
**Matsch,** Charles Leo AmMWSc 92
**Matsch,** L A 1935- AmMWSc 92
**Matsch,** Lee Allan 1935- WhoWest 92
**Matsch,** Richard P. 1930- WhoAmL 92
**Matschiner,** John Thomas 1927- AmMWSc 92
**Matsebula,** Mhlangano Stephen 1925- IntWW 91
**Matsen,** Bradford Conway 1944- WhoWest 92
**Matsen,** Jeffrey Robert 1939- WhoWest 92
**Matsen,** John M 1936- AmMWSc 92
**Matsen,** John Martin 1933- AmMWSc 92, WhoFI 92, WhoWest 92
**Matseshe,** John Wanyama 1941- WhoMW 92
**Matshikiza,** Todd 1921-1968 LiExTwC
**Matsko,** John G WhoAmP 91
**Matson,** Clive DrAPF 91
**Matson,** Dennis Ludwig 1942- AmMWSc 92
**Matson,** Howard John 1921- AmMWSc 92
**Matson,** James Herbert 1940- WhoFI 92
**Matson,** Jim WhoAmP 91
**Matson,** Leslie Emmet, Jr 1920- AmMWSc 92
**Matson,** Merwyn Dean 1937- WhoWest 92
**Matson,** Michael 1952- AmMWSc 92
**Matson,** Michael Steven 1948- AmMWSc 92
**Matson,** Norman 1893-1965 ScFEYrs
**Matson,** Ollie Adrian 1930- BlkOlyM
**Matson,** Ollie Genoa 1930- WhoBlA 92
**Matson,** Robert Bruce 1951- WhoFI 92
**Matson,** Sigfred Christian 1917- WhoEnt 92
**Matson,** Ted P 1929- AmMWSc 92
**Matson,** Virginia Mae Freeberg 1914- WhoMW 92
**Matson,** Wallace I. 1921- WrDr 92
**Matson,** Wesley Jennings 1924- WhoMW 92
**Matson,** William Robert 1927- WhoAmP 91
**Matsubara,** Hisako LiExTwC
**Matsuda,** Fujio 1924- AmMWSc 92, WhoWest 92
**Matsuda,** Ken 1920- AmMWSc 92
**Matsuda,** Kyoko 1932- AmMWSc 92
**Matsuda,** Naoharu 1960- WhoFI 92
**Matsuda,** Seigo 1925- AmMWSc 92
**Matsuda,** Yoshiyuki 1943- AmMWSc 92
**Matsudaira,** Yori-Aki 1931- ConCom 92
**Matsudaira,** Yoritsune 1907- ConCom 92
**Matsuguma,** Harold Joseph 1928- AmMWSc 92
**Matsui,** Masanao 1917- IntWW 91
**Matsui,** Robert T. 1941- AlmAP 92 [port]
**Matsui,** Robert Takeo 1941- WhoAmP 91, WhoWest 92
**Matsui,** Sei-Ichi AmMWSc 92
**Matsukata,** Masanobu 1907- IntWW 91
**Matsukawa,** Michiya 1924- IntWW 91, WhoFI 92
**Matsumae,** Shigeyoshi d1991 NewYTBS 91
**Matsumoto,** Charles 1932- AmMWSc 92
**Matsumoto,** Hiromu 1920- AmMWSc 92
**Matsumoto,** Hiroyuki 1948- AmMWSc 92
**Matsumoto,** Juro IntWW 91
**Matsumoto,** Keith Tadao 1957- WhoFI 92, WhoWest 92
**Matsumoto,** Ken 1935- IntWW 91
**Matsumoto,** Ken 1941- AmMWSc 92
**Matsumoto,** Lloyd H AmMWSc 92
**Matsumoto,** Paul Tetsuo 1927- WhoAmP 91
**Matsumoto,** Shigemi WhoEnt 92
**Matsumoto,** Yorimi 1926- AmMWSc 92
**Matsumura,** Kazuyoshi 1947- WhoWest 92
**Matsumura,** Kenneth N 1945- AmMWSc 92, WhoWest 92
**Matsumura,** Philip 1947- AmMWSc 92
**Matsumura,** Teizo 1929- ConCom 92
**Matsumura,** Vera Yoshi WhoEnt 92
**Matsunaga,** Geoffrey Dean 1949- WhoAmL 92, WhoFI 92, WhoWest 92
**Matsunaga,** Hikaru 1928- IntWW 91
**Matsunaga,** Kikuo 1933- WhoRel 92
**Matsunaga,** Masanao 1924- IntWW 91
**Matsunaga,** Spark Masayuki d1990 IntWW 91N
**Matsuno,** Raizo 1917- IntWW 91
**Matsuo,** Keizo 1942- AmMWSc 92
**Matsuo,** Robert R 1932- AmMWSc 92
**Matsuoka,** Eric Takao 1967- WhoWest 92
**Matsuoka,** Jeffery Shigeharu 1958- WhoWest 92
**Matsuoka,** Shiro 1930- AmMWSc 92
**Matsuoka,** Tats 1929- AmMWSc 92
**Matsuoka,** Yosuke 1880-1946 EncTR 91, FacFETw
**Matsusaka,** Teruhisha 1926- AmMWSc 92
**Matsushima,** John K 1920- AmMWSc 92
**Matsushima,** Satoshi 1923- AmMWSc 92
**Matsushita,** Konosuke 1894-1989 FacFETw
**Matsushita,** Masaharu 1912- IntWW 91, WhoFI 92
**Matsuura,** Richard M 1932- WhoAmP 91
**Matsuura,** Takeshi 1936- AmMWSc 92
**Matsuyama,** Akira 1912- IntWW 91
**Matsuyama,** George 1918- AmMWSc 92
**Matsuyama,** Yoshinori 1923- IntWW 91
**Matsuzaki,** Masaji AmMWSc 92
**Matsuzawa,** Takuji 1913- IntWW 91
**Matt,** Jayne Mary 1952- WhoMW 92
**Matta,** David Lyles 1945- WhoHisp 92
**Matta,** Frank B. 1945- WhoHisp 92
**Matta,** Joseph Edward 1948- AmMWSc 92
**Matta,** Michael Stanley 1940- AmMWSc 92
**Matta,** Roberto Sebastian 1911- DcTwDes
**Matta Echuarren,** Roberto Sebastiano 1912- FacFETw
**Mattaio** 1959- WhoEnt 92
**Mattaliano,** Christopher WhoEnt 92
**Mattano,** Leonard August 1917- AmMWSc 92
**Mattar,** Ahmad 1939- IntWW 91
**Mattar,** Farres Phillip 1947- AmMWSc 92
**Mattar,** Lawrence Joseph 1934- WhoAmL 92
**Mattarella,** Sergio 1941- IntWW 91
**Mattauch,** Robert Joseph 1940- AmMWSc 92
**Mattax,** Calvin Coolidge 1925- AmMWSc 92
**Matte,** Aaron M. 1948- WhoAmL 92
**Matte,** J Jacques 1955- AmMWSc 92
**Matte,** Joseph, III 1916- AmMWSc 92
**Matte,** Robert, Jr. DrAPF 91
**Mattea,** Kathy WhoEnt 92
**Mattei,** Janet Akyuz 1943- AmMWSc 92
**Mattei,** Robert Sylvester 1948- WhoFI 92
**Matten,** Lawrence Charles 1938- AmMWSc 92
**Mattenheimer,** Hermann G W 1921- AmMWSc 92
**Matteo,** Thomas Craig 1961- WhoEnt 92
**Matteoli,** Ralph, Jr. 1938- WhoWest 92
**Matteotti,** Giacomo 1885-1924 FacFETw
**Matteotti,** Gianmatteo 1921- IntWW 91
**Matter,** Edith Ann 1949- WhoRel 92
**Matter,** Herbert 1907-1984 DcTwDes
**Matter,** Raymond Wayne 1933- WhoAmP 91
**Mattera,** Philip 1953- ConAu 133
**Mattern,** Alexander Watson 1916- WhoRel 92
**Mattern,** Jack Roger 1960- WhoRel 92
**Mattern,** Keith Edward 1931- WhoAmL 92
**Mattern,** Michael Ross 1947- AmMWSc 92
**Mattern,** Paul Joseph 1922- AmMWSc 92
**Mattern,** Perry Chalmers 1950- WhoRel 92
**Mattern,** Rosalie Ruth 1942- WhoMW 92
**Mattersdorff,** Guenter Hans 1926- WhoWest 92
**Mattes,** Frederick Henry 1941- AmMWSc 92
**Mattes,** Hans George 1943- AmMWSc 92
**Mattes,** William Bustin 1953- AmMWSc 92
**Matteson,** Donald Stephen 1932- AmMWSc 92, WhoWest 92
**Matteson,** E. David 1939- WhoFI 92
**Matteson,** Michael Jude 1936- AmMWSc 92
**Matteson,** Sandra Anne 1956- WhoWest 92
**Matteson,** William Bleecker 1928- WhoAmL 92, WhoFI 92
**Matteucci,** Dominick Vincent 1924- WhoFI 92, WhoWest 92
**Mattfeld,** George Francis 1941- AmMWSc 92
**Mattfield,** Mary DrAPF 91
**Matthaei,** George L 1923- AmMWSc 92
**Matthau,** Charles 1964- IntMPA 92
**Matthau,** Charles Marcus 1964- WhoWest 92
**Matthau,** Walter 1920- IntMPA 92, IntWW 91, WhoEnt 92
**Matthei Aubel,** Fernando 1925- IntWW 91
**Mattheis,** Floyd E 1931- AmMWSc 92

**Mattheiss**, Leonard Francis 1931- *AmMWSc 92*
**Matthes**, Michael Taylor 1951- *AmMWSc 92*
**Matthes**, Ralph Kenneth, Jr 1935- *AmMWSc 92*
**Matthes**, Steven Allen 1950- *AmMWSc 92*
**Mattheson**, Johann 1681-1764 *NewAmDM*
**Matthew** *EncEarC*
**Matthew**, Chessor Lillie 1913- *Who 92*
**Matthew**, Christopher C. F. 1939- *WrDr 92*
**Matthew**, Christopher Charles Forrest 1939- *IntAu&W 91*
**Matthew**, Clifton, Jr. 1943- *WhoBlA 92*
**Matthew**, Colin Gray 1941- *IntWW 91*
**Matthew**, Henry Colin Gray 1941- *Who 92*
**Matthew**, Jean R. *DrAPF 91*
**Matthew**, Leodis Clyde 1949- *WhoAmL 92*
**Matthew**, Lyn 1936- *WhoWest 92*
**Matthew**, Robert Andrew James 1959- *IntAu&W 91*
**Matthew**, Wentworth Arthur 1892-1973 *RelLAm 91*
**Matthewman**, Keith 1936- *Who 92*
**Matthews** *Who 92*
**Matthews**, Baron 1919- *IntWW 91, Who 92*
**Matthews**, A Cynthia 1924- *WhoAmP 91*
**Matthews**, Albert D. 1923- *WhoBlA 92*
**Matthews**, Alden Ewart 1921- *WhoRel 92*
**Matthews**, Anthony 1925- *TwCPaSc*
**Matthews**, Aquilla E. *WhoBlA 92*
**Matthews**, Benjamin F *AmMWSc 92*
**Matthews**, Billie Watson 1930- *WhoBlA 92*
**Matthews**, Bonnie Hummel 1942- *WhoMW 92*
**Matthews**, Brad *WrDr 92*
**Matthews**, Brander 1852-1929 *BenetAL 91*
**Matthews**, Brian Wesley 1938- *AmMWSc 92*
**Matthews**, Burnita Shelton 1894-1988 *FacFETw*
**Matthews**, Burton Clare 1926- *AmMWSc 92*
**Matthews**, Caryl Eve 1937- *WhoEnt 92*
**Matthews**, Charles David 1946- *WhoMW 92*
**Matthews**, Charles Philo 1868-1907 *BiInAmS*
**Matthews**, Charles Robert 1946- *AmMWSc 92*
**Matthews**, Charles Sedwick 1920- *AmMWSc 92*
**Matthews**, Christian William, Jr. 1934- *WhoRel 92*
**Matthews**, Christopher John 1945- *WhoAmP 91*
**Matthews**, Clark Jio, II 1936- *WhoFI 92*
**Matthews**, Claude Lankford, Jr. 1941- *WhoBlA 92*
**Matthews**, Clay, Jr. 1956- *WhoBlA 92*
**Matthews**, Clifford Norman 1921- *AmMWSc 92, WhoMW 92*
**Matthews**, Colin 1946- *ConCom 92, Who 92*
**Matthews**, Craig Gerard 1943- *WhoFI 92*
**Matthews**, Cynthia Clark 1941- *WhoBlA 92*
**Matthews**, Dan Gus 1939- *WhoAmL 92*
**Matthews**, David 1920- *WhoBlA 92, WhoRel 92*
**Matthews**, David 1943- *ConCom 92*
**Matthews**, David 1951- *WhoAmP 91*
**Matthews**, David Allan 1943- *AmMWSc 92*
**Matthews**, David Eugene 1948- *WhoMW 92*
**Matthews**, David John 1943- *Who 92*
**Matthews**, David LeSueur 1928- *AmMWSc 92*
**Matthews**, David Livingston 1922- *AmMWSc 92*
**Matthews**, David Napier 1911- *Who 92*
**Matthews**, Demetreos Nestor 1928- *AmMWSc 92*
**Matthews**, Denis 1919- *IntAu&W 91*
**Matthews**, Dennis L 1948- *AmMWSc 92*
**Matthews**, Dolores Evelyn 1938- *WhoBlA 92*
**Matthews**, Dorothy 1962- *WhoBlA 92*
**Matthews**, Douglas 1927- *Who 92*
**Matthews**, Douglas Eugene 1953- *WhoAmL 92*
**Matthews**, Doyle Jensen 1926- *AmMWSc 92*
**Matthews**, Drexel Gene 1952- *WhoFI 92*
**Matthews**, Drummond Hoyle 1931- *IntWW 91, Who 92*
**Matthews**, Dwight Earl 1951- *AmMWSc 92*
**Matthews**, E K 1930- *AmMWSc 92*
**Matthews**, E W, Jr 1925- *AmMWSc 92*
**Matthews**, Edward E. 1931- *WhoFI 92*
**Matthews**, Edward Easton 1931- *WhoIns 92*
**Matthews**, Edward Whitehouse 1936- *AmMWSc 92*
**Matthews**, Edwin James Thomas 1915- *Who 92*
**Matthews**, Edwin Spencer, Jr. 1934- *WhoAmL 92*
**Matthews**, Elizabeth Woodfin 1927- *WhoAmL 92*
**Matthews**, Ellen *WrDr 92*
**Matthews**, Ernest 1904- *Who 92*
**Matthews**, Floyd V, Jr 1927- *AmMWSc 92*
**Matthews**, Frederick White 1915- *AmMWSc 92*
**Matthews**, Gail Thunberg 1938- *WhoFI 92*
**Matthews**, Gareth B. 1929- *ConAu 135*
**Matthews**, Gary Joseph 1942- *AmMWSc 92*
**Matthews**, Gary L *WhoAmP 91*
**Matthews**, Gary Nathaniel 1950- *WhoBlA 92*
**Matthews**, Geoffrey 1917- *Who 92*
**Matthews**, Geoffrey Vernon Townsend 1923- *Who 92*
**Matthews**, George Lloyd 1917- *Who 92*
**Matthews**, Gerald Eugene 1943- *WhoMW 92*
**Matthews**, Gilbert Elliott 1930- *WhoFI 92*
**Matthews**, Gordon 1908- *Who 92*
**Matthews**, Greg 1949- *ConAu 135*
**Matthews**, Gregory J. 1947- *WhoBlA 92*
**Matthews**, Harry Bradshaw 1952- *WhoBlA 92*
**Matthews**, Harry Roy 1942- *AmMWSc 92*
**Matthews**, Hazel Benton, Jr 1940- *AmMWSc 92*
**Matthews**, Henry Melvin 1926- *Who 92*
**Matthews**, Herbert Spencer 1921- *WhoAmP 91*
**Matthews**, Hewitt W. 1944- *WhoBlA 92*
**Matthews**, Hewitt William 1944- *AmMWSc 92*
**Matthews**, Horatio Keith 1917- *IntWW 91, Who 92*
**Matthews**, Jack *DrAPF 91*
**Matthews**, Jack 1925- *ConAu 15AS [port], ConNov 91, WhoMW 92, WrDr 92*
**Matthews**, Jack Beverly, Jr. 1951- *WhoEnt 92*
**Matthews**, James B 1933- *AmMWSc 92*
**Matthews**, James C., II *WhoMW 92*
**Matthews**, James Francis 1935- *AmMWSc 92*
**Matthews**, James Horace 1930- *AmMWSc 92*
**Matthews**, James Kenneth 1913- *RelLAm 91*
**Matthews**, James Lester 1926- *AmMWSc 92*
**Matthews**, James Vernon, II 1948- *WhoBlA 92*
**Matthews**, Jana B. 1940- *WhoFI 92, WhoWest 92*
**Matthews**, Jeanne Pearson 1941- *WhoFI 92*
**Matthews**, Jeffery Edward 1928- *Who 92*
**Matthews**, Jessie L. 1935- *WhoBlA 92*
**Matthews**, John 1930- *Who 92*
**Matthews**, John Burr Lumley 1935- *Who 92*
**Matthews**, John Duncan 1921- *Who 92*
**Matthews**, John Frederick 1940- *Who 92*
**Matthews**, John G 1917- *WhoAmP 91*
**Matthews**, John Louis 1932- *WhoWest 92*
**Matthews**, John Wesley, Jr 1940- *WhoAmP 91*
**Matthews**, June Lorraine 1939- *AmMWSc 92*
**Matthews**, Justus 1945- *WhoWest 92*
**Matthews**, Kathleen Shive 1945- *AmMWSc 92*
**Matthews**, Kenneth L *WhoAmP 91*
**Matthews**, Kevin *WhoEnt 92*
**Matthews**, L. White, III 1945- *WhoFI 92*
**Matthews**, Lee Drew 1943- *AmMWSc 92*
**Matthews**, Lena Dale *DrAPF 91*
**Matthews**, Leonard Louis 1930- *WhoBlA 92*
**Matthews**, Leslie Scott 1951- *AmMWSc 92*
**Matthews**, Linda Guerra 1949- *WhoHisp 92*
**Matthews**, Lori 1947- *WhoMW 92*
**Matthews**, Mallory Louis 1953- *WhoBlA 92*
**Matthews**, Margaret Rejean 1935- *BlkOlyM*
**Matthews**, Marjorie Swank 1916-1986 *RelLAm 91*
**Matthews**, Markia Anne 1956- *WhoWest 92*
**Matthews**, Martin, Jr 1926- *WhoAmP 91*
**Matthews**, Martin David 1938- *AmMWSc 92*
**Matthews**, Mary Eileen 1938- *AmMWSc 92*
**Matthews**, Mary Joan 1945- *WhoBlA 92*
**Matthews**, Merritt Stewart 1939- *WhoBlA 92*
**Matthews**, Michael 1930- *Who 92*
**Matthews**, Michael Gough 1931- *Who 92*
**Matthews**, Miriam 1905- *WhoBlA 92*
**Matthews**, Murray Albert 1943- *AmMWSc 92*
**Matthews**, N F J 1931- *AmMWSc 92*
**Matthews**, Norman Sherwood, Jr. 1944- *WhoWest 92*
**Matthews**, Norman Stuart 1933- *WhoFI 92*
**Matthews**, Pamela Winifred 1914- *Who 92*
**Matthews**, Patricia 1927- *WrDr 92*
**Matthews**, Patricia Anne 1927- *IntAu&W 91*
**Matthews**, Paul Aaron 1952- *WhoAmL 92*
**Matthews**, Paul Chandler 1926- *WhoAmL 92*
**Matthews**, Percy 1921- *Who 92*
**Matthews**, Peter 1922- *Who 92*
**Matthews**, Peter 1934- *WrDr 92*
**Matthews**, Peter, Mrs. *Who 92*
**Matthews**, Peter Alec 1922- *IntWW 91*
**Matthews**, Peter Bryan Conrad 1928- *IntWW 91, Who 92*
**Matthews**, Peter Hugoe 1934- *IntWW 91, Who 92*
**Matthews**, Peter Jack 1917- *Who 92*
**Matthews**, Peter John 1945- *IntAu&W 91*
**Matthews**, Philip 1916-1984 *TwCPaSc*
**Matthews**, R B 1942- *AmMWSc 92*
**Matthews**, Richard Bonnar 1915- *Who 92*
**Matthews**, Richard Carroll 1926- *WhoAmP 91*
**Matthews**, Richard David 1933- *WhoRel 92*
**Matthews**, Richard Ellis Ford 1921- *IntWW 91, Who 92*
**Matthews**, Richard Finis 1929- *AmMWSc 92*
**Matthews**, Richard John, Jr 1927- *AmMWSc 92*
**Matthews**, Robert A 1926- *AmMWSc 92*
**Matthews**, Robert C. O. 1927- *WrDr 92*
**Matthews**, Robert Charles Oliver 1927- *IntWW 91, Who 92*
**Matthews**, Robert L. 1930- *WhoBlA 92*
**Matthews**, Robert Wendell 1942- *AmMWSc 92*
**Matthews**, Robley Knight 1935- *AmMWSc 92*
**Matthews**, Roderick Jon 1946- *WhoFI 92*
**Matthews**, Ronald Alan 1952- *WhoEnt 92*
**Matthews**, Ronald Sydney 1922- *Who 92*
**Matthews**, Rowena Green 1938- *AmMWSc 92*
**Matthews**, Ruth H 1926- *AmMWSc 92*
**Matthews**, Sampson 1933- *WhoRel 92*
**Matthews**, Samuel Arthur *AmMWSc 92*
**Matthews**, Stanley 1915- *ConAu 134, Who 92*
**Matthews**, Stephen M 1938- *AmMWSc 92*
**Matthews**, Steven Dee 1946- *WhoEnt 92*
**Matthews**, T.S. d1991 *NewYTBS 91 [port]*
**Matthews**, T. S. 1901-1991 *ConAu 133, CurBio 91N*
**Matthews**, Thomas Robert 1939- *AmMWSc 92*
**Matthews**, Thomas Stanley d1991 *Who 92N*
**Matthews**, Thomas Stanley 1901- *IntAu&W 91*
**Matthews**, Timothy John 1907- *Who 92*
**Matthews**, Tom *WhoAmP 91*
**Matthews**, Victoria Earle 1861-1907 *NotBlAW 92 [port]*
**Matthews**, Vincent 1947- *WhoBlA 92*
**Matthews**, Vincent Edward 1947- *BlkOlyM*
**Matthews**, Virgil E. 1928- *WhoBlA 92*
**Matthews**, Virgil Edison 1928- *AmMWSc 92*
**Matthews**, W. W. *WhoRel 92*
**Matthews**, Walter Bryan 1920- *Who 92*
**Matthews**, Walter Charles John 1950- *WhoRel 92*
**Matthews**, Warren Wayne 1939- *WhoAmL 92, WhoWest 92*
**Matthews**, Washington 1843-1905 *BenetAL 91, BiInAmS*
**Matthews**, Westina Lomax 1948- *WhoBlA 92*
**Matthews**, William *DrAPF 91*
**Matthews**, William 1942- *ConPo 91, WrDr 92*
**Matthews**, William Gordon 1943- *WhoEnt 92*
**Matthews**, William Henry 1945- *WhoFI 92*
**Matthews**, William Henry, III 1919- *AmMWSc 92*
**Matthews**, William John 1919- *WhoWest 92*
**Matthews**, William John 1946- *AmMWSc 92*
**Matthews**, Zachariah Keodirelang 1901-1968 *DcEcMov*
**Matthews**, Zachary E 1956- *WhoAmP 91*
**Matthias**, John *DrAPF 91*
**Matthias**, John 1941- *ConPo 91, IntAu&W 91, WrDr 92*
**Matthias**, Judson S 1931- *AmMWSc 92*
**Matthias**, Judson Stillman 1931- *WhoWest 92*
**Matthias**, Ronald Stephen 1956- *WhoAmL 92*
**Matthies**, Joyce Muriel 1948- *WhoEnt 92*
**Matthies**, Mary Constance T. 1948- *WhoAmL 92*
**Matthiesen**, Garvin C. 1928- *WhoFI 92*
**Matthiesen**, Leroy Theodore 1921- *WhoRel 92*
**Matthiessen**, F. O. 1902-1950 *BenetAL 91, FacFETw*
**Matthiessen**, Peter *DrAPF 91*
**Matthiessen**, Peter 1927- *BenetAL 91, ConNov 91, IntAu&W 91, IntWW 91, WrDr 92*
**Matthiessen**, Poul Christian 1933- *IntWW 91*
**Matthijssen**, Charles 1931- *AmMWSc 92*
**Matthis**, James L., III 1955- *WhoBlA 92*
**Matthofer**, Hans 1925- *IntWW 91, Who 92*
**Matthus**, Siegfried 1934- *IntWW 91*
**Matthy**, Peter Douglas 1946- *WhoFI 92*
**Matthys**, Eric Francois 1956- *AmMWSc 92*
**Matthys**, Victor Hubert 1914-1947 *BiDExR*
**Matthysse**, Ann Gale 1939- *AmMWSc 92*
**Matthysse**, Steven William 1939- *AmMWSc 92*
**Mattice**, Jack Shafer 1941- *AmMWSc 92*
**Mattice**, Paul M 1913- *WhoIns 92*
**Mattice**, Wayne Lee 1940- *AmMWSc 92*
**Mattick**, Joseph Francis 1918- *AmMWSc 92*
**Mattics**, Leon Eugene 1940- *AmMWSc 92*
**Mattielli**, Louis 1949- *WhoAmL 92*
**Matties**, Charles R *WhoAmP 91*
**Mattila**, Edward Charles 1927- *WhoEnt 92*
**Mattila**, John Peter 1943- *WhoFI 92, WhoMW 92*
**Mattila**, Karita Marjatta 1960- *IntWW 91*
**Mattina**, Charles Frederick 1944- *AmMWSc 92*
**Mattina**, Mary Jane Incorvia 1944- *AmMWSc 92*
**Mattingley**, Christobel 1931- *ChlLR 24 [port], WrDr 92*
**Mattingley**, Christobel Rosemary 1931- *IntAu&W 91*
**Mattingly**, Alan 1949- *Who 92*
**Mattingly**, George *DrAPF 91*
**Mattingly**, Glen E 1932- *AmMWSc 92*
**Mattingly**, Loren James 1954- *WhoFI 92*
**Mattingly**, Mack Francis 1931- *IntWW 91, WhoAmP 91*
**Mattingly**, Richard Francis 1925- *AmMWSc 92*
**Mattingly**, Robert Kerker 1921- *WhoMW 92*
**Mattingly**, Steele F 1927- *AmMWSc 92*
**Mattingly**, Stephen 1922- *Who 92*
**Mattingly**, Stephen Joseph 1943- *AmMWSc 92*
**Mattinson**, James Meikle 1944- *AmMWSc 92*
**Mattioni**, Dante 1930- *WhoAmL 92*
**Mattioni**, John 1935- *WhoAmL 92*
**Mattis**, Allen Francis 1947- *AmMWSc 92*
**Mattis**, Daniel Charles 1932- *AmMWSc 92*
**Mattis**, James Melvin 1942- *WhoAmL 92*
**Mattison**, Alice *DrAPF 91*
**Mattison**, Charles Albert 1939- *WhoRel 92, WhoWest 92*
**Mattison**, Donald Roger 1944- *AmMWSc 92*
**Mattison**, Dorothy Love 1927- *WhoAmP 91*
**Mattison**, Elisa Sheri 1952- *WhoWest 92*
**Mattison**, Jack Lloyd 1939- *WhoAmL 92*
**Mattison**, Jackie R 1951- *WhoAmP 91*
**Mattison**, Louis Emil 1927- *AmMWSc 92*
**Mattison**, Priscilla Jane 1960- *WhoEnt 92*
**Mattison**, Ronald Paul, Sr. 1951- *WhoRel 92*
**Mattison**, Stanley Barron 1943- *WhoFI 92*
**Mattix-Wand**, Paula Jane 1967- *WhoRel 92*
**Mattlage**, Karl P 1940- *WhoAmP 91*
**Mattlin**, Benjamin Michael 1962- *WhoWest 92*
**Mattlin**, Sharon *DrAPF 91*
**Mattman**, Lida Holmes 1912- *AmMWSc 92*
**Matto**, Kenneth Bruce 1953- *WhoRel 92*
**Matto de Turner**, Clorinda 1852-1909 *SpAmWW*
**Mattoli**, Craig Leon 1952- *WhoFI 92*
**Matton**, Roger 1929- *NewAmDM*
**Mattone**, Joseph Michael 1931- *WhoFI 92*
**Mattone**, Vincent J. *WhoFI 92*
**Mattoon**, James Richard 1930- *AmMWSc 92*
**Mattoon**, Sara Halsey 1947- *WhoFI 92, WhoWest 92*
**Mattor**, John Alan 1932- *AmMWSc 92*

**Mattos,** James George 1932- *WhoAmP 91*
**Mattox,** Edward Irvin, Jr. 1956- *WhoMW 92, WhoRel 92*
**Mattox,** James Albon 1943- *WhoAmP 91*
**Mattox,** Joseph Edward 1950- *WhoRel 92*
**Mattox,** Karl 1936- *AmMWSc 92*
**Mattox,** Richard Benjamin 1921- *AmMWSc 92*
**Mattson,** Brian Jay 1948- *WhoFI 92*
**Mattson,** Carol Linnette 1946- *WhoMW 92*
**Mattson,** Catherine Marie 1935- *WhoAmP 91*
**Mattson,** Dale Edward 1934- *AmMWSc 92*
**Mattson,** Donald Eugene 1934- *AmMWSc 92*
**Mattson,** Doug Leif 1955- *WhoAmP 91*
**Mattson,** Edna O'Neill 1936- *WhoAmP 91*
**Mattson,** Fred Hugh 1918- *AmMWSc 92*
**Mattson,** Geraldine Ellen 1932- *WhoAmP 91*
**Mattson,** Guy C 1927- *AmMWSc 92*
**Mattson,** Harold F, Jr 1930- *AmMWSc 92*
**Mattson,** Helmi *DcAmImH*
**Mattson,** James Allen 1949- *WhoWest 92*
**Mattson,** James Stewart 1945- *WhoAmL 92*
**Mattson,** Jeffrey Mark 1965- *WhoFI 92*
**Mattson,** Joan C 1935- *AmMWSc 92*
**Mattson,** Karen Eleanor 1952- *WhoMW 92*
**Mattson,** Kenneth Michael 1951- *WhoAmL 92*
**Mattson,** Margaret Ellen 1947- *AmMWSc 92*
**Mattson,** Marlin Roy Albin 1939- *AmMWSc 92*
**Mattson,** Peter Humphrey 1932- *AmMWSc 92*
**Mattson,** Raymond Harding 1920- *AmMWSc 92*
**Mattson,** Richard Lewis 1935- *AmMWSc 92*
**Mattson,** Robert Bernard 1963- *WhoRel 92*
**Mattson,** Roy Henry 1927- *AmMWSc 92, WhoWest 92*
**Mattson,** Shawn Richard 1949- *WhoFI 92*
**Mattson,** Steven Roald 1955- *WhoMW 92*
**Mattson,** Vernon Williams 1934- *WhoRel 92*
**Mattson,** William Royce, Jr. 1946- *WhoMW 92*
**Mattuck,** Arthur Paul 1930- *AmMWSc 92*
**Matukas,** Victor John 1933- *AmMWSc 92*
**Matula,** David William 1937- *AmMWSc 92*
**Matula,** Dennis Lee 1949- *WhoRel 92*
**Matula,** Edward Paul, Jr. 1941- *WhoWest 92*
**Matula,** Richard A 1939- *AmMWSc 92*
**Matula,** Richard Allen 1938- *AmMWSc 92*
**Matulevicius,** Edward S 1942- *AmMWSc 92*
**Matulic,** Ljubomir Francisco 1923- *AmMWSc 92*
**Matulionis,** Daniel H 1938- *AmMWSc 92*
**Matulis,** Raymond M 1939- *AmMWSc 92*
**Matumoto,** Tosimatu 1926- *AmMWSc 92*
**Matune,** Frank Joseph 1948- *WhoAmL 92*
**Matura,** Mustapha 1939- *IntAu&W 91, WrDr 92*
**Matura,** Raymond Carl 1948- *WhoMW 92*
**Mature,** Victor 1916- *IntMPA 92*
**Maturen,** Michael Andrew 1964- *WhoRel 92*
**Maturi,** Vincent Francis 1916- *AmMWSc 92*
**Maturin,** Charles Robert 1780-1824 *RfGEnL 91*
**Maturin,** Fred, Mrs. *ScFEYrs*
**Maturo,** Frank J S, Jr 1929- *AmMWSc 92*
**Maturo,** Joseph Martin, III 1942- *AmMWSc 92*
**Matus,** Wayne Charles 1950- *WhoAmL 92*
**Matushin,** Michael Francis, Sr. 1934- *WhoEnt 92*
**Matusse,** Bento Bartolomeu *WhoRel 92*
**Matuszak,** Alice Jean Boyer 1935- *AmMWSc 92*
**Matuszak,** Charles A 1932- *AmMWSc 92*
**Matuszak,** David Robert 1934- *AmMWSc 92*
**Matuszczak,** Bernadetta 1933- *ConCom 92*
**Matuszek,** John Michael, Jr 1935- *AmMWSc 92*
**Matuszewski,** Stanley 1915- *WhoRel 92*
**Matuszko,** Anthony Joseph 1926- *AmMWSc 92*
**Matute Ausejo,** Ana Maria 1925- *IntAu&W 91, IntWW 91*
**Matutes Juan,** Abel 1941- *IntWW 91, Who 92*
**Matveev,** Aleksandr Terent'evich 1878-1960 *SovUnBD*
**Matveeva,** Novella Nikolaevna 1934- *SovUnBD*
**Matveyev,** Aleksey Nikolayevich 1922- *IntWW 91*
**Matveyeva,** Novella Nikolaevna 1934- *IntWW 91*
**Matwiyoff,** Nicholas Alexander 1937- *AmMWSc 92*
**Matyas,** E Leslie 1932- *AmMWSc 92*
**Matyas,** Gary Ralph 1956- *AmMWSc 92*
**Matyas,** Marsha Lakes 1957- *AmMWSc 92*
**Matyas,** Tom 1956- *WhoAmP 91*
**Matyjaszewski,** Krzysztof 1950- *AmMWSc 92*
**Matz,** Jeffrey Allan 1942- *WhoAmL 92*
**Matz,** Mary Dill 1931- *WhoRel 92*
**Matz,** Merton J. 1922- *WhoFI 92*
**Matz,** Milton 1927- *WhoRel 92*
**Matz,** Peter S. 1928- *WhoEnt 92*
**Matz,** Robert 1931- *AmMWSc 92*
**Matz,** Samuel Adam 1924- *AmMWSc 92*
**Matzdorff,** James Arthur 1956- *WhoFI 92, WhoWest 92*
**Matzeder,** Jean Marie Znidarsic 1948- *WhoAmL 92*
**Matzen,** Maurice Keith 1947- *AmMWSc 92*
**Matzen,** Robert T 1924- *WhoIns 92*
**Matzen,** Vernon Charles *AmMWSc 92*
**Matzen,** Walter T 1922- *AmMWSc 92*
**Matzer,** John Wayne 1945- *WhoWest 92*
**Matzinger,** Dale Frederick 1929- *AmMWSc 92*
**Matziorinis,** Kenneth N. 1954- *WhoFI 92*
**Matzkanin,** George Andrew 1938- *AmMWSc 92*
**Matzke,** Bruce Carter 1951- *WhoAmL 92*
**Matzner,** Edwin Arthur 1928- *AmMWSc 92*
**Matzner,** Markus 1929- *AmMWSc 92*
**Matzner,** Richard Alfred 1942- *AmMWSc 92*
**Mau,** Dwayne Holger 1942- *WhoRel 92*
**Mauceri,** Albert 1931- *WhoIns 92*
**Mauceri,** John 1945- *NewAmDM*
**Mauceri,** John Conrad 1958- *WhoEnt 92*
**Mauceri,** John Francis 1945- *Who 92, WhoEnt 92*
**Mauche,** Christopher W 1958- *AmMWSc 92*
**Mauchline,** Lord 1942- *Who 92*
**Mauchly,** John William 1907-1980 *FacFETw*
**Mauck,** Henry Page, Jr 1926- *AmMWSc 92*
**Mauck,** William M., Jr. 1938- *WhoFI 92*
**Mauclair,** Camille 1872-1945 *ThHEIm*
**Maud,** Empress *EncAmaz 91*
**Maud,** Humphrey John Hamilton 1934- *IntWW 91, Who 92*
**Maude** *Who 92*
**Maude,** Francis Anthony Aylmer 1953- *Who 92*
**Maude,** Frederick N 1854-1933 *ScFEYrs*
**Maude Of Stratford-Upon-Avon,** Baron 1912- *IntWW 91, Who 92*
**Maude-Roxby,** Alice *TwCPaSc*
**Mauderli,** Walter 1924- *AmMWSc 92*
**Mauderly,** Joe L 1943- *AmMWSc 92*
**Maudlin,** Lloyd Z 1924- *AmMWSc 92*
**Maudling,** Reginald 1917-1979 *FacFETw*
**Maudsley,** David V 1940- *AmMWSc 92*
**Maue-Dickson,** Wilma 1943- *AmMWSc 92*
**Mauer,** Alvin Marx 1928- *AmMWSc 92*
**Mauer,** Arlin Arthur 1930- *WhoWest 92*
**Mauer,** David Michael 1948- *WhoFI 92, WhoMW 92*
**Mauer,** Irving 1927- *AmMWSc 92*
**Mauer,** S Michael *AmMWSc 92*
**Mauer,** William F 1930- *WhoAmP 91*
**Mauerman,** Douglas Vern 1940- *WhoWest 92*
**Mauersberger,** Konrad 1938- *AmMWSc 92*
**Mauet,** Thomas Anton 1945- *WhoAmL 92*
**Mauga,** Seali'itu F 1947- *WhoAmP 91*
**Maugans,** Edgar Hurley 1935- *WhoFI 92*
**Maugans,** John Conrad 1938- *WhoMW 92*
**Mauger,** John William 1942- *AmMWSc 92*
**Mauger,** Patricia Ann 1937- *WhoEnt 92*
**Mauger,** Richard L 1936- *AmMWSc 92*
**Maugham,** Robin 1916- *IntAu&W 91*
**Maugham,** Robin 1916-1981 *LiExTwC*
**Maugham,** Syrie 1879-1955 *DcTwDes, FacFETw*
**Maugham,** W. Somerset 1874-1965 *CnDBLB 6 [port], ConLC 67 [port], FacFETw [port], LiExTwC, RfGEnL 91, ShSCr 8 [port]*
**Maughan,** Anne Margery *WrDr 92*
**Maughan,** Charles Gilbert 1923- *Who 92*
**Maughan,** Deryck C. *WhoFI 92*
**Maughan,** Edwin Kelly 1926- *AmMWSc 92*
**Maughan,** George Burwell 1910- *AmMWSc 92*
**Maughan,** Owen Eugene 1943- *AmMWSc 92*
**Maughan,** W Lowell *AmMWSc 92*
**Maughan,** Willard Zinn 1944- *WhoWest 92*
**Maughmer,** Karrol June *WhoAmP 91*
**Maughn,** James David 1947- *WhoIns 92*
**Mauk,** Arthur Grant 1947- *AmMWSc 92*
**Mauk,** Marcia Rokus 1947- *AmMWSc 92*
**Mauk,** Pamela Anne 1953- *WhoWest 92*
**Mauk,** Richard Kenneth 1953- *WhoAmP 91*
**Mauksch,** Ingeborg G *AmMWSc 92*
**Maul,** George A 1938- *AmMWSc 92*
**Maul,** Gerd G 1940- *AmMWSc 92*
**Maul,** James Joseph 1938- *AmMWSc 92*
**Maul,** Richard James 1947- *WhoEnt 92*
**Maul,** Stephen Bailey 1942- *WhoFI 92*
**Maul,** Terry Lee 1946- *WhoWest 92*
**Maulbetsch,** John Stewart 1939- *AmMWSc 92*
**Maulde,** Bruno Guy Andre Jean de 1934- *IntWW 91*
**Mauldin,** Bill 1921- *BenetAL 91*
**Mauldin,** Jean 1923- *WhoAmP 91*
**Mauldin,** Jean Humphries 1923- *WhoFI 92*
**Mauldin,** John Inglis 1947- *WhoAmL 92*
**Mauldin,** Kenneth Laurence 1918- *WhoRel 92*
**Mauldin,** Michael Douglas 1947- *WhoEnt 92*
**Mauldin,** Patricia Jarman 1939- *WhoFI 92*
**Mauldin,** Richard Daniel 1943- *AmMWSc 92*
**Maulding,** Barry Clifford 1945- *WhoAmL 92*
**Maulding,** Donald Roy 1936- *AmMWSc 92*
**Maulding,** Hawkins Valliant, Jr 1935- *AmMWSc 92*
**Mauldon,** James Grenfell 1920- *AmMWSc 92*
**Maule,** Albert R. *WhoBlA 92*
**Maule,** Henry 1915-1981 *ConAu 133*
**Maule,** James Edward 1951- *WhoAmL 92*
**Maule,** Michael 1921- *WhoEnt 92*
**Maule,** Randy William 1954- *WhoEnt 92*
**Maule,** William 1690-1726 *DcNCBi 4*
**Mauleverer,** Bruce 1946- *Who 92*
**Maull,** George Marriner 1947- *WhoEnt 92*
**Maullar,** Marci E. 1953- *WhoEnt 92*
**Maulnier,** Thierry 1909- *BiDExR*
**Maulsby,** Allen Farish 1922- *WhoAmL 92*
**Maulsby,** Ruhl 1923- *WhoAmP 91*
**Maultsby,** Dorothy M. 1927- *WhoBlA 92*
**Maultsby,** Portia K. 1947- *WhoBlA 92*
**Maultsby,** Sylvester 1935- *WhoBlA 92*
**Maulupe,** Saofa'igaoalii *WhoAmP 91*
**Maumela,** Titus Ntsieni 1924- *IntAu&W 91*
**Maumenee,** Alfred Edward 1913- *IntWW 91*
**Maumenee,** Irene Hussels 1940- *AmMWSc 92*
**Maund,** John Arthur Arrowsmith 1909- *Who 92*
**Maunder,** A Bruce 1934- *AmMWSc 92*
**Maunder,** Leonard 1927- *Who 92*
**Maundrell,** Wolseley David 1920- *Who 92*
**Maune,** David Francis 1939- *AmMWSc 92*
**Mauney,** Donald Wallace, Jr. 1942- *WhoBlA 92*
**Mauney,** Thomas Lee 1967- *WhoEnt 92*
**Maung,** Mohamed Ismael Khin 1932- *WhoMW 92*
**Maung Maung Gyee,** U. 1921- *IntWW 91*
**Maung Maung Kha,** U. *IntWW 91*
**Maunsell,** Susan Pamela 1942- *Who 92*
**Maunz,** Theodor 1901- *EncTR 91*
**Maupassant,** Guy de 1850-1893 *GuFrLit 1*
**Maupertuis,** Pierre Louis Moreau de 1698-1759 *BlkwCEP*
**Maupin,** Armistead 1944- *WrDr 92*
**Maupin,** Aubigny 1673?-1703 *EncAmaz 91*
**Maupin,** Pamela *AmMWSc 92*
**Maupin,** Virginia Lee 1924- *WhoRel 92*
**Maura,** Carmen 1946- *IntMPA 92*
**Maurel,** Victor 1848-1923 *NewAmDM*
**Maurer,** Adah Electra 1905- *WhoWest 92*
**Maurer,** Alan H 1947- *AmMWSc 92*
**Maurer,** Armand Augustine 1915- *WhoRel 92*
**Maurer,** Arthur James 1942- *AmMWSc 92*
**Maurer,** Bruce Anthony 1936- *AmMWSc 92*
**Maurer,** David L. 1945- *WhoAmL 92*
**Maurer,** Donald Leo 1934- *AmMWSc 92*
**Maurer,** E Robert 1921- *AmMWSc 92*
**Maurer,** Edward Lance 1937- *WhoMW 92*
**Maurer,** Evan Maclyn 1944- *WhoMW 92*
**Maurer,** Fred Dry 1909- *AmMWSc 92*
**Maurer,** Frederic George, III 1952- *WhoFI 92*
**Maurer,** Friedrich C 1936- *WhoAmP 91*
**Maurer,** Gernant E 1949- *AmMWSc 92*
**Maurer,** Hans Andreas 1913- *AmMWSc 92, WhoWest 92*
**Maurer,** Ion Gheorghe 1902- *IntWW 91*
**Maurer,** Ira Mark 1954- *WhoAmL 92*
**Maurer,** James Richardson 1930- *WhoAmL 92*
**Maurer,** John Edward 1923- *AmMWSc 92, WhoWest 92*
**Maurer,** Jose Clemente d1990 *IntWW 91N*
**Maurer,** Jose Clemente 1900- *WhoRel 92*
**Maurer,** Karl Gustav 1929- *AmMWSc 92*
**Maurer,** Leon H. 1924- *WhoEnt 92*
**Maurer,** Paul Herbert 1923- *AmMWSc 92*
**Maurer,** Paul Reed 1937- *WhoFI 92*
**Maurer,** Pauline Gardiner 1947- *WhoEnt 92*
**Maurer,** Pierre 1924- *WhoIns 92*
**Maurer,** Ralph Rudolf 1941- *AmMWSc 92*
**Maurer,** Richard Allen 1947- *AmMWSc 92*
**Maurer,** Robert Distler 1924- *AmMWSc 92*
**Maurer,** Robert Eugene 1925- *AmMWSc 92*
**Maurer,** Robert Joseph 1913- *AmMWSc 92*
**Maurer,** Robert Michael 1952- *WhoFI 92*
**Maurer,** Terry Scott 1953- *WhoMW 92, WhoRel 92*
**Maurer,** Wolfdieter L.R. 1941- *WhoEnt 92*
**Mauretti,** Gerald Joseph 1943- *WhoFI 92*
**Maurey,** Nicole 1926- *IntMPA 92*
**Mauriac,** Claude 1914- *GuFrLit 1, IntWW 91*
**Mauriac,** Francois 1885-1970 *GuFrLit 1, WhoNob 90*
**Maurice,** D V *AmMWSc 92*
**Maurice,** David Myer 1922- *AmMWSc 92*
**Maurice,** Michael 1889- *ScFEYrs*
**Maurice,** Rita Joy 1929- *Who 92*
**Mauricio,** Joao *WhoEnt 92*
**Maurin,** Peter Aristide 1877-1949 *AmPeW*
**Maurin,** Ray 1924- *WhoEnt 92*
**Maurina,** Zenta 1897-1978 *LiExTwC*
**Mauritz,** Marcus N 1936- *WhoAmP 91*
**Maurizi,** Michael R *AmMWSc 92*
**Maurmeyer,** Evelyn Mary 1951- *AmMWSc 92*
**Mauro,** Alexander 1921- *AmMWSc 92*
**Mauro,** Garry Paul 1948- *WhoAmP 91*
**Mauro,** Humberto 1897- *IntDcF 2-2 [port]*
**Mauro,** Jack Anthony 1916- *AmMWSc 92*
**Mauro,** John Rocco, Jr. 1945- *WhoWest 92*
**Mauro,** Kenneth 1947- *WhoAmL 92*
**Mauro,** Richard Frank 1945- *WhoAmL 92, WhoWest 92*
**Maurois,** Andre 1885-1967 *FacFETw, ScFEYrs, TwCSFW 91A*
**Mauroy,** Pierre 1928- *IntWW 91, Who 92*
**Maurras,** Charles 1868-1952 *EncTR 91, FacFETw, GuFrLit 1*
**Maurras,** Charles Marie Photius 1862-1952 *BiDExR*
**Maurrasse,** Florentin Jean-Marie Robert 1940- *AmMWSc 92*
**Maurstad,** Toralv 1926- *IntWW 91*
**Maury,** John Minor 1912- *WhoAmP 91*
**Maury,** Lucien Garnett 1923- *AmMWSc 92*
**Maury,** Matthew Fontaine 1806-1873 *BiInAmS*
**Maus,** Connie 1945- *WhoWest 92*
**Maus,** John Andrew 1945- *WhoWest 92*
**Maus,** Octave 1856-1919 *ThHEIm*
**Maus,** Ralph Dale 1903- *WhoFI 92*
**Maus,** Robert Nikolaus 1958- *WhoMW 92*
**Mausel,** Paul Warner 1936- *AmMWSc 92*
**Mausi,** Shahida Andrea 1954- *WhoBlA 92*
**Mausner,** Jack 1932- *AmMWSc 92*
**Mausner,** Leonard Franklin 1947- *AmMWSc 92*
**Maust,** Ezma Minnie 1914- *WhoEnt 92*
**Mauston,** Glenn Warren 1935- *AmMWSc 92*
**Maute,** Robert Edgar 1947- *AmMWSc 92*
**Maute,** Robert Lewis 1924- *AmMWSc 92*
**Mautino,** Richard A 1938- *WhoAmP 91*
**Mautner,** Henry George 1925- *AmMWSc 92*
**Mautz,** Charles William 1917- *AmMWSc 92*
**Mautz,** William Ward 1943- *AmMWSc 92*
**Mauzerall,** David Charles 1929- *AmMWSc 92*
**Mauzey,** Peter T 1930- *AmMWSc 92*
**Mauzy,** Michael P *AmMWSc 92*
**Mauzy,** Michael Philip 1928- *WhoMW 92*
**Mauzy,** Oscar Holcombe 1926- *WhoAmL 92, WhoAmP 91*
**Mauzy,** Robert Larry 1949- *WhoIns 92*
**Mauzy,** Thames L 1908- *WhoAmP 91*
**Mavar,** Victor V 1926- *WhoAmP 91*
**Maven,** Max 1950- *WhoEnt 92*
**Maverick,** Andrew William 1955- *AmMWSc 92*
**Maverick,** Fontaine Maury 1895-1954 *AmPolLe*
**Maverick,** Samuel 1602?-1676? *BenetAL 91*
**Maves,** David Walter 1937- *WhoEnt 92*
**Mavia** *EncAmaz 91*

**Maviglio,** Steven R 1958- *WhoAmP 91*
**Mavin,** John *ConAu 36NR*
**Mavis,** Demetra 1961- *WhoEnt 92*
**Mavis,** James Osbert 1925- *AmMWSc 92*
**Mavis,** Richard David 1943- *AmMWSc 92*
**Mavity,** Victor T, Jr 1920- *AmMWSc 92*
**Mavligit,** Giora M *AmMWSc 92*
**Mavor,** Elizabeth 1927- *ConNov 91, IntAu&W 91, WrDr 92*
**Mavor,** Huntington 1927- *AmMWSc 92*
**Mavor,** John 1942- *Who 92*
**Mavor,** Leslie 1916- *Who 92*
**Mavor,** Michael Barclay 1947- *Who 92*
**Mavor,** Ronald Henry Moray 1925- *Who 92*
**Mavretic,** Anton 1934- *AmMWSc 92*
**Mavretic,** Josephus L 1934- *WhoAmP 91*
**Mavrikes,** George Paul 1955- *WhoFI 92*
**Mavrina,** Tat'yana Alekseevna 1902- *SovUnBD*
**Mavriplis,** F 1920- *AmMWSc 92*
**Mavrodes,** George Ion 1926- *WhoRel 92*
**Mavroides,** John George 1922- *AmMWSc 92*
**Mavrommatis,** Andreas V. 1932- *IntWW 91*
**Mavros,** George 1909- *IntWW 91*
**Mavros,** George S. 1957- *WhoFI 92*
**Mavros,** Glenn Scott 1948- *WhoFI 92*
**Mavros,** Paul Scott 1937- *WhoIns 92*
**Mavroules,** Nicholas 1929- *AlmAP 92 [port], WhoAmP 91*
**Mavroyannis,** Constantine 1927- *AmMWSc 92*
**Maw,** Herbert B. 1893-1990 *CurBio 91N*
**Maw,** James Gordon 1936- *WhoFI 92*
**Maw,** Nicholas 1935- *ConCom 92, NewAmDM, Who 92*
**Maw,** Peter 1954- *TwCPaSc*
**Mawardi,** Osman Kamel 1917- *AmMWSc 92*
**Mawby,** Colin 1936- *Who 92*
**Mawby,** Janet *ConAu 36NR*
**Mawer,** Philip John Courtney 1947- *Who 92*
**Mawer,** Ronald K. *Who 92*
**Mawhinney,** Brian Stanley 1940- *Who 92*
**Mawhinney,** Fara Schneider 1961- *WhoAmL 92*
**Mawhinney,** John Q *ScFEYrs*
**Mawhinney,** John Thomas 1937- *WhoAmP 91, WhoWest 92*
**Mawhinney,** King 1947- *WhoFI 92*
**Mawhinney,** Michael G 1945- *AmMWSc 92*
**Mawhinney,** Paul Charles 1939- *WhoEnt 92*
**Mawia** *EncAmaz 91*
**Mawicke,** Albert Thomas 1921- *WhoMW 92*
**Mawrey,** Richard Brooks 1942- *Who 92*
**Mawson,** David 1924- *Who 92*
**Mawson,** Stuart Radcliffe 1918- *Who 92*
**Max,** Alphonse E 1929- *IntAu&W 91*
**Max,** Buddy *WhoEnt 92*
**Max,** Claire Ellen 1946- *AmMWSc 92*
**Max,** Edward E 1945- *AmMWSc 92*
**Max,** Herbert B. 1931- *WhoAmL 92*
**Max,** Nicholas *WrDr 92*
**Max,** Rodney Andrew 1947- *WhoAmL 92*
**Max,** Stephen Richard 1940- *AmMWSc 92*
**Maxam,** Allan M *AmMWSc 92*
**Maxam,** William Pierce 1932- *WhoAmP 91*
**Maxell,** Charles A. 1934- *WhoBlA 92*
**Maxence,** Jean-Pierre 1906-1956 *BiDExR*
**Maxentius** 279?-312 *EncEarC*
**Maxey,** Brian William 1939- *AmMWSc 92*
**Maxey,** Brigitte Latrecia 1967- *WhoBlA 92*
**Maxey,** Carl 1924- *WhoBlA 92*
**Maxey,** Diane Meadows 1943- *WhoWest 92*
**Maxey,** E James 1935- *AmMWSc 92*
**Maxey,** Gary 1955- *WhoAmP 91*
**Maxey,** Glen *WhoAmP 91*
**Maxey,** James, III 1943- *WhoBlA 92*
**Maxey,** Jo Ann *WhoBlA 92*
**Maxey,** Kirk Michael 1955- *WhoMW 92*
**Maxey,** Peter Malcolm 1930- *Who 92*
**Maxey,** Randall Allen 1960- *WhoMW 92*
**Maxey,** Thomas Fleming 1937- *WhoFI 92*
**Maxfield,** Bruce Wright 1939- *AmMWSc 92*
**Maxfield,** Conrad 1931- *WhoAmP 91*
**Maxfield,** Dale Allen 1952- *WhoRel 92*
**Maxfield,** Frederick Rowland 1949- *AmMWSc 92*
**Maxfield,** Guy Budd 1933- *WhoAmL 92*
**Maxfield,** James William 1948- *WhoAmL 92*
**Maxfield,** John Edward 1927- *AmMWSc 92*
**Maxfield,** Lori Rochelle 1959- *WhoMW 92*
**Maxfield,** Margaret Waugh 1926- *AmMWSc 92*
**Maxfield,** Michael Gerald 1954- *WhoFI 92*
**Maxfield,** Richard L 1925- *WhoAmP 91*
**Maxheim,** John Howard 1934- *WhoFI 92*
**Maxie,** Peggy Joan 1936- *WhoAmP 91, WhoBlA 92*
**Maxim,** Hiram Stevens 1840-1916 *BiInAmS*
**Maxim,** Leslie Daniel 1941- *AmMWSc 92*
**Maxim,** Robert Morgan 1940- *WhoAmP 91*
**Maximianus** d434 *EncEarC*
**Maximilian** d295 *EncEarC*
**Maximinus** *EncEarC*
**Maximinus Daia** d313 *EncEarC*
**Maximo,** Antonieta Elizabeth 1942- *WhoHisp 92*
**Maximos,** Bishop 1935- *WhoRel 92*
**Maximos V,** Hakim 1908- *IntWW 91*
**Maximov,** Vladimir 1932- *LiExTwC*
**Maximovich,** John 1896-1966 *RelLAm 91*
**Maximus Confessor** 580-662 *EncEarC*
**Maximus of Turin** d408? *EncEarC*
**Maxin,** Jacob *WhoEnt 92*
**Maxman,** John Henry 1949- *WhoFI 92*
**Maxmen,** Mimi 1945- *WhoEnt 92*
**Maxmin,** Jody Lewis *WhoWest 92*
**Maxner,** Joyce 1929- *ConAu 133*
**Maxon,** Arthur Ray 1881?-1911 *BiInAmS*
**Maxon,** H L *ScFEYrs*
**Maxon,** Marshall Stephen 1937- *AmMWSc 92*
**Maxon,** William Densmore 1926- *AmMWSc 92*
**Maxson,** Albert Leroy 1935- *WhoFI 92*
**Maxson,** Carlton J 1936- *AmMWSc 92*
**Maxson,** Carol Ann 1951- *WhoMW 92*
**Maxson,** Donald Robert 1924- *AmMWSc 92*
**Maxson,** Harry A. *DrAPF 91*
**Maxson,** Jim 1947- *WhoAmP 91*
**Maxson,** John Eugene 1945- *WhoMW 92*
**Maxson,** Linda Ellen R 1943- *AmMWSc 92*
**Maxson,** Mark Bradfield 1953- *WhoIns 92*
**Maxson,** Reed Barnard 1945- *WhoEnt 92*
**Maxson,** Robert E, Jr 1951- *AmMWSc 92*
**Maxson,** Stephen C 1938- *AmMWSc 92*
**Maxton,** John Alston 1936- *Who 92*
**Maxum,** Bernard J 1931- *AmMWSc 92*
**Maxvill,** Dal 1939- *WhoMW 92*
**Maxwell** *Who 92*
**Maxwell,** Lord 1919- *Who 92*
**Maxwell,** A. E. *WrDr 92*
**Maxwell,** Allen Jay 1873-1946 *DcNCBi 4*
**Maxwell,** Ann Elizabeth *WrDr 92*
**Maxwell,** Arthur Eugene 1925- *AmMWSc 92*
**Maxwell,** Arthur Graham 1921- *WhoRel 92*
**Maxwell,** Bertha Lyons *WhoBlA 92*
**Maxwell,** Bruce Edward 1951- *WhoMW 92*
**Maxwell,** Bryce 1919- *AmMWSc 92*
**Maxwell,** Carla Lena 1945- *WhoEnt 92*
**Maxwell,** Cedric 1955- *WhoBlA 92*
**Maxwell,** Charles Henry 1923- *AmMWSc 92*
**Maxwell,** Charles Neville 1927- *AmMWSc 92, WhoMW 92*
**Maxwell,** Chester Arthur 1930- *WhoEnt 92*
**Maxwell,** Christine 1950- *WhoFI 92*
**Maxwell,** D E S 1925- *IntAu&W 91, WrDr 92*
**Maxwell,** David Campbell F. *Who 92*
**Maxwell,** David E. 1944- *WhoWest 92*
**Maxwell,** David Ogden 1930- *WhoFI 92*
**Maxwell,** David Randal 1949- *WhoRel 92*
**Maxwell,** David Samuel 1931- *AmMWSc 92*
**Maxwell,** Debra Elizabeth 1952- *WhoAmP 91*
**Maxwell,** Donald 1877-1936 *TwCPaSc*
**Maxwell,** Donald A 1938- *AmMWSc 92*
**Maxwell,** Donald Robert 1929- *AmMWSc 92*
**Maxwell,** Donald Stanley 1930- *WhoFI 92, WhoWest 92*
**Maxwell,** Douglas Paul 1941- *AmMWSc 92*
**Maxwell,** Dwight Thomas 1937- *AmMWSc 92*
**Maxwell,** Emanuel 1912- *AmMWSc 92*
**Maxwell,** Florence Hinshaw 1914- *WhoMW 92*
**Maxwell,** Fred Baldwin 1862-1907 *BiInAmS*
**Maxwell,** Gavin 1914-1969 *SmATA 65 [port]*
**Maxwell,** George Ralph, II 1935- *AmMWSc 92*
**Maxwell,** Gerald 1862- *ScFEYrs*
**Maxwell,** Glenn 1931- *AmMWSc 92*
**Maxwell,** Gordon Stirling 1938- *IntAu&W 91*
**Maxwell,** Grant *TwCWW 91*
**Maxwell,** Gregory William 1917- *WhoFI 92, WhoMW 92*
**Maxwell,** Hamilton 1830-1923 *TwCPaSc*
**Maxwell,** Hamish 1926- *WhoFI 92*
**Maxwell,** Hazel B. 1905- *WhoBlA 92*
**Maxwell,** Ian *NewYTBS 91 [port]*
**Maxwell,** Ian 1956- *IntWW 91*
**Maxwell,** Ian Robert 1923- *Who 92*
**Maxwell,** Ian Robert Charles 1956- *Who 92, WhoFI 92*
**Maxwell,** Isabel S. 1950- *WhoWest 92*
**Maxwell,** J d1889 *DcLB 106 [port]*
**Maxwell,** James Donald 1940- *AmMWSc 92*
**Maxwell,** Jerome Eugene 1944- *WhoFI 92*
**Maxwell,** Joe 1957- *WhoAmP 91*
**Maxwell,** John *IntAu&W 91X, WrDr 92*
**Maxwell,** John d1895 *DcLB 106 [port]*
**Maxwell,** John 1905-1962 *TwCPaSc*
**Maxwell,** John Alfred 1921- *AmMWSc 92*
**Maxwell,** John Crawford 1914- *AmMWSc 92*
**Maxwell,** John Daniel 1950- *WhoEnt 92*
**Maxwell,** John Gary 1933- *AmMWSc 92*
**Maxwell,** John L. *WhoFI 92*
**Maxwell,** John Lucian 1948- *WhoEnt 92*
**Maxwell,** Joyce Bennett 1941- *AmMWSc 92*
**Maxwell,** Kenneth Eugene 1908- *AmMWSc 92*
**Maxwell,** Kenneth Robert 1941- *WrDr 92*
**Maxwell,** Kevin *NewYTBS 91 [port]*
**Maxwell,** Kevin F. H. 1959- *WhoFI 92*
**Maxwell,** Kevin Francis Herbert 1959- *Who 92*
**Maxwell,** Lee M 1930- *AmMWSc 92*
**Maxwell,** Leo C 1941- *AmMWSc 92*
**Maxwell,** Louis 1948- *WhoAmP 91*
**Maxwell,** Louis R 1900- *AmMWSc 92*
**Maxwell,** Marcella J. 1927- *WhoBlA 92*
**Maxwell,** Marta Montidoro *WhoHisp 92*
**Maxwell,** Martha 1831-1881 *BiInAmS*
**Maxwell,** Mary Delene Brownlee 1910- *WhoMW 92*
**Maxwell,** Melton Craig 1942- *WhoEnt 92*
**Maxwell,** Melvin Larry 1938- *WhoAmL 92*
**Maxwell,** Michael 1943- *Who 92*
**Maxwell,** Neal A. *WhoRel 92, WhoWest 92*
**Maxwell,** Nigel Mellor H. *Who 92*
**Maxwell,** Patricia Anne 1942- *IntAu&W 91, WrDr 92*
**Maxwell,** Patricia Joy 1937- *WhoMW 92*
**Maxwell,** Patrick 1909- *Who 92*
**Maxwell,** Peggy Kirsch *WhoWest 92*
**Maxwell,** Perriton 1867-1947 *ScFEYrs*
**Maxwell,** Peter *Who 92*
**Maxwell,** R *DcLB 106*
**Maxwell,** Richard 1943- *Who 92*
**Maxwell,** Richard Elmore 1921- *AmMWSc 92*
**Maxwell,** Richard Willis 1946- *WhoMW 92*
**Maxwell,** Robert *Who 92*
**Maxwell,** Robert 1906- *Who 92*
**Maxwell,** Robert 1923- *IntWW 91, WhoFI 92*
**Maxwell,** Robert 1923-1991 *ConAu 135, NewYTBS 91 [port], News 92-2*
**Maxwell,** Robert Arthur 1927- *AmMWSc 92*
**Maxwell,** Robert Earl 1924- *WhoAmL 92*
**Maxwell,** Robert Ian 1923- *FacFETw*
**Maxwell,** Robert James 1934- *Who 92*
**Maxwell,** Robert L 1920- *AmMWSc 92*
**Maxwell,** Robert Lee 1937- *WhoAmP 91*
**Maxwell,** Robert Patrick 1944- *WhoAmL 92*
**Maxwell,** Roger Allan 1932- *WhoBlA 92*
**Maxwell,** Ronald F. 1947- *IntMPA 92*
**Maxwell,** Stephen Lloyd 1921- *WhoBlA 92*
**Maxwell,** Terence d1991 *Who 92N*
**Maxwell,** Thad James 1945- *WhoEnt 92*
**Maxwell,** Thomas Heron 1912- *Who 92*
**Maxwell,** Thomas Knight 1943- *WhoFI 92*
**Maxwell,** Vera 1903- *DcTwDes*
**Maxwell,** Vernon 1965- *WhoBlA 92*
**Maxwell,** Vicky *WrDr 92*
**Maxwell,** Walter Henry 1935- *WhoAmP 91*
**Maxwell,** William *DrAPF 91, IntAu&W 91X, WrDr 92*
**Maxwell,** William 1908- *ConNov 91, WrDr 92*
**Maxwell,** William Davis 1949- *WhoEnt 92*
**Maxwell,** William H. 1852-1920 *DcAmImH*
**Maxwell,** William Hall Christie 1936- *AmMWSc 92*
**Maxwell,** William Keepers 1908- *BenetAL 91*
**Maxwell,** William L 1934- *AmMWSc 92*
**Maxwell,** William Sutherland 1874-1952 *RelLAm 91*
**Maxwell-Brogdon,** Florence Morency 1929- *WhoWest 92*
**Maxwell Davies,** Peter *IntWW 91, NewAmDM*
**Maxwell-Doherty,** Melissa Margaret 1955- *WhoRel 92*
**Maxwell-Hyslop,** Robert John 1931- *Who 92*
**Maxwell of Ardwell,** Frederick Gordon 1905- *Who 92*
**Maxwell-Reid,** Daphne Etta 1948- *WhoBlA 92*
**Maxwell Scott,** Dominic James 1968- *Who 92*
**Maxwell-Scott,** Jean 1923- *Who 92*
**Maxworthy,** Tony 1933- *AmMWSc 92*
**Maxx,** Dave Frank 1955- *WhoWest 92*
**May** *Who 92*
**May,** Baron 1931- *Who 92*
**May,** Adolf D, Jr 1927- *AmMWSc 92*
**May,** Adolf Darlington 1927- *WhoWest 92*
**May,** Alan Alfred 1942- *WhoAmL 92, WhoAmP 91, WhoMW 92*
**May,** Anthony 1940- *Who 92*
**May,** Aviva Rabinowitz *WhoEnt 92*
**May,** Benjamin 1736-1808 *DcNCBi 4*
**May,** Bill B *AmMWSc 92*
**May,** Brian Albert 1936- *Who 92*
**May,** Bruce Barnett 1948- *WhoAmL 92*
**May,** Calvin Walter, Jr. 1938- *WhoRel 92*
**May,** Cecil, Jr. *WhoRel 92*
**May,** Charles Alan Maynard 1924- *Who 92*
**May,** Charles Kent 1939- *WhoAmL 92*
**May,** Charles W. 1940- *WhoBlA 92*
**May,** Cornelius Wallace 1943- *WhoBlA 92*
**May,** Daniel John 1956- *WhoMW 92*
**May,** David Joe 1951- *WhoRel 92*
**May,** Dennis James 1947- *WhoAmP 91*
**May,** Derwent 1930- *WrDr 92*
**May,** Derwent James 1930- *IntAu&W 91*
**May,** Dickey R. 1950- *WhoBlA 92*
**May,** Donald Curtis, Jr 1917- *AmMWSc 92*
**May,** Douglas James 1946- *Who 92*
**May,** Earle B., Jr. 1930- *WhoAmL 92*
**May,** Edward James 1929- *WhoRel 92*
**May,** Edwin Hyland, Jr 1924- *WhoAmP 91*
**May,** Elaine *ReelWom*
**May,** Elaine 1932- *FacFETw, IntMPA 92, IntWW 91, WhoEnt 92, WrDr 92*
**May,** Ernest 1845-1925 *ThHEIm*
**May,** Ernest Dewey 1942- *WhoEnt 92*
**May,** Ernest Max 1913- *WhoRel 92*
**May,** Ernest R. 1928- *WrDr 92*
**May,** Everette Lee 1914- *AmMWSc 92*
**May,** Everette Lee, Jr 1944- *AmMWSc 92*
**May,** Felton Edwin 1935- *WhoRel 92*
**May,** Floyd O'Lander 1946- *WhoBlA 92*
**May,** Frank Pierce 1920- *AmMWSc 92*
**May,** Fred O 1919- *WhoAmP 91*
**May,** Geoffrey Crampton 1930- *Who 92*
**May,** Georges 1920- *IntWW 91*
**May,** Gerald Ware 1940- *AmMWSc 92*
**May,** Gerald William 1941- *IntWW 91, WhoWest 92*
**May,** Gita 1929- *IntAu&W 91, WrDr 92*
**May,** Gordon Leslie 1921- *Who 92*
**May,** Graham 1923- *Who 92*
**May,** Gregory Evers 1953- *WhoAmL 92*
**May,** Harold E 1920- *AmMWSc 92*
**May,** Harold H. 1928- *WhoFI 92*
**May,** Harry Blight d1991 *Who 92N*
**May,** Henry 1921- *WhoEnt 92*
**May,** Henry F. 1915- *WrDr 92*
**May,** Ira Philip 1954- *AmMWSc 92*
**May,** Irving 1918- *AmMWSc 92*
**May,** J Peter 1939- *AmMWSc 92*
**May,** James Aubrey, Jr 1942- *AmMWSc 92*
**May,** James David 1940- *AmMWSc 92*
**May,** James F. 1938- *WhoBlA 92*
**May,** James Shelby 1934- *WhoBlA 92*
**May,** Jerry Russell 1942- *AmMWSc 92*
**May,** Joan Christine *AmMWSc 92*
**May,** John 1912- *Who 92*
**May,** John 1923- *Who 92*
**May,** John Elliott, Jr 1921- *AmMWSc 92*
**May,** John H 1922- *WhoAmP 91*
**May,** John L. 1922- *CurBio 91 [port]*
**May,** John Lawrence 1922- *WhoRel 92*
**May,** John Otto 1913- *Who 92*
**May,** John Walter 1936- *AmMWSc 92*
**May,** Joseph Leserman 1929- *WhoAmL 92*
**May,** Joseph Myles 1930- *WhoAmL 92*
**May,** Julian 1931- *IntAu&W 91, TwCSFW 91, WrDr 92*
**May,** Karl 1842-1912 *EncTR 91 [port]*
**May,** Kenneth Nathaniel 1930- *AmMWSc 92, WhoFI 92*
**May,** Kenneth Spencer 1914- *Who 92*
**May,** Larry A. 1949- *WhoFI 92*
**May,** Lawrence Edward 1947- *WhoAmL 92*
**May,** Lee Andrew 1943- *WhoBlA 92*
**May,** Leonard Joseph 1947- *WhoMW 92*
**May,** Leopold 1923- *AmMWSc 92*
**May,** Louis Philip, III 1958- *WhoRel 92*
**May,** Mark 1959- *WhoBlA 92*
**May,** Melanie Ann 1955- *WhoRel 92*
**May,** Michael Melville 1925- *AmMWSc 92*
**May,** Michael Patrick 1954- *WhoAmL 92*
**May,** Michael Wayne 1949- *WhoWest 92*
**May,** Paul 1907- *Who 92*
**May,** Paul S 1931- *AmMWSc 92*
**May,** Paul W, Jr 1928- *WhoAmP 91*

**May**, Peter Barker Howard 1929- *Who 92*
**May**, Phyllis Jean 1932- *WhoFI 92, WhoMW 92*
**May**, Ralph Forrest 1941- *AmMWSc 92*
**May**, Richard Edward 1946- *WhoAmL 92*
**May**, Richard George 1938- *Who 92*
**May**, Richard Paul 1946- *WhoWest 92*
**May**, Robert A. 1911- *WhoAmL 92*
**May**, Robert McCredie 1936- *AmMWSc 92, IntWW 91, Who 92*
**May**, Robin 1929- *IntAu&W 91, WrDr 92*
**May**, Rollo 1909- *FacFETw, WrDr 92*
**May**, Ronald Alan 1928- *WhoAmL 92*
**May**, Ronald Varnelle 1946- *WhoWest 92*
**May**, Samuel J. 1797-1871 *AmPeW*
**May**, Samuel Joseph 1797-1871 *BenetAL 91*
**May**, Scott 1954- *BlkOlyM*
**May**, Sheldon William 1946- *AmMWSc 92*
**May**, Sherry Jan *AmMWSc 92*
**May**, Stephen 1931- *WhoAmP 91*
**May**, Stephen 1946- *IntAu&W 91*
**May**, Sterling Randolph 1946- *AmMWSc 92*
**May**, Stuart *Who 92*
**May**, Stuart Lamphear 1920- *WhoFI 92*
**May**, Thomas 1595?-1650 *RfGEnL 91*
**May**, Thomas Christopher 1964- *WhoWest 92*
**May**, Timothy James 1932- *WhoAmP 91*
**May**, Valentine Gilbert Delabere 1927- *Who 92*
**May**, Veronica Stewart 1920- *WhoBlA 92*
**May**, Walter Grant 1918- *AmMWSc 92, WhoMW 92*
**May**, Walter Ruch 1937- *AmMWSc 92*
**May**, William Eugene 1928- *WhoRel 92*
**May**, William G 1937- *AmMWSc 92*
**May**, William Hathaway *WhoAmL 92*
**May**, William Herbert Stuart 1937- *Who 92*
**May**, William John 1946- *WhoFI 92*
**May**, William Lee 1936- *BlkOlyM*
**May**, William Leopold, Jr. 1942- *WhoAmL 92*
**May**, Willie Eugene 1947- *AmMWSc 92*
**May**, Woodford F 1929- *WhoAmP 91*
**May**, Wynne *WrDr 92*
**Maya**, Dora Elssy 1955- *WhoHisp 92*
**Maya**, Gloria M. *WhoHisp 92*
**Maya**, Leon 1938- *AmMWSc 92*
**Maya**, Stephanie 1968- *WhoHisp 92*
**Maya**, Tristan 1926- *IntAu&W 91*
**Maya**, Walter 1929- *AmMWSc 92*
**Mayadas**, A Frank 1939- *AmMWSc 92*
**Mayakovsky**, Vladimir 1893-1930 *TwCSFW 91A*
**Mayakovsky**, Vladimir Vladimirovich 1893-1930 *SovUnBD*
**Mayakovsky**, Vladimir Vladimirovich 1894-1930 *FacFETw*
**Mayali**, Laurent 1956- *WhoAmL 92*
**Mayall**, Brian Holden 1932- *AmMWSc 92*
**Mayall**, John 1933- *ConMus 7 [port]*
**Mayall**, John Brumwell 1933- *WhoEnt 92*
**Mayall**, Lees 1915- *Who 92*
**Mayall**, Nicholas Ulrich 1906- *AmMWSc 92, IntWW 91*
**Maybank**, John 1930- *AmMWSc 92*
**Maybeck**, Bernard 1862-1957 *DcTwDes*
**Maybee**, John Stanley 1928- *AmMWSc 92*
**Mayberger**, Harold Woodrow 1919- *AmMWSc 92*
**Mayberry**, Claude A., Jr. 1933- *WhoBlA 92*
**Mayberry**, Donald Alan 1951- *WhoEnt 92*
**Mayberry**, John Patterson 1929- *AmMWSc 92*
**Mayberry**, Lillian Faye 1943- *AmMWSc 92*
**Mayberry**, Rena Hancox 1941- *WhoFI 92*
**Mayberry**, Thomas Carlyle 1925- *AmMWSc 92*
**Mayberry**, William Eugene 1929- *AmMWSc 92*
**Mayberry**, William Roy 1938- *AmMWSc 92*
**Mayberry-Stewart**, Melodie Irene 1948- *WhoWest 92*
**Maybray-King**, Lord 1901-1986 *FacFETw*
**Mayburg**, Sumner 1926- *AmMWSc 92*
**Maybury**, Anne *IntAu&W 91, WrDr 92*
**Maybury**, Paul Calvin 1924- *AmMWSc 92*
**Maybury**, Robert H 1923- *AmMWSc 92*
**Maybury**, Robert Vincent 1937- *WhoMW 92*
**Maycen**, Dale F. 1938- *WhoFI 92*
**Maycock**, Ian David 1935- *WhoFI 92*
**Maycock**, John Norman 1937- *AmMWSc 92*
**Maycock**, Paul Dean 1935- *AmMWSc 92*
**Maycock**, Paul Frederick 1930- *AmMWSc 92*
**Maydak**, Dawna M. *DrAPF 91*
**Maydan**, Dan 1935- *AmMWSc 92*
**Maydar**, Damdinjavyn 1916- *IntWW 91*
**Mayden**, Ruth Wyatt 1946- *WhoBlA 92*
**Maydew**, Randall C 1924- *AmMWSc 92*
**Maye**, Beatrice Carr Jones *WhoBlA 92*
**Maye**, Richard 1933- *WhoBlA 92*
**Maye**, Richard Boykin 1933- *WhoRel 92*
**Mayeda**, Cynthia Joy Yoshiko 1949- *WhoAmP 91*
**Mayeda**, Kazutoshi 1928- *AmMWSc 92*
**Mayeda**, Wataru 1928- *AmMWSc 92*
**Mayehoff**, Eddie 1914- *IntMPA 92*
**Mayell**, Jaspal Singh 1929- *AmMWSc 92*
**Mayenkar**, Krishna Vaman 1943- *WhoWest 92*
**Mayer**, Adrian C. 1922- *WrDr 92*
**Mayer**, Alan Eugene 1925- *WhoAmP 91*
**Mayer**, Albert 1897-1981 *FacFETw*
**Mayer**, Alfred Marshall 1836-1897 *BiInAmS*
**Mayer**, Anne 1953- *IntAu&W 91*
**Mayer**, Anne Brestel 1935- *WhoEnt 92*
**Mayer**, Arno J. 1926- *WrDr 92*
**Mayer**, Arthur Loeb 1886-1981 *FacFETw*
**Mayer**, Augustin 1911- *IntWW 91*
**Mayer**, Barbara J. *DrAPF 91*
**Mayer**, Ben 1925- *IntMPA 92*
**Mayer**, Bena Frank 1898-1991 *NewYTBS 91*
**Mayer**, Bernadette *DrAPF 91*
**Mayer**, Bernadette 1945- *IntAu&W 91, WrDr 92*
**Mayer**, Brantz 1809-1879 *BenetAL 91*
**Mayer**, Carl Joseph 1959- *WhoAmL 92*
**Mayer**, Charles James 1936- *IntWW 91, WhoFI 92*
**Mayer**, Christian 1922- *IntWW 91*
**Mayer**, Colin Peter 1953- *Who 92*
**Mayer**, Cornell Henry 1921- *AmMWSc 92*
**Mayer**, David Jonathan 1942- *AmMWSc 92*
**Mayer**, Debby *DrAPF 91*
**Mayer**, Dennis T *AmMWSc 92*
**Mayer**, Endre Agoston 1929- *WhoMW 92*
**Mayer**, Erich Anton 1930- *WhoFI 92*
**Mayer**, Eugene Stephen 1938- *AmMWSc 92*
**Mayer**, Ferdinand F d1866? *BiInAmS*
**Mayer**, Foster Lee, Jr 1942- *AmMWSc 92*
**Mayer**, Francis X 1930- *AmMWSc 92*
**Mayer**, Frederick Joseph 1940- *AmMWSc 92*
**Mayer**, Frederick Robert 1951- *WhoEnt 92*
**Mayer**, Garry Franklin 1945- *AmMWSc 92*
**Mayer**, George 1934- *AmMWSc 92*
**Mayer**, George Emil 1941- *AmMWSc 92*
**Mayer**, Gerald *IntMPA 92*
**Mayer**, Gerald Douglas 1933- *AmMWSc 92*
**Mayer**, Gerda 1927- *ConPo 91, IntAu&W 91, WrDr 92*
**Mayer**, H Robert 1941- *WhoAmP 91*
**Mayer**, Haldane Robert 1941- *WhoAmL 92*
**Mayer**, Hans 1907- *ConAu 133, IntWW 91*
**Mayer**, Harold Albert, III 1954- *WhoRel 92*
**Mayer**, Harris Louis 1921- *AmMWSc 92*
**Mayer**, Helene 1910- *EncAmaz 91*
**Mayer**, Helene 1910-1953 *EncTR 91 [port]*
**Mayer**, Henry 1914- *WhoEnt 92*
**Mayer**, Herbert Carleton, Jr. 1922- *WhoWest 92*
**Mayer**, J K 1907- *AmMWSc 92*
**Mayer**, James Hock 1935- *WhoAmL 92*
**Mayer**, James Joseph 1938- *WhoAmL 92*
**Mayer**, James Lamoine 1951- *WhoMW 92*
**Mayer**, James W 1930- *AmMWSc 92*
**Mayer**, Jean 1920- *AmMWSc 92, WhoAmP 91*
**Mayer**, Jeffrey Lowell 1947- *WhoMW 92*
**Mayer**, Jerome F 1947- *AmMWSc 92*
**Mayer**, Joe 1949- *WhoAmP 91*
**Mayer**, Joerg Werner Peter 1929- *AmMWSc 92*
**Mayer**, John 1948- *WhoAmL 92*
**Mayer**, John Anton, Jr. 1940- *WhoFI 92*
**Mayer**, John Edward 1952- *WhoMW 92*
**Mayer**, Joseph Leo 1933- *WhoAmL 92*
**Mayer**, Julian Richard 1929- *AmMWSc 92*
**Mayer**, Klaus 1924- *AmMWSc 92*
**Mayer**, Lawrence Arnold 1918- *WhoFI 92*
**Mayer**, Lawrence Michael 1949- *AmMWSc 92*
**Mayer**, Lawrence S. 1946- *WhoWest 92*
**Mayer**, Leonard William 1944- *WhoWest 92*
**Mayer**, Louis B 1885-1957 *FacFETw, RComAH*
**Mayer**, Maria Goeppert 1906-1972 *WhoNob 90*
**Mayer**, Marion Sidney 1935- *AmMWSc 92*
**Mayer**, Martin Prager 1928- *WhoFI 92*
**Mayer**, Meinhard Edwin 1929- *AmMWSc 92, WhoWest 92*
**Mayer**, Michael 1932- *TwCPaSc*
**Mayer**, Michael F. 1917- *IntMPA 92*
**Mayer**, Michael John 1941- *WhoMW 92*
**Mayer**, Musa 1943- *ConAu 135*
**Mayer**, Patricia Jayne 1950- *WhoFI 92, WhoWest 92*
**Mayer**, Paul Augustin 1911- *WhoRel 92*
**Mayer**, Peter *IntWW 91*
**Mayer**, Peter Conrad 1938- *WhoFI 92*
**Mayer**, Ramona Ann 1929- *AmMWSc 92*
**Mayer**, Raymond 1924- *WrDr 92*
**Mayer**, Richard F 1929- *AmMWSc 92*
**Mayer**, Richard Thomas 1945- *AmMWSc 92*
**Mayer**, Robert Anthony 1933- *WhoMW 92*
**Mayer**, Robert Glenn 1950- *WhoAmL 92*
**Mayer**, Robert James 1952- *WhoRel 92*
**Mayer**, Robert Nathan 1949- *WhoMW 92*
**Mayer**, Robert Steven 1954- *WhoMW 92*
**Mayer**, Roger Laurance 1926- *IntMPA 92*
**Mayer**, Ronald Franklin 1947- *WhoFI 92*
**Mayer**, Rupert 1876-1945 *EncTR 91*
**Mayer**, Seymour R. 1912- *IntMPA 92*
**Mayer**, Stanley Wallace 1916- *AmMWSc 92*
**Mayer**, Stephen Edward 1954- *WhoMW 92*
**Mayer**, Steven Edward 1929- *AmMWSc 92*
**Mayer**, Steven M. 1946- *WhoFI 92*
**Mayer**, Theodore Jack 1933- *AmMWSc 92*
**Mayer**, Thomas *IntWW 91*
**Mayer**, Thomas 1928- *Who 92*
**Mayer**, Thomas C 1931- *AmMWSc 92*
**Mayer**, Thomas King 1955- *WhoFI 92*
**Mayer**, Tom G 1943- *AmMWSc 92*
**Mayer**, Uri *WhoEnt 92A, WhoWest 92*
**Mayer**, Vernon William, Jr 1939- *AmMWSc 92*
**Mayer**, Vicki Lynn 1962- *WhoFI 92*
**Mayer**, Victor James 1933- *AmMWSc 92*
**Mayer**, Virginia Anne 1929- *WhoFI 92*
**Mayer**, Walter Georg 1927- *AmMWSc 92*
**Mayer**, William Dixon 1928- *AmMWSc 92*
**Mayer**, William Emilio 1940- *WhoFI 92*
**Mayer**, William John 1921- *AmMWSc 92*
**Mayer**, William Joseph 1939- *AmMWSc 92*
**Mayer**, William Vernon 1920- *AmMWSc 92*
**Mayer Brown**, Howard *Who 92*
**Mayer-Koenig**, Wolfgang 1946- *IntAu&W 91*
**Mayer-Kuckuk**, Theo 1927- *IntWW 91*
**Mayeri**, Earl Melchior 1940- *AmMWSc 92*
**Mayerle**, James Joseph 1945- *AmMWSc 92*
**Mayernik**, David John 1952- *WhoAmP 91*
**Mayernik**, John Joseph 1916- *AmMWSc 92*
**Mayeron**, Carol Ann 1951- *WhoRel 92*
**Mayers**, George Louis 1938- *AmMWSc 92*
**Mayers**, Howard Alex 1946- *WhoMW 92*
**Mayers**, Jean 1920- *AmMWSc 92*
**Mayers**, Richard Ralph 1925- *AmMWSc 92, WhoMW 92*
**Mayers**, Ronald Burton 1940- *WhoRel 92*
**Mayersohn**, Nettie 1926- *WhoAmP 91*
**Mayerson**, Anna *TwCPaSc*
**Mayerson**, Hy 1937- *WhoAmL 92*
**Mayerson**, Hymen Samuel 1900- *AmMWSc 92*
**Mayerson**, Sandra Elaine 1952- *WhoAmL 92*
**Mayes**, Bernard Duncan 1929- *WhoEnt 92*
**Mayes**, Billy Woods, II 1941- *AmMWSc 92*
**Mayes**, Christopher Thomas 1956- *WhoFI 92*
**Mayes**, Clinton, Jr. *WhoBlA 92*
**Mayes**, David Lee 1947- *WhoWest 92*
**Mayes**, David Lincoln 1942- *WhoMW 92*
**Mayes**, Doris Miriam 1928- *WhoBlA 92*
**Mayes**, Frances *DrAPF 91*
**Mayes**, Frederick Brian 1934- *Who 92*
**Mayes**, Helen M. 1918- *WhoBlA 92*
**Mayes**, Ila Laverne 1934- *WhoRel 92*
**Mayes**, Jesse J 1914- *WhoAmP 91*
**Mayes**, McKinley 1930- *AmMWSc 92, WhoBlA 92*
**Mayes**, Nathaniel H., Jr. 1941- *WhoBlA 92*
**Mayes**, Paul E 1928- *AmMWSc 92*
**Mayes**, Paul Eugene 1928- *WhoMW 92*
**Mayes**, Rueben 1963- *WhoBlA 92*
**Mayes**, Terrill W 1941- *AmMWSc 92*
**Mayes**, Wendell 1919- *IntMPA 92*
**Mayes**, Wendell Curran 1919- *WhoEnt 92*
**Mayesh**, Jay Philip 1947- *WhoAmL 92*
**Mayeux**, Jerry Vincent 1937- *AmMWSc 92*
**Mayewski**, Paul Andrew 1946- *AmMWSc 92*
**Mayfield**, Lord 1921- *Who 92*
**Mayfield**, Alease Marie 1933- *WhoIns 92*
**Mayfield**, Andrew 1950- *TwCPaSc*
**Mayfield**, Bruce DeWitt 1960- *WhoAmP 91*
**Mayfield**, Christopher John *Who 92*
**Mayfield**, Curtis 1942- *ConBlB 2 [port], NewAmDM, WhoBlA 92*
**Mayfield**, Curtis Lee 1942- *WhoEnt 92*
**Mayfield**, Darwin Lyell 1920- *AmMWSc 92*
**Mayfield**, David Merkley 1942- *WhoWest 92*
**Mayfield**, Earle Byron 1923- *AmMWSc 92*
**Mayfield**, Harold Ford 1911- *AmMWSc 92*
**Mayfield**, JoAnn H.O. 1932- *WhoBlA 92*
**Mayfield**, John Emory 1937- *AmMWSc 92*
**Mayfield**, John Eric 1941- *AmMWSc 92*
**Mayfield**, Julia *WrDr 92*
**Mayfield**, Lewis G 1922- *AmMWSc 92*
**Mayfield**, Maurice Kent 1938- *WhoMW 92*
**Mayfield**, Melburn Ross 1921- *AmMWSc 92*
**Mayfield**, Michael Douglas 1951- *WhoRel 92*
**Mayfield**, Richard Dean 1944- *WhoIns 92*
**Mayfield**, Richard Heverin 1921- *WhoAmL 92*
**Mayfield**, Vance Glen 1947- *WhoFI 92*
**Mayfield**, William S. 1919- *WhoBlA 92*
**Mayhall**, Jane *DrAPF 91*
**Mayhall**, John Tarkington 1937- *AmMWSc 92*
**Mayhall**, William McDonald 1947- *WhoFI 92*
**Mayhams**, Norridge Bryant 1903- *WhoBlA 92*
**Mayhan**, Robert J 1938- *AmMWSc 92*
**Mayhan**, Robert Joseph 1938- *WhoMW 92*
**Mayhar**, Ardath 1930- *IntAu&W 91, TwCSFW 91, WrDr 92*
**Mayhew** *Who 92*
**Mayhew**, Baron 1915- *IntWW 91, Who 92*
**Mayhew**, Aubrey 1927- *WhoEnt 92*
**Mayhew**, Christopher 1915- *WrDr 92*
**Mayhew**, David Raymond 1937- *WrDr 92*
**Mayhew**, Eric George 1938- *AmMWSc 92*
**Mayhew**, Experience 1673-1758 *BenetAL 91*
**Mayhew**, Henry 1812-1887 *NinCLC 31 [port]*
**Mayhew**, Jonathan 1720-1766 *BenetAL 91, BlkwCEP*
**Mayhew**, Josephine 1924- *WhoAmP 91*
**Mayhew**, Kenneth 1947- *Who 92*
**Mayhew**, Kenneth Edwin, Jr. 1934- *WhoFI 92*
**Mayhew**, Patrick 1929- *Who 92*
**Mayhew**, Patrick Barnabas Burke 1929- *IntWW 91*
**Mayhew**, Thomas, Jr. 1621?-1657 *BenetAL 91*
**Mayhew**, Thomas R 1935- *AmMWSc 92*
**Mayhew**, Wilbur Waldo 1920- *AmMWSc 92*
**Mayhew-Sanders**, John 1931- *Who 92*
**Mayka**, Stephen Paul 1946- *WhoAmL 92*
**Maykowski**, Elaine Marie 1962- *WhoEnt 92*
**Maykuth**, D J 1923- *AmMWSc 92*
**Mayland**, Bertrand Jesse 1916- *AmMWSc 92*
**Mayland**, Henry Frederick 1935- *AmMWSc 92*
**Mayland**, Henry Fredrick 1935- *WhoWest 92*
**Mayland**, Paul Fletcher 1942- *WhoFI 92*
**Mayland**, Ralph 1927- *Who 92*
**Maylem**, John 1739-1762? *BenetAL 91*
**Maylie-Pfenninger**, M F *AmMWSc 92*
**Maynard**, Alister 1903- *TwCPaSc*
**Maynard**, Allegra d1991 *NewYTBS 91*
**Maynard**, Andrew 1964- *BlkOlyM*
**Maynard**, Benjamin Hall 1960- *WhoFI 92*
**Maynard**, Brian Alfred 1917- *Who 92*
**Maynard**, Buddy Ira 1928- *WhoMW 92*
**Maynard**, Carl Wesley, Jr 1913- *AmMWSc 92*
**Maynard**, Charles Alvin 1951- *AmMWSc 92*
**Maynard**, Charles Douglas 1934- *AmMWSc 92*
**Maynard**, Christopher 1949- *IntAu&W 91*
**Maynard**, Edward Samuel 1930- *WhoBlA 92*
**Maynard**, Edwin Francis George 1921- *Who 92*
**Maynard**, Fredelle Bruser 1922- *IntAu&W 91*
**Maynard**, Geoffrey 1921- *WrDr 92*
**Maynard**, Geoffrey Walter 1921- *Who 92*
**Maynard**, George William 1839-1913 *BiInAmS*
**Maynard**, Harry Lee 1927- *WhoWest 92*
**Maynard**, James Barry 1946- *AmMWSc 92*
**Maynard**, Jerry Allen 1937- *AmMWSc 92*
**Maynard**, Joan *Who 92*
**Maynard**, Joan 1932- *WhoMW 92*
**Maynard**, John Herbert 1935- *WhoWest 92*
**Maynard**, John Howard, Jr 1945- *WhoAmP 91*
**Maynard**, John M 1929- *WhoAmP 91*

**Maynard**, John Ralph 1942- *WhoAmL 92, WhoFI 92*
**Maynard**, Julian Decatur 1945- *AmMWSc 92*
**Maynard**, Michael Anthony 1953- *WhoFI 92*
**Maynard**, Nan 1910- *WrDr 92*
**Maynard**, Nancy Gray 1941- *AmMWSc 92*
**Maynard**, Nancy Hicks 1946- *WhoWest 92*
**Maynard**, Nancy Kathleen Brazier 1910- *IntAu&W 91*
**Maynard**, Nigel 1921- *Who 92*
**Maynard**, Olivia Benedict 1936- *WhoAmP 91*
**Maynard**, Peter Montmorency 1929- *WhoFI 92*
**Maynard**, Richard 1936- *IntAu&W 91*
**Maynard**, Riley Henderson 1947- *WhoEnt 92*
**Maynard**, Robert C. 1937- *WhoBlA 92*
**Maynard**, Robert Clyve 1937- *WhoWest 92*
**Maynard**, Robert Edgerton *WhoIns 92*
**Maynard**, Roger Paul 1943- *Who 92*
**Maynard**, Theodore 1890-1956 *BenetAL 91*
**Maynard**, Theodore Roberts 1938- *AmMWSc 92*
**Maynard**, Valerie J. 1937- *WhoBlA 92*
**Maynard**, Vera Joan 1921- *Who 92*
**Maynard Smith**, John 1920- *Who 92*
**Mayne**, Berger C 1920- *AmMWSc 92*
**Mayne**, David Quinn 1930- *IntWW 91, Who 92*
**Mayne**, Diane 1934- *WhoAmL 92*
**Mayne**, Eric 1928- *Who 92*
**Mayne**, Ferdinand Philipp 1923- *WhoWest 92*
**Mayne**, Jasper 1604?-1672 *RfGEnL 91*
**Mayne**, John Fraser 1932- *Who 92*
**Mayne**, Michael Clement Otway 1929- *Who 92*
**Mayne**, Richard 1926- *IntAu&W 91, Who 92, WrDr 92*
**Mayne**, Roger 1929- *IntWW 91*
**Mayne**, Roger, Mrs. *Who 92*
**Mayne**, Seymour 1944- *ConPo 91, IntAu&W 91, WrDr 92*
**Mayne**, William 1928- *ChlLR 25 [port], IntAu&W 91, SmATA 68 [port], Who 92*
**Mayne**, William 1929- *WrDr 92*
**Maynert**, Everett William 1920- *AmMWSc 92*
**Maynes**, Albion Donald 1929- *AmMWSc 92*
**Maynes**, Charles William 1938- *WhoAmP 91*
**Maynes**, Gordon George 1946- *AmMWSc 92*
**Maynez**, Bernice H. *WhoHisp 92*
**Maynor**, Dorothy 1910- *NotBlAW 92, WhoBlA 92*
**Maynor**, Jeff 1945- *WhoMW 92*
**Maynor**, Kevin Elliott 1954- *WhoBlA 92*
**Maynor**, Peggy Thompson 1929- *WhoAmP 91*
**Mayo**, Earl of 1929- *Who 92*
**Mayo**, Barbara Shuler 1945- *AmMWSc 92*
**Mayo**, Barry Alan 1952- *WhoBlA 92*
**Mayo**, Cathy *DrAPF 91*
**Mayo**, Charles Atkins, III 1943- *AmMWSc 92*
**Mayo**, Clara 1931-1981 *WomPsyc*
**Mayo**, Clyde Calvin 1940- *WhoFI 92*
**Mayo**, Dana Walker 1928- *AmMWSc 92*
**Mayo**, De Paul 1924- *AmMWSc 92*
**Mayo**, Donald Glenn 1946- *WhoWest 92*
**Mayo**, Edward John 1931- *Who 92*
**Mayo**, Eileen 1906- *Who 92*
**Mayo**, Eli 1933- *WhoFI 92*
**Mayo**, Faye Nuell 1936- *WhoEnt 92*
**Mayo**, Frank 1839-1896 *BenetAL 91*
**Mayo**, Frank Rea 1908- *AmMWSc 92*
**Mayo**, Gerald Edgar 1932- *WhoIns 92*
**Mayo**, Harry D., III 1939- *WhoBlA 92*
**Mayo**, James *IntAu&W 91X, WrDr 92*
**Mayo**, James H. *WhoRel 92*
**Mayo**, James Wellington 1930- *WhoBlA 92*
**Mayo**, Jim *TwCWW 91*
**Mayo**, John *Who 92*
**Mayo**, John S 1930- *AmMWSc 92*
**Mayo**, John Sullivan 1930- *WhoFI 92*
**Mayo**, Joseph W *WhoAmP 91*
**Mayo**, Joseph William 1941- *AmMWSc 92*
**Mayo**, Julia A. 1926- *WhoBlA 92*
**Mayo**, Katherine 1867-1940 *BenetAL 91*
**Mayo**, Patricia Elton 1915- *WrDr 92*
**Mayo**, Ralph Elliott 1940- *AmMWSc 92*
**Mayo**, Robert William 1909- *Who 92*
**Mayo**, Santos 1928- *AmMWSc 92*
**Mayo**, Simon Herbert 1937- *Who 92*
**Mayo**, Thomas O 1930- *WhoAmP 91*
**Mayo**, Thomas Tabb, IV 1932- *AmMWSc 92*
**Mayo**, Thomas William 1949- *WhoAmL 92*
**Mayo**, Virginia 1920- *IntMPA 92*
**Mayo**, Virginia Clara 1920- *WhoEnt 92*
**Mayo**, William 1684?-1744 *BiInAmS*
**Mayo**, William Starbuck 1811-1895 *BenetAL 91*
**Mayo**, William Starbuck 1812-1895 *ScFEYrs*
**Mayo**, Z B 1943- *AmMWSc 92*
**Mayo-Smith**, Richmond 1854-1901 *BiInAmS*
**Mayock**, Robert Lee 1917- *AmMWSc 92*
**Mayoe**, Marian and Franklin 1856- *ScFEYrs*
**Mayoh**, Raymond Blanchflower 1925- *Who 92*
**Mayol**, Pedro Magdiel 1933- *WhoHisp 92*
**Mayol**, Richard Thomas 1949- *WhoWest 92*
**Mayol**, Robert Francis 1941- *AmMWSc 92*
**Mayor**, Archer *ConAu 134*
**Mayor**, Archer H. 1950- *ConAu 134*
**Mayor**, Fred 1865-1916 *TwCPaSc*
**Mayor**, Gilbert Harold 1939- *AmMWSc 92*
**Mayor**, Heather Donald 1930- *AmMWSc 92*
**Mayor**, Hugh Robert 1941- *Who 92*
**Mayor**, John Roberts 1906- *AmMWSc 92*
**Mayor**, Louis Enrique 1937- *WhoHisp 92*
**Mayor**, Rowland Herbert 1920- *AmMWSc 92*
**Mayor Zaragoza**, Federico 1934- *IntWW 91, Who 92*
**Mayoras**, Donald Eugene 1939- *WhoFI 92*
**Mayorets**, Anatoly Ivanovich 1929- *IntWW 91*
**Mayorga**, Dennis D. 1957- *WhoHisp 92*
**Mayorga**, Oscar Danilo 1949- *WhoHisp 92*
**Mayorga**, Rene N. 1956- *WhoHisp 92*
**Mayoux**, Jacques Georges Maurice Sylvain 1924- *IntWW 91*
**Mayper**, Jeffrey Bruce 1947- *WhoFI 92*
**Mayper**, V, Jr 1928- *AmMWSc 92*
**Maypole**, Donald Eugene 1934- *WhoMW 92*
**Mayr**, Andreas 1949- *AmMWSc 92*
**Mayr**, Ernst 1904- *AmMWSc 92, IntWW 91, WrDr 92*
**Mayr**, James Jerome 1942- *WhoMW 92*
**Mayr**, Kay Faystine 1939- *WhoEnt 92*
**Mayr**, Simon 1763-1845 *NewAmDM*
**Mayrhofer**, Manfred 1926- *IntWW 91*
**Mayrocker**, Friederike 1924- *IntAu&W 91*
**Mayron**, Lewis Walter 1932- *AmMWSc 92, WhoWest 92*
**Mayron**, Melanie 1952- *IntMPA 92, WhoEnt 92*
**Mayrovitz**, Harvey N 1944- *AmMWSc 92*
**Mays**, Alfred Thomas 1947- *WhoBlA 92*
**Mays**, Benjamin E 1895-1984 *FacFETw*
**Mays**, Benjamin Elijah 1895-1984 *RelLAm 91*
**Mays**, Bob D. 1942- *WhoMW 92*
**Mays**, Carol Jean 1933- *WhoAmP 91*
**Mays**, Carrie J. 1928- *WhoBlA 92*
**Mays**, Charles Edwin 1938- *AmMWSc 92*
**Mays**, Charles William 1930- *AmMWSc 92*
**Mays**, Charles William 1940- *WhoRel 92*
**Mays**, Colin Garth 1931- *IntWW 91, Who 92*
**Mays**, David 1949- *WhoBlA 92*
**Mays**, David Paul 1955- *WhoMW 92*
**Mays**, Dewey Orvric, Jr. 1929- *WhoBlA 92*
**Mays**, Edward Everett 1930- *WhoBlA 92*
**Mays**, George Francis 1956- *WhoRel 92*
**Mays**, Jack Edwin 1948- *WhoRel 92*
**Mays**, James A. 1939- *WhoBlA 92*
**Mays**, Jeffrey 1952- *WhoAmP 91*
**Mays**, John Rushing 1934- *AmMWSc 92*
**Mays**, L. Lowry 1935- *WhoEnt 92*
**Mays**, Larry Wesley 1948- *AmMWSc 92*
**Mays**, M Douglas 1950- *WhoAmP 91*
**Mays**, Robert, Jr 1947- *AmMWSc 92*
**Mays**, Rolland Lee 1920- *AmMWSc 92*
**Mays**, Sandra Denise 1953- *WhoBlA 92*
**Mays**, Thomas Joseph 1954- *WhoWest 92*
**Mays**, Tom *WhoAmP 91*
**Mays**, Travis Cortez 1968- *WhoBlA 92*
**Mays**, Vernon Lee 1933- *WhoBlA 92*
**Mays**, Vickie M. 1952- *WhoBlA 92*
**Mays**, W. Roy, III 1946- *WhoBlA 92*
**Mays**, William, Jr. 1929- *WhoBlA 92*
**Mays**, William O. 1934- *WhoBlA 92*
**Mays**, Willie 1931- *RComAH*
**Mays**, Willie Howard, Jr 1931- *FacFETw [port], WhoBlA 92*
**Mayse**, Marilyn Ann 1941- *WhoRel 92*
**Mayshark**, Cyrus 1926-1976 *ConAu 134*
**Maysles**, Albert 1926- *IntDcF 2-2, IntMPA 92*
**Maysles**, Albert 1933- *FacFETw*
**Maysles**, Albert H. 1926- *WhoEnt 92*
**Maysles**, David 1932-1987 *IntDcF 2-2*
**Maysles**, David 1933-1987 *FacFETw*
**Maystadt**, Philippe 1948- *IntWW 91*
**Maytag**, Frederick Lewis 1857-1937 *FacFETw*
**Mayton**, William Ty 1941- *WhoAmL 92*
**Mayuzumi**, Toshiro 1929- *ConCom 92, NewAmDM*
**Mazac**, Charles James 1940- *AmMWSc 92*
**Mazaheri**, Mohammad 1927- *AmMWSc 92*
**Mazak**, Richard Allan 1932- *WhoRel 92*
**Mazander**, Charles A, Jr 1927- *WhoAmP 91*
**Mazankowski**, Donald Frank 1935- *IntWW 91, Who 92, WhoFI 92*
**Mazar**, Benjamin 1906- *IntWW 91*
**Mazarak**, John Philip 1930- *WhoEnt 92*
**Mazarakis**, Michael Gerassimos 1947- *AmMWSc 92*
**Mazawey**, Louis Thomas *WhoAmL 92*
**Maze**, Jack Reiser 1937- *AmMWSc 92*
**Maze**, Paul 1887-1979 *TwCPaSc*
**Maze**, Robert Craig 1934- *AmMWSc 92*
**Maze**, Thomas Harold 1951- *AmMWSc 92*
**Mazeaud**, Pierre 1929- *IntWW 91*
**Mazel**, Joseph Lucas 1939- *WhoFI 92*
**Mazel**, Paul 1925- *AmMWSc 92*
**Mazelis**, Mendel 1922- *AmMWSc 92, WhoWest 92*
**Mazenko**, Donald Michael 1925- *WhoWest 92*
**Mazer**, Anne 1953- *ConAu 135, SmATA 67 [port]*
**Mazer**, Elliot Frederic 1941- *WhoEnt 92*
**Mazer**, Harry *DrAPF 91*
**Mazer**, Harry 1925- *SmATA 67 [port]*
**Mazer**, Lawrence 1937- *WhoAmL 92*
**Mazer**, Norma Fox *DrAPF 91*
**Mazer**, Norma Fox 1931- *SmATA 67 [port], WrDr 92*
**Mazeres**, Reginald Merle 1934- *AmMWSc 92*
**Mazerolle**, Alfred D 1943- *WhoAmP 91*
**Mazeski**, Edward James, Jr. 1929- *WhoAmL 92*
**Mazess**, Richard B 1939- *AmMWSc 92*
**Mazia**, Daniel 1912- *AmMWSc 92, IntWW 91*
**Maziarz**, Edward Anthony 1915- *WhoRel 92*
**Maziarz**, Lucille A 1924- *WhoAmP 91*
**Maziarz**, Marysia *DrAPF 91*
**Mazie**, Marvin Edward 1930- *WhoFI 92*
**Mazikowski**, Kevin J. 1966- *WhoFI 92*
**Mazin**, Ruth 1935- *WhoFI 92*
**Mazique**, Frances Margurite *WhoBlA 92*
**Mazlish**, Bruce 1923- *IntAu&W 91*
**Mazo**, James Emery 1937- *AmMWSc 92*
**Mazo**, Mark Elliott 1950- *WhoAmL 92, WhoFI 92*
**Mazo**, Robert Marc 1930- *AmMWSc 92*
**Mazola**, Ted *WhoAmP 91*
**Mazon**, Larri Wayne 1945- *WhoBlA 92*
**Mazon**, Manuel Reyes 1929- *WhoHisp 92*
**Mazor**, Julian *DrAPF 91*
**Mazowiecki**, Tadeusz *IntWW 91*
**Mazowiecki**, Tadeusz 1927- *FacFETw*
**Mazrui**, Ali A. 1933- *IntWW 91, Who 92, WrDr 92*
**Mazujian**, David Aram 1960- *WhoFI 92*
**Mazumdar**, Mainak 1935- *AmMWSc 92*
**Mazumdar**, Maxim William 1953- *IntAu&W 91*
**Mazumder**, Bibhuti R 1924- *AmMWSc 92*
**Mazumder**, Rajarshi *AmMWSc 92*
**Mazur**, Abraham 1911- *AmMWSc 92*
**Mazur**, Barry 1937- *AmMWSc 92*
**Mazur**, Bridget *DrAPF 91*
**Mazur**, D Bennett 1924- *WhoAmP 91*
**Mazur**, Eric 1957- *AmMWSc 92*
**Mazur**, Gail *DrAPF 91*
**Mazur**, Jacob 1921- *AmMWSc 92*
**Mazur**, James Andrew 1941- *WhoAmL 92, WhoAmP 91, WhoMW 92*
**Mazur**, John 1920- *WhoAmP 91*
**Mazur**, John Mark *DrAPF 91*
**Mazur**, Meredith Margie Handley 1941- *WhoWest 92*
**Mazur**, Peter 1928- *AmMWSc 92*
**Mazur**, Philip Daniel 1949- *WhoWest 92*
**Mazur**, Rita Z. *DrAPF 91*
**Mazur**, Robert Henry 1924- *AmMWSc 92*
**Mazur**, Stephen 1945- *AmMWSc 92*
**Mazura**, Adrianne C. 1951- *WhoAmL 92*
**Mazurek**, Joseph P 1948- *WhoAmP 91*
**Mazurek**, Thaddeus John 1942- *AmMWSc 92*
**Mazurki**, Mike 1909- *ConTFT 9*
**Mazurkiewicz**, Gregory Allen 1950- *WhoMW 92*
**Mazurkiewicz**, Joseph Edward 1942- *AmMWSc 92*
**Mazurkiewicz-Kwilecki**, Irena Maria *AmMWSc 92*
**Mazurov**, Kirill Trofimovich 1914-1989 *SovUnBD*
**Mazursky**, Paul 1930- *FacFETw, IntDcF 2-2 [port], IntMPA 92, IntWW 91, WhoEnt 92*
**Mazza**, Cris *DrAPF 91*
**Mazza**, Frank Carl 1945- *WhoEnt 92*
**Mazza**, John Gamble 1945- *WhoWest 92*
**Mazza**, Richard T 1939- *WhoAmP 91*
**Mazza**, Sergio *DcTwDes*
**Mazza**, Vito Michael 1935- *WhoAmP 91*
**Mazzaferri**, Katherine Aquino 1947- *WhoAmL 92*
**Mazzanti**, Geno M, Jr 1929- *WhoAmP 91*
**Mazzarella**, Andrew James 1950- *WhoFI 92*
**Mazzaro**, Jerome *DrAPF 91*
**Mazzaro**, Jerome 1934- *WrDr 92*
**Mazzaro**, Jerome Louis 1934- *IntAu&W 91*
**Mazze**, Edward Mark 1941- *WhoFI 92*
**Mazzei**, Philip 1730-1816 *DcAmImH*
**Mazzeno**, Laurence William 1921- *AmMWSc 92*
**Mazzini**, Giuseppe 1805-1872 *NinCLC 34 [port]*
**Mazzitelli**, Frederick R 1924- *AmMWSc 92*
**Mazzitelli**, John Patrick 1944- *WhoAmL 92*
**Mazzocchi**, Domenico 1592-1665 *NewAmDM*
**Mazzocchi**, Paul Henry 1939- *AmMWSc 92*
**Mazzocchi**, Virgilio 1597-1646 *NewAmDM*
**Mazzoccoli**, Sylvester Anthony 1939- *WhoRel 92*
**Mazzola**, Christian Larsen 1939- *WhoMW 92*
**Mazzola**, Eugene 1948- *WhoEnt 92*
**Mazzola**, John Glennon 1946- *WhoFI 92*
**Mazzola**, John William 1928- *WhoEnt 92*
**Mazzola**, Robert Allen 1948- *WhoWest 92*
**Mazzoleni**, Alberto 1927- *AmMWSc 92*
**Mazzoleni**, Ettore 1905-1968 *NewAmDM*
**Mazzoli**, Romano L. 1932- *AlmAP 92 [port]*
**Mazzoli**, Romano Louis 1932- *WhoAmP 91*
**Mazzolini**, Anthony I 1934- *WhoMW 92*
**Mazzolla**, Dan Patrick 1947- *WhoFI 92*
**Mazzone**, A. David 1928- *WhoAmL 92*
**Mazzone**, Horace M 1930- *AmMWSc 92*
**Mazzorin**, Carlos E. *WhoHisp 92*
**Mazzotta**, Vincent C *WhoAmP 91*
**Mazzotti**, Richard Rene 1937- *WhoMW 92*
**Mazzucato**, Ernesto 1937- *AmMWSc 92*
**Mazzucato**, Palo Vigilio 1966- *WhoEnt 92*
**Mazzuchelli**, Samuel 1806-1864 *DcAmImH*
**Mazzullo**, James Michael 1955- *AmMWSc 92*
**Mbang**, Sunday Coffie 1936- *WhoRel 92*
**Mbasogo**, Teodoro Obiang Nguema *IntWW 91*
**Mbaya**, Robert B. 1933- *IntWW 91*
**M'baye**, Keba 1924- *IntWW 91*
**Mbekeani**, Nyemba W. 1929- *Who 92*
**Mbeki**, Thabo 1942- *IntWW 91*
**Mbere**, Aggrey Mxolisi 1939- *WhoBlA 92*
**M'bow**, Amadou-Mahtar 1921- *IntWW 91, Who 92*
**Mboya**, Tom 1930-1969 *FacFETw*
**Mbugua**, Samuel 1946- *BlkOlyM*
**Mbure**, Sam 1950- *IntAu&W 91*
**Mburumba**, Kerina 1932- *IntAu&W 91*
**MC5** *NewAmDM*
**McAbee**, Jennings G 1944- *WhoAmP 91*
**McAboy**, Thomas Hatfield 1930- *WhoFI 92*
**McAdam**, Douglas John 1951- *IntAu&W 91*
**McAdam**, Ian 1917- *Who 92*
**McAdam**, James 1930- *Who 92*
**McAdam**, Keith Paul William James 1945- *Who 92*
**McAdam**, Kevin Terrance 1942- *WhoMW 92*
**McAdam**, Thomas Hugh 1955- *WhoWest 92*
**McAdam**, Will 1921- *AmMWSc 92*
**McAdam Clark**, James *Who 92*
**McAdams**, Anne Farron 1953- *WhoEnt 92*
**McAdams**, Arthur James 1923- *AmMWSc 92*
**McAdams**, Charles *TwCWW 91*
**McAdams**, David 1931- *WhoBlA 92*
**McAdams**, Harry Mayhew 1916- *WhoEnt 92*
**McAdams**, Linnie M. 1938- *WhoBlA 92*
**McAdams**, Michael Joseph 1949- *WhoFI 92*
**McAdams**, Patricia Daniels 1936- *WhoEnt 92*
**McAdams**, Peter Cooper 1940- *WhoEnt 92*
**McAdams**, Robert Eli 1929- *AmMWSc 92*
**McAdams**, Robert L. 1927- *WhoBlA 92*
**McAdams**, William Lee 1953- *WhoAmL 92*
**McAden**, Hugh 1720?-1781 *DcNCBi 4*
**McAden**, Rufus Yancey 1833-1889 *DcNCBi 4*
**McAdie**, Henry George 1930- *AmMWSc 92*
**McAdoo**, Bob 1951- *WhoBlA 92*

**McAdoo,** David J 1941- *AmMWSc 92*
**McAdoo,** Harriette P. 1940- *WhoBlA 92*
**McAdoo,** Henry Allen 1951- *WhoBlA 92*
**McAdoo,** Henry Robert 1916- *Who 92*
**McAdoo,** John Hart 1945- *AmMWSc 92*
**McAdoo,** William Gibbs 1863-1941 *AmPolLe, FacFETw*
**McAfee,** Alexander 1927- *WhoMW 92*
**McAfee,** Billy H 1931- *WhoAmP 91*
**McAfee,** Carrie R. 1931- *WhoBlA 92*
**McAfee,** Charles Francis 1932- *WhoBlA 92*
**McAfee,** David *WhoAmP 91*
**McAfee,** Donald A 1941- *AmMWSc 92*
**McAfee,** Jerry 1916- *AmMWSc 92, IntWW 91*
**McAfee,** John Gilmour 1926- *AmMWSc 92*
**McAfee,** Kenneth Bailey, Jr 1924- *AmMWSc 92*
**McAfee,** Leo C., Jr. 1945- *WhoBlA 92*
**McAfee,** Paul *TwCWW 91*
**McAfee,** Robert Dixon 1925- *AmMWSc 92*
**McAfee,** Walter S. 1914- *WhoBlA 92*
**McAfee,** Walter Samuel 1914- *AmMWSc 92*
**McAfee,** Wayne 1951- *WhoRel 92*
**McAfee,** William Gage 1943- *WhoFI 92*
**McAfee,** William Small 1929- *WhoWest 92*
**McAlack,** Matthew Mark 1961- *WhoRel 92*
**McAlack,** Robert Francis 1940- *AmMWSc 92*
**McAlduff,** Edward J 1939- *AmMWSc 92*
**McAlear,** Peter James Patrick 1949- *WhoWest 92*
**McAleavey,** David *DrAPF 91*
**McAleece,** Donald John *AmMWSc 92*
**Mc Aleer,** Felicia Lockhart 1952- *WhoFI 92*
**McAleer,** Kevin William 1950- *WhoFI 92*
**McAlester,** Arcie Lee, Jr 1933- *AmMWSc 92*
**McAlester,** J. D. 1946- *WhoFI 92*
**McAlexander,** James Albert 1958- *WhoFI 92*
**McAlice,** Bernard John 1930- *AmMWSc 92*
**McAlindon,** Thomas 1932- *WrDr 92*
**McAlindon,** Thomas Edward 1932- *IntAu&W 91*
**McAliskey,** Bernadette 1947- *Who 92*
**McAlister,** Albert *WhoAmP 91*
**McAlister,** Alexander Worth 1862-1946 *DcNCBi 4*
**McAlister,** Dean Ferdinand 1910- *AmMWSc 92*
**McAlister,** Elizabeth 1939- *AmPeW*
**McAlister,** Harold Alister 1949- *AmMWSc 92*
**McAlister,** Joe Michael 1955- *WhoBlA 92*
**McAlister,** Luther Durwood 1927- *ConAu 134*
**McAlister,** Maurice L. 1925- *WhoFI 92, WhoWest 92*
**McAlister,** Michael Ian 1930- *Who 92*
**McAlister,** Robert Beaton 1932- *WhoAmP 91*
**McAlister,** Robert Edward d1953 *RelLAm 91*
**McAlister,** Ronald William Lorne 1923- *Who 92*
**McAlister,** Sean Patrick 1945- *AmMWSc 92*
**McAlister,** Thomas Preston 1957- *WhoAmL 92*
**McAlister,** William Bruce 1929- *AmMWSc 92*
**McAlister,** William Harle Nelson 1940- *Who 92*
**McAllaster,** Richard Emerson 1951- *WhoFI 92*
**McAllion,** John 1948- *Who 92*
**McAllister,** Alan Jackson 1945- *AmMWSc 92*
**McAllister,** Arnold Lloyd 1921- *AmMWSc 92*
**McAllister,** Bruce 1946- *IntAu&W 91, TwCSFW 91, WrDr 92*
**McAllister,** Bruce H. *DrAPF 91*
**McAllister,** Byron Leon 1929- *AmMWSc 92*
**McAllister,** Chase Judson 1942- *WhoWest 92*
**McAllister,** Claire *DrAPF 91*
**McAllister,** David Franklin 1941- *AmMWSc 92*
**McAllister,** Donald Evan 1934- *AmMWSc 92*
**McAllister,** Francis Ralph 1942- *WhoFI 92*
**Mc Allister,** Gerald Nicholas 1923- *WhoRel 92*
**McAllister,** Gregory Thomas, Jr 1934- *AmMWSc 92*
**McAllister,** Howard Conlee 1924- *AmMWSc 92*
**McAllister,** Jane Ellen 1899- *NotBlAW 92*
**McAllister,** Jeannette Marie 1960- *WhoAmL 92*
**McAllister,** Jerome Watt 1944- *AmMWSc 92*
**McAllister,** John Brian 1941- *Who 92*
**McAllister,** Joy Torstrup 1927- *WhoWest 92*
**McAllister,** Kenneth Wayne 1949- *WhoAmL 92*
**McAllister,** LeRay L 1930- *WhoAmP 91*
**McAllister,** Leroy Timothy, Sr. 1918- *WhoBlA 92*
**McAllister,** Marcia A 1951- *WhoIns 92*
**McAllister,** Marialuisa N 1939- *AmMWSc 92*
**McAllister,** Mary E *WhoAmP 91*
**McAllister,** Orlando Antonio 1953- *WhoEnt 92*
**McAllister,** Peter Michael 1938- *WhoWest 92*
**McAllister,** Raymond Francis 1923- *AmMWSc 92*
**McAllister,** Richard *WhoAmP 91*
**McAllister,** Robert Cowden 1940- *WhoFI 92*
**McAllister,** Robert Joseph 1918- *WhoRel 92*
**McAllister,** Robert Milton 1922- *AmMWSc 92*
**McAllister,** Robert Wallace 1929- *AmMWSc 92*
**McAllister,** Warren Alexander 1941- *AmMWSc 92*
**McAllister,** William T 1944- *AmMWSc 92*
**McAlmon,** Robert 1896-1956 *BenetAL 91*
**McAloon,** Richard A. 1942- *WhoFI 92*
**McAlpin,** America Lenore 1950- *WhoAmL 92*
**McAlpin,** Art 1963- *WhoEnt 92*
**McAlpin,** Harry S. 1906- *WhoBlA 92*
**McAlpin,** John Harris 1933- *AmMWSc 92*
**McAlpin,** Kirk Martin 1923- *WhoAmL 92*
**McAlpine** *Who 92*
**McAlpine,** Christopher *Who 92*
**McAlpine,** George Albert 1933- *AmMWSc 92*
**McAlpine,** James Bruce 1939- *AmMWSc 92*
**McAlpine,** James Francis 1922- *AmMWSc 92*
**McAlpine,** Kenneth Donald 1953- *AmMWSc 92*
**McAlpine,** Phyllis Jean 1941- *AmMWSc 92*
**McAlpine,** Rachel 1940- *ConPo 91, WrDr 92*
**McAlpine,** Robert 1937- *WhoBlA 92*
**McAlpine,** Robert Douglas Christopher 1919- *Who 92*
**McAlpine,** Robert James 1932- *Who 92*
**McAlpine,** Robin 1906- *Who 92*
**McAlpine,** Stephen A. 1949- *WhoAmL 92, WhoWest 92*
**McAlpine,** Stephen Alan 1949- *WhoAmP 91*
**McAlpine,** William 1936- *Who 92*
**McAlpine,** William H. 1847- *RelLAm 91*
**McAlpine of Moffat,** Lord 1907-1990 *AnObit 1990*
**McAlpine of West Green,** Baron 1942- *Who 92*
**McAmis,** Edwin Earl 1934- *WhoAmL 92*
**McAnally,** Don 1913- *WhoWest 92*
**McAnally,** John Sackett 1918- *AmMWSc 92*
**McAnally,** Mary *DrAPF 91*
**McAnally,** Ray 1926-1989 *FacFETw*
**McAnally-Knight,** Mary *DrAPF 91*
**McAndrew,** Anne E. Battle 1951- *WhoBlA 92*
**McAndrew,** David Wayne 1952- *AmMWSc 92*
**McAndrew,** William Patrick, Jr. 1958- *WhoFI 92*
**McAndrew,** William R. d1968 *LesBEnT 92*
**McAndrews,** John Henry 1933- *AmMWSc 92*
**McAndrews,** Victoria Costa 1956- *WhoFI 92*
**McAnelly,** John Kitchel 1931- *AmMWSc 92*
**McAneny,** Laurence Raymond 1926- *AmMWSc 92*
**McAniff,** Edward John 1934- *WhoAmL 92*
**McAninch,** Arthur Neal, Jr. 1935- *WhoRel 92*
**McAninch,** Lloyd Nealson 1920- *AmMWSc 92*
**McAnuff,** Des 1952- *WhoEnt 92, WhoWest 92*
**McAnulty,** Brenda Hart 1949- *WhoBlA 92*
**McArdle,** Eugene W 1931- *AmMWSc 92*
**McArdle,** John Edward 1928- *WhoMW 92*
**McArdle,** Joseph John 1945- *AmMWSc 92*
**McArdle,** Stanley Lawrence 1922- *Who 92*
**McArthur,** Barbara Jean *WhoBlA 92*
**McArthur,** Charles Stewart 1908- *AmMWSc 92*
**McArthur,** Charles Wilson 1921- *AmMWSc 92*
**McArthur,** Colin Richard 1935- *AmMWSc 92*
**McArthur,** David Samuel 1941- *AmMWSc 92*
**McArthur,** E. J. 1958- *WhoAmL 92*
**McArthur,** Eldon Durant 1941- *AmMWSc 92, WhoWest 92*
**McArthur,** Harvey King 1912- *WrDr 92*
**McArthur,** James Duncan 1937- *WhoWest 92*
**McArthur,** Janet W 1914- *AmMWSc 92*
**McArthur,** John Dickson, Jr. 1955- *WhoRel 92*
**McArthur,** John Duncan 1938- *Who 92*
**McArthur,** John Hector 1934- *WhoFI 92*
**McArthur,** John William, Jr. 1955- *WhoAmL 92*
**McArthur,** Neil *DcNCBi 4*
**McArthur,** Richard Edward 1915- *AmMWSc 92*
**McArthur,** Thomas Burns 1938- *Who 92*
**McArthur,** Victoria Holloway 1949- *WhoEnt 92*
**McArthur,** William George 1940- *AmMWSc 92*
**McArthur,** William P 1943- *AmMWSc 92*
**McArthur,** William Pope 1814-1850 *BiInAmS*
**McAssey,** Edward V, Jr 1935- *AmMWSc 92*
**McAtee,** Dennis Paul 1958- *WhoMW 92*
**McAtee,** James Lee, Jr 1924- *AmMWSc 92*
**McAtee,** James Wayne 1945- *WhoFI 92*
**McAtee,** Lloyd Thomas 1939- *AmMWSc 92*
**McAtee,** Thomas Pearson 1939- *WhoFI 92*
**McAtee,** William J 1947- *WhoAmP 91*
**McAtee,** Yolanda Martinez 1940- *WhoHisp 92*
**McAulay,** Robert J 1939- *AmMWSc 92*
**McAulay,** Sara *DrAPF 91*
**McAuley,** Alexander *AmMWSc 92*
**McAuley,** James 1917-1976 *RfGEnL 91*
**McAuley,** James 1936- *ConPo 91*
**McAuley,** James J. *DrAPF 91*
**McAuley,** James J 1936- *IntAu&W 91, WrDr 92*
**McAuley,** Joanne Elaine 1932- *WhoFI 92*
**McAuley,** John P 1952- *WhoIns 92*
**McAuley,** Louis Floyd 1924- *AmMWSc 92*
**McAuley,** Patricia Tulley 1935- *AmMWSc 92*
**McAuley,** Paul J 1955- *TwCSFW 91*
**McAuley,** Van Alfon 1926- *AmMWSc 92*
**McAuliffe,** Anthony C 1898-1975 *FacFETw*
**McAuliffe,** Christa 1948-1986 *FacFETw*
**McAuliffe,** Clayton Doyle 1918- *AmMWSc 92*
**McAuliffe,** Cornelius James 1934- *WhoAmL 92*
**McAuliffe,** Cornelius James 1949- *WhoAmP 91*
**McAuliffe,** Daniel Joseph 1945- *WhoAmL 92, WhoFI 92*
**McAuliffe,** Elizabeth Ann 1945- *WhoRel 92*
**McAuliffe,** James Robert 1944- *WhoIns 92*
**McAuliffe,** John F *WhoAmP 91*
**McAuliffe,** John F. 1932- *WhoAmL 92*
**McAuliffe,** Joseph Robert 1950- *WhoRel 92*
**Mc Auliffe,** Michael F. 1920- *WhoRel 92*
**McAuliffe,** Roger P 1938- *WhoAmP 91*
**McAuliffe,** Rosemary 1927- *WhoAmL 92*
**McAuliffe,** William Geoffrey 1948- *AmMWSc 92*
**McAuslan,** Alexander d1793 *DcNCBi 4*
**McAvity,** Thomas A. d1972 *LesBEnT 92*
**McAvoy,** Brian Vincent 1958- *WhoAmL 92*
**McAvoy,** Bruce Ronald 1933- *AmMWSc 92*
**McAvoy,** Heather M. 1961- *WhoEnt 92*
**McAvoy,** James Arthur, Jr. 1926- *WhoAmL 92*
**McAvoy,** Joseph 1910- *Who 92*
**McAvoy,** Rita Cloutier 1917- *WhoAmP 91*
**McAvoy,** Thomas J. *WhoAmL 92*
**McAvoy,** Thomas John 1940- *AmMWSc 92*
**McAvoy,** Thomas McLaughlin 1943- *Who 92*
**McBain,** David Malcolm 1928- *Who 92*
**McBain,** Diane Jean 1941- *WhoEnt 92*
**McBain,** Ed *DrAPF 91, IntAu&W 91X, IntWW 91, Who 92, WrDr 92*
**McBain,** Laurie 1949- *IntAu&W 91, WrDr 92*
**Mc Bain,** LeRoy Doward 1917- *WhoRel 92*
**McBain,** Malcolm *Who 92*
**McBain,** Robert Mark 1946- *WhoEnt 92*
**McBarnette,** Bruce Olvin 1957- *WhoAmL 92*
**McBay,** Arthur John 1919- *AmMWSc 92*
**McBay,** Henry Cecil *WhoBlA 92*
**McBay,** Henry Cecil 1914- *AmMWSc 92*
**McBean,** Angus 1904-1990 *AnObit 1990*
**McBean,** Angus Rowland d1990 *IntWW 91N*
**McBean,** Edward A 1945- *AmMWSc 92*
**McBean,** Lois D *AmMWSc 92*
**McBean,** Robert Parker 1939- *AmMWSc 92*
**McBean,** Sharon Elizabeth 1937- *WhoRel 92*
**McBeath,** Elena R *AmMWSc 92*
**McBeath,** Gerald Alan 1942- *WhoWest 92*
**McBee,** Frank W, Jr 1920- *AmMWSc 92*
**McBee,** George Gilbert 1929- *AmMWSc 92*
**McBee,** Richard Harding 1916- *WhoRel 92*
**McBee,** Robert Levi 1927- *WhoMW 92*
**McBee,** Silas 1853-1924 *DcNCBi 4*
**McBee,** Vardry 1775-1864 *DcNCBi 4*
**McBee,** Vardry Alexander 1818-1904 *DcNCBi 4*
**McBee,** Vincent Clermont 1946- *WhoBlA 92*
**McBee,** W D 1925- *AmMWSc 92*
**McBee,** William K 1932- *WhoAmP 91*
**McBeth,** Veronica Simmons 1947- *WhoBlA 92*
**McBeth-Reynolds,** Sandra Kay 1950- *WhoBlA 92*
**McBey,** James 1883-1959 *TwCPaSc*
**McBirney,** Alexander Robert 1924- *AmMWSc 92*
**McBirnie,** William Steuart 1920- *WhoRel 92*
**McBlain,** David Alexander 1940- *WhoAmP 91*
**McBlair,** William 1917- *AmMWSc 92*
**McBrady,** John J 1916- *AmMWSc 92*
**McBratney,** George 1927- *Who 92*
**McBrayer,** James Franklin 1941- *AmMWSc 92*
**McBrayer,** Louis Burgin 1868-1938 *DcNCBi 4*
**McBrayer,** W. Neal 1963- *WhoAmL 92*
**McBreairty,** James *WhoAmP 91*
**McBrearty,** Denise Dewenter 1952- *WhoAmP 91*
**McBrearty,** James Connell 1941- *WhoAmL 92, WhoWest 92*
**McBrearty,** John Jarrett 1960- *WhoEnt 92*
**McBrearty,** Tony 1946- *Who 92*
**McBreen,** James 1938- *AmMWSc 92*
**McBreen,** Maura Ann *WhoAmL 92*
**McBride,** Abel Ernest 1933- *WhoAmP 91*
**McBride,** Angela Barron 1941- *AmMWSc 92, WhoMW 92*
**McBride,** Barry Clarke 1940- *AmMWSc 92*
**McBride,** Clifford Hoyt 1926- *AmMWSc 92*
**McBride,** Daniel Hatton 1945- *WhoEnt 92*
**McBride,** David B 1942- *WhoAmP 91*
**McBride,** Duncan Eldridge 1945- *AmMWSc 92*
**McBride,** Earle Francis 1932- *AmMWSc 92*
**McBride,** Frances *WhoBlA 92*
**McBride,** Frank E 1943- *WhoAmP 91*
**McBride,** Gordon Williams 1910- *AmMWSc 92*
**McBride,** J W 1915- *AmMWSc 92*
**McBride,** Jack J. 1936- *WhoFI 92*
**McBride,** James 1784-1817 *BiInAmS*
**McBride,** James Allan 1953- *WhoEnt 92*
**McBride,** James Francis 1946- *WhoAmL 92*
**McBride,** James Michael 1940- *AmMWSc 92*
**McBride,** Jerry E 1939- *WhoAmP 91*
**McBride,** Jim 1941- *IntMPA 92*
**McBride,** John Barton 1943- *AmMWSc 92*
**McBride,** Jonathan Evans 1942- *WhoFI 92*
**McBride,** Joseph James, Jr 1922- *AmMWSc 92*
**McBride,** Kathleen 1952- *WhoAmP 91*
**McBride,** Keith L. 1947- *WhoFI 92*
**McBride,** Kenneth Eugene 1948- *WhoAmL 92*
**McBride,** Lois Allene Fenner 1953- *WhoAmL 92*
**McBride,** Lyle E, Jr 1929- *AmMWSc 92*
**McBride,** Mary E. 1950- *WhoMW 92*
**McBride,** Mekeel *DrAPF 91*
**McBride,** Michael Flynn 1951- *WhoAmL 92*
**McBride,** Milford Lawrence, Jr. 1923- *WhoFI 92*
**McBride,** Mollie Elizabeth 1929- *AmMWSc 92*
**McBride,** Murdoch 1955- *WhoEnt 92*
**McBride,** Orlando W 1932- *AmMWSc 92*
**McBride,** Ralph Book 1928- *AmMWSc 92*
**McBride,** Ralph Harold 1932- *WhoRel 92*
**McBride,** Raymond Andrew 1927- *AmMWSc 92*
**McBride,** Regina *DrAPF 91*

**McBride,** Robert 1911- NewAmDM
**McBride,** Robert 1941- WrDr 92
**McBride,** Sara Vonla 1921- Who 92
**McBride,** Shelia Ann 1947- WhoBlA 92
**McBride,** Sherry Loueen 1937- WhoWest 92
**McBride,** Teresa 1962- WhoHisp 92
**McBride,** Thomas Matthew, III 1923- WhoAmL 92
**McBride,** Ullysses 1938- WhoBlA 92
**McBride,** Vonla Who 92
**McBride,** William 1928- WhoWest 92
**McBride,** William Griffith 1927- IntWW 91, Who 92
**McBride,** William H 1944- AmMWSc 92
**McBride,** William James 1940- IntWW 91
**McBride,** William Joseph 1938- AmMWSc 92
**McBride,** William Robert 1928- AmMWSc 92
**McBride,** Woodrow H 1918- AmMWSc 92
**McBrien,** Richard P. 1936- WrDr 92
**McBrien,** Richard Peter 1936- IntWW 91, WhoRel 92
**McBrien,** Vincent Owen 1916- AmMWSc 92
**McBrier,** Vivian Flagg WhoBlA 92
**McBroom,** Edward WhoAmP 91
**McBroom,** F. Pearl WhoBlA 92
**McBroom,** Marvin Jack 1941- AmMWSc 92
**McBroom,** Robert Sean 1964- WhoWest 92
**McBrown,** Gertrude P. 1898?-1989 NotBlAW 92
**McBryde,** Archibald 1766-1837 DcNCBi 4
**McBryde,** F Webster 1908- AmMWSc 92
**McBryde,** Jim WhoAmP 91
**McBryde,** Neill Gregory, Jr. 1944- WhoAmL 92
**McBryde,** Thomas Henry 1925- WhoAmL 92
**McBryde,** Vernon E 1933- AmMWSc 92
**McBryde,** William Arthur Evelyn 1917- AmMWSc 92
**McBurney,** Charles 1845-1913 BiInAmS
**McBurney,** Charles Walker, Jr. 1957- WhoAmL 92
**McBurney,** George William 1926- WhoAmL 92
**McBurney,** John Francis, III 1950- WhoAmP 91
**McBurney,** Ralph Edward 1906- Who 92
**McBurney,** Wendell Faris 1933- WhoMW 92
**McBurnie,** Tony 1929- Who 92
**McCaa,** Connie Smith 1937- AmMWSc 92
**McCaa,** John K. 1954- WhoBlA 92
**McCaa,** Michelle Denise 1965- WhoWest 92
**McCabe,** Brian Francis 1926- AmMWSc 92
**McCabe,** Catherine Cone 1942- WhoEnt 92
**McCabe,** Charles Cardwell 1836-1906 RelLAm 91
**McCabe,** Charles Henry, Jr. 1937- WhoFI 92
**McCabe,** Charles Kevin 1952- WhoAmL 92
**McCabe,** Christopher John 1956- WhoAmP 91
**McCabe,** Daniel Marie 1924- WhoRel 92
**McCabe,** David Michael 1956- WhoMW 92
**McCabe,** Donald James 1932- WhoMW 92
**McCabe,** Eamon Patrick 1948- IntWW 91
**McCabe,** Eamonn Patrick 1948- Who 92
**McCabe,** Edward Aeneas 1917- WhoFI 92
**McCabe,** Eugene 1930- WrDr 92
**McCabe,** Eugene Louis 1937- WhoBlA 92
**McCabe,** George Paul, Jr 1945- AmMWSc 92
**McCabe,** Gregory James, Jr 1956- AmMWSc 92
**McCabe,** James Bernard 1940- WhoAmL 92
**McCabe,** James J. 1929- WhoAmL 92
**McCabe,** James Walter, Sr 1917- WhoAmP 91
**McCabe,** Jewell Jackson 1924- NotBlAW 92
**McCabe,** Jewell Jackson 1945- WhoBlA 92
**McCabe,** John 1939- ConCom 92, IntWW 91, Who 92
**McCabe,** John C., III 1920- WrDr 92
**McCabe,** John Patrick 1935- AmMWSc 92
**McCabe,** Joseph D. WhoWest 92
**McCabe,** Joseph E. 1912- WhoRel 92
**McCabe,** Judith Hardin 1964- WhoFI 92
**McCabe,** Lawrence James 1935- WhoAmL 92
**McCabe,** Michael G. 1950- WhoFI 92
**McCabe,** Michael J. 1945- WhoFI 92
**McCabe,** Monica Petraglia 1959- WhoAmL 92
**McCabe,** Neil 1946- WhoMW 92
**McCabe,** R Tyler 1959- AmMWSc 92
**McCabe,** Richard Edmund 1929- WhoRel 92
**McCabe,** Robert Albert 1914- AmMWSc 92
**McCabe,** Robert James 1953- WhoFI 92
**McCabe,** Robert Lyden 1936- AmMWSc 92
**McCabe,** Stephen Michael 1941- WhoAmL 92
**McCabe,** Steven Lee 1950- AmMWSc 92
**McCabe,** William R 1928- AmMWSc 92
**McCachern,** Cynthia Cornwell 1964- WhoRel 92
**McCadam,** Paul Rutherford 1948- WhoFI 92, WhoIns 92
**McCadden,** John Edward, III 1949- WhoFI 92
**McCafferty,** Edward 1937- AmMWSc 92
**McCafferty,** John Martin 1956- WhoMW 92
**McCafferty,** Michael Gilbert 1938- WhoFI 92
**McCafferty,** Owen Edward 1952- WhoMW 92
**McCafferty,** Taylor 1946- ConAu 134
**McCafferty,** William Patrick 1945- AmMWSc 92
**McCaffery,** Margo 1938- WrDr 92
**McCaffree,** Edward D 1931- WhoAmP 91
**McCaffree,** William G. 1934- WhoAmL 92
**McCaffrey,** Anne 1926- ConAu 35NR, IntAu&W 91, TwCSFW 91, WrDr 92
**McCaffrey,** David Saxer, Jr 1942- AmMWSc 92
**McCaffrey,** Helen Theresa 1950- WhoAmL 92
**McCaffrey,** James Ambose 1939- WhoAmL 92
**McCaffrey,** Joann Wilkinson 1929- WhoAmP 91
**McCaffrey,** Joseph Peter 1951- AmMWSc 92
**McCaffrey,** Kevin John 1950- WhoFI 92
**McCaffrey,** Leigh Graffam 1958- WhoRel 92
**McCaffrey,** Phillip DrAPF 91
**McCaffrey,** Rita Whalen 1937- WhoAmP 91
**McCaffrey,** Robert Henry, Jr. 1927- WhoFI 92
**Mc Caffrey,** Stanley Eugene 1917- WhoWest 92
**McCaffrey,** Teresa Gayle 1964- WhoMW 92
**Mc Caffrey,** Thomas R. WhoMW 92
**McCaffrey,** Thomas Vincent 1948- AmMWSc 92
**McCaffrey,** Thos Daniel 1922- Who 92
**McCaffrey,** Timothy T 1939- WhoIns 92
**McCaffrey,** Walter 1949- WhoAmP 91
**McCaffrey,** William R 1934- WhoAmP 91
**McCaffrey,** William Thomas 1936- WhoFI 92
**McCaghren,** Marty Don 1953- WhoFI 92
**McCagney,** Nancy WhoRel 92
**McCahill,** Patrick Philip 1943- WhoRel 92
**McCaig,** Joseph J. 1944- WhoFI 92
**McCaig,** Robert 1907-1982 TwCWW 91
**McCain,** Arthur Hamilton 1925- AmMWSc 92
**McCain,** Betty 1931- WhoAmP 91
**McCain,** Claude, Jr. 1931- WhoBlA 92
**McCain,** David Bradford 1961- WhoAmL 92
**McCain,** Douglas C AmMWSc 92
**McCain,** Ella Byrd 1925- WhoBlA 92
**McCain,** Francis Saxon 1921- AmMWSc 92
**McCain,** George Howard 1924- AmMWSc 92
**McCain,** Hugh White 1882-1922 DcNCBi 4
**McCain,** James Herndon 1941- AmMWSc 92
**McCain,** John 1936- AlmAP 92 [port]
**McCain,** John Charles 1939- AmMWSc 92
**McCain,** John S 1936- WhoAmP 91
**McCain,** John Sidney, III 1936- IntWW 91, WhoWest 92
**McCain,** John Sidney, Jr 1911-1981 FacFETw
**McCain,** Martin George 1951- WhoRel 92
**McCain,** Mary Eloise 1958- WhoAmP 91
**McCain,** Paul Pressly 1884-1946 DcNCBi 4
**McCain,** Thomas Charlie 1939- WhoAmP 91
**McCain,** Warren Earl 1925- WhoFI 92, WhoWest 92
**McCain,** Wilbur Teal 1913- WhoAmP 91
**McCain,** William Frederick 1931- WhoAmP 91
**McCain,** William S 1953- WhoAmP 91
**McCalden,** Thomas A AmMWSc 92
**McCaldin,** J O 1922- AmMWSc 92
**McCaleb,** David Clanence 1938- WhoMW 92
**McCaleb,** Greg WhoAmP 91
**McCaleb,** Joe Wallace 1941- WhoAmL 92
**McCaleb,** Kirtland Edward 1926- AmMWSc 92
**McCaleb,** Stanley B 1919- AmMWSc 92
**McCalips,** Merle Leroy, Jr 1946- WhoAmP 91
**McCall,** Adeline Denham 1901-1989 DcNCBi 4
**McCall,** Aidan M. WhoBlA 92
**McCall,** Barbara Collins 1942- WhoBlA 92
**McCall,** Brian Patrick 1959- WhoFI 92
**McCall,** Bruce P. G. WhoFI 92
**McCall,** Carl WhoBlA 92
**McCall,** Charles 1907-1989 TwCPaSc
**McCall,** Charles Anthony 1965- WhoRel 92
**McCall,** Charles B 1928- AmMWSc 92
**McCall,** Charles Emory 1935- AmMWSc 92
**McCall,** Charles Patrick 1910- Who 92
**McCall,** Chester Hayden, Jr 1927- AmMWSc 92
**McCall,** Christopher Hugh 1944- Who 92
**McCall,** Dan 1940- ConAu 135
**McCall,** Daniel Thompson, Jr. 1909- WhoAmL 92
**McCall,** David Slesser 1934- Who 92
**McCall,** David Warren 1928- AmMWSc 92
**McCall,** Douglas Mark 1951- WhoAmL 92
**McCall,** Duke Kimbrough 1914- WhoRel 92
**McCall,** Edward Huffaker 1938- WhoMW 92
**McCall,** Emmanuel Lemuel 1936- WhoRel 92
**McCall,** Emmanuel Lemuel, Sr. 1936- WhoBlA 92
**McCall,** Eugene 1921- WhoAmP 91
**McCall,** Frederick Bays 1893-1973 DcNCBi 4
**McCall,** G. Daniel 1932- WhoRel 92
**McCall,** George Aloysius 1939- WhoIns 92
**McCall,** George Archibald 1802-1868 BiInAmS
**McCall,** H. Carl 1936- NewYTBS 91
**McCall,** Howard Weaver, Jr. 1907- WhoFI 92
**McCall,** James Lodge 1935- AmMWSc 92
**McCall,** Jerry C 1927- AmMWSc 92
**McCall,** Joan IntMPA 92, WhoEnt 92
**McCall,** John Armstrong Grice 1913- Who 92
**McCall,** John Donald 1911- Who 92
**McCall,** John Michael 1944- AmMWSc 92
**McCall,** John Patrick 1927- WhoMW 92
**McCall,** John Temple 1921- AmMWSc 92
**McCall,** Keith Bradley 1919- AmMWSc 92
**McCall,** Keith R 1959- WhoAmP 91
**McCall,** Mabel Bunny 1923- IntAu&W 91
**McCall,** Marion G., Jr. 1930- WhoBlA 92
**McCall,** Marsh Howard, Jr. 1939- WrDr 92
**McCall,** Marvin Anthony 1918- AmMWSc 92
**McCall,** Michael M. 1963- WhoFI 92
**McCall,** Nancy 1948- WhoEnt 92
**McCall,** Nelda Dunn 1945- WhoFI 92
**McCall,** Patrick Who 92
**McCall,** Peter Law 1948- AmMWSc 92
**McCall,** Richard C 1929- AmMWSc 92
**McCall,** Robert B AmMWSc 92
**McCall,** Robert B. 1940- WrDr 92
**McCall,** Robert Donnell 1927- WhoRel 92
**McCall,** Robert G 1913- AmMWSc 92
**McCall,** Robert H. 1938- WhoWest 92
**McCall,** Robin Home 1912- Who 92
**McCall,** Robin Louise 1957- WhoEnt 92
**McCall,** Thomas A 1950- WhoIns 92
**McCall,** Thomas J WhoAmP 91
**McCall,** Wendell ConAu 135
**McCall,** William 1929- Who 92
**McCall,** William Calder 1906- WhoWest 92
**McCall,** William David Hair Who 92
**McCall,** William Kent 1940- WhoMW 92
**McCalla,** Albert 1846-1918 BiInAmS
**McCalla,** Dennis Robert 1934- AmMWSc 92
**McCalla,** Erwin Stanley 1928- WhoBlA 92
**McCalley,** Barbara Vaglia Dougherty 1939- WhoWest 92
**McCalley,** Henry 1852-1904 BiInAmS
**McCalley,** Robert B, Jr 1922- AmMWSc 92
**McCalley,** Roderick Canfield 1943- AmMWSc 92
**McCallin,** Thomas Frederick 1966- WhoFI 92
**McCallion,** Anne Dewey 1954- WhoWest 92
**McCallion,** James d1991 NewYTBS 91
**McCallion,** William James 1918- AmMWSc 92
**McCallion,** William P. 1951- WhoFI 92
**McCallister,** Gary Dean 1947- WhoRel 92
**McCallister,** Lawrence P 1943- AmMWSc 92
**McCallister,** Richard Anthony 1937- WhoFI 92
**McCallister,** Todd Lee 1959- WhoFI 92
**McCallister,** Wren Vance 1969- WhoWest 92
**McCallon,** Larry Keith 1939- WhoWest 92
**McCallum,** Archibald Duncan Dugald 1914- Who 92
**McCallum,** Bennett Tarlton 1935- WhoFI 92
**McCallum,** Charles Alexander, Jr 1925- AmMWSc 92
**Mc Callum,** Charles Edward 1939- WhoAmL 92, WhoFI 92, WhoMW 92
**McCallum,** Charles John, Jr 1943- AmMWSc 92
**McCallum,** Daniel Vern 1952- WhoMW 92
**McCallum,** David 1933- IntMPA 92, WhoEnt 92
**McCallum,** Dean Ames 1929- WhoAmL 92
**McCallum,** Donald 1922- Who 92
**McCallum,** Donald Roy 1930- WhoAmL 92, WhoMW 92
**McCallum,** George Walter 1919- WhoAmP 91
**McCallum,** Googie Who 92
**McCallum,** Ian Who 92
**McCallum,** Ian Stewart 1936- Who 92
**McCallum,** James 1806-1889 DcNCBi 4
**McCallum,** James Neal 1939- WhoWest 92
**McCallum,** James Scott 1950- WhoMW 92
**McCallum,** John 1918- IntMPA 92
**McCallum,** John 1920- Who 92
**McCallum,** John Neil 1918- Who 92
**McCallum,** John Stuart 1944- WhoFI 92
**McCallum,** Keith Stuart 1919- AmMWSc 92
**McCallum,** Kenneth James 1918- AmMWSc 92
**McCallum,** Leo 1929- WhoBlA 92
**McCallum,** Malcolm E 1934- AmMWSc 92
**McCallum,** Mary Caroline 1929- WhoAmP 91
**McCallum,** Michael Dean 1953- WhoRel 92
**McCallum,** Milne Rhiannon 1957- WhoFI 92
**McCallum,** Napoleon Ardel 1963- WhoBlA 92
**McCallum,** Phyllis 1911- IntAu&W 91, WrDr 92
**McCallum,** Robert Ian 1920- Who 92
**McCallum,** Roderick Eugene 1944- AmMWSc 92
**McCallum,** Scott 1950- WhoAmP 91
**McCallum,** Scott Belden 1959- WhoFI 92
**McCallum,** Walter Edward 1936- WhoBlA 92
**McCally,** Charles David 1935- WhoEnt 92
**McCally,** Charles Richard 1958- WhoFI 92
**McCally,** Russell Lee 1940- AmMWSc 92
**McCalmon,** Jeffrey Alan 1955- WhoMW 92
**McCalmon,** Robert T, Jr 1943- AmMWSc 92
**McCalpin,** James P 1950- AmMWSc 92
**McCaman,** Marilyn Wales 1928- AmMWSc 92
**McCaman,** Richard Eugene 1930- AmMWSc 92
**McCambridge,** Mercedes 1918- IntMPA 92, WhoEnt 92
**McCamley,** Graham 1932- Who 92
**McCammon,** Bob WhoWest 92
**McCammon,** Dan 1944- AmMWSc 92
**Mc Cammon,** David Noel 1934- WhoFI 92, WhoMW 92
**McCammon,** Helen Mary 1933- AmMWSc 92
**McCammon,** James Andrew 1947- AmMWSc 92
**McCammon,** Lewis B, Jr 1920- AmMWSc 92
**McCammon,** Mary 1927- AmMWSc 92
**McCammon,** Richard B 1932- AmMWSc 92
**McCammon,** Robert Desmond 1932- AmMWSc 92
**McCammond,** David 1941- AmMWSc 92
**McCampbell,** Ray Irvin 1959- WhoBlA 92
**McCamus,** David Robert 1931- WhoFI 92
**McCamy,** Calvin S 1924- AmMWSc 92
**McCamy,** Jean DrAPF 91
**McCance,** Robert Alexander 1898- IntWW 91, Who 92
**McCance,** William 1894-1970 TwCPaSc
**McCandless,** Alfred A. 1927- AlmAP 92 [port], WhoAmP 91, WhoFI 92, WhoWest 92
**McCandless,** Barbara J. 1931- WhoMW 92
**McCandless,** Bruce, II 1937- IntWW 91
**McCandless,** Carolyn Keller 1945- WhoFI 92
**McCandless,** David Wayne 1941- AmMWSc 92

**McCandless**, Frank Philip 1932- *AmMWSc 92*
**McCandless**, Jane Bardarah 1925- *WhoRel 92*
**McCandless**, John R 1935- *WhoAmP 91*
**McCandless**, Sally 1939- *WhoAmP 91*
**McCandless**, Thomas Duncan 1956- *WhoFI 92*
**McCandlish**, Matthew Dean 1955- *WhoMW 92*
**McCandliss**, Russell John 1948- *AmMWSc 92*
**McCane**, Charles Anthony 1899- *WhoBlA 92*
**McCane**, Charlotte Antoinette *WhoBlA 92*
**McCanles**, Michael Frederick 1936- *WhoMW 92*
**McCann**, Anthony Francis 1940- *WhoFI 92*
**McCann**, Arthur *ConAu 34NR*
**McCann**, Bonnie Lou 1944- *WhoAmP 91*
**McCann**, Cathy *WhoEnt 92*
**McCann**, Daisy S 1927- *AmMWSc 92*
**McCann**, David DeWitt 1943- *WhoEnt 92*
**McCann**, David R. *DrAPF 91*
**McCann**, Dean Merton 1927- *WhoAmL 92, WhoFI 92*
**McCann**, Dorothy H *WhoAmP 91*
**McCann**, Edson *IntAu&W 91X, WrDr 92*
**McCann**, Edward 1943- *WhoFI 92*
**McCann**, Elizabeth Ireland 1931- *WhoEnt 92*
**McCann**, Frances Veronica 1927- *AmMWSc 92*
**McCann**, Francis X *WhoAmP 91*
**McCann**, Gerald 1950- *WhoAmP 91*
**McCann**, Gilbert Donald, Jr 1912- *AmMWSc 92*
**McCann**, Graham 1961- *ConAu 134*
**McCann**, Jack Arland 1926- *WhoWest 92*
**McCann**, James A 1924- *WhoAmP 91*
**McCann**, James Alwyn 1934- *AmMWSc 92*
**McCann**, Janet *DrAPF 91*
**McCann**, Jerry Clinton, Jr. 1951- *WhoRel 92*
**McCann**, John Francis 1937- *WhoFI 92*
**Mc Cann**, John Joseph 1937- *WhoAmL 92*
**McCann**, John Patrick 1956- *WhoMW 92*
**McCann**, John W 1923- *WhoAmP 91*
**McCann**, Joseph Leo 1948- *WhoAmL 92*
**McCann**, Lester J 1915- *AmMWSc 92*
**McCann**, Matthew 1960- *WhoEnt 92*
**McCann**, Maurice Joseph 1950- *WhoAmL 92*
**McCann**, Michael Francis 1943- *AmMWSc 92*
**McCann**, Norman *IntWW 91*
**McCann**, Owen 1907- *IntWW 91, Who 92, WhoRel 92*
**McCann**, Peter Paul 1943- *AmMWSc 92*
**McCann**, Peter Toland McAree 1924- *Who 92*
**McCann**, Raymond J. 1934- *WhoAmL 92, WhoFI 92*
**McCann**, Richard *DrAPF 91*
**McCann**, Robert *WhoAmP 91*
**McCann**, Robert Walter 1951- *WhoAmL 92*
**McCann**, Roger C 1942- *AmMWSc 92*
**McCann**, Samuel McDonald 1925- *AmMWSc 92*
**McCann**, Sean 1929- *ConAu 134*
**McCann**, Taylor Lee 1943- *WhoIns 92*
**McCann**, Thomas Ryland, Jr. 1944- *WhoRel 92*
**McCann**, William H, Jr 1945- *WhoAmP 91*
**McCann**, William Peter 1924- *AmMWSc 92*
**McCann**, William Vern, Jr. 1943- *WhoAmL 92*
**McCann-Collier**, Marjorie Dolores 1937- *AmMWSc 92*
**McCann-Vissepo**, Patricia 1951- *WhoHisp 92*
**McCannon**, Dindga Fatima 1947- *WhoBlA 92*
**McCanse**, Alan Ross 1938- *WhoEnt 92*
**McCants**, Charles Bernard 1924- *AmMWSc 92*
**McCants**, Clyde Taft 1933- *WhoRel 92*
**McCants**, Coolidge N. 1925- *WhoBlA 92*
**McCants**, Derek Michael 1953- *WhoEnt 92*
**McCants**, Jesse Lee, Sr. 1936- *WhoBlA 92*
**McCants**, Joyce Ray 1953- *WhoMW 92*
**McCants**, Keith 1968- *WhoBlA 92*
**McCants**, Louise Spears 1924- *WhoMW 92*
**McCants**, Odell 1942- *WhoBlA 92*
**McCardell**, Claire 1905-1958 *DcTwDes*
**McCardell**, Harriett Wynn 1922- *WhoWest 92*
**McCardell**, W M 1923- *AmMWSc 92*
**Mc Cardle**, Randall Raymond 1931- *WhoWest 92*
**McCarey**, Leo 1898-1969 *IntDcF 2-2 [port]*
**McCarl**, F. James 1947- *WhoFI 92*
**McCarl**, Henry N. 1941- *WhoFI 92*
**McCarl**, Henry Newton 1941- *AmMWSc 92*
**McCarl**, James Curtis 1928- *WhoMW 92*
**McCarl**, Richard Lawrence 1927- *AmMWSc 92*
**McCarley**, Harold Bell, Jr. 1953- *WhoAmL 92*
**McCarley**, Robert Eugene 1931- *AmMWSc 92*
**McCarley**, Robert William 1937- *AmMWSc 92*
**McCarley**, Victor J. 1950- *WhoMW 92*
**McCarley**, Wardlow Howard 1926- *AmMWSc 92*
**McCarn**, Davis Barton 1928- *AmMWSc 92*
**McCarney**, Howard John 1921- *WhoRel 92*
**McCarraher**, David 1922- *Who 92*
**McCarrell**, Clark Gabriel, Jr. 1958- *WhoBlA 92*
**McCarrell**, William 1886-1979 *RelLAm 91*
**McCarren**, Patricia Ann 1953- *WhoEnt 92*
**Mc Carrick**, Theodore Edgar 1930- *WhoRel 92*
**McCarriston**, Linda *DrAPF 91*
**McCarroll**, Bruce 1933- *AmMWSc 92*
**McCarroll**, Dave *WhoAmP 91*
**McCarroll**, Earl 1939- *WhoEnt 92*
**McCarroll**, Patricia Anne 1943- *WhoAmL 92*
**McCarroll**, William Henry 1930- *AmMWSc 92*
**McCarron**, Harold Edwin 1930- *WhoMW 92*
**McCarron**, Margaret Mary *AmMWSc 92*
**McCarron**, Paul *WhoAmP 91*
**McCarron**, Richard M *AmMWSc 92*
**McCarry**, Charles *DrAPF 91*
**McCarry**, Charles 1930- *IntAu&W 91, WrDr 92*
**McCarry**, Charles Eugene 1956- *WhoEnt 92*
**McCart**, Bruce Ronald 1938- *AmMWSc 92*
**McCartan**, Lucy 1942- *AmMWSc 92*
**McCarter**, James Thomas 1932- *AmMWSc 92*
**McCarter**, John Alexander 1918- *AmMWSc 92*
**McCarter**, Louis Eugene 1940- *WhoAmL 92*
**McCarter**, Mercedes Anita 1939- *WhoAmP 91*
**McCarter**, Neely D. *WhoRel 92, WhoWest 92*
**McCarter**, Roger John Moore 1941- *AmMWSc 92*
**McCarter**, States Marion 1937- *AmMWSc 92*
**Mc Carter**, Thomas N., III 1929- *WhoFI 92*
**McCarter**, William J. *LesBEnT 92*
**McCarthy** *Who 92*
**McCarthy**, Baron 1925- *Who 92*
**McCarthy**, Adolf Charles 1922- *Who 92*
**McCarthy**, Alan J. 1947- *WhoFI 92*
**McCarthy**, Andrew 1962- *IntMPA 92*
**McCarthy**, Barry Thomas 1943- *WhoMW 92*
**McCarthy**, Beatrice C 1935- *WhoAmP 91*
**McCarthy**, Beverly Fitch 1933- *WhoWest 92*
**McCarthy**, Brian Joseph 1953- *WhoAmL 92*
**McCarthy**, Brian Nelson 1945- *WhoWest 92*
**McCarthy**, Carol Lee 1948- *WhoMW 92*
**McCarthy**, Catherine Frances 1921- *WhoAmL 92*
**McCarthy**, Catherine Theresa 1957- *WhoRel 92*
**McCarthy**, Charles Alan 1936- *AmMWSc 92, WhoMW 92*
**McCarthy**, Charles Francis, Jr. 1926- *WhoAmL 92*
**McCarthy**, Charles R 1926- *AmMWSc 92*
**McCarthy**, Charlotte Marie 1937- *AmMWSc 92*
**McCarthy**, Colman 1938- *AmPeW*
**McCarthy**, Cormac *DrAPF 91*
**McCarthy**, Cormac 1933- *BenetAL 91, IntAu&W 91, TwCWW 91*
**McCarthy**, Daniel James 1932- *WhoFI 92*
**McCarthy**, Daniel M 1966- *WhoAmP 91*
**McCarthy**, Danny W 1950- *AmMWSc 92*
**McCarthy**, Darrin Michael 1966- *WhoWest 92*
**McCarthy**, Darry 1930- *ConAu 35NR*
**McCarthy**, David Bruce 1955- *WhoRel 92*
**McCarthy**, Deidre Ann 1961- *WhoEnt 92*
**Mc Carthy**, Denis Michael 1942- *WhoFI 92*
**McCarthy**, Dennis Dean 1942- *AmMWSc 92*
**McCarthy**, Dennis Joseph 1953- *AmMWSc 92*
**McCarthy**, Dennis Patrick 1943- *WhoMW 92*
**McCarthy**, Donal John 1922- *Who 92*
**McCarthy**, Donald John 1938- *AmMWSc 92*
**McCarthy**, Douglas Robert 1943- *AmMWSc 92*
**McCarthy**, Edward Anthony 1918- *WhoRel 92*
**McCarthy**, Edward David, Jr. 1955- *WhoFI 92*
**McCarthy**, Edward Paul 1945- *WhoAmP 91*
**McCarthy**, Eugene 1916- *FacFETw [port], WrDr 92*
**McCarthy**, Eugene Gregory 1934- *AmMWSc 92*
**McCarthy**, Eugene Joseph 1916- *AmPeW, AmPolLe, IntWW 91, Who 92, WhoAmP 91*
**McCarthy**, F D 1953- *AmMWSc 92*
**McCarthy**, Francis Davey 1943- *AmMWSc 92*
**McCarthy**, Francis Desmond 1936- *AmMWSc 92, WhoFI 92*
**McCarthy**, Frank John 1928- *AmMWSc 92*
**McCarthy**, Fred 1924- *WhoBlA 92*
**McCarthy**, Frederick William 1941- *WhoFI 92*
**McCarthy**, Gary 1943- *TwCWW 91, WrDr 92*
**McCarthy**, Gary W 1943- *IntAu&W 91*
**McCarthy**, George Daniel 1949- *WhoAmL 92*
**McCarthy**, Gerald *DrAPF 91*
**McCarthy**, Gerald Michael 1941- *WhoMW 92*
**McCarthy**, Gerald T 1909- *AmMWSc 92*
**McCarthy**, Grace Mary 1927- *WhoWest 92*
**McCarthy**, Gregory Joseph 1943- *AmMWSc 92*
**McCarthy**, Harold C 1926- *WhoIns 92*
**McCarthy**, J. Donald 1942- *WhoAmL 92*
**McCarthy**, J. Howard, Jr. 1927- *WhoWest 92*
**McCarthy**, J. Thomas 1937- *WhoAmL 92*
**McCarthy**, James Benjamin *AmMWSc 92*
**McCarthy**, James Francis 1914- *AmMWSc 92*
**McCarthy**, James Francis 1949- *AmMWSc 92*
**McCarthy**, James Francis, Sr. 1933- *WhoMW 92*
**McCarthy**, James Joseph 1944- *AmMWSc 92*
**McCarthy**, James Patrick 1930- *WhoWest 92*
**McCarthy**, James Patrick 1935- *WhoAmP 91*
**Mc Carthy**, Jean Jerome 1929- *WhoMW 92*
**McCarthy**, Joanne *DrAPF 91*
**McCarthy**, JoAnne Elizabeth 1943- *WhoWest 92*
**McCarthy**, Joanne Haftle 1935- *WhoWest 92*
**McCarthy**, John 1927- *AmMWSc 92*
**McCarthy**, John 1942- *AmMWSc 92*
**Mc Carthy**, John Edward 1930- *WhoRel 92*
**McCarthy**, John F 1920- *AmMWSc 92*
**McCarthy**, John F 1947- *AmMWSc 92*
**McCarthy**, John Francis 1911- *WhoAmP 91*
**McCarthy**, John J, Jr 1930- *WhoAmP 91*
**McCarthy**, John Joseph 1923- *AmMWSc 92*
**McCarthy**, John Lawrence, Jr 1929- *AmMWSc 92*
**McCarthy**, John Lockhart 1943- *AmMWSc 92*
**McCarthy**, John Michael 1952- *AmMWSc 92*
**McCarthy**, John Paul 1948- *WhoRel 92*
**McCarthy**, John Randolph 1915- *AmMWSc 92*
**McCarthy**, John T 1939- *WhoAmP 91*
**McCarthy**, Joseph 1908-1957 *BenetAL 91*
**McCarthy**, Joseph L 1913- *AmMWSc 92*
**McCarthy**, Joseph R 1908-1957 *FacFETw [port], RComAH*
**McCarthy**, Joseph Raymond 1908-1957 *AmPolLe [port]*
**McCarthy**, Joseph Vincent 1887-1978 *FacFETw*
**McCarthy**, Karen 1947- *WhoAmP 91*
**McCarthy**, Karen Delcambre 1959- *WhoAmL 92*
**McCarthy**, Kathleen 1958- *WhoEnt 92*
**McCarthy**, Kathryn Agnes 1924- *AmMWSc 92*
**McCarthy**, Kevin 1914- *IntMPA 92*
**McCarthy**, Kevin 1947- *WhoEnt 92*
**McCarthy**, Kevin Bart 1948- *WhoAmL 92*
**McCarthy**, Kevin Michael 1954- *WhoAmL 92*
**McCarthy**, Laurence James 1934- *WhoWest 92*
**McCarthy**, Lawrence E *AmMWSc 92*
**McCarthy**, Lawrence Joseph 1958- *WhoAmL 92*
**McCarthy**, Leo T 1930- *WhoAmP 91*
**McCarthy**, Leo Tarcisius 1930- *WhoWest 92*
**McCarthy**, Lillah *WhoEnt 92*
**McCarthy**, Luke Kilduff 1940- *WhoFI 92*
**McCarthy**, Mark T. 1960- *WhoFI 92*
**McCarthy**, Martin 1923- *AmMWSc 92*
**McCarthy**, Mary 1912- *IntAu&W 91*
**McCarthy**, Mary 1912-1989 *BenetAL 91, FacFETw, HanAmWH, ModAWWr*
**McCarthy**, Mary Ann 1938- *WhoMW 92*
**McCarthy**, Mary Ann Bartley 1923- *WhoWest 92*
**McCarthy**, Mary Anne 1939- *AmMWSc 92*
**McCarthy**, Matthew M. *WhoAmL 92*
**McCarthy**, Michael 1940- *WhoWest 92*
**McCarthy**, Michael Gerard 1962- *WhoEnt 92*
**McCarthy**, Michael Ward 1936- *WhoAmL 92*
**McCarthy**, Miles Duffield 1914- *AmMWSc 92*
**McCarthy**, Neil Justin, Jr 1939- *AmMWSc 92*
**McCarthy**, Neil M. 1957- *WhoFI 92*
**McCarthy**, Nicholas Melvyn 1938- *Who 92*
**McCarthy**, Nobu *WhoEnt 92*
**McCarthy**, Patricia Jean 1927- *WhoAmP 91*
**Mc Carthy**, Patricia Margaret 1943- *WhoWest 92*
**McCarthy**, Patrick Charles 1940- *AmMWSc 92*
**McCarthy**, Patrick John 1954- *WhoAmL 92*
**McCarthy**, Paul 1956- *WhoEnt 92*
**McCarthy**, Paul Edward 1956- *WhoAmP 91*
**McCarthy**, Paul James 1924- *AmMWSc 92*
**McCarthy**, Paul Joseph 1928- *AmMWSc 92*
**McCarthy**, Peter 1919- *Who 92*
**McCarthy**, Peter Charles 1941- *WhoAmP 91*
**McCarthy**, Philip John 1918- *AmMWSc 92*
**McCarthy**, Raymond Lawrence 1920- *AmMWSc 92*
**McCarthy**, Richard Dean 1927- *WhoAmP 91*
**McCarthy**, Robert Elmer 1926- *AmMWSc 92*
**McCarthy**, Robert Emmett 1940- *WhoAmP 91*
**McCarthy**, Robert Emmett 1951- *WhoAmL 92*
**McCarthy**, Robert John 1953- *WhoEnt 92*
**McCarthy**, Rosemary P 1928- *IntAu&W 91*
**McCarthy**, Scott 1947- *WhoRel 92*
**McCarthy**, Shaun 1928- *IntAu&W 91, WrDr 92*
**McCarthy**, Shaun Leaf 1939- *AmMWSc 92*
**McCarthy**, Susan Stacy 1962- *WhoFI 92*
**McCarthy**, Thaddeus 1907- *IntWW 91, Who 92*
**McCarthy**, Thomas 1954- *ConAu 133*
**McCarthy**, Thomas J, Jr 1932- *WhoIns 92*
**McCarthy**, Thomas William, II 1945- *WhoAmP 91*
**McCarthy**, Tim *DrAPF 91*
**McCarthy**, Timothy 1929- *WhoRel 92*
**McCarthy**, Vincent Paul 1940- *WhoAmL 92*
**McCarthy**, Walter Charles 1922- *AmMWSc 92*
**McCarthy**, Walter J, Jr 1925- *AmMWSc 92*
**Mc Carthy**, Walter John, Jr. 1925- *WhoFI 92, WhoMW 92*
**McCarthy**, William E J 1925- *IntAu&W 91, WrDr 92*
**McCarthy**, William Edward 1924- *WhoFI 92*
**McCarthy**, William Francis 1944- *WhoAmL 92*
**McCarthy**, William J. 1919- *WhoFI 92*
**McCarthy**, William John 1934- *WhoRel 92*
**McCarthy**, William John 1941- *AmMWSc 92*
**McCarthy**, William Robert 1941- *WhoRel 92*
**McCartie**, Leo *Who 92*
**McCartin**, Brian James 1951- *AmMWSc 92*
**McCartin**, James T. *DrAPF 91*

**McCartney**, Charles Edward, Jr 1947- *WhoAmP 91*
**McCartney**, Diane Louise 1951- *WhoFI 92*
**McCartney**, Dorothy *DrAPF 91*
**McCartney**, Dorothy Eleanor Wilson 1914- *IntAu&W 91*
**McCartney**, George F 1946- *WhoIns 92*
**McCartney**, Gordon Arthur 1937- *Who 92*
**McCartney**, Hugh 1920- *Who 92*
**McCartney**, Ian 1951- *Who 92*
**McCartney**, James Wilson 1929- *WhoAmL 92*
**McCartney**, John Joseph 1943- *WhoFI 92*
**McCartney**, Mike 1959- *WhoAmP 91*
**McCartney**, Morley Gordon 1917- *AmMWSc 92*
**McCartney**, Paul 1942- *FacFETw, IntMPA 92, IntWW 91, NewAmDM, Who 92, WhoEnt 92*
**Mc Cartney**, Ralph Farnham 1924- *WhoMW 92*
**McCartney**, Washington 1812-1856 *BiInAmS*
**McCartney**, William Hugh 1951- *WhoMW 92*
**McCartney-Francis**, Nancy L 1950- *AmMWSc 92*
**McCarty**, Billy Dean 1923- *AmMWSc 92*
**McCarty**, Charles Barry 1953- *WhoRel 92*
**McCarty**, Clark William 1916- *AmMWSc 92*
**McCarty**, Clifford 1929- *WrDr 92*
**McCarty**, Daniel J, Jr 1928- *AmMWSc 92*
**McCarty**, Daryl John 1930- *WhoAmP 91*
**McCarty**, Doran Chester 1931- *WhoRel 92*
**McCarty**, Frank William 1941- *WhoMW 92*
**McCarty**, Frederick Joseph 1927- *AmMWSc 92*
**McCarty**, Gale A *AmMWSc 92*
**McCarty**, Gil 1934- *WhoIns 92*
**McCarty**, Harvey Dwight 1932- *WhoRel 92*
**McCarty**, James T 1947- *WhoIns 92*
**McCarty**, Jesse Louis Henry *DrAPF 91*
**McCarty**, John Albert 1951- *WhoMW 92*
**McCarty**, John Edward 1928- *AmMWSc 92*
**McCarty**, John Jacob 1926- *WhoMW 92*
**McCarty**, Jon Gilbert 1946- *AmMWSc 92*
**McCarty**, Kenneth Scott 1922- *AmMWSc 92*
**McCarty**, Leslie Paul 1925- *AmMWSc 92, WhoMW 92*
**McCarty**, Lewis Vernon 1919- *AmMWSc 92*
**McCarty**, Lisa Joanne 1953- *WhoMW 92*
**McCarty**, Maclyn 1911- *AmMWSc 92, IntWW 91*
**McCarty**, Michiel Cleve 1951- *WhoFI 92*
**McCarty**, Nancy Jackobs 1940- *WhoFI 92*
**McCarty**, Perry L 1931- *AmMWSc 92*
**McCarty**, Richard Charles 1947- *AmMWSc 92*
**McCarty**, Richard Earl 1938- *AmMWSc 92*
**McCarty**, Roger Leland 1953- *WhoFI 92*
**McCarty**, Ron *WhoAmP 91*
**McCarty**, Stephen Robert 1948- *WhoRel 92*
**Mc Carty**, Theodore Milson 1909- *WhoMW 92*
**McCarty**, Virginia Dill 1924- *WhoAmP 91*
**McCarty**, William Bonner, Jr. 1921- *WhoFI 92*
**McCarty**, William Britt 1953- *WhoFI 92*
**McCarty**, William Dennis 1943- *WhoAmP 91*
**McCarty-Cooper**, William A. d1991 *NewYTBS 91*
**McCarver**, Tim *LesBEnT 92*
**McCarville**, Michael Edward 1936- *AmMWSc 92, WhoMW 92*
**McCary**, Deanna Brewer 1943- *WhoAmL 92*
**McCary**, Richard O 1926- *AmMWSc 92*
**McCasey**, Michael Patrick 1946- *WhoAmL 92*
**McCaskey**, A E 1909- *AmMWSc 92*
**McCaskey**, Daphne Theophilia 1912- *WhoBlA 92*
**McCaskey**, Douglas William 1942- *WhoIns 92*
**McCaskey**, Edward *WhoMW 92*
**McCaskey**, Michael 1943- *WhoMW 92*
**McCaskey**, Thomas Andrew 1928- *AmMWSc 92*
**McCaskill**, Charles 1935- *WhoMW 92*
**McCaskill**, Claire 1953- *WhoAmP 91*
**McCaskill**, Earle 1937- *WhoBlA 92*
**McCaskill**, Richard Sherwin 1961- *WhoRel 92*
**McCaslin**, Bob 1926- *WhoAmP 91*
**McCaslin**, Darrell 1951- *AmMWSc 92*
**McCaslin**, Nellie 1914- *IntAu&W 91, WhoEnt 92, WrDr 92*
**McCaslin**, Teresa Eve 1949- *WhoWest 92*
**McCaslin**, Thomas Wilbert 1947- *WhoWest 92*
**McCaughan**, Donald 1929- *AmMWSc 92*
**McCaughan**, Janice Elise 1957- *WhoAmL 92*
**McCaughan**, John F. 1935- *WhoFI 92*
**Mc Caughey**, Andrew Gilmour 1922- *WhoFI 92*
**McCaughey**, Davis 1914- *IntWW 91*
**McCaughey**, John Davis 1914- *Who 92*
**McCaughey**, Joseph M 1921- *AmMWSc 92*
**McCaughey**, William Frank 1921- *AmMWSc 92*
**McCaughran**, Donald Alistair 1932- *AmMWSc 92*
**McCaughren**, Geraldine 1951- *WrDr 92*
**McCaughren**, Tom 1936- *WrDr 92*
**McCaul**, Joseph Patrick 1952- *WhoMW 92*
**McCauley**, Barbara *DrAPF 91*
**McCauley**, Brian 1941- *WhoAmP 91*
**McCauley**, Carole Spearin *DrAPF 91*
**McCauley**, Cleyburn Lycurgus 1929- *WhoAmL 92*
**McCauley**, David Evan 1950- *AmMWSc 92*
**McCauley**, David W. 1958- *WhoAmL 92*
**McCauley**, Gerald Brady 1935- *AmMWSc 92*
**McCauley**, H Berton 1913- *AmMWSc 92*
**McCauley**, Howard W 1919- *AmMWSc 92*
**McCauley**, James A 1941- *AmMWSc 92*
**McCauley**, James Weymann 1940- *AmMWSc 92*
**McCauley**, Janie Caves 1946- *WhoEnt 92*
**McCauley**, John Francis 1932- *AmMWSc 92*
**McCauley**, John J, Jr *WhoAmP 91*
**McCauley**, John Paul, Jr. 1964- *WhoFI 92*
**McCauley**, Joseph Lee 1943- *AmMWSc 92*
**McCauley**, Kevin Bruce 1954- *WhoRel 92*
**McCauley**, Martin 1934- *IntAu&W 91, WrDr 92*
**McCauley**, Mary Ludwig Hays 1754?-1832 *BlkwEAR*
**McCauley**, Motly Ranke *ScFEYrs*
**McCauley**, Raynor 1949- *WhoRel 92*
**McCauley**, Rhea Darcelle 1952- *WhoMW 92*
**McCauley**, Richard Gray 1940- *WhoAmL 92, WhoFI 92*
**McCauley**, Robbie *DrAPF 91*
**McCauley**, Robert F 1913- *AmMWSc 92*
**McCauley**, Robert William 1926- *AmMWSc 92*
**McCauley**, Roy B, Jr 1919- *AmMWSc 92*
**McCauley**, Roy Barnard 1943- *AmMWSc 92*
**McCauley**, Sue 1941- *ConNov 91*
**McCauley**, William John 1920- *AmMWSc 92*
**McCauley Chapman**, Karen *AmMWSc 92*
**McCaulley**, James Alan, III 1948- *WhoBlA 92*
**McCaully**, Ronald James 1936- *AmMWSc 92*
**McCausland**, Benedict Maurice Perronet T. *Who 92*
**McCausland**, Ian 1929- *AmMWSc 92*
**McCausland**, Timothy Jon 1961- *WhoWest 92*
**McCavanagh**, James R *WhoAmP 91*
**McCave**, Ian Nicholas 1941- *Who 92*
**McCaw**, Kenneth 1907- *Who 92*
**McCaw**, Lyle Steven 1960- *WhoRel 92*
**McCaw**, Robert Bruce 1943- *WhoAmL 92*
**McCawley**, Elton Leeman 1915- *AmMWSc 92*
**McCawley**, Frank X 1924- *AmMWSc 92*
**McCay**, Charles Francis 1810-1889 *BiInAmS*
**McCay**, Paul Baker 1924- *AmMWSc 92*
**McCay**, Winsor 1867-1934 *FacFETw*
**McCay**, Winsor 1886-1934 *BenetAL 91*
**McChane**, Daniel Ray 1948- *WhoMW 92*
**McCheeney** d1876 *BiInAmS*
**McChesney**, Clifton Marsh 1929- *WhoMW 92*
**McChesney**, James Dewey 1939- *AmMWSc 92*
**McChesney**, Samuel Parker, III 1945- *WhoMW 92*
**McClafferty**, John Joseph 1906- *WhoRel 92*
**McClafferty**, Monica Harrison 1964- *WhoHisp 92*
**McClain**, Alva J. 1888-1968 *RelLAm 91*
**McClain**, Andrew Bradley 1948- *WhoBlA 92*
**McClain**, Charles James 1931- *WhoMW 92*
**McClain**, Charles Joseph, Jr. 1943- *WhoAmL 92*
**McClain**, Dan David 1955- *WhoAmL 92*
**McClain**, David H 1933- *WhoAmP 91*
**McClain**, Dorothy Mae 1931- *WhoBlA 92*
**McClain**, Earsalean J. 1910- *WhoBlA 92*
**McClain**, Edward B *WhoAmP 91*
**McClain**, Edward Ferrell 1935- *WhoAmP 91*
**McClain**, Eugene Fredrick 1926- *AmMWSc 92*
**McClain**, Gerald Ray 1941- *AmMWSc 92*
**McClain**, Gregory David 1957- *WhoRel 92*
**McClain**, James Lewis 1931- *WhoMW 92*
**McClain**, James W. 1939- *WhoBlA 92*
**McClain**, Jerome Gerald 1939- *WhoBlA 92*
**McClain**, John William 1928- *AmMWSc 92*
**McClain**, Katrina 1965- *BlkOlyM*
**McClain**, Larry French 1937- *WhoFI 92*
**McClain**, Luther, Jr. 1949- *WhoMW 92*
**McClain**, Marlon L. 1955- *WhoBlA 92*
**McClain**, Michael F 1947- *WhoAmP 91*
**McClain**, Michael William 1952- *WhoWest 92*
**McClain**, Paula Denice 1950- *WhoBlA 92, WhoWest 92*
**McClain**, Richard Allen 1960- *WhoRel 92*
**McClain**, Richard Stan 1951- *WhoEnt 92, WhoWest 92*
**McClain**, Ronald Theodore 1948- *WhoWest 92*
**McClain**, Shirla R. 1935- *WhoBlA 92*
**McClain**, Thomas E. 1950- *WhoMW 92*
**McClain**, Tomey Van 1952- *WhoRel 92*
**McClain**, William Andrew 1913- *WhoAmL 92, WhoBlA 92, WhoMW 92*
**McClain**, William B. 1938- *WhoRel 92*
**McClain**, William L. 1958- *WhoBlA 92*
**McClammy**, Charles Washington 1839-1896 *DcNCBi 4*
**McClammy**, Thad C. 1942- *WhoBlA 92*
**McClammy**, Thad C, Jr 1942- *WhoAmP 91*
**McClamroch**, N Harris 1942- *AmMWSc 92*
**McClanahan**, Larry Duncan 1938- *WhoFI 92*
**McClanahan**, Marian 1926- *WhoAmP 91*
**McClanahan**, Maurice Edward 1930- *WhoFI 92*
**McClanahan**, Molly 1937- *WhoAmP 91*
**McClanahan**, Ollin David 1956- *WhoEnt 92*
**McClanahan**, Rue *IntMPA 92, WhoEnt 92*
**McClanan**, Glenn Brooks 1934- *WhoAmP 91*
**McClane**, A. J. d1991 *NewYTBS 91 [port]*
**McClane**, Kenneth A, Jr 1951- *IntAu&W 91*
**McClane**, Kenneth Anderson *DrAPF 91*
**McClane**, Kenneth Anderson, Jr. 1951- *WhoBlA 92*
**McClane**, Robert Sanford 1939- *WhoFI 92*
**McClaran**, Ray E. *WhoRel 92*
**McClard**, Ronald Wayne 1951- *AmMWSc 92*
**McClaren**, Mike E. 1946- *WhoMW 92*
**McClary**, Andrew 1927- *AmMWSc 92*
**McClary**, Cecil Fay 1913- *AmMWSc 92*
**McClary**, David Lynn 1950- *WhoRel 92*
**McClary**, Jane McIlvaine *DrAPF 91*
**McClary**, Jane Stevenson McIlvaine 1919- *IntAu&W 91*
**McClary**, Jim Marston 1949- *WhoFI 92*
**McClaskey**, William H. 1912- *WhoBlA 92*
**McClatchey**, Al William 1949- *WhoMW 92*
**McClatchey**, Frank Sandy 1956- *WhoAmP 91*
**McClatchey**, John Francis 1929- *WhoAmL 92*
**McClatchey**, Kenneth D 1942- *AmMWSc 92*
**McClatchey**, Robert Alan 1938- *AmMWSc 92*
**McClatchy**, J.D. *DrAPF 91*
**McClatchy**, J. D. 1945- *WrDr 92*
**McClatchy**, James B. *WhoWest 92*
**McClatchy**, Joseph Kenneth 1939- *AmMWSc 92*
**McClatchy**, Richard A, Jr 1929- *WhoAmP 91*
**McClaugherty**, Joe L. 1951- *WhoAmL 92*
**McClaughry**, John 1937- *WhoAmP 91*
**McClaurin**, Irma *DrAPF 91*
**McClave**, Donald Silsbee 1941- *WhoFI 92, WhoWest 92*
**McClave**, William H., Jr. 1943- *WhoFI 92*
**McClay**, Harvey Curtis 1939- *WhoFI 92*
**McClay**, James J. 1926- *WhoWest 92*
**McClay**, Michael Howard 1949- *WhoMW 92*
**McClean**, David 1939- *Who 92*
**McClean**, Kathleen *Who 92*
**McClean**, L. Robert *WhoRel 92*
**McClean**, Vernon E. 1941- *WhoBlA 92*
**McCleary**, Harold Russell 1913- *AmMWSc 92*
**McCleary**, James A 1917- *AmMWSc 92*
**McCleary**, Jefferson Rand 1948- *AmMWSc 92*
**McCleary**, Mary Gilkeson 1920- *WhoEnt 92*
**McCleary**, Michael L 1944- *WhoAmP 91*
**McCleary**, Paul Frederick 1930- *WhoFI 92*
**McCleary**, Robert A. 1923-1973 *ConAu 134*
**McCleary**, Stephen Hill 1941- *AmMWSc 92*
**McCleave**, James David 1939- *AmMWSc 92*
**McCleave**, Mansel Philip 1926- *WhoBlA 92*
**McCleave**, Mildred Atwood Poston 1919- *WhoBlA 92*
**McCleery**, Nancy *DrAPF 91*
**McCleery**, Richard Grimes 1928- *WhoWest 92*
**Mc Cleery**, William Thomas 1911- *WhoEnt 92*
**McCleister**, Thom 1949- *WhoEnt 92*
**McClellan**, Aubrey Lester 1923- *AmMWSc 92*
**McClellan**, Betty Jane 1932- *AmMWSc 92*
**McClellan**, Bobby Ewing 1937- *AmMWSc 92*
**McClellan**, C W *WhoAmP 91*
**McClellan**, Craig Rene 1947- *WhoAmL 92, WhoWest 92*
**McClellan**, Craig Thomas 1948- *WhoRel 92*
**McClellan**, Edward J. 1921- *WhoBlA 92*
**McClellan**, Frank Madison 1945- *WhoBlA 92*
**McClellan**, George 1796-1847 *BiInAmS*
**McClellan**, George 1849-1913 *BiInAmS*
**McClellan**, George B. 1826-1885 *BenetAL 91, RComAH*
**McClellan**, George Brinton 1826-1885 *AmPolLe*
**McClellan**, Gerard 1913- *Who 92*
**McClellan**, Guerry Hamrick 1939- *AmMWSc 92*
**McClellan**, James E 1926- *WhoAmP 91*
**McClellan**, James Harold 1947- *AmMWSc 92*
**McClellan**, John Forbes 1917- *AmMWSc 92*
**McClellan**, John Forrest 1932- *Who 92*
**McClellan**, Karen A. 1960- *WhoFI 92*
**McClellan**, Kari Lee 1951- *WhoRel 92*
**McClellan**, Kenneth Allen 1955- *WhoWest 92*
**McClellan**, Larry Allen 1944- *WhoRel 92*
**McClellan**, Mark Howell 1957- *WhoWest 92*
**McClellan**, Mildred Nolte 1922- *WhoEnt 92*
**McClellan**, Richard Augustus 1930- *WhoFI 92*
**McClellan**, Roger Orville 1937- *AmMWSc 92*
**McClellan**, Stephen T. 1942- *ConAu 133*
**McClellan**, Tara J. 1962- *WhoEnt 92*
**McClellan**, Thomas Lee 1942- *WhoRel 92*
**McClelland**, Alan Lindsey 1925- *AmMWSc 92*
**McClelland**, Bernard Riley 1935- *AmMWSc 92*
**McClelland**, Bramlette 1920- *AmMWSc 92*
**McClelland**, Bruce *DrAPF 91*
**McClelland**, Charles Edgar 1940- *WrDr 92*
**McClelland**, Douglas *Who 92*
**McClelland**, Douglas 1926- *IntWW 91*
**McClelland**, Eddie L. 1957- *WhoFI 92*
**McClelland**, Emmy 1940- *WhoAmP 91*
**McClelland**, George Anderson Hugh 1931- *AmMWSc 92*
**McClelland**, George Ewart 1927- *Who 92*
**McClelland**, Grigor 1922- *Who 92*
**McClelland**, Isaac Holland 1907- *WhoBlA 92*
**McClelland**, Ivy Lillian 1908- *WrDr 92*
**McClelland**, James Morris 1943- *WhoFI 92*
**McClelland**, John Frederick 1941- *AmMWSc 92*
**McClelland**, John Morris 1915- *WhoWest 92*
**Mc Clelland**, John Peter 1933- *WhoWest 92*
**McClelland**, Karen Elizabeth 1954- *WhoMW 92*
**McClelland**, Marguerite Marie 1919- *WhoBlA 92*
**McClelland**, Michael 1956- *AmMWSc 92*
**McClelland**, Muriel 1941- *WhoAmL 92*
**McClelland**, Nannette Evette 1956- *WhoWest 92*
**McClelland**, Nina Irene 1929- *AmMWSc 92*
**McClelland**, Patricia G. 1944- *WhoRel 92*
**McClelland**, Raymond Cecil 1925- *WhoAmP 91*
**McClelland**, Rex Arnold 1936- *WhoFI 92*
**McClelland**, Robert Bruce 1961- *WhoFI 92*
**McClelland**, Robert Nelson 1929- *AmMWSc 92*
**McClelland**, Sandra Lynn 1960- *WhoFI 92*
**McClelland**, Vincent Alan 1933- *WrDr 92*
**McClelland**, W. Clark 1939- *WhoFI 92*
**McClelland**, W. Craig 1934- *IntWW 91*

**McClelland**, William Craig 1934- *WhoFI 92*
**McClement**, John Henry 1918- *AmMWSc 92*
**McClements**, Robert, Jr. 1928- *WhoFI 92*
**McClenachan**, Ellsworth C 1934- *AmMWSc 92*
**McClenaghan**, Leroy Ritter, Jr 1948- *AmMWSc 92*
**McClenahan**, William St Clair 1912- *AmMWSc 92*
**McClenathen**, William Richard 1915- *WhoAmL 92*
**McClendon**, Burwell Beeman, Jr 1930- *WhoAmP 91*
**McClendon**, Carol A. 1942- *WhoBlA 92*
**McClendon**, Ernestine d1991 *NewYTBS 91*
**McClendon**, Ernestine 1924- *WhoBlA 92*
**McClendon**, Franklin Eugene 1960- *WhoFI 92*
**Mc Clendon**, Fred Vernon *WhoFI 92*
**McClendon**, Irvin Lee, Sr. 1945- *WhoWest 92*
**McClendon**, James Fred 1938- *AmMWSc 92*
**McClendon**, John Haddaway 1921- *AmMWSc 92, WhoWest 92*
**McClendon**, Kellen 1944- *WhoBlA 92*
**McClendon**, Moses C. 1934- *WhoBlA 92*
**McClendon**, Rosalie 1884-1936 *NotBlAW 92 [port]*
**Mc Clendon**, Sarah Newcomb 1910- *WhoEnt 92*
**McClenic**, David A. 1926- *WhoBlA 92*
**McClenic**, Patricia Dickson 1947- *WhoBlA 92*
**McClennen**, Miriam J. 1923- *WhoWest 92*
**McClennen**, Sandra Elaine 1942- *WhoMW 92*
**McClenney**, Earl Hampton 1907- *WhoBlA 92*
**McClenny**, Patsy 1950- *WhoEnt 92*
**McClenon**, John R 1937- *AmMWSc 92*
**McCleskey**, Dale Wade 1952- *WhoRel 92*
**McCleverty**, Jon Armistice 1937- *Who 92*
**McCline**, Richard L. 1944- *WhoBlA 92*
**McClintic**, Denise Arcand 1958- *WhoAmL 92*
**McClintic**, Joseph Robert 1928- *AmMWSc 92*
**McClintic**, T B 1873?-1912 *BiInAmS*
**McClintock**, Barbara 1902- *AmMWSc 92, IntWW 91, WhoNob 90*
**McClintock**, Charles Michael 1949- *WhoAmP 91*
**McClintock**, Cyril Lawson Tait 1916- *Who 92*
**McClintock**, David 1913- *IntAu&W 91, Who 92*
**McClintock**, David K 1938- *AmMWSc 92*
**McClintock**, Elizabeth 1912- *AmMWSc 92*
**McClintock**, Emory 1840-1916 *BiInAmS*
**McClintock**, Eric 1918- *Who 92*
**McClintock**, Frank A 1921- *AmMWSc 92*
**McClintock**, George Vernon, Jr. 1944- *WhoEnt 92*
**McClintock**, Michael *DrAPF 91*
**McClintock**, Muriel Aymer 1909- *WhoAmP 91*
**McClintock**, Nicholas Cole 1916- *Who 92*
**McClintock**, Nivea Hernandez 1931- *WhoAmP 91*
**McClintock**, Patrick Ralph *AmMWSc 92*
**McClintock**, Thomas Miller, II 1956- *WhoAmP 91*
**McClintock-Bunbury** *Who 92*
**McClintock-Hernandez**, Kenneth D 1957- *WhoAmP 91*
**McClintock-Hernandez**, Kenneth Davison 1957- *WhoHisp 92*
**McClinton**, Curtis R., Jr. *WhoBlA 92*
**McClinton**, Danny Gardner 1944- *WhoRel 92*
**McClinton**, Delbert Ross 1940- *WhoEnt 92*
**McClomb**, George E. 1940- *WhoBlA 92*
**McClory**, Sean 1924- *IntMPA 92*
**McClory**, Sean Joseph 1924- *WhoEnt 92*
**McCloskey**, Allen Lyle 1922- *AmMWSc 92*
**McCloskey**, Bernard Mary 1924- *Who 92*
**McCloskey**, Chester Martin 1918- *AmMWSc 92*
**McCloskey**, Francis X. 1939- *AlmAP 92 [port]*
**McCloskey**, Frank 1939- *WhoAmP 91, WhoMW 92*
**McCloskey**, Gary Neil 1951- *WhoRel 92*
**McCloskey**, Jack *WhoMW 92*
**McCloskey**, James Augustus, Jr 1936- *AmMWSc 92*
**McCloskey**, John 1810-1885 *RelLAm 91*
**McCloskey**, John W 1938- *AmMWSc 92*
**McCloskey**, Lawrence Richard 1939- *AmMWSc 92*
**McCloskey**, Linda Louise 1946- *WhoWest 92*
**McCloskey**, Mark *DrAPF 91*
**McCloskey**, Mark 1938- *WrDr 92*
**McCloskey**, Michael James 1932- *WhoAmP 91*
**McCloskey**, Michael Joseph 1951- *WhoMW 92*
**McCloskey**, Paul Norton, Jr 1927- *WhoAmP 91*
**McCloskey**, Richard John 1944- *WhoAmP 91, WhoWest 92*
**McCloskey**, Richard Vensel 1933- *AmMWSc 92*
**McCloskey**, Robert 1914- *BenetAL 91, WrDr 92*
**McCloskey**, Robert James 1922- *IntWW 91, WhoAmP 91*
**McCloskey**, Teresemarie 1926- *AmMWSc 92*
**Mc Closkey**, William Robert 1918- *WhoMW 92*
**McCloud**, Aaron C. 1933- *WhoBlA 92*
**McCloud**, Anece Faison 1937- *WhoBlA 92*
**McCloud**, Darell Edison 1920- *AmMWSc 92*
**McCloud**, George Aaron 1967- *WhoBlA 92*
**McCloud**, Hal Emerson, Jr 1938- *AmMWSc 92*
**McCloud**, J. Oscar 1936- *WhoBlA 92*
**McCloud**, Jed *TwCWW 91*
**McCloud**, Ronnie 1947- *WhoBlA 92*
**McCloud**, Ruth 1921- *WhoAmP 91*
**McCloud**, Thomas Henry 1948- *WhoBlA 92*
**McCloy**, Carter James 1931- *WhoFI 92*
**McCloy**, Helen 1904- *IntAu&W 91, WrDr 92*
**McCloy**, James Murl 1934- *AmMWSc 92*
**McCloy**, John J 1895-1989 *FacFETw*
**McCloy**, John Jay 1895- *AmPolLe*
**McCluer**, Robert Hampton 1928- *AmMWSc 92*
**McCluggage**, Kerry *LesBEnT 92 [port]*
**McClun**, Maurice Craig 1954- *WhoRel 92*
**McClune**, James 1921- *Who 92*
**McCluney**, Ian 1937- *Who 92*
**McClung**, Alexander Keith, Jr. 1934- *WhoFI 92*
**McClung**, Andrew Colin 1923- *AmMWSc 92*
**McClung**, Arthur J 1912- *WhoAmP 91*
**McClung**, J Keith 1954- *AmMWSc 92*
**Mc Clung**, Jim Hill 1936- *WhoFI 92*
**McClung**, John A. 1804-1859 *BenetAL 91*
**McClung**, Kenneth Austin, Jr. 1947- *WhoFI 92*
**McClung**, Leland Swint 1910- *AmMWSc 92*
**McClung**, Leon Darrell, Jr. 1953- *WhoMW 92*
**McClung**, Marvin Richard 1917- *AmMWSc 92*
**McClung**, Merle Steven 1943- *WhoAmL 92*
**McClung**, Norvel Malcolm 1916- *AmMWSc 92*
**McClung**, Paul Joffre 1918- *WhoAmL 92*
**McClung**, Robert M. 1916- *SmATA 68 [port]*
**McClung**, Robert Marshall 1916- *WrDr 92*
**McClung**, Robert W 1920- *AmMWSc 92*
**McClung**, Ronald Allen 1958- *WhoRel 92*
**McClung**, Ronald Edwin Dawson 1941- *AmMWSc 92*
**McClung**, Willie David 1939- *WhoBlA 92*
**McClure**, Albert Bonner 1905-1972 *DcNCBi 4*
**McClure**, Alexander Doak 1850-1920 *DcNCBi 4*
**McClure**, Alexander K. 1828-1909 *BenetAL 91*
**McClure**, Allan Howard 1925- *WhoWest 92*
**McClure**, Alvin Bruce 1953- *WhoMW 92*
**McClure**, Ann 1950- *WhoAmL 92*
**McClure**, Anna Jo 1928- *WhoAmP 91*
**McClure**, Benjamin Thompson 1925- *AmMWSc 92*
**McClure**, Bruce Edward 1954- *WhoRel 92*
**McClure**, C H Barney 1941- *WhoAmP 91*
**Mc Clure**, Charles Alfred 1923- *WhoEnt 92*
**McClure**, Charles Micheal 1943- *WhoAmL 92*
**McClure**, Clair Wylie 1927- *AmMWSc 92*
**McClure**, Daniel M. 1952- *WhoAmL 92*
**McClure**, Daphne *TwCPaSc*
**McClure**, David 1926- *TwCPaSc, Who 92*
**McClure**, David Warren 1936- *AmMWSc 92*
**McClure**, Donald Ernest 1944- *AmMWSc 92*
**McClure**, Donald John 1940- *WhoAmL 92*
**McClure**, Donald Leon 1952- *WhoBlA 92*
**McClure**, Donald S. 1920- *IntWW 91*
**McClure**, Donald Stuart 1920- *AmMWSc 92*
**McClure**, Doug 1935- *IntMPA 92*
**McClure**, Earie *WhoBlA 92*
**McClure**, Edgar d1897 *BiInAmS*
**McClure**, Eldon Ray 1933- *AmMWSc 92*
**McClure**, Frederick Donald 1954- *WhoBlA 92*
**McClure**, Gene Benjamin 1941- *WhoAmL 92*
**McClure**, Gillian Mary 1948- *IntAu&W 91, WrDr 92*
**McClure**, Gordon 1922- *WhoFI 92*
**McClure**, Gordon Wallace 1923- *AmMWSc 92*
**McClure**, Harold Monroe 1937- *AmMWSc 92*
**McClure**, Howe Elliott 1910- *WhoWest 92*
**McClure**, J Doyle 1935- *AmMWSc 92*
**McClure**, James *DrAPF 91*
**McClure**, James 1939- *IntAu&W 91, WrDr 92*
**McClure**, James A. 1924- *IntWW 91, WhoAmP 91, WhoWest 92*
**McClure**, James Gore King, Jr. 1884-1956 *DcNCBi 4*
**Mc Clure**, James J., Jr. 1920- *WhoAmL 92, WhoAmP 91*
**McClure**, Janice *WhoAmP 91*
**McClure**, Janice Lee 1941- *WhoMW 92*
**McClure**, Jerry Weldon 1933- *AmMWSc 92*
**McClure**, Joel William, Jr 1927- *AmMWSc 92*
**McClure**, John *WhoAmP 91*
**McClure**, John Arthur 1934- *AmMWSc 92*
**McClure**, John Michael 1942- *WhoWest 92*
**McClure**, Joseph A 1951- *AmMWSc 92*
**McClure**, Joseph Andrew, Jr 1934- *AmMWSc 92*
**McClure**, Joseph Robert 1923- *Who 92*
**McClure**, Judson P 1934- *AmMWSc 92*
**McClure**, Kenneth Allen 1947- *WhoIns 92*
**McClure**, Marc 1957- *IntMPA 92*
**McClure**, Mark Stephen 1948- *AmMWSc 92*
**McClure**, Mary Anne 1939- *WhoAmP 91*
**McClure**, Michael *DrAPF 91*
**McClure**, Michael 1932- *BenetAL 91, ConPo 91, WrDr 92*
**McClure**, Michael Allen 1938- *AmMWSc 92*
**McClure**, Michael Edward 1941- *AmMWSc 92*
**McClure**, Michael Lawrence 1952- *WhoRel 92*
**McClure**, Michal Clyde 1940- *WhoFI 92*
**McClure**, Mitchell Lee 1957- *WhoRel 92*
**McClure**, Polley Ann 1943- *AmMWSc 92, WhoMW 92*
**McClure**, Richard Mark 1934- *AmMWSc 92*
**McClure**, Robert Charles 1932- *AmMWSc 92, WhoMW 92*
**McClure**, Roger John 1943- *WhoAmL 92*
**McClure**, S. S. 1857-1949 *BenetAL 91*
**McClure**, Stevan Terrance 1962- *WhoRel 92*
**McClure**, Theodore Dean 1936- *AmMWSc 92*
**McClure**, Thomas Edward 1954- *WhoAmL 92*
**McClure**, Thomas Fulton 1920- *WhoWest 92*
**McClure**, Thomas James 1955- *WhoAmL 92*
**McClure**, Victor 1887-1963 *ScFEYrs*
**McClure**, Wesley Allan 1959- *WhoAmL 92*
**McClure**, Wesley Cornelious *WhoBlA 92*
**McClure**, Wilbert James 1938- *BlkOlyM*
**McClure**, William Earl 1946- *WhoFI 92*
**McClure**, William Owen 1937- *AmMWSc 92, WhoWest 92*
**McClure**, William Robert 1941- *AmMWSc 92*
**McClurg**, Charles Alan 1944- *AmMWSc 92*
**McClurg**, Edie 1950- *IntMPA 92*
**McClurg**, James Edward 1945- *AmMWSc 92*
**McClurg**, Patricia A. 1939- *WhoRel 92*
**McClurkin**, Arlan Wilbur 1917- *AmMWSc 92*
**McClurkin**, Iola Taylor 1930- *AmMWSc 92*
**McClurkin**, Johnson Thomas 1929- *WhoBlA 92*
**McCluskey** *Who 92*
**McCluskey**, Baron 1929- *Who 92*
**McCluskey**, Dorothy Soest 1928- *WhoAmP 91*
**McCluskey**, Edward Joseph 1929- *AmMWSc 92*
**McCluskey**, Elwood Sturges 1925- *AmMWSc 92*
**McCluskey**, George E, Jr 1938- *AmMWSc 92*
**McCluskey**, John A. *DrAPF 91*
**McCluskey**, John A., Jr. 1944- *WhoBlA 92*
**McCluskey**, Robert Timmons 1923- *AmMWSc 92*
**McCluskie**, John Cameron 1946- *Who 92*
**McCluskie**, Samuel Joseph 1932- *Who 92*
**McClymer**, James P 1958- *AmMWSc 92*
**McClymonds**, Jean Ellen *WhoFI 92*
**Mc Clymont**, Hamilton 1944- *WhoEnt 92*
**McClymont**, John Wilbur 1925- *AmMWSc 92*
**McClymont**, Kenneth 1924- *AmMWSc 92*
**McCobb**, John Bradford, Jr. 1939- *WhoAmL 92*
**McCobb**, Paul 1917-1969 *DcTwDes*
**McCoid**, Donald J. 1943- *WhoRel 92*
**Mc Coin**, John Mack 1931- *WhoFI 92, WhoMW 92*
**McColl** *Who 92*
**McColl**, Colin 1932- *Who 92*
**McColl**, Hugh Francis 1938- *WhoFI 92*
**McColl**, Hugh Leon, Jr. 1935- *WhoFI 92*
**McColl**, Ian 1915- *Who 92*
**McColl**, James Renfrew 1940- *AmMWSc 92*
**McColl**, John Angus 1928- *WhoAmP 91*
**McColl**, John Duncan 1925- *AmMWSc 92*
**McColl**, Malcolm 1933- *AmMWSc 92*
**McColl**, William Duncan 1933- *WhoEnt 92*
**McColl Of Dulwich**, Baron 1933- *IntWW 91, Who 92*
**McCollester**, Duncan L 1925- *AmMWSc 92*
**McColley**, Denise Adele Herman 1953- *WhoAmL 92*
**McCollin**, Russ *DrAPF 91*
**McCollister**, John Y 1921- *WhoAmP 91*
**McCollister**, Robert John 1928- *AmMWSc 92*
**McColloch**, John Kearney 1946- *WhoFI 92*
**McColloch**, Murray Michael 1926- *WhoAmL 92, WhoIns 92*
**McColloch**, Robert James 1920- *AmMWSc 92*
**McCollom**, Alan Tompkins 1950- *WhoAmL 92*
**McCollom**, John Hildreth 1843-1915 *BiInAmS*
**McCollom**, Kenneth A 1922- *AmMWSc 92*
**McCollom**, Walter Raymond, Jr. 1949- *WhoMW 92*
**McCollough**, Fred, Jr 1928- *AmMWSc 92*
**McCollough**, Lucille Hanna 1905- *WhoAmP 91*
**McCollough**, Parker 1950- *WhoAmP 91*
**McCollough**, Patrick Hanna 1942- *WhoAmP 91*
**McCollough**, Walter 1915- *RelLAm 91*
**McCollough**, Walter 1915-1991 *WhoBlA 92N*
**McCollow**, Thomas James 1925- *WhoFI 92*
**McCollum**, Alice Odessa 1947- *WhoBlA 92*
**McCollum**, Alvin August 1920- *WhoWest 92*
**McCollum**, Anita LaVerne 1960- *WhoBlA 92*
**McCollum**, Anthony Wayne 1944- *AmMWSc 92*
**McCollum**, Bill 1944- *AlmAP 92 [port], WhoAmP 91*
**McCollum**, Charles Edward 1942- *WhoBlA 92*
**McCollum**, Clifford Glenn 1919- *AmMWSc 92*
**McCollum**, Dannel 1937- *WhoAmP 91*
**McCollum**, Donald Carruth, Jr 1930- *AmMWSc 92*
**McCollum**, Donald E 1927- *AmMWSc 92*
**McCollum**, Gilbert Dewey, Jr 1929- *AmMWSc 92*
**McCollum**, Gin *AmMWSc 92*
**McCollum**, Herbert W. *WhoFI 92*
**McCollum**, James Fountain 1946- *WhoAmL 92*
**McCollum**, John David 1929- *AmMWSc 92*
**McCollum**, John Edward 1930- *WhoAmL 92*
**McCollum**, John Morris 1922- *WhoEnt 92*
**McCollum**, Liam *Who 92*
**McCollum**, Linda Carlyle 1942- *WhoEnt 92*
**McCollum**, Odell 1926- *WhoRel 92*
**McCollum**, Richard Alton, II 1959- *WhoRel 92*
**McCollum**, Robert Edmund 1922- *AmMWSc 92*
**McCollum**, Robert Wayne 1925- *AmMWSc 92*
**McCollum**, William 1933- *Who 92*
**McCollum**, William Howard 1923- *AmMWSc 92*
**McColly**, Howard F 1902- *AmMWSc 92*
**McColm**, Douglas Woodruff 1933- *AmMWSc 92*
**McColman**, William Ernest 1947- *WhoFI 92*
**McColough**, Charles Peter 1922- *IntWW 91, WhoAmP 91*
**McColough**, Peter 1922- *Who 92*

**McComas**, David John 1958- *AmMWSc 92*
**McComas**, Stuart T 1932- *AmMWSc 92*
**McComb**, Jackie Roy 1940- *WhoRel 92*
**McComb**, John Christopher 1957- *WhoFI 92*
**McComb**, Leonard 1930- *TwCPaSc*
**McComb**, Leonard William Joseph 1930- *Who 92*
**McComb**, Mark Anthony 1958- *WhoFI 92*
**McCombe**, Bruce Douglas 1938- *AmMWSc 92*
**McCombe**, Richard George Bramwell 1952- *Who 92*
**McCombs**, Candace Cragen 1947- *AmMWSc 92*
**McCombs**, Charles Allan 1948- *AmMWSc 92*
**McCombs**, Freda Siler 1933- *AmMWSc 92*
**McCombs**, H Louis 1932- *AmMWSc 92*
**McCombs**, Judith *DrAPF 91*
**McCombs**, Richard N. 1946- *WhoFI 92*
**McCombs**, Robert Matthew *AmMWSc 92*
**McCombs**, Shirley Ann 1937- *WhoAmP 91*
**McComis**, William T 1938- *AmMWSc 92*
**McComis**, William Thomas 1938- *WhoMW 92*
**McComiskey**, Thomas Edward 1928- *WhoRel 92*
**McComsey**, Robert Ronald 1944- *WhoFI 92*
**McConachie**, Alexander Scot 1942- *WhoFI 92*
**McConachie**, Michael Paul 1956- *WhoRel 92*
**McConaghy**, John Stead, Jr 1942- *AmMWSc 92*
**McConaghy**, Richard Dene 1955- *WhoWest 92*
**McConahey**, William McConnell, Jr 1916- *AmMWSc 92*
**McConatha**, Barry Joe 1954- *WhoEnt 92*
**McConathy**, James Leslie, Jr 1956- *WhoAmP 91*
**McConathy**, Walter James 1941- *AmMWSc 92*
**McConchie**, Irving H 1923- *WhoAmP 91*
**McCone**, John A. d1991 *Who 92N*
**McCone**, John A. 1902-1991 *CurBio 91N, NewYTBS 91 [port]*
**McCone**, Selma J. *DcAmImH*
**McConeghey**, Nelljean *DrAPF 91*
**McConica**, James Kelsey 1930- *IntAu&W 91, WrDr 92*
**McConkey**, David Dale 1949- *WhoRel 92*
**McConkey**, James *DrAPF 91*
**McConkey**, James 1921- *BenetAL 91, WrDr 92*
**McConkey**, James Rodney 1921- *IntAu&W 91*
**McConkey**, John William *AmMWSc 92*
**McConkie**, James Wilson, II 1946- *WhoAmP 91*
**McConkie**, Oscar Walter 1926- *WhoAmL 92*
**McConnachie**, Brian 1942- *WhoEnt 92*
**McConnachie**, Peter Ross 1940- *AmMWSc 92*
**McConnaughey**, Bayard Harlow 1916- *AmMWSc 92*
**McConnaughey**, George C. d1966 *LesBEnT 92*
**Mc Connaughey**, George Carlton, Jr. 1925- *WhoAmL 92, WhoFI 92*
**McConnaughey**, James Walter 1951- *WhoFI 92*
**McConnaughey**, Mona M 1951- *AmMWSc 92*
**McConnaughy**, Thomas Bowen, Jr. 1942- *WhoFI 92*
**Mcconnel**, Frances Ruhlen *DrAPF 91*
**McConnel**, George Hunt 1947- *WhoRel 92*
**McConnel**, John Ludlnum 1826-1862 *BenetAL 91*
**McConnel**, Patricia *DrAPF 91*
**McConnel**, Patricia 1931- *ConAu 133*
**McConnel**, Richard Appleton 1933- *WhoWest 92*
**McConnel**, Robert Merriman 1936- *AmMWSc 92*
**McConnell**, A Mitchell, Jr 1942- *WhoAmP 91*
**McConnell**, Albert Joseph 1903- *IntWW 91, Who 92*
**McConnell**, Barbara Wright 1936- *WhoAmP 91*
**McConnell**, Bruce 1932- *AmMWSc 92*
**McConnell**, C W 1912- *AmMWSc 92*
**McConnell**, Calvin Dale 1928- *WhoRel 92, WhoWest 92*
**McConnell**, Charles Goodloe 1943- *WhoFI 92*
**McConnell**, Charles Michael 1959- *WhoMW 92*
**McConnell**, Conrad 1952- *WhoBlA 92*
**McConnell**, Dale Alan 1952- *WhoRel 92*
**McConnell**, David Graham 1926- *AmMWSc 92*
**McConnell**, David John 1944- *IntWW 91*
**McConnell**, David Kelso 1932- *WhoAmL 92*
**McConnell**, David Moffatt 1912- *WhoAmL 92*
**McConnell**, Dennis Brooks 1938- *AmMWSc 92*
**McConnell**, Dorothy Hughes *WhoBlA 92*
**McConnell**, Dudley d1991 *NewYTBS 91*
**McConnell**, Duncan 1909- *AmMWSc 92*
**McConnell**, E. Hoy, II 1941- *WhoFI 92, WhoMW 92*
**Mc Connell**, Edward Bosworth 1920- *WhoAmL 92*
**McConnell**, Ernest Eugene 1937- *AmMWSc 92*
**McConnell**, Francis John 1871-1953 *RelLAm 91*
**McConnell**, Freeman Erton 1914- *AmMWSc 92*
**McConnell**, Gary Dwain 1948- *WhoAmL 92*
**McConnell**, Glenn Fant 1947- *WhoAmP 91*
**McConnell**, Grant 1915- *WrDr 92*
**McConnell**, H M 1924- *AmMWSc 92*
**McConnell**, Harden M. 1927- *IntWW 91*
**McConnell**, Harden Marsden 1927- *AmMWSc 92*
**McConnell**, J C d1904 *BiInAmS*
**McConnell**, Jack Baylor 1925- *AmMWSc 92*
**McConnell**, Jack Lewis 1934- *WhoAmL 92*
**McConnell**, James Desmond Caldwell 1930- *IntWW 91, Who 92*
**McConnell**, James Francis 1936- *AmMWSc 92*
**McConnell**, James Guy 1947- *WhoAmL 92*
**McConnell**, James Rogers 1887-1917 *DcNCBi 4*
**McConnell**, John 1939- *Who 92*
**McConnell**, John Charles 1945- *AmMWSc 92*
**McConnell**, John Thomas 1945- *WhoMW 92*
**McConnell**, Johnny Duff 1961- *WhoRel 92*
**McConnell**, Joseph H. *LesBEnT 92*
**McConnell**, Kenneth G 1934- *AmMWSc 92*
**McConnell**, Kenneth Paul 1911- *AmMWSc 92*
**McConnell**, Melissa 1953- *WhoEnt 92*
**McConnell**, Michael Theodore 1954- *WhoAmL 92*
**Mc Connell**, Michael W. 1955- *WhoAmL 92*
**McConnell**, Mitch 1942- *AlmAP 92 [port]*
**McConnell**, Patricia Ann 1935- *WhoMW 92*
**McConnell**, Richard *WhoAmP 91*
**McConnell**, Richard Leon 1926- *AmMWSc 92*
**McConnell**, Robert A 1914- *AmMWSc 92*
**McConnell**, Robert A 1944- *WhoAmP 91*
**McConnell**, Robert Kendall 1937- *AmMWSc 92*
**McConnell**, Robert Shean *Who 92*
**McConnell**, Robert William Brian 1922- *Who 92*
**McConnell**, Roland C. 1910- *WhoBlA 92*
**McConnell**, Samuel Winfield, Jr 1940- *WhoAmP 91*
**McConnell**, Scott Rushton 1955- *WhoMW 92*
**McConnell**, Stewart 1923- *AmMWSc 92*
**McConnell**, Suzanne *DrAPF 91*
**McConnell**, Viola Carlberg 1903- *WhoMW 92*
**McConnell**, Wilbur Ross 1881-1920 *BiInAmS*
**McConnell**, Will *IntAu&W 91X*
**McConnell**, William Ray 1943- *AmMWSc 92*
**McConnell**, William Thomas, III 1946- *WhoRel 92*
**McConnell Barrett**, Barbara 1950- *WhoAmP 91*
**McConner**, Dorothy 1929- *WhoBlA 92*
**McConner**, Ora B. 1929- *WhoMW 92*
**McConner**, Stanley Jay, Sr. 1929- *WhoMW 92*
**McConnon**, James Charles 1926- *WhoAmP 91*
**McConomy**, James Herbert 1937- *WhoAmL 92*
**McConoughey**, Samuel R 1924- *AmMWSc 92*
**McConville**, Brian John 1933- *AmMWSc 92*
**McConville**, David Raymond 1946- *AmMWSc 92*
**McConville**, George T 1934- *AmMWSc 92*
**McConville**, John Frank 1936- *WhoWest 92*
**McConville**, John Theodore 1927- *AmMWSc 92*
**McConville**, Michael Anthony 1925- *Who 92*
**Mc Conville**, Sean Daniel Michael 1943- *WhoMW 92*
**McCoo**, Marilyn *WhoBlA 92*
**McCooe**, Terry Alan 1950- *WhoMW 92*
**McCook**, George Patrick 1937- *AmMWSc 92*
**McCook**, Henry Christopher 1837-1911 *BiInAmS*
**McCook**, Kathleen de la Pena *WhoHisp 92*
**McCook**, Robert Devon 1929- *AmMWSc 92*
**McCool**, D K 1937- *AmMWSc 92*
**McCool**, John Macalpine 1930- *AmMWSc 92*
**McCool**, Naomi Ellen 1922- *WhoAmP 91*
**McCool**, Richard Bunch 1925- *WhoFI 92, WhoMW 92*
**McCorcle**, Marcus Duane 1951- *WhoMW 92*
**McCord**, Anne 1942- *IntAu&W 91*
**McCord**, Colin Wallace 1928- *AmMWSc 92*
**McCord**, David 1897- *BenetAL 91, IntAu&W 91*
**McCord**, Howard *DrAPF 91*
**McCord**, Howard Lawrence 1932- *WhoMW 92*
**McCord**, James Neil 1946- *WhoAmL 92*
**McCord**, Joe M 1945- *AmMWSc 92*
**McCord**, Joe Milton 1945- *AmMWSc 92*
**Mc Cord**, John Harrison 1934- *WhoAmL 92*
**McCord**, Kent 1942- *WhoEnt 92*
**McCord**, Mervyn Noel Samuel 1929- *Who 92*
**McCord**, Michael Campbell 1936- *AmMWSc 92*
**McCord**, Thomas Bard 1939- *AmMWSc 92*
**McCord**, Thomas J. 1957- *WhoAmL 92*
**McCord**, Tommy Joe 1932- *AmMWSc 92*
**McCord**, Vincent Abbott, Jr. 1946- *WhoWest 92*
**McCord**, Whip *IntAu&W 91X, TwCWW 91*
**McCord**, William Charles 1928- *WhoFI 92*
**McCord**, William Mellen 1907- *AmMWSc 92*
**McCorduck**, Pamela 1940- *ConAu 36NR*
**McCorkell**, Don 1947- *WhoAmP 91*
**McCorkell**, Michael William 1925- *Who 92*
**McCorkindale**, Barry Clarke 1958- *WhoEnt 92*
**McCorkindale**, Douglas Hamilton 1939- *WhoFI 92*
**McCorkindale**, Laura Ann 1966- *WhoEnt 92*
**McCorkle**, Eddie Dale 1963- *WhoRel 92*
**McCorkle**, George Maston 1921- *AmMWSc 92*
**McCorkle**, Jill 1958- *WrDr 92*
**McCorkle**, Lutie Andrews *DcNCBi 4*
**McCorkle**, Richard Anthony 1940- *AmMWSc 92*
**McCorkle**, Robert Ellsworth 1938- *WhoWest 92*
**McCorkle**, Ruth *AmMWSc 92*
**McCorkle**, Samuel Eusebius 1746-1811 *DcNCBi 4*
**McCorkle**, Sarah Tallulah Andrews 1858-1939 *DcNCBi 4*
**McCorkle**, Sherman *WhoWest 92*
**McCorkle**, William Parsons 1855-1933 *DcNCBi 4*
**McCormac**, Billy Murray 1920- *AmMWSc 92*
**McCormac**, Jack Clark 1927- *AmMWSc 92*
**McCormac**, Mary Christine 1962- *WhoAmL 92*
**Mc Cormac**, Weston Arthur 1911- *WhoWest 92*
**McCormack**, Arthur Gerard 1911- *Who 92*
**McCormack**, Charles Elwin 1938- *AmMWSc 92*
**McCormack**, Curt 1952- *WhoAmP 91*
**McCormack**, Dennis K. *WhoWest 92*
**McCormack**, Donald Eugene 1930- *AmMWSc 92*
**McCormack**, Edward G. 1948- *WhoBlA 92*
**McCormack**, Edward Joseph, Jr. 1923- *WhoAmL 92*
**McCormack**, Elizabeth Frances 1960- *AmMWSc 92*
**McCormack**, Francis Joseph 1938- *AmMWSc 92*
**Mc Cormack**, Francis Xavier 1929- *WhoAmL 92, WhoFI 92*
**McCormack**, Gavan 1937- *WrDr 92*
**McCormack**, Grace 1908- *AmMWSc 92*
**McCormack**, Harold Robert 1922- *AmMWSc 92*
**McCormack**, James Patrick 1960- *WhoAmL 92*
**McCormack**, John 1884-1943 *FacFETw [port]*
**McCormack**, John 1884-1945 *NewAmDM*
**McCormack**, John 1921- *Who 92*
**McCormack**, John J, Jr 1944- *WhoIns 92*
**McCormack**, John Joseph, Jr 1938- *AmMWSc 92*
**McCormack**, John Joseph, Jr. 1944- *WhoFI 92*
**McCormack**, John P. 1923- *Who 92*
**McCormack**, John W 1891-1980 *FacFETw*
**McCormack**, John William 1891-1980 *AmPolLe*
**McCormack**, Joseph Andrew 1944- *WhoWest 92*
**McCormack**, Mark *LesBEnT 92*
**McCormack**, Mark H 1930- *WrDr 92*
**McCormack**, Mark Hume 1930- *IntWW 91, Who 92*
**McCormack**, Mike 1921- *AmMWSc 92, WhoAmP 91*
**McCormack**, Norman Albert 1951- *WhoMW 92*
**McCormack**, Richard J 1947- *WhoAmP 91*
**McCormack**, Richard Thomas Fox 1941- *WhoAmP 91, WhoFI 92*
**McCormack**, Robert Cornelius 1939- *WhoFI 92*
**McCormack**, Robert Joseph, Jr. 1957- *WhoAmL 92*
**McCormack**, Stanley Eugene 1949- *WhoFI 92*
**McCormack**, William Brewster 1923- *AmMWSc 92*
**McCormick**, Adele von Rust 1929- *WhoWest 92*
**McCormick**, Anna M 1949- *AmMWSc 92*
**McCormick**, Bailie Jack 1937- *AmMWSc 92, WhoMW 92*
**McCormick**, Barnes W, Jr 1926- *AmMWSc 92*
**McCormick**, Betty Jean 1950- *WhoEnt 92*
**McCormick**, Carroll Charles 1933- *WhoWest 92*
**McCormick**, Clyde Truman 1908- *AmMWSc 92*
**McCormick**, Curtiss Dean 1938- *WhoRel 92*
**McCormick**, Cyrus 1809-1884 *RComAH*
**McCormick**, Dale 1947- *WhoAmP 91*
**McCormick**, David Arthur 1946- *WhoAmL 92*
**McCormick**, David Herman 1954- *WhoAmL 92*
**McCormick**, David Loyd 1953- *AmMWSc 92*
**McCormick**, Donald 1911- *WrDr 92*
**McCormick**, Donald Bruce 1932- *AmMWSc 92*
**McCormick**, Donald E. 1941- *WhoEnt 92*
**McCormick**, Donald F. 1931- *WhoFI 92*
**McCormick**, Douglas Walter 1949- *WhoEnt 92*
**McCormick**, Edward Harrington 1935- *WhoAmP 91*
**McCormick**, Edward T. 1911-1991 *CurBio 91N*
**McCormick**, Eric Hall 1906- *WrDr 92*
**McCormick**, Floyd Guy, Jr. 1927- *WhoWest 92*
**McCormick**, Frank Andrew 1913-1982 *FacFETw*
**McCormick**, Fred C 1926- *AmMWSc 92*
**McCormick**, Frederick Bossert, Jr. 1959- *WhoMW 92*
**McCormick**, George R 1936- *AmMWSc 92*
**McCormick**, Geraldine *WhoAmP 91*
**McCormick**, Ginger G. 1962- *WhoRel 92*
**McCormick**, Harold L 1918- *WhoAmP 91*
**McCormick**, Hugh Thomas 1944- *WhoAmL 92*
**McCormick**, J Frank 1935- *AmMWSc 92*
**McCormick**, J Justin 1933- *AmMWSc 92*
**McCormick**, J. Luke 1949- *WhoMW 92*
**McCormick**, J Robert D 1921- *AmMWSc 92*
**McCormick**, James *DrAPF 91*
**McCormick**, James Clarence 1924- *WhoFI 92*
**McCormick**, James Edward 1927- *WhoFI 92*
**McCormick**, James Stevenson 1926- *Who 92*
**McCormick**, John 1944- *Who 92*
**McCormick**, John E 1923- *AmMWSc 92*
**McCormick**, John Francis 1933- *WhoFI 92*
**McCormick**, John O. 1918- *WrDr 92*
**McCormick**, John Ormsby 1916- *Who 92*
**McCormick**, John Owen 1918- *IntAu&W 91*
**McCormick**, John Pauling 1943- *AmMWSc 92, WhoMW 92*
**McCormick**, John S, Jr *WhoAmP 91*
**McCormick**, Jon Michael 1941- *AmMWSc 92*
**McCormick**, Judith Ann 1957- *WhoAmL 92*
**McCormick**, Kathleen Ann 1947- *AmMWSc 92*

**McCormick,** Kenneth James 1937- *AmMWSc 92*
**McCormick,** Larry David 1950- *WhoRel 92*
**McCormick,** Larry William 1933- *WhoBlA 92*
**McCormick,** Leander James 1819-1900 *BiInAmS*
**McCormick,** Lloyd J 1917- *WhoAmP 91*
**McCormick,** Loyd Weldon 1928- *WhoAmL 92*
**McCormick,** Michael Edward 1936- *AmMWSc 92*
**McCormick,** Michael Patrick 1940- *AmMWSc 92*
**McCormick,** Michael Scott 1966- *WhoMW 92*
**McCormick,** Michael Thomas 1962- *WhoAmL 92*
**McCormick,** Nancy Louise *WhoWest 92*
**McCormick,** Neil Glenn 1927- *AmMWSc 92*
**McCormick,** Norman Joseph 1938- *AmMWSc 92*
**McCormick,** Pamela Ann 1948- *WhoEnt 92*
**McCormick,** Patricia *EncAmaz 91*
**McCormick,** Paul R 1925- *AmMWSc 92*
**McCormick,** Paulette Jean 1951- *AmMWSc 92*
**McCormick,** Philip Thomas 1926- *AmMWSc 92*
**McCormick,** Richard Arthur 1922- *WhoRel 92*
**McCormick,** Richard David 1940- *WhoFI 92, WhoWest 92*
**McCormick,** Robert H 1914- *AmMWSc 92*
**McCormick,** Robert T 1951- *AmMWSc 92*
**McCormick,** Roy L 1929- *AmMWSc 92*
**McCormick,** Sharon Smith 1943- *WhoWest 92*
**McCormick,** Stephen Daniel 1955- *AmMWSc 92*
**McCormick,** Stephen Fahrney 1944- *AmMWSc 92*
**McCormick,** Steven Thomas 1955- *WhoFI 92*
**McCormick,** Timothy Brian Beer 1959- *WhoAmL 92*
**McCormick,** Tom 1923- *WhoAmP 91*
**McCormick,** William Charles 1933- *WhoWest 92*
**McCormick,** William Devlin 1931- *AmMWSc 92*
**McCormick,** William Edward 1912- *WhoFI 92, WhoMW 92*
**McCormick,** William F 1933- *AmMWSc 92*
**McCormick,** William Thomas, Jr. 1944- *WhoMW 92*
**McCormick,** Zachary Lorne 1952- *WhoWest 92*
**McCormick-Ray,** M Geraldine 1943- *AmMWSc 92*
**McCorquodale,** Barbara *ConAu 34NR, Who 92*
**McCorquodale,** Dan 1934- *WhoAmP 91*
**McCorquodale,** Dan A. 1934- *WhoWest 92*
**McCorquodale,** Donald James 1927- *AmMWSc 92*
**McCorquodale,** John Alexander 1938- *AmMWSc 92*
**McCorquodale,** Joseph Charles, Jr 1920- *WhoAmP 91*
**McCorriston,** James Roland 1919- *AmMWSc 92*
**McCorvey,** Antoinette Jenese Pete 1957- *WhoMW 92*
**McCosh,** Earl Curtis 1933- *WhoRel 92*
**McCosh,** James 1811-1894 *BenetAL 91*
**McCosker,** John E 1945- *AmMWSc 92*
**McCosker,** John Edward 1945- *WhoWest 92*
**McCotter,** Burney R 1920- *WhoIns 92*
**McCotter,** James Rawson 1943- *WhoAmL 92, WhoWest 92*
**McCoubrey,** Arthur Orlando 1920- *AmMWSc 92*
**McCouch,** Donald Grayson 1942- *WhoFI 92*
**McCoun,** Richard Allen 1941- *WhoWest 92*
**McCourt,** A W 1924- *AmMWSc 92*
**McCourt,** Frederick Richard Wayne 1940- *AmMWSc 92*
**McCourt,** James *DrAPF 91*
**McCourt,** James 1941- *WrDr 92*
**McCourt,** James P 1924- *WhoAmP 91*
**McCourt,** Robert Perry 1929- *AmMWSc 92*
**McCourt,** Robert Reilly 1935- *WhoRel 92*
**McCovey,** Willie 1938- *FacFETw*
**McCovey,** Willie Lee 1938- *WhoBlA 92*
**McCowan,** Anthony 1928- *Who 92*
**McCowan,** Archibald *ScFEYrs*
**McCowan,** Hew Cargill 1930- *Who 92*
**McCowan,** James Robert 1923- *AmMWSc 92*
**McCowan,** Otis Blakely 1934- *AmMWSc 92*
**McCowen,** Alec 1925- *IntMPA 92, IntWW 91, Who 92*
**McCowen,** Max Creager 1915- *AmMWSc 92*
**McCowen,** Sara Moss 1944- *AmMWSc 92*
**McCown,** Brent Howard 1943- *AmMWSc 92*
**McCown,** David Henry 1933- *WhoAmP 91*
**McCown,** John Daly 1954- *WhoFI 92*
**McCown,** John Joseph 1929- *AmMWSc 92*
**McCown,** Joseph Dana 1940- *AmMWSc 92*
**McCown,** Lowrie Bruce 1952- *WhoRel 92*
**McCown,** Malcolm G 1919- *AmMWSc 92*
**McCown,** Robert Bruce 1939- *AmMWSc 92*
**McCown,** Wayne Gordon 1942- *WhoRel 92*
**McCoy,** Barbara S. 1950- *WhoFI 92*
**McCoy,** Barry 1940- *AmMWSc 92*
**McCoy,** Barry Malcolm 1940- *WhoAmP 91*
**McCoy,** Ben Wade, Jr. 1952- *WhoFI 92*
**McCoy,** Benjamin J 1941- *AmMWSc 92*
**McCoy,** Bertie Elizabeth 1922- *WhoRel 92*
**McCoy,** Bob Parsons *WhoEnt 92*
**McCoy,** Brent Alan 1961- *WhoEnt 92*
**McCoy,** Brian Lloyd 1946- *WhoAmL 92*
**McCoy,** Carol Todman 1947- *WhoBlA 92*
**McCoy,** Carroll Pierce 1920- *WhoRel 92*
**McCoy,** Charles Ralph 1927- *AmMWSc 92*
**McCoy,** Charles Sherwood 1923- *IntAu&W 91*
**McCoy,** Charles Wallace 1920- *WhoFI 92*
**McCoy,** Charles Walter 1945- *WhoMW 92*
**McCoy,** Clarence John, Jr 1935- *AmMWSc 92*
**McCoy,** Clayton William 1938- *AmMWSc 92*
**McCoy,** David Ross 1942- *AmMWSc 92*
**McCoy,** Dennis Charles 1942- *WhoAmP 91*
**McCoy,** Dorothy 1903- *AmMWSc 92*
**McCoy,** Earl Donald 1948- *AmMWSc 92*
**McCoy,** Elaine Jean 1946- *WhoWest 92*
**McCoy,** Ernest E 1923- *AmMWSc 92*
**McCoy,** Eugene Lynn 1926- *WhoWest 92*
**McCoy,** Floyd W, Jr 1936- *AmMWSc 92*
**McCoy,** Frank Milton *WhoBlA 92*
**McCoy,** Frederick Douglass, Jr. 1936- *WhoBlA 92*
**McCoy,** George H. 1930- *WhoBlA 92*
**McCoy,** Gerald Edward 1944- *WhoWest 92*
**McCoy,** Gladys 1928- *WhoAmP 91, WhoBlA 92*
**McCoy,** Glenn Wesley 1933- *WhoRel 92*
**McCoy,** Hank *IntAu&W 91X*
**McCoy,** Horace 1897-1955 *BenetAL 91*
**McCoy,** Howard Bruce 1956- *WhoRel 92*
**McCoy,** Jack 1940- *WhoAmP 91*
**McCoy,** James Ernest 1941- *AmMWSc 92*
**McCoy,** James F. 1925- *WhoBlA 92*
**McCoy,** James Nelson 1955- *WhoBlA 92*
**McCoy,** Janet Yvonne 1939- *WhoWest 92*
**McCoy,** Jerry Dan 1941- *WhoRel 92*
**McCoy,** Jerry Jack 1941- *WhoAmL 92*
**McCoy,** Jessie Haynes 1955- *WhoBlA 92*
**McCoy,** Jim Wayne 1931- *WhoMW 92*
**McCoy,** Jimmy Jewell 1943- *AmMWSc 92*
**McCoy,** Joe Aaron 1927- *WhoRel 92*
**McCoy,** Joenne Rae 1941- *WhoMW 92*
**Mc Coy,** John Bonnet 1943- *WhoFI 92, WhoMW 92*
**McCoy,** John Harold 1935- *AmMWSc 92*
**McCoy,** John J 1936- *AmMWSc 92*
**McCoy,** John Philip, Jr *AmMWSc 92*
**McCoy,** John Roger 1916- *AmMWSc 92*
**McCoy,** Joseph Clifton 1930- *WhoBlA 92*
**McCoy,** Joseph Hamilton 1934- *AmMWSc 92*
**McCoy,** Judith Anne 1943- *WhoMW 92*
**McCoy,** Katherine Braden 1945- *WhoEnt 92*
**McCoy,** Layton Leslie 1927- *AmMWSc 92*
**McCoy,** Leamon M. *WhoBlA 92*
**Mc Coy,** Lee Berard 1925- *WhoFI 92*
**Mc Coy,** Lois Clark 1920- *WhoWest 92*
**McCoy,** Lowell Eugene 1937- *AmMWSc 92*
**McCoy,** Marshall *TwCWW 91*
**McCoy,** Mary Eleanora 1846-1923 *NotBlAW 92*
**McCoy,** Mich *TwCWW 91*
**McCoy,** Michael Dale 1944- *WhoEnt 92*
**McCoy,** Michael Franklin 1953- *WhoAmL 92*
**McCoy,** Michael Ryan 1950- *WhoRel 92*
**McCoy,** Millie-Christine 1851-1912 *DcNCBi 4*
**McCoy,** Millington F. 1941- *WhoFI 92*
**McCoy,** Neal S. 1940- *WhoAmL 92*
**McCoy,** Ralph E. 1915- *WrDr 92*
**McCoy,** Ralph Hines 1940- *AmMWSc 92*
**McCoy,** Rawley D 1914- *AmMWSc 92*
**McCoy,** Reagan Scott 1945- *WhoAmL 92*
**McCoy,** Robert *WhoAmP 91*
**McCoy,** Robert A 1942- *AmMWSc 92*
**McCoy,** Robert Allyn 1939- *AmMWSc 92*
**McCoy,** Roger Michael 1933- *AmMWSc 92*
**McCoy,** Scott, Jr 1939- *AmMWSc 92*
**McCoy,** Steven Wayne 1953- *WhoRel 92*
**McCoy,** Sue 1935- *AmMWSc 92*
**McCoy,** Susan Douglas 1944- *WhoWest 92*
**McCoy,** Thomas Joseph 1950- *AmMWSc 92*
**McCoy,** Thomas LaRue 1933- *AmMWSc 92*
**McCoy,** Thomas Raymond 1943- *WhoAmL 92*
**McCoy,** Tidal Windham 1945- *WhoAmP 91*
**McCoy,** Tun-Hsu 1944- *WhoAmP 91*
**McCoy,** V Eugene, Jr 1933- *AmMWSc 92*
**McCoy,** Viola 1900?-1956? *NotBlAW 92*
**McCoy,** Walter D. 1930- *WhoBlA 92*
**McCoy,** Wayne A. 1941- *WhoAmL 92*
**McCoy,** Wayne Anthony 1941- *WhoBlA 92*
**McCoy,** Wesley Lawrence 1935- *WhoEnt 92*
**McCoy,** William *WhoBlA 92*
**McCoy,** William, Jr 1921- *WhoAmP 91*
**McCoy,** William Charles, Jr. 1923- *WhoAmL 92*
**McCoy,** William J 1942- *WhoAmP 91*
**McCrabb,** Donald R. *WhoRel 92*
**McCracken,** Alexander Walker 1931- *AmMWSc 92*
**McCracken,** Derek Albert 1943- *AmMWSc 92*
**McCracken,** Francis Irvin 1935- *AmMWSc 92*
**McCracken,** Frank D. 1949- *WhoBlA 92*
**McCracken,** James 1926-1988 *FacFETw, NewAmDM*
**McCracken,** Jeffrey Adam *WhoEnt 92*
**McCracken,** Joe 1951- *WhoAmP 91*
**McCracken,** John Aitken 1934- *AmMWSc 92*
**McCracken,** John David 1939- *AmMWSc 92, WhoMW 92*
**McCracken,** Leslie G, Jr 1925- *AmMWSc 92*
**McCracken,** Michael Dwayne 1941- *AmMWSc 92*
**McCracken,** Mike 1943- *WhoAmP 91*
**McCracken,** Paul Winston 1915- *IntWW 91, WhoAmP 91, WhoMW 92*
**McCracken,** Philip Glen 1928- *AmMWSc 92*
**Mc Cracken,** Philip Trafton 1928- *WhoWest 92*
**McCracken,** Ralph Joseph 1921- *AmMWSc 92*
**McCracken,** Richard Owen 1939- *AmMWSc 92*
**McCracken,** Robert Eugene, Sr. 1930- *WhoMW 92*
**McCracken,** Robert James 1904-1973 *RelLAm 91*
**McCracken,** Shirley Ann Ross 1937- *WhoRel 92, WhoWest 92*
**McCracken,** Steven Carl 1950- *WhoAmL 92*
**McCracken,** Thomas James, Jr 1952- *WhoAmP 91*
**McCracken,** Thomas Osmer 1945- *WhoWest 92*
**McCracken,** Walter John 1953- *AmMWSc 92*
**McCrackin,** Bobbie Humenny 1944- *WhoFI 92*
**McCrackin,** Olympia F. 1950- *WhoBlA 92*
**McCrackin,** William K. 1933- *WhoFI 92*
**McCrady,** Edward, III 1933- *AmMWSc 92*
**McCrady,** Howard C. 1931- *WhoFI 92, WhoWest 92*
**McCrady,** James David 1930- *AmMWSc 92*
**McCrady,** John 1831-1881 *BiInAmS*
**McCrady,** William B 1933- *AmMWSc 92*
**McCrae,** Alister Geddes 1909- *Who 92*
**McCrae,** David Anthony 1950- *WhoMW 92*
**McCrae,** John 1872-1918 *BenetAL 91*
**McCrae,** John Leonidas 1917- *AmMWSc 92*
**McCrae,** William 1934- *WhoIns 92*
**McCraith,** Patrick James Danvers 1916- *Who 92*
**McCranie,** Erasmus James 1915- *AmMWSc 92*
**McCrary,** Anne Bowden 1926- *AmMWSc 92*
**McCrary,** Doctor Bulla 1875-1946 *DcNCBi 4*
**McCrary,** Giles Connell 1919- *WhoAmP 91*
**McCrary,** Thomas *WhoAmP 91*
**McCrary-Simmons,** Shirley Denise 1956- *WhoBlA 92*
**McCraven,** Carl Clarke 1926- *WhoBlA 92, WhoWest 92*
**McCraven,** Eva Stewart Mapes 1936- *WhoWest 92*
**McCraven,** Gladys L 1923- *WhoAmP 91*
**McCraven,** Marcus R. 1923- *WhoBlA 92*
**McCraw,** E Dewitt *WhoAmP 91*
**McCraw,** James Alvin 1929- *WhoRel 92*
**McCraw,** John Randolph, Jr 1942- *WhoAmP 91*
**McCraw,** Leslie Gladstone 1934- *WhoFI 92, WhoWest 92*
**McCraw,** Thomas K 1940- *IntAu&W 91, WrDr 92*
**McCraw,** Tom 1940- *WhoBlA 92*
**McCray,** Arthur Howard 1880-1919 *BiInAmS*
**McCray,** Billy Quincy 1927- *WhoAmP 91*
**McCray,** Billy Quincy 1929- *WhoBlA 92*
**McCray,** Christopher Columbus 1925- *WhoBlA 92*
**McCray,** Curtis Lee 1938- *WhoWest 92*
**McCray,** Joe Richard 1928- *WhoBlA 92*
**McCray,** Maceo E. 1935- *WhoBlA 92*
**McCray,** Melvin 1946- *WhoBlA 92*
**McCray,** Richard A 1937- *AmMWSc 92*
**McCray,** Rodney Earl 1961- *WhoBlA 92*
**McCray,** Ronald David 1957- *WhoFI 92*
**McCray,** Roy Howard 1946- *WhoBlA 92*
**McCray,** Thomas L. 1928- *WhoBlA 92*
**McCray,** William Joel *WhoBlA 92*
**McCrea,** Jane 1752?-1777 *BlkwEAR*
**McCrea,** Joel 1905-1990 *AnObit 1990, FacFETw, News 91*
**McCrea,** Kenneth Duncan 1953- *AmMWSc 92*
**McCrea,** Robert Thomas William 1948- *Who 92*
**McCrea,** Stephen Brian 1949- *WhoWest 92*
**McCrea,** William 1904- *Who 92, WrDr 92*
**McCrea,** William Hunter 1904- *IntWW 91*
**McCready,** Jack *IntAu&W 91X, WrDr 92*
**McCready,** Kenneth Frank 1939- *WhoFI 92, WhoWest 92*
**McCready,** Ronald Glen Lang 1939- *AmMWSc 92*
**McCready,** Thomas Arthur 1940- *AmMWSc 92*
**McCreary,** Bill 1933- *WhoBlA 92*
**McCreary,** David Neal 1945- *WhoRel 92*
**McCreary,** Frank E., III 1943- *WhoAmL 92*
**McCreary,** Paul Robert 1947- *WhoMW 92*
**McCredie,** Andrew Dalgarno 1930- *IntWW 91*
**McCredie,** John A 1923- *AmMWSc 92*
**McCredie,** Kenneth Blair 1935- *AmMWSc 92*
**McCree,** Donald Hanna, Jr. 1936- *WhoFI 92*
**McCree,** Edward L. 1942- *WhoBlA 92*
**McCree,** Floyd J. 1923-1988 *WhoBlA 92N*
**McCree,** Samuel W. *WhoBlA 92*
**McCreery,** Charles Anthony Selby 1942- *WrDr 92*
**McCreery,** Glenn Ernest 1943- *WhoWest 92*
**McCreery,** Lewis 1920- *Who 92*
**McCreery,** Richard Louis 1948- *AmMWSc 92*
**McCreery,** William 1931- *WhoEnt 92*
**McCreesh,** Donald S. *WhoRel 92*
**McCreight,** Charles Edward 1913- *AmMWSc 92*
**McCreight,** Edward M *AmMWSc 92*
**McCreight,** Louis R 1922- *AmMWSc 92*
**McCreless,** Thomas Griswold 1927- *AmMWSc 92, WhoWest 92*
**McCrery,** Jim 1949- *AlmAP 92 [port], WhoAmP 91*
**McCrickard,** Donald Cecil 1936- *Who 92*
**McCrimmon,** Donald Alan, Jr 1944- *AmMWSc 92*
**McCrimon,** Audrey L. 1954- *WhoBlA 92*
**McCrindle,** Robert 1929- *Who 92*
**McCrirrick,** Bryce 1927- *Who 92*
**McCrone,** Alistair William 1931- *AmMWSc 92*
**McCrone,** John David 1934- *AmMWSc 92*
**McCrone,** Robert Gavin Loudon 1933- *Who 92*
**McCrone,** Walter C 1916- *AmMWSc 92*
**McCroom,** Eddie Winther 1932- *WhoBlA 92*
**McCrorey,** H. Lawrence 1927- *WhoBlA 92*
**McCrorey,** Henry Lawrence 1927- *AmMWSc 92*
**McCrorie,** Edward *DrAPF 91*
**McCrorie,** Linda Esther *Who 92*
**McCrory,** E Cecil, Jr 1951- *WhoAmP 91*
**McCrory,** Martha *WhoEnt 92*
**McCrory,** Moy 1953- *WrDr 92*
**McCrory,** Robert Lee, Jr 1946- *AmMWSc 92*
**McCrory,** Sarah Graydon 1921- *WhoRel 92*
**McCrory,** Steve 1964- *BlkOlyM*

**McCrory**, Wallace Willard 1920- *AmMWSc 92*
**McCroskey**, James Allen 1949- *WhoAmP 91*
**McCroskey**, Robert Lee 1924- *AmMWSc 92*
**McCrosky**, Richard Eugene 1924- *AmMWSc 92*
**McCrossan**, Mary 1864?-1934 *TwCPaSc*
**McCrosson**, F Joseph 1940- *AmMWSc 92*
**McCrum**, Michael William 1924- *IntWW 91, Who 92*
**McCrumb**, Sharyn *DrAPF 91*
**McCrumm**, J D 1912- *AmMWSc 92*
**McCuaig**, Malcolm Adams 1936- *WhoRel 92*
**McCuan**, William Patrick 1941- *WhoFI 92*
**McCubbin**, Carrol J 1920- *WhoAmP 91*
**McCubbin**, David 1929- *Who 92*
**McCubbin**, Donald Gene 1930- *AmMWSc 92*
**McCubbin**, Henry Bell 1942- *Who 92*
**McCubbin**, Horace W *WhoIns 92*
**McCubbin**, Margaret Ann 1952- *WhoEnt 92*
**McCubbin**, Susan Brubeck 1948- *WhoWest 92*
**McCubbin**, Thomas King, Jr 1925- *AmMWSc 92*
**McCubbrey**, James Bruce 1936- *WhoAmL 92*
**McCue**, Carolyn M 1916- *AmMWSc 92*
**McCue**, Dennis Michael 1952- *WhoFI 92*
**McCue**, Donna Caprari *WhoEnt 92*
**McCue**, Edmund Bradley 1929- *AmMWSc 92*
**McCue**, Edward Patrick *DrAPF 91*
**McCue**, Howard McDowell, III 1946- *WhoAmL 92*
**McCue**, John Francis 1933- *AmMWSc 92*
**McCue**, Lillian Bueno *WrDr 92*
**McCue**, Lisa 1959- *SmATA 65*
**McCue**, Martin Thomas 1951- *WhoAmL 92*
**McCue**, Robert Owen 1947- *AmMWSc 92*
**McCue**, Steven J 1957- *WhoAmP 91*
**McCuen**, Jay Ross 1952- *WhoEnt 92*
**McCuen**, John Francis, Jr. 1944- *WhoAmL 92*
**McCuen**, John Joachim 1926- *WhoFI 92, WhoMW 92*
**McCuen**, R. David 1953- *WhoRel 92*
**McCuen**, Robert William 1940- *AmMWSc 92*
**McCuen**, W J 1943- *WhoAmP 91*
**McCuistion**, Robert Wiley 1927- *WhoRel 92*
**McCuistion**, Willis Lloyd 1937- *AmMWSc 92*
**McCuiston**, Frederick Douglass, Jr. 1940- *WhoBlA 92*
**McCuiston**, Lloyd Carlisle, Jr 1918- *WhoAmP 91*
**McCuiston**, Pat M 1917- *WhoAmP 91*
**McCuiston**, Stonewall, Jr. 1959- *WhoBlA 92*
**McCulla**, William Harvey 1941- *AmMWSc 92*
**McCullagh**, Grant Gibson 1951- *WhoFI 92, WhoMW 92*
**McCullagh**, Sheila K. 1920- *WrDr 92*
**McCullagh**, Sheila Kathleen 1920- *IntAu&W 91*
**McCullen**, Allie Ray 1944- *WhoAmP 91*
**McCullen**, John Douglas 1932- *AmMWSc 92*
**McCullen**, Joseph Thomas, Jr 1935- *WhoAmP 91*
**McCuller**, James 1940- *WhoBlA 92*
**McCullers**, Carson 1917-1967 *BenetAL 91, FacFETw [port], HanAmWH, ModAWWr, ShSCr 9 [port]*
**McCullers**, Eugene 1941- *WhoBlA 92*
**McCulley**, Johnston 1883-1958 *BenetAL 91, ScFEYrs, TwCWW 91*
**McCulley**, Michael Wilson 1953- *WhoEnt 92*
**McCullin**, Donald 1935- *IntWW 91, Who 92*
**McCulloch**, Alan McLeod 1907- *IntAu&W 91*
**McCulloch**, Alexander d1798 *DcNCBi 4*
**McCulloch**, Archibald Wilson 1940- *AmMWSc 92*
**McCulloch**, Ernest Armstrong 1926- *AmMWSc 92*
**McCulloch**, Frank W 1905- *WhoAmP 91*
**McCulloch**, Frank Walter, Jr. 1920- *WhoWest 92*
**McCulloch**, Frank Waugh 1905- *IntWW 91*
**McCulloch**, Henry d1755 *DcNCBi 4*
**McCulloch**, James Huston 1945- *WhoFI 92*
**McCulloch**, John Cameron 1942- *WhoAmP 91*
**McCulloch**, John Vincent 1927- *WhoIns 92*
**McCulloch**, Joseph 1908-1990 *AnObit 1990*
**McCulloch**, Joseph Flavius 1856-1934 *DcNCBi 4*
**McCulloch**, Joseph Howard 1946- *AmMWSc 92*
**McCulloch**, Joseph Matthew, Jr. 1952- *WhoAmL 92*
**McCulloch**, Nigel Simeon *Who 92*
**McCulloch**, Rachel 1942- *WhoFI 92*
**McCulloch**, Robert Winslow 1910- *WhoAmP 91*
**McCulloch**, Scott T 1958- *WhoAmP 91*
**McCulloch**, Thomas 1776-1843 *BenetAL 91*
**McCulloch**, William Henry 1941- *WhoWest 92*
**McCulloh**, Gerald William 1941- *WhoRel 92*
**McCulloh**, Henry 1700?-1779 *DcNCBi 4*
**McCulloh**, Henry Eustace 1737?-1810? *DcNCBi 4*
**McCulloh**, Richard Sears 1818-1894 *BiInAmS*
**McCulloh**, Thane H 1926- *AmMWSc 92*
**McCullough**, Benjamin Franklin 1934- *AmMWSc 92*
**McCullough**, C Bruce 1944- *AmMWSc 92*
**McCullough**, Charles *Who 92*
**McCullough**, Charles Franklin 1952- *WhoRel 92*
**McCullough**, Colleen 1937- *IntWW 91, WrDr 92*
**McCullough**, D. Patrick 1944- *WhoAmL 92*
**McCullough**, Dale Richard 1933- *AmMWSc 92*
**McCullough**, Darryl J 1951- *AmMWSc 92*
**McCullough**, David James 1962- *WhoRel 92*
**McCullough**, Donald Wayne 1949- *WhoRel 92*
**McCullough**, Dorothy 1934- *WhoEnt 92*
**McCullough**, Edgar Joseph, Jr 1931- *AmMWSc 92*
**McCullough**, Edwin Charles 1942- *AmMWSc 92*
**McCullough**, Elizabeth Ann 1952- *AmMWSc 92*
**McCullough**, Frances Louise 1941- *WhoBlA 92*
**McCullough**, Frank V 1920- *WhoIns 92*
**McCullough**, Frank Witcher, III 1945- *WhoAmL 92*
**McCullough**, Frederick Douglas 1897- *WhoBlA 92*
**McCullough**, Geraldine 1922- *WhoBlA 92*
**McCullough**, Henry Glenn Luther 1939- *WhoMW 92*
**McCullough**, Herbert Alfred 1914- *AmMWSc 92*
**McCullough**, Iain Charles 1931- *Who 92*
**McCullough**, Jack Dennis 1931- *AmMWSc 92*
**McCullough**, James Douglas, Jr 1938- *AmMWSc 92*
**McCullough**, James Howard 1955- *WhoAmP 91*
**McCullough**, James Richey 1949- *WhoAmP 91*
**McCullough**, Jefferson Walker 1944- *WhoFI 92*
**McCullough**, John A 1932- *WhoAmP 91*
**McCullough**, John James 1937- *AmMWSc 92*
**McCullough**, John Jeffrey 1938- *AmMWSc 92*
**McCullough**, John Martin 1940- *AmMWSc 92*
**McCullough**, John Price 1925- *AmMWSc 92*
**McCullough**, Julie Michelle 1965- *WhoEnt 92*
**McCullough**, Ken *DrAPF 91*
**McCullough**, Kim Ileen 1954- *WhoAmL 92*
**McCullough**, Leland Graves, III 1954- *WhoRel 92*
**McCullough**, Marshall Edward 1924- *AmMWSc 92*
**McCullough**, Michael William, Jr. 1950- *WhoRel 92*
**McCullough**, Murray Lester 1943- *WhoRel 92*
**McCullough**, R. Michael 1938- *WhoFI 92*
**Mc Cullough**, Ralph Clayton, II 1941- *WhoAmL 92*
**McCullough**, Richard Donald 1941- *AmMWSc 92*
**McCullough**, Richard Lawrence 1937- *WhoEnt 92*
**McCullough**, Robert Frederick, Jr. 1950- *WhoFI 92*
**McCullough**, Robert Spencer 1944- *WhoAmL 92*
**McCullough**, Robert William 1947- *AmMWSc 92*
**McCullough**, Roy Lynn 1934- *AmMWSc 92*
**Mc Cullough**, Samuel Alexander 1938- *WhoFI 92*
**McCullough**, Thomas F 1922- *AmMWSc 92*
**McCullough**, Timothy Joel 1945- *WhoMW 92*
**McCullough**, W.S. *ConAu 135*
**McCullough**, W. Stewart 1902-1982 *ConAu 135*
**McCullough**, Willard George 1914- *AmMWSc 92*
**McCullough-Wiggins**, Lydia Statoria 1948- *WhoMW 92*
**McCullum**, Donald Pitts 1928- *WhoBlA 92*
**McCully**, Emily Arnold *DrAPF 91*
**McCully**, John Raymond, Jr. 1935- *WhoRel 92*
**McCully**, Joseph C 1924- *AmMWSc 92*
**McCully**, Kilmer Serjus 1933- *AmMWSc 92*
**McCully**, Margaret E 1934- *AmMWSc 92*
**McCully**, Wayne Gunter 1922- *AmMWSc 92*
**McCumber**, Charles Allen 1956- *WhoFI 92*
**McCumber**, Dean Everett 1930- *AmMWSc 92, WhoFI 92*
**McCummings**, LeVerne 1932- *WhoBlA 92*
**McCumons**, Brenda K. 1951- *WhoRel 92*
**McCune**, Amy Reed 1954- *AmMWSc 92*
**McCune**, Barbara Ann 1934- *WhoEnt 92*
**Mc Cune**, Barron Patterson 1915- *WhoAmL 92*
**McCune**, Barry Lynn 1952- *WhoRel 92*
**McCune**, Conwell Clayton 1932- *AmMWSc 92*
**McCune**, Delbert Charles 1934- *AmMWSc 92*
**McCune**, Duncan Chalmers 1925- *AmMWSc 92*
**McCune**, Ellis E. 1921- *WhoWest 92*
**McCune**, Emmett L 1927- *AmMWSc 92*
**McCune**, Francis K 1906- *AmMWSc 92*
**McCune**, Francis Kimber 1906- *IntWW 91*
**McCune**, George Edward 1933- *WhoMW 92*
**McCune**, George Washington, Jr. 1921- *WhoRel 92*
**McCune**, Homer Wallace 1923- *AmMWSc 92*
**McCune**, James E 1931- *AmMWSc 92*
**McCune**, John Brian 1960- *WhoEnt 92*
**McCune**, John Robison 1926- *WhoAmP 91*
**McCune**, Leroy K 1917- *AmMWSc 92*
**McCune**, Mary Joan Huxley 1932- *AmMWSc 92*
**McCune**, Ronald William 1938- *AmMWSc 92*
**McCune**, Susan K 1958- *AmMWSc 92*
**McCune**, Sylvia Ann 1944- *AmMWSc 92, WhoMW 92*
**McCune**, William James, Jr 1915- *AmMWSc 92, IntWW 91*
**McCunn**, Peter Alexander 1922- *Who 92*
**McCunn**, Ruthanne Lum 1946- *IntAu&W 91*
**McCurdy**, Alan Hugh 1959- *AmMWSc 92, WhoWest 92*
**McCurdy**, Alexander 1905-1983 *NewAmDM*
**McCurdy**, Brenda Wright 1946- *WhoBlA 92*
**McCurdy**, Dave 1950- *AlmAP 92 [port], WhoAmP 91*
**McCurdy**, David Harold 1930- *AmMWSc 92*
**McCurdy**, Howard Douglas, Jr 1932- *AmMWSc 92*
**McCurdy**, John Andrew, Jr. 1945- *WhoWest 92*
**McCurdy**, John Dennis 1942- *AmMWSc 92*
**McCurdy**, Karen Marie 1957- *WhoMW 92*
**McCurdy**, Karen Rea 1938- *WhoRel 92*
**McCurdy**, Keith G 1937- *AmMWSc 92*
**McCurdy**, Kurt Basquin 1952- *WhoMW 92*
**McCurdy**, Larry Wayne 1935- *WhoFI 92*
**McCurdy**, Layton 1935- *AmMWSc 92*
**McCurdy**, M. A. 1852- *NotBlAW 92 [port]*
**McCurdy**, Matt 1959- *TwCPaSc*
**McCurdy**, Paul Ranney 1925- *AmMWSc 92*
**McCurdy**, Richard Clark 1909- *IntWW 91*
**McCurdy**, Wallace Hutchinson, Jr 1926- *AmMWSc 92*
**McCurley**, Anna Anderson 1943- *Who 92*
**McCurley**, Carl Michael 1946- *WhoAmL 92*
**McCurley**, Foster R., Jr. 1937- *ConAu 134*
**Mc Curley**, Robert Lee, Jr. 1941- *WhoAmL 92*
**McCurley**, Tom 1941- *WhoRel 92*
**McCurn**, Neal Peters 1926- *WhoAmL 92*
**McCurry**, Alan Brian 1953- *WhoMW 92*
**McCurry**, Margaret Irene 1942- *WhoMW 92*
**McCurry**, Patrick Matthew, Jr 1944- *AmMWSc 92*
**McCurry**, William Jeffery 1947- *WhoFI 92*
**McCurtin**, Peter *TwCWW 91*
**McCusker**, J. Stephen 1946- *WhoWest 92*
**McCusker**, James 1913- *Who 92*
**McCusker**, Jane 1943- *AmMWSc 92*
**McCusker**, Thomas *ScFEYrs*
**McCusker**, William LaValle 1918- *WhoAmL 92*
**McCuskey**, Lowell 1930- *WhoAmP 91*
**McCuskey**, Robert Scott 1938- *AmMWSc 92, WhoWest 92*
**McCutchan**, Gordon E 1935- *WhoIns 92*
**McCutchan**, Gordon Eugene 1935- *WhoAmL 92, WhoFI 92*
**McCutchan**, Philip 1920- *WrDr 92*
**McCutchan**, Philip Donald 1920- *IntAu&W 91*
**McCutchan**, Roy T 1918- *AmMWSc 92*
**McCutchan**, William Mark 1954- *WhoMW 92*
**McCutchen**, Charles Walter 1929- *AmMWSc 92*
**McCutchen**, David Johnstone 1951- *WhoEnt 92*
**McCutchen**, Edna Elizabeth 1914- *WhoWest 92*
**McCutchen**, Samuel P 1928- *AmMWSc 92*
**McCutcheon**, Andrew H, Jr 1927- *WhoAmP 91*
**McCutcheon**, Chester Myers 1907- *WhoFI 92*
**McCutcheon**, Elsie 1937- *ConAu 133*
**McCutcheon**, Elwyn Donovan 1912- *WhoRel 92*
**McCutcheon**, Ernest P 1933- *AmMWSc 92*
**McCutcheon**, George Barr 1866-1928 *BenetAL 91*
**McCutcheon**, Holly Marie 1950- *WhoMW 92*
**McCutcheon**, Hugh Davie-Martin 1909- *IntAu&W 91, WrDr 92*
**McCutcheon**, James Norton 1929- *WhoRel 92*
**McCutcheon**, John T. 1870-1949 *BenetAL 91, FacFETw*
**McCutcheon**, Lawrence 1950- *WhoBlA 92*
**McCutcheon**, Martin J 1941- *AmMWSc 92*
**McCutcheon**, Rob Stewart 1908- *AmMWSc 92*
**McCutcheon**, William *WhoMW 92*
**McCutcheon**, William Alan 1934- *Who 92, WrDr 92*
**McCutcheon**, William Henry 1940- *AmMWSc 92*
**McDade**, Donald Alan 1959- *WhoFI 92*
**McDade**, James Russell 1925- *WhoFI 92*
**McDade**, Joseph Edward 1940- *AmMWSc 92*
**McDade**, Joseph M. 1931- *AlmAP 92 [port]*
**McDade**, Joseph Michael 1931- *WhoAmP 91*
**McDade**, Robert Gary 1951- *WhoRel 92*
**McDade**, Sandy S 1947- *WhoAmP 91*
**McDade**, Thomas Rambaut 1933- *WhoAmL 92*
**McDaniel**, Adam Theodore 1925- *WhoBlA 92*
**McDaniel**, Anthony Lamar 1965- *WhoRel 92*
**McDaniel**, Arlie Leo 1915- *WhoRel 92*
**McDaniel**, Benjamin Thomas 1935- *AmMWSc 92*
**McDaniel**, Billy Ray 1943- *WhoBlA 92*
**McDaniel**, Boyce Dawkins 1917- *AmMWSc 92, IntWW 91*
**McDaniel**, Burruss, Jr 1927- *AmMWSc 92*
**McDaniel**, Carl Nimitz 1942- *AmMWSc 92*
**McDaniel**, Carl Vance 1929- *AmMWSc 92*
**McDaniel**, Charles Edwin 1937- *WhoRel 92*
**McDaniel**, Charles William 1927- *WhoBlA 92*
**McDaniel**, Clair Michael 1944- *WhoFI 92*
**McDaniel**, Dennis R. 1950- *WhoFI 92*
**McDaniel**, Drew Overton 1941- *WhoEnt 92*
**McDaniel**, Earl Wadsworth 1926- *AmMWSc 92*
**McDaniel**, Edgar Lamar, Jr 1931- *AmMWSc 92*
**McDaniel**, Elizabeth 1952- *WhoBlA 92*
**McDaniel**, Floyd Delbert, Sr 1942- *AmMWSc 92*
**McDaniel**, Gayner Raiford 1929- *AmMWSc 92*
**McDaniel**, George William 1942- *WhoRel 92*
**McDaniel**, Gerald Green Goforth 1945- *IntAu&W 91*
**McDaniel**, Hattie 1895-1952 *NotBlAW 92 [port]*
**McDaniel**, Inez Eugenia 1917- *WhoBlA 92*
**McDaniel**, Inga 1962- *WhoEnt 92*

**McDaniel**, Ivan Noel 1928- *AmMWSc 92*
**McDaniel**, James 1803-1869 *DcNCBi 4*
**McDaniel**, James Berkley, Jr. 1925- *WhoBlA 92*
**Mc Daniel**, James Edwin 1931- *WhoAmL 92*
**McDaniel**, Jarrel Dave 1930- *WhoAmL 92*
**McDaniel**, Jeff Anthony 1961- *WhoAmL 92*
**McDaniel**, Joseph Chandler 1950- *WhoAmL 92, WhoWest 92*
**McDaniel**, Judith *DrAPF 91*
**McDaniel**, June E. 1952- *WhoRel 92*
**McDaniel**, Lloyd Everett 1914- *AmMWSc 92*
**McDaniel**, Mark Steven 1958- *WhoAmL 92*
**McDaniel**, Marlin K *WhoAmP 91*
**McDaniel**, Max Paul 1947- *AmMWSc 92*
**McDaniel**, Michael Conway Dixon 1929- *WhoRel 92*
**McDaniel**, Michael Keith 1948- *WhoMW 92*
**McDaniel**, Michael Lynn *AmMWSc 92*
**McDaniel**, Mildred Louise 1933- *BlkOlyM*
**McDaniel**, Milton Edward 1938- *AmMWSc 92*
**McDaniel**, Myra A 1932- *WhoAmP 91*
**McDaniel**, Myra Atwell 1932- *WhoAmL 92, WhoBlA 92*
**McDaniel**, Neil Blake 1954- *WhoRel 92*
**McDaniel**, Paul Anderson 1930- *WhoBlA 92*
**McDaniel**, Paul William 1916- *WhoWest 92*
**McDaniel**, Preston Woods, Sr. 1916- *WhoFI 92*
**McDaniel**, Rebecca Maureen 1948- *WhoMW 92*
**McDaniel**, Reuben R. 1936- *WhoBlA 92*
**McDaniel**, Robert Anthony 1952- *WhoBlA 92*
**McDaniel**, Robert Gene 1941- *AmMWSc 92*
**Mc Daniel**, Roderick Rogers 1926- *WhoFI 92*
**McDaniel**, Roger Lanier, Jr 1952- *AmMWSc 92*
**McDaniel**, Sharon A. 1950- *WhoBlA 92*
**McDaniel**, Steve K 1951- *WhoAmP 91*
**McDaniel**, Susan Griffith 1938- *AmMWSc 92*
**McDaniel**, Terrence Lee 1965- *WhoBlA 92*
**McDaniel**, Tom *DrAPF 91*
**McDaniel**, Van Rick 1945- *AmMWSc 92*
**McDaniel**, Walter F *WhoAmP 91*
**McDaniel**, Wayne Logan 1955- *WhoFI 92*
**McDaniel**, Willard Rich 1934- *AmMWSc 92*
**McDaniel**, William Foster 1940- *WhoEnt 92*
**McDaniel**, William Franklin 1951- *AmMWSc 92*
**McDaniel**, William T., Jr. 1945- *WhoBlA 92*
**McDaniel**, Willie L, Jr 1932- *AmMWSc 92*
**McDaniel**, Xavier Maurice 1959- *WhoBlA 92*
**McDaniels**, Alfred F. 1940- *WhoBlA 92*
**McDaniels**, B. T. *WhoRel 92*
**McDaniels**, David K 1929- *AmMWSc 92*
**McDaniels**, John Edward, Sr. 1921- *WhoBlA 92*
**McDaniels**, Orrin Hunter 1939- *WhoBlA 92*
**McDaniels**, Sharin 1965- *WhoWest 92*
**Mc Dannald**, Clyde Elliott, Jr. 1923- *WhoFI 92*
**McDarrah**, Fred W. 1926- *WrDr 92*
**McDavid**, J. Gary 1947- *WhoAmL 92*
**McDavid**, James Michael 1945- *AmMWSc 92*
**McDavid**, Janet Louise 1950- *WhoAmL 92*
**Mc David**, Joel Duncan 1916- *WhoRel 92*
**McDavid**, William Henry 1946- *WhoAmL 92, WhoFI 92*
**McDermed**, John Dale 1941- *AmMWSc 92*
**McDermid**, John Fairbanks 1946- *WhoAmL 92*
**McDermid**, John Horton 1940- *WhoFI 92*
**McDermid**, Norman George Lloyd Roberts 1927- *Who 92*
**McDermid**, Richard Thomas Wright 1929- *Who 92*
**McDermitt**, Edward Vincent 1953- *WhoAmL 92*
**McDermot**, Murtagh *ScFEYrs*
**McDermott**, Alice *DrAPF 91*
**McDermott**, Cheryl Lynn 1953- *WhoEnt 92, WhoWest 92*
**McDermott**, Dana Paul 1948- *AmMWSc 92*
**McDermott**, Daniel J *AmMWSc 92*
**McDermott**, David Francis 1945- *WhoMW 92*
**McDermott**, Dirk Wade 1956- *WhoWest 92*
**McDermott**, Edward Aloysious 1920- *IntWW 91, WhoAmP 91*
**McDermott**, Elaine Mary 1937- *WhoRel 92*
**McDermott**, Emmet *Who 92*
**McDermott**, Francis Owen 1933- *WhoAmL 92*
**McDermott**, Helena E 1911- *WhoAmP 91*
**McDermott**, James 1936- *WhoAmP 91*
**McDermott**, James A. 1936- *AlmAP 92 [port], WhoWest 92*
**McDermott**, James Alexander 1938- *WhoAmL 92*
**McDermott**, James Edward 1955- *WhoAmL 92*
**McDermott**, James Patrick 1939- *WhoAmP 91*
**McDermott**, James T *WhoAmP 91*
**McDermott**, James T. 1926- *WhoAmL 92*
**McDermott**, John Aloysius, II 1943- *WhoAmL 92*
**McDermott**, John Francis 1929- *AmMWSc 92*
**McDermott**, John Harrison 1929- *WhoEnt 92*
**McDermott**, John Henry 1931- *WhoAmL 92*
**McDermott**, John Joseph 1927- *AmMWSc 92*
**McDermott**, John Richard, Jr. 1953- *WhoFI 92*
**McDermott**, Katherine Buck 1937- *WhoAmP 91*
**McDermott**, Kevin Daniel 1954- *WhoFI 92*
**McDermott**, Kevin J 1935- *AmMWSc 92*
**McDermott**, Lawrence Emmet 1911- *Who 92*
**McDermott**, Lillian Christie 1931- *AmMWSc 92*
**McDermott**, Mark Nordman 1930- *AmMWSc 92*
**McDermott**, Mark Rundle *AmMWSc 92*
**McDermott**, Michael Edward 1948- *WhoMW 92*
**McDermott**, Patricia L *WhoAmP 91*
**McDermott**, Patricia Louise *WhoAmL 92*
**McDermott**, Patrick Anthony 1941- *Who 92*
**McDermott**, Peter Paul, II 1950- *WhoMW 92*
**McDermott**, Richard P 1928- *AmMWSc 92*
**McDermott**, Robert B. 1927- *WhoAmL 92*
**McDermott**, Robert Emmet 1920- *AmMWSc 92*
**Mc Dermott**, Robert Francis 1920- *WhoFI 92, WhoIns 92*
**McDermott**, Robert Francis, Jr. 1945- *WhoAmL 92*
**McDermott**, Robert H 1931- *WhoIns 92*
**McDermott**, Robert Hogan 1931- *WhoAmP 91*
**McDermott**, Robert James 1932- *WhoAmP 91*
**McDermott**, Robert W 1943- *WhoIns 92*
**McDermott**, Shirley Ann 1964- *WhoAmL 92*
**McDermott**, Thomas *LesBEnT 92*
**McDermott**, Thomas John, Jr. 1931- *WhoAmL 92*
**McDermott**, Thomas M 1948- *WhoAmP 91*
**McDermott**, Vincent 1933- *WhoEnt 92*
**McDermott**, William Thomas 1945- *WhoFI 92*
**McDermott**, William Vincent, Jr 1917- *AmMWSc 92*
**McDevitt**, Charles *WhoAmL 92*
**McDevitt**, Charles E 1939- *WhoAmP 91*
**McDevitt**, Charles F 1932- *WhoAmP 91, WhoWest 92*
**McDevitt**, Daniel Bernard 1927- *AmMWSc 92*
**McDevitt**, David Stephen 1940- *AmMWSc 92*
**McDevitt**, Diane Marie 1955- *WhoAmL 92*
**McDevitt**, Hugh O'Neill 1930- *AmMWSc 92*
**McDevitt**, Jack 1935- *TwCSFW 91*
**McDevitt**, Noel Bruce, Jr. 1964- *WhoAmL 92*
**McDevitt**, Sheila Marie 1947- *WhoAmP 91*
**McDiarmid**, Donald Ralph 1937- *AmMWSc 92*
**McDiarmid**, Dorothy Shoemaker 1906- *WhoAmP 91*
**McDiarmid**, Ian *ConTFT 9*
**McDiarmid**, Ian Bertrand 1928- *AmMWSc 92*
**McDiarmid**, Robert Campbell 1937- *WhoAmL 92*
**McDiarmid**, Roy Wallace 1940- *AmMWSc 92*
**McDiarmid**, Ruth 1938- *AmMWSc 92*
**McDiffett**, Wayne Francis 1939- *AmMWSc 92*
**McDill**, Robert Lee 1944- *WhoEnt 92*
**McDill**, Thomas Allison 1926- *WhoRel 92*
**McDivitt**, James 1929- *FacFETw*
**McDivitt**, James Alton 1929- *WhoFI 92*
**McDivitt**, Maxine Estelle 1912- *AmMWSc 92*
**McDivitt**, Robert William 1931- *AmMWSc 92*
**McDole**, Marilyn Hayes 1950- *WhoMW 92*
**McDole**, Robert E 1930- *AmMWSc 92*
**McDonagh**, Enda 1930- *IntWW 91*
**McDonagh**, Jan M 1942- *AmMWSc 92*
**McDonagh**, John 1954- *WhoMW 92*
**McDonagh**, Robert 1924- *IntWW 91*
**McDonagh**, Thomas Joseph 1932- *WhoFI 92*
**McDonald**, Lord 1916- *Who 92*
**McDonald**, Alan Angus 1927- *WhoAmL 92*
**McDonald**, Alan James 1946- *WhoAmL 92*
**McDonald**, Alan T 1938- *AmMWSc 92*
**McDonald**, Albert 1930- *WhoAmP 91*
**McDonald**, Alden J., Jr. *WhoBlA 92*
**McDonald**, Alex Gordon 1921- *Who 92*
**McDonald**, Alexander Gordon *Who 92*
**McDonald**, Alexander John 1919- *Who 92*
**McDonald**, Alice 1940- *WhoAmP 91*
**McDonald**, Alistair 1925- *Who 92*
**McDonald**, Alistair Ian 1921- *Who 92*
**McDonald**, Allan Stuart 1922- *Who 92*
**McDonald**, Alonzo L. 1928- *IntWW 91*
**McDonald**, Alonzo Lowry, Jr. 1928- *WhoRel 92*
**Mc Donald**, Andrew J. 1923- *WhoRel 92*
**McDonald**, Angus Morris 1901-1977 *DcNCBi 4*
**McDonald**, Anita Dunlop 1929- *WhoBlA 92*
**McDonald**, Anne *WhoAmP 91*
**McDonald**, Arthur 1903- *Who 92*
**McDonald**, Arthur Bruce 1943- *AmMWSc 92*
**McDonald**, B J 1933- *WhoAmP 91*
**McDonald**, Barbara Brown 1924- *AmMWSc 92*
**McDonald**, Bernard 1942- *WhoBlA 92*
**McDonald**, Bernard Robert 1940- *AmMWSc 92*
**McDonald**, Bill 1954- *WhoMW 92*
**McDonald**, Bradley G. *WhoAmL 92*
**McDonald**, Brian Robert 1952- *WhoAmP 91*
**McDonald**, Bruce Eugene 1933- *AmMWSc 92*
**McDonald**, Charles J. 1931- *WhoBlA 92*
**McDonald**, Charles Joseph 1941- *AmMWSc 92*
**McDonald**, Charles Morris 1948- *WhoRel 92*
**McDonald**, Charles Raymond 1927- *WhoMW 92*
**McDonald**, Claire Michele 1955- *WhoEnt 92*
**McDonald**, Clarence Eugene 1926- *AmMWSc 92*
**McDonald**, Craydon Dean 1946- *WhoRel 92*
**McDonald**, Curtis W. 1934- *WhoBlA 92*
**McDonald**, Daniel James 1925- *AmMWSc 92*
**McDonald**, Daniel Patrick 1946- *AmMWSc 92*
**McDonald**, Daniel Robert 1944- *WhoAmP 91*
**McDonald**, Danny Lee *WhoAmP 91*
**McDonald**, David Arthur 1940- *Who 92*
**McDonald**, David J 1936- *WhoIns 92*
**McDonald**, David William 1923- *AmMWSc 92*
**McDonald**, David Wylie 1927- *Who 92*
**McDonald**, Dennis A 1938- *WhoAmP 91*
**McDonald**, Desmond P. 1927- *WhoFI 92*
**McDonald**, Donald 1930- *AmMWSc 92*
**McDonald**, Donald Burt 1932- *AmMWSc 92*
**McDonald**, Donald C 1919- *AmMWSc 92*
**McDonald**, Donald Michael 1947- *WhoRel 92*
**McDonald**, Douglas Hugh 1945- *WhoMW 92*
**McDonald**, Duncan 1921- *IntWW 91, Who 92*
**McDonald**, Edmund Morris 1917- *WhoBlA 92*
**McDonald**, Edward Lawson 1918- *IntWW 91, Who 92*
**McDonald**, Edward Richard 1873- *ScFEYrs*
**McDonald**, Edward Richard & R A Leger *ScFEYrs*
**McDonald**, Elaine Maria 1943- *Who 92*
**McDonald**, Elvin 1937?- *ConAu 34NR*
**McDonald**, Erroll 1954?- *ConBlB 1 [port]*
**McDonald**, Eugene, Jr. d1958 *LesBEnT 92*
**McDonald**, Eva Rose *WrDr 92*
**McDonald**, Eva Rose 1909- *IntAu&W 91*
**McDonald**, Forrest 1927- *IntAu&W 91, IntWW 91, WrDr 92*
**McDonald**, Francis James 1922- *IntWW 91, Who 92*
**McDonald**, Francis Michael 1931- *WhoAmL 92*
**McDonald**, Francis Raymond 1924- *AmMWSc 92*
**McDonald**, Frank Alan 1937- *AmMWSc 92*
**McDonald**, Frank Bethune 1925- *AmMWSc 92*
**McDonald**, Frank F, II *WhoAmP 91*
**McDonald**, Frank F., II 1951- *WhoMW 92*
**McDonald**, Gabrielle K. 1942- *WhoBlA 92*
**McDonald**, Gary Eugene 1943- *WhoRel 92*
**McDonald**, George 1936- *WhoAmL 92*
**McDonald**, George Gordon 1944- *AmMWSc 92*
**McDonald**, Geral Irving 1935- *AmMWSc 92*
**McDonald**, Gerald O 1922- *AmMWSc 92*
**McDonald**, Gerald Thomas 1933- *WhoAmL 92*
**McDonald**, Glena June 1947- *WhoMW 92*
**McDonald**, Graeme Patrick Daniel 1930- *Who 92*
**McDonald**, Greg Guy 1953- *WhoMW 92*
**McDonald**, Gregory 1937- *IntAu&W 91, WrDr 92*
**McDonald**, Guillermo Jurado *WhoHisp 92*
**McDonald**, H S 1927- *AmMWSc 92*
**McDonald**, Harl 1899-1955 *NewAmDM*
**McDonald**, Harry Sawyer 1930- *AmMWSc 92*
**McDonald**, Hector O 1930- *AmMWSc 92*
**McDonald**, Henry C 1928- *AmMWSc 92*
**McDonald**, Herbert G. 1929- *WhoBlA 92*
**McDonald**, Heyward Elliott 1925- *WhoAmP 91*
**McDonald**, Hugh Joseph 1913- *AmMWSc 92*
**McDonald**, Ian 1933- *ConPo 91, WrDr 92*
**McDonald**, Ian 1960- *TwCSFW 91*
**McDonald**, Ian Cameron Crawford 1939- *AmMWSc 92*
**McDonald**, Ian MacLaren 1928- *AmMWSc 92, WhoWest 92*
**McDonald**, Iverach 1908- *IntAu&W 91, Who 92*
**McDonald**, J. Chris 1954- *WhoEnt 92*
**McDonald**, J David 1942- *WhoIns 92*
**McDonald**, Jack H 1932- *WhoAmP 91*
**McDonald**, Jack Raymond 1944- *AmMWSc 92*
**McDonald**, James *Who 92, WhoRel 92*
**McDonald**, James 1940- *IntWW 91*
**McDonald**, James Bott 1942- *WhoFI 92, WhoWest 92*
**McDonald**, James Clifton 1930- *AmMWSc 92*
**McDonald**, James Francis 1940- *WhoFI 92*
**McDonald**, James Frederick 1939- *AmMWSc 92*
**McDonald**, James Grover 1886-1964 *AmPeW*
**McDonald**, James Joseph 1930- *WhoAmP 91*
**McDonald**, James Lee, Jr 1939- *AmMWSc 92*
**McDonald**, James Louis 1936- *WhoMW 92*
**McDonald**, Jamie *WrDr 92*
**McDonald**, Jay M *AmMWSc 92*
**McDonald**, Jeanne Stana 1942- *WhoRel 92*
**McDonald**, Jerry Lee 1950- *WhoMW 92*
**McDonald**, Jimmie Reed 1942- *AmMWSc 92*
**McDonald**, Joel Mark 1951- *WhoMW 92*
**McDonald**, John Alexander *AmMWSc 92*
**Mc Donald**, John B., Mrs. 1917- *WhoEnt 92, WhoWest 92*
**McDonald**, John C *AmMWSc 92*
**McDonald**, John C. 1936- *WhoFI 92*
**McDonald**, John Cecil 1924- *WhoAmP 91*
**McDonald**, John Charles 1936- *AmMWSc 92*
**McDonald**, John Cooper 1936- *WhoAmP 91*
**McDonald**, John Corbett 1918- *Who 92*
**McDonald**, John F 1942- *AmMWSc 92*
**McDonald**, John Francis Patrick 1942- *WhoFI 92*
**McDonald**, John Freeman 1943- *WhoFI 92, WhoMW 92*
**McDonald**, John Gregory 1937- *WhoFI 92*
**McDonald**, John Kennely 1930- *AmMWSc 92*
**McDonald**, John N 1942- *AmMWSc 92*
**McDonald**, John R. 1933- *WhoAmL 92*
**McDonald**, John Steven 1942- *WhoMW 92*
**McDonald**, John Stoner 1932- *AmMWSc 92*
**McDonald**, John W., Jr. 1922- *IntWW 91*

**McDonald,** John William 1945- *AmMWSc 92*
**McDonald,** John William David 1938- *AmMWSc 92*
**McDonald,** Jon Franklin 1946- *WhoBlA 92*
**McDonald,** Joseph Benedict 1958- *WhoAmL 92*
**McDonald,** Joseph Paul 1914- *WhoAmP 91*
**McDonald,** Julie *DrAPF 91*
**McDonald,** Kay Adair 1962- *WhoMW 92*
**McDonald,** Keith Leon 1923- *AmMWSc 92, WhoWest 92*
**McDonald,** Kenneth James 1930- *WhoAmP 91*
**McDonald,** Kenneth Malcolm 1954- *WhoRel 92*
**McDonald,** Kirk Thomas 1945- *AmMWSc 92*
**McDonald,** Larry Allen 1954- *WhoEnt 92*
**McDonald,** Larry Marvin 1952- *WhoBlA 92*
**McDonald,** Larry Steven 1956- *WhoRel 92*
**McDonald,** Larry William 1928- *AmMWSc 92*
**McDonald,** Lauren Wylie, Jr 1938- *WhoAmP 91*
**McDonald,** Lawson *Who 92*
**McDonald,** Lee J 1962- *AmMWSc 92*
**McDonald,** Leslie Ernest 1923- *AmMWSc 92*
**McDonald,** Lewis Newton 1937- *WhoRel 92*
**McDonald,** Lil F. 1960- *WhoEnt 92*
**McDonald,** Lynn 1940- *WrDr 92*
**McDonald,** Lynn Dale 1942- *AmMWSc 92*
**McDonald,** Malcolm Edwin 1915- *AmMWSc 92*
**McDonald,** Malcolm S. 1938- *WhoFI 92*
**McDonald,** Marguerite Bridget 1950- *AmMWSc 92*
**McDonald,** Marianne 1937- *WhoWest 92*
**McDonald,** Mark T. 1935- *WhoBlA 92*
**McDonald,** Marshall 1835-1895 *BiInAmS*
**McDonald,** Mary Ann Melody 1944- *WhoFI 92*
**McDonald,** Matthew 1970- *WhoEnt 92*
**McDonald,** Mavis 1944- *Who 92*
**McDonald,** Megan 1959- *ConAu 135, SmATA 67 [port]*
**McDonald,** Michael Joseph 1954- *WhoAmL 92*
**McDonald,** Mike 1958- *WhoBlA 92*
**McDonald,** Miles F. d1991 *NewYTBS 91*
**McDonald,** Miller Baird 1920- *WhoAmP 91*
**McDonald,** Nancy Hanks 1934- *WhoAmP 91*
**McDonald,** Oonagh *Who 92*
**McDonald,** P H, Jr 1924- *AmMWSc 92*
**McDonald,** Parker Lee 1924- *WhoAmL 92, WhoAmP 91*
**Mc Donald,** Patrick Allen 1936- *WhoAmL 92*
**McDonald,** Peggy Ann Stimmel 1931- *WhoFI 92*
**McDonald,** Perry Frank 1933- *AmMWSc 92*
**McDonald,** Peyton Dean 1936- *WhoFI 92*
**McDonald,** Philip Michael 1936- *AmMWSc 92*
**McDonald,** Phillip Wayne 1951- *WhoRel 92*
**McDonald,** R. Timothy 1940- *WhoBlA 92*
**McDonald,** Ralph Earl 1920- *AmMWSc 92, WhoMW 92*
**McDonald,** Ralph Waldo 1903-1977 *DcNCBi 4*
**McDonald,** Randy 1947- *WhoRel 92*
**McDonald,** Ray Locke 1931- *AmMWSc 92*
**McDonald,** Raymond *ScFEYrs*
**McDonald,** Richard E. 1929- *WhoBlA 92*
**McDonald,** Richard Norman 1931- *AmMWSc 92*
**McDonald,** Robert *ScFEYrs*
**McDonald,** Robert 1933- *WhoWest 92*
**McDonald,** Robert Garland 1942- *WhoWest 92*
**McDonald,** Robert H, Jr 1933- *AmMWSc 92*
**McDonald,** Robert Howat *Who 92*
**McDonald,** Robert James, Jr. 1958- *WhoMW 92*
**McDonald,** Robert Lendol 1924- *WhoAmP 91*
**McDonald,** Robert Skillings 1918- *AmMWSc 92*
**McDonald,** Roger 1941- *IntAu&W 91, WrDr 92*
**McDonald,** Roy Phillip 1928- *WhoMW 92*
**McDonald,** Scott Irwin 1958- *WhoFI 92*
**McDonald,** Stephen Lynn 1956- *WhoMW 92*
**McDonald,** Stephen Matthew 1969- *WhoRel 92*
**McDonald,** Susan Clark 1948- *WhoWest 92*
**McDonald,** Susann Hackett 1935- *WhoEnt 92*
**McDonald,** T W 1929- *AmMWSc 92*
**McDonald,** Tanny *WhoEnt 92*
**McDonald,** Ted Painter 1930- *AmMWSc 92*
**McDonald,** Terence Francis 1943- *AmMWSc 92*
**McDonald,** Terrence John 1949- *WhoAmP 91*
**McDonald,** Theresa Beatrice Pierce 1929- *WhoRel 92*
**McDonald,** Thomas Alexander 1942- *WhoAmL 92*
**McDonald,** Thomas Edward 1955- *WhoAmL 92*
**McDonald,** Thomas Edwin, Jr. 1939- *WhoWest 92*
**McDonald,** Timothy, III 1954- *WhoBlA 92*
**McDonald,** Timothy Louis 1955- *WhoEnt 92*
**McDonald,** Timothy Scott 1946- *AmMWSc 92*
**McDonald,** Tom 1923- *Who 92*
**McDonald,** Verna Pagenstecher 1923- *WhoWest 92*
**McDonald,** Virgil Lee 1957- *WhoWest 92*
**McDonald,** W John 1936- *AmMWSc 92*
**McDonald,** W. R. 1929- *WhoFI 92, WhoMW 92*
**McDonald,** Walter *DrAPF 91, WhoAmP 91*
**McDonald,** Walter 1934- *DcLB DS9 [port]*
**McDonald,** Walter R 1934- *IntAu&W 91*
**McDonald,** William 1929- *Who 92*
**McDonald,** William Andrew 1913- *WrDr 92*
**McDonald,** William Brice 1945- *WhoMW 92*
**McDonald,** William Charles 1933- *AmMWSc 92*
**McDonald,** William Emory 1924- *WhoBlA 92*
**McDonald,** William H. *WhoRel 92*
**McDonald,** William James Gilmour 1924- *Who 92*
**McDonald,** William John Farquhar 1911- *Who 92*
**McDonald,** William True 1935- *AmMWSc 92*
**McDonald,** William Ulma, Jr. 1927- *WhoMW 92*
**McDonald,** Willie Ruth Davis 1931- *WhoBlA 92*
**McDonald-Jonsson,** Laurie Jean 1949- *WhoWest 92*
**McDonaugh,** James 1912- *Who 92*
**McDonel,** Everett Timothy 1933- *AmMWSc 92*
**McDonell,** Horace George, Jr. 1928- *WhoFI 92*
**McDonell,** William Robert 1925- *AmMWSc 92*
**McDonnel,** Gerald M 1919- *AmMWSc 92*
**McDonnel,** William George 1952- *WhoWest 92*
**McDonnell** *Who 92*
**McDonnell,** Archie Joseph 1936- *AmMWSc 92*
**McDonnell,** Christopher Thomas 1931- *Who 92*
**McDonnell,** David Croft 1943- *Who 92*
**McDonnell,** David Keith 1950- *WhoAmL 92*
**McDonnell,** Denis Lane 1914- *Who 92*
**McDonnell,** Dennis J. 1942- *WhoFI 92*
**McDonnell,** Donald Raymond 1952- *WhoEnt 92*
**McDonnell,** Francis Nicholas 1940- *AmMWSc 92*
**McDonnell,** Hector 1947- *TwCPaSc*
**McDonnell,** James Kevin 1941- *WhoMW 92*
**McDonnell,** James S, Jr 1899-1980 *FacFETw*
**McDonnell,** John 1951- *Who 92*
**McDonnell,** John Beresford William 1940- *Who 92*
**McDonnell,** John Finney 1938- *WhoFI 92, WhoMW 92*
**McDonnell,** John Michael 1954- *WhoRel 92*
**McDonnell,** Kevin Lee 1932- *WrDr 92*
**McDonnell,** Kevin Paul 1958- *WhoFI 92*
**McDonnell,** Kilian 1921- *ConAu 34NR*
**McDonnell,** Leo F 1926- *AmMWSc 92*
**McDonnell,** Lois Eddy *WrDr 92*
**McDonnell,** Mark Jeffery 1953- *AmMWSc 92*
**McDonnell,** Mary 1952- *IntMPA 92*
**McDonnell,** Mary 1953?- *ConTFT 9*
**McDonnell,** Michael T., Jr. 1936- *WhoAmL 92*
**McDonnell,** Rex Graham, Jr 1924- *WhoAmP 91*
**McDonnell,** Sanford 1922- *AmMWSc 92*
**McDonnell,** Sanford N. 1922- *IntWW 91*
**McDonnell,** William Vincent 1922- *AmMWSc 92*
**McDonnold,** Steven Bradley 1958- *WhoFI 92*
**McDonogh,** Gary Wray 1952- *IntAu&W 91*
**McDonough,** Brian James 1956- *WhoAmL 92*
**McDonough,** Bridget Ann 1956- *WhoEnt 92*
**McDonough,** Dixie Jean 1935- *WhoFI 92*
**McDonough,** Edward Francis 1932- *WhoAmP 91*
**McDonough,** Eugene Stowell 1905- *AmMWSc 92*
**McDonough,** James Edward 1959- *AmMWSc 92*
**McDonough,** James Francis 1939- *AmMWSc 92*
**McDonough,** John Edward 1953- *WhoAmP 91*
**McDonough,** John Michael 1944- *WhoAmL 92*
**McDonough,** Joseph Edward 1937- *WhoAmL 92*
**McDonough,** Kathleen H 1947- *AmMWSc 92*
**McDonough,** Lawrence 1942- *WhoAmL 92*
**McDonough,** Leslie Marvin 1930- *AmMWSc 92*
**McDonough,** Martha Rose 1944- *WhoMW 92*
**McDonough,** Mary Joan 1957- *WhoAmL 92, WhoAmP 91*
**McDonough,** Patrick Dennis 1942- *WhoMW 92*
**McDonough,** Patrick Kevin 1949- *WhoWest 92*
**McDonough,** Reginald Milton 1936- *WhoRel 92*
**Mc Donough,** Richard Doyle 1931- *WhoFI 92*
**McDonough,** Robert E. *DrAPF 91*
**McDonough,** Robert Newton 1935- *AmMWSc 92*
**McDonough,** Russell 1924- *WhoAmP 91*
**McDonough,** Russell Charles 1924- *WhoAmL 92, WhoWest 92*
**McDonough,** Sheila Doreen 1928- *WhoRel 92*
**McDonough,** Thomas David 1952- *WhoAmL 92*
**McDonough,** Thomas Joseph 1940- *AmMWSc 92*
**McDonough,** Thomas Redmond *AmMWSc 92*
**McDonough,** Thomas Redmond 1945- *WhoFI 92*
**McDormand,** Frances 1958- *IntMPA 92*
**McDougal,** Alfred Leroy 1931- *WhoMW 92*
**McDougal,** David Blean, Jr 1923- *AmMWSc 92*
**McDougal,** Dennis Edward 1947- *WhoWest 92*
**McDougal,** Genevieve Guerra 1947- *WhoWest 92*
**McDougal,** Luther L. 1959- *WhoFI 92*
**McDougal,** Marie Patricia 1946- *WhoMW 92*
**McDougal,** Robert Nelson 1920- *AmMWSc 92*
**McDougal,** Stuart Yeatman 1942- *WhoMW 92*
**McDougald,** Archibald *DcNCBi 4*
**McDougald,** Larry Robert 1941- *AmMWSc 92*
**McDougald,** Michael Hall 1931- *WhoEnt 92*
**McDougald,** Samuel *DcNCBi 4*
**McDougall,** Alexander 1732-1786 *BlkwEAR*
**McDougall,** Barbara Jean 1937- *IntWW 91, Who 92, WhoFI 92*
**McDougall,** Dugald George 1942- *WhoAmP 91*
**McDougall,** George Douglas 1930- *WhoWest 92*
**McDougall,** I. Ross 1943- *WhoWest 92*
**McDougall,** James K *AmMWSc 92*
**McDougall,** Joyce 1926- *ConAu 36NR*
**McDougall,** Kenneth J 1935- *AmMWSc 92*
**McDougall,** Robert I 1929- *AmMWSc 92*
**McDougall,** Sharon L 1959- *WhoIns 92*
**McDougall,** Walter H 1858-1938 *ScFEYrs*
**McDougall,** William 1871-1938 *DcNCBi 4*
**McDougle,** Paul E 1928- *AmMWSc 92*
**McDouogall,** Walter A 1946- *IntAu&W 91*
**McDow,** John J 1925- *AmMWSc 92*
**Mc Dow,** Malcolm Ray 1936- *WhoRel 92*
**McDowall,** Betty *IntMPA 92*
**McDowall,** Brenda *Who 92*
**McDowall,** Keith Desmond 1929- *Who 92*
**McDowall,** Robert John Stewart d1990 *IntWW 91N*
**McDowall,** Roddy 1928- *IntMPA 92, IntWW 91, WhoEnt 92*
**McDowall,** Stuart 1926- *Who 92*
**McDowell,** Archibald 1818-1881 *DcNCBi 4*
**McDowell,** Benjamin A. 1939- *WhoBlA 92*
**McDowell,** Billy M. L. 1935- *WhoEnt 92*
**McDowell,** Bob 1940- *WhoAmP 91*
**McDowell,** Bobbie G *WhoAmP 91*
**McDowell,** Bobby Allen 1958- *WhoAmP 91*
**McDowell,** Carla Christine 1958- *WhoMW 92*
**McDowell,** Charles 1743-1815 *DcNCBi 4*
**McDowell,** Charles Alexander 1918- *AmMWSc 92*
**McDowell,** Claudia Shaw 1957- *WhoWest 92*
**McDowell,** Cleve 1941- *WhoBlA 92*
**McDowell,** Coulter *Who 92*
**McDowell,** Daniel E. 1959- *WhoRel 92*
**McDowell,** Daniel Quince, Jr. 1949- *WhoMW 92*
**McDowell,** David Keith 1937- *IntWW 91*
**McDowell,** Dawson Clayborn 1913- *AmMWSc 92*
**McDowell,** Donna Schultz 1946- *WhoAmL 92*
**McDowell,** E. Crosby 1942- *WhoWest 92*
**McDowell,** Edward Homer, Jr. 1949- *WhoBlA 92*
**McDowell,** Edwin S. 1935- *IntAu&W 91*
**McDowell,** Edwin Stewart 1935- *WrDr 92*
**McDowell,** Elizabeth Mary 1940- *AmMWSc 92*
**McDowell,** Eric 1925- *Who 92*
**McDowell,** Esther Arias 1948- *WhoHisp 92*
**McDowell,** Fletcher Hughes 1923- *AmMWSc 92*
**McDowell,** Fred Wallace 1939- *AmMWSc 92*
**McDowell,** Frederick P. W. 1915- *WrDr 92*
**McDowell,** George Edward 1944- *WhoMW 92*
**McDowell,** George Roy Colquhoun 1922- *Who 92*
**McDowell,** Harding Keith 1944- *AmMWSc 92*
**McDowell,** Harris B, III 1940- *WhoAmP 91*
**McDowell,** Henry 1910- *Who 92*
**McDowell,** Hershel 1930- *AmMWSc 92*
**McDowell,** James E 1924- *WhoAmP 91*
**McDowell,** Jeffrey Steven 1954- *WhoWest 92*
**McDowell,** Jennifer 1936- *WhoFI 92, WhoWest 92*
**McDowell,** John 1942- *WrDr 92*
**Mc Dowell,** John B. 1921- *WhoRel 92*
**McDowell,** John Henry 1942- *Who 92*
**McDowell,** John Parmelee 1931- *AmMWSc 92*
**McDowell,** John Willis 1921- *AmMWSc 92*
**McDowell,** Joseph 1756-1801 *DcNCBi 4*
**McDowell,** Joseph 1758-1795 *DcNCBi 4*
**McDowell,** Joseph Jefferson 1800-1877 *DcNCBi 4*
**McDowell,** Karen Ann 1945- *WhoAmL 92*
**McDowell,** Lee Russell 1941- *AmMWSc 92*
**McDowell,** Malcolm 1943- *IntMPA 92, IntWW 91, Who 92, WhoEnt 92*
**McDowell,** Marion Edward 1921- *AmMWSc 92*
**McDowell,** Martin Rastall Coulter 1932- *Who 92*
**McDowell,** Maurice James 1922- *AmMWSc 92*
**McDowell,** Michael 1950- *IntAu&W 91, WrDr 92*
**McDowell,** Michael David 1948- *WhoAmL 92, WhoFI 92*
**McDowell,** Peter Lee 1938- *WhoAmP 91*
**McDowell,** Robert *DrAPF 91*
**McDowell,** Robert Carter 1935- *AmMWSc 92*
**McDowell,** Robert E, Jr 1921- *AmMWSc 92*
**McDowell,** Robert Hull 1927- *AmMWSc 92*
**McDowell,** Robin Scott 1934- *AmMWSc 92, WhoWest 92*
**McDowell,** Sam Booker 1928- *AmMWSc 92*
**McDowell,** Silas 1795-1879 *DcNCBi 4*
**McDowell,** Stanley 1941- *Who 92*
**McDowell,** Susan *WhoAmP 91*
**McDowell,** Thomas David Smith 1823-1898 *DcNCBi 4*
**McDowell,** Timothy Hill 1946- *WhoAmP 91*
**McDowell,** W. Stuart 1947- *WhoEnt 92*
**McDowell,** Wilbur Benedict 1920- *AmMWSc 92*
**McDowell,** William D 1927- *WhoAmP 91*
**McDowell,** William Fraser 1858-1937 *RelLAm 91*
**McDowell,** William H 1953- *AmMWSc 92*
**McDowell,** William Jackson 1925- *AmMWSc 92*

**McDowell,** William Wallis 1823-1893 *DcNCBi 4*
**McDowell-Head,** Lelia M. 1953- *WhoBlA 92*
**McDowney,** Sheryl Blowe 1955- *WhoRel 92*
**McDuff,** Charles Robert 1929- *AmMWSc 92*
**McDuff,** Dusa Margaret 1945- *AmMWSc 92*
**McDuff,** Odis P 1931- *AmMWSc 92*
**McDuffie,** Bruce 1921- *AmMWSc 92*
**McDuffie,** David Wayne 1960- *WhoFI 92*
**McDuffie,** Deborah 1950- *WhoBlA 92*
**McDuffie,** Deborah Jeanne 1950- *WhoEnt 92*
**McDuffie,** Dwayne Glenn 1962- *WhoBlA 92*
**McDuffie,** Frederic Clement 1924- *AmMWSc 92*
**McDuffie,** George E, Jr 1925- *AmMWSc 92*
**McDuffie,** Hinfred 1949- *WhoBlA 92*
**McDuffie,** James Doyle 1929- *WhoAmP 91*
**McDuffie,** Joseph deLeon, Jr. 1950- *WhoBlA 92*
**McDuffie,** Norton G, Jr 1930- *AmMWSc 92*
**McEachen,** Richard Edward 1933- *WhoFI 92*
**McEachern,** Allan 1926- *Who 92, WhoWest 92*
**McEachern,** Bob 1927- *WhoAmP 91*
**McEachern,** Katherine Verdell McNeill 1930- *WhoBlA 92*
**McEachern,** Maceo R. 1946- *WhoBlA 92*
**McEachern,** William Archibald 1945- *WhoFI 92*
**McEachern-Ulmer,** Sylvia L. 1934- *WhoBlA 92*
**McEachin,** Daniel Malloy, Jr 1950- *WhoAmP 91*
**McEachin,** James 1930- *WhoBlA 92*
**McEachran,** Colin Neil 1940- *Who 92*
**McEachran,** John D 1941- *AmMWSc 92*
**McElderry,** Betty *WhoAmP 91*
**McEldowney,** Richard Dennis 1926- *IntAu&W 91, WrDr 92*
**McElfresh,** Adeline 1918- *IntAu&W 91, WrDr 92*
**McElfresh,** Paul Keith 1956- *WhoRel 92*
**McElgunn,** James Douglas 1939- *AmMWSc 92*
**McElhaney,** James Harry 1933- *AmMWSc 92*
**Mc Elhaney,** John Hess 1934- *WhoAmL 92*
**McElhaney,** Ronald Nelson 1942- *AmMWSc 92*
**McElhannon,** Charles Edward 1956- *WhoRel 92*
**McElhannon,** James R. 1944- *WhoRel 92*
**McElheney,** Jane 1836-1874 *BenetAL 91*
**McElheny,** Richard Lee 1936- *WhoAmP 91*
**McElheran,** Brock 1918- *WhoEnt 92*
**McElheran,** John 1929- *Who 92*
**McElhinney,** John 1921- *AmMWSc 92*
**McElhinney,** Margaret M *AmMWSc 92*
**McElhinney,** Robert Stanley 1933- *IntWW 91*
**McElhoe,** Forrest Lester, Jr 1923- *AmMWSc 92*
**McEligot,** Donald M 1931- *AmMWSc 92*
**McElligott,** Ann Theresa 1942- *WhoWest 92*
**McElligott,** James George 1938- *AmMWSc 92*
**McElligott,** Mary Ann 1953- *AmMWSc 92*
**McElligott,** Peter Edward 1935- *AmMWSc 92*
**McElligott,** Thomas James 1943- *WhoFI 92*
**McEllistrem,** Marcus Thomas 1926- *AmMWSc 92*
**McElmurray,** Jeanne Frances 1921- *WhoAmP 91*
**McElrath,** Charles Thomas 1946- *WhoRel 92*
**McElrath,** Frances *TwCWW 91*
**McElrath,** Gayle W 1915- *AmMWSc 92*
**McElrath,** Jack Howard 1933- *WhoEnt 92*
**McElrath,** Randall M. 1946- *WhoEnt 92*
**McElrath,** William N. 1932- *ConAu 35NR, SmATA 65*
**McElree,** Helen 1925- *AmMWSc 92*
**McElroy,** Albert Dean 1922- *AmMWSc 92*
**McElroy,** Alfred Z. 1930- *WhoBlA 92*
**McElroy,** Benjamin Roland 1944- *WhoAmP 91*
**McElroy,** Bernard Patrick 1938- *WhoMW 92*
**McElroy,** Bert Colyar 1943- *WhoAmL 92*
**McElroy,** Charles Dwayne 1967- *WhoBlA 92*
**McElroy,** Colleen J. *DrAPF 91*
**McElroy,** Colleen J 1935- *IntAu&W 91, WhoBlA 92, WrDr 92*
**McElroy,** David L 1930- *AmMWSc 92*
**McElroy,** Gavin Daniel 1960- *WhoAmL 92*
**McElroy,** George A. 1922- *WhoBlA 92*
**McElroy,** George Beamish 1824-1907 *BiInAmS*
**McElroy,** Jerome Lathrop 1937- *WhoFI 92*
**McElroy,** John 1846-1929 *ScFEYrs*
**McElroy,** Joseph *DrAPF 91*
**McElroy,** Joseph 1930- *BenetAL 91, ConNov 91, IntAu&W 91, WrDr 92*
**McElroy,** Joseph Elton 1949- *WhoMW 92*
**McElroy,** Kevin 1958- *WhoAmL 92*
**McElroy,** Laurince Larry Dean 1962- *WhoEnt 92*
**McElroy,** Lee *ConAu 36NR, IntAu&W 91X, TwCWW 91, WrDr 92*
**McElroy,** Lee A., Jr. 1948- *WhoBlA 92*
**McElroy,** Leo Francis 1932- *WhoWest 92*
**McElroy,** Michael Brendan 1939- *AmMWSc 92*
**McElroy,** Paul Tucker 1931- *AmMWSc 92*
**McElroy,** Roy Granville 1907- *Who 92*
**McElroy,** Sam M 1921- *WhoAmP 91*
**McElroy,** Wilbur Renfrew 1914- *AmMWSc 92*
**McElroy,** William David 1917- *AmMWSc 92, IntWW 91, WhoAmP 91*
**McElroy,** William Nordell 1926- *AmMWSc 92*
**McElroy,** William Tyndell, Jr 1924- *AmMWSc 92*
**McElvain,** David Plowman 1937- *WhoFI 92*
**McElvain,** W Lee 1939- *WhoAmP 91*
**McElvane,** Pamela Anne 1958- *WhoBlA 92*
**McElveen,** Gail Marie 1954- *WhoRel 92*
**McElveen,** H Donald 1935- *WhoAmP 91*
**McElveen,** Joseph T, Jr 1946- *WhoAmP 91*
**McElveen,** Junius Carlisle, Jr. 1947- *WhoAmL 92*
**McElvein,** Thomas I., Jr. 1936- *WhoAmL 92*
**McElwain,** David Bruce 1947- *WhoRel 92*
**Mc Elwain,** Joseph Arthur 1919- *WhoWest 92*
**McElwain,** Joseph Mitchell 1941- *WhoAmP 91*
**Mc Elwain,** Lester Stafford 1910- *WhoAmL 92*
**McElwain,** Timmie McKinnon 1939- *WhoRel 92*
**McElwaine,** Guy *WhoEnt 92*
**McElwaine,** Guy 1936- *IntMPA 92*
**McElwee,** Edgar Warren 1907- *AmMWSc 92*
**McElwee,** John Harvey 1834-1926 *DcNCBi 4*
**McElwee,** Robert L 1927- *AmMWSc 92*
**McElya,** Mitchel Roberts 1930- *WhoMW 92*
**McElyea,** Ulysses, Jr. 1941- *WhoWest 92*
**McEnally,** Terence Ernest, Jr 1927- *AmMWSc 92*
**McEnelly,** Minerva Perez 1955- *WhoHisp 92*
**McEnery,** John H. 1925- *ConAu 134*
**McEnery,** John Hartnett 1925- *Who 92*
**McEnery,** Peter 1940- *Who 92*
**McEnery,** Thomas *WhoAmP 91*
**McEnery,** Thomas 1945- *WhoWest 92*
**McEniry,** Robert Francis 1918- *WhoMW 92*
**McEnroe,** Harry A 1931- *WhoAmP 91*
**Mc Enroe,** James Joseph 1946- *WhoRel 92*
**McEnroe,** John 1959- *FacFETw*
**McEnroe,** John Patrick 1959- *IntWW 91*
**McEnrue,** Mary Pat 1953- *WhoWest 92*
**McEntee,** Kenneth 1921- *AmMWSc 92*
**McEntee,** Michael J 1952- *WhoAmP 91*
**McEntee,** Peter Donovan 1920- *IntWW 91, Who 92*
**McEntee,** Thomas Edwin 1943- *AmMWSc 92*
**McEntire,** Billy Ray 1960- *WhoRel 92*
**McEntire,** James Edward 1944- *WhoWest 92*
**McEntire,** Maleta Mae 1957- *WhoWest 92*
**McEntire,** Reba N. 1955- *WhoEnt 92*
**McEntire,** Richard Willian 1942- *AmMWSc 92*
**McEntyre,** John G 1920- *AmMWSc 92*
**McErlane,** Joseph James 1948- *WhoMW 92*
**McEssy,** Earl F 1913- *WhoAmP 91*
**McEvedy,** Colin 1930- *IntAu&W 91, WrDr 92*
**McEveety,** Bernard *IntMPA 92, LesBEnT 92*
**McEveety,** Vincent *IntMPA 92*
**McEver,** Harold Bruce 1944- *WhoFI 92*
**McEvilly,** James J *ScFEYrs*
**McEvilly,** James Lawrence 1926- *WhoAmP 91*
**McEvilly,** James Patrick, Jr. 1943- *WhoAmL 92*
**McEvilly,** Thomas V 1934- *AmMWSc 92*
**Mc Evilly,** Thomas Vincent 1934- *WhoWest 92*
**McEvily,** Arthur Joseph, Jr 1924- *AmMWSc 92*
**McEvily,** John Vincent, Jr. 1949- *WhoFI 92*
**McEvoy,** Ambrose 1878-1927 *TwCPaSc*
**McEvoy,** Brian Ralph 1952- *WhoEnt 92*
**McEvoy,** Charles Lucien 1917- *WhoFI 92*
**McEvoy,** David Dand 1938- *Who 92*
**McEvoy,** J. P. 1895-1958 *BenetAL 91*
**McEvoy,** James Edward 1920- *AmMWSc 92*
**McEvoy,** John Thomas 1937- *WhoAmP 91*
**McEvoy,** Joseph Edward 1942- *WhoFI 92*
**McEvoy,** Marjorie *IntAu&W 91, WrDr 92*
**McEvoy,** Mary 1870-1941 *TwCPaSc*
**McEvoy,** Mike *WhoAmP 91*
**McEvoy,** Nion Tucker 1952- *WhoWest 92*
**McEvoy,** Paul Nigel 1948- *WhoEnt 92*
**McEvoy,** Theodore Newman 1904- *Who 92*
**McEwan,** Alan Thomas 1940- *AmMWSc 92*
**McEwan,** Angus David 1937- *IntWW 91*
**McEwan,** Bruce 1937- *WhoAmP 91*
**McEwan,** Geraldine 1932- *IntWW 91, Who 92*
**McEwan,** Ian 1948- *ConLC 66 [port], ConNov 91, IntWW 91, WrDr 92*
**McEwan,** Ian Russell 1948- *IntAu&W 91, Who 92*
**McEwan,** Robert Neal 1949- *WhoMW 92*
**McEwan,** Robin Gilmour 1943- *Who 92*
**McEwan,** Rory 1932-1982 *TwCPaSc*
**McEwen,** Barry Allyn 1946- *WhoMW 92*
**McEwen,** Bob 1950- *AlmAP 92 [port], WhoAmP 91, WhoMW 92*
**McEwen,** Bruce F 1945- *AmMWSc 92*
**McEwen,** Bruce Sherman 1938- *AmMWSc 92*
**McEwen,** C Richard 1925- *AmMWSc 92*
**McEwen,** Charles Milton, Jr *AmMWSc 92*
**McEwen,** Charles Nehemiah 1942- *AmMWSc 92*
**McEwen,** Currier 1902- *AmMWSc 92*
**McEwen,** David John 1930- *AmMWSc 92*
**McEwen,** Everett E 1932- *AmMWSc 92*
**McEwen,** Freeman Lester 1926- *AmMWSc 92*
**McEwen,** Gerald Noah, Jr 1943- *AmMWSc 92*
**McEwen,** James Stevenson 1910- *Who 92*
**McEwen,** Joan Elizabeth 1952- *AmMWSc 92*
**McEwen,** John 1868-1948 *NewAmDM*
**McEwen,** John 1900-1980 *FacFETw*
**McEwen,** John 1965- *Who 92*
**McEwen,** John L *WhoAmP 91*
**McEwen,** Mark 1954- *WhoBlA 92*
**McEwen,** Robert B 1934- *AmMWSc 92*
**McEwen,** Robert Cameron 1920- *WhoAmP 91*
**McEwen,** Robert Joseph 1916- *WhoFI 92*
**McEwen,** Ruth Geibel 1912- *AmPeW*
**McEwen,** Terence Alexander 1929- *WhoEnt 92*
**McEwen,** William Edwin 1922- *AmMWSc 92*
**McEwing,** Mitchell Dalton 1935- *WhoBlA 92*
**McFadden,** Arthur B. 1940- *WhoBlA 92*
**McFadden,** Bruce Alden 1930- *AmMWSc 92*
**McFadden,** Cora C. 1945- *WhoBlA 92*
**McFadden,** Daniel Little 1937- *WhoFI 92*
**McFadden,** David 1940- *ConPo 91, IntAu&W 91, WrDr 92*
**McFadden,** David Lee 1945- *AmMWSc 92*
**McFadden,** David Wayne 1942- *WhoFI 92*
**McFadden,** Douglas Bruce 1940- *WhoAmL 92*
**McFadden,** Edward Regis *AmMWSc 92*
**McFadden,** Frank Hampton 1925- *WhoAmL 92, WhoFI 92*
**McFadden,** Frederick C., Jr. 1927- *WhoBlA 92*
**McFadden,** Geoffrey Bey 1953- *AmMWSc 92*
**McFadden,** Gerald Thomas 1965- *WhoMW 92*
**McFadden,** Gregory L. 1958- *WhoBlA 92*
**McFadden,** Harry Webber, Jr 1919- *AmMWSc 92*
**McFadden,** Jack Louis *WhoEnt 92*
**McFadden,** James Douglas 1934- *AmMWSc 92*
**McFadden,** James Frederick, Jr. 1920- *WhoMW 92*
**McFadden,** James L. 1929- *WhoBlA 92*
**McFadden,** Jean Alexandra 1941- *Who 92*
**McFadden,** Jeff 1957- *WhoFI 92*
**McFadden,** Jo Beth 1938- *WhoWest 92*
**Mc Fadden,** John Volney 1931- *WhoFI 92*
**McFadden,** Joseph Patrick 1939- *WhoFI 92, WhoIns 92*
**McFadden,** Leon Lambert 1920- *WhoWest 92*
**McFadden,** Lorne Austin 1926- *AmMWSc 92*
**McFadden,** Lucy-Ann Adams 1952- *AmMWSc 92*
**McFadden,** Mary 1936- *DcTwDes*
**McFadden,** Mary 1938- *IntWW 91*
**McFadden,** Mary F. 1944- *WhoMW 92*
**McFadden,** Nathaniel James 1946- *WhoAmP 91, WhoBlA 92*
**McFadden,** Peter W 1932- *AmMWSc 92*
**McFadden,** Robert B 1934- *AmMWSc 92*
**McFadden,** Roy 1921- *ConPo 91, IntAu&W 91, WrDr 92*
**McFadden,** Samuel Wilton 1935- *WhoBlA 92*
**McFadden,** Terry Ted 1936- *WhoWest 92*
**Mc Fadden,** Wilmot Curnow Hamm 1919- *WhoWest 92*
**McFaddin,** Theresa Garrison 1943- *WhoBlA 92*
**McFadyean,** Colin William 1943- *Who 92*
**McFadyen,** Jock *TwCPaSc*
**McFadzean** *Who 92*
**McFadzean,** Baron 1903- *IntWW 91, Who 92*
**McFadzean Of Kelvinside,** Baron 1915- *IntWW 91, Who 92, WrDr 92*
**McFall,** Andrew Calhoun, IV 1965- *WhoFI 92*
**McFall,** David 1919-1988 *TwCPaSc*
**McFall,** Elizabeth 1928- *AmMWSc 92*
**McFall,** Gardner *DrAPF 91*
**McFall,** John 1944- *Who 92*
**McFall,** Kay Lynn 1966- *WhoRel 92*
**McFall,** Mary 1938- *WhoBlA 92*
**McFall,** Richard Graham 1920- *IntWW 91, Who 92*
**McFalls,** Richard T 1932- *WhoIns 92*
**McFarlan,** Duncan d1816 *DcNCBi 4*
**McFarlan,** Edward, Jr 1921- *AmMWSc 92*
**McFarland,** Alan Roberts 1942- *WhoFI 92*
**McFarland,** Allen Keith 1953- *WhoAmL 92*
**McFarland,** Arthur C. 1947- *WhoBlA 92*
**McFarland,** Barbara Graves 1949- *WhoRel 92*
**McFarland,** Bob 1941- *WhoAmP 91*
**McFarland,** C. K. 1934- *WrDr 92*
**McFarland,** Charles Elwood 1927- *AmMWSc 92*
**McFarland,** Charles Manter 1920- *AmMWSc 92*
**McFarland,** Charles R 1927- *AmMWSc 92*
**McFarland,** Charles Warren 1942- *AmMWSc 92*
**McFarland,** Claudette 1935- *WhoBlA 92*
**McFarland,** Dalton E. 1919- *WrDr 92*
**McFarland,** David John 1938- *Who 92*
**McFarland,** Dennis *DrAPF 91*
**McFarland,** Dennis 1950- *ConLC 65 [port]*
**McFarland,** Dennis Claude 1942- *WhoAmP 91*
**McFarland,** Dennis L. 1947- *WhoFI 92*
**McFarland,** Douglas Dale, Jr. 1946- *WhoAmL 92*
**McFarland,** Duncan d1816 *DcNCBi 4*
**McFarland,** Edward Melvin 1944- *WhoWest 92*
**McFarland,** George Conrad, Jr. 1959- *WhoAmL 92*
**McFarland,** Gwen Nation 1930- *WhoAmP 91*
**Mc Farland,** H. Richard 1930- *WhoMW 92*
**McFarland,** Henry F *AmMWSc 92*
**McFarland,** J Ruth 1925- *WhoAmP 91*
**McFarland,** James 1947- *WhoAmP 91*
**McFarland,** James Donald 1929- *WhoMW 92*
**McFarland,** James Thomas 1942- *AmMWSc 92*
**McFarland,** James W. *WhoFI 92*
**McFarland,** James William 1931- *AmMWSc 92*
**McFarland,** James William 1948- *WhoFI 92*
**McFarland,** John *DrAPF 91*
**McFarland,** John 1927- *Who 92*
**McFarland,** John Alexander, Jr 1942- *WhoAmP 91*
**McFarland,** John Bernard 1943- *WhoFI 92*
**McFarland,** John T 1941- *WhoIns 92*
**McFarland,** John William 1923- *AmMWSc 92*
**McFarland,** Jon Weldon 1938- *WhoWest 92*
**McFarland,** Joseph Edward 1945- *WhoWest 92*
**McFarland,** Kay *WhoAmP 91*
**McFarland,** Kay Eleanor 1935- *WhoAmL 92, WhoMW 92*
**McFarland,** Kay Flowers 1942- *AmMWSc 92*
**McFarland,** Kevin John 1958- *WhoFI 92, WhoWest 92*
**McFarland,** Mack 1947- *AmMWSc 92*
**McFarland,** N R *ScFEYrs*

**Mc Farland,** Norman Francis 1922- WhoRel 92, WhoWest 92
**McFarland,** Ollie Franklin 1918- WhoBlA 92
**McFarland,** Richard Herbert 1929- AmMWSc 92
**McFarland,** Richard M. 1923- WhoFI 92
**McFarland,** Robert Edwin 1946- WhoAmL 92
**McFarland,** Robert Harold 1918- AmMWSc 92
**McFarland,** Robert Phillips 1943- WhoBlA 92
**McFarland,** Robert White 1825-1910 BiInAmS
**McFarland,** Ron DrAPF 91
**McFarland,** Thomas Robert 1952- WhoAmL 92
**McFarland,** Violet Sweet 1908- IntAu&W 91
**McFarland,** William D 1945- AmMWSc 92
**McFarland,** William Joseph 1929- WhoFI 92
**McFarland,** William Norman 1925- AmMWSc 92
**McFarland McNeil,** Marianne 1929- IntAu&W 91
**McFarlane,** Adrian Anthony 1946- WhoRel 92
**McFarlane,** Beth Lucetta Troester 1918- WhoFI 92
**McFarlane,** Duncan d1816 DcNCBi 4
**McFarlane,** Ellen Sandra 1938- AmMWSc 92
**McFarlane,** Finley Eugene 1940- AmMWSc 92
**McFarlane,** Franklin E. 1933- WhoBlA 92
**McFarlane,** Harold Finley 1945- AmMWSc 92
**McFarlane,** Ian 1923- Who 92
**McFarlane,** Ian Dalrymple 1915- IntWW 91, Who 92
**McFarlane,** James Sinclair 1925- Who 92
**McFarlane,** James Walter 1920- IntAu&W 91, Who 92, WrDr 92
**McFarlane,** Joanna 1961- AmMWSc 92
**McFarlane,** John Elwood 1929- AmMWSc 92
**McFarlane,** John Spencer 1915- AmMWSc 92
**Mc Farlane,** Karen Elizabeth 1942- WhoEnt 92
**McFarlane,** Kenneth Walter 1937- AmMWSc 92
**McFarlane,** Robert Carl 1937- IntWW 91, WhoAmP 91
**McFarlane,** Ross Alexander 1931- AmMWSc 92
**McFarlane,** Susan Sawin 1962- WhoAmL 92
**McFarlane,** Walter Alexander 1940- WhoAmL 92
**McFarlane of Llandaff,** Baroness 1926- Who 92
**McFarlin,** Dale Elroy AmMWSc 92
**McFarlin,** Emma Daniels 1921- WhoBlA 92
**McFarlin,** Kernaa D'Offert, Jr. 1946- WhoBlA 92
**McFarlin,** Richard Francis 1929- AmMWSc 92
**McFarren,** Earl Francis 1919- AmMWSc 92
**McFarron,** Gary Wayne 1948- WhoAmL 92
**McFate,** Kenneth L 1924- AmMWSc 92
**McFate,** Kenneth Leverne 1924- WhoMW 92
**McFatridge,** Keith William, Jr. 1946- WhoFI 92
**McFaul,** Michael L. 1948- WhoWest 92
**McFeat,** Tom Farrar Scott 1919- AmMWSc 92
**McFedries,** Robert, Jr 1930- AmMWSc 92, WhoFI 92
**McFee,** Alfred Frank 1931- AmMWSc 92
**McFee,** Arthur Storer 1932- AmMWSc 92
**McFee,** Donald Ray 1929- AmMWSc 92
**McFee,** Michael DrAPF 91
**McFee,** Raymond Herbert 1916- AmMWSc 92
**McFee,** Richard 1925- AmMWSc 92
**McFee,** Shirley Miller 1929- WhoAmP 91
**McFee,** Thomas S 1930- WhoAmP 91
**McFee,** William 1881-1966 BenetAL 91
**McFee,** William Warren 1935- AmMWSc 92, WhoMW 92
**McFeeley,** James Calvin 1940- AmMWSc 92
**McFeely,** Clarence Edward 1929- WhoFI 92
**McFeely,** Elizabeth Sarah Anne C. Who 92
**McFeely,** Richard Aubrey 1933- AmMWSc 92
**McFeeters,** Tom Lee 1938- WhoWest 92
**McFeron,** D E 1923- AmMWSc 92
**McFerren,** Johnny C 1933- WhoAmP 91
**McFerren,** Martha DrAPF 91
**McFerrin,** Bobby WhoEnt 92
**McFerrin,** Bobby 1950- WhoBlA 92
**McFerrin,** Robert 1921- WhoBlA 92
**McFerrin,** Sara Elizabeth Copper 1924- WhoBlA 92
**McFerson,** D Richard 1937- WhoIns 92
**McFerson,** D. Richard 1952- WhoFI 92
**McFerson,** Thomas Kimball 1943- WhoWest 92
**McFeters,** Gordon Alwyn 1939- AmMWSc 92
**McFetrich,** Alan 1940- Who 92
**McFetridge,** Mary Isabel 1969- WhoEnt 92
**McGaffey,** Deborah Lee 1950- WhoEnt 92
**Mc Gaffey,** Jere D. 1935- WhoAmL 92
**McGagh,** William Gilbert 1929- WhoFI 92
**McGahan,** Sharon Helen Rochelle 1943- WhoMW 92
**McGahern,** John 1934- ConNov 91, IntAu&W 91, IntWW 91, Who 92, WrDr 92
**McGahren,** William James 1924- AmMWSc 92
**McGair,** Joseph J 1945- WhoAmP 91
**McGalliard,** John D 1943- WhoIns 92
**McGandy,** Edward Lewis 1930- AmMWSc 92
**McGanity,** William James 1923- AmMWSc 92
**McGann,** Andrew 1925- WhoAmP 91
**McGann,** Eileen Elizabeth 1948- WhoAmL 92
**McGann,** John Milton 1948- WhoFI 92, WhoWest 92
**McGann,** John Raymond 1924- WhoRel 92
**McGann,** Locksley Earl 1946- AmMWSc 92
**McGanno,** Michael WrDr 92
**McGannon,** Donald H. d1984 LesBEnT 92 [port]
**McGargill,** Pamela Sue 1955- WhoMW 92
**McGarigle,** William John 1932- WhoEnt 92
**McGarity,** Arthur Edwin 1951- AmMWSc 92
**McGarity,** William Cecil 1921- AmMWSc 92
**McGarr,** Arthur 1940- AmMWSc 92
**McGarrell,** Patrick Bynon 1936- WhoFI 92
**McGarrity,** Gerard John 1940- AmMWSc 92
**McGarrity,** J. Forsyth 1921- Who 92
**McGarrity,** Joseph 1874-1940 DcAmImH
**McGarrity,** Mark 1943- IntAu&W 91, WrDr 92
**McGarry,** Alexander Banting 1940- WhoAmL 92
**McGarry,** Daniel Edward, Jr. 1947- WhoFI 92
**McGarry,** Dorothy 1929- WhoWest 92
**McGarry,** Frederick J 1927- AmMWSc 92
**McGarry,** Ian 1941- Who 92
**McGarry,** Jean DrAPF 91
**McGarry,** Jean 1952- IntAu&W 91
**McGarry,** John Denis 1940- AmMWSc 92
**McGarry,** John Warren WhoAmP 91
**McGarry,** Kevin Vincent 1929- WhoMW 92
**McGarry,** Margaret 1928- AmMWSc 92
**McGarry,** Michael P 1942- AmMWSc 92
**McGarry,** Paul Anthony 1928- AmMWSc 92
**McGarvey,** Alan 1942- Who 92
**McGarvey,** Bruce Ritchie 1928- AmMWSc 92
**McGarvey,** Dennis George 1949- WhoWest 92
**McGarvey,** Diane 1964- WhoFI 92
**McGarvey,** Donald Leroy 1953- WhoRel 92
**McGarvey,** Francis X 1919- AmMWSc 92
**McGarvey,** John William 1829-1911 RelLAm 91
**McGarvey,** William K. 1937- WhoMW 92
**McGarvin,** Eugene Edward 1940- WhoWest 92
**McGary,** Austin 1846-1928 RelLAm 91
**McGary,** Betty Winstead 1936- WhoRel 92
**McGary,** Carl T 1961- AmMWSc 92
**McGary,** Charles Wesley, Jr 1929- AmMWSc 92
**Mc Gary,** Thomas Hugh 1938- WhoMW 92
**McGathon,** Carrie M. 1936- WhoBlA 92
**McGaugh,** James L 1931- AmMWSc 92
**Mc Gaugh,** James Lafayette 1931- WhoWest 92
**McGaugh,** John Wesley 1938- AmMWSc 92
**McGaughan,** Henry S 1917- AmMWSc 92
**McGaughey,** Charles Gilbert 1925- AmMWSc 92
**McGaughey,** Douglas R. 1947- WhoRel 92
**McGaughey,** Florence Helen 1904- IntAu&W 91
**McGaughey,** James W 1935- WhoAmP 91
**McGaughey,** Miriam WhoEnt 92
**McGaughey,** Robert Howe, III 1943- WhoEnt 92
**McGaughey,** Robert William 1941- WhoWest 92
**McGaughy,** Lane Clifford 1940- WhoRel 92
**McGaughy,** Will 1933- WhoBlA 92
**McGauley,** Jacquelyne Sue 1951- WhoWest 92
**McGavick,** Phyllis Ann 1949- WhoAmP 91
**McGavin,** Darren 1922- IntMPA 92, WhoEnt 92
**McGavin,** Jock Campbell 1917- WhoWest 92
**McGavin,** Matthew Donald 1930- AmMWSc 92
**McGavin,** Raymond E 1921- AmMWSc 92
**McGavock,** Walter Donald 1933- AmMWSc 92
**McGavran,** Malcolm Howard 1929- AmMWSc 92
**McGaw,** Kenneth Roy 1926- WhoFI 92
**McGaw,** Sidney Edwin 1908- WhoWest 92
**McGeachin,** Robert Lorimer 1917- AmMWSc 92
**McGeachy,** Daniel Patrick, III 1929- WhoRel 92
**McGeachy,** Neill Roderick 1909-1979 DcNCBi 4
**McGeady,** Leon Joseph 1921- AmMWSc 92
**McGeady,** Paul Joseph 1920- WhoEnt 92
**McGean,** Thomas J 1937- AmMWSc 92
**McGeary,** David F R 1940- AmMWSc 92
**McGee,** Adolphus Stewart 1941- WhoBlA 92
**McGee,** Arthur Lee 1933- WhoBlA 92
**McGee,** Ben Lelon 1943- WhoAmP 91
**McGee,** Benjamin Lelon 1943- WhoBlA 92
**McGee,** Buford Lamar 1960- WhoBlA 92
**McGee,** Charles E 1935- AmMWSc 92
**McGee,** Corlis Ann 1954- WhoFI 92, WhoMW 92
**McGee,** Dawn Kathleen 1962- WhoAmL 92
**McGee,** Donna Johnson 1942- WhoAmP 91
**McGee,** Dorothy Horton 1913- WhoFI 92
**McGee,** Edward WhoAmP 91
**McGee,** Edward James 1947- WhoFI 92
**McGee,** Effie Mary 1928- WhoFI 92, WhoMW 92
**McGee,** Eva M. 1942- WhoBlA 92
**McGee,** Frank d1974 LesBEnT 92
**McGee,** Gale William 1915- IntWW 91, WhoAmP 91
**McGee,** Greg 1950- WrDr 92
**McGee,** Hansel Leslie 1926- WhoBlA 92
**McGee,** Henry A, Jr 1929- AmMWSc 92
**McGee,** Henry W., Jr. 1932- WhoAmL 92, WhoBlA 92
**McGee,** Henry Wadsworth, III 1953- WhoBlA 92
**McGee,** Hubert, Jr 1928- WhoAmP 91
**McGee,** Jacqueline T 1952- WhoAmP 91
**McGee,** James H. 1918- WhoBlA 92
**McGee,** James Howell 1918- WhoAmP 91
**McGee,** James Madison 1940- WhoBlA 92
**McGee,** James O'Donnell 1939- Who 92
**McGee,** James Patrick 1941- AmMWSc 92
**McGee,** James Sears 1942- WhoWest 92
**McGee,** JoAnn WhoBlA 92
**McGee,** John B. 1922- WhoWest 92
**McGee,** John Edward 1928- WhoMW 92
**McGee,** John Paul, Jr 1950- WhoAmP 91
**McGee,** Joseph H. 1929- WhoAmL 92
**McGee,** Joseph J, Jr 1919- WhoIns 92
**McGee,** Karen Ann 1950- WhoWest 92
**McGee,** Lawrence Ray 1952- AmMWSc 92
**McGee,** Leonard E 1952- WhoAmP 91
**McGee,** Lewis A. 1893-1979 RelLAm 91
**McGee,** M. Kevin 1950- WhoFI 92
**McGee,** Mark ConAu 134
**McGee,** Mark T. 1947- ConAu 134
**McGee,** Michael Jay 1952- WhoWest 92
**McGee,** Mike Ray 1959- WhoBlA 92
**McGee,** Pamela Denise 1962- BlkOlyM
**McGee,** Patricia I WhoAmP 91
**McGee,** Patrick Edgar 1944- IntAu&W 91
**McGee,** Rebecca E. 1943- WhoBlA 92
**McGee,** Rose N. 1921- WhoBlA 92
**McGee,** Terence Gary 1936- WrDr 92
**McGee,** Terrence James 1955- WhoMW 92
**McGee,** Thomas Donald 1925- AmMWSc 92
**McGee,** Thomas Howard 1941- AmMWSc 92
**McGee,** Thomas W. WhoRel 92
**McGee,** Thomas W 1924- WhoAmP 91
**McGee,** Timothy Dwayne 1964- WhoBlA 92
**McGee,** Timothy Sean 1947- WhoMW 92
**McGee,** Vonetta WhoBlA 92
**McGee,** Walter Hayden 1952- WhoAmL 92
**McGee,** William F 1937- AmMWSc 92
**McGee,** William John 1853-1912 BiInAmS
**McGee,** William Sears 1917- WhoAmP 91
**McGee,** William Stephen 1949- WhoAmL 92
**McGee,** William Walter 1939- AmMWSc 92
**McGee,** Willie Dean 1958- WhoBlA 92
**McGee-Russell,** Samuel M 1927- AmMWSc 92
**McGeehan,** Michael P 1960- WhoAmP 91
**McGeeney,** John Stephen 1934- WhoAmL 92
**McGeer,** Edith Graef 1923- AmMWSc 92
**McGeer,** James Peter 1922- AmMWSc 92
**McGeer,** Patrick L 1927- AmMWSc 92
**McGeezer,** Mark ConAu 134
**Mc Gehee,** Carden Coleman 1924- WhoFI 92
**Mc Gehee,** H. Coleman, Jr. 1923- WhoMW 92, WhoRel 92
**McGehee,** Lucius Polk 1868-1923 DcNCBi 4
**McGehee,** Maurice Edward 1914- WhoBlA 92
**McGehee,** Michael David 1952- WhoRel 92
**McGehee,** Montford 1822-1895 DcNCBi 4
**McGehee,** Nan E. 1928- WhoBlA 92
**McGehee,** Oscar Carruth 1939- AmMWSc 92
**McGehee,** Ralph Marshall 1921- AmMWSc 92
**McGehee,** Randy Gene 1952- WhoRel 92
**McGehee,** Richard Paul 1943- AmMWSc 92
**McGehee,** Richard Vernon 1934- AmMWSc 92
**McGehee,** Thomas Rives 1924- WhoFI 92
**McGeoch,** Ian 1914- Who 92
**McGeorge,** A, Jr 1921- AmMWSc 92
**McGeorge,** Robert Lloyd 1945- WhoAmL 92
**McGeough,** John TwCWW 91
**McGeough,** Joseph Anthony 1940- Who 92
**McGeough,** Laura Marie 1960- WhoAmL 92
**McGeown,** Mary Graham 1923- Who 92
**McGerity,** Joseph Loehr 1928- AmMWSc 92
**McGervey,** John Donald 1931- AmMWSc 92, WhoMW 92
**McGervey,** Paul John, III 1947- WhoFI 92
**McGettigan,** Charles Carroll, Jr. 1945- WhoFI 92
**McGhan,** William Frederick 1946- AmMWSc 92
**McGhee,** Charles Robert 1934- AmMWSc 92
**McGhee,** David Wesson 1945- WhoMW 92
**McGhee,** George C. 1912- IntWW 91
**McGhee,** George Crews 1912- Who 92, WhoAmP 91
**McGhee,** George Rufus, Jr 1951- AmMWSc 92
**McGhee,** Georgia Mae 1934- WhoBlA 92
**McGhee,** Howard 1918-1987 FacFETw
**McGhee,** James Leon 1948- WhoBlA 92
**McGhee,** Jerry Roger 1941- AmMWSc 92
**McGhee,** Nancy Bullock 1908- WhoBlA 92
**McGhee,** Nelson 1931- WhoAmP 91
**McGhee,** Odell Gene 1952- WhoMW 92
**McGhee,** Reginald D. 1927- WhoBlA 92
**McGhee,** Robert B 1929- AmMWSc 92
**McGhee,** Samuel T. 1940- WhoBlA 92
**McGhee,** Terence Joseph 1936- AmMWSc 92
**McGhee,** Walter Brownie 1915- WhoBlA 92
**McGhie,** James Ironside 1915- Who 92
**McGhie,** James Marshall 1944- Who 92
**McGhie,** Kirsty 1959- TwCPaSc
**McGibony,** Thomas Richard 1934- WhoEnt 92
**McGiff,** John C 1927- AmMWSc 92
**McGiffen,** Thomas Glenn 1964- WhoWest 92
**McGiffert,** Arthur Cushman 1851-1933 RelLAm 91
**Mc Giffert,** David Eliot 1926- WhoAmL 92
**McGiffin,** Robert Floyd, Jr. 1942- WhoWest 92
**McGill,** Angus WrDr 92
**McGill,** Angus 1927- Who 92
**McGill,** Archie Joseph, Jr. 1931- IntWW 91
**McGill,** Charles Beatty 1922- WhoIns 92
**McGill,** Dan M. 1919- ConAu 134
**McGill,** Dan Mays 1919- WhoIns 92
**McGill,** David A 1930- AmMWSc 92
**McGill,** David Edward 1963- WhoEnt 92
**McGill,** David John 1939- AmMWSc 92

McGill, David Park 1919- AmMWSc 92
McGill, Dorothy June 1930- WhoWest 92
McGill, Douglas B 1929- AmMWSc 92
McGill, George Emmert 1931- AmMWSc 92
McGill, Gilbert William 1947- WhoAmL 92
McGill, Henry Coleman, Jr 1921- AmMWSc 92
McGill, Ian IntAu&W 91X
McGill, James T 1940- WhoIns 92
McGill, John Y 1952- WhoAmP 91
McGill, Julian Edward 1932- AmMWSc 92
McGill, Kenneth Alan 1955- WhoRel 92
McGill, Lawrence David 1944- AmMWSc 92, WhoWest 92
McGill, Lovette Eunice 1953- WhoAmP 91
McGill, Mary Alice R 1951- WhoAmP 91
McGill, Maurice Leon 1936- WhoFI 92
McGill, Nigel Harry Duncan 1916- Who 92
McGill, O. J. 1928- WhoFI 92
Mc Gill, Robert Ernest, III 1931- WhoFI 92
McGill, Robert Mayo 1925- AmMWSc 92
McGill, Stephen 1912- Who 92
McGill, Suzanne 1944- AmMWSc 92
McGill, Thomas Conley, Jr 1942- AmMWSc 92
McGill, Thomas L., Jr. 1946- WhoBlA 92
McGill, William Bruce 1945- AmMWSc 92
McGill, William James 1922- IntWW 91
McGillem, C D 1923- AmMWSc 92
McGilley, Mary Janet 1924- WhoRel 92
McGilliard, A Dare 1926- AmMWSc 92
McGilliard, Lance Mason 1952- WhoFI 92
McGilliard, Lon Dee 1921- AmMWSc 92
McGilliard, Michael Lon 1947- AmMWSc 92
McGillicuddy, Joan Marie 1952- WhoWest 92
McGillicuddy, John Francis 1930- IntWW 91, WhoFI 92
McGilligan, Denis Brian 1921- Who 92
McGillis, Kelly IntWW 91
McGillis, Kelly 1957- IntMPA 92
McGillis, Kelly 1958- ConTFT 9
McGillivray, Alexander 1759?-1793 BlkwEAR, RComAH
McGillivray, Robert 1931- Who 92
McGilvary, Daniel 1828-1911 DcNCBi 4
McGilvery, Robert Warren 1920- AmMWSc 92
McGilvra, Albert Wayne 1961- WhoMW 92
McGilvray, Andrew Robert 1933- WhoRel 92
McGilvray, James William 1938- Who 92
McGinley, Donald F 1920- WhoAmP 91
McGinley, Edward Stillman, II 1939- WhoFI 92
McGinley, Mark Kennedy 1959- WhoEnt 92
McGinley, Michael James 1949- WhoIns 92
McGinley, Nancy Elizabeth 1952- WhoAmL 92
McGinley, Phyllis 1905-1978 BenetAL 91
McGinn, Bernard John 1937- WhoRel 92
McGinn, Clifford 1922- AmMWSc 92
McGinn, Donald Joseph 1905- WhoEnt 92
McGinn, James Thomas 1932- WhoEnt 92
McGinn, John Charlton 1943- WhoAmL 92
McGinn, Mary Lyn 1949- WhoFI 92
McGinn, Sarah Cass 1717- BlkwEAR
McGinnes, Burd Sheldon 1921- AmMWSc 92
McGinnes, Edgar Allan, Jr 1926- AmMWSc 92
McGinness, James Donald 1930- AmMWSc 92
McGinness, Joseph M 1947- WhoAmP 91
McGinness, William George, III 1948- AmMWSc 92
McGinness, William Scott, Jr. 1947- WhoAmL 92
McGinnies, William Grovenor 1899- AmMWSc 92
McGinnies, William Joseph 1927- AmMWSc 92
McGinnis, Alfred Chester, Sr 1930- WhoAmP 91
Mc Ginnis, Arthur Joseph 1911- WhoFI 92
McGinnis, Bob 1931- WhoAmP 91
McGinnis, Charles Henry, Jr 1934- AmMWSc 92
McGinnis, David Franklin, Jr 1944- AmMWSc 92
McGinnis, Denise Rochelle 1953- WhoMW 92
McGinnis, Donald Edward 1917- WhoEnt 92
McGinnis, Edward Charles, Jr. 1934- WhoMW 92
McGinnis, Eugene A 1921- AmMWSc 92
McGinnis, Gary David 1940- AmMWSc 92
McGinnis, George S. 1950- WhoBlA 92
McGinnis, James 1918- AmMWSc 92
McGinnis, James Allan 1931- WhoAmP 91
McGinnis, James F 1941- AmMWSc 92
McGinnis, James John 1948- WhoEnt 92
McGinnis, James Lee 1945- AmMWSc 92
McGinnis, James Michael 1944- WhoAmP 91
McGinnis, James W. 1940- WhoBlA 92
McGinnis, John Oldham 1957- WhoAmL 92
McGinnis, John Thurlow 1934- AmMWSc 92
McGinnis, John William 1943- WhoFI 92
McGinnis, Lyle David 1931- AmMWSc 92
McGinnis, Marlene LesBEnT 92
McGinnis, Michael Patrick 1950- WhoWest 92
McGinnis, Michael Randy 1942- AmMWSc 92
McGinnis, Michael Robert 1947- WhoAmP 91
McGinnis, Pamela Ann 1954- WhoEnt 92
McGinnis, Robert Cameron 1925- AmMWSc 92
McGinnis, Robert William 1936- WhoFI 92, WhoWest 92
McGinnis, Sean William 1955- WhoFI 92
McGinnis, Sheila 1938- WhoRel 92
McGinnis, Timothy 1940- WhoFI 92
McGinnis, W. Patrick WhoMW 92
McGinnis, William Joseph 1923- AmMWSc 92
McGinniss, Joe SourALJ
McGinniss, Joe 1942- IntAu&W 91, WrDr 92
McGinniss, Vincent Daniel 1942- AmMWSc 92
McGinty, Brian Donald 1937- WhoAmL 92
McGinty, Doris Evans 1925- WhoBlA 92
McGinty, Gayle Maxine 1960- WhoMW 92
McGinty, John C., Jr. 1950- WhoMW 92
McGinty, William Thomas 1952- WhoAmL 92
McGirk, Richard Heath 1945- AmMWSc 92
McGirr, Edward McCombie 1916- Who 92
McGirr, Jackelen Richardson 1941- WhoWest 92
McGirt, James Ephraim 1874-1930 DcNCBi 4
McGiverin, Arthur A. 1928- WhoAmL 92, WhoAmP 91, WhoMW 92
McGivern, Arthur J. 1947- WhoAmL 92
McGivern, Eugene 1938- Who 92
McGivern, William T. WhoAmL 92
McGivney, John J. 1956- WhoAmL 92
McGlade, Anne Mary 1960- WhoRel 92
McGlade, Thomas Michael 1959- WhoFI 92
McGlamery, Marshal Dean 1932- AmMWSc 92
McGlashan and Gill DcLB 106
McGlashan, John Reid Curtis 1921- Who 92
McGlashan, M. L. 1924- WrDr 92
McGlashan, Maxwell Len 1924- Who 92
McGlasson, Alvin Garnett 1925- AmMWSc 92
McGlaughlin, Daniel W WhoIns 92
McGlaughlin, William WhoEnt 92A
McGlennon, John Joseph 1949- WhoAmP 91
McGlinchey, Dermot Sheehan 1933- WhoAmL 92
McGlinchey, Joseph Dennis 1938- WhoFI 92
McGlinn, Francis Michael 1945- WhoIns 92
McGlinn, Frank C P 1914- WhoAmP 91
McGlinn, William David 1930- AmMWSc 92
McGlohon, Loonis Reeves 1921- WhoEnt 92
McGloin, Joseph Thaddeus 1917- WhoRel 92
McGloin, Paul Arthur 1923- AmMWSc 92
McGlone, Frank Bartlett 1913- WhoWest 92
McGlothan, Ernest 1937- WhoBlA 92
McGlothen, Goree 1915- WhoBlA 92
McGlothen, Lynn Everett 1950-1984 WhoBlA 92N
McGlothen, Steven Raymond 1951- WhoEnt 92
McGlothlin, Donald Allen, Sr 1926- WhoAmP 91
McGlothlin, James Dwayne 1951- WhoMW 92
McGlothlin, James Ira 1947- WhoRel 92
McGlynn, Betty Hoag 1914- WhoWest 92
McGlynn, Margaret L WhoAmP 91
McGlynn, Michael J WhoAmP 91
McGlynn, Sean Patrick 1931- AmMWSc 92
McGlynn, Stephen Patrick 1962- WhoAmL 92
McGoldrick, John Lewis 1941- WhoAmL 92
McGoldrick, Ruth Frances 1934- WhoRel 92
McGolrick, J. Edward, Jr. 1932- WhoAmL 92
McGonagle, Richard Francis 1946- WhoEnt 92
McGonagle, Stephen 1914- Who 92
McGonagle, Thomas G. 1959- WhoFI 92
McGonegle, Timothy Joseph 1952- WhoMW 92
McGonigal, Edgar R. 1953- WhoFI 92
McGonigal, William E 1939- AmMWSc 92
McGonigle, James Gregory 1945- WhoFI 92
McGonigle, Thomas Patrick 1960- WhoMW 92
McGoodwin, Jim 1953- WhoAmP 91
McGoodwin, Roland C. 1933- WhoBlA 92
McGoohan, Patrick 1928- IntMPA 92
McGookey, Donald Paul 1928- AmMWSc 92
McGorrill, Bruce Courtney 1931- WhoEnt 92
McGorry, Kenneth V. 1951- WhoEnt 92
McGough, Hugh Richard 1931- WhoAmL 92
McGough, Roger 1937- ConPo 91, IntAu&W 91, Who 92, WrDr 92
McGough, Walter Thomas 1919- WhoAmL 92
McGough, Walter Thomas, Jr. 1953- WhoAmL 92
McGough, William Edward 1928- AmMWSc 92
McGovern, Ann 1930- IntAu&W 91
McGovern, Cassandra Jane 1942- WhoMW 92
McGovern, Catherine Bigley 1939- WhoMW 92
McGovern, Charles Joseph 1920- WhoAmL 92
McGovern, Cynthia Ann 1948- WhoAmP 91
McGovern, Dianne 1948- WhoMW 92
McGovern, Elizabeth 1961- IntMPA 92, WhoEnt 92
McGovern, George 1922- WhoAmP 91
McGovern, George S 1922- FacFETw [port]
McGovern, George Stanley 1922- AmPolLe, IntWW 91, Who 92
McGovern, John James 1932- WhoIns 92
McGovern, John Joseph 1920- AmMWSc 92
McGovern, John Phillip 1921- AmMWSc 92, WrDr 92
McGovern, Lawrence T. 1944- WhoWest 92
Mc Govern, Maureen Therese 1949- WhoEnt 92
McGovern, Michael Patrick 1951- WhoWest 92
McGovern, Michael Trevor 1955- WhoMW 92
McGovern, Patricia WhoAmP 91
McGovern, Patricia Eileen 1954- WhoAmP 91
McGovern, Peter John 1938- WhoAmL 92
McGovern, R. Gordon 1926- IntWW 91
McGovern, Ricky James 1948- WhoWest 92
McGovern, Robert DrAPF 91
McGovern, Seann Eugene 1963- WhoMW 92, WhoRel 92
McGovern, Sheila Elizabeth 1936- WhoAmL 92
McGovern, Terence Joseph 1942- AmMWSc 92
McGovern, Terrence Phillip 1930- AmMWSc 92
McGovern, Tim WhoEnt 92
Mc Govern, Walter T. 1922- WhoAmL 92, WhoWest 92
McGovern, Wayne Ernest 1937- AmMWSc 92
McGovren, James Patrick 1947- AmMWSc 92
McGowan Who 92
McGowan, Baron 1938- Who 92
McGowan, Alan Patrick 1928- Who 92
McGowan, Blaine, Jr 1921- AmMWSc 92
McGowan, Bruce Henry 1924- Who 92
McGowan, Cynthia 1961- WhoMW 92
McGowan, David Allen 1952- WhoMW 92
McGowan, Dennis Edward 1952- WhoMW 92
McGowan, Edgar Leon 1920- WhoAmP 91
McGowan, Eleanor Brookens 1944- AmMWSc 92
McGowan, Elsie Henderson 1947- WhoBlA 92
McGowan, Francis Keith 1921- AmMWSc 92
McGowan, George Vincent 1928- WhoFI 92
McGowan, Ian Duncan 1945- Who 92
McGowan, Inez TwCSFW 91
McGowan, Jackie Elwood 1929- WhoMW 92
McGowan, James DrAPF 91, WhoFI 92
McGowan, James William 1931- AmMWSc 92
McGowan, Joan A 1944- AmMWSc 92
McGowan, Joe A., Jr. ConAu 133
McGowan, John Arthur 1924- AmMWSc 92
McGowan, John Barrie 1947- WhoAmL 92
McGowan, John Evans 1933- WhoFI 92
McGowan, John Joseph 1951- AmMWSc 92
McGowan, John P. 1953- ConAu 135
McGowan, Jon Gerald 1939- AmMWSc 92
McGowan, Joseph A., Jr. 1931- ConAu 133
McGowan, Joseph Augustine, III 1942- WhoFI 92
McGowan, Michael 1940- Who 92
McGowan, Michael James 1952- AmMWSc 92
McGowan, Nora McLin 1934- WhoFI 92
McGowan, Patrick D 1951- WhoAmP 91
McGowan, Patrick Francis 1940- WhoAmL 92
McGowan, Patrick K 1956- WhoAmP 91
McGowan, Robert Oliver 1944- IntAu&W 91
McGowan, Sherry A 1946- WhoAmP 91
McGowan, Steven Paul 1955- WhoAmL 92
McGowan, Thomas Randolph 1926- WhoBlA 92
McGowan, Whitman Ott 1950- WhoEnt 92
McGowan, William Courtney, Jr 1937- AmMWSc 92
Mc Gowan, William George 1927- WhoFI 92
McGowen, Ernest B, Sr WhoAmP 91
McGowin, David, Jr. 1942- WhoRel 92
McGown, Anne Catherine 1950- WhoAmL 92
McGown, Evelyn L 1944- AmMWSc 92
McGown, Jill 1947- WrDr 92
McGrady, Angele Vial 1941- AmMWSc 92
McGrady, Eddie James 1928- WhoBlA 92
McGrady, Edward Kevin 1935- Who 92
McGrady, Sandra Jean 1958- WhoRel 92
McGrady, Thomas 1863- ScFEYrs
McGrail, David Wayne 1944- AmMWSc 92
McGrail, Jeane Kathryn 1947- WhoMW 92
McGrail, Sean Francis 1928- Who 92
McGrail, Susan King 1952- WhoMW 92
McGranahan, Larry Clayton, Jr. 1971- WhoRel 92
McGrane, Bernard 1947- ConAu 133
McGrath, Abigail Hubbell Rosen 1941- WhoEnt 92
McGrath, Alister E. 1953- ConAu 134
McGrath, Arthur Kevin AmMWSc 92
McGrath, Barry 1932- WhoAmL 92
McGrath, Brian Henry 1925- Who 92
McGrath, Charles Morris 1943- AmMWSc 92
McGrath, Christopher Thomas 1958- WhoAmL 92
McGrath, Clarice Hobgood 1951- WhoBlA 92
McGrath, David Peter 1949- WhoAmP 91
McGrath, Donald G. 1933- WhoAmL 92
McGrath, Edward A. 1930- WhoFI 92
McGrath, Edward Joseph 1935- WhoAmL 92
McGrath, Eugene R AmMWSc 92
McGrath, Eugene R. 1942- WhoFI 92
McGrath, James A. 1932- IntWW 91
McGrath, James Edward 1934- AmMWSc 92
McGrath, James J 1931- AmMWSc 92
McGrath, James Joseph AmMWSc 92
McGrath, James Joseph 1931- WhoMW 92
McGrath, James W 1912- AmMWSc 92
McGrath, Jim DrAPF 91
McGrath, John 1935- IntAu&W 91, WrDr 92
McGrath, John Anthony 1935- WhoRel 92
McGrath, John Christie 1949- Who 92
McGrath, John F 1927- AmMWSc 92
McGrath, John F 1954- WhoIns 92
McGrath, John Joseph 1949- AmMWSc 92
McGrath, John Peter 1935- Who 92
McGrath, John Thomas 1918- AmMWSc 92
McGrath, Joseph Edward 1927- WhoMW 92
McGrath, Juliet Kaufmann DrAPF 91
McGrath, Kathryn Bradley 1944- WhoFI 92
McGrath, Kristina DrAPF 91

**McGrath**, Leonard Joseph 1945- *WhoAmP 91*
**McGrath**, Marcos Gregorio *WhoRel 92*
**McGrath**, Marcos Gregorio 1924- *IntWW 91*
**McGrath**, Mary F. 1954- *WhoFI 92*
**McGrath**, Maureen Eileen 1939- *WhoAmL 92*
**McGrath**, Michael Alan 1942- *WhoAmP 91, WhoMW 92*
**McGrath**, Michael Glennon 1941- *AmMWSc 92*
**McGrath**, Morgan *IntAu&W 91X*
**McGrath**, Patrick 1950- *ConNov 91*
**McGrath**, Patrick Gerard 1916- *Who 92*
**McGrath**, Patrick J. 1934- *WhoFI 92*
**McGrath**, Peter William d1990 *Who 92N*
**McGrath**, Raymond J. 1942- *AlmAP 92 [port], WhoAmP 91*
**McGrath**, Robert L 1938- *AmMWSc 92*
**McGrath**, Thomas *DrAPF 91*
**McGrath**, Thomas 1916- *ConPo 91*
**McGrath**, Thomas 1916-1990 *SmATA 66*
**McGrath**, Thomas Augustine 1919- *WhoRel 92*
**McGrath**, Thomas F, III 1947- *WhoIns 92*
**McGrath**, Thomas Frederick 1929- *AmMWSc 92*
**McGrath**, Thomas J. *IntMPA 92*
**McGrath**, Thomas J. 1932- *WhoAmL 92*
**McGrath**, Tom 1940- *WrDr 92*
**McGrath**, William Joseph 1943- *WhoAmL 92*
**McGrath**, William Robert 1933- *AmMWSc 92*
**McGrath**, William Thomas 1933- *AmMWSc 92*
**McGraw**, Burl David, III 1947- *WhoRel 92*
**McGraw**, Charles Patrick 1942- *AmMWSc 92*
**McGraw**, Darrell Vivian, Jr 1936- *WhoAmP 91*
**McGraw**, Delford Armstrong 1917- *AmMWSc 92*
**McGraw**, Elois Jarvis 1915- *SmATA 67 [port]*
**McGraw**, Eloise Jarvis 1915- *ConAu 36NR, IntAu&W 91, WrDr 92*
**McGraw**, Gary Earl 1940- *AmMWSc 92*
**McGraw**, Gerald Earl 1932- *WhoRel 92*
**McGraw**, Gerald Wayne 1943- *AmMWSc 92*
**Mc Graw**, Harold Whittlesey, Jr. 1918- *WhoFI 92*
**McGraw**, James Carmichael 1928- *AmMWSc 92*
**McGraw**, John Leon, Jr 1940- *AmMWSc 92*
**McGraw**, John Patrick 1947- *WhoEnt 92, WhoWest 92*
**McGraw**, John Thomas 1946- *WhoWest 92*
**McGraw**, Lavinia Morgan 1924- *WhoFI 92*
**McGraw**, Leslie Daniel 1920- *AmMWSc 92*
**McGraw**, Michael Gerard 1957- *WhoMW 92*
**McGraw**, Patrick John 1956- *WhoAmL 92*
**McGraw**, Richard Lyle 1936- *WhoFI 92*
**McGraw**, Robert Leonard 1949- *AmMWSc 92*
**McGraw**, Timothy E *AmMWSc 92*
**McGraw**, Vincent DePaul 1930- *WhoMW 92*
**McGraw**, Warren Randolph 1939- *WhoAmP 91*
**McGraw**, William Corbin 1916- *ConAu 36NR*
**McGraw**, William Ralph 1930- *WhoEnt 92*
**McGready**, James 1763-1817 *DcNCBi 4*
**McGreer**, Elizabeth Lawrence 1951- *WhoWest 92*
**McGreer**, Keith Ross 1946- *WhoMW 92*
**McGreevey**, James E 1957- *WhoAmP 91*
**McGreevey**, Mark F *WhoIns 92*
**McGreevy**, Brian Kenneth 1957- *WhoAmL 92*
**Mc Greevy**, John Charles 1938- *WhoMW 92*
**McGreevy**, Martin Kenneth 1931- *WhoIns 92*
**McGreevy**, Susan Brown 1934- *IntAu&W 91*
**McGreevy**, Terrence Gerard 1932- *WhoAmL 92*
**McGreevy**, William Joseph 1940- *WhoAmP 91*
**McGregor** *Who 92*
**McGregor**, Alistair Gerald Crichton 1937- *Who 92*
**McGregor**, Angus 1926- *Who 92*
**McGregor**, Bonnie A 1942- *AmMWSc 92*
**McGregor**, Cecelia Jean 1952- *WhoAmL 92*
**McGregor**, Charles 1927- *IntMPA 92*
**McGregor**, Chris 1936- *NewAmDM*
**McGregor**, Constance Leonard *WhoAmP 91*
**McGregor**, Dennis Nicholas 1943- *AmMWSc 92*
**McGregor**, Donald Neil 1936- *AmMWSc 92*
**McGregor**, Douglas D 1932- *AmMWSc 92*
**McGregor**, Douglas H 1939- *AmMWSc 92*
**McGregor**, Douglas Ian 1942- *AmMWSc 92*
**McGregor**, Duncan J 1921- *AmMWSc 92*
**McGregor**, Edna M. *WhoBlA 92*
**McGregor**, Frank Bobbitt, Jr. 1952- *WhoAmL 92*
**McGregor**, Gordon Peter 1932- *Who 92*
**McGregor**, Harvey 1926- *IntWW 91, Who 92*
**McGregor**, Ian 1922- *Who 92*
**McGregor**, Ian Alexander 1921- *Who 92*
**McGregor**, Ian Alexander 1922- *IntWW 91*
**McGregor**, Iona 1929- *IntAu&W 91, WrDr 92*
**McGregor**, James Stalker 1927- *Who 92*
**McGregor**, John Robert 1936- *WhoMW 92*
**McGregor**, Malcolm Francis 1910- *IntAu&W 91, WrDr 92*
**McGregor**, Maurice *AmMWSc 92*
**McGregor**, Murray Hugh 1936- *WhoFI 92*
**McGregor**, Nancy Rohwer 1930- *WhoAmP 91*
**McGregor**, Oran B. 1925- *WhoBlA 92*
**McGregor**, Peter 1926- *Who 92*
**McGregor**, Ronald Leighton 1919- *AmMWSc 92*
**McGregor**, Stanley Dane 1938- *AmMWSc 92*
**McGregor**, Theodore Anthony 1944- *WhoFI 92*
**McGregor**, Timothy Crary 1953- *WhoMW 92*
**McGregor**, Walter 1937- *AmMWSc 92*
**McGregor**, Wheeler Kesey, Jr 1929- *AmMWSc 92*
**McGregor**, William Henry Davis 1927- *AmMWSc 92*
**McGregor Of Durris**, Baron 1921- *IntWW 91, Who 92*
**McGrew**, Elizabeth Anne 1916- *AmMWSc 92*
**McGrew**, Ivey 1922- *WhoMW 92*
**McGrew**, James Hall 1944- *WhoAmL 92*
**McGrew**, Janice Olive Waggener *IntAu&W 91*
**McGrew**, Kathleen Alice 1952- *IntAu&W 91*
**McGrew**, Leroy Albert 1938- *AmMWSc 92*
**McGrew**, Michael Bruce 1950- *WhoRel 92*
**McGrew**, Thomas James 1942- *WhoAmL 92*
**McGrier**, Jerry, Sr. 1955- *WhoBlA 92*
**McGriff**, Deborah M. 1949- *WhoBlA 92*
**McGriff**, Frederick Stanley 1963- *WhoBlA 92*
**McGriff**, Jack 1920- *WhoAmP 91*
**McGriff**, Richard Bernard 1935- *AmMWSc 92*
**McGrigor**, Charles Edward 1922- *Who 92*
**McGroarty**, Estelle Josephine 1945- *AmMWSc 92, WhoMW 92*
**McGroddy**, James Cleary 1937- *AmMWSc 92*
**McGrogan**, James P. *WhoRel 92*
**McGrory**, Edward 1921- *IntAu&W 91*
**McGrory**, Joseph Bennett 1934- *AmMWSc 92*
**McGrory**, Larry James 1957- *WhoAmL 92*
**McGrouther**, Angus 1946- *Who 92*
**McGruder**, Charles E. 1925- *WhoBlA 92*
**McGruder**, Elaine 1949- *WhoAmP 91*
**McGruder**, James Patrick 1926- *WhoWest 92*
**McGuane**, Frank L., Jr. 1939- *WhoAmL 92*
**McGuane**, Thomas *DrAPF 91*
**McGuane**, Thomas 1939- *BenetAL 91, ConNov 91, TwCWW 91, WrDr 92*
**McGuckian**, Medbh 1950- *ConPo 91, FacFETw, IntAu&W 91, WrDr 92*
**McGuff**, Joe *WhoMW 92*
**McGuffee**, George Orville 1908- *WhoAmP 91*
**McGuffey**, Kenneth Duane 1932- *WhoAmP 91*
**McGuffey**, William Holmes 1800-1873 *BenetAL 91*
**McGuffie**, Ginger 1944- *WhoAmL 92*
**McGuffin**, Dorothy Brown 1944- *WhoBlA 92*
**McGuffin**, Mark *ConAu 134*
**McGuffin**, Peter 1949- *Who 92*
**McGuigan**, F. J. 1924- *WrDr 92*
**McGuigan**, Frank Joseph 1924- *AmMWSc 92, WhoWest 92*
**McGuigan**, James Charles 1894-1974 *RelLAm 91*
**McGuigan**, James E 1931- *AmMWSc 92*
**McGuigan**, Robert Alister, Jr 1942- *AmMWSc 92*
**McGuigan**, Robert Vincent 1931- *WhoIns 92*
**McGuigan**, Thomas Malcolm 1921- *IntWW 91*
**McGuigan Burns**, Simon Hugh *Who 92*
**Mc Guinn**, Martin Gregory 1942- *WhoAmL 92, WhoFI 92*
**McGuinness**, Barbara Sue 1947- *WhoFI 92, WhoMW 92*
**McGuinness**, Bradley Michael 1961- *WhoFI 92*
**McGuinness**, Brendan Peter 1931- *Who 92*
**McGuinness**, Deborah Louise 1958- *AmMWSc 92*
**McGuinness**, Eugene T 1927- *AmMWSc 92*
**McGuinness**, Frank 1953- *IntWW 91*
**McGuinness**, James Anthony 1941- *AmMWSc 92*
**McGuinness**, James Joseph *Who 92*
**McGuinness**, Kenneth Danner 1951- *WhoIns 92*
**McGuinness**, Norah 1903- *TwCPaSc*
**McGuinness**, Owen P 1956- *AmMWSc 92*
**McGuinness**, Vincent R. 1957- *WhoAmL 92*
**McGuire**, Anne Marie 1951- *WhoRel 92*
**McGuire**, Anthony Bartholomew 1945- *WhoMW 92*
**McGuire**, Brian Lyle 1959- *WhoFI 92*
**McGuire**, Carol Ann 1950- *WhoMW 92*
**McGuire**, Charles Francis 1929- *AmMWSc 92*
**McGuire**, Chester C., Jr. 1936- *WhoBlA 92*
**McGuire**, Christine H 1918- *AmMWSc 92*
**McGuire**, Cyril A. 1926- *WhoBlA 92*
**McGuire**, Daniel Thomas 1949- *WhoMW 92*
**McGuire**, David Kelty 1934- *AmMWSc 92*
**McGuire**, Dennis Lee 1957- *WhoRel 92*
**McGuire**, Don 1919- *IntMPA 92*
**McGuire**, Don Loye 1934- *WhoAmP 91*
**McGuire**, Donald Michael 1948- *WhoIns 92*
**McGuire**, Dorothy 1919- *IntMPA 92*
**Mc Guire**, Dorothy Hackett 1916- *WhoEnt 92*
**McGuire**, E. James 1914- *WhoAmL 92*
**McGuire**, Edith Marie 1944- *BlkOlyM [port]*
**McGuire**, Edward 1948- *ConCom 92*
**McGuire**, Edward David, Jr. 1948- *WhoAmL 92*
**McGuire**, Eugene Guenard 1945- *WhoAmL 92*
**McGuire**, Eugene J 1938- *AmMWSc 92*
**McGuire**, Francis Joseph 1932- *AmMWSc 92*
**McGuire**, George 1940- *AmMWSc 92*
**McGuire**, George Alexander 1866-1934 *RelLAm 91*
**McGuire**, Gerald 1918- *Who 92*
**McGuire**, Harvey Paul 1939- *WhoAmP 91*
**McGuire**, James Anthony 1941- *WhoAmL 92*
**McGuire**, James Charles 1917- *WhoWest 92*
**McGuire**, James Grant 1955- *WhoAmL 92*
**McGuire**, James Horton 1942- *AmMWSc 92*
**McGuire**, James Marcus 1935- *AmMWSc 92*
**McGuire**, James Michael 1940- *WhoFI 92*
**McGuire**, Jean Mitchell 1931- *WhoBlA 92*
**McGuire**, Jeanne Marie 1956- *WhoMW 92*
**McGuire**, John Albert 1931- *AmMWSc 92*
**McGuire**, John C *WhoAmP 91*
**McGuire**, John Francis 1945- *WhoAmL 92*
**McGuire**, John J 1930- *AmMWSc 92*
**McGuire**, John Joseph 1949- *AmMWSc 92*
**McGuire**, John L 1942- *AmMWSc 92*
**McGuire**, John Murray 1929- *AmMWSc 92*
**McGuire**, Joseph Clive 1920- *AmMWSc 92*
**McGuire**, Joseph Deakins 1842-1916 *BiInAmS*
**McGuire**, Joseph Smith, Jr 1931- *AmMWSc 92*
**McGuire**, Joseph William 1925- *WrDr 92*
**McGuire**, Judith Marie 1944- *WhoAmP 91*
**McGuire**, Martin Cyril 1933- *WhoFI 92*
**McGuire**, Mary Jo 1956- *WhoAmP 91*
**McGuire**, Michael *DrAPF 91*
**Mc Guire**, Michael John 1947- *WhoWest 92*
**McGuire**, Michael Thomas Francis 1926- *Who 92*
**McGuire**, Odell 1927- *AmMWSc 92*
**McGuire**, Patricia A. 1952- *WhoAmL 92*
**McGuire**, Paul M., Jr. 1935- *WhoBlA 92*
**McGuire**, Richard A 1946- *WhoIns 92*
**McGuire**, Richard Allen 1946- *WhoFI 92*
**McGuire**, Richard Oliver 1936- *WhoWest 92*
**McGuire**, Robert Ely d1991 *Who 92N*
**McGuire**, Robert Frank 1937- *AmMWSc 92*
**McGuire**, Rosalie J. *WhoBlA 92*
**McGuire**, Shirley Elizabeth 1944- *WhoRel 92*
**McGuire**, Stephen Craig 1948- *AmMWSc 92*
**McGuire**, Stephen Edward 1942- *AmMWSc 92*
**McGuire**, Terry Russell 1950- *AmMWSc 92*
**McGuire**, Thomas *DcNCBi 4*
**McGuire**, Thomas Joseph 1963- *WhoAmL 92*
**McGuire**, Thomas Peter 1945- *WhoEnt 92*
**McGuire**, Timothy James 1959- *WhoMW 92*
**McGuire**, Timothy Stuart 1954- *WhoFI 92*
**McGuire**, Timothy William 1938- *WhoFI 92*
**McGuire**, Travis Clinton *AmMWSc 92*
**McGuire**, William 1920- *AmMWSc 92*
**McGuire**, William Benedict 1929- *WhoAmL 92*
**McGuire**, William Dennis 1943- *WhoMW 92*
**McGuire**, William L 1937- *AmMWSc 92*
**McGuirk**, John F, Sr *WhoAmP 91*
**McGuirk**, Terrence 1925- *WhoEnt 92*
**McGuirk**, William Joseph 1944- *AmMWSc 92*
**McGuirl**, Marlene Dana Callis 1938- *WhoAmL 92*
**McGuirl**, Susan Elizabeth 1952- *WhoAmL 92*
**McGuirt**, Milford W. 1956- *WhoBlA 92*
**McGuite**, Donald Michael 1948- *WhoIns 92*
**McGulpin**, Elizabeth Jane 1932- *WhoWest 92*
**Mcgunagle**, George F. Patrick 1950- *WhoFI 92*
**McGunegill**, Mark Richard 1955- *WhoEnt 92*
**McGurk**, Colin Thomas 1922- *Who 92*
**McGurk**, Donald J 1940- *AmMWSc 92*
**McGurk**, Eugene David, Jr. 1951- *WhoAmL 92*
**Mc Gurk**, James Henry 1936- *WhoFI 92*
**McGurn**, Barrett 1914- *IntAu&W 91, WrDr 92*
**McGurn**, George William 1914- *WhoAmL 92, WhoMW 92*
**McGwire**, Thomas *DcNCBi 4*
**McHale**, Brian K *WhoAmP 91*
**McHale**, Craig 1963- *WhoWest 92*
**McHale**, Edward Thomas 1932- *AmMWSc 92*
**Mc Hale**, John Joseph 1921- *WhoRel 92*
**McHale**, John T 1933- *AmMWSc 92*
**McHale**, Keith Michael 1928- *Who 92*
**McHale**, M. Martin de Porres 1931- *WhoFI 92*
**McHale**, M. Perpetua 1920- *WhoRel 92*
**McHale**, Mary Cecilia 1956- *WhoAmL 92*
**McHale**, Maureen Bernadette Kenny 1955- *WhoFI 92*
**McHale**, Paul 1950- *WhoAmP 91*
**McHale**, Robert Michael 1932- *WhoAmL 92*
**McHale**, Sheila A 1940- *WhoAmP 91*
**McHann**, James Clark, Jr. 1950- *WhoRel 92*
**McHardy**, George Gordon 1910- *AmMWSc 92*
**McHardy**, Louis William 1930- *WhoWest 92*
**McHardy**, William Duff 1911- *IntWW 91, Who 92*
**McHarg**, Robert Elwood 1923- *WhoFI 92, WhoMW 92*
**McHargue**, Carl J 1926- *AmMWSc 92*
**McHargue**, Daniel Stephen, II 1945- *WhoAmP 91*
**McHargue**, Wayne Orval 1937- *WhoFI 92*
**McHarris**, William Charles 1937- *AmMWSc 92*
**McHatten**, Mary Timothy 1931- *WhoRel 92*
**McHattie**, Howard Hope 1937- *WhoFI 92*
**McHattie**, Stephen *IntMPA 92*
**McHatton**, Henry 1856-1917 *BiInAmS*
**McHenry**, Charles S 1948- *AmMWSc 92*
**McHenry**, Donald F. 1936- *IntWW 91, Who 92, WhoBlA 92*
**McHenry**, Edward A 1940- *WhoAmP 91*
**McHenry**, F Douglas *ScFEYrs*
**McHenry**, Henry Malcolm 1944- *AmMWSc 92*
**McHenry**, Hugh Lansden 1937- *AmMWSc 92*
**McHenry**, James 1785-1845 *BenetAL 91*
**McHenry**, James O'Neal 1940- *WhoBlA 92*
**McHenry**, K W, Jr 1928- *AmMWSc 92*
**McHenry**, Keith Welles, Jr. 1928- *WhoFI 92*
**McHenry**, Kelly David 1952- *AmMWSc 92*

**Mc Henry,** Martin Christopher 1932- *WhoMW 92*
**McHenry,** Mary Williamson 1933- *WhoBlA 92*
**Mc Henry,** Powell 1926- *WhoAmL 92, WhoFI 92*
**McHenry,** Richard Lewis 1955- *WhoAmL 92*
**McHenry,** Robert Dale 1945- *WhoMW 92*
**McHenry,** William Earl 1950- *AmMWSc 92*
**McHill,** Thomas Andrew 1953- *WhoAmL 92*
**McHugh,** Alexander E 1904- *AmMWSc 92*
**McHugh,** Arona *DrAPF 91*
**McHugh,** Brian Joseph 1959- *WhoRel 92*
**McHugh,** Connie 1938- *WhoAmP 91*
**McHugh,** Earl Stephen 1936- *WhoMW 92*
**McHugh,** Edward Francis, Jr. 1932- *WhoAmL 92*
**McHugh,** Frank 1954- *TwCPaSc*
**McHugh,** Heather *DrAPF 91*
**McHugh,** Heather 1948- *ConPo 91, WrDr 92*
**McHugh,** James 1915- *IntMPA 92*
**McHugh,** James 1930- *Who 92*
**McHugh,** James Anthony, Jr 1937- *AmMWSc 92*
**McHugh,** James Joseph 1930- *WhoAmL 92, WhoWest 92*
**McHugh,** Jimmy 1894-1969 *NewAmDM*
**McHugh,** Joan Bleckwell 1936- *WhoMW 92*
**McHugh,** John *WhoAmP 91*
**McHugh,** John 1927- *WrDr 92*
**McHugh,** John Francis 1927- *IntAu&W 91*
**McHugh,** John Laurence 1911- *AmMWSc 92*
**McHugh,** John M 1948- *WhoAmP 91*
**McHugh,** Joseph C 1928- *WhoIns 92*
**McHugh,** Josephine Flaherty 1947- *WhoWest 92*
**McHugh,** Kenneth Laurence 1927- *AmMWSc 92*
**Mc Hugh,** Margaret Ann Gloe 1920- *WhoWest 92*
**McHugh,** Mary Patricia 1915- *Who 92*
**McHugh,** Matthew F. 1938- *AlmAP 92 [port]*
**McHugh,** Matthew Francis 1938- *WhoAmP 91*
**McHugh,** Michael Sean 1968- *WhoEnt 92*
**McHugh,** Miles William 1964- *WhoFI 92*
**McHugh,** Paul Rodney 1931- *AmMWSc 92*
**McHugh,** Richard B 1923- *AmMWSc 92*
**Mc Hugh,** Robert Clayton 1928- *WhoWest 92*
**McHugh,** Stuart *TwCWW 91*
**McHugh,** Stuart Lawrence 1949- *AmMWSc 92*
**McHugh,** Thomas E 1936- *WhoAmP 91*
**McHugh,** Thomas Edward 1936- *WhoAmL 92*
**McHugh,** Tom Edward *WhoAmP 91*
**McHugh,** Vincent 1904-1983 *BenetAL 91*
**McHugh,** William Dennis 1929- *AmMWSc 92*
**McHuron,** Clark Ernest *AmMWSc 92*
**McIlhenny,** Hugh M 1938- *AmMWSc 92*
**Mc Ilhenny,** James Harrison 1927- *WhoFI 92*
**McIlhone,** James Patrick 1948- *WhoRel 92*
**McIlrath,** Paul E. 1954- *WhoAmL 92*
**McIlrath,** Thomas James 1938- *AmMWSc 92*
**McIlrath,** Wayne Jackson 1921- *AmMWSc 92*
**McIlrath,** William Oliver 1936- *AmMWSc 92*
**McIlreath,** Fred J 1929- *AmMWSc 92*
**McIlroy,** Harry Alexander 1940- *WhoFI 92*
**McIlroy,** M Douglas 1932- *AmMWSc 92*
**McIlvain,** Bill D 1932- *WhoAmP 91*
**McIlvain,** Jess Hall 1933- *AmMWSc 92*
**McIlvaine,** Charles 1840-1909 *BiInAmS*
**McIlvaine,** Joseph Peter 1948- *WhoWest 92*
**McIlvaine,** Stephen Brownlee 1953- *WhoAmL 92*
**McIlvanney,** William 1936- *IntAu&W 91, WrDr 92*
**Mc Ilveen,** Walter 1927- *WhoFI 92*
**McIlveene,** Charles Steele 1928- *WhoRel 92*
**McIlvenna,** John Antony 1919- *Who 92*
**McIlvenna,** Robert James 1950- *WhoFI 92*
**McIlwain,** Albert Hood 1936- *WhoBlA 92*
**McIlwain,** Alexander Edward 1933- *Who 92*
**McIlwain,** Carl Edwin 1931- *AmMWSc 92*
**McIlwain,** Clara Evans 1919- *WhoFI 92*
**McIlwain,** David Lee 1938- *AmMWSc 92*
**McIlwain,** Don Curtis 1938- *WhoMW 92*
**McIlwain,** Henry 1912- *IntWW 91, Who 92, WrDr 92*
**McIlwain,** James Terrell 1936- *AmMWSc 92*
**McIlwain,** Jeaneen J. 1960- *WhoBlA 92*
**McIlwain,** Nadine Williams 1943- *WhoBlA 92*
**McIlwain,** Robert Leslie, Jr 1929- *AmMWSc 92*
**McIlwain,** William Clarence, Jr 1926- *WhoIns 92*
**McIlwaine,** Deborah P 1923- *WhoAmP 91*
**McIlwraith,** Arthur Renwick 1914- *Who 92*
**McIlwraith,** Cyril Wayne 1947- *WhoWest 92*
**McInally,** Michael Lee 1957- *WhoEnt 92*
**McIndoe,** Darrell W 1930- *AmMWSc 92*
**McIndoe,** William Ian 1929- *Who 92*
**McInerney,** Brian *DrAPF 91*
**McInerney,** Eugene F 1938- *AmMWSc 92*
**McInerney,** Gary John 1948- *WhoAmP 91*
**McInerney,** Jay 1955- *BenetAL 91, ConNov 91, WrDr 92*
**McInerney,** John Gerard 1959- *AmMWSc 92, WhoWest 92*
**McInerney,** John Peter 1939- *Who 92*
**McInerney,** Murray Vincent d1988 *Who 92N*
**McInerney,** Thomas J. *WhoWest 92*
**McInerny,** Jay 1955- *IntAu&W 91*
**McInerny,** John S. 1928- *WhoAmL 92*
**McInerny,** Ralph 1929- *ConAu 34NR, IntAu&W 91, WrDr 92*
**McInerny,** Ralph Matthew 1929- *WhoMW 92*
**McIngvale,** Wesley A 1933- *WhoAmP 91*
**McInnes,** Allen T. 1937- *WhoFI 92*
**McInnes,** Donald Gordon 1940- *WhoMW 92*
**McInnes,** Harold A. 1927- *WhoFI 92*
**McInnes,** John Colin 1938- *Who 92*
**McInnes,** Miles d1818 *DcNCBi 4*
**McInnes,** Stewart D. 1937- *IntWW 91*
**McInnes,** Val Ambrose Gordon 1929- *WhoRel 92*
**McInnis,** David Fairley 1934- *WhoAmP 91*
**McInnis,** Kenneth John 1948- *WhoAmP 91*
**McInnis,** Scott Steve 1953- *WhoAmP 91*
**McInnis,** Susan MusE 1955- *WhoWest 92*
**McInnis,** William Donald 1932- *WhoAmP 91*
**McInroy,** Elmer Eastwood 1921- *AmMWSc 92*
**McIntee,** Dixie J 1913- *WhoAmP 91*
**McInteer,** Jack Scott 1947- *WhoAmL 92*
**McInteer,** Jim Bill 1921- *WhoRel 92*
**McIntire,** Carl 1906- *RelLAm 91*
**McIntire,** Charles David 1932- *AmMWSc 92*
**McIntire,** Frank E *WhoAmP 91*
**McIntire,** John d1991 *LesBEnT 92, NewYTBS 91 [port]*
**McIntire,** Junius Merlin 1918- *AmMWSc 92*
**McIntire,** Kenneth Robert 1933- *AmMWSc 92*
**McIntire,** Larry Richmond 1935- *WhoFI 92*
**McIntire,** Larry V 1943- *AmMWSc 92*
**McIntire,** Leanne 1957- *WhoEnt 92, WhoWest 92*
**McIntire,** Louis V 1925- *AmMWSc 92*
**McIntire,** Matilda S 1920- *AmMWSc 92*
**McIntire,** Sumner Harmon 1912- *AmMWSc 92*
**McIntire,** William Allan 1946- *WhoEnt 92*
**McIntire,** William S 1949- *AmMWSc 92*
**McIntosh** *Who 92*
**McIntosh,** Alan William 1944- *AmMWSc 92*
**McIntosh,** Alexander Omar 1913- *AmMWSc 92*
**McIntosh,** Alice T. 1933- *WhoBlA 92*
**McIntosh,** Angus 1914- *Who 92*
**McIntosh,** Anne Caroline Ballingall 1954- *Who 92*
**McIntosh,** Arthur Herbert Cranstoun 1934- *AmMWSc 92*
**McIntosh,** Bruce Andrew 1929- *AmMWSc 92*
**McIntosh,** Calvin Eugene 1926- *WhoMW 92*
**McIntosh,** Christopher 1943- *IntAu&W 91, WrDr 92*
**McIntosh,** Donald d1915 *BiInAmS*
**McIntosh,** Donald Edward 1930- *WhoMW 92*
**McIntosh,** Elaine Nelson 1924- *AmMWSc 92*
**McIntosh,** Elaine Virginia 1924- *WhoMW 92*
**McIntosh,** Frankie L. 1949- *WhoBlA 92*
**McIntosh,** Genista Mary 1946- *IntWW 91, Who 92*
**McIntosh,** Harold Leroy 1931- *AmMWSc 92*
**McIntosh,** Henry Deane 1921- *AmMWSc 92*
**McIntosh,** Hugh 1914- *Who 92*
**McIntosh,** Hugh Maurice 1945- *WhoAmL 92*
**McIntosh,** Ian 1919- *Who 92*
**McIntosh,** J. T. *WrDr 92*
**McIntosh,** J T 1925- *TwCSFW 91*
**McIntosh,** James Albert 1933- *WhoAmL 92*
**McIntosh,** James E. 1942- *WhoBlA 92*
**McIntosh,** Jay Richard 1968- *WhoRel 92*
**McIntosh,** Joan *DrAPF 91*
**McIntosh,** John McLennan 1940- *AmMWSc 92*
**McIntosh,** John Richard 1939- *AmMWSc 92*
**McIntosh,** John Stanton 1923- *AmMWSc 92*
**McIntosh,** Kinn Hamilton *WrDr 92*
**McIntosh,** Kinn Hamilton 1930- *IntAu&W 91*
**McIntosh,** Lee 1949- *AmMWSc 92*
**McIntosh,** Malcolm Kenneth 1945- *Who 92*
**McIntosh,** Martha E. 1848-1922 *RelLAm 91*
**McIntosh,** Michael Dean 1950- *WhoEnt 92*
**McIntosh,** Naomi Ellen Sargant 1933- *Who 92*
**McIntosh,** Neil Scott Wishart 1947- *Who 92*
**McIntosh,** Peter C. 1915- *WrDr 92*
**McIntosh,** Peter Chisholm 1915- *IntAu&W 91*
**McIntosh,** Rhodina Covington 1947- *WhoBlA 92*
**McIntosh,** Robert Edward 1940- *AmMWSc 92*
**McIntosh,** Robert Patrick 1920- *AmMWSc 92*
**McIntosh,** Ronald 1919- *Who 92*
**McIntosh,** Ronald Robert Duncan 1919- *IntWW 91*
**McIntosh,** Sandy *DrAPF 91*
**McIntosh,** Simeon Charles 1944- *WhoBlA 92*
**McIntosh,** T. Richard 1948- *WhoAmL 92*
**McIntosh,** Thomas Henry 1930- *AmMWSc 92*
**McIntosh,** Thomas James 1947- *AmMWSc 92*
**McIntosh,** Waldo Emerson d1991 *NewYTBS 91*
**McIntosh,** Walter Cordell 1927- *WhoBlA 92*
**McIntosh,** William David 1936- *AmMWSc 92*
**McIntosh,** William E., Jr. 1945- *WhoBlA 92*
**McIntosh,** William M 1918- *WhoAmP 91*
**McIntosh of Haringey,** Baron 1933- *Who 92*
**Mc Inturf,** Faith Mary 1917- *WhoMW 92*
**McInturff,** Alfred D 1937- *AmMWSc 92*
**McInturff,** Don A 1939- *WhoIns 92*
**McInturff,** Floyd M. 1923- *WhoMW 92*
**McIntyre,** Adelbert 1929- *AmMWSc 92*
**McIntyre,** Alasdair Duncan 1926- *Who 92*
**McIntyre,** Andrew 1931- *AmMWSc 92*
**McIntyre,** Carl Henry, Jr. 1958- *WhoAmL 92*
**McIntyre,** Carlene Virginia 1954- *WhoAmL 92*
**McIntyre,** Carolyn 1939- *WhoWest 92*
**McIntyre,** Colin 1944- *WhoEnt 92*
**McIntyre,** David John 1949- *WhoMW 92*
**McIntyre,** Deborah Vennette 1955- *WhoEnt 92*
**McIntyre,** Dennis 1943?-1990 *ConTFT 9*
**McIntyre,** Dianne Ruth 1946- *WhoBlA 92*
**McIntyre,** Donald 1923- *TwCPaSc*
**McIntyre,** Donald 1928- *AmMWSc 92*
**McIntyre,** Donald B 1923- *AmMWSc 92*
**McIntyre,** Donald Conroy 1934- *IntWW 91, Who 92, WhoEnt 92*
**McIntyre,** Douglas Alexander 1955- *WhoFI 92*
**McIntyre,** Douglas Carmichael, II 1956- *WhoAmL 92*
**McIntyre,** Gary A 1938- *AmMWSc 92*
**McIntyre,** Gene Earl 1932- *WhoAmP 91*
**McIntyre,** Hugh Baxter 1935- *WhoWest 92*
**McIntyre,** Ian James 1931- *Who 92*
**McIntyre,** James Douglass Edmonson 1934- *AmMWSc 92*
**McIntyre,** James Francis Aloysius 1886-1979 *RelLAm 91*
**McIntyre,** James T., Jr. 1940- *IntWW 91, WhoAmP 91*
**McIntyre,** John 1916- *IntWW 91, Who 92*
**McIntyre,** John A 1942- *AmMWSc 92*
**McIntyre,** John Armin 1920- *AmMWSc 92*
**McIntyre,** John Henry, Sr. 1925- *WhoBlA 92*
**McIntyre,** John Lee 1947- *WhoFI 92*
**McIntyre,** John T. 1871-1951 *BenetAL 91*
**McIntyre,** Joseph B 1957- *WhoAmP 91*
**McIntyre,** Judith Watland 1930- *AmMWSc 92*
**McIntyre,** Keith 1959- *TwCPaSc*
**McIntyre,** Kenneth J. 1944- *WhoAmL 92*
**McIntyre,** Laurence Cook, Jr 1934- *AmMWSc 92*
**McIntyre,** Marie Claire 1961- *AmMWSc 92*
**McIntyre,** Michael 1950- *WhoWest 92*
**McIntyre,** Michael Edgeworth 1941- *Who 92*
**McIntyre,** Michael John 1942- *WhoMW 92*
**McIntyre,** Michael John 1946- *WhoMW 92*
**McIntyre,** Mildred J. *WhoBlA 92*
**McIntyre,** Neil 1934- *Who 92*
**McIntyre,** Oscar Odd 1881-1938 *FacFETw*
**McIntyre,** Oswald Ross 1932- *AmMWSc 92*
**McIntyre,** Patricia Ann 1926- *AmMWSc 92*
**McIntyre,** Patrick Lynn 1955- *WhoWest 92*
**McIntyre,** Ralph Jackson 1923- *WhoRel 92*
**McIntyre,** Robert Douglas 1913- *Who 92*
**McIntyre,** Robert Francis 1954- *WhoWest 92*
**McIntyre,** Robert Gerald 1924- *AmMWSc 92*
**McIntyre,** Robert John 1928- *AmMWSc 92*
**McIntyre,** Robert Malcolm 1923- *WhoWest 92*
**McIntyre,** Robert Walker 1944- *WhoAmL 92*
**Mc Intyre,** Robert Walter 1922- *WhoRel 92*
**McIntyre,** Robert Wheeler 1936- *WhoWest 92*
**McIntyre,** Ronald Llewellyn 1934- *WhoMW 92*
**McIntyre,** Russell Theodore 1925- *AmMWSc 92*
**McIntyre,** Scott Campbell 1950- *WhoWest 92*
**McIntyre,** Thomas J *WhoAmP 91*
**McIntyre,** Thomas William 1941- *AmMWSc 92*
**McIntyre,** Vonda N 1948- *ConAu 34NR, TwCSFW 91, WrDr 92*
**McIntyre,** W David 1932- *IntAu&W 91, WrDr 92*
**McIntyre,** William Ernest, Jr 1925- *AmMWSc 92*
**McIntyre,** William Ian Mackay 1919- *Who 92*
**McIntyre-Ivy,** Joan Carol 1939- *WhoFI 92*
**McIrvine,** Edward Charles 1933- *AmMWSc 92*
**McIsaac,** Paul R 1926- *AmMWSc 92*
**McIsaac,** Paul William 1941- *WhoFI 92*
**McIsaac,** Robert James 1923- *AmMWSc 92*
**McIver,** Alexander 1822-1902 *DcNCBi 4*
**McIver,** Bruce Cooley 1940- *WhoFI 92*
**McIver,** Charles Duncan 1860-1906 *DcNCBi 4*
**McIver,** Colin 1784-1850 *DcNCBi 4*
**McIver,** David William 1960- *WhoRel 92*
**McIver,** George Willcox 1858-1947 *DcNCBi 4*
**McIver,** Guy Harding 1939- *WhoRel 92*
**McIver,** John Douglas 1941- *WhoBlA 92*
**McIver,** Loren 1909- *FacFETw*
**McIver,** Lula Verlinda Martin 1864-1944 *DcNCBi 4*
**McIver,** Margaret Hill 1925- *WhoBlA 92*
**McIver,** Neil Frederick 1950- *WhoAmP 91*
**McIver,** Norman L 1931- *AmMWSc 92*
**McIver,** Robert Thomas, Jr 1945- *AmMWSc 92*
**McIver,** Susan Bertha 1940- *AmMWSc 92*
**McIvor,** Basil *Who 92*
**McIvor,** Donald K. 1928- *IntWW 91*
**McIvor,** Donald Kenneth 1928- *Who 92, WhoFI 92*
**McIvor,** Frances Jill 1930- *Who 92*
**McIvor,** Keith L *AmMWSc 92*
**McIvor,** William Basil 1928- *Who 92*
**McJunkin,** Louis M 1931- *WhoAmP 91*
**McKague,** Allan Bruce 1940- *AmMWSc 92*
**McKague,** Herbert Lawrence 1935- *AmMWSc 92*
**McKague,** Thomas R. *DrAPF 91*
**McKaig,** Rae 1922- *Who 92*
**McKain,** David *DrAPF 91*
**McKain,** David 1937- *ConAu 14AS [port]*
**McKain,** Mary Margaret 1940- *WhoEnt 92, WhoWest 92*
**McKanders,** Julius A., II 1941- *WhoBlA 92*
**McKanders,** Kenneth Andre 1950- *WhoBlA 92*
**McKandes,** Dorothy Dell 1937- *WhoBlA 92, WhoMW 92*
**McKane,** Alice Woodby 1865-1948 *NotBlAW 92*

**McKane,** Terry John 1941- *WhoAmP 91, WhoMW 92*
**McKane,** William 1921- *IntWW 91, Who 92*
**McKannan,** Eugene Charles 1928- *AmMWSc 92*
**McKaskle,** Larry *WhoAmP 91*
**McKasy,** Bert J *WhoAmP 91*
**Mc Kaughan,** Howard Paul 1922- *WhoWest 92*
**McKaveney,** James P 1925- *AmMWSc 92*
**McKay,** Alexander Gordon 1924- *Who 92, WrDr 92*
**McKay,** Alexander Matthew 1921- *Who 92*
**McKay,** Alice Vitalich 1947- *WhoWest 92*
**McKay,** Allan George 1935- *Who 92*
**McKay,** Allen 1927- *Who 92*
**McKay,** Antonio Ricardo 1964- *BlkOlyM*
**McKay,** Archibald Charles 1929- *Who 92*
**McKay,** Brian 1945- *WhoAmP 91*
**McKay,** Charles Douglas 1957- *WhoRel 92*
**McKay,** Charles Leslie d1883 *BiInAmS*
**McKay,** Claude 1889-1948 *BenetAL 91, BlkLC [port], LiExTwC, TwCLC 41 [port]*
**McKay,** Claude 1890-1948 *AfrAmW, DcAmImH*
**McKay,** D. Brian 1945- *WhoAmL 92, WhoWest 92*
**McKay,** Dale Robert 1946- *AmMWSc 92*
**McKay,** David Oman 1873-1970 *RelLAm 91*
**McKay,** Donald Arthur 1931- *WhoFI 92*
**McKay,** Donald Edward 1938- *AmMWSc 92*
**McKay,** Donald George 1921- *AmMWSc 92*
**McKay,** Donald M. 1932- *WhoMW 92*
**McKay,** Douglas William 1927- *AmMWSc 92*
**McKay,** Edward Donald, III 1949- *AmMWSc 92*
**McKay,** Eugene Henry, Jr. 1929- *WhoFI 92*
**McKay,** Frederick *Who 92*
**McKay,** Glenn Reed 1936- *WhoEnt 92*
**McKay,** Jack Alexander 1942- *AmMWSc 92*
**McKay,** James A. *WhoRel 92*
**McKay,** James Brian 1940- *AmMWSc 92*
**McKay,** James Edgar 1939- *WhoFI 92*
**McKay,** James Frederick 1907- *Who 92*
**McKay,** James Harold 1928- *AmMWSc 92*
**McKay,** James Iver 1792-1853 *DcNCBi 4*
**McKay,** James Wilson 1912- *Who 92*
**McKay,** Janet Holmgren 1948- *WhoWest 92*
**McKay,** Jerry Bruce 1935- *AmMWSc 92*
**McKay,** Jim *LesBEnT 92*
**McKay,** John *NewYTBS 91 [port]*
**McKay,** John 1912- *Who 92*
**McKay,** John 1922-1975 *FacFETw*
**McKay,** John 1948- *WhoAmP 91*
**McKay,** John 1956- *WhoWest 92*
**McKay,** John Douglas 1960- *WhoAmL 92*
**McKay,** John Edward 1951- *WhoAmL 92*
**McKay,** John Henderson 1929- *Who 92*
**McKay,** John Judson, Jr. 1939- *WhoAmL 92*
**McKay,** John Patrick 1931- *WhoMW 92*
**McKay,** John Sophronus 1850-1917 *BiInAmS*
**McKay,** Juan Bautista 1957- *WhoEnt 92*
**McKay,** Julius Walker, II 1952- *WhoAmL 92*
**McKay,** Karen Nimmons 1947- *WhoBlA 92*
**McKay,** Kelsey Babcock 1924- *WhoFI 92*
**McKay,** Ken Carroll 1932- *WhoFI 92*
**McKay,** Kenneth Gardiner 1917- *AmMWSc 92*
**McKay,** Koln Gunn 1925- *WhoAmP 91*
**McKay,** Larry Lee 1943- *AmMWSc 92*
**McKay,** Margaret 1911- *Who 92*
**McKay,** Margo Marquita 1946- *WhoAmL 92*
**McKay,** Mark Patrick 1959- *WhoEnt 92*
**McKay,** Martha Clampitt 1920- *WhoAmP 91*
**McKay,** Michael Darrell 1944- *AmMWSc 92*
**McKay,** Michael Dennis 1951- *WhoAmL 92*
**McKay,** Michael S. 1958- *WhoAmL 92*
**McKay,** Monroe G *WhoAmP 91*
**McKay,** Monroe Gunn 1928- *WhoAmL 92*
**McKay,** Neill 1816-1893 *DcNCBi 4*
**McKay,** Richard A 1927- *AmMWSc 92*
**McKay,** Robert Connally 1950- *WhoAmL 92*
**McKay,** Robert Harvey 1927- *AmMWSc 92*
**McKay,** Robert James, Jr 1917- *AmMWSc 92*
**McKay,** Roy 1900- *Who 92*
**Mc Kay,** Samuel Leroy 1913- *WhoRel 92*
**McKay,** Sandra J 1947- *AmMWSc 92*
**McKay,** Sandy 1945- *WhoEnt 92*
**McKay,** Sharon Cline 1946- *WhoWest 92*
**Mc Kay,** Stephen Michael 1953- *WhoFI 92*
**McKay,** Steve 1964- *WhoEnt 92*
**McKay,** Susan Richards *AmMWSc 92*
**Mc Kay,** Thomas, Jr. 1920- *WhoAmL 92*
**McKay,** Thomas Lee 1941- *WhoWest 92*
**McKay,** Todd L. 1963- *WhoWest 92*
**McKay,** William Robert 1939- *Who 92*
**McKay,** Woodrow M 1941- *WhoAmP 91*
**McKaye,** Kenneth Robert 1947- *AmMWSc 92*
**McKayle,** Donald Cohen 1930- *WhoBlA 92, WhoEnt 92*
**McKeachie,** Wilbert J. 1921- *WrDr 92*
**McKeachnie,** Gayle F *WhoAmP 91*
**McKeachnie,** Gayle F. 1943- *WhoAmL 92*
**McKeage,** Donald William 1925- *WhoMW 92*
**McKeague,** David William 1946- *WhoAmL 92*
**McKeague,** Justin Alexander 1924- *AmMWSc 92*
**McKean,** Andrew 1949- *WhoAmP 91*
**McKean,** Charles Alexander 1946- *Who 92*
**McKean,** David Jesse 1946- *AmMWSc 92*
**McKean,** Douglas 1917- *Who 92*
**McKean,** Henry P 1930- *AmMWSc 92*
**McKean,** J. M. 1943- *WrDr 92*
**McKean,** James *DrAPF 91*
**McKean,** James Daniel 1946- *WhoMW 92*
**McKean,** John Maule Laurie 1943- *IntAu&W 91*
**McKean,** Joseph Walter, Jr 1944- *AmMWSc 92*
**Mc Kean,** Michael *WhoEnt 92*
**McKean,** Michael 1947- *IntMPA 92*
**McKean,** Philip Frick 1936- *WhoFI 92*
**McKean,** Robert d1991 *NewYTBS 91*
**McKean,** Robert B. 1943- *ConAu 135*
**McKean,** Thomas Arthur 1941- *AmMWSc 92, WhoWest 92*
**McKean,** Thomas Edward 1948- *WhoWest 92*
**McKean,** William Thomas, Jr 1938- *AmMWSc 92*
**McKearn,** Thomas Joseph 1948- *AmMWSc 92*
**McKearney,** James William 1938- *AmMWSc 92*
**McKearney,** Philip 1926- *Who 92*
**McKechnie,** Ed 1963- *WhoAmP 91*
**McKechnie,** Sheila Marshall 1948- *Who 92*
**McKechnie,** William Elliott 1952- *WhoAmP 91*
**McKee,** Adam E., Jr. 1932- *WhoBlA 92*
**Mc Kee,** Allen Page 1941- *WhoFI 92*
**McKee,** Bob *WhoAmP 91*
**McKee,** Bruce Welcher 1934- *WhoAmL 92*
**McKee,** Carol B 1942- *WhoAmP 91*
**McKee,** Cecil *Who 92*
**McKee,** Christopher Fulton 1942- *AmMWSc 92*
**McKee,** Clarence Vanzant 1942- *WhoBlA 92*
**McKee,** Claude Gibbons 1930- *AmMWSc 92*
**McKee,** Cynthia W 1915- *WhoAmP 91*
**McKee,** David *WrDr 92*
**McKee,** David Edward 1938- *AmMWSc 92*
**McKee,** David John 1947- *AmMWSc 92*
**McKee,** David Lannen 1936- *WhoFI 92, WhoMW 92*
**McKee,** Douglas William 1930- *AmMWSc 92*
**McKee,** Edith Merritt 1918- *AmMWSc 92*
**McKee,** Edward Ray 1941- *WhoFI 92*
**McKee,** Francis John 1943- *WhoAmL 92, WhoFI 92*
**McKee,** Frederick 1945- *WhoWest 92*
**Mc Kee,** George Moffitt, Jr. 1924- *WhoFI 92, WhoMW 92*
**McKee,** Gertrude Dills 1885-1948 *DcNCBi 4*
**McKee,** Graydon Samuel, III 1937- *WhoAmL 92*
**McKee,** Guy William 1919- *AmMWSc 92*
**McKee,** Harold Earl 1937- *WhoAmL 92*
**McKee,** Herbert C 1920- *AmMWSc 92*
**McKee,** Ira Keith 1950- *WhoAmL 92*
**McKee,** J Chester, Jr 1923- *AmMWSc 92*
**McKee,** James 1844-1912 *DcNCBi 4*
**McKee,** James Stanley Colton 1930- *AmMWSc 92*
**McKee,** James W 1932- *AmMWSc 92*
**McKee,** James W., Jr. 1922- *IntWW 91*
**McKee,** John Angus 1935- *IntWW 91*
**McKee,** John Carothers 1912- *WhoWest 92*
**McKee,** Kathryn Dian Grant 1937- *WhoFI 92*
**McKee,** Keith Earl 1928- *AmMWSc 92, WhoMW 92*
**McKee,** Lonette *WhoBlA 92*
**McKee,** Louis *DrAPF 91*
**McKee,** M Jean 1929- *WhoAmP 91*
**McKee,** Margaret Jean 1929- *WhoFI 92*
**McKee,** Mary Elizabeth 1949- *WhoEnt 92*
**McKee,** Melanie Bailey 1958- *WhoMW 92*
**McKee,** Michael Geoffrey 1931- *AmMWSc 92*
**McKee,** Michael Leland 1949- *AmMWSc 92*
**McKee,** Patrick Allen 1937- *AmMWSc 92*
**McKee,** Ralph Dyer, Jr. 1925- *WhoAmL 92*
**McKee,** Ralph Wendell 1912- *AmMWSc 92*
**Mc Kee,** Raymond Walter 1899- *WhoWest 92*
**McKee,** Robert B, Jr 1924- *AmMWSc 92*
**McKee,** Robert Stanley 1943- *WhoAmP 91*
**McKee,** Rodney Allen 1947- *AmMWSc 92*
**McKee,** Susan Park 1945- *WhoFI 92*
**McKee,** Terri Toth 1955- *WhoAmL 92*
**McKee,** Theodore A. *WhoBlA 92*
**McKee,** Thomas Benjamin 1935- *AmMWSc 92*
**McKee,** Thomas Frederick 1948- *WhoAmL 92*
**McKee,** Timothy Carlton 1944- *WhoFI 92*
**McKee,** W Dean, Jr 1920- *AmMWSc 92*
**McKee,** William Cecil 1905- *Who 92*
**McKee,** William Henry 1814-1875 *DcNCBi 4*
**McKee,** William James Ernest 1929- *Who 92*
**McKee,** William Lee 1946- *WhoFI 92*
**McKee-Velasquez,** Patrick 1953- *WhoHisp 92*
**McKeegan,** Pete P 1915- *WhoAmP 91*
**McKeehan,** Charles Wayne 1929- *AmMWSc 92*
**McKeehan,** Larry O., III 1953- *WhoEnt 92*
**McKeehan,** Mark Warren 1960- *WhoFI 92*
**McKeehan,** Wallace Lee 1944- *AmMWSc 92*
**McKeel,** R. Bruce 1942- *WhoWest 92*
**Mc Keel,** Sam Stewart 1926- *WhoMW 92*
**McKeel,** Thomas Burl 1944- *WhoBlA 92*
**McKeeman,** William Marshall 1934- *AmMWSc 92*
**McKeen,** Alexander C. 1927- *WhoMW 92*
**Mc Keen,** Chester M., Jr. 1923- *WhoFI 92*
**McKeen,** Colin Douglas 1916- *AmMWSc 92*
**McKeen,** Elden *WhoAmP 91*
**McKeen,** P. Douglas 1956- *WhoMW 92*
**McKeen,** Wilbert Ezekiel 1922- *AmMWSc 92*
**McKeever,** Brian Evans 1949- *WhoFI 92*
**McKeever,** Charles H 1912- *AmMWSc 92*
**McKeever,** Francis Dennis 1944- *WhoFI 92*
**McKeever,** Ian 1946- *TwCPaSc*
**McKeever,** James M. 1929- *WhoFI 92, WhoRel 92, WhoWest 92*
**McKeever,** L Dennis 1941- *AmMWSc 92*
**McKeever,** Paul Edward 1946- *AmMWSc 92*
**McKeever,** Stephen William Spencer 1950- *AmMWSc 92*
**McKeever,** Sturgis 1921- *AmMWSc 92*
**McKeever,** Thomas Joseph, Jr. 1949- *WhoAmL 92*
**McKeever,** Timothy A 1950- *WhoAmP 91*
**McKeith,** Floyd Kenneth 1955- *AmMWSc 92*
**McKeith,** Malissa Hathaway 1959- *WhoAmL 92*
**McKeithen,** John Julian 1918- *WhoAmP 91*
**McKeithen,** Walter Fox 1946- *WhoAmP 91*
**McKeldin,** Harry White, Jr. 1915- *WhoBlA 92*
**McKell,** Cyrus M. 1926- *WhoWest 92*
**McKell,** Cyrus Milo 1926- *AmMWSc 92*
**McKellar,** Bruce Harold John 1941- *AmMWSc 92*
**McKellar,** Darlene Iris 1945- *WhoWest 92*
**McKellar,** Henry Northington, Jr 1947- *AmMWSc 92*
**McKellar,** Stephen Alexander 1956- *WhoBlA 92*
**McKellen,** Ian 1939- *IntMPA 92, Who 92*
**McKellen,** Ian Murray 1939- *IntWW 91*
**McKeller,** Thomas Lee 1940- *WhoBlA 92*
**McKellips,** Gordon Wayne, Jr. 1941- *WhoWest 92*
**McKellips,** Roger *WhoAmP 91*
**McKellips,** Terral Lane 1938- *AmMWSc 92*
**McKelpin,** Joseph P. 1914- *WhoBlA 92*
**McKelvey,** Carole A. 1942- *ConAu 135*
**McKelvey,** Donald Richard 1938- *AmMWSc 92*
**McKelvey,** Edward Neil 1925- *IntWW 91*
**McKelvey,** Eugene Mowry 1934- *AmMWSc 92*
**McKelvey,** Forrest L *WhoAmP 91*
**McKelvey,** George Irwin, III 1925- *WhoWest 92*
**McKelvey,** Gerald John 1946- *WhoAmP 91*
**McKelvey,** James M 1925- *AmMWSc 92*
**McKelvey,** John Murray 1937- *AmMWSc 92*
**McKelvey,** John Philip 1926- *AmMWSc 92*
**McKelvey,** John Wesley 1914- *Who 92*
**McKelvey,** Joseph Harold, Jr. 1952- *WhoRel 92*
**McKelvey,** Robert William 1929- *AmMWSc 92*
**McKelvey,** Ronald Deane 1944- *AmMWSc 92*
**McKelvey,** William 1934- *Who 92*
**McKelvie,** Douglas H 1927- *AmMWSc 92*
**McKelvie,** Neil 1930- *AmMWSc 92*
**McKelvie,** Peter 1932- *Who 92*
**McKelvy,** Jeffrey F *AmMWSc 92*
**McKelway,** Alexander Jeffrey 1866-1918 *DcNCBi 4*
**McKelway,** Benjamin Mosby 1895-1976 *DcNCBi 4*
**McKemy,** David Scott 1962- *WhoRel 92*
**McKemy,** Wrenshall Vancel *WhoAmP 91*
**Mckendry,** Francis James 1957- *WhoFI 92*
**McKendry,** John H., Jr. 1950- *WhoAmL 92*
**McKenley,** Herbert 1922- *BlkOlyM [port]*
**McKenna,** Alvin James 1943- *WhoMW 92*
**McKenna,** Andrew James 1929- *WhoMW 92*
**McKenna,** Bernard James 1933- *WhoFI 92*
**McKenna,** Charles Edward 1944- *AmMWSc 92*
**McKenna,** Charles Nicholas 1965- *WhoFI 92*
**McKenna,** Dave 1930- *NewAmDM*
**McKenna,** David 1911- *Who 92*
**Mc Kenna,** David Loren 1929- *WhoRel 92*
**McKenna,** Denis L 1922- *WhoAmP 91*
**McKenna,** Edward J 1958- *AmMWSc 92*
**McKenna,** Edward James, Jr. 1950- *WhoAmL 92*
**McKenna,** Fay Ann 1944- *WhoFI 92*
**McKenna,** Francis Joseph 1948- *Who 92*
**McKenna,** Frank Joseph 1948- *IntWW 91*
**McKenna,** Frederick Gregory 1952- *WhoAmL 92*
**McKenna,** George J., III 1940- *WhoBlA 92*
**McKenna,** Hugh Francis 1921- *WhoIns 92*
**McKenna,** Jack F 1955- *AmMWSc 92*
**McKenna,** James *DrAPF 91*
**McKenna,** James 1929- *AmMWSc 92*
**McKenna,** Janice Lynn 1949- *WhoAmP 91*
**McKenna,** John Dennis 1940- *AmMWSc 92*
**McKenna,** John Dwaine 1946- *WhoWest 92*
**McKenna,** John Emory 1935- *WhoRel 92*
**McKenna,** John Holcomb 1936- *WhoRel 92*
**McKenna,** John Joseph 1932- *WhoMW 92*
**McKenna,** John Morgan 1927- *AmMWSc 92*
**McKenna,** Joseph 1843-1925 *FacFETw*
**McKenna,** Kenneth F, Jr 1943- *WhoAmP 91*
**McKenna,** Keven A 1945- *WhoAmP 91*
**McKenna,** Laura Marie 1959- *WhoAmL 92*
**McKenna,** Malcolm Carnegie 1930- *AmMWSc 92*
**McKenna,** Marian C 1926- *IntAu&W 91*
**Mc Kenna,** Marian Cecilia 1926- *WhoWest 92, WrDr 92*
**McKenna,** Mary Catherine 1945- *AmMWSc 92*
**McKenna,** Mary Jane *WhoAmP 91*
**McKenna,** Michael J. 1946- *WhoMW 92*
**McKenna,** Michael Joseph 1946- *AmMWSc 92*
**McKenna,** Olivia Cleveland 1939- *AmMWSc 92*
**McKenna,** Patrick James 1951- *WhoWest 92*
**McKenna,** Quentin Carnegie 1926- *WhoFI 92*
**McKenna,** Richard Henry 1927- *WhoMW 92*
**McKenna,** Richard M. 1913-1964 *TwCSFW 91*
**McKenna,** Richard Milton 1913-1964 *DcNCBi 4*
**McKenna,** Robert Charles 1936- *WhoWest 92*
**McKenna,** Robert J 1931- *WhoAmP 91*
**McKenna,** Robert Wilson 1940- *AmMWSc 92*
**McKenna,** Shirley Lee 1935- *WhoMW 92*
**Mc Kenna,** Sidney F. 1922- *WhoFI 92*
**McKenna,** Siobhan 1922- *WhoEnt 92*
**McKenna,** Siobhan 1923-1986 *FacFETw*
**McKenna,** Stephen 1939- *TwCPaSc*
**McKenna,** Stephen Francis 1939- *IntWW 91*
**McKenna,** Terence Patrick 1928- *WhoFI 92*
**McKenna,** Thomas Francis, Sr. 1921- *WhoAmL 92*
**McKenna,** Thomas Michael 1947- *AmMWSc 92*

**McKenna,** Thomas Patrick 1931- *IntWW 91*
**McKenna,** Virginia 1931- *IntWW 91*
**McKenna,** Willafay H 1936- *WhoAmP 91*
**Mc Kenna,** William A., Jr. *WhoFI 92*
**McKenna,** William Gerard 1956- *WhoFI 92*
**McKenna,** William Gillies 1949- *AmMWSc 92*
**McKenna,** William John 1926- *WhoMW 92*
**McKenna,** William P 1946- *WhoAmP 91*
**McKenney,** Charles Emerson 1932- *WhoAmL 92*
**McKenney,** Charles Lynn, Jr 1945- *AmMWSc 92*
**McKenney,** Dean Brinton 1940- *AmMWSc 92*
**McKenney,** Donald Joseph 1933- *AmMWSc 92*
**McKenney,** Frank Meath 1934- *WhoAmP 91*
**McKenney,** Katherine 1932- *WhoAmP 91*
**McKenney,** Keith Hollis *AmMWSc 92*
**McKenney,** Ruth 1911-1972 *BenetAL 91*
**Mc Kenney,** Walter Gibbs, Jr. 1913- *WhoFI 92*
**McKennon,** Keith Robert 1933- *IntWW 91, WhoFI 92, WhoMW 92*
**McKenny,** Stephen Richard 1959- *WhoFI 92*
**McKenny,** William D 1940- *WhoIns 92*
**McKently,** Alexandra H 1956- *AmMWSc 92*
**McKenzie,** Alexander 1896- *IntWW 91, Who 92*
**McKenzie,** Allan Dean 1930- *WhoWest 92*
**McKenzie,** Allister Roy *AmMWSc 92*
**McKenzie,** Arthur Leroy 1930- *WhoAmP 91*
**McKenzie,** Barbara 1934- *WrDr 92*
**McKenzie,** Basil Everard 1935- *AmMWSc 92*
**McKenzie,** Dan Peter 1942- *IntWW 91, Who 92*
**McKenzie,** David Bruce 1954- *AmMWSc 92*
**McKenzie,** Donald Edward 1924- *AmMWSc 92*
**McKenzie,** Donald Francis 1931- *Who 92*
**McKenzie,** Doug John 1951- *WhoEnt 92*
**McKenzie,** Douglas C. 1936- *WhoMW 92*
**McKenzie,** Edna B. 1923- *WhoBlA 92*
**McKenzie,** Eli, Jr. 1947- *WhoBlA 92*
**McKenzie,** Elijah George 1964- *WhoRel 92*
**McKenzie,** Floretta D. 1935- *WhoBlA 92*
**McKenzie,** Garry Donald 1941- *AmMWSc 92*
**McKenzie,** Gerald Malcolm *AmMWSc 92*
**McKenzie,** Gwendolyn Veron *WhoFI 92*
**Mc Kenzie,** Hilton Eugene 1921- *WhoFI 92*
**McKenzie,** James Franklin 1948- *WhoAmL 92*
**McKenzie,** James Montgomery 1925- *AmMWSc 92*
**McKenzie,** Jerry Howard 1935- *WhoEnt 92*
**McKenzie,** Jess Mack 1932- *AmMWSc 92*
**McKenzie,** Jo 1931- *WhoAmP 91*
**McKenzie,** John Cormack 1927- *Who 92*
**McKenzie,** John Crawford 1937- *Who 92*
**McKenzie,** John F. 1947- *WhoAmL 92*
**McKenzie,** John Foster 1923- *Who 92*
**McKenzie,** John L. 1910-1991 *ConAu 133, NewYTBS 91 [port]*
**McKenzie,** John Lawrence 1910- *IntWW 91*
**McKenzie,** John Maxwell 1927- *AmMWSc 92*
**McKenzie,** John Michael 1954- *WhoAmP 91*
**McKenzie,** John Ward 1918- *AmMWSc 92*
**McKenzie,** Joseph Addison 1930- *AmMWSc 92*
**McKenzie,** Joyce Nadine 1950- *WhoEnt 92*
**McKenzie,** Julia Kathleen 1941- *Who 92*
**McKenzie,** Katherine Jane 1954- *WhoFI 92*
**McKenzie,** Kent 1969- *WhoEnt 92*
**McKenzie,** Kevin Patrick 1954- *WhoEnt 92*
**McKenzie,** Lewis H *WhoAmP 91*
**McKenzie,** Malcolm Arthur 1903- *AmMWSc 92*
**McKenzie,** Mary Ellen 1928- *IntAu&W 91*
**McKenzie,** Mary Etna 1925- *WhoAmP 91*
**McKenzie,** Merle 1954- *WhoWest 92*
**McKenzie,** Michael 1943- *Who 92*
**McKenzie,** Paige *WrDr 92*
**McKenzie,** Paul Ross 1953- *WhoFI 92*
**McKenzie,** Ralph Nelson 1941- *AmMWSc 92*
**McKenzie,** Reginald 1950- *WhoBlA 92*
**McKenzie,** Rita Laurette 1947- *WhoEnt 92*
**McKenzie,** Robert Lawrence *AmMWSc 92*
**McKenzie,** Ronald Eugene 1949- *WhoAmP 91*
**McKenzie,** Ronald Ian Hector 1930- *AmMWSc 92*
**McKenzie,** Roy 1922- *Who 92*
**McKenzie,** Sally Freeman 1928- *WhoAmP 91*
**McKenzie,** Therman, Sr. 1949- *WhoBlA 92*
**McKenzie,** Wendell Herbert 1942- *AmMWSc 92*
**McKenzie,** Wilford Clifton 1913- *WhoBlA 92*
**McKenzie,** William Camacho 1954- *WhoWest 92*
**McKenzie,** William F 1941- *AmMWSc 92*
**McKenzie Johnston,** Henry Butler 1921- *Who 92*
**McKenzie Smith,** Ian 1935- *Who 92*
**McKeon,** Catherine 1953- *AmMWSc 92*
**McKeon,** Doug 1966- *IntMPA 92*
**McKeon,** Elizabeth Fairbanks 1931- *WhoFI 92*
**McKeon,** George A 1937- *WhoIns 92*
**McKeon,** James Edward 1930- *AmMWSc 92*
**McKeon,** Mary Gertrude 1926- *AmMWSc 92*
**McKeon,** Robert B. 1954- *WhoWest 92*
**McKeon,** Zahava Karl 1927- *IntAu&W 91*
**McKeough,** William Darcy 1933- *WhoFI 92*
**McKeown,** Allan John 1946- *WhoEnt 92*
**McKeown,** Gerrie Margaret 1955- *WhoEnt 92*
**McKeown,** James Edward 1940- *WhoFI 92*
**McKeown,** James John 1930- *AmMWSc 92*
**McKeown,** James Preston 1937- *AmMWSc 92*
**McKeown,** John Matthews, Jr. 1941- *WhoWest 92*
**McKeown,** Martin 1943- *WhoFI 92*
**McKeown,** Mary Elizabeth *WhoMW 92*
**McKeown,** Patricia Lucas 1939- *WhoEnt 92*
**McKeown,** Patrick Arthur 1930- *Who 92*
**McKeown,** Thomas S 1937- *IntAu&W 91*
**McKeown,** Thomas W. *WhoFI 92*
**McKeown,** Tom *DrAPF 91*
**McKeown,** Tom 1937- *ConPo 91, WrDr 92*
**McKeown-Longo,** Paula Jean *AmMWSc 92*
**McKercher,** Robert Hamilton 1930- *IntWW 91*
**McKern,** Leo *ConAu 134*
**McKern,** Leo 1920- *IntMPA 92, Who 92*
**McKern,** Leo Reginald 1920- *IntWW 91*
**McKern,** Reginald 1920- *ConAu 134*
**McKernan,** John *DrAPF 91*
**McKernan,** John R., Jr. 1948- *AlmAP 92 [port], WhoAmP 91*
**McKernan,** John Rettie 1948- *IntWW 91*
**McKernan,** Leo Joseph 1938- *WhoFI 92, WhoMW 92*
**McKernan,** Llewellyn T. *DrAPF 91*
**McKerns,** Kenneth 1919- *AmMWSc 92*
**McKerracher,** William James 1944- *WhoMW 92*
**McKerrow,** Amanda *WhoEnt 92*
**McKerson,** Effie M. 1924- *WhoBlA 92*
**McKerson,** Hayward *WhoAmP 91*
**McKerson,** Mazola 1921- *WhoBlA 92*
**McKesson,** Charles L *ScFEYrs*
**McKethan,** Alfred Augustus 1809-1890 *DcNCBi 4*
**McKetta,** John J, Jr 1915- *AmMWSc 92*
**McKevitt,** Gerald Lawrence 1939- *WhoRel 92, WhoWest 92*
**McKevlin,** Anthony John 1902-1946 *DcNCBi 4*
**McKey,** Derrick Wayne 1966- *WhoBlA 92*
**McKhann,** Charles Fremont 1930- *AmMWSc 92*
**McKhann,** Guy Mead 1932- *AmMWSc 92*
**McKibben,** Bill 1961- *IntAu&W 91*
**McKibben,** Billy J *WhoAmP 91*
**McKibben,** Gerald Hopkins 1939- *AmMWSc 92*
**McKibben,** Howard D. 1940- *WhoAmL 92, WhoWest 92*
**McKibben,** John Scott 1937- *AmMWSc 92*
**McKibben,** Joseph L 1912- *AmMWSc 92*
**McKibben,** Richard Alan 1951- *WhoMW 92*
**McKibben,** Robert Bruce 1943- *AmMWSc 92*
**McKibbin,** John Mead 1915- *AmMWSc 92*
**McKibbin,** William Alex 1940- *WhoMW 92*
**McKibbins,** Samuel Wayne 1931- *AmMWSc 92*
**McKiddy,** Gary Edward 1947- *WhoMW 92*
**McKie,** Edward Foss 1924- *WhoAmL 92*
**McKie,** John David 1909- *Who 92*
**McKiernan,** Francis J. *Who 92*
**McKiernan,** Franklin Mark 1940- *WhoMW 92*
**McKiernan,** Michel Amedee 1930- *AmMWSc 92*
**McKiernan,** Philip Brendan 1952- *WhoAmL 92*
**McKiernan,** Thomas Eugene 1940- *WhoFI 92*
**McKillip,** Patricia 1948- *WrDr 92*
**McKillip,** Patricia A. 1948- *TwCSFW 91*
**McKillip,** Patricia Claire *WhoEnt 92*
**McKillop,** Alexander Joseph *WhoAmL 92*
**McKillop,** Allan A 1925- *AmMWSc 92*
**McKillop,** J H 1927- *AmMWSc 92*
**McKillop,** Lucille Mary 1924- *AmMWSc 92*
**McKillop,** M. Lucille *WhoRel 92*
**McKillop,** Malcolm C *WhoAmP 91*
**McKillop,** William L M 1933- *AmMWSc 92*
**McKim,** Adele W 1914- *WhoAmP 91*
**McKim,** Donald Keith 1950- *WhoRel 92*
**McKim,** Elizabeth *DrAPF 91*
**McKim,** Frank Hastings 1945- *WhoFI 92, WhoMW 92*
**McKim,** Harlan L 1937- *AmMWSc 92*
**McKim,** Harriet Megchelsen 1919- *WhoWest 92*
**McKim,** Herbert Pope 1928- *WhoAmP 91*
**McKim,** Samuel John, III 1938- *WhoAmL 92, WhoFI 92, WhoMW 92*
**McKimmon,** Jane Simpson 1867-1957 *DcNCBi 4*
**McKimmy,** Milford D 1923- *AmMWSc 92*
**McKinlay,** Brian John 1933- *IntAu&W 91, WrDr 92*
**McKinlay,** Bruce 1936- *WhoFI 92*
**McKinless,** Kathy Jean 1954- *WhoFI 92*
**McKinley,** Bernie 1928- *WhoAmP 91*
**McKinley,** Brunson 1943- *WhoAmP 91*
**McKinley,** Camille Dombrowski 1922- *WhoMW 92*
**McKinley,** Carolyn May 1945- *AmMWSc 92*
**McKinley,** Clyde 1917- *AmMWSc 92*
**McKinley,** David Bennett 1947- *WhoAmP 91*
**McKinley,** David Cecil 1913- *Who 92*
**McKinley,** Ellen Bacon 1929- *WhoRel 92*
**McKinley,** Ernest Coleman 1955- *WhoRel 92*
**McKinley,** Hugh 1924- *IntAu&W 91*
**McKinley,** James *DrAPF 91*
**McKinley,** James Frank, Jr. 1943- *WhoFI 92*
**McKinley,** John Clark 1960- *WhoAmL 92*
**McKinley,** John K. 1920- *IntWW 91*
**McKinley,** John Key 1920- *Who 92, WhoFI 92*
**McKinley,** John McKeen 1930- *AmMWSc 92, WhoMW 92*
**McKinley,** Joseph Warner 1943- *WhoWest 92*
**McKinley,** Kathryn Rae 1954- *WhoWest 92*
**McKinley,** Mark Lee 1953- *WhoWest 92*
**McKinley,** Marvin Dyal 1937- *AmMWSc 92*
**McKinley,** Michael P 1946- *AmMWSc 92*
**McKinley,** Ray 1910- *NewAmDM*
**McKinley,** Ray E. 1925- *WhoBlA 92*
**McKinley,** Robin 1952- *WrDr 92*
**McKinley,** Susan Margaret 1947- *WhoMW 92*
**McKinley,** Vicky L 1957- *AmMWSc 92*
**McKinley,** William 1843-1901 *BenetAL 91, FacFETw, RComAH*
**McKinley,** William, Jr. 1843-1901 *AmPolLe [port]*
**McKinley,** William, Jr. 1924- *WhoBlA 92*
**McKinley,** William Albert 1917- *AmMWSc 92*
**McKinley,** William E. 1940- *WhoFI 92*
**McKinley,** William Frank 1961- *WhoFI 92*
**McKinne,** Barnabas 1673?-1740? *DcNCBi 4*
**McKinne,** Richard 1752-1800 *DcNCBi 4*
**McKinnell,** James Charles 1933- *WhoRel 92*
**McKinnell,** Letha Miriam 1929- *WhoRel 92*
**McKinnell,** Robert Gilmore 1926- *AmMWSc 92*
**McKinnell,** W P, Jr 1924- *AmMWSc 92*
**McKinney,** Alfred Lee 1937- *AmMWSc 92*
**McKinney,** Alma Swilley 1930- *WhoBlA 92*
**McKinney,** B. *WhoRel 92*
**McKinney,** Betsy 1939- *WhoAmP 91*
**McKinney,** Bob Wayne 1939- *WhoRel 92*
**McKinney,** Charles Dana, Jr 1920- *AmMWSc 92*
**McKinney,** Chester Meek 1920- *AmMWSc 92*
**McKinney,** Cobby Dee 1939- *WhoAmP 91*
**McKinney,** Cynthia *WhoAmP 91*
**McKinney,** David Scroggs 1902- *AmMWSc 92*
**McKinney,** Dennis Keith 1952- *WhoMW 92*
**McKinney,** Douglas L. 1955- *WhoMW 92*
**McKinney,** Douglas Ward 1953- *WhoRel 92*
**McKinney,** E. Doris 1921- *WhoBlA 92*
**McKinney,** Earl H 1929- *AmMWSc 92*
**McKinney,** Edgar Dean 1952- *WhoRel 92*
**McKinney,** Eloise Vaughn *WhoBlA 92*
**McKinney,** Ernest Lee, Sr. 1923- *WhoBlA 92*
**Mc Kinney,** Frank Edward, Jr. 1938- *WhoMW 92*
**McKinney,** Frank Kenneth 1943- *AmMWSc 92*
**McKinney,** Fred 1908-1981 *ConAu 135*
**McKinney,** George Dallas, Jr. 1932- *WhoBlA 92*
**McKinney,** Gordon R 1923- *AmMWSc 92*
**McKinney,** Gregory L. 1953- *WhoBlA 92*
**McKinney,** Irene *DrAPF 91*
**McKinney,** J E 1927- *WhoAmP 91*
**McKinney,** J. P., Mrs. *Who 92*
**McKinney,** Jacob K. 1920- *WhoBlA 92*
**Mc Kinney,** James Carroll 1921- *WhoEnt 92, WhoRel 92*
**McKinney,** James David 1941- *AmMWSc 92*
**McKinney,** James DeVaine, Jr. 1931- *WhoAmL 92*
**McKinney,** James L. 1946- *WhoMW 92*
**McKinney,** James Ray 1942- *WhoBlA 92*
**McKinney,** James Russell 1925- *IntWW 91*
**McKinney,** James T 1938- *AmMWSc 92*
**McKinney,** Jean 1935- *WhoRel 92*
**McKinney,** Jesse Doyle 1934- *WhoBlA 92*
**McKinney,** Jill Louise 1944- *WhoFI 92*
**McKinney,** John Benjamin 1932- *WhoMW 92*
**McKinney,** John Edward 1925- *AmMWSc 92*
**McKinney,** Johnny Frank 1952- *WhoRel 92*
**McKinney,** Joseph Arthur 1943- *WhoFI 92*
**Mc Kinney,** Joseph Crescent 1928- *WhoRel 92*
**McKinney,** Kennedy 1966- *BlkOlyM*
**McKinney,** Kenneth N. 1936- *WhoAmL 92*
**McKinney,** Larry Emmett 1949- *WhoRel 92*
**McKinney,** Larry J. 1944- *WhoAmL 92, WhoMW 92*
**McKinney,** Luther C. 1931- *WhoAmL 92, WhoFI 92*
**McKinney,** Max Terral 1935- *AmMWSc 92*
**McKinney,** Michael 1950- *AmMWSc 92*
**McKinney,** Michael LeRoy 1946- *WhoRel 92*
**McKinney,** Mike 1951- *WhoAmP 91*
**McKinney,** Nina Mae 1912-1967 *NotBlAW 92*
**McKinney,** Norma J. 1941- *WhoBlA 92*
**McKinney,** Paul 1923- *WhoBlA 92*
**McKinney,** Paul, Sr *WhoAmP 91*
**McKinney,** Paul Caylor 1930- *AmMWSc 92*
**McKinney,** Peter 1934- *AmMWSc 92*
**McKinney,** Ralph Vincent, Jr 1933- *AmMWSc 92*
**McKinney,** Richard D. 1942- *WhoMW 92*
**McKinney,** Richard Ishmael 1906- *WhoBlA 92*
**McKinney,** Richard Leroy 1928- *AmMWSc 92*
**McKinney,** Robert Christian 1856?-1918 *BiInAmS*
**McKinney,** Robert Hurley 1925- *WhoAmP 91*
**McKinney,** Robert M 1910- *WhoAmP 91*
**McKinney,** Robert Moody 1910- *IntWW 91*
**McKinney,** Robert Wesley 1931- *AmMWSc 92*
**McKinney,** Roger Minor 1926- *AmMWSc 92*
**McKinney,** Ronald James 1949- *AmMWSc 92*
**McKinney,** Rosemary Kasul 1941- *WhoMW 92*
**McKinney,** Ross E 1926- *AmMWSc 92*
**McKinney,** Rufus William 1930- *WhoBlA 92*
**McKinney,** Samuel Berry 1926- *WhoBlA 92*
**McKinney,** Sheila Mary Deirdre 1928- *Who 92*
**McKinney,** Ted Meredith 1938- *AmMWSc 92*
**McKinney,** Theophilus Elisha, Jr. 1933- *WhoBlA 92*
**McKinney,** Thurman Dwight 1947- *AmMWSc 92*
**McKinney,** Venora Ware 1937- *WhoBlA 92*
**McKinney,** Wade H., III 1925- *WhoBlA 92*
**McKinney,** Wayne 1950- *WhoAmP 91*
**McKinney,** Whitt 1946- *WhoEnt 92*
**McKinney,** William 1946- *WhoRel 92*
**McKinney,** William Alan 1927- *AmMWSc 92*
**McKinney,** William Douthitt, Jr. 1955- *WhoFI 92*

**McKinney**, William Mark 1923- *AmMWSc 92*
**McKinney**, William Markley 1930- *AmMWSc 92*
**McKinney**, William Scranton, III 1942- *WhoMW 92*
**McKinney Goldin**, Kathleen 1943- *IntAu&W 91*
**McKinney's Cotton Pickers** *NewAmDM*
**McKinnie**, Michael Brundred 1949- *WhoFI 92*
**McKinnie**, William Dennis 1957- *WhoAmL 92*
**McKinnis**, Charles Leslie 1923- *AmMWSc 92*
**McKinnon**, Arnold Borden 1927- *WhoFI 92*
**McKinnon**, Christine Emily 1951- *WhoEnt 92*
**McKinnon**, Clinton Dan 1934- *WhoAmP 91, WhoEnt 92*
**McKinnon**, Clinton Dotson 1906- *WhoAmP 91*
**McKinnon**, David M 1938- *AmMWSc 92*
**McKinnon**, Dennis Lewis 1961- *WhoBlA 92*
**McKinnon**, Don *IntWW 91*
**McKinnon**, Donald Charles 1939- *Who 92*
**McKinnon**, Edward Kurt 1956- *WhoRel 92*
**McKinnon**, Floyd Wingfield 1942- *WhoFI 92*
**McKinnon**, James 1929- *Who 92*
**McKinnon**, James Buckner 1916- *WhoFI 92, WhoWest 92*
**McKinnon**, James William 1932- *WhoEnt 92*
**McKinnon**, Karen Quelle *DrAPF 91*
**McKinnon**, Kenneth Richard 1931- *Who 92*
**McKinnon**, Robert Donald 1952- *WhoEnt 92*
**McKinnon**, Robert Harold 1927- *WhoFI 92*
**McKinnon**, Stuart 1938- *Who 92*
**McKinnon**, Walter Sneddon 1910- *Who 92*
**McKinnon**, William Beall 1954- *AmMWSc 92*
**McKinsey**, Elizabeth 1947- *WhoMW 92*
**McKinsey**, Richard Davis 1921- *AmMWSc 92*
**McKinstrie**, Colin J 1960- *AmMWSc 92*
**McKinstry**, Arthur Raymond d1991 *NewYTBS 91*
**McKinstry**, Donald Michael 1939- *AmMWSc 92*
**McKinstry**, Doris Naomi 1936- *AmMWSc 92*
**McKinstry**, Herbert Alden 1925- *AmMWSc 92*
**Mc Kinstry**, John Rothrock 1914- *WhoRel 92*
**McKinstry**, Karl Alexander 1943- *AmMWSc 92*
**McKinstry**, Michael McCoy 1947- *WhoAmL 92*
**McKinstry**, Robert 1944- *WhoRel 92*
**McKinstry**, Ronald Eugene 1926- *WhoAmL 92*
**McKintosh**, Ian 1938- *Who 92*
**McKinzie-Harper**, Barbara A. 1954- *WhoBlA 92*
**McKissack**, Jimmie Don 1937- *WhoAmP 91*
**McKissack**, Leatrice B. 1930- *WhoBlA 92*
**McKissack**, William Deberry 1925- *WhoBlA 92*
**McKissick**, Evelyn Williams 1923- *WhoBlA 92*
**McKissick**, Floyd B d1991 *NewYTBS 91 [port]*
**McKissick**, Floyd B. 1922-1991 *CurBio 91N, WhoBlA 92N*
**McKissick**, Floyd Bixler 1922-1991 *ConAu 134*
**McKissick**, Floyd Bixler, Sr. 1922-1991 *IntWW 91, -91N*
**McKissick**, Mabel F. Rice 1921- *WhoBlA 92*
**McKissock**, David Lee 1933- *WhoFI 92*
**McKissock**, Wylie 1906- *Who 92*
**McKisson**, R L 1922- *AmMWSc 92*
**McKitrick**, Mary Caroline 1955- *AmMWSc 92*
**McKittrick**, Daniel Patrick 1941- *WhoAmP 91*
**McKittrick**, J. Joseph 1943- *WhoAmL 92*
**McKittrick**, Neil Alastair 1948- *Who 92*
**McKittrick**, Neil Vincent 1961- *WhoAmL 92*
**McKlveen**, John William 1943- *AmMWSc 92*
**McKnab**, Paul Allen 1941- *WhoMW 92*
**McKneally**, Martin F *AmMWSc 92*
**McKnight**, Albert J. *WhoBlA 92*
**McKnight**, Billy Edward 1956- *WhoRel 92*
**McKnight**, Colbert Augustus 1916-1986 *DcNCBi 4*
**McKnight**, James E. *WhoRel 92*
**McKnight**, James Pope 1921- *AmMWSc 92*
**McKnight**, Joe Nip 1933- *WhoAmP 91*
**McKnight**, John James 1948- *WhoIns 92*
**McKnight**, John Lacy 1931- *AmMWSc 92*
**McKnight**, Joseph Webb 1925- *WhoAmL 92*
**McKnight**, Joy Fowler 1947- *WhoFI 92*
**McKnight**, Lancess 1901- *WhoBlA 92*
**McKnight**, Lee Cassell 1942- *WhoBlA 92*
**McKnight**, Lee Graves 1933- *AmMWSc 92*
**McKnight**, Lee Warren 1956- *AmMWSc 92*
**McKnight**, Lenore Ravin 1943- *WhoWest 92*
**McKnight**, Michael Lance 1939- *WhoMW 92*
**McKnight**, Oscar Tilden, Jr. 1956- *WhoMW 92*
**McKnight**, Philip Charles, II 1941- *WhoMW 92*
**McKnight**, Randy Sherwood 1943- *AmMWSc 92*
**McKnight**, Reginald 1956- *WhoBlA 92*
**McKnight**, Richard D 1944- *AmMWSc 92*
**McKnight**, Rick James 1956- *WhoMW 92*
**McKnight**, Robert Allen 1943- *WhoAmP 91*
**McKnight**, Robert Wayne 1944- *WhoAmP 91*
**McKnight**, Ronald 1948- *WhoBlA 92*
**McKnight**, Stephen Alen 1944- *WhoAmP 91*
**McKnight**, Steven L 1949- *AmMWSc 92*
**McKnight**, Thomas John 1906- *AmMWSc 92*
**McKnight**, Tom Lee 1928- *WrDr 92*
**McKnight**, William Baldwin 1923- *AmMWSc 92*
**McKnight**, William Edwin 1938- *WhoRel 92*
**McKnight**, William Hunter 1940- *IntWW 91*
**Mc Kone**, Don T. 1921- *WhoFI 92, WhoMW 92*
**McKone**, Thomas Christopher 1917- *WhoAmL 92*
**McKone**, Thomas Edward 1951- *AmMWSc 92*
**McKool**, Pat 1927- *WhoEnt 92*
**McKoon**, James Robert 1956- *WhoAmL 92*
**McKowen**, Dorothy Keeton 1948- *WhoMW 92*
**McKowen**, Gary R. 1945- *WhoFI 92*
**McKown**, Cora F 1943- *AmMWSc 92*
**McKown**, David John 1959- *WhoFI 92*
**McKown**, Steve 1948- *WhoRel 92*
**McKoy**, Allmand Alexander 1825-1885 *DcNCBi 4*
**McKoy**, Basil Vincent 1938- *AmMWSc 92*
**McKoy**, Clemencio Agustino 1928- *WhoBlA 92*
**McKoy**, James Benjamin, Jr 1927- *AmMWSc 92*
**McKoy**, John H. 1944- *WhoBlA 92*
**McKoy**, William Berry 1852-1928 *DcNCBi 4*
**McKuen**, Rod 1933- *BenetAL 91, IntAu&W 91, IntWW 91, NewAmDM, Who 92, WrDr 92*
**McKusick**, Victor Almon 1921- *AmMWSc 92*
**McKusick**, Vincent L 1921- *WhoAmP 91*
**Mc Kusick**, Vincent Lee 1921- *WhoAmL 92*
**McKyes**, Edward 1944- *AmMWSc 92*
**McLachlan**, Alexander 1818-1896 *BenetAL 91*
**McLachlan**, Andrew David 1935- *Who 92*
**McLachlan**, Angus Henry 1908- *Who 92*
**McLachlan**, Dan, Jr 1905- *AmMWSc 92*
**McLachlan**, Gordon 1918- *Who 92*
**McLachlan**, Ian Dougald 1911- *Who 92*
**McLachlan**, Jack 1930- *AmMWSc 92*
**McLachlan**, John Alan 1943- *AmMWSc 92*
**McLachlan**, Peter John 1936- *Who 92*
**McLachlan**, Richard Scott 1946- *AmMWSc 92*
**McLachlin**, Jeanne Ruth *AmMWSc 92*
**McLaen**, Donald Francis 1942- *AmMWSc 92*
**McLafferty**, Fred Warren 1923- *AmMWSc 92*
**McLafferty**, George H, Jr 1926- *AmMWSc 92*
**McLafferty**, John J, Jr 1929- *AmMWSc 92*
**McLagan**, Patricia Ann 1945- *WhoMW 92*
**McLaggan**, Murray Adams 1929- *Who 92*
**McLaglen**, Andrew V. 1920- *IntMPA 92, IntWW 91*
**Mc Laglen**, Andrew Victor 1920- *WhoEnt 92*
**McLaglen**, John J. *TwCWW 91, WrDr 92*
**McLain**, David Kenneth 1937- *AmMWSc 92*
**McLain**, Douglas Robert 1938- *AmMWSc 92*
**McLain**, Eric Robbins 1943- *WhoRel 92*
**McLain**, John 1937- *WhoEnt 92*
**McLain**, Maurice Clayton 1929- *WhoAmL 92*
**McLain**, Michael Durley 1950- *WhoMW 92*
**McLain**, Robert Malcolm 1931- *WhoEnt 92*
**McLain**, Stephan James 1953- *AmMWSc 92*
**McLain**, Susan Lynn 1949- *WhoAmL 92*
**McLain**, Will King 1937- *WhoWest 92*
**McLain**, William Harvey *AmMWSc 92*
**McLamore**, William Merrill 1921- *AmMWSc 92*
**McLanathan**, Richard 1916- *IntAu&W 91*
**McLandburgh**, Florence 1850- *ScFEYrs*
**McLandress**, Herschel *ConAu 34NR*
**McLane**, Frederick Berg 1941- *WhoAmL 92*
**McLane**, George Francis 1938- *AmMWSc 92*
**McLane**, Harry H 1925- *WhoAmP 91*
**McLane**, James Ray 1941- *WhoIns 92*
**McLane**, James Woods 1801-1864 *DcNCBi 4*
**McLane**, James Woods 1839-1912 *BiInAmS*
**McLane**, James Woods 1939- *WhoFI 92*
**McLane**, Jean 1926- *WhoAmP 91*
**McLane**, Louis 1786-1857 *AmPolLe*
**McLane**, Malcolm 1924- *WhoAmP 91*
**McLane**, Michael Nelson 1958- *WhoEnt 92*
**McLane**, Peter John 1941- *AmMWSc 92*
**McLane**, Robert Clayton 1924- *AmMWSc 92*
**McLane**, Robert Joel 1944- *WhoWest 92*
**McLane**, Susan B R 1948- *WhoAmP 91*
**McLane**, Susan Margaret 1956- *WhoWest 92*
**McLane**, Susan Neidlinger 1929- *WhoAmP 91*
**McLane**, Victoria 1939- *AmMWSc 92*
**McLaren** *Who 92*
**McLaren**, Anne Laura 1927- *Who 92*
**McLaren**, Archie Campbell, Jr 1942- *WhoWest 92*
**McLaren**, Charles Benjamin Bright 1850-1934 *BiDBrF 2*
**McLaren**, Clare *Who 92*
**McLaren**, Colin Andrew 1940- *IntAu&W 91*
**McLaren**, Derryl 1949- *WhoAmP 91*
**McLaren**, Digby Johns 1919- *AmMWSc 92, IntWW 91, Who 92*
**McLaren**, Douglas Earl 1948- *WhoBlA 92*
**McLaren**, Eugene Herbert 1924- *AmMWSc 92*
**McLaren**, Fred B. 1934- *WhoWest 92*
**McLaren**, Ian Alexander 1931- *AmMWSc 92*
**McLaren**, Ian Francis 1912- *WrDr 92*
**McLaren**, J Philip 1941- *AmMWSc 92*
**McLaren**, John 1932- *WrDr 92*
**McLaren**, John David 1932- *IntAu&W 91*
**McLaren**, Laura Elizabeth 1855?-1933 *BiDBrF 2*
**McLaren**, Leroy Clarence 1924- *AmMWSc 92*
**McLaren**, Malcolm G 1928- *AmMWSc 92*
**McLaren**, Marilyn Patricia 1942- *WhoFI 92*
**McLaren**, Mary Lee 1919- *WhoWest 92*
**McLaren**, Norman 1914-1987 *FacFETw*
**McLaren**, Robert Alexander 1946- *AmMWSc 92*
**McLaren**, Robert Wayne 1936- *AmMWSc 92*
**McLaren**, Robin John Taylor 1934- *Who 92*
**McLaren-Throckmorton**, Clare *Who 92*
**McLario**, John J., Jr. 1925- *WhoAmL 92*
**McLarnan**, Donald Edward 1906- *WhoFI 92, WhoWest 92*
**McLarney**, Charles Patrick 1942- *WhoAmL 92*
**McLarry**, Newman Ray 1923- *WhoRel 92*
**McLauchlan**, D C Ramsay 1962- *WhoAmP 91*
**McLauchlan**, Madeline Margaret Nicholls 1922- *Who 92*
**McLauchlan**, Thomas Joseph 1917- *Who 92*
**McLaughin**, Thomas Ford 1944- *WhoWest 92*
**McLaughlan**, Ian David 1919- *Who 92*
**McLaughlin**, Alan Charles 1945- *AmMWSc 92*
**McLaughlin**, Alexander C. J. 1925- *WhoFI 92*
**McLaughlin**, Andree N. *ConAu 133*
**McLaughlin**, Andree Nicola 1948- *ConAu 133, WhoBlA 92*
**McLaughlin**, Ann Dore 1941- *IntWW 91*
**McLaughlin**, Ann L. 1928- *ConAu 135*
**McLaughlin**, Ann Landis *DrAPF 91*
**McLaughlin**, Barbara Connor 1931- *WhoAmP 91*
**McLaughlin**, Barbara Jean 1941- *AmMWSc 92*
**McLaughlin**, Benjamin Wayne 1947- *WhoBlA 92*
**McLaughlin**, Bernard J. 1912- *WhoRel 92*
**McLaughlin**, Bernice 1931- *WhoEnt 92*
**McLaughlin**, Brian James 1964- *WhoEnt 92*
**McLaughlin**, Calvin Sturgis 1936- *AmMWSc 92*
**McLaughlin**, Carol Lynn *AmMWSc 92*
**McLaughlin**, Charles Albert 1926- *AmMWSc 92*
**McLaughlin**, Charles P 1937- *WhoAmP 91*
**McLaughlin**, Charles William, Jr 1906- *AmMWSc 92*
**McLaughlin**, Clara J. *WhoBlA 92*
**McLaughlin**, David 1934- *AmMWSc 92, WhoBlA 92*
**McLaughlin**, Dean 1931- *IntAu&W 91, TwCSFW 91, WrDr 92*
**McLaughlin**, Dolphy T. 1922- *WhoBlA 92*
**McLaughlin**, Donald Reed 1938- *AmMWSc 92*
**McLaughlin**, Dorothy Claire *WhoWest 92*
**McLaughlin**, Edward 1928- *AmMWSc 92*
**McLaughlin**, Eleanor Thomson 1938- *Who 92*
**McLaughlin**, Ellen Winnie 1937- *AmMWSc 92*
**McLaughlin**, Eurphan 1936- *WhoBlA 92*
**McLaughlin**, Florence Patricia 1916- *Who 92*
**McLaughlin**, Foil William 1923- *AmMWSc 92*
**McLaughlin**, Francis X 1930- *AmMWSc 92*
**McLaughlin**, Frank Charles 1931- *WhoFI 92*
**McLaughlin**, Gary James 1934- *WhoMW 92*
**McLaughlin**, George W. 1932- *WhoBlA 92*
**McLaughlin**, Gerald Wayne 1942- *AmMWSc 92*
**McLaughlin**, Glen 1934- *WhoFI 92*
**McLaughlin**, Harry Wright 1937- *AmMWSc 92*
**McLaughlin**, J F 1927- *AmMWSc 92*
**McLaughlin**, Jack A *AmMWSc 92*
**McLaughlin**, Jack Enloe 1923- *AmMWSc 92*
**McLaughlin**, Jacquelyn Snow 1943- *WhoBlA 92*
**McLaughlin**, James Daniel 1942- *WhoFI 92*
**McLaughlin**, James Daniel 1947- *WhoFI 92, WhoWest 92*
**McLaughlin**, James Daniel 1956- *WhoAmL 92*
**McLaughlin**, James Hugh 1953- *WhoAmP 91*
**McLaughlin**, James L 1942- *AmMWSc 92*
**McLaughlin**, James Patrick 1953- *WhoAmL 92*
**McLaughlin**, Jean Ann 1950- *WhoEnt 92*
**McLaughlin**, Jerry Loren 1939- *AmMWSc 92*
**McLaughlin**, Joe Anne *DrAPF 91*
**McLaughlin**, John *WhoEnt 92*
**McLaughlin**, John 1942- *NewAmDM*
**McLaughlin**, John Bell 1925- *WhoAmP 91*
**McLaughlin**, John Belton 1903- *WhoBlA 92*
**McLaughlin**, John H 1926- *WhoAmP 91*
**McLaughlin**, John J A 1924- *AmMWSc 92*
**McLaughlin**, John Joseph 1927- *WhoEnt 92*
**McLaughlin**, John Ross 1939- *AmMWSc 92*
**McLaughlin**, John Sherman 1932- *WhoAmL 92*
**McLaughlin**, Joseph *DrAPF 91*
**McLaughlin**, Joseph C. 1934-1984 *WhoBlA 92N*
**McLaughlin**, Joseph M 1933- *WhoAmP 91*
**McLaughlin**, Joseph Michael 1943- *WhoRel 92*
**McLaughlin**, Joyce Rogers *AmMWSc 92*
**McLaughlin**, Katye H. 1933- *WhoBlA 92*
**McLaughlin**, LaVerne Laney 1952- *WhoBlA 92*
**McLaughlin**, Linden Dale 1956- *WhoRel 92*
**McLaughlin**, Marguerite Pearl 1928- *WhoAmP 91*
**McLaughlin**, Martin Michael 1918- *WhoFI 92*
**McLaughlin**, Megan E. *WhoBlA 92*
**McLaughlin**, Michael Angelo 1950- *WhoFI 92*
**McLaughlin**, Michael Edward 1945- *WhoAmP 91*
**McLaughlin**, Michael Edward 1954- *WhoAmL 92*
**McLaughlin**, Michael James 1952- *WhoRel 92, WhoWest 92*

**McMillian,** Jimmy, Jr. 1953- *WhoBlA 92*
**McMillian,** Josie 1940- *WhoBlA 92*
**McMillian,** Theodore *WhoAmP 91*
**McMillian,** Theodore 1919- *WhoAmL 92, WhoBlA 92, WhoMW 92*
**McMillin,** Carl Richard 1946- *AmMWSc 92*
**McMillin,** Charles W 1932- *AmMWSc 92*
**McMillin,** David Robert 1948- *AmMWSc 92*
**McMillin,** Glenn Reinhard 1930- *WhoFI 92*
**McMillin,** James Craig 1949- *WhoAmL 92*
**McMillin,** Jeanie 1939- *AmMWSc 92*
**McMillin,** Raymond Craig 1947- *WhoAmL 92*
**McMillin,** Sheila Dawne 1945- *WhoFI 92, WhoMW 92*
**McMillion,** Leslie Glen, Sr 1930- *AmMWSc 92*
**McMillon,** Lynn A. 1941- *WhoRel 92*
**McMillon,** R L 1921- *WhoIns 92*
**McMinn,** B C 1921- *WhoAmP 91*
**McMinn,** Curtis J 1929- *AmMWSc 92*
**McMinn,** Richard Lynn 1957- *WhoRel 92*
**McMinn,** Robert Matthew Hay 1923- *Who 92*
**McMinn,** Trevor James 1921- *AmMWSc 92*
**McMinn,** William Lowell, Jr. 1943- *WhoMW 92*
**McMinnies,** John Gordon 1919- *Who 92*
**McMonagle,** Gerald F 1936- *WhoAmP 91*
**McMonies,** Walter Wittenberg, Jr. 1947- *WhoAmL 92*
**McMorran,** J. Burch 1899-1991 *NewYTBS 91 [port]*
**McMorris,** F Arthur 1944- *AmMWSc 92*
**McMorris,** Fred Raymond 1943- *AmMWSc 92*
**McMorris,** Jacqueline Williams 1936- *WhoBlA 92*
**McMorris,** Samuel Carter 1920- *WhoBlA 92*
**McMorrow,** Kathryn Ann 1962- *WhoWest 92*
**McMorrow,** Thomas *ScFEYrs*
**McMorrow,** Thomas 1886- *ScFEYrs*
**McMorrow,** Thomas Ray 1963- *WhoAmL 92*
**McMorrow,** Will F *ScFEYrs*
**McMullan,** Gordon *Who 92*
**McMullan,** James Burroughs 1934- *WhoEnt 92*
**McMullan,** James F, Jr 1931- *WhoAmP 91*
**McMullan,** James Franklin 1928- *WhoFI 92*
**McMullan,** James Patrick, Jr. 1936- *WhoEnt 92*
**McMullan,** John J *WhoAmP 91*
**McMullan,** Michael Brian 1926- *Who 92*
**McMullan,** Thomas Shelton 1868-1954 *DcNCBi 4*
**McMullan,** William Patrick, III 1952- *WhoFI 92*
**McMullen,** Archie Robert 1938- *WhoEnt 92*
**McMullen,** Betty A 1936- *IntAu&W 91*
**McMullen,** Bryce H 1921- *AmMWSc 92*
**McMullen,** Cynthia Diane 1954- *WhoFI 92*
**McMullen,** Daniel Robert 1948- *WhoMW 92*
**McMullen,** David 1963- *WhoFI 92*
**McMullen,** David Lawrence 1939- *Who 92*
**McMullen,** Francis Lee 1926- *WhoMW 92*
**McMullen,** Harry, Sr. 1884-1955 *DcNCBi 4*
**McMullen,** Horace Martin 1913- *WhoRel 92*
**McMullen,** James Clinton 1942- *AmMWSc 92*
**McMullen,** James Robert 1942- *AmMWSc 92*
**McMullen,** Jay *LesBEnT 92*
**McMullen,** Jeremy 1948- *WrDr 92*
**McMullen,** John Henry, Jr. 1944- *WhoFI 92*
**McMullen,** Mary 1920- *IntAu&W 91, WrDr 92*
**McMullen,** Patrick R *WhoAmP 91*
**McMullen,** Richard E. *DrAPF 91*
**McMullen,** Robert David 1930- *AmMWSc 92*
**McMullen,** Warren Anthony 1907- *AmMWSc 92*
**Mc Mullian,** Amos Ryals 1937- *WhoFI 92*
**McMullin,** C. David 1955- *WhoMW 92, WhoRel 92*
**McMullin,** Craig Stephen 1957- *WhoFI 92*
**McMullin,** Dix Holt 1933- *WhoAmP 91*
**McMullin,** Duncan 1927- *Who 92*
**McMullin,** Robert Joseph 1946- *WhoEnt 92*
**McMullin,** Ruth Roney 1942- *WhoFI 92*
**McMullins,** Tommy 1942- *WhoBlA 92*
**McMunn,** Earl William 1910- *WhoAmP 91*
**McMunn,** Richard E 1949- *WhoRel 92*
**McMurchie,** Lyle William 1928- *WhoFI 92*
**McMurchy,** Robert Connell 1902- *AmMWSc 92*
**McMurdie,** Howard Francis 1905- *AmMWSc 92*
**McMurdo,** C Gregory 1946- *WhoAmP 91*
**McMurdo,** Mary-Jane 1924- *WhoAmP 91, WhoWest 92*
**McMurphy,** Wilfred E 1934- *AmMWSc 92*
**McMurran,** Lewis Archer, Jr 1914- *WhoAmP 91*
**McMurran,** Stockton Mosby 1887-1920 *BiInAmS*
**McMurray,** Birch Lee 1931- *AmMWSc 92*
**McMurray,** Cecil Hugh 1942- *Who 92*
**McMurray,** David Bruce 1937- *Who 92*
**McMurray,** David Claude 1927- *AmMWSc 92*
**McMurray,** David N *AmMWSc 92*
**McMurray,** Jose Daniel 1949- *WhoHisp 92*
**McMurray,** Joseph Patrick Brendan 1912- *IntWW 91*
**McMurray,** Kay 1918- *WhoAmP 91*
**McMurray,** Loren Robert 1931- *AmMWSc 92*
**McMurray,** Walter Joseph 1935- *AmMWSc 92*
**McMurray,** William Colin Campbell 1931- *AmMWSc 92*
**McMurray,** William Josiah 1842-1905 *BiInAmS*
**McMurrey,** Frank Lynn 1939- *WhoEnt 92*
**McMurry,** John Edward 1942- *AmMWSc 92*
**McMurry,** Kermit Roosevelt, Jr. 1945- *WhoBlA 92*
**McMurry,** L. L. 1927- *WhoWest 92*
**McMurry,** Merley Lee 1949- *WhoBlA 92*
**McMurry,** Walter M., Jr. 1934- *WhoBlA 92*
**McMurry,** William 1929- *AmMWSc 92*
**McMurry,** William Scott 1921- *WhoMW 92*
**McMurtrey,** Lawrence J 1924- *AmMWSc 92*
**McMurtrie,** Alexander B, Jr *WhoAmP 91*
**McMurtrie,** Richard Angus 1909- *Who 92*
**McMurtrie,** William 1851-1913 *BiInAmS*
**McMurtry,** Carl Hewes 1931- *AmMWSc 92*
**McMurtry,** George James 1932- *AmMWSc 92*
**McMurtry,** Ivan Fredrick *AmMWSc 92*
**McMurtry,** James A 1932- *AmMWSc 92*
**McMurtry,** Larry *DrAPF 91*
**McMurtry,** Larry 1936- *BenetAL 91, ConNov 91, IntAu&W 91, TwCWW 91, WrDr 92*
**McMurtry,** Robert Gerald 1906- *IntAu&W 91*
**McMurtry,** Roy 1932- *Who 92*
**McMurtry,** Vanda Bruce 1949- *WhoAmL 92*
**McMurty,** Burton J *AmMWSc 92*
**McNab,** Jeb *TwCWW 91*
**McNab,** John Stanley 1937- *Who 92*
**McNab Jones,** Robin Francis 1922- *Who 92*
**McNabb,** Clarence Duncan, Jr 1928- *AmMWSc 92*
**McNabb,** Edward Timberlake, Jr. 1951- *WhoRel 92*
**McNabb,** F M Anne 1939- *AmMWSc 92*
**McNabb,** Frank William 1936- *WhoFI 92*
**McNabb,** Harold Sanderson, Jr 1927- *AmMWSc 92*
**McNabb,** Robert Henry 1917- *WhoRel 92*
**McNabb,** Roger Allen 1938- *AmMWSc 92*
**McNabb,** Talmadge Ford 1924- *WhoRel 92*
**McNail,** Stanley *DrAPF 91*
**McNair** *Who 92*
**McNair,** Baron 1958- *Who 92*
**McNair,** Archie 1919- *Who 92*
**McNair,** Barbara J. 1939- *WhoBlA 92*
**McNair,** Dennis M 1945- *AmMWSc 92*
**McNair,** Douglas McIntosh 1927- *AmMWSc 92*
**McNair,** Evander 1820-1902 *DcNCBi 4*
**McNair,** Harold Monroe 1933- *AmMWSc 92*
**McNair,** Irving M, Jr 1932- *AmMWSc 92*
**McNair,** J Christopher *WhoAmP 91*
**McNair,** James Jamieson d1990 *Who 92N*
**McNair,** John Calvin 1823-1858 *DcNCBi 4*
**McNair,** John Franklin, III 1927- *WhoFI 92*
**McNair,** Joseph *DrAPF 91*
**McNair,** Robert Evander 1923- *WhoAmP 91*
**McNair,** Robert J, Jr 1918- *AmMWSc 92*
**McNair,** Ronald E 1950-1986 *FacFETw*
**McNair,** Russell Arthur, Jr. 1934- *WhoAmL 92*
**McNair,** Ruth Davis 1921- *AmMWSc 92*
**Mc Nair,** Sylvia *WhoEnt 92*
**McNair,** Thomas Jaffrey 1927- *Who 92*
**McNair,** Wesley *DrAPF 91*
**McNair-Wilson,** Michael *Who 92*
**McNair-Wilson,** Patrick 1929- *Who 92*
**McNair-Wilson,** Robert Michael 1930- *Who 92*
**McNairn,** Caroline 1955- *TwCPaSc*
**McNairn,** Robert Blackwood 1940- *AmMWSc 92*
**McNairy,** Francine G. 1946- *WhoBlA 92*
**McNairy,** John 1762-1837 *DcNCBi 4*
**McNairy,** Sidney A. 1937- *WhoBlA 92*
**McNairy,** Sidney A, Jr 1937- *AmMWSc 92*
**McNall,** Bruce *WhoWest 92*
**McNall,** Lester R 1927- *AmMWSc 92*
**McNall,** P.E. 1888-1981 *ConAu 135*
**McNally,** Andrew, III 1909- *WhoFI 92*
**McNally,** Andrew, IV 1939- *WhoFI 92, WhoMW 92*
**McNally,** Chris 1960- *WhoAmP 91*
**McNally,** David Wendell 1956- *WhoEnt 92*
**McNally,** Derek 1934- *IntWW 91*
**McNally,** Elizabeth Mary *AmMWSc 92*
**McNally,** James F. 1932- *WhoFI 92*
**McNally,** James Henry 1936- *AmMWSc 92, WhoWest 92*
**McNally,** James Michael 1934- *WhoAmL 92*
**McNally,** James Nelson 1957- *WhoAmL 92*
**McNally,** James Rand, III 1944- *WhoAmP 91*
**McNally,** James Rand, Jr 1917- *AmMWSc 92*
**McNally,** Jeanne Margaret 1931- *WhoRel 92*
**McNally,** John G 1932- *AmMWSc 92*
**McNally,** John Joseph, Jr. 1955- *WhoAmL 92*
**McNally,** Karen Cook *AmMWSc 92*
**McNally,** Marla Lee 1958- *WhoEnt 92*
**McNally,** Mary Sarah 1937- *WhoRel 92*
**McNally,** Pierce Aldrich 1949- *WhoMW 92*
**McNally,** Richard Patrick 1950- *WhoRel 92*
**McNally,** Shaun M 1957- *WhoAmP 91*
**McNally,** Stephen 1913- *IntMPA 92*
**McNally,** Stephen Randall 1957- *WhoMW 92*
**McNally,** Terrence 1939- *BenetAL 91, IntAu&W 91, WhoEnt 92, WrDr 92*
**McNally,** Timothy Francis 1952- *WhoFI 92*
**McNally,** Timothy John 1954- *WhoAmP 91*
**McNally,** Tom 1943- *Who 92*
**McNamar,** David Fred 1940- *WhoAmL 92*
**McNamara,** A. J. 1936- *WhoAmL 92*
**McNamara,** Allen Garnet 1926- *AmMWSc 92*
**McNamara,** Anne H. 1947- *WhoAmL 92*
**McNamara,** Carole Dee Gonda 1950- *WhoMW 92*
**McNamara,** Colleen Marie 1949- *WhoEnt 92*
**McNamara,** Dan Goodrich 1922- *AmMWSc 92*
**McNamara,** David Joseph 1951- *WhoMW 92*
**McNamara,** Delbert Harold 1923- *AmMWSc 92*
**McNamara,** Dennis B 1942- *AmMWSc 92*
**McNamara,** Donald J 1944- *AmMWSc 92*
**McNamara,** Edward Howard 1926- *WhoAmP 91*
**McNamara,** Edward P 1910- *AmMWSc 92*
**McNamara,** Elsa Mae Broesamle 1958- *WhoFI 92*
**McNamara,** Eugene *DrAPF 91*
**McNamara,** Eugene Joseph 1930- *IntAu&W 91, WrDr 92*
**McNamara,** Francis T *WhoAmP 91*
**McNamara,** Henry P 1934- *WhoAmP 91*
**McNamara,** James Alyn, Jr 1943- *AmMWSc 92*
**McNamara,** James O'Connell 1942- *AmMWSc 92*
**McNamara,** John 1932- *WhoMW 92*
**McNamara,** John 1939- *WhoAmP 91*
**McNamara,** John F *WhoAmP 91*
**McNamara,** John F. 1935- *WhoFI 92*
**McNamara,** John Regis 1941- *AmMWSc 92*
**McNamara,** Joseph Burk 1930- *WhoAmL 92*
**Mc Namara,** Joseph Donald 1934- *WhoWest 92*
**McNamara,** Joseph Judson 1936- *AmMWSc 92*
**McNamara,** Julia Mary 1941- *WhoRel 92*
**McNamara,** Kathleen Michele 1957- *WhoEnt 92, WhoMW 92*
**McNamara,** Keith 1928- *WhoAmP 91*
**McNamara,** Kevin 1934- *Who 92*
**Mc Namara,** Lawrence J. 1928- *WhoRel 92*
**McNamara,** Mary Colleen 1947- *AmMWSc 92*
**McNamara,** Maureen Ann 1923- *WhoAmP 91*
**McNamara,** Michael John 1948- *WhoAmL 92*
**McNamara,** Michael Joseph 1929- *AmMWSc 92*
**McNamara,** Nan *WhoEnt 92*
**McNamara,** Neville 1923- *Who 92*
**McNamara,** Pamela Dee 1943- *AmMWSc 92*
**McNamara,** Patrick James 1959- *WhoAmL 92*
**McNamara,** Patrick Joseph 1961- *WhoAmL 92*
**Mc Namara,** Rieman, Jr. 1928- *WhoFI 92*
**McNamara,** Robert *DrAPF 91*
**McNamara,** Robert 1916- *WrDr 92*
**McNamara,** Robert B. *WhoFI 92*
**McNamara,** Robert Edward 1956- *WhoFI 92*
**McNamara,** Robert Strange 1916- *AmPolLe, FacFETw, IntWW 91, Who 92*
**McNamara,** Rosalee Miller 1956- *WhoAmL 92*
**McNamara,** Stephen Joseph 1952- *WhoEnt 92*
**McNamara,** Thomas E. 1940- *IntWW 91*
**McNamara,** Thomas Edmund 1940- *WhoAmP 91*
**McNamara,** Thomas Francis 1928- *AmMWSc 92*
**McNamara,** Thomas Michael 1955- *WhoWest 92*
**McNamara,** Thomas Neal 1930- *WhoAmL 92*
**McNamara,** Timothy Kevin 1955- *WhoAmL 92*
**McNamara,** William 1965- *IntMPA 92*
**McNamee,** Bernard M 1930- *AmMWSc 92*
**McNamee,** Catherine 1931- *WhoRel 92*
**McNamee,** Dennis Patrick 1952- *WhoAmL 92*
**McNamee,** Evelyn Haynes 1947- *WhoWest 92*
**McNamee,** James *WhoMW 92*
**McNamee,** James Emerson 1946- *AmMWSc 92*
**McNamee,** Kathleen 1949- *WhoMW 92*
**McNamee,** Lawrence Paul 1934- *AmMWSc 92*
**McNamee,** Louise *WhoFI 92*
**McNamee,** Mark G 1946- *AmMWSc 92*
**McNamee,** Thomas *DrAPF 91*
**McNamee,** Victoria Ann 1956- *WhoEnt 92*
**McNamer,** Elizabeth Forster 1936- *WhoRel 92*
**McNaney,** Robert Trainor 1934- *WhoAmL 92*
**McNary,** Gene 1935- *WhoAmL 92*
**Mcnary,** Kent Douglas 1947- *WhoFI 92*
**McNary,** Oscar Lee 1944- *WhoBlA 92*
**McNary,** Robert Reed 1903- *AmMWSc 92*
**McNatt,** Isaac G. 1916- *WhoBlA 92*
**McNaught,** Donald Curtis 1934- *AmMWSc 92*
**McNaught,** John Graeme 1941- *Who 92*
**McNaught,** Judith 1944- *WrDr 92*
**McNaughton,** Alexander Bryant 1948- *WhoAmL 92*
**McNaughton,** Anne Elizabeth 1952- *WhoAmP 91*
**McNaughton,** Duncan A 1910- *AmMWSc 92*
**McNaughton,** H. D. 1945- *WrDr 92*
**McNaughton,** Ian Kenneth Arnold 1920- *Who 92*
**McNaughton,** James Larry 1948- *AmMWSc 92*
**McNaughton,** John 1950- *IntMPA 92*
**McNaughton,** Mary Anne 1935- *WhoEnt 92*
**McNaughton,** Michael Walford 1943- *AmMWSc 92*
**McNaughton,** Robert 1924- *AmMWSc 92*
**McNaughton,** Robert Douglas 1936- *WhoRel 92*
**McNaughton,** Robert Lee 1935- *WhoFI 92*
**McNaughton,** Samuel J 1939- *AmMWSc 92*
**McNaughton,** Stanley O 1921- *WhoIns 92*
**McNay,** John Leeper *AmMWSc 92*
**McNeal,** Brian Lester 1938- *AmMWSc 92*
**McNeal,** Clark E 1942- *WhoAmP 91*
**McNeal,** Dale William, Jr 1939- *AmMWSc 92*
**McNeal,** Don 1958- *WhoBlA 92*
**McNeal,** Dorothy N. 1922- *WhoBlA 92*
**McNeal,** Francis H 1920- *AmMWSc 92*
**Mc Neal,** Harley John *WhoAmL 92*
**Mc Neal,** James Hector, Jr. 1927- *WhoFI 92*
**McNeal,** John Alex, Jr. 1932- *WhoBlA 92*
**McNeal,** Palmer Craig 1950- *WhoAmP 91*

**McNeal,** Ralph Leroy 1935- *WhoFI 92*
**McNeal,** Robert Joseph 1937- *AmMWSc 92*
**McNeal,** Sylvia Ann 1947- *WhoBlA 92*
**McNeal,** Travis S. 1967- *WhoBlA 92*
**McNeal,** William Clark 1930- *WhoAmP 91*
**Mc Nealy,** Scott 1954- *WhoWest 92*
**McNear,** Barbara Baxter 1939- *WhoFI 92*
**McNeary,** Joseph Allen 1948- *WhoFI 92*
**McNeary,** Peggy Drake 1937- *WhoMW 92*
**McNee,** David 1925- *Who 92*
**McNee,** David Blackstock 1925- *IntWW 91*
**McNeel,** Pleasant Jackson, III 1939- *WhoEnt 92*
**McNeel,** Synott Lance 1923- *WhoIns 92*
**McNeel,** Van Louis 1925- *WhoFI 92*
**McNeelege,** Matthew Kenneth 1958- *WhoWest 92*
**McNeely,** Carol J. 1954- *WhoBlA 92*
**McNeely,** Charles E. 1951- *WhoBlA 92*
**McNeely,** James Braden 1933- *AmMWSc 92*
**McNeely,** James Powell 1953- *WhoMW 92*
**McNeely,** Jerry C. *LesBEnT 92*
**McNeely,** Jim Madison 1956- *WhoWest 92*
**McNeely,** John W. 1950- *WhoEnt 92*
**McNeely,** Matthew 1920- *WhoBlA 92*
**McNeely,** Michael Dale 1955- *WhoIns 92*
**McNeely,** Richard Irving 1928- *WhoRel 92*
**McNeely,** Robert Lewis 1938- *AmMWSc 92*
**McNeely,** Sharon Lynn 1955- *WhoMW 92*
**McNeely-Johnson,** Kathy Ann 1957- *WhoFI 92*
**Mc Neer,** Charles Selden 1926- *WhoFI 92*
**McNees,** Caryl 1938- *WhoWest 92*
**McNees,** Roger Wayne 1944- *AmMWSc 92*
**McNeese,** Leonard Eugene 1935- *AmMWSc 92*
**McNeese,** Patrick Martin 1953- *WhoEnt 92*
**McNeice,** Gregory Malcolm 1939- *AmMWSc 92*
**McNeice,** Percy 1901- *Who 92*
**McNeil,** Alvin J. 1920- *WhoBlA 92*
**McNeil,** Barbara Joyce 1941- *AmMWSc 92*
**McNeil,** Bill *ConAu 133*
**McNeil,** Claudia Mae 1917- *WhoBlA 92*
**McNeil,** David John 1937- *Who 92*
**McNeil,** DeeDee *WhoBlA 92*
**McNeil,** Dennis Michael 1949- *WhoMW 92, WhoRel 92*
**McNeil,** Ernest Duke 1936- *WhoBlA 92*
**McNeil,** Everett 1862-1929 *ScFEYrs*
**McNeil,** Florence 1940- *ConPo 91, WrDr 92*
**McNeil,** Florence Ann 1940- *IntAu&W 91*
**McNeil,** Frank 1937- *WhoBlA 92*
**McNeil,** Frank William 1948- *WhoBlA 92*
**McNeil,** Frederick Harold 1916- *IntWW 91*
**McNeil,** Freeman 1959- *WhoBlA 92*
**McNeil,** Ian Robert 1932- *Who 92*
**McNeil,** Jeremy Nichol 1944- *AmMWSc 92*
**McNeil,** John *Who 92, WhoEnt 92*
**McNeil,** John C *WhoAmP 91*
**McNeil,** John D 1934- *WhoIns 92*
**McNeil,** John Struthers 1907- *Who 92*
**McNeil,** Kenneth Martin 1941- *AmMWSc 92*
**McNeil,** Kevin Michael 1954- *WhoAmL 92*
**McNeil,** Laurie Elizabeth 1956- *AmMWSc 92*
**McNeil,** Lori 1964?- *ConBlB 1 [port]*
**McNeil,** Lori Michelle 1963- *WhoBlA 92*
**McNeil,** Malcolm Ray 1947- *WhoMW 92*
**McNeil,** Marianne McFarland *DrAPF 91*
**McNeil,** Mark Frasher 1954- *WhoRel 92*
**McNeil,** Mark Sanford 1950- *WhoAmL 92*
**McNeil,** Mary *ConAu 134*
**McNeil,** Michael Brewer 1938- *AmMWSc 92*
**McNeil,** Nellie Miller 1937- *WhoAmP 91*
**McNeil,** Ogretta V. 1932- *WhoBlA 92*
**McNeil,** Paul L *AmMWSc 92*
**McNeil,** Phillip Eugene 1941- *AmMWSc 92*
**McNeil,** Raymond 1936- *AmMWSc 92*
**McNeil,** Richard Jerome 1932- *AmMWSc 92*
**McNeil,** Richard John 1959- *WhoAmL 92*
**McNeil,** Robert Duell 1935- *WhoWest 92*
**McNeil,** Thomas Kerney 1949- *WhoEnt 92*
**McNeil,** William K. 1940- *WhoEnt 92*
**McNeil,** William Russell 1924- *ConAu 133*
**McNeill,** Alfred Thomas, Jr. 1936- *WhoFI 92*
**McNeill,** Anthony *DrAPF 91*
**McNeill,** Anthony 1941- *ConPo 91, WrDr 92*
**McNeill,** Archibald 1796?-1849 *DcNCBi 4*
**Mc Neill,** Carmen Mary *WhoFI 92, WhoIns 92*
**McNeill,** Daniel 1752-1818 *DcNCBi 4*
**McNeill,** Douglas Arthur 1942- *WhoRel 92, WhoWest 92*
**McNeill,** Elisabeth *ConAu 135*
**McNeill,** Frederick Wallace 1932- *WhoFI 92*
**McNeill,** Gordon Keith 1953- *Who 92*
**McNeill,** Harry J. *WhoEnt 92*
**McNeill,** Ian 1947- *WhoIns 92*
**McNeill,** James Hipkins 1825-1865 *DcNCBi 4*
**McNeill,** James Walker 1952- *Who 92*
**McNeill,** Janet 1907- *IntAu&W 91, WrDr 92*
**McNeill,** John 1933- *AmMWSc 92, Who 92*
**McNeill,** John Charles 1874-1907 *DcNCBi 4*
**McNeill,** John Henderson 1941- *WhoAmL 92*
**McNeill,** John Hugh 1938- *AmMWSc 92*
**McNeill,** John J 1922- *AmMWSc 92*
**McNeill,** John L. *WhoBlA 92*
**McNeill,** John Malcolm 1909- *Who 92*
**McNeill,** John Scott 1960- *WhoEnt 92*
**McNeill,** Keith *Who 92*
**McNeill,** Kenneth Gordon 1926- *AmMWSc 92*
**McNeill,** Kenny Earl 1946- *AmMWSc 92*
**McNeill,** Kevin Michael 1956- *WhoWest 92*
**McNeill,** Michael John 1942- *AmMWSc 92*
**McNeill,** Nolan G 1934- *WhoAmP 91*
**McNeill,** Odessa M. 1945- *WhoRel 92*
**McNeill,** Paul Spurgeon, Jr. 1948- *WhoAmL 92*
**McNeill,** Peter Grant Brass 1929- *Who 92*
**McNeill,** Richard Charles 1957- *WhoAmL 92*
**McNeill,** Robert Bradley 1941- *AmMWSc 92*
**McNeill,** Robert Patrick 1941- *WhoFI 92*
**McNeill,** Thomas B. 1934- *WhoAmL 92*
**McNeill,** Thomas Ray 1952- *WhoAmL 92*
**McNeill,** Timothy J. 1955- *WhoMW 92*
**McNeill,** William Gibbs 1801-1853 *DcNCBi 4*
**McNeill,** William Hardy 1917- *WrDr 92*
**McNeill-Huntley,** Esther Mae 1921- *WhoBlA 92*
**McNeilly,** John Richard 1944- *WhoMW 92*
**McNeish,** Alexander Stewart 1938- *Who 92*
**McNeish,** James 1931- *IntAu&W 91, WrDr 92*
**McNelis,** Edward Joseph 1930- *AmMWSc 92*
**Mc Nelly,** Frederick Wright, Jr. 1947- *WhoMW 92*
**McNelly,** Patricia Colligan 1930- *WhoMW 92*
**McNelly,** Theodore Hart 1919- *WrDr 92*
**McNelly,** Trenton Chester 1962- *WhoEnt 92*
**McNelty,** Harry *WhoBlA 92*
**McNenny,** Kenneth G *WhoAmP 91*
**McNerney,** Daniel P 1920- *WhoAmP 91*
**McNerney,** James Murtha 1927- *AmMWSc 92*
**McNerney,** Joan *DrAPF 91*
**McNerney,** Walter J. 1925- *IntWW 91*
**McNesby,** James Robert 1922- *AmMWSc 92*
**McNett,** John Cameron 1944- *WhoAmL 92*
**McNett,** Margaret Ruth 1962- *WhoAmL 92*
**McNevin,** Susan Clardy 1947- *AmMWSc 92*
**McNevin-Petersen,** Valerie Joan 1953- *WhoFI 92*
**McNew,** Patrick Leon 1945- *WhoMW 92*
**McNey,** Craig Stewart 1946- *WhoWest 92*
**McNichol,** Kristy 1962- *IntMPA 92, WhoEnt 92*
**McNicholas,** David Paul 1941- *WhoFI 92*
**McNicholas,** James J 1934- *AmMWSc 92*
**McNicholas,** John Vincent 1936- *AmMWSc 92*
**McNicholas,** Laura T *AmMWSc 92*
**McNichols,** Bruce Smith 1939- *WhoEnt 92*
**McNichols,** Charles L. 1887- *TwCWW 91*
**McNichols,** Gerald Robert 1943- *AmMWSc 92, WhoFI 92*
**McNichols,** Roger J 1938- *AmMWSc 92*
**McNichols,** Roger Jeffrey 1938- *WhoMW 92*
**McNichols,** William H, Jr 1910- *WhoAmP 91*
**McNickle,** D'Arcy 1904-1977 *BenetAL 91, TwCWW 91*
**McNickle,** Michael M. *WhoFI 92*
**McNicol,** Bruce R. *WhoRel 92*
**McNicol,** David Williamson 1913- *Who 92*
**McNicol,** Donald 1939- *IntWW 91, Who 92*
**Mc Nicol,** Donald Edward 1921- *WhoAmL 92*
**McNicol,** George Paul 1929- *IntWW 91, Who 92*
**McNicol,** Lore Anne *AmMWSc 92*
**McNider,** James Small, III 1956- *WhoAmL 92*
**McNiece,** James Taylor 1948- *WhoAmL 92*
**McNiel,** James S, Jr 1921- *AmMWSc 92*
**McNiff,** Edward J, Jr 1935- *AmMWSc 92*
**McNiff,** Russell John 1943- *WhoFI 92*
**McNinch,** Frank Ramsay 1873-1950 *DcNCBi 4*
**McNish,** Althea Marjorie *Who 92*
**McNish,** James L. 1946- *WhoAmL 92*
**McNish,** Susan Kirk 1940- *WhoAmL 92*
**McNitt,** James R 1932- *AmMWSc 92*
**McNitt,** Richard Paul 1935- *AmMWSc 92*
**McNitt,** Willard Charles, III 1948- *WhoFI 92*
**McNiven,** Hugh D 1922- *AmMWSc 92*
**McNorriell,** Mozell M. 1922- *WhoBlA 92*
**McNorton,** Bruce Edward 1959- *WhoBlA 92*
**McNown,** John S 1916- *AmMWSc 92*
**McNulty,** Alfred Peter 1924- *WhoFI 92*
**McNulty,** Anthony 1911- *IntWW 91*
**McNulty,** Charles Lee, Jr 1918- *AmMWSc 92*
**McNulty,** Dermot 1949- *WhoFI 92*
**McNulty,** Faith 1918- *IntAu&W 91, WrDr 92*
**McNulty,** Frank John 1926- *WhoRel 92*
**McNulty,** George Frank 1945- *AmMWSc 92*
**McNulty,** Irving Bazil 1918- *AmMWSc 92*
**McNulty,** James F, Jr 1925- *WhoAmP 91*
**McNulty,** James F M *WhoIns 92*
**McNulty,** John 1896?-1956 *BenetAL 91*
**McNulty,** John Alexander 1946- *AmMWSc 92*
**McNulty,** John Kent 1934- *WhoAmL 92*
**McNulty,** Kristy Lee Ann 1958- *WhoWest 92*
**McNulty,** Marcia Ann 1944- *WhoMW 92*
**McNulty,** Matthew Francis, Jr. 1914- *WhoFI 92*
**McNulty,** Michael R. 1947- *AlmAP 92 [port]*
**McNulty,** Michael Robert 1947- *WhoAmP 91*
**McNulty,** Peter J 1941- *AmMWSc 92*
**McNulty,** Raymond Francis 1946- *WhoFI 92*
**McNulty,** Richard Paul 1946- *AmMWSc 92*
**McNulty,** Roy 1937- *Who 92*
**McNulty,** Samuel J. 1964- *WhoAmL 92*
**McNulty,** Thomas Aloysius 1933- *WhoFI 92*
**McNulty,** Ulrich Roy 1961- *WhoAmL 92*
**McNulty,** Wilbur Palmer 1925- *AmMWSc 92*
**McNutt,** Charles Harrison 1928- *AmMWSc 92*
**McNutt,** Charlie Fuller, Jr. 1931- *WhoRel 92*
**McNutt,** Clarence Wallace 1913- *AmMWSc 92*
**McNutt,** Douglas P 1935- *AmMWSc 92*
**McNutt,** Jack Wray 1934- *WhoFI 92*
**McNutt,** James 1935- *WhoAmP 91*
**McNutt,** Kristen W 1941- *AmMWSc 92*
**McNutt,** Marcia Kemper 1952- *AmMWSc 92*
**McNutt,** Michael John 1947- *AmMWSc 92*
**McNutt,** Ralph Leroy, Jr 1953- *AmMWSc 92*
**McNutt,** Robert Harold 1937- *AmMWSc 92*
**McNutt,** Ronald Clay 1929- *AmMWSc 92*
**McNutt,** Ronald Wallace 1956- *WhoAmL 92*
**McNutt,** Stephen Russell 1954- *WhoWest 92*
**McNutt,** Sue Irene 1932- *WhoMW 92*
**McOsker,** Charles C 1954- *AmMWSc 92*
**McOwen,** Robert C 1951- *AmMWSc 92*
**McPartland,** Jimmy 1907-1991 *NewAmDM, NewYTBS 91 [port]*
**McPartland,** Marian 1920- *NewAmDM*
**McPartland,** Mark Owen 1951- *WhoEnt 92*
**McPartlin,** Dennis William 1951- *WhoAmP 91*
**McPartlin,** Noel 1939- *Who 92*
**McPeak,** Merrill Anthony 1936- *IntWW 91*
**McPeek,** Max E. 1941- *WhoFI 92*
**McPeek,** Robert William 1951- *WhoEnt 92*
**McPeters,** Arnold Lawrence 1925- *AmMWSc 92*
**McPeters,** Richard Douglas 1947- *AmMWSc 92*
**McPetrie,** James Carnegie d1991 *Who 92N*
**McPhail,** Andrew Tennent 1937- *AmMWSc 92*
**McPhail,** Bartley Alan 1956- *WhoWest 92*
**McPhail,** Clark 1936- *WhoMW 92*
**McPhail,** Douglas H. 1962- *WhoMW 92*
**McPhail,** Edward Stan 1960- *WhoEnt 92*
**McPhail,** Evelyn W 1930- *WhoAmP 91*
**McPhail,** Irving P. 1949- *WhoBlA 92*
**McPhail,** Jasper Lewis 1930- *AmMWSc 92*
**McPhail,** Sharon 1948- *ConBlB 2 [port]*
**McPhail,** Sharon M. 1948- *WhoBlA 92*
**McPhail,** Weldon 1944- *WhoBlA 92*
**Mc Phail,** William K. V. 1960- *WhoWest 92*
**McPhatter,** Thomas H. 1923- *WhoBlA 92*
**McPhee,** Glenn Anne *WhoRel 92*
**McPhee,** John *IntAu&W 91, SourALJ*
**McPhee,** John 1931- *WrDr 92*
**McPhee,** John A. 1931- *BenetAL 91*
**McPhee,** Jonathan *WhoEnt 92*
**McPhee,** Roderick Fulton 1929- *WhoWest 92*
**McPhee,** Ronald P 1933- *WhoIns 92*
**McPhee,** Ronald Paul 1933- *WhoFI 92*
**McPhee,** W. R. 1956- *WhoEnt 92*
**McPhee,** William Miller 1906- *WhoWest 92*
**McPheeters,** Annie Lou 1908- *WhoBlA 92*
**McPheeters,** Jean McNiff 1951- *WhoAmP 91*
**McPheeters,** Kenneth Dale 1952- *AmMWSc 92*
**McPheeters,** Samuel Brown 1819-1870 *DcNCBi 4*
**McPheeters,** William 1778-1842 *DcNCBi 4*
**McPheron,** Alan Beaumont 1914- *WhoAmL 92*
**McPherron,** Robert Lloyd 1937- *AmMWSc 92*
**McPherson,** Aimee Semple 1890-1944 *FacFETw, HanAmWH, RelLAm 91*
**McPherson,** Alexander 1944- *AmMWSc 92*
**McPherson,** Alvadus Bradley 1937- *AmMWSc 92*
**McPherson,** Charles William *AmMWSc 92*
**McPherson,** Clara 1922- *AmMWSc 92*
**McPherson,** Clinton Marsud 1918- *AmMWSc 92*
**McPherson,** David E 1942- *WhoIns 92*
**McPherson,** Donald J 1921- *AmMWSc 92*
**McPherson,** Eric Scott 1951- *WhoAmP 91*
**Mc Pherson,** Frank Alfred 1933- *WhoFI 92*
**McPherson,** Gail *WhoFI 92*
**McPherson,** George, Jr 1921- *AmMWSc 92*
**McPherson,** Guy Randall 1960- *AmMWSc 92*
**McPherson,** Harold James 1939- *AmMWSc 92*
**McPherson,** Harriet A *WhoAmP 91*
**McPherson,** Harry Cummings, Jr. 1929- *IntWW 91*
**McPherson,** James A 1943- *ConNov 91, WrDr 92*
**McPherson,** James Alan *DrAPF 91*
**McPherson,** James Alan 1943- *BenetAL 91, WhoBlA 92*
**McPherson,** James Alexander Strachan 1927- *Who 92*
**McPherson,** James Allen 1943- *IntAu&W 91*
**McPherson,** James Aubrey 1931- *WhoAmL 92*
**McPherson,** James C, Jr 1926- *AmMWSc 92*
**McPherson,** James King 1937- *AmMWSc 92*
**McPherson,** James Louis 1922- *AmMWSc 92*
**McPherson,** James M. 1936- *IntWW 91*
**McPherson,** James Munro 1936- *IntAu&W 91, WrDr 92*
**McPherson,** James Willis, III 1956- *WhoWest 92*
**McPherson,** Jeffery David 1953- *WhoWest 92*
**McPherson,** John Edwin 1941- *AmMWSc 92*
**McPherson,** John G 1947- *AmMWSc 92*
**McPherson,** John M 1948- *AmMWSc 92*
**McPherson,** M Peter 1940- *WhoAmP 91*
**McPherson,** Melville Peter 1940- *IntWW 91*
**McPherson,** Michael *DrAPF 91*
**McPherson,** Michael Claude 1949- *WhoWest 92*
**McPherson,** Michael Dale 1952- *WhoWest 92*
**McPherson,** Natalie Jean 1944- *WhoFI 92*

**McPherson,** Orland Gordon 1930- *WhoAmP 91*
**McPherson,** Richard Willis 1948- *WhoRel 92*
**McPherson,** Robert Merrill 1948- *AmMWSc 92*
**McPherson,** Robert W *AmMWSc 92*
**McPherson,** Robert Wayne 1953- *WhoAmL 92*
**Mc Pherson,** Rolf Kennedy *WhoRel 92*
**McPherson,** Roosevelt Hill 1948- *WhoBlA 92*
**McPherson,** Ross 1934- *AmMWSc 92*
**McPherson,** Sandra *DrAPF 91*
**McPherson,** Sandra 1943- *BenetAL 91, ConPo 91, IntAu&W 91, WrDr 92*
**McPherson,** Thomas Alexander 1939- *AmMWSc 92*
**McPherson,** Thomas Allen 1935- *WhoAmP 91*
**McPherson,** Thomas C 1922- *AmMWSc 92*
**McPherson,** William H. 1927- *WhoBlA 92*
**McPherson,** William Hauhuth 1922- *WhoAmP 91*
**McPherson,** William Joseph, Jr 1950- *WhoAmP 91*
**McPhie,** Peter 1942- *AmMWSc 92*
**McPhilimy,** Robert O. 1942- *WhoMW 92*
**McPhillips,** Charles Vincent 1959- *WhoAmL 92*
**McPhillips,** Julian Lenwood, Jr 1946- *WhoAmP 91*
**McPhillips,** Mary Margaret 1945- *WhoAmP 91*
**McPike,** Jim 1943- *WhoAmP 91*
**McPike,** Martin John, Jr. 1946- *WhoFI 92*
**McQuade,** Ann Aikman 1928- *ConAu 34NR*
**McQuade,** Eugene M. *WhoFI 92*
**McQuade,** Henry Alonzo 1915- *AmMWSc 92*
**McQuade,** J Stanley 1932- *WhoAmP 91*
**Mc Quade,** Lawrence Carroll 1927- *WhoFI 92*
**McQuaid,** James 1939- *Who 92*
**McQuaid,** Phyllis W 1928- *WhoAmP 91*
**McQuaid,** Richard William 1923- *AmMWSc 92*
**McQuaid,** Salli Lou 1943- *WhoWest 92*
**McQuail,** Paul Christopher 1934- *Who 92*
**McQuain,** Ronald Jay 1952- *WhoMW 92*
**McQuarrie,** Albert 1918- *Who 92*
**McQuarrie,** Bruce Cale 1929- *AmMWSc 92*
**McQuarrie,** Claude Monroe, III 1950- *WhoAmL 92*
**McQuarrie,** Donald Allan 1937- *AmMWSc 92*
**McQuarrie,** Donald G 1931- *AmMWSc 92*
**McQuarrie,** Irvine Gray 1939- *AmMWSc 92*
**McQuate,** John Truman 1921- *AmMWSc 92*
**McQuate,** Robert Samuel 1947- *AmMWSc 92*
**McQuater,** Patricia A. 1951- *WhoBlA 92*
**McQuay,** James Phillip 1924- *WhoBlA 92*
**McQuay,** Mike 1949- *TwCSFW 91, WrDr 92*
**McQueen,** Anjetta 1966- *WhoBlA 92*
**McQueen,** Butterfly 1911- *WhoBlA 92*
**McQueen,** Charlene A 1947- *AmMWSc 92*
**McQueen,** Cilla 1949- *ConPo 91, WrDr 92*
**McQueen,** Cyrus B. 1951- *ConAu 135*
**McQueen,** Donald James 1943- *AmMWSc 92*
**McQueen,** Douglas Van 1958- *WhoRel 92*
**McQueen,** George W 1932- *WhoIns 92*
**McQueen,** Hugh 1800?-1855 *DcNCBi 4*
**McQueen,** Hugh J 1933- *AmMWSc 92*
**McQueen,** John 1804-1867 *DcNCBi 4*
**McQueen,** John Donald 1923- *AmMWSc 92*
**McQueen,** Justice Ellis 1927- *WhoEnt 92*
**McQueen,** Kevin Paige 1958- *WhoBlA 92*
**McQueen,** Michael Anthony 1956- *WhoBlA 92*
**McQueen,** Paul Dennis 1945- *WhoRel 92*
**McQueen,** Ralph Edward *AmMWSc 92*
**McQueen,** Scott Robert 1946- *WhoEnt 92*
**McQueen,** Stanley Eugene 1946- *WhoWest 92*
**McQueen,** Steve 1930-1980 *FacFETw*
**McQueen,** Thelma 1911- *NotBlAW 92*
**McQueen,** Trina *LesBEnT 92*
**McQueeney,** Thomas A. 1937- *WhoFI 92*
**McQuerrey,** Shirleen Mary 1948- *WhoMW 92*
**McQuerry,** Wayne Harrison 1922- *WhoWest 92*
**McQuigg,** John Dolph 1931- *WhoAmL 92*
**McQuigg,** Robert Duncan 1936- *AmMWSc 92*
**McQuiggan,** John 1922- *Who 92*
**McQuilkin,** Frank *DrAPF 91*
**McQuilkin,** John Robertson 1927- *WhoRel 92*
**McQuilkin,** Rennie *DrAPF 91*
**McQuilkin,** Robert Crawford, Jr. 1886-1952 *RelLAm 91*
**McQuilkin,** Robert Rennie *DrAPF 91*
**Mc Quillan,** Joseph Michael 1931- *WhoFI 92*
**McQuillan,** Karin 1950- *ConAu 133*
**Mc Quillan,** Margaret Mary *WhoFI 92*
**McQuillan,** William Rodger 1930- *Who 92*
**McQuillen,** Gordon Emmett 1943- *WhoMW 92*
**McQuillen,** Harry A. *WhoFI 92*
**McQuillen,** Howard Raymond 1924- *AmMWSc 92*
**McQuillen,** Jeremiah Joseph 1941- *WhoFI 92*
**McQuillen,** Mary Theresa 1932- *WhoAmP 91*
**McQuillen,** Michael Paul 1932- *AmMWSc 92*
**McQuillin,** Mahlon Brice, II 1950- *WhoEnt 92, WhoWest 92*
**McQuillin,** Richard Ross 1956- *WhoWest 92*
**McQuillin,** Robert 1935- *IntWW 91*
**McQuistan,** Richmond Beckett 1927- *AmMWSc 92*
**McQuiston,** Faye C 1928- *AmMWSc 92*
**McQuiston,** John Ward, II 1943- *WhoAmL 92*
**McQuiston,** Robert Earl 1936- *WhoAmL 92*
**McQuown,** Eloise *WhoAmP 91*
**McQuown,** Judith H. 1941- *WrDr 92*
**McQuown,** Judith Hershkowitz 1941- *WhoFI 92*
**McQuown,** Norman Anthony 1914- *IntAu&W 91*
**McRae,** Carmen *WhoEnt 92*
**McRae,** Carmen 1922- *NewAmDM, NotBlAW 92, WhoBlA 92*
**McRae,** Cefus Elton 1956- *WhoEnt 92*
**McRae,** Chuck 1939- *WhoAmP 91*
**McRae,** Colin John 1812-1877 *DcNCBi 4*
**McRae,** Cornelius *WhoRel 92*
**McRae,** Daniel George 1938- *AmMWSc 92*
**McRae,** Duncan Kirkland 1820-1888 *DcNCBi 4*
**McRae,** Eion Grant 1930- *AmMWSc 92*
**McRae,** Emmett N. 1943- *WhoBlA 92*
**McRae,** Frances Anne *Who 92*
**McRae,** Hal 1945- *WhoBlA 92*
**McRae,** Hamilton Eugene, III 1937- *WhoAmL 92, WhoWest 92*
**McRae,** Hamish Malcolm Donald 1943- *IntAu&W 91, Who 92*
**McRae,** Harold Abraham 1945- *WhoMW 92*
**McRae,** Helene Williams *WhoBlA 92*
**McRae,** Jack Ardon 1953- *WhoWest 92*
**McRae,** John Jones 1815-1868 *DcNCBi 4*
**McRae,** Karen K 1944- *WhoAmP 91*
**McRae,** Kenneth Douglas 1925- *WrDr 92*
**McRae,** Lorin Post 1936- *AmMWSc 92*
**McRae,** Nancy Elizabeth 1943- *WhoEnt 92*
**McRae,** Robert James 1931- *AmMWSc 92*
**McRae,** Robert Malcolm, Jr. 1921- *WhoAmL 92*
**McRae,** Ronald Edward 1955- *WhoBlA 92*
**McRae,** Thomas W. 1924- *WhoBlA 92*
**McRae,** Vincent Vernon 1918- *AmMWSc 92*
**McRae,** Wayne A 1925- *AmMWSc 92*
**McRaith,** John Jeremiah 1934- *WhoRel 92*
**McRaney,** Gerald *LesBEnT 92, WhoEnt 92*
**McRaney,** Gerald 1948- *IntMPA 92*
**McRay,** John Robert 1931- *WhoRel 92*
**McRay,** Paul *DrAPF 91*
**McRee,** Celia *WhoEnt 92*
**McRee,** Donald Ikerd 1934- *AmMWSc 92*
**McRee,** G J, Jr 1934- *AmMWSc 92*
**McRee,** Griffith John 1819-1872 *DcNCBi 4*
**McRee,** James Fergus 1794-1869 *DcNCBi 4*
**McRee,** William 1787-1833 *DcNCBi 4*
**McReynolds,** Allen, Jr. 1909- *WhoFI 92, WhoMW 92*
**McReynolds,** David Ernest 1929- *AmPeW*
**McReynolds,** Elaine A. 1948- *WhoBlA 92*
**McReynolds,** James C 1862-1946 *FacFETw*
**McReynolds,** Keith Marvin 1941- *WhoMW 92*
**McReynolds,** Larry Austin 1946- *AmMWSc 92*
**McReynolds,** Mary Armilda 1946- *WhoAmL 92*
**McReynolds,** Paul Robert 1936- *WhoRel 92*
**McReynolds,** R. Bruce 1940- *WhoWest 92*
**McReynolds,** Richard A 1944- *AmMWSc 92*
**McReynolds,** Ronald W. *DrAPF 91*
**McReynolds,** Stephen Paul 1938- *WhoAmL 92*
**McRight,** Paige Maxwell 1946- *WhoRel 92*
**McRipley,** G. Whitney 1957- *WhoBlA 92*
**McRitchie,** Bruce Dean 1938- *WhoFI 92*
**McRobbie,** Bonnie Jean 1949- *WhoAmL 92*
**McRobert,** Gussie 1933- *WhoAmP 91*
**McRobert,** Rosemary Dawn Teresa 1927- *Who 92*
**McRoberts,** Darrel Sherman 1938- *WhoAmP 91*
**McRoberts,** J William 1932- *AmMWSc 92*
**McRoberts,** Jeffrey 1954- *WhoEnt 92*
**McRoberts,** Joyce 1941- *WhoAmP 91*
**McRoberts,** Keith L 1931- *AmMWSc 92*
**McRoberts,** Robert *DrAPF 91*
**McRorie,** Robert Anderson 1924- *AmMWSc 92*
**McRorie,** William Edward 1940- *WhoIns 92*
**McRowe,** Arthur Watkins 1937- *AmMWSc 92*
**McRoy,** C Peter 1941- *AmMWSc 92*
**McRoy,** Gary Lewis 1959- *WhoMW 92*
**McRoy,** Ruth Gail 1947- *WhoBlA 92*
**McRuer,** Duane Torrance 1925- *AmMWSc 92*
**McShane,** Dennis Patrick 1951- *WhoWest 92*
**McShane,** Edward James d1989 *IntWW 91N*
**McShane,** Edward James 1904- *AmMWSc 92*
**McShane,** Ian 1942- *IntMPA 92*
**McShane,** James Henry, III 1950- *WhoMW 92*
**McShane,** Mark 1929- *IntAu&W 91, WrDr 92*
**McShann,** James Columbus 1916- *FacFETw*
**McSharry,** Deirdre 1932- *IntAu&W 91, Who 92*
**McSharry,** Deirdre Mary 1932- *IntWW 91*
**McSharry,** James John 1942- *AmMWSc 92*
**McSharry,** William Owen 1939- *AmMWSc 92*
**McShefferty,** John 1929- *AmMWSc 92, WhoFI 92*
**McSherry,** Charles K 1931- *AmMWSc 92*
**McSherry,** Diana Hartridge *AmMWSc 92*
**McSherry,** G X *WhoAmP 91*
**McSherry,** James Francis 1953- *WhoFI 92*
**McSherry,** Michael Anthony 1963- *WhoWest 92*
**McSherry,** Walter Clinton 1929- *WhoAmP 91*
**McSherry,** William John, Jr. 1947- *WhoAmL 92*
**McShine,** Arthur Hugh 1906- *Who 92*
**McShine,** Kynaston *ConAu 134*
**McShine,** Kynaston L. 1935- *ConAu 134*
**McSmith,** Blanche Preston 1920- *WhoBlA 92*
**McSorley,** Cisco 1950- *WhoAmP 91*
**McSorley,** Jean Sarah 1958- *ConAu 133*
**McSorley,** Robert 1949- *AmMWSc 92*
**McSpadden,** Clem Rogers 1925- *WhoAmP 91*
**McSpadden,** Donna Casity 1934- *WhoAmP 91*
**McStallworth,** Paul 1910- *WhoBlA 92*
**McStay,** James P 1945- *WhoAmP 91*
**McSwain,** Berah D. 1935- *WhoBlA 92*
**McSwain,** David L. 1928- *WhoBlA 92*
**McSwain,** Douglas Lawrence 1958- *WhoAmL 92*
**McSwain,** Larry Lee 1940- *WhoRel 92*
**McSwain,** Marc Daniell 1965- *WhoWest 92*
**McSwain,** Richard Horace 1949- *AmMWSc 92*
**McSwain,** Rick Dean 1944- *WhoFI 92*
**McSwain,** Rodney 1962- *WhoBlA 92*
**McSween,** Allen Crews, Jr. 1943- *WhoRel 92*
**McSween,** Cirilo A. 1929- *WhoBlA 92*
**McSween,** Harold B. *DrAPF 91*
**McSween,** Harry Y, Jr 1945- *AmMWSc 92*
**McSweeney,** E Douglas, Jr *WhoAmP 91*
**McSweeney,** Frances Kaye 1948- *AmMWSc 92*
**McSweeney,** John *WhoAmP 91*
**McSweeney,** Maurice J. 1938- *WhoAmL 92*
**McSweeny,** Edward Shearman 1934- *AmMWSc 92*
**McSweeny,** John Edward 1936- *WhoMW 92*
**McSweeny,** William Francis 1929- *WhoFI 92*
**McSwiney,** Charles Ronald 1943- *WhoAmL 92*
**McSwiney,** James Wilmer 1915- *IntWW 91*
**McTaggart,** Kenneth C 1919- *AmMWSc 92*
**McTaggart,** Linda Kay 1961- *WhoMW 92*
**McTaggart,** Terry Bruce 1954- *WhoFI 92*
**McTaggart-Cowan,** Patrick Duncan 1912- *AmMWSc 92*
**McTague,** James Aloysius 1949- *WhoFI 92*
**McTague,** John Paul 1938- *AmMWSc 92, WhoFI 92*
**McTate,** Gabriella Angel 1948- *WhoMW 92*
**McTeague,** Bertrand Luke 1935- *WhoFI 92*
**McTeague,** David 1952- *WhoAmP 91*
**McTeer,** Douglas E, Jr 1951- *WhoAmP 91*
**McTeer,** George Calvin 1938- *WhoBlA 92*
**McTeer,** Janet 1961- *ConTFT 9*
**McTell,** Blind Willie 1898?-1959 *NewAmDM*
**McTernan,** Edmund J 1930- *AmMWSc 92*
**McTernan,** Maureen E 1955- *WhoIns 92*
**McThomas,** Dorothy B. *WhoBlA 92*
**McTier,** Roselyn Jones 1916- *WhoBlA 92*
**McTier,** Samuel Eldon 1926- *WhoMW 92*
**McTiernan,** Edward A. d1990 *IntWW 91N*
**McTiernan,** Miriam 1952- *WhoWest 92*
**McTighe,** John Joseph 1946- *WhoFI 92*
**McTighe,** Teresa Wright 1949- *WhoWest 92*
**McTigue,** David Francis 1952- *AmMWSc 92*
**McTigue,** Frank Henry 1919- *AmMWSc 92*
**McTigue,** James Joseph 1951- *WhoEnt 92*
**McTurnan,** Lee Bowes 1937- *WhoAmL 92*
**McTyeire,** Holland Nimmons 1824-1889 *RelLAm 91*
**McTyeire,** Robert Adams 1949- *WhoEnt 92*
**McTyre,** Robert Earl, Sr. 1955- *WhoBlA 92*
**McVann,** Mark E. 1950- *WhoRel 92*
**McVaugh,** Rogers 1909- *AmMWSc 92*
**McVay,** Doris Elaine 1955- *WhoFI 92, WhoMW 92*
**McVay,** Francis Edward 1917- *AmMWSc 92*
**McVay,** Glen A *WhoAmP 91*
**McVea,** Emilie Watts 1867-1928 *DcNCBi 4*
**McVean,** Duncan Edward 1936- *AmMWSc 92, WhoMW 92*
**McVean,** James *WrDr 92*
**McVeigh,** Margaret Mary 1952- *WhoAmL 92*
**McVeigh,** Norman Shaw, III 1951- *WhoAmP 91*
**McVeigh-Pettigrew,** Sharon Christine 1949- *WhoWest 92*
**McVerry,** Terrence F 1943- *WhoAmP 91*
**McVey,** Eugene Steven 1927- *AmMWSc 92*
**McVey,** Henry Hanna, III 1935- *WhoAmL 92*
**McVey,** James Paul 1943- *AmMWSc 92*
**McVey,** James William 1931- *WhoMW 92*
**McVey,** Jeanne Howard 1935- *WhoAmP 91*
**McVey,** Jeffrey King 1950- *AmMWSc 92*
**McVey,** Lucille 1890-1925 *ReelWom*
**McVey,** Vernie Luther 1917- *WhoRel 92*
**McVey,** Walter Lewis, Jr 1922- *WhoAmP 91*
**McVicar,** John West 1928- *AmMWSc 92*
**McVicar,** Kenneth E 1920- *AmMWSc 92*
**McVicker,** H Keith 1943- *WhoIns 92*
**McVicker,** Mary Ellen Harshbarger 1951- *WhoMW 92*
**Mc Vie,** Christine Perfect 1943- *WhoEnt 92, WhoWest 92*
**McVoy,** Kirk Warren 1928- *AmMWSc 92*
**McWade,** Charles P. 1944- *WhoFI 92*
**McWatters,** George Edward 1922- *Who 92*
**McWatters,** Stephen John 1921- *Who 92*
**McWay,** Dana Christine 1959- *WhoAmL 92*
**McWeeney,** Laura C. 1952- *WhoAmL 92*
**McWeeny,** Roy 1924- *Who 92*
**McWhan,** Denis B 1935- *AmMWSc 92*
**McWherter,** Ned 1930- *AlmAP 92 [port]*
**McWherter,** Ned R. 1930- *IntWW 91, WhoAmP 91*
**McWhinney,** Henry G. *WhoFI 92*
**McWhinney,** Ian Renwick 1926- *AmMWSc 92*
**McWhinnie,** Dolores J 1933- *AmMWSc 92*
**McWhirter,** David Ian 1937- *WhoRel 92*
**McWhirter,** George 1939- *ConPo 91, IntAu&W 91, WrDr 92*
**McWhirter,** Ishbel 1927- *TwCPaSc*
**McWhirter,** James Herman 1924- *AmMWSc 92*
**McWhirter,** James Jeffries 1938- *WhoWest 92*
**McWhirter,** Norris Dewar 1925- *IntAu&W 91, IntWW 91, Who 92*
**McWhirter,** Robert 1904- *Who 92*
**McWhorter,** Alan L 1930- *AmMWSc 92*
**McWhorter,** Chester Gray 1927- *AmMWSc 92*
**McWhorter,** Clarence Austin 1918- *AmMWSc 92*

**McWhorter,** Earl James 1929- *AmMWSc 92*
**McWhorter,** Grace Agee 1948- *WhoBlA 92*
**McWhorter,** Hobart Amory, Jr. 1931- *WhoAmL 92*
**McWhorter,** John Francis 1941- *WhoMW 92*
**McWhorter,** Malcolm M 1926- *AmMWSc 92*
**McWhorter,** Millard Henry, III 1954- *WhoBlA 92*
**McWiggan,** Thomas Johnstone 1918- *Who 92*
**McWilliam,** Edward 1909- *IntWW 91, Who 92*
**McWilliam,** F.E. 1909- *TwCPaSc*
**McWilliam,** Joanne Elizabeth 1928- *WhoRel 92*
**McWilliam,** John David 1941- *Who 92*
**McWilliam,** Michael Douglas 1933- *Who 92*
**McWilliams,** Alfred E., Jr. 1938- *WhoBlA 92*
**McWilliams,** Alfred Edeard 1911- *WhoBlA 92*
**McWilliams,** Arthur Thomas 1927- *WhoAmP 91*
**McWilliams,** Carey 1905-1980 *BenetAL 91*
**McWilliams,** Debora Beck 1958- *WhoAmL 92*
**McWilliams,** Edward Lacaze 1941- *AmMWSc 92*
**McWilliams,** Francis 1926- *Who 92*
**McWilliams,** James Cyrus 1946- *AmMWSc 92*
**McWilliams,** James D. 1932- *WhoBlA 92*
**McWilliams,** Jim 1938- *WhoAmP 91*
**McWilliams,** John Lawrence, III 1943- *WhoAmL 92*
**McWilliams,** Joseph E. 1904- *BiDExR*
**McWilliams,** Karen 1943- *ConAu 133, SmATA 65 [port]*
**McWilliams,** Margaret 1929- *WrDr 92*
**McWilliams,** Margaret Ann Edgar 1929- *AmMWSc 92*
**McWilliams,** Margaret Edgar 1929- *IntAu&W 91*
**McWilliams,** Ralph David 1930- *AmMWSc 92*
**McWilliams,** Robert Gene 1939- *AmMWSc 92*
**McWilliams,** Robert Hugh 1916- *WhoAmL 92, WhoWest 92*
**McWilliams,** Roger Dean 1954- *AmMWSc 92*
**McWilliams,** Thomas F 1957- *WhoIns 92*
**McWilliams,** Warren Leigh 1946- *WhoRel 92*
**McWorter,** Gerald A. 1942- *WhoBlA 92*
**McWright,** Carter C. 1950- *WhoBlA 92*
**McWright,** Cornelius Glen 1929- *AmMWSc 92*
**McWright,** Glen Martin 1958- *AmMWSc 92*
**McZier,** Arthur 1935- *WhoBlA 92*
**Meace,** Jeffrey Gregory 1941- *WhoFI 92*
**Meacham,** Bobby 1960- *WhoBlA 92*
**Meacham,** Christopher Lee 1943- *WhoAmP 91*
**Meacham,** Ellis K. *DrAPF 91*
**Meacham,** Ellis K. 1913- *WrDr 92*
**Meacham,** Henry W. 1924- *WhoBlA 92*
**Meacham,** Margaret *DrAPF 91*
**Meacham,** Michael Allen 1948- *WhoEnt 92*
**Meacham,** Michael Robert 1953- *WhoAmP 91, WhoMW 92*
**Meacham,** Rebecca D 1943- *WhoAmP 91*
**Meacham,** Robert B. 1933- *WhoBlA 92*
**Meacham,** Robert Colegrove 1920- *AmMWSc 92*
**Meacham,** Roger Hening, Jr 1942- *AmMWSc 92*
**Meacham,** Standish 1932- *ConAu 135*
**Meacham,** William Feland 1913- *AmMWSc 92*
**Meacham,** William Ross 1923- *AmMWSc 92*
**Meacher,** Michael Hugh 1939- *IntWW 91, Who 92*
**Meachin,** David James Percy 1941- *WhoFI 92*
**Mead,** Albert Raymond 1915- *AmMWSc 92*
**Mead,** Bob *WhoAmP 91*
**Mead,** Carver Andress 1934- *AmMWSc 92*
**Mead,** Chester Alden 1932- *AmMWSc 92*
**Mead,** Dana George 1936- *WhoFI 92*
**Mead,** Darwin James 1910- *AmMWSc 92*
**Mead,** Edward Jairus 1928- *AmMWSc 92*
**Mead,** Edwin Doak 1849-1937 *AmPeW*
**Mead,** Frank Waldreth 1922- *AmMWSc 92*
**Mead,** George Wilson, II 1927- *WhoFI 92*
**Mead,** Gilbert Dunbar 1930- *AmMWSc 92*
**Mead,** Giles Willis 1928- *AmMWSc 92*
**Mead,** Gordon Sterling 1920- *WhoMW 92*
**Mead,** Hyrum Anderson, Jr. 1947- *WhoFI 92*
**Mead,** James Franklyn 1916- *AmMWSc 92*
**Mead,** James Irving 1952- *AmMWSc 92*
**Mead,** James Matthew 1945- *WhoFI 92*
**Mead,** Jaylee Montague 1929- *AmMWSc 92*
**Mead,** Jere *AmMWSc 92*
**Mead,** John *WhoFI 92*
**Mead,** Jude 1919- *WhoRel 92*
**Mead,** Judith Lee 1933- *WhoRel 92*
**Mead,** Judson 1917- *AmMWSc 92*
**Mead,** Larry Edward 1938- *WhoAmP 91*
**Mead,** Lawrence Myers 1918- *AmMWSc 92*
**Mead,** Loren Benjamin 1930- *WhoRel 92*
**Mead,** Lucia True Ames 1856-1936 *AmPeW*
**Mead,** Margaret 1901-1978 *BenetAL 91, FacFETw [port], HanAmWH, PorAmW [port], RComAH*
**Mead,** Marshall Walter 1921- *AmMWSc 92*
**Mead,** Matthew 1924- *ConPo 91, IntAu&W 91, WrDr 92*
**Mead,** Millard Wilmer 1930- *WhoRel 92*
**Mead,** Patrick Allen 1956- *WhoRel 92*
**Mead,** Philip 1948- *TwCPaSc*
**Mead,** Richard Wilson 1941- *AmMWSc 92*
**Mead,** Robert *LesBEnT 92*
**Mead,** Robert 1948- *WhoAmP 91*
**Mead,** Robert Charles 1957- *WhoMW 92*
**Mead,** Robert Warren 1940- *AmMWSc 92*
**Mead,** Rodney A 1938- *AmMWSc 92*
**Mead,** S Warren 1923- *AmMWSc 92*
**Mead,** Samuel B d1880 *BiInAmS*
**Mead,** Sedgwick 1911- *WhoWest 92*
**Mead,** Shepherd 1914- *IntAu&W 91, WrDr 92*
**Mead,** Sidney Moko 1927- *IntAu&W 91, WrDr 92*
**Mead,** Taylor *DrAPF 91*
**Mead,** Terry Eileen 1950- *WhoWest 92*
**Mead,** Wayland McCon 1931- *WhoIns 92*
**Mead,** William C 1946- *AmMWSc 92*
**Mead,** William J 1927- *AmMWSc 92*
**Mead,** William Richard 1915- *Who 92*
**Meade** *Who 92*
**Meade,** Alston B. 1930- *WhoBlA 92*
**Meade,** Alston Bancroft 1930- *AmMWSc 92*
**Meade,** Dale M 1939- *AmMWSc 92*
**Meade,** Daniel J. 1942- *WhoFI 92*
**Meade,** Danny Joe 1947- *WhoMW 92*
**Meade,** David Glenn 1950- *WhoRel 92*
**Meade,** David H. 1957- *WhoAmL 92*
**Meade,** E. Kidder, Jr. *LesBEnT 92*
**Meade,** Edward Pennington, II 1940- *WhoWest 92*
**Meade,** Eric Cubitt 1923- *Who 92*
**Meade,** Erica Helm *DrAPF 91*
**Meade,** Geoffrey *Who 92*
**Meade,** Grayson Eichelberger 1912- *AmMWSc 92*
**Meade,** James 1907- *IntAu&W 91, WrDr 92*
**Meade,** James Edward 1907- *IntWW 91, Who 92, WhoFI 92, WhoNob 90*
**Meade,** James Horace, Jr 1932- *AmMWSc 92*
**Meade,** John Arthur 1928- *AmMWSc 92*
**Meade,** Kenneth Albert 1935- *WhoRel 92*
**Meade,** Kenneth John 1925- *WhoWest 92*
**Meade,** Kevin R 1956- *WhoAmP 91*
**Meade,** L T 1854-1914 *ScFEYrs*
**Meade,** L.T., and Eustace, Robert *ScFEYrs*
**Meade,** Mary *ConAu 135*
**Meade,** Melvin C. 1929- *WhoBlA 92*
**Meade,** Patrick John 1913- *Who 92*
**Meade,** Randy Lee 1953- *WhoWest 92*
**Meade,** Reginald Eson 1911- *AmMWSc 92*
**Meade,** Richard *TwCWW 91*
**Meade,** Richard Geoffrey 1902- *Who 92*
**Meade,** Richard John Hannay 1938- *Who 92*
**Meade,** Robert Dale 1927- *WhoWest 92*
**Meade,** Robert Heber, Jr 1930- *AmMWSc 92*
**Meade,** Thomas Gerald 1937- *AmMWSc 92*
**Meade,** Thomas Leroy 1920- *AmMWSc 92*
**Meade,** Thomas Wilson 1936- *Who 92*
**Meade,** William d1833 *BiInAmS*
**Meade,** William F. 1925- *WhoBlA 92*
**Meade,** William Wayne 1965- *WhoRel 92*
**Meade-Hariri,** Margaret Regina 1959- *WhoFI 92*
**Meade-King,** Charles Martin 1913- *Who 92*
**Meade-Tollin,** Linda C. *WhoBlA 92*
**Meade-Tollin,** Linda Celida 1944- *WhoWest 92*
**Meader,** Arthur Lloyd, Jr 1920- *AmMWSc 92*
**Meader,** Bruce Ian 1955- *WhoEnt 92*
**Meader,** George 1907- *WhoAmP 91*
**Meader,** John Daniel 1931- *WhoAmL 92, WhoFI 92*
**Meader,** Paul G *WhoAmP 91*
**Meader,** Ralph Gibson 1904- *AmMWSc 92*
**Meader,** Willard L. 1933- *WhoWest 92*
**Meaders,** Ansley Little 1945- *WhoFI 92*
**Meaders,** Paul Le Sourd 1930- *WhoAmL 92*
**Meadmore,** Jean Georges 1922- *IntWW 91*
**Meador,** Daniel John 1926- *WhoAmL 92, WhoAmP 91*
**Meador,** Joseph Douglas 1958- *WhoRel 92*
**Meador,** Neil Franklin 1938- *AmMWSc 92*
**Meador,** Prentice Avery, Jr. 1938- *WhoRel 92*
**Meador,** Richard Lewis 1934- *WhoAmP 91*
**Meadors,** Gayle Marleen 1946- *WhoMW 92*
**Meadors,** Marshall LeRoy, Jr. 1933- *WhoRel 92*
**Meadow,** Charles T. 1929- *WrDr 92*
**Meadow,** Lynne 1946- *WhoEnt 92*
**Meadow,** Roy 1933- *Who 92*
**Meadowcroft,** Michael James 1942- *Who 92*
**Meadowcroft,** William Howarth 1929- *WhoAmP 91*
**Meadows,** Anna T 1931- *AmMWSc 92*
**Meadows,** Arthur Jack 1934- *Who 92*
**Meadows,** Audrey *LesBEnT 92, WhoEnt 92*
**Meadows,** Bernard 1915- *TwCPaSc*
**Meadows,** Bernard William 1915- *IntWW 91, Who 92*
**Meadows,** Brian T 1940- *AmMWSc 92*
**Meadows,** Brian Terry 1949- *WhoMW 92*
**Meadows,** Charles Milton 1912- *AmMWSc 92*
**Meadows,** Cheryl R. 1948- *WhoBlA 92*
**Meadows,** David John 1953- *WhoAmL 92*
**Meadows,** Ferguson Booker, Jr. 1942- *WhoBlA 92*
**Meadows,** Frank Pleasants, III 1961- *WhoFI 92*
**Meadows,** Gary Glenn 1945- *AmMWSc 92*
**Meadows,** Geoffrey Walsh 1921- *AmMWSc 92*
**Meadows,** Graham David 1941- *Who 92*
**Meadows,** Guy Allen 1950- *AmMWSc 92*
**Meadows,** Henry E, Jr 1931- *AmMWSc 92*
**Meadows,** James Wallace, Jr 1923- *AmMWSc 92*
**Meadows,** John Frederick 1926- *WhoAmL 92*
**Meadows,** Kevin Blane 1965- *WhoRel 92*
**Meadows,** Laura Lou 1932- *WhoAmL 92*
**Meadows,** Leonard R 1926- *WhoAmP 91*
**Meadows,** Lucile Smallwood 1918- *WhoAmP 91, WhoBlA 92*
**Meadows,** Mark Allan 1957- *AmMWSc 92*
**Meadows,** Peter *IntAu&W 91X*
**Meadows,** Richard H. 1928- *WhoBlA 92*
**Meadows,** Robert 1902- *Who 92*
**Meadows,** Sharon Marie 1950- *WhoFI 92*
**Meadows,** Stanley Howard 1945- *WhoAmL 92*
**Meadows,** Swithin Pinder 1902- *Who 92*
**Meadows,** W Robert 1919- *AmMWSc 92*
**Meadows-Rogers,** Arabella Thomas 1949- *WhoRel 92*
**Meads,** Jon A *AmMWSc 92*
**Meads,** Kat *DrAPF 91*
**Meads,** Manson 1918- *AmMWSc 92*
**Meads,** Philip F 1907- *AmMWSc 92*
**Meads,** Philip Francis, Jr 1937- *AmMWSc 92*
**Meadway,** John 1944- *Who 92*
**Meager,** Michael Anthony 1931- *Who 92*
**Meagher,** Blanche Margaret 1911- *IntWW 91*
**Meagher,** Donald Joseph 1949- *AmMWSc 92*
**Meagher,** Gary J. 1952- *WhoEnt 92*
**Meagher,** James Francis 1946- *AmMWSc 92*
**Meagher,** Michael Brannon 1950- *WhoMW 92*
**Meagher,** Michael Desmond 1933- *AmMWSc 92*
**Meagher,** Richard Brian 1947- *AmMWSc 92*
**Meagher,** Thomas Francis 1823-1867 *DcAmImH*
**Meagher,** Thomas Francis Vincent 1935- *WhoWest 92*
**Meagher,** Walter L., Jr. 1939- *WhoAmL 92*
**Meakem,** Carolyn Soliday 1936- *WhoFI 92*
**Meakin,** James William 1929- *AmMWSc 92*
**Meakin,** John C 1946- *AmMWSc 92*
**Meakin,** John David 1934- *AmMWSc 92*
**Meakin,** Paul 1944- *AmMWSc 92*
**Meakin,** Wilfred 1925- *Who 92*
**Meal,** Harlan C 1925- *AmMWSc 92*
**Meal,** Janet Hawkins 1927- *AmMWSc 92*
**Meal,** Larie 1939- *WhoMW 92*
**Meal,** Larie L 1939- *AmMWSc 92*
**Meale,** Alan 1949- *Who 92*
**Mealey,** Edward H 1925- *AmMWSc 92*
**Mealey,** Edward Hanly 1925- *WhoWest 92*
**Mealey,** John, Jr 1928- *AmMWSc 92*
**Mealey,** Linda Jeanne 1955- *WhoMW 92*
**Mealman,** Glenn Edward 1934- *WhoFI 92*
**Mealy,** Dennis C 1952- *WhoIns 92*
**Mealy,** Rosemari *DrAPF 91*
**Mean,** John D. *WhoRel 92*
**Meana,** Mitchell A. 1958- *WhoHisp 92*
**Meaney,** Donald V. *IntMPA 92*
**Meaney,** Patrick 1925- *Who 92*
**Meaney,** Patrick Michael 1925- *IntWW 91*
**Means,** Alexander 1801-1883 *DcNCBi 4*
**Means,** Anthony R 1941- *AmMWSc 92*
**Means,** Bertha E. 1920- *WhoBlA 92*
**Means,** Craig R. 1922- *WhoBlA 92*
**Means,** Craig Ray 1922- *AmMWSc 92*
**Means,** D Bruce 1941- *AmMWSc 92*
**Means,** David Scott 1947- *WhoMW 92*
**Means,** Donald Fitzgerald 1966- *WhoBlA 92*
**Means,** Elbert Lee 1945- *WhoBlA 92*
**Means,** Fred E. *WhoBlA 92*
**Means,** Gary Edward 1940- *AmMWSc 92, WhoMW 92*
**Means,** Gaston Bullock 1879-1938 *DcNCBi 4*
**Means,** Gordon Paul 1927- *WrDr 92*
**Means,** James Andrew 1937- *WhoWest 92*
**Means,** Jeffrey Lynn 1952- *AmMWSc 92*
**Means,** John Michael 1947- *WhoAmP 91*
**Means,** Kevin Michael 1955- *WhoBlA 92*
**Means,** L L *WhoAmP 91*
**Means,** Lane Lewis 1951- *WhoEnt 92*
**Means,** Lynn L 1914- *AmMWSc 92*
**Means,** Paul Barringer 1845-1910 *DcNCBi 4*
**Means,** Richard Dennis 1947- *WhoFI 92*
**Means,** Russell 1940- *FacFETw*
**Means,** Stephen Arden 1946- *WhoAmP 91*
**Means,** Terry Robert 1948- *WhoAmL 92*
**Means,** Winthrop D 1933- *AmMWSc 92*
**Meany,** David Van Dyke 1952- *WhoAmL 92*
**Meany,** George 1894-1980 *FacFETw*
**Meany,** Neill Richard 1923- *WhoRel 92, WhoWest 92*
**Meara,** Anne *WhoEnt 92*
**Meara,** Anne 1929- *IntMPA 92*
**Meares,** Claude Francis 1946- *AmMWSc 92*
**Meares,** John Levin 1920- *RelLAm 91*
**Meares,** Oliver Pendleton 1818-1906 *DcNCBi 4*
**Meares,** Paula G. Allen 1948- *WhoBlA 92*
**Meares,** William Belvidere 1787-1841 *DcNCBi 4*
**Meares,** William Belvidere, II 1826-1896 *DcNCBi 4*
**Mearian,** Judy Frank 1936- *WhoEnt 92*
**Mearns,** Alan John 1943- *AmMWSc 92*
**Mearns,** Edgar Alexander 1856-1916 *BiInAmS*
**Mearns,** William Skipwith 1745-1805 *DcNCBi 4*
**Mears,** A Garland *ScFEYrs*
**Mears,** Adrian Leonard 1944- *Who 92*
**Mears,** Brainerd, Jr 1921- *AmMWSc 92*
**Mears,** Charlotte *DrAPF 91*
**Mears,** Dana Christopher 1940- *AmMWSc 92*
**Mears,** David Elliott 1939- *AmMWSc 92*
**Mears,** David R 1936- *AmMWSc 92*
**Mears,** Gerald John 1938- *AmMWSc 92*
**Mears,** Gerald Joseph 1939- *WhoMW 92*
**Mears,** Henrietta Cornelia 1890-1963 *RelLAm 91*
**Mears,** James Austin 1944- *AmMWSc 92*
**Mears,** James Ewing 1838-1919 *BiInAmS*
**Mears,** John Cledan *Who 92*
**Mears,** Leverett 1850-1917 *BiInAmS*
**Mears,** Orum Glenn, III 1958- *WhoMW 92*
**Mears,** Patrick Edward 1951- *WhoAmL 92, WhoMW 92*
**Mears,** Roger Clifton, Jr 1925- *WhoAmP 91*
**Mears,** Whitney Harris 1912- *AmMWSc 92*
**Measamer,** S G 1913- *AmMWSc 92*
**Measday,** David Frederick 1937- *AmMWSc 92*
**Mease,** James 1771-1846 *BiInAmS*
**Mease,** Quentin R. 1917- *WhoBlA 92*
**Mease,** Ronald Franklin 1929- *WhoRel 92*
**Measel,** John William 1940- *AmMWSc 92*
**Measelle,** Richard L. 1938- *WhoFI 92*
**Measham,** Donald Charles 1932- *IntAu&W 91, WrDr 92*
**Measure,** Bruce 1951- *WhoAmP 91*
**Measures,** Raymond Massey 1938- *AmMWSc 92*
**Meath,** Bishop of 1940- *Who 92*
**Meath,** Earl of 1910- *Who 92*
**Meath,** William John 1936- *AmMWSc 92*
**Meath And Kildare,** Bishop of 1934- *Who 92*

**Meaton,** Jeffrey Carl 1957- *WhoMW 92*
**Meats,** Stephen *DrAPF 91*
**Meaux,** Alan Douglas 1951- *WhoWest 92*
**Meaux,** Ronald 1942- *WhoBlA 92*
**Meaux,** Thomas W 1954- *WhoAmP 91*
**Mebane,** Alexander 1744-1795 *DcNCBi 4*
**Mebane,** Benjamin Franklin 1823-1884 *DcNCBi 4*
**Mebane,** Benjamin Franklin, Jr. 1865-1926 *DcNCBi 4*
**Mebane,** Charles Harden 1862-1926 *DcNCBi 4*
**Mebane,** David Alexander 1959- *WhoAmL 92*
**Mebane,** George Allen 1850- *DcNCBi 4*
**Mebane,** Giles 1809-1899 *DcNCBi 4*
**Mebane,** James 1774-1857 *DcNCBi 4*
**Mebane,** John Harrison 1909- *WrDr 92*
**Mebane,** Mary E. *DrAPF 91*
**Mebiame,** Leon 1934- *IntWW 91*
**Mebus,** Charles Albert 1932- *AmMWSc 92*
**Mebus,** Robert Gwynne 1940- *WhoAmL 92*
**Mecabe,** Edwin Joseph 1956- *WhoFI 92*
**Mecca,** Christyna Emma 1936- *AmMWSc 92*
**Mecca,** Joseph A 1956- *WhoAmP 91*
**Mecca,** Stephen Joseph 1943- *AmMWSc 92*
**Mech,** L. David 1937- *WrDr 92*
**Mech,** Lucyan David 1937- *AmMWSc 92*
**Mech,** William Paul 1942- *AmMWSc 92*
**Mecham,** Evan 1924- *WhoAmP 91, WhoWest 92*
**Mecham,** Glenn Jefferson 1935- *WhoAmL 92, WhoWest 92*
**Mecham,** John Stephen 1928- *AmMWSc 92*
**Mecham,** Merlin J 1923- *AmMWSc 92*
**Mecham,** Paul F 1937- *WhoAmP 91*
**Mecham,** Robert P 1948- *AmMWSc 92*
**Mechanic,** Bill *IntMPA 92*
**Mechanic,** David 1936- *AmMWSc 92, IntWW 91*
**Mechanic,** Gerald 1927- *AmMWSc 92*
**Mechanic,** William M. *WhoEnt 92*
**Mechem,** Charles Stanley, Jr. 1930- *WhoMW 92*
**Mechem,** Joseph W 1942- *WhoIns 92*
**Mecherikunnel,** Ann Pottanat 1934- *AmMWSc 92*
**Mecherle,** G. Robert 1930- *WhoFI 92*
**Mechetti,** Fabio 1957- *WhoEnt 92*
**Mechigian,** Nancy Lee 1941- *WhoMW 92*
**Mechler,** Mark Vincent 1925- *AmMWSc 92*
**Mechlin,** George Francis, Jr 1923- *AmMWSc 92*
**Mechling,** Elizabeth 1945- *WhoWest 92*
**Mechling,** Paul Parks 1919- *WhoAmP 91*
**Mechling,** Paul Parks, II 1949- *WhoMW 92*
**Mechnikov,** Ilya Ilyich 1845-1916 *WhoNob 90*
**Mecholsky,** John Joseph, Jr 1944- *AmMWSc 92*
**Mechoso,** Carlos Roberto 1942- *WhoHisp 92*
**Mechtly,** Eugene A 1931- *AmMWSc 92*
**Mechur,** Robert Franklin 1945- *WhoAmL 92*
**Meciar,** Vladimir 1942- *IntWW 91*
**Meck,** Lynette *WhoRel 92*
**Meckauer,** Robert Monroe 1950- *WhoWest 92*
**Meckel,** Peter Timothy 1941- *WhoEnt 92*
**Meckel,** Richard A. 1948- *ConAu 135*
**Mecklenburg,** Roy Albert 1933- *AmMWSc 92*
**Meckler,** Alvin 1926- *AmMWSc 92*
**Meckler,** Milton 1932- *WhoWest 92*
**Mecklinger,** Ludwig 1919- *IntWW 91*
**Meckseper,** Friedrich 1936- *IntWW 91*
**Meckstroth,** George R 1935- *AmMWSc 92*
**Meckstroth,** Wilma Koenig 1929- *AmMWSc 92*
**Mecom,** Jane 1712-1794 *BenetAL 91*
**Meconi,** Vincent P 1951- *WhoAmP 91*
**Meda** *EncAmaz 91*
**Medairy,** Mark Curtis, Jr 1953- *WhoAmP 91*
**Medak,** Herman 1914- *AmMWSc 92*
**Medak,** Peter *IntMPA 92, IntWW 91*
**Medak,** Peter 1937- *WhoEnt 92*
**Medak,** Walter Hans 1915- *WhoWest 92*
**Medal,** Eduardo Antonio 1950- *WhoHisp 92*
**Medalia,** Avrom Izak 1923- *AmMWSc 92*
**Medalie,** Jack Harvey 1922- *AmMWSc 92*
**Medaris,** Edward Gene 1929- *WhoRel 92*
**Medaris,** Florence Isabel *WhoMW 92*
**Medaris,** J. Bruce 1902- *IntWW 91*
**Medaris,** John Bruce 1902- *WhoRel 92*
**Medaris,** L Gordon, Jr 1936- *AmMWSc 92*
**Medaris,** Levi Gordon, Jr. 1936- *WhoMW 92*
**Medavoy,** Mike 1941- *IntMPA 92, WhoEnt 92*
**Medavoy,** Patricia Duff 1955- *WhoEnt 92*
**Medawar,** Jean 1913- *ConAu 134*
**Medawar,** Nicholas Antoine Macbeth 1933- *Who 92*
**Medawar,** Peter Brian 1915- *WhoNob 90*
**Medawar,** Peter Brian 1915-1987 *FacFETw*
**Medberry,** Chauncey Joseph, III 1917- *IntWW 91*
**Medcalf,** Darrell Gerald 1937- *AmMWSc 92*
**Medcalf,** Robert Randolph, Jr. *DrAPF 91*
**Medcalf,** William Edwin, Jr. 1939- *WhoWest 92*
**Medcraf,** James Howard 1948- *WhoAmL 92*
**Medd,** Patrick William 1919- *Who 92*
**Medders,** Clarence E *WhoAmP 91, WhoWest 92*
**Medders,** Marion Wardner 1925- *WhoAmP 91*
**Medders,** Vernon S 1919- *WhoAmP 91*
**Meddings,** William Thomas, Jr. 1945- *WhoMW 92*
**Medearis,** Donald N, Jr 1927- *AmMWSc 92*
**Medearis,** Donald Norman, Jr. 1927- *IntWW 91*
**Medearis,** Kenneth Gordon 1930- *AmMWSc 92*
**Medearis,** Robert Park 1930- *WhoAmP 91*
**Medearis,** Victor L. 1921- *WhoBlA 92*
**Medebach,** Girolamo 1706-1790 *BlkwCEP*
**Medeiros,** Edward Alvin 1939- *WhoEnt 92*
**Medeiros,** Humberto Sousa 1915-1983 *RelLAm 91*
**Medeiros,** John J 1929- *WhoAmP 91*
**Medeiros,** Matthew Francis 1945- *WhoAmL 92*
**Medeiros,** Robert Whippen 1931- *AmMWSc 92*
**Medeiros,** Rosemary Hambly 1957- *WhoEnt 92*
**Medelci,** Mourad 1943- *IntWW 91*
**Medellin,** Jose H. 1941- *WhoHisp 92*
**Medema,** David Luke 1953- *WhoMW 92*
**Meder,** Mark Alan 1960- *WhoEnt 92*
**Mederos,** Julio *WhoHisp 92*
**Medford,** Don *WhoEnt 92*
**Medford,** Don 1917- *IntMPA 92*
**Medford,** Isabel *WhoBlA 92*
**Medhurst,** Brian 1935- *Who 92*
**Medici,** Cosimo de *DcNCBi 4*
**Medici,** Emilio Garrastazu 1905-1985 *FacFETw*
**Medici,** Giuseppe 1907- *IntWW 91*
**Medici,** Paul T 1919- *AmMWSc 92*
**Medici,** Stelios Prince Castanos de' 1927- *WhoRel 92*
**Medici,** Stephen Francis 1952- *WhoFI 92*
**Medick,** James Thomas 1946- *WhoFI 92*
**Medick,** Matthew A 1927- *AmMWSc 92*
**Medico,** Frank 1924- *WhoAmP 91*
**Medicraft,** Rodney Horace 1931- *WhoFI 92, WhoMW 92*
**Medicus,** Heinrich Adolf 1918- *AmMWSc 92*
**Medin,** A Louis 1925- *AmMWSc 92*
**Medin,** Lowell Ansgard 1932- *WhoFI 92, WhoMW 92*
**Medina,** Agustin 1950- *WhoHisp 92*
**Medina,** Agustin, Jr. 1946- *WhoHisp 92*
**Medina,** Andino, Jr. 1950- *WhoHisp 92*
**Medina,** Angel 1932- *WhoHisp 92*
**Medina,** Cesar Hjalmar 1963- *WhoHisp 92*
**Medina,** Cris 1951- *WhoHisp 92*
**Medina,** Daniel 1941- *AmMWSc 92*
**Medina,** David Jonathan 1951- *WhoHisp 92*
**Medina,** Enrique 1953- *WhoHisp 92*
**Medina,** Evelio *WhoHisp 92*
**Medina,** George O. *WhoHisp 92*
**Medina,** Gilbert M. *WhoHisp 92*
**Medina,** Harold 1888-1990 *AnObit 1990*
**Medina,** Harold R., Jr. d1991 *NewYTBS 91*
**Medina,** Harold Raymond 1888-1990 *FacFETw*
**Medina,** Isabel 1932- *WhoHisp 92*
**Medina,** Jeremy Todd 1972- *WhoEnt 92*
**Medina,** Jim 1940- *WhoHisp 92*
**Medina,** John A. 1942- *WhoHisp 92*
**Medina,** Jorge 1951- *WhoHisp 92*
**Medina,** Jose Enrique 1926- *AmMWSc 92, WhoHisp 92*
**Medina,** Juan de 158-?-1635 *HisDSpE*
**Medina,** Julian Phillip 1949- *WhoHisp 92*
**Medina,** Leopoldo Ocampo 1937- *WhoEnt 92*
**Medina,** Manuel *WhoHisp 92*
**Medina,** Manuel 1940- *WhoHisp 92*
**Medina,** Manuel, Jr. 1952- *WhoHisp 92*
**Medina,** Marjorie B 1945- *AmMWSc 92*
**Medina,** Mel *WhoHisp 92*
**Medina,** Miguel A., Jr. 1946- *WhoHisp 92*
**Medina,** Miguel Angel 1932- *AmMWSc 92*
**Medina,** Miguel Angel, Jr 1946- *AmMWSc 92*
**Medina,** Pablo *DrAPF 91*
**Medina,** Pablo 1948- *LiExTwC, WhoHisp 92*
**Medina,** Patricia 1921- *IntMPA 92*
**Medina,** Robert C. 1924- *WhoHisp 92*
**Medina,** Ruben Anthony 1957- *WhoFI 92*
**Medina,** Rubens *WhoHisp 92*
**Medina,** Ruth M. 1957- *WhoHisp 92*
**Medina,** Sandra Sellman 1947- *WhoWest 92*
**Medina,** Sandrale Olivia 1942- *WhoHisp 92*
**Medina,** Standish Forde, Jr. 1940- *WhoAmL 92*
**Medina,** Thomas Julian 1928- *WhoWest 92*
**Medina,** Tina Marie 1965- *WhoHisp 92*
**Medina,** Vicente 1955- *WhoHisp 92*
**Medina-Juarbe,** Arturo 1951- *WhoHisp 92*
**Medina-Ruiz,** Arturo 1941- *WhoHisp 92*
**Meding,** Charles W. *WhoFI 92*
**Medinger,** Charles Wynn 1950- *WhoEnt 92*
**Medinger,** John Donald 1948- *WhoAmP 91*
**Meditch,** James S 1934- *AmMWSc 92*
**Meditch,** James Stephen 1934- *WhoWest 92*
**Medland,** William James 1944- *WhoMW 92*
**Medler,** John Thomas 1914- *AmMWSc 92*
**Medley,** Charles Robert 1905- *Who 92*
**Medley,** Charles Robert Owen 1905- *IntWW 91*
**Medley,** George Julius 1930- *Who 92*
**Medley,** James Robert 1940- *WhoAmP 91*
**Medley,** Landon Daryle 1949- *WhoAmP 91*
**Medley,** Robert 1905- *TwCPaSc*
**Medley,** Sherrilyn 1946- *WhoFI 92*
**Medley,** Sidney S 1941- *AmMWSc 92*
**Medley,** Steven Paul 1949- *WhoWest 92*
**Medlicott,** Michael Geoffrey 1943- *Who 92*
**Medlin,** Dennis B 1942- *WhoIns 92*
**Medlin,** Gary Lewis 1957- *WhoAmL 92*
**Medlin,** Gene Woodard 1925- *AmMWSc 92*
**Medlin,** John Grimes, Jr. 1933- *WhoFI 92*
**Medlin,** Julie Anne Jones 1936- *AmMWSc 92*
**Medlin,** William Louis 1928- *AmMWSc 92*
**Medlinsky,** Albert Stanley 1932- *WhoWest 92*
**Medlock,** Ann 1933- *WhoWest 92*
**Medlock,** Eugene Shields 1954- *WhoWest 92*
**Medlock,** T. Travis 1934- *WhoBlA 92*
**Medlock,** Thomas Travis 1934- *WhoAmL 92, WhoAmP 91*
**Medlycott,** Mervyn 1947- *Who 92*
**Medman,** Edward A. 1937- *IntMPA 92*
**Medman,** Edward Alan 1937- *WhoEnt 92*
**Mednick,** Murray *DrAPF 91*
**Mednick,** Murray 1939- *IntAu&W 91, WhoEnt 92, WrDr 92*
**Mednick,** Robert 1940- *WhoFI 92*
**Mednieks,** Maija *AmMWSc 92*
**Mednikoff,** Reuben 1906-1976 *TwCPaSc*
**Medof,** Sandra Gwyn 1955- *WhoAmP 91*
**Medoff,** Gerald 1936- *AmMWSc 92*
**Medoff,** Judith *AmMWSc 92*
**Medoff,** Mark 1940- *IntAu&W 91, WrDr 92*
**Medoff,** Marshall Hilary 1945- *WhoFI 92*
**Medora,** Rustem Sohrab 1934- *AmMWSc 92*
**Medrano,** Ambrosia *WhoAmP 91*
**Medrano,** Ambrosio 1953- *WhoHisp 92*
**Medrano,** Bill N. 1939- *WhoHisp 92*
**Medrano,** Evangeline M. 1944- *WhoHisp 92*
**Medrano,** Francisco 1920- *WhoAmP 91*
**Medrano,** Manuel F., Jr. 1949- *WhoHisp 92*
**Medrano,** Pauline 1955- *WhoAmP 91*
**Medrud,** Ronald Curtis 1934- *AmMWSc 92*
**Medtner** *NewAmDM*
**Meduski,** Jerzy Wincenty 1918- *WhoWest 92*
**Medve,** Richard J 1936- *AmMWSc 92*
**Medvecky,** Thomas Edward 1937- *WhoAmL 92*
**Medved,** Aleksander Vasil'evich 1937- *SovUnBD*
**Medved',** Aleksandr Vasilevich 1937- *IntWW 91*
**Medved,** Jane Elizabeth Schecter 1948- *IntAu&W 91*
**Medved,** Michael 1948- *WhoEnt 92*
**Medvedev,** Nikolay Nikolaevich 1933- *SovUnBD*
**Medvedev,** Roy 1925- *IntAu&W 91, WrDr 92*
**Medvedev,** Roy Aleksandrovich 1925- *IntWW 91, SovUnBD*
**Medvedev,** Vadim Andreevich 1929- *SovUnBD*
**Medvedev,** Vadim Andreyevich 1929- *IntWW 91*
**Medvedev,** Zhores 1925- *IntAu&W 91, WrDr 92*
**Medvedev,** Zhores Aleksandrovich 1925- *IntWW 91, SovUnBD*
**Medvedkin,** Aleksandr Ivanovich 1900-1989 *SovUnBD*
**Medvei,** Victor Cornelius 1905- *IntAu&W 91, WrDr 92*
**Medvin,** Harvey N 1936- *WhoIns 92*
**Medwadowski,** Stefan J *AmMWSc 92*
**Medwall,** Henry 1461- *RfGEnL 91*
**Medway,** Lord 1968- *Who 92*
**Medway,** William 1927- *AmMWSc 92*
**Medwed,** Mameve S. *DrAPF 91*
**Medwick,** Thomas 1929- *AmMWSc 92*
**Medwin,** Herman 1920- *AmMWSc 92*
**Medwin,** Michael 1925- *IntMPA 92*
**Medwin,** Robert Joseph G. *Who 92*
**Medzigian,** Michael George 1960- *WhoFI 92*
**Medzihradsky,** Fedor 1932- *AmMWSc 92*
**Medzon,** Edward Lionel 1936- *AmMWSc 92*
**Mee,** Huan *ScFEYrs*
**Mee,** John Lawrence 1950- *WhoFI 92*
**Mee,** Susie *DrAPF 91*
**Meece,** Bernard Clayton 1927- *WhoRel 92*
**Meech,** John Athol 1947- *AmMWSc 92*
**Meech,** Levi Witter 1821-1912 *BiInAmS*
**Meech,** Norma M 1936- *WhoAmP 91*
**Meech,** Sonja Rosemary 1950- *WhoWest 92*
**Meecham,** William Coryell 1928- *AmMWSc 92, WhoWest 92*
**Meechan,** Charles James 1928- *AmMWSc 92*
**Meechan,** Robert John 1926- *AmMWSc 92*
**Meechie,** Helen Guild 1938- *Who 92*
**Meedel,** Thomas Huyck 1949- *AmMWSc 92*
**Meeder,** Jeanne Elizabeth 1950- *AmMWSc 92*
**Meeds,** Lloyd 1927- *WhoAmP 91*
**Meegan,** Charles Anthony 1944- *AmMWSc 92*
**Meegan,** Elizabeth *WhoRel 92*
**Meehan,** Edward Joseph 1912- *AmMWSc 92*
**Meehan,** Joan Barbara 1959- *WhoMW 92*
**Meehan,** John *WhoEnt 92*
**Meehan,** John Patrick 1923- *AmMWSc 92*
**Meehan,** Joseph Edward 1947- *WhoMW 92*
**Meehan,** Joseph Gerard 1931- *WhoFI 92*
**Meehan,** Martin Thomas 1956- *WhoAmP 91*
**Meehan,** Maude *DrAPF 91*
**Meehan,** Nancy Catherine 1931- *WhoEnt 92*
**Meehan,** Richard Thomas 1949- *WhoWest 92*
**Meehan,** Robert Henry 1946- *WhoFI 92*
**Meehan,** Thomas 1826-1901 *BiInAmS*
**Meehan,** Thomas 1942- *AmMWSc 92*
**Meehan,** William Robert 1931- *AmMWSc 92*
**Meek,** Alexander Beaufort 1814-1865 *BenetAL 91*
**Meek,** Brian Alexander 1939- *Who 92*
**Meek,** Carrie P 1926- *WhoAmP 91*
**Meek,** Charles Innes 1920- *Who 92*
**Meek,** Charles Richard 1941- *WhoEnt 92*
**Meek,** Devon Walter 1936- *AmMWSc 92*
**Meek,** Fielding Bradford 1817-1876 *BiInAmS*
**Meek,** Jack Wayne 1952- *WhoWest 92*
**Meek,** James Latham 1937- *AmMWSc 92*
**Meek,** Jay *DrAPF 91*
**Meek,** Jay 1937- *IntAu&W 91*
**Meek,** John E 1950- *WhoAmP 91*
**Meek,** John Martin 1929- *WhoFI 92*
**Meek,** John Millar 1912- *Who 92*
**Meek,** John Sawyers 1918- *AmMWSc 92*
**Meek,** Joseph *WrDr 92*
**Meek,** Joseph Chester, Jr 1931- *AmMWSc 92*
**Meek,** M. R. D. 1918- *WrDr 92*
**Meek,** Marcellus Robert 1929- *WhoWest 92*
**Meek,** Marshall 1925- *Who 92*
**Meek,** Paul Derald 1930- *IntWW 91, WhoFI 92*
**Meek,** Peter Hunt 1943- *WhoRel 92*
**Meek,** Phillip Joseph 1937- *WhoEnt 92*
**Meek,** Russell Charles 1937- *WhoBlA 92*
**Meek,** S P 1894-1972 *TwCSFW 91*
**Meek,** Seth Eugene 1859-1914 *BiInAmS*
**Meek,** Susan Jane 1944- *WhoRel 92*
**Meek,** Violet Imhof 1939- *AmMWSc 92*
**Meeker,** Anthony 1939- *WhoAmP 91, WhoWest 92*
**Meeker,** Arlene Dorothy Hallin 1935- *WhoFI 92*
**Meeker,** Charles R. *IntMPA 92*
**Meeker,** David Anthony 1939- *WhoAmP 91*

**Meeker,** David Lynn 1950- *AmMWSc 92*
**Meeker,** Ezra 1830-1928 *BenetAL 91*
**Meeker,** Guy Bentley 1945- *WhoFI 92*
**Meeker,** Loren David 1932- *AmMWSc 92*
**Meeker,** Milton Shy 1933- *WhoFI 92*
**Meeker,** Nathan Cook 1817-1879 *BenetAL 91*
**Meeker,** Ralph Dennis 1945- *AmMWSc 92*
**Meeker,** Thrygve Richard 1929- *AmMWSc 92*
**Meeker,** William Maurice 1915- *WhoFI 92*
**Meeker,** William Quackenbush, Jr 1949- *AmMWSc 92*
**Meekins,** Daniel Victor 1897-1964 *DcNCBi 4*
**Meekins,** Isaac Melson 1875-1946 *DcNCBi 4*
**Meekins,** John Fred 1937- *AmMWSc 92*
**Meekins,** Russ, Jr *WhoAmP 91*
**Meekison,** MaryFran 1919- *WhoMW 92*
**Meeks,** Benjamin Spencer, Jr 1924- *AmMWSc 92*
**Meeks,** Cordell David, Jr. 1942- *WhoBlA 92*
**Meeks,** D. Michael 1943- *WhoFI 92*
**Meeks,** Esther MacBain 1921- *IntAu&W 91, WrDr 92*
**Meeks,** Frank Robert 1928- *AmMWSc 92, WhoMW 92*
**Meeks,** James Donald 1920- *WhoWest 92*
**Meeks,** John Neal 1931- *WhoAmP 91*
**Meeks,** Joni Marsh 1931- *WhoAmP 91*
**Meeks,** Larry Gillette 1944- *WhoBlA 92*
**Meeks,** Mark Anthony 1946- *WhoRel 92*
**Meeks,** Merrill Douglas, II 1941- *WhoRel 92*
**Meeks,** Perker L., Jr. 1943- *WhoBlA 92*
**Meeks,** Reginald Kline 1954- *WhoAmP 91, WhoBlA 92*
**Meeks,** Robert G 1942- *AmMWSc 92*
**Meeks,** Robert L 1934- *WhoAmP 91*
**Meeks,** Wayne A. 1932- *WhoRel 92, WrDr 92*
**Meeks,** Wilkison 1915- *AmMWSc 92*
**Meelheim,** Richard Young 1925- *AmMWSc 92*
**Meem,** J Lawrence, Jr 1915- *AmMWSc 92*
**Meen,** Ronald Hugh 1925- *AmMWSc 92*
**Meenan,** Alan John 1946- *WhoRel 92*
**Meenan,** Patrick Henry 1927- *WhoAmP 91, WhoWest 92*
**Meenan,** Peter Michael 1942- *AmMWSc 92*
**Meendsen,** Fred Charles 1933- *WhoFI 92*
**Meentemeyer,** Vernon George 1942- *AmMWSc 92*
**Meer,** Fatima *IntAu&W 91*
**Meer,** Fatima 1929- *WrDr 92*
**Meer,** Jon Douglas 1963- *WhoWest 92*
**Meer,** Y. S. *WrDr 92*
**Meerbaum,** Samuel 1919- *AmMWSc 92*
**Meerbott,** William Keddie 1918- *AmMWSc 92*
**Meeres,** Norman Victor 1913- *Who 92*
**Meerovitch,** Eugene 1919- *AmMWSc 92*
**Meese,** Celia Edwards *WhoFI 92, WhoWest 92*
**Meese,** Edwin 1931- *IntWW 91*
**Meese,** Edwin, III 1931- *Who 92, WhoAmP 91*
**Meese,** Ernest Harold 1929- *WhoMW 92*
**Meese,** Gregory David 1956- *WhoAmL 92*
**Meese,** Jon Michael 1938- *AmMWSc 92*
**Meese,** Robert Allen 1956- *WhoMW 92*
**Meester,** Anneus Daniel 1937- *WhoMW 92*
**Meeter,** Dean Ray 1947- *WhoRel 92*
**Meeter,** Duane Anthony 1937- *AmMWSc 92*
**Meetz,** Gerald David 1937- *AmMWSc 92*
**Meetze,** George Elias 1909- *WhoAmP 91*
**Meeuse,** Bastiaan J D 1916- *AmMWSc 92*
**Meeuwig,** Richard O'Bannon 1927- *AmMWSc 92*
**Meezan,** Elias 1942- *AmMWSc 92*
**Mefferd,** Roy B, Jr 1920- *AmMWSc 92*
**Meffert,** Chris 1943- *WhoAmP 91*
**Mefford,** David Allen 1928- *AmMWSc 92*
**Mefford,** Dean A. *WhoMW 92*
**Mega,** Christopher John 1930- *WhoAmP 91*
**Megahan,** Walter Franklin 1935- *AmMWSc 92*
**Megahed,** Sid A 1941- *AmMWSc 92*
**Megahey,** Leslie 1944- *Who 92*
**Megahy,** Thomas 1929- *Who 92*
**Megapolensis,** Johannes 1603?-1670 *BenetAL 91*
**Megard,** Robert O 1933- *AmMWSc 92*
**Megargle,** Robert G 1941- *AmMWSc 92*
**Megarry,** Robert 1910- *IntWW 91, Who 92*
**Megaw,** Arthur Hubert Stanley 1910- *Who 92*
**Megaw,** John 1909- *Who 92*
**Megaw,** Neill *DrAPF 91*
**Megaw,** William James 1924- *AmMWSc 92*
**Megel,** Herbert 1926- *AmMWSc 92, WhoMW 92*
**Megennis,** June Katherine 1941- *WhoEnt 92*
**Megert,** Peter 1937- *WhoEnt 92*
**Megged,** Aharon 1920- *IntAu&W 91, WrDr 92*
**Meggers,** Betty J. 1921- *WrDr 92*
**Meggers,** William F, Jr 1924- *AmMWSc 92*
**Meggeson,** Michael 1930- *Who 92*
**Meggison,** David Laurence 1928- *AmMWSc 92*
**Meggitt,** Mervyn John 1924- *WrDr 92*
**Meggitt,** William Fredric 1928- *AmMWSc 92*
**Meggs,** Betty Sugg 1934- *WhoAmP 91*
**Meggs,** Brown 1930- *IntAu&W 91, WrDr 92*
**Meggs,** Margaret L. 1953- *WhoRel 92*
**Meghoo,** Gregory 1965- *BlkOlyM*
**Meghreblian,** Robert V 1922- *AmMWSc 92*
**Megibben,** Charles Kimbrough 1936- *AmMWSc 92*
**Megill,** David Wayne 1947- *WhoEnt 92*
**Megill,** Lawrence Rexford 1925- *AmMWSc 92*
**Megirian,** Robert 1926- *AmMWSc 92*
**Meglio,** Cheryl Ann 1964- *WhoEnt 92*
**Mego,** John L 1922- *AmMWSc 92*
**Megrath,** Kimberley Lewis 1953- *WhoWest 92*
**Megraw,** Robert Arthur 1939- *AmMWSc 92*
**Megraw,** Robert Ellis 1930- *AmMWSc 92*
**Megrue,** George Henry 1936- *AmMWSc 92*
**Megson,** Claude Walter 1936- *IntWW 91*
**Meguerian,** Garbis H 1922- *AmMWSc 92*
**Mehaffey,** James *Who 92*
**Mehaffey,** John Allen *WhoFI 92*
**Mehaffey,** Leathem, III 1941- *AmMWSc 92*
**Mehaignerie,** Pierre 1939- *IntWW 91*
**Mehalchin,** John Joseph 1937- *WhoFI 92*
**Mehalko,** Kenneth George 1938- *WhoMW 92*
**Meharry,** Ronald Lee 1950- *WhoMW 92*
**Mehboob Khan** 1909-1964 *IntDcF 2-2 [port]*
**Mehdizadeh,** Mostafa 1949- *WhoFI 92*
**Mehdizadeh,** Parviz 1934- *WhoFI 92, WhoWest 92*
**Mehedebi,** Bahsir 1912- *IntWW 91*
**Mehegan,** Constance M *WhoAmP 91*
**Mehendale,** Harihara Mahadeva 1942- *AmMWSc 92*
**Meher Baba** 1894-1969 *RelLAm 91*
**Meheriuk,** Michael 1936- *AmMWSc 92*
**Mehew,** Peter 1931- *Who 92*
**Mehl,** Douglas Wayne 1948- *WhoWest 92*
**Mehl,** James Bernard 1939- *AmMWSc 92*
**Mehl,** Jeffrey *WhoFI 92*
**Mehl,** John Edwards 1936- *WhoRel 92*
**Mehlburger,** Donald Lee, Sr 1937- *WhoAmP 91*
**Mehlenbacher,** Dohn Harlow 1931- *WhoFI 92*
**Mehler,** Alan Haskell 1922- *AmMWSc 92*
**Mehler,** Ernest Louis 1938- *AmMWSc 92*
**Mehlhaff,** Harvey *WhoRel 92*
**Mehlhaff,** Leon Curtis 1940- *AmMWSc 92*
**Mehlig,** Donald Homer 1935- *WhoIns 92*
**Mehlinger,** Kermit Thorpe 1918- *WhoBlA 92*
**Mehlis,** David Lee *WhoRel 92*
**Mehlman,** Lon Douglas 1959- *WhoWest 92*
**Mehlman,** Myron A 1934- *AmMWSc 92*
**Mehlschau,** Robert Eugene 1960- *WhoWest 92*
**Mehltretter,** Glenn William, Jr. 1942- *WhoFI 92*
**Mehlum,** Johan Arnt 1928- *WhoFI 92*
**Mehm,** George Joseph, Jr. 1956- *WhoFI 92*
**Mehne,** Wendy Herbener 1954- *WhoEnt 92*
**Mehner,** John Frederick 1921- *AmMWSc 92*
**Mehner,** William Michel 1943- *WhoFI 92*
**Mehr,** Cyrus B 1927- *AmMWSc 92*
**Mehr,** Rochelle Hope *DrAPF 91*
**Mehr,** Samuel Harry 1947- *WhoMW 92*
**Mehr,** Sheldon Marshall 1931- *WhoWest 92*
**Mehr,** Vern Conrad 1949- *WhoRel 92*
**Mehr,** William John 1941- *WhoAmL 92*
**Mehra,** Mool Chand 1936- *AmMWSc 92*
**Mehra,** Vinodkumar S 1935- *AmMWSc 92*
**Mehrabian,** Albert 1939- *WhoWest 92, WrDr 92*
**Mehrabian,** Robert 1941- *AmMWSc 92*
**Mehran,** Farrokh 1936- *AmMWSc 92*
**Mehren,** Lawrence Lindsay 1944- *WhoFI 92, WhoWest 92*
**Mehreteab,** Ghebre-Selassie 1941- *WhoBlA 92*
**Mehring,** Arnon Lewis, Jr 1915- *AmMWSc 92*
**Mehring,** Clinton Warren 1924- *WhoWest 92*
**Mehring,** Jeffrey Scott 1942- *AmMWSc 92*
**Mehring,** Walter 1896-1981 *EncTR 91*
**Mehringer,** Peter Joseph, Jr 1933- *AmMWSc 92*
**Mehrkam,** Quentin D 1921- *AmMWSc 92*
**Mehrkens,** Lyle 1937- *WhoAmP 91*
**Mehrle,** Paul Martin, Jr 1945- *AmMWSc 92*
**Mehrlich,** Ferdinand Paul 1905- *AmMWSc 92*
**Mehrotra,** Arvind Krishna 1947- *ConPo 91, WrDr 92*
**Mehrotra,** Bam Deo 1933- *AmMWSc 92*
**Mehrotra,** Kishan Gopal 1941- *AmMWSc 92*
**Mehrotra,** Prakash Chandra 1925- *Who 92*
**Mehrotra,** Ram Charan 1922- *IntWW 91, Who 92*
**Mehrotra,** Sriram 1931- *WrDr 92*
**Mehrtens,** Kit *WhoAmP 91*
**Mehrtens,** William Osborne, Jr. 1945- *WhoAmL 92*
**Mehs,** Doreen Margaret 1944- *AmMWSc 92*
**Mehta,** Atul Mansukhbhai 1949- *AmMWSc 92*
**Mehta,** Avinash C 1931- *AmMWSc 92*
**Mehta,** Bharat Ambalal 1947- *WhoMW 92*
**Mehta,** Bipin Mohanlal 1935- *AmMWSc 92*
**Mehta,** Gurmukh D 1945- *AmMWSc 92*
**Mehta,** Jatinder S 1939- *AmMWSc 92*
**Mehta,** Kishor Singh 1941- *AmMWSc 92*
**Mehta,** M Paul 1936- *WhoAmP 91*
**Mehta,** Mahendra 1952- *AmMWSc 92*
**Mehta,** Mehli 1908- *NewAmDM*
**Mehta,** N C 1938- *AmMWSc 92*
**Mehta,** Nariman Bomanshaw 1920- *AmMWSc 92*
**Mehta,** Narinder Kumar 1938- *WhoFI 92*
**Mehta,** Povindar Kumar *AmMWSc 92*
**Mehta,** Prakash V 1946- *AmMWSc 92*
**Mehta,** Rajendra 1955- *WhoMW 92*
**Mehta,** Rajendra G 1947- *AmMWSc 92*
**Mehta,** Sandeep 1966- *WhoFI 92*
**Mehta,** Shailesh J. 1949- *WhoFI 92*
**Mehta,** Sudhir 1946- *AmMWSc 92*
**Mehta,** Ved 1934- *BenetAL 91, Who 92, WrDr 92*
**Mehta,** Ved Parkash *DrAPF 91*
**Mehta,** Ved Parkash 1934- *IntAu&W 91, LiExTwC*
**Mehta,** Xerxes Jal 1940- *WhoEnt 92*
**Mehta,** Zarin 1938- *WhoEnt 92, WhoMW 92*
**Mehta,** Zubin 1936- *IntWW 91, NewAmDM, Who 92, WhoEnt 92*
**Mehul,** Etienne-Nicolas 1763-1817 *NewAmDM*
**Mehuron,** William Otto 1937- *WhoFI 92*
**Mei Yi** 1913- *IntWW 91*
**Mei,** Chiang C 1935- *AmMWSc 92*
**Mei,** Kenneth K 1932- *AmMWSc 92*
**Meibach,** Judith Karen 1937- *WhoEnt 92*
**Meibeyer,** Charles William, Jr. 1951- *WhoAmL 92*
**Meibeyer,** Shirley Ann 1932- *WhoAmP 91*
**Meibohm,** Edgar Paul Hubert 1915- *AmMWSc 92*
**Meiboom,** Saul 1916- *AmMWSc 92*
**Meibuhr,** Stuart Gene 1934- *AmMWSc 92*
**Meidinger,** Ingeborg Lucie 1923- *IntAu&W 91*
**Meidinger,** Miles John 1950- *WhoMW 92*
**Meidl,** Kevin 1960- *WhoMW 92*
**Meidner,** Else 1901- *TwCPaSc*
**Meienhofer,** Johannes Arnold 1929- *AmMWSc 92*
**Meier** *EncTR 91*
**Meier,** Albert Henry 1929- *AmMWSc 92*
**Meier,** August 1923- *WhoBlA 92*
**Meier,** Ben 1918- *WhoAmP 91*
**Meier,** Charles Frederick, Jr 1949- *AmMWSc 92*
**Meier,** Dale Joseph 1922- *AmMWSc 92*
**Meier,** David Benjamin 1938- *Who 92*
**Meier,** Diane Patricia 1957- *WhoWest 92*
**Meier,** Edward Daniel 1841-1914 *BiInAmS*
**Meier,** Eugene Paul 1942- *AmMWSc 92*
**Meier,** France Arnett 1928- *AmMWSc 92*
**Meier,** Gerald Herbert 1942- *AmMWSc 92*
**Meier,** Gerry Holden 1949- *WhoAmL 92*
**Meier,** Gregory Guilbert 1948- *WhoAmP 91*
**Meier,** Gustav 1929- *NewAmDM*
**Meier,** Harold Ellswith 1932- *WhoAmL 92, WhoAmP 91*
**Meier,** Henry N., Jr. 1948- *WhoAmL 92*
**Meier,** James Archibald 1936- *AmMWSc 92*
**Meier,** John Paul 1942- *WhoRel 92*
**Meier,** Joseph Francis 1936- *AmMWSc 92*
**Meier,** Karen Lorene 1942- *WhoMW 92*
**Meier,** Manfred John 1929- *AmMWSc 92*
**Meier,** Margaret Kitchen 1931- *WhoAmP 91*
**Meier,** Margaret Shelton 1936- *WhoEnt 92*
**Meier,** Mark Frederick 1925- *AmMWSc 92*
**Meier,** Mark Stephan 1959- *AmMWSc 92*
**Meier,** Michael McDaniel 1940- *AmMWSc 92*
**Meier,** Paul 1924- *AmMWSc 92, WhoMW 92*
**Meier,** Peter Gustav 1937- *AmMWSc 92*
**Meier,** Richard 1934- *DcTwDes*
**Meier,** Richard Alan 1934- *IntWW 91*
**Meier,** Richard Arthur 1953- *WhoAmL 92*
**Meier,** Robert R 1940- *AmMWSc 92*
**Meier,** Rudolf H 1918- *AmMWSc 92*
**Meier,** Wilbur L, Jr 1939- *AmMWSc 92*
**Meier,** William Edward 1966- *WhoMW 92*
**Meier,** William Henry 1904- *WhoAmP 91*
**Meier-Graefe,** Julius 1867-1935 *DcTwDes, FacFETw*
**Meieran,** Eugene Stuart 1937- *AmMWSc 92, WhoWest 92*
**Meiere,** Forrest T 1937- *AmMWSc 92*
**Meierhenry,** Mark V 1944- *WhoAmP 91*
**Meierhoefer,** Alan W 1944- *AmMWSc 92*
**Meighen,** Arthur 1874-1960 *FacFETw*
**Meighen,** Edward Arthur 1942- *AmMWSc 92*
**Meigs,** Arthur Vincent 1850-1912 *BiInAmS*
**Meigs,** Charles Delucena 1792-1869 *BiInAmS*
**Meigs,** James Aitken 1829-1879 *BiInAmS*
**Meigs,** Josiah 1757-1822 *BiInAmS*
**Meigs,** Montgomery Cunningham 1816-1892 *BiInAmS*
**Meigs,** Peveril 1903-1979 *ConAu 133*
**Meijer,** Arend 1947- *AmMWSc 92*
**Meijer,** Arnold Joseph 1905-1965 *BiDExR*
**Meijer,** Douglas 1954- *WhoFI 92*
**Meijer,** Frederik 1919- *WhoFI 92*
**Meijer,** Paul Herman Ernst 1921- *AmMWSc 92*
**Meijler,** Frits Louis 1925- *IntWW 91*
**Meike,** Annemarie *AmMWSc 92*
**Meikle,** Andrew 1719-1811 *BlkwCEP*
**Meikle,** Clive *IntAu&W 91X*
**Meikle,** Mary B 1934- *AmMWSc 92*
**Meikle,** Richard William 1922- *AmMWSc 92*
**Meikle,** Susan Elizabeth 1956- *WhoRel 92*
**Meikle,** William MacKay 1933- *WhoAmL 92*
**Meiklejohn,** Al 1923- *WhoAmP 91*
**Meiklejohn,** Alvin J., Jr. 1923- *WhoWest 92*
**Meiklejohn,** Donald Stuart 1950- *WhoAmL 92*
**Meiklejohn,** Lorraine J 1929- *WhoAmP 91*
**Meiklejohn,** Paul Thomas 1944- *WhoAmL 92*
**Meiklejohn,** Raymond Harry 1935- *WhoWest 92*
**Meiklejohn,** William 1903-1981 *FacFETw*
**Meiksin,** Zvi H 1926- *AmMWSc 92*
**Meiling,** Dean S 1948- *WhoIns 92*
**Meiling,** George Robert Lucas 1942- *WhoFI 92*
**Meiling,** Gerald Stewart 1936- *AmMWSc 92*
**Meiling,** Richard L 1908- *AmMWSc 92*
**Meilleur,** Brien Adrien 1949- *WhoWest 92*
**Meillon,** Alfonso 1926- *WhoHisp 92*
**Meiman,** James R 1933- *AmMWSc 92*
**Meincke,** P P M 1936- *AmMWSc 92*
**Meindl,** James D 1933- *AmMWSc 92*
**Meindl,** Robert James 1936- *WhoWest 92*
**Meine,** Evelyn de Vivo 1926- *WhoEnt 92*
**Meinecke,** Eberhard A 1933- *AmMWSc 92*
**Meinecke,** Friedrich 1862-1954 *EncTR 91*
**Meineke,** Howard Albert 1921- *AmMWSc 92*
**Meinel,** Aden Baker 1922- *AmMWSc 92*
**Meinel,** Marjorie Pettit 1922- *AmMWSc 92, WhoWest 92*
**Meiner,** Richard 1918- *IntWW 91*
**Meiner,** Sue Ellen Thompson 1943- *WhoMW 92*
**Meiners,** Henry C 1916- *AmMWSc 92*
**Meiners,** Jack Pearson 1919- *AmMWSc 92*
**Meiners,** John Alfred 1950- *WhoAmP 91*
**Meiners,** Phyllis A. 1940- *WhoFI 92, WhoMW 92*
**Meiners,** R.K. *DrAPF 91*
**Meinert,** Patricia Ann 1949- *WhoMW 92*
**Meinert,** Walter Theodore 1922- *AmMWSc 92*
**Meinertzhagen,** Daniel d1991 *Who 92N*
**Meinertzhagen,** Peter 1920- *Who 92*
**Meinertzhagen,** Peter Richard *Who 92*
**Meinhard,** James Edgar 1919- *AmMWSc 92*
**Meinhardt,** Erica *WhoEnt 92*
**Meinhardt,** Norman Anthony 1919- *AmMWSc 92*
**Meinhardt,** Peter 1903- *WrDr 92*
**Meinhold,** Arndt 1941- *WhoRel 92*

**Meinhold**, Charles Boyd 1934- *AmMWSc 92*
**Meinick**, Gary Steven 1950- *WhoFI 92*
**Meininger**, Gerald A 1952- *AmMWSc 92*
**Meininger**, Robert Allen 1938- *WhoMW 92*
**Meinke**, Alan Douglas 1963- *WhoMW 92*
**Meinke**, Geraldine Chciuk 1944- *AmMWSc 92*
**Meinke**, Peter *DrAPF 91*
**Meinke**, Peter 1932- *ConPo 91*, *IntAu&W 91*, *WrDr 92*
**Meinke**, William John 1942- *AmMWSc 92*
**Meinkoth**, Norman August 1913- *AmMWSc 92*
**Meins**, Frederick, Jr 1942- *AmMWSc 92*
**Meinschein**, Warren G 1920- *AmMWSc 92*
**Meinscher**, Kimothy Leigh 1965- *WhoFI 92*
**Meinster**, David Robert 1941- *WhoFI 92*
**Meints**, Clifford Leroy 1930- *AmMWSc 92*
**Meints**, Russel H 1939- *AmMWSc 92*
**Meints**, Vernon W 1948- *AmMWSc 92*
**Meintzer**, Roger Bruce 1927- *AmMWSc 92*
**Meinvielle**, Julio 1905-1973 *BiDExR*
**Meinwald**, Jerrold 1927- *AmMWSc 92*, *IntWW 91*
**Meinwald**, Yvonne Chu 1929- *AmMWSc 92*
**Meir**, Golda 1898-1978 *DcAmImH*, *FacFETw [port]*
**Meirion-Jones**, Gwyn Idris 1933- *Who 92*
**Meirovitch**, L 1928- *AmMWSc 92*
**Meis**, Jack Wayne 1957- *WhoMW 92*
**Meisburg**, John Marshall, Jr. 1946- *WhoAmL 92*
**Meisburg**, Steve *WhoAmP 91*
**Meisel**, Dan 1943- *AmMWSc 92*
**Meisel**, David Dering 1940- *AmMWSc 92*
**Meisel**, George Vincent 1933- *WhoAmL 92*
**Meisel**, Jerome 1934- *AmMWSc 92*
**Meisel**, Seymour Lionel 1922- *AmMWSc 92*
**Meiselman**, Herbert Joel 1940- *AmMWSc 92*
**Meiselman**, Neal J. 1953- *WhoAmL 92*
**Meiselman**, Newton 1930- *AmMWSc 92*
**Meisels**, Alexander 1926- *AmMWSc 92*
**Meisels**, Gerhard George 1931- *AmMWSc 92*
**Meisen**, Axel 1943- *AmMWSc 92*
**Meisenheimer**, John Long 1933- *AmMWSc 92*
**Meisenheimer**, Robert E 1930- *WhoIns 92*
**Meiser**, Hans 1888-1956 *EncTR 91 [port]*
**Meiser**, John H 1938- *AmMWSc 92*
**Meiser**, K D 1909- *AmMWSc 92*
**Meiser**, Michael David 1953- *AmMWSc 92*
**Meiser**, Richard Johannes 1931- *IntWW 91*
**Meisinger**, John Joseph 1945- *AmMWSc 92*
**Meiske**, Jay C 1930- *AmMWSc 92*
**Meisler**, Arnold Irwin *AmMWSc 92*
**Meisler**, Harold 1931- *AmMWSc 92*
**Meisler**, Miriam Horowitz 1943- *AmMWSc 92*
**Meisler**, Stanley 1931- *IntAu&W 91*
**Meislich**, Herbert 1920- *AmMWSc 92*
**Meisling**, Torben 1923- *AmMWSc 92*
**Meisner**, Dee Dolores Annette 1936- *WhoMW 92*
**Meisner**, Gerald Warren 1938- *AmMWSc 92*
**Meisner**, Joachim 1933- *IntWW 91*, *WhoRel 92*
**Meisner**, Lorraine Faxon 1931- *AmMWSc 92*
**Meisner**, Sanford 1905- *CurBio 91 [port]*
**Meiss**, Alfred Nelson 1918- *AmMWSc 92*
**Meiss**, James Donald *AmMWSc 92*
**Meiss**, Richard Alan 1943- *AmMWSc 92*
**Meissinger**, Hans F 1918- *AmMWSc 92*
**Meissner**, Bill *DrAPF 91*
**Meissner**, Charles Roebling, Jr 1923- *AmMWSc 92*
**Meissner**, Gerhard 1937- *AmMWSc 92*
**Meissner**, Hans Walter 1922- *AmMWSc 92*
**Meissner**, Loren Phillip 1928- *AmMWSc 92*, *WhoWest 92*
**Meissner**, Loren Phillip 1953- *WhoWest 92*
**Meissner**, Otto 1880-1953 *EncTR 91 [port]*
**Meister**, Alton 1922- *AmMWSc 92*, *IntWW 91*
**Meister**, Charles William 1940- *AmMWSc 92*
**Meister**, Frederick William 1938- *WhoAmL 92*
**Meister**, John Edward, Jr. 1956- *WhoWest 92*
**Meister**, Nancy Orear 1929- *WhoAmP 91*
**Meister**, Peter Dietrich 1920- *AmMWSc 92*
**Meister**, Robert 1925- *AmMWSc 92*
**Meister**, Verle Martin 1937- *WhoWest 92*
**Meisterman**, Bruce Ira 1946- *WhoEnt 92*
**Meistermann**, Georg *IntWW 91N*
**Meisters**, Gary Hosler 1932- *AmMWSc 92*
**Meistrich**, Marvin Lawrence 1941- *AmMWSc 92*
**Meites**, Joseph 1913- *AmMWSc 92*
**Meites**, Louis 1926- *AmMWSc 92*
**Meites**, Samuel 1921- *AmMWSc 92*
**Meitin**, Jose Garcia, Jr 1950- *AmMWSc 92*
**Meitler**, Carolyn Louise 1938- *AmMWSc 92*
**Meitner**, Lise 1878-1968 *FacFETw*
**Meitzen**, Manfred Otto 1930- *WhoRel 92*
**Meitzler**, Allen Henry 1928- *AmMWSc 92*
**Meitzler**, Carolyn Faith 1966- *WhoMW 92*
**Meixell**, Mabel Florence 1917- *WhoAmP 91*
**Meixler**, Lewis Donald 1941- *AmMWSc 92*
**Meixner**, Helen Ann Elizabeth 1941- *Who 92*
**Meixner**, Josef 1908- *IntWW 91*
**Meizel**, Stanley 1938- *AmMWSc 92*
**Mejeur**, Steven John 1955- *WhoMW 92*
**Mejia**, Alfred H. 1931- *WhoHisp 92*
**Mejia**, Barbara 1946- *WhoHisp 92*
**Mejia**, Feliciana 1943- *WhoRel 92*
**Mejia**, Georgiann Joan 1937- *WhoMW 92*
**Mejia**, Ignacia *WhoHisp 92*
**Mejia**, J. Ricardo 1961- *WhoWest 92*
**Mejia**, Joaquin 1951- *WhoHisp 92*
**Mejia**, Paul *WhoHisp 92*
**Mejia**, Paul Roman 1947- *WhoEnt 92*
**Mejia**, Santiago 1947- *WhoHisp 92*
**Mejia Rebollo**, Jose Angel 1932- *WhoHisp 92*
**Mejia Vallejo**, Manuel 1923- *DcLB 113 [port]*
**Mejias Franqui**, Diego E. 1953- *WhoHisp 92*
**Mejias-Lopez**, William 1959- *WhoHisp 92*
**Mejides**, Andres Aurelio 1939- *WhoAmP 91*
**Mekas**, Jonas 1922- *IntDcF 2-2 [port]*
**Mekhlis**, Lev Zakharovich 1889-1953 *SovUnBD*
**Mekjian**, Aram Zareh 1941- *AmMWSc 92*
**Mekk**, Nikolay Karlovich 1863-1929 *SovUnBD*
**Mekler**, Alan 1947- *AmMWSc 92*
**Mekler**, Arlen B 1932- *AmMWSc 92*
**Mel**, Howard Charles 1926- *AmMWSc 92*
**Mela**, David Jason 1958- *AmMWSc 92*
**Mela-Riker**, Leena Marja 1935- *AmMWSc 92*
**Melachrino**, George 1909-1965 *NewAmDM*
**Melack**, John Michael 1947- *AmMWSc 92*
**Melady**, Thomas 1927- *WrDr 92*
**Melady**, Thomas P *WhoAmP 91*
**Melamed**, Arthur Douglas 1945- *WhoAmL 92*
**Melamed**, David J. 1911- *IntMPA 92*
**Melamed**, Myron Roy 1927- *AmMWSc 92*
**Melamed**, Nathan T 1923- *AmMWSc 92*
**Melamed**, Richard 1952- *WhoAmL 92*
**Melamed**, Sidney 1920- *AmMWSc 92*
**Melamed**, Stephen Barry 1951- *WhoMW 92*
**Melamid**, Aleksandr 1943- *IntWW 91*
**Melan**, Melissa A 1958- *AmMWSc 92*
**Melancon**, Charles J 1947- *WhoAmP 91*
**Melancon**, Donald 1939- *WhoBlA 92*
**Melancon**, Mark J 1939- *AmMWSc 92*
**Melancon**, Norman 1939- *WhoBlA 92*
**Meland**, Bernard Eugene 1899- *WhoRel 92*
**Meland**, Margaret Welsh 1962- *WhoEnt 92*
**Melander**, Wayne Russell 1943- *AmMWSc 92*
**Melanesia**, Archbishop of 1944- *Who 92*
**Melanesia Central**, Bishop of *Who 92*
**Melania The Elder** 342?-410? *EncEarC*
**Melania The Younger** 383?-439 *EncEarC*
**Melanson**, Anne M. *WhoFI 92*
**Melashenko**, E. Lonnie 1947- *WhoRel 92*
**Melba**, Nellie 1859-1931 *FacFFTw*
**Melba**, Nellie 1861-1931 *NewAmDM*
**Melbardis**, Wolfgang Alexander 1946- *WhoAmL 92*
**Melbinger**, Michael S. 1958- *WhoAmL 92*
**Melbourne**, Archbishop of 1925- *Who 92*
**Melbourne**, Archbishop of 1929- *Who 92*
**Melbourne**, Assistant Bishops of *Who 92*
**Melby**, Arthur *WhoAmP 91*
**Melby**, Claire Arlene 1931- *WhoFI 92*
**Melby**, Edward C, Jr 1929- *AmMWSc 92*
**Melby**, James Christian 1928- *AmMWSc 92*
**Melby**, John B. 1941- *WhoEnt 92*
**Melby**, Robert Eugene 1928- *WhoAmP 91*
**Melby**, Steven Gene 1957- *WhoMW 92*
**Melcher**, Antony Henry *AmMWSc 92*
**Melcher**, Charles L 1952- *AmMWSc 92*
**Melcher**, James Russell 1936- *AmMWSc 92*
**Melcher**, John 1924- *IntWW 91*, *WhoAmP 91*
**Melcher**, Martin *LesBEnT 92*
**Melcher**, Robert Lee 1940- *AmMWSc 92*
**Melcher**, Ulrich Karl 1945- *AmMWSc 92*
**Melchers**, Georg 1906- *IntWW 91*
**Melchert**, Bruce Barnes 1934- *WhoAmP 91*
**Melchett**, Baron 1948- *Who 92*
**Melching**, J Stanley 1923- *AmMWSc 92*
**Melching**, Thomas Ray 1956- *WhoMW 92*
**Melchione**, Janet Burak 1950- *WhoIns 92*
**Melchior**, Bent 1929- *WhoRel 92*
**Melchior**, Donald L 1945- *AmMWSc 92*
**Melchior**, Ib 1917- *IntAu&W 91*, *IntMPA 92*, *WrDr 92*
**Melchior**, Ib J. *DrAPF 91*
**Melchior**, Ib Jorgen 1917- *WhoEnt 92*
**Melchior**, Jacklyn Butler 1918- *AmMWSc 92*
**Melchior**, Lauritz 1890-1973 *FacFETw*, *NewAmDM*
**Melchior**, Robert Charles 1933- *AmMWSc 92*
**Melchior**, Wayne Robert 1951- *WhoMW 92*
**Melchior-Bonnet**, Christian 1904- *Who 92*
**Melconian**, Linda Jean *WhoAmP 91*
**Melczek**, Dale J. 1938- *WhoRel 92*
**Meldau**, R F 1929- *AmMWSc 92*
**Meldman**, Burton Alan 1933- *WhoFI 92*, *WhoWest 92*
**Meldman**, Clifford Kay 1931- *WhoAmL 92*
**Meldman**, Robert Edward *WhoAmL 92*
**Meldner**, Heiner Walter 1939- *AmMWSc 92*
**Meldon**, Jerry Harris 1947- *AmMWSc 92*
**Meldrim**, John Waldo 1941- *AmMWSc 92*
**Meldrum**, Alan Hayward 1913- *AmMWSc 92*
**Meldrum**, Andrew 1909- *Who 92*
**Meldrum**, Bruce 1938- *Who 92*
**Meldrum**, James *IntAu&W 91X*, *WrDr 92*
**Meldrum**, Keith Cameron 1937- *Who 92*
**Mele**, Frank Michael 1935- *AmMWSc 92*
**Mele**, Joanne Theresa 1943- *WhoMW 92*
**Meleca**, C Benjamin 1937- *AmMWSc 92*
**Melechen**, Norman Edward 1924- *AmMWSc 92*
**Melehy**, Mahmoud Ahmed 1926- *AmMWSc 92*
**Meleisea**, F T *WhoAmP 91*
**Melen**, Ferit 1906-1988 *FacFETw*
**Melena**, Suzanne Theresa 1956- *WhoEnt 92*
**Melendez**, Al, Jr. 1932- *WhoHisp 92*
**Melendez**, Anibal *WhoHisp 92*
**Melendez**, Bill *LesBEnT 92*, *WhoHisp 92*
**Melendez**, Christian D. *WhoHisp 92*
**Melendez**, Gerardo Javier, Sr. 1959- *WhoHisp 92*
**Melendez**, Jesus Papoleto *DrAPF 91*
**Melendez**, Jose A. *WhoHisp 92*
**Melendez**, Jose Luis 1965- *WhoHisp 92*
**Melendez**, Luis Enrique 1939- *WhoAmP 91*
**Melendez**, Manuel J. 1942- *WhoHisp 92*
**Melendez**, Melinda Ramona 1948- *WhoHisp 92*
**Melendez**, Michael Paul 1952- *WhoHisp 92*
**Melendez**, Michael Sean 1962- *WhoRel 92*
**Melendez**, Mildred Corinne 1940- *WhoHisp 92*
**Melendez**, Richard 1954- *WhoHisp 92*
**Melendez**, Shirley Lola 1941- *WhoEnt 92*
**Melendez Rivera**, Hiram *WhoAmP 91*
**Melendez-Tate**, Gladys E. 1949- *WhoHisp 92*
**Melendres**, Carlos Arciaga 1939- *AmMWSc 92*
**Melendrez**, Sonny *WhoHisp 92*
**Melendy**, Mark Eastman 1955- *WhoAmP 91*
**Melendy**, Rita B 1939- *WhoAmP 91*
**Melera**, Peter William 1942- *AmMWSc 92*
**Meles Zenawi** *NewYTBS 91 [port]*
**Melese**, Gilbert B 1926- *AmMWSc 92*
**Melese**, Gilbert Bernard 1926- *WhoWest 92*
**Melfi**, Leonard 1935- *IntAu&W 91*, *WrDr 92*
**Melfi**, Leonard Theodore, Jr 1937- *AmMWSc 92*
**Melford**, Joel Eugene 1951- *WhoRel 92*
**Melford**, Michael 1944- *WhoAmL 92*
**Melford**, Sara Steck 1942- *AmMWSc 92*
**Melgar**, Myriam Del C. *WhoHisp 92*
**Melgard**, Rodney 1936- *AmMWSc 92*
**Melgarejo**, Juan Arturo 1957- *WhoMW 92*
**Melges**, Frederick Towne 1935- *AmMWSc 92*
**Melgoza Osorio**, Jose 1912- *WhoRel 92*
**Melgund**, Viscount 1953- *Who 92*
**Melhado**, L Lee 1945- *AmMWSc 92*
**Melhem**, D.H. *DrAPF 91*
**Melhorn**, Wilton Newton 1920- *AmMWSc 92*
**Melhuish**, Michael Ramsay 1932- *Who 92*
**Meli**, Alberto L G 1921- *AmMWSc 92*
**Meli**, Salvatore Andrew 1947- *WhoAmL 92*
**Melia**, Fulvio 1956- *AmMWSc 92*
**Melia**, Michael Brendan 1949- *AmMWSc 92*
**Melia**, Terence Patrick 1934- *Who 92*
**Melican**, James Patrick, Jr. 1940- *WhoAmL 92*, *WhoFI 92*
**Melich**, Michael Edward 1940- *AmMWSc 92*
**Melich**, Mitchell 1912- *WhoAmL 92*, *WhoAmP 91*
**Melich**, Tanya Marie 1936- *WhoAmP 91*
**Melicher**, Ronald William 1941- *WhoFI 92*, *WhoWest 92*
**Melick**, William F 1914- *AmMWSc 92*
**Melickian**, Gary Edward 1935- *AmMWSc 92*, *WhoFI 92*
**Melies**, Georges 1861-1938 *FacFETw*, *IntDcF 2-2 [port]*
**Melignano**, Carmine 1936- *WhoEnt 92*, *WhoFI 92*
**Melik-Pashaev**, Aleksandr Shamil'evich 1905-1964 *SovUnBD*
**Melikishvili**, Georgiy Aleksandrovich 1918- *IntWW 91*
**Melikov**, Arif Dzhangirovich 1933- *SovUnBD*
**Melikova**, Genia *WhoEnt 92*
**Melillo**, David Gregory 1947- *AmMWSc 92*
**Melin**, Brian Edward 1943- *AmMWSc 92*
**Melin**, Robert Arthur 1940- *WhoAmL 92*, *WhoMW 92*
**Meline**, Robert S 1919- *AmMWSc 92*
**Melino**, James John 1957- *WhoAmL 92*
**Melinsky**, Hugh 1924- *Who 92*
**Melinson**, James Robert 1939- *WhoAmL 92*
**Melio**, Anthony 1932- *WhoAmP 91*
**Melis**, Anastasios 1947- *AmMWSc 92*
**Melish**, John 1771-1822 *BenetAL 91*, *BiInAmS*
**Melissinos**, Adrian Constantin 1929- *AmMWSc 92*
**Melitius of Antioch** d381 *EncEarC*
**Melitius of Lycopolis** *EncEarC*
**Melito** *EncEarC*
**Meliton** 1913-1989 *DcEcMov*
**Melius**, Paul 1927- *AmMWSc 92*
**Melkanoff**, Michel Allan 1923- *AmMWSc 92*
**Melko**, Michaela 1938- *WhoMW 92*
**Melkonian**, Edward 1920- *AmMWSc 92*
**Mell**, Galen P 1934- *AmMWSc 92*
**Mell**, Patrick Hues 1850-1918 *BiInAmS*
**Mell**, Richard F 1939- *WhoAmP 91*
**Mella**, Arthur J 1937- *WhoIns 92*
**Mella**, Arthur John 1937- *WhoFI 92*
**Mella**, Diego L. 1949- *WhoHisp 92*
**Mellaart**, James 1925- *Who 92*
**Mellado**, Carmela Castaneda *WhoHisp 92*
**Mellado**, Raymond G. 1948- *WhoHisp 92*
**Mellanby**, Kenneth 1908- *IntWW 91*, *Who 92*, *WrDr 92*
**Melland**, Sylvia 1929- *TwCPaSc*
**Mellander**, G. A. 1935- *WrDr 92*
**Mellander**, Gustavo A. *WhoHisp 92*
**Mellars**, Paul Anthony 1939- *Who 92*
**Mellberg**, James Richard 1932- *AmMWSc 92*
**Mellberg**, Leonard Evert 1935- *AmMWSc 92*
**Mellberg**, William Franklin 1952- *WhoMW 92*
**Melle**, Chris F. 1956- *WhoWest 92*
**Mellegard**, Kirby Dean 1949- *WhoMW 92*
**Mellen**, Grenville 1799-1841 *BenetAL 91*
**Mellen**, Joan 1941- *IntAu&W 91*, *WrDr 92*
**Mellen**, Kirk A 1939- *WhoIns 92*
**Mellen**, Kirk Anthony 1939- *WhoFI 92*
**Mellen**, Robert Harrison 1919- *AmMWSc 92*
**Mellen**, Walter Roy 1928- *AmMWSc 92*
**Mellenbruch**, Giles Edward 1911- *WhoEnt 92*
**Mellencamp**, John 1951- *WhoEnt 92*
**Meller**, Norman 1913- *WrDr 92*
**Mellers**, Wilfrid 1914- *ConCom 92*, *WrDr 92*
**Mellers**, Wilfrid Howard 1914- *IntAu&W 91*, *IntWW 91*, *Who 92*
**Mellersh**, Francis Richard Lee 1922- *Who 92*
**Melles**, Carl 1926- *IntWW 91*
**Mellett**, James Silvan 1936- *AmMWSc 92*
**Mellette**, David C. 1909- *WhoBlA 92*
**Mellette**, Russell Ramsey, Jr 1927- *AmMWSc 92*
**Melley**, Steven Michael 1950- *WhoAmL 92*
**Melley**, William J., III 1953- *WhoAmL 92*
**Mellgren**, Ronald Lee 1946- *AmMWSc 92*
**Melli**, Marygold Shire 1926- *WhoAmL 92*
**Melliere**, Alvin L 1939- *AmMWSc 92*
**Mellies**, Margot J 1942- *AmMWSc 92*
**Mellin**, Gilbert Wylie 1925- *AmMWSc 92*

Mellin, James Patrick 1935- WhoMW 92
Mellin, Theodore Nelson 1937- AmMWSc 92
Melling, Cecil Thomas 1899- Who 92
Mellinger, Clair 1942- AmMWSc 92
Mellinger, Debra Keen 1954- WhoIns 92
Mellinger, Frederick 1914-1990 AnObit 1990
Mellinger, Gary Andreas 1943- AmMWSc 92
Mellinger, Larry K 1944- WhoAmP 91
Mellinger, Michael Vance 1945- AmMWSc 92
Mellini, Lou WhoFI 92
Mellink, Machteld Johanna 1917- IntWW 91
Mellinkoff, Sherman Mussoff 1920- AmMWSc 92
Mellins, Harry Zachary 1921- AmMWSc 92
Mellins, Robert B 1928- AmMWSc 92
Mellis, Margaret 1914- TwCPaSc
Mellish Who 92
Mellish, Baron 1913- IntWW 91, Who 92
Mellish, Gordon Hartley 1940- WhoFI 92
Mellish, John Mark 1952- WhoRel 92
Mellits, E David 1937- AmMWSc 92
Mellitt, Brian 1940- Who 92
Mellizo, Carlos 1942- WhoHisp 92
Mellman, Leonard 1924- WhoFI 92
Mellman, Myer W. 1917- WhoMW 92
Mellnas, Arne 1933- ConCom 92
Mellnik, David Carl 1955- WhoRel 92
Mello, Dawn 1938?- News 92-2 [port]
Mello, Donald R. 1934- WhoWest 92
Mello, Donald Ray 1934- WhoAmP 91
Mello, Henry J 1924- WhoAmP 91
Mello, Nancy K 1935- AmMWSc 92
Mello, Renee Lorraine 1964- WhoWest 92
Melloan, Erma Jean 1937- WhoAmP 91
Melloch, Michael Raymond 1953- AmMWSc 92
Mellon, Andrew 1855-1937 RComAH
Mellon, Andrew 1885-1937 ThHElm
Mellon, Andrew William 1855-1937 AmPolLe, FacFETw
Mellon, Bradley Floyd 1949- WhoRel 92
Mellon, Campbell A. 1876-1955 TwCPaSc
Mellon, David Duane 1931- WhoRel 92
Mellon, Dawn Marie 1964- WhoMW 92
Mellon, DeForest, Jr 1934- AmMWSc 92
Mellon, Edward Knox, Jr 1936- AmMWSc 92
Mellon, George Barry 1931- AmMWSc 92
Mellon, James 1929- IntWW 91, Who 92
Mellon, Paul 1907- IntWW 91, NewYTBS 91 [port], ThHElm, Who 92
Mellon, Wesley Jon 1945- WhoWest 92
Mellon, William Knox 1925- WhoWest 92
Mellon, William Robert 1957- WhoFI 92
Mellor, Arthur M 1942- AmMWSc 92
Mellor, David 1930- DcTwDes, Who 92
Mellor, David 1949- IntWW 91
Mellor, David Bridgwood 1929- AmMWSc 92
Mellor, David Hugh 1938- IntWW 91, Who 92
Mellor, David John 1940- Who 92
Mellor, David John 1949- Who 92
Mellor, Derrick 1926- Who 92
Mellor, George Lincoln, Jr 1929- AmMWSc 92
Mellor, Hugh Wright 1920- Who 92
Mellor, James Frederick McLean 1912- Who 92
Mellor, James Robb 1930- WhoFI 92, WhoMW 92
Mellor, John 1933- AmMWSc 92
Mellor, John Francis d1990 Who 92N
Mellor, John W. 1928- WrDr 92
Mellor, John Walter 1927- Who 92
Mellor, John Williams 1928- AmMWSc 92, WhoFI 92
Mellor, Kenneth Wilson Who 92
Mellor, Malcolm 1933- AmMWSc 92
Mellor, Robert Sydney 1931- AmMWSc 92
Mellor, Ronald William 1930- Who 92
Mellors, Alan 1940- AmMWSc 92
Mellors, Robert Charles 1916- AmMWSc 92
Mellott, Cloyd Rowe 1923- WhoAmL 92
Mellott, Leland DrAPF 91
Mellott, Robert Vernon 1928- WhoFI 92, WhoMW 92
Mellow, Ernest W 1918- AmMWSc 92
Mellow, James R. 1926- DcLB 111 [port], IntAu&W 91
Mellow, Mary Anne 1957- WhoAmL 92
Mellow, Robert James 1942- WhoAmP 91
Mellows, Anthony 1936- WrDr 92
Mellows, Anthony Roger 1936- Who 92
Mellum, Gale Robert 1942- WhoAmL 92
Melly, George 1926- IntAu&W 91, Who 92, WrDr 92
Mellyne, Robert 1666?-1708? DcNCBi 4
Melman, Philip Steven 1954- WhoWest 92
Melman, Richard WhoFI 92, WhoMW 92
Melmon, Kenneth 1934- IntWW 91
Melmon, Kenneth Lloyd 1934- AmMWSc 92
Melmoth, Christopher George Frederick F 1912- Who 92
Melngailis, Ivars 1933- AmMWSc 92
Melngailis, John 1939- AmMWSc 92
Melnichenko, Afanasiy Kondratevich 1923- IntWW 91
Melnick, Daniel 1934- IntMPA 92
Melnick, Daniel 1942- AmMWSc 92
Melnick, David DrAPF 91
Melnick, Edward Lawrence 1938- AmMWSc 92, WhoFI 92
Melnick, John Latane 1935- WhoAmP 91
Melnick, Joseph Jamie 1958- WhoMW 92
Melnick, Joseph Louis 1914- AmMWSc 92
Melnick, Laben Morton 1926- AmMWSc 92
Melnick, Robert Russell 1956- WhoAmL 92
Melnick, Ronald L 1943- AmMWSc 92
Melnick, Rowell Shep 1951- WhoAmP 91
Melnick, Roy E 1954- WhoAmP 91
Melnick, Saul IntMPA 92
Melnick, Vijaya L AmMWSc 92
Melnicove, Mark DrAPF 91
Melnik, Bertha WhoEnt 92
Melnik, Selinda A. 1951- WhoAmL 92
Melniker, Benjamin IntMPA 92
Melnikoff, Sarah Ann 1936- WhoMW 92
Melnikov, Aleksandr Grigorevich 1930- IntWW 91
Mel'nikov, Konstantin Stepanovich 1890-1974 SovUnBD
Mel'nikov, Leonid Grigor'evich 1906- SovUnBD
Melnikov, Vitaly Vyacheslavovich 1928- IntWW 91
Melnikov, Vladimir Ivanovich 1935- IntWW 91
Mel'nikov, Yakov Fedorovich 1896-1960 SovUnBD
Melnizky, Walter 1928- IntWW 91
Melnykovych, George 1924- AmMWSc 92
Meloan, Clifton E 1931- AmMWSc 92
Meloan, Taylor Wells 1919- WhoWest 92
Meloche, Henry Paul 1928- AmMWSc 92
Melodia, Paul Vincent 1939- WhoAmL 92
Melone, Joseph J 1931- WhoIns 92
Melone, Joseph James 1931- WhoFI 92
Melone, Victor Joseph 1933- WhoFI 92
Meloni, Edward George 1932- AmMWSc 92
Meloon, Daniel Thomas, Jr 1935- AmMWSc 92
Meloon, David Rand 1948- AmMWSc 92
Meloon, Robert A. 1928- WhoMW 92
Melosh, Henry Jay, IV 1947- AmMWSc 92, WhoWest 92
Melott, Ronald K. 1939- WhoWest 92
Melouk, Hassan A 1941- AmMWSc 92
Meloy, Carl Ridge 1912- AmMWSc 92
Meloy, Peter Michael 1942- WhoAmP 91
Meloy, Thomas Phillips 1925- AmMWSc 92
Melrose, Denis Graham 1921- Who 92
Melrose, Donald Blair 1940- IntWW 91
Melrose, James C 1922- AmMWSc 92
Melrose, Richard B 1949- AmMWSc 92
Melrose, Thomas S. 1922- WhoBlA 92
Melsa, James Louis 1938- AmMWSc 92
Melser, Harold Alfred 1942- WhoMW 92
Melsheimer, Frank Murphy 1940- AmMWSc 92
Melsheimer, Friedrich Valentin 1749-1814 BiInAmS
Melsheimer, Harold 1927- WhoWest 92
Melsheimer, Stephen Samuel 1943- AmMWSc 92
Melson, Gordon Anthony 1937- AmMWSc 92
Melson, Richard David 1957- WhoRel 92
Melsop, James William 1939- WhoFI 92
Melter, Robert Alan 1935- AmMWSc 92
Melton, Andrew Joseph, Jr. 1920- WhoFI 92
Melton, Arthur Richard 1943- AmMWSc 92
Melton, Barry 1947- WhoAmL 92
Melton, Billy Alexander, Jr 1932- AmMWSc 92
Melton, Bob 1943- WhoAmP 91
Melton, Bryant 1940- WhoAmP 91, WhoBlA 92
Melton, Buckner Franklin 1923- WhoAmP 91
Melton, Carlton E, Jr 1924- AmMWSc 92
Melton, Charles Estel 1924- AmMWSc 92
Melton, David 1934- IntAu&W 91
Melton, Emory L 1923- WhoAmP 91
Melton, Emory Leon 1923- WhoMW 92
Melton, Frank E. WhoBlA 92
Melton, Frank LeRoy 1921- WhoBlA 92
Melton, Gary Bentley 1952- WhoMW 92
Melton, Gary Warren 1952- WhoWest 92
Melton, Grant Kemp 1929- WhoAmP 91
Melton, Harry S. 1915- WhoBlA 92
Melton, Howell Webster 1923- WhoAmL 92
Melton, James Ray 1940- AmMWSc 92
Melton, John Gordon 1942- WhoWest 92
Melton, Johnny 1952- WhoRel 92
Melton, Laurie Alison 1964- WhoFI 92
Melton, Lee Joseph, III 1944- AmMWSc 92
Melton, Lynn Ayres 1944- AmMWSc 92
Melton, Margaret Belle 1925- WhoAmP 91
Melton, Marilyn Anders 1944- AmMWSc 92
Melton, Maurice Edward 1925- WhoFI 92
Melton, Michael Eric 1958- WhoAmL 92
Melton, Rex Eugene 1921- AmMWSc 92
Melton, Richard H WhoAmP 91
Melton, Sid 1925- WhoEnt 92
Melton, Stanley Emory 1951- WhoMW 92
Melton, Stephen Reid 1949- WhoFI 92
Melton, Thomas Mason 1927- AmMWSc 92
Melton, Wade Anthony 1957- WhoRel 92
Melton, William Allen Bill, Sr. 1939- WhoFI 92
Melton, William Grover, Jr 1923- AmMWSc 92
Meltz, Martin Lowell 1942- AmMWSc 92
Meltzer, Alan David 1963- WhoAmL 92
Meltzer, Alan Sidney 1932- AmMWSc 92
Meltzer, Allan H. 1928- WhoFI 92
Meltzer, Arnold Charles 1936- AmMWSc 92
Meltzer, Daniel J. 1951- WhoAmL 92
Meltzer, David DrAPF 91
Meltzer, David 1937- ConAu 35NR, ConPo 91, TwCSFW 91, WrDr 92
Meltzer, Debra Marie 1954- WhoFI 92
Meltzer, Herbert Lewis 1921- AmMWSc 92
Meltzer, Herbert Yale 1937- AmMWSc 92
Meltzer, Jay H. 1944- WhoFI 92
Meltzer, Larry Alan 1959- WhoFI 92
Meltzer, Martin Isaac AmMWSc 92
Meltzer, Milton 1915- Au&Arts 8 [port]
Meltzer, Monte Sean 1943- AmMWSc 92
Meltzer, Richard S 1942- AmMWSc 92
Meltzer, Richard Stuart 1948- AmMWSc 92
Meltzer, Samuel James 1851-1920 BiInAmS
Meltzer, Stephen Elliott 1948- WhoWest 92
Meltzer, Yale Leon 1931- WhoFI 92
Meltzoff, Andrew N. 1950- WhoWest 92
Meluch, R M 1956- TwCSFW 91, WrDr 92
Melveger, Alvin Joseph 1937- AmMWSc 92
Melvill Jones, Geoffrey 1923- IntWW 91, Who 92
Melville Who 92
Melville, Viscount 1937- Who 92
Melville, Anne IntAu&W 91X, WrDr 92
Melville, Anthony Edwin 1929- Who 92
Melville, Arabella 1948- WrDr 92
Melville, Arthur 1855-1904 TwCPaSc
Melville, Donald Burton 1914- AmMWSc 92
Melville, George Wallace 1841-1912 BiInAmS
Melville, Harry 1908- IntWW 91, Who 92
Melville, Herman 1819-1891 BenetAL 91, RComAH
Melville, James Who 92
Melville, James 1931- IntAu&W 91
Melville, Jean-Pierre 1917-1973 IntDcF 2-2 [port]
Melville, Jennie IntAu&W 91X, WrDr 92
Melville, Joel George 1943- AmMWSc 92
Melville, John 1902-1986 TwCPaSc
Melville, John Akin 1947- WhoFI 92
Melville, John W. 1909- WhoAmL 92
Melville, Leslie Galfreid 1902- IntWW 91, Who 92
Melville, Margarita WhoHisp 92
Melville, Marjorie Harris 1927- AmMWSc 92
Melville, Robert S 1913- AmMWSc 92
Melville, Ronald 1912- Who 92
Melville, William George 1927- WhoMW 92
Melville-Ross, Timothy David 1944- Who 92
Melvin, Alonzo Dorus 1862-1917 BiInAmS
Melvin, Billy Alfred 1929- WhoMW 92, WhoRel 92
Melvin, Bob Raymond 1934- WhoRel 92
Melvin, Cruse Douglas 1942- AmMWSc 92
Melvin, Donald Walter 1929- AmMWSc 92
Melvin, Dorothy Mae AmMWSc 92
Melvin, E A 1919- AmMWSc 92
Melvin, Gregory Mark 1956- WhoFI 92
Melvin, Harold James 1941- WhoBlA 92
Melvin, John A 1944- WhoIns 92
Melvin, John L 1935- AmMWSc 92
Melvin, John Turcan 1916- Who 92
Melvin, Jonathan David 1947- AmMWSc 92
Melvin, Joseph M. 1950- WhoFI 92
Melvin, June Louise 1960- WhoAmL 92
Melvin, Kenneth Ronald 1952- WhoAmP 91
Melvin, Lawrence Sherman, Jr 1947- AmMWSc 92
Melvin, Mael Avramy 1913- AmMWSc 92
Melvin, Stewart W 1941- AmMWSc 92
Melvin, Theresa J WhoAmP 91
Melvold, Roger Wayne 1946- AmMWSc 92
Melvyn Howe, George Who 92
Melwood, Mary IntAu&W 91, WrDr 92
Melzack, Ronald 1929- AmMWSc 92, WrDr 92
Melzer, Simon 1945- WhoEnt 92
Melzer, William C. WhoFI 92, WhoMW 92
Melzoni, Thomas, Jr. 1952- WhoRel 92
Membiela, Roymi Victoria 1957- WhoHisp 92
Memedova, Mary 1933- WhoWest 92
Memeger, Wesley, Jr 1939- AmMWSc 92
Memel, Sherwin Leonard 1930- WhoAmL 92
Memmi, Albert 1920- IntWW 91, LiExTwC
Memminger, Christopher Gustavus 1803-1888 DcNCBi 4
Memmott, David DrAPF 91
Memory, Jasper Durham 1936- AmMWSc 92
Memphis Minnie 1896-1973 NewAmDM
Memphis Slim 1915- NewAmDM
Men Huifeng 1937- IntWW 91
Mena, David L. 1945- WhoHisp 92
Mena, Roberto Abraham 1946- AmMWSc 92
Mena, Xavier WhoHisp 92
Mena De Quevedo, Margarita IntWW 91
Menahan, William Thomas 1935- WhoAmP 91
Menaker, Edward Goward 1919- WhoAmP 91
Menaker, Frank H., Jr. 1940- WhoAmL 92, WhoFI 92
Menaker, Jerome Seymour 1916- WhoMW 92
Menaker, Lewis 1942- AmMWSc 92
Menaker, Michael 1934- AmMWSc 92
Menaker, Richard Glen 1947- WhoAmL 92
Menander EncEarC
Menapace, Lawrence William 1937- AmMWSc 92
Menard, Albert Louis 1937- WhoFI 92
Menard, Albert Robert, III 1943- AmMWSc 92
Menard, Curt WhoAmP 91
Menard, David W. 1938- WhoFI 92
Menard, E. Dean 1933- WhoWest 92
Menard, Elizabeth Delia 1940- WhoRel 92
Menard, Jayne Bush 1946- WhoFI 92
Menard, Joan M 1935- WhoAmP 91
Menard, Orville D. 1933- WrDr 92
Menard, Orville Duane 1933- WhoMW 92
Menard, Rene R 1957- WhoAmP 91
Menas EncEarC
Menas of Constantinople d552 EncEarC
Menashe, Samuel DrAPF 91
Menashe, Victor D 1929- AmMWSc 92
Menashi, Jameel 1938- AmMWSc 92
Menatonon DcNCBi 4
Mencer, Charles David 1944- WhoIns 92
Mencer, Ernest James 1945- WhoBlA 92
Mencer, Glenn Everell 1925- WhoAmL 92
Mencer, Jetta 1959- WhoAmP 91
Mencer, Nellie T 1924- WhoAmP 91
Menchel, Donald 1932- WhoEnt 92
Mencher, Stuart Alan 1939- WhoFI 92
Mencin, Alan Jay 1957- WhoWest 92
Mencken, H. L. 1880-1956 BenetAL 91, RComAH
Mencken, Henry Louis 1880-1956 FacFETw [port]
Mencl, John Richard 1956- WhoAmL 92
Menco, Bernard 1946- AmMWSc 92
Menczel, Jehuda H 1936- AmMWSc 92
Mendal, Geoffrey Owen 1961- WhoWest 92
Mendales, Richard Ephraim 1950- WhoAmL 92
Mendall, Howard Lewis 1909- AmMWSc 92
Mendana de Neira, Alvaro de 1542-1595 HisDSpE
Mende, Erich 1916- IntWW 91, Who 92
Mende, Thomas Julius 1922- AmMWSc 92
Mendel, Arthur 1931- AmMWSc 92
Mendel, Barry M. 1950- WhoMW 92
Mendel, Elizabeth Ullmer 1957- WhoAmL 92
Mendel, Frank C 1946- AmMWSc 92
Mendel, Gerald Alan 1929- AmMWSc 92
Mendel, Jerry M 1938- AmMWSc 92
Mendel, John Richard 1936- AmMWSc 92
Mendel, Julius Louis 1925- AmMWSc 92
Mendel, Mark DrAPF 91

**Mendel**, Maurice I 1942- AmMWSc 92
**Mendel**, Roberta DrAPF 91
**Mendel**, Verne Edward 1923- AmMWSc 92
**Mendel**, Werner Max 1927- AmMWSc 92
**Mendelberg**, Hava Eva 1942- WhoMW 92
**Mendelhall**, Von Thatcher 1937- AmMWSc 92
**Mendell**, Henry Ross 1950- WhoWest 92
**Mendell**, Jay Stanley 1936- AmMWSc 92
**Mendell**, Lorne Michael 1941- AmMWSc 92
**Mendell**, Nancy Role 1944- AmMWSc 92
**Mendell**, Rosalind B 1920- AmMWSc 92
**Mendelowitz**, Allan Irwin 1943- WhoFI 92
**Mendelowitz**, Daniel M. 1905-1980 ConAu 135
**Mendelsohn**, Charles Jastrow 1880-1939 DcNCBi 4
**Mendelsohn**, Erich 1887-1953 DcTwDes, FacFETw
**Mendelsohn**, Jack 1918- WhoRel 92
**Mendelsohn**, Lawrence Barry 1934- AmMWSc 92
**Mendelsohn**, Loren David 1954- WhoMW 92
**Mendelsohn**, Louis Benjamin 1948- WhoFI 92
**Mendelsohn**, Marshall H 1946- AmMWSc 92
**Mendelsohn**, Martin 1935- IntAu&W 91, WrDr 92
**Mendelsohn**, Martin 1942- WhoAmL 92
**Mendelsohn**, Morris A 1928- AmMWSc 92
**Mendelsohn**, Mortimer Lester 1925- AmMWSc 92
**Mendelsohn**, Nathan Saul 1917- AmMWSc 92
**Mendelsohn**, Richard 1946- AmMWSc 92
**Mendelsohn**, Samuel 1850-1922 DcNCBi 4
**Mendelsohn**, Walter 1897- WhoAmL 92
**Mendelsohn**, Zehavah Whitney 1956- WhoMW 92
**Mendelson**, Bert 1926- AmMWSc 92
**Mendelson**, Carl Victor 1953- AmMWSc 92
**Mendelson**, Carole Ruth AmMWSc 92
**Mendelson**, David Frey 1925- WhoMW 92
**Mendelson**, Elliott 1931- AmMWSc 92
**Mendelson**, Emanuel Share 1909- AmMWSc 92
**Mendelson**, Jack H 1929- AmMWSc 92
**Mendelson**, Kenneth Samuel 1933- AmMWSc 92
**Mendelson**, Lee, and Melendez, Bill LesBEnT 92
**Mendelson**, Lee M. 1933- WhoEnt 92
**Mendelson**, Leonard M. 1923- WhoAmL 92, WhoFI 92
**Mendelson**, Martin 1937- AmMWSc 92
**Mendelson**, Morris 1922- WhoFI 92, WrDr 92
**Mendelson**, Myer 1920- AmMWSc 92
**Mendelson**, Neil Harland 1937- AmMWSc 92
**Mendelson**, Robert Alexander, Jr 1941- AmMWSc 92
**Mendelson**, Robert Allen 1930- AmMWSc 92
**Mendelson**, Steven Earle 1948- WhoAmL 92
**Mendelson**, Wilford Lee 1937- AmMWSc 92
**Mendelssohn**, Fanny 1805-1847 NewAmDM
**Mendelssohn**, Felix 1809-1847 NewAmDM
**Mendelssohn**, Moses 1729-1786 BlkwCEP
**Mendelssohn**, Roy 1949- AmMWSc 92
**Mendelssohn-Bartholdy**, Fanny 1805-1847 NewAmDM
**Mendelssohn-Bartholdy**, Felix 1809-1847 NewAmDM
**Mendelwager**, Greg H. 1950- WhoEnt 92
**Mendenhall**, Carrol Clay 1916- WhoWest 92
**Mendenhall**, Charles L 1931- AmMWSc 92
**Mendenhall**, Corwin 1916- ConAu 134
**Mendenhall**, George David 1945- AmMWSc 92
**Mendenhall**, George Emery 1916- WhoRel 92, WrDr 92
**Mendenhall**, John Rufus 1948- WhoBlA 92
**Mendenhall**, John Ryan 1928- WhoAmL 92, WhoFI 92
**Mendenhall**, Laura Shelton 1946- WhoRel 92
**Mendenhall**, N. Dale 1951- WhoRel 92
**Mendenhall**, Nereus 1819-1893 DcNCBi 4
**Mendenhall**, Robert Alan 1952- WhoRel 92
**Mendenhall**, Robert Vernon 1920- AmMWSc 92, WhoMW 92
**Mendenhall**, William, III 1925- AmMWSc 92
**Mender**, Mona Siegler 1926- WhoEnt 92
**Menderes**, Adnan 1899-1961 FacFETw
**Mendes**, Alfred H. 1897- LiExTwC
**Mendes**, Donna M. 1951- WhoBlA 92
**Mendes**, Helen Althia 1935- WhoBlA 92
**Mendes**, Henry Pereira 1852-1937 RelLAm 91
**Mendes**, Robert Laurence 1947- WhoIns 92
**Mendes**, Robert W 1938- AmMWSc 92
**Mendes-France**, Pierre 1907-1982 FacFETw
**Mendez**, Albert Orlando 1935- WhoFI 92
**Mendez**, Alfred WhoHisp 92
**Mendez**, C. Teresa 1960- WhoHisp 92
**Mendez**, Celestino Galo 1944- WhoWest 92
**Mendez**, Celia Marie 1965- WhoAmL 92
**Mendez**, Charlotte DrAPF 91
**Mendez**, David B. 1960- WhoHisp 92
**Mendez**, Elena 1956- WhoHisp 92
**Mendez**, Emilio Eugenio 1949- AmMWSc 92
**Mendez**, Eustorgio 1927- AmMWSc 92
**Mendez**, George 1956- WhoHisp 92
**Mendez**, Hector WhoHisp 92
**Mendez**, Hermann 1949- WhoHisp 92
**Mendez**, Hugh B. 1933- WhoBlA 92
**Mendez**, Hugo Saul 1954- WhoHisp 92
**Mendez**, Ileana Maria 1952- WhoEnt 92, WhoHisp 92
**Mendez**, Jana 1944- WhoAmP 91
**Mendez**, Jesus 1951- WhoHisp 92
**Mendez**, Julio Enrique 1948- WhoHisp 92
**Mendez**, Julio F. 1960- WhoHisp 92
**Mendez**, Mauricio David 1944- WhoHisp 92
**Mendez**, Michelle Annette 1961- WhoAmL 92
**Mendez**, Miguel A. WhoHisp 92
**Mendez**, Miguel Morales 1930- WhoHisp 92
**Mendez**, Olga WhoAmP 91, WhoHisp 92
**Mendez**, Rafael WhoHisp 92
**Mendez**, Ramon Ignacio 1775-1839 HisDSpE
**Mendez**, Raul H. WhoHisp 92
**Mendez**, Raymond A. 1947- SmATA 66
**Mendez**, Rogelio Francisco, Jr. 1948- WhoHisp 92
**Mendez**, Ruben Homero 1957- WhoHisp 92
**Mendez**, Thomas 1952- WhoRel 92
**Mendez**, Veronica 1942- WhoHisp 92
**Mendez**, Victor Manuel 1944- AmMWSc 92, WhoHisp 92
**Mendez**, William, Jr. 1948- WhoAmL 92, WhoHisp 92
**Mendez**, Yasmine M. 1960- WhoHisp 92
**Mendez-Longoria**, Miguel Angel 1942- WhoAmL 92
**Mendez Montenegro**, Julio Cesar 1915- IntWW 91
**Mendez-Polo**, Ceferino Anastasio 1913- WhoHisp 92
**Mendez Santiago**, Edwin 1954- WhoHisp 92
**Mendez-Smith**, Freda Ann 1939- WhoHisp 92
**Mendez Urrutia**, F. Vinicio 1957-1991 WhoHisp 92N
**Mendham**, Peter Miller 1944- WhoRel 92
**Mendham**, Robert William, Jr. 1956- WhoMW 92
**Mendicino**, Jane 1934- WhoAmP 91
**Mendicino**, Joseph Frank 1930- AmMWSc 92
**Mendieta**, Ana 1948-1985 WorArt 1980
**Mendieta**, Geronimo de 1525-1604 HisDSpE
**Mendillo**, Michael 1944- AmMWSc 92
**Mendini**, Douglas A. DrAPF 91
**Mendiola**, James Masga 1949- WhoAmP 91
**Mendiola-McLain**, Emma Lilia 1956- WhoHisp 92
**Mendis**, Devamitta Asoka 1936- AmMWSc 92
**Mendis**, Eustace Francis 1937- AmMWSc 92
**Mendis**, Vernon Lorraine Benjamin 1925- IntWW 91, Who 92
**Mendius**, Patricia Dodd Winter 1924- WhoWest 92
**Mendivil**, Fernando Quihuiz 1937- WhoHisp 92
**Mendizabal**, Maritza S. 1941- WhoHisp 92
**Mendl**, Lady DcTwDes
**Mendl**, James Henry Embleton 1927- Who 92
**Mendler**, Oliver J 1927- AmMWSc 92
**Mendlowitz**, Harold 1927- AmMWSc 92
**Mendlowitz**, Milton 1906- AmMWSc 92
**Mendosa**, Rick 1935- WhoHisp 92
**Mendoza**, Agapito 1946- WhoHisp 92
**Mendoza**, Al, Jr. 1943- WhoHisp 92
**Mendoza**, Antonio de 1490-1552 HisDSpE
**Mendoza**, Arturo Eugenio 1954- WhoWest 92
**Mendoza**, Candelario Jose 1919- WhoHisp 92
**Mendoza**, Celso Enriquez 1933- AmMWSc 92
**Mendoza**, David Vasquez 1948- WhoHisp 92
**Mendoza**, Ecce Iei, II 1963- WhoHisp 92
**Mendoza**, Ernest A. WhoHisp 92
**Mendoza**, Eva 1950- WhoHisp 92
**Mendoza**, Fernando Sanchez 1948- WhoHisp 92
**Mendoza**, George 1934- WhoHisp 92
**Mendoza**, George 1955- WhoHisp 92
**Mendoza**, George John 1955- WhoWest 92
**Mendoza**, Gilbert Reyes 1939- WhoHisp 92
**Mendoza**, Harry R. 1953- WhoHisp 92
**Mendoza**, Henry C. WhoHisp 92
**Mendoza**, Henry Trevino, III 1947- WhoHisp 92
**Mendoza**, Juan A. 1955- WhoHisp 92
**Mendoza**, Julian Nava 1934- WhoHisp 92
**Mendoza**, June IntWW 91
**Mendoza**, June Yvonne Who 92
**Mendoza**, Leticia Sanchez 1956- WhoHisp 92
**Mendoza**, Lisa 1958- WhoHisp 92
**Mendoza**, Luis WhoHisp 92
**Mendoza**, Lydia 1916- WhoHisp 92
**Mendoza**, Maria Luisa 1938- SpAmWW
**Mendoza**, Maurice 1921- Who 92
**Mendoza**, Michael Dennis 1944- WhoHisp 92
**Mendoza**, Nicolas WhoHisp 92
**Mendoza**, O. Nicholas 1941- WhoWest 92
**Mendoza**, Pablo, Jr. WhoHisp 92
**Mendoza**, Pedro de 1487- HisDSpE
**Mendoza**, Roberto G., Jr. 1945- WhoFI 92
**Mendoza**, Sylvia D. 1954- WhoHisp 92
**Mendoza**, Vivian P. Who 92
**Mendoza-Acosta**, Felix 1929- Who 92
**Mendoza Waszkowski**, Denise Yvette WhoEnt 92
**Mendrinas**, Konstantine 1943- WhoRel 92
**Menduke**, Hyman 1921- AmMWSc 92
**Mendybaev**, Marat Samievich 1936- SovUnBD
**Mendybayev**, Marat Samiyevich 1936- IntWW 91
**Mendyk**, Stan A.E. 1953- ConAu 135
**Mendyka**, Walter Adam, Jr. 1955- WhoMW 92
**Menebroker**, Ann DrAPF 91
**Meneely**, David Mark 1952- WhoMW 92
**Meneely**, George Rodney 1911- AmMWSc 92
**Menees**, James H 1929- AmMWSc 92
**Menefee**, Emory 1929- AmMWSc 92
**Menefee**, Frederick Lewis 1932- WhoMW 92
**Menefee**, Max Gene 1925- AmMWSc 92
**Menefee**, Robert William 1929- AmMWSc 92
**Menefee**, Samuel Pyeatt 1950- WhoAmL 92, WhoFI 92
**Meneghetti**, David 1923- AmMWSc 92
**Menegos**, Melanie Marie 1963- WhoMW 92
**Menell**, Peter Seth 1958- WhoWest 92
**Menem**, Carlos Saul 1935- IntWW 91
**Menemencioglu**, Turgut 1914- IntWW 91, Who 92
**Menen**, Aubrey 1912- IntAu&W 91
**Menendez**, Albert J 1942- IntAu&W 91, WrDr 92
**Menendez**, Albert John 1942- WhoHisp 92
**Menendez**, Ana Maria 1970- WhoHisp 92
**Menendez**, Carlos 1938- WhoHisp 92
**Menendez**, Catherine A 1959- WhoIns 92
**Menendez**, Jose 1957- WhoHisp 92
**Menendez**, Manuel, Jr. 1947- WhoAmL 92
**Menendez**, Manuel E. WhoHisp 92
**Menendez**, Manuel Gaspar 1935- AmMWSc 92
**Menendez**, Maria de los Angeles 1950- WhoHisp 92
**Menendez**, Michael Joseph 1949- WhoHisp 92
**Menendez**, Robert 1954- WhoAmP 91, WhoHisp 92
**Menendez-Monroig**, Jose M 1917- WhoAmP 91
**Menes**, Meir 1925- AmMWSc 92
**Menes**, Pauline H 1924- WhoAmP 91
**Meneses**, Adalberto 1926- WhoHisp 92
**Meneses**, Walter Eduardo 1953- WhoHisp 92
**Menevia**, Bishop of 1929- Who 92
**Meneweather**, Earl W. 1917- WhoBlA 92
**Menez**, Ernani Guingona 1931- AmMWSc 92
**Menezes**, Jose Piedade Caetano Agnelo 1939- AmMWSc 92
**Menezes**, Victor J. WhoFI 92
**Meng Ying** 1913- IntWW 91
**Meng**, H C AmMWSc 92
**Meng**, Heinz Karl 1924- AmMWSc 92
**Meng**, Karl H 1911- AmMWSc 92
**Meng**, Shien-Yi 1929- AmMWSc 92
**Mengali**, Umberto 1936- AmMWSc 92
**Mengarini**, Gregory 1811-1886 DcAmImH
**Menge**, Alan C 1934- AmMWSc 92
**Menge**, Bruce Allan 1943- AmMWSc 92
**Menge**, John Arthur 1945- AmMWSc 92
**Menge**, Richard Cramer 1935- WhoFI 92
**Mengebier**, William Louis 1921- AmMWSc 92
**Mengel**, Christopher Emile 1952- WhoAmL 92
**Mengel**, David Bruce 1948- AmMWSc 92, WhoMW 92
**Mengel**, J T 1918- AmMWSc 92
**Mengel**, Michael John 1956- WhoWest 92
**Mengel**, Robert Morrow 1921- AmMWSc 92
**Mengel**, Ronald Keith 1934- WhoMW 92
**Mengelberg**, Willem 1871-1951 FacFETw, NewAmDM
**Mengele**, Josef 1911-1978? FacFETw
**Mengele**, Josef 1911-1979 EncTR 91 [port]
**Mengeling**, William Lloyd 1933- AmMWSc 92, WhoMW 92
**Mengenhauser**, James Vernon 1933- AmMWSc 92
**Menger**, Eva L 1943- AmMWSc 92
**Menger**, Fred M 1937- AmMWSc 92
**Menger**, Harold Charles, Jr. 1952- WhoMW 92
**Mengers**, Sue 1938- IntMPA 92
**Menges**, Charles Philip, Jr. 1942- WhoFI 92
**Menges**, Chris IntWW 91
**Menges**, Chris 1940- IntMPA 92, WhoEnt 92
**Menges**, John Kenneth, Jr. 1957- WhoAmL 92
**Mengistu Haile Mariam** IntWW 91
**Mengistu Haile Mariam** 1937- FacFETw
**Mengoli**, Henry Francis 1928- AmMWSc 92
**Mengs**, Anton-Raphael 1728-1779 BlkwCEP
**Menguy**, Rene 1926- AmMWSc 92
**Menhennet**, David 1928- Who 92
**Menhinick**, Edward Fulton 1935- AmMWSc 92
**Menicucci**, Bruno P 1937- WhoAmP 91
**Menig**, Beatrice Quay 1923- WhoAmP 91
**Menikoff**, Barry 1939- WhoWest 92
**Menin**, Malcolm James Who 92
**Meninsky**, Bernard 1891-1950 TwCPaSc
**Meninsky**, Philip TwCPaSc
**Menius**, Arthur Clayton, III 1955- WhoEnt 92
**Menius**, Arthur Clayton, Jr 1916- AmMWSc 92
**Menk**, Carl William 1921- WhoFI 92
**Menk**, Charles George 1935- WhoMW 92
**Menk**, Louis W. 1918- IntWW 91
**Menkart**, John 1922- AmMWSc 92
**Menke**, Andrew G 1944- AmMWSc 92
**Menke**, David Hugh 1951- AmMWSc 92
**Menke**, Gareld Glenn 1958- WhoRel 92
**Menke**, Lester D 1918- WhoAmP 91
**Menke**, William Charles 1939- WhoFI 92
**Menkel-Meadow**, Carrie Joan 1949- WhoAmL 92
**Menken**, Adah Isaacs 1835?-1868 BenetAL 91, EncAmaz 91, NotBlAW 92
**Menken**, Marie 1909-1970 ReelWom
**Menken**, Robin Morna 1946- WhoEnt 92
**Menkes**, David 1922- WhoFI 92
**Menkes**, Harold A 1938- AmMWSc 92
**Menkes**, John H 1928- AmMWSc 92
**Menkes**, Sherwood Bradford 1921- AmMWSc 92
**Menkes**, Suzy Peta 1943- Who 92
**Menkin**, Christopher 1942- WhoWest 92
**Menkis**, Jonathan WhoEnt 92
**Menkiti**, Ifeanyi DrAPF 91
**Menlove**, Howard Olsen 1936- AmMWSc 92
**Menn**, Julius Joel 1929- AmMWSc 92
**Menne**, Thomas Joseph 1934- AmMWSc 92
**Mennear**, John Hartley 1935- AmMWSc 92
**Menneer**, Stephen Snow 1910- Who 92
**Mennega**, Aaldert 1930- AmMWSc 92
**Mennell**, Robert L. 1934- WhoAmL 92
**Mennella**, Vincent Alfred 1922- WhoWest 92
**Mennen**, Dorothy Runk 1915- WhoEnt 92
**Mennen**, Frederick C. d1991 NewYTBS 91
**Mennen**, Leonard 1938- WhoMW 92
**Mennenga**, Gordon W. DrAPF 91
**Mennicke**, Victor Ottomar 1927- WhoRel 92
**Mennin**, Peter 1923-1983 FacFETw, NewAmDM
**Menning**, Arnold J. 1930- WhoMW 92
**Menning**, J. H. 1915-1973 ConAu 134
**Menning**, Marion 1945- WhoAmP 91
**Menninga**, Alvin 1932- WhoMW 92
**Menninga**, Clarence 1928- AmMWSc 92
**Menninger Family** FacFETw

**Menninger,** Charles Frederick 1862-1953 *FacFETw*
**Menninger,** John Robert 1935- *AmMWSc 92*
**Menninger,** Karl 1893-1990 *AnObit 1990, News 91*
**Menninger,** Karl Augustus d1990 *IntWW 91N*
**Menninger,** Karl Augustus 1893- *AmMWSc 92*
**Menninger,** Karl Augustus 1893-1990 *FacFETw*
**Menninger,** Roy Wright 1926- *WhoMW 92*
**Menninger,** William *FacFETw*
**Menninger,** William Walter 1931- *AmMWSc 92*
**Mennis,** Edmund Addi 1919- *WhoFI 92*
**Mennitt,** Philip Gary 1937 *AmMWSc 92*
**Mennone,** Kate 1956- *WhoEnt 92*
**Meno,** John Peter 1942- *WhoRel 92*
**Menocal,** Armando M., III *WhoHisp 92*
**Menocal,** Armando Mato, III 1941- *WhoAmL 92*
**Menocal,** Mario 1866-1941 *HisDSpE*
**Menon,** Mambillikalathil Govind Kumar 1928- *IntWW 91, Who 92*
**Menon,** Manchery Prabhakara 1928- *AmMWSc 92*
**Menon,** Premachandran R 1931- *AmMWSc 92*
**Menon,** Thuppalay K 1928- *AmMWSc 92*
**Menon,** Vatakke Kurupath Narayana 1911- *IntWW 91*
**Menon,** Vijaya Bhaskar 1934- *WhoEnt 92*
**Menor,** Ron Christopher 1955- *WhoAmP 91*
**Menos,** Gus G 1920- *WhoAmP 91*
**Menotti,** Gian Carlo 1911- *BenetAL 91, ConCom 92, FacFETw, IntWW 91, NewAmDM, Who 92, WhoEnt 92*
**Menpes,** Mortimer 1855-1938 *TwCPaSc*
**Menq,** Chia-Hsiang 1956- *AmMWSc 92*
**Mensah,** Albert Addo 1959- *WhoWest 92*
**Mensah,** E. Kwaku 1945- *WhoBlA 92*
**Mensah,** Joseph Henry 1928- *IntWW 91*
**Mensah,** Patricia Lucas 1948- *AmMWSc 92*
**Mensch,** Homer 1913- *WhoEnt 92*
**Mensch,** Linda Susan 1951- *WhoEnt 92*
**Mensch,** Martin 1927- *WhoAmL 92*
**Mensch,** P Calvin d1901 *BiInAmS*
**Menscher,** Barnet Gary 1940- *WhoFI 92*
**Mensching,** Horst Georg 1921- *IntWW 91*
**Mensendiek,** Charles William 1925- *WhoRel 92*
**Menser,** Harry Alvin, Jr 1930- *AmMWSc 92*
**Mensforth,** Charlotte 1936- *TwCPaSc*
**Mensforth,** Eric 1906- *Who 92*
**Mensh,** Ivan Norman 1915- *WhoWest 92*
**Menshouse,** Alyssa Tefs 1947- *WhoRel 92*
**Menshov,** Vladimir Valentinovich 1939- *IntWW 91*
**Mensing,** Richard Walter 1936- *AmMWSc 92*
**Mensing,** Stephen Gustav 1946- *WhoRel 92*
**Mensinger,** Michael Christian 1950- *WhoMW 92*
**Mensinger,** Peggy 1923- *WhoAmP 91*
**Menson,** Richard L. 1943- *WhoAmL 92*
**Mente,** Glen Allen 1938- *AmMWSc 92*
**Menteer,** David Hilton 1939- *WhoEnt 92*
**Menter,** James 1921- *Who 92*
**Menter,** James Woodham 1921- *IntWW 91*
**Menter,** William George 1934- *WhoRel 92*
**Mentes,** Cevdet 1915- *IntWW 91*
**Menteshashvili,** Tengiz Nikolayevich *IntWW 91*
**Menteth,** James Stuart- 1922- *Who 92*
**Menton,** David Norman 1938- *AmMWSc 92*
**Menton,** Robert Thomas 1942- *AmMWSc 92*
**Menton,** William Joseph *WhoAmP 91*
**Mentone,** Pat Francis 1942- *AmMWSc 92*
**Mentor,** Lillian Francis *ScFEYrs*
**Mentre,** Paul 1935- *IntWW 91*
**Mentz,** Donald 1933- *Who 92*
**Mentz,** Henry Alvan, Jr. 1920- *WhoAmL 92*
**Mentz,** J Roger 1942- *WhoAmP 91*
**Mentz,** John Roger 1942- *WhoAmL 92*
**Mentz,** Lawrence 1946- *WhoAmL 92, WhoFI 92*
**Mentze,** Robert William 1952- *WhoRel 92*
**Mentzer,** John R 1916- *AmMWSc 92*
**Mentzer,** Richard Lynn, Jr. 1946- *WhoWest 92*
**Menudin,** Ibrahim 1948- *IntWW 91*
**Menuez,** D. Barry 1933- *WhoRel 92*
**Menuhin,** Hepzibah 1920-1981 *NewAmDM*
**Menuhin,** Yalta 1922- *NewAmDM*
**Menuhin,** Yehudi 1916- *FacFETw [port], IntWW 91, NewAmDM, Who 92, WhoEnt 92, WrDr 92*
**Menut,** Albert D. 1894-1981 *ConAu 135*
**Menyhert,** William Robert 1935- *AmMWSc 92*
**Menz,** Fredric Carl 1943- *WhoFI 92*
**Menz,** Leo Joseph 1927- *AmMWSc 92*
**Menza,** Greg 1950- *WhoEnt 92*
**Menzbier,** Mikhail Aleksandrovich 1855-1935 *SovUnBD*
**Menzbir,** Mikhail Aleksandrovich 1855-1935 *SovUnBD*
**Menze,** Clemens 1928- *IntWW 91*
**Menzel,** Bruce Willard 1942- *AmMWSc 92*
**Menzel,** Daniel B 1934- *AmMWSc 92*
**Menzel,** David Washington 1928- *AmMWSc 92*
**Menzel,** Erhard Roland *AmMWSc 92*
**Menzel,** Gerhard 1894-1966 *EncTR 91*
**Menzel,** Herybert 1906-1945 *EncTR 91*
**Menzel,** Jiri 1938- *IntDcF 2-2, IntWW 91*
**Menzel,** Joerg H 1939- *AmMWSc 92*
**Menzel,** Robert Winston 1920- *AmMWSc 92*
**Menzel,** Ronald George 1924- *AmMWSc 92*
**Menzel,** Wolfgang Paul 1945- *AmMWSc 92*
**Menzer,** Fred J 1933- *AmMWSc 92*
**Menzer,** Robert Everett 1938- *AmMWSc 92*
**Menzhinsky,** Vyacheslav Rudol'fovich 1874-1934 *SovUnBD*
**Menzie,** Beckie Jo 1957- *WhoEnt 92*
**Menzie,** Donald E 1922- *AmMWSc 92*
**Menzies,** Arthur Redpath 1916- *IntWW 91*
**Menzies,** Carl Stephen 1932- *AmMWSc 92*
**Menzies,** Jean Storke 1904- *WhoWest 92*
**Menzies,** John 1949- *AmMWSc 92*
**Menzies,** John Maxwell 1926- *Who 92*
**Menzies,** Pattie 1899- *Who 92*
**Menzies,** Peter 1912- *IntWW 91, Who 92*
**Menzies,** Robert Allen 1935- *AmMWSc 92*
**Menzies,** Robert Gordon 1894-1978 *FacFETw [port]*
**Menzies,** Robert Thomas 1943- *AmMWSc 92*
**Menzies,** Thomas Neal 1945- *WhoWest 92*
**Menzies-Wilson,** William Napier 1926- *Who 92*
**Menzin,** Margaret Schoenberg 1942- *AmMWSc 92*
**Meo,** Jean Alfred Emile Edouard 1927- *IntWW 91*
**Meola,** Robert Ralph 1927- *AmMWSc 92*
**Meola,** Roger Walker 1934- *AmMWSc 92*
**Meola,** Shirlee May 1935- *AmMWSc 92*
**Meotti,** Michael Patrick 1953- *WhoAmP 91*
**Meppen,** Adrian Joseph 1940- *WhoEnt 92*
**Mer,** Francis Paul 1939- *IntWW 91*
**Meranus,** Arthur Richard 1934- *WhoFI 92*
**Meranus,** Leonard Stanley 1928- *WhoAmL 92*
**Meraz,** Micheal J. 1954- *WhoHisp 92*
**Merbah,** Kasdi 1938- *IntWW 91*
**Merbecke,** John 1510?-1585? *NewAmDM*
**Merbs,** Charles Francis 1936- *AmMWSc 92*
**Mercadante,** Linda Angela *WhoMW 92, WhoRel 92*
**Mercadante,** Saverio 1795-1870 *NewAmDM*
**Mercader,** Caridad *EncAmaz 91*
**Mercader,** Ramon 1914-1978 *FacFETw*
**Mercado,** Albert William 1961- *WhoHisp 92*
**Mercado,** Andrea Morgan 1960- *WhoAmL 92*
**Mercado,** Camelia 1928- *WhoHisp 92*
**Mercado,** Carlos 1949- *WhoHisp 92*
**Mercado,** Edward 1937- *WhoHisp 92*
**Mercado,** Luis Fidel 1925- *WhoRel 92*
**Mercado,** Ralph 1941- *WhoHisp 92*
**Mercado,** Rich 1945- *WhoHisp 92*
**Mercado,** Roger 1967- *WhoHisp 92*
**Mercado,** Romelia 1962- *WhoHisp 92*
**Mercado,** Teresa I 1921- *AmMWSc 92*
**Mercado Irizarry,** Aurelio, Jr. 1948- *WhoHisp 92*
**Mercado Jarrin,** Luis Edgardo 1919- *IntWW 91*
**Mercado-Jimenez,** Teodoro 1935- *AmMWSc 92*
**Mercado y Villacorta,** Alonso de 1620?-1681 *HisDSpE*
**Mercaldo,** Daniel 1939- *WhoRel 92*
**Merced,** Nelson 1948- *WhoHisp 92*
**Merced,** Orlando Luis 1966- *WhoHisp 92*
**Merced,** Victor 1956- *WhoHisp 92*
**Merced-Reyes,** Josue 1950- *WhoHisp 92*
**Mercer,** Alan 1931- *Who 92*
**Mercer,** Alexander McDowell 1931- *AmMWSc 92*
**Mercer,** Arthur, Sr. 1921- *WhoBlA 92*
**Mercer,** Barney, III 1937- *WhoFI 92*
**Mercer,** Bernard 1912- *WhoIns 92*
**Mercer,** Calvin Richard 1953- *WhoRel 92*
**Mercer,** Courtney Eason 1949- *WhoAmL 92*
**Mercer,** David 1928-1980 *RfGEnL 91*
**Mercer,** David Robinson 1938- *WhoMW 92*
**Mercer,** Donna Eileen 1965- *WhoEnt 92*
**Mercer,** Edward Everett 1934- *AmMWSc 92*
**Mercer,** Edward King 1931- *AmMWSc 92*
**Mercer,** Edwin Wayne 1940- *WhoAmL 92*
**Mercer,** Eric Arthur John 1917- *Who 92*
**Mercer,** George 1733-1784 *DcNCBi 4*
**Mercer,** Henry Chapman 1856-1930 *DcTwDes*
**Mercer,** Henry Dwight 1939- *AmMWSc 92*
**Mercer,** Ian Dews 1933- *Who 92*
**Mercer,** James Wayne 1947- *AmMWSc 92*
**Mercer,** Jesse 1769-1841 *DcNCBi 4*
**Mercer,** Joe 1914-1990 *AnObit 1990*
**Mercer,** John A 1957- *WhoAmP 91*
**Mercer,** John Charles Kenneth 1917- *Who 92*
**Mercer,** John Edward 1946- *WhoAmP 91*
**Mercer,** John Herndon 1909-1976 *FacFETw*
**Mercer,** Johnny 1909-1976 *NewAmDM*
**Mercer,** Joseph Henry 1937- *WhoAmP 91, WhoWest 92*
**Mercer,** Kermit R 1933- *AmMWSc 92*
**Mercer,** Leo *WhoAmP 91*
**Mercer,** Leonard Preston, II 1941- *AmMWSc 92*
**Mercer,** Linda Lou 1945- *IntAu&W 91*
**Mercer,** Lloyd John 1936- *WhoWest 92*
**Mercer,** Mabel 1900-1984 *FacFETw*
**Mercer,** Malcolm Clarence 1944- *AmMWSc 92*
**Mercer,** Margaret Francis 1936- *WhoRel 92*
**Mercer,** Marian 1935- *WhoEnt 92*
**Mercer,** Mark Kent 1953- *WhoRel 92*
**Mercer,** Paul Frederick 1936- *AmMWSc 92*
**Mercer,** Ray 1961- *BlkOlyM*
**Mercer,** Robert Allen 1942- *AmMWSc 92*
**Mercer,** Robert B. *WhoAmL 92*
**Mercer,** Robert Edward 1924- *IntWW 91*
**Mercer,** Robert Giles Graham 1949- *Who 92*
**Mercer,** Robert Leroy 1946- *AmMWSc 92*
**Mercer,** Robert S 1925- *WhoAmP 91*
**Mercer,** Robert William *AmMWSc 92*
**Mercer,** Robert William Stanley 1935- *Who 92*
**Mercer,** Roger James 1944- *Who 92*
**Mercer,** Ronald L. 1934- *WhoFI 92*
**Mercer,** Samuel, Jr 1920- *AmMWSc 92*
**Mercer,** Sherwood Rocke 1907- *AmMWSc 92*
**Mercer,** Thomas T 1920- *AmMWSc 92*
**Mercer,** Valerie June 1947- *WhoBlA 92*
**Mercer,** Walter Ronald 1941- *AmMWSc 92*
**Mercer,** William A. 1927- *WhoBlA 92*
**Mercer,** William Parker 1855-1919 *DcNCBi 4*
**Mercer Nairne Petty-Fitzmaurice** *Who 92*
**Mercer-Pryor,** Diana 1950- *WhoBlA 92*
**Mercer-Smith,** James A 1953- *AmMWSc 92*
**Mercereau,** James Edgar 1930- *AmMWSc 92*
**Merchand,** Hernando 1942- *WhoHisp 92*
**Merchand,** Leslie A 1900- *IntAu&W 91*
**Merchant,** Bruce 1935- *AmMWSc 92*
**Merchant,** Christopher d1698? *DcNCBi 4*
**Merchant,** Donald Joseph 1921- *AmMWSc 92*
**Merchant,** Donna Rae 1948- *WhoFI 92*
**Merchant,** Henry Clifton 1942- *AmMWSc 92*
**Merchant,** Howard Carl 1935- *AmMWSc 92*
**Merchant,** Ismail 1936- *IntMPA 92, IntWW 91, Who 92*
**Merchant,** John F. 1933- *WhoBlA 92*
**Merchant,** John Richard 1945- *Who 92*
**Merchant,** Michael Brian 1963- *WhoAmL 92*
**Merchant,** Mylon Eugene 1913- *AmMWSc 92, WhoFI 92, WhoMW 92*
**Merchant,** Philip, Jr 1943- *AmMWSc 92*
**Merchant,** Piers Rolf Garfield 1951- *Who 92*
**Merchant,** Robert Wilson 1950- *WhoEnt 92*
**Merchant,** Roland Samuel, Sr 1929- *AmMWSc 92, WhoFI 92, WhoWest 92*
**Merchant,** Sabeeha 1959- *AmMWSc 92*
**Merchant,** Tom James 1959- *WhoEnt 92*
**Merchant,** Vijay 1911-1987 *FacFETw*
**Merchant,** William Moelwyn 1913- *IntAu&W 91, Who 92*
**Mercieca,** Joseph *Who 92*
**Mercieca,** Joseph 1928- *IntWW 91, WhoRel 92*
**Mercier,** Desire 1851-1926 *DcEcMov*
**Mercier,** Jacques Louis 1933- *WhoFI 92*
**Mercier,** Jean-Louis 1934- *WhoFI 92*
**Mercier,** Louis-Sebastien 1740-1814 *BlkwCEP, ScFEYrs*
**Mercier,** Richard Louis 1947- *WhoAmP 91*
**Merckx,** Eddy 1945- *FacFETw*
**Merckx,** Kenneth R 1926- *AmMWSc 92*
**Mercorella,** Anthony Joseph 1927- *WhoAmL 92*
**Mercouri,** Melina 1925- *IntMPA 92, IntWW 91*
**Mercouris,** George S. 1886-1943 *BiDExR*
**Mercur,** James 1842-1896 *BiInAmS*
**Mercure,** Jean 1909- *IntWW 91*
**Mercure,** Pierre 1927-1966 *NewAmDM*
**Mercurio,** Edward Peter 1944- *WhoWest 92*
**Mercury,** Freddie d1991 *NewYTBS 91 [port]*
**Mercury,** Freddie 1946-1991 *News 92-2*
**Mercy,** Leland, Jr. 1942- *WhoBlA 92*
**Merdinger,** Charles 1918- *WrDr 92*
**Merdinger,** Charles J 1918- *AmMWSc 92*
**Merdinger,** Emanuel 1906- *AmMWSc 92*
**Merdinger,** Steven Marc 1954- *WhoFI 92*
**Merdinger,** Susan 1943- *WhoFI 92*
**Mereday,** Richard F. 1929- *WhoBlA 92*
**Meredith,** Amituana'i 1912- *WhoAmP 91*
**Meredith,** Bevan *Who 92*
**Meredith,** Burgess 1909- *IntMPA 92, WhoEnt 92*
**Meredith,** Carol N 1948- *AmMWSc 92*
**Meredith,** Christopher 1954- *IntAu&W 91*
**Meredith,** Dale Dean 1940- *AmMWSc 92*
**Meredith,** David Bruce 1950- *AmMWSc 92*
**Meredith,** David Robert 1940- *WhoFI 92*
**Meredith,** Don *DrAPF 91, LesBEnT 92*
**Meredith,** Donald Lloyd 1941- *WhoRel 92*
**Meredith,** Doris 1944- *IntAu&W 91*
**Meredith,** Edwin Thomas, III 1933- *WhoFI 92*
**Meredith,** Ellis *ScFEYrs*
**Meredith,** Farris Ray 1929- *AmMWSc 92*
**Meredith,** Frank Homer 1953- *WhoRel 92*
**Meredith,** George 1828-1909 *CnDBLB 4 [port], RfGEnL 91, TwCLC 43 [port]*
**Meredith,** George Marlor 1923- *WhoFI 92*
**Meredith,** Hugh 1697?-1749? *DcNCBi 4*
**Meredith,** James 1933- *FacFETw [port]*
**Meredith,** James Harris 1947- *WhoAmP 91*
**Meredith,** James Howard 1933- *WhoBlA 92*
**Meredith,** Jesse Hedgepeth 1923- *AmMWSc 92*
**Meredith,** Jody Berry 1946- *WhoAmP 91*
**Meredith,** John Michael 1934- *Who 92*
**Meredith,** Leslie Hugh 1927- *AmMWSc 92*
**Meredith,** Orsell Montgomery 1923- *AmMWSc 92*
**Meredith,** Richard Alban Creed 1935- *Who 92*
**Meredith,** Richard C 1937-1979 *TwCSFW 91*
**Meredith,** Robert E 1928- *AmMWSc 92*
**Meredith,** Ronald Edward 1946- *WhoAmL 92*
**Meredith,** Ruby Frances 1948- *AmMWSc 92*
**Meredith,** Scott 1923- *WrDr 92*
**Meredith,** Solomon 1810-1875 *DcNCBi 4*
**Meredith,** Stephen Charles *AmMWSc 92*
**Meredith,** Thomas 1795-1850 *DcNCBi 4*
**Meredith,** Wanda Marie 1936- *WhoAmP 91*
**Meredith,** William *DrAPF 91*
**Meredith,** William 1919- *ConAu 14AS [port], ConPo 91, IntWW 91, WrDr 92*
**Meredith,** William Edward 1932- *AmMWSc 92*
**Meredith,** William G 1933- *AmMWSc 92*
**Meredith Davies,** Brian *Who 92*
**Merenbloom,** Robert Barry 1947- *WhoFI 92*
**Merendino,** Frank James 1955- *WhoWest 92*
**Merenivitch,** Jarrow 1942- *WhoBlA 92*
**Meresz,** Otto 1932- *AmMWSc 92*
**Meretskov,** Kirill Afanas'evich 1897-1968 *SovUnBD*
**Mereu,** Robert Frank 1930- *AmMWSc 92*
**Merezhkovsky,** Dmitry Sergeyevich 1865-1941 *LiExTwC*
**Mergen,** Dorothy Ann 1932- *WhoAmP 91*
**Mergen,** Francois 1925- *AmMWSc 92*
**Mergenhagen,** Stephan Edward 1930- *AmMWSc 92*
**Mergenovich,** Shirley Ann 1938- *WhoMW 92*
**Mergens,** William Joseph 1942- *AmMWSc 92*
**Mergentime,** Max 1914- *AmMWSc 92*
**Mergler,** H. Kent 1940- *WhoFI 92, WhoMW 92*
**Mergler,** H W 1924- *AmMWSc 92*
**Merhige,** Robert Reynold, Jr. 1919- *WhoAmL 92*
**Meriam,** James Lathrop 1917- *AmMWSc 92*

**Merickel**, Michael Gene 1952- *WhoMW 92*
**Mericle**, Morris H 1925- *AmMWSc 92*
**Mericle**, R Bruce 1938- *AmMWSc 92*
**Mericola**, Francis Carl 1911- *AmMWSc 92*
**Mericourt**, Theroigne de 1759?-1817 *EncAmaz 91*
**Meriden**, Terry 1946- *WhoMW 92*
**Merideth**, Charles Waymond 1940- *WhoBlA 92*
**Merideth**, H L, Jr 1930- *WhoAmP 91*
**Meridith**, Denise P. 1952- *WhoBlA 92*
**Meridor**, Dan 1947- *IntWW 91*
**Merifield**, Anthony James 1934- *Who 92*
**Merifield**, Paul M 1932- *AmMWSc 92, WhoWest 92*
**Merigan**, Thomas Charles, Jr 1934- *AmMWSc 92, WhoWest 92*
**Merikas**, George 1911- *IntWW 91*
**Merila**, Edith F. 1950- *WhoAmL 92*
**Merilan**, Charles Preston 1926- *AmMWSc 92*
**Merilan**, Jean Elizabeth 1962- *WhoMW 92*
**Merillon**, Jean-Marie 1926- *IntWW 91*
**Merilo**, Mati 1944- *AmMWSc 92*
**Merimee**, Prosper 1803-1870 *GuFrLit 1*
**Merin**, Peter *ConAu 34NR*
**Merin**, Robert Gillespie 1933- *AmMWSc 92*
**Merin**, Robert Lynn 1946- *WhoWest 92*
**Meriney**, Stephen D 1960- *AmMWSc 92*
**Merino**, Alfredo 1931- *WhoHisp 92*
**Merino Castro**, Jose Toribio 1915- *IntWW 91*
**Meritt**, Eldon Ray 1938- *WhoAmP 91*
**Merivale**, John 1917-1990 *AnObit 1990*
**Meriweather**, Melvin, Jr. 1937- *WhoBlA 92*
**Meriwether**, Heath J. 1944- *WhoMW 92*
**Meriwether**, John R 1937- *AmMWSc 92*
**Meriwether**, John W. *WhoFI 92*
**Meriwether**, John Williams, Jr 1942- *AmMWSc 92*
**Meriwether**, Lee 1862-1964 *ScFEYrs*
**Meriwether**, Lee 1935- *WhoEnt 92*
**Meriwether**, Lewis Smith 1930- *AmMWSc 92*
**Meriwether**, Louise *DrAPF 91*
**Meriwether**, Louise 1923- *NotBlAW 92, WhoBlA 92*
**Meriwether**, Roy Dennis 1943- *WhoBlA 92*
**Merjos**, Stavros Peter 1959- *WhoEnt 92*
**Merkel**, Frederick Karl 1936- *AmMWSc 92*
**Merkel**, George 1929- *AmMWSc 92*
**Merkel**, Jacek 1954- *IntWW 91*
**Merkel**, Joseph Robert 1924- *AmMWSc 92*
**Merkel**, Paul Barrett 1945- *AmMWSc 92*
**Merkel**, Robert Anthony 1926- *AmMWSc 92*
**Merkel**, Timothy Franklin 1942- *AmMWSc 92*
**Merkelbach**, Reinhold 1918- *IntWW 91*
**Merkelo**, Henri 1939- *AmMWSc 92*
**Merken**, Henry 1929- *AmMWSc 92*
**Merken**, Melvin 1927- *AmMWSc 92*
**Merker**, George Edward 1952- *WhoAmL 92*
**Merker**, Milton 1941- *AmMWSc 92*
**Merker**, Philip Charles 1922- *AmMWSc 92*
**Merker**, Stephen Louis 1941- *AmMWSc 92*
**Merkert**, George *WhoEnt 92*
**Merkes**, Edward Peter 1929- *AmMWSc 92*
**Merkin**, Daphne *DrAPF 91*
**Merkin**, William Leslie 1929- *WhoAmL 92*
**Merkl**, Neil Matthew 1931- *WhoAmL 92*
**Merkle**, Alan Ray 1947- *WhoAmL 92*
**Merkle**, Barbara Ramos 1954- *WhoHisp 92*
**Merkle**, F Henry 1931- *AmMWSc 92*
**Merkle**, Helen Louise 1950- *WhoMW 92*
**Merkle**, Judith A *ConAu 35NR*
**Merkle**, Patrick Guy 1956- *WhoAmL 92*
**Merkle**, Roberta K 1955- *AmMWSc 92*
**Merklein**, Helmut Martin 1940- *WhoRel 92*
**Merkley**, Clark Mortensen 1959- *WhoAmL 92*
**Merkley**, David Frederick 1945- *AmMWSc 92*
**Merkley**, Wayne Bingham 1941- *AmMWSc 92*
**Merklin**, Marc Bryan 1960- *WhoAmL 92*
**Merkling**, Frank 1924- *WhoEnt 92*
**Merkorewos**, Abune *WhoRel 92*
**Merkt**, John L 1946- *WhoAmP 91*
**Merkuriev**, Stanislav 1945- *IntWW 91*
**Merkurov**, Sergey Dmitrievich 1881-1952 *SovUnBD*
**Merkus**, Jenny *EncAmaz 91*
**Merle**, H. Etienne 1944- *WhoFI 92*
**Merle**, Robert 1908- *Who 92*
**Merleau-Ponty**, Maurice 1908-1961 *GuFrLit 1*
**Merley**, Bruce Michael 1946- *WhoEnt 92*
**Merlie**, John Paul 1945- *AmMWSc 92*
**Merlin**, Arthur *SmATA 66*
**Merlin**, Christina *IntAu&W 91X, WrDr 92*
**Merlin**, David *WrDr 92*
**Merlin**, Jan 1925- *WhoEnt 92*
**Merlin**, Peter Helmuth 1928- *WhoAmL 92*
**Merlin**, Robert Joseph 1954- *WhoAmL 92*
**Merlin**, Roberto Daniel 1950- *AmMWSc 92*
**Merlin-Jones**, Sally Barbara 1946- *WhoEnt 92*
**Merlini**, Giampaolo 1951- *AmMWSc 92*
**Merlino**, Glenn T 1953- *AmMWSc 92*
**Merlino**, Joseph Piedmont 1922- *WhoAmP 91*
**Merlis**, George 1940- *WhoEnt 92*
**Merlis**, Iris 1939- *WhoEnt 92*
**Merlis**, Robert 1948- *WhoEnt 92*
**Merlo**, Andrew Eugene 1942- *WhoFI 92*
**Merlo**, David 1931- *Who 92*
**Merlo**, Harry Angelo 1925- *WhoFI 92, WhoWest 92*
**Merloni**, Vittorio 1933- *IntWW 91*
**Merlotti**, Frank Henry 1926- *WhoFI 92*
**Mermagen**, Herbert Waldemar 1912- *Who 92*
**Mermagen**, William Henry 1935- *AmMWSc 92*
**Merman**, Ethel 1909-1984 *FacFETw, NewAmDM*
**Mermaz**, Louis 1931- *IntWW 91*
**Mermel**, Thaddeus Walter 1907- *AmMWSc 92*
**Mermelstein**, Jules Joshua 1955- *WhoAmL 92*
**Mermelstein**, Paula 1947- *WhoEnt 92*
**Mermelstein**, Robert *AmMWSc 92*
**Mermin**, N David 1935- *AmMWSc 92*
**MernaLyn** *WhoEnt 92*
**Merne**, Oscar James 1943- *WrDr 92*
**Merner**, Richard Raymond 1918- *AmMWSc 92*
**Mernit**, Susan *DrAPF 91*
**Mero**, Marjorie Anne 1940- *WhoFI 92*
**Merola**, A John 1931- *AmMWSc 92*
**Merola**, Gaetano 1881-1953 *NewAmDM*
**Merola**, Joseph Salvatore 1952- *AmMWSc 92*
**Meron**, Theodor 1930- *WhoAmL 92*
**Meroney**, Robert N 1937- *AmMWSc 92*
**Meroney**, Robert Nelson 1937- *WhoWest 92*
**Meroney**, William Hyde, III 1917- *AmMWSc 92*
**Merow**, Florence Lombardi 1932- *WhoAmP 91*
**Merow**, James F. 1932- *WhoAmL 92*
**Merow**, John Edward 1929- *WhoAmL 92*
**Merquior**, Jose Guilherme 1941- *IntAu&W 91*
**Merrell**, David John 1919- *AmMWSc 92*
**Merrell**, James Lee 1930- *WhoRel 92*
**Merrell**, Norman L 1924- *WhoAmP 91*
**Merrell**, Robert Bruce 1945- *WhoWest 92*
**Merrell**, Victor Dallas 1936- *WhoWest 92*
**Merren**, John Jay 1940- *WhoWest 92*
**Merrett**, Charles Edwin 1923- *Who 92*
**Merriam**, Charles Wolcott, III 1931- *AmMWSc 92*
**Merriam**, Daniel Francis 1927- *AmMWSc 92*
**Merriam**, Esther Virginia 1940- *AmMWSc 92*
**Merriam**, Eve *DrAPF 91*
**Merriam**, Eve 1916- *WrDr 92*
**Merriam**, Gene 1944- *WhoAmP 91*
**Merriam**, George Rennell, Jr 1913- *AmMWSc 92*
**Merriam**, Howard Gray 1932- *AmMWSc 92*
**Merriam**, John L 1911- *AmMWSc 92*
**Merriam**, John Roger 1940- *AmMWSc 92*
**Merriam**, Lawrence Campbell, Jr 1923- *AmMWSc 92*
**Merriam**, Marshal F 1932- *AmMWSc 92*
**Merriam**, Robert Arnold 1927- *AmMWSc 92*
**Merriam**, Robert William 1923- *AmMWSc 92*
**Merriam**, Sharan B. 1943- *ConAu 135*
**Merrick**, Arthur West 1917- *AmMWSc 92*
**Merrick**, David 1912- *IntMPA 92, IntWW 91, WhoEnt 92*
**Merrick**, Gordon 1916- *IntAu&W 91*
**Merrick**, John 1859-1919 *DcNCBi 4*
**Merrick**, John Robert 1941- *WhoAmL 92*
**Merrick**, John Vaughan 1828-1906 *BiInAmS*
**Merrick**, Joseph M 1930- *AmMWSc 92*
**Merrick**, Keith Leon 1923- *WhoFI 92*
**Merrick**, Lew 1953- *WhoFI 92, WhoWest 92*
**Merrick**, Lyda Moore 1890-1987 *NotBlAW 92*
**Merrick**, Mark *TwCWW 91*
**Merrick**, Richard A. 1930- *WhoWest 92*
**Merrick**, Stephen M. 1941- *WhoAmL 92*
**Merrick-Fairweather**, Norma 1928- *WhoBlA 92*
**Merricks**, Walter Hugh 1945- *Who 92*
**Merriell**, David McCray 1919- *AmMWSc 92*
**Merrier**, Helen 1932- *WhoEnt 92, WhoMW 92*
**Merrifield**, Bruce 1921- *IntWW 91*
**Merrifield**, Carldean 1924- *WhoMW 92, WhoRel 92*
**Merrifield**, D Bruce 1921- *AmMWSc 92*
**Merrifield**, Paul Elliott 1922- *AmMWSc 92*
**Merrifield**, Richard Ebert 1929- *AmMWSc 92*
**Merrifield**, Robert Bruce 1921- *AmMWSc 92, Who 92, WhoNob 90*
**Merrifield**, Robert G 1930- *AmMWSc 92*
**Merrigan**, Eugene T 1933- *WhoIns 92*
**Merrigan**, Joseph A 1940- *AmMWSc 92*
**Merrigan**, Mary Ellen 1951- *WhoWest 92*
**Merrigan**, William Joseph 1934- *WhoAmL 92*
**Merril**, Carl R 1936- *AmMWSc 92*
**Merril**, Judith 1923- *TwCSFW 91, WrDr 92*
**Merrill**, Abel Jay 1938- *WhoAmL 92*
**Merrill**, Albert Adams *ScFEYrs*
**Merrill**, Alvin Seymour 1930- *WhoAmP 91*
**Merrill**, Amanda A 1951- *WhoAmP 91*
**Merrill**, Arthur Lewis 1930- *WhoRel 92*
**Merrill**, Betty J. S. 1927- *WhoFI 92*
**Merrill**, Charles Merton 1907- *WhoAmL 92*
**Merrill**, Christopher *DrAPF 91*
**Merrill**, Claire Birsh 1924- *WhoEnt 92*
**Merrill**, Cynthia Tucker 1944- *WhoEnt 92*
**Merrill**, Dana Noyes 1934- *WhoFI 92*
**Merrill**, Dina *WhoEnt 92*
**Merrill**, Dina 1928- *IntMPA 92*
**Merrill**, Dorothy 1927- *AmMWSc 92*
**Merrill**, E W 1923- *AmMWSc 92*
**Merrill**, Eugene Haines 1934- *WhoRel 92*
**Merrill**, Frances Hatch 1939- *WhoAmP 91*
**Merrill**, Frank Edward 1948- *WhoEnt 92*
**Merrill**, Frank Harrison 1953- *WhoWest 92*
**Merrill**, Frederick James Hamilton 1861-1916 *BiInAmS*
**Merrill**, Gary 1915-1990 *AnObit 1990*
**Merrill**, Gary Frank 1947- *AmMWSc 92*
**Merrill**, Gary Lane Smith 1939- *AmMWSc 92*
**Merrill**, George Vanderneth 1947- *WhoAmL 92, WhoFI 92*
**Merrill**, Gerald P 1926- *WhoAmP 91*
**Merrill**, Glen Kenton 1935- *AmMWSc 92*
**Merrill**, Helen 1918- *WhoEnt 92*
**Merrill**, Howard Emerson 1930- *AmMWSc 92*
**Merrill**, Hugh Davis 1913- *WhoAmP 91*
**Merrill**, Jaies 1926- *IntAu&W 91*
**Merrill**, James 1926- *BenetAL 91, ConPo 91, FacFETw, IntWW 91, WrDr 92*
**Merrill**, James Allen 1925- *AmMWSc 92*
**Merrill**, James Cushing 1853-1902 *BiInAmS*
**Merrill**, James I. *DrAPF 91*
**Merrill**, Jean 1923- *WrDr 92*
**Merrill**, Jean Fairbanks 1923- *IntAu&W 91*
**Merrill**, Jerald Carl 1940- *AmMWSc 92*
**Merrill**, John Ellsworth 1902- *AmMWSc 92*
**Merrill**, John Jay 1933- *AmMWSc 92*
**Merrill**, John Putnam 1917- *AmMWSc 92*
**Merrill**, John Raymond 1939- *AmMWSc 92*
**Merrill**, John Russell 1931- *WhoWest 92*
**Merrill**, John T 1946- *AmMWSc 92*
**Merrill**, Joseph Hartwell 1903- *WhoRel 92*
**Merrill**, Joseph Melton 1923- *AmMWSc 92*
**Merrill**, Joshua 1820-1904 *BiInAmS*
**Merrill**, Judith 1923- *IntAu&W 91*
**Merrill**, Kathryn D *WhoAmP 91*
**Merrill**, Kenneth Coleman 1930- *WhoFI 92, WhoMW 92*
**Merrill**, Lee *DrAPF 91*
**Merrill**, Leland, Jr 1920- *AmMWSc 92*
**Merrill**, Lindsey 1925- *WhoEnt 92*
**Merrill**, Marcia Lee 1945- *WhoEnt 92*
**Merrill**, Marion 1929- *WhoEnt 92*
**Merrill**, Mary H. 1929- *WhoWest 92*
**Merrill**, Michael 1922- *WhoAmP 91*
**Merrill**, Michael Bradley 1953- *WhoRel 92*
**Merrill**, Michael H. 1954- *WhoMW 92*
**Merrill**, Nathan Frederick 1849?-1915 *BiInAmS*
**Merrill**, Odessa Norwood *WhoMW 92*
**Merrill**, Philip L 1945- *WhoAmP 91*
**Merrill**, Richard Austin 1937- *IntWW 91, WhoAmL 92*
**Merrill**, Richard Thomas 1928- *WhoFI 92, WhoMW 92*
**Merrill**, Robert 1917- *NewAmDM*
**Merrill**, Robert 1919- *IntWW 91, WhoEnt 92*
**Merrill**, Robert Clifford, Jr 1958- *AmMWSc 92*
**Merrill**, Robert Edward 1933- *WhoFI 92, WhoWest 92*
**Merrill**, Robert Hull 1922- *WhoWest 92*
**Merrill**, Robert Kimball 1945- *AmMWSc 92*
**Merrill**, Robert P 1934- *AmMWSc 92*
**Merrill**, Ronald Eugene 1947- *AmMWSc 92*
**Merrill**, Ronald Thomas 1938- *AmMWSc 92*
**Merrill**, Samuel, III 1939- *AmMWSc 92*
**Merrill**, Stephen Day 1939- *AmMWSc 92*
**Merrill**, Steven 1946- *WhoAmP 91*
**Merrill**, Steven William 1944- *WhoWest 92*
**Merrill**, Stuart 1863-1915 *BenetAL 91*
**Merrill**, Susan *DrAPF 91*
**Merrill**, Susan Lee 1942- *IntAu&W 91*
**Merrill**, Thomas F. 1932- *WrDr 92*
**Merrill**, Thomas Wendell 1949- *WhoAmL 92*
**Merrill**, Walter Hilson 1947- *AmMWSc 92*
**Merrill**, Warner Jay, Jr 1923- *AmMWSc 92*
**Merrill**, William 1933- *AmMWSc 92*
**Merrill**, William George 1931- *AmMWSc 92*
**Merrill**, William Meredith 1918- *AmMWSc 92*
**Merrill**, William Stanley 1798-1880 *BiInAmS*
**Merrill-Widick**, Marsha Lynn 1950- *WhoEnt 92*
**Merrills**, Roy 1934- *WhoFI 92*
**Merriman**, Alan *Who 92*
**Merriman**, Alex *ConAu 36NR*
**Merriman**, Basil Mandeville 1911- *Who 92*
**Merriman**, Chad *TwCWW 91*
**Merriman**, Henry Alan 1929- *Who 92*
**Merriman**, James Earl 1946- *WhoAmL 92*
**Merriman**, James Henry Herbert 1915- *Who 92*
**Merriman**, John d1974 *LesBEnT 92*
**Merriman**, John A 1942- *WhoAmP 91*
**Merriman**, Margarita Leonor 1927- *WhoEnt 92*
**Merriman**, Marion 1909- *ConAu 133*
**Merriman**, Nan 1920- *NewAmDM*
**Merriman**, Robert Douglas 1954- *WhoAmL 92*
**Merriman**, Robert E 1929- *WhoIns 92*
**Merriman**, Willis J. *WhoRel 92*
**Merrimon**, Augustus Summerfield 1830-1892 *DcNCBi 4*
**Merrin**, Seymour 1931- *AmMWSc 92*
**Merriner**, John Vennor 1941- *AmMWSc 92*
**Merris**, Russell Lloyd 1943- *AmMWSc 92*
**Merriss**, Philip Ramsay, Jr. 1948- *WhoFI 92*
**Merrithew**, Gerald S. 1931- *IntWW 91*
**Merritt**, A. 1884-1943 *BenetAL 91, ScFEYrs, TwCSFW 91*
**Merritt**, Abraham 1884-1943 *FacFETw*
**Merritt**, Alfred M, II 1937- *AmMWSc 92*
**Merritt**, Anthony Lewis 1940- *WhoBlA 92*
**Merritt**, Bishetta Dionne 1947- *WhoBlA 92*
**Merritt**, Bruce Gordon 1946- *WhoAmL 92, WhoWest 92*
**Merritt**, Charles, Jr 1919- *AmMWSc 92*
**Merritt**, Clair 1922- *AmMWSc 92*
**Merritt**, Dawana Denean 1966- *WhoBlA 92*
**Merritt**, Doris Honig 1923- *AmMWSc 92*
**Merritt**, E B *IntAu&W 91X*
**Merritt**, Emma F. G. 1860-1933 *NotBlAW 92*
**Merritt**, Frank Samuel 1943- *WhoAmL 92*
**Merritt**, Gilbert S *WhoAmP 91*
**Merritt**, Gilbert Stroud 1936- *WhoAmL 92*
**Merritt**, H Houston 1902-1979 *FacFETw*
**Merritt**, Henry Neyron 1919- *AmMWSc 92*
**Merritt**, Hiram Houston, Jr. 1902-1979 *DcNCBi 4*
**Merritt**, J L, Jr 1931- *AmMWSc 92*
**Merritt**, Jack 1918- *AmMWSc 92*
**Merritt**, James Edward 1938- *WhoAmL 92*
**Merritt**, James Francis 1944- *AmMWSc 92*
**Merritt**, James Gregory, Sr. 1952- *WhoRel 92*
**Merritt**, James W, Jr 1959- *WhoAmP 91*
**Merritt**, John 1930- *WhoAmP 91*
**Merritt**, John C. 1940- *WhoFI 92*
**Merritt**, John Edward 1926- *Who 92*
**Merritt**, Joseph, Jr 1934- *WhoAmP 91, WhoBlA 92*
**Merritt**, Jymie 1926- *WhoEnt 92*
**Merritt**, Karl Francis 1938- *WhoMW 92*
**Merritt**, Katharine 1938- *AmMWSc 92*
**Merritt**, Kenni Barrett 1950- *WhoAmL 92*
**Merritt**, LaVere Barrus 1936- *AmMWSc 92*

**Merritt**, Lynn G 1930- *WhoIns 92*
**Merritt**, Lynne Lionel, Jr 1915- *AmMWSc 92, WhoMW 92*
**Merritt**, Margaret Virginia 1942- *AmMWSc 92*
**Merritt**, Melody Beth 1953- *WhoMW 92*
**Merritt**, Melvin Leroy 1921- *AmMWSc 92*
**Merritt**, Michael Grady 1962- *WhoRel 92*
**Merritt**, Nancy-Jo 1942- *WhoAmL 92*
**Merritt**, Paul Burwell 1924- *WhoAmP 91*
**Merritt**, Paul Eugene 1920- *AmMWSc 92*
**Merritt**, R W 1913- *AmMWSc 92*
**Merritt**, Reuben Asa 1928- *WhoBlA 92*
**Merritt**, Richard Howard 1933- *AmMWSc 92*
**Merritt**, Richard William 1945- *AmMWSc 92*
**Merritt**, Robert Buell 1942- *AmMWSc 92*
**Merritt**, Robert Charles 1962- *WhoMW 92*
**Merritt**, Robert Edward 1930- *AmMWSc 92*
**Merritt**, Robert Edward 1941- *WhoAmL 92*
**Merritt**, Robert J. 1942- *WhoFI 92*
**Merritt**, Thomas Butler 1939- *WhoAmL 92*
**Merritt**, Thomas Mack 1949- *WhoBlA 92*
**Merritt**, Willette T. *WhoBlA 92*
**Merritt**, William D *AmMWSc 92*
**Merritt**, William E 1935- *WhoIns 92*
**Merritt-Cummings**, Annette 1946- *WhoBlA 92*
**Merrivale**, Baron 1917- *Who 92*
**Merriweather**, Barbara Christine 1948- *WhoBlA 92*
**Merriweather**, Michael Lamar 1960- *WhoBlA 92*
**Merriweather**, Robert Eugene 1948- *WhoBlA 92*
**Merriweather**, Thomas L. 1932- *WhoBlA 92*
**Merrow**, Douglas Alan 1958- *WhoAmL 92*
**Merrow**, George W 1928- *WhoAmP 91*
**Merrow-Hopp**, Susan B 1917- *AmMWSc 92*
**Merry**, James Ralph 1927- *WhoAmP 91*
**Merry**, Mildred R 1905- *WhoAmP 91*
**Merryman**, Carmen F *AmMWSc 92*
**Merryman**, John Henry 1920- *WhoAmL 92*
**Mersch**, Carol Linda 1938- *WhoFI 92*
**Mersel**, Marjorie Kathryn Pedersen 1923- *WhoFI 92, WhoWest 92*
**Mersereau**, Joanna Hayes 1928- *WhoEnt 92*
**Mersereau**, Paul Edward 1939- *WhoAmL 92*
**Mersereau**, Russell Manning 1946- *AmMWSc 92*
**Mersereau**, Stephen Crocker 1950- *WhoFI 92*
**Mersereau**, Susan 1946- *WhoFI 92*
**Mersey**, Viscount 1934- *Who 92*
**Mershart**, Eileen DeGrand 1944- *WhoAmP 91*
**Mershon**, Jeffrey Bruce 1940- *WhoFI 92*
**Mershon**, Melissa A 1953- *WhoAmP 91*
**Merskey**, Harold 1929- *AmMWSc 92*
**Mersky**, Roy Martin 1925- *WhoAmL 92*
**Mersmann**, Harry John 1936- *AmMWSc 92*
**Merson**, Marc 1931- *IntMPA 92*
**Merson**, Michael 1945- *IntWW 91*
**Mersten**, Gerald Stuart 1942- *AmMWSc 92*
**Merszei**, Zoltan 1922- *IntWW 91*
**Merta**, Douglas Ronald 1962- *WhoEnt 92*
**Merta**, Paul James 1939- *WhoEnt 92, WhoWest 92*
**Merte**, Herman, Jr 1929- *AmMWSc 92, WhoMW 92*
**Mertel**, Holly Edgar 1920- *AmMWSc 92*
**Merten**, Alan Gilbert 1941- *AmMWSc 92, WhoFI 92*
**Merten**, Harold Adams, Jr. 1927- *WhoMW 92*
**Merten**, Helmut L 1922- *AmMWSc 92*
**Merten**, Helmut Ludwig 1922- *WhoFI 92, WhoMW 92*
**Merten**, Ulrich 1930- *AmMWSc 92*
**Mertens**, Charles Franklin 1933- *WhoAmP 91*
**Mertens**, Christopher John 1958- *WhoAmL 92*
**Mertens**, David Roy 1947- *AmMWSc 92*
**Mertens**, Frederick Paul 1935- *AmMWSc 92*
**Mertens**, Glenn Charles 1957- *WhoRel 92*
**Mertens**, Lawrence E 1929- *AmMWSc 92*
**Mertens**, Mary Sue 1944- *WhoRel 92*
**Mertens**, Thomas M. 1949- *WhoEnt 92*
**Mertens**, Thomas Robert 1930- *AmMWSc 92, WhoMW 92*
**Mertens De Wilmars**, Josse 1912- *Who 92*
**Mertens De Wilmars**, Josse Marie Honore C 1912- *IntWW 91*
**Mertes**, Arthur Edward 1966- *WhoMW 92*
**Mertes**, David H 1929- *AmMWSc 92*
**Mertes**, Frank Peter, Jr 1935- *AmMWSc 92*
**Mertes**, Kristin Bowman 1946- *AmMWSc 92*
**Mertes**, Mathias Peter 1932- *AmMWSc 92*
**Merthyr**, Barony of *Who 92*
**Mertin**, Klaus 1922- *IntWW 91*
**Mertins**, Gustave Frederick 1872- *ScFEYrs*
**Mertins**, James Walter 1943- *AmMWSc 92*
**Merton**, Viscount 1971- *Who 92*
**Merton**, John Ralph 1913- *Who 92*
**Merton**, Joseph Lee 1923- *WhoBlA 92*
**Merton**, Patrick Anthony 1920- *IntWW 91, Who 92*
**Merton**, Robert K 1910- *AmMWSc 92, IntAu&W 91, IntWW 91, WrDr 92*
**Merton**, Thomas 1915-1968 *AmPeW, FacFETw*
**Merton**, Thomas 1915-1969 *BenetAL 91*
**Merton**, Thomas James 1915-1968 *RelLAm 91*
**Merts**, Athel Lavelle 1925- *AmMWSc 92*
**Mertz**, Barbara 1927- *ConAu 36NR*
**Mertz**, Barbara Louise Gross 1927- *IntAu&W 91*
**Mertz**, Dan 1928- *AmMWSc 92*
**Mertz**, David B 1934- *AmMWSc 92*
**Mertz**, Dolores M 1928- *WhoAmP 91*
**Mertz**, Edwin Theodore 1909- *AmMWSc 92, IntWW 92*
**Mertz**, Fred J. 1938- *WhoMW 92*
**Mertz**, Janet Elaine 1949- *AmMWSc 92*
**Mertz**, LuEsther T. d1991 *NewYTBS 91 [port]*
**Mertz**, Orville Richard 1918- *WhoMW 92*
**Mertz**, Paul Andrew 1961- *WhoFI 92*
**Mertz**, Robert Leroy 1934- *AmMWSc 92*
**Mertz**, Robert Ralph 1953- *WhoMW 92*
**Mertz**, Walter 1923- *AmMWSc 92*
**Mertz**, William J 1945- *AmMWSc 92*
**Meruelo**, Alex 1962- *WhoHisp 92*
**Meruelo**, Daniel 1947- *AmMWSc 92*
**Meruelo**, Raul Pablo 1955- *WhoAmL 92*
**Merula**, Tarquinio 1594?-1665 *NewAmDM*
**Merulo**, Claudio 1533-1604 *NewAmDM*
**Merva**, George E 1932- *AmMWSc 92*
**Mervielle**, Edgardo Jorge 1955- *WhoHisp 92*
**Mervine**, Edward Allen 1956- *WhoAmL 92*
**Mervyn Davies**, David Herbert *Who 92*
**Merwin**, David 1932- *WhoRel 92*
**Merwin**, Edwin Preston 1927- *WhoWest 92*
**Merwin**, Harmon Turner 1920- *WhoMW 92*
**Merwin**, Sam, Jr 1910- *TwCSFW 91*
**Merwin**, Samuel 1874-1936 *BenetAL 91*
**Merwin**, W.S. *DrAPF 91*
**Merwin**, W. S. 1927- *BenetAL 91, ConPo 91, WrDr 92*
**Meryman**, Charles Dale 1951- *AmMWSc 92*
**Meryman**, Harold Thayer 1921- *AmMWSc 92*
**Merz**, James L 1936- *AmMWSc 92*
**Merz**, Kenneth M, Jr 1922- *AmMWSc 92*
**Merz**, Mario 1925- *WorArt 1980*
**Merz**, Mary Catherine 1962- *WhoAmL 92*
**Merz**, Paul Louis 1918- *AmMWSc 92*
**Merz**, Richard A 1948- *AmMWSc 92*
**Merz**, Rollande *DrAPF 91*
**Merz**, Stuart Oscar Harold 1930- *WhoAmL 92*
**Merz**, Timothy 1927- *AmMWSc 92*
**Merz**, Walter John 1920- *AmMWSc 92*
**Merz**, William George 1941- *AmMWSc 92*
**Merzagora**, Cesare 1898- *IntWW 91*
**Merzbacher**, Claude F 1917- *AmMWSc 92*
**Merzbacher**, Eugen 1921- *AmMWSc 92*
**Merzban**, Mohammed Abdullah 1918- *IntWW 91*
**Merzenich**, Michael Matthias 1942- *AmMWSc 92*
**Merzer**, Allan Jay 1957- *WhoEnt 92*
**Mes**, Hans 1944- *AmMWSc 92*
**Mesa**, Dennis 1954- *WhoHisp 92*
**Mesa**, James Patrick 1943- *WhoHisp 92*
**Mesa**, Jose Ramon 1966- *WhoHisp 92*
**Mesa**, Mayra L. 1949- *WhoBlA 92*
**Mesa**, Raquel Chavez 1942- *WhoHisp 92*
**Mesa**, Reynaldo Rene 1959- *WhoHisp 92*
**Mesa**, Richard *WhoHisp 92*
**Mesa-Lago**, Carmelo 1934- *WhoHisp 92, WrDr 92*
**Mesa-Tejada**, Ricardo 1942- *AmMWSc 92*
**Mescall**, Eloise Therese *WhoWest 92*
**Meschan**, Isadore 1914- *AmMWSc 92*
**Mescheloff**, Moses 1909- *WhoRel 92*
**Mescher**, Anthony Louis 1949- *AmMWSc 92*
**Mescher**, Matthew F *AmMWSc 92*
**Meschi**, David John 1924- *AmMWSc 92*
**Meschia**, Giacomo 1926- *AmMWSc 92, WhoWest 92*
**Meschino**, Joseph Albert 1932- *AmMWSc 92*
**Meschke**, Herbert L 1928- *WhoAmP 91*
**Meschke**, Herbert Leonard 1928- *WhoAmL 92, WhoMW 92*
**Mesec**, Donald Francis 1936- *WhoWest 92*
**Mesecar**, Roderick Smit 1933- *AmMWSc 92*
**Meseke**, Marguerite Arvis *WhoAmP 91*
**Meselson**, Matthew Stanley 1930- *AmMWSc 92, IntWW 91*
**Meserve**, Bruce Elwyn 1917- *AmMWSc 92, WhoWest 92*
**Meserve**, Charles Francis 1850-1936 *DcNCBi 4*
**Meserve**, John H 1947- *WhoAmP 91*
**Meserve**, Lee Arthur 1944- *AmMWSc 92*
**Meserve**, Peter Lambert 1945- *AmMWSc 92*
**Meserve**, Richard Andrew 1944- *WhoAmL 92*
**Meserve**, Walter Joseph, Jr 1923- *IntAu&W 91, WrDr 92*
**Meservey**, Robert H 1921- *AmMWSc 92*
**Meseth**, Earl Herbert 1938- *AmMWSc 92*
**Meshack**, Lula M. *WhoBlA 92*
**Meshack**, Sheryl Hodges 1944- *WhoBlA 92*
**Meshberg**, Lev 1933- *IntWW 91*
**Meshbesher**, Ronald I. 1933- *WhoAmL 92, WhoMW 92*
**Meshel**, Harry *WhoAmP 91*
**Meshel**, Yeruham 1912- *IntWW 91*
**Meshii**, Masahiro 1931- *AmMWSc 92*
**Meshkov**, Aleksandr Grigorevich 1927- *IntWW 91*
**Meshkov**, Sydney 1927- *AmMWSc 92*
**Meshowski**, Frank Robert 1930- *WhoFI 92*
**Meshri**, Dayaldas Tanumal 1936- *AmMWSc 92*
**Mesiah**, Raymond N. 1932- *WhoBlA 92*
**Mesic**, Michael *DrAPF 91*
**Mesirca**, Sieglinde 1915- *WhoEnt 92*
**Mesirov**, Jill Portner 1950- *AmMWSc 92*
**Meskill**, David Thomas 1917- *WhoMW 92*
**Meskill**, Thomas J. 1928- *WhoAmL 92, WhoAmP 91*
**Meskill**, Thomas Joseph 1928- *IntWW 91*
**Meskin**, Lawrence Henry 1935- *AmMWSc 92*
**Mesko**, Zoltan 1883-1959 *BiDExR*
**Mesle**, Barbara Jalon 1950- *WhoMW 92*
**Mesler**, Corey J. *DrAPF 91*
**Mesler**, R B 1927- *AmMWSc 92*
**Meslier**, Jean 1664?-1729 *BlkwCEP*
**Mesloh**, Warren Henry 1949- *WhoWest 92*
**Meslow**, E Charles 1937- *AmMWSc 92*
**Mesmer**, Franz Anton 1734-1815 *BlkwCEP*
**Mesner**, Max H 1912- *AmMWSc 92*
**Mesney**, Dorothy Taylor 1916- *WhoEnt 92*
**Mesnikoff**, Alvin Murray 1925- *AmMWSc 92*
**Mesnil Du Buisson**, Robert Du 1895- *IntWW 91*
**Mesolella**, Vincent James, Jr 1949- *WhoAmP 91*
**Mesple**, Mady 1931- *NewAmDM*
**Mesquita**, Rosalyn Esther 1935- *WhoWest 92*
**Mesrob** *EncEarC*
**Mesrobian**, Robert Benjamin 1924- *AmMWSc 92*
**Messager**, Andre 1853-1929 *NewAmDM*
**Messager**, Annette 1943- *IntWW 91*
**Messal**, Edward Emil 1937- *AmMWSc 92*
**Messam**, Leroy Anthony 1923- *WhoFI 92*
**Messel**, Harry 1922- *Who 92, WrDr 92*
**Messemer**, Glenn Matthew 1947- *WhoAmL 92*
**Messene** *EncAmaz 91*
**Messenger**, Donald Burdett White 1935- *WhoAmP 91*
**Messenger**, George Clement 1930- *AmMWSc 92*
**Messenger**, Hiram John 1855-1913 *BiInAmS*
**Messenger**, James Robert 1948- *WhoEnt 92*
**Messenger**, Joseph Umlah 1913- *AmMWSc 92*
**Messenger**, Michael Scott 1945- *WhoAmP 91*
**Messenger**, Richard Bryan 1953- *WhoRel 92*
**Messenger**, Roger Alan 1943- *AmMWSc 92*
**Messenlehner**, Joanne Stofko 1939- *WhoAmP 91*
**Messens**, Mark Richard 1952- *WhoMW 92*
**Messer**, Arnold William 1946- *WhoEnt 92*
**Messer**, Charles Edward 1915- *AmMWSc 92*
**Messer**, Cholmeley Joseph 1929- *Who 92*
**Messer**, Donald Edward 1941- *WhoAmP 91, WhoRel 92, WhoWest 92*
**Messer**, Howard Francis 1945- *WhoAmL 92*
**Messer**, John Robert 1938- *WhoRel 92*
**Messer**, Michael F. 1954- *WhoMW 92*
**Messer**, Ralph Richardson 1945- *WhoEnt 92*
**Messer**, Thomas M 1920- *IntAu&W 91, IntWW 91, WrDr 92*
**Messer**, Wayne Ronald 1942- *AmMWSc 92*
**Messer**, William Alexander, III 1951- *WhoAmP 91*
**Messer**, William Sherwood, Jr 1958- *AmMWSc 92*
**Messerer**, Asaf Mikhaylovich 1903- *SovUnBD*
**Messerle**, Louis 1953- *AmMWSc 92*
**Messerli**, Douglas *DrAPF 91*
**Messerli**, Douglas John 1947- *IntAu&W 91*
**Messerli**, Franz Hannes 1942- *AmMWSc 92*
**Messerli**, Robbin Lance 1960- *WhoMW 92*
**Messerly**, Chris Alan 1958- *WhoAmL 92*
**Messerschmitt**, David G *AmMWSc 92*
**Messerschmitt**, Willy 1898-1978 *EncTR 91 [port], FacFETw*
**Messersmith**, Donald Howard 1928- *AmMWSc 92*
**Messersmith**, Frank S 1942- *WhoAmP 91*
**Messersmith**, James David 1931- *AmMWSc 92*
**Messersmith**, Lanny Dee 1942- *WhoAmL 92*
**Messersmith**, Robert E 1930- *AmMWSc 92*
**Messervy**, Godfrey 1924- *Who 92*
**Messia de la Cerda**, Pedro 1700-1783 *HisDSpE*
**Messiaen**, Olivier 1908- *ConCom 92, FacFETw, IntWW 91, NewAmDM, Who 92*
**Messiah**, Sonceria Von 1953- *WhoBlA 92*
**Messick**, Don 1926- *ConTFT 9, IntMPA 92, WhoEnt 92*
**Messick**, Kevin James 1963- *WhoEnt 92*
**Messick**, Neil Tilden 1949- *WhoAmP 91*
**Messick**, Roger E 1929- *AmMWSc 92*
**Messier**, Bernard 1926- *AmMWSc 92*
**Messier**, Donald R 1956- *WhoAmP 91*
**Messier**, Donald Royal 1932- *AmMWSc 92*
**Messier**, Irene M 1923- *WhoAmP 91*
**Messier**, Mark 1961- *WhoWest 92*
**Messier**, Russell 1944- *AmMWSc 92*
**Messiha**, Fathy S 1936- *AmMWSc 92*
**Messina**, Anthony John 1946- *WhoEnt 92*
**Messina**, Carla Gretchen 1937- *AmMWSc 92*
**Messina**, Edward Joseph 1937- *AmMWSc 92*
**Messina**, Frank James 1955- *AmMWSc 92*
**Messina**, Jerome Anthony 1941- *WhoAmL 92*
**Messina**, John Louis 1939- *WhoAmL 92*
**Messineo**, Luigi 1926- *AmMWSc 92*
**Messing**, David Joseph 1944- *WhoEnt 92, WhoFI 92*
**Messing**, Frank J 1929- *WhoIns 92*
**Messing**, Fredric 1948- *AmMWSc 92*
**Messing**, Harold 1935- *WhoEnt 92*
**Messing**, Joachim W 1946- *AmMWSc 92*
**Messing**, John Howard 1943- *WhoAmL 92*
**Messing**, Karen 1943- *AmMWSc 92*
**Messing**, Ralph Allan 1927- *AmMWSc 92*
**Messing**, Rita Bailey 1945- *AmMWSc 92*
**Messing**, Robin *DrAPF 91*
**Messing**, Sheldon Harold 1947- *AmMWSc 92*
**Messing**, Shelley *DrAPF 91*
**Messing**, Simon D 1922- *AmMWSc 92*
**Messinger**, Donald Hathaway 1943- *WhoAmL 92, WhoFI 92*
**Messinger**, Henry Peter 1921- *AmMWSc 92*
**Messinger**, J. Henry 1944- *WhoAmL 92*
**Messinger**, James Peter 1953- *WhoIns 92*
**Messinger**, Paul Raymond 1929- *WhoAmP 91*
**Messinger**, Richard C 1930- *AmMWSc 92*
**Messinger**, Ruth W 1940- *WhoAmP 91*
**Messinger**, Sheldon Leopold 1925- *WhoAmL 92*
**Messinger**, William Clifford 1915- *WhoFI 92*
**Messiter**, Herbert Lindsell *Who 92*
**Messitte**, Peter Jo 1941- *WhoAmL 92, WhoAmP 91*
**Messman**, John *TwCWW 91*
**Messman**, Ron A. 1937- *WhoMW 92*
**Messmer**, Dale Duwayne 1949- *WhoEnt 92*
**Messmer**, Dennis A 1937- *AmMWSc 92*
**Messmer**, Donald D 1926- *WhoIns 92*
**Messmer**, Michaeline 1954- *WhoFI 92*
**Messmer**, Pierre Auguste Joseph 1916- *IntWW 91, Who 92*

**Messmer**, Richard Paul 1941- *AmMWSc 92*
**Messmore**, Charlotte K 1948- *WhoAmP 91*
**Messmore**, Jack Merton 1952- *WhoMW 92*
**Messmore**, Thomas E *WhoIns 92*
**Messmore**, Thomas Ellison 1945- *WhoFI 92*
**Messner**, Douglas Robert 1964- *WhoFI 92*
**Messner**, Gerald Michael 1935- *WhoWest 92*
**Messner**, Howard Myron 1937- *WhoAmP 91*
**Messner**, Kathryn Hertzog 1915- *WhoWest 92*
**Messner**, Reinhold 1944- *ConAu 35NR*
**Messner**, Robert Thomas 1938- *WhoAmL 92*
**Messner**, Thomas G. 1944- *WhoFI 92*
**Messner**, William George 1950- *WhoEnt 92*
**Messner**, Zbigniew 1929- *IntWW 91*
**Messter**, Oskar 1866-1943 *FacFETw*
**Messuri**, Anthony Paul 1955- *WhoMW 92*
**Mestad**, Orville Laverne 1923- *WhoFI 92*
**Mestas**, Jean-Paul 1925- *IntAu&W 91*
**Mestecky**, Jiri 1941- *AmMWSc 92*
**Mestel**, Leon 1927- *IntWW 91*, *Who 92*
**Mestel**, Mark David 1951- *WhoAmL 92*
**Mester**, Jorge 1935- *NewAmDM*, *WhoHisp 92*
**Mester**, Loretta Jean 1958- *WhoFI 92*
**Mester**, Robert Loyd 1948- *WhoWest 92*
**Mestice**, Anthony F. 1923- *WhoRel 92*
**Mestiri**, Mahmoud 1929- *IntWW 91*
**Mestman**, Steven A 1946- *WhoIns 92*
**Meston** *Who 92*
**Meston**, Baron 1950- *Who 92*
**Mestral**, Georges de 1907-1990 *AnObit 1990*
**Mestre**, Goar *LesBEnT 92*
**Mestre**, Mercedes A. 1947- *WhoHisp 92*
**Mestres**, Ricardo 1958- *IntMPA 92*
**Mestres**, Ricardo Angelo, Jr. 1933- *WhoAmL 92*
**Mestrovic**, Ivan *DcAmImH*
**Mestvirishvili**, Mirian Alekseyevich 1934- *IntWW 91*
**Mesyats**, Gennady Andreyevich 1936- *IntWW 91*
**Mesyats**, Valentin Karpovich 1928- *IntWW 91*, *SovUnBD*
**Meszaros**, Howard Bradley 1956- *WhoMW 92*
**Meszaros**, Marta *ReelWom*
**Meszaros**, Marta 1931- *IntDcF 2-2 [port]*, *IntWW 91*
**Meszler**, Richard M 1942- *AmMWSc 92*
**Meszoely**, Charles Aladar Maria 1933- *AmMWSc 92*
**Meszoly**, Miklos 1921- *IntWW 91*
**Met**, Leon 1942- *WhoFI 92*
**Metacomet** *BenetAL 91*
**Metaksa**, Tanya K 1937- *WhoAmP 91*
**Metallica** *ConMus 7 [port]*
**Metanomski**, Wladyslaw Val 1923- *AmMWSc 92*
**Metastasio**, Pietro 1698-1782 *BlkwCEP*, *NewAmDM*
**Metaxakis**, Meletios 1871-1935 *RelLAm 91*
**Metaxas**, Ioannis 1871-1941 *BiDExR*, *EncTR 91*
**Metaxas**, Joannis 1871-1941 *FacFETw*
**Metaxas**, John C. 1958- *WhoEnt 92*
**Metayer**, Elizabeth Nener 1911- *WhoAmP 91*
**Metcalf**, Andrew Lee, Jr. 1944- *WhoBlA 92*
**Metcalf**, Artie Lou 1929- *AmMWSc 92*
**Metcalf**, Brian Walter 1945- *AmMWSc 92*
**Metcalf**, Darrell Arthur 1962- *WhoFI 92*
**Metcalf**, David Halstead 1957- *AmMWSc 92*
**Metcalf**, David Michael 1933- *Who 92*
**Metcalf**, DaVinci Carver 1955- *WhoBlA 92*
**Metcalf**, Donald 1929- *Who 92*, *WrDr 92*
**Metcalf**, Elizabeth 1921- *WhoAmP 91*
**Metcalf**, Eric Quinn 1968- *WhoBlA 92*
**Metcalf**, Frederic Thomas 1935- *AmMWSc 92*
**Metcalf**, Frederick Thomas 1921- *WhoEnt 92*
**Metcalf**, Harold 1940- *AmMWSc 92*
**Metcalf**, Helen Elizabeth 1942- *WhoWest 92*
**Metcalf**, Isaac Stevens Halstead 1912- *AmMWSc 92*
**Metcalf**, Jack 1927- *WhoAmP 91*, *WhoWest 92*
**Metcalf**, Janet 1935- *WhoAmP 91*
**Metcalf**, Jerald L 1936- *WhoAmP 91*
**Metcalf**, Jerry D. 1938- *WhoFI 92*
**Metcalf**, John 1938- *ConNov 91*, *IntWW 91*, *WrDr 92*
**Metcalf**, John Wesley 1938- *IntAu&W 91*
**Metcalf**, Laurie *IntMPA 92*
**Metcalf**, Lynnette Carol 1955- *WhoWest 92*
**Metcalf**, Malcolm 1917- *Who 92*
**Metcalf**, Michael Richard 1956- *WhoBlA 92*
**Metcalf**, Michael W 1946- *WhoAmP 91*
**Metcalf**, Paul *DrAPF 91*
**Metcalf**, Robert Gerald 1937- *WhoFI 92*
**Metcalf**, Robert Harker 1943- *AmMWSc 92*
**Metcalf**, Robert John Elmer 1919- *WhoFI 92*
**Metcalf**, Robert Lee 1916- *AmMWSc 92*, *IntWW 91*
**Metcalf**, Rosanne Elaine 1941- *WhoMW 92*
**Metcalf**, Suzanne *ConAu 133*
**Metcalf**, Virgil Alonzo 1936- *WhoWest 92*
**Metcalf**, Wayne 1952- *WhoAmP 91*
**Metcalf**, William 1838-1909 *BiInAmS*
**Metcalf**, William 1907- *AmMWSc 92*
**Metcalf**, William Evans 1944- *WhoAmL 92*
**Metcalf**, William Kenneth 1921- *AmMWSc 92*
**Metcalf**, William Lewis, Jr. 1932- *WhoMW 92*
**Metcalf**, Zeno Payne 1885-1956 *DcNCBi 4*
**Metcalf**, Zubie West, Jr. 1930- *WhoBlA 92*
**Metcalfe**, Adrian Peter 1942- *Who 92*
**Metcalfe**, Darrel Seymour 1913- *AmMWSc 92*
**Metcalfe**, David Henry Harold 1930- *Who 92*
**Metcalfe**, Dean Darrel 1944- *AmMWSc 92*
**Metcalfe**, Eloise Lopez 1942- *WhoAmP 91*
**Metcalfe**, Hugh 1928- *Who 92*
**Metcalfe**, James 1922- *AmMWSc 92*
**Metcalfe**, Joan 1923- *Who 92*
**Metcalfe**, Joseph Edward, III 1938- *AmMWSc 92*
**Metcalfe**, Lincoln Douglas 1921- *AmMWSc 92*, *WhoMW 92*
**Metcalfe**, Ralph Harold 1910- *BlkOlyM [port]*
**Metcalfe**, Ray H 1950- *WhoAmP 91*
**Metcalfe**, Robert Davis, III 1956- *WhoAmL 92*
**Metcalfe**, Samuel Lytler 1798-1856 *BiInAmS*
**Metcalfe**, Stanley Gordon 1932- *IntWW 91*, *Who 92*
**Metchnikoff**, Elie 1845-1916 *WhoNob 90*
**Metcoff**, Jack 1917- *AmMWSc 92*
**Metcoff**, Ronald M. 1941- *WhoFI 92*
**Meteer**, James William 1921- *AmMWSc 92*
**Metelica**, Michael J. 1950- *RelLAm 91*
**Meter**, Donald M 1931- *AmMWSc 92*
**Metesky**, George *ConAu 35NR*
**Metevier**, James F. 1941- *WhoFI 92*
**Meteyard**, Sidney Harold 1869-1947 *TwCPaSc*
**Metford**, John Callan James 1916- *Who 92*
**Metge**, Alice Joan 1930- *WrDr 92*
**Metge**, Joan 1930- *Who 92*
**Meth**, David L. *DrAPF 91*
**Meth**, Irving Marvin 1929- *AmMWSc 92*
**Metheney**, Twila S 1947- *WhoAmP 91*
**Methenitis**, Timothy Scott 1958- *WhoWest 92*
**Metheny**, Pat 1954- *NewAmDM*
**Metheny**, Patrick Bruce 1954- *WhoEnt 92*
**Metherell**, Alexander Franz 1939- *AmMWSc 92*
**Methfessel**, John D. 1935- *WhoAmL 92*
**Methlie**, William Russell, Jr. 1940- *WhoMW 92*
**Methodios of Boston**, Bishop 1946- *WhoRel 92*
**Methodius** d311? *EncEarC*
**Methot**, Maurice Ernest 1955- *WhoEnt 92*
**Methuen** *Who 92*
**Methuen and Company** *DcLB 112*
**Methuen**, Baron 1925- *Who 92*
**Methuen**, Lord 1886- *TwCPaSc*
**Methven**, Margaret Peterson 1918- *WhoWest 92*
**Metiu**, Horia I 1940- *AmMWSc 92*
**Metner**, Nikolay Karlovich 1880-1951 *NewAmDM*
**Metos**, Thomas Harry 1932- *WhoWest 92*
**Metoyer**, Carl B. 1925- *WhoBlA 92*
**Metoyer**, Rosia G. 1930- *WhoBlA 92*
**Metrano**, Art 1937- *WhoEnt 92*
**Metras**, Gary *DrAPF 91*
**Metras**, Gary 1947- *IntAu&W 91*
**Metreveli**, Aleksander Irakl'evich 1944- *SovUnBD*
**Metrick**, Richard Lee, Jr. 1958- *WhoRel 92*
**Metrione**, Robert M 1933- *AmMWSc 92*
**Metro**, James J 1942- *WhoAmP 91*
**Metropolis**, Nicholas Constantine 1915- *AmMWSc 92*, *WhoWest 92*
**Metry**, Amir Alfi 1942- *AmMWSc 92*
**Mets**, Laurens Jan 1946- *AmMWSc 92*
**Metsch**, Steven Gary 1960- *WhoEnt 92*
**Metsger**, Robert William 1920- *AmMWSc 92*
**Metsopoulos**, John G *WhoAmP 91*
**Metta**, David Keith 1953- *WhoMW 92*
**Mettam**, Roger C. *WrDr 92*
**Mette**, Herbert L 1925- *AmMWSc 92*
**Metteauer**, Michael Scott 1963- *WhoAmL 92*
**Mettee**, Howard Dawson 1939- *AmMWSc 92*
**Mettee**, Maurice Ferdinand 1943- *AmMWSc 92*
**Metter**, Bertram Milton 1927- *WhoFI 92*
**Metter**, Dean Edward 1932- *AmMWSc 92*
**Metter**, Gerald Edward 1944- *AmMWSc 92*
**Metter**, Ronald Elliot 1945- *WhoAmL 92*
**Metters**, Jeremy Stanley 1939- *Who 92*
**Metting**, Patricia J 1954- *AmMWSc 92*
**Mettle-Nunoo**, Nii Ahene 1945- *WhoBlA 92*
**Mettler**, Ken Glen 1948- *WhoRel 92*
**Mettler**, Pamela 1954- *WhoMW 92*
**Mettler**, Robert L. *WhoWest 92*
**Mettler**, Ruben Frederick 1924- *AmMWSc 92*, *IntWW 91*, *WhoWest 92*
**Mettrick**, David Francis 1932- *AmMWSc 92*
**Metts**, Harold M 1947- *WhoAmP 91*
**Metts**, John Van Bokkelen 1876-1959 *DcNCBi 4*
**Metts**, Sandy *WhoAmP 91*
**Metts**, Wallis C. 1932- *WhoRel 92*
**Metuzals**, Janis 1921- *AmMWSc 92*
**Metz**, Charles Edgar 1942- *AmMWSc 92*, *WhoMW 92*
**Metz**, Clyde 1940- *AmMWSc 92*
**Metz**, Craig Huseman 1955- *WhoAmL 92*, *WhoAmP 91*
**Metz**, David A 1933- *AmMWSc 92*
**Metz**, David J. 1933- *WhoFI 92*
**Metz**, Don 1940- *ConAu 135*
**Metz**, Donald C 1908- *AmMWSc 92*
**Metz**, Donald J 1924- *AmMWSc 92*
**Metz**, Donald S. 1916- *WhoRel 92*
**Metz**, Douglas Wilber 1934- *WhoAmL 92*
**Metz**, Edmund Joseph 1943- *WhoMW 92*
**Metz**, Edward 1921- *WhoFI 92*
**Metz**, Emmanuel Michael 1928- *WhoFI 92*
**Metz**, Florence Irene 1929- *AmMWSc 92*
**Metz**, Frank Andrew, Jr. 1934- *WhoFI 92*
**Metz**, Fred L 1935- *AmMWSc 92*
**Metz**, Jerred *DrAPF 91*
**Metz**, Jerred 1943- *IntAu&W 91*
**Metz**, Johann Baptist 1928- *IntWW 91*
**Metz**, John Thomas 1947- *AmMWSc 92*
**Metz**, Joseph Anthony 1937- *WhoWest 92*
**Metz**, Larry Edward 1955- *WhoAmL 92*
**Metz**, Leon C. 1930- *ConAu 36NR*
**Metz**, Mary Seawell 1937- *WhoWest 92*
**Metz**, Michael Bernum 1953- *WhoEnt 92*
**Metz**, Mike *DrAPF 91*
**Metz**, Paul 1918- *IntWW 91*
**Metz**, Peter Robert 1934- *AmMWSc 92*
**Metz**, Philip Steven 1945- *WhoMW 92*
**Metz**, Robert 1938- *AmMWSc 92*
**Metz**, Robert John Samuel 1929- *AmMWSc 92*
**Metz**, Roberta *DrAPF 91*
**Metz**, Robin *DrAPF 91*
**Metz**, Roger N 1938- *AmMWSc 92*
**Metz**, Ronald Irwin 1921- *WhoRel 92*
**Metze**, George M 1950- *AmMWSc 92*
**Metze**, Gernot 1930- *AmMWSc 92*
**Metzelaars**, Gretchen Jane 1953- *WhoEnt 92*
**Metzen**, James P 1943- *WhoAmP 91*
**Metzenbacher**, Gary William 1953- *WhoRel 92*
**Metzenbaum**, Howard M. 1917- *AlmAP 92 [port]*
**Metzenbaum**, Howard Morton 1917- *IntWW 91*, *NewYTBS 91 [port]*, *WhoAmP 91*, *WhoMW 92*
**Metzenberg**, Robert Lee 1930- *AmMWSc 92*
**Metzer**, Patricia Ann 1941- *WhoAmL 92*
**Metzgar**, Don P 1929- *AmMWSc 92*
**Metzgar**, Gary Philip 1956- *WhoMW 92*
**Metzgar**, Lee Hollis 1941- *AmMWSc 92*
**Metzgar**, Richard Stanley 1930- *AmMWSc 92*
**Metzger**, A J 1909- *AmMWSc 92*
**Metzger**, Albert E 1928- *AmMWSc 92*
**Metzger**, Boyd Ernest 1934- *AmMWSc 92*
**Metzger**, Bruce M. 1914- *WrDr 92*
**Metzger**, Bruce Manning 1914- *Who 92*, *WhoRel 92*
**Metzger**, Charles O 1923- *AmMWSc 92*
**Metzger**, Daniel Schaffer 1936- *AmMWSc 92*
**Metzger**, Darryl E 1937- *AmMWSc 92*
**Metzger**, Deena *DrAPF 91*
**Metzger**, Deena 1936- *IntAu&W 91*
**Metzger**, Dennis W 1951- *AmMWSc 92*
**Metzger**, Diane Hamill *DrAPF 91*
**Metzger**, Diane Hamill 1949- *WhoFI 92*
**Metzger**, Ernest Hugh 1923- *AmMWSc 92*
**Metzger**, Gershon 1935- *AmMWSc 92*
**Metzger**, H Peter 1931- *AmMWSc 92*
**Metzger**, Henry 1932- *AmMWSc 92*
**Metzger**, J. Kirk 1947- *WhoEnt 92*
**Metzger**, James David 1952- *AmMWSc 92*
**Metzger**, James Douglas 1942- *AmMWSc 92*
**Metzger**, James Edward 1950- *WhoFI 92*
**Metzger**, Jeffrey Paul 1950- *WhoAmL 92*
**Metzger**, John Mackay 1948- *WhoAmL 92*
**Metzger**, John U 1935- *WhoIns 92*
**Metzger**, Katherine H 1923- *WhoAmP 91*
**Metzger**, Kathleen Ann 1949- *WhoFI 92*
**Metzger**, Lewis Albert 1952- *WhoFI 92*
**Metzger**, Mark Christopher 1964- *WhoAmL 92*
**Metzger**, Marvin 1920- *AmMWSc 92*
**Metzger**, Max Joseph 1887-1944 *EncTR 91*
**Metzger**, Michael M. 1935- *WrDr 92*
**Metzger**, Radley 1930- *IntMPA 92*
**Metzger**, Raphael 1965- *WhoHisp 92*
**Metzger**, Robert Melville 1940- *AmMWSc 92*
**Metzger**, Robert P 1940- *AmMWSc 92*
**Metzger**, Robert Streicher 1950- *WhoAmL 92*
**Metzger**, Roger Edward 1936- *WhoFI 92*
**Metzger**, Sidney 1917- *AmMWSc 92*
**Metzger**, Sidney Henry, Jr 1929- *AmMWSc 92*
**Metzger**, Stanley D. 1916- *WrDr 92*
**Metzger**, Thomas Andrew 1944- *AmMWSc 92*
**Metzger**, Vernon Arthur 1918- *WhoFI 92*, *WhoWest 92*
**Metzger**, William John 1935- *AmMWSc 92*
**Metzler**, Carl Maust 1931- *AmMWSc 92*
**Metzler**, Charles Virgil 1929- *AmMWSc 92*
**Metzler**, David Everett 1924- *AmMWSc 92*
**Metzler**, Dwight F 1916- *AmMWSc 92*
**Metzler**, Eric Harold 1945- *WhoMW 92*
**Metzler**, Glenn Elam 1945- *WhoRel 92*
**Metzler**, Jim *IntMPA 92*
**Metzler**, Richard Clyde 1937- *AmMWSc 92*
**Metzler**, Yvonne Leete 1930- *WhoFI 92*
**Metzner**, Arthur B 1927- *AmMWSc 92*
**Metzner**, Carroll E 1919- *WhoAmP 91*
**Metzner**, Charles Miller 1912- *WhoAmL 92*
**Metzner**, Ernest Kurt 1949- *AmMWSc 92*
**Metzner**, Jerome 1911- *AmMWSc 92*
**Metzner**, John J 1932- *AmMWSc 92*
**Metzner**, Richard Joel 1942- *WhoWest 92*
**Meudt**, Edna 1906- *WrDr 92*
**Meudt**, Edna Kritz 1906- *IntAu&W 91*
**Meuleman**, Gezinus Evert 1925- *WhoRel 92*
**Meulemans**, Ludovicus 1924- *IntWW 91*
**Meuly**, Walter C 1898- *AmMWSc 92*
**Meunier**, Michel 1956- *AmMWSc 92*
**Meurant**, Georges 1948- *ConAu 135*
**Meurent**, Victorine 1844-1885? *ThHEIm [port]*
**Meurer**, William Henry 1956- *WhoEnt 92*
**Meuschke**, Paul John 1927- *WhoRel 92*
**Meussner**, R A 1920- *AmMWSc 92*
**Meuten**, Donald John 1948- *AmMWSc 92*
**Meuth**, Patterson Carl 1953- *WhoAmL 92*
**Meuwissen**, Lawrence Eugene 1947- *WhoAmL 92*
**Meux**, John Wesley 1928- *AmMWSc 92*
**Meverden**, James Robert 1954- *WhoMW 92*
**Mew**, Calvin Marshall 1947- *WhoFI 92*
**Mew**, Charlotte 1869-1928 *RfGEnL 91*
**Mewborn**, Ancel Clyde 1932- *AmMWSc 92*
**Mewborne**, James Marion 1848-1924 *DcNCBi 4*
**M'Ewen**, Ewen 1916- *Who 92*
**Mewes**, Horst 1940- *WhoWest 92*
**Mewhinney**, James Albert 1939- *AmMWSc 92*
**Mewissen**, Dieudonne Jean 1924- *AmMWSc 92*
**Mews**, Kurt Frederick 1962- *WhoRel 92*
**Mewshaw**, Michael 1943- *IntAu&W 91*, *WrDr 92*
**Mexal**, John Gregory 1946- *AmMWSc 92*
**Mexandeau**, Louis Jean 1931- *IntWW 91*
**Mexborough**, Earl of 1931- *Who 92*
**Meyberg**, Bernhard Ulrich 1917- *WhoFI 92*
**Meyboom**, Peter 1934- *AmMWSc 92*
**Meyburg**, Arnim Hans 1939- *AmMWSc 92*
**Meydrech**, Edward Frank 1943- *AmMWSc 92*
**Meye**, Robert Paul 1929- *WhoWest 92*
**Meyendorff**, John 1926- *WrDr 92*
**Meyer**, Albert Gregory 1903-1965 *RelLAm 91*
**Meyer**, Albert Ronald 1941- *AmMWSc 92*
**Meyer**, Albert William 1906- *AmMWSc 92*

**Meyer**, Alfred d1990 Who 92N
**Meyer**, Alfred 1891-1945 EncTR 91
**Meyer**, Alice Virginia 1922- WhoAmP 91
**Meyer**, Alvin F, Jr 1920- AmMWSc 92
**Meyer**, Andrea Peroutka 1963- WhoFI 92
**Meyer**, Andrew C., Jr. 1949- WhoAmL 92
**Meyer**, Andrew Hays 1963- WhoAmL 92
**Meyer**, Andrew U 1927- AmMWSc 92
**Meyer**, Annie Nathan 1867-1951 BenetAL 91, HanAmWH
**Meyer**, Anthony 1920- ConAu 134
**Meyer**, Anthony John Charles 1920- Who 92
**Meyer**, Armin Henry 1914- IntWW 91, WhoAmP 91
**Meyer**, Arnold Oskar 1877-1944 EncTR 91
**Meyer**, August Christopher 1900- WhoEnt 92
**Meyer**, August Christopher, Jr. 1937- WhoEnt 92
**Meyer**, Axel 1926- AmMWSc 92
**Meyer**, Barry M. IntMPA 92
**Meyer**, Ben F 1927- IntAu&W 91
**Meyer**, Ben Franklin 1927- WrDr 92
**Meyer**, Bernard Henry 1941- AmMWSc 92
**Meyer**, Bernard Sandler 1901- AmMWSc 92
**Meyer**, Bernhard O 1933- WhoIns 92
**Meyer**, Betty Michelson AmMWSc 92
**Meyer**, Bill 1925- WhoFI 92, WhoMW 92
**Meyer**, Brad Anthony 1952- AmMWSc 92
**Meyer**, Bruce Karl 1962- WhoRel 92
**Meyer**, Burnett Chandler 1921- AmMWSc 92
**Meyer**, C. M., Mrs. 1934- WhoMW 92
**Meyer**, Carl Beat 1934- AmMWSc 92
**Meyer**, Carl Dean, Jr 1942- AmMWSc 92
**Meyer**, Carl Sheaff 1932- WhoFI 92
**Meyer**, Catherine Dieffenbach 1951- WhoAmL 92
**Meyer**, Charles Howard 1952- WhoAmL 92
**Meyer**, Charles J. 1945- WhoMW 92
**Meyer**, Charles Robert 1920- WrDr 92
**Meyer**, Christian 1943- AmMWSc 92
**Meyer**, Christopher John Rome 1944- Who 92
**Meyer**, Clare Stephen 1942- WhoMW 92
**Meyer**, Conrad John Eustace 1922- Who 92
**Meyer**, Cord, Jr. 1920- AmPeW
**Meyer**, Dale Thomas 1948- WhoWest 92
**Meyer**, Daniel J 1936- WhoAmP 91
**Meyer**, Daniel Joseph 1936- WhoFI 92, WhoMW 92
**Meyer**, Daniel P 1954- WhoAmP 91
**Meyer**, David Bernard 1923- AmMWSc 92
**Meyer**, David Cooke 1955- WhoFI 92
**Meyer**, David Lachlan 1943- AmMWSc 92
**Meyer**, Dean J WhoAmP 91
**Meyer**, Delbert Henry 1926- AmMWSc 92
**Meyer**, Dennis Irwin 1935- WhoAmL 92
**Meyer**, Dennis W. 1947- WhoFI 92
**Meyer**, Diane Hutchins 1937- AmMWSc 92
**Meyer**, Donald Irwin 1926- AmMWSc 92
**Meyer**, Donald Ray 1924- WhoMW 92
**Meyer**, Donald Robert 1942- WhoAmL 92
**Meyer**, Douglas Edward 1942- WhoEnt 92
**Meyer**, Douglas LeRoy 1951- WhoRel 92
**Meyer**, Dwain Wilber 1944- AmMWSc 92
**Meyer**, Dwaine Fredric 1929- WhoEnt 92
**Meyer**, E Y 1946- IntAu&W 91
**Meyer**, Edgar F 1935- AmMWSc 92
**Meyer**, Edmond Gerald 1919- AmMWSc 92
**Meyer**, Edward C. 1928- IntWW 91
**Meyer**, Edward Dell 1941- AmMWSc 92
**Meyer**, Edward Henry 1927- WhoFI 92
**Meyer**, Edward Paul 1949- WhoFI 92
**Meyer**, Edwin F 1937- AmMWSc 92
**Meyer**, Emmanuel R. 1918- IntWW 91
**Meyer**, Eric G. 1953- WhoWest 92
**Meyer**, Eugene L. 1942- ConAu 135
**Meyer**, F. Arnold 1910- WhoMW 92
**Meyer**, Frank Henry 1915- AmMWSc 92
**Meyer**, Frank Joseph 1924- WhoFI 92
**Meyer**, Frank Nicholas 1875-1918 BiInAmS
**Meyer**, Franz 1923- AmMWSc 92
**Meyer**, Franz O 1945- AmMWSc 92
**Meyer**, Fred Jay 1963- WhoAmL 92
**Meyer**, Fred Josef 1931- WhoEnt 92
**Meyer**, Fred Paul 1931- AmMWSc 92
**Meyer**, Fred William, Jr. 1924- WhoFI 92, WhoMW 92
**Meyer**, Fred Wolfgang 1947- AmMWSc 92
**Meyer**, Frederick Gustav 1917- AmMWSc 92
**Meyer**, Frederick Jacobs 1931- WhoFI 92
**Meyer**, Frederick Ray 1927- WhoAmP 91
**Meyer**, Frederick Richard 1938- AmMWSc 92
**Meyer**, Frederick William 1943- WhoIns 92
**Meyer**, George G 1931- AmMWSc 92
**Meyer**, George Herbert 1928- WhoAmL 92
**Meyer**, George Wilbur 1941- AmMWSc 92
**Meyer**, Gerald Christopher 1948- WhoAmL 92
**Meyer**, Geraldine L 1927- WhoAmP 91
**Meyer**, Gerard G L 1941- AmMWSc 92
**Meyer**, Glenn Arthur 1934- AmMWSc 92, WhoMW 92
**Meyer**, Gregory Carl 1918- AmMWSc 92
**Meyer**, Gregory James 1949- WhoRel 92
**Meyer**, Gunter Hubert 1939- AmMWSc 92
**Meyer**, H. Theodore 1935- WhoAmL 92
**Meyer**, Hank 1920- WhoFI 92
**Meyer**, Hannes 1889-1954 DcTwDes, FacFETw
**Meyer**, Hans-Otto 1943- AmMWSc 92
**Meyer**, Harold David 1939- AmMWSc 92
**Meyer**, Harold Louis 1916- WhoFI 92, WhoMW 92
**Meyer**, Harry Martin, Jr 1928- AmMWSc 92
**Meyer**, Haruko 1929- AmMWSc 92
**Meyer**, Harvey John 1935- AmMWSc 92
**Meyer**, Heinz Friedrich 1932- AmMWSc 92
**Meyer**, Henry John 1927- WhoFI 92
**Meyer**, Henry Oostenwald Albertijn 1937- AmMWSc 92
**Meyer**, Herbert Eugene 1945- WhoFI 92
**Meyer**, Herbert Frederick Reichert, Jr. 1950- WhoFI 92
**Meyer**, Heribert 1913- AmMWSc 92
**Meyer**, Hermann 1927- AmMWSc 92
**Meyer**, Horst 1926- AmMWSc 92
**Meyer**, Howard Robert 1938- WhoAmL 92
**Meyer**, Irving 1920- AmMWSc 92
**Meyer**, Irwin Stephan 1941- WhoAmL 92, WhoFI 92
**Meyer**, Ivah Gene 1935- WhoWest 92
**Meyer**, J. Theodore 1936- WhoAmL 92, WhoAmP 91, WhoFI 92, WhoMW 92
**Meyer**, Jacob Owen 1934- WhoRel 92
**Meyer**, James Henry 1922- AmMWSc 92
**Meyer**, James Henry 1928- AmMWSc 92
**Meyer**, James Melvin 1943- AmMWSc 92
**Meyer**, James Wagner 1920- AmMWSc 92
**Meyer**, Jean Leon Andre 1914- IntWW 91
**Meyer**, Jean-Pierre 1929- AmMWSc 92
**Meyer**, Jeanette R. 1928- WhoMW 92
**Meyer**, Jerold Alan 1952- WhoMW 92
**Meyer**, Jerome J. 1938- WhoWest 92
**Meyer**, Johannes 1929- WhoIns 92
**Meyer**, John Austin 1919- AmMWSc 92
**Meyer**, John Michael 1947- WhoAmL 92
**Meyer**, John Phillip 1920- WhoAmL 92
**Meyer**, John R. 1927- WrDr 92
**Meyer**, John Richard 1948- AmMWSc 92
**Meyer**, John Sigmund 1937- AmMWSc 92
**Meyer**, John Stirling 1924- AmMWSc 92
**Meyer**, Joseph 1894-1987 NewAmDM
**Meyer**, Joseph B. 1941- WhoAmL 92, WhoAmP 91, WhoWest 92
**Meyer**, Joseph J, Jr 1925- WhoIns 92
**Meyer**, Joseph Urban 1948- WhoAmP 91
**Meyer**, Judy Lynn 1946- AmMWSc 92
**Meyer**, June IntAu&W 91X, WrDr 92
**Meyer**, Karl 1899- AmMWSc 92
**Meyer**, Kenneth J WhoAmP 91
**Meyer**, Kenneth Marven 1932- WhoRel 92
**Meyer**, Kent Alan 1955- WhoRel 92
**Meyer**, Kevin Lee 1963- WhoWest 92
**Meyer**, Klaus 1928- IntWW 91
**Meyer**, Krzysztof 1943- ConCom 92
**Meyer**, Laurence Louis 1940- WhoRel 92
**Meyer**, Lawrence 1941- ConAu 34NR, IntAu&W 91, WrDr 92
**Meyer**, Lawrence Donald 1933- AmMWSc 92
**Meyer**, Lawrence George 1940- WhoAmL 92, WhoFI 92
**Meyer**, Lee Gordon 1943- WhoAmL 92
**Meyer**, Leo Francis 1929- AmMWSc 92
**Meyer**, Leo Martin 1906- AmMWSc 92
**Meyer**, Leon Herbert 1926- AmMWSc 92
**Meyer**, Leonard B. 1918- WhoEnt 92, WrDr 92
**Meyer**, Lester Allen 1923- WhoRel 92
**Meyer**, Lhary 1947- AmMWSc 92, WhoEnt 92
**Meyer**, Louis B. 1933- WhoAmL 92
**Meyer**, Louis B, Jr 1933- WhoAmP 91
**Meyer**, Lucy Rider 1849-1922 RelLAm 91
**Meyer**, M. E. Joseph, III WhoFI 92, WhoWest 92
**Meyer**, Marilyn L. 1951- WhoFI 92
**Meyer**, Marshall Theodore 1930- WhoRel 92
**Meyer**, Martin Jay 1932- WhoAmL 92
**Meyer**, Martin Marinus, Jr 1936- AmMWSc 92
**Meyer**, Marvin Chris 1941- AmMWSc 92
**Meyer**, Marvin Clinton 1907- AmMWSc 92
**Meyer**, Marvin Godfrey 1938- WhoMW 92
**Meyer**, Marvin Wayne 1948- WhoRel 92, WhoWest 92
**Meyer**, Mary Jean 1947- WhoAmP 91
**Meyer**, Maurice Wesley 1925- AmMWSc 92
**Meyer**, Max Earl 1918- WhoAmL 92
**Meyer**, Michael 1921- IntAu&W 91, WrDr 92
**Meyer**, Michael Albert 1937- WhoMW 92, WhoRel 92
**Meyer**, Michael Broeker 1946- WhoAmL 92
**Meyer**, Michael C. 1956- WhoFI 92
**Meyer**, Michael Leverson 1921- Who 92
**Meyer**, Michael Martin 1945- WhoRel 92
**Meyer**, Michael Siegfried 1950- Who 92
**Meyer**, Michael W. WhoAmL 92
**Meyer**, Nancy Jo 1942- WhoMW 92
**Meyer**, Natalie 1930- WhoAmP 91, WhoWest 92
**Meyer**, Nicholas 1945- IntAu&W 91, IntMPA 92, WhoEnt 92, WrDr 92
**Meyer**, Norman James 1926- AmMWSc 92
**Meyer**, Norman Joseph 1930- AmMWSc 92
**Meyer**, Orville R 1926- AmMWSc 92
**Meyer**, Paul 1925- AmMWSc 92
**Meyer**, Paul A 1947- AmMWSc 92
**Meyer**, Paul Reims WhoMW 92
**Meyer**, Paul Richard 1930- AmMWSc 92
**Meyer**, Paul William 1924- WhoRel 92
**Meyer**, Peter 1920- AmMWSc 92
**Meyer**, Peter Bert 1943- WhoFI 92
**Meyer**, Philip Gilbert 1945- WhoAmL 92
**Meyer**, R Peter 1943- AmMWSc 92
**Meyer**, Ralph A, Jr 1943- AmMWSc 92
**Meyer**, Ralph O 1938- AmMWSc 92
**Meyer**, Ralph Roger 1940- AmMWSc 92
**Meyer**, Ramon Eugene 1933- WhoEnt 92, WhoMW 92
**Meyer**, Raymond W 1939- WhoAmP 91
**Meyer**, Rich Bakke, Jr 1943- AmMWSc 92
**Meyer**, Richard Adlin 1933- AmMWSc 92
**Meyer**, Richard Arthur 1946- AmMWSc 92
**Meyer**, Richard Charles 1930- AmMWSc 92
**Meyer**, Richard Christopher 1948- WhoRel 92
**Meyer**, Richard David 1943- AmMWSc 92
**Meyer**, Richard Edward 1939- WhoEnt 92
**Meyer**, Richard Edwin 1939- WhoWest 92
**Meyer**, Richard Ernst 1919- AmMWSc 92
**Meyer**, Richard Fastabend 1921- AmMWSc 92
**Meyer**, Richard Jonah 1933- WhoEnt 92
**Meyer**, Richard Lee 1931- AmMWSc 92
**Meyer**, Richard Lee 1937- AmMWSc 92
**Meyer**, Richard Neff 1945- WhoWest 92
**Meyer**, Rita A AmMWSc 92
**Meyer**, Robert Alan 1946- WhoFI 92
**Meyer**, Robert Bruce 1943- AmMWSc 92
**Meyer**, Robert Dean 1934- WhoIns 92
**Meyer**, Robert Earl 1932- AmMWSc 92
**Meyer**, Robert F 1925- AmMWSc 92
**Meyer**, Robert J., Jr. WhoFI 92
**Meyer**, Robert Jay 1949- AmMWSc 92
**Meyer**, Robert Kenneth 1932- IntWW 91
**Meyer**, Robert Paul 1924- AmMWSc 92
**Meyer**, Robert Paul 1945- WhoMW 92
**Meyer**, Robert Walter 1939- AmMWSc 92
**Meyer**, Roberta WhoRel 92
**Meyer**, Roger Arnold 1935- WhoMW 92
**Meyer**, Roger J 1928- AmMWSc 92
**Meyer**, Roger Jess Christian 1928- WhoWest 92
**Meyer**, Roger Paul 1950- WhoWest 92
**Meyer**, Roland Harry 1927- WhoFI 92, WhoMW 92
**Meyer**, Rollo John Oliver d1991 Who 92N
**Meyer**, Ronald 1952- ConAu 135
**Meyer**, Ronald Anthony AmMWSc 92
**Meyer**, Ronald Harmon 1929- AmMWSc 92
**Meyer**, Ronald Warren 1929- AmMWSc 92
**Meyer**, Russ 1922- IntMPA 92
**Meyer**, Russell William, Jr. 1932- WhoFI 92, WhoMW 92
**Meyer**, Ruth Kraemer 1945- WhoFI 92
**Meyer**, Ruth Krueger 1940- WhoMW 92
**Meyer**, Sally Cave 1937- WhoWest 92
**Meyer**, Samuel Gordon 1937- WhoMW 92
**Meyer**, Stephen Alan 1949- WhoFI 92
**Meyer**, Stephen Frederick 1947- AmMWSc 92
**Meyer**, Stephen Leonard 1948- WhoAmP 91
**Meyer**, Stuart Lloyd 1937- AmMWSc 92
**Meyer**, Stuart Philip 1960- WhoAmL 92
**Meyer**, Thomas DrAPF 91
**Meyer**, Thomas 1946- AmMWSc 92
**Meyer**, Thomas J. WhoAmL 92
**Meyer**, Thomas J 1941- AmMWSc 92
**Meyer**, Thomas J. 1949- WhoMW 92
**Meyer**, Thomas Robert 1936- WhoWest 92
**Meyer**, Ursula 1927- WhoWest 92
**Meyer**, Vern WhoAmP 91
**Meyer**, Vernon M 1924- AmMWSc 92
**Meyer**, Victor Bernard 1920- AmMWSc 92
**Meyer**, Vincent D 1932- AmMWSc 92
**Meyer**, W Keith 1929- AmMWSc 92
**Meyer**, Walter WhoAmP 91
**Meyer**, Walter 1932- AmMWSc 92
**Meyer**, Walter Edward 1929- AmMWSc 92
**Meyer**, Walter H 1922- AmMWSc 92
**Meyer**, Walter Joseph 1943- AmMWSc 92
**Meyer**, Walter Leslie 1931- AmMWSc 92
**Meyer**, Wilfred H WhoIns 92
**Meyer**, William Ellis 1936- AmMWSc 92
**Meyer**, William Guthrie 1947- WhoAmL 92
**Meyer**, William Laros 1936- AmMWSc 92
**Meyer**, William Louis 1956- WhoMW 92
**Meyer**, William Trenholm 1937- WhoWest 92
**Meyer**, Wolfgang E 1910- AmMWSc 92
**Meyer-Arendt**, Jurgen Richard 1921- AmMWSc 92, WhoWest 92
**Meyer-Cording**, Ulrich 1911- IntWW 91
**Meyer-Landrut**, Andreas 1929- IntWW 91
**Meyerand**, Russell Gilbert, Jr 1933- AmMWSc 92
**Meyerbeer**, Giacomo 1791-1864 NewAmDM
**Meyerhardt**, Richard Louis 1936- WhoMW 92
**Meyerhof**, Otto 1884-1951 EncTR 91 [port]
**Meyerhof**, Otto Fritz 1884-1951 FacFETw, WhoNob 90
**Meyerhof**, Walter Ernst 1922- AmMWSc 92
**Meyerhofer**, Dietrich 1931- AmMWSc 92
**Meyerhoff**, Arthur Augustus 1928- AmMWSc 92
**Meyerhoff**, Mark Elliot 1953- AmMWSc 92
**Meyerhold**, Vsevolod Yemilyevich 1874-1942 FacFETw
**Meyering**, Christopher Paul 1958- WhoAmL 92
**Meyering**, Ralph, Jr. 1951- WhoEnt 92
**Meyerkhol'd**, Vsevolod Emil'evich 1874-1940 SovUnBD
**Meyerman**, Harold John 1938- WhoWest 92
**Meyerott**, Roland Edward 1916- AmMWSc 92
**Meyerowitz**, Elliot Martin 1951- AmMWSc 92
**Meyerowitz**, Jan 1913- NewAmDM
**Meyerowitz**, Joel 1938- IntWW 91
**Meyerowitz**, Patricia 1933- IntAu&W 91, WrDr 92
**Meyers**, Abbey Sue 1944- WhoFI 92
**Meyers**, Al WhoAmP 91
**Meyers**, Alan Gordon 1947- WhoRel 92
**Meyers**, Albert Irving 1932- AmMWSc 92
**Meyers**, Anthony James 1950- WhoAmL 92
**Meyers**, Ari 1969- WhoHisp 92
**Meyers**, Bernard Leonard 1937- AmMWSc 92
**Meyers**, Bonnie 1948- WhoWest 92
**Meyers**, Bruce A. WhoFI 92
**Meyers**, Bruce Kemp 1943- WhoWest 92
**Meyers**, Cal Yale 1927- AmMWSc 92
**Meyers**, Carol Lyons 1942- WhoRel 92
**Meyers**, Carolyn Winstead 1946- AmMWSc 92
**Meyers**, Charles Richard 1930- WhoAmP 91
**Meyers**, Christene Cosgriffe 1948- WhoEnt 92
**Meyers**, Darryl Lee 1955- WhoAmL 92
**Meyers**, Donald Bates 1922- AmMWSc 92
**Meyers**, Earl Lawrence 1907- AmMWSc 92
**Meyers**, Edward 1927- AmMWSc 92
**Meyers**, Edward Alexander 1959- WhoFI 92
**Meyers**, Emil, Jr 1927- WhoAmP 91
**Meyers**, Ernest S. d1991 NewYTBS 91
**Meyers**, Frederick H 1918- AmMWSc 92
**Meyers**, Gail Helene 1962- WhoWest 92
**Meyers**, Gene Howard 1942- AmMWSc 92
**Meyers**, George Edward 1928- WhoFI 92
**Meyers**, Gerald Carl 1928- IntWW 91
**Meyers**, Gina Rose 1960- WhoMW 92
**Meyers**, Gregory Paul 1951- WhoMW 92
**Meyers**, Hannes, Jr 1932- WhoAmP 91
**Meyers**, Herbert 1931- AmMWSc 92, WhoWest 92
**Meyers**, Howard Craig 1951- WhoAmL 92, WhoWest 92
**Meyers**, Ishmael Alexander 1939- WhoBlA 92
**Meyers**, James Edward 1953- WhoFI 92
**Meyers**, James Harlan 1945- AmMWSc 92
**Meyers**, James Joseph 1923- WhoIns 92
**Meyers**, James Leonard 1947- WhoEnt 92

**Meyers**, James William 1942- WhoWest 92
**Meyers**, Jan WhoMW 92
**Meyers**, Jan 1928- AlmAP 92 [port], WhoAmP 91
**Meyers**, Jean Brewer 1939- WhoAmP 91
**Meyers**, Jeffrey 1939- DcLB 111 [port], IntAu&W 91, WrDr 92
**Meyers**, Jeffrey 1952- WhoAmL 92
**Meyers**, Jerry Ivan 1946- WhoAmL 92
**Meyers**, Joel D. d1991 NewYTBS 91
**Meyers**, John Charles 1950- WhoFI 92
**Meyers**, John Thomas, Jr. 1963- WhoFI 92
**Meyers**, Joyce Selber 1942- WhoAmL 92
**Meyers**, Karen Hopkins 1948- WhoMW 92
**Meyers**, Katherine May 1916- WhoAmP 91
**Meyers**, Kenneth Purcell AmMWSc 92
**Meyers**, Kenneth Raymond 1954- WhoFI 92
**Meyers**, Leroy Frederick 1927- AmMWSc 92
**Meyers**, Lou 1955- WhoFI 92
**Meyers**, Louis Jay 1955- WhoEnt 92
**Meyers**, Lynn Betty 1952- WhoMW 92
**Meyers**, M Douglas 1933- AmMWSc 92
**Meyers**, Marc Andre 1946- AmMWSc 92
**Meyers**, Marian Bennett 1938- AmMWSc 92
**Meyers**, Martin Bernard 1933- AmMWSc 92
**Meyers**, Maurice 1932- WhoAmP 91
**Meyers**, Merle Cooper 1951- WhoAmL 92
**Meyers**, Michael 1950- WhoBlA 92
**Meyers**, Norman George 1930- AmMWSc 92
**Meyers**, Ouidga Loris Moore 1944- WhoRel 92
**Meyers**, Philip Alan 1941- AmMWSc 92
**Meyers**, Philip Henry 1933- AmMWSc 92
**Meyers**, Pieter, Jr. 1941- WhoWest 92
**Meyers**, Raymond Francis, Jr. 1960- WhoRel 92
**Meyers**, Richard DrAPF 91
**Meyers**, Richard Milton 1935- WhoAmL 92
**Meyers**, Richard Stuart 1938- WhoWest 92
**Meyers**, Robert 1934- IntMPA 92
**Meyers**, Robert Allen 1936- AmMWSc 92
**Meyers**, Roger Joseph 1955- WhoWest 92
**Meyers**, Ron WhoAmP 91
**Meyers**, Ronald Roy 1944- WhoRel 92
**Meyers**, Rose M. 1945- WhoBlA 92
**Meyers**, Samuel Philip 1925- AmMWSc 92
**Meyers**, Stephen John 1960- WhoEnt 92
**Meyers**, Susan 1942- WrDr 92
**Meyers**, Theda Maria WhoWest 92
**Meyers**, Vernon J 1933- AmMWSc 92
**Meyers**, Victor Aloysius d1991 NewYTBS 91
**Meyers**, Wayne Marvin 1924- AmMWSc 92
**Meyers**, William C 1931- AmMWSc 92
**Meyers-Elliott**, Roberta Hart 1937- AmMWSc 92
**Meyersick**, Sharon Kay 1945- WhoMW 92
**Meyerson**, Arthur Lee 1938- AmMWSc 92
**Meyerson**, Bernard Steele 1954- AmMWSc 92
**Meyerson**, Charles 1955- WhoEnt 92
**Meyerson**, Ivan D. WhoAmL 92
**Meyerson**, Mark Daniel 1949- AmMWSc 92
**Meyerson**, Martin 1922- IntWW 91
**Meyerson**, Seymour 1916- AmMWSc 92
**Meyerson**, Stanley Phillip 1916- WhoAmL 92
**Meyjes**, Richard 1918- Who 92
**Meylan**, Maurice Andre 1942- AmMWSc 92
**Meyn**, Raymond Everett, Jr 1942- AmMWSc 92
**Meynell**, Alice 1847-1922 RfGEnL 91
**Meynell**, Alix 1903- Who 92
**Meynell**, Benedict William 1930- Who 92
**Meynell**, Hugo A. 1936- WrDr 92
**Meyner**, Helen Stevenson 1929- WhoAmP 91
**Meyo**, Robert Joseph 1936- WhoMW 92
**Meyrick**, Barbara O AmMWSc 92
**Meyrick**, David 1926- Who 92
**Meyrick**, George 1941- Who 92
**Meyrose**, Thomas Alexander 1954- WhoMW 92
**Meyrowitz**, Alan Lester 1945- AmMWSc 92
**Meysey-Thompson**, Simon 1935- Who 92
**Meystel**, Alexander Michael 1935- AmMWSc 92
**Meza**, Beatrice 1953- WhoHisp 92
**Meza**, Bruce-Aaron Jedidiah 1952- WhoEnt 92
**Meza**, Carlos J. 1958- WhoHisp 92
**Meza**, Roberto 1937- IntWW 91
**Meza-Overstreet**, Mark Lee 1950- WhoHisp 92
**Mezei**, Catherine 1931- AmMWSc 92
**Mezei**, Michael 1927- AmMWSc 92
**Mezei**, Mihaly 1944- AmMWSc 92
**Mezer**, Steven Henry 1954- WhoAmL 92
**Mezey**, Eugene Julius 1926- AmMWSc 92
**Mezey**, Kalman C 1909- AmMWSc 92
**Mezey**, Paul G 1943- AmMWSc 92
**Mezey**, Robert DrAPF 91
**Mezey**, Robert 1935- ConPo 91, WhoWest 92, WrDr 92
**Mezger**, Fritz Walter William 1928- AmMWSc 92
**Mezger-Freed**, Liselotte 1926- AmMWSc 92
**Mezhelaitis**, Eduardas 1919- IntWW 91
**Mezhirov**, Aleksandr Petrovich 1923- IntWW 91
**Mezhlauk**, Ivan Ivanovich 1891-1938 SovUnBD
**Mezhlauk**, Valeriy Ivanovich 1893-1938 SovUnBD
**Mezick**, James Andrew 1939- AmMWSc 92
**Mezquita**, Cristobal 1944- AmMWSc 92
**Mezrow**, Steven Milton 1960- WhoAmL 92
**Mezvinsky**, Edward M 1937- WhoAmP 91
**Mezzasoma**, Fernando 1907-1945 BiDExR
**Mezzatesta**, Jerry L 1946- WhoAmP 91
**Mezzich**, Juan Enrique 1945- WhoHisp 92
**Mezzino**, Michael Joseph, Jr 1940- AmMWSc 92
**Mfume**, Kweisi WhoBlA 92
**Mfume**, Kweisi 1948- AlmAP 92 [port], WhoAmP 91
**Mgrdechian**, Raffee 1927- AmMWSc 92, WhoFI 92
**Mhelan**, Muhammad WhoRel 92
**Mi**, Ming-Pi 1933- AmMWSc 92
**Miakwe**, Akepa 1934- Who 92
**Miale**, Joseph Nicolas 1919- AmMWSc 92
**Miall**, Andrew D 1944- AmMWSc 92
**Miall**, Leonard 1914- Who 92
**Miall**, Robert IntAu&W 91X
**Miank**, David Charles 1946- WhoWest 92
**Miano**, Louis Stephen 1934- WhoFI 92
**Miano**, Steven Thomas 1960- WhoAmL 92
**Miao Shan** EncAmaz 91
**Miari**, Suhail 1944- WhoMW 92
**Miatech**, Gerald James 1922- AmMWSc 92
**Mica**, Daniel Andrew 1944- WhoAmP 91
**Mica**, John L 1943- WhoAmP 91
**Mica**, Robert Leonard 1936- WhoAmP 91
**Micale**, Fortunato Joseph 1932- AmMWSc 92
**Micallef**, Daniel 1928- IntWW 91
**Micallef**, Francis WhoRel 92
**Micallef**, Joseph Vincent Raymond 1957- WhoWest 92
**Micciche**, Daniel John 1956- WhoAmL 92
**Miceika**, Gene 1947- WhoIns 92
**Miceli**, Angelo Sylvestro 1913- AmMWSc 92
**Miceli**, Ignatius 1918- WhoRel 92, WhoWest 92
**Miceli**, James R 1935- WhoAmP 91
**Miceli**, Joseph N 1945- AmMWSc 92
**Miceli**, Michael Vincent 1951- AmMWSc 92
**Miceli**, Vincent Peter d1991 NewYTBS 91
**Micetich**, Ronald George 1931- AmMWSc 92
**Mich**, Thomas Frederick 1939- AmMWSc 92
**Micha**, David Allan AmMWSc 92
**Michael**, Archbishop 1892-1958 RelLAm 91
**Michael**, King 1921- IntWW 91
**Michael of Kent**, Prince 1942 Who 92R
**Michael**, Alfred Frederick, Jr 1928- AmMWSc 92
**Michael**, Alun Edward 1943- Who 92
**Michael**, Ann E. DrAPF 91
**Michael**, Arthur B 1923- AmMWSc 92
**Michael**, Charlene Belton WhoBlA 92
**Michael**, Charles Reid 1939- AmMWSc 92
**Michael**, Charles Richard 1955- WhoRel 92
**Michael**, Dale R. 1942- WhoBlA 92
**Michael**, Donald F 1929- WhoAmP 91
**Michael**, Douglas Charles 1957- WhoAmL 92
**Michael**, Duncan 1937- Who 92
**Michael**, Edwin Daryl 1938- AmMWSc 92
**Michael**, Ellis LeRoy 1881-1920 BiInAmS
**Michael**, Ernest Arthur 1925- AmMWSc 92
**Michael**, Ernest Denzil, Jr 1922- AmMWSc 92
**Michael**, Frederick William 1943- WhoMW 92
**Michael**, Gary G. 1940- WhoFI 92
**Michael**, George WhoEnt 92
**Michael**, George 1963- IntWW 91
**Michael**, Harold K 1943- WhoAmP 91
**Michael**, Harold Kaye Bud 1955- WhoWest 92
**Michael**, Harold Louis 1920- AmMWSc 92
**Michael**, Helen Cecilia DeSilver Abbott 1857-1904 BiInAmS
**Michael**, Helen Katherine 1959- WhoAmL 92
**Michael**, I. D. L. 1936- WrDr 92
**Michael**, Ian David Lewis 1936- Who 92
**Michael**, Ian Lockie 1915- Who 92
**Michael**, Irving 1929- AmMWSc 92
**Michael**, Jacob Gabriel 1931- AmMWSc 92
**Michael**, James Harry, Jr. 1918- WhoAmL 92
**Michael**, James Henry 1920- IntWW 91
**Michael**, Joe Victor 1935- AmMWSc 92
**Michael**, Joel Allen 1940- AmMWSc 92, WhoMW 92
**Michael**, John A. 1921- ConAu 133
**Michael**, John Steven 1955- WhoEnt 92
**Michael**, Leslie William 1933- AmMWSc 92
**Michael**, Lloyd Hal 1942- AmMWSc 92
**Michael**, Mark A. 1948- WhoAmL 92
**Michael**, Mark D. 1951- WhoFI 92
**Michael**, Martha Ann 1956- WhoMW 92
**Michael**, Max, Jr 1916- AmMWSc 92
**Michael**, Norman 1931- AmMWSc 92
**Michael**, Patrick Doyle 1952- WhoWest 92
**Michael**, Paul Andrew 1928- AmMWSc 92
**Michael**, Peter 1938- Who 92
**Michael**, Phyllis Callender 1908- WhoEnt 92
**Michael**, Randall Blake 1948- WhoRel 92
**Michael**, Richard Phillip 1924- AmMWSc 92
**Michael**, Robert Roy 1946- WhoAmL 92
**Michael**, Sandra Dale 1945- AmMWSc 92
**Michael**, Stanley Reginald 1944- WhoRel 92
**Michael**, Stanley Vermont 1928- WhoRel 92
**Michael**, Thomas Hugh Glynn 1918- AmMWSc 92
**Michael**, Toby WhoAmP 91, WhoHisp 92
**Michael**, William Herbert, Jr 1926- AmMWSc 92
**Michael**, William R 1930- AmMWSc 92
**Michael-Kenney**, Shari Ann 1957- WhoFI 92
**Michaeli**, Dov 1935- AmMWSc 92
**Michaelides**, Constantinos M. 1937- IntWW 91
**Michaelis**, Arthur Frederick 1941- AmMWSc 92
**Michaelis**, Carl I 1918- AmMWSc 92
**Michaelis**, Elias K 1944- AmMWSc 92
**Michaelis**, Johann David 1717-1791 BlkwCEP
**Michaelis**, Lynn Otto 1944- WhoFI 92
**Michaelis**, Mary Louise 1943- AmMWSc 92
**Michaelis**, Michael 1919- AmMWSc 92
**Michaelis**, Otho Ernest, IV 1936- AmMWSc 92
**Michaelis**, Paul Charles 1935- AmMWSc 92
**Michaelis**, Richard C 1839-1909 ScFEYrs
**Michaels**, Adlai Eldon 1913- AmMWSc 92
**Michaels**, Al LesBEnT 92 [port]
**Michaels**, Alan Sherman 1922- AmMWSc 92
**Michaels**, Allan 1944- AmMWSc 92
**Michaels**, Andrice 1950- WhoAmP 91
**Michaels**, Barbara ConAu 36NR
**Michaels**, Barbara 1927- WrDr 92
**Michaels**, Brenda Hillman DrAPF 91
**Michaels**, Claire DrAPF 91
**Michaels**, Dale WrDr 92
**Michaels**, David D 1925- AmMWSc 92
**Michaels**, Fern WrDr 92
**Michaels**, Gary David 1955- WhoAmL 92
**Michaels**, Geneva Lane 1929- WhoRel 92
**Michaels**, George 1923- WhoAmL 92
**Michaels**, James E. WhoRel 92
**Michaels**, James Walker 1921- WhoFI 92
**Michaels**, Jane 1947- WhoAmL 92
**Michaels**, Joel B. 1938- IntMPA 92
**Michaels**, John Edward 1939- AmMWSc 92
**Michaels**, John Patrick, Jr. 1944- WhoFI 92
**Michaels**, Jon 1957- WhoEnt 92
**Michaels**, Joseph Eugene 1951- WhoEnt 92
**Michaels**, Kevan 1955- WhoEnt 92
**Michaels**, Kristin TwCWW 91, WrDr 92
**Michaels**, Larry DrAPF 91
**Michaels**, Leonard DrAPF 91
**Michaels**, Leonard 1933- ConNov 91, WrDr 92
**Michaels**, Leslie 1925- Who 92
**Michaels**, Lorne LesBEnT 92 [port], WhoEnt 92
**Michaels**, Lorne 1944- ConTFT 9, IntMPA 92
**Michaels**, Mark 1949- WhoEnt 92
**Michaels**, Mark David 1949- WhoMW 92
**Michaels**, Michael Israel 1908- Who 92
**Michaels**, Patrick Francis 1925- WhoEnt 92, WhoWest 92
**Michaels**, Peter J. 1958- WhoEnt 92
**Michaels**, Ray 1953- WhoEnt 92
**Michaels**, Richard 1936- IntMPA 92
**Michaels**, Richard Edward 1952- WhoAmL 92
**Michaels**, Richard Morton 1927- WhoMW 92
**Michaels**, Steve WrDr 92
**Michaels**, Willard A. 1917- WhoEnt 92
**Michaelsen**, April Lynn 1957- WhoRel 92
**Michaelsen**, Rachel Beth 1963- WhoWest 92
**Michaelsen**, Terje E 1942- AmMWSc 92
**Michaelson**, Benjamin, Jr. 1936- WhoAmL 92, WhoFI 92
**Michaelson**, Henry d1904 BiInAmS
**Michaelson**, I Arthur 1925- AmMWSc 92
**Michaelson**, Jerry Dean 1943- AmMWSc 92
**Michaelson**, John Charles 1953- WhoFI 92
**Michaelson**, Julius Cooley 1922- WhoAmP 91
**Michaelson**, Martin 1943- WhoAmL 92
**Michaelson**, Melvin 1928- WhoAmL 92
**Michaelson**, Merle Edward 1921- AmMWSc 92
**Michaelson**, S D 1913- AmMWSc 92
**Michaelson**, Solomon M 1922- AmMWSc 92
**Michak**, Helen Barbara 1926- WhoMW 92
**Michal**, Edwin Keith 1932- AmMWSc 92
**Michal**, Eugene J 1922- AmMWSc 92
**Michalak**, Charles 1946- WhoFI 92
**Michalak**, Craig Lance 1947- WhoFI 92
**Michalak**, Edward Francis 1937- WhoAmL 92
**Michalak**, Joseph T 1932- AmMWSc 92
**Michalak**, Robert Albert 1945- WhoAmL 92
**Michalak**, Thomas Ireneusz AmMWSc 92
**Michalek**, Gary Louis 1948- WhoWest 92
**Michalek**, Joel Edmund 1944- AmMWSc 92
**Michalek**, Suzanne M 1944- AmMWSc 92
**Michaletz**, William John 1964- WhoMW 92
**Michalik**, Edmund Richard 1915- AmMWSc 92
**Michalik**, Gregory James 1956- WhoFI 92
**Michalik**, John James 1945- WhoAmL 92, WhoWest 92
**Michalko**, Jan 1912-1990 WhoRel 92
**Michalko**, Ruth Grupe 1927- WhoRel 92
**Michalopoulos**, Andre Who 92N
**Michalopoulos**, George AmMWSc 92
**Michalowicz**, Joseph C 1916- AmMWSc 92
**Michalowicz**, Joseph Victor 1941- AmMWSc 92
**Michalowski**, Jerzy 1909- Who 92
**Michalowski**, Joseph Thomas 1943- AmMWSc 92
**Michalowski**, Radoslaw Lucas 1951- AmMWSc 92
**Michals**, George Francis 1935- WhoFI 92
**Michalske**, Terry Arthur 1953- AmMWSc 92
**Michalski**, Chester James 1942- AmMWSc 92
**Michalski**, Jan 1920- IntWW 91
**Michalski**, Joseph Potter 1945- AmMWSc 92
**Michalski**, Ryszard Spencer 1937- AmMWSc 92
**Michalsky**, Joseph Jan, Jr 1947- AmMWSc 92
**Michalson**, Edgar Lloyd 1929- AmMWSc 92
**Michaud**, Alphee Martial 1938- WhoFI 92
**Michaud**, Georges Joseph 1940- AmMWSc 92
**Michaud**, Gerald Fredrick 1949- WhoEnt 92
**Michaud**, Hilda Jean 1937- WhoRel 92
**Michaud**, Howard H 1902- AmMWSc 92
**Michaud**, Jean-Claude Georges 1933- IntWW 91
**Michaud**, Michael Herman 1955- WhoAmP 91
**Michaud**, Peter Paul 1950- WhoAmL 92
**Michaud**, Ronald Normand 1937- AmMWSc 92
**Michaud**, Ted C 1929- AmMWSc 92
**Michaud**, Ted Corneille 1929- WhoMW 92
**Michaux**, Andre 1746-1802 BiInAmS, DcNCBi 4
**Michaux**, Eric Coates 1941- WhoBlA 92
**Michaux**, Francois Andre 1770-1855 BiInAmS, DcNCBi 4
**Michaux**, Henri 1899-1984 GuFrLit 1
**Michaux**, Henry G. 1934- WhoBlA 92
**Michaux**, Henry M, Jr 1930- WhoAmP 91, WhoBlA 92

**Michaux**, Lightfoot Solomon 1884-1968 *RelLAm 91*
**Micheau**, Jack Bradford 1955- *WhoAmL 92*
**Micheaux**, Oscar 1884- *IntDcF 2-2*
**Micheaux**, Oscar 1884-1951 *TwCWW 91*
**Michejda**, Christopher Jan 1937- *AmMWSc 92*
**Michejda**, Oskar 1922- *AmMWSc 92*
**Michel**, Aaron Edmund 1957- *WhoAmL 92*
**Michel**, Anthony Nikolaus 1935- *AmMWSc 92, WhoMW 92*
**Michel**, Athenia Marie 1942- *WhoAmP 91*
**Michel**, Benoit 1940- *WhoFI 92*
**Michel**, Burlyn Everett 1923- *AmMWSc 92*
**Michel**, Clemence Louise 1830-1905 *EncAmaz 91*
**Michel**, Clifford Lloyd 1939- *WhoAmL 92*
**Michel**, D. Daniel, Jr. 1946- *WhoFI 92*
**Michel**, Daniel John 1949- *WhoEnt 92*
**Michel**, David John 1942- *AmMWSc 92*
**Michel**, F Curtis 1934- *AmMWSc 92*
**Michel**, Francois Claude 1928- *IntWW 91*
**Michel**, Frantz Ludwig 1680?-1714? *DcNCBi 4*
**Michel**, Gerd Wilhelm 1930- *AmMWSc 92*
**Michel**, Harding B 1924- *AmMWSc 92*
**Michel**, Harriet Richardson 1942- *WhoBlA 92*
**Michel**, Hartmut 1948- *AmMWSc 92, Who 92, WhoNob 90*
**Michel**, Henry Ludwig 1924- *WhoFI 92*
**Michel**, James H *WhoAmP 91*
**Michel**, Joseph 1925- *IntWW 91*
**Michel**, Karl Heinz 1929- *AmMWSc 92*
**Michel**, Kenneth Earl 1930- *AmMWSc 92*
**Michel**, Lester Allen 1919- *AmMWSc 92*
**Michel**, Louis 1923- *IntWW 91*
**Michel**, Mary Ann Kedzuf 1939- *WhoWest 92*
**Michel**, Milton Scott 1916- *WrDr 92*
**Michel**, Patricia Owen 1955- *WhoFI 92*
**Michel**, Paul R *WhoAmP 91*
**Michel**, Paul Redmond 1941- *WhoAmL 92*
**Michel**, Philip Martin 1939- *WhoFI 92, WhoMW 92*
**Michel**, Richard Edwin 1928- *AmMWSc 92, WhoMW 92*
**Michel**, Robert George 1949- *AmMWSc 92*
**Michel**, Robert H. 1923- *AlmAP 92 [port]*
**Michel**, Robert Henry 1923- *IntWW 91, WhoAmP 91, WhoMW 92*
**Michel**, Thomas Francis 1941- *WhoRel 92*
**Michel**, Victor James, Jr. 1927- *WhoWest 92*
**Michel**, Werner *IntMPA 92*
**Michel**, William Middleton 1822-1894 *BiInAmS*
**Michelakis**, Andrew M 1927- *AmMWSc 92*
**Michelangeli** 1920- *IntWW 91*
**Michelangeli**, Arturo Benedetti 1920- *NewAmDM*
**Michelbacher**, Abraham E 1899- *AmMWSc 92*
**Michelena**, Juan A. 1939- *WhoHisp 92*
**Michelet**, Jules 1798-1874 *GuFrLit 1, NinCLC 31 [port]*
**Michelet**, Michel 1899- *IntMPA 92*
**Micheli**, Frank James 1930- *WhoAmL 92*
**Micheli**, James Carl 1956- *WhoAmL 92*
**Micheli**, Joseph Ronald 1948- *WhoAmP 91*
**Micheli**, Lyle Joseph 1940- *AmMWSc 92*
**Micheli**, Robert Angelo 1922- *AmMWSc 92*
**Micheli**, Roger Paul 1949- *AmMWSc 92, WhoFI 92*
**Michelin**, Francois 1926- *IntWW 91*
**Michelin**, Reginald Townend 1903- *Who 92*
**Micheline**, Jack *DrAPF 91*
**Michelini**, Arturo 1909-1969 *BiDExR*
**Michelini**, Linda Katharine 1949- *WhoWest 92*
**Michelini**, Sylvia Hamilton 1946- *WhoFI 92*
**Michell**, Allan Henry 1930- *IntWW 91*
**Michell**, Keith *Who 92*
**Michell**, Keith 1926- *IntMPA 92*
**Michell**, Keith 1928- *IntWW 91*
**Michell**, Michael John 1942- *Who 92*
**Michell**, Robert H. 1941- *IntWW 91*
**Michell**, Robert Hall 1941- *Who 92*
**Michelman**, Frank I. 1936- *WhoAmL 92*
**Michelman**, Henry D. *WhoRel 92*
**Michelman**, Irving Simon 1917- *WhoFI 92*
**Michelman**, John S 1938- *AmMWSc 92*
**Michelmore**, Clifford Arthur 1919- *Who 92*
**Michelmore**, Laurence 1909- *IntWW 91*
**Michels**, Alan 1950- *WhoMW 92*
**Michels**, Corinne Anthony 1943- *AmMWSc 92*
**Michels**, Donald Joseph 1932- *AmMWSc 92*
**Michels**, H Harvey 1932- *AmMWSc 92*
**Michels**, John Rudolf 1944- *WhoAmP 91*
**Michels**, Lester David 1948- *AmMWSc 92*
**Michels**, Lloyd R 1916- *AmMWSc 92*
**Michels**, Oren William 1963- *WhoFI 92*
**Michels**, Robert 1936- *AmMWSc 92*
**Michels**, Ronald G. d1991 *NewYTBS 91*
**Michels**, Roy Samuel 1932- *WhoFI 92*
**Michels**, Stanley E 1933- *WhoAmP 91*
**Michelsen**, Arve 1923- *AmMWSc 92*
**Michelsen**, Axel 1940- *IntWW 91*
**Michelsen**, Clifford Stanley 1913- *WhoRel 92*
**Michelsen**, Hans Gunter 1920- *IntWW 91*
**Michelsen**, John Ernest 1946- *WhoFI 92, WhoMW 92*
**Michelson**, A. Rawle 1955- *WhoFI 92*
**Michelson**, Albert 1852-1931 *RComAH*
**Michelson**, Albert Abraham 1852-1931 *WhoNob 90*
**Michelson**, David Richard 1955- *WhoAmL 92*
**Michelson**, Douglas Jerome 1942- *WhoWest 92*
**Michelson**, Edward Harlan 1926- *AmMWSc 92*
**Michelson**, Ellen Beth 1951- *WhoFI 92*
**Michelson**, Eric L 1947- *AmMWSc 92*
**Michelson**, Gertrude Geraldine 1925- *WhoFI 92*
**Michelson**, Irving 1922- *AmMWSc 92*
**Michelson**, Joan *DrAPF 91*
**Michelson**, Larry 1952- *AmMWSc 92*
**Michelson**, Leslie Paul 1943- *AmMWSc 92*
**Michelson**, Lillian 1928- *WhoEnt 92*
**Michelson**, Louis 1919- *AmMWSc 92*
**Michelson**, Miriam 1870- *ScFEYrs*
**Michelson**, Peter *DrAPF 91*
**Michelson**, Reuben 1927- *WhoMW 92*
**Michelson**, Richard *DrAPF 91*
**Michelson**, Robert 1944- *WhoAmP 91*
**Michelson**, Robert Henry 1957- *WhoMW 92*
**Michelson**, Sonia 1928- *WhoWest 92*
**Michelson**, William Michael 1940- *WrDr 92*
**Michelstetter**, Stanley Hubert 1946- *WhoAmL 92*
**Michelucci**, Giovanni 1891-1990 *AnObit 1990*
**Michener**, Carroll K 1885-1970 *ScFEYrs*
**Michener**, Charles Duncan 1918- *AmMWSc 92, IntWW 91*
**Michener**, Charles Edward 1907- *AmMWSc 92*
**Michener**, Daniel Roland 1900- *IntWW 91*
**Michener**, David Lawrence, Jr. 1962- *WhoRel 92*
**Michener**, Ezra 1794-1887 *AmPeW, BiInAmS*
**Michener**, H David 1912- *AmMWSc 92*
**Michener**, James *DrAPF 91*
**Michener**, James A. 1907- *BenetAL 91, ConNov 91, FacFETw, TwCWW 91, WrDr 92*
**Michener**, James Albert 1907- *IntAu&W 91, IntWW 91, Who 92*
**Michener**, John William 1924- *AmMWSc 92*
**Michener**, Roland *IntWW 91*
**Michener**, Roland d1991 *Who 92N*
**Michener**, Roland 1900-1991 *CurBio 91N*
**Michenfelder**, John D 1931- *AmMWSc 92*
**Michetti**, Susan Jane 1948- *WhoFI 92, WhoMW 92*
**Michie**, Daniel Boorse, Jr. 1922- *WhoAmL 92*
**Michie**, David Alan Redpath 1928- *IntWW 91, Who 92*
**Michie**, David Doss 1936- *AmMWSc 92*
**Michie**, Donald 1923- *Who 92*
**Michie**, Donald Michael 1934- *WhoMW 92*
**Michie**, James 1927- *ConPo 91, IntAu&W 91, WrDr 92*
**Michie**, Jarvis D *AmMWSc 92*
**Michie**, Peter Smith 1839-1901 *BiInAmS*
**Michie**, Ray 1934- *Who 92*
**Michie**, Thomas Johnson, Jr 1931- *WhoAmP 91*
**Michie**, William 1935- *Who 92*
**Michieli**, Ronald Antonio 1934- *WhoWest 92*
**Michielli**, Donald Warren 1934- *AmMWSc 92*
**Michiels**, Leo Paul 1928- *AmMWSc 92*
**Michigan**, Alan 1945- *WhoAmL 92*
**Michik**, Robert Duane 1942- *WhoWest 92*
**Michl**, Josef 1939- *AmMWSc 92*
**Michlin**, Arnold Sidney 1920- *WhoMW 92*
**Michlmayr**, Manfred 1943- *AmMWSc 92*
**Michlovic**, Thomas A 1946- *WhoAmP 91*
**Michon**, Hubert *WhoRel 92*
**Michon**, John Albertus 1935- *IntWW 91*
**Michurin**, Ivan Vladimirovich 1855-1935 *SovUnBD*
**Michurina-Samoilova**, Vera Arkad'evna 1866-1948 *SovUnBD*
**Mick**, Paul 1956- *WhoEnt 92*
**Mick**, Thomas Eugene 1950- *WhoEnt 92*
**Mickal**, Abe 1913- *AmMWSc 92*
**Mickel**, Emanuel J 1937- *IntAu&W 91*
**Mickel**, Emanuel J., Jr. 1937- *WrDr 92*
**Mickel**, Hubert Sheldon 1937- *AmMWSc 92*
**Mickel**, John Thomas 1934- *AmMWSc 92*
**Mickel**, Joseph Thomas 1951- *WhoAmL 92*
**Mickel**, Ronald Eldon 1935- *WhoMW 92*
**Mickelberry**, William C. 1933- *WhoWest 92*
**Mickelberry**, William Charles 1933- *AmMWSc 92*
**Mickelsen**, Colleen 1949- *WhoRel 92*
**Mickelsen**, Einer Bjegaard 1922- *WhoAmL 92*
**Mickelsen**, John Raymond 1928- *AmMWSc 92*
**Mickelsen**, Olaf 1912- *AmMWSc 92*
**Mickelson**, Anastasia A. *WhoMW 92*
**Mickelson**, Arnold Rust 1922- *WhoRel 92*
**Mickelson**, Bob J 1921- *WhoAmP 91*
**Mickelson**, George S. 1941- *AlmAP 92 [port], IntWW 91, WhoMW 92*
**Mickelson**, George Speaker 1941- *WhoAmP 91*
**Mickelson**, Gordon M *WhoAmP 91*
**Mickelson**, Jerry *WhoEnt 92*
**Mickelson**, John Chester 1920- *AmMWSc 92*
**Mickelson**, John Clair 1929- *AmMWSc 92*
**Mickelson**, Michael Eugene 1940- *AmMWSc 92*
**Mickelson**, Milo Norval 1911- *AmMWSc 92*
**Mickelson**, Pamela Carlene Luebke 1952- *WhoMW 92*
**Mickelson**, Richard W 1930- *AmMWSc 92*
**Mickelson**, Rome H 1931- *AmMWSc 92*
**Mickelson**, Sig *LesBEnT 92*
**Mickelson**, Sig 1913- *WhoEnt 92*
**Mickens**, Maxine 1948- *WhoBlA 92*
**Mickens**, Ronald Elbert 1943- *AmMWSc 92, WhoBlA 92*
**Mickey**, Donald Lee 1943- *AmMWSc 92*
**Mickey**, George Henry 1910- *AmMWSc 92*
**Mickey**, Glen Franck 1945- *WhoFI 92*
**Mickey**, Gordon Eugene *WhoBlA 92*
**Mickey**, John Wesley 1942- *WhoAmP 91*
**Mickey**, Max Ray, Jr 1923- *AmMWSc 92*
**Mickey**, Paul Albert 1937- *WhoRel 92*
**Mickey**, Rosie Cheatham *WhoBlA 92*
**Mickins**, Andel W. 1924- *WhoBlA 92*
**Mickle**, Andrea Denise 1952- *WhoBlA 92*
**Mickle**, Ann Marie 1945- *AmMWSc 92*
**Mickle**, Billy A 1945- *WhoAmP 91*
**Mickle**, Elva L. 1949- *WhoBlA 92*
**Mickle**, Marlin Homer 1936- *AmMWSc 92*
**Mickle**, William 1735-1788 *RfGEnL 91*
**Micklejohn**, George 1717?-1818 *DcNCBi 4*
**Micklem**, Mark Cunningham 1958- *WhoFI 92*
**Mickler**, Randell Robert, Jr. 1948- *WhoRel 92*
**Mickles**, James 1923- *AmMWSc 92*
**Micklethwait**, Robert 1902- *Who 92*
**Mickley**, Harold S 1918- *AmMWSc 92*
**Mickley**, Richard Stroud 1939- *WhoRel 92*
**Micklin Silver**, Joan *IntDcF 2-2*
**Micklon**, Stephanie 1947- *WhoAmP 91*
**Micklow**, Craig Woodward 1947- *WhoFI 92*
**Micko**, Michael M 1935- *AmMWSc 92*
**Mickolus**, Edward 1950- *WrDr 92*
**Micks**, Deitra R. H. 1945- *WhoBlA 92*
**Mico**, Elva Jeanne 1940- *WhoEnt 92*
**Micou**, E. Venable 1945- *WhoFI 92*
**Micozzi**, Marc S 1953- *AmMWSc 92*
**Micozzie**, Nicholas Anthony 1930- *WhoAmP 91*
**Miczek**, Klaus A 1944- *AmMWSc 92*
**Miczuga**, Mark N. 1962- *WhoMW 92*
**Midanek**, Deborah Hicks 1954- *WhoFI 92*
**Midda**, Sara 1951- *ConAu 135, IntAu&W 91*
**Middaugh**, Alan Russell 1929- *WhoWest 92*
**Middaugh**, Benjamin D. 1934- *WhoEnt 92*
**Middaugh**, Jack Kendall, II 1949- *WhoFI 92*
**Middaugh**, James 1946- *WhoAmP 91*
**Middaugh**, Richard Lowe 1938- *AmMWSc 92*
**Middelkamp**, John Neal 1925- *AmMWSc 92*
**Middendorf**, Donald Floyd 1931- *AmMWSc 92*
**Middendorf**, Helmut 1953- *WorArt 1980*
**Middendorf**, Henry Stump, Jr 1923- *WhoAmP 91*
**Middendorf**, J. William, II 1924- *IntWW 91*
**Middendorf**, John William, II 1924- *WhoAmP 91*
**Middendorf**, Max Harold 1941- *WhoAmP 91*
**Middendorf**, Michael Paul 1959- *WhoRel 92*
**Middendorf**, William H 1921- *AmMWSc 92*
**Middlebrook**, Grace Irene 1927- *WhoWest 92*
**Middlebrook**, John Leslie 1946- *AmMWSc 92*
**Middlebrook**, Martin 1932- *WrDr 92*
**Middlebrook**, R D 1929- *AmMWSc 92*
**Middlebrook**, Stephen B., Sr. *WhoAmL 92*
**Middlebrook**, Stephen Beach 1937- *WhoIns 92*
**Middlebrooks**, Eddie Joe 1932- *AmMWSc 92, WhoFI 92*
**Middlebrooks**, Felicia 1957- *WhoBlA 92*
**Middlebrooks**, Mary Jo 1951- *WhoAmL 92*
**Middleditch**, Brian Stanley 1945- *AmMWSc 92*
**Middleditch**, Edward 1923- *IntWW 91*
**Middleditch**, Edward 1923-1987 *TwCPaSc*
**Middlehurst**, Barbara Mary 1915- *AmMWSc 92*
**Middlemas**, David Alan 1955- *WhoMW 92*
**Middlemas**, Robert Keith 1935- *Who 92*
**Middlemass**, Keith 1935- *WrDr 92*
**Middlemiss**, Robert William *DrAPF 91*
**Middlesbrough**, Auxiliary Bishop of *Who 92*
**Middlesbrough**, Bishop of 1917- *Who 92*
**Middlesex**, Archdeacon of *Who 92*
**Middleswart**, James Ira 1912- *WhoAmP 91*
**Middleton**, Baron 1921- *Who 92*
**Middleton**, Bishop Suffragan of 1925- *Who 92*
**Middleton**, Alex Lewis Aitken 1938- *AmMWSc 92*
**Middleton**, Anthony Wayne, Jr. 1939- *WhoWest 92*
**Middleton**, Arthur Everts 1919- *AmMWSc 92*
**Middleton**, Bernice Bryant 1922- *WhoBlA 92*
**Middleton**, Beth Ann 1955- *AmMWSc 92*
**Middleton**, Charles Cheavens 1930- *AmMWSc 92*
**Middleton**, Charles G, III 1947- *WhoAmP 91*
**Middleton**, Christopher *DrAPF 91*
**Middleton**, Christopher 1926- *ConPo 91, IntAu&W 91, IntWW 91, WrDr 92*
**Middleton**, Clyde William 1928- *WhoAmP 91*
**Middleton**, Conyers 1683-1750 *BlkwCEP*
**Middleton**, David 1920- *AmMWSc 92*
**Middleton**, David Andrew 1966- *WhoEnt 92*
**Middleton**, Donald King 1922- *IntWW 91, Who 92*
**Middleton**, Drew 1913- *IntAu&W 91*
**Middleton**, Drew 1913-1990 *AnObit 1990*
**Middleton**, Earl Matthew *WhoAmP 91*
**Middleton**, Edward Bernard 1948- *Who 92*
**Middleton**, Edward L. *WhoFI 92*
**Middleton**, Edwin Lee 1866-1928 *DcNCBi 4*
**Middleton**, Elliott, Jr 1925- *AmMWSc 92*
**Middleton**, Elwyn Linton 1914- *WhoAmL 92*
**Middleton**, Ernest J. 1937- *WhoBlA 92*
**Middleton**, Foster H 1922- *AmMWSc 92*
**Middleton**, Francis 1913- *Who 92*
**Middleton**, George 1880-1967 *BenetAL 91*
**Middleton**, George 1910- *Who 92*
**Middleton**, George Humphrey 1910- *IntWW 91*
**Middleton**, Gerard Viner 1931- *AmMWSc 92*
**Middleton**, Henry Moore, III 1943- *AmMWSc 92*
**Middleton**, Herman David, Sr. 1925- *WhoEnt 92*
**Middleton**, Ian 1928- *IntAu&W 91*
**Middleton**, Jack Baer 1929- *WhoAmL 92*
**Middleton**, James Arthur 1936- *WhoFI 92, WhoWest 92*
**Middleton**, James Boland 1934- *WhoAmL 92*
**Middleton**, Joan Kirkland 1936- *WhoRel 92*
**Middleton**, John A 1915- *WhoAmP 91*
**Middleton**, John Francis Marchment 1921- *WhoRel 92*
**Middleton**, John Patrick Windsor 1938- *Who 92*
**Middleton**, John Ross, Jr. 1940- *WhoFI 92*
**Middleton**, John T 1912- *AmMWSc 92*
**Middleton**, Kenneth William Bruce 1905- *Who 92*
**Middleton**, Lawrence John 1930- *Who 92*

**Middleton,** Linley Eric *Who 92*
**Middleton,** Lucy Laura 1941- *WhoRel 92*
**Middleton,** Marc Stephen 1950- *WhoFI 92, WhoMW 92*
**Middleton,** Michael A. 1947- *WhoBlA 92*
**Middleton,** Michael Humfrey 1917- *Who 92*
**Middleton,** Michael John 1953- *WhoWest 92*
**Middleton,** O. E. 1925- *ConNov 91, WrDr 92*
**Middleton,** Osman Edward 1925- *IntAu&W 91*
**Middleton,** Paulette Bauer 1946- *AmMWSc 92*
**Middleton,** Peter d1781 *BiInAmS*
**Middleton,** Peter 1934- *Who 92*
**Middleton,** Peter Edward 1934- *IntWW 91*
**Middleton,** Peter Tyler 1947- *WhoAmL 92*
**Middleton,** Richard B 1936- *AmMWSc 92*
**Middleton,** Richard Temple, III 1942- *WhoBlA 92*
**Middleton,** Robert 1920- *WhoEnt 92*
**Middleton,** Robert Gordon 1908- *WhoWest 92*
**Middleton,** Roger 1955- *IntAu&W 91*
**Middleton,** Ronald George 1913- *Who 92*
**Middleton,** Rose Nixon 1932- *WhoBlA 92*
**Middleton,** Roy 1927- *AmMWSc 92*
**Middleton,** Stanley 1919- *ConNov 91, IntAu&W 91, Who 92, WrDr 92*
**Middleton,** Stephen Hugh 1909- *Who 92*
**Middleton,** Thomas 1580?-1627 *RfGEnL 91*
**Middleton,** Thomas F 1945- *WhoAmP 91*
**Middleton,** Vertelle Delores 1942- *WhoBlA 92*
**Middleton,** Vincent Francis 1951- *WhoFI 92*
**Middleton,** Wayne Arthur 1945- *WhoFI 92*
**Middleton,** William Joseph 1927- *AmMWSc 92*
**Middlewood,** Martin Eugene 1947- *WhoWest 92*
**Middour,** Dean Lee 1943- *WhoWest 92*
**Midei,** Richard Allen 1947- *WhoMW 92*
**Midgett,** James Clayton, Jr. 1950- *WhoAmL 92*
**Midgett,** John Allen, Jr. 1876-1938 *DcNCBi 4*
**Midgett,** Levene Westcott 1891-1973 *DcNCBi 4*
**Midgett,** Little Bannister, III 1852-1928 *DcNCBi 4*
**Midgett,** Vance Llewellyn 1959- *WhoRel 92*
**Midgley,** A Rees, Jr 1933- *AmMWSc 92*
**Midgley,** Eric Atkinson 1913- *Who 92*
**Midgley,** James Eardley 1934- *AmMWSc 92*
**Midgley,** Leslie *LesBEnT 92*
**Midkiff,** Eleanor Elizabeth 1943- *WhoMW 92*
**Midkiff,** Kimberly Ann 1958- *WhoAmL 92*
**Midkiff,** Robert Richards 1920- *WhoFI 92*
**Midland,** Michael Mark 1946- *AmMWSc 92*
**Midlarsky,** Elizabeth *AmMWSc 92*
**Midler,** Bette 1945- *IntMPA 92, IntWW 91, WhoEnt 92*
**Midler,** Michael, Jr 1936- *AmMWSc 92*
**Midleton,** Viscount 1949- *Who 92*
**Midlige,** Frederick Horstmann, Jr 1935- *AmMWSc 92*
**Midori** 1971- *ConMus 7 [port], NewYTBS 91 [port]*
**Midteide,** Per J. *WhoRel 92*
**Midura,** Thaddeus 1931- *AmMWSc 92*
**Midwig,** William Carroll, Jr. 1951- *WhoFI 92*
**Midwinter,** Eric 1932- *WrDr 92*
**Midwinter,** Eric Clare 1932- *Who 92*
**Midwinter,** John Edwin 1938- *IntWW 91, Who 92*
**Midwinter,** Stanley Walter 1922- *Who 92*
**Midwood,** Bart A. *DrAPF 91*
**Midyett,** Michael Lyons 1946- *WhoAmL 92*
**Miech,** Allen C. 1939- *WhoFI 92*
**Miech,** Ralph Patrick 1933- *AmMWSc 92*
**Miech,** Ronald Joseph 1935- *AmMWSc 92*
**Mieczkowski,** Rondo *DrAPF 91*
**Mied,** Richard Paul 1946- *AmMWSc 92*
**Miedusiewski,** American Joe 1949- *WhoAmP 91*
**Miegel,** Agnes 1879-1964 *EncTR 91 [port]*
**Miehle,** William 1915- *AmMWSc 92*
**Miehls,** Donald Edward 1959- *WhoAmL 92*
**Miekka,** Richard G 1933- *AmMWSc 92*
**Miel,** Alice Marie 1906- *WrDr 92*
**Miel,** George J 1943- *AmMWSc 92*
**Miel,** Vicky Ann 1951- *WhoWest 92*
**Mielcuszny,** Albert John 1941- *WhoFI 92*
**Mielczarek,** Eugenie V 1931- *AmMWSc 92*
**Miele,** Angelo 1922- *AmMWSc 92, WrDr 92*
**Miele,** Frank Daniel 1955- *WhoEnt 92*
**Mielenz,** Jonathan Richard 1948- *AmMWSc 92*
**Mielenz,** Klaus Dieter 1929- *AmMWSc 92*
**Mielert,** Fritz Josef Maria 1879-1947 *EncTR 91*
**Mielke,** Clarence Harold, Jr. 1936- *WhoWest 92*
**Mielke,** Erich 1907- *IntWW 91*
**Mielke,** Eugene Albert 1946- *AmMWSc 92*
**Mielke,** Frederick William, Jr. 1921- *IntWW 91, WhoWest 92*
**Mielke,** James Edward 1940- *AmMWSc 92*
**Mielke,** Marvin V 1939- *AmMWSc 92*
**Mielke,** Paul Theodore 1920- *AmMWSc 92*
**Mielke,** Paul W, Jr 1931- *AmMWSc 92*
**Mielke,** Robert L *AmMWSc 92*
**Mielke,** Todd W *WhoAmP 91*
**Mielke,** William John 1947- *WhoFI 92*
**Mientka,** Walter Eugene 1925- *AmMWSc 92*
**Mier,** Millard George 1935- *AmMWSc 92*
**Mier,** Myra Esther 1951- *WhoEnt 92*
**Mier Noriega y Guerra,** Servando T de 1763-1827 *HisDSpE*
**Mier-y-Teran,** Maria Guadalupe 1950- *WhoRel 92*
**Miera,** Rick *WhoAmP 91, WhoHisp 92*
**Miereanu,** Costin 1943- *ConCom 92*
**Mierendorff,** Carlo 1897-1943 *EncTR 91 [port]*
**Miernyk,** Jan Andrew 1947- *AmMWSc 92*
**Miernyk,** William Henry 1918- *WrDr 92*
**Miers,** Christopher *TwCPaSc*
**Miers,** David 1937- *IntWW 91, Who 92*
**Miers,** Earl Schenck 1910-1972 *BenetAL 91*
**Miersma,** John Peter 1957- *WhoFI 92*
**Mierzwa,** Joseph William 1951- *WhoAmL 92*
**Mies,** Frederick Henry 1932- *AmMWSc 92*
**Mies,** Gregory Gerard 1967- *WhoMW 92*
**Mies,** John Charles 1946- *WhoFI 92*
**Mies van der Rode,** Ludwig 1886-1969 *FacFETw*
**Mies van der Rohe,** Ludwig 1886-1969 *DcTwDes*
**Miesch,** Alfred Thomas 1927- *AmMWSc 92*
**Miescher,** Guido 1921- *AmMWSc 92*
**Miesel,** John Louis 1941- *AmMWSc 92*
**Miesel,** Karl 1933- *IntWW 91*
**Miesel,** Ralph E. 1950- *WhoMW 92*
**Miesowicz,** Marian 1907- *IntWW 91*
**Miessler,** Gary Lee 1949- *AmMWSc 92*
**Mietlowski,** William Leonard 1947- *AmMWSc 92*
**Miettinen,** Mauri Kalevi 1941- *IntWW 91*
**Mieure,** James Philip 1941- *AmMWSc 92*
**Mieyal,** John Joseph 1944- *AmMWSc 92*
**Miffitt,** Donald Charles 1944- *AmMWSc 92*
**Mifflin,** Lloyd 1846-1921 *BenetAL 91*
**Mifflin,** Mark Jonathon 1957- *WhoEnt 92*
**Mifflin,** Martin David 1937- *AmMWSc 92*
**Mifflin,** Theodore Edward 1946- *AmMWSc 92*
**Mifsud Bonnici,** Carmelo 1933- *IntWW 91, Who 92*
**Mifsud Bonnici,** Ugo 1932- *IntWW 91*
**Mifune,** Toshiro 1920- *FacFETw, IntMPA 92, IntWW 91*
**Migaki,** James M. 1931- *WhoWest 92*
**Migala,** Joseph 1913- *WhoMW 92*
**Migala,** Lucyna Jozefa 1944- *WhoEnt 92, WhoMW 92*
**Migdal,** Arkadiy Baynusovich 1911- *IntWW 91*
**Migdal,** Sheldon Paul 1936- *WhoAmL 92*
**Migdalof,** Bruce Howard 1941- *AmMWSc 92*
**Migden,** Chester L. 1921- *IntMPA 92*
**Migdol,** Marvin Jacob 1937- *WhoFI 92*
**Migel,** Christopher James 1951- *WhoIns 92*
**Migenes,** Julia 1945- *WhoHisp 92*
**Migeon,** Barbara Ruben 1931- *AmMWSc 92*
**Migeon,** Claude Jean 1923- *AmMWSc 92*
**Miget,** Russell John 1942- *AmMWSc 92*
**Mighell,** Kenneth John 1931- *WhoAmL 92*
**Mighels,** Philip Verrill 1869-1911 *ScFEYrs*
**Mighton,** Charles Joseph 1913- *AmMWSc 92*
**Mighton,** Harold Russell 1919- *AmMWSc 92*
**Mighty Sparrow,** The 1935- *ConPo 91*
**Migliaccio,** Robert Anthony 1956- *WhoAmL 92*
**Migliaro,** Eugene Alphonse, Jr 1925- *WhoAmP 91*
**Migliaro,** Marco William 1948- *AmMWSc 92*
**Migliore,** Herman James 1946- *AmMWSc 92*
**Migliore,** Philip Joseph 1931- *AmMWSc 92*
**Migliori,** Jay 1930- *WhoEnt 92*
**Migliorino,** Robert Roy 1941- *WhoMW 92*
**Mignacca,** Egidio Carmen 1931- *WhoMW 92*
**Mignanelli,** Thomas D. *WhoWest 92*
**Mignault,** Jean De L 1924- *AmMWSc 92*
**Migne,** Jacques Paul 1800-1875 *EncEarC*
**Mignerey,** Alice Cox 1949- *AmMWSc 92*
**Mignery,** Arnold Louis 1918- *AmMWSc 92*
**Mignone,** Robert Joseph 1945- *AmMWSc 92*
**Migoya,** James Angel 1932- *WhoHisp 92*
**Miguel,** Aurelio *BlkOlyM*
**Miguel,** Mario Firmino d1991 *IntWW 91N*
**Miguez-Bonino,** Jose 1924- *IntWW 91*
**Migulin,** Vladimir Vasiliyevich 1911- *IntWW 91*
**Mihailoff,** Gregory A 1945- *AmMWSc 92*
**Mihailovic,** Draza 1893-1946 *FacFETw*
**Mihailovich,** Melita Jasmina 1963- *WhoMW 92*
**Mihailovski,** Alexander 1937- *AmMWSc 92*
**Mihajlov,** Mihajlo 1934- *IntWW 91, LiExTwC*
**Mihajlov,** Vsevolod S 1925- *AmMWSc 92*
**Mihalas,** Barbara R Weibel 1939- *AmMWSc 92*
**Mihalas,** Dimitri 1939- *AmMWSc 92*
**Mihalcik,** Eleanor 1929- *WhoAmP 91*
**Mihalczo,** John Thomas 1931- *AmMWSc 92*
**Mihalich,** Herman 1930- *WhoAmP 91*
**Mihalick,** Charles Rautze 1945- *WhoEnt 92*
**Mihalik,** Vojtech 1926- *IntAu&W 91, IntWW 91*
**Mihalisin,** John Raymond 1924- *AmMWSc 92*
**Mihalisin,** Ted Warren 1940- *AmMWSc 92*
**Mihalov,** John Donald 1937- *AmMWSc 92*
**Mihaly,** Andras 1917- *IntWW 91*
**Mihaly,** Eugene Bramer 1934- *WhoWest 92*
**Mihalyi,** Elemer 1919- *AmMWSc 92*
**Mihan,** Richard 1925- *WhoWest 92*
**Mihanovich,** Clement Simon 1913- *WrDr 92*
**Mihara,** Asao 1909- *IntWW 91*
**Mihelich,** Edward David 1950- *WhoMW 92*
**Mihelich,** Jeffery C. 1954- *WhoRel 92*
**Mihelich,** John L 1937- *AmMWSc 92*
**Mihelich,** John William 1922- *AmMWSc 92*
**Mihich,** Enrico 1928- *AmMWSc 92*
**Mihina,** Joseph Stephen 1918- *AmMWSc 92*
**Mihlbaugh,** Robert Holleran *WhoAmP 91*
**Mihm,** Martin C, Jr *AmMWSc 92*
**Mihm,** Michael Martin 1943- *WhoAmL 92, WhoMW 92*
**Mihopoulos,** Effie *DrAPF 91*
**Mihram,** George Arthur 1939- *AmMWSc 92*
**Mihran,** Theodore Gregory 1924- *AmMWSc 92*
**Mihursky,** Joseph Anthony 1933- *AmMWSc 92*
**Miick,** Rudy McGinnis *WhoWest 92*
**Miikkulainen,** Risto Pekka 1961- *AmMWSc 92*
**Mijalis,** Gus Sam 1934- *WhoAmP 91*
**Mijares,** Percival S. 1949- *WhoFI 92*
**Mijatovic,** Cvijetin 1913- *IntWW 91*
**Mijovic,** Jovan 1948- *AmMWSc 92*
**Mika,** Joseph John 1948- *WhoMW 92*
**Mika,** Leonard Aloysius 1917- *AmMWSc 92*
**Mika,** Thomas Stephen 1941- *AmMWSc 92*
**Mika,** Walter V. 1939- *WhoWest 92*
**Mikalow,** Alfred Alexander, II 1921- *WhoWest 92*
**Mikami,** Harry M 1915- *AmMWSc 92*
**Mikardo,** Ian 1908- *Who 92*
**Mikat,** Eileen M *AmMWSc 92*
**Mike,** Valerie 1934- *AmMWSc 92*
**Mikeal,** Patricia Ann 1960- *WhoWest 92*
**Mikel,** Thomas Kelly, Jr 1946- *AmMWSc 92, WhoWest 92*
**Mikelberg,** Arnold 1937- *WhoFI 92*
**Mikell,** Charles Donald 1934- *WhoBlA 92*
**Mikell,** George *IntMPA 92*
**Mikell,** Mike *WhoAmP 91*
**Mikell,** Richard Bruce 1946- *WhoFI 92*
**Mikes,** Gyorgy 1912-1987 *LiExTwC*
**Mikes,** John Andrew 1922- *AmMWSc 92*
**Mikes,** Peter 1938- *AmMWSc 92*
**Mikesell,** Jan Erwin 1943- *AmMWSc 92*
**Mikesell,** Janice H. *DrAPF 91*
**Mikesell,** Sharell Lee 1943- *AmMWSc 92*
**Mikesic,** David Paul 1944- *WhoAmP 91*
**Mikeska,** Emory Eugene 1927- *AmMWSc 92*
**Mikhail,** Adel Ayad 1934- *AmMWSc 92*
**Mikhail,** Edward H 1928- *IntAu&W 91, WrDr 92*
**Mikhail,** Mary Attalla 1945- *WhoWest 92*
**Mikhail,** Nabih N 1933- *AmMWSc 92*
**Mikhalchenko,** Alla Anatolevna 1957- *IntWW 91*
**Mikhalevich,** Vladimir Sergeyevich 1930- *IntWW 91*
**Mikhalkov,** Nikita 1945- *IntMPA 92*
**Mikhalkov,** Nikita Sergeevich 1945- *SovUnBD*
**Mikhalkov,** Nikita Sergeyevich 1945- *IntWW 91*
**Mikhalkov,** Sergey Vladimirovich 1913- *IntAu&W 91, IntWW 91*
**Mikhalkov-Konchalovsky,** Andrei 1937- *IntDcF 2-2 [port]*
**Mikhalkov-Konchalovsky,** Andrey S. 1937- *IntWW 91, SovUnBD*
**Mikhashoff,** Yvar Emilian 1944- *WhoEnt 92*
**Mikhaylov,** Nikolay Aleksandrovich 1906- *SovUnBD*
**Mikhaylov,** Vasiliy Mikhaylovich 1894-1937 *SovUnBD*
**Mikheyev,** Vladimir Andreyevich 1942- *IntWW 91*
**Mikhoels,** Solomon Mikhaylovich 1890-1948 *SovUnBD*
**Miki,** Takeo 1907-1988 *FacFETw*
**Mikic,** Bora 1932- *AmMWSc 92*
**Mikiewicz,** Anna Daniella 1960- *WhoFI 92*
**Mikita,** Joseph Karl 1918- *WhoEnt 92*
**Mikiten,** Terry Michael 1937- *AmMWSc 92*
**Mikitka,** Taras Ostapovich 1939- *WhoEnt 92*
**Mikkelsen,** Charles Roy 1954- *WhoFI 92*
**Mikkelsen,** David Robert 1949- *AmMWSc 92*
**Mikkelsen,** Duane Soren 1921- *AmMWSc 92*
**Mikkelsen,** Richard 1920- *IntWW 91*
**Mikkelsen,** Ricki Barner 1944- *WhoWest 92*
**Mikkelsen,** Robert Eugene 1942- *WhoWest 92*
**Mikkelsen,** William Mitchell 1923- *AmMWSc 92*
**Mikkelson,** Raymond Charles 1937- *AmMWSc 92*
**Mikkelson,** Ruth Lynn 1946- *WhoMW 92*
**Mikkola,** Donald E 1938- *AmMWSc 92*
**Mikkola,** Donald Emil 1938- *WhoMW 92*
**Mikkola,** Marja-Leena 1939- *IntAu&W 91*
**Miklas,** Wilhelm 1872-1956 *EncTR 91 [port]*
**Miklavcic,** Milan 1954- *AmMWSc 92, WhoMW 92*
**Miklave,** Matthew Thaddeus 1959- *WhoAmL 92*
**Mikle,** Janos J 1942- *AmMWSc 92*
**Miklich,** Thomas Robert 1947- *WhoFI 92*
**Miklofsky,** Haaren A 1920- *AmMWSc 92*
**Miklosko,** Jozef 1939- *IntWW 91*
**Miklowitz,** Gloria D 1927- *IntAu&W 91, SmATA 68 [port], WrDr 92*
**Miklowitz,** Julius 1919- *AmMWSc 92*
**Miknis,** Francis Paul 1940- *AmMWSc 92*
**Miko,** Andras 1922- *IntWW 91*
**Mikol,** Leslie Maria 1963- *WhoEnt 92*
**Mikolaizyk,** Marian *WhoRel 92*
**Mikolaj,** Paul G 1936- *AmMWSc 92*
**Mikolajcik,** Emil Michael 1926- *AmMWSc 92*
**Mikolajczak,** Alojzy Antoni 1935- *AmMWSc 92*
**Mikolasek,** Douglas Gene 1930- *AmMWSc 92, WhoMW 92*
**Mikolite,** Carl Frederick 1927- *WhoFI 92*
**Mikolowski,** Ken *DrAPF 91*
**Mikoyan,** Anastas Ivanovich 1895-1978 *SovUnBD*
**Mikoyan,** Anastas Ivanovich 1896-1978 *FacFETw*
**Mikoyan,** Artem Ivanovich 1905-1970 *SovUnBD*
**Mikrut,** John Joseph, Jr. 1944- *WhoMW 92*
**Miksad,** Richard Walter 1940- *AmMWSc 92*
**Miksch,** Eileen Evans 1926- *WhoAmP 91*
**Miksche,** Jerome Phillip 1930- *AmMWSc 92*
**Mikula,** Alan 1946- *WhoAmP 91*
**Mikula,** Bernard C 1924- *AmMWSc 92*
**Mikula,** Kenneth Richard 1950- *WhoIns 92*
**Mikulanis,** Dennis L. *WhoRel 92*
**Mikulcik,** E C 1936- *AmMWSc 92*
**Mikulcik,** John D 1936- *AmMWSc 92*
**Mikulec,** Richard Andrew 1928- *AmMWSc 92, WhoMW 92*
**Mikulecky,** Donald C 1936- *AmMWSc 92*
**Mikulic,** Branko 1928- *IntWW 91*

**Mikulic**, Donald George 1949- *AmMWSc 92*
**Mikulski**, Barbara A. 1936- *AlmAP 92 [port]*
**Mikulski**, Barbara Ann 1936- *IntWW 91, WhoAmP 91*
**Mikulski**, Chester Mark 1946- *AmMWSc 92*
**Mikulski**, James J 1934- *AmMWSc 92*
**Mikulski**, Piotr W 1925- *AmMWSc 92*
**Mikva**, Abner J 1926- *WhoAmP 91*
**Mikva**, Abner Joseph 1926- *WhoAmL 92*
**Mila**, Pablo Jose 1938- *WhoHisp 92*
**Milakofsky**, Louis 1941- *AmMWSc 92*
**Milakovic**, John George 1956- *WhoAmL 92*
**Milam**, Christine Marie 1956- *WhoRel 92*
**Milam**, David Kelton, Sr. 1932- *WhoHisp 92*
**Milam**, John D 1933- *AmMWSc 92*
**Milam**, June Matthews 1931- *WhoFI 92*
**Milam**, Lloyd Keith 1950- *WhoAmL 92*
**Milam**, Susan Storey 1947- *WhoAmP 91*
**Milam**, Wade 1918- *WhoAmP 91*
**Milam**, William B *WhoAmP 91*
**Milan**, Archbishop of *Who 92*
**Milan**, Edgar J. 1934- *WhoHisp 92*
**Milan**, Eduardo 1952- *ConSpAP*
**Milan**, Edwin Ramon 1950- *WhoHisp 92*
**Milan**, Frederick Arthur 1924- *AmMWSc 92*
**Milan**, Luis de 1500?-1565? *NewAmDM*
**Milan**, Ray 1942- *WhoEnt 92*
**Milani**, Victor John 1945- *AmMWSc 92*
**Milano**, Dominic David 1955- *WhoEnt 92*
**Milano**, Eugene John 1927- *WhoFI 92*
**Milano**, James Edward 1909- *WhoAmP 91*
**Milanov**, Zinka 1906-1989 *NewAmDM*
**Milanovich**, Fred Paul 1944- *AmMWSc 92*
**Milanovich**, Norma JoAnne 1945- *WhoWest 92*
**Milantoni**, John Vincent 1932- *WhoFI 92*
**Milaski**, John Joseph 1959- *WhoFI 92*
**Milavsky**, Harold Phillip 1931- *WhoWest 92*
**Milazzo**, Francis Henry 1928- *AmMWSc 92*
**Milbank**, Anthony 1939- *Who 92*
**Milberg**, Morton Edwin 1926- *AmMWSc 92*
**Milberger**, Ernest Carl 1921- *AmMWSc 92*
**Milbert**, Alfred Nicholas 1946- *AmMWSc 92*
**Milbert**, Robert P 1949- *WhoAmP 91*
**Milbert**, Roger P 1940- *WhoIns 92*
**Milbocker**, Daniel Clement 1931- *AmMWSc 92*
**Milbocker**, Michael 1962- *AmMWSc 92*
**Milborne-Swinnerton-Pilkington**, T. H. *Who 92*
**Milbourn**, Graham Maurice 1930- *Who 92*
**Milbourne**, Larry William 1951- *WhoBlA 92*
**Milbourne**, Walter Robertson 1933- *WhoAmL 92*
**Milbrath**, Earlon L 1941- *WhoIns 92*
**Milbrath**, Gene McCoy 1941- *AmMWSc 92*
**Milbrath**, Stephen Douglas 1950- *WhoAmL 92*
**Milbrodt**, Walter Frederick 1920- *WhoAmP 91*
**Milburn**, Anthony 1947- *Who 92*
**Milburn**, Bryan L. d1991 *NewYTBS 91*
**Milburn**, Colin 1941-1990 *AnObit 1990*
**Milburn**, Corinne M. 1930- *WhoBlA 92*
**Milburn**, Donald B. *Who 92*
**Milburn**, Frank Pierce 1868-1926 *DcNCBi 4*
**Milburn**, Gary L 1952- *AmMWSc 92*
**Milburn**, George 1906-1966 *TwCWW 91*
**Milburn**, Herbert Theodore 1931- *WhoAmL 92, WhoAmP 91*
**Milburn**, Jackie 1924-1988 *FacFETw*
**Milburn**, Nancy Stafford 1927- *AmMWSc 92*
**Milburn**, Richard Henry 1928- *AmMWSc 92*
**Milburn**, Robert Leslie Pollington 1907- *Who 92*
**Milburn**, Rodney, Jr 1950- *BlkOlyM*
**Milburn**, Ronald McRae 1928- *AmMWSc 92*
**Milby**, Thomas Hutchinson 1931- *AmMWSc 92*
**Milcarek**, Christine 1946- *AmMWSc 92*
**Milch**, Erhard 1892-1972 *EncTR 91 [port]*
**Milch**, Lawrence Jacques 1918- *AmMWSc 92*
**Milch**, Paul R 1934- *AmMWSc 92*
**Milch**, Robert Austin d1991 *NewYTBS 91*
**Milchan**, Arnon 1944- *IntMPA 92*
**Milchsack**, Lilo *Who 92*
**Milcinski**, Janez 1913- *IntWW 91*
**Mild**, Edward E. 1943- *WhoWest 92*
**Milder**, Alvin Sherman 1932- *WhoEnt 92*
**Milder**, Fredric Lloyd 1949- *AmMWSc 92*
**Mildon**, Arthur Leonard 1923- *Who 92*
**Mildren**, Jack 1949- *WhoAmP 91*
**Mildvan**, Albert S 1932- *AmMWSc 92*
**Mile**, Chuck Edward 1952- *WhoEnt 92*
**Miledi**, Ricardo 1927- *AmMWSc 92, IntWW 91, Who 92*
**Milefsky**, Norman R. 1933- *WhoFI 92*
**Mileikovsky**, Abram Gerasimovich 1911- *IntWW 91*
**Mileikowsky**, Curt 1923- *IntWW 91*
**Milenski**, Paul *DrAPF 91*
**Miler**, George Gibbon, Jr 1940- *AmMWSc 92*
**Miles** *ScFEYrs*
**Miles**, Baron d1991 *Who 92N*
**Miles**, Baron 1907- *IntWW 91*
**Miles**, Albert Edward William 1912- *Who 92*
**Miles**, Alfred Lee 1913- *WhoFI 92, WhoMW 92*
**Miles**, Anthony John 1930- *Who 92*
**Miles**, Anthony Lawrence 1932- *WhoAmP 91*
**Miles**, Barry 1943- *ConAu 134*
**Miles**, Bernard d1991 *NewYTBS 91 [port]*
**Miles**, Bernard 1907- *ConAu 133*
**Miles**, Betty *DrAPF 91*
**Miles**, Betty 1928- *IntAu&W 91, WrDr 92*
**Miles**, Bradley Robert 1944- *WhoWest 92*
**Miles**, Brian 1937- *Who 92*
**Miles**, Bruce Alan 1957- *WhoEnt 92*
**Miles**, Carlotta G. 1937- *WhoBlA 92*
**Miles**, Caroline Mary 1929- *Who 92*
**Miles**, Charlene 1928- *WhoMW 92*
**Miles**, Charles David 1926- *AmMWSc 92*
**Miles**, Charles Donald 1938- *AmMWSc 92*
**Miles**, Charles Gentry 1950- *WhoAmP 91*
**Miles**, Charles P 1922- *AmMWSc 92*
**Miles**, Charles William Noel 1915- *Who 92*
**Miles**, Christopher 1939- *IntMPA 92*
**Miles**, Christopher John 1939- *Who 92*
**Miles**, Corbin I 1940- *AmMWSc 92*
**Miles**, Daniel Davis 1942- *WhoWest 92*
**Miles**, Daniel S *AmMWSc 92*
**Miles**, David H 1928- *AmMWSc 92*
**Miles**, David Michael 1954- *WhoAmL 92, WhoFI 92*
**Miles**, Debra Ileen 1951- *WhoMW 92*
**Miles**, Delbert Howard 1943- *AmMWSc 92*
**Miles**, Dillwyn 1916- *Who 92*
**Miles**, Donald Orval 1939- *AmMWSc 92, WhoMW 92*
**Miles**, Dorothy Marie 1950- *WhoBlA 92*
**Miles**, Douglas Irving 1949- *WhoRel 92*
**Miles**, E. W. 1934- *WhoBlA 92*
**Miles**, Edith Wilson 1937- *AmMWSc 92*
**Miles**, Edward Lancelot 1939- *AmMWSc 92, WhoBlA 92, WhoWest 92*
**Miles**, Elton 1917- *WrDr 92*
**Miles**, Ernest Percy, Jr 1919- *AmMWSc 92*
**Miles**, Frank Belsley 1940- *AmMWSc 92*
**Miles**, Frank Edward 1930- *WhoAmP 91*
**Miles**, Frank J. W. 1944- *WhoBlA 92*
**Miles**, Frank Stephen 1920- *IntWW 91, Who 92*
**Miles**, Frederick Augustus 1928- *WhoBlA 92*
**Miles**, Geoffrey 1922- *Who 92*
**Miles**, George Benjamin 1926- *AmMWSc 92*
**Miles**, George H. 1824-1871 *BenetAL 91*
**Miles**, Hamish Alexander Drummond 1925- *Who 92*
**Miles**, Harry Todd 1926- *AmMWSc 92*
**Miles**, Harry V 1914- *AmMWSc 92*
**Miles**, Henry Harcourt Waters 1915- *AmMWSc 92*
**Miles**, Henry Michael 1936- *Who 92*
**Miles**, Jackie Dwain 1932- *WhoFI 92*
**Miles**, James Lowell 1937- *AmMWSc 92*
**Miles**, James S 1921- *AmMWSc 92*
**Miles**, James Tandy 1925- *WhoFI 92*
**Miles**, James William 1918- *AmMWSc 92*
**Miles**, Jeffrey Stuart 1944- *WhoEnt 92*
**Miles**, Jesse Mc Lane 1932- *WhoFI 92*
**Miles**, Jim *WhoAmP 91*
**Miles**, Jim 1935- *WhoAmP 91*
**Miles**, Joan 1949- *WhoAmP 91*
**Miles**, JoAnn Joyce 1934- *WhoAmP 91*
**Miles**, Joanna 1940- *WhoEnt 92*
**Miles**, John *IntAu&W 91X, WrDr 92*
**Miles**, John Arthur Reginald 1913- *IntWW 91*
**Miles**, John B 1933- *AmMWSc 92*
**Miles**, John E *WhoAmP 91*
**Miles**, John Edwin Alfred 1919- *Who 92*
**Miles**, John Martin 1947- *WhoAmL 92*
**Miles**, John P. 1929- *WhoRel 92*
**Miles**, John Seeley 1931- *Who 92*
**Miles**, John Thomas, Jr. 1932- *WhoMW 92*
**Miles**, John Wilder 1920- *AmMWSc 92, IntWW 91*
**Miles**, Joseph Belsley 1942- *AmMWSc 92*
**Miles**, Josephine 1911-1985 *BenetAL 91*
**Miles**, Kenneth L. 1937- *WhoBlA 92*
**Miles**, Lawrence Preston *WhoEnt 92*
**Miles**, Leland 1924- *IntAu&W 91, WrDr 92*
**Miles**, Leo Fidelis 1931- *WhoBlA 92*
**Miles**, Lindsey Anne *AmMWSc 92*
**Miles**, Manly 1826-1898 *BiInAmS*
**Miles**, MarCine Miller 1942- *WhoAmL 92*
**Miles**, Margaret 1911- *Who 92, WrDr 92*
**Miles**, Margaret Ruth 1937- *WhoRel 92*
**Miles**, Marion Lawrence 1929- *AmMWSc 92*
**Miles**, Marjorie Mae 1922- *WhoAmP 91*
**Miles**, Marsha Lynn 1955- *WhoMW 92*
**Miles**, Mary Alice 1948- *WhoBlA 92*
**Miles**, Matthew B. 1926- *ConAu 36NR*
**Miles**, Maurice Howard 1933- *AmMWSc 92*
**Miles**, Maurice Jarvis 1907- *AmMWSc 92*
**Miles**, Melvin Henry 1937- *AmMWSc 92*
**Miles**, Michael *Who 92*
**Miles**, Michael Arnold 1939- *WhoFI 92, WhoMW 92*
**Miles**, Michael Duffield 1955- *WhoWest 92*
**Miles**, Michael Wade 1945- *WrDr 92*
**Miles**, Michele Gae 1958- *WhoAmL 92*
**Miles**, Neil Wayne 1937- *AmMWSc 92*
**Miles**, Norman Kenneth 1946- *WhoBlA 92*
**Miles**, Oliver *Who 92*
**Miles**, Patricia Louise 1947- *WhoRel 92*
**Miles**, Peter Charles H. *Who 92*
**Miles**, Peter Tremayne 1924- *Who 92*
**Miles**, Philip Giltner 1922- *AmMWSc 92*
**Miles**, Rachel Jean 1945- *WhoBlA 92*
**Miles**, Ralph Fraley, Jr 1933- *AmMWSc 92, WhoWest 92*
**Miles**, Randall Jay 1952- *AmMWSc 92*
**Miles**, Raymond Edward 1932- *WhoFI 92*
**Miles**, Richard Bryant 1943- *AmMWSc 92*
**Miles**, Richard David 1947- *AmMWSc 92*
**Miles**, Richard Oliver 1936- *Who 92*
**Miles**, Robert D 1924- *AmMWSc 92*
**Miles**, Roger Steele 1937- *Who 92*
**Miles**, Roy Brian Edward 1935- *IntWW 91*
**Miles**, Sage B *ScFEYrs*
**Miles**, Samuel Israel 1949- *WhoWest 92*
**Miles**, Sara *DrAPF 91*
**Miles**, Sarah 1941- *IntMPA 92, IntWW 91*
**Miles**, Sheila Lee 1952- *WhoWest 92*
**Miles**, Stephen *Who 92*
**Miles**, Sylvia 1932- *IntMPA 92*
**Miles**, Thomas James *WhoAmP 91*
**Miles**, Thomas Timothy 1940- *WhoMW 92*
**Miles**, Travis Anthony 1937- *WhoAmP 91*
**Miles**, Vera 1930- *IntMPA 92, WhoEnt 92*
**Miles**, Vera M. 1932- *WhoBlA 92*
**Miles**, Vic 1931- *WhoBlA 92*
**Miles**, Wendell A. 1916- *WhoMW 92*
**Miles**, Wendy Ann *Who 92*
**Miles**, William 1913- *Who 92*
**Miles**, William 1933- *Who 92*
**Miles**, William Henry 1828-1892 *RelLAm 91*
**Miles**, Willie Leanna *WhoBlA 92*
**Miles**, Wyndham Davies 1916- *AmMWSc 92*
**Miles-LaGrange**, Vicki 1953- *WhoAmP 91*
**Milesi**, Luca *WhoRel 92*
**Milestone**, Lewis 1895-1980 *FacFETw, IntDcF 2-2 [port]*
**Milewich**, Leon 1927- *AmMWSc 92*
**Milewski**, John Vincent 1928- *AmMWSc 92*
**Milewski**, Piotr *WhoEnt 92*
**Milewski**, Stanley E. *WhoRel 92*
**Miley**, Anthony James 1942- *WhoEnt 92*
**Miley**, Bubber 1903-1932 *NewAmDM*
**Miley**, Debra Charlet 1963- *WhoBlA 92*
**Miley**, Frank Paul 1929- *WhoWest 92*
**Miley**, G H 1933- *AmMWSc 92*
**Miley**, Hugh Howard 1902- *WhoMW 92*
**Miley**, James Allen 1950- *WhoMW 92*
**Miley**, John Wulbern 1942- *AmMWSc 92*
**Miley**, Leslie, Jr. 1934- *WhoMW 92*
**Miley**, Robert Andrew 1962- *WhoAmL 92*
**Milford**, Baron 1902- *Who 92*
**Milford**, Frederick John 1926- *AmMWSc 92*
**Milford**, George Noel, Jr 1924- *AmMWSc 92*
**Milford**, H.C. 1932- *WhoMW 92*
**Milford**, John Tillman 1946- *Who 92*
**Milford**, John Wharton 1950- *WhoAmP 91*
**Milford**, Murray Hudson 1934- *AmMWSc 92*
**Milford Haven**, Marquess of 1961- *Who 92*
**Milgate**, Rodney Armour 1934- *IntAu&W 91*
**Milgram**, Gail Gleason 1942- *WrDr 92*
**Milgram**, Hank 1926- *IntMPA 92*
**Milgram**, Morris 1916- *WhoFI 92*
**Milgram**, Richard James 1939- *AmMWSc 92*
**Milgrim**, Darrow A. 1945- *WhoWest 92*
**Milgrim**, Hale A. 1948- *WhoEnt 92*
**Milgrom**, Felix 1919- *AmMWSc 92*
**Milgrom**, Jack 1927- *AmMWSc 92*
**Milham**, Robert Carr 1922- *AmMWSc 92*
**Milhander**, Marc Thomas 1958- *WhoMW 92*
**Milhaud**, Darius 1892-1974 *FacFETw, NewAmDM*
**Milhaven**, John Giles 1927- *WhoRel 92, WrDr 92*
**Milhoan**, Gene Roger 1942- *WhoFI 92*
**Milhouse**, Paul William 1910- *WhoRel 92, WrDr 92*
**Mili**, Jude Joseph 1931- *WhoRel 92*
**Mili**, Mohamed Ezzedine 1917- *IntWW 91*
**Milian**, Alwin S, Jr 1932- *AmMWSc 92*
**Milian**, Arsenio 1945- *WhoHisp 92*
**Milian**, Evarist, Jr. 1958- *WhoHisp 92*
**Milic-Emili**, Joseph 1931- *AmMWSc 92*
**Milici**, Anthony J 1954- *AmMWSc 92*
**Milici**, Robert Calvin 1931- *AmMWSc 92*
**Milicic**, Dragan 1948- *AmMWSc 92*
**Millman**, David Jay 1957- *WhoAmL 92*
**Milingo**, Emanuel 1930- *Who 92*
**Milingo**, Emmanuel 1930- *IntWW 91*
**Milionis**, Jerry Peter 1926- *AmMWSc 92*
**Miliora**, Maria Teresa 1938- *AmMWSc 92*
**Militant** *ConAu 35NR*
**Militello**, Clifford Paul 1954- *WhoEnt 92*
**Militello**, Samuel Philip 1947- *WhoAmL 92*
**Militz**, Annie Rix 1856-1924 *RelLAm 91*
**Milius**, John 1944- *IntMPA 92*
**Milius**, John Frederick 1944- *IntWW 91*
**Miljanich**, George Paul 1950- *AmMWSc 92*
**Milkey**, Robert William 1944- *AmMWSc 92*
**Milkey**, Virginia 1950- *WhoAmP 91*
**Milkina**, Nina 1919- *Who 92*
**Milkis**, Edward 1931- *IntMPA 92*
**Milkis**, Edward K. *WhoEnt 92*
**Milkman**, Martin Irving 1960- *WhoFI 92*
**Milkman**, Roger Dawson 1930- *AmMWSc 92*
**Milko**, Jean Ann 1934- *WhoAmP 91*
**Milkomane**, G. A. M. *Who 92*
**Milkovic**, Miran 1928- *AmMWSc 92*
**Mill**, James 1773-1836 *DcLB 107 [port]*
**Mill**, Jerry Wayne 1945- *WhoFI 92*
**Mill**, John Stuart 1806-1873 *CnDBLB 4 [port], RfGEnL 91*
**Mill**, Robert Duguid Forrest P. *Who 92*
**Mill**, Theodore 1931- *AmMWSc 92*
**Milla**, Roger 1952- *ConBlB 2 [port]*
**Millage**, David A 1953- *WhoAmP 91*
**Millais**, Ralph 1905- *Who 92*
**Millan**, Angel, Jr. 1945- *WhoHisp 92*
**Millan**, Bruce 1927- *IntWW 91, Who 92*
**Millan**, Gonzalo 1947- *ConSpAP*
**Millan**, Jose Luis 1952- *AmMWSc 92*
**Millan**, Steven Ajeet 1964- *WhoEnt 92*
**Milland**, Ray 1905-1986 *FacFETw*
**Millane**, John Vaughan, Jr. 1926- *WhoAmL 92*
**Millar** *Who 92*
**Millar**, Andrew 1707-1768 *BlkwCEP*
**Millar**, Anthony Bruce 1941- *Who 92*
**Millar**, Betty Phyllis Joy 1929- *Who 92*
**Millar**, Brad Stewart 1961- *WhoRel 92*
**Millar**, C Kay 1934- *AmMWSc 92*
**Millar**, Dan Pyle 1938- *WhoMW 92*
**Millar**, David Alan 1956- *WhoEnt 92*
**Millar**, David B *AmMWSc 92*
**Millar**, Fergus Graham Burtholme 1935- *IntWW 91, Who 92*
**Millar**, George 1910- *WrDr 92*
**Millar**, George Reid 1910- *Who 92*
**Millar**, Gordon Halstead 1923- *AmMWSc 92*
**Millar**, Ian Alastair D. *Who 92*
**Millar**, Jack William 1922- *AmMWSc 92*
**Millar**, Jeffery Lynn 1942- *WhoEnt 92*
**Millar**, Jocelyn Grenville 1954- *AmMWSc 92*
**Millar**, John 1735-1801 *BlkwCEP*
**Millar**, John David 1921- *AmMWSc 92*
**Millar**, John Donald 1934- *AmMWSc 92*
**Millar**, John Robert 1927- *AmMWSc 92*
**Millar**, John Stanley 1925- *Who 92*
**Millar**, Kenneth *BenetAL 91*
**Millar**, Margaret 1915- *BenetAL 91, ConNov 91, IntAu&W 91, WrDr 92*
**Millar**, Mark Kenneth 1959- *WhoMW 92*
**Millar**, Oliver 1923- *WrDr 92*
**Millar**, Oliver Nicholas 1923- *IntWW 91, Who 92*
**Millar**, Peter Carmichael 1927- *Who 92*
**Millar**, Raymond Irving 1930- *WhoAmP 91*
**Millar**, Richard William 1899-1990 *FacFETw*
**Millar**, Richard William, Jr. 1938- *WhoAmL 92*
**Millar**, Robert Fyfe 1928- *AmMWSc 92*
**Millar**, Ronald 1919- *IntAu&W 91, Who 92, WrDr 92*
**Millar**, Stuart 1929- *IntMPA 92*
**Millar**, Wayne Norval 1942- *AmMWSc 92*
**Millar**, William Malcolm 1913- *Who 92*
**Millard**, Alan Ralph 1937- *WrDr 92*

**Millard,** Charles Allen 1942- *WhoWest 92*
**Millard,** Charles Phillip 1948- *WhoMW 92*
**Millard,** Donald Rex 1947- *WhoFI 92*
**Millard,** Elizabeth Sanborn 1944- *WhoAmP 91*
**Millard,** Esther Lound 1909- *WhoFI 92*
**Millard,** Frank Bailey 1859-1941 *ScFEYrs*
**Millard,** Frederick William 1931- *AmMWSc 92*
**Millard,** George Buente 1917- *AmMWSc 92*
**Millard,** George Richard 1914- *WhoRel 92, WhoWest 92*
**Millard,** Guy 1917- *Who 92*
**Millard,** Guy Elwin 1917- *IntWW 91*
**Millard,** Herbert Charles 1938- *WhoAmP 91*
**Millard,** Herbert Dean 1924- *AmMWSc 92*
**Millard,** James Kemper 1948- *WhoFI 92*
**Millard,** Joseph 1908- *TwCWW 91*
**Millard,** Kenneth E. 1946- *WhoFI 92*
**Millard,** Kenneth Reimann 1930- *WhoWest 92*
**Millard,** Lavergne Harriet 1925- *WhoWest 92*
**Millard,** Malcolm Stuart 1914- *WhoWest 92*
**Millard,** Naomi Adeline Helen 1914- *IntWW 91*
**Millard,** Neal Steven 1947- *WhoAmL 92, WhoWest 92*
**Millard,** Patrick 1902- *TwCPaSc*
**Millard,** Raymond Spencer 1920- *Who 92*
**Millard,** Richard James 1918- *AmMWSc 92*
**Millard,** Ronald Wesley 1941- *AmMWSc 92*
**Millard,** Thomas Lewis 1927- *WhoBlA 92*
**Millard,** William James 1949- *AmMWSc 92*
**Millay,** Edna St. Vincent 1892-1950 *BenetAL 91, FacFETw, HanAmWH, ModAWWr*
**Mille,** Herve 1909- *IntWW 91*
**Milledge,** Luetta Upshur *WhoBlA 92*
**Millemann,** Raymond Eagan 1928- *AmMWSc 92*
**Millen,** Anthony Tristram Patrick 1928- *Who 92*
**Millen,** Jane 1953- *AmMWSc 92*
**Millen,** John Clyde 1941- *WhoRel 92*
**Millen,** Mathew Lloyd 1947- *WhoAmL 92*
**Millen,** Matt G. 1958- *WhoBlA 92*
**Millender,** Dharathula H. 1920- *WhoBlA 92*
**Millender,** Mallory Kimerling 1942- *WhoBlA 92*
**Millener,** David John 1944- *AmMWSc 92*
**Millenson,** Elliott J. 1955- *WhoFI 92*
**Millenson,** Roy Handen 1921- *WhoAmP 91*
**Miller,** A. Edward d1991 *NewYTBS 91*
**Miller,** A Eugene 1929- *AmMWSc 92*
**Miller,** A Kathrine 1913- *AmMWSc 92*
**Miller,** A. McA. *DrAPF 91*
**Miller,** Abraham 1940- *WrDr 92*
**Miller,** Adam David *DrAPF 91*
**Miller,** Adolphus James 1912- *AmMWSc 92*
**Miller,** Aileen Etta Martha 1924- *WhoMW 92*
**Miller,** Akeley 1926- *AmMWSc 92*
**Miller,** Alain 1961- *TwCPaSc*
**Miller,** Alan 1941- *TwCPaSc*
**Miller,** Alan B. 1937- *WhoFI 92*
**Miller,** Alan Cameron 1913- *Who 92*
**Miller,** Alan Charles 1945- *AmMWSc 92*
**Miller,** Alan Dale 1931- *AmMWSc 92*
**Miller,** Alan Gershon 1931- *WhoAmL 92*
**Miller,** Alan John McCulloch 1914- *Who 92*
**Miller,** Alan R 1932- *AmMWSc 92*
**Miller,** Alan Scott 1942- *WhoMW 92*
**Miller,** Alastair Cheape 1912- *Who 92*
**Miller,** Albert 1911- *AmMWSc 92*
**Miller,** Albert Eugene 1938- *AmMWSc 92*
**Miller,** Albert Thomas 1939- *AmMWSc 92*
**Miller,** Alex 1925- *AmMWSc 92*
**Miller,** Alexander 1928- *AmMWSc 92*
**Miller,** Alexander Calizance 1780?-1831 *DcNCBi 4*
**Miller,** Alexander Ronald 1915- *Who 92*
**Miller,** Alfred Charles 1947- *AmMWSc 92*
**Miller,** Alfred Eugene, III 1948- *WhoFI 92*
**Miller,** Alfred Montague 1940- *WhoAmL 92*
**Miller,** Alice Duer 1874-1942 *BenetAL 91*
**Miller,** Alice M *WhoAmP 91*
**Miller,** Alistair Ian 1940- *AmMWSc 92*
**Miller,** Allan 1929- *WhoEnt 92*
**Miller,** Allan George 1940- *WhoWest 92*
**Miller,** Allan Stephen 1928- *AmMWSc 92*
**Miller,** Allen Blair 1953- *WhoWest 92*
**Miller,** Allen H 1932- *AmMWSc 92*
**Miller,** Allen Terry, Jr. 1954- *WhoAmL 92*
**Miller,** Alvin V 1921- *WhoAmP 91*
**Miller,** Alvin Verle 1921- *WhoMW 92*
**Miller,** Ambrose Michael 1950- *WhoEnt 92*
**Miller,** Amelia *Who 92*
**Miller,** Amos W. 1927- *WhoRel 92*
**Miller,** Ancil 1944- *WhoAmP 91*
**Miller,** Andrea Lewis 1954- *WhoBlA 92*
**Miller,** Andrew 1936- *IntWW 91*
**Miller,** Andrew Gordon 1958- *WhoMW 92*
**Miller,** Andrew Lawrence 1956- *WhoAmL 92*
**Miller,** Andrew Pickens 1932- *WhoAmL 92, WhoAmP 91*
**Miller,** Anita 1931- *WhoAmP 91*
**Miller,** Ann *WhoEnt 92*
**Miller,** Ann 1919- *IntMPA 92*
**Miller,** Anna E. 1938- *WhoEnt 92*
**Miller,** Anna M. 1923- *WhoBlA 92*
**Miller,** Anne Elizabeth-Jalkanen 1958- *WhoMW 92*
**Miller,** Anne Kathleen 1942- *WhoWest 92*
**Miller,** Anthony 1965- *WhoBlA 92*
**Miller,** Anthony Bernard 1931- *AmMWSc 92*
**Miller,** Anthony Douglas 1958- *WhoWest 92*
**Miller,** Archibald Elliot Haswell 1887- *TwCPaSc*
**Miller,** Archie Randolph 1955- *WhoRel 92*
**Miller,** Arden Thomas 1950- *WhoMW 92*
**Miller,** Arild Justesen 1918- *AmMWSc 92*
**Miller,** Arjay 1916- *IntWW 91, Who 92, WhoWest 92*
**Miller,** Arlyn Ronald 1937- *WhoEnt 92*
**Miller,** Arnold 1928- *AmMWSc 92*
**Miller,** Arnold 1931- *WhoMW 92*
**Miller,** Arnold I 1956- *AmMWSc 92*
**Miller,** Arnold Joseph, Jr. 1957- *WhoWest 92*
**Miller,** Arnold Reed 1944- *AmMWSc 92*
**Miller,** Arthur *DrAPF 91*
**Miller,** Arthur 1915- *BenetAL 91, DramC 1 [port], FacFETw [port], IntAu&W 91, IntMPA 92, IntWW 91, RComAH, Who 92, WhoEnt 92, WrDr 92*
**Miller,** Arthur 1930- *AmMWSc 92*
**Miller,** Arthur Dusty 1952- *WhoWest 92*
**Miller,** Arthur I 1940- *AmMWSc 92*
**Miller,** Arthur J. 1934- *WhoBlA 92*
**Miller,** Arthur J, Jr 1946- *WhoAmP 91*
**Miller,** Arthur James 1950- *AmMWSc 92*
**Miller,** Arthur Joseph 1943- *AmMWSc 92*
**Miller,** Arthur R 1915- *AmMWSc 92*
**Miller,** Arthur Raphael 1934- *WhoAmL 92*
**Miller,** Arthur Simard 1935- *AmMWSc 92*
**Miller,** Audrey 1937- *AmMWSc 92*
**Miller,** August 1933- *AmMWSc 92*
**Miller,** Augustus Taylor, Jr 1910- *AmMWSc 92*
**Miller,** Banner Isom 1917-1976 *DcNCBi 4*
**Miller,** Barbara Darlene *WhoWest 92*
**Miller,** Barbara Rogalle 1939- *WhoAmP 91*
**Miller,** Barbara Stallcup 1919- *WhoWest 92*
**Miller,** Barry 1933- *AmMWSc 92*
**Miller,** Barry 1942- *AmMWSc 92, Who 92*
**Miller,** Barry 1958- *IntMPA 92*
**Miller,** Barry Joseph 1954- *WhoAmL 92*
**Miller,** Beatrice Ellen 1946- *WhoFI 92*
**Miller,** Ben 1936- *WhoAmL 92, WhoAmP 91, WhoMW 92*
**Miller,** Bence C. *WhoRel 92*
**Miller,** Benjamin Reid 1962- *WhoFI 92*
**Miller,** Benjamin Robertson, Jr. 1937- *WhoAmL 92*
**Miller,** Benjamin T. 1934- *WhoBlA 92*
**Miller,** Bennett F. 1948- *WhoRel 92*
**Miller,** Bernard *Who 92*
**Miller,** Bernard 1927- *AmMWSc 92*
**Miller,** Bernard 1930- *AmMWSc 92*
**Miller,** Bernard Keith 1953- *WhoRel 92, WhoWest 92*
**Miller,** Bernice J. 1920- *WhoMW 92*
**Miller,** Bernice Johnson *WhoBlA 92*
**Miller,** Berns 1946- *WhoAmP 91*
**Miller,** Bertin 1936- *WhoMW 92, WhoRel 92*
**Miller,** Betty 1928- *WhoAmP 91*
**Miller,** Betty G 1918- *WhoAmP 91*
**Miller,** Betty Jean 1958- *WhoWest 92*
**Miller,** Betty M 1930- *AmMWSc 92*
**Miller,** Beverly B. 1933- *WhoMW 92*
**Miller,** Beverly Jean 1955- *WhoRel 92*
**Miller,** Bill *DrAPF 91*
**Miller,** Bill 1923- *WhoMW 92*
**Miller,** Bill 1933- *WhoWest 92*
**Miller,** Billie Lynn 1934- *AmMWSc 92*
**Miller,** Bloomfield Jackson 1849-1905 *BiInAmS*
**Miller,** Bob 1945- *AlmAP 92 [port]*
**Miller,** Bobby Joe 1934- *AmMWSc 92*
**Miller,** Bonnie L. 1942- *WhoRel 92*
**Miller,** Bradley Adam 1959- *WhoFI 92*
**Miller,** Brian Henry 1948- *WhoAmL 92*
**Miller,** Brinton Marshall 1926- *AmMWSc 92*
**Miller,** Bronlow Kirk 1957- *WhoEnt 92*
**Miller,** Brown *DrAPF 91*
**Miller,** Bruce *Who 92*
**Miller,** Bruce A 1927- *WhoAmP 91*
**Miller,** Bruce Barnett, II 1961- *WhoRel 92*
**Miller,** Bruce Linn 1923- *AmMWSc 92*
**Miller,** Bruce Neil 1941- *AmMWSc 92*
**Miller,** Bruce R. 1955- *WhoMW 92*
**Miller,** Byron F 1931- *AmMWSc 92*
**Miller,** C Arden 1924- *AmMWSc 92, IntWW 91*
**Miller,** C Dan 1941- *AmMWSc 92*
**Miller,** C David 1931- *AmMWSc 92*
**Miller,** C Eugene 1928- *AmMWSc 92*
**Miller,** C. Ray *WhoRel 92*
**Miller,** Callix Edwin 1924- *WhoMW 92*
**Miller,** Calvin F 1947- *AmMWSc 92*
**Miller,** Cameron *Who 92*
**Miller,** Carl Elmer 1937- *AmMWSc 92*
**Miller,** Carl George 1942- *WhoFI 92*
**Miller,** Carl Henry, Jr 1920- *AmMWSc 92*
**Miller,** Carl Lawrence 1957- *WhoMW 92*
**Miller,** Carl Lewis 1939- *WhoWest 92*
**Miller,** Carlos Oakley 1923- *AmMWSc 92*
**Miller,** Carol Ann 1943- *AmMWSc 92*
**Miller,** Carol Raymond 1938- *AmMWSc 92*
**Miller,** Carole Ann 1942- *WhoAmP 91*
**Miller,** Carole Ann Lyons *WhoWest 92*
**Miller,** Caroll S 1926- *WhoAmP 91*
**Miller,** Carolyn Handler 1941- *WhoEnt 92*
**Miller,** Carroll Lee 1909- *WhoBlA 92*
**Miller,** Char *ConAu 34NR*
**Miller,** Charles A *AmMWSc 92*
**Miller,** Charles A. 1935- *WhoAmL 92*
**Miller,** Charles A. 1937- *WrDr 92*
**Miller,** Charles Allen 1937- *WhoMW 92*
**Miller,** Charles Benedict 1940- *AmMWSc 92*
**Miller,** Charles Daly 1928- *WhoWest 92*
**Miller,** Charles Edward 1925- *AmMWSc 92*
**Miller,** Charles Frederick, III 1941- *AmMWSc 92*
**Miller,** Charles G 1940- *AmMWSc 92*
**Miller,** Charles Gary 1957- *WhoAmL 92*
**Miller,** Charles Henry, Jr. 1933- *WhoRel 92*
**Miller,** Charles Leo, Jr. 1959- *WhoAmL 92*
**Miller,** Charles Leslie 1929- *AmMWSc 92*
**Miller,** Charles Maurice 1948- *WhoAmL 92*
**Miller,** Charles P 1918- *WhoAmP 91*
**Miller,** Charles William 1942- *AmMWSc 92*
**Miller,** Charles William 1945- *WhoMW 92*
**Miller,** Cheryl 1943- *IntMPA 92*
**Miller,** Cheryl De Ann 1964- *BlkOlyM [port]*
**Miller,** Cheryl Denise 1958- *WhoBlA 92*
**Miller,** Cheryl Thompson 1951- *WhoWest 92*
**Miller,** Chris H 1942- *AmMWSc 92*
**Miller,** Christian 1920- *IntAu&W 91, WrDr 92*
**Miller,** Christoper Lee 1949- *WhoEnt 92*
**Miller,** Christopher Charles 1956- *WhoRel 92*
**Miller,** Cincinnatus Hiner *BenetAL 91*
**Miller,** Clara Burr 1912- *WhoWest 92*
**Miller,** Clarence A 1938- *AmMWSc 92*
**Miller,** Clarence E. 1917- *AlmAP 92 [port], WhoAmP 91, WhoMW 92*
**Miller,** Clark Alvin 1934- *WhoFI 92*
**Miller,** Clark Lloyd 1954- *WhoRel 92*
**Miller,** Claude 1942- *IntDcF 2-2*
**Miller,** Cliff D. 1944- *WhoRel 92*
**Miller,** Clifford Albert 1928- *WhoFI 92, WhoWest 92*
**Miller,** Clifford Joel 1947- *WhoAmL 92*
**Miller,** Clifford Michael 1955- *WhoAmL 92*
**Miller,** Clinton 1939- *WhoAmP 91*
**Miller,** Colin 1943- *TwCPaSc*
**Miller,** Conrad Henry 1926- *AmMWSc 92*
**Miller,** Craig *WhoFI 92*
**Miller,** Craig Arthur 1956- *WhoMW 92*
**Miller,** Craig Johnson 1950- *WhoEnt 92*
**Miller,** Craig Russell 1949- *WhoEnt 92*
**Miller,** Curtis C 1935- *AmMWSc 92*
**Miller,** Curtis Herman 1947- *WhoMW 92, WhoRel 92*
**Miller,** D.D. 1864-1944 *RelLAm 91*
**Miller,** D Eugene 1941- *WhoIns 92*
**Miller,** Dale Andrew 1949- *WhoAmP 91, WhoMW 92*
**Miller,** Dale L 1941- *AmMWSc 92*
**Miller,** Dale Maurice 1948- *WhoRel 92*
**Miller,** Daniel James 1958- *WhoWest 92*
**Miller,** Daniel Long 1841-1921 *RelLAm 91*
**Miller,** Daniel Mark 1964- *WhoAmL 92*
**Miller,** Daniel Newton, Jr 1924- *AmMWSc 92*
**Miller,** Daniel Weber 1926- *AmMWSc 92, WhoMW 92*
**Miller,** Darrell Alvin 1932- *AmMWSc 92, WhoMW 92*
**Miller,** Darryl Ray 1949- *WhoRel 92*
**Miller,** Darvin Lowell 1929- *WhoMW 92*
**Miller,** David 1909- *IntMPA 92*
**Miller,** David 1928- *AmMWSc 92*
**Miller,** David 1946- *WrDr 92*
**Miller,** David A B 1954- *AmMWSc 92*
**Miller,** David Anthony 1946- *WhoAmL 92*
**Miller,** David Arthur 1942- *AmMWSc 92*
**Miller,** David Benedict 1909- *WhoAmP 91*
**Miller,** David Brian 1954- *WhoEnt 92*
**Miller,** David Bruce 1958- *WhoEnt 92*
**Miller,** David Burke 1930- *AmMWSc 92*
**Miller,** David Clair 1955- *WhoEnt 92*
**Miller,** David E 1945- *WhoAmP 91*
**Miller,** David Edwin 1931- *Who 92*
**Miller,** David G 1949- *WhoAmP 91*
**Miller,** David Harry 1939- *AmMWSc 92*
**Miller,** David Hewitt 1918- *AmMWSc 92*
**Miller,** David Jacob 1910- *AmMWSc 92*
**Miller,** David Jonathan 1944- *WhoAmL 92*
**Miller,** David L 1947- *WhoIns 92*
**Miller,** David Lee 1938- *AmMWSc 92*
**Miller,** David Lee 1955- *WhoEnt 92*
**Miller,** David LeRoy 1936- *WhoRel 92*
**Miller,** David Merlin 1934- *WhoMW 92*
**Miller,** David P. 1955- *WhoFI 92*
**Miller,** David Powell 1942- *WhoWest 92*
**Miller,** David Quentin 1936- *Who 92*
**Miller,** David Randolph 1953- *WhoEnt 92*
**Miller,** David Russell 1948- *WhoMW 92*
**Miller,** David S 1945- *AmMWSc 92*
**Miller,** David Teekell 1956- *WhoRel 92*
**Miller,** David Walter 1957- *WhoAmL 92, WhoWest 92*
**Miller,** David Wayne 1949- *WhoWest 92*
**Miller,** David Wayne 1961- *WhoRel 92*
**Miller,** David Wilkinson 1937- *WhoAmL 92*
**Miller,** Dawn Marie 1963- *WhoFI 92*
**Miller,** Dean Arthur 1931- *WhoRel 92*
**Miller,** Dean Charles 1928- *WhoEnt 92*
**Miller,** Dean Harold 1940- *WhoEnt 92*
**Miller,** Dean Jeffrey 1951- *WhoAmL 92*
**Miller,** Debbie 1951- *ConAu 133*
**Miller,** Deborah *DrAPF 91*
**Miller,** Deborah Jean 1951- *WhoFI 92, WhoMW 92*
**Miller,** Denis R. 1934- *WhoMW 92*
**Miller,** Dennis Dean 1945- *AmMWSc 92*
**Miller,** Dennis Dixon 1950- *WhoFI 92*
**Miller,** Dennis James 1954- *WhoWest 92*
**Miller,** Dennis Neil 1959- *WhoWest 92*
**Miller,** Dennis Weldon 1949- *WhoBlA 92*
**Miller,** Denny Marvin 1939- *WhoAmP 91*
**Miller,** Denzil Ray 1946- *WhoRel 92*
**Miller,** Derek Harry 1923- *AmMWSc 92*
**Miller,** Devin Lee 1965- *WhoRel 92*
**Miller,** Dexter J., Jr. 1934- *WhoBlA 92*
**Miller,** Diane Marie Wynne 1948- *WhoRel 92*
**Miller,** Diane Wilmarth 1940- *WhoWest 92*
**Miller,** Dick 1928- *IntMPA 92*
**Miller,** Dixon Fullerton 1948- *WhoAmL 92*
**Miller,** Don Curtis 1935- *AmMWSc 92*
**Miller,** Don Dalzell 1913- *AmMWSc 92*
**Miller,** Don K 1935- *WhoIns 92*
**Miller,** Don Wilson 1942- *AmMWSc 92*
**Miller,** Donald 1927- *Who 92*
**Miller,** Donald C. *Who 92*
**Miller,** Donald C. 1920- *IntWW 91*
**Miller,** Donald E. 1930- *WhoFI 92, WhoWest 92*
**Miller,** Donald Edward 1945- *WhoFI 92*
**Miller,** Donald Elbert 1906- *AmMWSc 92*
**Miller,** Donald Eugene 1929- *WhoRel 92*
**Miller,** Donald F 1924- *AmMWSc 92*
**Miller,** Donald Gabriel 1927- *AmMWSc 92*
**Miller,** Donald George 1909- *IntAu&W 91, WrDr 92*
**Miller,** Donald Kenneth, Jr. 1966- *WhoRel 92*
**Miller,** Donald Lesessne 1932- *WhoBlA 92*
**Miller,** Donald Morton 1930- *AmMWSc 92*
**Miller,** Donald Muxlow 1924- *WhoMW 92*
**Miller,** Donald Nelson 1923- *AmMWSc 92*
**Miller,** Donald Piguet 1927- *AmMWSc 92*
**Miller,** Donald Richard 1936- *AmMWSc 92*
**Miller,** Donald Spencer 1932- *AmMWSc 92*
**Miller,** Donald Wright 1927- *AmMWSc 92*
**Miller,** Donna Rita 1959- *WhoFI 92*
**Miller,** Doris Jean 1933- *WhoBlA 92*
**Miller,** Dorothea Starbuck 1908- *AmMWSc 92*
**Miller,** Dorothy Anne Smith 1931- *AmMWSc 92, WhoMW 92*

**Miller**, Douglas *Who 92*
**Miller**, Douglas 1906- *Who 92*
**Miller**, Douglas Charles 1956- *AmMWSc 92*
**Miller**, Douglas John 1952- *WhoEnt 92*
**Miller**, Douglas Kenneth 1947- *AmMWSc 92*
**Miller**, Douglas Lee 1942- *WhoAmP 91*
**Miller**, Douglas T. *WrDr 92*
**Miller**, Douglas Taylor 1937- *IntAu&W 91, WhoMW 92*
**Miller**, Douglass Ross 1942- *AmMWSc 92*
**Miller**, Duane David 1930- *WhoWest 92*
**Miller**, Duane Douglas 1943- *AmMWSc 92*
**Miller**, Duane L 1937- *WhoIns 92*
**Miller**, Dusty Campbell 1920- *WhoFI 92*
**Miller**, Dwane Gene 1934- *AmMWSc 92*
**Miller**, Dwight Richard 1943- *WhoMW 92*
**Miller**, Dwight Whittemore 1940- *WhoAmL 92*
**Miller**, E 1922- *AmMWSc 92*
**Miller**, E. Ethelbert *DrAPF 91*
**Miller**, E. Ethelbert 1950- *ConPo 91, IntAu&W 91, WhoBlA 92, WrDr 92*
**Miller**, E. Robert 1930- *WhoFI 92*
**Miller**, Earl Lewis 1925- *WhoAmP 91*
**Miller**, Earl Vonnidore 1923- *WhoBlA 92*
**Miller**, Eddie LeRoy 1937- *WhoRel 92, WhoWest 92*
**Miller**, Edith *WhoBlA 92*
**Miller**, Edmund *DrAPF 91*
**Miller**, Edmund Howd 1869-1906 *BiInAmS*
**Miller**, Edmund K 1935- *AmMWSc 92*
**Miller**, Edmund Kenneth 1935- *WhoWest 92*
**Miller**, Edward 1915- *IntWW 91, Who 92*
**Miller**, Edward 1922- *AmMWSc 92*
**Miller**, Edward 1930- *Who 92*
**Miller**, Edward 1932- *AmMWSc 92*
**Miller**, Edward Albert 1931- *WhoAmL 92*
**Miller**, Edward Andrew 1953- *WhoEnt 92*
**Miller**, Edward Boone 1922- *WhoAmP 91*
**Miller**, Edward Daniel 1940- *WhoFI 92*
**Miller**, Edward George 1934- *AmMWSc 92*
**Miller**, Edward Godfrey, Jr 1941- *AmMWSc 92*
**Miller**, Edward Isaac 1946- *WhoEnt 92*
**Miller**, Edward Jay 1946- *WhoMW 92*
**Miller**, Edward Joseph 1935- *AmMWSc 92*
**Miller**, Edward Lyle 1928- *WhoAmP 91*
**Miller**, Edward Manuel 1930- *WhoAmL 92*
**Miller**, Edwin Walter 1922- *WhoRel 92*
**Miller**, Eldon H. 1937- *WhoRel 92*
**Miller**, Eleanora *DrAPF 91*
**Miller**, Elena Diana 1941- *WhoEnt 92*
**Miller**, Elizabeth Eshelman 1919- *AmMWSc 92*
**Miller**, Elizabeth Rodriguez 1954- *WhoHisp 92*
**Miller**, Elizabeth Ruby 1905- *WhoAmP 91*
**Miller**, Elliott Cairns 1934- *WhoFI 92*
**Miller**, Elmon A, Jr *WhoAmP 91*
**Miller**, Elva Ruby Connes *WhoWest 92*
**Miller**, Elwood Morton 1907- *AmMWSc 92*
**Miller**, Elwyn Ritter 1923- *AmMWSc 92*
**Miller**, Emerson Waldo 1920- *WhoFI 92, WhoWest 92*
**Miller**, Emery B 1925- *AmMWSc 92*
**Miller**, Emilie Feiza 1936- *WhoAmP 91*
**Miller**, Emmett Gene 1929- *WhoRel 92*
**Miller**, Erenest Eugene 1948- *WhoBlA 92*
**Miller**, Eric Daniel 1956- *WhoAmL 92*
**Miller**, Ernest Arthur 1925- *WhoRel 92*
**Miller**, Ervin Dean 1939- *WhoAmP 91*
**Miller**, Estelle Lee 1929- *WhoAmP 91*
**Miller**, Esther Scobie Powers 1929- *WhoMW 92*
**Miller**, Ethel Jackson 1916- *WhoBlA 92*
**Miller**, Eugene 1922- *AmMWSc 92*
**Miller**, Eugene 1925- *WhoFI 92, WhoMW 92*
**Miller**, Eugene 1928- *WhoAmP 91*
**Miller**, Eugene Albert *WhoFI 92, WhoMW 92*
**Miller**, Eugene D 1931- *AmMWSc 92*
**Miller**, Eugene E. 1930- *ConAu 135*
**Miller**, Evan 1956- *WhoAmL 92*
**Miller**, Evans Royce 1932- *WhoBlA 92*
**Miller**, Evelyn B. *WhoBlA 92*
**Miller**, Everett George, Sr. 1921- *WhoRel 92*
**Miller**, F. Hudson 1957- *WhoEnt 92*
**Miller**, Floyd Glenn 1935- *AmMWSc 92*
**Miller**, Foil Allan 1916- *AmMWSc 92*
**Miller**, Forest Leonard, Jr 1936- *AmMWSc 92*
**Miller**, Forest R 1940- *AmMWSc 92*
**Miller**, Frances A. 1937- *WrDr 92*
**Miller**, Francis Joseph 1917- *AmMWSc 92*
**Miller**, Francis Marion 1925- *AmMWSc 92*
**Miller**, Francis Pickens 1895-1978 *ConAu 135*
**Miller**, Frank *TwCWW 91, WhoAmP 91*
**Miller**, Frank 1927- *IntWW 91*
**Miller**, Frank Ellsworth 1862-1919 *BiInAmS*
**Miller**, Frank L 1910- *WhoAmP 91*
**Miller**, Frank L 1930- *AmMWSc 92*
**Miller**, Frank L., IV 1951- *ConAu 34NR*
**Miller**, Frank Lee, Jr. 1944- *WhoBlA 92*
**Miller**, Frank Lloyd 1947- *WhoMW 92*
**Miller**, Frank Nelson 1919- *AmMWSc 92*
**Miller**, Frank Robert 1908- *Who 92*
**Miller**, Franklin, Jr 1912- *AmMWSc 92*
**Miller**, Franklin Emrick 1946- *WhoWest 92*
**Miller**, Franklin Stuart 1906- *AmMWSc 92*
**Miller**, Fred R 1943- *AmMWSc 92*
**Miller**, Frederick 1937- *AmMWSc 92*
**Miller**, Frederick A. 1946- *WhoBlA 92*
**Miller**, Frederick Arnold 1926- *AmMWSc 92*
**Miller**, Frederick E. 1931- *WhoBlA 92*
**Miller**, Frederick Gene 1936- *WhoMW 92*
**Miller**, Frederick N *AmMWSc 92*
**Miller**, Frederick Powell 1936- *AmMWSc 92*
**Miller**, Frederick Richard, Jr. 1940- *WhoRel 92*
**Miller**, Frederick Staten 1930- *WhoEnt 92, WhoMW 92*
**Miller**, Frederick Walter Gascoyne 1904- *IntAu&W 91, WrDr 92*
**Miller**, Frederick William 1912- *WhoMW 92*
**Miller**, Fredric N 1941- *AmMWSc 92*
**Miller**, Freeman Devold 1909- *AmMWSc 92*
**Miller**, G H 1924- *AmMWSc 92*
**Miller**, G. William 1925- *IntWW 91, Who 92*
**Miller**, Gabriel Lorimer 1928- *AmMWSc 92*
**Miller**, Gail Lorenz 1913- *AmMWSc 92*
**Miller**, Gale Timothy 1946- *WhoAmL 92*
**Miller**, Gareth B. 1928- *WhoRel 92*
**Miller**, Garfield Lankard, III 1950- *WhoFI 92*
**Miller**, Gary A 1945- *AmMWSc 92*
**Miller**, Gary Arthur 1950- *AmMWSc 92*
**Miller**, Gary Lee 1948- *WhoFI 92*
**Miller**, Gary Robert 1944- *WhoRel 92*
**Miller**, Gary Stephen 1953- *WhoFI 92*
**Miller**, Gary W 1940- *WhoIns 92*
**Miller**, Gay Davis 1947- *WhoAmL 92*
**Miller**, Gayle Joan 1944- *WhoEnt 92*
**Miller**, Gene Edward 1954- *WhoRel 92*
**Miller**, Gene Walker 1925- *AmMWSc 92*
**Miller**, Geoffrey Parsons 1950- *WhoAmL 92*
**Miller**, George *IntMPA 92*
**Miller**, George 1945- *AlmAP 92 [port], IntDcF 2-2 [port], IntMPA 92, IntWW 91, WhoAmP 91, WhoWest 92*
**Miller**, George A. 1920- *IntWW 91*
**Miller**, George Alford 1925- *AmMWSc 92*
**Miller**, George Armitage 1920- *AmMWSc 92*
**Miller**, George C 1925- *AmMWSc 92*
**Miller**, George Carroll, Jr. 1949- *WhoBlA 92*
**Miller**, George DeWitt, Jr. 1928- *WhoAmL 92*
**Miller**, George E 1937- *AmMWSc 92*
**Miller**, George F. *WhoFI 92*
**Miller**, George Maurice 1929- *AmMWSc 92*
**Miller**, George Milton 1943- *WhoAmL 92*
**Miller**, George N., Jr. 1951- *WhoBlA 92*
**Miller**, George Noyes 1845-1904 *ScFEYrs*
**Miller**, George Paul 1951- *AmMWSc 92*
**Miller**, George Russell 1945- *WhoAmL 92*
**Miller**, George Sutcliffe 1928- *WhoAmL 92*
**Miller**, George W, Jr *WhoAmP 91*
**Miller**, George William 1925- *WhoFI 92*
**Miller**, Gerald 1927- *WhoEnt 92*
**Miller**, Gerald Alan 1947- *AmMWSc 92*
**Miller**, Gerald E. *WhoRel 92*
**Miller**, Gerald E 1950- *AmMWSc 92*
**Miller**, Gerald Foster 1941- *WhoAmL 92*
**Miller**, Gerald H 1941- *WhoIns 92*
**Miller**, Gerald Joseph 1955- *WhoAmP 91*
**Miller**, Gerald Keith 1947- *WhoWest 92*
**Miller**, Gerald Lewis 1938- *WhoMW 92*
**Miller**, Gerald R 1934- *AmMWSc 92*
**Miller**, Gerald R 1939- *AmMWSc 92*
**Miller**, Gerald Ray 1936- *AmMWSc 92*
**Miller**, Glen A 1930- *AmMWSc 92*
**Miller**, Glendon Richard 1938- *AmMWSc 92, WhoMW 92*
**Miller**, Glenn 1904-1944 *FacFETw [port], NewAmDM*
**Miller**, Glenn 1909?-1944 *ConMus 6 [port], CurBio 91N*
**Miller**, Glenn Harry 1922- *AmMWSc 92*
**Miller**, Glenn Joseph 1925- *AmMWSc 92*
**Miller**, Glenn Marsh 1950- *WhoWest 92*
**Miller**, Gordon Allen 1941- *WhoWest 92*
**Miller**, Gordon Holman 1916- *WhoWest 92*
**Miller**, Gordon James 1960- *AmMWSc 92*
**Miller**, Gordon Lee 1938- *AmMWSc 92*
**Miller**, Gregory Alan 1946- *WhoEnt 92*
**Miller**, Gregory David 1953- *WhoFI 92*
**Miller**, Gregory Duane 1955- *AmMWSc 92*
**Miller**, Gregory James 1959- *WhoAmL 92*
**Miller**, Gregory Keith 1957- *WhoAmL 92*
**Miller**, Gregory Kent 1950- *WhoMW 92*
**Miller**, Grover Cleveland 1927- *AmMWSc 92*
**Miller**, Guthrie 1942- *AmMWSc 92*
**Miller**, Hainon A 1930- *WhoAmP 91*
**Miller**, Harold A 1921- *AmMWSc 92*
**Miller**, Harold Joseph, Jr 1938- *WhoAmP 91*
**Miller**, Harold Richard 1930- *WhoRel 92*
**Miller**, Harold T. 1923- *IntWW 91*
**Miller**, Harold William 1920- *WhoWest 92*
**Miller**, Harriet Evelyn 1919- *WhoWest 92*
**Miller**, Harriet Mann 1831-1918 *BiInAmS*
**Miller**, Harris N 1951- *WhoAmP 91*
**Miller**, Harry 1915- *AmMWSc 92*
**Miller**, Harry Benjamin 1924- *WhoAmL 92*
**Miller**, Harry Brill 1924- *WhoEnt 92*
**Miller**, Harry Brown 1913- *AmMWSc 92*
**Miller**, Harry Galen 1937- *AmMWSc 92*
**Miller**, Harvey 1942- *WhoFI 92*
**Miller**, Harvey Alfred 1928- *AmMWSc 92*
**Miller**, Harvey I 1932- *AmMWSc 92*
**Miller**, Hayward Laywon 1954- *WhoRel 92*
**Miller**, Heather Ross *DrAPF 91*
**Miller**, Heidi Ann 1954- *WhoWest 92*
**Miller**, Helen Carter 1925- *AmMWSc 92*
**Miller**, Helen Hill 1899- *WrDr 92*
**Miller**, Helen S. 1917- *WhoBlA 92*
**Miller**, Helen Topping 1884-1960 *DcNCBi 4*
**Miller**, Helena Agnes 1913- *AmMWSc 92*
**Miller**, Henry 1891-1980 *BenetAL 91, FacFETw [port], LiExTwC*
**Miller**, Henry B., Jr. 1940- *WhoBlA 92*
**Miller**, Henry Franklin 1938- *WhoAmL 92*
**Miller**, Henry Siefke 1901- *WhoFI 92*
**Miller**, Herbert A 1875-1951 *DcAmImH*
**Miller**, Herbert Chauncey 1907- *AmMWSc 92*
**Miller**, Herbert Crawford 1944- *AmMWSc 92*
**Miller**, Herbert Dell 1919- *WhoFI 92*
**Miller**, Herbert John, Jr. 1924- *WhoAmL 92*
**Miller**, Herbert Kenneth 1921- *AmMWSc 92*
**Miller**, Herman *DcTwDes*
**Miller**, Herman Lunden 1924- *AmMWSc 92*
**Miller**, Herman T 1931- *AmMWSc 92*
**Miller**, Hilary Duppa 1929- *Who 92*
**Miller**, Hillard Craig 1932- *AmMWSc 92*
**Miller**, Holmes *Who 92*
**Miller**, Holmes d1986 *Who 92N*
**Miller**, Horatio C. 1949- *WhoBlA 92*
**Miller**, Horrie, Mrs. *Who 92*
**Miller**, Howard *DcTwDes*
**Miller**, Howard Charles 1917- *AmMWSc 92*
**Miller**, Howard G 1955- *WhoAmP 91*
**Miller**, Howard M. 1929- *WhoBlA 92*
**Miller**, Howard Mark 1944- *WhoAmL 92*
**Miller**, Hugh 1937- *IntAu&W 91, WrDr 92*
**Miller**, Hugh Hunt 1925- *AmMWSc 92*
**Miller**, Hugh Thomas 1951- *WhoFI 92, WhoMW 92*
**Miller**, Hyman M *WhoAmP 91*
**Miller**, I George, Jr 1937- *AmMWSc 92*
**Miller**, Ian *WrDr 92*
**Miller**, Ian Douglas 1900- *Who 92*
**Miller**, Inglis J, Jr 1943- *AmMWSc 92*
**Miller**, Irvin Alexander 1932- *AmMWSc 92*
**Miller**, Irving F 1934- *AmMWSc 92*
**Miller**, Irwin 1928- *AmMWSc 92*
**Miller**, Isaac H., Jr. 1920- *WhoBlA 92*
**Miller**, Isadore *WhoEnt 92*
**Miller**, Israel 1918- *WhoRel 92*
**Miller**, Ivan Keith 1921- *AmMWSc 92*
**Miller**, Izetta Jewel 1884?-1978 *FacFETw*
**Miller**, J. Carter, Sr. 1920- *WhoFI 92*
**Miller**, J. D. Bruce 1922- *WrDr 92*
**Miller**, J Hillis 1928- *IntAu&W 91, WrDr 92*
**Miller**, J J 1947- *WhoIns 92*
**Miller**, J. Philip 1937- *WhoEnt 92*
**Miller**, J Sturgis 1923- *WhoAmP 91*
**Miller**, Jack 1945- *TwCPaSc*
**Miller**, Jack Culbertson 1925- *AmMWSc 92*
**Miller**, Jack David 1945- *WhoIns 92*
**Miller**, Jack Edmond 1944- *WhoFI 92*
**Miller**, Jack Everett 1921- *WhoAmL 92*
**Miller**, Jack Martin 1940- *AmMWSc 92*
**Miller**, Jack Pershing 1931- *WhoMW 92*
**Miller**, Jack Richard 1916- *IntWW 91, WhoAmL 92*
**Miller**, Jack W 1925- *AmMWSc 92*
**Miller**, Jacqueline Elizabeth 1935- *WhoBlA 92*
**Miller**, Jacques Francis 1931- *IntWW 91*
**Miller**, Jacques Francis Albert Pierre 1931- *Who 92*
**Miller**, Jake C. 1929- *WhoBlA 92*
**Miller**, James 1934- *Who 92*
**Miller**, James, Sr. 1944- *WhoBlA 92*
**Miller**, James Albert, Jr 1907- *AmMWSc 92*
**Miller**, James Alexander 1915- *AmMWSc 92*
**Miller**, James Alvin 1944- *WhoRel 92*
**Miller**, James Angus 1946- *AmMWSc 92*
**Miller**, James Arthur 1944- *WhoBlA 92*
**Miller**, James Avery 1932- *AmMWSc 92*
**Miller**, James Blaine 1883-1915 *BiInAmS*
**Miller**, James C, III *WhoAmP 91*
**Miller**, James Clifford, III 1942- *IntWW 91, WhoFI 92*
**Miller**, James Davis *WhoFI 92*
**Miller**, James E. *WhoFI 92*
**Miller**, James E 1927- *WhoAmP 91*
**Miller**, James Edward 1940- *AmMWSc 92*
**Miller**, James Edward 1942- *AmMWSc 92*
**Miller**, James Edward 1945- *ConAu 135*
**Miller**, James Edwin 1920- *WrDr 92*
**Miller**, James Edwin, III 1947- *WhoEnt 92*
**Miller**, James Eugene 1938- *AmMWSc 92*
**Miller**, James Franklin 1912- *AmMWSc 92*
**Miller**, James Frederick 1943- *AmMWSc 92*
**Miller**, James Gegan 1942- *AmMWSc 92*
**Miller**, James Gilbert 1946- *AmMWSc 92*
**Miller**, James H. 1932- *WhoFI 92*
**Miller**, James Henry 1938- *WhoEnt 92*
**Miller**, James Kincheloe 1932- *AmMWSc 92*
**Miller**, James L 1935- *AmMWSc 92*
**Miller**, James Lynn 1951- *WhoAmL 92, WhoWest 92*
**Miller**, James Monroe 1933- *AmMWSc 92*
**Miller**, James Monroe 1948- *WhoAmL 92*
**Miller**, James Nathaniel 1926- *AmMWSc 92*
**Miller**, James Patrick 1954- *WhoWest 92*
**Miller**, James Paul 1946- *AmMWSc 92*
**Miller**, James Q 1926- *AmMWSc 92*
**Miller**, James R *IntMPA 92*
**Miller**, James Ray 1948- *AmMWSc 92*
**Miller**, James Reginald 1928- *AmMWSc 92*
**Miller**, James Richard 1922- *AmMWSc 92*
**Miller**, James Robert 1922- *AmMWSc 92*
**Miller**, James Robert 1941- *AmMWSc 92*
**Miller**, James Roland 1921- *AmMWSc 92*
**Miller**, James Roland 1929- *AmMWSc 92*
**Miller**, James S. 1923- *WhoBlA 92*
**Miller**, James S. 1924- *WhoBlA 92*
**Miller**, James Taggert, Jr 1943- *AmMWSc 92*
**Miller**, James Woodell 1927- *AmMWSc 92*
**Miller**, Jan Dean 1942- *AmMWSc 92*
**Miller**, Jane *DrAPF 91*
**Miller**, Jane 1925-1989 *ConAu 34NR*
**Miller**, Jane Alsobrook 1928- *AmMWSc 92*
**Miller**, Janet Jenkins 1937- *WhoAmP 91*
**Miller**, Janice Margaret Lilly 1938- *AmMWSc 92*
**Miller**, Jarrell E 1913- *AmMWSc 92*
**Miller**, Jason 1932- *WrDr 92*
**Miller**, Jason 1939- *IntMPA 92, WhoEnt 92*
**Miller**, Jay Alan 1928- *WhoMW 92*
**Miller**, Jay Anthony 1959- *WhoRel 92*
**Miller**, Jean Carolyn Wilder 1932- *WhoBlA 92*
**Miller**, Jean Ruth 1927- *WhoWest 92*
**Miller**, Jeanne-Marie A. 1937- *WhoBlA 92*
**Miller**, Jeff 1941- *WhoAmP 91*
**Miller**, Jeffrey Charles 1954- *WhoAmP 91*
**Miller**, Jeffrey Clark 1943- *WhoAmL 92*
**Miller**, Jeffrey Grant 1941- *WhoAmL 92*
**Miller**, Jeffrey Robert 1941- *WhoWest 92*
**Miller**, Jeffrey Scott 1953- *WhoAmL 92*
**Miller**, Jerome K. 1931- *WhoWest 92*
**Miller**, Jerry A. 1935- *WhoWest 92*
**Miller**, Jerry Brian 1961- *WhoEnt 92*
**Miller**, Jerry D 1942- *WhoAmP 91*
**Miller**, Jerry Huber 1931- *WhoFI 92, WhoWest 92*
**Miller**, Jerry J 1933- *WhoAmP 91*
**Miller**, Jerry K 1934- *AmMWSc 92*
**Miller**, Jerry Lee 1952- *WhoEnt 92*
**Miller**, Jesse L, Jr 1942- *WhoAmP 91*
**Miller**, Jesse P. 1920- *WhoBlA 92*
**Miller**, Jim *TwCWW 91*
**Miller**, Jim Wayne *DrAPF 91*
**Miller**, Jim Wayne 1936- *ConAu 15AS [port], IntAu&W 91, WrDr 92*
**Miller**, Joan Marie Nonnenmocher 1935- *WhoRel 92*

**Miller**, Joaquin 1837-1913 *BenetAL 91*
**Miller**, Joel Steven 1944- *AmMWSc 92*
**Miller**, Joella *WhoRel 92*
**Miller**, John *TwCPaSc*
**Miller**, John A 1927- *WhoIns 92*
**Miller**, John Adalbert 1927- *WhoFI 92*
**Miller**, John Allen 1866-1935 *RelLAm 91*
**Miller**, John Antonio 1942- *WhoRel 92*
**Miller**, John Bryan Peter Duppa- 1903- *Who 92*
**Miller**, John C. d1991 *NewYTBS 91*
**Miller**, John Cameron 1949- *AmMWSc 92*
**Miller**, John Campbell 1938- *WhoAmL 92*
**Miller**, John D. Bruce 1922- *Who 92*
**Miller**, John David 1923- *AmMWSc 92*
**Miller**, John E. *DrAPF 91*
**Miller**, John E 1929- *WhoAmP 91*
**Miller**, John Eddie 1945- *WhoAmL 92*
**Miller**, John Francis C. *Who 92*
**Miller**, John Frederick 1928- *AmMWSc 92*
**Miller**, John Fulenwider 1834-1906 *DcNCBi 4*
**Miller**, John George 1908- *AmMWSc 92*
**Miller**, John Grider 1935- *ConAu 133*
**Miller**, John Grier 1943- *AmMWSc 92*
**Miller**, John Griffin 1956- *WhoEnt 92*
**Miller**, John H. 1917- *WhoBlA 92*
**Miller**, John Harmsworth 1930- *Who 92*
**Miller**, John Harold 1925- *WhoMW 92, WhoRel 92*
**Miller**, John Henry 1917- *WhoRel 92*
**Miller**, John Henry 1933- *AmMWSc 92*
**Miller**, John Holmes 1925- *Who 92*
**Miller**, John Howard 1943- *AmMWSc 92*
**Miller**, John Howard 1959- *WhoFI 92*
**Miller**, John Ireland 1912- *Who 92*
**Miller**, John James 1918- *AmMWSc 92*
**Miller**, John Jerry 1937- *WhoFI 92*
**Miller**, John Johnston, III 1934- *AmMWSc 92*
**Miller**, John Joseph 1928- *Who 92*
**Miller**, John Kent 1944- *WhoAmL 92*
**Miller**, John Leed 1949- *WhoAmL 92*
**Miller**, John Mansel 1919- *Who 92*
**Miller**, John Michael 1954- *AmMWSc 92*
**Miller**, John Nelson 1948- *WhoFI 92*
**Miller**, John Philip 1957- *WhoFI 92*
**Miller**, John R. 1938- *AlmAP 92 [port], WhoAmP 91, WhoWest 92*
**Miller**, John Robert 1944- *AmMWSc 92*
**Miller**, John Ronald 1938- *WhoRel 92*
**Miller**, John Stewart Abercromby Smith 1928- *WhoRel 92*
**Miller**, John T., Jr. 1922- *WhoAmL 92*
**Miller**, John Ulman 1914- *WhoRel 92*
**Miller**, John Walcott 1930- *AmMWSc 92*
**Miller**, John Wesley, III 1941- *WhoAmL 92*
**Miller**, John Wesley, Jr 1935- *AmMWSc 92*
**Miller**, John William, Jr. 1942- *WhoEnt 92*
**Miller**, Jon Cristofer 1938- *WhoMW 92*
**Miller**, Jon H. 1938- *IntWW 91*
**Miller**, Jon Hamilton 1938- *WhoFI 92, WhoWest 92*
**Miller**, Jon Philip 1944- *AmMWSc 92, WhoWest 92*
**Miller**, Jonathan 1934- *FacFETw, IntAu&W 91, WrDr 92*
**Miller**, Jonathan Wolfe 1934- *IntWW 91, Who 92, WhoEnt 92*
**Miller**, Jordan *DrAPF 91*
**Miller**, Jordan Yale 1919- *WrDr 92*
**Miller**, Josef Mayer 1937- *AmMWSc 92*
**Miller**, Joseph 1937- *AmMWSc 92*
**Miller**, Joseph Arthur 1933- *WhoWest 92*
**Miller**, Joseph Edward, Jr. 1945- *WhoWest 92*
**Miller**, Joseph Edwin 1942- *AmMWSc 92*
**Miller**, Joseph Henry 1924- *AmMWSc 92*
**Miller**, Joseph Herman 1930- *WhoBlA 92*
**Miller**, Joseph Holmes 1919- *Who 92*
**Miller**, Joseph Howard 1925- *WhoEnt 92*
**Miller**, Joseph Irwin 1909- *WhoFI 92, WhoMW 92*
**Miller**, Joseph James 1912- *WhoAmP 91*
**Miller**, Joseph Owen 1949- *WhoAmP 91*
**Miller**, Joseph Quinter 1899-1983 *RelLAm 91*
**Miller**, Josephine *AmMWSc 92*
**Miller**, Josephine Welder 1942- *WhoAmP 91*
**Miller**, Joshua d1901 *BiInAmS*
**Miller**, Joyce Fiddick 1939- *AmMWSc 92*
**Miller**, Joyce Mary 1945- *AmMWSc 92*
**Miller**, JP *LesBEnT 92*
**Miller**, JP 1919- *IntMPA 92, WhoEnt 92*
**Miller**, Judea Bennett 1930- *WhoRel 92*
**Miller**, Judith 1936- *WhoAmP 91*
**Miller**, Judith Ann 1941- *WhoRel 92*
**Miller**, Judith Ann 1952- *WhoRel 92*
**Miller**, Judith Evelyn 1951- *AmMWSc 92*
**Miller**, Judith Henderson 1951- *Who 92*
**Miller**, Judy Statman 1938- *WhoFI 92*
**Miller**, Julian Creighton, Jr 1940- *AmMWSc 92*
**Miller**, Julian Sidney 1886-1946 *DcNCBi 4*
**Miller**, K. Bruce 1927- *WrDr 92*
**Miller**, Karen Lewis 1942- *WhoEnt 92*
**Miller**, Karin R. 1964- *WhoFI 92*
**Miller**, Karl 1931- *IntAu&W 91, WrDr 92*
**Miller**, Karl A. 1931- *WhoFI 92*
**Miller**, Karl Fergus Connor 1931- *IntWW 91, Who 92*
**Miller**, Kathleen Roberts 1947- *WhoAmP 91*
**Miller**, Kathryn J. Blind 1953- *WhoWest 92*
**Miller**, Keith 1938- *WhoFI 92*
**Miller**, Keith Allan 1953- *WhoEnt 92*
**Miller**, Keith Lloyd 1951- *WhoMW 92*
**Miller**, Keith Wyatt 1941- *AmMWSc 92*
**Miller**, Ken Leroy 1933- *WhoRel 92*
**Miller**, Kenneth A. 1944- *WhoWest 92*
**Miller**, Kenneth Allan Glen 1926- *Who 92*
**Miller**, Kenneth Bernard 1951- *WhoBlA 92*
**Miller**, Kenneth E. 1926- *WrDr 92*
**Miller**, Kenneth Edward 1951- *WhoWest 92*
**Miller**, Kenneth Eugene 1926- *WhoEnt 92*
**Miller**, Kenneth James 1950- *WhoMW 92*
**Miller**, Kenneth Jay 1924- *AmMWSc 92*
**Miller**, Kenneth John 1939- *AmMWSc 92*
**Miller**, Kenneth L 1943- *AmMWSc 92*
**Miller**, Kenneth Lehr 1961- *WhoAmL 92*
**Miller**, Kenneth M, Sr 1921- *AmMWSc 92*
**Miller**, Kenneth Melvin 1943- *AmMWSc 92*
**Miller**, Kenneth Michael 1921- *WhoFI 92*
**Miller**, Kenneth Philip 1915- *AmMWSc 92*
**Miller**, Kenneth Raymond 1948- *AmMWSc 92*
**Miller**, Kenneth Sielke 1922- *AmMWSc 92*
**Miller**, Kenneth William 1947- *WhoFI 92*
**Miller**, Kent D 1925- *AmMWSc 92*
**Miller**, Kent Dunkerton 1941- *WhoWest 92*
**Miller**, Kevin D. 1949- *WhoMW 92*
**Miller**, Kevin D. 1966- *WhoBlA 92*
**Miller**, Kevin Grey 1930- *WhoAmP 91*
**Miller**, Kim Irving 1936- *AmMWSc 92*
**Miller**, Kim Sandra 1961- *WhoEnt 92*
**Miller**, Kimberly Ann 1963- *WhoEnt 92*
**Miller**, Kimberly Clarke 1965- *WhoMW 92*
**Miller**, Kirk 1949- *AmMWSc 92*
**Miller**, L. Martin 1939- *WhoFI 92*
**Miller**, Laird O'Neil, Jr. 1915- *WhoRel 92*
**Miller**, Lajos 1940- *IntWW 91*
**Miller**, Lamar Perry 1925- *WhoBlA 92*
**Miller**, Lane Franklin 1949- *WhoFI 92*
**Miller**, Larry Brent 1960- *WhoAmL 92*
**Miller**, Larry David 1945- *WhoMW 92*
**Miller**, Larry Gene 1946- *AmMWSc 92*
**Miller**, Larry H. *WhoWest 92*
**Miller**, Larry Joe 1954- *WhoRel 92*
**Miller**, Larry O'Dell 1939- *AmMWSc 92*
**Miller**, Laura Ariane 1954- *WhoAmL 92*
**Miller**, Laurel Milton 1935- *WhoBlA 92*
**Miller**, Lauren Levy 1958- *WhoAmL 92*
**Miller**, Laurence Herbert 1934- *AmMWSc 92*
**Miller**, Lawrence A., Jr. 1951- *WhoBlA 92*
**Miller**, Lawrence Daniel, Jr. 1934- *WhoWest 92*
**Miller**, Lawrence Edward 1944- *WhoAmL 92*
**Miller**, Lawrence Edward 1950- *WhoBlA 92*
**Miller**, Lawrence G *WhoAmP 91*
**Miller**, Lawrence Ingram 1914- *AmMWSc 92*
**Miller**, Lawrence Marvin 1962- *WhoMW 92*
**Miller**, Lawrence Richard 1943- *WhoIns 92*
**Miller**, Lee Robert 1951- *WhoEnt 92*
**Miller**, Lee Stephen 1930- *AmMWSc 92*
**Miller**, Leland Bishop, Jr. 1931- *WhoFI 92*
**Miller**, Lennox V 1946- *BlkOlyM*
**Miller**, Lenore 1932- *WhoFI 92*
**Miller**, Leo E 1887-1952 *ScFEYrs*
**Miller**, Leon Lee 1912- *AmMWSc 92*
**Miller**, Leonard David 1930- *AmMWSc 92*
**Miller**, Leonard Robert 1933- *AmMWSc 92*
**Miller**, Leroy Jesse 1933- *AmMWSc 92*
**Miller**, Lesley James, Jr. 1951- *WhoBlA 92*
**Miller**, Leslie Adrienne *DrAPF 91*
**Miller**, Leslie Anne 1951- *WhoAmL 92*
**Miller**, Lester Leon 1935- *WhoWest 92*
**Miller**, Lester Livingston, Jr. 1930- *WhoWest 92*
**Miller**, Lily Poritz 1938- *IntAu&W 91*
**Miller**, Linda Jean 1958- *AmMWSc 92*
**Miller**, Linda Patterson 1946- *ConAu 135*
**Miller**, Lisa Ann 1956- *WhoAmL 92*
**Miller**, Lisa Lynn Morris 1962- *WhoRel 92*
**Miller**, Lloyd George 1934- *AmMWSc 92*
**Miller**, Lloyd Lawrence 1938- *WhoMW 92, WhoRel 92*
**Miller**, Lois Kathryn 1945- *AmMWSc 92*
**Miller**, Loren, Jr. 1937- *WhoBlA 92*
**Miller**, Loren Solomon 1949- *WhoEnt 92*
**Miller**, Lori E. 1959- *WhoBlA 92*
**Miller**, Lorraine Theresa 1931- *AmMWSc 92*
**Miller**, Lou Ann Margaret 1952- *WhoMW 92*
**Miller**, Louis C. 1952- *WhoFI 92*
**Miller**, Louis Howard 1935- *AmMWSc 92*
**Miller**, Louise 1936- *WhoAmP 91*
**Miller**, Louise T. 1919- *WhoBlA 92*
**Miller**, Lowell D 1933- *AmMWSc 92*
**Miller**, Ludlow 1935- *WhoFI 92*
**Miller**, Luvenia C. 1909- *WhoBlA 92*
**Miller**, Lydia J *WhoAmP 91*
**Miller**, Lyle Devon 1938- *AmMWSc 92, WhoMW 92*
**Miller**, Lyle G. *WhoRel 92*
**Miller**, Lynn 1932- *AmMWSc 92*
**Miller**, Lynn C 1938- *WhoIns 92*
**Miller**, Lynn H. 1937- *WrDr 92*
**Miller**, Lynne Marie 1951- *WhoFI 92*
**Miller**, Lyster Keith 1932- *AmMWSc 92, WhoWest 92*
**Miller**, M H 1928- *AmMWSc 92*
**Miller**, M. Joy 1934- *WhoFI 92*
**Miller**, M. Sammye 1947- *WhoBlA 92*
**Miller**, Malcolm Henry 1934- *WhoMW 92*
**Miller**, Maposure T. 1934- *WhoBlA 92*
**Miller**, Marc A. 1952- *WhoEnt 92*
**Miller**, Marc William 1947- *IntAu&W 91*
**Miller**, Marc William 1948- *WhoAmL 92*
**Miller**, Marcia M. 1948- *WhoBlA 92*
**Miller**, Marcia Madsen 1944- *AmMWSc 92*
**Miller**, Marcus Hay 1941- *Who 92*
**Miller**, Margaret 1940- *WhoAmP 91*
**Miller**, Margaret Elizabeth 1934- *WhoBlA 92*
**Miller**, Margaret Greer 1934- *WhoBlA 92*
**Miller**, Margaret J *IntAu&W 91X*
**Miller**, Mariko Terasaki *WhoAmP 91*
**Miller**, Marilyn 1898-1936 *NewAmDM*
**Miller**, Marilyn Suzanne 1950- *WhoEnt 92*
**Miller**, Marion 1913- *WhoWest 92*
**Miller**, Marjorie 1922- *WhoAmP 91*
**Miller**, Mark *WhoFI 92, WhoMW 92*
**Miller**, Mark Andrew 1943- *WhoRel 92*
**Miller**, Mark Edward 1957- *WhoAmL 92*
**Miller**, Mark Fred 1948- *WhoEnt 92*
**Miller**, Mark I. 1927- *WhoRel 92*
**Miller**, Marlin Eugene 1938- *WhoRel 92*
**Miller**, Martha Escabi 1945- *WhoHisp 92*
**Miller**, Martin Eugene 1945- *WhoRel 92*
**Miller**, Martin John 1946- *Who 92*
**Miller**, Martin Stuart 1949- *WhoAmL 92*
**Miller**, Martin Wesley 1925- *AmMWSc 92*
**Miller**, Marvin *ConAu 133, SmATA 65*
**Miller**, Marvin E 1945- *WhoAmP 91*
**Miller**, Marvin Eugene 1927- *WhoAmP 91*
**Miller**, Mary *WrDr 92*
**Miller**, Mary 1942- *WhoAmP 91*
**Miller**, Mary A. 1941- *WhoWest 92*
**Miller**, Mary Alice 1954- *WhoMW 92*
**Miller**, Mary Elizabeth 1947- *WhoEnt 92*
**Miller**, Mary Elizabeth H. *Who 92*
**Miller**, Mary Hotchkiss 1936- *WhoRel 92*
**Miller**, Mary Jeannette 1912- *WhoFI 92*
**Miller**, Mary Rita 1918- *WhoAmP 91*
**Miller**, Mary Stephanie 1940- *WhoRel 92*
**Miller**, Maryanne Cunningham 1931- *WhoAmP 91*
**Miller**, Matthew Jeffrey 1940- *WhoFI 92*
**Miller**, Matthew John 1958- *WhoAmL 92*
**Miller**, Mattie Sherryl 1933- *WhoBlA 92*
**Miller**, Maurice Dean 1946- *WhoMW 92*
**Miller**, Maurice Max 1929- *AmMWSc 92*
**Miller**, Maurice Solomon 1920- *Who 92*
**Miller**, Max B. *IntMPA 92*
**Miller**, Max Dunham, Jr. 1946- *WhoAmL 92*
**Miller**, Max K 1934- *AmMWSc 92*
**Miller**, Maxwell A. 1948- *WhoAmL 92*
**Miller**, May *DrAPF 91*
**Miller**, May 1899- *NotBlAW 92*
**Miller**, Maynard Malcolm 1921- *AmMWSc 92, WhoWest 92*
**Miller**, Melton M, Jr 1933- *AmMWSc 92*
**Miller**, Melvin Allen 1950- *WhoBlA 92*
**Miller**, Melvin B. 1934- *WhoBlA 92*
**Miller**, Melvin Eugene 1949- *WhoFI 92*
**Miller**, Melvin Howard 1939- *WhoAmP 91*
**Miller**, Melvin J 1940- *AmMWSc 92*
**Miller**, Melvin P 1935- *AmMWSc 92*
**Miller**, Meredith 1922- *AmMWSc 92*
**Miller**, Merle 1919-1986 *BenetAL 91*
**Miller**, Merton 1923- *WrDr 92*
**Miller**, Merton Howard 1923- *ConAu 134, IntWW 91, WhoFI 92, WhoMW 92, WhoNob 90*
**Miller**, Michael 1933- *Who 92*
**Miller**, Michael 1937- *WhoAmL 92*
**Miller**, Michael A. *Who 92*
**Miller**, Michael Barbree 1938- *WhoFI 92*
**Miller**, Michael Carl 1955- *WhoMW 92*
**Miller**, Michael Charles 1942- *AmMWSc 92*
**Miller**, Michael Daniel 1948- *WhoEnt 92*
**Miller**, Michael E 1937- *AmMWSc 92*
**Miller**, Michael J. 1958- *WhoFI 92*
**Miller**, Michael M. 1948- *WhoEnt 92*
**Miller**, Michael Patiky 1944- *WhoAmL 92*
**Miller**, Michael Paul 1938- *WhoFI 92*
**Miller**, Michael Paul 1963- *WhoFI 92*
**Miller**, Michael Richard 1946- *WhoAmL 92*
**Miller**, Michael William 1966- *WhoMW 92*
**Miller**, Michelle Avanda 1948- *WhoAmL 92*
**Miller**, Mike *WhoAmP 91*
**Miller**, Mildred *WhoEnt 92*
**Miller**, Millage Clinton, III 1932- *AmMWSc 92*
**Miller**, Milton Allen 1954- *WhoAmL 92*
**Miller**, Milton David 1911- *WhoWest 92*
**Miller**, Milton H 1927- *AmMWSc 92*
**Miller**, Miriam Turteltaub 1924- *WhoAmL 92*
**Miller**, Mitch 1911- *NewAmDM*
**Miller**, Morris 1924- *IntWW 91*
**Miller**, Morris Gary 1954- *WhoAmL 92*
**Miller**, Mortimer Michael 1929- *WhoAmP 91*
**Miller**, Morton W 1936- *AmMWSc 92*
**Miller**, Moses William, Jr. 1950- *WhoRel 92*
**Miller**, Murray Henry 1931- *AmMWSc 92*
**Miller**, Myke Rhodes 1955- *WhoEnt 92*
**Miller**, Myron 1933- *AmMWSc 92*
**Miller**, Nancy E 1947- *AmMWSc 92*
**Miller**, Nancy Gail 1953- *WhoAmL 92*
**Miller**, Nathan 1927- *WrDr 92*
**Miller**, Nathan C 1937- *AmMWSc 92*
**Miller**, Nathan H 1943- *WhoAmP 91*
**Miller**, Neal Elgar 1909- *AmMWSc 92, IntWW 91*
**Miller**, Neil Austin 1932- *AmMWSc 92*
**Miller**, Neil Richard 1945- *AmMWSc 92*
**Miller**, Neil Stuart 1958- *WhoFI 92*
**Miller**, Newton E 1919- *WhoAmP 91*
**Miller**, Nicholas Carl 1942- *AmMWSc 92*
**Miller**, Norman 1926- *TwCPaSc*
**Miller**, Norman Calvin 1939- *WhoFI 92*
**Miller**, Norman E 1931- *AmMWSc 92*
**Miller**, Norman Gustav 1925- *AmMWSc 92*
**Miller**, Norman L. 1928- *WhoBlA 92*
**Miller**, Norman Richard 1948- *WhoAmL 92*
**Miller**, Norman Samuel 1943- *WhoFI 92*
**Miller**, Norton George 1942- *AmMWSc 92*
**Miller**, Oliver O. 1944- *WhoBlA 92*
**Miller**, Orie Otis 1892-1977 *AmPeW*
**Miller**, Orlando Jack 1927- *AmMWSc 92*
**Miller**, Orlo 1911- *IntAu&W 91, WrDr 92*
**Miller**, Orson K, Jr 1930- *AmMWSc 92*
**Miller**, Oscar Lee 1887-1970 *DcNCBi 4*
**Miller**, Oscar Lee, Jr 1925- *AmMWSc 92*
**Miller**, Oswald Bernard 1904- *Who 92*
**Miller**, Ovvie 1935- *WhoAmL 92*
**Miller**, Owen Thomas 1927- *WhoAmP 91*
**Miller**, Owen Winston 1922- *AmMWSc 92*
**Miller**, P Schuyler 1912-1974 *TwCSFW 91*
**Miller**, Pam 1938- *WhoAmP 91*
**Miller**, Pamela *DrAPF 91*
**Miller**, Park Hays, Jr 1916- *AmMWSc 92*
**Miller**, Patricia 1936- *WhoAmP 91*
**Miller**, Patricia 1947- *WhoAmP 91*
**Miller**, Patrick Dwight, Jr. 1935- *WhoRel 92*
**Miller**, Patrick William 1947- *WhoMW 92*
**Miller**, Patsy Ruth 1904- *WhoEnt 92*
**Miller**, Paul *WhoAmL 92*
**Miller**, Paul 1906-1991 *NewYTBS 91 [port]*
**Miller**, Paul 1922- *AmMWSc 92*
**Miller**, Paul Albert 1924- *WhoFI 92, WhoWest 92*
**Miller**, Paul Allen 1955- *WhoRel 92*
**Miller**, Paul Christian 1948- *WhoFI 92*
**Miller**, Paul Dean 1941- *AmMWSc 92*
**Miller**, Paul George 1941- *AmMWSc 92*
**Miller**, Paul Henderson 1928- *WhoRel 92*
**Miller**, Paul J. 1929- *WhoAmL 92*
**Miller**, Paul James 1939- *WhoFI 92*
**Miller**, Paul Leroy, Jr 1934- *AmMWSc 92*
**Miller**, Paul Lukens 1919- *IntWW 91*
**Miller**, Paul Martin 1914- *WhoRel 92*
**Miller**, Paul Neil 1950- *WhoWest 92*
**Miller**, Paul R., Jr. d1991 *NewYTBS 91*
**Miller**, Paul Scott 1943- *AmMWSc 92*
**Miller**, Paul Thomas 1944- *AmMWSc 92*
**Miller**, Paul William 1901- *AmMWSc 92*
**Miller**, Paul William 1918- *Who 92*
**Miller**, Pauline Monz 1931- *AmMWSc 92*
**Miller**, Penelope Ann 1964- *IntMPA 92*
**Miller**, Percy Hugh 1922- *AmMWSc 92*
**Miller**, Perry 1905-1963 *BenetAL 91, FacFETw*
**Miller**, Peter 1939- *TwCPaSc*
**Miller**, Peter Francis Nigel 1924- *Who 92*
**Miller**, Peter J 1919- *WhoAmP 91*
**Miller**, Peter North 1930- *IntWW 91, Who 92*

Miller, Peter Spencer 1938- WhoAmP 91
Miller, Petr 1941- IntWW 91
Miller, Philip DrAPF 91
Miller, Philip Arthur 1923- AmMWSc 92
Miller, Philip Dixon 1932- AmMWSc 92
Miller, Philip Francis 1921- WhoFI 92
Miller, Philip Joseph 1941- AmMWSc 92
Miller, Philip Vernon 1948- WhoRel 92
Miller, Philip William 1948- WhoMW 92
Miller, Phillip Allen 1954- WhoRel 92
Miller, R. Craig 1946- ConAu 135
Miller, Raeburn DrAPF 91
Miller, Ralph English 1933- AmMWSc 92
Miller, Ralph LeRoy 1909- AmMWSc 92
Miller, Ralph Menno 1925- WhoRel 92, WhoWest 92
Miller, Ralph Ross 1934- WhoAmP 91
Miller, Randal Howard 1947- WhoMW 92
Miller, Randall Martin 1945- ConAu 34NR
Miller, Randall Robert 1949- WhoMW 92
Miller, Randolph Crump 1910- WhoRel 92, WrDr 92
Miller, Randolph Latourette 1947- WhoFI 92
Miller, Randy Smarr 1958- WhoWest 92
Miller, Randy W R 1946- WhoAmP 91
Miller, Ray 1949- WhoAmP 91
Miller, Ray, Jr. 1949- WhoBlA 92
Miller, Raymond Earl 1956- AmMWSc 92
Miller, Raymond Edward 1928- AmMWSc 92
Miller, Raymond Edwin 1937- AmMWSc 92
Miller, Raymond Jarvis 1934- AmMWSc 92
Miller, Raymond Michael 1945- AmMWSc 92
Miller, Raymond Vincent, Jr. 1954- WhoAmL 92
Miller, Raymond Woodruff 1928- AmMWSc 92
Miller, Reed 1918- WhoAmL 92
Miller, Reed P. WhoFI 92
Miller, Reginald Wayne 1965- WhoBlA 92
Miller, Reid C AmMWSc 92
Miller, Rene H 1916- AmMWSc 92
Miller, Richard 1930- WorArt 1980 [port]
Miller, Richard A. 1940- WhoRel 92
Miller, Richard Alan 1931- WhoFI 92
Miller, Richard Alan 1944- WhoWest 92
Miller, Richard Albert 1912- AmMWSc 92
Miller, Richard Allan 1947- WhoAmL 92
Miller, Richard Allen 1944- AmMWSc 92
Miller, Richard Allen 1945- WhoAmL 92
Miller, Richard Allen 1953- WhoAmL 92
Miller, Richard Arthur 1927- WhoMW 92
Miller, Richard Avery 1911- AmMWSc 92
Miller, Richard Charles, Jr. 1947- WhoBlA 92
Miller, Richard David 1942- WhoMW 92
Miller, Richard Edward 1937- AmMWSc 92
Miller, Richard Franklin 1927- WhoWest 92
Miller, Richard Graham 1938- AmMWSc 92
Miller, Richard H 1926- WhoAmP 91
Miller, Richard Harold 1942- WhoAmP 91
Miller, Richard Harris 1943- WhoIns 92
Miller, Richard Henry 1926- AmMWSc 92, WhoMW 92
Miller, Richard I. 1929- WhoAmL 92
Miller, Richard J 1937- AmMWSc 92
Miller, Richard Jerome 1939- WhoFI 92
Miller, Richard Keith 1939- AmMWSc 92
Miller, Richard Keith 1949- AmMWSc 92
Miller, Richard Kermit 1946- AmMWSc 92
Miller, Richard King 1949- Who 92
Miller, Richard Lawrence 1949- ConAu 134
Miller, Richard Lee 1940- AmMWSc 92
Miller, Richard Lee 1942- AmMWSc 92
Miller, Richard Leslie 1944- WhoMW 92
Miller, Richard Linn 1933- AmMWSc 92
Miller, Richard Lloyd 1931- AmMWSc 92
Miller, Richard Lynn 1945- AmMWSc 92
Miller, Richard Morgan WhoFI 92
Miller, Richard Morgan 1931- Who 92
Miller, Richard Nelson 1929- WhoFI 92
Miller, Richard Roy 1941- AmMWSc 92
Miller, Richard Samuel 1922- AmMWSc 92
Miller, Richard Sherwin 1930- WhoAmL 92
Miller, Richard Steven 1951- WhoAmL 92
Miller, Richard William 1947- AmMWSc 92
Miller, Richard Wilson 1934- AmMWSc 92
Miller, Rick Dean 1954- WhoRel 92
Miller, Rick Larry 1961- WhoRel 92
Miller, Rob Dale 1954- WhoFI 92
Miller, Rob Hollis DrAPF 91
Miller, Robert A 1939- WhoAmP 91
Miller, Robert Alan 1943- AmMWSc 92
Miller, Robert Alan 1949- WhoWest 92
Miller, Robert Alexander Gavin D. Who 92
Miller, Robert Allan 1944- WhoRel 92
Miller, Robert Allen 1932- WhoFI 92
Miller, Robert Alon 1948- AmMWSc 92
Miller, Robert Arthur 1939- WhoAmL 92, WhoMW 92
Miller, Robert B 1938- WhoIns 92
Miller, Robert Burnham 1942- AmMWSc 92
Miller, Robert Carl 1938- AmMWSc 92
Miller, Robert Carl 1943- WhoFI 92
Miller, Robert Carmi, Jr 1942- AmMWSc 92
Miller, Robert Charles 1925- AmMWSc 92
Miller, Robert Charles 1927- WhoAmP 91
Miller, Robert Christopher 1935- AmMWSc 92
Miller, Robert Daniel 1960- WhoAmL 92, WhoFI 92
Miller, Robert David 1932- WhoFI 92, WhoMW 92
Miller, Robert David 1941- WhoAmP 91
Miller, Robert Demorest 1919- AmMWSc 92
Miller, Robert Dennis 1941- AmMWSc 92
Miller, Robert DuWayne 1912- AmMWSc 92
Miller, Robert Earl 1932- AmMWSc 92
Miller, Robert Earl, Jr 1955- WhoAmP 91
Miller, Robert Ellis 1932- IntMPA 92
Miller, Robert Ernest 1936- AmMWSc 92
Miller, Robert Gary 1941- WhoWest 92
Miller, Robert Gerard 1925- AmMWSc 92
Miller, Robert Gerry 1944- AmMWSc 92
Miller, Robert H 1925- AmMWSc 92
Miller, Robert H 1930- AmMWSc 92
Miller, Robert Harold 1933- AmMWSc 92
Miller, Robert Harold 1957- AmMWSc 92
Miller, Robert Harry 1896-1979 WhoBlA 92N
Miller, Robert Haskins 1919- WhoAmL 92, WhoAmP 91, WhoMW 92
Miller, Robert Hopkins 1927- WhoAmP 91
Miller, Robert Hugh 1944- WhoAmP 91
Miller, Robert Hyland 1937- WhoWest 92
Miller, Robert J 1945- WhoAmP 91
Miller, Robert James 1944- WhoWest 92
Miller, Robert James, II 1933- AmMWSc 92
Miller, Robert Jeffrey 1961- WhoEnt 92
Miller, Robert Johnstone 1758-1834 DcNCBi 4
Miller, Robert Joseph 1939- AmMWSc 92
Miller, Robert Joseph 1941- AmMWSc 92
Miller, Robert Joseph 1945- WhoWest 92
Miller, Robert Keith 1949- ConAu 35NR
Miller, Robert L 1926- AmMWSc 92
Miller, Robert L., Jr. 1950- WhoAmL 92
Miller, Robert Laverne 1953- WhoBlA 92
Miller, Robert Lindsey 1933- WhoRel 92
Miller, Robert Llewellyn 1929- AmMWSc 92
Miller, Robert Llewelyn 1957- WhoEnt 92
Miller, Robert Lynn 1948- WhoFI 92
Miller, Robert Martin 1922- WhoEnt 92
Miller, Robert Morrison, Jr. 1856-1925 DcNCBi 4
Miller, Robert Oran WhoRel 92
Miller, Robert Palm 1931- WhoAmL 92
Miller, Robert Ray 1954- WhoRel 92
Miller, Robert Royce 1944- WhoRel 92
Miller, Robert Rush 1916- AmMWSc 92
Miller, Robert Scott 1947- WhoWest 92
Miller, Robert Steven 1963- WhoWest 92
Miller, Robert Stevens, Jr. 1941- IntWW 91, WhoFI 92
Miller, Robert T WhoAmP 91
Miller, Robert Verne 1945- AmMWSc 92
Miller, Robert W 1931- AmMWSc 92
Miller, Robert Walker, Jr 1941- AmMWSc 92
Miller, Robert Warren 1931- WhoAmL 92
Miller, Robert Warwick 1921- AmMWSc 92
Miller, Robert William 1922- WhoFI 92
Miller, Robert Witherspoon 1918- AmMWSc 92
Miller, Robin Anthony 1937- Who 92
Miller, Roderick Joseph 1953- WhoRel 92
Miller, Rodger Muckerman 1938- WhoFI 92
Miller, Roger 1936- NewAmDM
Miller, Roger Dean 1936- WhoEnt 92
Miller, Roger Ervin 1952- AmMWSc 92
Miller, Roger Frederick 1950- WhoMW 92, WhoRel 92
Miller, Roger Heering 1931- AmMWSc 92
Miller, Ron 1932- WhoAmP 91, WhoMW 92
Miller, Ronald Andrew Baird 1937- Who 92
Miller, Ronald Baxter 1948- WhoBlA 92
Miller, Ronald David 1962- WhoAmL 92
Miller, Ronald Eldon 1941- AmMWSc 92
Miller, Ronald Kinsman 1929- Who 92
Miller, Ronald Knox 1943- WhoAmP 91
Miller, Ronald Lee 1936- AmMWSc 92
Miller, Ronald S. Who 92
Miller, Ronald W. 1933- IntMPA 92
Miller, Ross M. 1954- WhoFI 92
Miller, Ross M., Jr. 1928- WhoBlA 92
Miller, Roswell Kenfield 1932- AmMWSc 92
Miller, Roy F 1912- WhoAmP 91
Miller, Roy Frank 1935- Who 92
Miller, Roy Glenn 1933- AmMWSc 92
Miller, Roy Phillip 1945- WhoAmP 91
Miller, Roy Raymond 1929- WhoMW 92
Miller, Royal DeVere, Jr. 1938- WhoWest 92
Miller, Rudolph J 1934- AmMWSc 92
Miller, Rupert Griel 1933- AmMWSc 92
Miller, Russell 1938- ConAu 133
Miller, Russell Bensley 1946- AmMWSc 92
Miller, Russell Bryan 1940- AmMWSc 92
Miller, Russell Edmund 1942- WhoRel 92
Miller, Russell L., Jr. 1939- WhoBlA 92
Miller, Russell Lee 1922- AmMWSc 92
Miller, Russell Loyd, Jr 1939- AmMWSc 92
Miller, Russell Rowland 1937- WhoIns 92, WhoWest 92
Miller, Ruth 1931- WhoAmL 92
Miller, Ruth Carol 1934- WhoEnt 92
Miller, Sally Ann 1954- AmMWSc 92
Miller, Sam Foster 1957- WhoEnt 92
Miller, Samuel Aaron 1952- WhoEnt 92
Miller, Samuel Almond 1836-1897 BiInAmS
Miller, Samuel Martin 1938- WhoFI 92
Miller, Samuel O. 1931- WhoBlA 92
Miller, Sandra Carol 1946- AmMWSc 92
Miller, Sanford Allen 1951- WhoIns 92
Miller, Sanford Arthur 1931- AmMWSc 92
Miller, Sanford Stuart 1938- AmMWSc 92
Miller, Sarah Pearl 1938- WhoRel 92
Miller, Saul Edward 1930- WhoWest 92
Miller, Scott Cannon 1947- AmMWSc 92
Miller, Scott Gerald 1956- WhoWest 92
Miller, Selwyn Emerson 1960- WhoEnt 92
Miller, Sharron WhoEnt 92
Miller, Sharyl Kay 1945- WhoFI 92
Miller, Shelby A 1914- AmMWSc 92
Miller, Shelley DrAPF 91
Miller, Sherri Schimke 1965- WhoMW 92
Miller, Sherwood Robert 1932- AmMWSc 92
Miller, Sidney 1926- WhoFI 92
Miller, Sidney Israel 1923- AmMWSc 92
Miller, Sidney James 1943- Who 92
Miller, Smith 1804-1872 DcNCBi 4
Miller, Sol 1914- AmMWSc 92
Miller, Stacy Lynn 1964- WhoMW 92
Miller, Stanley Allen 1928- WhoAmP 91
Miller, Stanley Frank 1935- AmMWSc 92
Miller, Stanley Lloyd 1930- AmMWSc 92, FacFETw, IntWW 91
Miller, Stanley Ray 1940- WhoEnt 92, WhoWest 92
Miller, Stephen 1915- Who 92
Miller, Stephen Douglas 1946- AmMWSc 92
Miller, Stephen Douglas 1948- AmMWSc 92
Miller, Stephen Duane 1952- WhoRel 92
Miller, Stephen Franks 1805-1873 DcNCBi 4
Miller, Stephen Grant Ross 1959- WhoFI 92
Miller, Stephen Herschel 1941- AmMWSc 92
Miller, Stephen M. DrAPF 91
Miller, Stephen M. M. 1947- WhoFI 92
Miller, Stephen Paul DrAPF 91
Miller, Stephen Ralph 1950- WhoAmL 92
Miller, Stephen Wiley 1958- WhoAmL 92
Miller, Steve WhoEnt 92
Miller, Steve 1943- NewAmDM
Miller, Steve 1949- WhoAmP 91
Miller, Steve P F 1956- AmMWSc 92
Miller, Steven 1953- WhoAmL 92
Miller, Steven Daniel 1956- WhoAmL 92
Miller, Steven Lawrence 1940- WhoAmP 91
Miller, Steven Ralph 1936- AmMWSc 92
Miller, Steven Richard 1953- WhoAmL 92
Miller, Stewart E 1918- AmMWSc 92
Miller, Stuart C. 1927- WrDr 92
Miller, Stuart Creighton 1927- IntAu&W 91
Miller, Sue 1943- WrDr 92
Miller, Sue Ann 1947- AmMWSc 92
Miller, Susan 1944- WrDr 92
Miller, Susan Elizabeth 1951- WhoAmP 91
Miller, Susan Mary 1955- AmMWSc 92
Miller, Sylvia Alberta Gregory 1919- WhoBlA 92
Miller, Telly Hugh 1939- WhoBlA 92
Miller, Terence George 1918- IntWW 91, Who 92
Miller, Teresa Nell 1955- WhoFI 92
Miller, Terry Alan 1943- AmMWSc 92
Miller, Terry Dennis 1941- WhoWest 92
Miller, Terry James 1949- WhoAmP 91
Miller, Terry Keith 1959- WhoRel 92
Miller, Terry Lee 1940- AmMWSc 92
Miller, Terry Lynn 1945- AmMWSc 92
Miller, Terry Morrow 1947- WhoAmL 92
Miller, Thelma Delmoor 1921- WhoBlA 92
Miller, Theodore Charles 1933- AmMWSc 92
Miller, Theodore Curtis 1953- WhoEnt 92, WhoRel 92
Miller, Theodore H. 1905- WhoBlA 92
Miller, Theodore Lee 1940- AmMWSc 92
Miller, Theresa Ann 1945- WhoMW 92
Miller, Thomas d1685? DcNCBi 4
Miller, Thomas d1694 DcNCBi 4
Miller, Thomas 1932- AmMWSc 92
Miller, Thomas Albert 1940- AmMWSc 92
Miller, Thomas B WhoAmP 91
Miller, Thomas B. 1933- WhoMW 92
Miller, Thomas Burk 1929- WhoAmL 92
Miller, Thomas Cecil 1951- WhoWest 92
Miller, Thomas Earl, Jr. 1936- WhoRel 92
Miller, Thomas Edward 1957- WhoEnt 92
Miller, Thomas Eugene 1929- WhoAmL 92, WhoWest 92
Miller, Thomas F. 1941- WhoEnt 92
Miller, Thomas Gore 1924- AmMWSc 92
Miller, Thomas Hudelson 1934- WhoWest 92
Miller, Thomas J 1944- WhoAmP 91
Miller, Thomas L. 1950- WhoMW 92
Miller, Thomas Lee 1935- AmMWSc 92
Miller, Thomas Marshall 1940- AmMWSc 92
Miller, Thomas Marshall, Sr. 1948- WhoRel 92
Miller, Thomas Milton 1930- WhoFI 92, WhoMW 92
Miller, Thomas R. 1949- WhoFI 92
Miller, Thomas V Mike, Jr WhoAmP 91
Miller, Thomas William 1929- AmMWSc 92
Miller, Thomasene 1942- WhoBlA 92
Miller, Tice Lewis 1938- WhoEnt 92, WhoMW 92
Miller, Timothy Alan 1944- WhoRel 92
Miller, Timothy Alan 1955- WhoEnt 92
Miller, Timothy Curtis 1954- WhoRel 92
Miller, Timothy Ivan 1951- WhoMW 92
Miller, Timothy Peters 1927- WhoWest 92
Miller, Timothy Wayne 1962- WhoRel 92
Miller, Tom H 1925- WhoAmP 91
Miller, Toni Lynn 1959- WhoMW 92
Miller, Tony 1927- IntAu&W 91, WhoEnt 92
Miller, Tracy Bertram 1927- AmMWSc 92
Miller, Trudy Joyce WhoMW 92
Miller, Vassar DrAPF 91
Miller, Vassar 1924- ConPo 91, IntAu&W 91, WrDr 92
Miller, Vernon Dallace 1932- WhoRel 92
Miller, Vernon Richard 1939- WhoAmP 91
Miller, Vic 1951- WhoAmP 91
Miller, Victor Charles 1922- AmMWSc 92
Miller, Vincent Joseph WhoAmP 91
Miller, W E 1913- AmMWSc 92
Miller, Wade WrDr 92
Miller, Wade Elliott, II 1932- AmMWSc 92
Miller, Walter Charles 1918- AmMWSc 92
Miller, Walter D 1925- WhoAmP 91
Miller, Walter Dale 1925- WhoMW 92
Miller, Walter E 1914- AmMWSc 92
Miller, Walter Geoffrey Thomas 1934- IntWW 91
Miller, Walter George 1932- Who 92
Miller, Walter James DrAPF 91
Miller, Walter M 1922- IntAu&W 91
Miller, Walter M, Jr 1922- TwCSFW 91, WrDr 92
Miller, Walter M., Jr. 1923- BenetAL 91
Miller, Walter Neal 1929- WhoFI 92
Miller, Walter Peter 1932- AmMWSc 92
Miller, Walter Richard, Jr. 1934- WhoFI 92
Miller, Wanda Gough 1934- WhoAmP 91
Miller, Ward Beecher 1954- WhoBlA 92
Miller, Ward MacLaughlin, Jr. 1933- WhoAmL 92
Miller, Warne TwCWW 91
Miller, Warren WhoRel 92
Miller, Warren Baker 1917- WhoAmP 91
Miller, Warren C. DrAPF 91
Miller, Warren Canfield 1893- WhoMW 92
Miller, Warren E. 1924- WrDr 92
Miller, Warren F., Jr. 1943- WhoBlA 92
Miller, Warren Fletcher, Jr 1943- AmMWSc 92
Miller, Warren James 1931- AmMWSc 92
Miller, Warren M ScFEYrs A
Miller, Warren Victor 1944- AmMWSc 92
Miller, Warren William 1954- WhoRel 92
Miller, Watkins Wilford 1947- AmMWSc 92

**Miller**, Wayne 1951- *WhoEnt 92*
**Miller**, Wayne Clayton 1949- *WhoMW 92*
**Miller**, Wayne L 1924- *AmMWSc 92*
**Miller**, Wayne Rubin 1955- *WhoEnt 92*
**Miller**, Wendell Smith 1925- *WhoWest 92*
**Miller**, Wesley A *WhoAmP 91*
**Miller**, Wilbur Hobart 1915- *AmMWSc 92, WhoFI 92*
**Miller**, Wilbur J. 1928- *WhoBlA 92*
**Miller**, Willard, Jr 1937- *AmMWSc 92*
**Miller**, William *IntWW 91, Who 92*
**Miller**, William 1782-1849 *BenetAL 91*
**Miller**, William 1783?-1825 *DcNCBi 4*
**Miller**, William 1922- *AmMWSc 92*
**Miller**, William A. *WhoMW 92*
**Miller**, William Amos *ScFEYrs*
**Miller**, William Anton 1935- *AmMWSc 92*
**Miller**, William Augustus 1910- *WhoWest 92*
**Miller**, William B 1917- *AmMWSc 92*
**Miller**, William Brunner 1923- *AmMWSc 92*
**Miller**, William Charles 1937- *WhoAmL 92, WhoFI 92*
**Miller**, William Charles 1947- *WhoRel 92*
**Miller**, William Clare 1940- *WhoWest 92*
**Miller**, William Dawes 1919- *WhoFI 92*
**Miller**, William E. *LesBEnT 92*
**Miller**, William E. 1914-1983 *FacFETw*
**Miller**, William Eldon 1930- *AmMWSc 92*
**Miller**, William Elwood 1919- *WhoWest 92*
**Miller**, William Eugene 1916- *AmMWSc 92*
**Miller**, William F. 1943- *WhoEnt 92*
**Miller**, William Franklin 1920- *AmMWSc 92*
**Miller**, William Frederick 1925- *AmMWSc 92, WhoFI 92, WhoWest 92*
**Miller**, William Frederick 1935- *WhoFI 92*
**Miller**, William Frederick 1946- *WhoAmL 92*
**Miller**, William Green 1931- *WhoAmP 91*
**Miller**, William Henry 1926- *AmMWSc 92*
**Miller**, William Hughes 1941- *AmMWSc 92, WhoWest 92*
**Miller**, William Ian 1946- *WhoAmL 92*
**Miller**, William J. *WhoFI 92*
**Miller**, William Jack 1927- *AmMWSc 92*
**Miller**, William James 1942- *WhoMW 92*
**Miller**, William Kenneth 1940- *WhoMW 92*
**Miller**, William Knight 1918- *AmMWSc 92*
**Miller**, William Laubach 1943- *AmMWSc 92*
**Miller**, William Lawrence 1937- *AmMWSc 92*
**Miller**, William Lee, Jr. 1926- *WhoRel 92*
**Miller**, William Lloyd 1935- *AmMWSc 92*
**Miller**, William Louis 1925- *AmMWSc 92*
**Miller**, William Nathaniel 1947- *WhoBlA 92*
**Miller**, William O. 1934- *WhoBlA 92*
**Miller**, William Paul 1943- *WhoMW 92*
**Miller**, William Peters 1927- *WhoMW 92*
**Miller**, William Preston 1930- *BlkOlyM*
**Miller**, William Ralph 1917- *AmMWSc 92*
**Miller**, William Reynolds, Jr 1939- *AmMWSc 92*
**Miller**, William Robert 1924- *AmMWSc 92*
**Miller**, William Robert 1928- *WhoFI 92*
**Miller**, William Robert 1943- *AmMWSc 92*
**Miller**, William Robert, Jr 1934- *AmMWSc 92*
**Miller**, William Ronald d1991 *Who 92N*
**Miller**, William Shannon 1926- *WhoRel 92*
**Miller**, William Stan 1955- *WhoEnt 92*
**Miller**, William Taylor 1911- *AmMWSc 92*
**Miller**, William Theodore 1925- *AmMWSc 92*
**Miller**, William Vencill 1940- *WhoMW 92*
**Miller**, William Wadd, III 1932- *AmMWSc 92*
**Miller**, William Walter 1941- *AmMWSc 92*
**Miller**, William Weaver 1933- *AmMWSc 92*
**Miller**, Willie 1942- *AmMWSc 92*
**Miller**, Willie James 1902- *WhoBlA 92*
**Miller**, Willoughby Dayton 1853-1907 *BiInAmS*
**Miller**, Wilma Hildruth 1936- *WrDr 92*
**Miller**, Wilmer Glenn 1932- *AmMWSc 92*
**Miller**, Wilmer Jay 1925- *AmMWSc 92*
**Miller**, Yvonne Bond 1934- *WhoAmP 91, WhoBlA 92*
**Miller**, Zell Bryan 1932- *AlmAP 92 [port], IntWW 91, WhoAmP 91*
**Miller**, Zoya Dickins 1923- *WhoWest 92*
**Miller-Boyette** *LesBEnT 92*
**Miller-Duggan**, Devon *DrAPF 91*
**Miller-Graziano**, Carol L *AmMWSc 92*
**Miller Jones**, Mrs. *Who 92*
**Miller-Jones**, Dalton 1940- *WhoBlA 92*
**Miller-Lewis**, S. Jill 1957- *WhoBlA 92*
**Miller of Glenlee**, Macdonald d1991 *Who 92N*
**Miller of Glenlee**, Stephen 1953- *Who 92*
**Miller Parker**, Agnes *Who 92*
**Miller-Reid**, Dora Alma *WhoBlA 92*
**Miller-Stevens**, Louise Teresa 1919- *AmMWSc 92*
**Millerick**, Eugene J *WhoAmP 91*
**Millero**, Frank Joseph, Jr 1939- *AmMWSc 92*
**Millerson**, Gerald 1923- *WrDr 92*
**Milles-Lade** *Who 92*
**Milleson**, Ronald Kinsey 1934- *WhoAmP 91*
**Millet**, Blaine William 1954- *WhoFI 92*
**Millet**, Jean-Francois 1814-1875 *ThHEIm*
**Millet**, Peter J 1940- *AmMWSc 92*
**Millet**, Pierre Georges Louis 1922- *IntWW 91*
**Millett**, Allan Reed 1937- *WhoMW 92*
**Millett**, Anthea Christine 1941- *Who 92*
**Millett**, Francis Spencer 1943- *AmMWSc 92*
**Millett**, John *IntAu&W 91, WrDr 92*
**Millett**, Kate 1934- *BenetAL 91, ConLC 67 [port], IntAu&W 91, WrDr 92*
**Millett**, Kenneth Cary 1941- *AmMWSc 92*
**Millett**, Knolly E. 1922- *WhoBlA 92*
**Millett**, Martin 1955- *ConAu 133*
**Millett**, Martin J. 1955- *WrDr 92*
**Millett**, Merlin Lyle 1923- *WhoWest 92*
**Millett**, Merrill Albert 1915- *AmMWSc 92*
**Millett**, Mervyn 1910- *WrDr 92*
**Millett**, Peter 1932- *Who 92*
**Millett**, Ricardo A. 1945- *WhoBlA 92*
**Millett**, Walter Elmer 1917- *AmMWSc 92*
**Millette**, Clarke Francis 1947- *AmMWSc 92*
**Millette**, Robert Loomis 1933- *AmMWSc 92*
**Millette**, Ted J 1930- *WhoAmP 91*
**Milley**, David Clark 1941- *WhoRel 92*
**Millgate**, Michael Henry 1929- *Who 92*
**Millgram**, Abraham E 1901- *WrDr 92*
**Millgram**, Abraham Ezra 1901- *WhoRel 92*
**Millham**, Charles Blanchard 1936- *AmMWSc 92*
**Millhauser**, Marguerite Sue 1953- *WhoAmL 92*
**Millhauser**, Steven 1943- *BenetAL 91*
**Millheim**, Keith K *AmMWSc 92*
**Millhiser**, Marlys 1938- *IntAu&W 91, WrDr 92*
**Millhouse**, Edward W, Jr 1922- *AmMWSc 92*
**Millhouse**, Oliver Eugene 1941- *AmMWSc 92*
**Millian**, Stephen Jerry 1927- *AmMWSc 92*
**Millican**, Arthenia J Bates 1920- *IntAu&W 91, WhoBlA 92*
**Millican**, Mike *WhoAmP 91*
**Millich**, Frank 1928- *AmMWSc 92*
**Millich**, Nancy Anne 1943- *WhoAmL 92*
**Millichap**, J Gordon 1918- *AmMWSc 92*
**Millichip**, Frederick Albert 1914- *Who 92*
**Millichip**, Paul 1929- *TwCPaSc*
**Millie-Christine** *DcNCBi 4*
**Millier**, William F 1921- *AmMWSc 92*
**Milligan**, Lord 1934- *Who 92*
**Milligan**, Barton 1929- *AmMWSc 92*
**Milligan**, Bruce R 1956- *WhoIns 92*
**Milligan**, Charles Stuart 1918- *WhoRel 92*
**Milligan**, Frederick James 1906- *WhoMW 92*
**Milligan**, George Clinton 1919- *AmMWSc 92*
**Milligan**, Hugh D. 1931- *WhoBlA 92*
**Milligan**, Iain Anstruther 1950- *Who 92*
**Milligan**, James George *Who 92*
**Milligan**, John H 1933- *AmMWSc 92*
**Milligan**, John Padgett, Jr. 1943- *WhoAmL 92*
**Milligan**, John Vorley 1936- *AmMWSc 92*
**Milligan**, Larry Patrick 1940- *AmMWSc 92*
**Milligan**, Lawrence Drake, Jr. 1936- *WhoFI 92*
**Milligan**, Mancil W 1934- *AmMWSc 92*
**Milligan**, Merle Wallace 1922- *AmMWSc 92*
**Milligan**, Robert Lee, Jr. 1934- *WhoFI 92, WhoMW 92*
**Milligan**, Robert T 1919- *AmMWSc 92*
**Milligan**, Spike 1918- *FacFETw, IntAu&W 91, IntWW 91, WrDr 92*
**Milligan**, Terence Alan 1918- *Who 92*
**Milligan**, Terry Wilson 1935- *AmMWSc 92*
**Milligan**, Thomas *DrAPF 91*
**Milligan**, Thomas Kenneth 1941- *WhoAmL 92*
**Milligan**, Thomas Stuart 1934- *WhoAmP 91*
**Milligan**, Unav Opal Wade *WhoBlA 92*
**Milligan**, Veronica Jean Kathleen 1926- *Who 92*
**Milligan**, Walter Jay 1931- *WhoEnt 92*
**Milligan**, Wilbert Harvey, III 1945- *AmMWSc 92*
**Milligan**, Wyndham Macbeth Moir 1907- *Who 92*
**Milligram**, Steven Irwin 1953- *WhoAmL 92*
**Millikan**, Allan G 1927- *AmMWSc 92*
**Millikan**, Clark Harold 1915- *AmMWSc 92*
**Millikan**, Daniel Franklin, Jr 1918- *AmMWSc 92*
**Millikan**, James Rolens 1950- *WhoFI 92*
**Millikan**, Kim Yaeger 1954- *WhoRel 92*
**Millikan**, Larry Edward 1936- *AmMWSc 92*
**Millikan**, Robert Andrews 1868-1953 *FacFETw, WhoNob 90*
**Millikan**, Robert C. 1946- *WhoAmL 92*
**Millikan**, Roger Conant 1931- *AmMWSc 92*
**Milliken**, Charles Buckland 1931- *WhoAmL 92*
**Milliken**, Frank R. d1991 *NewYTBS 91 [port]*
**Milliken**, Frank R 1914- *AmMWSc 92*
**Milliken**, Herselle E Jackson 1915- *WhoAmP 91*
**Milliken**, John Andrew 1923- *AmMWSc 92*
**Milliken**, John Geddes 1945- *WhoAmP 91*
**Milliken**, John Gordon 1927- *WhoAmP 91, WhoWest 92*
**Milliken**, Roger 1915- *WhoFI 92*
**Milliken**, Spencer Rankin 1924- *AmMWSc 92*
**Milliken**, W F, Jr 1911- *AmMWSc 92*
**Milliken**, William Grawn 1922- *WhoAmP 91*
**Millikin**, Benjamin Love 1851-1916 *BiInAmS*
**Milliman**, George Elmer 1937- *AmMWSc 92*
**Milliman**, John D 1938- *AmMWSc 92*
**Millimet**, Erwin 1925- *WhoAmL 92*
**Millimet**, Joseph Allen 1914- *WhoAmL 92*
**Millimet**, Stanley 1928- *WhoFI 92*
**Millin**, Henry Allan *WhoBlA 92*
**Milliner**, Edward Lee, Jr. 1951- *WhoRel 92*
**Milliner**, Eric Killmon 1945- *AmMWSc 92*
**Milling** *Who 92*
**Milling**, Jens Andreas 1951- *WhoMW 92*
**Milling**, Marcus Eugene 1938- *AmMWSc 92*
**Milling**, Peter Francis *Who 92*
**Millinger**, Donald Michael 1954- *WhoEnt 92*
**Millington**, Alaric 1922- *WrDr 92*
**Millington**, Anthony Nigel Raymond 1945- *Who 92*
**Millington**, Ernest Rogers 1916- *Who 92*
**Millington**, John 1779-1868 *BiInAmS*
**Millington**, William Frank 1922- *AmMWSc 92*
**Million**, E Z 1940- *WhoAmP 91*
**Million**, Kenneth Rhea 1939- *WhoMW 92*
**Million**, Rodney Reiff 1929- *AmMWSc 92*
**Million**, Ruth Hatfield 1923- *WhoEnt 92*
**Milliones**, Jake 1940- *WhoBlA 92*
**Milliren**, Claudia Jean 1950- *WhoMW 92*
**Milliron**, John Patrick 1947- *WhoAmP 91*
**Millirons**, Vivian Sue 1942- *WhoAmP 91*
**Millis**, Albert Jason Taylor 1941- *AmMWSc 92*
**Millis**, David Howard 1958- *WhoBlA 92*
**Millis**, James Edward 1884-1961 *DcNCBi 4*
**Millis**, James Henry 1849-1913 *DcNCBi 4*
**Millis**, John Schoff 1903- *AmMWSc 92*
**Millis**, Mark Matthew 1940- *WhoAmP 91*
**Millis**, Robert Lowell 1941- *AmMWSc 92*
**Millius**, Dean Robert 1963- *WhoEnt 92, WhoMW 92*
**Millman**, Barry Mackenzie 1934- *AmMWSc 92*
**Millman**, Bruce Russell 1948- *WhoAmL 92*
**Millman**, George Harold 1919- *AmMWSc 92*
**Millman**, Howard J. 1931- *WhoEnt 92*
**Millman**, Irving 1923- *AmMWSc 92*
**Millman**, Jacob d1991 *NewYTBS 91*
**Millman**, Joan *DrAPF 91*
**Millman**, Joan 1931- *ConAu 135*
**Millman**, Jode Susan 1954- *WhoAmL 92*
**Millman**, Linda Josephson 1960- *WhoAmL 92*
**Millman**, Peter MacKenzie 1906- *AmMWSc 92*
**Millman**, Richard Steven 1945- *AmMWSc 92*
**Millman**, Robert Barnet 1939- *AmMWSc 92*
**Millman**, Sheila Kay 1943- *WhoAmP 91*
**Millman**, Sidney 1908- *AmMWSc 92*
**Millner**, Aubrey Howard, Jr. 1961- *WhoFI 92*
**Millner**, Cork 1931- *ConAu 134*
**Millner**, Dianne Maxine 1949- *WhoBlA 92*
**Millner**, Elaine Stone *AmMWSc 92*
**Millner**, John Jeffrey 1951- *WhoMW 92*
**Millner**, Ralph 1912- *Who 92*
**Millner**, Wallace B., III 1939- *WhoFI 92*
**Millo**, Aprile Elizabeth 1958- *WhoEnt 92*
**Millo**, Frank Ronald 1951- *WhoAmL 92*
**Millocker**, Karl 1842-1899 *NewAmDM*
**Millon**, Charles 1945- *IntWW 91*
**Millon**, Delecta Gay 1943- *WhoMW 92*
**Millot**, Georges 1917- *IntWW 91*
**Milloy**, Frank Joseph, Jr. 1924- *WhoMW 92*
**Mills** *Who 92*
**Mills and Boon** *DcLB 112*
**Mills**, Viscount 1956- *Who 92*
**Mills**, A. R. *WrDr 92*
**Mills**, Adelbert Philo 1883-1918 *BiInAmS*
**Mills**, Alan Oswald Gawler 1914- *Who 92*
**Mills**, Alfred Preston 1922- *AmMWSc 92*
**Mills**, Allen Paine, Jr 1940- *AmMWSc 92*
**Mills**, Alley *WhoEnt 92*
**Mills**, Alvin M. 1922- *WhoEnt 92*
**Mills**, Ann *EncAmaz 91*
**Mills**, Anna M. 1949- *WhoMW 92*
**Mills**, Anthony David 1918- *Who 92*
**Mills**, Anthony Francis 1938- *AmMWSc 92*
**Mills**, Anthony John 1940- *WhoFI 92*
**Mills**, Armon Leroi 1940- *WhoFI 92*
**Mills**, B D, Jr 1912- *AmMWSc 92*
**Mills**, Barbara Jean Lyon 1940- *Who 92*
**Mills**, Benjamin Fay 1857-1916 *RelLAm 91*
**Mills**, Bernard Yarnton 1920- *Who 92*
**Mills**, Billy G. 1929- *WhoBlA 92*
**Mills**, Bradford A. 1954- *WhoWest 92*
**Mills**, Bruce Randall 1963- *WhoFI 92*
**Mills**, C. Wright 1916-1962 *BenetAL 91*
**Mills**, Carol Andrews 1943- *WhoAmP 91*
**Mills**, Carol Margaret 1943- *WhoFI 92, WhoWest 92*
**Mills**, Cassandra E. 1959- *WhoBlA 92*
**Mills**, Cecil E 1934- *WhoAmP 91*
**Mills**, Charles 1914- *Who 92*
**Mills**, Charles Gardner 1940- *WhoAmL 92*
**Mills**, Charles Wright 1916-1962 *AmPeW*
**Mills**, Claudia 1954- *IntAu&W 91*
**Mills**, Claudia Eileen 1950- *AmMWSc 92*
**Mills**, Columbus 1808-1882 *DcNCBi 4*
**Mills**, Craig David 1953- *WhoAmL 92*
**Mills**, Dallice Ivan 1939- *AmMWSc 92*
**Mills**, David Edward 1953- *AmMWSc 92*
**Mills**, Debra 1963- *WhoAmP 91*
**Mills**, Denise 1965- *WhoRel 92*
**Mills**, Don Harper 1927- *AmMWSc 92*
**Mills**, Donald 1915- *WhoBlA 92*
**Mills**, Donald Owen 1921- *IntWW 91*
**Mills**, Donna *WhoEnt 92*
**Mills**, Donna 1944- *IntMPA 92*
**Mills**, Dorothy 1889-1959 *ScFEYrs*
**Mills**, Douglas Leon 1940- *AmMWSc 92*
**Mills**, Earl Lee 1925- *WhoAmP 91*
**Mills**, Earl Ronald 1943- *AmMWSc 92*
**Mills**, Edward 1915- *Who 92*
**Mills**, Edward D. 1915- *WrDr 92*
**Mills**, Edward James 1954- *WhoAmL 92*
**Mills**, Eldon S. 1926- *WhoWest 92*
**Mills**, Eleanor Pendleton 1937- *WhoAmP 91*
**Mills**, Elliott 1935- *AmMWSc 92*
**Mills**, Eric Leonard 1936- *AmMWSc 92*
**Mills**, Eric Robertson 1918- *Who 92*
**Mills**, Eric William 1920- *Who 92*
**Mills**, Florence 1896-1927 *NotBlAW 92 [port]*
**Mills**, Frances Jones *WhoAmP 91*
**Mills**, Frank 1923- *IntWW 91, Who 92*
**Mills**, Frank D 1937- *AmMWSc 92*
**Mills**, Frederick Eugene 1928- *AmMWSc 92*
**Mills**, G J 1924- *AmMWSc 92*
**Mills**, Gary Kenith 1946- *AmMWSc 92*
**Mills**, George Alexander 1914- *AmMWSc 92*
**Mills**, George Hiilani 1921- *AmMWSc 92*
**Mills**, George Ian 1935- *Who 92*
**Mills**, George Marshall 1923- *WhoFI 92*
**Mills**, George William 1939- *WhoAmP 91*
**Mills**, Giles Hallam 1922- *Who 92*
**Mills**, Gladys Hunter 1923- *WhoBlA 92*
**Mills**, Glenn B., Jr. 1948- *WhoBlA 92*
**Mills**, Gordon Candee 1924- *AmMWSc 92*
**Mills**, Graham *Who 92*
**Mills**, Harold Hernshaw 1938- *Who 92*
**Mills**, Harry Arvin 1946- *AmMWSc 92*
**Mills**, Harvey Wayland 1926- *WhoAmP 91*
**Mills**, Hayley 1946- *IntMPA 92*
**Mills**, Hayley Cathrine Rose Vivien 1946- *IntWW 91, WhoEnt 92*
**Mills**, Henry 1813-1889 *BiInAmS*
**Mills**, Herbert 1913- *WhoBlA 92*
**Mills**, Howard Leonard 1920- *AmMWSc 92*

Mills, Huey Allen 1946- WhoRel 92
Mills, Hughie E. 1924- WhoBlA 92
Mills, Iain Campbell 1940- Who 92
Mills, Ian Who 92
Mills, Ira Kelly 1921- AmMWSc 92
Mills, Irving 1894-1985 FacFETw
Mills, Ivor 1929- Who 92
Mills, Ivor Henry 1921- Who 92
Mills, Jack Burl 1920- WhoWest 92
Mills, Jack F 1928- AmMWSc 92
Mills, Jacqueline Warner 1948- WhoAmL 92
Mills, James 1932- WrDr 92
Mills, James Eugene 1935- WhoAmP 91
Mills, James Herbert Lawrence 1933- AmMWSc 92
Mills, James Ignatius 1944- AmMWSc 92
Mills, James Louis 1947- AmMWSc 92
Mills, James Wilson 1942- AmMWSc 92
Mills, Janet E 1943- AmMWSc 92
Mills, Janet Marsico 1924- WhoAmP 91
Mills, Janet Trafton 1947- WhoAmP 91
Mills, Jeffery N WhoAmP 91
Mills, Jerry L. 1948- WhoAmL 92
Mills, Jerry Lee 1943- AmMWSc 92
Mills, Joan Marie 1926- WhoMW 92
Mills, Joey Richard 1950- WhoBlA 92
Mills, John ScFEYrs, Who 92
Mills, John 1908- FacFETw, IntMPA 92, IntWW 91, WhoEnt 92
Mills, John 1956- WhoBlA 92
Mills, John Blakely, III 1939- AmMWSc 92
Mills, John F. F. P. Who 92
Mills, John Francis 1949- WhoFI 92
Mills, John Haymes 1831-1898 DcNCBi 4
Mills, John James 1939- AmMWSc 92
Mills, John L. WhoBlA 92
Mills, John Lewis Ernest Watts 1908- Who 92
Mills, John Norman 1932- AmMWSc 92
Mills, John Robert 1916- Who 92
Mills, John T 1937- AmMWSc 92
Mills, John William 1914- Who 92
Mills, Jon L 1947- WhoAmP 91
Mills, Juan J. 1956- WhoHisp 92
Mills, Juliet 1941- IntMPA 92
Mills, Karen R 1940- WhoAmP 91
Mills, Kenneth Eugene 1946- WhoRel 92
Mills, King Louis, Jr 1916- AmMWSc 92
Mills, Laurence John 1920- Who 92
Mills, Lawrence 1932- WhoAmL 92, WhoFI 92, WhoWest 92
Mills, Lawrence Donald, Jr. 1946- WhoRel 92
Mills, Lawrence William Robert 1934- Who 92
Mills, Lee Allen 1948- WhoAmL 92
Mills, Leif Anthony 1936- Who 92
Mills, Leonard Sidney 1914- Who 92
Mills, Leslie Lee 1943- WhoRel 92
Mills, Lewis Craig, Jr 1923- AmMWSc 92
Mills, Lillian Magdalene WhoEnt 92
Mills, Linda S. 1951- WhoFI 92
Mills, Liston Oury 1928- WhoRel 92
Mills, Lloyd L. DrAPF 91
Mills, Lois Terrell 1958- WhoBlA 92
Mills, Luther Rice 1840-1920 DcNCBi 4
Mills, Madolia Massey 1919- AmMWSc 92
Mills, Marcus Max 1952- WhoAmL 92
Mills, Martha Alice 1941- WhoAmL 92
Mills, Mary Bell McMillan Who 92
Mills, Mary Elizabeth 1926- WhoBlA 92
Mills, Mary Lee 1912- WhoBlA 92
Mills, Mervyn 1906- WrDr 92
Mills, Michael James 1951- WhoFI 92
Mills, Michael Paul 1956- WhoAmP 91
Mills, Miriam Naomi 1949- WhoEnt 92
Mills, Morris Hadley 1927- WhoAmP 91
Mills, Nancy Stewart 1950- AmMWSc 92
Mills, Neil McLay 1923- Who 92
Mills, Nigel 1932- Who 92
Mills, Osborne, Jr. 1947- WhoAmL 92
Mills, Patricia Hughes 1957- WhoAmL 92
Mills, Patrick Leo, Sr 1952- AmMWSc 92
Mills, Paul L. DrAPF 91
Mills, Peter 1921- Who 92
Mills, Peter 1924- Who 92
Mills, Peter William 1942- Who 92
Mills, Phyllis Joy 1930- WhoRel 92
Mills, Quincy Sharpe 1884-1918 DcNCBi 4
Mills, Ralph J., Jr. 1931- WrDr 92
Mills, Ralph Joseph, Jr 1931- IntAu&W 91
Mills, Richard 1949- ConCom 92
Mills, Richard Henry 1929- WhoAmL 92, WhoMW 92
Mills, Richard Lewis 1941- WhoFI 92
Mills, Richard Michael 1931- Who 92
Mills, Robert 1936- WhoBlA 92
Mills, Robert Barney 1922- AmMWSc 92
Mills, Robert Ferris 1939- Who 92
Mills, Robert Gail 1924- AmMWSc 92
Mills, Robert Laurence 1927- AmMWSc 92
Mills, Robert Leroy 1922- AmMWSc 92
Mills, Robert Lorimier 1937- WhoEnt 92
Mills, Robert Paul 1956- WhoRel 92
Mills, Robert Scott 1949- WhoEnt 92
Mills, Roger Edward 1930- AmMWSc 92
Mills, Rosalie Jane Gregory 1947- WhoRel 92, WhoWest 92
Mills, Russell 1952- TwCPaSc
Mills, Russell Clarence 1918- AmMWSc 92
Mills, Stanley Edwin Druce 1913- Who 92
Mills, Stanley Richard 1947- WhoAmL 92
Mills, Stanley Robert, Jr. 1929- WhoFI 92
Mills, Stephanie 1959- WhoBlA 92, WhoEnt 92
Mills, Steven Harlon 1945- AmMWSc 92
Mills, Steven Reynard 1957- WhoRel 92
Mills, Stratton Who 92
Mills, Terry Richard 1967- WhoBlA 92
Mills, Thomas C. H. 1949- WhoWest 92
Mills, Thomas K 1942- AmMWSc 92
Mills, Thomas Marshall 1938- AmMWSc 92
Mills, Wendell Holmes, Jr 1945- AmMWSc 92
Mills, Wilbur 1909- FacFETw
Mills, Wilbur D 1909- WhoAmP 91
Mills, Wilbur Daigh 1909- IntWW 91, Who 92
Mills, William 1923- TwCPaSc
Mills, William Andy 1929- AmMWSc 92
Mills, William Douglas 1959- WhoRel 92
Mills, William Graham 1917- Who 92
Mills, William Harold 1921- AmMWSc 92
Mills, William J, Jr 1918- AmMWSc 92
Mills, William P 1947- WhoAmP 91
Mills, William Raymond 1930- AmMWSc 92
Mills, William Ronald 1947- AmMWSc 92
Mills, William Stratton 1932- Who 92
Millsap, John E 1960- WhoAmP 91
Millsap, Mike 1948- WhoAmP 91
Millsaps, Bryant 1947- WhoAmP 91
Millsaps, Knox 1921- AmMWSc 92, IntWW 91
Millsaps, Luther Lee 1926- WhoAmP 91
Millson, Henry Edmond, Jr. 1928- WhoWest 92
Millson, John Albert 1918- Who 92
Millson, John Arthur 1952- WhoMW 92
Millson, Rory Oliver 1950- WhoAmL 92
Millspaugh, Gregory Lowell 1947- WhoAmP 91
Millspaugh, Lynda 1945- WhoAmL 92
Millspaugh, Thomas E.D. 1960- WhoAmL 92
Millstein, David J. 1953- WhoAmL 92
Millstein, Ira M. 1926- WhoAmL 92
Millstein, Jeffrey Alan 1957- AmMWSc 92
Millstein, Julian Stuart 1944- WhoAmL 92
Millstein, Lloyd Gilbert 1932- AmMWSc 92
Millum, Trevor WrDr 92
Millward, Eric 1935- ConPo 91, WrDr 92
Millward, William 1909- Who 92
Millward Kest, Sally Dee 1947- WhoAmL 92
Milman, Andree Who 92
Milman, Derek 1918- Who 92
Milman, Donald S. 1924- ConAu 134
Milman, Doris H 1917- AmMWSc 92
Milman, Gregory AmMWSc 92
Milman, Harry Abraham 1943- AmMWSc 92
Milmine, Douglas 1921- Who 92
Milmo, John Boyle Martin 1943- Who 92
Milmo, Patrick Helenus 1938- Who 92
Milmore, John Edward 1943- AmMWSc 92
Miln, Louise 1864-1933 BenetAL 91
Milne Who 92
Milne, Baron 1909- Who 92
Milne, A.A. 1882-1956 ChlLR 26 [port], ConAu 133, FacFETw, RfGEnL 91
Milne, Alasdair David Gordon 1930- IntWW 91, Who 92
Milne, Alexander Berkeley 1924- Who 92
Milne, Alexander Taylor 1906- Who 92
Milne, Alisdair LesBEnT 92
Milne, Andrew McNicoll 1937- Who 92
Milne, Berkeley Who 92
Milne, Bruce Thomas 1957- WhoWest 92
Milne, Christopher Robin 1920- IntAu&W 91, WrDr 92
Milne, Dale Stewart 1945- WhoRel 92, WhoWest 92
Milne, David 1882-1953 FacFETw
Milne, David Bayard 1940- AmMWSc 92
Milne, David Calder 1945- Who 92
Milne, David Hall 1939- AmMWSc 92
Milne, Denys Gordon 1926- IntWW 91, Who 92
Milne, Donald George 1934- WhoAmP 91
Milne, Douglas Graeme 1919- Who 92
Milne, Edmund Alexander 1927- AmMWSc 92
Milne, Eric Campbell 1929- AmMWSc 92
Milne, George McLean, Jr 1943- AmMWSc 92
Milne, George William Anthony 1937- AmMWSc 92
Milne, Gordon Gladstone 1916- AmMWSc 92
Milne, Ian Innes 1912- Who 92
Milne, James L. Who 92
Milne, John 1924- Who 92
Milne, John 1931- TwCPaSc
Milne, John 1952- WrDr 92
Milne, John Drummond 1924- IntWW 91
Milne, Kenneth Lancelot 1915- Who 92
Milne, Larry WrDr 92
Milne, Lorus J. WrDr 92
Milne, Lorus Johnson 1912- AmMWSc 92
Milne, Malcolm 1887-1954 TwCPaSc
Milne, Malcolm Davenport d1991 Who 92N
Milne, Malcolm Davenport 1915- IntWW 91
Milne, Margery AmMWSc 92, WrDr 92
Milne, Maurice 1916- Who 92
Milne, Norman 1915- Who 92
Milne, Peter Alexander 1935- Who 92
Milne, Robert Duncan 1844-1899 ScFEYrs
Milne, Seumas 1958- ConAu 135
Milne, Stephen Carl 1949- WhoMW 92
Milne, Susan Belisle 1948- WhoFI 92
Milne, Teddy 1930- IntAu&W 91
Milne, Thomas Anderson 1927- AmMWSc 92
Milne, W Gordon 1921- IntAu&W 91
Milne, William James 1843-1914 BiInAmS
Milne Home, Archibald John Fitzwilliam 1909- Who 92
Milne Home, John Gavin 1916- Who 92
Milne-Watson, Michael 1910- IntWW 91, Who 92
Milner Who 92
Milner and Sowerby DcLB 106
Milner, Alice N 1925- AmMWSc 92
Milner, Anthony 1925- ConCom 92
Milner, Anthony Francis Dominic 1925- IntWW 91
Milner, Arthur John Robin Gorell 1934- Who 92
Milner, Arthur Neil 1936- WhoFI 92
Milner, Brenda 1918- AmMWSc 92, Who 92
Milner, Charles Fremont, Jr. 1942- WhoFI 92
Milner, Clifford E 1928- AmMWSc 92
Milner, Curtis Dean 1947- WhoFI 92
Milner, Daniel Paul 1952- WhoEnt 92
Milner, David 1938- AmMWSc 92
Milner, Eddie James, Jr. 1955- WhoBlA 92
Milner, Eric Charles 1928- AmMWSc 92
Milner, Esther 1918- WrDr 92
Milner, George Edward Mordaunt 1911- Who 92
Milner, H M ScFEYrs
Milner, H M and Mary Shelley ScFEYrs
Milner, Harold William 1934- WhoMW 92
Milner, Ian Frank George 1911- IntAu&W 91, WrDr 92
Milner, Jack 1910- IntMPA 92
Milner, James 1735?-1772 DcNCBi 4
Milner, Jay ConAu 133
Milner, Joanne R 1957- WhoAmP 91
Milner, Joe W. 1929- WhoWest 92
Milner, John Austin 1947- AmMWSc 92
Milner, Joseph 1922- Who 92
Milner, Lewis Marion 1945- WhoMW 92
Milner, Marion 1900- IntAu&W 91, TwCPaSc, WrDr 92
Milner, Martin 1931- IntMPA 92
Milner, Martin 1952- WhoWest 92
Milner, Max 1914- AmMWSc 92
Milner, Michael Edwin 1952- WhoBlA 92
Milner, Mordaunt Who 92
Milner, Paul Chambers 1931- AmMWSc 92
Milner, Peter 1951- TwCPaSc
Milner, Ralph Who 92
Milner, Reid Thompson 1903- AmMWSc 92, WhoMW 92
Milner, Ron 1938- BlkLC [port], WrDr 92
Milner, Ronald DrAPF 91
Milner, Ronald James Who 92
Milner, Thirman L. 1933- WhoBlA 92
Milner, William 1803-1850 DcLB 106
Milner-Barry, Stuart 1906- Who 92
Milner of Leeds, Baron 1923- Who 92
Milnes, Arthur G 1922- AmMWSc 92
Milnes, Jennifer 1936- TwCPaSc
Milnes, Margaret 1908- TwCPaSc
Milnes, Rodney Who 92
Milnes, Sherill 1935- IntWW 91
Milnes, Sherrill 1935- NewAmDM
Milnes, Sherrill Eustace 1935- WhoEnt 92
Milnes, William Robert, Jr. 1946- WhoFI 92
Milnes Coates, Anthony 1948- Who 92
Milnes-Smith, John 1912- TwCPaSc
Milnor, John Willard 1931- AmMWSc 92
Milnor, Tilla Savanuck Klotz 1934- AmMWSc 92
Milnor, William Robert 1920- AmMWSc 92
Milo, Albert Javier, Jr. 1951- WhoHisp 92
Milo, George Edward 1932- AmMWSc 92
Milo, Ronnie 1949- IntWW 91
Milone, Anthony M. 1932- WhoRel 92, WhoWest 92
Milone, Charles Robert 1913- AmMWSc 92
Milone, Eugene Frank 1939- AmMWSc 92
Milone, Francis Michael 1947- WhoAmL 92
Milosevic, Slobodan 1941- IntWW 91, NewYTBS 91 [port]
Miloslavsky, Dimitry T. Who 92
Milosz, Czeslaw 1911- BenetAL 91, IntAu&W 91, IntWW 91, LiExTwC, Who 92, WhoNob 90, WhoWest 92
Milota, William John 1941- WhoAmL 92
Milow, Keith 1945- IntWW 91, TwCPaSc
Milrod, Eve Meredith 1962- WhoFI 92
Milroy, Dominic Liston 1932- Who 92
Milroy, Jack 1938- TwCPaSc
Milroy, Lisa 1959- TwCPaSc
Milsap, Ronnie WhoEnt 92
Milsom, Charles Henry 1926- WrDr 92
Milsom, Robert Cortlandt 1924- WhoFI 92
Milsom, Stroud Francis Charles 1923- IntWW 91, Who 92, WrDr 92
Milsom, William Kenneth 1947- AmMWSc 92
Milsted, Amy 1944- AmMWSc 92
Milstein, Alan Carl 1953- WhoAmL 92
Milstein, Cesar 1927- AmMWSc 92, IntWW 91, Who 92, WhoNob 90
Milstein, Elliott Steven 1944- WhoAmL 92
Milstein, Frederick 1939- AmMWSc 92
Milstein, Nathan 1904- FacFETw, IntWW 91, NewAmDM, Who 92, WhoEnt 92
Milstein, Richard Craig 1946- WhoAmL 92
Milstein, Richard Sherman 1926- WhoAmL 92
Milstein, Stanley Richard 1944- AmMWSc 92
Milstoc, Mayer 1920- AmMWSc 92
Milsum, John H 1925- AmMWSc 92
Miltiades EncEarC
Milton, Albert Fenner 1940- AmMWSc 92
Milton, Barbara DrAPF 91
Milton, Charles 1896- AmMWSc 92
Milton, Christian Michel 1947- WhoFI 92
Milton, Daniel Jeremy 1934- AmMWSc 92
Milton, David Q. DrAPF 91
Milton, David Scott 1934- WhoEnt 92
Milton, Derek Francis 1935- IntWW 91, Who 92
Milton, Douglas 1924- IntWW 91
Milton, Edith DrAPF 91
Milton, Henry 1918- WhoBlA 92
Milton, Henry Benford 1961- WhoBlA 92
Milton, Howard William, Jr. 1946- WhoRel 92
Milton, Israel Henry 1929- WhoBlA 92
Milton, J. Margaret 1934- WhoRel 92
Milton, James E 1934- AmMWSc 92
Milton, John 1608-1674 CnDBLB 2 [port], RfGEnL 91
Milton, John Charles Douglas 1924- AmMWSc 92
Milton, John R. DrAPF 91
Milton, John R. 1924- WrDr 92
Milton, Joyce DrAPF 91
Milton, Joyce 1946- WrDr 92
Milton, Kimball Alan 1944- AmMWSc 92
Milton, Kirby Mitchell 1923- AmMWSc 92
Milton, LeRoy 1924- WhoBlA 92
Milton, Morris Wilbert 1943- WhoAmP 91
Milton, Nancy Melissa 1942- AmMWSc 92
Milton, Nathan Monroe 1961- WhoRel 92
Milton, Octavia Washington 1933- WhoBlA 92
Milton, Osborne 1920- AmMWSc 92
Milton, Robert Mitchell 1920- AmMWSc 92
Milton, Roy Charles 1934- AmMWSc 92
Milton, Samuel Byron 1902- WhoBlA 92
Milton, Sue 1942- WhoAmP 91
Milton-Thompson, Godfrey 1930- Who 92
Milton-Thompson, Godfrey James 1930- IntWW 91
Milverton, Baron 1930- Who 92
Milverton, Charles A. ConAu 35NR
Milward, Alan S. 1935- WrDr 92
Milward, Alan Steele 1935- IntAu&W 91, Who 92
Milward, Frith 1906- TwCPaSc
Milyutin, Vladimir Petrovich 1884-1937 SovUnBD
Milz, Wendell Collins 1918- AmMWSc 92
Milzoff, Joel Robert 1944- AmMWSc 92
Mimaroglu, Sait Kemal 1929- WhoFI 92
Mimiaga, Robert Joaquin 1937- WhoHisp 92

**Mimieux**, Yvette 1939- *IntMPA 92*
**Mimmack**, William Edward 1926- *AmMWSc 92*
**Mimms**, Maxine Buie 1929- *WhoBlA 92*
**Mimna**, Curtis John 1943- *WhoFI 92*
**Mimnaugh**, Michael Neil 1949- *AmMWSc 92*
**Mims**, Albert 1924- *WhoMW 92*
**Mims**, Billy Burns, Jr. 1946- *WhoRel 92*
**Mims**, Cedric Arthur 1924- *IntWW 91, Who 92*
**Mims**, Charles Wayne 1944- *AmMWSc 92*
**Mims**, Edwin 1872-1959 *DcNCBi 4*
**Mims**, Gary Brooks 1952- *WhoAmL 92*
**Mims**, George E. 1932- *WhoBlA 92*
**Mims**, George L. 1934- *WhoBlA 92*
**Mims**, Hornsby 1926- *WhoIns 92*
**Mims**, Lambert Carter 1930- *WhoAmP 91*
**Mims**, Madeline 1948- *BlkOlyM*
**Mims**, Madeline Manning 1948- *WhoBlA 92*
**Mims**, Marjorie Joyce 1926- *WhoBlA 92*
**Mims**, Michael Gene 1963- *WhoWest 92*
**Mims**, Oscar Lugrie 1934- *WhoBlA 92*
**Mims**, Robert Bradford 1934- *WhoBlA 92*
**Mims**, Thomas Jerome 1899- *WhoFI 92, WhoIns 92*
**Mims**, William B 1922- *AmMWSc 92*
**Mims**, William Thomas 1963- *WhoAmP 91*
**Mims-Rich**, Robin Eleanor 1965- *WhoWest 92*
**Min**, Elizabeth 1954- *WhoEnt 92*
**Min**, Hokey 1954- *WhoFI 92*
**Min**, Kongki 1931- *AmMWSc 92*
**Min**, Kwang-Shik 1927- *AmMWSc 92*
**Min**, Kyung-Whan 1937- *AmMWSc 92*
**Min**, Sung Sik 1942- *WhoFI 92*
**Min**, Tony C 1923- *AmMWSc 92*
**Minac**, Vladimir 1922- *IntWW 91*
**Minah**, Francis Misheck 1929- *IntWW 91*
**Minah**, Glenn Ernest 1939- *AmMWSc 92*
**Minahan**, Daniel F. 1929- *WhoAmL 92*
**Minahan**, Peter M 1945- *WhoAmP 91*
**Minami**, Isamu 1922- *WhoWest 92*
**Minar**, Paul Gerald 1932- *WhoWest 92*
**Minar**, Rudolf John 1966- *WhoFI 92*
**Minarcin**, Milton William, Jr. 1945- *WhoEnt 92*
**Minard**, Joseph M 1932- *WhoAmP 91*
**Minard**, Robert David 1941- *AmMWSc 92*
**Minard**, Thomas Michael 1944- *WhoFI 92*
**Minarik**, Carman John 1959- *WhoMW 92*
**Minarik**, Else H 1920- *IntAu&W 91, WrDr 92*
**Minarik**, John Paul *DrAPF 91*
**Minarik**, John Paul 1947- *IntAu&W 91*
**Minassian**, Donald Paul 1935- *AmMWSc 92, WhoMW 92*
**Minassian**, Michael G. *DrAPF 91*
**Minatoya**, Hiroaki 1911- *AmMWSc 92*
**Minc**, Henryk 1919- *AmMWSc 92*
**Mincer**, Allen I 1957- *AmMWSc 92*
**Mincer**, Jacob 1922- *IntWW 91, WhoFI 92*
**Mincey**, W. James 1947- *WhoBlA 92*
**Minch**, Edwin Wilton 1951- *AmMWSc 92*
**Minch**, Michael Joseph 1943- *AmMWSc 92*
**Minch**, Walter Edward 1926- *WhoAmP 91*
**Minchak**, Robert John 1929- *AmMWSc 92*
**Mincher**, Bruce J 1957- *AmMWSc 92*
**Minchew**, John Randall 1957- *WhoAmL 92*
**Minchinton**, Walter Edward 1921- *Who 92, WrDr 92*
**Mincieli**, Robert Michael 1956- *WhoEnt 92*
**Minck**, Richard V 1932- *WhoIns 92*
**Minck**, Robert W 1934- *AmMWSc 92*
**Minckler**, Jeff 1912- *AmMWSc 92*
**Minckler**, Leon Sherwood, Jr 1930- *AmMWSc 92*
**Minckler**, Tate Muldown 1934- *AmMWSc 92*
**Minckley**, Wendell Lee 1935- *AmMWSc 92*
**Minckwitz**, Bernard von 1944- *IntWW 91*
**Minczeski**, John *DrAPF 91*
**Minczeski**, John 1947- *IntAu&W 91*
**Minda**, Carl David 1943- *AmMWSc 92*
**Mindach**, Rex Allen 1957- *WhoRel 92*
**Mindadze**, Aleksandr Anatol'evich 1949- *SovUnBD*
**Mindak**, Robert Joseph 1925- *AmMWSc 92*
**Minde**, Karl Klaus 1933- *AmMWSc 92*
**Mindel**, David Alan 1949- *WhoFI 92*
**Mindel**, Joseph 1912- *AmMWSc 92*
**Mindel**, Laurence Brisker 1937- *WhoFI 92*
**Mindell**, Earl Lawrence 1940- *WhoWest 92*
**Mindell**, Eugene R 1922- *AmMWSc 92*
**Minden**, Henry Thomas 1923- *AmMWSc 92*
**Mindess**, Sidney 1940- *AmMWSc 92*
**Mindich**, Leonard Eugene 1936- *AmMWSc 92*
**Mindiola**, Tatcho, Jr. *WhoHisp 92*
**Mindlin**, Harold 1930- *AmMWSc 92*
**Mindlin**, Michael 1923- *ConAu 133*
**Mindlin**, Raymond D 1906- *AmMWSc 92*
**Mindlin**, Rowland L 1912- *AmMWSc 92*
**Mindling**, Martin John 1947- *WhoFI 92*
**Mindreau**, Carlos Anthony 1944- *WhoMW 92*
**Mindrum**, Thomas Leigh 1949- *WhoFI 92*
**Mindszenty**, Jozsef 1892-1975 *FacFETw*
**Mine**, Andrew Stephen 1961- *WhoAmL 92*
**Minear**, Judith *WhoRel 92*
**Minear**, Paul Sevier 1906- *WhoRel 92, WrDr 92*
**Minear**, Richard H 1938- *IntAu&W 91*
**Minear**, Richard Hoffman 1938- *WrDr 92*
**Minear**, Roger Allan 1939- *AmMWSc 92*
**Minear**, William Loris 1910- *WhoWest 92*
**Mineau**, Wendy Jayne 1963- *WhoAmL 92*
**Minehart**, Ralph Conrad 1935- *AmMWSc 92*
**Miner**, Bryant Albert 1934- *AmMWSc 92*
**Miner**, David Morris 1962- *WhoAmP 91*
**Miner**, Donald 1913- *WhoAmP 91*
**Miner**, Doris P *WhoAmP 91*
**Miner**, Earl 1927- *WrDr 92*
**Miner**, Earl Roy 1927- *IntAu&W 91*
**Miner**, Ellis Devere, Jr 1937- *AmMWSc 92*
**Miner**, Frend John 1928- *AmMWSc 92*
**Miner**, Gary David 1942- *AmMWSc 92*
**Miner**, George Kenneth 1936- *AmMWSc 92*
**Miner**, Gordon Stanley 1940- *AmMWSc 92*
**Miner**, J Ronald 1938- *AmMWSc 92*
**Miner**, James Edward 1953- *WhoRel 92*
**Miner**, James Joshua 1928- *AmMWSc 92*
**Miner**, Jan 1917- *WhoEnt 92*
**Miner**, John 1947- *WhoEnt 92*
**Miner**, John Burnham 1926- *WhoFI 92*
**Miner**, John Edward 1937- *WhoWest 92*
**Miner**, John Ronald 1938- *WhoWest 92*
**Miner**, Karen Mills *AmMWSc 92*
**Miner**, Lawrence Brent 1952- *WhoWest 92*
**Miner**, Lenworth Robert, Jr. 1946- *WhoRel 92*
**Miner**, Matthew *ConAu 35NR*
**Miner**, Merthyr Leilani 1912- *AmMWSc 92*
**Miner**, Robert Scott, Jr 1918- *AmMWSc 92*
**Miner**, Roger Jeffrey 1934- *WhoAmL 92, WhoAmP 91*
**Miner**, Ruth 1920- *WhoAmP 91*
**Miner**, Stephen *ConTFT 9*
**Miner**, Steve 1951- *ConTFT 9, IntMPA 92*
**Miner**, Terry Lee 1953- *WhoMW 92*
**Miner**, Valerie *DrAPF 91*
**Miner**, William Gerard 1950- *WhoBlA 92*
**Miner**, Worthington *LesBEnT 92*
**Minerbi**, Luciano Mario Lauro 1941- *WhoWest 92*
**Minerbo**, Gerald N 1939- *AmMWSc 92*
**Minerbo**, Grace Moffat *AmMWSc 92*
**Mines**, Allan Howard 1936- *AmMWSc 92*
**Mines**, Michael 1929- *WhoAmL 92, WhoWest 92*
**Minet**, Ronald G 1922- *AmMWSc 92*
**Mineta**, Norman Y. 1931- *AlmAP 92 [port]*
**Mineta**, Norman Yoshio 1931- *WhoAmP 91, WhoWest 92*
**Minette**, Dennis Jerome 1937- *WhoFI 92*
**Minette**, William F 1921- *WhoAmP 91*
**Minford**, James Dean 1923- *AmMWSc 92*
**Minford**, Patrick 1943- *IntWW 91, Who 92*
**Ming**, Donald George K. *WhoBlA 92*
**Ming**, Li Chung 1945- *AmMWSc 92*
**Ming**, Si-Chun 1922- *AmMWSc 92*
**Mingay**, G. E. 1923- *WrDr 92*
**Mingay**, Gordon Edmund 1923- *IntAu&W 91*
**Mingay**, Ray 1938- *Who 92*
**Mingee**, James Clyde, III 1943- *WhoAmL 92*
**Minger**, Terrell John 1942- *WhoFI 92, WhoWest 92*
**Minges**, Merrill Loren 1937- *AmMWSc 92*
**Minghella**, Anthony 1954- *WrDr 92*
**Mingilton**, Dale Matthew 1963- *WhoWest 92*
**Mingle**, John O 1931- *AmMWSc 92*
**Minglin**, Michael Alan 1951- *WhoAmP 91*
**Mingo**, Frank L. 1939-1989 *WhoBlA 92N*
**Mingo**, Pauline Hylton 1945- *WhoBlA 92*
**Mingori**, Diamond Lewis 1938- *AmMWSc 92*
**Mingrone**, Louis V 1940- *AmMWSc 92*
**Mings**, William Thor 1956- *WhoEnt 92*
**Mingus**, Charles 1922-1979 *FacFETw [port], NewAmDM*
**Mingus**, David R. 1960- *WhoMW 92*
**Minhas**, Faqir Ullah 1924- *WhoWest 92*
**Minhinnick**, Gordon 1902- *Who 92*
**Minhinnick**, Robert 1952- *ConPo 91, IntAu&W 91, WrDr 92*
**Miniats**, Olgerts Pauls 1923- *AmMWSc 92*
**Minic**, Milos 1914- *IntWW 91*
**Minich**, Marlin 1938- *AmMWSc 92*
**Minich**, Marlin Don 1938- *WhoMW 92*
**Minick**, Charles Richard 1936- *AmMWSc 92*
**Minicucci**, Daryl Sharp 1954- *WhoRel 92*
**Minicucci**, Robert A. 1952- *WhoFI 92*
**Minicucci**, Steven Anthony 1964- *WhoAmL 92*
**Minin**, Viktor Ivanovich 1926- *IntWW 91*
**Minion**, Mia 1960- *WhoBlA 92*
**Minion**, Stephen d1990 *Who 92N*
**Miniscalco**, William J 1946- *AmMWSc 92*
**Minish**, Joseph George 1916- *WhoAmP 91*
**Minisi**, Anthony S. 1926- *WhoAmL 92*
**Minium**, Edward W. 1917- *WrDr 92*
**Miniutti**, John Roberts 1937- *WhoFI 92*
**Miniutti**, Patrick Michael 1947- *WhoFI 92*
**Mink**, Gaylord Ira 1931- *AmMWSc 92*
**Mink**, Irving Bernard 1927- *AmMWSc 92*
**Mink**, James Walter 1935- *AmMWSc 92*
**Mink**, Lawrence Albright 1936- *AmMWSc 92*
**Mink**, Lawrence B. 1943- *WhoAmL 92*
**Mink**, Patsy T. 1927- *AlmAP 92 [port]*
**Mink**, Patsy Takemoto 1927- *WhoAmP 91, WhoWest 92*
**Minkel**, Herbert Philip, Jr. 1947- *WhoAmL 92*
**Minker**, Gary Alan 1955- *WhoEnt 92*
**Minker**, Jack 1927- *AmMWSc 92*
**Minkiewicz**, Vincent Joseph 1938- *AmMWSc 92*
**Minkin**, Jean Albert 1925- *AmMWSc 92*
**Minkin**, Michael 1945- *WhoAmL 92*
**Minkin**, Stephen *DrAPF 91*
**Minkin**, Thomas 1941- *WhoAmL 92*
**Minkler**, John Archer 1938- *WhoWest 92*
**Minkoff**, Eli Cooperman 1943- *AmMWSc 92*
**Minkow**, Rosalie 1927- *ConAu 135*
**Minkowitz**, Martin 1939- *WhoAmL 92*
**Minkowitz**, Stanley 1928- *AmMWSc 92*
**Minkowski**, Alexandre 1915- *IntWW 91*
**Minkowski**, Jan Michael 1916- *AmMWSc 92*
**Minkowycz**, W J 1937- *AmMWSc 92*
**Minks**, Wilfried 1930- *IntWW 91*
**Minn**, Fredrick Louis 1935- *AmMWSc 92*
**Minna**, John *AmMWSc 92*
**Minnard**, Lawrence Robert 1943- *WhoAmL 92*
**Minne**, Lona A *WhoAmP 91*
**Minne**, Ronn N 1924- *AmMWSc 92*
**Minnear**, William Paul 1946- *AmMWSc 92*
**Minnelli**, Liza 1946- *IntMPA 92, IntWW 91, NewAmDM, WhoEnt 92*
**Minnelli**, Vincente 1910-1986 *FacFETw, IntDcF 2-2 [port]*
**Minneman**, Kenneth Paul 1952- *AmMWSc 92*
**Minneman**, Michael Paul 1959- *WhoFI 92, WhoMW 92*
**Minneman**, Milton J 1923- *AmMWSc 92*
**Minnemeyer**, Harry Joseph 1932- *AmMWSc 92*
**Minner**, Ruth Ann 1935- *WhoAmP 91*
**Minners**, Howard Alyn 1931- *AmMWSc 92*
**Minneste**, Viktor, Jr. 1932- *WhoMW 92*
**Minnett**, Harry Clive 1917- *IntWW 91*
**Minney**, Bruce Kevin 1958- *WhoRel 92*
**Minney**, Michael Jay 1948- *WhoAmL 92, WhoAmP 91*
**Minnich**, Edward Rolland 1961- *WhoEnt 92, WhoFI 92*
**Minnich**, John Edwin 1942- *AmMWSc 92*
**Minnich**, Joseph Edward 1932- *WhoFI 92, WhoWest 92*
**Minnich**, Margaret Wharton 1954- *WhoWest 92*
**Minnich**, Martha Jean 1921- *WhoRel 92*
**Minnick**, Bruce Alexander 1943- *WhoAmL 92*
**Minnick**, Carlton Printess, Jr. 1927- *WhoRel 92*
**Minnick**, Craig Alan 1951- *WhoFI 92*
**Minnick**, Daniel James, Jr 1925- *WhoAmP 91*
**Minnick**, Danny Richard 1937- *AmMWSc 92*
**Minnick**, Donald Edward 1935- *WhoRel 92*
**Minnick**, Joseph H *WhoAmP 91*
**Minnick**, Robert C 1926- *AmMWSc 92*
**Minnick**, Terry Jay 1951- *WhoFI 92*
**Minnie**, Mary Virginia 1922- *WhoWest 92*
**Minnifield**, Nita Michele 1960- *AmMWSc 92*
**Minnigerode**, Gunther von 1929- *IntWW 91*
**Minnis**, M John *WhoAmP 91*
**Minnitt**, Robert John 1913- *Who 92*
**Minnix**, Bruce Milton 1923- *WhoEnt 92*
**Minnix**, Richard Bryant 1933- *AmMWSc 92*
**Minno**, Matthew Fraher 1959- *WhoAmL 92*
**Mino**, Carlos Felix 1932- *WhoHisp 92*
**Minoca**, Subhash C 1947- *AmMWSc 92*
**Minocha**, Harish C 1932- *AmMWSc 92*
**Minock**, Michael Edward 1937- *AmMWSc 92*
**Minogue**, John Patrick d1989 *Who 92N*
**Minogue**, Kenneth Robert 1930- *Who 92, WrDr 92*
**Minogue**, Patrick John O'Brien 1922- *Who 92*
**Minor**, Bernice F 1932- *WhoAmP 91*
**Minor**, Billy Joe 1938- *WhoBlA 92*
**Minor**, Carl Allen 1917- *WhoMW 92*
**Minor**, Charles Daniel 1927- *WhoAmL 92*
**Minor**, Charles Oscar 1920- *AmMWSc 92*
**Minor**, David M. 1947- *WhoBlA 92*
**Minor**, Deborah Ann 1951- *WhoBlA 92*
**Minor**, Edward Colquitt 1942- *WhoAmL 92, WhoFI 92*
**Minor**, Emma Lucille 1925- *WhoBlA 92*
**Minor**, George Gilmer, Jr. 1912- *WhoFI 92*
**Minor**, James *DrAPF 91*
**Minor**, James E 1919- *AmMWSc 92*
**Minor**, Jessica *WhoBlA 92*
**Minor**, John A. *WhoBlA 92*
**Minor**, John S. 1948- *WhoBlA 92*
**Minor**, John Thomas 1939- *WhoRel 92*
**Minor**, John Threecivelous 1950- *AmMWSc 92*
**Minor**, Melvin G 1937- *WhoAmP 91*
**Minor**, Philip d1991 *NewYTBS 91*
**Minor**, Raleigh Colston 1936- *WhoFI 92*
**Minor**, Richard Allen 1951- *WhoMW 92*
**Minor**, Robert Neil 1945- *WhoRel 92*
**Minor**, Ronald R 1936- *AmMWSc 92*
**Minor**, Ronald Ray 1944- *WhoRel 92*
**Minor**, Rudiger Rainer 1939- *WhoRel 92*
**Minor**, Vicki Beize 1938- *WhoBlA 92*
**Minor**, William *WhoAmP 91*
**Minor**, Willie 1951- *WhoBlA 92*
**Minore**, Don 1931- *AmMWSc 92*
**Minoso**, Minnie 1922- *WhoHisp 92*
**Minot**, Charles Sedgwick 1852-1914 *BiInAmS*
**Minot**, George Richards 1758-1802 *BenetAL 91*
**Minot**, George Richards 1885-1950 *WhoNob 90*
**Minot**, Henry Davis 1859-1890 *BiInAmS*
**Minot**, Michael Jay 1946- *AmMWSc 92*
**Minot**, Stephen *DrAPF 91*
**Minot**, Stephen 1927- *WrDr 92*
**Minot**, Susan 1956- *ConAu 134, WrDr 92*
**Minot**, Susan Anderson 1956- *IntAu&W 91*
**Minotis**, Alexis d1990 *IntWW 91N*
**Minotti**, Peter Lee 1935- *AmMWSc 92*
**Minow**, Charles Thomas 1958- *WhoEnt 92*
**Minow**, Martha L. 1954- *WhoAmL 92*
**Minow**, Nell 1952- *WhoAmL 92*
**Minow**, Newton N. *LesBEnT 92*
**Minow**, Newton N. 1926- *IntWW 91, WrDr 92*
**Minow**, Newton Norman 1926- *WhoAmL 92, WhoAmP 91, WhoMW 92*
**Minowa**, Noboru 1924- *IntWW 91*
**Minowada**, Jun 1927- *AmMWSc 92*
**Minowitz**, Abraham A. 1920- *WhoMW 92*
**Minsavage**, Edward Joseph 1918- *AmMWSc 92*
**Minshall**, Brinton Paynter 1943- *WhoRel 92*
**Minshall**, Gerry Wayne 1938- *AmMWSc 92*
**Minshall**, Vera 1924- *WrDr 92*
**Minshall**, William Harold 1911- *AmMWSc 92*
**Minsinger**, William Elliot 1950- *AmMWSc 92*
**Minsker**, David Harry 1938- *AmMWSc 92*
**Minsker**, Eliot A. 1933- *WhoEnt 92*
**Minsker**, Robert Stanley 1911- *WhoFI 92*
**Minsky**, Betty Jane 1932- *WrDr 92*
**Minsky**, Howard G. *IntMPA 92*
**Minsky**, Marvin Lee 1927- *AmMWSc 92, IntWW 91*
**Minsky**, Morton 1902-1987 *ConAu 135*
**Minta**, Joe Oduro 1942- *AmMWSc 92*
**Mintaredja**, Mohamad Sjafa'at 1921- *IntWW 91*
**Mintchell**, Gary Alan 1947- *WhoFI 92, WhoMW 92*
**Mintel**, William August 1947- *WhoAmL 92*
**Minter**, Alan 1951- *IntWW 91*
**Minter**, Alfred Leon 1951- *WhoFI 92*
**Minter**, Charles Laskey 1941- *WhoFI 92*
**Minter**, David Lee 1935- *IntAu&W 91, WrDr 92*
**Minter**, Eloise Devada 1928- *WhoBlA 92*
**Minter**, James Lewis 1954- *WhoMW 92*
**Minter**, Jerry Burnett 1913- *AmMWSc 92*
**Minter**, Kendall Arthur 1952- *WhoBlA 92, WhoEnt 92*
**Minter**, Michael Kent 1950- *WhoFI 92*
**Minter**, Otto Douglas 1923- *WhoFI 92*
**Minter**, Steven Alan 1938- *WhoBlA 92*
**Minter**, Thomas Kendall 1924- *WhoBlA 92*

**Minter**, Wilbert Douglas, Sr. 1946- *WhoBlA 92*
**Minthorn**, Martin Lloyd, Jr 1922- *AmMWSc 92*
**Minto**, Earl of 1928- *Who 92*
**Minto**, Alfred 1928- *Who 92*
**Minto**, Barbara Lee *WhoFI 92*
**Minto**, Walter 1753-1796 *BiInAmS*
**Minto**, William 1845-1893 *ScFEYrs*
**Mintoff**, Dominic 1916- *IntWW 91, Who 92*
**Minton**, Allen Paul 1943- *AmMWSc 92*
**Minton**, George Raymond 1953- *WhoEnt 92*
**Minton**, Helena *DrAPF 91*
**Minton**, James Dale 1950- *WhoEnt 92*
**Minton**, John 1917-1957 *TwCPaSc*
**Minton**, Joseph Kelly, Sr. 1943- *WhoRel 92*
**Minton**, Norman A 1924- *AmMWSc 92*
**Minton**, Paul Christopher 1933- *WhoMW 92*
**Minton**, Paul Dixon 1918- *AmMWSc 92*
**Minton**, Russell Farbeux, Sr. 1900- *WhoBlA 92*
**Minton**, Sherman 1890-1965 *FacFETw*
**Minton**, Sherman Anthony 1919- *AmMWSc 92, WhoMW 92*
**Minton**, Yvonne 1938- *NewAmDM*
**Minton**, Yvonne Fay *Who 92, WhoEnt 92*
**Minton**, Yvonne Fay 1938- *IntWW 91*
**Mints**, Isaak Izrailovich 1896- *SovUnBD*
**Mints**, Paul Stephen 1966- *WhoRel 92*
**Minty**, Judith *DrAPF 91*
**Minty**, Keith Larry 1933- *WhoFI 92, WhoWest 92*
**Mintz**, A Aaron 1922- *AmMWSc 92*
**Mintz**, Albert 1929- *WhoAmL 92*
**Mintz**, Beatrice 1921- *AmMWSc 92*
**Mintz**, Daniel Gordon 1948- *WhoAmP 91*
**Mintz**, Daniel Harvey 1930- *AmMWSc 92*
**Mintz**, Donald Monturean 1929- *WhoEnt 92*
**Mintz**, Douglas C *WhoAmP 91*
**Mintz**, Esther Uress 1907- *AmMWSc 92*
**Mintz**, Florinda 1951- *IntAu&W 91*
**Mintz**, Fred 1918- *AmMWSc 92*
**Mintz**, Jacqueline Wei 1937- *WhoAmL 92*
**Mintz**, Jeffry Alan 1943- *WhoAmL 92*
**Mintz**, Joel Alan 1949- *WhoAmL 92*
**Mintz**, Joseph David 1933- *WhoAmL 92*
**Mintz**, Leigh Wayne 1939- *AmMWSc 92, WhoWest 92*
**Mintz**, Phil *DrAPF 91*
**Mintz**, Reginold Lee *WhoBlA 92*
**Mintz**, Ronald Steven 1947- *WhoAmL 92*
**Mintz**, Ruth Finer *DrAPF 91*
**Mintz**, Ruth Finer 1919- *WrDr 92*
**Mintz**, Samuel I 1923- *IntAu&W 91, WrDr 92*
**Mintz**, Shlomo 1957- *IntWW 91, WhoEnt 92*
**Mintz**, Stephen Allan 1943- *WhoFI 92*
**Mintz**, Stephen Larry 1943- *AmMWSc 92*
**Mintz**, Stuart Alan 1956- *WhoWest 92*
**Mintzer**, David 1926- *AmMWSc 92*
**Mintzer**, Edward Carl, Jr. 1949- *WhoAmL 92*
**Mintzer**, Yvette *DrAPF 91*
**Minucius Felix** *EncEarC*
**Minudri**, Regina Ursula 1937- *WhoWest 92*
**Minuit**, Peter 1580-1638 *BenetAL 91*
**Minus**, Homer Wellington 1931- *WhoBlA 92*
**Minuse**, Catherine Jean 1951- *WhoAmL 92*
**Minyard**, Handsel B. 1943- *WhoBlA 92*
**Minyard**, James Patrick 1929- *AmMWSc 92*
**Minythyia** *EncAmaz 91*
**Minz**, Alexander *WhoEnt 92*
**Minzner**, Dean Frederick 1945- *WhoWest 92*
**Minzner**, Dick 1943- *WhoAmP 91*
**Minzner**, Raymond Arthur 1915- *AmMWSc 92*
**Miodowicz**, Alfred 1929- *IntWW 91*
**Miota**, Margaret Elizabeth 1940- *WhoMW 92*
**Miou Miou** 1950- *IntMPA 92*
**Miovic**, Margaret Lancefield 1943- *AmMWSc 92*
**Miquel**, Jaime 1929- *AmMWSc 92*
**Miquel**, Pierre Gabriel Roger 1930- *IntWW 91*
**Miquel**, Raymond Clive 1931- *Who 92*
**Mir**, Carl J. 1956- *WhoHisp 92*
**Mir**, Gasper, III 1946- *WhoHisp 92*
**Mir**, Ghulam Nabi 1939- *AmMWSc 92*
**Mir**, John Walter 1954- *WhoEnt 92*
**Mir**, Leon 1938- *AmMWSc 92*
**Mir**, Pedro 1913- *ConSpAP*
**Mira** *EncAmaz 91*
**Mirabal**, Carlos G. 1947- *WhoHisp 92*
**Mirabal**, George G. 1949- *WhoHisp 92*
**Mirabaud**, Jean-Baptiste 1675-1760 *BlkwCEP*
**Mirabeau**, Victor de Riqueti, marquis de 1715-1789 *BlkwCEP*
**Mirabella**, Francis Michael, Jr 1943- *AmMWSc 92*
**Mirabella**, Grace 1930- *CurBio 91 [port]*
**Mirabelli**, Christopher Kevin *AmMWSc 92*
**Mirabelli**, Eugene *DrAPF 91*
**Mirabelli**, Eugene, Jr 1931- *IntAu&W 91, WrDr 92*
**Mirabello**, Francis Joseph 1954- *WhoAmL 92*
**Mirabile**, Charles Samuel, Jr 1937- *AmMWSc 92*
**Mirabito**, John A 1917- *AmMWSc 92*
**Mirabito**, Paul S. d1991 *NewYTBS 91 [port]*
**Mirabito**, Richard 1956- *WhoAmL 92*
**Mirachi**, Joseph d1991 *NewYTBS 91*
**Miracle**, Bianca Jutta 1965- *WhoRel 92*
**Miracle**, Chester Lee 1934- *AmMWSc 92*
**Miracle**, Gordon Eldon 1930- *WhoMW 92*
**Miraglia**, Gennaro J 1929- *AmMWSc 92*
**Mirakhor**, Abbas *IntWW 91*
**Miraldi**, Floro D 1931- *AmMWSc 92*
**Mirand**, Edwin Albert 1926- *AmMWSc 92*
**Miranda**, Andres, Jr. 1940- *WhoHisp 92*
**Miranda**, Armand F 1935- *AmMWSc 92*
**Miranda**, Carmen 1909-1955 *NewAmDM*
**Miranda**, Constancio F 1926- *AmMWSc 92*
**Miranda**, Francesco de 1750-1816 *BlkwCEP*
**Miranda**, Francisco 1750-1816 *BenetAL 91*
**Miranda**, Francisco de 1750-1816 *HisDSpE*
**Miranda**, Frank Joseph 1946- *AmMWSc 92*
**Miranda**, Frederick Ralph 1940- *WhoHisp 92*
**Miranda**, Gary *DrAPF 91*
**Miranda**, Gilbert A 1943- *AmMWSc 92*
**Miranda**, Guillermo, Jr. *WhoHisp 92*
**Miranda**, Hector, Sr. 1960- *WhoHisp 92*
**Miranda**, Henry A, Jr 1924- *AmMWSc 92*
**Miranda**, Lourdes *WhoHisp 92*
**Miranda**, Malvin L. 1939- *WhoHisp 92*
**Miranda**, Manuel Robert 1939- *WhoHisp 92*
**Miranda**, Maria de L. 1960- *WhoHisp 92*
**Miranda**, Maria T. 1936- *WhoHisp 92*
**Miranda**, Mario Javier 1954- *WhoFI 92*
**Miranda**, Quirinus Ronnie 1939- *AmMWSc 92*
**Miranda**, Rafael 1961- *WhoWest 92*
**Miranda**, Robert A. *WhoHisp 92*
**Miranda**, Robert Julian 1952- *WhoHisp 92*
**Miranda**, Robert Nicholas 1934- *WhoFI 92*
**Miranda**, Ruben Michael 1952- *WhoAmP 91*
**Miranda**, Thomas Joseph 1927- *AmMWSc 92, WhoMW 92*
**Miranda**, William 1951- *WhoHisp 92*
**Mirando**, Louis Patrick 1953- *WhoAmL 92*
**Miranker**, Willard Lee 1932- *AmMWSc 92*
**Mirante**, Arthur J., II 1943- *WhoFI 92*
**Mirante**, Thomas Anthony 1931- *WhoEnt 92*
**Miranti**, Santi Vincent 1952- *WhoMW 92*
**Mirarchi**, Ralph Edward 1950- *AmMWSc 92*
**Mirbeau**, Octave 1848-1917 *GuFrLit 1, ThHEIm*
**Mircetich**, Srecko M 1926- *AmMWSc 92*
**Mirchandaney**, Arjan Sobhraj 1923- *WhoMW 92*
**Mirchin**, David Martin 1957- *WhoAmL 92*
**Mirdha**, Ram Niwas 1924- *IntWW 91*
**Mire**, Nathan 1946- *WhoFI 92*
**Mirel**, Jeffrey 1948- *WhoMW 92*
**Mireles**, Andy 1950- *WhoHisp 92*
**Mireles**, Oscar *DrAPF 91*
**Mireles**, R. Christina 1961- *WhoHisp 92*
**Mireles**, Raymond D. *WhoHisp 92*
**Mirels**, Harold 1924- *AmMWSc 92*
**Mirenberg**, Anita *DrAPF 91*
**Mirenburg**, Barry L 1952- *IntAu&W 91*
**Mires**, Raymond William 1933- *AmMWSc 92*
**Mires**, Ronald E. 1930- *WhoWest 92*
**Mirhej**, Michael Edward 1931- *AmMWSc 92*
**Miricioiu**, Nelly 1952- *IntWW 91*
**Mirikitani**, Janice *DrAPF 91*
**Mirisch**, David 1935- *IntMPA 92*
**Mirisch**, Marvin E. 1918- *IntMPA 92*
**Mirisch**, Marvin Elliot 1918- *WhoEnt 92*
**Mirisch**, Walter 1921- *IntMPA 92*
**Mirisch**, Walter Mortimer 1921- *WhoEnt 92*
**Mirk**, Judy Ann 1944- *WhoWest 92*
**Mirkes**, Philip Edmund 1943- *AmMWSc 92*
**Mirkin**, Bernard Leo 1928- *AmMWSc 92*
**Mirkin**, L David *AmMWSc 92*
**Mirkin**, Meyer 1914- *WhoWest 92*
**Mirko**, Rosemary Natalya 1958- *WhoWest 92*
**Mirkovich**, Joseph Allen 1954- *WhoRel 92*
**Mirman**, Joel Harvey 1941- *WhoAmL 92*
**Mirman**, Sophie 1956- *Who 92*
**Miro**, Joan 1893-1983 *FacFETw*
**Miro Romero**, Pilar 1940- *IntWW 91*
**Mirocha**, Chester Joseph 1930- *AmMWSc 92*
**Miron**, Gaston 1928- *BenetAL 91*
**Miron**, Wilfrid Lyonel 1913- *Who 92*
**Mironenko**, Viktor Ivanovich 1953- *IntWW 91*
**Mironescu**, Stefan Gheorghe Dan 1932- *AmMWSc 92*
**Miroshkin**, Oleg Semenovich 1928- *IntWW 91*
**Mirowitz**, Howard David 1951- *WhoFI 92*
**Mirowitz**, L I 1923- *AmMWSc 92*
**Mirowski**, Philip Edward 1951- *WhoFI 92, WhoMW 92*
**Mirra** *WhoEnt 92*
**Mirren**, Helen 1945- *IntWW 91*
**Mirren**, Helen 1946- *IntMPA 92*
**Mirrlees**, James Alexander 1936- *IntWW 91, Who 92*
**Mirrlees**, Robin Ian Evelyn Stuart DeLaL- 1925- *Who 92*
**Mirro**, Richard Allen 1951- *WhoFI 92*
**Mirsky**, Allan Franklin 1929- *AmMWSc 92*
**Mirsky**, Arthur 1927- *AmMWSc 92*
**Mirsky**, D.S. 1890-1939 *SovUnBD*
**Mirsky**, Mark *DrAPF 91*
**Mirsky**, Mark 1939- *ConNov 91, WrDr 92*
**Mirsky**, Norman Barry 1937- *WhoRel 92*
**Mirsky**, W 1922- *AmMWSc 92*
**Mirtallo**, Jay Matthew 1953- *WhoMW 92*
**Mirucki**, Patrick Michael 1959- *WhoEnt 92*
**Mirvis**, Ephraim Yitzchak 1956- *WhoRel 92*
**Mirvish**, Edwin 1914- *Who 92*
**Mirvish**, Robert F 1921- *IntAu&W 91*
**Mirvish**, Sidney Solomon 1929- *AmMWSc 92*
**Mirviss**, Stanley Burton 1922- *AmMWSc 92*
**Mirza Ali Khan** 1901?-1960 *FacFETw*
**Mirza**, David Brown 1936- *WhoFI 92, WhoMW 92*
**Mirza**, John 1922- *AmMWSc 92*
**Mirza**, Mohd Z Ahan Azurdah 1945- *IntAu&W 91*
**Mirzabekov**, Andrei D. 1937- *IntWW 91*
**Mirzai**, Mohammed 1945- *WhoFI 92*
**Mirzoyan**, Edvard 1921- *ConCom 92*
**Mirzoyan**, Edvard Mikhailovich 1921- *IntWW 91*
**Misa**, Kenneth Franklin 1939- *WhoWest 92*
**Misasi**, Riccardo 1932- *IntWW 91*
**Miscampbell**, Norman Alexander 1925- *Who 92*
**Misch**, Donald William 1929- *AmMWSc 92*
**Misch**, Herbert Louis 1917- *AmMWSc 92*
**Misch**, Peter 1909- *AmMWSc 92*
**Mischak**, Robert Michael, Jr. 1958- *WhoWest 92*
**Mischakoff**, Mischa 1896-1981 *NewAmDM*
**Mischell**, Patricia Lucille 1936- *WhoRel 92*
**Mischer**, Don 1941- *IntMPA 92*
**Mischke**, Carl Herbert 1922- *WhoRel 92*
**Mischke**, Charles R 1927- *AmMWSc 92*
**Mischke**, Charles Russell 1927- *WhoMW 92*
**Mischke**, Frederick Charles 1930- *WhoFI 92*
**Mischke**, Richard E 1940- *AmMWSc 92*
**Mischke**, Roland A 1930- *AmMWSc 92*
**Mischler**, Harland Louis *WhoFI 92*
**Mischler**, Norman Martin 1920- *Who 92*
**Mischnick**, Wolfgang 1921- *IntWW 91*
**Mischou**, Gregory Lee 1961- *WhoFI 92*
**Miscoll**, James P. *WhoFI 92*
**Misconi**, Nebil Yousif 1939- *AmMWSc 92*
**Miscovich**, Timothy Joseph 1958- *WhoMW 92*
**Misek**, Bernard 1930- *AmMWSc 92*
**Miselis**, Richard Robert 1945- *AmMWSc 92*
**Miselson**, Alex J. Jacob 1926- *WhoFI 92*
**Misenheimer**, Barry Kay 1953- *WhoFI 92*
**Misenheimer**, Patricia Mobley 1943- *WhoRel 92*
**Miser**, Randall E 1938- *WhoAmP 91*
**Miserendino**, Leo Joseph 1950- *WhoMW 92*
**Misfeldt**, Michael Lee 1950- *AmMWSc 92*
**Mish**, Jo *DrAPF 91*
**Mish**, Lawrence Bronislaw 1923- *AmMWSc 92*
**Mishan**, E J 1917- *IntAu&W 91, WrDr 92*
**Mishcon** *Who 92*
**Mishcon**, Baron 1915- *Who 92*
**Misheff**, Sue Ellen 1951- *WhoMW 92*
**Mishel**, Lawrence *WhoFI 92*
**Misheloff**, Michael Norman 1944- *AmMWSc 92*
**Mishima**, Yukio 1925-1970 *BiDExR, DramC 1 [port], FacFETw*
**Mishin**, Vasiliy Pavlovich 1917- *IntWW 91*
**Mishin**, Viktor Maksimovich 1943- *IntWW 91*
**Mishkin**, Barbara Friedman 1936- *WhoAmL 92*
**Mishkin**, Edwin B. 1937- *WhoAmL 92*
**Mishkin**, Eli Absalom 1917- *AmMWSc 92*
**Mishkin**, Frederic S. 1951- *WhoFI 92*
**Mishkin**, Jeffrey Alan 1948- *WhoAmL 92*
**Mishkin**, Julia *DrAPF 91*
**Mishkin**, Marjorie Wong 1940- *WhoWest 92*
**Mishkin**, Mortimer 1926- *AmMWSc 92*
**Mishkin**, Paul J. 1927- *WhoAmL 92*
**Mishkin**, Philip 1915- *WhoAmP 91*
**Mishler**, John Milton, IV 1946- *AmMWSc 92*
**Mishmash**, Harold Edward 1942- *AmMWSc 92*
**Mishoe**, Luna I 1917- *AmMWSc 92*
**Mishoe**, Luna I, II 1948- *WhoAmP 91*
**Mishra**, Brajesh Chandra 1928- *IntWW 91*
**Mishra**, Dinesh S 1961- *AmMWSc 92*
**Mishra**, Jayakanta 1922- *IntAu&W 91*
**Mishra**, Karen Elizabeth 1963- *WhoMW 92*
**Mishra**, Ram K 1945- *AmMWSc 92*
**Mishra**, Ramamurti S. *RelLAm 91*
**Mishra**, Satya Narayan 1947- *AmMWSc 92*
**Mishra**, Vishwa Mohan 1937- *WhoMW 92*
**Mishuck**, Eli 1923- *AmMWSc 92*
**Mishur**, Dave Francis 1941- *WhoMW 92*
**Misiaita**, Asora *WhoAmP 91*
**Misiaszek**, Edward T 1928- *AmMWSc 92*
**Misiek**, Martin 1919- *AmMWSc 92*
**Miskel**, John Albert 1919- *AmMWSc 92*
**Miskel**, John Joseph, Jr 1933- *AmMWSc 92*
**Miskell**, William Charles 1926- *WhoEnt 92*
**Miskiewicz**, Benon 1930- *IntWW 91*
**Miskimen**, Carmen Rivera 1933- *AmMWSc 92*
**Miskimen**, George William 1930- *AmMWSc 92*
**Miskimen**, James Burt 1942- *WhoEnt 92*
**Miskimen**, Mark Allan 1955- *WhoEnt 92*
**Miskin**, James 1925- *Who 92*
**Miskin**, Raymond John 1928- *Who 92*
**Miskovsky**, George, Sr. 1910- *WhoAmL 92*
**Miskovsky**, Nicholas Matthew 1940- *AmMWSc 92*
**Miskus**, Michael Anthony 1950- *WhoFI 92, WhoWest 92*
**Misla Aldarondo**, Edison *WhoAmP 91, WhoHisp 92*
**Mislan**, Scott Thomas 1966- *WhoEnt 92*
**Mislevy**, Paul 1941- *AmMWSc 92*
**Mislin**, Kim Marie 1959- *WhoRel 92*
**Mislivec**, Philip Brian 1939- *AmMWSc 92*
**Mislove**, Michael William 1944- *AmMWSc 92*
**Mislow**, Kurt Martin 1923- *AmMWSc 92*
**Misner**, Charles William 1932- *AmMWSc 92*
**Misner**, Paul 1936- *WhoRel 92*
**Misner**, Robert David 1920- *AmMWSc 92*
**Misner**, Robert E 1941- *AmMWSc 92*
**Misner**, Steven John 1949- *WhoAmL 92*
**Misono**, Kunio Shiraishi 1946- *AmMWSc 92*
**Misra**, Alok C 1950- *AmMWSc 92*
**Misra**, Anand Lal 1928- *AmMWSc 92*
**Misra**, Dhirendra N 1936- *AmMWSc 92*
**Misra**, Dwarika Nath 1933- *AmMWSc 92*
**Misra**, Hara Prasad 1940- *AmMWSc 92*
**Misra**, Prabhakar 1955- *AmMWSc 92*
**Misra**, Prabhat Kumar 1940- *WhoMW 92*
**Misra**, Raghunath P 1928- *AmMWSc 92*
**Misra**, Raj Pratap 1919- *AmMWSc 92*
**Misra**, Ram-Bilas 1940- *IntAu&W 91*
**Misra**, Renuka 1940- *AmMWSc 92*
**Misra**, Sudhan Sekher 1938- *AmMWSc 92*
**Misra**, Sushil 1940- *AmMWSc 92*
**Misrach**, Richard 1949- *News 91 [port]*
**Misrock**, S. Leslie 1928- *WhoAmL 92*
**Misrok**, Irwin Roger 1932- *WhoFI 92*
**Missal**, Joshua Morton 1915- *WhoWest 92*
**Missan**, Richard Sherman 1933- *WhoAmL 92*
**Misselbeck**, Theodore Albert 1950- *WhoRel 92*
**Misselbrook**, Desmond 1913- *Who 92*
**Missen**, R W 1928- *AmMWSc 92*
**Misshore**, Joseph O., Jr. *WhoBlA 92*
**Missman**, Jeffrey Stephan 1944- *WhoMW 92*

Missoffe, Francois 1919- IntWW 91
Mister, Melvin Anthony 1938- WhoBlA 92
Mistler, Linda Corinne 1946- WhoFI 92
Mistler, Richard Edward 1935- AmMWSc 92
Mistral, Frederic 1830-1914 GuFrLit 1, WhoNob 90
Mistral, Gabriela 1889-1957 BenetAL 91, FacFETw [port], SpAmWW, WhoNob 90
Mistree, Farrokh AmMWSc 92
Mistretta, Charlotte Mae 1944- AmMWSc 92
Mistretta, Michael Anthony 1964- WhoMW 92
Mistry, Cyrus Dhanjishaw 1951- WhoEnt 92
Mistry, Dhruva 1957- IntWW 91, TwCPaSc, Who 92
Mistry, Nariman Burjor 1937- AmMWSc 92
Mistry, Pradip Keshavlal 1942- WhoMW 92
Mistry, Rohinton 1952- LiExTwC
Mistry, Sorab Pirozshah 1920- AmMWSc 92
Misugi, Takahiko 1927- AmMWSc 92
Mita, Katsushige 1924- IntWW 91
Mitacek, Eugene Jaroslav 1935- AmMWSc 92
Mitacek, Paul, Jr 1932- AmMWSc 92
Mitala, Joseph Jerrold 1947- AmMWSc 92
Mitalas, Romas 1933- AmMWSc 92
Mitch, Frank Allan 1920- AmMWSc 92
Mitch, William Evans 1941- AmMWSc 92
Mitchal, Saundra Marie 1949- WhoBlA 92
Mitcham, Donald 1921- AmMWSc 92
Mitcham, Heather 1941- Who 92
Mitcham, Julius Jerome 1941- WhoFI 92
Mitcham, Richard I. 1923- WhoWest 92
Mitchel, John Purroy 1879-1919 DcAmImH
Mitchel, Ormsby MacKnight 1809-1862 BiInAmS
Mitchell, A Richard 1939- AmMWSc 92
Mitchell, Abbie 1884-1960 NotBlAW 92
Mitchell, Adrian 1932- ConPo 91, IntAu&W 91, Who 92, WrDr 92
Mitchell, Albert William 1944- WhoRel 92
Mitchell, Alec Burton 1924- Who 92
Mitchell, Alexander Graham 1923- Who 92
Mitchell, Alexander Rebar 1938- AmMWSc 92
Mitchell, Alfred S ScFEYrs
Mitchell, Anderson 1800-1876 DcNCBi 4
Mitchell, Andrew John Bower 1956- Who 92
Mitchell, Angus Who 92
Mitchell, Ann Denman 1939- AmMWSc 92
Mitchell, Arthur 1934- ConBlB 2 [port], IntWW 91, WhoBlA 92, WhoEnt 92
Mitchell, Arthur Dennis 1918- Who 92
Mitchell, Augustus William 1913- WhoBlA 92
Mitchell, Austin Vernon 1934- Who 92
Mitchell, Basil George 1917- IntWW 91, Who 92
Mitchell, Bennie Robert, Jr. 1948- WhoBlA 92
Mitchell, Benson Doyle, Sr. 1913- WhoBlA 92
Mitchell, Bert Norman 1938- WhoBlA 92
Mitchell, Billy Joel 1934- WhoAmP 91
Mitchell, Billy M. 1926- WhoBlA 92
Mitchell, Bob Who 92
Mitchell, Bradford W 1927- WhoIns 92
Mitchell, Bradford William 1927- WhoFI 92
Mitchell, Brenda K. 1943- WhoBlA 92
Mitchell, Brian James 1936- AmMWSc 92
Mitchell, Brian Stokes WhoEnt 92
Mitchell, Briane Nelson 1953- WhoAmL 92
Mitchell, Bruce Logan 1947- WhoFI 92
Mitchell, Bruce Tyson 1928- WhoAmP 91
Mitchell, Bryan Franklin 1927- WhoAmP 91
Mitchell, Burley Bayard, Jr. 1940- WhoAmL 92, WhoAmP 91
Mitchell, Bush P. 1921- WhoBlA 92
Mitchell, Byron Lynwood 1936- WhoBlA 92
Mitchell, Cameron 1918- IntMPA 92
Mitchell, Carl Gene 1926- WhoRel 92
Mitchell, Carlton S. 1950- WhoBlA 92
Mitchell, Carol Ann 1957- WhoAmL 92
Mitchell, Carol Greene 1960- WhoBlA 92
Mitchell, Cary Arthur 1943- AmMWSc 92
Mitchell, Charles, Jr. 1938- WhoBlA 92
Mitchell, Charles Archie 1926- WhoFI 92
Mitchell, Charles Brauer 1937- WhoFI 92
Mitchell, Charles E. 1925- WhoBlA 92
Mitchell, Charles Elliott 1941- AmMWSc 92, WhoWest 92
Mitchell, Charles Julian Humphrey Who 92
Mitchell, Charles Summers 1934- WhoWest 92
Mitchell, Charles Wellman 1954- WhoAmP 91
Mitchell, Cheryl Elaine 1951- WhoFI 92
Mitchell, Christopher Wright 1957- WhoRel 92
Mitchell, Clarence M 1911-1984 FacFETw
Mitchell, Clifford L 1930- AmMWSc 92
Mitchell, Clyde ConAu 36NR
Mitchell, Clyde T TwCSFW 91
Mitchell, Colin Campbell 1925- Who 92
Mitchell, Corinne Howard 1914- WhoBlA 92
Mitchell, Cranston J. 1946- WhoBlA 92
Mitchell, Daniel B. 1941- WhoBlA 92
Mitchell, Daniel Roy 1942- WhoRel 92
Mitchell, David 1924- WrDr 92
Mitchell, David 1928- Who 92
Mitchell, David C. 1941- WhoFI 92
Mitchell, David Campbell 1957- WhoWest 92
Mitchell, David E. WhoWest 92
Mitchell, David Farrar 1918- AmMWSc 92
Mitchell, David Guy, Jr. 1943- WhoMW 92
Mitchell, David Hillard 1945- AmMWSc 92
Mitchell, David John 1924- IntAu&W 91
Mitchell, David Walker 1935- WhoAmL 92
Mitchell, David Wesley 1913- AmMWSc 92
Mitchell, David William 1933- Who 92
Mitchell, Dean 1942- WhoEnt 92
Mitchell, Dean Lewis 1929- AmMWSc 92
Mitchell, Denis 1911-1990 AnObit 1990
Mitchell, Denis 1912- TwCPaSc
Mitchell, Dennis Who 92
Mitchell, Dennis Keith 1946- AmMWSc 92
Mitchell, Derek 1922- IntWW 91, Who 92
Mitchell, Dolphus Burl 1922- WhoBlA 92
Mitchell, Don DrAPF 91
Mitchell, Donald 1943- WhoBlA 92
Mitchell, Donald Gilman 1917- AmMWSc 92
Mitchell, Donald Grant 1822-1908 BenetAL 91
Mitchell, Donald J 1923- WhoAmP 91
Mitchell, Donald J 1938- AmMWSc 92
Mitchell, Donald W 1923- AmMWSc 92
Mitchell, Donald Wayne 1946- WhoFI 92
Mitchell, Doug WhoRel 92
Mitchell, Douglas 1948- WhoBlA 92
Mitchell, Douglas Channing 1964- WhoRel 92
Mitchell, Douglas Graham 1938- WhoFI 92
Mitchell, Douglas Svard 1918- Who 92
Mitchell, Duncan 1941- IntWW 91
Mitchell, Dwayne Oscar 1959- WhoBlA 92
Mitchell, E P 1852-1927 ScFEYrs
Mitchell, Earl Bruce 1927- AmMWSc 92
Mitchell, Earl Dean 1939- WhoWest 92
Mitchell, Earl Douglass, Jr 1938- AmMWSc 92, WhoBlA 92
Mitchell, Earl Nelson 1926- AmMWSc 92
Mitchell, Edgar 1930- FacFETw
Mitchell, Edgar William 1925- Who 92
Mitchell, Edgar William John 1925- IntWW 91
Mitchell, Edward James 1949- WhoMW 92
Mitchell, Edward Lee 1932- WhoIns 92
Mitchell, Edward Milton 1924- WhoMW 92
Mitchell, Edwin H., Sr. 1921- WhoBlA 92
Mitchell, Elisha 1793-1857 BiInAmS, DcNCBi 4
Mitchell, Elizabeth H 1940- WhoAmP 91
Mitchell, Ella Pearson 1917- WhoBlA 92
Mitchell, Elyne 1913- WrDr 92
Mitchell, Elyne Keith 1913- IntAu&W 91
Mitchell, Emerson Blackhorse DrAPF 91
Mitchell, Emmitt W. WhoBlA 92
Mitchell, Enid 1919- IntAu&W 91
Mitchell, Eric, Mrs. Who 92
Mitchell, Eric Ignatius 1948- WhoBlA 92
Mitchell, Eva Purnell 1953- WhoWest 92
Mitchell, Everett Royal 1936- AmMWSc 92
Mitchell, Ewan Who 92
Mitchell, Frank Who 92
Mitchell, Gary C 1950- WhoAmP 91
Mitchell, Gary Earl 1935- AmMWSc 92
Mitchell, Gary Everett 1954- WhoAmL 92
Mitchell, Gary Lee 1953- WhoFI 92
Mitchell, Geneva Brooke 1929- WhoWest 92
Mitchell, Geoffrey Charles 1921- Who 92
Mitchell, Geoffrey Duncan IntAu&W 91, WrDr 92
Mitchell, George Archibald Grant 1906- Who 92
Mitchell, George B 1940- WhoIns 92
Mitchell, George Ernest, Jr 1930- AmMWSc 92
Mitchell, George Francis 1912- IntWW 91, Who 92
Mitchell, George Frank 1950- WhoFI 92
Mitchell, George J. 1933- AlmAP 92 [port]
Mitchell, George John 1933- IntWW 91, WhoAmP 91
Mitchell, George Joseph 1925- AmMWSc 92
Mitchell, George L. WhoBlA 92
Mitchell, George Redmond, Jr 1917- AmMWSc 92
Mitchell, George Trice 1914- WhoMW 92
Mitchell, Gerald Raymond 1939- WhoMW 92
Mitchell, Geraldine Vaughn 1940- AmMWSc 92
Mitchell, Gregory Roderick 1960- WhoFI 92
Mitchell, Grover WhoBlA 92
Mitchell, H Rees 1908- AmMWSc 92
Mitchell, Harold Charles d1991 Who 92N
Mitchell, Harold Hugh 1916- AmMWSc 92
Mitchell, Harry 1930- Who 92
Mitchell, Harry 1940- WhoAmP 91
Mitchell, Harry E. 1940- WhoWest 92
Mitchell, Helen C AmMWSc 92
Mitchell, Helen Josephine Who 92
Mitchell, Henry 1830-1902 BiInAmS
Mitchell, Henry Allen, Jr. 1935- WhoAmL 92
Mitchell, Henry Andrew 1936- AmMWSc 92
Mitchell, Henry B. 1918- WhoBlA 92
Mitchell, Henry Heywood 1919- WhoBlA 92, WhoRel 92
Mitchell, Henry Maurice 1925- WhoAmL 92
Mitchell, Herschel Kenworthy 1913- AmMWSc 92
Mitchell, Homer DrAPF 91
Mitchell, Horace 1944- WhoBlA 92
Mitchell, Howard 1911-1988 NewAmDM
Mitchell, Huey P. 1935- WhoBlA 92
Mitchell, Hugh Bertron 1923- AmMWSc 92
Mitchell, Hugh Burnton 1907- WhoAmP 91
Mitchell, Ian Edward 1932- Who 92
Mitchell, Irvin Sharp 1934- WhoRel 92
Mitchell, Irving Nelson 1850-1918 BiInAmS
Mitchell, Isaac BenetAL 91
Mitchell, Iverson O., III 1943- WhoBlA 92
Mitchell, J A 1845-1918 ScFEYrs
Mitchell, Jack Harris, Jr 1911- AmMWSc 92
Mitchell, Jacob Bill 1932- WhoBlA 92
Mitchell, James 1926- Who 92, WrDr 92
Mitchell, James 1943- WhoAmP 91
Mitchell, James A. WhoFI 92
Mitchell, James Alfred 1852-1902 BiInAmS
Mitchell, James Austin 1941- WhoFI 92, WhoIns 92
Mitchell, James Benjamin 1924- WhoAmP 91
Mitchell, James Clyde 1918- Who 92
Mitchell, James Emmett 1939- AmMWSc 92
Mitchell, James Fitzallen 1931- IntWW 91, Who 92
Mitchell, James George 1943- AmMWSc 92
Mitchell, James H. 1948- WhoBlA 92
Mitchell, James Herbert 1946- WhoWest 92
Mitchell, James K 1930- AmMWSc 92
Mitchell, James Kenneth 1930- WhoWest 92
Mitchell, James Lachlan Martin 1929- Who 92
Mitchell, James Leslie RfGEnL 91
Mitchell, James Richard 1946- IntWW 91
Mitchell, James Wesley 1950- WhoAmP 91
Mitchell, James Winfield 1943- AmMWSc 92, WhoBlA 92
Mitchell, Janet Elizabeth 1951- WhoAmL 92
Mitchell, Janet Joyce 1941- WhoEnt 92
Mitchell, Jeffrey Thomas 1946- WhoMW 92
Mitchell, Jerald Andrew 1941- AmMWSc 92
Mitchell, Jere Holloway 1928- AmMWSc 92
Mitchell, Jeremy George Swale Hamilton 1929- Who 92
Mitchell, Jerome 1935- IntAu&W 91, WrDr 92
Mitchell, Jerome Robert 1957- WhoFI 92
Mitchell, Jerome Wilk 1953- WhoMW 92
Mitchell, Jerry R 1941- AmMWSc 92
Mitchell, Joan 1926- FacFETw, IntWW 91, NewYTBS 91 [port]
Mitchell, Joan E. 1920- WrDr 92
Mitchell, Joan Eileen 1920- Who 92
Mitchell, Joan LaVerne 1947- AmMWSc 92
Mitchell, Joann 1956- WhoBlA 92
Mitchell, Joanne 1938- WhoBlA 92
Mitchell, Joe H. DrAPF 91
Mitchell, John 1680?-1750? BenetAL 91
Mitchell, John 1711-1768 BiInAmS
Mitchell, John 1826-1906 DcNCBi 4
Mitchell, John 1942- TwCPaSc
Mitchell, John, Jr 1913- AmMWSc 92
Mitchell, John Alexander 1945- AmMWSc 92
Mitchell, John Ames 1845-1918 BenetAL 91
Mitchell, John Angus 1924- Who 92
Mitchell, John Anthony 1940- WhoFI 92
Mitchell, John Charles 1932- AmMWSc 92
Mitchell, John Clifford 1955- AmMWSc 92, WhoWest 92
Mitchell, John Douglas 1944- AmMWSc 92
Mitchell, John Edwards 1917- AmMWSc 92
Mitchell, John Francis 1928- WhoFI 92
Mitchell, John Gall 1931- Who 92
Mitchell, John Henderson 1933- WhoFI 92
Mitchell, John Howard 1921- WrDr 92
Mitchell, John Jacob 1917- AmMWSc 92
Mitchell, John Kearsley 1793-1858 BiInAmS
Mitchell, John Kearsley 1859-1917 BiInAmS
Mitchell, John Laurin Amos 1944- AmMWSc 92, WhoMW 92
Mitchell, John Logan 1947- Who 92
Mitchell, John Matthew 1925- Who 92
Mitchell, John Murray, Jr 1928- AmMWSc 92
Mitchell, John Newton 1913-1988 AmPolLe, FacFETw
Mitchell, John Noyes, Jr. 1930- WhoWest 92
Mitchell, John Peter 1932- AmMWSc 92
Mitchell, John Phillimore 1918- WrDr 92
Mitchell, John Richard Anthony d1991 Who 92N
Mitchell, John Taylor 1931- AmMWSc 92
Mitchell, John Thomas 1958- WhoAmL 92
Mitchell, John W 1928- WhoIns 92
Mitchell, John Wesley 1913- AmMWSc 92, Who 92
Mitchell, John William 1944- WhoWest 92
Mitchell, John Wright 1935- AmMWSc 92
Mitchell, Joni 1943- FacFETw, IntWW 91, NewAmDM, News 91 [port], WhoEnt 92
Mitchell, Joseph 1908- ConNov 91, IntWW 91, SourALJ, WrDr 92
Mitchell, Joseph A 1942- WhoAmP 91
Mitchell, Joseph Christopher 1922- AmMWSc 92, WhoBlA 92
Mitchell, Joseph Nathan 1922- WhoIns 92
Mitchell, Joseph Patrick 1939- WhoWest 92
Mitchell, Joseph Rodney 1914- Who 92
Mitchell, Joseph Rudolph 1938- WhoBlA 92
Mitchell, Joseph Shannon Baird 1959- AmMWSc 92
Mitchell, Josephine Margaret AmMWSc 92
Mitchell, Juanita 1913- NotBlAW 92
Mitchell, Judson, Jr. 1941- WhoBlA 92
Mitchell, JudyLynn 1951- WhoBlA 92
Mitchell, Julia L. 1933- WhoFI 92
Mitchell, Julian 1935- ConNov 91, IntAu&W 91, IntWW 91, Who 92, WrDr 92
Mitchell, Juliet 1940- IntAu&W 91, WrDr 92
Mitchell, Julius P. 1941- WhoBlA 92
Mitchell, K L IntAu&W 91X
Mitchell, Kathleen Ann 1948- WhoWest 92
Mitchell, Keith Clarudius IntWW 91
Mitchell, Keith Kirkman 1927- Who 92
Mitchell, Kelly Karnale 1928- WhoBlA 92
Mitchell, Kendall WhoMW 92
Mitchell, Kenneth Frank 1940- AmMWSc 92
Mitchell, Kenneth John 1938- AmMWSc 92
Mitchell, Kenneth Reece 1930- WhoRel 92
Mitchell, Kim Sarahjane 1954- WhoAmL 92
Mitchell, Langdon 1862-1935 BenetAL 91
Mitchell, Lansing Leroy 1914- WhoAmL 92
Mitchell, Larry WhoAmP 91
Mitchell, Larry Randell 1950- WhoAmP 91
Mitchell, Lawrence Gustave 1942- AmMWSc 92
Mitchell, Leah Jean 1965- WhoFI 92

**Mitchell**, Lee Hartley 1941- *WhoFI 92*
**Mitchell**, Lee Mark 1943- *WhoMW 92*
**Mitchell**, LeMonte Felton 1939- *WhoBlA 92*
**Mitchell**, Leona 1949- *WhoBlA 92*
**Mitchell**, Leonel Lake 1930- *WhoRel 92*
**Mitchell**, LeRoy 1921-1990 *WhoBlA 92N*
**Mitchell**, Lilyann Jackson 1933- *WhoBlA 92*
**Mitchell**, Lindell Marvin 1937- *WhoFI 92*
**Mitchell**, Loften 1919- *WhoBlA 92, WrDr 92*
**Mitchell**, Louise *WhoBlA 92*
**Mitchell**, Lucius Quinn 1959- *WhoFI 92*
**Mitchell**, Lynn Lee 1945- *WhoWest 92*
**Mitchell**, Madeleine Enid 1941- *AmMWSc 92, WhoWest 92*
**Mitchell**, Malcolm Stuart 1937- *AmMWSc 92*
**Mitchell**, Margaret 1900-1949 *BenetAL 91, FacFETw*
**Mitchell**, Margaretta 1935- *WrDr 92*
**Mitchell**, Margaretta Meyer Kuhlthau 1935- *IntAu&W 91*
**Mitchell**, Maria *DrAPF 91*
**Mitchell**, Maria 1818-1889 *BiInAmS, HanAmWH*
**Mitchell**, Marian Bartlett 1941- *WhoBlA 92*
**Mitchell**, Mark Randolph 1955- *WhoBlA 92*
**Mitchell**, Martha Mallard 1940- *WhoBlA 92*
**Mitchell**, Martin *Who 92*
**Mitchell**, Marvin Harry 1937- *WhoAmL 92*
**Mitchell**, Maryann *WhoAmP 91*
**Mitchell**, Maurice Clayton 1952- *WhoFI 92*
**Mitchell**, Maurice McClellan, Jr 1929- *AmMWSc 92*
**Mitchell**, Melvin J. 1904- *WhoBlA 92*
**Mitchell**, Melvin Lester 1939- *WhoBlA 92*
**Mitchell**, Memory F. 1924- *WrDr 92*
**Mitchell**, Michael A 1941- *AmMWSc 92*
**Mitchell**, Michael Allan 1956- *WhoMW 92*
**Mitchell**, Michael Ernst 1943- *AmMWSc 92*
**Mitchell**, Michael Roger 1941- *AmMWSc 92*
**Mitchell**, Michael William 1937- *WhoAmL 92*
**Mitchell**, Mike Anthony 1956- *WhoBlA 92*
**Mitchell**, Mike P 1925- *WhoAmP 91*
**Mitchell**, Mozella Gordon 1936- *WhoRel 92*
**Mitchell**, Myron James 1947- *AmMWSc 92*
**Mitchell**, Myrtle L. *WhoRel 92*
**Mitchell**, Nelli L. *WhoBlA 92*
**Mitchell**, Nora *DrAPF 91*
**Mitchell**, Norman L 1928- *AmMWSc 92*
**Mitchell**, Olga Mary Mracek 1933- *AmMWSc 92*
**Mitchell**, Orlan E. 1933- *WhoRel 92*
**Mitchell**, Ormond Glenn 1927- *AmMWSc 92*
**Mitchell**, Orrin Dwight 1946- *WhoBlA 92*
**Mitchell**, Oscar Howard 1852?-1889 *BiInAmS*
**Mitchell**, Ossie Ware 1919- *WhoBlA 92*
**Mitchell**, Owen Robert 1945- *AmMWSc 92*
**Mitchell**, Parren James 1922- *WhoAmP 91, WhoBlA 92*
**Mitchell**, Patricia Ann 1943- *WhoAmL 92, WhoFI 92*
**Mitchell**, Patrick Denis 1955- *WhoMW 92*
**Mitchell**, Patrick Reynolds 1930- *Who 92*
**Mitchell**, Patsy Malier 1948- *WhoRel 92*
**Mitchell**, Peter 1920- *AmMWSc 92*
**Mitchell**, Peter Denis 1920- *WhoNob 90*
**Mitchell**, Peter Dennis 1920- *IntWW 91, Who 92*
**Mitchell**, Peter W. 1942- *WhoWest 92*
**Mitchell**, Philip W 1941- *WhoIns 92*
**Mitchell**, Quitman J. *WhoBlA 92*
**Mitchell**, R Clayton, Jr *WhoAmP 91*
**Mitchell**, Ralph 1934- *AmMWSc 92*
**Mitchell**, Ralph David 1934- *WhoMW 92, WhoRel 92*
**Mitchell**, Reginald 1895-1937 *FacFETw*
**Mitchell**, Reginald Eugene 1947- *AmMWSc 92*
**Mitchell**, Reginald Harry 1943- *AmMWSc 92*
**Mitchell**, Richard Charles 1927- *Who 92*
**Mitchell**, Richard Charles 1953- *WhoMW 92*
**Mitchell**, Richard Lee 1938- *AmMWSc 92*
**Mitchell**, Richard Leigh 1941- *WhoAmL 92*
**Mitchell**, Richard Scott 1929- *AmMWSc 92*
**Mitchell**, Richard Shepard 1938- *AmMWSc 92*
**Mitchell**, Richard Sibley 1932- *AmMWSc 92*
**Mitchell**, Richard Warren 1923- *AmMWSc 92*
**Mitchell**, Rick 1946- *WhoEnt 92*
**Mitchell**, Robby K 1916- *IntAu&W 91, WrDr 92*
**Mitchell**, Robert 1913- *Who 92*
**Mitchell**, Robert A 1922- *AmMWSc 92*
**Mitchell**, Robert Alexander 1935- *AmMWSc 92*
**Mitchell**, Robert Arthur 1926- *WhoMW 92*
**Mitchell**, Robert Bruce 1942- *AmMWSc 92*
**Mitchell**, Robert C. 1935- *WhoBlA 92*
**Mitchell**, Robert Campbell 1940- *WhoWest 92*
**Mitchell**, Robert Curtis 1928- *AmMWSc 92*
**Mitchell**, Robert Dalton 1923- *AmMWSc 92*
**Mitchell**, Robert Deatrick 1929- *WhoEnt 92*
**Mitchell**, Robert Everitt 1929- *WhoAmL 92*
**Mitchell**, Robert Imrie 1916- *Who 92*
**Mitchell**, Robert Ira 1950- *WhoWest 92*
**Mitchell**, Robert L. *WhoBlA 92*
**Mitchell**, Robert L 1923- *AmMWSc 92*
**Mitchell**, Robert Lee, III 1957- *WhoFI 92*
**Mitchell**, Robert Lee, Sr. 1932- *WhoBlA 92*
**Mitchell**, Robert P. 1951- *WhoBlA 92*
**Mitchell**, Roberta King 1951- *WhoRel 92*
**Mitchell**, Roderick Bernard 1955- *WhoBlA 92*
**Mitchell**, Rodger 1926- *AmMWSc 92*
**Mitchell**, Roger *DrAPF 91*
**Mitchell**, Roger 1935- *IntAu&W 91, WrDr 92*
**Mitchell**, Roger Harold 1946- *AmMWSc 92*
**Mitchell**, Roger L 1932- *AmMWSc 92*
**Mitchell**, Roger Lowry 1932- *WhoFI 92*
**Mitchell**, Roger W 1937- *AmMWSc 92*
**Mitchell**, Roma 1913- *Who 92*
**Mitchell**, Roma Flinders 1913- *IntWW 91*
**Mitchell**, Ronnie Monroe 1952- *WhoAmL 92*
**Mitchell**, Roscoe 1940- *NewAmDM*
**Mitchell**, Roscoe E. 1934- *WhoBlA 92*
**Mitchell**, Ross Galbraith 1920- *Who 92*
**Mitchell**, Roy Ernest 1936- *AmMWSc 92*
**Mitchell**, Roy Shaw 1934- *WhoAmL 92*
**Mitchell**, S. Weir 1829-1914 *BenetAL 91*
**Mitchell**, Sadie Stridiron 1922- *WhoRel 92*
**Mitchell**, Sam M 1929- *WhoAmP 91*
**Mitchell**, Samuel Augustus 1792-1868 *BiInAmS*
**Mitchell**, Samuel E., Jr. 1963- *WhoBlA 92*
**Mitchell**, Samuel Robert 1938- *WhoFI 92*
**Mitchell**, Samuel Underhill 1931- *WhoFI 92*
**Mitchell**, Sanford Carveth 1942- *WhoRel 92*
**Mitchell**, Scoey 1930- *WhoBlA 92*
**Mitchell**, Scott Eugene 1936- *WhoRel 92*
**Mitchell**, Sidney Alexander 1895-1966 *ConAu 134*
**Mitchell**, Silas Weir 1829-1914 *BiInAmS*
**Mitchell**, Stanley Henryk 1949- *WhoBlA 92*
**Mitchell**, Stephen A. 1946- *ConAu 133*
**Mitchell**, Stephen George 1941- *Who 92*
**Mitchell**, Stephen Keith 1942- *AmMWSc 92*
**Mitchell**, Stephen Milton 1943- *WhoFI 92*
**Mitchell**, Steven Thomas 1953- *WhoMW 92*
**Mitchell**, Susan *DrAPF 91*
**Mitchell**, Tandie Vera 1942- *WhoWest 92*
**Mitchell**, Terence Croft 1929- *Who 92*
**Mitchell**, Terence Edward 1937- *AmMWSc 92, WhoWest 92*
**Mitchell**, Terry Eugene 1939- *WhoAmL 92*
**Mitchell**, Tex Dwayne 1949- *WhoBlA 92*
**Mitchell**, Theo W. 1938- *WhoBlA 92*
**Mitchell**, Theo Walker 1938- *WhoAmP 91*
**Mitchell**, Theodore 1926- *AmMWSc 92*
**Mitchell**, Thomas Brian 1957- *WhoEnt 92*
**Mitchell**, Thomas Duche 1791-1865 *BiInAmS*
**Mitchell**, Thomas George 1927- *AmMWSc 92*
**Mitchell**, Thomas Greenfield 1941- *AmMWSc 92*
**Mitchell**, Thomas Noel 1939- *IntWW 91*
**Mitchell**, Thomas Owen 1944- *AmMWSc 92*
**Mitchell**, Thomas Robert 1937- *WhoFI 92*
**Mitchell**, Timothy Charles 1950- *WhoRel 92*
**Mitchell**, Timothy P 1949- *WhoIns 92*
**Mitchell**, Timothy Papin 1949- *WhoFI 92*
**Mitchell**, Tittica Roberts 1939- *WhoEnt 92*
**Mitchell**, Tom M *AmMWSc 92*
**Mitchell**, Val Leonard 1938- *AmMWSc 92*
**Mitchell**, Valery J 1942- *WhoAmP 91*
**Mitchell**, Vernice Virginia 1921- *WhoMW 92*
**Mitchell**, Virgil Allen 1914- *WhoRel 92*
**Mitchell**, W 1943- *WhoAmP 91*
**Mitchell**, W. O. 1914- *BenetAL 91, ConNov 91, WrDr 92*
**Mitchell**, Wallace Clark 1920- *AmMWSc 92*
**Mitchell**, Walter Edmund, Jr 1925- *AmMWSc 92*
**Mitchell**, Warren 1926- *Who 92*
**Mitchell**, Warren I. 1937- *WhoFI 92, WhoWest 92*
**Mitchell**, Wayne Lee 1937- *WhoWest 92*
**Mitchell**, Wendell Wilkie 1940- *WhoAmP 91*
**Mitchell**, Wiley Francis, Jr 1932- *WhoAmP 91*
**Mitchell**, William *Who 92*
**Mitchell**, William 1791-1869 *BiInAmS*
**Mitchell**, William 1879-1936 *FacFETw*
**Mitchell**, William 1912-1988 *DcTwDes*
**Mitchell**, William Alexander 1911- *AmMWSc 92*
**Mitchell**, William Cobbey 1939- *AmMWSc 92*
**Mitchell**, William Eric Marcus d1990 *Who 92N*
**Mitchell**, William Graham Champion 1946- *WhoAmL 92*
**Mitchell**, William Grant 1921- *WhoEnt 92*
**Mitchell**, William Grayson 1950- *WhoBlA 92*
**Mitchell**, William H 1921- *AmMWSc 92*
**Mitchell**, William John *AmMWSc 92*
**Mitchell**, William John Thomas 1942- *IntAu&W 91*
**Mitchell**, William Joseph 1936- *Who 92*
**Mitchell**, William O 1914- *IntAu&W 91*
**Mitchell**, William P. 1912- *WhoBlA 92*
**Mitchell**, William Randolph 1944- *WhoFI 92*
**Mitchell**, William Richard 1930- *WhoEnt 92*
**Mitchell**, William Warren 1923- *AmMWSc 92*
**Mitchell**, William Watson 1810-1897 *DcNCBi 4*
**Mitchell**, Willis *ScFEYrs*
**Mitchell**, Windell T. 1941- *WhoBlA 92*
**Mitchell**, Zinora M. 1957- *WhoBlA 92*
**Mitchell-Ball**, Dianne *WhoWest 92*
**Mitchell-Bateman**, Mildred 1922- *WhoBlA 92*
**Mitchell Cotts**, R. C. *Who 92*
**Mitchell-Esteva**, Byron 1944- *WhoHisp 92*
**Mitchell-Hayes**, Minnie Marie 1948- *IntAu&W 91*
**Mitchell-Kernan**, Claudia 1941- *WhoWest 92*
**Mitchell-Kernan**, Claudia Irene 1941- *WhoBlA 92*
**Mitchell-Thomson** *Who 92*
**Mitchelson**, Marvin Morris 1928- *WhoAmL 92*
**Mitchelson**, Tom *DrAPF 91*
**Mitchem**, Arnold Levy 1938- *WhoBlA 92*
**Mitchem**, Hinton 1938- *WhoAmP 91*
**Mitchem**, John Alan 1940- *AmMWSc 92*
**Mitchem**, John Clifford *WhoBlA 92*
**Mitchem**, Mary Teresa 1944- *WhoFI 92*
**Mitchem-Davis**, Anne *WhoBlA 92*
**Mitchener**, Leoma Donis *WhoAmP 91*
**Mitchenson**, Francis Joseph Blackett *Who 92*
**Mitchill**, Samuel Latham 1764-1831 *BiInAmS*
**Mitchison**, Avrion *Who 92*
**Mitchison**, Denis Anthony 1919- *Who 92*
**Mitchison**, John Murdoch 1922- *IntWW 91, Who 92*
**Mitchison**, Naomi 1897- *ConNov 91, IntAu&W 91, IntWW 91, TwCSFW 91, WrDr 92*
**Mitchison**, Naomi Margaret 1897- *Who 92*
**Mitchison**, Nicholas Avrion 1928- *IntWW 91, Who 92*
**Mitchison**, Rosalind 1919- *WrDr 92*
**Mitchison**, Rosalind Mary 1914- *IntAu&W 91*
**Mitchler**, Robert W 1920- *WhoAmP 91*
**Mitchner**, Hyman 1930- *AmMWSc 92*
**Mitchner**, Morton 1926- *AmMWSc 92*
**Mitchum**, Hank *IntAu&W 91X, TwCWW 91, WrDr 92*
**Mitchum**, Jim 1941- *IntMPA 92*
**Mitchum**, Robert 1917- *FacFETw, IntMPA 92*
**Mitchum**, Robert Charles Duran 1917- *IntWW 91, WhoEnt 92*
**Mitchum**, Ronald Kem 1946- *AmMWSc 92*
**Mitchum**, Tommy E 1949- *WhoAmP 91*
**Mitchusson**, Thomas Joseph 1957- *WhoMW 92*
**Mitdank**, Joachim 1931- *Who 92*
**Mitescu**, Catalin Dan 1938- *AmMWSc 92*
**Mitford** *Who 92*
**Mitford sisters** *FacFETw*
**Mitford**, Deborah *FacFETw*
**Mitford**, Diana 1910- *FacFETw*
**Mitford**, Jessica 1917- *FacFETw, IntAu&W 91, IntWW 91, WrDr 92*
**Mitford**, Jessica Lucy 1917- *Who 92*
**Mitford**, Mary Russell 1787-1855 *DcLB 110 [port], RfGEnL 91*
**Mitford**, Nancy 1904-1973 *FacFETw, RfGEnL 91*
**Mitford**, Pamela *FacFETw*
**Mitford**, Rupert Leo Scott B. *Who 92*
**Mitford**, Unity 1914-1948 *FacFETw*
**Mitford**, Unity Valkyrie 1914-1948 *EncTR 91 [port]*
**Mitford-Slade**, Patrick Buxton 1936- *Who 92*
**Mitgang**, Alix Susan 1959- *WhoWest 92*
**Mitgang**, Herbert 1920- *WrDr 92*
**Mithcell**, William Marvin 1935- *AmMWSc 92*
**Mithen**, Dallas Alfred 1923- *Who 92*
**Mithoff**, Richard Warren *WhoAmL 92*
**Mithun**, Robert James 1949- *WhoWest 92*
**Mitiguy**, Arthur Andrew 1957- *WhoAmL 92*
**Mitilier**, Terry John 1949- *WhoIns 92*
**Mitio**, John, III 1950- *WhoWest 92*
**Mitlak**, Stefany Lynn 1958- *WhoAmL 92*
**Mitler**, Henri Emmanuel 1930- *AmMWSc 92*
**Mitnick**, Harold 1923- *WhoAmL 92*
**Mitoff**, S P 1924- *AmMWSc 92*
**Mitoma**, Chozo 1922- *AmMWSc 92*
**Mitra**, Ashesh Prosad 1927- *Who 92*
**Mitra**, Chittaranjan 1926- *IntWW 91*
**Mitra**, Grihapati 1927- *AmMWSc 92*
**Mitra**, Jyotirmay 1921- *AmMWSc 92*
**Mitra**, Sanjit K 1935- *AmMWSc 92*
**Mitra**, Sankar 1937- *AmMWSc 92*
**Mitra**, Shashanka S 1932- *AmMWSc 92*
**Mitra**, Sombhu 1915- *IntWW 91*
**Mitra**, Sunanda 1936- *AmMWSc 92*
**Mitrano**, Joseph Charles 1940- *WhoWest 92*
**Mitrano**, Peter Paul 1951- *WhoAmL 92*
**Mitre**, Eduardo 1943- *ConSpAP*
**Mitro**, James Edward 1942- *WhoFI 92*
**Mitrokhin**, Dmitriy Isidorovich 1883-1973 *SovUnBD*
**Mitropolsky**, Yuriy Alekseyevich 1917- *IntWW 91*
**Mitropoulos**, Dimitri 1896-1960 *NewAmDM*
**Mitrovich**, Stephen N. *DcAmImH*
**Mitruka**, Brij Mohan 1937- *AmMWSc 92*
**Mitsakis**, Kariofilis 1932- *Who 92*
**Mitsch**, William Joseph 1947- *AmMWSc 92, WhoMW 92*
**Mitscher**, Lester Allen 1931- *AmMWSc 92, WhoMW 92*
**Mitson**, Eileen N. 1930- *WrDr 92*
**Mitson**, Eileen Nora 1930- *IntAu&W 91*
**Mitsotakis**, Constantine 1918- *IntWW 91*
**Mitsoulis**, Evan 1954- *AmMWSc 92*
**Mitsubayashi**, Yataro 1918- *IntWW 91*
**Mitsuda**, Hisateru 1914- *IntWW 91*
**Mitsui**, Akira 1929- *AmMWSc 92*
**Mitsui**, James Masao *DrAPF 91*
**Mitsui**, Patricia Teruko 1946- *WhoEnt 92*
**Mitsutomi**, T 1923- *AmMWSc 92*
**Mitsuya**, Hiroaki 1950- *AmMWSc 92*
**Mitsuzuka**, Hiroshi *IntWW 91*
**Mittag**, Gunter 1926- *IntWW 91*
**Mittag**, Thomas Waldemar 1937- *AmMWSc 92*
**Mittal**, Balraj 1951- *AmMWSc 92*
**Mittal**, Gauri S 1947- *AmMWSc 92*
**Mittal**, Kamal Kant 1935- *AmMWSc 92*
**Mittal**, Kashmiri Lal 1945- *AmMWSc 92*
**Mittal**, Yashaswini Deval 1941- *AmMWSc 92*
**Mittel**, John J. *WhoFI 92*
**Mitteldorf**, Darryl 1955- *WhoEnt 92*
**Mittelholzer**, Edgar 1909-1965 *LiExTwC, RfGEnL 91*
**Mittelholzer**, Edgar Austin 1909-1965 *BenetAL 91*
**Mittelman**, Arnold 1924- *AmMWSc 92*
**Mittelman**, Phillip Sidney 1925- *WhoWest 92*
**Mittelstaedt**, Stanley George 1909- *AmMWSc 92*
**Mitten**, David Gordon 1935- *WhoRel 92*
**Mitten**, Loring G 1920- *AmMWSc 92*
**Mittendorf**, Theodor Henry 1895- *WhoFI 92*
**Mittenthal**, Barry Steven 1952- *WhoAmL 92*
**Mittenthal**, Jay Edward 1941- *AmMWSc 92*
**Mittenthal**, Richard 1926- *WhoAmL 92*
**Mitter**, Sanjoy 1933- *AmMWSc 92*
**Mitterer**, Otto 1911- *IntWW 91*
**Mitterer**, Richard Max 1938- *AmMWSc 92*
**Mitterling**, Richard Alan 1961- *WhoRel 92*
**Mitterrand**, Francois 1916- *FacFETw [port]*

**Mitterrand**, Francois Maurice Marie 1916- *IntWW 91, Who 92*
**Mitterrand**, Jacques 1918- *IntWW 91*
**Mitting**, John Edward 1947- *Who 92*
**Mittleman**, John *AmMWSc 92*
**Mittleman**, Marvin Harold 1928- *AmMWSc 92*
**Mittleman**, Philip Stewart 1951- *WhoFI 92*
**Mittler**, Arthur 1943- *AmMWSc 92*
**Mittler**, Diana 1941- *WhoEnt 92*
**Mittler**, James Carlton 1935- *AmMWSc 92*
**Mittler**, James Emmett 1943- *WhoFI 92*
**Mittler**, Peter Joseph 1930- *Who 92*
**Mittler**, Robert S *AmMWSc 92*
**Mittlestaedt**, James Michael 1964- *WhoMW 92*
**Mittman**, Alan Lee 1949- *WhoAmL 92*
**Mittman**, Benjamin 1928- *AmMWSc 92*
**Mittnik**, Stefan 1954- *WhoFI 92*
**Mitton**, Charles Leslie 1907- *Who 92*
**Mitton**, Jacqueline 1948- *SmATA 66*
**Mitton**, Jeffry Bond 1947- *AmMWSc 92*
**Mitton**, Michael Anthony 1947- *WhoFI 92*
**Mitton**, Simon 1946- *SmATA 66*
**Mittra**, Sid 1930- *WhoFI 92*
**Miturich**, Petr Vasil'evich 1887-1956 *SovUnBD*
**Mitus**, Wladyslaw J 1920- *AmMWSc 92*
**Mityagin**, Boris Samuel 1937- *AmMWSc 92*
**Mitylene** *EncAmaz 91*
**Mitze**, Thomas Clark *WhoEnt 92*
**Mitzen**, Nancy Elizabeth 1955- *WhoEnt 92*
**Mitzman**, Nancy Jane 1938- *WhoAmP 91*
**Mitzman**, Richard 1945- *TwCPaSc*
**Mitzner**, Donald H. 1940- *WhoFI 92*
**Mitzner**, Kenneth Martin 1938- *AmMWSc 92*
**Mitzner**, Miles Leemon 1957- *WhoAmL 92*
**Miura**, Carole K Masutani 1938- *AmMWSc 92*
**Miura**, Chizuko 1931- *ConAu 133*
**Miura**, George Akio 1942- *AmMWSc 92*
**Miura**, Robert Mitsuru 1938- *AmMWSc 92*
**Miura-Atcheson**, Susan Mitsuko 1955- *WhoEnt 92*
**Miwa**, Gerald T 1945- *AmMWSc 92*
**Mix**, Dwight Franklin 1932- *AmMWSc 92*
**Mix**, Michael Cary 1941- *AmMWSc 92*
**Mix**, Richard Irwin 1931- *WhoEnt 92*
**Mix**, Tom 1880-1940 *FacFETw*
**Mixan**, Craig Edward 1946- *AmMWSc 92*
**Mixer**, Charles E *ScFEYrs*
**Mixer**, Dennis Lynn 1952- *WhoRel 92*
**Mixer**, Ronald Wayne 1954- *WhoMW 92, WhoRel 92*
**Mixon**, Alan 1933- *WhoEnt 92*
**Mixon**, Aubrey Clifton 1924- *AmMWSc 92*
**Mixon**, Clarence W. 1934- *WhoBlA 92*
**Mixon**, Forest Orion 1931- *AmMWSc 92*
**Mixon**, Forrest Orion 1900-1956 *DcNCBi 4*
**Mixon**, Roy Darvin 1922- *WhoRel 92*
**Mixon**, Veronica 1948- *WhoBlA 92*
**Mixon**, Wehlan Eugene 1952- *WhoWest 92*
**Mixson**, Wayne 1922- *WhoAmP 91*
**Mixter**, Russell Lowell 1906- *AmMWSc 92*
**Miya**, Tom Saburo 1923- *AmMWSc 92*
**Miyada**, Don Shuso 1925- *AmMWSc 92*
**Miyagawa**, Ichiro 1922- *AmMWSc 92*
**Miyai**, Jinnosuke 1921- *IntWW 91*
**Miyai**, Katsumi 1931- *AmMWSc 92*
**Miyake**, Issey 1938- *IntWW 91*
**Miyake**, Shigemitsu 1911- *IntWW 91*
**Miyakoda**, Kikuro 1927- *AmMWSc 92*
**Miyamoto**, Craig Toyoki 1944- *WhoFI 92*
**Miyamoto**, Kenji 1908- *IntAu&W 91, IntWW 91*
**Miyamoto**, Michael Dwight 1945- *AmMWSc 92*
**Miyamoto**, Michael Masao 1955- *AmMWSc 92*
**Miyamoto**, Richard Takashi 1944- *WhoMW 92*
**Miyamoto**, Seiichi 1944- *AmMWSc 92*
**Miyamoto**, Wayne Akira 1947- *WhoWest 92*
**Miyano**, Kenjiro 1947- *AmMWSc 92*
**Miyao**, Stanley K 1946- *WhoIns 92*
**Miyao**, Stanley Kenji 1946- *WhoFI 92*
**Miyares**, Marcelino 1937- *WhoHisp 92*
**Miyasaka**, Kyoko 1950- *AmMWSc 92*
**Miyasaka**, Naomi 1963- *WhoWest 92*
**Miyasaki**, Shuichi 1928- *WhoAmL 92, WhoWest 92*
**Miyashiro**, Akiho 1920- *AmMWSc 92*
**Miyata**, Gen 1933- *WhoRel 92*
**Miyata**, Keijiro 1951- *WhoWest 92*
**Miyawaki**, Edison Hiroyuki 1929- *WhoWest 92*
**Miyazaki**, Hiromichi 1921- *IntWW 91*
**Miyazaki**, Kagayaki 1909- *IntWW 91*
**Miyazawa**, Kiichi 1919- *IntWW 91, NewYTBS 91, News 92-2 [port]*
**Miyoshi**, Akira 1933- *ConCom 92*
**Miyoshi**, David Masao 1944- *WhoFI 92*
**Miyoshi**, Kazuhisa 1946- *AmMWSc 92*
**Mize**, Charles Edward 1934- *AmMWSc 92*
**Mize**, Craig Dalton 1963- *WhoEnt 92*
**Mize**, Dwight Workman 1929- *WhoAmP 91*
**Mize**, Jack Pitts 1923- *AmMWSc 92*
**Mize**, Joe H 1934- *AmMWSc 92*
**Mize**, Ricky Dane 1959- *WhoEnt 92*
**Mize**, Robert Herbert, Jr. 1907- *WhoRel 92, WhoWest 92*
**Mizejewski**, Gerald Jude 1939- *AmMWSc 92*
**Mizel**, Larry A. 1942- *WhoWest 92*
**Mizel**, Steven B 1947- *AmMWSc 92*
**Mizell**, Andrew Hooper, III 1926- *WhoFI 92*
**Mizell**, Louis Richard 1918- *AmMWSc 92*
**Mizell**, Merle 1927- *AmMWSc 92*
**Mizell**, Sherwin 1931- *AmMWSc 92*
**Mizell**, Wilmer David 1931- *WhoAmP 91*
**Mizer**, Richard Anthony 1952- *WhoWest 92*
**Mizere**, N. T. 1940- *IntWW 91*
**Mizeres**, Nicholas James 1924- *AmMWSc 92*
**Mizioch**, Gregory John 1952- *WhoWest 92*
**Miziolek**, Andrzej Wladyslaw 1950- *AmMWSc 92*
**Miziorko**, Henry Michael 1947- *AmMWSc 92*
**Mizma**, Edward John 1934- *AmMWSc 92*
**Mizner**, Wilson 1876-1933 *BenetAL 91*
**Mizoguchi**, Kenji 1898-1956 *FacFETw, IntDcF 2-2 [port]*
**Mizokawa**, Donald Tsuneo 1943- *WhoWest 92*
**Mizrahi**, Gerard 1952- *WhoFI 92*
**Mizrahi**, Isaac 1961- *CurBio 91 [port], News 91 [port]*
**Mizuguchi**, Norman 1939- *WhoAmP 91*
**Mizukami**, Hiroshi 1932- *AmMWSc 92*
**Mizuno**, Kiyoshi *IntWW 91*
**Mizuno**, Nobuko S 1916- *AmMWSc 92*
**Mizuno**, Nobuko Shimotori 1916- *WhoWest 92*
**Mizuno**, Seiichi 1905- *IntWW 91*
**Mizuno**, Shigeki 1936- *AmMWSc 92*
**Mizuno**, William George *AmMWSc 92*
**Mizushima**, Masataka 1923- *AmMWSc 92*
**Mizutani**, Satoshi 1937- *AmMWSc 92*
**Mizzell**, Mary Elizabeth 1952- *WhoRel 92*
**Mizzell**, William Clarence 1949- *WhoBlA 92*
**Mjolnir** *EncTR 91*
**Mjolsness**, Raymond C 1933- *AmMWSc 92*
**Mkapa**, Benjamin William 1938- *IntWW 91*
**Mkhatshwa**, Smangaliso 1939- *IntWW 91*
**Mkona**, Callisto Matekenya 1930- *Who 92*
**Mladenov**, Peter Toshev 1936- *IntWW 91*
**Mlekush**, Kenneth C 1938- *WhoIns 92*
**Mleziva**, Dennis John 1950- *WhoAmP 91*
**Mlinaric**, David 1939- *Who 92*
**Mlodozeniec**, Arthur Roman 1937- *AmMWSc 92*
**Mlotek**, Herman Victor 1922- *WhoMW 92*
**Mlsna**, Kathryn Kimura 1952- *WhoAmL 92*
**Mlsna**, Timothy Martin 1947- *WhoAmL 92*
**Mlynar**, Linda Herren *DrAPF 91*
**Mlynczak**, Tadeusz Witold 1934- *IntWW 91*
**Mnookin**, Robert Harris 1942- *WhoAmL 92*
**Mnookin**, Wendy M. *DrAPF 91*
**Mnuchin**, Robert E. *WhoFI 92*
**Mo Wenxiang** 1923- *IntWW 91*
**Mo**, Charles Tse Chin 1943- *AmMWSc 92*
**Mo**, Luke Wei 1934- *AmMWSc 92*
**Mo**, Timothy 1950- *ConNov 91*
**Mo**, Timothy 1953- *IntAu&W 91, WrDr 92*
**Mo**, Timothy Peter 1950- *Who 92*
**Moad**, M F 1928- *AmMWSc 92*
**Moaddeli**, Hoshang 1938- *WhoEnt 92*
**Moak**, Charles Dexter 1922- *AmMWSc 92*
**Moak**, James Emanuel 1916- *AmMWSc 92*
**Moak**, Robert Warren 1958- *WhoAmP 91*
**Moakley**, John Joseph 1927- *AlmAP 92 [port], WhoAmP 91*
**Moalla**, Mansour 1930- *IntWW 91*
**Moan**, Raymond Charles 1942- *WhoAmP 91*
**Moaney**, Eric R. 1934- *WhoBlA 92*
**Moat**, Albert Groombridge 1926- *AmMWSc 92*
**Moat**, Douglas Clarkson 1931- *WhoIns 92*
**Moat**, John 1936- *ConPo 91, IntAu&W 91, WrDr 92*
**Moate**, Roger Denis 1938- *Who 92*
**Moates**, G. Paul 1947- *WhoAmL 92*
**Moates**, Robert Franklin 1938- *AmMWSc 92*
**Moats**, Harold 1939- *WhoWest 92*
**Moats**, William Alden 1928- *AmMWSc 92*
**Moatts**, Morris 1930- *WhoAmP 91*
**Moavenzadeh**, Fred 1935- *AmMWSc 92*
**Moawad**, Atef H 1935- *AmMWSc 92*
**Moazami**, Ali 1961- *WhoFI 92*
**Moazed**, K L 1930- *AmMWSc 92*
**Mobarhan**, Sohrab 1941- *AmMWSc 92*
**Mobbs**, Nigel 1937- *IntWW 91, Who 92*
**Moberg**, David O. 1922- *WrDr 92*
**Moberg**, David Oscar 1922- *WhoMW 92, WhoRel 92*
**Moberg**, Dorothy Rood 1924- *WhoAmP 91*
**Moberg**, Gary Philip 1941- *AmMWSc 92*
**Moberg**, Vilhelm *BenetAL 91*
**Moberg**, William Karl 1948- *AmMWSc 92*
**Moberger**, George Carl 1925- *WhoAmL 92*
**Moberly**, Harry, Jr 1950- *WhoAmP 91*
**Moberly**, John 1925- *Who 92*
**Moberly**, John Campbell 1925- *IntWW 91*
**Moberly**, Linden Emery 1923- *WhoWest 92*
**Moberly**, Mervyn Eugene 1936- *WhoRel 92*
**Moberly**, Michael D. 1956- *WhoAmL 92*
**Moberly**, Patrick 1928- *Who 92*
**Moberly**, Patrick Hamilton 1928- *IntWW 91*
**Moberly**, Ralph M 1929- *AmMWSc 92*
**Moberly**, Richard James 1906- *Who 92*
**Moberly**, Robert Blakely 1941- *WhoFI 92*
**Moberly**, Stephen C 1941- *WhoAmP 91*
**Mobley**, Bert A *AmMWSc 92*
**Mobley**, Carroll Edward 1941- *AmMWSc 92*
**Mobley**, Charles Alfred 1943- *WhoAmP 91*
**Mobley**, Charles Lamar 1932- *WhoBlA 92*
**Mobley**, Clifton Arvil 1922- *WhoAmP 91*
**Mobley**, Curtis Dale 1947- *AmMWSc 92*
**Mobley**, Edward David 1932- *WhoFI 92*
**Mobley**, Emily Ruth *WhoMW 92*
**Mobley**, Emily Ruth 1942- *WhoBlA 92*
**Mobley**, Eugenia L. 1921- *WhoBlA 92*
**Mobley**, Forrest Causey, Jr. 1941- *WhoRel 92*
**Mobley**, George Melton, Jr. 1948- *WhoAmL 92*
**Mobley**, Hank 1930-1986 *NewAmDM*
**Mobley**, Jean Bellingrath 1927- *AmMWSc 92*
**Mobley**, Joan Thompson 1944- *WhoBlA 92*
**Mobley**, John Homer, II 1930- *WhoAmL 92, WhoFI 92*
**Mobley**, John O, Jr *WhoAmP 91*
**Mobley**, Jonniepat 1932- *WhoWest 92*
**Mobley**, Karen Ruth 1961- *WhoWest 92*
**Mobley**, Lenora Washington 1940- *WhoAmP 91*
**Mobley**, Mark 1964- *WhoEnt 92*
**Mobley**, Norma Mason Garland 1923- *WhoFI 92*
**Mobley**, Ralph Claude *AmMWSc 92*
**Mobley**, Richard Allan 1952- *WhoMW 92*
**Mobley**, Stacey J. 1945- *WhoBlA 92*
**Mobley**, Sybil C. 1925- *WhoBlA 92*
**Mobley**, Taze Russell, Jr. 1946- *WhoAmL 92*
**Mobraaten**, Larry Edward 1938- *AmMWSc 92*
**Moburg**, Kenneth Dean 1925- *WhoMW 92*
**Mobutu Sese Seko** 1930- *ConBlB 1 [port], FacFETw, IntWW 91*
**Mobyed**, Robert T 1943- *WhoIns 92*
**Mocabee**, James David 1958- *WhoAmP 91*
**Mocarski**, Richard Peter 1947- *WhoFI 92*
**Mocatta**, Alan Abraham d1990 *Who 92N*
**Moch**, Irving, Jr 1927- *AmMWSc 92*
**Moch**, Jules 1893-1985 *FacFETw*
**Moch**, Lawrence E. 1929- *WhoBlA 92*
**Moch**, Mary Inez 1943- *WhoMW 92, WhoRel 92*
**Moch**, Robert Gaston 1914- *WhoAmL 92*
**Mochalin**, Fyodor Ivanovich 1920- *IntWW 91*
**Mochan**, Eugene *AmMWSc 92*
**Mocharla**, Raman 1953- *AmMWSc 92, WhoMW 92*
**Mochary**, Mary Veronica 1942- *WhoFI 92*
**Mochel**, Jack McKinney 1939- *AmMWSc 92*
**Mochel**, Myron George 1905- *AmMWSc 92*
**Mochel**, Virgil Dale 1930- *AmMWSc 92*
**Mochizuki**, Diane Yukiko 1952- *AmMWSc 92*
**Mochon**, John 1958- *WhoMW 92*
**Mochrie**, Richard D 1928- *AmMWSc 92*
**Mocilnikar**, Frank Charles 1950- *WhoMW 92*
**Mociuk**, Yar W. 1927- *IntMPA 92*
**Mock**, Alois 1934- *IntWW 91*
**Mock**, David Clinton, Jr 1922- *AmMWSc 92*
**Mock**, Dean R *WhoAmP 91*
**Mock**, Douglas Wayne 1947- *AmMWSc 92*
**Mock**, Gordon Duane 1927- *AmMWSc 92*
**Mock**, James Allen 1953- *WhoMW 92*
**Mock**, James E. 1940- *WhoBlA 92*
**Mock**, James Joseph 1943- *AmMWSc 92*
**Mock**, James Richard 1951- *WhoFI 92*
**Mock**, John E 1925- *AmMWSc 92*
**Mock**, Lawrence Edward, Jr. 1946- *WhoFI 92*
**Mock**, Leilani Ann 1944- *WhoRel 92*
**Mock**, Orin Bailey 1938- *AmMWSc 92*
**Mock**, Patrick Joseph 1957- *WhoWest 92*
**Mock**, Rick Jim 1958- *WhoEnt 92*
**Mock**, Robert Claude 1928- *WhoFI 92*
**Mock**, Steven James 1934- *AmMWSc 92*
**Mock**, William L 1938- *AmMWSc 92*
**Mockett**, Alfred T. 1949- *WhoFI 92*
**Mockett**, Paul M 1936- *AmMWSc 92*
**Mockford**, Edward Lee 1930- *AmMWSc 92*
**Mockler**, Colman M, Jr. d1991 *NewYTBS 91 [port]*
**Mockler**, Edward Joseph 1954- *WhoFI 92*
**Mockler**, Franklin 1935- *WhoAmL 92*
**Mocko**, George Paul 1934- *WhoRel 92*
**Mockovak**, Paul William, II 1955- *WhoEnt 92*
**Mockrin**, Stephen Charles 1946- *AmMWSc 92*
**Mockros**, Lyle F 1933- *AmMWSc 92*
**Moctezuma** *HisDSpE*
**Moczulski**, Leszek 1930- *IntWW 91*
**Moczygemba**, George A 1939- *AmMWSc 92*
**Modabber**, Farrokh Z 1940- *AmMWSc 92*
**Modafferi**, Anthony Kenneth, III 1960- *WhoAmL 92*
**Modafferi**, Judy Hall 1943- *AmMWSc 92*
**Modai**, Itzhak 1926- *IntWW 91*
**Modak**, Arvind T *AmMWSc 92*
**Modak**, Ashok Trimbak 1946- *AmMWSc 92*
**Modarressi**, Taghi 1931- *ConAu 134*
**Moddel**, Garret R 1954- *AmMWSc 92*
**Modderman**, John Philip 1944- *AmMWSc 92*
**Mode**, Charles J 1927- *AmMWSc 92*
**Mode**, Paul J., Jr. 1938- *WhoAmL 92*
**Mode**, Vincent Alan 1940- *AmMWSc 92*
**Model**, Frank Steven 1942- *AmMWSc 92*
**Model**, Peter 1933- *AmMWSc 92*
**Model**, Walter 1891-1945 *EncTR 91 [port]*
**Model**, Walther 1891-1945 *FacFETw*
**Modell**, Arthur B. 1925- *WhoMW 92*
**Modell**, Jack Gary 1956- *WhoMW 92*
**Modell**, Jerome Herbert 1932- *AmMWSc 92*
**Modell**, Walter 1907- *AmMWSc 92*
**Moder**, Joseph J 1924- *AmMWSc 92*
**Modern Jazz Quartet** *NewAmDM*
**Moderow**, Joseph R. 1948- *WhoAmL 92*
**Moderson**, Christopher Paul 1959- *WhoMW 92*
**Modery**, Richard Gillman 1941- *WhoFI 92*
**Modesitt**, Donald Ernest 1936- *AmMWSc 92*
**Modesitt**, Ricky Wayne 1955- *WhoEnt 92*
**Modest**, Edward Julian 1923- *AmMWSc 92*
**Modeste**, Leon Edgar 1926- *WhoBlA 92*
**Modesto**, Phillip *WhoHisp 92*
**Modi**, V J 1930- *AmMWSc 92*
**Modi**, Vinay Kumar 1943- *IntWW 91*
**Modiano**, Patrick Jean 1945- *IntAu&W 91, IntWW 91*
**Modiano-Revah**, Manuel 1957- *WhoHisp 92*
**Modic**, Frank Joseph 1922- *AmMWSc 92*
**Modica**, Michael Angelo 1952- *WhoRel 92*
**Modica**, Steven Vincent 1961- *WhoAmL 92*
**Modie**, Ruth Rowell 1905- *WhoAmP 91*
**Modigliani**, Amedeo 1884-1920 *FacFETw*
**Modigliani**, Franco 1918- *IntWW 91, Who 92, WhoFI 92, WhoNob 90, WrDr 92*
**Modine**, Franklin Arthur 1936- *AmMWSc 92*
**Modine**, Matthew 1959- *IntMPA 92*
**Modisane**, Bloke 1923-1986 *LiExTwC*
**Modise**, Joe 1929- *IntWW 91*
**Modisette**, Jerry L 1934- *AmMWSc 92*
**Modjeska**, Helena 1840-1909 *DcAmImH*
**Modjeski**, Ralph 1861-1940 *DcTwDes, FacFETw*
**Modjtahedi**, Parviz M. 1939- *WhoFI 92*
**Modl**, Martha *IntWW 91*
**Modlin**, Herbert Charles 1913- *AmMWSc 92*
**Modlin**, Howard S. 1931- *WhoAmL 92, WhoFI 92*
**Modlin**, Irvin M 1946- *AmMWSc 92*
**Modlin**, Richard Frank 1937- *AmMWSc 92*

**Modrak,** John Bruce 1943- AmMWSc 92
**Modreski,** Peter John 1946- AmMWSc 92
**Modrey,** Joseph 1916- AmMWSc 92
**Modrich,** Paul L 1946- AmMWSc 92
**Modrow,** Hans 1928- IntWW 91
**Modrzakowski,** Malcolm Charles 1952- AmMWSc 92
**Modthryth** EncAmaz 91
**Modugno,** Victor Joseph 1949- WhoWest 92
**Modzelewski,** Kazimierz 1934- IntWW 91
**Moe,** Aaron Jay 1955- AmMWSc 92
**Moe,** Andrew Irving 1927- WhoWest 92
**Moe,** Chesney Rudolph 1908- AmMWSc 92
**Moe,** Christian H. 1929- WrDr 92
**Moe,** Christian Hollis 1929- WhoEnt 92
**Moe,** Dennis L 1917- AmMWSc 92
**Moe,** Donald Edward 1942 WhoFI 92
**Moe,** Donald M 1942- WhoAmP 91
**Moe,** George 1925- AmMWSc 92
**Moe,** George Cecil Rawle 1932- IntWW 91
**Moe,** George Wylbur 1942- AmMWSc 92
**Moe,** Gregory Robert 1956- AmMWSc 92
**Moe,** James Burton 1940- AmMWSc 92
**Moe,** Lawrence Henry 1917- WhoEnt 92
**Moe,** Maynard L 1935- AmMWSc 92
**Moe,** Michael K 1937- AmMWSc 92
**Moe,** Mildred Minasian 1929- AmMWSc 92
**Moe,** Orville Leroy 1936- WhoWest 92
**Moe,** Osborne Kenneth 1925- AmMWSc 92
**Moe,** Richard 1936- WhoAmP 91
**Moe,** Richard Palmer 1936- WhoAmL 92
**Moe,** Robert Anthony 1923- AmMWSc 92
**Moe,** Roger Deane 1944- WhoAmP 91
**Moe,** Thorvald 1940- IntWW 91
**Moeck,** Walter F. 1922- WhoEnt 92
**Moeckel,** Richard Thorpe 1952- WhoFI 92
**Moeckel,** W E 1922- AmMWSc 92
**Moedritzer,** Kurt 1929- AmMWSc 92, WhoMW 92
**Moehlman,** Patricia des Roses 1943- AmMWSc 92
**Moehlman,** Robert Stevens 1910- AmMWSc 92
**Moehlmann,** Nicholas Bruce 1938- WhoAmP 91
**Moehring,** Fred Adolph 1935- WhoFI 92
**Moehring,** Joan Marquart 1935- AmMWSc 92
**Moehring,** Thomas John 1936- AmMWSc 92
**Moehs,** Peter John 1940- AmMWSc 92
**Moeling,** Walter Goos, IV 1943- WhoAmL 92, WhoFI 92
**Moellenberg,** R D 1936- WhoAmP 91
**Moeller,** A. Diane 1935- WhoMW 92
**Moeller,** Achim Ferdinand Gerd 1942- WhoFI 92
**Moeller,** Arthur Charles 1919- AmMWSc 92
**Moeller,** Bernd 1931- IntWW 91
**Moeller,** Carl William, Jr 1924- AmMWSc 92
**Moeller,** Charles 1912-1986 DcEcMov
**Moeller,** D W 1927- AmMWSc 92
**Moeller,** David E. 1952- WhoWest 92
**Moeller,** Eileen DrAPF 91
**Moeller,** Elnora Frances 1948- WhoMW 92
**Moeller,** Floyd Douglas 1949- WhoAmL 92
**Moeller,** Henry William 1937- AmMWSc 92
**Moeller,** James WhoAmP 91
**Moeller,** James 1933- WhoAmL 92, WhoWest 92
**Moeller,** Jeanette 1926- WhoAmP 91
**Moeller,** Michael 1947- WhoAmP 91
**Moeller,** Michael W. 1953- WhoFI 92
**Moeller,** Peter H 1939- WhoIns 92
**Moeller,** Philip 1880-1958 BenetAL 91
**Moeller,** Philip Theodore 1946- WhoFI 92
**Moeller,** Philip Williams 1941- WhoFI 92
**Moeller,** Robert Charles 1954- WhoWest 92
**Moeller,** Robert Lynn 1955- WhoMW 92
**Moeller,** Theodore William 1943- AmMWSc 92
**Moeller van den Bruck,** Arthur 1876-1925 BiDExR, EncTR 91 [port]
**Moellering,** Richard William 1940- WhoFI 92
**Moellmann,** Gisela E Bielitz 1929- AmMWSc 92
**Moelter,** Gregory Martin 1919- AmMWSc 92
**Moen,** Allen LeRoy 1933- AmMWSc 92
**Moen,** Donne P. WhoFI 92
**Moen,** Rodney C 1937- WhoAmP 91
**Moen,** Rodney Charles 1937- WhoMW 92
**Moen,** Walter B 1920- AmMWSc 92
**Moench,** Robert Borden 1954- WhoEnt 92
**Moench,** Robert Hadley 1926- AmMWSc 92
**Moench,** Robert William 1927- WhoFI 92, WhoWest 92
**Moennig** NewAmDM
**Moens,** Peter B 1931- AmMWSc 92
**Moenssens,** Andre A. 1930- WrDr 92
**Moeran,** Edward Warner 1903- Who 92
**Moerbeek,** Stanley Leonard 1951- WhoWest 92
**Moerdani,** Leonardus Benjamin 1932- IntWW 91
**Moerdler,** Charles Gerard 1934- WhoAmL 92, WhoFI 92
**Moermond,** Curtis Roghair 1941- WhoRel 92
**Moermond,** Timothy Creighton 1947- AmMWSc 92
**Moerner,** William Esco 1953- AmMWSc 92
**Moersch,** Karl 1926- IntWW 91
**Moertel,** Charles George 1927- AmMWSc 92, IntWW 91
**Moertono,** Amir IntWW 91
**Moeschberger,** Melvin Lee 1940- AmMWSc 92
**Moesel,** Rodd Alan 1954- WhoAmP 91
**Moeslein,** Frank A. 1943- WhoFI 92
**Moessbauer,** Rudolf Ludwig 1929- WhoNob 90
**Moessinger,** David 1930- WhoEnt 92
**Moeves,** Edward Charles 1947- WhoMW 92
**Moevs,** Robert 1920- NewAmDM
**Moevs,** Robert Walter 1920- WhoEnt 92
**Mofenson,** David J. 1943- WhoAmL 92
**Mofenson,** David Joel 1943- WhoAmP 91
**Moffa,** David Joseph 1942- AmMWSc 92
**Moffa-White,** Andrea Marie 1949- AmMWSc 92
**Moffat,** Alexander 1943- TwCPaSc
**Moffat,** Anthony Frederick John 1943- AmMWSc 92
**Moffat,** Cameron 1929- Who 92
**Moffat,** Donald 1930- IntMPA 92
**Moffat,** Gwen 1924- IntAu&W 91, WrDr 92
**Moffat,** James 1921- AmMWSc 92
**Moffat,** John Blain 1930- AmMWSc 92
**Moffat,** John Keith 1943- AmMWSc 92
**Moffat,** John Lawrence 1916- WrDr 92
**Moffat,** John William 1932- AmMWSc 92
**Moffat,** Kenneth M 1932- WhoIns 92
**Moffat,** MaryBeth 1951- WhoFI 92
**Moffat,** Richard Howe 1931- WhoAmL 92
**Moffat,** Robert J 1927- AmMWSc 92
**Moffatt,** Betty Clare 1936- IntAu&W 91
**Moffatt,** David John 1939- AmMWSc 92
**Moffatt,** David Lloyd AmMWSc 92
**Moffatt,** Henry Keith 1935- IntWW 91, Who 92
**Moffatt,** Hugh McCulloch, Jr. 1933- WhoWest 92
**Moffatt,** John 1922- IntWW 91, Who 92
**Moffatt,** John Gilbert 1930- AmMWSc 92
**Moffatt,** John Myrick 1940- WhoFI 92
**Moffatt,** Joyce Anne 1936- WhoEnt 92, WhoWest 92
**Moffatt,** Katy 1950- WhoEnt 92
**Moffatt,** Robert Henry 1930- WhoWest 92
**Moffatt,** William Craig 1933- AmMWSc 92
**Moffeit,** Kenneth Charles 1939- AmMWSc 92
**Moffeit,** Tony DrAPF 91
**Moffeit,** Tony A IntAu&W 91
**Moffet,** Alan Theodore 1936- AmMWSc 92
**Moffet,** Hugh L 1932- AmMWSc 92
**Moffet,** Kenneth William 1959- WhoAmL 92
**Moffet,** Robert Bruce AmMWSc 92
**Moffett,** Anthony 1944- WhoAmP 91
**Moffett,** Benjamin Charles, Jr 1923- AmMWSc 92
**Moffett,** Cleveland 1863-1926 ScFEYrs
**Moffett,** David Franklin, Jr 1947- AmMWSc 92
**Moffett,** Frank Cardwell 1931- WhoFI 92, WhoWest 92
**Moffett,** Jonathan Phillip 1954- WhoEnt 92, WhoWest 92
**Moffett,** Judith DrAPF 91
**Moffett,** Judith 1942- ConPo 91, IntAu&W 91, TwCSFW 91, WrDr 92
**Moffett,** Robert Bruce 1914- AmMWSc 92
**Moffett,** Samuel Hugh 1916- WhoRel 92, WrDr 92
**Moffett,** Stacia Brandon AmMWSc 92
**Moffett,** William Andrew 1933- WhoWest 92
**Moffie,** Robert Wayne 1950- WhoWest 92
**Moffit,** William C. 1925- WhoEnt 92
**Moffitt,** Dale Edwin 1934- WhoEnt 92
**Moffitt,** Donald Eugene 1932- WhoWest 92
**Moffitt,** Elvira Worth Jackson Walker 1836-1930 DcNCBi 4
**Moffitt,** Emerson Amos 1924- AmMWSc 92
**Moffitt,** H Lee 1941- WhoAmP 91
**Moffitt,** Harold Roger 1934- AmMWSc 92
**Moffitt,** John Jacob 1930- WhoEnt 92
**Moffitt,** Karin Anderson 1963- WhoAmL 92
**Moffitt,** Robert Allan 1918- AmMWSc 92
**Moffitt,** Terry Ervin WhoRel 92
**Moffo,** Anna IntWW 91
**Moffo,** Anna 1927- WhoEnt 92
**Moffo,** Anna 1935- NewAmDM
**Mofford,** Rose 1922- IntWW 91, WhoAmP 91, WhoWest 92
**Mofield,** William Ray 1921- WhoEnt 92
**Mofolo,** Thomas 1876-1948 BlkLC [port]
**Mog,** David Michael 1942- AmMWSc 92
**Mogab,** Nancy Robin 1956- WhoAmL 92
**Mogabgab,** William Joseph 1921- AmMWSc 92
**Mogae,** Festus Gontebanye 1939- IntWW 91
**Mogel,** William Allen 1942- WhoAmL 92
**Mogensen,** Borge 1914-1972 DcTwDes
**Mogensen,** Hans Lloyd 1938- AmMWSc 92
**Mogenson,** Gordon James 1931- AmMWSc 92
**Moger,** Art IntMPA 92
**Moger,** Stanley H. 1936- IntMPA 92
**Mogerman,** Veronica Linda 1954- WhoFI 92
**Mogford,** James A 1930- AmMWSc 92
**Mogg** Who 92
**Mogg,** Donald Whitehead 1924- WhoWest 92
**Mogg,** John 1913- Who 92
**Mogg,** John Frederick 1943- Who 92
**Moggach,** Deborah 1948- WrDr 92
**Moggie,** Leo 1941- IntWW 91
**Moggio,** Mary Virginia 1947- AmMWSc 92
**Moggridge,** Harry Traherne 1936- Who 92
**Moghadam,** Omid A 1968- AmMWSc 92
**Moghissi,** Kamran S 1925- AmMWSc 92, WhoMW 92
**Mogil,** H Michael 1945- AmMWSc 92
**Moglen,** Eben 1959- WhoAmL 92
**Moglen,** Leland Louis 1944- WhoAmL 92
**Moglia,** James John 1959- WhoFI 92
**Mogol,** Alan Jay 1946- WhoAmL 92
**Mogren,** Edwin Walfred 1921- AmMWSc 92
**Mogro-Campero,** Antonio 1940- AmMWSc 92
**Mogrovejo,** Toribio Alfonso de 1538-1606 HisDSpE
**Mogulescu,** Joseph DcTwDes
**Mogulescu,** Maurice DcTwDes
**Mogulof,** Melvin Bernard 1926- WhoWest 92
**Mogus,** Mary Ann AmMWSc 92
**Mogwe,** Archibald Mooketsa 1921- IntWW 91
**Mogyordy,** Laura Jane 1960- WhoRel 92
**Mohabir,** Vishundyal Ramotar 1951- WhoWest 92
**Mohacsi,** Erno 1929- AmMWSc 92
**Mohal,** Brij Raj 1961- WhoMW 92
**Mohale,** Albert Steerforth 1928- IntWW 91
**Mohamad,** Encik Mustaffa Bin 1941- IntWW 91
**Mohamed,** Aly Hamed 1924- AmMWSc 92
**Mohamed,** Farghalli Abdelrahman 1943- AmMWSc 92
**Mohamed,** Gerald R., Jr. 1948- WhoBlA 92
**Mohamed,** N P 1929- IntAu&W 91
**Mohamed,** Ollie 1925- WhoAmP 91
**Mohamed Ali,** Ibrahim 1932- Who 92
**Mohamed Kamil,** Abdallah 1936- IntWW 91
**Mohammad,** Najand 1955- WhoFI 92
**Mohammad,** Nazar 1935- IntWW 91
**Mohammad,** Syed Fazal 1942- AmMWSc 92
**Mohammed Sidi Ibrahim Bassiri** HisDSpE
**Mohammed Zahir Shah** 1914- IntWW 91
**Mohammed,** Ali Mahdi IntWW 91
**Mohammed,** Amadu Nayaya 1935- IntWW 91
**Mohammed,** Auyuab 1928- AmMWSc 92
**Mohammed,** Kamaluddin 1927- IntWW 91
**Mohammed,** Kasheed 1930- AmMWSc 92
**Mohan,** Arthur G 1935- AmMWSc 92
**Mohan,** Chandra 1950- AmMWSc 92
**Mohan,** D. Mike 1945- WhoWest 92
**Mohan,** J C, Jr 1921- AmMWSc 92
**Mohan,** Narendra 1946- AmMWSc 92
**Mohan,** Prem 1954- AmMWSc 92
**Mohan,** Ramesh 1920- IntWW 91
**Mohan,** Subburaman 1951- WhoWest 92
**Mohan,** Tungesh Nath 1949- WhoEnt 92
**Mohan,** V. Joseph S. WhoWest 92
**Mohan,** William F 1943- WhoAmP 91
**Mohanakumar,** Thalachallour AmMWSc 92
**Mohandas,** Thuluvancheri 1946- AmMWSc 92
**Mohanti,** Prafulla 1936- ConAu 134
**Mohanty,** Ganesh Prasad 1934- AmMWSc 92
**Mohanty,** Gopal 1933- AmMWSc 92
**Mohanty,** Sashi B 1932- AmMWSc 92
**Mohapatra,** Pramoda Kumar 1955- AmMWSc 92
**Mohapatra,** Rabindra Nath 1944- AmMWSc 92
**Mohar,** John 1949- WhoAmP 91
**Mohasseb,** Saeed 1960- WhoFI 92
**Mohat,** John Theodore 1924- AmMWSc 92
**Mohberg,** Joyce 1931- AmMWSc 92
**Mohberg,** Noel Ross 1939- AmMWSc 92, WhoMW 92
**Mohel,** Sidney Karl 1956- WhoAmL 92
**Mohelnitzky,** Gerald J 1942- WhoIns 92
**Mohen,** Peter James 1947- WhoEnt 92
**Moher,** Francis Anthony Peter 1955- ConAu 133
**Moher,** Frank ConAu 133
**Mohieddin,** Ahmed Fuad 1926-1984 FacFETw
**Mohieddin,** Zakaria 1918- IntWW 91
**Mohilner,** David Morris 1930- AmMWSc 92
**Mohiuddin,** A. H. G. 1940- IntWW 91
**Mohiuddin,** Syed M 1934- AmMWSc 92
**Mohl,** Anthony Steven 1961- WhoFI 92
**Mohl,** Ruth 1891- IntAu&W 91
**Mohla,** Suresh 1943- AmMWSc 92
**Mohlajee,** Prem N. 1935- WhoMW 92
**Mohlenbrock,** Robert H, Jr 1931- AmMWSc 92
**Mohlenkamp,** Marvin Joseph, Jr 1940- AmMWSc 92
**Mohler,** Irvin C, Jr 1925- AmMWSc 92
**Mohler,** James Aylward 1923- IntAu&W 91, WhoMW 92, WhoRel 92, WrDr 92
**Mohler,** James Dawson 1926- AmMWSc 92
**Mohler,** James William 1955- WhoRel 92, WhoWest 92
**Mohler,** Johann Adam 1796-1838 EncEarC
**Mohler,** John George 1932- AmMWSc 92
**Mohler,** Orren 1908- AmMWSc 92
**Mohler,** Richard Albert, Jr. 1959- WhoRel 92
**Mohler,** Ronald Rutt 1931- AmMWSc 92
**Mohler,** Stanley Ross 1927- AmMWSc 92
**Mohler,** Terence John WhoMW 92
**Mohler,** William C 1927- AmMWSc 92
**Mohlke,** Byron Henry 1938- AmMWSc 92
**Mohmand,** Abdul Ahad 1959- FacFETw
**Mohn,** James Frederic 1922- AmMWSc 92
**Mohn,** Melvin P 1926- AmMWSc 92
**Mohn,** Reinhard 1921- IntWW 91
**Mohn,** Walter Rosing 1948- AmMWSc 92
**Mohnen,** Volker A 1937- AmMWSc 92
**Mohney,** Nell W. 1921- WhoRel 92
**Mohney,** Ralph Wilson 1918- WhoRel 92
**Moholland,** Fred W WhoAmP 91
**Moholy,** Noel Francis 1916- WhoRel 92, WhoWest 92
**Moholy-Nagy,** Laszlo 1895-1946 DcTwDes
**Moholy-Nagy,** Lazlo 1895-1946 FacFETw
**Mohorita,** Vasil 1952- IntWW 91
**Mohos,** Steven Charles 1918- AmMWSc 92
**Mohr,** Anthony James 1947- WhoAmL 92
**Mohr,** Bill DrAPF 91
**Mohr,** Charles Theodore 1824-1901 BiInAmS
**Mohr,** Charlotte Lorraine 1922- WhoAmP 91
**Mohr,** Cristina A. 1956- WhoFI 92
**Mohr,** David Allen 1950- WhoRel 92
**Mohr,** Diane Louise 1951- WhoBlA 92
**Mohr,** Ellen G. 1942- WhoMW 92
**Mohr,** James LeGrand 1950- WhoMW 92
**Mohr,** Jay Preston 1937- AmMWSc 92
**Mohr,** Jeffrey Dignan 1960- WhoFI 92
**Mohr,** Jeffrey Jon 1947- WhoRel 92
**Mohr,** Jeffrey Thomas 1950- WhoFI 92
**Mohr,** John Luther 1911- AmMWSc 92, WhoWest 92
**Mohr,** John Richard 1944- WhoMW 92
**Mohr,** Karen 1963- WhoMW 92
**Mohr,** Kimberley Kelley 1959- WhoAmL 92
**Mohr,** Milton Ernst 1915- AmMWSc 92
**Mohr,** Nicholasa 1935- Au&Arts 8 [port], HanAmWH, WhoHisp 92
**Mohr,** Paul B. 1931- WhoBlA 92
**Mohr,** Raymond Phillip 1959- WhoMW 92
**Mohr,** Roger John 1931- WhoFI 92
**Mohr,** Scott Chalmers 1940- AmMWSc 92
**Mohr,** Selby 1918- WhoWest 92
**Mohr,** Siegfried Heinrich 1930- WhoWest 92
**Mohr,** Steffen 1942- IntAu&W 91
**Mohr,** Steven August 1955- WhoRel 92
**Mohraz,** Bijan 1937- AmMWSc 92
**Mohrdick,** Eunice Marie WhoWest 92

**Mohrenweiser**, Harvey W. 1940- *WhoWest 92*
**Mohrenweiser**, Harvey Walter 1940- *AmMWSc 92*
**Mohrig**, Jerry R 1936- *AmMWSc 92*
**Mohring**, Herbert 1928- *WhoFI 92, WhoMW 92*
**Mohrland**, J Scott 1950- *AmMWSc 92*
**Mohrman**, Harold W 1917- *AmMWSc 92*
**Mohrmann**, Corinne Marie 1944- *WhoWest 92*
**Mohrt**, Michel 1914- *IntAu&W 91, IntWW 91*
**Mohs**, Frederic Edward 1910- *AmMWSc 92, WhoMW 92*
**Mohsenin**, Nuri N 1923- *AmMWSc 92*
**Mohtadi**, Farhang 1926- *AmMWSc 92*
**Mohtashemi**, Ali Akbar 1946- *IntWW 91*
**Mohyeddin**, Zia 1931- *Who 92*
**Moi**, Daniel 1924- *ConBlB 1 [port]*
**Moi**, Daniel arap 1924- *IntWW 91, Who 92*
**Moilanen**, Robert Dean 1938- *WhoAmL 92*
**Moilanen**, Thomas Alfred 1944- *WhoFI 92, WhoMW 92*
**Moinet**, Eric Emil 1952- *WhoFI 92*
**Moinot**, Pierre 1920- *IntWW 91*
**Moiola**, Richard James 1937- *AmMWSc 92*
**Moir**, David Chandler 1947- *AmMWSc 92*
**Moir**, Edward 1932- *WhoIns 92*
**Moir**, Ernest Ian Royds 1925- *Who 92*
**Moir**, Guthrie 1917- *Who 92*
**Moir**, James 1710?-1767 *DcNCBi 4*
**Moir**, James William Charles 1941- *Who 92*
**Moir**, Kevin Scott 1955- *WhoWest 92*
**Moir**, Ralph Wayne 1940- *AmMWSc 92*
**Moir**, Robert Young 1920- *AmMWSc 92*
**Moir**, Ronald Brown, Jr 1953- *AmMWSc 92*
**Moir Carey**, D. M. *Who 92*
**Moira**, Gerald 1867-1959 *TwCPaSc*
**Moise**, Edwin Evariste 1918- *AmMWSc 92*
**Moise**, Leslie 1959- *WhoRel 92*
**Moise**, Mary 1850-1930 *RelLAm 91*
**Moise**, Nancy Sydney 1954- *AmMWSc 92*
**Moise**, Penina 1797-1880 *BenetAL 91*
**Moise**, Robert Christian 1960- *WhoFI 92*
**Moiseenko**, Yevsey Yevseevich 1916- *SovUnBD*
**Moiseev**, Igor' Aleksandrovich 1906- *SovUnBD*
**Moiseev**, Mikhail Alekseevich 1939- *SovUnBD*
**Moiseiwitsch**, Benjamin Lawrence 1927- *IntWW 91, Who 92*
**Moiseiwitsch**, Benno 1890-1963 *FacFETw*
**Moiseiwitsch**, Tanya 1914- *Who 92*
**Moiseyev**, Alexis N 1932- *AmMWSc 92*
**Moiseyev**, Igor Aleksandrovich 1906- *IntWW 91*
**Moiseyev**, Igor Alexandrovich 1906- *FacFETw*
**Moiseyev**, Mikhail 1939- *IntWW 91*
**Moiseyev**, Nikolay Andreyevich 1934- *IntWW 91*
**Moiseyeva**, Olga Nikolayevna 1928- *IntWW 91*
**Moison**, Robert Leon 1929- *AmMWSc 92*
**Moissan**, Ferdinand Frederick Henri 1852-1907 *WhoNob 90*
**Moissides-Hines**, Lydia Elizabeth 1948- *AmMWSc 92*
**Moiz**, Syed Abdul 1937- *AmMWSc 92*
**Mojica**, Aurora 1939- *WhoHisp 92*
**Mojica-a**, Tobias 1943- *AmMWSc 92*
**Mojonnier**, Joyce F 1943- *WhoAmP 91*
**Mojsov**, Lazar 1920- *IntWW 91*
**Mojtabai**, A.G. *DrAPF 91*
**Mok**, Carson Kwok-Chi 1932- *WhoFI 92*
**Mok**, Machteld Cornelia 1947- *AmMWSc 92*
**Mokadam**, Anita Raghunathrao 1962- *WhoMW 92*
**Mokadam**, Raghunath G 1923- *AmMWSc 92*
**Mokae**, Zakes 1935- *IntMPA 92*
**Mokama**, Moleleki Didwell 1933- *Who 92*
**Mokanu**, Aleksandr Aleksandrovich 1934- *IntWW 91, SovUnBD*
**Moke**, Charles Burdette 1910- *AmMWSc 92*
**Mokhanto**, Philip Monyane 1946- *IntWW 91*
**Mokhayesh**, Carl 1941- *WhoMW 92*
**Mokhtari**, Manouchehr 1955- *WhoFI 92*
**Mokler**, Brian Victor 1936- *AmMWSc 92*
**Mokler**, Corwin Morris 1925- *AmMWSc 92*
**Mokma**, Delbert Lewis 1942- *AmMWSc 92*
**Mokodopo**, Jean-Paul *IntWW 91*
**Mokoroane**, Morena Moletsane 1932- *IntWW 91*
**Mokotoff**, Michael 1939- *AmMWSc 92*
**Mokrasch**, Lewis Carl 1930- *AmMWSc 92*
**Mokrosch**, Reinhold Erich 1940- *WhoRel 92*
**Mokrzynski**, Jerzy Boguslaw 1909- *IntWW 91*
**Mokuku**, Philip Stanley *WhoRel 92*
**Mokulis**, Paula 1947- *WhoEnt 92*
**Mol**, Johannis J. 1922- *WrDr 92*
**Mola**, Richard Arthur 1936- *WhoAmP 91*
**Molan**, John Edward 1927- *WhoRel 92*
**Molan**, Richard Edward 1947- *WhoAmL 92*
**Moland**, Willie C. 1931- *WhoBlA 92*
**Molander**, Gustaf 1888-1973 *IntDcF 2-2*
**Molapo**, Charles Dube 1918- *IntWW 91*
**Molapo**, Mooki Motsarapane 1928- *Who 92*
**Molapo**, Mooki Vitus 1937- *IntWW 91*
**Molau**, Gunther Erich 1932- *AmMWSc 92*
**Molberg**, Maxine 1921- *WhoAmP 91*
**Molchior**, Carol Joyce 1953- *WhoAmL 92*
**Mold**, Carolyn *AmMWSc 92*
**Mold**, James Davis 1920- *AmMWSc 92*
**Moldanado**, Swarnalatha Adusumilli *WhoWest 92*
**Moldave**, Kivie 1923- *AmMWSc 92*
**Moldaw**, Stuart G. 1927- *WhoWest 92*
**Moldawer**, Marc 1922- *AmMWSc 92*
**Molday**, Robert S 1943- *AmMWSc 92*
**Molde**, David Lawrence 1959- *WhoWest 92*
**Moldea**, Dan E. 1950- *WrDr 92*
**Moldenhauer**, Judith A. 1951- *WhoEnt 92*
**Moldenhauer**, Paul 1876-1947 *EncTR 91*
**Moldenhauer**, Ralph Roy 1935- *AmMWSc 92*
**Moldenhauer**, William Calvin 1923- *AmMWSc 92*
**Molder**, S 1935- *AmMWSc 92*
**Molders**, Werner 1913-1941 *EncTR 91 [port]*
**Moldo**, Julie G. 1949- *WhoEnt 92*
**Moldon**, Peter Leonard 1937- *IntAu&W 91*
**Moldovan**, Roman 1911- *IntWW 91*
**Moldover**, Michael Robert 1940- *AmMWSc 92*
**Moldt**, Ewald 1927- *IntWW 91*
**Mole**, David Richard Penton 1943- *Who 92*
**Mole**, John 1941- *ConPo 91, WrDr 92*
**Mole**, John Douglas 1941- *IntAu&W 91*
**Mole**, John Edwin 1944- *AmMWSc 92*
**Mole**, Miff 1898-1961 *NewAmDM*
**Mole**, Paul Angelo 1938- *AmMWSc 92*
**Molecke**, Martin A 1945- *AmMWSc 92*
**Molefe**, Popo Simon 1952- *IntWW 91*
**Molek**, Mary 1909-1982 *DcAmImH*
**Molen**, Gerald Robert 1935- *WhoEnt 92*
**Molenbeek**, Robert Gerrit 1944- *WhoMW 92*
**Molenda**, John R 1931- *AmMWSc 92*
**Molenda**, Linda Marie 1957- *WhoMW 92*
**Molenda**, Michael Charles 1956- *WhoEnt 92*
**Molendorp**, Dayton H 1947- *WhoIns 92*
**Molenkamp**, Charles Richard 1941- *AmMWSc 92, WhoWest 92*
**Moler**, Cleve B 1939- *AmMWSc 92*
**Moler**, Donald Lewis 1918- *WhoMW 92*
**Moles**, Randall Carl 1946- *WhoMW 92*
**Molesworth** *Who 92*
**Molesworth**, Viscount 1907- *Who 92*
**Molesworth**, Allen Henry Neville 1931- *Who 92*
**Molesworth**, Charles *DrAPF 91*
**Molesworth**, Charles 1941- *WrDr 92*
**Molesworth**, Ted Allen, II 1954- *WhoAmP 91*
**Molesworth-St Aubyn**, Arscott 1926- *Who 92*
**Molette**, Barbara J. 1940- *WhoBlA 92*
**Molette**, Carlton Woodard, II 1939- *WhoBlA 92*
**Molette**, Willie L. 1919- *WhoBlA 92*
**Moley**, Raymond 1886-1975 *FacFETw*
**Molfese**, Dennis Lee 1946- *WhoMW 92*
**Molgaard**, Johannes 1936- *AmMWSc 92*
**Molhave**, Lars 1944- *AmMWSc 92*
**Molho**, Lazaros Errikos 1953- *WhoFI 92*
**Moliere**, Jeffrey Michael 1948- *WhoMW 92*
**Moliga**, Letalu M *WhoAmP 91*
**Molin**, Adrian Leopold 1880-1942 *BiDExR*
**Molin**, Charles *SmATA 68*
**Molin**, Peggy Ann 1926- *WhoAmP 91*
**Molin**, Rune 1931- *IntWW 91*
**Molin**, Yuriy Nikolaevich 1934- *IntWW 91*
**Molina**, Alfred 1953- *IntMPA 92*
**Molina**, Carla Maria 1965- *WhoWest 92*
**Molina**, Carlos M. 1940- *WhoEnt 92*
**Molina**, David Jude 1954- *WhoHisp 92*
**Molina**, Enrique 1910- *ConSpAP*
**Molina**, Gloria 1948- *NewYTBS 91 [port], WhoAmP 91, WhoHisp 92*
**Molina**, J. Ernesto 1935- *WhoHisp 92*
**Molina**, John Charles 1929- *WhoWest 92*
**Molina**, John Francis 1950- *AmMWSc 92*
**Molina**, Jose Efren 1929- *WhoHisp 92*
**Molina**, Julio Alfredo 1948- *WhoHisp 92*
**Molina**, Magdalena T. 1928- *WhoHisp 92*
**Molina**, Maria Christine 1945- *WhoHisp 92*
**Molina**, Mario Jose 1943- *AmMWSc 92*
**Molina**, Matilda *WhoAmP 91*
**Molina**, Pedro 1777-1854 *HisDSpE*
**Molina**, Randolph John 1951- *AmMWSc 92*
**Molina**, Robert 1951- *WhoHisp 92*
**Molina**, Steve 1957- *WhoHisp 92*
**Molina**, William Henry 1962- *WhoEnt 92*
**Molina Barraza**, Arturo Armando 1927- *IntWW 91*
**Molinari**, Guy Victor 1928- *WhoAmP 91*
**Molinari**, John A *AmMWSc 92*
**Molinari**, Pietro Filippo 1923- *AmMWSc 92*
**Molinari**, Ricardo E. 1898- *IntWW 91*
**Molinari**, Robert James 1952- *AmMWSc 92*
**Molinari**, Susan 1958- *AlmAP 92 [port], WhoAmP 91*
**Molinari**, William R. *WhoFI 92*
**Molinari-Pradelli**, Francesco 1911- *NewAmDM*
**Molinaro**, Edouard 1928- *IntMPA 92*
**Molinaro**, Thomas Edward 1957- *WhoWest 92*
**Molinaro**, Ursule *DrAPF 91*
**Molinder**, John Irving 1941- *AmMWSc 92*
**Moline**, Harold Emil 1939- *AmMWSc 92*
**Moline**, Jack Louis 1952- *WhoRel 92*
**Moline**, Sheldon Walter 1931- *AmMWSc 92*
**Moline**, Waldemar John 1934- *AmMWSc 92*
**Molines**, Joseph S. *WhoHisp 92*
**Molineux**, Roland Burnham 1866-1917 *BiInAmS*
**Molinoff**, Perry Brown 1940- *AmMWSc 92*
**Molins**, Lorraine 1953- *TwCPaSc*
**Molis**, Todd Alan 1947- *WhoMW 92*
**Molitch**, Mark E 1943- *AmMWSc 92*
**Molitor**, Edouard 1931- *Who 92*
**Molitor**, Margaret Anne 1920- *WhoRel 92*
**Molitor**, Thomas R. 1957- *WhoAmL 92*
**Molitoris**, Bruce Albert 1951- *WhoWest 92*
**Molk**, Ulrich 1937- *IntWW 91*
**Moll Cutpurse** *EncAmaz 91*
**Moll**, Albert James 1937- *AmMWSc 92*
**Moll**, David Carter 1948- *WhoFI 92*
**Moll**, Edward Owen 1939- *AmMWSc 92*
**Moll**, Gary Daniel 1950- *WhoMW 92*
**Moll**, Harold Wesbrook 1914- *AmMWSc 92*
**Moll**, John Edgar 1934- *WhoFI 92*
**Moll**, John L 1921- *AmMWSc 92*
**Moll**, Jonathan Lawrence 1958- *WhoAmL 92*
**Moll**, Kenneth Leon 1932- *AmMWSc 92*
**Moll**, Kurt 1938- *IntWW 91, NewAmDM*
**Moll**, Magnus 1928- *AmMWSc 92*
**Moll**, Patricia Peyser 1946- *AmMWSc 92*
**Moll**, Richard A 1935- *AmMWSc 92*
**Moll**, Robert Harry 1927- *AmMWSc 92*
**Moll**, Russell Addison 1946- *AmMWSc 92*
**Moll**, William Francis, Jr 1931- *AmMWSc 92*
**Mollard**, Emile d1991 *NewYTBS 91*
**Mollard**, John D 1924- *AmMWSc 92*
**Mollat du Jourdin**, Michel Jacques 1911- *IntWW 91*
**Molldrem**, Mark Jerome 1947- *WhoRel 92*
**Mollemann**, Jurgen W. 1945- *IntWW 91*
**Mollen**, Robert Paul 1955- *WhoAmL 92*
**Mollenauer**, Linn F 1937- *AmMWSc 92*
**Mollenhoff**, Clark R. 1921-1991 *ConAu 133, CurBio 91N, NewYTBS 91*
**Mollenkamp**, Gayle L *WhoAmP 91*
**Mollenkopf**, Janet Arlene 1931- *WhoAmP 91*
**Mollenkott**, Virginia Ramey 1932- *IntAu&W 91, WrDr 92*
**Moller**, Erwin 1939- *IntWW 91*
**Moller**, Hans Bjerrum 1932- *IntWW 91*
**Moller**, Karlind Theodore 1942- *AmMWSc 92*
**Moller**, Louis C 1943- *WhoIns 92*
**Moller**, Maersk Mc-Kinney 1913- *IntWW 91*
**Moller**, Peter 1941- *AmMWSc 92*
**Moller**, Peter C 1938- *AmMWSc 92*
**Moller**, Raymond William 1920- *AmMWSc 92*
**Moller**, William Richard, Jr. 1941- *WhoFI 92*
**Mollere**, Phillip David 1944- *AmMWSc 92*
**Molles**, Manuel Carl, Jr 1948- *AmMWSc 92*
**Mollet**, Guy 1905-1975 *FacFETw*
**Mollhausen**, Heinrich Balduin 1825-1905 *BenetAL 91*
**Mollica**, Joseph Anthony 1940- *AmMWSc 92*
**Mollica**, Santo 1958- *WhoEnt 92*
**Mollicone**, Henry Joseph 1946- *WhoEnt 92*
**Mollin**, Douglas Edward 1962- *WhoFI 92*
**Mollin**, Richard Anthony 1947- *AmMWSc 92*
**Molling**, Charles Francis 1940- *WhoAmL 92*
**Mollinger**, Judith Ellen 1943- *WhoAmL 92*
**Mollison**, Patrick Loudon 1914- *IntWW 91, Who 92*
**Mollner**, Frederick Richard 1946- *WhoWest 92*
**Mollo**, Joe Kaibe 1944- *IntWW 91*
**Mollo**, Joseph Molelekoa Kaibe 1944- *Who 92*
**Mollo-Christensen**, Erik Leonard 1923- *AmMWSc 92*
**Mollohan**, Alan B. 1943- *AlmAP 92 [port], WhoAmP 91*
**Mollohan**, Robert H 1909- *WhoAmP 91*
**Mollow**, Benjamin R 1938- *AmMWSc 92*
**Molloy** *Who 92*
**Molloy**, Baron 1918- *Who 92*
**Molloy**, Andrew A 1930- *AmMWSc 92*
**Molloy**, Arthur Eugene 1955- *WhoFI 92*
**Molloy**, Charles Thomas 1914- *AmMWSc 92*
**Molloy**, James Haggin 1933- *WhoAmP 91*
**Molloy**, M. 1917- *WrDr 92*
**Molloy**, Marilyn 1931- *AmMWSc 92*
**Molloy**, Michael 1917- *IntAu&W 91*
**Molloy**, Michael John 1940- *IntAu&W 91, Who 92*
**Molloy**, Neil 1948- *WhoAmP 91*
**Molloy**, Robert 1906-1977 *BenetAL 91*
**Molloy**, Robert Jacques 1964- *WhoFI 92*
**Molloy**, Robert M. 1936- *IntWW 91*
**Molloy**, Robert Stephen 1959- *WhoAmL 92*
**Mollura**, Carlos A. 1934- *WhoHisp 92*
**Mollwo**, Erich 1909- *IntWW 91*
**Molly Pitcher** *BenetAL 91*
**Molly Pitcher** 1760-1843 *EncAmaz 91*
**Molmud**, Paul 1923- *AmMWSc 92*
**Molnar**, Charles Edwin 1935- *AmMWSc 92*
**Molnar**, Daniel Edwin 1949- *WhoMW 92*
**Molnar**, Ferenc 1878-1952 *LiExTwC*
**Molnar**, George D 1922- *AmMWSc 92*
**Molnar**, George William 1914- *AmMWSc 92*
**Molnar**, Imre 1906- *AmMWSc 92*
**Molnar**, Janos 1927- *AmMWSc 92*
**Molnar**, Lawrence 1927- *WhoAmL 92*
**Molnar**, Michael Robert 1945- *AmMWSc 92*
**Molnar**, Peter Hale 1943- *AmMWSc 92*
**Molnar**, Stephen P 1935- *AmMWSc 92*
**Molnar**, Zelma Villanyi 1931- *AmMWSc 92*
**Molner**, Mary E *WhoAmP 91*
**Molnia**, Bruce Franklin 1945- *AmMWSc 92*
**Molof**, Alan H 1928- *AmMWSc 92*
**Molofsky**, Merle *DrAPF 91*
**Molom**, Tsendiyn 1932- *IntWW 91*
**Molomjamts**, Demchigiyn 1920- *IntWW 91*
**Moloney**, John Bromley 1924- *AmMWSc 92*
**Moloney**, Michael J 1936- *AmMWSc 92*
**Moloney**, Michael R 1941- *WhoAmP 91*
**Moloney**, Thomas Joseph 1952- *WhoAmL 92*
**Moloney**, Thomas W *AmMWSc 92*
**Moloney**, Thomas Walter 1946- *IntWW 91*
**Moloney**, William Curry 1907- *AmMWSc 92*
**Molony**, Michael Janssens, Jr. 1922- *WhoAmL 92, WhoFI 92*
**Molony**, Thomas Desmond *Who 92*
**Molotov**, Viacheslav Mikhailovich 1890-1986 *EncTR 91 [port]*
**Molotov**, Vyacheslav Mikhailovich 1890-1986 *FacFETw*
**Molotov**, Vyacheslav Mikhaylovich 1890-1986 *SovUnBD*
**Molotsky**, Hyman Max 1919- *AmMWSc 92*
**Molpus**, Dick 1949- *WhoAmP 91*
**Mols**, Jean-Baptiste Bello-Portu 1964- *WhoEnt 92*
**Molson** *Who 92*
**Molson**, Baron 1903- *Who 92*
**Molson**, Eric H. 1937- *IntWW 91, WhoFI 92*
**Molt**, Cynthia Marylee 1957- *WhoFI 92, WhoWest 92*
**Molt**, James Teunis 1947- *AmMWSc 92*
**Molta**, Linda Anne 1960- *WhoAmL 92*
**Molteni**, Agostino 1933- *AmMWSc 92*
**Molteni**, Richard A 1944- *AmMWSc 92*
**Molter**, Lynne Ann 1957- *AmMWSc 92*
**Moltke**, Helmuth James, Count von 1907-1945 *EncTR 91 [port]*
**Moltmann**, Gunter 1926- *IntWW 91*
**Moltyaner**, Grigory 1943- *AmMWSc 92*
**Moltz**, Ira Alexander 1949- *WhoAmL 92*

**Moltz,** James Edward 1932- WhoFI 92
**Moltz,** Marshall Jerome 1930- WhoAmL 92, WhoMW 92
**Moltzan,** Herbert John 1933- AmMWSc 92
**Moltzon,** Richard Francis 1941- WhoFI 92
**Moluf,** Robert Timothy 1955- WhoRel 92
**Molumby,** Robert Eugene 1936- WhoMW 92
**Molvik,** Arthur Warren 1943- AmMWSc 92
**Molyneaux,** David Glenn 1945- WhoMW 92
**Molyneaux,** James Henry 1920- IntWW 91, Who 92
**Molyneux,** Edward 1891-1974 DcTwDes, FacFETw
**Molyneux,** James Robert M. Who 92
**Molyneux,** John Ecob 1935- AmMWSc 92
**Molyneux,** Russell John 1938- AmMWSc 92
**Molyneux,** Wilfrid 1910- Who 92
**Molyneux,** William 1656-1698 BlkwCEP
**Molz,** Fred John, III 1943- AmMWSc 92
**Molzon,** Justina Ann 1950- WhoAmL 92
**Momaday,** N. Scott DrAPF 91
**Momaday,** N. Scott 1934- BenetAL 91, ConAu 34NR, ConNov 91, TwCWW 91, WrDr 92
**Momaday,** Navarre Scott 1934- IntAu&W 91, WhoWest 92
**Mombach,** Patti Ann 1958- WhoWest 92
**Momberg,** Harold Leslie 1929- AmMWSc 92
**Momen,** Moojan 1950- IntAu&W 91
**Momeni,** Michael Hoshang 1938- WhoMW 92
**Moment,** Gairdner Bostwick 1905- AmMWSc 92
**Momi,** Balbir Singh 1935- IntAu&W 91
**Momin,** Abdul 1921- IntWW 91
**Mommaerts,** Wilfried 1917- AmMWSc 92
**Mommer,** Anthony William 1944- WhoAmL 92
**Mommsen,** Christian Matthias Theodor 1817-1903 WhoNob 90
**Mommsen,** Katharina 1925- WhoWest 92
**Mommsen,** Katharina Zimmer 1925- IntAu&W 91
**Momoh,** Joseph Saidu 1937- IntWW 91
**Momot,** Walter Thomas 1938- AmMWSc 92
**Momparler,** Richard Lewis 1935- AmMWSc 92
**Momper,** Arthur William 1950- WhoWest 92
**Momper,** Stephen Edward 1959- WhoMW 92
**Momper,** Walter 1945- IntWW 91
**Mon,** Joseph John Gerard 1930- WhoRel 92
**Monacella,** Vincent Joseph 1926- AmMWSc 92
**Monacelli,** Amleto Andres 1961- WhoHisp 92
**Monacelli,** Richard Arnold 1935- WhoAmP 91
**Monacelli-Johnson,** Linda DrAPF 91
**Monach,** Andrew E. 1954- WhoAmL 92
**Monachelli,** Frank Joseph 1948- WhoAmP 91
**Monachino,** Francis Leonard WhoEnt 92
**Monack,** A J 1904- AmMWSc 92
**Monaco,** Anthony Peter 1932- AmMWSc 92
**Monaco,** Ferdinand Roger 1940- WhoWest 92
**Monaco,** James 1942- WrDr 92
**Monaco,** James Frederick 1942- IntAu&W 91
**Monaco,** Lawrence Henry 1925- AmMWSc 92
**Monaco,** Mario del NewAmDM
**Monaco,** Michael P. WhoFI 92
**Monaco,** Michelle Anne 1962- WhoWest 92
**Monaco,** Paul J 1952- AmMWSc 92
**Monagan,** Alfrieta Parks 1945- WhoBlA 92
**Monagas,** Lionel John 1921- WhoBlA 92
**Monaghan,** David 1944- ConAu 133
**Monaghan,** Henry P. 1934- WhoAmL 92
**Monaghan,** James 1914- Who 92
**Monaghan,** James Edward, Jr. 1947- WhoWest 92
**Monaghan,** Jeanne Mary 1960- WhoMW 92
**Monaghan,** Jessine Adrienne 1953- WhoAmL 92
**Monaghan,** Patricia DrAPF 91
**Monaghan,** Patricia 1946- WhoRel 92
**Monaghan,** Patrick Henry 1922- AmMWSc 92
**Monaghan,** Peter Gerard 1949- WhoAmL 92
**Monaghan,** Robert Lee 1923- WhoAmP 91
**Monaghan,** Thomas NewYTBS 91 [port]
**Monaghan,** Thomas Stephen 1937- WhoFI 92, WhoMW 92
**Monaghan,** Tom WhoAmP 91
**Monagle,** Daniel J 1936- AmMWSc 92
**Monagle,** John Joseph, Jr 1929- AmMWSc 92
**Monahan,** Alan Richard 1939- AmMWSc 92
**Monahan,** Casey James 1959- WhoEnt 92
**Monahan,** Catherine E 1949- WhoIns 92
**Monahan,** Denis Coleman 1949- WhoAmL 92
**Monahan,** Edward Charles 1936- AmMWSc 92
**Monahan,** Edward James 1931- AmMWSc 92
**Monahan,** Edward Joseph, III 1942- WhoMW 92
**Monahan,** George Lennox, Jr. 1933- WhoEnt 92
**Monahan,** Hubert Harvey 1922- AmMWSc 92
**Monahan,** James Emmett 1925- AmMWSc 92
**Monahan,** John Francis 1964- WhoWest 92
**Monahan,** John T. 1946- WhoAmL 92
**Monahan,** Laurie WhoEnt 92
**Monahan,** Leonard Francis 1948- WhoEnt 92, WhoMW 92
**Monahan,** Marie Terry 1927- WhoAmL 92
**Monahan,** Mary WhoAmP 91
**Monahan,** Michael 1865-1933 BenetAL 91
**Monahan,** Raymond John 1951- WhoAmP 91
**Monahan,** Rita Short 1954- WhoWest 92
**Monahan,** Thomas Andrew, Jr. 1920- WhoFI 92
**Monahan,** Willian Welsh, Jr 1929- WhoAmP 91
**Monajemi,** Mehdi 1954- WhoWest 92
**Monaldo,** Francis Michael 1956- AmMWSc 92
**Monan,** Gerald E 1933- AmMWSc 92
**Monarchi,** David Edward 1944- WhoWest 92
**Monard,** Joyce Anne 1946- AmMWSc 92
**Monarrez,** Alicia 1964- WhoHisp 92
**Monash,** Curt Alfred 1960- WhoFI 92
**Monash,** Paul LesBEnT 92
**Monash,** Paul 1917- IntMPA 92
**Monastra,** Carl C. 1953- WhoAmL 92
**Monath,** Thomas P 1940- AmMWSc 92
**Monberg,** Jay Peter 1935- WhoFI 92, WhoMW 92
**Monberg,** Torben Axel 1929- IntWW 91
**Monboddo,** James Burnett 1714-1799 BlkwCEP
**Moncada,** Salvador Enrique 1944- Who 92
**Monce,** Michael Nolen 1952- AmMWSc 92
**Monce,** Raymond Eugene 1924- WhoAmP 91
**Moncel,** Robert William 1917- Who 92
**Monchamp,** Roch Robert 1931- AmMWSc 92
**Moncher,** Daniel Joseph 1960- WhoMW 92
**Monchick,** Louis 1927- AmMWSc 92
**Moncivais,** Emil Ray 1942- WhoHisp 92
**Monck** Who 92
**Monck,** Viscount Who 92
**Monck,** Harry Nelson, IV 1958- WhoAmL 92
**Monck,** Nicholas Jeremy 1935- Who 92
**Monck,** Sarah Knight 1961- WhoFI 92
**Monckton** Who 92
**Monckton,** Christopher Walter 1952- Who 92
**Monckton-Arundell** Who 92
**Monckton of Brenchley,** Viscount 1915- Who 92
**Moncreiff** Who 92
**Moncreiff,** Baron 1915- Who 92
**Moncrief,** Eugene Charles 1932- AmMWSc 92
**Moncrief,** John William 1941- AmMWSc 92
**Moncrief,** Michael J 1943- WhoAmP 91
**Moncrief,** Nancy D 1957- AmMWSc 92
**Moncrief,** Shelly, Jr. 1948- WhoEnt 92
**Moncrief,** Sidney 1957- WhoBlA 92
**Moncrieff,** William S. Who 92
**Moncrieff,** William Thomas 1794-1857 RfGEnL 91
**Moncton,** Archbishop of 1930- Who 92
**Moncton,** David Eugene 1948- AmMWSc 92
**Moncure,** Albert F. 1924- WhoBlA 92
**Moncure,** Henry, Jr 1930- AmMWSc 92
**Moncure,** Jane Belk 1926- IntAu&W 91
**Moncure,** Thomas McCarty, Jr 1951- WhoAmP 91
**Moncus,** Mary Lynn 1934- WhoWest 92
**Mond** Who 92
**Mond,** Bertram 1931- AmMWSc 92
**Mond,** James Jacob 1946- AmMWSc 92
**Mondal,** Kalyan 1951- AmMWSc 92
**Mondale,** Ted A 1957- WhoAmP 91
**Mondale,** Theodore Adams 1957- WhoMW 92
**Mondale,** Walter F 1928- FacFETw [port]
**Mondale,** Walter Frederick 1928- AmPolLe, IntWW 91, Who 92, WhoAmL 92, WhoAmP 91
**Mondanaro,** Philip J 1950- WhoIns 92
**Mondani,** Thomas P 1934- WhoAmP 91
**Mondavi,** Robert Gerald WhoWest 92
**Monday,** Derrell Wayne 1948- WhoRel 92
**Monday,** Horace Reginald 1907- Who 92
**Monday,** John Christian 1925- WhoWest 92
**Monday,** Jon Ellis 1947- WhoEnt 92
**Monday,** Kenny 1961- BlkOlyM
**Monde,** David Moss 1959- WhoAmL 92
**Mondell,** Cynthia B. Frances 1946- WhoEnt 92
**Mondello,** John Paul 1948- WhoFI 92
**Mondello,** Joseph N 1938- WhoAmP 91, WhoHisp 92
**Monden,** Vince LaMonte 1961- WhoRel 92
**Monder,** Carl 1928- AmMWSc 92
**Mondjo,** Nicolas 1933- IntWW 91
**Mondl,** Mark Christopher 1948- WhoMW 92
**Mondlin,** Marvin 1927- WhoFI 92
**Mondolfo,** L F 1910- AmMWSc 92
**Mondon,** Carl Erwin AmMWSc 92
**Mondonville,** Jean-Joseph Cassanea de 1711-1772 NewAmDM
**Mondragon,** Chris 1936- WhoHisp 92
**Mondragon,** Clarence 1940- WhoHisp 92
**Mondragon,** Delfi 1941- WhoHisp 92
**Mondragon,** Fred Eloy 1942- WhoAmP 91
**Mondragon,** James I. WhoHisp 92
**Mondragon,** Nadine 1945- WhoAmP 91
**Mondragon,** Norbert L. 1960- WhoHisp 92
**Mondragon,** Roberto A. 1940- WhoHisp 92
**Mondrian,** Piet 1872-1944 DcTwDes, FacFETw
**Mondschean,** Thomas Herbert 1957- WhoFI 92
**Mondshein,** Lee Julian 1944- WhoAmL 92
**Mondul,** Donald David 1945- WhoAmL 92, WhoMW 92
**Mondy,** Nell Irene 1921- AmMWSc 92
**Mone,** Bernard J 1940- WhoIns 92
**Mone,** John Aloysius Who 92
**Mone,** Louis Carmen 1936- WhoWest 92
**Mone,** Peter John 1940- WhoAmL 92
**Mone,** Robert Paul 1934- WhoAmL 92
**Monell,** Joseph Tarrigan 1857?-1915 BiInAmS
**Moner,** John George 1928- AmMWSc 92
**Monerawela,** Chandra 1937- IntWW 91, Who 92
**Mones,** James J 1952- IntAu&W 91
**Monesson,** Harry S. 1935- ConAu 133
**Monestier,** Marc 1959- AmMWSc 92
**Monet,** Claude 1840-1926 FacFETw, ThHEIm [port]
**Monet,** Jacques 1930- IntAu&W 91, WhoRel 92, WrDr 92
**Monet,** Maria Pereira 1949- WhoFI 92
**Moneta,** Ernesto Teodoro 1833-1918 WhoNob 90
**Moneti,** Giancarlo 1931- AmMWSc 92
**Monette,** Francis C 1941- AmMWSc 92
**Monette,** John Wesley 1803-1851 BenetAL 91
**Monette,** Madeleine 1951- IntAu&W 91
**Monette,** Paul Raoul 1910- WhoRel 92
**Money,** David Charles 1918- IntAu&W 91, WrDr 92
**Money,** Eldon A 1930- WhoAmP 91
**Money,** Ernle 1931- Who 92
**Money,** George Gilbert 1914- Who 92
**Money,** Henry Thomas 1933- WhoRel 92
**Money,** J B 1921- WhoAmP 91
**Money,** James 1918- ConAu 133
**Money,** John William 1921- AmMWSc 92
**Money,** Keith 1935- IntAu&W 91, WrDr 92
**Money,** Kenneth Eric 1935- AmMWSc 92
**Money,** Lloyd J 1920- AmMWSc 92
**Money,** Peter DrAPF 91
**Money-Coutts** Who 92
**Money-Coutts,** David Burdett 1931- IntWW 91, Who 92
**Monfore,** Gervaise Edwin 1910- AmMWSc 92
**Monfort,** Elias Riggs, III 1929- WhoWest 92
**Monfort,** Kenneth 1928- WhoWest 92
**Monfort,** Richard L. 1954- WhoFI 92, WhoMW 92, WhoWest 92
**Monfort,** Silvia 1923- IntWW 91
**Monforte,** John Ford 1954- WhoEnt 92
**Monforton,** Gerard Roland 1938- AmMWSc 92
**Monfred,** Richard Alan 1961- WhoAmL 92
**Mongan,** Edwin Lawrence, Jr 1919- AmMWSc 92
**Mongchi** EncAmaz 91
**Monge,** Luis Alberto 1925- IntWW 91
**Monge,** Pedro R. 1943- WhoHisp 92
**Mongell,** Susan Jane 1958- WhoFI 92
**Mongelli,** Thomas Guy 1952- WhoEnt 92
**Mongeluzzi,** Robert James 1956- WhoAmL 92
**Monger,** George William 1937- Who 92
**Monger,** James William Heron 1937- AmMWSc 92
**Mongini,** Patricia Katherine Ann 1950- AmMWSc 92
**Mongo Beti** 1932- IntWW 91
**Mongue,** Robert Edward 1951- WhoAmL 92
**Monguno,** Alhaji Shettima Ali 1926- IntWW 91
**Monheit,** Alan G 1949- AmMWSc 92
**Moniba,** Harry Fumba 1937- Who 92
**Monica** 331?-387 EncEarC
**Monica,** John C. 1941- WhoAmL 92
**Monical,** Robert Duane 1925- WhoMW 92
**Monicelli,** Mario 1915- IntDcF 2-2, IntMPA 92, IntWW 91
**Monick,** John Carl, Jr. 1958- WhoEnt 92
**Monie,** Ian Whitelaw 1918- AmMWSc 92
**Monier,** Louis Marcel 1956- AmMWSc 92
**Monier-Williams,** Evelyn Faithfull 1920- Who 92
**Monin,** Lawrence Owen 1942- WhoFI 92, WhoIns 92
**Moniot,** Robert Keith 1950- AmMWSc 92
**Monippallil,** Matthew M. 1938- WhoFI 92
**Monismith,** Carl L 1926- AmMWSc 92
**Moniuszko,** Stanislaw 1819-1872 NewAmDM
**Moniz,** Egas 1874-1955 FacFETw
**Moniz,** Ernest Jeffrey 1944- AmMWSc 92
**Moniz,** William B 1932- AmMWSc 92
**Monjan,** Andrew Arthur 1938- AmMWSc 92
**Monjar,** Harvey WhoRel 92
**Monje,** Andrew, Jr. 1928- WhoHisp 92
**Monjo,** John C 1931- WhoAmP 91
**Monk,** Alec Who 92
**Monk,** Allan James 1942- WhoEnt 92
**Monk,** Anthony John 1923- Who 92
**Monk,** Archibald 1788?-1869 DcNCBi 4
**Monk,** Art 1957- WhoBlA 92
**Monk,** Arthur James 1924- Who 92
**Monk,** Carl Douglas 1933- AmMWSc 92
**Monk,** Clayborne Morris 1938- AmMWSc 92
**Monk,** David Alec 1942- Who 92
**Monk,** Edd Dudley 1948- WhoBlA 92
**Monk,** Gregory Brittain 1942- WhoWest 92
**Monk,** James Donald 1930- AmMWSc 92
**Monk,** James Russell 1947- WhoAmP 91
**Monk,** Janice Jones 1937- WhoWest 92
**Monk,** John Carr 1827-1877 DcNCBi 4
**Monk,** Maria 1817?-1849 BenetAL 91
**Monk,** Meredith NewYTBS 91
**Monk,** Meredith 1942- ConCom 92
**Monk,** Meredith 1943- NewAmDM
**Monk,** Meredith Jane 1942- WhoEnt 92
**Monk,** Robert C. 1930- WrDr 92
**Monk,** Robert Clarence 1930- WhoRel 92
**Monk,** Thelonious 1917-1982 ConBlB 1 [port], ConMus 6 [port], NewAmDM
**Monk,** Thelonious Sphere 1917-1982 DcNCBi 4
**Monk,** Thelonius 1917-1982 FacFETw [port]
**Monk,** William Henry 1823-1889 NewAmDM
**Monk,** William Hoover 1930- WhoRel 92
**Monk Bretton,** Baron 1924- Who 92
**Monke,** Edwin J 1925- AmMWSc 92
**Monkees,** The ConMus 7 [port]
**Monkewitz,** Peter Alexis 1943- AmMWSc 92
**Monkhorst,** Hendrik J 1938- AmMWSc 92
**Monkhouse,** Bob 1928- IntMPA 92
**Monkman,** Richard Drake 1954- WhoWest 92
**Monks,** John WhoAmP 91
**Monks,** John 1954- TwCPaSc
**Monks,** John, Jr. IntMPA 92
**Monks,** John, Jr. 1910- WhoEnt 92
**Monks,** John Stephen 1945- Who 92
**Monks,** Robert A G 1933- WhoAmP 91
**Monkswell,** Baron 1947- Who 92
**Monlux,** Andrew W 1920- AmMWSc 92
**Monmonier,** Mark 1943- AmMWSc 92
**Monmouth,** Bishop of 1922- Who 92
**Monmouth,** Dean of Who 92
**Monn,** Donald Edgar 1938- AmMWSc 92
**Monn,** Matthias Georg 1717-1750 NewAmDM
**Monnahan,** John Edwin 1951- WhoMW 92
**Monnar,** Marlene Mercedes 1953- WhoHisp 92
**Monnard,** Jean-Francois 1941- WhoEnt 92
**Monne,** Noelia 1948- WhoHisp 92
**Monnerville,** Gaston 1897-1991 NewYTBS 91
**Monnerville,** Gaston Charles Francois 1897- IntWW 91
**Monnet,** Elizabeth Rose 1952- WhoAmL 92
**Monnet,** Jean 1888-1979 FacFETw

**Monnier,** Claude Michel 1938- *IntWW 91*
**Monnington,** Thomas 1902-1976 *TwCPaSc*
**Monod,** Jacques 1927- *NewAmDM*
**Monod,** Jacques Lucien 1910-1976 *FacFETw, WhoNob 90*
**Monod,** Jaques-Louis *WhoEnt 92*
**Monod,** Jerome 1930- *IntWW 91*
**Monod,** Theodore 1902- *Who 92*
**Monod,** Theodore Andre 1902- *IntWW 91*
**Monopoli,** Daniel Marco 1939- *WhoMW 92*
**Monopoli,** Richard V 1930- *AmMWSc 92*
**Monory,** Jacques 1934- *IntWW 91*
**Monory,** Rene Claude Aristide 1923- *IntWW 91*
**Monos,** Emil 1935- *AmMWSc 92*
**Monoson,** Herbert L 1936- *AmMWSc 92*
**Monostori,** Benedict Joseph 1919- *AmMWSc 92*
**Monrad,** Ditlev 1949- *AmMWSc 92*
**Monreal Luque,** Alberto 1928- *IntWW 91*
**Monro,** Andrew Hugh 1950- *Who 92*
**Monro,** David Hector 1911- *IntWW 91*
**Monro,** Harold 1879-1932 *RfGEnL 91*
**Monro,** Hector 1922- *Who 92*
**Monro,** Hugh *Who 92*
**Monro,** Nicholas 1936- *TwCPaSc*
**Monro Davies,** William Llewellyn 1927- *Who 92*
**Monroe,** Annie Lucky 1933- *WhoBlA 92*
**Monroe,** Barbara Samson Granger 1913- *AmMWSc 92*
**Monroe,** Bill *LesBEnT 92*
**Monroe,** Bill 1911- *NewAmDM*
**Monroe,** Bruce Malcolm 1940- *AmMWSc 92*
**Monroe,** Burt Leavelle, Jr 1930- *AmMWSc 92*
**Monroe,** Carl Dean, III 1960- *WhoAmL 92*
**Monroe,** Charles Edward 1950- *WhoBlA 92*
**Monroe,** Chauncey 1950- *WhoEnt 92*
**Monroe,** Debra 1958- *ConAu 134*
**Monroe,** Earl 1944- *WhoBlA 92*
**Monroe,** Early D., Jr. 1944- *WhoBlA 92*
**Monroe,** Elizabeth McLeister 1940- *AmMWSc 92*
**Monroe,** Eric George 1944- *WhoWest 92*
**Monroe,** Eugene Alan 1934- *AmMWSc 92*
**Monroe,** Eugene Crosby 1880-1961 *RelLAm 91*
**Monroe,** Gerald J *WhoAmP 91*
**Monroe,** Harriet 1860-1936 *BenetAL 91, FacFETw*
**Monroe,** Haskell M., Jr. 1931- *WhoMW 92*
**Monroe,** Hunter Kelly 1962- *WhoFI 92*
**Monroe,** James 1758-1831 *AmPolLe [port], BenetAL 91, RComAH*
**Monroe,** James H. 1946- *WhoBlA 92*
**Monroe,** John George d1991 *Who 92N*
**Monroe,** John Roger 1949- *WhoRel 92*
**Monroe,** Kendyl Kurth 1936- *WhoAmL 92*
**Monroe,** Kenneth Edward, Jr 1928- *WhoAmP 91*
**Monroe,** Laverne 1945- *WhoMW 92*
**Monroe,** Lee Alexander 1932- *WhoAmL 92*
**Monroe,** Lillie Mae 1948- *WhoBlA 92*
**Monroe,** Linda Roach 1952- *WhoHisp 92*
**Monroe,** Marilyn 1926-1962 *FacFETw [port], HanAmWH, RComAH*
**Monroe,** Marion 1898-1983 *FacFETw*
**Monroe,** Melrose 1919- *WhoFI 92*
**Monroe,** Michael Blane 1954- *WhoRel 92*
**Monroe,** Michael James 1948- *WhoFI 92*
**Monroe,** Michael Leo 1951- *WhoFI 92*
**Monroe,** Robert Alex *WhoBlA 92*
**Monroe,** Robert James 1918- *AmMWSc 92*
**Monroe,** Ronald Eugene 1933- *AmMWSc 92*
**Monroe,** Russell Ronald 1920- *AmMWSc 92*
**Monroe,** Stacey Weller 1962- *WhoRel 92*
**Monroe,** Stanley Edwin 1902- *WhoWest 92*
**Monroe,** Stuart Benton 1934- *AmMWSc 92*
**Monroe,** Sylvester 1951- *WhoWest 92*
**Monroe,** Thomas Frank 1944- *WhoFI 92*
**Monroe,** W Rod 1942- *WhoAmP 91*
**Monroe,** Walter Harris, III 1944- *WhoAmL 92*
**Monroe,** Watson Hiner 1907- *AmMWSc 92*
**Monroe,** William Eugene 1930- *WhoFI 92*
**Monroe,** William Lewis 1941- *WhoFI 92*
**Monroe,** William R, Jr *WhoAmP 91*
**Monroig,** Antonio 1944- *WhoAmP 91, WhoHisp 92*
**Monsaraz,** Alberto de 1889-1959 *BiDExR*
**Monsarrat,** Ann Whitelaw 1937- *IntAu&W 91, WrDr 92*
**Monse,** Ernst Ulrich 1927- *AmMWSc 92*
**Monsees,** James E 1937- *AmMWSc 92*
**Monsees,** Janet Louise 1943- *WhoAmP 91*
**Monsell,** Viscount 1905- *Who 92*
**Monsen,** David Elmer 1946- *WhoRel 92*
**Monsen,** Elaine R 1935- *AmMWSc 92*
**Monsen,** Harry 1924- *AmMWSc 92*
**Monserrat,** Leonardo G. 1948- *WhoHisp 92*
**Monsieur Croche** *NewAmDM*
**Monsimer,** Harold Gene 1928- *AmMWSc 92*
**Monsky,** Michael David Wolf Von Sommer 1947- *WhoFI 92*
**Monsman,** Gerald 1940- *WhoWest 92*
**Monson** *Who 92*
**Monson,** Baron 1932- *Who 92*
**Monson,** Angela Zoe 1955- *WhoAmP 91*
**Monson,** Arch, Jr 1913- *WhoAmP 91*
**Monson,** David S 1945- *WhoAmP 91*
**Monson,** Dianne Lynn 1934- *WhoMW 92*
**Monson,** Douglas Marion 1955- *WhoAmL 92*
**Monson,** Frederick Carlton 1939- *AmMWSc 92*
**Monson,** Harry O 1919- *AmMWSc 92*
**Monson,** James Edward 1932- *AmMWSc 92, WhoWest 92*
**Monson,** Joyce Loraine 1938- *WhoAmP 91*
**Monson,** Kerry William 1957- *WhoMW 92*
**Monson,** Leslie 1912- *Who 92*
**Monson,** Paul Herman 1925- *AmMWSc 92*
**Monson,** Richard Stanley 1937- *AmMWSc 92*
**Monson,** Thomas Spencer 1927- *WhoRel 92, WhoWest 92*
**Monson,** Warren Glenn 1926- *AmMWSc 92*
**Monson,** William Bonnar Leslie 1912- *IntWW 91*
**Monson,** William Joye 1927- *AmMWSc 92*
**Monsor,** Barbara Allen 1923- *WhoAmP 91*
**Monsos,** Michael Trevor 1960- *WhoWest 92*
**Monsour,** Michael Anton 1952- *WhoHisp 92*
**Monsour,** Victor 1922- *AmMWSc 92*
**Monstein,** Marline Berta 1955- *WhoHisp 92*
**Monstery,** Thomas Hoyer 1824-1902 *ScFEYrs*
**Mont,** George Edward 1935- *AmMWSc 92*
**Monta,** Marian Frances 1932- *WhoEnt 92*
**Montag,** David Moses 1939- *WhoWest 92*
**Montag,** Kenneth Girard 1948- *WhoMW 92*
**Montag,** Mordechai 1925- *AmMWSc 92*
**Montag,** Tom 1947- *IntAu&W 91, WrDr 92*
**Montagna,** Gilberto Luis Humberto 1936- *IntWW 91*
**Montagna,** William 1913- *AmMWSc 92*
**Montagne,** Edward J. *IntMPA 92*
**Montagne,** John 1920- *WhoWest 92*
**Montagne,** John M 1920- *AmMWSc 92*
**Montagne Sanchez,** Ernesto 1916- *IntWW 91*
**Montagnier,** Luc 1932- *IntWW 91, Who 92*
**Montagu** *Who 92*
**Montagu,** Alexander Victor 1906- *Who 92*
**Montagu,** Ashley 1905- *Who 92, WrDr 92*
**Montagu,** Elizabeth 1720-1800 *BlkwCEP*
**Montagu,** Ewen 1901-1985 *FacFETw*
**Montagu,** Jennifer 1931- *WrDr 92*
**Montagu,** Jennifer Iris Rachel 1931- *Who 92*
**Montagu,** John Edward Hollister 1943- *Who 92*
**Montagu,** Mary Wortley 1689-1762 *BlkwCEP, RfGEnL 91*
**Montagu,** Montague Francis Ashley *Who 92*
**Montagu,** Nicholas Lionel John 1944- *Who 92*
**Montagu,** Robert 1949- *IntAu&W 91*
**Montagu,** Victor *Who 92*
**Montagu Douglas Scott** *Who 92*
**Montagu of Beaulieu,** Baron 1926- *Who 92*
**Montagu Of Beaulieu,** Lord 1926- *WrDr 92*
**Montagu of Beaulieu,** Edward John B 1926- *IntAu&W 91*
**Montagu-Pollock,** Giles Hampden *Who 92*
**Montagu-Pollock,** William H. 1903- *Who 92*
**Montagu-Stuart-Wortley** *Who 92*
**Montague** *Who 92*
**Montague,** Barbara Ann 1929- *AmMWSc 92*
**Montague,** Charles Howard 1858-1889 *ScFEYrs*
**Montague,** Charles Howard & Hammond, C M *ScFEYrs*
**Montague,** Daniel Grover 1937- *AmMWSc 92*
**Montague,** Diana 1953- *IntWW 91*
**Montague,** Drogo K 1942- *AmMWSc 92*
**Montague,** Eleanor D 1926- *AmMWSc 92*
**Montague,** Francis Arnold d1991 *Who 92N*
**Montague,** Frank Douglas, Jr. 1925- *WhoAmL 92*
**Montague,** Fredrick Howard, Jr 1945- *AmMWSc 92*
**Montague,** Gary Leslie 1939- *WhoWest 92*
**Montague,** George T. 1929- *ConAu 133*
**Montague,** Harriet Frances 1905- *AmMWSc 92*
**Montague,** Jeanne Ann 1951- *WhoFI 92*
**Montague,** John 1929- *ConPo 91, IntAu&W 91, RfGEnL 91, WrDr 92*
**Montague,** John H 1925- *AmMWSc 92*
**Montague,** Kenneth C, Jr 1942- *WhoAmP 91*
**Montague,** L David *AmMWSc 92*
**Montague,** Lee 1929- *WhoBlA 92*
**Montague,** Margaret Prescott 1878-1955 *ScFEYrs*
**Montague,** Michael Jacob 1932- *Who 92*
**Montague,** Michael James 1947- *AmMWSc 92*
**Montague,** Nelson C. 1929- *WhoBlA 92*
**Montague,** Owen Douglas 1962- *WhoEnt 92*
**Montague,** Patricia Tucker 1937- *AmMWSc 92*
**Montague,** Ruth Mary Bryceson 1939- *Who 92*
**Montague,** Sidney James 1950- *WhoWest 92*
**Montague,** Stephen 1940- *AmMWSc 92*
**Montague,** Stephen 1943- *ConCom 92*
**Montague Browne,** Anthony Arthur Duncan 1923- *Who 92*
**Montague-Jones,** Ronald 1909- *Who 92*
**Montaigne,** Ortiz *WhoBlA 92*
**Montalban,** Carlos d1991 *NewYTBS 91 [port]*
**Montalban,** Ricardo 1920- *IntMPA 92, WhoEnt 92, WhoHisp 92*
**Montalban-Anderssen,** Romero Anton, XIV 1960- *WhoHisp 92*
**Montalbano,** Joseph A *WhoAmP 91*
**Montalbano,** Mark M *WhoAmP 91*
**Montalbetti,** Raymon 1924- *AmMWSc 92*
**Montale,** Eugenio 1896-1981 *DcLB 114 [port], FacFETw [port], WhoNob 90*
**Montalenti,** Giuseppe *IntWW 91N*
**Montali,** Dennis 1940- *WhoAmL 92*
**Montalto,** Joseph Gerard 1951- *WhoAmP 91*
**Montalto,** Richard Michael 1951- *WhoEnt 92*
**Montalvo,** Ana E. 1948- *WhoHisp 92*
**Montalvo,** Consuelo *WhoHisp 92*
**Montalvo,** Evelyn 1950- *WhoFI 92*
**Montalvo,** Frank A. 1950- *WhoHisp 92*
**Montalvo,** Harry 1961- *WhoHisp 92*
**Montalvo,** Jose Luis 1946- *WhoHisp 92*
**Montalvo,** Jose Miguel 1928- *AmMWSc 92*
**Montalvo,** Joseph G, Jr 1937- *AmMWSc 92*
**Montalvo,** Juan 1832-1889 *BenetAL 91*
**Montalvo,** Leo *WhoHisp 92*
**Montalvo,** Louis Anthony 1922- *WhoHisp 92*
**Montalvo,** Maria Antonia 1951- *WhoHisp 92*
**Montalvo,** Ramiro A 1937- *AmMWSc 92*
**Montalvo,** Socorro Inmaculada 1954- *WhoHisp 92*
**Montana,** Andrew Frederick 1930- *AmMWSc 92*
**Montana,** Anthony J 1950- *AmMWSc 92*
**Montana,** Claude *IntWW 91*
**Montana,** James Samuel, Jr. 1943- *WhoAmL 92*
**Montana,** Joe 1956- *FacFETw*
**Montana,** Jordi 1949- *WhoFI 92*
**Montana,** Joseph C., Jr. 1956- *WhoWest 92*
**Montana,** Lewis 1952- *WhoAmL 92*
**Montana,** Patsy *WhoEnt 92*
**Montana,** Priscila A. C. 1948- *WhoHisp 92*
**Montana,** Vanni B. d1991 *NewYTBS 91*
**Montanaro,** Frank A 1961- *WhoAmP 91*
**Montand,** Yves 1921- *FacFETw, IntMPA 92, IntWW 91*
**Montand,** Yves 1921-1991 *NewYTBS 91 [port], News 92-2*
**Montane,** Diana *WhoHisp 92*
**Montane,** Olga Gonzalez 1927- *WhoHisp 92*
**Montanelli,** Indro 1909- *IntWW 91*
**Montanez,** Pablo I. 1958- *WhoHisp 92*
**Montanez,** William Joseph 1952- *WhoHisp 92*
**Montange,** Charles H. 1951- *WhoAmL 92*
**Montani,** Jean-Pierre 1951- *AmMWSc 92*
**Montano,** Carlos Xavier 1955- *WhoHisp 92*
**Montano,** George John 1927- *WhoAmP 91*
**Montano,** Johnnie Anthony 1936- *WhoHisp 92*
**Montano,** Jorge 1945- *IntWW 91*
**Montano,** Louis R. 1928- *WhoHisp 92*
**Montano,** Mary 1949- *WhoHisp 92*
**Montano,** Mary L. *WhoHisp 92*
**Montano,** Pedro Antonio 1940- *AmMWSc 92*
**Montanus,** Arnoldus 1625?-1683 *BenetAL 91*
**Montanus,** Edward d1981 *LesBEnT 92*
**Montayne,** John D *WhoAmP 91*
**Montazer,** G Hosein 1961- *AmMWSc 92*
**Montazeri,** Hossein Ali *WhoRel 92*
**Montazeri,** Hussein Ali 1923?- *IntWW 91*
**Montcalm deSaint-Vean,** Louis, Marquis de 1712-1759 *BenetAL 91*
**Monte,** Bryan Robert 1957- *IntAu&W 91*
**Monte,** Elisa *WhoEnt 92*
**Monte,** Eric *WhoEnt 92*
**Monte,** Hilda 1914-1945 *EncTR 91*
**Monte,** Philippe de 1521-1603 *NewAmDM*
**Monte,** Ralph 1960- *WhoHisp 92*
**Monteagle of Brandon,** Baron 1926- *Who 92*
**Monteagudo,** Eduardo 1953- *WhoHisp 92*
**Monteagudo,** Gene M. 1966- *WhoHisp 92*
**Monteagudo,** Lourdes Maria 1955- *WhoHisp 92*
**Montealegre,** Lily Bendana 1961- *WhoHisp 92*
**Montecalvo,** Robert Louis 1963- *WhoFI 92*
**Montedonico,** Joseph 1937- *WhoAmL 92*
**Montefiore,** Harold Henry S. *Who 92*
**Montefiore,** Hugh 1920- *ConAu 133*
**Montefiore,** Hugh William 1920- *IntWW 91, Who 92*
**Montefusco,** Cheryl Marie 1948- *AmMWSc 92*
**Montegriffo,** Peter Cecil Patrick 1960- *IntWW 91*
**Monteguado,** Bernardo 1785-1825 *HisDSpE*
**Montei,** Elizabeth Loveton 1954- *WhoEnt 92*
**Montei,** William Tuttle 1952- *WhoMW 92*
**Monteiro,** Antonio Mascarenhas *IntWW 91*
**Monteiro,** Edward J. 1948- *WhoEnt 92*
**Monteiro,** Geraldine Marie 1965- *WhoMW 92*
**Monteiro,** Manuel James 1926- *WhoFI 92*
**Monteiro,** Marilyn D.S. 1941- *WhoBlA 92*
**Monteiro,** Thomas 1939- *WhoBlA 92*
**Monteith,** Charles Montgomery 1921- *Who 92*
**Monteith,** David Yates, III 1935- *WhoAmL 92*
**Monteith,** George Rae 1904- *Who 92*
**Monteith,** Henry C. 1937- *WhoBlA 92*
**Monteith,** John Lennox 1929- *Who 92*
**Monteith,** Katherine Simmons 1957- *WhoEnt 92*
**Monteith,** Larry King 1933- *AmMWSc 92*
**Monteith,** Robert Charles Michael 1914- *Who 92*
**Montejano,** Rodolfo 1938- *WhoHisp 92*
**Montejo,** Eugenio 1938- *ConSpAP*
**Montejo,** Francisco de 1484-1550 *HisDSpE*
**Montelaro,** James 1921- *AmMWSc 92*
**Monteleone,** Joseph Peter 1951- *WhoFI 92*
**Monteleone,** Thomas F 1946- *TwCSFW 91, WrDr 92*
**Monteleone,** Thomas Francis 1946- *IntAu&W 91*
**Montell,** Craig 1955- *AmMWSc 92*
**Montella,** William Everett, Jr. 1943- *WhoEnt 92*
**Montelongo,** Delia C. 1940- *WhoHisp 92*
**Montemayor,** Carlos Rene 1945- *WhoHisp 92*
**Montemayor,** Edilberto F. 1950- *WhoHisp 92*
**Montemayor,** Raymond 1941- *WhoHisp 92*
**Montemezzi,** Italo 1875-1952 *NewAmDM*
**Montemurro,** Donald Gilbert 1930- *AmMWSc 92*
**Montenegro,** Robert 1935- *WhoMW 92*
**Montenyohl,** Victor Irl 1921- *AmMWSc 92*
**Montero,** Ana M. 1949- *WhoHisp 92*
**Montero,** Carlos Esteban, Jr. 1963- *WhoEnt 92*
**Montero,** Darrel Martin 1946- *WhoWest 92*
**Montero,** Emily Bernal 1953- *WhoHisp 92*
**Montero,** Faustino, Jr. 1963- *WhoHisp 92*
**Montero,** Fernan Gonzalo 1948- *WhoHisp 92*
**Montero,** Jorge Humberto 1937- *WhoEnt 92*
**Monterrosa,** Jose Napoleon 1953- *WhoWest 92*
**Monterroso,** Amalia *WhoHisp 92*
**Monterrosso de Lavelleja,** Ana *EncAmaz 91*
**Monterroza,** Adiel Abisay 1957- *WhoHisp 92*
**Montes,** Diego J. 1955- *WhoHisp 92*
**Montes,** Jess Henry 1944- *WhoHisp 92*

**Montes,** Maria Eugenia 1952- *AmMWSc 92*
**Montes,** Mary *WhoHisp 92*
**Montes,** Pablo 1944- *BlkOlyM*
**Montes,** Richard *WhoHisp 92*
**Montes,** Virginia E. 1943- *WhoHisp 92*
**Montes De Oca,** Alberto R. 1952- *WhoHisp 92*
**Montes de Oca,** Marco Antonio 1932- *ConSpAP*
**Montes de Oca Ricks,** Maria Helena 1947- *WhoHisp 92*
**Montes Huidobro,** Matias 1931- *WhoHisp 92*
**Montesano,** Frank Anthony 1939- *WhoMW 92*
**Montesco,** Liliana 1934- *WhoHisp 92*
**Montesi,** Jorge 1949- *WhoEnt 92*
**Montesino,** Orlando C. 1950- *WhoFI 92*
**Montesino,** Paul V. 1937- *WhoHisp 92*
**Montesquieu** *BlkwEAR*
**Montesquieu,** Charles-Louis Secondat 1689-1755 *BlkwCEP*
**Montessori,** Maria 1870-1952 *FacFETw, WomPsyc*
**Montet,** George Louis 1919- *AmMWSc 92*
**Monteux,** Claude 1920- *NewAmDM*
**Monteux,** Pierre 1875-1964 *FacFETw, NewAmDM*
**Monteverde,** Ronald Peter 1947- *WhoWest 92*
**Monteverde,** Terrence Michael 1961- *WhoFI 92*
**Monteverdi,** Claudio 1567-1643 *NewAmDM*
**Monteverdi,** Mark Victor 1963- *WhoBlA 92*
**Montevilla,** Julio Vargas 1943- *WhoRel 92*
**Montez,** Bettina L. *WhoEnt 92*
**Montez,** Chris 1943- *WhoHisp 92*
**Montez,** Noel Pena 1965- *WhoHisp 92*
**Montezuma** *HisDSpE*
**Montezuma** 1480?-1520 *BenetAL 91*
**Montezuma II** *HisDSpE*
**Montezuma,** Carlos 1865?-1923 *RComAH*
**Montfaucon,** Bernard de 1655-1741 *BlkwCEP*
**Montford,** John T 1943- *WhoAmP 91*
**Montfort,** Joseph d1776 *DcNCBi 4*
**Montfort,** Norbert 1925- *IntWW 91*
**Montfort,** Thomas P *ScFEYrs*
**Montgomerie** *Who 92*
**Montgomerie,** Lord 1966- *Who 92*
**Montgomerie,** Alexander 1550?-1598 *RfGEnL 91*
**Montgomerie,** Robert Dennis 1947- *AmMWSc 92*
**Montgomery** *Who 92*
**Montgomery,** Alan Everard 1938- *Who 92*
**Montgomery,** Alpha LeVon, Sr. 1919- *WhoBlA 92*
**Montgomery,** Andrew Stuart 1960- *WhoFI 92, WhoMW 92*
**Montgomery,** Baby Peggy 1918- *WhoEnt 92*
**Montgomery,** Barbara Curry 1939- *WhoBlA 92*
**Montgomery,** Basil Henry David 1931- *Who 92*
**Montgomery,** Bernard Law 1887-1976 *EncTR 91 [port], FacFETw [port]*
**Montgomery,** Betty D *WhoAmP 91*
**Montgomery,** Billy W 1937- *WhoAmP 91*
**Montgomery,** Bob 1938- *WhoEnt 92*
**Montgomery,** Brian 1962- *WhoMW 92*
**Montgomery,** Brian Walter 1957- *WhoBlA 92*
**Montgomery,** C. Barry 1937- *WhoMW 92*
**Montgomery,** Carl Halloway, Jr. 1952- *WhoRel 92*
**Montgomery,** Carl Robert 1939- *WhoAmP 91*
**Montgomery,** Carol Artman *DrAPF 91*
**Montgomery,** Carrie Judd 1858-1945 *RelLAm 91*
**Montgomery,** Catherine Lewis *WhoBlA 92*
**Montgomery,** Charles Gray 1937- *AmMWSc 92, WhoMW 92*
**Montgomery,** Charles John 1917- *IntWW 91, Who 92*
**Montgomery,** Clark Taylor 1941- *WhoFI 92*
**Montgomery,** Daniel Michael 1943- *AmMWSc 92*
**Montgomery,** Darlene Thelma 1929- *WhoRel 92*
**Montgomery,** David *Who 92*
**Montgomery,** David 1927- *Who 92*
**Montgomery,** David 1937- *IntWW 91*
**Montgomery,** David 1948- *IntAu&W 91*
**Montgomery,** David Bruce 1938- *IntAu&W 91, WrDr 92*
**Montgomery,** David Campbell 1936- *AmMWSc 92*
**Montgomery,** David Carey 1938- *AmMWSc 92*
**Montgomery,** David John 1948- *Who 92*
**Montgomery,** David Rogers 1947- *WhoAmL 92*
**Montgomery,** Deane 1909- *AmMWSc 92, IntWW 91*
**Montgomery,** Derek *IntAu&W 91X*
**Montgomery,** Desmond Alan Dill 1916- *Who 92*
**Montgomery,** Dillard Brewster 1936- *WhoEnt 92*
**Montgomery,** Don W 1925- *WhoIns 92*
**Montgomery,** Donald Bruce 1933- *AmMWSc 92*
**Montgomery,** Donald Joseph 1917- *AmMWSc 92*
**Montgomery,** Donald L *WhoAmP 91*
**Montgomery,** Douglas C 1943- *AmMWSc 92*
**Montgomery,** Dwight Ray 1950- *WhoBlA 92*
**Montgomery,** Earline 1944- *WhoBlA 92*
**Montgomery,** Earline Robertson 1944- *WhoBlA 92*
**Montgomery,** Edmund Duncan 1835-1911 *BiInAmS*
**Montgomery,** Edward Harry 1939- *AmMWSc 92*
**Montgomery,** Edward Taylor 1946- *WhoEnt 92*
**Montgomery,** Elizabeth 1933- *IntMPA 92*
**Montgomery,** Errol Lee 1939- *AmMWSc 92*
**Montgomery,** Ethel Constance 1931- *WhoBlA 92*
**Montgomery,** Evangeline Juliet 1933- *WhoBlA 92*
**Montgomery,** Felix Bowden, Jr. 1930- *WhoFI 92*
**Montgomery,** Fergus *Who 92*
**Montgomery,** Frances Trego 1858-1925 *ScFEYrs*
**Montgomery,** Fred O. 1922- *WhoBlA 92*
**Montgomery,** G Franklin 1921- *AmMWSc 92*
**Montgomery,** G. V. 1920- *AlmAP 92 [port]*
**Montgomery,** Gary 1957- *WhoMW 92*
**Montgomery,** Gary Lee 1942- *WhoAmP 91*
**Montgomery,** George *DrAPF 91*
**Montgomery,** George 1916- *IntMPA 92*
**Montgomery,** George Cranwell 1944- *WhoAmP 91*
**Montgomery,** George Lightbody 1905- *Who 92*
**Montgomery,** George Louis, Jr. 1934- *WhoBlA 92*
**Montgomery,** George Paul, Jr 1943- *AmMWSc 92*
**Montgomery,** George Rodgers 1910- *Who 92*
**Montgomery,** Gillespie V *WhoAmP 91*
**Montgomery,** Glenn A. *WhoFI 92*
**Montgomery,** Gregory B. 1946- *WhoBlA 92*
**Montgomery,** Harold Ronnie 1938- *WhoAmP 91*
**Montgomery,** Harry J. 1939- *WhoBlA 92*
**Montgomery,** Harry Sheffie 1926- *WhoAmP 91*
**Montgomery,** Helen Barrett 1861-1934 *RelLAm 91*
**Montgomery,** Henry 1848- *BiInAmS*
**Montgomery,** Henry Irving 1924- *WhoFI 92, WhoMW 92*
**Montgomery,** Hugh 1904- *AmMWSc 92*
**Montgomery,** Hugh Bryan Greville 1929- *Who 92*
**Montgomery,** Hugh Lowell 1944- *AmMWSc 92*
**Montgomery,** Ilene Nowicki 1942- *AmMWSc 92, WhoMW 92*
**Montgomery,** James C. 1918- *WhoBlA 92*
**Montgomery,** James Douglas 1937- *AmMWSc 92*
**Montgomery,** James Ervin 1951- *WhoRel 92*
**Montgomery,** James Fischer 1934- *WhoFI 92, WhoWest 92*
**Montgomery,** James Watson 1959- *WhoFI 92*
**Montgomery,** James Winchester 1921- *WhoRel 92*
**Montgomery,** Janice Sondra *WhoMW 92*
**Montgomery,** Jim 1937- *WhoAmP 91*
**Montgomery,** Joe Elliott 1942- *WhoBlA 92*
**Montgomery,** John *IntWW 91, Who 92*
**Montgomery,** John d1744 *DcNCBi 4*
**Montgomery,** John Atterbury 1924- *AmMWSc 92*
**Montgomery,** John D. 1920- *WrDr 92*
**Montgomery,** John Darrell 1947- *WhoAmL 92*
**Montgomery,** John Duncan 1928- *Who 92*
**Montgomery,** John Henry 1937- *WhoFI 92*
**Montgomery,** John Joseph 1858-1911 *BiInAmS*
**Montgomery,** John Matthew 1930- *Who 92*
**Montgomery,** John Osborn 1921- *WhoFI 92*
**Montgomery,** John R 1934- *AmMWSc 92*
**Montgomery,** John Rupert Patrick 1913- *Who 92*
**Montgomery,** John Warwick 1931- *IntWW 91, WhoAmL 92*
**Montgomery,** Joseph William 1951- *WhoFI 92*
**Montgomery,** Keesler H. 1917- *WhoBlA 92*
**Montgomery,** Kenneth 1943- *NewAmDM*
**Montgomery,** Kirby Vincent 1953- *WhoIns 92*
**Montgomery,** L. M. 1874-1942 *BenetAL 91, RfGEnL 91*
**Montgomery,** Lawrence Kernan 1935- *AmMWSc 92*
**Montgomery,** Leslie D 1939- *AmMWSc 92*
**Montgomery,** Linda Kay 1951- *WhoAmP 91*
**Montgomery,** Lisa A. 1959- *WhoAmL 92*
**Montgomery,** M Susan 1943- *AmMWSc 92*
**Montgomery,** Marion *DrAPF 91*
**Montgomery,** Marion 1925- *IntAu&W 91, WrDr 92*
**Montgomery,** Marjorie Ann 1941- *WhoAmL 92*
**Montgomery,** Michael B 1936- *WhoAmP 91*
**Montgomery,** Michael Bruce 1936- *WhoAmL 92*
**Montgomery,** Michael Davis 1936- *AmMWSc 92*
**Montgomery,** Michael Hart 1960- *WhoAmL 92*
**Montgomery,** Michael Henry 1955- *WhoRel 92*
**Montgomery,** Michael J. 1954- *WhoFI 92*
**Montgomery,** Michael Lee 1956- *WhoMW 92*
**Montgomery,** Mildred M. 1929- *WhoBlA 92*
**Montgomery,** Monty J 1939- *AmMWSc 92*
**Montgomery,** Morris William 1929- *AmMWSc 92*
**Montgomery,** Olive 1909- *WhoEnt 92*
**Montgomery,** Oliver R. 1929- *WhoBlA 92*
**Montgomery,** Oscar Lee 1949- *WhoBlA 92*
**Montgomery,** Patrick E. 1949- *WhoEnt 92*
**Montgomery,** Patrick Matthew 1957- *WhoIns 92*
**Montgomery,** Paul Charles 1944- *AmMWSc 92*
**Montgomery,** Payne 1933- *WhoBlA 92*
**Montgomery,** Peter Williams 1935- *AmMWSc 92*
**Montgomery,** Philip O'Bryan, Jr 1921- *AmMWSc 92*
**Montgomery,** Ray Hillman 1935- *WhoAmP 91*
**Montgomery,** Raymond Braislin 1910- *AmMWSc 92*
**Montgomery,** Rex 1923- *AmMWSc 92*
**Montgomery,** Richard 1738-1775 *BlkwEAR*
**Montgomery,** Richard A 1919- *AmMWSc 92*
**Montgomery,** Richard Calvin 1957- *WhoEnt 92*
**Montgomery,** Richard Glee 1938- *AmMWSc 92*
**Montgomery,** Richard Millar 1941- *AmMWSc 92*
**Montgomery,** Richard Paul 1959- *WhoWest 92*
**Montgomery,** Richard R *ScFEYrs*
**Montgomery,** Robert d1981 *LesBEnT 92*
**Montgomery,** Robert Alvin 1956- *WhoMW 92*
**Montgomery,** Robert Harold 1959- *WhoAmL 92*
**Montgomery,** Robert Humphrey, Jr. 1923- *WhoAmL 92*
**Montgomery,** Robert L 1935- *AmMWSc 92*
**Montgomery,** Robert Lew 1941- *WhoMW 92*
**Montgomery,** Robert Louis 1935- *WhoWest 92*
**Montgomery,** Robert Raynor 1943- *WhoFI 92*
**Montgomery,** Ronald Eugene 1937- *AmMWSc 92*
**Montgomery,** Royce Lee 1933- *AmMWSc 92*
**Montgomery,** Ruth 1927- *WhoAmP 91*
**Montgomery,** Rutherford 1894-1985 *TwCWW 91*
**Montgomery,** Seth *WhoAmP 91*
**Montgomery,** Seth David 1937- *WhoAmL 92, WhoWest 92*
**Montgomery,** Sheryl Elizabeth 1958- *WhoEnt 92*
**Montgomery,** Stewart Robert 1924- *AmMWSc 92*
**Montgomery,** Sy 1958- *ConAu 135*
**Montgomery,** Theodore Ashton 1923- *AmMWSc 92*
**Montgomery,** Thomas Harrison, Jr 1873-1912 *BiInAmS*
**Montgomery,** Toni-Marie 1956- *WhoBlA 92*
**Montgomery,** Trent *WhoBlA 92*
**Montgomery,** Velmanette *WhoAmP 91*
**Montgomery,** Walter Alexander 1845-1921 *DcNCBi 4*
**Montgomery,** Walter Alexander 1872-1949 *DcNCBi 4*
**Montgomery,** Wes 1925-1968 *NewAmDM*
**Montgomery,** William 1789-1844 *DcNCBi 4*
**Montgomery,** William Fergus 1927- *Who 92*
**Montgomery,** William J. 1930- *WhoFI 92*
**Montgomery,** William Jackson 1929- *WhoMW 92*
**Montgomery,** William R. 1924- *WhoBlA 92*
**Montgomery,** William Wayne 1923- *AmMWSc 92*
**Montgomery,** Willie Henry 1939- *WhoBlA 92*
**Montgomery,** Willson Linn 1946- *AmMWSc 92*
**Montgomery Cuninghame,** John Christopher 1935- *Who 92*
**Montgomery of Alamein,** Viscount 1928- *Who 92*
**Montgomery Watt,** William *Who 92*
**Montgoris,** William J. *WhoFI 92*
**Month,** Melvin 1936- *AmMWSc 92*
**Montherlant,** Henri de 1896-1972 *FacFETw*
**Montherlant,** Henry de 1896-1972 *GuFrLit 1*
**Monti,** Innocenzo 1909- *IntWW 91*
**Monti,** John Anthony 1949- *AmMWSc 92*
**Monti,** Luigi 1830-1903 *BenetAL 91*
**Monti,** Stephen Arion 1939- *AmMWSc 92*
**Monticciolo,** Joseph Domenick 1937- *WhoFI 92*
**Montie,** Thomas C 1934- *AmMWSc 92*
**Montiel,** Jose R. *WhoHisp 92*
**Montiel,** Jose Ramon *WhoHisp 92*
**Montiel,** Miguel 1942- *WhoHisp 92*
**Montiel,** Roberto C. *WhoHisp 92*
**Montiel,** Susan Purcell 1960- *WhoAmL 92*
**Montierth,** Max Romney 1938- *AmMWSc 92*
**Montieth,** Richard Voorhees 1913- *AmMWSc 92*
**Montijo,** Ben 1940- *WhoFI 92, WhoHisp 92*
**Montijo,** Ralph Elias, Jr. 1928- *WhoFI 92, WhoHisp 92*
**Montilla,** Cesar Alberto, Jr 1942- *WhoAmP 91*
**Montion,** Louis Herrera, Jr. 1943- *WhoHisp 92*
**Montis,** John Michael 1957- *WhoMW 92*
**Montisci,** Marcello Giovanni 1954- *WhoFI 92*
**Montjar,** Monty Jack 1924- *AmMWSc 92*
**Montlake,** Henry Joseph 1930- *Who 92*
**Montmorency,** Arnold Geoffrey de *Who 92*
**Monto,** Arnold Simon 1933- *AmMWSc 92*
**Monton,** Anthony Allen 1951- *WhoAmL 92*
**Montone,** Kenneth Alan 1938- *WhoWest 92*
**Montoni,** Lorin Marc 1962- *WhoAmP 91*
**Montoro,** Rafael 1852-1933 *HisDSpE*
**Montoure,** John Ernest 1927- *AmMWSc 92*
**Montovani,** Edward James, Sr. 1938- *WhoFI 92*
**Montoya,** A. R. *WhoHisp 92*
**Montoya,** Abran Felipe, Jr. 1948- *WhoHisp 92*
**Montoya,** Alfredo C. 1921- *WhoHisp 92*
**Montoya,** Alicia Navarro 1947- *WhoAmP 91*
**Montoya,** Alvaro 1942- *WhoHisp 92*
**Montoya,** Benjamin F. *WhoHisp 92*
**Montoya,** Carlos 1903- *NewAmDM*
**Montoya,** Carlos Garcia 1903- *WhoEnt 92*
**Montoya,** Charles William 1937- *WhoHisp 92*
**Montoya,** David *WhoHisp 92*
**Montoya,** David, Jr 1934- *WhoHisp 92*
**Montoya,** Delilah M. 1955- *WhoHisp 92*
**Montoya,** Demetrio H. 1937- *WhoHisp 92*
**Montoya,** Dennis William 1954- *WhoAmL 92*
**Montoya,** Frieda M. 1923- *WhoHisp 92*
**Montoya,** Hector R. 1954- *WhoFI 92*
**Montoya,** Herbert Patricio 1942- *WhoAmP 91*
**Montoya,** Isaac D. 1950- *WhoHisp 92*
**Montoya,** John J. 1945- *WhoHisp 92*
**Montoya,** Jorge P. 1946- *WhoHisp 92*
**Montoya,** Jose *DrAPF 91*
**Montoya,** Joseph O. 1945- *WhoHisp 92*
**Montoya,** Julio Cesar 1942- *WhoHisp 92*
**Montoya,** Linda Just 1941- *WhoEnt 92*
**Montoya,** Linda L. 1947- *WhoHisp 92*
**Montoya,** Louis *WhoHisp 92*

**Montoya,** Malaquias 1938- *WhoHisp 92*
**Montoya,** Max *WhoHisp 92*
**Montoya,** Nancy Lucero 1954- *WhoHisp 92*
**Montoya,** Pres L. 1954- *WhoHisp 92*
**Montoya,** Regina T. 1953- *WhoAmL 92, WhoHisp 92*
**Montoya,** Richard 1960- *WhoHisp 92*
**Montoya,** Ruben Ortiz 1923- *WhoHisp 92*
**Montoya,** Sam John 1946- *WhoHisp 92*
**Montoya,** Thomas Paul 1953- *WhoHisp 92*
**Montoya,** Velma *WhoHisp 92*
**Montpensier,** Anne Marie Louise d'Orleans 1627-1693 *EncAmaz 91*
**Montreal,** Bishop of 1938- *Who 92*
**Montremy,** Philipe Marie Waldruche de 1913- *IntWW 91*
**Montrone,** Paul Michael 1941- *WhoFI 92, WhoWest 92*
**Mont'Ros-Mendoza,** Theresa 1952- *WhoHisp 92*
**Montrose,** Duke of 1907- *Who 92*
**Montrose,** Charles Joseph 1942- *AmMWSc 92*
**Montrose,** Donald W. 1923- *WhoRel 92, WhoWest 92*
**Montross,** Franklin, IV 1956- *WhoIns 92*
**Montross,** W. Scott 1947- *WhoAmL 92*
**Monts,** David Lee 1951- *AmMWSc 92*
**Montsalvatge,** Xavier 1912- *ConCom 92, NewAmDM*
**Montsalvatge Bassols,** Xavier 1912- *ConCom 92*
**Montufar,** Carlos de 1780-1816 *HisDSpE*
**Montufar y Coronado,** Manuel 1791-1844 *HisDSpE*
**Montufar y Larrea,** Juan Pio de 1759-1818 *HisDSpE*
**Montupet,** Jean-Paul Leon 1947- *WhoFI 92*
**Montville,** Thomas Joseph 1953- *AmMWSc 92*
**Montwill,** Alexander 1935- *IntWW 91*
**Monty Python** *Au&Arts 7 [port], ConAu 35NR, IntMPA 92, SmATA 67*
**Monty,** Barbara Sue 1949- *WhoAmL 92*
**Monty,** Gloria *WhoEnt 92*
**Monty,** Jean Claude 1947- *WhoFI 92*
**Monty,** Kenneth James 1930- *AmMWSc 92*
**Monty,** Robert 1944- *WhoAmP 91*
**Montz,** Florence Stolte 1924- *WhoRel 92*
**Montzingo,** Lloyd J, Jr 1927- *AmMWSc 92*
**Monyak,** Wendell Peter 1931- *WhoMW 92*
**Monyake,** Lengolo Bureng 1930- *IntWW 91*
**Monyek,** Harice Kinsler 1937- *WhoMW 92*
**Monyer,** Pete, Jr. 1944- *WhoHisp 92*
**Monzen,** Mitsugi 1918- *IntWW 91*
**Monzon-Aguirre,** Victor J. 1949- *WhoHisp 92*
**Monzyk,** Bruce Francis *AmMWSc 92*
**Moo-Young,** Louise L. 1942- *WhoBlA 92*
**Moo-Young,** Murray *AmMWSc 92*
**Mooberry,** Jared Ben 1942- *AmMWSc 92*
**Moock,** Andrew William 1958- *WhoMW 92*
**Mood,** Alexander McFarlane 1913- *AmMWSc 92*
**Moodera,** Jagadeesh Subbaiah *AmMWSc 92*
**Moodey,** James R. 1932- *WhoMW 92, WhoRel 92*
**Moodie,** Dahlia Maria 1959- *WhoBlA 92*
**Moodie,** Donald 1892-1963 *TwCPaSc*
**Moodie,** Graeme Cochrane 1924- *IntAu&W 91, WrDr 92*
**Moodie,** Susanna 1803-1885 *BenetAL 91*
**Moody Blues** *NewAmDM*
**Moody Blues,** The *FacFETw*
**Moody,** Anne 1940- *BenetAL 91, WhoBlA 92*
**Moody,** Anthony Merald 1932- *WhoAmP 91*
**Moody,** Arnold Ralph 1941- *AmMWSc 92*
**Moody,** Charles David, Sr. 1932- *WhoBlA 92*
**Moody,** Charles Edward, Jr 1948- *AmMWSc 92*
**Moody,** Charles Russell 1956- *WhoWest 92*
**Moody,** Daniel McPherson 1962- *WhoEnt 92*
**Moody,** David Burritt 1940- *AmMWSc 92, WhoMW 92*
**Moody,** David Coit, III 1948- *AmMWSc 92*
**Moody,** David Edward 1950- *AmMWSc 92, WhoWest 92*
**Moody,** David Edward 1952- *WhoWest 92*
**Moody,** David George 1953- *WhoEnt 92*
**Moody,** David John 1947- *WhoEnt 92*
**Moody,** David Wright 1937- *AmMWSc 92*
**Moody,** Dwight Laymond, Jr. 1929- *WhoEnt 92*
**Moody,** Dwight Lyman 1837-1899 *BenetAL 91*
**Moody,** Dwight Lyman Ryther 1837-1899 *RelLAm 91*
**Moody,** Edward Grant 1919- *AmMWSc 92*
**Moody,** Edward H *WhoAmP 91*
**Moody,** Elizabeth Anne 1948- *AmMWSc 92*
**Moody,** Eric 1946- *TwCPaSc*
**Moody,** Eric Edward Marshall 1938- *AmMWSc 92*
**Moody,** Eric Orlando 1951- *WhoBlA 92*
**Moody,** Evelyn Wilie *WhoFI 92*
**Moody,** Frank Gordon 1928- *AmMWSc 92*
**Moody,** Fredreatha E. 1941- *WhoBlA 92*
**Moody,** G. William 1928- *WhoFI 92*
**Moody,** George Franklin 1930- *IntWW 91*
**Moody,** Gregory 1966- *WhoRel 92*
**Moody,** H A *ScFEYrs*
**Moody,** Harold L. 1932- *WhoBlA 92*
**Moody,** Harry John 1926- *AmMWSc 92*
**Moody,** Helen Newington Wills 1905- *FacFETw*
**Moody,** Helen Wills *Who 92*
**Moody,** Howard Craig 1951- *WhoAmP 91*
**Moody,** J William 1947- *WhoAmP 91*
**Moody,** James Maxwell 1940- *WhoAmL 92*
**Moody,** James Montraville 1858-1903 *DcNCBi 4*
**Moody,** James P 1935- *WhoAmP 91*
**Moody,** James Tyne 1938- *WhoAmL 92*
**Moody,** Jay I. 1961- *WhoRel 92*
**Moody,** Jim 1935- *AlmAP 92 [port], WhoMW 92*
**Moody,** John Charles 1936- *WhoMW 92*
**Moody,** John Henry 1945- *WhoRel 92*
**Moody,** John Percivale 1906- *Who 92*
**Moody,** John Robert 1942- *AmMWSc 92*
**Moody,** Joseph Charles 1958- *WhoEnt 92*
**Moody,** Joseph M 1928- *WhoAmP 91*
**Moody,** Judith Barbara 1942- *AmMWSc 92*
**Moody,** Kenton J 1954- *AmMWSc 92*
**Moody,** Larry Alan 1945- *WhoRel 92*
**Moody,** Leroy Stephen 1918- *AmMWSc 92*
**Moody,** Leslie Howard 1922- *Who 92*
**Moody,** Linda Ann 1954- *WhoRel 92*
**Moody,** Lundsford *WhoAmP 91*
**Moody,** Lynne Gatlin *WhoBlA 92*
**Moody,** Martin L 1925- *AmMWSc 92*
**Moody,** Mary Blair 1837-1919 *BiInAmS*
**Moody,** Max Dale 1924- *AmMWSc 92*
**Moody,** Michael Eugene 1952- *AmMWSc 92*
**Moody,** Michael Jay 1958- *WhoWest 92*
**Moody,** Nancy Drummelsmith 1946- *WhoAmL 92*
**Moody,** Patrick Jess 1952- *WhoEnt 92*
**Moody,** Peter Edward 1918- *Who 92*
**Moody,** Peter Richard, Jr. 1943- *WhoMW 92*
**Moody,** R. Bruce *DrAPF 91*
**Moody,** Randall Douglas 1962- *WhoRel 92*
**Moody,** Robert Adams 1934- *AmMWSc 92*
**Moody,** Robert Alan 1951- *WhoEnt 92*
**Moody,** Robert Arthur 1956- *WhoRel 92*
**Moody,** Robert J 1942- *WhoAmP 91*
**Moody,** Robert L. 1936- *WhoFI 92*
**Moody,** Robert Leon 1944- *WhoFI 92*
**Moody,** Rodger *DrAPF 91*
**Moody,** Ron 1924- *WhoEnt 92*
**Moody,** Sheryl A. 1955- *WhoAmL 92*
**Moody,** Shirley *DrAPF 91*
**Moody,** Susan *WrDr 92*
**Moody,** Willard James, Jr. 1957- *WhoAmL 92*
**Moody,** Willard James, Sr. 1924- *WhoAmL 92, WhoAmP 91*
**Moody,** William Dennis 1948- *WhoBlA 92*
**Moody,** William Glenn 1933- *AmMWSc 92*
**Moody,** William H 1853-1917 *FacFETw*
**Moody,** William Ralph 1919- *WhoRel 92*
**Moody,** William Vaughn 1869-1910 *BenetAL 91*
**Moody,** Willis E, Jr 1924- *AmMWSc 92*
**Mooers,** Calvin Northrup 1919- *AmMWSc 92*
**Mooers,** Christopher Northrup Kennard 1935- *AmMWSc 92*
**Mooers,** Daniel William 1943- *WhoAmL 92*
**Mooers,** Douglas Francis 1949- *WhoWest 92*
**Mooers,** Emma Wilson Davidson d1911 *BiInAmS*
**Mooers,** Howard T 1921- *AmMWSc 92*
**Mooers,** Malcolm Minter 1924- *WhoRel 92*
**Mooers,** Philip F 1940- *WhoIns 92*
**Moog,** Mary Ann Pimley 1952- *WhoAmL 92*
**Moog,** Robert A. 1934- *NewAmDM*
**Moog,** Robert Arthur 1934- *WhoEnt 92*
**Mook,** David Gerard 1952- *WhoEnt 92*
**Mook,** Dean Tritschler 1935- *AmMWSc 92*
**Mook,** Delo Emerson, II 1942- *AmMWSc 92*
**Mook,** Herbert Arthur, Jr 1939- *AmMWSc 92*
**Mookerjea,** Sailen 1930- *AmMWSc 92*
**Mookerjee,** Birendra Nath 1899- *Who 92*
**Mookherji,** Tripty Kumar 1938- *AmMWSc 92*
**Mookini,** Esther T. 1928- *ConAu 135*
**Moolenaar,** Robert John 1931- *AmMWSc 92*
**Moolgavkar,** Suresh Hiraji 1943- *AmMWSc 92*
**Moollan,** Abdool Hamid 1933- *Who 92*
**Moollan,** Cassam 1927- *Who 92*
**Moolten,** Frederick London 1932- *AmMWSc 92*
**Moolten,** Sylvan E 1904- *AmMWSc 92*
**Moomau,** Pamela Hooper 1954- *WhoFI 92*
**Moomaw,** James Aubrey 1955- *WhoAmL 92*
**Moomaw,** Jon Leslie 1945- *WhoMW 92*
**Moomaw,** Max *WhoAmP 91*
**Moomaw,** William Renken 1938- *AmMWSc 92*
**Moon,** Brenda Elizabeth 1931- *Who 92*
**Moon,** Byong Hoon 1926- *AmMWSc 92*
**Moon,** Chang Keuk 1948- *WhoFI 92*
**Moon,** Deug Woon *AmMWSc 92*
**Moon,** Donald W 1934- *AmMWSc 92*
**Moon,** Elizabeth 1945- *ConAu 134*
**Moon,** Francis C 1939- *AmMWSc 92*
**Moon,** George D, Jr 1927- *AmMWSc 92*
**Moon,** Geraldine N. d1991 *NewYTBS 91*
**Moon,** Gordon Ray *WhoAmP 91*
**Moon,** Harley W 1936- *AmMWSc 92*
**Moon,** Jeremy 1934-1973 *TwCPaSc*
**Moon,** John Henry, Sr. 1937- *WhoFI 92*
**Moon,** John Paul 1952- *WhoEnt 92*
**Moon,** John Scafa 1960- *WhoRel 92, WhoWest 92*
**Moon,** John Wesley *AmMWSc 92*
**Moon,** John Wesley 1940- *WhoWest 92*
**Moon,** Keith 1947-1978 *FacFETw*
**Moon,** Kunduck 1953- *WhoFI 92*
**Moon,** Lauren Gwinn 1960- *WhoMW 92*
**Moon,** Maria Elena 1945- *WhoHisp 92*
**Moon,** Marjorie Ruth 1926- *WhoAmP 91*
**Moon,** Mary Marjorie 1932- *Who 92*
**Moon,** Mick 1937- *TwCPaSc*
**Moon,** Milton Lewis 1922- *AmMWSc 92*
**Moon,** Mollie 1912-1990 *NotBlAW 92*
**Moon,** Peter Clayton 1940- *AmMWSc 92*
**Moon,** Peter James Scott d1991 *Who 92N*
**Moon,** Peter Wilfred Giles Graham- 1942- *Who 92*
**Moon,** Philip Burton 1907- *Who 92*
**Moon,** R. Bruce 1959- *WhoAmL 92*
**Moon,** Ralph Marks, Jr 1929- *AmMWSc 92*
**Moon,** Richard C 1926- *AmMWSc 92*
**Moon,** Robert John 1942- *AmMWSc 92*
**Moon,** Robert Preston 1958- *WhoRel 92*
**Moon,** Roger 1914- *Who 92*
**Moon,** Ronald T *WhoAmP 91*
**Moon,** Ronald T. Y. 1940- *WhoAmL 92, WhoWest 92*
**Moon,** Spencer 1948- *WhoEnt 92*
**Moon,** Sun Myung 1920- *FacFETw, RelLAm 91*
**Moon,** Sung 1928- *AmMWSc 92*
**Moon,** Tag Young 1931- *AmMWSc 92*
**Moon,** Tessie Jo 1961- *AmMWSc 92*
**Moon,** Thomas Charles 1940- *AmMWSc 92*
**Moon,** Thomas Edward 1943- *AmMWSc 92*
**Moon,** Thomas William 1944- *AmMWSc 92*
**Moon,** Walter D. 1940- *WhoBlA 92*
**Moon,** Warren 1956- *CurBio 91 [port], News 91 [port], -91-3 [port], WhoBlA 92*
**Moon,** Wilchor David 1933- *AmMWSc 92*
**Moonan,** Timothy James 1959- *WhoFI 92*
**Moone,** James Clark 1940- *WhoBlA 92*
**Moone,** Wanda Renee 1956- *WhoBlA 92*
**Mooney,** Bel 1946- *IntAu&W 91, Who 92*
**Mooney,** Charles Michael 1951- *BlkOlyM*
**Mooney,** Christopher Francis 1925- *WrDr 92*
**Mooney,** David Samuel 1928- *AmMWSc 92*
**Mooney,** David Walton 1955- *WhoFI 92*
**Mooney,** Debra *WhoEnt 92*
**Mooney,** Donald James 1926- *WhoFI 92*
**Mooney,** Edward, Jr 1942- *AmMWSc 92*
**Mooney,** Edward Francis 1882-1958 *RelLAm 91*
**Mooney,** Edward Joseph, Jr. 1941- *WhoMW 92*
**Mooney,** Harold A 1932- *AmMWSc 92*
**Mooney,** Harold Alfred 1932- *IntWW 91*
**Mooney,** James Pierce 1943- *WhoEnt 92*
**Mooney,** Jerome Henri 1944- *WhoAmL 92*
**Mooney,** John Allen 1918- *WhoFI 92, WhoMW 92*
**Mooney,** John Bernard 1926- *AmMWSc 92*
**Mooney,** John Bradford, Jr 1931- *AmMWSc 92*
**Mooney,** John Joseph 1930- *WhoAmP 91*
**Mooney,** John Murray 1928- *WhoWest 92*
**Mooney,** Jon Randolph 1957- *WhoFI 92*
**Mooney,** Justin David 1932- *WhoFI 92*
**Mooney,** Kevin Sean 1953- *WhoEnt 92*
**Mooney,** Kevin Xavier 1933- *WhoIns 92*
**Mooney,** Larry Albert 1936- *AmMWSc 92*
**Mooney,** Margaret L 1929- *AmMWSc 92*
**Mooney,** Mary Margaret 1939- *WhoRel 92*
**Mooney,** Michael Edward 1945- *WhoAmL 92*
**Mooney,** Michael Morse 1939- *IntAu&W 91*
**Mooney,** Patricia May 1945- *AmMWSc 92*
**Mooney,** Richard T 1925- *AmMWSc 92*
**Mooney,** Richard Warren 1923- *AmMWSc 92*
**Mooney,** Thomas Burt *WhoAmL 92*
**Mooney,** Vicki 1949- *WhoEnt 92*
**Mooney,** Walter D 1951- *AmMWSc 92*
**Mooney,** William M. *WhoFI 92*
**Mooney,** William Piatt 1936- *WhoEnt 92*
**Mooneyham,** W. Stanley d1991 *NewYTBS 91 [port]*
**Mooneyham,** W. Stanley 1926-1991 *ConAu 134*
**Moonie,** Lewis George 1947- *Who 92*
**Moonjean,** Hank *IntMPA 92*
**Moonman,** Eric 1929- *IntAu&W 91, Who 92, WrDr 92*
**Moons,** Charles M. J. A. 1917- *IntWW 91*
**Moonves,** Leslie *LesBEnT 92*
**Moonves,** Leslie 1949- *WhoEnt 92*
**Moor,** Dmitriy Stakhievich 1883-1946 *SovUnBD*
**Moor,** James Talley 1948- *WhoRel 92*
**Moor,** William C 1941- *AmMWSc 92*
**Moor,** William Chattle 1941- *WhoWest 92*
**Moor-Jankowski,** J 1924- *AmMWSc 92*
**Mooradian,** Arshag Dertad 1953- *AmMWSc 92*
**Moorbath,** Stephen Erwin 1929- *IntWW 91, Who 92*
**Moorcock,** Michael 1939- *ConNov 91, IntAu&W 91, TwCSFW 91, WrDr 92*
**Moorcraft,** Dennis Harry 1921- *Who 92*
**Moorcroft,** Donald Ross 1935- *AmMWSc 92*
**Moorcroft,** William Herbert 1944- *AmMWSc 92*
**Moore** *Who 92*
**Moore,** Viscount 1983- *Who 92*
**Moore,** A Donald 1923- *AmMWSc 92*
**Moore,** Aaron McDuffie 1863-1923 *DcNCBi 4*
**Moore,** Acel 1940- *WhoBlA 92*
**Moore,** Ada d1991 *NewYTBS 91*
**Moore,** Aimee N 1918- *AmMWSc 92*
**Moore,** Alan Edward 1936- *Who 92*
**Moore,** Albert 1952- *WhoBlA 92*
**Moore,** Albert J. 1948- *WhoAmL 92*
**Moore,** Alexander Mazyck 1917- *AmMWSc 92*
**Moore,** Alexander Wyndham Hume S. *Who 92*
**Moore,** Alfred 1755-1810 *DcNCBi 4*
**Moore,** Alfred 1956- *WhoBlA 92*
**Moore,** Alice Evelyn 1933- *WhoBlA 92*
**Moore,** Allen Murdoch 1940- *AmMWSc 92*
**Moore,** Alstork Edward 1940- *WhoBlA 92*
**Moore,** Alton Wallace 1916- *AmMWSc 92*
**Moore,** Alvy 1925- *ConTFT 9*
**Moore,** Amos 1884-1958 *TwCWW 91*
**Moore,** Ana Maria 1942- *AmMWSc 92*
**Moore,** Andrew G T, II 1935- *WhoAmP 91*
**Moore,** Andrew Given Tobias, II 1935- *WhoAmL 92*
**Moore,** Andrew Michael, Jr. 1940- *WhoFI 92*
**Moore,** Anne *WhoRel 92*
**Moore,** Annie Carroll 1871-1961 *HanAmWH*
**Moore,** Annie Jewell 1919- *WhoBlA 92*
**Moore,** Anon *ScFEYrs*
**Moore,** Anthony Louis 1946- *WhoBlA 92*
**Moore,** Antony Ross 1918- *Who 92*
**Moore,** Arch Alfred, Jr. 1923- *IntWW 91*
**Moore,** Archibald Lee Wright 1916- *WhoBlA 92*
**Moore,** Archie 1913- *FacFETw*
**Moore,** Archie Bradford, Jr. 1933- *WhoBlA 92*
**Moore,** Arnold D. 1916- *WhoBlA 92*
**Moore,** Arnold Robert 1923- *AmMWSc 92*
**Moore,** Arthur C. 1894- *WhoBlA 92*
**Moore,** Arthur James 1888-1974 *RelLAm 91*
**Moore,** Arthur William 1920- *WhoAmL 92*
**Moore,** Arthur William 1937- *AmMWSc 92*
**Moore,** Audley 1898- *NotBlAW 92 [port]*

**Moore,** Barbara 1934- IntAu&W 91, WrDr 92

**Moore,** Barry Newton 1941- AmMWSc 92

**Moore,** Bartholomew Figures 1801-1878 DcNCBi 4

**Moore,** Benita Ann 1931- WhoMW 92, WhoRel 92

**Moore,** Benjamin LaBree 1915- AmMWSc 92

**Moore,** Berrien, III 1941- AmMWSc 92

**Moore,** Betty Clark 1915- AmMWSc 92

**Moore,** Betty Jo WhoWest 92

**Moore,** Beverly Ann 1934- WhoWest 92

**Moore,** Beverly Cooper 1909- WhoAmL 92

**Moore,** Beverly Cooper, Jr. 1945- WhoAmL 92

**Moore,** Bill C 1907- AmMWSc 92

**Moore,** Billie Lee 1931- WhoFI 92

**Moore,** Billy Don 1956- WhoEnt 92

**Moore,** Blaine H. 1931- WhoWest 92

**Moore,** Blake William 1926- AmMWSc 92

**Moore,** Bob Loyce 1932- WhoEnt 92

**Moore,** Bob Stahly 1936- WhoFI 92

**Moore,** Bobby IntWW 91, Who 92

**Moore,** Bobby 1949- WhoBlA 92

**Moore,** Bobby Graham 1940- AmMWSc 92

**Moore,** Brenda Carol 1945- WhoBlA 92

**Moore,** Brian DrAPF 91

**Moore,** Brian 1921- BenetAL 91, ConNov 91, FacFETw, IntAu&W 91, IntWW 91, LiExTwC, RfGEnL 91, Who 92, WrDr 92

**Moore,** Brian Baden 1932- Who 92

**Moore,** Brian Clive 1945- WhoFI 92

**Moore,** Bruce Alan 1952- WhoMW 92

**Moore,** C Bradley 1939- AmMWSc 92, WhoWest 92

**Moore,** C Fred 1936- AmMWSc 92

**Moore,** C L 1911-1988 TwCSFW 91

**Moore,** C. Thomas 1930- WhoRel 92

**Moore,** Calvin 1951- WhoAmP 91

**Moore,** Calvin C 1936- AmMWSc 92

**Moore,** Carey Armstrong 1930- WrDr 92

**Moore,** Carl 1919- AmMWSc 92

**Moore,** Carl Edward 1915- AmMWSc 92

**Moore,** Carl R 1930- WhoAmP 91

**Moore,** Carla Jean 1950- AmMWSc 92

**Moore,** Carleton Bryant 1932- AmMWSc 92, WhoWest 92

**Moore,** Carman 1936- IntAu&W 91, WrDr 92

**Moore,** Carman Leroy 1936- WhoBlA 92

**Moore,** Carol Louise 1943- WhoBlA 92

**Moore,** Carol Wood 1943- AmMWSc 92

**Moore,** Carole Rinne 1944- IntWW 91

**Moore,** Carolyn Dabbs 1931- WhoAmP 91

**Moore,** Carolyn Lannin 1945- WhoMW 92

**Moore,** Celesta Rose 1944- WhoMW 92

**Moore,** Charleen Morizot 1944- AmMWSc 92

**Moore,** Charles B 1927- AmMWSc 92

**Moore,** Charles D. 1906- WhoBlA 92

**Moore,** Charles Godat 1927- AmMWSc 92

**Moore,** Charles Hewes, Jr. 1929- WhoMW 92

**Moore,** Charles Hilary 1956- IntAu&W 91, Who 92

**Moore,** Charles Leonard 1854-1923 BenetAL 91

**Moore,** Charles Stuart 1910- Who 92

**Moore,** Charles W. 1923- WhoBlA 92

**Moore,** Charles W. 1925- WrDr 92

**Moore,** Charles Willard 1930- WhoEnt 92

**Moore,** Charlie W. 1926- WhoBlA 92

**Moore,** Christine James 1930- WhoBlA 92

**Moore,** Christopher Hugh 1950- IntAu&W 91

**Moore,** Christopher W. 1964- WhoWest 92

**Moore,** Cicely Frances Who 92

**Moore,** Clarence L 1931- AmMWSc 92

**Moore,** Clark WhoRel 92

**Moore,** Claude Henry 1923- AmMWSc 92

**Moore,** Clement Clarke 1779-1863 BenetAL 91

**Moore,** Cleotha Franklin 1942- WhoBlA 92

**Moore,** Clifton Leonard 1900-1966 DcNCBi 4

**Moore,** Clyde H, Jr 1933- AmMWSc 92

**Moore,** Coban Cheek 1922- WhoAmP 91

**Moore,** Colin A. 1944- WhoBlA 92

**Moore,** Colleen 1902-1988 FacFETw

**Moore,** Condict 1916- AmMWSc 92

**Moore,** Constance 1922- IntMPA 92

**Moore,** Cornell Leverette 1939- WhoBlA 92

**Moore,** Craig Damon 1942- AmMWSc 92

**Moore,** Cynthia M. 1963- WhoBlA 92

**Moore,** Cynthia Rich 1964- WhoMW 92

**Moore,** Cyril L 1928- AmMWSc 92

**Moore,** Dalton, Jr. 1918- WhoFI 92

**Moore,** Dan Houston 1909- AmMWSc 92

**Moore,** Dan Houston, II 1941- AmMWSc 92

**Moore,** Daniel A., Jr. 1934- WhoAmL 92, WhoAmP 91, WhoWest 92

**Moore,** Daniel Charles 1918- AmMWSc 92

**Moore,** Daniel Elliott 1953- WhoFI 92

**Moore,** Daniel Horatio 1959- WhoFI 92

**Moore,** Daniel Michael 1954- WhoAmL 92

**Moore,** Daniel Thomas 1953- WhoRel 92

**Moore,** David A 1917- AmMWSc 92

**Moore,** David Austin 1935- WhoFI 92, WhoWest 92

**Moore,** David Bernard, II 1940- WhoBlA 92

**Moore,** David C 1941- WhoIns 92

**Moore,** David Guy 1952- WhoAmL 92

**Moore,** David James Ladd 1937- Who 92

**Moore,** David Jay 1936- AmMWSc 92

**Moore,** David Joseph 1941- WhoMW 92

**Moore,** David Laidley, Jr. 1952- WhoFI 92

**Moore,** David Lee 1940- AmMWSc 92

**Moore,** David M. 1955- WhoBlA 92

**Moore,** David Mark 1958- WhoFI 92

**Moore,** David Max 1949- WhoMW 92

**Moore,** David Sheldon 1940- AmMWSc 92

**Moore,** David Warren 1939- AmMWSc 92

**Moore,** Deborah Dash 1946- WhoRel 92

**Moore,** Demi NewYTBS 91 [port]

**Moore,** Demi 1962- IntMPA 92, WhoEnt 92

**Moore,** Demi 1963?- News 91 [port]

**Moore,** Dennis Eugene 1948- WhoMW 92

**Moore,** Dennis Paul 1946- WhoFI 92

**Moore,** Derek William 1931- Who 92

**Moore,** Derick Colden 1956- WhoEnt 92

**Moore,** Derry Who 92

**Moore,** Dian L. 1953- WhoWest 92

**Moore,** Dianne Lea 1949- WhoWest 92

**Moore,** Dickie 1925- IntMPA 92

**Moore,** Dolores Wickline 1932- WhoFI 92

**Moore,** Don A 1928- WhoAmP 91

**Moore,** Donald WhoAmP 91

**Moore,** Donald Bruce 1941- WhoRel 92

**Moore,** Donald L. 1933- WhoRel 92

**Moore,** Donald R 1933- AmMWSc 92

**Moore,** Donald Richard 1921- AmMWSc 92

**Moore,** Donald Torian 1933- WhoBlA 92

**Moore,** Donald Vincent 1915- AmMWSc 92

**Moore,** Donald Walter 1942- WhoWest 92

**Moore,** Donald Willard 1928- WhoWest 92

**Moore,** Doris Langley 1902- IntAu&W 91

**Moore,** Dorothy A 1929- WhoAmP 91

**Moore,** Dorothy Price 1910- WhoAmP 91

**Moore,** Dorothy Rudd 1940- NewAmDM

**Moore,** Douglas 1893-1969 BenetAL 91

**Moore,** Douglas Bryant 1946- WhoEnt 92

**Moore,** Douglas Dewain 1948- WhoMW 92

**Moore,** Douglas Houston 1920- AmMWSc 92

**Moore,** Douglas S. 1893-1969 NewAmDM

**Moore,** Duane Grey 1929- AmMWSc 92

**Moore,** Duane Milton 1933- AmMWSc 92

**Moore,** Dudley 1935- FacFETw, IntMPA 92

**Moore,** Dudley L, Jr 1936- WhoIns 92

**Moore,** Dudley Lester, Jr. 1936- WhoFI 92

**Moore,** Dudley Stuart John 1935- IntWW 91, Who 92, WhoEnt 92

**Moore,** Duncan Thomas 1946- AmMWSc 92

**Moore,** Dwayne Harrison 1958- WhoBlA 92

**Moore,** E. Harris WhoRel 92

**Moore,** E Neil 1932- AmMWSc 92

**Moore,** Earl B. 1930- WhoBlA 92

**Moore,** Earl Neil 1904- AmMWSc 92

**Moore,** Eddie C. d1991 NewYTBS 91 [port]

**Moore,** Eddie N., Jr. WhoBlA 92

**Moore,** Edgar Tilden, Jr 1937- AmMWSc 92

**Moore,** Edmund Wright 1938- WhoEnt 92

**Moore,** Edna Ruth 1911- WhoAmP 91

**Moore,** Edward 1712-1757 RfGEnL 91

**Moore,** Edward D WhoAmP 91

**Moore,** Edward Forrest 1925- AmMWSc 92

**Moore,** Edward Francis Butler 1906- Who 92

**Moore,** Edward Lee 1929- AmMWSc 92

**Moore,** Edward Stanton 1910- Who 92

**Moore,** Edward T 1937- AmMWSc 92

**Moore,** Edward Weldon 1930- AmMWSc 92

**Moore,** Edwin Forrest 1912- AmMWSc 92

**Moore,** Edwin Granville 1950- AmMWSc 92

**Moore,** Edwin Lewis 1916- AmMWSc 92

**Moore,** Edwin Neal 1934- AmMWSc 92

**Moore,** Elaine 1947- WhoBlA 92

**Moore,** Elaine Susan 1951- WhoMW 92

**Moore,** Elizabeth IntAu&W 91X

**Moore,** Elizabeth A 1938- WhoAmP 91

**Moore,** Elizabeth Jane 1940- WhoWest 92

**Moore,** Elliott Paul 1936- AmMWSc 92

**Moore,** Ellis 1924- IntMPA 92

**Moore,** Emanuel A. 1941- WhoBlA 92

**Moore,** Emerson J. 1938- WhoBlA 92

**Moore,** Emerson John 1938- WhoRel 92

**Moore,** Emily Allyn 1950- WhoMW 92

**Moore,** Emily Louise 1946- WhoMW 92

**Moore,** Emmett Burris, Jr 1929- AmMWSc 92

**Moore,** Enoch William 1868-1952 DcNCBi 4

**Moore,** Erin Colleen 1924- AmMWSc 92

**Moore,** Ernest C 1922- WhoAmP 91

**Moore,** Ernest Carroll, III 1944- WhoAmL 92, WhoWest 92

**Moore,** Ernest J 1919- AmMWSc 92

**Moore,** Eugene WhoAmP 91

**Moore,** Eugene Roger 1933- AmMWSc 92

**Moore,** Evan Gregory 1923- WhoBlA 92

**Moore,** Evelyn Dzurilla 1962- WhoMW 92

**Moore,** Evelyn K. 1937- WhoBlA 92

**Moore,** Evelyn Tournoy 1957- WhoMW 92

**Moore,** F. Richard 1944- WhoEnt 92

**Moore,** Fenton Daniel 1938- AmMWSc 92

**Moore,** Feryall Rahman 1961- WhoEnt 92

**Moore,** Fletcher Brooks 1926- AmMWSc 92

**Moore,** Frances Faye 1943- IntAu&W 91

**Moore,** Francis Bertram 1905- AmMWSc 92

**Moore,** Francis Daniels 1913- AmMWSc 92, IntWW 91

**Moore,** Frank 1828-1904 BenetAL 91

**Moore,** Frank Archer 1920- AmMWSc 92

**Moore,** Frank Devitt, III 1931- AmMWSc 92

**Moore,** Frank Frankfurt 1855-1931 ScFEYrs

**Moore,** Frank Ludwig 1945- AmMWSc 92

**Moore,** Frank Timothy 1951- WhoRel 92

**Moore,** Franklin Hall, Jr. 1937- WhoAmL 92

**Moore,** Franklin K 1922- AmMWSc 92

**Moore,** Franklin Shearer 1960- WhoFI 92, WhoMW 92

**Moore,** Fred Edward 1923- AmMWSc 92

**Moore,** Fred Henderson 1934- WhoBlA 92

**Moore,** Fred Thurman 1921- WhoAmP 91

**Moore,** Frederick Alvin 1952- WhoBlA 92

**Moore,** Frederick David 1902- Who 92

**Moore,** G E 1873-1958 FacFETw

**Moore,** Gabriel 1785-1844 DcNCBi 4

**Moore,** Garry LesBEnT 92

**Moore,** Garry 1915- IntMPA 92, WhoEnt 92

**Moore,** Garry 1949- WhoAmP 91

**Moore,** Garry Edgar 1948- AmMWSc 92

**Moore,** Gary E. 1962- WhoBlA 92

**Moore,** Gary Richard 1945- WhoFI 92

**Moore,** Gary T 1945- AmMWSc 92

**Moore,** Gary Thomas 1942- AmMWSc 92

**Moore,** Geoffrey Herbert 1920- Who 92

**Moore,** George 1715-1778 DcNCBi 4

**Moore,** George 1852-1933 RfGEnL 91, ThHElm

**Moore,** George 1913- Who 92

**Moore,** George 1923- Who 92

**Moore,** George A 1913- AmMWSc 92

**Moore,** George Anthony 1914- WhoBlA 92

**Moore,** George Augustus 1852-1933 FacFETw

**Moore,** George Crawford Jackson WhoAmL 92

**Moore,** George Eagleton 1927- WhoRel 92

**Moore,** George Edgar 1907- Who 92

**Moore,** George Edward 1922- AmMWSc 92

**Moore,** George Edward 1946- WhoAmL 92

**Moore,** George Emerson, Jr 1914- AmMWSc 92

**Moore,** George Emory, Jr. 1949- WhoFI 92

**Moore,** George Eugene 1920- AmMWSc 92

**Moore,** George Henry 1823-1892 BenetAL 91

**Moore,** George Herbert 1903- Who 92

**Moore,** George K 1927- WhoIns 92

**Moore,** George Thomas 1945- WhoBlA 92

**Moore,** George W. 1926-1991 NewYTBS 91 [port]

**Moore,** George Wayne 1949- WhoFI 92, WhoWest 92

**Moore,** George William 1928- AmMWSc 92

**Moore,** Georgina Mary 1930- IntWW 91, Who 92

**Moore,** Gerald 1899-1987 FacFETw, NewAmDM

**Moore,** Gerald L. 1933- WhoBlA 92

**Moore,** Gerald L 1939- AmMWSc 92

**Moore,** Gideon Emmet 1842-1895 BiInAmS

**Moore,** Glenn D 1923- AmMWSc 92

**Moore,** Godwin Cotton 1806-1880 DcNCBi 4

**Moore,** Gordon Charles 1928- Who 92

**Moore,** Gordon E. 1929- WhoFI 92, WhoWest 92

**Moore,** Gordon Earle 1929- AmMWSc 92

**Moore,** Gordon George 1935- AmMWSc 92

**Moore,** Grace 1898-1947 NewAmDM

**Moore,** Graham John 1946- AmMWSc 92

**Moore,** Greg David 1967- WhoFI 92

**Moore,** Gregory Frank 1951- AmMWSc 92

**Moore,** Gwen WhoAmP 91, WhoBlA 92

**Moore,** Gwendolynne Sophia 1951- WhoAmP 91

**Moore,** Gwyneth WrDr 92

**Moore,** Hal G 1929- AmMWSc 92, WhoWest 92, WrDr 92

**Moore,** Harold Arthur 1925- AmMWSc 92

**Moore,** Harold Beveridge 1928- AmMWSc 92

**Moore,** Harold LeRoy 1915- WhoMW 92

**Moore,** Harold W 1936- AmMWSc 92

**Moore,** Harry 1915- Who 92

**Moore,** Harry Ballard, Jr 1928- AmMWSc 92

**Moore,** Harry Russell 1921- WhoAmL 92

**Moore,** Hazel Stamps 1924- WhoBlA 92

**Moore,** Helen Boulware 1936- WhoBlA 92

**Moore,** Helen D. S. 1932- WhoBlA 92

**Moore,** Helen Elizabeth 1920- WhoMW 92

**Moore,** Helen Miller 1942- WhoRel 92

**Moore,** Henderson Alfred, Jr. 1912- WhoFI 92

**Moore,** Henry 1898-1986 FacFETw, TwCPaSc

**Moore,** Henry J. 1949- WhoBlA 92

**Moore,** Henry J, II 1928- AmMWSc 92

**Moore,** Henry Roderick Who 92

**Moore,** Henry Rogers 1916- WhoFI 92

**Moore,** Henry Trumbull, Jr. 1932- WhoAmL 92

**Moore,** Henry Wylie 1923- Who 92

**Moore,** Herff Leo, Jr. 1937- WhoFI 92

**Moore,** Hight C. 1871-1957 DcNCBi 4

**Moore,** Hilliard T., Sr. 1925- WhoBlA 92

**Moore,** Hiram Beene 1914- WhoBlA 92

**Moore,** Honor DrAPF 91

**Moore,** Howard, Jr. 1932- WhoBlA 92

**Moore,** Howard Francis 1948- AmMWSc 92

**Moore,** Howard Roswald, Jr. 1932- WhoAmL 92

**Moore,** Hugh Jacob, Jr. 1944- WhoAmL 92

**Moore,** J Lawrence 1917- WhoAmP 91

**Moore,** J. Owen BenetAL 91

**Moore,** J. Richard 1934- WhoAmL 92

**Moore,** J Strother 1947- AmMWSc 92

**Moore,** Jack Kenneth 1921- WhoAmP 91

**Moore,** Jack Leslie 1947- WhoFI 92, WhoMW 92

**Moore,** Jack Lynne 1920- WhoRel 92

**Moore,** James DrAPF 91

**Moore,** James 1737-1777 DcNCBi 4

**Moore,** James Alexander 1923- AmMWSc 92

**Moore,** James Alfred 1939- AmMWSc 92

**Moore,** James Alfred 1957- WhoRel 92

**Moore,** James Allan 1939- AmMWSc 92

**Moore,** James Arthur 1951- WhoMW 92

**Moore,** James C WhoAmP 91

**Moore,** James Carlton 1923- AmMWSc 92

**Moore,** James Clark 1935- WhoMW 92

**Moore,** James E 1935- WhoAmP 91

**Moore,** James Edward 1852-1918 BiInAmS

**Moore,** James Edward 1934- WhoFI 92

**Moore,** James Everett, Jr. 1950- WhoAmL 92

**Moore,** James F 1928- WhoIns 92

**Moore,** James Fraser 1946- WhoRel 92

**Moore,** James Frederick, Jr 1938- AmMWSc 92

**Moore,** James Gregory 1930- AmMWSc 92

**Moore,** James Kelly 1950- WhoEnt 92

**Moore,** James L. WhoBlA 92

**Moore,** James Mack, Jr. 1945- WhoAmL 92

**Moore,** James Mendon 1925- AmMWSc 92

**Moore,** James Norman 1931- AmMWSc 92

**Moore,** James Osborne 1909-1988 DcNCBi 4

**Moore,** James Russell 1962- WhoRel 92

**Moore,** James Sam, Jr. 1930- WhoAmL 92

**Moore,** James Thomas 1952- AmMWSc 92

**Moore,** James Thomas, III 1942- WhoAmL 92

**Moore,** James W 1844-1909 BiInAmS

**Moore,** James W I 1923- AmMWSc 92

**Moore,** James William 1936- WhoEnt 92

**Moore,** Jane Bond 1938- WhoBlA 92

**Moore,** Janet 1935- WhoAmP 91

**Moore,** Janice Townley DrAPF 91

**Moore,** Jay Winston 1942- AmMWSc 92

**Moore,** Jean E. WhoBlA 92

**Moore,** Jean Oliver 1925- WhoAmL 92, WhoMW 92

**Moore,** Jeffrey Clyde 1962- WhoWest 92

**Moore,** Jellether Marie 1949- WhoBlA 92

**Moore,** Jeremy Who 92

**Moore,** Jerry A., Jr. 1918- WhoBlA 92

**Moore,** Jerry Lamar 1942- AmMWSc 92

Moore, Jerry Lee 1945- *WhoRel 92*
Moore, Joan Elizabeth 1951- *WhoFI 92*
Moore, Joanna Patterson 1832-1916 *RelLAm 91*
Moore, Joanne Iweita 1928- *AmMWSc 92*
Moore, John 1729-1802 *RfGEnL 91*
Moore, John 1753?-1781? *DcNCBi 4*
Moore, John 1858-1929 *BenetAL 91*
Moore, John 1915- *Who 92*
Moore, John 1937- *Who 92*
Moore, John A. 1915- *IntWW 91*
Moore, John Alexander 1915- *AmMWSc 92*
Moore, John Arthur 1939- *AmMWSc 92*
Moore, John Ashton 1940- *WhoWest 92*
Moore, John Atkin 1931- *WhoAmL 92*
Moore, John Baily, Jr 1944- *AmMWSc 92*
Moore, John Byron 1963- *WhoAmL 92*
Moore, John Carman Gailey 1916- *AmMWSc 92*
Moore, John Coleman 1923- *AmMWSc 92*
Moore, John D. 1937- *WhoWest 92*
Moore, John Douglas 1939- *AmMWSc 92*
Moore, John Douglas 1943- *AmMWSc 92*
Moore, John Duain 1913- *AmMWSc 92*
Moore, John Edward 1920- *WhoFI 92, WhoMW 92*
Moore, John Edward 1935- *AmMWSc 92*
Moore, John Edward Michael 1937- *IntWW 91*
Moore, John Edwin, Jr. 1942- *WhoMW 92*
Moore, John Evelyn 1921- *IntAu&W 91, IntWW 91, Who 92*
Moore, John Ezra 1931- *AmMWSc 92*
Moore, John Fitzallen 1928- *AmMWSc 92*
Moore, John Hays 1941- *AmMWSc 92*
Moore, John Henry, II 1929- *WhoAmL 92*
Moore, John Jeremy 1928- *IntWW 91, Who 92*
Moore, John Jeremy 1944- *AmMWSc 92*
Moore, John Marshall, Jr 1935- *AmMWSc 92*
Moore, John Michael 1921- *Who 92*
Moore, John Michael 1935- *Who 92, WrDr 92*
Moore, John N. 1937- *WrDr 92*
Moore, John Norton 1937- *IntAu&W 91, WhoFI 92*
Moore, John P *WhoAmP 91*
Moore, John Parker, Jr. 1942- *WhoEnt 92*
Moore, John Porfilio 1934- *WhoAmL 92, WhoWest 92*
Moore, John R 1916- *AmMWSc 92*
Moore, John Richard 1921- *WhoMW 92*
Moore, John Robert 1934- *AmMWSc 92*
Moore, John Royston 1921- *Who 92*
Moore, John Sterling, Jr. 1918- *WhoRel 92*
Moore, John Ward 1939- *AmMWSc 92*
Moore, John Wesley, Jr. 1948- *WhoBlA 92*
Moore, John Wheeler 1833-1906 *DcNCBi 4*
Moore, John Wilson 1920- *AmMWSc 92*
Moore, Johnes Kittelle 1931- *AmMWSc 92*
Moore, Johnnie Adolph 1929- *WhoBlA 92*
Moore, Johnnie Nathan 1947- *AmMWSc 92*
Moore, Johnny Brian 1958- *WhoBlA 92*
Moore, Jonathan 1932- *WhoAmP 91*
Moore, Jonathan Guy J. *Who 92*
Moore, Joseph 1832-1905 *DcNCBi 4*
Moore, Joseph 1920- *WhoFI 92*
Moore, Joseph B 1926- *AmMWSc 92*
Moore, Joseph Curtis 1914- *AmMWSc 92*
Moore, Joseph Herbert 1922- *AmMWSc 92*
Moore, Joseph Howard 1965- *WhoMW 92*
Moore, Joseph Kendall 1957- *WhoRel 92*
Moore, Joseph L. 1935- *WhoBlA 92*
Moore, Joseph Neal 1948- *AmMWSc 92*
Moore, Josephine Carroll 1925- *AmMWSc 92*
Moore, Jossie A. 1947- *WhoBlA 92*
Moore, Joyce West 1936- *WhoWest 92*
Moore, Juanita 1922- *WhoBlA 92*
Moore, Julia A. 1847-1920 *BenetAL 91*
Moore, Julian Keith 1945- *Who 92*
Moore, Justin Edward 1952- *WhoWest 92*
Moore, Karen E. *WhoBlA 92*
Moore, Karen Nelson 1948- *WhoAmL 92*
Moore, Kathleen Carter 1866-1920 *BilnAmS*
Moore, Keith Albert 1947- *WhoRel 92*
Moore, Keith Leon 1925- *AmMWSc 92*
Moore, Kelly Lynn 1958- *WhoWest 92*
Moore, Kenneth Cameron 1947- *WhoAmL 92*
Moore, Kenneth Edwin 1933- *AmMWSc 92*
Moore, Kenneth Howard 1907- *AmMWSc 92*
Moore, Kenneth J 1957- *AmMWSc 92*
Moore, Kenneth Virgil 1933- *AmMWSc 92*
Moore, Kenneth Wayne 1950- *WhoRel 92*
Moore, Kermit 1929- *WhoBlA 92*
Moore, Kieron 1925- *IntMPA 92*
Moore, Kimberly C. 1962- *WhoEnt 92*
Moore, Kris 1941- *AmMWSc 92*
Moore, Lance Wayne 1957- *WhoRel 92*
Moore, Lane Reynolds 1958- *WhoRel 92*
Moore, Larry Eugene 1947- *WhoAmP 91*
Moore, Larry Louis 1954- *WhoBlA 92*
Moore, Larry Wallace 1937- *AmMWSc 92*
Moore, Laureen Rachel 1961- *WhoMW 92*
Moore, Laurence Dale 1937- *AmMWSc 92*
Moore, Lawrence Edward 1938- *AmMWSc 92*
Moore, Lawrence Jack 1926- *WhoAmL 92*
Moore, Lawrence William 1946- *WhoAmL 92*
Moore, Lee E 1938- *AmMWSc 92*
Moore, Lenard D. *DrAPF 91*
Moore, Lenard Duane 1958- *WhoBlA 92*
Moore, Lenny Edward 1933- *WhoBlA 92*
Moore, Leon 1931- *AmMWSc 92*
Moore, Leonard Oro 1931- *AmMWSc 92*
Moore, Leslie 1913-1976 *TwCPaSc*
Moore, Leslie Rowsell 1912- *Who 92*
Moore, Lewis Calvin 1935- *WhoBlA 92*
Moore, Libbie Ann 1960- *WhoAmL 92*
Moore, Lillian Virginia Holdeman 1929- *AmMWSc 92*
Moore, Lloyd Evans 1931- *WhoAmL 92*
Moore, Lois Jean 1935- *WhoBlA 92*
Moore, Lorna Grindlay *AmMWSc 92*
Moore, Lorrie *DrAPF 91*
Moore, Lorrie 1957- *ConLC 68 [port], ConNov 91, WrDr 92*
Moore, Louis Doyle, Jr 1926- *AmMWSc 92*
Moore, Louis Toomer 1885-1961 *DcNCBi 4*
Moore, Lucille Sanders 1920- *WhoBlA 92*
Moore, M. Elizabeth Gibbs *WhoBlA 92*
Moore, M. Joanne 1945- *WhoRel 92*
Moore, M Louise and Beauchamp, M *ScFEYrs*
Moore, Majorie Louise 1917- *WhoAmP 91*
Moore, Malcolm A S 1944- *AmMWSc 92*
Moore, Marcellus Harrison 1939- *WhoBlA 92*
Moore, Margaret Anne 1939- *WhoFI 92*
Moore, Margaret Perlin 1935- *WhoWest 92*
Moore, Marian J. *WhoBlA 92*
Moore, Marianne 1887-1972 *BenetAL 91, FacFETw [port], ModAWWr, PoeCrit 4 [port], RComAH*
Moore, Marianne Craig 1887-1972 *HanAmWH*
Moore, Marie 1933- *WhoRel 92*
Moore, Marion E 1934- *AmMWSc 92*
Moore, Marshall Walter 1929- *WhoAmP 91*
Moore, Martha May 1949- *AmMWSc 92*
Moore, Marvin G 1908- *AmMWSc 92*
Moore, Mary *Who 92, WhoFI 92*
Moore, Mary 1938- *WhoAmP 91*
Moore, Mary Ann 1940- *WhoWest 92*
Moore, Mary Elizabeth 1930- *AmMWSc 92*
Moore, Mary French 1938- *WhoWest 92*
Moore, Mary Tyler *LesBEnT 92 [port]*
Moore, Mary Tyler 1936- *IntMPA 92, WhoEnt 92*
Moore, Maureen 1943- *ConAu 135*
Moore, Maureen Terence 1942- *WhoWest 92*
Moore, Maurice 1682?-1743 *DcNCBi 4*
Moore, Maurice, Jr. 1735-1777 *DcNCBi 4*
Moore, Maurice Lee 1909- *AmMWSc 92*
Moore, Mavor 1919- *WhoEnt 92, WrDr 92*
Moore, McPherson Dorsett 1947- *WhoAmL 92, WhoMW 92*
Moore, Mechlin Dongan 1930- *WhoFI 92*
Moore, Melanie Anne 1950- *WhoBlA 92*
Moore, Melba 1945- *ConMus 7 [port], NotBlAW 92, WhoBlA 92*
Moore, Melba 1947- *WhoEnt 92*
Moore, Melinda 1971- *WhoEnt 92*
Moore, Melita Holly 1909- *AmMWSc 92*
Moore, Merijeanne Anne 1958- *WhoWest 92*
Moore, Merrill 1903-1957 *BenetAL 91*
Moore, Michael Antony Claes 1942- *Who 92*
Moore, Michael Arthur 1943- *Who 92*
Moore, Michael B. 1947- *WhoAmL 92*
Moore, Michael D. 1939- *WhoFI 92*
Moore, Michael David 1939- *WhoMW 92*
Moore, Michael Edward 1948- *WhoWest 92*
Moore, Michael Kenneth 1949- *IntWW 91, Who 92*
Moore, Michael Rodney Newton 1936- *Who 92*
Moore, Michael S. *Who 92*
Moore, Michael Scott 1943- *WhoAmL 92*
Moore, Michael Stanley 1930- *AmMWSc 92*
Moore, Michael T. 1948- *WhoAmL 92*
Moore, Michael Thomas 1934- *WhoFI 92*
Moore, Michal Charles 1947- *WhoWest 92*
Moore, Mike *WhoAmL 92, WhoAmP 91*
Moore, Milo Anderson 1942- *WhoFI 92*
Moore, Milton Donald, Jr. 1953- *WhoBlA 92*
Moore, Mitchell Jay 1954- *WhoAmL 92*
Moore, Monica Margaret 1942- *WhoWest 92*
Moore, Mortimer Norman 1927- *AmMWSc 92*
Moore, N. Webster 1913- *WhoBlA 92*
Moore, Nadine Hanson 1941- *AmMWSc 92*
Moore, Nancy Jean 1946- *WhoAmP 91*
Moore, Nat 1951- *WhoBlA 92*
Moore, Nathan 1931- *WhoBlA 92*
Moore, Nelson Jay 1941- *AmMWSc 92*
Moore, Nicholas 1918- *IntAu&W 91*
Moore, Nicholas 1958- *TwCPaSc*
Moore, Noah Watson, Jr. 1902- *WhoBlA 92*
Moore, Noel E 1934- *AmMWSc 92*
Moore, Noel Ernest Ackroyd 1928- *Who 92*
Moore, Nolan John 1938- *WhoFI 92*
Moore, Norman Winfrid 1923- *Who 92*
Moore, Olive B 1916- *WhoAmP 91*
Moore, Omar Khayyam 1920- *WhoWest 92*
Moore, Oscar James, Jr. *WhoBlA 92*
Moore, Oscar William, Jr. 1938- *WhoBlA 92*
Moore, Osler Kendall 1962- *WhoAmL 92*
Moore, Pamela Eleen 1968- *WhoFI 92*
Moore, Parlett Longworth 1907- *WhoBlA 92*
Moore, Patrick 1923- *TwCSFW 91, WrDr 92*
Moore, Patrick Alfred Caldwell- 1923- *Who 92*
Moore, Patrick Caldwell 1923- *IntAu&W 91, IntWW 91*
Moore, Paul, Jr. 1919- *WhoRel 92*
Moore, Paul Brian 1940- *AmMWSc 92*
Moore, Paul Harris 1938- *AmMWSc 92*
Moore, Percival 1886-1964 *TwCPaSc*
Moore, Peter Bartlett 1939- *AmMWSc 92*
Moore, Peter Clement 1924- *Who 92*
Moore, Peter Francis 1936- *AmMWSc 92*
Moore, Peter Gerald 1928- *Who 92*
Moore, Peter John 1942- *WhoWest 92*
Moore, Peter Weddick 1859-1934 *DcNCBi 4*
Moore, Philip John 1943- *Who 92*
Moore, Philip Walsh 1920- *WhoFI 92*
Moore, Phyllis Maie 1929- *WhoAmP 91*
Moore, Powell Allen 1938- *WhoAmP 91*
Moore, Ralph Bishop 1941- *AmMWSc 92*
Moore, Ralph Leslie 1924- *AmMWSc 92*
Moore, Ralph O. 1941- *WhoRel 92*
Moore, Randall Keith 1958- *WhoRel 92*
Moore, Randy 1949- *WhoAmP 91*
Moore, Randy 1954- *AmMWSc 92*
Moore, Ray A 1912- *WhoAmP 91*
Moore, Rayburn Sabatzky 1920- *WrDr 92*
Moore, Raylyn *DrAPF 91*
Moore, Raymond A 1927- *AmMWSc 92*
Moore, Raymond F, Jr 1927- *AmMWSc 92*
Moore, Raymond H 1918- *AmMWSc 92*
Moore, Raymond Kenworthy 1942- *AmMWSc 92*
Moore, Raymond Knox 1944- *AmMWSc 92*
Moore, Raymond Lionel 1932- *WhoEnt 92*
Moore, Raymond S. 1915- *WrDr 92*
Moore, Reginald George 1932- *AmMWSc 92*
Moore, Reid Francis, Jr 1934- *WhoAmP 91*
Moore, Richard *DrAPF 91*
Moore, Richard 1927- *AmMWSc 92, WhoWest 92, WrDr 92*
Moore, Richard A. *LesBEnT 92*
Moore, Richard A. 1914- *IntWW 91*
Moore, Richard Alan 1948- *WhoMW 92*
Moore, Richard Allan 1924- *AmMWSc 92*
Moore, Richard Anthony 1914- *WhoAmP 91*
Moore, Richard Anthony 1928- *AmMWSc 92*
Moore, Richard B 1815-1885 *BilnAmS*
Moore, Richard Baxter 1943- *WhoBlA 92*
Moore, Richard Dana 1926- *AmMWSc 92*
Moore, Richard Davis 1932- *AmMWSc 92*
Moore, Richard Donald 1924- *AmMWSc 92*
Moore, Richard E 1933- *AmMWSc 92*
Moore, Richard Earle 1916- *WhoBlA 92*
Moore, Richard Joseph 1948- *WhoEnt 92*
Moore, Richard K 1923- *AmMWSc 92*
Moore, Richard Lee 1918- *AmMWSc 92*
Moore, Richard Newton 1926- *AmMWSc 92*
Moore, Richard Thomas 1943- *WhoAmP 91*
Moore, Richard V. 1906- *WhoBlA 92*
Moore, Richard Valentine 1916- *Who 92*
Moore, Richard W. 1949- *WhoFI 92*
Moore, Robert 1915- *Who 92*
Moore, Robert 1941- *Who 92*
Moore, Robert Alonzo 1931- *AmMWSc 92*
Moore, Robert Andrew 1953- *WhoBlA 92*
Moore, Robert Avery 1932- *AmMWSc 92*
Moore, Robert B 1935- *AmMWSc 92*
Moore, Robert Blaine *AmMWSc 92*
Moore, Robert Byron 1929- *AmMWSc 92*
Moore, Robert E 1923- *AmMWSc 92*
Moore, Robert Earl 1923- *AmMWSc 92*
Moore, Robert Edmund 1925- *AmMWSc 92*
Moore, Robert Emmett 1931- *AmMWSc 92*
Moore, Robert F. 1941- *IntWW 91*
Moore, Robert F. 1944- *WhoBlA 92*
Moore, Robert Forrest 1931- *WhoFI 92*
Moore, Robert George 1949- *WhoRel 92*
Moore, Robert H 1930- *AmMWSc 92*
Moore, Robert Haldane 1940- *WhoEnt 92*
Moore, Robert Henry 1906- *WhoRel 92*
Moore, Robert Henry 1940- *WhoFI 92, WhoIns 92*
Moore, Robert Henry, Jr. 1923- *WhoFI 92*
Moore, Robert J 1917- *AmMWSc 92*
Moore, Robert Laurens 1945- *AmMWSc 92*
Moore, Robert Lee 1870-1949 *DcNCBi 4*
Moore, Robert Lee 1920- *AmMWSc 92*
Moore, Robert Lowell, Jr. 1925- *WhoEnt 92*
Moore, Robert Madison 1925- *WhoAmL 92*
Moore, Robert Michael 1961- *WhoMW 92*
Moore, Robert Rood 1937- *WhoRel 92*
Moore, Robert Stephens 1933- *AmMWSc 92*
Moore, Robert Thompson 1937- *WhoAmL 92*
Moore, Robert Yates 1931- *AmMWSc 92*
Moore, Robin 1950- *ConAu 134*
Moore, Robin James 1934- *IntWW 91*
Moore, Rodney Gregory 1960- *WhoEnt 92*
Moore, Roger 1694-1751 *DcNCBi 4*
Moore, Roger 1839-1900 *DcNCBi 4*
Moore, Roger 1927- *IntMPA 92, IntWW 91, Who 92*
Moore, Roger George 1927- *WhoEnt 92*
Moore, Ronald 1939- *WhoRel 92*
Moore, Ronald Bruce 1945- *WhoEnt 92*
Moore, Ronald Clark 1949- *WhoWest 92*
Moore, Ronald Glen 1952- *WhoWest 92*
Moore, Ronald Lee 1942- *AmMWSc 92*
Moore, Ronald Quentin 1939- *WhoRel 92*
Moore, Rosalie *DrAPF 91*
Moore, Roscoe Michael, Jr 1944- *AmMWSc 92, WhoBlA 92*
Moore, Rourke A *WhoAmP 91*
Moore, Rowena Geneva 1910- *WhoAmP 91*
Moore, Roy 1908- *Who 92*
Moore, Roy Worsham, III 1941- *WhoAmL 92*
Moore, Royal Walker 1938- *WhoAmL 92*
Moore, Rufus Adolphus 1923- *AmMWSc 92*
Moore, Russell Eugene 1965- *WhoFI 92*
Moore, Russell Thomas 1943- *AmMWSc 92*
Moore, Ruth Nulton 1923- *IntAu&W 91*
Moore, Ruth Tillinghast 1938- *WhoWest 92*
Moore, Sally 1962- *TwCPaSc*
Moore, Samuel Clark 1924- *WhoAmL 92*
Moore, Sanford Earl 1928- *WhoFI 92*
Moore, Scott *WhoAmP 91*
Moore, Scott Michael 1958- *WhoFI 92*
Moore, Sean 1926- *AmMWSc 92*
Moore, Sean Breanndan 1944- *AmMWSc 92*
Moore, Shelley Lorraine 1950- *WhoBlA 92*
Moore, Sidney Dwayne 1938- *WhoWest 92*
Moore, Sonia 1902- *WhoEnt 92*
Moore, Stanford 1913-1982 *WhoNob 90*
Moore, Stephen 1734-1799 *DcNCBi 4*
Moore, Stephen Lee 1955- *WhoMW 92*
Moore, Steven Carroll 1949- *WhoFI 92, WhoRel 92, WhoWest 92*
Moore, Steven Richard 1942- *WhoEnt 92*
Moore, Susie M. 1918- *WhoBlA 92*
Moore, T. Inglis *ConAu 135*
Moore, T. Sturge 1870-1944 *RfGEnL 91*
Moore, Terence 1931- *Who 92*
Moore, Terry 1932- *IntMPA 92*
Moore, Terry Lee 1962- *WhoAmL 92*
Moore, Thaddeus Thomson 1945- *WhoMW 92*
Moore, Theodore Carlton, Jr 1938- *AmMWSc 92*
Moore, Theral Orvis 1927- *AmMWSc 92*
Moore, Theron Langford 1934- *AmMWSc 92*
Moore, Thomas 1779-1852 *RfGEnL 91*
Moore, Thomas Andrew 1944- *AmMWSc 92*
Moore, Thomas Carrol 1936- *AmMWSc 92*
Moore, Thomas Clarence 1943- *WhoAmP 91*
Moore, Thomas E. *WhoMW 92*
Moore, Thomas Edward 1942- *WhoRel 92*
Moore, Thomas Edwin 1918- *AmMWSc 92*

**Moore,** Thomas Edwin 1930- *AmMWSc 92*
**Moore,** Thomas Francis 1922- *AmMWSc 92*
**Moore,** Thomas H. 1927- *WhoBlA 92*
**Moore,** Thomas James, III 1942- *WhoMW 92*
**Moore,** Thomas Joseph 1943- *WhoFI 92*
**Moore,** Thomas L. 1926- *WhoBlA 92*
**Moore,** Thomas L 1950- *WhoAmP 91*
**Moore,** Thomas Longworth 1842-1926 *DcNCBi 4*
**Moore,** Thomas Matthew *AmMWSc 92*
**Moore,** Thomas Overton 1804-1876 *DcNCBi 4*
**Moore,** Thomas Paul 1928- *WhoEnt 92*
**Moore,** Thomas R. 1932- *WhoAmL 92*
**Moore,** Thomas Stephen, Jr 1942- *AmMWSc 92*
**Moore,** Thomas Terrell, Jr. 1954- *WhoEnt 92*
**Moore,** Thomas W. *IntMPA 92, LesBEnT 92*
**Moore,** Thomas Warner 1928- *AmMWSc 92*
**Moore,** Thomas William 1925- *Who 92*
**Moore,** Thomasine Elizabeth 1949- *WhoAmP 91*
**Moore,** Timothy James 1949- *WhoFI 92, WhoMW 92*
**Moore,** Timothy Paul 1958- *WhoEnt 92*
**Moore,** Todd *DrAPF 91*
**Moore,** Tom 1943- *WhoEnt 92*
**Moore,** Tom D. 1928- *WhoRel 92*
**Moore,** Tom Inglis 1901-1978? *ConAu 135*
**Moore,** Tom Loyd 1926- *WhoWest 92*
**Moore,** Trudy S. 1957- *WhoBlA 92*
**Moore,** U A Presnell 1925- *WhoAmP 91*
**Moore,** Undine Smith 1904-1989 *NotBlAW 92*
**Moore,** Undine Smith 1905-1988 *NewAmDM*
**Moore,** Undine Smith 1907- *WhoBlA 92*
**Moore,** Vaughn Clayton 1934- *AmMWSc 92*
**Moore,** Vernon John, Jr. 1942- *WhoMW 92*
**Moore,** Vernon Leon 1936- *AmMWSc 92*
**Moore,** Virgil Clinton 1933- *WhoAmP 91*
**Moore,** W Allen 1945- *WhoAmP 91*
**Moore,** W. E. C. 1927- *IntWW 91*
**Moore,** W Edgar 1910- *WhoAmP 91*
**Moore,** W Henson 1939- *WhoAmP 91*
**Moore,** W. Henson, III 1939- *WhoFI 92*
**Moore,** W Taylor 1939- *WhoAmP 91*
**Moore,** Walter Calvin 1910- *AmMWSc 92*
**Moore,** Walter Dengel 1936- *WhoWest 92*
**Moore,** Walter Edward C 1927- *AmMWSc 92*
**Moore,** Walter Emil, Jr. 1925- *WhoMW 92*
**Moore,** Walter Guy 1913- *AmMWSc 92*
**Moore,** Walter John 1918- *AmMWSc 92*
**Moore,** Walter L 1916- *AmMWSc 92*
**Moore,** Walter Louis 1946- *WhoBlA 92*
**Moore,** Walter M 1920- *WhoAmP 91*
**Moore,** Walter P, Jr *AmMWSc 92*
**Moore,** Walter William 1857-1926 *DcNCBi 4*
**Moore,** Ward 1903-1978 *TwCSFW 91*
**Moore,** Ward Wilfred 1924- *AmMWSc 92*
**Moore,** Warfield, Jr. 1934- *WhoBlA 92*
**Moore,** Warren Keith 1923- *AmMWSc 92*
**Moore,** Wayne Elden 1919- *AmMWSc 92*
**Moore,** Wenda Weekes 1941- *WhoBlA 92, WhoMW 92*
**Moore,** Wesley Benjamin 1926- *WhoMW 92*
**Moore,** Wesley Earl 1956- *WhoEnt 92*
**Moore,** Wesley Sanford 1935- *AmMWSc 92*
**Moore,** Wilbert E 1914- *IntAu&W 91*
**Moore,** Wilfred Eugene 1954- *WhoRel 92*
**Moore,** Wilfred G 1907- *IntAu&W 91*
**Moore,** Willard S 1941- *AmMWSc 92*
**Moore,** William 1927- *Who 92*
**Moore,** William Armistead 1831-1884 *DcNCBi 4*
**Moore,** William D, Jr 1917- *WhoAmP 91*
**Moore,** William David 1949- *WhoEnt 92, WhoRel 92*
**Moore,** William E, III 1934- *WhoAmP 91*
**Moore,** William Edward 1949- *WhoIns 92*
**Moore,** William Evan 1925- *WhoFI 92*
**Moore,** William Graham 1922- *WhoAmP 91*
**Moore,** William Grover, Jr. *WhoFI 92*
**Moore,** William J *WhoAmP 91*
**Moore,** William John 1837-1901? *DcNCBi 4*
**Moore,** William Leonard 1943- *WhoWest 92*
**Moore,** William Marshall 1930- *AmMWSc 92*
**Moore,** William Robert 1928- *AmMWSc 92*
**Moore,** William Rudy, Jr 1943- *WhoAmP 91*
**Moore,** William S, Jr 1947- *WhoAmP 91*
**Moore,** William Samuel 1942- *AmMWSc 92*
**Moore,** William Stockman 1944- *WhoAmL 92*
**Moore,** William W 1912- *AmMWSc 92*
**Moore,** William Wilson 1937- *WhoFI 92*
**Moore,** Willis Henry Allphin 1940- *WhoWest 92*
**Moore,** Winston E. *WhoBlA 92*
**Moore,** Yvette 1958- *ConAu 135*
**Moore-Bick,** Martin James 1946- *Who 92*
**Moore-Brabazon** *Who 92*
**Moore-Ede,** Martin C 1945- *AmMWSc 92*
**Moore of Wolvercote,** Baron 1921- *Who 92*
**Moore-Rinvolucri,** Mina Josephine 1902- *IntAu&W 91*
**Moore-Stovall,** Joyce 1948- *WhoBlA 92*
**Moorefield,** Herbert Hughes 1918- *AmMWSc 92*
**Moorehead,** Bobbie Wooten 1937- *WhoBlA 92*
**Moorehead,** Caroline 1944- *IntAu&W 91, WrDr 92*
**Moorehead,** Emery Matthew 1954- *WhoBlA 92*
**Moorehead,** Eric K. 1958- *WhoBlA 92*
**Moorehead,** Justin Leslie 1947- *WhoBlA 92*
**Moorehead,** Ralph Glen 1949- *WhoMW 92*
**Moorehead,** Thomas A. 1944- *WhoBlA 92*
**Moorehead,** Thomas Allen 1944- *WhoMW 92*
**Moorehead,** Thomas J 1947- *AmMWSc 92*
**Moorehead,** Timothy Lucas 1957- *WhoAmL 92*
**Moorehead,** Wells Rufus 1931- *AmMWSc 92*
**Moorer,** Thomas Hinman 1912- *IntWW 91, Who 92*
**Moorer,** William Bowling 1935- *WhoRel 92*
**Moores,** Brian, Mrs. *Who 92*
**Moores,** Eldridge Morton 1938- *AmMWSc 92*
**Moores,** Frank Duff 1933- *IntWW 91, Who 92*
**Moores,** Hervey Cuthrell 1926- *WhoAmP 91*
**Moores,** John 1896- *IntWW 91, Who 92*
**Moores,** Peter 1932- *Who 92*
**Moores,** Russell R 1935- *AmMWSc 92*
**Moores,** Yvonne 1941- *Who 92*
**Moorey,** Adrian Edward 1946- *Who 92*
**Moorey,** Peter Roger Stuart 1937- *WrDr 92*
**Moorey,** Roger 1937- *IntWW 91, Who 92*
**Moorhead,** Andrea *DrAPF 91*
**Moorhead,** Carlos J. 1922- *AlmAP 92 [port], WhoAmP 91, WhoWest 92*
**Moorhead,** Diana 1940- *WrDr 92*
**Moorhead,** Edward Darrell 1930- *AmMWSc 92*
**Moorhead,** John Couper 1949- *WhoWest 92*
**Moorhead,** John Dane 1941- *WhoFI 92, WhoMW 92*
**Moorhead,** John Leslie 1942- *WhoBlA 92*
**Moorhead,** John Wilbur 1942- *AmMWSc 92*
**Moorhead,** Joseph H. 1921- *WhoBlA 92*
**Moorhead,** Max L. 1914-1981 *ConAu 135*
**Moorhead,** Michael Jonathan 1944- *WhoAmL 92*
**Moorhead,** Paul Sidney 1924- *AmMWSc 92*
**Moorhead,** Philip Darwin 1933- *AmMWSc 92*
**Moorhead,** Thomas Burch 1934- *WhoAmL 92*
**Moorhead,** William Dean 1936- *AmMWSc 92*
**Moorhouse,** Cecil James 1924- *Who 92*
**Moorhouse,** Douglas C *AmMWSc 92*
**Moorhouse,** Frank 1938- *ConNov 91, IntAu&W 91*
**Moorhouse,** Geoffrey 1931- *IntAu&W 91, Who 92, WrDr 92*
**Moorhouse,** James *Who 92*
**Moorhouse,** John A 1926- *AmMWSc 92*
**Moorhouse,** Linda Virginia 1945- *WhoMW 92*
**Moorhouse,** Tessa 1938- *Who 92*
**Mooring,** Francis Paul 1921- *AmMWSc 92*
**Mooring,** John Stuart 1926- *AmMWSc 92*
**Mooring,** Kittye D. 1932- *WhoBlA 92*
**Mooring,** Paul K 1923- *AmMWSc 92*
**Moorjani,** Kishin 1935- *AmMWSc 92*
**Moorman,** Charlotte 1933- *NewAmDM*
**Moorman,** Charlotte 1933-1991 *NewYTBS 91 [port]*
**Moorman,** Clinton R. 1924- *WhoBlA 92*
**Moorman,** Gary William 1949- *AmMWSc 92*
**Moorman,** Holsey Alexander 1938- *WhoBlA 92*
**Moorman,** James Watt 1937- *WhoAmP 91*
**Moorman,** John Richard Humpidge 1905- *IntAu&W 91*
**Moorman,** Mary Caroline 1905- *Who 92*
**Moorman,** Michael F. 1942- *WhoFI 92*
**Moorman,** Richard Hal, IV 1950- *WhoAmL 92*
**Moorman,** Robert Bruce 1916- *AmMWSc 92*
**Moorman,** Robert Crain 1933- *WhoMW 92*
**Moorman,** William Joseph 1942- *WhoMW 92*
**Moorman van Kappen,** Olav 1937- *IntWW 91*
**Moorrees,** Coenraad Frans August 1916- *AmMWSc 92*
**Moorshead,** John Earl 1939- *WhoMW 92*
**Moorthy,** Arambamoorthy Thedchana 1928- *IntWW 91, Who 92*
**Moos,** Anthony Manuel 1913- *AmMWSc 92*
**Moos,** Carl 1930- *AmMWSc 92*
**Moos,** Gilbert Ellsworth 1915- *AmMWSc 92*
**Moos,** Henry Warren 1936- *AmMWSc 92*
**Moos,** Michael *DrAPF 91*
**Moos,** Walter Hamilton 1954- *AmMWSc 92*
**Moosa,** Roy 1953- *WhoEnt 92*
**Moose,** Elton LeRoy 1935- *WhoRel 92*
**Moose,** George E 1944- *WhoAmP 91, WhoBlA 92*
**Moose,** Mary Immaculette 1921- *WhoRel 92*
**Moose,** Richard M. *WhoFI 92*
**Moose,** Ruth *DrAPF 91*
**Moosman,** Darvan Albert *AmMWSc 92*
**Moosonee,** Bishop of 1941- *Who 92*
**Moossy,** John 1925- *AmMWSc 92*
**Moot,** John Rutherford 1922- *WhoAmP 91*
**Moot,** Welles Van Ness, Jr. 1917- *WhoFI 92*
**Moote,** A. Lloyd 1931- *WrDr 92*
**Mootham,** Orby Howell 1901- *Who 92*
**Mootry,** Charles 1948- *WhoBlA 92*
**Mooty,** John William 1922- *WhoMW 92*
**Mooz,** Elizabeth Dodd 1939- *AmMWSc 92*
**Mooz,** William E., Jr. 1960- *WhoAmL 92*
**Mooz,** William Ernst 1929- *AmMWSc 92*
**Mopper,** Kenneth 1947- *AmMWSc 92*
**Moppett,** Charles Edward 1941- *AmMWSc 92*
**Mopsik,** Frederick Israel 1938- *AmMWSc 92*
**Mora,** David Richard 1945- *WhoHisp 92*
**Mora,** E Kelly *WhoAmP 91, WhoHisp 92*
**Mora,** Emilio Chavez 1928- *AmMWSc 92*
**Mora,** Homer *WhoHisp 92*
**Mora,** Jose Maria Luis 1794-1850 *HisDSpE*
**Mora,** Jose O *AmMWSc 92*
**Mora,** Kathleen Rita 1948- *WhoFI 92*
**Mora,** Maria-Alicia 1959- *WhoHisp 92*
**Mora,** Narciso Andres 1934- *WhoHisp 92*
**Mora,** Pat 1942- *WhoHisp 92*
**Mora,** Peter T 1924- *AmMWSc 92*
**Mora,** Philippe 1949- *WhoEnt 92*
**Mora,** Thomas, Jr. 1954- *WhoHisp 92*
**Morabito,** Bruno P 1922- *AmMWSc 92*
**Morabito,** Joseph Michael 1941- *AmMWSc 92*
**Morabito,** Rocco 1920- *ConAu 134*
**Morack,** John Ludwig *AmMWSc 92*
**Morado,** David F. 1949- *WhoHisp 92*
**Moraes,** Dom 1938- *ConPo 91, LiExTwC, RfGEnL 91, Who 92, WrDr 92*
**Moraes,** Dominic 1938- *IntAu&W 91, IntWW 91*
**Moraff,** Barbara *DrAPF 91*
**Moraff,** Howard *AmMWSc 92*
**Moraga,** Cherrie *DrAPF 91*
**Moraga,** Cherrie 1952- *WhoHisp 92*
**Moraga,** Peter 1926- *WhoHisp 92*
**Moragne,** Lenora *WhoBlA 92*
**Moragne,** Rudolph 1933- *WhoBlA 92*
**Morahan,** Christopher Thomas 1929- *Who 92*
**Morahan,** Daniel Michael 1940- *WhoFI 92*
**Morahan,** John Roger 1954- *WhoFI 92*
**Morahan,** Page Smith 1940- *AmMWSc 92*
**Morahan,** Thomas P *WhoAmP 91*
**Morain,** Mary Stone Dewing 1911- *WhoWest 92*
**Morais,** Manuel Antonio 1939- *WhoFI 92*
**Morais,** Rejean 1938- *AmMWSc 92*
**Moraitis,** Georgios 1942- *IntWW 91*
**Moraitis,** Nicoclis George 1924- *WhoEnt 92*
**Morales,** Alejandro 1944- *WhoHisp 92*
**Morales,** Alex 1966- *WhoHisp 92*
**Morales,** Alvino 1950- *WhoHisp 92*
**Morales,** Angel E. 1953- *WhoHisp 92*
**Morales,** Angel L. 1952- *WhoHisp 92*
**Morales,** Anthony Russell 1960- *WhoHisp 92*
**Morales,** Antonio 1937- *WhoHisp 92*
**Morales,** Antonio Gil *WhoHisp 92*
**Morales,** Armando 1927- *IntWW 91*
**Morales,** Armando 1932- *WhoWest 92*
**Morales,** Carl E. *WhoFI 92*
**Morales,** Cecilio Jose, Jr. 1952- *WhoHisp 92*
**Morales,** Charles S. 1946- *WhoHisp 92*
**Morales,** Claudio H. 1945- *WhoHisp 92*
**Morales,** Cristobal de 1500?-1553 *NewAmDM*
**Morales,** Dan *WhoAmL 92*
**Morales,** Dan 1956- *WhoHisp 92*
**Morales,** Daniel C 1956- *WhoAmP 91*
**Morales,** Daniel Richard 1929- *AmMWSc 92*
**Morales,** David *WhoHisp 92*
**Morales,** David 1953- *WhoHisp 92*
**Morales,** Deborah 1952- *WhoHisp 92*
**Morales,** Dionicio *WhoHisp 92*
**Morales,** Ed 1956- *WhoHisp 92*
**Morales,** Esai 1963- *WhoHisp 92*
**Morales,** Esai Manuel 1962- *WhoEnt 92*
**Morales,** Felicita 1951- *WhoHisp 92*
**Morales,** Frank 1941- *WhoHisp 92*
**Morales,** Fred 1924- *WhoHisp 92*
**Morales,** Fred, Jr. 1951- *WhoEnt 92*
**Morales,** George John 1945- *AmMWSc 92*
**Morales,** Gilbert 1965- *WhoHisp 92*
**Morales,** Ibra 1945- *WhoHisp 92*
**Morales,** Jenny 1949- *WhoHisp 92*
**Morales,** Jorge Francisco 1948- *WhoHisp 92*
**Morales,** Jorge Juan 1945- *WhoHisp 92*
**Morales,** Jorge Luis 1930- *WhoHisp 92*
**Morales,** Jose 1945- *WhoHisp 92*
**Morales,** Jose 1952- *WhoHisp 92*
**Morales,** Jose Alberto *WhoHisp 92*
**Morales,** Joseph M. 1955- *WhoHisp 92*
**Morales,** Juan 1948- *BlkOlyM*
**Morales,** Juan de Dios 1767-1810 *HisDSpE*
**Morales,** Juan M. 1928- *WhoHisp 92*
**Morales,** Juan M. 1956- *WhoHisp 92*
**Morales,** Judy 1941- *WhoHisp 92*
**Morales,** Julio, Jr. 1942- *WhoHisp 92*
**Morales,** Julio K. 1948- *WhoAmL 92*
**Morales,** Magda Hernandez 1943- *WhoHisp 92*
**Morales,** Manuel Francisco 1919- *WhoHisp 92*
**Morales,** Manuel Frank 1919- *AmMWSc 92*
**Morales,** Manuel Sabastian 1956- *WhoEnt 92*
**Morales,** Michael 1963- *WhoHisp 92*
**Morales,** Mike 1949- *WhoAmP 91*
**Morales,** Milsa 1952- *WhoHisp 92*
**Morales,** Nancy Barbara 1950- *WhoHisp 92*
**Morales,** Nestor 1909- *WhoAmL 92*
**Morales,** Nydia 1955- *WhoHisp 92*
**Morales,** Ophelia C. 1928- *WhoHisp 92*
**Morales,** Pete, Jr. 1950- *WhoHisp 92*
**Morales,** Rafael 1919- *DcLB 108 [port]*
**Morales,** Ralph, Jr. 1940- *WhoHisp 92*
**Morales,** Raul 1935- *AmMWSc 92, WhoHisp 92*
**Morales,** Raymond C. *WhoHisp 92*
**Morales,** Raymond Chacon 1946- *WhoHisp 92*
**Morales,** Richard 1938- *WhoHisp 92*
**Morales,** Richard 1949- *WhoHisp 92*
**Morales,** Sylvia *WhoHisp 92*
**Morales,** Thomas Frime, Jr. 1947- *WhoHisp 92*
**Morales Bermudez,** Francisco 1921- *IntWW 91*
**Morales Bermudez Pedraglio,** Remigio 1947- *IntWW 91*
**Morales-Couvertier,** Angel Luis 1919- *WhoHisp 92*
**Morales-Galarreta,** Julio 1936- *WhoMW 92*
**Morales-Lebron,** Mariano 1935- *WhoHisp 92*
**Morales Lemus,** Jose 1808-1870 *HisDSpE*
**Morales-Loebl,** Maria 1953- *WhoHisp 92*
**Morales-Nadal,** Milga 1947- *WhoHisp 92*
**Morales-Nieves,** Alfredo 1956- *WhoHisp 92*
**Morales-Pereira,** Antonio 1928- *WhoHisp 92*
**Morales Reyes,** Luis 1936- *WhoRel 92*
**Morales-Rivas,** Alice 1961- *WhoHisp 92*
**Moralez,** Joselyn Hope 1966- *WhoHisp 92*
**Moran,** Baron 1924- *IntWW 91, Who 92*
**Moran,** Charles A. 1943- *WhoFI 92*
**Moran,** Charles F, Jr 1931- *WhoAmP 91*
**Moran,** Christopher Andrew 1957- *WhoFI 92*
**Moran,** Daniel Austin 1936- *AmMWSc 92*
**Moran,** David Dunstan *AmMWSc 92*
**Moran,** David John 1951- *WhoMW 92*
**Moran,** David Taylor 1940- *AmMWSc 92*
**Moran,** Denis Joseph 1942- *AmMWSc 92*
**Moran,** Edward Francis, Jr 1932- *AmMWSc 92*
**Moran,** Edward V 1953- *WhoAmP 91*
**Moran,** Edwin T, Jr *AmMWSc 92*
**Moran,** Emilio Federico 1946- *WhoMW 92*

**Moran**, James 1929- *WhoAmP 91*
**Moran**, James Byron 1930- *WhoAmL 92, WhoMW 92*
**Moran**, James Michael, Jr 1943- *AmMWSc 92*
**Moran**, James P 1945- *WhoAmP 91*
**Moran**, James P., Jr. 1945- *AlmAP 92 [port]*
**Moran**, Jeffrey Chris 1954- *AmMWSc 92*
**Moran**, Jeffrey W 1946- *WhoAmP 91*
**Moran**, Jerry *WhoAmP 91*
**Moran**, John *WhoRel 92*
**Moran**, John 1929- *Who 92*
**Moran**, John A. 1932- *WhoFI 92*
**Moran**, John Charles 1942- *IntAu&W 91*
**Moran**, John J 1927- *AmMWSc 92*
**Moran**, John P 1934- *AmMWSc 92*
**Moran**, Joseph Michael 1944- *AmMWSc 92*
**Moran**, Joseph Milbert 1929- *WhoAmL 92*
**Moran**, Joyce E. 1948- *WhoBlA 92*
**Moran**, Juliette May 1917- *AmMWSc 92*
**Moran**, Kim 1935- *WhoAmP 91*
**Moran**, Lois 1909-1990 *AnObit 1990*
**Moran**, Manus Francis 1927- *Who 92*
**Moran**, Martin Joseph 1930- *WhoFI 92*
**Moran**, Mary *DrAPF 91*
**Moran**, Mary Chapar *WhoAmP 91*
**Moran**, Michael 1912- *IntWW 91*
**Moran**, Michael Edward 1963- *WhoFI 92*
**Moran**, Neil Clymer 1924- *AmMWSc 92*
**Moran**, Patty Ann 1947- *WhoEnt 92*
**Moran**, Paul Richard 1936- *AmMWSc 92*
**Moran**, Peggy 1918- *WhoEnt 92*
**Moran**, Philip David 1937- *WhoAmL 92*
**Moran**, Rachel 1956- *WhoAmL 92*
**Moran**, Reid 1916- *AmMWSc 92*
**Moran**, Robert 1937- *NewAmDM*
**Moran**, Robert Daniel 1929- *WhoAmL 92*
**Moran**, Robert E., Sr. 1921- *WhoBlA 92*
**Moran**, Robert Russell 1926- *WhoAmL 92*
**Moran**, Robert Stephen, Jr. 1953- *WhoAmL 92*
**Moran**, Ronald P. *WhoAmL 92*
**Moran**, Sheila Kathleeen *WhoEnt 92*
**Moran**, Thomas Francis 1936- *AmMWSc 92*
**Moran**, Thomas Francis 1943- *WhoWest 92*
**Moran**, Thomas Harry 1937- *WhoWest 92*
**Moran**, Thomas Irving 1930- *AmMWSc 92*
**Moran**, Thomas J 1920- *WhoAmP 91*
**Moran**, Thomas J 1938- *AmMWSc 92*
**Moran**, Thomas James 1912- *AmMWSc 92*
**Moran**, Thomas Joseph 1920- *WhoAmL 92, WhoMW 92*
**Moran**, Thomas Patrick 1937- *WhoFI 92*
**Moran**, Thomas Patrick 1941- *AmMWSc 92*
**Moran**, Timothy 1918- *WhoAmP 91*
**Moran**, Timothy Lawrence 1957- *WhoMW 92*
**Moran**, Victor John, III 1951- *WhoIns 92*
**Moran**, Vincent 1932- *IntWW 91*
**Moran**, Walter Harrison, Jr 1930- *AmMWSc 92*
**Moran**, William Madison 1948- *WhoFI 92*
**Moran**, William Rodes 1919- *AmMWSc 92*
**Moran Lopez**, Fernando 1926- *IntWW 91*
**Morancie**, Horace L. *WhoBlA 92*
**Morancy**, Elizabeth 1941- *WhoAmP 91*
**Morand**, Blaise E. 1932- *WhoRel 92, WhoWest 92*
**Morand**, C. Morey de 1944- *TwCPaSc*
**Morand**, James M 1938- *AmMWSc 92*
**Morand**, Jeffrey Peter 1955- *WhoFI 92*
**Morand**, Peter 1935- *AmMWSc 92*
**Morandi**, Giorgio 1890-1964 *FacFETw*
**Moranis**, Rick 1954- *IntMPA 92*
**Morano**, Carl John 1958- *WhoEnt 92*
**Morano**, Michael L 1915- *WhoAmP 91*
**Morant**, Mack Bernard 1946- *WhoBlA 92*
**Morant**, Trente 1952- *WhoEnt 92*
**Morante**, Elsa 1918-1985 *ConAu 35NR, FacFETw*
**Morante**, Rosemary Anne 1949- *WhoAmP 91*
**Morantes**, Rafael Ernesto 1954- *WhoHisp 92*
**Morari**, Manfred 1951- *AmMWSc 92*
**Morash**, Ronald 1945- *AmMWSc 92*
**Morasko**, Robert A. 1960- *WhoFI 92*
**Morata**, Larry P. 1953- *WhoHisp 92*
**Morath**, Max 1926- *NewAmDM*
**Morath**, Max Edward 1926- *WhoEnt 92*
**Morath**, Richard Joseph 1925- *AmMWSc 92*
**Morauta**, Mekere 1946- *Who 92*
**Moravcsik**, Michael Julius 1928- *AmMWSc 92*
**Moravec**, Hans Peter 1948- *AmMWSc 92*
**Moravec**, Lisa Kay 1962- *WhoMW 92*
**Moravia**, Alberto d1990 *IntWW 91N, Who 92N*
**Moravia**, Alberto 1907-1990 *AnObit 1990, FacFETw, LiExTwC*
**Moravy**, L. Joe 1950- *WhoFI 92*
**Morawa**, Arnold Peter 1940- *AmMWSc 92*
**Morawetz**, Cathleen Synge 1923- *AmMWSc 92*
**Morawetz**, Herbert 1915- *AmMWSc 92*
**Morawetz**, Oskar 1917- *NewAmDM*
**Morawitz**, Hans 1935- *AmMWSc 92*
**Morawski**, Kazimierz 1929- *IntWW 91*
**Moray**, Earl of 1928- *Who 92*
**Moray**, Edward Bruce D. *Who 92*
**Moray**, Neville Peter 1935- *AmMWSc 92*
**Moray**, Sherry 1963- *WhoEnt 92, WhoMW 92*
**Moray Ross And Caithness**, Bishop of 1928- *Who 92*
**Moray Ross And Caithness**, Dean of *Who 92*
**Moray Williams**, Ursula 1911- *IntAu&W 91, WrDr 92*
**Morazan**, Francisco 1792-1842 *HisDSpE*
**Morbey**, Graham Kenneth 1935- *AmMWSc 92*
**Morch**, Dea Trier 1941- *IntAu&W 91*
**Morck**, Paul *TwCWW 91*
**Morck**, Roland Anton 1913- *AmMWSc 92*
**Morck**, Timothy Anton 1949- *AmMWSc 92*
**Morcock**, Robert Edward 1938- *AmMWSc 92*
**Morcom**, Anthony John 1916- *Who 92*
**Morcom**, Christopher 1939- *Who 92*
**Morcom**, Claudia House *WhoBlA 92*
**Morcom**, John Brian 1925- *Who 92*
**Morcos-Asaad**, Fikry Naguib 1930- *Who 92*
**Morcott**, Southwood J. 1939- *WhoFI 92, WhoMW 92*
**Morcroft**, Heather 1958- *WhoAmL 92*
**Mord**, Allan John 1943- *WhoWest 92*
**Mord**, Irving Conrad, II 1950- *WhoAmL 92*
**Morda Evans**, Raymond John *Who 92*
**Mordasky**, John David 1925- *WhoAmP 91*
**Mordaunt**, Richard 1940- *Who 92*
**Mordaunt**, Walter J. d1991 *NewYTBS 91*
**Mordden**, Ethan 1947- *WrDr 92*
**Mordeaux**, Elaine *EncAmaz 91*
**Mordecai**, Alfred 1804-1887 *BiInAmS, DcNCBi 4*
**Mordecai**, Benjamin 1944- *WhoEnt 92*
**Mordecai**, David *WhoWest 92*
**Mordecai**, Ellen 1790-1884 *DcNCBi 4*
**Mordecai**, Ellen Mordecai 1820-1916 *DcNCBi 4*
**Mordecai**, George Washington 1801-1871 *DcNCBi 4*
**Mordecai**, Jacob 1762-1838 *DcNCBi 4*
**Mordecai**, Moses 1785-1824 *DcNCBi 4*
**Mordecai**, Pamela 1942- *ConAu 134*
**Mordecai**, Samuel Fox, II 1852-1927 *DcNCBi 4*
**Morden**, John Grant 1925- *WhoRel 92*
**Mordes**, John Peter 1947- *AmMWSc 92*
**Mordeson**, John N 1934- *AmMWSc 92*
**Mordfin**, Leonard 1929- *AmMWSc 92*
**Mordkovitch**, Lydia 1944- *IntWW 91*
**Mordler**, John Michael 1938- *WhoEnt 92*
**Mordo**, Jean Henri 1945- *WhoFI 92*
**Morduchow**, Morris 1921- *AmMWSc 92*
**Morduchowitz**, Abraham 1933- *AmMWSc 92*
**Mordue**, Dale Lewis 1933- *AmMWSc 92*
**Mordue**, Richard Eric 1941- *Who 92*
**Mordukhovich**, Boris S 1948- *AmMWSc 92*
**Mordukhovich**, Boris Sholimovich 1948- *WhoMW 92*
**Mordy**, James Calvin 1927- *WhoFI 92, WhoMW 92*
**More**, Carolina *IntAu&W 91X*
**More**, Caroline *WrDr 92*
**More**, Douglas McLochlan 1926- *WhoAmL 92*
**More**, Eduardo A. 1929- *WhoHisp 92*
**More**, Hannah 1745-1833 *BlkwCEP, DcLB 107 [port], -109 [port], RfGEnL 91*
**More**, Kenneth Riddell 1910- *AmMWSc 92*
**More**, Mary Thomas 1916- *WhoRel 92*
**More**, Norman 1921- *Who 92*
**More**, Paul Elmer 1864-1937 *BenetAL 91*
**More**, Richard Michael 1942- *AmMWSc 92*
**More**, Thomas *BiInAmS*
**More**, Thomas 1478-1535 *RfGEnL 91, ScFEYrs*
**More-Gordon**, Harry *TwCPaSc*
**More-Molyneux**, James Robert 1920- *Who 92*
**Morean**, Gary Arnold 1955- *WhoAmL 92*
**Moreas**, Jean 1856-1910 *GuFrLit 1*
**Moreau** *DcNCBi 4*
**Moreau**, David Merlin 1927- *IntAu&W 91, WrDr 92*
**Moreau**, Gustave 1826-1898 *ThHEIm*
**Moreau**, James William 1948- *WhoEnt 92*
**Moreau**, Jean Raymond 1924- *AmMWSc 92*
**Moreau**, Jeanne 1928- *FacFETw, IntMPA 92, IntWW 91, Who 92*
**Moreau**, Joseph Anthony 1962- *WhoEnt 92*
**Moreau**, Robert Arthur 1952- *AmMWSc 92*
**Moreau**, Rudolf von 1910-1939 *EncTR 91*
**Moreau de Saint-Mery**, Mederic-Louis-Elie 1750-1819 *BenetAL 91*
**Moreell**, Ben 1892-1978 *FacFETw*
**Morefield**, Michael Thomas 1956- *WhoFI 92*
**Morehart**, Allen L 1933- *AmMWSc 92*
**Morehart**, Lori Kiko 1963- *WhoMW 92*
**Morehart**, Thomas Berton 1942- *WhoWest 92*
**Morehead**, Andrew Jay 1938- *WhoFI 92*
**Morehead**, Charles Richard 1947- *WhoIns 92*
**Morehead**, Eugene Lindsay 1845-1889 *DcNCBi 4*
**Morehead**, Florida Mae 1948- *WhoBlA 92*
**Morehead**, Frederick Ferguson, Jr 1929- *AmMWSc 92*
**Morehead**, James Turner 1799-1875 *DcNCBi 4*
**Morehead**, James Turner 1840-1908 *DcNCBi 4*
**Morehead**, James Turner, Jr. 1838-1919 *DcNCBi 4*
**Morehead**, John Lindsay 1894-1964 *DcNCBi 4*
**Morehead**, John Motley 1796-1866 *DcNCBi 4*
**Morehead**, John Motley, II 1866-1923 *DcNCBi 4*
**Morehead**, John Motley, III 1870-1965 *DcNCBi 4*
**Morehead**, John Woodson 1948- *WhoMW 92*
**Morehead**, Patricia S 1936- *WhoAmP 91*
**Morehouse**, Alpha L 1923- *AmMWSc 92*
**Morehouse**, Carl Edward 1951- *WhoWest 92*
**Morehouse**, Chauncey Anderson 1926- *AmMWSc 92*
**Morehouse**, Clarence Kopperl 1917- *AmMWSc 92*
**Morehouse**, Clifford P. 1904-1977 *ConAu 134*
**Morehouse**, David C. *WhoAmL 92*
**Morehouse**, Henry Lyman 1834-1917 *RelLAm 91*
**Morehouse**, James Ernest 1944- *WhoFI 92*
**Morehouse**, Laurence Englemohr 1913- *AmMWSc 92*
**Morehouse**, Lawrence G 1925- *AmMWSc 92*
**Morehouse**, Margaret Gulick 1904- *AmMWSc 92*
**Morehouse**, Neal Francis 1908- *AmMWSc 92*
**Morein**, Joseph A. *WhoFI 92*
**Moreira**, Antonio R 1950- *AmMWSc 92*
**Moreira**, Domingo R. *WhoHisp 92*
**Moreira**, Jorge Eduardo 1943- *AmMWSc 92*
**Moreira**, Jorge Washington 1955- *WhoHisp 92*
**Moreira**, Marcio Martins 1947- *WhoFI 92*
**Moreira Neves**, Lucas 1925- *IntWW 91, WhoRel 92*
**Morejon**, Clara Baez 1940- *AmMWSc 92*
**Morejon**, Nancy 1944- *SpAmWW*
**Morel**, Jean 1903-1975 *NewAmDM*
**Morel**, Raymond Victor 1949- *WhoFI 92*
**Morel**, Thomas 1943- *AmMWSc 92*
**Morel-Seytoux**, Hubert Jean 1932- *AmMWSc 92*
**Morelan**, Paula Kay 1949- *WhoEnt 92*
**Moreland**, Alvin Franklin 1931- *AmMWSc 92*
**Moreland**, C L *WhoAmP 91*
**Moreland**, Charles Glen 1936- *AmMWSc 92*
**Moreland**, Dana A 1951- *WhoAmP 91*
**Moreland**, Donald Edwin 1919- *AmMWSc 92*
**Moreland**, Ferrin Bates 1909- *AmMWSc 92*
**Moreland**, Jane P. *DrAPF 91*
**Moreland**, Lois Baldwin *WhoBlA 92*
**Moreland**, Parker Elbert, Jr 1931- *AmMWSc 92*
**Moreland**, Raymond Theodore, Jr. 1944- *WhoRel 92*
**Moreland**, Richard C. 1953- *ConAu 135*
**Moreland**, Robert John 1941- *Who 92*
**Moreland**, Sallie V. *WhoBlA 92*
**Moreland**, Suzanne 1951- *AmMWSc 92*
**Moreland**, Walter Thomas, Jr 1926- *AmMWSc 92*
**Moreland**, William John 1916- *WhoMW 92*
**Moreland-Young**, Curtina 1949- *WhoBlA 92*
**Morell**, Pierre 1941- *AmMWSc 92*
**Morell**, Theo 1886-1948 *EncTR 91 [port]*
**Morell**, Tim 1957- *WhoAmL 92*
**Morell de Santa Cruz**, Pedro Agustin 1694-1768 *HisDSpE*
**Morella**, Constance A. 1931- *AlmAP 92 [port]*
**Morella**, Constance Albanese 1931- *WhoAmP 91*
**Morelle**, Joseph D *WhoAmP 91*
**Morellet**, Francois Charles Alexis Albert 1926- *IntWW 91*
**Morelli**, Anthony Frank 1956- *WhoMW 92*
**Morelli**, Carmen 1922- *WhoAmL 92, WhoAmP 91, WhoFI 92*
**Morelli**, Joseph Gabriel, Jr. 1953- *WhoWest 92*
**Morelli**, William Annibale, Sr. 1938- *WhoMW 92*
**Morello**, Edwin Francis 1928- *AmMWSc 92*
**Morello**, Joe 1928- *NewAmDM*
**Morello**, Joseph Albert 1928- *WhoEnt 92*
**Morello**, Josephine A 1936- *AmMWSc 92*
**Morelly** *BlkwCEP*
**Morelock**, Jack 1928- *AmMWSc 92*
**Morelos**, Alfredo, Jr. 1952- *WhoHisp 92*
**Morelos**, Raymond Perez, Jr. 1944- *WhoHisp 92*
**Morelos y Pavon**, Jose Maria 1765-1815 *HisDSpE*
**Moremen**, William Merrill 1927- *WhoRel 92*
**Moren**, Leslie Arthur 1914- *WhoWest 92*
**Moren**, Sergio R. 1944- *WhoHisp 92*
**Morency**, Paula J. 1955- *WhoAmL 92*
**Moreng**, Robert Edward 1922- *AmMWSc 92*
**Moreno**, Abraham, Jr. 1948- *WhoFI 92*
**Moreno**, Alejandro, Jr 1947- *WhoAmP 91, WhoHisp 92*
**Moreno**, Alfredo A., Jr. 1919- *WhoHisp 92*
**Moreno**, Anthony Ernest 1954- *WhoWest 92*
**Moreno**, Antonio 1918- *WrDr 92*
**Moreno**, Antonio Elosegui 1918- *WhoHisp 92*
**Moreno**, Antonio L., Sr. 1945- *WhoHisp 92*
**Moreno**, Armando 1932- *IntAu&W 91*
**Moreno**, Arturo 1934- *WhoHisp 92*
**Moreno**, Carlos Julio 1946- *AmMWSc 92, WhoHisp 92*
**Moreno**, Carlos W. 1936- *WhoHisp 92*
**Moreno**, Cecilia May *WhoHisp 92*
**Moreno**, Clara Triay 1942- *WhoHisp 92*
**Moreno**, Dario Vincent 1958- *WhoHisp 92*
**Moreno**, Dorinda *DrAPF 91*
**Moreno**, Elida 1944- *WhoHisp 92*
**Moreno**, Ernest Henry 1946- *WhoHisp 92*
**Moreno**, Esteban 1926- *AmMWSc 92*
**Moreno**, Federico Antonio, Sr. 1952- *WhoHisp 92*
**Moreno**, Fernando *WhoHisp 92*
**Moreno**, Fernando 1946- *WhoHisp 92*
**Moreno**, Frank *IntMPA 92*
**Moreno**, Frank Javier 1961- *WhoWest 92*
**Moreno**, Frank Javier, Jr. 1961- *WhoHisp 92*
**Moreno**, Gilberto 1936- *WhoHisp 92*
**Moreno**, Glen Richard 1943- *WhoFI 92*
**Moreno**, Guillermo Fernandez 1948- *WhoRel 92*
**Moreno**, H. Paul *WhoHisp 92*
**Moreno**, Hernan 1939- *AmMWSc 92*
**Moreno**, Jaime Ricardo 1958- *WhoHisp 92*
**Moreno**, Jose Antonio 1928- *WhoHisp 92*
**Moreno**, Jose Guillermo 1951- *WhoHisp 92*
**Moreno**, Juan Carlos 1954- *WhoHisp 92*
**Moreno**, Luis Fernando 1951- *WhoHisp 92*
**Moreno**, Luis G., Jr. 1955- *WhoHisp 92*
**Moreno**, Luisa *HanAmWH*
**Moreno**, Luisa 1906- *RComAH*
**Moreno**, Lydia Holguin *WhoRel 92*
**Moreno**, Manuel 1945- *WhoHisp 92*
**Moreno**, Manuel D. 1930- *WhoHisp 92, WhoRel 92, WhoWest 92*
**Moreno**, Marcelino, Jr. 1961- *WhoHisp 92*
**Moreno**, Mariano 1778-1811 *BlkwCEP, HisDSpE*
**Moreno**, Mario Francisco, Jr. 1953- *WhoHisp 92*
**Moreno**, Mark Charles 1958- *WhoEnt 92*
**Moreno**, Mary A. *WhoHisp 92*
**Moreno**, Michael Anthony 1958- *WhoWest 92*
**Moreno**, Michael Rafael 1954- *WhoHisp 92*
**Moreno**, Miguel Angel *WhoHisp 92*
**Moreno**, Myriam 1959- *WhoAmL 92*
**Moreno**, Orlando Julio 1944- *WhoHisp 92*
**Moreno**, Oscar *WhoHisp 92*
**Moreno**, Oscar 1946- *AmMWSc 92*
**Moreno**, Patricia Jean *WhoAmP 91*
**Moreno**, Paul 1931- *WhoHisp 92*
**Moreno**, Paul Cruz 1931- *WhoAmP 91*

Moreno, Rachael E. 1941- WhoHisp 92
Moreno, Rafael 1949- WhoHisp 92
Moreno, Richard WhoHisp 92
Moreno, Richard D. 1940- WhoHisp 92
Moreno, Richard Frank, Jr. 1955- WhoWest 92
Moreno, Richard Mills 1938- WhoWest 92
Moreno, Rita ReelWom
Moreno, Rita 1931- IntMPA 92, WhoEnt 92, WhoHisp 92
Moreno, Rogelio WhoHisp 92
Moreno, Rudolfo 1933- WhoHisp 92
Moreno, Vaughn Michael 1947- WhoHisp 92
Moreno, Victor John 1955- WhoHisp 92
Moreno, William WhoHisp 92
Moreno Barbera, Fernando 1913- WhoFI 92
Moreno-Black, Geraldine 1946- WhoHisp 92
Moreno-Black, Geraldine S 1946- AmMWSc 92
Moreno Martinez, Alfonso 1922- IntWW 91
Moreno Rodriguez, Gilberto 1936- WhoAmP 91
Moreno-Salcedo, Luis 1918- IntWW 91
Morenzoni, Richard Anthony 1946- AmMWSc 92
Morera, Osvaldo Francisco 1966- WhoHisp 92
Moreri, Louis 1653-1680 BlkwCEP
Mores, Antoine Amadee Marie Vincent M 1858-1896 BiDExR
Mores, Steven Frederick 1945- WhoMW 92
Moreschi, Roger P 1938- WhoIns 92
Moreschi, Roger Patrick 1938- WhoFI 92
Moresky, Lana 1946- WhoAmP 91
Moress, Helen Rae 1934- WhoAmP 91
Morest, Donald Kent 1934- AmMWSc 92
Moret, Louis F 1944- WhoAmP 91, WhoHisp 92
Moreton Who 92
Moreton, Lord 1951- Who 92
Moreton, Eleanor 1956- TwCPaSc
Moreton, John IntAu&W 91X, WrDr 92
Moreton, John 1917- Who 92
Moreton, Julian Edward 1943- AmMWSc 92
Moreton, N. Edwina 1950- ConAu 135
Moreton, Robert Dulaney 1913- AmMWSc 92
Moreton, Thomas Hugh 1917- WhoRel 92
Moreton, Vic 1951- TwCPaSc
Morett, Angela Marie 1952- WhoHisp 92
Moretti, G 1917- AmMWSc 92
Moretti, Marino 1885-1979 DcLB 114 [port]
Moretti, Peter M 1935- AmMWSc 92
Moretti, Richard Leo 1929- AmMWSc 92
Moretto, Luciano G 1940- AmMWSc 92
Moretz, Roger C 1942- AmMWSc 92
Moretz, William Henry 1914- AmMWSc 92
Morewitz, Harry Alan 1923- AmMWSc 92
Morey, Ann-Janine 1951- WhoRel 92
Morey, Anthony Bernard Nicholas 1936- Who 92
Morey, Booker Williams 1941- AmMWSc 92
Morey, Carl Reginald 1934- WhoEnt 92
Morey, Charles Leonard, III 1947- WhoEnt 92
Morey, Darrell Dorr 1914- AmMWSc 92
Morey, Donald Roger 1907- AmMWSc 92
Morey, George L. 1954- WhoRel 92
Morey, Glenn Bernhardt 1935- AmMWSc 92
Morey, Robert Hardy 1956- WhoEnt 92, WhoWest 92
Morey, Robert Vance 1945- AmMWSc 92
Morey, Samuel 1762-1843 BiInAmS
Morey, Walt 1907- IntAu&W 91, WrDr 92
Morey-Holton, Emily Rene 1936- AmMWSc 92
Morf, Darrel Arle 1943- WhoMW 92
Morfit, Campbell 1820-1897 BiInAmS
Morfit, Thomas Garrison 1915- WhoEnt 92
Morfopoulos, Vassilis C P 1937- AmMWSc 92
Morford, Henry 1823-1881 BenetAL 91
Morford-Burg, JoAnn Marie 1956- WhoAmP 91
Morga Sanchez Garay y Lopez, Antonio de 1559-1636 HisDSpE
Morgado, Arnold 1952- WhoAmP 91
Morgado, Richard Joseph 1946- WhoFI 92
Morgado, Robert WhoEnt 92, WhoFI 92
Morgal, Paul Walter 1911- AmMWSc 92
Morgali, James R 1932- AmMWSc 92
Morgan Who 92
Morgan, Lady RfGEnL 91
Morgan, Alan Raymond 1955- AmMWSc 92
Morgan, Alan Wyndham Who 92
Morgan, Alice Johnson Parham 1943- WhoBlA 92
Morgan, Alison M. 1930- WrDr 92
Morgan, Alison Mary 1930- IntAu&W 91
Morgan, Allen Lewis WhoAmL 92
Morgan, Alvin H 1908- AmMWSc 92
Morgan, Andre 1952- IntMPA 92
Morgan, Andrew Price 1836-1906 BiInAmS
Morgan, Angela 1873-1957 AmPeW
Morgan, Annette N 1938- WhoAmP 91
Morgan, Anthony Hugh 1931- Who 92
Morgan, Anthony Thomas 1950- WhoEnt 92
Morgan, Anthony Wayne 1943- WhoWest 92
Morgan, Antony Richard 1940- AmMWSc 92
Morgan, Ardys Nord 1946- WhoMW 92
Morgan, Arthur 1944- TwCPaSc
Morgan, Arthur and Brown, Charles R ScFEYrs
Morgan, Arthur I, Jr 1923- AmMWSc 92
Morgan, Arthur William Crawford 1931- Who 92
Morgan, Audrey 1931- WhoWest 92
Morgan, Austen 1949- WrDr 92
Morgan, Bassett ScFEYrs
Morgan, Ben 1953- WhoEnt 92
Morgan, Bernard S, Jr 1927- AmMWSc 92
Morgan, Beverly Carver 1927- AmMWSc 92
Morgan, Bill Who 92
Morgan, Booker T. 1926- WhoBlA 92
Morgan, Brinley John 1916- Who 92
Morgan, Bruce 1945- Who 92
Morgan, Bruce Blake 1946- WhoFI 92, WhoMW 92
Morgan, Bruce Harry 1931- AmMWSc 92
Morgan, Bryan Edward 1919- AmMWSc 92
Morgan, Bryan McLaury 1955- WhoRel 92
Morgan, Carl William 1916- AmMWSc 92
Morgan, Carol Ellis 1954- WhoAmL 92
Morgan, Carol M. 1944- WhoHisp 92
Morgan, Carole DrAPF 91
Morgan, Chandos Clifford Hastings Mansel 1920- Who 92
Morgan, Charles 1894-1958 RfGEnL 91
Morgan, Charles, Jr. 1930- WhoAmL 92
Morgan, Charles Christopher 1939- Who 92
Morgan, Charles D 1934- AmMWSc 92
Morgan, Charles Edward Phillip 1916- WhoWest 92
Morgan, Charles Linwood, Jr. 1956- WhoAmL 92
Morgan, Charles Robert 1934- AmMWSc 92
Morgan, Charlie O 1931- WhoAmP 91
Morgan, Charlotte Theresa 1938- WhoBlA 92
Morgan, Claire WrDr 92
Morgan, Clarence Edward, III 1945- WhoAmP 91
Morgan, Clifford Isaac 1930- Who 92
Morgan, Clyde Alafiju 1940- WhoBlA 92
Morgan, Clyde Nathaniel 1923- WhoAmP 91
Morgan, Cyril Dion 1917- Who 92
Morgan, Dale Eugene 1930- WhoAmP 91
Morgan, Dan WhoAmP 91
Morgan, Dan 1925- IntAu&W 91, TwCSFW 91, WrDr 92
Morgan, Daniel 1735?-1802 BlkwEAR
Morgan, Daniel Davies 1939- WhoWest 92
Morgan, Daniel Joseph 1957- WhoEnt 92
Morgan, Daniel Melvin 1946- WhoWest 92
Morgan, David Allen 1962- WhoWest 92
Morgan, David Dudley 1914- Who 92
Morgan, David Forbes 1930- WhoRel 92, WhoWest 92
Morgan, David Gethin 1929- Who 92
Morgan, David Glyn 1933- Who 92
Morgan, David John H. Who 92
Morgan, David Thomas 1946- Who 92
Morgan, David Zackquill 1925- AmMWSc 92
Morgan, Debbi WhoBlA 92
Morgan, Dennis 1910- IntMPA 92
Morgan, Dennis Brent 1949- WhoMW 92, WhoRel 92
Morgan, Dennis Del 1949- WhoAmL 92
Morgan, Dennis Lee 1947- WhoRel 92
Morgan, Dennis Raymond 1942- AmMWSc 92
Morgan, Dennis Richard 1942- WhoAmL 92, WhoMW 92
Morgan, Dennis William 1952- WhoEnt 92
Morgan, Dewi 1916- Who 92, WrDr 92
Morgan, Dolores Parker WhoBlA 92
Morgan, Donald Crane 1940- WhoAmL 92
Morgan, Donald E 1917- AmMWSc 92
Morgan, Donald Lee 1934- WhoAmL 92
Morgan, Donald Lee 1946- AmMWSc 92
Morgan, Donald O'Quinn 1934- AmMWSc 92
Morgan, Donald Pryse AmMWSc 92
Morgan, Donald R 1933- AmMWSc 92
Morgan, Donn Farley 1943- WhoRel 92
Morgan, Douglas 1936- Who 92
Morgan, Dudley Who 92
Morgan, Eddie Mack, Jr AmMWSc 92
Morgan, Edward WhoEnt 92
Morgan, Edward L, Jr 1943- WhoIns 92
Morgan, Edward P. LesBEnT 92
Morgan, Edwin 1920- ConPo 91, IntAu&W 91, Who 92, WrDr 92
Morgan, Edwin John 1927- Who 92
Morgan, Elaine 1920- IntAu&W 91, WrDr 92
Morgan, Eldridge Gates 1925- WhoBlA 92
Morgan, Elizabeth DrAPF 91
Morgan, Elliott Wayne 1957- WhoWest 92
Morgan, Ellis 1916- Who 92
Morgan, Ernest 1896- Who 92
Morgan, Evan 1930- AmMWSc 92
Morgan, Fletcher, Jr. 1920- WhoBlA 92
Morgan, Frances Irene 1958- WhoFI 92
Morgan, Frank TwCWW 91
Morgan, Frank Edward, II 1952- WhoAmL 92
Morgan, Frank J. 1925- WhoFI 92
Morgan, Frank Leslie 1926- Who 92
Morgan, Frank Stanley 1893- Who 92
Morgan, Frank W 1915- AmMWSc 92
Morgan, Fred William 1945- WhoMW 92
Morgan, Frederick 1922- ConPo 91, WrDr 92
Morgan, Frederick William 1943- WhoWest 92
Morgan, G.J. TwCWW 91
Morgan, Gail 1953- IntAu&W 91
Morgan, Garrett 1877-1963 ConBlB 1 [port]
Morgan, Gary B. 1943- WhoWest 92
Morgan, Gemmell Who 92
Morgan, Geoffrey Thomas 1931- Who 92
Morgan, George Carl 1931- WhoMW 92
Morgan, George Douglas 1953- WhoWest 92
Morgan, George Edwards 1962- WhoEnt 92
Morgan, George Emir, III 1953- WhoFI 92
Morgan, George Frederick 1922- IntAu&W 91
Morgan, George L 1937- AmMWSc 92
Morgan, George Lewis Bush 1925- Who 92
Morgan, George Wallace 1941- AmMWSc 92
Morgan, George Wesley 1941- WhoRel 92
Morgan, George William, III 1944- WhoEnt 92
Morgan, Geraint Who 92
Morgan, Glyn 1926- TwCPaSc
Morgan, Gordon D. 1931- WhoBlA 92
Morgan, Gregory Paul 1958- WhoFI 92
Morgan, Gretna Faye 1927- WhoFI 92
Morgan, Gwenda d1991 Who 92N
Morgan, Gwyn Who 92
Morgan, H. G. 1934- WrDr 92
Morgan, H Keith 1942- AmMWSc 92
Morgan, Harold George 1943- WhoAmP 91
Morgan, Harry 1915- IntMPA 92
Morgan, Harry 1926- WhoBlA 92
Morgan, Harry Clark 1916- AmMWSc 92
Morgan, Harvey Bland 1930- WhoAmP 91
Morgan, Haywood, Sr. 1936- WhoBlA 92
Morgan, Hazel C. Brown 1930- WhoBlA 92
Morgan, Helen 1900-1941 NewAmDM
Morgan, Helen 1921- WrDr 92
Morgan, Henry 1635?-1688 BenetAL 91
Morgan, Henry 1915- WhoEnt 92
Morgan, Henry Coke, Jr 1935- WhoAmP 91
Morgan, Henry Gemmell 1922- Who 92
Morgan, Henry J. 1924- WhoAmL 92
Morgan, Henry Lewis 1818-1881 BenetAL 91
Morgan, Henry Victor 1865-1952 RelLAm 91
Morgan, Herbert Doyle 1929- WhoAmP 91
Morgan, Herbert R 1914- AmMWSc 92
Morgan, Horace C 1928- AmMWSc 92
Morgan, Howard 1949- TwCPaSc
Morgan, Howard Campbell 1935- WhoFI 92, WhoMW 92
Morgan, Howard E 1927- AmMWSc 92
Morgan, Hugh Allan 1933- WhoMW 92
Morgan, Hywel Rhodri 1939- Who 92
Morgan, Ira Lon 1926- AmMWSc 92
Morgan, J P 1837-1913 FacFETw
Morgan, J P, Jr 1867-1943 FacFETw
Morgan, J. Pierpont 1837-1913 BenetAL 91, RComAH
Morgan, Jack Gray 1940- WhoEnt 92
Morgan, Jack M. 1924- WhoWest 92
Morgan, Jack Mac Gee 1924- WhoAmP 91
Morgan, Jack Pearson 1947- WhoEnt 92
Morgan, Jacque ScFEYrs
Morgan, Jacque Lloyd 1873- ScFEYrs
Morgan, James 1914- WhoBlA 92
Morgan, James A. WhoAmL 92
Morgan, James Allen 1934- WhoFI 92
Morgan, James Dudley 1862-1919 BiInAmS
Morgan, James Durward 1936- WhoFI 92
Morgan, James Ethelwyn 1952- WhoEnt 92
Morgan, James Francis 1950- WhoEnt 92
Morgan, James Franklin 1943- WhoAmP 91
Morgan, James Frederick 1915- AmMWSc 92
Morgan, James Frederick 1941- AmMWSc 92
Morgan, James Hanly 1937- WhoAmP 91
Morgan, James Jay 1942- WhoFI 92
Morgan, James John 1932- AmMWSc 92
Morgan, James Leonard, III 1958- WhoAmP 91
Morgan, James N. 1918- IntWW 91
Morgan, James Philip 1948- AmMWSc 92
Morgan, James Richard 1953- AmMWSc 92
Morgan, James Thomas, Jr. 1911- WhoFI 92
Morgan, Jane Hale 1925- WhoBlA 92
Morgan, Janet 1945- Who 92, WrDr 92
Morgan, Jeffrey David 1959- WhoMW 92
Morgan, Jim 1937- WhoAmP 91
Morgan, Jimmy D 1945- WhoAmP 91
Morgan, Jo Valentine, Jr. 1920- WhoAmL 92
Morgan, Joe 1943- WhoBlA 92
Morgan, Joe Peter 1931- AmMWSc 92
Morgan, John DrAPF 91, TwCWW 91
Morgan, John 1735-1789 BenetAL 91
Morgan, John 1929- Who 92
Morgan, John Alfred 1931- Who 92
Morgan, John Ambrose 1934- Who 92
Morgan, John C. d1991 NewYTBS 91
Morgan, John Clifford, II 1938- AmMWSc 92
Morgan, John D 1921- AmMWSc 92
Morgan, John Davis, III 1955- AmMWSc 92
Morgan, John Derald 1939- AmMWSc 92, WhoWest 92
Morgan, John Gwyn 1934- Who 92
Morgan, John Jordan 1947- WhoAmP 91
Morgan, John Joseph, Jr. 1934- WhoAmL 92
Morgan, John Lewis 1919- Who 92
Morgan, John Lorenz 1951- WhoMW 92
Morgan, John P 1940- AmMWSc 92
Morgan, John Paul 1929- WhoBlA 92
Morgan, John Pierpont 1948- WhoRel 92
Morgan, John Stephen 1963- WhoAmP 91
Morgan, John Walter 1932- AmMWSc 92
Morgan, John William Harold 1927- Who 92
Morgan, Joseph 1671-1745 BenetAL 91
Morgan, Joseph 1909- AmMWSc 92
Morgan, Joseph C. 1921- WhoBlA 92
Morgan, Joseph L. 1936- WhoBlA 92
Morgan, Juanita Kennedy 1911- WhoBlA 92
Morgan, Juliet 1937- AmMWSc 92
Morgan, June Elloie 1949- WhoBlA 92
Morgan, Karen D. 1953- WhoRel 92
Morgan, Karen J 1945- AmMWSc 92
Morgan, Karl Ziegler 1907- AmMWSc 92
Morgan, Kathleen Greive 1950- AmMWSc 92
Morgan, Kathryn A 1922- AmMWSc 92
Morgan, Keith John 1929- Who 92
Morgan, Kenneth 1928- Who 92
Morgan, Kenneth Owen 1934- IntWW 91, Who 92
Morgan, Kenneth Robb 1952- AmMWSc 92
Morgan, Kenneth Smith 1925- Who 92
Morgan, Kenneth Wilbur 1944- WhoRel 92
Morgan, Kermit I. 1942- WhoBlA 92
Morgan, Kevin Thomas 1943- AmMWSc 92
Morgan, La Belle EncAmaz 91
Morgan, Lael 1936- WrDr 92
Morgan, Larry Ronald 1936- WhoRel 92
Morgan, Laura Dana Puffer 1874-1962 AmPeW
Morgan, Laura Frances 1961- WhoAmL 92
Morgan, Lee Laverne 1920- IntWW 91
Morgan, Lee Roy, Jr 1936- AmMWSc 92
Morgan, Leland J WhoAmP 91
Morgan, Leon Alford 1934- WhoFI 92
Morgan, Leon M. 1940- WhoBlA 92
Morgan, Leon Owen 1919- AmMWSc 92
Morgan, Leonard Amos 1926- WhoFI 92
Morgan, Leonard Eugene 1946- WhoFI 92
Morgan, Leslie Who 92
Morgan, Lewis Henry 1818-1881 BiInAmS
Morgan, Lucian L 1928- AmMWSc 92
Morgan, Lucy 1961- WhoMW 92
Morgan, Lucy Calista 1889-1981 DcNCBi 4

**Morgan,** Lynda M 1949- *WhoAmP 91*
**Morgan,** Lynn Marie 1947- *WhoEnt 92*
**Morgan,** M Granger 1941- *AmMWSc 92*
**Morgan,** Marilynne Ann 1946- *Who 92*
**Morgan,** Marjorie *WrDr 92*
**Morgan,** Marjorie Susan 1956- *AmMWSc 92*
**Morgan,** Mark *WrDr 92*
**Morgan,** Mark 1837-1916 *DcNCBi 4*
**Morgan,** Mark Allen 1957- *WhoWest 92*
**Morgan,** Mark Bryan 1957- *WhoRel 92*
**Morgan,** Mark Douglas 1952- *AmMWSc 92*
**Morgan,** Mark Quenten 1950- *WhoWest 92*
**Morgan,** Marvin Thomas 1921- *AmMWSc 92*
**Morgan,** Mary H. Ethel 1912- *WhoBlA 92*
**Morgan,** Meli'sa 1964- *WhoBlA 92*
**Morgan,** Melvin 1918- *WhoAmP 91*
**Morgan,** Meredith Walter 1912- *AmMWSc 92*
**Morgan,** Merle L 1919- *AmMWSc 92*
**Morgan,** Michael 1957- *WhoBlA 92*
**Morgan,** Michael Allen 1948- *AmMWSc 92, WhoEnt 92*
**Morgan,** Michael David 1942- *Who 92*
**Morgan,** Michael Dean 1941- *AmMWSc 92*
**Morgan,** Michael Hugh 1925- *Who 92*
**Morgan,** Michele 1920- *IntMPA 92, IntWW 91*
**Morgan,** Monica Alise 1963- *WhoBlA 92*
**Morgan,** Monroe Talton, Sr 1933- *AmMWSc 92*
**Morgan,** Morris Herbert 1950- *AmMWSc 92*
**Morgan,** Murray Cromwell 1916- *WhoWest 92*
**Morgan,** Nancy H 1933- *AmMWSc 92*
**Morgan,** Neil 1924- *WrDr 92*
**Morgan,** Omar Drennan, Jr 1913- *AmMWSc 92*
**Morgan,** Ora Billy, Jr 1930- *AmMWSc 92*
**Morgan,** P J *WhoAmP 91*
**Morgan,** Page Wesley 1933- *AmMWSc 92*
**Morgan,** Patricia 1944- *IntAu&W 91, WrDr 92*
**Morgan,** Patrick John 1956- *WhoWest 92*
**Morgan,** Paul E 1923- *AmMWSc 92*
**Morgan,** Paul Winthrop 1911- *AmMWSc 92*
**Morgan,** Perry 1884-1955 *DcNCBi 4*
**Morgan,** Pete 1939- *ConAu 133, ConPo 91, WrDr 92*
**Morgan,** Peter Trevor Hopkin 1919- *Who 92*
**Morgan,** Peter William Lloyd 1936- *IntWW 91, Who 92*
**Morgan,** Philip 1930- *IntWW 91, Who 92*
**Morgan,** R John 1923- *AmMWSc 92*
**Morgan,** Raleigh, Jr. 1916- *WhoBlA 92*
**Morgan,** Randall Collins, Sr. 1917- *WhoBlA 92*
**Morgan,** Raymond P 1943- *AmMWSc 92*
**Morgan,** Raymond Scott 1949- *WhoFI 92*
**Morgan,** Raymond Victor, Jr 1942- *AmMWSc 92*
**Morgan,** Rebecca Q 1938- *WhoAmP 91*
**Morgan,** Rebecca Quinn 1938- *WhoWest 92*
**Morgan,** Relbue Marvin 1939- *AmMWSc 92*
**Morgan,** Rhelda Elnola 1947- *WhoMW 92*
**Morgan,** Rhodri *Who 92*
**Morgan,** Ric 1950- *WhoMW 92*
**Morgan,** Richard *DrAPF 91, WhoAmP 91*
**Morgan,** Richard Greer 1943- *WhoAmL 92*
**Morgan,** Richard H., Jr. 1944- *WhoBlA 92*
**Morgan,** Richard Joseph, IV 1945- *WhoAmP 91*
**Morgan,** Richard Martin 1940- *Who 92*
**Morgan,** Richard Thomas 1937- *WhoFI 92*
**Morgan,** Robert *DrAPF 91*
**Morgan,** Robert 1921- *ConPo 91, WrDr 92*
**Morgan,** Robert 1922- *IntAu&W 91*
**Morgan,** Robert 1944- *ConPo 91, WrDr 92*
**Morgan,** Robert, Jr 1954- *WhoBlA 92*
**Morgan,** Robert B. 1934- *WhoFI 92, WhoMW 92*
**Morgan,** Robert Bruce 1934- *WhoIns 92*
**Morgan,** Robert Burren 1925- *IntWW 91, WhoAmP 91*
**Morgan,** Robert Crawley 1933- *WhoRel 92*
**Morgan,** Robert Dale 1912- *WhoAmL 92, WhoMW 92*
**Morgan,** Robert Edward 1924- *WhoAmL 92, WhoMW 92*
**Morgan,** Robert George 1941- *WhoFI 92*
**Morgan,** Robert Hall 1950- *WhoAmL 92*
**Morgan,** Robert Lee 1934- *WhoBlA 92*
**Morgan,** Robert P 1934- *AmMWSc 92, WhoEnt 92*
**Morgan,** Robert W., II 1932- *WhoBlA 92*
**Morgan,** Robin *DrAPF 91*
**Morgan,** Robin 1941- *News 91 [port]*
**Morgan,** Robin Milne 1930- *Who 92*
**Morgan,** Robin Richard 1953- *Who 92*
**Morgan,** Roger Hugh Vaughan Charles 1926- *Who 92*
**Morgan,** Roger John 1942- *AmMWSc 92*
**Morgan,** Roger Pearce 1932- *Who 92*
**Morgan,** Ronald Keith 1934- *WhoRel 92*
**Morgan,** Rose *NotBlAW 92, WhoBlA 92*
**Morgan,** Roy Edward 1908- *WhoEnt 92*
**Morgan,** Rudolph Courtney 1950- *WhoBlA 92*
**Morgan,** Sally 1951- *ConAu 134*
**Morgan,** Samuel Pope 1923- *AmMWSc 92, WhoFI 92*
**Morgan,** Samuel Tate 1857-1920 *DcNCBi 4*
**Morgan,** Sarah 1959- *SmATA 68*
**Morgan,** Seth 1949-1990 *AnObit 1990, ConLC 65 [port]*
**Morgan,** Shawn Trent 1963- *WhoWest 92*
**Morgan,** Sherli Jo 1953- *WhoRel 92*
**Morgan,** Speer *DrAPF 91*
**Morgan,** Stanley 1955- *WhoBlA 92*
**Morgan,** Stanley L 1918- *AmMWSc 92*
**Morgan,** Stanley Leins 1918- *WhoMW 92*
**Morgan,** Stephen Charles 1946- *WhoWest 92*
**Morgan,** Stephen Harold 1954- *WhoEnt 92*
**Morgan,** Susan Wright 1967- *WhoEnt 92*
**Morgan,** Ted 1932- *IntAu&W 91, LiExTwC, WrDr 92*
**Morgan,** Terence 1921- *IntMPA 92*
**Morgan,** Theodore 1910- *WhoFI 92, WrDr 92*
**Morgan,** Thomas D. 1942- *WhoAmL 92*
**Morgan,** Thomas Daniel 1953- *WhoFI 92*
**Morgan,** Thomas Edward 1943- *AmMWSc 92*
**Morgan,** Thomas Ellsworth 1906- *WhoAmP 91*
**Morgan,** Thomas Hunt 1866-1945 *FacFETw, WhoNob 90*
**Morgan,** Thomas J. 1847-1912 *DcAmImH*
**Morgan,** Thomas Joseph 1943- *AmMWSc 92*
**Morgan,** Thomas Kenneth, Jr 1949- *AmMWSc 92*
**Morgan,** Thomas Oliver *Who 92*
**Morgan,** Thomas Oliver 1944- *WhoRel 92, WhoWest 92*
**Morgan,** Timi Sue 1953- *WhoAmL 92*
**Morgan,** Timothy Gale 1959- *WhoRel 92*
**Morgan,** Timothy Ian 1955- *WhoMW 92*
**Morgan,** Tom 1914- *Who 92*
**Morgan,** Tony *Who 92*
**Morgan,** Travis C 1929- *WhoIns 92*
**Morgan,** Troy R. 1960- *WhoFI 92*
**Morgan,** Vaughan Frederick John 1931- *Who 92*
**Morgan,** Virginia *ConAu 34NR*
**Morgan,** Walter Clifford 1921- *AmMWSc 92*
**Morgan,** Walter L 1930- *AmMWSc 92*
**Morgan,** Walter Thomas James 1900- *IntWW 91, Who 92*
**Morgan,** Warren W. *WhoBlA 92*
**Morgan,** Wayne Philip 1942- *WhoWest 92*
**Morgan,** William Basil 1927- *Who 92*
**Morgan,** William Bruce 1926- *AmMWSc 92*
**Morgan,** William Geraint 1920- *Who 92*
**Morgan,** William Gwyn 1914- *Who 92*
**Morgan,** William James 1914- *Who 92*
**Morgan,** William Jason 1935- *AmMWSc 92*
**Morgan,** William Keith C 1929- *AmMWSc 92*
**Morgan,** William L, Jr 1927- *AmMWSc 92*
**Morgan,** William Perry 1961- *WhoEnt 92*
**Morgan,** William R 1922- *AmMWSc 92*
**Morgan,** William T. 1928- *WhoFI 92*
**Morgan,** William T 1941- *AmMWSc 92*
**Morgan,** William Wilson 1906- *AmMWSc 92, IntWW 91*
**Morgan,** Willie, Jr. 1951- *WhoBlA 92*
**Morgan,** Winfield Scott 1921- *AmMWSc 92*
**Morgan,** Winifred Alice 1938- *WhoMW 92*
**Morgan,** Wm Lowell 1946- *AmMWSc 92*
**Morgan,** Wyman 1941- *AmMWSc 92*
**Morgan-Giles,** Morgan 1914- *Who 92*
**Morgan-Grenville,** Gerard 1931- *IntAu&W 91, WrDr 92*
**Morgan Hughes,** David *Who 92*
**Morgan-Lee,** Veronica 1948- *WhoRel 92*
**Morgan-Owen,** John Gethin 1914- *Who 92*
**Morgan-Pond,** Caroline G *AmMWSc 92, WhoMW 92*
**Morgan-Price,** Veronica Elizabeth 1945- *WhoBlA 92*
**Morgan-Smith,** Sylvia *WhoBlA 92*
**Morgan-Washington,** Barbara 1953- *WhoBlA 92*
**Morgan-Welch,** Beverly Ann 1952- *WhoBlA 92*
**Morgan-Witts,** Max 1931- *WrDr 92*
**Morgan-Witts,** Maxwell 1931- *IntAu&W 91*
**Morgane,** Peter J 1927- *AmMWSc 92*
**Morganroth,** Fred 1938- *WhoAmL 92, WhoMW 92*
**Morganroth,** Joel 1945- *AmMWSc 92*
**Morganroth,** Mayer 1931- *WhoAmL 92, WhoMW 92*
**Morgans,** David Edward 1951- *WhoAmL 92*
**Morgans,** Leland Foster 1939- *AmMWSc 92*
**Morganstern,** Daniel Robert 1940- *WhoEnt 92*
**Morganstern,** Mark *DrAPF 91*
**Morgante,** John-Paul 1962- *WhoRel 92, WhoWest 92*
**Morgen,** John Donald 1953- *WhoMW 92*
**Morgenbesser,** Henry Ives 1956- *WhoAmL 92*
**Morgenroth,** Earl Eugene 1936- *WhoWest 92*
**Morgenroth,** Robert William 1957- *WhoEnt 92*
**Morgens,** Howard J. 1910- *IntWW 91*
**Morgenstein,** William 1933- *WhoFI 92*
**Morgenstern,** Alan Lawrence 1933- *AmMWSc 92*
**Morgenstern,** Christian 1871-1914 *FacFETw*
**Morgenstern,** Dan Michael 1929- *WhoEnt 92*
**Morgenstern,** Matthew *AmMWSc 92*
**Morgenstern,** N R 1935- *AmMWSc 92*
**Morgenstern,** Sheldon Jon 1938- *WhoEnt 92*
**Morgenthal,** Becky Holz 1947- *WhoFI 92*
**Morgenthaler,** Alisa Marie 1960- *WhoAmL 92*
**Morgenthaler,** Frederic R 1933- *AmMWSc 92*
**Morgenthaler,** George William 1926- *AmMWSc 92*
**Morgenthau,** Hans Joachim 1904-1980 *AmPeW, FacFETw*
**Morgenthau,** Henry, Jr. 1891-1967 *AmPolLe, EncTR 91 [port], FacFETw*
**Morgenthau,** Robert Morris 1919- *IntWW 91, WhoAmL 92*
**Morgera,** Salvatore Domenic 1946- *AmMWSc 92*
**Morgison,** F. Edward 1940- *WhoFI 92*
**Morgun,** Fyodor Trofimovich 1924- *IntWW 91*
**Morhaim,** Abraham 1932- *WhoRel 92*
**Mori,** Allen Anthony 1947- *WhoWest 92*
**Mori,** Erik Jun 1962- *AmMWSc 92*
**Mori,** Hanae *IntWW 91*
**Mori,** Haruki 1911- *IntWW 91, Who 92*
**Mori,** Hideo 1925- *IntWW 91*
**Mori,** Jun 1929- *WhoAmL 92*
**Mori,** Kazuhisa 1926- *IntWW 91*
**Mori,** Peter Taketoshi 1925- *AmMWSc 92*
**Mori,** Raymond I 1926- *AmMWSc 92*
**Mori,** Scott Alan 1941- *AmMWSc 92*
**Mori,** Taisuke 1920- *IntWW 91*
**Mori,** Toshio 1910- *BenetAL 91*
**Mori,** William Guido 1929- *WhoAmP 91*
**Morial,** Ernest Nathan 1929- *WhoAmP 91*
**Morial,** Ernest Nathan 1929-1989 *WhoBlA 92N*
**Morial,** Marc Haydel 1958- *WhoAmL 92*
**Morial,** Sybil Haydel 1932- *WhoBlA 92*
**Moriarty,** Brian David 1942- *WhoMW 92*
**Moriarty,** Brian James 1956- *WhoEnt 92*
**Moriarty,** C Michael 1941- *AmMWSc 92*
**Moriarty,** Cathy 1960- *IntMPA 92*
**Moriarty,** Daniel Delmar, Jr 1946- *AmMWSc 92*
**Moriarty,** David John 1948- *AmMWSc 92*
**Moriarty,** Donald Peter, II 1935- *WhoWest 92*
**Moriarty,** Frederic Barstow 1940- *WhoAmL 92*
**Moriarty,** Frederick L 1913- *IntAu&W 91, WrDr 92*
**Moriarty,** Gerald Evelyn 1928- *Who 92*
**Moriarty,** Herbert Bernard, Jr. 1929- *WhoAmL 92*
**Moriarty,** James Francis 1957- *WhoAmL 92*
**Moriarty,** Joan Olivia Elsie 1923- *Who 92*
**Moriarty,** John 1930- *WhoEnt 92, WhoWest 92*
**Moriarty,** John Alan 1944- *AmMWSc 92*
**Moriarty,** John Lawrence, Jr 1932- *AmMWSc 92*
**Moriarty,** Kevin Joseph 1940- *AmMWSc 92*
**Moriarty,** Marshall Theodore 1948- *WhoAmL 92*
**Moriarty,** Michael 1941- *IntMPA 92, WhoEnt 92*
**Moriarty,** Michael Gerald 1960- *WhoRel 92*
**Moriarty,** Michael John 1930- *Who 92*
**Moriarty,** Robert Brian 1940- *WhoAmL 92*
**Moriarty,** Robert M 1933- *AmMWSc 92*
**Moriarty,** William E, Jr. 1952- *WhoIns 92*
**Moriber,** Louis G 1917- *AmMWSc 92*
**Morice,** Dave *DrAPF 91*
**Morice,** Peter Beaumont 1926- *Who 92*
**Morici,** Peter George, Jr. 1948- *WhoFI 92*
**Morie,** G. Glen *WhoAmL 92*
**Morie,** Gerald Prescott 1939- *AmMWSc 92*
**Morie,** Scott 1956- *WhoRel 92*
**Morien,** Lyle J 1944- *WhoIns 92*
**Morihara,** David *WhoAmP 91*
**Morii,** Kiyoji *WhoFI 92*
**Morillo y Morillo,** Pablo 1778-1837 *HisDSpE*
**Morimoto,** Akiko Charlene 1948- *WhoWest 92*
**Morimoto,** Carl Noboru 1942- *WhoWest 92*
**Morin,** Carlton Paul 1932- *WhoFI 92*
**Morin,** Charles Raymond 1947- *AmMWSc 92, WhoMW 92*
**Morin,** Dornis Clinton 1923- *AmMWSc 92*
**Morin,** Edgar 1921- *IntWW 91*
**Morin,** Edward *DrAPF 91*
**Morin,** Francis Joseph 1917- *AmMWSc 92*
**Morin,** George Cardinal Albert 1943- *AmMWSc 92*
**Morin,** James Gunnar 1942- *AmMWSc 92*
**Morin,** Jean 1916- *IntWW 91*
**Morin,** John Edward 1951- *AmMWSc 92*
**Morin,** Lamar Howard 1962- *WhoRel 92*
**Morin,** Leo Gregory 1941- *AmMWSc 92*
**Morin,** Nancy Ruth 1948- *AmMWSc 92*
**Morin,** Paul 1889-1963 *BenetAL 91*
**Morin,** Penny B. *WhoHisp 92*
**Morin,** Peter B 1955- *WhoAmP 91*
**Morin,** Peter Jay 1953- *AmMWSc 92*
**Morin,** Richard Dudley 1918- *AmMWSc 92*
**Morin,** Robert B. *IntMPA 92*
**Morin,** Roland Louis 1932- *IntWW 91*
**Morin,** Thomas Lee 1943- *AmMWSc 92*
**Morin,** Walter Arthur 1933- *AmMWSc 92*
**Morin,** William Raymond 1949- *WhoMW 92*
**Morin,** Wollaston Gerald 1936- *WhoFI 92*
**Morinaga,** Teiichiro 1910- *IntWW 91*
**Morine,** Bruce Phillip 1947- *WhoFI 92*
**Morine,** Hoder *SmATA 65*
**Morini,** Erica 1910- *Who 92*
**Morinigo,** Fernando Bernardino 1936- *AmMWSc 92*
**Morinigo,** Higinio 1897- *IntWW 91*
**Morino,** Luigi 1938- *AmMWSc 92*
**Morioka,** Ted T 1921- *WhoAmP 91*
**Morios,** Armando *WhoHisp 92*
**Morisawa,** Marie 1919- *AmMWSc 92*
**Morisey,** Patricia Garland 1921- *WhoBlA 92*
**Morishima,** Akira 1930- *AmMWSc 92*
**Morishima,** Hisayo Oda 1929- *AmMWSc 92*
**Morishima,** Michio 1923- *IntWW 91, Who 92*
**Morishita,** Motoharu 1922- *IntWW 91*
**Morishita,** Yoko 1948- *NewYTBS 91 [port]*
**Morison,** Lord 1931- *Who 92*
**Morison,** George Shattuck 1842-1903 *BiInAmS*
**Morison,** Hugh 1943- *Who 92*
**Morison,** Ian George 1928- *AmMWSc 92*
**Morison,** Jack 1954- *WhoWest 92*
**Morison,** John A. 1942- *WhoMW 92*
**Morison,** Richard Trevor *Who 92*
**Morison,** Samuel Eliot 1887-1976 *BenetAL 91, FacFETw*
**Morison,** Stanley 1889-1967 *FacFETw*
**Morison,** Thomas Richard Atkin 1939- *Who 92*
**Morisot,** Berthe 1841-1895 *ThHEIm [port]*
**Morisseau,** Gerald Paul 1942- *WhoAmP 91*
**Morisset,** Pierre 1938- *AmMWSc 92*
**Morita,** Akio 1921- *IntWW 91, Who 92, WhoEnt 92, WhoFI 92*
**Morita,** Hirokazu 1926- *AmMWSc 92*
**Morita,** James Masami 1913- *WhoWest 92*
**Morita,** Noriyuki 1932- *IntMPA 92*
**Morita,** Pat 1932- *WhoEnt 92*
**Morita,** Richard Yukio 1923- *AmMWSc 92*
**Morita,** Toshiko N 1926- *AmMWSc 92*
**Morits,** Yunna Petrovna 1937- *IntWW 91*
**Moritsugu,** Toshio 1925- *AmMWSc 92*
**Moritz,** Albert F. *DrAPF 91*
**Moritz,** Barry Kyler 1941- *AmMWSc 92*
**Moritz,** Carl Albert 1914- *AmMWSc 92*
**Moritz,** Charles Worthington 1936- *WhoFI 92*
**Moritz,** Claire Louise 1954- *WhoFI 92*
**Moritz,** J. Kenneth 1962- *WhoAmL 92*
**Moritz,** John Joseph, Jr. 1947- *WhoMW 92*
**Moritz,** John Matthew, Jr. 1962- *WhoFI 92*
**Moritz,** Karl-Philip 1757-1793 *BlkwCEP*
**Moritz,** Milton Edward 1931- *WhoFI 92*
**Moritz,** Milton I. 1933- *IntMPA 92*
**Moritz,** Reiner *LesBEnT 92*

Moritz, Roger Homer 1937- AmMWSc 92
Moritz, Terry Francis 1942- WhoAmL 92
Moriwaki, Melvin M 1952- AmMWSc 92
Moriyama, Iwao Milton 1909- AmMWSc 92
Moriyama, Mayumi 1928- IntWW 91
Moriyama, Raymond 1929- IntWW 91
Morizet, Jacques 1921- IntWW 91
Morizot-Young, Carol Ann 1944- IntAu&W 91
Morizumi, S James 1923- AmMWSc 92
Mork, David Peter Sogn 1942- AmMWSc 92, WhoMW 92
Mork, Gordon Robert 1938- WhoMW 92
Mork, Loren Leslie 1956- WhoEnt 92
Morkan, John F. 1955- WhoAmL 92
Morken, Donald A 1922- AmMWSc 92
Morkoc, Hadis 1947- AmMWSc 92
Morkovin, Mark V 1917- AmMWSc 92
Morlan, George K. 1904- WrDr 92
Morland, Dick WrDr 92
Morland, Francis 1934- TwCPaSc
Morland, Martin Robert 1933- Who 92
Morland, Michael 1929- Who 92
Morland, Peter Henry TwCWW 91
Morland, Robert 1935- Who 92
Morlang, Barbara Louise AmMWSc 92
Morley Who 92
Morley, Earl of 1923- Who 92
Morley, Alfred Charles, Jr. 1927- WhoFI 92
Morley, Bobbie Mary 1952- WhoFI 92
Morley, Cecil Denis 1911- Who 92
Morley, Christopher 1890-1957 BenetAL 91, FacFETw
Morley, Colin Godfrey Dennis 1941- AmMWSc 92
Morley, David 1923- IntAu&W 91, WrDr 92
Morley, Don 1937- IntAu&W 91
Morley, Elliot Anthony 1952- Who 92
Morley, Eric Douglas Who 92
Morley, Gayle L 1936- AmMWSc 92
Morley, George W 1923- AmMWSc 92
Morley, Guy Andrew 1959- WhoAmL 92
Morley, Harold Hall 1943- WhoFI 92
Morley, Harold Victor 1927- AmMWSc 92
Morley, Harry 1881-1943 TwCPaSc
Morley, Henry 1822-1894 ScFEYrs
Morley, Herbert 1919- Who 92
Morley, Hilda DrAPF 91
Morley, Jeffrey Joshua 1953- WhoEnt 92
Morley, John 1924- Who 92
Morley, John 1942- TwCPaSc
Morley, John David 1948- IntAu&W 91
Morley, John E 1946- AmMWSc 92
Morley, John Harwood 1933- Who 92
Morley, Lawrence Whitaker 1920- AmMWSc 92
Morley, Lloyd Albert 1940- AmMWSc 92
Morley, Malcolm 1931- IntWW 91, TwCPaSc
Morley, Malcolm A. 1931- Who 92
Morley, Michael Darwin 1930- AmMWSc 92
Morley, Patricia Marlow 1929- IntAu&W 91
Morley, Robert 1908- IntMPA 92, IntWW 91, Who 92
Morley, Robert Emmett, Jr 1951- AmMWSc 92
Morley, Roger Hubert 1931- IntWW 91
Morley, Ruth d1991 NewYTBS 91
Morley, Sheridan 1941- WrDr 92
Morley, Sheridan Robert 1941- IntAu&W 91, Who 92
Morley, Thomas 1557?-1602 NewAmDM
Morley, Thomas Paterson 1920- AmMWSc 92
Morley, Wilfred Owen TwCSFW 91
Morley, William Fenton 1912- Who 92
Morley-John, Michael 1923- Who 92
Morling, Leonard Francis 1904- Who 92
Morling, Norton Arthur 1909- Who 92
Morlino, Bruce 1953- WhoFI 92
Morlock, Carl G 1906- AmMWSc 92
Morman, Kenneth N 1940- AmMWSc 92
Morman, Michael T 1945- AmMWSc 92
Morneau, Louis 1961- WhoEnt 92
Morneau, Robert Fealey 1938- WhoRel 92
Mornel, Ted 1936- WhoEnt 92
Morneweck, Samuel 1939- AmMWSc 92
Morning, John Frew, Jr. 1932- WhoBlA 92
Mornington, Earl of 1978- Who 92
Moro DcNCBi 4
Moro, Aldo 1916-1978 FacFETw [port]
Moro, Cesar 1903-1956 BenetAL 91
Moro, Peter 1911- IntWW 91, Who 92
Moro, Vincenzo 1922- IntWW 91
Morocco, King of IntWW 91
Moroi, David S 1926- AmMWSc 92
Moroles, Jesus Bautista 1950- WhoHisp 92, WorArt 1980 [port]
Morones, Anthony 1955- WhoHisp 92
Moroney, Kristalia Stavrolakis 1954- WhoFI 92
Moroney, Linda L. S. Muffie 1943- WhoAmL 92
Moroney, Michael John 1940- WhoAmL 92
Moroney, Michael Vincent 1930- WhoWest 92
Moroney, Robert Emmet 1903- WhoFI 92
Morong, C. Oscar, Jr. WhoFI 92
Morong, C Oscar, Jr 1935- WhoIns 92
Morong, Thomas 1827-1894 BiInAmS
Moroni, Antonio 1953- AmMWSc 92
Moroni, Eneo C 1923- AmMWSc 92
Moros, Stephen Andrew 1928- AmMWSc 92
Morosco, B. Anthony 1936- WhoAmL 92
Morosin, Bruno 1934- AmMWSc 92
Moross, Jerome 1913-1983 NewAmDM
Moross, Manfred David 1931- IntWW 91
Moroux, Anthony Drexel, Sr. 1948- WhoAmL 92
Morowitz, Harold J IntAu&W 91, WrDr 92
Morowitz, Harold Joseph 1927- AmMWSc 92
Moroz, Leonard Arthur 1935- AmMWSc 92
Moroz, William James 1927- AmMWSc 92
Morozov, Ivan 1871-1921 ThHEIm
Morozov, Mikhail 1870-1903 ThHEIm
Morozov, Vladimir Mikhailovich 1933- IntWW 91
Morozowich, Walter 1933- AmMWSc 92
Morozzi, Massimo DcTwDes
Morpeth, Viscount 1949- Who 92
Morpeth, Douglas 1924- Who 92
Morphet, David Ian 1940- Who 92
Morphet, Richard Edward 1938- Who 92
Morphew, Ronald R. 1933- WhoFI 92
Morphonios, Ellen James 1929- WhoAmL 92
Morphos, Evangeline Mary 1949- WhoEnt 92
Morpurgo, J. E. 1918- WrDr 92
Morpurgo, Jack Eric 1918- IntAu&W 91, Who 92
Morpurgo Davies, Anna Elbina Who 92
Morr, Charles Vernon 1927- AmMWSc 92
Morr, James Earl 1946- WhoAmL 92
Morra, Joyce Ann 1941- WhoRel 92
Morra, Lawrence Anthony 1951- WhoEnt 92
Morrah, Dave ConAu 134
Morrah, David Wardlaw, Jr. 1914-1991 ConAu 134
Morrah, Ruth d1990 Who 92N
Morral, F R 1907- AmMWSc 92
Morral, Frank Rolf 1937- WhoMW 92
Morral, John Eric 1939- AmMWSc 92
Morran, Donald Keith 1950- WhoMW 92
Morrar, Atef Ismail 1950- WhoEnt 92, WhoFI 92
Morre, D James 1935- AmMWSc 92
Morre, Dorothy Marie 1935- AmMWSc 92
Morreale, Ben DrAPF 91
Morreale, Joseph Constantino 1944- WhoFI 92
Morreau, James Earl, Jr. 1955- WhoAmL 92
Morrel, Bernard Baldwin 1940- AmMWSc 92
Morrel, William Griffin, Jr. 1933- WhoFI 92
Morrell, Arthur A 1943- WhoAmP 91
Morrell, Benjamin 1797-1839 BenetAL 91
Morrell, David DrAPF 91
Morrell, David Cameron 1929- Who 92
Morrell, Frances Maine 1937- Who 92
Morrell, Frank 1926- AmMWSc 92
Morrell, Gareth 1956- WhoEnt 92
Morrell, George Walter 1946- WhoMW 92
Morrell, Herbert William 1915- Who 92
Morrell, James George 1923- Who 92
Morrell, James Herbert Lloyd 1907- Who 92
Morrell, Leslie James 1931- Who 92
Morrell, Robert Ellis 1930- WhoRel 92
Morrell, Steve 1952- WhoEnt 92
Morrell, William Who 92
Morrell, William Egbert 1909- AmMWSc 92
Morressy, John DrAPF 91
Morressy, John 1930- IntAu&W 91, TwCSFW 91, WrDr 92
Morrette, Thomas John 1950- WhoRel 92
Morrey, John Rolph 1930- AmMWSc 92, WhoWest 92
Morrical, Daniel Gene 1955- AmMWSc 92
Morrice, Norman Who 92
Morrice, Norman Alexander 1931- IntWW 91
Morrice, Philip 1943- Who 92
Morricone, Ennio 1928- IntMPA 92, IntWW 91
Morril, Mark Charles 1947- WhoAmL 92
Morrill, Bernard 1910- AmMWSc 92
Morrill, Callis Gary 1938- AmMWSc 92
Morrill, Charles D 1919- AmMWSc 92
Morrill, Geary Steven 1953- WhoEnt 92
Morrill, Gene A 1931- AmMWSc 92
Morrill, James Lawrence, Jr 1930- AmMWSc 92
Morrill, John Barstow, Jr 1929- AmMWSc 92
Morrill, John Elliott 1935- AmMWSc 92
Morrill, John Stephen 1946- WrDr 92
Morrill, Lawrence George 1929- AmMWSc 92
Morrill, Michael Dean 1955- WhoRel 92
Morrill, Park 1860-1898 BiInAmS
Morrill, Richard L 1934- ConAu 35NR
Morrill, Robert Burns 1937- WhoAmL 92
Morrill, Terence Clark 1940- AmMWSc 92
Morrill, Wendell Lee 1941- AmMWSc 92
Morrin, Peter Arthur Francis 1931- AmMWSc 92
Morrin, Virginia White 1913- WhoWest 92
Morris Who 92
Morris 1961-1978 FacFETw
Morris, Baron 1937- Who 92
Morris, A Burr 1924- WhoAmP 91
Morris, Aaron Paul 1956- WhoWest 92
Morris, Alan 1931- AmMWSc 92
Morris, Albert Jeff 1945- WhoMW 92
Morris, Albert William, Jr. 1946- WhoEnt 92
Morris, Alec 1926- Who 92
Morris, Alfred ScFEYrs
Morris, Alfred 1928- Who 92
Morris, Alfred Cosier 1941- Who 92
Morris, Alfred L. 1933-1989 WhoBlA 92N
Morris, Alvin Leonard 1927- AmMWSc 92
Morris, Anita IntMPA 92
Morris, Anthony 1938- TwCPaSc
Morris, Anthony Lee 1957- WhoAmP 91
Morris, Anthony Paul 1948- Who 92
Morris, Archie, III 1938- WhoBlA 92
Morris, Arnold Alec Who 92
Morris, Arthur Edward 1935- AmMWSc 92
Morris, Arthur Joseph 1881-1973 DcNCBi 4
Morris, Barry Livingston 1947- WhoFI 92
Morris, Benjamin Stephen d1990 IntWW 91N
Morris, Bernard Alexander 1937- WhoBlA 92
Morris, Betty Sue 1941- WhoAmP 91
Morris, Bill 1924- WhoAmP 91
Morris, Bill 1945- WhoAmP 91
Morris, Brooks T 1913- AmMWSc 92
Morris, Bruce L WhoAmP 91
Morris, Burlene 1935- WhoAmP 91
Morris, C. Robert 1928- WhoAmL 92
Morris, C Timothy 1950- WhoIns 92
Morris, Calvin S. 1941- WhoBlA 92
Morris, Carol DrAPF 91
Morris, Catherine Elizabeth 1949- AmMWSc 92
Morris, Cecelia 1916- IntAu&W 91
Morris, Cecil Arthur, Sr 1943- AmMWSc 92
Morris, Cedric 1889-1982 TwCPaSc [port]
Morris, Charel 1949- WhoEnt 92
Morris, Charles 1833-1922 BenetAL 91
Morris, Charles 1901- WrDr 92
Morris, Charles 1901-1979 ConAu 135
Morris, Charles C. 1943- WhoFI 92
Morris, Charles Dennison 1948- WhoRel 92
Morris, Charles Edward 1940- WhoAmL 92
Morris, Charles Edward 1941- AmMWSc 92
Morris, Charles Edward, Jr. 1931- WhoBlA 92
Morris, Charles Elliot 1929- AmMWSc 92
Morris, Charles Gould 1940- WhoMW 92
Morris, Charles L. d1991 NewYTBS 91
Morris, Charles R. WrDr 92
Morris, Charles Richard 1926- Who 92
Morris, Chris 1946- ConAu 133, SmATA 66
Morris, Christopher Who 92
Morris, Christopher Hugh 1938- IntAu&W 91, WrDr 92
Morris, Christopher Vernard 1966- WhoBlA 92
Morris, Claude C 1958- AmMWSc 92
Morris, Cletus Eugene 1935- AmMWSc 92
Morris, Clifton 1937- WhoBlA 92
Morris, Clyde 1963- WhoEnt 92
Morris, Colin IntAu&W 91
Morris, Colin 1929- Who 92
Morris, Dana Earl 1955- WhoAmL 92
Morris, Daniel Henry ScFEYrs
Morris, Daniel Joseph 1951- AmMWSc 92
Morris, Daniel Luzon 1907- AmMWSc 92
Morris, Daniel Wayne 1950- WhoMW 92
Morris, David Who 92
Morris, David 1933- AmMWSc 92
Morris, David Albert 1936- AmMWSc 92
Morris, David Alexander Nathaniel 1944- AmMWSc 92
Morris, David Clinton 1941- WhoMW 92
Morris, David Elwyn 1920- Who 92
Morris, David Griffiths 1940- Who 92
Morris, David Hugh 1941- WhoFI 92, WhoMW 92
Morris, David John 1945- WhoWest 92
Morris, David Julian 1939- AmMWSc 92
Morris, David Mark 1949- WhoFI 92
Morris, David Richard 1930- Who 92
Morris, David Richard 1934- Who 92
Morris, David Robert 1939- AmMWSc 92
Morris, David Rowland 1930- AmMWSc 92
Morris, David William 1937- Who 92
Morris, Denis Edward 1907- Who 92
Morris, Derek 1930- AmMWSc 92
Morris, Derek James 1945- Who 92
Morris, Desmond 1928- TwCPaSc, WrDr 92
Morris, Desmond John 1928- IntAu&W 91, IntWW 91, Who 92
Morris, Desmond Victor 1926- Who 92
Morris, DeWitt Talmage 1962- WhoRel 92
Morris, Dolores N. 1948- WhoBlA 92
Morris, Dolores Orinskia WhoBlA 92
Morris, Donald 1945- WhoFI 92
Morris, Donald Charles 1951- WhoWest 92
Morris, Donald E. WhoMW 92
Morris, Donald Eugene 1940- AmMWSc 92
Morris, Donald Wayne 1941- WhoAmP 91
Morris, Earle E, Jr 1928- WhoAmP 91
Morris, Edmund 1940- WrDr 92
Morris, Edward Allan 1910- Who 92
Morris, Edward C 1916- AmMWSc 92
Morris, Edward James 1915- Who 92
Morris, Edward James, Jr. 1936- WhoFI 92
Morris, Edward Knox, Jr. 1948- WhoMW 92
Morris, Edward Lyman 1870-1913 BiInAmS
Morris, Edward William, Jr. 1943- WhoAmL 92
Morris, Edwin Bateman, III 1939- WhoFI 92
Morris, Effie Lee WhoBlA 92
Morris, Elias C. 1855-1922 RelLAm 91
Morris, Elise L. 1916- WhoBlA 92
Morris, Elizabeth J. DrAPF 91
Morris, Elizabeth Treat 1936- WhoWest 92
Morris, Ella Lucille 1923- WhoBlA 92
Morris, Elliot Cobia 1926- AmMWSc 92
Morris, Ellwood 1813?-1872 BiInAmS
Morris, Ellwood 1814?-1872 DcNCBi 4
Morris, Eric 1940- IntAu&W 91, WrDr 92
Morris, Ernest B. d1991 NewYTBS 91
Morris, Ernest Roland 1942- WhoBlA 92
Morris, Eugene 1939- WhoBlA 92
Morris, Eugene Ray 1930- AmMWSc 92
Morris, Everett Franklin 1924- AmMWSc 92
Morris, Frank Charles, Jr. 1948- WhoAmL 92
Morris, Frank Eugene 1923- WhoFI 92
Morris, Frank Lorenzo, Sr. 1939- WhoBlA 92
Morris, Fred 1934- WhoRel 92
Morris, Fred W 1922- AmMWSc 92
Morris, G. Ronald 1936- WhoFI 92
Morris, Gareth Who 92
Morris, Gareth 1920- Who 92
Morris, Garrett 1937- WhoBlA 92
Morris, Gary Alan 1943- WhoFI 92
Morris, Gene Franklin 1934- AmMWSc 92
Morris, Gene Ray 1927- AmMWSc 92
Morris, Geoffrey F. 1962- WhoEnt 92
Morris, George Cooper, Jr 1924- AmMWSc 92
Morris, George Michael 1952- AmMWSc 92
Morris, George N 1930- WhoIns 92
Morris, George Pope 1802-1864 BenetAL 91
Morris, George V 1930- AmMWSc 92
Morris, George Walter 1935- WhoMW 92
Morris, George William 1921- AmMWSc 92
Morris, Gerald Brooks 1933- AmMWSc 92
Morris, Gerald Patrick 1939- AmMWSc 92
Morris, Gerard 1955- TwCPaSc
Morris, Gertrude Elaine 1924- WhoBlA 92
Morris, Gordon James 1942- WhoFI 92
Morris, Gouverneur 1752-1816 BenetAL 91, BlkwEAR [port], RComAH
Morris, Gouverneur 1876-1953 ScFEYrs
Morris, Grace Kirschbaum 1933- WhoMW 92
Morris, Greg 1933- WhoBlA 92
Morris, Greg Arthur 1953- WhoAmL 92
Morris, H Ramsey, Jr 1940- WhoAmP 91
Morris, Hal Tryon 1920- AmMWSc 92
Morris, Halcyon Ellen McNeil 1927- AmMWSc 92

Morris, Harold Hollingsworth, Jr 1917- AmMWSc 92
Morris, Harold Robert 1943- WhoMW 92
Morris, Harry DrAPF 91
Morris, Harry 1924- IntAu&W 91, WrDr 92
Morris, Harvey 1946- ConAu 134
Morris, Henry Arthur, Jr. 1923- WhoWest 92
Morris, Henry Madison, III 1942- WhoFI 92
Morris, Henry Madison, Jr 1918- AmMWSc 92, WhoRel 92
Morris, Herbert 1928- WhoAmL 92
Morris, Herbert Allen 1919- AmMWSc 92
Morris, Herbert Comstock 1917- AmMWSc 92
Morris, Herman, Jr. 1951- WhoBlA 92
Morris, Horace W. 1928- WhoBlA 92
Morris, Horton Harold 1922- AmMWSc 92
Morris, Howard 1919- IntMPA 92
Morris, Howard Arthur 1919- AmMWSc 92
Morris, Howard Redfern 1946- Who 92
Morris, Hubert Andrew 1946- WhoMW 92
Morris, Hughlett Lewis 1931- AmMWSc 92
Morris, Hunter Mason 1933- WhoRel 92
Morris, Ivor Gray 1911- Who 92
Morris, J William 1918- AmMWSc 92
Morris, James IntWW 91, Who 92, WrDr 92
Morris, James 1936- Who 92
Morris, James Albert 1942- AmMWSc 92
Morris, James Allen 1929- AmMWSc 92
Morris, James Baker 1953- WhoMW 92
Morris, James C. DrAPF 91
Morris, James Daniel 1957- WhoMW 92
Morris, James Edward 1937- WhoFI 92
Morris, James F 1922- AmMWSc 92
Morris, James G 1928- AmMWSc 92
Morris, James Grant 1930- AmMWSc 92, WhoWest 92
Morris, James Joseph, Jr 1933- AmMWSc 92
Morris, James Malachy 1952- WhoAmL 92, WhoFI 92
Morris, James Paxton 1935- WhoAmP 91
Morris, James Peter 1926- Who 92
Morris, James Richard 1925- Who 92
Morris, James Russell 1941- AmMWSc 92
Morris, James Russell 1944- WhoFI 92
Morris, James Shepherd 1931- Who 92
Morris, James T 1950- AmMWSc 92
Morris, James Thomas 1960- WhoIns 92
Morris, Jamie Walter 1965- WhoBlA 92
Morris, Jan 1926- IntAu&W 91, IntWW 91, Who 92, WrDr 92
Morris, Jan Charles 1950- WhoAmL 92
Morris, Jane Elizabeth 1940- WhoMW 92
Morris, Janet 1946- ConAu 35NR, SmATA 66
Morris, Janet E. 1946- TwCSFW 91, WrDr 92
Morris, Janet Ellen 1946- IntAu&W 91
Morris, Jean 1924- WrDr 92
Morris, Jeffrey Lee 1959- WhoWest 92
Morris, Jeffrey Thomas 1955- WhoAmL 92
Morris, Jerald Vinson 1931- WhoRel 92
Morris, Jeremy Noah 1910- Who 92
Morris, Jerome 1944- WhoEnt 92
Morris, Jerry Lee, Jr 1952- AmMWSc 92
Morris, Jimmie Wayne 1944- WhoWest 92
Morris, Joan Clair 1943- WhoEnt 92
Morris, Joe WhoEnt 92
Morris, Joe 1960- WhoBlA 92
Morris, Joel M. 1944- WhoBlA 92
Morris, John IntMPA 92, WrDr 92
Morris, John 1926- WhoEnt 92
Morris, John 1931- IntWW 91, Who 92
Morris, John Barton 1910- WhoFI 92
Morris, John Burnett 1930- WhoRel 92
Morris, John Carl 1948- WhoMW 92
Morris, John E. 1916- WhoAmL 92
Morris, John Edward 1936- AmMWSc 92
Morris, John Emory 1937- AmMWSc 92
Morris, John Evan A. Who 92
Morris, John F 1928- AmMWSc 92
Morris, John Francis 1956- WhoAmL 92
Morris, John Gareth 1932- Who 92
Morris, John Gottlieb 1803-1895 BiInAmS
Morris, John Lee 1924- WhoEnt 92
Morris, John Leonard 1929- AmMWSc 92
Morris, John Lewis 1842-1905 BiInAmS
Morris, John McLean 1914- AmMWSc 92
Morris, John N. DrAPF 91
Morris, John Nickerson 1942- WhoWest 92
Morris, John Rayl 1939- WhoFI 92
Morris, John Richard 1958- WhoFI 92
Morris, John Robert 1955- WhoAmL 92
Morris, John S. DrAPF 91
Morris, John Steven 1947- WhoFI 92
Morris, John Theodore 1929- WhoWest 92
Morris, John William, Jr 1943- AmMWSc 92
Morris, John Woodland 1921- AmMWSc 92
Morris, Johnny 1935- WhoEnt 92
Morris, Jorden Walter 1967- WhoEnt 92
Morris, Joseph Allan 1951- WhoAmL 92, WhoAmP 91, WhoMW 92
Morris, Joseph Anthony 1918- AmMWSc 92, WhoFI 92
Morris, Joseph Anthony 1953- WhoRel 92
Morris, Joseph Burton 1925- AmMWSc 92
Morris, Joseph Richard 1935- AmMWSc 92
Morris, Julian IntAu&W 91X, WrDr 92
Morris, Justin Roy 1937- AmMWSc 92
Morris, Katharine WrDr 92
Morris, Kathleen Elizabeth 1949- WhoEnt 92
Morris, Keith Elliot Hedley 1934- Who 92
Morris, Kelso B. WhoBlA 92
Morris, Kenneth Donald 1946- WhoAmL 92
Morris, Kenton 1947- WhoEnt 92
Morris, Kristine Anne 1954- WhoWest 92
Morris, Kyra H. 1957- WhoFI 92
Morris, L. Daniel, Jr. 1939- WhoAmL 92
Morris, Larry Allen 1944- WhoMW 92
Morris, Larry Arthur 1937- AmMWSc 92
Morris, Larry Brungard 1939- WhoAmP 91
Morris, Lawrence Robert 1942- AmMWSc 92
Morris, Lawretta Goudy 1937- WhoFI 92
Morris, LeAnne Allen 1949- WhoWest 92
Morris, Leibert Wayne 1950- WhoBlA 92
Morris, Leigh Edward 1934- WhoMW 92
Morris, Leo Raymond 1922- AmMWSc 92
Morris, Leon Lamb 1914- WrDr 92
Morris, Leonard Leslie 1914- AmMWSc 92
Morris, Lester Joseph 1915- WhoFI 92
Morris, Lewis R. 1926- WhoBlA 92
Morris, Lucien Ellis 1914- AmMWSc 92
Morris, Major 1921- WhoBlA 92
Morris, Mali 1945- TwCPaSc
Morris, Manford D 1926- AmMWSc 92
Morris, Margaret Elizabeth 1962- WhoMW 92
Morris, Margaret Lindsay 1950- WhoBlA 92
Morris, Margaretta Hare 1797-1867 BiInAmS
Morris, Maria Antonia 1940- WhoWest 92
Morris, Marilyn Emily AmMWSc 92
Morris, Marion Clyde 1932- AmMWSc 92
Morris, Mark WhoEnt 92
Morris, Mark 1956- News 91 [port]
Morris, Mark Ronald 1941- WhoFI 92
Morris, Mark Root 1947- AmMWSc 92
Morris, Mark William 1956- IntWW 91
Morris, Marlene C. 1933- WhoBlA 92
Morris, Marlene Cook 1933- AmMWSc 92
Morris, Mary DrAPF 91
Morris, Mary Lou A. 1941- WhoRel 92
Morris, Mary Rosalind 1920- AmMWSc 92
Morris, Max Who 92
Morris, Mellasenah Y. 1947- WhoBlA 92
Morris, Melvin 1937- WhoBlA 92
Morris, Melvin L 1929- AmMWSc 92
Morris, Melvin Lewis 1914- AmMWSc 92
Morris, Melvin Solomon AmMWSc 92
Morris, Mervyn 1937- ConPo 91, WrDr 92
Morris, Michael 1940- WrDr 92
Morris, Michael D 1939- AmMWSc 92
Morris, Michael D 1941- WhoAmP 91
Morris, Michael Edward 1962- WhoEnt 92
Morris, Michael Roy 1953- WhoEnt 92
Morris, Michael Sachs 1924- Who 92
Morris, Michael Thomas 1949- WhoRel 92
Morris, Michael Wolfgang Laurence 1936- Who 92
Morris, Milton Curtis 1936- WhoBlA 92N
Morris, N Ronald 1933- AmMWSc 92
Morris, Nancy Mitchell 1940- AmMWSc 92
Morris, Naomi Elizabeth 1921-1986 DcNCBi 4
Morris, Nicholas Benjamin 1965- WhoEnt 92
Morris, Nigel Godfrey 1908- Who 92
Morris, Norma Frances 1935- Who 92
Morris, Norman Frederick 1920- Who 92
Morris, Norval 1923- WhoAmL 92
Morris, Oran Wilkinson 1798-1877 BiInAmS
Morris, Oswald 1915- IntMPA 92
Morris, Owen G 1927- AmMWSc 92
Morris, Owen Humphrey 1921- Who 92
Morris, Patrick Nicholas 1939- WhoRel 92
Morris, Patrick Wayne 1955- WhoRel 92
Morris, Peter Who 92
Morris, Peter Alan 1945- AmMWSc 92
Morris, Peter Christopher West 1937- Who 92
Morris, Peter Craig 1937- AmMWSc 92
Morris, Peter Frederick 1932- IntWW 91
Morris, Peter John 1934- IntWW 91, Who 92
Morris, Peter T. Who 92
Morris, Ralph ScFEYrs
Morris, Ralph Dennis 1940- AmMWSc 92
Morris, Ralph William 1928- AmMWSc 92
Morris, Randal Edward 1945- AmMWSc 92
Morris, Randal Edward 1952- WhoWest 92
Morris, Richard Who 92
Morris, Richard 1924- IntMPA 92
Morris, Richard 1939- WrDr 92
Morris, Richard 1944- WhoEnt 92
Morris, Richard Herbert 1928- AmMWSc 92
Morris, Richard Joel 1945- WhoEnt 92
Morris, Richard Louis 1940- WhoMW 92
Morris, Richard W. DrAPF 91
Morris, Richard Ward 1939- WhoWest 92
Morris, Rick Gene 1959- WhoEnt 92
Morris, Robert AmMWSc 92
Morris, Robert 1734-1806 BlkwEAR [port], RComAH
Morris, Robert 1910- AmMWSc 92
Morris, Robert 1913- Who 92
Morris, Robert 1923- WhoIns 92
Morris, Robert Alan 1958- AmMWSc 92
Morris, Robert C. 1942- ConAu 135
Morris, Robert Carter 1943- AmMWSc 92
Morris, Robert Clarence 1928- AmMWSc 92
Morris, Robert Craig 1944- AmMWSc 92
Morris, Robert Gemmill 1929- AmMWSc 92
Morris, Robert James, Jr. 1953- WhoAmL 92
Morris, Robert John 1950- WhoFI 92
Morris, Robert Julian, Jr. 1932- WhoMW 92
Morris, Robert K 1933- IntAu&W 91, WrDr 92
Morris, Robert Matthew 1937- Who 92
Morris, Robert Renly 1938- WhoRel 92
Morris, Robert Steven 1951- WhoWest 92
Morris, Robert V., Sr. 1958- WhoBlA 92
Morris, Robert Wharton 1920- AmMWSc 92
Morris, Robert William 1941- AmMWSc 92
Morris, Roger Oliver 1932- Who 92
Morris, Ronald James Arthur 1915- Who 92
Morris, Ronald Patrick 1955- WhoMW 92
Morris, Rosemary Shull 1929- AmMWSc 92
Morris, Ross Eugene 1922- WhoAmL 92
Morris, Roy Owen 1934- AmMWSc 92
Morris, Russell Norman, Jr 1951- WhoAmP 91
Morris, Samuel Cary, III 1942- AmMWSc 92
Morris, Samuel Solomon 1916-1989 WhoBlA 92N
Morris, Samuel W 1918- WhoAmP 91
Morris, Sara IntAu&W 91X, WrDr 92
Morris, Sharon Kay 1946- WhoAmL 92
Morris, Shirley Lou 1930- WhoAmP 91
Morris, Sidney Machen, Jr 1946- AmMWSc 92
Morris, Simon C. Who 92
Morris, Stanley E 1942- WhoAmP 91
Morris, Stanley E., Jr. 1944- WhoBlA 92
Morris, Stanley P 1937- AmMWSc 92
Morris, Stephen 1935- IntAu&W 91, WrDr 92
Morris, Stephen James Michael 1934- WhoAmL 92
Morris, Tammy Mynetta 1959- WhoWest 92
Morris, Terence Patrick 1931- Who 92
Morris, Terry 1914- IntAu&W 91
Morris, Thomas 1914- Who 92
Morris, Thomas Dallam 1913- WhoAmP 91
Morris, Thomas Jack 1947- AmMWSc 92
Morris, Thomas Wendell 1930- AmMWSc 92
Morris, Thomas Wilde 1943- AmMWSc 92
Morris, Thomas William 1944- WhoEnt 92, WhoMW 92
Morris, Timothy Denis 1935- Who 92
Morris, Tom Howard 1942- WhoMW 92
Morris, Trefor Alfred 1934- Who 92
Morris, Trevor Raymond 1930- Who 92
Morris, Valerie Bonita 1947- WhoEnt 92
Morris, Vance Blom, II 1949- WhoAmP 91
Morris, W Patrick 1940- WhoAmP 91
Morris, Walter Frederick 1914- Who 92
Morris, Wayne Lee 1954- WhoBlA 92
Morris, William WhoAmP 91
Morris, William 1834-1896 CnDBLB 4 [port], DcTwDes, RfGEnL 91, ScFEYrs, TwCSFW 91
Morris, William 1938- Who 92
Morris, William 1941- WhoAmL 92
Morris, William Collins 1936- WhoRel 92
Morris, William David 1936- Who 92
Morris, William Edward 1913- IntAu&W 91
Morris, William Frederick 1943- WhoEnt 92
Morris, William Guy 1940- AmMWSc 92
Morris, William H, Jr 1929- WhoAmP 91
Morris, William Henry 1931- WhoMW 92
Morris, William Ian Clinch 1907- Who 92
Morris, William James 1925- Who 92
Morris, William Joseph 1923- AmMWSc 92
Morris, William L. DrAPF 91
Morris, William Lewis 1931- AmMWSc 92
Morris, William Wesley 1937- WhoBlA 92
Morris, William Woodson 1956- WhoEnt 92
Morris, Willie 1934- IntAu&W 91, IntWW 91, WrDr 92
Morris, Wright DrAPF 91
Morris, Wright 1910- BenetAL 91, ConNov 91, TwCWW 91, WrDr 92
Morris, Wyn 1929- Who 92
Morris-Archinal, Gretchen Suzanne 1963- WhoMW 92
Morris-Hale, Walter 1933- WhoBlA 92
Morris Hooke, Anne 1939- AmMWSc 92
Morris-Jones, Ifor Henry 1922- Who 92
Morris-Jones, Wyndraeth Humphreys 1918- Who 92, WrDr 92
Morris-Kramer, Anthony 1950- WhoEnt 92
Morris of Castle Morris, Baron 1930- Who 92
Morris of Kenwood, Baron 1928- Who 92
Morris-Suzuki, Tessa Irene Jessica 1951- IntAu&W 91
Morris Williams, Christine Margaret Who 92
Morrisett, Joel David 1942- AmMWSc 92
Morrisey, Jimmy 1922- WhoBlA 92
Morrisey, Michael A. 1952- WhoFI 92
Morrisey, Sean 1943- TwCPaSc
Morrish, Allan Henry 1924- AmMWSc 92
Morrish, John Edwin 1915- Who 92
Morrison Who 92
Morrison, Baron 1914- Who 92
Morrison, Adrian Russel 1935- AmMWSc 92
Morrison, Alexander 1717-1805 DcNCBi 4
Morrison, Alexander John Henderson 1927- Who 92
Morrison, Alice Louise 1921- WhoAmP 91
Morrison, Andrew 1941- DcTwDes
Morrison, Angus Hugh 1935- WhoAmP 91
Morrison, Anthony James 1936- IntAu&W 91
Morrison, Arthur 1863-1945 RfGEnL 91, ScFEYrs
Morrison, Ashton Byrom 1922- AmMWSc 92
Morrison, Aubrey Rohan 1943- WhoMW 92
Morrison, Barton Douglas 1965- WhoRel 92
Morrison, Benjamin Franklin, III 1943- WhoAmP 91
Morrison, Bill 1935- ConAu 135, SmATA 66
Morrison, Bill 1940- IntAu&W 91, WrDr 92
Morrison, Blake Who 92
Morrison, Blake 1950- ConPo 91, IntAu&W 91, WrDr 92
Morrison, Boone 1941- WhoWest 92
Morrison, Bruce A 1944- WhoAmP 91
Morrison, Cameron 1869-1953 DcNCBi 4
Morrison, Carleton Henry 1942- WhoWest 92
Morrison, Charles 1932- Who 92
Morrison, Charles Clayton 1874-1966 AmPeW, RelLAm 91
Morrison, Charles Edward 1943- WhoBlA 92
Morrison, Charles Freeman, Jr 1929- AmMWSc 92
Morrison, Clarence C 1932- AmMWSc 92
Morrison, Clarence Christopher 1939- WhoBlA 92
Morrison, Connie 1935- WhoAmP 91
Morrison, Curtis Angus 1945- WhoBlA 92
Morrison, David Campbell 1941- AmMWSc 92
Morrison, David Lee 1933- AmMWSc 92
Morrison, De Lesseps S, Jr 1944- WhoAmP 91
Morrison, Denise Sue 1958- WhoMW 92
Morrison, Dennis John 1942- Who 92
Morrison, Donald Alexander Campbell 1916- Who 92
Morrison, Donald Allen 1936- AmMWSc 92

Morrison, Donald Franklin 1931- AmMWSc 92
Morrison, Donald Ross 1922- AmMWSc 92
Morrison, Donald Thomas 1928- WhoAmL 92
Morrison, Dorothy Jean Allison 1933- IntAu&W 91
Morrison, Douglas Wildes 1947- AmMWSc 92
Morrison, Dudley Butler 1937- WhoFI 92
Morrison, Eston Odell 1932- AmMWSc 92
Morrison, Frank Albert, Jr 1943- AmMWSc 92
Morrison, Frank Brenner, Jr 1937- WhoAmP 91
Morrison, Fred LaMont 1939- WhoAmL 92
Morrison, Fred Wilson 1890-1985 DcNCBi 4
Morrison, Garfield E., Jr. 1939- WhoBlA 92
Morrison, Gary William WhoMW 92
Morrison, George Harold 1921- AmMWSc 92
Morrison, George Leroy 1928- WhoEnt 92
Morrison, George Thornton 1924- WhoWest 92
Morrison, Glenn C 1933- AmMWSc 92
Morrison, Glenn Leslie 1929- WhoRel 92
Morrison, Gordon Mackay, Jr. 1930- WhoFI 92
Morrison, Gwendolyn Christine Caldwell 1949- WhoBlA 92
Morrison, Harry 1937- AmMWSc 92
Morrison, Harry L. 1932- WhoBlA 92
Morrison, Harry Lee 1932- AmMWSc 92
Morrison, Harvey Lee, Jr. 1947- WhoAmL 92
Morrison, Helen Dubino 1926- WhoAmP 91
Morrison, Henry Clay 1857-1942 RelLAm 91
Morrison, Henry T., Jr. 1939- IntMPA 92
Morrison, Herbert 1906-1989 FacFETw
Morrison, Herbert Knowles 1854-1885 BilnAmS
Morrison, Herbert Stanley 1888-1965 FacFETw
Morrison, Howard 1935- Who 92
Morrison, Howard B. 1960- WhoRel 92
Morrison, Howard Clark 1958- WhoRel 92
Morrison, Hugh A 1935- WhoAmP 91
Morrison, Hugh MacGregor 1936- AmMWSc 92
Morrison, Huntly Frank 1938- AmMWSc 92
Morrison, Ian Gordon 1914- Who 92
Morrison, Ian Kenneth 1939- AmMWSc 92
Morrison, James 1932- TwCPaSc
Morrison, James Alexander 1918- AmMWSc 92
Morrison, James Barbour 1943- AmMWSc 92
Morrison, James Daniel 1936- AmMWSc 92
Morrison, James Douglas 1924- IntWW 91
Morrison, James Ian 1930- Who 92
Morrison, James Ian 1952- WhoWest 92
Morrison, James S. 1929- WhoFI 92
Morrison, James W., Jr. 1936- WhoBlA 92
Morrison, James Wayne 1957- WhoAmL 92
Morrison, Jeanette Helen 1927- ConAu 134, WhoEnt 92
Morrison, Joan 1922- ConAu 133, SmATA 65 [port]
Morrison, John Agnew 1932- AmMWSc 92
Morrison, John Alan 1955- WhoRel 92
Morrison, John Albert 1924- AmMWSc 92
Morrison, John Allan 1927- AmMWSc 92
Morrison, John Anthony 1938- Who 92
Morrison, John B 1938- AmMWSc 92
Morrison, John Coulter 1943- AmMWSc 92
Morrison, John Dittgen 1921- WhoAmL 92
Morrison, John Eddy, Jr 1939- AmMWSc 92
Morrison, John Emerson, III 1941- WhoRel 92
Morrison, John Horton 1933- WhoAmL 92
Morrison, John Lamb Murray 1906- Who 92
Morrison, John Sinclair 1913- Who 92
Morrison, John Stuart 1947- AmMWSc 92
Morrison, Johnny Edward 1952- WhoBlA 92
Morrison, Joseph 1848- BilnAmS
Morrison, Joseph Young 1951- WhoFI 92
Morrison, Joy South WhoEnt 92
Morrison, Juan LaRue, Sr. 1943- WhoBlA 92
Morrison, Julia DrAPF 91
Morrison, K. C. 1946- WhoBlA 92
Morrison, K Jaydene 1933- WhoAmP 91
Morrison, Keith Anthony 1942- WhoBlA 92
Morrison, Kenneth Jess 1921- AmMWSc 92
Morrison, Kermit Charles, Jr. 1947- WhoAmL 92
Morrison, Kristin Diane 1934- IntAu&W 91, WrDr 92
Morrison, Larry Ellis 1955- WhoRel 92
Morrison, Lester M. 1907-1991 ConAu 134
Morrison, Lillian DrAPF 91
Morrison, Linda Smith 1950- WhoAmP 91
Morrison, Lloyd Richard 1959- WhoRel 92
Morrison, Lorena Ann 1943- WhoRel 92
Morrison, Madison DrAPF 91
Morrison, Malcolm Cameron 1942- AmMWSc 92
Morrison, Marcy Gail 1958- WhoEnt 92
Morrison, Margaret 1924- Who 92
Morrison, Martin 1921- AmMWSc 92
Morrison, Mary Alice AmMWSc 92
Morrison, Mary Anne 1937- Who 92
Morrison, Mary Jane 1944- WhoAmL 92
Morrison, Michael Frank 1951- WhoEnt 92
Morrison, Michael Gordon 1937- WhoMW 92
Morrison, Michael Ian Donald 1929- WhoIns 92
Morrison, Michelle Williams 1947- WhoWest 92
Morrison, Milton Edward 1939- AmMWSc 92
Morrison, Murdo Donald 1919- WhoWest 92
Morrison, Nancy Dunlap 1946- AmMWSc 92
Morrison, Nathan 1912- AmMWSc 92
Morrison, Nigel Murray Paton 1948- Who 92
Morrison, Nona Lou 1930- WhoAmP 91
Morrison, Perry 1959- ConAu 134
Morrison, Peter 1944- Who 92
Morrison, Peter Reed 1919- AmMWSc 92
Morrison, Philip 1915- AmMWSc 92
Morrison, Philip Blake 1950- Who 92
Morrison, R.H. 1915- ConAu 135
Morrison, Ralph M 1932- AmMWSc 92
Morrison, Reginald Joseph Gordon 1909- Who 92
Morrison, Richard TwCSFW 91
Morrison, Richard Allan 1938- WhoFI 92
Morrison, Richard Charles 1938- AmMWSc 92
Morrison, Richard David 1910- WhoBlA 92
Morrison, Richard Neely 1947- WhoRel 92
Morrison, Rick 1957- WhoBlA 92
Morrison, Rickman James 1946- WhoMW 92
Morrison, Robert B., Jr. 1954- WhoBlA 92
Morrison, Robert Dean 1915- AmMWSc 92
Morrison, Robert Edwin 1942- WhoEnt 92
Morrison, Robert Hall 1798-1889 DcNCBi 4
Morrison, Robert Haywood 1927- WrDr 92
Morrison, Robert Scheck 1942- WhoFI 92
Morrison, Robert W, Jr 1938- AmMWSc 92
Morrison, Robert William 1941- WhoIns 92
Morrison, Roberta WrDr 92
Morrison, Roger Barron 1914- AmMWSc 92, WhoWest 92
Morrison, Rollin John 1937- AmMWSc 92
Morrison, Ronald E. 1949- WhoBlA 92
Morrison, Samuel F. 1936- WhoBlA 92
Morrison, Sara Antoinette Sibell Frances 1934- Who 92
Morrison, Shaun Francis AmMWSc 92
Morrison, Shelley 1936- WhoEnt 92, WhoHisp 92
Morrison, Sherie Leaver 1942- AmMWSc 92
Morrison, Shirley Linden 1935- WhoWest 92
Morrison, Sid 1933- AlmAP 92 [port], WhoAmP 91, WhoWest 92
Morrison, Sidonie A 1947- AmMWSc 92
Morrison, Spencer Horton 1919- AmMWSc 92
Morrison, Stanley Roy 1926- AmMWSc 92
Morrison, Stephen Roger 1947- Who 92
Morrison, Steven Eugene 1947- WhoRel 92
Morrison, Steven Howard 1945- WhoMW 92
Morrison, Stuart Love 1922- Who 92
Morrison, Susan M. WhoRel 92
Morrison, Theodore 1901- IntAu&W 91
Morrison, Theodore V, Jr 1935- WhoAmP 91
Morrison, Thomas Golden 1918- AmMWSc 92
Morrison, Thomas L WhoAmP 91
Morrison, Thomas Truxton WhoMW 92
Morrison, Timothy WhoEnt 92
Morrison, Timothy Arthur 1949- WhoRel 92
Morrison, Toni DrAPF 91
Morrison, Toni 1931- AfrAmW, BenetAL 91, BlkLC [port], ConBlB 2 [port], ConNov 91, FacFETw, HanAmWH, IntWW 91, ModAWWr, NotBlAW 92 [port], WhoBlA 92, WrDr 92
Morrison, Tony 1936- WrDr 92
Morrison, Travis 1948- WhoAmP 91
Morrison, Trudi Michelle 1950- WhoBlA 92
Morrison, Van 1945- NewAmDM, WhoEnt 92
Morrison, Walton Stephen 1907- WhoAmL 92, WhoFI 92
Morrison, Wanda Stalcup 1934- WhoAmP 91
Morrison, Wilbur H. 1915- WrDr 92
Morrison, Wilbur Howard 1915- IntAu&W 91
Morrison, William Alfred 1948- AmMWSc 92
Morrison, William Charles Carnegie 1938- Who 92
Morrison, William D 1927- AmMWSc 92
Morrison, William Edward 1951- WhoWest 92
Morrison, William Fosdick 1935- WhoWest 92
Morrison, William Garth 1943- Who 92
Morrison, William Joseph 1942- AmMWSc 92
Morrison, William Lawrence 1928- IntWW 91
Morrison-Bell, William 1956- Who 92
Morrison-Low, James Who 92
Morrison-Scott, Terence Charles Stuart 1908- IntWW 91, Who 92
Morriss, Cynthia Matus 1953- WhoHisp 92
Morriss, Frank 1923- IntAu&W 91, WrDr 92
Morriss, Frank Howard, Jr 1940- AmMWSc 92
Morriss, J-H ConAu 34NR
Morrissette, Maurice Corlette 1921- AmMWSc 92
Morrissette, Roland A 1916- WhoAmP 91
Morrissette, Rosemary D. WhoFI 92
Morrissey, Bruce William 1942- AmMWSc 92
Morrissey, David Joseph 1953- AmMWSc 92
Morrissey, Francis Daniel 1930- WhoAmL 92
Morrissey, George Michael 1941- WhoAmL 92
Morrissey, J Edward 1932- AmMWSc 92
Morrissey, J L TwCSFW 91
Morrissey, James Henry 1953- AmMWSc 92
Morrissey, John Carroll 1914- WhoWest 92
Morrissey, John F 1924- AmMWSc 92
Morrissey, Kymberlee Anne 1957- WhoWest 92
Morrissey, Mary Jane 1951- WhoAmP 91
Morrissey, Michael W 1954- WhoAmP 91
Morrissey, Paul 1939- IntMPA 92
Morrissey, Peter A. 1953- WhoFI 92
Morrissey, Philip John AmMWSc 92
Morrissey, Spencer W 1951- WhoAmP 91
Morrissey, Thomas Jerome WhoFI 92
Morrissey, William Thomas 1950- WhoWest 92
Morrissy, Mary Jule 1952- WhoMW 92
Morritt, Andrew 1938- Who 92
Morritt, Hope 1930- IntAu&W 91, WrDr 92
Morrocco, Alberto 1917- TwCPaSc, Who 92
Morrocco, Alfred Frederick, Jr 1947- WhoAmP 91
Morrogh, Henton 1917- Who 92
Morrone, Edward P 1950- WhoAmP 91
Morrone, Samuel R. WhoFI 92
Morrone, Terry 1936- AmMWSc 92
Morroni, William 1948- WhoEnt 92
Morrow, Andrew Glenn 1922- AmMWSc 92
Morrow, Barry Albert 1939- AmMWSc 92
Morrow, Barry Nelson 1948- WhoEnt 92
Morrow, Bradford DrAPF 91
Morrow, Bruce 1937- WhoEnt 92
Morrow, Charles G., III 1956- WhoBlA 92
Morrow, Charles Gay, III 1956- WhoAmP 91
Morrow, Charles T 1941- AmMWSc 92
Morrow, Charles Tabor 1917- AmMWSc 92
Morrow, Charlie DrAPF 91
Morrow, Charlie 1942- NewAmDM
Morrow, Christopher Brian 1955- WhoFI 92
Morrow, Danny Ray 1957- WhoRel 92
Morrow, David Austin 1935- AmMWSc 92
Morrow, Dean Huston 1931- AmMWSc 92
Morrow, Debbie Marie 1962- WhoEnt 92
Morrow, Dennis Robert 1951- WhoMW 92
Morrow, Dion Griffith 1932- WhoBlA 92
Morrow, Duane Francis 1933- AmMWSc 92
Morrow, Dwight W. 1873-1931 BenetAL 91
Morrow, Dwight Whitney 1873-1931 AmPeW, AmPolLe
Morrow, E. Frederic 1909- WhoBlA 92
Morrow, Elizabeth 1873-1955 BenetAL 91
Morrow, Elizabeth 1947- WhoMW 92
Morrow, Floyd Lee 1933- WhoAmP 91
Morrow, Fred C 1926- WhoIns 92
Morrow, G E 1840?-1900 BilnAmS
Morrow, Grant, III 1933- AmMWSc 92
Morrow, Honore Willsie 1880-1940 BenetAL 91, TwCWW 91
Morrow, Hugh 1915-1991 NewYTBS 91
Morrow, Ian 1912- Who 92
Morrow, Ian Thomas 1912- IntWW 91
Morrow, J. Paul 1932- WhoAmL 92
Morrow, Jack I 1933- AmMWSc 92
Morrow, James 1947- TwCSFW 91
Morrow, James Allen, Jr 1941- AmMWSc 92
Morrow, James Franklin 1944- WhoAmL 92
Morrow, James Ward 1964- WhoAmL 92, WhoAmP 91
Morrow, Janet Ruth 1957- AmMWSc 92
Morrow, Jeff WhoEnt 92
Morrow, Jeff 1917- IntMPA 92
Morrow, Jesse WhoBlA 92
Morrow, JoDean 1929- AmMWSc 92
Morrow, John Charles, III 1924- AmMWSc 92
Morrow, John Ellsworth 1943- WhoAmL 92
Morrow, John Howard, Jr. 1944- WhoBlA 92
Morrow, John L WhoAmP 91
Morrow, John W, Jr 1922- WhoAmP 91
Morrow, John Watson 1931- IntWW 91
Morrow, Johnny M WhoAmP 91
Morrow, Jon S AmMWSc 92
Morrow, Kenneth John, Jr 1938- AmMWSc 92
Morrow, Kevin Paul 1963- WhoFI 92
Morrow, Larry Alan 1938- AmMWSc 92
Morrow, Laverne 1954- WhoBlA 92
Morrow, Leslie Ann 1965- WhoEnt 92
Morrow, Lowell Howard ScFEYrs
Morrow, Martin S. 1923- Who 92
Morrow, Nebraska 1927- WhoBlA 92
Morrow, Norman Louis 1942- AmMWSc 92
Morrow, Norman Robert 1937- AmMWSc 92
Morrow, Paul Edward 1922- AmMWSc 92
Morrow, Phillip Henry 1943- WhoBlA 92
Morrow, Prince Albert 1846-1913 BilnAmS
Morrow, Richard Alexander 1937- AmMWSc 92
Morrow, Richard Joseph 1928- AmMWSc 92
Morrow, Richard M 1926- AmMWSc 92
Morrow, Richard Martin 1926- WhoFI 92, WhoMW 92
Morrow, Richard Raymond 1939- WhoAmP 91
Morrow, Rob 1962- WhoEnt 92
Morrow, Roy Wayne 1942- AmMWSc 92
Morrow, Samuel P., Jr. 1928- WhoBlA 92
Morrow, Samuel Roy, III 1949- WhoFI 92
Morrow, Scott 1920- AmMWSc 92
Morrow, Scott Douglas 1954- WhoEnt 92
Morrow, Stephen Mark 1952- WhoAmL 92
Morrow, Susan Dagmar 1932- WhoWest 92
Morrow, Terry Oran 1947- AmMWSc 92
Morrow, Thomas F 1944- WhoIns 92
Morrow, Thomas John 1946- AmMWSc 92
Morrow, W C 1852-1923 ScFEYrs
Morrow, Walter E, Jr 1928- AmMWSc 92
Morrow, William Earl, Jr 1930- WhoAmP 91
Morrow, William John Woodroofe AmMWSc 92
Morrow, William Owen 1927- WhoFI 92
Morrow, William Scot 1931- AmMWSc 92
Morrow, Winston Vaughan 1924- WhoFI 92, WhoWest 92
Mors, Walter B. 1920- IntWW 91
Mors, William George 1920- WhoEnt 92
Morsberger, Emory WhoAmP 91
Morsberger, Louis Phillip 1929- WhoAmP 91

**Morsch,** Thomas Harvey 1931- WhoAmL 92
**Morse,** A. Reynolds 1914- WhoMW 92
**Morse,** Alan Richard, Jr. 1938- WhoFI 92
**Morse,** Andrew Richard 1946- WhoFI 92
**Morse,** Annie Ruth W. WhoBlA 92
**Morse,** Arthur D. d1971 LesBEnT 92
**Morse,** Bernard S 1934- AmMWSc 92
**Morse,** Bradford IntWW 91
**Morse,** Burt Jules 1926- AmMWSc 92
**Morse,** Carl DrAPF 91
**Morse,** Carmel Lei 1953- WhoEnt 92
**Morse,** Carol WrDr 92
**Morse,** Christopher Jeremy 1928- IntWW 91, Who 92
**Morse,** Daniel E 1941- AmMWSc 92
**Morse,** David A. d1990 IntWW 91N, Who 92N
**Morse,** David A. 1907-1990 CurBio 91N
**Morse,** David Abner 1907-1990 FacFETw
**Morse,** Dennis Ervin 1947- AmMWSc 92
**Morse,** Donald E. 1936- WrDr 92
**Morse,** Duane Dale 1950- WhoAmL 92
**Morse,** Edward A ScFEYrs
**Morse,** Edward Everett 1932- AmMWSc 92
**Morse,** Edward Lewis 1942- WhoFI 92
**Morse,** Eleanor R. 1912- WhoMW 92
**Morse,** Elisha Wilson 1866-1915 BiInAmS
**Morse,** Ernest Lee 1922- WhoAmP 91
**Morse,** Erskine Vance 1921- AmMWSc 92
**Morse,** Eva Mae 1938- WhoAmP 91
**Morse,** F. Bradford 1921- IntWW 91
**Morse,** Francis 1917- AmMWSc 92
**Morse,** Frank Bradford 1921- WhoAmP 91
**Morse,** Fred A 1937- AmMWSc 92
**Morse,** Frederick Addison 1937- WhoWest 92
**Morse,** Gerald Ira 1909- WhoAmP 91
**Morse,** Harmon Northrop 1848-1920 BiInAmS
**Morse,** Harold E. 1938- WhoEnt 92
**Morse,** Helvise Glessner 1925- AmMWSc 92
**Morse,** Herbert Carpenter, III 1943- AmMWSc 92
**Morse,** Herbert E. WhoFI 92
**Morse,** Ivan E, Jr 1925- AmMWSc 92
**Morse,** J G 1921- AmMWSc 92
**Morse,** J. Mitchell 1912- WrDr 92
**Morse,** Jack Craig 1936- WhoAmL 92
**Morse,** James L WhoAmP 91
**Morse,** James L. 1940- WhoAmL 92
**Morse,** James Lewis 1940- WhoAmP 91
**Morse,** Jane H 1929- AmMWSc 92
**Morse,** Jedidiah 1761-1826 BenetAL 91, BiInAmS, BlkwEAR
**Morse,** Jeremy IntWW 91, Who 92
**Morse,** JoAnn T 1919- WhoAmP 91
**Morse,** John Thomas 1935- AmMWSc 92
**Morse,** John Walker 1940- WhoWest 92
**Morse,** John Wilbur 1946- AmMWSc 92
**Morse,** Joseph Ervin 1940- WhoBlA 92
**Morse,** Joseph Grant 1939- AmMWSc 92
**Morse,** Joseph Grant 1953- AmMWSc 92
**Morse,** Karen W 1940- AmMWSc 92
**Morse,** L. A. 1945- WrDr 92
**Morse,** Leon William 1912- WhoFI 92, WhoMW 92
**Morse,** Lewis David 1924- AmMWSc 92
**Morse,** Lowell Wesley 1937- WhoWest 92
**Morse,** Luis C 1940- WhoAmP 91, WhoHisp 92
**Morse,** M Patricia 1938- AmMWSc 92
**Morse,** Marvin Henry 1929- WhoAmL 92
**Morse,** Maryanne H 1944- WhoAmP 91
**Morse,** Melvin Laurance 1921- AmMWSc 92
**Morse,** Michael David 1952- WhoWest 92
**Morse,** Mildred S. 1942- WhoBlA 92
**Morse,** N L 1917- AmMWSc 92
**Morse,** Oliver 1922- WhoBlA 92
**Morse,** Peter Hodges 1935- WhoMW 92
**Morse,** R A 1920- AmMWSc 92
**Morse,** R.C. DrAPF 91
**Morse,** Richard Jay 1933- WhoWest 92
**Morse,** Richard McGee 1922- WrDr 92
**Morse,** Richard Stetson 1911- AmMWSc 92
**Morse,** Robert 1931- IntMPA 92
**Morse,** Robert Alan 1931- WhoEnt 92
**Morse,** Robert Emmett, III 1950- WhoAmL 92
**Morse,** Robert Harry 1941- WhoAmL 92
**Morse,** Robert Malcolm 1938- AmMWSc 92
**Morse,** Robert Warren 1921- AmMWSc 92
**Morse,** Roger Alfred 1927- AmMWSc 92
**Morse,** Ronald Loyd 1940- AmMWSc 92
**Morse,** Rory DrAPF 91
**Morse,** Roy E 1916- AmMWSc 92
**Morse,** Samuel F. B. 1791-1872 BenetAL 91, DcAmImH, RComAH
**Morse,** Samuel Finley Breese 1791-1872 BiInAmS
**Morse,** Saul Julian 1948- WhoMW 92
**Morse,** Sidney Edwards 1794-1871 BenetAL 91
**Morse,** Stearns Anthony 1931- AmMWSc 92
**Morse,** Stephan A 1947- WhoAmP 91
**Morse,** Stephen Allen 1942- AmMWSc 92
**Morse,** Stephen J. 1945- WhoAmL 92
**Morse,** Stephen Scott 1951- AmMWSc 92
**Morse,** Steven 1957- WhoAmP 91
**Morse,** Susan E. ReelWom
**Morse,** Terry Wayne 1946- WhoRel 92
**Morse,** Theodore Frederick 1932- AmMWSc 92
**Morse,** Warren W. 1912- WhoBlA 92
**Morse,** Wayne Lyman 1900-1974 AmPolLe [port]
**Morse,** William Charles 1915- WhoMW 92
**Morse,** William Herbert 1928- AmMWSc 92
**Morse,** William M 1947- AmMWSc 92
**Morse Riley,** Barbara Lyn 1958- WhoBlA 92
**Morson,** Basil Clifford 1921- Who 92
**Morson,** Hugh 1850-1925 DcNCBi 4
**Morss,** Tony Dean 1957- WhoWest 92
**Mort,** Andrew James 1951- AmMWSc 92
**Mort,** Jo-Ann DrAPF 91
**Mort,** John Ernest Llewelyn 1915- Who 92
**Mort,** Joseph 1936- AmMWSc 92
**Mort,** Marion 1937- Who 92
**Mortada,** Mohamed 1925- AmMWSc 92
**Mortara,** Lorne B 1932- AmMWSc 92
**Mortarotti,** Franco Antonio 1964- WhoFI 92
**Mortazavi,** Saeed 1947- WhoFI 92
**Mortel,** Rodrigue 1933- AmMWSc 92, WhoBlA 92
**Mortell,** Robert Thomas 1946- WhoWest 92
**Morten,** Stanley Wilbur 1943- WhoFI 92
**Mortensen,** Arvid LeGrande 1941- WhoAmL 92, WhoFI 92
**Mortensen,** David Soren 1942- WhoAmL 92
**Mortensen,** Earl Miller 1933- AmMWSc 92, WhoMW 92
**Mortensen,** Glen Albert 1933- AmMWSc 92
**Mortensen,** H Grant WhoAmP 91
**Mortensen,** Harley Eugene 1931- AmMWSc 92
**Mortensen,** James Michael 1937- WhoIns 92
**Mortensen,** John Alan 1929- AmMWSc 92
**Mortensen,** Kjeld 1925- IntWW 91
**Mortensen,** Knud 1939- AmMWSc 92
**Mortensen,** Philip Stephen 1947- WhoEnt 92
**Mortensen,** Richard E 1935- AmMWSc 92
**Mortensen,** Richard Edgar 1935- WhoWest 92
**Mortensen,** Stanley John 1949- WhoMW 92
**Mortensen,** Steve Lawrence 1964- WhoEnt 92
**Mortensen,** Susan Marie 1950- WhoWest 92
**Mortenson,** James L. 1944- WhoMW 92
**Mortenson,** Kenneth Ernest 1926- AmMWSc 92
**Mortenson,** Leonard Earl 1928- AmMWSc 92
**Mortenson,** Theadore Hampton 1934- AmMWSc 92
**Mortenson,** Thomas Theodore 1934- WhoFI 92
**Morter,** Raymond Lione 1920- AmMWSc 92, WhoMW 92
**Mortham,** Sandra Barringer 1951- WhoAmP 91
**Morthland,** Mark Stephen 1958- WhoAmL 92
**Mortiboy,** Clara Louise Beck 1928- WhoMW 92
**Mortier,** Gerard 1943- CurBio 91 [port], IntWW 91, WhoEnt 92
**Mortier,** Roland F. J. 1920- IntWW 91
**Mortimer,** Anita Louise 1950- WhoAmL 92
**Mortimer,** Averell Harriman 1956- WhoFI 92
**Mortimer,** Barry Who 92
**Mortimer,** Chapman IntAu&W 91X
**Mortimer,** Charles IntAu&W 91X
**Mortimer,** Charles Edgar 1921- AmMWSc 92
**Mortimer,** Clifford Hiley 1911- AmMWSc 92, Who 92
**Mortimer,** Delores M. WhoBlA 92
**Mortimer,** Edward Albert, Jr 1922- AmMWSc 92
**Mortimer,** G F WhoAmP 91
**Mortimer,** Gerald James 1918- IntWW 91, Who 92
**Mortimer,** Gregory Keith 1954- WhoAmP 91
**Mortimer,** J Thomas 1939- AmMWSc 92
**Mortimer,** James Arthur 1944- AmMWSc 92
**Mortimer,** James Edward 1921- IntWW 91, Who 92, WrDr 92
**Mortimer,** John 1923- CnDBLB 8 [port], ConNov 91, ConTFT 9, FacFETw, RfGEnL 91, WrDr 92
**Mortimer,** John Barry 1931- Who 92
**Mortimer,** John Clifford 1923- IntAu&W 91, IntWW 91, Who 92
**Mortimer,** John L. 1908-1977 ConAu 135
**Mortimer,** Katharine Mary Hope 1946- Who 92
**Mortimer,** Kenneth 1922- AmMWSc 92
**Mortimer,** Penelope 1918- ConNov 91, IntAu&W 91, Who 92, WrDr 92
**Mortimer,** Penelope Ruth 1918- IntWW 91
**Mortimer,** Richard W 1936- AmMWSc 92
**Mortimer,** Robert George 1933- AmMWSc 92
**Mortimer,** Robert Keith 1927- AmMWSc 92
**Mortimer,** Roger 1914- Who 92
**Mortimer,** Rory Dixon 1950- WhoAmL 92
**Mortimer,** William James 1932- WhoWest 92
**Mortimore,** Glenn Edward 1925- AmMWSc 92
**Mortimore,** Simon Anthony 1950- Who 92
**Mortkowitz,** Barbara 1946- WhoWest 92
**Mortland,** Max Merle 1923- AmMWSc 92
**Mortlock,** Herbert Norman 1926- Who 92
**Mortlock,** Robert Paul 1931- AmMWSc 92
**Mortman,** Doris IntAu&W 91
**Mortman-Friedman,** Beth-Lynn 1950- WhoEnt 92
**Mortola,** Jacopo Prospero 1949- AmMWSc 92
**Morton** Who 92
**Morton,** Earl of 1927- Who 92
**Morton,** A S ScFEYrs
**Morton,** Alastair IntWW 91, Who 92
**Morton,** Alastair 1910-1963 TwCPaSc
**Morton,** Albert G WhoAmP 91
**Morton,** Alexander A., III WhoFI 92
**Morton,** Andrew Queen 1919- Who 92
**Morton,** Anthony 1923- Who 92
**Morton,** Arthur 1908- IntMPA 92
**Morton,** Arthur 1915- Who 92
**Morton,** Azie B. 1936- WhoBlA 92
**Morton,** Brenda WrDr 92
**Morton,** Brian d1991 Who 92N
**Morton,** Brian 1912- IntWW 91
**Morton,** Bridget Balthrop DrAPF 91
**Morton,** Bruce LesBEnT 92
**Morton,** Bruce Eldine 1938- AmMWSc 92
**Morton,** Bruce Rutherfurd 1926- WrDr 92
**Morton,** Carlos DrAPF 91
**Morton,** Carlos 1947- WhoHisp 92
**Morton,** Carolyn Kay 1951- WhoFI 92
**Morton,** Charles 1627-1698 BenetAL 91
**Morton,** Charles Brinkley 1926- WhoRel 92
**Morton,** Charles E. 1926- WhoBlA 92
**Morton,** Chesley Venable, Jr 1951- WhoAmP 91
**Morton,** Craig Richard 1942- WhoMW 92
**Morton,** Crichton Charles 1912- Who 92
**Morton,** Cynthia Neverdon 1944- WhoBlA 92
**Morton,** David WhoRel 92
**Morton,** David 1929- IntWW 91, WhoFI 92, WhoMW 92
**Morton,** Don Townley 1933- WhoWest 92
**Morton,** Donald Charles 1933- AmMWSc 92, IntWW 91
**Morton,** Donald John 1931- AmMWSc 92
**Morton,** Donald Lee 1934- AmMWSc 92, WhoWest 92
**Morton,** Douglas M 1935- AmMWSc 92
**Morton,** E James 1926- WhoIns 92
**Morton,** Edward James 1926- WhoFI 92
**Morton,** Francis J. 1949- WhoAmL 92
**Morton,** Frank 1906- Who 92
**Morton,** Frederic 1925- LiExTwC
**Morton,** G A 1903- AmMWSc 92
**Morton,** Garnett Fry 1947- WhoAmP 91
**Morton,** Gary LesBEnT 92
**Morton,** Gene L. 1939- WhoFI 92
**Morton,** George 1585-1628? BenetAL 91
**Morton,** George Martin 1940- Who 92
**Morton,** Glen TwCWW 91
**Morton,** Harrison Leon 1938- AmMWSc 92
**Morton,** Harry B WhoAmP 91
**Morton,** Harry E 1906- AmMWSc 92
**Morton,** Harvey Leon 1941- WhoAmP 91
**Morton,** Henrietta Olive 1937- WhoWest 92
**Morton,** Henry 1836-1902 BiInAmS
**Morton,** Henry Albert 1925- IntAu&W 91
**Morton,** Henry W. 1929- IntAu&W 91, WrDr 92
**Morton,** Howard LeRoy 1924- AmMWSc 92
**Morton,** Hughes Gregory 1923- WhoFI 92, WhoWest 92
**Morton,** James 1938- ConAu 133
**Morton,** James A. 1929- WhoBlA 92
**Morton,** Jeffrey Bruce 1941- AmMWSc 92
**Morton,** Jelly Roll 1885?-1941 ConMus 7 [port]
**Morton,** Jelly Roll 1890-1941 FacFETw, NewAmDM
**Morton,** John, Jr. 1967- WhoBlA 92
**Morton,** John Dudley 1914- AmMWSc 92
**Morton,** John Duggan, Sr 1937- WhoAmP 91
**Morton,** John Hall 1940- WhoAmL 92
**Morton,** John Henderson 1923- AmMWSc 92
**Morton,** John Kenneth 1928- AmMWSc 92
**Morton,** John Robert, III 1929- AmMWSc 92
**Morton,** John West, Jr 1925- AmMWSc 92
**Morton,** Joseph Chandler 1932- WhoMW 92
**Morton,** Joseph James Pandozzi 1941- AmMWSc 92
**Morton,** Joyce Helmick 1956- WhoAmL 92
**Morton,** Katy TwCPaSc
**Morton,** Keith William 1930- Who 92
**Morton,** Kenneth Valentine Freeland 1907- Who 92
**Morton,** Leona M. 1912- WhoBlA 92
**Morton,** Levi Parsons 1824-1920 AmPolLe
**Morton,** Margaret E. 1924- WhoBlA 92
**Morton,** Margaret E Woods 1924- WhoAmP 91
**Morton,** Marie Etta 1926- WhoAmP 91
**Morton,** Marilyn M. 1946- WhoBlA 92
**Morton,** Mark Edward 1956- WhoFI 92
**Morton,** Martin Lewis 1934- AmMWSc 92
**Morton,** Maurice 1913- AmMWSc 92
**Morton,** Nathaniel 1613-1685 BenetAL 91
**Morton,** Newton Ennis 1929- AmMWSc 92
**Morton,** Patsy Jennings 1951- WhoBlA 92
**Morton,** Paul Gustav 1938- WhoFI 92
**Morton,** Perry Wilkes, Jr 1923- AmMWSc 92
**Morton,** Perry Williams 1939- WhoFI 92
**Morton,** Phillip A AmMWSc 92
**Morton,** R. James P. 1953- WhoFI 92
**Morton,** Randall Eugene 1950- AmMWSc 92
**Morton,** Raymond John, Jr. 1961- WhoEnt 92
**Morton,** Richard Alan 1938- AmMWSc 92
**Morton,** Richard Everett 1930- IntAu&W 91, WrDr 92
**Morton,** Richard G 1918- WhoAmP 91
**Morton,** Robert Alastair 1938- IntWW 91, Who 92
**Morton,** Robert Alex 1942- AmMWSc 92
**Morton,** Robert L. 1889-1976 ConAu 134
**Morton,** Robert Steel 1917- WrDr 92
**Morton,** Roger David 1935- AmMWSc 92
**Morton,** Roger Roy Adams 1941- AmMWSc 92
**Morton,** Russell Scott 1954- WhoRel 92
**Morton,** Samuel George 1799-1851 BiInAmS
**Morton,** Sarah Wentworth 1759-1846 BenetAL 91
**Morton,** Stephen Alastair 1913- Who 92
**Morton,** Stephen Dana 1932- AmMWSc 92, WhoMW 92
**Morton,** Thomas 1575?-1646? BenetAL 91
**Morton,** Thomas 1764-1838 RfGEnL 91
**Morton,** Thomas Hellman 1947- AmMWSc 92, WhoWest 92
**Morton,** W.C. DrAPF 91
**Morton,** Walter Graydon 1946- WhoWest 92
**Morton,** Warren Allen 1924- WhoAmP 91
**Morton,** William 1926- Who 92
**Morton,** William Edwards 1929- AmMWSc 92, WhoWest 92
**Morton,** William Gilbert, Jr. 1937- WhoFI 92
**Morton,** William Stanley 1947- WhoBlA 92
**Morton,** William Thomas Green 1819-1868 BiInAmS
**Morton Boyd,** John Who 92
**Morton-Finney,** John 1889- WhoBlA 92
**Morton Jack,** David 1935- Who 92
**Morton of Shuna,** Baron 1930- Who 92
**Morton-Saner,** Robert 1911- Who 92
**Mortonson,** Stephen Hansen 1945- WhoMW 92
**Mortus,** Cynthia A. DrAPF 91
**Mortvedt,** Howard William 1942- WhoWest 92
**Mortvedt,** John Jacob 1932- AmMWSc 92
**Morvis,** George Michael 1940- WhoFI 92, WhoMW 92
**Morwick,** Carolyn Hammond 1942- WhoAmP 91
**Moryl,** Richard 1929- NewAmDM
**Mosak,** Barbara Marcia 1950- WhoEnt 92, WhoMW 92
**Mosak,** Harold H. 1921- WhoMW 92

**Mosak**, Richard David 1945- AmMWSc 92
**Mosakowski**, Kenneth Robert 1946- WhoAmP 91
**Mosar**, Nicolas 1927- IntWW 91, Who 92
**Mosbach**, Erwin Heinz 1920- AmMWSc 92
**Mosbacher**, Emil, Jr. 1922- IntWW 91, WhoAmP 91
**Mosbacher**, Martin Bruce 1951- WhoFI 92
**Mosbacher**, Robert A, Jr 1951- WhoAmP 91
**Mosbacher**, Robert A, Sr 1927- WhoAmP 91
**Mosbacher**, Robert Adam 1927- IntWW 91, WhoFI 92
**Mosbakk**, Kurt 1934- IntWW 91
**Mosberg**, Arnold T 1946- AmMWSc 92
**Mosbo**, John Alvin 1947- AmMWSc 92
**Mosborg**, Robert J 1924- AmMWSc 92
**Mosburg**, Earl R, Jr 1928- AmMWSc 92
**Mosby**, Carolyn Brown 1932-1990 WhoBlA 92N
**Mosby**, Carolyn Lewis 1937- WhoBlA 92
**Mosby**, Dorothea Susan 1948- WhoWest 92
**Mosby**, Esvan Scott 1910- WhoBlA 92
**Mosby**, Hakon d1989 IntWW 91N
**Mosby**, James Francis 1937- AmMWSc 92
**Mosby**, John Davenport, III 1956- WhoFI 92
**Mosby**, John Oliver 1917- WhoFI 92
**Mosby**, John Singleton 1833-1916 BenetAL 91
**Mosby**, John Singleton, Jr. 1950- WhoMW 92
**Mosby**, Nathaniel 1929- WhoBlA 92
**Mosby**, Ralph Joseph 1931- WhoRel 92
**Mosby**, William Lindsay 1921- AmMWSc 92
**Mosca**, Salvatore Joseph 1927- WhoEnt 92
**Mosca**, Ugo 1914- IntWW 91
**Moscatelli**, David Anthony 1949- AmMWSc 92
**Moscatelli**, Ezio Anthony 1926- AmMWSc 92
**Moscatelli**, Frank A 1951- AmMWSc 92
**Moscato**, Nicholas, Jr. 1942- WhoFI 92
**Moschandreas**, Demetrios J 1943- AmMWSc 92
**Moschel**, Robert Carl AmMWSc 92
**Moscheles**, Ignaz 1794-1870 NewAmDM
**Mosches**, Julio Cesar 1912- WhoHisp 92
**Moschetta**, Luciano 1959- WhoFI 92
**Moschopedis**, Speros E 1926- AmMWSc 92
**Moschos**, Demitrios Mina 1941- WhoAmL 92
**Moschovakis**, Joan Rand 1937- AmMWSc 92
**Moschovakis**, Yiannis N 1938- AmMWSc 92
**Moscicki**, Eve Karin 1948- AmMWSc 92
**Mosco**, Maisie IntAu&W 91
**Mosco**, Vincent 1948- ConAu 35NR
**Moscona**, Aron Arthur 1922- AmMWSc 92, WhoMW 92
**Moscona**, Jodi Anthony 1953- WhoAmP 91
**Mosconi**, Roger Paul 1945- WhoFI 92
**Mosconi**, William J. 1913- WhoEnt 92
**Moscony**, John Joseph 1929- AmMWSc 92
**Moscoso**, Eloy 1935- WhoHisp 92
**Moscoso**, Pedro Fermin 1928- WhoHisp 92
**Moscoso Del Prado Y Munoz**, Javier 1934- IntWW 91
**Moscovici**, Carlo 1925- AmMWSc 92
**Moscovici**, Henri 1944- AmMWSc 92
**Moscowitz**, Albert 1929- AmMWSc 92
**Mosdell**, Lionel Patrick 1912- Who 92
**Mose**, Douglas George 1942- AmMWSc 92
**Mosebar**, Donald Howard 1961- WhoBlA 92
**Moseby**, Lloyd Anthony 1959- WhoBlA 92
**Mosee**, Jean C. 1927- WhoBlA 92
**Moseka**, Aminata WhoBlA 92, WhoEnt 92
**Mosel**, Tad LesBEnT 92
**Mosel**, Tad 1922- BenetAL 91, WrDr 92
**Moseley**, Barbara M. 1938- WhoBlA 92
**Moseley**, Calvin Edwin, Jr. 1906- WhoBlA 92
**Moseley**, Carlos DuPre 1914- WhoEnt 92
**Moseley**, Dorcas Jean 1939- WhoRel 92
**Moseley**, Edward 1682?-1749 DcNCBi 4
**Moseley**, Frances Kenney 1949- WhoBlA 92
**Moseley**, Frederick Strong, III 1928- WhoFI 92
**Moseley**, George 1925- Who 92
**Moseley**, George Van Horn 1874-1960 BiDExR
**Moseley**, Harley Sutherland Lewis 1919- IntWW 91
**Moseley**, Harrison Miller 1921- AmMWSc 92
**Moseley**, Harry Edward 1929- AmMWSc 92
**Moseley**, Hywel 1936- Who 92
**Moseley**, Jack 1931- WhoFI 92
**Moseley**, James Francis 1936- WhoAmL 92, WhoFI 92
**Moseley**, James Orville B. 1909- WhoBlA 92
**Moseley**, James R 1948- WhoAmP 91
**Moseley**, Jerry Lynn 1957- WhoAmP 91
**Moseley**, John Travis 1942- AmMWSc 92
**Moseley**, Lloyd Winfred 1908- WhoFI 92
**Moseley**, Lynn Johnson 1948- AmMWSc 92
**Moseley**, Martin Edward 1930- WhoAmP 91
**Moseley**, Maynard Fowle 1918- AmMWSc 92
**Moseley**, Patterson B 1918- AmMWSc 92
**Moseley**, Phillip Duane 1946- WhoAmP 91
**Moseley**, Roger Lester 1949- WhoIns 92
**Moseley**, Sherrard Thomas 1921- AmMWSc 92
**Moseley**, Spencer Dumaresq d1991 NewYTBS 91 [port]
**Moseley**, William DrAPF 91
**Moseley**, William David, Jr 1936- AmMWSc 92
**Moseley**, William Dunn 1795-1863 DcNCBi 4
**Moseley Braun**, Carol E. 1947- WhoBlA 92
**Mosely**, Jack Meredith 1917- WhoWest 92
**Mosely**, John de Sola 1933- WhoWest 92
**Mosely**, Ralph Ellington, III 1944- WhoRel 92
**Moseman**, John Gustav 1921- AmMWSc 92
**Moseman**, Robert Fredrick 1941- AmMWSc 92
**Mosen**, Arthur Walter 1922- AmMWSc 92
**Moser**, Alma P 1935- AmMWSc 92
**Moser**, Bruno Carl 1940- AmMWSc 92
**Moser**, Charles R 1939- AmMWSc 92
**Moser**, Chris Van 1949- WhoEnt 92
**Moser**, Claus 1922- Who 92
**Moser**, Claus Adolf 1922- IntWW 91
**Moser**, Craig Lawrence 1946- WhoFI 92
**Moser**, Dean Joseph 1942- WhoWest 92
**Moser**, Donald Eugene 1925- AmMWSc 92
**Moser**, Frank 1927- AmMWSc 92
**Moser**, Frank Hans 1907- AmMWSc 92
**Moser**, Gene Wendell 1930- AmMWSc 92
**Moser**, Glenn Allen 1943- AmMWSc 92
**Moser**, Herbert Charles 1929- AmMWSc 92
**Moser**, James Howard 1928- AmMWSc 92
**Moser**, John Richard 1927- WhoAmP 91
**Moser**, John William, Jr 1936- AmMWSc 92
**Moser**, Joseph M 1930- AmMWSc 92
**Moser**, Jurgen 1928- AmMWSc 92
**Moser**, Jurgen K. 1928- IntWW 91
**Moser**, Justus 1720-1794 BlkwCEP
**Moser**, Kenneth Bruce 1933- AmMWSc 92
**Moser**, Kenneth Miles 1929- AmMWSc 92
**Moser**, Koloman 1868-1918 DcTwDes, FacFETw
**Moser**, Louise Elizabeth 1943- AmMWSc 92
**Moser**, Lowell E 1940- AmMWSc 92
**Moser**, Martin Peter 1928- WhoAmL 92
**Moser**, Norman DrAPF 91
**Moser**, Paul E 1942- AmMWSc 92
**Moser**, Paul H 1931- AmMWSc 92
**Moser**, Raymond 1931- WhoAmP 91
**Moser**, Robert E 1939- AmMWSc 92
**Moser**, Robert Harlan 1923- AmMWSc 92
**Moser**, Roger Alden 1929- WhoFI 92
**Moser**, Roy Edgar 1922- AmMWSc 92
**Moser**, Royce, Jr 1935- AmMWSc 92, WhoWest 92
**Moser**, Sigward Markus 1962- WhoEnt 92
**Moser**, Stephen Adcock 1946- AmMWSc 92
**Moser**, Suzan Anne 1959- WhoMW 92
**Moser**, Virginia Clayton 1954- AmMWSc 92
**Moser**, William Daniel 1945- WhoMW 92
**Moser**, William O J 1927- AmMWSc 92
**Moser**, William Ray 1935- AmMWSc 92
**Moser-Proell**, Annemarie 1953- FacFETw
**Moser-Veillon**, Phylis B 1947- AmMWSc 92
**Moses** EncEarC
**Moses**, Alan George 1945- Who 92
**Moses**, Alfred Henry 1929- WhoAmL 92
**Moses**, Alfred Joseph 1859-1920 BiInAmS
**Moses**, Alice J. 1929- WhoBlA 92
**Moses**, Andrew M. 1926- WhoBlA 92
**Moses**, Bonnie Smith 1955- WhoAmL 92
**Moses**, Campbell, Jr 1917- AmMWSc 92
**Moses**, Charles Alexander 1923- IntMPA 92, WhoEnt 92
**Moses**, Don V 1936- WhoEnt 92
**Moses**, Edward Joel 1938- AmMWSc 92
**Moses**, Edward Pearson 1857-1948 DcNCBi 4
**Moses**, Edwin DrAPF 91
**Moses**, Edwin 1953- WhoBlA 92
**Moses**, Edwin 1955- IntWW 91
**Moses**, Edwin Corley 1955- BlkOlyM [port]
**Moses**, Elbert Raymond, Jr 1908- IntAu&W 91, WhoWest 92, WrDr 92
**Moses**, Eric George Rufus 1914- Who 92
**Moses**, Francis Guy 1937- AmMWSc 92
**Moses**, Gilbert 1942- IntMPA 92, WhoBlA 92
**Moses**, Gregory Allen 1950- AmMWSc 92
**Moses**, Gregory Hayes, Jr. 1933- WhoFI 92, WhoMW 92
**Moses**, Hal Lynwood 1934- AmMWSc 92
**Moses**, Hamilton, Jr. 1909- WhoAmL 92
**Moses**, Harold Webster 1949- WhoBlA 92
**Moses**, Harry Elecks 1922- AmMWSc 92
**Moses**, Henry A 1939- AmMWSc 92, WhoBlA 92
**Moses**, Herbert A 1929- AmMWSc 92
**Moses**, Joel 1941- AmMWSc 92
**Moses**, John Henry 1938- Who 92
**Moses**, Johnnie, Jr. 1939- WhoBlA 92
**Moses**, Kenneth 1931- Who 92
**Moses**, Lincoln Ellsworth 1921- AmMWSc 92, IntWW 91
**Moses**, Linda Karen 1957- WhoFI 92
**Moses**, Lionel Elliott 1949- WhoRel 92
**Moses**, MacDonald 1936- WhoBlA 92
**Moses**, Michael Howard 1940- WhoIns 92
**Moses**, Michael James 1956- WhoFI 92
**Moses**, Milton E. 1939- WhoBlA 92
**Moses**, Montrose James 1919- AmMWSc 92
**Moses**, Nancy Lee Heise 1947- WhoEnt 92
**Moses**, Otto A 1846-1906 BiInAmS
**Moses**, Ray Napoleon, Jr 1936- AmMWSc 92
**Moses**, Robert WhoEnt 92
**Moses**, Robert 1888-1981 FacFETw
**Moses**, Ronald Elliot 1930- AmMWSc 92
**Moses**, Saul 1921- AmMWSc 92
**Moses**, Thomas Freeman 1836-1917 BiInAmS
**Moses**, W.R. DrAPF 91
**Moses**, Wilson Jeremiah 1942- WhoBlA 92
**Moses**, Winfield C, Jr 1943- WhoAmP 91
**Moseson**, Richard S. 1955- WhoEnt 92
**Mosesson**, Michael W 1934- AmMWSc 92
**Mosettig**, Michael David 1942- WhoEnt 92
**Mosevics**, Mark 1920- IntWW 91
**Mosgrove**, Reed Wesley 1963- WhoEnt 92
**Moshaver**, Cyrus Ali 1955- WhoFI 92
**Mosheim**, Johann Lorenz Von 1694-1755 EncEarC
**Moshell**, Alan N 1947- AmMWSc 92
**Mosher**, Carol Walker 1921- AmMWSc 92
**Mosher**, Clifford Coleman, III 1927- AmMWSc 92
**Mosher**, Deane Fremont, Jr 1943- AmMWSc 92
**Mosher**, Don R 1921- AmMWSc 92
**Mosher**, Donna Patricia 1941- AmMWSc 92
**Mosher**, Gerold Lynn 1956- WhoMW 92
**Mosher**, Gregory Dean 1949- WhoEnt 92
**Mosher**, Harold Elwood 1920- AmMWSc 92
**Mosher**, Harry Stone 1915- AmMWSc 92
**Mosher**, James Arthur 1942- AmMWSc 92
**Mosher**, John Carpenter 1948- WhoWest 92
**Mosher**, John Ivan 1933- AmMWSc 92
**Mosher**, Loren Cameron 1938- AmMWSc 92, WhoWest 92
**Mosher**, Loren Richard 1933- AmMWSc 92
**Mosher**, Melville Calvin 1945- AmMWSc 92
**Mosher**, Melvyn Wayne 1940- AmMWSc 92
**Mosher**, Richard Arthur 1946- AmMWSc 92
**Mosher**, Robert Eugene 1920- AmMWSc 92
**Mosher**, Sally Ekenberg 1934- WhoWest 92
**Mosher**, Sharon 1951- AmMWSc 92
**Mosher**, Sol 1928- WhoAmP 91
**Mosher**, William John 1961- WhoAmL 92
**Moshey**, Edward A AmMWSc 92
**Moshier**, John Thomas 1957- WhoAmL 92
**Moshier**, Terry Allen 1936- WhoAmP 91
**Moshinsky**, Elijah 1946- Who 92
**Moshiri**, Gerald Alexander 1929- AmMWSc 92
**Moshman**, Jack 1924- AmMWSc 92
**Moshoeshoe II** 1938- IntWW 91
**Moshy**, Raymond Joseph 1925- AmMWSc 92
**Mosier**, Arvin Ray 1945- AmMWSc 92
**Mosier**, Benjamin 1926- AmMWSc 92
**Mosier**, Edward Bert 1947- WhoRel 92
**Mosier**, Gary Gene 1947- WhoMW 92
**Mosier**, H David, Jr 1925- AmMWSc 92
**Mosier**, Jacob Eugene 1924- AmMWSc 92
**Mosier**, Stephen R 1942- AmMWSc 92
**Mosig**, Gisela 1930- AmMWSc 92
**Mosimann**, Anton 1947- IntWW 91, Who 92
**Mosimann**, James Emile 1930- AmMWSc 92
**Mosk**, Richard Mitchell 1939- WhoAmL 92
**Mosk**, Stanley 1912- WhoAmL 92, WhoAmP 91, WhoWest 92
**Moskal**, Joseph Russell 1950- AmMWSc 92
**Moskal**, Robert M. 1937- WhoRel 92
**Moskalenko**, Kirill Semenovich 1902-1985 SovUnBD
**Moskalik**, Andrew James 1967- WhoMW 92
**Moskalski**, Elton Alfred 1939- WhoWest 92
**Moskalyk**, Richard Edward 1936- AmMWSc 92
**Mosko**, Sigmund W 1936- AmMWSc 92
**Moskos**, Charles C. 1934- WhoMW 92
**Moskovic**, Steven 1963- WhoEnt 92
**Moskovis**, L. Michael 1933- WhoMW 92
**Moskovits**, Martin 1943- AmMWSc 92
**Moskovitz**, Stuart Jeffrey 1949- WhoAmL 92
**Moskow**, Michael H. 1938- WrDr 92
**Moskowitz**, Bette Ann DrAPF 91
**Moskowitz**, David William 1952- WhoMW 92
**Moskowitz**, Faye DrAPF 91
**Moskowitz**, Gerard Jay 1940- AmMWSc 92
**Moskowitz**, Gordon David 1934- AmMWSc 92
**Moskowitz**, Harold Louis 1953- WhoAmL 92
**Moskowitz**, Joel Steven 1947- WhoAmL 92
**Moskowitz**, Jules Warren 1934- AmMWSc 92
**Moskowitz**, Kenneth Paul 1948- WhoFI 92
**Moskowitz**, Leah 1960- WhoAmL 92
**Moskowitz**, Mark Lewis 1925- AmMWSc 92
**Moskowitz**, Martin A 1935- AmMWSc 92
**Moskowitz**, Merwin 1921- AmMWSc 92
**Moskowitz**, Michael Arthur 1942- AmMWSc 92
**Moskowitz**, Norman 1922- AmMWSc 92
**Moskowitz**, Robert 1935- WorArt 1980
**Moskowitz**, Ronald 1939- AmMWSc 92
**Moskowitz**, Sam 1920- ScFEYrs
**Moskowitz**, Seymour 1930- WhoRel 92
**Moskowitz**, Stanley Alan 1956- WhoFI 92
**Moskowitz**, Stuart Stanley 1955- WhoAmL 92
**Moskus**, Jerry Ray 1942- WhoWest 92
**Moskvin**, Andrey Nikolaevich 1901-1961 SovUnBD
**Moskvin**, Ivan Mikhaylovich 1874-1946 SovUnBD
**Moskvin**, Ivan Mikhaylovich 1890-1939 SovUnBD
**Mosler**, Hermann 1912- IntWW 91
**Mosley** Who 92
**Mosley**, Charles E. 1937- WhoBlA 92
**Mosley**, Daniel Joseph 1947- WhoMW 92
**Mosley**, Daniel Lynn 1956- WhoAmL 92
**Mosley**, Edna Wilson 1925- WhoBlA 92
**Mosley**, Edward R. WhoBlA 92
**Mosley**, Elwood A. 1943- WhoBlA 92
**Mosley**, Eugene Lyter 1942- WhoAmP 91
**Mosley**, Geraldine B. 1920- WhoBlA 92
**Mosley**, Glenn Richard 1935- WhoRel 92
**Mosley**, Godfrey Thomas 1953- WhoRel 92
**Mosley**, James W 1929- AmMWSc 92
**Mosley**, John Colbert 1935- WhoBlA 92
**Mosley**, John Ross 1922- AmMWSc 92
**Mosley**, John William WhoBlA 92
**Mosley**, Lawrence Edward, Sr. 1953- WhoBlA 92
**Mosley**, Leonard 1913- WrDr 92
**Mosley**, Leonard 1931- IntAu&W 91
**Mosley**, Linda Kay 1948- WhoAmL 92
**Mosley**, Maurice B 1946- WhoAmP 91, WhoBlA 92
**Mosley**, Nicholas IntWW 91, Who 92
**Mosley**, Nicholas 1923- ConNov 91, IntAu&W 91, WrDr 92
**Mosley**, Oswald 1896-1980 EncTR 91 [port], FacFETw
**Mosley**, Oswald Ernald 1896-1980 BiDExR
**Mosley**, Roger E. IntMPA 92
**Mosley**, Roy Edward 1963- WhoRel 92
**Mosley**, Stephen T 1949- AmMWSc 92
**Mosley**, Steven 1952- ConAu 133
**Mosley**, Thomas Edmond, Jr. 1950- WhoFI 92
**Mosley**, Tracey Ray 1960- WhoBlA 92
**Mosley**, Weldon V 1924- WhoIns 92
**Mosley**, Wilbur Clanton, Jr 1938- AmMWSc 92
**Moslin**, Helen 1956- TwCPaSc

**Mosman,** Craig William 1959- *WhoWest 92*
**Mosoeunyane,** Khethang Aloysius 1942- *IntWW 91*
**Mosqueda,** Joe J. 1954- *WhoHisp 92*
**Mosqueira,** Charlotte Marianne 1937- *WhoWest 92*
**Moss,** Alfred A., Jr. 1943- *WhoBlA 92*
**Moss,** Alfred Allinson d1990 *Who 92N*
**Moss,** Alfred Jefferson, Jr 1940- *AmMWSc 92*
**Moss,** Ambler Holmes, Jr 1937- *WhoAmP 91*
**Moss,** Arthur Henshey 1930- *WhoAmL 92*
**Moss,** Barbara 1946- *WrDr 92*
**Moss,** Barry L. 1943- *WhoAmL 92*
**Moss,** Basil Stanley 1918- *Who 92*
**Moss,** Bernard 1937- *AmMWSc 92*
**Moss,** Bill Ralph 1950- *WhoAmL 92, WhoFI 92*
**Moss,** Buelon Rexford 1937- *AmMWSc 92*
**Moss,** Calvin E 1939- *AmMWSc 92*
**Moss,** Charles 1938- *WhoFI 92*
**Moss,** Charles B., Jr. 1944- *IntMPA 92*
**Moss,** Charles James 1917- *Who 92*
**Moss,** Charles Norman 1914- *WhoWest 92*
**Moss,** Claude Wayne 1935- *AmMWSc 92*
**Moss,** Colin William 1914- *TwCPaSc*
**Moss,** Crayton Lee 1954- *WhoMW 92*
**Moss,** Cynthia J. 1940- *WrDr 92*
**Moss,** Dale Nelson 1930- *AmMWSc 92*
**Moss,** Daniel Calvin, Jr. 1933- *WhoBlA 92*
**Moss,** David Christopher 1946- *Who 92*
**Moss,** David Earl 1952- *WhoFI 92*
**Moss,** David Francis 1927- *Who 92*
**Moss,** David John E. *Who 92*
**Moss,** David Joseph 1938- *Who 92*
**Moss,** Debra Lee 1952- *WhoWest 92*
**Moss,** Donna Anderson 1954- *WhoAmP 91*
**Moss,** Donovan Dean 1926- *AmMWSc 92*
**Moss,** Douglas Mabbett 1954- *WhoWest 92*
**Moss,** Duane Reid 1925- *WhoWest 92*
**Moss,** Edward Herbert St George 1918- *Who 92*
**Moss,** Elaine Dora 1924- *Who 92*
**Moss,** Estella Mae 1928- *WhoBlA 92*
**Moss,** Faryl Sims 1944- *WhoAmL 92*
**Moss,** Frank Edward 1911- *WhoAmP 91*
**Moss,** Frank Edward 1934- *AmMWSc 92*
**Moss,** Frank L. *IntMPA 92*
**Moss,** Gabriel Stephen 1949- *Who 92*
**Moss,** Gary Paul 1957- *WhoEnt 92*
**Moss,** George Joseph, Jr. 1938- *WhoFI 92*
**Moss,** Gerald 1931- *AmMWSc 92*
**Moss,** Gerald Allen 1940- *AmMWSc 92*
**Moss,** Gerald L. 1936- *WhoAmL 92*
**Moss,** Gerald S 1935- *AmMWSc 92*
**Moss,** Ginger Lee 1961- *WhoEnt 92*
**Moss,** Gordon Ervin 1937- *WhoMW 92*
**Moss,** Harry Mark 1919- *WhoAmP 91*
**Moss,** Harvey 1951- *WhoAmP 91*
**Moss,** Henry Samuel 1926- *WhoMW 92*
**Moss,** Herbert Irwin 1932- *AmMWSc 92*
**Moss,** Howard 1922- *BenetAL 91*
**Moss,** Irwin *IntMPA 92*
**Moss,** J Eliot B 1954- *AmMWSc 92*
**Moss,** Jack Irwin 1930- *WhoEnt 92*
**Moss,** James A. 1920-1990 *WhoBlA 92N*
**Moss,** James B, Jr 1924- *WhoAmP 91*
**Moss,** James Burke 1933- *WhoMW 92*
**Moss,** James Edward 1949- *WhoBlA 92*
**Moss,** James Lamar 1956- *WhoFI 92*
**Moss,** James R *WhoAmP 91*
**Moss,** James Richard Frederick 1916- *Who 92*
**Moss,** Jane Hope *Who 92*
**Moss,** Jeffrey Arnold 1942- *WhoEnt 92*
**Moss,** Jeffrey B. 1945- *WhoEnt 92*
**Moss,** Joe Albaugh 1925- *WhoAmL 92*
**Moss,** Joel 1946- *AmMWSc 92*
**Moss,** Joel Charles 1949- *WhoEnt 92*
**Moss,** John Frederick 1943- *WhoMW 92*
**Moss,** John Michael 1936- *Who 92*
**Moss,** John Ringer 1920- *Who 92*
**Moss,** Justin Leslie 1947- *WhoEnt 92*
**Moss,** Lawrence Kenneth 1927- *WhoEnt 92*
**Moss,** Leo D 1911- *AmMWSc 92*
**Moss,** Leonard Godfrey 1932- *Who 92*
**Moss,** Leslie Otha 1952- *WhoMW 92*
**Moss,** Lloyd Glenn 1947- *WhoRel 92*
**Moss,** Lloyd Kent 1924- *AmMWSc 92*
**Moss,** Malcolm Douglas 1943- *Who 92*
**Moss,** Marlow 1890-1958 *TwCPaSc*
**Moss,** Martin Grenville 1923- *Who 92*
**Moss,** Marvin 1929- *AmMWSc 92, WhoWest 92*
**Moss,** Melvin Lane 1915- *AmMWSc 92*
**Moss,** Melvin Lionel 1923- *AmMWSc 92*
**Moss,** Michael *Who 92*
**Moss,** Michael 1943- *WhoFI 92*
**Moss,** Morton Herbert 1914- *WhoWest 92*
**Moss,** Myra E. 1937- *WhoWest 92*
**Moss,** N. Henry d1990 *NewYTBS 91*
**Moss,** Nancy *WrDr 92*
**Moss,** Norman Bernard 1928- *IntAu&W 91*
**Moss,** Norman J. *Who 92*
**Moss,** Otis, Jr. *WhoRel 92*
**Moss,** Otis, Jr. 1935- *WhoBlA 92*
**Moss,** Peter *IntAu&W 91, WrDr 92*
**Moss,** Peter 1947- *WhoEnt 92*
**Moss,** Peyton Howard 1914- *WhoAmL 92*
**Moss,** Ralph Walter *WhoEnt 92*
**Moss,** Randy Hays 1953- *AmMWSc 92*
**Moss,** Raymond Lloyd 1959- *WhoAmL 92, WhoFI 92*
**Moss,** Richard 1947- *AmMWSc 92*
**Moss,** Richard Maurice 1925- *WhoWest 92*
**Moss,** Richard Wallace 1941- *AmMWSc 92*
**Moss,** Robert *WrDr 92*
**Moss,** Robert A. 1915- *WhoRel 92*
**Moss,** Robert Allen 1940- *AmMWSc 92*
**Moss,** Robert C., Jr. 1939- *WhoBlA 92*
**Moss,** Robert Earl 1940- *WhoAmP 91*
**Moss,** Robert Henry 1922- *AmMWSc 92*
**Moss,** Robert L 1940- *AmMWSc 92*
**Moss,** Robert Thomas 1949- *WhoMW 92*
**Moss,** Robert Verelle, Jr. 1922-1976 *DcNCBi 4*
**Moss,** Robert Wayne 1938- *WhoFI 92*
**Moss,** Roberta *WrDr 92*
**Moss,** Rodney Dale 1927- *AmMWSc 92*
**Moss,** Ronald Trevor 1942- *Who 92*
**Moss,** Rose *DrAPF 91*
**Moss,** Rose 1937- *LiExTwC, WrDr 92*
**Moss,** Scott Francis 1954- *WhoFI 92*
**Moss,** Simeon F. 1920- *WhoBlA 92*
**Moss,** Simon Charles 1934- *AmMWSc 92*
**Moss,** Stanley *DrAPF 91*
**Moss,** Stanley 1935- *ConPo 91, WrDr 92*
**Moss,** Stephen Edward 1940- *WhoAmL 92*
**Moss,** Steven C 1948- *AmMWSc 92*
**Moss,** Steven David 1955- *WhoWest 92*
**Moss,** Stewart 1937- *WhoEnt 92*
**Moss,** Stirling 1929- *IntWW 91, Who 92, WrDr 92*
**Moss,** Sylvia *DrAPF 91*
**Moss,** Sylvia Elise 1935- *WhoEnt 92*
**Moss,** Tanya Jill 1958- *WhoBlA 92*
**Moss,** Terry 1946- *WhoEnt 92*
**Moss,** Thomas Edward, Sr. 1934- *WhoBlA 92*
**Moss,** Thomas Henry 1939- *WhoAmP 91*
**Moss,** Thomas Warren, Jr 1928- *WhoAmP 91*
**Moss,** Trevor Simpson 1921- *Who 92*
**Moss,** Truett W 1930- *WhoAmP 91*
**Moss,** Virginia E. 1875-1919 *RelLAm 91*
**Moss,** Wayne B. 1960- *WhoBlA 92*
**Moss,** William John 1921- *WhoAmL 92*
**Moss,** William W. 1935- *WhoFI 92*
**Moss,** William Wayne 1937- *AmMWSc 92*
**Moss,** Wilmar Burnett, Jr. 1928- *WhoBlA 92*
**Moss,** Winston *WhoBlA 92*
**Moss-Salentijn,** Letty 1943- *AmMWSc 92*
**Mossack,** Robert Alan 1956- *WhoRel 92*
**Mossadeq,** Mohammed 1881-1967 *FacFETw*
**Mossakowski,** Miroslaw 1929- *IntWW 91*
**Mossavar-Rahmani,** Bijan 1952- *WhoWest 92*
**Mossawir,** Harve H., Jr. 1942- *WhoAmL 92*
**Mossbauer,** Rudolf 1929- *IntWW 91*
**Mossbauer,** Rudolf L. 1929- *Who 92*
**Mossberg,** Thomas William 1951- *AmMWSc 92*
**Mossbrucker,** Tom *WhoEnt 92*
**Mosse,** George L. 1918- *WrDr 92*
**Mosse,** Peter John Charles 1947- *WhoFI 92*
**Mosse,** Spencer 1945- *WhoEnt 92*
**Mossell,** Gertrude Bustill 1855-1948 *NotBlAW 92 [port]*
**Mosselmans,** Carel Maurits 1929- *Who 92*
**Mosser,** John Snavely 1928- *AmMWSc 92*
**Mosser,** Thomas Joseph 1944- *WhoFI 92*
**Mossiman,** Ary 1925- *WhoFI 92*
**Mossinghoff,** Gerald Joseph 1935- *WhoAmL 92, WhoAmP 91*
**Mossman,** Albert Pruitt 1937- *WhoWest 92*
**Mossman,** Archie Stanton 1926- *AmMWSc 92*
**Mossman,** Brooke T 1947- *AmMWSc 92*
**Mossman,** Burt *TwCWW 91*
**Mossman,** David John 1938- *AmMWSc 92*
**Mossman,** Deborah Jean 1956- *WhoMW 92*
**Mossman,** Hugh Vaughan 1946- *WhoAmL 92*
**Mossman,** Kenneth Leslie 1946- *AmMWSc 92, WhoWest 92*
**Mossman,** Robert Gillis, IV 1960- *WhoMW 92*
**Mossman,** Thomas Mellish, Jr. 1938- *WhoEnt 92*
**Mossop,** Grant Dilworth 1948- *AmMWSc 92*
**Mossop,** Irene *ConAu 34NR*
**Most,** David S 1929- *AmMWSc 92*
**Most,** Don 1953- *WhoEnt 92*
**Most,** Jack Lawrence 1935- *WhoAmL 92*
**Most,** Joseph Morris 1943- *AmMWSc 92*
**Most,** Robert Bernard 1952- *WhoWest 92*
**Mostafapour,** M Kazem 1937- *AmMWSc 92*
**Mostardi,** Richard Albert 1938- *AmMWSc 92*
**Mostart,** August Egbert Laurent Marie 1951- *WhoEnt 92, WhoWest 92*
**Mostel,** Josh 1946- *IntMPA 92*
**Mosteller,** C Frederick 1916- *AmMWSc 92*
**Mosteller,** Frederick 1916- *IntWW 91*
**Mosteller,** Henry Walter 1932- *AmMWSc 92*
**Mosteller,** James Wilbur, III 1940- *WhoWest 92*
**Mosteller,** Raymond Dee 1941- *AmMWSc 92*
**Mosteller,** Robert Cobb 1938- *AmMWSc 92*
**Mosteller,** Robert P. 1948- *WhoAmL 92*
**Moster,** Mark Leslie 1953- *AmMWSc 92*
**Moster,** Mary Clare 1950- *WhoMW 92*
**Mostert,** P. S. 1927- *WrDr 92*
**Mostert,** Paul Stallings 1927- *AmMWSc 92*
**Mostiler,** John L 1923- *WhoAmP 91*
**Mostoff,** Allan Samuel 1932- *WhoAmL 92*
**Mostofi,** F Ksh *AmMWSc 92*
**Mostofi,** Khosrow 1921- *WhoWest 92*
**Mostoller,** Mark Ellsworth 1941- *AmMWSc 92*
**Mostov,** George Daniel 1923- *AmMWSc 92*
**Mostov,** Keith Elliot 1956- *WhoWest 92*
**Mostow,** George Daniel 1923- *AmMWSc 92, IntWW 91*
**Mostow,** Jonathan Carl 1961- *WhoEnt 92*
**Mostyn,** Baron 1920- *Who 92*
**Mostyn,** David *Who 92*
**Mostyn,** Joseph David 1928- *Who 92*
**Mostyn,** William Basil John 1975- *Who 92*
**Mostyn-Owen,** Gaia *IntAu&W 91X*
**Moszkowski,** Alexander 1851-1934 *ScFEYrs*
**Moszkowski,** Steven Alexander 1927- *AmMWSc 92*
**Mota,** Hector D. *WhoHisp 92*
**Mota,** Ion 1902-1936 *BiDExR*
**Mota,** Manny 1938- *WhoHisp 92*
**Mota-Altman,** Norma Patricia 1952- *WhoHisp 92*
**Mota de Freitas,** Duarte Emanuel 1957- *AmMWSc 92*
**Mota y Escobar,** Alonso de la 1556-1625 *HisDSpE*
**Motard,** R L 1925- *AmMWSc 92*
**Mote,** C D, Jr 1937- *AmMWSc 92*
**Mote,** Clayton Daniel, Jr. 1937- *WhoWest 92*
**Mote,** Dennis K. 1952- *WhoRel 92*
**Mote,** Harold Trevor 1919- *Who 92*
**Mote,** James Curtis 1945- *WhoFI 92*
**Mote,** Jimmy Dale 1930- *AmMWSc 92*
**Mote,** Michael Isnardi 1935- *AmMWSc 92*
**Mote,** Paul Steven 1947- *WhoWest 92*
**Motecuhzoma I** *HisDSpE*
**Motecuhzoma II** *HisDSpE*
**Motejunas,** Gerald William 1950- *WhoAmL 92*
**Moten,** Bennie 1894-1935 *NewAmDM*
**Moten,** Birdia B. 1934- *WhoBlA 92*
**Moten,** Chauncey Donald 1933- *WhoBlA 92*
**Moten,** Emmett S., Jr. 1944- *WhoBlA 92*
**Moten,** Lucy Ellen 1851-1933 *NotBlAW 92*
**Motenko,** Neil Philip 1951- *WhoAmL 92*
**Motes,** Dennis Roy 1950- *AmMWSc 92*
**Motesiczky,** Marie-Louise von 1906- *IntWW 91, TwCPaSc*
**Mother Jones** *RComAH*
**Mother Ross** *EncAmaz 91*
**Mothers of Invention** *NewAmDM*
**Mothershead,** Charles Ivan, III 1948- *WhoAmP 91*
**Mothershead,** John Gates 1932- *WhoMW 92*
**Mothershed,** Spaesio W. 1925- *WhoBlA 92*
**Mothersill,** John Sydney 1931- *AmMWSc 92*
**Motherway,** Joseph E 1930- *AmMWSc 92*
**Motherway,** Robert T *WhoAmP 91*
**Motherwell,** Bishop of 1937- *Who 92*
**Motherwell,** Jonathan Thomas 1952- *WhoFI 92*
**Motherwell,** Robert 1915- *IntWW 91*
**Motherwell,** Robert 1915-1991 *CurBio 91N, FacFETw, NewYTBS 91 [port], News 92-1*
**Mothopeng,** Zephania Lekoane d1990 *IntWW 91N*
**Mothopeng,** Zephania Lekoane 1913-1990 *FacFETw*
**Moticka,** Edward James 1944- *AmMWSc 92*
**Motier,** Marie Joseph Paul Yves Roch G 1757-1834 *BlkwEAR*
**Motiff,** James P 1943- *AmMWSc 92*
**Motiff,** James Peter 1943- *WhoMW 92*
**Motil,** Joseph Sylvester 1910- *WhoWest 92*
**Motion,** Andrew *WrDr 92*
**Motion,** Andrew 1952- *ConPo 91, IntWW 91, Who 92*
**Motion,** Andrew Peter 1952- *IntAu&W 91*
**Motl,** Gerald Patrick 1946- *WhoFI 92*
**Motlagh,** Mojtaba Rastgar 1940- *WhoWest 92*
**Motley,** Annette *WrDr 92*
**Motley,** Constance Baker 1921- *NotBlAW 92 [port], WhoAmL 92, WhoBlA 92*
**Motley,** David Lynn 1958- *WhoBlA 92*
**Motley,** David Malcolm 1929- *AmMWSc 92*
**Motley,** John H. 1942- *WhoBlA 92*
**Motley,** John Lothrop 1814-1877 *BenetAL 91*
**Motley,** John Paul 1927- *WhoFI 92*
**Motley,** Langhorne A 1938- *WhoAmP 91*
**Motley,** Ronald Clark 1954- *WhoBlA 92*
**Motley,** Willard 1912-1965 *BenetAL 91*
**Motolinia,** Benavente *HisDSpE*
**Moton,** McKinley, III 1957- *WhoMW 92*
**Motoyama,** Etsuro K 1932- *AmMWSc 92*
**Motrico,** Conde de *HisDSpE*
**Motsavage,** Vincent Andrew 1934- *AmMWSc 92*
**Motschall,** Jon Mark 1954- *WhoMW 92*
**Motschenbacher,** Steven Peter 1956- *WhoWest 92*
**Motsett,** Charles Bourke 1949- *WhoFI 92*
**Motsinger,** John Kings 1947- *WhoAmL 92*
**Motsinger,** Lawrence Ralph 1953- *WhoMW 92*
**Motsinger,** Linda Sue 1947- *WhoMW 92*
**Motsuenyane,** Samuel Mokgethi 1927- *IntWW 91*
**Mott,** Alyce Evelyn 1946- *WhoEnt 92*
**Mott,** Elaine *DrAPF 91*
**Mott,** Frank Luther 1886-1964 *BenetAL 91*
**Mott,** Gregory George Sidney 1925- *Who 92*
**Mott,** Harold 1928- *AmMWSc 92*
**Mott,** Henry Augustus, Jr 1852-1896 *BiInAmS*
**Mott,** J Thomas 1949- *WhoAmP 91*
**Mott,** Jack Edward 1937- *AmMWSc 92*
**Mott,** James 1788-1868 *AmPeW*
**Mott,** Joe Leonard 1937- *AmMWSc 92*
**Mott,** John 1865-1955 *FacFETw*
**Mott,** John Charles Spencer 1926- *Who 92*
**Mott,** John Harmar 1922- *Who 92*
**Mott,** John James 1834-1919 *DcNCBi 4*
**Mott,** John R. 1865-1955 *DcEcMov [port], RelLAm 91, WhoNob 90*
**Mott,** John Raleigh 1865-1955 *AmPeW*
**Mott,** Julian Edward 1929- *AmMWSc 92*
**Mott,** June Marjorie 1920- *WhoWest 92*
**Mott,** Lucretia 1793-1880 *RComAH*
**Mott,** Lucretia Coffin 1793-1880 *AmPeW, BenetAL 91, HanAmWH*
**Mott,** Michael *DrAPF 91*
**Mott,** Michael Charles Alston 1930- *IntAu&W 91*
**Mott,** Michael Duncan 1940- *Who 92*
**Mott,** Nevill 1905- *Who 92*
**Mott,** Nevill Francis 1905- *AmMWSc 92, FacFETw, IntWW 91, WhoNob 90*
**Mott,** Philip Charles 1948- *Who 92*
**Mott,** Ralph Lionel 1937- *AmMWSc 92*
**Mott,** Robert Lewis 1924- *WhoEnt 92*
**Mott,** Roger Alan 1950- *WhoAmP 91*
**Mott,** Stokes E., Jr. 1947- *WhoBlA 92*
**Mott,** Thomas 1926- *AmMWSc 92*
**Mott,** Victor Raymond 1915- *WhoAmP 91*
**Mott-Radclyffe,** Charles 1911- *Who 92*
**Motta,** Dick 1931- *ConAu 134*
**Motta,** Jerome J 1933- *AmMWSc 92*
**Motta,** John Joseph 1949- *WhoFI 92, WhoWest 92*
**Motta,** John Richard 1931- *WhoWest 92*
**Motte,** Mary Margaret 1936- *WhoRel 92*
**Motteck,** Carl T. 1928- *WhoWest 92*
**Motteler,** Zane Clinton 1935- *AmMWSc 92*
**Mottelson,** Ben R. 1926- *Who 92*
**Mottelson,** Benjamin Roy 1926- *WhoNob 90*
**Motter,** Charlotte Kay 1922- *WhoWest 92*
**Motter,** James Wilson 1940- *WhoMW 92*
**Motter,** Roberta Lee 1936- *WhoWest 92*
**Mottershead,** Frank William 1911- *Who 92*
**Mottet,** Norman Karle 1924- *AmMWSc 92, WhoWest 92*
**Mottice,** Susan Louise 1954- *WhoWest 92*
**Mottinger,** John P 1938- *AmMWSc 92*
**Mottistone,** Baron 1920- *Who 92*
**Mottl,** Felix 1856-1911 *NewAmDM*
**Mottl,** Ronald M, Sr 1934- *WhoAmP 91*
**Mottley,** Carolyn 1947- *AmMWSc 92*
**Mottley,** Wendell 1941- *BlkOlyM*
**Mottmann,** John 1944- *AmMWSc 92*

**Motto,** Jerome 1921- AmMWSc 92
**Mottola,** Gary F. 1947- WhoAmL 92
**Mottola,** Horacio Antonio 1930- AmMWSc 92
**Mottola,** John T 1945- WhoIns 92
**Mottram,** Eric ConPo 91, WrDr 92
**Mottram,** John Frederick 1930- Who 92
**Mottram,** Norman James 1959- WhoWest 92
**Mottram,** Richard Clive 1946- Who 92
**Mottram,** Richard Donald, Jr. 1943- WhoRel 92
**Motts,** Ward Sundt 1924- AmMWSc 92
**Mottur,** George Preston 1950- AmMWSc 92
**Mottus,** Edward Hugo 1922- AmMWSc 92
**Motulsky,** Arno Gunther 1923- AmMWSc 92, IntWW 91
**Motupalli,** Satyanarayana 1928- WhoMW 92
**Motwani,** Nalini M AmMWSc 92
**Motycka,** Toby Gregg 1956- WhoMW 92
**Motyer,** John Alexander 1924- Who 92
**Motz,** Diana Gribbon 1943- WhoAmL 92
**Motz,** Henry Thomas 1923- AmMWSc 92
**Motz,** John Frederick 1942- WhoAmL 92
**Motz,** Joseph William 1918- AmMWSc 92
**Motz,** Kaye La Marr 1932- AmMWSc 92
**Motz,** Lloyd 1910- AmMWSc 92
**Motz,** Paul John 1950- WhoMW 92
**Motz,** Robin Owen 1939- AmMWSc 92
**Motz,** Simion 1926- WhoRel 92
**Motzel,** Jacqueline Mary 1936- WhoMW 92, WhoRel 92
**Motzer,** Paul D. WhoRel 92
**Motzkin,** Shirley M 1927- AmMWSc 92
**Mou,** Duen-Gang 1948- AmMWSc 92
**Mou,** Lan 1957- WhoWest 92
**Mouchly-Weiss,** Harriet 1942- WhoFI 92
**Mouchy,** Duchesse de 1935- WhoFI 92
**Mouck,** Norman Garrison, Jr. 1928- WhoWest 92
**Moudgil,** Brij Mohan 1945- AmMWSc 92
**Moudgil,** Virinder Kumar AmMWSc 92
**Mouery,** David Douglas 1958- WhoEnt 92
**Mouftah,** Hussein T 1947- AmMWSc 92
**Moughler,** John Harvey 1923- WhoAmP 91
**Mougianis,** Nick Anthony 1925- WhoMW 92
**Moujaes,** Samir Farid 1949- WhoWest 92
**Mouk,** Robert Watts 1940- AmMWSc 92
**Moukawsher,** Thomas G WhoAmP 91
**Moul,** Francis Dean 1940- WhoAmP 91
**Moul,** Maxine WhoMW 92
**Moul,** Maxine B WhoAmP 91
**Moul,** William Charles 1940- WhoAmL 92
**Moulay Hassan Ben El Mehdi** 1912- IntWW 91
**Moulaye,** Mohamed 1936- IntWW 91
**Mould,** Daphne 1920- WrDr 92
**Mould,** Daphne Desire Charlotte Pochin 1920- IntAu&W 91
**Mould,** Edwin WrDr 92
**Mould,** Richard A 1927- AmMWSc 92
**Moulden,** Trevor Holmes 1939- AmMWSc 92
**Moulder,** James William 1921- AmMWSc 92
**Moulder,** Jerry Wright 1942- AmMWSc 92
**Moulder,** Peter Vincent, Jr 1921- AmMWSc 92
**Moulder,** Victor ScFEYrs
**Moulder,** Wilton Arlyn 1931- WhoRel 92
**Moulds,** William Joseph 1933- AmMWSc 92
**Moule,** Charles Francis Digby 1908- IntWW 91, Who 92, WrDr 92
**Moule,** Claire Marie 1963- WhoFI 92
**Moule,** David 1933- AmMWSc 92
**Moulin,** Jean 1899-1943 FacFETw
**Moulins,** Max 1914- IntWW 91
**Moulis,** Edward Jean, Jr 1940- AmMWSc 92
**Moulton,** Alexander Eric 1920- IntWW 91, Who 92
**Moulton,** Arthur B 1920- AmMWSc 92
**Moulton,** Bruce Carl 1940- AmMWSc 92
**Moulton,** Carl TwCSFW 91
**Moulton,** Charles Wesley 1927- WhoMW 92
**Moulton,** Edward Q 1926- AmMWSc 92
**Moulton,** Grace Charbonnet 1923- AmMWSc 92
**Moulton,** Herbert F 1936- WhoIns 92
**Moulton,** Herbert L ScFEYrs
**Moulton,** Hugh Geoffrey 1933- WhoAmL 92, WhoFI 92
**Moulton,** James Frank, Jr 1921- AmMWSc 92
**Moulton,** James Louis 1906- Who 92, WrDr 92
**Moulton,** James Roger 1950- WhoFI 92
**Moulton,** Leslie Howard 1915- Who 92
**Moulton,** Linda Ann 1955- WhoFI 92
**Moulton,** Peter Franklin 1946- AmMWSc 92
**Moulton,** Phillips Prentice 1909- WhoRel 92
**Moulton,** Richard Way 1948- WhoRel 92
**Moulton,** Robert Henry 1925- AmMWSc 92
**Moulton,** Russell Dana 1965- AmMWSc 92
**Moulton,** William Alfred 1931- WhoWest 92
**Moulton,** William G 1925- AmMWSc 92
**Moulton,** William Scott 1953- WhoEnt 92
**Moultrie,** James Bertram 1944- IntWW 91
**Moultrie,** John Wesley, Jr. 1904- WhoMW 92
**Moultrie,** Roy D WhoAmP 91
**Moultrup,** James Patrick 1957- WhoWest 92
**Mouly,** Eileen Louise 1955- WhoFI 92
**Mouly,** Raymond J 1922- AmMWSc 92
**Moumin,** Amini Ali 1944- IntWW 91
**Mounajjed,** Moudacer Seif-El-Dine 1963- WhoMW 92
**Mounce,** Donald Arthur 1955- WhoMW 92
**Mound,** Fred 1932- IntMPA 92
**Mound,** Laurence Alfred 1934- Who 92
**Mound,** Trevor Ernest John 1930- Who 92
**Mounds,** Leona Mae Reed 1945- WhoWest 92
**Mounsey,** John Patrick David 1914- Who 92
**Mount,** Benjamin Wakefield 1949- WhoAmL 92
**Mount,** Bertha Lauritzen 1940- AmMWSc 92
**Mount,** Christopher John 1913- Who 92
**Mount,** David Allen 1943- WhoEnt 92
**Mount,** David William Alexander 1938- AmMWSc 92
**Mount,** Donald I 1931- AmMWSc 92
**Mount,** Eldridge Milford, III 1950- AmMWSc 92
**Mount,** Ferdinand Who 92
**Mount,** Ferdinand 1939- IntWW 91
**Mount,** Gary Arthur 1936- AmMWSc 92
**Mount,** James 1908- Who 92
**Mount,** John Brian 1958- WhoMW 92
**Mount,** John Meredith 1942- WhoFI 92
**Mount,** John Wallace 1946- WhoEnt 92, WhoWest 92
**Mount,** Karl A. 1945- WhoFI 92
**Mount,** Kenneth R 1933- AmMWSc 92
**Mount,** Lloyd Gordon 1916- AmMWSc 92
**Mount,** Margaret Elizabeth Doyle 1926- WhoRel 92
**Mount,** Mark Samuel 1940- AmMWSc 92
**Mount,** Paul 1922- TwCPaSc
**Mount,** Ramon Albert 1939- AmMWSc 92
**Mount,** Robert Hughes 1931- AmMWSc 92
**Mount,** Thom 1948- IntMPA 92
**Mount,** Thomas Henderson 1948- WhoEnt 92
**Mount,** William 1904- Who 92
**Mount,** William Robert Ferdinand 1939- IntAu&W 91, Who 92
**Mount Charles,** Earl of 1951- Who 92
**Mount Edgcumbe,** Earl of 1939- Who 92
**Mountain Wolf Woman** 1884-1960 RelLAm 91
**Mountain,** Clifton Fletcher 1924- AmMWSc 92
**Mountain,** David Charles, Jr 1946- AmMWSc 92
**Mountain,** Denis Mortimer 1929- Who 92
**Mountain,** Jon Keskula 1944- WhoEnt 92
**Mountain,** Joseph D & Gleason, C Sterling ScFEYrs
**Mountain,** Raymond Dale 1937- AmMWSc 92
**Mountbatten** Who 92
**Mountbatten,** Louis 1900-1979 ConAu 133, FacFETw [port]
**Mountbatten,** Richard ConAu 35NR
**Mountbatten of Burma,** Countess 1924- Who 92
**Mountcastle,** Kenneth Franklin, Jr. 1928- WhoFI 92
**Mountcastle,** Vernon Benjamin 1918- AmMWSc 92
**Mountcastle,** Vernon Benjamin, Jr. 1918- IntWW 91
**Mountcastle,** William R, Jr 1921- AmMWSc 92
**Mountcastle,** William Wallace, Jr. 1925- WhoRel 92
**Mounter,** Julian D'Arcy 1944- IntWW 91
**Mountevans,** Baron 1943- Who 92
**Mountfield,** David ConAu 34NR, WrDr 92
**Mountfield,** Peter 1935- Who 92
**Mountfield,** Robin 1939- Who 92
**Mountflorence,** James Cole 1745?-1817? DcNCBi 4
**Mountford,** Arnold Robert 1922- Who 92
**Mountford,** Kent 1938- AmMWSc 92
**Mountfort,** Guy Reginald 1905- Who 92
**Mountgarret,** Viscount 1936- Who 92
**Mountjoy,** Eric W 1931- AmMWSc 92
**Mountjoy,** Richard 1932- WhoAmP 91
**Mounts,** Richard Duane 1941- AmMWSc 92
**Mounts,** Timothy Lee 1937- AmMWSc 92
**Mounts,** William David 1959- WhoEnt 92
**Mountsier,** William Wallace 1932- WhoMW 92
**Mountstuart,** Lord 1989- Who 92
**Mountz,** Louise Carson Smith 1911- WhoMW 92
**Mountz,** Timothy Wilson 1955- WhoAmL 92
**Mountzoures,** H.L. DrAPF 91
**Moura,** Paul E 1956- WhoAmP 91
**Mourad,** A George 1931- AmMWSc 92
**Mourad,** Joumana 1954- TwCPaSc
**Mourant,** A. E. 1904- WrDr 92
**Mourant,** Arthur Ernest 1904- IntWW 91, Who 92
**Mourant,** Walter Byron 1910- WhoEnt 92
**Mourany,** Hamid Antoine WhoRel 92
**Mourdoukoutas,** Panos 1955- WhoFI 92
**Moure,** Erin 1955- ConPo 91
**Moureaux,** Philippe 1939- IntWW 91
**Mourek,** Joseph Edward 1910- WhoEnt 92
**Moureu,** Henri 1899-1978 FacFETw
**Mourgue,** Olivier 1939- DcTwDes
**Mouri,** Michael Patrick 1955- WhoWest 92
**Mouritsen,** T Edgar 1926- AmMWSc 92
**Mourning,** Michael Charles 1940- AmMWSc 92
**Mouron,** Adolphe Jean-Marie 1901-1968 DcTwDes
**Moursund,** Albert Wadel, III 1919- WhoAmL 92, WhoFI 92
**Moursund,** David G 1936- AmMWSc 92
**Moury,** John David 1960- AmMWSc 92
**Mouschovias,** Telemachos Charalambous 1945- AmMWSc 92
**Mousel,** Craig Lawrence 1947- WhoAmL 92
**Mousel,** Donald Kee 1932- WhoWest 92
**Moushegian,** George 1923- AmMWSc 92
**Moushoutas,** Constantine 1928- IntWW 91
**Mousnier,** Roland Emile 1907- IntWW 91
**Moussa,** Pierre L. 1922- IntWW 91
**Moussavi,** Mir Hussein 1942- IntWW 91
**Mousseau,** Doris Naomi Barton 1934- WhoMW 92
**Mousseau,** Phillip Jean 1938- WhoMW 92
**Moussorgsky** NewAmDM
**Moussouris,** Harry AmMWSc 92
**Moustakas,** Theodore D 1940- AmMWSc 92
**Moustiers,** Pierre Jean 1924- IntWW 91
**Mout,** Marianne Elisabeth Henriette N. 1945- IntWW 91
**Mouton,** Barbara Anne WhoBlA 92
**Mouton,** Charles Peter 1960- WhoBlA 92
**Mouton,** Jean 1459-1522 NewAmDM
**Moutoussamy,** John Warren 1922- WhoBlA 92
**Mouw,** David Richard 1942- AmMWSc 92
**Mouyassar,** James Jamil Redick 1960- WhoMW 92
**Mouzon,** Alphonse 1948- WhoEnt 92
**Mouzon,** Edwin DuBose 1869-1937 DcNCBi 4
**Mouzon,** Henry, Jr. 1741-1807 DcNCBi 4
**Movat,** Henry Zoltan 1923- AmMWSc 92
**Moverley,** Gerald Who 92
**Movius,** Geoffrey DrAPF 91
**Movius,** William Gust 1943- AmMWSc 92
**Movshon,** J Anthony 1950- AmMWSc 92
**Movshovitz,** Howard Paul 1944- WhoEnt 92
**Movsisian,** Vladimir Migranovich 1933- IntWW 91
**Movsisyan,** Vladimir Migranovich 1933- SovUnBD
**Mow,** C C 1930- AmMWSc 92
**Mow,** Maurice 1940- AmMWSc 92
**Mow,** Robert Henry, Jr. 1938- WhoAmL 92
**Mow,** Van C 1939- AmMWSc 92
**Mowat,** Barry Alan 1947- WhoEnt 92
**Mowat,** David 1943- WrDr 92
**Mowat,** David McIvor 1939- Who 92
**Mowat,** David William 1943- IntAu&W 91
**Mowat,** Farley 1921- BenetAL 91, WrDr 92
**Mowat,** Farley McGill 1921- IntAu&W 91, IntWW 91
**Mowat,** J Richard 1943- AmMWSc 92
**Mowat,** John Stuart 1923- Who 92
**Mowatt,** Anna BenetAL 91
**Mowatt,** Oswald Victor WhoBlA 92
**Mowatt,** Thomas C 1936- AmMWSc 92
**Mowatt,** Zeke 1961- WhoBlA 92
**Mowbray,** Baron 1923- Who 92
**Mowbray,** A.R. 1824-1875 DcLB 106
**Mowbray,** Donald F 1937- AmMWSc 92
**Mowbray,** John 1916- Who 92
**Mowbray,** John Code 1918- WhoAmL 92, WhoAmP 91, WhoWest 92
**Mowbray,** John Robert 1932- Who 92
**Mowbray,** Thomas Bruce 1940- AmMWSc 92
**Mowbray,** William John 1928- Who 92
**Mowell,** John Byard 1934- WhoFI 92
**Mowen,** Maryanne Myers 1948- WhoFI 92
**Mower,** Brian Leonard 1934- Who 92
**Mower,** Howard Frederick 1929- AmMWSc 92
**Mower,** Lyman 1927- AmMWSc 92
**Mower,** Robert G 1928- AmMWSc 92
**Mower,** Scarlett Sue 1941- WhoAmP 91
**Mowery,** Anna Renshaw 1931- WhoAmP 91
**Mowery,** Dwight Fay, Jr 1915- AmMWSc 92
**Mowery,** Harold F, Jr 1930- WhoAmP 91
**Mowery,** Michael William 1952- WhoAmL 92
**Mowery,** Morris Everett 1942- WhoAmP 91
**Mowery,** Norman Glenn 1947- WhoRel 92
**Mowery,** Richard Allen, Jr 1938- AmMWSc 92
**Mowery,** Robert Long 1934- WhoRel 92
**Mowery,** William Byron 1899-1957 TwCWW 91
**Mowitz,** Arnold Martin 1923- AmMWSc 92
**Mowl,** Colin John 1947- Who 92
**Mowlam,** Marjorie 1949- Who 92
**Mowle,** Frederic J 1937- AmMWSc 92
**Mowles,** Thomas Francis 1934- AmMWSc 92
**Mowll,** Christopher Martyn 1932- Who 92
**Mowrer,** Edgar Ansel 1892-1971 AmPeW
**Mowrer,** Gordon Brown 1936- WhoAmP 91
**Mowrer,** Lilian Thomson 1889?-1990 CurBio 91N
**Mowrer,** Paul Scott 1887-1971 AmPeW, BenetAL 91
**Mowrey,** Gary Lee 1947- AmMWSc 92
**Mowrey,** Timothy James 1958- WhoFI 92
**Mowrey,** Valla Bryan, Jr. 1935- WhoAmL 92
**Mowry,** David Thomas 1917- AmMWSc 92
**Mowry,** George Barton 1952- WhoAmL 92
**Mowry,** Jess 1960- ConAu 133
**Mowry,** John L. 1905- WhoMW 92
**Mowry,** Robert Wilbur 1923- AmMWSc 92
**Mowry,** Samuel Orin 1923- WhoAmP 91
**Mowshowitz,** Abbe 1939- AmMWSc 92
**Moxham,** Douglas Grant 1942- WhoAmL 92
**Moxley,** Frank O. 1908- WhoBlA 92
**Moxley,** John H, III 1935- AmMWSc 92
**Moxley,** John Howard, III 1935- IntWW 91, WhoAmP 91
**Moxley,** Joseph M. DrAPF 91
**Moxley,** Robert Thomas 1953- WhoAmL 92
**Moxness,** Karen AmMWSc 92
**Moxon,** Alvin Lloyd 1909- WhoMW 92
**Moxon,** Edward 1801-1858 DcLB 106
**Moxon,** Edward, Son, and Company DcLB 106
**Moxon,** Edward Richard 1941- Who 92
**Moxon,** James 1920- WrDr 92
**Moxon,** John Sawyer 1939- WhoFI 92
**Moxon,** Michael Anthony 1942- Who 92
**Moxon,** Richard 1941- IntWW 91
**Moxon Browne,** Robert William 1946- Who 92
**Moy,** Celeste Marie 1950- WhoBlA 92
**Moy,** Curt Wayne 1961- WhoAmL 92
**Moy,** Dan 1955- AmMWSc 92
**Moy,** James Hee 1929- AmMWSc 92
**Moy,** Mamie Wong 1929- AmMWSc 92
**Moy,** Richard Henry 1931- AmMWSc 92
**Moy,** Russell Glenn 1953- WhoRel 92
**Moy,** Stephen David 1966- WhoFI 92
**Moy,** William A 1931- AmMWSc 92
**Moya,** Hidalgo 1920- IntWW 91, Who 92
**Moya,** P. Robert 1944- WhoHisp 92
**Moya,** Patrick Robert 1944- WhoAmL 92
**Moya,** Sara Dreier 1945- WhoWest 92
**Moya Palencia,** Mario 1933- IntWW 91
**Moye,** Anthony Joseph 1933- AmMWSc 92, WhoWest 92
**Moye,** Carla Johnson 1955- WhoBlA 92
**Moye,** Donald Wayne 1950- WhoRel 92
**Moye,** Eric Vaughn 1954- WhoAmL 92
**Moye,** Hugh Anson 1938- AmMWSc 92
**Moye,** James M 1921- WhoAmP 91
**Moye,** Judy Henley 1944- WhoAmP 91
**Moye,** Ulysses Grant, II 1942- WhoRel 92
**Moyed,** Dean 1969- WhoEnt 92
**Moyed,** Harris S 1925- AmMWSc 92
**Moyer,** Alan Dean 1928- WhoWest 92
**Moyer,** Arthur Lynn 1938- WhoMW 92
**Moyer,** Bruce A 1952- AmMWSc 92
**Moyer,** Bruce Eugene 1953- WhoRel 92
**Moyer,** Bruce Frederick 1950- WhoEnt 92
**Moyer,** Calvin Lyle 1941- AmMWSc 92
**Moyer,** Carl Edward 1926- AmMWSc 92
**Moyer,** Charles Milton 1937- WhoRel 92

**Moyer,** Craig Alan 1955- *WhoAmL 92, WhoWest 92*
**Moyer,** David S. 1952- *WhoFI 92*
**Moyer,** Dean La Roche 1925- *AmMWSc 92*
**Moyer,** Denise Joy DeGeorge 1963- *WhoMW 92*
**Moyer,** Geoffrey H 1938- *AmMWSc 92*
**Moyer,** Glenn Roydon 1929- *WhoAmP 91*
**Moyer,** H C 1918- *AmMWSc 92*
**Moyer,** Harlan Ernest 1926- *WhoFI 92, WhoWest 92*
**Moyer,** Holley Marker 1947- *WhoAmL 92*
**Moyer,** Homer Edward, Jr. 1942- *WhoAmL 92*
**Moyer,** James Carroll 1941- *WhoRel 92*
**Moyer,** James D. 1949- *WhoAmL 92*
**Moyer,** James Robert 1942- *AmMWSc 92*
**Moyer,** Jay Edward 1940- *WhoAmL 92*
**Moyer,** Jennifer *DrAPF 91*
**Moyer,** Jerry Mills 1940- *WhoFI 92*
**Moyer,** John A *WhoAmP 91*
**Moyer,** John Allen 1951- *AmMWSc 92*
**Moyer,** John Clarence 1946- *AmMWSc 92*
**Moyer,** John Henry 1919- *AmMWSc 92*
**Moyer,** John Raymond 1931- *AmMWSc 92*
**Moyer,** K. E. 1919- *WrDr 92*
**Moyer,** Kenneth Evan 1919- *AmMWSc 92*
**Moyer,** Kenneth Harold 1929- *AmMWSc 92*
**Moyer,** Leroy 1942- *AmMWSc 92*
**Moyer,** Margaret Ellen Dempsey 1938- *WhoRel 92*
**Moyer,** Mark Henry 1955- *WhoRel 92*
**Moyer,** Mary Pat Sutter 1951- *AmMWSc 92*
**Moyer,** Melvin Isaac 1921- *AmMWSc 92*
**Moyer,** Patricia Helen 1927- *AmMWSc 92*
**Moyer,** Ralph Owen, Jr 1936- *AmMWSc 92*
**Moyer,** Ray Allen 1946- *WhoEnt 92*
**Moyer,** Raymond J *WhoAmP 91*
**Moyer,** Rex Carlton 1935- *AmMWSc 92*
**Moyer,** Richard W 1940- *AmMWSc 92*
**Moyer,** Robert 1937- *AmMWSc 92*
**Moyer,** Samuel Edward 1934- *AmMWSc 92*
**Moyer,** Thomas 1939- *WhoAmP 91*
**Moyer,** Thomas E 1952- *WhoAmP 91*
**Moyer,** Thomas J. 1939- *WhoAmL 92, WhoMW 92*
**Moyer,** Vance Edwards 1914- *AmMWSc 92*
**Moyer,** Walter Allen, Jr 1922- *AmMWSc 92*
**Moyer,** Wayne A 1930- *AmMWSc 92*
**Moyer,** William C, Jr 1937- *AmMWSc 92*
**Moyerman,** Robert Max 1925- *AmMWSc 92*
**Moyers,** Bill 1934- *IntMPA 92, News 91 [port]*
**Moyers,** Bill D. *LesBEnT 92 [port]*
**Moyers,** Bill D. 1934- *IntWW 91, Who 92*
**Moyers,** Jack 1921- *AmMWSc 92*
**Moyers,** Jarvis Lee 1943- *AmMWSc 92*
**Moyers,** Robert M. 1948- *WhoAmL 92*
**Moyers,** Sam 1939- *WhoMW 92*
**Moyers,** William Taylor 1916- *WhoWest 92*
**Moyersoen,** Ludovic Marie Odilon 1904- *IntWW 91*
**Moyes,** Gertrude Patricia 1923- *IntAu&W 91*
**Moyes,** Henry 1750-1807 *BiInAmS*
**Moyes,** Kenneth Jack 1918- *Who 92*
**Moyes,** Patricia 1923- *WrDr 92*
**Moylan,** David 1915- *Who 92*
**Moylan,** James E., Jr. 1951- *WhoFI 92*
**Moylan,** James Harold 1930- *WhoAmP 91*
**Moylan,** James Joseph 1948- *WhoAmL 92*
**Moylan,** Kurt S 1939- *WhoAmP 91*
**Moylan,** Stephen Craig 1952- *WhoMW 92*
**Moyle,** Bennett Isaac 1946- *WhoFI 92*
**Moyle,** Colin James 1929- *IntWW 91*
**Moyle,** David Douglas 1942- *AmMWSc 92*
**Moyle,** Oscar Wood, III 1938- *WhoAmL 92, WhoFI 92*
**Moyle,** Peter Briggs 1942- *AmMWSc 92*
**Moyle,** Richard W 1930- *AmMWSc 92*
**Moyle,** Roland 1928- *Who 92*
**Moyler,** Freeman William, Jr. 1931- *WhoBlA 92*
**Moyles,** Lois *DrAPF 91*
**Moyls,** Benjamin Nelson 1919- *AmMWSc 92*
**Moynahan,** John Daniel, Jr. 1935- *WhoFI 92*
**Moynahan,** Julian 1925- *WrDr 92*
**Moynahan,** Molly 1957- *ConAu 133*
**Moynahan,** Thomas A 1938- *WhoAmP 91*
**Moyne,** Baron 1905- *IntWW 91, Who 92*
**Moyne,** John Abel 1920- *AmMWSc 92*
**Moynet,** Andre 1921- *IntWW 91*
**Moynihan** *Who 92*
**Moynihan,** Baron 1936- *Who 92*
**Moynihan,** Colin Berkeley 1955- *IntWW 91, Who 92*
**Moynihan,** Cornelius Timothy 1939- *AmMWSc 92*
**Moynihan,** Daniel Patrick 1927- *AlmAP 92 [port], AmPolLe, FacFETw, IntAu&W 91, IntWW 91, Who 92, WhoAmP 91, WrDr 92*
**Moynihan,** David Stanton 1942- *WhoWest 92*
**Moynihan,** George Edward 1927- *WhoEnt 92*
**Moynihan,** James Francis 1952- *WhoAmP 91*
**Moynihan,** John Bignell 1933- *WhoAmL 92*
**Moynihan,** John Dominic 1932- *IntAu&W 91, WrDr 92*
**Moynihan,** Kenneth James 1944- *WhoAmP 91*
**Moynihan,** Martin Humphrey 1928- *AmMWSc 92*
**Moynihan,** Martin John 1916- *Who 92*
**Moynihan,** Maurice 1902- *WrDr 92*
**Moynihan,** Noel 1916- *Who 92*
**Moynihan,** Rodrigo d1990 *IntWW 91N, Who 92N*
**Moynihan,** Rodrigo 1910- *TwCPaSc*
**Moynihan,** Rodrigo 1910-1990 *AnObit 1990*
**Moynihan,** Rosemary 1943- *WhoAmP 91*
**Moynihan,** Timothy 1941- *WhoAmP 91*
**Moyola,** Baron 1923- *IntWW 91, Who 92*
**Moyse,** Alexis 1912- *IntWW 91*
**Moyse,** Louis 1912- *NewAmDM*
**Moyse,** Marcel 1889-1984 *NewAmDM*
**Moyser,** George H. 1945- *ConAu 134*
**Moyski,** Stephen Marek 1965- *WhoWest 92*
**Moyssiadis,** James David 1948- *WhoEnt 92*
**Mozart,** Leopold 1719-1787 *NewAmDM*
**Mozart,** Wolfgang Amadeus 1756-1791 *BlkwCEP [port], NewAmDM*
**Mozden,** Stanley Walter, Jr 1940- *WhoAmP 91*
**Mozell,** Maxwell Mark 1929- *AmMWSc 92*
**Mozena,** John Daniel 1956- *WhoWest 92*
**Mozer,** Bernard 1925- *AmMWSc 92*
**Mozer,** Forrest S 1929- *AmMWSc 92*
**Mozer,** Paul W. *NewYTBS 91 [port]*
**Mozersky,** Samuel M 1924- *AmMWSc 92*
**Mozeson,** Isaac Elchanan *DrAPF 91*
**Mozgovoi,** Ivan Alekseyevich 1927- *IntWW 91*
**Mozhaev,** Pavel Petrovich 1930- *IntWW 91*
**Mozhayev,** Boris Andreyevich 1923- *IntWW 91*
**Mozingo,** Hugh Nelson 1925- *AmMWSc 92*
**Mozley,** James Marshall, Jr 1922- *AmMWSc 92*
**Mozley,** Patricia Joann 1948- *WhoMW 92*
**Mozley,** Robert Fred 1917- *AmMWSc 92*
**Mozley,** Samuel Clifford 1943- *AmMWSc 92*
**Mozumder,** Asokendu 1931- *AmMWSc 92*
**Mozurkewich,** George 1953- *AmMWSc 92*
**Mozzi,** Robert Lewis 1931- *AmMWSc 92*
**Mpetha,** Oscar 1909- *IntWW 91*
**Mphahlele,** Es'kia 1919- *ConNov 91, IntWW 91, LiExTwC*
**Mphahlele,** Ezekiel *DrAPF 91*
**Mphahlele,** Ezekiel 1919- *BlkLC [port], IntAu&W 91, WrDr 92*
**M'Pherson,** Philip Keith 1927- *Who 92*
**Mpinga Kasenda** 1937- *IntWW 91*
**Mpuchane,** Samuel Akuna 1943- *IntWW 91, Who 92*
**Mqhayi,** S.E.K. 1875-1945 *BlkLC*
**Mr. X** *ScFEYrs*
**Mracky,** Ronald Sydney 1932- *WhoFI 92, WhoWest 92*
**Mramor,** James Plummer 1943- *WhoMW 92*
**Mravinsky,** Yevgeniy Aleksandrovich 1903-1988 *SovUnBD*
**Mravinsky,** Yevgeny Alexandrovich 1903-1988 *FacFETw*
**Mraw,** Stephen Charles 1950- *AmMWSc 92*
**Mrazek,** James E. 1914- *WrDr 92*
**Mrazek,** Robert J. 1945- *AlmAP 92 [port], WhoAmP 91*
**Mrazek,** Robert Vernon 1936- *AmMWSc 92*
**Mrazek,** Rudolph G 1922- *AmMWSc 92*
**Mrkonic,** Emil *WhoAmP 91*
**Mrkonic,** George Ralph, Jr. 1952- *WhoFI 92*
**Mrkonich,** Marko J. 1954- *WhoAmL 92*
**Mroczkowski,** Stanley 1925- *AmMWSc 92*
**Mrotek,** James Joseph 1939- *AmMWSc 92*
**Mroudjae,** Ali *IntWW 91*
**Mrouweh,** Adnan 1936- *IntWW 91*
**Mrovka,** David Anthony 1949- *WhoRel 92*
**Mrowca,** Jerome 1949- *WhoAmL 92*
**Mrowca,** Joseph J 1939- *AmMWSc 92*
**Mroz,** Kenneth S. 1954- *WhoAmL 92*
**Mrozek,** Slawomir 1930- *IntWW 91, LiExTwC*
**Mrozik,** Helmut 1931- *AmMWSc 92*
**Mrozinski,** Peter Matthew 1947- *AmMWSc 92*
**Mrtek,** Robert George 1940- *AmMWSc 92*
**Mruk,** Eugene Robert 1927- *WhoFI 92*
**Mrvan,** Frank, Jr *WhoAmP 91*
**Mshonaji,** Bibi 1939- *WhoBlA 92*
**Msuya,** Cleopa David 1931- *IntWW 91*
**Mtawali,** Bernard Brenm 1935- *Who 92*
**Mtei,** Edwin Isaac Mbiliewi 1932- *IntWW 91*
**Mtekateka,** Josiah 1903- *Who 92*
**Mtoto,** Pepo 1935- *WhoBlA 92*
**Mtshali,** Mbuyiseni Oswald Joseph 1940- *LiExTwC*
**Mtshali,** Oswald 1940- *ConPo 91, WrDr 92*
**Mu Guiying** *EncAmaz 91*
**Mu Qing** 1921- *IntWW 91*
**Mu,** Albert T. 1959- *WhoWest 92*
**Mua'au,** Aulava *WhoAmP 91*
**Mualla,** Rashid bin Ahmad Al 1930- *IntWW 91*
**Muamba,** Muepu 1946- *IntAu&W 91*
**Muan,** Arnulf 1923- *AmMWSc 92*
**Mubako,** Simbi Veke 1936- *IntWW 91*
**Mubarak,** Hosni 1928- *FacFETw [port], IntWW 91, News 91 [port]*
**Mucci,** Joseph Francis *AmMWSc 92*
**Mucci,** Richard Joseph 1950- *WhoWest 92*
**Muccia,** Joseph William 1948- *WhoFI 92*
**Mucciano,** Stephanie Lyons 1944- *WhoFI 92*
**Muccilli,** Jay Edward 1941- *WhoWest 92*
**Muce,** Paul Maximilian 1940- *WhoWest 92*
**Mucenieks,** Paul Raimond 1921- *AmMWSc 92*
**Mucha,** Alphonse 1860-1939 *DcTwDes*
**Mucha,** Jiri 1915- *IntAu&W 91, WrDr 92*
**Mucha,** Jiri 1915-1991 *ConAu 134*
**Mucha,** Patty *DrAPF 91*
**Mucha,** Susan Elizabeth 1958- *WhoWest 92*
**Muchin,** Arden Archie 1920- *WhoAmL 92*
**Muchmore,** Harold Gordon 1920- *AmMWSc 92*
**Muchmore,** John Michael 1936- *WhoMW 92*
**Muchmore,** Robert B 1917- *AmMWSc 92*
**Muchmore,** William Breuleux 1920- *AmMWSc 92*
**Muchovej,** James John 1953- *AmMWSc 92*
**Muchow,** Gordon Mark 1921- *AmMWSc 92*
**Muchow,** Reinhold 1905-1933 *EncTR 91 [port]*
**Muchowski,** Joseph Martin 1937- *AmMWSc 92*
**Muck,** Darrel Lee 1938- *AmMWSc 92*
**Muck,** David Wesley 1939- *WhoRel 92*
**Muck,** George A 1937- *AmMWSc 92*
**Muck,** Karl 1859-1940 *NewAmDM*
**Muck,** Terry Charles 1947- *WhoRel 92*
**Muckelroy,** William Lawrence 1945- *WhoBlA 92*
**Muckenfuss,** Cantwell Faulkner, III 1945- *WhoAmL 92*
**Muckenfuss,** Charles 1927- *AmMWSc 92*
**Muckenhoupt,** Benjamin 1933- *AmMWSc 92*
**Muckenthaler,** Florian August 1933- *AmMWSc 92*
**Muckerheide,** Annette *AmMWSc 92*
**Muckerman,** Ann *WhoRel 92*
**Muckerman,** Norman James 1917- *WhoRel 92*
**Muckler,** Carl Henry 1941- *WhoAmP 91*
**Mucowski,** Richard John 1944- *WhoRel 92*
**Mudarra,** Alonso 1510?-1580 *NewAmDM*
**Mudawar,** Issam 1955- *WhoMW 92*
**Mudd,** David 1933- *Who 92*
**Mudd,** Emily H. 1898- *WrDr 92*
**Mudd,** J Gerard 1921- *AmMWSc 92*
**Mudd,** John Brian 1929- *AmMWSc 92*
**Mudd,** John Philip 1932- *WhoAmL 92, WhoFI 92*
**Mudd,** Louis L. 1943- *WhoBlA 92*
**Mudd,** Michael Sidney 1951- *WhoMW 92*
**Mudd,** Roger *LesBEnT 92*
**Mudd,** Roger 1928- *IntMPA 92*
**Mudd,** Roger Harrison 1928- *IntWW 91*
**Mudd,** Stephen Wayne 1949- *WhoMW 92*
**Mudd,** Stuart Harvey 1927- *AmMWSc 92*
**Mudd,** Susan Elizabeth 1955- *WhoEnt 92*
**Mudd,** Therese M 1931- *WhoAmP 91*
**Muddersnook,** Blyde, Professor *ScFEYrs*
**Muddy Waters** 1915- *NewAmDM*
**Muddy Waters** 1915-1983 *FacFETw*
**Mudenda,** Elijah Haatukali Kaiba 1927- *IntWW 91*
**Mudenge,** Isack Stanislaus Gorerazvo 1941- *IntWW 91*
**Muderick,** Michael 1946- *WhoEnt 92*
**Mudge,** Benjamin Franklin 1817-1879 *BiInAmS*
**Mudge,** Dirk *IntWW 91*
**Mudge,** Gilbert Horton 1915- *AmMWSc 92*
**Mudge,** Lewis Seymour 1929- *WhoRel 92*
**Mudge,** Michael Allen 1958- *WhoRel 92*
**Mudgett,** Theresa Inez 1952- *WhoAmP 91*
**Mudholkar,** Govind S 1934- *AmMWSc 92*
**Mudie,** Ian 1911-1976 *ConAu 135*
**Mudrey,** Michael George, Jr 1945- *AmMWSc 92*
**Mudroch,** Alena 1930- *AmMWSc 92*
**Mudry,** Karen Michele 1948- *AmMWSc 92*
**Mudry,** Michael 1926- *WhoFI 92*
**Muecke,** Charles Andrew 1918- *WhoWest 92*
**Muecke,** Herbert Oscar 1940- *AmMWSc 92*
**Mueckler,** Mike Max 1953- *AmMWSc 92*
**Muegel,** Glenn Allen 1934- *WhoEnt 92*
**Muegge,** Paul 1936- *WhoAmP 91*
**Mueggler,** Walter Frank 1926- *AmMWSc 92*
**Mueh,** Hans Juergen 1944- *WhoWest 92*
**Muehl,** Lois Baker 1920- *IntAu&W 91, WrDr 92*
**Muehlbauer,** James Herman 1940- *WhoFI 92*
**Muehlbauer,** Renice Ann 1947- *WhoWest 92*
**Muehlbauer,** Stephen Leslie 1949- *WhoIns 92*
**Muehlberger,** William Rudolf 1923- *AmMWSc 92*
**Muehlenberg,** Ekkehard Friedrich Wilhelm 1938- *WhoRel 92*
**Muehlenberg,** Heinrich Melchior 1711-1787 *DcAmImH*
**Muehling,** Arthur J 1928- *AmMWSc 92*
**Muehrcke,** Robert C 1921- *AmMWSc 92*
**Mueller,** Alfred H 1939- *AmMWSc 92*
**Mueller,** Allan George 1942- *WhoAmP 91*
**Mueller,** Andrew Gerard 1961- *WhoMW 92*
**Mueller,** Anne Elisabeth 1930- *Who 92*
**Mueller,** Anne O'Quin 1929- *WhoAmP 91*
**Mueller,** August P 1933- *AmMWSc 92*
**Mueller,** Bernard 1950- *WhoMW 92*
**Mueller,** Bonnie Mae 1944- *WhoWest 92*
**Mueller,** Bruno J W 1934- *AmMWSc 92*
**Mueller,** Carl Richard 1931- *WhoEnt 92*
**Mueller,** Charles Carsten 1937- *AmMWSc 92*
**Mueller,** Charles Frederick 1939- *AmMWSc 92*
**Mueller,** Charles Leonard 1939- *WhoAmP 91*
**Mueller,** Charles Richard 1925- *AmMWSc 92*
**Mueller,** Charles W 1912- *AmMWSc 92*
**Mueller,** Charles William 1938- *WhoFI 92*
**Mueller,** Claus 1941- *WhoEnt 92*
**Mueller,** Dale M J 1939- *AmMWSc 92*
**Mueller,** David Livingstone 1929- *WhoRel 92*
**Mueller,** Delbert Dean 1933- *AmMWSc 92*
**Mueller,** Dennis *AmMWSc 92*
**Mueller,** Dennis W 1949- *AmMWSc 92*
**Mueller,** Diane Mayne 1934- *WhoAmL 92*
**Mueller,** Don Sheridan 1927- *WhoMW 92*
**Mueller,** Donald Dean 1937- *WhoWest 92*
**Mueller,** Edward E 1924- *AmMWSc 92*
**Mueller,** Francis E. *WhoRel 92*
**Mueller,** Fred Michael 1938- *AmMWSc 92*
**Mueller,** Gail Delories 1957- *WhoWest 92*
**Mueller,** Gary Alfred 1950- *WhoWest 92*
**Mueller,** Gene Leon 1950- *WhoRel 92*
**Mueller,** George Bernard 1939- *WhoMW 92*
**Mueller,** George E 1918- *AmMWSc 92, IntWW 91*
**Mueller,** George Peter 1918- *AmMWSc 92*
**Mueller,** Gerald Conrad 1920- *AmMWSc 92*
**Mueller,** Gerd Dieter 1936- *WhoFI 92*
**Mueller,** Gerhard G. 1930- *ConAu 36NR*
**Mueller,** Harold 1920- *WhoEnt 92*
**Mueller,** Helmut 1926- *AmMWSc 92*
**Mueller,** Helmut Charles 1931- *AmMWSc 92*
**Mueller,** Henrietta Waters 1915- *WhoWest 92*
**Mueller,** Henry Edward 1946- *WhoAmL 92*
**Mueller,** Herbert Adolph 1914- *WhoRel 92*
**Mueller,** Hiltrud S 1926- *AmMWSc 92*
**Mueller,** Inez Lee 1916- *WhoAmP 91*
**Mueller,** Irene Marian 1904- *AmMWSc 92*
**Mueller,** Ivan I 1930- *AmMWSc 92*
**Mueller,** James Paul 1954- *WhoWest 92*
**Mueller,** Jeffrey Guy 1954- *WhoMW 92*
**Mueller,** Joerg 1942- *SmATA 67*
**Mueller,** John Alfred 1906- *WhoRel 92*
**Mueller,** John Frederick 1922- *AmMWSc 92*

**Mueller**, John Frederick Jack 1941- *WhoAmP 91*
**Mueller**, John McKay 1955- *WhoFI 92*
**Mueller**, John Nicholas 1951- *WhoEnt 92*
**Mueller**, Justus Frederick 1902- *AmMWSc 92*
**Mueller**, Karl Alexander 1927- *AmMWSc 92*
**Mueller**, Karl Hugo, Jr 1943- *AmMWSc 92*
**Mueller**, Kimberly Sue 1960- *WhoWest 92*
**Mueller**, Linda Carol 1957- *WhoMW 92*
**Mueller**, Lisa Marie 1966- *WhoMW 92*
**Mueller**, Lisel *DrAPF 91*
**Mueller**, Lisel 1924- *WrDr 92*
**Mueller**, Mark Christopher 1945- *WhoAmL 92*
**Mueller**, Marnie *DrAPF 91*
**Mueller**, Marvin Martin 1928- *AmMWSc 92*
**Mueller**, Mary Kay 1953- *WhoRel 92*
**Mueller**, Melinda *DrAPF 91*
**Mueller**, Melvin H 1918- *AmMWSc 92*
**Mueller**, Merrill *LesBEnT 92*
**Mueller**, Michael Lewis 1952- *WhoFI 92*
**Mueller**, Nancy Schneider 1933- *AmMWSc 92*
**Mueller**, Paul Allen 1945- *AmMWSc 92*
**Mueller**, Paul Henry 1917- *WhoFI 92*
**Mueller**, Paulette 1953- *WhoAmL 92*
**Mueller**, Peggy Jean 1952- *WhoEnt 92*
**Mueller**, Peter Klaus 1926- *AmMWSc 92*
**Mueller**, Raymond Jay 1959- *WhoWest 92*
**Mueller**, Raymond Karl 1941- *AmMWSc 92*
**Mueller**, Raymond Terence 1947- *WhoAmL 92*
**Mueller**, Reid Vance 1960- *WhoWest 92*
**Mueller**, Reuben Herbert 1897-1982 *RelLAm 91*
**Mueller**, Richard Allan 1961- *WhoFI 92*
**Mueller**, Richard Edward 1927- *WhoAmL 92*
**Mueller**, Rita Marie 1918- *AmMWSc 92*
**Mueller**, Robert Andrew 1952- *AmMWSc 92*
**Mueller**, Robert Arthur 1938- *AmMWSc 92*
**Mueller**, Robert Emmett 1925- *IntAu&W 91, WrDr 92*
**Mueller**, Robert Kirk 1913- *AmMWSc 92*
**Mueller**, Robert Swan, III 1944- *WhoAmP 91*
**Mueller**, Rolf Karl 1914- *AmMWSc 92*
**Mueller**, Ronald James 1935- *WhoMW 92*
**Mueller**, Roy Clement 1930- *WhoEnt 92, WhoFI 92*
**Mueller**, Sabina Gertrude 1940- *AmMWSc 92*
**Mueller**, Shirley Anne 1950- *WhoFI 92*
**Mueller**, Stephen Neil 1947- *AmMWSc 92*
**Mueller**, Theodore Arnold 1938- *AmMWSc 92*
**Mueller**, Theodore Rolf 1928- *AmMWSc 92*
**Mueller**, Thomas J 1934- *AmMWSc 92*
**Mueller**, Thomas Joseph 1946- *AmMWSc 92*
**Mueller**, Virginia Rumely 1949- *WhoMW 92*
**Mueller**, Walt 1925- *WhoAmP 91*
**Mueller**, Walter Carl 1934- *AmMWSc 92*
**Mueller**, Walter L 1930- *WhoIns 92*
**Mueller**, Wayne Paul 1933- *AmMWSc 92*
**Mueller**, Wendelin Henry, III 1941- *AmMWSc 92*
**Mueller**, Wendy Ann 1963- *WhoFI 92*
**Mueller**, Werner Diebolt 1925- *WhoMW 92*
**Mueller**, Willard Fritz 1925- *WhoFI 92, WhoMW 92*
**Mueller**, William Ludwig 1951- *WhoAmL 92*
**Mueller**, William M 1917- *AmMWSc 92*
**Mueller**, William R. 1916- *WrDr 92*
**Mueller**, Willys Francis, Jr. 1934- *WhoMW 92*
**Mueller-Dombois**, Dieter 1925- *AmMWSc 92*
**Muellner**, John Phillip 1936- *WhoMW 92*
**Muench**, Aloisius 1889-1962 *RelLAm 91*
**Muench**, Donald Leo 1934- *AmMWSc 92*
**Muench**, Karl Hugo 1934- *AmMWSc 92*
**Muench**, Linda Jo 1943- *WhoEnt 92*
**Muench**, Nils Lilienberg 1928- *AmMWSc 92*
**Muench**, Paul Georg 1877- *ScFEYrs*
**Muench**, Robin Davie 1942- *AmMWSc 92*
**Muendel**, Carl H 1930- *AmMWSc 92*
**Muendel**, Hans-Henning 1942- *AmMWSc 92*
**Muenich**, George Raynor 1939- *WhoRel 92*
**Muenow**, David W 1939- *AmMWSc 92*
**Muenster**, Karen *WhoAmP 91*
**Muentener**, Donald Arthur 1926- *AmMWSc 92*
**Muenter**, Annabel Adams 1944- *AmMWSc 92*
**Muenter**, John Stuart 1938- *AmMWSc 92*
**Muenzenberger**, Thomas Bourque 1943- *AmMWSc 92, WhoMW 92*
**Muesing-Ellwood**, Edith E. *DrAPF 91*
**Muessen**, Henry J. d1991 *NewYTBS 91*
**Muessig**, Paul Henry 1949- *AmMWSc 92*
**Muessig**, Siegfried 1922- *WhoWest 92*
**Muessig**, Siegfried Joseph 1922- *AmMWSc 92*
**Muether**, Herbert Robert 1921- *AmMWSc 92*
**Mueting**, Ann Marie 1956- *AmMWSc 92*
**Muezzinoglu**, Ziya 1919- *IntWW 91*
**Muff** *Who 92*
**Muff**, Stephen Carl 1962- *WhoFI 92*
**Muffat**, Georg 1653-1704 *NewAmDM*
**Muffat**, Gottlieb 1690-1770 *NewAmDM*
**Muffler**, Leroy John Patrick 1937- *AmMWSc 92*
**Muffley**, Harry Chilton 1921- *AmMWSc 92*
**Mufson**, Daniel 1942- *AmMWSc 92*
**Mufson**, R Allan 1946- *AmMWSc 92*
**Mufson**, Stuart Lee 1946- *AmMWSc 92*
**Mufti**, Izhar H 1931- *AmMWSc 92*
**Mufti**, Siraj I. 1938- *WhoWest 92*
**Muftic**, Michael 1933- *WhoAmP 91*
**Muga**, Marvin Luis 1932- *AmMWSc 92*
**Mugabe**, Robert 1924- *FacFETw [port]*
**Mugabe**, Robert Gabriel 1924- *IntWW 91, Who 92*
**Mugabi**, John *BlkOlyM*
**Mugalian**, Richard Aram 1922- *WhoAmP 91*
**Mugan**, Daniel Joseph 1933- *WhoHisp 92*
**Mugavero**, Francis J. 1914-1991 *NewYTBS 91 [port]*
**Mugford**, Alfred George 1928- *WhoFI 92*
**Mugge**, Joel Dalton 1946- *WhoMW 92*
**Muggenburg**, Bruce Al 1937- *AmMWSc 92, WhoWest 92*
**Muggeridge**, Derek Brian 1943- *AmMWSc 92*
**Muggeridge**, Malcolm d1990 *IntWW 91N, Who 92N*
**Muggeridge**, Malcolm 1903-1990 *AnObit 1990, CurBio 91N, FacFETw*
**Muggeson**, Margaret Elizabeth 1942- *IntAu&W 91, WrDr 92*
**Muggli**, Agatha 1943- *WhoMW 92*
**Muggli**, Robert Zeno 1929- *AmMWSc 92*
**Muggs**, J. Fred *LesBEnT 92*
**Mughabghab**, Said F 1934- *AmMWSc 92*
**Mughni**, Mohammad A. Riaz 1950- *WhoMW 92*
**Mugica**, Richard *WhoHisp 92*
**Mugica Herzog**, Enrique 1932- *IntWW 91*
**Mugler**, Dale H 1948- *AmMWSc 92*
**Mugler**, Frederick, Jr. *DrAPF 91*
**Mugler**, Larry George 1946- *WhoWest 92*
**Mugler**, Thierry 1946- *IntWW 91*
**Mugnaini**, Enrico 1937- *AmMWSc 92*
**Mugno**, Christina Marie 1946- *WhoEnt 92*
**Mugnozza**, Carlo S. *Who 92*
**Muguruza**, Francisco J. *WhoHisp 92*
**Mugwira**, Luke Makore 1940- *AmMWSc 92*
**Muhajir**, El *DrAPF 91*
**Muhammad**, Ali Nasser 1939- *IntWW 91*
**Muhammad**, Angel Saladdin Abdullah 1941- *WhoEnt 92*
**Muhammad**, Askiaa 1945- *WhoBlA 92*
**Muhammad**, Elijah 1897-1975 *FacFETw [port], RelLAm 91*
**Muhammad**, M. Akbar 1951- *WhoBlA 92*
**Muhammad**, Marita 1943- *WhoBlA 92*
**Muhammad**, Raquel Annissa 1932- *WhoWest 92*
**Muhammad**, Shirley M. 1938- *WhoBlA 92*
**Muhammad**, Wallace D. 1933- *WhoBlA 92, WhoRel 92*
**Muhammad**, Warith Deen 1933- *WhoBlA 92*
**Muhammadullah** 1921- *IntWW 91*
**Muheim**, Franz Emmanuel 1931- *IntWW 91, Who 92*
**Muhieddin** *IntWW 91*
**Muhl**, Edward E. 1907- *IntMPA 92*
**Muhl**, Edward J 1945- *WhoIns 92*
**Muhlanger**, Erich 1941- *WhoFI 92*
**Muhlbach**, Robert Arthur 1946- *WhoAmL 92*
**Muhlbauer**, Karlheinz Christoph 1930- *AmMWSc 92*
**Muhlbauer**, Louis J 1929- *WhoAmP 91*
**Muhlbauer**, Michael Christoph 1957- *WhoMW 92*
**Muhleman**, Duane Owen 1931- *AmMWSc 92*
**Muhlenberg**, Frederick Augustus Conrad 1750-1801 *AmPolLe*
**Muhlenberg**, Gotthilf Henry Ernest 1753-1815 *BiInAmS*
**Muhlenbruch**, Carl W 1915- *AmMWSc 92, WhoFI 92, WhoMW 92*
**Muhler**, Joseph Charles 1923- *AmMWSc 92*
**Muhringer**, Doris Agathe Annemarie 1920- *IntAu&W 91*
**Muhs**, Beth Ann 1957- *WhoRel 92*
**Muhs**, Merrill Arthur 1926- *AmMWSc 92*
**Muhs**, Robert Keith, Sr 1926- *WhoAmP 91*
**Muhsam**, Erich 1878-1934 *EncTR 91 [port]*
**Mui**, Jimmy Kun 1958- *WhoFI 92*
**Mui**, Lorna H. 1915- *ConAu 133*
**Muir**, Alec Andrew 1909- *Who 92*
**Muir**, Alexander Laird 1937- *Who 92*
**Muir**, Arthur H, Jr 1931- *AmMWSc 92*
**Muir**, Barry Sinclair 1932- *AmMWSc 92*
**Muir**, Charles S *ScFEYrs*
**Muir**, Derek Charles G 1949- *AmMWSc 92*
**Muir**, Donald Ridley 1929- *AmMWSc 92*
**Muir**, Douglas 1937- *TwCPaSc*
**Muir**, Douglas William 1940- *AmMWSc 92*
**Muir**, E. Roger 1918- *IntMPA 92*
**Muir**, Edwin 1887-1959 *FacFETw, RfGEnL 91*
**Muir**, Frank 1920- *IntAu&W 91, Who 92, WrDr 92*
**Muir**, Helen 1920- *IntWW 91, Who 92*
**Muir**, Helen 1937- *SmATA 65 [port]*
**Muir**, J. Dapray 1936- *WhoAmL 92*
**Muir**, James A. *TwCWW 91*
**Muir**, James Alexander 1938- *AmMWSc 92*
**Muir**, Jean Elizabeth *IntWW 91, Who 92*
**Muir**, John 1838-1914 *BenetAL 91, BiInAmS, DcAmImH, FacFETw*
**Muir**, John 1910- *Who 92*
**Muir**, John Gerald Grainger d1990 *Who 92N*
**Muir**, John Todd, Jr. 1936- *WhoRel 92*
**Muir**, Kenneth 1907- *IntAu&W 91, IntWW 91, Who 92, WrDr 92*
**Muir**, Laurence 1925- *Who 92*
**Muir**, Malcolm 1914- *WhoAmL 92*
**Muir**, Mariel Meents 1939- *AmMWSc 92*
**Muir**, Melvin K 1932- *AmMWSc 92*
**Muir**, Patrick Fred 1960- *AmMWSc 92*
**Muir**, Richard 1943- *IntAu&W 91, WrDr 92*
**Muir**, Richard John Sutherland 1942- *Who 92*
**Muir**, Robert Eugene 1934- *WhoAmL 92*
**Muir**, Robert Mathew 1917- *AmMWSc 92*
**Muir**, Thomas Gustave, Jr 1938- *AmMWSc 92*
**Muir**, Tom 1936- *Who 92*
**Muir**, Ward 1878-1927 *ScFEYrs*
**Muir**, William A 1937- *AmMWSc 92*
**Muir**, William Ernest 1940- *AmMWSc 92*
**Muir**, William Ker, Jr. 1931- *WhoWest 92*
**Muir**, William W, III 1946- *AmMWSc 92*
**Muir**, Wilson Burnett 1932- *AmMWSc 92*
**Muir Beddall**, Hugh Richard *Who 92*
**Muir Mackenzie**, Alexander 1955- *Who 92*
**Muir Wood**, Alan 1921- *IntWW 91, Who 92*
**Muirden**, Bruce Wallace 1928- *WrDr 92*
**Muirhead**, David 1918- *Who 92*
**Muirhead**, E Eric 1916- *AmMWSc 92*
**Muirhead**, Robb John 1946- *AmMWSc 92*
**Muirhead**, Vincent Uriel 1919- *AmMWSc 92*
**Muirshiel**, Viscount 1905- *IntWW 91, Who 92*
**Muizeck**, Marina *EncAmaz 91*
**Mujaji** *EncAmaz 91*
**Mujica**, Mauro E. 1941- *WhoFI 92*
**Mujica Lainez**, Manuel 1910-1984 *FacFETw*
**Mujumdar**, Arun Sadashiv 1945- *AmMWSc 92*
**Mujumdar**, Vilas Sitaram 1941- *WhoWest 92*
**Mujuru**, Joyce Teurai-Ropa 1955- *IntWW 91*
**Muka**, Arthur Allen 1924- *AmMWSc 92*
**Muka**, Betty Loraine Oakes 1929- *WhoFI 92*
**Mukai**, Cromwell Daisaku 1917- *AmMWSc 92*
**Mukamal**, Steven Sasoon 1940- *WhoAmL 92*
**Mukamal**, Stuart Sasson 1951- *WhoAmP 91*
**Mukasey**, Michael B. 1941- *WhoAmL 92*
**Mukashev**, Salamat 1927- *IntWW 91*
**Mukaya** *EncAmaz 91*
**Mukerjee**, Barid 1928- *AmMWSc 92*
**Mukerjee**, Pasupati 1932- *AmMWSc 92*
**Mukerjee**, Rahul 1953- *WhoFI 92*
**Mukerji**, Mukul Kumar 1938- *AmMWSc 92*
**Mukha**, Stepan Nesterovich *IntWW 91*
**Mukhamedov**, Irek *IntWW 91*
**Mukhedkar**, Dinkar 1936- *AmMWSc 92*
**Mukherjea**, Arunava 1941- *AmMWSc 92*
**Mukherjee**, Amal 1944- *AmMWSc 92*
**Mukherjee**, Amiya K 1936- *AmMWSc 92*
**Mukherjee**, Asit B *AmMWSc 92*
**Mukherjee**, Bharati 1932- *LiExTwC*
**Mukherjee**, Bharati 1940- *BenetAL 91, ConNov 91, IntAu&W 91, WrDr 92*
**Mukherjee**, Bharati 1950- *IntWW 91*
**Mukherjee**, Debi Prasad 1939- *AmMWSc 92*
**Mukherjee**, Kalinath 1932- *AmMWSc 92, WhoMW 92*
**Mukherjee**, Pranab Kumar 1935- *IntWW 91, Who 92*
**Mukherjee**, Pritish 1955- *AmMWSc 92*
**Mukherjee**, Ranesh Kumar 1964- *WhoMW 92*
**Mukherjee**, Tapan Kumar 1929- *AmMWSc 92*
**Mukherjee**, Tara Kumar 1923- *Who 92*
**Mukherji**, Kalyan Kumar 1939- *AmMWSc 92*
**Mukhina**, Vera Ignat'evna 1889-1953 *SovUnBD*
**Mukhitdinov**, Nuritdin Akramovich 1917- *SovUnBD*
**Mukhopadhyay**, Nimai Chand 1942- *AmMWSc 92*
**Mukhopadhyay**, Nitis 1950- *AmMWSc 92*
**Mukhtar**, Hasan 1947- *AmMWSc 92*
**Mukhtar**, Mallam Abdul-Muhyi Mohammed 1944- *IntWW 91*
**Muki**, Rokuro 1928- *AmMWSc 92*
**Mukkada**, Antony Job *AmMWSc 92*
**Muktananda**, Paramahansa 1908-1982 *RelLAm 91*
**Mukunnemkeril**, George Mathew 1939- *AmMWSc 92*
**Mukwanga**, Eridari 1943- *BlkOlyM*
**Mula**, Frank Charles *WhoEnt 92*
**Mula**, Tom 1951- *WhoEnt 92*
**Mulac**, Pamela Ann 1944- *WhoRel 92*
**Mulaik**, Stanley B 1902- *AmMWSc 92*
**Mulamba Nyunyi Wa Kadima** 1928- *IntWW 91*
**Mular**, A L 1930- *AmMWSc 92*
**Mularie**, William Mack 1938- *AmMWSc 92*
**Mularz**, Edward Julius 1943- *AmMWSc 92*
**Mularz**, Theodore Leonard 1933- *WhoFI 92*
**Mulas**, Pablo Marcelo 1939- *AmMWSc 92*
**Mulase**, Motohico 1954- *WhoWest 92*
**Mulay**, Laxman Nilakantha 1923- *AmMWSc 92*
**Mulay**, Shree 1941- *AmMWSc 92*
**Mulberry**, Richard 1920- *WhoAmP 91*
**Mulcahey**, Patricia *WhoRel 92*
**Mulcahey**, Richard Thomas 1935- *WhoAmP 91*
**Mulcahey**, Thomas P 1931- *AmMWSc 92*
**Mulcahy**, Daniel J 1947- *WhoIns 92*
**Mulcahy**, David Louis 1937- *AmMWSc 92*
**Mulcahy**, Edward William 1921- *WhoAmP 91*
**Mulcahy**, Gabriel Michael 1929- *AmMWSc 92*
**Mulcahy**, Geoffrey John 1942- *IntWW 91, Who 92*
**Mulcahy**, John 1950- *WhoAmL 92*
**Mulcahy**, John J. 1922- *WhoRel 92*
**Mulcahy**, John Joseph 1941- *AmMWSc 92*
**Mulcahy**, Robert Charles 1940- *WhoRel 92*
**Mulcahy**, Robert William 1951- *WhoAmL 92*
**Mulcare**, Donald J 1938- *AmMWSc 92*
**Mulchi**, Charles Lee 1941- *AmMWSc 92*
**Mulcrone**, Thomas Francis 1912- *AmMWSc 92*
**Muldaur**, Diana 1938- *IntMPA 92*
**Muldaur**, Diana Charlton 1938- *WhoEnt 92*
**Muldawer**, Leonard 1920- *AmMWSc 92*
**Mulder**, Carel 1928- *AmMWSc 92*
**Mulder**, Cornelius Petrus 1925-1988 *FacFETw*
**Mulder**, Dennis Marlin 1943- *WhoMW 92, WhoRel 92*
**Mulder**, Donald William 1917- *AmMWSc 92*
**Mulder**, Edwin George 1929- *WhoRel 92*
**Mulder**, John Bastian 1932- *AmMWSc 92*
**Mulder**, John Mark 1946- *WhoRel 92*
**Mulder**, Martin Jan 1923- *WhoRel 92*
**Mulder**, Nanny 1948- *TwCPaSc*
**Mulder**, Robert Udo 1952- *AmMWSc 92*
**Mulderig**, Robert A 1953- *WhoIns 92*
**Muldoon**, Brian 1947- *WhoAmL 92*
**Muldoon**, Catherine Riesgo *WhoHisp 92*
**Muldoon**, Gary 1950- *WhoAmL 92*
**Muldoon**, Jane Katherine 1938- *WhoRel 92*
**Muldoon**, John William 1933- *WhoMW 92*
**Muldoon**, Martin E 1939- *AmMWSc 92*
**Muldoon**, Nancy Knight 1938- *WhoWest 92*
**Muldoon**, Paul 1951- *ConPo 91, IntAu&W 91, WrDr 92*
**Muldoon**, Paul Benedict 1951- *IntWW 91*
**Muldoon**, Robert 1921- *Who 92*
**Muldoon**, Robert David 1921- *IntWW 91*
**Muldoon**, Robert Joseph, Jr. 1936- *WhoAmL 92*

**Muldoon,** Thomas George 1938- *AmMWSc 92*
**Muldoon,** William Henry, III 1935- *WhoWest 92*
**Muldowney,** Dominic 1952- *ConCom 92*
**Muldowney,** Dominic John 1952- *IntWW 91, Who 92*
**Muldowney,** James 1939- *AmMWSc 92*
**Muldowney,** Jerome Thomas 1945- *WhoIns 92*
**Muldrew,** Donald Boyd 1934- *AmMWSc 92*
**Muldrow,** Catherine 1931- *WhoBlA 92*
**Muldrow,** Charles Norment, Jr 1930- *AmMWSc 92*
**Muldrow,** James Christopher 1945- *WhoBlA 92*
**Mule,** Anthony Vincent 1943- *WhoFI 92*
**Mule,** Margaret Mary Falcon 1941- *WhoAmP 91*
**Mule,** Salvatore Joseph 1932- *AmMWSc 92*
**Mulford,** Clarence E. 1883-1956 *BenetAL 91, TwCWW 91*
**Mulford,** David Campbell 1937- *WhoAmP 91*
**Mulford,** Dwight James 1911- *AmMWSc 92*
**Mulford,** John Garland 1941- *WhoAmL 92*
**Mulford,** Maxene Fabe *DrAPF 91*
**Mulford,** Michael K 1954- *WhoAmP 91*
**Mulford,** Prentice 1834-1891 *BenetAL 91*
**Mulford,** Rand Perry 1943- *WhoWest 92*
**Mulford,** Robert Alan 1947- *AmMWSc 92*
**Mulford,** Robert Neal Ramsay 1922- *AmMWSc 92*
**Mulford,** Wendy 1941- *ConPo 91, WrDr 92*
**Mulgan,** John 1911-1945 *RfGEnL 91*
**Mulgrave,** Earl of 1954- *Who 92*
**Mulgrew,** John Christopher, Jr. 1939- *WhoAmL 92*
**Mulgrew,** Kate 1955- *IntMPA 92*
**Mulhausen,** Hedy Ann 1940- *AmMWSc 92, WhoMW 92*
**Mulhausen,** Robert Oscar 1930- *AmMWSc 92*
**Mulhern,** Edwin Joseph 1927- *WhoAmL 92*
**Mulhern,** Elsa Paine 1909- *WhoAmP 91*
**Mulhern,** Harriet Guber 1933- *WhoAmL 92*
**Mulhern,** John E, Jr 1926- *AmMWSc 92*
**Mulhern,** Joseph Patrick 1921- *WhoAmL 92*
**Mulhern,** Matt 1960- *IntMPA 92*
**Mulhern,** Maureen *DrAPF 91*
**Mulhollan,** Paige Elliott 1934- *WhoMW 92*
**Mulholland** *Who 92*
**Mulholland,** Allan E 1949- *WhoIns 92*
**Mulholland,** Angela Broadway 1957- *WhoAmL 92*
**Mulholland,** Clare 1939- *Who 92*
**Mulholland,** George 1938- *AmMWSc 92*
**Mulholland,** James Stephan *WhoEnt 92, WhoWest 92*
**Mulholland,** John Derral 1934- *AmMWSc 92*
**Mulholland,** Michael 1915- *Who 92*
**Mulholland,** Robert E. *LesBEnT 92*
**Mulholland,** Robert E. 1933- *IntMPA 92*
**Mulholland,** Robert J 1940- *AmMWSc 92*
**Mulholland,** William David, Jr. 1926- *IntWW 91*
**Mulich,** Steve Francis 1934- *WhoMW 92*
**Mulich,** William *WhoAmP 91*
**Mulick,** James Anton 1948- *AmMWSc 92*
**Mulieri,** Berthann Scubon 1937- *AmMWSc 92*
**Mulieri,** Louis A 1935- *AmMWSc 92*
**Mulinos,** Michael George 1897- *AmMWSc 92*
**Mulitauaopele,** Alamoana S *WhoAmP 91*
**Mulitauaopele,** Ivi *WhoAmP 91*
**Mulkearns,** Ronald Austin *Who 92*
**Mulkern,** John 1931- *Who 92*
**Mulkerrin,** Paul Francis 1956- *WhoFI 92*
**Mulks,** Martha Huard 1950- *AmMWSc 92*
**Mull,** Charles Gilbert 1935- *WhoWest 92*
**Mull,** Gale W. 1945- *WhoAmL 92*
**Mull,** Gerald S. *Who 92*
**Mull,** Martin *LesBEnT 92, WhoRel 92*
**Mull,** Martin 1943- *IntMPA 92, WhoEnt 92*
**Mull,** Odus McCoy 1880-1962 *DcNCBi 4*
**Mulla,** Mir Subhan *AmMWSc 92*
**Mullally,** Pierce Harry 1918- *WhoFI 92, WhoMW 92*
**Mullaly,** Terence Frederick Stanley 1927- *Who 92*
**Mullan,** Bob 1947- *WrDr 92*
**Mullan,** Charles Heron 1912- *Who 92*
**Mullan,** Colette 1961- *TwCPaSc*
**Mullan,** Dermott Joseph 1944- *AmMWSc 92*
**Mullan,** John F 1925- *AmMWSc 92*
**Mullane,** Denis Francis 1930- *WhoFI 92, WhoIns 92*
**Mullane,** Robert Terrance 1952- *WhoMW 92*
**Mullaney,** Joseph E. 1933- *WhoAmL 92, WhoFI 92*
**Mullaney,** Paul F 1938- *AmMWSc 92*
**Mullaney,** Steven 1951- *WhoMW 92*
**Mullaney,** Thomas Joseph 1946- *WhoAmL 92*
**Mullard,** Chris 1944- *IntAu&W 91, WrDr 92*
**Mullare,** Thomas Kenwood, Jr. 1939- *WhoAmL 92*
**Mullarkey,** Mary J *WhoAmP 91*
**Mullarkey,** Mary J. 1943- *WhoAmL 92, WhoWest 92*
**Mullavey,** Greg 1939- *WhoEnt 92*
**Mullen,** Ann A 1935- *WhoAmP 91*
**Mullen,** Anthony J 1927- *AmMWSc 92*
**Mullen,** Barbara J *AmMWSc 92*
**Mullen,** Claude Robert, Jr. 1931- *WhoWest 92*
**Mullen,** Eileen Anne 1943- *WhoFI 92*
**Mullen,** Frank Albert 1931- *WhoRel 92*
**Mullen,** Gary Lee 1947- *AmMWSc 92*
**Mullen,** Gary Richard 1945- *AmMWSc 92*
**Mullen,** Harryette *DrAPF 91*
**Mullen,** James A 1928- *AmMWSc 92*
**Mullen,** James G 1933- *AmMWSc 92*
**Mullen,** James L 1942- *AmMWSc 92*
**Mullen,** James Madison 1845-1931 *DcNCBi 4*
**Mullen,** John Edward, III 1951- *WhoFI 92*
**Mullen,** John Frederick 1962- *WhoEnt 92*
**Mullen,** John W 1947- *WhoIns 92*
**Mullen,** Joseph David 1934- *AmMWSc 92*
**Mullen,** Joseph Matthew 1944- *AmMWSc 92*
**Mullen,** Kenneth 1939- *AmMWSc 92*
**Mullen,** Laura *DrAPF 91*
**Mullen,** Martin P 1921- *WhoAmP 91*
**Mullen,** Michael Francis 1915- *WhoFI 92*
**Mullen,** Michael J *WhoIns 92*
**Mullen,** Michael John 1939- *WhoAmL 92*
**Mullen,** Michael Patrick 1942- *WhoAmL 92*
**Mullen,** Patricia Ann 1935- *AmMWSc 92*
**Mullen,** Regina Marie 1952- *WhoEnt 92*
**Mullen,** Richard Joseph 1941- *AmMWSc 92*
**Mullen,** Robert Terrence 1935- *AmMWSc 92*
**Mullen,** Robert Welch, Jr. 1955- *WhoAmL 92*
**Mullen,** Thomas Edgar 1936- *WhoMW 92*
**Mullen,** Thomas John 1945- *WhoWest 92*
**Mullenbach,** Linda Herman 1948- *WhoAmL 92*
**Mullendore,** A W 1928- *AmMWSc 92*
**Mullendore,** Herbert Jack 1920- *WhoAmP 91*
**Mullendore,** James Alan 1932- *AmMWSc 92*
**Mullendore,** James Myers 1919- *AmMWSc 92*
**Mullendore,** John W 1934- *WhoIns 92*
**Mullendore,** Mark Edward 1960- *WhoMW 92*
**Mullenix,** Kenneth Eugene 1947- *WhoEnt 92*
**Mullenix,** Ted 1945- *WhoAmP 91*
**Mullenix,** Travis H. 1931- *WhoWest 92*
**Mullens,** Anthony 1936- *Who 92*
**Mullens,** Delbert W. 1944- *WhoBlA 92*
**Mullens,** William Leonard 1919- *WhoRel 92*
**Muller,** Alex *Who 92*
**Muller,** Alfred 1940- *WhoEnt 92*
**Muller,** Burton Harlow 1924- *AmMWSc 92*
**Muller,** Claudya Barbara 1946- *WhoMW 92*
**Muller,** Claus 1920- *IntWW 91*
**Muller,** Cornelius Herman 1909- *AmMWSc 92*
**Muller,** David Eugene 1924- *AmMWSc 92*
**Muller,** Dietrich 1936- *AmMWSc 92*
**Muller,** Earl Cannon 1947- *WhoRel 92*
**Muller,** Emilio Eduardo 1945- *WhoRel 92*
**Muller,** Eric Rene 1938- *AmMWSc 92*
**Muller,** Ernest Hathaway 1923- *AmMWSc 92*
**Muller,** Franz Joseph 1938- *Who 92*
**Muller,** Fritz 1889-1942 *EncTR 91*
**Muller,** Gary William *WhoFI 92*
**Muller,** George Heinz 1919- *AmMWSc 92*
**Muller,** Gerhard 1929- *IntWW 91*
**Muller,** Heinrich 1900-1945 *BiDExR, EncTR 91 [port]*
**Muller,** Hermann 1876-1931 *EncTR 91 [port]*
**Muller,** Hermann Joseph 1890-1967 *FacFETw, WhoNob 90*
**Muller,** James Alan 1955- *WhoFI 92*
**Muller,** James Waldemar 1953- *WhoWest 92*
**Muller,** Jennifer 1944- *WhoEnt 92*
**Muller,** Jerome Kenneth 1934- *WhoWest 92*
**Muller,** Johannes von 1752-1809 *BlkwCEP*
**Muller,** John E *TwCSFW 91, WrDr 92*
**Muller,** John J. H. *WhoEnt 92*
**Muller,** John Paul 1940- *WhoMW 92*
**Muller,** Jon Loring 1956- *WhoAmP 91*
**Muller,** Jorg *SmATA 67*
**Muller,** Josef 1898-1979 *EncTR 91*
**Muller,** K. Alex 1927- *IntWW 91*
**Muller,** Karl Alex 1927- *Who 92, WhoNob 90*
**Muller,** Karl Alexander von 1882-1964 *EncTR 91*
**Muller,** Karl Frederick 1935- *AmMWSc 92*
**Muller,** Kenneth Joseph 1945- *AmMWSc 92*
**Muller,** Kurt Alexander 1955- *WhoAmL 92*
**Muller,** Lawrence Dean 1941- *AmMWSc 92*
**Muller,** Ludwig 1883-1945 *EncTR 91 [port]*
**Muller,** Lyle Dean 1935- *WhoRel 92*
**Muller,** Marcel Wettstein 1922- *AmMWSc 92*
**Muller,** Marcia 1944- *IntAu&W 91, WrDr 92*
**Muller,** Mervin Edgar 1928- *AmMWSc 92, WhoMW 92*
**Muller,** Michael J. 1944- *WhoHisp 92*
**Muller,** Michael J. 1947- *WhoAmL 92*
**Muller,** Miklos 1930- *AmMWSc 92*
**Muller,** Norbert 1929- *AmMWSc 92*
**Muller,** Olaf 1938- *AmMWSc 92*
**Muller,** Otto 1870-1944 *EncTR 91*
**Muller,** Otto Helmuth 1946- *AmMWSc 92*
**Muller,** Paul Hermann 1899-1965 *WhoNob 90*
**Muller,** Paul Johannes 1944- *WhoFI 92*
**Muller,** Paul William 1958- *WhoFI 92*
**Muller,** Peter 1947- *IntMPA 92, WhoEnt 92*
**Muller,** Ralph Louis Junius 1933- *Who 92*
**Muller,** Richard A 1944- *AmMWSc 92*
**Muller,** Richard August 1944- *WhoWest 92*
**Muller,** Richard S 1933- *AmMWSc 92*
**Muller,** Robby 1940- *IntMPA 92*
**Muller,** Robert, Mrs. *Who 92*
**Muller,** Robert Albert 1928- *AmMWSc 92*
**Muller,** Robert E 1921- *AmMWSc 92*
**Muller,** Robert Neil 1946- *AmMWSc 92*
**Muller,** Roger Wayne 1947- *WhoWest 92*
**Muller,** Rolf Hugo 1929- *AmMWSc 92*
**Muller,** Scott William 1950- *WhoAmL 92*
**Muller,** Steven 1927- *IntWW 91*
**Muller,** Uwe Richard *AmMWSc 92*
**Muller,** William A 1942- *AmMWSc 92*
**Muller,** William Henry, Jr 1919- *AmMWSc 92*
**Muller-Carioba,** Joao Bertoldo Jacob 1929- *WhoEnt 92*
**Muller-Eberhard,** Hans Joachim 1927- *AmMWSc 92*
**Muller-Eberhard,** Ursula 1928- *AmMWSc 92*
**Muller-Munk,** Peter 1904-1967 *DcTwDes*
**Muller-Ortega,** Paul Eduardo 1949- *WhoRel 92*
**Muller-Parker,** Gisele 1953- *WhoWest 92*
**Muller-Parker,** Gisele Therese *AmMWSc 92*
**Muller-Schwarze,** Dietland *AmMWSc 92*
**Muller-Seidel,** Walter 1918- *IntWW 91*
**Muller-Sieburg,** Christa E *AmMWSc 92*
**Muller-Warmuth,** Werner 1929- *IntWW 91*
**Mullet,** Maurice Eugene 1937- *WhoAmP 91*
**Mullett,** Aidan Anthony 1933- *Who 92*
**Mullett,** Donald L. 1929- *WhoBlA 92*
**Mullett,** John McLaughlin 1950- *WhoFI 92*
**Mullett,** John St. Hilary 1925- *WrDr 92*
**Mullett,** Leslie Baden 1920- *Who 92*
**Mullett,** Melinda F. 1960- *WhoWest 92*
**Mullett,** Michael Alan 1945- *WhoAmL 92*
**Mullett,** Tony *Who 92*
**Mulley** *Who 92*
**Mulley,** Baron 1918- *IntWW 91, Who 92*
**Mullhaupt,** Joseph Timothy 1932- *AmMWSc 92*
**Mullican,** Moon 1909-1967 *NewAmDM*
**Mulligan,** Andrew Armstrong 1936- *Who 92*
**Mulligan,** Annette Marie 1959- *WhoRel 92, WhoWest 92*
**Mulligan,** Anthony Christopher 1963- *WhoWest 92*
**Mulligan,** Benjamin Edward 1936- *AmMWSc 92*
**Mulligan,** Bernard 1934- *AmMWSc 92*
**Mulligan,** Carol Harris 1954- *WhoBlA 92*
**Mulligan,** David Keith 1951- *WhoFI 92*
**Mulligan,** Donald Edward 1933- *WhoWest 92*
**Mulligan,** Eugene Worth 1926- *WhoFI 92*
**Mulligan,** Geoffrey C 1958- *AmMWSc 92*
**Mulligan,** Gerald Joseph 1927- *WhoEnt 92*
**Mulligan,** Gerry 1927- *NewAmDM*
**Mulligan,** James Anthony 1924- *AmMWSc 92*
**Mulligan,** James H, Jr 1920- *AmMWSc 92*
**Mulligan,** John Mosher d1991 *NewYTBS 91*
**Mulligan,** Joseph Francis 1920- *AmMWSc 92*
**Mulligan,** Kathleen Ann *WhoEnt 92*
**Mulligan,** Kevin T 1959- *WhoAmP 91*
**Mulligan,** Martha Elizabeth 1939- *WhoRel 92*
**Mulligan,** Michael R. 1950- *WhoBlA 92*
**Mulligan,** Patrick 1912- *Who 92*
**Mulligan,** Raymond A. 1914- *WrDr 92*
**Mulligan,** Richard 1932- *IntMPA 92*
**Mulligan,** Richard M. 1932- *WhoEnt 92*
**Mulligan,** Robert 1925- *IntDcF 2-2 [port], IntMPA 92*
**Mulligan,** Robert Joseph 1948- *WhoAmP 91*
**Mulligan,** Timothy James 1955- *AmMWSc 92*
**Mulligan,** William 1921- *Who 92*
**Mulligan,** William G. d1991 *NewYTBS 91*
**Mulligan,** William Hughes 1918- *WhoAmL 92*
**Mulliken,** Robert Sanderson 1896-1986 *WhoNob 90*
**Mullikin,** H F 1908- *AmMWSc 92*
**Mullikin,** Richard V 1923- *AmMWSc 92*
**Mullikin,** Thomas Wilson 1928- *AmMWSc 92, WhoMW 92*
**Mullin,** Beth Conway 1945- *AmMWSc 92*
**Mullin,** Brian Robert 1945- *AmMWSc 92*
**Mullin,** Chris John *IntAu&W 91*
**Mullin,** Christopher John 1947- *Who 92*
**Mullin,** Constance Hammond 1939- *WhoEnt 92*
**Mullin,** J. Shan 1934- *WhoAmL 92*
**Mullin,** James Michael 1954- *AmMWSc 92*
**Mullin,** John William 1925- *Who 92*
**Mullin,** Leo Francis 1943- *WhoFI 92*
**Mullin,** Michael Mahlon 1937- *AmMWSc 92*
**Mullin,** Patricia E *WhoIns 92*
**Mullin,** Patrick Allen 1950- *WhoAmL 92*
**Mullin,** Randy Gene 1964- *WhoRel 92*
**Mullin,** Robert Spencer 1912- *AmMWSc 92*
**Mullin,** Ronald Cleveland 1936- *AmMWSc 92*
**Mullin,** Ronald K 1949- *WhoAmP 91*
**Mullin,** Willard 1902-1978 *FacFETw*
**Mullin,** William Jesse 1934- *AmMWSc 92*
**Mullinax,** Michael Frederick 1945- *WhoAmP 91*
**Mullinax,** Perry Franklin 1931- *AmMWSc 92*
**Mullineaux,** Donal Ray 1925- *AmMWSc 92*
**Mullineaux,** Richard Denison 1923- *AmMWSc 92*
**Mullinix,** Edward Wingate 1924- *WhoAmL 92*
**Mullinix,** Kathleen Patricia 1944- *AmMWSc 92*
**Mullinix,** Mark Lorin 1955- *WhoFI 92*
**Mullinix,** Raymond G 1948- *WhoAmP 91*
**Mullinix,** Steve 1949- *WhoEnt 92*
**Mullins,** Ann *IntAu&W 91X*
**Mullins,** Anna Carrolle 1945- *WhoWest 92*
**Mullins,** Chucky d1991 *NewYTBS 91*
**Mullins,** Dail W, Jr 1944- *AmMWSc 92*
**Mullins,** Daniel Joseph *Who 92*
**Mullins,** David W., Jr. *NewYTBS 91 [port]*
**Mullins,** David W., Jr. 1946- *WhoFI 92*
**Mullins,** Deborra E *AmMWSc 92*
**Mullins,** Donald Eugene 1944- *AmMWSc 92*
**Mullins,** Edgar Young 1860-1928 *RelLAm 91*
**Mullins,** Edward Lee 1944- *WhoRel 92*
**Mullins,** Edward Wade, Jr. 1936- *WhoAmL 92*
**Mullins,** Edwin 1933- *IntAu&W 91, WrDr 92*
**Mullins,** Edwin Brandt 1933- *Who 92*
**Mullins,** Helene *DrAPF 91*
**Mullins,** Henry Thomas 1951- *AmMWSc 92*
**Mullins,** James B 1934- *WhoIns 92*
**Mullins,** James Michael 1945- *AmMWSc 92*
**Mullins,** Jeanette Somerville 1932- *AmMWSc 92*
**Mullins,** Jeremiah Andrew 1936- *WhoFI 92*
**Mullins,** Jerome Joseph 1925- *WhoMW 92*
**Mullins,** John A 1931- *AmMWSc 92*
**Mullins,** John Thomas 1932- *AmMWSc 92*

**Mullins,** Joseph Chester 1931- *AmMWSc 92*
**Mullins,** Joseph Francis, Jr 1927- *WhoAmP 91*
**Mullins,** Kenny R. 1956- *WhoEnt 92*
**Mullins,** Larry A. 1949- *WhoWest 92*
**Mullins,** Lawrence J 1921- *AmMWSc 92*
**Mullins,** Leonard 1918- *Who 92*
**Mullins,** Leslie Morris 1917- *WhoAmL 92*
**Mullins,** Lorin John 1917- *AmMWSc 92*
**Mullins,** Margaret Ann Frances 1953- *WhoAmL 92*
**Mullins,** Melinda Roberta 1958- *WhoEnt 92*
**Mullins,** Nancy Claire 1946- *WhoEnt 92*
**Mullins,** Norman Reid 1927- *WhoAmP 91*
**Mullins,** Richard James *AmMWSc 92*
**Mullins,** Robert Emmet 1937- *AmMWSc 92*
**Mullins,** Ruth Gladys 1943- *WhoWest 92*
**Mullins,** Sonia E. 1961- *WhoHisp 92*
**Mullins,** Traci Lerae 1960- *WhoWest 92*
**Mullins,** William D *WhoAmP 91*
**Mullins,** William Wilson 1927- *AmMWSc 92*
**Mullis,** Carol Bea 1923- *WhoAmP 91*
**Mullis,** H Thomas 1943- *WhoAmP 91*
**Mullis,** Kary Banks 1944- *WhoWest 92*
**Mullis,** M. Joyce 1953- *WhoRel 92*
**Mullis,** Madeline Gail Herman 1936- *WhoRel 92*
**Mullison,** Wendell Roxby 1913- *AmMWSc 92*
**Mullner,** Timothy Paul 1959- *WhoRel 92*
**Mulloney,** Brian 1942- *AmMWSc 92*
**Mullooly,** John P 1937- *AmMWSc 92*
**Mullova,** Viktoria 1959- *IntWW 91*
**Mulloy,** Patrick Aloysius 1941- *WhoFI 92*
**Mulock,** Dinah Maria 1826-1887 *RfGEnL 91*
**Mulock,** Edwin Thomas 1943- *WhoAmL 92*
**Mulrane,** Scott H. *DrAPF 91*
**Mulready,** Richard T *WhoAmP 91*
**Mulready,** Thomas James, Jr. 1958- *WhoEnt 92*
**Mulrennan,** Cecilia Agnes 1925- *AmMWSc 92*
**Mulrennan,** John Andrew, Jr 1934- *AmMWSc 92*
**Mulroney,** Brian 1939- *FacFETw [port], IntWW 91, Who 92*
**Mulroney,** Dermot *IntMPA 92*
**Mulroney,** John Patrick 1935- *WhoFI 92*
**Mulrow,** Patrick J 1926- *AmMWSc 92*
**Mulroy,** Bertrand Clair 1913- *WhoRel 92*
**Mulroy,** Juliana Catherine 1948- *AmMWSc 92*
**Mulroy,** Michael Joseph 1931- *AmMWSc 92*
**Mulroy,** Thomas Robert, Jr. 1946- *WhoAmL 92*
**Mulroy,** Thomas Wilkinson 1946- *AmMWSc 92*
**Mulson,** Joseph F 1929- *AmMWSc 92*
**Multasuo,** Eija Elina 1958- *WhoFI 92*
**Multauaopele,** Ivi S 1939- *WhoAmP 91*
**Multer,** H Gray 1926- *AmMWSc 92*
**Multz,** Carroll Edward 1936- *WhoAmP 91*
**Mulukutla,** Sarma Sreerama 1938- *AmMWSc 92*
**Mulvaney,** Dallas Edward 1946- *WhoMW 92*
**Mulvaney,** Derek John 1925- *Who 92*
**Mulvaney,** James Edward 1929- *AmMWSc 92*
**Mulvaney,** James Michael 1949- *WhoAmL 92*
**Mulvaney,** Thomas Francis 1949- *WhoAmL 92*
**Mulvaney,** Thomas Francis 1950- *WhoAmL 92*
**Mulvaney,** Thomas Richard 1933- *AmMWSc 92*
**Mulvany,** Nancy Claire 1952- *WhoWest 92*
**Mulvee,** Robert Edward 1930- *WhoRel 92*
**Mulverhill,** Robert Clarence, Jr. 1954- *WhoWest 92*
**Mulvey,** Dennis Michael 1938- *AmMWSc 92, WhoWest 92*
**Mulvey,** James Patrick 1947- *AmMWSc 92*
**Mulvey,** Margaret 1952- *AmMWSc 92*
**Mulvey,** Philip Francis, Jr 1931- *AmMWSc 92*
**Mulvey,** Richard I. 1929- *WhoAmL 92*
**Mulvihill,** David James 1946- *WhoRel 92*
**Mulvihill,** John Edward 1939- *WhoRel 92*
**Mulvihill,** John Joseph 1943- *AmMWSc 92*
**Mulvihill,** Mary Lou Jolie 1928- *AmMWSc 92*
**Mulvihill,** Maureen E. 1944- *ConAu 134, -135*
**Mulvihill,** Paul Laurence 1938- *WhoAmL 92*
**Mulvihill,** Peter James 1956- *WhoWest 92*
**Mulvihill,** Terence Joseph 1931- *WhoFI 92*
**Mulvihill,** William *DrAPF 91*
**Muly,** Emil Christopher, Jr 1934- *AmMWSc 92*
**Muma,** Martin Hammond 1916- *AmMWSc 92*
**Muma,** Nancy A 1958- *AmMWSc 92*
**Mumaugh,** Brian Michael 1957- *WhoAmL 92*
**Mumaw,** Kathleen Elizabeth 1952- *WhoFI 92*
**Mumba,** Stephen *WhoRel 92*
**Mumbach,** Norbert R 1920- *AmMWSc 92*
**Mumford,** Bernard C. 1930- *RelLAm 91*
**Mumford,** Brian Frederick 1941- *WhoAmL 92*
**Mumford,** David Bryant 1937- *AmMWSc 92, IntWW 91*
**Mumford,** David Louis 1932- *AmMWSc 92*
**Mumford,** Enid *Who 92*
**Mumford,** Ethel Watts 1878-1940 *BenetAL 91, ScFEYrs*
**Mumford,** George d1818 *DcNCBi 4*
**Mumford,** George 1927- *AmMWSc 92*
**Mumford,** George Saltonstall 1928- *AmMWSc 92*
**Mumford,** James Gregory 1863-1914 *BiInAmS*
**Mumford,** Lawrence Quincy 1903-1982 *DcNCBi 4*
**Mumford,** Lewis 1895- *IntAu&W 91*
**Mumford,** Lewis 1895-1990 *AnObit 1990, BenetAL 91, DcTwDes, FacFETw*
**Mumford,** Patricia Rae 1932- *WhoRel 92, WhoWest 92*
**Mumford,** Peter 1922- *Who 92*
**Mumford,** Russell Eugene 1922- *AmMWSc 92*
**Mumford,** Ruth *WrDr 92*
**Mumford,** Tex *TwCWW 91*
**Mumford,** Thaddeus Quentin, Jr. 1951- *WhoBlA 92*
**Mumford,** Willard R 1933- *AmMWSc 92*
**Mumford,** William Frederick 1930- *Who 92*
**Mumm,** Dave 1950- *WhoWest 92*
**Mumm,** Robert Franklin 1935- *AmMWSc 92*
**Mumma,** Albert G 1906- *AmMWSc 92*
**Mumma,** Gordon 1935- *ConCom 92, NewAmDM, WhoEnt 92*
**Mumma,** Martin Dale 1936- *AmMWSc 92*
**Mumma,** Michael Jon 1941- *AmMWSc 92*
**Mumma,** Ralph O 1934- *AmMWSc 92*
**Mumme,** James Horace 1926- *WhoAmP 91, WhoRel 92*
**Mumme,** Judith E 1943- *AmMWSc 92*
**Mumme,** Kenneth Irving *AmMWSc 92*
**Mummert,** Jack R. 1962- *WhoMW 92*
**Mummery,** Christopher John L. *Who 92*
**Mummery,** John Frank 1938- *Who 92*
**Mumphrey,** Jerry Wayne 1952- *WhoBlA 92*
**Mumpton,** Frederick Albert 1932- *AmMWSc 92*
**Mumtaz,** Mohammad Moizuddin 1949- *AmMWSc 92*
**Mumy,** Bill 1954- *IntMPA 92*
**Mumy,** Billy 1954- *WhoEnt 92*
**Mun,** Alton M 1923- *AmMWSc 92*
**Muna,** Nadeem Mitri 1928- *AmMWSc 92*
**Muna,** Solomon Tandeng 1912- *IntWW 91*
**Munan,** Louis 1921- *AmMWSc 92*
**Munari,** Bruno 1907- *DcTwDes*
**Munarriz,** Lazaro R. *WhoHisp 92*
**Munasinghe,** Mohan 1945- *WhoFI 92*
**Munasinghe,** Mohan P 1945- *AmMWSc 92*
**Munby,** John Latimer 1937- *Who 92*
**Muncaster,** Claude Grahame 1903-1974 *TwCPaSc*
**Muncey,** Barbara Deane 1952- *WhoMW 92*
**Munch,** Charles 1891-1968 *FacFETw, NewAmDM*
**Munch,** Edvard 1863-1944 *FacFETw*
**Munch,** G 1921- *AmMWSc 92*
**Munch,** Jesper 1945- *AmMWSc 92*
**Munch,** John Howard 1938- *AmMWSc 92*
**Munch,** Ralph Howard 1911- *AmMWSc 92*
**Munch,** Robert Joseph 1951- *WhoFI 92*
**Munch,** Theodore 1919- *AmMWSc 92*
**Munchausen,** Linda Lou 1946- *AmMWSc 92*
**Munchhausen,** Borries, Baron von 1874-1945 *EncTR 91*
**Munchinger,** Karl 1915- *NewAmDM*
**Munchmeyer,** Alwin 1908- *IntWW 91*
**Munchmeyer,** Frederick Clarke 1922- *AmMWSc 92*
**Munck,** Allan Ulf 1925- *AmMWSc 92*
**Muncy,** Bobby W. 1931- *WhoRel 92*
**Muncy,** Martha Elizabeth 1919- *WhoMW 92*
**Muncy,** Robert Jess 1929- *AmMWSc 92*
**Munczeu,** Herman J 1927- *AmMWSc 92*
**Mund,** Harold Hugh 1945- *WhoAmP 91*
**Mundadan,** Anthony Mathias 1923- *WhoRel 92*
**Munday,** Anthony 1560?-1633? *RfGEnL 91*
**Munday,** Cheryl Casselberry 1950- *WhoBlA 92*
**Munday,** J C 1907- *AmMWSc 92*
**Munday,** John 1924- *Who 92*
**Munday,** John Clingman, Jr 1940- *AmMWSc 92*
**Munday,** Robert Stevenson 1954- *WhoRel 92*
**Munday,** Theodore F 1937- *AmMWSc 92*
**Munde,** Paul Fortunatus 1846-1902 *BiInAmS*
**Mundebo,** Ingemar 1930- *IntWW 91*
**Mundel,** August B 1911- *AmMWSc 92*
**Mundel,** Marvin Everett 1916- *WrDr 92*
**Mundelein,** George William 1872-1939 *RelLAm 91*
**Mundell,** David Edward 1931- *WhoFI 92*
**Mundell,** John Andrew, Jr. 1923- *WhoAmL 92*
**Mundell,** Percy Meldrum 1921- *AmMWSc 92*
**Mundell,** Robert David 1936- *AmMWSc 92*
**Mundell,** William A 1952- *WhoAmP 91*
**Munden,** Robin Ghezzi 1947- *WhoAmL 92, WhoFI 92*
**Munder,** Terrie Hollowed 1930- *WhoMW 92*
**Mundey,** Paul Eston Risser 1951- *WhoRel 92*
**Mundheim,** Robert Harry 1933- *WhoAmL 92, WhoAmP 91*
**Mundie,** Lloyd George 1916- *AmMWSc 92*
**Mundis,** Hester *DrAPF 91*
**Mundis,** Hester 1938- *ConAu 34NR, IntAu&W 91, WrDr 92*
**Mundis,** Hester Jane 1938- *WhoEnt 92*
**Mundis,** Jerrold *DrAPF 91*
**Mundkur,** Balaji 1924- *AmMWSc 92*
**Mundo,** Oto *ScFEYrs*
**Mundorff,** Sheila Ann 1945- *AmMWSc 92*
**Mundschenk,** Paul Ernest 1938- *WhoRel 92*
**Mundstock,** Karl 1915- *IntAu&W 91*
**Mundt,** Brian Daniel 1959- *WhoMW 92*
**Mundt,** Donald K 1923- *WhoIns 92*
**Mundt,** Gary Harold 1943- *WhoAmP 91*
**Mundt,** Gerald D 1936- *WhoIns 92*
**Mundt,** Philip A 1927- *AmMWSc 92*
**Mundt,** Ray B. 1928- *WhoFI 92*
**Mundt,** William Frank 1942- *WhoAmL 92*
**Mundy,** Bradford Philip 1938- *AmMWSc 92*
**Mundy,** Gardner Marshall 1934- *WhoAmL 92*
**Mundy,** Gregory Robert 1942- *AmMWSc 92*
**Mundy,** Henry 1919- *TwCPaSc*
**Mundy,** John 1555?-1630 *NewAmDM*
**Mundy,** John Francis 1946- *WhoFI 92*
**Mundy,** Max *WrDr 92*
**Mundy,** Phyllis 1948- *WhoAmP 91*
**Mundy,** Roy Lee 1922- *AmMWSc 92*
**Mundy,** Talbot 1879-1940 *BenetAL 91, ScFEYrs*
**Mundy,** William 1529?-1591 *NewAmDM*
**Muneta,** Paul 1931- *AmMWSc 92*
**Munford,** Dillard 1918- *WhoAmP 91, WhoFI 92*
**Munford,** Joan Hardie 1933- *WhoAmP 91*
**Munford,** John Durburrow 1928- *WhoFI 92*
**Munford,** Paul Stanley 1949- *WhoBlA 92*
**Munford,** Robert 1730?-1784 *BenetAL 91*
**Munford,** William 1775-1825 *BenetAL 91*
**Munford,** William Arthur 1911- *Who 92, WrDr 92*
**Mungai,** Joseph James 1943- *IntWW 91*
**Mungai,** Njoroge 1926- *IntWW 91*
**Mungall,** Allan George 1928- *AmMWSc 92*
**Mungall,** William Stewart 1945- *AmMWSc 92*
**Mungan,** Necmettin 1934- *AmMWSc 92*
**Mungandu,** Adrian *WhoRel 92*
**Munger,** Bryce Leon 1933- *AmMWSc 92*
**Munger,** Charles Galloway 1912- *AmMWSc 92*
**Munger,** Edwin Stanton 1921- *WhoWest 92*
**Munger,** Harold Hawley, II 1947- *WhoMW 92*
**Munger,** John Francis 1946- *WhoAmP 91*
**Munger,** Paul R 1932- *AmMWSc 92*
**Munger,** Stanley H 1920- *AmMWSc 92*
**Munger,** Willard M 1911- *WhoAmP 91*
**Mungia,** Sal Alejo, Jr. 1959- *WhoAmL 92*
**Mungin,** Horace *DrAPF 91*
**Mungo,** M. Stewart 1952- *WhoFI 92*
**Mungo,** Michael J. 1928- *WhoFI 92*
**Mung'omba,** Wila D'Israeli 1939- *IntWW 91*
**Munguia,** Gus *WhoHisp 92*
**Munhall,** Ruth Beatrice 1929- *WhoFI 92*
**Muni,** Indu A 1942- *AmMWSc 92*
**Muni,** Paul 1896-1967 *FacFETw*
**Muniappan,** Rangaswamy Naicker 1941- *AmMWSc 92*
**Munic,** Martin Daniel 1959- *WhoAmL 92*
**Munich,** John Robert 1955- *WhoAmL 92*
**Munigle,** Jo Anne 1934- *AmMWSc 92*
**Munik,** Janusz 1950- *WhoFI 92*
**Munim,** Mohammad Abdul 1935- *IntWW 91*
**Munir,** Ashley Edward 1934- *Who 92*
**Munir,** Zuhair A 1934- *AmMWSc 92*
**Munisteri,** Arthur Angelo 1939- *WhoAmL 92*
**Munitz,** Barry Allen 1941- *WhoWest 92*
**Munitz,** Milton K. 1913- *ConAu 36NR*
**Munive Escobar,** Luis 1920- *WhoRel 92*
**Munive y Aspee,** Lope Antonio de 1630-1689 *HisDSpE*
**Muniz,** Carlos Manuel 1922- *IntWW 91*
**Muniz,** Eddy 1960- *WhoHisp 92*
**Muniz,** Herminio 1928- *WhoHisp 92*
**Muniz Arrambide,** Isabel 1960- *WhoHisp 92*
**Muniz-Huberman,** Angelina 1936- *IntAu&W 91*
**Muniz Rivera,** Edgardo Luis 1964- *WhoHisp 92*
**Muniz-Torres,** Oscar 1947- *WhoHisp 92*
**Munizzi,** Pamela Annette 1954- *WhoAmP 91*
**Munk,** Andrzej 1921-1961 *IntDcF 2-2 [port]*
**Munk,** Benedikt Aage 1929- *AmMWSc 92*
**Munk,** Chris *WhoBlA 92*
**Munk,** Frank 1901- *IntWW 91*
**Munk,** Miner Nelson 1934- *AmMWSc 92*
**Munk,** Petr 1932- *AmMWSc 92*
**Munk,** Vladimir 1925- *AmMWSc 92*
**Munk,** Walter Heinrich 1917- *AmMWSc 92, IntWW 91, WhoWest 92*
**Munk Andersen,** Jens 1928- *IntWW 91*
**Munk Olsen,** Birger 1935- *IntWW 91*
**Munkacsi,** Istvan 1927- *AmMWSc 92*
**Munkejord,** Svein 1948- *IntWW 91*
**Munkres,** James Raymond 1930- *AmMWSc 92*
**Munley,** Annette E 1936- *WhoAmP 91*
**Munn,** David Alan 1947- *AmMWSc 92*
**Munn,** George Edward 1924- *AmMWSc 92*
**Munn,** H T *ScFEYrs*
**Munn,** H Warner 1903-1982 *ScFEYrs*
**Munn,** James 1920- *Who 92*
**Munn,** John Irvin 1922- *AmMWSc 92*
**Munn,** John Symonds 1933- *WhoMW 92*
**Munn,** Lewis Edwin 1944- *WhoEnt 92*
**Munn,** Robert Edward 1919- *AmMWSc 92*
**Munn,** Robert James 1937- *AmMWSc 92*
**Munn,** Susan Ann 1961- *WhoMW 92*
**Munn,** William Charles, II 1938- *WhoWest 92*
**Munnecke,** Donald Edwin 1920- *AmMWSc 92*
**Munneke,** Russell Edward 1946- *WhoEnt 92, WhoMW 92*
**Munnell,** Alicia Haydock 1942- *WhoFI 92*
**Munnell,** Equinn W 1913- *AmMWSc 92*
**Munnich,** Lee William, Jr 1945- *WhoAmP 91*
**Munninger,** Michael Joseph 1948- *WhoWest 92*
**Munnings,** Alfred 1878-1959 *TwCPaSc*
**Munno,** Frank J 1936- *AmMWSc 92*
**Munno,** Maurice William 1948- *WhoAmL 92*
**Munns,** Donald Neville 1931- *AmMWSc 92*
**Munns,** Paul Robert 1963- *WhoAmP 91*
**Munns,** Theodore Willard 1941- *AmMWSc 92*
**Munns,** Victor George 1926- *Who 92*
**Munns,** W O 1926- *AmMWSc 92*
**Munonye,** John 1929- *ConNov 91, WrDr 92*
**Munos Marin,** Luis 1898-1980 *HisDSpE*
**Munoz,** Adan, Jr. 1948- *WhoHisp 92*
**Munoz,** Anthony 1958- *WhoBlA 92, WhoHisp 92*
**Munoz,** Artemio Zaragosa 1944- *WhoHisp 92*
**Munoz,** Aurelio *WhoHisp 92*
**Munoz,** Braulio 1946- *WhoHisp 92*
**Munoz,** Carlos, Jr. 1939- *WhoHisp 92*
**Munoz,** Carlos Ramon *WhoHisp 92*
**Munoz,** Carlos Ramon 1935- *WhoFI 92*
**Munoz,** Carmen 1936- *WhoHisp 92*
**Munoz,** Celia Alvarez 1937- *WhoHisp 92*
**Munoz,** Dorothy D. 1927- *WhoRel 92*
**Munoz,** Edward 1927- *WhoHisp 92*
**Munoz,** Edward H. 1944- *WhoHisp 92*
**Munoz,** Elias Miguel 1954- *WhoHisp 92*
**Munoz,** Frances *WhoHisp 92*
**Munoz,** George 1951- *WhoHisp 92*
**Munoz,** Grisel 1957- *WhoHisp 92*
**Munoz,** James Loomis 1939- *AmMWSc 92*
**Munoz,** Joanne Maura *WhoHisp 92*
**Munoz,** John Anthony *WhoHisp 92*
**Munoz,** John Joaquin 1918- *AmMWSc 92, WhoHisp 92*
**Munoz,** John Joseph 1932- *WhoWest 92*

**Munoz**, John Richard 1948- *WhoHisp 92*
**Munoz**, Jose Francisco 1946- *WhoHisp 92*
**Munoz**, Jose Luis 1945- *WhoHisp 92*
**Munoz**, Joseph 1940- *WhoHisp 92*
**Munoz**, Juan H. 1944- *WhoHisp 92*
**Munoz**, Julian Daniel 1946- *WhoFI 92*
**Munoz**, Julio Alex 1922- *WhoHisp 92*
**Munoz**, Leonel 1953- *WhoHisp 92*
**Munoz**, Manuel Anthony 1945- *WhoFI 92, WhoHisp 92*
**Munoz**, Maria De Lourdes 1952- *AmMWSc 92*
**Munoz**, Mario Alejandro 1928- *WhoMW 92*
**Munoz**, Memo 1955- *WhoHisp 92*
**Munoz**, Michael John 1963- *WhoHisp 92*
**Munoz**, Moises Garcia 1922- *WhoHisp 92*
**Munoz**, Pedro Javier 1968- *WhoHisp 92*
**Munoz**, Raul 1932- *WhoHisp 92*
**Munoz**, Raul Enrique 1939- *WhoHisp 92*
**Munoz**, Ricardo Felipe 1950- *WhoWest 92*
**Munoz**, Robert Francis 1953- *WhoAmL 92*
**Munoz**, Robert I. *WhoHisp 92*
**Munoz**, Romeo Solano 1933- *WhoMW 92*
**Munoz**, Victoria *WhoHisp 92*
**Munoz**, Willy Oscar 1949- *WhoHisp 92, WhoMW 92*
**Munoz-Blanco**, Maria M. 1963- *WhoHisp 92*
**Munoz-Dones**, Eloisa 1922- *WhoHisp 92*
**Munoz Grandes**, Agustin 1896-1970 *BiDExR*
**Munoz Ledo**, Porfirio 1933- *IntWW 91*
**Munoz Marin**, Luis 1898-1980 *FacFETw, RComAH*
**Munoz Mendoza**, Victoria 1940- *WhoAmP 91*
**Munoz Nunez**, Rafael 1925- *WhoRel 92*
**Munoz-Rivera**, Luis 1916- *WhoAmP 91*
**Munoz-Sandoval**, Ana Felicia 1947- *WhoHisp 92*
**Munoz-Sola**, Haydee S. 1943- *WhoHisp 92*
**Munoz Vega**, Pablo 1903- *IntWW 91*
**Munro**, Alan 1935- *Who 92*
**Munro**, Alice 1931- *BenetAL 91, ConNov 91, IntAu&W 91, RfGEnL 91, WrDr 92*
**Munro**, Alison *Who 92*
**Munro**, Charles Rowcliffe 1902- *Who 92*
**Munro**, Colin William Gordon R. *Who 92*
**Munro**, Cristina Stirling 1940- *WhoEnt 92*
**Munro**, Dana G. d1990 *IntWW 91N*
**Munro**, David Mackenzie 1950- *IntAu&W 91*
**Munro**, Donald J. 1931- *ConAu 133*
**Munro**, Donald W, Jr 1937- *AmMWSc 92*
**Munro**, Graeme Neil 1944- *Who 92*
**Munro**, H. H. 1870-1916 *CnDBLB 5 [port]*
**Munro**, Hamish N 1915- *AmMWSc 92*
**Munro**, Hamish Nisbet 1915- *IntWW 91*
**Munro**, Hector Hugh *RfGEnL 91*
**Munro**, Hedi 1916- *WhoEnt 92*
**Munro**, Ian Arthur Hoyle 1923- *Who 92*
**Munro**, J. Richard *LesBEnT 92*
**Munro**, J. Richard 1931- *IntWW 91, WhoFI 92*
**Munro**, James *WrDr 92*
**Munro**, James Ian 1947- *AmMWSc 92*
**Munro**, James Lionel 1938- *WhoMW 92*
**Munro**, John 1849-1930 *ScFEYrs*
**Munro**, John Bennet Lorimer 1905- *Who 92*
**Munro**, John Carr 1931- *IntWW 91*
**Munro**, John Cummings 1858-1910 *BiInAmS*
**Munro**, John M. 1932- *WrDr 92*
**Munro**, John Murchison 1932- *IntAu&W 91*
**Munro**, Joseph Barnes, Jr. 1930- *WhoAmL 92*
**Munro**, Margaret S 1920- *WhoAmP 91*
**Munro**, Martha 1947- *WhoEnt 92*
**Munro**, Mary *IntAu&W 91X, WrDr 92*
**Munro**, Michael Brian 1948- *AmMWSc 92*
**Munro**, Ralph Davies 1943- *WhoAmP 91, WhoWest 92*
**Munro**, Richard Harding 1943- *AmMWSc 92*
**Munro**, Robert 1907- *Who 92*
**Munro**, Robert Allan 1932- *WhoMW 92*
**Munro**, Roderick Anthony 1955- *WhoMW 92*
**Munro**, Ronald Eadie *IntAu&W 91X, WrDr 92*
**Munro**, Ronald Gordon *AmMWSc 92*
**Munro**, Sydney Douglas G. *Who 92*
**Munro**, William 1900- *Who 92*
**Munro**, William Delmar 1916- *AmMWSc 92*
**Munro**, Winsome 1925- *WhoRel 92*
**Munro of Foulis**, Patrick 1912- *Who 92*
**Munro of Foulis-Obsdale**, Ian Talbot 1929- *Who 92*
**Munro of Lindertis**, Alasdair 1927- *Who 92*
**Munroe**, David A 1938- *WhoAmP 91*
**Munroe**, Donna Scott 1945- *WhoFI 92, WhoWest 92*
**Munroe**, Eugene Gordon 1919- *AmMWSc 92*
**Munroe**, George d1896 *BiInAmS*
**Munroe**, John Peter 1857-1940 *DcNCBi 4*
**Munroe**, Lorne *WhoEnt 92*
**Munroe**, Lydia Darlene 1933- *WhoWest 92*
**Munroe**, Marshall Evans 1918- *AmMWSc 92*
**Munroe**, Ralph William Taylor 1951- *WhoFI 92*
**Munroe**, Stephen Horner 1946- *AmMWSc 92*
**Munrow**, David 1942-1976 *NewAmDM*
**Munrow**, Roger Davis 1929- *Who 92*
**Muns Albuixech**, Joaquin 1935- *IntWW 91*
**Munsch**, Kenneth Michael 1947- *WhoFI 92*
**Munsch**, Robert 1945- *IntAu&W 91, WrDr 92*
**Munsch**, Terri Sue 1953- *WhoFI 92*
**Munse**, William H 1919- *AmMWSc 92*
**Munse**, William Herman 1919- *WhoMW 92*
**Munsee**, Jack Howard 1934- *AmMWSc 92*
**Munsel**, Patrice 1925- *NewAmDM*
**Munsell**, Albert 1858-1918 *DcTwDes*
**Munsell**, Charles Edward 1858-1918 *BiInAmS*
**Munsell**, Monroe Wallwork 1925- *AmMWSc 92*
**Munsell**, Susan Grimes *WhoAmP 91*
**Munsey**, Everard 1933- *WhoAmP 91*
**Munsey**, Frank A. 1854-1925 *BenetAL 91*
**Munsey**, Frank Andrew 1854-1925 *FacFETw*
**Munsey**, Frank Torrance 1922- *WhoRel 92*
**Munsey**, Rodney Roundy 1932- *WhoAmL 92*
**Munsick**, Robert Alliot 1928- *AmMWSc 92*
**Munson**, Albert Enoch 1934- *AmMWSc 92*
**Munson**, Albert G 1931- *AmMWSc 92*
**Munson**, Alex Robert 1941- *WhoAmL 92*
**Munson**, Arthur Julius 1907- *WhoAmP 91*
**Munson**, Arvid W 1933- *AmMWSc 92*
**Munson**, Benjamin Ray 1937- *AmMWSc 92*
**Munson**, Burnaby 1933- *AmMWSc 92*
**Munson**, Charlie E. 1877-1975 *ConAu 134*
**Munson**, Cheryl Denise 1954- *WhoBIA 92*
**Munson**, Darrell E 1933- *AmMWSc 92*
**Munson**, David Roy 1942- *WhoAmP 91*
**Munson**, Don 1908-1978 *ConAu 133*
**Munson**, Donald Albert 1941- *AmMWSc 92*
**Munson**, Donald Francis 1937- *WhoAmP 91*
**Munson**, Eddie Ray 1950- *WhoBIA 92*
**Munson**, Edwin Sterling 1933- *AmMWSc 92*
**Munson**, Eneas 1734-1826 *BiInAmS*
**Munson**, Gorham 1896-1969 *BenetAL 91*
**Munson**, H Randall, Jr 1934- *AmMWSc 92*
**Munson**, Howard G. 1924- *WhoAmL 92*
**Munson**, J C 1926- *AmMWSc 92*
**Munson**, James William 1943- *AmMWSc 92*
**Munson**, John B 1914- *WhoAmP 91*
**Munson**, John Bacon 1932- *AmMWSc 92*
**Munson**, Lucille Marguerite 1914- *WhoFI 92, WhoWest 92*
**Munson**, Nancy Kay 1936- *WhoAmL 92, WhoFI 92*
**Munson**, Norma Frances 1923- *WhoMW 92*
**Munson**, Paul Lewis 1910- *AmMWSc 92*
**Munson**, Ralph Andrew 1950- *WhoWest 92*
**Munson**, Ray Eugene 1927- *WhoWest 92*
**Munson**, Robert Dean 1927- *AmMWSc 92*
**Munson**, Robert H. 1931- *WhoBIA 92*
**Munson**, Roger L. *WhoRel 92*
**Munson**, Ronald Alfred 1933- *AmMWSc 92*
**Munson**, Thomas Nolan 1924- *WrDr 92*
**Munson**, Thomas Volney 1843-1913 *BiInAmS*
**Munson**, Thurman 1947-1979 *FacFETw*
**Munson**, Virginia Aldrich 1932- *WhoMW 92*
**Munster**, Earl of 1926- *Who 92*
**Munster**, Edward W *WhoAmP 91*
**Munsterberg**, Hugo 1863-1916 *BiInAmS*
**Munstermann**, Leonard Elmer 1942- *WhoMW 92*
**Munsterteiger**, Kay Diane 1956- *WhoWest 92*
**Munt**, Donna S 1950- *WhoIns 92*
**Muntean**, George 1950- *WhoRel 92*
**Muntean**, Richard August 1949- *AmMWSc 92*
**Munter**, Pamela Osborne 1943- *WhoFI 92*
**Munts**, Mary Louise 1924- *WhoAmP 91*
**Munts**, Steven Rowe 1949- *WhoWest 92*
**Muntyan**, Mikhail Ivanovich 1943- *IntWW 91*
**Muntz**, Eric Phillip 1934- *AmMWSc 92*
**Muntz**, Kathryn Howe *AmMWSc 92*
**Muntz**, Richard Robert 1941- *AmMWSc 92*
**Muntz**, Ronald Lee 1945- *AmMWSc 92*
**Muntzner**, Gregory Charles 1952- *WhoWest 92*
**Munu**, Momodu 1938- *IntWW 91*
**Munushian**, Jack 1923- *AmMWSc 92*
**Munves**, Elizabeth Douglass *AmMWSc 92*
**Munyer**, Edward Arnold 1936- *AmMWSc 92*
**Munyon**, William Harry, Jr. 1945- *WhoFI 92*
**Munz**, Peter 1921- *IntAu&W 91, WrDr 92*
**Munzenberg**, Willi 1889-1940 *EncTR 91 [port]*
**Munzer**, Annette Elizabeth 1944- *WhoEnt 92*
**Munzer**, Cynthia Brown 1948- *WhoEnt 92*
**Munzer**, Martha E. 1899- *WrDr 92*
**Munzer**, Rudolph James 1918- *WhoFI 92*
**Munzer**, Stephen Ira 1939- *WhoAmL 92*
**Munzer**, Stephen R. 1944- *WhoAmL 92*
**Munzinger**, Judith Montgomery 1944- *WhoMW 92*
**Muoto**, Oliver Chukwudi 1965- *WhoWest 92*
**Mur**, Lazaro Jesus, Jr. 1957- *WhoAmL 92*
**Mura**, David *DrAPF 91*
**Mura**, Toshio 1925- *AmMWSc 92*
**Muraca**, Ralph John 1935- *AmMWSc 92*
**Murad**, Edmond 1934- *AmMWSc 92*
**Murad**, Emil Moise 1926- *AmMWSc 92*
**Murad**, Ferid 1936- *AmMWSc 92*
**Murad**, John Louis 1932- *AmMWSc 92*
**Murad**, Sohail 1953- *AmMWSc 92*
**Murad**, Turhon Allen 1944- *AmMWSc 92*
**Muradeli**, Vano Il'ich 1908-1970 *SovUnBD*
**Muradyan**, Sarkis Mambreevich 1927- *SovUnBD*
**Murai**, Kotaro 1925- *AmMWSc 92*
**Murai**, Miyeko Mary 1913- *AmMWSc 92*
**Murail**, Tristan 1947- *ConCom 92*
**Murakami**, Masanori 1940- *AmMWSc 92*
**Murakami**, Masanori 1943- *AmMWSc 92*
**Murakami**, Takio 1921- *AmMWSc 92*
**Murakami**, Toshio *WhoRel 92*
**Murakhovsky**, Vsevolod Serafimovich 1926- *IntWW 91, SovUnBD*
**Murakishi**, Harry Haruo 1917- *AmMWSc 92*
**Muramoto**, Hiroshi 1922- *AmMWSc 92*
**Muranaka**, Hideo 1946- *WhoWest 92*
**Murano**, Genesio 1941- *AmMWSc 92*
**Murany**, Ernest Elmer 1923- *AmMWSc 92*
**Muraoka**, Sadakatsu 1910- *IntWW 91*
**Muraoka**, Takamitsu 1938- *IntWW 91*
**Murashige**, Toshio 1930- *AmMWSc 92*
**Muraski**, Anthony Augustus 1946- *WhoAmL 92, WhoFI 92, WhoMW 92*
**Muraskin**, Murray 1935- *AmMWSc 92*
**Murasko**, Donna Marie 1950- *AmMWSc 92*
**Murasugi**, Kunio 1929- *AmMWSc 92*
**Murat**, Achille, Prince 1801-1847 *BenetAL 91*
**Murat**, Joachim 1767-1815 *BenetAL 91*
**Murat**, William M 1957- *WhoAmP 91*
**Murata**, Alice Kishiye 1940- *WhoMW 92*
**Murata**, Keijiro 1924- *IntWW 91*
**Murata**, Kiyoaki 1922- *IntAu&W 91, IntWW 91*
**Murata**, Makoto 1926- *IntWW 91*
**Murata**, Masachika 1906- *IntWW 91*
**Murata**, Ryohei 1929- *IntWW 91*
**Murata**, Tadao 1938- *AmMWSc 92*
**Muratori**, Fred *DrAPF 91*
**Muratori**, Jack R 1929- *WhoAmP 91*
**Muratori**, Ludovico Antonio 1672-1750 *BlkwCEP*
**Muravin**, Victor 1929- *LiExTwC*
**Murawski**, Elisabeth *DrAPF 91*
**Murawski**, Thomas Frank 1945- *WhoFI 92*
**Muray**, Julius J 1931- *AmMWSc 92*
**Murayama**, Makio 1912- *AmMWSc 92*
**Murayama**, Takayuki 1932- *AmMWSc 92*
**Murayama**, Tatsuo *IntWW 91*
**Murbach**, Earl Wesley 1922- *AmMWSc 92*
**Murch**, Everett Lloyd 1935- *WhoFI 92, WhoMW 92*
**Murch**, Laurence Everett 1942- *AmMWSc 92*
**Murch**, Robert Matthews 1924- *AmMWSc 92*
**Murch**, S Allan 1929- *AmMWSc 92*
**Murch**, Walter *ConTFT 9*
**Murch**, Walter Scott 1943- *WhoEnt 92*
**Murchake**, John 1922- *WhoFI 92*
**Murchie**, Guy 1907- *WrDr 92*
**Murchie**, John Ivor 1928- *Who 92*
**Murchison**, Claudius Temple 1889-1968 *DcNCBi 4*
**Murchison**, Craig Brian 1943- *AmMWSc 92*
**Murchison**, David Claudius 1923- *WhoAmL 92, WhoFI 92*
**Murchison**, David Reid 1837-1882 *DcNCBi 4*
**Murchison**, David Roderick 1948- *WhoAmL 92, WhoFI 92*
**Murchison**, Ira 1933- *BlkOlyM*
**Murchison**, Kenneth McKenzie 1831-1904 *DcNCBi 4*
**Murchison**, Pamela W 1943- *AmMWSc 92*
**Murchison**, Thomas Edgar 1932- *AmMWSc 92*
**Murcia**, Joey *WhoEnt 92*
**Murciano**, Marianne 1957- *WhoHisp 92*
**Murcko**, Donald Leroy 1953- *WhoMW 92*
**Murcray**, David Guy 1924- *AmMWSc 92*
**Murcray**, Frank James 1950- *AmMWSc 92*
**Murdaugh**, Herschel Victor, Jr 1928- *AmMWSc 92*
**Murday**, James Stanley 1942- *AmMWSc 92*
**Murden**, W P, Jr 1924- *AmMWSc 92*
**Murden**, William Roland, Jr 1922- *AmMWSc 92*
**Murdeshwar**, Mangesh Ganesh 1933- *AmMWSc 92*
**Murdic**, Thomas Edward 1953- *WhoAmP 91*
**Murdick**, Philip W 1928- *AmMWSc 92*
**Murdin**, Paul Geoffrey 1942- *Who 92*
**Murdoch**, Arthur 1934- *AmMWSc 92*
**Murdoch**, Arthur Roy 1934- *WhoMW 92*
**Murdoch**, Bruce Thomas 1940- *AmMWSc 92*
**Murdoch**, Charles Loraine 1932- *AmMWSc 92*
**Murdoch**, David Armor 1942- *WhoAmL 92, WhoFI 92*
**Murdoch**, David Carruthers 1912- *AmMWSc 92*
**Murdoch**, Elisabeth 1909- *Who 92*
**Murdoch**, Francis Johnstone 1846-1909 *DcNCBi 4*
**Murdoch**, Frank Hitchcock 1843-1872 *BenetAL 91*
**Murdoch**, H J *TwCSFW 91*
**Murdoch**, Iris *Who 92*
**Murdoch**, Iris 1919- *CnDBLB 8 [port], ConNov 91, IntAu&W 91, IntWW 91, RfGEnL 91, WrDr 92*
**Murdoch**, Iris 1922- *FacFETw*
**Murdoch**, Jean Iris 1919- *Who 92*
**Murdoch**, John Derek Walter 1945- *Who 92*
**Murdoch**, Joseph B 1927- *AmMWSc 92*
**Murdoch**, Keith Rupert 1931- *Who 92*
**Murdoch**, Mary Charlotte 1864-1916 *BiDBrF 2*
**Murdoch**, Richard 1907-1990 *AnObit 1990*
**Murdoch**, Richard Bernard d1990 *Who 92N*
**Murdoch**, Robert 1911- *Who 92*
**Murdoch**, Robert Whitten 1937- *WhoAmL 92, WhoFI 92*
**Murdoch**, Rupert *LesBEnT 92 [port], Who 92*
**Murdoch**, Rupert 1931- *FacFETw, IntAu&W 91, IntMPA 92, IntWW 91, WhoFI 92*
**Murdoch**, William Richard 1931- *WhoWest 92*
**Murdoch**, William Ridley Morton 1917- *Who 92*
**Murdoch**, William W 1939- *AmMWSc 92*
**Murdoch-Kitt**, Jonathan Michael 1948- *WhoAmL 92*
**Murdock**, Archie Lee 1933- *AmMWSc 92*
**Murdock**, Barbara Walker 1951- *WhoAmL 92*
**Murdock**, Beatrice K *WhoAmP 91*
**Murdock**, Charles William 1935- *WhoAmL 92*
**Murdock**, David H. 1923- *WhoFI 92, WhoWest 92*
**Murdock**, Deborah Dale 1943- *WhoAmP 91*
**Murdock**, Delmar Curtis 1952- *WhoRel 92*
**Murdock**, Denis Ray 1948- *WhoWest 92*
**Murdock**, Donald Dean 1928- *WhoAmP 91*
**Murdock**, Eugene C. 1921- *WrDr 92*
**Murdock**, Eugene Converse 1921- *IntAu&W 91*
**Murdock**, Fenoi R 1917- *AmMWSc 92*
**Murdock**, Gary Allen 1960- *WhoMW 92*
**Murdock**, Gordon Alfred 1923- *AmMWSc 92*
**Murdock**, Gordon Robert 1943- *AmMWSc 92*
**Murdock**, Harold Russell 1919- *AmMWSc 92*
**Murdock**, Jamie Lee 1953- *WhoAmL 92*
**Murdock**, Joann 1955- *WhoEnt 92*
**Murdock**, John Edgar, III 1947- *WhoAmL 92*
**Murdock**, John Thomas 1927- *AmMWSc 92*

**Murdock**, Joseph Patrick 1928- *WhoAmL 92*
**Murdock**, Keith Chadwick 1928- *AmMWSc 92*
**Murdock**, Mickey L 1942- *WhoIns 92*
**Murdock**, Norman A 1931- *WhoAmP 91*
**Murdock**, Norman Anthony 1931- *WhoAmL 92*
**Murdock**, Pamela Ervilla 1940- *WhoWest 92*
**Murdock**, Phelps Dubois, Jr. 1944- *WhoFI 92, WhoMW 92*
**Murdock**, Steven Kent 1946- *WhoWest 92*
**Murdock**, Veronica 1963- *WhoEnt 92, WhoWest 92*
**Murdy**, Louise Baughan 1935- *WrDr 92*
**Murdy**, William Henry 1928- *AmMWSc 92*
**Mure**, David 1912-1986 *ConAu 134*
**Mure**, Kenneth Nisbet 1947- *Who 92*
**Mureika**, Roman A 1944- *AmMWSc 92*
**Muren**, Dennis E. 1946- *WhoEnt 92*
**Murena**, H. A. 1923- *IntWW 91*
**Murensky**, Rick, III 1953- *WhoAmP 91*
**Murer**, Erik Homann 1931- *AmMWSc 92*
**Murer**, Eugene 1845-1906 *ThHEIm*
**Murerwa**, Herbert Muchemwa 1941- *IntWW 91, Who 92*
**Murff**, Henry Dwayne 1951- *WhoEnt 92*
**Murfin**, Jane 1893-1955 *ReelWom [port]*
**Murfin**, Michael 1954- *TwCPaSc*
**Murfree**, Hardy 1752-1809 *DcNCBi 4*
**Murfree**, Mary Noailles 1850-1922 *BenetAL 91*
**Murfree**, William Hardy 1781-1826 *DcNCBi 4*
**Murga**, Jesse SantiEsteban 1958- *WhoAmL 92*
**Murgatroyd**, Eric Neal 1950- *WhoFI 92*
**Murgatroyd**, Walter 1921- *Who 92*
**Murger**, Henry 1822-1862 *GuFrLit 1*
**Murgie**, Samuel A 1957- *AmMWSc 92*
**Murgita**, Robert Anthony 1942- *AmMWSc 92*
**Murgola**, Emanuel J 1937- *AmMWSc 92*
**Murguia**, Alejandro *DrAPF 91*
**Murguia**, D. Edward 1943- *WhoHisp 92*
**Murguia**, Dana M. 1967- *WhoHisp 92*
**Murguia**, Filiberto 1932- *WhoHisp 92*
**Murgulescu**, Ilie 1902- *IntWW 91*
**Murie**, Jan O 1939- *AmMWSc 92*
**Murie**, Margaret E. 1902- *WrDr 92*
**Murie**, Richard A 1923- *AmMWSc 92*
**Murieta**, Joaquin 1829?-1853 *BenetAL 91*
**Murillo**, Alice 1954- *WhoHisp 92*
**Murillo**, John J., Jr. 1964- *WhoHisp 92*
**Murillo**, Pedro Domingo 1757-1810 *HisDSpE*
**Murillo-Rohde**, Ildaura M. *WhoHisp 92*
**Murino**, Clifford John 1929- *AmMWSc 92*
**Murino**, Vincent S 1924- *AmMWSc 92*
**Muris**, Timothy Joseph 1949- *WhoAmP 91*
**Murison**, Gerald Leonard 1939- *AmMWSc 92*
**Murk**, Lyndon Keith 1926- *WhoRel 92*
**Murkowski**, Frank H. 1933- *AlmAP 92 [port], WhoAmP 91*
**Murkowski**, Frank Hughes 1933- *IntWW 91, WhoWest 92*
**Murley**, John Tregarthen 1928- *Who 92*
**Murley**, Reginald 1916- *Who 92*
**Murli**, Hemalatha *AmMWSc 92*
**Murman**, Earll Morton 1942- *AmMWSc 92*
**Murmann**, Robert Kent 1927- *AmMWSc 92*
**Murnaghan**, Francis D, Jr *WhoAmP 91*
**Murnaghan**, Francis Dominic, Jr. 1920- *WhoAmL 92*
**Murnane**, Edward David 1944- *WhoMW 92*
**Murnane**, George Thomas, Jr. 1921- *WhoFI 92*
**Murnane**, Gerald 1939- *ConNov 91, TwCSFW 91, WrDr 92*
**Murnane**, Thomas George 1926- *AmMWSc 92*
**Murnane**, Thomas William 1936- *AmMWSc 92*
**Murnau**, F. W. 1888-1931 *IntDcF 2-2 [port]*
**Murnick**, Daniel E 1941- *AmMWSc 92*
**Murnighan**, John Keith 1948- *WhoMW 92*
**Murnik**, James Michael 1934- *WhoMW 92*
**Murnik**, Mary Rengo 1942- *AmMWSc 92, WhoMW 92*
**Muro**, Gertrude Hilda 1939- *WhoHisp 92*
**Muro**, Roy Alfred 1942- *WhoFI 92*
**Muroga**, Saburo 1925- *AmMWSc 92*
**Murov**, Steven Lee 1940- *AmMWSc 92*
**Murovich**, Vincent Charles 1932- *WhoAmL 92*
**Murphey**, Archibald DeBow 1777?-1832 *DcNCBi 4*
**Murphey**, Arthur Gage, Jr. 1927- *WhoAmL 92*
**Murphey**, Byron Freeze 1918- *AmMWSc 92*
**Murphey**, Joseph Colin *DrAPF 91*
**Murphey**, Patrick Allen 1950- *WhoAmL 92*
**Murphey**, Rhoads 1919- *IntAu&W 91, WrDr 92*
**Murphey**, Robert Stafford 1921- *AmMWSc 92*
**Murphey**, Robert William 1933- *WhoWest 92*
**Murphey**, Rodney Keith 1942- *AmMWSc 92*
**Murphey**, Wayne K 1927- *AmMWSc 92*
**Murphey**, Will B 1928- *WhoIns 92*
**Murphree**, A Linn 1945- *AmMWSc 92*
**Murphree**, Henry Bernard Scott 1927- *AmMWSc 92*
**Murphree**, Jon Tal 1936- *WhoRel 92*
**Murphree**, Sharon Ann 1949- *WhoAmL 92*
**Murphy**, Alexander James 1939- *AmMWSc 92*
**Murphy**, Alfred Henry 1918- *AmMWSc 92*
**Murphy**, Allan Hunt 1931- *AmMWSc 92*
**Murphy**, Allen Emerson 1921- *AmMWSc 92*
**Murphy**, Allen Forrest, III 1954- *WhoFI 92*
**Murphy**, Alvin Hugh 1930- *WhoBlA 92*
**Murphy**, Andrew John 1946- *Who 92*
**Murphy**, Andrew Phillip, Jr. 1922- *WhoAmL 92*
**Murphy**, Anthony 1962- *WhoFI 92*
**Murphy**, Anthony Albert 1924- *Who 92*
**Murphy**, Arthur 1727-1805 *RfGEnL 91*
**Murphy**, Arthur G. 1929- *WhoBlA 92*
**Murphy**, Arthur Patrick 1917- *IntAu&W 91*
**Murphy**, Arthur Thomas 1929- *AmMWSc 92*
**Murphy**, Arthur William 1922- *WhoAmL 92*
**Murphy**, Audie 1924-1971 *FacFETw*
**Murphy**, Austin de la Salle 1917- *WhoFI 92*
**Murphy**, Austin J. 1927- *AlmAP 92 [port]*
**Murphy**, Austin John 1927- *WhoAmP 91*
**Murphy**, Barbara Beasley *DrAPF 91*
**Murphy**, Barbara Joan 1936- *WhoAmP 91*
**Murphy**, Beatrice M. 1908- *WhoBlA 92*
**Murphy**, Ben 1942- *IntMPA 92*
**Murphy**, Benjamin Edward 1942- *WhoEnt 92*
**Murphy**, Benjamin Thomas 1962- *WhoFI 92*
**Murphy**, Bernard T 1932- *AmMWSc 92*
**Murphy**, Bette Jane Manion 1931- *WhoAmP 91*
**Murphy**, Betty Jane Southard *WhoAmL 92*
**Murphy**, Betty Southard *WhoAmP 91*
**Murphy**, Brian Boru 1947- *AmMWSc 92*
**Murphy**, Brian Donal 1939- *AmMWSc 92*
**Murphy**, Brian James 1956- *WhoMW 92*
**Murphy**, Brian Logan 1939- *AmMWSc 92*
**Murphy**, Brian Taunton, Mrs. *Who 92*
**Murphy**, Brianne *ReelWom*
**Murphy**, Brianne 1937- *WhoEnt 92A*
**Murphy**, Bruce Daniel 1941- *AmMWSc 92*
**Murphy**, C H, Jr 1927- *AmMWSc 92*
**Murphy**, Calvin Jerome 1948- *WhoBlA 92*
**Murphy**, Carol Rozier 1916- *WhoRel 92*
**Murphy**, Carolyn Louise 1944- *WhoIns 92*
**Murphy**, Catherine Mary 1940- *AmMWSc 92*
**Murphy**, Charles A. 1932- *WhoBlA 92*
**Murphy**, Charles Bernard 1950- *WhoMW 92*
**Murphy**, Charles Franklin 1933- *AmMWSc 92*
**Murphy**, Charles Franklin 1940- *AmMWSc 92*
**Murphy**, Charles Haywood, Jr. 1920- *WhoFI 92*
**Murphy**, Charles Joseph 1947- *WhoFI 92*
**Murphy**, Charles Thornton 1938- *AmMWSc 92*
**Murphy**, Charles William 1929- *WhoBlA 92, WhoMW 92*
**Murphy**, Charles William 1961- *WhoFI 92*
**Murphy**, Chris Allan 1953- *WhoMW 92*
**Murphy**, Christopher Philip Yorke 1947- *Who 92*
**Murphy**, Clarence John 1934- *AmMWSc 92*
**Murphy**, Claude Wayne 1946- *WhoRel 92*
**Murphy**, Clifford Elyman 1912- *AmMWSc 92*
**Murphy**, Clyde Everett 1948- *WhoBlA 92*
**Murphy**, Colleen Patricia 1943- *WhoMW 92*
**Murphy**, Collin Grisseau 1940- *AmMWSc 92*
**Murphy**, Cornelius Bernard 1918- *AmMWSc 92*
**Murphy**, Cornelius McCaffrey 1936- *Who 92*
**Murphy**, Daniel Barker 1928- *AmMWSc 92*
**Murphy**, Daniel Hayes, II 1941- *WhoAmL 92*
**Murphy**, Daniel Howard 1944- *WhoBlA 92*
**Murphy**, Daniel Ignatius 1927- *WhoAmL 92*
**Murphy**, Daniel James 1947- *WhoAmL 92*
**Murphy**, Daniel John 1912- *AmMWSc 92*
**Murphy**, Daniel John 1935- *AmMWSc 92*
**Murphy**, Daniel Joseph d1991 *NewYTBS 91*
**Murphy**, Daniel L 1929- *AmMWSc 92*
**Murphy**, Daniel Patrick 1947- *WhoFI 92*
**Murphy**, Daniel R. 1954- *WhoAmL 92*
**Murphy**, David E. 1939- *WhoMW 92*
**Murphy**, David James, III 1963- *WhoEnt 92*
**Murphy**, David Ridgeway 1945- *WhoFI 92*
**Murphy**, Deborah June 1955- *WhoAmL 92*
**Murphy**, Deborah Lask 1946- *WhoAmP 91*
**Murphy**, Delbert S 1929- *WhoAmP 91*
**Murphy**, Della Mary 1935- *WhoBlA 92*
**Murphy**, Denis J. 1938- *WhoAmL 92*
**Murphy**, Dennis L 1936- *AmMWSc 92*
**Murphy**, Dervla 1931- *IntAu&W 91, Who 92*
**Murphy**, Dervla Mary 1931- *IntWW 91, WrDr 92*
**Murphy**, Diana E. 1934- *WhoAmL 92, WhoMW 92*
**Murphy**, Diane Alyce 1949- *WhoMW 92*
**Murphy**, Donal B 1944- *AmMWSc 92*
**Murphy**, Donald G 1934- *AmMWSc 92*
**Murphy**, Donald Paul 1937- *WhoMW 92*
**Murphy**, Donald Richard 1938- *WhoBlA 92*
**Murphy**, Donn Brian 1930- *WhoEnt 92*
**Murphy**, Donna Lee 1941- *WhoEnt 92*
**Murphy**, Douglas Blakeney 1945- *AmMWSc 92*
**Murphy**, Dwayne Keith 1955- *WhoBlA 92*
**Murphy**, E. Jefferson 1926- *WrDr 92*
**Murphy**, Eddie *LesBEnT 92*
**Murphy**, Eddie 1951- *IntWW 91*
**Murphy**, Eddie 1961- *IntMPA 92, WhoBlA 92, WhoEnt 92*
**Murphy**, Edgar Gardner 1869-1913 *BiInAmS*
**Murphy**, Edward Francis 1947- *WhoMW 92*
**Murphy**, Edward G 1921- *AmMWSc 92*
**Murphy**, Edward P. *WhoEnt 92*
**Murphy**, Elaine *WhoEnt 92*
**Murphy**, Elaine Romaine *DrAPF 91*
**Murphy**, Elbridge Norris 1943- *WhoMW 92*
**Murphy**, Eleanor M *WhoAmP 91*
**Murphy**, Elizabeth *WhoAmP 91*
**Murphy**, Ellis *WhoFI 92, WhoMW 92*
**Murphy**, Eugene F 1913- *AmMWSc 92*
**Murphy**, Eugene F. 1936- *WhoFI 92*
**Murphy**, Evelyn F 1940- *WhoAmP 91*
**Murphy**, Ewell Edward, Jr. 1928- *WhoAmL 92*
**Murphy**, Frances L., II *WhoBlA 92*
**Murphy**, Francis Patrick 1950- *WhoAmL 92*
**Murphy**, Francis Seward 1914- *WhoWest 92*
**Murphy**, Francis Xavier, Jr. 1948- *WhoFI 92*
**Murphy**, Frank *DrAPF 91*
**Murphy**, Frank 1890-1949 *FacFETw*
**Murphy**, Frank 1893-1949 *AmPolLe*
**Murphy**, Franklin David 1916- *IntWW 91, WhoWest 92*
**Murphy**, Frederick A 1934- *AmMWSc 92*
**Murphy**, Frederick James 1949- *WhoRel 92*
**Murphy**, Frederick Vernon 1938- *AmMWSc 92*
**Murphy**, G Read 1856-1925 *ScFEYrs*
**Murphy**, Gene 1956- *WhoBlA 92*
**Murphy**, George 1902- *IntMPA 92*
**Murphy**, George A 1923- *WhoAmP 91*
**Murphy**, George B., Jr. 1905- *WhoBlA 92*
**Murphy**, George E. *DrAPF 91*
**Murphy**, George Earl 1922- *AmMWSc 92, WhoMW 92*
**Murphy**, George Earl 1945- *WhoMW 92*
**Murphy**, George Graham 1943- *AmMWSc 92*
**Murphy**, George L *WhoAmP 91*
**Murphy**, George Moseley 1903-1968 *DcNCBi 4*
**Murphy**, George Washington 1919- *AmMWSc 92*
**Murphy**, George William 1941- *WhoIns 92*
**Murphy**, Gerald 1938- *WhoFI 92*
**Murphy**, Gerald Stephen, Sr. 1922- *WhoAmL 92*
**Murphy**, Gervase *Who 92*
**Murphy**, Gordon J. *WrDr 92*
**Murphy**, Gordon J 1927- *AmMWSc 92*
**Murphy**, Grattan Patrick 1935- *AmMWSc 92*
**Murphy**, Harold George 1934- *WhoFI 92*
**Murphy**, Harold Loyd 1927- *WhoAmL 92*
**Murphy**, Harriet Louise M. *WhoBlA 92*
**Murphy**, Henry D 1929- *AmMWSc 92*
**Murphy**, Ira H. 1928- *WhoBlA 92*
**Murphy**, Irene Helen *WhoRel 92*
**Murphy**, J. Allen 1953- *WhoAmL 92*
**Murphy**, Jack Redmond 1912- *WhoAmP 91*
**Murphy**, Jacqueline Adell 1948- *WhoWest 92*
**Murphy**, James 1937- *WhoFI 92*
**Murphy**, James A 1935- *AmMWSc 92*
**Murphy**, James Allan, Jr. 1929- *WhoAmL 92*
**Murphy**, James Bryson, Jr. 1932- *WhoFI 92*
**Murphy**, James Bumgardner 1884-1950 *DcNCBi 4*
**Murphy**, James Clair 1931- *AmMWSc 92*
**Murphy**, James F. 1933- *WhoFI 92, WhoMW 92*
**Murphy**, James Francis 1938- *WhoAmL 92*
**Murphy**, James Gilbert 1919- *AmMWSc 92*
**Murphy**, James Henry 1959- *WhoRel 92*
**Murphy**, James Jerome 1923- *WhoWest 92*
**Murphy**, James Jerome, Jr 1936- *WhoAmP 91*
**Murphy**, James John 1939- *AmMWSc 92*
**Murphy**, James Joseph 1938- *AmMWSc 92*
**Murphy**, James L. 1939- *WhoFI 92*
**Murphy**, James Lawson 1951- *WhoWest 92*
**Murphy**, James Lee 1940- *AmMWSc 92*
**Murphy**, James Michael 1943- *WhoAmL 92*
**Murphy**, James Patrick 1932- *Who 92*
**Murphy**, James Paul 1925- *WhoAmL 92*
**Murphy**, James Paul 1944- *WhoAmL 92*
**Murphy**, James S. 1934- *ConAu 134*
**Murphy**, James Slater 1921- *AmMWSc 92*
**Murphy**, James W 1936- *WhoIns 92*
**Murphy**, James William 1936- *WhoAmP 91*
**Murphy**, Jane *WhoAmP 91*
**Murphy**, Jeanette Carol 1931- *WhoMW 92*
**Murphy**, Jeanne Claire 1929- *WhoBlA 92*
**Murphy**, Jeremiah P 1930- *WhoAmP 91*
**Murphy**, Jill *IntAu&W 91*
**Murphy**, Jill 1949- *WrDr 92*
**Murphy**, Jim 1925- *WhoAmP 91*
**Murphy**, Joanne Wharton 1934- *WhoAmL 92*
**Murphy**, John 1785-1841 *DcNCBi 4*
**Murphy**, John 1945- *TwCPaSc*
**Murphy**, John A. 1905- *Who 92*
**Murphy**, John A. 1929- *IntWW 91*
**Murphy**, John Albert 1837-1892? *DcNCBi 4*
**Murphy**, John Aloysius 1905- *IntWW 91*
**Murphy**, John Arthur 1929- *WhoFI 92*
**Murphy**, John Benjamin 1857-1916 *BiInAmS*
**Murphy**, John Carter 1921- *WhoFI 92*
**Murphy**, John Condron, Jr. 1945- *WhoAmL 92*
**Murphy**, John Cornelius 1936- *AmMWSc 92*
**Murphy**, John E, Jr 1943- *WhoAmP 91*
**Murphy**, John F. 1905- *IntMPA 92*
**Murphy**, John Francis 1922- *AmMWSc 92*
**Murphy**, John Francis 1923- *WhoAmP 91, WhoRel 92*
**Murphy**, John Francis 1938- *WhoAmP 91*
**Murphy**, John Gervase 1926- *Who 92*
**Murphy**, John H., III 1916- *WhoBlA 92*
**Murphy**, John J 1928- *WhoIns 92*
**Murphy**, John J, Jr 1946- *WhoIns 92*
**Murphy**, John Joseph 1920- *AmMWSc 92*
**Murphy**, John Joseph 1931- *WhoFI 92*
**Murphy**, John Joseph 1936- *WhoIns 92*
**Murphy**, John Joseph 1940- *AmMWSc 92*
**Murphy**, John Joseph, Jr. 1951- *WhoFI 92*
**Murphy**, John Leonard 1950- *WhoEnt 92*
**Murphy**, John Matthew, Jr. 1935- *WhoBlA 92*
**Murphy**, John Michael 1935- *AmMWSc 92*
**Murphy**, John Michael 1945- *IntWW 91*
**Murphy**, John N 1939- *AmMWSc 92*
**Murphy**, John Patrick 1945- *WhoIns 92*
**Murphy**, John R 1941- *AmMWSc 92*
**Murphy**, John Riffe 1942- *AmMWSc 92*
**Murphy**, John Thomas 1932- *WhoAmL 92, WhoWest 92*
**Murphy**, John Thomas 1938- *AmMWSc 92*
**Murphy**, John W. 1937- *WhoFI 92*
**Murphy**, Joseph 1898-1981 *RelLAm 91*
**Murphy**, Joseph 1932- *AmMWSc 92*
**Murphy**, Joseph E., Jr. 1930- *ConAu 133, SmATA 65 [port]*

**Murphy**, Joseph Edward, Jr. 1930- *WhoFI 92*
**Murphy**, Joseph Richard 1947- *WhoEnt 92*
**Murphy**, Joseph Robison 1925- *AmMWSc 92*
**Murphy**, Juneann Wadsworth 1937- *AmMWSc 92*
**Murphy**, Kathleen Mary 1945- *WhoAmL 92, WhoFI 92*
**Murphy**, Kathryn Alice 1949- *WhoAmL 92*
**Murphy**, Kay A. *DrAPF 91*
**Murphy**, Keirnan James *WhoFI 92*
**Murphy**, Keith Lawson 1932- *AmMWSc 92*
**Murphy**, Kenneth Robert 1940- *AmMWSc 92*
**Murphy**, Kevin Dion 1963- *WhoBlA 92*
**Murphy**, Kevin James 1957- *WhoFI 92*
**Murphy**, Kevin Palmer, Sr. 1957- *WhoFI 92*
**Murphy**, Larry 1952- *WhoAmP 91*
**Murphy**, Larry S 1937- *AmMWSc 92*
**Murphy**, Laura Sunstein 1947- *WhoAmL 92*
**Murphy**, Lawrence Martin 1941- *WhoWest 92*
**Murphy**, Lea Frances 1954- *AmMWSc 92*
**Murphy**, Leslie 1915- *Who 92*
**Murphy**, Leslie Frederick 1915- *IntWW 91*
**Murphy**, Lester Fuller 1936- *WhoAmL 92*
**Murphy**, Lewis Curtis 1933- *WhoAmP 91*
**Murphy**, Lorenzo Dow, Jr. 1929- *WhoWest 92*
**Murphy**, Lyle 1908- *WhoEnt 92*
**Murphy**, Margaret H *WhoAmP 91*
**Murphy**, Margaret Humphries *WhoBlA 92*
**Murphy**, Marjory Beth 1925- *AmMWSc 92*
**Murphy**, Mark 1942- *WhoRel 92*
**Murphy**, Martha Arman 1948- *WhoWest 92*
**Murphy**, Martin Joseph, Jr 1942- *AmMWSc 92*
**Murphy**, Mary Ann 1943- *WhoWest 92*
**Murphy**, Mary Catherine *WhoAmP 91*
**Murphy**, Mary Eileen 1954- *AmMWSc 92*
**Murphy**, Mary Ellen 1928- *AmMWSc 92*
**Murphy**, Mary Kathryn 1941- *WhoFI 92, WhoMW 92*
**Murphy**, Mary Lillie 1919- *WhoAmP 91*
**Murphy**, Mary Lois 1916- *AmMWSc 92*
**Murphy**, Mary Nadine 1933- *AmMWSc 92*
**Murphy**, Mary Zimmerman 1953- *WhoMW 92*
**Murphy**, Matthew J, Jr 1926- *WhoAmP 91*
**Murphy**, Maurice J, Jr *WhoAmP 91*
**Murphy**, Maurice Thomas 1935- *WhoAmP 91*
**Murphy**, Max Ray 1934- *WhoAmL 92, WhoMW 92*
**Murphy**, Michael *DrAPF 91*
**Murphy**, Michael 1938- *IntMPA 92*
**Murphy**, Michael A 1925- *AmMWSc 92*
**Murphy**, Michael Denis 1956- *WhoEnt 92*
**Murphy**, Michael Edward 1948- *WhoMW 92*
**Murphy**, Michael Emmett 1936- *WhoFI 92, WhoMW 92*
**Murphy**, Michael George 1938- *WhoEnt 92*
**Murphy**, Michael John *AmMWSc 92*
**Murphy**, Michael Jon 1950- *WhoEnt 92*
**Murphy**, Michael Joseph 1915- *WhoRel 92*
**Murphy**, Michael Joseph 1923- *AmMWSc 92*
**Murphy**, Michael Joseph 1953- *AmMWSc 92*
**Murphy**, Michael McKay 1946- *WhoBlA 92*
**Murphy**, Michael Ross 1953- *AmMWSc 92*
**Murphy**, Michael Terrence 1946- *WhoAmL 92*
**Murphy**, Michelle 1927- *WhoRel 92*
**Murphy**, Mike 1932- *WhoAmP 91*
**Murphy**, Monte Lillian *WhoMW 92*
**Murphy**, Nancey Claire 1951- *WhoRel 92*
**Murphy**, Nancy L 1929- *WhoAmP 91*
**Murphy**, Napoleon Bonapart 1921- *WhoAmP 91*
**Murphy**, Neil *Who 92*
**Murphy**, Nyla A 1931- *WhoAmP 91*
**Murphy**, P.D. *DrAPF 91*
**Murphy**, Pat *DrAPF 91*
**Murphy**, Pat 1955- *TwCSFW 91*
**Murphy**, Pat 1959- *WhoAmP 91*
**Murphy**, Patricia A 1951- *AmMWSc 92*
**Murphy**, Patrick Aidan 1937- *AmMWSc 92*
**Murphy**, Patrick Francis 1960- *WhoAmP 91*
**Murphy**, Patrick Hale 1948- *WhoAmP 91*
**Murphy**, Patrick James 1931- *Who 92*
**Murphy**, Patrick Joseph 1940- *AmMWSc 92*
**Murphy**, Patrick Joseph 1949- *WhoFI 92*
**Murphy**, Patrick Livingston 1848-1907 *DcNCBi 4*
**Murphy**, Patrick M *WhoAmP 91*
**Murphy**, Patrick Wallace 1944- *Who 92*
**Murphy**, Paul Bailey 1963- *WhoAmL 92*
**Murphy**, Paul Henry 1942- *AmMWSc 92*
**Murphy**, Paul Joseph 1957- *WhoAmL 92*
**Murphy**, Paul Peter 1948- *Who 92*
**Murphy**, Paula Christine 1950- *WhoBlA 92*
**Murphy**, Peter 1942- *TwCPaSc*
**Murphy**, Peter Connacher, Jr 1936- *WhoAmP 91*
**Murphy**, Peter E. *DrAPF 91*
**Murphy**, Peter George 1942- *AmMWSc 92*
**Murphy**, Peter John 1939- *AmMWSc 92*
**Murphy**, Philip Edward 1945- *WhoWest 92*
**Murphy**, Philip Francis 1933- *WhoRel 92*
**Murphy**, Ramon Birkett 1935- *WhoFI 92*
**Murphy**, Randall Bertrand 1954- *AmMWSc 92*
**Murphy**, Randall Kent 1943- *WhoFI 92*
**Murphy**, Ray Bradford 1922- *AmMWSc 92*
**Murphy**, Raymond 1937- *WhoAmP 91*
**Murphy**, Raymond M. 1927- *WhoBlA 92*
**Murphy**, Regina 1945- *WhoRel 92*
**Murphy**, Ric 1951- *WhoBlA 92*
**Murphy**, Rich *DrAPF 91*
**Murphy**, Richard *WhoEnt 92*
**Murphy**, Richard 1912- *IntMPA 92*
**Murphy**, Richard 1927- *ConPo 91, IntAu&W 91, WrDr 92*
**Murphy**, Richard Alan 1938- *AmMWSc 92*
**Murphy**, Richard Allan 1941- *AmMWSc 92*
**Murphy**, Richard Arthur *AmMWSc 92*
**Murphy**, Richard Carden 1947- *WhoFI 92*
**Murphy**, Richard E 1931- *WhoAmP 91*
**Murphy**, Richard Holmes 1915- *Who 92*
**Murphy**, Richard James 1929- *WhoAmP 91*
**Murphy**, Richard Patrick 1954- *WhoAmL 92*
**Murphy**, Richard Thomas 1908- *WrDr 92*
**Murphy**, Richard Vanderburgh 1951- *WhoAmL 92*
**Murphy**, Richard William 1929- *IntWW 91, WhoAmP 91*
**Murphy**, Robert Blair 1931- *WhoFI 92*
**Murphy**, Robert Brady Lawrence 1905- *WhoAmL 92*
**Murphy**, Robert C 1926- *WhoAmP 91*
**Murphy**, Robert Carl 1919- *AmMWSc 92*
**Murphy**, Robert Carl 1944- *AmMWSc 92, WhoWest 92*
**Murphy**, Robert Charles 1926- *WhoAmL 92*
**Murphy**, Robert E 1918- *WhoAmP 91*
**Murphy**, Robert Francis 1953- *AmMWSc 92*
**Murphy**, Robert G. *WhoFI 92*
**Murphy**, Robert Grant 1952- *WhoMW 92*
**Murphy**, Robert Harry 1938- *WhoFI 92*
**Murphy**, Robert Joseph 1958- *WhoAmL 92*
**Murphy**, Robert L. 1935- *WhoBlA 92*
**Murphy**, Robert Owen, Sr. 1926- *WhoFI 92*
**Murphy**, Robert Patrick 1943- *AmMWSc 92*
**Murphy**, Roderick Patrick 1939- *WhoAmP 91*
**Murphy**, Roland Edmund 1917- *IntAu&W 91, WhoRel 92, WrDr 92*
**Murphy**, Romallus O. 1928- *WhoBlA 92*
**Murphy**, Rosemary *WhoEnt 92*
**Murphy**, Roy Emerson 1926- *AmMWSc 92*
**Murphy**, Royse Peak 1914- *AmMWSc 92*
**Murphy**, Ruth Ann *AmMWSc 92*
**Murphy**, Sandra Robison 1949- *WhoAmL 92*
**Murphy**, Sean David 1960- *WhoAmL 92*
**Murphy**, Sean Patrick 1957- *WhoAmL 92*
**Murphy**, Sean Patrick 1963- *WhoAmL 92*
**Murphy**, Sharon Margaret 1940- *WhoRel 92*
**Murphy**, Shaun Edward 1961- *WhoFI 92*
**Murphy**, Sheila E. *DrAPF 91*
**Murphy**, Sheila M. 1937- *WhoAmL 92*
**Murphy**, Sheldon Douglas 1933- *AmMWSc 92*
**Murphy**, Shirley R 1928- *IntAu&W 91, WrDr 92*
**Murphy**, Spencer 1904-1964 *DcNCBi 4*
**Murphy**, Stanley Reed 1924- *AmMWSc 92*
**Murphy**, Stephen Edward 1944- *WhoEnt 92*
**Murphy**, Stephen Vincent 1945- *WhoFI 92*
**Murphy**, Steven *WhoEnt 92*
**Murphy**, Steven R. 1939- *WhoWest 92*
**Murphy**, Sylvia 1937- *IntAu&W 91, WrDr 92*
**Murphy**, Ted Daniel 1936- *AmMWSc 92*
**Murphy**, Terence Martin 1942- *AmMWSc 92*
**Murphy**, Teresa Ann 1957- *WhoWest 92*
**Murphy**, Terrence John 1920- *WhoRel 92*
**Murphy**, Terry Laurence 1942- *WhoAmP 91*
**Murphy**, Thomas 1915- *IntWW 91*
**Murphy**, Thomas 1928- *Who 92*
**Murphy**, Thomas 1935- *IntAu&W 91, WrDr 92*
**Murphy**, Thomas A. 1915- *Who 92*
**Murphy**, Thomas A 1937- *AmMWSc 92*
**Murphy**, Thomas Aquinas 1915- *IntWW 91*
**Murphy**, Thomas Aquinas 1951- *WhoMW 92*
**Murphy**, Thomas Austin 1911- *WhoRel 92*
**Murphy**, Thomas Bailey 1924- *WhoAmP 91*
**Murphy**, Thomas Daniel 1934- *AmMWSc 92*
**Murphy**, Thomas DuPont, II 1960- *WhoAmL 92*
**Murphy**, Thomas Francis 1905- *WhoAmL 92*
**Murphy**, Thomas J 1930- *WhoAmP 91*
**Murphy**, Thomas J 1944- *WhoIns 92*
**Murphy**, Thomas James 1942- *AmMWSc 92*
**Murphy**, Thomas James 1956- *Who 92, WhoAmL 92*
**Murphy**, Thomas Jewell 1939- *WhoAmL 92*
**Murphy**, Thomas Joseph 1930- *WhoAmL 92*
**Murphy**, Thomas Joseph 1932- *WhoRel 92, WhoWest 92*
**Murphy**, Thomas Joseph 1941- *AmMWSc 92*
**Murphy**, Thomas Joseph 1944- *WhoAmP 91*
**Murphy**, Thomas S. *LesBEnT 92 [port]*
**Murphy**, Thomas S. 1925- *WhoEnt 92, WhoFI 92*
**Murphy**, Thomas S 1932- *WhoIns 92*
**Murphy**, Thomas W 1953- *WhoAmP 91*
**Murphy**, Thomas William, Jr 1942- *WhoAmP 91*
**Murphy**, Timothy Donald 1950- *WhoAmP 91*
**Murphy**, Timothy F 1950- *AmMWSc 92*
**Murphy**, Timothy James 1946- *WhoAmP 91*
**Murphy**, Timothy Randall 1953- *WhoAmL 92*
**Murphy**, Tom 1935- *IntWW 91*
**Murphy**, Turk 1915-1987 *NewAmDM*
**Murphy**, Vanissa Dawn 1953- *WhoEnt 92*
**Murphy**, Walter 1872-1946 *DcNCBi 4*
**Murphy**, Walter Francis 1929- *IntAu&W 91, WrDr 92*
**Murphy**, Walter Thomas 1928- *AmMWSc 92*
**Murphy**, Warren Burton 1933- *WhoEnt 92*
**Murphy**, Wendell H 1938- *WhoAmP 91*
**Murphy**, William Beverly 1907- *IntWW 91*
**Murphy**, William Edward, Jr. 1941- *WhoBlA 92*
**Murphy**, William F. 1940- *WhoRel 92*
**Murphy**, William Francis 1906- *WrDr 92*
**Murphy**, William Frederick 1939- *AmMWSc 92*
**Murphy**, William G 1921- *AmMWSc 92*
**Murphy**, William Host 1926- *WhoMW 92*
**Murphy**, William J 1927- *AmMWSc 92*
**Murphy**, William John 1958- *WhoEnt 92*
**Murphy**, William K. *DrAPF 91*
**Murphy**, William Malcolm, Jr 1927- *WhoAmP 91*
**Murphy**, William Michael 1941- *AmMWSc 92*
**Murphy**, William Parry 1892- *WhoNob 90*
**Murphy**, William Parry, Jr 1923- *AmMWSc 92*
**Murphy**, William R 1928- *AmMWSc 92*
**Murphy**, William Robert 1927- *WhoAmL 92*
**Murphy**, William Tayloe, Jr 1933- *WhoAmP 91*
**Murphy-Barrera**, Linda Frances 1956- *WhoHisp 92*
**Murphy-O'Connor**, Cormac *Who 92*
**Murphy-O'Connor**, Cormac 1932- *IntWW 91*
**Murr**, Brown L, Jr 1931- *AmMWSc 92*
**Murr**, Lawrence Eugene 1939- *AmMWSc 92*
**Murr**, Wilhelm 1888-1945 *EncTR 91 [port]*
**Murrain**, Godfrey H. 1927- *WhoBlA 92*
**Murrain**, Samuel Urbane, Sr. 1930- *WhoHisp 92*
**Murrain**, William A. 1945- *WhoBlA 92*
**Murray** *Who 92*
**Murray**, Bishop of The 1931- *Who 92*
**Murray**, Lord 1922- *Who 92*
**Murray**, A. Rosemary 1913- *IntWW 91*
**Murray**, Alan Edward 1946- *WhoEnt 92*
**Murray**, Albert 1916- *IntAu&W 91, WrDr 92*
**Murray**, Albert L. 1916- *WhoBlA 92*
**Murray**, Albert R. 1946- *WhoBlA 92*
**Murray**, Alice Pearl 1932- *WhoFI 92*
**Murray**, Alice Rosemary 1913- *Who 92*
**Murray**, Allen Edward 1929- *IntWW 91, WhoFI 92*
**Murray**, Andrew Robin 1941- *Who 92*
**Murray**, Anna Martin *WhoBlA 92*
**Murray**, Anne 1934- *WhoRel 92*
**Murray**, Anne 1945- *WhoEnt 92*
**Murray**, Anne 1946- *NewAmDM*
**Murray**, Antony *Who 92*
**Murray**, Archibald R. 1933- *WhoBlA 92*
**Murray**, Arthur 1895-1991 *CurBio 91N, NewYTBS 91 [port], News 91, -91-3*
**Murray**, Athol Laverick 1930- *Who 92*
**Murray**, Barbara 1929- *IntMPA 92*
**Murray**, Barbara Ann 1948- *WhoRel 92*
**Murray**, Barbara Ann 1953- *WhoMW 92*
**Murray**, Barbara Bateman 1933- *WhoFI 92*
**Murray**, Beatrice *IntAu&W 91X, WrDr 92*
**Murray**, Bernard Joseph 1915- *WhoRel 92*
**Murray**, Bertram George, Jr 1933- *AmMWSc 92*
**Murray**, Bill *LesBEnT 92*
**Murray**, Bill 1950- *IntMPA 92, IntWW 91, WhoEnt 92*
**Murray**, Brian 1933- *Who 92*
**Murray**, Brian Stewart d1991 *Who 92N*
**Murray**, Bruce C 1931- *AmMWSc 92*
**Murray**, Bryan Clarence 1942- *WhoMW 92*
**Murray**, Calvin Clyde 1907- *AmMWSc 92*
**Murray**, Carole *DrAPF 91*
**Murray**, Cecil James Boyd d1991 *Who 92N*
**Murray**, Cecil Wayne 1950- *WhoFI 92*
**Murray**, Charles 1894-1954 *TwCPaSc*
**Murray**, Charles 1943- *WrDr 92*
**Murray**, Charles Alan 1943- *IntWW 91*
**Murray**, Charles B. 1948- *WhoRel 92*
**Murray**, Charles Edward 1928- *WhoAmP 91*
**Murray**, Charles Henry 1917- *IntWW 91, Who 92*
**Murray**, Christopher Brock 1937- *AmMWSc 92*
**Murray**, Dan *DrAPF 91*
**Murray**, Daniel Augustine 1937- *WhoRel 92*
**Murray**, Daniel T. *WhoFI 92*
**Murray**, D'Arcy Shannon 1959- *WhoWest 92*
**Murray**, David 1830-1905 *BiInAmS*
**Murray**, David 1945- *ConAu 133*
**Murray**, David 1953- *WhoMW 92, WhoRel 92*
**Murray**, David Alexander 1947- *WhoRel 92*
**Murray**, David Christie 1847-1907 *ScFEYrs*
**Murray**, David Edward 1951- *Who 92*
**Murray**, David Keith 1955- *WhoBlA 92*
**Murray**, David Michael 1940- *WhoRel 92*
**Murray**, David William 1930- *AmMWSc 92*
**Murray**, Delbert Milton 1941- *WhoFI 92, WhoMW 92*
**Murray**, Dennis Lynn 1948- *WhoMW 92*
**Murray**, Don 1929- *IntMPA 92*
**Murray**, Donald 1923- *Who 92*
**Murray**, Donald 1924- *Who 92*
**Murray**, Donald Shipley 1916- *AmMWSc 92*
**Murray**, Eddie Clarence 1956- *WhoBlA 92*
**Murray**, Edna McClain 1918- *WhoBlA 92*
**Murray**, Edward Conley 1931- *AmMWSc 92*
**Murray**, E'Lane Carlisle *DrAPF 91*
**Murray**, Elizabeth 1940- *NewYTBS 91 [port], WorArt 1980 [port]*
**Murray**, Ethel Ann 1932- *WhoAmP 91*
**Murray**, Ferne Hannah 1918- *WhoRel 92*
**Murray**, Finnie Ardrey, Jr 1943- *AmMWSc 92*
**Murray**, Fiona *WrDr 92*
**Murray**, Florence K 1916- *WhoAmP 91*
**Murray**, Florence Kerins 1916- *WhoAmL 92*
**Murray**, Frances 1928- *IntAu&W 91, WrDr 92*
**Murray**, Francis E 1918- *AmMWSc 92*
**Murray**, Francis Joseph 1911- *AmMWSc 92*
**Murray**, Francis Joseph 1920- *AmMWSc 92*
**Murray**, Francis William 1921- *WhoWest 92*
**Murray**, Francis Wisner, III 1928- *WhoFI 92*
**Murray**, Fred E *WhoAmP 91*
**Murray**, Frederick Franklin 1950- *WhoAmL 92, WhoFI 92*

**Murray**, Frederick Nelson 1935- *AmMWSc 92*
**Murray**, G.E. *DrAPF 91*
**Murray**, G G A 1866-1957 *ScFEYrs*
**Murray**, Galen Keith 1950- *WhoMW 92*
**Murray**, Gary Joseph 1950- *AmMWSc 92*
**Murray**, George Cloyd 1934- *AmMWSc 92*
**Murray**, George E 1923- *WhoAmP 91*
**Murray**, George Sargent 1924- *Who 92*
**Murray**, George T 1927- *AmMWSc 92*
**Murray**, George William 1945- *WhoRel 92*
**Murray**, Glen A 1939- *AmMWSc 92*
**Murray**, Gordon 1935- *Who 92*
**Murray**, Grover Elmer 1916- *AmMWSc 92*
**Murray**, Harlan W. *WhoFI 92*
**Murray**, Harold Dixon 1931- *AmMWSc 92*
**Murray**, Haydn Herbert 1924- *AmMWSc 92, WhoMW 92*
**Murray**, Helen 1938- *WhoEnt 92*
**Murray**, Herbert Frazier 1923- *WhoAmL 92*
**Murray**, Hubert 1861-1940 *FacFETw*
**Murray**, Hugh Leander 1925- *WhoRel 92*
**Murray**, Hugh Thomas 1938- *IntAu&W 91*
**Murray**, Hyde H 1930- *WhoAmP 91*
**Murray**, Ian Stewart 1951- *WhoEnt 92*
**Murray**, J. Ralph 1931- *WhoBlA 92*
**Murray**, Jack R 1929- *WhoAmP 91*
**Murray**, James 1713-1781 *DcNCBi 4*
**Murray**, James 1919- *Who 92*
**Murray**, James Alan 1942- *WhoFI 92*
**Murray**, James Bryan 1953- *WhoMW 92*
**Murray**, James C. 1939- *WhoFI 92*
**Murray**, James Dickson 1931- *Who 92*
**Murray**, James Doyle 1938- *WhoFI 92*
**Murray**, James F. *WhoFI 92*
**Murray**, James Gordon 1927- *AmMWSc 92*
**Murray**, James Hamilton 1933- *WhoBlA 92*
**Murray**, James J. *WhoRel 92*
**Murray**, James Kirtis, Jr. 1935- *WhoFI 92*
**Murray**, James Michael 1944- *WhoAmL 92*
**Murray**, James P. 1946- *WhoBlA 92*
**Murray**, James Patrick 1906- *Who 92*
**Murray**, James Patrick 1919- *ConAu 34NR*
**Murray**, James Patrick 1946- *WhoEnt 92*
**Murray**, James W 1933- *AmMWSc 92*
**Murray**, Jan 1917- *IntMPA 92*
**Murray**, Jane Ellen *WhoEnt 92*
**Murray**, Jay Clarence 1929- *AmMWSc 92*
**Murray**, Jean Carolyn 1927- *WhoRel 92*
**Murray**, Jeanne *WhoEnt 92*
**Murray**, Jeanne Morris 1925- *AmMWSc 92*
**Murray**, Jennifer Susan 1950- *Who 92*
**Murray**, Jim *ConAu 34NR*
**Murray**, Jo Bumbarger 1945- *WhoWest 92*
**Murray**, Joan *DrAPF 91*
**Murray**, Joan 1941- *NotBlAW 92*
**Murray**, Joan Baird 1926- *AmMWSc 92*
**Murray**, Joan Elizabeth 1941- *WhoEnt 92*
**Murray**, Joan Nina 1938- *WhoWest 92*
**Murray**, John *Who 92*
**Murray**, John 1730-1809 *BlkwEAR*
**Murray**, John Antony 1921- *Who 92*
**Murray**, John Arnaud Robin Grey *Who 92*
**Murray**, John Courtney 1904-1967 *RelLAm 91*
**Murray**, John D *WhoIns 92*
**Murray**, John Edward, Jr. 1932- *WhoAmL 92*
**Murray**, John Frederic 1927- *AmMWSc 92*
**Murray**, John Gardner 1857-1929 *RelLAm 91*
**Murray**, John George 1962- *WhoWest 92*
**Murray**, John Joseph 1915- *WrDr 92*
**Murray**, John Joseph 1937- *AmMWSc 92*
**Murray**, John Joseph, Jr 1914- *WhoAmP 91*
**Murray**, John Randolph 1916- *AmMWSc 92*
**Murray**, John Roberts 1943- *AmMWSc 92*
**Murray**, John Stevenson 1939- *WhoAmP 91*
**Murray**, John W. 1921- *WhoBlA 92*
**Murray**, John Wolcott 1909- *AmMWSc 92*
**Murray**, Joseph Buford 1933- *AmMWSc 92*
**Murray**, Joseph E 1919- *AmMWSc 92, WhoNob 90*
**Murray**, Joseph Edward 1919- *IntWW 91*
**Murray**, Joseph James, Jr 1930- *AmMWSc 92*
**Murray**, Joseph Lawrence 1960- *WhoMW 92*
**Murray**, Judith Sargent 1751-1820 *BlkwEAR*
**Murray**, Katherine Maud Elisabeth 1909- *Who 92*
**Murray**, Kathleen Ann 1952- *WhoIns 92*
**Murray**, Kathleen Ellen 1946- *WhoFI 92*
**Murray**, Kathryn Hazel 1906- *WhoEnt 92*
**Murray**, Kay L. 1938- *WhoBlA 92*
**Murray**, Ken *LesBEnT 92*
**Murray**, Kenneth 1930- *Who 92*
**Murray**, Kenneth Alexander George 1916- *Who 92*
**Murray**, Kenneth Richard 1938- *WhoFI 92*
**Murray**, Larry James 1945- *WhoRel 92*
**Murray**, Lawrence 1939- *WhoFI 92*
**Murray**, Lawrence P, Jr 1930- *AmMWSc 92*
**Murray**, Leo Joseph 1927- *Who 92*
**Murray**, Leo Thomas 1937- *AmMWSc 92*
**Murray**, Les 1938- *ConPo 91, FacFETw, RfGEnL 91, WrDr 92*
**Murray**, Les A 1938- *IntAu&W 91*
**Murray**, Lewellyn St. Elmo 1926- *WhoRel 92*
**Murray**, Linda *WrDr 92*
**Murray**, Lowell 1936- *IntWW 91*
**Murray**, M John 1922- *AmMWSc 92*
**Murray**, Mabel Lake 1935- *WhoBlA 92*
**Murray**, Marion 1937- *AmMWSc 92*
**Murray**, Martha Bowman 1951- *WhoRel 92*
**Murray**, Martin L *WhoAmP 91*
**Murray**, Marvin 1927- *AmMWSc 92*
**Murray**, Mary Agnes 1913- *IntAu&W 91*
**Murray**, Mary Aileen 1914- *AmMWSc 92*
**Murray**, Mary Jeanette *WhoAmP 91*
**Murray**, Michael Dennis 1947- *WhoMW 92*
**Murray**, Michael Patrick 1930- *WhoAmL 92*
**Murray**, Michael Peter 1946- *WhoFI 92*
**Murray**, Michael Webster 1935- *WhoAmP 91*
**Murray**, Nevada 1920-1990 *WhoBlA 92N*
**Murray**, Nigel 1944- *Who 92*
**Murray**, Noreen Elizabeth 1935- *IntWW 91, Who 92*
**Murray**, O. Russel 1951- *WhoAmL 92*
**Murray**, Obie Dale 1950- *WhoRel 92*
**Murray**, Ouima Slate 1927- *WhoMW 92*
**Murray**, Patrick 1965- *Who 92*
**Murray**, Patrick Brian 1964- *WhoAmL 92*
**Murray**, Patrick Robert 1948- *AmMWSc 92*
**Murray**, Patty L 1950- *WhoAmP 91*
**Murray**, Paul Brady 1923- *WhoFI 92*
**Murray**, Pauli 1901-1985 *NotBlAW 92 [port]*
**Murray**, Peter 1915- *Who 92*
**Murray**, Peter 1920- *AmMWSc 92, Who 92, WhoFI 92, WrDr 92*
**Murray**, Peter Tom 1941- *WhoFI 92*
**Murray**, Phillip 1886-1952 *FacFETw*
**Murray**, R. A. 1947- *WhoBlA 92*
**Murray**, Ralbern Hugh 1929- *WhoFI 92*
**Murray**, Raymond Carl 1929- *AmMWSc 92*
**Murray**, Raymond Gorbold 1916- *AmMWSc 92*
**Murray**, Raymond Harold 1925- *AmMWSc 92*
**Murray**, Raymond L 1920- *AmMWSc 92*
**Murray**, Richard Bennett 1928- *AmMWSc 92*
**Murray**, Richard Charles 1949- *WhoAmP 91*
**Murray**, Richard Henry 1954- *WhoFI 92*
**Murray**, Robb 1953- *WhoEnt 92*
**Murray**, Robert A 1948- *WhoAmP 91*
**Murray**, Robert Allen 1929- *WrDr 92*
**Murray**, Robert C. 1945- *WhoFI 92*
**Murray**, Robert Drake 1845-1903 *BiInAmS*
**Murray**, Robert Eugene 1926- *WhoRel 92*
**Murray**, Robert F. 1931- *WhoBlA 92*
**Murray**, Robert Fox 1952- *WhoAmL 92*
**Murray**, Robert Fulton, Jr 1931- *AmMWSc 92*
**Murray**, Robert G 1952- *WhoIns 92*
**Murray**, Robert George Everitt 1919- *AmMWSc 92*
**Murray**, Robert Hale, III 1953- *WhoMW 92*
**Murray**, Robert Kincaid 1932- *AmMWSc 92*
**Murray**, Robert Wallace 1928- *AmMWSc 92*
**Murray**, Robert William 1936- *WhoFI 92*
**Murray**, Robin MacGregor 1944- *Who 92*
**Murray**, Rodney Brent 1949- *AmMWSc 92*
**Murray**, Roger 1936- *Who 92*
**Murray**, Roger Kenneth, Jr 1942- *AmMWSc 92*
**Murray**, Rona 1924- *ConPo 91, WrDr 92*
**Murray**, Ronald 1931- *WhoFI 92*
**Murray**, Ronald King *Who 92*
**Murray**, Ronald Ormiston 1912- *Who 92*
**Murray**, Rosemary *IntWW 91, Who 92*
**Murray**, Rowland William Patrick 1910- *Who 92*
**Murray**, Royce Wilton 1937- *AmMWSc 92*
**Murray**, Russell, II 1925- *WhoAmP 91*
**Murray**, Simon 1940- *IntWW 91, WhoFI 92*
**Murray**, Spencer J., III 1964- *WhoBlA 92*
**Murray**, Stephen James 1943- *WhoAmL 92*
**Murray**, Stephen Patrick 1938- *AmMWSc 92*
**Murray**, Stephen S 1944- *AmMWSc 92*
**Murray**, Steven Nelsen 1944- *AmMWSc 92*
**Murray**, Sunny 1937- *NewAmDM*
**Murray**, Susan Elizabeth 1952- *WhoAmL 92*
**Murray**, Sylvester 1941- *WhoBlA 92*
**Murray**, T J 1938- *AmMWSc 92*
**Murray**, Terrence 1939- *WhoFI 92*
**Murray**, Thad S 1919- *WhoAmP 91*
**Murray**, Thomas Allan 1952- *WhoMW 92*
**Murray**, Thomas Azel 1929- *WhoBlA 92*
**Murray**, Thomas Edward 1956- *WhoMW 92*
**Murray**, Thomas Francis *AmMWSc 92*
**Murray**, Thomas Henry 1946- *AmMWSc 92*
**Murray**, Thomas Mantle 1943- *WhoEnt 92*
**Murray**, Thomas Pinkney 1942- *AmMWSc 92*
**Murray**, Thomas W., Jr. 1935- *WhoBlA 92*
**Murray**, Timothy Vincent 1930- *IntWW 91*
**Murray**, Tracy 1940- *WhoFI 92*
**Murray**, V T 1874- *ScFEYrs*
**Murray**, Vernon Gay 1945- *WhoRel 92*
**Murray**, Virgie W. 1931- *WhoBlA 92*
**Murray**, Virginia R. *DrAPF 91*
**Murray**, Virginia R 1914- *IntAu&W 91*
**Murray**, Wallace Jasper 1940- *AmMWSc 92*
**Murray**, Willard H, Jr *WhoAmP 91*
**Murray**, William *DrAPF 91*
**Murray**, William D. 1935- *WhoFI 92*
**Murray**, William Daniel 1908- *WhoAmL 92*
**Murray**, William David 1908-1986 *DcNCBi 4*
**Murray**, William Douglas 1950- *AmMWSc 92*
**Murray**, William Hutchison 1913- *IntAu&W 91, WrDr 92*
**Murray**, William J 1933- *AmMWSc 92*
**Murray**, William J 1948- *WhoIns 92*
**Murray**, William Joseph 1946- *WhoRel 92*
**Murray**, William Michael 1953- *WhoAmL 92*
**Murray**, William Peter 1924- *WhoAmL 92*
**Murray**, William R 1924- *AmMWSc 92*
**Murray**, William Sparrow 1926- *AmMWSc 92*
**Murray**, Winston Lloyd, Jr. 1952- *WhoBlA 92*
**Murray of Blackbarony**, Nigel Andrew D 1944- *Who 92*
**Murray Of Epping Forest**, Baron 1922- *IntWW 91, Who 92*
**Murray Of Newhaven**, Baron 1903- *IntWW 91, Who 92*
**Murrell**, Barbara Curry 1938- *WhoBlA 92*
**Murrell**, Charlayne E. 1951- *WhoBlA 92*
**Murrell**, Geoffrey David George 1934- *Who 92*
**Murrell**, Hugh Jerry 1937- *AmMWSc 92*
**Murrell**, James Thomas, Jr 1942- *AmMWSc 92*
**Murrell**, Janice Marie 1937- *WhoEnt 92*
**Murrell**, John 1945- *WrDr 92*
**Murrell**, John Norman 1932- *Who 92*
**Murrell**, Kenneth Darwin 1940- *AmMWSc 92*
**Murrell**, Leonard Richard 1933- *AmMWSc 92*
**Murrell**, Peter C. 1920- *WhoBlA 92*
**Murrell**, Robert George 1932- *WhoAmL 92*
**Murrell**, Sylvia Marilyn 1947- *WhoBlA 92*
**Murren**, Douglas Edward 1951- *WhoRel 92, WhoWest 92*
**Murrey**, John Woodall 1942- *WhoAmL 92*
**Murrey**, Joseph Huffmaster, Jr 1926- *WhoAmP 91*
**Murrie**, William 1903- *Who 92*
**Murrieta**, Joaquin 1829?-1853 *BenetAL 91*
**Murrill**, Evelyn A 1930- *AmMWSc 92*
**Murrill**, Lena Freeman 1950- *WhoEnt 92*
**Murrill**, Paul W 1934- *AmMWSc 92*
**Murrin**, Leonard Charles 1943- *AmMWSc 92*
**Murrin**, Regis Doubet 1930- *WhoAmL 92*
**Murrin**, Thomas E 1923- *WhoIns 92*
**Murrin**, Thomas J 1929- *AmMWSc 92*
**Murrish**, David Earl 1937- *AmMWSc 92*
**Murrish**, Stephanie Susan 1966- *WhoEnt 92*
**Murrmann**, Richard P 1940- *AmMWSc 92*
**Murrow**, Edward R. d1965 *LesBEnT 92 [port]*
**Murrow**, Edward R 1908-1965 *FacFETw [port]*
**Murrow**, Edward Roscoe 1908-1965 *DcNCBi 4*
**Murrow**, Liza Ketchum *DrAPF 91*
**Murry**, Colin Middleton *TwCSFW 91*
**Murry**, Colin Middleton 1926- *WrDr 92*
**Murry**, Harold David, Jr. 1943- *WhoAmL 92*
**Murry**, John Middleton 1889-1957 *FacFETw*
**Murry**, Katherine Middleton 1925- *ConAu 133*
**Mursell**, Peter 1913- *Who 92*
**Mursky**, Gregory 1929- *AmMWSc 92*
**Murta**, Jack Burnett *IntWW 91*
**Murta**, Kenneth Hall 1929- *Who 92*
**Murtagh**, Christopher Matthew 1955- *WhoWest 92*
**Murtagh**, Frederick Reed 1944- *AmMWSc 92*
**Murtagh**, James P. 1911- *WhoAmL 92*
**Murtagh**, Marion *Who 92*
**Murtaugh**, Christopher David 1945- *WhoAmL 92*
**Murtaugh**, Jack *WhoRel 92*
**Murtaugh**, John Brian 1937- *WhoAmP 91*
**Murtfeldt**, Mary Esther 1848-1913 *BiInAmS*
**Murtha**, Brian T. 1942- *WhoAmL 92*
**Murtha**, David Thomas 1957- *WhoMW 92*
**Murtha**, John Francis 1930- *WhoRel 92*
**Murtha**, John P. 1932- *AlmAP 92 [port]*
**Murtha**, John Patrick *WhoAmP 91*
**Murtha**, Joseph P 1931- *AmMWSc 92*
**Murthy**, A S Krishna 1932- *AmMWSc 92*
**Murthy**, Andiappan Kumaresa Sundara *AmMWSc 92*
**Murthy**, Krishna K *AmMWSc 92*
**Murthy**, Mahadi Raghavandrarao Ven 1929- *AmMWSc 92*
**Murthy**, Raman Chittaram *AmMWSc 92*
**Murthy**, Srinivasa K R 1949- *AmMWSc 92*
**Murthy**, Vadiraja Venkatesa 1940- *AmMWSc 92*
**Murthy**, Varanasi Rama 1933- *AmMWSc 92*
**Murthy**, Veeraraghavan Krishna 1934- *AmMWSc 92, WhoWest 92*
**Murthy**, Vishnubhakta Shrinivas 1942- *AmMWSc 92*
**Murti**, Kuruganti Gopalakrishna 1943- *AmMWSc 92*
**Murto**, Patty Lila 1950- *WhoAmP 91*
**Murton** *Who 92*
**Murton of Lindisfarne**, Baron 1914- *Who 92*
**Murty**, Dangety Satyanarayana 1927- *AmMWSc 92*
**Murty**, Dasika Radha Krishna 1931- *AmMWSc 92*
**Murty**, Katta Gopalakrishna 1936- *AmMWSc 92, WhoMW 92*
**Murty**, Rama Chandra 1928- *AmMWSc 92*
**Murty**, Tadepalli Satyanarayana 1938- *AmMWSc 92*
**Murumbi**, Joseph A. d1990 *IntWW 91N*
**Murunga**, Dick *BlkOlyM*
**Murvosh**, Chad M 1931- *AmMWSc 92*
**Muryasz**, Jacqueline Marie 1955- *WhoRel 92*
**Musa**, John D 1933- *AmMWSc 92*
**Musa**, Luis Giordano 1958- *WhoAmL 92*
**Musa**, Mahmoud Nimir 1943- *AmMWSc 92*
**Musa**, Samuel A *AmMWSc 92*
**Musabayev**, Isak Kurbanovich 1910- *IntWW 91*
**Musacchia**, X J 1923- *AmMWSc 92*
**Musacchio**, Theodore Alphonsus 1934- *WhoWest 92*
**Musakhanov**, Mirzakhamud M. 1912- *SovUnBD*
**Musal**, Henry M, Jr 1931- *AmMWSc 92*
**Musante**, Catherine Antoinette 1911- *WhoRel 92*
**Musante**, Jacqueline Muriel 1926- *WhoRel 92*
**Musante**, Jane Sparkes 1937- *WhoEnt 92*
**Musante**, Tony *IntMPA 92, WhoEnt 92*
**Musaphia**, Joseph 1935- *IntAu&W 91, WrDr 92*
**Musburger**, Brent *LesBEnT 92 [port]*
**Muscarella**, Patricia A 1952- *WhoAmP 91*
**Muscari**, Joseph A 1935- *AmMWSc 92*
**Muscatello**, Anthony Curtis 1950- *AmMWSc 92*
**Muscatine**, Leonard 1932- *AmMWSc 92*
**Muscato**, Andrew 1953- *WhoAmL 92*
**Muscato**, Joseph James 1949- *WhoMW 92*
**Musch**, David C 1954- *AmMWSc 92*
**Muschalek**, Caroline Creel 1952- *WhoFI 92*
**Muschamp**, George Morris, Jr. 1944- *WhoMW 92*
**Muschek**, Lawrence David 1943- *AmMWSc 92*
**Muschel**, Louis Henry 1916- *AmMWSc 92*

**Muschg**, Adolf 1934- *IntWW 91*
**Muschik**, Gary Mathew 1944- *AmMWSc 92*
**Muschio**, Henry M, Jr 1931- *AmMWSc 92*
**Muschler**, James Arthur 1958- *WhoFI 92*
**Muschlitz**, Earle Eugene, Jr 1921- *AmMWSc 92*
**Muscoplat**, Charles Craig 1948- *AmMWSc 92*
**Muscroft**, Harold Colin 1924- *Who 92*
**Muse**, Dan T. 1882-1950 *RelLAm 91*
**Muse**, Helen Elizabeth 1917- *IntAu&W 91*
**Muse**, Joel, Jr 1941- *AmMWSc 92*
**Muse**, Patricia *DrAPF 91*
**Muse**, Stephen H. 1947- *WhoAmL 92*
**Muse**, William Brown, Jr. 1918- *WhoBlA 92*
**Muse**, William Van 1939- *WhoMW 92*
**Musen**, Mark Alan 1956- *WhoWest 92*
**Muser**, Marc 1954- *AmMWSc 92*
**Muserlian**, Charles A. 1932- *WhoAmL 92, WhoFI 92*
**Muses**, C.A. *ConAu 135*
**Muses**, Charles Arthur 1919- *ConAu 135*
**Museus**, Robert Allen 1955- *WhoMW 92*
**Museveni**, Yoweri Kaguta 1944- *IntWW 91*
**Museveni**, Yoweri Kaguta 1945- *Who 92*
**Musfelt**, Duane Clark 1951- *WhoAmL 92*
**Musgrave**, Albert Wayne 1923- *AmMWSc 92*
**Musgrave**, Charles Edward 1932- *WhoEnt 92, WhoMW 92*
**Musgrave**, Christopher 1949- *Who 92*
**Musgrave**, Dennis Charles 1921- *Who 92*
**Musgrave**, F Story 1935- *AmMWSc 92*
**Musgrave**, Mary Elizabeth 1954- *AmMWSc 92*
**Musgrave**, R. Kenton 1927- *WhoAmL 92*
**Musgrave**, Richard James 1922- *Who 92*
**Musgrave**, Rosanne Kimble 1952- *Who 92*
**Musgrave**, Stanley Dean 1919- *AmMWSc 92*
**Musgrave**, Susan 1951- *ConPo 91, IntAu&W 91, WrDr 92*
**Musgrave**, Thea *WhoEnt 92*
**Musgrave**, Thea 1928- *ConCom 92, IntWW 91, NewAmDM, Who 92*
**Musgrave**, William Kenneth Rodgerson 1918- *Who 92*
**Musgrove**, D Ronald 1956- *WhoAmP 91*
**Musgrove**, Frank 1922- *IntAu&W 91, Who 92, WrDr 92*
**Musgrove**, Harold John 1930- *Who 92*
**Musgrove**, John 1920- *Who 92*
**Musgrove**, Margaret Wynkoop 1943- *WhoBlA 92*
**Mushak**, Paul 1935- *AmMWSc 92*
**Mushegan-Watson**, Janet 1955- *WhoRel 92*
**Mushen**, Robert Linton 1943- *WhoWest 92*
**Musher**, Daniel Michael 1938- *AmMWSc 92*
**Mushett**, Charles Wilbur 1914- *AmMWSc 92*
**Mushik**, Corliss Dodge *WhoAmP 91*
**Mushin**, William W. 1910- *Who 92*
**Mushinski**, J Frederic 1938- *AmMWSc 92*
**Mushinsky**, Mary M *WhoAmP 91*
**Mushketik**, Yuri Mikhailovich 1929- *IntWW 91*
**Mushotzky**, Richard Fred 1947- *AmMWSc 92*
**Musial**, Stan 1920- *FacFETw*
**Music**, John Farris 1921- *AmMWSc 92*
**Music**, Lorenzo *LesBEnT 92*
**Musick**, Gerald Joe 1940- *AmMWSc 92*
**Musick**, Jack T 1927- *AmMWSc 92*
**Musick**, James R 1946- *AmMWSc 92*
**Musick**, John A 1941- *AmMWSc 92*
**Musick**, Robert Lawrence, Jr. 1947- *WhoAmL 92*
**Musidora** 1884-1957 *ReelWom*
**Musiek**, Frank Edward 1947- *AmMWSc 92*
**Musihin**, Konstantin K. 1927- *WhoWest 92*
**Musiker**, Reuben 1931- *IntWW 91, WrDr 92*
**Musil**, Robert 1880-1942 *FacFETw*
**Musil**, Robert Edler 1880-1942 *LiExTwC*
**Musilli**, John d1991 *NewYTBS 91*
**Musin**, Dmitri Petrovich *IntWW 91*
**Musin**, Donald Jeline 1936- *WhoRel 92*
**Musin**, Stephen A. 1958- *WhoFI 92*
**Musinski**, Donald Louis 1946- *AmMWSc 92*
**Muska**, Carl Frank 1948- *AmMWSc 92*
**Muskat**, Joseph Baruch 1935- *AmMWSc 92*
**Muskat**, Morris 1906- *AmMWSc 92*
**Muskatt**, Herman S 1931- *AmMWSc 92*
**Muske**, Carol *DrAPF 91*
**Muske-Dukes**, Carol Anne 1946- *WhoWest 92*
**Muskelly**, Anna Marie *WhoBlA 92*
**Musker**, John 1906- *Who 92*
**Musker**, Warren Kenneth 1934- *AmMWSc 92*
**Muskerry**, Baron 1948- *Who 92*
**Musket**, Ronald George 1940- *WhoWest 92*
**Muskie**, Edmund Sixtus 1914- *AmPolLe, FacFETw, IntWW 91, Who 92, WhoAmP 91*
**Muskin**, Victor Philip 1942- *WhoAmL 92*
**Muskovitz**, Susannah 1959- *WhoAmL 92*
**Musler**, George T 1929- *WhoAmP 91*
**Musokotwane**, Kebby Sililo Kambulu 1946- *IntWW 91*
**Musolf**, DeAnne Margaret 1960- *WhoWest 92*
**Musolf**, Lloyd D. 1919- *WrDr 92*
**Musolf**, Lloyd Daryl 1919- *IntAu&W 91*
**Musolino**, Joseph Richard 1937- *WhoFI 92*
**Musone**, Fred James 1944- *WhoMW 92*
**Muss**, Daniel R 1928- *AmMWSc 92*
**Mussasa** *EncAmaz 91*
**Musschenbroek**, Pieter van 1692-1761 *BlkwCEP*
**Mussehl**, Allan Arthur 1942- *WhoMW 92*
**Mussell**, Harry W 1941- *AmMWSc 92*
**Musselman**, Darwin B 1916- *WhoWest 92*
**Musselman**, Elizabeth Ann 1954- *WhoWest 92*
**Musselman**, John J. 1926- *WhoFI 92*
**Musselman**, Lois *WhoWest 92*
**Musselman**, Nelson Page 1917- *AmMWSc 92*
**Musselman**, Raymond *WhoAmP 91*
**Musselman**, Robert Carl 1942- *WhoWest 92*
**Musselman**, Victor Paul 1946- *WhoFI 92*
**Musselmann**, Kenneth George 1946- *WhoWest 92*
**Musselwhite**, Marvin D, Jr 1938- *WhoAmP 91*
**Mussen**, Eric Carnes 1944- *AmMWSc 92*
**Musser**, Alice 1929- *WhoAmP 91*
**Musser**, Benjamin 1889-1951 *BenetAL 91*
**Musser**, C. Walton 1909- *WhoWest 92*
**Musser**, Daniel 1810-1877 *AmPeW*
**Musser**, David Musselman 1909- *AmMWSc 92*
**Musser**, David Rea 1944- *AmMWSc 92*
**Musser**, Joe 1936- *IntAu&W 91, WrDr 92*
**Musser**, John H 1949- *AmMWSc 92*
**Musser**, John Herr 1856-1912 *BiInAmS*
**Musser**, Joseph White 1872-1954 *RelLAm 91*
**Musser**, Michael Tuttle 1942- *AmMWSc 92*
**Musser**, Terry M 1947- *WhoAmP 91*
**Musser**, Tharon 1925- *WhoEnt 92*
**Musser**, William Wesley, Jr. 1918- *WhoAmL 92*
**Musserian**, John R. 1961- *WhoFI 92*
**Mussert**, Anton Adriaan 1894-1946 *BiDExR, EncTR 91*
**Musset**, Alfred de 1810-1857 *GuFrLit 1*
**Musset**, Paul de 1804-1880 *GuFrLit 1*
**Mussey**, Joseph Arthur 1948- *WhoFI 92*
**Mussey**, Virginia T H *IntAu&W 91X, WrDr 92*
**Mussi**, Mary 1907- *IntAu&W 91*
**Mussinan**, Cynthia June 1946- *AmMWSc 92*
**Mussman**, William Edward 1919- *WhoAmL 92*
**Mussman**, William Edward, III 1951- *WhoAmL 92*
**Mussolini**, Benito 1883-1945 *EncTR 91 [port], FacFETw [port]*
**Mussolini**, Benito Amilcare Andrea 1883-1945 *BiDExR*
**Musson**, Alfred Henry 1900- *Who 92*
**Musson**, Alfred Lyman 1911- *AmMWSc 92*
**Musson**, Geoffrey 1910- *Who 92*
**Musson**, John Geoffrey Robin 1939- *Who 92*
**Musson**, John Nicholas Whitaker 1927- *Who 92*
**Musson**, Robert A *AmMWSc 92*
**Musson**, Samuel Dixon 1908- *Who 92*
**Mussorgsky**, Modest Petrovich 1839-1881 *NewAmDM*
**Mustacchi**, Henry 1930- *AmMWSc 92*
**Mustacchi**, Piero 1920- *WhoWest 92*
**Mustacchi**, Piero Omar de Zamalek 1920- *AmMWSc 92*
**Mustaf**, Jerrod 1949- *WhoBlA 92*
**Mustafa**, Mohammad Ghulam 1940- *WhoWest 92*
**Mustafa**, Mohammed G 1941- *AmMWSc 92*
**Mustafa**, Nasr El-Din 1930- *Who 92*
**Mustafa**, Shams 1952- *AmMWSc 92*
**Mustafa**, Syed Jamal 1946- *AmMWSc 92*
**Mustansir**, Ali 1952- *WhoFI 92*
**Mustapha Bin Datu Harun** 1918- *IntWW 91*
**Mustapha**, Alhaji Mohamed Sanusi 1903- *WhoRel 92*
**Mustard**, James Fraser 1927- *AmMWSc 92*
**Mustard**, Margaret Jean 1920- *AmMWSc 92*
**Mustard**, William Thornton 1914-1987 *FacFETw*
**Muste**, Abraham Johannes 1885-1967 *AmPeW, RelLAm 91*
**Mustel**, Victor 1815-1890 *NewAmDM*
**Muster**, Douglas Frederick 1918- *AmMWSc 92*
**Muster**, John Joseph 1958- *WhoAmP 91*
**Mustill**, Michael 1931- *Who 92*
**Musto**, Barry 1930- *IntAu&W 91, WrDr 92*
**Musto**, Joseph J. 1943- *WhoAmL 92*
**Musto**, Michael J. *IntMPA 92*
**Musto**, Raphael J 1929- *WhoAmP 91*
**Mustoe**, Anne 1933- *Who 92*
**Mustoe**, David Winston 1930- *WhoFI 92*
**Muston**, Gerald Bruce *Who 92*
**Mustone**, Amelia P 1928- *WhoAmP 91*
**Musy**, Jean Edouard 1938- *IntWW 91*
**Musyoki**, Michael 1956- *BlkOlyM*
**Mut**, Stuart Creighton 1924- *AmMWSc 92*
**Mutai**, Mitsuo d1991 *NewYTBS 91*
**Mutale**, Elaine Butler 1943- *WhoBlA 92*
**Mutalibov**, Ayaz Niyazi Ogly 1938- *IntWW 91, SovUnBD*
**Mutallab**, Alhaji Umaru Abdul 1939- *IntWW 91*
**Mutch**, Duane Ollen 1925- *WhoAmP 91*
**Mutch**, George William 1943- *AmMWSc 92*
**Mutch**, Patricia Black 1943- *AmMWSc 92*
**Mutcheruon**, James Albertus, Jr. 1941- *WhoBlA 92*
**Mutchler**, Calvin Kendal 1926- *AmMWSc 92*
**Mutchler**, Edward Michael 1935- *WhoFI 92, WhoMW 92*
**Mutchler**, Gordon Sinclair 1938- *AmMWSc 92*
**Mutchmor**, John A 1929- *AmMWSc 92*
**Mutel**, Robert Lucien 1946- *AmMWSc 92, WhoMW 92*
**Muth**, Chester William 1922- *AmMWSc 92*
**Muth**, Eginhard Joerg 1928- *AmMWSc 92*
**Muth**, Eric Anthony 1948- *AmMWSc 92*
**Muth**, Gilbert Jerome 1938- *AmMWSc 92*
**Muth**, John Fraser 1930- *WhoFI 92, WhoMW 92*
**Muth**, Michael Kelsey 1959- *WhoFI 92*
**Muth**, Richard F. 1927- *WrDr 92*
**Muth**, Richard Ferris 1927- *WhoFI 92*
**Muth**, Wayne Allen 1932- *AmMWSc 92*
**Mutharasan**, Rajakkannu 1947- *AmMWSc 92*
**Muthel**, Lothar 1896-1964 *EncTR 91 [port]*
**Muthesius**, Hermann 1861-1927 *DcTwDes, FacFETw*
**Muthukrishnan**, Subbaratnam 1942- *AmMWSc 92, WhoMW 92*
**Muthukumar**, Murugappan *AmMWSc 92*
**Muthuswamy**, Petham Padayatchi 1945- *WhoMW 92*
**Muti**, Ettore 1902-1943 *BiDExR*
**Muti**, Riccardo 1941- *IntWW 91, NewAmDM, Who 92, WhoEnt 92*
**Mutis**, Alvaro 1923- *ConSpAP*
**Mutis-Duplat**, Emilio 1932- *AmMWSc 92*
**Mutmansky**, Jan Martin 1941- *AmMWSc 92*
**Muto**, Kabun 1926- *IntWW 91*
**Muto**, Peter 1924- *AmMWSc 92, WhoAmP 91*
**Muto**, Susan Annette 1942- *WhoRel 92*
**Mutsch**, Edward L 1939- *AmMWSc 92*
**Mutschlecner**, Joseph Paul 1930- *AmMWSc 92*
**Mutschler**, Carlfried 1926- *IntWW 91*
**Mutschler**, Herbert Frederick 1919- *WhoWest 92*
**Mutschmann**, Martin 1879-1948 *EncTR 91 [port]*
**Mutsu**, Ian Yonosuke 1907- *IntMPA 92*
**Mutt**, Mihkel 1953- *IntAu&W 91*
**Muttalib**, Khandker Abdul 1952- *AmMWSc 92*
**Mutter**, Anne-Sophie 1963- *IntWW 91*
**Mutter**, Walter Edward 1921- *AmMWSc 92*
**Mutter**, William Hugh 1934- *AmMWSc 92*
**Mutterperl**, William Charles 1946- *WhoAmL 92*
**Mutti**, Albert Frederick 1938- *WhoRel 92*
**Mutti**, John Harmon 1947- *WhoFI 92*
**Mutton**, Donald Barrett 1927- *AmMWSc 92*
**Mutty**, Paul Roland 1939- *WhoMW 92*
**Mutz**, John M *WhoAmP 91*
**Mutz**, Steven Herbert 1958- *WhoAmL 92*
**Mutzebaugh**, Richard Frances 1933- *WhoAmP 91*
**Mutzenberger**, Marv *WhoAmP 91*
**Mutziger**, Judy Lynn 1947- *WhoFI 92*
**Muul**, Illar 1938- *AmMWSc 92*
**Muus**, Jytte Marie 1904- *AmMWSc 92*
**Muuss**, Rolf Eduard 1924- *WrDr 92*
**Muvdi**, Bichara B 1927- *AmMWSc 92*
**Muwakkil**, Salim 1947- *WhoBlA 92*
**Muwanga**, Paulo d1991 *IntWW 91, -91N, NewYTBS 91*
**Muxlow**, Keith 1933- *WhoAmP 91*
**Muybridge**, Eadweard *ThHEIm*
**Muybridge**, Eadweard 1830-1904 *BenetAL 91*
**Muys**, Jerome Christian 1932- *WhoAmL 92*
**Muyskens**, John David 1934- *WhoRel 92*
**Muyumba**, Francois N. 1939- *WhoBlA 92*
**Muzenda**, Simon Vengai 1922- *IntWW 91*
**Muzik**, Thomas J 1919- *AmMWSc 92*
**Muzio**, Claudia 1889-1936 *NewAmDM*
**Muzorewa**, Abel 1925- *FacFETw*
**Muzorewa**, Abel Tendekayi 1925- *IntWW 91*
**Muzyczko**, Thaddeus Marion 1936- *AmMWSc 92*
**Muzyka**, Donald Richard 1938- *AmMWSc 92*
**Muzzey**, David Saville 1870-1965 *RelLAm 91*
**Muzzy**, James F 1939- *WhoIns 92*
**Mveng**, Engelbert 1930- *IntWW 91*
**Mwaanga**, Vernon Johnson 1939- *IntWW 91*
**Mwakawago**, Daudi Ngelautwa 1939- *IntWW 91*
**Mwale**, Siteke Gibson 1929- *IntWW 91*
**Mwalozi**, Chilyalya 1936- *WhoWest 92*
**Mwamba**, Zuberi I. 1937- *WhoBlA 92*
**Mwanakatwe**, John Mupanga 1926- *IntWW 91*
**Mwanza**, Jacob Mumbi 1937- *Who 92*
**Mwinyi**, Ali Hassan 1925- *ConBlB 1 [port], IntWW 91*
**Mwinyi**, Ndugu Ali Hassan 1925- *Who 92*
**Mya Han**, Andrew *WhoRel 92*
**Myakota**, Aleksey Sergeyevich 1932- *IntWW 91*
**Myart**, James Willie, Jr 1954- *WhoAmP 91*
**Myaskovsky**, Nicholas Yakovlevich 1881-1950 *FacFETw*
**Myaskovsky**, Nikolai 1881-1950 *NewAmDM*
**Myaskovsky**, Nikolay Yakovlevich 1881-1950 *SovUnBD*
**Myatt**, Gordon J. 1928- *WhoBlA 92*
**Mybeck**, Richard Raymond 1928- *WhoWest 92*
**Myburgh**, Albert Tertius d1990 *IntWW 91N*
**Myburgh**, Albert Tertius 1934- *IntAu&W 91*
**Mycek**, Mary J 1926- *AmMWSc 92*
**Mychajlonka**, Myron 1947- *AmMWSc 92*
**Mycielski**, Jan 1932- *AmMWSc 92*
**Mycock**, Frederick Charles 1943- *WhoAmL 92*
**Mycue**, Edward *DrAPF 91*
**Mydland**, Brent 1952-1990 *AnObit 1990*
**Mydland**, M LaVonne 1923- *WhoAmP 91*
**Myer**, Albert James 1829-1880 *BiInAmS*
**Myer**, Carole Wendy 1944- *AmMWSc 92*
**Myer**, Dillon S 1891-1982 *FacFETw*
**Myer**, Donal Gene 1930- *AmMWSc 92*
**Myer**, Donald Beekman 1937- *WhoFI 92*
**Myer**, George Henry 1937- *AmMWSc 92*
**Myer**, Glenn Evans 1941- *AmMWSc 92*
**Myer**, John Andrew 1956- *WhoFI 92*
**Myer**, Jon Harold 1922- *AmMWSc 92, WhoWest 92*
**Myer**, Paul Joseph 1954- *WhoMW 92*
**Myer**, Sidney Baillieu 1926- *Who 92*
**Myer**, Yash Paul 1932- *AmMWSc 92*
**Myerberg**, Marcia 1945- *WhoFI 92*
**Myerholtz**, Ralph W, Jr 1926- *AmMWSc 92*
**Myers**, Adam Jerome, III 1951- *WhoAmL 92, WhoFI 92*
**Myers**, Adrian Marvyn 1951- *WhoIns 92*
**Myers**, Al 1922- *WhoFI 92, WhoWest 92*
**Myers**, Alan Louis 1932- *AmMWSc 92*
**Myers**, Albert Edwin 1931- *WhoRel 92*
**Myers**, Albert Gallatin 1880-1976 *DcNCBi 4*
**Myers**, Alton J. 1934- *WhoRel 92*
**Myers**, Andrew Daniel 1953- *WhoAmL 92*
**Myers**, Anne Boone 1958- *AmMWSc 92*
**Myers**, Arno Rhodes 1907- *WhoFI 92*
**Myers**, Arthur John 1918- *AmMWSc 92*
**Myers**, Barton 1934- *IntWW 91, WhoFI 92, WhoWest 92*
**Myers**, Basil R 1922- *AmMWSc 92*
**Myers**, Benjamin Franklin, Jr 1926- *AmMWSc 92*
**Myers**, Bernard *IntAu&W 91*
**Myers**, Bernard Samuel 1949- *WhoBlA 92*
**Myers**, Beth Ann 1957- *WhoAmL 92*
**Myers**, Betty June 1928- *AmMWSc 92*
**Myers**, Blake 1923- *AmMWSc 92*
**Myers**, Bob *DrAPF 91*
**Myers**, Bradley Lawrence 1961- *WhoWest 92*

**Myers,** Bryan D 1936- AmMWSc 92
**Myers,** Carole Lynn WhoEnt 92
**Myers,** Caroline Elizabeth Clark 1887-1980 ConAu 134
**Myers,** Carrol Bruce 1943- AmMWSc 92
**Myers,** Carroll Jean 1928- WhoAmP 91
**Myers,** Charles 1943- AmMWSc 92
**Myers,** Charles Christopher 1934- AmMWSc 92
**Myers,** Charles Edwin 1940- AmMWSc 92
**Myers,** Charles Kendell 1938- WhoWest 92
**Myers,** Charles R 1956- AmMWSc 92
**Myers,** Charles William 1936- AmMWSc 92
**Myers,** Clay 1927- WhoAmP 91
**Myers,** Clifford Earl 1929- AmMWSc 92
**Myers,** Connie Jean 1946- WhoWest 92
**Myers,** Corrine 1936- WhoRel 92
**Myers,** Craig Alan 1964- WhoRel 92
**Myers,** Dale D 1922- WhoAmP 91
**Myers,** Dale Dehaven 1922- AmMWSc 92, IntWW 91
**Myers,** Dane Jacob 1948- WhoAmL 92
**Myers,** Daniel N. 1942- WhoAmL 92
**Myers,** Darlene Marie 1950- WhoEnt 92
**Myers,** Darrell R. 1940- WhoWest 92
**Myers,** David 1906- AmMWSc 92
**Myers,** David Daniel 1932- AmMWSc 92
**Myers,** David L 1933- WhoIns 92
**Myers,** David Milton 1911- Who 92
**Myers,** David Richard 1948- AmMWSc 92, WhoFI 92
**Myers,** Deborah Elizabeth 1954- WhoWest 92
**Myers,** Debra J. 1952- WhoBlA 92
**Myers,** Dennis Gillford 1953- WhoWest 92
**Myers,** Dennis Joseph 1953- WhoAmL 92
**Myers,** Denys Peter 1884-1972 AmPeW
**Myers,** Dirck V 1935- AmMWSc 92
**Myers,** Donald Albin 1936- AmMWSc 92
**Myers,** Donald Arthur 1921- AmMWSc 92
**Myers,** Donald Earl 1931- AmMWSc 92, WhoWest 92
**Myers,** Donald Royal 1913- AmMWSc 92
**Myers,** Douglas George 1949- WhoWest 92
**Myers,** Douglas Mark 1946- WhoAmP 91
**Myers,** Duane George 1954- WhoFI 92
**Myers,** Earl A 1929- AmMWSc 92
**Myers,** Earl Eugene 1924- AmMWSc 92
**Myers,** Earl T. 1930- WhoBlA 92
**Myers,** Edmund Charles Wolf 1906- Who 92
**Myers,** Elisabeth P. 1918- WrDr 92
**Myers,** Elizabeth Rouse 1923- WhoWest 92
**Myers,** Elliot H AmMWSc 92
**Myers,** Elmer 1926- WhoWest 92
**Myers,** Emma McGraw 1953- WhoBlA 92
**Myers,** Eric Lee 1962- WhoRel 92
**Myers,** Ernest Paul 1938- WhoMW 92
**Myers,** Ernest Ray WhoBlA 92
**Myers,** Eugene Nicholas 1933- AmMWSc 92
**Myers,** Frances Althea 1957- WhoBlA 92
**Myers,** Franklin 1952- WhoAmL 92
**Myers,** Gardiner Hubbard 1939- AmMWSc 92
**Myers,** Gary Elsworth 1942- WhoEnt 92
**Myers,** Gary Lynn 1951- WhoRel 92
**Myers,** Gene Jay 1931- WhoWest 92
**Myers,** Geoffrey 1930- Who 92
**Myers,** Geoffrey Morris Price 1927- Who 92
**Myers,** George, Jr. DrAPF 91
**Myers,** George E 1926- AmMWSc 92
**Myers,** George Henry 1930- AmMWSc 92
**Myers,** George Scott, Jr 1934- AmMWSc 92
**Myers,** Gerald Andy 1928- AmMWSc 92
**Myers,** Glen E 1934- AmMWSc 92
**Myers,** Glenn Alexander 1949- AmMWSc 92
**Myers,** Gordon Elliot 1929- Who 92
**Myers,** Grant G 1930- AmMWSc 92
**Myers,** Gregory Edwin 1960- WhoFI 92, WhoWest 92
**Myers,** Gretchen Hardy Godar 1958- WhoAmL 92
**Myers,** Gustavus 1872-1942 BenetAL 91
**Myers,** Gwen McHaney 1925- WhoAmP 91
**Myers,** Hardy 1939- WhoAmP 91
**Myers,** Harry Eric 1914- Who 92
**Myers,** Harvey Nathaniel 1946- AmMWSc 92, WhoMW 92
**Myers,** Helen Dee WhoWest 92
**Myers,** Holly WhoAmP 91
**Myers,** Howard 1928- AmMWSc 92
**Myers,** Howard Benjaman 1937- WhoFI 92
**Myers,** Howard M 1923- AmMWSc 92
**Myers,** Ira Lee 1924- AmMWSc 92
**Myers,** Israel 1950- WhoFI 92
**Myers,** J. Kenneth 1949- WhoAmL 92
**Myers,** Jack DrAPF 91
**Myers,** Jack 1941- WrDr 92
**Myers,** Jack Charles 1947- WhoEnt 92
**Myers,** Jack Dennis 1944- WhoMW 92
**Myers,** Jack Duane 1913- AmMWSc 92
**Myers,** Jack Edgar 1913- AmMWSc 92
**Myers,** Jack Elliott 1941- IntAu&W 91
**Myers,** Jack Kay 1946- WhoFI 92
**Myers,** Jacke Duane 1913- IntWW 91
**Myers,** Jacob M. 1904- WrDr 92
**Myers,** Jacob Martin 1919- AmMWSc 92
**Myers,** Jacqualine Desmona 1951- WhoBlA 92
**Myers,** James E. 1919- WhoEnt 92
**Myers,** James Harlan 1925- WhoFI 92
**Myers,** James Hurley 1940- AmMWSc 92
**Myers,** James R 1933- AmMWSc 92
**Myers,** James Robert 1954- AmMWSc 92
**Myers,** James Woodrow, III 1954- WhoAmL 92
**Myers,** Jay Scott 1921- WhoAmP 91
**Myers,** Jeffrey 1932- AmMWSc 92
**Myers,** Jeffrey Donald 1955- WhoWest 92
**Myers,** Jeffrey Rayner 1953- WhoEnt 92
**Myers,** Jerome Joseph WhoFI 92
**Myers,** Jerry D. 1963- WhoMW 92
**Myers,** Jesse J 1876?-1914 BiInAmS
**Myers,** John Adams 1932- AmMWSc 92
**Myers,** John Albert 1943- AmMWSc 92
**Myers,** John Arthur 1946- WhoAmL 92
**Myers,** John David 1937- Who 92
**Myers,** John E 1923- AmMWSc 92
**Myers,** John Eldridge 1917- WhoMW 92
**Myers,** John Holt 1923- WhoAmL 92
**Myers,** John Joseph 1941- WhoRel 92
**Myers,** John Leslie 1950- WhoAmP 91
**Myers,** John Martin 1935- AmMWSc 92
**Myers,** John Moore 1946- WhoMW 92
**Myers,** John Myers 1906- TwCWW 91
**Myers,** John T. 1927- AlmAP 92 [port], WhoAmP 91
**Myers,** John Thomas 1927- WhoMW 92
**Myers,** Jon D WhoAmP 91
**Myers,** Julian F. 1918- IntMPA 92
**Myers,** Kenneth 1907- Who 92
**Myers,** Kenneth Ellis 1932- WhoMW 92
**Myers,** Kenneth Morton 1933- WhoAmP 91
**Myers,** Kenneth Raymond 1939- WhoAmL 92
**Myers,** Kevin Rice 1956- WhoRel 92
**Myers,** L.H. 1881-1944 RfGEnL 91
**Myers,** L. Leonard 1933- WhoBlA 92
**Myers,** Larry Allen 1947- WhoFI 92
**Myers,** Larry Wayne 1946- WhoRel 92
**Myers,** Laura Elizabeth 1965- WhoEnt 92
**Myers,** Lawrence Stanley, Jr 1919- AmMWSc 92
**Myers,** Lee Earl 1932- WhoFI 92
**Myers,** Lena Wright WhoBlA 92
**Myers,** Leslie Reese 1955- WhoEnt 92
**Myers,** Lewis Horace 1946- WhoBlA 92
**Myers,** Lonn William 1946- WhoAmL 92
**Myers,** Lou 1945- WhoEnt 92
**Myers,** Louis Michael 1930- WhoFI 92
**Myers,** Lowell Jack 1930- WhoAmL 92
**Myers,** Lyle Leslie 1938- AmMWSc 92
**Myers,** Marcus Norville 1928- AmMWSc 92
**Myers,** Marilyn Virginia 1954- WhoFI 92
**Myers,** Mark d1990 Who 92N
**Myers,** Mark B 1938- AmMWSc 92
**Myers,** Mark Eden 1953- WhoMW 92
**Myers,** Mark L. WhoFI 92
**Myers,** Martin Trevor 1941- Who 92
**Myers,** Maureen 1943- AmMWSc 92
**Myers,** Max H 1936- AmMWSc 92
**Myers,** Melvil Bertrand, Jr 1928- AmMWSc 92
**Myers,** Michael Alan 1964- WhoMW 92
**Myers,** Michael Kenneth 1939- AmMWSc 92
**Myers,** Michael Mark 1958- WhoMW 92
**Myers,** Michele Tolela 1941- WhoMW 92
**Myers,** Miller Franklin 1929- WhoFI 92
**Myers,** Minor, Jr. 1942- ConAu 133, WhoMW 92
**Myers,** Morey M. 1927- WhoAmL 92
**Myers,** Morgan Frank 1936- WhoWest 92
**Myers,** Nancy Lee 1946- WhoMW 92
**Myers,** Neil DrAPF 91
**Myers,** Neill WhoFI 91
**Myers,** Norman Allan 1935- WhoFI 92
**Myers,** Norman W WhoAmP 91
**Myers,** Oval, Jr 1933- AmMWSc 92, WhoMW 92
**Myers,** Patricia Ann 1955- WhoIns 92
**Myers,** Paul 1932- WrDr 92
**Myers,** Paul Walter 1923- AmMWSc 92
**Myers,** Pennie M. 1939- WhoMW 92
**Myers,** Peter Briggs 1926- AmMWSc 92
**Myers,** Peter Hamilton 1812-1878 BenetAL 91
**Myers,** Peter S. 1923- IntMPA 92
**Myers,** Philip 1931- Who 92
**Myers,** Philip 1947- AmMWSc 92
**Myers,** Philip Cherdak 1944- AmMWSc 92
**Myers,** Phillip Fenton 1935- WhoFI 92, WhoWest 92
**Myers,** Phillip S 1916- AmMWSc 92
**Myers,** Phillip Samuel 1916- WhoMW 92
**Myers,** R Thomas 1921- AmMWSc 92
**Myers,** Raymond Harold 1937- AmMWSc 92
**Myers,** Raymond Reever 1920- AmMWSc 92
**Myers,** Richard Alan 1953- WhoWest 92
**Myers,** Richard F 1931- AmMWSc 92
**Myers,** Richard F. 1944- WhoRel 92
**Myers,** Richard Hepworth 1947- AmMWSc 92
**Myers,** Richard K. 1956- WhoFI 92
**Myers,** Richard Lee 1944- AmMWSc 92
**Myers,** Richard Showse 1942- AmMWSc 92
**Myers,** Robert Anthony 1937- AmMWSc 92
**Myers,** Robert Durant 1931- AmMWSc 92
**Myers,** Robert Eugene 1928- WhoMW 92
**Myers,** Robert Eugene 1953- WhoMW 92
**Myers,** Robert Frederick 1916- AmMWSc 92
**Myers,** Robert Gilbert 1932- WhoFI 92
**Myers,** Robert Jay 1934- WhoFI 92
**Myers,** Robert Julius 1912- WhoAmP 91
**Myers,** Robert L., Jr. WhoBlA 92
**Myers,** Robert Lee, III 1928- WhoAmP 91
**Myers,** Robert Manson 1921- IntAu&W 91, WrDr 92
**Myers,** Robert Norman, Jr. 1949- WhoFI 92
**Myers,** Robert Page 1900- WhoMW 92
**Myers,** Rolland Graham 1945- WhoFI 92
**Myers,** Rollie John, Jr 1924- AmMWSc 92
**Myers,** Ronald Berl 1944- AmMWSc 92
**Myers,** Ronald Elwood 1929- AmMWSc 92
**Myers,** Ronald Eugene 1947- AmMWSc 92, WhoMW 92
**Myers,** Ronald Fenner 1930- AmMWSc 92
**Myers,** Ronald G 1933- AmMWSc 92
**Myers,** Roy Maurice 1911- AmMWSc 92
**Myers,** Rufus, Jr 1942- WhoAmP 91
**Myers,** Rupert 1921- Who 92
**Myers,** Ruth Elois 1922- WhoWest 92
**Myers,** Samuel L. 1919- WhoBlA 92
**Myers,** Samuel L., Jr. 1949- WhoBlA 92
**Myers,** Samuel Maxwell, Jr 1943- AmMWSc 92
**Myers,** Sara Alice WhoWest 92
**Myers,** Sere Spaulding 1930- WhoBlA 92
**Myers,** Stanley IntMPA 92
**Myers,** Stephen Bruce 1949- WhoFI 92
**Myers,** Stephen Hawley 1953- WhoAmL 92
**Myers,** Steven Richard 1956- AmMWSc 92
**Myers,** Suzanne Carey 1953- WhoMW 92
**Myers,** Theldon 1927- WhoEnt 92
**Myers,** Thomas DeWitt 1938- AmMWSc 92
**Myers,** Thomas Edward 1954- WhoFI 92
**Myers,** Thomas Oscar 1936- WhoRel 92
**Myers,** Thomas Perkins 1941- WhoMW 92
**Myers,** Thomas Wilmer 1939- AmMWSc 92
**Myers,** Timothy Halter 1940- WhoMW 92
**Myers,** Verne Steele 1907- AmMWSc 92
**Myers,** Vernon W 1919- AmMWSc 92
**Myers,** Victor 1921- AmMWSc 92
**Myers,** Victoria Christina 1943- WhoBlA 92
**Myers,** Walter Dean DrAPF 91
**Myers,** Walter Dean 1937- BlkLC [port], WhoBlA 92, WrDr 92
**Myers,** Walter Loy 1933- AmMWSc 92
**Myers,** Walter M. WrDr 92
**Myers,** Warren Powers Laird 1921- AmMWSc 92
**Myers,** Wayne Lawrence 1942- AmMWSc 92
**Myers,** Willard Glazier, Jr 1935- AmMWSc 92
**Myers,** William Carl 1950- WhoFI 92
**Myers,** William Charles 1963- WhoRel 92
**Myers,** William George 1930- WhoAmP 91
**Myers,** William George 1938- WhoRel 92
**Myers,** William Graydon AmMWSc 92
**Myers,** William Howard 1908- AmMWSc 92
**Myers,** William Howard 1946- AmMWSc 92
**Myers,** William Rayford 1818-1901 DcNCBi 4
**Myers,** Woodrow Augustus, Jr. 1954- WhoBlA 92
**Myers Brown,** Joan 1931- WhoEnt 92
**Myers-May,** Yvette WhoBlA 92
**Myers Medeiros,** Patricia Jo 1942- WhoWest 92
**Myerson,** Alan 1936- WhoEnt 92
**Myerson,** Albert Leon 1919- AmMWSc 92
**Myerson,** Arthur Levey 1928- Who 92
**Myerson,** Bernard 1918- IntMPA 92
**Myerson,** David Henry 1948- WhoWest 92
**Myerson,** David J. 1939- WhoEnt 92
**Myerson,** Eleanor 1922- WhoAmP 91
**Myerson,** Gerald 1951- AmMWSc 92, WhoWest 92
**Myerson,** Jacob M. 1926- IntWW 91
**Myerson,** Paul E. 1922- WhoFI 92
**Myerson,** Ralph M 1918- AmMWSc 92
**Myerson,** Raymond King 1917- WhoWest 92
**Myerson,** Roger Bruce 1951- WhoFI 92, WhoMW 92
**Myerson,** Toby Salter 1949- WhoAmL 92
**Mygatt,** Tracy Dickinson 1885-1973 AmPeW
**Mygrant,** John W. 1952- WhoAmL 92
**Myhand,** Dennis Monroe 1957- WhoRel 92
**Myhre,** Byron Arnold 1928- AmMWSc 92
**Myhre,** David V 1932- AmMWSc 92
**Myhre,** Philip C 1933- AmMWSc 92
**Myhre-Hollerman,** Janet M 1932- AmMWSc 92
**Myhre-Hollerman,** Janet Marlene 1932- WhoWest 92
**Myhren,** Trygve Edward 1937- WhoFI 92, WhoWest 92
**Myhrum,** Christopher Bentley 1953- WhoAmL 92
**Myint Maung,** U. 1921- IntWW 91
**Mykietyn,** Stephanie 1953- WhoEnt 92
**Mykkanen,** Donald L 1932- AmMWSc 92
**Mykkanen,** Donald Lee 1932- WhoWest 92
**Mykles,** Donald Lee 1950- AmMWSc 92
**Myland,** Howard David 1929- Who 92
**Myles,** Charles Wesley 1947- AmMWSc 92
**Myles,** David Fairlie 1925- Who 92
**Myles,** Diana Gold 1944- AmMWSc 92
**Myles,** Eileen DrAPF 91
**Myles,** Elliott Andrew 1960- WhoAmL 92
**Myles,** Ernestine 1921- WhoBlA 92
**Myles,** Herbert John 1923- WhoBlA 92
**Myles,** Joseph W. 1941- WhoMW 92
**Myles,** Kevin Michael 1934- AmMWSc 92
**Myles,** Stan, Jr. 1943- WhoBlA 92
**Myles,** Symon WrDr 92
**Myles,** Wilbert 1935- WhoBlA 92
**Myles,** William 1936- WhoBlA 92
**Myllent,** Peter Who 92
**Mylne,** Nigel James 1939- Who 92
**Mylnechuk,** Larry Herbert 1948- WhoFI 92
**Myl'nikov,** Andrey Andreevich 1919- SovUnBD
**Mylod,** Robert Joseph 1939- WhoFI 92, WhoMW 92
**Mylonas,** Constantine 1916- AmMWSc 92
**Mylrea,** Kenneth C 1935- AmMWSc 92
**Mylroie,** John Eglinton 1949- AmMWSc 92
**Mylroie,** Victor L 1937- AmMWSc 92
**Mylroie,** Willa W 1917- AmMWSc 92
**Myman,** Harvey Lewis 1948- WhoEnt 92
**Mynors,** Richard 1947- Who 92
**Mynsberge,** Richard Charles 1934- WhoFI 92
**Myntti,** Jon Nicholas 1940- WhoMW 92
**Myoda,** Toshio Timothy 1929- AmMWSc 92
**Myrberg,** Arthur August, Jr 1933- AmMWSc 92
**Myrdal,** Alva 1902-1986 FacFETw, WomSoc
**Myrdal,** Alva Reimer 1902-1986 WhoNob 90
**Myrdal,** Gunnar 1898-1987 FacFETw
**Myrdal,** Jan 1927- IntWW 91
**Myrdal,** Karl Gunnar 1898-1987 WhoNob 90
**Myrdal,** Rosemarie C 1929- WhoAmP 91
**Myren,** David James 1960- WhoMW 92
**Myrene** EncAmaz 91
**Myres,** John Antony Lovell 1936- Who 92
**Myres,** Miles Timothy 1931- AmMWSc 92
**Myrianthopoulos,** Ntinos 1921- AmMWSc 92
**Myrick,** Albert Charles, Jr 1939- AmMWSc 92
**Myrick,** Clarissa 1954- WhoBlA 92
**Myrick,** David WrDr 92
**Myrick,** Henry Nugent 1935- AmMWSc 92
**Myrick,** Howard A., Jr. 1934- WhoBlA 92
**Myrick,** Michael Lenn 1961- AmMWSc 92
**Myrick,** Steven Dale 1956- WhoRel 92
**Myrick,** Sue 1941- WhoAmP 91
**Myricks,** Larry 1956- BlkOlyM
**Myricks,** Noel 1935- WhoBlA 92
**Myrin,** Alarik F 1946- WhoAmP 91
**Myrin,** N. Alarik 1946- WhoWest 92
**Myrina** EncAmaz 91
**Myrold,** David Douglas 1955- AmMWSc 92
**Myron,** Duane R 1943- AmMWSc 92
**Myron,** Harold William 1947- AmMWSc 92
**Myron,** Thomas L 1923- AmMWSc 92
**Myronuk,** Donald Joseph AmMWSc 92

**Myrover**, James Henry 1843-1908 *DcNCBi 4*
**Myrtales** *EncAmaz 91*
**Myrtetus**, William Kane 1934- *WhoAmP 91*
**Myrtle**, Andrew Dewe 1932- *Who 92*
**Myrvik**, Norman *WhoEnt 92*
**Myrvik**, Quentin N 1921- *AmMWSc 92*
**Myrvoll**, Ole 1911- *IntWW 91*
**Mysak**, Lawrence Alexander 1940- *AmMWSc 92*
**Myse**, Gordon George 1935- *WhoAmL 92*
**Mysels**, Estella Katzenellenbogen 1921- *AmMWSc 92*
**Mysels**, Karol Joseph 1914- *AmMWSc 92, WhoWest 92*
**Mysen**, Bjorn O. 1947- *IntWW 91*
**Mysen**, Bjorn Olav 1947- *AmMWSc 92*
**Myser**, Willard C 1923- *AmMWSc 92*
**Myslik**, Edward Joseph, Jr. 1932- *WhoFI 92*
**Myslinski**, Norbert Raymond 1947- *AmMWSc 92*
**Myslobodsky**, M S 1937- *AmMWSc 92*
**Mysnichenko**, Vladislav Petrovich 1929- *IntWW 91*
**Mytelka**, Alan Ira 1935- *AmMWSc 92*
**Mytelka**, Arnold Krieger 1937- *WhoAmL 92*
**Mytton**, James W 1927- *AmMWSc 92*
**Myuus**, Andrew 1935- *TwCPaSc*
**Mzali**, Mohamed 1925- *IntWW 91*
**Mzamane**, Mbuelelo Vizikhungo 1948- *LiExTwC*
**Mzhavanadze**, Vasiliy Pavlovich 1902- *SovUnBD*

# N

**N.W.A.** *ConMus 6 [port]*
**Na Renhua** 1962- *IntWW 91*
**Na,** George Chao 1947- *AmMWSc 92*
**Naaden,** Lawrence L *WhoAmP 91*
**Naae,** Douglas Gene 1946- *AmMWSc 92*
**Naake,** Hans Joachim 1925- *AmMWSc 92*
**Naam,** Nashaat H. 1946- *WhoMW 92*
**Naar,** Jacques 1930- *AmMWSc 92*
**Naar,** Joseph Thomas 1925- *WhoEnt 92, WhoWest 92*
**Naar,** Raymond Zacharias *AmMWSc 92*
**Naas,** Lord 1953- *Who 92*
**Naas,** Jolinda 1937- *WhoRel 92*
**Naas,** Joseph Edwin 1947- *WhoFI 92*
**Naatanen,** Risto Kalervo 1939- *IntWW 91*
**Nabakowski,** Ronald Lee 1942- *WhoAmP 91*
**Nabakowski,** Timothy Jay 1947- *WhoRel 92*
**Nabarro,** Frank Reginald Nunes 1916- *IntWW 91, Who 92*
**Nabarro,** John 1915- *Who 92*
**Nabb,** Magdalen 1947- *WrDr 92*
**Nabbes,** Thomas 1605?-1641? *RfGEnL 91*
**Nabelek,** Anna K 1934- *AmMWSc 92*
**Naber,** Cynthia Sheridan 1949- *WhoWest 92*
**Naber,** Edward Carl 1926- *AmMWSc 92*
**Nabers,** Drayton, Jr 1940- *WhoIns 92*
**Nabers,** Lynn 1940- *WhoAmP 91*
**Nabeshima,** Toshitaka 1943- *AmMWSc 92*
**Nabi,** Mohamed 1935- *IntWW 91*
**Nabiev,** Rakhman 1930- *IntWW 91*
**Nabighian,** Misac N 1931- *AmMWSc 92*
**Nabinger,** David Earl 1939- *WhoMW 92*
**Nable,** Eugenie *DrAPF 91*
**Nabokov,** Nicholas 1903-1978 *NewAmDM*
**Nabokov,** Peter 1940- *WrDr 92*
**Nabokov,** Vera 1902-1991 *DcLB Y91N [port]*
**Nabokov,** Vladimir d1977 *DcLB Y91*
**Nabokov,** Vladimir 1899-1977 *BenetAL 91*
**Nabokov,** Vladimir Vladimirovich 1899-1977 *FacFETw, LiExTwC*
**Nabonne,** Ronald P. 1947- *WhoBlA 92*
**Nabor,** George W 1929- *AmMWSc 92*
**Nabors,** Charles J, Jr 1934- *AmMWSc 92, WhoBlA 92*
**Nabors,** Charlotte DeVinney 1938- *WhoRel 92*
**Nabors,** Eugene 1931- *WhoAmL 92*
**Nabors,** James Thurston 1930- *WhoEnt 92*
**Nabors,** Jesse Lee, Sr. 1940- *WhoBlA 92*
**Nabors,** Jim 1932- *IntMPA 92*
**Nabors,** Michael C. R. 1959- *WhoRel 92*
**Nabors,** Murray Wayne 1943- *AmMWSc 92*
**Nabours,** Robert Eugene 1934- *AmMWSc 92*
**Nabrit,** Henry Clarke 1915- *WhoBlA 92*
**Nabrit,** James M., III 1932- *WhoBlA 92*
**Nabrit,** James M., Jr. 1900- *WhoBlA 92*
**Nabrit,** Samuel M. 1905- *WhoBlA 92*
**Nabrit,** Samuel Milton 1905- *AmMWSc 92*
**Nabseth,** Lars 1928- *IntWW 91*
**Nabuco,** Joaquim 1849-1910 *BenetAL 91*
**Nabulsi,** Mohammed Said 1928- *IntWW 91*
**Nabulsi,** Omar N. 1936- *IntWW 91*
**Nacamu,** Robert Larry 1944- *AmMWSc 92*
**Nace,** Donald Miller 1924- *AmMWSc 92*
**Nace,** Harold Russ 1921- *AmMWSc 92*
**Nace,** Paul Foley 1917- *AmMWSc 92*
**Nace,** Theodore Keifer 1925- *WhoAmP 91*
**Nachamkin,** Jack 1940- *AmMWSc 92*
**Nachbar,** Martin Stephen 1937- *AmMWSc 92*
**Nachbar,** William 1923- *AmMWSc 92*
**Nachbin,** Leopoldo 1922- *AmMWSc 92*
**Nachlinger,** R Ray 1944- *AmMWSc 92*
**Nachman,** Arje 1946- *AmMWSc 92*
**Nachman,** David Charles 1944- *WhoFI 92*
**Nachman,** Joseph F 1918- *AmMWSc 92*
**Nachman,** Norman Harry *WhoAmL 92*
**Nachman,** Ralph Louis 1931- *AmMWSc 92*
**Nachman,** Richard Joseph 1944- *WhoWest 92*
**Nachman,** Ronald James 1954- *AmMWSc 92*
**Nachmias,** Vivianne T *AmMWSc 92*
**Nachreiner,** Michael Leo 1944- *WhoAmP 91*
**Nachreiner,** Raymond F 1942- *AmMWSc 92*
**Nachshin,** Robert Jay 1950- *WhoAmL 92*
**Nacht,** Sergio 1934- *AmMWSc 92, WhoWest 92*
**Nacht,** Steve Jerry 1948- *WhoWest 92*
**Nachtigal,** Patricia 1946- *WhoAmL 92*
**Nachtigal,** Ralph E 1933- *WhoAmP 91*
**Nachtigall,** Dieter 1927- *IntWW 91*
**Nachtigall,** Guenter Willi 1929- *AmMWSc 92*
**Nachtman,** Elliot Simon 1923- *AmMWSc 92, WhoMW 92*
**Nachtmann,** Francis Weldon 1913-1982 *ConAu 133*
**Nachtrieb,** Norman Harry 1916- *AmMWSc 92*
**Nachtsheim,** Philip Robert 1928- *AmMWSc 92*
**Nachtwey,** David Stuart 1929- *AmMWSc 92*
**Nachwalter,** Michael 1940- *WhoAmL 92*
**Nack,** John Eduard 1934- *WhoMW 92*
**Nacmias,** Joseph 1945- *WhoFI 92*
**Nacol,** Mae 1944- *WhoAmL 92, WhoFI 92*
**Nacozy,** Paul E 1942- *AmMWSc 92*
**Nacy,** Carol Anne 1948- *AmMWSc 92*
**Nad,** Leon M. d1991 *NewYTBS 91*
**Nadal,** Edward Morse 1843-1896 *DcNCBi 4*
**Nadal,** Jose Miguel, Jr. 1947- *WhoHisp 92*
**Nadal-Ginard,** Bernardo 1942- *AmMWSc 92*
**Nadar** 1820-1910 *GuFrLit 1, ThHEIm*
**Nadas,** Alexander Sandor 1913- *AmMWSc 92*
**Nadas,** John Adalbert 1949- *WhoMW 92*
**Nadasdy,** Leonard John 1930- *WhoAmP 91*
**Nadasen,** Aruna *AmMWSc 92*
**Naddy,** Badie Ihrahim 1933- *AmMWSc 92*
**Nadeau,** Allan J. 1935- *WhoFI 92*
**Nadeau,** Bertin F. 1940- *WhoFI 92*
**Nadeau,** Betty Kellett 1965- *AmMWSc 92*
**Nadeau,** Denise Melanie *WhoMW 92*
**Nadeau,** Gregory Guy 1957- *WhoAmP 91*
**Nadeau,** Guy R 1956- *WhoAmP 91*
**Nadeau,** Herbert Gerard 1928- *AmMWSc 92*
**Nadeau,** James Lee 1961- *WhoRel 92*
**Nadeau,** John 1934- *WhoFI 92*
**Nadeau,** Joseph Eugene 1937- *WhoFI 92*
**Nadeau,** Reginald Antoine 1932- *AmMWSc 92*
**Nadel,** Edwin 1928- *WhoIns 92*
**Nadel,** Elliott 1945- *WhoFI 92*
**Nadel,** Ethan Richard 1941- *AmMWSc 92*
**Nadel,** Jay A 1929- *AmMWSc 92*
**Nadel,** Norman A 1927- *AmMWSc 92*
**Nadelbach,** Jay 1952- *WhoAmL 92*
**Nadelhaft,** Irving 1928- *AmMWSc 92*
**Nadell,** Andrew Thomas 1946- *WhoWest 92*
**Nadelman,** Elie 1882-1946 *FacFETw*
**Nadelson,** Eileen Nora 1938- *WhoAmL 92*
**Naden,** Vernon Dewitt 1947- *WhoMW 92*
**Nader,** Allan E 1937- *AmMWSc 92*
**Nader,** Bassam Salim 1952- *AmMWSc 92*
**Nader,** G. A. 1940- *WrDr 92*
**Nader,** George 1921- *IntMPA 92*
**Nader,** John S 1921- *AmMWSc 92*
**Nader,** Ralph 1934- *DcTwDes, FacFETw [port], IntWW 91, RComAH, Who 92, WrDr 92*
**Nader,** Robert Alexander 1928- *WhoAmL 92, WhoAmP 91*
**Naderi,** Jamie Benedict 1951- *WhoFI 92*
**Naderpur,** Nader *LiExTwC*
**Nadesan,** Pararajasingam 1917- *Who 92*
**Nadherny,** Ferdinand *WhoFI 92*
**Nadich,** Judah 1912- *IntAu&W 91, WhoRel 92*
**Nadig,** Gerald George 1945- *WhoMW 92*
**Nadim,** Mohammad Reza 1948- *WhoAmL 92*
**Nadir,** Zakee *DrAPF 91*
**Nadiradze,** Aleksandr Davidovich 1914-1987 *SovUnBD*
**Nadiri,** M. Ishaq 1936- *WhoFI 92*
**Nadkarni,** Girish Vishwanath 1957- *WhoFI 92*
**Nadkarni,** Ramachandra Anand 1938- *AmMWSc 92*
**Nadkarni,** Suresh Shankar 1934- *IntWW 91*
**Nadler,** Allan Lawrence 1954- *WhoRel 92*
**Nadler,** Charles Fenger 1929- *AmMWSc 92*
**Nadler,** Charles H. 1940- *WhoAmL 92*
**Nadler,** Gerald 1924- *AmMWSc 92*
**Nadler,** Henry Louis 1936- *AmMWSc 92, WhoMW 92*
**Nadler,** J Victor *AmMWSc 92*
**Nadler,** Jerrold Lewis 1947- *WhoAmP 91*
**Nadler,** Josef 1884-1963 *EncTR 91*
**Nadler,** Kenneth David 1942- *AmMWSc 92*
**Nadler,** Marjorie Keeshan 1954- *WhoMW 92*
**Nadler,** Mark Alan 1948- *WhoMW 92*
**Nadler,** Melvin Philip 1940- *AmMWSc 92*
**Nadler,** Norman Jacob 1927- *AmMWSc 92*
**Nadler,** Ronald D 1936- *AmMWSc 92*
**Nadler,** Sheila June 1943- *WhoEnt 92*
**Nadol,** Bronislaw Joseph, Jr 1943- *AmMWSc 92*
**Nadolney,** Carlton H 1933- *AmMWSc 92*
**Nadolny,** Rose Faye 1933- *WhoMW 92*
**Nadolny,** Rudolf 1873-1953 *EncTR 91*
**Nadolny,** Sten 1942- *IntAu&W 91*
**Nadolski,** Linda *WhoAmP 91*
**Nady,** John 1945- *WhoEnt 92, WhoWest 92*
**Nadybal,** Jonathan David 1948- *WhoFI 92*
**Nadzick,** Judith Ann 1948- *WhoFI 92*
**Naef,** Kurt *DcTwDes*
**Naegele,** Edward Wister, Jr 1923- *AmMWSc 92*
**Naegele,** Eugene Alexander 1946- *WhoMW 92*
**Naegele,** Philipp Otto 1928- *WhoEnt 92*
**Naegele,** Timothy Duncan 1941- *WhoFI 92*
**Naegeli,** Cynthia Ann 1956- *WhoMW 92*
**Naeger,** Leonard L 1941- *AmMWSc 92*
**Naeser,** Charles Rudolph 1910- *AmMWSc 92*
**Naeser,** Charles Wilbur 1940- *AmMWSc 92, WhoWest 92*
**Naeser,** Nancy Dearien 1944- *AmMWSc 92*
**Naeseth,** Gerhard Brandt 1913- *WhoMW 92*
**Naeve,** Clifford M. 1947- *WhoAmL 92*
**Naeve,** Clifford Milo 1947- *WhoAmP 91*
**Naeye,** Richard L 1929- *AmMWSc 92*
**Nafe,** John Elliott 1914- *AmMWSc 92*
**Naff,** John Davis 1918- *AmMWSc 92*
**Naff,** Marion Benton 1918- *AmMWSc 92*
**Naffah,** Eli A. 1950- *WhoWest 92*
**Naffah,** Fouad Georges 1925- *IntWW 91*
**Naficy,** Hamid 1944- *WhoWest 92*
**Nafie,** Laurence Allen 1945- *AmMWSc 92*
**Nafissi-Varchei,** Mohammad Mehdi 1936- *AmMWSc 92*
**Nafpaktitis,** Basil G 1929- *AmMWSc 92*
**Naftalis,** Gary Philip 1941- *WhoAmL 92, WhoFI 92*
**Naftolin,** Frederick 1936- *AmMWSc 92*
**Nafziger,** Estel Wayne 1938- *WhoFI 92, WhoMW 92*
**Nafziger,** Pattie Lois *WhoAmP 91*
**Nafziger,** Ralph Hamilton 1937- *AmMWSc 92*
**Nag,** Asish Chandra 1932- *AmMWSc 92*
**Nagai,** Jiro 1927- *AmMWSc 92*
**Nagai,** Michio 1923- *IntWW 91*
**Nagakura,** Saburo 1920- *IntWW 91*
**Nagamatsu,** Henry T 1916- *AmMWSc 92*
**Nagan,** Winston Percival 1941- *WhoBlA 92*
**Nagano,** Kent George *WhoEnt 92*
**Nagano,** Shigeo 1900-1984 *FacFETw*
**Nagao,** Alvin Takashi 1953- *WhoAmL 92*
**Nagarajan,** Ramamurthy 1960- *WhoWest 92*
**Nagarkatti,** Mitzi 1952- *AmMWSc 92*
**Nagarkatti,** Prakash S 1952- *AmMWSc 92*
**Nagasawa,** Herbert Tsukasa 1927- *AmMWSc 92*
**Nagashima,** Yoichiro 1945- *WhoFI 92*
**Nagata,** Isao 1942- *WhoMW 92*
**Nagata,** Kazuhiro 1947- *AmMWSc 92*
**Nagata,** Russel 1951- *WhoAmP 91*
**Nagata,** Takao 1911- *IntWW 91*
**Nagata,** Takesi 1913- *IntWW 91*
**Nagayama,** Mokuo 1929- *IntAu&W 91*
**Nagda,** Kanti 1946- *Who 92*
**Nagel,** Alexander 1945- *AmMWSc 92*
**Nagel,** Candice *WhoAmP 91*
**Nagel,** Carol 1937- *WhoAmP 91*
**Nagel,** Charles William 1926- *AmMWSc 92*
**Nagel,** Chris B., Jr. 1952- *WhoRel 92*
**Nagel,** David Charles 1951- *WhoRel 92*
**Nagel,** Donald Lewis 1941- *AmMWSc 92*

**Nagel,** Edgar Herbert 1938- *AmMWSc 92*
**Nagel,** Eugene L 1924- *AmMWSc 92*
**Nagel,** Fritz John 1919- *AmMWSc 92*
**Nagel,** G W 1915- *AmMWSc 92*
**Nagel,** Glenn M 1944- *AmMWSc 92*
**Nagel,** Gunter 1936- *IntWW 91*
**Nagel,** Harold G. 1940- *WhoMW 92*
**Nagel,** Harold George 1940- *AmMWSc 92*
**Nagel,** Harry Leslie 1943- *AmMWSc 92*
**Nagel,** Ivan 1931- *IntWW 91*
**Nagel,** Jerome Kaub 1923- *WhoWest 92*
**Nagel,** Louis 1908- *IntWW 91*
**Nagel,** Paul C 1926- *IntAu&W 91, WrDr 92*
**Nagel,** Robert Earl, Jr. 1924- *WhoEnt 92*
**Nagel,** Robert Forder 1947- *WhoAmL 92*
**Nagel,** Ronald Curtis 1961- *WhoWest 92*
**Nagel,** Ronald Lafuente 1936- *AmMWSc 92*
**Nagel,** Scott Alan 1953- *WhoEnt 92*
**Nagel,** Sidney Robert 1948- *AmMWSc 92*
**Nagel,** Stanley Blair 1928- *WhoWest 92*
**Nagel,** Stuart 1934- *WrDr 92*
**Nagel,** Stuart Samuel 1934- *WhoMW 92*
**Nagel,** Terry Marvin 1943- *AmMWSc 92*
**Nagel,** Thomas 1937- *WhoAmL 92*
**Nagel,** William Lee 1949- *WhoFI 92*
**Nagele,** Daniel Alan 1962- *WhoRel 92*
**Nageli,** Hans Georg 1773-1836 *NewAmDM*
**Nagell,** Raymond H 1927- *AmMWSc 92*
**Nageotte,** Richard Russell 1936- *WhoAmL 92*
**Nager,** Elizabeth Eileen 1956- *WhoMW 92*
**Nager,** George Theodore 1917- *AmMWSc 92*
**Nager,** Larry Mark 1953- *WhoEnt 92*
**Nager,** Norman 1936- *WhoWest 92*
**Nager,** Steve 1949- *WhoWest 92*
**Nager,** Terry Edward 1949- *WhoFI 92*
**Nager,** Urs Felix 1922- *AmMWSc 92*
**Nagera,** Humberto 1927- *AmMWSc 92*
**Naghdi,** P M 1924- *AmMWSc 92*
**Nagi,** Anterdhyan Singh 1933- *AmMWSc 92*
**Nagibin,** Yuriy Markovich 1920- *IntWW 91, SovUnBD*
**Nagin,** Lawrence M. 1941- *WhoAmL 92*
**Nagin,** Stephen E. 1946- *WhoAmL 92*
**Nagle,** Barbara Tomassone 1947- *AmMWSc 92*
**Nagle,** Darragh 1919- *AmMWSc 92*
**Nagle,** David R. 1943- *AlmAP 92 [port], WhoAmP 91, WhoMW 92*
**Nagle,** Dennis Charles 1945- *AmMWSc 92*
**Nagle,** Edward John 1941- *AmMWSc 92*
**Nagle,** Francis J 1924- *AmMWSc 92*
**Nagle,** Frederick, Jr 1937- *AmMWSc 92*
**Nagle,** Friend Richard 1930- *WhoIns 92*
**Nagle,** H Troy 1942- *AmMWSc 92*
**Nagle,** James F 1929- *WhoAmP 91*
**Nagle,** James John 1937- *AmMWSc 92*
**Nagle,** John F 1939- *AmMWSc 92*
**Nagle,** M. Steve 1953- *WhoAmL 92*
**Nagle,** Nancy Elizabeth 1951- *WhoFI 92*
**Nagle,** Patricia Anne 1928- *WhoAmP 91*
**Nagle,** Ray Burdell 1939- *AmMWSc 92*
**Nagle,** Raymond J. d1991 *NewYTBS 91*
**Nagle,** Richard Kent 1947- *AmMWSc 92*
**Nagle,** Robert David 1935- *WhoMW 92*
**Nagle,** Thomas Ja 1957- *WhoWest 92*
**Nagle,** William Arthur 1943- *AmMWSc 92*
**Nagle,** William P, Jr *WhoAmP 91*
**Nagler,** Arnold Leon 1932- *AmMWSc 92*
**Nagler,** Charles Arthur 1916- *AmMWSc 92, WhoMW 92*
**Nagler,** Leon Gregory 1932- *WhoFI 92*
**Nagler,** Robert Carlton 1923- *AmMWSc 92*
**Nagler,** Stewart Gordon 1943- *WhoFI 92, WhoIns 92, WhoWest 92*
**Nagler-Anderson,** Cathryn 1957- *AmMWSc 92*
**Naglestad,** Frederic Allen 1929- *WhoWest 92*
**Naglich,** Donald Ray 1951- *WhoMW 92*
**Naglieri,** Anthony N 1930- *AmMWSc 92*
**Nagodawithana,** Tilak Walter *AmMWSc 92*
**Nagode,** Larry Allen 1938- *AmMWSc 92*
**Nagurski,** Bronislau 1908-1990 *FacFETw*
**Nagurski,** Bronko 1908-1990 *AnObit 1990*
**Nagy,** Andrew F 1932- *AmMWSc 92*
**Nagy,** Bartholomew Stephen 1927- *AmMWSc 92*
**Nagy,** Bela Ferenc 1926- *AmMWSc 92*
**Nagy,** Dennis J 1950- *AmMWSc 92*
**Nagy,** Ferenc Jozsef 1923- *IntWW 91*
**Nagy,** George 1937- *AmMWSc 92*
**Nagy,** Gyula 1918- *WhoRel 92*
**Nagy,** Imre 1896-1958 *FacFETw*
**Nagy,** Ivan *WhoEnt 92*
**Nagy,** Janos L. *Who 92*
**Nagy,** Julius G 1925- *AmMWSc 92*
**Nagy,** Kenneth Alex 1943- *AmMWSc 92*
**Nagy,** Melinda McCorkle 1959- *WhoMW 92*
**Nagy,** Robert David 1929- *WhoEnt 92*
**Nagy,** Robert John 1945- *WhoFI 92*
**Nagy,** Stephen Mears, Jr 1939- *AmMWSc 92*
**Nagy,** Steven 1936- *AmMWSc 92*
**Nagy,** Theresa Ann 1946- *AmMWSc 92*
**Nagy,** Zoltan 1933- *AmMWSc 92*
**Nagylaki,** Thomas Andrew 1944- *AmMWSc 92, WhoMW 92*
**Nagyvary,** Joseph 1934- *AmMWSc 92*
**Naha,** Ed 1950- *TwCSFW 91, WrDr 92*
**Nahabedian,** Kevork Vartan 1928- *AmMWSc 92*
**Nahai,** Hamid 1952- *WhoAmL 92*
**Nahal,** Chamal 1927- *IntAu&W 91*
**Nahal,** Chaman 1927- *ConNov 91, WrDr 92*
**Naharro-Calderon,** Jose Maria 1953- *WhoHisp 92*
**Nahas,** Gabriel G. 1920- *WrDr 92*
**Nahas,** Gabriel Georges 1920- *AmMWSc 92*
**Nahat,** Dennis F. 1946- *WhoEnt 92, WhoMW 92, WhoWest 92*
**Nahata,** Milap Chand 1950- *AmMWSc 92, WhoMW 92*
**Nahay,** Paul 1958- *WhoEnt 92*
**Nahayan,** Zayed bin al- 1918- *IntWW 91*
**Nahhas,** Fuad Michael 1927- *AmMWSc 92*
**Nahigian,** Alma Louise 1936- *WhoFI 92*
**Nahigian,** Robert John 1956- *WhoFI 92*
**Nahikian,** William O. *WhoFI 92*
**Nahill,** Charles F, Jr 1938- *WhoAmP 91*
**Nahm,** Milton C. 1903-1991 *ConAu 133*
**Nahm,** Moon H 1948- *AmMWSc 92*
**Nahm,** Steve Kisum, Sr. 1936- *WhoFI 92*
**Nahm-Mijo,** Trina 1949- *WhoWest 92*
**Nahman,** Norris S 1925- *AmMWSc 92*
**Nahman,** Norris Stanley 1925- *WhoWest 92*
**Nahmias,** Andre Joseph 1930- *AmMWSc 92*
**Nahmias,** Steven 1945- *AmMWSc 92*
**Nahnybida,** Simon T. 1945- *WhoFI 92*
**Nahon,** Paul G 1933- *WhoAmP 91*
**Nahory,** Robert Edward 1938- *AmMWSc 92*
**Nahrwold,** David Lange 1935- *AmMWSc 92, WhoMW 92*
**Nahrwold,** James Lange 1939- *WhoIns 92*
**Nahrwold,** Michael L 1943- *AmMWSc 92*
**Naib,** Farid A. 1960- *WhoFI 92*
**Naib,** Zuher M 1927- *AmMWSc 92*
**Naibert,** Zane Elvin 1931- *AmMWSc 92*
**Naide,** Meyer 1907- *AmMWSc 92*
**Naiden,** James 1943- *WrDr 92*
**Naider,** Fred R 1945- *AmMWSc 92*
**Naides,** Phillip 1930- *WhoFI 92*
**Naidin,** James *DrAPF 91*
**Naidoo,** Jay 1954- *IntWW 91*
**Naidu,** Angi Satyanarayan 1936- *AmMWSc 92*
**Naidu,** Janakiram Ramaswamy 1931- *AmMWSc 92*
**Naidu,** Sarojini 1879-1949 *RfGEnL 91*
**Naidu,** Seetala V 1957- *AmMWSc 92*
**Naidus,** Harold 1921- *AmMWSc 92*
**Naifeh,** Jimmy 1939- *WhoAmP 91*
**Naify,** Marshall 1920- *IntMPA 92*
**Naify,** Robert *IntMPA 92*
**Naigeon,** Jacques-Andre 1738-1810 *BlkwCEP*
**Naik,** Datta Vittal 1947- *AmMWSc 92*
**Naik,** Tarun Ratilal 1940- *AmMWSc 92*
**Nail,** Billy Ray 1933- *AmMWSc 92*
**Nail,** Kathy Sue *WhoEnt 92*
**Nail,** Olin Wesley 1930- *WhoFI 92*
**Nailatikau,** Epeli 1941- *Who 92*
**Naille,** Richard Allen, II 1945- *WhoWest 92*
**Nailor,** Jerry L 1946- *WhoAmP 91*
**Nailor,** Peter 1928- *Who 92*
**Nails,** Kenneth H 1942- *WhoIns 92*
**Nails,** Odell 1929- *WhoBlA 92*
**Naim,** Choudhri Mohammed 1936- *WhoMW 92*
**Naiman,** Cara B. 1964- *WhoEnt 92*
**Naiman,** Jason Reeves 1945- *WhoFI 92*
**Naiman,** Robert Joseph 1947- *AmMWSc 92*
**Naimark,** George Modell 1925- *AmMWSc 92, WhoFI 92*
**Naimark,** Richard Wythes 1951- *WhoFI 92*
**Naimg,** Mikhail *DcAmImH*
**Naimi,** Shapur *AmMWSc 92*
**Naimoli,** Vincent Joseph 1937- *WhoFI 92*
**Naimpally,** Somashekhar Amrith 1931- *AmMWSc 92*
**Naimy,** Mikhail *DcAmImH*
**Naini,** Majid M *AmMWSc 92*
**Naini,** Mariam Jafari 1963- *WhoAmL 92*
**Nainoa,** Sam K., Jr. 1944- *WhoHisp 92*
**Naipaul,** Shiva 1945-1985 *FacFETw, LiExTwC*
**Naipaul,** V. S. 1932- *BenetAL 91, CnDBLB 8 [port], ConNov 91, FacFETw, LiExTwC, RfGEnL 91, WrDr 92*
**Naipaul,** Vidiadhar S *NewYTBS 91 [port]*
**Naipaul,** Vidiadhar Surajprasad 1932- *IntAu&W 91, IntWW 91, Who 92*
**Naipawer,** Richard Edward 1945- *AmMWSc 92*
**Nair,** C Rajagopalan *AmMWSc 92*
**Nair,** C. V. Devan *IntWW 91*
**Nair,** Chandra Kunju 1944- *AmMWSc 92*
**Nair,** Chengara Veetil Devan 1923- *Who 92*
**Nair,** Gangadharan V M 1930- *AmMWSc 92*
**Nair,** Garyth 1943- *WhoEnt 92*
**Nair,** K Aiyappan 1936- *AmMWSc 92*
**Nair,** Kumaran Manikantan 1933- *WhoFI 92*
**Nair,** Madhavan G 1940- *AmMWSc 92*
**Nair,** Mia 1957- *IntMPA 92*
**Nair,** Padmanabhan 1931- *AmMWSc 92*
**Nair,** Pankajam K *AmMWSc 92*
**Nair,** Ramachandran Mukundalayam Sivarama 1938- *AmMWSc 92*
**Nair,** Shankar P 1926- *AmMWSc 92*
**Nair,** Sreedhar 1928- *AmMWSc 92*
**Nair,** Vasavan N P 1934- *AmMWSc 92*
**Nair,** Vasu 1939- *AmMWSc 92*
**Nair,** Velayudhan 1928- *AmMWSc 92*
**Nair,** Vijay 1941- *AmMWSc 92*
**Nairn,** Alan Eben Mackenzie 1927- *AmMWSc 92*
**Nairn,** Charles Edward 1926- *WhoRel 92*
**Nairn,** James Francis 1945- *WhoMW 92*
**Nairn,** John Graham 1928- *AmMWSc 92*
**Nairn,** Kenneth Gordon 1898- *Who 92*
**Nairn,** Margaret 1924- *Who 92*
**Nairn,** Martin John L. *Who 92*
**Nairn,** Michael 1938- *Who 92*
**Nairn,** Robert Arnold S. *Who 92*
**Nairn,** Roderick 1951- *AmMWSc 92*
**Nairn,** Thomas Allen 1948- *WhoRel 92*
**Nairne,** Lady 1912- *Who 92*
**Nairne,** Alexander Robert 1953- *Who 92*
**Nairne,** Patrick 1921- *Who 92*
**Nairne,** Patrick Dalmahoy 1921- *IntWW 91*
**Nairne,** Sandy *Who 92*
**Nairobi,** Archbishop of 1923- *Who 92*
**Naisbitt,** John 1929- *WrDr 92*
**Naiser,** Rick James, Jr. 1957- *WhoEnt 92*
**Naishtat,** Elliott 1945- *WhoAmP 91*
**Naismith,** James Pomeroy 1936- *AmMWSc 92*
**Naistat,** Samuel Solomon 1917- *AmMWSc 92*
**Naito,** Herbert K 1942- *AmMWSc 92*
**Naito,** Lisa 1955- *WhoAmP 91*
**Naitoh,** Paul Yoshimasa 1931- *AmMWSc 92*
**Naitove,** Arthur 1926- *AmMWSc 92*
**Najafi,** Ahmad 1950- *AmMWSc 92*
**Najar,** Leo Michael 1953- *WhoMW 92*
**Najar,** Maryse 1957- *WhoEnt 92*
**Najar,** Rudolph Michael 1931- *AmMWSc 92*
**Najarian,** Haig Hagop 1925- *AmMWSc 92*
**Najarian,** John Sarkis 1927- *AmMWSc 92, IntWW 91*
**Najarian,** Peter *DrAPF 91, WrDr 92*
**Najarian,** Robert 1942- *WhoEnt 92*
**Najder,** Zdzislaw 1930- *IntWW 91, LiExTwC*
**Najera,** Edmund L. 1936- *WhoHisp 92*
**Najera,** Richard *WhoHisp 92*
**Najera,** Richard Almeraz 1937- *WhoHisp 92*
**Najibullah,** Maj.-Gen. 1947- *IntWW 91*
**Najjar,** Edward Robert 1951- *WhoHisp 92*
**Najjar,** Talib A 1938- *AmMWSc 92*
**Najjar,** Victor Assad 1914- *AmMWSc 92*
**Naka,** Atsuyuki 1952- *WhoFI 92*
**Naka,** F Robert 1923- *AmMWSc 92*
**Nakabayashi,** Nicholas Takateru 1920- *WhoWest 92*
**Nakada,** Henry Isao 1922- *AmMWSc 92*
**Nakada,** Minoru Paul 1921- *AmMWSc 92*
**Nakada,** Yoshinao 1918- *AmMWSc 92*
**Nakadomari,** Hisamitsu 1935- *AmMWSc 92*
**Nakae,** Toshitada 1929- *IntWW 91*
**Nakae,** Yosuke 1922- *IntWW 91*
**Nakagawa,** Allen Donald 1955- *WhoWest 92*
**Nakagawa,** Julie *WhoEnt 92*
**Nakagawa,** Shizutoshi 1947- *AmMWSc 92*
**Nakagawa,** Yasushi *AmMWSc 92*
**Nakahara,** Nobuyuki 1934- *IntWW 91*
**Nakahara,** Shohei 1942- *AmMWSc 92*
**Nakahata,** Tadaka 1924- *WhoWest 92*
**Nakai,** Minoru *WhoFI 92*
**Nakai,** Shuryo 1926- *AmMWSc 92*
**Nakajima,** Fumio 1904- *IntWW 91*
**Nakajima,** Gentaro 1929- *IntWW 91*
**Nakajima,** Hiroshi 1928- *IntWW 91, Who 92*
**Nakajima,** Motowo 1951- *AmMWSc 92*
**Nakajima,** Nobuyuki 1923- *AmMWSc 92*
**Nakajima,** Shigehiro 1931- *AmMWSc 92*
**Nakajima,** Takeshi 1924- *IntWW 91*
**Nakajima,** Yasuko 1932- *AmMWSc 92*
**Nakamoto,** Jon Masao 1958- *WhoWest 92*
**Nakamoto,** Kazuo 1922- *AmMWSc 92*
**Nakamoto,** Tetsuo 1939- *AmMWSc 92*
**Nakamoto,** Tokumasa 1928- *AmMWSc 92*
**Nakamura,** Eugene Leroy 1926- *AmMWSc 92*
**Nakamura,** Hajime 1912- *IntWW 91*
**Nakamura,** Hisao 1923- *IntWW 91*
**Nakamura,** Ichiro 1926- *IntWW 91*
**Nakamura,** Kaneo 1922- *IntWW 91*
**Nakamura,** Karl Yukio 1958- *WhoWest 92*
**Nakamura,** Leonard Isamu 1948- *WhoFI 92*
**Nakamura,** Mitsuru J 1926- *AmMWSc 92*
**Nakamura,** Motohiko 1929- *IntMPA 92*
**Nakamura,** Robert Masao 1935- *AmMWSc 92*
**Nakamura,** Robert Motoharu 1927- *AmMWSc 92*
**Nakamura,** Sachiko Jane 1938- *WhoWest 92*
**Nakamura,** Shoichiro 1935- *AmMWSc 92*
**Nakamura,** Taro 1920- *IntWW 91*
**Nakamura,** Yoshiro 1926- *WhoAmP 91*
**Nakane,** Paul K 1935- *AmMWSc 92*
**Nakanishi,** Keith Koji 1947- *AmMWSc 92*
**Nakanishi,** Koji 1925- *AmMWSc 92*
**Nakano,** Desmond *ConAu 134*
**Nakano,** James Hiroto 1922- *AmMWSc 92*
**Nakano,** Kenneth Rikuji 1915- *WhoWest 92*
**Nakano-Matsumoto,** Naomi Namiko 1960- *WhoWest 92*
**Nakao,** Eiichi 1930- *IntWW 91*
**Nakaoka,** James Tatsumi 1952- *WhoWest 92*
**Nakaoka,** John Tatsuya 1952- *WhoFI 92*
**Nakasato,** Dennis M 1947- *WhoAmP 91*
**Nakashima,** George 1905-1990 *DcTwDes*
**Nakashima,** Joanne P 1937- *WhoAmP 91*
**Nakashima,** Joanne Pumphrey 1937- *WhoWest 92*
**Nakashima,** Nobuo 1931- *WhoAmP 91*
**Nakashima,** Patricia Hatsuye 1943- *WhoWest 92*
**Nakashima,** Tadayoshi 1922- *AmMWSc 92*
**Nakashimada,** Bonnie Charlene 1960- *WhoRel 92*
**Nakasone,** Henry Yoshiki 1920- *AmMWSc 92*
**Nakasone,** Yasuhiro 1917- *IntWW 91*
**Nakasone,** Yasuhiro 1918- *FacFETw [port], Who 92*
**Nakata,** Herbert Minoru 1930- *AmMWSc 92*
**Nakatani,** Roy E 1918- *AmMWSc 92*
**Nakato,** Tatsuaki 1942- *AmMWSc 92*
**Nakatsu,** Kanji 1945- *AmMWSc 92*
**Nakatsugawa,** Tsutomu 1933- *AmMWSc 92*
**Nakatsukasa,** Pedro Taiskan 1943- *WhoAmP 91*
**Nakayama,** Francis Shigeru 1930- *AmMWSc 92*
**Nakayama,** Fuji *WhoRel 92*
**Nakayama,** Komei 1910- *IntWW 91*
**Nakayama,** Masaaki 1932- *IntWW 91*
**Nakayama,** Roy Minoru 1923- *AmMWSc 92*
**Nakayama,** Shigeru 1928- *IntAu&W 91, WrDr 92*
**Nakayama,** Tadashi 1932- *WhoFI 92*
**Nakayama,** Takao 1913- *AmMWSc 92*
**Nakayama,** Taro 1924- *IntWW 91*
**Nakayama,** Tommy 1928- *AmMWSc 92*
**Nakayama,** Yoshihiro 1914- *IntWW 91*
**Nakell,** Mark *DrAPF 91*
**Naker,** Mary Leslie 1954- *WhoMW 92*
**Nakhasi,** Hira Lal 1950- *AmMWSc 92*
**Nakhjavani,** Ali-Yullah 1919- *WhoRel 92*
**Nakhnikian,** George 1920- *WrDr 92*
**Nakib,** Ahmad Abdul Wahab al- 1933- *IntWW 91*
**Nakon,** Robert Steven 1944- *AmMWSc 92*
**Nakovich,** Steven B., Jr. 1945- *WhoMW 92*
**Nalbandian,** John 1932- *AmMWSc 92*
**Nalbandyan,** Dmitriy Arkad'evich 1906- *SovUnBD*
**Nalbandyan,** Dmitriy Arkadiyevich 1906- *IntWW 91*
**Nalcioglu,** Orhan 1944- *WhoWest 92*
**Nalder,** Crawford David 1910- *Who 92*
**Nalder,** Eric Christopher 1946- *WhoWest 92*
**Naldrett,** Anthony James 1933- *AmMWSc 92*
**Nalecz,** Maciej 1922- *IntWW 91*
**Nalepka,** John Carmen 1965- *WhoFI 92*
**Nalewaja,** Donna *WhoAmP 91*
**Nalewaja,** John Dennis 1930- *AmMWSc 92*
**Nall,** Barry T 1948- *AmMWSc 92*
**Nall,** Michael 1921- *Who 92*
**Nall,** Ray W 1939- *AmMWSc 92*
**Nall-Cain** *Who 92*
**Nalle,** Billy *IntMPA 92*
**Nallet,** Henri Pierre 1939- *IntWW 91*

**Nash,** Diane 1938- *NotBlAW 92*
**Nash,** Donald Joseph 1930- *AmMWSc 92*
**Nash,** Donald Robert 1938- *AmMWSc 92*
**Nash,** Dorris Valentine 1913- *WhoAmP 91*
**Nash,** Douglas B 1932- *AmMWSc 92*
**Nash,** Edmund Garrett 1936- *AmMWSc 92*
**Nash,** Edward Thomas 1943- *AmMWSc 92*
**Nash,** Ellison 1913- *Who 92*
**Nash,** Eva L. 1925- *WhoBlA 92*
**Nash,** Eveleigh 1873-1956 *DcLB 112 [port]*
**Nash,** Francis 1742?-1777 *DcNCBi 4*
**Nash,** Francis 1855-1932 *DcNCBi 4*
**Nash,** Francis Marion 1948- *WhoEnt 92*
**Nash,** Franklin Richard 1934- *AmMWSc 92*
**Nash,** Frederick 1781-1858 *DcNCBi 4*
**Nash,** Gary B 1933- *IntAu&W 91, WrDr 92*
**Nash,** George T., III 1935- *WhoBlA 92*
**Nash,** Gerald D. 1928- *WrDr 92*
**Nash,** Gerald David 1928- *IntAu&W 91*
**Nash,** Gordon Bernard, Jr. 1944- *WhoAmL 92*
**Nash,** Graham William 1942- *WhoEnt 92*
**Nash,** Harold Anthony 1918- *AmMWSc 92*
**Nash,** Harold Earl 1914- *AmMWSc 92*
**Nash,** Harry Charles 1927- *AmMWSc 92*
**Nash,** Helen E. 1921- *WhoBlA 92*
**Nash,** Henry 1932- *WhoBlA 92*
**Nash,** Henry Gary 1952- *WhoBlA 92*
**Nash,** Howard Allen 1937- *AmMWSc 92*
**Nash,** Howard P., Jr. 1900-1981 *ConAu 133*
**Nash,** Isabel Jackson 1934- *BenetAL 91*
**Nash,** J Thomas 1941- *AmMWSc 92*
**Nash,** James Lewis, Jr 1926- *AmMWSc 92*
**Nash,** James Richard 1931- *AmMWSc 92*
**Nash,** John 1893-1977 *TwCPaSc*
**Nash,** John Christopher 1947- *AmMWSc 92*
**Nash,** John Edward 1925- *Who 92*
**Nash,** Jonathon Michael 1942- *AmMWSc 92*
**Nash,** Justina Davis Dobbs *DcNCBi 4*
**Nash,** Kathleen Cecilia Black 1948- *WhoEnt 92*
**Nash,** Kenneth Laverne 1950- *AmMWSc 92, WhoMW 92*
**Nash,** Knowlton 1927- *ConAu 135*
**Nash,** Larry Duane 1947- *WhoAmP 91*
**Nash,** Lawrence F 1937- *WhoAmP 91*
**Nash,** Lee J. 1939- *WhoFI 92*
**Nash,** Lee Marten 1927- *WhoWest 92*
**Nash,** Leon Albert 1912- *WhoBlA 92*
**Nash,** Leonard Kollender 1918- *AmMWSc 92*
**Nash,** Leonidas Lydwell 1846-1917 *DcNCBi 4*
**Nash,** LeRoy T. 1925- *WhoBlA 92*
**Nash,** Maria Jane 1819-1907 *DcNCBi 4*
**Nash,** Mary Godfrey 1942- *WhoAmL 92*
**Nash,** Matthew 1952- *WhoEnt 92*
**Nash,** Michaux, Jr. 1933- *WhoFI 92*
**Nash,** Mildred J. *DrAPF 91*
**Nash,** Murray L 1917- *AmMWSc 92*
**Nash,** N. Richard 1913- *IntMPA 92*
**Nash,** Nancy Trice 1943- *WhoRel 92*
**Nash,** Newlyn *WrDr 92*
**Nash,** Ogden 1902-1971 *BenetAL 91, ConAu 34NR, FacFETw*
**Nash,** Patrick Gerard 1933- *WrDr 92*
**Nash,** Paul 1889-1946 *DcTwDes, FacFETw, TwCPaSc*
**Nash,** Paul 1924- *IntAu&W 91, WrDr 92*
**Nash,** Paul 1948- *WhoEnt 92*
**Nash,** Paul LeNoir 1931- *WhoAmL 92*
**Nash,** Peter 1945- *AmMWSc 92*
**Nash,** Peter Gillette 1937- *WhoAmL 92, WhoAmP 91*
**Nash,** Peter Howard 1917- *AmMWSc 92*
**Nash,** Philip 1930- *Who 92*
**Nash,** Philip Curtis 1890-1947 *AmPeW*
**Nash,** Ralph Glen 1930- *AmMWSc 92*
**Nash,** Ralph Robert 1916- *AmMWSc 92*
**Nash,** Reginald George 1922- *AmMWSc 92*
**Nash,** Richard Eugene 1954- *WhoWest 92*
**Nash,** Richard Mark 1958- *WhoMW 92, WhoRel 92*
**Nash,** Robert Arnold 1930- *AmMWSc 92*
**Nash,** Robert Fred 1933- *WhoMW 92*
**Nash,** Robert Joseph 1939- *AmMWSc 92*
**Nash,** Robert T 1929- *AmMWSc 92*
**Nash,** Roderick 1939- *WrDr 92*
**Nash,** Ronald Herman 1936- *WhoRel 92*
**Nash,** Ronald Peter 1946- *Who 92*
**Nash,** Royston Hulbert 1933- *WhoEnt 92*
**Nash,** Sally Kollock 1811-1893 *DcNCBi 4*
**Nash,** Spencer James 1938- *WhoMW 92*
**Nash,** Stephen Michael 1947- *WhoFI 92, WhoMW 92*
**Nash,** Steven Boyd 1955- *WhoRel 92*
**Nash,** Steven G 1938- *WhoAmP 91*
**Nash,** Sylvia Dotseth 1945- *WhoRel 92*
**Nash,** Thomas 1919- *WhoBlA 92*
**Nash,** Thomas Arthur Manly 1905- *Who 92*
**Nash,** Tom 1931- *TwCPaSc*
**Nash,** Trevor Gifford 1930- *Who 92*
**Nash,** Valery *DrAPF 91*
**Nash,** Victor E 1928- *AmMWSc 92*
**Nash,** Victoria C 1915- *WhoAmP 91*
**Nash,** William A 1922- *AmMWSc 92*
**Nash,** William Donald 1947- *AmMWSc 92*
**Nash,** William George 1920- *WrDr 92*
**Nash,** William Hart 1925- *AmMWSc 92*
**Nash,** William Purcell 1944- *AmMWSc 92*
**Nasha,** Margaret Nnananyana 1947- *Who 92*
**Nashashibi,** Nasser Eddin 1924- *IntWW 91*
**Nashe,** Thomas 1567?-1601 *RfGEnL 91*
**Nashed,** Mohammed Zuhair Zaki 1936- *AmMWSc 92*
**Nashed,** Wilson 1919- *AmMWSc 92*
**Nashman,** Alvin E 1926- *AmMWSc 92*
**Nashold,** Blaine S 1923- *AmMWSc 92*
**Nashua** 1952-1982 *FacFETw*
**Nasi,** Giovanni 1918- *IntWW 91*
**Nasio,** Brenda *DrAPF 91*
**Nasir,** Agha 1937- *IntWW 91*
**Nasir,** Amin Ibrahim 1926- *FacFETw*
**Nasir,** Amir Ibrahim 1926- *IntWW 91*
**Nasjletti,** Alberto *AmMWSc 92*
**Naskali,** Richard John 1935- *AmMWSc 92*
**Nasky,** Harold Gregory 1942- *WhoAmL 92*
**Naslund,** Sena Jeter *DrAPF 91*
**Nasman,** Stephen Kent 1949- *WhoWest 92*
**Nasmith** *Who 92*
**Nasmyth,** George William 1882-1920 *AmPeW*
**Nasmyth,** Kim Ashley 1952- *Who 92*
**Naso,** Valerie Joan 1941- *WhoWest 92*
**Nason,** Charles T 1946- *WhoIns 92*
**Nason,** Charles Tuckey 1946- *WhoFI 92*
**Nason,** Dolores Irene 1934- *WhoFI 92, WhoWest 92*
**Nason,** Freda Lee 1944- *WhoFI 92*
**Nason,** Henry Bradford 1831-1895 *BiInAmS*
**Nason,** Howard King 1913- *AmMWSc 92*
**Nason,** John Charles 1945- *WhoAmP 91*
**Nason,** John William 1905- *IntWW 91*
**Nason,** Justin Patrick Pearse 1937- *Who 92*
**Nason,** Leonard Yoshimoto 1954- *WhoAmL 92*
**Nason,** Robert Dohrmann 1939- *AmMWSc 92*
**Nason,** Tema *DrAPF 91, IntAu&W 91*
**Nason,** William Abbot 1841- *BiInAmS*
**Nasr,** Farouk Sayf an- 1922- *IntWW 91*
**Nasr,** Kameel Bassam 1949- *IntAu&W 91*
**Nasr,** Seyyed Hossein 1933- *WrDr 92*
**Nasra,** George Yousef 1947- *WhoFI 92*
**Nasrallah,** Henry A 1947- *AmMWSc 92*
**Nasrallah,** Mikhail Elia 1939- *AmMWSc 92*
**Nasriddinova,** Yadgar Sadykovna 1920- *SovUnBD*
**Nass,** David Alan, Jr. 1956- *WhoFI 92*
**Nass,** Herbert Evan 1959- *WhoAmL 92*
**Nass,** Margit M K 1931- *AmMWSc 92*
**Nass,** Roger Donald 1932- *AmMWSc 92*
**Nass,** Stephen L *WhoAmP 91*
**Nassar,** Eugene Paul 1935- *IntAu&W 91, WrDr 92*
**Nassar,** George Joseph, Jr. 1954- *WhoAmL 92*
**Nassar,** Nahoum Philip 1942- *WhoIns 92*
**Nassau,** Kurt 1927- *AmMWSc 92*
**Nassau,** Michael Jay 1935- *WhoAmL 92*
**Nassau,** Robert Hamill 1941- *WhoFI 92*
**Nassauer,** Rudolf 1924- *IntAu&W 91, WrDr 92*
**Nassberg,** Richard T. 1942- *WhoAmL 92*
**Nasser,** DeLill 1929- *AmMWSc 92*
**Nasser,** Gamal Abdel 1918-1970 *FacFETw [port]*
**Nasser,** Karim Wade 1926- *AmMWSc 92*
**Nasser,** Tourai 1944- *AmMWSc 92*
**Nasser,** William Kaleel 1933- *WhoMW 92*
**Nassersharif,** Bahram 1960- *AmMWSc 92*
**Nassi,** Isaac Robert 1949- *AmMWSc 92*
**Nassif,** Bradley Louis 1954- *WhoRel 92*
**Nassif,** Christopher 1959- *WhoWest 92*
**Nassif,** Edward George 1949- *WhoMW 92*
**Nassif,** Robin Stoltz 1953- *WhoEnt 92*
**Nassikas,** John Nicholas 1917- *WhoAmP 91*
**Nassivera,** John C. 1950- *WhoEnt 92*
**Nasson,** Ronald *WhoRel 92*
**Nassos,** Patricia Saima 1951- *AmMWSc 92*
**Nassour,** Ellis 1941- *WhoEnt 92*
**Nast,** Conde 1873-1942 *FacFETw*
**Nast,** Dianne Martha 1944- *WhoAmL 92*
**Nast,** Thomas 1840-1902 *BenetAL 91, RComAH*
**Nastanovich,** Robert Andrew 1937- *WhoAmP 91*
**Nastas,** George, III 1944- *WhoFI 92, WhoMW 92*
**Nastase,** Adrian *IntWW 91*
**Nastase,** Ilie 1946- *IntWW 91*
**Nastri,** Kathleen Lenehan 1961- *WhoAmL 92*
**Nasution,** Abdul Haris 1918- *IntWW 91*
**Nat,** Yves 1890-1956 *NewAmDM*
**Natal,** Bishop of 1934- *Who 92*
**Natale,** Nicholas Robert 1953- *AmMWSc 92*
**Natalini,** John Joseph 1944- *AmMWSc 92, WhoMW 92*
**Natani,** Kirmach 1935- *AmMWSc 92*
**Natansohn,** Samuel 1929- *AmMWSc 92*
**Natanson,** Maurice 1924- *WrDr 92*
**Natanson,** Paul Steven 1949- *WhoEnt 92*
**Natapoff,** Marshall 1925- *AmMWSc 92*
**Natarajan,** Balas Kausik 1959- *WhoWest 92*
**Natarajan,** Kottayam Viswanathan 1933- *AmMWSc 92*
**Natarajan,** Viswanathan 1948- *AmMWSc 92*
**Natarus,** Burton F 1933- *WhoAmP 91*
**Natcher,** Stephen Darlington 1940- *WhoAmL 92, WhoFI 92*
**Natcher,** William H *WhoAmP 91*
**Natcher,** William H. 1909- *AlmAP 92 [port]*
**Natchez,** Gladys 1915- *WrDr 92*
**Natelson,** Benjamin Henry *AmMWSc 92*
**Natelson,** Samuel 1909- *AmMWSc 92*
**Nates,** Jerome Harvey 1945- *WhoAmL 92*
**Nath,** Amar 1929- *AmMWSc 92*
**Nath,** Dhurma Gian 1934- *IntWW 91*
**Nath,** Dilip K 1933- *AmMWSc 92*
**Nath,** Gian 1934- *Who 92*
**Nath,** Jayasree 1939- *AmMWSc 92*
**Nath,** Joginder 1932- *AmMWSc 92*
**Nath,** K Rajinder 1937- *AmMWSc 92*
**Nath,** Nrapendra 1940- *AmMWSc 92*
**Nath,** Pran 1939- *AmMWSc 92*
**Nath,** Ravinder Katyal 1942- *AmMWSc 92*
**Nathan** *Who 92*
**Nathan,** Baron 1922- *Who 92*
**Nathan,** Alan Marc 1946- *AmMWSc 92*
**Nathan,** Charles C 1919- *AmMWSc 92*
**Nathan,** David 1926- *IntAu&W 91, WrDr 92*
**Nathan,** David G 1929- *AmMWSc 92*
**Nathan,** Edward Leonard 1924- *IntAu&W 91*
**Nathan,** Ernest d1991 *NewYTBS 91*
**Nathan,** Frederic Solis 1922- *WhoAmL 92*
**Nathan,** Geoffrey Steven 1949- *WhoMW 92*
**Nathan,** George Jean 1882-1958 *BenetAL 91*
**Nathan,** Henry C 1924- *AmMWSc 92*
**Nathan,** Janet 1938- *TwCPaSc*
**Nathan,** Jody Rae 1957- *WhoAmL 92*
**Nathan,** John Edward 1937- *WhoEnt 92*
**Nathan,** John Edward 1949- *WhoMW 92*
**Nathan,** Johnnie Alma 1950- *WhoRel 92*
**Nathan,** Kandiah Shanmuga d1990 *Who 92N*
**Nathan,** Kurt 1920- *AmMWSc 92*
**Nathan,** Lawrence Charles 1944- *AmMWSc 92, WhoWest 92*
**Nathan,** Leonard *DrAPF 91*
**Nathan,** Leonard 1924- *ConPo 91, WrDr 92*
**Nathan,** Leonard Edward 1924- *WhoWest 92*
**Nathan,** Marc A 1937- *AmMWSc 92*
**Nathan,** Mark Ryan 1971- *WhoEnt 92*
**Nathan,** Marshall I 1933- *AmMWSc 92*
**Nathan,** Maud 1862-1946 *DcAmImH*
**Nathan,** Nancy Button 1946- *WhoEnt 92*
**Nathan,** Norman *DrAPF 91*
**Nathan,** Norman 1915- *WrDr 92*
**Nathan,** Ove 1926- *IntWW 91*
**Nathan,** Paul 1924- *AmMWSc 92*
**Nathan,** Peter 1914- *WrDr 92*
**Nathan,** Richard Arnold 1944- *AmMWSc 92, WhoFI 92*
**Nathan,** Richard D *AmMWSc 92*
**Nathan,** Richard Perle 1935- *WhoAmP 91*
**Nathan,** Robert 1894-1985 *BenetAL 91*
**Nathan,** Robert Burton 1917- *WhoMW 92*
**Nathan,** Robert Stuart *DrAPF 91*
**Nathan,** Robert Stuart 1948- *WhoEnt 92*
**Nathan,** Ronald Gene 1951- *AmMWSc 92*
**Nathan,** Ronald Jay 1945- *WhoFI 92*
**Nathan,** Theodora Nathalia 1923- *WhoAmP 91*
**Nathan,** Tony Curtis 1956- *WhoBlA 92*
**Nathaniel,** His Grace Bishop 1940- *WhoRel 92*
**Nathaniel,** Edward J H 1928- *AmMWSc 92*
**Nathaniel,** Isabel *DrAPF 91*
**Nathans,** Daniel 1928- *AmMWSc 92, IntWW 91, Who 92, WhoNob 90*
**Nathanson,** A. Lynn 1955- *WhoEnt 92*
**Nathanson,** Benjamin 1929- *AmMWSc 92*
**Nathanson,** Fred E 1933- *AmMWSc 92*
**Nathanson,** H C 1936- *AmMWSc 92*
**Nathanson,** James E *WhoAmP 91*
**Nathanson,** Leonard Mark 1929- *WhoAmL 92*
**Nathanson,** Linda Sue 1946- *WhoFI 92*
**Nathanson,** Marc Bennett 1945- *WhoFI 92*
**Nathanson,** Melvyn Bernard 1944- *AmMWSc 92*
**Nathanson,** Nancy Louise 1951- *WhoAmP 91*
**Nathanson,** Neal 1927- *AmMWSc 92*
**Nathanson,** Neil Marc 1948- *AmMWSc 92*
**Nathanson,** Rosanne 1946- *WhoAmL 92*
**Nathanson,** Tenney *DrAPF 91*
**Nathanson,** Theodore Herzl 1923- *WhoWest 92*
**Nathanson,** Wayne Richard 1934- *WhoMW 92*
**Nathanson,** Weston Irwin 1938- *AmMWSc 92*
**Nathe,** Dennis Gerhardt 1938- *WhoAmP 91, WhoWest 92*
**Nathenson,** Manuel 1944- *AmMWSc 92*
**Nathenson,** Stanley G 1933- *AmMWSc 92*
**Nather,** Roy Edward 1926- *AmMWSc 92*
**Nathwani,** Bharat N 1945- *AmMWSc 92*
**Nathwani,** Bharat Narottam 1945- *WhoWest 92*
**Nation,** Carry 1846-1911 *BenetAL 91*
**Nation,** Floyd Reuben 1946- *WhoAmL 92*
**Nation,** James Edward 1933- *AmMWSc 92*
**Nation,** James Lamar 1936- *AmMWSc 92*
**Nation,** John 1935- *AmMWSc 92*
**Nation,** Joseph Edward 1956- *WhoWest 92*
**Nation,** Royce W. 1925- *WhoEnt 92*
**Nations,** Claude 1929- *AmMWSc 92*
**Nations,** Jack Dale 1934- *AmMWSc 92*
**Nations,** Opal Louis *DrAPF 91*
**Nations,** Wayne Edward 1933- *WhoFI 92*
**Native Dancer** 1950-1967 *FacFETw*
**Natividad,** Irene 1948- *WhoAmP 91*
**Natke,** Ernest, Jr *AmMWSc 92*
**Natkie,** John L. *DrAPF 91*
**Natkiewicz,** Jan *DrAPF 91*
**Natkin,** Jory Alan 1960- *WhoMW 92*
**Natoli,** Gary R. 1962- *WhoEnt 92*
**Natoli,** John 1950- *AmMWSc 92*
**Natowitz,** Joseph Bernard 1936- *AmMWSc 92*
**Natowsky,** Sheldon 1944- *AmMWSc 92*
**Natrella,** Joseph 1919- *AmMWSc 92*
**Natsuki,** Shizuko 1938- *IntAu&W 91*
**Natta,** Alessandro 1917- *IntWW 91*
**Natta,** Clayton Lyle 1932- *AmMWSc 92*
**Natta,** Giulio 1903-1979 *WhoNob 90*
**Natter,** Jeff 1956- *WhoWest 92*
**Nattie,** Eugene Edward 1944- *AmMWSc 92*
**Nattiel,** Christine Henry 1939- *WhoRel 92*
**Nattiel,** Ricky Rennard 1966- *WhoBlA 92*
**Nattier,** Frank Emile, Jr. 1915- *WhoAmL 92*
**Nattkemper,** C Don 1947- *WhoAmP 91*
**Nattress,** John Andrew 1920- *AmMWSc 92*
**Natuk,** Robert James 1956- *AmMWSc 92*
**Natusch,** Sheila 1926- *WrDr 92*
**Natusch,** Sheila Ellen 1926- *IntAu&W 91*
**Natwar-Singh,** K. 1931- *WrDr 92*
**Natwar-Singh,** Kanwar 1931- *Who 92*
**Natwick,** Grim 1890-1990 *AnObit 1990*
**Natwick,** Mildred 1908- *IntMPA 92*
**Natwick,** Myron 1890-1990 *FacFETw*
**Natzke,** Roger Paul 1939- *AmMWSc 92*
**Nau,** Arlo *WhoRel 92*
**Nau,** Carl August 1903- *AmMWSc 92*
**Nau,** Dana S 1951- *AmMWSc 92*
**Nau,** Henry R. 1941- *ConAu 135*
**Nau,** Henry Richard 1941- *WhoFI 92*
**Nau,** Richard William 1941- *AmMWSc 92*
**Nau,** Robert H 1913- *AmMWSc 92*
**Naud,** Robert Armstead *WhoEnt 92*
**Naudascher,** Eduard 1929- *AmMWSc 92*
**Naude,** Beyers 1915- *IntWW 91*
**Naude,** Christiaan Frederick Beyers 1915- *DcEcMov*
**Naudot,** Jacques-Christophe 1690?-1762 *NewAmDM*
**Nauen,** Elinor *DrAPF 91*
**Nauenberg,** Michael 1934- *AmMWSc 92*
**Nauenberg,** Uriel 1938- *AmMWSc 92*
**Nauert,** Peter W 1943- *WhoIns 92*
**Nauert,** Roger Charles 1943- *WhoMW 92*
**Naughten,** John Charles 1942- *AmMWSc 92*
**Naughten,** Robert Norman 1928- *WhoWest 92*
**Naughter,** Patrick M 1943- *WhoIns 92*
**Naughtie,** James 1951- *Who 92*
**Naughton,** Alan Jack 1952- *WhoMW 92*
**Naughton,** Bill *ConAu 36NR*
**Naughton,** Bill 1910- *ConNov 91, IntAu&W 91, WrDr 92*
**Naughton,** David 1951- *IntMPA 92*
**Naughton,** James 1945- *IntMPA 92, WhoEnt 92*
**Naughton,** John *AmMWSc 92*
**Naughton,** John M. 1936- *WhoFI 92*
**Naughton,** Michael A 1926- *AmMWSc 92*

**Naughton**, Philip Anthony 1943- *Who 92*
**Naughton**, Steven Joseph 1954- *WhoMW 92*
**Naughton**, William John 1910- *ConAu 36NR*
**Naugle**, Donald 1936- *AmMWSc 92*
**Naugle**, Jim 1954- *WhoAmP 91*
**Naugle**, John J, Jr 1922- *WhoAmP 91*
**Naugle**, Norman Wakefield 1931- *AmMWSc 92*
**Naugle**, Robert Paul 1951- *WhoMW 92*
**Naujocks**, Alfred Helmut 1911-1966 *EncTR 91*
**Nault**, Fernand 1921- *WhoEnt 92*
**Naum**, Thomas J. 1944- *WhoFI 92*
**Nauman**, Bruce 1941- *IntWW 91*
**Nauman**, Charles Hartley 1937- *AmMWSc 92*
**Nauman**, Craig Jeffrey 1945- *WhoMW 92*
**Nauman**, Edward Bruce 1937- *AmMWSc 92*
**Nauman**, Edward Franklin 1915- *AmMWSc 92*
**Nauman**, Gerald Marston 1931- *WhoIns 92*
**Nauman**, Robert Karl 1941- *AmMWSc 92*
**Nauman**, Robert Vincent 1923- *AmMWSc 92*
**Naumann**, Alfred Wayne 1928- *AmMWSc 92*
**Naumann**, Hans Richard Ernst 1936- *WhoFI 92*
**Naumann**, Hugh Donald 1923- *AmMWSc 92*
**Naumann**, Johann Gottlieb 1741-1801 *NewAmDM*
**Naumann**, Max 1875-1939 *EncTR 91*
**Naumann**, Michael 1941- *IntWW 91*
**Naumann**, Richard Walter 1946- *WhoFI 92*
**Naumann**, Robert Alexander 1929- *AmMWSc 92*
**Naumann**, Robert Jordan 1935- *AmMWSc 92*
**Naumann**, William Carl 1938- *WhoFI 92*
**Naumann**, William L. 1911- *IntWW 91*
**Naumburg**, Walter W. 1867-1959 *NewAmDM*
**Naumoff**, Lawrence *IntAu&W 91*
**Naumov**, Vladimir Naumovich 1927- *IntWW 91*
**Naunas**, John S. 1941- *WhoMW 92*
**Naunas**, Thomas Ash 1951- *WhoEnt 92*
**Naunton**, Ralph Frederick 1921- *AmMWSc 92*
**Naus**, Joseph Irwin 1938- *AmMWSc 92*
**Nauseef**, William Michael *AmMWSc 92*
**Nausica** d1890 *EncAmaz 91*
**Nausin**, Frank Gilbert 1948- *WhoRel 92*
**Nauss**, Kathleen Minihan 1940- *AmMWSc 92*
**Nauta**, Walle J H 1916- *AmMWSc 92*
**Nauta**, Walle Jetze Harinx 1916- *IntWW 91*
**Nava**, Julian 1927- *WhoHisp 92*
**Nava**, Michael 1954- *WhoHisp 92*
**Nava**, Robert Joseph, Jr. 1954- *WhoHisp 92*
**Nava-Carrillo**, German 1930- *IntWW 91*
**Nava Hamaker**, Mary Lou *WhoHisp 92*
**Nava-Villarreal**, Hector Rolando 1943- *WhoHisp 92*
**Navab**, Farhad 1938- *AmMWSc 92*
**Navajas-Mogro**, Hugo 1923- *IntWW 91*
**Naval Officer**, A *ScFEYrs*
**Navalkar**, Ram G 1924- *AmMWSc 92*
**Navangul**, Himanshoo Vishnu 1940- *AmMWSc 92*
**Navar**, Luis Gabriel 1941- *AmMWSc 92*
**Navaratnam**, Siva 1961- *WhoFI 92*
**Navarra**, Andre 1911-1988 *NewAmDM*
**Navarra**, John Gabriel 1927- *AmMWSc 92*
**Navarre**, Henri 1898-1983 *FacFETw*
**Navarre**, James Earl 1931- *WhoWest 92*
**Navarre**, Mike 1956- *WhoAmP 91*
**Navarre**, William Francis 1937- *WhoAmL 92*
**Navarre**, Yves 1940- *ConAu 133*
**Navarre**, Yves Henri Michel 1940- *IntWW 91*
**Navarrete**, Jorge Eduardo 1940- *Who 92*
**Navarrette**, Llorente Fred 1966- *WhoHisp 92*
**Navarro**, Antonio 1922- *WhoHisp 92*
**Navarro**, Artemio Edward 1950- *WhoHisp 92*, *WhoWest 92*
**Navarro**, Bruce Charles 1954- *WhoAmL 92*
**Navarro**, Carlos Salvador 1946- *WhoHisp 92*
**Navarro**, Conrado Enrique 1954- *WhoRel 92*
**Navarro**, Edward Fernando 1950- *WhoHisp 92*
**Navarro**, Eugenia Marie 1944- *WhoAmL 92*
**Navarro**, Fats 1923-1950 *NewAmDM*
**Navarro**, Flor Hernandez 1939- *WhoHisp 92*
**Navarro**, Garcia 1941- *WhoEnt 92*
**Navarro**, Georgie *WhoAmP 91*
**Navarro**, Jeffery Michael 1953- *WhoAmL 92*
**Navarro**, Jose 1944- *WhoHisp 92*
**Navarro**, Joseph Anthony 1927- *AmMWSc 92*
**Navarro**, Luis A. 1958- *WhoHisp 92*
**Navarro**, Mary Louise 1933- *WhoHisp 92*
**Navarro**, Miguel 1928- *WhoHisp 92*
**Navarro**, Mireya 1957- *WhoHisp 92*
**Navarro**, Nestor J., Jr. 1947- *WhoHisp 92*
**Navarro**, Octavio R. 1959- *WhoHisp 92*
**Navarro**, Pedro 1948- *WhoHisp 92*
**Navarro**, Rafael A. 1935- *WhoHisp 92*
**Navarro**, Richard A. 1955- *WhoHisp 92*
**Navarro**, Richard H. 1951- *WhoHisp 92*
**Navarro**, Robert 1939- *WhoHisp 92*
**Navarro**, Robert David 1941- *WhoHisp 92*
**Navarro**, Samara Heros 1956- *WhoHisp 92*
**Navarro**, Steven Raymond 1948- *WhoFI 92*
**Navarro**, Victoria *WhoHisp 92*
**Navarro-Alicea**, Jorge L. 1937- *WhoHisp 92*
**Navarro-Bermudez**, Francisco Jose 1935- *AmMWSc 92*, *WhoHisp 92*
**Navas**, Deborah *DrAPF 91*
**Navas**, Linda Moore 1949- *WhoFI 92*
**Navas**, William A., Jr. *WhoHisp 92*
**Navashin**, Sergey Gavrilovich 1857-1930 *SovUnBD*
**Navasky**, Victor 1932- *WrDr 92*
**Navasky**, Victor Saul 1932- *IntWW 91*
**Navatta**, Anna Paula 1956- *WhoAmL 92*
**Nave**, Carl R 1939- *AmMWSc 92*
**Nave**, Floyd Roger 1925- *AmMWSc 92*
**Nave**, Paul Michael 1943- *AmMWSc 92*
**Nave**, Thomas George 1950- *WhoAmL 92*
**Navedo**, Angel C., Sr. 1941- *WhoHisp 92*
**Naveira de Rodon**, Miriam *WhoAmP 91*
**Navejas**, Kathleen Mello 1954- *WhoHisp 92*
**Navero**, William *DrAPF 91*
**Navia**, Juan M. 1927- *WhoHisp 92*
**Navia**, Juan Marcelo 1927- *AmMWSc 92*
**Navia**, Luis E. 1940- *WhoHisp 92*
**Naviasky**, Philip 1894- *TwCPaSc*
**Navin**, MaryAnn Elizabeth 1951- *WhoFI 92*
**Navlakha**, Jainendra K 1950- *AmMWSc 92*
**Navon**, David H 1924- *AmMWSc 92*
**Navon**, Itzhak 1921- *IntWW 91*
**Navratil**, Gerald Anton 1951- *AmMWSc 92*
**Navratil**, James Dale 1941- *AmMWSc 92*
**Navratil**, Robert Norman *WhoAmP 91*
**Navratilova**, Martina 1956- *FacFETw [port]*, *IntWW 91*
**Navrotsky**, Alexandra 1943- *AmMWSc 92*
**Nawaisky**, Mechtild 1906- *TwCPaSc*
**Nawar**, Tewfik 1939- *AmMWSc 92*
**Nawar**, Wassef W 1926- *AmMWSc 92*
**Nawara**, Mark 1962- *WhoEnt 92*
**Nawaschin**, Sergey Gavrilovich 1857-1930 *SovUnBD*
**Nawaz**, S. Shah 1917- *IntWW 91*
**Naworski**, Joseph Sylvester, Jr 1937- *AmMWSc 92*
**Nawrath**, William Michael 1947- *WhoAmP 91*
**Nawrocki**, Aleksander 1940- *IntAu&W 91*
**Nawrocki**, Jerzy d1990 *IntWW 91N*
**Nawrocky**, Roman Jaroslaw 1932- *AmMWSc 92*
**Nawy**, Edward George 1926- *AmMWSc 92*
**Nay**, Barbara Lee 1951- *WhoAmL 92*
**Nayak**, Debi Prosad 1937- *AmMWSc 92*
**Nayak**, Harogadde Manappa 1931- *IntAu&W 91*
**Nayak**, Ramesh Kadbet 1934- *AmMWSc 92*
**Nayak**, Tapan Kumar 1957- *AmMWSc 92*
**Nayan**, Teofilo Manaloto 1926- *WhoMW 92*
**Nayar**, Jai Krishen 1933- *AmMWSc 92*
**Nayar**, Kuldip 1924- *Who 92*
**Nayar**, Sushila 1914- *IntWW 91*
**Nayashkov**, Ivan Semyonovich 1924- *IntWW 91*
**Nayden**, Denis J. 1954- *WhoFI 92*
**Nayder**, Linda Ann 1962- *WhoMW 92*
**Nayef Ibn Abdul Aziz** 1933- *IntWW 91*
**Nayer**, Louise *DrAPF 91*
**Nayfeh**, Ali Hasan 1933- *AmMWSc 92*
**Nayfeh**, Munir Hasan 1945- *AmMWSc 92*
**Nayfeh**, Shihadeh Nasri *AmMWSc 92*
**Nayler**, Georgina Ruth 1959- *Who 92*
**Naylor**, Alfred F 1927- *AmMWSc 92*
**Naylor**, Aubrey Willard 1915- *AmMWSc 92*
**Naylor**, Benjamin Franklin 1917- *AmMWSc 92*
**Naylor**, Bernard 1938- *Who 92*
**Naylor**, Bruce Gordon 1950- *AmMWSc 92*
**Naylor**, C. Bruce *WhoRel 92*
**Naylor**, Carter Graham 1942- *AmMWSc 92*
**Naylor**, Charles John 1943- *Who 92*
**Naylor**, Charles Robert, Jr. 1944- *WhoMW 92*
**Naylor**, David L 1959- *AmMWSc 92*
**Naylor**, David Murray 1938- *Who 92*
**Naylor**, Denny Ve 1937- *AmMWSc 92*
**Naylor**, Derek 1929- *AmMWSc 92*
**Naylor**, Ernest 1931- *Who 92*
**Naylor**, Frank W, Jr 1939- *WhoAmP 91*
**Naylor**, George LeRoy 1915- *WhoAmL 92*, *WhoFI 92*, *WhoMW 92*
**Naylor**, Gerald Wayne 1922- *AmMWSc 92*
**Naylor**, Gloria *DrAPF 91*
**Naylor**, Gloria 1950- *AfrAmW*, *BenetAL 91*, *BlkLC [port]*, *ConNov 91*, *HanAmWH*, *IntAu&W 91*, *WhoBlA 92*, *WrDr 92*
**Naylor**, Harry Brooks 1914- *AmMWSc 92*
**Naylor**, James Lora, Jr. 1927- *WhoRel 92*
**Naylor**, Jean Ann 1948- *WhoFI 92*
**Naylor**, John *Who 92*
**Naylor**, John Albert 1940- *WhoFI 92*, *WhoMW 92*
**Naylor**, Keith d1990 *Who 92N*
**Naylor**, Lauretta *WhoBlA 92*
**Naylor**, Malcolm Neville 1926- *Who 92*
**Naylor**, Marcus A, Jr 1920- *AmMWSc 92*
**Naylor**, Margot Ailsa 1907-1972 *ConAu 134*
**Naylor**, Martin 1944- *TwCPaSc*
**Naylor**, Maurice *Who 92*
**Naylor**, Paul Henry 1948- *AmMWSc 92*
**Naylor**, Peter Brian 1933- *Who 92*
**Naylor**, Phyllis *SmATA 66 [port]*
**Naylor**, Phyllis Reynolds *DrAPF 91*
**Naylor**, Phyllis Reynolds 1933- *SmATA 66 [port]*, *WrDr 92*
**Naylor**, Richard Stevens 1939- *AmMWSc 92*
**Naylor**, Robert Ernest, Jr 1932- *AmMWSc 92*
**Naylor**, Robert Wesley 1944- *WhoAmP 91*
**Naylor**, William Edward 1943- *WhoWest 92*
**Naylor**, William Maurice 1920- *Who 92*
**Naylor-Jackson**, Jerry 1939- *WhoWest 92*
**Naylor-Leyland**, Philip 1953- *Who 92*
**Nayman**, Robbie L. 1937- *WhoBlA 92*
**Naymark**, Sherman 1920- *AmMWSc 92*
**Naymik**, Daniel Allan 1922- *AmMWSc 92*
**Nayudu**, Y Rammohanroy 1922- *AmMWSc 92*
**Nayyar**, Rajinder 1936- *AmMWSc 92*
**Nazarbaev**, Nursultan Abishevich 1940- *IntWW 91*, *SovUnBD*
**Nazarenko**, Tat'yana Grigor'evna 1944- *SovUnBD*
**Nazareth** *NewAmDM*
**Nazareth**, Gerald Paul 1932- *Who 92*
**Nazareth**, Peter 1940- *LiExTwC*
**Nazarian**, Girair Mihran 1926- *AmMWSc 92*
**Nazario**, Carlos D., Jr. 1951- *WhoHisp 92*
**Nazario-Guirau**, Armando L. 1954- *WhoHisp 92*
**Nazaroff**, George Vasily 1938- *AmMWSc 92*
**Nazaroff**, William W 1955- *AmMWSc 92*
**Nazem**, Faramarz Franz 1943- *AmMWSc 92*
**Nazer**, Hisham Mohi ed-Din 1932- *IntWW 91*
**Nazerian**, Keyvan 1934- *AmMWSc 92*
**Nazir-Ali**, Michael 1949- *Who 92*
**Nazir-Ali**, Michael James 1949- *IntWW 91*
**Nazos**, Demetri Eleftherios 1949- *WhoMW 92*
**Nazri**, Gholam-Abbas 1951- *AmMWSc 92*
**Nazy**, John Robert 1933- *AmMWSc 92*, *WhoFI 92*
**Nazzaro**, David Alfred 1940- *WhoWest 92*
**Nazzaro**, Lou Paul 1930- *WhoEnt 92*
**Ncamiso Ndlovu**, Louis *WhoRel 92*
**Ncozana**, Silas S. *WhoRel 92*
**Ndamase**, Tutor Nyangilizwe 1921- *IntWW 91*
**N'Dayen**, Joachim *WhoRel 92*
**Ndegwa**, Duncan Nderitu 1925- *IntWW 91*
**N'diaye**, Babacar 1937- *IntWW 91*
**Ndinisa**, Jeremiah *WhoRel 92*
**Ndlovu**, Callistus P. 1936- *WhoBlA 92*
**N'dong**, Leon 1935- *IntWW 91*
**N'Dour**, Youssou 1959- *ConBlB 1 [port]*, *ConMus 6 [port]*
**Ndungane**, Winston Njongo 1941- *IntWW 91*
**Ne Win**, U 1911- *FacFETw*, *IntWW 91*
**Neaderhouser Purdy**, Carla Cecilia 1945- *AmMWSc 92*
**Neagle**, Anna 1904-1986 *FacFETw*
**Neagle**, Lyle H 1931- *AmMWSc 92*
**Neagley**, Ross 1907- *WrDr 92*
**Neagu**, Paul 1938- *IntWW 91*, *TwCPaSc*
**Neal**, A. Curtis 1922- *WhoAmL 92*
**Neal**, Albert Aiken 1945- *WhoRel 92*
**Neal**, Albert Harvey 1925- *WhoRel 92*
**Neal**, Alimam Butler 1947- *WhoBlA 92*
**Neal**, Arthur 1951- *TwCPaSc*
**Neal**, Bernard George 1922- *Who 92*
**Neal**, Brenda Jean 1952- *WhoBlA 92*
**Neal**, Bruce Walter 1931- *WhoRel 92*
**Neal**, C Leon 1938- *AmMWSc 92*
**Neal**, Constance 1942- *WhoMW 92*
**Neal**, Curly 1942- *WhoBlA 92*
**Neal**, David Grant 1949- *WhoAmP 91*
**Neal**, David Wayne 1955- *WhoAmL 92*
**Neal**, Donald Wade 1951- *AmMWSc 92*
**Neal**, Donn C. 1940- *WhoMW 92*
**Neal**, Earl 1928- *WhoAmP 91*
**Neal**, Earl Langdon 1928- *WhoBlA 92*
**Neal**, Eddie 1943- *WhoBlA 92*
**Neal**, Edna D. 1943- *WhoBlA 92*
**Neal**, Edward Garrison 1940- *WhoAmL 92*
**Neal**, Edwin Patterson 1933- *WhoMW 92*
**Neal**, Eric 1924- *Who 92*
**Neal**, Eric James 1924- *IntWW 91*
**Neal**, Ernest Gordon 1911- *IntAu&W 91*, *WrDr 92*
**Neal**, Frank 1932- *WrDr 92*
**Neal**, Fred Warner 1915- *IntAu&W 91*, *WrDr 92*
**Neal**, Frederic Douglas 1942- *WhoBlA 92*
**Neal**, Frederick Albert 1932- *Who 92*
**Neal**, Gerald A 1945- *WhoAmP 91*
**Neal**, Green Belton 1946- *WhoBlA 92*
**Neal**, Harry Edward 1906- *IntAu&W 91*, *WrDr 92*
**Neal**, Harry Morton 1931- *Who 92*
**Neal**, Herman Joseph 1923- *WhoBlA 92*
**Neal**, Homer Alfred 1942- *AmMWSc 92*, *WhoBlA 92*
**Neal**, Ira Tinsley 1931- *WhoBlA 92*
**Neal**, J P, III 1908- *AmMWSc 92*
**Neal**, James *TwCPaSc*
**Neal**, James F. 1929- *WhoAmL 92*
**Neal**, James Preston 1935- *WhoAmP 91*
**Neal**, James S. 1922- *WhoBlA 92*
**Neal**, James Thomas 1921- *WhoAmP 91*
**Neal**, James Thomas 1936- *AmMWSc 92*
**Neal**, Joe M, Jr 1935- *WhoAmP 91*
**Neal**, John 1793-1876 *BenetAL 91*
**Neal**, John Alexander 1940- *AmMWSc 92*
**Neal**, John Alva 1938- *AmMWSc 92*
**Neal**, John Anthony 1955- *WhoAmP 91*
**Neal**, John E. 1959- *WhoMW 92*
**Neal**, John Lloyd, Jr 1937- *AmMWSc 92*
**Neal**, John William, Jr 1937- *AmMWSc 92*
**Neal**, Joseph C., Jr. 1941- *WhoBlA 92*
**Neal**, Joseph Clay 1807-1847 *BenetAL 91*
**Neal**, Kenneth Alton 1953- *WhoFI 92*
**Neal**, Larry Dwight 1941- *WhoFI 92*, *WhoMW 92*
**Neal**, LaVelle E., III 1965- *WhoBlA 92*
**Neal**, Leonard 1913- *Who 92*
**Neal**, Leonard Francis 1913- *IntWW 91*
**Neal**, Lynwood 1932- *WhoBlA 92*
**Neal**, Malcolm John 1940- *WhoEnt 92*
**Neal**, Marcus Pinson, Jr 1927- *AmMWSc 92*
**Neal**, Marie Augusta 1921- *ConAu 35NR*, *IntAu&W 91*, *WrDr 92*
**Neal**, Marjorie Esther Herman 1935- *WhoRel 92*
**Neal**, Michael David 1927- *Who 92*
**Neal**, Michael James 1956- *WhoEnt 92*
**Neal**, Michael William 1946- *AmMWSc 92*
**Neal**, Montford Lee 1942- *WhoRel 92*
**Neal**, Patricia 1926- *IntMPA 92*, *IntWW 91*, *WhoEnt 92*
**Neal**, Patricia Harley 1930- *WhoWest 92*
**Neal**, Perry David 1941- *WhoRel 92*
**Neal**, Philip Mark 1940- *WhoFI 92*
**Neal**, Randall Stranton 1952- *WhoRel 92*
**Neal**, Richard Allan 1939- *AmMWSc 92*
**Neal**, Richard B 1917- *AmMWSc 92*
**Neal**, Richard E. 1949- *AlmAP 92 [port]*
**Neal**, Richard Edmund 1949- *WhoAmP 91*
**Neal**, Richard Edward 1925- *WhoFI 92*
**Neal**, Robert A 1928- *AmMWSc 92*
**Neal**, Robert B 1938- *WhoIns 92*
**Neal**, Robert Paul 1939- *WhoAmP 91*
**Neal**, Sarah Lee 1924- *WhoAmP 91*
**Neal**, Scotty Ray 1937- *AmMWSc 92*
**Neal**, Shirley Anne 1936- *WhoAmP 91*
**Neal**, Stephen L. 1934- *AlmAP 92 [port]*
**Neal**, Stephen Lybrook 1934- *WhoAmP 91*
**Neal**, Sylvester 1943- *WhoBlA 92*
**Neal**, Thomas Edward 1942- *AmMWSc 92*
**Neal**, Tom Wright, Jr. 1946- *WhoRel 92*
**Neal**, Victor Thomas 1924- *AmMWSc 92*
**Neal**, William Joseph 1939- *AmMWSc 92*
**Neale**, Alan 1918- *Who 92*
**Neale**, Betty Irene 1930- *WhoAmP 91*
**Neale**, Chinyere 1953- *WhoBlA 92*
**Neale**, Elaine Anne 1944- *AmMWSc 92*
**Neale**, Ernest Richard Ward 1923- *AmMWSc 92*
**Neale**, Gerrard Anthony 1941- *Who 92*
**Neale**, John Robert Geoffrey 1926- *Who 92*
**Neale**, Keith Douglas 1947- *Who 92*
**Neale**, Kenneth James 1922- *Who 92*
**Neale**, Michael Cooper 1929- *Who 92*
**Neale**, Robert S 1936- *AmMWSc 92*

**Neale,** Walter Castle 1925- *WrDr 92*
**Nealey,** Darwin R *WhoAmP 91*
**Nealey,** Richard H 1936- *AmMWSc 92*
**Neall,** Ralph Eugene 1927- *WhoRel 92*
**Neall,** Robert Raymond 1948- *WhoAmP 91*
**Nealon,** Catherina Theresa *Who 92*
**Nealon,** Thomas F, Jr 1920- *AmMWSc 92*
**Nealon,** William Joseph, Jr. 1923- *WhoAmL 92*
**Neals,** Felix 1929- *WhoBlA 92*
**Neals,** Huerta C. 1914- *WhoBlA 92*
**Nealson,** Kenneth Henry 1943- *AmMWSc 92*
**Nealy,** Carson Louis 1938- *AmMWSc 92*
**Nealy,** David Lewis 1936- *AmMWSc 92*
**Neaman,** Brycene Allen 1955- *WhoWest 92*
**Neame,** Alan John 1924- *WrDr 92*
**Neame,** Robert Harry Beale 1934- *Who 92*
**Neame,** Ronald 1911- *IntMPA 92, IntWW 91, Who 92, WhoEnt 92*
**Neander,** August 1789-1850 *EncEarC*
**Neaoutiyne,** Paul 1952- *IntWW 91*
**Near,** Timothy 1945- *ConTFT 9*
**Nearing,** Helen Knothe 1904- *AmPeW*
**Nearing,** Scott 1883-1983 *AmPeW, BenetAL 91, FacFETw*
**Nearing,** Vivienne W. *WhoAmL 92*
**Nears,** Colin Gray 1933- *Who 92*
**Neary,** Brian Joseph 1951- *WhoAmL 92*
**Neary,** Dennis Patrick 1944- *WhoAmP 91, WhoMW 92*
**Neary,** Dennis Roy 1952- *WhoEnt 92*
**Neary,** Jeffrey Andrew 1958- *WhoAmP 91*
**Neary,** Joseph Thomas 1943- *AmMWSc 92*
**Neary,** Martin Gerard James 1940- *IntWW 91, Who 92*
**Neary,** Patricia Elinor *WhoEnt 92*
**Neary,** Robert D. *WhoFI 92*
**Neary,** Terrence Joseph 1957- *WhoMW 92*
**Neas,** John Theodore 1940- *WhoFI 92*
**Neas,** Ralph Graham 1946- *NewYTBS 91 [port]*
**Neas,** Ralph Graham, Jr 1946- *WhoAmP 91*
**Neas,** Robert Edwin 1935- *AmMWSc 92*
**Nease,** Martha LeAnn 1955- *WhoAmP 91*
**Nease,** Robert F 1931- *AmMWSc 92*
**Neathery,** James Arthur 1961- *WhoRel 92*
**Neathery,** Milton White 1928- *AmMWSc 92*
**Neathery,** Raymond Franklin 1939- *AmMWSc 92*
**Neathery,** Thornton Lee 1931- *AmMWSc 92*
**Neaton,** Robert Alan 1956- *WhoAmP 91*
**Neave,** Airey 1916-1979 *FacFETw*
**Neave,** Arundell Thomas Clifton 1916- *Who 92*
**Neave,** Julius Arthur Sheffield 1919- *Who 92*
**Neave Airey** *Who 92*
**Neavel,** Richard Charles 1931- *AmMWSc 92*
**Neaves,** J. Clark, Jr. *WhoFI 92*
**Neaves,** William Barlow 1943- *AmMWSc 92*
**Neavon,** Joseph Roy 1928- *WhoBlA 92*
**Nebbia,** Fernando 1945- *IntWW 91*
**Nebe,** Arthur 1894-1945 *BiDExR, EncTR 91 [port]*
**Nebeker,** Alan V 1938- *AmMWSc 92*
**Nebeker,** Frank Quill 1930- *WhoAmP 91*
**Nebeker,** Thomas Evan 1945- *AmMWSc 92*
**Nebel,** Carl Walter 1937- *AmMWSc 92*
**Nebel,** Kai Allen 1932- *WhoAmL 92*
**Nebelkopf,** Ethan 1946- *WhoWest 92*
**Nebenzahl,** Linda Levine 1949- *AmMWSc 92*
**Nebergall,** Donald Charles 1928- *WhoFI 92, WhoMW 92*
**Nebert,** Daniel Walter 1938- *AmMWSc 92*
**Nebgen,** John William 1935- *AmMWSc 92*
**Nebiker,** John Herbert 1936- *AmMWSc 92*
**Neblett,** Carol 1946- *NewAmDM*
**Neblett,** Richard F. 1925- *WhoBlA 92*
**Neblett,** Thomas Randolph 1928- *WhoMW 92*
**Nebolsine,** Peter Eugene 1945- *AmMWSc 92*
**Nebreda,** Vicente 1930- *WhoEnt 92*
**Nece,** Ronald Elliott 1927- *AmMWSc 92*
**Nechay,** Bohdan Roman *AmMWSc 92*
**Nechitaylo,** Vasiliy Kirillovich 1915-1980 *SovUnBD*
**Nechkina,** Militsa Vasil'evna 1901- *SovUnBD*
**Necker de Saussure,** Albertine Adrienne 1766-1841 *BlkwCEP*
**Neckermann,** Josef Carl 1912- *IntWW 91*
**Neckermann,** Peter J 1935- *WhoIns 92*
**Neckers,** Douglas 1938- *AmMWSc 92*
**Nectarius** *EncEarC*
**Nedd,** Archibald 1916- *Who 92*
**Nedd,** Johnnie Colemon *WhoBlA 92*
**Nedd,** Priscilla Anne 1955- *WhoEnt 92, WhoMW 92*
**Neddenriep,** Richard Joe 1930- *AmMWSc 92*
**Nedderman,** Howard Charles 1919- *AmMWSc 92*
**Neddo,** Francis Jackson 1921- *WhoRel 92*
**Nedeljkovich,** Mihajlo 1953- *WhoMW 92*
**Nedelsky,** Leo 1903- *AmMWSc 92*
**Nederlander,** James Laurence 1960- *WhoEnt 92*
**Nederlander,** James M. 1922- *CurBio 91 [port]*
**Nederlander,** James Morton 1922- *WhoEnt 92*
**Nederlander,** Marjorie Smith 1922- *WhoMW 92*
**Nederlander,** Robert E 1933- *WhoAmP 91, WhoEnt 92*
**Nederlander,** Sarah d1991 *NewYTBS 91*
**Nederveld,** Ruth Elizabeth 1933- *WhoFI 92*
**Nedich,** Ronald Lee 1941- *AmMWSc 92*
**Nedoluha,** Alfred K 1928- *AmMWSc 92*
**Nedswick,** Leonard Michael 1946- *WhoFI 92*
**Nedwek,** Thomas Wayne 1933- *WhoAmL 92, WhoMW 92*
**Nedwick,** John Joseph 1922- *AmMWSc 92*
**Nedza,** Edward A 1927- *WhoAmP 91*
**Nee,** M Coleman 1917- *AmMWSc 92*
**Nee,** Michael Wei-Kuo 1955- *AmMWSc 92*
**Nee,** Victor W 1935- *AmMWSc 92*
**Nee,** Watchman 1903-1972 *RelLAm 91*
**Neeb,** Martin John 1933- *WhoWest 92*
**Neece,** Evelyn Ruth 1926- *WhoRel 92*
**Neece,** George A 1939- *AmMWSc 92*
**Neece,** Robert Barry 1948- *WhoAmL 92*
**Needell,** Russell Lawrence 1956- *WhoAmL 92*
**Needels,** Theodore S 1922- *AmMWSc 92*
**Needham** *Who 92*
**Needham,** Charles D 1937- *AmMWSc 92*
**Needham,** Daniel 1922- *WhoAmP 91*
**Needham,** George Austin 1943- *WhoFI 92*
**Needham,** Gerald Morton 1917- *AmMWSc 92*
**Needham,** Glen Ray 1951- *AmMWSc 92*
**Needham,** Hal 1931- *IntMPA 92*
**Needham,** James J. 1926- *IntWW 91*
**Needham,** John Turberville 1713-1781 *BlkwCEP*
**Needham,** Joseph 1900- *ConAu 34NR, IntAu&W 91, IntWW 91, Who 92*
**Needham,** Kathleen Ann 1944- *WhoMW 92*
**Needham,** Nancy Jean 1941- *WhoFI 92*
**Needham,** Noel Joseph Terence Montgomery *Who 92*
**Needham,** Phillip 1940- *Who 92*
**Needham,** Richard Francis 1942- *Who 92*
**Needham,** Richard Henshaw 1926- *WhoMW 92*
**Needham,** Roger Michael 1935- *Who 92*
**Needham,** Thomas E, Jr 1942- *AmMWSc 92*
**Needham,** William Felix, Jr 1926- *WhoAmP 91*
**Needle,** Jan 1943- *IntAu&W 91, WrDr 92*
**Needleman,** Alan 1944- *AmMWSc 92*
**Needleman,** Herbert L *AmMWSc 92*
**Needleman,** Jacob 1934- *IntWW 91, WrDr 92*
**Needleman,** Michael S. 1958- *WhoWest 92*
**Needleman,** Philip 1939- *AmMWSc 92*
**Needleman,** Saul Ben 1927- *AmMWSc 92*
**Needler,** George Treglohan 1935- *AmMWSc 92*
**Needler,** Martin Cyril 1933- *WhoWest 92*
**Needles,** Howard Lee 1937- *AmMWSc 92*
**Neefe,** Douglas Charles 1944- *WhoWest 92*
**Neefe,** John R 1943- *AmMWSc 92*
**Neel,** Alice 1900-1984 *FacFETw, HanAmWH*
**Neel,** Boyd 1905-1981 *NewAmDM*
**Neel,** Charles Norman 1941- *WhoAmP 91*
**Neel,** David William 1958- *WhoAmL 92*
**Neel,** Harry Bryan, III 1939- *WhoMW 92*
**Neel,** James Van Gundia 1915- *AmMWSc 92, IntWW 91, WhoMW 92*
**Neel,** James William 1925- *AmMWSc 92*
**Neel,** Joe Kendall, Sr 1915- *AmMWSc 92*
**Neel,** Louis Eugene Felix 1904- *AmMWSc 92, IntWW 91, Who 92, WhoNob 90*
**Neel,** Peggy Sue 1934- *WhoRel 92*
**Neel,** Thomas H 1941- *AmMWSc 92*
**Neel,** William Wallace 1918- *AmMWSc 92*
**Neeland,** Roger Philip 1942- *WhoWest 92*
**Neeld,** Judith *DrAPF 91*
**Neeld,** Vaughn DeLeath 1943- *WhoMW 92*
**Neeley,** Charles Mack 1942- *AmMWSc 92*
**Neeley,** Mark E. 1952- *WhoRel 92*
**Neeley,** Robert Andrew 1960- *WhoEnt 92*
**Neelin,** J. David 1959- *WhoWest 92*
**Neelin,** James Michael 1930- *AmMWSc 92*
**Neelon,** Daniel Paul 1959- *WhoAmL 92*
**Neels,** Betty *WrDr 92*
**Neels,** John Thomas 1958- *WhoFI 92*
**Neely,** Brock Wesley 1926- *AmMWSc 92*
**Neely,** Charles Lea, Jr 1927- *AmMWSc 92*
**Neely,** David E. *WhoBlA 92*
**Neely,** Henry Mason 1942- *WhoBlA 92*
**Neely,** Jack Lynn 1949- *WhoMW 92*
**Neely,** Mary Ruth 1928- *WhoAmP 91*
**Neely,** Noel Anne 1943- *WhoAmP 91*
**Neely,** Peter Munro 1927- *AmMWSc 92*
**Neely,** Richard *IntAu&W 91, WrDr 92*
**Neely,** Richard 1941- *WhoAmL 92, WhoAmP 91*
**Neely,** Robert Dan 1928- *AmMWSc 92*
**Neely,** Stanley Carrell 1937- *AmMWSc 92*
**Neely,** Ted Kenneth, II 1961- *WhoFI 92*
**Neely,** Thomas Emerson 1943- *WhoAmL 92*
**Neely,** Walter E. *WhoAmL 92*
**Neely,** William Charles 1931- *AmMWSc 92*
**Neeman,** Moshe 1919- *AmMWSc 92*
**Ne'eman,** Yuval 1925- *IntWW 91*
**Neenan,** John Patrick 1943- *AmMWSc 92*
**Neeper,** Donald Andrew 1937- *AmMWSc 92*
**Neeper,** Frederic Allen 1946- *WhoWest 92*
**Neeper,** Ralph Arnold 1940- *AmMWSc 92*
**Neer,** Eva Julia *AmMWSc 92*
**Neer,** Keith Lowell 1949- *AmMWSc 92*
**Neer,** Robert M 1935- *AmMWSc 92*
**Neesby,** Torben Emil 1909- *AmMWSc 92*
**Neese,** Ronald Dwain 1948- *WhoWest 92*
**Neese,** Sandra Forbes 1943- *WhoEnt 92*
**Neeson,** John Francis 1936- *AmMWSc 92*
**Neeson,** Liam 1952- *IntMPA 92*
**Neeson,** Richard G 1946- *WhoAmP 91*
**Neet,** Kenneth Edward 1936- *AmMWSc 92*
**Neetzel,** Raymond John 1937- *WhoMW 92*
**Nef,** Isabelle 1898-1976 *NewAmDM*
**Nef,** John Ulric 1862-1915 *BiInAmS*
**Nefedov,** Oleg Matveyevich 1931- *IntWW 91*
**Neff,** Alven William 1923- *AmMWSc 92*
**Neff,** Bonita Dostal 1942- *WhoMW 92*
**Neff,** Bruce Lyle 1950- *AmMWSc 92*
**Neff,** Carole Cukell 1951- *WhoAmL 92*
**Neff,** Carroll Forsyth 1908- *AmMWSc 92*
**Neff,** Deenie Kinder 1957- *WhoMW 92*
**Neff,** Edwin, Jr. 1942- *WhoFI 92*
**Neff,** Francine Irving 1925- *WhoAmP 91*
**Neff,** Fred Leonard 1948- *WhoAmL 92, WhoFI 92, WhoMW 92*
**Neff,** Gregory Wayne 1955- *WhoEnt 92*
**Neff,** Herbert Preston, Jr 1930- *AmMWSc 92*
**Neff,** Hildegarde 1925- *IntMPA 92*
**Neff,** James Larry 1945- *WhoMW 92*
**Neff,** John 1951- *WhoEnt 92*
**Neff,** John David 1926- *AmMWSc 92*
**Neff,** John Michael 1932- *WhoWest 92*
**Neff,** John S 1934- *AmMWSc 92*
**Neff,** Laurence D 1938- *AmMWSc 92*
**Neff,** Lester Leroy 1923- *WhoRel 92, WhoWest 92*
**Neff,** Loren Lee 1918- *AmMWSc 92*
**Neff,** Mark Edward 1950- *WhoAmL 92*
**Neff,** Mary Muskoff 1930- *AmMWSc 92*
**Neff,** P. Sherrill 1951- *WhoFI 92*
**Neff,** Peter 1827-1903 *BiInAmS*
**Neff,** Peter John 1938- *WhoFI 92*
**Neff,** Ray Quinn 1928- *WhoFI 92*
**Neff,** Raymond Kenneth 1942- *AmMWSc 92, WhoMW 92*
**Neff,** Richard D 1932- *AmMWSc 92*
**Neff,** Richmond C 1923- *AmMWSc 92*
**Neff,** Robert Clark 1921- *WhoAmL 92, WhoMW 92*
**Neff,** Robert Jack 1921- *AmMWSc 92*
**Neff,** Robert Matthew 1955- *WhoAmL 92*
**Neff,** Robert Wilbur 1936- *WhoRel 92*
**Neff,** Stuart Edmund 1926- *AmMWSc 92*
**Neff,** Thomas Joseph 1937- *WhoFI 92*
**Neff,** Thomas O'Neil 1909- *AmMWSc 92*
**Neff,** Thomas Rodney 1937- *AmMWSc 92*
**Neff,** Vern C 1927- *WhoAmP 91*
**Neff,** Vernon Duane 1932- *AmMWSc 92*
**Neff,** Walter Perry 1927- *WhoFI 92*
**Neff,** William David 1945- *AmMWSc 92*
**Neff,** William Duwayne 1912- *AmMWSc 92, IntWW 91*
**Neff,** William H 1931- *AmMWSc 92*
**Neff,** William Medina 1929- *AmMWSc 92*
**Neff-Davis,** Carol Ann *AmMWSc 92*
**Neffati,** Chedly 1946- *IntWW 91*
**Nefkens,** Bernard Marie 1934- *AmMWSc 92*
**Nefske,** Donald Joseph 1938- *AmMWSc 92, WhoMW 92*
**Neft,** Nivaed 1922- *AmMWSc 92*
**Neft,** Rhoda Shear *WhoAmL 92*
**Nefzger,** Anna Marie 1926- *WhoAmP 91*
**Negahban,** Ezatollah 1926- *IntWW 91*
**Negandhi,** Anant 1929- *WrDr 92*
**Negara Brunei Darussalam,** Sultan of 1946- *Who 92*
**Negari,** Edmond 1947- *WhoFI 92*
**Negele,** John William 1944- *AmMWSc 92*
**Neggers,** Joseph 1940- *AmMWSc 92*
**Negin,** Michael 1942- *AmMWSc 92*
**Negishi,** Ei-ichi 1935- *AmMWSc 92*
**Negishi,** Masahiko *AmMWSc 92*
**Negishi,** Takashi 1933- *IntWW 91*
**Negley,** Glenn 1907- *ScFEYrs*
**Negley,** Glenn and Patrick, J Max *ScFEYrs*
**Negre,** Louis-Pascal 1928- *IntWW 91*
**Negrepontis,** Michael 1928- *WhoMW 92, WhoRel 92*
**Negrete,** Louis Richard 1934- *WhoHisp 92*
**Negri,** Ada 1870-1945 *DcLB 114 [port]*
**Negri Sembilan,** Yang di-Pertuan Besar 1922- *IntWW 91*
**Negrier,** Francois Charles 1928- *WhoIns 92*
**Negrin,** Carl Michael 1958- *WhoHisp 92*
**Negrin,** Michael Barry 1956- *WhoEnt 92*
**Negro-Vilar,** Andres F 1940- *AmMWSc 92*
**Negron,** Edna *WhoAmP 91, WhoHisp 92*
**Negron,** Victor 1949- *WhoAmP 91*
**Negron,** Yolanda 1963- *WhoHisp 92*
**Negron-Garcia,** Antonio S *WhoAmP 91*
**Negron-Garcia,** Antonio S. 1940- *WhoAmL 92*
**Negron-Olivieri,** Francisco A. 1933- *WhoHisp 92*
**Negron Santana,** Hermin 1937- *WhoRel 92*
**Negroponte,** John D *WhoAmP 91*
**Negroponte,** John Dimitri 1939- *IntWW 91*
**Negstad,** Richard B *WhoAmP 91*
**Negulesco,** Jean 1900- *IntDcF 2-2 [port], IntMPA 92*
**Negus,** Norma Florence 1932- *Who 92*
**Negus,** Norman Curtiss 1926- *AmMWSc 92*
**Negus,** Richard 1927- *Who 92*
**Negus-de Wys,** Jane Biesterfeld 1924- *WhoWest 92*
**Nehamkin,** Arieh 1925- *IntWW 91*
**Nehanda** 1862?-1898 *EncAmaz 91*
**Nehart,** William James 1954- *WhoMW 92*
**Neher,** Carola 1905-1942 *EncTR 91*
**Neher,** Clarence M 1916- *AmMWSc 92*
**Neher,** David Daniel 1923- *AmMWSc 92*
**Neher,** Dean Royce 1929- *AmMWSc 92*
**Neher,** Erwin 1944- *AmMWSc 92, IntWW 91*
**Neher,** Fred Wendell 1903- *WhoWest 92*
**Neher,** George Martin 1921- *AmMWSc 92*
**Neher,** James Edward 1953- *WhoRel 92*
**Neher,** Leland K 1920- *AmMWSc 92*
**Neher,** Leonardo 1922- *WhoAmP 91*
**Neher,** Leslie Irwin 1906- *WhoFI 92, WhoMW 92*
**Neher,** Maynard Bruce 1923- *AmMWSc 92*
**Neher,** Raymond Edwin 1925- *WhoWest 92*
**Neher,** Richard P *WhoAmP 91*
**Neher,** Robert Trostle 1930- *AmMWSc 92*
**Neher,** Timothy Pyper 1947- *WhoFI 92*
**Nehls,** James Warwick 1926- *AmMWSc 92*
**Nehorai,** Arye 1951- *AmMWSc 92*
**Nehra,** Gerald Peter 1940- *WhoAmL 92*
**Nehring,** William H 1915- *WhoAmP 91*
**Nehrkorn,** Thomas 1957- *AmMWSc 92*
**Nehrling,** Arno Herbert, Jr. 1928- *WhoFI 92*
**Nehrt,** Lee C. 1926- *WrDr 92*
**Nehru,** Arun *IntWW 91*
**Nehru,** Braj Kumar 1909- *IntWW 91, Who 92*
**Nehru,** Jawaharlal 1889-1964 *ConAu 34NR, FacFETw [port]*
**Nei,** Masatoshi 1931- *AmMWSc 92*
**Neibacher,** Albert L. d1991 *NewYTBS 91*
**Neibaur,** Mack William 1922- *WhoAmP 91*
**Neibel,** John Brewster 1930- *WhoAmL 92*
**Neibel,** Oliver Joseph, Jr. 1927- *WhoMW 92*
**Neibling,** William Howard 1952- *AmMWSc 92*
**Neiburg,** Dale Alan 1945- *WhoEnt 92*
**Neiburger,** Judith A *WhoAmP 91*
**Neiburger,** Morris 1910- *AmMWSc 92*
**Neiburger,** Orrin M 1925- *WhoIns 92*
**Neideffer,** Carole Elaine 1944- *WhoAmP 91*
**Neideffer,** David Lee 1944- *WhoAmP 91*
**Neidell,** Martin H. 1946- *WhoAmL 92*
**Neidell,** Norman Samson 1939- *AmMWSc 92*
**Neiderbach,** Shelley *DrAPF 91*
**Neiderhiser,** Dewey Harold 1935- *AmMWSc 92*
**Neiderhiser,** Frederick Gerald 1951- *WhoRel 92*
**Neiders,** Mirdza Erika 1933- *AmMWSc 92*
**Neidert,** Kalo Edward 1918- *WhoFI 92*
**Neidhardt,** Frederick Carl 1931- *AmMWSc 92*

**Neidhardt**, Richard Joseph 1942- *WhoFI 92*
**Neidhardt**, Walter Jim 1934- *AmMWSc 92, WhoRel 92*
**Neidich**, Charles *WhoEnt 92*
**Neidich**, George Arthur 1950- *WhoAmL 92*
**Neidig**, Donald Foster 1944- *AmMWSc 92*
**Neidig**, Donald Foster, Jr. 1944- *WhoWest 92*
**Neidig**, Howard Anthony 1923- *AmMWSc 92*
**Neidigh**, Kim L. *DrAPF 91*
**Neidinger**, Richard Dean 1955- *AmMWSc 92*
**Neidle**, Enid Anne 1924- *AmMWSc 92*
**Neidleman**, Saul L 1929- *AmMWSc 92*
**Neidlinger**, Gustav 1910- *IntWW 91*
**Neidlinger**, Hermann H 1944- *AmMWSc 92*
**Neidpath**, Lord 1948- *Who 92*
**Neie**, Van E 1938- *AmMWSc 92*
**Neiers**, David Francis 1960- *WhoAmL 92*
**Neighbors**, Charlette 1941- *WhoEnt 92*
**Neighbors**, John Newton 1928- *WhoFI 92*
**Neighbour**, Oliver Wray 1923- *Who 92*
**Neighbour**, Ralph W 1906- *IntAu&W 91, WrDr 92*
**Neighbour**, Ralph Webster, Sr. 1906- *WhoRel 92*
**Neihardt**, Joanne Eve 1945- *WhoMW 92*
**Neihardt**, John G. 1881-1973 *BenetAL 91, TwCWW 91*
**Neihart**, Carlene Rose 1929- *WhoEnt 92*
**Neiheisel**, James 1927- *AmMWSc 92*
**Neiheisel**, Thomas Henry 1953- *WhoFI 92, WhoMW 92*
**Neihof**, John Eldon 1934- *WhoRel 92*
**Neihof**, Rex A 1921- *AmMWSc 92*
**Neikirk**, Dean P 1957- *AmMWSc 92*
**Neikirk**, Joseph Randolph 1928- *WhoFI 92*
**Neikirk**, William Robert 1938- *WhoFI 92*
**Neikrug**, Marc 1946- *ConCom 92, NewAmDM*
**Neil**, Andrew Ferguson 1949- *IntWW 91, Who 92*
**Neil**, Andrew G. 1949- *WhoAmL 92*
**Neil**, Cleveland Oswald 1931- *WhoBlA 92*
**Neil**, Frances *IntAu&W 91X*
**Neil**, G. Eugene 1940- *WhoAmL 92*
**Neil**, Gary Lawrence 1940- *AmMWSc 92*
**Neil**, George Randall 1948- *AmMWSc 92*
**Neil**, Herbert Edward, Jr. 1931- *WhoFI 92, WhoMW 92*
**Neil**, Iain Alexander 1956- *WhoWest 92*
**Neil**, J. Meredith 1937- *WrDr 92*
**Neil**, Matthew 1917- *Who 92*
**Neil**, Richard H 1932- *WhoIns 92*
**Neil**, Ronald John Baille 1942- *Who 92*
**Neil**, Thanet *IntAu&W 91X*
**Neil**, Thomas 1913- *Who 92*
**Neil**, Thomas C 1934- *AmMWSc 92*
**Neil**, William 1954- *WhoEnt 92*
**Neilan**, Marshall 1891-1958 *IntDcF 2-2*
**Neilan**, Sarah *IntAu&W 91, WrDr 92*
**Neiland**, Bonita J 1928- *AmMWSc 92*
**Neiland**, Brendan 1941- *TwCPaSc*
**Neiland**, Kenneth Alfred 1929- *AmMWSc 92*
**Neilands**, John Brian 1921- *AmMWSc 92*
**Neild**, Ralph E 1924- *AmMWSc 92*
**Neild**, Robert Ralph 1924- *IntWW 91, Who 92*
**Neiler**, John Henry 1922- *AmMWSc 92*
**Neill**, A S 1883-1973 *FacFETw*
**Neill**, Alexander Bold 1919- *AmMWSc 92*
**Neill**, Alistair 1932- *Who 92*
**Neill**, Brian 1923- *Who 92*
**Neill**, Brian Neill 1923- *IntWW 91*
**Neill**, Bruce Ferguson 1941- *Who 92*
**Neill**, Denis Michael 1943- *WhoAmL 92*
**Neill**, Derrick James 1922- *Who 92*
**Neill**, Don Samuel 1949- *WhoAmP 91*
**Neill**, Francis Patrick 1926- *IntWW 91, Who 92*
**Neill**, Gary Alvis 1951- *WhoAmP 91*
**Neill**, Hugh *Who 92*
**Neill**, Ivan 1906- *Who 92*
**Neill**, Ivan Delacherois 1912- *Who 92*
**Neill**, James Hugh 1921- *Who 92*
**Neill**, Jimmy Dyke 1939- *AmMWSc 92*
**Neill**, John Robert Winder *Who 92*
**Neill**, Patrick *Who 92*
**Neill**, Peter *DrAPF 91*
**Neill**, Robert Harold 1930- *WhoWest 92*
**Neill**, Robert Lee 1941- *AmMWSc 92*
**Neill**, Sam 1947- *IntMPA 92*
**Neill**, Stephen Charles 1900-1984 *DcEcMov*
**Neill**, William Alexander *AmMWSc 92*
**Neill**, William Harold 1943- *AmMWSc 92*
**Neilly**, Thomas Dayton 1957- *WhoAmL 92*
**Neils**, Betty Jo 1919- *WhoAmP 91*
**Neils**, Howard William 1929- *WhoAmP 91*
**Neilsen**, Gerald Henry 1948- *AmMWSc 92*
**Neilsen**, Ivan Robert 1915- *AmMWSc 92*
**Neilsen**, Tom *WhoAmP 91*
**Neilson**, Andrew 1946- *IntAu&W 91*
**Neilson**, Archibald 1745?-1805 *DcNCBi 4*
**Neilson**, Benjamin Reath 1938- *WhoAmL 92*
**Neilson**, Bruce John 1943- *WhoAmP 91*
**Neilson**, Denny Woodall *WhoAmP 91*
**Neilson**, Francis 1867-1961 *AmPeW*
**Neilson**, George Croydon 1928- *AmMWSc 92*
**Neilson**, George Francis, Jr 1930- *AmMWSc 92*
**Neilson**, Ian 1918- *Who 92*
**Neilson**, James Maxwell 1912- *AmMWSc 92*
**Neilson**, James Warren 1933- *WrDr 92*
**Neilson**, John Warrington 1918- *AmMWSc 92*
**Neilson**, John Wilbert Tennant 1944- *WhoWest 92*
**Neilson**, Nigel Fraser 1919- *Who 92*
**Neilson**, Richard Alvin 1937- *Who 92*
**Neilson**, Robert Hugh 1948- *AmMWSc 92*
**Neilson**, Ronald Price 1949- *AmMWSc 92*
**Neilson**, Shaw 1872-1942 *RfGEnL 91*
**Neiman**, Gary Scott 1947- *AmMWSc 92*
**Neiman**, Jeffrey Charles 1953- *WhoAmL 92*
**Neiman**, Tanya Marie 1949- *WhoAmL 92*
**Neimann**, Albert Alexander 1939- *WhoWest 92*
**Neimark**, Anne E. 1935- *ConAu 36NR*
**Neimark**, Harold Carl 1932- *AmMWSc 92*
**Neimark**, Paul G. 1934- *ConAu 135*
**Neimark**, Philip John 1939- *WhoFI 92, WhoMW 92*
**Neimark**, Vassa 1954- *WhoMW 92*
**Neims**, Allen Howard 1938- *AmMWSc 92*
**Nein**, Lawrence Frederick 1936- *WhoFI 92*
**Nein**, Scott R *WhoAmP 91*
**Neiner**, Andrew Joseph 1950- *WhoFI 92, WhoMW 92*
**Neipris**, Janet 1936- *WhoEnt 92*
**Neira**, Daniel Alejandro 1955- *WhoHisp 92*
**Neira**, Gail Elizabeth *WhoHisp 92*
**Neis**, Arthur Veral 1940- *WhoFI 92, WhoMW 92*
**Neis**, John Peter 1955- *WhoFI 92*
**Neisendorfer**, Joseph 1945- *AmMWSc 92*
**Neiser**, Brent Allen 1954- *WhoFI 92, WhoWest 92*
**Neish**, Francis Edward 1925- *WhoFI 92*
**Neish**, Gordon Arthur 1949- *AmMWSc 92*
**Neiss**, Edgar 1939- *WhoEnt 92*
**Neiswanger**, Marjorie Bull 1929- *WhoFI 92*
**Neiswender**, David Daniel 1930- *AmMWSc 92*
**Neith-hetep** *EncAmaz 91*
**Neithamer**, Richard Walter 1929- *AmMWSc 92*
**Neitzel**, George Paul 1947- *AmMWSc 92*
**Neitzke**, Eric Karl 1955- *WhoAmL 92*
**Neizer**, Meredith Ann 1956- *WhoBlA 92*
**Neizvestny**, Ernst 1925- *FacFETw*
**Neizvestny**, Ernst Iosifovich 1925- *IntWW 91*
**Neizvestny**, Ernst Iosifovich 1926- *SovUnBD*
**Nejad**, Ebrahim 1942- *WhoEnt 92*
**Nejaime**, Nabih 1935- *WhoAmP 91*
**Nejelski**, Paul Arthur 1938- *WhoAmL 92*
**Nekimken**, Albert 1944- *WhoFI 92*
**Nekola**, Louis William 1954- *WhoMW 92*
**Nekrasov**, Viktor 1911- *LiExTwC*
**Nekrasov**, Viktor Platonovich 1911-1987 *SovUnBD*
**Nekrich**, Aleksandr Moiseyevich 1920- *IntWW 91*
**Nel**, Louis Daniel 1934- *AmMWSc 92*
**Nelb**, Gary William 1952- *AmMWSc 92*
**Nelb**, Robert Gilman 1923- *AmMWSc 92*
**Nelder**, John Ashworth 1924- *IntWW 91, Who 92*
**Neldner**, Hal M. 1938- *WhoWest 92*
**Neligan**, Desmond West Edmund 1906- *Who 92*
**Neligan**, Michael Hugh Desmond 1936- *Who 92*
**Nelipovich**, Sandra Grassi 1939- *WhoWest 92*
**Nelissen**, Roelof J. 1931- *IntWW 91*
**Nelkin**, Mark 1931- *AmMWSc 92*
**Nell**, Craig Arthur 1952- *WhoRel 92*
**Nell**, William Cooper 1816-1874 *BenetAL 91*
**Nell-Breuning**, Oswald von 1890-1991 *NewYTBS 91*
**Nellams**, Jane Harris 1955- *WhoWest 92*
**Nellemose**, Knud 1908- *IntWW 91*
**Nelles**, John Sumner 1920- *AmMWSc 92*
**Nelli**, D. James 1917- *WhoFI 92*
**Nelligan**, Emile 1879-1941 *BenetAL 91*
**Nelligan**, Kate 1951- *IntMPA 92, IntWW 91, WhoEnt 92*
**Nelligan**, William Bryon 1920- *AmMWSc 92*
**Nellis**, Jennifred Gene 1948- *WhoMW 92*
**Nellis**, Lois Fonda 1926- *AmMWSc 92*
**Nellis**, Stephen H 1942- *AmMWSc 92*
**Nellis**, William J *AmMWSc 92*
**Nellis**, William John 1937- *WhoAmL 92*
**Nellist**, David 1952- *Who 92*
**Nellor**, John Ernest 1922- *AmMWSc 92*
**Nellum**, Albert L. 1932- *WhoBlA 92*
**Nellums**, Robert 1921- *AmMWSc 92*
**Nelms**, George E 1927- *AmMWSc 92*
**Nelms**, Ommie Lee 1942- *WhoBlA 92*
**Nelms**, Sheryl L. *DrAPF 91*
**Nelp**, Will B 1929- *AmMWSc 92*
**Nelsen**, Betty Jo 1935- *WhoAmP 91*
**Nelsen**, Newell Stewart 1941- *WhoRel 92*
**Nelsen**, Richard Harry 1962- *WhoMW 92*
**Nelsen**, Roger Bain 1942- *AmMWSc 92, WhoWest 92*
**Nelsen**, Stephen Flanders 1940- *AmMWSc 92*
**Nelsen**, Thomas Sloan 1926- *AmMWSc 92*
**Nelsestuen**, Gary Lee 1944- *AmMWSc 92*
**Nelson** *Who 92*
**Nelson**, Earl 1941- *Who 92*
**Nelson**, A Carl, Jr 1926- *AmMWSc 92*
**Nelson**, A Gene 1942- *AmMWSc 92*
**Nelson**, Alan C 1933- *WhoAmP 91*
**Nelson**, Alan Jan 1944- *WhoRel 92*
**Nelson**, Alan R 1933- *AmMWSc 92*
**Nelson**, Albert Louis, III 1938- *WhoFI 92, WhoMW 92*
**Nelson**, Albert Wendell 1935- *AmMWSc 92*
**Nelson**, A'Lelia 1918- *WhoBlA 92*
**Nelson**, Alfred Thomas 1942- *WhoFI 92*
**Nelson**, Alfred W *WhoAmP 91*
**Nelson**, Allen Charles 1932- *AmMWSc 92*
**Nelson**, Anna 1943- *WhoAmP 91*
**Nelson**, Annie Greene 1902- *NotBlAW 92*
**Nelson**, Anthony *Who 92*
**Nelson**, Antonya *DrAPF 91*
**Nelson**, Arlene B 1925- *WhoAmP 91*
**Nelson**, Arnold Bernard 1922- *AmMWSc 92*
**Nelson**, Arthur A *ScFEYrs*
**Nelson**, Arthur Alexander, Jr 1946- *AmMWSc 92, WhoWest 92*
**Nelson**, Arthur Edward *AmMWSc 92*
**Nelson**, Arthur Hunt 1923- *WhoFI 92*
**Nelson**, Arthur Kendall 1932- *AmMWSc 92*
**Nelson**, Arthur L 1915- *AmMWSc 92*
**Nelson**, Artie Cortez 1955- *WhoBlA 92*
**Nelson**, Barbara Jane 1960- *WhoAmL 92*
**Nelson**, Barbara Lord 1930- *WhoEnt 92*
**Nelson**, Barry *WhoEnt 92*
**Nelson**, Barry 1923- *IntMPA 92*
**Nelson**, Barry A. 1954- *WhoAmL 92*
**Nelson**, Benjamin K. 1946- *WhoMW 92*
**Nelson**, Bernard Clinton 1934- *AmMWSc 92*
**Nelson**, Bernard W 1935- *AmMWSc 92*
**Nelson**, Bertram James 1925- *Who 92*
**Nelson**, Betty Henry 1932- *WhoAmP 91*
**Nelson**, Betty Palmer 1938- *ConAu 134*
**Nelson**, Bill 1942- *WhoAmP 91*
**Nelson**, Brent Alan 1962- *WhoMW 92, WhoRel 92*
**Nelson**, Brent Christopher 1957- *WhoWest 92*
**Nelson**, Brian W. 1960- *WhoMW 92*
**Nelson**, Bruce *WhoAmP 91*
**Nelson**, Bruce Sherman 1951- *WhoFI 92*
**Nelson**, Bruce Warren 1929- *AmMWSc 92*
**Nelson**, Bryan Eugene 1946- *WhoAmL 92*
**Nelson**, Bryan Herbert 1956- *WhoWest 92*
**Nelson**, Bryant McNeill 1932- *WhoRel 92*
**Nelson**, Burt 1922- *AmMWSc 92*
**Nelson**, Campbell Louis d1991 *Who 92N*
**Nelson**, Carl Vincent 1947- *WhoMW 92*
**Nelson**, Carlton Hans 1937- *AmMWSc 92*
**Nelson**, Carolyn Callenbach 1937- *WhoAmP 91*
**Nelson**, Carolyn Marie 1945- *WhoWest 92*
**Nelson**, Charles 1925- *WhoAmP 91*
**Nelson**, Charles A 1936- *AmMWSc 92*
**Nelson**, Charles Arnold 1943- *AmMWSc 92*
**Nelson**, Charles G 1933- *AmMWSc 92*
**Nelson**, Charles Henry 1941- *AmMWSc 92*
**Nelson**, Charles J. 1920- *WhoBlA 92*
**Nelson**, Charles Lamar 1917- *IntAu&W 91*
**Nelson**, Charles William 1944- *WhoMW 92*
**Nelson**, Christopher Bruce 1948- *WhoAmL 92*
**Nelson**, Christopher John 1953- *WhoMW 92*
**Nelson**, Clair L 1940- *WhoAmP 91*
**Nelson**, Clarence Norman 1909- *AmMWSc 92*
**Nelson**, Clayton H 1937- *WhoIns 92*
**Nelson**, Cleopatra McClellan 1914- *WhoBlA 92*
**Nelson**, Clifford Lee, Jr. 1936- *WhoWest 92*
**Nelson**, Clifford Melvin, Jr 1937- *AmMWSc 92*
**Nelson**, Clifford Vincent 1915- *AmMWSc 92*
**Nelson**, Cordner 1918- *WrDr 92*
**Nelson**, Craig 1956- *WhoFI 92*
**Nelson**, Craig Alan 1961- *WhoWest 92*
**Nelson**, Craig Eugene 1940- *AmMWSc 92*
**Nelson**, Craig T. *WhoEnt 92*
**Nelson**, Craig T. 1946- *IntMPA 92*
**Nelson**, Curtis Elton 1939- *WhoWest 92*
**Nelson**, Curtis Jerome 1940- *AmMWSc 92*
**Nelson**, Curtis Norman 1941- *AmMWSc 92*
**Nelson**, D Kent 1939- *AmMWSc 92*
**Nelson**, Dan Karl 1947- *WhoAmL 92*
**Nelson**, Daniel 1941- *IntAu&W 91, WrDr 92*
**Nelson**, Daniel Barlow 1959- *WhoFI 92*
**Nelson**, Daniel K. 1957- *WhoMW 92*
**Nelson**, Darby *WhoAmP 91*
**Nelson**, Darrell Wayne 1939- *AmMWSc 92*
**Nelson**, Darren Melvin 1925- *AmMWSc 92*
**Nelson**, Darrin 1959- *WhoBlA 92*
**Nelson**, Darryl James 1950- *WhoWest 92*
**Nelson**, Davey d1991 *NewYTBS 91*
**Nelson**, David 1918- *AmMWSc 92*
**Nelson**, David 1936- *IntMPA 92*
**Nelson**, David A *WhoAmP 91*
**Nelson**, David A 1961- *AmMWSc 92*
**Nelson**, David Alan 1931- *AmMWSc 92*
**Nelson**, David Aldrich 1932- *WhoAmL 92, WhoMW 92*
**Nelson**, David Brian 1940- *AmMWSc 92*
**Nelson**, David C. 1953- *WhoRel 92*
**Nelson**, David Charles 1944- *WhoEnt 92*
**Nelson**, David E. 1944- *WhoBlA 92*
**Nelson**, David Edward 1930- *WhoAmL 92*
**Nelson**, David Elmer 1933- *AmMWSc 92*
**Nelson**, David Herman 1943- *AmMWSc 92*
**Nelson**, David J. *DrAPF 91*
**Nelson**, David Joe 1942- *WhoMW 92*
**Nelson**, David Kenneth 1949- *WhoFI 92*
**Nelson**, David L 1944- *AmMWSc 92*
**Nelson**, David L 1948- *AmMWSc 92*
**Nelson**, David Larry 1953- *WhoAmL 92*
**Nelson**, David Lee 1942- *AmMWSc 92*
**Nelson**, David Leonard 1930- *WhoFI 92*
**Nelson**, David Lloyd 1948- *AmMWSc 92*
**Nelson**, David Lowell 1957- *WhoEnt 92*
**Nelson**, David Lynn 1942- *AmMWSc 92*
**Nelson**, David Michael 1946- *AmMWSc 92*
**Nelson**, David Robert 1951- *AmMWSc 92*
**Nelson**, David S. 1933- *WhoAmL 92, WhoBlA 92*
**Nelson**, David Torrison 1927- *AmMWSc 92*
**Nelson**, David Wallace 1951- *WhoEnt 92, WhoFI 92*
**Nelson**, David William 1949- *WhoFI 92*
**Nelson**, David William 1958- *WhoWest 92*
**Nelson**, Deane Frederick 1938- *WhoRel 92*
**Nelson**, Deborah Jeanne 1952- *WhoEnt 92*
**Nelson**, Debra J. 1957- *WhoBlA 92*
**Nelson**, Debra L. 1958- *WhoFI 92*
**Nelson**, Dennis Gene 1955- *WhoMW 92*
**Nelson**, Dennis Raymond 1936- *AmMWSc 92*
**Nelson**, Diana Walker 1941- *WhoAmP 91*
**Nelson**, Diane Roddy 1944- *AmMWSc 92*
**Nelson**, Diedrik Arlen 1934- *WhoRel 92*
**Nelson**, Doeg M. 1931- *WhoBlA 92*
**Nelson**, Don Alden 1927- *WhoWest 92*
**Nelson**, Don Harry 1925- *AmMWSc 92*
**Nelson**, Don Jerome 1930- *AmMWSc 92*
**Nelson**, Donald Arvid 1940- *WhoWest 92*
**Nelson**, Donald Carl 1931- *AmMWSc 92*
**Nelson**, Donald Clifford 1926- *WhoFI 92*
**Nelson**, Donald Frederick 1930- *AmMWSc 92*
**Nelson**, Donald J 1938- *AmMWSc 92*
**Nelson**, Donald John 1945- *AmMWSc 92*
**Nelson**, Donald Lloyd 1923- *WhoEnt 92*
**Nelson**, Donald Marr 1888-1959 *AmPolLe*
**Nelson**, Donald R 1939- *WhoAmP 91*
**Nelson**, Donald T 1935- *WhoAmP 91*
**Nelson**, Donie Alberta 1942- *WhoEnt 92*
**Nelson**, Dorothy *WhoRel 92*
**Nelson**, Dorothy W *WhoAmP 91*
**Nelson**, Dorothy Wright 1928- *WhoAmL 92, WhoRel 92*
**Nelson**, Dotson McGinnis, Jr. 1915- *WhoRel 92*
**Nelson**, Douglas A 1927- *AmMWSc 92*
**Nelson**, Douglas O *AmMWSc 92*
**Nelson**, Drew Vernon 1947- *WhoWest 92*
**Nelson**, Duane Juan 1939- *WhoRel 92*
**Nelson**, E. Benjamin 1941- *AlmAP 92 [port], WhoAmP 91, WhoIns 92, WhoMW 92*
**Nelson**, Earl Edward 1935- *AmMWSc 92*
**Nelson**, Edward Blake 1943- *AmMWSc 92*
**Nelson**, Edward Bryant 1916- *AmMWSc 92*
**Nelson**, Edward L., Jr. *WhoFI 92*
**Nelson**, Edward O. 1925- *WhoBlA 92*
**Nelson**, Edward Sheffield 1941- *WhoAmL 92*
**Nelson**, Edward Thomson d1897 *BiInAmS*

**Nelson,** Edwin L. 1940- *WhoAmL 92*
**Nelson,** Edwin Stafford 1928- *WhoEnt 92*
**Nelson,** Edwin Sterling 1943- *WhoRel 92*
**Nelson,** Eileen F. *WhoBlA 92*
**Nelson,** Eldon Carl 1935- *AmMWSc 92*
**Nelson,** Eldon Lane, Jr 1942- *AmMWSc 92*
**Nelson,** Eldred 1917- *AmMWSc 92*
**Nelson,** Elof G. 1924- *ConAu 35NR*
**Nelson,** Elton Glen 1910- *AmMWSc 92*
**Nelson,** Eric Alan 1949- *AmMWSc 92*
**Nelson,** Eric Douglas Mackinlay 1912- *Who 92*
**Nelson,** Eric Loren 1924- *AmMWSc 92*
**Nelson,** Eric Mark 1959- *WhoAmL 92*
**Nelson,** Eric V 1940- *AmMWSc 92*
**Nelson,** Eric Victor 1927- *Who 92*
**Nelson,** Erland 1928- *AmMWSc 92*
**Nelson,** Ernest William 1896-1974 *DcNCBi 4*
**Nelson,** Eulah Mae 1933- *WhoRel 92*
**Nelson,** Eustace John 1912- *Who 92*
**Nelson,** Evelyn Merle *AmMWSc 92*
**Nelson,** Flora Sue 1930- *WhoBlA 92*
**Nelson,** Frank Eugene 1909- *AmMWSc 92, WhoWest 92*
**Nelson,** Frank Lovell 1873-1947 *ScFEYrs*
**Nelson,** Frank V 1919- *WhoAmP 91*
**Nelson,** Frans Edward 1933- *WhoRel 92*
**Nelson,** Frederick *ScFEYrs*
**Nelson,** Frederick Carl 1932- *AmMWSc 92*
**Nelson,** Gailon Walker 1931- *WhoRel 92*
**Nelson,** Garrett R. *WhoFI 92, WhoWest 92*
**Nelson,** Gary Alfred 1936- *WhoAmP 91*
**Nelson,** Gary Dean 1935- *WhoAmP 91*
**Nelson,** Gary J *WhoAmP 91*
**Nelson,** Gary Joe 1933- *AmMWSc 92*
**Nelson,** Gayle Herbert 1926- *AmMWSc 92*
**Nelson,** Gaylord Anton 1916- *IntWW 91, WhoAmP 91*
**Nelson,** Gene *LesBEnT 92*
**Nelson,** Gene 1920- *IntMPA 92*
**Nelson,** Geoffrey Kenneth 1923- *IntAu&W 91, WrDr 92*
**Nelson,** George 1908-1934 *FacFETw*
**Nelson,** George 1908-1986 *DcTwDes*
**Nelson,** George 1942- *AmMWSc 92*
**Nelson,** George Driver 1950- *AmMWSc 92*
**Nelson,** George H. 1924- *WhoBlA 92*
**Nelson,** George Humphry 1930- *AmMWSc 92*
**Nelson,** George Leonard 1943- *AmMWSc 92*
**Nelson,** George Martin 1964- *WhoMW 92*
**Nelson,** George N. 1932- *WhoWest 92*
**Nelson,** George William 1938- *AmMWSc 92*
**Nelson,** Gerald Clifford 1940- *AmMWSc 92*
**Nelson,** Gerald Duane 1933- *AmMWSc 92*
**Nelson,** Gilbert Harry 1927- *AmMWSc 92*
**Nelson,** Gilbert L. 1942- *WhoBlA 92*
**Nelson,** Gordon Albert 1925- *AmMWSc 92*
**Nelson,** Gordon L 1919- *AmMWSc 92*
**Nelson,** Gordon Lee 1936- *WhoAmP 91*
**Nelson,** Gordon Leigh 1943- *AmMWSc 92, WhoFI 92*
**Nelson,** Gordon M 1941- *WhoAmP 91*
**Nelson,** Gregory A 1952- *AmMWSc 92*
**Nelson,** Gregory James 1965- *WhoWest 92*
**Nelson,** Gregory Victor 1943- *AmMWSc 92*
**Nelson,** H H 1912- *WhoIns 92*
**Nelson,** H. Viscount, Jr. 1939- *WhoBlA 92*
**Nelson,** Harlan Frederick 1938- *AmMWSc 92, WhoMW 92*
**Nelson,** Harold D 1921- *WhoAmP 91*
**Nelson,** Harold Melvin 1946- *WhoMW 92*
**Nelson,** Harold Stanley 1930- *AmMWSc 92*
**Nelson,** Harriet 1914- *IntMPA 92*
**Nelson,** Harriet Hilliard 1914- *WhoEnt 92*
**Nelson,** Harry David 1939- *WhoMW 92*
**Nelson,** Harry Ernest 1913- *AmMWSc 92*
**Nelson,** Harry Gladstone 1922- *AmMWSc 92, WhoMW 92*
**Nelson,** Harvard G 1919- *AmMWSc 92*
**Nelson,** Harvey F, Jr 1924- *WhoAmP 91*
**Nelson,** Hedwig Potok 1954- *WhoFI 92*
**Nelson,** Herbert Leroy 1922- *AmMWSc 92*
**Nelson,** Homer Mark 1932- *AmMWSc 92*
**Nelson,** Howard *DrAPF 91*
**Nelson,** Howard 1923- *WhoBlA 92*
**Nelson,** Howard A d1915 *BiInAmS*
**Nelson,** Howard Gustave 1938- *AmMWSc 92*
**Nelson,** Hubert John Arthur 1935- *WhoRel 92*
**Nelson,** Iral Clair 1927- *AmMWSc 92*
**Nelson,** Israel James Douglas 1944- *WhoRel 92*
**Nelson,** Ivory Vance 1934- *AmMWSc 92, WhoBlA 92*
**Nelson,** J. Bryan 1932- *WrDr 92*
**Nelson,** J Byron 1937- *AmMWSc 92*
**Nelson,** J Garnett 1939- *WhoIns 92*
**Nelson,** J. Robert 1920- *WrDr 92*
**Nelson,** Jack Ewald 1936- *WhoFI 92*
**Nelson,** Jack H 1930- *WhoIns 92*
**Nelson,** Jack Lee 1932- *WrDr 92*
**Nelson,** Jack Raymond 1934- *AmMWSc 92, WhoWest 92*
**Nelson,** Jack Russell 1929- *WhoWest 92*
**Nelson,** James 1932- *WhoEnt 92*
**Nelson,** James Alan 1950- *WhoWest 92*
**Nelson,** James Arly 1943- *AmMWSc 92*
**Nelson,** James Donald 1943- *AmMWSc 92*
**Nelson,** James F. 1927- *WhoRel 92, WhoWest 92*
**Nelson,** James Frederick, Jr 1945- *WhoAmP 91*
**Nelson,** James Graham 1929- *WrDr 92*
**Nelson,** James H, Jr 1926- *AmMWSc 92*
**Nelson,** James Harold 1936- *AmMWSc 92*
**Nelson,** James Lee 1935- *WhoAmP 91*
**Nelson,** James Milton 1957- *WhoAmL 92*
**Nelson,** James Randall 1955- *WhoAmL 92*
**Nelson,** James S 1933- *AmMWSc 92*
**Nelson,** Jamie 1949- *Who 92*
**Nelson,** Janet Kathryn 1954- *WhoEnt 92*
**Nelson,** Jay Edward 1957- *WhoEnt 92*
**Nelson,** Jay Phillip 1950- *WhoMW 92*
**Nelson,** Jeffrey David 1963- *WhoEnt 92*
**Nelson,** Jeffrey Owen 1956- *WhoMW 92*
**Nelson,** Jeremy E *WhoAmP 91*
**Nelson,** Jerry Allen 1923- *AmMWSc 92*
**Nelson,** Jerry Earl 1944- *AmMWSc 92*
**Nelson,** Jerry Rees 1947- *AmMWSc 92*
**Nelson,** Jo *DrAPF 91*
**Nelson,** John 1936- *WhoAmP 91*
**Nelson,** John 1941- *NewAmDM*
**Nelson,** John Archibald 1916- *AmMWSc 92*
**Nelson,** John Arthur 1938- *AmMWSc 92*
**Nelson,** John Bernard 1930- *WhoAmL 92*
**Nelson,** John Carl 1958- *WhoFI 92*
**Nelson,** John D 1930- *AmMWSc 92*
**Nelson,** John Daniel 1950- *AmMWSc 92*
**Nelson,** John David 1939- *WhoWest 92*
**Nelson,** John Douglas 1951- *WhoRel 92*
**Nelson,** John Franklin 1934- *AmMWSc 92*
**Nelson,** John Graeme 1947- *Who 92*
**Nelson,** John Henry 1919- *WhoAmP 91*
**Nelson,** John Henry 1940- *AmMWSc 92*
**Nelson,** John Howard 1926- *AmMWSc 92, WhoMW 92*
**Nelson,** John Howard 1930- *AmMWSc 92*
**Nelson,** John Keith 1943- *AmMWSc 92*
**Nelson,** John Martin 1931- *WhoFI 92*
**Nelson,** John Marvin, Jr 1933- *AmMWSc 92*
**Nelson,** John Robert 1920- *WhoRel 92*
**Nelson,** John Robert 1951- *WhoAmL 92*
**Nelson,** John Walter, Jr. 1923- *WhoFI 92*
**Nelson,** John Wilhelm, III 1937- *WhoFI 92*
**Nelson,** John William 1926- *AmMWSc 92*
**Nelson,** Jonathan P. 1939- *WhoBlA 92*
**Nelson,** Jonathan Robert 1956- *WhoAmL 92*
**Nelson,** Joni Lysett 1938- *WhoAmL 92*
**Nelson,** Joseph Edward 1932- *AmMWSc 92*
**Nelson,** Joseph Schieser 1937- *AmMWSc 92*
**Nelson,** Judd 1959- *ConTFT 9, IntMPA 92*
**Nelson,** Judd Owen 1947- *AmMWSc 92*
**Nelson,** Judith 1939- *IntWW 91*
**Nelson,** Julius 1858-1916 *BiInAmS*
**Nelson,** Karen Ann 1948- *AmMWSc 92, WhoWest 92*
**Nelson,** Karin Becker *AmMWSc 92*
**Nelson,** Karl Marcus *AmMWSc 92*
**Nelson,** Kathleen Veenstra 1932- *WhoWest 92*
**Nelson,** Kay LeRoi 1926- *AmMWSc 92*
**Nelson,** Keith 1934- *AmMWSc 92*
**Nelson,** Keith A 1953- *AmMWSc 92*
**Nelson,** Keithe Eugene 1935- *WhoAmL 92*
**Nelson,** Ken 1936- *WhoAmP 91*
**Nelson,** Kenneth Arthur 1942- *WhoWest 92*
**Nelson,** Kenneth Fred 1942- *AmMWSc 92*
**Nelson,** Kenneth Sigurd 1943- *WhoRel 92*
**Nelson,** Kenneth William 1917- *AmMWSc 92*
**Nelson,** Kent *DrAPF 91*
**Nelson,** Kent Earl 1940- *WhoEnt 92*
**Nelson,** Kevin Alfred 1958- *WhoAmL 92*
**Nelson,** Kim L 1948- *WhoAmP 91*
**Nelson,** Kirk Richard 1956- *WhoWest 92*
**Nelson,** Klayton Edward 1917- *AmMWSc 92*
**Nelson,** Knox 1926- *WhoAmP 91*
**Nelson,** Knut 1843-1923 *DcAmImH*
**Nelson,** Kurt Herbert 1924- *AmMWSc 92*
**Nelson,** Kyler Fischer 1938- *AmMWSc 92*
**Nelson,** L Clair 1918- *WhoAmP 91*
**Nelson,** L. Scott *WhoWest 92*
**Nelson,** Larry Ardean 1952- *WhoAmP 91*
**Nelson,** Larry Dean 1937- *AmMWSc 92*
**Nelson,** Lawrence Barclay 1931- *AmMWSc 92*
**Nelson,** Lawrence Emerson 1893-1978 *ConAu 134*
**Nelson,** Lawrence Olaf 1926- *WhoWest 92*
**Nelson,** Lenis Alton 1940- *AmMWSc 92*
**Nelson,** Leon Sydney 1942- *WhoMW 92*
**Nelson,** Leonard 1920- *AmMWSc 92*
**Nelson,** Leonard C 1920- *AmMWSc 92*
**Nelson,** Leonard Earl 1944- *WhoFI 92*
**Nelson,** Linda Ann 1955- *WhoAmP 91*
**Nelson,** Linda Ann 1959- *WhoWest 92*
**Nelson,** Linda J 1942- *WhoAmP 91*
**Nelson,** Linda Ruth 1944- *WhoWest 92*
**Nelson,** Lisa Elena 1964- *WhoEnt 92*
**Nelson,** Lloyd Steadman 1922- *AmMWSc 92*
**Nelson,** Lois Craswell 1934- *WhoMW 92*
**Nelson,** Lori 1933- *IntMPA 92*
**Nelson,** Louis 1902-1990 *AnObit 1990*
**Nelson,** Louise Mary 1951- *AmMWSc 92*
**Nelson,** Lowry, Jr. 1926- *WrDr 92*
**Nelson,** Lyle Engnar 1921- *AmMWSc 92*
**Nelson,** Lynn Anne 1952- *WhoMW 92*
**Nelson,** Magnus Charles 1938- *WhoWest 92*
**Nelson,** Manfred R. 1933- *WhoWest 92*
**Nelson,** Margaret Christina 1943- *AmMWSc 92*
**Nelson,** Marguerite *IntAu&W 91X*
**Nelson,** Marita Lee *AmMWSc 92*
**Nelson,** Marjorie Ann 1920- *WhoRel 92*
**Nelson,** Mark *WrDr 92*
**Nelson,** Mark Adams 1949- *AmMWSc 92*
**Nelson,** Mark Allen 1954- *WhoAmL 92*
**Nelson,** Mark David 1949- *WhoAmP 91*
**Nelson,** Mark James 1952- *AmMWSc 92*
**Nelson,** Mark K 1942- *WhoAmP 91*
**Nelson,** Martha 1923- *WrDr 92*
**Nelson,** Marvin R 1926- *WhoIns 92*
**Nelson,** Mary Anne 1952- *AmMWSc 92*
**Nelson,** Mary Bernice *WhoRel 92*
**Nelson,** Mary Carroll 1929- *WhoWest 92*
**Nelson,** Mary Ellen Dickson 1933- *WhoMW 92*
**Nelson,** Mary Lockett 1914- *AmMWSc 92*
**Nelson,** Mary Lou 1932- *WhoAmP 91*
**Nelson,** Mary S 1943- *WhoAmP 91*
**Nelson,** Merced 1948- *WhoAmP 91*
**Nelson,** Merle Royte 1935- *WhoAmP 91*
**Nelson,** Merrill F 1955- *WhoAmP 91*
**Nelson,** Merritt Richard 1932- *AmMWSc 92*
**Nelson,** Mervyn d1991 *NewYTBS 91*
**Nelson,** Michael Bryan 1950- *WhoFI 92*
**Nelson,** Michael Earl 1953- *WhoMW 92*
**Nelson,** Michael Edward 1929- *Who 92*
**Nelson,** Michael Fall 1950- *WhoAmP 91*
**Nelson,** Michael John 1955- *WhoEnt 92*
**Nelson,** Michael Richard 1947- *WhoEnt 92*
**Nelson,** Michael Roy 1954- *WhoMW 92*
**Nelson,** Michael Underhill 1932- *WhoMW 92*
**Nelson,** Mike 1947- *WhoAmP 91*
**Nelson,** Mildred *DrAPF 91*
**Nelson,** Nancy Eleanor 1933- *WhoWest 92*
**Nelson,** Nate 1932-1984 *FacFETw*
**Nelson,** Nathan 1938- *AmMWSc 92*
**Nelson,** Nathaniel W. 1921- *WhoBlA 92*
**Nelson,** Neal Stanley 1934- *AmMWSc 92*
**Nelson,** Neil Douglas 1944- *AmMWSc 92*
**Nelson,** Nels M 1919- *AmMWSc 92*
**Nelson,** Nels Robert 1923- *WhoEnt 92*
**Nelson,** Nevin Mary 1941- *WhoWest 92*
**Nelson,** Nicholas 1947- *Who 92*
**Nelson,** Nils Keith 1926- *AmMWSc 92*
**Nelson,** Noelle Cross 1947- *WhoWest 92*
**Nelson,** Norman Allan 1927- *AmMWSc 92*
**Nelson,** Norman Augustine 1926- *WhoRel 92*
**Nelson,** Norman Crooks 1929- *AmMWSc 92*
**Nelson,** Norman Neibuhr 1937- *AmMWSc 92*
**Nelson,** Norton 1910- *AmMWSc 92*
**Nelson,** Norvell John *AmMWSc 92*
**Nelson,** Novella C. 1939- *WhoBlA 92*
**Nelson,** O. Edward 1935- *WhoWest 92*
**Nelson,** Oliver Evans, Jr 1920- *AmMWSc 92*
**Nelson,** Orville Alfonzo 1925- *WhoBlA 92*
**Nelson,** Ozzie d1975 *LesBEnT 92*
**Nelson,** Pamela A *WhoAmP 91*
**Nelson,** Patricia Ann 1955- *WhoBlA 92*
**Nelson,** Paul *DrAPF 91*
**Nelson,** Paul 1895- *DcTwDes*
**Nelson,** Paul Donald 1932- *WhoBlA 92*
**Nelson,** Paul Douglas 1948- *WhoAmL 92*
**Nelson,** Paul Edward 1927- *AmMWSc 92*
**Nelson,** Paul James 1932- *WhoFI 92*
**Nelson,** Paul Thomas 1952- *WhoRel 92*
**Nelson,** Paul Victor 1939- *AmMWSc 92*
**Nelson,** Paula Morrison Bronson 1944- *WhoWest 92*
**Nelson,** Peter *ConAu 135*
**Nelson,** Peter E. *DrAPF 91*
**Nelson,** Peter Reid 1949- *AmMWSc 92*
**Nelson,** Philip Adel 1903- *WhoRel 92*
**Nelson,** Philip Bradford 1951- *WhoFI 92*
**Nelson,** Philip Edwin 1934- *AmMWSc 92*
**Nelson,** Phillip Gillard 1931- *AmMWSc 92*
**Nelson,** Prince Rogers 1958- *WhoBlA 92*
**Nelson,** R P *WhoAmP 91*
**Nelson,** R William 1931- *AmMWSc 92*
**Nelson,** Ralph *LesBEnT 92*
**Nelson,** Ralph A 1927- *AmMWSc 92*
**Nelson,** Ralph Alfred 1927- *IntWW 91, WhoMW 92*
**Nelson,** Ralph Francis 1945- *AmMWSc 92*
**Nelson,** Ralph Norman 1921- *WhoMW 92*
**Nelson,** Randall Bruce 1948- *AmMWSc 92*
**Nelson,** Randall Cleaver 1945- *WhoAmL 92*
**Nelson,** Randall Erland 1948- *WhoWest 92*
**Nelson,** Randy Scott 1952- *WhoAmL 92*
**Nelson,** Ray 1931- *TwCSFW 91, WrDr 92*
**Nelson,** Ray Faraday *DrAPF 91*
**Nelson,** Raymond Adolph 1926- *AmMWSc 92*
**Nelson,** Raymond John 1917- *AmMWSc 92*
**Nelson,** Raymond S. 1921- *ConAu 36NR*
**Nelson,** Rebecca Elaine 1960- *WhoMW 92*
**Nelson,** Rex Roland 1924- *AmMWSc 92*
**Nelson,** Rhonna Lynn 1957- *WhoMW 92*
**Nelson,** Richard *Who 92*
**Nelson,** Richard 1938- *WhoEnt 92*
**Nelson,** Richard 1950- *IntAu&W 91, WrDr 92*
**Nelson,** Richard Anthony 1948- *Who 92*
**Nelson,** Richard Arthur 1947- *WhoAmL 92*
**Nelson,** Richard Bartel 1940- *AmMWSc 92*
**Nelson,** Richard Burton 1911- *AmMWSc 92*
**Nelson,** Richard Carl 1915- *AmMWSc 92*
**Nelson,** Richard Carroll 1938- *WhoMW 92*
**Nelson,** Richard D 1941- *AmMWSc 92*
**Nelson,** Richard David 1940- *WhoMW 92*
**Nelson,** Richard Earl 1926- *WhoRel 92*
**Nelson,** Richard Henry 1939- *WhoFI 92*
**Nelson,** Richard K 1941- *SmATA 65*
**Nelson,** Richard L 1934- *AmMWSc 92*
**Nelson,** Richard Leedom, Jr. 1939- *WhoFI 92*
**Nelson,** Richard M 1925- *WhoAmP 91*
**Nelson,** Richard R. *WhoAmL 92*
**Nelson,** Richard Robert *AmMWSc 92*
**Nelson,** Richard Stuart 1937- *Who 92*
**Nelson,** Richard W. 1961- *WhoWest 92*
**Nelson,** Richard William 1945- *WhoFI 92*
**Nelson,** Richard Y., Jr. 1939- *WhoBlA 92*
**Nelson,** Ricky 1940-1985 *FacFETw*
**Nelson,** Ricky Eugene 1956- *WhoFI 92*
**Nelson,** Ricky Lee 1959- *WhoBlA 92*
**Nelson,** Robert *WhoAmP 91*
**Nelson,** Robert A 1935- *AmMWSc 92*
**Nelson,** Robert Andrew 1943- *AmMWSc 92*
**Nelson,** Robert B 1929- *AmMWSc 92*
**Nelson,** Robert B 1935- *AmMWSc 92*
**Nelson,** Robert Bruce 1935- *WhoAmL 92*
**Nelson,** Robert Carmichael 1926- *WhoEnt 92*
**Nelson,** Robert D *AmMWSc 92*
**Nelson,** Robert Earl, Jr. 1938- *WhoFI 92*
**Nelson,** Robert Eddinger 1928- *WhoMW 92*
**Nelson,** Robert Franklyn 1942- *Who 92*
**Nelson,** Robert George 1928- *WhoRel 92*
**Nelson,** Robert John 1926- *WhoFI 92*
**Nelson,** Robert Leon 1945- *AmMWSc 92*
**Nelson,** Robert Louis 1931- *WhoAmL 92*
**Nelson,** Robert M *AmMWSc 92*
**Nelson,** Robert Mellinger 1918- *AmMWSc 92*
**Nelson,** Robert Norton 1941- *AmMWSc 92*
**Nelson,** Robert S 1911- *AmMWSc 92*
**Nelson,** Robert Wales, Sr. 1925- *WhoBlA 92*
**Nelson,** Robert William 1942- *WhoFI 92, WhoWest 92*
**Nelson,** Roberta Jean 1960- *WhoRel 92*
**Nelson,** Rodney *DrAPF 91*
**Nelson,** Roger Edwin 1940- *AmMWSc 92*
**Nelson,** Roger Lee 1948- *WhoEnt 92*
**Nelson,** Roger Mederic 1935- *WhoFI 92*
**Nelson,** Roger Peter 1942- *AmMWSc 92*
**Nelson,** Roger William 1947- *WhoEnt 92*
**Nelson,** RoJean Evelyn 1927- *WhoAmP 91*
**Nelson,** Ron 1929- *WhoEnt 92*
**Nelson,** Ronald Digby 1935- *WhoMW 92*
**Nelson,** Ronald Duncan 1931- *WhoBlA 92*
**Nelson,** Ronald Harvey 1918- *AmMWSc 92, WhoMW 92*
**Nelson,** Roscoe Conkling, III 1948- *WhoAmL 92*
**Nelson,** Roy Gunnar 1951- *WhoWest 92*
**Nelson,** Roy P. 1923- *WrDr 92*
**Nelson,** Russell Andrew 1913- *AmMWSc 92*
**Nelson,** Russell C 1925- *AmMWSc 92*
**Nelson,** Russell Marion 1924- *AmMWSc 92, WhoWest 92*
**Nelson,** S O 1927- *AmMWSc 92*
**Nelson,** Samuel James 1925- *AmMWSc 92*

**Nelson**, Sarah Milledge 1931- *WhoWest 92*
**Nelson**, Scott D. 1959- *WhoMW 92*
**Nelson**, Sheffield *WhoAmP 91*
**Nelson**, Sheila Diane 1948- *WhoAmP 91*
**Nelson**, Sheldon Douglas 1943- *AmMWSc 92*
**Nelson**, Sherlee Stanford 1934- *WhoAmL 92*
**Nelson**, Shirley *DrAPF 91*
**Nelson**, Sidney D 1945- *AmMWSc 92*
**Nelson**, Sidney Richard 1907- *Who 92*
**Nelson**, Sigurd Oscar, Jr 1937- *AmMWSc 92*
**Nelson**, St Elmo Dudley 1919- *Who 92*
**Nelson**, Stanley *DrAPF 91*
**Nelson**, Stanley Reid 1928- *AmMWSc 92*
**Nelson**, Stephen Charles 1942- *WhoAmL 92*
**Nelson**, Stephen Clarke 1952- *WhoEnt 92*
**Nelson**, Stephen Glen 1947- *AmMWSc 92*
**Nelson**, Stephen Richard 1958- *WhoWest 92*
**Nelson**, Steven 1961- *TwCPaSc*
**Nelson**, Steven Craig 1944- *WhoAmL 92*
**Nelson**, Steven Dwayne 1950- *WhoAmL 92*
**Nelson**, Stuart *Who 92*
**Nelson**, Susan Emilie 1944- *WhoEnt 92*
**Nelson**, Syd G 1932- *WhoAmP 91*
**Nelson**, Sydney B. 1935- *WhoAmL 92, WhoAmP 91*
**Nelson**, Talmadge Seab 1928- *AmMWSc 92*
**Nelson**, Ted S *WhoAmP 91*
**Nelson**, Terence John 1939- *AmMWSc 92*
**Nelson**, Terrell Mark 1960- *WhoRel 92*
**Nelson**, Terry Ellan Elisabeth 1954- *WhoRel 92*
**Nelson**, Theodora S 1913- *AmMWSc 92*
**Nelson**, Thomas d1892 *DcLB 106*
**Nelson**, Thomas 1780-1861 *DcLB 106*
**Nelson**, Thomas, and Sons *DcLB 106*
**Nelson**, Thomas Charles 1923- *AmMWSc 92*
**Nelson**, Thomas Clifford 1925- *AmMWSc 92*
**Nelson**, Thomas E 1934- *WhoAmP 91*
**Nelson**, Thomas Edward *AmMWSc 92*
**Nelson**, Thomas Eustis, Jr 1922- *AmMWSc 92*
**Nelson**, Thomas Evar 1934- *AmMWSc 92*
**Nelson**, Thomas G *WhoAmP 91*
**Nelson**, Thomas George 1949- *WhoMW 92*
**Nelson**, Thomas Howard 1944- *WhoAmL 92*
**Nelson**, Thomas Lothian 1922- *AmMWSc 92*
**Nelson**, Todd Arthur 1955- *WhoMW 92*
**Nelson**, Tom *WhoAmP 91*
**Nelson**, Vera Joyce *DrAPF 91*
**Nelson**, Vernon A 1939- *AmMWSc 92*
**Nelson**, Vernon Ronald 1921- *AmMWSc 92*
**Nelson**, Victor Eugene 1936- *AmMWSc 92*
**Nelson**, Vincent Carl 1941- *WhoWest 92*
**Nelson**, Vita Joy 1937- *WhoFI 92*
**Nelson**, W L 1927- *AmMWSc 92*
**Nelson**, Walter Garnet 1950- *AmMWSc 92*
**Nelson**, Walter Ralph 1937- *AmMWSc 92*
**Nelson**, Walter William 1954- *WhoWest 92*
**Nelson**, Wanda Jean 1938- *WhoBlA 92*
**Nelson**, Wanda Lee 1952- *WhoBlA 92*
**Nelson**, Warren Bryant 1922- *WhoFI 92*
**Nelson**, Warren Louis 1940- *WhoAmP 91, WhoFI 92*
**Nelson**, Wayne Bryce 1936- *AmMWSc 92*
**Nelson**, Wayne Franklin 1920- *AmMWSc 92*
**Nelson**, Wendel Lane 1939- *AmMWSc 92*
**Nelson**, Werner Lind 1914- *AmMWSc 92*
**Nelson**, Wilbur C 1913- *AmMWSc 92*
**Nelson**, Wilfred H 1936- *AmMWSc 92*
**Nelson**, Willard Gregory 1937- *WhoWest 92*
**Nelson**, William Arnold 1918- *AmMWSc 92*
**Nelson**, William Bradley 1944- *WhoWest 92*
**Nelson**, William Curtis 1937- *WhoFI 92*
**Nelson**, William Edward 1926- *WhoFI 92*
**Nelson**, William Edward 1940- *WhoAmL 92*
**Nelson**, William Edward, Jr. 1941- *WhoBlA 92*
**Nelson**, William Eugene 1927- *WhoAmL 92*
**Nelson**, William Frank 1924- *AmMWSc 92*
**Nelson**, William George, IV 1934- *WhoMW 92*
**Nelson**, William Harris Morehead, III 1951- *WhoFI 92*
**Nelson**, William Henry 1943- *AmMWSc 92*
**Nelson**, William Hoyt 1930- *WhoRel 92*
**Nelson**, William Nathan 1956- *WhoMW 92*
**Nelson**, William Pierrepont, III 1920- *AmMWSc 92*
**Nelson**, William Rankin 1921- *WhoWest 92*
**Nelson**, William Vernon Hope d1991 *Who 92N*
**Nelson**, William W. 1917-1988 *WhoBlA 92N*
**Nelson**, Willie 1933- *IntMPA 92, NewAmDM, WhoEnt 92*
**Nelson-Holgate**, Gail Evangelyn 1944- *WhoBlA 92*
**Nelson-Humphries**, Tessa *IntAu&W 91, WrDr 92*
**Nelson NZ**, Bishop of 1941- *Who 92*
**Nelson Of Stafford**, Baron 1917- *IntWW 91, Who 92*
**Nelson-Rees**, Walter Anthony 1929- *AmMWSc 92*
**Nelsova**, Zara *WhoEnt 92*
**Nelsova**, Zara 1918- *NewAmDM*
**Nelting**, George *WhoRel 92*
**Neltnor**, Donald Alan 1949- *WhoAmP 91*
**Neman**, Beth S. 1931- *WhoMW 92*
**Nemapare**, Esau Thomas Jan 1903- *WhoRel 92*
**Nemat-Nasser**, Siavouche 1936- *AmMWSc 92*
**Nematollahi**, Jay 1925- *AmMWSc 92*
**Nemchinov**, Vasiliy Sergeevich 1894-1964 *SovUnBD*
**Nemec**, Corin 1971- *IntMPA 92*
**Nemec**, David *DrAPF 91*
**Nemec**, Jan 1936- *IntDcF 2-2*
**Nemec**, Jaroslav 1921- *IntWW 91*
**Nemec**, Josef 1929- *AmMWSc 92*
**Nemec**, Joseph William 1922- *AmMWSc 92*
**Nemec**, Stanley 1935- *AmMWSc 92*
**Nemec**, Vernita *DrAPF 91*
**Nemecek**, Georgina Marie 1946- *AmMWSc 92*
**Nemecek**, Randolph Michael 1956- *WhoMW 92*
**Nemeiry**, Gaafar Mohammed al- *IntWW 91*
**Nemenzo**, Francisco 1905- *AmMWSc 92*
**Nemer**, Martin Joseph 1929- *AmMWSc 92*
**Nemere**, Ilka M 1953- *AmMWSc 92*
**Nemeroff**, Charles Barnet 1949- *AmMWSc 92*
**Nemeroff**, Michael Alan 1946- *WhoAmL 92*
**Nemerov**, Donald Scott 1950- *WhoMW 92*
**Nemerov**, Howard *DrAPF 91*
**Nemerov**, Howard 1920- *BenetAL 91, ConPo 91, IntAu&W 91, IntWW 91, WrDr 92*
**Nemerov**, Howard 1920-1991 *ConAu 134, CurBio 91N, FacFETw, NewYTBS 91 [port], News 92-1*
**Nemerow**, Nelson L 1923- *AmMWSc 92*
**Nemerson**, Matthew L 1956- *WhoAmP 91*
**Nemerson**, Roy Edward 1946- *WhoEnt 92*
**Nemerson**, Yale 1931- *AmMWSc 92*
**Nemery**, Gaafar Mohammed al- 1930- *IntWW 91*
**Nemes**, Graciela P. *WhoHisp 92*
**Nemes Nagy**, Agnes 1922- *IntWW 91*
**Nemesius** *EncEarC*
**Nemet-Nejat**, Murat *DrAPF 91*
**Nemeth**, Abraham 1918- *AmMWSc 92*
**Nemeth**, Andrew Martin 1926- *AmMWSc 92*
**Nemeth**, Edward Joseph 1938- *AmMWSc 92*
**Nemeth**, Evi 1940- *AmMWSc 92*
**Nemeth**, Joseph 1940- *AmMWSc 92*
**Nemeth**, Karoly 1922- *IntWW 91*
**Nemeth**, Laszlo K 1932- *AmMWSc 92*
**Nemeth**, Margaret Ann *AmMWSc 92*
**Nemeth**, Miklos 1948- *IntWW 91*
**Nemeth**, Patricia Marie 1959- *WhoAmL 92*
**Nemeth**, Peter John 1941- *WhoAmP 91*
**Nemeth**, Ronald Louis 1941- *AmMWSc 92*
**Nemeth**, Zoltan Anthony 1931- *AmMWSc 92, WhoMW 92*
**Nemethy**, George 1934- *AmMWSc 92*
**Nemetz**, Nathaniel Theodore 1913- *Who 92*
**Nemhauser**, George L 1937- *AmMWSc 92*
**Nemia**, Frank Anthony 1932- *WhoAmL 92*
**Nemir**, Donald Philip 1931- *WhoAmL 92, WhoWest 92*
**Nemir**, Paul, Jr 1920- *AmMWSc 92*
**Nemir**, Rosa Lee 1905- *AmMWSc 92*
**Nemiro**, Beverly Mirium Anderson 1925- *WhoWest 92*
**Nemiroff**, Maxine Celia 1935- *WhoWest 92*
**Nemiroff**, Robert B. d1991 *NewYTBS 91*
**Nemirovich-Danchenko**, Vasily Ivanovich 1848-1936 *FacFETw*
**Nemirovich-Danchenko**, Vladimir Ivanovich 1858-1943 *SovUnBD*
**Nemirow**, Arnold Myles 1943- *WhoFI 92, WhoMW 92*
**Nemirow**, Joel Alan 1951- *WhoMW 92*
**Nemitsas**, Takis 1930- *IntWW 91*
**Nemitz**, William Charles 1928- *AmMWSc 92*
**Nemo**, Omen *ScFEYrs*
**Nemon**, Oscar 1905-1985 *FacFETw*
**Nemoto**, Takuma *AmMWSc 92*
**Nemphos**, Speros Peter 1930- *AmMWSc 92*
**Nemschoff**, Louise 1950- *WhoEnt 92*
**Nemser**, Cindy *DrAPF 91*
**Nemser**, Earl Harold 1947- *WhoAmL 92*
**Nemtchinova**, Vera 1899-1984 *FacFETw*
**Nemzoff**, Ruth 1940- *WhoAmP 91*
**Nenashev**, Mikhail Fyodovovich 1929- *IntWW 91*
**Nendick**, David Alan Challoner 1932- *Who 92*
**Nenni**, Pietro 1891-1980 *FacFETw*
**Nenno**, Robert Peter 1922- *AmMWSc 92*
**Nenno**, Stephen Kenney 1942- *WhoEnt 92*
**Nepean**, Evan Yorke 1909- *Who 92*
**Nephew**, F. Theresa 1958- *WhoAmL 92*
**Nepil**, Frantisek 1929- *IntAu&W 91*
**Nepo**, Mark *DrAPF 91*
**Neppe**, Vernon Michael 1951- *WhoWest 92*
**Nepple**, James Anthony 1945- *WhoAmL 92*
**Neprintsev**, Yuriy Mikhaylovich 1909- *SovUnBD*
**Neptune**, John Addison 1919- *AmMWSc 92*
**Neptune**, William Everett 1928- *AmMWSc 92*
**Nequette**, Merritt Charles 1938- *WhoMW 92*
**Nerbun**, Robert Charles, Jr 1946- *AmMWSc 92*
**Nercessian**, Yeghia Toros 1931- *WhoWest 92*
**Nereim**, Anders 1947- *WhoMW 92*
**Nerem**, Robert Michael 1937- *AmMWSc 92*
**Nerenberg**, Aaron 1940- *WhoAmL 92*
**Nerenberg**, Morton Abraham 1936- *AmMWSc 92*
**Nereson**, Norris 1918- *AmMWSc 92*
**Nereus and Achilleus** *EncEarC*
**Nergard**, Charles L 1929- *WhoAmP 91*
**Neri**, Aldo 1930- *IntWW 91*
**Neri**, Anthony 1948- *AmMWSc 92*
**Neri**, Manuel 1930- *WhoHisp 92*
**Neri**, Pompeo 1706-1776 *BlkwCEP*
**Neri**, Rudolph Orazio 1928- *AmMWSc 92*
**Neri**, Umberto 1939- *AmMWSc 92*
**Nerina**, Nadia 1927- *Who 92*
**Nering**, Evar Dare 1921- *AmMWSc 92*
**Nerio**, Mark Anthony 1955- *WhoHisp 92*
**Nerio**, Yolanda Paramo 1943- *WhoHisp 92*
**Nerken**, Albert 1912- *AmMWSc 92*
**Nerken**, Ruth Moira 1952- *WhoEnt 92*
**Nerland**, Donald Eugene 1946- *AmMWSc 92*
**Nerlich**, Graham C. 1929- *WrDr 92*
**Nerlich**, Graham Charles 1929- *IntWW 91*
**Nerlich**, William Edward 1923- *AmMWSc 92*
**Nerlove**, Marc L. 1933- *IntWW 91, WhoFI 92*
**Nern**, Michael Glenn 1960- *WhoMW 92*
**Nernst**, Walther Hermann 1864-1941 *WhoNob 90*
**Nero** 37-68 *EncEarC*
**Nero**, Anthony V, Jr 1942- *AmMWSc 92*
**Nero**, David M., Jr. 1924- *WhoBlA 92*
**Nero**, Franco 1941- *IntMPA 92, IntWW 91*
**Nero**, Peter 1934- *WhoEnt 92*
**Nero**, Robert Anthony 1946- *WhoMW 92*
**Neroda**, Georgiy Vasil'evich 1895-1983 *SovUnBD*
**Nerode**, Anil 1932- *AmMWSc 92*
**Nersasian**, Arthur 1924- *AmMWSc 92*
**Neruda**, Pablo 1904-1973 *BenetAL 91, FacFETw, LiExTwC, PoeCrit 4 [port], WhoNob 90*
**Nerval**, Gerard de 1808-1855 *GuFrLit 1*
**Nervi**, Pier Luigi 1891- *DcTwDes*
**Nervi**, Pier Luigi 1891-1979 *FacFETw*
**Nervo**, Amado Ruiz de 1870-1919 *BenetAL 91*
**Nerzig**, Myron Hy 1936- *WhoMW 92*
**Nes**, William David 1953- *AmMWSc 92*
**Nes**, William Robert 1926- *AmMWSc 92*
**Nesbeda**, Paul 1921- *AmMWSc 92*
**Nesbet**, Robert Kenyon 1930- *AmMWSc 92*
**Nesbit**, E. 1858-1924 *RfGEnL 91*
**Nesbit**, Edith 1858-1924 *ScFEYrs*
**Nesbit**, Lee Cleeton 1950- *WhoMW 92*
**Nesbit**, Phyllis Schneider 1919- *WhoAmL 92*
**Nesbit**, Richard Allison 1935- *AmMWSc 92*
**Nesbit**, Troy *IntAu&W 91X, WrDr 92*
**Nesbit**, Wilbur D 1871-1927 *ScFEYrs*
**Nesbit**, William Reed 1930- *WhoFI 92*
**Nesbitt**, Alexander John 1901- *WhoEnt 92*
**Nesbitt**, Benjamin Clark 1944- *WhoFI 92*
**Nesbitt**, Bruce Edward 1951- *AmMWSc 92*
**Nesbitt**, Carl C 1958- *AmMWSc 92*
**Nesbitt**, Cecil James 1912- *AmMWSc 92*
**Nesbitt**, Charles Rudolph 1921- *WhoAmL 92*
**Nesbitt**, Frank Wilbur 1916- *WhoAmL 92*
**Nesbitt**, Gordon Morley 1961- *WhoMW 92*
**Nesbitt**, Herbert Hugh John 1913- *AmMWSc 92*
**Nesbitt**, John Arthur 1933- *WhoMW 92*
**Nesbitt**, John B 1924- *AmMWSc 92*
**Nesbitt**, Joseph Henderson 1921- *WhoAmP 91*
**Nesbitt**, Lenore Carrero *WhoAmL 92*
**Nesbitt**, Lowell 1933- *IntWW 91*
**Nesbitt**, Martin L 1946- *WhoAmP 91*
**Nesbitt**, Paul Edward 1943- *WhoWest 92*
**Nesbitt**, Prexy-Rozell William 1944- *WhoBlA 92*
**Nesbitt**, Robert Edward Lee, Jr 1924- *AmMWSc 92*
**Nesbitt**, Rosemary Sinnett 1924- *WhoEnt 92*
**Nesbitt**, Stuart Stoner 1921- *AmMWSc 92*
**Nesbitt**, William Belton 1932- *AmMWSc 92*
**Nesby**, Donald Ray, Sr. 1937- *WhoBlA 92*
**Neschling**, John Luciano 1947- *WhoEnt 92*
**Nesenbergs**, Martin 1928- *AmMWSc 92*
**Nesgos**, Peter Dimaratos 1957- *WhoAmL 92*
**Nesheim**, David James 1944- *WhoMW 92*
**Nesheim**, Malden Charles 1931- *AmMWSc 92*
**Nesheim**, Michael Ernest 1945- *AmMWSc 92*
**Nesheim**, Obed John 1929- *WhoRel 92*
**Nesheim**, Robert Olaf 1921- *AmMWSc 92, WhoWest 92*
**Nesheim**, Stanley 1930- *AmMWSc 92*
**Neshyba**, Steve 1927- *AmMWSc 92*
**Nesius**, Karen Elizabeth 1961- *WhoRel 92*
**Neslen**, Richard Rockwood 1939- *WhoAmL 92*
**Nesler**, Joanne 1932- *WhoFI 92*
**Nesline**, Frederick William, Jr 1926- *AmMWSc 92*
**Nesmeyanov**, Aleksandr Nikolaevich 1899-1980 *SovUnBD*
**Nesmith**, Dorothy Edna 1923- *WhoWest 92*
**Nesmith**, Michael 1942- *IntMPA 92*
**Nesmith**, Richard Duey 1929- *WhoRel 92*
**Nesnow**, Stephen Charles 1941- *AmMWSc 92*
**Nespole**, Joseph James 1936- *WhoAmL 92*
**Nespral**, Jackie Frances 1966- *WhoHisp 92*
**Ness** *EncAmaz 91*
**Ness**, Andrew David 1952- *WhoAmL 92*
**Ness**, Charles *Who 92*
**Ness**, Charles Allen 1947- *WhoRel 92*
**Ness**, Diane *WhoAmP 91*
**Ness**, Eliot 1902-1957 *FacFETw*
**Ness**, Gary Gene 1948- *WhoMW 92*
**Ness**, Gene Charles 1944- *AmMWSc 92*
**Ness**, Harald Maurets, Jr. 1932- *WhoMW 92*
**Ness**, Julius B *WhoAmP 91*
**Ness**, Linda Ann 1947- *AmMWSc 92*
**Ness**, Nathan 1916- *AmMWSc 92*
**Ness**, Norman Frederick 1933- *AmMWSc 92*
**Ness**, Philip Wahmann, Jr. 1936- *WhoFI 92, WhoIns 92*
**Ness**, Robert Kiracofe 1922- *AmMWSc 92*
**Ness**, Thomas Patrick 1960- *WhoMW 92*
**Nessa** *EncAmaz 91*
**Nessan**, Craig Lee 1952- *WhoRel 92*
**Nessel**, Robert J 1936- *AmMWSc 92*
**Nessel**, Robert Jay 1936- *WhoMW 92*
**Nessel**, William Joseph 1929- *WhoRel 92*
**Nessellhauf**, Lois Lucille 1938- *WhoEnt 92*
**Nesselson**, Eugene J 1928- *AmMWSc 92*
**Nesselson**, Eugene Joseph 1938- *WhoMW 92*
**Nessen**, Greta von 1900?-1978? *DcTwDes*
**Nessen**, Ron *LesBEnT 92*
**Nessen**, Walter von d1942 *DcTwDes*
**Nessen**, Ward Henry 1909- *WhoFI 92*
**Nesser**, Joan Kay 1938- *WhoRel 92*
**Nessi**, Jose M. *WhoHisp 92*
**Nessler**, Walter 1912- *TwCPaSc*
**Nessmith**, Josh T, Jr 1923- *AmMWSc 92*
**Nesson**, Charles R. 1939- *WhoAmL 92*
**Nestande**, Bruce 1938- *WhoAmP 91*
**Neste**, Sherman Lester 1943- *AmMWSc 92*
**Nestell**, Merlynd Keith 1937- *AmMWSc 92*
**Nester**, Eugene William 1930- *AmMWSc 92*
**Nesterenko**, Aleksey Yefremovich 1915- *IntWW 91*

**Nesterenko,** Yevgeniy Yevgeniyevich 1938- *IntWW 91*
**Nesterenko,** Yevgeny Yevgen'evich 1938- *SovUnBD*
**Nesterikhin,** Yuri Efremovich 1930- *IntWW 91*
**Nesterov,** Mikhail Vasil'evich 1862-1942 *SovUnBD*
**Nesterova,** Natal'ya Igon'eva 1944- *SovUnBD*
**Nestico,** Pasquale Francesco 1945- *AmMWSc 92*
**Nestle,** Joan *DrAPF 91*
**Nestler,** Louis Baepler 1912- *WhoMW 92*
**Nestor,** Bishop 1825-1882 *RelLAm 91*
**Nestor,** Agnes 1880-1948 *DcAmImH*
**Nestor,** Basil 1960- *WhoEnt 92*
**Nestor,** C William, Jr 1931- *AmMWSc 92*
**Nestor,** Charles Bernard 1947- *WhoRel 92*
**Nestor,** Jack *DrAPF 91*
**Nestor,** John Joseph, Jr 1945- *AmMWSc 92*
**Nestor,** Karl Elwood 1937- *AmMWSc 92*
**Nestor,** Ontario Horia 1922- *AmMWSc 92*
**Nestor,** Susan E. 1956- *WhoMW 92*
**Nestor,** Tod Andrew 1963- *WhoFI 92*
**Nestor,** Wayne Allen 1953- *WhoRel 92*
**Nestorius** 381?-451 *EncEarC*
**Nestrick,** Dwight L. 1947- *WhoFI 92*
**Nestrick,** Terry John *AmMWSc 92*
**Nestvold,** Elwood Olaf 1932- *AmMWSc 92*
**Nesty,** Anthony *BlkOlyM*
**Nesty,** Glenn Albert 1911- *WhoWest 92*
**Nesvadba,** Josef 1926- *TwCSFW 91A*
**Nesvan,** Geraldine Root *WhoMW 92*
**Nesvarba,** Lonnie Ray 1954- *WhoMW 92*
**Net,** Juan Antonio *WhoHisp 92*
**Neta,** Pedatsur 1938- *AmMWSc 92*
**Neta,** Ruth *AmMWSc 92*
**Netanyahu,** Benjamin 1949- *IntWW 91*
**Neter,** John 1923- *AmMWSc 92*
**Nethaway,** David Robert 1929- *AmMWSc 92*
**Nethercot,** Arthur Hobart, Jr 1923- *AmMWSc 92*
**Nethercut,** Philip Edwin 1921- *AmMWSc 92*
**Netherland,** Joel Bernard 1935- *WhoAmP 91*
**Netherlands,** Prince of the 1911- *IntWW 91*
**Netherthorpe,** Baron 1964- *Who 92*
**Netherton,** Jane 1945- *WhoFI 92*
**Netherton,** Lowell Edwin 1922- *AmMWSc 92*
**Nethery,** Arthur Alan 1938- *WhoMW 92*
**Nething,** David E *WhoAmP 91*
**Neti,** Radhakrishna Murty 1933- *AmMWSc 92*
**Neto,** Agostinho Antonio 1922-1979 *FacFETw*
**Netravali,** Arun Narayan 1946- *AmMWSc 92*
**Netsch,** Dawn Clark 1926- *WhoAmL 92, WhoAmP 91, WhoMW 92*
**Netsky,** Hankus 1955- *WhoEnt 92*
**Netsky,** Martin George 1917- *AmMWSc 92*
**Nett,** Carl Anthony 1941- *WhoAmP 91*
**Nett,** John Bernard 1940- *WhoMW 92*
**Nett,** T M *AmMWSc 92*
**Nettel,** Stephen J E 1932- *AmMWSc 92*
**Nettelhorst,** Robin Paul 1957- *WhoRel 92*
**Nettels,** George E, Jr 1927- *WhoAmP 91*
**Netter,** Cornelia Ann 1933- *WhoFI 92*
**Netter,** Douglas *IntMPA 92*
**Netter,** Frank H. 1906-1991 *NewYTBS 91 [port]*
**Netter,** Kurt Fred 1919- *WhoFI 92*
**Netter,** Mildrette 1948- *BlkOlyM*
**Netter,** Miriam Maccoby 1935- *WhoAmL 92*
**Netters,** Tyrone Homer 1954- *WhoBlA 92*
**Netterstrom,** Henrik Munck 1924- *IntWW 91*
**Netterville,** George Bronson 1929- *WhoRel 92*
**Netterville,** George Leon, Jr. 1907- *WhoBlA 92*
**Netterville,** Luke 1846-1928 *ScFEYrs*
**Nettesheim,** Christine Cook 1944- *WhoAmL 92*
**Nettesheim,** Paul 1933- *AmMWSc 92*
**Nettle,** Robert Dale 1924- *WhoAmP 91, WhoMW 92*
**Nettleford,** Rex Milton 1933- *WhoBlA 92*
**Nettles,** A. Bentley 1963- *WhoAmL 92*
**Nettles,** Clem M 1930- *WhoAmP 91*
**Nettles,** Eugene Leroy, Jr 1954- *WhoAmP 91*
**Nettles,** John Barnwell 1922- *AmMWSc 92*
**Nettles,** John Leonard 1925- *WhoAmL 92*
**Nettles,** John Spratt 1943- *WhoBlA 92*
**Nettles,** Larry Wade 1956- *WhoAmL 92*
**Nettles,** Willard, Jr. 1944- *WhoBlA 92*
**Nettles,** William Carl, Jr 1934- *AmMWSc 92*
**Nettleton,** Donald Edward, Jr 1930- *AmMWSc 92*
**Nettleton,** Edwin S 1831-1901 *BiInAmS*
**Nettleton,** G Stephen 1946- *AmMWSc 92*
**Nettleton,** James H. 1940- *WhoEnt 92*
**Nettleton,** Janeva Ann 1952- *WhoFI 92*
**Nettleton,** Lois *IntMPA 92, WhoEnt 92*
**Nettleton,** Wiley Dennis 1932- *AmMWSc 92*
**Netto,** Igor Alexandrovich 1930- *SovUnBD*
**Netzel,** Daniel Anthony 1934- *AmMWSc 92*
**Netzel,** Paul Arthur 1941- *WhoFI 92, WhoWest 92*
**Netzel,** Richard G 1928- *AmMWSc 92*
**Netzel,** Thomas Leonard 1946- *AmMWSc 92*
**Netzer,** David Willis 1939- *AmMWSc 92*
**Netzky-Jolly,** Wendy Heather 1955- *WhoWest 92*
**Netzley,** Robert E 1922- *WhoAmP 91*
**Neu,** Arthur Alan 1933- *WhoAmP 91*
**Neu,** Carl Herbert, Jr. 1937- *WhoWest 92*
**Neu,** Ernest Ludwig 1915- *AmMWSc 92*
**Neu,** Harold Conrad 1934- *AmMWSc 92*
**Neu,** John Ternay 1920- *AmMWSc 92*
**Neu,** Kenneth G. 1955- *WhoFI 92*
**Neubacher,** Hermann 1893-1960 *BiDExR*
**Neubarth,** Sanford L 1948- *WhoIns 92*
**Neubauer,** Alex 1959- *ConAu 135*
**Neubauer,** Benedict Francis 1938- *AmMWSc 92*
**Neubauer,** Florence Butler 1955- *WhoEnt 92*
**Neubauer,** James Emmanuel 1952- *WhoWest 92*
**Neubauer,** Jeffrey S 1955- *WhoAmP 91*
**Neubauer,** Joseph 1941- *WhoFI 92*
**Neubauer,** L W 1904- *AmMWSc 92*
**Neubauer,** Michael Gerald 1954- *WhoWest 92*
**Neubauer,** Paul *WhoEnt 92*
**Neubauer,** Russell Howard 1944- *AmMWSc 92*
**Neubauer,** Werner George 1930- *AmMWSc 92*
**Neubeck,** Clifford Edward 1917- *AmMWSc 92*
**Neubecker,** Robert Duane 1925- *AmMWSc 92*
**Neuber,** Friedel 1935- *IntWW 91*
**Neuberger,** Albert 1908- *IntWW 91, Who 92*
**Neuberger,** Dan 1929- *AmMWSc 92*
**Neuberger,** David Edmond 1948- *Who 92*
**Neuberger,** Egon 1925- *WhoFI 92*
**Neuberger,** Hans Hermann 1910- *AmMWSc 92*
**Neuberger,** Jacob 1927- *AmMWSc 92*
**Neuberger,** John Stephen 1938- *AmMWSc 92, WhoMW 92*
**Neuberger,** John William 1934- *AmMWSc 92*
**Neuberger,** Julia 1950- *ConAu 135*
**Neuberger,** Julia Babette Sarah 1950- *IntWW 91, Who 92*
**Neuberger,** Mark Joseph 1955- *WhoAmL 92*
**Neuberger,** Maurine Brown *WhoAmP 91*
**Neubert,** Jerome Arthur 1938- *AmMWSc 92*
**Neubert,** Karen Marie 1958- *WhoFI 92*
**Neubert,** Michael 1933- *Who 92*
**Neubert,** Ralph Lewis 1922- *WhoFI 92*
**Neubert,** Theodore John 1917- *AmMWSc 92*
**Neubert,** Vernon H 1927- *AmMWSc 92*
**Neubig,** Herbert F. 1934- *WhoFI 92*
**Neubig,** Richard Robert 1953- *AmMWSc 92*
**Neuborne,** Burt 1941- *WhoAmL 92*
**Neubort,** Shimon 1942- *AmMWSc 92*
**Neucere,** Joseph Navin 1932- *AmMWSc 92*
**Neudeck,** Gerold W 1936- *AmMWSc 92*
**Neudeck,** Gerold Walter 1936- *WhoMW 92*
**Neudeck,** Lowell Donald 1937- *AmMWSc 92*
**Neudoerffer,** Volkmar Caj 1941- *WhoIns 92*
**Neue,** Uwe Dieter 1948- *AmMWSc 92*
**Neuefeind,** Wilhelm 1939- *WhoFI 92, WhoMW 92*
**Neuendorffer,** Joseph Alfred 1918- *AmMWSc 92*
**Neuenschwander,** Bob 1948- *WhoAmP 91*
**Neuer,** Kathleen *DrAPF 91*
**Neuer,** Philip David 1946- *WhoAmL 92*
**Neufeld,** Abram Herman 1907- *AmMWSc 92*
**Neufeld,** Amos *DrAPF 91*
**Neufeld,** Arline E. 1952- *WhoHisp 92*
**Neufeld,** Berney Roy 1941- *AmMWSc 92*
**Neufeld,** Daniel Arthur 1945- *AmMWSc 92*
**Neufeld,** Elizabeth Fondal 1928- *AmMWSc 92*
**Neufeld,** Gaylen Jay 1939- *AmMWSc 92*
**Neufeld,** Gordon R 1937- *AmMWSc 92*
**Neufeld,** Harold Alex 1924- *AmMWSc 92*
**Neufeld,** Herb *WhoRel 92*
**Neufeld,** Jerry Don 1940- *AmMWSc 92*
**Neufeld,** Mace 1928- *ConTFT 9, WhoEnt 92*
**Neufeld,** Melvin J *WhoAmP 91*
**Neufeld,** Peter Lorenz 1931- *IntAu&W 91*
**Neufeld,** Ronald David 1947- *AmMWSc 92*
**Neufeld,** Timothy Lee 1947- *WhoAmL 92*
**Neufeld,** Victor *LesBEnT 92*
**Neuffer,** Myron Gerald 1922- *AmMWSc 92*
**Neufville,** Mortimer H. 1939- *WhoBlA 92*
**Neugarten,** Bernice L *AmMWSc 92*
**Neugarten,** Bernice L 1916- *WomPsyc*
**Neugarten,** Bernice Levin 1916- *IntWW 91*
**Neugebauer,** Christoph Johannes 1927- *AmMWSc 92*
**Neugebauer,** Constantine Aloysius 1930- *AmMWSc 92*
**Neugebauer,** Gerry 1932- *AmMWSc 92*
**Neugebauer,** Joy Lois 1927- *WhoAmP 91*
**Neugebauer,** Otto E *AmMWSc 92*
**Neugebauer,** Richard 1944- *AmMWSc 92*
**Neugeboren,** Jay *DrAPF 91*
**Neugeboren,** Jay 1938- *BenetAL 91, ConNov 91, IntAu&W 91, WrDr 92*
**Neuger,** Edwin 1924- *WhoFI 92*
**Neuger,** Sanford 1925- *WhoMW 92*
**Neugroschel,** Joachim *DrAPF 91*
**Neugroschl,** Daniel 1966- *AmMWSc 92*
**Neuhalfen,** Andrew J 1961- *AmMWSc 92*
**Neuharth,** Allen H. 1924- *IntWW 91*
**Neuhaus,** Cable 1947- *WhoEnt 92, WhoWest 92*
**Neuhaus,** Francis Clemens 1932- *AmMWSc 92*
**Neuhaus,** Genrikh Gustavovich 1888-1964 *SovUnBD*
**Neuhaus,** Joseph Emanuel 1957- *WhoAmL 92*
**Neuhaus,** Max 1939- *NewAmDM*
**Neuhaus,** Otto Wilhelm 1922- *AmMWSc 92*
**Neuhaus,** Richard J. 1936- *WrDr 92*
**Neuhaus,** Richard John 1936- *WhoRel 92*
**Neuhauser,** Charles William, Jr. 1952- *WhoFI 92*
**Neuhauser,** Duncan B 1939- *AmMWSc 92*
**Neuhauser,** Duncan von Briesen 1939- *IntWW 91*
**Neuhauser,** Mary 1934- *WhoAmP 91*
**Neuhauser,** Philipp Danton 1929- *WhoEnt 92*
**Neuhold,** John Mathew 1928- *AmMWSc 92*
**Neuhouser,** David Lee 1933- *AmMWSc 92*
**Neulinger,** John 1924-1991 *ConAu 134*
**Neumaier,** Gerhard John 1937- *WhoFI 92*
**Neumaier,** Mark Adam 1958- *WhoAmL 92*
**Neumaier,** Robert Harold 1942- *WhoMW 92*
**Neumaier,** Robert Joseph 1951- *WhoAmP 91*
**Neuman,** Alan *LesBEnT 92*
**Neuman,** Charles Herbert 1937- *AmMWSc 92*
**Neuman,** Charles P 1940- *AmMWSc 92*
**Neuman,** Daniel Moses 1944- *WhoEnt 92*
**Neuman,** E. Jack *LesBEnT 92*
**Neuman,** George Anthony 1945- *WhoMW 92*
**Neuman,** Isaac 1922- *WhoRel 92*
**Neuman,** K. Sidney 1936- *WhoAmL 92*
**Neuman,** Linda 1948- *WhoAmP 91*
**Neuman,** Linda Kinney *WhoAmL 92, WhoMW 92*
**Neuman,** Maxine Darcy 1948- *WhoEnt 92*
**Neuman,** Michael R 1938- *AmMWSc 92*
**Neuman,** Peter Herbert 1938- *WhoAmL 92*
**Neuman,** Richard Stephen 1945- *AmMWSc 92*
**Neuman,** Robert Ballin 1920- *AmMWSc 92*
**Neuman,** Robert C, Jr 1938- *AmMWSc 92*
**Neuman,** Rosalind Joyce 1938- *AmMWSc 92*
**Neuman,** Shlomo Peter 1938- *AmMWSc 92*
**Neuman,** Ted 1946- *WhoAmP 91*
**Neumann,** A Conrad 1933- *AmMWSc 92*
**Neumann,** Alfred 1909- *IntWW 91*
**Neumann,** Arie Zodok 1961- *WhoFI 92*
**Neumann,** Bernhard Hermann 1909- *IntWW 91, Who 92*
**Neumann,** Bruce Eduard 1958- *WhoMW 92*
**Neumann,** Calvin Lee 1938- *AmMWSc 92*
**Neumann,** David Allan 1950- *WhoEnt 92*
**Neumann,** Fred William 1918- *AmMWSc 92*
**Neumann,** Frederick Lloyd 1949- *WhoMW 92*
**Neumann,** Frederick Loomis 1930- *WhoFI 92*
**Neumann,** Gerhard 1917- *AmMWSc 92*
**Neumann,** Heinz 1902-1937 *EncTR 91*
**Neumann,** Helmut Carl 1916- *AmMWSc 92*
**Neumann,** Henry Matthew 1924- *AmMWSc 92*
**Neumann,** Herman Ernest 1931- *WhoWest 92*
**Neumann,** Herschel 1930- *AmMWSc 92, WhoWest 92*
**Neumann,** Joachim Peter 1931- *AmMWSc 92*
**Neumann,** Marguerite 1914- *AmMWSc 92*
**Neumann,** Nancy Ruth 1948- *WhoWest 92*
**Neumann,** Norbert Paul 1931- *AmMWSc 92*
**Neumann,** Otto Colby 1936- *WhoAmP 91*
**Neumann,** Paul Gerhard 1911- *AmMWSc 92*
**Neumann,** Peter A. 1962- *WhoAmL 92*
**Neumann,** Peter G 1932- *AmMWSc 92*
**Neumann,** Peter Gabriel 1932- *WhoWest 92*
**Neumann,** Rita 1944- *WhoAmL 92*
**Neumann,** Robert 1897-1975 *LiExTwC*
**Neumann,** Robert Gerhard 1916- *IntWW 91, WhoAmP 91*
**Neumann,** Ronald D 1947- *AmMWSc 92*
**Neumann,** Roy Covert 1921- *WhoMW 92*
**Neumann,** Stephen Michael 1952- *AmMWSc 92*
**Neumann,** Steve Michael 1950- *WhoEnt 92*
**Neumann,** Vaclav 1920- *IntWW 91, NewAmDM*
**Neumann,** William 1934- *WhoMW 92*
**Neumark,** Frederick Allan 1942- *WhoMW 92*
**Neumark,** Gertrude Fanny 1927- *AmMWSc 92*
**Neumark,** Michael Harry 1945- *WhoAmL 92, WhoMW 92*
**Neumeier,** John 1942- *CurBio 91 [port], IntWW 91, WhoEnt 92*
**Neumeier,** Leander Anthony 1933- *AmMWSc 92*
**Neumeier,** Matthew Michael 1954- *WhoAmL 92, WhoMW 92*
**Neumeier,** Richard L. 1946- *WhoAmL 92*
**Neumeyer,** John L 1930- *AmMWSc 92*
**Neumeyer,** Peter *DrAPF 91*
**Neumeyer,** Peter 1929- *WrDr 92*
**Neumeyer,** Peter F 1929- *IntAu&W 91*
**Neumeyer,** Peter Florian 1929- *WhoWest 92*
**Neumiller,** Harry Jacob, Jr 1929- *AmMWSc 92, WhoMW 92*
**Neumoegen,** Berthold 1845-1895 *BiInAmS*
**Neuner,** George William 1943- *WhoAmL 92*
**Neuner,** Kirk 1954- *WhoAmL 92*
**Neunzig,** Herbert Henry 1927- *AmMWSc 92*
**Neupert,** Werner Martin 1931- *AmMWSc 92*
**Neurath,** Alexander Robert 1933- *AmMWSc 92*
**Neurath,** Hans 1909- *AmMWSc 92, IntWW 91*
**Neurath,** Konstantin, Baron von 1873-1956 *EncTR 91 [port]*
**Neureiter,** Norman Paul 1932- *AmMWSc 92*
**Neuringer,** Joseph Louis 1922- *AmMWSc 92*
**Neuringer,** Leo J 1928- *AmMWSc 92*
**Neuroth,** William C. *WhoRel 92*
**Neurrisse,** Andre 1916- *IntWW 91*
**Neus,** Daniel Duane 1966- *WhoFI 92*
**Neuschel,** Sherman K 1913- *AmMWSc 92*
**Neuse,** Eberhard Wilhelm 1925- *AmMWSc 92*
**Neuser,** Kenneth Joseph 1938- *WhoMW 92*
**Neushul,** Michael, Jr 1933- *AmMWSc 92*
**Neusiedler,** Hans 1508?-1563 *NewAmDM*
**Neusiedler,** Melchior 1531-1590 *NewAmDM*
**Neusner,** Jacob 1932- *WhoRel 92, WrDr 92*
**Neusom,** Thomas G. 1922- *WhoBlA 92*
**Neustadt,** Bernard Ray 1943- *AmMWSc 92*
**Neustadt,** Richard E 1919- *IntAu&W 91, WrDr 92*
**Neustadt,** Richard Elliott 1919- *IntWW 91*
**Neustadt,** Shirley Vivien Teresa Brittain *Who 92*
**Neustadter,** Siegfried Friedrich 1923- *AmMWSc 92*
**Neustatter,** Angela Lindesay 1943- *IntAu&W 91*
**Neutra,** Marian R 1938- *AmMWSc 92*
**Neutra,** Richard Josef 1892-1970 *DcTwDes, FacFETw*
**Neuts,** Marcel Fernand 1935- *AmMWSc 92, WhoWest 92*
**Neuvar,** Erwin W 1930- *AmMWSc 92*
**Neuville,** Thomas M 1950- *WhoAmP 91*

**Neuvo**, Yrjo A. 1943- *IntWW 91*
**Neuwirth**, Alan James 1943- *WhoAmL 92*
**Neuwirth**, Allan Charles 1956- *WhoEnt 92*
**Neuwirth**, Bebe *WhoEnt 92*
**Neuwirth**, Eric 1957- *WhoFI 92*
**Neuwirth**, Jerome H 1931- *AmMWSc 92*
**Neuwirth**, Lucien 1924- *IntWW 91*
**Neuwirth**, Maria 1944- *AmMWSc 92*
**Neuwirth**, Robert Samuel 1933- *AmMWSc 92*
**Neuzil**, Edward F 1930- *AmMWSc 92*
**Neuzil**, John Paul 1942- *AmMWSc 92*
**Neuzil**, Richard William 1924- *AmMWSc 92*
**Neva**, Franklin Allen 1922- *AmMWSc 92*
**Nevada**, Emma 1859-1940 *NewAmDM*
**Nevada**, Mignon 1886-1971 *NewAmDM*
**Nevai**, Lucia *DrAPF 91*
**Nevai**, Paul 1948- *AmMWSc 92*
**Nevalainen**, David Eric 1944- *AmMWSc 92*
**Nevanlinna**, Eero Olavi 1948- *IntWW 91*
**Nevarez**, Hector O. 1940- *WhoHisp 92*
**Nevarez**, Juan A. 1951- *WhoHisp 92*
**Nevarez**, Miguel A. 1937- *WhoHisp 92*
**Nevas**, Alan Harris 1928- *WhoAmL 92*
**Neve**, David Lewis 1920- *Who 92*
**Neve**, Richard Anthony 1923- *AmMWSc 92*
**Neveloff**, Jay A. 1950- *WhoAmL 92*
**Nevels**, Robert Dudley 1946- *AmMWSc 92*
**Nevels**, Zebedee James 1926-1988 *WhoBlA 92N*
**Nevelson**, Louise 1900-1988 *FacFETw, RComAH*
**Neverson**, Norman Carl 1943- *WhoAmP 91*
**Neves**, Richard Joseph *AmMWSc 92*
**Neves-Perman**, Maria 1937- *WhoHisp 92*
**Neveu**, Darwin D 1933- *AmMWSc 92*
**Neveu**, Maurice C 1929- *AmMWSc 92*
**Neveu**, Raymond Philip 1938- *WhoFI 92*
**Nevid**, Jeffrey Steven *AmMWSc 92*
**Nevile**, Henry Nicholas 1920- *Who 92*
**Nevill** *Who 92*
**Nevill**, Bernard Richard 1934- *Who 92*
**Nevill**, Cosmo Alexander Richard 1907- *Who 92*
**Nevill**, Gale E, Jr 1933- *AmMWSc 92*
**Nevill**, William Albert 1929- *AmMWSc 92*
**Neville** *Who 92*
**Neville**, Aaron *WhoEnt 92*
**Neville**, Adam Matthew 1923- *Who 92*
**Neville**, Alexander Munro 1935- *Who 92*
**Neville**, Art *WhoEnt 92*
**Neville**, Charles *WhoEnt 92*
**Neville**, Cyril *WhoEnt 92*
**Neville**, David Michael, Jr *AmMWSc 92*
**Neville**, Donald Edward 1936- *AmMWSc 92*
**Neville**, Emily Cheney 1919- *WrDr 92*
**Neville**, Graham 1933- *Who 92*
**Neville**, Gwen Kennedy 1938- *ConAu 35NR*
**Neville**, James Morton 1939- *WhoAmL 92, WhoFI 92*
**Neville**, James Ryan 1925- *AmMWSc 92*
**Neville**, Janice Nelson 1930- *AmMWSc 92*
**Neville**, John 1925- *IntWW 91, Who 92, WhoEnt 92*
**Neville**, John Oliver 1929- *Who 92*
**Neville**, Joseph P 1934- *WhoIns 92*
**Neville**, Kris 1925-1980 *TwCSFW 91*
**Neville**, Margaret Cobb 1934- *AmMWSc 92*
**Neville**, Mary Jo 1957- *WhoAmP 91*
**Neville**, Munro *Who 92*
**Neville**, Patrick 1932- *Who 92*
**Neville**, Phoebe 1941- *WhoEnt 92*
**Neville**, Richard 1921- *Who 92*
**Neville**, Robert C. 1939- *WrDr 92*
**Neville**, Robert Cummings 1939- *IntAu&W 91*
**Neville**, Roger Albert Gartside 1931- *Who 92*
**Neville**, Royce Robert 1914- *Who 92*
**Neville**, Susan *DrAPF 91*
**Neville**, Tam Lin *DrAPF 91*
**Neville**, Walter Edward, Jr 1924- *AmMWSc 92*
**Neville**, William E 1919- *AmMWSc 92*
**Neville-Jones**, Pauline 1939- *Who 92*
**Neville-Rolfe**, Marianne Teresa 1944- *Who 92*
**Nevin**, Arthur 1871-1943 *NewAmDM*
**Nevin**, Cindy Creighton 1957- *WhoAmP 91*
**Nevin**, Crocker 1923- *WhoWest 92*
**Nevin**, David 1927- *TwCWW 91, WrDr 92*
**Nevin**, David Wright 1947- *WhoWest 92*
**Nevin**, Edward Thomas 1925- *WrDr 92*
**Nevin**, Ethelbert 1862-1901 *NewAmDM*
**Nevin**, Evelyn C. 1910- *WrDr 92*
**Nevin**, James B *ScFEYrs*
**Nevin**, John Joseph 1927- *IntWW 91*
**Nevin**, John Robert 1943- *WhoMW 92*
**Nevin**, Leonard Verne 1943- *WhoAmP 91*
**Nevin**, Pete 1952- *TwCPaSc*
**Nevin**, Richard 1916- *Who 92*
**Nevin**, Robert Stephen 1933- *AmMWSc 92*
**Nevins**, Allan 1890-1971 *BenetAL 91, FacFETw*
**Nevins**, Arthur Gerard, Jr. 1948- *WhoAmL 92*
**Nevins**, Arthur James 1937- *AmMWSc 92*
**Nevins**, Claudette *WhoEnt 92*
**Nevins**, Donald James 1937- *AmMWSc 92*
**Nevins**, Francis M, Jr 1943- *IntAu&W 91, WrDr 92*
**Nevins**, John J. 1932- *WhoRel 92*
**Nevins**, John Mitchell 1954- *WhoAmL 92*
**Nevins**, Richard, Jr. 1947- *WhoFI 92*
**Nevins**, Sheila 1939- *WhoEnt 92*
**Nevins**, William McCay 1948- *AmMWSc 92*
**Nevinson**, Christopher R.W. 1889-1946 *TwCPaSc*
**Nevis**, Arnold Hastings 1931- *AmMWSc 92*
**Nevison**, Christopher H 1945- *AmMWSc 92*
**Nevitt**, George Allen 1940- *WhoIns 92*
**Nevitt**, Michael Vogt 1923- *AmMWSc 92*
**Nevitt**, Thomas D 1925- *AmMWSc 92*
**Nevius**, Timothy Alfred 1952- *AmMWSc 92*
**Nevling**, Lorin Ives, Jr 1930- *AmMWSc 92*
**Nevo**, Eviatar 1929- *AmMWSc 92*
**Nevo**, Ruth 1924- *IntWW 91*
**Nevola**, Paul Thomas 1942- *WhoAmP 91*
**New Kids on the Block** *News 91*
**New Orleans Rhythm Kings** *NewAmDM*
**New York Dolls** *NewAmDM*
**New**, Anthony 1924- *WrDr 92*
**New**, Anthony Sherwood Brooks 1924- *IntAu&W 91*
**New**, John Coy, Jr 1948- *AmMWSc 92*
**New**, Kenneth Dean 1938- *WhoAmP 91*
**New**, Laurence 1932- *Who 92*
**New**, Lori Lynne 1964- *WhoEnt 92*
**New**, Maria Iandolo 1928- *AmMWSc 92*
**New**, Rosetta Holbrock 1921- *WhoMW 92*
**New Westminster**, Archbishop of 1927- *Who 92*
**New Zealand**, Primate And Archbishop of 1934- *Who 92*
**Newacheck**, David John 1953- *WhoAmL 92, WhoWest 92*
**Newall** *Who 92*
**Newall**, Baron 1930- *Who 92*
**Newall**, J. E. *IntWW 91*
**Newall**, James Edward Malcolm 1935- *WhoFI 92, WhoWest 92*
**Newall**, Paul Henry 1934- *Who 92*
**Newall**, Robert Henry 1924- *WhoEnt 92*
**Newall**, Venetia June 1935- *IntAu&W 91, WrDr 92*
**Newark**, Archdeacon of *Who 92*
**Neway**, Julie Marlaine 1954- *WhoFI 92*
**Newball**, Harold Harcourt 1942- *AmMWSc 92*
**Newbegin**, Robert d1991 *NewYTBS 91*
**Newberg**, Dorothy Beck 1919- *WhoWest 92*
**Newberg**, Ellen Joyce 1941- *WhoWest 92*
**Newberg**, Howard Scott 1961- *WhoWest 92*
**Newberg**, William Charles 1910- *WhoFI 92, WhoWest 92*
**Newberger**, Arthur Ruben 1939- *WhoEnt 92*
**Newberger**, Barry Stephen 1945- *AmMWSc 92*
**Newberger**, Edward 1940- *AmMWSc 92*
**Newberger**, Mark 1942- *AmMWSc 92*
**Newberger**, Stuart Marshall 1938- *AmMWSc 92*
**Newbern**, Captolia Dent 1902- *WhoBlA 92*
**Newbern**, Walter P. 1907- *WhoBlA 92*
**Newberne**, James Wilson 1923- *AmMWSc 92*
**Newberne**, Paul M 1920- *AmMWSc 92*
**Newberry**, Alan John Hesson 1937- *WhoWest 92*
**Newberry**, Andrew Todd 1935- *AmMWSc 92*
**Newberry**, Brian Michael 1963- *WhoMW 92*
**Newberry**, Cedric Charles 1953- *WhoBlA 92*
**Newberry**, Conrad Floyde 1931- *WhoWest 92*
**Newberry**, Elizabeth Carter 1921- *WhoFI 92*
**Newberry**, J. Stuart 1949- *WhoAmL 92*
**Newberry**, James Henry, Jr. 1956- *WhoAmL 92*
**Newberry**, John Coverdale 1934- *TwCPaSc*
**Newberry**, John Strong 1822-1892 *BilnAmS*
**Newberry**, Raymond Scudamore 1935- *Who 92*
**Newberry**, Richard Alan 1954- *WhoFI 92*
**Newberry**, Trudell McClelland 1939- *WhoBlA 92*
**Newberry**, Walter Loomis 1804-1868 *BenetAL 91*
**Newberry**, William Marcus 1938- *AmMWSc 92*
**Newbert**, Russell Anderson 1937- *WhoRel 92*
**Newbery**, A Chris 1923- *AmMWSc 92*
**Newbery**, Charles Bruce *IntMPA 92*
**Newbery**, David Michael Garrood 1943- *IntWW 91, Who 92*
**Newbery**, Francis 1855-1946 *TwCPaSc*
**Newbery**, John 1713-1767 *BenetAL 91, BlkwCEP, FacFETw*
**Newbery**, Randi Friedman 1952- *WhoAmL 92*
**Newbigging**, David Kennedy 1934- *IntWW 91, Who 92*
**Newbigin**, Lesslie 1909- *DcEcMov, IntWW 91, Who 92*
**Newbill**, Sallie Puller 1940- *WhoAmP 91*
**Newblatt**, Stewart Albert 1927- *WhoAmL 92*
**Newbold**, Charles Demoree 1909- *Who 92*
**Newbold**, John Lowe 1935- *WhoFI 92*
**Newbold**, Nathan Carter 1871-1957 *DcNCBi 4*
**Newbold**, Robert Thomas 1920- *WhoBlA 92*
**Newbolt**, William Barlow 1934- *AmMWSc 92*
**Newborg**, Gerald Gordon 1942- *WhoMW 92*
**Newborg**, Michael Foxx 1948- *AmMWSc 92*
**Newborn**, Ernest *WhoRel 92*
**Newborn**, Jud 1952- *IntAu&W 91*
**Newborn**, Monroe M 1938- *AmMWSc 92*
**Newborn**, Odie Vernon, Jr. 1947- *WhoBlA 92*
**Newborn**, Phineas, Jr. 1931-1989 *NewAmDM*
**Newborn**, Phineas Lajette, Jr. 1931- *WhoBlA 92*
**Newborough**, Baron 1917- *Who 92*
**Newborough**, Bruce A. 1957- *WhoAmL 92*
**Newbould**, Mary Benet 1955- *WhoAmP 91*
**Newbould**, Peter Edmond 1954- *WhoAmP 91*
**Newbound**, Kenneth Bateman *AmMWSc 92*
**Newbrook**, Peter 1920- *IntMPA 92*
**Newbrun**, Ernest 1932- *AmMWSc 92, WhoWest 92*
**Newburg**, Andre W. G. 1928- *WhoAmL 92*
**Newburg**, Edward A 1929- *AmMWSc 92*
**Newburger**, Jerold 1923- *AmMWSc 92*
**Newburger**, May W *WhoAmP 91*
**Newburgh**, Earl of 1942- *Who 92*
**Newburgh**, Robert Warren 1922- *AmMWSc 92*
**Newburgh**, Ronald Gerald 1926- *AmMWSc 92*
**Newburn**, David *WhoAmP 91*
**Newburn**, Ray Leon, Jr 1933- *AmMWSc 92*
**Newbury**, Dale Elwood 1947- *AmMWSc 92*
**Newbury**, Robert W 1939- *AmMWSc 92*
**Newby**, Eric 1919- *IntWW 91, Who 92, WrDr 92*
**Newby**, Frank Armon, Jr 1932- *AmMWSc 92*
**Newby**, Gabriel d1735 *DcNCBi 4*
**Newby**, Gene *WhoAmP 91*
**Newby**, Howard 1918- *IntAu&W 91, IntWW 91*
**Newby**, Howard Joseph 1947- *Who 92*
**Newby**, James Richard 1949- *WhoMW 92, WhoRel 92*
**Newby**, Jill Jeanine 1960- *WhoWest 92*
**Newby**, John M. *WhoRel 92*
**Newby**, John R 1923- *AmMWSc 92*
**Newby**, Neal D 1899- *AmMWSc 92*
**Newby**, Neal Dow, Jr 1926- *AmMWSc 92*
**Newby**, Olin Carris 1939- *WhoAmP 91*
**Newby**, P. H. 1918- *ConNov 91, RfGEnL 91, WrDr 92*
**Newby**, Percy Howard 1918- *Who 92*
**Newby**, Richard L. *DrAPF 91*
**Newby**, Richard Mark 1953- *Who 92*
**Newby**, Sarah Clark 1936- *WhoRel 92*
**Newby**, Thomas Cautley 1798?-1882 *DcLB 106*
**Newby**, Thomas Paul 1958- *WhoMW 92*
**Newby**, William Edward 1923- *AmMWSc 92*
**Newcastle**, Bishop of 1929- *Who 92*
**Newcastle**, Duchess of *RfGEnL 91*
**Newcastle**, Provost of *Who 92*
**Newcastle**, Margaret, Duchess Of 1624-1674 *ScFEYrs*
**Newcastle NSW**, Bishop of 1927- *Who 92*
**Newcom**, Charles W. 1948- *WhoAmL 92*
**Newcom**, James E. 1907- *IntMPA 92*
**Newcomb**, Bruce 1940- *WhoAmP 91*
**Newcomb**, Danforth 1943- *WhoAmL 92*
**Newcomb**, Douglas David 1957- *WhoRel 92*
**Newcomb**, Eldon Henry 1919- *AmMWSc 92*
**Newcomb**, Harvey Russell 1916- *AmMWSc 92*
**Newcomb**, James Edward 1934- *WhoAmP 91*
**Newcomb**, Martin 1946- *AmMWSc 92*
**Newcomb**, Robert Lewis 1932- *AmMWSc 92*
**Newcomb**, Robert Wayne 1933- *AmMWSc 92*
**Newcomb**, Russell W *WhoAmP 91*
**Newcomb**, Simon 1835-1909 *BilnAmS, ScFEYrs*
**Newcomb**, Thomas F 1927- *AmMWSc 92*
**Newcomb**, Wesley 1808-1892 *BilnAmS*
**Newcomb**, William A 1927- *AmMWSc 92*
**Newcombe**, David S 1929- *AmMWSc 92*
**Newcombe**, Edward Jeffrey 1944- *WhoAmP 91*
**Newcombe**, George Michael 1947- *WhoAmL 92*
**Newcombe**, Howard Borden 1914- *AmMWSc 92*
**Newcombe**, John David 1944- *IntWW 91*
**Newcome**, Marshall Millar 1926- *AmMWSc 92*
**Newcomer**, Clarence Charles 1923- *WhoAmL 92*
**Newcomer**, James W. 1912- *WrDr 92*
**Newcomer**, James William 1912- *IntAu&W 91*
**Newcomer**, Wilbur Stanley 1919- *AmMWSc 92*
**Newdegate** *Who 92*
**Newe**, Gerard Benedict *Who 92N*
**Newell**, Allen 1927- *AmMWSc 92*
**Newell**, Arlo Frederic 1926- *WhoFI 92, WhoRel 92*
**Newell**, Benjamin C 1910- *WhoAmP 91*
**Newell**, Byron Bruce, Jr. 1932- *WhoRel 92*
**Newell**, Castle Skip, III 1940- *WhoWest 92*
**Newell**, Christopher William Paul 1950- *Who 92*
**Newell**, Crosby *IntAu&W 91X, WrDr 92*
**Newell**, Darrell E 1926- *AmMWSc 92*
**Newell**, David Alexander, Jr. 1938- *WhoEnt 92*
**Newell**, David R 1946- *WhoAmP 91*
**Newell**, Frank William 1916- *AmMWSc 92*
**Newell**, Gordon Frank 1925- *AmMWSc 92*
**Newell**, Gordon Wilfred 1921- *AmMWSc 92*
**Newell**, Gregory John 1949- *WhoAmP 91*
**Newell**, James Robert 1957- *WhoFI 92*
**Newell**, Jimmy Randall 1941- *WhoFI 92*
**Newell**, Jon Albert 1941- *AmMWSc 92*
**Newell**, Jonathan Clark 1943- *AmMWSc 92*
**Newell**, Kathleen 1922- *AmMWSc 92*
**Newell**, Marjorie Pauline *AmMWSc 92*
**Newell**, Matthias Gregory 1927- *WhoBlA 92*
**Newell**, Michael Stephen 1949- *WhoWest 92*
**Newell**, Mike 1942- *IntMPA 92*
**Newell**, Nanette 1951- *AmMWSc 92*
**Newell**, Norman Dennis 1909- *AmMWSc 92, IntWW 91*
**Newell**, Phillip Keith *Who 92*
**Newell**, Reginald Edward 1931- *AmMWSc 92*
**Newell**, Richard Nelson 1932- *WhoFI 92*
**Newell**, Richard S. 1933- *ConAu 134*
**Newell**, Robert Henry 1836-1901 *BenetAL 91*
**Newell**, Robert Paul 1936- *WhoEnt 92*
**Newell**, Virginia K. *WhoBlA 92*
**Newell**, William 1938- *WhoBlA 92*
**Newell**, William H. 1922- *WrDr 92*
**Newell**, William Henry 1943- *WhoMW 92*
**Newell**, William T. 1929- *WrDr 92*
**Newell**, William Thurlo 1943- *WhoWest 92*
**Newell-Morris**, Laura 1933- *AmMWSc 92*
**Newens**, Stanley 1930- *Who 92*
**Newey**, Herbert Alfred 1916- *AmMWSc 92*
**Newey**, John Henry Richard 1923- *Who 92*
**Newey**, Paul Davis 1914- *WhoAmL 92*
**Newey**, Sidney Brian 1937- *Who 92*
**Newfang**, Oscar 1875-1943 *AmPeW*
**Newfoundland Central**, Bishop of 1935- *Who 92*
**Newfoundland Eastern & Labrador**, Bishop 1929- *Who 92*
**Newfoundland Western**, Archbishop of 1932- *Who 92*
**Newhall**, Beaumont 1908- *WrDr 92*
**Newhall**, Charles Watson, III 1944- *WhoFI 92*
**Newhall**, David, III 1937- *WhoAmP 91*
**Newhall**, Frederick Augustus, Jr. 1918- *WhoFI 92*
**Newhall**, Patricia 1927- *WhoEnt 92*
**Newhart**, Bob *LesBEnT 92*
**Newhart**, Bob 1929- *ConTFT 9, IntMPA 92, WhoEnt 92, WhoWest 92*
**Newhart**, M Joan *AmMWSc 92*

**Newhart**, Robert Lincoln, II 1948- WhoEnt 92
**Newhauser**, Judy Ann 1965- WhoMW 92
**Newhoff**, Stanley Neal 1944- WhoWest 92
**Newhouse**, Albert 1914- AmMWSc 92
**Newhouse**, Edward 1911- BenetAL 91
**Newhouse**, Edward, Mrs. 1917- WhoEnt 92
**Newhouse**, Frederick Vaughn 1948- BlkOlyM
**Newhouse**, Gerald Francis 1940- WhoAmP 91
**Newhouse**, Irving R 1920- WhoAmP 91
**Newhouse**, Joseph Paul 1942- AmMWSc 92, WhoFI 92
**Newhouse**, Keith N 1924- AmMWSc 92
**Newhouse**, Kevin Thomas 1955- WhoMW 92
**Newhouse**, Richard H. 1924- WhoBlA 92
**Newhouse**, Richard H, Jr 1924- WhoAmP 91
**Newhouse**, Robert F. 1950- WhoBlA 92
**Newhouse**, Robert John Darrell 1911- Who 92
**Newhouse**, Russell C 1906- AmMWSc 92
**Newhouse**, S. I., Jr. IntWW 91
**Newhouse**, Samuel 1895-1979 FacFETw
**Newhouse**, Shelby Ziel 1926- WhoEnt 92
**Newhouse**, Verne Frederic 1930- AmMWSc 92
**Newhouse**, Vernon Leopold 1928- AmMWSc 92
**Newill**, James Wagner 1934- WhoFI 92, WhoMW 92
**Newill**, Robert 1921- WrDr 92
**Newing**, John Frederick 1940- Who 92
**Newing**, Kenneth Albert 1923- Who 92
**Newington**, Michael John 1932- Who 92
**Newinski**, Dennis R 1944- WhoAmP 91
**Newirth**, Terry L 1945- AmMWSc 92
**Newis**, Kenneth 1916- Who 92
**Newitt**, Edward James 1927- AmMWSc 92
**Newitt**, John Garwood, Jr. 1941- WhoAmL 92, WhoFI 92
**Newkirk**, C C 1878-1938 ScFEYrs
**Newkirk**, Frank, Jr 1957- WhoAmP 91
**Newkirk**, Gary Francis 1946- AmMWSc 92
**Newkirk**, George L 1941- WhoAmP 91
**Newkirk**, Glen Alton 1931- WhoMW 92
**Newkirk**, Gordon Allen, Jr 1928- AmMWSc 92
**Newkirk**, Gwendolyn WhoBlA 92
**Newkirk**, Herbert William 1928- AmMWSc 92
**Newkirk**, Inez Doris 1921- WhoBlA 92
**Newkirk**, John Burt 1920- AmMWSc 92
**Newkirk**, Lester Leroy 1920- AmMWSc 92
**Newkirk**, Newton ScFEYrs
**Newkirk**, Queenie Hortense WhoBlA 92
**Newkirk**, Raymond Leslie 1944- WhoFI 92, WhoWest 92
**Newkirk**, Thomas H. 1929- WhoBlA 92
**Newkome**, George Richard 1938- AmMWSc 92
**Newland**, David Edward 1936- Who 92
**Newland**, Gordon Clay 1927- AmMWSc 92
**Newland**, Herman William 1917- AmMWSc 92
**Newland**, John 1917- IntMPA 92
**Newland**, Larry J. 1935- WhoEnt 92
**Newland**, Leo Winburne 1940- AmMWSc 92
**Newland**, Robert Joe 1946- AmMWSc 92
**Newland**, Ruth Laura 1949- WhoWest 92
**Newland**, William Calhoun 1860-1938 DcNCBi 4
**Newland**, Zachary Jonas 1954- WhoBlA 92
**Newlands**, Michael John 1931- AmMWSc 92
**Newlands**, Willy 1934- IntAu&W 91
**Newler**, Jerome Marc 1947- WhoFI 92
**Newley**, Anthony 1931- IntMPA 92, WhoEnt 92
**Newley**, Edward Frank 1913- Who 92
**Newley**, George Anthony 1931- Who 92
**Newlin**, Charles Fremont 1953- WhoAmL 92
**Newlin**, Charles W 1924- AmMWSc 92
**Newlin**, Douglas Randal 1940- WhoWest 92
**Newlin**, Glenn Stutzman 1962- WhoMW 92
**Newlin**, Jeffrey John 1951- WhoRel 92
**Newlin**, John 1776-1867 DcNCBi 4
**Newlin**, Julye Gail 1967- WhoEnt 92
**Newlin**, Lyman Wilbur 1910- WhoFI 92
**Newlin**, Margaret Rudd 1925- WrDr 92
**Newlin**, Michael H 1926- WhoAmP 91
**Newlin**, Owen Jay 1928- AmMWSc 92
**Newlin**, Philip Blaine 1923- AmMWSc 92
**Newlin**, Rufus K. WhoBlA 92
**Newlin**, William Rankin 1940- WhoAmL 92
**Newling**, John 1952- TwCPaSc
**Newlove**, John 1938- BenetAL 91, ConPo 91, IntAu&W 91, WrDr 92
**Newman**, Abraham 1907- TwCPaSc
**Newman**, Albert Henry 1852-1933 RelLAm 91
**Newman**, Alfred 1900-1970 NewAmDM
**Newman**, Alfred S. 1940- IntMPA 92
**Newman**, Andrea 1938- IntAu&W 91, WrDr 92
**Newman**, Andrew 1938- WhoAmL 92
**Newman**, Andrew Edison 1944- WhoFI 92, WhoMW 92
**Newman**, Anthony 1941- NewAmDM
**Newman**, Arnold 1918- FacFETw
**Newman**, Aubrey N 1927- IntAu&W 91, WrDr 92
**Newman**, Avis 1946- TwCPaSc
**Newman**, B G 1926- AmMWSc 92
**Newman**, Barbara IntAu&W 91X
**Newman**, Barbara Pollock 1939- WhoEnt 92
**Newman**, Barnett 1905-1971 FacFETw
**Newman**, Barry 1938- IntMPA 92
**Newman**, Barry Foster 1938- WhoEnt 92
**Newman**, Barry Hilton 1926- Who 92
**Newman**, Barry Marc 1951- WhoMW 92
**Newman**, Bernard 1913- AmMWSc 92
**Newman**, Bertha L 1926- AmMWSc 92
**Newman**, Bobby Gene 1926- WhoAmP 91
**Newman**, Bruce Allen 1943- WhoAmP 91
**Newman**, Bruce Lee 1960- WhoFI 92
**Newman**, C. J. 1935- ConNov 91, WrDr 92
**Newman**, Carol L. 1949- WhoAmL 92
**Newman**, Charles 1938- ConNov 91, WrDr 92
**Newman**, Charles Andrew 1949- WhoAmL 92, WhoMW 92
**Newman**, Charles Forrest 1937- WhoAmL 92
**Newman**, Charles Michael 1946- AmMWSc 92
**Newman**, Christopher Joseph 1952- WhoEnt 92
**Newman**, Clarence Benton 1921- WhoAmP 91
**Newman**, Clarence Walter 1932- AmMWSc 92
**Newman**, Cliff 1942- WhoAmP 91
**Newman**, Colleen A. 1942- WhoBlA 92
**Newman**, Constance Berry 1935- WhoBlA 92
**Newman**, Cynthia 1960- WhoWest 92
**Newman**, Cynthia Stair 1922- WhoAmP 91
**Newman**, Cyril Wilfred Francis 1937- Who 92
**Newman**, Daisy WrDr 92
**Newman**, Daisy 1904- IntAu&W 91
**Newman**, Daniel F WhoAmP 91
**Newman**, Darrell Francis 1940- AmMWSc 92
**Newman**, David 1937- IntMPA 92
**Newman**, David, Jr. 1932- WhoBlA 92
**Newman**, David Bruce, Jr 1948- AmMWSc 92
**Newman**, David Edward 1947- AmMWSc 92
**Newman**, David S 1936- AmMWSc 92
**Newman**, David William 1933- AmMWSc 92
**Newman**, Della M 1932- WhoAmP 91
**Newman**, Denis 1930- WhoFI 92
**Newman**, Dennis Nathan 1946- WhoAmL 92
**Newman**, Donald John 1939- WhoMW 92
**Newman**, Donna Ann 1957- WhoMW 92
**Newman**, Dorothy G 1917- WhoAmP 91
**Newman**, Douglas Frederick 1953- WhoFI 92
**Newman**, Edgar Leon 1939- WhoWest 92
**Newman**, Edward 1953- Who 92
**Newman**, Edwin LesBEnT 92 [port]
**Newman**, Edwin 1919- IntMPA 92, WrDr 92
**Newman**, Edwin Harold 1919- IntAu&W 91, IntWW 91
**Newman**, Eric Allan 1950- AmMWSc 92
**Newman**, Ernest 1868-1959 ScFEYrs
**Newman**, Ernest Wilbur 1928- WhoBlA 92
**Newman**, Eugene 1930- AmMWSc 92
**Newman**, Ezra 1929- AmMWSc 92
**Newman**, Felice DrAPF 91
**Newman**, Francis 1963- Who 92
**Newman**, Franklin Scott 1931- AmMWSc 92
**Newman**, Fred C 1931- WhoIns 92
**Newman**, Frederick Edward Fry 1916- Who 92
**Newman**, Fredric Samuel 1945- WhoAmL 92
**Newman**, G F 1945- IntAu&W 91, WrDr 92
**Newman**, Gary Len 1947- WhoRel 92
**Newman**, Geary Thomas 1953- WhoEnt 92
**Newman**, Geoffrey 1947- Who 92
**Newman**, Geoffrey W. 1946- WhoBlA 92
**Newman**, George Allen 1941- AmMWSc 92
**Newman**, George Michael 1941- Who 92
**Newman**, Gerald 1931- WhoFI 92
**Newman**, Gerald 1945- TwCPaSc
**Newman**, Gordon Harold 1933- WhoAmL 92, WhoFI 92
**Newman**, Graham Reginald 1924- Who 92
**Newman**, Gwill Linderme 1932- WhoMW 92
**Newman**, Harold Tolman 1916- WhoAmP 91
**Newman**, Harry Alan 1956- WhoFI 92
**Newman**, Harry Alexander 1928- WhoRel 92
**Newman**, Herbert S. 1934- WhoFI 92
**Newman**, Howard Abraham Ira 1929- AmMWSc 92
**Newman**, J Nicholas 1935- AmMWSc 92
**Newman**, J. Robert 1928- WhoWest 92
**Newman**, Jack 1902- Who 92
**Newman**, Jack Huff 1929- AmMWSc 92
**Newman**, James 1932- WhoWest 92
**Newman**, James Charles, Jr 1942- AmMWSc 92
**Newman**, James Edward 1920- AmMWSc 92
**Newman**, James Michael 1946- WhoAmL 92
**Newman**, James Michael 1949- WhoFI 92
**Newman**, James Roy 1948- WhoFI 92
**Newman**, Jan Bristow 1951- WhoWest 92
**Newman**, Jane 1947- WhoFI 92
**Newman**, Jeanne Louise 1946- WhoFI 92
**Newman**, Jeffrey Brian 1954- WhoAmL 92
**Newman**, Jeffrey K. 1951- WhoEnt 92
**Newman**, Jerrold Mitchell 1954- WhoFI 92
**Newman**, Jewel J WhoAmP 91
**Newman**, Joe 1922- NewAmDM
**Newman**, Joel DrAPF 91
**Newman**, John Alexander 1932- AmMWSc 92
**Newman**, John B 1938- AmMWSc 92
**Newman**, John Henry 1801-1890 RfGEnL 91
**Newman**, John Hughes 1945- AmMWSc 92
**Newman**, John Joseph 1936- AmMWSc 92
**Newman**, John Kevin 1928- WhoMW 92
**Newman**, John Scott 1938- AmMWSc 92
**Newman**, John Sylvester, Jr. 1963- WhoBlA 92
**Newman**, Jon O WhoAmP 91
**Newman**, Jon O. 1932- WhoAmL 92
**Newman**, JoNel 1961- WhoAmL 92
**Newman**, Joseph H. 1928- WhoMW 92
**Newman**, Joseph Herbert 1925- AmMWSc 92, WhoFI 92
**Newman**, Joseph James 1933- WhoFI 92
**Newman**, Joseph M. 1909- IntMPA 92
**Newman**, Julian M 1927- WhoIns 92
**Newman**, Karl Max 1919- Who 92
**Newman**, Karl Robert 1931- AmMWSc 92
**Newman**, Katharine Dealy 1911- WhoWest 92
**Newman**, Kathryn Bereano d1991 NewYTBS 91
**Newman**, Kenneth IntWW 91
**Newman**, Kenneth 1926- Who 92
**Newman**, Kenneth J. 1944- WhoBlA 92
**Newman**, Kenneth Wilfred AmMWSc 92
**Newman**, Kenya Maria 1963- WhoBlA 92
**Newman**, L. Michael 1937- WhoMW 92
**Newman**, Laraine 1952- IntMPA 92
**Newman**, Lawrence 1931- WhoAmL 92
**Newman**, Lawrence Walker 1935- WhoAmL 92, WhoFI 92
**Newman**, LeGrand 1940- WhoBlA 92
**Newman**, Leonard 1931- AmMWSc 92
**Newman**, Leonard Jay 1927- WhoFI 92
**Newman**, Leslea DrAPF 91
**Newman**, Leslea 1955- IntAu&W 91
**Newman**, Leslie DrAPF 91
**Newman**, Lester Joseph 1933- AmMWSc 92
**Newman**, Linnaea Rose 1953- WhoMW 92
**Newman**, Lloyd Norton 1931- WhoFI 92
**Newman**, Lois Mae 1942- WhoWest 92
**Newman**, Lotte Therese 1929- Who 92
**Newman**, Louis Benjamin AmMWSc 92, WhoMW 92
**Newman**, M M 1909- AmMWSc 92
**Newman**, M. W. 1917- WhoMW 92
**Newman**, Malcolm 1946- Who 92
**Newman**, Marc Alan 1955- WhoWest 92
**Newman**, Margaret IntAu&W 91X, WrDr 92
**Newman**, Mark M 1935- WhoAmP 91
**Newman**, Max WhoAmP 91
**Newman**, Melvin Micklin 1921- AmMWSc 92
**Newman**, Melvin Spencer 1908- AmMWSc 92, IntWW 91
**Newman**, Michael Charles 1951- AmMWSc 92
**Newman**, Michael J 1948- AmMWSc 92
**Newman**, Michael Rodney 1945- WhoAmL 92, WhoWest 92
**Newman**, Miller Maurice 1941- WhoBlA 92
**Newman**, Morris 1924- AmMWSc 92
**Newman**, Murray Arthur 1924- AmMWSc 92
**Newman**, Nancy Marilyn 1941- WhoWest 92
**Newman**, Nancy Noziska 1950- WhoFI 92
**Newman**, Nanette IntWW 91
**Newman**, Nanette 1934- IntMPA 92
**Newman**, Nanette 1939- Who 92
**Newman**, Nathaniel 1942- WhoBlA 92
**Newman**, Nicholas C. 1939- WhoAmL 92
**Newman**, Norman 1939- AmMWSc 92
**Newman**, Norman 1952- WhoAmL 92
**Newman**, Oscar 1935- WrDr 92
**Newman**, P.B. DrAPF 91
**Newman**, P. B. 1919- WrDr 92
**Newman**, Paul 1925- FacFETw [port], IntMPA 92, IntWW 91, Who 92, WhoEnt 92
**Newman**, Paul 1941- WhoAmL 92
**Newman**, Paul Dean 1938- WhoBlA 92
**Newman**, Paul Harold 1933- AmMWSc 92
**Newman**, Pauline WhoAmP 91
**Newman**, Pauline 1927- AmMWSc 92, WhoAmL 92
**Newman**, Peter 1929- WrDr 92
**Newman**, Peter C. 1929- IntWW 91
**Newman**, Peter Charles 1929- IntAu&W 91
**Newman**, Peter Ross 1952- WhoEnt 92
**Newman**, Philip Harker 1911- Who 92
**Newman**, Philip Robert 1942- WhoMW 92
**Newman**, Phyllis 1933- ConAu 134
**Newman**, R W 1914- AmMWSc 92
**Newman**, Randy 1943- ConTFT 9, WhoEnt 92
**Newman**, Randy 1945- IntMPA 92
**Newman**, Rebecca DrAPF 91
**Newman**, Richard Holt 1932- AmMWSc 92
**Newman**, Robert Alwin 1948- AmMWSc 92
**Newman**, Robert Chapman 1941- WhoRel 92
**Newman**, Robert Douglas 1961- WhoFI 92
**Newman**, Robert Weidenthal 1914- AmMWSc 92
**Newman**, Roger 1925- AmMWSc 92
**Newman**, Rogers J 1926- AmMWSc 92
**Newman**, Rosalind 1946- WhoEnt 92
**Newman**, Roy Thomas 1936- Who 92
**Newman**, Samuel 1938- WhoFI 92
**Newman**, Samuel Mark 1957- WhoEnt 92
**Newman**, Samuel Tyler 1964- WhoRel 92
**Newman**, Sandy Kay 1951- WhoRel 92
**Newman**, Sarah Winans 1941- AmMWSc 92
**Newman**, Scott David 1947- WhoAmL 92
**Newman**, Seraine Dianne 1942- WhoEnt 92
**Newman**, Seymour 1922- AmMWSc 92, WhoMW 92
**Newman**, Sharan 1949- WrDr 92
**Newman**, Sharon Ann 1952- WhoEnt 92
**Newman**, Simon Louis 1947- AmMWSc 92
**Newman**, Simon M 1906- AmMWSc 92
**Newman**, Sol DrAPF 91
**Newman**, Stephen Alexander 1938- AmMWSc 92
**Newman**, Stephen Michael 1945- WhoAmL 92
**Newman**, Stephen Scott 1964- WhoFI 92
**Newman**, Steven Barry 1952- AmMWSc 92
**Newman**, Steven H 1943- WhoIns 92
**Newman**, Stuart Alan 1945- AmMWSc 92
**Newman**, Sydney IntMPA 92, LesBEnT 92
**Newman**, Sydney Cecil 1917- Who 92
**Newman**, Theodore R, Jr 1934- WhoAmP 91
**Newman**, Theodore Roosevelt, Jr. 1934- WhoAmL 92, WhoBlA 92
**Newman**, Thomas Daniel 1922- WhoRel 92
**Newman**, Thomas G 1931- WhoAmP 91
**Newman**, Thomas Rubin 1933- WhoAmL 92
**Newman**, Tillman Eugene, Jr. 1938- WhoFI 92
**Newman**, Wade DrAPF 91
**Newman**, Wade Davis 1936- WhoMW 92
**Newman**, Walter Brown 1920- IntMPA 92
**Newman**, Walter Hayes 1938- AmMWSc 92
**Newman**, Wiley Clifford, Jr 1931- AmMWSc 92
**Newman**, William Alexander 1934- AmMWSc 92
**Newman**, William Anderson 1927- AmMWSc 92
**Newman**, William Bernard, Jr. 1950- WhoAmL 92, WhoFI 92
**Newman**, William C. 1928- WhoRel 92
**Newman**, William Guy 1952- WhoEnt 92
**Newman**, William L 1920- AmMWSc 92
**Newman**, William S. 1912- WrDr 92
**Newman**, William Stein 1912- WhoEnt 92
**Newman**, William Thomas, Jr. 1950- WhoBlA 92
**Newmar**, Julie 1933- IntMPA 92
**Newmar**, Julie Chalane WhoEnt 92

**Newmarch**, Michael George 1938- *IntWW 91, Who 92*
**Newmark**, Harold Leon 1918- *AmMWSc 92*
**Newmark**, Jonathan *AmMWSc 92*
**Newmark**, Leonard 1929- *WrDr 92*
**Newmark**, Milton Maxwell 1916- *WhoAmL 92*
**Newmark**, Philip Barnard 1946- *WhoEnt 92*
**Newmark**, Richard Alan 1940- *AmMWSc 92*
**Newmark**, Stephen 1943- *AmMWSc 92*
**Newmiller**, Ronda Marie 1962- *WhoWest 92*
**Newnam**, Brian Emerson 1941- *WhoWest 92*
**Newnam**, Thomas d1723 *DcNCBi 4*
**Newnan**, Daniel 1780?-1851 *DcNCBi 4*
**Newnan**, John 1773?-1833 *DcNCBi 4*
**Newnes**, George 1851-1910 *DcLB 112 [port]*
**Newnham**, Ian Frederick Montague 1911- *Who 92*
**Newnham**, Robert Everest 1929- *AmMWSc 92*
**Newnham**, Robert Montague 1934- *AmMWSc 92*
**Newns**, Foley 1909- *Who 92*
**Newpher**, James Alfred, Jr. 1930- *WhoMW 92*
**Newpol**, Joseph James 1944- *WhoAmL 92*
**Newport**, Viscount 1980- *Who 92*
**Newport**, James William 1945- *WhoEnt 92*
**Newport**, John Paul 1917- *WhoRel 92*
**Newport**, John Paul, Jr. 1954- *ConAu 135*
**Newport**, Walter Augustus 1917- *WhoAmL 92*
**Newquist**, Donald Stewart 1953- *WhoWest 92*
**Newquist**, Gary Melville 1938- *WhoWest 92*
**Newquist**, Jerreld L. 1919-1976 *ConAu 134*
**Newrock**, Kenneth Matthew 1944- *AmMWSc 92*
**Newrock**, Richard Sandor 1942- *AmMWSc 92*
**Newroth**, Peter Russell 1945- *AmMWSc 92*
**Newry And Morne**, Viscount 1966- *Who 92*
**Newsam**, John M *AmMWSc 92*
**Newsam**, Peter 1928- *Who 92*
**Newsom**, Bernard Dean 1924- *AmMWSc 92*
**Newsom**, Dallas Walton 1873-1949 *DcNCBi 4*
**Newsom**, David D 1918- *WhoAmP 91*
**Newsom**, David Dunlop 1918- *IntWW 91*
**Newsom**, Donald Wilson 1918- *AmMWSc 92*
**Newsom**, George Edward 1919- *WhoAmP 91*
**Newsom**, George Harold 1909- *Who 92*
**Newsom**, Gerald Higley 1939- *AmMWSc 92*
**Newsom**, Herbert Charles 1931- *AmMWSc 92*
**Newsom**, John Edward, Sr. 1944- *WhoMW 92*
**Newsom**, Leo Dale 1915- *AmMWSc 92*
**Newsom**, Lionel H. 1919- *WhoBlA 92N*
**Newsom**, Raymond A 1931- *AmMWSc 92*
**Newsom**, Tommy 1929- *WhoEnt 92*
**Newsom**, William S, Jr 1918- *AmMWSc 92*
**Newsom-Davis**, John Michael 1932- *Who 92*
**Newsome**, Albert Ray 1894-1951 *DcNCBi 4*
**Newsome**, Burnell 1938- *WhoBlA 92*
**Newsome**, Clarence Geno 1950- *WhoBlA 92*
**Newsome**, Cola King 1925- *WhoBlA 92*
**Newsome**, David Anthony 1942- *AmMWSc 92*
**Newsome**, David Hay 1929- *Who 92, WrDr 92*
**Newsome**, Effie Lee 1885-1979 *NotBlAW 92*
**Newsome**, Elisa C. 1964- *WhoBlA 92*
**Newsome**, Emanuel T. 1942- *WhoBlA 92*
**Newsome**, George Marvin 1919- *WhoAmL 92*
**Newsome**, Jay Anand 1962- *WhoWest 92*
**Newsome**, Joseph E *WhoAmP 91*
**Newsome**, Moses, Jr. 1944- *WhoBlA 92*
**Newsome**, Ozzie 1956- *WhoBlA 92*
**Newsome**, Paula Renee 1955- *WhoBlA 92*
**Newsome**, Randall Jackson 1950- *WhoWest 92*
**Newsome**, Richard Duane 1931- *AmMWSc 92*
**Newsome**, Ross Whitted 1935- *AmMWSc 92*
**Newsome**, Steven Cameron 1952- *WhoBlA 92*
**Newsome**, Victor 1935- *TwCPaSc*
**Newsome**, Vincent Karl 1961- *WhoBlA 92*
**Newsome**, William Antony 1919- *Who 92*
**Newson**, Ben Lee, Jr. 1949- *WhoMW 92*
**Newson**, David Hughes 1917- *WhoRel 92*
**Newson**, Harold Don 1924- *AmMWSc 92*
**Newson**, Henry Byron 1860-1910 *BiInAmS*
**Newson**, Roosevelt, Jr. 1946- *WhoBlA 92*
**Newson-Smith**, John 1911- *Who 92*
**Newstadt**, David Roland 1930- *WhoFI 92*
**Newstead**, James Duncan MacInnes 1930- *AmMWSc 92*
**Newstead**, Robert Richard 1935- *WhoWest 92*
**Newstein**, Herman 1918- *AmMWSc 92*
**Newstein**, Maurice 1926- *AmMWSc 92*
**Newswanger**, Carl Keeport 1941- *WhoRel 92*
**Newte**, Horace 1870-1949 *ScFEYrs*
**Newth**, Rebecca *DrAPF 91*
**Newton**, Baron 1915- *Who 92*
**Newton**, A. Edward 1863-1940 *BenetAL 91*
**Newton**, Alexander Worthy 1930- *WhoAmL 92*
**Newton**, Algernon 1880-1968 *TwCPaSc*
**Newton**, Amos Sylvester 1916- *AmMWSc 92*
**Newton**, Andrew E., Jr. 1943- *WhoBlA 92*
**Newton**, Antony Harold 1937- *Who 92*
**Newton**, Arthur R 1951- *AmMWSc 92*
**Newton**, Austin *AmMWSc 92*
**Newton**, Barry Hamilton 1932- *Who 92*
**Newton**, Bradford Curtis 1957- *WhoRel 92*
**Newton**, Charles, Jr. 1907- *WhoWest 92*
**Newton**, Charles Oliver 1947- *WhoAmP 91*
**Newton**, Charles Wilfrid 1928- *IntWW 91, Who 92*
**Newton**, Chester Whittier 1920- *AmMWSc 92*
**Newton**, Christopher *WhoEnt 92*
**Newton**, Christopher 1936- *IntWW 91*
**Newton**, Christopher Carl 1942- *WhoEnt 92*
**Newton**, Clive Trevor 1931- *Who 92*
**Newton**, D B 1916- *IntAu&W 91, TwCWW 91, WrDr 92*
**Newton**, Dan C. 1952- *WhoMW 92*
**Newton**, David C 1939- *AmMWSc 92*
**Newton**, David E. 1933- *ConAu 135, SmATA 67 [port]*
**Newton**, David G 1935- *WhoAmP 91*
**Newton**, Demetrius C *WhoAmP 91*
**Newton**, Demetrius C. 1928- *WhoBlA 92*
**Newton**, Derek Henry 1933- *Who 92*
**Newton**, Douglas 1884-1951 *ScFEYrs*
**Newton**, Douglas Anthony 1915- *Who 92*
**Newton**, Elisabeth G 1933- *AmMWSc 92*
**Newton**, Ernest E., II 1956- *WhoBlA 92*
**Newton**, Ernest Eugene, II 1956- *WhoAmP 91*
**Newton**, Floyd Childs, III 1955- *WhoAmL 92*
**Newton**, Frank Cota-Robles 1946- *WhoHisp 92*
**Newton**, Gale JoAnn 1954- *WhoFI 92*
**Newton**, George 1765-1840 *DcNCBi 4*
**Newton**, George Durfee, Jr. 1931- *WhoAmL 92*
**Newton**, George Larry 1945- *AmMWSc 92*
**Newton**, Geralynn Marie 1964- *WhoEnt 92*
**Newton**, Gordon *Who 92*
**Newton**, Harry Michael 1923- *Who 92*
**Newton**, Helmut 1920- *CurBio 91 [port]*
**Newton**, Henry 1845-1877 *BiInAmS*
**Newton**, Howard Edwin 1929- *WhoRel 92*
**Newton**, Howard Joseph 1949- *AmMWSc 92*
**Newton**, Hubert Anson 1830-1896 *BiInAmS*
**Newton**, Huey 1942-1989 *ConBlB 2 [port]*
**Newton**, Huey P. 1942-1989 *FacFETw*
**Newton**, Isaac 1642-1727 *BlkwCEP*
**Newton**, Jack W *AmMWSc 92*
**Newton**, Jacqueline L. *WhoBlA 92*
**Newton**, James Douglas, Jr. 1949- *WhoBlA 92*
**Newton**, James E. 1941- *WhoBlA 92*
**Newton**, Jean S. 1952- *WhoMW 92*
**Newton**, John 1823-1895 *BiInAmS*
**Newton**, John 1925- *WhoEnt 92*
**Newton**, John Anthony 1930- *Who 92*
**Newton**, John David 1921- *Who 92*
**Newton**, John Marshall 1913- *AmMWSc 92*
**Newton**, John Michael 1935- *Who 92*
**Newton**, John Oswald 1924- *IntWW 91*
**Newton**, John Paul 1947- *WhoMW 92*
**Newton**, John S 1908- *AmMWSc 92*
**Newton**, John Skillman 1908- *WhoMW 92*
**Newton**, John Wharton, III 1953- *WhoAmL 92*
**Newton**, Jonathan Brooks 1950- *WhoEnt 92*
**Newton**, Joseph Emory O'Neal 1927- *AmMWSc 92*
**Newton**, Joseph Fort 1876-1950 *RelLAm 91*
**Newton**, Juice *WhoEnt 92*
**Newton**, Kenneth 1918- *Who 92*
**Newton**, Kenneth 1940- *WrDr 92*
**Newton**, Leslie Gordon 1907- *IntAu&W 91, IntWW 91, Who 92*
**Newton**, Margaret 1927- *Who 92*
**Newton**, Marshall Dickinson 1940- *AmMWSc 92*
**Newton**, Maxwell 1929-1990 *AnObit 1990*
**Newton**, Melvin Gary 1939- *AmMWSc 92*
**Newton**, Melvin T. *WhoBlA 92*
**Newton**, Michael *Who 92*
**Newton**, Michael 1932- *AmMWSc 92*
**Newton**, Mike 1951- *TwCWW 91*
**Newton**, Norman Lewis 1929- *WrDr 92*
**Newton**, Oliver A., Jr. 1925- *WhoBlA 92*
**Newton**, Oscar Lee, Jr 1927- *WhoIns 92*
**Newton**, Paul Edward 1945- *AmMWSc 92*
**Newton**, Paul Kenneth 1959- *WhoMW 92*
**Newton**, Peter Marcus 1942- *Who 92*
**Newton**, Ray 1953- *WhoEnt 92*
**Newton**, Rhonwen Leonard 1940- *WhoFI 92*
**Newton**, Richard Howard 1932- *WhoWest 92*
**Newton**, Richard James 1927- *Who 92*
**Newton**, Richard Matthew 1952- *WhoIns 92*
**Newton**, Richard Wayne 1948- *AmMWSc 92*
**Newton**, Robert 1944- *WhoBlA 92*
**Newton**, Robert Andrew 1922- *AmMWSc 92*
**Newton**, Robert Chaffer 1933- *AmMWSc 92*
**Newton**, Robert D., Jr. 1928- *WhoMW 92, WhoRel 92*
**Newton**, Robert George 1948- *WhoEnt 92*
**Newton**, Robert Morgan 1948- *AmMWSc 92*
**Newton**, Robert R. 1918- *WrDr 92*
**Newton**, Robin Caprice 1957- *WhoBlA 92*
**Newton**, Roger Gerhard 1924- *AmMWSc 92*
**Newton**, Ronald Gordon 1912- *IntWW 91*
**Newton**, Russell William 1956- *WhoFI 92*
**Newton**, Saul B. d1991 *NewYTBS 91*
**Newton**, Sheila A 1954- *AmMWSc 92*
**Newton**, Stephen Bruington 1934- *AmMWSc 92*
**Newton**, Steven Robert 1960- *WhoMW 92*
**Newton**, Suzanne *DrAPF 91*
**Newton**, Suzanne 1936- *IntAu&W 91, WrDr 92*
**Newton**, Thomas Allen 1943- *AmMWSc 92*
**Newton**, Thomas Hans 1925- *AmMWSc 92*
**Newton**, Thomas Howard 1962- *WhoFI 92*
**Newton**, Thomas William 1923- *AmMWSc 92*
**Newton**, Tyre Alexander 1921- *AmMWSc 92*
**Newton**, Victor Joseph 1937- *AmMWSc 92*
**Newton**, Warren S, Jr 1938- *WhoIns 92*
**Newton**, Wayne 1942- *WhoEnt 92, WhoWest 92*
**Newton**, Wilfrid *Who 92*
**Newton**, William Allen, Jr 1923- *AmMWSc 92*
**Newton**, William Edward 1938- *AmMWSc 92*
**Newton**, William H., III 1945- *WhoAmL 92*
**Newton-Clare**, Herbert Mitchell 1922- *Who 92*
**Newton Dunn**, William Francis 1941- *Who 92*
**Newton-John**, Olivia 1948- *IntMPA 92, IntWW 91, WhoEnt 92*
**Newton-Skelley**, Martha Louise 1949- *WhoFI 92*
**Nexo**, Martin Andersen 1869-1954 *TwCLC 43 [port]*
**Nexsen**, Julian Jacobs 1924- *WhoAmL 92*
**Ney**, Edward 1920- *IntWW 91*
**Ney**, Edward N 1925- *WhoAmP 91*
**Ney**, Edward Noonan 1925- *IntWW 91*
**Ney**, Edward Purdy 1920- *AmMWSc 92*
**Ney**, Michael Vincent 1947- *WhoMW 92*
**Ney**, Peter E 1930- *AmMWSc 92*
**Ney**, Peter H. 1931- *WhoAmL 92*
**Ney**, Peter Stewart d1846 *DcNCBi 4*
**Ney**, Richard 1917- *IntMPA 92*
**Ney**, Robert William 1954- *WhoAmP 91*
**Ney**, Roman 1931- *IntWW 91*
**Ney**, Ronald E, Jr *AmMWSc 92*
**Ney**, Wilbert Roger 1929- *AmMWSc 92*
**Neyer**, Jerome Charles 1938- *WhoFI 92*
**Neygauz**, Genrikh Gustavovich 1888-1964 *SovUnBD*
**Neyhart**, Phillip Ray 1956- *WhoRel 92*
**Neylan**, Kathleen Mary 1944- *WhoAmP 91*
**Neyland**, Leedell Wallace 1921- *WhoBlA 92*
**Neylon**, James M *DrAPF 91*
**Neylon**, Martin Joseph 1920- *WhoRel 92, WhoWest 92*
**Neynaber**, Roy H 1926- *AmMWSc 92*
**Nezeritis**, Andreas 1897- *IntWW 91*
**Nezrick**, Frank Albert 1937- *AmMWSc 92*
**Nezval**, Vitezslav 1900-1958 *TwCLC 44 [port]*
**Ng Miu** *EncAmaz 91*
**Ng Nui** *EncAmaz 91*
**Ng**, Ah-Kau *AmMWSc 92*
**Ng**, Bartholomew Sung-Hong 1946- *AmMWSc 92*
**Ng**, Edward Wai-Kwok *AmMWSc 92*
**Ng**, Fae Myenne *DrAPF 91*
**Ng**, Gerald Joe Lup 1946- *WhoWest 92*
**Ng**, Kam Wing 1951- *AmMWSc 92*
**Ng**, Lawrence Chen-Yim 1946- *AmMWSc 92, WhoWest 92*
**Ng**, Lawrence Ming-Loy 1940- *WhoWest 92*
**Ng**, Simon S F *AmMWSc 92*
**Ng**, Tai-Kai 1959- *AmMWSc 92*
**Ng**, Terry Kaleung 1955- *WhoMW 92*
**NG**, Thomson Kwan-Ting 1955- *WhoFI 92*
**Ng**, Timothy J 1950- *AmMWSc 92*
**Ng**, Waikit John 1948- *WhoEnt 92*
**Ng**, Wing Chiu 1947- *WhoFI 92*
**Ng**, Wing-Fai 1956- *AmMWSc 92*
**Ng Cheng Kiat**, Encik 1941- *IntWW 91*
**Ngai**, Kia Ling 1940- *AmMWSc 92*
**Ngai**, Shih Hsun 1920- *AmMWSc 92*
**Ngaiza**, Christopher Pastor 1930- *Who 92*
**Ngakinar**, Mamari Djime *IntWW 91*
**Ngala**, Ronald G 1923-1972 *FacFETw*
**Ngapo Ngawang-Jigme** *IntWW 91*
**Ngapoi Ngawang Jigmi** 1911- *IntWW 91*
**Ngata**, Henare Kohere 1917- *Who 92*
**Ngau**, Harrison *News 91 [port], -91-3 [port]*
**Ngei**, Paul 1923- *IntWW 91*
**Ngema**, Mbongeni 1955- *ConTFT 9*
**Ng'ethe Njoroge** *Who 92*
**Nghean**, Gregory Yong Sool *WhoRel 92*
**Ngo Dinh Nhu**, Madame *IntWW 91*
**Ngo**, Ratanamuny 1964- *WhoWest 92*
**Ngo**, That Tjien 1944- *AmMWSc 92*
**Ngonda**, Putteho Muketoi 1936- *IntWW 91, Who 92*
**Ngoyi**, Lillian 1911-1980 *FacFETw*
**Nguelouoli**, Aboubakar 1953- *WhoRel 92*
**Nguema Mbasogo**, Teodoro Obiang *IntWW 91*
**Ngugi wa Thiong'o** 1938- *BlkLC [port], ConNov 91, LiExTwC, RfGEnL 91*
**Ngugi**, J T 1938- *IntAu&W 91, WrDr 92*
**Ngugi**, John 1962- *BlkOlyM [port]*
**Ngugi**, Wa Thiong'o *WrDr 92*
**Ngugi**, Wa Thiong'o 1938- *IntWW 91*
**Nguyen Cao Ky** 1930- *IntWW 91*
**Nguyen Co Thach** 1923- *IntWW 91*
**Nguyen Huu Tho** 1910- *IntWW 91*
**Nguyen Khanh** 1927- *IntWW 91*
**Nguyen Phu Duc** 1924- *IntWW 91*
**Nguyen Thi Binh**, Madame 1927- *IntWW 91*
**Nguyen Van Hieu** d1991 *NewYTBS 91*
**Nguyen Van Linh** 1913- *IntWW 91*
**Nguyen Van Linh** 1915- *FacFETw*
**Nguyen Van Loc** 1922- *IntWW 91*
**Nguyen Van Thieu** 1923- *IntWW 91*
**Nguyen Van Vy** 1916- *IntWW 91*
**Nguyen**, Ann Cac Khue *WhoWest 92*
**Nguyen**, Caroline Phuongdung *AmMWSc 92*
**Nguyen**, Charles Cuong 1956- *AmMWSc 92, WhoFI 92*
**Nguyen**, Henry Thien 1954- *AmMWSc 92*
**Nguyen**, Hien Vu 1943- *AmMWSc 92*
**Nguyen**, Huan Dinh 1962- *WhoFI 92*
**Nguyen**, Hung 1961- *WhoMW 92*
**Nguyen**, King Xuan 1930- *WhoWest 92*
**Nguyen**, Lan Kim 1960- *WhoWest 92*
**Nguyen**, Luu Thanh 1954- *AmMWSc 92*
**Nguyen**, Ngoc Huy 1924- *IntAu&W 91*
**Nguyen**, Paul Dung Quoc 1943- *WhoAmL 92*
**Nguyen**, Tang Dinh 1948- *WhoWest 92*
**Nguyen**, Thuan Van 1929- *AmMWSc 92*
**Nguyen**, Trung Duc 1951- *WhoWest 92*
**Nguyen**, Trung Hung 1952- *WhoFI 92*
**Nguyen**, Truyen Thanh 1930- *WhoFI 92*
**Nguyen**, Tuan Anh 1935- *WhoFI 92*
**Nguyen**, Tuan Anh 1956- *WhoWest 92*
**Nguyen-Dinh**, Phuc 1949- *AmMWSc 92*
**Nguyen-Doyne**, Jean Quyen 1963- *WhoWest 92*
**Nguza Karl-I-Bond** 1938- *IntWW 91*
**Nhongo**, Teurai Ropa *EncAmaz 91*
**Nhu**, Madame *IntWW 91*
**Ni Chih-Fu** *IntWW 91*
**Ni Zhengyu** 1906- *IntWW 91*
**Ni Zhifu** 1933- *IntWW 91*
**Ni**, Chen-Chou 1927- *AmMWSc 92*
**Ni**, I-Hsun 1946- *AmMWSc 92*
**Ni**, Wayne Weijen 1961- *WhoWest 92*
**Ni Chuilleanain**, Eilean 1942- *ConPo 91, IntAu&W 91, WrDr 92*
**Niall**, Horace Lionel Richard 1904- *Who 92*
**Niarchos**, Stavros Spyros 1909- *IntWW 91, Who 92*

**Niare**, Seydou 1933- *IntWW 91*
**Niasse**, Cheikh Moustapha 1939- *IntWW 91*
**Niatum**, Duane *DrAPF 91*
**Niazi**, Maulana Kausar 1934- *IntWW 91*
**Nibbe**, Susan Marlene 1961- *WhoMW 92*
**Nibbelink**, Cynthia *DrAPF 91*
**Nibbelink**, Gary Wayne 1944- *WhoRel 92*
**Nibbering**, Nicolaas Martinus Maria 1938- *IntWW 91*
**Nibbs**, Alphonse, Sr. 1947- *WhoBlA 92*
**Nibbs**, Monsell Morrison 1961- *WhoWest 92*
**Nibert**, James Garland 1950- *WhoMW 92*
**Niblack**, John Franklin 1939- *AmMWSc 92*
**Nibler**, Joseph William 1941- *AmMWSc 92*
**Niblett**, Charles Leslie 1943- *AmMWSc 92*
**Niblett**, William Roy *WrDr 92*
**Niblett**, William Roy 1906- *Who 92*
**Nibley**, Robert Ricks 1913- *WhoWest 92*
**Nibley**, Sloan *IntMPA 92*
**Niblo**, Fred 1874-1948 *IntDcF 2-2 [port]*
**Niblock**, Henry 1911- *Who 92*
**Niblock**, Phill 1933- *NewAmDM*
**Niblock**, William Robert 1928- *WhoFI 92*
**Nicandros**, Constantine Stavros 1933- *WhoFI 92*
**Nicastro**, David Harlan *AmMWSc 92*
**Nicastro**, Lawrence William 1953- *WhoEnt 92*
**Nicco-Annan**, Lionel *WhoBlA 92*
**Niccol**, Kathleen Agnes *Who 92*
**Niccolai**, Nilo Anthony 1940- *AmMWSc 92*
**Niccum**, Robert Frederick 1925- *WhoAmL 92*
**Niccum**, Stephen Duane 1959- *WhoRel 92*
**Nice**, Carter 1940- *WhoEnt 92, WhoWest 92*
**Nice**, Charles Monroe, Jr 1919- *AmMWSc 92*
**Nice**, Geoffrey 1945- *Who 92*
**Nice**, James William 1948- *WhoWest 92*
**Nice**, Robert Joseph 1959- *WhoAmL 92*
**Nice-Hood**, Bonita Collette 1954- *WhoEnt 92*
**Niceley**, Frank S 1947- *WhoAmP 91*
**Nicely**, Kenneth Aubrey 1938- *AmMWSc 92*
**Nicely**, Kip W 1954- *WhoAmP 91*
**Nicely**, Timothy 1944- *WhoWest 92*
**Nicely**, Vincent Alvin 1943- *AmMWSc 92*
**Nicely**, William Abbott 1930- *WhoAmL 92*
**Nicely**, William Perry Amos 1922- *WhoAmP 91*
**Niceta of Remesiana** d414? *EncEarC*
**Nichaman**, Milton Z 1931- *AmMWSc 92*
**Nichol**, B P 1944- *IntAu&W 91*
**Nichol**, B. P. 1944-1988 *SmATA 66*
**Nichol**, Barry P. 1944- *BenetAL 91*
**Nichol**, Charles Adam 1922- *AmMWSc 92*
**Nichol**, Doyle L 1952- *WhoAmP 91*
**Nichol**, Duncan Kirkbride 1941- *Who 92*
**Nichol**, Francis David 1897-1966 *RelLAm 91*
**Nichol**, Francis Richard, Jr 1942- *AmMWSc 92*
**Nichol**, Fred Joseph 1912- *WhoAmL 92*
**Nichol**, Gene Ray, Jr. 1951- *WhoAmL 92*
**Nichol**, James Charles 1922- *AmMWSc 92*
**Nichol**, Lawrence Walter 1935- *IntWW 91, Who 92*
**Nichol**, Muriel Edith *Who 92*
**Nichol**, William E 1918- *WhoAmP 91*
**Nichol**, William Edison 1918- *WhoMW 92*
**Nicholaides**, John J, III 1944- *AmMWSc 92*
**Nicholas II** 1868-1918 *FacFETw*
**Nicholas**, Archbishop *WhoRel 92*
**Nicholas**, Bishop 1851-1915 *RelLAm 91*
**Nicholas**, Bishop 1936- *WhoRel 92*
**Nicholas**, Grand Duke 1856-1929 *FacFETw*
**Nicholas of Cusa** 1401-1464 *DcLB 115 [port]*
**Nicholas**, St. *EncEarC*
**Nicholas**, Angela Jane 1929- *Who 92*
**Nicholas**, Barry *Who 92*
**Nicholas**, Carol Lynn 1938- *WhoAmL 92*
**Nicholas**, David 1930- *IntAu&W 91, IntWW 91, Who 92*
**Nicholas**, David Durell 1930- *WhoAmP 91*
**Nicholas**, David M. 1939- *WrDr 92*
**Nicholas**, David R 1941- *WhoAmP 91*
**Nicholas**, David Robert 1941- *WhoRel 92*
**Nicholas**, Denise 1944- *WhoBlA 92*
**Nicholas**, Eugene J *WhoAmP 91*
**Nicholas**, Fayard Antonio 1914- *WhoBlA 92*
**Nicholas**, Frederick M. 1920- *WhoAmL 92*
**Nicholas**, Gwendolyn Smith 1951- *WhoBlA 92*
**Nicholas**, Harold Joseph 1919- *AmMWSc 92*
**Nicholas**, Harry *Who 92*
**Nicholas**, Herbert George 1911- *IntAu&W 91, IntWW 91, Who 92, WrDr 92*
**Nicholas**, Herbert Richard 1905- *IntWW 91, Who 92*
**Nicholas**, James A 1921- *AmMWSc 92*
**Nicholas**, James Hayden 1956- *WhoEnt 92*
**Nicholas**, Jane *Who 92*
**Nicholas**, John Keiran Barry 1919- *IntWW 91, Who 92*
**Nicholas**, John William 1924- *IntWW 91, Who 92*
**Nicholas**, Kenneth M 1947- *AmMWSc 92*
**Nicholas**, Laurie Stevens 1959- *WhoWest 92*
**Nicholas**, Lawrence Bruce 1945- *WhoFI 92*
**Nicholas**, Leslie 1913- *AmMWSc 92*
**Nicholas**, Mary Burke *WhoBlA 92*
**Nicholas**, N. J. *LesBEnT 92*
**Nicholas**, Nicholas John, Jr. 1939- *IntWW 91, WhoFI 92*
**Nicholas**, Paul Peter 1938- *AmMWSc 92*
**Nicholas**, Ralph Wallace 1934- *WhoMW 92*
**Nicholas**, Stephen Wayne 1956- *WhoAmL 92*
**Nicholas**, Thomas Peter 1948- *WhoWest 92*
**Nicholas**, William Ford 1923- *Who 92*
**Nicholes**, Paul Scott 1916- *AmMWSc 92*
**Nicholl**, Anthony John David 1935- *Who 92*
**Nicholl**, Don d1980 *LesBEnT 92*
**Nicholl**, Nobes Einsel, Jr. 1936- *WhoFI 92*
**Nicholls** *Who 92*
**Nicholls**, Bertram 1883-1974 *TwCPaSc*
**Nicholls**, Brian 1928- *Who 92*
**Nicholls**, C. S. 1943- *ConAu 133*
**Nicholls**, Christine Stephanie 1943- *Who 92*
**Nicholls**, Clive Victor 1932- *Who 92*
**Nicholls**, Colin Alfred Arthur 1932- *Who 92*
**Nicholls**, David Alan *Who 92*
**Nicholls**, David Herbert 1942- *WhoAmL 92*
**Nicholls**, Donald 1933- *Who 92*
**Nicholls**, Doris McEwen 1927- *AmMWSc 92*
**Nicholls**, Francis Brian B *Who 92*
**Nicholls**, Gerald P 1943- *AmMWSc 92*
**Nicholls**, Grant T 1946- *WhoIns 92*
**Nicholls**, J A 1921- *AmMWSc 92*
**Nicholls**, John *Who 92*
**Nicholls**, John Graham 1929- *Who 92*
**Nicholls**, John Moreton 1926- *Who 92*
**Nicholls**, Nigel Hamilton 1938- *Who 92*
**Nicholls**, Patrick Charles Martyn 1948- *Who 92*
**Nicholls**, Peter 1935- *AmMWSc 92*
**Nicholls**, Peter John 1945- *AmMWSc 92*
**Nicholls**, Philip 1914- *Who 92*
**Nicholls**, Ralph William 1926- *AmMWSc 92*
**Nicholls**, Richard H. 1938- *WhoAmL 92*
**Nicholls**, Robert Lee 1929- *AmMWSc 92*
**Nicholls**, Robert Michael 1939- *Who 92*
**Nicholls**, Vernon Sampson 1917- *Who 92*
**Nichols**, Adelaide *ConAu 134*
**Nichols**, Albert L. 1951- *WhoFI 92*
**Nichols**, Albert Myron 1914- *WhoRel 92*
**Nichols**, Alexander Vladimir 1924- *AmMWSc 92*
**Nichols**, Alfred Glen 1952- *WhoBlA 92*
**Nichols**, Ambrose Reuben, Jr 1914- *AmMWSc 92*
**Nichols**, Andrew Livingston 1936- *WhoFI 92*
**Nichols**, Andrew Wilkinson 1937- *WhoWest 92*
**Nichols**, Anne *BenetAL 91*
**Nichols**, Avis Belle 1913- *WhoAmP 91*
**Nichols**, Barbara Ann 1921- *AmMWSc 92*
**Nichols**, Benjamin 1920- *AmMWSc 92*
**Nichols**, Billy Nick 1938- *WhoRel 92*
**Nichols**, Buford Lee, Jr 1931- *AmMWSc 92*
**Nichols**, C. Walter, III 1937- *WhoFI 92*
**Nichols**, Carl William 1924- *AmMWSc 92*
**Nichols**, Charles Harold 1919- *WhoBlA 92*
**Nichols**, Chester Encell 1935- *AmMWSc 92*
**Nichols**, Chet, II 1948- *WhoEnt 92*
**Nichols**, Clement Roy 1909- *Who 92*
**Nichols**, Courtland Geoffrey 1934- *AmMWSc 92*
**Nichols**, Daniel Joseph 1948- *WhoRel 92*
**Nichols**, David 1956- *ConAu 133*
**Nichols**, David A 1917- *WhoAmP 91*
**Nichols**, David Allen 1939- *WhoMW 92*
**Nichols**, David Arthur 1917- *WhoAmL 92*
**Nichols**, David Earl 1944- *AmMWSc 92, WhoMW 92*
**Nichols**, David Eugene 1953- *WhoRel 92*
**Nichols**, David Lawrence 1947- *WhoRel 92*
**Nichols**, David Norton 1954- *WhoWest 92*
**Nichols**, Davis Betz 1940- *AmMWSc 92*
**Nichols**, Delton 1953- *WhoRel 92*
**Nichols**, Dick 1926- *AlmAP 92 [port]*
**Nichols**, Dimaggio 1951- *WhoBlA 92*
**Nichols**, Dinah Alison 1943- *Who 92*
**Nichols**, Donald Arthur 1940- *WhoFI 92, WhoMW 92*
**Nichols**, Donald Ray 1927- *AmMWSc 92*
**Nichols**, Donald Richardson 1911- *AmMWSc 92*
**Nichols**, Dorothy Naddelle 1923- *WhoAmP 91*
**Nichols**, Douglas James 1942- *AmMWSc 92*
**Nichols**, Duane Guy 1937- *AmMWSc 92*
**Nichols**, Edie Diane 1939- *WhoFI 92*
**Nichols**, Edward 1911- *Who 92*
**Nichols**, Edward K., Jr. 1918- *WhoBlA 92*
**Nichols**, Edwin J. 1931- *WhoBlA 92*
**Nichols**, Elaine 1952- *WhoBlA 92*
**Nichols**, Eugene Douglas 1923- *AmMWSc 92*
**Nichols**, Evelin Gertraud 1931- *WhoAmP 91*
**Nichols**, Francis Neale, II 1935- *WhoMW 92*
**Nichols**, Francis William 1930- *WhoRel 92*
**Nichols**, Frederic Hone 1937- *AmMWSc 92*
**Nichols**, Frederick Harris 1936- *WhoAmL 92*
**Nichols**, G Starr 1918- *AmMWSc 92*
**Nichols**, Galen Loy 1946- *WhoEnt 92*
**Nichols**, George Leon, Jr. 1938- *WhoRel 92*
**Nichols**, George Thomas 1948- *WhoMW 92*
**Nichols**, Grace 1950- *ConPo 91, WrDr 92*
**Nichols**, Harold James 1945- *WhoEnt 92, WhoMW 92*
**Nichols**, Henry Eliot 1924- *WhoAmL 92, WhoFI 92*
**Nichols**, Henry H. 1916- *WhoBlA 92*
**Nichols**, Herbert Wayne 1937- *AmMWSc 92*
**Nichols**, Howard Eugene 1940- *WhoWest 92*
**Nichols**, Huey Paul 1934- *WhoRel 92*
**Nichols**, Hugh 1936- *WhoWest 92*
**Nichols**, J Hugh 1930- *WhoAmP 91*
**Nichols**, J Wylie *AmMWSc 92*
**Nichols**, Jack Loran 1939- *AmMWSc 92*
**Nichols**, Jackie Jordan 1947- *WhoEnt 92*
**Nichols**, James Carlile 1950- *AmMWSc 92*
**Nichols**, James Dale 1949- *AmMWSc 92*
**Nichols**, James Phillip 1944- *WhoFI 92*
**Nichols**, James R. *DrAPF 91*
**Nichols**, James Randall 1931- *AmMWSc 92*
**Nichols**, James Robbs 1926- *AmMWSc 92*
**Nichols**, James Robinson 1819-1888 *BiInAmS*
**Nichols**, James Ross 1944- *AmMWSc 92*
**Nichols**, James T 1930- *AmMWSc 92*
**Nichols**, Janet 1952- *ConAu 135, SmATA 67 [port]*
**Nichols**, Jeremy Gareth Lane 1943- *Who 92*
**Nichols**, Joan Kane *DrAPF 91*
**Nichols**, Joe Dean 1931- *AmMWSc 92*
**Nichols**, Joel Martin, Jr. *ScFEYrs*
**Nichols**, John *Who 92*
**Nichols**, John 1834-1917 *DcNCBi 4*
**Nichols**, John 1940- *BenetAL 91, IntAu&W 91, TwCWW 91, WrDr 92*
**Nichols**, John C 1939- *AmMWSc 92*
**Nichols**, John D. 1930- *WhoFI 92, WhoMW 92*
**Nichols**, John Gordon 1930- *WrDr 92*
**Nichols**, John Julian 1941- *WhoAmL 92*
**Nichols**, John Treadwell 1940- *WhoEnt 92*
**Nichols**, John Winfrith de Lisle 1919- *Who 92*
**Nichols**, Johnnie Juanita 1908- *WhoAmP 91*
**Nichols**, Jon Preston 1950- *WhoEnt 92*
**Nichols**, Joseph 1917- *AmMWSc 92*
**Nichols**, Kathleen Mary 1948- *AmMWSc 92*
**Nichols**, Kathryn Marion 1946- *AmMWSc 92*
**Nichols**, Kay Bailey 1908- *WhoBlA 92*
**Nichols**, Kenneth David 1907- *AmMWSc 92*
**Nichols**, Kenneth E 1920- *AmMWSc 92*
**Nichols**, Kenneth John 1923- *Who 92*
**Nichols**, Kyra 1959- *WhoEnt 92*
**Nichols**, L.T. 1844-1912 *RelLAm 91*
**Nichols**, Larry A., Jr. 1956- *WhoRel 92*
**Nichols**, Lee L, Jr 1923- *AmMWSc 92*
**Nichols**, Leigh *ConAu 36NR, WrDr 92*
**Nichols**, LeRoy 1924- *WhoBlA 92*
**Nichols**, Linda Lipford 1957- *WhoAmL 92*
**Nichols**, Mark Edward 1961- *WhoAmL 92*
**Nichols**, Mary Gove 1810-1884 *HanAmWH*
**Nichols**, Mary Perot 1926- *WhoEnt 92*
**Nichols**, Michael Charles 1951- *AmMWSc 92*
**Nichols**, Mike *LesBEnT 92*
**Nichols**, Mike 1931- *BenetAL 91, FacFETw, IntDcF 2-2 [port], IntMPA 92, IntWW 91, WhoEnt 92*
**Nichols**, Nancy Jean 1939- *WhoAmP 91*
**Nichols**, Nathan Lankford 1917- *AmMWSc 92*
**Nichols**, Nichelle *WhoBlA 92*
**Nichols**, Nick 1944- *WhoBlA 92*
**Nichols**, Nina Da Vinci *DrAPF 91*
**Nichols**, Norman J 1928- *WhoIns 92*
**Nichols**, Othniel Foster 1845-1908 *BiInAmS*
**Nichols**, Owen D. 1929- *WhoBlA 92*
**Nichols**, Pamela Marjorie *Who 92*
**Nichols**, Paul 1939- *WhoBlA 92*
**Nichols**, Peter 1927- *ConLC 65 [port], WrDr 92*
**Nichols**, Peter Richard 1927- *IntAu&W 91, Who 92*
**Nichols**, Philip Vance 1934- *WhoAmP 91*
**Nichols**, R. Eugene 1914- *WrDr 92*
**Nichols**, Randall Wayne 1962- *WhoAmL 92*
**Nichols**, Red 1905-1965 *NewAmDM*
**Nichols**, Richard Dale 1926- *WhoAmP 91, WhoMW 92*
**Nichols**, Robert 1893-1944 *ScFEYrs*
**Nichols**, Robert and Browne, Maurice *ScFEYrs*
**Nichols**, Robert Edmund 1925- *WhoWest 92*
**Nichols**, Robert Lee 1924- *WhoFI 92*
**Nichols**, Robert Leslie 1904- *AmMWSc 92*
**Nichols**, Robert Loring 1946- *AmMWSc 92*
**Nichols**, Robert Ted 1925- *AmMWSc 92*
**Nichols**, Roger 1939- *WrDr 92*
**Nichols**, Roger Louis 1933- *WhoWest 92*
**Nichols**, Roger Loyd 1926- *AmMWSc 92*
**Nichols**, Ron *WhoAmP 91*
**Nichols**, Ronald Augustus 1956- *WhoBlA 92*
**Nichols**, Roy Calvin 1918- *WhoBlA 92*
**Nichols**, Roy Elwyn 1909- *AmMWSc 92*
**Nichols**, Rudolph Henry 1911- *AmMWSc 92*
**Nichols**, Rudy J 1945- *WhoAmP 91*
**Nichols**, Ruth 1948- *WrDr 92*
**Nichols**, Scott *TwCSFW 91*
**Nichols**, Scott Huntington 1952- *WhoAmL 92*
**Nichols**, Sylvia A. 1925- *WhoBlA 92*
**Nichols**, Teresa Ann 1956- *WhoRel 92*
**Nichols**, Thomas Low 1815-1901 *BenetAL 91*
**Nichols**, Timothy Robert 1956- *WhoRel 92*
**Nichols**, Vance Everett 1959- *WhoRel 92*
**Nichols**, Vincent Gerard 1945- *IntWW 91, Who 92*
**Nichols**, Walter L. *WhoBlA 92*
**Nichols**, Walter LaPlora 1938- *WhoBlA 92*
**Nichols**, Warren Wesley 1929- *AmMWSc 92*
**Nichols**, Willard R. *WhoAmL 92*
**Nichols**, William 1777?-1853 *DcNCBi 4*
**Nichols**, William H. 1928- *WhoMW 92*
**Nichols**, William Henry 1913- *Who 92*
**Nichols**, William Herbert 1928- *AmMWSc 92*
**Nichols**, William Howard, Jr. 1942- *WhoRel 92*
**Nichols**, William Kenneth 1943- *AmMWSc 92*
**Nichols**, William Reginald 1912- *Who 92*
**Nichols**, William Ripley 1847-1886 *BiInAmS*
**Nichols**, Wilmer Wayne 1934- *AmMWSc 92*
**Nichols-Elliott**, Ruth L. 1948- *WhoBlA 92*
**Nicholsen**, James Therman 1950- *WhoMW 92*
**Nicholson**, Alfred 1936- *WhoBlA 92*
**Nicholson**, Angus Archibald Norman 1919- *Who 92*
**Nicholson**, Anthony Thomas Cuthbertson 1929- *Who 92*
**Nicholson**, Arnold Eugene 1930- *AmMWSc 92*
**Nicholson**, Ben 1894-1982 *FacFETw, TwCPaSc*
**Nicholson**, Betty *WhoRel 92*
**Nicholson**, Bradford L *WhoAmP 91*
**Nicholson**, Brent Bentley 1954- *WhoAmL 92*
**Nicholson**, Brian Thomas Graves 1930- *Who 92*
**Nicholson**, Bruce *WhoEnt 92*
**Nicholson**, Bruce Lee 1943- *AmMWSc 92*
**Nicholson**, Bryan Hubert 1932- *IntWW 91, Who 92*
**Nicholson**, Charles Gordon 1935- *Who 92*
**Nicholson**, Charles Graham 1933- *WhoIns 92*
**Nicholson**, Christina *IntAu&W 91X, WrDr 92*
**Nicholson**, Claude Wilson, Jr. 1930- *WhoMW 92*
**Nicholson**, D Allan 1939- *AmMWSc 92*

**Nicholson,** Daniel Elbert 1926- *AmMWSc 92*
**Nicholson,** Daniel Francis 1949- *WhoMW 92*
**Nicholson,** David 1904- *Who 92*
**Nicholson,** David Bosworth 1950- *WhoEnt 92*
**Nicholson,** David John 1944- *Who 92*
**Nicholson,** David Lee 1947- *WhoAmP 91*
**Nicholson,** Donald Paul 1930- *AmMWSc 92*
**Nicholson,** Douglas Gillison 1908- *AmMWSc 92*
**Nicholson,** Dwight Roy 1947- *AmMWSc 92*
**Nicholson,** E.Q. 1908- *TwCPaSc*
**Nicholson,** E. W. 1938- *WrDr 92*
**Nicholson,** Earl G *WhoAmP 91*
**Nicholson,** Edna Elizabeth 1907- *WhoMW 92*
**Nicholson,** Edward Max 1904- *Who 92*
**Nicholson,** Edward Rupert 1909- *Who 92*
**Nicholson,** Emma Harriet 1941- *Who 92*
**Nicholson,** Ernest Wilson 1938- *IntWW 91, Who 92*
**Nicholson,** Eugene Haines 1907- *AmMWSc 92*
**Nicholson,** Francis Joseph 1921- *WhoAmL 92*
**Nicholson,** Geoffrey 1929- *IntAu&W 91, WrDr 92*
**Nicholson,** George Alexander, III 1961- *WhoFI 92*
**Nicholson,** Gerald Lee 1944- *WhoMW 92*
**Nicholson,** Godfrey d1991 *Who 92N*
**Nicholson,** Gordon *Who 92*
**Nicholson,** Howard 1912- *Who 92*
**Nicholson,** Howard White, Jr 1944- *AmMWSc 92*
**Nicholson,** Hubert 1908- *IntAu&W 91, WrDr 92*
**Nicholson,** Isadore 1925- *WhoWest 92*
**Nicholson,** J Charles 1942- *AmMWSc 92*
**Nicholson,** J W G 1931- *AmMWSc 92*
**Nicholson,** Jack 1937- *FacFETw, IntMPA 92, IntWW 91, Who 92, WhoEnt 92*
**Nicholson,** James Frederick 1945- *Who 92*
**Nicholson,** James Lloyd 1943- *WhoMW 92*
**Nicholson,** James Michael 1933- *Who 92*
**Nicholson,** Jessie Ree 1952- *WhoAmL 92*
**Nicholson,** John 1911- *IntWW 91, Who 92*
**Nicholson,** John Patrick 1936- *WhoMW 92*
**Nicholson,** John Wayne, Jr. 1967- *WhoRel 92*
**Nicholson,** Joseph *DrAPF 91*
**Nicholson,** Joseph Milford 1935- *WhoMW 92*
**Nicholson,** Joseph Shield 1850-1927 *ScFEYrs*
**Nicholson,** Joseph Thomas 1961- *WhoEnt 92*
**Nicholson,** Kate 1929- *TwCPaSc*
**Nicholson,** Larry Michael 1941- *AmMWSc 92*
**Nicholson,** Lawrence E. 1915- *WhoBlA 92*
**Nicholson,** Leonard d1990 *Who 92N*
**Nicholson,** Lewis Frederick 1918- *Who 92*
**Nicholson,** Luther Beal 1921- *WhoFI 92*
**Nicholson,** Margie May 1925- *AmMWSc 92*
**Nicholson,** Marion Crawford 1917- *WhoAmP 91, WhoMW 92*
**Nicholson,** Mark William 1960- *WhoAmL 92*
**Nicholson,** Max *Who 92*
**Nicholson,** Meredith 1866-1947 *BenetAL 91*
**Nicholson,** Michael *Who 92*
**Nicholson,** Michael 1936- *WhoAmL 92*
**Nicholson,** Michael Constantine 1932- *Who 92*
**Nicholson,** Morris E, Jr 1916- *AmMWSc 92*
**Nicholson,** Nicholas 1938- *AmMWSc 92*
**Nicholson,** Norman 1914-1987 *RfGEnL 91*
**Nicholson,** Patrick Stephen 1936- *AmMWSc 92*
**Nicholson,** Paul *WhoEnt 92, WhoWest 92*
**Nicholson,** Paul Douglas 1938- *Who 92*
**Nicholson,** R James 1938- *WhoAmP 91*
**Nicholson,** Ralph Lambton Robb 1924- *Who 92*
**Nicholson,** Ralph Lester 1942- *AmMWSc 92*
**Nicholson,** Ranald 1931- *WrDr 92*
**Nicholson,** Richard Benjamin 1928- *AmMWSc 92*
**Nicholson,** Richard Selindh 1938- *AmMWSc 92*
**Nicholson,** Robert 1920- *Who 92*
**Nicholson,** Robert Clyde 1926- *WhoFI 92*
**Nicholson,** Robin 1934- *Who 92*
**Nicholson,** Robin Buchanan 1934- *IntWW 91*
**Nicholson,** Roy S. 1903- *WhoRel 92*
**Nicholson,** Rupert *Who 92*
**Nicholson,** Ruth *WhoAmP 91*
**Nicholson,** Shirley Jean 1925- *WhoRel 92*
**Nicholson,** Simon 1934-1990 *TwCPaSc*
**Nicholson,** Theodore H. 1929- *WhoMW 92*
**Nicholson,** Thomas D. 1922-1991 *NewYTBS 91 [port]*
**Nicholson,** Thomas Dominic 1922- *AmMWSc 92*
**Nicholson,** Timothy 1828-1924 *DcNCBi 4*
**Nicholson,** Victor Alvin 1941- *AmMWSc 92*
**Nicholson,** W J 1938- *AmMWSc 92*
**Nicholson,** Wayne Lowell 1958- *AmMWSc 92*
**Nicholson,** Wesley Lathrop 1929- *AmMWSc 92*
**Nicholson,** Will Faust, Jr. 1929- *WhoFI 92, WhoWest 92*
**Nicholson,** William 1872-1949 *TwCPaSc*
**Nicholson,** William Jamieson 1930- *AmMWSc 92*
**Nicholson,** William McNeal 1905-1974 *DcNCBi 4*
**Nicholson,** William Noel 1936- *WhoMW 92*
**Nicholson,** William Robert 1925- *AmMWSc 92*
**Nicholson,** Winifred 1893-1981 *TwCPaSc*
**Nicholson-Guthrie,** Catherine Shirley *AmMWSc 92*
**Nichtern,** Claire Joseph *WhoEnt 92*
**Nichting,** Ann Louise 1940- *WhoRel 92*
**Nick,** Dagmar 1926- *IntAu&W 91*
**Nick,** Eugene Anthony 1951- *WhoEnt 92*
**Nickander,** Rodney Carl 1938- *AmMWSc 92*
**Nickel,** Albert George 1943- *WhoFI 92*
**Nickel,** Charles Lynn 1946- *WhoMW 92*
**Nickel,** Dieter H 1936- *WhoAmP 91*
**Nickel,** George H 1937- *AmMWSc 92*
**Nickel,** Herman W. 1928- *IntWW 91, WhoAmP 91*
**Nickel,** James Alvin 1925- *AmMWSc 92*
**Nickel,** James Wesley 1943- *WhoWest 92*
**Nickel,** Jeffrey David 1962- *WhoAmL 92*
**Nickel,** Phillip Arnold 1937- *AmMWSc 92*
**Nickel,** Susan Earlene 1951- *WhoWest 92*
**Nickel,** Vernon L 1918- *AmMWSc 92*
**Nickell,** Cecil D 1941- *AmMWSc 92*
**Nickell,** Christopher Shea 1959- *WhoAmL 92*
**Nickell,** James A. 1931- *WhoMW 92*
**Nickell,** Louis G 1921- *AmMWSc 92*
**Nickell,** Paul *IntMPA 92*
**Nickell,** Stephen John 1944- *Who 92*
**Nickell,** William Everett 1916- *AmMWSc 92*
**Nickels,** Gregory James 1955- *WhoAmP 91*
**Nickelsburg,** George William Elmer 1934- *WhoRel 92*
**Nickelsen,** Richard Peter 1925- *AmMWSc 92*
**Nickelson,** Robert L 1927- *AmMWSc 92*
**Nickens,** Jacks Clarence 1949- *WhoAmL 92*
**Nickerson,** Albert Lindsay 1911- *IntWW 91, Who 92*
**Nickerson,** Bruce Greenwood 1950- *AmMWSc 92*
**Nickerson,** Bruce William 1941- *WhoAmL 92*
**Nickerson,** Camille 1888-1982 *NotBlAW 92*
**Nickerson,** Eugene Hoffman 1918- *WhoAmP 91*
**Nickerson,** Gary Lee 1942- *WhoMW 92*
**Nickerson,** Helen Kelsall 1918- *AmMWSc 92*
**Nickerson,** John David 1927- *AmMWSc 92*
**Nickerson,** John Lester 1903- *AmMWSc 92*
**Nickerson,** John Munro *AmMWSc 92*
**Nickerson,** Kenneth Warwick 1942- *AmMWSc 92*
**Nickerson,** Mark 1916- *AmMWSc 92*
**Nickerson,** Mark William 1948- *WhoAmL 92*
**Nickerson,** Norton Hart 1926- *AmMWSc 92*
**Nickerson,** Peter Ayers 1941- *AmMWSc 92*
**Nickerson,** Richard G 1927- *AmMWSc 92*
**Nickerson,** Robert Fletcher 1930- *AmMWSc 92*
**Nickerson,** Roy 1927- *ConAu 35NR*
**Nickerson,** Roy I *WhoAmP 91*
**Nickerson,** Sheila *DrAPF 91*
**Nickerson,** Stephen Clark 1950- *AmMWSc 92*
**Nickerson,** William H 1939- *WhoAmP 91*
**Nickerson,** Willie Curtis 1926- *WhoBlA 92*
**Nickinello,** Louis R 1940- *WhoAmP 91*
**Nickisch,** Willard Wayne 1939- *WhoMW 92*
**Nicklas,** Robert Bruce 1932- *AmMWSc 92*
**Nicklas,** Tori Jane 1960- *WhoWest 92*
**Nicklaus,** Charles Edward 1915- *WhoMW 92*
**Nicklaus,** Frederick *DrAPF 91*
**Nicklaus,** Jack William 1940- *FacFETw, IntWW 91, Who 92*
**Nickle,** David Allan 1944- *AmMWSc 92*
**Nickle,** Dennis Edwin 1936- *WhoFI 92, WhoRel 92*
**Nickle,** William R 1935- *AmMWSc 92*
**Nickles,** Don 1948- *AlmAP 92 [port]*
**Nickles,** Donald Lee 1948- *IntWW 91, WhoAmP 91*
**Nickles,** Robert Jerome 1940- *AmMWSc 92*
**Nickless,** David Morgan 1952- *WhoAmL 92*
**Nickless,** Will 1902-1979? *SmATA 66 [port]*
**Nicklow,** Robert Merle 1936- *AmMWSc 92*
**Nickol,** Brent Bonner 1940- *AmMWSc 92*
**Nickol,** Steven R 1950- *WhoAmP 91*
**Nickolas,** George Tom 1933- *WhoMW 92*
**Nickolay,** Timothy John 1964- *WhoMW 92*
**Nickolls,** John Richard 1950- *AmMWSc 92*
**Nickoloff,** Brian 1959- *WhoEnt 92*
**Nickols,** G Allen 1951- *AmMWSc 92*
**Nickols,** Herbert Arthur 1926- *Who 92*
**Nickols,** Norris Allan 1928- *AmMWSc 92*
**Nickon,** Alex 1927- *AmMWSc 92*
**Nicks,** Oran Wesley 1925- *AmMWSc 92*
**Nicks,** Stevie 1948- *WhoEnt 92*
**Nicks,** William James, Sr. 1905- *WhoBlA 92*
**Nicksay,** David *IntMPA 92*
**Nicksay,** David A. *WhoEnt 92*
**Nicksich,** Paul Nick 1951- *WhoWest 92*
**Nickson,** Arthur 1902?-1974 *TwCWW 91*
**Nickson,** David 1929- *Who 92*
**Nickson,** David Wigley 1929- *IntWW 91*
**Nickson,** Francis 1929- *Who 92*
**Nickson,** Milton Scott, Jr. 1934- *WhoAmL 92*
**Nickson,** Richard *DrAPF 91*
**Nickson,** Sheila Joan 1936- *WhoBlA 92*
**Nickum,** Gary John 1948- *WhoFI 92*
**Nickum,** John Gerald 1935- *AmMWSc 92*
**Niclas Krebs** 1401-1464 *DcLB 115 [port]*
**Niclas von Cusse** 1401-1464 *DcLB 115 [port]*
**Nico,** William Raymond 1940- *AmMWSc 92*
**Nicodemus,** David Bowman 1916- *AmMWSc 92*
**Nicodemus,** Fred E 1911- *AmMWSc 92*
**Nicodemus,** William Byron 1943- *WhoMW 92*
**Nicodim** 1929-1978 *DcEcMov*
**Nicodim,** Ion 1932- *IntWW 91*
**Nicol** *Who 92*
**Nicol,** Baroness 1923- *Who 92*
**Nicol,** Abioseh 1924- *IntAu&W 91, WrDr 92*
**Nicol,** Alex 1919- *IntMPA 92*
**Nicol,** Andrew William 1933- *Who 92*
**Nicol,** Angus Sebastian Torquil Eyers 1933- *Who 92*
**Nicol,** Betty Lou 1922- *WhoAmP 91*
**Nicol,** C W *IntAu&W 91*
**Nicol,** Charles Albert 1925- *AmMWSc 92*
**Nicol,** David 1915- *AmMWSc 92*
**Nicol,** Davidson Sylvester Hector W. 1924- *IntWW 91, Who 92*
**Nicol,** Dominik 1930- *IntAu&W 91*
**Nicol,** Donald MacGillivray 1923- *IntAu&W 91, IntWW 91, Who 92, WrDr 92*
**Nicol,** Eric 1919- *ConAu 36NR*
**Nicol,** James 1921- *AmMWSc 92*
**Nicol,** Joseph Arthur Colin 1915- *IntWW 91, Who 92*
**Nicol,** Malcolm F. 1939- *WhoWest 92*
**Nicol,** Malcolm Foertner 1939- *AmMWSc 92*
**Nicol,** Susan Elizabeth 1941- *AmMWSc 92*
**Nicol-Cole,** Silvanus B. 1920- *IntWW 91*
**Nicola,** Andree *ConAu 133*
**Nicola,** James B. 1958- *WhoEnt 92*
**Nicoladis,** Michael Frank 1960- *WhoFI 92*
**Nicolae,** George G 1943- *AmMWSc 92*
**Nicolaeff,** Ariadne 1915- *IntAu&W 91, WrDr 92*
**Nicolaenko,** Basil 1942- *AmMWSc 92*
**Nicolai,** Christoph Friedrich 1733-1811 *BlkwCEP*
**Nicolai,** Eugene Ralph 1911- *WhoWest 92*
**Nicolai,** Otto 1810-1849 *NewAmDM*
**Nicolai,** Paul Peter 1953- *WhoAmL 92*
**Nicolai,** Van Olin 1924- *AmMWSc 92*
**Nicolaides,** Cristino 1925- *IntWW 91*
**Nicolaides,** John Dudley 1923- *AmMWSc 92*
**Nicolaides,** Mary 1927- *WhoAmL 92*
**Nicolaides,** R A 1946- *AmMWSc 92*
**Nicolaisen,** B H 1920- *AmMWSc 92*
**Nicolanti,** David Raymond 1947- *WhoFI 92*
**Nicolas,** F R E *IntAu&W 91X*
**Nicolas,** Georges Spiridon 1952- *WhoFI 92*
**Nicolau,** Gabriela 1928- *AmMWSc 92*
**Nicolaus Cusanus** 1401-1464 *DcLB 115 [port]*
**Nicolay,** Dana Eugene 1953- *WhoEnt 92*
**Nicolay,** J. G. 1832-1901 *BenetAL 91*
**Nicolay,** Janice *WhoAmP 91*
**Nicolaysen,** Bruce 1934- *IntAu&W 91, WrDr 92*
**Nicolazzi,** Franco 1924- *IntWW 91*
**Nicole,** Christopher 1930- *WrDr 92*
**Nicole,** Christopher Robin 1930- *IntAu&W 91*
**Nicolet,** Aurele 1926- *NewAmDM*
**Nicolet,** Claude 1930- *IntWW 91*
**Nicolette,** Archie John 1918- *WhoMW 92*
**Nicolette,** John Anthony 1935- *AmMWSc 92*
**Nicoletti,** Francois-Xavier 1936- *WhoFI 92*
**Nicoletti,** Geoffrey Louis 1949- *WhoRel 92*
**Nicoletti,** Joseph 1947- *WhoWest 92*
**Nicoletti,** Joseph Daniel 1930- *WhoFI 92*
**Nicoli,** Eric Luciano 1950- *Who 92*
**Nicolin,** Curt Rene 1921- *IntWW 91*
**Nicolini** 1673-1732 *NewAmDM*
**Nicoll,** Charles S 1937- *AmMWSc 92*
**Nicoll,** Douglas Robertson 1920- *Who 92*
**Nicoll,** Helen 1937- *WrDr 92*
**Nicoll,** Jeffrey Fancher 1948- *AmMWSc 92*
**Nicoll,** Roger Andrew 1941- *AmMWSc 92*
**Nicoll,** Ronald Ewart 1921- *Who 92*
**Nicoll,** William 1927- *Who 92*
**Nicolle,** Anthony William 1935- *Who 92*
**Nicolle,** Charles Jules Henri 1866-1936 *WhoNob 90*
**Nicolle,** Francois Marcel Andre 1937- *AmMWSc 92*
**Nicolle,** Rachelle Joye 1954- *WhoAmL 92*
**Nicollet,** Joseph Nicholas *BenetAL 91*
**Nicollet,** Joseph Nicolas 1786-1843 *BiInAmS*
**Nicolls,** Ken E 1935- *AmMWSc 92*
**Nicoloff,** Demetre M 1933- *AmMWSc 92*
**Nicolosi,** Gregory Ralph 1943- *AmMWSc 92*
**Nicolosi,** Joseph Anthony 1950- *AmMWSc 92*
**Nicolosi,** Vincent F *WhoAmP 91*
**Nicolson** *Who 92*
**Nicolson,** David 1922- *Who 92*
**Nicolson,** David Lancaster 1922- *IntWW 91*
**Nicolson,** Ian 1928- *WrDr 92*
**Nicolson,** Malise Allen 1921- *Who 92*
**Nicolson,** Nigel 1917- *IntAu&W 91, Who 92, WrDr 92*
**Nicolson,** Paul Clement 1938- *AmMWSc 92*
**Nicolson,** Roy Macdonald 1944- *Who 92*
**Nicosia,** Joseph A. 1943- *WhoFI 92*
**Nicosia,** Santo Valerio 1943- *AmMWSc 92*
**Nicuesa,** Diego de 1465-1511? *HisDSpE*
**Niculescu,** Bogdan Nicolae *IntWW 91*
**Niculescu,** Stefan 1927- *ConCom 92, IntWW 91*
**Nida,** Eugene Albert 1914- *WhoRel 92*
**Nida,** Robert Hale 1940- *WhoAmL 92*
**Niday,** James Barker 1917- *AmMWSc 92*
**Niden,** Albert H 1927- *AmMWSc 92*
**Nidetz,** Myron Philip 1935- *WhoFI 92, WhoMW 92*
**Nido,** Rafael Juan, III 1969- *WhoHisp 92*
**Nie Bichu** 1928- *IntWW 91*
**Nie Fengzhi** 1914- *IntWW 91*
**Nie Gongcheng** *IntWW 91*
**Nie Kuiju** 1929- *IntWW 91*
**Nie Li** 1932- *IntWW 91*
**Nie Rongzhen** 1899- *IntWW 91*
**Niebanck,** Harold F. 1957- *WhoFI 92*
**Niebauer,** John J 1914- *AmMWSc 92*
**Niebel,** B W 1918- *AmMWSc 92*
**Niebergall,** Paul J 1932- *AmMWSc 92*
**Nieberlein,** Vernon Adolph 1918- *AmMWSc 92*
**Niebla,** Elvia Elisa 1945- *WhoHisp 92*
**Niebla,** J. Fernando 1939- *WhoHisp 92*
**Niebuhr,** Helmut Richard 1894-1962 *RelLAm 91*
**Niebuhr,** Reinhold 1892-1971 *AmPeW, BenetAL 91, DcEcMov, FacFETw, RComAH, RelLAm 91*
**Niebuhr,** Richard Reinhold 1926- *WhoRel 92*
**Nieburg,** H. L. 1927- *WrDr 92*
**Niebyl,** Jennifer Robinson 1942- *AmMWSc 92*
**Niedbalski,** Joseph S *AmMWSc 92*
**Niedecker,** Charles William 1913- *WhoIns 92*
**Niedecker,** Lorine 1903-1970 *BenetAL 91*
**Nieden,** Wilhelm zur 1878-1945 *EncTR 91*
**Niedenfuhr,** Francis W 1926- *AmMWSc 92*
**Niedenzu,** Kurt 1930- *AmMWSc 92*

**Nieder**, Rhonda Michele 1957- *WhoFI 92*
**Niedergeses**, James D. 1917- *WhoRel 92*
**Niederhauser**, Warren Dexter 1918- *AmMWSc 92*
**Niederhoffer**, Roy Gary 1966- *WhoFI 92*
**Niederjohn**, Russell James 1944- *AmMWSc 92, WhoMW 92*
**Niederkorn**, Jerry Young 1946- *AmMWSc 92*
**Niederland**, William G 1904- *AmMWSc 92*
**Niederman**, James Corson 1924- *AmMWSc 92*
**Niederman**, Kim 1951- *WhoMW 92*
**Niederman**, Richard *AmMWSc 92*
**Niederman**, Robert Aaron 1937- *AmMWSc 92*
**Niedermayer**, Alfred O 1921- *AmMWSc 92*
**Niedermeier**, Robert Paul 1918- *AmMWSc 92*
**Niedermeier**, Thomas Paul 1943- *WhoMW 92*
**Niedermeier**, William 1923- *AmMWSc 92*
**Niedermeyer**, Ernst F 1920- *AmMWSc 92*
**Niederpruem**, Donald J 1928- *AmMWSc 92*
**Niederstadt**, Roland G 1943- *WhoAmP 91*
**Niedner**, Frederick Arthur, Jr. 1945- *WhoMW 92, WhoRel 92*
**Niedrach**, Leonard William 1921- *AmMWSc 92*
**Nieduszynski**, Anthony John 1939- *Who 92*
**Niedzielski**, Edmund Luke 1917- *AmMWSc 92*
**Niedzielski**, Henri Zygmunt 1931- *WhoWest 92*
**Niedzielski**, Henryk Zygmunt 1931- *IntAu&W 91*
**Niedzwiecki**, Alexandra 1948- *WhoWest 92*
**Niefeld**, Jaye Sutter 1924- *WhoFI 92*
**Niefeld**, Jo Ann R 1929- *WhoAmP 91*
**Nieforth**, Karl Allen 1936- *AmMWSc 92*
**Nieh Jung-Chen** *IntWW 91*
**Nieh K'uei-Chu** *IntWW 91*
**Niehans**, Daniel 1949- *WhoAmL 92*
**Niehans**, Juerg 1919- *ConAu 133*
**Niehans**, Jurg *ConAu 133*
**Niehaus**, Chloe Mae 1929- *WhoMW 92*
**Niehaus**, James William 1955- *WhoMW 92*
**Niehaus**, Keith Allen 1964- *WhoMW 92*
**Niehaus**, Merle H. 1933- *WhoWest 92*
**Niehaus**, Merle Hinson 1933- *AmMWSc 92*
**Niehaus**, Robert James 1930- *WhoFI 92*
**Niehaus**, Walter G, Jr 1937- *AmMWSc 92*
**Niehaus-Kleinman**, Agnes 1925- *WhoEnt 92*
**Niehauser**, Gregory Anthony 1963- *WhoMW 92*
**Niehenke**, John Joseph 1944- *WhoFI 92*
**Niehoff**, K. Richard B. 1943- *WhoFI 92*
**Niehoff**, Leonard Marvin 1957- *WhoAmL 92*
**Niehoff**, Philip John 1959- *WhoAmL 92*
**Niehoff**, William Joseph 1960- *WhoAmL 92*
**Niehouse**, Oliver Leslie 1920- *WhoFI 92*
**Niekamp**, Carl William 1943- *AmMWSc 92*
**Niekisch**, Ernst 1889-1967 *BiDExR, EncTR 91*
**Nielan**, Paul E 1957- *AmMWSc 92*
**Nield**, Basil Edward 1903- *Who 92*
**Nield**, David A 1938- *WhoIns 92*
**Nield**, Howard 1949- *ConAu 135*
**Nield**, William 1913- *Who 92*
**Niell**, Arthur Edwin 1942- *AmMWSc 92*
**Nielsen**, A.C., Jr. *LesBEnT 92*
**Nielsen**, Aksel Christopher W. *Who 92*
**Nielsen**, Alan Walter 1946- *WhoEnt 92*
**Nielsen**, Albert Kramer 1920- *WhoRel 92*
**Nielsen**, Alvin Herborg 1910- *AmMWSc 92*
**Nielsen**, Arnold Thor 1923- *AmMWSc 92*
**Nielsen**, Arthur C., Sr. d1980 *LesBEnT 92*
**Nielsen**, Arthur Hansen 1914- *WhoAmL 92*
**Nielsen**, Arthur R 1942- *WhoIns 92*
**Nielsen**, Barbara *WhoAmP 91*
**Nielsen**, Ben R 1945- *WhoAmP 91*
**Nielsen**, Boje Turin 1944- *WhoWest 92*
**Nielsen**, Carl 1865-1931 *FacFETw, NewAmDM*
**Nielsen**, Carl Eby 1915- *AmMWSc 92*
**Nielsen**, Christian Bayard 1954- *WhoAmL 92*
**Nielsen**, Christian Eric 1960- *WhoFI 92*
**Nielsen**, Corbett A *WhoIns 92*
**Nielsen**, David Gary 1943- *AmMWSc 92*
**Nielsen**, Dennis E. 1937- *WhoFI 92*
**Nielsen**, Donald R 1930- *AmMWSc 92*
**Nielsen**, Donald R 1931- *AmMWSc 92*
**Nielsen**, Donald Rodney 1931- *WhoWest 92*
**Nielsen**, Erik H. 1924- *IntWW 91, Who 92*
**Nielsen**, Forrest Harold 1941- *AmMWSc 92, WhoMW 92*
**Nielsen**, Gerald Alan 1934- *AmMWSc 92*
**Nielsen**, Glade 1926- *WhoAmP 91*
**Nielsen**, Greg Ross 1947- *WhoAmL 92*
**Nielsen**, Harald Christian 1930- *AmMWSc 92*
**Nielsen**, Helen 1918- *IntAu&W 91, WrDr 92*
**Nielsen**, Helge 1918- *IntWW 91*
**Nielsen**, Helmer L 1921- *AmMWSc 92*
**Nielsen**, James Wiley 1944- *WhoAmP 91*
**Nielsen**, John Mark 1951- *WhoMW 92*
**Nielsen**, John Merle 1928- *AmMWSc 92*
**Nielsen**, John P 1911- *AmMWSc 92*
**Nielsen**, Joyce 1933- *WhoAmP 91*
**Nielsen**, Kaj Leo 1914- *AmMWSc 92*
**Nielsen**, Kenneth Burton 1929- *WhoAmP 91*
**Nielsen**, Kent Christopher 1945- *AmMWSc 92*
**Nielsen**, Kirsten 1943- *WhoRel 92*
**Nielsen**, Klaus H B 1945- *AmMWSc 92*
**Nielsen**, Lawrence Arthur 1934- *AmMWSc 92*
**Nielsen**, Lawrence Ernie 1917- *AmMWSc 92*
**Nielsen**, Leland C. 1919- *WhoAmL 92*
**Nielsen**, Leslie 1926- *IntMPA 92, WhoEnt 92*
**Nielsen**, Lewis Thomas 1920- *AmMWSc 92*
**Nielsen**, Mark Joseph 1959- *WhoFI 92, WhoWest 92*
**Nielsen**, Merlyn Keith 1948- *AmMWSc 92*
**Nielsen**, Milo Alfred 1938- *AmMWSc 92*
**Nielsen**, N Norby 1928- *AmMWSc 92*
**Nielsen**, N Ole 1930- *AmMWSc 92*
**Nielsen**, Niels Christian 1921- *IntAu&W 91*
**Nielsen**, Niels Christian 1942- *AmMWSc 92*
**Nielsen**, Niels Christian, Jr. 1921- *WhoRel 92, WrDr 92*
**Nielsen**, Niels F, Jr 1927- *WhoAmP 91*
**Nielsen**, Norman L 1935- *WhoAmP 91*
**Nielsen**, Norman Russell 1941- *AmMWSc 92, WhoWest 92*
**Nielsen**, Paul Herron 1943- *AmMWSc 92*
**Nielsen**, Peter Adams 1926- *AmMWSc 92*
**Nielsen**, Peter James 1938- *AmMWSc 92*
**Nielsen**, Peter Tryon 1933- *AmMWSc 92*
**Nielsen**, Philip Edward 1944- *AmMWSc 92*
**Nielsen**, Ray 1916- *WhoAmP 91*
**Nielsen**, Sivert Andreas 1916- *IntWW 91*
**Nielsen**, Stephen James 1951- *WhoWest 92*
**Nielsen**, Stu *WhoAmP 91*
**Nielsen**, Stuart Dee 1932- *AmMWSc 92, WhoWest 92*
**Nielsen**, Surl L 1936- *AmMWSc 92*
**Nielsen**, Susan Thomson 1947- *AmMWSc 92*
**Nielsen**, Svend Woge 1926- *AmMWSc 92*
**Nielsen**, Tage 1929- *ConCom 92*
**Nielsen**, Tore Rynning 1960- *WhoFI 92*
**Nielsen**, William F. 1934- *WhoAmL 92*
**Nielson**, Clair W 1935- *AmMWSc 92*
**Nielson**, Dennis Lon 1948- *AmMWSc 92*
**Nielson**, Eldon Denzel 1920- *AmMWSc 92*
**Nielson**, George Marius 1934- *AmMWSc 92*
**Nielson**, Howard C 1924- *WhoAmP 91*
**Nielson**, Howard Curtis 1924- *AmMWSc 92, WhoWest 92*
**Nielson**, Jane Ellen 1943- *AmMWSc 92*
**Nielson**, John Williams 1968- *WhoRel 92*
**Nielson**, Mervin William 1927- *AmMWSc 92*
**Nielson**, Read R 1928- *AmMWSc 92*
**Niem**, Alan Randolph 1944- *AmMWSc 92*
**Niem**, Wendy Adams 1946- *AmMWSc 92*
**Nieman**, Frank Bernard 1932- *WhoRel 92*
**Nieman**, Gary Frank *AmMWSc 92*
**Nieman**, George Carroll 1938- *AmMWSc 92*
**Nieman**, Nancy Dale 1939- *WhoWest 92*
**Nieman**, Richard Hovey 1922- *AmMWSc 92, WhoWest 92*
**Nieman**, Timothy Alan 1948- *AmMWSc 92, WhoMW 92*
**Niemann**, August 1839-1919 *ScFEYrs*
**Niemann**, Harry C 1932- *WhoIns 92*
**Niemann**, Linda 1946- *ConAu 133*
**Niemann**, Marilyn Anne *AmMWSc 92*
**Niemann**, Nicholas Kent 1956- *WhoMW 92*
**Niemann**, Ralph Henry 1922- *AmMWSc 92*
**Niemann**, Theodore Frank 1939- *AmMWSc 92*
**Niemczyk**, Harry D 1929- *AmMWSc 92*
**Niemczyk**, Julian M *WhoAmP 91*
**Niemczyk**, Thomas M 1947- *AmMWSc 92*
**Niemeier**, Richard William 1945- *AmMWSc 92*
**Niemeth**, Charles Frederick 1939- *WhoAmL 92*
**Niemeyer**, Daniel Charles 1939- *WhoEnt 92*
**Niemeyer**, George Lewis 1939- *WhoMW 92*
**Niemeyer**, Gerhart 1907- *IntWW 91*
**Niemeyer**, Kenneth H 1928- *AmMWSc 92*
**Niemeyer**, Oscar 1907- *IntWW 91, Who 92*
**Niemeyer**, Paul Victor 1941- *WhoAmL 92, WhoAmP 91*
**Niemeyer**, Sidney 1951- *AmMWSc 92*
**Niemeyer**, Theodore Michael 1949- *WhoFI 92*
**Niemi**, Alfred Otto 1915- *AmMWSc 92*
**Niemi**, Bruce Edward 1949- *WhoAmP 91*
**Niemi**, Irmeli 1931- *IntWW 91*
**Niemi**, Janice *WhoAmP 91*
**Niemi**, Janice 1928- *WhoWest 92*
**Niemi**, Nicole *DrAPF 91*
**Niemi**, Peter G. 1937- *WhoMW 92*
**Niemi**, Robert John 1961- *WhoWest 92*
**Niemiec**, Peter Jude 1951- *WhoAmL 92*
**Nieminen**, Kai Tapani 1950- *IntAu&W 91*
**Nieminski**, Joseph Ignatius 1926- *WhoRel 92*
**Niemira**, Michael Paul 1955- *WhoFI 92*
**Niemitz**, Jeffrey William 1950- *AmMWSc 92*
**Niemoeller**, John Arthur 1957- *WhoAmL 92*
**Niemoeller**, Martin 1892-1984 *FacFETw*
**Niemoller**, Arthur B. 1912- *WhoFI 92, WhoMW 92*
**Niemoller**, Klaus 1929- *IntWW 91*
**Niemoller**, Martin 1892-1984 *DcEcMov, EncTR 91 [port]*
**Niemuth**, Todd Roger 1963- *WhoMW 92*
**Nien Te-Hsiang** *IntWW 91*
**Nienburg**, George Frank 1938- *WhoFI 92*
**Nienhouse**, Everett J 1936- *AmMWSc 92*
**Nienhuis**, Arthur Wesley 1941- *AmMWSc 92*
**Nienstaedt**, Hans 1922- *AmMWSc 92*
**Nieporte**, William Michael 1963- *WhoRel 92*
**Nier**, Alfred O. C. 1911- *IntWW 91*
**Nier**, Alfred Otto Carl 1911- *AmMWSc 92*
**Nierenberg**, Gerard I. 1923- *WrDr 92*
**Nierenberg**, Norman 1919- *WhoFI 92, WhoWest 92*
**Nierenberg**, Roger 1947- *WhoEnt 92*
**Nierenberg**, William Aaron 1919- *AmMWSc 92, IntWW 91, WhoWest 92*
**Niering**, William Albert 1924- *AmMWSc 92*
**Nierlich**, Donald P 1935- *AmMWSc 92*
**Nierman**, Lyndy Ann 1947- *WhoMW 92*
**Niermann**, Thomas Arthur 1941- *WhoRel 92*
**Niersbach**, Donald Charles 1928- *WhoMW 92*
**Nierste**, Joseph Paul 1952- *WhoMW 92*
**Nies**, Alan Sheffer 1937- *AmMWSc 92*
**Nies**, Helen W *WhoAmP 91*
**Nies**, Helen Wilson *WhoAmL 92*
**Niese**, Harry Allan 1945- *WhoFI 92*
**Niesen**, Thomas Marvin 1944- *AmMWSc 92*
**Niesluchowski**, Witold S. 1944- *WhoWest 92*
**Niesse**, John Edgar 1927- *AmMWSc 92*
**Nieto**, Ernesto *WhoHisp 92*
**Nieto**, Eva Margarita *WhoHisp 92*
**Nieto**, Eva Maria 1922- *WhoHisp 92*
**Nieto**, Juan Maria 1936- *WhoMW 92*
**Nieto**, Luis P., Jr. 1955- *WhoHisp 92*
**Nieto**, Maria Refugio 1949- *WhoHisp 92*
**Nieto**, Michael Martin 1940- *AmMWSc 92, WhoHisp 92*
**Nieto**, Minerva 1948- *WhoHisp 92*
**Nieto**, Ramon Dante 1957- *WhoHisp 92*
**Nieto**, Rebecca Ann 1962- *WhoHisp 92*
**Nieto**, Rey J. *WhoHisp 92*
**Nieto**, Sonia 1943- *WhoHisp 92*
**Nieto Del Rio**, Juan Carlos 1962- *WhoHisp 92*
**Nieto Gallo**, Gratiniano 1917- *IntWW 91*
**Nietzsche**, Friedrich 1844-1900 *EncTR 91 [port]*
**Nieuwerkerke**, Emilien, Comte de 1811-1892 *ThHEIm*
**Nieuwsma**, Milton John 1941- *WhoFI 92, WhoMW 92*
**Nievergelt**, Jurg 1938- *AmMWSc 92*
**Nievergelt**, Yves 1954- *AmMWSc 92*
**Nieves**, Agustin Alberto 1963- *WhoHisp 92*
**Nieves**, Alvaro Lezcano 1944- *WhoHisp 92*
**Nieves**, Evelyn J. 1960- *WhoHisp 92*
**Nieves**, Felix D. 1942- *WhoHisp 92*
**Nieves**, Juan Manuel 1965- *WhoHisp 92*
**Nieves**, Marysol 1965- *WhoHisp 92*
**Nieves**, Robert 1945- *WhoHisp 92*
**Nieves**, Theresa 1952- *WhoHisp 92*
**Nieves**, Wilfredo 1949- *WhoHisp 92*
**Nieves-Cruz**, Bedford 1961- *WhoHisp 92*
**Nieviera**, Else 1891-1944 *EncTR 91*
**Nieweg**, Clinton Fairlamb 1937- *WhoEnt 92*
**Niewenhuis**, Robert James 1936- *AmMWSc 92*
**Niewiarowski**, Stefan 1928- *AmMWSc 92*
**Niewood**, Gerard Joseph 1943- *WhoEnt 92*
**Niezabitowska**, Malgorzata 1948- *IntWW 91*
**Niezabitowska**, Malgorzata 1949?- *News 91 [port], -91-3 [port]*
**Niezer**, Thomas Maurice 1959- *WhoAmL 92*
**Niffenegger**, Daniel Arvid 1930- *AmMWSc 92*
**Niflis**, Michael *DrAPF 91*
**Nigam**, Anjul 1965- *WhoEnt 92*
**Nigam**, Bishan Perkash 1928- *AmMWSc 92, WhoWest 92*
**Nigam**, Lakshmi Narayan 1934- *AmMWSc 92*
**Nigeria**, Metropolitan Archbishop of *Who 92*
**Nigg**, Herbert Nicholas 1941- *AmMWSc 92*
**Nigg**, Joe *ConAu 35NR*
**Nigg**, Joseph E 1938- *ConAu 35NR*
**Nigg**, Joseph Eugene 1938- *IntAu&W 91*
**Nigg**, Serge 1924- *ConCom 92, NewAmDM*
**Niggemann**, Richard Everett 1938- *WhoMW 92*
**Niggli**, Josephina 1910-1983 *BenetAL 91*
**Nigh**, Edward Leroy, Jr 1927- *AmMWSc 92*
**Nigh**, George 1927- *IntWW 91*
**Nigh**, George Patterson 1927- *WhoAmP 91*
**Nigh**, Harold Eugene 1932- *AmMWSc 92*
**Nighswander**, Esther R *WhoAmP 91*
**Nighswonger**, Paul Floyd 1923- *AmMWSc 92*
**Nighswonger**, Terri Kay 1962- *WhoMW 92*
**Nightingale**, Arthur Esten 1919- *AmMWSc 92*
**Nightingale**, Barbra *DrAPF 91*
**Nightingale**, Ben *DrAPF 91*
**Nightingale**, Benedict *Who 92*
**Nightingale**, Benedict 1939- *IntWW 91*
**Nightingale**, Charles 1947- *Who 92*
**Nightingale**, Charles Henry 1939- *AmMWSc 92*
**Nightingale**, Dorothy Virginia 1902- *AmMWSc 92*
**Nightingale**, Edmund Anthony 1903- *WhoMW 92*
**Nightingale**, Edmund Joseph 1941- *WhoMW 92*
**Nightingale**, Edward Humphrey 1904- *Who 92*
**Nightingale**, Elena Ottolenghi 1932- *AmMWSc 92*
**Nightingale**, Geoffrey Joseph 1938- *WhoFI 92*
**Nightingale**, Jesse Phillip 1919- *WhoBlA 92*
**Nightingale**, John 1913- *Who 92*
**Nightingale**, Paula *TwCPaSc*
**Nightingale**, Richard Edwin 1926- *AmMWSc 92*
**Nightingale**, Roger Daniel 1945- *Who 92*
**Nightingale**, William Benedict 1939- *Who 92*
**Nightingale of Cromarty**, Michael David 1927- *Who 92*
**Nigra**, John Dominick 1931- *WhoFI 92*
**Nigrelli**, Ross Franco 1903- *AmMWSc 92*
**Nigro**, Armand Michael 1928- *WhoRel 92*
**Nigro**, Bernard Angelo, Jr. 1960- *WhoAmL 92*
**Nigro**, Felix A. 1914- *WrDr 92*
**Nigro**, Joseph Ben 1946- *WhoAmP 91*
**Nigro**, Nicholas J 1934- *AmMWSc 92*
**Nigrovic**, Vladimir 1934- *AmMWSc 92*
**Nihal Singh**, Surendra 1929- *IntAu&W 91, IntWW 91*
**Nihart**, Ruth Lucille *WhoMW 92*
**Nihil**, Marlys Lenz 1925- *WhoMW 92*
**Nihill**, Julian Dumontiel 1950- *WhoAmL 92*
**Niilus**, Leopoldo Juan 1930- *IntWW 91*
**Niitamo**, Olavi Ensio 1926- *IntWW 91*
**Nijdam**, Christophe Andre Francois 1956- *WhoFI 92*
**Nijenhuis**, Albert 1926- *AmMWSc 92*
**Nijenhuis**, Emmie te 1931- *IntWW 91*
**Nijhout**, H Frederik 1947- *AmMWSc 92*
**Nijinska**, Bronislava 1891-1972 *FacFETw*
**Nijinska**, Irina 1913-1991 *NewYTBS 91 [port]*
**Nijinsky**, Vaslav 1890-1950 *FacFETw [port]*
**Nijpels**, Eduardus Hermannes Theresia M. 1950- *IntWW 91*
**Nikaido**, Hiroshi 1932- *AmMWSc 92*
**Nikaido**, Susumu 1909- *IntWW 91*
**Nikander**, Juho Kustaa 1855-1919 *DcAmImH*
**Nikelly**, John G 1929- *AmMWSc 92*
**Nikezic**, Marko d1991 *NewYTBS 91*
**Niki**, Hiromi *AmMWSc 92*

**Nikich**, Anatoliy Yur'evich 1918- SovUnBD
**Nikich-Krilichevsky**, Anatoliy Yur'evich 1918- SovUnBD
**Nikiforov**, Valentin Mikhailovich 1934- IntWW 91
**Nikiforuk**, Gordon 1922- AmMWSc 92
**Nikiforuk**, P N 1930- AmMWSc 92
**Nikisch**, Arthur 1855-1922 FacFETw, NewAmDM
**Nikitin**, Aleksey Vasil'evich 1937-1984 SovUnBD
**Nikitin**, Sergey Konstantinovich 1926- IntWW 91
**Nikitin**, Vladilen Valentinovich 1936- IntWW 91
**Nikitovitch-Winer**, Miroslava B 1929- AmMWSc 92
**Nikkel**, Henry 1922- AmMWSc 92
**Nikkel**, Ronald Wilbert 1946- WhoRel 92
**Niklas**, Karl Joseph 1948- AmMWSc 92
**Niklasson**, Bertil, Frau Who 92
**Niklaus**, Robert 1910- IntAu&W 91, Who 92, WrDr 92
**Niklaus**, Thelma 1912-1970 ConAu 134
**Niklowitz**, Werner Johannes 1923- AmMWSc 92
**Niklus**, Mart-Olav 1934- SovUnBD
**Nikodem**, Robert Bruce 1939- AmMWSc 92
**Nikodim**, Metropolitan 1929-1978 SovUnBD
**Nikoi**, Amon 1930- IntWW 91
**Nikolaeva**, Galina Yevgen'evna 1911-1963 SovUnBD
**Nikolaeva**, Klavdiya Ivanovna 1893-1944 SovUnBD
**Nikolai**, Paul John 1931- AmMWSc 92
**Nikolai**, Robert Joseph 1937- AmMWSc 92
**Nikolais**, Alwin Theodore 1910- WhoEnt 92
**Nikolayev**, Andrian 1929- FacFETw
**Nikolayeva**, Tatiana Petrovna 1924- IntWW 91
**Nikolayeva-Tereshkova**, Valentina V 1937- Who 92
**Nikolic**, Nikola M 1927- AmMWSc 92
**Nikolsky**, Sergey Ivanovich 1923- IntWW 91
**Nikonov**, Aleksandr Aleksandrovich 1918- SovUnBD
**Nikonov**, Viktor Petrovich 1929- IntWW 91, SovUnBD
**Nikora**, Allen P 1955- AmMWSc 92
**Nikoui**, Hossein Reza 1949- WhoMW 92
**Nikoui**, Nik 1938- AmMWSc 92
**Nikulin**, Ivan Ivanovich IntWW 91
**Nil**, Guven 1944- WhoFI 92
**Nilan**, Robert Arthur 1923- AmMWSc 92
**Nilan**, Thomas George 1926- AmMWSc 92
**Nile**, Dorothea WrDr 92
**Niles**, Alban I. 1933- WhoBlA 92
**Niles**, Alban Isaac 1933- WhoWest 92
**Niles**, Anita Gale 1919- WhoAmP 91
**Niles**, Blair 1888?-1959 BenetAL 91
**Niles**, Charles Lannon, Jr 1924- WhoIns 92
**Niles**, Daniel Thambyrajah 1908-1970 DcEcMov [port]
**Niles**, George Alva 1926- AmMWSc 92
**Niles**, James Alfred 1945- AmMWSc 92
**Niles**, John Edward 1945- WhoEnt 92
**Niles**, John Gilbert 1943- WhoAmL 92
**Niles**, John Jacob 1892-1980 FacFETw, NewAmDM
**Niles**, John Stanley 1946- WhoFI 92
**Niles**, Lyndrey Arnaud 1936- WhoBlA 92
**Niles**, Nelson Robinson 1924- AmMWSc 92
**Niles**, Philip William Benjamin 1936- AmMWSc 92
**Niles**, Samuel 1674-1762 BenetAL 91
**Niles**, Thomas M T 1939- WhoAmP 91
**Niles**, Thomas Michael Tolliver 1939- IntWW 91
**Niles**, Walter Dulany, II 1953- WhoMW 92
**Niles**, Wesley F 1932- AmMWSc 92
**Niles**, William Harmon 1838-1910 BiInAmS
**Nilges**, Al J 1929- WhoAmP 91
**Nilges**, Mark J 1952- AmMWSc 92
**Nilin**, Pavel Filippovich 1908-1981 SovUnBD
**Nill**, Kimball Roy 1958- WhoMW 92
**Nilles**, John Mathias 1932- WhoWest 92
**Nilles**, John Michael 1930- WhoAmL 92
**Nilon**, Charles Hampton 1916- WhoBlA 92
**Nilon**, Laura Ann 1960- WhoEnt 92
**Nilsen**, Aileen Pace 1936- WhoWest 92
**Nilsen**, Clifford Theodore 1932- WhoFI 92
**Nilsen**, Curt Alan 1965- WhoWest 92
**Nilsen**, Don Lee Fred 1934- WhoWest 92
**Nilsen**, Nels William 1954- WhoRel 92
**Nilsen**, Nicholas 1937- WhoFI 92
**Nilsen**, Richard DrAPF 91
**Nilsen**, Vladimir Semenovich 1905-1938 SovUnBD
**Nilsen**, Walter Grahn 1927- AmMWSc 92
**Nilson**, Arthur H 1926- AmMWSc 92
**Nilson**, Douglas Carlyle 1944- WhoWest 92
**Nilson**, Douglas Carlyle, Jr 1944- WhoAmP 91
**Nilson**, Edwin Norman 1917- AmMWSc 92
**Nilson**, Erick Bogseth 1927- AmMWSc 92
**Nilson**, John Anthony 1936- AmMWSc 92
**Nilson**, Jon 1943- WhoRel 92
**Nilson**, Linda Burzotta 1949- WhoAmP 91
**Nilson**, Maria June 1942- WhoAmP 91
**Nilsson**, Birgit 1918- FacFETw, IntWW 91, NewAmDM, WhoEnt 92
**Nilsson**, Birgit 1922- Who 92
**Nilsson**, Bo 1937- NewAmDM
**Nilsson**, Bruce Eugene 1942- WhoMW 92
**Nilsson**, Goran W. WhoEnt 92
**Nilsson**, Gosta 1912- IntWW 91
**Nilsson**, Harry 1941- WhoEnt 92
**Nilsson**, Nic 1933- WhoFI 92
**Nilsson**, Nils John 1933- AmMWSc 92
**Nilsson**, Robert 1938- IntWW 91
**Nilsson**, William A 1931- AmMWSc 92
**Nilus of Ancyra** d430? EncEarC
**Nilva**, Leonid 1956- WhoWest 92
**Nimah**, Hassan Ali Hussain al- 1940- IntWW 91
**Niman**, John 1938- AmMWSc 92
**Nimatallah**, Yusuf A. 1936- IntWW 91
**Nimer**, Edward Lee 1923- AmMWSc 92
**Nimeri**, Gaafar Mohammed al- IntWW 91
**Nimetz**, Matthew 1939- WhoAmP 91
**Nimitz**, Chester 1885-1966 RComAH
**Nimitz**, Chester William 1885-1966 FacFETw [port]
**Nimitz**, Walter W von AmMWSc 92
**Nimkin**, Bernard William 1923- WhoAmL 92
**Nimmo**, Anthony 1954- WhoAmL 92
**Nimmo**, Bruce Glen 1938- AmMWSc 92
**Nimmo**, Derek Robert 1932- Who 92
**Nimmo**, Herbert Lee 1934- WhoFI 92
**Nimmo**, Jenny 1944- WrDr 92
**Nimmo**, John 1909- Who 92
**Nimmo**, Thomas Dewey 1938- WhoIns 92
**Nimmo Smith**, William Austin 1942- Who 92
**Nimmons**, Julius WhoBlA 92
**Nimmons**, Phillip Rista 1923- WhoEnt 92
**Nimni**, Marcel Efraim 1931- AmMWSc 92
**Nimnicht**, Nona DrAPF 91
**Nimocks**, Michael Frederick 1942- WhoRel 92
**Nimoy**, Leonard LesBEnT 92
**Nimoy**, Leonard 1931- IntMPA 92, IntWW 91, WhoEnt 92
**Nimptsch**, Uli 1897-1977 TwCPaSc
**Nimr**, Nabih al- 1931- IntWW 91
**Nims**, Arthur Lee, III 1923- WhoAmL 92
**Nims**, Gary Alan 1952- WhoRel 92
**Nims**, John Buchanan 1924- AmMWSc 92
**Nims**, John Frederick DrAPF 91
**Nims**, John Frederick 1913- ConAu 35NR, ConPo 91, IntAu&W 91, WrDr 92
**Nims**, Stuart V 1921- WhoAmP 91
**Nims**, Theodore, Jr. 1942- WhoBlA 92
**Nims**, Walter Worthington 1949- WhoMW 92
**Nimsgern**, Siegmund 1940- NewAmDM
**Nin**, Anais 1903-1977 BenetAL 91, FacFETw, HanAmWH, LiExTwC, ModAWWr
**Nin**, Joaquin 1879-1949 NewAmDM
**Nin-Culmell**, Joaquin Maria 1908- IntWW 91, NewAmDM
**Nin y Castellanos**, Joaquin 1879-1949 NewAmDM
**Ninburg**, Daniel Harvey 1928- WhoAmP 91
**Nind**, Philip Frederick 1918- Who 92
**Nine**, Harmon D 1931- AmMWSc 92
**Nineham**, Dennis Eric 1921- IntWW 91, Who 92, WhoRel 92, WrDr 92
**Ning**, Robert Y 1939- AmMWSc 92
**Ning**, Tak Hung 1943- AmMWSc 92
**Ninian** 360?-432? EncEarC
**Nininger**, Robert D 1919- AmMWSc 92
**Ninis**, Richard Betts 1931- Who 92
**Ninke**, Arthur Albert 1909- WhoFI 92, WhoMW 92
**Ninke**, William Herbert 1937- AmMWSc 92
**Ninkovich-Steinbach**, Dana Suzanne 1952- WhoWest 92
**Ninn-Hansen**, Erik 1922- IntWW 91
**Ninneman**, Richard Canney 1936- WhoAmL 92
**Nino** EncEarC
**Nino**, Hipolito V 1924- AmMWSc 92
**Nino**, Jose WhoHisp 92
**Ninos**, Nicholas Peter 1936- WhoWest 92
**Niordson**, Frithiof Igor Niord 1922- IntWW 91
**Nip**, Wai Kit 1941- AmMWSc 92, WhoWest 92
**Nipkow**, Karl-Ernst Heinrich 1928- WhoRel 92
**Nipper**, Henry Carmack 1940- AmMWSc 92
**Nipper**, John Michael 1944- WhoAmP 91
**Nipperdey**, Hans Carl 1895-1968 EncTR 91
**Nippes**, Ernest F 1918- AmMWSc 92
**Nippo**, Murn Marcus 1944- AmMWSc 92
**Nipps**, Randall Cramer 1955- WhoMW 92
**Nipson**, Herbert 1916- WhoBlA 92
**Niquette**, James Randall 1948- WhoAmP 91
**Niquette**, Russell Frank, Sr 1907- WhoAmP 91
**Nirdosh**, Inderjit 1943- AmMWSc 92
**Nirenberg**, Darryl D. 1959- WhoAmL 92
**Nirenberg**, Louis 1925- AmMWSc 92, IntWW 91
**Nirenberg**, Marshall Warren 1927- AmMWSc 92, FacFETw, IntWW 91, Who 92, WhoNob 90
**Nirschl**, Joseph Peter 1945- AmMWSc 92
**Nisari**, Joseph 1942- WhoRel 92
**Nisbet**, Alex Richard 1938- AmMWSc 92
**Nisbet**, Andrew WhoAmP 91
**Nisbet**, Gerald D 1941- WhoAmP 91
**Nisbet**, Hugh Barr 1940- Who 92
**Nisbet**, Hume 1848-1921 ScFEYrs
**Nisbet**, Jerry J 1924- AmMWSc 92
**Nisbet**, Joanne 1931- WhoEnt 92
**Nisbet**, John 1738-1817 DcNCBi 4
**Nisbet**, John Donald 1922- Who 92
**Nisbet**, John S 1927- AmMWSc 92
**Nisbet**, Robin George Murdoch 1925- IntWW 91, Who 92
**Nisbet**, Stanley Donald 1912- Who 92, WrDr 92
**Nisbet-Brown**, Eric Robert 1956- AmMWSc 92
**Nisbet-Smith**, Dugal 1935- Who 92
**Nise**, Michael 1943- WhoEnt 92
**Nisenoff**, Martin 1928- AmMWSc 92
**Nish**, Albert Raymond, Jr. 1922- WhoWest 92
**Nish**, Ian Hill 1926- IntAu&W 91, WrDr 92
**Nishanov**, Rafik Nishanovich 1926- IntWW 91, SovUnBD
**Nishi**, Shunji Forrest 1917- WhoRel 92
**Nishi**, Yoshio 1940- AmMWSc 92
**Nishibayashi**, Masaru 1923- AmMWSc 92
**Nishida**, Mamoru 1928- IntWW 91
**Nishida**, Melody Yae 1957- WhoEnt 92
**Nishida**, Toshiro 1926- AmMWSc 92
**Nishiguchi**, Don Jerry 1955- WhoWest 92
**Nishikawa**, Alfred Hirotoshi 1938- AmMWSc 92
**Nishikawa**, Shojiro 1913- IntWW 91
**Nishikawara**, Margaret T 1923- AmMWSc 92
**Nishikubo**, Duane Tamotsu 1959- WhoWest 92
**Nishimoto**, Roy Katsuto 1944- AmMWSc 92
**Nishimura**, Jonathan Sei 1931- AmMWSc 92
**Nishimura**, Joseph Yo 1933- WhoFI 92
**Nishimura**, Ken 1934- WhoRel 92
**Nishio**, Suehiro 1891-1981 FacFETw
**Nishioka**, David Jitsuo 1945- AmMWSc 92
**Nishioka**, Richard Seiji 1933- AmMWSc 92
**Nishioka**, Teruo 1945- WhoWest 92
**Nishioka**, Yutaka 1948- AmMWSc 92
**Nishitani**, Martha 1920- WhoEnt 92
**Nisi**, Vittoria Eufemia 1943- WhoRel 92
**Nisibori**, Masahiro 1918- IntWW 91
**Niskanen**, Paul McCord 1943- WhoWest 92
**Nisonoff**, Alfred 1923- AmMWSc 92
**Niss**, Hamilton Frederick 1923- AmMWSc 92
**Nissan**, Alfred H 1914- AmMWSc 92
**Nissan**, Alfred Heskel 1914- Who 92
**Nissan**, Michael 1955- WhoAmL 92
**Nissel**, Siegmund 1922- IntWW 91
**Nissel**, Stanley N. 1930 WhoAmL 92
**Nisselbaum**, Jerome Seymour 1925- AmMWSc 92
**Nissen**, Carl Andrew, Jr. 1930- WhoRel 92
**Nissen**, David Edgar Joseph 1942- Who 92
**Nissen**, George Maitland 1930- Who 92
**Nissen**, John Philip 1813-1874 DcNCBi 4
**Nissen**, Judy Kay 1942- WhoFI 92
**Nissen**, Karl Iversen 1906- Who 92
**Nissen**, William John 1947- WhoAmL 92
**Nissenbaum**, Robert Jay 1952- WhoAmL 92
**Nissenson**, Hugh DrAPF 91
**Nissenson**, Hugh 1933- BenetAL 91, ConNov 91, WrDr 92
**Nissenson**, Robert A 1949- AmMWSc 92
**Nissim**, Moshe 1935- IntWW 91
**Nissim-Sabat**, Charles 1938- AmMWSc 92
**Nissinen**, Mikko Pekka 1962- WhoEnt 92
**Nissiotis**, Nikos Angelos 1925-1986 DcEcMov
**Nissky**, Georgiy Grigor'evich 1903- SovUnBD
**Nissley**, Eleanore Steffens WhoAmP 91
**Nissley**, M. John 1949- WhoRel 92
**Nissley**, S Peter AmMWSc 92
**Nissman**, Albert 1930- IntAu&W 91, WrDr 92
**Nissman**, Blossom S. 1928- WrDr 92
**Nist**, John 1925- IntAu&W 91
**Nisteruk**, Chester Joseph 1928- AmMWSc 92
**Nisula**, Bruce Carl 1945- AmMWSc 92
**Niswander**, Calvin Elroy 1925- WhoAmP 91
**Niswander**, Jerry David 1930- AmMWSc 92
**Niswender**, Gordon Dean 1940- AmMWSc 92
**Nitchie**, George Wilson 1921- IntAu&W 91, WrDr 92
**Nitchke**, Howard Dean 1949- WhoFI 92
**Nitecki**, Danute Emilija 1927- AmMWSc 92
**Nitecki**, Matthew H 1925- AmMWSc 92, WhoMW 92
**Nitecki**, Zbigniew 1946- AmMWSc 92
**Nitenson**, Sheldon 1927- WhoFI 92
**Nithman**, Charles Joseph 1937- AmMWSc 92
**Nitikman**, Franklin W. 1940- WhoAmL 92
**Nitisastro**, Widjojo 1927- IntWW 91
**Nitocris** EncAmaz 91
**Nitowsky**, Harold Martin 1925- AmMWSc 92
**Nitsche**, Amy Sowden 1960- WhoWest 92
**Nitsche**, Erik 1908- DcTwDes
**Nitsche**, Johannes Carl Christian AmMWSc 92
**Nitschke**, J Michael 1939- AmMWSc 92
**Nitske**, W. Robert 1909- WrDr 92
**Nitsos**, Ronald Eugene 1937- AmMWSc 92
**Nitta**, Eugene Tadashi 1946- WhoWest 92
**Nitterhouse**, Denise 1950- WhoMW 92
**Nittis**, Guiseppe de 1846-1884 ThHEIm
**Nittler**, LeRoy Walter 1921- AmMWSc 92
**Nittolo**, Raymond Allen 1954- WhoEnt 92
**Nittrouer**, Charles A 1950- AmMWSc 92
**Nitty Gritty Dirt Band**, The ConMus 6 [port]
**Nitty-Gritty Dirt Band** NewAmDM
**Nitz**, David F 1950- AmMWSc 92
**Nitz**, Frederic William 1943- WhoWest 92
**Nitz**, Otto William Julius 1905- AmMWSc 92
**Nitz**, P Kenneth, Jr 1940- WhoIns 92
**Nitzchke**, Oscar d1991 NewYTBS 91
**Nitze**, Paul Henry 1907- IntWW 91, WhoAmP 91
**Nitze**, William Albert 1942- WhoAmL 92
**Nitzschke**, James Lloyd 1951- WhoMW 92
**Niu Shucai** 1908- IntWW 91
**Niu**, David 1960- WhoAmL 92
**Niu**, Mann Chiang 1914- AmMWSc 92
**Niukula**, Paula Nayala 1937- WhoRel 92
**Niumata**, Malo L WhoAmP 91
**Niven**, Alastair 1944- WrDr 92
**Niven**, Alastair Neil Robertson 1944- IntAu&W 91, Who 92
**Niven**, Cecil Rex 1898- Who 92
**Niven**, David, Jr. 1942- IntMPA 92
**Niven**, Donald Ferries 1947- AmMWSc 92
**Niven**, Frederick 1878-1944 BenetAL 91, TwCWW 91
**Niven**, Ian Who 92
**Niven**, John Robertson 1919- Who 92
**Niven**, Larry DrAPF 91
**Niven**, Larry 1938- IntAu&W 91, TwCSFW 91, WrDr 92
**Niven**, Margaret Graeme 1906- TwCPaSc, Who 92
**Niven**, Rex Who 92
**Niven**, Rex 1898- IntAu&W 91, WrDr 92
**Nivens**, Beatryce Thomasinia 1948- WhoBlA 92
**Niver**, Millard Benjamin 1934- WhoMW 92
**Nivert**, Judith A 1949- WhoIns 92
**Nivinsky**, Ignatiy Ignat'evich 1881-1933 SovUnBD
**Nivison** Who 92
**Niwa**, Hyosuke d1990 IntWW 91N
**Niwano**, Nikkyo 1906- IntWW 91
**Nix**, Arthur Wayne 1955- WhoFI 92
**Nix**, Beverly Ann 1951- WhoEnt 92
**Nix**, Charles Ray WhoAmP 91
**Nix**, Dennis Keith 1941- WhoWest 92
**Nix**, Gary William 1941- WhoWest 92
**Nix**, James Kelly 1934- WhoAmP 91
**Nix**, James Rayford 1938- AmMWSc 92, WhoWest 92
**Nix**, Joe Franklin 1939- AmMWSc 92
**Nix**, John Sydney 1927- Who 92
**Nix**, Kenneth Owen 1939- WhoAmP 91
**Nix**, Nancy Jean WhoWest 92
**Nix**, Pat 1931- WhoAmP 91
**Nix**, Rick 1950- WhoBlA 92
**Nix**, Robert Lynn 1940- WhoRel 92

**Nix,** Robert N C, Jr 1928- *WhoAmP 91, WhoBlA 92*
**Nix,** Robert Nelson Cornelius, Jr. 1928- *WhoAmL 92*
**Nix,** Roscoe Russa 1921- *WhoBlA 92*
**Nix,** Sunder 1961- *BlkOlyM*
**Nix,** Theophilus Richard 1925- *WhoBlA 92*
**Nix,** Theophilus Richard, Jr. 1953- *WhoBlA 92*
**Nix,** William Dale 1936- *AmMWSc 92*
**Nix,** William Gaines 1926- *WhoRel 92*
**Nix,** William Patterson 1948- *IntMPA 92*
**Nixon,** Agnes *LesBEnT 92*
**Nixon,** Agnes 1927- *IntMPA 92*
**Nixon,** Agnes Eckhardt *WhoEnt 92*
**Nixon,** Alan Charles 1908- *AmMWSc 92*
**Nixon,** Alfred 1856-1924 *DcNCBi 4*
**Nixon,** Anne Nims 1916- *WhoAmP 91*
**Nixon,** Barbara Elizabeth 1954- *WhoRel 92*
**Nixon,** Baunita T 1932- *WhoAmP 91*
**Nixon,** Carol Holladay 1937- *WhoAmP 91*
**Nixon,** Charles Melville 1935- *AmMWSc 92*
**Nixon,** Charles William 1925- *AmMWSc 92*
**Nixon,** Charles William 1929- *AmMWSc 92*
**Nixon,** Corwin M 1916- *WhoAmP 91*
**Nixon,** Cynthia 1966- *IntMPA 92*
**Nixon,** David *WhoEnt 92*
**Nixon,** David Michael *DrAPF 91*
**Nixon,** Donald Merwin 1935- *AmMWSc 92*
**Nixon,** Edwin 1925- *Who 92*
**Nixon,** Edwin Ronald 1925- *IntWW 91*
**Nixon,** Elray S 1931- *AmMWSc 92*
**Nixon,** Eugene Ray 1919- *AmMWSc 92*
**Nixon,** Felix Nathaniel 1918- *WhoBlA 92*
**Nixon,** George W. 1935- *WhoBlA 92*
**Nixon,** Gladys 1920- *WhoBlA 92*
**Nixon,** Glenford Delacy 1956- *WhoBlA 92*
**Nixon,** Henry Barber 1857-1916 *BiInAmS*
**Nixon,** James Joseph, III 1947- *WhoWest 92*
**Nixon,** James Melvin *WhoBlA 92*
**Nixon,** Jeremiah Willson 1956- *WhoAmP 91*
**Nixon,** Joan Lowery 1927- *ChlLR 24 [port], WrDr 92*
**Nixon,** John 1623?-1692 *DcNCBi 4*
**Nixon,** John Trice 1933- *WhoAmL 92*
**Nixon,** John V 1940- *AmMWSc 92*
**Nixon,** John William 1922- *WhoBlA 92*
**Nixon,** Kenneth Michael John Basil 1919- *Who 92*
**Nixon,** Leslie C 1956- *WhoAmP 91*
**Nixon,** Marni 1930- *NewAmDM, WhoEnt 92*
**Nixon,** Nicholas Nichols 1800-1868 *DcNCBi 4*
**Nixon,** Nick 1945- *WhoEnt 92*
**Nixon,** Norm Ellard 1955- *WhoBlA 92*
**Nixon,** Patrick Michael 1944- *Who 92*
**Nixon,** Paul R 1924- *AmMWSc 92*
**Nixon,** Peter James 1928- *IntWW 91*
**Nixon,** Ray, Jr 1956- *WhoWest 92*
**Nixon,** Richard 1913- *IntAu&W 91, WrDr 92*
**Nixon,** Richard M. 1913- *BenetAL 91, FacFETw, RComAH, Who 92, WhoAmP 91*
**Nixon,** Richard Milhous 1913- *AmPolLe [port], IntWW 91*
**Nixon,** Robert d1794 *DcNCBi 4*
**Nixon,** Robert Henry 1954- *WhoEnt 92*
**Nixon,** Robert Obey, Sr. 1922- *WhoWest 92*
**Nixon,** Roger 1921- *NewAmDM*
**Nixon,** Sallie *DrAPF 91*
**Nixon,** Scott West 1943- *AmMWSc 92*
**Nixon,** Tamara Friedman 1938- *WhoFI 92*
**Nixon,** Wilfrid Austin 1959- *AmMWSc 92*
**Nixson,** Frederick Ian 1943- *IntAu&W 91, WrDr 92*
**Niyazov,** Saparmurad Ataevich 1940- *SovUnBD*
**Niyazov,** Saparmurad Atayevich 1940- *IntWW 91*
**Niyogi,** Salil Kumar 1932- *AmMWSc 92*
**Niyungeko,** Jonathas 1946- *IntWW 91*
**Niza,** Marcos de 1500?-1558 *HisDSpE*
**Nizalowski,** Edward Michael 1947- *IntAu&W 91*
**Nizami,** Tariq Ahmed 1958- *WhoWest 92*
**Nizan,** Paul 1905-1940 *GuFrLit 1*
**Nizel,** Abraham Edward 1917- *AmMWSc 92*
**Nizer,** Louis 1902- *IntMPA 92*
**Niziurski,** Edmund Stanislaw 1925- *IntAu&W 91*
**Nizovtseva,** Alla Afanasyeva 1930- *IntWW 91*
**Nizza,** Matthew G. 1928- *WhoAmL 92*
**Nizzoli,** Marcello 1887-1969 *DcTwDes*
**Njemoga Kolar,** Ana 1951- *IntAu&W 91*
**Njiiri,** Ruth Stutts 1929- *WhoBlA 92*
**Njoku,** Eni 1917- *IntWW 91*
**Njonjo,** Charles E. G. H. 1920- *IntWW 91*
**Njoroge,** Mbugua J. 1944- *WhoBlA 92*
**Njoroge,** Ng'ethe *IntWW 91*
**Njus,** David Lars 1948- *AmMWSc 92*
**Nkabinde,** Thulani *DrAPF 91*
**Nkala,** Enos 1933- *IntWW 91*
**Nkomo,** Joshua 1917- *FacFETw [port], IntWW 91*
**Nkomo,** Wendy Renee 1962- *WhoFI 92*
**Nkongola,** Muyumba Wa 1939- *WhoBlA 92*
**Nkonyansa,** Osafuhin Kwaku 1938- *WhoBlA 92*
**Nkosi,** Lewis 1936- *BlkLC, IntAu&W 91, LiExTwC, WrDr 92*
**Nkrumah,** Kwame 1909-1972 *FacFETw [port]*
**Nnadozie,** Emmanuel Uzoma A. 1956- *WhoMW 92*
**N'Namdi,** Carmen Ann 1949- *WhoBlA 92*
**N'Namdi,** George Richard 1946- *WhoBlA 92*
**Nnolim,** Charles E. 1939- *WhoBlA 92*
**Noack,** Carol Lynn 1935- *WhoFI 92*
**Noack,** Fritz 1935- *NewAmDM*
**Noack,** Harold Quincy, Jr. 1931- *WhoAmL 92*
**Noack,** Manfred Gerhard 1936- *AmMWSc 92*
**Noad,** Kenneth 1900- *Who 92*
**Noah** *EncEarC*
**Noah,** Eric Linnaeus 1955- *WhoWest 92*
**Noah,** Harold J. 1925- *WrDr 92*
**Noah,** Harold Julius 1925- *IntWW 91*
**Noah,** Leroy Edward 1934- *WhoBlA 92*
**Noah,** Mordecai M. 1785-1851 *BenetAL 91, DcAmImH*
**Noah,** Raymond Douglas 1932- *WhoAmP 91*
**Noah,** Sheri Lynn 1954- *WhoRel 92*
**Noah,** Steven Craig 1948- *WhoAmP 91*
**Noailles,** Anna de 1876-1933 *FrenWW*
**Noakes,** David Lloyd George 1942- *AmMWSc 92*
**Noakes,** George 1924- *IntWW 91, Who 92, WhoRel 92*
**Noakes,** John Edward 1930- *AmMWSc 92*
**Noakes,** John Edward 1935- *Who 92*
**Noakes,** Michael 1933- *IntWW 91, TwCPaSc, Who 92*
**Noakes,** Philip Reuben 1915- *Who 92*
**Noakes,** Roy *TwCPaSc*
**Noakes,** Sheila Valerie *Who 92*
**Noakes,** Sidney Henry 1905- *Who 92*
**Noakes,** Susan Jeanne 1945- *WhoMW 92*
**Noakes,** Vivien 1937- *IntAu&W 91, WrDr 92*
**Noall,** Matthew Wilcox 1924- *AmMWSc 92*
**Noback,** Charles Robert 1916- *AmMWSc 92*
**Noback,** Richardson K 1923- *AmMWSc 92*
**Nobay,** Robert 1942- *Who 92*
**Nobbs,** David Gordon 1935- *Who 92*
**Nobbs,** Kenneth John 1938- *WhoFI 92*
**Nobe,** Ken 1925- *AmMWSc 92*
**Nobel,** Alfred 1833-1896 *FacFETw*
**Nobel,** Jerry 1937- *WhoAmP 91*
**Nobel,** Joel J 1934- *AmMWSc 92*
**Nobel,** Park S 1938- *AmMWSc 92*
**Nobel,** Phil *TwCSFW 91, WrDr 92*
**Nobes,** Patrick 1933- *Who 92*
**Nobes,** Peter John 1935- *Who 92*
**Nobile,** Umberto 1885-1978 *FacFETw*
**Nobis,** Elizabeth Ann 1916- *WhoAmP 91*
**Nobis,** John Francis 1921- *AmMWSc 92*
**Noble,** Adrian Keith 1950- *IntWW 91, Who 92*
**Noble,** Alfred 1844-1914 *BiInAmS*
**Noble,** Alfred J 1858?-1916 *BiInAmS*
**Noble,** Allen G 1930- *AmMWSc 92*
**Noble,** Ann Curtis 1943- *AmMWSc 92*
**Noble,** Barrie Paul 1938- *Who 92*
**Noble,** Bernice *AmMWSc 92*
**Noble,** Beulah Catherine 1924- *WhoBlA 92*
**Noble,** Charles *WrDr 92*
**Noble,** Charles Carmin 1916- *AmMWSc 92*
**Noble,** Charles Edward 1930- *WhoFI 92*
**Noble,** Charles Norman 1935- *WhoFI 92*
**Noble,** Dan D *WhoAmP 91*
**Noble,** David 1923- *Who 92*
**Noble,** David 1929- *Who 92*
**Noble,** David 1961- *Who 92*
**Noble,** David J 1931- *WhoIns 92*
**Noble,** David Jeff 1931- *WhoFI 92, WhoMW 92*
**Noble,** Dean Lawrence 1961- *WhoMW 92*
**Noble,** Denis 1936- *IntWW 91, Who 92*
**Noble,** Edward J. d1958 *LesBEnT 92*
**Noble,** Edwin Austin 1922- *AmMWSc 92*
**Noble,** Elmer Ray 1909- *AmMWSc 92*
**Noble,** Fraser *Who 92*
**Noble,** Gilbert E. 1932- *WhoBlA 92*
**Noble,** Glenn Arthur 1909- *AmMWSc 92*
**Noble,** Gordon Albert 1927- *AmMWSc 92*
**Noble,** Guy 1959- *TwCPaSc*
**Noble,** Haven Douglas 1941- *WhoMW 92*
**Noble,** Howard Earl 1909- *WhoFI 92*
**Noble,** Iain 1935- *Who 92*
**Noble,** James 1919- *TwCPaSc*
**Noble,** James Kendrick, Jr. 1928- *WhoFI 92*
**Noble,** James Wilkes 1922- *WhoEnt 92*
**Noble,** Jeffrey V. *WhoBlA 92*
**Noble,** John Appelbe 1914- *IntAu&W 91*
**Noble,** John Charles 1941- *WhoBlA 92*
**Noble,** John Dale 1934- *AmMWSc 92*
**Noble,** John Pritchard 1931- *WhoBlA 92*
**Noble,** John Robert 1953- *WhoWest 92*
**Noble,** Julian Victor 1940- *AmMWSc 92*
**Noble,** Kenneth Albert *Who 92*
**Noble,** Marc Brunel d1991 *Who 92N*
**Noble,** Marcus Cicero Stephens 1855-1942 *DcNCBi 4*
**Noble,** Mitzi McAlexander 1941- *WhoRel 92*
**Noble,** Nancy Lee 1922- *AmMWSc 92*
**Noble,** Norma Lynette 1944- *WhoBlA 92*
**Noble,** Paul, Jr 1922- *AmMWSc 92*
**Noble,** Paul Ronald 1935- *WhoEnt 92*
**Noble,** Peter *IntMPA 92*
**Noble,** Peter 1953- *TwCPaSc*
**Noble,** Phillip Ray 1945- *WhoEnt 92*
**Noble,** R Elaine 1944- *WhoAmP 91*
**Noble,** Ray 1903-1978 *FacFETw, NewAmDM*
**Noble,** Reginald Duston 1935- *AmMWSc 92, WhoMW 92*
**Noble,** Richard Barry 1963- *WhoFI 92*
**Noble,** Richard Daniel 1946- *AmMWSc 92*
**Noble,** Richard Lloyd 1939- *WhoAmL 92, WhoFI 92, WhoWest 92*
**Noble,** Robert Hamilton 1916- *AmMWSc 92*
**Noble,** Robert Laing 1910- *AmMWSc 92, IntWW 91*
**Noble,** Robert Lee 1923- *AmMWSc 92*
**Noble,** Robert Tyrol 1940- *WhoFI 92*
**Noble,** Robert Vernon 1923- *AmMWSc 92*
**Noble,** Robert Warren, Jr 1937- *AmMWSc 92*
**Noble,** Ronald Kenneth 1956- *WhoAmL 92*
**Noble,** Russell Edwin 1923- *WhoAmL 92*
**Noble,** Sherwood d1991 *NewYTBS 91*
**Noble,** T. Tertius 1867-1953 *NewAmDM*
**Noble,** Ted Eugene 1945- *WhoWest 92*
**Noble,** Thomas Alexander Fraser 1918- *Who 92*
**Noble,** Vincent Edward 1933- *AmMWSc 92*
**Noble,** Weston Henry 1922- *WhoEnt 92, WhoMW 92*
**Noble,** William Charles 1935- *WrDr 92*
**Nobles,** Edward *DrAPF 91*
**Nobles,** Laurence Hewit 1927- *AmMWSc 92*
**Nobles,** Patricia Joyce 1955- *WhoBlA 92*
**Nobles,** William Lewis 1925- *AmMWSc 92*
**Noblesse,** Francis 1946- *AmMWSc 92*
**Noblet,** Raymond 1943- *AmMWSc 92*
**Noblin,** Bobby Gene 1937- *WhoAmP 91*
**Noblit,** Betty Jean 1948- *WhoWest 92*
**Noblitt,** Floyd Wilson 1923- *WhoAmP 91*
**Noboa,** Junior 1964- *WhoHisp 92*
**Noboa-Polanco,** Julio 1949- *WhoHisp 92*
**Nobre,** Marlos 1939- *ConCom 92*
**Nobs,** Claude *WhoEnt 92*
**Nobusawa,** Nobuo 1930- *AmMWSc 92*
**Nocenti,** Mero Raymond 1928- *AmMWSc 92*
**Nocera,** John Anthony 1952- *WhoAmL 92*
**Nocera,** Robert Anthony 1959- *WhoFI 92*
**Nocerino,** Kathryn *DrAPF 91*
**Nocerino,** Patricia Ann 1946- *WhoWest 92*
**Noceti,** Richard Paul 1947- *AmMWSc 92*
**Nochevkin,** Anatoliy Petrovich 1928- *IntWW 91*
**Nochimson,** David 1943- *WhoAmL 92, WhoEnt 92*
**Nochlin,** Linda Weinberg 1931- *WrDr 92*
**Nock,** Albert Jay 1873-1945 *BenetAL 91*
**Nock,** George Roy, III 1938- *WhoAmL 92*
**Nock,** Norman Lindfield d1990 *Who 92N*
**Nock,** O. S. 1905- *WrDr 92*
**Nockels,** Cheryl Ferris 1935- *AmMWSc 92*
**Nockolds,** Stephen Robert d1990 *IntWW 91N*
**Noda,** Kaoru 1924- *AmMWSc 92*
**Noda,** Lafayette Hachiro 1916- *AmMWSc 92*
**Nodar,** Richard enry 1935- *AmMWSc 92*
**Nodarse Chao,** Olga I. 1944- *WhoFI 92*
**Nodder,** Timothy Edward 1930- *Who 92*
**Nodelman,** Jared Robert 1937- *WhoFI 92*
**Nodier,** Charles 1780-1844 *GuFrLit 1*
**Nodiff,** Edward Albert 1926- *AmMWSc 92*
**Nodset,** Joan L. *WrDr 92*
**Nodtvedt,** Magnus 1924- *WhoIns 92*
**Nodulman,** Lawrence Jay 1947- *AmMWSc 92*
**Nodvik,** John S 1930- *AmMWSc 92*
**Noe,** Bryan Dale 1943- *AmMWSc 92*
**Noe,** David Clifford 1964- *WhoFI 92, WhoWest 92*
**Noe,** Elnora 1928- *WhoMW 92*
**Noe,** Eric Arden 1943- *AmMWSc 92*
**Noe,** Frances Elsie 1923- *AmMWSc 92, WhoMW 92*
**Noe,** James Kirby 1951- *WhoMW 92*
**Noe,** Jerre D 1923- *AmMWSc 92*
**Noe,** Lewis John 1941- *AmMWSc 92*
**Noe,** Randolph 1939- *WhoAmL 92*
**Noe,** Roger C 1949- *WhoAmP 91*
**Noe,** Sally Woodworth 1926- *WhoWest 92*
**Noe,** Virgilio 1922- *WhoRel 92*
**Noebel,** David Arthur 1936- *WhoRel 92*
**Noehren,** Robert 1910- *NewAmDM*
**Noehren,** Theodore Henry 1917- *AmMWSc 92*
**Noel** *Who 92*
**Noel,** Ann Harting 1944- *WhoAmP 91*
**Noel,** Barbara Hughes McMurtry 1929- *WhoEnt 92*
**Noel,** Bruce William 1934- *AmMWSc 92*
**Noel,** Dale Leon 1936- *AmMWSc 92*
**Noel,** Eldon Keith 1929- *WhoAmP 91*
**Noel,** Emile 1922- *IntWW 91*
**Noel,** Gambier John Byng 1914- *Who 92*
**Noel,** Geoffrey Lindsay James 1923- *Who 92*
**Noel,** Gerald Thomas *WhoMW 92*
**Noel,** Gerald Thomas 1934- *AmMWSc 92*
**Noel,** Gerard Eyre Wriothesley 1926- *IntAu&W 91, Who 92*
**Noel,** James A 1922- *AmMWSc 92*
**Noel,** James Latane, Jr. 1909- *WhoAmL 92*
**Noel,** Jan Christina 1949- *AmMWSc 92*
**Noel,** John *WrDr 92*
**Noel,** Laurent 1920- *WhoRel 92*
**Noel,** Lloyd Staton, Jr. 1941- *WhoWest 92*
**Noel,** Margery McCullough 1937- *WhoWest 92*
**Noel,** Patrick Adolphus 1940- *WhoBlA 92*
**Noel,** Randall Deane 1953- *WhoAmL 92*
**Noel,** Tallulah Ann 1945- *WhoMW 92*
**Noel-Baker,** Francis Edward 1920- *Who 92*
**Noel-Baker,** Philip 1889-1982 *FacFETw*
**Noel-Baker,** Philip John 1889-1982 *WhoNob 90*
**Noel-Buxton** *Who 92*
**Noel-Buxton,** Baron 1940- *Who 92*
**Noel-Hume,** Ivor 1927- *IntAu&W 91, SmATA 65, WrDr 92*
**Noel-Paton** *Who 92*
**Noel-Paton,** Ranald 1938- *Who 92*
**Noelke,** Paul 1915- *WhoAmL 92*
**Noelken,** Milton Edward 1935- *AmMWSc 92*
**Noell,** John Summers, Jr. 1941- *WhoAmL 92*
**Noelle-Neumann,** Elisabeth 1916- *IntWW 91*
**Noelte,** Rudolf 1921- *IntWW 91*
**Noer,** Richard Juul 1937- *AmMWSc 92*
**Noer,** Rudolf Juul 1904- *AmMWSc 92*
**Noerdlinger,** Peter David 1935- *AmMWSc 92*
**Noest,** Peter John 1948- *Who 92*
**Noeth,** Carolyn Frances 1924- *WhoMW 92*
**Noeth,** Louise Ann 1954- *WhoWest 92*
**Noether,** Emmy 1882-1935 *HanAmWH*
**Noether,** Gottfried Emanuel 1915- *AmMWSc 92*
**Noetus** *EncEarC*
**Noetzel,** Arthur Jerome 1916- *WhoFI 92, WhoMW 92*
**Noetzel,** David Martin 1929- *AmMWSc 92*
**Nof,** Shimon Y 1946- *AmMWSc 92, ConAu 135*
**Nofal,** Sayed 1910- *IntWW 91*
**Nofer,** George Hancock 1926- *WhoAmL 92*
**Noffsinger,** Ella Mae 1934- *AmMWSc 92*
**Noftle,** Ronald Edward 1939- *AmMWSc 92*
**Noftz,** Philip Thomas 1962- *WhoEnt 92*
**Nofziger,** David Lynn 1944- *AmMWSc 92*
**Noga,** Charles Frank 1942- *WhoAmP 91*
**Noga,** Edward Joseph 1953- *AmMWSc 92*
**Nogales,** Luis Guerrero 1943- *WhoEnt 92, WhoFI 92*
**Nogami,** Yukihisa 1929- *AmMWSc 92*
**Nogar,** Nicholas Stephen 1950- *AmMWSc 92*
**Nogawa,** Shoji 1927- *IntWW 91*
**Nogee,** Jeffrey Laurence 1952- *WhoAmL 92*
**Nogee,** Joseph L 1929- *IntAu&W 91, WrDr 92*
**Nogene,** Endel Jaan 1950- *WhoEnt 92*
**Noges,** Endrik 1927- *AmMWSc 92*
**Nogg,** Donald Irwin 1930- *WhoFI 92*
**Nogg,** L. Randall 1955- *WhoEnt 92*
**Nogg,** Manya Elaine *WhoEnt 92*
**Noggle,** Burl L. 1924- *ConAu 134*
**Noggle,** Joseph Henry 1936- *AmMWSc 92*
**Nogrady,** Thomas 1925- *AmMWSc 92*
**Noguchi,** Hideo 1945- *WhoFI 92, WhoWest 92*
**Noguchi,** Isamu 1904- *FacFETw*

**Noguchi,** Isamu 1904-1988 *DcTwDes, RComAH*
**Noguchi,** Philip D 1949- *AmMWSc 92*
**Noguchi,** Teruo 1917- *IntWW 91*
**Noguchi,** Thomas Tsunetomi 1927- *WhoEnt 92, WhoWest 92*
**Nogueira,** Albano Pires Fernandes 1911- *IntWW 91, Who 92*
**Nogueira,** Alberto Franco 1918- *IntWW 91*
**Nogueira,** Denio Chagas 1920- *IntWW 91*
**Nogueira-Batista,** Paulo 1929- *IntWW 91*
**Noguera,** Pedro Antonio 1959- *WhoBlA 92*
**Nogueras,** Nicolas, Jr *WhoAmP 91*
**Noguere,** Suzanne *DrAPF 91*
**Nogueres,** Henri d1990 *IntWW 91N*
**Nogues,** Alexander Omar, Sr. 1926- *WhoHisp 92*
**Nogues,** Juan Francisco 1925-1990 *WhoHisp 92N*
**Noh,** Laird 1938- *WhoAmP 91*
**Nohel,** John Adolph 1924- *AmMWSc 92*
**Nohl,** Thomas Jon 1955- *WhoMW 92*
**Nohren,** Richard Lee 1952- *WhoAmP 91*
**Noid,** Donald William 1949- *AmMWSc 92*
**Noiret,** Philippe 1930- *IntMPA 92, IntWW 91*
**Noisette,** Ruffin N. 1923- *WhoBlA 92*
**Noiseux,** Claude Francois 1953- *AmMWSc 92*
**Nojgaard,** Morten 1934- *IntWW 91*
**Nokes,** Richard Francis 1934- *AmMWSc 92*
**Nokin,** Max 1907- *IntWW 91*
**Nola,** Frank Joseph 1930- *AmMWSc 92*
**Nolan,** Alan Tucker 1923- *WhoAmL 92*
**Nolan,** Arthur E 1919- *WhoIns 92*
**Nolan,** Bob 1908-1980 *NewAmDM*
**Nolan,** Carol Elizabeth 1932- *WhoMW 92*
**Nolan,** Carole Rita 1932- *WhoEnt 92, WhoMW 92*
**Nolan,** Catherine *WhoAmP 91*
**Nolan,** Chris 1930- *AmMWSc 92*
**Nolan,** Christopher 1965- *WrDr 92*
**Nolan,** Chuck *TwCWW 91*
**Nolan,** Clifford N 1925- *AmMWSc 92*
**Nolan,** Daniel F 1932- *WhoAmP 91*
**Nolan,** David Brian 1951- *WhoAmL 92*
**Nolan,** Dennis R. 1945- *WhoAmL 92*
**Nolan,** Edward J *AmMWSc 92*
**Nolan,** Eileen Joan 1920- *Who 92*
**Nolan,** Elizabeth Joan 1946- *WhoFI 92*
**Nolan,** Frederick *WrDr 92*
**Nolan,** George Junior 1935- *AmMWSc 92*
**Nolan,** Howard Charles, Jr 1932- *WhoAmP 91*
**Nolan,** Jack 1959- *WhoEnt 92*
**Nolan,** James *DrAPF 91*
**Nolan,** James Francis 1931- *AmMWSc 92*
**Nolan,** James Martin 1950- *WhoWest 92*
**Nolan,** James P 1929- *AmMWSc 92*
**Nolan,** James Robert 1923- *AmMWSc 92*
**Nolan,** Janiece Simmons *AmMWSc 92*
**Nolan,** John D 1946- *WhoIns 92*
**Nolan,** John Edward 1927- *WhoAmL 92*
**Nolan,** John Gavin 1924- *WhoRel 92*
**Nolan,** John Michael 1948- *WhoAmL 92, WhoFI 92*
**Nolan,** John Thomas, Jr 1930- *AmMWSc 92*
**Nolan,** Joseph R 1925- *WhoAmP 91*
**Nolan,** Joseph Richard 1925- *WhoAmL 92*
**Nolan,** Joseph Stuart 1939- *WhoMW 92*
**Nolan,** Keith W. 1964- *ConAu 36NR, WrDr 92*
**Nolan,** Mark Gregory 1958- *WhoWest 92*
**Nolan,** Michael 1928- *Who 92*
**Nolan,** Michael Francis 1947- *AmMWSc 92*
**Nolan,** Patricia A *WhoAmP 91*
**Nolan,** Patricia Ann 1955- *WhoWest 92*
**Nolan,** Patrick 1933- *IntAu&W 91*
**Nolan,** Patrick James 1950- *WhoAmP 91*
**Nolan,** Patrick Joseph 1933- *WhoEnt 92*
**Nolan,** Patrick Joseph 1938- *WhoFI 92*
**Nolan,** Paul T. 1919- *WrDr 92*
**Nolan,** Peter Andrew 1950- *WhoAmL 92*
**Nolan,** Peter Francis 1943- *WhoAmL 92*
**Nolan,** Raymond Patrick 1944- *WhoWest 92*
**Nolan,** Richard Arthur 1937- *AmMWSc 92*
**Nolan,** Richard Thomas 1937- *WhoRel 92*
**Nolan,** Robert L. 1912- *WhoBlA 92*
**Nolan,** Sidney 1917- *Who 92*
**Nolan,** Sidney Robert 1917- *IntWW 91*
**Nolan,** Stanton Peelle 1933- *AmMWSc 92*
**Nolan,** Terrance Joseph, Jr. 1950- *WhoAmL 92*
**Nolan,** Thomas Brennan 1901- *AmMWSc 92, IntWW 91*
**Nolan,** Val, Jr 1920- *AmMWSc 92*
**Nolan,** Victoria Holmes 1952- *WhoEnt 92, WhoMW 92*
**Nolan,** William F 1928- *IntAu&W 91, TwCSFW 91, WrDr 92*
**Noland,** Clarence D, Jr 1937- *WhoAmP 91*
**Noland,** Douglas Eugene 1957- *WhoRel 92*
**Noland,** Gary Lloyd 1942- *WhoMW 92*
**Noland,** James Ellsworth 1920- *WhoAmL 92, WhoMW 92*
**Noland,** James Sterling 1933- *AmMWSc 92*
**Noland,** Jerre Lancaster 1921- *AmMWSc 92*
**Noland,** Josh 1938- *WhoEnt 92*
**Noland,** Kenneth 1924- *FacFETw*
**Noland,** Kenneth Clifton 1927- *IntWW 91*
**Noland,** N Duane 1956- *WhoAmP 91*
**Noland,** Paul Robert 1924- *AmMWSc 92*
**Noland,** Wayland E. *WhoMW 92*
**Noland,** Wayland Evan 1926- *AmMWSc 92*
**Nolasco,** Jesus Bautista 1917- *AmMWSc 92*
**Nolasco,** Margarita 1948- *WhoHisp 92*
**Nolcini,** Edmond *ScFEYrs*
**Nold,** Daniel Ray 1962- *WhoMW 92, WhoRel 92*
**Nolde,** Emil 1867-1956 *EncTR 91 [port], FacFETw*
**Nolde,** Nancy *WhoRel 92*
**Nolde,** Otto Frederick 1899-1972 *AmPeW*
**Nole,** Phyllis Rose *WhoEnt 92*
**Nolen,** David Jackson *WhoAmP 91*
**Nolen,** Frank William 1939- *WhoAmP 91*
**Nolen,** Granville Abraham 1926- *AmMWSc 92*
**Nolen,** Jerry A, Jr 1940- *AmMWSc 92*
**Nolen,** Jerry Aften, Jr. 1940- *WhoMW 92*
**Nolen,** Lynn Dean 1940- *WhoAmL 92*
**Nolen,** Roy Lemuel 1937- *WhoAmL 92*
**Noles,** Eva M. 1919- *WhoBlA 92*
**Nolf,** Luther Owen 1902- *AmMWSc 92*
**Nolfi,** Edward Anthony 1958- *WhoAmL 92*
**Noli,** Fan *DcAmImH*
**Noli,** Theophan S. 1882-1965 *RelLAm 91*
**Nolin,** Gail Amy 1944- *WhoAmP 91*
**Nolin,** Janet M *AmMWSc 92*
**Noll,** Clifford Raymond, Jr 1922- *AmMWSc 92*
**Noll,** Francis Charles, Jr. 1952- *WhoFI 92*
**Noll,** Hans 1924- *AmMWSc 92*
**Noll,** John Stephen 1944- *AmMWSc 92*
**Noll,** Kenneth E 1936- *AmMWSc 92*
**Noll,** Leo Albert 1932- *AmMWSc 92*
**Noll,** Martin *ConAu 134*
**Noll,** Richard 1959- *ConAu 134*
**Noll,** Walter 1925- *AmMWSc 92*
**Noll,** William Niven 1942- *WhoWest 92*
**Nolland,** Christopher Marc 1951- *WhoAmL 92*
**Nollau,** Lee Gordon 1950- *WhoAmL 92*
**Nolle,** Alfred Wilson 1919- *AmMWSc 92*
**Nollen,** Paul Marion 1934- *AmMWSc 92*
**Noller,** David Conrad 1923- *AmMWSc 92*
**Noller,** Harry Francis, Jr 1939- *AmMWSc 92*
**Nollet,** Jean-Antoine 1700-1770 *BlkwCEP*
**Nolley,** J Robert, Jr. 1929- *WhoIns 92*
**Nollman,** James M. 1947- *WhoWest 92*
**Nolt,** Douglas Eugene 1957- *WhoRel 92*
**Nolte,** C. Elmer, Jr. 1905- *IntMPA 92*
**Nolte,** Carol M. 1939- *WhoEnt 92*
**Nolte,** Edgard Frank 1931- *WhoFI 92*
**Nolte,** George Washington 1904- *WhoFI 92*
**Nolte,** John Michael 1941- *WhoWest 92*
**Nolte,** Kenneth George 1941- *AmMWSc 92*
**Nolte,** Lawrence William 1905- *WhoWest 92*
**Nolte,** Loren W 1933- *AmMWSc 92*
**Nolte,** Nick 1941- *IntMPA 92, NewYTBS 91 [port]*
**Nolte,** Nick 1942- *IntWW 91, WhoEnt 92*
**Noltimier,** Hallan Costello 1937- *AmMWSc 92*
**Nolting,** Billy J. 1947- *WhoMW 92*
**Nolting,** Earl 1937- *WhoMW 92, WhoRel 92*
**Nolting,** Frederick William 1950- *WhoMW 92*
**Nolting,** Henry Frederick 1916- *AmMWSc 92*
**Nolting,** Henry Frederick, Jr. 1916- *WhoMW 92*
**Nolting,** Ronald William 1937- *WhoIns 92*
**Noltingk,** Bernard Edward 1918- *IntAu&W 91, WrDr 92*
**Nomani,** M Zafar 1935- *AmMWSc 92*
**Nomura,** Kaworu Carl 1922- *AmMWSc 92*
**Nomura,** Masayasu 1927- *AmMWSc 92, IntWW 91*
**Nomura,** Yasumasa 1921- *AmMWSc 92*
**Nomura,** Yoshihiro 1941- *IntWW 91*
**Nonaka,** Makoto 1948- *WhoWest 92*
**Noname** *ScFEYrs*
**Noname** 1854-1927 *ScFEYrs*
**Noname** 1865-1939 *ScFEYrs*
**Nondahl,** Thomas Arthur 1951- *AmMWSc 92*
**Nonet,** Philippe 1939- *WhoAmL 92*
**Nong** 1930- *WhoWest 92*
**Nonhebel,** Clare 1953- *IntAu&W 91*
**Nonnecke,** Ib Libner 1922- *AmMWSc 92*
**Nonnenmann,** Uwe 1961- *AmMWSc 92*
**Nonnus of Panopolis** 400?- *EncEarC*
**Nono,** Luigi 1924-1990 *AnObit 1990, FacFETw, NewAmDM*
**Nono,** Luigi 1924-1991 *ConCom 92*
**Nonoyama,** Meihan 1938- *AmMWSc 92*
**Nonweiler,** Terence Reginald Forbes 1925- *Who 92*
**Nooden,** Larry Donald 1936- *AmMWSc 92*
**Nooker,** Eugene L 1922- *AmMWSc 92*
**Noolandi,** Jaan 1942- *AmMWSc 92*
**Noon,** David 1946- *WhoEnt 92*
**Noon,** James Anthony, Jr. 1949- *WhoMW 92*
**Noon,** James Peter 1956- *WhoMW 92*
**Noon,** Terri J. 1951- *WhoMW 92*
**Noonan,** Charles D 1928- *AmMWSc 92*
**Noonan,** Donald 1935- *WhoAmP 91*
**Noonan,** Gerald M 1945- *WhoAmP 91*
**Noonan,** Guy Francis 1949- *WhoRel 92*
**Noonan,** Jacqueline Anne 1928- *AmMWSc 92*
**Noonan,** James Waring 1944- *AmMWSc 92*
**Noonan,** John Ford 1943- *WrDr 92*
**Noonan,** John Robert 1946- *AmMWSc 92*
**Noonan,** John T *WhoAmP 91*
**Noonan,** John T., Jr. 1926- *WhoAmL 92*
**Noonan,** Kenneth Daniel 1948- *AmMWSc 92*
**Noonan,** Lowell G. 1922- *WrDr 92*
**Noonan,** Lowell Gerald 1922- *IntAu&W 91*
**Noonan,** Mary M 1950- *WhoIns 92*
**Noonan,** Michael Dennis 1941- *WhoAmL 92*
**Noonan,** Michael Joseph 1935- *IntWW 91*
**Noonan,** Norine Elizabeth 1948- *AmMWSc 92*
**Noonan,** Rose Mary Madden 1918- *WhoAmL 92*
**Noonan,** Thomas Robert 1912- *AmMWSc 92*
**Noonan,** Thomas Wyatt 1933- *AmMWSc 92*
**Noonan,** William Francis 1932- *WhoFI 92*
**Noonan,** William Moss 1942- *WhoFI 92*
**Noone,** Edwina *WrDr 92*
**Noone,** Jimmie 1895-1944 *NewAmDM*
**Noone,** Lana Mae 1946- *WhoEnt 92*
**Noone,** Thomas Patrick 1937- *WhoAmL 92*
**Noonkester,** James Ralph 1924- *WhoFI 92*
**Noor al-Hussein,** Queen of Jordan 1951- *CurBio 91 [port]*
**Noor,** Ahmed Khairy 1938- *AmMWSc 92*
**Noor,** Mohamad Yusof 1941- *IntWW 91*
**Noor,** Rusli 1927- *Who 92*
**Noorbakhsh,** Mohsen 1948- *IntWW 91*
**Noorda,** Bob 1927- *DcTwDes*
**Noordergraaf,** Abraham 1929- *AmMWSc 92*
**Noordung,** Hermann 1892-1929 *FacFETw*
**Nopar,** Alan Scott 1951- *WhoAmL 92, WhoFI 92, WhoWest 92*
**Nopper,** Ralph Jacob 1916- *WhoMW 92*
**Noppinger,** John George 1913- *WhoFI 92*
**Nor,** Genghis 1946- *WhoBlA 92*
**Nora,** Audrey Hart 1936- *AmMWSc 92*
**Nora,** Gerald Ernest, Jr. 1951- *WhoAmL 92*
**Nora,** James Jackson 1928- *AmMWSc 92, WhoWest 92*
**Nora,** Simon 1921- *IntWW 91*
**Nora,** Wendy Alison 1951- *WhoAmL 92*
**Noragon,** Jack LeRoy 1937- *WhoMW 92*
**Norall,** Frank 1918- *ConAu 133*
**Norat,** Manuel Eric 1950- *WhoHisp 92*
**Norat-Phillips,** Sarah L. 1956- *WhoHisp 92*
**Norback,** Diane Hagemen 1946- *AmMWSc 92*
**Norbeck,** Edward 1915- *WrDr 92*
**Norbeck,** Edwin 1930- *AmMWSc 92*
**Norbeck,** Edwin, Jr. 1930- *WhoMW 92*
**Norberg,** Arthur Lawrence 1938- *AmMWSc 92*
**Norberg,** Arthur Lawrence, Jr. 1938- *WhoMW 92*
**Norberg,** Charles Robert 1912- *WhoAmL 92*
**Norberg,** Dag 1909- *IntWW 91*
**Norberg,** Eric Gunnar 1943- *WhoEnt 92*
**Norberg,** Richard Edwin 1922- *AmMWSc 92*
**Norbom,** Jon Ola 1923- *IntWW 91*
**Norburn,** David 1941- *Who 92*
**Norburn,** Susan Joyce *Who 92*
**Norbury,** Earl of 1939- *Who 92*
**Norbury,** Brian Martin 1938- *Who 92*
**Norbury,** Thom 1942- *WhoMW 92*
**Norby,** Christopher 1949- *WhoAmP 91, WhoWest 92*
**Norby,** Mark Alan 1955- *WhoAmL 92*
**Norby,** Rockford Douglas 1935- *WhoEnt 92, WhoWest 92*
**Norby,** Rodney Dale 1945- *AmMWSc 92*
**Norcia,** Leonard Nicholas 1916- *AmMWSc 92*
**Norcia,** Stephen William 1941- *WhoFI 92*
**Norcom,** James, Sr. 1778-1850 *DcNCBi 4*
**Norcross,** Bruce Edward 1935- *AmMWSc 92*
**Norcross,** David F 1937- *WhoAmP 91*
**Norcross,** David Warren 1941- *AmMWSc 92*
**Norcross,** John *SmATA 65*
**Norcross,** Lawrence John Charles 1927- *Who 92*
**Norcross,** Lisabet 1924- *WrDr 92*
**Norcross,** Marvin Augustus 1931- *AmMWSc 92*
**Norcross,** Neil Linwood 1928- *AmMWSc 92*
**Nord,** Beryl Annette 1948- *WhoAmL 92*
**Nord,** Carol Ann *DrAPF 91*
**Nord,** Gordon Ludwig, Jr 1942- *AmMWSc 92*
**Nord,** Hans Robert 1919- *IntWW 91*
**Nord,** Harold Emil, Jr. 1928- *WhoFI 92*
**Nord,** John C 1938- *AmMWSc 92*
**Nord,** Robert Eamor 1945- *WhoMW 92*
**Nord,** Sheldon Carl 1960- *WhoWest 92*
**Nordahl,** Thomas Edward 1948- *WhoWest 92*
**Nordal,** Johannes 1924- *IntWW 91*
**Nordan,** Harold Cecil 1925- *AmMWSc 92*
**Nordberg,** Ivar 1933- *IntWW 91*
**Nordberg,** John Albert 1926- *WhoAmL 92, WhoMW 92*
**Nordberg,** Michael Charles 1946- *WhoFI 92*
**Nordberg,** Nils Lovering 1934- *WhoAmP 91*
**Nordbrandt,** Henrik 1945- *IntAu&W 91*
**Nordby,** Gene M 1926- *AmMWSc 92*
**Nordby,** Gordon Lee 1929- *AmMWSc 92*
**Nordby,** Harold Edwin 1931- *AmMWSc 92*
**Nordby,** Virginia Cecile 1929- *WhoAmL 92*
**Nordbye,** Richard Arthur 1919- *WhoAmL 92*
**Norddahl,** Birgir Valson 1947- *WhoFI 92*
**Nordeen,** David Charles 1952- *WhoAmL 92*
**Nordell,** William James 1930- *AmMWSc 92*
**Norden,** Allan James 1924- *AmMWSc 92*
**Norden,** Carroll Raymond 1923- *AmMWSc 92*
**Norden,** Christer Bjorn 1951- *WhoEnt 92*
**Norden,** Denis 1922- *Who 92*
**Norden,** Dennis Arthur 1945- *WhoAmL 92*
**Norden,** Gerald *TwCPaSc*
**Norden,** Jeanette Jean 1948- *AmMWSc 92*
**Norden,** K. Elis 1921- *WhoFI 92*
**Nordenberg,** Mark Alan 1948- *WhoAmL 92*
**Nordenfalk,** Carl 1907- *IntWW 91*
**Nordenflycht,** Hedvig Charlotta 1718-1763 *BlkwCEP*
**Nordeng,** Stephan C 1923- *AmMWSc 92*
**Nordgren,** Gerald Paul 1954- *WhoAmL 92*
**Nordgren,** Pehr Henrik 1944- *ConCom 92*
**Nordgren,** Peter David 1952- *WhoEnt 92*
**Nordgren,** Ronald P 1936- *AmMWSc 92*
**Nordgren,** Sharon L 1943- *WhoAmP 91*
**Nordgren,** William Bennett 1960- *WhoWest 92*
**Nordhagen,** Per Jonas 1929- *IntWW 91*
**Nordhaus,** Jean *DrAPF 91*
**Nordhaus,** Robert Riggs 1937- *WhoAmL 92*
**Nordhausen,** Joan Katharine 1937- *WhoFI 92*
**Nordheim,** Arne 1931- *ConCom 92, NewAmDM*
**Nordheim,** Richard J. 1959- *WhoEnt 92*
**Nordhoff,** Charles 1830-1901 *BenetAL 91*
**Nordhoff,** Charles Bernard 1887-1947 *BenetAL 91*
**Nordhoff,** Charles Gilbert 1959- *WhoWest 92*
**Nordholm,** Gregory Eynon 1952- *WhoWest 92*
**Nordica,** Lillian 1857-1914 *NewAmDM*
**Nordicus** *ConAu 34NR*
**Nordin,** Albert Andrew 1934- *AmMWSc 92*
**Nordin,** Diane Carol 1958- *WhoFI 92*
**Nordin,** Gerald LeRoy 1944- *AmMWSc 92*
**Nordin,** Ivan Conrad 1932- *AmMWSc 92, WhoMW 92*
**Nordin,** John Hoffman 1934- *AmMWSc 92*
**Nordin,** Paul 1929- *AmMWSc 92*
**Nordin,** Philip 1922- *AmMWSc 92*
**Nordin,** Richard Nels 1947- *AmMWSc 92*
**Nordin,** Vidar John 1924- *AmMWSc 92*
**Nordine,** Paul Clemens 1940- *AmMWSc 92*
**Nordlander,** John Eric 1934- *AmMWSc 92*
**Nordlander,** Peter Jan Arne 1955- *AmMWSc 92*
**Nordli,** Odvar 1927- *IntWW 91*
**Nordlie,** Bert Edward 1935- *AmMWSc 92*
**Nordlie,** Frank Gerald 1932- *AmMWSc 92*

**Nordlie,** Robert Conrad 1930- *AmMWSc 92*
**Nordlie,** Robert Leland 1949- *WhoRel 92*
**Nordling,** Bernard Erick 1921- *WhoAmL 92, WhoFI 92*
**Nordling,** Carl 1931- *IntWW 91*
**Nordlinger,** Douglas Edward 1956- *WhoAmL 92*
**Nordlund,** Donald Craig 1949- *WhoAmL 92, WhoFI 92, WhoWest 92*
**Nordlund,** Donald Elmer 1922- *WhoFI 92*
**Nordlund,** James John 1939- *AmMWSc 92, WhoMW 92*
**Nordlund,** R L 1929- *AmMWSc 92*
**Nordlund,** William Chalmers 1954- *WhoAmL 92*
**Nordman,** Christer Eric 1925- *AmMWSc 92*
**Nordman,** James Emery 1934- *AmMWSc 92*
**Nordman,** Jeanne Kay 1948- *WhoMW 92*
**Nordman,** Richard D. 1946- *WhoMW 92*
**Nordmann,** Ronald Maurice 1941- *WhoFI 92*
**Nordmeyer,** Francis R 1940- *AmMWSc 92*
**Nordmeyer,** Mary Betsy 1939- *WhoWest 92*
**Nordquist,** Edwin C 1921- *AmMWSc 92*
**Nordquist,** Paul Edgard Rudolph, Jr 1936- *AmMWSc 92*
**Nordquist,** Robert Ersel 1938- *AmMWSc 92*
**Nordquist,** Sandralee Rahn 1940- *WhoRel 92*
**Nordqvist,** Erik Askbo 1943- *WhoFI 92*
**Nordschow,** Carleton Deane 1926- *AmMWSc 92*
**Nordskog,** Arne William 1913- *AmMWSc 92*
**Nordstedt,** Roger Arlo 1942- *AmMWSc 92*
**Nordstrand,** Raymond William 1932- *WhoEnt 92, WhoFI 92*
**Nordstrom,** Brian Hoyt 1949- *AmMWSc 92*
**Nordstrom,** Bruce A. 1933- *WhoWest 92*
**Nordstrom,** Darrell Kirk 1946- *AmMWSc 92*
**Nordstrom,** J David 1937- *AmMWSc 92*
**Nordstrom,** James F. 1940- *WhoWest 92*
**Nordstrom,** John N. 1937- *WhoFI 92*
**Nordstrom,** Richard Dean 1933- *WhoWest 92*
**Nordstrom,** Torkel 1910- *IntWW 91*
**Nordstrom,** Wayne Jerome 1950- *WhoMW 92*
**Nordt,** Paul Winfried, Jr. 1914- *WhoFI 92*
**Nordtvedt,** Kenneth L 1939- *AmMWSc 92*
**Nordtvedt,** Kenneth L, Jr 1939- *WhoAmP 91*
**Nordtvedt,** Matilda 1926- *SmATA 67*
**Nordyke,** Ellis Larrimore 1942- *AmMWSc 92*
**Noreika,** Alexander Joseph 1935- *AmMWSc 92*
**Noreika,** Joseph Casimir 1950- *WhoMW 92*
**Noreika,** Louise A 1923- *WhoAmP 91*
**Norek,** Frances Therese 1947- *WhoAmL 92, WhoMW 92*
**Norek,** Mark Gregory 1962- *WhoFI 92*
**Norell,** Jacob Solomon 1927- *Who 92*
**Norell,** John Reynolds 1937- *AmMWSc 92*
**Norell,** Norman 1900-1972 *DcTwDes*
**Norem,** Allen John 1941- *WhoAmP 91*
**Norem,** Richard Frederick, Sr. 1931- *WhoEnt 92*
**Noren,** Gerry Karl 1942- *AmMWSc 92*
**Noren,** Paul Harold Andreas 1910- *WhoRel 92*
**Norena,** Maria Claudia 1963- *WhoHisp 92*
**Norenberg,** Curtis Duane 1931- *WhoMW 92*
**Norfleet,** Fred L., Jr. 1950- *WhoBlA 92*
**Norfleet,** Janet 1933- *WhoBlA 92*
**Norfleet,** Morris L 1930- *AmMWSc 92*
**Norfolk,** Archdeacon of *Who 92*
**Norfolk,** Duke of 1915- *IntWW 91, Who 92*
**Norfolk,** Edward Matheson 1921- *Who 92*
**Norfolk,** Lavinia, Duchess of 1916- *Who 92*
**Norfolk,** Leslie William 1911- *Who 92*
**Norfolk,** Neveda Brooks 1929- *WhoAmP 91*
**Norfolk,** William Ray 1941- *WhoAmL 92*
**Norford,** Brian Seeley 1932- *AmMWSc 92*
**Norford,** George E. 1918- *WhoBlA 92*
**Norgaard,** Carl Aage 1924- *IntWW 91*
**Norgaard,** Ivar 1922- *IntWW 91*
**Norgaard,** Nicholas J 1943- *AmMWSc 92*
**Norgaard,** Richard Bruce 1943- *WhoWest 92*
**Norgard,** John Davey 1914- *Who 92*
**Norgard,** Mark David 1952- *WhoMW 92*
**Norgard,** Per 1932- *ConCom 92, NewAmDM*
**Norgle,** Charles Ronald, Sr. 1937- *WhoAmL 92, WhoMW 92*
**Norgren,** C. Neil 1923- *WhoWest 92*
**Norgren,** Constance *DrAPF 91*
**Norheim,** Neil Martin 1943- *WhoRel 92*
**Norholm,** Ib 1931- *ConCom 92, NewAmDM*
**Norick,** Ronald J 1941- *WhoAmP 91*
**Noriega,** Antonio 1940- *IntWW 91*
**Noriega,** Edward Manuel L 1960- *WhoHisp 92*
**Noriega,** Norman Joseph 1942- *WhoRel 92*
**Noriega,** Richard, Jr. 1950- *WhoHisp 92*
**Noriega,** Roger F. A. 1959- *WhoHisp 92*
**Noriega,** Saturnino N. 1939- *WhoHisp 92*
**Noriega Morena,** Manuel Antonio *FacFETw*
**Noriega Rodriguez,** David *WhoAmP 91, WhoHisp 92*
**Norin,** Allen Joseph 1944- *AmMWSc 92*
**Noring,** Jon Everett 1954- *AmMWSc 92*
**Norins,** Arthur Leonard 1928- *AmMWSc 92, WhoMW 92*
**Nork,** William Edward 1934- *AmMWSc 92*
**Norkeh,** Frederick Benedict 1956- *WhoMW 92*
**Norkin,** Cynthia Clair 1932- *WhoMW 92*
**Norkin,** Mark Mitchell 1955- *WhoWest 92*
**Norkin,** Sam 1917- *WhoEnt 92*
**Norkunas,** Mykolas *DcAmImH*
**Norkus,** Herbert 1916-1932 *EncTR 91*
**Norland,** Otto Realf 1930- *Who 92*
**Norland,** Rodney Lee 1949- *IntAu&W 91*
**Norling,** Bengt Olov 1925- *IntWW 91*
**Norling,** Bernard 1924- *IntAu&W 91, WrDr 92*
**Norling,** Irwin Denison 1916- *WhoMW 92*
**Norling,** Parry McWhinnie 1939- *AmMWSc 92*
**Norling,** Richard A. 1945- *WhoMW 92*
**Norlyn,** Jack David 1931- *AmMWSc 92*
**Norman,** Baroness d1991 *Who 92N*
**Norman,** Albert George, Jr. 1929- *WhoAmL 92, WhoFI 92*
**Norman,** Alex 1923- *AmMWSc 92*
**Norman,** Alex James 1931- *WhoBlA 92*
**Norman,** Alexander Vesey 1930- *Who 92*
**Norman,** Amos 1921- *AmMWSc 92*
**Norman,** Anne 1937- *TwCPaSc*
**Norman,** Anthony Mansfeldt 1934- *Who 92*
**Norman,** Anthony Westcott 1938- *AmMWSc 92*
**Norman,** Antony Dilworth 1963- *WhoRel 92*
**Norman,** Archibald Percy 1912- *Who 92*
**Norman,** Arlan Dale 1940- *AmMWSc 92*
**Norman,** Arthur 1917- *Who 92*
**Norman,** Arthur Gordon 1917- *IntWW 91*
**Norman,** Barry *IntMPA 92*
**Norman,** Barry 1933- *Who 92*
**Norman,** Barry Leslie 1933- *IntAu&W 91, IntWW 91*
**Norman,** Billy Ray 1935- *AmMWSc 92*
**Norman,** Bobby Don 1933- *WhoBlA 92*
**Norman,** Bruce 1936- *IntAu&W 91, WrDr 92*
**Norman,** Bruce 1936-1990 *AnObit 1990*
**Norman,** Calvin Haines 1923- *WhoBlA 92*
**Norman,** Carl Edgar 1931- *AmMWSc 92*
**Norman,** Charles 1904- *DcLB 111 [port]*
**Norman,** Clarence, Jr 1951- *WhoAmP 91*
**Norman,** Clifford P. 1943- *WhoBlA 92*
**Norman,** D. F. 1935- *WhoRel 92*
**Norman,** David 1942- *AmMWSc 92*
**Norman,** David Mark 1941- *WhoFI 92*
**Norman,** David Ray 1957- *WhoAmL 92*
**Norman,** Denis 1931- *IntWW 91*
**Norman,** Dennis Paul 1961- *WhoMW 92*
**Norman,** Desmond *Who 92*
**Norman,** Diana 1935- *ConAu 135*
**Norman,** Donald Arthur 1935- *WhoWest 92*
**Norman,** Douglas James 1946- *AmMWSc 92*
**Norman,** E. Gladys 1933- *WhoWest 92*
**Norman,** Edward 1932- *AmMWSc 92*
**Norman,** Edward Cobb 1913- *AmMWSc 92*
**Norman,** Edward R. 1938- *WrDr 92*
**Norman,** Edward Robert 1938- *Who 92*
**Norman,** Eliane Meyer 1931- *AmMWSc 92*
**Norman,** Eric B 1951- *AmMWSc 92*
**Norman,** Eric Edlund 1944- *WhoFI 92*
**Norman,** Floyd 1911- *AmMWSc 92*
**Norman,** Gary L 1950- *AmMWSc 92*
**Norman,** Geoffrey *Who 92*
**Norman,** Geoffrey 1935- *Who 92*
**Norman,** George Alfred B. *Who 92*
**Norman,** George E. 1933- *WhoBlA 92*
**Norman,** Georgette M. 1946- *WhoBlA 92*
**Norman,** Geraldine 1940- *IntAu&W 91*
**Norman,** Greg 1955- *ConAu 133*
**Norman,** Gurney *DrAPF 91*
**Norman,** Hilary *IntAu&W 91*
**Norman,** Homer Howard 1933- *WhoRel 92*
**Norman,** Horace Geoffrey 1896- *Who 92*
**Norman,** Howard Duane 1942- *AmMWSc 92*
**Norman,** Jack C 1938- *AmMWSc 92*
**Norman,** James Everett, Jr 1939- *AmMWSc 92*
**Norman,** James H. 1948- *WhoBlA 92*
**Norman,** Jeremiah 1771-1843 *DcNCBi 4*
**Norman,** Jessye 1945- *ConMus 7 [port], FacFETw, IntWW 91, NewAmDM, NotBlAW 92, Who 92, WhoBlA 92, WhoEnt 92*
**Norman,** Jim 1935- *WhoAmP 91*
**Norman,** Joe G, Jr 1947- *AmMWSc 92*
**Norman,** John 1912- *IntAu&W 91*
**Norman,** John 1931- *TwCSFW 91, WrDr 92*
**Norman,** John Barstow, Jr. 1940- *WhoEnt 92, WhoWest 92*
**Norman,** John C. 1930- *WhoBlA 92*
**Norman,** John E. 1936- *WhoWest 92*
**Norman,** John Edward 1922- *WhoWest 92*
**Norman,** John Harris 1929- *AmMWSc 92*
**Norman,** John Matthew 1942- *AmMWSc 92*
**Norman,** Julie Anne 1943- *WhoMW 92*
**Norman,** Kenneth Darnel 1964- *WhoBlA 92*
**Norman,** Kenneth Roy 1925- *Who 92*
**Norman,** L A, Jr 1908- *AmMWSc 92*
**Norman,** Larry Ellis 1952- *WhoAmP 91*
**Norman,** Lilith 1927- *WrDr 92*
**Norman,** Lindsay Dean, Jr. 1937- *WhoWest 92*
**Norman,** Maidie Ruth 1912- *WhoBlA 92*
**Norman,** Marc *DrAPF 91*
**Norman,** Margaret 1908-1976 *TwCPaSc*
**Norman,** Mark 1927- *Who 92*
**Norman,** Mark Richard 1910- *Who 92*
**Norman,** Marsha 1947- *BenetAL 91, IntAu&W 91, WhoEnt 92, WrDr 92*
**Norman,** Merrick Joseph 1954- *WhoAmL 92*
**Norman,** Michael 1947- *IntAu&W 91, WhoMW 92*
**Norman,** Moses C. *WhoBlA 92*
**Norman,** Nigel Desmond 1929- *Who 92*
**Norman,** Norman B. d1991 *NewYTBS 91 [port]*
**Norman,** Orval Gene 1937- *WhoMW 92*
**Norman,** Oscar Loris 1925- *AmMWSc 92*
**Norman,** P. Roosevelt 1933- *WhoBlA 92*
**Norman,** Patricia 1947- *WhoBlA 92*
**Norman,** Peter Minert 1932- *WhoMW 92*
**Norman,** Philip Sidney 1924- *AmMWSc 92*
**Norman,** Ray Marshall 1960- *WhoEnt 92*
**Norman,** Reid Lynn 1944- *AmMWSc 92*
**Norman,** Richard 1932- *Who 92*
**Norman,** Richard Daviess 1927- *AmMWSc 92, WhoMW 92*
**Norman,** Richard Oswald Chandler 1932- *IntWW 91*
**Norman,** Robert 1912- *Who 92*
**Norman,** Robert 1914- *Who 92*
**Norman,** Robert Daniel 1938- *AmMWSc 92*
**Norman,** Robert Zane 1924- *AmMWSc 92*
**Norman,** Roger Atkinson, Jr 1946- *AmMWSc 92*
**Norman,** Ronald Michael 1952- *WhoEnt 92*
**Norman,** Ronald Victor 1929- *WhoMW 92*
**Norman,** Ronnie Lee 1957- *WhoRel 92*
**Norman,** Roy A. 1941- *WhoBlA 92*
**Norman,** Seth Michael 1953- *WhoWest 92*
**Norman,** Sherry Lynn 1958- *WhoWest 92*
**Norman,** Stephen Peckham 1942- *WhoFI 92*
**Norman,** Steve Albert 1948- *WhoEnt 92*
**Norman,** Timothy Joe 1962- *WhoRel 92*
**Norman,** Vesey *Who 92*
**Norman,** Wallace 1962- *WhoBlA 92*
**Norman,** Wesley P 1928- *AmMWSc 92*
**Norman,** Wesley W d1899 *BiInAmS*
**Norman,** William H. 1946- *WhoBlA 92*
**Norman,** William James 1922- *WhoAmP 91*
**Norman,** William S. 1938- *WhoBlA 92*
**Norman,** William Stanley 1938- *WhoFI 92*
**Norman,** Willoughby Rollo *Who 92*
**Norman,** Willoughby Rollo 1909- *IntWW 91*
**Norman,** Wyatt Thomas, III 1952- *WhoFI 92*
**Normanby,** Marquis of 1912- *Who 92*
**Normand,** James Arthur 1953- *WhoAmP 91*
**Normand,** Mabel 1894-1930 *ReelWom*
**Normand,** Robert 1940- *WhoFI 92*
**Normandin,** Kurt A 1957- *WhoAmP 91*
**Normandin,** Raymond O 1930- *AmMWSc 92*
**Normandin,** Robert F 1927- *AmMWSc 92*
**Normann,** Richard A 1943- *AmMWSc 92*
**Normann,** Sigurd Johns 1935- *AmMWSc 92*
**Normansell,** David E 1938- *AmMWSc 92*
**Normant,** Henri 1907- *IntWW 91*
**Normanton,** Earl of 1945- *Who 92*
**Normanton,** Tom 1917- *Who 92*
**Normark,** William Raymond 1943- *AmMWSc 92*
**Norment,** Beverly Ray 1941- *AmMWSc 92*
**Norment,** Hillyer Gavin 1928- *AmMWSc 92*
**Normile,** Hubert Clarence 1906- *AmMWSc 92*
**Normington,** David John 1951- *Who 92*
**Norminton,** Edward Joseph 1938- *AmMWSc 92*
**Nornes,** Howard Onsgaard 1931- *AmMWSc 92*
**Nornes,** Sherman Berdeen 1929- *AmMWSc 92*
**Norniella,** Jesus, Jr. 1940- *WhoHisp 92*
**Noro,** Kyoichi 1919- *IntWW 91*
**Norodom Sihanouk** 1922- *NewYTBS 91 [port]*
**Norodom Sihanouk,** Samdech Preah 1922- *IntWW 91*
**Noronha,** Fernando M Oliveira 1924- *AmMWSc 92*
**Norquest,** Carrol 1901-1981 *ConAu 133*
**Norquist,** John O 1949- *WhoAmP 91*
**Norquist,** John Olof 1949- *WhoMW 92*
**Norrback,** Johan Ole 1941- *IntWW 91*
**Norrbin,** Stefan Christer 1959- *WhoFI 92*
**Norrbom,** Allen Lee 1957- *AmMWSc 92*
**Norrdin,** Robert W 1937- *AmMWSc 92*
**Norred,** William Preston 1945- *AmMWSc 92*
**Norrell,** Mitchell Abbott 1961- *WhoAmL 92*
**Norrell-Nance,** Rosalind Elizabeth 1950- *WhoBlA 92*
**Norrell-Thomas,** Sondra 1941- *WhoBlA 92*
**Norreys,** Lord 1958- *Who 92*
**Norrgard,** Clyde L *WhoAmP 91*
**Norrie** *Who 92*
**Norrie,** Baron 1936- *Who 92*
**Norrie,** D H 1929- *AmMWSc 92*
**Norrie,** Marian Farrow 1940- *Who 92*
**Norrington,** Humphrey Thomas 1936- *Who 92*
**Norrington,** Roger 1934- *NewAmDM*
**Norrington,** Roger Arthur Carver 1934- *IntWW 91, Who 92, WhoEnt 92*
**Norris,** A R 1937- *AmMWSc 92*
**Norris,** Alan E 1935- *WhoAmP 91*
**Norris,** Alan Eugene 1935- *WhoAmL 92, WhoMW 92*
**Norris,** Albert Stanley 1926- *AmMWSc 92*
**Norris,** Andrea Spaulding 1945- *WhoMW 92*
**Norris,** Andrew Edward 1937- *AmMWSc 92*
**Norris,** Arlyn C. 1949- *WhoRel 92*
**Norris,** Arthur Mae 1911- *WhoBlA 92*
**Norris,** Brent Lee 1952- *WhoFI 92*
**Norris,** Carroll Boyd, Jr 1941- *AmMWSc 92*
**Norris,** Charles Glenn 1906- *IntMPA 92*
**Norris,** Charles L., Sr. 1926- *WhoBlA 92*
**Norris,** Charles R 1925- *WhoAmP 91*
**Norris,** Chester E, Jr 1927- *WhoAmP 91*
**Norris,** Christopher 1955- *WhoEnt 92*
**Norris,** Christopher Neil F. *Who 92*
**Norris,** Chuck *WhoEnt 92*
**Norris,** Chuck 1940- *IntMPA 92*
**Norris,** Clarence E 1910- *WhoAmP 91*
**Norris,** Curtis H. 1913- *WhoBlA 92*
**Norris,** Cynthia Clarice 1956- *WhoBlA 92, WhoRel 92*
**Norris,** D. Wayne 1939- *WhoWest 92*
**Norris,** Dale Melvin, Jr 1930- *AmMWSc 92*
**Norris,** Daniel Howard 1933- *AmMWSc 92, WhoWest 92*
**Norris,** Dave Noel 1942- *WhoAmP 91*
**Norris,** David Byrd 1933- *WhoAmP 91*
**Norris,** David Joseph 1922- *Who 92*
**Norris,** David Otto 1939- *AmMWSc 92*
**Norris,** David Randolph 1952- *WhoEnt 92*
**Norris,** Dean Rayburn 1937- *AmMWSc 92*
**Norris,** Donald Earl, Jr 1940- *AmMWSc 92*
**Norris,** Donna M. 1943- *WhoBlA 92*
**Norris,** Earl Ray 1937- *WhoRel 92*
**Norris,** Edwin Oscar, Jr. 1926- *WhoAmL 92*
**Norris,** Eric 1918- *Who 92*
**Norris,** Eric Amexander 1959- *WhoWest 92*
**Norris,** Eric George 1918- *IntWW 91*
**Norris,** Ethel Maureen 1956- *WhoBlA 92*
**Norris,** Eugene Michael 1938- *AmMWSc 92*
**Norris,** Fletcher R 1934- *AmMWSc 92*
**Norris,** Forbes Holten, Jr 1928- *AmMWSc 92*
**Norris,** Frances McMurtray 1946- *WhoAmP 91*
**Norris,** Frank 1870-1902 *BenetAL 91, TwCWW 91*
**Norris,** Frank Arthur 1913- *AmMWSc 92*
**Norris,** Fred Arthur, Jr. 1945- *WhoBlA 92*
**Norris,** Frederick Walter 1941- *WhoRel 92*
**Norris,** Geoffrey 1937- *AmMWSc 92*

**Norris,** Geoffrey 1947- *WrDr 92*
**Norris,** George William 1861-1944 *AmPolLe, FacFETw*
**Norris,** Gilbert Frank 1916- *Who 92*
**Norris,** Graham Alexander 1913- *Who 92*
**Norris,** Gunilla *DrAPF 91*
**Norris,** H Thomas 1934- *AmMWSc 92*
**Norris,** Herbert Walter 1904- *Who 92*
**Norris,** James Alexander 1938- *WhoIns 92*
**Norris,** James Ellsworth Chiles 1932- *WhoBlA 92*
**Norris,** James Newcome, IV 1942- *AmMWSc 92*
**Norris,** James Scott 1943- *AmMWSc 92*
**Norris,** James W 1930- *WhoAmP 91*
**Norris,** Jane 1960- *TwCPaSc*
**Norris,** Joan *DrAPF 91*
**Norris,** John *WhoRel 92*
**Norris,** John 1657-1711 *BlkwCEP*
**Norris,** John Anthony 1946- *WhoFI 92*
**Norris,** John David 1947- *WhoAmL 92*
**Norris,** John Franklyn 1887-1952 *RelLAm 91*
**Norris,** John Hallam Mercer 1929- *Who 92*
**Norris,** John Robert 1932- *Who 92*
**Norris,** John Windsor, Jr. 1936- *WhoFI 92*
**Norris,** Joni *WhoEnt 92*
**Norris,** Joseph Brian 1955- *WhoMW 92*
**Norris,** Joy Cole 1958- *WhoRel 92*
**Norris,** June 1922- *WhoRel 92*
**Norris,** Karl H 1921- *AmMWSc 92*
**Norris,** Kathleen *DrAPF 91*
**Norris,** Kathleen 1878-1966 *FacFETw*
**Norris,** Kathleen 1880-1966 *BenetAL 91*
**Norris,** Kathleen Thompson 1880-1966 *AmPeW*
**Norris,** Ken 1951- *ConPo 91, WrDr 92*
**Norris,** Kenneth Stafford 1924- *AmMWSc 92*
**Norris,** Leslie 1921- *ConPo 91, WrDr 92*
**Norris,** Logan Allen 1936- *AmMWSc 92*
**Norris,** Max Edwin 1940- *WhoMW 92*
**Norris,** Michael Kelvin 1955- *WhoBlA 92*
**Norris,** Neal Albert 1951- *WhoFI 92*
**Norris,** Norman 1932- *TwCPaSc*
**Norris,** Patricia Ann 1932- *AmMWSc 92*
**Norris,** Paul Edmund 1918- *AmMWSc 92, WhoMW 92*
**Norris,** Paul Robert 1948- *WhoEnt 92*
**Norris,** Philip Eugene 1954- *WhoEnt 92*
**Norris,** Phyllis Irene 1909- *WrDr 92*
**Norris,** Pippa 1953- *ConAu 134*
**Norris,** Richard C 1935- *AmMWSc 92*
**Norris,** Richard Patrick 1944- *WhoMW 92*
**Norris,** Robert Francis 1938- *AmMWSc 92*
**Norris,** Robert Matheson 1921- *AmMWSc 92*
**Norris,** Robert Michael 1951- *WhoRel 92*
**Norris,** Ronald Michael 1938- *WhoFI 92*
**Norris,** Roy Howard 1930- *AmMWSc 92*
**Norris,** Russell Bradner, Jr. 1942- *WhoRel 92*
**Norris,** Steven James 1951- *AmMWSc 92*
**Norris,** Steven John 1945- *Who 92*
**Norris,** Sydney George 1937- *Who 92*
**Norris,** Terry *NewYTBS 91 [port]*
**Norris,** Terry Orban 1922- *AmMWSc 92*
**Norris,** Thomas Hughes 1916- *AmMWSc 92*
**Norris,** Tracy Hopkins 1927- *WhoMW 92*
**Norris,** Victor Snyder 1944- *WhoRel 92*
**Norris,** Walter, Jr. 1945- *WhoBlA 92*
**Norris,** Walter Blaine, Jr. 1949- *WhoEnt 92*
**Norris,** Wayne Oren 1952- *WhoWest 92*
**Norris,** Wilfred Glen 1932- *AmMWSc 92*
**Norris,** William A *WhoAmP 91*
**Norris,** William Albert 1927- *WhoAmL 92*
**Norris,** William C 1911- *AmMWSc 92*
**Norris,** William Elmore, Jr 1921- *AmMWSc 92*
**Norris,** William Fisher 1839-1901 *BiInAmS*
**Norris,** William Penrod 1920- *AmMWSc 92, WhoMW 92*
**Norris,** William Warren 1927- *AmMWSc 92*
**Norris,** Wyman 1959- *WhoEnt 92*
**Norrish,** Ronald George Wreyford 1897-1978 *FacFETw, WhoNob 90*
**Norse,** Harold *DrAPF 91*
**Norse,** Harold 1916- *ConPo 91, WrDr 92*
**Norse,** Harold George 1916- *IntAu&W 91*
**Norstad,** Lauris 1907-1988 *FacFETw*
**Norstadt,** Fred A 1926- *AmMWSc 92*
**Norstein,** Yuriy Borisovich 1941- *SovUnBD*
**Norstog,** Knut Jonson 1921- *AmMWSc 92*
**Norstrand,** Hans Peter 1940- *WhoFI 92*
**Norsworthy,** Elizabeth Krassovsky 1943- *WhoAmL 92*
**Norsworthy,** John Randolph 1939- *WhoFI 92*
**Norsworthy,** Naomi 1877-1916 *BiInAmS*
**North** *Who 92*
**North,** Lord 1971- *Who 92*
**North,** Alastair Macarthur 1932- *IntWW 91*
**North,** Alex d1991 *NewYTBS 91 [port]*
**North,** Alex 1910- *IntWW 91, NewAmDM*
**North,** Andrew *TwCSFW 91, WrDr 92*
**North,** Anne Via 1939- *WhoWest 92*
**North,** Anthony *ConAu 36NR*
**North,** Charles *DrAPF 91*
**North,** Charles A 1932- *AmMWSc 92*
**North,** Charles A 1941- *WhoIns 92*
**North,** Colin *IntAu&W 91X, TwCWW 91*
**North,** Edward D 1918- *AmMWSc 92*
**North,** Elizabeth 1932- *IntAu&W 91, WrDr 92*
**North,** Erasmus Darwin 1806-1858 *BiInAmS*
**North,** Eric 1884- *ScFEYrs*
**North,** Frank Mason 1850-1935 *RelLAm 91*
**North,** Franklin H *ScFEYrs*
**North,** Frederick 1732-1792 *BlkwEAR [port]*
**North,** Gerald D.W. 1951- *WhoAmL 92*
**North,** Gil *IntAu&W 91X, WrDr 92*
**North,** Harper Qua 1917- *AmMWSc 92*
**North,** Henry *ScFEYrs*
**North,** Henry E T 1931- *AmMWSc 92*
**North,** James A 1934- *AmMWSc 92*
**North,** John David 1934- *IntWW 91*
**North,** John David 1949- *WhoAmL 92*
**North,** John Joseph 1926- *Who 92*
**North,** Jonathan *Who 92*
**North,** Keith Allen 1938- *WhoFI 92*
**North,** Kenneth Earl 1945- *WhoAmL 92, WhoFI 92, WhoMW 92*
**North,** Kevin A 1952- *WhoIns 92*
**North,** Leo 1942- *WhoEnt 92*
**North,** Mark Huntington 1946- *WhoWest 92*
**North,** Mary Hayne *DrAPF 91*
**North,** Oliver L. 1943- *IntWW 91*
**North,** Paul 1940- *AmMWSc 92*
**North,** Peter Machin 1936- *IntWW 91, Who 92*
**North,** R Alan 1944- *AmMWSc 92*
**North,** Richard Bernard, Jr. 1957- *WhoAmL 92*
**North,** Richard Ralph 1934- *AmMWSc 92*
**North,** Robert 1916- *WrDr 92*
**North,** Robert 1945- *Who 92*
**North,** Robert J 1935- *AmMWSc 92*
**North,** Roger 1651?-1734 *BlkwCEP*
**North,** Ross Stafford 1930- *WhoRel 92*
**North,** Sara *IntAu&W 91X*
**North,** Sheree 1933- *IntMPA 92*
**North,** Sterling 1906-1974 *BenetAL 91*
**North,** Steve 1953- *WhoEnt 92*
**North,** Thomas 1919- *Who 92*
**North,** W Paul Tuisku 1934- *AmMWSc 92*
**North,** Wheeler James 1922- *AmMWSc 92*
**North,** William Charles 1925- *AmMWSc 92*
**North,** William Gordon 1942- *AmMWSc 92*
**North,** William Jonathan 1931- *Who 92*
**North-Eastern Caribbean & Aruba,** Bishop *Who 92*
**North-Root,** Helen May 1947- *AmMWSc 92*
**Northam,** Edward Stafford 1927- *AmMWSc 92*
**Northampton,** Archdeacon of *Who 92*
**Northampton,** Bishop of 1925- *Who 92*
**Northampton,** Marquess of 1946- *Who 92*
**Northard,** John Henry 1926- *IntWW 91, Who 92*
**Northbourne,** Baron 1926- *Who 92*
**Northbrook,** Baron d1990 *Who 92N*
**Northbrook,** Baron 1954- *Who 92*
**Northcliffe,** Viscount 1865-1922 *FacFETw*
**Northcliffe,** Lee Conrad 1926- *AmMWSc 92*
**Northcote** *Who 92*
**Northcote,** Donald Henry 1921- *IntWW 91, Who 92*
**Northcote,** Peter Colston 1920- *Who 92*
**Northcott,** Douglas 1916- *WrDr 92*
**Northcott,** Douglas Geoffrey 1916- *Who 92*
**Northcott,** Jean 1926- *AmMWSc 92*
**Northcross,** David C. 1917- *WhoBlA 92*
**Northcross,** Deborah Ametra 1951- *WhoBlA 92*
**Northcross,** Wilson Hill, Jr. 1946- *WhoBlA 92*
**Northcutt,** Clarence Dewey 1916- *WhoAmL 92*
**Northcutt,** Helene Louise Berking 1916- *WhoWest 92*
**Northcutt,** Richard Glenn 1941- *AmMWSc 92*
**Northcutt,** Robert Allan 1937- *AmMWSc 92*
**Northcutt,** Wanda L 1937- *WhoAmP 91*
**Northenor,** Doris Jean 1932- *WhoAmP 91*
**Northern Dancer** 1961-1990 *FacFETw*
**Northern,** Glenn Eric 1967- *WhoMW 92*
**Northern,** Jerry Lee 1940- *AmMWSc 92*
**Northern,** Richard 1948- *WhoAmL 92*
**Northern,** Robert A. 1934- *WhoBlA 92*
**Northern Argentina,** Bishop of 1937- *Who 92*
**Northern Territory,** Bishop of the 1936- *Who 92*
**Northesk,** Earl of 1926- *Who 92*
**Northey,** William T 1928- *AmMWSc 92*
**Northfelt,** Merlyn Winfield 1915- *WhoRel 92*
**Northfield,** Baron 1923- *Who 92*
**Northington,** Dewey Jackson, Jr 1946- *AmMWSc 92*
**Northington,** Glyn Ray 1957- *WhoMW 92*
**Northland,** Viscount *Who 92*
**Northnagel,** E.W. *DrAPF 91*
**Northolt,** Archdeacon of *Who 92*
**Northouse,** Richard A 1938- *AmMWSc 92*
**Northover,** John 1937- *AmMWSc 92*
**Northover,** Vernon Keith 1934- *WhoBlA 92*
**Northrip,** John Willard 1934- *AmMWSc 92*
**Northrop,** Charles Porter 1941- *WhoAmL 92*
**Northrop,** David A 1938- *AmMWSc 92*
**Northrop,** Edward H. 1943- *WhoFI 92*
**Northrop,** Edward Skottowe 1911- *WhoAmL 92*
**Northrop,** Filmer S. C. 1893- *Who 92*
**Northrop,** John 1923- *AmMWSc 92*
**Northrop,** John Howard 1891- *FacFETw*
**Northrop,** John Howard 1891-1987 *WhoNob 90*
**Northrop,** John Isaiah 1861-1891 *BiInAmS*
**Northrop,** John Knudsen 1895-1981 *FacFETw*
**Northrop,** Robert Burr 1935- *AmMWSc 92*
**Northrop,** Theodore George 1924- *AmMWSc 92*
**Northrup,** Clyde John Marshall, Jr 1938- *AmMWSc 92*
**Northrup,** Jack Von 1935- *WhoMW 92*
**Northrup,** Jeri Renee 1963- *WhoFI 92*
**Northrup,** Sandra Joan 1938- *WhoWest 92*
**Northrup,** William Kelly 1942- *WhoMW 92*
**Northshield,** Robert *LesBEnT 92 [port]*
**Northumberland,** Archdeacon of *Who 92*
**Northumberland,** Duke of 1953- *Who 92*
**Northup,** Anne Meagher 1948- *WhoAmP 91*
**Northup,** Larry L 1940- *AmMWSc 92*
**Northup,** Melvin Lee 1941- *AmMWSc 92*
**Northup,** Sharon Joan 1942- *AmMWSc 92*
**Northway,** Eileen Mary 1931- *Who 92*
**Northwood,** Derek Owen 1943- *AmMWSc 92*
**Nortje,** Arthur 1942-1970 *LiExTwC*
**Norton** *Who 92*
**Norton,** Baron 1915- *Who 92*
**Norton,** Andre 1912- *IntAu&W 91, TwCSFW 91, WrDr 92*
**Norton,** Andrew McCall 1962- *WhoAmP 91*
**Norton,** Andrews 1786-1853 *BenetAL 91*
**Norton,** Augustus Richard 1946- *IntAu&W 91, WrDr 92*
**Norton,** Aurelia Evangeline 1932- *WhoBlA 92*
**Norton,** C. McKim 1907-1991 *NewYTBS 91 [port]*
**Norton,** Charles Albert 1920- *IntAu&W 91*
**Norton,** Charles Eliot 1827-1908 *BenetAL 91*
**Norton,** Charles Lawrence 1917- *AmMWSc 92*
**Norton,** Charles Warren 1944- *AmMWSc 92*
**Norton,** Clifford John d1990 *Who 92N*
**Norton,** Cynthia Friend 1940- *AmMWSc 92*
**Norton,** Daniel Remsen 1922- *AmMWSc 92*
**Norton,** Daryl Edward 1957- *WhoRel 92*
**Norton,** Dave Kenneth 1949- *WhoFI 92*
**Norton,** David Jerry 1940- *AmMWSc 92*
**Norton,** David William 1944- *AmMWSc 92*
**Norton,** Denis Locklin 1939- *AmMWSc 92*
**Norton,** Diana Mae 1945- *WhoMW 92*
**Norton,** Don Carlos 1922- *AmMWSc 92*
**Norton,** Donald 1920- *Who 92*
**Norton,** Donald Alan 1920- *AmMWSc 92*
**Norton,** Douglas Ray 1933- *WhoFI 92, WhoWest 92*
**Norton,** Edward 1823-1894 *BiInAmS*
**Norton,** Edward W D 1922- *AmMWSc 92*
**Norton,** Edward Worthington 1938- *WhoBlA 92*
**Norton,** Eleanor Holmes *WhoAmP 91*
**Norton,** Eleanor Holmes 1937- *AlmAP 92 [port], WhoAmL 92*
**Norton,** Eleanor Holmes 1938- *NotBlAW 92, WhoBlA 92*
**Norton,** Elinor Frances 1929- *AmMWSc 92*
**Norton,** Elliot 1903- *WhoEnt 92*
**Norton,** Eunice 1908- *WhoEnt 92*
**Norton,** Frank Louis 1942- *WhoAmP 91*
**Norton,** Fred Carl 1938- *WhoAmP 91*
**Norton,** Gale 1954- *WhoAmL 92, WhoWest 92*
**Norton,** Gale Ann 1954- *WhoAmP 91*
**Norton,** George Haseltine, Jr. 1914- *WhoFI 92*
**Norton,** George Mosse 1942- *WhoMW 92*
**Norton,** Gerald Patrick 1940- *WhoAmL 92*
**Norton,** Gerard Ross 1915- *Who 92*
**Norton,** H. Don 1945- *WhoFI 92*
**Norton,** H. Gaither 1918- *WhoFI 92*
**Norton,** Herbert Steven 1934- *WhoFI 92*
**Norton,** Hugh Edward 1936- *IntWW 91, Who 92*
**Norton,** James Augustus, Jr 1921- *AmMWSc 92*
**Norton,** James J. 1930- *WhoFI 92*
**Norton,** James Jennings 1918- *AmMWSc 92*
**Norton,** James Michael 1946- *AmMWSc 92*
**Norton,** Jeffrey Joseph 1958- *WhoAmL 92*
**Norton,** Jenny 1945- *WhoAmP 91*
**Norton,** Joe L. 1942- *WhoAmL 92*
**Norton,** John *DrAPF 91*
**Norton,** John 1606-1663 *BenetAL 91*
**Norton,** John Henry 1955- *WhoAmL 92*
**Norton,** John Hise 1952- *WhoAmL 92*
**Norton,** John L *WhoAmP 91*
**Norton,** John Leslie 1945- *AmMWSc 92*
**Norton,** John Lindsey 1935- *Who 92*
**Norton,** John Pitkin 1822-1852 *BiInAmS*
**Norton,** John William Roy 1898-1974 *DcNCBi 4*
**Norton,** Joseph Daniel 1927- *AmMWSc 92*
**Norton,** Joseph R 1915- *AmMWSc 92*
**Norton,** Karen Ann 1950- *WhoWest 92*
**Norton,** Karl Kenneth 1938- *AmMWSc 92*
**Norton,** Kenneth Howard, Jr. 1966- *WhoBlA 92*
**Norton,** Larry 1947- *AmMWSc 92*
**Norton,** Lewis Franklin 1930- *WhoIns 92*
**Norton,** Lewis Mills 1855-1893 *BiInAmS*
**Norton,** Lilburn Lafayette 1927- *AmMWSc 92*
**Norton,** Louis Arthur 1937- *AmMWSc 92*
**Norton,** Mahlon H 1922- *AmMWSc 92*
**Norton,** Margaret *TwCPaSc*
**Norton,** Mark Charles 1952- *WhoEnt 92*
**Norton,** Mary 1903- *IntAu&W 91, Who 92, WrDr 92*
**Norton,** Mary Katherine *WhoAmL 92*
**Norton,** Michael Jeffrey 1938- *WhoAmL 92, WhoAmP 91*
**Norton,** Omar P *WhoAmP 91*
**Norton,** Peter Bowes 1929- *WhoFI 92, WhoMW 92*
**Norton,** Philip 1951- *WrDr 92*
**Norton,** Richard E 1928- *AmMWSc 92*
**Norton,** Richard Vail 1940- *AmMWSc 92*
**Norton,** Robert Alan 1926- *AmMWSc 92*
**Norton,** Robert Anthony 1939- *IntWW 91*
**Norton,** Robert James 1914- *AmMWSc 92*
**Norton,** Robert W 1923- *WhoAmP 91*
**Norton,** Roy 1869-1942 *ScFEYrs*
**Norton,** Scott J 1936- *AmMWSc 92*
**Norton,** Sidney Augustus 1835-1918 *BiInAmS*
**Norton,** Stata Elaine 1922- *AmMWSc 92*
**Norton,** Stephen Allen 1940- *AmMWSc 92*
**Norton,** Ted Raymond 1919- *AmMWSc 92*
**Norton,** Thomas 1532-1584 *RfGEnL 91*
**Norton,** Thomas C 1934- *WhoAmP 91*
**Norton,** Thomas Edmond 1940- *WhoWest 92*
**Norton,** Tom E 1940- *WhoAmP 91*
**Norton,** Virginia Marino 1934- *AmMWSc 92*
**Norton,** William Augustus 1810-1883 *BiInAmS*
**Norton,** William George 1951- *WhoAmP 91*
**Norton,** William Thompson 1929- *AmMWSc 92*
**Norton-Griffiths,** John 1938- *Who 92*
**Norton-Smith,** John 1931- *IntAu&W 91*
**Norton-Taylor,** Judy *WhoEnt 92*
**Nortz,** H Robert 1932- *WhoAmP 91*
**Norusis,** Marija Jurate 1948- *AmMWSc 92*
**Norval,** Richard Andrew 1950- *AmMWSc 92*
**Norvel,** William Leonard 1935- *WhoBlA 92*
**Norvell,** James David 1939- *WhoAmP 91*
**Norvell,** John Charles 1940- *AmMWSc 92*
**Norvell,** John Edmondson, III 1929- *AmMWSc 92*
**Norvell,** Ralph, Jr. 1921- *WhoAmL 92*
**Norvell,** Thomas Vernon 1955- *WhoRel 92*
**Norvil,** Manning *TwCSFW 91*
**Norville,** Craig Hubert 1944- *WhoAmL 92*
**Norville,** Deborah *LesBEnT 92*
**Norvitch,** Mary Ellen 1955- *AmMWSc 92*
**Norvo,** Red 1908- *NewAmDM*
**Norwalk,** Thomas Kent 1954- *WhoRel 92*
**Norway,** Kate 1913- *IntAu&W 91*
**Norwich,** Archdeacon of *Who 92*
**Norwich,** Bishop of 1933- *Who 92*

**Norwich**, Dean of Who 92
**Norwich**, Viscount 1929- Who 92
**Norwich**, Anne 1929- TwCPaSc
**Norwich**, John Julius 1929- IntAu&W 91, WrDr 92
**Norwich**, Kenneth Howard 1939- AmMWSc 92
**Norwood**, Audrianne WhoEnt 92
**Norwood**, Bernice N. 1917- WhoBlA 92
**Norwood**, Calvin Coolidge 1927- WhoBlA 92
**Norwood**, Charles Arthur 1938- AmMWSc 92
**Norwood**, Elizabeth Lee 1912- WhoBlA 92
**Norwood**, Frederick Reyes 1939- AmMWSc 92
**Norwood**, Gerald 1938- AmMWSc 92
**Norwood**, Jack Mitchell 1930- WhoAmP 91
**Norwood**, Jack Roy 1926- WhoFI 92
**Norwood**, James Alan 1944- WhoFI 92
**Norwood**, James S 1932- AmMWSc 92
**Norwood**, Janet L WhoAmP 91
**Norwood**, Janet Lippe 1923- WhoFI 92
**Norwood**, Jennifer 1961- WhoFI 92
**Norwood**, John F. 1927- WhoBlA 92
**Norwood**, John Wall 1803-1885 DcNCBi 4
**Norwood**, Joseph Granville 1807-1895 BiInAmS
**Norwood**, Joy Janell 1936- WhoMW 92
**Norwood**, Matthew A. WhoRel 92
**Norwood**, Peter 1929- TwCPaSc
**Norwood**, Philip Weltner 1947- WhoFI 92
**Norwood**, Richard E 1934- AmMWSc 92
**Norwood**, Ronald Eugene 1952- WhoFI 92, WhoWest 92
**Norwood**, Suzanne Freda 1926- Who 92
**Norwood**, Tom 1943- WhoBlA 92
**Norwood**, V.G.C. 1920-1983 TwCWW 91
**Norwood**, Victor George Charles 1920- IntAu&W 91
**Norwood**, Walter 1907- Who 92
**Norwood**, Warren DrAPF 91
**Norwood**, Warren 1945- IntAu&W 91, TwCSFW 91, WrDr 92
**Norwood**, William 1767-1842 DcNCBi 4
**Norwood**, William 1806-1887 DcNCBi 4
**Norwood**, William R. 1936- WhoBlA 92
**Nosacek**, Gary John 1955- WhoEnt 92
**Nosal**, Eugene Adam 1942- AmMWSc 92
**Nosanow**, Lewis H 1931- AmMWSc 92
**Nosco**, Dennis Lawrence 1953- WhoMW 92
**Nosek**, Thomas Michael 1947- AmMWSc 92
**Noshay**, Allen 1933- AmMWSc 92
**Noshpitz**, Joseph Dove 1922- AmMWSc 92
**Nosiglia**, Enrique 1949- IntWW 91
**Noske**, Gustav 1868-1946 EncTR 91 [port]
**Noskowiak**, Arthur Fredrick 1920- AmMWSc 92
**Nosler**, Brad Miller 1960- WhoEnt 92
**Nosler**, Robert Amos 1946- WhoWest 92
**Nosov**, Yevgeny Ivanovich 1925- IntWW 91
**Noss**, John Bramble 1935- IntWW 91, Who 92
**Noss**, Richard Robert 1950- AmMWSc 92
**Nossal**, Gustav 1931- Who 92, WrDr 92
**Nossal**, Gustav Joseph Victor 1931- IntWW 91
**Nossal**, Nancy 1937- AmMWSc 92
**Nossal**, Ralph J 1937- AmMWSc 92
**Nossaman**, Norman L 1932- AmMWSc 92
**Nosseck**, Noel 1943- IntMPA 92, WhoEnt 92
**Nossiter**, Bernard Daniel 1926- IntAu&W 91, Who 92, WhoFI 92
**Nostbakken**, Roger Wesley 1930- WhoRel 92
**Nostradamus**, Merlin 1822-1904 ScFEYrs A
**Nostrand**, Howard Lee 1910- WrDr 92
**Nostrand**, Jennifer DrAPF 91
**Nostrand**, S. DrAPF 91
**Nosworthy**, Darlene Marie 1948- WhoEnt 92
**Nosworthy**, Harold George 1908- Who 92
**Nota**, Ronald John 1948- WhoFI 92, WhoMW 92
**Notarianni**, Philip Frank 1948- WhoWest 92
**Notarnicola**, James 1951- WhoFI 92
**Notaro**, Anthony 1956- AmMWSc 92
**Notation**, Albert David 1935- AmMWSc 92
**Notch**, James Stephen 1950- WhoFI 92
**Noteboom**, William Duane 1933- AmMWSc 92
**Noterdaeme**, Paul M. J. 1929- IntWW 91
**Noterman**, M. Patrice WhoRel 92
**Notestein**, Barbara 1949- WhoAmP 91
**Notestein**, David Albert 1953- WhoIns 92
**Notestine**, Wilbur Edmund 1931- WhoAmL 92
**Notev**, Georgy WhoEnt 92
**Noth**, Heinrich 1928- IntWW 91
**Nothaft**, Frank Emile 1956- WhoFI 92
**Nothdurft**, Robert Ray 1939- AmMWSc 92
**Nothmann**, Rudolf S. 1907- WhoAmL 92, WhoFI 92, WhoWest 92
**Nothnagel**, Eugene Alfred 1952- AmMWSc 92
**Nothnagel**, Paul E. 1934- WhoFI 92
**Nothomb**, Charles Ferdinand 1936- IntWW 91
**Nothomb**, Pierre 1887-1966 BiDExR
**Notice**, Guy Symour 1929- WhoBlA 92
**Notides**, Angelo C 1936- AmMWSc 92
**Notkin**, Nathan Thomas 1917- WhoAmL 92
**Notkin**, Richard T. 1948- WhoWest 92
**Notkins**, Abner Louis 1932- AmMWSc 92
**Notley**, Alice DrAPF 91
**Notley**, Alice 1945- ConPo 91, IntAu&W 91, WrDr 92
**Notley**, Norman Thomas 1928- AmMWSc 92
**Noto**, Anthony Carmen 1933- WhoMW 92
**Noto**, John Edward 1947- WhoMW 92
**Noto**, Lore 1923- ConAu 134
**Noto**, Robert Arthur 1952- WhoAmL 92
**Noto**, Thomas Anthony 1931- AmMWSc 92
**Notosusanto**, Nugroho 1931- IntWW 91
**Nott**, Charles Robert Harley 1904- Who 92
**Nott**, Henry Junius 1797-1837 BenetAL 91
**Nott**, John 1932- Who 92
**Nott**, John William Frederic 1932- IntWW 91
**Nott**, Josiah Clark 1804-1873 BiInAmS
**Nott**, Kathleen Cecilia Who 92
**Nott**, Peter John Who 92
**Nott**, Peter John 1933- IntWW 91
**Nottage**, Raymond Frederick Tritton 1916- Who 92
**Nottebohm**, Fernando AmMWSc 92
**Notter**, David Anthony 1959- WhoMW 92
**Notter**, Mary Frances 1947- AmMWSc 92
**Nottingham**, Archdeacon of Who 92
**Nottingham**, Bishop of 1925- Who 92
**Nottingham**, Edward Willis, Jr. 1948- WhoAmL 92
**Nottingham**, R Kendall 1938- WhoIns 92
**Nottingham**, William Jesse 1927- WhoRel 92
**Notz**, William Irwin 1951- AmMWSc 92
**Nouel**, Philippe 1926- IntWW 91
**Noufi**, Rommel 1947- AmMWSc 92
**Nouira**, Hedi 1911- IntWW 91
**Noujaim**, Antoine Akl 1937- AmMWSc 92
**Noulles**, Richard Billings 1949- WhoAmL 92
**Noulton**, John David 1939- Who 92
**Noumazalay**, Ambroise 1933- IntWW 91
**Noun**, Robert Jeff 1948- WhoAmL 92
**Nouri**, Michael 1945- IntMPA 92
**Nourissier**, Francois 1927- IntWW 91
**Nourrit**, Adolphe 1802-1839 NewAmDM
**Nourse**, Alan E 1928- TwCSFW 91, WrDr 92
**Nourse**, Hugh Oliver 1933- WhoFI 92
**Nourse**, Martin 1932- Who 92
**Nourse**, Thomas Miller 1922- WhoFI 92
**Nousiainen**, Jaakko Ilmari 1931- IntWW 91
**Nouwen**, Henri J. 1932- WrDr 92
**Nova**, Craig DrAPF 91
**Nova Scotia**, Assistant Bishop of Who 92
**Nova Scotia**, Bishop of 1935- Who 92
**Novacek**, Dale Robert 1957- WhoMW 92
**Novacek**, Jack Emil 1957- WhoMW 92
**Novacek**, Michael John 1948- AmMWSc 92
**Novack**, Gary Dean 1953- AmMWSc 92
**Novack**, George 1905- WrDr 92
**Novack**, Joseph 1928- AmMWSc 92
**Novaco**, Anthony Dominic 1943- AmMWSc 92
**Novaes**, Guillomar 1895-1979 NewAmDM
**Novaes**, Guiomar 1896-1979 FacFETw
**Novak**, Alfred 1915- AmMWSc 92
**Novak**, Ann-Nadine 1951- WhoFI 92
**Novak**, Barbara Ellen 1949- WhoEnt 92
**Novak**, Ben 1943- WhoAmL 92
**Novak**, Bruce Michael AmMWSc 92
**Novak**, Darwin Albert, Jr. 1935- WhoFI 92
**Novak**, David 1941- WhoRel 92
**Novak**, Dianne Irene 1959- WhoMW 92
**Novak**, Edward John 1922- WhoMW 92
**Novak**, Ernest Richard 1940- AmMWSc 92
**Novak**, Estelle Gershgoren DrAPF 91
**Novak**, Glenn David 1947- WhoEnt 92
**Novak**, Gordon Shaw, Jr 1947- AmMWSc 92
**Novak**, Irwin Daniel 1942- AmMWSc 92
**Novak**, James B, III 1913- WhoAmP 91
**Novak**, James Lawrence 1961- AmMWSc 92
**Novak**, Jan 1921- NewAmDM
**Novak**, Jan 1953- LiExTwC
**Novak**, Jo-Ann Stout 1956- WhoFI 92
**Novak**, John Christopher 1964- WhoMW 92
**Novak**, John Philip 1946- WhoAmP 91
**Novak**, Josef 1905- IntWW 91
**Novak**, Josef Frantisek 1942- AmMWSc 92
**Novak**, Joseph ConAu 134
**Novak**, Joseph 1959- WhoRel 92
**Novak**, Joseph Donald 1930- AmMWSc 92
**Novak**, Kim 1933- IntMPA 92, WhoEnt 92
**Novak**, Ladislav Peter 1922- AmMWSc 92
**Novak**, Lawrence Peter 1951- WhoAmP 91
**Novak**, Marie Marta 1940- AmMWSc 92
**Novak**, Mary Ann 1944- WhoMW 92
**Novak**, Maximillian Erwin 1930- IntAu&W 91, WrDr 92
**Novak**, Michael DrAPF 91
**Novak**, Michael 1933- IntAu&W 91, IntWW 91, WrDr 92
**Novak**, Michael John 1933- WhoRel 92
**Novak**, Michael John 1948- WhoMW 92
**Novak**, Michael Paul DrAPF 91
**Novak**, Milos 1925- AmMWSc 92
**Novak**, Paul Ernest 1946- WhoMW 92
**Novak**, Paul M. WhoAmL 92
**Novak**, Raymond Francis AmMWSc 92
**Novak**, Robert Eugene 1949- AmMWSc 92
**Novak**, Robert Louis 1937- AmMWSc 92
**Novak**, Robert Otto 1930- AmMWSc 92
**Novak**, Robert William 1939- AmMWSc 92
**Novak**, Ronald William 1942- AmMWSc 92
**Novak**, Stephen Robert 1939- AmMWSc 92
**Novak**, Steven F. 1955- WhoEnt 92
**Novak**, Steven G 1949- WhoAmP 91
**Novak**, Sylvestre Louis 1946- WhoEnt 92
**Novak**, Terry Lee 1940- WhoWest 92
**Novak**, Thaddeus John 1940- AmMWSc 92
**Novak**, Victor Anthony 1930- WhoFI 92
**Novak**, Vitezslav 1870-1949 NewAmDM
**Novakovich**, Josip DrAPF 91
**Noval**, Michele M. 1954- WhoHisp 92
**Novales**, Ronald Richards 1928- AmMWSc 92, WhoMW 92
**Novalis** 1772-1801 BlkwCEP
**Novanglus** BenetAL 91
**Novarina**, Maurice Paul Joseph 1907- IntWW 91
**Novaro**, Mario 1868-1944 DcLB 114 [port]
**Novatian** EncEarC
**Nove**, Alec 1915- IntAu&W 91, WrDr 92
**Nove**, Alexander 1915- IntWW 91, Who 92
**Novek**, Minda DrAPF 91
**Novello**, Alfred 1810-1896 NewAmDM
**Novello**, Antonia 1944- News 91 [port]
**Novello**, Antonia Coello 1944- AmMWSc 92, WhoHisp 92
**Novello**, Clara 1818-1908 NewAmDM
**Novello**, Don 1943- IntMPA 92, WhoEnt 92
**Novello**, Frederick Charles 1916- AmMWSc 92
**Novello**, Ivor 1893-1951 FacFETw, NewAmDM
**Novello**, Joseph Nunzio 1949- WhoFI 92
**Novello**, Vincent 1781-1861 NewAmDM
**Novello-Davies**, Clara 1861-1943 NewAmDM
**November**, Sharyn DrAPF 91
**Noven**, Daniel Albert 1955- WhoFI 92
**Novenstern**, Samuel 1926- WhoFI 92
**Noventa**, Giacomo 1898-1960 DcLB 114 [port]
**Noverre**, Jean-Georges 1727-1810 BlkwCEP
**Novetzke**, Sally Johnson 1932- WhoAmP 91
**Novick**, Aaron 1919- AmMWSc 92
**Novick**, Alvin 1925- AmMWSc 92
**Novick**, Barbara 1960- WhoFI 92
**Novick**, David d1991 NewYTBS 91
**Novick**, Julius Lerner 1939- WhoEnt 92
**Novick**, Leah Engel 1932- WhoAmP 91
**Novick**, Marian DrAPF 91
**Novick**, Marvin 1931- WhoAmP 91
**Novick**, Richard P 1932- AmMWSc 92
**Novick**, Robert 1923- AmMWSc 92
**Novick**, Rudolph G 1910- AmMWSc 92
**Novick**, Stewart Eugene 1945- AmMWSc 92
**Novick**, Stuart Allan 1944- WhoWest 92
**Novick**, Tom 1957- WhoAmP 91
**Novick**, William Joseph, Jr 1931- AmMWSc 92
**Noviello**, Betty L 1954- WhoIns 92
**Novik**, Jay A 1944- WhoIns 92
**Novikoff**, Harold Stephen 1951- WhoAmL 92
**Novikoff**, Phyllis Marie AmMWSc 92
**Novikov**, Aleksandr Aleksandrovich 1900-1976 SovUnBD
**Novikov**, Ignatiy Trofimovich 1906- SovUnBD
**Novikov**, Igor' Aleksandrovich 1929- SovUnBD
**Novikov**, Nikolai Ivanovich 1744-1818 BlkwCEP
**Novikov**, Sergey Petrovich 1938- IntWW 91
**Novikov**, Vladimir Nikolaevich 1907- SovUnBD
**Novis**, Derrick A. 1950- WhoFI 92
**Novitch**, Mark 1932- WhoFI 92
**Novitski**, Edward 1918- AmMWSc 92
**Novitsky**, James Alan 1951- AmMWSc 92
**Novitz**, Charles Richard 1934- WhoEnt 92
**Novlan**, David John 1947- AmMWSc 92
**Novoa**, Jose I. WhoHisp 92
**Novoa**, Luis Ernesto 1958- WhoRel 92
**Novoa**, William Brewster 1930- AmMWSc 92
**Novoa-Sancho**, Nydia Marle 1944- WhoHisp 92
**Novodvorsky**, Mark Benjamin 1946- AmMWSc 92
**Novogradac**, Michael Joseph 1961- WhoFI 92
**Novosad**, Robert S 1920- AmMWSc 92
**Novotny**, Anthony James 1932- AmMWSc 92
**Novotny**, Antonin 1904-1975 FacFETw
**Novotny**, Charles 1936- AmMWSc 92
**Novotny**, David Joseph 1953- WhoAmL 92
**Novotny**, Deborah Ann 1964- WhoFI 92, WhoMW 92
**Novotny**, Donald Bob 1937- AmMWSc 92
**Novotny**, Donald Wayne 1934- AmMWSc 92
**Novotny**, James Frank 1937- AmMWSc 92
**Novotny**, Jaroslav 1924- AmMWSc 92
**Novotny**, Kevin 1966- WhoEnt 92
**Novotny**, Robert Thomas 1924- AmMWSc 92
**Novotny**, Vlad Joseph 1944- AmMWSc 92
**Novovich**, Serge 1932- WhoAmL 92
**Novozhilov**, Viktor Valentinovich 1892-1970 SovUnBD
**Novy**, Brett Arthur 1957- WhoFI 92
**Novy**, Miles Joseph 1937- AmMWSc 92
**Nowack**, Virginia Berglund 1944- WhoRel 92
**Nowack**, William J 1945- AmMWSc 92
**Nowacki**, James Nelson 1947- WhoAmL 92
**Nowaczek**, Frank Huxley 1930- WhoMW 92
**Nowaczyk**, Timothy Irvin 1953- WhoMW 92
**Nowaczynski**, Wojciech 1925- AmMWSc 92
**Nowak**, Anthony Victor 1938- AmMWSc 92
**Nowak**, Arthur John 1937- AmMWSc 92
**Nowak**, Chester John, Jr. 1941- WhoMW 92
**Nowak**, Chester Joseph 1923- WhoMW 92
**Nowak**, David Alan 1949- WhoMW 92
**Nowak**, Edward J. WhoAmL 92
**Nowak**, Edwin James 1936- AmMWSc 92
**Nowak**, Gregory Joseph 1959- WhoAmL 92
**Nowak**, Henry J. 1935- AlmAP 92 [port]
**Nowak**, Henry James 1935- WhoAmP 91
**Nowak**, Henry Julius 1931- WhoEnt 92
**Nowak**, James Michael 1956- WhoEnt 92
**Nowak**, John E. 1947- WhoAmL 92, WhoMW 92
**Nowak**, Joseph Anthony 1948- WhoMW 92
**Nowak**, Lionel 1911- NewAmDM
**Nowak**, Mark Andrew 1955- WhoAmL 92
**Nowak**, Patricia Rose 1946- WhoMW 92
**Nowak**, Robert John 1956- WhoMW 92
**Nowak**, Robert Michael 1930- AmMWSc 92, WhoMW 92
**Nowak**, Tadeusz 1930- IntAu&W 91, IntWW 91
**Nowak**, Thaddeus Stanley, Jr 1949- AmMWSc 92
**Nowak**, Thomas 1942- AmMWSc 92
**Nowak**, Thomas L. 1942- WhoMW 92
**Nowak**, Welville B 1921- AmMWSc 92
**Nowar**, Ma'an Abu 1928- Who 92
**Nowatzki**, Edward Alexander 1936- AmMWSc 92
**Nowatzki**, Robert E WhoAmP 91
**Nowell**, John William 1919- AmMWSc 92
**Nowell**, Ken 1956- WhoAmP 91
**Nowell**, Lucille Terry 1951- WhoEnt 92
**Nowell**, Peter Carey 1928- AmMWSc 92
**Nowell**, Wesley Raymond 1924- AmMWSc 92
**Nowell-Smith**, Patrick Horace 1914- Who 92
**Nowell-Smith**, Simon Harcourt 1909- Who 92
**Nower**, Leon 1927- AmMWSc 92
**Nowick**, A S 1923- AmMWSc 92
**Nowicke**, Joan Weiland AmMWSc 92
**Nowicki**, Maciej 1941- IntWW 91
**Nowicki**, Matthew 1910-1950 DcNCBi 4
**Nowina-Konopka**, Piotr 1949- IntWW 91
**Nowinski**, Jerzy L 1905- AmMWSc 92
**Nowlan**, Alden 1933-1983 BenetAL 91
**Nowlan**, George Joseph 1925- WhoEnt 92

**Nowlan,** Philip Francis 1888-1940 *TwCSFW 91*
**Nowland,** James Ferrell 1942- *WhoAmL 92*
**Nowland,** Matthew Stephen 1959- *WhoFI 92*
**Nowlin,** Charles Henry 1932- *AmMWSc 92*
**Nowlin,** Duane Dale 1937- *AmMWSc 92*
**Nowlin,** James Robertson 1937- *WhoAmL 92*
**Nowlin,** William Gerard, Jr. 1945- *WhoEnt 92*
**Nowlin,** Worth D, Jr 1935- *AmMWSc 92*
**Nowlis,** David Peter 1937- *AmMWSc 92*
**Nowogrodzki,** M 1920- *AmMWSc 92*
**Noworyta,** Eugeniusz 1935- *IntWW 91*
**Nowotny,** Alois Henry Andre 1922- *AmMWSc 92*
**Nowotny,** Hans 1911- *AmMWSc 92*
**Nowotny,** Kurt A 1931- *AmMWSc 92*
**Nowra,** Louis 1950- *IntWW 91, WrDr 92*
**Noxon,** Nicolas *LesBEnT 92*
**Noxon,** Nicolas Lane 1936- *WhoEnt 92*
**Noya,** Francisco *WhoEnt 92*
**Noyce,** Donald Sterling 1923- *AmMWSc 92*
**Noyce,** Gaylord Brewster 1926- *WhoRel 92*
**Noyce,** James William 1955- *WhoIns 92*
**Noyce,** Philip 1950- *IntMPA 92*
**Noyce,** Robert 1927-1990 *AnObit 1990*
**Noyce,** Robert Norton d1990 *IntWW 91N*
**Noyce,** Robert Norton 1927- *AmMWSc 92*
**Noyce,** Robert Norton 1927-1990 *FacFETw*
**Noyd,** Roy Allen 1941- *WhoRel 92*
**Noye,** Fred Charles 1946- *WhoAmP 91*
**Noyer-Weidner,** Alfred 1921- *IntWW 91*
**Noyes,** Alfred 1880-1958 *RfGEnL 91*
**Noyes,** Alfred 1880-1959 *FacFETw*
**Noyes,** Charles Kelby 1952- *WhoEnt 92*
**Noyes,** Claudia Margaret 1940- *AmMWSc 92*
**Noyes,** Dan 1958- *WhoEnt 92*
**Noyes,** David Holbrook 1935- *AmMWSc 92*
**Noyes,** Dorothy Rae 1927- *WhoRel 92*
**Noyes,** Eliot 1910-1977 *DcTwDes*
**Noyes,** H Pierre 1923- *AmMWSc 92*
**Noyes,** Henry 1910- *ConAu 133*
**Noyes,** Howard Ellis 1922- *AmMWSc 92*
**Noyes,** John Humphrey 1811-1886 *AmPeW, BenetAL 91*
**Noyes,** Keven Scott 1956- *WhoMW 92*
**Noyes,** Paul R 1928- *AmMWSc 92*
**Noyes,** Pierrepont B 1870-1959 *ScFEYrs*
**Noyes,** Ralph Norton 1923- *Who 92*
**Noyes,** Richard Francis 1952- *WhoMW 92*
**Noyes,** Richard Macy 1919- *AmMWSc 92, IntWW 91*
**Noyes,** Robert Wilson 1934- *AmMWSc 92*
**Noyes,** Russell, Jr 1934- *AmMWSc 92, WhoMW 92*
**Noyes,** Stanley *DrAPF 91*
**Noyes,** Stanley 1924- *ConAu 35NR, WrDr 92*
**Noyes,** Ward David 1927- *AmMWSc 92*
**Noyes,** William 1857-1915 *BiInAmS*
**Noyes-Taylor,** Stephanie 1964- *WhoEnt 92*
**Noz,** Marilyn E 1939- *AmMWSc 92*
**Nozaki,** Kenzie 1916- *AmMWSc 92*
**Nozaki,** Yasuhiko 1913- *AmMWSc 92*
**Nozick,** Robert 1938- *IntWW 91, WrDr 92*
**Nozieres,** Philippe Pierre Gaston F. 1932- *IntWW 91*
**Nozik,** Arthur Jack 1936- *AmMWSc 92*
**Noziska,** Charles Brant 1953- *WhoAmL 92, WhoWest 92*
**Nozzolillo,** Constance 1926- *AmMWSc 92*
**Nozzolio,** Michael F 1951- *WhoAmP 91*
**Nriagu,** Jerome O. 1942- *ConAu 135*
**Nriagu,** Jerome Okonkwo 1942- *AmMWSc 92*
**Nsekela,** Amon James 1930- *IntWW 91, Who 92*
**Nsengiyumva,** Vincent *WhoRel 92*
**N'singa Udjuu Ongwabeki Untube** 1934- *IntWW 91*
**Nsubuga,** Emmanuel 1914- *IntWW 91*
**Nsubuga,** Emmanuel Kiwanuka d1991 *NewYTBS 91*
**Ntiwane,** Nkomeni Douglas 1933- *Who 92*
**Nu,** U. 1907- *IntWW 91*
**Nua,** Mailo S T *WhoAmP 91*
**Nua,** Sao T 1948- *WhoAmP 91*
**Nuber,** Richard H 1943- *WhoAmP 91*
**Nucci,** John A 1952- *WhoAmP 91*
**Nucci,** Joseph E., Jr. 1962- *WhoWest 92*
**Nucci,** Leo 1942- *WhoEnt 92*
**Nuccio,** Richard Harold 1946- *WhoMW 92*
**Nuccitelli,** Richard Lee 1948- *AmMWSc 92*
**Nuccitelli,** Saul Arnold 1928- *WhoFI 92, WhoMW 92*
**Nuchow,** William Haywood 1928- *WhoAmP 91*
**Nucifora,** Alfred John 1946- *WhoFI 92*
**Nuckles,** Douglas Boyd 1931- *AmMWSc 92*
**Nucklos,** Shirley 1949- *WhoMW 92*
**Nuckolls,** Billie Jean 1943- *WhoAmP 91*
**Nuckolls,** Hugh Paul 1941- *WhoAmP 91*
**Nuckolls,** Joe Allen 1929- *AmMWSc 92*
**Nuckolls,** John Hopkins 1930- *AmMWSc 92, WhoFI 92*
**Nuckolls,** Kenneth Russell 1921- *WhoAmP 91*
**Nuckols,** Robert Marshall 1937- *WhoFI 92*
**Nudel,** Ida 1931- *ConAu 134*
**Nudelman,** Sidney 1938- *WhoAmL 92*
**Nudelman,** Sol 1922- *AmMWSc 92*
**Nudelstejer,** Sergio 1924- *IntAu&W 91*
**Nuelle,** David William 1957- *WhoMW 92*
**Nuemaier,** Roger Laurence 1949- *WhoFI 92*
**Nuenke,** Richard Harold 1932- *AmMWSc 92*
**Nuernberger,** Phil 1942- *ConAu 35NR*
**Nuese,** Charles J 1939- *AmMWSc 92*
**Nuessle,** Albert Christian 1915- *AmMWSc 92*
**Nuessle,** Noel Oliver 1928- *AmMWSc 92*
**Nuetzel,** John Arlington 1925- *AmMWSc 92*
**Nuffield,** Edward Wilfrid 1914- *AmMWSc 92*
**Nugee,** Edward George 1928- *Who 92*
**Nugee,** Rachel Elizabeth 1926- *Who 92*
**Nugent** *Who 92*
**Nugent,** Catherine Marie 1966- *WhoEnt 92*
**Nugent,** Charles Arter, Jr 1924- *AmMWSc 92*
**Nugent,** Daniel Eugene 1927- *WhoFI 92, WhoMW 92*
**Nugent,** George Robert 1921- *AmMWSc 92*
**Nugent,** James E *WhoAmP 91*
**Nugent,** John 1933- *Who 92*
**Nugent,** John Andrew 1958- *WhoWest 92*
**Nugent,** John Hilliard 1944- *WhoFI 92*
**Nugent,** Johnny Wesley 1939- *WhoAmP 91*
**Nugent,** Leonard James 1930- *AmMWSc 92*
**Nugent,** Lori S. 1962- *WhoFI 92*
**Nugent,** Maurice Joseph, Jr 1937- *AmMWSc 92*
**Nugent,** Miriam 1940- *WhoRel 92*
**Nugent,** Neill 1947- *ConAu 133*
**Nugent,** Nelle 1939- *WhoEnt 92*
**Nugent,** Peter Walter James 1920- *Who 92*
**Nugent,** Robert Charles 1936- *AmMWSc 92*
**Nugent,** Robert Emmet 1955- *WhoAmP 91*
**Nugent,** Robert Emmet, III 1955- *WhoAmL 92*
**Nugent,** Robin 1925- *Who 92*
**Nugent,** Shane Vincent 1962- *WhoMW 92*
**Nugent,** Sherwin Thomas 1938- *AmMWSc 92*
**Nugent,** Theodore Anthony 1948- *WhoEnt 92*
**Nugent,** Walter T. K. 1935- *WrDr 92*
**Nugent of Guildford,** Baron 1907- *Who 92*
**Nuiry,** Octavio Emilio 1958- *WhoHisp 92*
**Nuite-Belleville,** Jo Ann 1945- *AmMWSc 92*
**Nujoma,** Sam Shafilshuna 1929- *IntWW 91*
**Nuki,** Klaus 1931- *AmMWSc 92*
**Null,** Earl Eugene 1936- *WhoFI 92*
**Null,** Harold R 1929- *AmMWSc 92*
**Null,** Jack Elton 1938- *WhoWest 92*
**Null,** Michael Elliot 1947- *WhoAmL 92*
**Null,** Paul Bryan 1944- *WhoRel 92*
**Null,** Thomas Blanton 1941- *WhoEnt 92*
**Nulman,** Seymour Shlomo 1921- *WhoRel 92*
**Nulton,** William Clements 1931- *WhoAmL 92*
**Numairi,** Gaafar al- *IntWW 91*
**Numan,** Yasin Said *IntWW 91*
**Numata,** Nobuo 1954- *WhoFI 92*
**Numenius** *EncEarC*
**Nummi,** Yki 1925- *DcTwDes*
**Numminen,** Juhani Mikko 1942 *WhoEnt 92*
**Nummy,** William Ralph 1921- *AmMWSc 92*
**Nunamaker,** Richard Allan 1951- *AmMWSc 92*
**Nunan,** Craig S 1918- *AmMWSc 92*
**Nunan,** Manus 1926- *Who 92*
**Nunburnholme,** Baron 1928- *Who 92*
**Nunchuck,** Mary Inez 1948- *WhoMW 92*
**Nuncio,** Pete N. 1942- *WhoHisp 92*
**Nunery,** Gladys Cannon 1904- *WhoBlA 92*
**Nunery,** Leroy David 1955- *WhoBlA 92*
**Nunes,** Anthony Charles 1942- *AmMWSc 92*
**Nunes,** Claude 1924- *ConAu 134*
**Nunes,** Emmanuel 1941- *ConCom 92*
**Nunes,** Manuel Jacinto 1926- *IntWW 91*
**Nunes,** Paul Donald 1944- *AmMWSc 92*
**Nunez Cabeza de Vaca** *BenetAL 91*
**Nunez,** Aguilar Daniel 1958- *BlkOlyM*
**Nunez,** Albert, Jr. 1946- *WhoHisp 92*
**Nunez,** Alex 1938- *WhoHisp 92*
**Nunez,** Ana Rosa 1926- *WhoHisp 92*
**Nunez,** Antonio Alberto 1948- *WhoHisp 92*
**Nunez,** Edwin 1963- *WhoHisp 92*
**Nunez,** Elpidio *WhoHisp 92*
**Nunez,** German 1948- *WhoHisp 92*
**Nunez,** Jose 1964- *WhoHisp 92*
**Nunez,** Juan Solomon, Jr. 1945- *WhoHisp 92*
**Nunez,** Julio V. 1960- *WhoHisp 92*
**Nunez,** Louis *WhoHisp 92*
**Nunez,** Loys Joseph 1926- *AmMWSc 92*
**Nunez,** Mario 1948- *WhoHisp 92*
**Nunez,** Paula *WhoEnt 92*
**Nunez,** Paulino A. *WhoHisp 92*
**Nunez,** Peter Kent 1942- *WhoHisp 92*
**Nunez,** Ralph *WhoHisp 92*
**Nunez,** Rene Jose 1941- *WhoHisp 92*
**Nunez,** Samuel B, Jr 1930- *WhoAmP 91, WhoHisp 92*
**Nunez,** William J, III 1944- *AmMWSc 92*
**Nunez,** William L. 1967- *WhoEnt 92*
**Nunez,** Yolanda 1952- *WhoHisp 92*
**Nunez Cabeza de Vaca,** Alvar *HisDSpE*
**Nunez de Balbao,** Vasco *HisDSpE*
**Nunez-del Toro,** Orlando 1940- *WhoHisp 92*
**Nunez de Pineda y Bascunan,** Francisco 1607-1682 *HisDSpE*
**Nunez de Vela,** Blasco 1490-1546 *HisDSpE*
**Nunez de Villavicencio,** Orlando 1940- *WhoHisp 92*
**Nunez-Lawton,** Miguel G. 1949- *WhoFI 92*
**Nunez Ledo,** Mercedes 1955- *WhoHisp 92*
**Nunez-Molina,** Mario A. 1957- *WhoHisp 92*
**Nunez-Wormack,** Elsa *WhoHisp 92*
**Nungesser,** Roland 1925- *IntWW 91*
**Nungesser,** William Aicklen 1929- *WhoAmP 91*
**Nunis,** Doyce B, Jr 1924- *IntAu&W 91, WrDr 92*
**Nunis,** Richard Arlen 1932- *WhoWest 92*
**Nunke,** Ronald John 1926- *AmMWSc 92*
**Nunley,** Robert Gray 1930- *AmMWSc 92*
**Nunn,** Arthur Sherman, Jr 1922- *AmMWSc 92*
**Nunn,** Bobbie B. *WhoBlA 92*
**Nunn,** David Oliver 1921- *WhoRel 92*
**Nunn,** Dorothy Mae *AmMWSc 92*
**Nunn,** Freddie Joe 1962- *WhoBlA 92*
**Nunn,** Frederick McKinley 1937- *IntAu&W 91, WrDr 92*
**Nunn,** G. Raymond 1918- *WrDr 92*
**Nunn,** George Harry 1935- *WhoRel 92*
**Nunn,** John 1955- *IntAu&W 91, WrDr 92*
**Nunn,** John, Jr. 1953- *WhoBlA 92*
**Nunn,** John Francis 1925- *IntWW 91, Who 92*
**Nunn,** John Richard Danford 1925- *Who 92*
**Nunn,** Leslie Edgar 1941- *WhoAmL 92, WhoWest 92*
**Nunn,** Louie B 1924- *WhoAmP 91*
**Nunn,** Randall Harrison 1945- *WhoAmL 92*
**Nunn,** Robert Harry 1933- *AmMWSc 92*
**Nunn,** Robinson S. 1944- *WhoBlA 92*
**Nunn,** Roland Cicero 1930- *AmMWSc 92*
**Nunn,** Sam 1938- *AlmAP 92 [port], IntWW 91, WhoAmP 91*
**Nunn,** Stephen R 1952- *WhoAmP 91*
**Nunn,** Trevor Robert 1940- *IntWW 91, Who 92, WhoEnt 92*
**Nunn,** Walter Gordon 1928- *WhoRel 92*
**Nunn,** Walter M, Jr 1925- *AmMWSc 92*
**Nunn,** William Curtis 1908- *IntAu&W 91, WrDr 92*
**Nunn,** William Goldwin, Jr. *WhoBlA 92*
**Nunnally,** David Ambrose 1934- *AmMWSc 92*
**Nunnally,** David H., Sr. 1929- *WhoBlA 92*
**Nunnally,** Huey Neal 1944- *AmMWSc 92*
**Nunnally,** James David 1945- *WhoAmP 91*
**Nunnally,** John Marshall 1965- *WhoAmP 91*
**Nunnally,** Knox Dillon 1943- *WhoAmL 92*
**Nunnally,** Nelson Rudolph 1935- *AmMWSc 92*
**Nunnally,** Stephens Watson 1927- *AmMWSc 92*
**Nunneley,** John Hewlett 1922- *Who 92*
**Nunneley,** Sarah A 1941- *AmMWSc 92*
**Nunnery,** Louis Wallace 1919- *WhoEnt 92*
**Nunnery,** Willie James 1948- *WhoBlA 92*
**Nunney,** Leonard Peter 1949- *AmMWSc 92*
**Nunoi,** Keijiro 1930- *WhoFI 92*
**Nunz,** Gregory Joseph 1934- *WhoWest 92*
**Nunziata,** Susan 1965- *WhoEnt 92*
**Nuorteva,** Santeri 1881-1929 *DcAmImH*
**Nuorvala,** Aarne Johannes 1912- *IntWW 91*
**Nuovo,** Betty A 1931- *WhoAmP 91*
**Nur Jehan** d1645 *EncAmaz 91*
**Nur,** Amos M 1938- *AmMWSc 92*
**Nur,** Hussain Sayid 1939- *AmMWSc 92*
**Nur,** Uzi 1928- *AmMWSc 92*
**Nur Khan,** M. 1923- *IntWW 91*
**Nurdin,** Mark Gregory 1961- *WhoFI 92*
**Nuremberg,** Michael R. 1944- *WhoFI 92*
**Nureyev,** Rudolf 1938- *IntMPA 92, IntWW 91, SovUnBD*
**Nureyev,** Rudolf Hametovich 1938- *Who 92, WhoEnt 92*
**Nureyev,** Rudolph 1938- *FacFETw*
**Nuriyev,** Ziya Nuriyevich 1915- *IntWW 91*
**Nurjadin,** Roesmin 1930- *IntWW 91, Who 92*
**Nurko,** Michael 1942- *WhoEnt 92*
**Nurkse,** D. *DrAPF 91*
**Nurmesniemi,** Antil 1927- *DcTwDes*
**Nurmi,** Maiju *DcAmImH*
**Nurmi,** Paavo 1897-1973 *FacFETw*
**Nurmi,** Ruth Swanson 1923- *WhoEnt 92*
**Nurmia,** Matti Juhani 1930- *AmMWSc 92*
**Nurnberg,** Walter 1907- *WrDr 92*
**Nurnberger,** John Ignatius, Sr 1916- *AmMWSc 92*
**Nurnberger,** Thomas Salisbury, Jr. 1918- *WhoFI 92*
**Nursall,** John Ralph 1925- *AmMWSc 92*
**Nursaw,** James 1932- *Who 92*
**Nursaw,** William George 1903- *Who 92*
**Nurse,** Paul Maxime 1949- *IntWW 91, Who 92*
**Nurse,** Rebecca 1621-1692 *HanAmWH*
**Nurse,** Richard A. 1939- *WhoBlA 92*
**Nurse,** Robert Earl 1942- *WhoBlA 92*
**Nursten,** Harry Erwin *Who 92*
**Nursten,** Jean Patricia *WrDr 92*
**Nusbickel,** Edward M, Jr 1930- *AmMWSc 92*
**Nuseibeh,** Hazem *IntWW 91*
**Nusim,** Stanley Herbert 1935- *AmMWSc 92*
**Nuss,** Clara Marie 1947- *WhoFI 92*
**Nuss,** Thomas Francis 1932- *WhoAmL 92*
**Nuss,** William Martin 1954- *WhoEnt 92*
**Nussbaum,** Adolf Edward 1925- *AmMWSc 92*
**Nussbaum,** Alexander Leopold 1925- *AmMWSc 92*
**Nussbaum,** Allen 1919- *AmMWSc 92*
**Nussbaum,** E. Michael 1960- *WhoWest 92*
**Nussbaum,** Elmer 1920- *AmMWSc 92*
**Nussbaum,** Martha Craven 1947- *ConAu 134, WrDr 92*
**Nussbaum,** Mirko 1930- *AmMWSc 92*
**Nussbaum,** Noel Sidney 1935- *AmMWSc 92*
**Nussbaum,** Roger David 1944- *AmMWSc 92*
**Nussbaum,** Ronald Archie 1942- *AmMWSc 92*
**Nussbaum,** Rudi Hans 1922- *AmMWSc 92*
**Nussbaum,** Stephen 1948- *WhoMW 92*
**Nussbaum,** Theodore Jay 1953- *WhoFI 92*
**Nussbaum,** V M, Jr 1919- *WhoAmP 91*
**Nussbaumer,** John 1950- *WhoAmL 92*
**Nussdorf,** Harry 1947- *WhoAmP 91*
**Nussenbaum,** Siegfried Fred 1919- *AmMWSc 92*
**Nussenblatt,** Robert Burton 1948- *AmMWSc 92*
**Nussenzveig,** Herch Moyses 1933- *AmMWSc 92*
**Nussenzweig,** Victor 1928- *AmMWSc 92*
**Nusser,** Wilford Lee 1924- *AmMWSc 92*
**Nussle,** James 1960- *WhoAmP 91*
**Nussle,** James Allen 1960- *WhoMW 92*
**Nussle,** Jim 1960- *AlmAP 92 [port]*
**Nusslein-Volhard,** Christiane 1942- *IntWW 91*
**Nussmann,** Adolph 1739-1794 *DcNCBi 4*
**Nussmann,** David George 1937- *AmMWSc 92*
**Nusynowitz,** Martin Lawrence 1933- *AmMWSc 92*
**Nutakki,** Dharma Rao 1937- *AmMWSc 92*
**Nutall,** James Edward 1933- *WhoBlA 92*
**Nute,** C Thomas 1945- *AmMWSc 92*
**Nute,** Helen Elizabeth 1897- *WhoAmP 91*
**Nute,** Peter Eric 1938- *AmMWSc 92*
**Nuth,** Timothy Edwin 1961- *WhoAmL 92*
**Nutley,** Hugh 1932- *AmMWSc 92*
**Nutman,** Phillip Sadler 1914- *IntWW 91, Who 92*
**Nutt,** Ambrose Benjamin 1920- *WhoBlA 92*
**Nutt,** David 1810-1863 *DcLB 106*
**Nutt,** Maurice Joseph 1962- *WhoBlA 92*
**Nutt,** Nan 1925- *WhoRel 92, WhoWest 92*
**Nutt,** Ruth Foelsche 1940- *AmMWSc 92*
**Nuttall,** Alfred L 1943- *AmMWSc 92*
**Nuttall,** Christopher Peter 1939- *Who 92*
**Nuttall,** Derek 1937- *Who 92*
**Nuttall,** Frank Q 1929- *AmMWSc 92*
**Nuttall,** Geoffrey Fillingham 1911- *Who 92*
**Nuttall,** Herbert Ericksen, Jr 1944- *AmMWSc 92*

# O

**O. Henry** BenetAL 91
**O. Henry** 1862-1910 FacFETw
**Oace,** Susan M 1941- AmMWSc 92
**Oade,** Kamile Preston 1946- WhoAmL 92
**Oak Ridge Boys,** The ConMus 7 [port]
**Oak,** Charles Walter 1941- WhoMW 92
**Oakar,** Mary Rose 1940- AlmAP 92 [port], WhoAmP 91, WhoMW 92
**Oakeley,** John 1932- Who 92
**Oakeley,** Mary 1913- Who 92
**Oakerson,** James F. 1921- WhoWest 92
**Oakes,** Billy Dean 1928- AmMWSc 92
**Oakes,** Calvin Hawley d1991 NewYTBS 91
**Oakes,** Christopher 1949- Who 92
**Oakes,** David 1947- AmMWSc 92
**Oakes,** Donald R 1940- WhoIns 92
**Oakes,** Gordon James 1931- Who 92
**Oakes,** Heather R 1959- BlkOlyM
**Oakes,** James 1953- IntAu&W 91, WrDr 92
**Oakes,** James L WhoAmP 91
**Oakes,** James L. 1924- WhoAmL 92
**Oakes,** John Bertram 1913- IntAu&W 91, IntWW 91
**Oakes,** John Morgan 1955- AmMWSc 92
**Oakes,** Joseph Stewart 1919- Who 92
**Oakes,** Lester C 1923- AmMWSc 92
**Oakes,** Melvin Ervin Louis 1936- AmMWSc 92
**Oakes,** Philip 1928- ConPo 91, IntAu&W 91, WrDr 92
**Oakes,** Robert Gibson 1918- WhoFI 92
**Oakes,** Robert James 1936- AmMWSc 92
**Oakes,** Robert Roy 1951- WhoMW 92
**Oakes,** Roy Sidney 1928- WhoAmP 91
**Oakes,** Terry Louis 1953- WhoWest 92
**Oakes,** Thomas Wyatt 1950- AmMWSc 92
**Oakes,** Urian 1631?-1681 BenetAL 91
**Oakes,** William 1799-1848 BiInAmS
**Oakes-Smith,** Elizabeth BenetAL 91
**Oakeshott,** Gordon B 1904- AmMWSc 92
**Oakeshott,** Gordon Blaisdell 1904- WhoWest 92
**Oakeshott,** Michael 1901-1990 AnObit 1990, ConAu 133
**Oakeshott,** Michael Joseph d1990 IntWW 91N, Who 92N
**Oakey,** John Martin, Jr. 1935- WhoAmL 92
**Oakford,** Robert Vernon 1917- AmMWSc 92
**Oakham,** Archdeacon of Who 92
**Oakley,** Alfred J. 1878-1959 TwCPaSc
**Oakley,** Ann 1944- IntAu&W 91, WrDr 92
**Oakley,** Annie 1860-1926 EncAmaz 91
**Oakley,** Berl Ray 1949- AmMWSc 92
**Oakley,** Brian Wynne 1927- IntWW 91, Who 92
**Oakley,** Bruce 1936- AmMWSc 92
**Oakley,** Carolyn Le 1942- WhoAmP 91
**Oakley,** Charles 1925- TwCPaSc
**Oakley,** Charles 1963- WhoBlA 92
**Oakley,** Charles Allen 1900- WrDr 92
**Oakley,** Cheri Lynn 1957- WhoRel 92
**Oakley,** Christopher John 1941- Who 92
**Oakley,** David Charles 1929- AmMWSc 92
**Oakley,** David Lyons, Jr. 1910- WhoAmL 92
**Oakley,** Godfrey Porter, Jr 1940- AmMWSc 92
**Oakley,** Graham 1929- IntAu&W 91, WrDr 92
**Oakley,** James Edwin 1948- WhoRel 92
**Oakley,** James William, Jr 1935- WhoAmP 91
**Oakley,** John Davidson 1921- Who 92
**Oakley,** Keith 1957- WhoAmP 91
**Oakley,** Lawrence Charles 1925- WhoFI 92
**Oakley,** Lezlee 1963- WhoMW 92
**Oakley,** Robert B WhoAmP 91
**Oakley,** Robert Bruce 1959- WhoRel 92
**Oakley,** Robert Lee, Jr. 1957- WhoEnt 92
**Oakley,** Robin Francis Leigh 1941- Who 92
**Oakley,** Stewart Philip 1931- WrDr 92
**Oakley,** Timothy Emrick 1957- WhoEnt 92
**Oakley,** Wilfrid George 1905- Who 92
**Oakman,** Douglas Edward 1953- WhoRel 92
**Oaks,** B Ann 1929- AmMWSc 92
**Oaks,** Dallin H. 1932- WrDr 92
**Oaks,** Dallin Harris 1932- WhoWest 92
**Oaks,** David Keith 1954- WhoAmP 91
**Oaks,** Emily Caywood Jordan 1939- AmMWSc 92
**Oaks,** Harold Rasmus 1926- WhoEnt 92
**Oaks,** J Howard 1930- AmMWSc 92
**Oaks,** John Adams 1942- AmMWSc 92
**Oaks,** Margaret Marlene 1940- WhoRel 92, WhoWest 92
**Oaks,** Nathaniel T WhoAmP 91
**Oaks,** Richard Lee 1944- WhoMW 92
**Oaks,** Robert Quincy, Jr 1938- AmMWSc 92
**Oaks,** Steven Clark 1938- WhoAmP 91
**Oaks,** Wilbur W 1928- AmMWSc 92
**Oaksey,** Baron 1929- Who 92
**Oaksey,** Lord 1929- WrDr 92
**Oakshott,** Anthony 1929- Who 92
**Oalmann,** Margaret Claire 1929- AmMWSc 92
**Oandasan,** William Cortes 1947- IntAu&W 91
**Oates,** Caleb E. 1917- WhoBlA 92
**Oates,** Carl Everette 1931- WhoAmL 92
**Oates,** David 1927- Who 92
**Oates,** Gordon Cedric 1932- AmMWSc 92
**Oates,** Jimmie C 1933- AmMWSc 92
**Oates,** John 1930- Who 92
**Oates,** John Alexander 1870-1958 DcNCBi 4
**Oates,** John Alexander 1932- AmMWSc 92
**Oates,** Joyce Carol DrAPF 91
**Oates,** Joyce Carol 1938- BenetAL 91, ConNov 91, ConPo 91, FacFETw, IntAu&W 91, IntWW 91, ModAWWr, WrDr 92
**Oates,** Keith 1942- Who 92
**Oates,** Laurence Campbell 1946- Who 92
**Oates,** Peter Joseph 1947- AmMWSc 92
**Oates,** Richard Patrick 1937- AmMWSc 92
**Oates,** Stephen B 1936- IntAu&W 91, WrDr 92
**Oates,** Thomas 1917- Who 92
**Oates,** Wallace Eugene 1937- IntAu&W 91, WhoFI 92, WrDr 92
**Oates,** Wanda Anita 1942- WhoBlA 92
**Oates-Nies,** Kathleen Ann 1957- WhoAmL 92
**Oatfield,** Harold 1910- AmMWSc 92
**Oatis,** Kathleen Ann 1951- WhoAmP 91
**Oatley,** Brian 1935- Who 92
**Oatley,** Charles 1904- IntWW 91, Who 92
**Oatley,** Michael Charles 1935- Who 92
**Oatman,** Earl R 1920- AmMWSc 92
**Oaxaca,** Fernando WhoAmP 91
**Oaxaca,** Fernando 1927- WhoHisp 92
**Oaxaca,** Jaime 1931- WhoHisp 92
**Obaid,** Fikri Makram 1916- IntWW 91
**Obaidi,** Mahdi M. Al- 1928- IntWW 91
**Obaldia,** Rene de 1918- ConAu 133
**O'Ballance,** Edgar 1918- IntAu&W 91, WrDr 92
**Oban,** Provost of Who 92
**Oban,** William Ernest 1947- WhoAmP 91
**Obando,** Jose Maria 1795-1860 HisDSpE
**Obando Bravo,** Miguel 1926- WhoRel 92
**Obando Y Bravo,** Miguel 1926- IntWW 91
**O'Banner-Owens,** Jeanette WhoBlA 92
**O'Bannon,** Daniel Thomas 1946- WhoEnt 92
**O'Bannon,** Don Tella, Jr. 1957- WhoAmL 92
**O'Bannon,** Frank Lewis 1930- WhoAmP 91, WhoMW 92
**O'Bannon,** John Horatio 1926- AmMWSc 92
**O'Barr,** Bobby Gene 1932- WhoAmL 92
**O'Barr,** Richard Dale 1932- AmMWSc 92
**O'Barr,** William McAlston 1942- AmMWSc 92
**Obarski,** Marek 1947- IntAu&W 91
**Obasanjo,** Olusegun 1937- IntWW 91, Who 92
**Obaseki,** Lovette I. 1953- WhoFI 92
**Obasi,** Godwin Olu Patrick 1933- Who 92
**Obayuwana,** Alphonsus Osarobo 1948- WhoBlA 92
**Obbink,** Russell C 1924- AmMWSc 92
**Obear,** Frederick W 1935- AmMWSc 92
**Obebe,** Joseph O. 1950- WhoMW 92
**Obee,** Thomas Francis 1943- WhoMW 92
**Obeegadoo,** Claude 1928- Who 92
**Obeid,** Atef IntWW 91
**Obeidat,** Ahmad Abdul-Majeed 1938- IntWW 91
**O'Beirne,** Andrew Jon 1944- AmMWSc 92
**O'Beirne,** Cornelius Banahan 1915- Who 92
**O'Beirne,** Julie Kay 1961- WhoMW 92
**O'Beirne Ranelagh,** John 1947- Who 92
**Obeji,** John T 1939- AmMWSc 92
**O'Benar,** John DeMarion 1943- AmMWSc 92
**Obenchain,** Carl F 1935- AmMWSc 92
**Obenchain,** Robert Lincoln 1941- AmMWSc 92
**Obendorf,** Ralph Louis 1938- AmMWSc 92
**Obenland,** Clayton O 1912- AmMWSc 92
**Obenshain,** Felix Edward 1928- AmMWSc 92
**Obenshain,** Helen Wilkins 1934- WhoAmP 91
**Obenshain,** Mark Dudley 1962- WhoAmP 91
**Obenshain,** Scott Alan 1964- WhoFI 92
**Ober,** Ann Morgan 1916- WhoAmP 91
**Ober,** Christopher Kemper 1954- AmMWSc 92
**Ober,** David Ray 1939- AmMWSc 92
**Ober,** Douglas Gary 1946- WhoFI 92
**Ober,** Eric LesBEnT 92 [port]
**Ober,** Eric W. WhoEnt 92A
**Ober,** Fred A 1849-1913 ScFEYrs
**Ober,** Frederick Albion 1849-1913 BiInAmS
**Ober,** Richard Francis, Jr. 1943- WhoAmL 92, WhoFI 92
**Ober,** Robert Elwood 1931- AmMWSc 92
**Ober,** Russell John, Jr. 1948- WhoAmL 92
**Ober,** Stephen Henry 1949- WhoWest 92
**Ober,** William B 1920- AmMWSc 92
**Oberdier,** Ronald Ray 1945- WhoAmL 92
**Oberding,** Dennis George 1935- AmMWSc 92
**Oberdorf,** Charles 1941- IntAu&W 91
**Oberdorfer,** Eugene, II 1932- WhoIns 92
**Oberdorfer,** Louis F. 1919- WhoAmL 92
**Oberdorfer,** Michael Douglas 1942- AmMWSc 92
**Oberdorster,** Gunter 1939- AmMWSc 92
**Oberender,** Frederick G 1933- AmMWSc 92
**Oberg,** Carl Albrecht 1897-1965 EncTR 91 [port]
**Oberg,** Danny 1951- WhoAmP 91
**Oberg,** Larry Reynold WhoMW 92
**Oberhausen,** Joyce Ann Wynn 1941- WhoFI 92
**Oberheim,** The Baron 1951- WhoWest 92
**Oberhellman,** Theodore Arnold, Jr. 1934- WhoFI 92
**Oberhelman,** Harry Alvin, Jr 1923- AmMWSc 92
**Oberhofer,** Edward Samuel 1939- AmMWSc 92
**Oberholtzer,** James Edward 1942- AmMWSc 92
**Oberholtzer,** James Scott 1953- WhoAmL 92
**Oberholtzer,** Jay Roy 1930- WhoFI 92
**Oberholtzer,** John H. 1809-1895 RelLAm 91
**Oberlander,** Herbert 1939- AmMWSc 92
**Oberlander,** Theodor 1905- EncTR 91 [port]
**Oberlander,** Theodore M 1933- AmMWSc 92
**Oberle,** Frank 1932- IntWW 91
**Oberle,** Thomas M 1930- AmMWSc 92
**Oberle,** William Albert, Jr 1949- WhoAmP 91
**Oberleas,** Donald 1933- AmMWSc 92
**Oberley,** Larry Wayne 1946- WhoMW 92
**Oberley,** Terry De Wayne 1946- AmMWSc 92
**Oberlin,** Daniel Malcolm 1948- AmMWSc 92
**Oberlin,** David W. 1920- IntWW 91, WhoAmP 91
**Oberlin,** Earl Clifford, III 1956- WhoFI 92
**Oberlin,** Russell 1928- NewAmDM
**Oberly,** Charles M, III WhoAmP 91
**Oberly,** Charles Monroe, III 1946- WhoAmL 92
**Oberly,** Dennis George 1935- WhoFI 92
**Oberly,** Gene Herman 1925- AmMWSc 92
**Oberly,** Ralph Edwin 1941- AmMWSc 92
**Obermaier,** Otto George 1936- WhoAmL 92
**Oberman,** Albert 1934- AmMWSc 92
**Oberman,** Carl Marc 1952- WhoFI 92
**Oberman,** Harold A 1932- AmMWSc 92

**Oberman,** Harold Austen 1932- *WhoMW 92*
**Oberman,** Larry 1940- *WhoFI 92*
**Oberman,** Michael Alan 1942- *WhoMW 92*
**Oberman,** Norman Charles 1929- *WhoWest 92*
**Obermann,** George 1935- *WhoMW 92*
**Obermann,** Richard Michael 1949- *WhoFI 92*
**Obermayer,** Arthur S 1931- *AmMWSc 92*
**Obermayer,** Herman Joseph 1924- *WhoFI 92*
**Obermeyer,** Susan White 1958- *WhoWest 92*
**Obermier,** Norman W 1915- *WhoAmP 91*
**Oberndorf,** Meyera E *WhoAmP 91*
**Oberpeul,** Debra Saul 1959- *WhoMW 92*
**Oberquell,** Diane *WhoAmP 91*
**Oberreit,** Walter William 1928- *WhoFI 92*
**O'Berry,** Annie Land 1885-1944 *DcNCBi 4*
**O'Berry,** Phillip Aaron 1933- *AmMWSc 92*
**Oberschlake,** Dwight W. *WhoMW 92*
**Oberst,** Fred William 1904- *AmMWSc 92*
**Oberst,** Paul 1914- *WhoAmL 92*
**Oberst,** Robert Clair 1952- *WhoMW 92*
**Oberst,** Robert John 1929- *WhoFI 92*
**Oberstar,** Helen Elizabeth 1923- *AmMWSc 92*
**Oberstar,** James L. 1934- *AlmAP 92 [port], WhoAmP 91, WhoMW 92*
**Oberstein,** Marydale 1942- *WhoWest 92*
**Oberster,** Arthur Eugene 1929- *AmMWSc 92, WhoMW 92*
**Obert,** Edward Fredric 1910- *AmMWSc 92*
**Obert,** Jessie C 1911- *AmMWSc 92*
**Obert,** Paul Richard 1928- *WhoAmL 92, WhoFI 92*
**Oberteuffer,** John Amiard 1940- *AmMWSc 92*
**Oberth,** Hermann 1894-1989 *FacFETw*
**Oberti,** Sylvia Marie Antoinette 1952- *WhoWest 92*
**Oberwager,** Frances Robertson 1923- *WhoAmP 91*
**Obeso Rivera,** Sergio 1931- *WhoRel 92*
**Obets,** Bob *TwCWW 91*
**Obey,** David R. 1938- *AlmAP 92 [port], WhoAmP 91*
**Obey,** David Ross 1938- *WhoMW 92*
**Obey,** James H 1916- *AmMWSc 92*
**Obi,** James E. 1942- *WhoBlA 92*
**Obi,** Onyeabo C. 1938- *IntWW 91*
**Obie,** Brian B *WhoAmP 91*
**Obiedo,** Ray Anthony 1952- *WhoHisp 92*
**O'Bier,** Don Micheal 1946- *WhoRel 92*
**Obijeski,** John Francis 1941- *AmMWSc 92*
**Obinna,** Eleazu S. 1934- *WhoBlA 92*
**O'Biso,** Carol 1953- *ConAu 133*
**Oblad,** Alex Golden 1909- *AmMWSc 92*
**Oblak,** Frank Anthony 1957- *WhoMW 92*
**Oblate Sisters of Providence** *NotBlAW 92*
**Obledo,** Mario Guerra 1932- *WhoHisp 92*
**Obligado,** Lilian 1931- *ConAu 134*
**Oblinger,** Diana Gelene 1954- *AmMWSc 92*
**Oblinger,** James Leslie 1945- *AmMWSc 92*
**Oblinger,** Josephine Kneidl 1913- *WhoAmP 91*
**Oblinger,** Nancy L 1945- *WhoIns 92*
**O'Block,** Robert Paul 1943- *WhoFI 92*
**Obninsky,** Victor Peter 1944- *WhoWest 92*
**Obodowski,** Janusz 1930- *IntWW 91*
**Obolensky,** Dimitri 1918- *IntWW 91, Who 92*
**Oboler,** Arch 1907-1987 *BenetAL 91*
**Obolsky,** Alexander Eduard 1962- *WhoMW 92*
**Oborin,** Lev 1907-1974 *NewAmDM*
**Oborin,** Lev Nikolaevich 1907-1974 *SovUnBD*
**Obote,** Milton 1924- *FacFETw, IntWW 91, Who 92*
**Oboukhov,** Alexei 1938- *IntWW 91*
**O'Boyle,** Patrick Aloysius 1896-1987 *RelLAm 91*
**Oboyski-Battelene,** Joanne Marie 1956- *WhoEnt 92*
**Obradovich,** John Dinko 1930- *AmMWSc 92*
**O'Brady,** Frederic 1903- *IntAu&W 91*
**Obraztsov,** Ivan Filoppovich 1920- *IntWW 91*
**Obraztsov,** Sergey Vladimirovich 1901- *SovUnBD*
**Obraztsova,** Elena 1937- *NewAmDM*
**Obraztsova,** Yelena Vasil'evna 1937- *SovUnBD*
**Obraztsova,** Yelena Vasiliyevna 1937- *IntWW 91*
**Obrecht,** Eldon Ross 1920- *WhoMW 92*
**Obrecht,** Jacob 1450?-1505 *NewAmDM*
**Obrecht,** James Carlton *ConAu 135*
**Obrecht,** Jas 1952- *ConAu 135*
**Obrecht,** Kenneth William 1933- *WhoMW 92*
**Obregon,** Alejandro 1920- *IntWW 91*
**Obregon,** Carlos Daniel 1959- *WhoHisp 92*
**Obregon,** Richard Rivera 1951- *WhoHisp 92*
**Obregon,** Valentin 1953- *WhoHisp 92*
**Obremski,** Henry J 1931- *AmMWSc 92*
**Obremski,** Robert John 1941- *AmMWSc 92*
**Obrentz,** Howard 1926- *WhoWest 92*
**O'Brian,** Frank *TwCWW 91, WrDr 92*
**O'Brian,** Hugh 1930- *IntMPA 92, WhoEnt 92*
**O'Brian,** William Daniel *WhoAmL 92*
**O'Briant,** Pat Wayne 1960- *WhoEnt 92*
**O'Briant,** Walter H. 1937- *WrDr 92*
**O'Brien** *Who 92*
**O'Brien,** Albert James 1914- *WhoMW 92*
**O'Brien,** Ana Colomar *WhoHisp 92*
**O'Brien,** Andrew M 1952- *WhoIns 92*
**O'Brien,** Anna Belle Clement *WhoAmP 91*
**O'Brien,** Anne Sibley 1952- *WrDr 92*
**O'Brien,** Anne T 1936- *AmMWSc 92*
**O'Brien,** Barbara Cooney *AmMWSc 92*
**O'Brien,** Beatrice *DrAPF 91*
**O'Brien,** Benedict Butler, Jr 1934- *AmMWSc 92*
**O'Brien,** Bernard Francis 1914- *WhoAmP 91*
**O'Brien,** Betty Alice 1932- *WhoRel 92*
**O'Brien,** Bonny Kathlene 1964- *WhoEnt 92*
**O'Brien,** Brian 1898- *AmMWSc 92, IntWW 91*
**O'Brien,** Brian Murrough Fergus 1931- *Who 92*
**O'Brien,** Brien Michael 1957- *WhoMW 92*
**O'Brien,** Carol Jean 1939- *WhoMW 92*
**O'Brien,** Charles H. 1920- *WhoAmL 92*
**O'Brien,** Charles Michael 1919- *Who 92*
**O'Brien,** Charles Patrick 1936- *WhoIns 92*
**O'Brien,** Charles Richard 1934- *WhoMW 92*
**O'Brien,** Christopher Edward 1955- *WhoAmL 92*
**O'Brien,** Clancy *TwCSFW 91*
**O'Brien,** Conor Cruise 1917- *FacFETw, IntAu&W 91, IntWW 91, Who 92, WrDr 92*
**O'Brien,** Daniel H 1932- *AmMWSc 92*
**O'Brien,** Daniel Joseph 1945- *WhoEnt 92*
**O'Brien,** Daniel William 1926- *WhoAmL 92, WhoMW 92*
**O'Brien,** Deborah A *AmMWSc 92*
**O'Brien,** Denis Patrick 1939- *Who 92*
**O'Brien,** Dennis Craig 1938- *AmMWSc 92*
**O'Brien,** Dennis M *WhoAmP 91*
**O'Brien,** Dermod Patrick 1939- *Who 92*
**O'Brien,** Donald Eugene 1923- *WhoAmL 92, WhoMW 92*
**O'Brien,** Donough 1923- *AmMWSc 92*
**O'Brien,** Dorothy Merrie 1936- *WhoAmP 91*
**O'Brien,** Edna *Who 92*
**O'Brien,** Edna 1932- *CnDBLB 8 [port], ConLC 65 [port], ConNov 91, FacFETw, LiExTwC, WrDr 92*
**O'Brien,** Edna 1936- *IntAu&W 91, IntWW 91*
**O'Brien,** Edward E 1933- *AmMWSc 92*
**O'Brien,** Edward J. 1890-1941 *BenetAL 91*
**O'Brien,** Edward Lee 1945- *WhoAmL 92*
**O'Brien,** Elizabeth Brooks *WhoAmL 92*
**O'Brien,** Ellen J. 1950- *WhoEnt 92*
**O'Brien,** Elmer 1911- *WrDr 92*
**O'Brien,** Elmer John 1932- *WhoRel 92*
**O'Brien,** Eugene 1945- *NewAmDM*
**O'Brien,** Fitz-James 1828?-1862 *BenetAL 91, ScFEYrs*
**O'Brien,** Flann 1911-1966 *RfGEnL 91*
**O'Brien,** Flann 1912-1966 *FacFETw*
**O'Brien,** Francis Joseph 1958- *WhoMW 92*
**O'Brien,** Francis Xavier 1935- *AmMWSc 92*
**O'Brien,** Frank Michael 1875-1943 *BenetAL 91*
**O'Brien,** Frederick 1869-1932 *BenetAL 91*
**O'Brien,** Frederick 1917- *Who 92*
**O'Brien,** Gregory Francis 1950- *WhoFI 92*
**O'Brien,** Gregory Michael St. Lawrence 1944- *IntWW 91*
**O'Brien,** Harold Aloysious, Jr 1936- *AmMWSc 92*
**O'Brien,** Harold Aloysius, Jr. 1936- *WhoWest 92*
**O'Brien,** Helene Jeannette 1946- *WhoFI 92*
**O'Brien,** Herbert John 1930- *WhoAmP 91*
**O'Brien,** Howard Vincent 1888-1947 *BenetAL 91*
**O'Brien,** J E *ScFEYrs*
**O'Brien,** Jack George 1939- *WhoWest 92*
**O'Brien,** Jacquelyn K 1931- *WhoAmP 91*
**O'Brien,** James Francis 1934- *AmMWSc 92*
**O'Brien,** James Francis 1941- *AmMWSc 92, WhoMW 92*
**O'Brien,** James J 1935- *AmMWSc 92*
**O'Brien,** James Joseph 1930- *Who 92*
**O'Brien,** James Patrick 1961- *WhoWest 92*
**O'Brien,** James Randall 1949- *WhoRel 92*
**O'Brien,** Janet W *WhoAmP 91*
**O'Brien,** Joan A *AmMWSc 92*
**O'Brien,** John *DrAPF 91*
**O'Brien,** John 1921- *WhoAmP 91*
**O'Brien,** John Aeneas 1920- *WhoAmP 91*
**O'Brien,** John C 1945- *AmMWSc 92*
**O'Brien,** John Edward 1929- *WhoFI 92*
**O'Brien,** John F 1943- *WhoIns 92*
**O'Brien,** John Feighan 1936- *WhoMW 92*
**O'Brien,** John Fitzgerald 1928- *WhoAmP 91*
**O'Brien,** John Graham 1948- *WhoAmL 92*
**O'Brien,** John Kevin 1958- *WhoEnt 92*
**O'Brien,** John L 1911- *WhoAmP 91*
**O'Brien,** John M. 1930- *WhoFI 92*
**O'Brien,** John Patrick 1926- *WhoAmL 92*
**O'Brien,** John Rusch 1935- *WhoFI 92*
**O'Brien,** John S 1934- *AmMWSc 92*
**O'Brien,** John W. 1931- *Who 92*
**O'Brien,** John William, Jr. 1937- *WhoFI 92*
**O'Brien,** Joseph E 1940- *WhoIns 92*
**O'Brien,** Joseph Edward, Jr. 1933- *WhoAmL 92*
**O'Brien,** Joseph Lewis 1929- *WhoMW 92, WhoRel 92*
**O'Brien,** Joseph M 1917- *WhoAmP 91*
**O'Brien,** Joseph Patrick, Jr. 1940- *WhoFI 92*
**O'Brien,** Joseph William, Jr 1929- *WhoAmP 91*
**O'Brien,** Justin *WhoRel 92*
**O'Brien,** Kate 1897-1974 *RfGEnL 91*
**O'Brien,** Katharine *DrAPF 91, IntAu&W 91*
**O'Brien,** Katharine E. 1901- *WrDr 92*
**O'Brien,** Kathleen Ann 1944- *WhoMW 92*
**O'Brien,** Kathleen Ann 1945- *WhoAmP 91*
**O'Brien,** Kathleen Mary 1951- *WhoRel 92*
**O'Brien,** Keith Michael 1954- *WhoWest 92*
**O'Brien,** Keith Michael Patrick *Who 92*
**O'Brien,** Keith Michael Patrick 1938- *IntWW 91*
**O'Brien,** Kenneth Alfred, Jr. 1956- *WhoAmL 92*
**O'Brien,** Kenneth Robert 1937- *WhoFI 92*
**O'Brien,** Keran 1931- *AmMWSc 92*
**O'Brien,** Kevin *Who 92*
**O'Brien,** Kevin Charles 1957- *WhoWest 92*
**O'Brien,** Larry Joe 1929- *AmMWSc 92*
**O'Brien,** Lawrence 1917-1990 *AnObit 1990*
**O'Brien,** Lawrence Francis d1990 *IntWW 91N*
**O'Brien,** Lawrence Francis, III 1945- *WhoAmL 92*
**O'Brien,** Lawrence Francis, Jr 1917-1990 *FacFETw*
**O'Brien,** Leo, Jr 1931- *WhoAmP 91*
**O'Brien,** Liam 1913- *IntMPA 92*
**O'Brien,** Lisa Marie 1969- *WhoHisp 92*
**O'Brien,** Margaret 1937- *WhoEnt 92*
**O'Brien,** Margaret 1938- *IntMPA 92*
**O'Brien,** Mark *DrAPF 91*
**O'Brien,** Mark D 1939- *WhoAmP 91*
**O'Brien,** Mary Devon 1944- *WhoFI 92*
**O'Brien,** Mary Ellen Atkins *WhoEnt 92*
**O'Brien,** Mary-Margaret 1946- *WhoRel 92*
**O'Brien,** Maureen Joan 1953- *WhoAmL 92*
**O'Brien,** Michael *DrAPF 91*
**O'Brien,** Michael 1918- *AmMWSc 92*
**O'Brien,** Michael Harvey 1942- *AmMWSc 92*
**O'Brien,** Michael J *WhoIns 92*
**O'Brien,** Michael J 1942- *WhoAmP 91*
**O'Brien,** Michael John 1950- *WhoMW 92*
**O'Brien,** Michael Vincent 1917- *IntWW 91, Who 92*
**O'Brien,** Morrough P *AmMWSc 92*
**O'Brien,** Neal Ray 1937- *AmMWSc 92*
**O'Brien,** Orin A. *WhoEnt 92*
**O'Brien,** Oswald 1928- *Who 92*
**O'Brien,** Patricia Jean 1937- *WhoAmP 91*
**O'Brien,** Patricia Joan 1935- *WhoMW 92*
**O'Brien,** Patrick 1932- *WrDr 92*
**O'Brien,** Patrick J 1947- *WhoIns 92*
**O'Brien,** Patrick John 1957- *WhoWest 92*
**O'Brien,** Patrick Karl 1932- *IntWW 91, Who 92*
**O'Brien,** Patrick William 1927- *WhoAmL 92*
**O'Brien,** Patrick William 1945- *Who 92*
**O'Brien,** Paul Charles 1939- *WhoFI 92*
**O'Brien,** Paul J 1933- *AmMWSc 92*
**O'Brien,** Paul Jerry 1925- *WhoWest 92*
**Obrien,** Peter Charles 1943- *AmMWSc 92, WhoMW 92*
**O'Brien,** Peter J 1937- *AmMWSc 92*
**O'Brien,** Philip Michael 1940- *WhoWest 92*
**O'Brien,** Raymond Francis 1922- *WhoFI 92, WhoWest 92*
**O'Brien,** Raymond Francis 1936- *Who 92*
**O'Brien,** Raymond Vincent, Jr. 1927- *WhoFI 92*
**O'Brien,** Rebecca L. 1956- *WhoWest 92*
**O'Brien,** Redmond R 1931- *AmMWSc 92*
**O'Brien,** Richard 1920- *Who 92*
**O'Brien,** Richard Desmond 1929- *AmMWSc 92*
**O'Brien,** Richard E. 1952- *WhoFI 92*
**O'Brien,** Richard John, Jr. 1954- *WhoAmL 92*
**O'Brien,** Richard Lee 1934- *AmMWSc 92*
**O'Brien,** Robert 1945- *AmMWSc 92*
**O'Brien,** Robert Emmet, Jr. 1949- *WhoFI 92*
**O'Brien,** Robert Felix 1921- *WhoEnt 92*
**O'Brien,** Robert L 1936- *AmMWSc 92*
**O'Brien,** Robert Neville 1921- *AmMWSc 92*
**O'Brien,** Robert Richard 1964- *WhoEnt 92*
**O'Brien,** Robert S. 1918- *WhoWest 92*
**O'Brien,** Robert Thomas 1925- *AmMWSc 92*
**O'Brien,** Robert Thomas 1941- *WhoFI 92*
**O'Brien,** Roger Gerard 1935- *WhoRel 92*
**O'Brien,** Ronald J 1932- *AmMWSc 92*
**O'Brien,** Rory Patrick 1954- *WhoFI 92*
**O'Brien,** Sean 1952- *ConPo 91, WrDr 92*
**O'Brien,** Shannon P *WhoAmP 91*
**O'Brien,** Stephen 1936- *Who 92*
**O'Brien,** Stephen James 1944- *AmMWSc 92*
**O'Brien,** Sue 1939- *WhoWest 92*
**O'Brien,** Terence John 1921- *IntWW 91, Who 92*
**O'Brien,** Terrence Leo 1943- *WhoAmL 92*
**O'Brien,** Terrence Patrick 1953- *WhoEnt 92*
**O'Brien,** Thomas C. d1991 *NewYTBS 91*
**O'Brien,** Thomas Doran 1910- *AmMWSc 92*
**O'Brien,** Thomas George, III 1942- *WhoAmL 92*
**O'Brien,** Thomas Henry 1937- *WhoFI 92*
**O'Brien,** Thomas Herbert 1921- *WhoFI 92*
**O'Brien,** Thomas Joseph 1935- *WhoRel 92, WhoWest 92*
**O'Brien,** Thomas Kevin 1923- *Who 92*
**O'Brien,** Thomas Michael 1950- *WhoMW 92*
**O'Brien,** Thomas V 1937- *AmMWSc 92*
**O'Brien,** Thomas W 1938- *AmMWSc 92*
**O'Brien,** Tim 1946- *BenetAL 91, ConNov 91, DcLB DS9 [port], WrDr 92*
**O'Brien,** Timothy Brian 1929- *Who 92*
**O'Brien,** Timothy James 1945- *WhoAmL 92*
**O'Brien,** Timothy John 1958- *Who 92*
**O'Brien,** Timothy Martin 1944- *WhoAmL 92*
**O'Brien,** TJ St. James 1972- *WhoEnt 92*
**O'Brien,** Turlough Aubrey 1907- *Who 92*
**O'Brien,** Vincent *IntWW 91, Who 92*
**O'Brien,** Virginia 1919- *IntMPA 92*
**O'Brien,** Vivian 1924- *AmMWSc 92*
**O'Brien,** Walter John 1951- *WhoEnt 92*
**O'Brien,** Walter Joseph, II 1939- *WhoAmL 92*
**O'Brien,** William 1916- *Who 92*
**O'Brien,** William 1929- *Who 92*
**O'Brien,** William Daniel, Jr 1942- *AmMWSc 92*
**O'Brien,** William Dermod 1865-1945 *TwCPaSc*
**O'Brien,** William E *AmMWSc 92*
**O'Brien,** William J. *WhoAmL 92*
**O'Brien,** William Jerome, II 1954- *WhoAmL 92*
**O'Brien,** William John 1932- *WhoFI 92, WhoIns 92*
**O'Brien,** William John 1942- *AmMWSc 92*
**O'Brien,** William Joseph 1935- *AmMWSc 92*
**O'Brien,** William Joseph 1940- *WhoMW 92*
**O'Brien,** William M 1931- *AmMWSc 92*
**O'Brien,** William P. *DrAPF 91*
**O'Brien,** William Thomas 1854-1906 *DcNCBi 4*
**O'Brien Of Lothbury,** Baron 1908- *IntWW 91, Who 92*
**O'Brien Quinn,** James Aiden *Who 92*
**O'Brien Quinn,** James Aiden 1932- *IntWW 91*
**O'Brien Smith,** Valerie Elizabeth 1954- *WhoEnt 92*
**O'Brient,** David Warren 1927- *WhoFI 92*
**Obrinsky,** Mark Henry 1950- *WhoFI 92*
**Obrist,** Hermann 1863-1927 *DcTwDes*
**O'Broin,** Leon 1902- *IntAu&W 91*
**Obrosov,** Igor' Pavlovich 1930- *SovUnBD*
**Obruchev,** Vladimir Afanasievich 1862-1956 *ScFEYrs*
**Obruzut,** Geoff *WhoAmP 91*
**O'Bryan,** James A, Jr 1956- *WhoAmP 91*
**O'Bryan,** James Alvanley, Jr. 1956- *WhoBlA 92*
**O'Bryan,** Janet 1957- *WhoMW 92*

**O'Bryan**, Michael Gavin 1961- *WhoAmL 92*
**O'Bryan**, William Hall 1919- *WhoIns 92*
**O'Bryant**, David Claude 1935- *AmMWSc 92*
**O'Bryant**, John D. 1931- *WhoBlA 92*
**O'Bryant**, Tilmon Bunche 1920- *WhoBlA 92*
**Observer** *AmPeW*
**Obst**, Andrew Wesley 1942- *AmMWSc 92*
**Obst**, George Jay 1939- *WhoMW 92*
**Obst**, Lynda Rosen 1950- *WhoEnt 92*
**Obst**, Norman Philip 1944- *WhoFI 92, WhoMW 92*
**Obst**, Richard Conrad, Jr. 1960- *WhoFI 92*
**Obstfeld**, Raymond *DrAPF 91*
**Obstfeld**, Raymond 1952- *IntAu&W 91*
**Obstler**, Harold 1925- *WhoFI 92*
**O Buachalla**, Breandan 1936- *IntWW 91*
**Obuchi**, Keizo 1937- *IntWW 91*
**Obuchowski**, Janice *LesBEnT 92*
**Obuchowski**, Michael John 1952- *WhoAmP 91*
**Obuchowski**, Raymond Joseph 1955- *WhoAmL 92*
**Obukhova**, Nadezhda Andreevna 1886-1961 *SovUnBD*
**O'Byrne**, Bryan Jay 1931- *WhoEnt 92*
**O'Byrne**, Christopher Lee 1953- *WhoMW 92*
**O'Byrne**, Paul J. 1922- *WhoRel 92, WhoWest 92*
**Obzina**, Jaromir 1929- *IntWW 91*
**O'Cain**, Barbara Rushing 1950- *WhoAmL 92*
**Ocain**, Timothy Donald *AmMWSc 92*
**O'Callaghan**, Dennis John 1940- *AmMWSc 92*
**O'Callaghan**, Donal N 1929- *WhoAmP 91*
**O'Callaghan**, James Patrick 1949- *AmMWSc 92*
**O'Callaghan**, John Joseph 1931- *WhoRel 92*
**O'Callaghan**, Michael James 1954- *AmMWSc 92*
**O'Callaghan**, Mike 1929- *IntWW 91*
**O'Callaghan**, Richard J 1944- *AmMWSc 92*
**O'Callaghan**, Robert Patrick 1924- *WhoAmL 92*
**O'Callaghan**, William Lawrence, Jr. 1941- *WhoEnt 92*
**Ocampo**, Sergio G. 1961- *WhoHisp 92*
**Ocampo**, Silvina 1903- *SpAmWW*
**Ocampo**, Victoria 1890-1979 *SpAmWW*
**Ocampo-Friedmann**, Roseli C 1937- *AmMWSc 92*
**Ocanas**, Gilberto S. 1953- *WhoHisp 92*
**O'Canto**, Raymond Jose, Jr. 1959- *WhoHisp 92*
**Ocasek**, Oliver Robert 1925- *WhoAmP 91*
**Ocasek**, Ric *WhoEnt 92*
**O'Casey**, Brenda *WrDr 92*
**O'Casey**, Breon 1928- *TwCPaSc*
**O'Casey**, Eileen 1903- *ConAu 133*
**O'Casey**, Sean 1880-1964 *CnDBLB 6 [port], FacFETw, LiExTwC, RfGEnL 91*
**Ocasio**, Edgardo 1955- *WhoHisp 92*
**Ocasio**, Nilda 1943- *WhoHisp 92*
**Ocasio**, Rafael 1960- *WhoHisp 92*
**Ocasio-Melendez**, Marcial E. 1942- *WhoHisp 92*
**Ocasio-Melendez**, Marcial Enrique 1942- *WhoMW 92*
**O'Cathain**, Baroness 1938- *Who 92*
**Occelli**, Mario Lorenzo 1942- *AmMWSc 92*
**Occhetto**, Achille 1936- *IntWW 91*
**Occhiato**, Michael A *WhoAmP 91*
**Occhiato**, Michael Anthony *WhoWest 92*
**Occhipinti**, Carl Joseph 1931- *WhoWest 92*
**Occhiuto**, Antonino 1912- *IntWW 91*
**Occhiuzzo**, Lucia Rajszel 1951- *WhoFI 92*
**Occolowitz**, John Lewis 1931- *AmMWSc 92*
**Occom**, Samson 1723-1792 *BenetAL 91*
**Occomy**, Marita B. 1899-1971 *BenetAL 91*
**Occum**, Samson 1723-1792 *BenetAL 91*
**Ocean**, Billy 1952- *WhoEnt 92*
**Ocean**, Humphrey 1951- *TwCPaSc*
**Ochab**, Edward 1906-1989 *FacFETw*
**Ochester**, Ed *DrAPF 91*
**O'Chester**, Harold Eugene 1927- *WhoRel 92*
**Ochi**, Ihei 1920- *IntWW 91*
**Ochiai**, Ei-Ichiro 1936- *AmMWSc 92*
**Ochiai**, Eiichi 1916- *IntWW 91*
**Ochiai**, Shinya 1935- *AmMWSc 92*
**Ochiltree**, Jamie 1952- *WhoIns 92*
**Ochiltree**, Stuart A. 1941- *WhoFI 92*
**Ochiltree**, William Beck 1811-1867 *DcNCBi 4*
**Ochirbat**, Gombojaviin 1929- *IntWW 91*
**Ochirbat**, Punsalmaagin 1942- *IntWW 91*
**Ochman**, Wieslaw 1937- *IntWW 91*
**Ochner**, Ronald William 1935- *WhoRel 92*
**Ochoa**, Antonio A., Jr. 1930- *WhoHisp 92*
**Ochoa**, Armando 1843- *WhoWest 92*
**Ochoa**, Armando 1943- *WhoRel 92*
**Ochoa**, Benjamin Gamino 1926- *WhoHisp 92*
**Ochoa**, Edgar 1953- *WhoHisp 92*
**Ochoa**, Eduardo Martin 1950- *WhoFI 92*
**Ochoa**, Ellen 1958- *WhoHisp 92*
**Ochoa**, Frank Joseph 1950- *WhoHisp 92*
**Ochoa**, Ignacio Garcia 1953- *WhoHisp 92*
**Ochoa**, James Edward 1950- *WhoWest 92*
**Ochoa**, Jesus Zeferino 1936- *WhoHisp 92*
**Ochoa**, John Robert 1947- *WhoAmP 91*
**Ochoa**, Ralph Michael 1941- *WhoHisp 92*
**Ochoa**, Ricardo 1945- *WhoHisp 92*
**Ochoa**, Richard 1955- *WhoHisp 92*
**Ochoa**, Sandor Rodolfo 1944- *WhoHisp 92*
**Ochoa**, Severo 1905- *AmMWSc 92, FacFETw, IntWW 91, Who 92, WhoNob 90*
**Ochoa**, Victor Orozco 1948- *WhoHisp 92*
**Ochoa Mejia**, Jose 1940- *WhoFI 92*
**Ochrymowycz**, Leo Arthur 1943- *AmMWSc 92*
**Ochs**, Adolph S. 1858-1935 *BenetAL 91*
**Ochs**, Carol 1939- *ConAu 36NR*
**Ochs**, David Alan 1965- *WhoMW 92*
**Ochs**, Gary Lee 1949- *WhoWest 92*
**Ochs**, Hans D 1936- *AmMWSc 92*
**Ochs**, Herman 1913- *WhoFI 92*
**Ochs**, John David 1950- *WhoAmP 91*
**Ochs**, Larabee Lars 1950- *WhoEnt 92*
**Ochs**, Peter Warren 1950- *WhoRel 92*
**Ochs**, Phil 1940-1976 *ConMus 7 [port], NewAmDM*
**Ochs**, Raymond S 1952- *AmMWSc 92*
**Ochs**, Sidney 1924- *AmMWSc 92*
**Ochs**, Stefan A 1922- *AmMWSc 92*
**Ochs**, Vanessa 1953- *ConAu 134*
**Ochs**, Vanessa L. *DrAPF 91*
**Ochsner**, John Lockwood 1927- *AmMWSc 92*
**Ochsner**, Othon Henry, II 1934- *WhoMW 92*
**Ochsner**, Seymour Fiske 1915- *AmMWSc 92*
**Ockeghem**, Johannes 1415?-1497 *NewAmDM*
**Ockenga**, Harold John 1905-1985 *RelLAm 91*
**Ockenga**, Starr 1938- *ConAu 134*
**Ockerbloom**, Richard C. 1929- *WhoFI 92*
**Ockerman**, Foster 1920- *WhoAmP 91*
**Ockerman**, Herbert W 1932- *AmMWSc 92*
**Ockerse**, Ralph 1933- *AmMWSc 92*
**Ockerse**, Thomas 1940- *WhoEnt 92*
**Ockerse**, Tom *DrAPF 91*
**Ockey**, Ronald J. 1934- *WhoAmL 92, WhoAmP 91, WhoWest 92*
**Ockham**, William of 1285?-1347 *DcLB 115 [port]*
**Ockman**, Nathan 1926- *AmMWSc 92*
**Ockrent**, Christine 1944- *IntWW 91*
**Ockum**, Samson 1723-1792 *BenetAL 91*
**O'Clair**, David Francis 1941- *WhoIns 92*
**O Cofaigh**, Tomas F. 1921- *IntWW 91*
**O'Collins**, Gerald Glynn 1931- *ConAu 34NR, WrDr 92*
**Ocone**, Luke Ralph 1925- *AmMWSc 92*
**O'Connell**, Ann 1934- *WhoAmP 91*
**O'Connell**, Brendan J *WhoIns 92*
**O'Connell**, Charles Francis 1955- *WhoFI 92*
**O'Connell**, Colman *WhoRel 92*
**O'Connell**, Daniel *DcAmImH*
**O'Connell**, Daniel Francis 1955- *WhoAmL 92*
**O'Connell**, Daniel James 1954- *WhoAmL 92*
**O'Connell**, David d1991 *NewYTBS 91*
**O'Connell**, David Paul 1940- *WhoAmP 91*
**O'Connell**, Denis J. 1849-1927 *DcAmImH*
**O'Connell**, Desmond Henry, Jr. 1936- *Who 92*
**O'Connell**, Edmond J, Jr 1939- *AmMWSc 92*
**O'Connell**, Edward Joseph, III 1952- *WhoMW 92*
**O'Connell**, Eilis 1953- *TwCPaSc*
**O'Connell**, Francis Joseph 1913- *WhoAmL 92*
**O'Connell**, Francis Vincent 1903- *WhoFI 92*
**O'Connell**, Frank Dennis 1927- *AmMWSc 92*
**O'Connell**, Frank J *WhoAmP 91*
**O'Connell**, Harold Patrick, Jr. 1933- *WhoMW 92*
**O'Connell**, Harry E 1916- *AmMWSc 92*
**O'Connell**, Helen G 1917- *WhoAmP 91*
**O'Connell**, Henry Francis 1922- *WhoAmL 92, WhoFI 92*
**O'Connell**, Jack *IntMPA 92*
**O'Connell**, Jack 1951- *WhoAmP 91*
**O'Connell**, James Jerome 1946- *WhoAmP 91*
**O'Connell**, James Joseph 1933- *WhoMW 92*
**O'Connell**, James S 1932- *AmMWSc 92*
**O'Connell**, Jeffrey 1928- *WhoAmL 92*
**O'Connell**, Jeremiah J. 1932- *WrDr 92*
**O'Connell**, Jeremiah John 1949- *WhoFI 92*
**O'Connell**, John Edward 1943- *WhoIns 92*
**O'Connell**, John Eugene Anthony 1906- *Who 92*
**O'Connell**, John P 1938- *AmMWSc 92*
**O'Connell**, John W. 1943- *WhoMW 92*
**O'Connell**, Joseph J 1866?-1916 *BiInAmS*
**O'Connell**, Kathleen Ann 1947- *WhoMW 92*
**O'Connell**, Kathy L. 1964- *WhoWest 92*
**O'Connell**, Kevin 1933- *WhoAmL 92*
**O'Connell**, Lawrence B. 1947- *WhoAmL 92*
**O'Connell**, Margaret Sullivan 1942- *WhoAmL 92*
**O'Connell**, Marvin R. 1930- *ConAu 134*
**O'Connell**, Mary Ann 1934- *WhoWest 92*
**O'Connell**, Maurice 1958- *Who 92*
**O'Connell**, Maurice Daniel 1929- *WhoAmL 92*
**O'Connell**, Neil James 1937- *WhoRel 92*
**O'Connell**, Patrick Francis 1926- *WhoRel 92*
**O'Connell**, Paul William 1922- *AmMWSc 92*
**O'Connell**, Richard *DrAPF 91*
**O'Connell**, Richard 1928- *IntAu&W 91*
**O'Connell**, Richard John 1941- *AmMWSc 92*
**O'Connell**, Richard Lawrence 1929- *WhoWest 92*
**O'Connell**, Robert F 1933- *AmMWSc 92*
**O'Connell**, Robert J 1943- *WhoIns 92*
**O'Connell**, Robert John 1943- *WhoFI 92*
**O'Connell**, Robert West 1943- *AmMWSc 92*
**O'Connell**, Thomas Patrick 1955- *WhoMW 92*
**O'Connell**, William 1859-1944 *RelLAm 91*
**O'Connell**, William Stephen 1953- *WhoMW 92*
**O'Connell-Thompson**, Margaret Mary 1962- *WhoFI 92*
**O'Conner**, Bert *TwCWW 91*
**O'Conner**, Clint *TwCWW 91*
**O'Connor**, Alan 1955- *ConAu 133*
**O'Connor**, Ann Patricia *WhoRel 92*
**O'Connor**, Anthony 1917- *Who 92*
**O'Connor**, Anthony Michael 1939- *IntAu&W 91, WrDr 92*
**O'Connor**, Bernard James 1953- *WhoFI 92*
**O'Connor**, Billy Keith 1942- *WhoRel 92*
**O'Connor**, Brenda Anne 1959- *WhoWest 92*
**O'Connor**, Brian Edward 1952- *WhoAmL 92*
**O'Connor**, Brian John 1955- *WhoWest 92*
**O'Connor**, Brian Lee 1944- *AmMWSc 92*
**O'Connor**, Brian Michael 1942- *Who 92*
**O'Connor**, Carol Alf 1948- *AmMWSc 92*
**O'Connor**, Carol Ann 1946- *WhoWest 92*
**O'Connor**, Carroll *LesBEnT 92*
**O'Connor**, Carroll 1924- *ConTFT 9, IntMPA 92, WhoEnt 92*
**O'Connor**, Catherine 1956- *WhoAmL 92*
**O'Connor**, Cecilian Leonard 1922- *AmMWSc 92*
**O'Connor**, Charles Aloysius, III 1942- *WhoAmL 92*
**O'Connor**, Charles E. *WhoRel 92*
**O'Connor**, Charles P. 1940- *WhoAmL 92*
**O'Connor**, Charles Timothy 1930- *AmMWSc 92*
**O'Connor**, Charmian Jocelyn 1937- *IntWW 91*
**O'Connor**, Colleen Mary 1956- *WhoFI 92*
**O'Connor**, Cormac Murphy *Who 92*
**O'Connor**, Daniel John 1914- *Who 92*
**O'Connor**, Daniel Patrick 1960- *WhoAmL 92*
**O'Connor**, Daniel Thomas *AmMWSc 92*
**O'Connor**, Daniel Thomas 1942- *WhoWest 92*
**O'Connor**, Daniel William 1925- *WhoRel 92*
**O'Connor**, David Evans 1932- *AmMWSc 92*
**O'Connor**, Davis Owen 1954- *WhoAmL 92*
**O'Connor**, Dennis 1930- *WhoAmP 91*
**O'Connor**, Donald 1925- *FacFETw, IntMPA 92*
**O'Connor**, Donald J 1922- *AmMWSc 92*
**O'Connor**, Donald Thomas 1935- *WhoAmL 92*
**O'Connor**, Earl Eugene 1922- *WhoAmL 92*
**O'Connor**, Edward Dennis 1922- *WhoRel 92*
**O'Connor**, Edward Gearing 1940- *WhoAmL 92*
**O'Connor**, Edward T, Jr 1942- *WhoAmP 91*
**O'Connor**, Edward Vincent, Jr. 1952- *WhoAmL 92*
**O'Connor**, Edwin 1918-1968 *BenetAL 91*
**O'Connor**, Flannery 1925-1964 *Au&Arts 7 [port], BenetAL 91, ConLC 66 [port], FacFETw, HanAmWH, ModAWWr*
**O'Connor**, Francis Brian 1932- *Who 92*
**O'Connor**, Francis P 1927- *WhoAmP 91*
**O'Connor**, Francis Patrick 1927- *WhoAmL 92*
**O'Connor**, Francis V. *DrAPF 91*
**O'Connor**, Francis V 1937- *WrDr 92*
**O'Connor**, Frank 1903-1966 *FacFETw, LiExTwC, RfGEnL 91*
**O'Connor**, Gayle McCormick 1956- *WhoAmL 92*
**O'Connor**, George Albert 1944- *AmMWSc 92*
**O'Connor**, George Aquin 1921- *WhoRel 92*
**O'Connor**, George Richard 1928- *AmMWSc 92*
**O'Connor**, Gillian Rose 1941- *Who 92*
**O'Connor**, Glynnis 1955- *IntMPA 92*
**O'Connor**, Gwendolyn Marie 1928- *WhoAmP 91*
**O'Connor**, Hubert Patrick 1928- *WhoRel 92*
**O'Connor**, Jack 1902-1978 *TwCWW 91*
**O'Connor**, Jack Francis 1959- *WhoWest 92*
**O'Connor**, James John 1937- *WhoFI 92, WhoMW 92*
**O'Connor**, James Michael 1942- *WhoAmL 92*
**O'Connor**, Joel Sturges 1937- *AmMWSc 92*
**O'Connor**, John 1913- *TwCPaSc*
**O'Connor**, John 1920- *IntWW 91*
**O'Connor**, John Dennis 1942- *AmMWSc 92*
**O'Connor**, John Francis 1935- *AmMWSc 92*
**O'Connor**, John Ignatius 1954- *WhoAmL 92*
**O'Connor**, John J. *LesBEnT 92*
**O'Connor**, John Joseph 1916- *AmMWSc 92*
**O'Connor**, John Joseph 1920- *RelLAm 91, WhoRel 92*
**O'Connor**, John Joseph 1959- *WhoWest 92*
**O'Connor**, John Joseph, III 1955- *WhoFI 92*
**O'Connor**, John Killeen 1932- *WhoAmL 92*
**O'Connor**, John Paul 1939- *WhoMW 92*
**O'Connor**, John Thomas 1933- *AmMWSc 92*
**O'Connor**, John Thomas 1944- *WhoFI 92*
**O'Connor**, Joseph A., Jr. 1937- *WhoAmL 92*
**O'Connor**, Joseph Michael 1925- *AmMWSc 92*
**O'Connor**, Joseph W 1942- *WhoIns 92*
**O'Connor**, Judith 1936- *WhoAmP 91*
**O'Connor**, Julie Montgomery 1957- *WhoAmL 92*
**O'Connor**, June Elizabeth 1941- *WhoRel 92*
**O'Connor**, Karl William 1931- *WhoAmL 92*
**O'Connor**, Kathleen Lucille 1944- *WhoWest 92*
**O'Connor**, Kevin d1991 *NewYTBS 91*
**O'Connor**, Kevin 1929- *Who 92*
**O'Connor**, Kevin James 1950- *WhoFI 92*
**O'Connor**, Kevin Patrick 1951- *WhoAmL 92*
**O'Connor**, Kevin Thomas 1950- *WhoWest 92*
**O'Connor**, Laurence P *WhoIns 92*
**O'Connor**, Lawrence Joseph, Jr. 1914- *WhoFI 92*
**O'Connor**, Lila Hunt 1936- *AmMWSc 92*
**O'Connor**, Marcel 1958- *TwCPaSc*
**O'Connor**, Margaret 1927- *WhoAmP 91*
**O'Connor**, Mary 1947- *ConAu 133*
**O'Connor**, Mary Beth *DrAPF 91*
**O'Connor**, Mary Patricia 1937- *WhoAmP 91*
**O'Connor**, Matthew James 1940- *AmMWSc 92*
**O'Connor**, Maureen 1946- *WhoWest 92*
**O'Connor**, Maureen Frances 1946- *WhoAmP 91*
**O'Connor**, Michael *Who 92, WhoAmP 91*
**O'Connor**, Michael 1944- *TwCPaSc*
**O'Connor**, Michael Arthur 1953- *WhoEnt 92*
**O'Connor**, Michael Gerard 1949- *WhoAmP 91*
**O'Connor**, Michael John 1946- *WhoFI 92*
**O'Connor**, Michael Joseph 1928- *WhoAmP 91*
**O'Connor**, Michael Kieran 1952- *AmMWSc 92, WhoMW 92*
**O'Connor**, Michael L 1938- *AmMWSc 92*
**O'Connor**, Michael Patrick *DrAPF 91*
**O'Connor**, Michael Patrick 1950- *WhoRel 92*

**O'Connor,** Nancy Morrison 1951- *WhoAmL 92*
**O'Connor,** Pat *IntMPA 92*
**O'Connor,** Patricia W. 1931- *WrDr 92*
**O'Connor,** Patrick 1925- *WhoEnt 92*
**O'Connor,** Patrick J 1954- *WhoAmP 91*
**O'Connor,** Patrick Joseph 1914- *Who 92*
**O'Connor,** Patrick Lyman 1956- *WhoAmP 91*
**O'Connor,** Patrick McCarthy 1914- *Who 92*
**O'Connor,** Philip F *DrAPF 91*
**O'Connor,** Raymond G. 1915- *WrDr 92*
**O'Connor,** Raymond James 1926- *IntWW 91*
**O'Connor,** Raymond Vincent, Jr. 1951- *WhoAmL 92*
**O'Connor,** Richard 1954- *WhoEnt 92*
**O'Connor,** Richard Dennis 1937- *WhoAmL 92*
**O'Connor,** Richard Donald 1931- *WhoFI 92*
**O'Connor,** Richard M 1953- *WhoAmP 91*
**O'Connor,** Robert Emmett 1945- *WhoAmP 91*
**O'Connor,** Rod 1934- *AmMWSc 92*
**O'Connor,** Rodney Earl 1950- *WhoBlA 92*
**O'Connor,** Rory 1925- *Who 92*
**O'Connor,** Ruth Elkinton 1927- *WhoWest 92*
**O'Connor,** Sandra Ann 1943- *WhoAmP 91*
**O'Connor,** Sandra Day 1930- *AmPolLe [port], FacFETw [port], IntWW 91, News 91 [port], RComAH, Who 92, WhoAmL 92, WhoAmP 91*
**O'Connor,** Sean Lenane 1955- *WhoFI 92*
**O'Connor,** Sinead 1966- *CurBio 91 [port]*
**O'Connor,** Stephen *DrAPF 91*
**O'Connor,** Sylvia Cannon 1934- *WhoMW 92*
**O'Connor,** Terrence John 1936- *WhoMW 92*
**O'Connor,** Terry Areatus 1945- *WhoMW 92*
**O'Connor,** Thomas F., Jr. 1947- *WhoBlA 92*
**O'Connor,** Thomas J. 1950- *WhoMW 92*
**O'Connor,** Thomas P 1944- *WhoIns 92*
**O'Connor,** Thomas Patrick 1944- *WhoFI 92*
**O'Connor,** Timothy Charles 1945- *WhoMW 92*
**O'Connor,** Timothy Edmond 1925- *AmMWSc 92*
**O'Connor,** Timothy J, Jr *WhoAmP 91*
**O'Connor,** William Brian 1940- *AmMWSc 92*
**O'Connor,** William Douglas 1832-1889 *BenetAL 91*
**O'Connor,** William E. 1922- *WrDr 92*
**O'Connor,** William F. *WhoFI 92*
**O'Connor,** William Matthew 1955- *WhoAmL 92*
**O'Connor,** William Michael 1942- *WhoWest 92*
**O'Connor,** William Michael 1947- *WhoFI 92, WhoMW 92*
**O'Connor,** William Stewart 1953- *WhoWest 92*
**O'Connor Fraser,** Susan Lee 1954- *WhoEnt 92*
**O'Connor Howe,** Josephine Mary 1924- *Who 92*
**O'Conor,** Roderic 1860-1940 *TwCPaSc*
**O'Conor,** Vincent John, Jr 1927- *AmMWSc 92*
**Ocque,** James Peter 1937- *WhoAmP 91*
**Octavia** d12BC *EncAmaz 91*
**Oda,** Beth Brown 1953- *IntAu&W 91*
**Oda,** Margaret Yuriko 1925- *WhoWest 92*
**Oda,** Randy Keith 1953- *WhoEnt 92*
**Oda,** Shigeru 1924- *IntWW 91*
**Oda,** Yoshio 1933- *WhoWest 92*
**Odaga,** Asenath 1938- *IntAu&W 91, SmATA 67 [port], WrDr 92*
**O Dalaigh,** Cearbhall 1911-1978 *FacFETw*
**O'Daly,** Lawrence Patrick 1936- *WhoEnt 92*
**Odam,** Joyce *DrAPF 91*
**O'Daniel,** Ed. Jr 1938- *WhoAmP 91*
**O'Daniel,** Janet *IntAu&W 91, WrDr 92*
**O'Daniel,** Therman B. 1908-1986 *ConAu 133*
**O'Daniel,** Therman Benjamin 1908-1986 *WhoBlA 92N*
**O'Daniel,** William L 1923- *WhoAmP 91*
**Odar,** Fuat 1934- *AmMWSc 92*
**Odasz,** F B, Jr 1922- *AmMWSc 92*
**O'Day,** Anita 1919- *NewAmDM*
**O'Day,** Anita Belle Colton 1919- *WhoEnt 92*
**O'Day,** Danton Harry 1946- *AmMWSc 92*
**O'Day,** Joseph F *WhoAmP 91*
**O'Day,** Molly 1923- *NewAmDM*
**O'Day,** Paul Thomas 1935- *WhoFI 92*
**Odd,** Gilbert 1902- *IntAu&W 91, WrDr 92*
**Oddi,** Marcia Jeanne 1941- *WhoAmL 92*
**Oddi,** Silvio 1910- *IntWW 91, WhoRel 92*
**Oddie,** Christopher Ripley 1929- *Who 92*
**Oddie,** Guy Barrie 1922- *Who 92*
**Oddis,** Joseph Anthony 1928- *AmMWSc 92*
**Oddis,** Leroy 1931- *AmMWSc 92*
**Oddone,** Piermaria Jorge 1944- *AmMWSc 92*
**Oddson,** John Keith 1935- *AmMWSc 92*
**Oddy,** Christine Margaret 1955- *Who 92*
**Oddy,** Revel 1922- *Who 92*
**Oddy,** William Andrew 1942- *Who 92*
**Ode,** Philip E 1935- *AmMWSc 92*
**Ode,** Richard Herman 1941- *AmMWSc 92*
**O'Dea,** Constance Louise 1948- *WhoFI 92*
**O'Dea,** Daniel Joseph 1949- *WhoFI 92*
**O'Dea,** Gail Ann 1954- *WhoEnt 92*
**O'Dea,** John 1965- *WhoAmP 91*
**O'Dea,** Patrick Jerad 1918- *Who 92*
**O'Dea,** Robert Francis *AmMWSc 92*
**Odegaard,** Charles 1911- *IntWW 91*
**Odegaard,** Charles E 1911- *AmMWSc 92*
**Odegaard,** Gary Martin 1940- *WhoAmP 91*
**Odegard,** Cindy Millard 1965- *WhoWest 92*
**Odegard,** Kevin Kerrick 1950- *WhoEnt 92*
**Odegard,** Mark Erie 1940- *WhoWest 92*
**Odeh,** A S 1925- *AmMWSc 92*
**Odeh,** Farouk M *AmMWSc 92*
**Odeh,** Robert Eugene 1930- *AmMWSc 92*
**Odekirk,** Bruce 1951- *WhoWest 92*
**Odell,** Alexandra Robinson 1947- *WhoWest 92*
**Odell,** Andrew Paul 1949- *AmMWSc 92*
**O'Dell,** Austin Almond, Jr 1933- *AmMWSc 92*
**O'Dell,** Boyd Lee 1916- *AmMWSc 92*
**O'Dell,** Charles Robert 1937- *AmMWSc 92*
**Odell,** Daniel Keith 1945- *AmMWSc 92*
**O'Dell,** David *DrAPF 91*
**Odell,** Donald Austin 1925- *WhoFI 92*
**Odell,** George Van, Jr *AmMWSc 92*
**Odell,** Herbert 1937- *WhoAmL 92*
**Odell,** James Alexander 1841-1930 *DcNCBi 4*
**O'Dell,** Jean Marland 1931- *AmMWSc 92*
**O'Dell,** Joan Elizabeth 1932- *WhoAmL 92*
**Odell,** John H. 1955- *WhoWest 92*
**Odell,** John Milton 1831-1910 *DcNCBi 4*
**Odell,** John William *Who 92*
**Odell,** Jonathan 1737-1818 *BenetAL 91*
**O'Dell,** June Patricia 1929- *Who 92*
**Odell,** Leonard C. d1991 *NewYTBS 91*
**Odell,** Leonard E 1945- *WhoIns 92*
**Odell,** Lois Dorothea 1915- *AmMWSc 92*
**O'Dell,** Lynn Marie Luegge 1938- *WhoMW 92*
**O'Dell,** Michael Lynn 1951- *WhoMW 92*
**Odell,** Norman Raymond 1927- *AmMWSc 92*
**Odell,** Patrick L 1930- *AmMWSc 92*
**Odell,** Peter R. 1930- *WrDr 92*
**Odell,** Peter Randon 1930- *IntAu&W 91, Who 92*
**O'Dell,** Ralph Douglas 1938- *AmMWSc 92*
**Odell,** Richard *WhoAmP 91*
**O'Dell,** Richard L. 1949- *WhoEnt 92*
**Odell,** Robert P, Jr 1943- *WhoAmP 91*
**Odell,** Robin Ian 1935- *IntAu&W 91, WrDr 92*
**Odell,** Stanley 1929- *Who 92*
**Odell,** Stuart Irwin 1940- *WhoAmL 92*
**O'Dell,** Thomas Beniah 1920- *AmMWSc 92*
**Odell,** Thomas Edwin 1953- *WhoMW 92*
**Odell,** Trevor Arthur 1954- *WhoEnt 92*
**O'Dell,** William H 1938- *WhoAmP 91*
**Odell Hodgson,** Luis E. 1912- *DcEcMov*
**O'Dell Smith,** Roberta Maxine 1930- *AmMWSc 92*
**Odelola,** Amos Oyetunji 1927- *IntWW 91*
**Oden,** Gloria *DrAPF 91*
**Oden,** Gloria C. 1923- *WhoBlA 92*
**Oden,** Jean Phifer 1936- *WhoMW 92*
**Oden,** John Tinsley 1936- *AmMWSc 92*
**Oden,** Kelly Michelle 1965- *WhoWest 92*
**Oden,** Peter Howland 1933- *AmMWSc 92*
**Oden,** Walter Eugene 1935- *WhoBlA 92*
**Oden,** William Bryant 1935- *WhoRel 92*
**Oden,** William Evert 1944- *WhoWest 92*
**Odencrantz,** Frederick Kirk 1921- *AmMWSc 92*
**Odenheimer,** Kurt John Sigmund 1911- *AmMWSc 92*
**Odense,** Paul Holger 1926- *AmMWSc 92*
**Oder,** Frederic Carl Emil 1919- *AmMWSc 92*
**Oder,** Robin Roy 1934- *AmMWSc 92*
**Oderman,** Stuart Douglas 1940- *WhoEnt 92*
**Odermatt,** Bruno George 1956- *WhoIns 92*
**Odermatt,** Robert Allen 1938- *WhoWest 92*
**Odescalchi,** Edmond Pery 1928- *WhoFI 92*
**Odesky,** Stanford H. 1937- *WhoMW 92*
**Odesser,** Rochelle 1951- *WhoFI 92*
**Odets,** Clifford 1906-1963 *BenetAL 91, FacFETw*
**Odetta** 1930- *ConMus 7 [port], NewAmDM, NotBlAW 92*
**Odette,** G Robert 1943- *AmMWSc 92*
**Odgers,** Christopher Reynold 1955- *WhoWest 92*
**Odgers,** Graeme David William 1934- *IntWW 91, Who 92*
**Odgers,** Paul Randell 1915- *Who 92*
**Odgers,** Richard William 1936- *WhoAmL 92, WhoFI 92*
**Odhams Limited** *DcLB 112*
**Odhams,** William *DcLB 112 [port]*
**Odian,** George G 1933- *AmMWSc 92*
**Odijk,** Pamela Agnes 1942- *IntAu&W 91*
**Odinet,** Kenneth L 1930- *WhoAmP 91*
**Odinga,** A. Oginga 1911- *IntWW 91*
**Odio,** Cesar H. *WhoHisp 92*
**Odio,** Eunice 1922-1974 *SpAmWW*
**Odiorne,** George Stanley 1920- *WhoFI 92*
**Odiorne,** Thomas 1769-1851 *BenetAL 91*
**Odiorne,** Truman J 1944- *AmMWSc 92*
**Odioso,** Raymond C 1923- *AmMWSc 92*
**Odland,** George Fisher 1922- *AmMWSc 92*
**Odland,** Paul Kenneth 1922- *WhoMW 92*
**Odle,** E V *ScFEYrs*
**Odle,** John William 1914- *AmMWSc 92*
**Odle,** Robert C, Jr 1944- *WhoAmP 91*
**Odle,** Robert Charles, Jr. 1944- *WhoAmL 92*
**Odling,** Thomas George 1911- *Who 92*
**Odling,** William 1909- *Who 92*
**Odling-Smee,** John Charles 1943- *Who 92*
**Odo,** Nadine Akemi 1963- *WhoWest 92*
**Odoacer** 434?-493 *EncEarC*
**O'Doherty,** Desmond Sylvester 1920- *AmMWSc 92*
**O'Doherty,** Eamonn 1918- *WrDr 92*
**O'Doherty,** George Oliver-Plunkett 1936- *AmMWSc 92*
**O'Doherty,** Kieran E. d1991 *NewYTBS 91*
**Odol,** Marilyn Elaine 1941- *WhoFI 92*
**Odom,** Carolyn 1944- *WhoBlA 92*
**Odom,** Cliff Louis 1958- *WhoBlA 92*
**Odom,** Darryl Eugene 1955- *WhoBlA 92*
**Odom,** David Russell 1950- *WhoRel 92*
**Odom,** Gary 1951- *WhoAmP 91*
**Odom,** George Cosby, Jr. 1922- *WhoRel 92*
**Odom,** Guy Leary 1911- *AmMWSc 92*
**Odom,** Homer Clyde, Jr 1942- *AmMWSc 92*
**Odom,** Ira Edgar 1932- *AmMWSc 92*
**Odom,** Jerome David 1942- *AmMWSc 92*
**Odom,** Kenneth Keith 1952- *WhoMW 92*
**Odom,** Linda Christine 1953- *WhoMW 92*
**Odom,** Robert, Jr. 1951- *WhoEnt 92*
**Odom,** Robert Fulton, Jr 1935- *WhoAmP 91*
**Odom,** Stonewall, II 1940- *WhoBlA 92*
**Odom,** Thomas LaFontine 1938- *WhoAmP 91*
**Odom,** Vernon Lane, Jr. 1948- *WhoBlA 92*
**Odom,** William E. 1936- *WhoMW 92*
**Odom,** William Eldridge 1932- *WhoAmP 91*
**Odom-Groh,** Larry Lea 1942- *WhoRel 92*
**Odomes,** Nathaniel Bernard 1965- *WhoBlA 92*
**O'Domirok,** Thomas Darrell 1955- *WhoEnt 92*
**Odoms,** Willie O. 1950- *WhoBlA 92*
**O'Donaghue,** Hughie 1953- *TwCPaSc*
**O'Donnell,** Allen 1931- *WhoAmP 91*
**O'Donnell,** Ashton Jay 1921- *AmMWSc 92*
**O'Donnell,** Augustine Thomas 1952- *IntWW 91, Who 92*
**O'Donnell,** Barry 1926- *Who 92*
**O'Donnell,** Bernard 1929-1983 *ConAu 133*
**O'Donnell,** Bill *WhoAmP 91*
**O'Donnell,** C F 1920- *AmMWSc 92*
**O'Donnell,** Christopher John 1940- *WhoMW 92*
**O'Donnell,** Cletus Francis 1917- *WhoRel 92*
**O'Donnell,** Clifford Robert 1939- *WhoWest 92*
**O'Donnell,** David Daniel 1941- *WhoWest 92*
**O'Donnell,** Donat *IntAu&W 91X*
**O'Donnell,** Edward 1938- *AmMWSc 92*
**O'Donnell,** Edward Francis, Jr. 1950- *WhoAmL 92*
**O'Donnell,** Edward J. d1991 *NewYTBS 91 [port]*
**O'Donnell,** Edward Joseph 1931- *WhoRel 92*
**O'Donnell,** Frank W 1922- *WhoAmP 91*
**O'Donnell,** James Anthony 1961- *Who 92*
**O'Donnell,** James Edward 1953- *WhoMW 92*
**O'Donnell,** James Francis 1928- *AmMWSc 92*
**O'Donnell,** James Howlett, III 1937- *WhoMW 92*
**O'Donnell,** James Maurice 1948- *WhoFI 92*
**O'Donnell,** James Vincent 1941- *WhoFI 92*
**O'Donnell,** John C. *WhoEnt 92*
**O'Donnell,** John Lawrence 1950- *WhoAmL 92*
**O'Donnell,** John Logan 1914- *WhoAmL 92*
**O'Donnell,** John Michael 1945- *WhoAmL 92*
**O'Donnell,** Joseph Allen, III 1947- *AmMWSc 92*
**O'Donnell,** Joseph Michael 1944- *WhoFI 92*
**O'Donnell,** Joseph Michael 1946- *WhoFI 92*
**O'Donnell,** K.M. *TwCSFW 91, WrDr 92*
**O'Donnell,** Kathleen 1949- *WhoAmP 91*
**O'Donnell,** Kevin 1925- *WhoFI 92*
**O'Donnell,** Kevin, Jr 1950- *IntAu&W 91, TwCSFW 91, WrDr 92*
**O'Donnell,** Lawrence, III 1957- *WhoAmL 92*
**O'Donnell,** Lawrence Allen 1952- *WhoFI 92*
**O'Donnell,** Lillian 1920- *IntAu&W 91*
**O'Donnell,** Lillian 1926- *WrDr 92*
**O'Donnell,** Lorena Mae 1929- *WhoBlA 92*
**O'Donnell,** Loretta Mary 1955- *WhoMW 92*
**O'Donnell,** M. R. *WrDr 92*
**O'Donnell,** Mark Joseph 1954- *WhoMW 92*
**O'Donnell,** Mark Patrick 1954- *WhoEnt 92*
**O'Donnell,** Martin James 1946- *AmMWSc 92*
**O'Donnell,** Martin Thomas 1967- *WhoWest 92*
**O'Donnell,** Michael 1928- *IntAu&W 91, Who 92*
**O'Donnell,** Michael James 1960- *WhoWest 92*
**O'Donnell,** Michael Joseph 1946- *WhoMW 92*
**O'Donnell,** Michael Paul 1956- *WhoFI 92*
**O'Donnell,** Michael Robert 1956- *WhoAmL 92*
**O'Donnell,** Neil Taney 1961- *WhoAmL 92*
**O'Donnell,** Patricia *DrAPF 91*
**O'Donnell,** Patrick Emmett 1937- *WhoAmP 91*
**O'Donnell,** Peadar 1893-1986 *ConAu 135, FacFETw*
**O'Donnell,** Peter 1920- *IntAu&W 91, WrDr 92*
**O'Donnell,** Peter Sean 1949- *WhoFI 92*
**O'Donnell,** Priscilla Sue 1937- *WhoAmL 92*
**O'Donnell,** Raymond Thomas 1931- *AmMWSc 92*
**O'Donnell,** Robert John 1943- *WhoAmL 92*
**O'Donnell,** Robert Patrick 1919- *WhoRel 92*
**O'Donnell,** Robert Paul 1959- *WhoMW 92*
**O'Donnell,** Robert W 1943- *WhoAmP 91*
**O'Donnell,** Ron 1952- *TwCPaSc*
**O'Donnell,** Sally Maria 1956- *WhoHisp 92*
**O'Donnell,** Terence J 1951- *AmMWSc 92*
**O'Donnell,** Terrence 1944- *WhoAmL 92*
**O'Donnell,** Thomas H. 1943- *WhoFI 92*
**O'Donnell,** Thomas Joseph 1918- *WhoRel 92*
**O'Donnell,** Thomas Lawrence Patrick 1926- *WhoAmL 92*
**O'Donnell,** Thomas Mitchell 1936- *WhoFI 92*
**O'Donnell,** Turlough 1924- *Who 92*
**O'Donnell,** William 1951- *WhoAmP 91*
**O'Donnell,** William David 1926- *WhoFI 92, WhoMW 92*
**O'Donnell,** William Thomas 1939- *WhoFI 92, WhoWest 92*
**O'Donoghue,** Aileen Ann 1958- *AmMWSc 92*
**O'Donoghue,** Bernadette 1958- *TwCPaSc*
**O'Donoghue,** John Lipomi 1947- *AmMWSc 92*
**O'Donoghue,** Michael 1929- *Who 92*
**O'Donoghue,** Philip Nicholas 1929- *Who 92*
**O'Donohue,** Cynthia H 1936- *AmMWSc 92*
**O'Donohue,** Daniel A 1931- *WhoAmP 91*
**O'Donovan,** Gerard Anthony 1937- *AmMWSc 92*
**O'Donovan,** Jerome X 1944- *WhoAmP 91*
**O'Donovan,** Joan Mary 1914- *IntAu&W 91, WrDr 92*
**O'Donovan,** Leo Jeremiah 1934- *WhoRel 92*
**O'Donovan,** Oliver Michael Timothy 1945- *Who 92*
**Odor,** David Lee 1943- *AmMWSc 92*
**Odor,** Dorothy Louise 1922- *AmMWSc 92*
**Odor,** Richard Lane 1954- *WhoMW 92*
**Odorizzi,** James Joseph 1947- *WhoFI 92*
**O'Dowd,** Carol W. 1952- *WhoWest 92*
**O'Dowd,** Donald Davy 1927- *WhoWest 92*

**Odrey,** Nicholas Gerald 1942- AmMWSc 92
**O'Driscoll,** Dennis 1954- ConPo 91, WrDr 92
**O'Driscoll,** Gerald P., Jr. 1947- ConAu 133
**O'Driscoll,** Gerald Patrick, Jr. 1947- WhoFI 92
**O'Driscoll,** Kenneth F 1931- AmMWSc 92
**O'Driscoll,** P. R. Who 92
**O'Driscoll,** Robert 1938- ConAu 35NR
**O'Driscoll,** Suzanne 1955- TwCPaSc
**O'Driscoll,** Timothy Joseph 1908- IntWW 91
**Odset,** Joan L IntAu&W 91X
**Oduber,** Nelson O. IntWW 91
**Oduber Quiros,** Daniel 1921- IntWW 91
**O'Duffy,** Eoin 1892-1944 BiDExR
**O Duinn,** Proinnsias 1941- WhoEnt 92
**Odum,** Eugene P. 1913- IntWW 91
**Odum,** Eugene Pleasants 1913- AmMWSc 92
**Odum,** Howard Thomas 1924- AmMWSc 92
**Odum,** Howard Washington 1884-1954 BenetAL 91, DcNCBi 4, FacFETw
**Odum,** William Eugene 1942- AmMWSc 92
**Odunmbaku,** Abiodun Olatunji 1952- WhoFI 92
**Oduyoye,** Mercy Amba 1934- WhoRel 92
**O'Dwyer,** Brian 1945- WhoAmL 92
**O'Dwyer,** John J 1925- AmMWSc 92
**Odya,** Charles E 1947- AmMWSc 92
**Odza,** Randall M. 1942- WhoAmL 92
**Oe,** Kenzaburo 1935- ConAu 36NR, IntWW 91
**Oechel,** Walter C 1945- AmMWSc 92
**Oecumenius** EncEarC
**Oegema,** Theodore Richard, Jr 1945- AmMWSc 92
**Oegerle,** Robin Olin 1952- WhoFI 92
**Oehlberg,** Richard N 1942- AmMWSc 92
**Oehler,** Hans 1888-1967 BiDExR
**Oehler,** Richard Dale 1925- WhoAmL 92
**Oehlers,** Gordon Richard 1933- Who 92
**Oehlke,** Mark Allan 1955- WhoMW 92
**Oehlschlager,** Allan Cameron 1940- AmMWSc 92
**Oehme,** Frederick Wolfgang 1933- AmMWSc 92, WhoMW 92
**Oehme,** Reinhard 1928- AmMWSc 92
**Oehmke,** Richard Wallace 1935- AmMWSc 92
**Oehmke,** Robert H 1927- AmMWSc 92
**Oehmler,** George Courtland 1926- WhoFI 92
**Oehser,** Paul Henry 1904- AmMWSc 92
**Oei,** Djong-Gie 1931- AmMWSc 92
**Oekber,** Norman Fred 1927- AmMWSc 92
**Oekerman,** Michael Allen 1956- WhoAmP 91
**Oelberg,** Thomas Jonathon 1956- AmMWSc 92
**Oelerich,** Francis Joseph, III 1960- WhoFI 92
**Oelfke,** William C 1941- AmMWSc 92
**Oelke,** Ervin Albert 1933- AmMWSc 92
**Oelman,** Michael 1941- TwCPaSc
**Oelman,** Robert Schantz 1909- IntWW 91
**Oels,** Helen C 1931- AmMWSc 92
**Oels,** Thomas William 1951- WhoWest 92
**Oelslager,** W Scott 1953- WhoAmP 91
**Oelssner,** Fred 1903-1977 EncTR 91
**Oemichen,** William Lee 1960- WhoAmL 92, WhoAmP 91, WhoMW 92
**Oen,** Ordean Silas 1927- AmMWSc 92
**Oeripan,** Soegiharto 1963- WhoFI 92
**Oerke,** Andrew DrAPF 91
**Oertel,** Donata 1947- AmMWSc 92
**Oertel,** Gerhard Friedrich 1920- AmMWSc 92
**Oertel,** Goetz K 1934- AmMWSc 92
**Oertel,** Goetz Kuno Heinrich 1934- AmMWSc 92
**Oertel,** Johannes Adam Simon 1823-1909 DcNCBi 4
**Oertel,** Richard Paul 1944- AmMWSc 92
**Oerter,** Al 1936- FacFETw
**Oerter,** Alfred A. 1936- IntWW 91
**Oertley,** Karen Oberlaender 1952- WhoEnt 92
**Oertli,** Johann Jakob 1927- AmMWSc 92
**Oertli-Cajacob,** Peter 1941- WhoFI 92
**Oesper,** Peter 1917- AmMWSc 92
**Oesterle,** Dale Arthur 1950- WhoAmL 92
**Oesterling,** Myrna Jane 1917- AmMWSc 92
**Oesterling,** Thomas O 1938- AmMWSc 92
**Oesterreich,** Roger Edward 1930- AmMWSc 92
**Oesterreicher,** Hans 1939- AmMWSc 92
**Oesterreicher,** John M. 1904- WrDr 92
**Oesterwinter,** Claus 1928- AmMWSc 92
**Oestreich,** Alan Emil 1939- AmMWSc 92
**Oestreich,** Paul Christopher 1963- WhoWest 92
**Oestreicher,** Hans Laurenz 1912- AmMWSc 92
**Oestreicher,** Martha Beatrice 1899- WhoWest 92
**Oestreicher,** Paul 1931- IntWW 91, Who 92
**Oetheimer,** Richard A. 1956- WhoAmL 92
**Oetinger,** David Frederick 1945- AmMWSc 92
**Oetker,** Rudolf-August 1916- IntWW 91
**Oetking,** Philip 1922- AmMWSc 92
**Oetter,** Bruce Christian 1949- WhoAmL 92
**Oettgen,** Herbert Friedrich 1923- AmMWSc 92
**Oetting,** Dave 1951- WhoAmP 91
**Oetting,** Franklin Lee 1930- AmMWSc 92
**Oetting,** Mildred Katherine WhoFI 92
**Oetting,** Richard Fleming 1931- WhoAmL 92
**Oetting,** Robert B 1933- AmMWSc 92
**Oetting,** Roger H. 1931- WhoAmL 92
**Oetting,** William Starr 1955- AmMWSc 92
**Oettinger,** Anthony Gervin 1929- AmMWSc 92
**Oettinger,** Elmer Rosenthal 1913- WhoAmL 92
**Oettinger,** Frank Frederic 1940- AmMWSc 92
**Oettinger,** Julian Alan WhoAmL 92
**Oettinger,** Peter Ernest 1937- AmMWSc 92
**of Mar** Who 92
**O'Fallon,** John Robert 1937- AmMWSc 92
**O'Fallon,** Nancy McCumber 1938- AmMWSc 92
**O'Fallon,** William M 1934- AmMWSc 92
**O'Faolain,** Julia WrDr 92
**O'Faolain,** Julia 1932- ConNov 91, IntAu&W 91
**O'Faolain,** Sean d1991 Who 92N
**O'Faolain,** Sean 1900- IntAu&W 91, IntWW 91, WrDr 92
**O'Faolain,** Sean 1900-1991 ConAu 134, CurBio 91N, FacFETw, NewYTBS 91 [port], RfGEnL 91
**O'Farrell,** Charles Patrick 1937- AmMWSc 92
**O'Farrell,** Michael John 1944- AmMWSc 92
**O'Farrell,** Padraic 1932- WrDr 92
**O'Farrell,** Patrick 1933- WrDr 92
**O'Farrell,** Patrick James 1933- IntAu&W 91, IntWW 91
**O'Farrell,** Thomas Paul 1936- AmMWSc 92
**O'Farrill,** Arturo 1921- WhoEnt 92
**Ofelt,** George Sterling 1937- AmMWSc 92
**Ofengand,** Edward James 1932- AmMWSc 92
**O'Ferral,** Margarita M. 1946- WhoHisp 92
**O'Ferrall,** Anne F. 1906- WhoBlA 92
**O'Ferrall,** Basil Arthur 1924- Who 92
**Offaly,** Earl of 1974- Who 92
**Offen,** George Richard AmMWSc 92
**Offen,** Henry William 1937- AmMWSc 92
**Offen,** Karen 1939- ConAu 34NR
**Offen,** Ron DrAPF 91
**Offen,** Yehuda 1922- IntAu&W 91
**Offenbach,** Jacques 1819-1880 NewAmDM
**Offenbacher,** Elmer Lazard 1923- AmMWSc 92
**Offenberger,** Allan Anthony 1938- AmMWSc 92
**Offenhauer,** Robert Dwight 1918- AmMWSc 92
**Offenhauser,** William H., Jr. 1904- IntMPA 92
**Offenhiser,** Andrew Brewster 1926- WhoMW 92
**Offenkrantz,** William Charles 1924- AmMWSc 92
**Offensend,** David Glenn 1953- WhoFI 92
**Offer,** Daniel 1929- AmMWSc 92
**Offergeld,** Rainer 1937- IntWW 91
**Offerman,** Jose Antonio Dono 1968- WhoHisp 92
**Officer,** Carl Edward 1952- WhoBlA 92
**Officer,** David Adrian 1938- IntWW 91
**Offield,** Terry Watson 1933- AmMWSc 92
**Offit,** Sidney DrAPF 91
**Offler,** Hilary Seton d1991 Who 92N
**Offner,** Franklin Faller 1911- AmMWSc 92
**Offner,** Gwynneth Davies 1955- AmMWSc 92
**Offner,** Halina 1945- WhoWest 92
**Offner,** Paul 1942- WhoAmP 91
**Offner,** Stacy Karen 1955- WhoRel 92
**Offner,** Stuart Addison 1953- WhoAmL 92
**Offodile,** Onyebuchi Felix 1949- WhoMW 92
**Offord,** Albert Cyril 1906- IntWW 91, Who 92
**Offord,** David Robert 1933- AmMWSc 92
**Offroy,** Raymond 1909- IntWW 91
**Offsey,** Sol DrAPF 91
**Offutt,** Andrew J IntAu&W 91
**Offutt,** Andrew J 1934?- TwCSFW 91, WrDr 92
**Offutt,** Narda Julie 1948- WhoBlA 92
**Offutt,** William Franklin 1919- AmMWSc 92
**O'Fiaich,** Tomas 1923-1990 AnObit 1990, FacFETw
**Ofiesh,** Abdullah 1880-1971 RelLAm 91
**Ofisa,** Asoau 1907- WhoAmP 91
**O'Flaherty,** Coleman Anthony 1933- Who 92
**O'Flaherty,** Edward Martin 1934- WhoRel 92
**O'Flaherty,** James Carneal 1914- WrDr 92
**O'Flaherty,** Larrance Michael Arthur 1941- AmMWSc 92
**O'Flaherty,** Liam 1896-1984 ConAu 35NR, LiExTwC, RfGEnL 91
**O'Flaherty,** Liam 1897-1984 FacFETw
**O'Flarity,** James P. 1923- WhoAmL 92
**O'Flinn,** Peter Russell 1953- WhoAmL 92
**O'Flynn,** Francis Duncan 1918- IntWW 91, Who 92
**O'Flynn,** Patrick S. 1934- WhoMW 92
**O'Flynn-Thomas,** Patricia 1939- WhoBlA 92
**Ofman,** Jose Omar 1943- WhoHisp 92
**Ofner,** Harald 1932- IntWW 91
**Ofner,** James Alan 1922- WhoFI 92
**Ofner,** Peter 1923- AmMWSc 92
**Ofner,** William Bernard 1929- WhoAmL 92, WhoFI 92
**Ofodile,** Ferdinand Azikiwe 1941- WhoBlA 92
**O'Foghludha,** Fearghus Tadhg 1927- AmMWSc 92
**Ofstead,** Eilert A 1934- AmMWSc 92
**Ofte,** Donald 1929- WhoWest 92
**Oftedahl,** Marvin Loren 1931- AmMWSc 92, WhoMW 92
**Ofverholm,** Stefan 1936- WhoFI 92
**Ogaki,** Masao 1958- WhoFI 92
**O'Gallagher,** Joseph James 1939- AmMWSc 92, WhoMW 92
**Oganesoff,** Igor Michael 1924- WhoEnt 92
**Ogar,** George W 1918- AmMWSc 92
**O'Gara,** Bartholomew Willis 1923- AmMWSc 92
**O'Gara,** William B WhoAmP 91
**Ogard,** Allen E 1931- AmMWSc 92
**Ogarkov,** Nikolay Vasil'evich 1917- SovUnBD
**Ogarkov,** Nikolay Vasiliyevich 1917- IntWW 91
**Ogasawara,** Frank X 1913- AmMWSc 92
**Ogata,** Akio 1927- AmMWSc 92
**Ogata,** Hisashi 1926- AmMWSc 92
**Ogata,** Katsuhiko 1925- AmMWSc 92
**Ogata,** Sadako IntWW 91
**Ogata,** Shijuro 1927- IntWW 91
**Ogawa,** Dennis 1943- WrDr 92
**Ogawa,** Hajimu 1931- AmMWSc 92
**Ogawa,** Heiji 1910- IntWW 91
**Ogawa,** Heishiro 1916- IntWW 91
**Ogawa,** Joseph Minoru 1925- AmMWSc 92
**Ogawa,** Masaru 1915- IntAu&W 91
**Ogawa,** Osamu 1945- WhoFI 92
**Ogawa,** Pelorhankhe Al DrAPF 91
**Ogawara,** Saburo 1931- IntWW 91
**Ogborn,** Lawrence L 1932- AmMWSc 92
**Ogborn,** Michael James 1947- WhoAmL 92, WhoWest 92
**Ogburn,** Charlton 1911- IntAu&W 91, WrDr 92
**Ogburn,** Clifton Alfred 1930- AmMWSc 92
**Ogburn,** Derial L 1949- WhoAmP 91
**Ogburn,** Phillip Nash 1940- AmMWSc 92
**Ogburn,** Roy 1942- WhoAmP 91
**Ogden,** C Robert 1923- WhoIns 92
**Ogden,** Charles Kay 1889-1957 BiDBrF 2
**Ogden,** Chester Robert 1923- WhoFI 92
**Ogden,** Chris 1945- ConAu 133
**Ogden,** Clint TwCWW 91
**Ogden,** David Anderson 1931- AmMWSc 92
**Ogden,** Dunbar Hunt 1935- WhoWest 92
**Ogden,** Edward Michael 1926- Who 92
**Ogden,** Eric 1923- Who 92
**Ogden,** Eva L ScFEYrs
**Ogden,** Geoff 1929- TwCPaSc
**Ogden,** Herbert Gouverneur 1846-1906 BiInAmS
**Ogden,** Ingram Wesley 1920- AmMWSc 92
**Ogden,** James Gordon, III 1928- AmMWSc 92
**Ogden,** Jean Lucille 1950- WhoWest 92
**Ogden,** Joanne 1941- WhoFI 92
**Ogden,** John Conrad 1940- AmMWSc 92
**Ogden,** John Hamilton 1951- WhoAmL 92
**Ogden,** Joseph Patrick 1956- WhoFI 92
**Ogden,** Lawrence 1919- AmMWSc 92
**Ogden,** Mark Clair 1956- WhoEnt 92
**Ogden,** Maureen B 1928- WhoAmP 91
**Ogden,** Michael Who 92
**Ogden,** Myron Waldo 1917- WhoWest 92
**Ogden,** Philip Myron 1938- AmMWSc 92
**Ogden,** Robert Newton 1952- WhoFI 92
**Ogden,** Robert Schuyler 1934- WhoAmL 92
**Ogden,** Robert Verl 1938- AmMWSc 92
**Ogden,** Schubert Miles 1928- WhoRel 92
**Ogden,** Steve 1950- WhoAmP 91
**Ogden,** Thomas E 1929- AmMWSc 92
**Ogden,** Tom 1951- WhoEnt 92
**Ogden,** Valeria M 1924- WhoAmP 91
**Ogden,** W. Edwin 1947- WhoAmL 92
**Ogden,** William Frederick 1942- AmMWSc 92
**Ogdon,** John 1937-1989 FacFETw, NewAmDM
**Ogdon,** Will 1921- NewAmDM
**Ogdon,** William D. d1991 NewYTBS 91 [port]
**Ogesen,** Robert Bruce 1934- WhoMW 92
**Ogg,** Alan WhoBlA 92
**Ogg,** Alex Grant, Jr 1941- AmMWSc 92
**Ogg,** Frank Chappell, Jr 1930- AmMWSc 92
**Ogg,** Jack Clyde 1933- WhoAmP 91
**Ogg,** James Elvis 1924- AmMWSc 92
**Ogg,** Wilson Reid 1928- WhoAmL 92, WhoFI 92, WhoWest 92
**Ogi,** Adolf 1942- IntWW 91
**Ogida,** Mikio 1938- WhoRel 92
**Ogier,** Walter Thomas 1925- AmMWSc 92
**Ogilby,** Peter Remsen 1955- AmMWSc 92
**Ogilvie,** Lady d1990 Who 92N
**Ogilvie,** Alec 1913- Who 92
**Ogilvie,** Bridget Margaret 1938- Who 92
**Ogilvie,** Bruce Campbell 1944- WhoFI 92, WhoMW 92
**Ogilvie,** Donald Gordon 1943- WhoFI 92
**Ogilvie,** Elisabeth 1917- WrDr 92
**Ogilvie,** Elizabeth 1917- IntAu&W 91
**Ogilvie,** Elizabeth 1946- TwCPaSc
**Ogilvie,** James 1775-1820 BenetAL 91
**Ogilvie,** James Louis 1929- AmMWSc 92
**Ogilvie,** James William, Jr 1925- AmMWSc 92
**Ogilvie,** Keith W 1926- AmMWSc 92
**Ogilvie,** Kelvin Kenneth 1942- AmMWSc 92
**Ogilvie,** Lloyd John 1930- WhoRel 92
**Ogilvie,** Marilyn Bailey 1936- AmMWSc 92
**Ogilvie,** Marvin Lee 1935- AmMWSc 92
**Ogilvie,** Richard Ian 1936- AmMWSc 92
**Ogilvie,** Robert Edward 1923- AmMWSc 92
**Ogilvie,** T Francis 1929- AmMWSc 92
**Ogilvie-Grant** Who 92
**Ogilvie-Laing of Kinkell,** Gerald 1936- Who 92
**Ogilvie Thompson,** Julian 1934- IntWW 91, Who 92
**Ogilvy** Who 92
**Ogilvy,** Lord 1958- Who 92
**Ogilvy,** Alexandra 1936- IntWW 91
**Ogilvy,** Angus 1928- Who 92
**Ogilvy,** C. Stanley 1913- WrDr 92
**Ogilvy,** David 1914- Who 92
**Ogilvy,** David Mackenzie 1911- IntWW 91, Who 92
**Ogilvy,** David Wallace 1945- WhoFI 92
**Ogilvy,** Winston Stowell 1918- AmMWSc 92
**Ogilvy-Wedderburn,** Andrew John Alexander 1952- Who 92
**Ogimachi,** Naomi Neil 1925- AmMWSc 92
**Oginsky,** Evelyn Lenore 1919- AmMWSc 92
**Ogle,** Alice Nichols 1925- WhoAmP 91
**Ogle,** Andrew Austin 1970- WhoEnt 92
**Ogle,** James D 1920- AmMWSc 92
**Ogle,** Pearl Rexford, Jr 1928- AmMWSc 92
**Ogle,** Robert Earl 1949- WhoFI 92
**Ogle,** Robert Joseph 1957- WhoAmL 92
**Ogle,** Thomas Frank 1942- AmMWSc 92
**Ogle,** Wayne LeRoy 1922- AmMWSc 92
**Ogle-Skan,** Peter Henry 1915- Who 92
**Oglesby,** Clarkson Hill 1908- AmMWSc 92
**Oglesby,** David Berger 1941- AmMWSc 92
**Oglesby,** Dennis Michael, Jr. 1960- WhoMW 92
**Oglesby,** Gayle Arden 1925- AmMWSc 92
**Oglesby,** James Robert 1941- WhoBlA 92
**Oglesby,** Joe 1947- WhoBlA 92
**Oglesby,** Larry Calmer 1936- AmMWSc 92
**Oglesby,** Mira-Lani DrAPF 91
**Oglesby,** Peter Rogerson 1922- Who 92
**Oglesby,** Ray Thurmond 1932- AmMWSc 92
**Oglesby,** Richard James, IV 1947- WhoWest 92
**Oglesby,** Sabert, Jr 1921- AmMWSc 92
**Oglesby,** Tony B. 1954- WhoBlA 92
**Oglesby,** Wendy Carol 1956- WhoEnt 92
**Oglethorpe,** James Edward 1696-1785 BenetAL 91
**Ogletree,** Charles J., Jr. 1952- WhoBlA 92

**Ogletree**, Thomas Warren 1933- *IntAu&W 91, WrDr 92*
**Ogletree-Bolden**, Yvonne Theresa 1955- *WhoEnt 92*
**Ogliaruso**, Michael Anthony 1938- *AmMWSc 92*
**Oglivie**, Benjamin A. 1949- *WhoBlA 92*
**Ogmore**, Baron 1931- *Who 92*
**Ognall**, Harry Henry 1934- *Who 92*
**O'Gorman**, Brian Stapleton d1991 *Who 92N*
**O'Gorman**, Frank 1940- *WrDr 92*
**O'Gorman**, James 1959- *AmMWSc 92*
**O'Gorman**, Leary 1948- *WhoWest 92*
**O'Gorman**, Ned *DrAPF 91*
**O'Gorman**, Ned 1929- *ConPo 91, IntAu&W 91, WrDr 92*
**O'Gorman**, Patricia Ann 1946- *WhoAmL 92*
**Ogra**, Pearay L *AmMWSc 92*
**O'Grady**, Dennis Joseph 1943- *WhoAmL 92*
**O'Grady**, Desmond 1935- *ConPo 91, WrDr 92*
**O'Grady**, Desmond James Bernard 1935- *IntAu&W 91*
**O'Grady**, Francis William 1925- *Who 92*
**O'Grady**, James John 1936- *WhoMW 92*
**O'Grady**, James Patrick 1936- *WhoAmL 92, WhoMW 92*
**O'Grady**, John Francis *WhoRel 92*
**O'Grady**, John Joseph, III 1933- *WhoAmL 92*
**O'Grady**, Richard Terence 1956- *AmMWSc 92*
**O'Grady**, Rohan 1922- *IntAu&W 91, WrDr 92*
**O'Grady**, Thomas Francis 1946- *WhoFI 92*
**O'Grady**, Thomas James 1942- *WhoAmL 92*
**O'Grady**, Tom *DrAPF 91*
**O'Grady**, Tom 1943- *IntAu&W 91*
**O'Grady**, Walter John 1926- *WhoAmP 91*
**O'Grady**, William Edward 1939- *AmMWSc 92*
**Ogrean**, David William 1953- *WhoWest 92*
**O'Green**, Frederick W. 1921- *IntWW 91*
**O'Green**, Frederick Wilbert 1921- *WhoWest 92*
**Ogren**, David Ernest 1930- *AmMWSc 92*
**Ogren**, Harold O. 1943- *WhoMW 92*
**Ogren**, Harold Olof 1943- *AmMWSc 92*
**Ogren**, Herman August 1925- *AmMWSc 92*
**Ogren**, Paul Anders 1951- *WhoAmP 91*
**Ogren**, Paul Joseph 1941- *AmMWSc 92*
**Ogren**, Robert Edward 1922- *AmMWSc 92*
**Ogren**, William Lewis 1938- *AmMWSc 92*
**Ogris**, Werner 1935- *IntWW 91*
**O'Grodnick**, Joseph Stanley 1945- *WhoFI 92*
**Ogryzlo**, Elmer Alexander 1933- *AmMWSc 92*
**Ogston**, Alexander George 1911- *IntWW 91, Who 92*
**Ogston**, Derek 1932- *Who 92*
**O'Guin**, Christopher Dwayne 1954- *WhoAmP 91*
**Ogunnaike**, Babatunde Ayodeji 1956- *AmMWSc 92*
**Ogura**, Joseph H 1915- *AmMWSc 92*
**Ogura**, Takekazu 1910- *IntWW 91*
**Oh**, Byungdu 1958- *AmMWSc 92*
**Oh**, Chan Soo 1938- *AmMWSc 92*
**Oh**, Hilario Lim 1936- *AmMWSc 92*
**Oh**, Jang Ok 1927- *AmMWSc 92, WhoWest 92*
**Oh**, Matthew InSoo 1938- *WhoAmL 92, WhoMW 92*
**Oh**, May Buong Yu Lau 1940- *WhoFI 92*
**Oh**, Se Jeung 1935- *AmMWSc 92*
**Oh**, Shin Joong 1936- *AmMWSc 92*
**Oh**, Soon-Teck 1933- *WhoEnt 92*
**Oh**, Tai Keun 1934- *WhoFI 92*
**Oh**, William 1931- *AmMWSc 92*
**O'Hagan**, Baron 1945- *Who 92*
**O'Hagan**, Desmond 1909- *Who 92*
**O'Hagan**, Howard 1902-1982 *BenetAL 91*
**O'Hagan**, Joan *WrDr 92*
**O'Hagan**, John T. 1925-1991 *NewYTBS 91 [port]*
**O'Hagan**, William Gordon 1943- *WhoWest 92*
**O'Hagin-Estrada**, Isabel Barbara 1954- *WhoHisp 92*
**O'Hair**, Madalyn Mays Murray 1919- *RelLAm 91*
**O'Hali**, Abdulaziz A. 1937- *IntWW 91*
**O'Hallion**, Sheila *ConAu 135*
**O'Halloran**, Charles 1924- *Who 92*
**O'Halloran**, Michael 1947- *WhoIns 92*
**O'Halloran**, Michael Joseph 1933- *Who 92*
**O'Halloran**, Shawn Patrick 1958- *WhoFI 92*
**O'Halloran**, Thomas A 1931- *AmMWSc 92*
**O'Halloran**, Thomas Alphonsus, Jr. 1931- *WhoMW 92*
**Ohana**, Maurice 1914- *ConCom 92, NewAmDM*
**Ohanian**, Hans C 1941- *AmMWSc 92*
**Ohanian**, Krekor 1925- *WhoEnt 92*
**Ohanian**, Thomas A. *WhoEnt 92*
**O'Hanlan**, Edward Vincent 1956- *WhoAmL 92*
**O'Hanlon**, James *LesBEnT 92*
**O'Hanlon**, James Barry 1927- *WhoAmL 92*
**O'Hanlon**, John 1821-1905 *DcAmImH*
**O'Hanlon**, Rory 1934- *IntWW 91*
**Ohannessian**, Harry Haroutune 1919- *WhoFI 92*
**O'Hara**, Alfred Peck 1919- *WhoAmL 92*
**O'Hara**, Anne *AmPeW*
**O'Hara**, Bill 1929- *Who 92*
**O'Hara**, Catherine 1954- *IntMPA 92*
**Ohara**, Coralee 1943- *WhoEnt 92*
**O'Hara**, Derek Ive 1928- *Who 92*
**O'Hara**, Edward 1937- *Who 92*
**O'Hara**, Francis Patrick 1951- *WhoFI 92*
**O'Hara**, Frank 1926-1966 *BenetAL 91*
**O'Hara**, Gerry 1924- *IntMPA 92*
**O'Hara**, James Edward 1844-1905 *DcNCBi 4*
**O'Hara**, James Thomas 1936- *WhoAmL 92*
**O'Hara**, Jessee A *WhoAmP 91*
**O'Hara**, John 1905-1970 *BenetAL 91, FacFETw*
**O'Hara**, John Francis 1888-1960 *RelLAm 91*
**O'Hara**, John Paul, III 1946- *WhoMW 92*
**Ohara**, Jun-Ichi 1950- *WhoWest 92*
**O'Hara**, Kenneth *WrDr 92*
**O'Hara**, Leon P. 1920- *WhoBlA 92*
**Ohara**, Maricarmen 1954- *WhoHisp 92*
**O'Hara**, Marion Malone 1932- *WhoIns 92*
**O'Hara**, Marjorie 1928- *ConAu 135*
**O'Hara**, Mary 1885-1980 *BenetAL 91, TwCWW 91*
**O'Hara**, Maureen *WhoEnt 92*
**O'Hara**, Maureen 1921- *IntMPA 92*
**O'Hara**, Maureen 1953- *WhoFI 92*
**O'Hara**, Michael James 1953- *WhoMW 92*
**O'Hara**, Michael James 1956- *WhoWest 92*
**O'Hara**, Michael John 1933- *IntWW 91, Who 92*
**O'Hara**, Norbert Wilhelm 1930- *AmMWSc 92*
**O'Hara**, Oscar Coleman 1918- *WhoMW 92*
**O'Hara**, Randolph 1940- *WhoEnt 92*
**O'Hara**, Richard Edward 1947- *WhoRel 92*
**O'Hara**, Steven Thomas 1957- *WhoAmL 92*
**O'Hara**, Theodore 1820-1867 *BenetAL 91*
**O'Hare**, Carrie Jane 1959- *WhoEnt 92*
**O'Hare**, Daniel John 1955- *WhoMW 92*
**O'Hare**, Dean Raymond 1942- *WhoFI 92, WhoIns 92*
**O'Hare**, J. Michael 1938- *WhoMW 92*
**O'Hare**, Jean A. 1950- *WhoAmL 92*
**O'Hare**, John Michael 1938- *AmMWSc 92*
**O'Hare**, Joseph Aloysius 1931- *IntWW 91*
**O'Hare**, Kate Richards 1876-1948 *HanAmWH*
**O'Hare**, Patrick 1936- *AmMWSc 92*
**O'Hare**, Robert Joseph Michael, Jr. 1943- *WhoFI 92, WhoIns 92*
**O'Hare**, Stephen T 1928- *WhoIns 92*
**Oharenko**, Maria T. 1950- *WhoWest 92*
**Ohashi**, Yoshikazu 1941- *AmMWSc 92*
**O'Haver**, Doreen J 1933- *WhoAmP 91*
**O'Haver**, Thomas Calvin 1941- *AmMWSc 92*
**O'Hea**, Eugene Kevin 1941- *AmMWSc 92*
**O'Hearn**, Daniel P. 1963- *WhoRel 92*
**O'Hearn**, George Thomas 1934- *AmMWSc 92*
**O'Hearn**, James William 1922- *WhoMW 92*
**O'Hearn**, Michael John 1952- *WhoAmL 92*
**O'Hearn**, Robert Raymond 1921- *WhoEnt 92*
**O'Hehir**, Diana *DrAPF 91*
**O'Hehir**, Diana 1922- *IntAu&W 91*
**O hEocha**, Colm 1926- *IntWW 91*
**O'Herlihy**, Dan 1919- *IntMPA 92*
**O'Hern**, Daniel J, Sr 1930- *WhoAmP 91*
**O'Hern**, Daniel Joseph 1930- *WhoAmL 92*
**O'Hern**, Elizabeth Moot 1913- *AmMWSc 92*
**O'Hern**, Eugene A 1927- *AmMWSc 92*
**O'Herron**, Jonathan 1929- *WhoFI 92*
**Ohga**, Norio 1930- *IntWW 91, WhoEnt 92*
**Ohi**, Seigo 1943- *AmMWSc 92*
**O'Higgins**, Bernardo 1778-1842 *HisDSpE*
**O'Higgins**, Harvey Jerrold 1876-1929 *BenetAL 91*
**O'Higgins**, James 1915- *WhoRel 92*
**O'Higgins**, Paul 1927- *Who 92, WrDr 92*
**O'Higgins**, Thomas Francis 1916- *Who 92*
**Ohira**, Kazuto 1933- *WhoEnt 92*
**Ohki**, Kenneth 1922- *AmMWSc 92*
**Ohki**, Shinpei 1933- *AmMWSc 92*
**Ohkuchi**, Shunichi 1918- *IntWW 91*
**Ohl**, Dana Alan 1958- *WhoMW 92*
**Ohl**, Donald Gordon 1915- *AmMWSc 92*
**Ohl**, Paul 1940- *IntAu&W 91*
**Ohl**, Robert Craig 1935- *WhoFI 92*
**Ohlberg**, Stanley Miles 1921- *AmMWSc 92*
**Ohle**, David *DrAPF 91*
**Ohle**, Ernest Linwood 1917- *AmMWSc 92*
**Ohle**, Lester C. 1921- *WhoMW 92*
**Ohlemiller**, Robert John, Jr. 1950- *WhoMW 92*
**Ohlenbusch**, Robert Eugene 1930- *AmMWSc 92*
**Ohlendorf**, Harry Max 1940- *AmMWSc 92*
**Ohlendorf**, Otto 1907-1951 *EncTR 91 [port]*
**Ohlendorf**, Otto 1908-1951 *BiDExR*
**Ohler**, Thomas Chester 1942- *WhoAmP 91*
**Ohlerking**, David Paul 1940- *WhoRel 92*
**Ohlgren**, Thomas Harold 1941- *WhoMW 92*
**Ohlin**, Bertil Gotthard 1899-1979 *WhoNob 90*
**Ohline**, Robert Wayne 1934- *AmMWSc 92*
**Ohlinger**, Marie Edna 1941- *WhoRel 92*
**Ohlmacher**, Albert Philip 1865-1916 *BiInAmS*
**Ohlman**, Douglas Ronald 1949- *WhoAmL 92, WhoFI 92*
**Ohlmeyer**, Don *LesBEnT 92*
**Ohlmeyer**, Donald W., Jr. 1945- *IntMPA 92*
**Ohlrogge**, Alvin John 1915- *AmMWSc 92*
**Ohlsen**, William David 1932- *AmMWSc 92*
**Ohlson**, Brian 1936- *Who 92*
**Ohlson**, John E 1940- *AmMWSc 92*
**Ohlsson**, Garrick 1948- *IntWW 91, NewAmDM*
**Ohlsson**, Oscar Olof, Jr. 1926- *WhoMW 92*
**Ohlsson**, Robert Louis 1915- *AmMWSc 92*
**Ohlsson-Wilhelm**, Betsy Mae 1942- *AmMWSc 92*
**Ohlwiler**, Robert Henry 1947- *WhoFI 92*
**Ohly**, D. Christopher 1950- *WhoAmL 92*
**Ohly**, Friedrich 1914- *IntWW 91*
**Ohm**, E A 1926- *AmMWSc 92*
**Ohm**, Frederick C 1858?-1916 *BiInAmS*
**Ohm**, Herbert Willis 1945- *AmMWSc 92, WhoMW 92*
**Ohm**, Jack Elton 1932- *AmMWSc 92*
**Ohm**, June Marie 1945- *IntAu&W 91*
**Ohm**, Peter H. d1991 *NewYTBS 91*
**Ohm**, Wilma Jean 1928- *WhoAmP 91*
**Ohman**, Diana J 1950- *WhoAmP 91*
**Ohman**, Gunnar P 1918- *AmMWSc 92*
**Ohman**, John Michael 1948- *WhoAmP 91*
**Ohman**, Richard W *WhoIns 92*
**Ohman**, Robert Baird 1934- *WhoRel 92*
**Ohman-Youngs**, Anne *DrAPF 91*
**Ohmart**, Dale Lynn 1959- *WhoRel 92*
**Ohmart**, Robert Dale 1938- *AmMWSc 92*
**Ohme**, Paul Adolph 1940- *AmMWSc 92*
**Ohmer**, Merlin Maurice 1923- *AmMWSc 92*
**Ohmer**, Thomas Joseph 1954- *WhoMW 92*
**Ohmoto**, Hiroshi 1941- *AmMWSc 92*
**Ohms**, Cosmo 1947- *WhoEnt 92*
**Ohms**, Jack Ivan 1930- *AmMWSc 92*
**Ohms**, Richard Earl 1927- *AmMWSc 92*
**Ohmstede**, Bryce Alton 1924- *WhoAmP 91*
**Ohmstede**, Frances Elizabeth 1926- *WhoAmP 91*
**Ohnemus**, Duane Alan 1960- *WhoMW 92*
**Ohnesorge**, Wilhelm 1872-1962 *EncTR 91*
**Ohnesorge**, William Edward 1931- *AmMWSc 92*
**Ohnishi**, Minoru 1925- *IntWW 91*
**Ohnishi**, Tomoko 1931- *AmMWSc 92*
**Ohnishi**, Tsuyoshi 1931- *AmMWSc 92*
**Ohnmacht**, Mark Walter 1956- *WhoEnt 92*
**Ohno**, Susumu 1928- *AmMWSc 92, IntWW 91*
**Ohno**, Talichi 1912-1990 *FacFETw*
**Ohnsman**, David Robert 1943- *WhoFI 92*
**Ohnuki**, Yasushi 1926- *AmMWSc 92*
**Ohnuma**, Shoroku 1928- *AmMWSc 92*
**Ohnuma**, Takao 1932- *AmMWSc 92*
**O'Hollaren**, John David 1922- *WhoWest 92*
**O'Hollaren**, Paul Joseph 1927- *WhoFI 92*
**O'Hora**, Nancy Jacobson 1937- *WhoAmP 91*
**O'Horgan**, Thomas Foster 1926- *WhoEnt 92*
**O'Horgan**, Tom 1926- *IntMPA 92*
**Ohr**, Eleonore A 1932- *AmMWSc 92*
**Ohrenstein**, Manfred 1925- *WhoAmP 91*
**Ohring**, George 1931- *AmMWSc 92*
**Ohring**, Milton 1936- *AmMWSc 92*
**Ohrn**, Nils Yngve 1934- *AmMWSc 92*
**Ohrstedt**, Robert James 1953- *WhoRel 92*
**Ohrstrom**, Ricard Riggs 1922- *WhoFI 92*
**Ohsfeldt**, Robert Lee 1956- *WhoFI 92*
**Ohsiek**, Frederick Charles 1937- *WhoRel 92*
**Ohta**, Masao 1919- *AmMWSc 92*
**Ohtake**, Takeshi 1926- *AmMWSc 92*
**Ohtani**, Hiroshi 1910- *IntMPA 92*
**Ohtani**, Ichiji 1912- *IntWW 91*
**Ohtani**, Monshu Koshin 1945- *IntWW 91*
**Ohuchi**, Teruyuki 1929- *IntWW 91*
**Ohyama**, Heiichiro 1947- *WhoEnt 92, WhoWest 92*
**Oi**, Walter Yasuo 1929- *WhoFI 92*
**Oien**, Arne 1928- *IntWW 91*
**Oien**, Helen Grossbeck 1940- *AmMWSc 92*
**Oien**, Hemming Olaf 1926- *WhoAmP 91*
**Oigme** *EncAmaz 91*
**Oiko** *EncAmaz 91*
**Oinas**, Felix J. 1911- *WrDr 92*
**Oishi**, Jitsoishi *WhoRel 92*
**Oishi**, Noboru 1928- *AmMWSc 92*
**Oishi**, Senpachi *IntWW 91*
**Oistad**, Leon L 1942- *WhoAmP 91*
**Oisteanu**, Valery *DrAPF 91*
**Oistrakh**, David 1908-1974 *FacFETw, NewAmDM*
**Oistrakh**, David Fedorovich 1908-1974 *SovUnBD*
**Oistrakh**, Igor 1931- *NewAmDM*
**Oistrakh**, Igor Davidovich 1931- *IntWW 91, SovUnBD, Who 92*
**Oizerman**, Teodor Ilyich 1914- *IntWW 91*
**Oja**, Carol J. 1953- *ConAu 135, WrDr 92*
**Oja**, Tonis 1937- *AmMWSc 92*
**Ojakaar**, Leo 1926- *AmMWSc 92*
**Ojala**, Ossi Arne Atos 1933- *IntAu&W 91*
**Ojalvo**, Irving U 1936- *AmMWSc 92*
**Ojalvo**, Morris 1924- *AmMWSc 92*
**Ojalvo**, Morris S 1923- *AmMWSc 92*
**Ojanen**, Risto Ensio 1927- *IntWW 91*
**Ojard**, Bruce Allen 1951- *WhoMW 92*
**Ojea**, Jose L., II 1930- *WhoHisp 92*
**Ojeda**, Alonso de 1468?-1515 *HisDSpE*
**Ojeda**, Bob 1957- *WhoHisp 92*
**Ojeda**, Sergio Raul 1946- *AmMWSc 92*
**Ojeda**, Virginia F. *WhoHisp 92*
**Ojeda Eiseley**, Jaime de 1933- *IntWW 91*
**Ojeda Paullada**, Pedro 1934- *IntWW 91*
**Ojetti**, Ugo 1871-1946 *DcAmImH*
**Ojiaku**, Alamezie Enwereaku 1947- *WhoFI 92*
**Ojile**, Joseph Michael 1959- *WhoMW 92*
**Ojima**, Iwao 1945- *AmMWSc 92*
**Ojinaga**, Raymond B. 1949- *WhoHisp 92*
**Ojukwu**, Chukwenmeka 1933- *FacFETw*
**Ojukwu**, Chukwuemeka Odumegwu 1933- *IntWW 91*
**Oka**, Hirono 1957- *WhoEnt 92*
**Oka**, Masamichi *AmMWSc 92*
**Oka**, Seishi William 1936- *AmMWSc 92*
**Oka**, Takami 1940- *AmMWSc 92*
**Oka**, Takashi 1924- *ConAu 135*
**Oka**, Takeshi 1932- *AmMWSc 92, Who 92*
**Okabayashi**, Michio 1939- *AmMWSc 92*
**Okabe**, Hideo 1923- *AmMWSc 92*
**Okada**, John 1923-1971 *BenetAL 91*
**Okada**, R H 1925- *AmMWSc 92*
**Okada**, Tadashi A 1928- *AmMWSc 92*
**Okai**, John *ConPo 91, WrDr 92*
**O'Kain**, Marie Jeanette *WhoBlA 92*
**O'Kain**, Roosevelt 1933- *WhoBlA 92*
**Okal**, Emile Andre 1950- *AmMWSc 92*
**Okamoto**, K Keith 1920- *AmMWSc 92*
**Okamoto**, Michiko 1932- *AmMWSc 92*
**Okamoto**, Naofumi 1947- *WhoEnt 92*
**Okamura**, Judy Paulette 1942- *AmMWSc 92*
**Okamura**, Kiyohisa 1935- *AmMWSc 92*
**Okamura**, Sogo 1918- *AmMWSc 92*
**Okamura**, Tom 1948- *WhoAmP 91*
**Okamura**, William H 1941- *AmMWSc 92*
**O'Kane**, Daniel Joseph 1919- *AmMWSc 92*
**O'Kane**, James Daniel 1951- *WhoAmP 91*
**O'Kane**, Joseph James 1952- *WhoEnt 92*
**O'Kane**, Kevin Charles 1946- *AmMWSc 92*
**O'Kane**, Michael James, Jr. 1960- *WhoFI 92*
**Okantah**, Mwatabu *DrAPF 91*
**Okara**, Gabriel 1921- *ConPo 91, RfGEnL 91, WrDr 92*
**Okasha**, Sarwat Mahmoud Fahmy 1921- *IntWW 91*
**Okashimo**, Katsumi 1929- *AmMWSc 92*
**Okawara**, Yoshio 1919- *IntWW 91*
**Okaya**, Yoshi Haru 1927- *AmMWSc 92*
**Okazaki**, Haruo 1926- *AmMWSc 92*
**Okazaki**, Tadao 1943- *IntAu&W 91*
**Okazaki**, Tadeo 1943- *IntAu&W 91*
**Okcun**, Gunduz 1936- *IntWW 91*
**Oke**, John Beverley 1928- *AmMWSc 92*
**Oke**, Kenneth Leo 1924- *WhoAmP 91*
**Oke**, Robert Eugene *WhoAmP 91*
**Oke**, Timothy Richard 1941- *AmMWSc 92*

O'Kean, Herman C 1933- AmMWSc 92
Okebugwu, Andrew Nkasiobi 1937- WhoFI 92
O'Keefe, Arthur F 1930- WhoIns 92
O'Keefe, Constance 1948- WhoAmL 92
O'Keefe, Daniel Francis, Jr. 1936- WhoAmL 92
O'Keefe, Dennis D AmMWSc 92
O'Keefe, Dennis Robert 1939- AmMWSc 92
O'Keefe, Edward John 1941- AmMWSc 92
O'Keefe, Eugene H AmMWSc 92
O'Keefe, Fredrick Rea 1944- WhoRel 92
O'Keefe, Gerald Francis 1918- WhoMW 92, WhoRel 92
O'Keefe, J George 1931- AmMWSc 92
O'Keefe, J. Redmond WhoRel 92
O'Keefe, John Aloysius 1916- AmMWSc 92
O'Keefe, John Dugan 1937- AmMWSc 92
O'Keefe, John Harold 1938- Who 92
O'Keefe, Joseph Ross 1954- WhoFI 92
O'Keefe, Joseph Thomas 1919- WhoRel 92
O'Keefe, Lloyd F. WhoRel 92
O'Keefe, Maria Magda 1938- WhoHisp 92
O'Keefe, Mark D 1952- WhoAmP 91
O'Keefe, Martha Anne 1938- WhoAmP 91
O'Keefe, Michael 1955- IntMPA 92
O'Keefe, Michael Adrian 1942- AmMWSc 92, WhoWest 92
O'Keefe, Michael Daniel 1938- WhoAmL 92
O'Keefe, Michael Hanley, Jr 1931- WhoAmP 91
O'Keefe, Raymond Peter 1928- WhoAmL 92
O'Keefe, Richard R. DrAPF 91
O'Keefe, Terence Michael 1959- WhoEnt 92
O'Keefe, Thomas Andrew 1961- WhoAmL 92
O'Keefe, Thomas Joseph 1935- AmMWSc 92
O'Keefe, Thomas Michael 1940- WhoMW 92
O'Keefe, Vincent Thomas 1920- WhoRel 92
O'Keefe, William John 1936- WhoIns 92
O'Keeffe, Charles B, Jr 1939- WhoAmP 91
O'Keeffe, David John 1930- AmMWSc 92
O'Keeffe, Georgia 1887-1986 FacFETw [port], HanAmWH, PorAmW [port], RComAH
O'Keeffe, John 1747-1833 RfGEnL 91
O'Keeffe, Laurence 1931- Who 92
O'Keeffe, Lawrence Eugene 1934- AmMWSc 92
O'Keeffe, Michael 1934- AmMWSc 92
O'Keeffe, Whitney Carter 1935- WhoAmP 91, WhoFI 92
O'Keeffe, William B. 1939- WhoAmL 92
O'Kehie, Collins Emeka 1952- WhoAmL 92
O'Kelley, Grover Davis 1928- AmMWSc 92
O'Kelley, Joseph Charles 1922- AmMWSc 92
O'Kelley, William Clark 1930- WhoAmL 92
O'Kelly, Berry 1861?-1931 DcNCBi 4
O'Kelly, Elizabeth 1915- WrDr 92
O'Kelly, Francis Joseph 1921- Who 92
O'Kelly, James 1741?-1826 DcNCBi 4
Oken, Donald 1928- AmMWSc 92
Oken, Martin Myron 1939- WhoMW 92
O'Kennedy, Michael 1936- IntWW 91
O'Kennedy, Michael E. 1936- Who 92
Okeover, Peter Ralph Leopold W. Who 92
Oker-Blom, Nils Christian Edgar 1919- IntWW 91
Okerholm, Richard Arthur 1941- AmMWSc 92
Okero, Isaac Edwin Omolo 1931- IntWW 91
Okeson, Thomas L. 1946- WhoMW 92
Okey, David William 1946- WhoMW 92
Okey, Eugene Paul 1923- WhoAmL 92
Okeyo, Michael George 1939- IntWW 91
Okezie, Josiah Onyebuchi Johnson 1924- IntWW 91
Okhamafe, E. Imafedia WhoBlA 92
Okhlopkov, Nikolay Pavlovich 1900-1967 SovUnBD
Okhotnikov, Nikolai Petrovich 1937- IntWW 91
O'Kieffe, Mike 1939- WhoAmP 91
Okigbo, Christopher 1932-1967 BlkLC [port], RfGEnL 91
Okiishi, Theodore Hisao 1939- AmMWSc 92
Okinaka, Yutaka 1926- AmMWSc 92
Okinda, Jerome 1933- IntWW 91
Okita, George Torao 1922- AmMWSc 92
Okita, Saburo 1914- IntWW 91
Oklak, Mark Anthony 1949- WhoMW 92
Oko, Andrew Jan 1946- WhoWest 92
Oko, Yuji 1949- TwCPaSc
Okogie, Anthony Olubunmi Who 92, WhoRel 92
Okogie, Anthony Olubunmi 1936- IntWW 91
O'Kon, James Alexander 1937- WhoFI 92
Okon, Longin Jan 1927- IntAu&W 91
Okon, Ted 1929- IntMPA 92
Okon, Zbigniew Waldemar 1945- IntAu&W 91
Okondo, Peter Habenga 1925- IntWW 91
O'Konski, Chester Thomas 1921- AmMWSc 92
Okore, Cynthia Ann 1945- WhoBlA 92
Okoro, Anezi 1929- WrDr 92
Okos, Martin Robert 1945- AmMWSc 92
Okoso, Yoshinori 1915- IntWW 91
Okoth, Yona Who 92, WhoRel 92
Okoye, Christian E. 1961- WhoBlA 92
Okpaku, Joseph 1943- IntAu&W 91
Okpara, Mzee Lasana 1941- WhoBlA 92
Okrasinski, Richard Joseph 1951- WhoWest 92
Okrasinski, Stanley John 1952- AmMWSc 92
Okrend, Harold 1934- AmMWSc 92
Okrent, Daniel 1948- IntAu&W 91
Okrent, David 1922- AmMWSc 92, WhoWest 92
Okress, Ernest Carl 1910- AmMWSc 92
Okri, Ben 1959- ConNov 91, IntWW 91
Okri, Ben 1960- LiExTwC
Oksenberg, Michel Charles 1938- WhoAmP 91
Oksnes, Oskar 1921- IntWW 91
Oktay, Erol 1938- AmMWSc 92
Okubo, Akira 1925- AmMWSc 92
Okubo, Susumu 1930- AmMWSc 92
Okuda, Keiwa IntWW 91
Okudzhava, Bulat Shalvovich 1924- IntWW 91, SovUnBD
Okulitch, Andrew Vladimir 1941- AmMWSc 92
Okulitch, Vladimir Joseph 1906- AmMWSc 92
Okulski, Thomas Alexander 1943- AmMWSc 92
Okuma, Albert Akira, Jr. 1946- WhoFI 92, WhoWest 92
Okumura, Kiyohisa 1935- WhoMW 92
Okumura, Mitchio 1957- AmMWSc 92
Okun, D A 1917- AmMWSc 92
Okun, Daniel A. 1917- IntWW 91
Okun, Eli 1947- WhoEnt 92
Okun, Lawrence M 1940- AmMWSc 92
Okun, Lev Borisovich 1929- IntWW 91
Okun, Ronald 1932- AmMWSc 92
Okunewick, James Philip 1934- AmMWSc 92
Okuni, Izumo no EncAmaz 91
Okuno, Seisuke 1913- IntWW 91
Okunor, Shiame 1937- WhoBlA 92
Okwit, Seymour 1929- AmMWSc 92
Okwumabua, Benjamin Nkem 1939- WhoBlA 92
Ol', Andrey Andreevich 1883-1958 SovUnBD
Olafson, Barry D 1949- AmMWSc 92
Olafsson, Olaf WhoEnt 92
Olafsson, Patrick Gordon 1920- AmMWSc 92
Olagbegi II, The Olowo of Owo 1910- Who 92
Olague, Ruben, Jr. 1957- WhoHisp 92
Olah, George Andrew 1927- AmMWSc 92
Olah, James Sander 1946- WhoRel 92
Olah, Judith Agnes 1929- AmMWSc 92
Olajuwon, Hakeem 1963- ConBlB 2 [port]
Olajuwon, Hakeem Abdul 1963- WhoBlA 92
Oland, S. M. WhoFI 92
Olander, Bradley Ward 1964- WhoEnt 92
Olander, Brett William 1959- WhoAmL 92
Olander, D R 1931- AmMWSc 92
Olander, Donald Edgar 1929- WhoWest 92
Olander, Donald Paul 1940- AmMWSc 92
Olander, Harvey Johan 1932- AmMWSc 92
Olander, James Alton 1944- AmMWSc 92
Olander, Ray Gunnar 1926- WhoFI 92
Olaneta, Pedro Antonio de d1825 HisDSpE
Olang', Festo Habakkuk 1914- IntWW 91, Who 92
O'Laoghaire, Liam IntAu&W 91X, WrDr 92
Olar, Terry Thomas 1947- WhoFI 92
O'Larkin, Sean ScFEYrs
Olasov, Brian Fredric 1959- WhoFI 92
Olasz, Richard D 1930- WhoAmP 91
O'Laughlin, Jeanne 1929- WhoRel 92
O'Laughlin, Marjorie H WhoAmP 91
O'Laughlin, Marjorie Hartley WhoMW 92
Olav V 1903-1991 FacFETw
Olav, King of Norway 1903-1991 News 91, -91-3
Olav V, King of Norway d1991 IntWW 91N
Olav V, King of Norway 1903-1991 NewYTBS 91 [port]
Olav V, King of Norway 1908-1991 CurBio 91N
Olaves, Jorge L. 1956- WhoHisp 92
Olawumi, Bertha Ann 1945- WhoBlA 92
Olayan, Suliman Saleh 1918- Who 92
Olazabal, Francisco 1886-1937 RelLAm 91
Olazagasti-Segovia, Elena 1952- WhoHisp 92
Olbrechts, Guy Robert 1935- WhoFI 92, WhoWest 92
Olbrich, Josef 1867-1908 DcTwDes
Olbrich, Steven Emil 1938- AmMWSc 92
Olbricht, Friedrich 1888-1944 EncTR 91 [port]
Olbricht, Thomas Henry 1929- WhoRel 92
Olcay, Osman 1924- IntWW 91
Olchak, Lawrence Larry Stephen 1955- WhoFI 92
Olcott, Chauncey 1858-1932 NewAmDM
Olcott, Chauncey 1860-1932 BenetAL 91
Olcott, Eugene L 1918- AmMWSc 92
Olcott, Frances Jenkins 1872?-1963 BenetAL 91
Olcott, James Louis 1944- WhoEnt 92
Olcott, Joanne Elizabeth 1958- WhoWest 92
Olcott, Sidney 1874-1949 IntDcF 2-2
Olczak, Janusz 1941- IntAu&W 91
Olczak, Joseph Marian 1940- WhoRel 92
Olczak, Paul Vincent 1943- AmMWSc 92
Old Scout, An ScFEYrs
Old, Bruce S 1913- AmMWSc 92
Old, Hughes Oliphant 1933- WhoRel 92
Old, Lloyd John 1933- AmMWSc 92
Old, Richard Robert 1953- WhoWest 92
Old, Thomas Eugene 1943- AmMWSc 92
Old-Lady-Grieves-the-Enemy EncAmaz 91
Oldale, Robert Nicholas AmMWSc 92
Oldberg, Carl Malcolm 1947- WhoMW 92
Oldberg, Oscar 1846-1913 BiInAmS
Oldemeyer, John Lee 1941- AmMWSc 92
Oldemeyer, Robert King 1922- AmMWSc 92
Olden, Diana Jean 1943- WhoFI 92
Olden, Walter L. 1953- WhoEnt 92
Oldenbourg, Zoe 1916- IntWW 91
Oldenbourg-Idalie, Zoe 1916- Who 92
Oldenburg, C C 1929- AmMWSc 92
Oldenburg, Claes 1929- FacFETw, IntWW 91
Oldenburg, Douglas W. WhoRel 92
Oldenburg, Douglas William 1946- AmMWSc 92
Oldenburg, Richard Erik 1933- IntWW 91, Who 92
Oldenburg, Theodore Richard 1932- AmMWSc 92
Oldenburg, William D 1958- WhoAmP 91
Oldendorf, William Henry 1925- AmMWSc 92
Oldenkamp, Richard D 1931- AmMWSc 92
Older, Julia DrAPF 91
Olderman, Gerald Myron 1933- WhoWest 92
Oldfather, Charles Eugene 1927- WhoAmL 92
Oldfield, Bruce 1950- IntWW 91, Who 92
Oldfield, Daniel G 1925- AmMWSc 92
Oldfield, E. Lawrence 1944- WhoAmL 92
Oldfield, Edward Hudson 1947- AmMWSc 92
Oldfield, Eric 1948- AmMWSc 92
Oldfield, George Newton 1936- AmMWSc 92
Oldfield, James Edmund 1921- AmMWSc 92
Oldfield, Jenny 1949- WrDr 92
Oldfield, John Richard Anthony 1899- Who 92
Oldfield, John Stewart 1940- WhoRel 92
Oldfield, Maurice 1915-1981 FacFETw
Oldfield, Michael 1950- ConAu 135
Oldfield, Michael Gordon 1953- Who 92
Oldfield, Mike ConAu 135
Oldfield, Pamela 1931- WrDr 92
Oldfield, Russell Miller 1946- WhoAmL 92
Oldfield, Thomas Edward 1947- AmMWSc 92
Oldham, Algie Sidney, Jr. 1927- WhoBlA 92
Oldham, Arthur Charles Godolphin 1905- Who 92
Oldham, Bill Wayne 1934- AmMWSc 92
Oldham, Darius Dudley 1941- WhoAmL 92
Oldham, Dortch 1919- WhoAmP 91
Oldham, Geoffrey 1929- Who 92
Oldham, George Ashton 1877-1963 AmPeW
Oldham, James Warren 1950- AmMWSc 92
Oldham, Jawann 1957- WhoBlA 92
Oldham, John 1653-1683 RfGEnL 91
Oldham, John William 1952- WhoAmP 91
Oldham, Joseph Houldsworth 1874-1969 DcEcMov [port]
Oldham, Keith Bentley 1929- AmMWSc 92
Oldham, Lea Leever 1931- WhoMW 92
Oldham, Lucian Kenneth 1922- WhoAmP 91
Oldham, Mary 1944- SmATA 65
Oldham, Maurice WhoBlA 92
Oldham, Maxine Jernigan 1923- WhoFI 92, WhoWest 92
Oldham, Perry DrAPF 91
Oldham, Phyllis Virginia Kidd 1926- WhoMW 92
Oldham, Robert Kenneth 1941- AmMWSc 92
Oldham, Ronald Wayne 1949- WhoAmP 91
Oldham, Stephen Richard 1944- WhoFI 92
Oldham, Susan Banks 1942- AmMWSc 92
Oldham, Warren WhoAmP 91
Oldham, William Edward 1948- WhoRel 92
Oldham, William G 1938- AmMWSc 92
Oldknow, Antony DrAPF 91
Oldknow, Antony 1939- IntAu&W 91
Oldman, Gary 1958- ConTFT 9, IntMPA 92, IntWW 91
Oldman, Oliver 1920- WhoAmL 92, WhoFI 92
Oldmeadow, Ernest 1867-1949 ScFEYrs
Oldmixon, John 1673-1742 BenetAL 91
Olds, Daniel Wayne 1935- AmMWSc 92
Olds, Durward 1921- AmMWSc 92
Olds, Elizabeth d1991 NewYTBS 91
Olds, Elizabeth 1896-1991 ConAu 133, SmATA 66
Olds, Elizabeth Fay 1933- WhoAmP 91
Olds, Frederick Augustus 1853-1935 DcNCBi 4
Olds, James Howard 1945- WhoRel 92
Olds, John Theodore 1943- WhoFI 92
Olds, Sharon DrAPF 91
Olds, Sharon 1942- ConPo 91, WrDr 92
Olds-Cihigoyenetche, Jennifer DrAPF 91
Olds-Clarke, Patricia Jean 1943- AmMWSc 92
Oldsey, Bernard DrAPF 91
Oldsey, Bernard 1923- IntAu&W 91
Oldsey, Bernard S. 1923- WrDr 92
Oldshue, J Y 1925- AmMWSc 92
Oldshue, James Y. 1925- WhoFI 92
Oldshue, Mary Holl 1951- WhoFI 92
Oldshue, Paul Frederick 1949- WhoFI 92, WhoWest 92
Oldstone, Michael Beaureguard Alan 1934- AmMWSc 92
Oldstyle, Jonathan BenetAL 91
Oldweiler, Thomas Patrick 1961- WhoAmL 92
Oldys, William 1696-1761 BlkwCEP
Ole-Luk-Oie 1868-1951 ScFEYrs
Olea, Greg Manuel 1959- WhoHisp 92
O'Leary WrDr 92
O'Leary, Anne K 1916- AmMWSc 92
O'Leary, Brian Todd 1940- AmMWSc 92
O'Leary, Con ScFEYrs
O'Leary, Cornelius Peter 1944- WhoAmP 91
O'Leary, Daniel Edmund 1950- WhoFI 92, WhoWest 92
O'Leary, Daniel Vincent, Jr. 1942- WhoAmL 92, WhoMW 92
O'Leary, Dawn DrAPF 91
O'Leary, Dennis 1934- WhoRel 92
O'Leary, Dennis Patrick 1939- AmMWSc 92
O'Leary, Edward Cornelius 1920- WhoRel 92
O'Leary, Gerard Paul, Jr 1940- AmMWSc 92
O'Leary, Gertrude Eileen 1941- WhoMW 92
O'Leary, Hazel R. 1937- WhoFI 92
O'Leary, James William 1938- AmMWSc 92
O'Leary, John Francis 1917- AmMWSc 92
O'Leary, John R 1954- WhoAmP 91
O'Leary, Joseph Evans 1945- WhoAmL 92
O'Leary, Kevin Joseph 1932- AmMWSc 92
O'Leary, Liam 1910- IntAu&W 91, WrDr 92
O'Leary, Marion Hugh 1941- AmMWSc 92
O'Leary, Michael 1936- Who 92
O'Leary, Michael 1938- IntWW 91
O'Leary, Michael D. 1949- WhoWest 92
O'Leary, Patrick 1920- ConAu 134
O'Leary, Paul Francis 1945- WhoAmP 91
O'Leary, Paul Gerard 1935- WhoFI 92
O'Leary, Peggy Rene 1951- WhoWest 92
O'Leary, Peter Leslie 1929- Who 92
O'Leary, Terence Daniel 1928- IntWW 91, Who 92
O'Leary, Thomas Howard 1934- WhoFI 92, WhoWest 92
O'Leary, Timothy F 1945- WhoAmP 91

**O'Leary,** Timothy Francis 1948- *WhoMW 92*
**O'Leary,** Timothy Joseph 1952- *AmMWSc 92*
**O' Leary,** Timothy Michael 1946- *WhoFI 92, WhoMW 92*
**Olechowski,** Jerome Robert 1931- *AmMWSc 92*
**Olechowski,** Tadeusz 1926- *IntWW 91*
**Oleck,** Howard L. 1911- *WrDr 92*
**Oleckno,** William Anton 1948- *AmMWSc 92*
**Oleen,** Lana P 1949- *WhoAmP 91*
**Oleesky,** Samuel S 1913- *AmMWSc 92*
**Oleinick,** Nancy Landy 1941- *AmMWSc 92*
**Oleinick,** Tracy Bender 1955- *WhoEnt 92*
**Olejniczak,** Julian Michael 1939- *WhoAmL 92*
**Olek,** John J. 1953- *WhoRel 92*
**Olem,** Harvey 1951- *AmMWSc 92*
**Olenchock,** Stephen Anthony 1946- *AmMWSc 92*
**Olender,** David Paul 1967- *WhoRel 92*
**Olendorf,** William Carr, Jr. 1945- *WhoFI 92*
**Olenick,** John George 1935- *AmMWSc 92*
**Olenick,** Richard Peter 1951- *AmMWSc 92*
**Oler,** Norman 1929- *AmMWSc 92*
**Oler-Kesler,** Mary Margaret 1952- *WhoWest 92*
**Olert,** Frederick Herman 1904- *WhoRel 92*
**Oles,** Carole *DrAPF 91*
**Oles,** Keith Floyd 1921- *AmMWSc 92*
**Oles',** Oleksander 1878-1944 *LiExTwC*
**Oles,** Paul Stevenson 1936- *WhoFI 92*
**Oles,** Stuart Gregory 1924- *WhoAmL 92, WhoWest 92*
**Olesen,** Aase 1934- *IntWW 91*
**Olesen,** Douglas Eugene 1939- *AmMWSc 92, WhoMW 92*
**Olesen,** Jens 1943- *WhoFI 92*
**Olesen,** Peter Filtenborg 1933- *WhoMW 92*
**Olesen,** Poul 1939- *IntWW 91*
**Olesen,** Virginia 1925- *WomSoc*
**Olesha,** Yuriy Karlovich 1899-1960 *SovUnBD*
**Olesiak,** Kazimierz 1937- *IntWW 91*
**Oleske,** James Matthew 1945- *AmMWSc 92*
**Oleskiewicz,** Francis S 1928- *WhoIns 92*
**Oleson,** Norman Lee 1912- *AmMWSc 92*
**Oleson,** Otto H 1915- *WhoAmP 91*
**Olexa,** Stephanie A 1950- *AmMWSc 92*
**Olexia,** Paul Dale 1939- *AmMWSc 92*
**Oleynik,** Boris Il'ich 1935- *SovUnBD*
**Oleynik,** Boris Ilyich 1935- *IntWW 91*
**Olf,** Heinz Gunther 1934- *AmMWSc 92*
**Olfe,** D 1935- *AmMWSc 92*
**Olford,** Stephen Frederick 1918- *WhoRel 92*
**Olga** *EncAmaz 91*
**Olgaard,** Anders 1926- *IntWW 91*
**Olguin,** Dolores C. 1939- *WhoHisp 92*
**Olguin,** M. Michael 1948- *WhoHisp 92*
**Olguin,** Michael *WhoAmP 91*
**Olguin,** Ronald G. 1941- *WhoHisp 92*
**Olguin,** Ronald Gerald 1941- *WhoAmP 91*
**Olhaye,** Roble 1944- *IntWW 91*
**Olhoeft,** Gary Roy 1949- *AmMWSc 92*
**Olhoft,** Wayne Lee 1951- *WhoAmP 91*
**Olian,** Robert Martin 1953- *WhoAmL 92*
**Oliansky,** Joel 1935- *ConAu 133*
**Oliart Saussol,** Alberto 1928- *IntWW 91*
**Olick,** Arthur Seymour 1931- *WhoAmL 92*
**Olick,** Philip Stewart 1936- *WhoAmL 92*
**Olid,** Cristobal de 1492-1524 *HisDSpE*
**Olien,** Neil Arnold 1935- *AmMWSc 92*
**Oliensis,** Sheldon 1922- *WhoAmL 92*
**Oliet,** Seymour 1927- *AmMWSc 92*
**Oliger,** Joseph Emmert 1941- *AmMWSc 92*
**Oliker,** Vladimir 1945- *AmMWSc 92*
**Olimpio,** J Lisbeth *WhoAmP 91*
**Olin,** Arthur David 1928- *AmMWSc 92*
**Olin,** Jacqueline S 1932- *AmMWSc 92*
**Olin,** James R. 1920- *AlmAP 92 [port]*
**Olin,** James Randolph 1920- *WhoAmP 91*
**Olin,** Jeffrey Lloyd 1962- *WhoAmL 92*
**Olin,** Ken 1954- *ConTFT 9*
**Olin,** Ken 1955- *WhoEnt 92*
**Olin,** Lena 1955- *IntMPA 92*
**Olin,** Lena 1956- *News 91 [port]*
**Olin,** Lena Maria Jonna 1955- *WhoEnt 92*
**Olin,** Philip 1941- *AmMWSc 92*
**Olin,** Robert 1948- *AmMWSc 92*
**Olin,** Thomas Franklin 1928- *WhoMW 92*
**Olin,** William, Sr 1924- *AmMWSc 92*
**Oline,** Larry Ward 1937- *AmMWSc 92*
**Oliner,** Arthur A 1921- *AmMWSc 92*
**Olinger,** Stella Marie 1943- *WhoEnt 92*
**Olinick,** Michael 1941- *AmMWSc 92*
**Olins,** Ada Levy 1938- *AmMWSc 92*
**Olins,** Donald Edward 1937- *AmMWSc 92*
**Olins,** Wallace 1930- *Who 92*
**Olinto,** Antonio 1919- *IntAu&W 91*
**Oliphant,** Ben R. *WhoRel 92*
**Oliphant,** Betty 1918- *WhoEnt 92*
**Oliphant,** Charles Frederick, III 1949- *WhoAmL 92*
**Oliphant,** Charles Romig 1917- *WhoWest 92*
**Oliphant,** Charles Winfield 1920- *AmMWSc 92*
**Oliphant,** Dave *DrAPF 91*
**Oliphant,** David Nigel Kington B. *Who 92*
**Oliphant,** Edward Eugene 1942- *AmMWSc 92*
**Oliphant,** Ernie L. 1934- *WhoWest 92*
**Oliphant,** James S. 1945- *WhoAmL 92*
**Oliphant,** Lynn Wesley 1942- *AmMWSc 92*
**Oliphant,** Malcolm William 1920- *AmMWSc 92*
**Oliphant,** Margaret 1828-1897 *RfGEnL 91*
**Oliphant,** Mark 1901- *Who 92*
**Oliphant,** Mark Laurence Elwin 1901- *IntWW 91*
**Oliphant,** Pat 1935- *CurBio 91 [port]*
**Oliphant,** Patrick 1935- *IntWW 91*
**Oliphant,** Robert *DrAPF 91*
**Oliphant,** Robert Thompson 1924- *WhoWest 92*
**Oliphint,** Benjamin Ray 1924- *WhoRel 92*
**Oliphint,** Scott 1955- *WhoRel 92*
**Olitski,** Jules 1922- *IntWW 91*
**Olitzky,** Kerry Marc 1954- *WhoRel 92*
**Oliva,** Dolores Maria 1944- *WhoHisp 92*
**Oliva,** L. Jay 1933- *WrDr 92*
**Oliva,** Nicholas Paul Michael 1953- *WhoEnt 92*
**Oliva,** Robert Rogelio 1946- *WhoHisp 92*
**Oliva,** Stephen Edward 1946- *WhoWest 92*
**Oliva,** Tony 1940- *WhoHisp 92*
**Olivares,** Julian, Jr. 1940- *WhoHisp 92*
**Olivares,** Mary Lou *WhoHisp 92*
**Olivares,** Olga 1939- *WhoHisp 92*
**Olivares,** Omar 1967- *WhoHisp 92*
**Olivas,** Adolf 1956- *WhoAmP 91*
**Olivas,** Daniel A. 1959- *WhoAmL 92*
**Olivas,** Guadalupe Soto 1952- *WhoHisp 92*
**Olivas,** Louis 1947- *WhoHisp 92*
**Olivas,** Ramon Rodriguez, Jr. 1949- *WhoHisp 92*
**Olive,** Aulsey Thomas 1931- *AmMWSc 92*
**Olive,** Chris Wiley 1958- *WhoAmP 91*
**Olive,** Dave 1952- *WhoEnt 92*
**Olive,** David Ian 1937- *IntWW 91, Who 92*
**Olive,** David Wolph 1927- *AmMWSc 92*
**Olive,** Diego Eduardo 1949- *WhoEnt 92, WhoHisp 92*
**Olive,** Eugene Irving 1890-1968 *DcNCBi 4*
**Olive,** Gloria 1923- *AmMWSc 92*
**Olive,** Hubert Ethridge, Sr. 1895-1972 *DcNCBi 4*
**Olive,** J Fred, II 1916- *WhoAmP 91*
**Olive,** John 1949- *WhoEnt 92*
**Olive,** John H 1929- *AmMWSc 92*
**Olive,** Joseph P 1941- *AmMWSc 92*
**Olive,** Lindsay Shepherd 1917- *AmMWSc 92*
**Olive,** Peggy Louise 1948- *AmMWSc 92*
**Oliveira,** Araken de *IntWW 91*
**Oliveira,** Elmar 1950- *WhoEnt 92*
**Oliveira,** Gaspar *WhoHisp 92*
**Oliveira,** Manoel de 1908- *IntDcF 2-2, IntWW 91*
**Oliveira,** Rene Orlando 1955- *WhoAmP 91, WhoHisp 92*
**Oliveira,** Sharon *WhoHisp 92*
**Oliver** *Who 92*
**Oliver,** Abe D, Jr 1925- *AmMWSc 92*
**Oliver,** Al, Jr. 1946- *WhoBlA 92*
**Oliver,** Andrew 1731-1799 *BiInAmS*
**Oliver,** Anthony 1922- *WrDr 92*
**Oliver,** Anthony Thomas, Jr. 1929- *WhoWest 92*
**Oliver,** Barbara Anne 1952- *WhoWest 92*
**Oliver,** Barry Gordon 1942- *AmMWSc 92*
**Oliver,** Benjamin Rhys 1928- *Who 92*
**Oliver,** Bennie F 1927- *AmMWSc 92*
**Oliver,** Bernard M 1916- *AmMWSc 92*
**Oliver,** Brian Darnell 1968- *WhoBlA 92*
**Oliver,** Bruce Lawrence 1951- *WhoFI 92*
**Oliver,** Calvin C 1932- *AmMWSc 92*
**Oliver,** Carl Edward 1943- *AmMWSc 92*
**Oliver,** Chad 1928- *IntAu&W 91, TwCSFW 91, WrDr 92*
**Oliver,** Charles Augustus 1853-1911 *BiInAmS*
**Oliver,** Christopher Lee 1961- *WhoMW 92*
**Oliver,** Clinton Paul 1922- *WhoAmP 91*
**Oliver,** Constance 1942- *AmMWSc 92*
**Oliver,** Cordelia *TwCPaSc*
**Oliver,** Covey T. 1913- *IntWW 91*
**Oliver,** Covey Thomas 1913- *WhoAmP 91*
**Oliver,** Daily E. 1942- *WhoBlA 92*
**Oliver,** Dale Hugh 1947- *WhoAmL 92*
**Oliver,** Dan David 1952- *WhoWest 92*
**Oliver,** Daniel 1939- *WhoAmP 91*
**Oliver,** Daphna R 1945- *AmMWSc 92*
**Oliver,** David John 1949- *AmMWSc 92*
**Oliver,** David Keightley Rideal 1949- *Who 92*
**Oliver,** David W 1932- *AmMWSc 92*
**Oliver,** Deborah Janell 1948- *WhoMW 92*
**Oliver,** Denis Richard 1941- *AmMWSc 92*
**Oliver,** Dennis Stanley 1926- *Who 92*
**Oliver,** Donald Raymond 1930- *AmMWSc 92*
**Oliver,** Douglas LeRoy 1955- *WhoMW 92*
**Oliver,** Earl Davis 1923- *AmMWSc 92*
**Oliver,** Edith 1913- *WhoEnt 92*
**Oliver,** Edward Carl 1930- *WhoFI 92*
**Oliver,** Egbert S. 1902- *WrDr 92*
**Oliver,** Elena 1942- *WhoHisp 92*
**Oliver,** Ernest 1900- *Who 92*
**Oliver,** Eugene Joseph 1941- *AmMWSc 92*
**Oliver,** Fernando 1949- *WhoHisp 92*
**Oliver,** Floyd Anthony 1927- *WhoWest 92*
**Oliver,** Francis Richard 1932- *WrDr 92*
**Oliver,** Frank Louis 1922- *WhoAmP 91, WhoBlA 92*
**Oliver,** G Charles 1931- *AmMWSc 92*
**Oliver,** Garold Lewis 1957- *WhoFI 92*
**Oliver,** Gene Leech 1929- *AmMWSc 92*
**Oliver,** George Benjamin 1938- *WhoMW 92*
**Oliver,** Glenn D. 1962- *WhoAmL 92*
**Oliver,** Halley Brooks 1921- *WhoRel 92*
**Oliver,** Harold Hunter 1930- *WhoRel 92*
**Oliver,** Hugh Patrick Hoblyn 1929- *IntAu&W 91*
**Oliver,** Jack Ertle 1923- *AmMWSc 92*
**Oliver,** Jack Wallace 1938- *AmMWSc 92*
**Oliver,** James Alexander d1990 *Who 92N*
**Oliver,** James Edward 1829-1895 *BiInAmS*
**Oliver,** James Henry, Jr 1931- *AmMWSc 92*
**Oliver,** James L. 1934- *WhoBlA 92*
**Oliver,** James Ray 1957- *WhoEnt 92*
**Oliver,** James Russell 1924- *AmMWSc 92*
**Oliver,** James V *WhoAmP 91*
**Oliver,** James William 1947- *WhoIns 92*
**Oliver,** Janet Mary 1945- *AmMWSc 92*
**Oliver,** Jerry Alton, Sr. 1947- *WhoBlA 92*
**Oliver,** Jesse Dean 1944- *WhoAmP 91, WhoBlA 92*
**Oliver,** Joe 1885-1938 *FacFETw*
**Oliver,** Joel Day 1945- *AmMWSc 92*
**Oliver,** John Andrew 1913- *Who 92*
**Oliver,** John E. 1933- *WrDr 92*
**Oliver,** John Edward 1933- *AmMWSc 92, IntAu&W 91*
**Oliver,** John Edward 1951- *WhoFI 92, WhoWest 92*
**Oliver,** John Eoff, Jr 1933- *AmMWSc 92*
**Oliver,** John J., Jr. 1945- *WhoBlA 92*
**Oliver,** John Keith *Who 92*
**Oliver,** John Laurence 1910- *IntAu&W 91, Who 92*
**Oliver,** John Oliver William 1911- *Who 92*
**Oliver,** John Parker 1939- *AmMWSc 92*
**Oliver,** John Percy, II 1942- *WhoAmL 92*
**Oliver,** John Preston 1934- *AmMWSc 92*
**Oliver,** John Sanford 1939- *WhoEnt 92*
**Oliver,** John William Posegate 1935- *WhoRel 92*
**Oliver,** Joyce Anne 1958- *WhoFI 92, WhoWest 92*
**Oliver,** Joyce Frizzell 1935- *WhoWest 92*
**Oliver,** Kelly Hoyet, Jr 1923- *AmMWSc 92*
**Oliver,** Ken 1948- *TwCPaSc*
**Oliver,** Kenneth A. 1912- *WrDr 92*
**Oliver,** Kenneth Nathaniel 1945- *WhoBlA 92*
**Oliver,** King 1885-1938 *NewAmDM*
**Oliver,** Lawrence Philip 1932- *WhoFI 92*
**Oliver,** LeAnn Michelle 1955- *WhoFI 92*
**Oliver,** Leslie Howard 1940- *AmMWSc 92*
**Oliver,** Madge 1874-1924 *TwCPaSc*
**Oliver,** Marian Parker 1924- *WhoAmP 91*
**Oliver,** Mark *IntAu&W 91X, WrDr 92*
**Oliver,** Mark 1957- *WhoFI 92*
**Oliver,** Mark A 1958- *WhoIns 92*
**Oliver,** Marshal 1843?-1900 *BiInAmS*
**Oliver,** Mary *DrAPF 91*
**Oliver,** Mary 1935- *ConPo 91, WrDr 92*
**Oliver,** Mary Anne McPherson 1935- *WhoRel 92*
**Oliver,** Mary Margaret *WhoAmP 91*
**Oliver,** Maureen 1947- *TwCPaSc*
**Oliver,** Melvin L. 1950- *WhoBlA 92*
**Oliver,** Michael Francis 1925- *Who 92*
**Oliver,** Michael Randolph 1961- *WhoWest 92*
**Oliver,** Michael Thomas 1943- *WhoFI 92*
**Oliver,** Montague 1919- *AmMWSc 92*
**Oliver,** Morris Albert 1918- *AmMWSc 92*
**Oliver,** Nyra J. 1951- *WhoMW 92*
**Oliver,** Owen 1863-1933 *ScFEYrs*
**Oliver,** Patrick 1933- *TwCPaSc*
**Oliver,** Paul 1927- *WrDr 92*
**Oliver,** Paul Alfred 1940- *AmMWSc 92*
**Oliver,** Paul H 1927- *IntAu&W 91*
**Oliver,** Peter 1927- *TwCPaSc*
**Oliver,** Peter Richard 1917- *Who 92*
**Oliver,** Raymond 1909-1990 *AnObit 1990*
**Oliver,** Reginald Rene St John 1952- *IntAu&W 91*
**Oliver,** Richard 1945- *IntAu&W 91*
**Oliver,** Richard Alexander Cavaye 1904- *Who 92*
**Oliver,** Richard Charles 1930- *AmMWSc 92*
**Oliver,** Richard Stanley 1936- *WhoEnt 92*
**Oliver,** Richard Wayne 1946- *WhoFI 92*
**Oliver,** Robert 1930- *WhoFI 92*
**Oliver,** Robert C 1925- *AmMWSc 92*
**Oliver,** Robert G 1927- *WhoAmP 91*
**Oliver,** Robert Marquam 1931- *AmMWSc 92*
**Oliver,** Robert Spencer 1937- *WhoAmL 92, WhoAmP 91*
**Oliver,** Robert Tarbell 1909- *WrDr 92*
**Oliver,** Robert W. 1922- *ConAu 135*
**Oliver,** Robert Warner 1922- *WhoFI 92, WhoWest 92*
**Oliver,** Roger W. *WhoEnt 92*
**Oliver,** Roland 1923- *IntWW 91*
**Oliver,** Roland Anthony 1923- *IntAu&W 91, WrDr 92*
**Oliver,** Ron 1947- *AmMWSc 92*
**Oliver,** Ronald Anthony 1923- *Who 92*
**Oliver,** Ronald Daniel 1946- *WhoBlA 92*
**Oliver,** Ronald Martin 1929- *Who 92*
**Oliver,** Ruby *ReelWom*
**Oliver,** Samuel William, Jr. 1935- *WhoAmL 92*
**Oliver,** Stephen 1950- *ConCom 92*
**Oliver,** Stephen John Lindsay 1938- *Who 92*
**Oliver,** Stephen Ronald 1947- *WhoWest 92*
**Oliver,** Steven Wiles 1947- *WhoFI 92*
**Oliver,** Sy 1910-1988 *FacFETw, NewAmDM*
**Oliver,** Terry D 1947- *WhoAmP 91*
**Oliver,** Thomas Albert 1924- *AmMWSc 92*
**Oliver,** Thomas K, Jr 1925- *AmMWSc 92*
**Oliver,** Thomas Kilbury 1922- *AmMWSc 92*
**Oliver,** William Albert, Jr 1926- *AmMWSc 92*
**Oliver,** William Henry 1915- *WhoBlA 92*
**Oliver,** William J 1925- *AmMWSc 92*
**Oliver,** William Parker 1940- *AmMWSc 92*
**Oliver-Gonzales,** Jose 1912- *AmMWSc 92*
**Oliver Leahy Tinen Kaehler,** Jeannette 1927- *WhoEnt 92*
**Oliver of Aylmerton,** Baron 1921- *IntWW 91, Who 92*
**Olivera,** Beatriz Maria 1956- *WhoHisp 92*
**Olivera,** Mercedes 1948- *WhoHisp 92*
**Oliveras,** Rene Martin 1943- *WhoHisp 92*
**Oliveras-Soto,** Gilberto 1959- *WhoHisp 92*
**Olivere,** Marilyn Hess 1949- *WhoWest 92*
**Oliverez,** Manuel *WhoHisp 92*
**Oliveri,** Sal *WhoAmP 91*
**Oliverio,** Vincent Thomas 1928- *AmMWSc 92*
**Olivero,** John Joseph, Jr 1941- *AmMWSc 92*
**Olivero,** Magda 1913?- *NewAmDM*
**Oliveros,** Chuck *DrAPF 91*
**Oliveros,** Gilda C. 1949- *WhoHisp 92*
**Oliveros,** Pauline 1932- *ConCom 92, NewAmDM, WhoEnt 92*
**Oliveto,** Eugene Paul 1924- *AmMWSc 92*
**Oliveto,** Frank Louis 1956- *WhoFI 92*
**Olivetti,** Angelo Oliviero 1874-1931 *BiDExR*
**Olivier,** Lady *Who 92*
**Olivier,** Andre 1938- *AmMWSc 92*
**Olivier,** Giorgio Borg 1911-1980 *FacFETw*
**Olivier,** Henry 1914- *Who 92*
**Olivier,** Henry Francis 1948- *WhoMW 92*
**Olivier,** Jay Charles 1947- *WhoEnt 92*
**Olivier,** Kenneth Leo 1932- *AmMWSc 92*
**Olivier,** Laurence 1907-1989 *FacFETw [port]*
**Olivier,** Lawrence Anthony 1960- *WhoEnt 92*
**Olivier,** Louis 1923- *IntWW 91*
**Olivo,** Dora F 1943- *WhoAmP 91*
**Olivo,** Efren 1936- *WhoHisp 92*
**Olivo,** Juan Ramiro 1946- *WhoHisp 92*
**Olivo,** Richard Francis 1942- *AmMWSc 92*
**Oliwa,** Dave 1954- *WhoEnt 92*
**Olken,** Melvin I 1935- *AmMWSc 92*
**Olken,** Samuel Robert 1960- *WhoAmL 92*
**Olkin,** Ingram 1924- *AmMWSc 92*
**Olkon,** Ellis 1939- *WhoAmP 91*
**Olkon,** Nancy Katherine 1941- *WhoAmP 91*
**Olkonen,** Elsie Swan 1917- *WhoAmP 91*
**Olla,** Bori Liborio 1937- *AmMWSc 92*
**Ollard,** Richard 1923- *IntAu&W 91, WrDr 92*
**Ollard,** Richard Laurence 1923- *Who 92*
**Ollee,** Mildred W. 1936- *WhoBlA 92*
**Olleman,** Roger D 1923- *AmMWSc 92*
**Ollenhauer,** Erich 1901-1963 *EncTR 91 [port]*
**Oller,** Mark Louis 1964- *WhoRel 92*
**Oller y Cestero,** Francisco 1833-1917 *ThHEIm*

**Ollerenshaw**, Kathleen 1912- Who 92, WrDr 92
**Ollerenshaw**, Neil Campbell 1933- AmMWSc 92
**Ollerhead**, Robin Wemp 1937- AmMWSc 92
**Ollerich**, Dwayne A 1934- AmMWSc 92
**Olley**, John William 1938- WhoRel 92
**Ollie**, C Arthur 1941- WhoAmP 91
**Ollier**, Cliff David 1931- WrDr 92
**Ollila**, Esko Juhani 1940- IntWW 91
**Ollis**, David F 1941- AmMWSc 92
**Ollis**, James Bruce 1934- WhoAmP 91
**Ollis**, William David 1924- Who 92
**Ollison**, Ida Bell 1926- WhoBlA 92
**Ollivant**, Alfred 1874-1927 ScFEYrs
**Olliver**, Denis G. 1940- WhoMW 92
**Olliver**, Paul 1949- WhoEnt 92
**Ollo**, Michael Anthony 1959- WhoRel 92
**Ollom**, John Frederick 1922- AmMWSc 92
**Olloqui**, Jose Juan de 1931- IntWW 91
**Ollor**, Walter Gbute 1950- WhoFI 92
**Olm**, Jeffrey Michael 1963- WhoEnt 92
**Olman**, Maryellen 1946- WhoFI 92
**Olmedo**, Irma Maria 1943- WhoHisp 92
**Olmedo**, Jose Joaquin 1780-1847 HisDSpE
**Olmedo**, Kim Ellen 1959- WhoHisp 92
**Olmer**, Jane Chasnoff AmMWSc 92
**Olmert**, Ehud 1945- IntWW 91
**Olmez**, Ilhan 1942- AmMWSc 92
**Olmi**, Ermanno 1931- IntDcF 2-2 [port], IntMPA 92, IntWW 91
**Olminsky**, Jami Kathleen 1965- WhoMW 92
**Olmo**, Ralph James 1946- WhoAmP 91
**Olmos**, Antonio Garcia 1963- WhoHisp 92
**Olmos**, David R. 1957- WhoHisp 92
**Olmos**, Edward James WhoEnt 92
**Olmos**, Edward James 1947- IntMPA 92, WhoHisp 92
**Olmstead**, Alan Mark 1948- WhoEnt 92
**Olmstead**, Dennis John 1957- WhoAmL 92
**Olmstead**, Gerald Eugene 1954- WhoRel 92
**Olmstead**, John Aaron 1930- AmMWSc 92
**Olmstead**, Marjorie A 1958- AmMWSc 92
**Olmstead**, Paul Smith 1897- AmMWSc 92
**Olmstead**, Robert 1954- WrDr 92
**Olmstead**, Tommy C 1929- WhoAmP 91
**Olmstead**, Van Dregge, Jr. 1943- WhoFI 92
**Olmstead**, William Carl 1946- WhoRel 92
**Olmstead**, William Edward 1936- AmMWSc 92
**Olmstead**, William N 1950- AmMWSc 92
**Olmsted**, Clinton Albert 1925- AmMWSc 92
**Olmsted**, David John 1939- WhoFI 92
**Olmsted**, Denison 1791-1859 BilnAmS, DcNCBi 4
**Olmsted**, Denison, Jr 1824-1846 BilnAmS
**Olmsted**, Franklin Howard 1921- AmMWSc 92
**Olmsted**, Frederick Law 1822-1903 BenetAL 91, DcTwDes
**Olmsted**, Joanna Belle 1947- AmMWSc 92
**Olmsted**, Mildred 1890- HanAmWH
**Olmsted**, Mildred Scott 1890-1990 AmPeW
**Olmsted**, Richard Dale 1947- AmMWSc 92
**Olmsted**, Robert W. 1936- WrDr 92
**Olmsted**, Sallie Lockwood 1959- WhoEnt 92
**Olness**, Alan 1941- AmMWSc 92
**Olness**, Dolores Urquiza 1935- AmMWSc 92
**Olness**, Fredrick Iver 1959- AmMWSc 92
**Olness**, John William 1929- AmMWSc 92
**Olness**, Karen Norma 1936- WhoMW 92
**Olness**, Robert James 1933- AmMWSc 92
**Olney**, Charles Edward 1924- AmMWSc 92
**Olney**, Jesse 1798-1872 BenetAL 91
**Olney**, John William 1931- AmMWSc 92
**Olney**, Kathryn Louise 1955- WhoWest 92
**Olney**, Richard 1835-1917 AmPolLe
**Olney**, Ross David 1951- AmMWSc 92
**Olney**, Ross R 1929- IntAu&W 91, WrDr 92
**Olney**, Stephen Thayer 1812-1878 BilnAmS
**O'Loane**, James Kenneth 1913- AmMWSc 92
**Olofson**, Roy Arne 1936- AmMWSc 92
**Olofson**, Tom William 1941- WhoFI 92, WhoMW 92
**Olofsson**, Daniel Joel 1954- WhoAmL 92
**Ologboni**, Tejumola F. 1945- WhoBlA 92
**O'Loghlen**, Colman 1916- Who 92
**Oloomi**, Hossein Mohammad 1959- WhoMW 92
**O'Looney**, Patricia Anne 1954- AmMWSc 92
**O'Loughlin**, Gerald Stuart 1921- IntMPA 92
**O'Loughlin**, James William, III 1955- WhoAmP 91
**O'Loughlin**, John Kirby 1929- WhoFI 92
**O'Loughlin**, Walter K 1910- AmMWSc 92
**Olovsson**, Ivar 1928- IntWW 91
**Olowu**, Dele 1952- ConAu 135
**Olp**, Anita Louise 1962- WhoWest 92
**Olphin**, Philip Bruce 1954- WhoFI 92
**Olpin**, Glen W. 1950- WhoFI 92
**Olpin**, Owen 1934- WhoAmL 92
**Olpin**, Robert Spencer 1940- WhoWest 92
**Olsby**, Gary Allen 1956- WhoRel 92
**Olsby**, Gregory Scott WhoWest 92
**Olscamp**, Paul James 1937- WhoMW 92
**Olschwang**, Alan Paul 1942- WhoAmL 92
**Olschwanger**, Paul Farley 1960- WhoFI 92
**Olsen**, Arthur Martin 1909- AmMWSc 92, WhoMW 92
**Olsen**, Bob 1884-1956 TwCSFW 91
**Olsen**, Carl John 1928- AmMWSc 92
**Olsen**, Carol M 1946- WhoIns 92
**Olsen**, Charles Edward 1943- AmMWSc 92
**Olsen**, Charles J., III 1951- WhoFI 92
**Olsen**, Clarence Wilmott 1903- AmMWSc 92
**Olsen**, Clifford Wayne 1936- WhoWest 92
**Olsen**, Curtiss Forrest 1958- WhoWest 92
**Olsen**, Dagne B 1933- WhoAmP 91
**Olsen**, Daniel Paul 1952- WhoWest 92
**Olsen**, David DrAPF 91
**Olsen**, David Magnor 1941- WhoWest 92
**Olsen**, Don B 1930- AmMWSc 92
**Olsen**, Don Lee 1928- WhoWest 92
**Olsen**, Douglas Alfred 1930- AmMWSc 92
**Olsen**, Edward John 1927- AmMWSc 92
**Olsen**, Edward Tait 1942- AmMWSc 92
**Olsen**, Edwin Carl, III 1932- AmMWSc 92
**Olsen**, Elaine 1925- WhoAmP 91
**Olsen**, Ernfred Michael 1957- WhoFI 92
**Olsen**, Eugene Donald 1933- AmMWSc 92
**Olsen**, Evan L 1932- WhoAmP 91
**Olsen**, Farrel John 1929- AmMWSc 92
**Olsen**, Frances Elisabeth 1945- WhoAmL 92
**Olsen**, Gary 1953- WhoEnt 92
**Olsen**, Gary Alvin 1949- WhoMW 92
**Olsen**, George Duane 1940- AmMWSc 92
**Olsen**, George Edward 1924- WhoMW 92
**Olsen**, Glenn W 1931- AmMWSc 92
**Olsen**, Glenn Warren 1938- WhoWest 92
**Olsen**, Gregory Hammond 1945- AmMWSc 92
**Olsen**, Hans Peter 1940- WhoAmL 92
**Olsen**, Harold Charles 1931- WhoRel 92
**Olsen**, Harold Fremont 1920- WhoAmL 92
**Olsen**, Harris Leland 1947- WhoWest 92
**Olsen**, James Calvin 1939- AmMWSc 92
**Olsen**, James Leroy 1930- AmMWSc 92
**Olsen**, James Roger 1956- WhoWest 92
**Olsen**, Janet Denney 1956- WhoAmL 92
**Olsen**, Janus Frederick, III 1942- WhoWest 92
**Olsen**, Jean Ann 1942- WhoMW 92
**Olsen**, John Stuart 1950- AmMWSc 92
**Olsen**, Kathie Lynn 1952- AmMWSc 92
**Olsen**, Kenneth 1926- AmMWSc 92
**Olsen**, Kenneth Allen 1953- WhoAmL 92
**Olsen**, Kenneth Harold 1930- AmMWSc 92
**Olsen**, Kenneth Harry 1926- WhoFI 92
**Olsen**, Kenneth Wayne 1944- AmMWSc 92
**Olsen**, Larry Carrol 1937- AmMWSc 92
**Olsen**, Lester Paul 1945- WhoRel 92
**Olsen**, M. Kent 1948- WhoAmL 92
**Olsen**, Mark Edward 1954- WhoEnt 92
**Olsen**, Marvin Elliott 1936- WhoMW 92
**Olsen**, Miles Jeffrey 1952- WhoRel 92
**Olsen**, Niels-Erik 1948- WhoFI 92
**Olsen**, Olaf 1928- IntWW 91
**Olsen**, Orvil Alva 1917- AmMWSc 92
**Olsen**, Oscar Marken 1925- WhoFI 92
**Olsen**, Otto H 1925- IntAu&W 91, WrDr 92
**Olsen**, Patricia Graciela 1951- WhoEnt 92
**Olsen**, Peter Fredric 1935- AmMWSc 92
**Olsen**, Ralph A 1925- AmMWSc 92
**Olsen**, Richard George 1937- AmMWSc 92
**Olsen**, Richard Kenneth 1935- AmMWSc 92
**Olsen**, Richard Standal 1936- AmMWSc 92
**Olsen**, Richard William 1944- AmMWSc 92
**Olsen**, Robert Arthur 1943- WhoFI 92, WhoWest 92
**Olsen**, Robert Gerner 1946- AmMWSc 92
**Olsen**, Robert John 1928- WhoFI 92
**Olsen**, Robert Thorvald 1915- AmMWSc 92
**Olsen**, Rodney L 1936- AmMWSc 92
**Olsen**, Ronald H 1932- AmMWSc 92
**Olsen**, Sally WhoAmP 91
**Olsen**, Samuel Richard, Jr. 1938- WhoMW 92
**Olsen**, Sheila Ann 1938- WhoAmP 91
**Olsen**, Sondra Spatt DrAPF 91
**Olsen**, Stanley John 1919- AmMWSc 92, WhoWest 92
**Olsen**, Stephen Lars 1942- AmMWSc 92
**Olsen**, Steven Lloyd 1950- WhoWest 92
**Olsen**, T. V. 1932- TwCWW 91, WrDr 92
**Olsen**, Theodore Victor 1932- IntAu&W 91
**Olsen**, Tillie DrAPF 91
**Olsen**, Tillie 1912?- ConNov 91
**Olsen**, Tillie 1913- BenetAL 91, HanAmWH, TwCWW 91, WrDr 92
**Olsen**, Torkil 1922- IntWW 91
**Olsen**, Violet 1922-1991 ConAu 134
**Olsen**, W. Scott DrAPF 91
**Olsen**, Ward Alan 1934- AmMWSc 92
**Olsen**, Wesley WhoRel 92
**Olsen**, William Charles 1933- AmMWSc 92
**Olsen**, William Michael 1945- WhoFI 92
**Olshan**, Kenneth S. 1932- WhoFI 92
**Olshansky**, Brian 1952- WhoMW 92
**Olshansky**, Norman 1946- WhoRel 92
**Olshen**, Abraham C 1913- AmMWSc 92
**Olshen**, Abraham Charles 1913- WhoFI 92, WhoWest 92
**Olshen**, Richard Allen 1942- AmMWSc 92
**Olsher**, Laura Nancy 1927- WhoEnt 92
**Olshove**, Dennis WhoAmP 91
**Olson**, Albert Lloyd 1924- AmMWSc 92
**Olson**, Alec Gehard 1930- WhoAmP 91
**Olson**, Alfred C 1926- AmMWSc 92
**Olson**, Alice Adele 1928- WhoAmP 91
**Olson**, Allan Theodore 1930- AmMWSc 92
**Olson**, Allen Ingvar 1938- IntWW 91, WhoAmP 91
**Olson**, Andrew Clarence, Jr 1917- AmMWSc 92
**Olson**, Ann Terrie 1959- WhoAmL 92
**Olson**, Arielle North 1932- ConAu 134, SmATA 67 [port]
**Olson**, Arthur Olaf 1942- AmMWSc 92
**Olson**, Arthur Russell 1919- AmMWSc 92
**Olson**, Austin C 1918- AmMWSc 92
**Olson**, Barbara Jeannette Sloan 1950- WhoEnt 92
**Olson**, Barry Gay 1933- WhoMW 92
**Olson**, Betty H 1947- AmMWSc 92
**Olson**, Bill 1953- WhoAmP 91
**Olson**, Bruce Allan 1947- WhoFI 92
**Olson**, Bruce Joseph 1949- WhoEnt 92
**Olson**, Carl 1910- AmMWSc 92
**Olson**, Carl 1941- ConAu 36NR
**Olson**, Carl Eric 1914- WhoAmL 92
**Olson**, Carol 1957- WhoAmP 91
**Olson**, Carol Ann 1945- WhoRel 92
**Olson**, Carter LeRoy 1935- AmMWSc 92
**Olson**, Charles 1910-1970 BenetAL 91, ConAu 35NR, FacFETw
**Olson**, Charles D. 1956- WhoAmL 92
**Olson**, Clifford Gerald 1942- AmMWSc 92
**Olson**, Clifford Larry 1946- WhoFI 92, WhoMW 92
**Olson**, Clinton L 1916- WhoAmP 91
**Olson**, Craig Alan 1960- WhoWest 92
**Olson**, Craig William 1934- WhoAmP 91
**Olson**, Craig William 1956- WhoMW 92
**Olson**, Dale C. 1934- IntMPA 92, WhoEnt 92
**Olson**, Dale Wilson 1941- AmMWSc 92
**Olson**, Dan 1955- WhoAmP 91
**Olson**, Dan Emil 1942- WhoMW 92
**Olson**, Danford Harold 1935- AmMWSc 92
**Olson**, Daniel Dwain 1953- WhoFI 92
**Olson**, Darryl Raynold 1940- WhoRel 92
**Olson**, David Carl 1954- WhoEnt 92
**Olson**, David Conrad 1949- WhoAmL 92
**Olson**, David Gardels 1940- AmMWSc 92
**Olson**, David Harold 1937- AmMWSc 92
**Olson**, David John 1941- IntAu&W 91, WhoWest 92
**Olson**, David LeRoy 1942- AmMWSc 92
**Olson**, David Richard 1935- WrDr 92
**Olson**, David Wendell 1938- WhoRel 92
**Olson**, David Wendell 1950- WhoMW 92
**Olson**, Dennis Thorald 1954- WhoRel 92
**Olson**, Donald B 1952- AmMWSc 92
**Olson**, Donald George 1941- WhoMW 92
**Olson**, Donald Richard 1917- AmMWSc 92
**Olson**, Douglas Bernard 1945- AmMWSc 92, WhoWest 92
**Olson**, Douglas Stuart 1960- WhoFI 92
**Olson**, Earl Burdette, Jr 1939- AmMWSc 92
**Olson**, Edgar L 1937- WhoAmP 91
**Olson**, Edward Cooper 1930- AmMWSc 92
**Olson**, Edwin Andrew 1925- AmMWSc 92
**Olson**, Edwin S 1937- AmMWSc 92
**Olson**, Edwin W, Jr WhoAmP 91
**Olson**, Elder 1909- BenetAL 91, ConPo 91, IntAu&W 91, WrDr 92
**Olson**, Elizabeth Kirk 1955- WhoFI 92
**Olson**, Emanuel A 1916- AmMWSc 92
**Olson**, Eric Ellis 1949- WhoEnt 92
**Olson**, Erik Joseph 1932- AmMWSc 92
**Olson**, Everett C. 1910- IntWW 91
**Olson**, Everett Claire 1910- AmMWSc 92
**Olson**, Ferron Allred 1921- AmMWSc 92
**Olson**, Frances Allene 1914- WhoAmP 91
**Olson**, Frank Albert 1932- WhoFI 92
**Olson**, Frank R 1922- AmMWSc 92
**Olson**, Gary Lee 1945- AmMWSc 92
**Olson**, Gary Miles 1931- WhoAmP 91
**Olson**, Gary Monroe 1944- WhoMW 92
**Olson**, Gen 1938- WhoAmP 91, WhoMW 92
**Olson**, Gene 1926- WhoAmP 91
**Olson**, George Gilbert 1924- AmMWSc 92
**Olson**, George LeRoy 1924- WhoRel 92
**Olson**, Gerald Allen 1944- AmMWSc 92
**Olson**, Gerald Lee 1933- WhoMW 92
**Olson**, Gerald Theodore 1928- WhoWest 92
**Olson**, Gordon Lee 1951- AmMWSc 92
**Olson**, Gordon W. 1936- WhoRel 92
**Olson**, Grace Cameron 1940- WhoRel 92
**Olson**, H M 1923- AmMWSc 92
**Olson**, Harold Cecil 1905- AmMWSc 92
**Olson**, Harold Dean 1946- WhoMW 92
**Olson**, Harry Andrew, Jr. 1923- WhoFI 92
**Olson**, Horace Andrew 1925- IntWW 91
**Olson**, Howard H 1927- AmMWSc 92
**Olson**, Howard Halfdan 1927- WhoAmP 91
**Olson**, Howard Stanley 1922- WhoRel 92
**Olson**, J S 1928- AmMWSc 92
**Olson**, Jack Benjamin 1920- WhoAmP 91
**Olson**, James 1930- IntMPA 92
**Olson**, James Allen 1924- AmMWSc 92
**Olson**, James Clifton 1917- WrDr 92
**Olson**, James Gordon 1940- AmMWSc 92
**Olson**, James Paul 1941- AmMWSc 92
**Olson**, James R. DrAPF 91
**Olson**, James Robert 1940- WhoFI 92
**Olson**, James Robert 1943- AmMWSc 92
**Olson**, Janice Lynn 1946- WhoWest 92
**Olson**, Jean L 1948- AmMWSc 92
**Olson**, Jerry Chipman 1917- AmMWSc 92, WhoWest 92
**Olson**, Jerry Dean, Jr. 1958- WhoRel 92
**Olson**, Jimmy Karl 1942- AmMWSc 92
**Olson**, John A. WhoRel 92
**Olson**, John Bennet 1917- AmMWSc 92
**Olson**, John Bernard 1931- AmMWSc 92
**Olson**, John Frederick 1939- WhoAmL 92
**Olson**, John Melvin 1929- AmMWSc 92
**Olson**, John Michael 1947- WhoAmL 92, WhoAmP 91, WhoMW 92
**Olson**, John Richard 1932- AmMWSc 92
**Olson**, John S 1946- AmMWSc 92
**Olson**, John Victor 1913- AmMWSc 92
**Olson**, Jon H 1934- AmMWSc 92
**Olson**, Judith Mary Reedy 1939- WhoMW 92
**Olson**, Judith Reedy 1939- WhoAmP 91
**Olson**, Karl William 1936- AmMWSc 92
**Olson**, Katy 1928- WhoAmP 91
**Olson**, Kenneth B 1908- AmMWSc 92
**Olson**, Kenneth Paul 1935- WhoWest 92
**Olson**, Kim L. 1956- WhoFI 92
**Olson**, Kirby DrAPF 91
**Olson**, Lance David 1951- WhoEnt 92
**Olson**, Larry Allan 1952- WhoMW 92
**Olson**, Lee Charles 1936- AmMWSc 92
**Olson**, Leonard Carl 1945- AmMWSc 92
**Olson**, LeRoy David 1929- AmMWSc 92
**Olson**, Leroy Justin 1926- AmMWSc 92
**Olson**, Lloyd Clarence 1935- AmMWSc 92, WhoMW 92
**Olson**, Lowell Eugene 1939- WhoMW 92
**Olson**, Lyndon Lowell, Jr 1947- WhoAmP 91
**Olson**, Lynne E AmMWSc 92
**Olson**, Magnus 1909- AmMWSc 92
**Olson**, Mancur, Jr. 1932- WrDr 92
**Olson**, Marian Katherine 1933- WhoWest 92
**Olson**, Mark Jack 1963- WhoRel 92
**Olson**, Mark Obed Jerome 1940- AmMWSc 92
**Olson**, Marlin Lee 1927- WhoMW 92
**Olson**, Matthew Wayne 1960- WhoRel 92
**Olson**, Maurice Alan 1926- WhoAmP 91
**Olson**, Maynard Victor 1943- AmMWSc 92
**Olson**, Melvin Martin 1915- AmMWSc 92
**Olson**, Merle Stratte 1940- AmMWSc 92
**Olson**, Myron J 1928- WhoAmP 91
**Olson**, Nancy 1929- IntMPA 92
**Olson**, Nancy Suzanne 1955- WhoWest 92
**Olson**, Norman Fredrick 1931- AmMWSc 92
**Olson**, Norman O 1914- AmMWSc 92
**Olson**, Orlin A 1926- WhoAmP 91
**Olson**, Oscar Edward 1914- AmMWSc 92
**Olson**, Paul Andrew 1932- WhoMW 92
**Olson**, Paul Leonard 1952- WhoRel 92
**Olson**, Paul Lester Herman 1950- WhoFI 92
**Olson**, Peter Lee 1950- AmMWSc 92
**Olson**, Peter Wesley 1950- WhoFI 92
**Olson**, Phyllis Arlene 1944- WhoMW 92
**Olson**, Randall J 1947- AmMWSc 92
**Olson**, Reuben Magnus 1919- AmMWSc 92

Olson, Richard David 1944- AmMWSc 92
Olson, Richard Dean 1949- WhoWest 92
Olson, Richard Earl 1953- WhoAmP 91
Olson, Richard Gottlieb 1922- WhoMW 92
Olson, Richard Hubbell 1928- AmMWSc 92
Olson, Richard Jeffrey 1953- WhoMW 92
Olson, Richard Louis 1932- AmMWSc 92
Olson, Rita Kaye 1948- WhoMW 92
Olson, Robert 1930- WhoAmP 91
Olson, Robert Earl 1947- WhoMW 92
Olson, Robert Eldon 1940- AmMWSc 92
Olson, Robert Eugene 1919- AmMWSc 92
Olson, Robert Howard 1944- WhoAmL 92, WhoWest 92
Olson, Robert Leroy 1932- AmMWSc 92
Olson, Robert Wyrick 1945- WhoAmL 92
Olson, Rodney Ellsworth 1912- WhoWest 92
Olson, Roger D. 1967- WhoFI 92
Olson, Ronald Charles 1937- WhoWest 92
Olson, Roy Arthur 1938- WhoMW 92
Olson, Roy E 1929- AmMWSc 92
Olson, Roy Edwin 1931- AmMWSc 92
Olson, Rue Eileen 1928- WhoMW 92
Olson, Russell A WhoAmP 91
Olson, Russell L. 1933- WhoFI 92
Olson, Scott Michael 1962- WhoEnt 92
Olson, Sharee 1941- WhoEnt 92
Olson, Sharon DrAPF 91
Olson, Stanley William 1914- AmMWSc 92
Olson, Stephen Edward 1941- WhoFI 92
Olson, Steven Darrel 1953- WhoRel 92
Olson, Steven Floyd 1953- WhoRel 92
Olson, Steven Stanley 1950- WhoWest 92
Olson, Steven T 1948- AmMWSc 92
Olson, Storrs Lovejoy 1944- AmMWSc 92
Olson, Terrence Leonard 1953- WhoEnt 92
Olson, Theodore Bevry 1940- WhoAmP 91
Olson, Thomas Charles 1949- WhoEnt 92
Olson, Thomas Jon 1953- WhoWest 92
Olson, Thomas Michael 1946- WhoIns 92
Olson, Timothy Allan 1952- WhoWest 92
Olson, Toby DrAPF 91
Olson, Toby 1937- ConPo 91, IntAu&W 91, WrDr 92
Olson, Vincent WhoAmP 91
Olson, Walter Harold 1945- AmMWSc 92
Olson, Walter K. 1954- ConAu 135
Olson, Walter T 1917- AmMWSc 92
Olson, Wanda 1957- WhoAmL 92
Olson, Wilbert Orin 1947- WhoMW 92
Olson, Willard Orvin 1933- AmMWSc 92
Olson, Willard Paul 1939- AmMWSc 92
Olson, William Arthur 1932- AmMWSc 92
Olson, William Bruce 1930- AmMWSc 92
Olson, William Jeffrey 1949- WhoAmL 92, WhoAmP 91
Olson, William Marvin 1929- AmMWSc 92
Olson, William Thomas 1940- WhoWest 92
Olson, Wilma King 1945- AmMWSc 92
Olsson, Alexis Bruno 1960- WhoMW 92
Olsson, Carl Alfred 1938- AmMWSc 92
Olsson, Curt G. 1927- IntWW 91
Olsson, Curt Gunnar 1927- Who 92
Olsson, George C.P. d1991 NewYTBS 91
Olsson, Julius 1864-1942 TwCPaSc
Olsson, Nils Ove 1932- AmMWSc 92
Olsson, Pehr Christopher 1947- WhoMW 92
Olsson, Ray Andrew 1931- AmMWSc 92
Olsson, Richard Keith 1931- AmMWSc 92
Olsson, Ronald Arthur 1955- WhoWest 92
Olsson-Seffer, Pehr Hjalmar 1873-1911 BiInAmS
Olstad, Brent Raymond 1960- WhoRel 92
Olstad, Charles 1932-1976 ConAu 134
Olstad, Roger Gale 1934- AmMWSc 92
Olsten, Jann L 1948- WhoAmP 91
Olsten, William d1991 NewYTBS 91 [port]
Olster, Elliot Frederick 1942- AmMWSc 92
Olstowski, Franciszek 1927- AmMWSc 92, WhoFI 92
Olszanski, Dennis John 1948- AmMWSc 92
Olszewski, Liliana 1965- WhoHisp 92
Olte, Andrejs 1927- AmMWSc 92
Oltenacu, Elizabeth Allison Branford 1947- AmMWSc 92
Olthof, Theodorus Hendrikus Antonius 1934- AmMWSc 92
Oltjen, Robert Raymond 1932- AmMWSc 92
Oltman, C. Dwight 1936- WhoEnt 92
Oltramare, Georges 1896-1960 BiDExR
Oltz, Richard John 1945- WhoRel 92
Oludhe-Macgoye, Marjorie 1928- ConAu 133
Olufosoye, Timothy 1918- Who 92
Olufosoye, Timothy Omotayo 1918- IntWW 91, WhoRel 92
Olugebefola, Ademola 1941- WhoBlA 92
Oluleye, James Johnson 1937- IntWW 91
Olum, Paul 1918- AmMWSc 92, WhoWest 92
Olver, Elwood Forrest 1922- AmMWSc 92
Olver, Frank William John 1924- AmMWSc 92
Olver, John 1936- AlmAP 92 [port]
Olver, John Walter 1936- AmMWSc 92, WhoAmP 91
Olver, Peter John 1952- AmMWSc 92
Olver, Stephen 1916- Who 92
Olvera, Joe DrAPF 91
Olvera, Joe E. 1944- WhoHisp 92
Olvera, Jose Jesus 1935- WhoHisp 92
Olvera-dela Cruz, Monica 1958- AmMWSc 92
Olyanova, Nadya d1991 NewYTBS 91
Olympias d314BC EncAmaz 91
Olympias 365?-410? EncEarC
Olympiodorus EncEarC
Olynyk, Paul 1918- AmMWSc 92
Olyott, Leonard Eric 1926- Who 92
Olyphant, Murray, Jr 1923- AmMWSc 92
Olzacki, James Joseph 1949- WhoIns 92
Omachi, Akira 1922- AmMWSc 92
Omahana, Robin Joseph 1950- WhoAmL 92
O'Mahoney, Michael Terrence 1943- WhoMW 92
O'Mahony, Audrey Madeline 1938- WhoRel 92
O'Mahony, Kevin Patrick 1957- WhoAmL 92
Omai 1753?-1780? BlkwCEP
O'Maley, David Boyers 1946- WhoIns 92
O'Malley, Alice T 1929- AmMWSc 92
O'Malley, Bert W 1936- AmMWSc 92
O'Malley, Carlon Martin 1929- WhoAmL 92
O'Malley, Cornelia Leary 1906- WhoAmL 92
O'Malley, David Patrick 1944- WhoEnt 92
O'Malley, Desmond Joseph 1939- IntWW 91
O'Malley, Dianemarie DrAPF 91
O'Malley, Edward Joseph, III 1948- WhoAmL 92
O'Malley, Edward Joseph, Jr. 1942- WhoFI 92
O'Malley, Edward Paul 1926- AmMWSc 92
O'Malley, Emanuela DrAPF 91
O'Malley, Eugene Francis 1950- WhoFI 92
O'Malley, Frank IntAu&W 91X
O'Malley, Frank Ward 1875-1932 BenetAL 91
O'Malley, Grace 1530?-1600? EncAmaz 91
O'Malley, Jack WhoAmL 92
O'Malley, James Joseph 1940- AmMWSc 92
O'Malley, James Patrick, III 1951- WhoEnt 92
O'Malley, John Richard 1928- AmMWSc 92
O'Malley, Joseph James 1923- WhoAmL 92
O'Malley, Joseph W WhoAmP 91
O'Malley, Mary 1941- IntAu&W 91, WrDr 92
O'Malley, Mary Therese AmMWSc 92
O'Malley, Matthew Joseph 1940- AmMWSc 92
O'Malley, Michael William 1947- WhoMW 92
O'Malley, Patrick IntAu&W 91X
O'Malley, Patrick Anthony 1942- WhoMW 92
O'Malley, Peter 1937- WhoWest 92
O'Malley, Richard John 1945- AmMWSc 92
O'Malley, Robert Edmund, Jr 1939- AmMWSc 92
O'Malley, Robert Francis 1918- AmMWSc 92
O'Malley, Scott 1946- WhoEnt 92
O'Malley, Sean 1944- WhoRel 92
O'Malley, Shaun F. WhoFI 92
O'Malley, Shelly Savard 1962- WhoEnt 92
O'Malley, Stephen Joseph 1965- WhoMW 92
O'Malley, Stephen Keppel 1940- Who 92
O'Malley, Terence Trumpy 1944- WhoAmP 91
O'Malley, Thomas Francis 1928- AmMWSc 92
O'Malley, Tony 1913- TwCPaSc
O'Malley, Walter F 1903-1979 FacFETw
O'Malley, William Charles 1937- WhoFI 92
Oman, Carl Henry 1938- AmMWSc 92
Oman, Charles McMaster 1944- AmMWSc 92
Oman, David A 1952- WhoAmP 91
Oman, Douglas A 1944- WhoAmP 91
Oman, Henry 1918- AmMWSc 92
Oman, Julia Trevelyan 1930- IntWW 91, Who 92
Oman, Paul Wilson 1908- AmMWSc 92
Oman, Paul Wilson, Jr. 1951- WhoWest 92
Oman, Ralph 1940- WhoAmL 92
Oman, Richard Heer 1926- WhoAmL 92, WhoMW 92
Oman, Robert Milton 1934- AmMWSc 92
Oman, Sidney Maynard 1928- WhoAmP 91
Omana, Julio Alfredo, Sr. 1938- WhoHisp 92
Omand, David Bruce 1947- Who 92
Omang, Joanne 1943- ConAu 135
Omann, Bernie WhoAmP 91
Omansky, Michael Laurence 1952- WhoEnt 92
Omar Moreau DcNCBi 4
Omar, Abu Hassan Bin Haj 1940- IntWW 91
Omar, Irfan 1965- WhoRel 92
Omar, Napsiah binti 1943- IntWW 91
O'Mara, James Herbert 1936- AmMWSc 92
O'Mara, James Wright 1940- WhoAmL 92
O'Mara, John Aloysius 1924- WhoRel 92
O'Mara, Marilyn Mae 1942- WhoMW 92
O'Mara, Michael Martin 1942- AmMWSc 92
O'Mara, Robert E 1933- AmMWSc 92
O'Mara, Stephen Paul 1951- WhoEnt 92
Omari, Dunstan Alfred 1922- IntWW 91
O'Marie, Carol Anne 1915- WrDr 92
Omata, Robert Rokuro 1920- AmMWSc 92
Omaye, Stanley Teruo 1945- AmMWSc 92
Omdah, Lloyd B. 1931- WhoMW 92
Omdahl, John L 1940- AmMWSc 92
Omdahl, Lloyd B 1931- WhoAmP 91
O'Mealia, James Paul 1958- WhoFI 92
O'Meara, David Lillis 1959- AmMWSc 92
O'Meara, Edward S WhoAmP 91
O'Meara, Edward Thomas 1921- WhoRel 92
O'Meara, Eileen Anne 1960- WhoEnt 92
O'Meara, George Francis 1941- AmMWSc 92
O'Meara, John Joseph 1915- WrDr 92
O'Meara, Marcian Thomas 1929- WhoRel 92
O'Meara, O Timothy 1928- AmMWSc 92
O'Meara, Thomas Franklin 1935- WhoRel 92
O'Meara, Walter A 1897-1989 SmATA 65 [port]
O'Melia, Charles R 1934- AmMWSc 92
Omenn, Gilbert S 1941- AmMWSc 92
Omer, George Elbert, Jr 1922- AmMWSc 92
Omer, Guy Clifton, Jr 1912- AmMWSc 92
Omer, Robert Wendell 1948- WhoFI 92, WhoMW 92
Omernick, Raymond John 1923- WhoAmP 91
Omholt, Bruce Donald 1943- WhoFI 92, WhoWest 92
Omholt, Elmer V 1920- WhoAmP 91
Omid, Ahmad 1931- AmMWSc 92
Omidvar, Kazem 1926- AmMWSc 92
Omilijonas, Vytas Albinas 1958- WhoMW 92
Ominami Pascual, Carlos 1951- IntWW 91
Ominsky, Alan Jay 1938- WhoAmL 92
Omiros, George James 1956- WhoFI 92
Ommerle, Harry G. d1976 LesBEnT 92
Ommodt, Donald Henry 1931- WhoMW 92
Omodt, Gary Wilson 1929- AmMWSc 92
Omolade, Barbara 1942- WhoBlA 92
Omole, Gabriel Gbolabo 1940- WhoFI 92
Omoleye, Mike 1940- IntAu&W 91
Omolodun, John Olatunji 1935- Who 92
O Morain, Donall 1923- IntWW 91
O'Morchoe, Charles C C 1931- AmMWSc 92
O'Morchoe, David Nial Creagh 1928- Who 92
O'Morchoe, Patricia Jean 1930- AmMWSc 92
Omorogbe, Oluyinka Osayame 1957- IntWW 91
O'Morrison, Kevin IntAu&W 91
O'Morrison, Kevin 1916- WhoEnt 92
Omran, Abdel Rahim 1925- AmMWSc 92
Omtvedt, Irvin T 1935- AmMWSc 92
O'Mullane, Tess De Araugo ConAu 135
Omura, Jimmie Matsumoto 1912- IntAu&W 91
Omura, Jimmy Kazuhiro 1940- AmMWSc 92, WhoWest 92
Omura, June Ellen 1964- WhoEnt 92
Ona, Pedro de 1570-1643? HisDSpE
Onak, Thomas Philip 1932- WhoWest 92
Onal, Ergun 1946- AmMWSc 92
O'Nan, Michael Ernest 1943- AmMWSc 92
Onana-Awana, Charles 1923- IntWW 91
Onassis, Aristotle 1906-1975 FacFETw
Onassis, Jacqueline FacFETw
Onassis, Jacqueline Lee Bouvier 1929- IntWW 91
Onat, E T 1925- AmMWSc 92
Onate, Juan De DcAmImH
Onate, Juan de 1549-1624 HisDSpE
Oncken, Henry Kuck 1938- WhoAmL 92
Oncley, John Lawrence 1910- AmMWSc 92
Oncley, Paul Bennett 1911- AmMWSc 92
Onda, Robert Jeffrey 1957- WhoAmL 92
Ondaatje, Michael 1943- BenetAL 91, ConNov 91, ConPo 91, IntAu&W 91, IntWW 91, LiExTwC, WrDr 92
Ondack, Daniel Lee 1952- WhoMW 92
Ondarts, Raul Agustin 1915- IntWW 91
Ondas, Susan Marie 1964- WhoMW 92
Ondeck, Thomas P. 1946- WhoAmL 92
Ondejko, Michael Raymond 1960- WhoMW 92
Onder, Melih Kamil 1966- WhoFI 92
Onderdonk, Mike WhoAmP 91
Ondetti, Miguel Angel 1930- AmMWSc 92
Ondik, Helen Margaret 1930- AmMWSc 92
Ondina, Jorge H 1931- WhoIns 92
Ondo, Jerome G 1939- AmMWSc 92
Ondov, John Michael 1948- AmMWSc 92
Ondrejka, Arthur Richard 1934- AmMWSc 92
Ondrejka, Ronald 1932- WhoEnt 92
One Of The Survivors ScFEYrs
One Who Saw It ScFEYrs
One, Ernest G 1929- WhoIns 92
O'Neal, Andrea Louise 1952- WhoMW 92
O'Neal, B F, Jr 1922- WhoAmP 91
O'Neal, Charles Edward 1950- WhoFI 92
O'Neal, Charles Harold 1936- AmMWSc 92
O'Neal, Charles Roy 1929- WhoMW 92
O'Neal, Connie Murry 1951- WhoBlA 92
O'Neal, Dale, Jr. 1957- WhoAmL 92
O'Neal, Eddie S. 1935- WhoBlA 92
Oneal, Elizabeth 1934- IntAu&W 91, WrDr 92
O'Neal, Ellis Eldridge, Jr. 1923- WhoRel 92
O'Neal, F. Hodge d1991 NewYTBS 91
O'Neal, Floyd Breland 1928- AmMWSc 92
O'Neal, Frederick 1905- IntMPA 92, WhoEnt 92
O'Neal, Frederick Douglas 1905- WhoBlA 92
O'Neal, Fredrick William, Jr. 1948- WhoBlA 92
O'Neal, Gerald Frederick 1933- WhoIns 92
Oneal, Glen, Jr 1917- AmMWSc 92
O'Neal, Hank 1940- ConAu 134, WhoEnt 92
O'Neal, Harriet Roberts 1952- WhoWest 92
O'Neal, Harry E 1931- AmMWSc 92
O'Neal, Harry Roger 1935- AmMWSc 92
O'Neal, Hubert Ronald 1937- AmMWSc 92
O'Neal, James Duane 1928- WhoFI 92
O'Neal, John Benjamin, Jr 1934- AmMWSc 92
O'Neal, John M. 1940- WhoBlA 92
O'Neal, Julia Caroline 1949- WhoWest 92
O'Neal, Kathleen Len 1953- WhoFI 92
O'Neal, Malinda King 1929- WhoBlA 92
O'Neal, Melinda Pauly 1950- WhoEnt 92
O'Neal, Michael R 1951- WhoAmP 91
O'Neal, Michael Ralph 1951- WhoAmL 92
O'Neal, Michael Scott, Sr. 1948- WhoAmL 92
O'Neal, Patricia L 1923- AmMWSc 92
O'Neal, Patrick 1927- IntMPA 92
O'Neal, Regina WhoBlA 92
O'Neal, Robert Munger 1922- AmMWSc 92
O'Neal, Ron 1937- IntMPA 92
O'Neal, Ronald Eugene 1942- WhoMW 92
O'Neal, Russell D 1914- AmMWSc 92
O'Neal, Ryan 1941- IntMPA 92, IntWW 91, WhoEnt 92
O'Neal, Shaquille 1972- News 92-1 [port]
O'Neal, Steven George 1947- AmMWSc 92
O'Neal, Tatum 1963- IntMPA 92, IntWW 91, WhoEnt 92
O'Neal, Thomas Denny 1941- AmMWSc 92
O'Neal, Thomas Norman 1938- AmMWSc 92
O'Neal, Tosha Dierdre 1961- WhoEnt 92
Oneal, Zibby WrDr 92
Oneda, Sadao 1923- AmMWSc 92
O'Neil, Alexander Henry Who 92
O'Neil, Bernerd Le Roy 1935- WhoMW 92
O'Neil, Brian Stephen 1952- WhoFI 92
O'Neil, Carol Elliot 1951- AmMWSc 92
O'Neil, Charles Albert 1952- WhoEnt 92
O'Neil, Daniel Joseph 1942- AmMWSc 92
O'Neil, Desmond 1920- Who 92

**O'Neil**, Elizabeth Jean 1942- *AmMWSc 92*
**O'Neil**, Ervin Raymond 1959- *WhoRel 92*
**O'Neil**, James E 1939- *WhoAmP 91*
**O'Neil**, James Edward 1939- *WhoAmL 92*
**O'Neil**, James R 1934- *AmMWSc 92*
**O'Neil**, John G A 1937- *WhoAmP 91*
**O'Neil**, John J 1928- *AmMWSc 92*
**O'Neil**, John J 1935- *AmMWSc 92*
**O'Neil**, John Joseph 1943- *WhoAmL 92, WhoFI 92*
**O'Neil**, Kelly Kenneth 1954- *WhoFI 92*
**O'Neil**, Leo E. 1928- *WhoRel 92*
**O'Neil**, Lisa M 1964- *WhoAmP 91*
**O'Neil**, Louis C 1930- *AmMWSc 92*
**O'Neil**, Michael Gerald 1922- *IntWW 91*
**O'Neil**, Patrick Eugene 1942- *AmMWSc 92*
**O'Neil**, Philip William 1958- *WhoWest 92*
**O'Neil**, Robert James 1955- *AmMWSc 92*
**O'Neil**, Robert Marchant 1934- *WhoAmL 92*
**O'Neil**, Roger 1938- *Who 92*
**O'Neil**, Russell 1927-1991 *NewYTBS 91*
**Oneil**, Stephen Vincent 1947- *AmMWSc 92*
**Oneil**, Susan Jean 1952- *WhoMW 92*
**O'Neil**, Terry *LesBEnT 92*
**O'Neil**, Thomas 1922- *WhoAmP 91*
**O'Neil**, Thomas F. 1915- *IntMPA 92*
**O'Neil**, Thomas Francis 1915- *IntWW 91*
**O'Neil**, Thomas Michael 1940- *AmMWSc 92*
**O'Neil**, William Andrew 1927- *IntWW 91*
**O'Neill** *Who 92*
**O'Neill**, Baron 1933- *Who 92*
**O'Neill**, Alan Albert 1916- *Who 92*
**O'Neill**, Arthur J *WhoAmP 91*
**O'Neill**, Arthur J. 1917- *WhoRel 92*
**O'Neill**, Beverly Lewis 1930- *WhoRel 92*
**O'Neill**, Brian 1940- *AmMWSc 92, WhoIns 92*
**O'Neill**, Brian Dennis 1946- *WhoAmL 92*
**O'Neill**, Brian Edward 1935- *WhoFI 92*
**O'Neill**, Christina Marie 1953- *WhoAmP 91*
**O'Neill**, Clifford 1964- *WhoEnt 92*
**O'Neill**, Daniel 1920-1974 *TwCPaSc*
**O'Neill**, Daniel 1938- *WhoHisp 92*
**O'Neill**, Dennis William 1939- *WhoFI 92*
**O'Neill**, Donald Edmund 1926- *WhoFI 92*
**O'Neill**, Edward John 1942- *AmMWSc 92*
**O'Neill**, Edward Leo 1927- *AmMWSc 92*
**O'Neill**, Edward True 1940- *AmMWSc 92*
**O'Neill**, Egan *IntAu&W 91X*
**O'Neill**, Eileen Jane 1955- *AmMWSc 92*
**O'Neill**, Eugene 1888-1953 *BenetAL 91, RComAH*
**O'Neill**, Eugene F 1918- *AmMWSc 92*
**O'Neill**, Eugene Gladstone 1888-1953 *FacFETw [port], WhoNob 90*
**O'Neill**, Finbarr Joseph 1952- *WhoAmL 92*
**O'Neill**, Francis X, Jr *WhoAmP 91*
**O'Neill**, Frank John 1940- *AmMWSc 92*
**O'Neill**, Gary Marshall 1952- *WhoFI 92, WhoWest 92*
**O'Neill**, George Francis 1922- *AmMWSc 92*
**O'Neill**, Gerard K 1927- *SmATA 65 [port]*
**O'Neill**, Hector *WhoAmP 91, WhoHisp 92*
**O'Neill**, Hugh 1939- *Who 92*
**O'Neill**, James A, Jr 1933- *AmMWSc 92*
**O'Neill**, James E, Jr 1929- *WhoAmP 91*
**O'Neill**, James F 1923- *AmMWSc 92*
**O'Neill**, James Michael 1954- *WhoAmP 91*
**O'Neill**, Jennifer 1949- *IntMPA 92*
**O'Neill**, Jennifer Lee 1948- *WhoEnt 92*
**O'Neill**, John Cornelius 1929- *AmMWSc 92*
**O'Neill**, John Dacey 1930- *AmMWSc 92*
**O'Neill**, John Francis 1937- *AmMWSc 92*
**O'Neill**, John H, Jr 1922- *AmMWSc 92*
**O'Neill**, John Joseph 1919- *AmMWSc 92*
**O'Neill**, John T. 1944- *WhoFI 92*
**O'Neill**, Joseph 1878-1952 *TwCSFW 91*
**ONeill**, Joseph Lawrence 1931- *AmMWSc 92*
**O'Neill**, Judith 1930- *WrDr 92*
**O'Neill**, June Ellenoff 1934- *WhoFI 92*
**O'Neill**, Katherine Templeton 1949- *WhoMW 92*
**O'Neill**, Lawrence Daniel 1946- *WhoAmL 92*
**O'Neill**, Lawrence T. *DrAPF 91*
**O'Neill**, Martin 1945- *Who 92*
**O'Neill**, Mary Teresa 1944- *WhoMW 92*
**O'Neill**, Matt 1937- *WhoAmP 91*
**O'Neill**, Michael 1953- *ConAu 133*
**O'Neill**, Michael Foy 1943- *WhoWest 92*
**O'Neill**, Michael Joseph 1956- *WhoFI 92*
**O'Neill**, Michael Joseph 1960- *WhoFI 92*
**O'Neill**, Michael Wayne 1940- *AmMWSc 92*
**O'Neill**, Norah Ellen 1949- *WhoWest 92*
**O'Neill**, Norris Lawrence 1926- *WhoAmL 92*
**O'Neill**, Patricia Lynn 1949- *AmMWSc 92*
**O'Neill**, Patrick Geoffrey 1924- *IntAu&W 91, Who 92, WrDr 92*
**O'Neill**, Patrick J *WhoIns 92*
**O'Neill**, Patrick Joseph 1949- *AmMWSc 92*
**O'Neill**, Patrick Joseph 1953- *WhoAmL 92*
**O'Neill**, Paul 1928- *IntAu&W 91*
**O'Neill**, Paul Edward 1945- *WhoMW 92*
**O'Neill**, Paul H. 1935- *IntWW 91*
**O'Neill**, Paul Henry 1935- *WhoFI 92*
**O'Neill**, Philip Daniel, Jr. 1951- *WhoAmL 92*
**O'Neill**, R R 1916- *AmMWSc 92*
**O'Neill**, Ralph A 1897-1980 *FacFETw*
**O'Neill**, Richard J 1923- *WhoAmP 91*
**O'Neill**, Richard Thomas 1933- *AmMWSc 92, WhoMW 92*
**O'Neill**, Richard Winslow, II 1954- *WhoEnt 92*
**O'Neill**, Robert James 1932- *IntWW 91, Who 92*
**O'Neill**, Robert John 1936- *Who 92, WrDr 92*
**O'Neill**, Robert Vincent 1940- *AmMWSc 92*
**O'Neill**, Ronald C 1929- *AmMWSc 92*
**O'Neill**, Sallie Boyd 1926- *WhoWest 92*
**O'Neill**, Shirley 1947- *TwCPaSc*
**O'Neill**, Terence Marne 1914-1990 *FacFETw*
**O'Neill**, Terence Patrick 1938- *IntWW 91*
**O'Neill**, Thomas Brendan 1923- *AmMWSc 92, WhoWest 92*
**O'Neill**, Thomas Hall Robinson 1923- *AmMWSc 92*
**O'Neill**, Thomas Newman, Jr. 1928- *WhoAmL 92*
**O'Neill**, Thomas P, III 1944- *WhoAmP 91*
**O'Neill**, Thomas P, Jr. 1912- *Who 92, WhoAmP 91*
**O'Neill**, Thomas Patrick 1957- *WhoMW 92*
**O'Neill**, Thomas Philip, Jr. 1912- *AmPolLe, IntWW 91*
**O'Neill**, Timothy Thomas 1934- *WhoWest 92*
**O'Neill**, Virginia Alice 1941- *WhoAmP 91*
**O'Neill**, William A 1930- *WhoAmP 91*
**O'Neill**, William Atchison 1930- *IntWW 91*
**O'Neill**, William D 1938- *AmMWSc 92*
**O'Neill**, William James, Jr. 1933- *WhoMW 92*
**O'Neill**, William L. 1935- *ConAu 34NR, WrDr 92*
**O'Neill**, William Patrick 1951- *WhoAmL 92*
**O'Neill**, William Robert 1950- *WhoAmL 92*
**O'Neill of the Maine**, Baron d1990 *IntWW 91N*
**O'Neill of the Maine**, Lord 1914-1990 *AnObit 1990*
**Onek**, Joseph N 1942- *WhoAmP 91*
**Onema**, Fama 1936- *WhoRel 92*
**Onetti**, Juan Carlos 1909- *BenetAL 91, DcLB 113 [port], IntWW 91, LiExTwC*
**Oney**, Alvin James 1943- *WhoRel 92*
**Ong Pang Boon** 1929- *IntWW 91*
**Ong Teng Cheong** 1936- *IntWW 91*
**Ong**, Chung-Jian Jerry 1944- *AmMWSc 92*
**Ong**, Colin Ghee Hock 1963- *WhoWest 92*
**Ong**, David Eugene 1943- *AmMWSc 92*
**Ong**, DeWitt G. 1947- *WhoWest 92*
**Ong**, Eng-Bee 1933- *AmMWSc 92*
**Ong**, H. K. 1957- *WhoWest 92*
**Ong**, James Shaujen 1957- *WhoMW 92*
**Ong**, John Doyle 1933- *IntWW 91, WhoFI 92, WhoMW 92*
**Ong**, John Nathan, Jr 1927- *AmMWSc 92*
**Ong**, John Tjoan Ho 1937- *AmMWSc 92*
**Ong**, Nai-Phuan 1948- *AmMWSc 92*
**Ong**, Omar Yoke-Lin 1917- *IntWW 91*
**Ong**, Poen Sing 1927- *AmMWSc 92*
**Ong**, Romualdo Anover 1939- *IntWW 91*
**Ong**, Sing-Cheong 1952- *WhoMW 92*
**Ong**, Sue *WhoRel 92*
**Ong**, Tong-man 1935- *AmMWSc 92*
**Ong**, Walter J. 1912- *WrDr 92*
**Ong**, Walter Jackson 1912- *IntAu&W 91*
**Ongania**, Juan Carlos 1914- *IntWW 91*
**Ongaro**, Mario Peter 1926- *WhoRel 92*
**Ongerth**, Henry J 1913- *AmMWSc 92*
**Ongley**, Joseph 1918- *Who 92*
**Ongman**, John Will 1951- *WhoAmL 92*
**Onik**, Gary M 1952- *AmMWSc 92*
**Onions**, Oliver 1873-1961 *ScFEYrs*
**O'Nions**, Robert Keith 1944- *IntWW 91, Who 92*
**Onischak**, Michael 1943- *AmMWSc 92*
**Onishi**, Akira 1929- *WhoFI 92*
**Onishi**, Yasuo 1943- *WhoWest 92*
**Onitri**, Herbert M. Adebola 1928- *IntWW 91*
**Onizuka**, Ellison 1946-1986 *FacFETw*
**Onken**, Arthur Blake 1935- *AmMWSc 92*
**Onken**, Henry Dralle 1932- *WhoMW 92*
**Onley**, David S 1934- *AmMWSc 92*
**Onley**, David Sutherland 1934- *WhoMW 92*
**Onley**, Ernest Edward, Jr. 1932- *WhoRel 92*
**Onley**, Francesca 1933- *WhoRel 92*
**Onli**, Turtel 1952- *WhoBlA 92*
**Onn**, David Goodwin 1937- *AmMWSc 92*
**Onnen**, Tony 1938- *WhoAmP 91*
**Onnerfors**, Alf 1925- *IntWW 91*
**Ono**, Akira 1928- *IntWW 91*
**Ono**, Jon Ryoichi 1946- *WhoAmP 91*
**Ono**, Kanji 1938- *AmMWSc 92*
**Ono**, Yoneo 1925- *WhoWest 92*
**Onoe**, Morio 1926- *AmMWSc 92, IntWW 91*
**Onofre Jarpa Reyes**, Sergio 1921- *IntWW 91*
**Onofrey**, Debra Anne Catherine 1956- *WhoFI 92*
**Onofri**, Arturo 1885-1928 *DcLB 114 [port]*
**O'Nolan**, Brian *RfGEnL 91*
**Ononye**, Daniel Chuka 1948- *WhoMW 92*
**Onopchenko**, Anatoli 1937- *AmMWSc 92*
**Onorato**, Alfred John 1939- *WhoAmP 91*
**Onorato**, George *WhoAmP 91*
**Onsager**, Jerome Andrew 1936- *AmMWSc 92*
**Onsager**, Lars 1903-1976 *WhoNob 90*
**Onslow** *Who 92*
**Onslow**, Earl of 1938- *Who 92*
**Onslow**, Cranley 1926- *Who 92*
**Onslow**, Cranley Gordon Douglas 1926- *IntWW 91*
**Onslow**, John 1932- *Who 92*
**Onstad**, Charles Arnold 1941- *AmMWSc 92*
**Onstine Wood**, Mary Louise 1963- *WhoWest 92*
**Onstott**, Edward Irvin 1922- *AmMWSc 92, WhoWest 92*
**Ontario**, Bishop of 1923- *Who 92*
**Ontario**, Metropolitan of *Who 92*
**Ontell**, Marcia 1937- *AmMWSc 92*
**Ontiveros**, Robert *WhoHisp 92*
**Ontiveros**, Steve 1961- *WhoHisp 92*
**Ontjes**, David A 1937- *AmMWSc 92*
**Ontkean**, Michael 1950- *IntMPA 92, WhoEnt 92*
**Ontko**, Joseph Andrew 1932- *AmMWSc 92*
**Onton**, Aare 1939- *AmMWSc 92*
**Onunkwo**, Emanuel Nwafor 1933- *WhoFI 92*
**Onuska**, Francis Ivan 1935- *AmMWSc 92*
**Onwin**, Glen 1947- *TwCPaSc*
**Onwood**, David P 1936- *AmMWSc 92*
**Onwudiwe**, Ebere 1952- *WhoBlA 92*
**Onwumechili**, Cyril Agodi 1932- *IntWW 91*
**Onyeama**, Charles Dadi 1917- *IntWW 91*
**Onyeama**, Dillibe 1951- *WrDr 92*
**Onyejekwe**, Chike Onyekachi 1960- *WhoBlA 92*
**Onyonka**, Zachary 1939- *IntWW 91*
**Onyshkevych**, Lubomyr S 1933- *AmMWSc 92*
**Onyszchuk**, Mario 1930- *AmMWSc 92*
**Onyszkiewicz**, Janusz 1937- *IntWW 91*
**Ooi**, Boon Seng 1940- *AmMWSc 92*
**Ooka**, Jeri Jean 1945- *AmMWSc 92*
**Ooka**, Shohei 1909- *IntAu&W 91*
**Oono**, Yoshitsugu 1948- *AmMWSc 92*
**Oort**, Abraham H 1934- *AmMWSc 92*
**Oort**, Jan Hendrik 1900- *IntWW 91*
**Oost**, Stewart Irvin 1921-1981 *ConAu 135*
**Oostdam**, Bernard Lodewijk 1932- *AmMWSc 92*
**Oosten**, Roger Lester 1937- *WhoFI 92*
**Oosterbaan**, Bennie 1906-1990 *CurBio 91N*
**Oosterhuis**, Derrick M 1947- *AmMWSc 92*
**OOsterhuis**, William Tenley 1940- *AmMWSc 92*
**Oosterwal**, Gottfried 1930- *WhoRel 92*
**Opabajo**, Olutoyin Olushina 1960- *WhoFI 92*
**Opacic**, George Richard 1957- *WhoWest 92*
**O'Pake**, Michael Allen 1940- *WhoAmP 91*
**Opal**, Chet Brian d1991 *NewYTBS 91*
**Opal**, Chet Brian 1942- *AmMWSc 92*
**Opala**, Marian P 1921- *WhoAmP 91*
**Opala**, Marian Peter 1921- *WhoAmL 92*
**Opalinski**, Fred Stanley 1948- *WhoRel 92*
**Opar**, David Paul 1952- *WhoFI 92*
**Oparil**, Suzanne 1941- *AmMWSc 92*
**Oparin**, Aleksandr Ivanovich 1894-1980 *SovUnBD*
**Oparin**, Alexander Ivanovich 1894-1976 *FacFETw*
**Opas**, Evan E 1953- *AmMWSc 92*
**Opatoshu**, David 1918- *IntMPA 92, WhoEnt 92*
**Opatrny**, Donald Charles 1952- *WhoFI 92*
**Opatrny**, Jaroslav 1946- *AmMWSc 92*
**Opava-Stitzer**, Susan C 1947- *AmMWSc 92*
**Opdahl**, Keith Michael 1934- *WhoMW 92*
**Opdyke**, David F *AmMWSc 92*
**Opdyke**, Neil 1933- *AmMWSc 92*
**Opechancanough** *BenetAL 91*
**Opechowski**, Wladyslaw 1911- *AmMWSc 92*
**Opedahl**, Olaf E 1912- *WhoAmP 91*
**Opel**, John R. 1925- *WhoFI 92*
**Opel**, John Roberts 1925- *IntWW 91*
**Opel**, Susan Margaret 1959- *WhoFI 92*
**Opell**, Brent Douglas 1949- *AmMWSc 92*
**Opella**, Stanley Joseph 1947- *AmMWSc 92*
**Opelt**, Rilla Anne *WhoAmP 91*
**Open**, Michael 1947- *WhoEnt 92*
**Openden**, Lori *WhoEnt 92*
**Opengart**, Bea *DrAPF 91*
**Openshaw**, Dale Kim 1950- *WhoWest 92*
**Openshaw**, Martin David 1940- *AmMWSc 92*
**Openshaw**, Peter 1947- *Who 92*
**Opfell**, John Burton 1924- *AmMWSc 92*
**Opfer**, Neil David 1954- *WhoWest 92*
**Opferkuch**, Paul Raymond 1938- *WhoAmP 91*
**Opferman**, Thomas F. 1962- *WhoEnt 92*
**Ophuls**, Marcel 1927- *FacFETw, IntDcF 2-2 [port], IntMPA 92, WhoEnt 92*
**Ophuls**, Max 1902-1957 *FacFETw, IntDcF 2-2 [port]*
**Ophuls**, Patrick 1934- *ConAu 135*
**Ophuls**, William *ConAu 135*
**Opie**, Alan John 1945- *Who 92*
**Opie**, Amelia 1769-1853 *RfGEnL 91*
**Opie**, Geoffrey James 1939- *Who 92*
**Opie**, Iona 1923- *IntAu&W 91, WrDr 92*
**Opie**, Iona Margaret Balfour 1923- *Who 92*
**Opie**, Joseph Wendell 1913- *AmMWSc 92*
**Opie**, Julian 1958- *TwCPaSc*
**Opie**, Julian Gilbert 1958- *IntWW 91*
**Opie**, June 1926- *WrDr 92*
**Opie**, Lionel Henry 1933- *IntWW 91*
**Opie**, Nancy D. *WhoMW 92*
**Opie**, Roger Gilbert 1927- *Who 92*
**Opie**, Thomas Ranson 1948- *AmMWSc 92*
**Opie**, William R 1920- *AmMWSc 92*
**Opiela**, Alexander David, Jr 1929- *AmMWSc 92*
**Opila**, Robert L, Jr 1951- *AmMWSc 92*
**Opitz**, Bernard Francis, Jr. 1947- *WhoFI 92*
**Opitz**, David Wilmer 1945- *WhoAmP 91*
**Opitz**, Herman Ernest 1929- *AmMWSc 92*
**Opitz**, John Marius 1935- *AmMWSc 92, WhoWest 92*
**Ople**, Blas F. 1927- *IntWW 91*
**Opler**, Marvin K. 1914-1981 *ConAu 133*
**Oplet**, David William 1936- *WhoMW 92*
**Oplinger**, Edward Scott 1943- *AmMWSc 92*
**Oplinger**, Janet Sue 1961- *WhoMW 92*
**Opoien**, Danny Lee 1955- *WhoMW 92*
**Opotowsky**, Maurice Leon 1931- *WhoWest 92*
**Opotowsky**, Stan *IntMPA 92*
**Opotowsky**, Stuart Berger 1935- *WhoFI 92*
**Opp**, Albert Geelmuyden 1931- *AmMWSc 92*
**Oppe**, Thomas Ernest 1925- *Who 92*
**Oppedahl**, Phillip Edward 1935- *WhoWest 92*
**Oppelt**, John Andrew 1937- *AmMWSc 92*
**Oppelt**, John Christian 1931- *AmMWSc 92*
**Oppen**, George 1908-1984 *BenetAL 91*
**Oppenheim**, A K 1915- *AmMWSc 92*
**Oppenheim**, Alan Victor 1937- *AmMWSc 92*
**Oppenheim**, Alexander 1903- *IntWW 91, Who 92*
**Oppenheim**, Bernard Edward 1937- *AmMWSc 92*
**Oppenheim**, David Jerome 1922- *WhoEnt 92*
**Oppenheim**, Dennis A. 1938- *IntWW 91*
**Oppenheim**, Duncan 1904- *TwCPaSc, Who 92*
**Oppenheim**, Duncan Morris 1904- *IntWW 91*
**Oppenheim**, E Phillips 1866-1946 *ScFEYrs*
**Oppenheim**, Felix E. 1913- *WrDr 92*
**Oppenheim**, Irwin 1929- *AmMWSc 92*
**Oppenheim**, James 1882-1932 *BenetAL 91*
**Oppenheim**, Joost J 1934- *AmMWSc 92*
**Oppenheim**, Joseph Harold 1926- *AmMWSc 92*
**Oppenheim**, Martha Kunkel 1935- *WhoEnt 92*
**Oppenheim**, Nathan 1865-1916 *BilnAmS*
**Oppenheim**, Phillip Anthony Charles L 1956- *Who 92*
**Oppenheim**, Ronald William 1938- *AmMWSc 92*
**Oppenheim**, Samuel Aaron 1940- *WhoWest 92*
**Oppenheim-Barnes**, Baroness 1930- *IntWW 91, Who 92*
**Oppenheimer**, Andres Miguel 1951- *WhoHisp 92*

**Oppenheimer**, Carl Henry, Jr 1921- *AmMWSc 92*
**Oppenheimer**, Frank 1912-1985 *FacFETw*
**Oppenheimer**, Franz Martin 1919- *WhoAmL 92*
**Oppenheimer**, Harry Frederick 1908- *IntWW 91, Who 92*
**Oppenheimer**, Helen 1926- *Who 92*
**Oppenheimer**, J Robert 1904-1967 *ConAu 34NR, FacFETw [port], RComAH*
**Oppenheimer**, Jack Hans 1927- *AmMWSc 92*
**Oppenheimer**, Jane Marion 1911- *AmMWSc 92*
**Oppenheimer**, Jerry L. 1937- *WhoAmL 92*
**Oppenheimer**, Joel 1930- *IntAu&W 91*
**Oppenheimer**, Larry Eric 1942- *AmMWSc 92*
**Oppenheimer**, Martin J. 1933- *WhoAmL 92*
**Oppenheimer**, Michael 1924- *Who 92*
**Oppenheimer**, Michael 1946- *AmMWSc 92*
**Oppenheimer**, Nicholas Frank 1945- *IntWW 91*
**Oppenheimer**, Norman Joseph 1946- *AmMWSc 92*
**Oppenheimer**, Peter Morris 1938- *Who 92*
**Oppenheimer**, Philip 1911- *Who 92*
**Oppenheimer**, Phillip R 1948- *AmMWSc 92*
**Oppenheimer**, Preston Carl 1958- *WhoWest 92*
**Oppenheimer**, Randolph Carl 1954- *WhoAmL 92*
**Oppenheimer**, Rex Maurice 1949- *WhoWest 92*
**Oppenheimer**, Steven Bernard 1944- *AmMWSc 92*
**Oppenheimer**, Suzi 1934- *WhoAmP 91*
**Oppenheimer**, Tom Lucius 1943- *WhoFI 92*
**Oppenhoff**, Franz 1902-1945 *EncTR 91*
**Oppenlander**, Fritz 1952- *WhoMW 92*
**Oppenlander**, Joseph Clarence 1931- *AmMWSc 92*
**Oppenlander**, Karl Heinrich 1932- *IntWW 91*
**Oppenlander**, Robert Kirk 1952- *WhoFI 92*
**Oppens**, Ursula 1944- *NewAmDM*
**Opper**, Frederick Burr 1857-1937 *BenetAL 91*
**Opper**, Susanna 1940- *WhoFI 92*
**Opperman**, Dwight Darwin 1923- *WhoFI 92*
**Opperman**, Hubert 1904- *Who 92*
**Opperman**, Jimmy Stuart 1957- *WhoEnt 92*
**Opperman**, Leonard 1928- *WhoAmL 92*
**Opperthauser**, Earl Charles 1925- *WhoAmP 91*
**Oprea**, Gheorghe 1927- *IntWW 91*
**Opsahl**, Torkel 1931- *IntWW 91*
**Opsal**, Philip Mason 1931- *WhoWest 92*
**Opsitnick**, Allan Joseph 1953- *WhoAmL 92*
**Optatus of Milevis** *EncEarC*
**Optic**, Oliver *BenetAL 91, SmATA 67*
**Oquendo**, Jorge Luis 1963- *WhoEnt 92*
**Oquendo**, Jose Manuel 1963- *WhoHisp 92*
**Oquendo**, Mateo Rosas de *HisDSpE*
**O'Quinn**, Terry *IntMPA 92*
**Orabona**, John 1943- *WhoAmP 91*
**Orahovats**, Peter Dimiter 1922- *AmMWSc 92*
**Oram** *Who 92*
**Oram**, Baron 1913- *Who 92*
**Oram**, Clifton 1917- *WrDr 92*
**Oram**, Kenneth Cyril 1919- *Who 92*
**Oram**, Samuel 1913- *Who 92*
**Orama Monroig**, Jorge *WhoAmP 91*
**Oramas-Oliva**, Oscar 1936- *IntWW 91*
**Oran**, Carl Franklin 1913- *WhoMW 92*
**Oran**, Elaine Surick 1946- *AmMWSc 92*
**Oran**, Stuart I. 1950- *WhoAmL 92*
**O'Rand**, Michael Gene 1945- *AmMWSc 92*
**Oranen**, Raija Helena 1948- *IntAu&W 91*
**Orange**, Larry Franklin 1943- *WhoRel 92*
**O'Rangers**, John Joseph 1936- *AmMWSc 92*
**Oranmore and Browne**, Baron 1901- *Who 92*
**Orano**, Paolo 1875-1945 *BiDExR*
**Oratz**, Murray 1927- *AmMWSc 92*
**Orava**, R Norman 1935- *AmMWSc 92*
**O'Rawe**, Anne 1955- *TwCPaSc*
**Oray**, Bedii *AmMWSc 92*
**Orayevsky**, Anatoli Nikolaevich 1934- *IntWW 91*
**Orazem**, Peter Francis 1955- *WhoFI 92, WhoMW 92*
**Orazio**, Angelo Frank 1926- *WhoAmP 91*
**Orazio**, Joan Politi 1930- *WhoFI 92*
**Orazio**, Paul Vincent 1957- *WhoFI 92*
**Orbach**, Jerry 1935- *IntMPA 92, WhoEnt 92*
**Orbach**, Raymond Lee 1934- *AmMWSc 92*
**Orban**, Edward 1915- *AmMWSc 92, WhoMW 92*
**Orban**, John Edward 1952- *AmMWSc 92*
**Orbe**, Monica Patricia 1968- *WhoHisp 92*
**Orbeck**, Edmund N 1915- *WhoAmP 91*
**Orbeli**, Leon Abgarovich 1882-1958 *SovUnBD*
**Orbelian**, Konstantin Agaparonovich 1928- *IntWW 91*
**Orben**, Jack Richard 1938- *WhoFI 92*
**Orben**, Robert 1927- *WhoEnt 92*
**Orbison**, Roy 1936-1988 *FacFETw*
**Orbison**, Roy 1936-1989 *NewAmDM*
**Orbon**, Julian d1991 *NewYTBS 91*
**Orbon**, Julian 1925- *ConCom 92*
**Orbon de Soto**, Julian 1925- *ConCom 92*
**Orbos**, Oscar *NewYTBS 91*
**Orchard**, Dennis Frank 1912- *IntAu&W 91, WrDr 92*
**Orchard**, Edward Eric 1920- *Who 92*
**Orchard**, Henry John 1922- *AmMWSc 92*
**Orchard**, Peter Francis 1927- *IntWW 91, Who 92*
**Orchard**, Robert John 1946- *WhoEnt 92*
**Orchard**, Stephen Michael 1944- *Who 92*
**Orchard-Lisle**, Paul David 1938- *Who 92*
**Orchin**, Milton 1914- *AmMWSc 92, WhoMW 92*
**Orci**, Norma 1944- *WhoHisp 92*
**Orcutt**, Bruce Call 1937- *AmMWSc 92*
**Orcutt**, David Michael 1943- *AmMWSc 92*
**Orcutt**, Donald Adelbert 1926- *AmMWSc 92*
**Orcutt**, Frederic Scott, Jr 1940- *AmMWSc 92*
**Orcutt**, Harold George 1918- *AmMWSc 92*
**Orcutt**, James A 1918- *AmMWSc 92*
**Orcutt**, JoEllen Lindh 1940- *WhoAmP 91*
**Orcutt**, John Arthur 1943- *AmMWSc 92*
**Orcutt**, John C 1927- *AmMWSc 92*
**Orcutt**, Richard G 1924- *AmMWSc 92*
**Orczy**, Emmuska 1865-1947 *ScFEYrs*
**Ord**, Andrew James B. *Who 92*
**Ord**, George 1781-1866 *BiInAmS*
**Ord**, John Allyn 1912- *AmMWSc 92*
**Ordahl**, Charles Philip 1945- *AmMWSc 92*
**Ordal**, George Winford 1943- *AmMWSc 92, WhoMW 92*
**Ordas**, Diego de 1480-1532 *HisDSpE*
**Ordaz**, Phillip A. 1934- *WhoHisp 92*
**Orde**, Alan C. C. *Who 92*
**Orde**, Denis Alan 1932- *Who 92*
**Orde**, John Campbell- 1943- *Who 92*
**Orde-Powlett** *Who 92*
**Orden**, Alex 1916- *AmMWSc 92*
**Orden**, Ted 1920- *WhoWest 92*
**Order**, Stanley Elias 1934- *AmMWSc 92*
**Ordille**, Carol Maria *AmMWSc 92*
**Ording**, Michael K. 1955- *WhoAmL 92*
**Ordish**, George 1904- *IntAu&W 91*
**Ordish**, George 1906- *WrDr 92*
**Ordish**, George 1908?-1991 *ConAu 133*
**Ordman**, Alfred Bram 1948- *AmMWSc 92*
**Ordman**, Edward Thorne 1944- *AmMWSc 92*
**Ordonez**, Michael Andrew 1954- *WhoHisp 92*
**Ordonez**, Nelson Gonzalo 1944- *AmMWSc 92*
**Ordonez**, Ricardo 1959- *WhoHisp 92*
**Ordonez**, Sedfrey A. 1921- *IntWW 91*
**Ordover**, Abraham Philip 1937- *WhoAmL 92*
**Ordronaux**, John 1830-1908 *BiInAmS*
**Ordung**, Philip F 1919- *AmMWSc 92*
**Orduno**, Robert Daniel 1933- *WhoWest 92*
**Orduno**, Robert Octavio 1933- *WhoHisp 92*
**Ordway**, Albert 1843-1897 *BiInAmS*
**Ordway**, Ellen 1927- *AmMWSc 92*
**Ordway**, Frederick I, III 1927- *IntAu&W 91, WrDr 92*
**Ordway**, George A 1943- *AmMWSc 92*
**Ordway**, John Morse 1823-1909 *BiInAmS*
**Ordway**, Nelson Kneeland 1912- *AmMWSc 92*
**Ordynska**, Stanislawa *EncAmaz 91*
**Ordynsky**, George 1944- *WhoWest 92*
**Ordzhonikidze**, Grigoriy Konstantinovich 1886-1937 *SovUnBD*
**Ordzhonikidze**, Grigory Konstantinovich 1866-1937 *FacFETw*
**Ore**, Cecilie 1954- *ConCom 92*
**Ore**, Fernando 1926- *AmMWSc 92*
**Ore**, Henry Thomas 1934- *AmMWSc 92*
**Ore**, Joyce L. 1939- *WhoMW 92*
**Ore**, Luis Geronimo de 1554-1630 *HisDSpE*
**Ore**, Rebecca 1948- *TwCSFW 91*
**Ore**, Robert 1951- *WhoEnt 92*
**O'Reagan**, Kevin Patrick 1960- *WhoFI 92*
**Oreamuno**, Yolanda 1916-1956 *SpAmWW*
**O'Rear**, Dennis John 1950- *AmMWSc 92*
**Orear**, Jay 1925- *AmMWSc 92*
**Orear**, Richard 1911- *IntMPA 92*
**O'Rear**, Steward William 1919- *AmMWSc 92*
**Orebaugh**, Errol Glen 1937- *AmMWSc 92*
**Orebaugh**, Phoebe May 1935- *WhoAmP 91*
**Orecchio**, John A. 1966- *WhoMW 92*
**Orechio**, Carl A 1914- *WhoAmP 91*
**Orechio**, Carmen A 1926- *WhoAmP 91*
**Oreffice**, Paul F. 1927- *IntWW 91*
**Oreffice**, Paul Fausto 1927- *WhoFI 92, WhoMW 92*
**O'Regan**, Barry 1915- *Who 92*
**O'Regan**, Brendan 1917- *IntWW 91*
**O'Regan**, Charles Robert *WhoAmP 91*
**Oregon** *NewAmDM*
**Orehotsky**, John Lewis 1934- *AmMWSc 92*
**O'Reilly**, Anthony J. F. 1936- *IntWW 91*
**O'Reilly**, Anthony John Francis 1936- *Who 92, WhoFI 92*
**O'Reilly**, Colm *Who 92*
**O'Reilly**, Edward 1948- *IntWW 91*
**O'Reilly**, Edward Joseph 1953- *WhoAmL 92*
**O'Reilly**, Francis Joseph 1922- *Who 92*
**O'Reilly**, Frank Warren, Jr. 1921- *WhoEnt 92*
**O'Reilly**, Hugh Joseph 1936- *WhoMW 92*
**O'Reilly**, James Emil 1945- *AmMWSc 92*
**O'Reilly**, James Michael 1934- *AmMWSc 92*
**O'Reilly**, John Bernard 1918- *WhoAmP 91*
**O'Reilly**, John Boyle 1844-1890 *BenetAL 91, DcAmImH*
**O'Reilly**, John F. 1945- *WhoAmL 92, WhoWest 92*
**O'Reilly**, Kelley Amanda 1962- *WhoWest 92*
**O'Reilly**, Patrick James 1965- *WhoWest 92*
**O'Reilly**, Richard 1943- *AmMWSc 92*
**O'Reilly**, Robert Maitland 1845-1912 *BiInAmS*
**O'Reilly**, Rosann Tagliaferro 1948- *WhoMW 92*
**O'Reilly**, Terence Joseph 1954- *WhoEnt 92*
**O'Reilly**, Thomas Patrick 1938- *WhoAmP 91*
**O'Reilly**, Timothy Patrick 1945- *WhoAmL 92*
**O'Reilly**, Wenda Brewster 1948- *WhoWest 92*
**O'Reilly**, William Edward 1945- *WhoMW 92*
**O'Reilly**, William John 1919- *Who 92*
**Oreja Aguirre**, Marcelino 1935- *IntWW 91, Who 92*
**Orejas-Miranda**, Braulio 1933- *AmMWSc 92*
**Orejon y Aparicio**, Jose de 1706-1765 *NewAmDM*
**Orek**, Osman Nuri 1925- *IntWW 91*
**Orel**, Harold 1926- *WhoEnt 92, WhoMW 92, WrDr 92*
**O'Rell**, Dennis Dee 1941- *AmMWSc 92*
**Orell**, Seth Rowell 1942- *WhoWest 92*
**Orellana**, Francisco de 1511?-1546 *HisDSpE*
**Orellana**, Manuel Antonio 1955- *WhoWest 92*
**Orellana**, Manuel M. 1947- *WhoHisp 92*
**Orellana**, Nicolas Alberto 1954- *WhoHisp 92*
**Orellana**, Rolando 1942- *WhoHisp 92*
**Orem**, Charles Annistone 1929- *WhoFI 92*
**Orem**, John *AmMWSc 92*
**Orem**, Michael William 1942- *AmMWSc 92*
**Orem**, Sandra Elizabeth 1940- *WhoFI 92*
**Oren**, Laurence Ross 1964- *WhoWest 92*
**Oren**, Shmuel Shimon 1944- *AmMWSc 92*
**Orendain**, Antonio 1930- *WhoHisp 92*
**Orendorff**, David Edward 1948- *WhoRel 92*
**Orenshein**, Herbert 1931- *WhoIns 92*
**Orenstein**, Albert *AmMWSc 92*
**Orenstein**, David M 1945- *AmMWSc 92*
**Orenstein**, Harold David 1936- *WhoAmP 91*
**Orenstein**, Howard 1955- *WhoAmP 91*
**Orenstein**, Jan Marc 1942- *AmMWSc 92*
**Orenstein**, Jeffrey Robert 1944- *WhoMW 92*
**Orenstein**, Michael 1939- *WhoWest 92*
**Orenstein**, Walter Albert 1948- *AmMWSc 92*
**Orent**, Gerard M. 1931- *WhoFI 92*
**Orentas**, Rodney Raymond 1958- *WhoFI 92*
**Orentlicher**, David 1955- *WhoAmL 92*
**Orentlicher**, John 1943- *WhoEnt 92*
**Oresanya**, Sasaenia Adedeji 1946- *IntWW 91*
**Orescanin**, Bogdan 1916- *Who 92*
**Oreshnikov**, Viktor Mikhaylovich 1904- *SovUnBD*
**Oresick**, Peter *DrAPF 91*
**Oresman**, Donald 1925- *WhoAmL 92*
**Orey**, Steven 1928- *AmMWSc 92*
**Orezzoli**, Hector d1991 *NewYTBS 91 [port]*
**Orf**, James Harold 1948- *WhoMW 92*
**Orf**, John W 1950- *AmMWSc 92*
**Orf**, Ted Eugene 1945- *WhoWest 92*
**Orfalea**, Gregory *DrAPF 91*
**Orff**, Carl 1895-1982 *EncTR 91, FacFETw, NewAmDM*
**Orfield**, Myron Willard, Jr 1961- *WhoAmP 91*
**Orfila**, Alejandro 1925- *IntWW 91*
**Orfila**, Ansley Ulm 1940- *WhoRel 92*
**Orgad**, Ben Zion 1926- *IntWW 91*
**Orgain**, Albert Marcellus, IV 1943- *WhoAmL 92*
**Organ**, Bryan 1935- *IntWW 91, TwCPaSc, Who 92*
**Organ**, Claude H., Jr. 1928- *WhoBlA 92*
**Organ**, James Albert 1931- *AmMWSc 92*
**Organ**, Margaret 1946- *TwCPaSc*
**Organ**, Troy Wilson 1912- *IntAu&W 91, WrDr 92*
**Organov**, Nikolay Nikolaevich 1901-1982 *SovUnBD*
**Organski**, A. F. K. 1923- *WrDr 92*
**Orgebin-Crist**, Marie-Claire 1936- *AmMWSc 92*
**Orgel**, Doris 1929- *IntAu&W 91, WrDr 92*
**Orgel**, Irene *DrAPF 91*
**Orgel**, Leslie E 1927- *AmMWSc 92*
**Orgel**, Leslie Eleazer 1927- *Who 92, WhoWest 92*
**Orgel**, Stephen Kitay 1933- *WhoWest 92*
**Orgell**, Wallace Herman 1928- *AmMWSc 92*
**Orgill**, Montie M 1929- *AmMWSc 92*
**Orheim**, Paul Joseph 1950- *WhoAmP 91*
**Orhon**, Necdet Kadri 1928- *WhoMW 92*
**Ori**, Joseph John 1955- *WhoFI 92*
**Oriaku**, Ebere Agwu 1951- *WhoFI 92*
**Oriani**, Ana Gloria 1953- *WhoHisp 92*
**Oriani**, Richard Anthony 1920- *AmMWSc 92*
**Orians**, Gordon Howell 1932- *AmMWSc 92*
**Oribe**, Manuel 1792-1857 *HisDSpE*
**Oriel**, Steven S 1923- *AmMWSc 92*
**Orien**, Raymond Cha 1970- *WhoEnt 92*
**Orient**, Jane Michel 1946- *AmMWSc 92*
**Orieux**, Jean 1907- *IntWW 91*
**Origen** 185?-251? *EncEarC*
**Original Dixieland Jazz Band** *FacFETw, NewAmDM*
**Orihel**, Thomas Charles 1929- *AmMWSc 92*
**O'Riley**, Warren *TwCWW 91*
**Oring**, Lewis Warren 1938- *AmMWSc 92*
**Oriol**, Jacques 1923- *IntAu&W 91*
**Orioles** *NewAmDM*
**O'Riordan**, John Patrick Bruce 1936- *Who 92*
**O'Riordan**, Timothy *Who 92*
**Orkand**, Donald Saul 1936- *WhoFI 92*
**Orkand**, Richard K 1936- *AmMWSc 92*
**Orkin**, Ad 1922- *IntMPA 92*
**Orkin**, Harvey d1975 *LesBEnT 92*
**Orkin**, Lazarus Allerton 1910- *AmMWSc 92*
**Orkin**, Louis R 1915- *AmMWSc 92*
**Orkin**, Ruth 1921-1985 *FacFETw*
**Orkin**, Stuart H 1946- *AmMWSc 92*
**Orkney**, Earl of 1919- *Who 92*
**Orkney**, G Dale 1936- *AmMWSc 92*
**Orland**, Frank J 1917- *AmMWSc 92*
**Orland**, George H 1924- *AmMWSc 92*
**Orland**, Henry 1918- *WhoEnt 92*
**Orland**, Ted Norcross 1941- *WhoWest 92*
**Orlandi Contucci**, Corrado 1914- *IntWW 91*
**Orlando**, Anthony Michael 1942- *AmMWSc 92*
**Orlando**, Carl *AmMWSc 92*
**Orlando**, Charles M 1935- *AmMWSc 92*
**Orlando**, Joe 1953- *WhoEnt 92*
**Orlando**, Joseph Alexander 1929- *AmMWSc 92*
**Orlando**, L. J. *WhoWest 92*
**Orlando**, Laurie 1962- *WhoAmL 92*
**Orlando**, Quentin R *WhoAmP 91*
**Orlando**, Terry Philip 1952- *AmMWSc 92*
**Orlando**, Tony 1944- *WhoHisp 92*
**Orlando**, Vittorio Emmanuele 1860-1952 *FacFETw*
**Orlans**, F Barbara 1928- *AmMWSc 92*
**Orlans**, Harold 1921- *WrDr 92*
**Orlanski**, Isidoro 1939- *AmMWSc 92*
**Orlansky**, Grace Suydam 1925- *WhoAmP 91*
**Orlansky**, Julian David 1930- *WhoAmL 92*
**Orlasky**, Cindy Lee 1951- *WhoMW 92*
**Orlean**, Susan 1955- *ConAu 134*
**Orleans**, James *WhoEnt 92*
**Orlebar**, Michael Keith Orlebar S. *Who 92*
**Orlebeke**, Charles J 1934- *WhoAmP 91*
**Orlebeke**, Lynn A. 1954- *WhoFI 92*
**Orlebeke**, William Ronald 1933- *WhoAmL 92, WhoWest 92*

**Orledge**, Robert 1948- *WrDr 92*
**Orlen**, Steve *DrAPF 91*
**Orlett**, Edward J 1933- *WhoAmP 91*
**Orlev**, Uri 1931- *ConAu 34NR*
**Orley**, Dean Paul 1941- *WhoMW 92*
**Orlic**, Donald 1932- *AmMWSc 92*
**Orlich**, Rose *DrAPF 91*
**Orlick**, Charles Alex 1927- *AmMWSc 92*
**Orlick**, Henry 1947- *TwCPaSc*
**Orlidge**, Alicia *AmMWSc 92*
**Orlik**, Peter Blythe 1944- *WhoEnt 92*
**Orlik**, Peter Paul 1938- *AmMWSc 92*
**Orlik**, Randy Phillip 1952- *WhoAmL 92*
**Orlik-Ruckemann**, Kazimierz Jerzy 1925- *AmMWSc 92*
**Orlin**, Hyman 1920- *AmMWSc 92*
**Orlins**, Stephen A. 1950- *WhoFI 92*
**Orlock**, Carol *DrAPF 91*
**Orloff**, Arthur Ellsworth 1908- *WhoEnt 92*
**Orloff**, David Ira 1944- *AmMWSc 92*
**Orloff**, Gary William 1946- *WhoAmL 92*
**Orloff**, Harold David 1915- *AmMWSc 92*
**Orloff**, Jack 1921- *AmMWSc 92*
**Orloff**, Jonathan H *AmMWSc 92*
**Orloff**, Lawrence 1941- *AmMWSc 92*
**Orloff**, Malcolm Kenneth 1939- *AmMWSc 92*
**Orloff**, Marshall Jerome 1927- *AmMWSc 92*
**Orloff**, Neil 1943- *AmMWSc 92, WhoAmL 92, WhoWest 92*
**Orloff**, Vladimir 1928- *NewAmDM*
**Orloski**, Richard John 1947- *WhoAmP 91*
**Orlov**, Vladimir Pavlovich 1921- *IntWW 91*
**Orlov**, Yuri Alexandrovich 1893-1966 *FacFETw*
**Orlov**, Yuri F. 1924- *IntWW 91*
**Orlov**, Yuriy Fedorovich 1924- *SovUnBD*
**Orlova**, Alexandra 1911- *ConAu 133*
**Orlova**, Lyubov' Petrovna 1902-1975 *SovUnBD*
**Orlovsky**, Peter *DrAPF 91*
**Orlowski**, Wladyslaw 1922- *IntAu&W 91*
**Orman**, Alan R. *WhoRel 92*
**Orman**, Arthur Allen 1932- *WhoWest 92*
**Orman**, Charles 1944- *AmMWSc 92*
**Orman**, John Leo 1949- *WhoWest 92*
**Orman**, Stanley 1935- *Who 92*
**Ormandy**, Eugene 1899-1985 *FacFETw, NewAmDM*
**Ormasa**, John 1925- *WhoAmL 92, WhoWest 92*
**Orme**, Antony R 1936- *ConAu 35NR*
**Orme**, Denis Arthur 1946- *WhoFI 92*
**Orme**, Gregory Keith 1953- *WhoAmL 92*
**Orme**, Jeremy David 1943- *Who 92*
**Orme**, Lila Morton *WhoAmP 91*
**Orme**, Maynard Evan 1936- *WhoEnt 92, WhoWest 92*
**Orme**, Stanley 1923- *IntWW 91, Who 92*
**Orme-Johnson**, Nanette Roberts 1937- *AmMWSc 92*
**Orme-Johnson**, William H 1938- *AmMWSc 92*
**Ormerod**, Alec William 1932- *Who 92*
**Ormerod**, Jan 1946- *ConAu 35NR*
**Ormerod**, Roger *IntAu&W 91, WrDr 92*
**Ormerod**, Roger 1920- *ConAu 35NR*
**Ormes**, Jonathan Fairfield *AmMWSc 92*
**Ormesson**, Jean d' 1925- *IntWW 91, Who 92*
**Ormond**, Clyde 1906-1985 *ConAu 36NR*
**Ormond**, John 1905- *Who 92*
**Ormond**, John Kevin 1965- *WhoRel 92*
**Ormond**, Richard 1939- *ConAu 35NR*
**Ormond**, Richard Louis 1939- *IntWW 91, Who 92*
**Ormond**, Wyriot, Jr. d1773 *DcNCBi 4*
**Ormond**, Wyriot, Sr. 1707?-1758? *DcNCBi 4*
**Ormonde**, Marquess of 1899- *Who 92*
**Ormondroyd**, Edward 1925- *WrDr 92*
**Ormont**, Louis Robert 1918- *ConAu 35NR*
**Ormos**, Claude Patrick 1951- *WhoRel 92*
**Ormrod**, Douglas Padraic 1934- *AmMWSc 92*
**Ormrod**, Roger 1911- *Who 92*
**Orms**, Howard Raymond 1920- *WhoMW 92*
**Ormsbee**, Allen I 1926- *AmMWSc 92*
**Ormsbee**, David *IntAu&W 91X, WrDr 92*
**Ormsby**, David G. 1933- *WhoAmL 92*
**Ormsby**, Frank 1947- *ConPo 91, IntAu&W 91, WrDr 92*
**Ormsby**, Michael Charles 1957- *WhoAmL 92*
**Ormsby**, Robert B. Jr *AmMWSc 92*
**Ormsby**, W Clayton 1924- *AmMWSc 92*
**Ormsby Gore** *Who 92*
**Ormson**, James Gabriel 1929- *WhoMW 92*
**Orn**, Michael Kent 1942- *WhoMW 92*
**Orna**, Mary Virginia 1934- *AmMWSc 92*
**Ornano**, Michel d' d1991 *IntWW 91N*
**Ornat**, Andrzej 1946- *IntWW 91*
**Ornati**, Oscar A. d1991 *NewYTBS 91*
**Ornato**, Joseph Pasquale 1947- *AmMWSc 92*
**Ornburn**, Kristee Jean 1956- *WhoMW 92*
**Orndorff**, Charles Lewis 1952- *WhoAmP 91*
**Orndorff**, Mark Christian 1957- *WhoAmL 92*
**Orndorff**, Roy Lee, Jr 1935- *AmMWSc 92*
**Ornduff**, Robert 1932- *AmMWSc 92*
**Orne**, Martin Theodore 1927- *AmMWSc 92*
**Ornelas**, Michael Raul 1952- *WhoHisp 92*
**Ornelas**, Victor F. 1948- *WhoHisp 92*
**Ornellas**, Donald Louis 1932- *WhoWest 92*
**Ornish**, Dean *NewYTBS 91 [port]*
**Ornithoparcus**, Andreas 1490?-1535? *NewAmDM*
**Ornitz**, Barry Louis 1949- *AmMWSc 92*
**Ornosky**, Paul M. 1961- *WhoMW 92*
**Ornstein**, Alexander Thomas 1944- *WhoAmL 92*
**Ornstein**, Donald Samuel 1934- *AmMWSc 92, IntWW 91, WhoWest 92*
**Ornstein**, Leo 1892- *NewAmDM*
**Ornstein**, Leonard 1926- *AmMWSc 92*
**Ornstein**, Robert 1925- *WrDr 92*
**Ornstein**, Robert E. 1942- *ConAu 35NR*
**Ornstein**, Stanley Irwin 1939- *WhoFI 92*
**Ornstein**, Wilhelm 1905- *AmMWSc 92*
**Ornston**, Leo Nicholas 1940- *AmMWSc 92*
**Ornt**, Daniel Burrows 1951- *AmMWSc 92*
**Oro**, Juan 1923- *AmMWSc 92*
**Orodenker**, Norman Gilbert 1933- *WhoAmL 92*
**Orofino**, Thomas Allan 1930- *AmMWSc 92*
**Orona**, Ernest Joseph 1942- *WhoWest 92*
**Orona**, Josef L. 1948- *WhoHisp 92*
**Orona**, Manuel Jimenez 1946- *WhoEnt 92, WhoHisp 92*
**Orona**, Nelly 1931- *WhoHisp 92*
**Oronsky**, Arnold Lewis 1940- *AmMWSc 92*
**Oropesa**, Daniel Thomas 1949- *WhoMW 92*
**O'Rorke**, Brian 1901-1974 *DcTwDes, FacFETw*
**O'Rorke**, James Francis, Jr. 1936- *WhoAmL 92*
**Oros**, Margaret Olava 1912- *AmMWSc 92*
**Orosco**, Jesse 1957- *WhoHisp 92*
**Oroshnik**, Jesse 1924- *AmMWSc 92*
**Orosius** *EncEarC*
**Orosz**, Charles George 1949- *AmMWSc 92*
**Oroszian**, Stephen 1927- *AmMWSc 92*
**O'Rourke**, Andrew 1931- *IntWW 91, Who 92*
**O'Rourke**, Andrew Patrick 1933- *IntAu&W 91*
**O'Rourke**, C. Larry 1937- *WhoAmL 92*
**O'Rourke**, Carl Edward 1935- *WhoRel 92*
**O'Rourke**, Edmund Newton, Jr 1923- *AmMWSc 92*
**O'Rourke**, Edward William 1917- *WhoRel 92*
**O'Rourke**, Frank 1916- *IntAu&W 91*
**O'Rourke**, Frank 1916-1989 *TwCWW 91*
**O'Rourke**, J. Tracy 1935- *WhoFI 92*
**O'Rourke**, James 1925- *AmMWSc 92*
**O'Rourke**, Jim *WhoAmP 91*
**O'Rourke**, Joan B. Doty Werthman 1933- *WhoMW 92*
**O'Rourke**, JoAnne A 1939- *WhoAmP 91*
**O'Rourke**, John Alvin 1924- *AmMWSc 92*
**O'Rourke**, John J. 1922- *IntMPA 92*
**O'Rourke**, John Raymond, Jr. 1951- *WhoAmL 92*
**O'Rourke**, Joseph *AmMWSc 92*
**O'Rourke**, Lawrence Michael 1938- *ConAu 35NR*
**O'Rourke**, Margaret Cookson 1927- *WhoAmP 91*
**O'Rourke**, Mary 1937- *IntWW 91*
**O'Rourke**, P J 1947- *IntAu&W 91, WrDr 92*
**O'Rourke**, Peter John 1946- *AmMWSc 92*
**O'Rourke**, Richard Clair 1930- *AmMWSc 92*
**O'Rourke**, Stephen Charles 1916- *WhoAmP 91*
**O'Rourke**, Thomas Denis 1948- *AmMWSc 92*
**O'Rourke**, William *DrAPF 91*
**O'Rourke**, William 1945- *ConAu 35NR, WrDr 92*
**O'Rourke**, William Henry, Jr. 1938- *WhoWest 92*
**Orovida** *TwCPaSc*
**Orowan**, Egon 1902- *AmMWSc 92*
**Oroyan**, Susanna 1942- *WhoWest 92*
**Oroza**, Ileana 1950- *WhoHisp 92*
**Orozco**, Carmen F. 1936- *WhoHisp 92*
**Orozco**, Frank *WhoHisp 92*
**Orozco**, John Alfred 1959- *WhoHisp 92*
**Orozco**, Jose A. 1949- *WhoHisp 92*
**Orozco**, Joseph William 1921- *WhoAmP 91*
**Orozco**, Luz Maria 1933- *WhoHisp 92*
**Orozco**, LuzMaria 1933- *WhoMW 92*
**Orozco**, Mary Lee 1933- *WhoHisp 92*
**Orozco**, Mauricio J. 1960- *WhoHisp 92*
**Orozco**, Olga 1920- *ConSpAP, SpAmWW*
**Orozco**, Raymond E. 1933- *WhoHisp 92*
**Orozco**, Ronald Avelino 1951- *WhoHisp 92*
**Orpen**, Rick Lee 1953- *WhoMW 92*
**Orpen**, William 1878-1931 *FacFETw, TwCPaSc [port]*
**Orphan**, Victor John 1940- *AmMWSc 92*
**Orphanides**, Gus George 1947- *AmMWSc 92*
**Orphanides**, Nora Charlotte 1951- *WhoEnt 92*
**Orphanos**, Demetrius George 1922- *AmMWSc 92*
**Orphanoudakis**, Stelios Constantine 1948- *AmMWSc 92*
**Orpheus C. Kerr** *BenetAL 91*
**Orpurt**, Philip Arvid 1921- *AmMWSc 92*
**Orr**, A Lorraine 1921- *WhoAmP 91*
**Orr**, Alan R 1936- *AmMWSc 92*
**Orr**, Alan Stewart d1991 *Who 92N*
**Orr**, Beatrice Yewer 1951- *AmMWSc 92*
**Orr**, Bradford Grant 1958- *WhoMW 92*
**Orr**, Carl Robert 1954- *WhoFI 92*
**Orr**, Charles Henry 1924- *AmMWSc 92*
**Orr**, Chris 1943- *TwCPaSc*
**Orr**, Clyde 1921- *WrDr 92*
**Orr**, Clyde, Jr 1921- *AmMWSc 92*
**Orr**, Clyde Hugh 1931- *WhoBlA 92*
**Orr**, Daniel 1933- *WhoFI 92*
**Orr**, Daniel B 1919- *WhoAmP 91*
**Orr**, David 1922- *Who 92*
**Orr**, David Alexander 1922- *IntWW 91*
**Orr**, David Duvall 1944- *WhoAmP 91*
**Orr**, Donald Eugene, Jr 1945- *AmMWSc 92*
**Orr**, Dorothy *WhoBlA 92*
**Orr**, E Wycliffe *WhoAmP 91*
**Orr**, Earl Lawton 1934- *WhoBlA 92*
**Orr**, Franklin M, Jr 1946- *AmMWSc 92*
**Orr**, Frederick William 1942- *AmMWSc 92*
**Orr**, George J *WhoAmP 91*
**Orr**, Gregory *DrAPF 91*
**Orr**, Gregory 1947- *ConPo 91, WrDr 92*
**Orr**, Henry Porter 1921- *AmMWSc 92*
**Orr**, Iain Campbell 1942- *Who 92*
**Orr**, Jack Edward 1918- *AmMWSc 92*
**Orr**, James Anthony 1948- *AmMWSc 92*
**Orr**, James Bernard Vivian 1917- *Who 92*
**Orr**, James Cameron 1930- *AmMWSc 92*
**Orr**, James Franklin, II 1949- *WhoMW 92*
**Orr**, James Henry 1927- *Who 92*
**Orr**, James Lawrence 1822-1873 *AmPolLe*
**Orr**, James Robert 1952- *WhoEnt 92*
**Orr**, Jean Fergus Henderson 1920- *Who 92*
**Orr**, Jeffery Lee 1961- *WhoRel 92*
**Orr**, John Berk 1933- *WhoRel 92*
**Orr**, John Boyd 1880-1971 *WhoNob 90*
**Orr**, John Henry 1918- *Who 92*
**Orr**, John R 1933- *AmMWSc 92*
**Orr**, Kay A. 1939- *IntWW 91, WhoAmP 91, WhoMW 92*
**Orr**, Larry G. 1948- *WhoRel 92*
**Orr**, Leighton 1907- *AmMWSc 92*
**Orr**, Linda *DrAPF 91*
**Orr**, Linda 1943- *ConAu 35NR*
**Orr**, Louis 1879-1966 *DcNCBi 4*
**Orr**, Louis M. 1958- *WhoBlA 92*
**Orr**, Lowell Preston 1930- *AmMWSc 92*
**Orr**, Marcia 1949- *WhoFI 92*
**Orr**, Marshall H 1942- *AmMWSc 92*
**Orr**, Mary Faith 1920- *AmMWSc 92*
**Orr**, Melanie 1950- *WhoAmL 92*
**Orr**, Michael P. 1947- *WhoWest 92*
**Orr**, Nancy Hoffner 1941- *AmMWSc 92*
**Orr**, Orty Edwin 1920- *AmMWSc 92*
**Orr**, Patricia Pepper 1954- *WhoRel 92*
**Orr**, Quinn Lindsay 1957- *WhoEnt 92*
**Orr**, Ray 1953- *WhoBlA 92*
**Orr**, Richard Clayton 1941- *AmMWSc 92*
**Orr**, Robert Dunkerson 1917- *IntWW 91, WhoAmP 91*
**Orr**, Robert Gordon 1948- *FacFETw*
**Orr**, Robert Richmond 1930- *WrDr 92*
**Orr**, Robert S 1937- *AmMWSc 92*
**Orr**, Robert Thomas 1908- *AmMWSc 92*
**Orr**, Robert William 1940- *AmMWSc 92*
**Orr**, Robin 1909- *ConCom 92, Who 92*
**Orr**, Robin Denise Moore 1934- *AmMWSc 92*
**Orr**, Roy Lee 1932- *WhoAmP 91*
**Orr**, San Watterson, Jr. 1941- *WhoFI 92*
**Orr**, Terrence S. 1943- *WhoEnt 92*
**Orr**, Theresa J. Castellana 1941- *WhoFI 92*
**Orr**, Verlena *DrAPF 91*
**Orr**, Virgil 1923- *WhoAmP 91*
**Orr**, Wendell Eugene 1930- *WhoEnt 92*
**Orr**, William Campbell 1920- *AmMWSc 92*
**Orr**, William N 1939- *AmMWSc 92*
**Orr**, William T. *LesBEnT 92*
**Orr**, William T. 1917- *IntMPA 92*
**Orr**, Wilson Lee 1923- *AmMWSc 92*
**Orr-Ewing** *Who 92*
**Orr-Ewing**, Baron 1912- *Who 92*
**Orr Ewing**, Edward Stuart 1931- *Who 92*
**Orr-Ewing**, Hamish 1924- *IntWW 91, Who 92*
**Orr Ewing**, Ronald Archibald 1912- *Who 92*
**Orrall**, Frank Quimby 1925- *AmMWSc 92*
**Orrego**, George Humberto 1950- *WhoHisp 92*
**Orrego**, Hector 1923- *AmMWSc 92*
**Orrego-Salas**, Juan Antonio 1919- *WhoEnt 92*
**Orrego Vicuna**, Francisco 1942- *IntWW 91, Who 92*
**Orrell**, James Francis Freestone 1944- *Who 92*
**Orrell**, John 1934- *ConAu 35NR*
**Orrell**, Marthavan 1963- *WhoEnt 92*
**Orrenius**, Sten 1937- *AmMWSc 92*
**Orrery**, Earl of *RfGEnL 91*
**Orrick**, William Horsley, Jr. 1915- *WhoAmL 92, WhoAmP 91, WhoWest 92*
**Orringer**, Shelly Genser *WhoEnt 92*
**Orris**, Daryl Joseph 1947- *WhoFI 92, WhoMW 92*
**Orris**, Neil Kenneth 1960- *WhoEnt 92*
**Orrison**, Carrol Payton 1929- *WhoAmP 91*
**Orrmont**, Arthur 1922- *ConAu 35NR*
**Orrock**, Nancy Gorgan *WhoAmP 91*
**Orrock**, R Dennis 1943- *WhoAmP 91*
**Orrock**, Robert Dickson 1955- *WhoAmP 91*
**Orrok**, Francene Feldman 1937- *WhoWest 92*
**Orrok**, George Timothy 1930- *AmMWSc 92*
**Ors**, Jose Alberto 1944- *AmMWSc 92*
**Orsatti**, Alfred Kendall 1932- *WhoWest 92*
**Orsatti**, Ernest Benjamin 1949- *WhoAmL 92*
**Orsatti**, Frank H. 1942- *WhoEnt 92*
**Orsborn**, JoAnn 1936- *WhoWest 92*
**Orsborn**, John F 1929- *AmMWSc 92*
**Orsenigo**, Joseph Reuter 1922- *AmMWSc 92*
**Orsetti**, Christian Ernest 1923- *IntWW 91*
**Orsi**, Ernest Vinicio 1922- *AmMWSc 92*
**Orsinger**, Richard Remington 1950- *WhoAmL 92*
**Orsini**, Frank R 1938- *AmMWSc 92*
**Orsini**, Louis *WhoAmP 91*
**Orsini**, Margaret Ward 1916- *AmMWSc 92*
**Orson**, Marshall David 1960- *WhoEnt 92*
**Orson**, Rasin Ward 1927- *Who 92*
**Orsy**, Ladislas 1921- *WhoRel 92*
**Orszag**, Steven Alan 1943- *AmMWSc 92*
**Orszulak**, Richard Stewart 1957- *WhoFI 92, WhoMW 92*
**Ort**, Carol 1947- *AmMWSc 92*
**Ort**, Donald Richard 1949- *AmMWSc 92*
**Ort**, Morris Richard 1927- *AmMWSc 92*
**Ort**, Rosalyn Maria 1942- *WhoWest 92*
**Ortal**, Jose Casimiro, Jr. 1952- *WhoHisp 92*
**Ortal-Miranda**, Yolanda *WhoHisp 92*
**Ortaldo**, John R *AmMWSc 92*
**Ortbal**, John David 1951- *WhoMW 92*
**Ortbals**, Alan Joseph 1952- *WhoMW 92*
**Ortega**, Anthony David 1958- *WhoHisp 92*
**Ortega**, Augusto Cesar 1927- *WhoHisp 92*
**Ortega**, Belen 1918- *WhoHisp 92*
**Ortega**, Blanca Rosa 1948- *WhoHisp 92*
**Ortega**, David Fernando 1940- *WhoHisp 92*
**Ortega**, Deborah L. 1955- *WhoHisp 92*
**Ortega**, Encarnacion Maria 1938- *WhoRel 92*
**Ortega**, Ernest Eugene 1940- *WhoHisp 92*
**Ortega**, German E. 1933- *WhoHisp 92*
**Ortega**, Ginka Gerova *WhoEnt 92*
**Ortega**, Gustavo Ramon 1945- *AmMWSc 92*
**Ortega**, Ildefonso B. 1935- *WhoFI 92*
**Ortega**, Jacobo 1929- *AmMWSc 92, WhoHisp 92*
**Ortega**, James *WhoHisp 92*
**Ortega**, James M 1932- *AmMWSc 92*
**Ortega**, Juan *BlkOlyM*
**Ortega**, Julio 1942- *IntAu&W 91, LiExTwC*
**Ortega**, Katherine Davalos *WhoHisp 92*
**Ortega**, Lawrence A. 1948- *WhoHisp 92*
**Ortega**, Linda Dolores 1951- *WhoHisp 92*
**Ortega**, Lorraine G 1940- *WhoAmP 91*
**Ortega**, M. Alice 1960- *WhoHisp 92*
**Ortega**, Manuel Anthony 1953- *WhoHisp 92*
**Ortega**, Manuel J., Jr. 1948- *WhoHisp 92*
**Ortega**, Oscar 1956- *WhoHisp 92*
**Ortega**, Oscar J. *WhoHisp 92*
**Ortega**, Patricia L. 1956- *WhoHisp 92*
**Ortega**, Rafael Enrique 1952- *WhoHisp 92*
**Ortega**, Ray 1940- *WhoHisp 92*
**Ortega**, Reuben A. *WhoHisp 92*
**Ortega**, Robert, Jr. 1947- *WhoHisp 92*
**Ortega**, Ruben *WhoAmP 91*
**Ortega**, Ruben Francisco, Jr. 1956- *WhoHisp 92*
**Ortega**, Silver 1949- *WhoHisp 92*
**Ortega**, Tony 1958- *WhoHisp 92*

**Ortega Carter,** Dolores 1950- *WhoHisp 92*
**Ortega Chamorro,** Guillermo 1909- *WhoHisp 92*
**Ortega-Davey,** Maria Belen 1918- *WhoHisp 92*
**Ortega Saavedra,** Daniel 1945- *FacFETw [port], IntWW 91*
**Ortega Y Alamino,** Jaime Lucas *WhoRel 92*
**Ortega y Gasset,** Jose 1883-1955 *FacFETw, LiExTwC*
**Ortego,** Gilda Baeza 1952- *WhoWest 92*
**Ortego,** James Dale 1941- *AmMWSc 92*
**Ortego,** Joseph John 1954- *WhoHisp 92*
**Ortego,** Philip D. *DrAPF 91*
**Ortego y Gasca,** Felipe de 1926- *WhoHisp 92*
**Ortel,** William Charles Gormley 1926- *AmMWSc 92*
**Orten,** Betty 1927- *WhoAmP 91*
**Orten,** James M 1904- *AmMWSc 92*
**Ortenberg,** Elisabeth Claiborne 1929- *WhoFI 92*
**Ortengren,** John 1931- *WhoFI 92*
**Ortez,** Donald Jeronimo 1941- *WhoHisp 92*
**Ortez Colindres,** Enrique 1931- *IntWW 91*
**Orth,** Charles Douglas 1942- *AmMWSc 92*
**Orth,** Charles Joseph 1930- *AmMWSc 92*
**Orth,** Daniel Adam, III 1937- *WhoIns 92*
**Orth,** George Otto, Jr 1913- *AmMWSc 92*
**Orth,** Joanne M *AmMWSc 92*
**Orth,** John C 1931- *AmMWSc 92*
**Orth,** Paul Gerhardt 1929- *AmMWSc 92*
**Orth,** Robert D 1935- *WhoAmP 91*
**Orth,** Robert Joseph 1947- *AmMWSc 92*
**Orth,** William Albert 1931- *AmMWSc 92*
**Orthel,** Susan Diane 1952- *WhoWest 92*
**Orthoefer,** John George 1932- *AmMWSc 92*
**Orthryth,** Queen of Mercia *EncAmaz 91*
**Orthwein,** W C 1924- *AmMWSc 92*
**Ortino,** Hector Ruben 1942- *WhoHisp 92*
**Ortique,** Revius Oliver, Jr. 1924- *WhoBlA 92*
**Ortiz,** A. Luis 1947- *WhoAmL 92*
**Ortiz,** Agustin 1954- *WhoWest 92*
**Ortiz,** Alfonso A. 1939- *WrDr 92*
**Ortiz,** Alfredo Tomas 1948- *WhoHisp 92*
**Ortiz,** Ana-Alicia *WhoEnt 92*
**Ortiz,** Angel L. *WhoHisp 92*
**Ortiz,** Antonio G. *DrAPF 91*
**Ortiz,** Antonio Ignacio 1961- *WhoEnt 92, WhoFI 92, WhoWest 92*
**Ortiz,** Araceli 1937- *AmMWSc 92, WhoHisp 92*
**Ortiz,** Augusto 1917- *WhoHisp 92*
**Ortiz,** Beatriz E. 1959- *WhoHisp 92*
**Ortiz,** Carlos A. 1946- *WhoHisp 92*
**Ortiz,** Carlos Guillermo 1956- *WhoHisp 92*
**Ortiz,** Carlos Roberto 1946- *WhoHisp 92*
**Ortiz,** Carmen D. *WhoHisp 92*
**Ortiz,** Charles Francis 1951- *WhoWest 92*
**Ortiz,** Charles Leo 1941- *WhoHisp 92*
**Ortiz,** Clemencia 1942- *WhoHisp 92*
**Ortiz,** Cristina 1950- *IntWW 91*
**Ortiz,** Daniel Zapata 1954- *WhoHisp 92*
**Ortiz,** Delia 1924- *WhoBlA 92*
**Ortiz,** Diego 1510?-1570? *NewAmDM*
**Ortiz,** Edgardo 1926- *WhoHisp 92*
**Ortiz,** Elisabeth Lambert 1928- *ConAu 35NR*
**Ortiz,** Emanuel *WhoHisp 92*
**Ortiz,** Enrique O. *WhoHisp 92*
**Ortiz,** Francis V., Jr. 1926- *WhoHisp 92*
**Ortiz,** Frank P. 1939- *WhoHisp 92*
**Ortiz,** Frank Vincent 1926- *IntWW 91*
**Ortiz,** Frank Xavier 1949- *WhoHisp 92*
**Ortiz,** George 1942- *WhoHisp 92*
**Ortiz,** Gus R. 1955- *WhoWest 92*
**Ortiz,** Hector *WhoHisp 92*
**Ortiz,** Herminio, Jr. 1949- *WhoHisp 92*
**Ortiz,** Isidro D. 1949- *WhoHisp 92*
**Ortiz,** Jack *WhoHisp 92*
**Ortiz,** James A. *WhoHisp 92*
**Ortiz,** Jay Richard Gentry 1945- *WhoAmL 92*
**Ortiz,** Jesus, Jr. 1942- *WhoHisp 92*
**Ortiz,** Jose G. 1950- *WhoHisp 92*
**Ortiz,** Jose Ramon *WhoHisp 92*
**Ortiz,** Joseph Vincent 1956- *WhoHisp 92*
**Ortiz,** Julia Cristina 1955- *WhoHisp 92*
**Ortiz,** Junior 1959- *WhoHisp 92*
**Ortiz,** Luis Tony 1955- *WhoHisp 92*
**Ortiz,** Manuel, Jr. 1938- *WhoHisp 92*
**Ortiz,** Maria C. 1959- *WhoHisp 92*
**Ortiz,** Maria de Los Angeles 1947- *WhoHisp 92*
**Ortiz,** Maria Elena 1946- *WhoHisp 92*
**Ortiz,** Maritza 1956- *WhoHisp 92*
**Ortiz,** Maritza 1958- *WhoHisp 92*
**Ortiz,** Melchor, Jr 1942- *AmMWSc 92*
**Ortiz,** Michael Guadalupe 1929- *WhoRel 92*
**Ortiz,** Miguel 1954- *WhoHisp 92*
**Ortiz,** Miguel A. *DrAPF 91*
**Ortiz,** Nelda Jean 1956- *WhoAmL 92*
**Ortiz,** Norma I. 1955- *WhoHisp 92*
**Ortiz,** Nydia 1951- *WhoHisp 92*
**Ortiz,** Olivia Frances 1926- *WhoHisp 92*
**Ortiz,** Pablo Francis 1948- *WhoHisp 92*
**Ortiz,** Pedro 1949- *WhoHisp 92*
**Ortiz,** Pedro Rene 1965- *WhoFI 92*
**Ortiz,** Peter *WhoAmP 91*
**Ortiz,** Peter J 1913-1988 *FacFETw*
**Ortiz,** Rachael 1941- *WhoHisp 92*
**Ortiz,** Rafael Montanez 1934- *WhoHisp 92*
**Ortiz,** Raquel 1945- *WhoHisp 92*
**Ortiz,** Raymond Z. 1953- *WhoHisp 92*
**Ortiz,** Rene Genaro 1941- *IntWW 91*
**Ortiz,** Reynaldo U. 1946- *WhoHisp 92*
**Ortiz,** Ronald Antonio 1930- *WhoHisp 92*
**Ortiz,** Ronald Gilbert 1953- *WhoMW 92*
**Ortiz,** S. M. *WhoHisp 92*
**Ortiz,** Samuel Luis 1950- *WhoHisp 92*
**Ortiz,** Simon J. *DrAPF 91*
**Ortiz,** Simon J. 1941- *BenetAL 91, ConAu 134, ConPo 91, IntAu&W 91, TwCWW 91, WrDr 92*
**Ortiz,** Solomon P. 1937- *AlmAP 92 [port], WhoAmP 91*
**Ortiz,** Solomon Porfirio 1937- *WhoHisp 92*
**Ortiz,** Sylvia Margarita 1968- *WhoHisp 92*
**Ortiz,** Tino G. *WhoHisp 92*
**Ortiz,** Vilma 1954- *WhoHisp 92*
**Ortiz,** William 1947- *WhoEnt 92*
**Ortiz-Alvarez,** Jorge L. 1952- *WhoHisp 92*
**Ortiz-Brunet,** Jorge 1940- *WhoHisp 92*
**Ortiz-Buonafina,** Marta 1933- *WhoHisp 92*
**Ortiz-Cotto,** Pablo 1929- *WhoHisp 92*
**Ortiz de Dominguez,** Josefa 1768-1829 *HisDSpE*
**Ortiz de Montellano,** Bernard Ramon, V 1938- *WhoHisp 92*
**Ortiz de Montellano,** Paul Richard *WhoHisp 92*
**Ortiz de Montellano,** Paul Richard 1942- *AmMWSc 92*
**Ortiz De Rozas,** Carlos 1926- *IntWW 91, Who 92*
**Ortiz Diaz,** Tomas 1944- *WhoHisp 92*
**Ortiz-Franco,** Luis 1946- *WhoHisp 92, WhoWest 92*
**Ortiz-Griffin,** Julia L. *WhoHisp 92*
**Ortiz-Macri,** Veronica Cecilia 1937- *WhoHisp 92*
**Ortiz Mena,** Antonio 1912- *IntWW 91*
**Ortiz-Patino,** Jaime 1930- *WhoFI 92*
**Ortiz-Suarez,** Humberto J. 1941- *WhoHisp 92*
**Ortiz Tinoco,** Cesar d1991 *NewYTBS 91*
**Ortiz-White,** Aleene J. 1953- *WhoHisp 92*
**Ortloff,** George Christian 1947- *WhoAmP 91*
**Ortman,** Eldon Emil 1934- *AmMWSc 92*
**Ortman,** Harold R 1917- *AmMWSc 92*
**Ortman,** Robert A 1926- *AmMWSc 92*
**Ortman,** Terry Lynn 1959- *WhoMW 92*
**Ortmann,** Dorothea 1912- *WhoEnt 92*
**Ortmann,** Jeffrey 1954- *WhoMW 92*
**Ortner,** Donald John 1938- *AmMWSc 92*
**Ortner,** Mary Joanne 1946- *AmMWSc 92*
**Ortner,** Robert 1927- *ConAu 135*
**Ortner,** Toni *DrAPF 91*
**Ortolani,** Benito 1928- *WhoEnt 92*
**Ortoleva,** Peter Joseph 1942- *AmMWSc 92*
**Ortoli,** Francois-Xavier 1925- *IntWW 91, Who 92*
**Ortoll,** Javier *WhoHisp 92*
**Orton,** Bill *WhoAmP 91*
**Orton,** Bill 1949- *WhoWest 92*
**Orton,** Colin George 1938- *AmMWSc 92, WhoMW 92*
**Orton,** Edward Francis Baxter 1829-1899 *BiInAmS*
**Orton,** George W 1919- *AmMWSc 92*
**Orton,** Glenn Scott 1948- *AmMWSc 92*
**Orton,** James 1830-1877 *BiInAmS*
**Orton,** Joe *ConAu 35NR*
**Orton,** Joe 1933-1967 *CnDBLB 8 [port], FacFETw, RfGEnL 91*
**Orton,** John Edward, III 1931- *WhoAmL 92*
**Orton,** John Kingsley 1933-1967 *ConAu 35NR*
**Orton,** John Paul 1925- *AmMWSc 92*
**Orton,** Robert Frank 1936- *WhoAmL 92*
**Orton,** Vrest 1897-1986 *ConAu 35NR*
**Orton,** William H. 1948- *AlmAP 92 [port]*
**Orton,** William R, Jr 1922- *AmMWSc 92*
**Ortona,** Egidio 1910- *IntWW 91*
**Orts,** Frank A 1931- *AmMWSc 92*
**Orttung,** William Herbert 1934- *AmMWSc 92*
**Ortwein,** John Lawrence 1944- *WhoRel 92*
**Ortwerth,** Beryl John 1937- *AmMWSc 92*
**Ortwerth,** Joseph Robert 1956- *WhoAmP 91*
**Ortynsky,** Stephen 1866-1916 *RelLAm 91*
**Orullian,** B. LaRae 1933- *WhoWest 92*
**Orvick,** George Myron 1929- *WhoRel 92*
**Orvig,** Chris *AmMWSc 92*
**Orville,** Harold Duvall 1932- *AmMWSc 92*
**Orville,** Philip Moore 1930- *AmMWSc 92*
**Orville,** Richard Edmonds 1936- *AmMWSc 92*
**Orwell,** George 1903-1950 *CnDBLB 7 [port], FacFETw [port], RfGEnL 91, TwCSFW 91*
**Orwig,** Eugene R, Jr 1919- *AmMWSc 92*
**Orwig,** Larry Eugene 1944- *AmMWSc 92*
**Orwig,** Matthew Dane 1959- *WhoAmL 92*
**Orwig,** Melvin Daryl 1940- *WhoFI 92*
**Orwoll,** Gregg S. K. 1926- *WhoAmL 92, WhoFI 92, WhoMW 92*
**Orwoll,** Robert Arvid 1940- *AmMWSc 92*
**Ory,** Edward 1886-1973 *FacFETw*
**Ory,** Horace Anthony 1932- *AmMWSc 92*
**Ory,** Kid 1886-1973 *NewAmDM*
**Ory,** Marcia Gail 1950- *AmMWSc 92*
**Ory,** Robert Louis 1925- *AmMWSc 92*
**Ory,** Susan Summer 1951- *WhoRel 92*
**Oryshkevich,** Roman Sviatoslav 1928- *WhoMW 92*
**Orza,** Vincent Frank 1950- *WhoFI 92*
**Orzech,** Ann Dorothy Wagner 1950- *WhoFI 92*
**Orzech,** Chester Eugene, Jr 1937- *AmMWSc 92*
**Orzech,** Morris 1942- *AmMWSc 92*
**Orzechowski,** Marian Odon 1931- *IntWW 91*
**Orzechowski,** Raymond Frank 1938- *AmMWSc 92*
**Orzel,** Michael Dale 1952- *WhoAmL 92*
**Orzel,** Ronald F. 1934- *WhoMW 92*
**Osacky,** John *WhoRel 92*
**Osaki,** Mark *DrAPF 91*
**Osakwe,** Christopher 1942- *WhoAmL 92, WhoBlA 92*
**Osann,** Edward William, Jr. 1918- *WhoAmL 92*
**Osar,** Karen Rohn 1949- *WhoFI 92*
**Osawa,** Yoshio 1930- *AmMWSc 92*
**Osbahr,** Albert J, Jr 1931- *AmMWSc 92*
**Osbaldeston,** Gordon Francis 1930- *IntWW 91*
**Osberg,** G L 1917- *AmMWSc 92*
**Osberg,** Philip Henry 1924- *AmMWSc 92*
**Osborg,** Hans 1901- *AmMWSc 92*
**Osborn,** Bonita Genevieve 1941- *WhoFI 92*
**Osborn,** Carolyn *DrAPF 91*
**Osborn,** Charles 1775-1850 *DcNCBi 4*
**Osborn,** Christopher Raymoln, Jr. 1950- *WhoRel 92*
**Osborn,** Claiborn Lee 1933- *AmMWSc 92*
**Osborn,** Clayton F *WhoAmP 91*
**Osborn,** Daniel Scott 1965- *WhoEnt 92*
**Osborn,** David 1923- *ConAu 134*
**Osborn,** DeVerle Ross 1925- *WhoMW 92*
**Osborn,** Donald Earl 1952- *AmMWSc 92*
**Osborn,** Donald Robert 1929- *WhoAmL 92*
**Osborn,** Dorothy Harris 1927- *WhoFI 92*
**Osborn,** Elburt Franklin 1911- *AmMWSc 92*
**Osborn,** Eric Francis 1922- *IntWW 91, WrDr 92*
**Osborn,** Frederic Adrian 1941- *Who 92*
**Osborn,** H James 1932- *AmMWSc 92*
**Osborn,** Henry H 1926- *AmMWSc 92*
**Osborn,** Henry Stafford 1823-1894 *BiInAmS*
**Osborn,** Herbert B 1929- *AmMWSc 92*
**Osborn,** Holly Ann 1959- *WhoMW 92*
**Osborn,** Howard Ashley 1928- *AmMWSc 92*
**Osborn,** J. Marshall 1930- *WhoMW 92*
**Osborn,** J Marshall, Jr 1930- *AmMWSc 92*
**Osborn,** J R 1924- *AmMWSc 92*
**Osborn,** James Andrew 1963- *WhoRel 92*
**Osborn,** James Lowell 1931- *WhoRel 92*
**Osborn,** James Maxwell 1929- *AmMWSc 92*
**Osborn,** Janet Lynn 1952- *WhoMW 92*
**Osborn,** Jeffrey L *AmMWSc 92*
**Osborn,** Jeffrey Whitaker 1930- *AmMWSc 92*
**Osborn,** John 1922- *Who 92*
**Osborn,** John David 1948- *WhoMW 92*
**Osborn,** John Edward 1936- *AmMWSc 92*
**Osborn,** John Edward 1957- *WhoAmL 92*
**Osborn,** John Jay *DrAPF 91*
**Osborn,** John Simcoe, Jr. 1926- *WhoAmL 92*
**Osborn,** John William 1936- *WhoRel 92*
**Osborn,** Jones *WhoAmP 91*
**Osborn,** June Elaine 1937- *AmMWSc 92*
**Osborn,** Kenneth Louis 1946- *WhoMW 92*
**Osborn,** Kenneth Wakeman 1937- *AmMWSc 92*
**Osborn,** La Donna Carol 1947- *WhoRel 92*
**Osborn,** Laughton 1809?-1878 *BenetAL 91*
**Osborn,** Lloyd William 1929- *WhoRel 92*
**Osborn,** Malcolm Everett 1928- *WhoAmL 92*
**Osborn,** Mark Eliot 1950- *WhoMW 92*
**Osborn,** Mary Jane 1927- *AmMWSc 92*
**Osborn,** Ralph Stephen 1952- *WhoWest 92*
**Osborn,** Richard 1958- *Who 92*
**Osborn,** Roger 1920- *AmMWSc 92*
**Osborn,** Ronald Edwin 1917- *WhoRel 92, WrDr 92*
**Osborn,** Ronald George 1948- *AmMWSc 92*
**Osborn,** Simeon James 1958- *WhoAmL 92*
**Osborn,** Terry Wayne 1943- *AmMWSc 92*
**Osborn,** Theodore L, Jr 1910- *WhoIns 92*
**Osborn,** Wayne Henry 1942- *AmMWSc 92*
**Osborne Brothers,** The *NewAmDM*
**Osborne,** Lord 1937- *Who 92*
**Osborne,** Adlai 1744-1814 *DcNCBi 4*
**Osborne,** Alexander 1709-1776 *DcNCBi 4*
**Osborne,** Alfred E., Jr. 1944- *WhoBlA 92*
**Osborne,** Allen 1949- *WhoFI 92*
**Osborne,** Anthony David 1935- *Who 92*
**Osborne,** Bartley P., Jr. 1934- *WhoFI 92*
**Osborne,** Carl Andrew 1940- *AmMWSc 92*
**Osborne,** Charles 1927- *ConAu 34NR, IntAu&W 91, Who 92, WrDr 92*
**Osborne,** Charles Edward 1929- *AmMWSc 92*
**Osborne,** Chester G 1915- *ConAu 35NR*
**Osborne,** Clayton Henriquez 1945- *WhoBlA 92*
**Osborne,** Coles Alexander 1896- *Who 92*
**Osborne,** David *ConAu 36NR, TwCSFW 91, WrDr 92*
**Osborne,** David Wendell 1935- *AmMWSc 92*
**Osborne,** Denis Gordon 1932- *IntWW 91, Who 92*
**Osborne,** Duffield 1858-1917 *ScFEYrs*
**Osborne,** Earl Thomas 1920- *WhoAmP 91*
**Osborne,** Edward Beryl 1919- *WhoAmP 91*
**Osborne,** Edwin Augustus 1837-1926 *DcNCBi 4*
**Osborne,** Ernest L. 1932- *WhoBlA 92*
**Osborne,** Estelle Massey 1901-1981 *WhoBlA 92N*
**Osborne,** F Edward 1925- *WhoAmP 91*
**Osborne,** Francis Irwin 1853-1920 *DcNCBi 4*
**Osborne,** Frank Harold 1944- *AmMWSc 92*
**Osborne,** Franklin Talmage 1939- *AmMWSc 92*
**Osborne,** Gayla Marlene 1956- *WhoFI 92*
**Osborne,** Gayle Ann 1951- *WhoWest 92*
**Osborne,** George *ConAu 36NR*
**Osborne,** George Delano 1938- *WhoEnt 92*
**Osborne,** George Edwin 1917- *AmMWSc 92*
**Osborne,** George H *WhoAmP 91*
**Osborne,** Gregory *WhoEnt 92*
**Osborne,** Gregory 1955- *IntWW 91*
**Osborne,** Gwendolyn Eunice 1949- *WhoBlA 92*
**Osborne,** H. Paul 1914- *WhoRel 92*
**Osborne,** Hamish Scott 1948- *WhoAmL 92*
**Osborne,** Helena *Who 92*
**Osborne,** Hugh Stancill 1918- *WhoBlA 92*
**Osborne,** J Scott, III 1951- *AmMWSc 92*
**Osborne,** James Alfred 1927- *WhoRel 92*
**Osborne,** James L 1928- *WhoIns 92*
**Osborne,** James Walker 1811-1869 *DcNCBi 4*
**Osborne,** James Walker 1859-1919 *DcNCBi 4*
**Osborne,** James William 1928- *AmMWSc 92*
**Osborne,** Jeffrey *WhoEnt 92*
**Osborne,** Jeffrey Linton 1948- *WhoBlA 92*
**Osborne,** Jerry L 1940- *AmMWSc 92*
**Osborne,** Jerry Ramon 1938- *WhoAmL 92*
**Osborne,** John 1929- *CnDBLB 7 [port], FacFETw, IntAu&W 91, IntMPA 92, RfGEnL 91, Who 92, WrDr 92*
**Osborne,** John Alan 1922- *AmMWSc 92*
**Osborne,** John Chevor d1819 *DcNCBi 4*
**Osborne,** John James 1929- *IntWW 91*
**Osborne,** Kenan Bernard 1930- *WhoRel 92*
**Osborne,** Kenneth Hilton *Who 92*
**Osborne,** Lance Smith 1949- *AmMWSc 92*
**Osborne,** Larry Walter 1939- *WhoWest 92*
**Osborne,** Louis Shreve 1923- *AmMWSc 92*
**Osborne,** Maggie 1941- *IntAu&W 91*
**Osborne,** Malcolm 1880-1963 *TwCPaSc*
**Osborne,** Mark Lewis 1952- *WhoEnt 92*
**Osborne,** Mary Pope 1949- *IntAu&W 91*
**Osborne,** MaryHelen 1936- *WhoMW 92*
**Osborne,** Melville 1922- *AmMWSc 92*
**Osborne,** Michael John *Who 92*
**Osborne,** Milton 1936- *WrDr 92*
**Osborne,** Morris Floyd 1931- *AmMWSc 92*
**Osborne,** Nigel 1948- *ConCom 92*
**Osborne,** Oliver Hilton 1931- *WhoBlA 92*
**Osborne,** Otis O. 1939- *WhoRel 92*
**Osborne,** Paul James 1921- *AmMWSc 92*
**Osborne,** Peter 1943- *Who 92*
**Osborne,** Phillip Lee 1959- *WhoWest 92*
**Osborne,** Quinton Albert 1951- *WhoMW 92*

**Osborne**, Richard de Jongh 1934- *IntWW 91, WhoFI 92*
**Osborne**, Richard Hazelet 1920- *AmMWSc 92*
**Osborne**, Richard Jay 1951- *WhoFI 92*
**Osborne**, Richard L. *DrAPF 91*
**Osborne**, Richard Vincent 1936- *AmMWSc 92*
**Osborne**, Robert Howard 1939- *AmMWSc 92*
**Osborne**, Robert Kidder 1921- *AmMWSc 92*
**Osborne**, Ronald Drake 1941- *WhoWest 92*
**Osborne**, Ronald Walter 1946- *WhoFI 92*
**Osborne**, Trevor 1943- *Who 92*
**Osborne**, William Arthur 1948- *WhoAmP 91*
**Osborne**, William Reginald, Jr. 1957- *WhoBlA 92*
**Osborne**, William Walter, Jr. 1948- *WhoAmL 92*
**Osborne**, William Wesley 1920- *AmMWSc 92*
**Osbourn**, Gordon Cecil 1954- *AmMWSc 92*
**Osbourne**, Ivor 1951- *WrDr 92*
**Osbourne**, Ivor Livingstone 1951- *IntAu&W 91*
**Osbourne**, Lloyd 1868-1947 *BenetAL 91*
**Osbourne**, Ozzy 1948- *WhoEnt 92*
**Osburn**, Bennie Irve 1937- *AmMWSc 92*
**Osburn**, Carroll Duane 1941- *WhoRel 92*
**Osburn**, Richard Lee 1940- *AmMWSc 92*
**Osby**, Robert Edward 1937- *WhoWest 92*
**Osby**, Simeon B., Jr. 1909- *WhoBlA 92*
**Oscai**, Lawrence B 1938- *AmMWSc 92*
**O'Scannlain**, Diarmuid F 1937- *WhoAmP 91*
**O'Scannlain**, Diarmuid Fionntain 1937- *WhoAmL 92*
**Oscar**, A. 1919- *TwCPaSc*
**Oscar**, Irving S 1923- *AmMWSc 92*
**Oscarson**, Kurt E 1948- *WhoAmP 91*
**Oscarsson**, Per Oscar Heinrich 1927- *IntWW 91*
**Osceola** 1800?-1838 *BenetAL 91*
**Oschal**, James Christopher 1961- *WhoAmL 92*
**Oschwald**, Don L 1923- *WhoAmP 91*
**Osdoby**, Philip 1949- *AmMWSc 92*
**Ose**, Peggy Jo 1951- *WhoMW 92*
**Oseasohn**, Robert 1924- *AmMWSc 92*
**Osebold**, John William 1921- *AmMWSc 92*
**Osedacz**, Richard Philip 1962- *WhoWest 92*
**Osegueda**, Laura Margaret 1955- *WhoHisp 92*
**Osei**, Edward Kofi 1959- *WhoFI 92*
**Osei-Gyimah**, Peter 1946- *AmMWSc 92*
**Osejo**, Rafael Francisco 1790-1848 *HisDSpE*
**Oseni**, Hakeem O. 1938- *WhoBlA 92*
**Osepchuk**, John M 1927- *AmMWSc 92*
**Oser**, Bernard Levussove 1899- *AmMWSc 92*
**Oser**, Hans Joerg 1929- *AmMWSc 92*
**Oserrah** *EncAmaz 91*
**Oseth**, John Marcus 1944- *WhoAmL 92*
**Osgood**, McIlvaine and Company *DcLB 112*
**Osgood**, Charles *LesBEnT 92 [port]*
**Osgood**, Charles Edgar 1938- *AmMWSc 92*
**Osgood**, Charles Freeman 1938- *AmMWSc 92*
**Osgood**, Christopher James 1949- *AmMWSc 92*
**Osgood**, David William 1940- *AmMWSc 92*
**Osgood**, Elmer Clayton 1906- *AmMWSc 92*
**Osgood**, Frances Sargent 1811-1850 *BenetAL 91*
**Osgood**, Frank William 1931- *WhoWest 92*
**Osgood**, Judy Kay 1952- *WhoMW 92*
**Osgood**, Patricia Fisher *AmMWSc 92*
**Osgood**, Peter Greer 1940- *WhoFI 92*
**Osgood**, Randall Mark 1951- *WhoWest 92*
**Osgood**, Richard Magee, Jr 1943- *AmMWSc 92*
**Osgood**, Robert Vernon 1941- *AmMWSc 92*
**Osgood**, Russell King 1947- *WhoAmL 92*
**Osgood**, Theodore Jesse 1940- *WhoRel 92*
**Osgood**, Wilfred Beede 1911- *WhoAmP 91*
**Oshanin**, Lev Ivanovich 1912- *SovUnBD*
**O'Shaughnessy**, Charles Dennis 1941- *AmMWSc 92*
**O'Shaughnessy**, James Patrick 1947- *WhoAmL 92, WhoFI 92, WhoMW 92*
**O'Shaughnessy**, William Joseph 1937- *WhoAmL 92*
**O'Shea**, Alexander Paterson d1990 *Who 92N*
**O'Shea**, Bob *WhoAmP 91*
**O'Shea**, Charles J 1958- *WhoAmP 91*
**O'Shea**, David Michael 1927- *Who 92*
**O'Shea**, Donald Charles 1938- *AmMWSc 92*
**O'Shea**, Francis Xavier 1932- *AmMWSc 92*
**O'Shea**, Joyce Burnett 1935- *WhoMW 92*
**O'Shea**, Kevin C. 1953- *WhoFI 92*
**O'Shea**, Martin Lester 1938- *WhoAmP 91*
**O'Shea**, Milo 1926- *IntMPA 92*
**O'Shea**, Neil Patrick 1961- *WhoMW 92*
**O'Shea**, Pat 1931- *WrDr 92*
**O'Shea**, Patrick John 1932- *WhoRel 92*
**O'Shea**, Patrick Joseph 1950- *WhoAmL 92*
**O'Shea**, Peter Joseph, Jr. 1937- *WhoFI 92*
**O'Shea**, Shawn Patrick 1957- *WhoWest 92*
**O'Shea**, Timothy Allan 1944- *AmMWSc 92*
**O'Sheel**, Shaemas 1886-1954 *BenetAL 91*
**Osheim**, Yvonne Nelson 1944- *AmMWSc 92*
**Osher**, John Edward 1929- *AmMWSc 92, WhoWest 92*
**Osher**, Stanley Joel 1942- *AmMWSc 92*
**Osheroff**, Douglas Dean 1945- *AmMWSc 92, WhoWest 92*
**Osheroff**, Neil 1952- *AmMWSc 92*
**Osheroff**, Phyllis Liu 1945- *WhoWest 92*
**O'Shields**, Dale Alvin 1955- *WhoRel 92*
**Oshiki**, Kaz 1924- *WhoAmP 91*
**Oshima**, Eugene Akio 1934- *AmMWSc 92*
**Oshima**, Nagisa 1932- *IntDcF 2-2 [port], IntMPA 92, IntWW 91*
**Oshiro**, Dennis Takemitsu 1944- *WhoFI 92*
**Oshiro**, George 1938- *AmMWSc 92*
**Oshiro**, Lyndon Satoru 1933- *AmMWSc 92*
**Oshiro**, Paul T 1955- *WhoAmP 91*
**Oshiro**, Yuki 1935- *AmMWSc 92*
**Oshiyoye**, Adekunle 1951- *WhoBlA 92*
**Oshiyoye**, Adekunle Emmanuel 1951- *WhoMW 92*
**Oshman**, M Kenneth *AmMWSc 92*
**Oshman**, Malin Kenneth 1940- *WhoFI 92*
**Osias**, Richard Allen 1938- *WhoFI 92*
**Osiatynski**, Jerzy 1941- *IntWW 91*
**Osibin**, Willard S. 1925- *WhoBlA 92*
**Osicki**, Kenneth John 1939- *WhoMW 92*
**Osiecka**, Agnieszka 1936- *IntAu&W 91*
**Osiecki**, Clarice A *WhoAmP 91*
**Osiek**, Carolyn Ann 1940- *WhoRel 92*
**Osifchin**, Nicholas 1924- *AmMWSc 92*
**Osifelo**, Frederick 1928- *Who 92*
**Osigweh**, Chimezie Anthony Baylon-Pascal 1955- *WhoFI 92*
**Osinchak**, Joseph 1937- *AmMWSc 92*
**Osing**, Gordon *DrAPF 91*
**Osinski**, Marek Andrzej 1948- *AmMWSc 92*
**Osinsky**, N. 1887-1938 *SovUnBD*
**Osipov**, Vladimir Nikolaevich 1938- *SovUnBD*
**Osipov**, Vladimir Vasilevich 1933- *IntWW 91*
**Osipow**, Lloyd Irving 1919- *AmMWSc 92*
**Osipow**, Samuel Herman 1934- *AmMWSc 92*
**Osipyan**, Yuri Andreyevich 1931- *IntWW 91*
**Osip'yan**, Yuriy Andreevich 1931- *SovUnBD*
**Osis**, Daiga Guntra 1943- *WhoAmL 92*
**Osisiogu**, William 1930- *IntWW 91*
**Osiyoye**, Adekunle 1951- *WhoMW 92*
**Oskarson**, Peter 1951- *IntWW 91*
**Oski**, Frank 1932- *AmMWSc 92*
**Oskvig**, Michael Wayne 1963- *WhoMW 92*
**Osler**, Dorothy K 1923- *WhoAmP 91*
**Osler**, Margaret J 1942- *AmMWSc 92*
**Osler**, Robert Donald 1924- *AmMWSc 92*
**Osler**, William 1849-1919 *BiInAmS*
**Oslin**, Kay Toinette *WhoEnt 92*
**Osman**, Abdillahi Said 1939- *IntWW 91*
**Osman**, Abdool Raman 1902- *IntWW 91, Who 92*
**Osman**, Ahmed 1930- *IntWW 91*
**Osman**, Amal Abd ar-Rahim *IntWW 91*
**Osman**, Betty B 1929- *ConAu 35NR*
**Osman**, Edith Gabriella 1949- *WhoAmL 92*
**Osman**, Elizabeth Mary 1915- *AmMWSc 92*
**Osman**, Herbert Eugene 1931- *WhoRel 92*
**Osman**, Jack D 1943- *ConAu 35NR*
**Osman**, Jack Douglas 1943- *AmMWSc 92*
**Osman**, Louis 1914- *Who 92*
**Osman**, M O M 1936- *AmMWSc 92*
**Osman**, Mohammad Kheir 1928- *Who 92*
**Osman**, Osman Ahmed 1917- *IntWW 91*
**Osman**, Raman *Who 92*
**Osman**, Richard William 1948- *AmMWSc 92*
**Osment**, Lamar Sutton 1924- *AmMWSc 92*
**Osmer**, Patrick Stewart 1943- *AmMWSc 92*
**Osmerkin**, Aleksandr Aleksandrovich 1892-1953 *SovUnBD*
**Osmers**, Herman Reinhard 1937- *AmMWSc 92*
**Osminin**, Stanislav Aleksandrovich 1934- *IntWW 91*
**Osmond**, Charles Barry 1939- *IntWW 91, Who 92*
**Osmond**, Daniel Harcourt 1934- *AmMWSc 92*
**Osmond**, Dennis Gordon 1930- *AmMWSc 92*
**Osmond**, Donald Clark 1957- *WhoEnt 92A*
**Osmond**, Donny 1957- *IntMPA 92*
**Osmond**, Douglas 1914- *Who 92*
**Osmond**, John C, Jr 1923- *AmMWSc 92*
**Osmond**, John Kenneth 1928- *AmMWSc 92*
**Osmond**, Lynn Joyce 1957- *WhoEnt 92*
**Osmond**, Marie 1959- *ConAu 134, IntMPA 92, WhoEnt 92*
**Osmond**, Mervyn Victor 1912- *Who 92*
**Osmond**, Michael William Massy 1918- *Who 92*
**Osmond**, Paul 1917- *Who 92*
**Osmond**, Russell Lowell 1945- *WhoFI 92*
**Osmonds**, The *LesBEnT 92*
**Osmotherly**, Edward Benjamin Crofton 1942- *Who 92*
**Osmun**, John Vincent 1918- *AmMWSc 92*
**Osmun**, Leighton *ScFEYrs*
**Osmycki**, Daniel A. 1931- *WhoMW 92*
**Osoba**, David 1932- *AmMWSc 92*
**Osoba**, Joseph Schiller 1919- *AmMWSc 92*
**Osofisan**, Femi 1946- *WrDr 92*
**Osofsky**, Barbara Langer 1937- *AmMWSc 92*
**Osofsky**, Howard J 1935- *AmMWSc 92*
**Osogo**, James Charles Nakhwanga 1932- *IntWW 91*
**Osol**, Arthur 1905- *AmMWSc 92*
**Osola**, John 1926- *Who 92*
**Osorio**, Irene Figueroa 1948- *WhoHisp 92*
**Osorio**, Mariano 1777-1819 *HisDSpE*
**Osorio Garcia**, Alfonso 1923- *IntWW 91*
**Osowiec**, Darlene Ann 1951- *WhoMW 92*
**Osowski**, Kenneth John 1958- *WhoMW 92*
**Ospina**, Sonia M. 1955- *WhoHisp 92*
**Osri**, Stanley M 1916- *AmMWSc 92*
**Ossakow**, Sidney Leonard 1938- *AmMWSc 92*
**Osserman**, Elliott Frederick 1925- *AmMWSc 92*
**Osserman**, Robert 1926- *AmMWSc 92*
**Ossesia**, Michel Germain 1929- *AmMWSc 92*
**Ossewaarde**, Anne Winkler 1957- *WhoFI 92, WhoWest 92*
**Ossietzky**, Carl von 1889-1938 *EncTR 91 [port], FacFETw, WhoNob 90*
**Ossler**, Charlene Claire 1949- *WhoMW 92*
**Ossoli**, Margaret *BenetAL 91*
**Ossovsky**, Petr Pavlovich 1925- *SovUnBD*
**Osswald**, Albert 1919- *IntWW 91*
**Ost**, Warren William 1926- *WhoRel 92*
**Ostaff**, William A 1914- *AmMWSc 92*
**Ostaffe**, Michael John 1964- *WhoMW 92*
**Ostapenko**, A 1923- *AmMWSc 92*
**Ostapuk**, David Ray 1948- *WhoAmL 92*
**Ostaszewski**, Alyce Vitella 1936- *WhoRel 92*
**Ostaszewski**, John Stephen 1959- *WhoFI 92*
**Ostaszewski**, Krzysztof Maciej 1957- *WhoFI 92*
**Ostazeski**, Stanley A 1926- *AmMWSc 92*
**Ostberg**, Ragnar 1866-1945 *DcTwDes*
**Ostby**, Elena Lizabeth 1959- *WhoAmL 92*
**Ostby**, Kevin Charles 1956- *WhoFI 92*
**Ostby**, Ronald 1937- *WhoFI 92*
**O'Steen**, Sam 1923- *IntMPA 92*
**O'Steen**, Van 1946- *WhoAmL 92*
**O'Steen**, Wendall Keith 1928- *AmMWSc 92*
**Osten**, Garlan Avon 1923- *WhoEnt 92*
**Osten Sacken**, Carl Robert R. Von Der 1828-1906 *BiInAmS*
**Ostendorf**, David William 1950- *AmMWSc 92*
**Ostendorf**, Frederick Otto 1913- *WhoWest 92*
**Ostendorf**, Lloyd 1921- *SmATA 65 [port]*
**Osteneco** 1705?-1777? *DcNCBi 4*
**Ostenso**, Brian Tang 1951- *WhoMW 92*
**Ostenso**, Grace Laudon 1932- *AmMWSc 92*
**Ostenso**, Martha 1900-1963 *BenetAL 91, TwCWW 91*
**Ostenso**, Ned Allen 1930- *AmMWSc 92, WhoAmP 91*
**Ostenson**, Jerome E *AmMWSc 92*
**Oster**, Bernard 1946- *WhoAmL 92*
**Oster**, Bernd 1926- *AmMWSc 92*
**Oster**, Clarence Alfred 1933- *AmMWSc 92*
**Oster**, Dean Howard 1929- *WhoMW 92*
**Oster**, Eugene Arthur 1929- *AmMWSc 92*
**Oster**, George F 1940- *AmMWSc 92*
**Oster**, Gerald 1918- *AmMWSc 92*
**Oster**, Hans 1888-1945 *EncTR 91 [port]*
**Oster**, James Donald 1937- *AmMWSc 92*
**Oster**, Jerry 1943- *ConAu 35NR, WhoEnt 92*
**Oster**, Leigh Ann Hussey 1961- *WhoWest 92*
**Oster**, Lewis Henry 1923- *WhoMW 92*
**Oster**, Ludwig Friedrich 1931- *AmMWSc 92*
**Oster**, Mark Otho 1937- *AmMWSc 92*
**Oster**, Martin William 1947- *AmMWSc 92*
**Oster**, Merrill James 1940- *WhoRel 92*
**Osterbauer**, Kevin Lee 1964- *WhoAmL 92*
**Osterbauer**, Ron Joseph 1952- *WhoMW 92*
**Osterberg**, Arnold Curtis 1921- *AmMWSc 92*
**Osterberg**, Charles Lamar 1920- *AmMWSc 92*
**Osterberg**, David 1943- *WhoAmP 91*
**Osterberg**, Donald Mouretz 1937- *AmMWSc 92*
**Osterberg**, Edward Charles, Jr. 1942- *WhoAmL 92*
**Osterberg**, J O 1915- *AmMWSc 92*
**Osterberg**, Max 1869-1904 *BiInAmS*
**Osterberg**, Robert Edward 1942- *AmMWSc 92*
**Osterberg**, Thomas Karl 1953- *WhoMW 92*
**Osterberger**, Kenneth E 1930- *WhoAmP 91*
**Osterbrock**, Carl H 1931- *AmMWSc 92*
**Osterbrock**, Donald E 1924- *AmMWSc 92, IntWW 91, WrDr 92*
**Osterburg**, James 1944- *AmMWSc 92*
**Ostercamp**, Daryl Lee 1932- *AmMWSc 92*
**Ostergaard**, Knud 1922- *IntWW 91*
**Ostergaard**, Kurt Filer 1963- *WhoMW 92*
**Ostergren**, Gregory V 1955- *WhoIns 92*
**Osterhaus**, William Eric 1935- *WhoEnt 92*
**Osterheld**, Robert Keith 1925- *AmMWSc 92*
**Osterhoff**, James Marvin 1936- *WhoFI 92*
**Osterholm**, Ronald Joseph 1958- *WhoMW 92*
**Osterholtz**, Frederick David 1938- *AmMWSc 92*
**Osterhoudt**, Hans Walter 1936- *AmMWSc 92*
**Osterhoudt**, Robert G 1942- *ConAu 35NR*
**Osterhoudt**, Walter Jabez 1906- *AmMWSc 92*
**Osterhout**, Michael Dennis 1948- *WhoEnt 92*
**Osterhout**, Raymond L 1931- *WhoIns 92*
**Osterhout**, Richard Cadwallader 1945- *WhoAmL 92*
**Osterhout**, Suydam 1925- *AmMWSc 92*
**Osterkamp**, Thomas Eugene *AmMWSc 92*
**Osterle**, J F 1925- *AmMWSc 92*
**Osterloh**, Henry Joe 1935- *WhoAmP 91*
**Osterman**, Frederic J. 1952- *WhoMW 92*
**Osterman**, Kathy *WhoAmP 91*
**Osterman**, Lawrence Jay 1956- *WhoEnt 92*
**Osterman**, Susan *DrAPF 91*
**Osterman-Olson**, Karen 1951- *WhoFI 92*
**Ostermann**, Russell Dean 1952- *AmMWSc 92*
**Ostermayer**, Frederick William, Jr 1937- *AmMWSc 92*
**Ostermeyer**, Cliff Ayers 1923- *WhoEnt 92*
**Ostermiller**, John Victor 1910- *WhoWest 92*
**Ostertag**, Robert Louis 1931- *WhoAmL 92*
**Osterud**, Harold T 1923- *AmMWSc 92*
**Osterwald**, Bibi 1920- *WhoEnt 92*
**Osterwald**, Frank William 1922- *AmMWSc 92*
**Osteryoung**, Janet G 1939- *AmMWSc 92*
**Osteryoung**, Jerome S. 1942- *WhoFI 92*
**Osteryoung**, Robert Allen 1927- *AmMWSc 92*
**Ostfeld**, Adrian Michael 1926- *AmMWSc 92*
**Ostfeld**, Franz Joseph Wilhelm 1915- *WhoWest 92*
**Osthoff**, Tom 1936- *WhoAmP 91*
**Osthus**, Mark Adrian 1945- *WhoRel 92*
**Ostle**, Bernard 1921- *AmMWSc 92*
**Ostler**, David Sorenson 1931- *WhoAmP 91*
**Ostlere**, Gordon *Who 92*
**Ostlind**, Dan A 1936- *AmMWSc 92*
**Ostling**, Paul James 1948- *WhoFI 92*
**Ostling**, Ralph A 1927- *WhoAmP 91*
**Ostling**, Richard N 1940- *ConAu 35NR*
**Ostling**, Richard Neil 1940- *WhoRel 92*
**Ostlund**, H Gote 1923- *AmMWSc 92*
**Ostlund**, John C 1927- *WhoAmP 91*
**Ostlund**, Neil Sinclair 1942- *AmMWSc 92*
**Ostmann**, Bernard George 1927- *AmMWSc 92*
**Ostmann**, James Buckley 1944- *WhoEnt 92*
**Ostmo**, David Charles 1959- *WhoEnt 92*
**Ostoja-Starzewski**, Martin 1954- *WhoMW 92*
**Ostow**, Mortimer 1918- *ConAu 35NR*

**Ostrach,** Simon 1923- *AmMWSc 92*
**Ostrand-Rosenberg,** Suzanne T 1948- *AmMWSc 92*
**Ostrander,** Charles Evans 1916- *AmMWSc 92*
**Ostrander,** Darl Reed 1935- *AmMWSc 92*
**Ostrander,** Lee E 1939- *AmMWSc 92*
**Ostrander,** Patricia *NewYTBS 91*
**Ostrander,** Peter Erling 1943- *AmMWSc 92*
**Ostrander,** Peter Harris 1950- *WhoWest 92*
**Ostrander,** Richard James, Jr. 1954- *WhoFI 92*
**Ostrau,** Norman 1938- *WhoAmP 91*
**Ostrem,** Donald Lee 1940- *WhoAmL 92*
**Ostrem,** Walter Martin 1930- *WhoMW 92*
**Ostriker,** Alicia *DrAPF 91*
**Ostriker,** Alicia 1937- *IntAu&W 91*
**Ostriker,** Jeremiah 1937- *IntWW 91*
**Ostriker,** Jeremiah P 1937- *AmMWSc 92*
**Ostroff,** Anton G 1925- *AmMWSc 92*
**Ostrofsky,** Benjamin 1925- *AmMWSc 92*
**Ostrofsky,** Bernard 1922- *AmMWSc 92*
**Ostrofsky,** Milton Lewis 1947- *AmMWSc 92*
**Ostrogorsky,** Michael 1951- *WhoWest 92*
**Ostrom,** Carl Eric 1912- *AmMWSc 92*
**Ostrom,** Donald Irving 1939- *WhoAmP 91*
**Ostrom,** Douglas Roy 1946- *WhoFI 92*
**Ostrom,** Hans *DrAPF 91*
**Ostrom,** John Harold 1928- *AmMWSc 92*
**Ostrom,** Meredith Eggers 1930- *AmMWSc 92*
**Ostrom,** Theodore Gleason 1916- *AmMWSc 92*
**Ostrom,** Thomas Ross 1924- *AmMWSc 92*
**Ostrov,** Eric 1941- *ConAu 34NR*
**Ostrovsky,** David Saul 1943- *AmMWSc 92*
**Ostrovsky,** Nikolay Alekseevich 1904-1936 *SovUnBD*
**Ostrovsky,** Rafail M *AmMWSc 92*
**Ostrow,** Bonnie Susan 1940- *WhoAmP 91*
**Ostrow,** David Henry 1953- *AmMWSc 92*
**Ostrow,** Jay Donald 1930- *AmMWSc 92*
**Ostrow,** Joseph W. 1933- *WhoFI 92*
**Ostrow,** Leib Sanford 1951- *WhoEnt 92*
**Ostrow,** Martin Ira 1947- *WhoEnt 92*
**Ostrow,** Michael Jay 1934- *WhoAmL 92*
**Ostrow,** Samuel David 1945- *WhoFI 92*
**Ostrow,** Stuart 1932- *WhoEnt 92*
**Ostrower,** Fayga 1920- *IntWW 91*
**Ostrowski,** Edward Joseph 1923- *AmMWSc 92*
**Ostrowski,** Joan Lorraine *Who 92*
**Ostrowski,** John Martin 1953- *WhoAmL 92*
**Ostrowski,** Ronald Stephen 1939- *AmMWSc 92*
**Ostrowski,** Wlodzimierz Stanislaw 1925- *IntWW 91*
**Ostroy,** Joan Patsy 1942- *WhoAmL 92*
**Ostroy,** Sanford Eugene 1939- *AmMWSc 92, WhoMW 92*
**Ostrum,** Dean Gardner 1922- *WhoEnt 92*
**Ostrum,** G Kenneth 1938- *AmMWSc 92*
**Ostry,** Sylvia 1927- *IntWW 91*
**Ostwald,** David Franklin 1943- *WhoEnt 92*
**Ostwald,** Friedrich Wilhelm 1853-1932 *WhoNob 90*
**Ostwald,** Martin 1922- *ConAu 35NR*
**Ostwald,** Peter Frederic 1928- *AmMWSc 92*
**Ostwald,** Phillip F 1931- *AmMWSc 92*
**Ostwald,** Venice Eloise Varner 1928- *WhoWest 92*
**Ostwald,** Wilhelm 1853-1932 *DcTwDes*
**Osuch,** Carl 1925- *AmMWSc 92*
**Osuch,** Christopher Erion 1951- *AmMWSc 92*
**Osuch,** Mary Ann V 1941- *AmMWSc 92*
**O'Sullevan,** Peter *IntAu&W 91*
**O'Sullevan,** Peter John 1918- *Who 92*
**O'Sullivan,** Brendan Patrick 1930- *WhoAmL 92*
**O'Sullivan,** Carrol Austin John 1915- *Who 92*
**O'Sullivan,** Gerald Joseph 1941- *WhoMW 92*
**O'Sullivan,** Gerry 1959- *ConAu 135*
**O'Sullivan,** James 1917- *Who 92*
**O'Sullivan,** John *Who 92*
**O'Sullivan,** John 1942- *AmMWSc 92, IntWW 91*
**O'Sullivan,** John Joseph 1949- *WhoMW 92*
**O'Sullivan,** John Patrick, Jr. 1942- *WhoFI 92*
**OSullivan,** Joseph 1945- *AmMWSc 92*
**O'Sullivan,** Kevin *WhoAmP 91*
**O'Sullivan,** Kevin P. 1928- *IntMPA 92*
**O'Sullivan,** Mary F. *DrAPF 91*
**O'Sullivan,** Mary Kenney 1864-1943 *HanAmWH*
**O'Sullivan,** Maureen 1911- *IntMPA 92, WhoEnt 92*
**O'Sullivan,** Neal 1959- *WhoFI 92*
**O'Sullivan,** Roger Francis 1946- *WhoAmP 91*
**O'Sullivan,** Sally Angela 1949- *Who 92*
**O'Sullivan,** Timothy 1945- *WrDr 92*
**O'Sullivan,** Timothy Patrick *WhoAmP 91*
**O'Sullivan,** Vincent 1937- *ConAu 35NR, ConPo 91, WrDr 92*
**O'Sullivan,** William John 1931- *AmMWSc 92*
**Osumi,** Kenichiro 1904- *IntWW 91*
**Osumi,** Masato 1942- *WhoFI 92*
**Osvath,** Ludovic Lajos 1938- *WhoRel 92*
**Oswald,** Delmont Richard 1940- *WhoWest 92*
**Oswald,** Edward Odell 1940- *AmMWSc 92*
**Oswald,** Ernest John *DrAPF 91*
**Oswald,** Felix Leopold 1845-1906 *BiInAmS*
**Oswald,** Gerd 1919- *WhoEnt 92*
**Oswald,** Gregory William 1945- *WhoEnt 92*
**Oswald,** Harold Nicholas, Jr. 1961- *WhoRel 92*
**Oswald,** James Marlin 1935- *WhoFI 92*
**Oswald,** John Julian Robertson 1933- *IntWW 91*
**Oswald,** John Wieland 1917- *AmMWSc 92*
**Oswald,** Julian 1933- *Who 92*
**Oswald,** Lee Harvey 1939-1964 *FacFETw [port]*
**Oswald,** Lori Jo *DrAPF 91*
**Oswald,** Louis Alfred, III 1963- *WhoWest 92*
**Oswald,** Marshall St John 1911- *Who 92*
**Oswald,** Michael Anthony 1949- *WhoAmL 92*
**Oswald,** Neville Christopher 1910- *Who 92*
**Oswald,** Richard 1959- *WhoEnt 92*
**Oswald,** Richard Anthony 1941- *Who 92*
**Oswald,** Robert B, Jr 1932- *AmMWSc 92*
**Oswald,** Rudolph A. 1932- *WhoFI 92*
**Oswald,** Russell G. 1908-1991 *NewYTBS 91 [port]*
**Oswald,** Terry 1959- *WhoMW 92*
**Oswald,** Therese Anne 1960- *WhoWest 92*
**Oswald,** Thomas d1990 *Who 92N*
**Oswald,** William J 1919- *AmMWSc 92*
**Oswald,** William Jack 1927- *WhoFI 92*
**Oswald,** William Richard Michael 1934- *Who 92*
**Oswalt,** Jesse Harrell 1923- *AmMWSc 92*
**Oswalt,** John Newell 1940- *WhoRel 92*
**Oswalt,** Wendell H 1927- *ConAu 35NR*
**Osweiler,** Gary D 1942- *AmMWSc 92*
**Ota,** Asher Kenhachiro 1934- *AmMWSc 92*
**Ota,** Henry Yasushi 1942- *WhoAmL 92*
**Ota,** Shuji John 1950- *WhoWest 92*
**Otaka,** Tadaaki 1947- *IntWW 91, WhoEnt 92*
**Otani,** Mike 1945- *WhoFI 92*
**Otani,** Sachio 1924- *IntWW 91*
**Otani,** Theodore Toshiro 1925- *AmMWSc 92*
**Otchakovsky-Laurens,** Paul 1944- *IntWW 91*
**Otchy,** Thomas Gerald 1943- *WhoFI 92*
**Oteiba,** Mana Saeed al- 1946- *IntWW 91*
**Otenasek,** Mildred 1914- *WhoAmP 91*
**Otero,** Agustin F. 1932- *WhoHisp 92*
**Otero,** Alejandro d1990 *IntWW 91N*
**Otero,** Antonio Jacinto 1938- *WhoHisp 92*
**Otero,** Carmen 1933- *WhoAmL 92, WhoHisp 92*
**Otero,** Ingrid 1959- *WhoHisp 92*
**Otero,** Jack 1934- *WhoAmP 91*
**Otero,** Joaquin Francisco 1934- *WhoHisp 92*
**Otero,** Jose Alejandro 1926- *WhoHisp 92*
**Otero,** Jose U. 1930- *WhoHisp 92*
**Otero,** Joseph A. 1926- *WhoHisp 92*
**Otero,** Manuel Ramos *DrAPF 91*
**Otero,** Maria del Pilar 1941- *WhoFI 92*
**Otero,** Phillip William 1955- *WhoWest 92*
**Otero,** Raymond B 1938- *AmMWSc 92*
**Otero,** Richard J. 1939- *WhoHisp 92*
**Otero,** Rolando 1957- *WhoHisp 92*
**Otero Rosario,** Ismael *WhoHisp 92*
**Otero Rosario,** Israel *WhoAmP 91*
**Otero-Smart,** Ingrid 1959- *WhoHisp 92*
**Otey,** Felix Harold 1927- *AmMWSc 92*
**Otey,** Flem B., III 1935- *WhoBlA 92*
**Otey,** James Hervey 1800-1863 *DcNCBi 4*
**Otey,** Orlando 1925- *WhoEnt 92*
**Othersen,** Cheryl Lee 1948- *WhoFI 92*
**Othersen,** Henry Biemann, Jr 1930- *AmMWSc 92*
**Othman Bin Wok** 1924- *IntWW 91*
**Othman,** Abdul Manan bin 1935- *IntWW 91*
**Othman,** Talat Mohamad 1936- *WhoMW 92*
**Othmer,** David Artman 1941- *WhoEnt 92*
**Othmer,** Donald F 1904- *AmMWSc 92*
**Othmer,** Donald Frederick 1904- *IntWW 91, WhoFI 92*
**Othmer,** Ekkehard 1933- *AmMWSc 92*
**Othmer,** Hans George 1943- *AmMWSc 92*
**Othmer,** Murray E 1907- *AmMWSc 92*
**Othon,** Art *WhoHisp 92*
**Otieno-Ayim,** Larban Allan 1940- *WhoBlA 92*
**Otis,** Amos Joseph 1947- *WhoBlA 92*
**Otis,** Arthur Brooks 1913- *AmMWSc 92*
**Otis,** Harrison Gray 1765-1848 *BenetAL 91*
**Otis,** James 1725- *BlkwEAR*
**Otis,** James 1725-1783 *AmPolLe, BenetAL 91*
**Otis,** James 1848-1912 *ScFEYrs*
**Otis,** Jerry Eugene 1941- *WhoAmL 92*
**Otis,** John James 1922- *WhoFI 92*
**Otis,** Lance Neville 1939- *WhoWest 92*
**Otis,** Leon Spelly 1924- *WhoWest 92*
**Otis,** Marshall Voigt 1919- *AmMWSc 92*
**Otis,** Michael John 1949- *WhoAmP 91*
**Otis,** Todd H 1945- *WhoAmP 91*
**Otken,** Charles Clay 1927- *AmMWSc 92*
**Otlowski,** George J 1912- *WhoAmP 91*
**Otman Assed,** Mohamed 1922- *IntWW 91*
**Otocka,** Edward Paul 1940- *AmMWSc 92*
**Otomo,** Stacy Akio 1955- *WhoWest 92*
**O'Toole,** Annette 1953- *IntMPA 92*
**O'Toole,** Austin Martin 1935- *WhoAmL 92, WhoFI 92*
**O'Toole,** Brian Joseph 1955- *WhoAmP 91*
**O'Toole,** David John 1944- *WhoMW 92*
**O'Toole,** Eugene Joseph 1952- *WhoRel 92*
**O'Toole,** Francis J. 1944- *WhoAmL 92*
**O'Toole,** James 1945- *IntAu&W 91*
**O'Toole,** James J 1943- *AmMWSc 92*
**O'Toole,** John E. 1929- *WhoFI 92*
**O'Toole,** Kathleen Mary 1958- *WhoEnt 92*
**O'Toole,** Patrick Francis 1948- *WhoAmP 91*
**O'Toole,** Peter 1932- *IntMPA 92, Who 92, WhoEnt 92*
**O'Toole,** Peter Seamus 1932- *IntWW 91*
**O'Toole,** Robert Francis 1936- *WhoRel 92*
**O'Toole,** Robert Joseph 1941- *WhoFI 92, WhoMW 92*
**O'Toole,** Stanley *IntMPA 92*
**O'Toole,** Thomas Elmer 1941- *WhoMW 92*
**O'Toole,** Timothy T. 1955- *WhoAmL 92*
**O'Toole,** William George 1934- *WhoAmL 92*
**Otoshi,** Tom Yasuo 1931- *WhoWest 92*
**Otrhalek,** Joseph V 1922- *AmMWSc 92, WhoMW 92*
**Otrusina,** Edward C. 1956- *WhoMW 92*
**Otsason,** Rein Augustovich 1931- *IntWW 91*
**Otsep,** Fedor Aleksandrovich 1895-1949 *SovUnBD*
**Otsuka,** Yuji 1929- *IntWW 91*
**Ott,** Alexander Reginald 1931- *WhoAmP 91*
**Ott,** Alvin Robert 1949- *WhoAmP 91*
**Ott,** Attiat Farag 1935- *WhoFI 92*
**Ott,** Billy Joe 1923- *AmMWSc 92*
**Ott,** Bob E *WhoAmP 91*
**Ott,** Cobern Erwin 1941- *AmMWSc 92*
**Ott,** David James 1946- *AmMWSc 92*
**Ott,** David Lee 1947- *WhoEnt 92*
**Ott,** David N 1937- *WhoAmP 91*
**Ott,** Donald George 1926- *AmMWSc 92*
**Ott,** Edgar Alton 1938- *AmMWSc 92*
**Ott,** Edward 1941- *AmMWSc 92*
**Ott,** Gil *DrAPF 91*
**Ott,** Gilbert Russell, Jr. 1943- *WhoFI 92*
**Ott,** Granville E 1935- *AmMWSc 92*
**Ott,** Harry 1933- *IntWW 91*
**Ott,** Henry C 1910- *AmMWSc 92*
**Ott,** Isaac 1847-1916 *BiInAmS*
**Ott,** J Bevan 1934- *AmMWSc 92*
**Ott,** Karen Jacobs 1939- *AmMWSc 92*
**Ott,** Karl O 1925- *AmMWSc 92*
**Ott,** Kent A 1955- *WhoAmP 91*
**Ott,** Mack 1943- *WhoFI 92*
**Ott,** Mel 1909-1958 *FacFETw*
**Ott,** R. Lyman 1940- *WhoMW 92*
**Ott,** R Lyman, Jr 1940- *AmMWSc 92*
**Ott,** Richard Albert 1932- *WhoMW 92*
**Ott,** Richard L *AmMWSc 92*
**Ott,** Roger Arthur, Sr. 1930- *WhoMW 92*
**Ott,** Sharon *WhoEnt 92*
**Ott,** Stanley Joseph 1927- *WhoRel 92*
**Ott,** Teunis Jan 1943- *AmMWSc 92*
**Ott,** Walter Richard 1943- *AmMWSc 92*
**Ott,** Wayne R 1940- *AmMWSc 92*
**Ott,** William Roger 1942- *AmMWSc 92*
**Ottawa,** Archbishop of 1915- *Who 92*
**Ottawa,** Bishop of *Who 92*
**Ottaway,** James Haller, Jr. 1938- *WhoFI 92*
**Ottaway,** Lois Marie 1931- *WhoRel 92*
**Ottaway,** Richard Geoffrey James 1945- *Who 92*
**Otte,** A Ray 1929- *WhoIns 92*
**Otte,** Carel 1922- *AmMWSc 92*
**Otte,** Carl 1923- *WhoAmP 91*
**Otte,** Daniel 1939- *AmMWSc 92*
**Otte,** Paul Joseph 1923- *WhoAmP 91*
**Otte,** Ray M, Jr 1946- *WhoAmP 91*
**Otte,** Ruth *LesBEnT 92*
**Otte,** Stephen B 1943- *WhoIns 92*
**Otten,** Arthur Edward, Jr. 1930- *WhoAmL 92*
**Otten,** Charlotte M 1915- *ConAu 35NR*
**Otten,** Leonard John, III 1944- *WhoWest 92*
**Otten,** Terry 1938- *ConAu 35NR*
**Otten,** Terry Ralph 1938- *WhoMW 92*
**Ottenbacher,** Kenneth John 1950- *AmMWSc 92*
**Ottenberg,** Simon 1923- *ConAu 35NR, WhoWest 92, WrDr 92*
**Ottenbrite,** Raphael Martin 1936- *AmMWSc 92*
**Ottenhoff,** Robert George 1948- *WhoEnt 92*
**Ottensmeyer,** Frank Peter 1939- *AmMWSc 92*
**Ottenstein,** Daniel 1930- *AmMWSc 92*
**Ottenweller,** Albert Henry 1916- *WhoMW 92, WhoRel 92*
**Otter,** Clement Leroy 1942- *WhoAmP 91, WhoWest 92*
**Otter,** Fred August 1928- *AmMWSc 92*
**Otter,** Richard Robert 1920- *AmMWSc 92*
**Otter,** Timothy 1953- *AmMWSc 92*
**Otter,** Victor Charles 1914- *Who 92*
**Otterbein,** Keith Frederick 1936- *ConAu 35NR*
**Otterby,** Donald Eugene 1932- *AmMWSc 92*
**Otterman,** Robert James 1932- *WhoAmP 91*
**Otterness,** Ivan George 1938- *AmMWSc 92*
**Ottersen,** Roger W. *WhoRel 92*
**Ottervik,** Kristine Joan 1951- *WhoFI 92*
**Ottesen,** Eric Albert 1943- *AmMWSc 92*
**Ottesen,** Realff Henry 1941- *WhoMW 92*
**Otteson,** Otto Harry 1931- *AmMWSc 92*
**Ottewill,** Ronald Harry 1927- *IntWW 91, Who 92*
**Ottey-Page,** Merlene 1960- *BlkOlyM*
**Otting,** William Joseph 1919- *AmMWSc 92*
**Ottinger,** Carol Blanche 1933- *AmMWSc 92*
**Ottinger,** Edward E 1934- *WhoAmP 91*
**Ottinger,** Nolen Ray, III 1961- *WhoEnt 92*
**Ottinger,** Richard Estes 1932- *WhoEnt 92*
**Ottinger,** Richard Lawrence 1929- *WhoAmP 91*
**Ottinger,** Ulrike 1942- *IntDcF 2-2*
**Ottino,** Julio Mario 1951- *AmMWSc 92, WhoMW 92*
**Ottke,** Robert Crittenden 1922- *AmMWSc 92*
**Ottley,** Agnes May d1990 *Who 92N*
**Ottley,** Athniel C 1941- *WhoAmP 91*
**Ottley,** Austin H. 1918- *WhoBlA 92*
**Ottley,** James H. *WhoRel 92*
**Ottley,** Jerold Don 1934- *WhoEnt 92, WhoWest 92*
**Ottley,** Neville 1926- *WhoBlA 92*
**Ottley,** Reginald Leslie 1909-1985 *ConAu 34NR*
**Ottley,** Roi 1906-1960 *BenetAL 91*
**Ottlik,** Geza d1990 *IntWW 91N*
**Ottman,** John Budlong 1922- *WhoFI 92*
**Ottman,** Ruth 1952- *AmMWSc 92*
**Otto,** A. Stuart, Jr. 1915- *WhoRel 92, WhoWest 92*
**Otto,** Albert Dean 1939- *AmMWSc 92*
**Otto,** Berthold 1859-1933 *EncTR 91*
**Otto,** Charlotte A 1946- *AmMWSc 92*
**Otto,** David A 1948- *AmMWSc 92*
**Otto,** David Arthur 1934- *AmMWSc 92*
**Otto,** Edgar John 1926- *WhoRel 92*
**Otto,** Fred Bishop 1934- *AmMWSc 92*
**Otto,** Fred Douglas 1935- *AmMWSc 92*
**Otto,** Frederick Joseph 1948- *WhoMW 92*
**Otto,** Frei 1925- *DcTwDes*
**Otto,** Frei P. 1925- *IntWW 91*
**Otto,** Gilbert Fred 1901- *AmMWSc 92*
**Otto,** Glenn E 1924- *WhoAmP 91*
**Otto,** Hans 1900-1933 *EncTR 91*
**Otto,** Harley John 1928- *AmMWSc 92*
**Otto,** Ingolf Helgi Elfried 1920- *WhoFI 92*
**Otto,** James V. 1923- *WhoFI 92*
**Otto,** Jeffery Lee 1955- *WhoWest 92*
**Otto,** John B, Jr 1918- *AmMWSc 92*
**Otto,** John Francis 1919- *WhoFI 92*
**Otto,** John Henry 1946- *WhoAmL 92*
**Otto,** Klaus 1929- *AmMWSc 92, WhoMW 92*
**Otto,** Lawrence James 1941- *WhoIns 92*
**Otto,** Lon *DrAPF 91*
**Otto,** Luther B. 1937- *ConAu 133*
**Otto,** Mary Castrop 1920- *WhoAmP 91*
**Otto,** Myron Lynn 1942- *WhoFI 92*
**Otto,** Richard E 1928- *WhoIns 92*
**Otto,** Robert Emil 1932- *AmMWSc 92*
**Otto,** Robert Simpson 1946- *WhoWest 92*
**Otto,** Roberta 1943- *WhoEnt 92*
**Otto,** Roland John 1946- *AmMWSc 92*
**Otto,** Svend *SmATA 67*
**Otto,** Vivian Wickey 1925- *WhoRel 92*
**Otto,** William Harvey 1936- *WhoRel 92*

**Otto**, Wolfgang Karl Ferdinand 1927- AmMWSc 92
**Otto-Rieke**, Gerd 1950- IntAu&W 91
**Ottoboni**, M Alice AmMWSc 92
**Ottolenghi**, Abramo Cesare 1931- AmMWSc 92
**Ottolenghi**, Athos 1923- AmMWSc 92
**Ottolengui**, Rodrigues 1861?-1937 ScFEYrs
**Otton**, Geoffrey 1927- Who 92
**Otton**, Philip 1933- Who 92
**Ottone**, Piero 1924- IntAu&W 91, IntWW 91
**Ottoson**, Harold 1930- AmMWSc 92
**Ottoson**, Joseph William 1929- WhoMW 92, WhoRel 92
**Ottoson**, R. Stanley WhoRel 92
**Otts**, James K 1930- WhoAmP 91
**Otts**, James Mitchell 1968- WhoRel 92
**Ottsen**, Lamar Edward, Jr. 1939- WhoAmL 92
**Ottumwa**, Salvador 1945- WhoHisp 92
**Otudeko**, Adebisi Olusoga 1935- WhoBlA 92
**Otumfuo Nana Opoku Ware II** 1919- IntWW 91
**Otunga**, Maurice Who 92
**Otunga**, Maurice 1923- IntWW 91, WhoRel 92
**Otvos**, Ervin George 1935- AmMWSc 92
**Otvos**, John William 1917- AmMWSc 92
**Otway**, Harry John 1935- AmMWSc 92
**Otway**, Thomas 1652-1685 RfGEnL 91
**Otwell**, Ronnie Ray 1929- IntMPA 92
**Otwell**, Walter Steven 1948- AmMWSc 92
**Ou**, Jing-hsiung James 1954- WhoWest 92
**Ou**, Jonathan Tsien-hsiong 1934- AmMWSc 92
**Ou**, Lo-Chang 1932- AmMWSc 92
**Ou**, Susan Ker-hwa WhoWest 92
**Ouano**, Augustus Ceniza 1936- AmMWSc 92
**Ouattara**, Alassane D. 1942- IntWW 91
**Oubradous**, Fernand 1903-1986 NewAmDM
**Oubre**, Hayward Louis WhoBlA 92
**Oubre**, Linda Seiffert 1958- WhoBlA 92, WhoWest 92
**Ouchi**, Tsutomu 1918- IntWW 91
**Oud**, Jacobus Johannes Pieter 1890-1963 DcTwDes
**Ouderkirk**, John Thomas 1931- AmMWSc 92
**Ouderkirk**, Mason James 1953- WhoAmL 92
**Oudovenko**, Guennadi I. 1931- IntWW 91
**Oueddei**, Goukouni 1944- IntWW 91
**Ouedraogo**, Gerard Kango 1925- IntWW 91
**Ouellet**, Andre 1939- IntWW 91
**Ouellet**, Gilles 1922- WhoRel 92
**Ouellet**, Henri 1938- AmMWSc 92
**Ouellet**, Ludovic 1923- AmMWSc 92
**Ouellet**, Marcel 1940- AmMWSc 92
**Ouellette**, Andre J 1946- AmMWSc 92
**Ouellette**, Gloria Marianne 1925- WhoRel 92
**Ouellette**, Janeyce Dawn 1955- WhoWest 92
**Ouellette**, Robert J 1938- AmMWSc 92
**Ouellette**, Robert O 1949- WhoAmP 91
**Ouellette**, Sue Ellen 1947- WhoMW 92
**Oughstun**, Kurt Edmund 1949- AmMWSc 92
**Oughton**, James Henry, Jr. 1913- WhoMW 92
**Ouida** 1839-1908 RfGEnL 91, TwCLC 43 [port]
**Ouimet**, Alfred J, Jr 1931- AmMWSc 92
**Ouimet**, Cecily Ramos WhoHisp 92
**Oujesky**, Helen Matusevich 1930- AmMWSc 92
**Ouko**, Robert 1948- BlkOlyM
**Oulahan**, Richard 1918-1985 ConAu 36NR
**Ould Hamody**, Mohamed-Said 1942- IntWW 91
**Ouless**, Walter William 1848-1933 TwCPaSc
**Oulman**, Charles S 1933- AmMWSc 92
**Oulton**, Derek 1927- Who 92
**Oulton**, Therese 1953- TwCPaSc
**Oulton**, Wilfrid Ewart 1911- Who 92
**Oulvey**, Joseph Michael 1965- WhoMW 92
**Oumarou**, Ide 1937- IntWW 91
**Oumarou**, Mamane IntWW 91
**Oumlil**, Abderrahman Ben 1957- WhoMW 92
**Ounjian**, Marilyn J. 1947- WhoFI 92
**Ounsted**, John 1919- Who 92
**Ourada**, Thomas D 1958- WhoAmP 91
**Ourisson**, Guy 1926- IntWW 91
**Oursler**, Clellie Curtis 1915- AmMWSc 92
**Oursler**, Fulton 1893-1952 BenetAL 91
**Oursler**, Will 1913-1985 ConAu 35NR
**Ourth**, Donald Dean 1939- AmMWSc 92
**Ousby**, Ian 1947- ConAu 35NR
**Ouseley**, William Norman 1935- WhoMW 92
**Ouseph**, Pullom John 1933- AmMWSc 92
**Ousler**, Charles Fulton, Sr. 1893-1952 RelLAm 91
**Ousley**, Harold Lomax 1929- WhoBlA 92
**Ousmane**, Sembene 1923- BlkLC [port], ConLC 66 [port], IntAu&W 91, IntWW 91, LiExTwC
**Oussani**, James John 1920- WhoFI 92
**Ousterhout**, Anne McCabe WhoMW 92
**Outcalt**, David L 1935- AmMWSc 92
**Outcalt**, David Lewis 1935- WhoMW 92
**Outcalt**, Samuel Irvine 1936- AmMWSc 92
**Outcault**, R. F. 1863-1928 BenetAL 91
**Outerbridge**, John Stuart 1936- AmMWSc 92
**Outerbridge**, Paul, Jr. 1891-1959 DcTwDes, FacFETw
**Outerbridge**, William Fulwood 1930- AmMWSc 92
**Outerino**, Felix C. Who 92
**Outhouse**, Edward Burton 1924- WhoWest 92
**Outhouse**, James Burton 1916- AmMWSc 92, WhoMW 92
**Outhwaite**, William 1949- WrDr 92
**Outka**, Darryll E 1929- AmMWSc 92
**Outka**, Gene Harold 1937- WhoRel 92
**Outlaw**, Arthur R 1926- WhoAmP 91
**Outlaw**, Arthur Robert 1926- WhoFI 92
**Outlaw**, David 1806-1868 DcNCBi 4
**Outlaw**, Dev 1960- WhoFI 92
**Outlaw**, George 1771-1825 DcNCBi 4
**Outlaw**, Henry Earl 1937- AmMWSc 92
**Outlaw**, Lucius T., Jr. 1944- WhoBlA 92
**Outlaw**, Patricia Anne WhoBlA 92
**Outlaw**, Ronald Allen 1937- AmMWSc 92
**Outlaw**, Warren Gregory 1951- WhoBlA 92
**Outler**, Albert Cook 1908-1989 RelLAm 91
**Outon**, Francisco Jose Arenaza WhoEnt 92
**Outram**, Alan James 1937- Who 92
**Outram**, Dorinda 1949- IntWW 91
**Outt**, Thomas 1953- WhoEnt 92
**Outten**, Elmer Stuart, Jr 1944- WhoAmP 91
**Outterbridge**, John Wilfred 1933- WhoBlA 92
**Outwater**, John O 1923- AmMWSc 92
**Outzen**, Henry Clair, Jr 1939- AmMWSc 92
**Ouvrieu**, Jean-Bernard 1939- IntWW 91
**Ouwehand**, William 1932- WhoWest 92
**Ouwinga**, Sidney WhoAmP 91
**Ouyang Shan** 1908- IntWW 91
**Ouzounian**, Armenuhi 1942- WhoMW 92
**Ouzts**, Dale Keith 1941- WhoEnt 92, WhoMW 92
**Ouzts**, Johnny Drew 1934- AmMWSc 92
**Ova**, Wayne Keith 1953- WhoRel 92
**Ovadia**, Jacques 1923- AmMWSc 92
**Ovalle**, Alonso de 1601-1651 HisDSpE
**Ovalle**, William Keith, Jr 1944- AmMWSc 92
**Ovando**, Nicolas de 1451?- HisDSpE
**Ovando Candia**, Alfredo 1918-1982 FacFETw
**Ovard**, A R 1921- WhoAmP 91
**Ovard**, Glen F. 1928- WrDr 92
**Ovary**, Zoltan 1907- AmMWSc 92
**Ovchinikov**, Vladimir 1958- IntWW 91
**Ovchinnikov**, Lev Nikolayevich 1913- IntWW 91
**Ovchinnikov**, Yurii Anatolevich 1934- IntWW 91
**Ovchinnikov**, Yuriy Anatol'evich 1934-1988 SovUnBD
**Ove**, Peter 1930- AmMWSc 92
**Ovechkin**, Valentin Vladimirovich 1904-1968 SovUnBD
**Ovenall**, Derick William 1930- AmMWSc 92
**Ovenden**, Graham 1943- TwCPaSc
**Ovenden**, Graham Stuart 1943- IntWW 91
**Ovenden**, John Frederick 1942- Who 92
**Ovenfors**, Carl-Olof Nils Sten 1923- AmMWSc 92
**Ovens**, Patrick John 1922- Who 92
**Ovens**, William George 1939- AmMWSc 92
**Ovenshine**, A Thomas 1936- AmMWSc 92
**Overall**, James Carney, Jr 1937- AmMWSc 92
**Overall**, John 1913- Who 92
**Overall**, Manard 1939- WhoBlA 92
**Overall**, Park WhoEnt 92
**Overbea**, Luix Virgil 1923- WhoBlA 92
**Overbeck**, Egon 1918- IntWW 91
**Overbeck**, Gene Edward 1929- WhoFI 92
**Overbeck**, Henry West 1930- AmMWSc 92
**Overbeck**, James A. 1940- WhoRel 92
**Overbeek**, Jan Theodoor Gerard 1911- IntWW 91
**Overberg**, Kenneth R 1944- ConAu 35NR
**Overberger**, Charles Gilbert 1920- AmMWSc 92
**Overberger**, James Edwin 1930- AmMWSc 92
**Overbury**, Colin 1931- Who 92
**Overby**, Ernestine Benita 1915-1985 WhoBlA 92N
**Overby**, Lacy Rasco 1920- AmMWSc 92
**Overcamp**, James Louis, Jr. 1947- WhoWest 92
**Overcamp**, Thomas Joseph 1946- AmMWSc 92
**Overcash**, Michael Ray 1944- AmMWSc 92
**Overcash**, Reece A., Jr. 1926- WhoFI 92
**Overdahl**, Curtis J 1917- AmMWSc 92
**Overdorf**, Margaret Veronica 1954- WhoFI 92
**Overend**, George 1921- Who 92
**Overend**, John J 1928- WhoIns 92
**Overend**, Ralph Phillips 1944- AmMWSc 92
**Overend**, William George 1921- WrDr 92
**Overfelt**, Lee 1923- WhoAmL 92
**Overgaard**, Mary Ann 1951- WhoAmL 92
**Overgaard**, Robert Milton 1929- WhoRel 92
**Overhage**, Carl F J 1910- AmMWSc 92
**Overhauser**, Albert Warner 1925- AmMWSc 92, IntWW 91
**Overhauser**, Paul B. 1957- WhoAmL 92
**Overholser**, Connie Sue 1954- WhoMW 92
**Overholser**, Knowles Arthur AmMWSc 92
**Overholser**, Wayne D 1906- IntAu&W 91, TwCWW 91, WrDr 92
**Overholt**, Darwin D. 1943- WhoRel 92
**Overholt**, Edward Lynn 1956- WhoRel 92
**Overholt**, John Lough 1909- AmMWSc 92
**Overholt**, Miles Harvard 1921- WhoFI 92, WhoWest 92
**Overholt**, Miles Harvard, III 1948- WhoFI 92
**Overhouse**, Madge Virginia 1924- WhoAmP 91
**Overing**, Michael Steven 1961- WhoAmL 92
**Overington**, John 1946- WhoAmP 91
**Overland**, James Edward 1947- AmMWSc 92
**Overley**, Jack Castle 1932- AmMWSc 92
**Overlock**, Frances Frost 1926- WhoAmP 91
**Overlund**, Ervin Kenneth 1928- WhoRel 92
**Overman**, Allen Ray 1937- AmMWSc 92
**Overman**, Amegda Jack 1920- AmMWSc 92
**Overman**, David Charles 1961- WhoEnt 92
**Overman**, Dean Lee 1943- WhoAmL 92
**Overman**, Dennis Orton 1943- AmMWSc 92
**Overman**, Edwin Scott 1922- WhoIns 92
**Overman**, Frederick 1803?-1852 BiInAmS
**Overman**, Germaine Tenkotte 1958- WhoMW 92
**Overman**, Joseph DeWitt 1918- AmMWSc 92
**Overman**, Larry Eugene 1943- AmMWSc 92
**Overman**, Lee Slater 1854-1930 DcNCBi 4
**Overman**, Ralph Theodore 1919- AmMWSc 92
**Overman**, Richard Hinson 1929- WhoRel 92
**Overman**, Timothy Lloyd 1943- AmMWSc 92
**Overmier**, J Bruce 1938- AmMWSc 92
**Overmyer**, Elizabeth Clark 1957- WhoEnt 92
**Overmyer**, Janet Elaine 1931- WhoMW 92
**Overmyer**, John Michael 1964- WhoEnt 92
**Overmyer**, Kathy Jo 1962- WhoMW 92
**Overmyer**, Kenneth Wayne 1931- WhoRel 92
**Overmyer**, Robert Franklin 1929- AmMWSc 92
**Overocker**, Elizabeth Ann 1951- WhoMW 92
**Overseth**, Oliver Enoch 1928- AmMWSc 92
**Overskei**, David Orvin 1948- AmMWSc 92
**Overson**, Brent C 1950- WhoAmP 91
**Overstreet**, Everett Louis WhoBlA 92
**Overstreet**, Harry L. 1938- WhoBlA 92
**Overstreet**, Morris WhoBlA 92
**Overstreet**, Raymond D 1942- WhoAmP 91
**Overstreet**, Reginald Larry 1941- WhoRel 92
**Overstreet**, Robin Miles 1939- AmMWSc 92
**Overstreet**, Tommy 1937- WhoEnt 92
**Overton**, Ben F 1926- WhoAmP 91
**Overton**, Benjamin Frederick 1926- WhoAmL 92
**Overton**, Betty Jean 1949- WhoBlA 92
**Overton**, David Thomas 1953- WhoMW 92
**Overton**, Donald A 1935- AmMWSc 92
**Overton**, Edward Beardslee 1942- AmMWSc 92
**Overton**, Edwin Dean 1939- WhoRel 92, WhoWest 92
**Overton**, George Washington 1918- WhoFI 92, WhoMW 92
**Overton**, Hal 1920-1972 NewAmDM
**Overton**, Hugh 1923- Who 92
**Overton**, James Ray 1936- AmMWSc 92
**Overton**, Jane Harper 1919- AmMWSc 92
**Overton**, Jenny 1942- WrDr 92
**Overton**, Jenny Margaret Mary 1942- IntAu&W 91
**Overton**, John Randall 1933- WhoWest 92
**Overton**, Lewis Marvin, Jr. 1937- WhoWest 92
**Overton**, Marcus Lee 1943- WhoEnt 92
**Overton**, Ron DrAPF 91
**Overton**, Volma Robert 1924- WhoBlA 92
**Overton**, William Calvin, Jr 1918- AmMWSc 92
**Overton**, William Samuels 1949- WhoFI 92
**Overturf**, Gary D 1943- AmMWSc 92
**Overturf**, Mark Anthony 1955- WhoWest 92
**Overturf**, Merrill L 1938- AmMWSc 92
**Overvold**, Roberta Joyce 1934- WhoWest 92
**Overway**, Kurt Randall 1959- WhoRel 92
**Overweg**, Norbert I A AmMWSc 92
**Overy**, Paul 1940- ConAu 35NR, IntAu&W 91, WrDr 92
**Overzet**, Lawrence John 1961- AmMWSc 92
**Ovesen**, Ellis DrAPF 91
**Ovesen**, Ellis 1923- IntAu&W 91
**Oveson**, W Val 1952- WhoAmP 91, WhoWest 92
**Ovett**, Stephen Michael 1955- IntWW 91
**Oviatt**, Boardman Lambert 1863-1889 BiInAmS
**Oviatt**, Candace Ann 1939- AmMWSc 92
**Oviatt**, Charles Dixon 1924- AmMWSc 92
**Oviatt**, Larry Andrew 1939- WhoWest 92
**Ovid** 43BC-18?AD ClMLC 7 [port]
**Oviedo**, Ollie O. 1956- WhoHisp 92
**Oviedo y Valdes**, Gonzalo Fernandez 1478-1557 HisDSpE
**Ovington**, Mary White DcAmImH
**Ovinnikov**, Richard Sergeyevich 1930- IntWW 91
**Ovitsky**, Steven Alan 1947- WhoEnt 92, WhoMW 92
**Ovitz**, Michael WhoEnt 92
**Ovitz**, Michael 1946- IntWW 91
**Ovsenik**, Edward Charles 1956- WhoAmL 92
**Ovshinsky**, Iris M 1927- AmMWSc 92
**Ovshinsky**, Stanford R 1922- AmMWSc 92
**Ovunc**, Bulent Ahmet 1927- AmMWSc 92
**Owada**, Hisashi 1932- IntWW 91
**Owades**, Joseph Lawrence 1919- AmMWSc 92
**Owcza**, Jurgen WhoFI 92
**Owczarek**, J A 1926- AmMWSc 92
**Owczarski**, William A 1934- AmMWSc 92
**Owczarzak**, Alfred 1923- AmMWSc 92
**Owellen**, Richard John 1935- AmMWSc 92
**Owen**, Alfred David 1936- Who 92
**Owen**, Alice Koning 1930- AmMWSc 92
**Owen**, Allen Ferdinand 1816-1865 DcNCBi 4
**Owen**, Alun 1919- Who 92
**Owen**, Alun 1925- ConAu 34NR, IntAu&W 91, IntMPA 92, Who 92, WrDr 92
**Owen**, Amy 1944- WhoWest 92
**Owen**, Aron 1919- Who 92
**Owen**, Benjamin Wade 1904-1983 DcNCBi 4
**Owen**, Bernard Laurence 1925- Who 92
**Owen**, Bernard Lawton 1929- AmMWSc 92, WhoMW 92
**Owen**, Bill 1914- IntMPA 92
**Owen**, Brad WhoAmP 91
**Owen**, Bruce Douglas 1927- AmMWSc 92
**Owen**, Bruce M 1943- ConAu 35NR
**Owen**, Carlos J. 1939- WhoRel 92
**Owen**, Carol Thompson 1944- WhoWest 92
**Owen**, Charles 1915- WrDr 92
**Owen**, Charles A., Jr. 1914- ConAu 36NR
**Owen**, Charles Archibald, Jr 1915- AmMWSc 92
**Owen**, Charles Scott 1942- AmMWSc 92
**Owen**, Claude Bernard, Jr. 1945- WhoFI 92
**Owen**, D F 1931- ConAu 35NR
**Owen**, Daniel Bruce 1950- WhoFI 92
**Owen**, Daniel Thomas 1947- WhoEnt 92
**Owen**, Dave 1931- WhoAmP 91
**Owen**, David Who 92
**Owen**, David 1898-1968 ConAu 36NR
**Owen**, David 1938- FacFETw, WrDr 92
**Owen**, David 1940- WhoAmP 91
**Owen**, David 1955- WrDr 92

**Owen,** David A 1937- *AmMWSc 92*
**Owen,** David Allan 1943- *AmMWSc 92*
**Owen,** David Anthony Llewellyn 1938- *IntWW 91, Who 92*
**Owen,** David Dale 1807-1860 *BiInAmS*
**Owen,** David Harold Owen 1933- *Who 92*
**Owen,** David Lanyon Ll. *Who 92*
**Owen,** David R 1942- *AmMWSc 92*
**Owen,** Dean *TwCWW 91*
**Owen,** Derwyn 1914- *WrDr 92*
**Owen,** Derwyn Trevor 1876-1947 *RelLAm 91*
**Owen,** Dolores B *ConAu 34NR*
**Owen,** Donald Bruce 1922- *AmMWSc 92*
**Owen,** Donald Edward 1936- *AmMWSc 92*
**Owen,** Donald Eugene 1928- *AmMWSc 92*
**Owen,** Douglas David Roy 1922- *ConAu 35NR, IntAu&W 91, WrDr 92*
**Owen,** Edwin 1910- *Who 92*
**Owen,** Eileen *DrAPF 91*
**Owen,** Eileen 1949- *IntAu&W 91*
**Owen,** Eric William 1964- *WhoWest 92*
**Owen,** Fletcher Bailey, Jr 1929- *AmMWSc 92*
**Owen,** Foster Gamble 1926- *AmMWSc 92*
**Owen,** Frances Lee 1949- *AmMWSc 92*
**Owen,** Frank 1893-1968 *ScFEYrs*
**Owen,** Frazer Nelson 1947- *AmMWSc 92*
**Owen,** Gareth 1922- *Who 92*
**Owen,** Gareth 1936- *SmATA 14AS [port], WrDr 92*
**Owen,** Gary 1944- *WhoAmP 91*
**Owen,** Gary Dean 1947- *WhoMW 92*
**Owen,** Gary Robert 1951- *WhoEnt 92, WhoMW 92*
**Owen,** Gene Scott 1943- *AmMWSc 92*
**Owen,** Geoffrey 1934- *IntWW 91, Who 92*
**Owen,** George Earle 1908- *WhoRel 92*
**Owen,** George Murdock 1930- *AmMWSc 92*
**Owen,** Gerald Victor 1922- *Who 92*
**Owen,** Gilbert Eugene 1949- *WhoWest 92*
**Owen,** Gordon Michael William 1937- *Who 92*
**Owen,** Guy 1925-1981 *ConAu 36NR, DcNCBi 4*
**Owen,** Gwilym Emyr, Jr 1933- *AmMWSc 92*
**Owen,** H. Martyn 1929- *WhoAmL 92, WhoFI 92*
**Owen,** Harry 1911- *Who 92*
**Owen,** Harry A, Jr 1919- *AmMWSc 92*
**Owen,** Henry David 1920- *WhoAmP 91*
**Owen,** Hugh *ScFEYrs, TwCWW 91*
**Owen,** Hugh 1915- *Who 92*
**Owen,** Hugo Dudley C. *Who 92*
**Owen,** Idris Wyn 1912- *Who 92*
**Owen,** Ivor Henry 1930- *Who 92*
**Owen,** James 1784-1865 *DcNCBi 4*
**Owen,** James Emmet 1935- *AmMWSc 92, WhoMW 92*
**Owen,** James Paige 1942- *WhoAmP 91*
**Owen,** James Robert 1914- *AmMWSc 92*
**Owen,** Jane 1965- *TwCPaSc*
**Owen,** Jeffrey Lynn 1951- *WhoWest 92*
**Owen,** Joel 1935- *AmMWSc 92*
**Owen,** John 1787-1841 *DcNCBi 4*
**Owen,** John 1925- *Who 92*
**Owen,** John Atkinson, Jr 1924- *AmMWSc 92*
**Owen,** John Aubrey 1945- *Who 92*
**Owen,** John Benjamin Brynmor 1910- *Who 92*
**Owen,** John Fletcher 1895-1976 *DcNCBi 4*
**Owen,** John Gethin M. *Who 92*
**Owen,** John Halliwell 1935- *Who 92*
**Owen,** John Harding 1931- *AmMWSc 92*
**Owen,** John Ivor Headon 1922- *Who 92*
**Owen,** John Joseph Thomas 1934- *Who 92*
**Owen,** John Simpson 1912- *Who 92*
**Owen,** John V. *Who 92*
**Owen,** John Wyn 1942- *Who 92*
**Owen,** Joslyn Grey 1928- *Who 92*
**Owen,** Karen Cordelia 1943- *WhoFI 92*
**Owen,** Kenneth Frederick 1935- *IntWW 91*
**Owen,** Loyd Eugene, Jr. 1943- *WhoAmL 92*
**Owen,** Lynn 1946- *WhoAmP 91*
**Owen,** Lynn Rasmussen *WhoEnt 92*
**Owen,** Marv d1991 *NewYTBS 91*
**Owen,** Maureen A. *DrAPF 91*
**Owen,** Michael *WhoEnt 92*
**Owen,** Nancy N 1935- *WhoAmP 91*
**Owen,** Nathan Richard 1919- *WhoFI 92*
**Owen,** Oliver Elon 1934- *AmMWSc 92*
**Owen,** Patricia *Who 92*
**Owen,** Paul Howard 1944- *AmMWSc 92*
**Owen,** Paul Robert d1990 *Who 92N*
**Owen,** Paul Robert 1920- *IntWW 91*
**Owen,** Peter *DcLB 112 [port]*
**Owen,** Peter Francis 1940- *Who 92*
**Owen,** Philip Loscombe Wintringham 1920- *Who 92*
**Owen,** Ray Bucklin, Jr 1937- *AmMWSc 92*
**Owen,** Ray David 1915- *AmMWSc 92, IntWW 91*
**Owen,** Raymond Harold 1932- *WhoRel 92*
**Owen,** Richard 1810-1890 *BiInAmS*
**Owen,** Richard 1922- *WhoAmL 92*
**Owen,** Richard Arthur James 1910- *Who 92*
**Owen,** Richard Wilfred 1932- *Who 92*
**Owen,** Robert *DcAmImH*
**Owen,** Robert 1771-1858 *DcLB 107 [port]*
**Owen,** Robert Barry 1943- *AmMWSc 92, WhoWest 92*
**Owen,** Robert Charles 1962- *WhoAmL 92*
**Owen,** Robert Dale 1801-1877 *AmPeW, BenetAL 91*
**Owen,** Robert John Richard 1940- *IntWW 91, Who 92*
**Owen,** Robert L 1940- *AmMWSc 92*
**Owen,** Robert Michael 1944- *Who 92*
**Owen,** Robert Michael 1946- *AmMWSc 92*
**Owen,** Robert Penrhyn 1918- *Who 92*
**Owen,** Robert W, Jr 1935- *AmMWSc 92*
**Owen,** Roberts Bishop 1926- *WhoAmL 92*
**Owen,** Roderic 1921- *WrDr 92*
**Owen,** Rowland Hubert 1903- *Who 92*
**Owen,** Samuel Griffith 1925- *Who 92*
**Owen,** Stanley Paul 1924- *AmMWSc 92*
**Owen,** Stephen Lee 1952- *WhoAmL 92*
**Owen,** Sue *DrAPF 91*
**Owen,** Sydney John Thomas *AmMWSc 92*
**Owen,** Terence Cunliffe 1930- *AmMWSc 92*
**Owen,** Thomas 1735-1806 *DcNCBi 4*
**Owen,** Thomas Arfon 1933- *Who 92*
**Owen,** Thomas E 1931- *AmMWSc 92*
**Owen,** Thomas Llewellyn 1928- *WhoFI 92*
**Owen,** Thomas Walker 1925- *WhoFI 92*
**Owen,** Tobias Chant 1936- *AmMWSc 92*
**Owen,** Trevor Bryan 1928- *Who 92*
**Owen,** W. J. B. 1916- *ConAu 134*
**Owen,** W Masters *WhoAmP 91*
**Owen,** Walter S 1920- *AmMWSc 92*
**Owen,** Walter Shepherd 1920- *Who 92*
**Owen,** Walter Wycliffe 1906- *AmMWSc 92*
**Owen,** Warren H 1927- *AmMWSc 92*
**Owen,** Warwick 1916- *IntAu&W 91, WrDr 92*
**Owen,** Wilfred 1893-1918 *CnDBLB 6 [port], FacFETw, RfGEnL 91*
**Owen,** Wilfred 1912- *ConAu 36NR, WhoFI 92*
**Owen,** William d1734 *DcNCBi 4*
**Owen,** William 1802-1842 *AmPeW*
**Owen,** William Bert 1903- *AmMWSc 92*
**Owen,** William Frederick 1947- *WhoWest 92*
**Owen,** William Hayes 1807?-1877? *DcNCBi 4*
**Owen,** William Lee 1915- *WhoAmL 92*
**Owen-Jones,** John Eryl 1912- *Who 92*
**Owen-Jones,** Lindsay 1946- *IntWW 91*
**Owen-Jones,** Lindsay Harwood 1946- *Who 92*
**Owen-Towle,** Carolyn Sheets 1935- *WhoRel 92*
**Owendoff,** Stephen Peter 1943- *WhoAmL 92*
**Owens,** Aaron James 1947- *AmMWSc 92*
**Owens,** Albert A. *DcAmImH*
**Owens,** Albert Henry, Jr 1926- *AmMWSc 92*
**Owens,** Albert Thomas 1948- *WhoFI 92*
**Owens,** Andi 1934- *WhoBlA 92*
**Owens,** Angle B., Jr. 1922- *WhoBlA 92*
**Owens,** Bernard Charles 1928- *Who 92*
**Owens,** Boone Bailey 1932- *AmMWSc 92*
**Owens,** Brigman 1943- *WhoBlA 92*
**Owens,** Buck 1929- *NewAmDM, WhoEnt 92, WhoWest 92*
**Owens,** Chandler David *WhoRel 92*
**Owens,** Charlene B. 1926-1990 *WhoBlA 92N*
**Owens,** Charles Allen 1945- *AmMWSc 92*
**Owens,** Charles Clinton 1942- *WhoBlA 92*
**Owens,** Charles David 1947- *WhoFI 92*
**Owens,** Charles Earl 1939- *WhoMW 92*
**Owens,** Charles Edward 1938- *WhoBlA 92*
**Owens,** Charles Franklin, Jr. 1956- *WhoRel 92*
**Owens,** Charles Wesley 1935- *AmMWSc 92*
**Owens,** Clarence Burgess 1926- *AmMWSc 92*
**Owens,** Clifford 1931- *AmMWSc 92*
**Owens,** Curtis 1938- *WhoBlA 92*
**Owens,** Daniel Walter 1948- *WhoBlA 92*
**Owens,** David Kenneth 1948- *WhoBlA 92*
**Owens,** David Kingston 1948- *AmMWSc 92*
**Owens,** David William 1946- *AmMWSc 92*
**Owens,** Debbie A. 1956- *WhoBlA 92*
**Owens,** Donald Phil 1942- *WhoRel 92*
**Owens,** Doris A. 1950- *WhoWest 92*
**Owens,** Douglas Wayne 1937- *WhoAmP 91*
**Owens,** Edward 1957- *WhoBlA 92*
**Owens,** Edward Henry 1945- *AmMWSc 92*
**Owens,** Edward Oliver 1948- *WhoBlA 92*
**Owens,** Edwin Chandler 1935- *WhoIns 92*
**Owens,** Emmett Hennington *WhoAmP 91*
**Owens,** Ernest Sibley, III 1945- *WhoWest 92*
**Owens,** Frank Arthur Robert 1912- *Who 92*
**Owens,** Frank James 1939- *AmMWSc 92*
**Owens,** Frederick Hammann 1928- *AmMWSc 92*
**Owens,** Fredric Newell 1941- *AmMWSc 92*
**Owens,** G Kay 1942- *AmMWSc 92*
**Owens,** Garland Chester 1922- *WhoFI 92*
**Owens,** Gary *WhoEnt 92, WhoWest 92*
**Owens,** Gary Keith *AmMWSc 92*
**Owens,** Gaylon 1934- *WhoAmP 91*
**Owens,** Genevra Irene 1917- *WhoAmP 91*
**Owens,** George A. 1919- *WhoBlA 92*
**Owens,** Glen Edward 1947- *WhoRel 92*
**Owens,** Guy 1926- *AmMWSc 92*
**Owens,** Harold Eston 1943- *WhoRel 92*
**Owens,** Howard T, Jr 1934- *WhoAmP 91*
**Owens,** Hugo Armstrong, Sr. 1916- *WhoBlA 92*
**Owens,** Ida S 1939- *AmMWSc 92*
**Owens,** Iris *DrAPF 91*
**Owens,** Isaiah H. 1920- *WhoBlA 92*
**Owens,** James Alvin, Jr. 1948- *WhoBlA 92*
**Owens,** James Carl 1937- *AmMWSc 92*
**Owens,** James Cleveland 1913-1980 *BlkOlyM [port]*
**Owens,** James E. 1937- *WhoBlA 92*
**Owens,** James Hilliard 1920- *WhoMW 92*
**Owens,** James Robert 1957- *WhoEnt 92, WhoRel 92*
**Owens,** James Robert, Jr. 1943- *WhoEnt 92*
**Owens,** James Samuel 1908- *AmMWSc 92*
**Owens,** Jana Jae 1943- *WhoEnt 92*
**Owens,** Janine Ann 1959- *WhoMW 92*
**Owens,** Jay R. 1944- *WhoBlA 92*
**Owens,** Jefferson Pleas 1917- *WhoBlA 92*
**Owens,** Jerry Sue 1947- *WhoBlA 92*
**Owens,** Jesse 1913-1980 *ConBlB 2 [port], FacFETw [port], RComAH*
**Owens,** Jimmy 1943- *WhoBlA 92*
**Owens,** Jo Ann Faye 1947- *WhoAmP 91*
**Owens,** Joan D. 1942- *WhoEnt 92*
**Owens,** Joan Murrell 1933- *WhoBlA 92*
**Owens,** John Charles 1944- *AmMWSc 92*
**Owens,** John Michael 1951- *AmMWSc 92*
**Owens,** John N 1936- *AmMWSc 92*
**Owens,** John Ridland 1932- *Who 92*
**Owens,** John William, Jr. 1946- *WhoEnt 92*
**Owens,** Joseph 1908- *IntAu&W 91, WhoRel 92, WrDr 92*
**Owens,** Joseph E *WhoAmP 91*
**Owens,** Joseph Francis, III 1946- *AmMWSc 92*
**Owens,** Judith Myoli 1940- *WhoBlA 92*
**Owens,** Kenneth Eugene 1926- *AmMWSc 92*
**Owens,** Kevin Glenn 1960- *AmMWSc 92*
**Owens,** Lillie Anne 1935- *WhoBlA 92*
**Owens,** Louis *DrAPF 91*
**Owens,** Lowell Davis 1931- *AmMWSc 92*
**Owens,** Luvie Moore 1933- *WhoMW 92*
**Owens,** Lynda Gayle 1956- *WhoBlA 92*
**Owens,** Major R. 1936- *AlmAP 92 [port], WhoAmP 91, WhoBlA 92*
**Owens,** Maxwell Allan 1959- *WhoWest 92*
**Owens,** Michael *WhoEnt 92*
**Owens,** Michael Ted 1952- *WhoRel 92*
**Owens,** Nancy Matchton 1962- *WhoEnt 92*
**Owens,** Nathaniel Davis 1948- *WhoBlA 92*
**Owens,** O'dell M. *WhoBlA 92*
**Owens,** Pamela Jean 1948- *WhoRel 92*
**Owens,** Patricia Ann *WhoMW 92*
**Owens,** Patti-Reba 1953- *WhoEnt 92*
**Owens,** Phyllis Eileen Padilla 1952- *WhoHisp 92*
**Owens,** Randal L. 1945- *WhoFI 92*
**Owens,** Richard Wilson 1941- *WhoRel 92*
**Owens,** Robert F. *WhoRel 92*
**Owens,** Robert Hunter 1921- *AmMWSc 92*
**Owens,** Robert Jessen, Jr. 1947- *WhoRel 92*
**Owens,** Robert Lee 1932- *WhoBlA 92*
**Owens,** Robert Leon, III 1925- *WhoBlA 92*
**Owens,** Robert Patrick 1954- *WhoAmL 92, WhoWest 92*
**Owens,** Robert Phillip 1931- *WhoWest 92*
**Owens,** Robin Shane 1954- *WhoRel 92*
**Owens,** Rochelle *DrAPF 91*
**Owens,** Rochelle 1936- *ConPo 91, WrDr 92*
**Owens,** Rodney Joe 1950- *WhoAmL 92*
**Owens,** Ronald 1930- *WhoBlA 92*
**Owens,** Ronald C. 1936- *WhoBlA 92*
**Owens,** Ronnie David 1945- *WhoRel 92*
**Owens,** Ruth Ann 1943- *WhoMW 92*
**Owens,** Scott Andrew 1958- *WhoMW 92*
**Owens,** Stephen Thomas 1948- *WhoAmL 92*
**Owens,** Thomas C. 1922- *WhoBlA 92*
**Owens,** Thomas Charles 1941- *AmMWSc 92*
**Owens,** Tim G. 1948- *WhoEnt 92*
**Owens,** Traci 1962- *WhoEnt 92*
**Owens,** Treka Elaine 1953- *WhoBlA 92*
**Owens,** V. Andre 1966- *WhoEnt 92*
**Owens,** Victor Allen 1945- *WhoBlA 92*
**Owens,** Vivian Ann 1948- *AmMWSc 92*
**Owens,** Wallace, Jr. *WhoBlA 92*
**Owens,** Walter *WhoAmP 91*
**Owens,** Warner Barry 1939- *WhoWest 92*
**Owens,** Wayne 1937- *AlmAP 92 [port], WhoWest 92*
**Owens,** Wilbur Dawson, Jr. 1930- *WhoAmL 92*
**Owens,** William 1937- *WhoAmP 91, WhoBlA 92*
**Owens,** William A. 1905-1990 *ConAu 133, -36NR*
**Owens,** William Clarence 1947- *WhoAmP 91*
**Owens,** William F 1950- *WhoAmP 91*
**Owens,** William Gregg Lee 1947- *WhoAmL 92*
**Owens,** William Leo 1930- *AmMWSc 92*
**Owens,** William Lewis 1949- *WhoAmL 92*
**Owens,** William Richard 1941- *AmMWSc 92*
**Owens-Hicks,** Shirley *WhoAmP 91*
**Owens-Hicks,** Shirley 1942- *WhoBlA 92*
**Owens-Smith,** Joyce Latrell 1949- *WhoBlA 92*
**Owensby,** Clenton Edgar 1940- *AmMWSc 92*
**Owensby,** Earl 1935- *IntMPA 92*
**Owensby,** Emmett C. 1918- *WhoRel 92*
**Owensby,** James Richard 1942- *WhoAmL 92*
**Owenson,** Sydney 1775?-1859 *RfGEnL 91*
**Ower,** David Cheyne 1931- *Who 92*
**Owers,** Anne Elizabeth 1947- *Who 92*
**Owers,** Noel Oscar 1926- *AmMWSc 92*
**Owings,** Addison Davis 1936- *AmMWSc 92*
**Owings,** George W, III 1945- *WhoAmP 91*
**Owings,** James Claggett, Jr 1940- *AmMWSc 92*
**Owings,** Margaret Wentworth 1913- *WhoWest 92*
**Owings,** Nathaniel Alexander 1903-1984 *ConAu 35NR*
**Owings,** Rachel Harriet 1926- *WhoEnt 92*
**Owings,** Timothy Lawrence 1953- *WhoRel 92*
**Ownbey,** Gerald Bruce 1916- *AmMWSc 92*
**Ownbey,** Lenore F. Daly *WhoFI 92*
**Ownby,** Charlotte Ledbetter 1947- *AmMWSc 92*
**Ownby,** Dennis Randall 1948- *AmMWSc 92, WhoMW 92*
**Ownby,** James Donald 1944- *AmMWSc 92*
**Ownby,** P Darrell 1935- *AmMWSc 92*
**Owo,** The Olowo of *Who 92*
**Owre,** Oscar Theodore 1917- *AmMWSc 92*
**Owren,** Michael J. 1955- *WhoWest 92*
**Owsley,** Betty Joan *WhoBlA 92*
**Owsley,** Dennis Clark 1943- *AmMWSc 92*
**Owsley,** Henry Furlow 1955- *WhoFI 92*
**Owsley,** Ray 1932- *WhoAmP 91*
**Owston,** Peyton Wood 1938- *AmMWSc 92*
**Owusu,** Kwame Nini 1942- *IntWW 91*
**Owusu,** Victor 1923- *IntWW 91*
**Owyang,** Gilbert Hsiaopin *AmMWSc 92*
**Oxborrow,** Gordon Squires 1939- *AmMWSc 92*
**Oxburgh,** Ernest Ronald 1934- *IntWW 91, Who 92*
**Oxbury,** Harold Frederick 1903- *Who 92*
**Oxenberg,** Catherine 1961- *IntMPA 92*
**Oxenburg,** Allen Sven 1927- *WhoEnt 92*
**Oxenbury,** Helen 1938- *ConAu 35NR, SmATA 68 [port]*
**Oxenden,** Ashton 1808-1892 *RelLAm 91*
**Oxender,** Dale LaVern 1932- *AmMWSc 92*
**Oxender,** Glenn S 1943- *WhoAmP 91*
**Oxender,** Richard Alan 1948- *WhoMW 92*
**Oxendine,** John Edward 1943- *WhoBlA 92*
**Oxenkrug,** Gregory Faiva 1941- *AmMWSc 92*
**Oxford,** Archdeacon of *Who 92*
**Oxford,** Bishop of 1936- *Who 92*
**Oxford,** C W 1921- *AmMWSc 92*
**Oxford,** Edwin 1939- *AmMWSc 92*
**Oxford,** Kenneth 1924- *Who 92*
**Oxford and Asquith,** Earl of 1916- *Who 92*
**Oxfuird,** Master of 1969- *Who 92*
**Oxfuird,** Viscount of 1934- *Who 92*
**Oxlade,** Zena Elsie 1929- *Who 92*
**Oxlee,** Colin Hamilton 1935- *Who 92*
**Oxley,** Humphrey Leslie Malcolm 1909- *Who 92*
**Oxley,** James Keith R. *Who 92*
**Oxley,** Joseph H 1929- *AmMWSc 92*
**Oxley,** Julian Christopher 1938- *Who 92*
**Oxley,** Lawrence Augustus 1887-1973 *DcNCBi 4*
**Oxley,** Leo Lionel 1934- *WhoBlA 92*
**Oxley,** Lucy Orintha 1912- *WhoBlA 92*
**Oxley,** Mark Edwin 1956- *WhoMW 92*
**Oxley,** Michael G. 1944- *AlmAP 92 [port]*

**Oxley**, Michael Garver 1944- *WhoAmP 91, WhoMW 92*
**Oxley**, Myron B *WhoAmP 91*
**Oxley**, Philip 1922- *AmMWSc 92, WhoWest 92*
**Oxley**, Theron D, Jr 1931- *AmMWSc 92*
**Oxley**, William 1939- *ConPo 91, IntAu&W 91, WrDr 92*
**Oxman**, Allan Shelly 1949- *WhoFI 92*
**Oxman**, Bernard Herbert 1941- *WhoAmL 92*
**Oxman**, David Craig 1941- *WhoAmL 92*
**Oxman**, Michael Allan 1935- *AmMWSc 92*
**Oxmantown**, Lord 1969- *Who 92*
**Oxnam**, Garfield Bromley 1891-1963 *AmPeW, RelLAm 91*
**Oxnard**, Charles Ernest 1933- *AmMWSc 92*
**Oxner**, Glenn Ruckman 1938- *WhoFI 92*
**Oxtoby**, David 1938- *TwCPaSc*
**Oxtoby**, David W 1951- *AmMWSc 92*
**Oxtoby**, David William 1951- *WhoMW 92*
**Oxtoby**, John Corning 1910- *AmMWSc 92*
**Oxtoby**, Willard Gurdon 1933- *WhoRel 92*
**Oyalowo**, Tunde O. 1953- *WhoBlA 92*
**Oyama**, Jiro 1925- *AmMWSc 92*
**Oyama**, Shigeo Ted 1955- *AmMWSc 92*
**Oyama**, Vance I 1922- *AmMWSc 92*
**Oyamada**, Paul Herbert 1921- *WhoWest 92*
**Oyamo** *DrAPF 91*
**Oyangen**, Gunhild 1947- *IntWW 91*
**Oye**, Harald Arnljot 1935- *IntWW 91*
**Oye-Mba**, Casimir 1942- *IntWW 91*
**Oyen**, Ordean James 1944- *AmMWSc 92*
**Oyer**, Alden Tremaine 1947- *AmMWSc 92*
**Oyer**, Herbert Joseph 1921- *AmMWSc 92, WhoMW 92*
**Oyer**, Kenneth Eldon 1939- *WhoMW 92*
**Oyeshiku**, Patricia Delores Worthy 1944- *WhoBlA 92*
**Oyewole**, Saundra Herndon 1943- *AmMWSc 92, WhoBlA 92*
**Oyler**, Alan Richard 1947- *AmMWSc 92*
**Oyler**, Dee Edward 1942- *AmMWSc 92*
**Oyler**, Glenn W 1923- *AmMWSc 92*
**Oyler**, J Mack 1926- *AmMWSc 92*
**Oyler**, James Russell, Jr. 1946- *WhoFI 92*
**Oyler**, W. Kent *WhoFI 92*
**Oyloe**, Turner Leo 1932- *WhoWest 92*
**Oyola**, Eliezer 1944- *WhoHisp 92*
**Oyono**, Ferdinand 1929- *LiExTwC*
**Oyono**, Ferdinand Leopold 1929- *IntWW 91*
**Oyoue**, Jean-Felix 1928- *IntWW 91*
**Oyster**, Clyde William 1940- *AmMWSc 92*
**Oz**, Amos 1939- *IntAu&W 91, IntWW 91, NewYTBS 91 [port]*
**Oz**, Frank 1944- *IntMPA 92*
**Oz**, Frank Richard 1944- *WhoEnt 92*
**Oza**, Dipak H 1954- *AmMWSc 92*
**Oza**, Kandarp Govindlal 1942- *AmMWSc 92*
**Ozag**, David 1962- *WhoFI 92*
**Ozaki**, Henry Yoshio 1923- *AmMWSc 92*
**Ozaki**, Robert S 1934- *ConAu 35NR*
**Ozaki**, Satoshi 1929- *AmMWSc 92*
**Ozal**, Turgut 1927- *FacFETw, IntWW 91*
**Ozan**, M Turgut 1919- *AmMWSc 92*
**Ozanich**, Charles George 1933- *WhoWest 92*
**Ozanne**, Dominic L. 1953- *WhoBlA 92*
**Ozanne**, James Herbert 1943- *WhoFI 92*
**Ozari**, Yehuda 1944- *AmMWSc 92*
**Ozarow**, Kent Jorgensen *DrAPF 91*
**Ozato**, Keiko *AmMWSc 92*
**Ozato**, Sadatoshi 1930- *IntWW 91*
**Ozawa**, Ichiro *IntWW 91*
**Ozawa**, Kenneth Susumu 1931- *AmMWSc 92*
**Ozawa**, Seiji 1935- *FacFETw, IntWW 91, NewAmDM, Who 92, WhoEnt 92*
**Ozawa**, Tatsuo *IntWW 91*
**Ozawa**, Terutomo 1935- *ConAu 34NR, WhoFI 92*
**Ozbek**, Rifat 1953- *IntWW 91*
**Ozbirn**, David Wade 1956- *WhoEnt 92*
**Ozbun**, Jim L. *WhoMW 92*
**Ozbun**, Jim L 1936- *AmMWSc 92*
**Ozburn**, George W *AmMWSc 92*
**Ozdas**, Mehmet Nimet 1921- *IntWW 91*
**Ozdowski**, Jerzy 1925- *IntWW 91*
**Ozelli**, Tunch 1938- *WhoFI 92*
**Ozenda**, Paul 1920- *IntWW 91*
**Ozendo**, Pierre L 1950- *WhoIns 92*
**Ozenfant**, Amedee 1886-1966 *DcTwDes*
**Ozenghar**, Laurie Ann 1962- *WhoEnt 92*
**Ozer**, Bernard d1991 *NewYTBS 91 [port]*
**Ozer**, Harvey Leon 1938- *AmMWSc 92*
**Ozer**, Mark Norman 1932- *AmMWSc 92*
**Ozere**, Rudolph L 1926- *AmMWSc 92*
**Ozernoy**, Leonid M 1939- *AmMWSc 92*
**Ozernoy**, Leonid Moissey 1939- *WhoWest 92*
**Ozga-Michalski**, Jozef 1919- *IntWW 91*
**Ozherelev**, Oleg 1941- *IntWW 91*
**Ozick**, Cynthia *DrAPF 91*
**Ozick**, Cynthia 1928- *BenetAL 91, ConNov 91, IntAu&W 91, WrDr 92*
**Ozier**, Irving 1938- *AmMWSc 92*
**Ozim**, Francis Taiino 1946- *WhoBlA 92*
**Ozim**, Igor 1931- *IntWW 91*
**Ozimek**, Edward Joseph 1945- *AmMWSc 92*
**Ozimkoski**, Raymond Edward 1927- *AmMWSc 92*
**Oziomek**, James 1941- *AmMWSc 92*
**Ozisik**, M Necati 1923- *AmMWSc 92*
**Ozkan**, Umit Sivrioglu 1954- *WhoMW 92*
**Ozment**, Dennis Dean 1945- *WhoAmP 91*
**Ozment**, Steven E 1939- *ConAu 35NR*
**Ozmon**, Howard 1935- *WrDr 92*
**Ozmun**, Scott Alan 1958- *WhoAmL 92*
**Ozog**, Francis Joseph 1922- *AmMWSc 92*
**Ozol**, Michael Arvid 1934- *AmMWSc 92*
**Ozolins**, Karlis Lotars 1923- *WhoRel 92*
**Ozols**, Juris *AmMWSc 92*
**Ozonoff**, David Michael 1942- *AmMWSc 92*
**Ozsvath**, Istvan 1928- *AmMWSc 92*
**Ozu**, Yasujiro 1903-1963 *FacFETw, IntDcF 2-2 [port]*
**Ozuna**, George, Jr. 1930- *WhoFI 92, WhoHisp 92*

# P

**Paabo**, Maya 1929- *AmMWSc 92*
**Paal**, Frank F 1930- *AmMWSc 92*
**Paananen**, Eloise Engle 1923- *IntAu&W 91*
**Paape**, Max J *AmMWSc 92*
**Paar**, Jack *LesBEnT 92*
**Paar**, Jack 1918- *IntMPA 92, IntWW 91*
**Paarsons**, James Delbert 1947- *AmMWSc 92*
**Paas**, Martha White 1946- *WhoMW 92*
**Paasio**, Pertti Kullervo 1939- *IntWW 91*
**Paaswell**, Robert E 1937- *AmMWSc 92*
**Paavola**, Laurie Gail *AmMWSc 92*
**Pabarcius**, Algis 1932- *WhoFI 92*
**Pabian**, Roger Karr 1935- *WhoMW 92*
**Pablos**, Rolando 1939- *WhoHisp 92*
**Pabon**, Darwin Peter 1958- *WhoFI 92*
**Pabon**, Velez Luis 1947- *WhoEnt 92*
**Pabon-Price**, Noemi 1950- *WhoHisp 92*
**Pabst**, Adolf 1899- *AmMWSc 92*
**Pabst**, G. W. 1885-1967 *IntDcF 2-2 [port]*
**Pabst**, Michael John 1945- *AmMWSc 92*
**Pabst**, Waldemar 1880-1970 *BiDExR*
**Pacala**, Leon 1926- *WhoRel 92*
**Pacana**, Nicolas Romo 1953- *WhoEnt 92*
**Pacansky**, Thomas John 1946- *AmMWSc 92*
**Pacavira**, Manuel Pedro 1939- *IntWW 91*
**Pacchiarotti**, Gasparo 1740-1821 *NewAmDM*
**Pacciardi**, Randolfo d1991 *NewYTBS 91*
**Pacciardi**, Randolfo 1899-1991 *CurBio 91N*
**Pace**, Alicia Guzman 1949- *WhoHisp 92*
**Pace**, Brooks 1942- *WhoWest 92*
**Pace**, Carlos Nick 1940- *AmMWSc 92*
**Pace**, Carolina Jolliff 1938- *WhoFI 92*
**Pace**, Caroline S 1942- *AmMWSc 92*
**Pace**, Charles Henry 1886-1963 *NewAmDM*
**Pace**, Daniel Gannon 1945- *AmMWSc 92*
**Pace**, Denny F. 1926- *WhoWest 92*
**Pace**, Eric 1936- *WrDr 92*
**Pace**, Frank Anthony 1950- *WhoEnt 92*
**Pace**, Henry Alexander 1914- *AmMWSc 92*
**Pace**, Henry Buford 1929- *AmMWSc 92*
**Pace**, Judith G 1949- *AmMWSc 92*
**Pace**, Kay Robertine *WhoBlA 92*
**Pace**, Lorin Nelson 1925- *WhoAmP 91, WhoWest 92*
**Pace**, Marshall Osteen 1941- *AmMWSc 92*
**Pace**, Marvin M 1944- *AmMWSc 92*
**Pace**, Nello 1916- *AmMWSc 92*
**Pace**, Norman R 1942- *AmMWSc 92*
**Pace**, Ralph C., Sr. *WhoEnt 92*
**Pace**, Richard Yost 1956- *WhoMW 92*
**Pace**, Rosalind *DrAPF 91*
**Pace**, Rosella *DrAPF 91*
**Pace**, Salvatore Joseph 1944- *AmMWSc 92*
**Pace**, Sheryl Lynn 1966- *WhoWest 92*
**Pace**, Stanley Carter 1921- *IntWW 91, WhoFI 92*
**Pace**, Stanley Dan 1947- *WhoAmL 92*
**Pace**, Thomas 1951- *WhoAmL 92*
**Pace**, Wesley Emory 1924- *AmMWSc 92*
**Pace**, William Greenville 1927- *AmMWSc 92*
**Pace**, William Roy 1951- *WhoEnt 92*
**Pace Asciak**, Cecil 1940- *AmMWSc 92*
**Pacea**, Ion 1924- *IntWW 91*
**Pacela**, Allan F 1938- *AmMWSc 92*
**Pacela**, Allan Fred 1938- *WhoWest 92*
**Pacelli**, Angela DeFlorio *WhoAmP 91*
**Pacelli**, Eugenio *EncTR 91*
**Pacelli**, Henry Paul *WhoAmP 91*
**Pacer**, John Charles 1947- *AmMWSc 92*
**Pacer**, Richard A 1939- *AmMWSc 92*
**Pacernick**, Gary Bernard *DrAPF 91*
**Pacetti**, James M. 1960- *WhoFI 92*
**Pacey**, Gilbert E 1952- *AmMWSc 92*
**Pacey**, Philip Desmond 1941- *AmMWSc 92*
**Pach**, Zsigmond Pal 1919- *IntWW 91*
**Pacha**, Robert Edward 1932- *AmMWSc 92*
**Pachariyangkun**, Upadit 1920- *IntWW 91*
**Pache**, Bernard 1934- *IntWW 91*
**Pachecho**, Rondon 1919- *IntWW 91*
**Pacheco**, Adonio W., Jr. 1956- *WhoHisp 92*
**Pacheco**, Alex *WhoHisp 92*
**Pacheco**, Ana M. 1943- *TwCPaSc*
**Pacheco**, Andres Leopoldo 1960- *WhoHisp 92*
**Pacheco**, Anthony Louis 1932- *AmMWSc 92*
**Pacheco**, Benny Sena, Jr. 1951- *WhoHisp 92*
**Pacheco**, Ceferino *WhoHisp 92*
**Pacheco**, Donald Norman, Jr. 1959- *WhoHisp 92*
**Pacheco**, Efrain Alcides 1934- *WhoHisp 92*
**Pacheco**, Evelyn 1950- *WhoHisp 92*
**Pacheco**, Javier *DrAPF 91*
**Pacheco**, Joe B. 1937- *WhoHisp 92*
**Pacheco**, Jose 1942- *WhoHisp 92*
**Pacheco**, Jose Emilio 1939- *ConSpAP*
**Pacheco**, Luis Novoa 1956- *WhoHisp 92*
**Pacheco**, Manuel Trinidad 1941- *WhoHisp 92, WhoWest 92*
**Pacheco**, Marc R *WhoAmP 91*
**Pacheco**, Mary Ann 1950- *WhoHisp 92*
**Pacheco**, Richard 1924- *WhoAmP 91, WhoHisp 92*
**Pacheco**, Richard, Jr. 1927- *WhoHisp 92*
**Pacheco**, Sammy Lawrence 1952- *WhoHisp 92*
**Pacheco Areco**, Jorge 1920- *IntWW 91*
**Pachelbel**, Charles Theodore 1690-1750 *NewAmDM*
**Pachelbel**, Johann 1653-1706 *NewAmDM*
**Pachelli**, Mike *WhoEnt 92*
**Pachence**, Ronald Anthony 1945- *WhoRel 92*
**Pachios**, Harold Christy 1936- *WhoAmP 91*
**Pachman**, Daniel James 1911- *AmMWSc 92*
**Pachman**, Lauren M 1937- *AmMWSc 92*
**Pachmann**, Vladimir de 1848-1933 *NewAmDM*
**Pacholczyk**, Andrzej Grzegorz 1935- *AmMWSc 92*
**Pacholka**, Kenneth 1926- *AmMWSc 92*
**Pachomius** 292?-346 *EncEarC*
**Pachon**, Harry 1945- *WhoHisp 92*
**Pachon**, Harry Peter 1945- *WhoAmP 91*
**Pachow**, Wang 1918- *WhoRel 92*
**Pachter**, Irwin Jacob 1925- *AmMWSc 92*
**Pachter**, Jonathan Alan 1957- *AmMWSc 92*
**Pachter**, Victor 1921- *WhoFI 92*
**Pachter**, Wendy Susan 1954- *WhoAmL 92*
**Pachut**, Joseph F 1950- *AmMWSc 92*
**Pacian of Barcelona** 310?-392? *EncEarC*
**Pacie**, Joni Nicole *WhoEnt 92*
**Pacific**, Joseph Nicholas, Jr. 1950- *WhoWest 92*
**Pacifici**, James Grady 1939- *AmMWSc 92*
**Pacifico**, Carl 1921- *WrDr 92*
**Pacifico**, Carl R 1921- *IntAu&W 91*
**Pacini**, Giovanni 1796-1867 *NewAmDM*
**Pacino**, Al 1940- *IntMPA 92, IntWW 91, WhoEnt 92*
**Paciorek**, Kazimiera J L 1931- *AmMWSc 92*
**Paciotti**, Michael Anthony 1942- *AmMWSc 92*
**Pack**, Albert Boyd 1919- *AmMWSc 92*
**Pack**, Allan I 1943- *AmMWSc 92*
**Pack**, Donald Cecil 1920- *Who 92*
**Pack**, Harry Samuel 1943- *WhoFI 92*
**Pack**, John Lee 1927- *AmMWSc 92*
**Pack**, Judy Kay Daniels 1943- *WhoAmP 91*
**Pack**, Merrill Raymond 1923- *AmMWSc 92*
**Pack**, Michael 1954- *WhoEnt 92*
**Pack**, Phoebe Katherine Finley 1907- *WhoWest 92*
**Pack**, Richard Morris 1915- *WhoEnt 92*
**Pack**, Robert *DrAPF 91*
**Pack**, Robert 1929- *BenetAL 91, ConPo 91, WrDr 92*
**Pack**, Roger A. 1907- *WrDr 92*
**Pack**, Russell T 1937- *AmMWSc 92, WhoWest 92*
**Pack**, Spencer J. 1953- *WhoFI 92*
**Pack**, Walter Frank 1916- *WhoRel 92*
**Packard**, Alpheus Spring, Jr 1839-1905 *BiInAmS*
**Packard**, Ann Nadia 1948- *WhoMW 92*
**Packard**, Barbara B K 1938- *AmMWSc 92*
**Packard**, Beverly Sue *AmMWSc 92*
**Packard**, Bonnie B 1946- *WhoAmP 91*
**Packard**, David 1912- *AmMWSc 92, IntWW 91, WhoFI 92, WhoWest 92*
**Packard**, Douglas 1903- *Who 92*
**Packard**, Frank L 1877-1942 *ScFEYrs*
**Packard**, Frederick A 1862?-1902 *BiInAmS*
**Packard**, Gary Claire 1938- *AmMWSc 92*
**Packard**, Harry 1914-1991 *NewYTBS 91*
**Packard**, Karle Sanborn, Jr 1921- *AmMWSc 92*
**Packard**, Martin Everett 1921- *AmMWSc 92*
**Packard**, Patricia Lois 1927- *AmMWSc 92*
**Packard**, Richard Darrell 1928- *AmMWSc 92*
**Packard**, Robert 1916- *ConAu 134*
**Packard**, Robert Charles 1919- *WhoAmL 92*
**Packard**, Robert Gay 1924- *AmMWSc 92*
**Packard**, Robert Goodale, III 1951- *WhoWest 92*
**Packard**, Ron 1931- *AlmAP 92 [port], WhoAmP 91*
**Packard**, Ronald 1931- *WhoWest 92*
**Packard**, Russell Calvert 1946- *WhoRel 92*
**Packard**, Sherman A 1949- *WhoAmP 91*
**Packard**, Sophia B. 1824-1891 *RelLAm 91*
**Packard**, Stephen Michael 1953- *WhoAmL 92*
**Packard**, Theodore Train 1942- *AmMWSc 92*
**Packard**, Vance 1914- *BenetAL 91, IntAu&W 91, IntWW 91, Who 92, WrDr 92*
**Packard**, Vernal Sidney, Jr 1930- *AmMWSc 92*
**Packard**, William *DrAPF 91*
**Packchanian**, Ardzroony 1900- *AmMWSc 92*
**Packel**, Edward Wesler 1941- *AmMWSc 92, WhoMW 92*
**Packenham**, Daniel J. *WhoRel 92*
**Packenham**, Jack 1938- *TwCPaSc*
**Packer**, Arnold Herman 1935- *WhoAmP 91*
**Packer**, B. L. 1947- *ConAu 133*
**Packer**, Barry Deal 1956- *WhoRel 92*
**Packer**, Beverly White 1930- *WhoAmP 91*
**Packer**, Billy *LesBEnT 92*
**Packer**, Charles M 1930- *AmMWSc 92*
**Packer**, Daniel Fredric, Jr. 1947- *WhoBlA 92*
**Packer**, Eve *DrAPF 91*
**Packer**, James Innell 1926- *IntAu&W 91, WrDr 92*
**Packer**, John Richard 1946- *Who 92*
**Packer**, Kenneth Frederick 1924- *AmMWSc 92*
**Packer**, Kenneth John 1938- *Who 92*
**Packer**, Kerry Francis Bullmore 1937- *IntWW 91, Who 92*
**Packer**, Lawrence Frank *WhoBlA 92*
**Packer**, Leo S 1920- *AmMWSc 92*
**Packer**, Lester 1929- *AmMWSc 92*
**Packer**, Lewis C 1893- *AmMWSc 92*
**Packer**, Mark Barry 1944- *WhoAmL 92, WhoWest 92*
**Packer**, Mark Steven 1957- *WhoAmL 92*
**Packer**, Mary A. 1952- *WhoFI 92*
**Packer**, R Allen 1914- *AmMWSc 92*
**Packer**, Randall Kent 1945- *AmMWSc 92*
**Packer**, Raymond Allen 1914- *WhoMW 92*
**Packer**, Richard John 1944- *Who 92*
**Packer**, Russell Howard 1951- *WhoFI 92*
**Packer**, Stephen Barry 1928- *WhoFI 92*
**Packer**, William John 1940- *Who 92*
**Packert**, Gayla Beth 1953- *WhoAmL 92*
**Packett**, Charles Neville 1922- *WrDr 92*
**Packett**, Leonard Vasco 1932- *AmMWSc 92*
**Packham**, Marian Aitchison 1927- *AmMWSc 92*
**Packman**, Albert M 1930- *AmMWSc 92*
**Packman**, Charles Henry 1942- *AmMWSc 92*
**Packman**, Elias Wolfe 1930- *AmMWSc 92*
**Packman**, Paul Frederick 1936- *AmMWSc 92*
**Packman**, Paul Michael 1938- *AmMWSc 92*
**Packman**, Seymour 1943- *AmMWSc 92*
**Packo**, Joseph John 1925- *WhoFI 92*
**Packo**, R.G. 1959- *WhoMW 92*
**Packshaw**, Robin David 1933- *Who 92*
**Packwood**, Bob 1932- *AlmAP 92 [port], IntWW 91, WhoAmP 91, WhoWest 92*
**Packwood**, William Theodore, III 1942- *WhoMW 92*
**Paco D'Arcos**, Joaquim 1908- *IntAu&W 91*
**Pacosz**, Christina V. *DrAPF 91*
**Pacquin**, Edward H *WhoAmP 91*
**Paczesny**, Edmunette 1933- *WhoRel 92*
**Paczynski**, Bohdan 1940- *AmMWSc 92*
**Padalino**, Joseph John 1922- *AmMWSc 92*

**Padalino,** Stephen John 1954- *AmMWSc 92*
**Padarathsingh,** Martin Lancelot *AmMWSc 92*
**Padavan,** Frank *WhoAmP 91*
**Padawer,** Jacques 1925- *AmMWSc 92*
**Padberg,** Harriet A 1922- *AmMWSc 92*
**Padberg,** Harriet Ann 1922- *WhoMW 92*
**Padberg,** Helen Swan *WhoEnt 92, WhoMW 92*
**Padberg,** John W. 1926- *WhoRel 92*
**Padberg,** Lawrence Frederick 1945- *WhoMW 92*
**Paddack,** Stephen J 1934- *AmMWSc 92*
**Padden,** Frank Joseph, Jr 1928- *AmMWSc 92*
**Padden,** Mike 1946- *WhoAmP 91*
**Paddio,** Gerald *WhoBlA 92*
**Paddio-Johnson,** Eunice Alice 1928- *WhoBlA 92*
**Paddison,** Fletcher C 1921- *AmMWSc 92*
**Paddison,** Richard Milton 1919- *AmMWSc 92*
**Paddock,** Elton Farnham 1913- *AmMWSc 92*
**Paddock,** Gary Vincent 1942- *AmMWSc 92*
**Paddock,** Jean K *AmMWSc 92*
**Paddock,** John *WhoMW 92*
**Paddock,** John Allen 1916- *WhoAmP 91*
**Paddock,** Paul Bradley 1942- *WhoFI 92*
**Paddock,** Robert Alton 1942- *AmMWSc 92*
**Paddock,** Ross Perry 1907- *RelLAm 91*
**Padegs,** Andris 1929- *AmMWSc 92*
**Padel,** Ruth 1946- *ConAu 134*
**Paden,** Carolyn Eileen Belknap 1953- *WhoMW 92*
**Paden,** Dallas Louis 1929- *WhoWest 92*
**Paden,** John Wilburn 1933- *AmMWSc 92*
**Paden,** Robert Charles 1942- *WhoMW 92*
**Pader,** Morton 1921- *AmMWSc 92*
**Paderewski,** Ignace Jan 1860-1941 *FacFETw, NewAmDM*
**Padfield,** Nicholas David 1947- *Who 92*
**Padfield,** Peter 1932- *WrDr 92*
**Padfield,** Peter Lawrence Notton 1932- *IntAu&W 91*
**Padgaonkar,** Dileep 1944- *IntWW 91*
**Padget,** John E. 1948- *WhoWest 92*
**Padgett,** Algie Ross 1911- *AmMWSc 92*
**Padgett,** Billie Lou 1930- *AmMWSc 92*
**Padgett,** Chester James 1942- *WhoFI 92*
**Padgett,** David Emerson 1945- *AmMWSc 92*
**Padgett,** David Ramon 1956- *WhoMW 92*
**Padgett,** Doran William 1925- *AmMWSc 92*
**Padgett,** Dorothy B 1927- *WhoAmP 91*
**Padgett,** Douglas Ralph Xavier 1942- *WhoAmL 92*
**Padgett,** Frank D 1923- *WhoAmP 91*
**Padgett,** Frank David 1923- *WhoAmL 92, WhoWest 92*
**Padgett,** George Arnold 1931- *AmMWSc 92*
**Padgett,** George Arthur 1932- *WhoAmL 92*
**Padgett,** James A. 1948- *WhoBlA 92*
**Padgett,** Kenneth W 1929- *WhoAmP 91*
**Padgett,** Lewis *TwCSFW 91*
**Padgett,** Mike 1923- *WhoAmP 91*
**Padgett,** Nina Hanenson 1956- *WhoEnt 92*
**Padgett,** Paul Marvin *WhoAmP 91*
**Padgett,** Ron *DrAPF 91*
**Padgett,** Ron 1942- *ConPo 91, WrDr 92*
**Padgett,** Shelton Edward 1948- *WhoAmL 92*
**Padgett,** Stanley Theodore 1957- *WhoAmL 92*
**Padgett,** Thomas Robert 1943- *WhoMW 92*
**Padgett,** Tom *DrAPF 91*
**Padgett,** William Jowayne 1943- *AmMWSc 92*
**Padgitt,** Dennis Darrell 1939- *AmMWSc 92*
**Padhi,** Sally Bulpitt 1944- *AmMWSc 92*
**Padia,** Anna Marie 1945- *WhoHisp 92*
**Padian,** Kevin 1951- *AmMWSc 92, WhoWest 92*
**Padilla,** Alonzo J. 1953- *WhoHisp 92*
**Padilla,** Amado Manuel 1942- *WhoHisp 92*
**Padilla,** Andrew, Jr 1937- *AmMWSc 92*
**Padilla,** Charlie B 1920- *WhoAmP 91*
**Padilla,** David Joseph, Jr. 1944- *WhoHisp 92*
**Padilla,** David P. 1949- *WhoHisp 92*
**Padilla,** Ernest A. *WhoHisp 92*
**Padilla,** Felix M. *WhoHisp 92*
**Padilla,** George Alonso 1945- *WhoHisp 92*
**Padilla,** George Jasso 1934- *WhoHisp 92*
**Padilla,** George M 1929- *AmMWSc 92*
**Padilla,** Geraro *WhoHisp 92*
**Padilla,** Gilbert 1929- *WhoHisp 92*
**Padilla,** Gilberto Cruz 1939- *WhoHisp 92*
**Padilla,** Heberto 1932- *ConSpAP, LiExTwC, WhoHisp 92*
**Padilla,** Hernan 1938- *WhoAmP 91, WhoHisp 92*
**Padilla,** Isaac F. *WhoHisp 92*
**Padilla,** James Earl 1953- *WhoAmL 92*
**Padilla,** James J. *WhoHisp 92*
**Padilla,** Kevin Joseph 1964- *WhoHisp 92*
**Padilla,** Leocadio Joseph 1927- *WhoHisp 92*
**Padilla,** Lorenzo Mamigo 1937- *WhoWest 92*
**Padilla,** Lorraine Marie 1952- *WhoFI 92*
**Padilla,** Lydia A. 1950- *WhoHisp 92*
**Padilla,** Maria Pacheco *EncAmaz 91*
**Padilla,** Mariam *WhoHisp 92*
**Padilla,** Michael A. *WhoHisp 92*
**Padilla,** Nancy A. 1950- *WhoHisp 92*
**Padilla,** Nancy Ann 1950- *WhoAmP 91*
**Padilla,** Patrick J. 1950- *WhoHisp 92*
**Padilla,** Paula Jeanette 1953- *WhoHisp 92*
**Padilla,** Raymond V. *WhoHisp 92*
**Padilla,** Richard 1949- *WhoHisp 92*
**Padilla,** Rudy 1940- *WhoHisp 92*
**Padilla,** Sally G. 1937- *WhoHisp 92*
**Padilla,** Wanda Maria 1948- *WhoHisp 92*
**Padilla,** William Joseph 1956- *WhoHisp 92*
**Padilla Arancibia,** David *IntWW 91*
**Padilla Lozano,** Jose Guadalupe 1920- *WhoRel 92*
**Padin,** Dion *WhoHisp 92*
**Padiyara,** Anthony 1921- *IntWW 91, WhoRel 92*
**Padlan,** Eduardo Agustin 1940- *AmMWSc 92*
**Padmanabhan,** G R 1935- *AmMWSc 92*
**Padmini** *EncAmaz 91*
**Padmore,** Lady *Who 92*
**Padmore,** Elaine Marguirite 1947- *Who 92*
**Padmore,** Gerald 1944- *WhoAmL 92*
**Padmore,** Joel M 1938- *AmMWSc 92*
**Padmore,** Thomas 1909- *Who 92*
**Padnos,** Norman 1937- *AmMWSc 92*
**Padoa-Schioppa,** Tommaso 1940- *IntWW 91*
**Padorr,** Laila 1929- *WhoEnt 92*
**Padovan,** John Mario Faskally 1938- *Who 92*
**Padovani,** Elaine Reeves 1938- *AmMWSc 92*
**Padovani,** Francois Antoine 1937- *AmMWSc 92*
**Padovano,** Annibale 1527-1575 *NewAmDM*
**Padovano,** Anthony T. 1934- *WrDr 92*
**Padovano,** Anthony Thomas *IntAu&W 91*
**Padovano,** Anthony Thomas 1934- *WhoRel 92*
**Padrick,** Richard Keith 1939- *WhoRel 92*
**Padrini,** Vittorio Arturo *AmMWSc 92*
**Padrnos,** Richard Scott 1957- *WhoWest 92*
**Padro,** Peter Louis, Jr. 1945- *WhoRel 92, WhoWest 92*
**Padron,** D. Lorenzo 1945- *WhoHisp 92*
**Padron,** Eduardo J. 1945- *WhoHisp 92*
**Padron,** Elida R. 1954- *WhoHisp 92*
**Padron,** Jorge Louis 1931- *AmMWSc 92*
**Padron,** Maria de Los Angeles 1955- *WhoHisp 92*
**Padron,** Peter E. *WhoHisp 92*
**Padrta,** Frank George 1930- *AmMWSc 92*
**Padua,** David A 1949- *AmMWSc 92*
**Padua,** Paul Mathias 1903-1981 *EncTR 91*
**Paduana,** Joseph A 1917- *AmMWSc 92*
**Padula,** Fred David 1937- *WhoEnt 92*
**Padula,** Mary L *WhoAmP 91*
**Padulo,** Louis 1936- *AmMWSc 92, WhoBlA 92*
**Padve,** Martha Bertonneau *WhoWest 92*
**Padwa,** Albert 1937- *AmMWSc 92*
**Padwa,** Allen Robert 1952- *AmMWSc 92*
**Padwater,** John Herrington 1966- *WhoFI 92*
**Padwe,** Carol 1944- *WhoWest 92*
**Pady,** Karen A. 1952- *WhoEnt 92*
**Padykula,** Helen Ann 1924- *AmMWSc 92*
**Pae Myung-In** 1932- *IntWW 91*
**Pae,** K D *AmMWSc 92*
**Paech,** Christian 1942- *AmMWSc 92*
**Paegle,** Julia Nogues 1943- *AmMWSc 92*
**Paer,** Ferdinando 1771-1839 *NewAmDM*
**Paesler,** Michael Arthur 1946- *AmMWSc 92*
**Paetkau,** Verner Henry 1941- *AmMWSc 92*
**Paetro,** Maxine 1946- *WrDr 92*
**Paez,** Jose Antonio 1790-1873 *HisDSpE*
**Paez,** Richard A. *WhoHisp 92*
**Paffard,** Michael 1928- *WrDr 92*
**Paffard,** Ronald Wilson 1904- *Who 92*
**Paffenbarger,** Ralph Seal, Jr 1922- *AmMWSc 92*
**Paffhouse,** Gregory Dale 1947- *WhoMW 92*
**Pafford,** John Henry Pyle 1900- *IntWW 91, Who 92, WrDr 92*
**Pafford,** William N 1929- *AmMWSc 92*
**Paffrath,** Hans-Georg 1922- *IntWW 91*
**Pagan,** Ana Ivelise 1957- *WhoHisp 92*
**Pagan,** Antonio 1963- *WhoHisp 92*
**Pagan,** Fernando L. 1943- *WhoHisp 92*
**Pagan,** John 1951- *WhoAmP 91*
**Pagan,** John Ruston 1951- *WhoAmL 92*
**Pagan,** Luz Maria 1928- *WhoFI 92*
**Pagan,** Michael Angel 1958- *WhoMW 92*
**Pagan,** Sam 1959- *WhoHisp 92*
**Pagan-Ayala,** Benjamin 1928- *WhoHisp 92*
**Pagan-Font,** Francisco Alfredo 1940- *AmMWSc 92*
**Paganelli,** Charles Victor 1929- *AmMWSc 92*
**Paganelli,** Robert P 1931- *WhoAmP 91*
**Pagani,** Albert Louis 1936- *WhoWest 92*
**Pagani,** Beverly Darlene 1937- *WhoWest 92*
**Paganini,** Emil Presley 1945- *WhoMW 92*
**Paganini,** Niccolo 1782-1840 *NewAmDM*
**Paganis,** K George 1937- *WhoIns 92*
**Pagano,** Alfred H 1930- *WhoAmP 91*
**Pagano,** Alfred Horton 1930- *AmMWSc 92*
**Pagano,** Anna Louise Reynolds 1933- *WhoRel 92*
**Pagano,** Anthony Frank 1948- *WhoAmL 92*
**Pagano,** Gino 1921- *IntWW 91*
**Pagano,** Joseph Frank 1919- *AmMWSc 92*
**Pagano,** Joseph Stephen 1931- *AmMWSc 92*
**Pagano,** Richard Emil 1944- *AmMWSc 92*
**Paganucci,** Paul Donnelly 1931- *WhoFI 92*
**Pagbalha Geleg Namgyai** 1940- *IntWW 91*
**Page** *Who 92*
**Page,** Alan Cameron 1942- *AmMWSc 92*
**Page,** Alan Cedric 1945- *WhoBlA 92*
**Page,** Albert Lee 1927- *AmMWSc 92*
**Page,** Alexander Warren 1914- *IntWW 91, Who 92*
**Page,** Alfred Emil, Jr. 1938- *WhoAmL 92*
**Page,** Aline Hammond 1946- *WhoWest 92*
**Page,** Ann 1958- *WhoFI 92*
**Page,** Annette 1932- *Who 92*
**Page,** Anthony 1935- *IntMPA 92, Who 92*
**Page,** Arthur John 1919- *Who 92*
**Page,** Arthur R 1930- *AmMWSc 92*
**Page,** Ashley 1956- *WhoEnt 92*
**Page,** Benjamin Ingrim 1940- *WhoMW 92*
**Page,** Benjamin Markham 1911- *AmMWSc 92*
**Page,** Bertram Samuel 1904- *Who 92*
**Page,** Bruce 1936- *IntAu&W 91, IntWW 91, Who 92*
**Page,** Carl Victor 1938- *AmMWSc 92*
**Page,** Catherine Anne 1963- *WhoMW 92*
**Page,** Cedric Daniel 1945- *WhoBlA 92*
**Page,** Charles Edward 1920- *Who 92*
**Page,** Charles Grafton 1812-1868 *BiInAmS*
**Page,** Charles H 1909- *IntAu&W 91, WrDr 92*
**Page,** Charles Henry 1941- *AmMWSc 92*
**Page,** Chester H 1912- *AmMWSc 92*
**Page,** Curtis Matthewson 1946- *WhoRel 92, WhoWest 92*
**Page,** Cyril Leslie 1916- *Who 92*
**Page,** D J 1937- *AmMWSc 92*
**Page,** David 1952- *WhoEnt 92*
**Page,** David L 1941- *AmMWSc 92*
**Page,** David Sanborn 1943- *AmMWSc 92*
**Page,** Dennis Fountain 1919- *Who 92*
**Page,** Derek Howard 1929- *AmMWSc 92*
**Page,** Diana 1946- *IntAu&W 91*
**Page,** Dozzie Lyons 1921- *WhoMW 92*
**Page,** Earl Michael 1950- *WhoFI 92*
**Page,** Edgar J 1919- *AmMWSc 92*
**Page,** Edwin Howard 1920- *AmMWSc 92*
**Page,** Edwin Kenneth 1898- *Who 92*
**Page,** Eleanor *IntAu&W 91X, SmATA 67*
**Page,** Elizabeth 1889- *BenetAL 91*
**Page,** Emma *IntAu&W 91, WrDr 92*
**Page,** Ernest 1927- *AmMWSc 92*
**Page,** Ewan Stafford 1928- *IntWW 91, Who 92*
**Page,** Frederick 1917- *Who 92*
**Page,** Frederick Forest 1943- *WhoEnt 92*
**Page,** Genevieve 1927- *IntWW 91*
**Page,** Geoff 1940- *ConAu 133, ConPo 91, WrDr 92*
**Page,** Gregory Oliver 1950- *WhoBlA 92*
**Page,** Harrison Eugene 1941- *WhoBlA 92*
**Page,** Hot Lips 1908-1954 *NewAmDM*
**Page,** Howard William Barrett 1943- *Who 92*
**Page,** Irvine H. 1901-1991 *CurBio 91N, NewYTBS 91 [port]*
**Page,** Irvine Heinly 1901- *AmMWSc 92, IntWW 91*
**Page,** J. Boyd 1948- *WhoAmL 92*
**Page,** Jack Randall 1956- *WhoAmL 92*
**Page,** Jake *ConAu 35NR*
**Page,** James Allen 1918- *WhoBlA 92*
**Page,** James Jefferson 1949- *WhoFI 92*
**Page,** James K, Jr. 1936- *ConAu 35NR*
**Page,** Jean-Guy 1926- *WhoRel 92*
**Page,** Jennifer Anne 1944- *Who 92*
**Page,** Jennifer Lorraine 1962- *WhoWest 92*
**Page,** Jerry 1961- *BlkOlyM*
**Page,** Joanna R Ziegler 1938- *AmMWSc 92*
**Page,** John *Who 92*
**Page,** John Boyd, Jr 1938- *AmMWSc 92*
**Page,** John Brangwyn 1923- *IntWW 91, Who 92*
**Page,** John C 1924- *WhoAmP 91*
**Page,** John David 1950- *WhoFI 92, WhoWest 92*
**Page,** John Gardner 1940- *AmMWSc 92*
**Page,** John Humphrey 1923- *Who 92*
**Page,** John Irwin 1930- *WhoRel 92*
**Page,** John Joseph Joffre 1915- *Who 92*
**Page,** John Kenneth 1924- *Who 92*
**Page,** John Sheridan, Jr. 1942- *WhoBlA 92*
**Page,** Joseph French, III 1942- *WhoAmL 92*
**Page,** Kathy 1958- *ConAu 133, WrDr 92*
**Page,** Kenneth *Who 92*
**Page,** Kirby 1890-1957 *AmPeW*
**Page,** Larry J 1941- *AmMWSc 92*
**Page,** Larry Waldron 1955- *WhoWest 92*
**Page,** Lawrence Merle 1944- *AmMWSc 92*
**Page,** Leslie Andrew 1924- *WhoWest 92*
**Page,** Lincoln Ridler 1910- *AmMWSc 92*
**Page,** Linda Kay 1943- *WhoFI 92*
**Page,** Logan Waller 1870-1918 *BiInAmS*
**Page,** Lorne Albert 1921- *AmMWSc 92*
**Page,** Lot Bates 1923- *AmMWSc 92*
**Page,** Louise *AmMWSc 92*
**Page,** Louise 1955- *IntAu&W 91, WrDr 92*
**Page,** Malcolm I 1930- *AmMWSc 92*
**Page,** Marguerite A. *WhoBlA 92*
**Page,** Marilyle Sweet 1942- *WhoRel 92*
**Page,** Matthew John 1929- *WhoAmP 91*
**Page,** Michel 1940- *AmMWSc 92*
**Page,** Nancy Rickards 1956- *WhoFI 92*
**Page,** Nelson Franklin 1938- *AmMWSc 92*
**Page,** Norbert Paul 1932- *AmMWSc 92*
**Page,** Norman 1930- *IntAu&W 91, WrDr 92*
**Page,** Norman J 1939- *AmMWSc 92*
**Page,** Oran Charles 1939- *WhoAmL 92*
**Page,** P. K. 1916- *BenetAL 91, ConPo 91, RfGEnL 91, WrDr 92*
**Page,** Patricia Kathleen 1916- *IntAu&W 91*
**Page,** Patti 1927- *IntMPA 92, NewAmDM*
**Page,** Peter Crozer 1946- *WhoWest 92*
**Page,** Ralph E. d1991 *NewYTBS 91*
**Page,** Raymond Ian 1924- *Who 92*
**Page,** Rebecca Hazel 1956- *WhoEnt 92*
**Page,** Rector Lee 1944- *AmMWSc 92*
**Page,** Richard Lewis 1941- *Who 92*
**Page,** Richard M 1926- *WhoIns 92*
**Page,** Robert Alan, Jr 1938- *AmMWSc 92*
**Page,** Robert Eugene, Jr 1949- *AmMWSc 92*
**Page,** Robert Griffith 1921- *AmMWSc 92*
**Page,** Robert Henry 1927- *AmMWSc 92*
**Page,** Robert Jeffress 1922- *WhoRel 92*
**Page,** Robert Leroy 1931- *AmMWSc 92*
**Page,** Robin 1943- *IntAu&W 91, WrDr 92*
**Page,** Rodney Fred 1946- *WhoAmL 92*
**Pages,** Rodney I. *WhoRel 92*
**Page,** Rosemary Saxton 1927- *WhoBlA 92*
**Page,** Roy Christopher 1932- *AmMWSc 92*
**Page,** Ruth 1899-1991 *CurBio 91N, FacFETw, NewYTBS 91 [port]*
**Page,** Ruth Joanne 1945- *WhoMW 92*
**Page,** Sally Jacquelyn 1943- *WhoMW 92*
**Page,** Samuel William 1945- *AmMWSc 92*
**Page,** Sandra Rector 1946- *WhoAmP 91*
**Page,** Simon Richard 1934- *Who 92*
**Page,** Stanley Stephen 1937- *AmMWSc 92*
**Page,** Stephen Allen 1952- *WhoAmP 91*
**Page,** Stephen Franklin 1940- *WhoFI 92*
**Page,** Steven Michael 1949- *WhoMW 92*
**Page,** Thomas Alexander 1933- *WhoFI 92, WhoWest 92*
**Page,** Thomas Cramer 1920- *WhoFI 92, WhoMW 92*
**Page,** Thomas Lee 1941- *AmMWSc 92*
**Page,** Thomas Nelson 1853-1922 *BenetAL 91*
**Page,** Thornton Leigh 1913- *AmMWSc 92*
**Page,** Tom *DrAPF 91*
**Page,** Vicky *IntAu&W 91X*
**Page,** Walter 1900-1957 *NewAmDM*
**Page,** Walter Hines 1855-1918 *BenetAL 91, FacFETw*
**Page,** William *DrAPF 91*
**Page,** William 1929- *ConAu 35NR*
**Page,** William Perren 1938- *WhoEnt 92*
**Page,** Willie F. 1929- *WhoBlA 92*
**Page,** Willis *WhoEnt 92*
**Page Wood,** Anthony John 1951- *Who 92*
**Pagel,** Bernard Ephraim Julius 1930- *Who 92*
**Pagel,** Josanne Kissel 1956- *WhoMW 92*
**Pagels,** Elaine *WrDr 92*
**Pagels,** Elaine Hiesey *WhoRel 92*
**Pagels,** Jurgen Heinrich 1925- *WhoEnt 92*
**Pagenkopf,** Andrea L 1942- *AmMWSc 92*
**Pagenkopf,** Gordon K 1941- *AmMWSc 92*
**Pageotte,** Donald P 1926- *WhoAmP 91*
**Pager,** David 1935- *AmMWSc 92*

Pages, Ernest Alexander 1959- WhoHisp 92
Pages, Robert Alex 1941- AmMWSc 92
Paget Who 92
Paget, Allen Maxwell 1919- WhoFI 92
Paget, David Christopher John 1942- Who 92
Paget, Debra 1933- IntMPA 92
Paget, John 1914- Who 92
Paget, John Arthur 1922- WhoWest 92
Paget, Julian 1921- Who 92, WrDr 92
Paget, Richard M d1991 NewYTBS 91
Paget De Beaudesert, Lord 1986- Who 92
Paget-Lowe, Henry ConAu 133
Paget-Wilkes, Michael Jocelyn James 1941- Who 92
Pagett, Betty Strathman 1941- WhoRel 92
Pagett, Nicola 1945- IntMPA 92
Pagis, Dan 1931-1986 FacFETw
Pagis, Dom 1930-1986 LiExTwC
Paglia, Camille 1947- ConLC 68 [port]
Pagliarini, Ronald James 1957- WhoAmP 91
Pagliaro, Frank Joseph, Jr 1940- WhoAmP 91
Pagliaro, James Domenic 1951- WhoAmL 92
Pagliughi, Gloria F WhoAmP 91
Pagnamenta, Antonio 1934- AmMWSc 92
Pagnamenta, Peter John 1941- Who 92
Pagni, Patrick John 1942- AmMWSc 92
Pagni, Richard 1941- AmMWSc 92
Pagnol, Marcel 1895-1974 GuFrLit 1, IntDcF 2-2 [port]
Pagnozzi, Richard Douglas 1947- WhoIns 92
Pagnucci, Gianfranco DrAPF 91
Pagoria, Michael Philip 1955- WhoFI 92
Pagosa, Dorothy Catherine 1954- WhoRel 92
Pagter, Carl Richard 1934- IntAu&W 91, WhoAmL 92
Pahang, Sultan of 1930- IntWW 91
Pahl, Herbert Bowen 1927- AmMWSc 92
Pahlavi, Farah Diba 1938- IntWW 91
Pahlevi, Muhammad Reza 1919-1980 FacFETw [port]
Pahlevi, Reza 1878-1944 FacFETw
Pahlmann, William C. 1900-1987 DcTwDes
Pahr, Willibald P. 1930- IntWW 91
Pahwa, Anil 1954- WhoMW 92
Pai Hsin-yung 1937- LiExTwC
Pai, Anantha M 1931- AmMWSc 92
Pai, Anna Chao 1935- AmMWSc 92
Pai, Damodar Mangalore AmMWSc 92
Pai, David H-C 1936- AmMWSc 92
Pai, Mangalore Anantha 1931- AmMWSc 92
Pai, Paul Tsu-Chiang 1941- WhoWest 92
Pai, S I 1913- AmMWSc 92
Pai, Sadanand V 1937- AmMWSc 92
Pai, Venkatrao K 1939- AmMWSc 92
Paiba, Denis Anthony 1926- Who 92
Paice, James Edward Thornton 1949- Who 92
Paice, Karlo Bruce 1906- Who 92
Paice, Michael 1949- AmMWSc 92
Paice, Philip Stuart 1884-1940 TwCPaSc
Paicopolos, Michael F 1920- WhoAmP 91
Paidoussis, Michael Pandeli 1935- AmMWSc 92
Paiewonsky, Ralph 1907- WhoAmP 91
Paiewonsky, Ralph M. d1991 NewYTBS 91
Paige, Alvin 1934- WhoBlA 92
Paige, David ConAu 36NR
Paige, David A 1957- AmMWSc 92
Paige, David M 1918- AmMWSc 92
Paige, David M 1939- AmMWSc 92
Paige, Edward George Sydney 1930- Who 92
Paige, Emmett, Jr. 1931- WhoBlA 92
Paige, Eugene 1929- AmMWSc 92
Paige, Frank Eaton, Jr 1944- AmMWSc 92
Paige, Hilliard W 1919- AmMWSc 92
Paige, Janis 1923- IntMPA 92
Paige, Janis 1925- WhoEnt 92
Paige, Leroy 1906?-1982 FacFETw
Paige, Lowell J. 1919- WhoWest 92
Paige, Norma 1922- WhoMW 92
Paige, Paul 1934- WhoWest 92
Paige, Richard ConAu 36NR
Paige, Richard Collings 1911- Who 92
Paige, Roderick 1935- WhoBlA 92
Paige, Russell Alston 1929- AmMWSc 92
Paige, Stephone 1961- WhoBlA 92
Paige, Victor Grellier 1925- IntWW 91, Who 92
Paigen, Beverly Joyce 1938- AmMWSc 92
Paigen, Kenneth 1927- AmMWSc 92
Paik Byung-dong 1936- ConCom 92
Paik, Ho Jung 1944- AmMWSc 92
Paik, Kun Woo 1946- IntWW 91
Paik, Nam June LesBEnT 92
Paik, Nam June 1932- NewAmDM, WorArt 1980 [port]
Paik, S F 1935- AmMWSc 92
Paik, Woon Ki 1925- AmMWSc 92
Paikoff, Myron 1932- AmMWSc 92
Pailen, Donald 1941- WhoBlA 92
Paillard, Jean-Francois 1928- NewAmDM
Pailthorp, John Raymond 1920- AmMWSc 92
Pailthorpe, Grace W. 1883-1971 TwCPaSc
Paim, Uno 1922- AmMWSc 92
Pain, Barry 1864-1928 ScFEYrs
Pain, Barry Newton 1931- Who 92
Pain, Horace Rollo 1921- Who 92
Pain, Peter 1913- Who 92
Pain, Philip BenetAL 91
Pain, Rollo Who 92
Paine, Albert Bigelow 1861-1937 BenetAL 91, ScFEYrs
Paine, Barbara Gordon DrAPF 91
Paine, Bruce Edwin 1933- WhoFI 92
Paine, Charles F. 1920- IntMPA 92
Paine, Clair Maynard 1930- AmMWSc 92
Paine, David Philip 1929- AmMWSc 92
Paine, Dwight Milton 1931- AmMWSc 92
Paine, George 1918- Who 92
Paine, James Carriger 1924- WhoAmL 92
Paine, John Alsop 1840-1912 BilnAmS
Paine, John Knowles 1839-1906 NewAmDM
Paine, Lauran 1916- TwCWW 91
Paine, Lee Alfred 1920- AmMWSc 92
Paine, Marylin J 1931- WhoAmP 91
Paine, Peter Stanley 1921- Who 92
Paine, Philip Lowell 1945- AmMWSc 92
Paine, Ralph D. 1871-1925 BenetAL 91
Paine, Ralph Delahaye, Jr. d1991 NewYTBS 91
Paine, Richard Bradford 1928- AmMWSc 92
Paine, Robert Madison 1925- AmMWSc 92
Paine, Robert T 1933- AmMWSc 92
Paine, Robert Treat 1731-1814 BenetAL 91
Paine, Robert Treat 1773-1811 BenetAL 91
Paine, Robert Treat 1803-1885 BilnAmS
Paine, Robert Treat, Jr 1944- AmMWSc 92
Paine, Roger Edward 1943- Who 92
Paine, Stephen Curtiss 1932- WhoMW 92
Paine, T O 1921- AmMWSc 92
Paine, Thomas 1737-1809 AmPolLe [port], BenetAL 91, BlkwCEP, BlkwEAR [port], RComAH, RfGEnL 91
Paine, Thomas 1921- FacFETw
Paine, Thomas Fite, Jr 1918- AmMWSc 92
Paine, Thomas Otten 1921- IntWW 91, Who 92, WhoWest 92
Paintal, Amreek Singh 1940- AmMWSc 92
Paintal, Autar Singh 1925- IntWW 91, Who 92
Paintal, Priti 1960- ConCom 92
Painter, Amelia Ann 1946- WhoWest 92
Painter, Ann B 1920- WhoAmP 91
Painter, Charlotte DrAPF 91, WrDr 92
Painter, Gayle Stanford 1941- AmMWSc 92
Painter, George Duncan 1914- Who 92
Painter, Helen 1913- WrDr 92
Painter, Jack T 1930- AmMWSc 92
Painter, James Howard 1935- AmMWSc 92
Painter, James Morgan 1952- WhoAmL 92
Painter, Jeffrey Farrar 1951- AmMWSc 92
Painter, John 1935- WrDr 92
Painter, Joseph H d1908 BilnAmS
Painter, Kent 1942- AmMWSc 92
Painter, Linda Robinson 1940- AmMWSc 92
Painter, Mark Philip 1947- WhoAmL 92, WhoMW 92
Painter, Nell Irvin 1942- NotBlAW 92, WhoBlA 92
Painter, Pamela DrAPF 91
Painter, Richard J 1931- AmMWSc 92
Painter, Robert Blair 1924- AmMWSc 92
Painter, Robert Hilton 1932- AmMWSc 92
Painter, Ronald Dean 1945- AmMWSc 92
Painter, Ruth Coburn Robbins 1910- AmMWSc 92
Painter, Terence James 1935- Who 92
Painter, Thomas Jay 1944- WhoFI 92
Painter, William Hall 1927- WhoAmL 92
Painter, William Ralph WhoRel 92
Painting, Rodger T 1938- WhoIns 92
Painton, Russell Elliott 1940- WhoAmL 92
Pair, Claude H 1911- AmMWSc 92
Paire, Newell J WhoAmP 91
Pais, Abraham 1918- AmMWSc 92, IntWW 91
Pais, Arie 1930- IntWW 91
Pais, Josh 1958- WhoEnt 92
Pais, Mara Devine 1959- WhoAmL 92
Paisano, Roberta Elizabeth 1957- WhoWest 92
Paisant, Immaculata WhoRel 92
Paisiello, Giovanni 1740-1816 BlkwCEP, NewAmDM
Paisley, Bishop of 1929- Who 92
Paisley, David M 1935- AmMWSc 92
Paisley, Ian 1926- FacFETw
Paisley, Ian Richard Kyle 1926- IntWW 91, Who 92
Paisley, Keith W 1928- WhoAmP 91
Paisley, Mark Alan 1949- WhoMW 92
Paisley, Melvyn R 1924- WhoAmP 91
Paisley, Nancy Sandelin 1936- AmMWSc 92
Paisley, Robert 1919- Who 92
Paisley, Tom 1932- WhoEnt 92
Paisner, Bruce LesBEnT 92
Paisner, Bruce Lawrence 1942- WhoEnt 92
Pait, Larry Richard 1954- WhoEnt 92
Pait, Royedon Gillispie 1956- WhoWest 92
Paiva, Joseph Moura 1955- WhoFI 92
Pajak, David Joseph 1956- WhoAmL 92
Pajak, Penelope Anne 1947- WhoAmP 91
Pajamies, Esko DcTwDes
Pajari, George Edward 1936- AmMWSc 92
Pajaud, William E. 1925- WhoBlA 92
Pajcic, Steve WhoAmP 91
Pajer, Robert John 1947- WhoFI 92
Pajestka, Jozef 1924- IntWW 91
Pajil, Cheryl V. 1949- WhoHisp 92
Pajka, Ralph Stanley 1952- WhoMW 92
Pajot, Gilles-Etienne 1958- WhoFI 92
Pak, Charles Y 1935- AmMWSc 92
Pak, Ronald Y S 1957- AmMWSc 92
Pak, William Louis 1932- AmMWSc 92
Pakdemirli, Ekrem IntWW 91
Pake, George Edward 1924- AmMWSc 92, IntWW 91
Pakenham Who 92
Pakenham, Elizabeth Who 92
Pakenham, Henry Desmond Verner 1911- Who 92
Pakenham, Michael Aidan 1943- Who 92
Pakenham, Thomas 1933- Who 92, WrDr 92
Pakenham-Walsh, John 1928- Who 92
Pakes, Steven P 1934- AmMWSc 92
Pakhmutova, Aleksandra Nikolaevna 1929- SovUnBD
Pakhomov, Aleksandr Fedorovich 1900-1973 SovUnBD
Pakington Who 92
Pakiser, Louis Charles, Jr 1919- AmMWSc 92, WhoWest 92
Pakman, Leonard Marvin 1933- AmMWSc 92
Pakula, Alan J. 1928- IntDcF 2-2 [port], IntMPA 92, IntWW 91, WhoEnt 92
Pakula, Hannah IntAu&W 91
Pakula, Leonard Anthony 1945- WhoEnt 92
Pakvasa, Sandip 1935- AmMWSc 92, WhoWest 92
Pal, Benjamin Peary d1989 IntWW 91N
Pal, Dhiraj 1948- AmMWSc 92
Pal, George 1908-1980 FacFETw
Pal, Lenard 1925- IntWW 91
Pal, Prabir Kumar 1936- WhoFI 92
Pal, Pratapaditya 1935- WrDr 92
Palabrica, Christopher Alan 1963- WhoMW 92
Palacas, James George 1930- AmMWSc 92
Palace, Kristin Munro 1957- WhoAmL 92
Palacino, John Michael 1959- WhoEnt 92
Palacio, Ernesto 1900-1979 BiDExR
Palacio, Jose Luis 1947- WhoFI 92
Palacios, Arturo 1961- WhoHisp 92
Palacios, Enrique 1935- WhoMW 92
Palacios, Gloria P. 1965- WhoRel 92
Palacios, Jeannette C. De 1946- WhoHisp 92
Palacios, Luis E. 1956- WhoHisp 92
Palacios, Magno WhoHisp 92
PaLacios, Omar Lawrence 1958- WhoWest 92
Palacios, Pedro Pablo 1953- WhoWest 92
Palacios, Raphael R. WhoHisp 92
Palacios, Vicente 1963- WhoHisp 92
Palacios De Vizzio, Sergio 1936- IntWW 91, WhoAmL 92
Palacioz, Joe John 1948- WhoHisp 92
Palacol, Cecilia Batnag 1941- WhoWest 92
Palade, George E 1912- AmMWSc 92
Palade, George Emil 1912- FacFETw, IntWW 91, Who 92, WhoNob 90, WhoWest 92
Paladino, Albert Edward 1932- WhoFI 92
Paladino, Daniel R. WhoAmL 92
Paladino, Frank Vincent 1952- AmMWSc 92, WhoMW 92
Palaeologina, Helen EncAmaz 91
Palaia, Joseph A 1927- WhoAmP 91
Palaic, Djuro 1937- AmMWSc 92
Palais, Joseph C 1936- AmMWSc 92
Palais, Richard Sheldon 1931- AmMWSc 92
Palamand, Suryanarayana Rao AmMWSc 92, WhoMW 92
Palamara, Joseph WhoAmP 91
Palance, Jack WhoEnt 92
Palance, Jack 1920- IntMPA 92
Palandech, John R. DcAmImH
Palandt, Otto 1877-1951 EncTR 91
Palaniswamy, Pachagounder 1945- AmMWSc 92
Palanker, Louise Gail 1956- WhoEnt 92
Palar, Lambertus N 1902-1981 FacFETw
Palas, Frank Joseph 1918- AmMWSc 92
Palaszek, Mary De Paul 1935- AmMWSc 92
Palatiello, John Michael 1955- WhoFI 92
Palatnick, Barton 1940- AmMWSc 92
Palaty, Vladimir 1933- AmMWSc 92
Palau, Luis 1934- IntWW 91, WhoHisp 92, WhoRel 92
Palay, Sanford Louis 1918- AmMWSc 92
Palayew, Max Jacob 1930- AmMWSc 92
Palazotto, Anthony Nicholas 1935- AmMWSc 92
Palazuelos, Ramon 1929- WhoHisp 92
Palazzeschi, Aldo 1885-1974 DcLB 114 [port]
Palazzi, Francis Andrew 1962- WhoEnt 92
Palazzi, Joseph Lazarro 1947- WhoFI 92
Palazzini, Pietro 1912- IntWW 91, WhoRel 92
Palazzo, Frank J 1917- WhoAmP 91
Palazzolo, Tom 1937- WhoEnt 92
Palchak, Robert Joseph Francis 1927- AmMWSc 92
Palchesko, David Alan 1955- WhoMW 92
Palchinsky, Peter Ioakimovich 1875-1929 FacFETw
Palcisko, Bernard Jerome 1951- WhoMW 92
Palcy, Euzhan ReelWom, WhoBlA 92
Palcy, Euzhan 1957- IntMPA 92
Palczuk, Nicholas C 1927- AmMWSc 92
Paldus, Josef 1935- AmMWSc 92
Paldy, Lester George 1934- AmMWSc 92
Palek, Jiri Frant AmMWSc 92
Palen, Jennie M. DrAPF 91
Palen, Joseph W 1935- AmMWSc 92
Palen, Theodore Edward 1954- WhoWest 92
Palencia, Elaine Fowler DrAPF 91
Palencia-Roth, Michael 1946- WhoHisp 92, WhoMW 92
Palenik, Gus J 1933- AmMWSc 92
Paleologos, Nicholas Arthur 1953- WhoAmP 91
Palepu, Krishna Gour 1954- WhoFI 92
Palermino, Anthony J WhoAmP 91
Palermo, Anthony Robert 1929- WhoAmL 92
Palermo, Felice Charles 1931- AmMWSc 92
Palermo, Joseph Leo 1958- WhoEnt 92
Palermo, Norman Anthony 1937- WhoAmL 92
Palestine, Alan G 1952- AmMWSc 92
Palestine, Charlemagne 1945- NewAmDM
Palestrina, Giovanni Pierluigi da 1525-1594 NewAmDM
Palethorpe-Todd, Richard Andrew Who 92
Palette, John 1928- Who 92
Paletti, Paul Raymond, Jr. 1950- WhoAmL 92
Palevitz, Barry Allan 1944- AmMWSc 92
Palevsky, Gerald 1926- AmMWSc 92
Paley, Grace DrAPF 91
Paley, Grace 1922- BenetAL 91, ConNov 91, HanAmWH, IntWW 91, ModAWWr, ShSCr 8 [port], WrDr 92
Paley, Hiram 1933- AmMWSc 92
Paley, Maggie DrAPF 91
Paley, Richard Thomas 1936- WhoFI 92
Paley, Vivian Gussin 1929- WrDr 92
Paley, William S. d1990 IntWW 91N, LesBEnT 92 [port]
Paley, William S. 1901-1990 AnObit 1990, CurBio 91N, FacFETw, News 91
Palffy, Fidel 1895-1946 BiDExR
Palffy-Muhoray, Peter 1944- AmMWSc 92
Palfree, Roger Grenville Eric 1946- AmMWSc 92
Palfrey, John Gorham 1796-1881 BenetAL 91
Palfrey, Thomas Rossman, Jr 1925- AmMWSc 92
Palfreyman, Michael Gavin 1945- WhoMW 92
Paliganoff, David James 1941- WhoMW 92
Palik, Edward Daniel 1928- AmMWSc 92
Palik, Emil Samuel 1923- AmMWSc 92
Palileo, Hazel Valencia 1951- WhoEnt 92
Palilla, Frank C 1925- AmMWSc 92
Palin, Michael 1943- ConAu 35NR, IntMPA 92, SmATA 67 [port], WrDr 92
Palin, Michael Edward 1943- IntAu&W 91, IntWW 91, Who 92
Palin, Roger Hewlett Who 92
Palincsar, Edward Emil 1920- AmMWSc 92
Paling, Helen Elizabeth 1933- Who 92
Paling, William Thomas 1892- Who 92
Palinkas, James Thomas 1945- WhoFI 92

**Palisano**, John Raymond 1947- *AmMWSc 92*
**Paliwal**, Bhudatt R 1938- *AmMWSc 92*
**Paliwal**, Yogesh Chandra 1942- *AmMWSc 92*
**Palizzi**, Anthony N. 1942- *WhoAmL 92, WhoFI 92*
**Palka**, John Milan 1939- *AmMWSc 92*
**Palke**, William England 1941- *AmMWSc 92*
**Palkhivala**, Nani Ardeshir 1920- *IntWW 91*
**Palkovitz**, Herbert 1942- *WhoAmL 92*
**Pall**, Cary David 1953- *WhoEnt 92*
**Pall**, David B *AmMWSc 92*
**Pall**, Ellen Jane 1952- *WhoEnt 92*
**Pall**, Martin L 1942- *AmMWSc 92*
**Palladino**, Madaline 1924- *WhoAmL 92*
**Palladino**, Nunzio J 1916- *AmMWSc 92*
**Palladino**, Richard Walter 1933- *AmMWSc 92*
**Palladino**, Vincent Oliver 1929- *WhoAmP 91*
**Palladino**, William Joseph 1947- *AmMWSc 92*
**Palladius** 365?-425 *EncEarC*
**Pallaev**, Gaibnazar 1929- *IntWW 91*
**Pallak**, Michael 1942- *AmMWSc 92*
**Pallam**, John James 1940- *WhoAmL 92, WhoFI 92*
**Pallander**, Edwin *ScFEYrs*
**Pallansch**, Michael J 1918- *AmMWSc 92*
**Pallant**, Cheryl *DrAPF 91*
**Pallant**, Layeh *DrAPF 91*
**Pallardy**, Stephen Gerard 1951- *AmMWSc 92*
**Pallardy**, Tom Patrick 1947- *WhoEnt 92*
**Pallares**, Mariano 1943- *WhoHisp 92*
**Pallas**, Gregory 1951- *WhoAmP 91*
**Pallasch**, B. Michael 1933- *WhoAmL 92, WhoMW 92*
**Pallasch**, Brian Thomas 1965- *WhoFI 92*
**Pallavicini**, Maria Georgina 1952- *AmMWSc 92*
**Paller**, Mark Stephen 1952- *AmMWSc 92*
**Pallett**, David Stephen 1938- *AmMWSc 92*
**Palley**, Claire Dorothea Taylor 1931- *Who 92*
**Palley**, Robert Lloyd 1958- *WhoMW 92*
**Palli**, Paolo Gaetano 1939- *WhoFI 92*
**Palliser**, Charles 1947- *ConNov 91, WrDr 92*
**Palliser**, Charles 1948?- *ConLC 65 [port]*
**Palliser**, Herbert William 1883-1963 *TwCPaSc*
**Palliser**, Michael 1922- *IntWW 91, Who 92*
**Pallister**, Janis *DrAPF 91*
**Pallmann**, Albert J 1926- *AmMWSc 92*
**Pallone**, Adrian Joseph 1928- *AmMWSc 92*
**Pallone**, Frank, Jr. 1951- *AlmAP 92 [port], WhoAmP 91*
**Pallone**, Joseph Andrew 1947- *WhoFI 92*
**Pallos**, Ferenc M 1933- *AmMWSc 92*
**Pallot**, Arthur Keith 1918- *Who 92*
**Pallot**, E. Albert 1908- *WhoAmL 92*
**Pallotta**, Barry S 1951- *AmMWSc 92*
**Pallotta**, Dominick John 1942- *AmMWSc 92*
**Pallottino**, Massimo 1909- *IntWW 91*
**Palluconi**, Frank Don 1939- *AmMWSc 92*
**Palm**, Charles Gilman 1944- *WhoWest 92*
**Palm**, Ed 1934- *WhoAmP 91*
**Palm**, Elmer Thurman 1927- *AmMWSc 92*
**Palm**, Gary Howard 1942- *WhoAmL 92*
**Palm**, Gerald Albert 1942- *WhoAmL 92*
**Palm**, John Daniel 1924- *AmMWSc 92*
**Palm**, John Milton, Jr. 1939- *WhoMW 92*
**Palm**, Marion *DrAPF 91*
**Palm**, Mary Egdahl 1954- *AmMWSc 92*
**Palm**, Nancy Cleone 1939- *WhoFI 92, WhoWest 92*
**Palm**, Sally Louise *AmMWSc 92*
**Palm**, Scott Kevin 1958- *WhoFI 92*
**Palm**, Siegfried 1927- *NewAmDM*
**Palm**, T. Arthur 1954- *WhoFI 92*
**Palm**, William John 1944- *AmMWSc 92*
**Palma**, Henry, Sr. 1933- *WhoHisp 92*
**Palma**, Michael John 1956- *WhoAmL 92*
**Palma**, Nicholas James 1953- *WhoAmL 92*
**Palma**, Raul Arnulfo 1925- *WhoHisp 92*
**Palma**, Ricardo 1833-1919 *BenetAL 91*
**Palmadesso**, Peter Joseph 1940- *AmMWSc 92*
**Palmanteer**, Ted *DrAPF 91*
**Palmar**, Derek 1919- *IntWW 91, Who 92*
**Palmarez**, Sulema E. 1957- *WhoHisp 92*
**Palmas**, Angelo 1914- *WhoRel 92*
**Palmatier**, Elmer Arthur 1912- *AmMWSc 92*
**Palmatier**, Everett Dyson 1917- *AmMWSc 92*
**Palmatier**, Malcolm Arthur 1922- *WhoWest 92*
**Palmblad**, Ivan G 1938- *AmMWSc 92*
**Palme**, Olof 1927-1986 *FacFETw*
**Palmedo**, Philip F 1934- *AmMWSc 92*
**Palmeira**, Ricardo Antonio Ribeiro 1930- *AmMWSc 92*
**Palmeiro**, Rafael Corrales 1964- *WhoHisp 92*
**Palmer** *Who 92*
**Palmer**, Baron 1951- *Who 92*
**Palmer**, Alan 1936- *AmMWSc 92, WhoWest 92*
**Palmer**, Alan Blakeslee 1934- *AmMWSc 92*
**Palmer**, Alan Kenneth 1941- *WhoAmL 92*
**Palmer**, Alan Warwick 1926- *IntAu&W 91, WrDr 92*
**Palmer**, Alexander Mitchell 1872-1936 *AmPolLe*
**Palmer**, Alfred 1877-1951 *TwCPaSc*
**Palmer**, Alice *WhoAmP 91*
**Palmer**, Alice Freeman 1855-1902 *BenetAL 91*
**Palmer**, Allison Ralph 1927- *AmMWSc 92*
**Palmer**, Andrew Eustace 1937- *Who 92*
**Palmer**, Ann Therese Darin 1951- *WhoAmL 92*
**Palmer**, Anthony Thomas Richard 1941- *Who 92*
**Palmer**, Anthony Wheeler 1936- *Who 92*
**Palmer**, Arnold 1929- *FacFETw*
**Palmer**, Arnold Daniel 1929- *IntWW 91, Who 92, WhoEnt 92*
**Palmer**, Arthur Montague Frank 1912- *Who 92*
**Palmer**, Arthur N 1940- *AmMWSc 92*
**Palmer**, Arthur William 1861-1904 *BiInAmS*
**Palmer**, Bernard 1914- *TwCWW 91*
**Palmer**, Bernard Harold Michael 1929- *Who 92*
**Palmer**, Berthina E. 1927- *WhoBlA 92*
**Palmer**, Betsy *LesBEnT 92*
**Palmer**, Betsy 1926- *IntMPA 92*
**Palmer**, Beverly B 1945- *AmMWSc 92*
**Palmer**, Beverly Blazey 1945- *WhoWest 92*
**Palmer**, Bob Gene 1932- *WhoWest 92*
**Palmer**, Brian Desmond 1939- *Who 92*
**Palmer**, Brian Eugene 1948- *WhoAmL 92*
**Palmer**, Bruce Robert 1946- *AmMWSc 92*
**Palmer**, Bryan D 1936- *AmMWSc 92*
**Palmer**, Byron Allen 1949- *AmMWSc 92*
**Palmer**, C. Everard 1930- *WrDr 92*
**Palmer**, Carey 1943- *WrDr 92*
**Palmer**, Catherine Gardella 1924- *AmMWSc 92*
**Palmer**, Charlene Noel *DrAPF 91*
**Palmer**, Charles A. 1945- *WhoEnt 92*
**Palmer**, Charles B 1935- *WhoAmP 91*
**Palmer**, Charles H *ScFEYrs*
**Palmer**, Charles Harvey 1919- *AmMWSc 92*
**Palmer**, Charles Mark 1941- *Who 92*
**Palmer**, Charles Mason, Jr. 1942- *WhoFI 92*
**Palmer**, Charles Patrick 1933- *Who 92*
**Palmer**, Charles Ray 1940- *WhoEnt 92, WhoWest 92*
**Palmer**, Charles Robert 1954- *WhoEnt 92*
**Palmer**, Charles Stuart William 1930- *Who 92*
**Palmer**, Charles William 1945- *Who 92*
**Palmer**, Christine *WhoEnt 92*
**Palmer**, Cleddie Allen 1917- *WhoAmL 92*
**Palmer**, Clinton Scott 1954- *WhoWest 92*
**Palmer**, Curtis Allyn 1948- *AmMWSc 92*
**Palmer**, Curtis Ray *WhoEnt 92, WhoMW 92*
**Palmer**, Daisy Ann *WhoFI 92*
**Palmer**, Darlene Tolbert 1946- *WhoBlA 92*
**Palmer**, Darwin L 1930- *AmMWSc 92*
**Palmer**, David *DrAPF 91*
**Palmer**, David Chris 1953- *WhoWest 92*
**Palmer**, David Erroll Prior 1941- *Who 92*
**Palmer**, David Gilbert 1945- *WhoAmL 92*
**Palmer**, David Vereker 1926- *Who 92*
**Palmer**, Dennis, III 1914- *WhoBlA 92*
**Palmer**, Dennis Alan 1953- *WhoWest 92*
**Palmer**, Dennis Dale 1945- *WhoAmL 92*
**Palmer**, Derek George 1928- *Who 92*
**Palmer**, Diana 1946- *WrDr 92*
**Palmer**, Don *ConAu 134, SmATA 65*
**Palmer**, Donald Curtis 1934- *WhoRel 92*
**Palmer**, Doreen P. 1949- *WhoBlA 92*
**Palmer**, Douglas Harold 1951- *WhoBlA 92*
**Palmer**, E Reed 1932- *WhoAmP 91*
**Palmer**, Edgar M 1934- *AmMWSc 92*
**Palmer**, Edgar Z. 1898-1977 *ConAu 135*
**Palmer**, Edward 1831-1911 *BiInAmS*
**Palmer**, Edward 1928- *WhoBlA 92*
**Palmer**, Edward 1937- *WhoBlA 92*
**Palmer**, Edward Eugene 1923- *WhoAmP 91*
**Palmer**, Edward Hurry 1912- *Who 92*
**Palmer**, Elliott B., Sr. 1933- *WhoBlA 92*
**Palmer**, Ellsworth Levi 1910- *WhoRel 92*
**Palmer**, Elmer Eugene 1931- *WhoAmL 92*
**Palmer**, Eugene *TwCPaSc*
**Palmer**, Eugene Charles 1938- *AmMWSc 92*
**Palmer**, Everett Vernon 1948- *WhoWest 92*
**Palmer**, Felicity Joan 1944- *Who 92*
**Palmer**, Francis Harvey 1930- *Who 92*
**Palmer**, Frank Robert 1922- *IntAu&W 91, IntWW 91, Who 92, WrDr 92*
**Palmer**, Frederick B St Clair 1938- *AmMWSc 92*
**Palmer**, G., Jr. *DrAPF 91*
**Palmer**, Garrick 1933- *TwCPaSc*
**Palmer**, Gay B. 1962- *WhoRel 92*
**Palmer**, Geoffrey 1936- *Who 92*
**Palmer**, Geoffrey 1942- *FacFETw, Who 92*
**Palmer**, Geoffrey Winston Russell 1942- *IntWW 91*
**Palmer**, George Herbert 1842-1933 *BenetAL 91*
**Palmer**, Glenn Earl 1935- *AmMWSc 92*
**Palmer**, Graham 1935- *AmMWSc 92*
**Palmer**, Grant H 1911- *AmMWSc 92*
**Palmer**, Gregg 1927- *IntMPA 92*
**Palmer**, Gretchen Everilde 1945- *WhoRel 92*
**Palmer**, H A 1919- *AmMWSc 92*
**Palmer**, H Currie 1935- *AmMWSc 92*
**Palmer**, Hap 1942- *SmATA 68 [port]*
**Palmer**, Harry William 1919- *WhoRel 92*
**Palmer**, Harvey Earl 1929- *AmMWSc 92*
**Palmer**, Harvey John 1946- *AmMWSc 92*
**Palmer**, Helen Virginia 1928- *WhoRel 92*
**Palmer**, Henry 1926-1990 *AnObit 1990*
**Palmer**, Horace Anthony 1937- *Who 92*
**Palmer**, Howard Benedict 1925- *AmMWSc 92*
**Palmer**, Howell M, III 1951- *WhoIns 92*
**Palmer**, J H *ScFEYrs*
**Palmer**, James D 1930- *AmMWSc 92*
**Palmer**, James E. 1938- *WhoBlA 92*
**Palmer**, James F 1950- *AmMWSc 92*
**Palmer**, James Frederick 1931- *AmMWSc 92*
**Palmer**, James Joseph 1943- *WhoMW 92*
**Palmer**, James Kenneth 1926- *AmMWSc 92*
**Palmer**, James L. D. 1928- *WhoBlA 92*
**Palmer**, James McLean 1937- *AmMWSc 92*
**Palmer**, Jay 1928- *AmMWSc 92*
**Palmer**, Jean May 1951- *WhoFI 92*
**Palmer**, Jeffress Gary 1921- *AmMWSc 92*
**Palmer**, Jim 1945- *News 91 [port]*
**Palmer**, Joe 1951- *WhoBlA 92*
**Palmer**, John *WhoAmP 91*
**Palmer**, John 1920- *Who 92*
**Palmer**, John 1926- *Who 92*
**Palmer**, John 1928- *Who 92*
**Palmer**, John A. 1926-1982 *ConAu 134*
**Palmer**, John A. 1944- *WhoBlA 92*
**Palmer**, John Albert, Jr 1933- *WhoAmP 91*
**Palmer**, John C., Jr. 1934- *WhoMW 92*
**Palmer**, John Davis 1931- *AmMWSc 92*
**Palmer**, John Derry 1932- *AmMWSc 92*
**Palmer**, John Frank, Jr 1915- *AmMWSc 92*
**Palmer**, John J 1939- *WhoIns 92*
**Palmer**, John M 1922- *AmMWSc 92*
**Palmer**, John Marshall 1906- *WhoAmL 92, WhoMW 92*
**Palmer**, John Parker 1939- *AmMWSc 92*
**Palmer**, John Warren 1908- *AmMWSc 92*
**Palmer**, Jon 1940- *AmMWSc 92*
**Palmer**, Joseph Michael 1928- *Who 92*
**Palmer**, Judith 1934- *WhoWest 92*
**Palmer**, Judith Grace 1948- *WhoAmL 92*
**Palmer**, Juliette 1930- *WrDr 92*
**Palmer**, Keith Henry 1928- *AmMWSc 92*
**Palmer**, Kenneth 1945- *AmMWSc 92*
**Palmer**, Kenneth A 1939- *WhoIns 92*
**Palmer**, Kenneth Charles 1944- *AmMWSc 92*
**Palmer**, Kent Friedley 1941- *AmMWSc 92*
**Palmer**, Kim Richard 1950- *WhoRel 92*
**Palmer**, Lance Eugene 1960- *WhoAmL 92*
**Palmer**, Larry Alan 1945- *AmMWSc 92*
**Palmer**, Larry Isaac 1944- *WhoAmL 92*
**Palmer**, Laura Olivia 1955- *WhoBlA 92*
**Palmer**, Laurence Clive 1932- *AmMWSc 92*
**Palmer**, Leigh Hunt 1935- *AmMWSc 92*
**Palmer**, Leonard A 1931- *AmMWSc 92*
**Palmer**, Leslie *DrAPF 91*
**Palmer**, Leslie Robert 1910- *Who 92*
**Palmer**, Lester Davis 1929- *WhoRel 92*
**Palmer**, Lilli *TwCPaSc*
**Palmer**, Linda L 1947- *WhoAmP 91*
**Palmer**, Linwood E, Jr 1921- *WhoAmP 91*
**Palmer**, Lori Winchell 1959- *WhoFI 92*
**Palmer**, Madelyn 1910- *IntAu&W 91*
**Palmer**, Marcia Ann 1951- *WhoMW 92*
**Palmer**, Mark *Who 92*
**Palmer**, Mark A *WhoAmP 91*
**Palmer**, Martin C. 1951- *WhoWest 92*
**Palmer**, Matthew David 1957- *WhoFI 92*
**Palmer**, Michael *DrAPF 91, Who 92*
**Palmer**, Michael 1942- *ConAu 35NR*
**Palmer**, Michael 1943- *ConPo 91, WrDr 92*
**Palmer**, Michael Denison 1933- *WrDr 92*
**Palmer**, Michael Julian Barham 1933- *Who 92*
**Palmer**, Michael Paul 1944- *WhoAmL 92*
**Palmer**, Michael Rule 1950- *AmMWSc 92*
**Palmer**, Mike *WhoAmP 91*
**Palmer**, Miley Embry 1937- *WhoRel 92*
**Palmer**, Miriam *DrAPF 91*
**Palmer**, Monroe Edward 1938- *Who 92*
**Palmer**, Nancy Swygert 1953- *WhoAmL 92*
**Palmer**, Noel 1926- *WhoBlA 92*
**Palmer**, Norman D. 1909- *WrDr 92*
**Palmer**, Norman Kitchener 1928- *Who 92*
**Palmer**, Patricia Ann Texter 1932- *WhoWest 92*
**Palmer**, Patrick *Who 92*
**Palmer**, Patrick 1936- *IntMPA 92*
**Palmer**, Patrick Asa 1943- *WhoFI 92*
**Palmer**, Patrick Edward 1940- *AmMWSc 92*
**Palmer**, Peter John 1932- *IntAu&W 91, WrDr 92*
**Palmer**, Philip Francis 1903- *Who 92*
**Palmer**, Philip Isham, Jr. 1929- *WhoAmL 92*
**Palmer**, Ralph Lee 1909- *AmMWSc 92*
**Palmer**, Ralph Simon 1914- *AmMWSc 92*
**Palmer**, Randall William 1955- *WhoWest 92*
**Palmer**, Ray 1808-1887 *BenetAL 91*
**Palmer**, Raymond A 1910-1977 *TwCSFW 91*
**Palmer**, Reid G 1941- *AmMWSc 92*
**Palmer**, Richard Alan 1935- *AmMWSc 92*
**Palmer**, Richard Carl 1931- *AmMWSc 92*
**Palmer**, Richard Everett 1944- *AmMWSc 92*
**Palmer**, Richard Hudson 1940- *WhoEnt 92*
**Palmer**, Richard Ware 1919- *WhoAmL 92*
**Palmer**, Robert 1915- *NewAmDM*
**Palmer**, Robert Alan 1948- *WhoAmL 92*
**Palmer**, Robert B 1934- *AmMWSc 92*
**Palmer**, Robert Gerald 1936- *AmMWSc 92*
**Palmer**, Robert Henry Stephen 1927- *Who 92*
**Palmer**, Robert Howard 1931- *AmMWSc 92*
**Palmer**, Robert L., II 1943- *WhoBlA 92*
**Palmer**, Robert Leslie 1957- *WhoAmL 92*
**Palmer**, Robert Montgomerie 1953- *WhoAmL 92*
**Palmer**, Robert R. 1950- *WhoEnt 92*
**Palmer**, Robert Towne 1947- *WhoAmL 92, WhoFI 92, WhoMW 92*
**Palmer**, Robie M H *WhoAmP 91*
**Palmer**, Robie Marcus Hooker 1941- *IntWW 91*
**Palmer**, Rodney James 1945- *WhoAmP 91*
**Palmer**, Roger 1931- *AmMWSc 92*
**Palmer**, Roger 1946- *TwCPaSc*
**Palmer**, Roger Clive 1946- *WhoWest 92*
**Palmer**, Ronald D 1932- *WhoAmP 91*
**Palmer**, Ronald DeWayne 1932- *WhoBlA 92*
**Palmer**, Ronald Leigh 1939- *WhoAmL 92*
**Palmer**, Rufus N 1902- *AmMWSc 92*
**Palmer**, Rupert Dewitt 1929- *AmMWSc 92*
**Palmer**, Russell Eugene 1934- *WhoFI 92*
**Palmer**, Shelton Leigh 1958- *WhoEnt 92*
**Palmer**, Sidney John 1913- *Who 92*
**Palmer**, Stanley H. 1944- *ConAu 135*
**Palmer**, Stephen Eugene 1896- *WhoRel 92*
**Palmer**, Sushma Mahyera 1944- *AmMWSc 92*
**Palmer**, Theodore W 1935- *AmMWSc 92*
**Palmer**, Theodore Windle 1935- *WhoWest 92*
**Palmer**, Thomas Adolph 1935- *AmMWSc 92*
**Palmer**, Thomas Earl 1939- *WhoAmL 92*
**Palmer**, Thomas Joseph 1931- *Who 92*
**Palmer**, Thomas Monroe 1931- *WhoRel 92*
**Palmer**, Thomas Stuart 1947- *WhoFI 92*
**Palmer**, Timothy Trow 1938- *AmMWSc 92*
**Palmer**, Tony Brian 1930- *Who 92*
**Palmer**, Vance 1885-1959 *RfGEnL 91*
**Palmer**, Vincent Allan 1913- *WhoWest 92*
**Palmer**, Warren K 1941- *AmMWSc 92*
**Palmer**, Wayne Lewis 1949- *WhoEnt 92*
**Palmer**, Willard Aldrich, III 1942- *WhoEnt 92*
**Palmer**, William Arthur 1946- *WhoRel 92*
**Palmer**, William Darrell 1935- *WhoAmP 91*
**Palmer**, William Franklin 1937- *AmMWSc 92, WhoMW 92*
**Palmer**, William J. 1943- *ConAu 134*
**Palmer**, William John 1909- *Who 92*
**Palmer**, William Joseph 1934- *WhoWest 92*
**Palmer**, William Rockne 1955- *WhoAmL 92*
**Palmer**, Winifred G *AmMWSc 92*
**Palmer-Hildreth**, Barbara Jean 1941- *WhoBlA 92*
**Palmere**, Raymond M 1925- *AmMWSc 92*
**Palmeri**, Victor R. 1926- *WhoHisp 92*

**Palmersheim,** Thomas Francis 1932- *WhoEnt 92*
**Palmes,** Edward Dannelly 1916- *AmMWSc 92*
**Palmes,** Peter Manfred Jerome 1920- *Who 92*
**Palmese,** Richard Dominick 1947- *WhoEnt 92, WhoFI 92*
**Palmeter,** N. David 1938- *WhoAmL 92*
**Palmgren,** Muriel Signe 1949- *AmMWSc 92*
**Palmgren,** Selim 1878-1951 *NewAmDM*
**Palmieri,** Anthony, III 1948- *WhoMW 92*
**Palmieri,** Carmen J. 1938- *WhoHisp 92*
**Palmieri,** Dennis Anthony 1956- *WhoAmL 92*
**Palmieri,** Guy Joseph 1936- *WhoMW 92*
**Palmieri,** James John, Sr 1913- *WhoAmP 91*
**Palmieri,** Joseph Nicholas 1932- *AmMWSc 92*
**Palmieri,** Nicola W. 1935- *WhoAmL 92*
**Palmieri,** Ralph J 1947- *WhoIns 92*
**Palmieri,** Robert Michael 1930- *WhoMW 92*
**Palmieri,** Rodney August 1944- *WhoWest 92*
**Palmisano,** Paul Anthony 1929- *AmMWSc 92*
**Palmiter,** Richard 1942- *AmMWSc 92*
**Palmore,** John Stanley, Jr 1917- *WhoAmP 91*
**Palmore,** Julian Ivanhoe, III 1938- *AmMWSc 92, WhoMW 92*
**Palmore,** Lynne A. Janifer 1952- *WhoBlA 92*
**Palmore,** William P 1934- *AmMWSc 92*
**Palmour,** Hayne, III 1925- *AmMWSc 92*
**Palmour,** Roberta Martin 1942- *AmMWSc 92*
**Palmquist,** Donald Leonard 1936- *AmMWSc 92*
**Palmquist,** John Charles 1934- *AmMWSc 92*
**Palmquist,** Robert Clarence 1938- *AmMWSc 92*
**Palmquist,** Robert Phillips 1951- *WhoFI 92*
**Palmquist,** Sven 1906- *DcTwDes*
**Palmroth,** John William 1939- *WhoFI 92*
**Palms,** John Michael 1935- *AmMWSc 92*
**Palms,** Peter John, IV 1934- *WhoFI 92*
**Palms,** Roger Curtis 1936- *WhoRel 92*
**Palo,** Nicholas Edwin 1945- *WhoMW 92*
**Palocz,** Istvan 1920- *AmMWSc 92*
**Palomarez,** Nat 1937- *WhoHisp 92*
**Palombi,** Barbara Jean 1949- *WhoWest 92*
**Palombi,** Richard Francis 1931- *WhoEnt 92*
**Palombo,** Bernardo Alfredo 1948- *WhoHisp 92*
**Palomino,** Angel 1929- *IntAu&W 91*
**Palomino,** Carlos 1950- *WhoHisp 92*
**Palomino Roedel,** Jose 1937- *IntWW 91*
**Palomo,** Antonio M 1931- *WhoAmP 91*
**Palomo,** Luis 1954- *WhoEnt 92*
**Palopoli,** Frank Patrick 1922- *AmMWSc 92*
**Palos,** Frank G. 1948- *WhoHisp 92*
**Palos,** James Joseph 1961- *WhoHisp 92*
**Palosuo,** Heikki Wilhelm 1951- *WhoFI 92*
**Palotay,** James Lajos 1922- *AmMWSc 92*
**Palotta,** Joseph Luke 1940- *AmMWSc 92*
**Palou,** Francisco 1722?-1789? *BenetAL 91*
**Palous,** Radim 1924- *IntWW 91*
**Paloyan,** Edward 1932- *AmMWSc 92*
**Pals,** Daniel L. 1946- *WhoRel 92*
**Pals,** Donald Theodore 1934- *AmMWSc 92*
**Palsce,** David Alan 1953- *WhoEnt 92*
**Palser,** Barbara Frances 1916- *AmMWSc 92*
**Palshaw,** John Louis 1932- *WhoFI 92*
**Palsma,** Mary Jacobson 1942- *WhoWest 92*
**Palsson,** Hermann 1921- *WrDr 92*
**Palsson,** Thorsteinn 1947- *IntWW 91*
**Paltenghi,** Julian 1955- *TwCPaSc*
**Palter,** N H 1921- *AmMWSc 92*
**Paltock,** Robert 1697-1767 *RfGEnL 91, ScFEYrs*
**Paltridge,** Garth William 1940- *IntWW 91*
**Paltrow,** Bruce 1943- *ConTFT 9, IntMPA 92*
**Palubicki,** Lynn Ann 1955- *WhoMW 92*
**Palubinskas,** Alphonse J 1922- *AmMWSc 92*
**Palubinskas,** Felix Stanley 1920- *AmMWSc 92*
**Paluch,** Edward Peter 1952- *AmMWSc 92*
**Paluga,** Pamela Joy 1963- *WhoWest 92*
**Palumbo** *Who 92*
**Palumbo,** Baron 1935- *IntWW 91, Who 92*
**Palumbo,** Dennis J. 1929- *WrDr 92*
**Palumbo,** Francis Xavier Bernard 1945- *AmMWSc 92*
**Palumbo,** James Fredrick 1950- *WhoFI 92*
**Palumbo,** Mario Joseph 1933- *WhoAmL 92, WhoAmP 91*
**Palumbo,** Michael Arnold 1945- *WhoWest 92*
**Palumbo,** Michael R. 1946- *WhoAmL 92*
**Palumbo,** Pasquale John 1932- *AmMWSc 92*
**Palumbo,** Richard A 1938- *WhoAmP 91*
**Palumbo,** Ruth Ann 1949- *WhoAmP 91*
**Palumbo,** Samuel Anthony 1939- *AmMWSc 92*
**Palumbo,** Terri Ann 1956- *WhoEnt 92*
**Palumbo,** Thomas G 1950- *WhoAmP 91*
**Palumbo,** Vincent J, Jr 1956- *WhoAmP 91*
**Palusamy,** Sam Subbu 1939- *AmMWSc 92*
**Palusinski,** Olgierd Aleksander 1937- *AmMWSc 92*
**Pam,** Jerry 1926- *IntMPA 92*
**Pama,** Cornelis 1916- *IntAu&W 91, WrDr 92*
**Pamer,** Treva Louise 1938- *AmMWSc 92*
**Pamidi,** Prabhakar Ramarao 1942- *AmMWSc 92*
**Pamnani,** Motilal Bhagwandas 1933- *AmMWSc 92*
**Pampanini,** Silvana 1925- *IntMPA 92*
**Pampe,** William R 1923- *AmMWSc 92*
**Pampel,** Martha Maria 1913- *IntAu&W 91*
**Pampeyan,** Earl H 1925- *AmMWSc 92*
**Pampeyan,** Earl Haig 1925- *WhoWest 92*
**Pamphiius** 240?-309 *EncEarC*
**Pamplin,** Robert Boisseau, Jr. 1941- *WhoFI 92, WhoWest 92*
**Pamplin,** Robert Boisseau, Sr. 1911- *WhoFI 92, WhoWest 92*
**Pan He** 1926- *IntWW 91*
**Pan Hong** 1954- *IntWW 91*
**Pan Rongwen** 1931- *IntWW 91*
**Pan,** Bingham Y K 1923- *AmMWSc 92*
**Pan,** Chai-Fu 1936- *AmMWSc 92*
**Pan,** Chuen Yong 1940- *AmMWSc 92*
**Pan,** Coda H T 1929- *AmMWSc 92*
**Pan,** David 1944- *AmMWSc 92*
**Pan,** Hermes 1910-1990 *AnObit 1990, ConTFT 9, FacFETw*
**Pan,** Huo-Hsi 1918- *AmMWSc 92*
**Pan,** Huo-Ping 1921- *AmMWSc 92*
**Pan,** In-Chang 1929- *AmMWSc 92*
**Pan,** Jiawei 1935- *WhoWest 92*
**Pan,** Kee-Chuan 1941- *AmMWSc 92*
**Pan,** Ko Chang 1939- *AmMWSc 92*
**Pan,** Poh-Hsi 1922- *AmMWSc 92*
**Pan,** Samuel Cheng 1912- *AmMWSc 92*
**Pan,** Steve Chia-Tung 1922- *AmMWSc 92*
**Pan,** Victor 1939- *AmMWSc 92*
**Pan,** Yu-Ching E 1945- *AmMWSc 92*
**Pan,** Yu-Li 1939- *AmMWSc 92*
**Pan,** Yuan-Siang *AmMWSc 92*
**Pan,** Yuh Kang 1937- *AmMWSc 92*
**Pana,** Doru *IntWW 91*
**Panagides,** John 1944- *AmMWSc 92*
**Panagiotopoulos,** Athanassios Z 1960- *AmMWSc 92*
**Panagiotopoulos,** Vasos-Peter John, II 1961- *WhoFI 92*
**Panagore,** Peter Baldwin 1959- *WhoRel 92*
**Panajotovic,** Ilija Svetislav 1932- *WhoEnt 92*
**Panalaks,** Thavil 1917- *AmMWSc 92*
**Panama,** Charles A. 1925- *IntMPA 92*
**Panama,** Norman *IntMPA 92*
**Panangala,** Victor S 1939- *AmMWSc 92*
**Panar,** Manuel 1935- *AmMWSc 92*
**Panard,** Pierre Marie Maurice 1916- *IntWW 91*
**Panarella,** Emilio 1933- *AmMWSc 92*
**Panaretos,** Basil Nicholas, Jr. 1940- *WhoWest 92*
**Panaretos,** John 1948- *WhoFI 92*
**Panarites,** John Peter 1939- *WhoFI 92*
**Panas,** Eustace G. 1924- *IntWW 91*
**Panasci,** Henry Anthony, Jr. 1928- *WhoFI 92*
**Panasci,** Nancy Ervin 1954- *WhoWest 92*
**Panasenko,** Sharon Muldoon 1950- *AmMWSc 92*
**Panasevich,** Robert Edward *AmMWSc 92*
**Panati,** Charles 1943- *SmATA 65 [port]*
**Panavision Kid,** The *IntAu&W 91X*
**Panayappan,** Ramanathan 1936- *AmMWSc 92*
**Panayides,** Tasos Christou 1934- *Who 92*
**Panayides Christou,** Tasos 1934- *IntWW 91*
**Panayotacos,** Constantine P. 1918- *IntWW 91*
**Panayotovich,** Sam 1946- *WhoAmP 91*
**Pancella,** John Raymond 1931- *AmMWSc 92*
**Pancero,** Jack Blocher 1923- *WhoMW 92*
**Panchal,** Shanti 1951- *TwCPaSc*
**Panciera,** Roger J 1929- *AmMWSc 92*
**Panciroli,** Romeo 1923- *IntWW 91*
**Panckoucke,** Charles-Joseph 1736-1798 *BlkwCEP*
**Pancoast,** Joseph 1805-1882 *BiInAmS*
**Pancoast,** Seth 1823-1889 *BiInAmS*
**Pancoast,** William Henry 1835-1897 *BiInAmS*
**Pancoe,** William Louis, Jr 1938- *AmMWSc 92*
**Pancratz,** Linda Marie 1955- *WhoMW 92*
**Panda,** Durga Prasad 1945- *WhoMW 92*
**Pandak,** Sharon Elizabeth 1953- *WhoAmL 92*
**Panday,** Kedar 1920- *IntWW 91*
**Pande,** Chandra Shekhar 1940- *AmMWSc 92*
**Pande,** Gyan Shanker 1932- *AmMWSc 92*
**Pande,** Krishna P *AmMWSc 92*
**Pande,** Shri Vardhan 1940- *AmMWSc 92*
**Pandell,** Alexander Jerry 1942- *AmMWSc 92*
**Pandey,** Ishwari Raj 1934- *Who 92*
**Pandey,** Jagdish Narayan 1936- *AmMWSc 92*
**Pandey,** Kailash N *AmMWSc 92*
**Pandey,** Raghvendra Kumar 1937- *AmMWSc 92*
**Pandey,** Ramesh Chandra 1938- *AmMWSc 92*
**Pandey,** Ras Bihari *AmMWSc 92*
**Pandey,** Surendra Nath 1945- *AmMWSc 92*
**Pandeya,** Nirmalendu Kumar 1940- *WhoMW 92*
**Pandeya,** Prakash N 1943- *AmMWSc 92*
**Pandharipande,** Vijay Raghunath 1940- *AmMWSc 92*
**Pandian,** Natesa G 1947- *AmMWSc 92*
**Pandian,** Ramaiah Devadoss 1942- *WhoMW 92*
**Pandit,** Hemchandra M 1924- *AmMWSc 92*
**Pandit,** Jasraj 1930- *IntWW 91*
**Pandit,** Sudhakar Madhavrao 1939- *AmMWSc 92*
**Pandit,** Vijaya 1900-1990 *AnObit 1990*
**Pandit,** Vijaya Lakshmi d1990 *IntWW 91N, Who 92N*
**Pandit,** Vijaya Lakshmi 1900-1990 *CurBio 91N, FacFETw*
**Pando,** Alan Oscar 1931- *WhoFI 92*
**Pando,** Robert Terry 1938- *WhoFI 92*
**Pandolf,** Kent Barry 1945- *AmMWSc 92*
**Pandolfe,** John Thomas, Jr. 1941- *WhoAmL 92*
**Pandolfe,** William David 1945- *AmMWSc 92*
**Pandolfi,** Filippo Maria 1927- *IntWW 91, Who 92*
**Pandolfo,** Joseph P 1930- *AmMWSc 92*
**Pandorf,** Robert Clay *AmMWSc 92*
**Pandres,** Dave, Jr 1928- *AmMWSc 92*
**Pandya,** Harish C. 1945- *WhoBlA 92*
**Pandya,** Krishnakant Hariprasad 1935- *AmMWSc 92*
**Panec,** William Joseph 1937- *WhoAmL 92*
**Panehal,** Francine Mary 1925- *WhoAmP 91*
**Panek,** Edward John 1941- *AmMWSc 92*
**Panek,** Louis A 1919- *AmMWSc 92*
**Panelli,** Edward A 1931- *WhoAmP 91*
**Panelli,** Edward Alexander 1931- *WhoAmL 92, WhoWest 92*
**Panelli,** Juan A. 1962- *WhoHisp 92*
**Panepinto,** James R. 1944- *WhoFI 92*
**Panero,** Leopoldo 1909-1962 *DcLB 108 [port]*
**Panessa-Warren,** Barbara Jean 1947- *AmMWSc 92*
**Paneth,** Nigel Sefton 1946- *AmMWSc 92*
**Panethiere,** Henry Andrea 1914- *WhoAmP 91*
**Panetta,** Charles Anthony 1932- *AmMWSc 92*
**Panetta,** Joseph Daniel 1954- *WhoWest 92*
**Panetta,** Leon E. 1938- *AlmAP 92 [port]*
**Panetta,** Leon Edward 1938- *WhoAmP 91, WhoFI 92, WhoWest 92*
**Paneyko,** Stephen Hobbs 1942- *WhoFI 92*
**Panferov,** Fedor Ivanovich 1896-1960 *FacFETw, SovUnBD*
**Panfilov,** Gleb 1933- *IntWW 91*
**Panfilov,** Gleb 1934- *SovUnBD*
**Panfilov,** Gleb 1937- *IntDcF 2-2 [port]*
**Pang,** Chan Yueh 1947- *AmMWSc 92*
**Pang,** Cho Yat *AmMWSc 92*
**Pang,** David C 1942- *AmMWSc 92*
**Pang,** Henrianna Yicksing 1952- *AmMWSc 92*
**Pang,** Herbert George 1922- *WhoWest 92*
**Pang,** Joshua Keun-Uk 1924- *WhoFI 92, WhoMW 92*
**Pang,** Kevin D. *WhoWest 92*
**Pang,** Kevin Dit Kwan *AmMWSc 92*
**Pang,** Kim-Ching Sandy *AmMWSc 92*
**Pang,** Peter Kai To 1941- *AmMWSc 92*
**Pang,** Wing Ning 1942- *WhoRel 92*
**Pang,** Yuan 1947- *AmMWSc 92*
**Pang-Ching,** Glenn K 1931- *AmMWSc 92*
**Pangalos,** Theodoros 1938- *IntWW 91*
**Pangborn,** Edgar 1909-1976 *TwCSFW 91*
**Pangborn,** Robert Northrup 1951- *AmMWSc 92*
**Pangborn,** Rose Marie Valdes 1932- *AmMWSc 92*
**Pangburn,** Charles Hales, III 1955- *WhoAmL 92*
**Pangelinan,** Edward DeLeon Guerrero 1941- *WhoAmP 91*
**Pangelinan,** Joaquin Ito 1942- *WhoAmP 91*
**Panger,** Gene Anthony 1961- *WhoMW 92*
**Pangerapan,** Bob George 1938- *WhoFI 92*
**Pangerl,** Susann M. 1951- *WhoRel 92*
**Panggabean,** Maraden Saur Halomoan 1922- *IntWW 91*
**Pangindian,** Gene Javier 1950- *WhoWest 92*
**Pangle,** Charles Lee 1941- *WhoAmP 91*
**Pango Vildoso,** Grover 1947- *IntWW 91*
**Panhofer,** Walter 1910- *IntWW 91*
**Paniagua,** Santos Donato *WhoHisp 92*
**Panicci,** Ronald J 1941- *AmMWSc 92*
**Paniccia,** Mario Domenic 1948- *WhoFI 92*
**Paniccia,** Patricia Lynn 1952- *WhoAmL 92*
**Panich,** Danuta Bembenista 1954- *WhoAmL 92*
**Panichas,** George A. 1930- *WrDr 92*
**Panichas,** George Andrew 1930- *IntAu&W 91, IntWW 91*
**Panici,** Charles *WhoAmP 91*
**Panigrahi,** Chintamani 1922- *IntWW 91*
**Panigrahi,** Sanjukta 1944- *IntWW 91*
**Paniker,** Ayyappa 1930- *IntAu&W 91*
**Paniker,** Salvador 1927- *IntAu&W 91*
**Panikkar,** Raimon 1918- *WhoRel 92*
**Panish,** Morton B 1929- *AmMWSc 92*
**Panisset,** Jean-Claude 1935- *AmMWSc 92*
**Paniszczyn,** John Francis 1958- *WhoAmL 92*
**Panitch,** Leo 1945- *WrDr 92*
**Panitz,** David Hirsh d1991 *NewYTBS 91 [port]*
**Panitz,** Janda Kirk Griffith 1945- *AmMWSc 92*
**Panitz,** Lawrence Herbert 1941- *WhoAmL 92*
**Pank,** David 1935- *Who 92*
**Pankavich,** John Anthony 1929- *AmMWSc 92*
**Panken,** Andrew I. 1953- *WhoAmL 92*
**Panken,** Peter Michael 1936- *WhoAmL 92*
**Pankey,** Eric Martin 1959- *WhoMW 92*
**Pankey,** George Atkinson 1933- *AmMWSc 92*
**Pankey,** Phil 1928- *WhoAmP 91*
**Pankey,** Ronald Arthur 1956- *WhoRel 92*
**Pankhurst,** Emmeline Goulden 1858-1928 *FacFETw*
**Pankhurst,** Leonard Thomas 1902- *Who 92*
**Pankhurst,** Richard 1927- *WrDr 92*
**Pankhurst,** Sylvia 1882-1960 *TwCPaSc*
**Pankin,** Boris D. *NewYTBS 91 [port]*
**Pankin,** Jayson Darryl 1957- *WhoFI 92*
**Pankiwskyj,** Kost Andrij 1936- *AmMWSc 92*
**Pankok,** Bernhard 1872-1943 *DcTwDes*
**Pankok,** Thomas A 1931- *WhoAmP 91*
**Pankopf,** Arthur, Jr 1931- *WhoAmP 91*
**Pankopf,** John F. 1935- *WhoMW 92*
**Pankov,** Gradimir Krunislav 1938- *WhoEnt 92*
**Pankove,** Jacques I 1922- *AmMWSc 92*
**Pankove,** Jacques Isaac 1922- *WhoWest 92*
**Pankovich,** Arsen M 1930- *AmMWSc 92*
**Pankow,** James Frederick 1951- *AmMWSc 92*
**Pankowski,** Elsie *DrAPF 91*
**Pankratova,** Anna Milhaylovna 1897-1957 *SovUnBD*
**Pankratz,** Ronald Ernest 1918- *AmMWSc 92, WhoMW 92*
**Panlener,** Ann Josephine 1926- *WhoMW 92*
**Panlilio,** Filadelfo 1918- *AmMWSc 92*
**Pannabecker,** Richard Floyd 1922- *AmMWSc 92*
**Pannell,** James H 1920- *WhoAmP 91*
**Pannell,** James L *WhoAmP 91*
**Pannell,** Keith Howard 1940- *AmMWSc 92*
**Pannell,** Lolita 1912- *AmMWSc 92*
**Pannell,** Patrick Weldon 1936- *WhoBlA 92*
**Pannell,** Randall J. 1950- *WhoRel 92*
**Pannell,** Richard Byron 1952- *AmMWSc 92*
**Pannell,** William E. 1929- *WhoBlA 92*
**Pannella,** Giorgio 1934- *AmMWSc 92*
**Pannenberg,** Wolfhart Ulrich 1928- *IntWW 91*
**Panner,** Bernard J 1928- *AmMWSc 92*
**Panner,** Owen M. 1924- *WhoAmL 92, WhoWest 92*
**Pannett,** Juliet Kathleen *Who 92*
**Panni,** Marcello 1940- *IntWW 91*
**Pannick,** David 1956- *WrDr 92*
**Pannier,** Clyde Robert 1930- *WhoFI 92*
**Pannill,** Fitzhugh Carter, Jr 1921- *AmMWSc 92*
**Pannill,** William Presley 1940- *WhoAmL 92*
**Panning,** Armin *WhoRel 92*
**Pannos,** Michael *WhoAmP 91*
**Pannozo,** Clint A. 1947- *WhoEnt 92*

**Paquet,** Jean Guy 1938- *AmMWSc 92, Who 92*
**Paquette,** David George 1945- *AmMWSc 92*
**Paquette,** Gerard Arthur 1926- *AmMWSc 92*
**Paquette,** Guy 1930- *AmMWSc 92*
**Paquette,** Joseph F., Jr. 1934- *WhoFI 92*
**Paquette,** Leo Armand 1934- *AmMWSc 92*
**Paquette,** Mario 1938- *WhoRel 92*
**Paquette,** Robert George 1915- *AmMWSc 92*
**Paquette,** Rudolphe G 1913- *WhoAmP 91*
**Paquin,** Jeffrey Dean 1960- *WhoAmL 92*
**Paquin,** Paul Peter 1943- *WhoFI 92*
**Parabellum** 1871-1935 *ScFEYrs*
**Paracer,** Surindar Mohan 1941- *AmMWSc 92*
**Paradice,** Sammy Irwin 1952- *WhoFI 92*
**Paradis,** Adrian A 1912- *SmATA 67 [port]*
**Paradis,** Adrian Alexis 1912- *WrDr 92*
**Paradis,** Eugene J 1923- *WhoAmP 91*
**Paradis,** Judy 1944- *WhoAmP 91*
**Paradis,** Maria Theresia von 1759-1824 *NewAmDM*
**Paradis,** Patrick Eugene 1953- *WhoAmP 91*
**Paradis,** Philip *DrAPF 91*
**Paradise,** Lois Jean 1928- *AmMWSc 92*
**Paradise,** Melvin 1925- *WhoAmL 92*
**Paradise,** Norman Francis 1943- *AmMWSc 92, WhoMW 92*
**Paradjanov,** Sergei 1924-1990 *AnObit 1990*
**Parady,** John Edward 1939- *WhoWest 92*
**Paradzhanov,** Sergei 1924-1990 *IntDcF 2-2 [port]*
**Paradzhanov,** Sergey Iosifovich 1924-1990 *SovUnBD*
**Paradzhyanov,** Sergey Iosifovich d1990 *IntWW 91N*
**Paraense,** Wladimir Lobato 1914- *IntWW 91*
**Paragano,** Vincent Dominick 1956- *WhoAmL 92*
**Paraguay,** Bishop of 1940- *Who 92*
**Parakkal,** Paul Fab 1931- *AmMWSc 92*
**Paramo,** Constanza Gisella 1956- *WhoHisp 92*
**Paran,** Mark Lloyd 1953- *WhoAmL 92, WhoFI 92*
**Paranchych,** William 1933- *AmMWSc 92*
**Paranjape,** Bhalachandra Vishwanath 1922- *AmMWSc 92*
**Pararajasingam,** Sangarapillai 1896- *Who 92*
**Paras,** Nicholas Andrew 1942- *WhoFI 92*
**Parascak,** John Joseph 1961- *WhoEnt 92*
**Parascandola,** John Louis 1941- *AmMWSc 92*
**Parascos,** Edward Themistocles 1931- *WhoFI 92*
**Paraskakis,** Michael Emanuel 1930- *WhoFI 92*
**Paraskevaidis,** Graciela 1940- *ConCom 92*
**Paraskevas,** Frixos 1928- *AmMWSc 92*
**Paraskevopoulos,** George 1929- *AmMWSc 92*
**Parasrampuria,** Jagdish 1958- *WhoMW 92*
**Parasuraman,** Raja 1950- *AmMWSc 92*
**Paraszczak,** Jurij Rostyslan 1952- *AmMWSc 92*
**Parate,** Natthu Sonbaji 1936- *AmMWSc 92*
**Paratje,** Mercedes *WhoFI 92*
**Parauda,** Joseph Ronald 1932- *WhoAmL 92*
**Paravisini-Gebert,** Lizabeth 1953- *WhoHisp 92*
**Paray,** Paul 1886-1979 *NewAmDM*
**Parayre,** Jean-Paul-Christophe 1937- *IntWW 91, Who 92*
**Parberry,** Ian 1959- *AmMWSc 92*
**Parbo,** Arvi 1926- *Who 92*
**Parbo,** Arvi Hillar 1926- *IntWW 91*
**Parcells,** Alan Jerome 1929- *AmMWSc 92*
**Parcells,** Bill 1941- *CurBio 91 [port]*
**Parcells,** Dayton Balcom, III 1960- *WhoAmL 92*
**Parcells,** Margaret R 1930- *WhoAmP 91*
**Parchen,** Frank Raymond, Jr 1923- *AmMWSc 92*
**Parcher,** James V 1920- *AmMWSc 92*
**Parchment,** John Gerald 1923- *AmMWSc 92*
**Parczewski,** Krzysztof I 1926- *AmMWSc 92*
**Pardee,** Arthur Beck 1921- *AmMWSc 92, IntWW 91*
**Pardee,** Candyce Beumler 1954- *WhoAmL 92*
**Pardee,** Jean *WhoAmP 91*
**Pardee,** Joel David 1947- *AmMWSc 92*
**Pardee,** Lenora Maxine 1937- *WhoRel 92*
**Pardee,** Margaret Ross 1920- *WhoEnt 92*
**Pardee,** Otway O'Meara 1920- *AmMWSc 92*
**Pardee,** Rodger John 1954- *WhoEnt 92*
**Pardee,** Scott Edward 1936- *WhoFI 92*
**Pardee,** William A 1914- *AmMWSc 92*
**Pardee,** William Durley 1929- *AmMWSc 92*
**Pardee,** William Joseph 1944- *AmMWSc 92*
**Parden,** Robert James 1922- *AmMWSc 92*
**Pardieck,** Roger Lee 1937- *WhoAmL 92*
**Pardinek,** Mary Therese 1958- *WhoFI 92, WhoMW 92*
**Pardini,** Ronald Shields 1938- *AmMWSc 92*
**Pardo,** Arvid 1914- *IntWW 91*
**Pardo,** Bruce Edward 1947- *WhoHisp 92*
**Pardo,** James William 1964- *WhoHisp 92*
**Pardo,** Luis Maria de Pablo 1914- *IntWW 91*
**Pardo,** Richard Claude 1947- *AmMWSc 92*
**Pardo,** Robert Edward 1951- *WhoMW 92*
**Pardo,** William Bermudez 1928- *AmMWSc 92*
**Pardoe,** Alan Douglas William 1943- *Who 92*
**Pardoe,** Geoffrey Keith Charles 1928- *Who 92*
**Pardoe,** John George Magrath *Who 92*
**Pardoe,** John Wentworth 1934- *Who 92*
**Pardoe,** M. 1902- *WrDr 92*
**Pardridge,** William M *AmMWSc 92*
**Pardue,** A. Michael 1931- *WhoWest 92*
**Pardue,** Dwight Edward 1928- *WhoFI 92*
**Pardue,** Harry L 1934- *AmMWSc 92*
**Pardue,** Howard Monroe 1942- *WhoEnt 92*
**Pardue,** Mary Lou 1933- *AmMWSc 92*
**Pardue,** William B 1930- *WhoIns 92*
**Pardue,** William M 1935- *AmMWSc 92*
**Pare,** J R Jocelyn 1959- *AmMWSc 92*
**Pare,** Marius 1903- *WhoRel 92*
**Pare,** Michael 1959- *IntMPA 92*
**Pare,** Philip Norris 1910- *Who 92*
**Pare,** Victor Kenneth 1928- *AmMWSc 92*
**Pare,** William Paul 1933- *AmMWSc 92*
**Paredes,** Americo 1915- *WhoHisp 92*
**Paredes,** Bert 1947- *WhoWest 92*
**Paredes,** Frank C., Jr. 1949- *WhoHisp 92*
**Paredes,** Ismael S. 1942- *WhoHisp 92*
**Paredes,** James Anthony 1939- *WhoHisp 92*
**Paredes,** Ruben Dario 1931- *IntWW 91*
**Parees,** David Marc 1950- *AmMWSc 92*
**Parejko,** Ronald Anthony 1940- *AmMWSc 92*
**Parekh,** Bhikhu Chhotalal 1935- *Who 92*
**Parekh,** Girish Girdhar 1939- *WhoMW 92*
**Parekh,** Hasmukh 1911- *IntWW 91*
**Parekh,** Parimal Vasantlal 1959- *WhoMW 92*
**Parella,** Gaetano D 1922- *WhoAmP 91*
**Parent,** Andre 1944- *AmMWSc 92*
**Parent,** Elizabeth Anne 1941- *WhoWest 92*
**Parent,** James E. 1939- *WhoFI 92*
**Parent,** Joseph D 1910- *AmMWSc 92*
**Parent,** Paul *WhoAmP 91*
**Parent,** Richard Alfred 1935- *AmMWSc 92*
**Parent,** Roger O *WhoAmP 91*
**Parente,** Daniel John 1954- *WhoEnt 92*
**Parente,** Marie J *WhoAmP 91*
**Parenti,** Kathy Ann 1957- *WhoWest 92*
**Parer,** Julian Thomas 1934- *WhoWest 92*
**Pares,** Peter 1908- *Who 92*
**Pares-Avila,** Jose Agustin 1964- *WhoHisp 92*
**Paresa,** Leonard Pomaikai, Jr. 1956- *WhoWest 92*
**Paresi,** Barbara Ann 1958- *WhoEnt 92*
**Paret,** Peter 1924- *IntWW 91*
**Parets,** Eric 1948- *WhoFI 92*
**Paretsky,** David 1918- *AmMWSc 92, WhoMW 92*
**Paretsky,** Sara 1947- *WrDr 92*
**Paretsky,** Sara N. 1947- *WhoMW 92*
**Parfenie,** Maria *ConAu 34NR*
**Parfenovich,** Vladimir Ivanovich 1958- *SovUnBD*
**Parfet,** William U. 1946- *WhoFI 92*
**Parfit,** Derek Antony 1942- *Who 92*
**Parfitt,** A M 1930- *AmMWSc 92*
**Parfitt,** Tudor 1944- *WrDr 92*
**Pargas,** Fernando A. *WhoEnt 92*
**Pargellis,** Andrew Nason 1952- *AmMWSc 92*
**Pargeter,** Edith 1913- *IntAu&W 91, IntWW 91, Who 92, WrDr 92*
**Pargeter,** Philip 1933- *Who 92*
**Pargman,** David 1937- *AmMWSc 92*
**Pargoff,** Robert Michael 1961- *WhoMW 92*
**Parham,** Bobby Eugene *WhoAmP 91*
**Parham,** Brenda Joyce 1944- *WhoBlA 92*
**Parham,** Charles Fox 1873-1929 *RelLAm 91*
**Parham,** Ellen Speiden 1938- *AmMWSc 92, WhoMW 92*
**Parham,** Frederick Robertson d1991 *Who 92N*
**Parham,** Frederick Russell 1953- *WhoBlA 92*
**Parham,** James Crowder, II 1938- *AmMWSc 92*
**Parham,** Johnny Eugene, Jr. 1937- *WhoBlA 92*
**Parham,** Joseph Byars 1919-1980 *ConAu 135*
**Parham,** Lloyd L 1928- *WhoIns 92*
**Parham,** Marc Ellous 1948- *AmMWSc 92*
**Parham,** Margaret Payne 1942- *AmMWSc 92*
**Parham,** Marjorie B. *WhoBlA 92*
**Parham,** Robert *DrAPF 91*
**Parham,** Samuel Levenus 1905- *WhoBlA 92*
**Parham,** Samuel M 1930- *WhoAmP 91*
**Parham,** Thomas David, Jr. 1920- *WhoBlA 92*
**Parham,** Walter Edward 1930- *AmMWSc 92*
**Parham,** William Thomas 1913- *WrDr 92*
**Parikh,** Hemant Bhupendra 1951- *AmMWSc 92*
**Parikh,** Indu *AmMWSc 92*
**Parikh,** Jekishan R 1922- *AmMWSc 92*
**Parikh,** Manoj Jayantilal 1957- *WhoFI 92*
**Parikh,** N M 1929- *AmMWSc 92*
**Parikh,** Parimal J. 1949- *WhoFI 92*
**Parikh,** Pravin Jayantilal 1942- *WhoFI 92*
**Parikh,** Rohit Jivanlal 1936- *AmMWSc 92*
**Parikh,** Sarvabhaum Sohanlal 1935- *AmMWSc 92*
**Parikh,** Shrikant Navnitlal 1956- *WhoFI 92*
**Parini,** Jay 1948- *WrDr 92*
**Parins,** Robert James 1918- *WhoMW 92*
**Paris,** Archbishop of *Who 92*
**Paris,** Bernard Jay 1931- *IntAu&W 91, WrDr 92*
**Paris,** Bubba 1960- *WhoBlA 92*
**Paris,** Calvin Rudolph 1932- *WhoBlA 92*
**Paris,** Clark Davis 1911- *AmMWSc 92*
**Paris,** David Andrew 1962- *WhoWest 92*
**Paris,** David Leonard 1944- *AmMWSc 92*
**Paris,** Demetrius T 1928- *AmMWSc 92*
**Paris,** Doris Fort 1924- *AmMWSc 92*
**Paris,** Erna 1938- *IntAu&W 91*
**Paris,** Felipe Sanchez 1941- *WhoHisp 92*
**Paris,** Franklin D 1933- *WhoAmP 91*
**Paris,** George M, Sr *WhoAmP 91*
**Paris,** Jean Philip 1935- *AmMWSc 92*
**Paris,** Jerry d1986 *LesBEnT 92*
**Paris,** Matthew *DrAPF 91*
**Paris,** Michael 1947- *WhoMW 92*
**Paris,** Michael 1949- *ConAu 135*
**Paris,** Mike *ConAu 135*
**Paris,** Olden Edwards 1927- *WhoMW 92*
**Paris,** Oscar Hall 1931- *AmMWSc 92*
**Paris,** Peter Junior 1933- *WhoRel 92*
**Paris,** Robert Steven 1957- *WhoEnt 92*
**Paris,** Steven Mark 1956- *WhoFI 92*
**Paris,** Theodore Ross 1950- *WhoMW 92*
**Paris de Bollardiere,** Jacques Marie Roch 1907-1986 *FacFETw*
**Parise,** Marc Robert 1953- *WhoFI 92*
**Pariseau,** Judy Louise 1941- *WhoAmP 91*
**Pariseau,** Patricia 1936- *WhoAmP 91*
**Parisek,** Charles Bruce 1931- *AmMWSc 92*
**Pariser,** Harry 1911- *AmMWSc 92*
**Pariser,** Michael David 1950- *WhoEnt 92*
**Pariser,** Rudolph 1923- *AmMWSc 92*
**Parish,** Barbara Shirk *DrAPF 91*
**Parish,** Charles 1927- *WhoMW 92*
**Parish,** Curtis Lee 1937- *AmMWSc 92*
**Parish,** Daniel M 1919- *WhoAmP 91*
**Parish,** Darrell Joe 1934- *AmMWSc 92*
**Parish,** David W. *Who 92*
**Parish,** Dorothy 1910- *NewYTBS 91 [port]*
**Parish,** Edward James 1943- *AmMWSc 92*
**Parish,** Elijah 1762-1825 *BenetAL 91*
**Parish,** Harlie Albert, Jr 1940- *AmMWSc 92*
**Parish,** Henry, II, Mrs. 1910- *DcTwDes, FacFETw*
**Parish,** James 1944- *IntAu&W 91, WrDr 92*
**Parish,** James Robert *IntMPA 92*
**Parish,** Jeffrey Lee 1945- *AmMWSc 92*
**Parish,** Peggy *IntAu&W 91*
**Parish,** Richard Lee 1945- *AmMWSc 92*
**Parish,** Robert 1953- *WhoBlA 92*
**Parish,** Roger Cook 1940- *AmMWSc 92*
**Parish,** Trueman Davis 1939- *AmMWSc 92*
**Parish,** William R 1920- *AmMWSc 92*
**Parisi,** Anthony J. d1991 *NewYTBS 91*
**Parisi,** George I 1931- *AmMWSc 92*
**Parisi,** Joseph Anthony 1944- *IntAu&W 91*
**Parisi,** Joseph Thomas 1934- *AmMWSc 92*
**Parisi,** Robert Arthur, Jr. 1963- *WhoAmL 92*
**Parisi,** Stephen Thomas 1940- *WhoAmL 92*
**Parisien,** Maurice Ray 1951- *WhoMW 92*
**Parisot,** Aldo 1920- *NewAmDM*
**Parisse,** Anthony John 1936- *AmMWSc 92*
**Pariza,** Michael Willard 1943- *AmMWSc 92*
**Pariza,** Richard James 1946- *AmMWSc 92*
**Parizean,** Alia 1930- *LiExTwC*
**Parizek,** Eldon Joseph 1920- *AmMWSc 92*
**Parizek,** Richard Rudolph 1934- *AmMWSc 92*
**Parizo,** Bernard Ernest 1932- *WhoAmP 91*
**Parizo,** Kevin Douglas 1952- *WhoRel 92*
**Parizo,** Mary Ann 1934- *WhoAmP 91*
**Park** *Who 92*
**Park Choong-Hoon** 1919- *IntWW 91*
**Park Chung Hee** 1917-1979 *FacFETw*
**Park Sung Sang** 1923- *IntWW 91*
**Park,** Alice Locke 1861-1961 *AmPeW*
**Park,** Alistair 1930-1984 *TwCPaSc*
**Park,** Andrew Edward Wilson 1939- *Who 92*
**Park,** Andrew Sung 1951- *WhoRel 92*
**Park,** Anne 1958- *WhoFI 92*
**Park,** Austin F 1825-1893 *BiInAmS*
**Park,** B J 1934- *AmMWSc 92*
**Park,** Carole Roper 1939- *WhoAmP 91*
**Park,** Chan H 1937- *AmMWSc 92*
**Park,** Chan Mo 1935- *AmMWSc 92*
**Park,** Charles Rawlinson 1916- *AmMWSc 92, IntWW 91*
**Park,** Chong Jin 1936- *AmMWSc 92*
**Park,** Chul 1934- *AmMWSc 92*
**Park,** Chull 1932- *AmMWSc 92*
**Park,** Chung Gun 1939- *AmMWSc 92*
**Park,** Chung Ho 1936- *AmMWSc 92*
**Park,** Chung Sun 1942- *AmMWSc 92*
**Park,** Conrad B 1919- *AmMWSc 92*
**Park,** Dabney Glenn, Jr. 1941- *WhoRel 92*
**Park,** David Allen 1919- *AmMWSc 92*
**Park,** David Duck-Young 1942- *WhoWest 92*
**Park,** Dorothy Goodwin Dent *WhoEnt 92*
**Park,** Duk-Won 1945- *AmMWSc 92*
**Park,** Edward C, Jr 1923- *AmMWSc 92*
**Park,** Edward Cahill, Jr. 1923- *WhoWest 92*
**Park,** Emma 1950- *TwCPaSc*
**Park,** Eung-Chun 1958- *WhoRel 92*
**Park,** Francis Wood, III 1932- *WhoRel 92*
**Park,** George Bennet 1946- *AmMWSc 92*
**Park,** George Maclean 1914- *Who 92*
**Park,** Gerald 1937- *TwCPaSc*
**Park,** Gerald L 1933- *AmMWSc 92*
**Park,** Gerald Leslie 1933- *WhoMW 92*
**Park,** Heebok 1933- *AmMWSc 92*
**Park,** Herbert William, III 1920- *AmMWSc 92*
**Park,** Hong Y. 1938- *WhoMW 92*
**Park,** Howard Mitchell 1922- *WhoRel 92*
**Park,** Hugh 1910- *Who 92*
**Park,** Ian Grahame 1935- *Who 92*
**Park,** Ian Michael 1938- *Who 92*
**Park,** Ida May d1954 *ReelWom*
**Park,** J Stephen 1941- *WhoAmP 91*
**Park,** Jae Young 1930- *AmMWSc 92*
**Park,** James Lemuel 1940- *AmMWSc 92*
**Park,** James Theodore 1922- *AmMWSc 92*
**Park,** James Wallace 1934- *WhoFI 92*
**Park,** Jane Harting 1925- *AmMWSc 92*
**Park,** Jeffrey Bryan 1951- *WhoFI 92*
**Park,** John 1880-1962 *TwCPaSc*
**Park,** John C. 1925- *WhoFI 92*
**Park,** John Edward, Jr. 1953- *WhoFI 92*
**Park,** John Faircloth 1930- *WhoRel 92*
**Park,** John Howard, Jr 1932- *AmMWSc 92*
**Park,** John Thornton 1935- *AmMWSc 92*
**Park,** Joon B 1944- *AmMWSc 92*
**Park,** Kiri *Who 92*
**Park,** Kisoon *AmMWSc 92*
**Park,** Kwangjai 1935- *AmMWSc 92*
**Park,** Lee Crandall 1926- *AmMWSc 92*
**Park,** Mary Caroline 1932- *WhoAmP 91*
**Park,** Merle 1937- *Who 92*
**Park,** Merle Florence 1937- *IntWW 91*
**Park,** Michael *Who 92*
**Park,** Myung Kun 1934- *AmMWSc 92*
**Park,** Paul 1954- *TwCSFW 91*
**Park,** Paul Heechung 1941- *AmMWSc 92*
**Park,** Paul Kilho 1931- *AmMWSc 92*
**Park,** Richard Avery, IV 1938- *AmMWSc 92*
**Park,** Richard Dee 1942- *AmMWSc 92*
**Park,** Richard Lee 1943- *WhoMW 92*
**Park,** Robert 1933- *IntWW 91*
**Park,** Robert Ezra 1864-1944 *DcAmImH*
**Park,** Robert H 1902- *AmMWSc 92*
**Park,** Robert H. 1916- *IntMPA 92*
**Park,** Robert L 1931- *AmMWSc 92*
**Park,** Robert Lynn 1932- *AmMWSc 92*
**Park,** Robert William 1929- *AmMWSc 92*
**Park,** Roderic Bruce 1932- *AmMWSc 92*
**Park,** Roger Cook 1942- *WhoAmL 92*
**Park,** Roswell 1852-1914 *BiInAmS*
**Park,** Roy Hampton 1910- *WhoEnt 92*
**Park,** Ruth *IntAu&W 91, WrDr 92*
**Park,** Sally Lease 1938- *WhoAmL 92*
**Park,** Samuel 1936- *AmMWSc 92*
**Park,** Seung Kook 1957- *WhoWest 92*
**Park,** Stanley William 1967- *WhoFI 92*
**Park,** Su-Moon 1941- *AmMWSc 92*

Park, Sung Jae 1937- WhoMW 92
Park, Taisoo 1929- AmMWSc 92
Park, Taylor Richard 1959- WhoRel 92
Park, Thomas 1908- AmMWSc 92
Park, Trevor 1927- Who 92
Park, Vernon Kee 1928- AmMWSc 92
Park, Virginia Lawhon 1937- WhoAmP 91
Park, William H 1929- AmMWSc 92
Park, William Wynnewood 1947- WhoAmL 92
Park, Won Joon 1935- AmMWSc 92
Park, Yoon Soo 1929- AmMWSc 92
Park, Young D 1932- AmMWSc 92
Park of Monmouth, Baroness 1921- Who 92
Parka, Stanley John 1935- AmMWSc 92
Parkany, John 1921- WhoFI 92
Parkanyi, Cyril 1933- AmMWSc 92
Parke, Andrew Butler 1960- WhoEnt 92
Parke, Clifford Thomas 1936- WhoRel 92
Parke, Dennis Vernon William 1922- Who 92
Parke, Grace Nakyung 1955- WhoAmL 92
Parke, John 1754-1789 BenetAL 91
Parke, Lowell William 1925- WhoAmP 91
Parke, Robert Leon 1940- WhoFI 92
Parke, Russell Frank 1932- AmMWSc 92
Parke, Terry R 1944- WhoAmP 91
Parke, Wesley Wilkin 1926- AmMWSc 92
Parke, William C 1941- AmMWSc 92
Parkening, Christopher 1947- ConMus 7 [port]
Parkening, Terry Arthur 1943- AmMWSc 92
Parker Who 92
Parker, Son, and Bourn DcLB 106
Parker, Viscount 1943- Who 92
Parker, A Miller 1895- Who 92
Parker, Agnes Miller 1895-1980 TwCPaSc
Parker, Alan 1944- IntDcF 2-2, IntMPA 92
Parker, Alan Douglas 1945- AmMWSc 92
Parker, Alan William 1944- IntWW 91, Who 92, WhoEnt 92
Parker, Albert John 1953- AmMWSc 92
Parker, Alice 1925- WhoEnt 92
Parker, Alice Cline 1948- AmMWSc 92
Parker, Allan Leslie 1938- WhoMW 92
Parker, Alton Brooks 1852-1926 AmPolLe
Parker, Angelo Pan 1945- WhoAmL 92
Parker, Antonina B 1921- WhoAmP 91
Parker, Arlynn Ann 1954- WhoAmL 92
Parker, Arnita Walden 1905- WhoBlA 92
Parker, Arthur Caswell 1881-1955 BenetAL 91
Parker, Arthur L 1950- AmMWSc 92
Parker, Averette Mhoon 1939- WhoBlA 92
Parker, B F 1924- AmMWSc 92
Parker, Barrett 1908- WrDr 92
Parker, Barrington D. 1915- WhoBlA 92
Parker, Barry James Charles 1947- WhoFI 92
Parker, Barry Lynn 1958- WhoRel 92
Parker, Barry Richard 1935- AmMWSc 92
Parker, Barry T 1932- WhoAmP 91
Parker, Bernard F., Jr. 1949- WhoBlA 92
Parker, Beulah Mae 1943- AmMWSc 92
Parker, Billie Ida 1952- WhoFI 92
Parker, Bonnie FacFETw
Parker, Bonnie 1910-1934 HanAmWH
Parker, Brent M 1927- AmMWSc 92
Parker, Brian Prescott 1929- WhoWest 92
Parker, Bruce C 1933- AmMWSc 92
Parker, Calvin Alfred 1931- AmMWSc 92
Parker, Cameron Holdsworth 1932- Who 92
Parker, Carl Allen 1934- WhoAmP 91
Parker, Carl Harold 1923- WhoAmP 91
Parker, Carol Elaine Greenberg 1947- AmMWSc 92
Parker, Caroline Jane Fairchild 1938- WhoRel 92
Parker, Catherine M 1921- WhoAmP 91
Parker, Catherine Susanne 1934- WhoWest 92
Parker, Charles Arthur 1961- WhoRel 92
Parker, Charles D 1924- AmMWSc 92
Parker, Charles Edward 1927- WhoAmL 92, WhoWest 92
Parker, Charles F 1820-1883 BiInAmS
Parker, Charles J, Jr 1930- AmMWSc 92
Parker, Charles McCrae 1930- WhoBlA 92
Parker, Charles Thomas 1918- WhoBlA 92
Parker, Charles W 1930- AmMWSc 92
Parker, Charlie 1920-1955 FacFETw [port], NewAmDM
Parker, Charlotte Blair 1868-1937 BenetAL 91
Parker, Christopher DrAPF 91
Parker, Christopher William 1947- WhoAmL 92
Parker, Christopher William Oxley 1920- Who 92
Parker, Claire 1906-1981 ReelWom [port]
Parker, Clara d1991 NewYTBS 91
Parker, Claude A. 1938- WhoBlA 92
Parker, Cleofus Varren, Jr 1937- AmMWSc 92
Parker, Clifford Frederick 1920- Who 92
Parker, Constance Anne TwCPaSc
Parker, Daniel 1925- WhoAmP 91
Parker, Daniel Louis 1924- WhoFI 92
Parker, Darwin Carey 1956- WhoBlA 92
Parker, David 1954- WhoAmP 91
Parker, David B. 1956- ConAu 135
Parker, David Charles 1945- AmMWSc 92
Parker, David Garland 1940- AmMWSc 92
Parker, David Gene 1951- WhoBlA 92
Parker, David H 1953- AmMWSc 92
Parker, David R. 1957- WhoMW 92
Parker, David Russell 1950- WhoBlA 92
Parker, Derek 1932- WrDr 92
Parker, Diana Jean 1932- Who 92
Parker, Don Earl 1932- AmMWSc 92
Parker, Donal C 1931- AmMWSc 92
Parker, Donald Dean 1899-1983 ConAu 34NR
Parker, Donald Emory 1933- WhoIns 92
Parker, Donald Irwin 1921- WhoAmP 91
Parker, Donald LaRue 1935- WhoFI 92
Parker, Donald Lester 1944- AmMWSc 92
Parker, Donald Samuel 1948- WhoAmL 92
Parker, Donn Blanchard 1929- AmMWSc 92
Parker, Doris S. 1931- WhoBlA 92
Parker, Doris Sims 1931- WhoMW 92
Parker, Dorothy 1893-1967 BenetAL 91, ConLC 68 [port], FacFETw, HanAmWH, ModAWWr, ReelWom
Parker, Dorothy Lundquist 1939- AmMWSc 92
Parker, Douglas D. Who 92
Parker, Douglas Granger 1919- Who 92
Parker, Douglas Irwin 1949- WhoMW 92
Parker, Douglas Martin 1935- WhoAmL 92
Parker, E T 1926- AmMWSc 92, WhoMW 92
Parker, Earl Elmer 1918- AmMWSc 92
Parker, Earl Randall 1912- AmMWSc 92
Parker, Earle Leroy 1943- WhoFI 92
Parker, Edna G. 1930- WhoAmL 92
Parker, Edna Mae 1910- IntAu&W 91
Parker, Edward Burns, II 1955- WhoAmL 92
Parker, Edward Everett 1941- WhoBlA 92
Parker, Ehi 1952- AmMWSc 92
Parker, Eleanor 1922- IntMPA 92
Parker, Ellis Jackson, III 1932- WhoFI 92
Parker, Eric 1933- Who 92
Parker, Eric Wilson 1933- IntWW 91
Parker, Eugene N. 1927- IntWW 91
Parker, Eugene Newman 1927- AmMWSc 92
Parker, Everett C. LesBEnT 92
Parker, Everett Carlton 1913- WhoRel 92
Parker, Fess 1925- IntMPA 92
Parker, Frances Lawrence 1906- AmMWSc 92
Parker, Francis Dunbar 1918- AmMWSc 92
Parker, Frank 1932- WhoWest 92
Parker, Frank C, III 1945- WhoAmP 91
Parker, Frank L 1926- AmMWSc 92
Parker, Frank S 1921- AmMWSc 92
Parker, Franklin 1921- IntAu&W 91, IntWW 91, WrDr 92
Parker, Fred Lee Cecil 1923- WhoBlA 92
Parker, Fred Wayne 1951- WhoAmP 91
Parker, Frederick John 1927- Who 92
Parker, Frederick John 1952- AmMWSc 92
Parker, Frederick L 1939- WhoAmP 91
Parker, G. John, Sr. 1941- WhoBlA 92
Parker, G Preston 1943- WhoAmP 91
Parker, Garald G, Sr 1905- AmMWSc 92
Parker, Garda May 1939- WhoEnt 92
Parker, Gary WhoAmP 91
Parker, Gary Wayne 1945- WhoIns 92
Parker, Geoffrey Who 92
Parker, Geoffrey Alan 1944- Who 92
Parker, Geoffrey John 1937- Who 92
Parker, George 1929- WhoAmP 91
Parker, George Anthony 1952- WhoBlA 92, WhoFI 92
Parker, George Daniel 1945- WhoMW 92
Parker, George Edgar 1946- WhoAmL 92
Parker, George Priestley, Jr. 1943- WhoAmL 92
Parker, George Ralph 1942- AmMWSc 92
Parker, George W 1939- AmMWSc 92
Parker, Gilbert 1862-1932 BenetAL 91
Parker, Glenn Charles 1928- WhoAmL 92
Parker, Gloria WhoEnt 92
Parker, Gordon 1940- IntAu&W 91, WrDr 92
Parker, Gordon Arthur 1936- AmMWSc 92, WhoMW 92
Parker, Gordon Rae 1935- WhoWest 92
Parker, Graham 1950- WhoEnt 92
Parker, Grant Dean 1958- WhoAmL 92
Parker, H Dennison 1941- AmMWSc 92
Parker, H. Wallace 1941- WhoBlA 92
Parker, Harold R 1920- AmMWSc 92
Parker, Harold W. 1924- WhoRel 92
Parker, Harry W 1932- AmMWSc 92
Parker, Helen Meister 1935- AmMWSc 92
Parker, Henry Ellsworth 1928- WhoBlA 92
Parker, Henry Griffith, III 1926- WhoIns 92
Parker, Henry H. 1933- WhoBlA 92
Parker, Henry Seabury, III 1944- AmMWSc 92
Parker, Henry Webster 1822?-1903 BiInAmS
Parker, Henry Whipple 1924- AmMWSc 92
Parker, Herbert Edmund 1919- AmMWSc 92
Parker, Herbert Gerald 1929- WhoBlA 92
Parker, Herbert John Harvey Who 92
Parker, Horatio 1863-1919 NewAmDM
Parker, Howard 1931- WhoAmP 91
Parker, Howard Ashley, Jr 1922- AmMWSc 92
Parker, Hugh 1919- Who 92
Parker, J. H. 1806-1884 DcLB 106
Parker, Jack Who 92
Parker, Jack Lindsay 1930- AmMWSc 92
Parker, Jack Steele 1918- AmMWSc 92
Parker, Jacquelyn Heath WhoBlA 92
Parker, Jacquelyn Susan 1960- WhoMW 92
Parker, James DcLB 106, IntAu&W 91X
Parker, James Aubrey 1937- WhoAmL 92, WhoWest 92
Parker, James E. WhoBlA 92
Parker, James Edward 1938- WhoFI 92
Parker, James Floyd 1946- WhoMW 92, WhoRel 92
Parker, James Francis 1947- WhoAmL 92
Parker, James Geoffrey 1933- Who 92
Parker, James Henry, Jr 1926- AmMWSc 92
Parker, James John 1947- WhoMW 92
Parker, James L. 1923- WhoBlA 92
Parker, James Mavin 1934- Who 92
Parker, James Ray 1956- WhoFI 92
Parker, James Roland Walter 1919- Who 92
Parker, James Stewart 1941- IntAu&W 91
Parker, James Thomas 1934- WhoBlA 92
Parker, James Watson 1951- WhoEnt 92
Parker, James Willard 1945- AmMWSc 92
Parker, Jameson 1947- IntMPA 92
Parker, Jane Marsh 1836-1913 BenetAL 91
Parker, Jannette WhoAmP 91
Parker, Jean Who 92
Parker, Jean L. 1923- WhoBlA 92
Parker, Jeff, Sr. 1927- WhoBlA 92
Parker, Jeffrey Scott 1952- WhoAmL 92
Parker, Jennifer Ware 1959- AmMWSc 92
Parker, Jerald D 1930- AmMWSc 92
Parker, Jerald Vawer 1939- AmMWSc 92, WhoWest 92
Parker, Jerry 1928- WhoAmP 91
Parker, Jerry L. 1957- WhoFI 92
Parker, Jerry P. 1943- WhoBlA 92
Parker, Jim 1944- WhoAmP 91
Parker, Joan Marie 1954- WhoFI 92
Parker, John Who 92
Parker, John 1906-1987 ConAu 34NR
Parker, John Basil 1946- WhoEnt 92
Parker, John Brian 1959- WhoWest 92
Parker, John C 1935- AmMWSc 92
Parker, John Curtis 1935- AmMWSc 92
Parker, John F 1907- WhoAmP 91
Parker, John Havelock 1929- IntWW 91
Parker, John Hill 1944- WhoAmL 92
Parker, John Hilliard 1941- AmMWSc 92
Parker, John Malcolm 1920- WhoFI 92
Parker, John Marchbank 1920- AmMWSc 92, WhoWest 92
Parker, John Mason, III 1906- AmMWSc 92
Parker, John Michael 1920- Who 92
Parker, John Orval 1930- AmMWSc 92
Parker, John Paul 1945- WhoAmP 91
Parker, John Rutledge 1946- WhoFI 92
Parker, John Victor 1928- WhoAmL 92
Parker, John W. 1792-1870 DcLB 106
Parker, John W. 1820-1860 DcLB 106
Parker, John W., and Sons DcLB 106
Parker, John William 1931- AmMWSc 92, WhoWest 92
Parker, Johnson 1917- AmMWSc 92
Parker, Jon Irving 1944- AmMWSc 92
Parker, Jonathan Frederic 1937- Who 92
Parker, Joseph B, Jr 1916- AmMWSc 92
Parker, Joseph Caiaphas, Jr. 1952- WhoAmL 92, WhoBlA 92
Parker, Joseph Mayon 1931- WhoAmP 91, WhoFI 92
Parker, Joseph R 1916- AmMWSc 92
Parker, Joyce Linda 1944- WhoBlA 92
Parker, Judith WhoEnt 92
Parker, Judith Koehler 1940- WhoAmP 91
Parker, Julie Ann 1963- WhoAmL 92
Parker, Junior 1927-1971 NewAmDM
Parker, Kai J. 1939- WhoBlA 92
Parker, Karl 1895- Who 92
Parker, Karl Theodore 1895- IntWW 91
Parker, Kathleen 1948- WhoEnt 92
Parker, Kathlyn Ann 1945- AmMWSc 92
Parker, Keith Dwight 1954- WhoBlA 92
Parker, Keith John 1940- IntAu&W 91, Who 92
Parker, Keith Krom 1950- AmMWSc 92
Parker, Kellis E. 1942- WhoAmL 92, WhoBlA 92
Parker, Kenneth Alfred Lamport 1912- Who 92
Parker, Kenneth D 1935- AmMWSc 92
Parker, Kenneth Dean 1935- WhoWest 92
Parker, Kinneth Owen 1937- WhoMW 92
Parker, Kit 1948- WhoEnt 92
Parker, Kristy Kay 1957- IntAu&W 91
Parker, Larry James 1942- WhoAmP 91
Parker, Larry Lee 1938- WhoFI 92
Parker, Larry Maynard 1951- WhoEnt 92
Parker, Lee 1949- WhoBlA 92
Parker, Lee Fischer 1932- WhoMW 92
Parker, Lee Ward 1923- AmMWSc 92
Parker, Leon Douglas 1920- WhoAmP 91
Parker, Leonard Emanuel 1938- AmMWSc 92
Parker, LeRoy A, Jr 1930- AmMWSc 92
Parker, Leslie 1939- AmMWSc 92
Parker, Lewis Wardlaw, Jr 1928- WhoAmP 91
Parker, Lisa Maureen 1955- WhoAmP 91
Parker, Lloyd Robinson, Jr 1950- AmMWSc 92
Parker, Lutrelle Fleming 1924- WhoBlA 92
Parker, Maceo ConMus 7 [port], WhoEnt 92
Parker, Margaret Annette McCrie Johnston Who 92
Parker, Margaret Maier 1950- AmMWSc 92
Parker, Marjorie Alice Collett d1991 Who 92N
Parker, Martin Leonard 1921- WhoAmP 91
Parker, Mary Ann 1953- WhoAmL 92
Parker, Mary Langston 1924- AmMWSc 92
Parker, Maryland Mike 1926- WhoBlA 92
Parker, Matthew 1945- WhoBlA 92, WhoRel 92
Parker, Maynard Michael 1940- IntAu&W 91, IntWW 91, WhoFI 92
Parker, Michael Who 92
Parker, Michael 1938- AmMWSc 92
Parker, Michael Clynes 1924- Who 92
Parker, Michael David 1954- WhoWest 92
Parker, Michael John 1941- Who 92
Parker, Michael Joseph Bennett 1931- Who 92
Parker, Michael St J. Who 92
Parker, Mike 1949- AlmAP 92 [port], WhoAmP 91
Parker, Murl Wayne 1939- AmMWSc 92
Parker, N F 1923- AmMWSc 92
Parker, Nancy Johanne Rentner 1937- AmMWSc 92
Parker, Nancy W. 1930- WrDr 92
Parker, Nick Charles 1943- AmMWSc 92
Parker, Noel Geoffrey 1943- Who 92
Parker, Omar Sigmund, Jr. 1945- WhoAmL 92
Parker, Patrick Evan 1951- WhoMW 92
Parker, Patrick Johnston 1931- WhoFI 92
Parker, Patrick LeGrand 1933- AmMWSc 92
Parker, Patrick Streeter 1929- WhoMW 92
Parker, Paul E. 1935- WhoBlA 92
Parker, Paul Michael 1928- AmMWSc 92
Parker, Peter Who 92
Parker, Peter 1924- IntWW 91, Who 92
Parker, Peter Donald MacDougall 1936- AmMWSc 92
Parker, Peter Eddy 1944- AmMWSc 92
Parker, Pierson 1905- WhoRel 92
Parker, Polly Jane 1961- WhoMW 92
Parker, Quanah 1845-1911 RelLAm 91
Parker, Ralph 1919- WhoAmP 91
Parker, Ray, Jr. 1954- WhoBlA 92
Parker, Reginald Boden 1901- Who 92
Parker, Richard 1915- IntAu&W 91
Parker, Richard Alan 1931- AmMWSc 92
Parker, Richard Bordeaux 1923- WhoAmP 91
Parker, Richard C 1939- AmMWSc 92
Parker, Richard Davies 1945- WhoAmL 92
Parker, Richard Garland 1956- WhoRel 92
Parker, Richard Ghrist 1941- AmMWSc 92
Parker, Richard H 1932- AmMWSc 92
Parker, Richard Hyde 1937- Who 92
Parker, Richard Langley 1929- AmMWSc 92
Parker, Richard W. 1945- WhoWest 92
Parker, Richard Wilson 1943- WhoAmL 92
Parker, Robert Allan Ridley 1936- AmMWSc 92
Parker, Robert Alton 1956- WhoEnt 92

Parker, Robert B 1932- IntAu&W 91, WrDr 92
Parker, Robert Brown 1932- WhoEnt 92
Parker, Robert C ScFEYrs
Parker, Robert Chauncey Humphrey 1941- WhoMW 92
Parker, Robert Daniel 1945- WhoWest 92
Parker, Robert Davis Rickard 1942- AmMWSc 92
Parker, Robert Frederic 1907- AmMWSc 92
Parker, Robert G 1925- AmMWSc 92
Parker, Robert Hallett 1922- AmMWSc 92
Parker, Robert Louis 1929- AmMWSc 92
Parker, Robert M. 1937- WhoAmL 92
Parker, Robert Marc 1952- WhoAmL 92
Parker, Robert Orion 1915- AmMWSc 92
Parker, Robert Rudolph 1927- WhoMW 92
Parker, Robert Samuel 1924- WhoAmL 92
Parker, Robert Stewart 1915- WrDr 92
Parker, Robert Stewart 1949- Who 92
Parker, Robert Tarbert 1919- AmMWSc 92
Parker, Robert Vernon 1931- WhoAmL 92
Parker, Robert Whittingham, Jr 1948- WhoAmP 91
Parker, Robin Leigh 1956- WhoAmL 92
Parker, Rodger D 1934- AmMWSc 92
Parker, Rodney Edwin 1931- WhoAmP 91
Parker, Roger 1923- Who 92
Parker, Roger A 1943- AmMWSc 92
Parker, Ronald Bruce 1932- AmMWSc 92
Parker, Ronald Keith 1949- WhoEnt 92
Parker, Ronald R AmMWSc 92
Parker, Ronald W 1950- AmMWSc 92
Parker, Ronald William 1909- Who 92
Parker, Roy Alfred 1930- WhoWest 92
Parker, Roy Denver, Jr 1943- AmMWSc 92
Parker, Samuel 1779-1866 BenetAL 91
Parker, Sarah Jessica 1965- IntMPA 92
Parker, Scott 1950- WhoEnt 92
Parker, Scott Jackson 1945- WhoEnt 92
Parker, Sherwood 1932- AmMWSc 92
Parker, Sidney G 1925- AmMWSc 92
Parker, Sidney Thomas 1913- AmMWSc 92
Parker, Stafford W. 1935- WhoBlA 92
Parker, Stanley R. 1927- WrDr 92
Parker, Stephen A. WhoBlA 92
Parker, Stephen Jan 1939- WhoMW 92
Parker, Steve H. 1950- WhoMW 92
Parker, Sue Ellen 1950- WhoAmP 91
Parker, Susan Elaine 1959- WhoMW 92
Parker, Suzy 1933- IntMPA 92
Parker, Sydney R 1923- AmMWSc 92
Parker, Theodore 1810-1860 AmPeW, BenetAL 91
Parker, Theodore Clifford 1929- WhoFI 92, WhoWest 92
Parker, Thomas 1595-1677 BenetAL 91
Parker, Thomas 1916- WrDr 92
Parker, Thomas C. 1959- WhoRel 92
Parker, Thomas Charles 1941- WhoEnt 92
Parker, Thomas Dunklin 1931- WhoRel 92
Parker, Thomas E., Jr. 1916- WhoBlA 92
Parker, Thomas Edwin, III 1944- WhoBlA 92
Parker, Thomas John 1942- IntWW 91, Who 92
Parker, Tim WhoAmP 91
Parker, Travis Jay 1913- AmMWSc 92
Parker, V M 1915- WhoAmP 91
Parker, Vincent Eveland 1914- AmMWSc 92
Parker, Virgil Jon 1925- WhoWest 92
Parker, Virgil Thomas 1951- AmMWSc 92
Parker, W. Dale 1925- WrDr 92
Parker, W. H. 1912- WrDr 92
Parker, Walteen Carter 1946- WhoAmP 91
Parker, Walter Gee 1933- WhoBlA 92
Parker, Wayne Charles 1956- WhoWest 92
Parker, Wilfred John 1915- Who 92
Parker, Willard Albert 1938- AmMWSc 92
Parker, William WhoAmP 91
Parker, William Alan d1990 Who 92N
Parker, William Arthur 1949- AmMWSc 92
Parker, William C., Jr. 1939- WhoBlA 92
Parker, William Elbridge 1913- WhoWest 92
Parker, William Evans 1940- AmMWSc 92
Parker, William Hartley 1947- WhoBlA 92
Parker, William Hayes, Jr. 1947- WhoBlA 92
Parker, William Henry 1941- AmMWSc 92
Parker, William James 1926- AmMWSc 92
Parker, William Lawrence 1939- AmMWSc 92
Parker, William Lawrence, Jr. 1931- WhoAmL 92
Parker, William Peter 1950- Who 92
Parker, William Skinker 1942- AmMWSc 92
Parker, William Thomas 1928- WhoAmP 91
Parker, Winifred Ellis 1960- AmMWSc 92
Parker-Jervis, Roger 1931- Who 92
Parker-Robinson, D. LaVerne 1949- WhoBlA 92
Parker-Sawyers, Paula WhoBlA 92
Parker-Scott, Susan Lee 1961- WhoFI 92
Parkerson, John 1945- WhoAmP 91
Parkerson, Michelle ReelWom [port]
Parkerson, William Francis, Jr 1920- WhoAmP 91
Parkes, Alan 1900-1990 AnObit 1990
Parkes, Alan Sterling d1990 IntWW 91N
Parkes, Basil 1907- Who 92
Parkes, Ed 1904- IntWW 91
Parkes, Edward 1926- IntWW 91, Who 92
Parkes, James Edward 1949- WhoMW 92
Parkes, John Alan 1939- Who 92
Parkes, John Hubert 1930- Who 92
Parkes, Kenneth Carroll 1922- AmMWSc 92
Parkes, Margaret 1925- Who 92
Parkes, Norman James 1912- Who 92
Parkes, Roger Graham 1933- IntAu&W 91, WrDr 92
Parkey, Glen WhoAmP 91
Parkhie, Mukund Raghunathrao 1933- AmMWSc 92
Parkhill, Harold Loyal 1928- WhoMW 92
Parkhill, Miriam May 1913- WhoMW 92
Parkhouse, James 1927- Who 92
Parkhouse, Peter 1927- Who 92
Parkhurst, Charlotte Livermore 1928- WhoEnt 92
Parkhurst, David Frank 1942- AmMWSc 92
Parkhurst, Henry Martyn 1825-1908 BiInAmS
Parkhurst, Lawrence John 1937- AmMWSc 92
Parkhurst, Raymond Thurston 1898- Who 92
Parkin, A.M. 1943- TwCPaSc
Parkin, Blaine R 1922- AmMWSc 92
Parkin, Don Merrill 1943- AmMWSc 92
Parkin, Evelyn Hope 1910- WhoFI 92
Parkin, James Lamar 1939- AmMWSc 92
Parkin, John Mackintosh 1920- Who 92
Parkin, Molly 1932- IntAu&W 91, WrDr 92
Parkin, Sally 1944- TwCPaSc
Parkin, Sara Lamb 1946- Who 92
Parkins, Barbara 1943- IntMPA 92
Parkins, Bowen Edward 1934- AmMWSc 92
Parkins, Charles Warren 1937- AmMWSc 92
Parkins, Frederick Milton 1935- AmMWSc 92
Parkins, Graham Charles 1942- Who 92
Parkins, John Alexander 1916- AmMWSc 92
Parkins, Robert Collings 1948- WhoEnt 92
Parkins, William Edward 1916- AmMWSc 92
Parkinson, Andrew 1954- AmMWSc 92
Parkinson, Bradford W AmMWSc 92, WhoWest 92
Parkinson, Bruce Alan 1951- AmMWSc 92
Parkinson, Cecil 1931- Who 92
Parkinson, Cecil Edward 1931- IntWW 91
Parkinson, Claire Lucille 1948- AmMWSc 92
Parkinson, Cyril Northcote 1909- IntAu&W 91, IntWW 91, Who 92, WrDr 92
Parkinson, Dan 1935- TwCWW 91, WrDr 92
Parkinson, David B. d1991 NewYTBS 91
Parkinson, David Hardress 1918- Who 92
Parkinson, David Lee 1949- WhoMW 92
Parkinson, Del R. 1948- WhoWest 92
Parkinson, Dennis 1927- AmMWSc 92
Parkinson, Desmond Frederick 1920- Who 92
Parkinson, Desmond John 1913- Who 92
Parkinson, Don 1942- WhoAmP 91
Parkinson, Don 1943- WhoFI 92
Parkinson, Dwight Maughan 1963- WhoFI 92
Parkinson, Ewart West 1926- Who 92
Parkinson, Fred 1929- WhoAmP 91
Parkinson, G Vernon 1924- AmMWSc 92
Parkinson, Georgina WhoEnt 92
Parkinson, Gerald 1926- TwCPaSc
Parkinson, Graham Edward 1937- Who 92
Parkinson, Howard Evans 1936- WhoFI 92
Parkinson, James Christopher 1920- Who 92
Parkinson, James Fendall, III 1948- WhoAmL 92
Parkinson, James Thomas, III 1940- WhoFI 92
Parkinson, John David 1929- WhoFI 92
Parkinson, John Stansfield 1944- AmMWSc 92
Parkinson, Maria Luisa 1951- WhoWest 92
Parkinson, Mark V 1957- WhoAmP 91
Parkinson, Michael WrDr 92
Parkinson, Michael 1935- IntAu&W 91, IntWW 91, Who 92
Parkinson, Nicholas 1925- Who 92
Parkinson, Norman 1913-1990 AnObit 1990
Parkinson, Paul K. 1952- WhoAmL 92
Parkinson, R E 1909- AmMWSc 92
Parkinson, Roger P. 1941- WhoMW 92
Parkinson, Ronald Dennis 1945- Who 92
Parkinson, Stuart Wicks 1955- WhoEnt 92
Parkinson, Thomas DrAPF 91
Parkinson, Thomas 1920- ConPo 91, WrDr 92
Parkinson, Thomas Brian 1935- WhoWest 92
Parkinson, Thomas Franklin 1925- AmMWSc 92
Parkinson, Thomas Harry 1907- Who 92
Parkinson, Thomas Ignatius, Jr. 1914- WhoFI 92
Parkinson, William Charles 1918- AmMWSc 92
Parkinson, William Hambleton 1932- AmMWSc 92
Parkinson, William Walker, Jr 1919- AmMWSc 92
Parkison, Roger C 1949- AmMWSc 92
Parkman, Francis 1823-1893 BenetAL 91, BiInAmS
Parkman, Paul Douglas 1932- AmMWSc 92
Parkman, Robertson AmMWSc 92
Parkman, Theodore 1837-1862 BiInAmS
Parkos, Gregory T. 1930- WhoWest 92
Parks, Albert Fielding 1909- AmMWSc 92
Parks, Albert Lauriston 1935- WhoAmL 92
Parks, Arnold Grant 1939- WhoBlA 92
Parks, Bernard 1944- WhoBlA 92
Parks, Bert LesBEnT 92
Parks, Bert 1914- IntMPA 92, WhoEnt 92
Parks, Bill WhoAmP 91
Parks, Carol C. 1949- WhoEnt 92
Parks, Carrie Anne 1955- WhoMW 92
Parks, Corrine Frances 1934- WhoMW 92
Parks, David Scott 1963- WhoRel 92
Parks, Del 1941- WhoAmP 91
Parks, Donald E 1931- AmMWSc 92
Parks, Donald Lee 1931- WhoWest 92
Parks, E K 1917- AmMWSc 92
Parks, Ed H. 1922- WhoAmL 92
Parks, Edna Dorintha 1910- WrDr 92
Parks, Elmer L. 1916- WhoRel 92
Parks, Eric K 1940- AmMWSc 92
Parks, Gailyn D. 1950- WhoEnt 92
Parks, George A 1931- AmMWSc 92
Parks, George B. 1925- WhoBlA 92
Parks, George Kung 1935- AmMWSc 92
Parks, Gerald Barttett DrAPF 91
Parks, Gerald Thomas, Jr. 1944- WhoWest 92
Parks, Gilbert R. 1944- WhoBlA 92
Parks, Gordon 1912- BlkLC [port], ConBlB 1 [port], FacFETw, IntMPA 92, WrDr 92
Parks, Gordon A. 1912- WhoBlA 92
Parks, Gordon Alexander Buchanan 1912- IntAu&W 91
Parks, Gordon Roger Alexander Buchanan 1912- WhoEnt 92
Parks, Grace Susan 1948- WhoFI 92
Parks, Graham Martin 1947- WhoAmL 92
Parks, Harold George 1942- AmMWSc 92
Parks, Harold Raymond 1949- AmMWSc 92, WhoWest 92
Parks, Herbert Louis 1925- WhoIns 92
Parks, James C 1942- AmMWSc 92
Parks, James Clinton, Jr. 1944- WhoBlA 92
Parks, James Dallas 1906- WhoBlA 92
Parks, James Edgar 1939- AmMWSc 92
Parks, James Edward 1946- WhoBlA 92
Parks, James Henry, III 1956- WhoFI 92
Parks, James Robert 1936- WhoEnt 92
Parks, James Thomas 1947- WhoFI 92
Parks, James Willard 1927- WhoRel 92
Parks, Jeffrey A 1948- WhoAmP 91
Parks, Joe B 1915- WhoAmP 91
Parks, John Gordon 1940- WhoMW 92
Parks, John Lindsay 1929- WhoIns 92
Parks, John S 1939- AmMWSc 92
Parks, Kenneth Lee 1931- AmMWSc 92
Parks, Larry Joseph 1955- WhoRel 92
Parks, Leo Wilburn 1930- AmMWSc 92
Parks, Lewis Arthur 1947- AmMWSc 92
Parks, Lloyd McClain 1912- AmMWSc 92
Parks, Martha J. 1952- WhoFI 92
Parks, Mary June 1926- WhoIns 92
Parks, Matthew William 1925- WhoAmL 92
Parks, Maxie Lander 1951- BlkOlyM
Parks, Michael 1938- IntMPA 92
Parks, Michael 1943- IntAu&W 91
Parks, Michael Christopher 1943- WhoWest 92
Parks, Michael William 1947- WhoRel 92
Parks, Neil Edward 1949- WhoMW 92
Parks, Norris Jim 1943- AmMWSc 92
Parks, Opal WhoAmP 91
Parks, Orlando Alvin, II 1961- WhoRel 92
Parks, Paul 1923- WhoBlA 92
Parks, Paul Blair 1934- AmMWSc 92
Parks, Paul Franklin 1933- AmMWSc 92
Parks, Raymond G 1939- WhoAmP 91
Parks, Richard Dee 1938- WhoEnt 92, WhoWest 92
Parks, Richard Keith 1947- WhoWest 92
Parks, Robert Emmett, Jr 1921- AmMWSc 92
Parks, Robert J 1922- AmMWSc 92
Parks, Robert Keith 1927- WhoRel 92
Parks, Robert Myers 1927- WhoFI 92
Parks, Ronald Dee 1935- AmMWSc 92
Parks, Rosa FacFETw
Parks, Rosa 1913- ConBlB 1 [port], HanAmWH, NotBlAW 92 [port], WhoBlA 92
Parks, Ross Lombard 1920- AmMWSc 92
Parks, Sandra Lenette Reeves 1950- WhoEnt 92
Parks, Sherman A. 1924- WhoBlA 92
Parks, Stephen J. 1957- WhoFI 92
Parks, Terry Everett 1941- AmMWSc 92
Parks, Thelma Reece 1923- WhoBlA 92
Parks, Thomas Merwin 1947- WhoFI 92
Parks, Thomas Norville 1950- WhoWest 92
Parks, Thomas Richard 1931- WhoFI 92
Parks, Thomas William 1939- AmMWSc 92
Parks, Tim 1954- IntAu&W 91, LiExTwC, WrDr 92
Parks, Tom Harris 1932- WhoWest 92
Parks, Vincent Joseph 1928- AmMWSc 92
Parks, William Anthony, Jr 1947- WhoAmP 91
Parks, William Frank 1938- AmMWSc 92
Parks, William Hamilton 1934- WhoWest 92
Parks-Duncanson, Louise 1929- WhoBlA 92
Parks-Gaddis, Catherine M WhoAmP 91
Parkyn, Brian 1923- Who 92
Parkyn, John Duwane 1944- WhoMW 92
Parla, JoAnn Oliveros 1948- WhoHisp 92
Parlakian, Nishan 1925- ConAu 133
Parlan, Ben Strebel WhoWest 92
Parlee, Mary Brown 1943- WhoFI 92
Parler, William Carlos 1929- WhoAmL 92
Parlett, Beresford 1932- AmMWSc 92
Parlett, James DrAPF 91
Parlett, John Knight 1937- WhoAmP 91
Parlette, Carol Holland 1944- WhoWest 92
Parlette, Thomas Joseph 1963- WhoRel 92
Parley, Peter BenetAL 91
Parli, C John AmMWSc 92
Parliament NewAmDM
Parliment, Thomas H 1939- AmMWSc 92
Parlin, Charles C., Jr. 1928- WhoAmL 92
Parloa, Maria 1843-1909 BiInAmS
Parlove, Linda Leigh 1962- WhoMW 92
Parlow, Albert Francis 1933- AmMWSc 92
Parlow, Kathleen 1890-1963 NewAmDM
Parma, David Hopkins 1940- AmMWSc 92
Parma, Florence Virginia 1940- WhoWest 92
Parma, Ildebrando da NewAmDM
Parmalee, Paul Woodburn 1926- AmMWSc 92
Parmar, Samuel L. 1921-1979 DcEcMov
Parmar, Surendra S AmMWSc 92
Parme, Alfred L 1909- AmMWSc 92
Parmele, Mary Platt 1843-1911 ScFEYrs
Parmelee, Carlton Edwin 1918- AmMWSc 92
Parmelee, David Freeland 1924- AmMWSc 92
Parmelee, Ken 1940- WhoAmP 91
Parmelee, Paul Frederick 1925- WhoEnt 92
Parmelee, Walker Michael 1952- WhoMW 92
Parmely, Michael J 1947- AmMWSc 92
Parment, William L 1942- WhoAmP 91
Parmenter, Charles Stedman 1933- AmMWSc 92
Parmenter, Lonnie LeRoy 1944- WhoMW 92
Parmenter, Robert Haley 1925- AmMWSc 92
Parmentier, Edgar M 1945- AmMWSc 92
Parmer, Anita Floy 1941- WhoMW 92
Parmer, Dan Gerald 1926- WhoMW 92
Parmer, Hugh Q 1939- WhoAmP 91
Parmerter, R Reid 1935- AmMWSc 92
Parmerter, Stanley Marshall 1920- AmMWSc 92
Parmet, Herbert S. 1929- WrDr 92
Parmet, Herbert Samuel 1929- IntAu&W 91

**Parmeter,** John Richard, Jr 1927- *AmMWSc 92*
**Parmley,** William W 1936- *AmMWSc 92*
**Parmly,** Charles Howard 1868-1917 *BiInAmS*
**Parmoor,** Baron 1929- *Who 92*
**Parms,** Edwin L. 1937- *WhoBlA 92*
**Parnaby,** John 1937- *Who 92*
**Parnall,** Theodore 1942- *WhoAmL 92*
**Parnas,** Leslie 1931- *NewAmDM*
**Parnell** *Who 92*
**Parnell,** Arnold W. 1936- *WhoBlA 92*
**Parnell,** David Russell 1925- *WhoAmP 91*
**Parnell,** Dennis Richard 1939- *AmMWSc 92*
**Parnell,** Donald Ray 1942- *AmMWSc 92*
**Parnell,** James Franklin 1934- *AmMWSc 92*
**Parnell,** John Vaze, III 1944- *WhoBlA 92*
**Parnell,** Pat *WhoAmP 91*
**Parnell,** Richard Michael 1956- *WhoWest 92*
**Parnell,** Thomas 1679-1718? *RfGEnL 91*
**Parnell,** Thomas Alfred 1931- *AmMWSc 92*
**Parnell,** William Cornelius, Jr. 1940- *WhoBlA 92*
**Parnell,** William Michael 1956- *WhoRel 92*
**Parnes,** Herbert S 1919- *ConAu 34NR*
**Parnes,** Irwin 1917- *WhoEnt 92*
**Parnes,** Milton N 1939- *AmMWSc 92*
**Parness,** Jeffrey Marc 1965- *WhoFI 92*
**Parnis,** Alexander Edward Libor 1911- *Who 92*
**Parnok,** Sofiya Yakovlevna 1885-1933 *SovUnBD*
**Parochetti,** James V 1940- *AmMWSc 92*
**Paroda,** David John, Jr. 1952- *WhoWest 92*
**Parode,** L C 1924- *AmMWSc 92*
**Parodi,** Anton Gaetano 1923- *IntAu&W 91, IntWW 91*
**Parodi,** Oscar S. 1932- *WhoHisp 92*
**Parola,** Fredrick Edson, Jr 1946- *WhoAmP 91*
**Paronetto,** Fiorenzo 1929- *AmMWSc 92*
**Paroni,** Genevieve Marie Swick 1926- *WhoWest 92*
**Paront,** George John 1953- *WhoRel 92*
**Parotti,** Phillip 1941- *WrDr 92*
**Parpia,** Jeevak Mahmud 1952- *AmMWSc 92*
**Parque,** Richard *DrAPF 91*
**Parr,** A. E. 1900-1991 *CurBio 91N*
**Parr,** Albert Clarence 1942- *AmMWSc 92*
**Parr,** Albert E. d1991 *NewYTBS 91 [port]*
**Parr,** Albert Eide 1900- *IntWW 91*
**Parr,** Carolyn Miller 1937- *WhoAmL 92*
**Parr,** Christopher Alan 1941- *AmMWSc 92*
**Parr,** Darryl Alan 1960- *WhoRel 92*
**Parr,** Donald 1930- *Who 92*
**Parr,** Ednapearl Flores 1916- *WhoAmP 91*
**Parr,** James Floyd, Jr 1929- *AmMWSc 92*
**Parr,** James Gordon 1927- *AmMWSc 92*
**Parr,** James Theodore 1934- *AmMWSc 92*
**Parr,** Phyllis Graham 1937- *AmMWSc 92*
**Parr,** Richard Arnold, II 1958- *WhoFI 92*
**Parr,** Robert Francis 1951- *WhoFI 92*
**Parr,** Robert Ghormley 1921- *AmMWSc 92, IntWW 91*
**Parr,** Thomas Randall 1957- *WhoRel 92*
**Parr,** William Chris 1953- *AmMWSc 92*
**Parra,** George Ernest 1957- *WhoEnt 92*
**Parra,** Jose *WhoHisp 92*
**Parra,** Mike *WhoHisp 92*
**Parra,** Nicanor 1914- *BenetAL 91, ConSpAP, FacFETw, IntWW 91, LiExTwC*
**Parra,** Teresa de la 1889-1936 *SpAmWW*
**Parra,** Teresa de la 1895-1936 *BenetAL 91*
**Parra,** Teresita J. 1934- *WhoHisp 92*
**Parra,** Tim *WhoHisp 92*
**Parra,** Violeta 1917-1967 *SpAmWW*
**Parra,** William Charles 1942- *WhoHisp 92*
**Parra Herrera,** German *IntWW 91*
**Parra Sanojo,** Ana Teresa 1889-1936 *SpAmWW*
**Parrack,** Richard M 1927- *IntAu&W 91*
**Parraguirre,** Ronald David 1959- *WhoAmL 92*
**Parramatta,** Bishop of *Who 92*
**Parran,** John Thomas, Jr 1926- *WhoAmP 91*
**Parras,** Toni 1966- *WhoEnt 92*
**Parratt,** James Roy 1933- *IntWW 91*
**Parratt,** Lyman George 1908- *AmMWSc 92*
**Parravano,** Carlo 1945- *AmMWSc 92*
**Parravicini,** Giannino 1910- *IntWW 91*
**Parreira,** Helio Correa 1926- *AmMWSc 92*
**Parrell,** Daniel Joseph 1968- *WhoMW 92*
**Parrenas,** Cecilia Salazar 1945- *WhoWest 92*
**Parrenin,** Jacques 1919- *NewAmDM*
**Parrent,** Allan Mitchell 1930- *WhoRel 92*
**Parrent,** George Burl, Jr. 1931- *WhoFI 92*
**Parrent,** Joanne Elizabeth 1948- *WhoEnt 92*
**Parrett,** Benjamin Leighton 1941- *WhoMW 92*
**Parrett,** John 1947- *Who 92*
**Parrett,** Ned Albert 1939- *AmMWSc 92*
**Parretti,** Giancarlo *LesBEnT 92*
**Parretti,** Giancarlo 1941- *IntMPA 92*
**Parretti,** Giancarlo 1942- *WhoEnt 92, WhoWest 92*
**Parri,** Ferruccio 1889-1981 *FacFETw*
**Parrill,** Irwin Homer 1909- *AmMWSc 92*
**Parrinder,** Geoffrey 1910- *Who 92*
**Parrington,** Vernon L. 1871-1929 *BenetAL 91*
**Parriott,** Joseph D 1933- *WhoAmP 91*
**Parris,** Alvin, III 1951- *WhoBlA 92*
**Parris,** Caroline Rolande 1942- *WhoMW 92*
**Parris,** Gregory Leroy 1953- *WhoRel 92*
**Parris,** Guichard 1903-1990 *ConAu 133, WhoBlA 92N*
**Parris,** Mark S. 1957- *WhoAmL 92*
**Parris,** Matthew 1949- *ConAu 134, IntWW 91*
**Parris,** Matthew Francis 1949- *Who 92*
**Parris,** Patricia Elizabeth 1950- *WhoWest 92*
**Parris,** Robert 1924- *WhoEnt 92*
**Parrish,** Alfred Sherwen d1990 *Who 92N*
**Parrish,** Alvin Edward 1922- *AmMWSc 92*
**Parrish,** Anne 1888-1957 *BenetAL 91*
**Parrish,** Barry Jay 1946- *WhoWest 92*
**Parrish,** Bobby Lee 1931- *WhoFI 92*
**Parrish,** Celestia Susannah 1853-1918 *BiInAmS*
**Parrish,** Charles Henry 1899- *WhoBlA 92*
**Parrish,** Cheryl Ann 1954- *WhoEnt 92*
**Parrish,** Clarence R. 1921- *WhoBlA 92*
**Parrish,** Clyde Franklin 1938- *AmMWSc 92*
**Parrish,** Dale Wayne 1924- *AmMWSc 92*
**Parrish,** David Joe 1943- *AmMWSc 92*
**Parrish,** David Keith 1944- *AmMWSc 92*
**Parrish,** David Walker, Jr. 1923- *WhoAmL 92*
**Parrish,** Donald Baker 1913- *AmMWSc 92*
**Parrish,** Edward Alton, Jr 1937- *AmMWSc 92*
**Parrish,** Frank *WrDr 92*
**Parrish,** Fred Kenneth 1927- *AmMWSc 92*
**Parrish,** Frederick Charles, Jr 1933- *AmMWSc 92*
**Parrish,** George Roderick 1943- *WhoWest 92*
**Parrish,** Harry Jacob 1922- *WhoAmP 91*
**Parrish,** Herbert Charles 1919- *AmMWSc 92*
**Parrish,** James Davis 1935- *AmMWSc 92*
**Parrish,** James W. 1908- *WhoBlA 92*
**Parrish,** James W 1946- *WhoAmP 91*
**Parrish,** Jemima G Buchanan 1906- *IntAu&W 91*
**Parrish,** Jimmy David 1947- *WhoAmP 91*
**Parrish,** John Albert 1939- *AmMWSc 92*
**Parrish,** John Henry 1924- *WhoBlA 92*
**Parrish,** John W, Jr 1941- *AmMWSc 92*
**Parrish,** John Wesley, Jr 1941- *AmMWSc 92*
**Parrish,** Judith Totman 1950- *AmMWSc 92*
**Parrish,** Kenneth Gene 1942- *WhoMW 92*
**Parrish,** Larry J *WhoAmP 91*
**Parrish,** Lemar 1947- *WhoBlA 92*
**Parrish,** Mary 1863?- *NotBlAW 92*
**Parrish,** Maurice Drue 1950- *WhoBlA 92*
**Parrish,** Maurice Lee 1917- *WhoWest 92*
**Parrish,** Maxfield 1870-1966 *BenetAL 91, FacFETw*
**Parrish,** Nancy Elaine 1948- *WhoAmP 91*
**Parrish,** Overton Burgin, Jr. 1933- *WhoFI 92*
**Parrish,** Patt *WrDr 92*
**Parrish,** Richard Henry 1939- *AmMWSc 92*
**Parrish,** Robert A, Jr 1930- *AmMWSc 92*
**Parrish,** Robert Ambrose 1927- *WhoAmP 91*
**Parrish,** Robert R. 1916- *IntMPA 92*
**Parrish,** Ron 1942- *WhoRel 92*
**Parrish,** Rufus H. *WhoBlA 92*
**Parrish,** Susan Burgess 1958- *WhoRel 92*
**Parrish,** Vicki Jo Payne 1948- *WhoEnt 92*
**Parrish,** Virginia Kay 1953- *WhoAmP 91*
**Parrish,** Wayne 1920- *AmMWSc 92*
**Parrish,** Wendy 1950-1977 *ConAu 133*
**Parrish,** William 1914- *AmMWSc 92*
**Parrish,** William E. 1931- *WrDr 92*
**Parrish-Harra,** Carol Williams 1935- *WhoRel 92*
**Parro,** Douglas Arthur 1954- *WhoWest 92*
**Parron,** Delores L. 1944- *WhoBlA 92*
**Parrot,** Kenneth D. 1947- *WhoFI 92*
**Parrot,** Kent Kane 1911- *WhoEnt 92*
**Parrott,** Andrew Haden 1947- *IntWW 91, Who 92*
**Parrott,** Billy James 1935- *WhoEnt 92*
**Parrott,** Charles Norman 1947- *WhoFI 92*
**Parrott,** Dean Allen 1922- *WhoRel 92*
**Parrott,** Dennis Alan 1953- *WhoMW 92*
**Parrott,** Dennis Beecher 1929- *WhoFI 92, WhoWest 92*
**Parrott,** Dennis Kirk 1954- *WhoAmP 91*
**Parrott,** Douglas Morris 1927- *WhoRel 92*
**Parrott,** Eugene Lee 1925- *AmMWSc 92, WhoMW 92*
**Parrott,** Ian 1916- *ConCom 92, WrDr 92*
**Parrott,** James Alfred 1952- *WhoFI 92*
**Parrott,** Jasper William 1944- *WhoEnt 92*
**Parrott,** John Harold 1946- *WhoWest 92*
**Parrott,** Marshall Ward 1927- *AmMWSc 92*
**Parrott,** Mary Ellen 1943- *WhoAmP 91*
**Parrott,** Nancy Sharon 1944- *WhoAmL 92*
**Parrott,** Richard Leslie 1952- *WhoRel 92*
**Parrott,** Robert Harold 1923- *AmMWSc 92*
**Parrott,** Rodney Lee 1942- *WhoRel 92*
**Parrott,** Stephen Kinsley 1941- *AmMWSc 92*
**Parrott,** Stephen Laurent 1949- *AmMWSc 92*
**Parrott,** William Lamar 1930- *AmMWSc 92*
**Parroy,** Michael Picton 1946- *Who 92*
**Parry** *Who 92*
**Parry,** Baron 1925- *Who 92*
**Parry,** Alan 1927- *Who 92*
**Parry,** Albert 1901- *IntAu&W 91, WrDr 92*
**Parry,** Anthony Joseph 1935- *Who 92*
**Parry,** Arthur Edward *WhoIns 92*
**Parry,** Atwell J., Jr. 1925- *WhoWest 92*
**Parry,** Atwell Junior 1925- *WhoAmP 91*
**Parry,** Carol Jacqueline 1941- *WhoFI 92*
**Parry,** Charles Christopher 1823-1890 *BiInAmS*
**Parry,** Charles J 1942- *AmMWSc 92*
**Parry,** Charles William 1924- *IntWW 91*
**Parry,** David M 1852-1915 *ScFEYrs*
**Parry,** Eldryd Hugh Owen 1930- *Who 92*
**Parry,** Ellwood C., III 1941- *WrDr 92*
**Parry,** Emyr Owen 1933- *Who 92*
**Parry,** Ernest J. *Who 92*
**Parry,** Gordon *AmMWSc 92*
**Parry,** Hubert 1848-1918 *NewAmDM*
**Parry,** Hubert Dean 1909- *AmMWSc 92*
**Parry,** Hugh 1911- *Who 92*
**Parry,** Hugh J. *DrAPF 91*
**Parry,** Hugh Jones 1916- *WrDr 92*
**Parry,** John Alderson 1934- *Who 92*
**Parry,** John Robert 1941- *WhoWest 92*
**Parry,** Margaret Joan 1919- *Who 92*
**Parry,** Marian *DrAPF 91*
**Parry,** Myron Gene 1933- *AmMWSc 92*
**Parry,** Pamela Jeffcott 1948- *WhoWest 92*
**Parry,** Robert 1933- *Who 92*
**Parry,** Robert Troutt 1939- *WhoFI 92, WhoWest 92*
**Parry,** Robert Walter 1917- *AmMWSc 92*
**Parry,** Ronald John 1942- *AmMWSc 92*
**Parry,** Timothy R. 1954- *WhoAmL 92*
**Parry,** Victor Thomas Henry 1927- *Who 92*
**Parry,** Walter P. *WhoRel 92*
**Parry,** William 1934- *Who 92*
**Parry,** William DeWitt 1941- *WhoAmL 92*
**Parry,** William Everett 1951- *WhoEnt 92*
**Parry,** William Lockhart 1924- *AmMWSc 92*
**Parry,** William Thomas 1935- *AmMWSc 92*
**Parry Brown,** Arthur Ivor *Who 92*
**Parry-Evans,** David 1935- *Who 92*
**Parry Evans,** Mary Alethea 1929- *Who 92*
**Parry Jones,** Terence Graham *Who 92*
**Pars,** Harry George 1928- *AmMWSc 92*
**Parsa,** Kooros 1938- *WhoWest 92*
**Parsa,** Zohreh *AmMWSc 92*
**Parsch,** Lucas Dean 1946- *AmMWSc 92*
**Parsch,** William Steven 1954- *WhoMW 92*
**Parsegian,** V Lawrence 1908- *AmMWSc 92*
**Parsegian,** Vozken Adrian 1939- *AmMWSc 92*
**Parshall,** Brian J 1945- *AmMWSc 92*
**Parshall,** Craig Littleton 1950- *WhoAmL 92*
**Parshall,** Donald Richard, Jr. 1954- *WhoMW 92*
**Parshall,** George William 1929- *AmMWSc 92*
**Parshin,** Aleksandr Yakovlevich 1939- *IntWW 91*
**Parshley,** Philip Ford, Jr. 1931- *WhoWest 92*
**Parsignault,** Daniel Raymond 1937- *AmMWSc 92*
**Parsky,** Gerald Lawrence 1942- *WhoAmL 92*
**Parsley,** David William 1958- *WhoWest 92*
**Parsley,** Frances Elaine 1924- *WhoAmP 91*
**Parsley,** Robert Charles 1956- *WhoRel 92*
**Parsley,** Ronald Lee 1937- *AmMWSc 92*
**Parsley,** Steven Dwayne 1959- *WhoFI 92*
**Parsloe,** Phyllida 1930- *Who 92*
**Parslow,** Philip Leo 1938- *WhoEnt 92, WhoWest 92*
**Parsly,** Lewis F, Jr 1918- *AmMWSc 92*
**Parson,** David 1924- *WhoAmL 92*
**Parson,** Houston 1925- *WhoBlA 92*
**Parson,** John Morris 1946- *AmMWSc 92*
**Parson,** Louise Alayne 1947- *AmMWSc 92*
**Parson,** Mary Jean 1934- *ConAu 133*
**Parson,** Robert Paul 1957- *AmMWSc 92*
**Parson,** Tom *DrAPF 91*
**Parson,** William Wood 1939- *AmMWSc 92*
**Parson,** Willie L. 1942- *WhoBlA 92*
**Parsonnet,** Victor 1924- *AmMWSc 92*
**Parsons** *Who 92*
**Parsons,** Adrian *Who 92*
**Parsons,** Alan *Who 92*
**Parsons,** Alfred 1847-1920 *TwCPaSc*
**Parsons,** Alfred Roy 1925- *Who 92*
**Parsons,** Alvin L 1949- *WhoIns 92*
**Parsons,** Andrew John 1943- *WhoFI 92*
**Parsons,** Anthony 1922- *Who 92*
**Parsons,** Anthony Derrick 1922- *IntWW 91*
**Parsons,** C. J. 1941- *WrDr 92*
**Parsons,** Carl Michael 1954- *AmMWSc 92*
**Parsons,** Charles Adrian 1929- *Who 92*
**Parsons,** Charles Allan, Jr. 1943- *WhoAmL 92, WhoMW 92*
**Parsons,** Charles H. 1940- *ConAu 134*
**Parsons,** Coleman O. 1905-1991 *ConAu 134*
**Parsons,** David Jerome 1947- *AmMWSc 92*
**Parsons,** Donald D. *WhoRel 92*
**Parsons,** Donald Frederick 1928- *AmMWSc 92*
**Parsons,** Donald James 1922- *WhoRel 92*
**Parsons,** Edwin Spencer 1919- *WhoRel 92*
**Parsons,** Elizabeth 1953- *TwCPaSc*
**Parsons,** Ellen *ConAu 36NR*
**Parsons,** Elmer Earl 1919- *WhoRel 92*
**Parsons,** Elsie Clews 1874-1941 *WomSoc*
**Parsons,** Elsie Clews 1875?-1941 *BenetAL 91*
**Parsons,** Elsie Worthington Clews 1875-1941 *AmPeW*
**Parsons,** Estelle 1927- *IntMPA 92, WhoEnt 92*
**Parsons,** Geoffrey 1929- *IntWW 91*
**Parsons,** Geoffrey Penwill 1929- *Who 92*
**Parsons,** Gibbe Hull 1942- *WhoWest 92*
**Parsons,** Gram 1946-1973 *ConMus 7 [port]*
**Parsons,** Harold Morris 1937- *WhoEnt 92*
**Parsons,** J. D., Mrs. *Who 92*
**Parsons,** J. Graham 1907-1991 *NewYTBS 91 [port]*
**Parsons,** Jack 1920- *WrDr 92*
**Parsons,** Jack 1930- *WhoAmP 91*
**Parsons,** James B. 1911- *WhoBlA 92*
**Parsons,** James Sidney 1922- *AmMWSc 92*
**Parsons,** Jerry Montgomery 1946- *AmMWSc 92*
**Parsons,** John Arthur 1932- *AmMWSc 92*
**Parsons,** John Christopher 1946- *Who 92*
**Parsons,** John David 1925- *AmMWSc 92*
**Parsons,** John David 1935- *Who 92*
**Parsons,** John G 1939- *AmMWSc 92*
**Parsons,** John Lawrence 1924- *AmMWSc 92*
**Parsons,** John Martin 1958- *WhoFI 92*
**Parsons,** John Michael 1915- *Who 92*
**Parsons,** John Thoren 1913- *AmMWSc 92, WhoMW 92*
**Parsons,** Jonathan Wayne 1955- *WhoWest 92*
**Parsons,** Keith 1957- *WhoAmL 92*
**Parsons,** Kenneth Charles 1921- *Who 92*
**Parsons,** L Claire 1933- *AmMWSc 92*
**Parsons,** Lawrence Reed 1944- *AmMWSc 92*
**Parsons,** Lindsley 1915- *IntMPA 92*
**Parsons,** Lindsley, Sr. *WhoEnt 92*
**Parsons,** Louella 1893-1972 *ReelWom*
**Parsons,** Louella O. 1893-1972 *BenetAL 91*
**Parsons,** Lucy Gonzalez 1852-1942 *HanAmWH*
**Parsons,** Mac 1943- *WhoAmP 91*
**Parsons,** Marcedes Marie 1927- *WhoWest 92*
**Parsons,** Margot Palaith 1942- *WhoEnt 92*
**Parsons,** Marilee Benore 1956- *WhoMW 92*
**Parsons,** Merribell Maddux *WhoMW 92*
**Parsons,** Michael *Who 92*
**Parsons,** Michael L 1940- *AmMWSc 92*
**Parsons,** Michael Loewen 1940- *WhoWest 92*
**Parsons,** Pauline 1912- *Who 92*
**Parsons,** Penelope 1955- *WhoEnt 92*
**Parsons,** Peter John 1936- *IntWW 91, Who 92*
**Parsons,** Philip I. 1941- *WhoBlA 92*
**Parsons,** Ralph L., II 1936- *WhoRel 92*
**Parsons,** Richard 1928- *Who 92*
**Parsons,** Richard 1949- *WhoBlA 92*

**Parsons,** Richard Curtis 1942- *WhoWest 92*
**Parsons,** Richard Edmund Clement Fownes 1928- *IntWW 91*
**Parsons,** Robert F 1926- *WhoAmP 91*
**Parsons,** Robert Hathaway 1941- *AmMWSc 92*
**Parsons,** Robert Jerome 1907- *AmMWSc 92*
**Parsons,** Robert W 1932- *AmMWSc 92*
**Parsons,** Rodney Lawrence 1939- *AmMWSc 92*
**Parsons,** Roger 1926- *IntWW 91, Who 92*
**Parsons,** Roger Bruce 1932- *AmMWSc 92*
**Parsons,** Stanley Monroe 1943- *AmMWSc 92*
**Parsons,** Stuart Nelson 1942- *WhoFI 92*
**Parsons,** Stuart Overton, Jr. 1926- *WhoWest 92*
**Parsons,** T. W. 1819-1892 *BenetAL 91*
**Parsons,** Talcott 1902-1979 *ConAu 35NR, FacFETw*
**Parsons,** Theophilus 1750-1813 *BlkwEAR*
**Parsons,** Theran Duane 1922- *AmMWSc 92*
**Parsons,** Thomas Alan 1924- *Who 92*
**Parsons,** Thomas Sturges 1930- *AmMWSc 92*
**Parsons,** Timothy F 1938- *AmMWSc 92*
**Parsons,** Timothy John 1962- *WhoRel 92*
**Parsons,** Timothy Richard 1932- *AmMWSc 92*
**Parsons,** Torrence Douglas 1941- *AmMWSc 92*
**Parsons,** Virginia Mae 1942- *WhoMW 92*
**Parsons,** Wayne Douglas 1943- *WhoAmL 92*
**Parsons,** Willard H *AmMWSc 92*
**Parsons,** William Belle, Jr 1924- *AmMWSc 92*
**Parsons,** William Earl, II 1948- *WhoAmL 92*
**Parsons,** William W. d1991 *NewYTBS 91*
**Parsons-Smith,** Gerald 1911- *Who 92*
**Parsuraman,** Armoogum 1951- *IntWW 91*
**Part,** Arvo 1935- *ConCom 92, IntWW 91, SovUnBD*
**Part,** Ronald Michael 1961- *WhoEnt 92*
**Partain,** Clarence Leon 1940- *AmMWSc 92*
**Partain,** Gerald Lavern 1925- *AmMWSc 92*
**Partanen,** Carl Richard 1921- *AmMWSc 92*
**Partanen,** Jouni Pekka 1957- *AmMWSc 92*
**Partch,** Harry 1901-1974 *NewAmDM*
**Partch,** Richard Earl 1936- *AmMWSc 92*
**Partee,** Cecil A. 1921- *WhoAmL 92, WhoAmP 91, WhoBlA 92*
**Parteli,** Carlos 1910- *IntWW 91*
**Partenheimer,** Walter 1941- *AmMWSc 92*
**Parter,** Seymour Victor 1927- *AmMWSc 92*
**Parthasarathi,** Manavasi Narasimhan 1924- *AmMWSc 92*
**Parthasarathy,** R. 1934- *ConPo 91, WrDr 92*
**Parthasarathy,** Rengachary 1936- *AmMWSc 92*
**Parthasarathy,** Sampath 1947- *AmMWSc 92*
**Parthasarathy,** Triplicane Asuri *AmMWSc 92*
**Parthemore,** Ronald Douglas 1951- *WhoAmP 91*
**Partheniades,** Emmanuel 1926- *AmMWSc 92*
**Parthenios** 1919- *WhoRel 92*
**Particular,** Pertinax *BenetAL 91*
**Partida,** Gregory John, Jr 1942- *AmMWSc 92*
**Partida,** Juan Ramon 1951- *WhoHisp 92*
**Partin,** Dale Lee 1949- *AmMWSc 92*
**Partin,** Jacqueline Surratt 1934- *AmMWSc 92*
**Partin,** John Calvin 1933- *AmMWSc 92*
**Partin,** Milton Douglas 1962- *WhoRel 92*
**Partin,** Ronald Lee 1946- *WhoMW 92*
**Partin,** Winfred 1946- *WhoRel 92*
**Partington,** Michael W 1926- *AmMWSc 92*
**Partington,** Ruth *BenetAL 91*
**Partington,** Thomas Martin 1944- *Who 92*
**Partington,** Tony 1957- *WhoEnt 92*
**Partlett,** David F. 1947- *WhoAmL 92*
**Partlow,** Frank Almond, Jr. 1938- *WhoWest 92*
**Partnoy,** Alicia *DrAPF 91*
**Partnoy,** Ronald Allen 1933- *WhoAmL 92*
**Parton,** Anthony 1959- *ConAu 133*
**Parton,** Dolly 1946- *IntMPA 92*
**Parton,** Dolly Rebecca 1946- *IntWW 91, WhoEnt 92*
**Parton,** Ethel 1862-1944 *BenetAL 91*
**Parton,** James 1822-1891 *BenetAL 91*
**Parton,** John Edwin 1912- *Who 92*
**Parton,** Mary Jean 1933- *WhoAmP 91*
**Parton,** Sara Payson Willis *BenetAL 91*
**Parton,** W Jeff 1925- *WhoIns 92*
**Parton,** William Brad 1960- *WhoWest 92*
**Parton,** William Julian, Jr 1944- *AmMWSc 92*
**Partos,** Oedoen 1907-1977 *NewAmDM*
**Partovi,** Afshin 1963- *AmMWSc 92*
**Partow-Navid,** Parviz 1950- *WhoWest 92*
**Partoyan,** Garo Arakel 1936- *WhoAmL 92*
**Partridge and Oakey** *DcLB 106*
**Partridge,** Arthur *Who 92*
**Partridge,** Arthur Dean 1927- *AmMWSc 92*
**Partridge,** Astley Cooper 1901- *IntAu&W 91, WrDr 92*
**Partridge,** Bellamy 1878-1960 *BenetAL 91*
**Partridge,** Benjamin Waring, III 1944- *WhoAmP 91*
**Partridge,** Bernard B. *Who 92*
**Partridge,** Derek 1935- *IntMPA 92*
**Partridge,** Derek 1945- *ConAu 135*
**Partridge,** Derek William 1931- *IntWW 91, Who 92*
**Partridge,** Dixie Lee *DrAPF 91*
**Partridge,** Harry Cowderoy d1990 *Who 92N*
**Partridge,** Ian Harold 1938- *Who 92*
**Partridge,** James Enoch 1942- *AmMWSc 92*
**Partridge,** Jenny 1947- *WrDr 92*
**Partridge,** Jerry Alvin 1939- *AmMWSc 92*
**Partridge,** John Albert 1924- *IntWW 91, Who 92*
**Partridge,** John Joseph 1942- *AmMWSc 92*
**Partridge,** Josh 1942- *TwCPaSc*
**Partridge,** L Donald 1945- *AmMWSc 92*
**Partridge,** Linda 1950- *Who 92*
**Partridge,** Lloyd Donald 1922- *AmMWSc 92*
**Partridge,** M.W. 1913-1973 *TwCPaSc*
**Partridge,** Marika Denham 1955- *WhoEnt 92*
**Partridge,** Mark Henry Heathcote 1922- *IntWW 91*
**Partridge,** Michael 1935- *Who 92*
**Partridge,** Miles 1913- *Who 92*
**Partridge,** Robert Bruce 1940- *AmMWSc 92*
**Partridge,** Samuel Wm. *DcLB 106*
**Partridge,** Sanborn 1915- *WhoAmP 91*
**Partridge,** Stanley Miles 1913- *IntWW 91*
**Partridge,** William Arthur 1912- *Who 92*
**Partridge,** William Franklin, Jr. 1945- *WhoAmL 92*
**Partsalides,** Dimitrios 1901-1980 *FacFETw*
**Party,** Lionel *WhoEnt 92*
**Partyka,** Robert Edward 1930- *AmMWSc 92*
**Parungo,** Farn Pwu 1932- *AmMWSc 92*
**Parvez,** Zaheer 1939- *AmMWSc 92*
**Parvin,** Betty 1916- *IntAu&W 91*
**Parvin,** Betty 1917- *WrDr 92*
**Parvin,** Landon 1948- *NewYTBS 91 [port], WhoAmP 91*
**Parvin,** Philip Eugene 1927- *AmMWSc 92*
**Parviz,** Azar-Mehr 1937- *WhoWest 92*
**Parvulescu,** Antares 1923- *AmMWSc 92*
**Parysek,** Linda M 1954- *AmMWSc 92*
**Parzen,** Emanuel 1929- *AmMWSc 92*
**Parzen,** George 1924- *AmMWSc 92*
**Parzen,** Philip *AmMWSc 92*
**Pas,** Eric Ivan 1948- *AmMWSc 92*
**Pasachoff,** Jay M 1943- *AmMWSc 92*
**Pasahow,** Lynn Harold 1947- *WhoAmL 92*
**Pasakarnis,** Pamela Ann 1949- *WhoFI 92*
**Pasamanick,** Benjamin 1914- *AmMWSc 92*
**Pasant,** David A. 1951- *WhoMW 92*
**Pasarell,** Enrique Antonio 1949- *WhoHisp 92*
**Pasarow,** Reinee Elizabeth 1950- *WhoFI 92, WhoWest 92*
**Pasatieri,** Thomas 1945- *NewAmDM*
**Pasby,** Brian 1937- *AmMWSc 92*
**Pascal,** Blaise 1623-1662 *BlkwCEP*
**Pascal,** Cecil Bennett 1926- *WhoWest 92*
**Pascal,** Felipe Antonio 1953- *WhoHisp 92*
**Pascal,** Francine 1938- *ChlLR 25 [port], IntAu&W 91*
**Pascal,** Gerald Ross 1907-1984 *ConAu 133*
**Pascal,** Harold Saunders 1934- *WhoFI 92, WhoMW 92*
**Pascal,** Jean-Baptiste Lucien 1930- *IntWW 91*
**Pascal-Trouillot,** Ertha 1943- *IntWW 91*
**Pascale,** Richard Tanner 1938- *WrDr 92*
**Pascarella,** Perry 1934- *WrDr 92*
**Pasceri,** Ralph Edward 1937- *AmMWSc 92*
**Paschal,** Beverly Jo 1955- *WhoAmL 92*
**Paschal,** Eloise Richardson 1936- *WhoBlA 92*
**Paschal,** Willie L. 1926- *WhoBlA 92*
**Paschall,** Eugene F 1922- *AmMWSc 92*
**Paschall,** Gael Penland 1949- *WhoFI 92*
**Paschall,** Homer Donald 1926- *AmMWSc 92*
**Paschang,** John Linus 1895- *WhoRel 92*
**Paschen,** Elise Maria 1959- *IntAu&W 91*
**Pascher,** Frances 1905- *AmMWSc 92*
**Paschke,** Donald Vernon 1929- *WhoEnt 92*
**Paschke,** Edward Ernest 1943- *AmMWSc 92*
**Paschke,** Edward F. 1939- *WhoMW 92*
**Paschke,** Fritz 1929- *IntWW 91*
**Paschke,** John Donald 1925- *AmMWSc 92*
**Paschke,** Richard Eugene 1937- *AmMWSc 92*
**Paschke,** William Lindall 1946- *AmMWSc 92*
**Paschkis,** Victor d1991 *NewYTBS 91*
**Paschos,** Emmanuel Anthony 1940- *AmMWSc 92*
**Pasciak,** Joseph Edward 1950- *AmMWSc 92*
**Pascin,** Jules 1885-1930 *FacFETw*
**Pasco,** Allan Humphrey 1937- *WhoMW 92*
**Pasco,** Richard Edward 1926- *IntWW 91, Who 92*
**Pasco,** Robert William 1947- *AmMWSc 92*
**Pasco,** Rowanne 1938- *Who 92*
**Pasco,** Tito E. 1930- *WhoRel 92*
**Pascoe,** Alan Peter 1947- *Who 92*
**Pascoe,** D Monte 1935- *WhoAmP 91*
**Pascoe,** Edmund Normoyle 1948- *WhoIns 92*
**Pascoe,** Edward Rudy 1948- *WhoMW 92*
**Pascoe,** Elise Mostyn 1939- *IntAu&W 91*
**Pascoe,** Jane 1955- *TwCPaSc*
**Pascoe,** Llewellyn Patrick 1939- *WhoFI 92*
**Pascoe,** Michael William 1930- *Who 92*
**Pascoe,** Nigel Spencer Knight 1940- *Who 92*
**Pascoe,** Pat *WhoAmP 91*
**Pascoe,** Patricia Hill 1935- *WhoWest 92*
**Pascoe,** Robert 1932- *Who 92*
**Pascotto,** Alvaro 1949- *WhoAmL 92*
**Pascrell,** William J, Jr 1937- *WhoAmP 91*
**Pascu,** Dan 1938- *AmMWSc 92*
**Pascu,** Ronald *WhoEnt 92*
**Pascu,** Stefan 1914- *IntAu&W 91*
**Pascual,** Hugo 1935- *WhoHisp 92*
**Pascual,** Ramon 1942- *IntWW 91*
**Pascual,** Roberto 1942- *AmMWSc 92*
**Pascual,** Virginia 1951- *WhoHisp 92*
**Pascucci,** Richard Anthony 1948- *WhoMW 92*
**Pascucci,** Scott 1958- *WhoEnt 92*
**Pascuito,** Joan Annette 1952- *WhoAmP 91*
**Pasdar,** Adrian *ConTFT 9*
**Pasdeloup,** Jules-Etienne 1819-1887 *NewAmDM*
**Paselk,** Richard Alan 1945- *AmMWSc 92*
**Pasetta,** Marty *LesBEnT 92*
**Pasetta,** Marty 1932- *IntMPA 92*
**Pasetti,** Peter 1916- *IntWW 91*
**Pasewark,** William R 1924- *ConAu 35NR*
**Pasewark,** William Robert 1924- *WrDr 92*
**Pasfield,** William Horton 1924- *AmMWSc 92*
**Pash,** Margaret *WhoEnt 92*
**Pash,** Mary Margaret 1934- *WhoMW 92*
**Pashan,** Mark Allen 1960- *WhoMW 92*
**Pashayan,** Charles, Jr 1941- *WhoAmP 91, WhoWest 92*
**Pashby,** Gary J. 1941- *WhoAmL 92*
**Pashley,** David Henry 1939- *AmMWSc 92*
**Pashley,** Donald William 1927- *IntWW 91, Who 92*
**Pashley,** Emil Frederick, Jr 1930- *AmMWSc 92*
**Pashley,** Eugene W., Jr. 1954- *WhoMW 92*
**Pashukanis,** Yevgeniy Bronislavovich 1891-1937 *SovUnBD*
**Pasic,** Nikola 1845-1926 *FacFETw*
**Pasick,** Robert 1946- *ConAu 134*
**Pasik,** Pedro 1926- *AmMWSc 92*
**Pasik,** Tauba 1927- *AmMWSc 92*
**Pasillas,** Diane *WhoHisp 92*
**Pasinetti,** Luigi Lodovico 1930- *IntWW 91*
**Pasini,** Roy 1927- *WhoIns 92*
**Pasionek,** Robert Anthony 1951- *WhoFI 92*
**Pasipoularides,** Ares D 1943- *AmMWSc 92*
**Pask,** Joseph Adam 1913- *AmMWSc 92*
**Pask,** Raymond Frank 1944- *IntAu&W 91, WrDr 92*
**Paskai,** Laszlo 1927- *IntWW 91, WhoRel 92*
**Paskar',** Petr Andreevich 1929- *SovUnBD*
**Paskar,** Pyotr Andreyevich 1929- *IntWW 91*
**Paskausky,** David Frank 1938- *AmMWSc 92*
**Paske,** William Charles 1944- *AmMWSc 92*
**Paskievici,** Wladimir 1930- *AmMWSc 92*
**Paskin,** Arthur 1924- *AmMWSc 92*
**Paskins-Hurlburt,** Andrea Jeanne 1943- *AmMWSc 92*
**Pasko,** Thomas Joseph, Jr 1937- *AmMWSc 92*
**Paskow,** Shimon 1932- *WhoRel 92*
**Paskusz,** Gerhard F 1922- *AmMWSc 92*
**Pasky,** Cynthia Jo 1959- *WhoMW 92*
**Pasley,** James Michael 1953- *WhoMW 92*
**Pasley,** James Neville 1939- *AmMWSc 92*
**Pasley,** Malcolm 1926- *Who 92*
**Pasley,** Robert S. 1912- *WhoAmL 92*
**Pasma,** James Jay 1933- *WhoAmP 91*
**Pasmanik,** Wolf *DrAPF 91*
**Pasmore,** Victor 1908- *IntWW 91, TwCPaSc, Who 92*
**Pasmore,** Wendy 1915- *TwCPaSc*
**Pasolini,** Pier Paolo 1922-1975 *FacFETw, IntDcF 2-2 [port]*
**Pasos,** Joaquin 1914-1947 *ConSpAP*
**Pasour,** Ernest Caleb, Jr. 1932- *WhoFI 92*
**Pasqua,** Charles Victor 1927- *IntWW 91*
**Pasqua,** Pietro F 1922- *AmMWSc 92*
**Pasqua,** Thomas Mario, Jr. 1938- *WhoWest 92*
**Pasquale,** Frank Anthony 1954- *WhoFI 92*
**Pasquarelli,** Joseph J. 1927- *WhoFI 92*
**Pasquill,** Frank 1914- *Who 92*
**Pasquini** *ConAu 34NR*
**Pasquini,** Bernardo 1637-1710 *NewAmDM*
**Pass,** Bobby Clifton 1931- *AmMWSc 92*
**Pass,** Donna Lee 1950- *WhoWest 92*
**Pass,** Douglas 1930- *TwCPaSc*
**Pass,** Joe 1929- *NewAmDM*
**Pass,** Robert Floyd 1947- *AmMWSc 92*
**Pass,** Thomas Emery 1945- *WhoRel 92*
**Passage,** David 1942- *WhoAmP 91*
**Passailaigue,** Ernest L, Jr 1947- *WhoAmP 91*
**Passalacqua,** Angela Virginia 1961- *WhoAmL 92*
**Passananti,** Gaetano Thomas 1925- *AmMWSc 92*
**Passaniti,** Antonino *AmMWSc 92*
**Passannante,** William F 1920- *WhoAmP 91*
**Passano,** Leonard Magruder 1924- *AmMWSc 92*
**Passante,** Dom *TwCSFW 91*
**Passarinho,** Jarbas Goncalves 1920- *IntWW 91*
**Passaro,** Vincent *DrAPF 91*
**Passavant,** William Alfred 1821-1894 *RelLAm 91*
**Passchier,** Arie Anton 1940- *AmMWSc 92*
**Passell,** Laurence 1925- *AmMWSc 92*
**Passell,** Thomas Oliver 1929- *AmMWSc 92*
**Passenheim,** Burr Charles 1941- *AmMWSc 92*
**Passer,** Ivan 1933- *IntDcF 2-2 [port], IntMPA 92*
**Passerello,** Chris Edward 1944- *AmMWSc 92*
**Passerello,** John B. *DrAPF 91*
**Passero,** James Joseph 1934- *WhoFI 92*
**Passey,** Richard Boyd 1937- *AmMWSc 92*
**Passicot Callier,** Andres 1937- *IntWW 91*
**Passino,** Barbara Joyce 1947- *WhoWest 92*
**Passino,** Dora R May 1940- *AmMWSc 92*
**Passino,** Nicholas Alfred 1940- *AmMWSc 92*
**Passion,** Robert *DrAPF 91*
**Passman,** Donald Steven 1940- *AmMWSc 92*
**Passman,** Frederick Jay 1948- *AmMWSc 92*
**Passman,** Sidney 1927- *AmMWSc 92*
**Passman,** Stephen Lee 1942- *AmMWSc 92, WhoWest 92*
**Passmore,** Edmund M 1931- *AmMWSc 92*
**Passmore,** Howard Clinton 1942- *AmMWSc 92*
**Passmore,** Jack 1940- *AmMWSc 92*
**Passmore,** Jan William 1940- *WhoWest 92*
**Passmore,** John Arthur 1914- *IntWW 91*
**Passmore,** John Charles *AmMWSc 92*
**Passmore,** Juanita Carter 1926- *WhoBlA 92*
**Passmore,** William A. 1929- *WhoBlA 92*
**Passner,** Albert 1938- *AmMWSc 92*
**Passoja,** Dann E 1941- *AmMWSc 92*
**Passon,** Betty Jane 1931- *WhoAmP 91*
**Passow,** A. Harry 1920- *WrDr 92*
**Passow,** Eli 1939- *AmMWSc 92*
**Passwater,** Richard Albert 1937- *AmMWSc 92*
**Passy,** Frederic 1822-1912 *WhoNob 90*
**Past,** Wallace Lyle 1924- *AmMWSc 92*
**Pasta,** Giuditta 1798-1865 *NewAmDM*
**Pastan,** Ira Harry 1931- *AmMWSc 92*
**Pastan,** Linda *DrAPF 91*
**Pastan,** Linda 1932- *ConPo 91, WrDr 92*
**Pasteelnick,** Louis Andre 1929- *AmMWSc 92*
**Pastega,** Richard Louis 1936- *WhoAmP 91, WhoWest 92*
**Pastell,** Daniel L 1922- *AmMWSc 92*
**Paster,** Gary M. 1943- *IntMPA 92*
**Paster,** Janice D 1942- *WhoAmP 91*
**Pasterczyk,** William Robert 1917- *AmMWSc 92*
**Pasterfield,** Philip John 1920- *Who 92*

**Pasternack**, Bernard Samuel 1932- *AmMWSc 92*
**Pasternack**, Robert Francis 1936- *AmMWSc 92*
**Pasternak**, Bogdan 1932- *IntAu&W 91*
**Pasternak**, Boris 1890-1960 *FacFETw [port]*
**Pasternak**, Boris Leonidovich 1890-1960 *SovUnBD, WhoNob 90*
**Pasternak**, Derick Peter 1941- *WhoWest 92*
**Pasternak**, Gavril William 1947- *AmMWSc 92*
**Pasternak**, Joe 1901- *IntMPA 92*
**Pasternak**, Joe 1901-1991 *NewYTBS 91*
**Pasternak**, Kathryn Ann 1961- *WhoEnt 92*
**Pasternak**, William M. 1942- *WhoWest 92*
**Pasteur**, Alfred Bernard 1947- *WhoBlA 92*
**Pastille**, Catherine L. 1958- *WhoRel 92*
**Pastin**, Mark Joseph 1949- *WhoWest 92*
**Pastinen**, Ilkka 1928- *Who 92*
**Pastinen**, Ilkka Olavi 1928- *IntWW 91*
**Pasto**, Arvid Eric 1944- *AmMWSc 92*
**Pasto**, Daniel Jerome 1936- *AmMWSc 92*
**Paston** *LitC 17*
**Paston-Bedingfeld**, Edmund George Felix 1915- *Who 92*
**Paston-Bedingfeld**, Henry Edgar 1943- *Who 92*
**Paston Brown**, Beryl 1909- *Who 92*
**Pastor**, Ed *WhoWest 92*
**Pastor**, Ed Lopez 1943- *WhoHisp 92*
**Pastor**, Edward Lopez 1943- *WhoAmP 91*
**Pastor**, Esti 1936- *WhoWest 92*
**Pastor**, Ned *DrAPF 91*
**Pastor**, Selma R *WhoAmP 91*
**Pastor De La Torre**, Celso 1914- *IntWW 91*
**Pastore**, John O. *LesBEnT 92*
**Pastore**, Nicholas *NewYTBS 91 [port]*
**Pastore**, Peter Nicholas 1907- *AmMWSc 92*
**Pastore**, Robert L 1946- *WhoAmP 91*
**Pastore**, Thomas Michael 1959- *WhoWest 92*
**Pastorelle**, Peter John 1933- *WhoEnt 92*
**Pastorelli**, Robert *WhoEnt 92*
**Pastorino Viscardi**, Enrique Juan 1918- *IntWW 91*
**Pastorius**, Carolee Gans 1945- *WhoEnt 92*
**Pastorius**, Francis Daniel 1651-1720 *BenetAL 91*
**Pastoriza**, Jorge 1952- *WhoHisp 92*
**Pastos**, Spero 1940- *IntAu&W 91*
**Pastrana Borrero**, Misael 1923- *IntWW 91*
**Pastreich**, Peter 1938- *WhoWest 92*
**Pastrick**, Robert A 1927- *WhoAmP 91*
**Pastrnak**, Candy Kay 1958- *WhoAmL 92*
**Pastrone**, Giovanni 1883-1959 *FacFETw, IntDcF 2-2*
**Pastuch**, Boris Max *WhoEnt 92*
**Pastukhiv**, Serhij Kindzeriavyj 1924- *WhoRel 92*
**Pastukhov**, Boris Nikolayevich 1933- *IntWW 91*
**Pastuszyn**, Andrzej 1940- *AmMWSc 92*
**Pasula**, Marlene Rose 1942- *WhoWest 92*
**Pasvolsky**, Leo 1893-1953 *AmPeW*
**Paszner**, Laszlo 1934- *AmMWSc 92*
**Pasztor**, Valerie Margaret 1936- *AmMWSc 92*
**Paszyc**, Aleksy Jerzy 1912- *AmMWSc 92*
**Paszynski**, Aleksander 1928- *IntWW 91*
**Patai**, Raphael 1910- *WrDr 92*
**Pataki**, Andrew 1927- *WhoRel 92*
**Pataki**, George 1945- *WhoAmP 91*
**Pataki**, Michael 1938- *ConTFT 9*
**Pataki**, Mike *ConTFT 9*
**Pataky**, Edward Francis 1956- *WhoEnt 92*
**Patalas**, Kazimierz 1925- *AmMWSc 92*
**Patallo**, Indalecio *WhoHisp 92*
**Patane**, Giuseppe 1931- *IntWW 91*
**Patane**, Giuseppe 1932-1989 *NewAmDM*
**Patane**, I Edward 1935- *WhoIns 92*
**Patanelli**, Dolores J 1932- *AmMWSc 92*
**Patasse**, Ange 1937- *FacFETw, IntWW 91*
**Patch**, David Clemens 1953- *WhoFI 92*
**Patch**, Lauren Nelson 1951- *WhoFI 92, WhoIns 92, WhoMW 92*
**Patchan**, Joseph 1922- *WhoAmL 92*
**Patchell**, William Joseph 1948- *WhoFI 92*
**Patchen**, Kenneth 1911-1972 *BenetAL 91, ConAu 35NR*
**Patchett**, Arthur Allan 1929- *AmMWSc 92*
**Patchett**, Mary Elwyn 1897- *IntAu&W 91*
**Patchett**, R Dale 1950- *WhoAmP 91*
**Patchett**, Terry 1940- *Who 92*
**Patching**, Thomas 1915- *AmMWSc 92*
**Pate**, Brian David 1928- *AmMWSc 92*
**Pate**, Findlay Moye 1941- *AmMWSc 92*
**Pate**, Gary Ray 1957- *WhoRel 92*
**Pate**, Henry Scott 1958- *WhoWest 92*
**Pate**, Jacqueline Hail 1930- *WhoFI 92*
**Pate**, James Leonard 1935- *WhoFI 92*
**Pate**, James Wynford 1928- *AmMWSc 92*
**Pate**, John Stewart 1932- *IntWW 91, Who 92*
**Pate**, John W., Sr. 1923- *WhoBlA 92*
**Pate**, Kenneth Randall 1968- *WhoRel 92*
**Pate**, Larry Dale 1946- *WhoRel 92*
**Pate**, Linda Kay 1949- *WhoFI 92*
**Pate**, Michael Glass 1955- *WhoFI 92*
**Pate**, Paul Danny 1958- *WhoAmP 91, WhoMW 92*
**Pate**, Ronald Everett 1952- *WhoMW 92, WhoRel 92*
**Pate**, Stephen Patrick 1958- *WhoAmL 92*
**Pate**, Sue *WhoAmP 91*
**Pate**, Thomas L 1927- *WhoAmP 91*
**Pate-Cornell**, Marie-Elisabeth Lucienne 1948- *WhoWest 92*
**Patel**, Anil S 1939- *AmMWSc 92*
**Patel**, Appasaheb Raojibhai 1931- *AmMWSc 92*
**Patel**, Arvindkumar Motibhai 1937- *AmMWSc 92*
**Patel**, Bhagwandas Mavjibhai 1938- *AmMWSc 92*
**Patel**, Chandra Kumar Naranbhai 1938- *AmMWSc 92*
**Patel**, Chiman Raojibhai 1932- *WhoMW 92*
**Patel**, Dali Jehangir *AmMWSc 92*
**Patel**, Deepak A. 1963- *WhoMW 92*
**Patel**, Ghanshyam K. 1949- *WhoMW 92*
**Patel**, Gieve 1940- *ConPo 91, WrDr 92*
**Patel**, Girishchandra Babubhai 1948- *AmMWSc 92*
**Patel**, Gordhan L 1936- *AmMWSc 92*
**Patel**, Gordhanbhai Nathalal 1942- *AmMWSc 92*
**Patel**, Goswami 1925- *TwCPaSc*
**Patel**, Hirubhai 1904- *IntWW 91*
**Patel**, Indraprasad Gordhanbhai 1924- *IntWW 91, Who 92*
**Patel**, Jamshed R 1925- *AmMWSc 92*
**Patel**, Janak Chhotubhai 1957- *WhoMW 92*
**Patel**, Jay Prahlad 1947- *WhoFI 92*
**Patel**, Jeram 1930- *IntWW 91*
**Patel**, Jitendra Balkrishna 1942- *AmMWSc 92*
**Patel**, Kalyanji U 1925- *AmMWSc 92*
**Patel**, Magan 1937- *WhoFI 92*
**Patel**, Marilyn Hall 1938- *WhoAmL 92*
**Patel**, Mayur 1955- *AmMWSc 92*
**Patel**, Mulchand Shambhubhai 1939- *AmMWSc 92*
**Patel**, Nagin K 1932- *AmMWSc 92*
**Patel**, Narayan Ganesh 1928- *AmMWSc 92*
**Patel**, Navin J. 1949- *WhoWest 92*
**Patel**, Nutankumar T *AmMWSc 92*
**Patel**, Popat-Lal Mulji-bhai *AmMWSc 92*
**Patel**, Praful Raojibhai Chaturbhai 1939- *IntWW 91, Who 92*
**Patel**, Prafull Raojibhai 1937- *AmMWSc 92*
**Patel**, Rajnikant V 1948- *AmMWSc 92*
**Patel**, Rutton Dinshaw 1942- *AmMWSc 92*
**Patel**, Sharad A 1925- *AmMWSc 92*
**Patel**, Siddharth Manilal 1933- *AmMWSc 92*
**Patel**, Sudhir 1961- *WhoWest 92*
**Patel**, Sunil 1959- *TwCPaSc*
**Patel**, Tarun B 1953- *AmMWSc 92*
**Patel**, Virendra C 1938- *AmMWSc 92*
**Patel**, Vithalbhai Ambalal 1936- *AmMWSc 92*
**Patel**, Vithalbhai L 1935- *AmMWSc 92*
**Pateman**, Jack Edward 1921- *Who 92*
**Pateman**, John Arthur 1926- *IntWW 91*
**Pateman**, John Arthur Joseph 1926- *Who 92*
**Pateman**, Trevor John 1947- *WrDr 92*
**Patenaude-Yarnell**, Joan 1945- *WhoEnt 92*
**Patent**, Dorothy Hinshaw 1940- *SmATA 13AS [port]*
**Patent**, Gregory Joseph 1939- *AmMWSc 92*
**Pater**, Elias *WrDr 92*
**Pater**, Michael John 1957- *WhoAmL 92*
**Pater**, Walter 1839-1894 *CnDBLB 4 [port], RfGEnL 91*
**Patera**, J 1936- *AmMWSc 92*
**Paterakis**, Yolanda 1934- *IntAu&W 91*
**Paterakos**, Nick Chris 1959- *WhoFI 92*
**Paterniti**, James R, Jr 1948- *AmMWSc 92*
**Paterniti**, Thomas H 1929- *WhoAmP 91*
**Paterno**, Pedro 1857-1911 *HisDSpE*
**Paternotte**, William Leslie 1945- *WhoFI 92*
**Paternotte DeLaVaillee**, Alexandre E M L 1923- *IntWW 91*
**Patero**, Joseph D 1932- *WhoAmP 91*
**Paterson**, Alan Robb Phillips 1923- *AmMWSc 92*
**Paterson**, Alexander Craig 1924- *Who 92*
**Paterson**, Alistair 1929- *ConPo 91, IntAu&W 91, WrDr 92*
**Paterson**, Andrew Barton 1864-1941 *RfGEnL 91*
**Paterson**, Arthur Renwick 1922- *AmMWSc 92*
**Paterson**, Basil Alexander 1926- *WhoAmP 91, WhoBlA 92*
**Paterson**, Betty 1916- *Who 92*
**Paterson**, David A 1955- *WhoAmP 91*
**Paterson**, Dennis 1930- *Who 92*
**Paterson**, Dennis Craig 1930- *IntWW 91*
**Paterson**, Donald Robert 1920- *AmMWSc 92*
**Paterson**, Francis 1930- *Who 92*
**Paterson**, Frank David 1918- *Who 92*
**Paterson**, George 1906- *Who 92*
**Paterson**, Ian Veitch 1911- *Who 92*
**Paterson**, James 1854-1932 *TwCPaSc*
**Paterson**, James Edmund Neil 1915- *Who 92*
**Paterson**, James Hunter 1947- *WhoMW 92*
**Paterson**, James Lenander 1941- *AmMWSc 92*
**Paterson**, James McEwan 1937- *AmMWSc 92*
**Paterson**, James Rupert 1932- *Who 92*
**Paterson**, James Veitch 1928- *Who 92*
**Paterson**, John 1801-1883 *BiInAmS*
**Paterson**, John Allan d1991 *Who 92N*
**Paterson**, John Mower Alexander 1920- *Who 92*
**Paterson**, John Munn Kirk 1922- *Who 92*
**Paterson**, John Thomas Farquhar 1938- *Who 92*
**Paterson**, John Valentine J. *Who 92*
**Paterson**, Katherine 1932- *WrDr 92*
**Paterson**, Laurie Ann 1957- *WhoFI 92*
**Paterson**, Mervyn Silas 1925- *IntWW 91*
**Paterson**, Neil *Who 92*
**Paterson**, Neil 1915- *IntAu&W 91*
**Paterson**, Neil 1916- *WrDr 92*
**Paterson**, Philip Y 1925- *AmMWSc 92*
**Paterson**, Robert Andrew 1926- *AmMWSc 92*
**Paterson**, Robert Lancelot 1918- *Who 92*
**Paterson**, Robert W 1939- *AmMWSc 92*
**Paterson**, Ronald 1933- *IntAu&W 91, WrDr 92*
**Paterson**, William 1745-1806 *AmPolLe, BlkwEAR*
**Paterson**, William Alexander *Who 92*
**Paterson**, William Gordon *AmMWSc 92*
**Paterson-Brown**, June 1932- *Who 92*
**Pates**, Anne Louise 1913- *AmMWSc 92*
**Pates**, Harold *WhoBlA 92*
**Pates**, James Morgan 1950- *WhoAmP 91*
**Patey**, Edward Henry 1915- *Who 92*
**Pathak**, Jayant Himatlal 1920- *IntAu&W 91*
**Pathak**, Madhukar 1927- *AmMWSc 92*
**Pathak**, Prabhakar H 1942- *AmMWSc 92*
**Pathak**, Raghunandan Swarup 1924- *Who 92*
**Pathak**, Rahunandan Swarup 1924- *IntWW 91*
**Pathak**, Sen 1940- *AmMWSc 92*
**Pathak**, Vibhav Gautam 1964- *WhoWest 92*
**Pathania**, Rajeshwar S *AmMWSc 92*
**Pathfinder**, Peter 1937- *RelLAm 91*
**Pathria**, Raj Kumar 1933- *AmMWSc 92*
**Pati**, Christopher Martin 1962- *WhoEnt 92*
**Pati**, Jogesh Chandra 1937- *AmMWSc 92*
**Patience**, Andrew 1941- *Who 92*
**Patience**, John Francis 1951- *AmMWSc 92*
**Patil**, Ganapati P 1934- *AmMWSc 92*
**Patil**, Kashinath Ziparu *AmMWSc 92*
**Patil**, Murlidhar P. 1942- *WhoMW 92*
**Patil**, Popat N 1934- *AmMWSc 92*
**Patil**, Suresh Siddheshwar 1935- *AmMWSc 92*
**Patil**, Veerendra 1924- *IntWW 91*
**Patin**, Joseph Patrick 1937- *WhoBlA 92*
**Patin**, Jude W. P. 1940- *WhoBlA 92*
**Patin**, Robert W 1942- *WhoIns 92*
**Patinkin**, Don 1922- *IntWW 91*
**Patinkin**, Mandy 1952- *IntMPA 92, WhoEnt 92*
**Patinkin**, Mark 1953- *ConAu 133*
**Patinkin**, Seymour Harold 1926- *AmMWSc 92*
**Patinkin**, Sheldon 1935- *WhoEnt 92, WhoMW 92*
**Patino**, Arthur, Jr. 1927- *WhoRel 92*
**Patino**, Isidro Frank 1943- *WhoWest 92*
**Patino**, Jose 1666-1736 *HisDSpE*
**Patire**, Anthony Paul 1941- *WhoMW 92*
**Patler**, Louis *DrAPF 91*
**Patman**, Carrin Mauritz 1932- *WhoAmP 91*
**Patman**, Harold C 1935- *WhoIns 92*
**Patman**, Philip Franklin 1937- *WhoAmL 92*
**Patman**, William N 1927- *WhoAmP 91*
**Patmon**, Claude 1941- *WhoBlA 92*
**Patmore**, Alan Barry 1940- *WhoWest 92*
**Patmore**, Allan 1931- *Who 92*
**Patmore**, Coventry 1823-1896 *RfGEnL 91*
**Patmore**, Edwin Lee 1934- *AmMWSc 92*
**Patmore**, Geraldine Mary *WhoWest 92*
**Patnaik**, Amiya Krishna 1930- *AmMWSc 92*
**Patnaik**, Bijoyanananda 1916- *IntWW 91*
**Patnaik**, Janaki Ballav 1927- *IntWW 91*
**Patnaik**, Pradeep Kumar 1944- *WhoFI 92*
**Patner**, Richard 1946- *WhoWest 92*
**Patnett**, John Henry 1948- *WhoBlA 92*
**Patnick**, Irvine 1929- *Who 92*
**Patnode**, Robert Arthur 1918- *AmMWSc 92*
**Patolichev**, Nikolay Semenovich 1908-1989 *SovUnBD*
**Paton** *Who 92*
**Paton**, Alan 1903- *IntAu&W 91*
**Paton**, Alan 1903-1988 *FacFETw, RfGEnL 91*
**Paton**, Alasdair Chalmers 1944- *Who 92*
**Paton**, Angus *IntWW 91, Who 92*
**Paton**, Ann *Who 92*
**Paton**, Boris Yevgeniyevich 1918- *IntWW 91*
**Paton**, Bruce Calder 1925- *AmMWSc 92*
**Paton**, David 1930- *AmMWSc 92*
**Paton**, David Macdonald 1913- *Who 92, WrDr 92*
**Paton**, David Murray 1938- *AmMWSc 92*
**Paton**, Douglas Shaw F. *Who 92*
**Paton**, Douglas Stuart 1926- *Who 92*
**Paton**, Michael John Macdonald 1922- *Who 92*
**Paton**, Neil 1938- *AmMWSc 92*
**Paton**, Russell Emerson 1960- *WhoRel 92*
**Paton**, Thomas Angus 1905- *IntWW 91, Who 92*
**Paton**, William 1886-1943 *DcEcMov [port]*
**Paton**, William 1917- *Who 92*
**Paton**, William A. d1991 *NewYTBS 91*
**Paton**, William Drummond Macdonald 1917- *IntWW 91*
**Paton Walsh**, Jill 1937- *IntAu&W 91, Who 92, WrDr 92*
**Patorski**, Janusz 1946- *IntWW 91*
**Patra**, Sushant Kumar 1939- *WhoFI 92*
**Patrascioiu**, Adrian Nicolae *AmMWSc 92*
**Patri**, Angelo 1876-1965 *DcAmImH*
**Patriarca**, Peter 1921- *AmMWSc 92*
**Patriarche**, Mercer Harding 1916- *AmMWSc 92*
**Patric**, James Holton 1922- *AmMWSc 92*
**Patric**, Jason 1966- *IntMPA 92*
**Patricio**, Rui Manuel de Medeiros d'E. 1932- *IntWW 91*
**Patrick** d460? *EncEarC*
**Patrick**, Alison Mary Houston 1921- *IntWW 91*
**Patrick**, Anne Estelle 1941- *WhoRel 92*
**Patrick**, Billy Wayne 1955- *WhoAmP 91*
**Patrick**, C.L. 1918- *IntMPA 92*
**Patrick**, Carl Lloyd 1918- *WhoEnt 92*
**Patrick**, Charles Namon, Jr. 1949- *WhoBlA 92*
**Patrick**, Charles Russell 1940- *AmMWSc 92*
**Patrick**, Douglas Franklin 1950- *WhoAmL 92*
**Patrick**, Edward Alfred *WhoMW 92*
**Patrick**, Edward Alfred 1937- *AmMWSc 92*
**Patrick**, George Edward 1851-1916 *BiInAmS*
**Patrick**, George Frederick 1942- *WhoMW 92*
**Patrick**, George Milton 1920- *WhoFI 92, WhoMW 92*
**Patrick**, Graham Abner 1946- *AmMWSc 92*
**Patrick**, Graham McIntosh 1921- *Who 92*
**Patrick**, H. Hunter 1939- *WhoAmL 92*
**Patrick**, Ida Hilda Acuna 1948- *WhoHisp 92*
**Patrick**, Isadore W., Jr. 1951- *WhoBlA 92*
**Patrick**, James Burns 1923- *AmMWSc 92*
**Patrick**, James Edward 1944- *AmMWSc 92*
**Patrick**, James L. 1919- *WhoBlA 92*
**Patrick**, James McIntosh 1907- *TwCPaSc, Who 92*
**Patrick**, James R 1931- *AmMWSc 92*
**Patrick**, Jane Austin 1930- *WhoFI 92, WhoMW 92*
**Patrick**, Jay 1949- *WhoEnt 92*
**Patrick**, Jennie R. 1949- *WhoBlA 92*
**Patrick**, Jim 1958- *WhoEnt 92*
**Patrick**, John 1905- *IntAu&W 91, IntWW 91*
**Patrick**, John 1906?- *BenetAL 91*
**Patrick**, John 1907- *WrDr 92*
**Patrick**, John Bowman 1916- *Who 92*
**Patrick**, Julius, Jr. 1938- *WhoBlA 92*
**Patrick**, Kerry *WhoAmP 91*
**Patrick**, Kevin 1953- *WhoEnt 92*
**Patrick**, Lawrence Clarence, Jr. 1945- *WhoBlA 92*
**Patrick**, Leslie Dayle 1951- *WhoWest 92*
**Patrick**, Lou 1953- *WhoEnt 92*
**Patrick**, Lynda Lee 1938- *WhoWest 92*
**Patrick**, Margaret Kathleen 1923- *Who 92*
**Patrick**, Mark Russell 1949- *WhoFI 92*
**Patrick**, Marty 1949- *WhoAmL 92*
**Patrick**, Matthew 1955- *IntMPA 92, WhoWest 92*
**Patrick**, Maxine *WrDr 92*
**Patrick**, Merrell Lee 1933- *AmMWSc 92*

**Patrick**, Michael Heath 1936- *AmMWSc 92, WhoMW 92*
**Patrick**, Michael W. 1950- *IntMPA 92*
**Patrick**, Odessa R. 1933- *WhoBlA 92*
**Patrick**, Opal Lee Young 1929- *WhoBlA 92*
**Patrick**, Rembert Wallace 1909-1967 *ConAu 134*
**Patrick**, Richard Montgomery 1928- *AmMWSc 92*
**Patrick**, Robert 1937- *IntAu&W 91, WrDr 92*
**Patrick**, Robert Alexander 1954- *WhoMW 92*
**Patrick**, Robert F 1921- *AmMWSc 92*
**Patrick**, Robert John, Jr. 1934- *WhoAmL 92*
**Patrick**, Robert L *AmMWSc 92*
**Patrick**, Robert McHenry 1928- *WhoFI 92*
**Patrick**, Ruth 1907- *AmMWSc 92, IntWW 91*
**Patrick**, Steven Joseph 1962- *WhoEnt 92*
**Patrick**, Susan *IntAu&W 91X, WrDr 92*
**Patrick**, Thomas *WhoEnt 92*
**Patrick**, Timothy Benson 1941- *AmMWSc 92*
**Patrick**, Vincent Jerome 1959- *WhoBlA 92*
**Patrick**, Wesley Clare 1951- *AmMWSc 92*
**Patrick**, William *DrAPF 91*
**Patrick**, William Banks, Jr. 1943- *WhoAmL 92*
**Patrick**, William Bradshaw 1923- *WhoAmL 92, WhoMW 92*
**Patrick**, William H, Jr 1925- *AmMWSc 92*
**Patrick**, William T., Jr. 1920- *WhoBlA 92*
**Patrick**, Zenon Alexander 1924- *AmMWSc 92*
**Patricola**, Steven Lawrence 1957- *WhoFI 92*
**Patrida**, Juan R. *WhoHisp 92*
**Patrides**, C A 1930- *IntAu&W 91, WrDr 92*
**Patrik**, Gary Steven 1944- *WhoIns 92*
**Patrik**, Maxine *IntAu&W 91X*
**Patriquin**, Edward Leroy, Jr. 1958- *WhoWest 92*
**Patriquin**, Redmond L. 1938- *WhoFI 92*
**Patronella**, David M 1957- *WhoAmP 91*
**Patronik**, Richard Stephen 1956- *WhoIns 92*
**Patronis**, Eugene Thayer, Jr 1932- *AmMWSc 92*
**Patrow-Rosene**, Kristine Lydal 1963- *WhoMW 92*
**Patsakos**, George 1942- *AmMWSc 92, WhoWest 92*
**Patsalides**, Andreas 1922- *IntWW 91*
**Patsayev**, Viktor 1933-1971 *FacFETw*
**Patsch**, Wolfgang 1946- *AmMWSc 92*
**Patsey**, Richard Lee 1935- *WhoAmL 92*
**Patsiga**, Robert A 1934- *AmMWSc 92*
**Patsis**, Angelos Vlasios 1928- *AmMWSc 92*
**Patt**, Gideon 1933- *IntWW 91*
**Patt**, Leonard Merton 1948- *AmMWSc 92*
**Patt**, Raymond Martin 1917- *WhoAmL 92*
**Patt**, Yale Nance 1939- *AmMWSc 92*
**Pattabhiraman**, Tammanur R 1934- *AmMWSc 92*
**Pattakos**, Stylianos 1912- *IntWW 91*
**Pattantyus**, Tamas Imre 1934- *WhoFI 92*
**Patte**, George David, Jr. 1945- *WhoAmL 92*
**Pattee**, Fred Lewis 1863-1950 *BenetAL 91*
**Pattee**, Harold Edward 1934- *AmMWSc 92*
**Pattee**, Howard Hunt, Jr 1926- *AmMWSc 92*
**Pattee**, Oliver Henry 1948- *AmMWSc 92*
**Pattee**, Peter A 1932- *AmMWSc 92*
**Patten**, Bebe Harrison 1913- *WhoRel 92*
**Patten**, Bebe Rebecca 1950- *WhoRel 92*
**Patten**, Bernard Clarence 1931- *AmMWSc 92*
**Patten**, Brian 1946- *ConPo 91, IntAu&W 91, Who 92, WrDr 92*
**Patten**, Charles Louis 1951- *WhoAmP 91*
**Patten**, Christopher 1944- *IntWW 91, Who 92*
**Patten**, David Stuart 1936- *WhoMW 92*
**Patten**, Duncan Theunissen 1934- *AmMWSc 92*
**Patten**, Edward Roy 1939- *WhoBlA 92*
**Patten**, Gaylord Penrod 1938- *AmMWSc 92*
**Patten**, Gilbert 1866-1945 *ScFEYrs*
**Patten**, John 1945- *Who 92*
**Patten**, Joseph Hurlbut 1801-1877 *BiInAmS*
**Patten**, Karl *DrAPF 91*
**Patten**, Lanny Ray 1934- *WhoFI 92*
**Patten**, Lewis B 1915-1981 *TwCWW 91*
**Patten**, Nicholas John 1950- *Who 92*
**Patten**, Raymond Alex 1937- *AmMWSc 92*
**Patten**, Richard E. 1953- *WhoWest 92*
**Patten**, Robert L *WhoAmP 91*
**Patten**, Thomas H. 1929- *WrDr 92*
**Patten**, Thomas Louis 1945- *WhoAmL 92*
**Patten**, Tom 1926- *Who 92*
**Patten**, W. George 1931- *WhoBlA 92*
**Patten**, William 1865-1945 *ScFEYrs*
**Patten**, William Gilbert 1866-1945 *BenetAL 91*
**Patten-Benham**, Priscilla Carla 1950- *WhoRel 92*
**Pattenden**, Gerald 1940- *Who 92*
**Pattengill**, Merle Dean 1942- *AmMWSc 92*
**Patterson**, Alonzo B. 1937- *WhoBlA 92*
**Patterson**, Andrew, Jr 1916- *AmMWSc 92*
**Patterson**, Anita Carol 1944- *WhoRel 92*
**Patterson**, Ann Ricene 1961- *WhoFI 92*
**Patterson**, Archibald Oscar 1908- *AmMWSc 92*
**Patterson**, Arthur 1906- *Who 92*
**Patterson**, Arthur Gordon 1917- *Who 92*
**Patterson**, Arthur Lawrence 1934- *WhoRel 92*
**Patterson**, Audrey 1926- *BlkOlyM*
**Patterson**, B. Leroy 1935- *WhoRel 92*
**Patterson**, Barbara Ann *WhoBlA 92*
**Patterson**, Barbara Boccia 1957- *WhoFI 92*
**Patterson**, Ben *Who 92*
**Patterson**, Beverley Pamela Grace 1956- *WhoFI 92*
**Patterson**, C Maurice 1913- *AmMWSc 92*
**Patterson**, Carlile Pollock 1816-1881 *BiInAmS*
**Patterson**, Cecil Booker, Jr. 1941- *WhoBlA 92*
**Patterson**, Cecil John 1908- *IntWW 91, Who 92*
**Patterson**, Cecil Lloyd 1917- *WhoBlA 92*
**Patterson**, Charles Jerry 1925- *WhoBlA 92*
**Patterson**, Charles Meade 1919- *AmMWSc 92*
**Patterson**, Christine Ann 1949- *WhoBlA 92*
**Patterson**, Christopher Warren 1946- *AmMWSc 92*
**Patterson**, Clair Cameron 1922- *AmMWSc 92*
**Patterson**, Clarence J. 1925- *WhoBlA 92*
**Patterson**, Clinton David 1936- *WhoBlA 92*
**Patterson**, Constance Marie 1934- *Who 92*
**Patterson**, Curtis Ray 1944- *WhoBlA 92*
**Patterson**, Dana Moore 1960- *WhoAmP 91*
**Patterson**, Daniel William 1948- *WhoWest 92*
**Patterson**, David 1944- *AmMWSc 92, WhoWest 92*
**Patterson**, David Andrew 1947- *WhoWest 92*
**Patterson**, David Leon 1949- *WhoBlA 92*
**Patterson**, David Thomas 1946- *AmMWSc 92*
**Patterson**, Dawn Marie *WhoWest 92*
**Patterson**, Day Lewis 1943- *WhoEnt 92*
**Patterson**, Dennis Bruce 1941- *AmMWSc 92, WhoWest 92*
**Patterson**, Dennis Glen 1948- *WhoWest 92*
**Patterson**, Dennis Ray 1946- *AmMWSc 92*
**Patterson**, Dessie Lee 1919- *WhoBlA 92*
**Patterson**, Donald Duke 1927- *AmMWSc 92*
**Patterson**, Donald Floyd 1931- *AmMWSc 92*
**Patterson**, Donald Lee 1947- *WhoEnt 92*
**Patterson**, Donald Ross 1939- *WhoAmL 92*
**Patterson**, Donis Dean 1930- *WhoRel 92*
**Patterson**, Dorothea *TwCPaSc*
**Patterson**, Doug 1945- *TwCPaSc*
**Patterson**, Douglas Reid 1945- *AmMWSc 92*
**Patterson**, Dwight Fleming, Jr. 1939- *WhoAmL 92*
**Patterson**, E G *WhoAmP 91*
**Patterson**, Earl Byron 1923- *AmMWSc 92*
**Patterson**, Earl E 1923- *AmMWSc 92*
**Patterson**, Earl Edgar 1923- *WhoAmP 91*
**Patterson**, Earl F 1930- *WhoAmP 91*
**Patterson**, Edward Matthew 1943- *AmMWSc 92*
**Patterson**, Edward Milton 1948- *WhoAmL 92*
**Patterson**, Edwin 1921- *WhoRel 92*
**Patterson**, Elizabeth Ann 1936- *WhoBlA 92*
**Patterson**, Elizabeth Chambers *AmMWSc 92*
**Patterson**, Elizabeth Hayes 1945- *WhoBlA 92*
**Patterson**, Elizabeth J. 1939- *AlmAP 92 [port]*
**Patterson**, Elizabeth Johnston 1939- *WhoAmP 91*
**Patterson**, Elizabeth Knight 1909- *AmMWSc 92*
**Patterson**, Emma L. 1904-1984 *ConAu 135*
**Patterson**, Eric 1930- *Who 92*
**Patterson**, Ernest Leonard 1918- *AmMWSc 92*
**Patterson**, Evelynne 1930- *WhoBlA 92*
**Patterson**, Floyd *WhoBlA 92*
**Patterson**, Floyd 1935- *FacFETw*
**Patterson**, Floyd P 1935- *BlkOlyM*
**Patterson**, Francine G. P. 1947- *WhoWest 92*
**Patterson**, Fred La Vern 1916- *AmMWSc 92*
**Patterson**, Gardner 1916- *IntWW 91*
**Patterson**, Gary David 1946- *AmMWSc 92*
**Patterson**, Gary Kent 1939- *AmMWSc 92*
**Patterson**, George Benjamin 1939- *Who 92*
**Patterson**, George Harold 1917- *AmMWSc 92*
**Patterson**, Gerald Robert 1956- *WhoEnt 92*
**Patterson**, Gerald William 1953- *WhoBlA 92*
**Patterson**, Glenn Wayne 1938- *AmMWSc 92*
**Patterson**, Gordon Derby, Jr 1923- *AmMWSc 92*
**Patterson**, Grace Limerick 1938- *WhoBlA 92*
**Patterson**, Grady Leslie, Jr 1924- *WhoAmP 91, WhoFI 92*
**Patterson**, Greg *WhoAmP 91*
**Patterson**, Gregory Matthew Leon 1954- *AmMWSc 92*
**Patterson**, Harlan Ray 1931- *WhoFI 92, WhoMW 92*
**Patterson**, Harold E *WhoAmP 91*
**Patterson**, Harry *WrDr 92*
**Patterson**, Harry 1929- *IntAu&W 91, IntWW 91, Who 92*
**Patterson**, Harry Robert 1921- *AmMWSc 92*
**Patterson**, Henry *IntAu&W 91X*
**Patterson**, Henry 1939- *WrDr 92*
**Patterson**, Howard Hugh 1938- *AmMWSc 92*
**Patterson**, Hugh Foggan 1924- *Who 92*
**Patterson**, Ian D 1897- *AmMWSc 92*
**Patterson**, J. O. *WhoRel 92*
**Patterson**, J O, Jr 1935- *WhoAmP 91*
**Patterson**, Jacqueline J. 1928- *WhoBlA 92*
**Patterson**, James 1935- *WhoBlA 92*
**Patterson**, James 1947- *ConAu 133*
**Patterson**, James A 1942- *WhoIns 92*
**Patterson**, James Aris 1935- *WhoEnt 92*
**Patterson**, James Deane 1934- *AmMWSc 92*
**Patterson**, James Douglas 1964- *AmMWSc 92*
**Patterson**, James F 1942- *WhoAmP 91*
**Patterson**, James Fulton 1918- *AmMWSc 92*
**Patterson**, James Gordon, III 1953- *WhoFI 92*
**Patterson**, James Hardy 1935- *WhoEnt 92*
**Patterson**, James Howard 1921- *AmMWSc 92*
**Patterson**, James Oglethorpe 1912-1989 *WhoBlA 92N*
**Patterson**, James Oglethorpe, Sr. 1912-1989 *RelLAm 91*
**Patterson**, James Reid 1918- *AmMWSc 92*
**Patterson**, James W 1940- *AmMWSc 92*
**Patterson**, Jane Smith 1940- *WhoAmP 91*
**Patterson**, Janet 1941- *TwCPaSc*
**Patterson**, Jerome Anthony, Jr. 1948- *WhoAmL 92*
**Patterson**, Jerry A 1942- *WhoAmP 91*
**Patterson**, Jerry Mumford 1934- *WhoAmP 91*
**Patterson**, Jim *WhoAmP 91*
**Patterson**, Jimmy Dale 1958- *WhoRel 92*
**Patterson**, Joan Delores 1944- *WhoBlA 92*
**Patterson**, John Allan 1931- *Who 92*
**Patterson**, John Legerwood, Jr 1913- *AmMWSc 92*
**Patterson**, John Malcolm 1921- *WhoAmP 91*
**Patterson**, John Miles 1926- *AmMWSc 92*
**Patterson**, John Reuben 1928- *WhoWest 92*
**Patterson**, John T., Jr. 1928- *WhoBlA 92*
**Patterson**, John W 1936- *AmMWSc 92*
**Patterson**, John Ward 1916- *AmMWSc 92*
**Patterson**, John William 1949- *WhoAmP 91*
**Patterson**, Joseph Cromwell 1928- *WhoFI 92*
**Patterson**, Joseph Gilbert 1926- *AmMWSc 92*
**Patterson**, Kathi 1950- *WhoEnt 92*
**Patterson**, Kay 1931- *WhoAmP 91, WhoBlA 92*
**Patterson**, L P 1934- *WhoAmP 91*
**Patterson**, Larry K 1937- *AmMWSc 92*
**Patterson**, Lawrence Patrick 1932- *WhoBlA 92*
**Patterson**, Leighton Paige 1942- *WhoRel 92*
**Patterson**, Lester Roy 1938- *WhoAmP 91*
**Patterson**, Linda Thomson 1949- *WhoFI 92*
**Patterson**, Lloyd 1931- *WhoBlA 92*
**Patterson**, Loyd Thomas 1930- *AmMWSc 92*
**Patterson**, Lucille Joan *WhoMW 92*
**Patterson**, Lydia R. 1936- *WhoBlA 92*
**Patterson**, Malcolm Robert 1935- *AmMWSc 92*
**Patterson**, Manford Kenneth, Jr 1926- *AmMWSc 92*
**Patterson**, Maria Jevitz 1944- *AmMWSc 92*
**Patterson**, Marian L *WhoAmP 91*
**Patterson**, Marie *Who 92*
**Patterson**, Mark Lister 1934- *Who 92*
**Patterson**, Mark Robert 1957- *AmMWSc 92*
**Patterson**, Mark Stribling 1952- *WhoMW 92*
**Patterson**, Mary Jane 1840-1894 *NotBlAW 92 [port]*
**Patterson**, Mary Lynn 1958- *WhoMW 92*
**Patterson**, Max E 1923- *AmMWSc 92*
**Patterson**, Michael 1939- *WrDr 92*
**Patterson**, Michael Duane 1949- *WhoBlA 92*
**Patterson**, Michael Milton 1942- *AmMWSc 92, WhoMW 92*
**Patterson**, Michael Wyndham 1939- *IntAu&W 91*
**Patterson**, Orlando 1940- *BenetAL 91, ConNov 91, WrDr 92*
**Patterson**, Orlando Horace 1940- *WhoBlA 92*
**Patterson**, Oscar, III 1945- *WhoEnt 92*
**Patterson**, Patricia Anne 1938- *WhoAmL 92*
**Patterson**, Paul 1926- *WhoBlA 92*
**Patterson**, Paul 1947- *ConCom 92*
**Patterson**, Paul A. 1929- *WhoBlA 92*
**Patterson**, Paul H 1943- *AmMWSc 92*
**Patterson**, Paul Leslie 1947- *Who 92*
**Patterson**, Pola Noah 1935- *WhoBlA 92*
**Patterson**, Raymond R. *DrAPF 91*
**Patterson**, Raymond R. 1929- *ConPo 91, WhoBlA 92, WrDr 92*
**Patterson**, Rex Alan 1927- *IntWW 91*
**Patterson**, Richard Austin 1942- *WhoAmL 92*
**Patterson**, Richard George 1929- *WhoAmP 91*
**Patterson**, Richard L 1932- *AmMWSc 92*
**Patterson**, Richard Rodney 1925- *WhoAmP 91*
**Patterson**, Richard Sheldon 1932- *AmMWSc 92*
**Patterson**, Rickey Lee 1952- *WhoRel 92*
**Patterson**, Robert 1743-1824 *BiInAmS*
**Patterson**, Robert Allen 1927- *AmMWSc 92*
**Patterson**, Robert Eugene 1932- *WhoFI 92*
**Patterson**, Robert Lynn 1939- *WhoFI 92*
**Patterson**, Robert Maskell 1787-1854 *BiInAmS*
**Patterson**, Robert Porter, Jr. 1923- *WhoAmL 92*
**Patterson**, Robert Preston 1939- *AmMWSc 92*
**Patterson**, Robertson Rush 1947- *WhoFI 92*
**Patterson**, Ronald Brinton 1941- *AmMWSc 92*
**Patterson**, Ronald E. *WhoBlA 92*
**Patterson**, Ronald James 1943- *AmMWSc 92*
**Patterson**, Ronald Paul 1941- *WhoRel 92*
**Patterson**, Rosalyn Mitchell 1939- *AmMWSc 92*
**Patterson**, Roy 1926- *AmMWSc 92*
**Patterson**, Russel Hugo, Jr 1929- *AmMWSc 92*
**Patterson**, Russell 1930- *WhoEnt 92*
**Patterson**, Russell Alfred 1947- *WhoFI 92*
**Patterson**, Russell Lee 1959- *WhoMW 92*
**Patterson**, Sam H 1918- *AmMWSc 92*
**Patterson**, Samuel S 1917- *AmMWSc 92*
**Patterson**, Scott G. 1946- *WhoAmL 92*
**Patterson**, Solon P. 1935- *WhoFI 92*
**Patterson**, Stephen F 1939- *WhoIns 92*
**Patterson**, Steven Leroy 1947- *AmMWSc 92*
**Patterson**, Theodore Carter Chavis 1932- *WhoBlA 92*
**Patterson**, Thomas C *WhoAmP 91*
**Patterson**, Thomas Edward 1953- *WhoAmL 92*
**Patterson**, Thomas Harvey 1941- *WhoFI 92*
**Patterson**, Tim J 1957- *AmMWSc 92*
**Patterson**, Troy B 1923- *AmMWSc 92*
**Patterson**, Truett Clifton 1937- *AmMWSc 92*
**Patterson**, Vance 1945- *WhoMW 92*
**Patterson**, Vernon Howe 1910- *AmMWSc 92*
**Patterson**, Veronica *DrAPF 91*
**Patterson**, Virginia Calvert 1958- *WhoAmL 92*
**Patterson**, Virginia Catharine 1931- *WhoRel 92*
**Patterson**, William A 1899-1980 *FacFETw*

**Patterson,** William Alexander 1915- *AmMWSc 92*
**Patterson,** William Benjamin 1931- *WhoBlA 92*
**Patterson,** William Bradford 1921- *AmMWSc 92*
**Patterson,** William Burr 1935- *WhoAmL 92*
**Patterson,** William Creigh, Jr 1921- *AmMWSc 92*
**Patterson,** William Frank 1936- *WhoMW 92*
**Patterson,** William James 1930- *Who 92*
**Patterson,** William Jerry 1939- *AmMWSc 92*
**Patterson,** Willis Charles 1930- *WhoBlA 92*
**Patterson,** Windell Ray 1930- *WhoRel 92*
**Patteson,** Carter *DrAPF 91*
**Patteson,** Roy Kinneer, Jr. 1928- *WhoRel 92*
**Patti,** Adelina 1843-1919 *NewAmDM*
**Patti,** Andrew S. 1940- *WhoWest 92*
**Patti,** Black *NewAmDM*
**Patti,** Frank J 1924- *WhoAmP 91*
**Patti,** Sandi 1956- *ConMus 7 [port]*
**Pattie,** Donald L 1933- *AmMWSc 92*
**Pattie,** Geoffrey 1936- *Who 92*
**Pattie,** James Ohio 1804-1850? *BenetAL 91*
**Pattie,** Kenton Harman 1939- *WhoFI 92*
**Pattillo,** Kaye Bridges 1940- *WhoEnt 92*
**Pattillo,** Nickles Keat 1947- *WhoFI 92*
**Pattillo,** Robert Allen 1951- *AmMWSc 92*
**Pattillo,** Roland A. 1933- *WhoBlA 92*
**Pattillo,** Rowland D 1923- *WhoAmP 91*
**Pattillo,** Walter Hugh, Jr 1930- *AmMWSc 92*
**Pattinson,** Baden 1899- *Who 92*
**Pattinson,** Derek *Who 92*
**Pattinson,** John Mellor 1899- *IntWW 91, Who 92*
**Pattinson,** Peter L. F. *Who 92*
**Pattinson,** William Derek 1930- *IntWW 91, Who 92*
**Pattisall,** Richard Chapman 1938- *WhoAmP 91*
**Pattishall,** Beverly Wyckliffe 1916- *WhoAmL 92, WhoMW 92*
**Pattison,** Abbott Lawrence 1916- *WhoEnt 92*
**Pattison,** Bruce 1908- *Who 92*
**Pattison,** David Arnold 1941- *Who 92*
**Pattison,** Edward W 1932- *WhoAmP 91*
**Pattison,** Eugene Hamilton 1935- *WhoMW 92*
**Pattison,** Fred Lewis 1932- *WhoRel 92*
**Pattison,** George Linsley 1950- *Who 92, WhoRel 92*
**Pattison,** Granville Sharp 1791?-1851 *BiInAmS*
**Pattison,** Michael Ambrose 1946- *Who 92*
**Pattison,** Orville Hoyt 1929- *WhoAmP 91*
**Pattman,** Virgil Thomas, Sr. 1940- *WhoBlA 92*
**Pattok,** Sandra Lee 1938- *WhoAmP 91*
**Patton,** Alton DeWitt 1935- *AmMWSc 92*
**Patton,** Audley Everett 1898- *WhoWest 92*
**Patton,** Barbara A *WhoAmP 91*
**Patton,** Barbara Weeks 1941- *WhoWest 92*
**Patton,** Bobby Ray 1935- *WhoEnt 92, WhoWest 92*
**Patton,** Bruce Riley 1944- *AmMWSc 92*
**Patton,** Carl E 1941- *AmMWSc 92*
**Patton,** Carl Elliott 1941- *WhoWest 92*
**Patton,** Carolyn Vannette *WhoBlA 92*
**Patton,** Charles C 1936- *AmMWSc 92*
**Patton,** Charley 1887?-1934 *NewAmDM*
**Patton,** Curtis L. 1935- *WhoBlA 92*
**Patton,** Curtis LeVerne 1935- *AmMWSc 92*
**Patton,** Daniel Craig 1952- *WhoFI 92*
**Patton,** Darla June Eaton 1948- *WhoAmL 92*
**Patton,** David Roger 1934- *AmMWSc 92*
**Patton,** Deanna Kay 1953- *WhoMW 92*
**Patton,** Dennis David 1930- *AmMWSc 92*
**Patton,** Edwin Guy 1904- *WhoAmP 91*
**Patton,** Elizabeth *DrAPF 91*
**Patton,** Elizabeth VanDyke 1944- *AmMWSc 92*
**Patton,** Ernest Gibbes 1924- *AmMWSc 92*
**Patton,** Frances Gray 1906- *BenetAL 91*
**Patton,** Francis Landley 1843-1932 *RelLAm 91*
**Patton,** Frank *TwCSFW 91*
**Patton,** Gary Lloyd 1954- *WhoRel 92*
**Patton,** George Erwin d1991 *NewYTBS 91*
**Patton,** George Mallory 1930- *WhoRel 92*
**Patton,** George S, Jr 1885-1945 *FacFETw [port]*
**Patton,** Georgia E. L. 1864-1900 *NotBlAW 92 [port]*
**Patton,** Gerald Wilson 1947- *WhoBlA 92*
**Patton,** Gerard B 1933- *WhoAmP 91*
**Patton,** Harry Dickson 1918- *AmMWSc 92*
**Patton,** Hugh Wilson 1921- *AmMWSc 92*
**Patton,** James Lloyd 1941- *AmMWSc 92*
**Patton,** James Richard, Jr. 1928- *WhoAmL 92*
**Patton,** James Winton 1929- *AmMWSc 92*
**Patton,** John Barratt 1915- *AmMWSc 92*
**Patton,** John F 1939- *AmMWSc 92*
**Patton,** John Stuart 1946- *AmMWSc 92*
**Patton,** John Thomas, Jr 1917- *AmMWSc 92*
**Patton,** John Tinsman 1931- *AmMWSc 92*
**Patton,** Jon Michael 1942- *AmMWSc 92*
**Patton,** Joseph Alexander 1936- *Who 92*
**Patton,** Joyce Bradford 1947- *WhoBlA 92*
**Patton,** Kenneth Roger 1957- *WhoRel 92*
**Patton,** Laura Jeanne 1959- *WhoWest 92*
**Patton,** Leo Wesley 1919- *AmMWSc 92*
**Patton,** Leroy 1944- *WhoBlA 92*
**Patton,** Matthew Henry 1936- *WhoAmP 91*
**Patton,** Michael Glenn 1944- *WhoAmP 91*
**Patton,** Nancy Jane 1936- *AmMWSc 92, WhoMW 92*
**Patton,** Peter C 1935- *AmMWSc 92*
**Patton,** Peter C 1949- *AmMWSc 92*
**Patton,** Phil 1952- *ConAu 133*
**Patton,** Ray Baker 1932- *WhoMW 92*
**Patton,** Rob *DrAPF 91*
**Patton,** Robert 1947- *WhoBlA 92*
**Patton,** Robert D 1933- *WhoAmP 91*
**Patton,** Robert Franklin 1919- *AmMWSc 92*
**Patton,** Robert Frederick 1927- *WhoFI 92*
**Patton,** Robert Lyle 1943- *AmMWSc 92*
**Patton,** Robert Thomas 1940- *WhoRel 92*
**Patton,** Ronald Kent 1938- *WhoFI 92*
**Patton,** Ronald L. 1941- *WhoRel 92*
**Patton,** Rosezelia L. 1934- *WhoBlA 92*
**Patton,** Samuel Catherwood 1923- *WhoAmL 92*
**Patton,** Sharon 1947- *AmMWSc 92*
**Patton,** Stuart 1920- *AmMWSc 92*
**Patton,** Tad LeMarre 1925- *AmMWSc 92*
**Patton,** Thomas Hudson 1934- *AmMWSc 92*
**Patton,** Thomas James 1948- *WhoMW 92*
**Patton,** Thomas Kirby 1954- *WhoFI 92*
**Patton,** Thomas William Saunderson 1914- *Who 92*
**Patton,** Wendell Keeler 1932- *AmMWSc 92*
**Patton,** Will 1954- *IntMPA 92*
**Patton,** William C. 1912- *WhoBlA 92*
**Patton,** William Hampton 1853-1918 *BiInAmS*
**Patton,** William Henry 1925- *AmMWSc 92*
**Patton,** William Robert 1960- *WhoFI 92*
**Patton,** William W. 1927- *WhoEnt 92*
**Patton,** William Wallace, Jr 1923- *AmMWSc 92, WhoWest 92*
**Pattullo,** Bruce 1938- *Who 92*
**Pattullo,** George 1879-1967 *TwCWW 91*
**Patty,** Clarence Wayne 1932- *AmMWSc 92*
**Patty,** Richard Roland 1933- *AmMWSc 92*
**Patty,** Seldon Elijah 1943- *WhoAmL 92*
**Pattyn,** Gerald J. 1958- *WhoWest 92*
**Paturis,** Emmanuel Michael 1933- *WhoAmL 92, WhoFI 92*
**Patwardhan,** Bhalchandra H 1947- *AmMWSc 92*
**Patz,** Arnall 1920- *AmMWSc 92*
**Patz,** Janice Maria 1963- *WhoAmL 92*
**Patz,** Lawrence Charles 1932- *WhoIns 92*
**Patzaichin,** Ivan 1949- *IntWW 91*
**Patzak,** Julius 1898-1974 *NewAmDM*
**Patzer,** Eric John 1949- *WhoWest 92*
**Patzer,** William Scott 1961- *WhoFI 92*
**Patzig,** Guenther 1926- *IntWW 91*
**Patzke,** Frank Thomas 1950- *WhoMW 92*
**Patzman,** Stephen Narr 1942- *WhoIns 92*
**Pau,** Louis F 1948- *AmMWSc 92, IntWW 91*
**Pau-Llosa,** Ricardo *DrAPF 91*
**Pau-Llosa,** Ricardo 1954- *LiExTwC*
**Pau-Llosa,** Ricardo Manuel 1954- *WhoHisp 92*
**Paucker,** Kurt 1924- *AmMWSc 92*
**Paudler,** William W 1932- *AmMWSc 92, WhoWest 92*
**Pauerstein,** Carl Joseph 1932- *AmMWSc 92*
**Pauk,** Gyorgy 1936- *IntWW 91, Who 92*
**Pauk,** Walter 1914- *WrDr 92*
**Pauken,** Robert John 1939- *AmMWSc 92*
**Pauken,** Thomas Weir 1944- *WhoAmP 91*
**Pauker,** John *DrAPF 91*
**Pauker,** John d1991 *NewYTBS 91*
**Pauker,** John 1920-1991 *ConAu 133*
**Pauker,** Stephen Gary 1942- *AmMWSc 92*
**Paukstelis,** Joseph V 1939- *AmMWSc 92*
**Paul** d65? *EncEarC [port]*
**Paul** 1754-1801 *BlkwCEP*
**Paul VI** 1897-1978 *DcEcMov*
**Paul of Samosata** *EncEarC*
**Paul VI,** Pope 1897-1978 *FacFETw*
**Paul Wilhelm,** Duke of Wurttemberg 1797-1860 *BiInAmS, DcAmImH*
**Paul,** Alan *WhoEnt 92*
**Paul,** Alan Roderick 1950- *Who 92*
**Paul,** Alice 1885-1977 *HanAmWH, PorAmW [port], RComAH*
**Paul,** Allen Edward 1945- *WhoAmP 91*
**Paul,** Alvin, III 1941- *WhoBlA 92*
**Paul,** Ara Garo 1929- *AmMWSc 92*
**Paul,** Arthur 1925- *WhoEnt 92*
**Paul,** Augustus John, III 1946- *AmMWSc 92*
**Paul,** B 1931- *AmMWSc 92*
**Paul,** Barbara *WrDr 92*
**Paul,** Barbara Jeanne 1931- *IntAu&W 91*
**Paul,** Beatrice 1943- *WhoBlA 92*
**Paul,** Benoy Bhushan 1936- *AmMWSc 92*
**Paul,** Bruno 1874-1968 *DcTwDes*
**Paul,** C. Kegan d1902 *DcLB 106 [port]*
**Paul,** Christian Thomas 1926- *WhoFI 92*
**Paul,** Daniel Opdyke 1927- *WhoAmP 91*
**Paul,** David Louis *AmMWSc 92*
**Paul,** David Manuel 1927- *Who 92*
**Paul,** David Patrick 1959- *WhoMW 92*
**Paul,** Derek 1929- *AmMWSc 92*
**Paul,** Dilip Kumar 1940- *AmMWSc 92*
**Paul,** Donald Ross 1939- *AmMWSc 92*
**Paul,** Donovan Jerald 1953- *WhoMW 92*
**Paul,** Douglas Allan 1949- *WhoFI 92*
**Paul,** Edward Gray 1931- *AmMWSc 92*
**Paul,** Edward Lane 1962- *WhoAmL 92*
**Paul,** Edward W 1944- *AmMWSc 92*
**Paul,** Eldor Alvin 1931- *AmMWSc 92*
**Paul,** Elliot 1891-1958 *BenetAL 91*
**Paul,** Eric S. *WhoFI 92*
**Paul,** Eve W. 1930- *WhoAmL 92*
**Paul,** Felix *WhoRel 92*
**Paul,** Frank Allen 1958- *WhoMW 92*
**Paul,** Frank W *AmMWSc 92*
**Paul,** Garrett Edward 1949- *WhoRel 92*
**Paul,** Gary Gene 1953- *WhoFI 92, WhoMW 92*
**Paul,** Geoffrey David 1929- *Who 92*
**Paul,** George, Jr 1937- *AmMWSc 92*
**Paul,** George William 1940- *Who 92*
**Paul,** Gerard John Christopher 1907- *Who 92*
**Paul,** Gilbert Ivan 1922- *AmMWSc 92*
**Paul,** Grace 1908- *WhoMW 92*
**Paul,** Harbhajan Singh 1937- *AmMWSc 92*
**Paul,** Herbert Morton *WhoAmL 92, WhoFI 92*
**Paul,** Herman Louis, Jr. 1912- *WhoFI 92*
**Paul,** Hugh Glencairn B. *Who 92*
**Paul,** Iain C 1938- *AmMWSc 92*
**Paul,** Igor 1936- *AmMWSc 92*
**Paul,** Jack Davis 1927- *WhoMW 92*
**Paul,** James Caverly Newlin 1926- *WhoAmL 92*
**Paul,** James Charles 1948- *WhoMW 92*
**Paul,** James Robert 1934- *WhoFI 92*
**Paul,** James William 1945- *WhoAmL 92*
**Paul,** Jeddeo 1929- *AmMWSc 92*
**Paul,** Jeremy 1939- *IntAu&W 91*
**Paul,** Jerome L 1937- *AmMWSc 92*
**Paul,** Jerome Thomas 1912- *AmMWSc 92*
**Paul,** Jerome Thomas 1933- *WhoFI 92*
**Paul,** Joel H. 1942- *WhoRel 92*
**Paul,** John *BenetAL 91*
**Paul,** John Douglas 1928- *Who 92*
**Paul,** John F. 1934- *WhoBlA 92*
**Paul,** John Joseph 1918- *WhoMW 92, WhoRel 92*
**Paul,** John Warburton 1916- *IntWW 91, Who 92*
**Paul,** Kamalendu Bikash 1937- *AmMWSc 92*
**Paul,** Kathleen Sharon 1959- *WhoMW 92*
**Paul,** Kegan, Trench, Trubner and Company *DcLB 106*
**Paul,** Larry Anthony 1946- *WhoEnt 92*
**Paul,** Lawrence Thomas 1933- *AmMWSc 92*
**Paul,** Leendert Cornelis 1946- *AmMWSc 92*
**Paul,** Les 1915- *NewAmDM, WhoEnt 92*
**Paul,** Louis 1901-1970 *BenetAL 91*
**Paul,** M.B. 1909- *IntMPA 92, WhoEnt 92*
**Paul,** Mary Melchior 1952- *WhoMW 92*
**Paul,** Maurice M. 1932- *WhoAmL 92*
**Paul,** Miles Richard 1940- *AmMWSc 92*
**Paul,** Milton Holiday 1926- *AmMWSc 92*
**Paul,** Noel Strange 1914- *Who 92*
**Paul,** Norman R 1927- *WhoAmP 91*
**Paul,** Oglesby 1916- *AmMWSc 92*
**Paul,** Pauline Constance 1912- *AmMWSc 92*
**Paul,** Peter 1932- *AmMWSc 92*
**Paul,** Prem Sagar 1947- *AmMWSc 92*
**Paul,** Reginald 1936- *AmMWSc 92*
**Paul,** Richard Jerome 1944- *AmMWSc 92*
**Paul,** Richard William 1937- *WhoWest 92*
**Paul,** Richard Wright 1953- *WhoAmL 92*
**Paul,** Robert Arthur 1937- *WhoFI 92*
**Paul,** Robert Cameron 1935- *IntWW 91, Who 92*
**Paul,** Robert Carey 1950- *WhoAmL 92*
**Paul,** Robert E, Jr 1927- *AmMWSc 92*
**Paul,** Robert Hugh 1927- *AmMWSc 92*
**Paul,** Robert Jaquish 1922- *WhoWest 92*
**Paul,** Robert Scott 1958- *WhoRel 92*
**Paul,** Robert William 1869-1943 *FacFETw*
**Paul,** Robert William, Jr 1946- *AmMWSc 92*
**Paul,** Roderick Sayers 1935- *Who 92*
**Paul,** Roland Arthur 1937- *WhoAmL 92, WhoFI 92*
**Paul,** Rolf 1930- *AmMWSc 92*
**Paul,** Ron 1935- *WhoAmP 91*
**Paul,** Ronald Ian S. *Who 92*
**Paul,** Ronald Stanley 1923- *AmMWSc 92*
**Paul,** Samuel Joseph, III 1952- *WhoEnt 92*
**Paul,** Sandra Koodin 1938- *WhoFI 92*
**Paul,** Shale 1931- *WhoWest 92*
**Paul,** Stanley *DcLB 112*
**Paul,** Steven 1958- *IntMPA 92*
**Paul,** Steven M *AmMWSc 92*
**Paul,** Swraj 1931- *Who 92*
**Paul,** Thomas Francis 1924- *WrDr 92*
**Paul,** Thomas William 1946- *WhoMW 92*
**Paul,** Vera Maxine 1940- *WhoBlA 92*
**Paul,** Vivian 1925- *WhoAmL 92*
**Paul,** William 1918- *AmMWSc 92*
**Paul,** William 1926- *AmMWSc 92*
**Paul,** William Erwin 1936- *AmMWSc 92*
**Paul,** William George 1930- *WhoAmL 92, WhoFI 92*
**Paul,** Wolfgang 1913- *IntWW 91, Who 92, WhoNob 90*
**Paul,** Wolfgang 1918- *AmMWSc 92*
**Paula** 374-404 *EncEarC*
**Paulay,** Gustav 1957- *AmMWSc 92*
**Paulding,** Hiram 1797-1878 *BenetAL 91*
**Paulding,** James Kirke 1778-1860 *BenetAL 91*
**Paule,** Lawrence David 1960- *WhoWest 92*
**Paule,** Merle Gale 1952- *AmMWSc 92*
**Paule,** Robert Charles 1932- *AmMWSc 92*
**Paule,** Wendelin Joseph 1927- *AmMWSc 92*
**Paulet** *Who 92*
**Pauley,** Gilbert Buckhannan 1939- *AmMWSc 92*
**Pauley,** James Donald 1941- *AmMWSc 92*
**Pauley,** James L 1925- *AmMWSc 92*
**Pauley,** Jane *LesBEnT 92*
**Pauley,** Jane 1950- *IntMPA 92*
**Pauley,** Jim G 1932- *WhoAmP 91*
**Pauley,** Rhoda Anne 1939- *WhoFI 92*
**Pauley,** Richard Heim 1932- *WhoFI 92*
**Pauley,** Robert Reinhold 1923- *WhoEnt 92*
**Pauley,** Thomas Kyle 1940- *AmMWSc 92*
**Pauley,** Timothy Oather 1932- *WhoMW 92*
**Pauli,** Chris Henry 1957- *WhoFI 92, WhoMW 92*
**Pauli,** Wolfgang 1900-1958 *FacFETw*
**Pauli,** Wolfgang Ernst 1900-1958 *WhoNob 90*
**Paulie** 1947- *IntAu&W 91*
**Paulie,** M Catherine Therese *AmMWSc 92*
**Paulien,** Jon 1949- *WhoRel 92*
**Paulik,** Frank Edward 1935- *AmMWSc 92*
**Paulikas,** George A 1936- *AmMWSc 92*
**Paulin,** Andrew 1955- *WhoWest 92*
**Paulin,** Donald J 1933- *WhoAmP 91*
**Paulin,** Gaston 1934- *AmMWSc 92*
**Paulin,** Jerome John 1936- *AmMWSc 92*
**Paulin,** Michael Vincent 1941- *WhoFI 92*
**Paulin,** Pierre 1927- *DcTwDes*
**Paulin,** Roger Cole 1937- *Who 92*
**Paulin,** Tom 1949- *ConPo 91, IntAu&W 91, WrDr 92*
**Paulinelli,** Allysson 1936- *IntWW 91*
**Pauling,** Edward Crellin 1937- *AmMWSc 92*
**Pauling,** Linus 1901- *AmPeW, FacFETw [port], Who 92, WrDr 92*
**Pauling,** Linus Carl 1901- *AmMWSc 92, IntWW 91, WhoWest 92*
**Pauling,** Linus Carl 1901-1981 *WhoNob 90*
**Paulino,** Cleotilde Camacho 1927- *WhoAmP 91*
**Paulinus of Nola** 355-431 *EncEarC*
**Paulish,** Daniel John 1949- *AmMWSc 92*
**Paulissen,** Leo John 1915- *AmMWSc 92*
**Paulk,** Bernice Herring 1926- *WhoBlA 92*
**Paulk,** Earl Pearly 1927- *WhoRel 92*
**Paulk,** Earl Pearly, Jr. 1927- *RelLAm 91*
**Paulk,** James Lane 1949- *WhoAmP 91*
**Paulk,** John Irvine 1928- *AmMWSc 92*
**Paulk,** Shirley Riva 1945- *WhoFI 92*
**Paulk,** William R 1931- *WhoAmP 91*
**Paull,** Allan E 1918- *AmMWSc 92*
**Paull,** Barberi Platt 1949- *WhoEnt 92*
**Paull,** Barry Richard 1947- *AmMWSc 92*
**Paull,** Kenneth Dywain 1942- *AmMWSc 92*
**Paull,** Mary 1940- *WhoAmP 91*
**Paull,** Rachel Krebs 1933- *AmMWSc 92*
**Paull,** Richard Allen 1930- *AmMWSc 92*
**Paull,** Willis K, Jr 1944- *AmMWSc 92*
**Paullin,** Joann Marie 1946- *WhoWest 92*
**Paulling,** J R, Jr 1930- *AmMWSc 92*
**Paulmier,** Frederick Clark 1873-1906 *BiInAmS*
**Paulnock,** Donna Marie *AmMWSc 92*
**Paulos,** John A. 1945- *WrDr 92*
**Paulos,** John Allen 1945- *AmMWSc 92*

**Pauls,** Raymond Voldemarovich *IntWW 91*
**Pauls,** Raymond Voldemarovich 1936- *SovUnBD*
**Pauls,** Rolf Friedemann 1915- *IntWW 91*
**Paulsell,** William Oliver 1935- *WhoRel 92*
**Paulsen,** Beverly Jo 1949- *WhoMW 92*
**Paulsen,** Borge Regnar 1915- *WhoFI 92*
**Paulsen,** Charles Alvin 1924- *AmMWSc 92*
**Paulsen,** Douglas F 1952- *AmMWSc 92*
**Paulsen,** Duane E 1937- *AmMWSc 92*
**Paulsen,** Elsa Proehl 1923- *AmMWSc 92*
**Paulsen,** Gaige Brue 1905- *WhoMW 92*
**Paulsen,** Gary 1939- *TwCCWW 91, WrDr 92*
**Paulsen,** Gary James *DrAPF 91*
**Paulsen,** Gary Melvin 1939- *AmMWSc 92*
**Paulsen,** Jan 1935- *WhoRel 92*
**Paulsen,** Joseph Charles, V 1925- *WhoFI 92*
**Paulsen,** Kathryn *DrAPF 91*
**Paulsen,** Kevin Michael 1960- *WhoFI 92*
**Paulsen,** Linda Grayson 1951- *WhoEnt 92*
**Paulsen,** Marvin Russell 1946- *AmMWSc 92*
**Paulsen,** Pat 1927- *WhoEnt 92*
**Paulsen,** Paul 1935- *AmMWSc 92*
**Paulsen,** Wayne Merrill 1941- *WhoRel 92*
**Paulshock,** Marvin 1923- *AmMWSc 92*
**Paulson,** A.B. *DrAPF 91*
**Paulson,** Allen Eugene 1922- *WhoFI 92*
**Paulson,** Boyd Colton, Jr 1946- *AmMWSc 92*
**Paulson,** Carlton 1934- *AmMWSc 92*
**Paulson,** Charles Maxwell, Jr 1936- *AmMWSc 92*
**Paulson,** Christopher Robert 1947- *WhoAmP 91*
**Paulson,** Clayton Arvid 1938- *AmMWSc 92*
**Paulson,** David E 1931- *WhoAmP 91*
**Paulson,** David F 1938- *AmMWSc 92*
**Paulson,** David J *AmMWSc 92*
**Paulson,** Dennis Roy 1937- *AmMWSc 92*
**Paulson,** Donald Lowell 1912- *AmMWSc 92*
**Paulson,** Donald Robert 1943- *AmMWSc 92*
**Paulson,** Edward 1915- *AmMWSc 92*
**Paulson,** Gaylord D 1937- *AmMWSc 92*
**Paulson,** Glenn 1941- *AmMWSc 92*
**Paulson,** Hendrik Pieter 1948- *WhoRel 92*
**Paulson,** James Carsten 1948- *AmMWSc 92*
**Paulson,** James M 1923- *AmMWSc 92*
**Paulson,** John Alfred 1955- *WhoFI 92*
**Paulson,** John Frederick 1929- *AmMWSc 92*
**Paulson,** Joseph Albert 1940- *WhoWest 92*
**Paulson,** Larry Jerome 1945- *AmMWSc 92*
**Paulson,** Lawrence Clifford 1951- *WhoAmL 92*
**Paulson,** Louis George 1947- *WhoAmL 92*
**Paulson,** Mark Clements 1913- *AmMWSc 92*
**Paulson,** Michael Dana 1943- *WhoMW 92*
**Paulson,** Oscar Lawrence 1930- *AmMWSc 92*
**Paulson,** Ronald 1930- *IntAu&W 91, WrDr 92*
**Paulson,** Scott 1953- *WhoRel 92*
**Paulson,** Terry Lee 1945- *WhoWest 92*
**Paulson,** Warren Lee 1932- *WhoRel 92*
**Paulson,** Wayne Lee 1934- *AmMWSc 92*
**Paulson,** William Arnold, Jr. 1927- *WhoMW 92*
**Paulson,** William H 1926- *AmMWSc 92*
**Paulson,** William Lee 1913- *WhoAmP 91*
**Paulson,** William Ross 1955- *WhoMW 92*
**Paulson-Ehrhardt,** Patricia Helen 1956- *WhoWest 92*
**Paulston,** Rolland G. 1929- *WrDr 92*
**Paulu,** Burton 1910- *IntAu&W 91, WrDr 92*
**Paulu,** Frances Brown 1920- *WhoMW 92*
**Paulus,** Albert 1927- *AmMWSc 92*
**Paulus,** Friedrich 1890-1957 *EncTR 91*
**Paulus,** Harold John 1914- *AmMWSc 92*
**Paulus,** Judith K. 1947- *WhoFI 92, WhoMW 92*
**Paulus,** Kenneth Scott, Sr. 1954- *WhoMW 92*
**Paulus,** Norma J 1933- *WhoAmP 91*
**Paulus,** Sharon Marie 1949- *WhoAmL 92*
**Paulus,** Stephen 1949- *ConCom 92, NewAmDM*
**Paulus,** Stephen Harrison 1949- *WhoEnt 92*
**Paulusz,** Jan Gilbert 1929- *Who 92*
**Pauly,** D. Tod 1954- *WhoFI 92*
**Pauly,** David F 1952- *WhoIns 92*
**Pauly,** Evelyn May Rockwell 1924- *WhoMW 92*
**Pauly,** James Ross 1927- *WhoWest 92*
**Pauly,** John Edward 1927- *AmMWSc 92*
**Pauly,** Nancy Marie 1936- *WhoRel 92*
**Pauly,** Sidney J 1933- *WhoAmP 91*
**Paulyuk,** Yanis Antonovich 1906- *SovUnBD*
**Paumgartner,** Bernhard 1887-1971 *NewAmDM*
**Paun,** Radu 1915- *IntWW 91*
**Pauncefort,** Bernard Edward 1926- *Who 92*
**Pauncefort-Duncombe,** Philip *Who 92*
**Paunio,** Jouko Juhani Kyosti 1928- *IntWW 91*
**Paup,** Martin Arnold 1930- *WhoWest 92*
**Paupini,** Giuseppe 1907- *IntWW 91, WhoRel 92*
**Paur,** Sandra Orley 1946- *AmMWSc 92*
**Pausch,** Jerry Bliss 1939- *AmMWSc 92*
**Paust,** Marian 1908- *WrDr 92*
**Paust,** Marian Pier 1908- *IntAu&W 91*
**Paustian,** Frederick Franz 1926- *AmMWSc 92*
**Paustian,** John Earle 1928- *AmMWSc 92*
**Paustovsky,** Konstantin Georg'evich 1892-1968 *SovUnBD*
**Pautler,** Eugene L 1931- *AmMWSc 92*
**Pautsch,** Charles William 1952- *WhoAmL 92*
**Pauw,** Peter George *AmMWSc 92*
**Pauwels,** Louis 1920- *IntWW 91*
**Pauzus,** Gerald Xavier 1943- *WhoAmP 91*
**Paval,** John 1958- *WhoAmL 92*
**Pavalon,** Eugene Irving 1933- *WhoAmL 92, WhoMW 92*
**Pavan,** Crodowaldo 1919- *AmMWSc 92*
**Pavan,** Marisa 1932- *IntMPA 92*
**Pavan,** Pietro 1903- *IntWW 91, WhoRel 92*
**Pavan,** Robert David John 1929- *WhoFI 92*
**Pavarini,** Peter Alfred 1952- *WhoAmL 92*
**Pavarotti,** Luciano 1935- *FacFETw [port], IntWW 91, NewAmDM, Who 92, WhoEnt 92*
**Pavek,** Charles Christopher 1955- *WhoFI 92*
**Pavek,** Joseph John 1927- *AmMWSc 92*
**Pavel Petrovich** 1754-1801 *BlkwCEP*
**Pavelic,** Ante 1889-1959 *BiDExR*
**Pavelic,** Ante 1898-1959 *EncTR 91 [port]*
**Pavelic,** Vjekoslav 1929- *AmMWSc 92*
**Pavelka,** Elaine Blanche *WhoMW 92*
**Pavelle,** Arthur 1934- *WhoIns 92*
**Pavese,** Cesare 1908-1950 *FacFETw, LiExTwC*
**Pavey,** Don 1922- *IntAu&W 91, WrDr 92*
**Pavey,** Martin Christopher 1940- *Who 92*
**Pavey,** Norman Curtis 1943- *WhoRel 92*
**Pavgi,** Sushama 1955- *AmMWSc 92*
**Pavia,** Donald Lee 1941- *AmMWSc 92*
**Pavia,** George M. 1928- *WhoAmL 92*
**Pavia,** Louis, Jr. 1950- *WhoFI 92*
**Pavich,** Emil Sam 1931- *WhoAmP 91*
**Pavilanis,** Vytautas 1920- *AmMWSc 92*
**Pavilon,** Michael Douglas 1945- *WhoFI 92*
**Pavini,** Paschal Joseph 1929- *WhoMW 92*
**Pavitt,** Edward 1918- *IntWW 91*
**Pavitt,** William Hesser, Jr. 1916- *WhoAmL 92*
**Pavkovic,** Stephen F 1932- *AmMWSc 92*
**Pavlasek,** Tomas J F 1923- *AmMWSc 92*
**Pavlath,** Attila Endre 1930- *AmMWSc 92, WhoWest 92*
**Pavlicek,** Frantisek 1923- *IntWW 91*
**Pavlich,** Walter *DrAPF 91*
**Pavlick,** Harvey Naylor 1942- *WhoFI 92, WhoWest 92*
**Pavlick,** Wendy Caroline 1967- *WhoMW 92*
**Pavlides,** Louis 1921- *AmMWSc 92*
**Pavlidis,** Theo 1934- *AmMWSc 92*
**Pavlik,** Edward John 1946- *AmMWSc 92*
**Pavlik,** James William 1937- *AmMWSc 92*
**Pavlik,** John M. 1939- *IntMPA 92*
**Pavlik,** John Michael 1939- *WhoEnt 92*
**Pavlin,** Edward George 1940- *AmMWSc 92*
**Pavlin,** Mark Stanley 1951- *AmMWSc 92*
**Pavlisko,** Joseph Anthony 1953- *AmMWSc 92*
**Pavlon,** Jerry 1958- *WhoEnt 92*
**Pavlonnis,** Rich *WhoAmP 91*
**Pavlopoulos,** Theodore G 1925- *AmMWSc 92*
**Pavlos,** John 1927- *AmMWSc 92*
**Pavlov,** Georgiy Sergeevich 1910- *SovUnBD*
**Pavlov,** Ivan Petrovich 1849-1936 *FacFETw [port], SovUnBD, WhoNob 90*
**Pavlov,** Sergey Pavlovich 1929- *IntWW 91*
**Pavlov,** Valentin *IntWW 91*
**Pavlov,** Vladimir Yakovlevich 1923- *IntWW 91*
**Pavlova,** Anna Pavlovna 1881-1931 *FacFETw [port]*
**Pavlovic,** Arthur Stephen 1925- *AmMWSc 92*
**Pavlovic,** Dusan M 1921- *AmMWSc 92*
**Pavlovich,** Michael Anthony 1964- *WhoWest 92*
**Pavlovich,** Raymond Doran 1934- *AmMWSc 92*
**Pavlovich,** Robert John 1929- *WhoAmP 91*
**Pavlovskis,** Olgerts Raimonds 1934- *AmMWSc 92*
**Pavlow,** Muriel 1921- *IntMPA 92*
**Pavlowitch,** Stevan K. 1933- *WrDr 92*
**Pavlychenko,** Dmytro Vasylovych 1929- *IntWW 91*
**Pavlychko,** Dmytro Vasyl'ovych 1929- *SovUnBD*
**Pavolini,** Alessandro 1903-1945 *BiDExR*
**Pavony,** William H. 1940- *WhoFI 92*
**Pavy,** Octave 1844-1884 *BiInAmS*
**Pawar,** Sharadchandra Govindrao 1940- *IntWW 91*
**Pawel,** Ernst 1920- *WrDr 92*
**Pawel,** Janet Elizabeth 1962- *AmMWSc 92*
**Pawel,** Richard E 1932- *AmMWSc 92*
**Pawelec,** William John 1917- *WhoFI 92*
**Pawelek,** John Mason 1942- *AmMWSc 92*
**Pawelkiewicz,** Jerzy 1922- *IntWW 91*
**Pawl,** Ronald Phillip 1935- *WhoMW 92*
**Pawlak,** Florian Boleslaus 1914- *WhoMW 92*
**Pawlak,** Mark *DrAPF 91*
**Pawlak,** Mark Joseph 1948- *IntAu&W 91*
**Pawle,** Gerald Strachan 1913-1991 *ConAu 135*
**Pawle,** John 1915- *TwCPaSc*
**Pawley,** Martin 1938- *WrDr 92*
**Pawley,** Robert John 1939- *Who 92*
**Pawley,** Thomas D., III 1917- *WhoBlA 92*
**Pawlicki,** Anthony Joseph 1944- *AmMWSc 92*
**Pawlicki,** Clarence Francis 1930- *WhoAmL 92*
**Pawliczko,** George Ihor 1950- *WhoFI 92*
**Pawlik,** Bernadette Marie 1953- *WhoMW 92*
**Pawlik,** James David 1958- *WhoAmL 92, WhoMW 92*
**Pawlikowski,** John Thaddeus 1940- *IntAu&W 91, WhoRel 92, WrDr 92*
**Pawlisch,** Paul E 1931- *AmMWSc 92*
**Pawlowicz,** Edmund F 1941- *AmMWSc 92*
**Pawlowicz,** Michael Wilson 1938- *WhoRel 92*
**Pawlowski,** Anthony T 1922- *AmMWSc 92*
**Pawlowski,** Eugene Ernest 1943- *WhoMW 92*
**Pawlowski,** Norman E 1938- *AmMWSc 92*
**Pawlowski,** Philip John 1943- *AmMWSc 92*
**Pawluk,** Steve 1930- *AmMWSc 92*
**Pawlyk,** William John 1941- *WhoWest 92*
**Pawsey,** James Francis 1933- *Who 92*
**Pawson,** Beverly Ann 1934- *AmMWSc 92*
**Pawson,** David Leo 1938- *AmMWSc 92*
**Pawula,** Kenneth John 1935- *WhoWest 92*
**Pawula,** Robert Francis 1936- *AmMWSc 92*
**Pax,** Ralph A 1934- *AmMWSc 92*
**Paxman,** Jeremy Dickson 1950- *IntWW 91, Who 92*
**Paxon,** Bill 1954- *AlmAP 92 [port], WhoAmP 91*
**Paxson,** Diana L. 1943- *RelLAm 91*
**Paxson,** James Malone 1912- *WhoAmP 91*
**Paxson,** John Ralph 1942- *AmMWSc 92*
**Paxson,** Thomas Dunning, Jr. 1943- *WhoMW 92*
**Paxton,** Albert Elwyn 1902- *WhoMW 92*
**Paxton,** Bill *IntMPA 92*
**Paxton,** Gertrude Garnes 1931- *WhoBlA 92*
**Paxton,** Glenn Gilbert 1931- *WhoEnt 92*
**Paxton,** H W 1927- *AmMWSc 92*
**Paxton,** Hugh Campbell 1909- *AmMWSc 92*
**Paxton,** Jack Dunmire 1936- *AmMWSc 92*
**Paxton,** Jane P *WhoAmP 91*
**Paxton,** Jay Lee 1947- *WhoAmL 92*
**Paxton,** John 1923- *Who 92, WrDr 92*
**Paxton,** John Wesley 1937- *WhoFI 92*
**Paxton,** K Bradley 1938- *AmMWSc 92*
**Paxton,** Lois *WrDr 92*
**Paxton,** Peter James 1923- *Who 92*
**Paxton,** Philip *BenetAL 91*
**Paxton,** Phyllis Ann 1942- *WhoBlA 92*
**Paxton,** R R 1920- *AmMWSc 92*
**Paxton,** Ralph 1950- *AmMWSc 92*
**Paxton,** Robert James 1928- *WhoAmP 91*
**Paxton,** Tom 1937- *WhoEnt 92*
**Pay,** Howard Richard 1951- *WhoWest 92*
**Pay,** William *IntMPA 92*
**Payack,** Paul J.J. *DrAPF 91*
**Payack,** Peter *DrAPF 91*
**Payan,** Art *WhoHisp 92*
**Payan,** Gustavo L. 1954- *WhoHisp 92*
**Payan,** Jean-Jacques 1935- *IntWW 91*
**Payant,** Vital Robert 1932- *WhoWest 92*
**Payden,** Henry J., Sr. 1923- *WhoBlA 92*
**Paye,** Jean-Claude 1934- *IntWW 91, Who 92*
**Payea,** Norman Philip, II 1949- *WhoWest 92*
**Payer,** Andrew Francis 1943- *AmMWSc 92*
**Payer,** Joe Howard 1943- *AmMWSc 92*
**Payerli,** Peter Leslie 1963- *WhoFI 92*
**Payet,** Marcel Daniel 1947- *AmMWSc 92*
**Paykel,** Eugene Stern 1934- *Who 92*
**Paylore,** Patricia Paquita 1909- *AmMWSc 92*
**Payment,** Kenneth Arnold 1941- *WhoAmL 92*
**Payn,** James 1830-1898 *ScFEYrs*
**Payne,** A R Middletoun *ScFEYrs*
**Payne,** Alan *WrDr 92*
**Payne,** Alan Jeffrey 1933- *Who 92*
**Payne,** Allen Douglas 1959- *WhoEnt 92*
**Payne,** Allison Griffin 1964- *WhoBlA 92*
**Payne,** Ancil Horace 1921- *WhoEnt 92*
**Payne,** Ancil Newton, Jr. 1935- *WhoAmL 92*
**Payne,** Anita H 1926- *AmMWSc 92*
**Payne,** Anita Hart 1926- *WhoMW 92*
**Payne,** Anthony 1927- *AmMWSc 92*
**Payne,** Anthony 1936- *ConCom 92*
**Payne,** Anthony Edward 1936- *IntWW 91*
**Payne,** Antony 1947- *WhoEnt 92*
**Payne,** Arthur Eddie, III 1955- *WhoEnt 92*
**Payne,** Arthur Lee 1946- *WhoAmP 91*
**Payne,** Arthur Stanley 1930- *Who 92*
**Payne,** Barbara Casteel 1940- *WhoAmL 92*
**Payne,** Basil *DrAPF 91*
**Payne,** Bertram R *AmMWSc 92*
**Payne,** Beverly *WhoBlA 92*
**Payne,** Brown H. 1915- *WhoBlA 92*
**Payne,** Bruce 1911- *WrDr 92*
**Payne,** Christopher Charles 1946- *Who 92*
**Payne,** Christopher Frederick 1930- *Who 92*
**Payne,** Claire Margaret 1943- *WhoWest 92*
**Payne,** Colleen Heafy 1958- *WhoFI 92*
**Payne,** Daniel Alexander 1811-1893 *RelLAm 91*
**Payne,** David Emer 1944- *WhoMW 92*
**Payne,** David Glenn 1950- *AmMWSc 92*
**Payne,** David Seth 1934- *WhoRel 92*
**Payne,** Deborah Anne 1952- *WhoFI 92*
**Payne,** DeWitt Allen 1944- *AmMWSc 92*
**Payne,** Don Andrew 1955- *WhoEnt 92*
**Payne,** Donald 1934- *WhoAmP 91*
**Payne,** Donald Glen 1956- *WhoRel 92*
**Payne,** Donald Gordon 1924- *IntAu&W 91, WrDr 92*
**Payne,** Donald M. 1934- *AlmAP 92 [port], ConBlB 2 [port], WhoBlA 92*
**Payne,** Donna L *AmMWSc 92*
**Payne,** Douglas G 1928- *WhoAmP 91*
**Payne,** Edward Carlton 1928- *WhoRel 92*
**Payne,** Ernest Alexander 1902-1980 *DcEcMov*
**Payne,** Ethel d1991 *NewYTBS 91*
**Payne,** Ethel 1911-1991 *NotBlAW 92 [port]*
**Payne,** Ethel Lois 1911-1991 *WhoBlA 92N*
**Payne,** Francis Xavier 1937- *WhoFI 92*
**Payne,** Fred R 1931- *AmMWSc 92*
**Payne,** Freda 1944- *WhoBlA 92*
**Payne,** Gareld Gene 1931- *WhoEnt 92*
**Payne,** Gary D. 1948- *WhoBlA 92*
**Payne,** George Lefevre 1911- *Who 92*
**Payne,** Georgia Ann 1945- *WhoMW 92*
**Payne,** Gerald Lew 1938- *AmMWSc 92*
**Payne,** Harold Timothy 1946- *WhoEnt 92*
**Payne,** Harrison H 1925- *AmMWSc 92*
**Payne,** Harry E, Jr *WhoAmP 91*
**Payne,** Henry Salusbury Legh D. *Who 92*
**Payne,** Holland I 1918- *AmMWSc 92*
**Payne,** Ian 1926- *Who 92*
**Payne,** Irene R 1921- *AmMWSc 92*
**Payne,** J. Gregory 1949- *WrDr 92*
**Payne,** James 1941- *AmMWSc 92*
**Payne,** James Earl 1963- *WhoMW 92*
**Payne,** James Edward 1944- *AmMWSc 92*
**Payne,** James Floyd 1943- *WhoBlA 92*
**Payne,** James Richmond 1921- *Who 92*
**Payne,** Jane Marian *Who 92*
**Payne,** Jeffrey Ford 1958- *WhoRel 92*
**Payne,** Jennifer Lynn 1965- *WhoMW 92*
**Payne,** Jerry Allen 1937- *AmMWSc 92*
**Payne,** Jerry Oscar 1953- *WhoBlA 92*
**Payne,** Jesse James 1947- *WhoBlA 92*
**Payne,** John Burnett *DrAPF 91*
**Payne,** John Howard 1791 1852 *BenetAL 91*
**Payne,** June Evelyn 1948- *WhoBlA 92*
**Payne,** Keith 1933- *Who 92*
**Payne,** Kenneth Victor 1966- *WhoBlA 92*
**Payne,** Kenyon Thomas 1918- *AmMWSc 92*
**Payne,** Kevin Clark 1957- *WhoRel 92*
**Payne,** Ladell 1933- *ConAu 134*
**Payne,** Laurence 1919- *IntAu&W 91, WrDr 92*
**Payne,** Lawrence Edward 1923- *AmMWSc 92*
**Payne,** Leonard Sidney 1925- *Who 92*
**Payne,** Leslie 1941- *WhoBlA 92*
**Payne,** Lewis F., Jr. 1945- *AlmAP 92 [port], WhoAmP 91*
**Payne,** Linda Lawson 1946- *AmMWSc 92*
**Payne,** Lisa R. 1962- *WhoBlA 92*
**Payne,** Lucy Ann Salsbury 1952- *WhoAmL 92*

**Payne,** Maggi D. 1945- *WhoEnt 92*
**Payne,** Margaret Anne 1947- *WhoAmL 92*
**Payne,** Margaret Berneta 1935- *WhoRel 92*
**Payne,** Margaret Ralston 1946- *WhoBlA 92, WhoMW 92*
**Payne,** Marita 1960- *BlkOlyM*
**Payne,** Marvin Gay 1936- *AmMWSc 92*
**Payne,** Melvin Monroe 1911-1990 *FacFETw*
**Payne,** Michael Wilkinson 1963- *WhoEnt 92*
**Payne,** Mitchell Howard 1950- *WhoBlA 92*
**Payne,** Myron William 1945- *AmMWSc 92*
**Payne,** N. Joyce 1941- *WhoBlA 92*
**Payne,** Nicholas Charles 1942- *AmMWSc 92*
**Payne,** Norman *IntMPA 92*
**Payne,** Norman 1921- *Who 92*
**Payne,** Norman John 1921- *IntWW 91*
**Payne,** Osborne Allen 1925- *WhoBlA 92*
**Payne,** Patty Anne 1961- *WhoHisp 92*
**Payne,** Paula Marie 1952- *WhoRel 92*
**Payne,** Peggy *DrAPF 91*
**Payne,** Peggy 1949- *IntAu&W 91*
**Payne,** Peter Charles John 1928- *Who 92*
**Payne,** Philip Barton 1948- *WhoRel 92*
**Payne,** Philip Warren 1950- *AmMWSc 92*
**Payne,** Richard Allen 1934- *WhoMW 92*
**Payne,** Richard Earl 1936- *AmMWSc 92*
**Payne,** Richard Steven 1943- *AmMWSc 92*
**Payne,** Robert B 1938- *AmMWSc 92*
**Payne,** Robert Somers *WhoIns 92*
**Payne,** Roderick Austin 1955- *WhoRel 92*
**Payne,** Rose Marise 1909- *AmMWSc 92*
**Payne,** Samuel, Sr. 1919- *WhoBlA 92*
**Payne,** Samuel B. d1991 *NewYTBS 91 [port]*
**Payne,** Shelby Dale 1959- *WhoEnt 92*
**Payne,** Sidney Stewart 1932- *WhoRel 92*
**Payne,** Stanley E 1939- *AmMWSc 92*
**Payne,** Stewart *Who 92*
**Payne,** Theodore M. 1949- *WhoFI 92, WhoMW 92*
**Payne,** Thomas Anthony 1943- *WhoAmP 91*
**Payne,** Thomas Gibson 1915- *AmMWSc 92*
**Payne,** Thomas Lee 1941- *AmMWSc 92*
**Payne,** Torrence P B *AmMWSc 92*
**Payne,** Trevor Ian *Who 92*
**Payne,** Vernon 1945- *WhoBlA 92*
**Payne,** Warren Gilbert 1954- *WhoWest 92*
**Payne,** Wilford Alexander 1945- *WhoBlA 92*
**Payne,** Willard William 1934- *AmMWSc 92*
**Payne,** William Haydon 1939- *WhoEnt 92*
**Payne,** William Jackson 1925- *AmMWSc 92*
**Payne,** William Lamar 1966- *WhoRel 92*
**Payne,** William Sanford 1946- *WhoFI 92*
**Payne,** William Thomas 1953- *WhoAmL 92*
**Payne,** William Walker 1913- *AmMWSc 92*
**Payne-Butler,** George William 1919- *Who 92*
**Payne-Gallwey,** Philip 1935- *Who 92*
**Paynter,** Camen Russell 1916- *AmMWSc 92*
**Paynter,** David H. 1921- *ConAu 135*
**Paynter,** Gerald C 1938- *AmMWSc 92*
**Paynter,** Henry M 1923- *AmMWSc 92*
**Paynter,** Howard L 1931- *AmMWSc 92*
**Paynter,** John, Jr 1936- *AmMWSc 92*
**Paynter,** John Frederick 1931- *Who 92*
**Paynter,** John Philip 1928- *WhoEnt 92*
**Paynter,** Malcolm James Benjamin 1937- *AmMWSc 92*
**Paynter,** Noel Stephen 1898- *Who 92*
**Paynter,** Raymond Andrew, Jr 1925- *AmMWSc 92*
**Paynter,** Robert 1928- *IntMPA 92*
**Pays,** Amanda 1959- *IntMPA 92*
**Payson,** Henry Edwards 1925- *AmMWSc 92*
**Payson,** Henry S 1921- *WhoIns 92*
**Payson,** Martin D. *IntMPA 92*
**Payson,** Martin David 1936- *WhoAmL 92*
**Payson,** Mary Wold 1915- *WhoAmP 91*
**Paysse,** Rachel Weaver 1946- *WhoWest 92*
**Payte,** J. Michael 1946- *WhoFI 92*
**Payton,** Albert Levern 1944- *AmMWSc 92, WhoBlA 92*
**Payton,** Arthur David 1935- *AmMWSc 92*
**Payton,** Benjamin Franklin 1932- *WhoBlA 92*
**Payton,** Brian Wallace *AmMWSc 92*
**Payton,** Carolyn Robertson 1925- *NotBlAW 92, WhoBlA 92, WomPsyc*
**Payton,** Cecil Warren 1942- *AmMWSc 92*
**Payton,** Daniel N, III 1940- *AmMWSc 92*
**Payton,** Gary Dwayne 1968- *WhoBlA 92*
**Payton,** Jeff 1946- *WhoBlA 92*
**Payton,** Joseph 1944- *WhoMW 92*
**Payton,** Michael A 1940- *WhoAmP 91*
**Payton,** Nolan H. 1919- *WhoBlA 92*
**Payton,** Otto D 1929- *AmMWSc 92*
**Payton,** Patrick Herbert 1941- *AmMWSc 92*
**Payton,** Ralph Reed 1926- *WhoEnt 92*
**Payton,** Renato Marcel 1955- *WhoEnt 92*
**Payton,** Robert Donald 1949- *WhoEnt 92*
**Payton,** Robert Gilbert 1929- *AmMWSc 92*
**Payton,** Roger Edward 1956- *WhoFI 92, WhoMW 92*
**Payton,** Sallyanne 1943- *WhoAmL 92*
**Payton,** Stanley Walden 1921- *Who 92*
**Payton,** Thomas William 1946- *WhoFI 92*
**Payton,** Victor Emmanuel 1948- *WhoBlA 92*
**Payton,** Walter 1954- *WhoMW 92*
**Payton,** Walter Jerry 1954- *FacFETw, WhoBlA 92*
**Payton,** Willis Conwell 1923- *WhoBlA 92*
**Paz,** Denis George 1945- *WhoHisp 92*
**Paz,** Francis Xavier 1931- *WhoHisp 92*
**Paz,** Juan Carlos 1901-1972 *NewAmDM*
**Paz,** Mario Meir 1924- *AmMWSc 92*
**Paz,** Mercedes Aurora 1928- *AmMWSc 92*
**Paz,** Octavio 1914- *BenetAL 91, ConLC 65 [port], ConSpAP, FacFETw [port], IntAu&W 91, IntWW 91, LiExTwC, News 91 [port], Who 92, WhoNob 90*
**Paz,** Rudy J. 1938- *WhoHisp 92*
**Paz Estenssoro,** Victor 1907- *IntWW 91*
**Paz Soldan,** Miguel Mateo 1945- *WhoWest 92*
**Paz Zamora,** Jaime 1939- *IntWW 91*
**Pazdan,** Mary Margaret 1942- *WhoRel 92*
**Pazdernik,** Thomas Lowell 1943- *AmMWSc 92*
**Pazich,** Philip Michael 1947- *AmMWSc 92*
**Pazirandeh,** Mahmood 1932- *WhoMW 92*
**Pazol,** James Leslie 1937- *WhoAmL 92*
**Pazoles,** Christopher James 1950- *AmMWSc 92*
**Pazos Kanki,** Vicente 1779-1845 *HisDSpE*
**Pazur,** John Howard 1922- *AmMWSc 92*
**p'Bitek,** Okot 1931-1982 *BlkLC [port], LiExTwC, RfGEnL 91*
**Pe,** Maung Hla 1920- *AmMWSc 92*
**Peabody,** Andrew Preston 1811-1893 *BenetAL 91*
**Peabody,** Dwight Van Dorn, Jr 1924- *AmMWSc 92*
**Peabody,** Elizabeth Palmer 1804-1894 *BenetAL 91, HanAmWH*
**Peabody,** Frank Robert 1920- *AmMWSc 92*
**Peabody,** George 1795-1869 *BiInAmS*
**Peabody,** George Foster 1852-1938 *AmPeW*
**Peabody,** George Lee 1922- *WhoFI 92*
**Peabody,** George Livingston 1850-1914 *BiInAmS*
**Peabody,** Josephine Preston 1874-1922 *BenetAL 91*
**Peabody,** Lucy Whitehead McGill Waterbury 1861-1949 *RelLAm 91*
**Peabody,** Richard *DrAPF 91*
**Peabody,** Robert Lee 1931- *WrDr 92*
**Peabody,** Selim Hobart 1829-1903 *BiInAmS*
**Peace,** Eula H. 1920- *WhoBlA 92*
**Peace,** Frank *TwCWW 91*
**Peace,** G. Earl, Jr. 1945- *WhoBlA 92*
**Peace,** George Earl, Jr 1945- *AmMWSc 92*
**Peace,** Scott Parker 1942- *WhoAmP 91*
**Peace,** Steve 1953- *WhoAmP 91*
**Peace,** Wallace O'Kelly 1943- *WhoMW 92*
**Peaceman,** Donald W 1926- *AmMWSc 92*
**Peach,** Charles Lindsay K. *Who 92*
**Peach,** Denis Alan 1928- *Who 92*
**Peach,** Leonard 1932- *Who 92*
**Peach,** Michael Edwin 1937- *AmMWSc 92*
**Peach,** Michael Joe 1940- *AmMWSc 92*
**Peach,** Peter Angus 1920- *AmMWSc 92*
**Peach,** Roy *AmMWSc 92*
**Peaches,** Daniel 1940- *WhoAmP 91*
**Peachey,** Keith Albert 1956- *WhoRel 92*
**Peachey,** Lee DeBorde 1932- *AmMWSc 92*
**Peacock,** Alan 1922- *IntWW 91, Who 92, WrDr 92*
**Peacock,** Alvin Ward 1929- *WhoFI 92*
**Peacock,** Andrew 1939- *FacFETw*
**Peacock,** Andrew Sharp 1939- *IntWW 91, Who 92*
**Peacock,** Brian 1934- *TwCPaSc*
**Peacock,** Burnie L. 1921- *WhoEnt 92*
**Peacock,** Cassius L, Jr 1920- *WhoAmP 91*
**Peacock,** Clarisse Loxton *TwCPaSc*
**Peacock,** Elizabeth Joan 1937- *Who 92*
**Peacock,** Erle Ewart 1926- *AmMWSc 92*
**Peacock,** Gary 1935- *NewAmDM*
**Peacock,** Gary, Jr. 1962- *WhoFI 92*
**Peacock,** Geoffrey Arden d1991 *Who 92N*
**Peacock,** Hugh Anthony 1928- *AmMWSc 92*
**Peacock,** Ian Michael *LesBEnT 92*
**Peacock,** Ian Michael 1929- *Who 92*
**Peacock,** John Talmer 1931- *AmMWSc 92*
**Peacock,** Joseph Henry 1918- *Who 92*
**Peacock,** Joseph N. *WhoRel 92*
**Peacock,** Judith Ann 1939- *WhoEnt 92*
**Peacock,** Lelon James 1928- *AmMWSc 92*
**Peacock,** Lucy 1785-1816 *BlkwCEP*
**Peacock,** Michael *Who 92*
**Peacock,** Milton O 1916- *AmMWSc 92*
**Peacock,** Molly *DrAPF 91*
**Peacock,** Molly 1947- *ConPo 91, WrDr 92*
**Peacock,** Percy 1953- *TwCPaSc*
**Peacock,** Peter N B 1921- *AmMWSc 92*
**Peacock,** Ralph 1868-1946 *TwCPaSc*
**Peacock,** Richard Beck 1933- *WhoWest 92*
**Peacock,** Richard Wesley 1939- *AmMWSc 92*
**Peacock,** Ronald 1907- *IntWW 91, Who 92, WrDr 92*
**Peacock,** Ronald Howard 1954- *WhoMW 92*
**Peacock,** Roy Norman 1930- *AmMWSc 92*
**Peacock,** Samuel Moore, Jr 1922- *AmMWSc 92*
**Peacock,** Thomas Love 1785-1866 *RfGEnL 91*
**Peacock,** Tom *DrAPF 91*
**Peacock,** Val Edward 1951- *AmMWSc 92*
**Peacock,** William James 1937- *IntWW 91, Who 92*
**Peacocke,** Arthur Robert 1924- *Who 92*
**Peacocke,** Christopher Arthur Bruce 1950- *IntWW 91, Who 92*
**Peacocke,** Cuthbert Irvine 1903- *Who 92*
**Peacor,** Donald Ralph 1937- *AmMWSc 92*
**Peaden,** Paul Allan 1955- *WhoWest 92*
**Peagler,** Frederick Douglass 1922- *WhoBlA 92*
**Peagler,** Owen F 1931- *WhoAmP 91*
**Peagler,** Owen F. 1935- *WhoBlA 92*
**Peak,** David 1941- *AmMWSc 92*
**Peak,** David 1953- *ConAu 133*
**Peak,** Meyrick James 1937- *AmMWSc 92*
**Peak,** Paul E. 1953- *WhoRel 92*
**Peak,** Wilferd Warner 1924- *AmMWSc 92*
**Peakall,** David B 1931- *AmMWSc 92*
**Peake** *Who 92*
**Peake,** Charles Franklin 1933- *WhoFI 92*
**Peake,** Clinton J 1932- *AmMWSc 92*
**Peake,** David Alphy Edward Raymond 1934- *Who 92*
**Peake,** Edmund James, Jr 1938- *AmMWSc 92*
**Peake,** Edward James, Jr. 1933- *WhoBlA 92*
**Peake,** Felicity 1913- *Who 92*
**Peake,** Harold J 1920- *AmMWSc 92*
**Peake,** John Fordyce 1933- *Who 92*
**Peake,** John Morris 1924- *Who 92*
**Peake,** Lilian *IntAu&W 91, WrDr 92*
**Peake,** Mary S. 1823-1862 *NotBlAW 92*
**Peake,** Mervyn 1911-1968 *RfGEnL 91, TwCPaSc, TwCSFW 91*
**Peake,** Mervyn L 1911-1968 *FacFETw*
**Peake,** Robert Lee 1935- *AmMWSc 92*
**Peake,** Thaddeus Andrew, III 1948- *AmMWSc 92*
**Peake,** William Alfred 1953- *WhoRel 92*
**Peake,** William Tower 1929- *AmMWSc 92*
**Peaker,** E.J. *IntMPA 92*
**Peaker,** Edra Jeanne 1944- *WhoEnt 92*
**Peaker,** Malcolm 1943- *Who 92*
**Peal,** Michael 1948- *WhoEnt 92*
**Peal,** S. Edward d1991 *NewYTBS 91*
**Peale Family** *HanAmWH*
**Peale,** Albert Charles 1849-1914 *BiInAmS*
**Peale,** Anna Claypoole 1791-1878 *HanAmWH*
**Peale,** Charles Willson 1741-1827 *BenetAL 91, BiInAmS, BlkwEAR [port]*
**Peale,** Harriet Cany 1800-1869 *HanAmWH*
**Peale,** Margaretta Angelica 1795-1882 *HanAmWH*
**Peale,** Mary Jane 1827-1902 *HanAmWH*
**Peale,** Norman Vincent 1898- *BenetAL 91, RelLAm 91, WhoRel 92, WrDr 92*
**Peale,** Rembrandt 1778-1860 *BenetAL 91, BiInAmS*
**Peale,** Rosalba Carriera 1799-1874 *HanAmWH*
**Peale,** Ruth Stafford 1906- *WhoRel 92*
**Peale,** Sarah Miriam 1800-1885 *HanAmWH*
**Peale,** Stanton Jerrold 1937- *AmMWSc 92*
**Peale,** Titian Ramsay 1799-1885 *BiInAmS*
**Peanasky,** Robert Joseph 1927- *AmMWSc 92*
**Peapples,** George Alan 1940- *WhoFI 92*
**Pearce** *Who 92*
**Pearce,** Baron d1990 *IntWW 91N, Who 92N*
**Pearce,** Lord 1901-1990 *AnObit 1990*
**Pearce,** Alan Marple 1949- *WhoFI 92*
**Pearce,** Andrew 1937- *Who 92*
**Pearce,** Ann Philippa *IntAu&W 91, SmATA 67 [port], Who 92*
**Pearce,** Ashley 1962- *TwCPaSc*
**Pearce,** Austin 1921- *Who 92*
**Pearce,** Austin William 1921- *IntWW 91*
**Pearce,** Brian *Who 92*
**Pearce,** Brian Louis 1933- *IntAu&W 91, WrDr 92*
**Pearce,** Bryan 1929- *TwCPaSc*
**Pearce,** Charles Maresco 1874-1964 *TwCPaSc*
**Pearce,** Charles Walter 1947- *AmMWSc 92*
**Pearce,** Christopher *IntMPA 92*
**Pearce,** Colman Cormac 1938- *WhoEnt 92*
**Pearce,** Daniel Norton Idris 1933- *Who 92*
**Pearce,** David Archibald 1920- *AmMWSc 92*
**Pearce,** David Harry 1943- *AmMWSc 92*
**Pearce,** Drue 1951- *WhoAmP 91*
**Pearce,** Eli M 1929- *AmMWSc 92*
**Pearce,** Eric 1905- *Who 92*
**Pearce,** Floyd Earl 1935- *IntAu&W 91*
**Pearce,** Frank G 1918- *AmMWSc 92*
**Pearce,** Frederick James *AmMWSc 92*
**Pearce,** Gary Douglas 1952- *WhoRel 92*
**Pearce,** George 1921- *Who 92*
**Pearce,** George Hamilton 1921- *WhoRel 92*
**Pearce,** George William 1942- *AmMWSc 92*
**Pearce,** H E, Jr 1936- *WhoAmP 91*
**Pearce,** Harry Jonathan 1942- *WhoAmL 92, WhoFI 92*
**Pearce,** Howard Spencer 1924- *Who 92*
**Pearce,** Idris *Who 92*
**Pearce,** Idris 1933- *IntWW 91*
**Pearce,** Jack B 1930- *AmMWSc 92*
**Pearce,** Janice 1931- *WhoWest 92*
**Pearce,** John Brian 1935- *Who 92*
**Pearce,** John Dalziel Wyndham 1904- *Who 92*
**Pearce,** John Stedman 1940- *WhoAmP 91*
**Pearce,** John Trevor Archdall 1916- *Who 92*
**Pearce,** John Y. 1948- *WhoAmL 92*
**Pearce,** Joseph Huske 1941- *WhoMW 92*
**Pearce,** Keith Ian 1927- *AmMWSc 92*
**Pearce,** Leslie Arthur 1918- *Who 92*
**Pearce,** Lester *WhoAmP 91*
**Pearce,** Lupe 1942- *WhoHisp 92*
**Pearce,** Martha Flores 1953- *WhoHisp 92*
**Pearce,** Mary E. 1932- *WrDr 92*
**Pearce,** Mary Emily 1932- *IntAu&W 91*
**Pearce,** Michael Leonard 1933- *WhoFI 92*
**Pearce,** Morton Lee 1920- *AmMWSc 92*
**Pearce,** Neville John Lewis 1933- *Who 92*
**Pearce,** Philippa *Who 92, WrDr 92*
**Pearce,** Philippa 1920- *SmATA 67 [port]*
**Pearce,** Richard 1943- *IntMPA 92*
**Pearce,** Richard Allen 1951- *WhoBlA 92*
**Pearce,** Richard Hugh 1924- *AmMWSc 92*
**Pearce,** Richard William, Jr. 1941- *WhoIns 92*
**Pearce,** Robert Brent 1936- *AmMWSc 92*
**Pearce,** Robert Penrose 1924- *Who 92*
**Pearce,** Robert Wayne 1944- *WhoWest 92*
**Pearce,** Roy Harvey 1919- *WrDr 92*
**Pearce,** Stephen Wade 1954- *WhoMW 92*
**Pearce,** Thomas Hulme 1938- *AmMWSc 92*
**Pearce,** Timothy Harold 1958- *WhoRel 92*
**Pearce,** William Joseph 1925- *WhoEnt 92*
**Pearce-McCall,** Debra Nore 1959- *WhoMW 92*
**Pearcy,** Carl Mark, Jr 1935- *AmMWSc 92*
**Pearcy,** Robert Woodwell 1941- *AmMWSc 92*
**Pearcy,** William Gordon 1929- *AmMWSc 92*
**Peard,** Kenyon 1902- *Who 92*
**Peard,** William John 1928- *AmMWSc 92*
**Peardon,** David Lee 1932- *AmMWSc 92*
**Pearincott,** Joseph V 1929- *AmMWSc 92*
**Pearl,** Barry Lee 1950- *WhoEnt 92*
**Pearl,** Bernard Harold 1933- *WhoMW 92*
**Pearl,** Burt 1957- *WhoEnt 92*
**Pearl,** Chaim 1919- *WhoRel 92*
**Pearl,** David 1944- *ConAu 133*
**Pearl,** Gary Steven 1949- *AmMWSc 92*
**Pearl,** Irwin Albert 1913- *AmMWSc 92, WhoMW 92*
**Pearl,** James G 1941- *WhoIns 92*
**Pearl,** John Christopher 1938- *AmMWSc 92*
**Pearl,** Judea 1936- *AmMWSc 92*
**Pearl,** Kenneth Leroy, Jr. 1957- *WhoWest 92*
**Pearl,** Laurence Dickson 1934- *WhoAmL 92*
**Pearl,** Martin Herbert 1928- *AmMWSc 92*
**Pearl,** Minnie 1912- *NewAmDM, WhoEnt 92*
**Pearl,** Ronald G 1949- *AmMWSc 92*
**Pearl,** Steven Barrack 1963- *WhoEnt 92*
**Pearl,** Steven Lawrence 1957- *WhoMW 92*
**Pearl,** Valerie Louise 1926- *IntWW 91, Who 92*
**Pearl,** W L 1921- *AmMWSc 92*
**Pearl,** William 1920- *AmMWSc 92*
**Pearle,** Philip Mark 1936- *AmMWSc 92*
**Pearlman,** Alan L 1936- *AmMWSc 92*
**Pearlman,** Bill *DrAPF 91*
**Pearlman,** Bruce A 1949- *AmMWSc 92*
**Pearlman,** Charlotte Blehert 1919- *WhoAmP 91*
**Pearlman,** Edith *DrAPF 91*

Pearlman, Jerry Kent 1939- WhoFI 92
Pearlman, Jodi Marie 1964- WhoMW 92
Pearlman, Louis, Jr. 1930- WhoAmL 92
Pearlman, Louis Jay 1954- WhoFI 92
Pearlman, Michael Allen 1946- WhoAmL 92
Pearlman, Michael R 1941- AmMWSc 92
Pearlman, Mickey 1938- ConAu 134
Pearlman, Moshe 1911- WrDr 92
Pearlman, Norman 1922- AmMWSc 92
Pearlman, Peter Steven 1946- WhoAmL 92
Pearlman, Rodney 1951- AmMWSc 92
Pearlman, Ronald Alan 1940- WhoAmL 92, WhoAmP 91
Pearlman, Ronald C 1944- AmMWSc 92
Pearlman, Ronald E 1941- AmMWSc 92
Pearlman, Samuel Segel 1942- WhoAmL 92
Pearlman, Stephen Mitchell 1960- WhoFI 92
Pearlman, Valerie Anne 1936- Who 92
Pearlman, William Henry 1914- AmMWSc 92
Pearlmutter, Anne Frances 1940- AmMWSc 92
Pearlson, Fredda S. DrAPF 91
Pearlson, Jordan 1924- WhoRel 92
Pearlson, Wilbur H 1915- AmMWSc 92
Pearlstein, Arne Jacob 1952- AmMWSc 92
Pearlstein, Brenda 1943- WhoFI 92
Pearlstein, Edgar Aaron 1927- AmMWSc 92
Pearlstein, Leon Donald 1932- AmMWSc 92
Pearlstein, Mark Edward 1948- WhoFI 92
Pearlstein, Robert David 1949- AmMWSc 92
Pearlstein, Robert Milton 1937- AmMWSc 92
Pearlstein, Sol 1930- AmMWSc 92
Pearlstine, Norman 1942- WhoFI 92
Pearman, G Timothy 1940- AmMWSc 92
Pearman, James 1904- Who 92
Pearman, James Elwood, Jr. 1948- WhoFI 92
Pearman, James Richard 1940- WhoAmL 92
Pearman, Raven-Symone Christina 1985- WhoBlA 92
Pearman, Virgil L 1933- WhoAmP 91
Pearn, Victor DrAPF 91
Pearne, George Reginald 1948- WhoWest 92
Pears, Coultas D 1925- AmMWSc 92
Pears, David Francis 1921- IntWW 91, Who 92
Pears, Edward Richard 1951- WhoRel 92
Pears, Peter 1910-1986 FacFETw, NewAmDM
Pearsall, Derek 1931- WrDr 92
Pearsall, Derek Albert 1931- IntAu&W 91
Pearsall, George W 1933- AmMWSc 92
Pearsall, Glenn Lincoln 1949- WhoFI 92
Pearsall, Harry James 1916- WhoMW 92
Pearsall, Phyllis 1906- TwCPaSc
Pearsall, Phyllis Isobel 1906- Who 92
Pearsall, R J ScFEYrs
Pearsall, Ronald 1927- IntAu&W 91, WrDr 92
Pearsall, Rosellen Dee 1945- WhoFI 92
Pearsall, S H 1923- AmMWSc 92
Pearsall, Thomas Perine 1945- WhoWest 92
Pearsall Stipek, Cathy Rae 1932- WhoAmP 91
Pearse, Anthony Guy Everson 1916- IntWW 91, Who 92
Pearse, Barbara Mary Frances 1948- IntWW 91, Who 92
Pearse, Brian Gerald 1933- IntWW 91, Who 92
Pearse, George Ancell, Jr 1930- AmMWSc 92
Pearse, John Barnard Swett 1842-1914 BiInAmS
Pearse, John Roger Southey G Who 92
Pearse, John Stuart 1936- AmMWSc 92
Pearse, Patrick Henry 1879-1916 FacFETw
Pearse, Richard DrAPF 91
Pearse, Vicki Buchsbaum 1942- AmMWSc 92
Pearse, Warren Harland 1927- AmMWSc 92
Pearson Who 92
Pearson, Alastair Stevenson 1915- Who 92
Pearson, Albert Marchant 1916- AmMWSc 92
Pearson, Allan Einar 1936- AmMWSc 92
Pearson, Allen Mobley 1909- AmMWSc 92
Pearson, Andrall E. 1925- IntWW 91
Pearson, Anthony Alan 1954- WhoRel 92
Pearson, Arthur David 1932- AmMWSc 92
Pearson, Barbara Joy 1942- WhoMW 92
Pearson, Bennie Jake 1929- AmMWSc 92
Pearson, Bill 1922- ConNov 91, WrDr 92
Pearson, Birger Albert 1934- WhoRel 92
Pearson, Brian William 1949- Who 92
Pearson, Carl E 1922- AmMWSc 92
Pearson, Carol Lynn 1939- ConAu 133
Pearson, Charles Thomas, Jr. 1929- WhoAmL 92
Pearson, Charles Warren 1952- WhoRel 92
Pearson, Christy Marie 1961- WhoEnt 92
Pearson, Clifton 1948- WhoBlA 92
Pearson, Colin Arthur 1935- AmMWSc 92
Pearson, Dale Sheldon 1942- AmMWSc 92
Pearson, Daniel Bester, III 1949- AmMWSc 92
Pearson, Daniel S. 1930- WhoAmL 92
Pearson, Dave 1937- TwCPaSc
Pearson, Dave Lee 1950- WhoAmP 91
Pearson, David Compton Froome 1931- Who 92
Pearson, David D 1938- AmMWSc 92
Pearson, David Leander 1943- AmMWSc 92
Pearson, Denning Who 92
Pearson, Derek Leslie 1921- Who 92
Pearson, Diane 1931- IntAu&W 91, WrDr 92
Pearson, Donald A 1921- AmMWSc 92
Pearson, Donald A 1931- AmMWSc 92
Pearson, Donald Emanual 1914- AmMWSc 92
Pearson, Donald Melvin 1917- WhoEnt 92
Pearson, Donald S. 1943- WhoMW 92
Pearson, Drew 1896-1969 FacFETw
Pearson, Drew 1951- WhoBlA 92
Pearson, Earl F 1941- AmMWSc 92
Pearson, Edmund Lester 1880-1937 BenetAL 91
Pearson, Edward John 1938- Who 92
Pearson, Edwin Forrest 1938- AmMWSc 92
Pearson, Elizabeth Maria 1953- WhoRel 92
Pearson, Erman A 1920- AmMWSc 92
Pearson, Erwin Gale 1932- WhoWest 92
Pearson, Frain Garfield 1936- WhoWest 92
Pearson, Francis Fenwick d1991 Who 92N
Pearson, Francis Nicholas 1943- Who 92
Pearson, Frederick Joseph 1935- AmMWSc 92
Pearson, Garry Allen 1934- WhoAmL 92
Pearson, Gary Dean 1952- WhoMW 92
Pearson, Gary Richard 1938- AmMWSc 92
Pearson, Gayle 1947- WrDr 92
Pearson, George 1875-1973 IntDcF 2-2 [port]
Pearson, George Burton, Jr. 1905- WhoFI 92
Pearson, George Denton 1941- AmMWSc 92
Pearson, George John 1928- AmMWSc 92
Pearson, Gertrude B WhoAmP 91
Pearson, Glen Hamilton 1948- AmMWSc 92
Pearson, Graham Scott 1935- Who 92
Pearson, Hans Lennart 1927- AmMWSc 92
Pearson, Henry Alexander 1933- AmMWSc 92
Pearson, Henry Clyde 1925- WhoAmL 92
Pearson, Herbert Macdonald 1908- Who 92
Pearson, Herbert William 1850-1916 BiInAmS
Pearson, Herman B. 1947- WhoBlA 92
Pearson, Howard Allen 1929- AmMWSc 92
Pearson, J Raymond 1912- AmMWSc 92
Pearson, J Richmond 1930- WhoAmP 91
Pearson, James A. 1925- WhoBlA 92
Pearson, James B WhoAmP 91
Pearson, James Boyd, Jr 1930- AmMWSc 92
Pearson, James Denning 1908- Who 92
Pearson, James Douglas 1911- Who 92
Pearson, James Edward 1956- WhoWest 92
Pearson, James Eldon 1926- AmMWSc 92
Pearson, James Joseph 1934- AmMWSc 92
Pearson, James Murray 1937- AmMWSc 92
Pearson, Jean DrAPF 91
Pearson, Jerome 1938- AmMWSc 92
Pearson, Jesse S. 1923- WhoBlA 92
Pearson, Jim Berry, Jr. 1948- WhoFI 92
Pearson, John Who 92
Pearson, John 1923- AmMWSc 92, WhoWest 92
Pearson, John 1930- WrDr 92
Pearson, John 1934- IntAu&W 91, WrDr 92
Pearson, John E 1927- WhoIns 92
Pearson, John Edgar 1927- WhoFI 92, WhoMW 92
Pearson, John Edward 1946- WhoAmL 92
Pearson, John Elliot 1916- WhoEnt 92
Pearson, John Michael 1933- AmMWSc 92
Pearson, John Richard 1938- AmMWSc 92
Pearson, John W 1918- AmMWSc 92
Pearson, John William 1920- Who 92
Pearson, John William 1935- AmMWSc 92
Pearson, Joseph T 1933- AmMWSc 92
Pearson, Karl Herbert 1934- AmMWSc 92
Pearson, Keir Gordon 1942- AmMWSc 92
Pearson, Keith David WrDr 92
Pearson, Keith Laurence 1929- WhoWest 92
Pearson, Keith Philip 1941- Who 92
Pearson, Kit 1947- ChlLR 26 [port]
Pearson, Kristine Ann 1956- WhoMW 92
Pearson, Kyle Gilbert 1959- WhoMW 92
Pearson, Lennart Jon 1942- WhoWest 92
Pearson, Leonard 1868-1909 BiInAmS
Pearson, Lester 1897-1972 FacFETw
Pearson, Lester Bowles 1897-1972 WhoNob 90
Pearson, Linley E WhoAmP 91
Pearson, Linley E. 1946- WhoAmL 92, WhoMW 92
Pearson, Lionel 1908- WrDr 92
Pearson, Lonnie Wilson 1946- AmMWSc 92
Pearson, Lorentz Clarence 1924- AmMWSc 92, WhoAmP 91
Pearson, Louise Mary 1919- WhoFI 92, WhoMW 92
Pearson, Marilyn Ruth 1955- WhoBlA 92
Pearson, Mark WhoEnt 92
Pearson, Mark Landell 1940- AmMWSc 92
Pearson, Mary Margaret 1922- WhoFI 92
Pearson, Max 1933- DcTwDes
Pearson, Michael David 1941- WhoAmP 91
Pearson, Michael J 1938- AmMWSc 92
Pearson, Michael Novel 1956- WhoBlA 92
Pearson, Myrna Schmidt 1936- AmMWSc 92
Pearson, Nels Kenneth 1918- WhoMW 92
Pearson, Nicholas Who 92
Pearson, Norman 1928- WhoFI 92, WhoMW 92
Pearson, Norman Charles 1909- Who 92
Pearson, Olof Hjalmer 1913- AmMWSc 92
Pearson, P. A. 1939- WhoFI 92
Pearson, Paul 1921- AmMWSc 92
Pearson, Paul Brown 1905- AmMWSc 92
Pearson, Paul David 1940- WhoAmL 92
Pearson, Paul Guy 1926- AmMWSc 92, WhoMW 92
Pearson, Philip Richardson, Jr 1927- AmMWSc 92
Pearson, Phillip T 1932- AmMWSc 92
Pearson, Phillip Theodore 1932- WhoMW 92
Pearson, Preston James 1945- WhoBlA 92
Pearson, R L 1930- AmMWSc 92
Pearson, Ra-Nelle Lynn 1952- WhoAmP 91
Pearson, Ralph E. d1991 NewYTBS 91
Pearson, Ralph Gottfrid 1919- AmMWSc 92
Pearson, Ralph Gottfried 1919- IntWW 91
Pearson, Ralph W 1920- WhoAmP 91
Pearson, Ramona Henderson 1952- WhoBlA 92
Pearson, Richard Jarvis 1925- WhoWest 92
Pearson, Ridley 1953- ConAu 135
Pearson, Robert Bernard AmMWSc 92
Pearson, Robert Melvin 1930- AmMWSc 92
Pearson, Robert Stanley 1927- AmMWSc 92
Pearson, Ronald Earl 1944- AmMWSc 92
Pearson, Ronald Gene 1955- WhoAmL 92
Pearson, Ronald Matthew 1925- Who 92
Pearson, Roy 1914- WrDr 92
Pearson, Roy Messer, Jr. 1914- WhoRel 92
Pearson, Scott Roberts 1938- WhoFI 92, WrDr 92
Pearson, Stanley E. 1949- WhoBlA 92
Pearson, Stephen Funk 1950- WhoEnt 92
Pearson, Steven Earl 1953- WhoRel 92
Pearson, T. R. 1956- WrDr 92
Pearson, Terrance Laverne 1937- AmMWSc 92
Pearson, Theodore Richard 1951- WhoAmP 91
Pearson, Thomas 1914- Who 92
Pearson, Thomas Arthur 1950- AmMWSc 92
Pearson, Thomas Dawson, Jr. 1939- WhoAmL 92
Pearson, Vernon R WhoAmP 91
Pearson, Walter Howard 1946- AmMWSc 92, WhoWest 92
Pearson, Warren Thomas 1929- WhoWest 92
Pearson, Wesley A 1932- AmMWSc 92
Pearson, William Dean 1941- AmMWSc 92
Pearson, William Harrison 1922- IntAu&W 91
Pearson, Willie Anthony 1963- WhoEnt 92
Pearson of Rannoch, Baron 1942- Who 92
Peart, Lord 1914-1988 FacFETw
Peart, Brian 1925- Who 92
Peart, Robert McDermand 1925- AmMWSc 92
Peart, Stanley 1922- IntWW 91, Who 92
Pearton, Stephen John 1957- AmMWSc 92
Peary, Robert Edwin 1856-1920 BenetAL 91, BiInAmS, FacFETw [port]
Peary, Timothy H 1943- WhoAmP 91
Peasback, David R. WhoFI 92
Peascoe, Warren Joseph 1943- AmMWSc 92
Pease Who 92
Pease, Alfred Vincent 1926- Who 92
Pease, Archie Granville 1908- WhoMW 92
Pease, Burton Frank 1928- AmMWSc 92
Pease, Deborah DrAPF 91
Pease, Denise Louise 1953- WhoBlA 92, WhoFI 92
Pease, Donald J. 1931- AlmAP 92 [port]
Pease, Donald James 1931- WhoAmP 91, WhoMW 92
Pease, Douglas Edward 1942- WhoFI 92
Pease, Edward Allan 1951- WhoAmP 91, WhoMW 92
Pease, Edwin Chapman, Jr. 1938- WhoRel 92
Pease, Howard 1894-1974 BenetAL 91
Pease, James Robert 1937- AmMWSc 92
Pease, Marshall Carleton, III 1920- AmMWSc 92
Pease, Michael Anthony 1964- WhoMW 92
Pease, Paul Lorin 1943- AmMWSc 92
Pease, Rendel Sebastian 1922- IntWW 91, Who 92
Pease, Richard Bruce 1957- WhoMW 92
Pease, Richard Thorn 1922- Who 92
Pease, Robert DrAPF 91
Pease, Robert John Claude 1922- Who 92
Pease, Robert Louis 1925- AmMWSc 92
Pease, Robert Wright 1917- AmMWSc 92
Pease, Roger Fabian Wedgwood 1936- AmMWSc 92
Pease, Roland F., Jr. DrAPF 91
Pease, Rosamund Dorothy Benson 1935- Who 92
Pease, Sara Gooding 1918- WhoRel 92
Pease, Vincent Who 92
Pease, W Harper d1872 BiInAmS
Peasland, Bruce Randall 1945- WhoFI 92
Peaslee, Alfred Tredway, Jr 1930- AmMWSc 92
Peaslee, Amos Jenkins 1887-1969 AmPeW
Peaslee, David Chase 1922- AmMWSc 92
Peaslee, Doyle E 1930- AmMWSc 92
Peaslee, James M. 1952- WhoAmL 92
Peaslee, Janice L 1935- WhoAmP 91
Peaslee, John Eric 1952- WhoMW 92
Peaslee, Margaret H 1935- AmMWSc 92
Peaslee, Maurice Keenan 1950- WhoAmL 92
Peaslee, Richard Cutts 1930- WhoEnt 92
Peasley, Lyle James 1954- WhoRel 92
Peat, Gerrard 1920- Who 92
Peat, Lawrence Joseph 1928- Who 92
Peat, Michael Charles Gerrard 1949- Who 92
Peat, Watson 1922- Who 92
Peatman, John B 1934- AmMWSc 92
Peatman, William Burling 1939- AmMWSc 92
Peattie, Donald Culross 1898-1964 BenetAL 91
Peavey, John T WhoAmP 91
Peavler, Terry J. 1942- ConAu 135
Peavy, Don Ezzard, Sr. 1950- WhoAmL 92
Peavy, Homer Louis, Jr. 1924- WhoFI 92, WhoMW 92
Peavy, Howard Sidney 1942- AmMWSc 92
Peavy, James Edwin 1920- WhoAmP 91
Peavy, John W., Jr. 1943- WhoBlA 92
Peavy, Linda DrAPF 91
Peavy, S Lanny 1938- WhoIns 92
Peay, Francis WhoBlA 92
Peay, Isaac Charles, Sr. 1910- WhoBlA 92
Peay, John Hurst 1935- WhoAmL 92
Peay, Samuel 1939- WhoBlA 92
Pebereau, Georges Alexandre 1931- IntWW 91
Pebly, Harry E 1923- AmMWSc 92
Peccei, Roberto Daniele 1942- AmMWSc 92, WhoWest 92
Pecci, Joseph 1930- AmMWSc 92
Pech, Lawrence Marion 1959- WhoEnt 92
Pechacek, Terry Frank 1947- AmMWSc 92
Pechan, Michael J 1950- AmMWSc 92
Pechel, Peter 1920- ConAu 135
Pechenik, Jan A 1950- AmMWSc 92
Pechet, Joy Elizabeth 1954- WhoWest 92
Pechet, Liberto 1926- AmMWSc 92
Pechmann, Cornelia Ann Rachel 1959- WhoWest 92
Pechous, Robert C WhoAmP 91
Pechstein, Max 1881-1955 FacFETw

**Pechtel,** Curtis Theodore 1920- *WhoWest 92*
**Pechter,** Richard S. *WhoFI 92*
**Pechter,** Steven Jerome 1958- *WhoFI 92*
**Pechukas,** Philip 1942- *AmMWSc 92*
**Pechuman,** LaVerne LeRoy 1913- *AmMWSc 92*
**Pecina,** Richard W 1935- *AmMWSc 92*
**Peck,** Alfred Dennis 1953- *WhoRel 92*
**Peck,** Ammon Broughton *AmMWSc 92*
**Peck,** Ann 1945- *WhoEnt 92*
**Peck,** Anne Elliott Roberts 1935- *WhoFI 92*
**Peck,** Annie Smith 1850-1935 *BenetAL 91*
**Peck,** Barbara May 1926- *WhoAmP 91*
**Peck,** Bob 1945- *ConTFT 9*
**Peck,** Bradford 1853-1935 *ScFEYrs*
**Peck,** Carl Curtis 1942- *AmMWSc 92*
**Peck,** Charles Edward 1925- *WhoFI 92*
**Peck,** Charles Horton 1833-1917 *BiInAmS*
**Peck,** Charles Karl, Jr. 1921- *WhoEnt 92, WhoWest 92*
**Peck,** Charles S. 1947- *WhoWest 92*
**Peck,** Charles William 1934- *AmMWSc 92*
**Peck,** Curtiss Steven 1947- *WhoMW 92*
**Peck,** D Stewart 1918- *AmMWSc 92*
**Peck,** Dallas Lynn 1929- *AmMWSc 92*
**Peck,** David 1917- *Who 92*
**Peck,** David W 1925- *AmMWSc 92*
**Peck,** Deana S. 1947- *WhoAmL 92*
**Peck,** Donald Harvey 1945- *WhoWest 92*
**Peck,** Donald Vincent 1930- *WhoEnt 92*
**Peck,** Douglas Robert 1960- *WhoBlA 92*
**Peck,** Edson Ruther 1915- *AmMWSc 92*
**Peck,** Edward 1915- *Who 92*
**Peck,** Edward Heywood 1915- *IntWW 91*
**Peck,** Edward Lionel 1929- *WhoAmP 91*
**Peck,** Elbert Eugene 1954- *WhoRel 92*
**Peck,** Ellie Enriquez 1934- *WhoAmP 91, WhoHisp 92, WhoWest 92*
**Peck,** Emily Mann 1946- *AmMWSc 92, WhoMW 92*
**Peck,** Ernest James, Jr 1941- *AmMWSc 92*
**Peck,** Eugene Lincoln 1922- *AmMWSc 92*
**Peck,** Fred Neil 1945- *WhoFI 92*
**Peck,** Gail J. *DrAPF 91*
**Peck,** Gaillard Ray, Jr. 1940- *WhoWest 92*
**Peck,** Garnet E 1930- *AmMWSc 92*
**Peck,** Garnet Edward 1930- *WhoMW 92*
**Peck,** George Wilbur 1840-1916 *BenetAL 91*
**Peck,** Gregory 1916- *IntMPA 92, IntWW 91, Who 92, WhoEnt 92*
**Peck,** Gregory Lester 1952- *WhoBlA 92*
**Peck,** Harry Dowd, Jr 1927- *AmMWSc 92*
**Peck,** Harry Thurston 1856-1914 *BenetAL 91*
**Peck,** James 1914- *AmPeW*
**Peck,** James Ingraham 1863-1898 *BiInAmS*
**Peck,** Joel Slonim 1948- *WhoFI 92*
**Peck,** John *DrAPF 91*
**Peck,** John 1913- *Who 92*
**Peck,** John 1941- *ConPo 91, WrDr 92*
**Peck,** John, Jr. 1943- *WhoFI 92*
**Peck,** John F 1936- *AmMWSc 92*
**Peck,** John Frederick 1941- *IntAu&W 91*
**Peck,** John H 1937- *AmMWSc 92*
**Peck,** John Howard 1913- *IntWW 91*
**Peck,** John Hubert 1942- *AmMWSc 92*
**Peck,** John Mason 1789-1858 *BenetAL 91*
**Peck,** John W. 1913- *WhoAmL 92, WhoMW 92*
**Peck,** Leontyne Clay 1958- *WhoBlA 92*
**Peck,** Louis P 1918- *WhoAmP 91*
**Peck,** Louis W 1851?-1898 *BiInAmS*
**Peck,** Lyman Colt 1920- *AmMWSc 92*
**Peck,** M. Scott 1936- *CurBio 91 [port], WrDr 92*
**Peck,** Merlin Larry 1940- *AmMWSc 92*
**Peck,** Merton Joseph 1925- *IntAu&W 91, WrDr 92*
**Peck,** Mira Paszko 1946- *WhoAmL 92*
**Peck,** Nathan Hiram 1923- *AmMWSc 92*
**Peck,** Neil 1939- *WhoAmL 92*
**Peck,** Newton Tenney 1937- *AmMWSc 92, WhoMW 92*
**Peck,** Paul Lachlan 1928- *WhoRel 92, WhoWest 92*
**Peck,** Ralph B 1912- *AmMWSc 92*
**Peck,** Ray L 1926- *WhoAmP 91*
**Peck,** Raymond A, Jr *WhoAmP 91*
**Peck,** Raymond Charles, Sr. 1937- *WhoWest 92*
**Peck,** Raymond Elliott 1904- *AmMWSc 92*
**Peck,** Richard *DrAPF 91*
**Peck,** Richard 1934- *IntAu&W 91, WrDr 92*
**Peck,** Richard Earl 1936- *WhoWest 92*
**Peck,** Richard J. 1958- *WhoEnt 92*
**Peck,** Richard Leslie 1937- *Who 92*
**Peck,** Richard Merle 1921- *AmMWSc 92*
**Peck,** Robert 1924- *WhoAmP 91*
**Peck,** Robert E 1947- *AmMWSc 92*
**Peck,** Robert Newton *IntAu&W 91, WrDr 92*
**Peck,** Russell Allen, Jr 1924- *AmMWSc 92*
**Peck,** Samuel Minturn 1854-1938 *BenetAL 91*
**Peck,** Stanley Edwards 1916- *Who 92*
**Peck,** Stephen John 1956- *WhoFI 92*
**Peck,** Stephen Joseph 1946- *WhoEnt 92*
**Peck,** Stewart Blaine 1942- *AmMWSc 92*
**Peck,** Suzanne Wexler 1945- *WhoMW 92*
**Peck,** Sylvia *DrAPF 91*
**Peck,** Sylvia 1953- *ConAu 135*
**Peck,** Theodore Richard 1931- *AmMWSc 92*
**Peck,** Vivian Rosetta 1924- *WhoAmP 91*
**Peck,** Wallace *ScFEYrs*
**Peck,** William Arno 1933- *AmMWSc 92*
**Peck,** William B 1920- *AmMWSc 92*
**Peck,** William Dandridge 1763-1822 *BiInAmS*
**Peck,** William Guy 1820-1892 *BiInAmS*
**Peck,** William R, III 1931- *WhoAmP 91*
**Pecka,** James Thomas 1932- *AmMWSc 92*
**Peckarsky,** Barbara Lynn 1947- *AmMWSc 92*
**Peckenpaugh,** Angela *DrAPF 91*
**Peckenpaugh,** Robert Earl 1926- *WhoFI 92*
**Pecker,** David J. 1951- *WhoFI 92*
**Pecker,** Jean-Claude 1923- *IntWW 91*
**Peckerman,** Bruce Martin 1949- *WhoAmL 92*
**Peckford,** Brian 1942- *IntWW 91, Who 92*
**Peckham,** Alan Embree 1931- *AmMWSc 92*
**Peckham,** Arthur John 1920- *Who 92*
**Peckham,** Donald 1932- *WhoFI 92, WhoWest 92*
**Peckham,** Donald Charles 1922- *AmMWSc 92*
**Peckham,** George Williams 1845-1914 *BiInAmS*
**Peckham,** Michael John 1935- *IntWW 91, Who 92*
**Peckham,** Morse 1914- *IntAu&W 91, WrDr 92*
**Peckham,** P Hunter 1944- *AmMWSc 92*
**Peckham,** Richard *BenetAL 91*
**Peckham,** Richard Stark 1924- *AmMWSc 92*
**Peckham,** Robert Francis 1920- *WhoAmL 92*
**Peckham,** Rufus W 1838-1909 *FacFETw*
**Peckham,** Rufus Wheeler, Jr 1928- *WhoAmP 91*
**Peckham,** Stephen Farnum 1839-1918 *BiInAmS*
**Peckham,** William Dierolf 1922- *AmMWSc 92*
**Peckinpah,** Sam 1925-1984 *IntDcF 2-2 [port]*
**Peckinpaugh,** Jack *WhoIns 92*
**Peckinpaugh,** Walter Stidger, Jr. 1943- *WhoMW 92*
**Peckman,** David Aaron 1960- *WhoFI 92*
**Pecknold,** Paul Carson 1942- *AmMWSc 92*
**Peckolick,** Alan 1940- *WhoEnt 92*
**Peckover,** Richard Stuart 1942- *Who 92*
**Pecora,** Frank Anthony 1930- *WhoAmP 91*
**Pecora,** Robert 1938- *AmMWSc 92*
**Pecoraro,** Joseph John 1949- *WhoAmL 92*
**Pecoraro,** Vincent L 1956- *AmMWSc 92*
**Pecorini,** Hector A 1924- *AmMWSc 92*
**Pecot,** Charles Matthew 1934- *WhoIns 92*
**Pecoux,** Olivier 1958- *WhoFI 92*
**Pecqueur,** Michel Andre Fernand 1931- *IntWW 91*
**Pecsenye,** Timothy 1952- *WhoMW 92*
**Pecsi,** Marton 1923- *IntWW 91*
**Pecsok,** Robert Louis 1918- *AmMWSc 92, WhoWest 92*
**Pectol,** Richard William, Jr. 1931- *WhoRel 92*
**Pectorius** *EncEarC*
**Pecze,** David Emery 1958- *WhoFI 92, WhoMW 92*
**Pedace,** William Bruno 1936- *WhoMW 92*
**Pedalino,** Joseph, Jr. 1957- *WhoEnt 92*
**Pedas,** Jim *IntMPA 92*
**Pedas,** Ted 1931- *IntMPA 92*
**Pedder,** Arthur 1904- *Who 92*
**Pedder,** Glenn Curtiss 1942- *WhoRel 92*
**Pedder,** Ian 1926- *Who 92*
**Peddicord,** Fred, III 1941- *WhoAmP 91*
**Peddicord,** Roland Dale 1936- *WhoMW 92*
**Peddie,** Robert Allan 1921- *Who 92*
**Peden,** Charles H F 1953- *AmMWSc 92*
**Peden,** Irene C 1925- *AmMWSc 92*
**Peden,** Mark Renick 1965- *WhoWest 92*
**Peden,** S. T., Jr. 1944- *WhoBlA 92*
**Peden,** William *DrAPF 91*
**Peden,** William 1913- *WrDr 92*
**Peden,** William Creighton 1935- *WhoFI 92*
**Pedersen,** Bernard Edwin 1925- *WhoAmP 91*
**Pedersen,** Carl Th. 1935- *IntWW 91*
**Pedersen,** Charles John 1904- *AmMWSc 92*
**Pedersen,** Charles John 1904-1989 *WhoNob 90*
**Pedersen,** Elizabeth Ann 1952- *WhoMW 92*
**Pedersen,** Ellis Hans 1948- *WhoMW 92*
**Pedersen,** Franklin D 1933- *AmMWSc 92*
**Pedersen,** Gaylen 1934- *WhoWest 92*
**Pedersen,** George 1931- *Who 92*
**Pedersen,** Gert K. 1940- *IntWW 91*
**Pedersen,** K. George 1931- *IntWW 91*
**Pedersen,** Katherine L 1937- *AmMWSc 92*
**Pedersen,** Knud B 1932- *AmMWSc 92*
**Pedersen,** Lee G 1938- *AmMWSc 92*
**Pedersen,** Leo Damborg 1946- *AmMWSc 92*
**Pedersen,** Martin Albert 1946- *WhoWest 92*
**Pedersen,** Miriam Swydan 1954- *WhoAmL 92*
**Pedersen,** Olaf 1920- *IntWW 91*
**Pedersen,** Peder Christian 1943- *AmMWSc 92*
**Pedersen,** Peer 1925- *WhoIns 92*
**Pedersen,** Peter L 1939- *AmMWSc 92*
**Pedersen,** R. Lane 1952- *WhoWest 92*
**Pedersen,** Richard F 1925- *WhoAmP 91*
**Pedersen,** Richard Foote 1925- *IntWW 91*
**Pedersen,** Roger Arnold 1944- *AmMWSc 92*
**Pedersen,** Svend Erik 1944- *WhoMW 92*
**Pedersen,** Thor 1945- *IntWW 91*
**Pedersen,** Vagn Moeller 1942- *WhoMW 92*
**Pedersen,** Walter 1924- *WhoRel 92*
**Pedersen,** Wesley Niels 1922- *WhoFI 92*
**Pedersen,** William 1938- *FacFETw*
**Pederson,** Audrey Jean 1926- *WhoAmP 91*
**Pederson,** Bruce Jean Pierre 1954- *WhoAmL 92*
**Pederson,** Clifton *WhoRel 92*
**Pederson,** Con *WhoEnt 92*
**Pederson,** Cynthia S. *DrAPF 91*
**Pederson,** Darryll Thoralf 1939- *AmMWSc 92*
**Pederson,** Donald O 1925- *AmMWSc 92*
**Pederson,** Donald Oscar 1925- *IntWW 91*
**Pederson,** Gordon Roy 1927- *WhoAmP 91*
**Pederson,** Howard Leslie 1914- *WhoFI 92*
**Pederson,** Kathryn Marie 1958- *WhoMW 92*
**Pederson,** Miriam *DrAPF 91*
**Pederson,** Richard Charles 1928- *WhoAmP 91*
**Pederson,** Robert Russell 1956- *WhoFI 92*
**Pederson,** Roger Noel 1930- *AmMWSc 92*
**Pederson,** Sanford Lloyd 1952- *WhoMW 92*
**Pederson,** Thoru Judd 1941- *AmMWSc 92*
**Pederson,** Vernon Clayton 1929- *AmMWSc 92*
**Pederson,** Wayne Allen 1947- *WhoRel 92*
**Pederzani,** Paul P, III 1957- *WhoAmP 91*
**Pederzani,** Paul Peter, Jr 1925- *WhoAmP 91*
**Pedicini,** Louis James 1926- *WhoMW 92*
**Pedigo,** Howard Kenneth 1931- *WhoMW 92*
**Pedigo,** Larry Preston 1938- *AmMWSc 92*
**Pedler,** Frederick 1908- *WrDr 92*
**Pedler,** Frederick Johnson d1991 *Who 92N*
**Pedler,** Frederick Johnson 1908-1991 *ConAu 134*
**Pedler,** Kit 1927-1981 *TwCSFW 91*
**Pedley,** Alan Sydney 1917- *Who 92*
**Pedley,** Geoffrey Stephen 1940- *Who 92*
**Pedley,** Hugh 1852-1923 *ScFEYrs*
**Pedley,** James Munro 1936- *WhoAmP 91*
**Pedley,** Stephen *Who 92*
**Pedlosky,** Joseph 1938- *AmMWSc 92*
**Pedneault,** Roch 1927- *WhoRel 92*
**Pedoe,** Daniel 1910- *AmMWSc 92, WrDr 92*
**Pedolsky,** Alan Robert 1946- *WhoFI 92, WhoWest 92*
**Pedoto,** Gerald Joseph 1948- *WhoMW 92*
**Pedowitz,** James M. 1915- *WhoAmL 92*
**Pedraja,** Rafael R 1929- *AmMWSc 92*
**Pedram,** Marilyn Beth 1937- *WhoMW 92*
**Pedrarias** *HisDSpE*
**Pedraza,** Manuel, Jr. 1951- *WhoHisp 92*
**Pedraza,** Pablo Martinez 1941- *WhoHisp 92*
**Pedraza,** Pedro, Jr. 1946- *WhoHisp 92*
**Pedrell,** Felipe 1841-1922 *NewAmDM*
**Pedrick,** Jean *DrAPF 91*
**Pedrotti,** Leno Stephano 1927- *AmMWSc 92*
**Pedroza,** Arturo 1937- *WhoHisp 92*
**Pedroza,** Gregorio Cruz 1941- *AmMWSc 92*
**Pedroza,** Javier Sergio 1953- *WhoHisp 92*
**Peebles,** Allene Kay 1938- *WhoMW 92*
**Peebles,** Allie Muse 1926- *WhoBlA 92*
**Peebles,** Alvin Roy 1884-1917 *BiInAmS*
**Peebles,** Anne *SmATA 66*
**Peebles,** Carol Lynn 1941- *WhoWest 92*
**Peebles,** Charles Robert 1929- *AmMWSc 92*
**Peebles,** Craig Lewis 1950- *AmMWSc 92*
**Peebles,** Daniel Percy, III 1966- *WhoBlA 92*
**Peebles,** Edward McCrady 1924- *AmMWSc 92*
**Peebles,** Gregory Allen 1963- *WhoWest 92*
**Peebles,** Hugh Oscar, Jr 1933- *AmMWSc 92*
**Peebles,** James Martin 1822-1922 *RelLAm 91*
**Peebles,** Jane 1951- *WhoAmL 92*
**Peebles,** Lucretia Neal Drane 1950- *WhoWest 92*
**Peebles,** Peyton Z, Jr 1934- *AmMWSc 92*
**Peebles,** Phillip J 1935- *AmMWSc 92*
**Peebles,** Phillip James Edwin 1935- *Who 92*
**Peebles-Meyers,** Helen Marjorie 1915- *WhoBlA 92*
**Peebles-Wilkins,** Wilma Cecelia 1945- *WhoBlA 92*
**Peech,** Alan James 1905- *Who 92*
**Peech,** Neil Malcolm 1908- *Who 92*
**Peek,** Booker C. 1940- *WhoBlA 92*
**Peek,** Brent William 1944- *WhoEnt 92*
**Peek,** Francis 1915- *Who 92*
**Peek,** H Milton 1928- *AmMWSc 92*
**Peek,** James Mack 1933- *AmMWSc 92, WhoWest 92*
**Peek,** James Merrell 1936- *AmMWSc 92*
**Peek,** Marvir E. 1940- *WhoBlA 92*
**Peek,** Neal Frazier 1929- *AmMWSc 92*
**Peek,** Richard 1914- *Who 92*
**Peek,** Willis Manco 1943- *WhoMW 92*
**Peekner,** Ray *DrAPF 91, WrDr 92*
**Peel** *Who 92*
**Peel,** Earl 1947- *Who 92*
**Peel,** Bruce Braden 1916- *WrDr 92*
**Peel,** David Alexander Robert 1940- *Who 92*
**Peel,** Deanna Lynn 1962- *WhoAmP 91*
**Peel,** Deborah Gayle 1954- *WhoMW 92*
**Peel,** Edwin 1911- *WrDr 92*
**Peel,** Edwin Arthur 1911- *Who 92*
**Peel,** H. M. 1930- *WrDr 92*
**Peel,** Hazel Mary 1930- *IntAu&W 91*
**Peel,** Jack Armitage 1921- *Who 92*
**Peel,** James Edwin 1924- *AmMWSc 92*
**Peel,** John *Who 92*
**Peel,** John David Yeadon 1941- *Who 92*
**Peel,** John Harold 1904- *Who 92*
**Peel,** Jonathan Sidney 1937- *Who 92*
**Peel,** Malcolm L. 1936- *WrDr 92*
**Peel,** William John 1912- *Who 92*
**Peele,** George 1556?-1596? *RfGEnL 91*
**Peele,** John E., Jr. 1934- *WhoBlA 92*
**Peele,** Luther Martin 1929- *WhoRel 92*
**Peeler,** Diane Faustina 1959- *WhoBlA 92*
**Peeler,** Dudley F, Jr 1931- *AmMWSc 92*
**Peeler,** Harvey S, Jr 1948- *WhoAmP 91*
**Peeler,** Joseph 1930- *Who 92*
**Peeler,** Stuart Thorne 1929- *WhoWest 92*
**Peelle,** Robert W 1929- *AmMWSc 92*
**Peeney,** James Doyle 1933- *WhoFI 92*
**Peeples,** Audrey Rone 1939- *WhoBlA 92*
**Peeples,** Darryl 1943- *WhoBlA 92*
**Peeples,** Earle Edward 1929- *AmMWSc 92*
**Peeples,** Edwin 1915- *WrDr 92*
**Peeples,** Johnston William 1948- *AmMWSc 92*
**Peeples,** Nia *WhoEnt 92*
**Peeples,** Samuel Anthony *TwCWW 91*
**Peeples,** Vernon 1930- *WhoAmP 91*
**Peeples,** Wade Alfred, Jr. 1947- *WhoEnt 92*
**Peeples,** Wayne Jacobson 1940- *AmMWSc 92*
**Peeples,** William Dewey, Jr 1928- *AmMWSc 92*
**Peeps,** Claire Victoria Calder 1956- *WhoWest 92*
**Peer,** Rakesh 1961- *WhoWest 92*
**Peer,** Wilbur Tyrone 1951- *WhoBlA 92*
**Peerce,** Jan 1904-1984 *FacFETw, NewAmDM*
**Peerce,** Larry *IntMPA 92*
**Peerce,** Larry 1935?- *ConTFT 9*
**Peercy,** Paul S 1940- *AmMWSc 92*
**Peerey,** Richard Lee 1948- *WhoRel 92*
**Peers,** Michael Geoffrey 1934- *IntWW 91, Who 92, WhoRel 92*
**Peerschke,** Ellinor Irmgard Barbara 1954- *AmMWSc 92*
**Peerson,** Martin 1571?-1651 *NewAmDM*
**Peerthum,** Satteeanund 1941- *IntWW 91*
**Peery,** Benjamin Franklin, Jr. 1922- *WhoBlA 92*
**Peery,** Charles Eugene 1933- *WhoAmL 92*
**Peery,** Clifford Young 1934- *AmMWSc 92*
**Peery,** Larry Joe 1941- *AmMWSc 92*
**Peery,** Thomas Martin 1909- *AmMWSc 92*
**Peery,** W Kim *WhoAmP 91*
**Peery,** William Whitley, II 1952- *WhoFI 92*
**Pees,** Samuel T 1926- *AmMWSc 92*
**Peet,** Bill 1915- *IntAu&W 91, WrDr 92*
**Peet,** John Carlisle, Jr. 1928- *WhoAmL 92*
**Peet,** Mary Monnig 1947- *AmMWSc 92*
**Peet,** Norton Paul 1944- *AmMWSc 92*

**Peet,** Robert G 1933- *AmMWSc 92*
**Peet,** Robert Krug 1947- *AmMWSc 92*
**Peet,** Ronald Hugh 1925- *Who 92*
**Peet,** Stephen Denison 1831-1914 *BiInAmS*
**Peete,** Calvin 1943- *WhoBlA 92*
**Peete,** Charles Henry, Jr 1924- *AmMWSc 92*
**Peete,** Rodney 1966- *WhoBlA 92*
**Peete,** William P J 1921- *AmMWSc 92*
**Peeters,** Anthony Marie 1944- *WhoFI 92*
**Peeters,** Flor 1903-1986 *NewAmDM*
**Peeters,** Randall Louis 1945- *AmMWSc 92*
**Peets,** Edwin Arnold 1929- *AmMWSc 92*
**Peevey,** Michael Robert 1938- *WhoFI 92*
**Peevy,** Donn M 1949- *WhoAmP 91*
**Peevy,** Walter Jackson 1914- *AmMWSc 92*
**Peffer,** John Roscoe 1928- *AmMWSc 92*
**Pefley,** Norman Gordon 1955- *WhoFI 92*
**Pefley,** Richard K 1921- *AmMWSc 92*
**Pegg,** Anthony Edward 1942- *AmMWSc 92*
**Pegg,** David John 1940- *AmMWSc 92*
**Pegg,** Michael Anstice 1931- *Who 92*
**Pegg,** Philip John 1936- *AmMWSc 92*
**Pegge,** Cecil Denis 1902- *IntAu&W 91, WrDr 92*
**Peggie,** Robert Galloway Emslie 1929- *Who 92*
**Peglar,** George W 1922- *AmMWSc 92*
**Pegler,** Alfred Ernest 1924- *Who 92*
**Pegler,** James Basil Holmes 1912- *Who 92*
**Pegler,** Westbrook 1894-1969 *FacFETw*
**Pegolotti,** James Alfred 1933- *AmMWSc 92*
**Pegorsch,** Dennis William 1941- *WhoRel 92*
**Pegram,** Dennis James 1954- *WhoRel 92*
**Pegram,** George Vernon, Jr 1937- *AmMWSc 92*
**Pegram,** John Braxton 1938- *WhoAmL 92*
**Pegues,** Robert L., Jr. 1936- *WhoBlA 92*
**Pegues,** W. Wesley 1956- *WhoRel 92*
**Pegues,** Wennette West 1936- *WhoBlA 92*
**Peguese,** Charles R. 1938- *WhoBlA 92*
**Peguy,** Charles 1873-1914 *FacFETw, GuFrLit 1*
**Pehl,** Jeffrey A. 1961- *WhoFI 92*
**Pehl,** Richard Henry 1936- *AmMWSc 92, WhoWest 92*
**Pehler,** James C 1942- *WhoAmP 91*
**Pehlke,** Robert Donald 1933- *AmMWSc 92*
**Pehnt,** Wolfgang 1931- *WrDr 92*
**Pehrson,** Joseph Ralph 1950- *WhoEnt 92*
**Pei Ieoh Ming** 1917- *IntWW 91*
**Pei Jianzhang** 1927- *IntWW 91*
**Pei Shengji** *IntWW 91*
**Pei,** David Chung-Tze 1929- *AmMWSc 92*
**Pei,** I M 1917- *FacFETw, RComAH*
**Pei,** Mario 1901-1978 *FacFETw*
**Pei,** Richard Yu-Sien 1927- *AmMWSc 92*
**Pei,** Shin-Shem 1949- *AmMWSc 92*
**Pei,** Wenzhong 1904-1982 *FacFETw*
**Peick,** Doris *WhoAmP 91*
**Peierls,** Ronald F 1935- *AmMWSc 92*
**Peierls,** Rudolf 1907- *Who 92*
**Peierls,** Rudolf Ernst 1907- *IntWW 91*
**Peifer,** James J 1924- *AmMWSc 92*
**Peifer,** Janet Marie 1945- *WhoRel 92*
**Peiffer,** Elizabeth Anne 1954- *WhoWest 92*
**Peiffer,** Howard R 1931- *AmMWSc 92*
**Peiffer,** Rober Louis, Jr 1947- *AmMWSc 92*
**Peightel,** William Edgar 1927- *AmMWSc 92*
**Peikari,** Behrouz 1938- *AmMWSc 92*
**Peil,** Kelly M *AmMWSc 92*
**Peil,** Timothy Scott 1952- *WhoMW 92*
**Peimbert,** Manuel 1941- *IntWW 91*
**Peinado,** Arnold B., Jr. 1931- *WhoHisp 92*
**Peinado,** Bernardo 1961- *WhoWest 92*
**Peinado,** Federico 1956- *WhoHisp 92*
**Peinado,** Luis Armando 1929- *WhoHisp 92*
**Peinado,** Rolando E 1938- *AmMWSc 92*
**Peine,** Ollie Campbell 1945- *WhoRel 92*
**Peinemann,** Edith 1939- *IntWW 91*
**Peiner,** Werner 1897- *EncTR 91*
**Peiper,** Joachim 1915-1976 *EncTR 91 [port]*
**Peirano,** Lawrence Edward 1929- *WhoWest 92*
**Peirce,** Benjamin 1809-1880 *BiInAmS*
**Peirce,** Benjamin Osgood 1854-1914 *BiInAmS*
**Peirce,** Charles Sanders 1839-1914 *BiInAmS*
**Peirce,** Charles Santiago Sanders 1839-1914 *BenetAL 91*
**Peirce,** Edmund Converse, II 1917- *AmMWSc 92*
**Peirce,** Frederick Fairbanks 1953- *WhoAmL 92*
**Peirce,** George 1883-1919 *BiInAmS*
**Peirce,** James Jeffrey 1949- *AmMWSc 92*
**Peirce,** James Mills 1834-1906 *BiInAmS*
**Peirce,** John Wentworth 1946- *AmMWSc 92*
**Peirce,** Lincoln Carret 1930- *AmMWSc 92*
**Peirce,** Martin 1936- *Who 92*
**Peirce,** Melusina Fay 1836- *BenetAL 91*
**Peirce,** Neal R 1932- *IntAu&W 91, WrDr 92*
**Peirce,** Robert Bentley 1939- *WhoEnt 92*
**Peirce,** Robert Neil, Jr 1938- *WhoAmP 91*
**Peirce,** William 1590?-1641 *BenetAL 91, BiInAmS*
**Peirce,** William Spangar 1938- *WhoFI 92, WhoMW 92*
**Peirent,** Robert John 1921- *AmMWSc 92*
**Peiris,** Gamini Lakshman 1946- *IntWW 91*
**Peirse,** Henry G. De La P. B. *Who 92*
**Peirse,** Richard 1931- *Who 92*
**Peirson,** Mrs. *EncAmaz 91*
**Peirson,** David Robert 1939- *AmMWSc 92*
**Peirson,** George Ewell 1957- *WhoEnt 92*
**Peirson,** Gwynne Walker 1921- *WhoBlA 92*
**Peirson,** Margaret Ellen 1942- *Who 92*
**Peisach,** Jack 1932- *AmMWSc 92*
**Peisach,** Max 1926- *IntWW 91*
**Peiser,** Herbert Steffen 1917- *AmMWSc 92*
**Peiser,** Judith Louise 1945- *WhoEnt 92*
**Peiser,** Richard Bondy 1948- *WhoWest 92*
**Peisinger,** Jon Robert 1947- *WhoEnt 92*
**Peiss,** Clarence Norman 1922- *AmMWSc 92*
**Peissner,** Lorraine C 1919- *AmMWSc 92*
**Peithman,** Roscoe Edward 1913- *AmMWSc 92*
**Peitz,** Betsy 1948- *AmMWSc 92*
**Peitz,** Earl F 1930- *WhoIns 92*
**Peitzman,** Lawrence 1947- *WhoAmL 92*
**Peixinho,** Jorge 1940- *ConCom 92*
**Pejic,** Dragoslav 1929- *IntWW 91*
**Pejovich,** Ted *DrAPF 91*
**Pejza,** John Philip 1934- *WhoRel 92*
**Pekala,** Phillip H *AmMWSc 92*
**Pekarek,** Robert Sidney 1940- *AmMWSc 92*
**Pekarsky,** Daniel *WhoRel 92*
**Pekas,** Jerome Charles 1936- *AmMWSc 92*
**Pekau,** Oscar A 1941- *AmMWSc 92*
**Pekeris,** Chaim L. 1908- *IntWW 91*
**Pekeris,** Chaim Leib 1908- *AmMWSc 92*
**Pekich,** Elizabeth Krams 1948- *WhoAmL 92*
**Pekkala,** Ahti Antti Johannes 1924- *IntWW 91*
**Peko,** James Anthony 1967- *WhoFI 92*
**Pekoz,** Teoman 1937- *AmMWSc 92*
**Peladeau,** Pierre 1925- *WhoFI 92*
**Pelaez,** Armantina R. 1948- *WhoRel 92*
**Pelaez,** Joaquin 1954- *WhoHisp 92*
**Pelagius** 350?-425? *EncEarC*
**Pelagius I** *EncEarC*
**Pelagius II** *EncEarC*
**Pelanda,** Kevin Lee 1956- *WhoAmL 92*
**Pelate,** Sharon Mabel 1940- *WhoEnt 92*
**Pelavin,** Michael Allen 1936- *WhoAmL 92*
**Pelayo,** Jose Alfonso Patino 1955- *WhoHisp 92*
**Pelc,** Karol I. 1935- *WhoMW 92*
**Pelcovits,** Robert Alan 1954- *AmMWSc 92*
**Pelczar,** Francis A 1939- *AmMWSc 92*
**Pelczarski,** Karen Ann 1960- *WhoAmL 92*
**Pele** 1940- *FacFETw [port], IntWW 91*
**Peled,** Abraham 1945- *AmMWSc 92*
**Peleg,** David 1923- *IntWW 91*
**Pelehac,** Kenneth Michael 1963- *WhoMW 92*
**Peletsis,** Georgy 1947- *ConCom 92*
**Pelfrey,** Lloyd Marvin 1931- *WhoRel 92*
**Pelham** *Who 92*
**Pelham,** Hugh Reginald Brentnall 1954- *IntWW 91, Who 92*
**Pelham,** Randy C. 1948- *WhoMW 92*
**Pelham,** William 1759-1827 *AmPeW*
**Pelham Burn,** Angus Maitland 1931- *Who 92*
**Pelicano,** Stephen Michael 1958- *WhoFI 92*
**Peligrad,** Costel 1945- *WhoMW 92*
**Pelikan,** Edward Warren 1926- *AmMWSc 92*
**Pelikan,** Jaroslav 1923- *IntWW 91, WrDr 92*
**Pelikan,** Jaroslav Jan 1923- *WhoRel 92*
**Pelikan,** Jaroslav Jan, Jr. 1923- *RelLAm 91*
**Peline,** Val P 1930- *AmMWSc 92*
**Pelisek,** Frank John 1930- *WhoFI 92*
**Pelishek,** Rick Charles 1955- *WhoMW 92*
**Pelissier,** Jacques Daniel Paul 1917- *IntWW 91*
**Pelíza,** Robert John 1920- *IntWW 91, Who 92*
**Peljee,** Myatavyn 1927- *IntWW 91*
**Pelka,** David Gerard 1943- *AmMWSc 92*
**Pelkie,** J W *TwCSFW 91*
**Pelkonen,** John Peter 1937- *WhoRel 92*
**Pell,** Claiborne 1918- *AlmAP 92 [port], WhoAmP 91*
**Pell,** Claiborne de Borda 1918- *IntWW 91*
**Pell,** Derek *DrAPF 91*
**Pell,** Douglas Stewart 1952- *WhoEnt 92*
**Pell,** Duane *WhoAmP 91*
**Pell,** Erik Mauritz 1923- *AmMWSc 92*
**Pell,** Ernest Eugene 1937- *WhoWest 92*
**Pell,** Eva Joy 1948- *AmMWSc 92*
**Pell,** Jonathan Laurence 1949- *WhoEnt 92*
**Pell,** Kynric M 1938- *AmMWSc 92*
**Pell,** Mary Chase 1915- *WhoMW 92*
**Pell,** Mel 1942- *AmMWSc 92*
**Pell,** Sidney 1922- *AmMWSc 92*
**Pell,** Wilbur Frank, Jr. 1915- *WhoAmL 92, WhoMW 92*
**Pella,** Jerome Jacob 1939- *AmMWSc 92, WhoWest 92*
**Pella,** Milton Orville 1914- *AmMWSc 92*
**Pellan,** Alfred 1906- *FacFETw*
**Pellar,** Ronald 1930- *WhoFI 92*
**Pellat,** Charles Lucien Paul 1914- *IntWW 91*
**Pellecchia,** John Michael 1958- *WhoAmL 92*
**Pelleg,** Amir 1944- *AmMWSc 92*
**Pellegrini,** Claudio 1935- *AmMWSc 92, WhoWest 92*
**Pellegrini,** Frank C 1940- *AmMWSc 92*
**Pellegrini,** John P, Jr 1926- *AmMWSc 92*
**Pellegrini,** Maria C 1947- *AmMWSc 92*
**Pellegrini,** Robert J 1941- *AmMWSc 92, WhoWest 92*
**Pellegrino,** Antonio Paulo 1966- *WhoEnt 92*
**Pellegrino,** Edmund Daniel 1920- *AmMWSc 92, IntWW 91*
**Pellegrino,** James Leonard 1938- *WhoAmP 91*
**Pellegrino,** Michele A 1940- *AmMWSc 92*
**Pellenbarg,** Robert Ernest 1949- *AmMWSc 92*
**Peller,** Leonard 1928- *AmMWSc 92*
**Pellerano,** Maria B. 1957- *ConAu 133*
**Pellereau,** Peter John Mitchell 1921- *Who 92*
**Pellerin,** Auguste 1852-1929 *ThHEIm*
**Pellerin,** Charles James, Jr 1944- *AmMWSc 92*
**Pellerite,** James John 1926- *WhoEnt 92*
**Pelletier,** Alcid Milton 1926- *WhoMW 92*
**Pelletier,** Charles A 1932- *AmMWSc 92*
**Pelletier,** Claude Henri 1941- *WhoFI 92*
**Pelletier,** Claudia Patricia 1960- *WhoFI 92*
**Pelletier,** Frederick H. 1916- *WhoRel 92*
**Pelletier,** Georges H 1939- *AmMWSc 92*
**Pelletier,** Gerard 1919- *IntWW 91*
**Pelletier,** Gerard Eugene 1930- *AmMWSc 92*
**Pelletier,** James Lewis 1930- *WhoAmL 92*
**Pelletier,** Joan Wick 1942- *AmMWSc 92*
**Pelletier,** Joseph J 1953- *WhoIns 92*
**Pelletier,** Nancy *DrAPF 91*
**Pelletier,** Omer 1929- *AmMWSc 92*
**Pelletier,** Pierre 1919- *IntWW 91*
**Pelletier,** R Marc 1946- *AmMWSc 92*
**Pelletier,** Raymond 1910- *IntWW 91*
**Pelletier,** S William 1924- *AmMWSc 92*
**Pelletier,** Wilfred 1896-1982 *NewAmDM*
**Pelletreau,** Robert H, Jr 1935- *WhoAmP 91*
**Pelletreau,** Robert Halsey, Jr. 1935- *IntWW 91*
**Pellett,** David Earl 1938- *AmMWSc 92*
**Pellett,** Harold M 1938- *AmMWSc 92*
**Pellett,** Norman Eugene 1934- *AmMWSc 92*
**Pellew** *Who 92*
**Pellew,** Mark Edward 1942- *Who 92*
**Pellew-Harvey,** Claughton 1890- *TwCPaSc*
**Pelley,** Janet R 1932- *WhoAmP 91*
**Pelley,** William Dudley 1890-1965 *BiDExR, RelLAm 91*
**Pelleya,** Roberto 1956- *WhoAmL 92*
**Pelli,** Cesar 1926- *FacFETw, IntWW 91*
**Pelli,** Cesar 1927?- *News 91 [port]*
**Pellicane,** Mary 1922- *WhoRel 92*
**Pelliciaro,** Edward Joseph 1921- *AmMWSc 92*
**Pellicer,** Angel 1948- *AmMWSc 92*
**Pellicer,** Baldo Alfredo 1955- *WhoFI 92*
**Pellier,** Laurence *AmMWSc 92*
**Pellinen,** Donald Gary 1939- *AmMWSc 92*
**Pelling,** Anthony Adair 1934- *Who 92*
**Pelling,** Henry Mathison 1920- *Who 92, WrDr 92*
**Pellini,** William S 1917- *AmMWSc 92*
**Pellino,** Charles Edward, Jr. 1943- *WhoAmL 92*
**Pellis,** Neal Robert 1944- *AmMWSc 92*
**Pellizzari,** Edo Domenico 1942- *AmMWSc 92*
**Pellon,** Joseph 1928- *AmMWSc 92*
**Pellone,** David Thomas 1944- *WhoFI 92, WhoWest 92*
**Pelloux,** Regis M N 1931- *AmMWSc 92*
**Pellow,** Dick 1931- *WhoAmP 91*
**Pellow,** William T *WhoAmP 91*
**Pelly,** Derek Roland 1929- *IntWW 91, Who 92*
**Pelly,** Frank Michael 1933- *WhoAmP 91*
**Pelly,** John 1918- *Who 92*
**Pelofsky,** Joel 1937- *WhoMW 92*
**Peloquin,** Bruce Simon 1936- *WhoAmP 91*
**Peloquin,** Robert Dolan 1929- *WhoFI 92*
**Peloquin,** Stanley J 1921- *AmMWSc 92*
**Pelosi,** Evelyn Tyminski 1938- *AmMWSc 92*
**Pelosi,** Lorenzo Fred 1944- *AmMWSc 92*
**Pelosi,** Nancy *WhoAmP 91*
**Pelosi,** Nancy 1940- *AlmAP 92 [port]*
**Pelosi,** Nancy 1941- *WhoWest 92*
**Pelosi,** Ronald 1934- *WhoAmP 91*
**Pelosi,** Stanford Salvatore, Jr 1938- *AmMWSc 92*
**Peloso,** John F. X. 1934- *WhoAmL 92*
**Peloso,** Joseph F 1946- *WhoIns 92*
**Pelote,** Dorothy B. 1929- *WhoBlA 92*
**Pelote,** Dorothy B 1934- *WhoAmP 91*
**Pelotte,** Donald Edmond 1945- *WhoRel 92, WhoWest 92*
**Peloubet,** Francis Nathan 1831-1920 *RelLAm 91*
**Pelowski,** Gene P, Jr 1952- *WhoAmP 91*
**Pelphrey,** Michael Wayne 1946- *WhoFI 92*
**Pel'she,** Arvid Yanovich 1899-1983 *SovUnBD*
**Pelt,** Roland J 1931- *AmMWSc 92*
**Peltason,** Jack W. 1923- *IntWW 91*
**Peltason,** Jack Walter 1923- *WhoWest 92*
**Peltier,** Arma Martin 1938- *WhoBlA 92*
**Peltier,** Charles Francis 1945- *AmMWSc 92*
**Peltier,** Eugene J 1910- *AmMWSc 92*
**Peltier,** Hubert Conrad 1925- *AmMWSc 92*
**Peltier,** Joseph 1929- *WhoAmP 91*
**Peltier,** Leonard Francis 1920- *AmMWSc 92*
**Peltier,** Mary Anne 1936- *WhoRel 92*
**Peltier,** Ronald James 1949- *WhoFI 92*
**Peltier,** Wanda Jo 1933- *WhoAmP 91*
**Peltier,** William Richard 1943- *AmMWSc 92*
**Pelto,** Jonathan W 1961- *WhoAmP 91*
**Pelton,** Harold Marcel 1922- *WhoWest 92*
**Pelton,** Horace Wilbur 1906- *WhoAmP 91*
**Pelton,** Joan Elisabeth Mason 1932- *WhoEnt 92*
**Pelton,** John Forrester 1924- *AmMWSc 92*
**Pelton,** Joseph Neal 1943- *WhoWest 92*
**Pelton,** Michael Ramsay 1940- *AmMWSc 92*
**Pelton,** Russell Meredith, Jr. 1938- *WhoAmL 92, WhoMW 92*
**Pelton,** Virginia Lue 1928- *WhoFI 92*
**Pelton,** Warren J. 1923- *ConAu 133*
**Pelton,** William Harvey 1946- *WhoFI 92*
**Peltser,** Tatiana Ivanovna 1904- *IntWW 91*
**Peltsman,** Michael 1947- *LiExTwC*
**Peltzer,** Douglas Lea 1938- *WhoFI 92*
**Peltzer,** Mary Kay 1924- *WhoAmP 91*
**Peltzman,** Alan 1937- *AmMWSc 92*
**Peltzman,** Sam 1940- *WhoFI 92, WhoMW 92*
**Peluffo,** Luisa 1941- *IntAu&W 91*
**Pelusa,** Joan-Ellen Michelle 1960- *WhoRel 92*
**Pelusi,** Philip Paul 1939- *WhoFI 92*
**Peluso,** Ada 1941- *AmMWSc 92*
**Peluso,** Theodore Louis 1933- *WhoFI 92*
**Pelz,** Dwight *WhoAmP 91*
**Pelzer,** Charles Francis 1935- *AmMWSc 92*
**Pelzer,** Christopher Victor 1954- *WhoEnt 92*
**Pember Reeves,** Maud d1953 *BiDBrF 2*
**Pemberton** *Who 92*
**Pemberton,** Alan Brooke 1923- *Who 92*
**Pemberton,** Alexander 1957- *TwCPaSc*
**Pemberton,** Bradley Powell 1952- *WhoMW 92*
**Pemberton,** Carol Ann 1939- *WhoMW 92*
**Pemberton,** David Melbert 1926- *WhoBlA 92*
**Pemberton,** Desmond Valdo 1927- *Who 92*
**Pemberton,** Donald Gordon 1934- *WhoAmP 91*
**Pemberton,** Francis 1916- *Who 92*
**Pemberton,** Henry 1694-1771 *BlkwCEP*
**Pemberton,** Henry 1826-1911 *BiInAmS*
**Pemberton,** Henry, Jr 1855-1913 *BiInAmS*
**Pemberton,** John 1912- *Who 92*
**Pemberton,** John, III 1928- *WhoRel 92*
**Pemberton,** Judith Ann 1947- *WhoAmL 92*
**Pemberton,** Larry Norvell 1932- *WhoMW 92*
**Pemberton,** Margaret 1943- *IntAu&W 91, WrDr 92*
**Pemberton,** Matthew Anthony 1947- *WhoWest 92*
**Pemberton,** Max 1863-1950 *ScFEYrs*
**Pemberton,** Nan *WrDr 92*
**Pemberton,** Priscilla Elizabeth 1919- *WhoBlA 92*
**Pemberton,** Ronald Ray 1950- *WhoFI 92*

**Pemble,** Richard Hoppe 1941- *AmMWSc 92*
**Pembroke,** Earl of 1939- *Who 92*
**Pembroke,** James Donald 1948- *WhoAmL 92*
**Pembroke,** Mary, Countess of *Who 92*
**Pembroke,** Richard C, Sr 1933- *WhoAmP 91*
**Pempel,** Amy Elizabeth 1960- *WhoEnt 92*
**Pemrick,** Raymond Edward 1920- *AmMWSc 92*
**Pemsler,** J Paul 1929- *AmMWSc 92*
**Pen,** Jan 1921- *WrDr 92*
**Pena,** Ada R. *WhoHisp 92*
**Pena,** Albar A. 1931- *WhoHisp 92*
**Pena,** Alejandro 1959- *WhoHisp 92*
**Pena,** Alvaro *WhoHisp 92*
**Pena,** Angel R. *WhoHisp 92*
**Pena,** Beatriz M. 1939- *WhoHisp 92*
**Pena,** Carmen Aida 1941- *WhoHisp 92*
**Pena,** Celinda Marie 1961- *WhoHisp 92*
**Pena,** Daniel Silva, Jr. 1937- *WhoHisp 92*
**Pena,** Eduardo 1935- *WhoHisp 92*
**Pena,** Elizabeth *WhoEnt 92*
**Pena,** Elizabeth 1959- *WhoHisp 92*
**Pena,** Elizabeth 1961- *IntMPA 92*
**Pena,** Emilio Thomas 1951- *WhoHisp 92*
**Pena,** Englantina Canales 1927- *WhoHisp 92*
**Pena,** Enrique H. *WhoHisp 92*
**Pena,** Ervie 1934- *WhoHisp 92*
**Pena,** Estela M. *WhoHisp 92*
**Pena,** Federico *WhoAmP 91*
**Pena,** Federico 1947- *WhoHisp 92*
**Pena,** Federico Fabian 1947- *WhoWest 92*
**Pena,** Fernando, Jr. 1937- *WhoHisp 92*
**Pena,** George A. *WhoHisp 92*
**Pena,** Geronimo 1967- *WhoHisp 92*
**Pena,** Gladys Violeta 1947- *WhoHisp 92*
**Pena,** Herman *WhoHisp 92*
**Pena,** Hilario S. 1910- *WhoHisp 92*
**Pena,** Hugo Gabriel 1928- *AmMWSc 92*
**Pena,** Jesus J. 1947- *WhoHisp 92*
**Pena,** Jesus Reyes 1949- *WhoHisp 92*
**Pena,** John J., Jr. 1954- *WhoHisp 92*
**Pena,** Jorge Augusto 1919- *AmMWSc 92*
**Pena,** Juan Jose 1945- *WhoAmP 91, WhoWest 92*
**Pena,** Juan-Paz 1942- *WhoHisp 92*
**Pena,** Maggie *WhoHisp 92*
**Pena,** Manuel *WhoHisp 92*
**Pena,** Manuel, Jr 1924- *WhoAmP 91, WhoHisp 92, WhoWest 92*
**Pena,** Manuel F. 1939- *WhoHisp 92*
**Pena,** Octavio G. 1941- *WhoHisp 92*
**Pena,** Paco 1942- *IntWW 91, Who 92*
**Pena,** Raymond 1938- *WhoHisp 92*
**Pena,** Raymundo *WhoHisp 92*
**Pena,** Raymundo Joseph 1934- *WhoRel 92*
**Pena,** Richard 1948- *WhoAmL 92*
**Pena,** Robert Bubba 1949- *WhoBlA 92*
**Pena,** Steve Andrew 1955- *WhoHisp 92*
**Pena,** Tony 1957- *WhoBlA 92, WhoHisp 92*
**Pena Clos,** Sergio *WhoAmP 91, WhoHisp 92*
**Pena Munoz,** Margarita 1937- *IntAu&W 91*
**Pena Pena,** Joaquin *WhoAmP 91, WhoHisp 92*
**Pena y Montenegro,** Alonso de 1596-1687 *HisDSpE*
**Penaherrera Padilla,** Blasco 1934- *IntWW 91*
**Penalosa,** Enrique 1930- *IntWW 91*
**Penaloza,** Charles Aaron 1948- *WhoHisp 92*
**Penaloza,** Lisa N. 1958- *WhoHisp 92*
**Penaloza,** Robert Louis 1955- *WhoHisp 92*
**Penaluna,** Carolyn Irene 1961- *WhoFI 92*
**Penaluna,** Daniel Thomas 1962- *WhoMW 92*
**Penalver,** Fernando de 1765-1837 *HisDSpE*
**Penalver,** Rafael A., Jr. 1951- *WhoHisp 92*
**Penalver y Cardenas,** Luis Ignacio 1749-1810 *HisDSpE*
**Penaranda,** Frank E. 1939- *WhoHisp 92*
**Penaranda,** Oscar *DrAPF 91*
**Penbera,** Joseph John 1947- *WhoWest 92*
**Pence,** Harry Edmond 1937- *AmMWSc 92*
**Pence,** Ira Wilson, Jr *AmMWSc 92*
**Pence,** Jeffrey Alan 1958- *WhoMW 92*
**Pence,** Jerry Glenn 1953- *WhoRel 92*
**Pence,** John Thomas 1941- *WhoMW 92*
**Pence,** Judith Ann 1933- *WhoEnt 92*
**Pence,** Leland Hadley 1911- *AmMWSc 92, WhoMW 92*
**Pence,** Patrick John 1954- *WhoMW 92*
**Penceal,** Bernadette Whitley 1944- *WhoBlA 92*
**Penchansky,** David 1951- *WhoRel 92*
**Penchas,** Shmuel 1939- *IntWW 91*
**Penchina,** Claude Michel 1939- *AmMWSc 92*
**Penck,** A. R. 1939- *IntWW 91, WorArt 1980 [port]*
**Pendell-Frantz,** Peggy Metzka 1947- *WhoMW 92*
**Pender,** Baron 1933- *Who 92*
**Pender,** Jack 1918- *TwCPaSc*
**Pender,** John H 1930- *WhoIns 92*
**Pender,** John Hurst 1930- *WhoFI 92*
**Pender,** Lydia 1907- *IntAu&W 91, WrDr 92*
**Pender,** Melvin 1937- *BlkOlyM, WhoBlA 92*
**Pender,** Michael Roger 1926- *WhoFI 92*
**Pender,** Thomas Raymond 1962- *WhoAmL 92*
**Pender,** William Clark 1955- *WhoRel 92*
**Penderecki,** Krzysztof 1933- *NewAmDM*
**Penderecki,** Krzysztof 1933- *ConCom 92, FacFETw, IntWW 91, Who 92*
**Pendered,** Richard Geoffrey 1921- *Who 92*
**Pendergast,** David R *AmMWSc 92*
**Pendergast,** Edward G 1938- *WhoIns 92*
**Pendergast,** Edward Gaylord 1938- *WhoFI 92*
**Pendergast,** James *DrAPF 91*
**Pendergast,** Thomas Joseph 1872-1945 *FacFETw*
**Penderghast,** Thomas Frederick 1936- *WhoWest 92*
**Pendergraft,** David William 1956- *WhoEnt 92*
**Pendergraft,** Michele M. 1954- *WhoBlA 92*
**Pendergraft,** Phyllis M 1937- *WhoAmP 91*
**Pendergrass,** Emma H. *WhoBlA 92*
**Pendergrass,** Levester 1946- *AmMWSc 92*
**Pendergrass,** Margaret E. 1912- *WhoBlA 92*
**Pendergrass,** Paula Ann 1938- *WhoMW 92*
**Pendergrass,** Robert Nixon 1918- *AmMWSc 92*
**Pendergrass,** Teddy 1950- *NewAmDM, WhoEnt 92*
**Pendergrass,** Theodore D. 1950- *WhoBlA 92*
**Pendergrass,** Thomas Wayne 1945- *AmMWSc 92*
**Penders,** John Patrick 1942- *WhoAmL 92*
**Pendexter,** Hugh 1875-1940 *BenetAL 91, ScFEYrs A, TwCWW 91*
**Pendexter,** Joan Marie 1947- *WhoAmP 91*
**Pendland,** Jacquelyn C *AmMWSc 92*
**Pendle,** Joseph 1933- *TwCPaSc*
**Pendlebury,** Edward 1925- *Who 92*
**Pendleton,** Austin 1940- *IntMPA 92*
**Pendleton,** Bill *WhoAmP 91*
**Pendleton,** Billy 1934- *WhoAmP 91*
**Pendleton,** Brian Clarke 1941- *WhoAmP 91*
**Pendleton,** Don 1927- *IntAu&W 91, WrDr 92*
**Pendleton,** Edmund 1721-1803 *BlkwEAR*
**Pendleton,** Edmund E 1922- *WhoAmP 91*
**Pendleton,** Edmund Monroe 1815-1884 *BiInAmS*
**Pendleton,** Florence Howard *WhoAmP 91*
**Pendleton,** Ford *TwCWW 91*
**Pendleton,** Gloria Bell 1927- *WhoRel 92*
**Pendleton,** Hugh Nelson, III 1935- *AmMWSc 92*
**Pendleton,** John Davis 1912- *AmMWSc 92*
**Pendleton,** Mark Edsel 1952- *WhoMW 92*
**Pendleton,** Moses Robert Andrew 1949- *WhoEnt 92*
**Pendleton,** Othniel Alsop 1911- *WhoFI 92, WhoWest 92*
**Pendleton,** Peggy A *WhoAmP 91*
**Pendleton,** Robert Grubb 1939- *AmMWSc 92*
**Pendleton,** Ronald Kenneth 1940- *WhoWest 92*
**Pendleton,** Terry Lee 1960- *WhoBlA 92*
**Pendleton,** Thelma Brown 1911- *WhoMW 92*
**Pendleton,** Verne H., Jr. 1945- *WhoWest 92*
**Pendleton,** Wesley William 1914- *AmMWSc 92*
**Pendleton,** William Kimbrough 1817-1899 *AmPeW*
**Pendley,** Larry M. 1942- *WhoMW 92*
**Pendower,** John Edward Hicks 1927- *Who 92*
**Pendower,** T.C.H. 1899-1976 *TwCWW 91*
**Pendray,** G Edward 1901-1987 *FacFETw*
**Pendred,** Piers Loughnan 1943- *Who 92*
**Pendrill,** Viviana *WhoHisp 92*
**Pendry,** John Brian 1943- *Who 92*
**Pendry,** Thomas 1934- *Who 92*
**Pendse,** Pratapsinha C *AmMWSc 92*
**Pendygraft,** George William 1946- *WhoAmL 92*
**Pene,** Jacques Jean 1937- *AmMWSc 92*
**Pene du Bois,** William 1916- *SmATA 68 [port]*
**Penelas,** Alex *WhoHisp 92*
**Penelton,** Barbara Spencer 1937- *WhoBlA 92*
**Penfield,** Janet G. Harbison 1916- *WhoRel 92*
**Penfield,** Marjorie Porter 1942- *AmMWSc 92*
**Penfield,** Paul, Jr 1933- *AmMWSc 92*
**Penfield,** Robert Harrison 1921- *AmMWSc 92*
**Penfield,** Samuel Lewis 1856-1906 *BiInAmS*
**Penfold,** Nita *DrAPF 91*
**Penfold,** Robert Bernard 1916- *Who 92*
**Peng Chong** 1933- *IntWW 91*
**Peng Deqing** 1915- *IntWW 91*
**Peng Huanwu** 1915- *IntWW 91*
**Peng Jiaqing** 1909- *IntWW 91*
**Peng Shilu** 1925- *IntWW 91*
**Peng Zhen** 1902- *IntWW 91*
**Peng,** Andrew Chung Yen 1924- *AmMWSc 92*
**Peng,** Fred Ming-Sheng 1936- *AmMWSc 92*
**Peng,** Jen-chieh 1949- *AmMWSc 92*
**Peng,** Liang-Chuan 1936- *WhoFI 92*
**Peng,** Shi-Kaung 1941- *AmMWSc 92*
**Peng,** Song-Tsuen 1937- *AmMWSc 92*
**Peng,** Syd Syh-Deng 1939- *AmMWSc 92*
**Peng,** Tai-Chan 1928- *AmMWSc 92*
**Peng,** Yeh-Shan 1936- *AmMWSc 92*
**Pengelley,** David John 1952- *AmMWSc 92*
**Pengelley,** Eric T 1919- *AmMWSc 92*
**Pengelly,** Richard Anthony 1925- *Who 92*
**Penger,** Christian 1850?-1902 *BiInAmS*
**Penglase,** Frank Dennis 1940- *WhoFI 92*
**Pengra,** James G 1933- *AmMWSc 92*
**Pengra,** Robert Monroe 1926- *AmMWSc 92*
**Pengreep,** William *IntAu&W 91X*
**Penha,** James W. *DrAPF 91*
**Penhale,** Polly Ann 1947- *AmMWSc 92*
**Penhallegon,** John Russell 1954- *WhoAmL 92*
**Penhallow,** David Pearce 1854-1910 *BiInAmS*
**Penhallow,** Richard 1906- *WhoAmP 91*
**Penhallow,** Samuel 1665-1726 *BenetAL 91*
**Penhallurick,** Kent Walker 1951- *WhoAmL 92*
**Penhoet,** Edward Etienne 1940- *AmMWSc 92*
**Penhollow,** John O 1934- *AmMWSc 92*
**Penhos,** Juan Carlos 1918- *AmMWSc 92*
**Penick,** George Dial 1922- *AmMWSc 92*
**Penick,** James Lal, Jr. 1932- *WrDr 92*
**Penick,** John Edgar 1944- *IntAu&W 91*
**Penick,** Nell Ann Inman 1944- *WhoMW 92*
**Penick,** Robert Douglas 1943- *WhoIns 92*
**Penico,** Anthony Joseph 1923- *AmMWSc 92*
**Penikett,** Antony David John 1945- *WhoWest 92*
**Penington,** David Geoffrey 1930- *IntWW 91, Who 92*
**Penisten,** Gary D 1931- *WhoAmP 91*
**Penisten,** Gary Dean 1931- *WhoFI 92*
**Peniston,** Louis Tandy 1919- *WhoAmP 91*
**Penix,** Bill 1922- *WhoAmP 91*
**Penjore,** Lyonpo Sangye 1928- *IntWW 91*
**Penk,** Anna Michaelides 1928- *AmMWSc 92*
**Penkoff,** Diane Witmer 1945- *WhoWest 92*
**Penkovsky,** Oleg 1919-1963 *FacFETw*
**Penland,** James Granville 1951- *AmMWSc 92*
**Penley,** William Henry 1917- *Who 92*
**Penlidis,** Alexander 1957- *AmMWSc 92*
**Penlington,** Ross Grange 1931- *Who 92*
**Penman,** Ian Dalgleish 1931- *Who 92*
**Penman,** John 1913- *Who 92*
**Penman,** Paul D 1937- *AmMWSc 92*
**Penman,** Sheldon 1930- *AmMWSc 92*
**Penn & Teller** *News 92-1 [port]*
**Penn,** Anna Belle Rhodes 1865- *NotBlAW 92*
**Penn,** Arthur 1922- *IntDcF 2-2, IntMPA 92, IntWW 91*
**Penn,** Arthur 1942- *AmMWSc 92*
**Penn,** Arthur Hiller 1922- *WhoEnt 92*
**Penn,** Benjamin Grant 1947- *AmMWSc 92*
**Penn,** Cecil Ray 1948- *WhoRel 92*
**Penn,** Charles E. 1928- *WhoBlA 92*
**Penn,** Christopher *IntMPA 92*
**Penn,** David Clyde 1953- *WhoRel 92*
**Penn,** David Joseph 1944- *WhoRel 92*
**Penn,** David Louis 1958- *WhoMW 92*
**Penn,** Eric 1916- *Who 92*
**Penn,** Howard Lewis 1946- *AmMWSc 92*
**Penn,** Irving 1917- *DcTwDes, FacFETw, IntWW 91*
**Penn,** J. B. 1944- *WhoFI 92*
**Penn,** John *WrDr 92*
**Penn,** John 1921- *TwCPaSc*
**Penn,** John Garrett 1932- *WhoAmL 92, WhoBlA 92*
**Penn,** John S 1926- *WhoAmP 91*
**Penn,** Luther 1924- *WhoBlA 92*
**Penn,** Lynn Sharon 1943- *AmMWSc 92*
**Penn,** Mindell Lewis 1944- *WhoBlA 92*
**Penn,** Nolan E. 1928- *WhoBlA 92*
**Penn,** Richard 1945- *Who 92*
**Penn,** Robert Clarence 1943- *WhoBlA 92*
**Penn,** Ronald Hulen 1951- *WhoMW 92*
**Penn,** Sean *NewYTBS 91 [port]*
**Penn,** Sean 1960- *IntMPA 92, WhoEnt 92*
**Penn,** Shelton C. 1925- *WhoBlA 92*
**Penn,** Thomas Clifton 1929- *AmMWSc 92*
**Penn,** William 1644-1718 *BenetAL 91*
**Penn,** William Albert 1943- *WhoEnt 92*
**Penn,** William B 1917- *AmMWSc 92*
**Penn,** William Charles 1877-1968 *TwCPaSc*
**Penn,** William S. *DrAPF 91*
**Penn-Atkins,** Barbara A. 1935- *WhoBlA 92*
**Penna,** Michael Anthony 1945- *AmMWSc 92*
**Penna,** Richard Paul 1935- *AmMWSc 92*
**Penna,** Sandro 1906-1977 *DcLB 114 [port]*
**Pennak,** Robert William 1912- *AmMWSc 92*
**Pennaneach,** Biova-Soumi 1941- *IntWW 91*
**Pennant** *Who 92*
**Pennant,** David Edward Thornton 1912- *Who 92*
**Pennant,** Edmund *DrAPF 91*
**Pennant-Rea,** Rupert Lascelles 1948- *IntAu&W 91, IntWW 91, Who 92*
**Pennario,** Leonard 1924- *NewAmDM*
**Penndorf,** Rudolf 1911- *AmMWSc 92*
**Pennebaker,** D.A. 1926- *IntMPA 92*
**Pennebaker,** Donn Alan 1925- *WhoEnt 92*
**Pennebaker,** James W 1950- *AmMWSc 92*
**Pennebaker,** John David 1943- *WhoAmP 91*
**Pennebaker,** William B, Jr 1935- *AmMWSc 92*
**Pennekamp,** Peter Henk 1952- *WhoEnt 92*
**Pennell,** Elizabeth Robins 1855-1936 *BenetAL 91*
**Pennell,** Joseph 1858-1926 *TwCPaSc*
**Pennell,** Joseph Stanley 1857-1926 *BenetAL 91*
**Pennell,** Joseph Stanley 1908-1963 *BenetAL 91*
**Pennell,** Leslie 1906- *Who 92*
**Pennell,** Maynard L 1910- *AmMWSc 92*
**Pennell,** Timothy Clinard 1933- *AmMWSc 92*
**Pennell,** William Brooke 1935- *WhoAmL 92*
**Pennell,** William Wayne 1939- *WhoRel 92*
**Pennella,** Joseph 1947- *WhoRel 92*
**Penneman,** Robert Allen 1919- *AmMWSc 92*
**Penner,** Alvin Paul 1947- *AmMWSc 92*
**Penner,** Donald 1936- *AmMWSc 92*
**Penner,** Fred 1946- *SmATA 67 [port]*
**Penner,** Glenn H 1960- *AmMWSc 92*
**Penner,** Hellmut Philip 1925- *AmMWSc 92*
**Penner,** Jonathan *DrAPF 91*
**Penner,** Jonathan 1940- *WrDr 92*
**Penner,** Joyce Elaine 1948- *AmMWSc 92*
**Penner,** Robyn Roxanne 1968- *WhoRel 92*
**Penner,** Rudolph Gerhard 1936- *WhoFI 92*
**Penner,** S S 1921- *AmMWSc 92*
**Penner,** Samuel 1930- *AmMWSc 92*
**Penner,** Siegfried Edmund 1923- *AmMWSc 92*
**Penner,** Stanford Solomon 1921- *WhoWest 92*
**Penner,** Vernon D 1939- *WhoAmP 91*
**Penner-Hahn,** James Edward 1957- *AmMWSc 92*
**Penney** *Who 92*
**Penney,** Baron d1991 *IntWW 91N, Who 92N*
**Penney,** Alphonsus Liguori *Who 92*
**Penney,** Alphonsus Liguori 1924- *WhoRel 92*
**Penney,** Carl Murray 1937- *AmMWSc 92*
**Penney,** Charles Rand 1923- *WhoAmL 92, WhoFI 92*
**Penney,** David Emory 1938- *AmMWSc 92*
**Penney,** David George 1940- *AmMWSc 92*
**Penney,** David P 1933- *AmMWSc 92*
**Penney,** Edmund Freeman 1926- *WhoEnt 92*
**Penney,** Gaylord W 1898- *AmMWSc 92*
**Penney,** J C 1875-1971 *FacFETw*
**Penney,** James Arthur 1954- *WhoAmL 92*
**Penney,** Jennifer Beverly 1946- *Who 92*
**Penney,** Reginald John 1919- *Who 92*
**Penney,** Richard Cole 1945- *AmMWSc 92*
**Penney,** William George d1991 *NewYTBS 91 [port]*
**Penney,** William George 1901-1991 *CurBio 91N*
**Penney,** William George 1909-1991 *FacFETw*
**Penney,** William Harry 1929- *AmMWSc 92*
**Penneys,** Raymond 1919- *AmMWSc 92*
**Penniall,** Ralph 1922- *AmMWSc 92*
**Pennick,** Aurie Alma 1947- *WhoBlA 92*
**Pennicott,** Brian Thomas 1938- *Who 92*
**Pennie,** Daniel R. *WhoAmL 92, WhoFI 92*
**Pennie,** Hester *ConAu 135*
**Pennie,** Michael 1936- *TwCPaSc*
**Pennie,** Michael William 1936- *IntWW 91*
**Pennie,** Nancy Loraine 1960- *WhoAmL 92*

**Penniman,** Nicholas Griffith, IV 1938- *WhoFI 92, WhoMW 92*
**Penniman,** Richard Wayne 1932- *WhoBlA 92, WhoEnt 92*
**Penniman,** William Howard 1948- *WhoAmL 92*
**Pennine,** Anthony P 1927- *WhoAmP 91*
**Penning,** John Russell, Jr 1922- *AmMWSc 92*
**Penning,** Richard Ted 1955- *WhoMW 92*
**Penning-Rowsell,** Edmund Lionel 1913- *Who 92*
**Penninger,** William Holt, Jr. 1954- *WhoAmL 92, WhoMW 92*
**Penningroth,** Stephen Meader 1944- *AmMWSc 92*
**Pennings,** Matt Daniel 1931- *WhoWest 92*
**Pennington,** Alyce Loraine 1953- *WhoAmL 92*
**Pennington,** Anna Ruth 1948- *WhoRel 92*
**Pennington,** Anthony James 1932- *AmMWSc 92*
**Pennington,** Beverly Melcher 1931- *WhoFI 92, WhoMW 92*
**Pennington,** Bruce Carter 1932- *WhoFI 92*
**Pennington,** Bruce Wilson, II 1947- *WhoWest 92*
**Pennington,** D. Ashley 1955- *WhoAmL 92*
**Pennington,** David Eugene 1939- *AmMWSc 92*
**Pennington,** Dorothy Carolyn 1921- *WhoWest 92*
**Pennington,** Edith Mae 1902-1974 *RelLAm 91*
**Pennington,** Eliberto Escamilla 1958- *WhoHisp 92*
**Pennington,** Frank Cook 1924- *AmMWSc 92*
**Pennington,** Hugh Allen, Jr. 1956- *WhoAmL 92*
**Pennington,** J Gordon 1927- *WhoAmP 91*
**Pennington,** Jean A T 1946- *AmMWSc 92*
**Pennington,** Jesse C. 1938- *WhoBlA 92*
**Pennington,** John Elton 1929- *WhoRel 92*
**Pennington,** Keith Samuel 1936- *AmMWSc 92*
**Pennington,** Lawrence Robert 1926- *WhoAmL 92*
**Pennington,** Lee *DrAPF 91*
**Pennington,** Leenette Morse 1936- *WhoBlA 92*
**Pennington,** Michael Vivian Fyfe 1943- *Who 92*
**Pennington,** Nathan Edward 1960- *WhoEnt 92*
**Pennington,** Ralph Hugh 1924- *AmMWSc 92*
**Pennington,** Randy 1940- *WhoAmP 91*
**Pennington,** Robert Elija 1926- *AmMWSc 92*
**Pennington,** Robert Roland 1927- *Who 92*
**Pennington,** Robert Varian 1932- *WhoFI 92*
**Pennington,** Sammy Noel 1941- *AmMWSc 92*
**Pennington,** Thomas K 1936- *WhoIns 92*
**Pennington,** Troy Duke 1947- *WhoEnt 92*
**Pennington,** Vicki Davis 1951- *WhoRel 92*
**Pennington,** Walter Carter 1957- *WhoFI 92*
**Pennington,** Wayne David 1950- *AmMWSc 92*
**Pennington,** William 1796-1862 *AmPolLe*
**Pennison,** Clifford Francis 1913- *Who 92*
**Pennisten,** John William 1939- *WhoFI 92*
**Penniston,** John Thomas 1935- *AmMWSc 92*
**Penno,** David Bruce 1952- *WhoFI 92*
**Pennock** *Who 92*
**Pennock,** Baron 1920- *IntWW 91, Who 92*
**Pennock,** Bernard Eugene 1938- *AmMWSc 92*
**Pennock,** Donald William 1915- *WhoFI 92*
**Pennock,** Gordon Robert 1947- *WhoMW 92*
**Pennoyer,** Russell Parsons 1951- *WhoFI 92*
**Pennsylvania Farmer** *BenetAL 91*
**Penny** *Who 92*
**Penny,** Christopher 1947- *TwCPaSc*
**Penny,** David 1918- *Who 92*
**Penny,** David Dickinson 1951- *WhoFI 92*
**Penny,** John Sloyan 1914- *AmMWSc 92*
**Penny,** Joseph Noel Bailey 1916- *Who 92*
**Penny,** Keith, Sr 1932- *AmMWSc 92*
**Penny,** Nicholas Beaver 1949- *Who 92*
**Penny,** Robert 1935- *WhoBlA 92*
**Penny,** Robert L. 1940- *WhoBlA 92*
**Penny,** Roger Pratt 1936- *WhoFI 92*
**Penny,** Timothy J. 1951- *AlmAP 92 [port], WhoAmP 91*
**Penny,** Timothy Joseph 1951- *WhoMW 92*
**Penny,** William Lewis 1953- *WhoAmL 92*
**Pennycuick,** Colin James 1933- *Who 92*
**Pennypacker,** Carlton Reese 1950- *AmMWSc 92*
**Pennywell,** Phillip, Jr. 1941- *WhoBlA 92*
**Penrhyn,** Baron 1908- *Who 92*
**Penrice,** Geoffrey 1923- *Who 92*
**Penrice,** Thomas James 1954- *WhoFI 92*
**Penrith,** Bishop Suffragan of 1928- *Who 92*
**Penrod,** Howard Leslie *WhoMW 92*
**Penrod,** James Wilford 1934- *WhoEnt 92*
**Penrod,** Steven David 1947- *WhoMW 92*
**Penrose,** Lord 1938- *Who 92*
**Penrose,** Cynthia C. 1939- *WhoFI 92*
**Penrose,** Edith Tilton 1914- *IntWW 91, Who 92*
**Penrose,** George William *Who 92*
**Penrose,** Gordon 1925- *SmATA 66 [port]*
**Penrose,** Gordon William Gavin 1925- *IntAu&W 91*
**Penrose,** John Hubert 1916- *Who 92*
**Penrose,** Oliver 1929- *IntWW 91, Who 92*
**Penrose,** Richard Alexander Fullerton 1827-1908 *BiInAmS*
**Penrose,** Roger 1931- *IntWW 91, News 91 [port], Who 92, WrDr 92*
**Penrose,** Roland 1900-1984 *FacFETw, TwCPaSc*
**Penrose,** Romania Pratt 1839-1932 *RelLAm 91*
**Penrose,** Thomas Neall 1835?-1902 *BiInAmS*
**Penrose,** William Roy 1943- *AmMWSc 92*
**Penry,** Walter E, Jr *WhoAmP 91*
**Penry-Davey,** David Herbert 1942- *Who 92*
**Pensack,** Joseph Michael 1916- *AmMWSc 92*
**Pensak,** David Alan 1948- *AmMWSc 92*
**Pense,** Alan Wiggins 1934- *AmMWSc 92*
**Pensinger,** John Lynn 1949- *WhoAmL 92*
**Pensis,** Henri Bram 1927- *WhoEnt 92, WhoMW 92*
**Penskar,** Mark Howard 1953- *WhoAmL 92*
**Pensky,** Jack 1924- *AmMWSc 92*
**Penstone,** S Robert 1930- *AmMWSc 92*
**Pentcheff,** Nicolas 1911- *WhoEnt 92*
**Pentecost,** David Henry 1938- *Who 92*
**Pentecost,** George Frederick 1842-1920 *RelLAm 91*
**Pentecost,** Hugh *BenetAL 91, IntAu&W 91X*
**Pentecost,** John Dwight 1915- *RelLAm 91*
**Pentecost,** Joseph L 1930- *AmMWSc 92*
**Pentecoste,** Joseph C. 1918- *WhoBlA 92*
**Pentiuk,** Randall Alan 1955- *WhoAmL 92, WhoMW 92*
**Pentland,** Barbara 1912- *NewAmDM*
**Pentland,** Barbara Lally 1912- *WhoEnt 92*
**Pentney,** Roberta Pierson 1936- *AmMWSc 92*
**Pento,** Joseph Thomas 1943- *AmMWSc 92*
**Penton,** Harold Roy, Jr 1947- *AmMWSc 92*
**Penton,** Zelda Eve 1939- *AmMWSc 92*
**Penwell,** Jones Clark 1921- *WhoWest 92*
**Penwell,** Richard Carlton 1942- *AmMWSc 92*
**Penz,** P Andrew 1939- *AmMWSc 92*
**Penza,** Jeffrey Alan 1957- *WhoFI 92*
**Penzavecchia,** James *DrAPF 91*
**Penzell,** David Stewart 1959- *WhoMW 92*
**Penzer,** Geoffrey Ronald 1943- *Who 92*
**Penzera,** David Alan 1970- *WhoFI 92*
**Penzi,** James *DrAPF 91*
**Penzias,** Arno A 1933- *AmMWSc 92*
**Penzias,** Arno Allan 1923- *WhoNob 90*
**Penzias,** Arno Allan 1933- *IntWW 91, Who 92, WhoFI 92*
**Penzien,** Joseph 1924- *AmMWSc 92*
**Penzler,** Otto 1942- *ConAu 35NR*
**Peo,** Ernest Ramy, Jr 1925- *AmMWSc 92*
**Peoples,** Don *WhoAmP 91*
**Peoples,** Dwayne Robert 1962- *WhoRel 92*
**Peoples,** Earl F., Sr. 1930- *WhoBlA 92*
**Peoples,** Erskine L. 1931- *WhoBlA 92*
**Peoples,** Florence W. 1940- *WhoBlA 92*
**Peoples,** Gregory Allan 1951- *WhoBlA 92*
**Peoples,** Harrison Promis, Jr. 1940- *WhoBlA 92*
**Peoples,** John *WhoAmP 91*
**Peoples,** John, Jr 1933- *AmMWSc 92*
**Peoples,** John Arthur, Jr. 1926- *WhoBlA 92*
**Peoples,** John Derrick, Jr. 1951- *WhoBlA 92*
**Peoples,** Joyce P. 1937- *WhoBlA 92*
**Peoples,** Morgan D. 1919- *ConAu 133*
**Peoples,** Sesser R. 1934- *WhoBlA 92*
**Peoples,** Stuart Anderson 1907- *AmMWSc 92*
**Peoples,** Veo, Jr. 1947- *WhoBlA 92*
**Pepe,** Barbara Eilene 1951- *WhoWest 92*
**Pepe,** Frank Albert 1931- *AmMWSc 92*
**Pepe,** Joseph Philip 1947- *AmMWSc 92*
**Pepe,** Louis Robert 1943- *WhoAmL 92, WhoAmP 91*
**Pepe,** Philip S. d1991 *NewYTBS 91*
**Pepe,** Stephen Phillip 1943- *WhoAmL 92*
**Peper,** Christian Baird 1910- *WhoAmL 92, WhoFI 92, WhoMW 92*
**Peper,** Erik 1944- *AmMWSc 92*
**Pepin,** Clermont 1926- *NewAmDM*
**Pepin,** Herbert Spencer 1928- *AmMWSc 92*
**Pepin,** Jean-Luc 1924- *IntWW 91*
**Pepin,** Lucie 1936- *IntWW 91*
**Pepin,** Robert Osborne 1933- *AmMWSc 92*
**Pepin,** Theodore John 1939- *AmMWSc 92*
**Pepin,** Timothy Leroy 1942- *WhoFI 92*
**Pepine,** Carl John 1941- *AmMWSc 92*
**Pepino,** Leo P 1927- *WhoAmP 91*
**Pepinsky,** Pauline Nichols 1919- *WhoMW 92*
**Pepinsky,** Raymond 1912- *AmMWSc 92*
**Pepkowitz,** Leonard Paul 1915- *AmMWSc 92*
**Peplinski,** Daniel Raymond 1951- *WhoWest 92*
**Peploe,** Clare *IntMPA 92*
**Peploe,** Denis 1914- *TwCPaSc, Who 92*
**Peploe,** Samuel John 1871-1935 *TwCPaSc*
**Peploe,** William Watson 1869-1933 *TwCPaSc*
**Peplow,** Ronald Dean 1948- *WhoMW 92*
**Peponis,** Harold Arthur 1928- *WhoMW 92*
**Pepoy,** Louis John 1938- *AmMWSc 92*
**Peppard,** Bradford Davies 1955- *WhoFI 92*
**Peppard,** George 1928- *IntMPA 92, IntWW 91, WhoEnt 92*
**Peppard,** Nadine Sheila 1922- *Who 92*
**Peppard,** Patrick Francis 1942- *WhoMW 92, WhoRel 92*
**Peppas,** Nikolaos Athanassiou 1948- *AmMWSc 92*
**Peppe,** M John 1941- *WhoIns 92*
**Peppe,** Rodney 1934- *WrDr 92*
**Peppe,** Rodney Darrell 1934- *IntAu&W 91*
**Peppel,** Heidi Karen Ross 1960- *WhoMW 92*
**Pepper,** Allan Michael 1943- *WhoAmL 92*
**Pepper,** Arnold Norman 1925- *WhoWest 92*
**Pepper,** Art 1925-1982 *NewAmDM*
**Pepper,** Beverly 1924- *WorArt 1980*
**Pepper,** Claude 1900-1989 *FacFETw*
**Pepper,** Claude Denson 1900-1989 *AmPolLe*
**Pepper,** Darrell Weldon 1946- *WhoWest 92*
**Pepper,** David Charles 1917- *IntWW 91*
**Pepper,** David M. 1949- *WhoWest 92*
**Pepper,** Donald Allen 1951- *WhoWest 92*
**Pepper,** Dorothy Mae 1932- *WhoWest 92*
**Pepper,** Evan Harold 1927- *AmMWSc 92*
**Pepper,** Gordon Terry 1934- *Who 92*
**Pepper,** James Morley 1920- *AmMWSc 92*
**Pepper,** John Roy 1937- *WhoWest 92*
**Pepper,** Kenneth Bruce 1913- *Who 92*
**Pepper,** Lawrence Anthony, Jr 1943- *WhoAmP 91*
**Pepper,** Louis Henry 1924- *WhoWest 92*
**Pepper,** Michael 1942- *IntWW 91, Who 92*
**Pepper,** Paul Milton 1909- *AmMWSc 92, WhoMW 92*
**Pepper,** Rollin E 1924- *AmMWSc 92*
**Pepper,** Thomas Mark 1939- *WhoFI 92*
**Pepper,** Thomas Peter 1918- *AmMWSc 92*
**Pepper,** William 1843-1898 *BiInAmS*
**Pepper,** William Donald 1935- *AmMWSc 92*
**Pepperberg,** David Roy 1944- *AmMWSc 92*
**Peppercorn,** Arthur Douglas 1847-1924 *TwCPaSc*
**Peppercorn,** John Edward 1937- *WhoWest 92*
**Pepperell,** William 1696-1759 *BenetAL 91*
**Pepperman,** Armand Bennett, Jr 1941- *AmMWSc 92*
**Pepperman,** Carla Rae 1959- *WhoAmL 92*
**Pepperman,** Lewis Jay 1952- *WhoAmL 92*
**Peppers,** Donald Alan 1950- *WhoFI 92*
**Peppers,** Russel A 1932- *AmMWSc 92*
**Peppiatt,** Hugh Stephen Kenneth 1930- *Who 92*
**Peppiatt-Aylesworth** *LesBEnT 92*
**Peppin,** Richard J 1943- *AmMWSc 92*
**Pepping,** Ernst 1901-1981 *NewAmDM*
**Peppitt,** John Raymond 1931- *Who 92*
**Pepple,** David Ralph 1943- *WhoIns 92*
**Pepple,** William Charles 1949- *WhoAmL 92*
**Peppler,** Henry James 1911- *AmMWSc 92*
**Peppler,** Richard Douglas 1943- *AmMWSc 92*
**Pepples,** Ernest 1935- *WhoFI 92*
**Pepusch,** Johann Christoph 1667-1752 *NewAmDM*
**Pepyne,** Edward Walter 1925- *WhoAmL 92*
**Pepys** *Who 92*
**Pepys,** Rachel 1905- *Who 92*
**Pepys,** Samuel 1633-1703 *CnDBLB 2 [port], RfGEnL 91*
**Pequegnat,** Linda Haithcock 1931- *WhoWest 92*
**Pequegnat,** Linda Lee Haithcock 1931- *AmMWSc 92*
**Pequegnat,** Willis Eugene 1914- *AmMWSc 92*
**Pequinot,** Mary K. 1955- *WhoMW 92*
**Pequito Rebelo,** Jose Adriano 1892-1983 *BiDExR*
**Per-Lee,** John H 1929- *AmMWSc 92*
**Pera,** John Dominic 1922- *AmMWSc 92*
**Pera,** Lucian T. 1960- *WhoAmL 92*
**Peracchi,** Franco 1952- *WhoFI 92*
**Peracchia,** Camillo 1938- *AmMWSc 92*
**Peracchio,** Aldo Anthony 1935- *AmMWSc 92*
**Perahia,** Murray 1947- *IntWW 91, NewAmDM, Who 92, WhoEnt 92*
**Peraino,** Carl 1935- *AmMWSc 92*
**Perak,** Sultan of 1928- *IntWW 91*
**Perakis,** Anastassios Nicholas 1953- *WhoMW 92*
**Perakis,** Robert Anthony 1953- *WhoAmP 91*
**Perakos,** Sperie P. 1915- *IntMPA 92*
**Perales,** Cesar A. 1940- *WhoHisp 92*
**Perales,** Christopher Oscar 1962- *WhoHisp 92*
**Perales,** Eduardo *WhoHisp 92*
**Perales,** Jorge Inocente 1951- *WhoHisp 92*
**Peralta,** Frank Carlos 1946- *WhoHisp 92*
**Peralta,** Frederick A *WhoAmP 91*
**Peralta,** Frederick A., Jr. *WhoHisp 92*
**Peralta,** Mauro G. 1947- *WhoHisp 92*
**Peralta,** Modesto Mangasi, Jr. 1941- *WhoMW 92*
**Peralta,** Richard Carl 1949- *AmMWSc 92, WhoHisp 92*
**Peralta Azurdia,** Enrique 1908- *IntWW 91*
**Peralta de la Vega,** Jose Maria 1763-1836 *HisDSpE*
**Peralta y Barnuevo,** Pedro de 1663-1743 *HisDSpE*
**Peranich,** Diane C 1940- *WhoAmP 91*
**Peranski,** Robert Zigmunt 1935- *WhoIns 92*
**Perara,** Mitchell Mebane 1924- *WhoBlA 92*
**Peraro,** James Salvatore 1935- *WhoMW 92*
**Perata,** Kathy Lois 1945- *WhoWest 92*
**Peratrovich,** Elizabeth 1911-1958 *HanAmWH*
**Peraza-Labrador,** Luis Francisco 1958- *WhoHisp 92*
**Percarpio,** Edward P 1934- *AmMWSc 92*
**Perce,** Elbert 1831-1869 *ScFEYrs*
**Percec,** Virgil 1946- *AmMWSc 92*
**Percell,** Emery A. 1933- *WhoRel 92*
**Percesepe,** Gary John 1954- *WhoRel 92*
**Perceval** *Who 92*
**Perceval,** Viscount 1934- *Who 92*
**Perceval,** John de Burgh 1923- *IntWW 91*
**Perceval,** Matthew 1945- *TwCPaSc*
**Perceval,** Michael 1936- *Who 92*
**Perceval,** Robert Westby 1914- *Who 92*
**Perch,** Philemon *BenetAL 91*
**Perchak,** Robert Matthew 1954- *WhoMW 92*
**Perchard,** Colin William 1940- *Who 92*
**Perche Rivas,** Emilio *WhoHisp 92*
**Perchik,** Simon *DrAPF 91*
**Perchonock,** Carl David 1946- *AmMWSc 92*
**Percich,** James Angelo 1944- *AmMWSc 92*
**Percival,** Allen Dain 1925- *Who 92*
**Percival,** Anthony 1910- *Who 92*
**Percival,** Douglas Franklin 1926- *AmMWSc 92*
**Percival,** Frank William 1948- *AmMWSc 92*
**Percival,** Harold Waldwin 1868-1953 *RelLAm 91*
**Percival,** Ian 1921- *Who 92*
**Percival,** Ian Colin 1931- *Who 92*
**Percival,** James Gates 1795-1856 *BenetAL 91, BiInAmS*
**Percival,** John 1937- *Who 92*
**Percival,** John A 1952- *AmMWSc 92*
**Percival,** Maurice 1906-1987 *TwCPaSc*
**Percival,** Robert C. 1908- *WrDr 92*
**Percival,** Robert Clarendon 1908- *Who 92*
**Percival,** Walter Ian *Who 92*
**Percival,** William Colony 1924- *AmMWSc 92*
**Percival-Prescott,** Westby William 1923- *Who 92*
**Percovich Roca,** Luis *IntWW 91*
**Percus,** Jerome K 1926- *AmMWSc 92*
**Percy** *Who 92*
**Percy,** Algernon Eustace Hugh H. *Who 92*
**Percy,** Charles Harting 1919- *IntWW 91, WhoAmP 91*
**Percy,** Charles Henry *ConAu 133, SmATA 65*
**Percy,** Douglas C 1914- *IntAu&W 91*
**Percy,** Florence *BenetAL 91*
**Percy,** George 1580-1632 *BenetAL 91*
**Percy,** John Pitkeathly 1942- *Who 92*
**Percy,** John Rees 1941- *AmMWSc 92*
**Percy,** John Smith 1938- *AmMWSc 92*
**Percy,** Jonathan Arthur 1943- *AmMWSc 92*
**Percy,** Lee Edward 1953- *WhoEnt 92, WhoWest 92*
**Percy,** Maire Ede 1939- *AmMWSc 92*

**Percy,** Rodney Algernon 1924- Who 92
**Percy,** Walker 1916- IntAu&W 91
**Percy,** Walker 1916-1990 AnObit 1990, BenetAL 91, ConLC 65 [port], FacFETw
**Percy,** William Alexander 1885-1942 BenetAL 91
**Perdew,** John Paul 1943- AmMWSc 92
**Perdigo,** Luisa Marina 1947- WhoHisp 92
**Perdomo,** Eduardo WhoHisp 92
**Perdomo,** George Luis 1961- WhoHisp 92
**Perdreau,** Connie WhoBlA 92
**Perdrisat,** Charles F 1932- AmMWSc 92
**Perdue,** Beverly Moore 1948- WhoAmP 91
**Perdue,** Charles L., Jr. 1930- ConAu 135
**Perdue,** Daniel Stephen 1952- WhoRel 92
**Perdue,** Edward Michael 1947- AmMWSc 92
**Perdue,** Franklin P WhoFI 92
**Perdue,** Franklin Roosevelt 1944- WhoBlA 92
**Perdue,** George WhoAmP 91, WhoBlA 92
**Perdue,** James F 1933- AmMWSc 92
**Perdue,** John F. 1912- WhoBlA 92
**Perdue,** Julia M. Ward 1938- WhoBlA 92
**Perdue,** Leo G. WhoRel 92
**Perdue,** Richard Dale 1955- WhoRel 92
**Perdue,** Richard Gordon 1910- Who 92
**Perdue,** Robert Edward, Jr 1924- AmMWSc 92
**Perdue,** Robert Eugene 1940- WhoBlA 92
**Perdue,** Sonny WhoAmP 91
**Perea,** Alicia 1955- WhoHisp 92
**Perea,** Juan F. 1955- WhoAmL 92, WhoHisp 92
**Perea,** Sylvia Jean 1941- WhoHisp 92
**Perea,** Toribio 1944- WhoHisp 92
**Perec,** Georges 1936-1982 GuFrLit 1
**Pereda,** Delfina Haydee 1921- WhoHisp 92
**Pereda,** Francisco Eugenio 1923- WhoHisp 92
**Pereda,** John WhoHisp 92
**Pereda,** Lucy 1944- WhoEnt 92
**Peregrin,** Magda Elizabeth 1923- WhoWest 92
**Peregrine,** Gwilym Rhys 1924- Who 92
**Peregrino,** Hugo WhoHisp 92
**Pereira da Silva** 1937- WhoEnt 92
**Pereira,** A. Nicolau Gracias 1926- WhoRel 92
**Pereira,** Alvaro Javier 1963- WhoHisp 92
**Pereira,** Aristides Maria 1923- IntWW 91
**Pereira,** Arthur Leonard 1906- Who 92
**Pereira,** Charles Who 92
**Pereira,** Edmund S 1921- WhoAmP 91
**Pereira,** Enrique A. WhoHisp 92
**Pereira,** Gerard P 1937- AmMWSc 92
**Pereira,** Helen Mary 1926- IntAu&W 91
**Pereira,** Helio Gelli 1918- IntWW 91, Who 92
**Pereira,** Herbert Charles 1913- IntWW 91, Who 92
**Pereira,** Joseph 1928- AmMWSc 92
**Pereira,** Julio Cesar 1944- WhoHisp 92
**Pereira,** Luis G. 1962- WhoHisp 92
**Pereira,** Margaret 1928- Who 92
**Pereira,** Martin Rodrigues 1920- AmMWSc 92
**Pereira,** Michael Alan 1944- AmMWSc 92
**Pereira,** Nino Rodrigues 1945- AmMWSc 92
**Pereira,** Peter 1952- WhoRel 92
**Pereira,** Robert William 1947- WhoRel 92
**Pereira,** Sarah Martin 1909- WhoBlA 92
**Pereira,** Sergio 1944- WhoHisp 92
**Pereira,** Teresinka DrAPF 91
**Pereira,** Teresinka 1934- IntAu&W 91
**Pereira Burgos,** Cesar 1929- IntWW 91
**Pereira Dos Santos,** Adalberto 1905- IntWW 91
**Pereira dos Santos,** Nelson 1928- IntDcF 2-2
**Pereira Gray,** Denis John Who 92
**Pereira Leite,** Sergio 1946- WhoFI 92
**Pereira Lira,** Paulo H. 1930- IntWW 91
**Pereira-Mendes,** Henry 1852-1937 ScFEYrs
**Pereira-Mendoza,** Vivian 1917- Who 92
**Pereiras Garcia,** Manuel 1950- WhoHisp 92
**Perek,** Lubos 1919- IntWW 91
**Perek,** Patricia Jean 1948- WhoFI 92
**Perel,** James Maurice 1933- AmMWSc 92
**Perel,** Jane Lunin DrAPF 91
**Perel,** Julius 1927- AmMWSc 92
**Perel,** William Morris 1927- AmMWSc 92
**Perell,** Edward Andrew 1940- WhoAmL 92
**Perella,** Joseph Robert 1941- WhoFI 92
**Perelman,** Bob 1947- ConPo 91, WrDr 92
**Perelman,** Leon Joseph 1911- WhoFI 92
**Perelman,** Lewis J. 1946- WrDr 92
**Perelman,** Melvin 1930- WhoFI 92, WhoMW 92
**Perelman,** Rachel Greenspan 1938- WhoAmP 91
**Perelman,** Ronald O. 1943- CurBio 91 [port]
**Perelman,** Ronald Owen 1943- IntWW 91, WhoFI 92
**Perelman,** S. J. 1904-1979 BenetAL 91, FacFETw
**Perelmuter,** Hayim Goren 1914- WhoRel 92
**Perelmuter,** Rosa 1948- WhoHisp 92
**Perels,** Friedrich Justus 1910-1945 EncTR 91
**Perelson,** Alan Stuart 1947- AmMWSc 92
**Perelson,** Glenn Howard 1954- WhoWest 92
**Perenchio,** Andrew J. 1930- IntMPA 92
**Perenchio,** Andrew Jerrold 1930- WhoEnt 92
**Pereny,** George DrAPF 91
**Perenyi,** Eleanor 1918- ConAu 133
**Perenyi,** Miklos 1948- IntWW 91
**Perera,** Ana Maria 1925- WhoHisp 92
**Perera,** Ed TwCPaSc
**Perera,** Hilda 1926- WhoHisp 92
**Perera,** Lawrence Thacher 1935- WhoAmL 92
**Perera,** Liyanage Henry Horace 1915- IntWW 91
**Perera,** Padma DrAPF 91
**Perera,** Ronald 1941- NewAmDM
**Perera,** Victor DrAPF 91
**Perera,** Victor Haim 1934- IntAu&W 91
**Perera,** Wahalatantrige D. R. 1928- IntWW 91
**Perera-Pfeifer,** Isabel WhoHisp 92
**Peres,** Shimon 1923- FacFETw [port], IntWW 91, Who 92
**Peress,** Maurice 1930- NewAmDM
**Peress,** Nancy E 1943- AmMWSc 92
**Peressini,** Anthony L 1934- AmMWSc 92
**Peressini,** William Edward 1956- WhoFI 92
**Peresson,** Sergio d1991 NewYTBS 91
**Perestiani,** Ivan Nikolaevich 1870-1959 SovUnBD
**Peresypkin,** Oleg Gerasimovich IntWW 91
**Pereszlenyi-Pinter,** Martha 1948- WhoMW 92
**Peret,** Benjamin 1899-1959 GuFrLit 1
**Peretti,** Ettore A 1913- AmMWSc 92
**Peretz,** Bertram AmMWSc 92
**Peretz,** David Lindsay Corbett 1943- Who 92
**Peretz,** Isaac Leib 1851-1915 LiExTwC
**Peretz,** Marc Harlan WhoEnt 92
**Peretz,** Yitzhak Haim 1939- IntWW 91
**Peretzian,** Michael 1941- WhoEnt 92
**Pereverzev,** Valeryan Fedorovich 1882-1968 SovUnBD
**Perey,** Bernard Jean Francois 1930- AmMWSc 92
**Perey,** Francis George 1932- AmMWSc 92
**Perey,** Ron Joseph 1943- WhoAmL 92
**Pereyra,** Diomedes De ScFEYrs
**Pereyra-Suarez,** Charles Albert 1947- WhoAmL 92, WhoWest 92
**Pereyra-Suarez,** Esther 1925- WhoHisp 92
**Perez,** Albert Pena 1940- WhoHisp 92
**Perez,** Alberto Julian 1948- WhoHisp 92
**Perez,** Alejandro 1940- WhoHisp 92
**Perez,** Alejandro Raymundo 1936- WhoHisp 92
**Perez,** Alicia 1953- WhoHisp 92
**Perez,** Alicia S. 1931- WhoHisp 92
**Perez,** Alonzo 1956- WhoHisp 92
**Perez,** Amanda Carrales 1932- WhoHisp 92
**Perez,** Angie Vigil WhoAmP 91
**Perez,** Anna 1951- ConBlB 1 [port]
**Perez,** Anna 1952- WhoBlA 92
**Perez,** Anthony Martin, Jr. 1953- WhoFI 92, WhoWest 92
**Perez,** Antonio WhoHisp 92
**Perez,** Arturo WhoHisp 92
**Perez,** Bernardo Matias 1939- WhoHisp 92
**Perez,** Bobbie M. Anthony 1923- WhoBlA 92
**Perez,** Carlos 1950- WhoHisp 92
**Perez,** Carlos A 1934- AmMWSc 92, WhoHisp 92
**Perez,** Carlos Jesus 1959- WhoHisp 92
**Perez,** Carmelo WhoHisp 92
**Perez,** Carmen WhoAmP 91, WhoHisp 92
**Perez,** Carmen Gonzalez 1956- WhoHisp 92
**Perez,** Carmen O. WhoHisp 92
**Perez,** Danny Edward 1963- WhoHisp 92
**Perez,** Dario 1941- WhoHisp 92
**Perez,** David 1948- WhoHisp 92
**Perez,** David Douglas 1937- WhoHisp 92
**Perez,** Donna Yvette 1961- WhoEnt 92
**Perez,** Edgar 1948- WhoHisp 92
**Perez,** Elio 1938- WhoHisp 92
**Perez,** Elva A. WhoHisp 92
**Perez,** Emiliano 1935- WhoHisp 92
**Perez,** Emilio 1940- WhoHisp 92
**Perez,** Enrique Manuel 1957- WhoHisp 92
**Perez,** Esteban d1515 HisDSpE
**Perez,** Estela Comilang 1929- WhoWest 92
**Perez,** Eustolia WhoHisp 92
**Perez,** Felix WhoHisp 92
**Perez,** Francisco Luis 1950- WhoHisp 92
**Perez,** Francisco R. 1938- WhoHisp 92
**Perez,** Frank WhoHisp 92
**Perez,** Frank S. 1929- WhoHisp 92
**Perez,** George WhoHisp 92
**Perez,** Gerard Vincent 1946- WhoFI 92, WhoMW 92
**Perez,** Gilbert Bernal 1950- WhoHisp 92
**Perez,** Gilberto Guillermo 1943- WhoHisp 92
**Perez,** Guido O 1938- AmMWSc 92
**Perez,** Guido Oscar 1938- WhoHisp 92
**Perez,** Guillermo 1957- WhoHisp 92
**Perez,** Gustavo 1928- WhoHisp 92
**Perez,** Hector 1957- WhoHisp 92
**Perez,** Hector Antonio Tico 1962- WhoAmL 92
**Perez,** Hector Daniel AmMWSc 92
**Perez,** Herbert John 1959- WhoHisp 92
**Perez,** Isidro WhoHisp 92
**Perez,** James Benito WhoHisp 92
**Perez,** James Rudolph 1936- WhoHisp 92
**Perez,** Jane R. 1943- WhoHisp 92
**Perez,** Jim 1957- WhoHisp 92
**Perez,** John Carlos 1941- AmMWSc 92
**Perez,** Jorge BlkOlyM
**Perez,** Jorge David 1964- WhoHisp 92
**Perez,** Jorge L. 1962- WhoHisp 92
**Perez,** Jose WhoHisp 92
**Perez,** Jose 1939- WhoHisp 92
**Perez,** Jose Luis 1951- WhoMW 92
**Perez,** Jose Manuel 1954- WhoRel 92
**Perez,** Jose Miguel WhoHisp 92
**Perez,** Jose R., Jr. 1948- WhoHisp 92
**Perez,** Joseph Dominique 1942- AmMWSc 92
**Perez,** Joseph E. 1946- WhoHisp 92
**Perez,** Joseph F. 1930- ConAu 36NR
**Perez,** Joseph Peter 1944- WhoHisp 92
**Perez,** Juan Ovidio 1954- WhoHisp 92
**Perez,** Julian Ernesto 1933- WhoHisp 92
**Perez,** Julio E. 1958- WhoHisp 92
**Perez,** Julio Edgardo 1950- WhoHisp 92
**Perez,** Laura Alonso 1962- WhoHisp 92
**Perez,** Leo 1958- WhoHisp 92
**Perez,** Lombardo WhoHisp 92
**Perez,** Louie WhoHisp 92
**Perez,** Louis G. 1946- WhoHisp 92
**Perez,** Luis 1928- WhoHisp 92
**Perez,** Luis 1940- WhoHisp 92
**Perez,** Luis A. 1947- WhoHisp 92
**Perez,** Luis Alberto 1956- WhoAmL 92, WhoHisp 92
**Perez,** Lydia 1947- WhoHisp 92
**Perez,** Lydia Tena 1955- WhoHisp 92
**Perez,** Manuel 1939- WhoHisp 92
**Perez,** Margaret 1949- WhoHisp 92
**Perez,** Maria E. 1928- WhoHisp 92
**Perez,** Mariano Martin 1964- WhoHisp 92
**Perez,** Marie Antoinette 1950- WhoAmL 92
**Perez,** Mario 1940- WhoHisp 92
**Perez,** Mario Alberto 1958- WhoHisp 92
**Perez,** Maritza E. 1947- WhoHisp 92
**Perez,** Maritza Ivonne 1957- WhoHisp 92
**Perez,** Marlene 1959- WhoHisp 92
**Perez,** Martin WhoHisp 92
**Perez,** Mary A. WhoHisp 92
**Perez,** Melido T. 1966- WhoHisp 92
**Perez,** Melvyn James 1936- WhoAmL 92, WhoHisp 92
**Perez,** Mike 1964- WhoHisp 92
**Perez,** Minerva 1955- WhoHisp 92
**Perez,** Nancy WhoHisp 92
**Perez,** Nicolas J 1943- WhoAmP 91, WhoHisp 92
**Perez,** Pablo 1936- WhoHisp 92
**Perez,** Pascual Gross 1957- WhoHisp 92
**Perez,** Pedro 1936- WhoHisp 92
**Perez,** Pedro L. 1935- WhoHisp 92
**Perez,** Pete WhoHisp 92
**Perez,** Peter Felix 1948- WhoAmP 91
**Perez,** Peter Manuel 1940- WhoFI 92
**Perez,** Rafael R. WhoHisp 92
**Perez,** Raul Ramon 1942- WhoHisp 92
**Perez,** Ray WhoHisp 92
**Perez,** Reinaldo Jesu 1957- WhoWest 92
**Perez,** Renato Eduardo 1937- WhoHisp 92
**Perez,** Rey WhoHisp 92
**Perez,** Ricardo 1959- AmMWSc 92
**Perez,** Richard 1947- WhoHisp 92
**Perez,** Richard Lee 1940- WhoHisp 92
**Perez,** Richard Lee 1946- WhoAmL 92, WhoWest 92
**Perez,** Richard Patrick 1941- WhoHisp 92
**Perez,** Richard Raymond 1934- WhoHisp 92
**Perez,** Robert WhoHisp 92
**Perez,** Robert 1942- WhoHisp 92
**Perez,** Robert Antony 1955- WhoHisp 92
**Perez,** Roger A. 1959- WhoHisp 92
**Perez,** Roland W. 1943- WhoHisp 92
**Perez,** Rolando 1957- WhoHisp 92
**Perez,** Romulo 1954- WhoHisp 92
**Perez,** Ronald 1949- WhoFI 92
**Perez,** Ronald A. 1949- WhoHisp 92
**Perez,** Rosie WhoHisp 92
**Perez,** Salvador Stephen 1965- WhoHisp 92
**Perez,** Santiago, Jr. 1938- WhoHisp 92
**Perez,** Segundo, Jr. 1949- WhoHisp 92
**Perez,** Severo 1941- WhoEnt 92
**Perez,** Severo, Jr. 1941- WhoHisp 92
**Perez,** Sory 1948- WhoHisp 92
**Perez,** Stephen Manuel 1947- WhoHisp 92
**Perez,** Tony 1942- WhoHisp 92
**Perez,** Toraldo Casimiro, Jr. 1936- WhoHisp 92
**Perez,** Victor O. 1947- WhoHisp 92
**Perez,** Vincent R. 1938- WhoHisp 92
**Perez,** Waldo D. 1946- WhoHisp 92
**Perez,** William Charles 1944- WhoHisp 92
**Perez,** Yorkis Miguel 1967- WhoHisp 92
**Perez-Aguilera,** Jose Raul 1961- WhoHisp 92
**Perez-Albuerne,** Evelio A 1939- AmMWSc 92
**Perez Alfonzo,** Juan Pablo 1904-1979 FacFETw
**Perez Armenteros,** Conrado 1950- BlkOlyM
**Perez Aucar,** Manuel A. 1922- WhoHisp 92
**Perez-Blanco,** Horacio 1951- WhoHisp 92
**Perez-Bustillo,** Camilo WhoHisp 92
**Perez Calama,** Jose 1740-1792 HisDSpE
**Perez-Captoe,** Juan M. 1938- WhoHisp 92
**Perez-Colon,** Roberto 1949- WhoHisp 92
**Perez-Cruet,** Jorge AmMWSc 92
**Perez de Cuellar,** Javier 1920- FacFETw, IntWW 91, News 91 [port], -91-3 [port], Who 92
**Perez del Rio,** Jose Joaquin 1941- WhoHisp 92
**Perez de Rivas,** Andres 1575-1655 HisDSpE
**Perez-Erdelyi,** Mireya 1942- WhoHisp 92
**Perez Esquivel,** Adolfo 1931- IntWW 91, Who 92, WhoNob 90
**Perez-Farfante,** Isabel C. 1916- WhoHisp 92
**Perez-Farfante,** Isabel Cristina 1916- AmMWSc 92
**Perez-Feria,** Richard M. 1964- WhoHisp 92
**Perez Fernandez,** Pedro 1949- IntWW 91
**Perez Firmat,** Gustavo 1950- WhoHisp 92
**Perez-Gimenez,** Juan Manuel 1941- WhoAmL 92, WhoHisp 92
**Perez Godoy,** Ricardo Pio 1905- IntWW 91
**Perez-Hernandez,** Manny WhoHisp 92
**Perez Jimenez,** Marcos 1914- IntWW 91
**Perez-Llorca,** Jose Pedro 1940- IntWW 91
**Perez-Lopez,** Rene 1945- WhoHisp 92
**Perez Marin,** Andres 1961- WhoHisp 92
**Perez-Mendez,** Victor 1923- AmMWSc 92, WhoHisp 92, WhoWest 92
**Perez-Mireles,** Guadalupe Louisa 1951- WhoHisp 92
**Perez Mon,** Coynthia 1958- WhoHisp 92
**Perez Oms,** Candido 1961- WhoFI 92
**Perez Rivera,** Harry Luis WhoAmP 91
**Perez Rodriguez,** Carlos Andres 1922- IntWW 91
**Perez-Rodriguez,** Carolyn Delfina 1951- WhoHisp 92
**Perez Rodriguez,** Roberto J. 1947- WhoHisp 92
**Perez-Stable,** Maria Adelaida 1954- WhoHisp 92
**Perez-Stansfield,** Maria Pilar WhoHisp 92
**Perez-Tamayo,** Ruheri 1926- AmMWSc 92
**Perez-Tulla,** Maritza Ivonne 1957- WhoHisp 92
**Perez-Vega,** Elsa 1953- WhoHisp 92
**Perez y Mena,** Andres I. 1948- WhoHisp 92
**Perfetti,** Patricia F 1952- AmMWSc 92
**Perfetti,** Randolph B 1949- AmMWSc 92
**Perfetti,** Thomas Albert 1952- AmMWSc 92
**Pergam,** Albert Steven 1938- WhoAmL 92
**Pergament,** Jeffrey Wayne 1951- WhoEnt 92
**Pergande,** Theodore 1840-1916 BiInAmS
**Pergericht,** Frances Lee 1952- WhoAmL 92
**Pergolesi,** Giovanni Battista 1710-1736 BlkwCEP, NewAmDM
**Perhac,** Ralph Matthew 1928- AmMWSc 92
**Perhach,** James Lawrence 1943- AmMWSc 92
**Perhacs,** Marylouise Helen 1944- WhoEnt 92
**Perham,** Lester R 1918- WhoAmP 91
**Perham,** Richard Nelson 1937- Who 92
**Peri,** Barbara Anne 1925- AmMWSc 92
**Peri,** Jacopo 1561-1633 NewAmDM
**Peri,** John Bayard 1923- AmMWSc 92
**Peri,** Peter 1899-1967 TwCPaSc
**Peri Fagerstrom,** Rene Alberto 1926- IntWW 91
**Peri Rossi,** Cristina 1941- SpAmWW
**Peric-Knowlton,** Wlatka 1955- AmMWSc 92
**Pericak-Spector,** Kathleen Anne 1954- AmMWSc 92

**Perich**, Robert Charles 1954- WhoMW 92
**Perier**, Francois 1919- IntWW 91
**Peries**, Lester James 1919- IntDcF 2-2 [port]
**Perigot**, Francois 1926- IntWW 91
**Perilla**, Alejandro 1965- WhoHisp 92
**Perilli**, Frank Ray 1925- WhoEnt 92
**Perillie**, Pasquale E 1926- AmMWSc 92
**Perillo**, Giulio 1946- WhoFI 92
**Perillo**, Lucia Maria DrAPF 91
**Perillo**, Phillip Alan 1949- WhoFI 92
**Perilloux**, Bruce Edgar 1961- WhoWest 92
**Perilman**, Nathan A. d1991 NewYTBS 91
**Periman**, Phillip 1938- AmMWSc 92
**Perin**, Francois 1921- IntWW 91
**Perin**, Roberto 1948- ConAu 133
**Perinat**, Marques de 1923- Who 92
**Perinat**, Luis Guillermo, Marques de 1923- IntWW 91
**Perine**, James L. 1943- WhoBlA 92
**Perine**, Martha Levingston 1948- WhoBlA 92
**Perini**, Jose 1928- AmMWSc 92
**Perino**, Janice Vinyard 1946- AmMWSc 92
**Perish**, Melanie DrAPF 91
**Perisho**, Clarence H 1924- AmMWSc 92
**Perisho**, Clarence R 1917- AmMWSc 92
**Perisic**, Zoran 1940- IntWW 91
**Perisin**, Ivo 1925- IntWW 91
**Perissinotto**, Giorgio 1942- WhoWest 92
**Perito**, Joseph Gerald, Jr. 1927- WhoWest 92
**Perkel**, Donald Howard 1930- AmMWSc 92
**Perkel**, Robert Jules 1926- AmMWSc 92
**Perkin**, James Russell Conway 1928- IntWW 91
**Perkins**, A Thomas 1942- AmMWSc 92
**Perkins**, Alfred J 1912- AmMWSc 92
**Perkins**, Alice Elizabeth 1949- Who 92
**Perkins**, Anne Scarlett 1937- WhoAmP 91
**Perkins**, Anthony 1932- IntMPA 92, WhoEnt 92
**Perkins**, Anthony C WhoAmP 91
**Perkins**, Anthony Lee 1942- WhoRel 92
**Perkins**, Arthur John 1931- WhoEnt 92
**Perkins**, Bernard James 1928- Who 92
**Perkins**, Bobby Frank 1929- AmMWSc 92
**Perkins**, Bradley Alan 1957- WhoAmL 92
**Perkins**, Brenda 1934- TwCPaSc
**Perkins**, Brenda Gail 1955- WhoMW 92
**Perkins**, Carl 1932- NewAmDM, WhoEnt 92
**Perkins**, Carl C. 1954- AlmAP 92 [port], WhoAmP 91
**Perkins**, Charles Windell 1946- WhoBlA 92
**Perkins**, Courtland D 1912- AmMWSc 92
**Perkins**, David DrAPF 91
**Perkins**, David D. 1919- IntWW 91
**Perkins**, David Dexter 1919- AmMWSc 92
**Perkins**, David Karl 1951- WhoMW 92
**Perkins**, Derek Duncombe S. Who 92
**Perkins**, Dian R 1946- WhoAmP 91
**Perkins**, Donald H. 1925- IntWW 91
**Perkins**, Donald Hill 1925- Who 92
**Perkins**, Donald Young 1923- AmMWSc 92
**Perkins**, Dorothy A 1926- WhoAmP 91, WhoWest 92
**Perkins**, Dwight Clark 1914- WhoIns 92
**Perkins**, Dwight Heald 1934- IntAu&W 91, WhoFI 92, WrDr 92
**Perkins**, E. Benson 1881-1964 ConAu 134
**Perkins**, Edward George 1934- AmMWSc 92
**Perkins**, Edward J. 1928- IntWW 91
**Perkins**, Edward Joseph 1928- WhoAmP 91, WhoBlA 92
**Perkins**, Eli BenetAL 91
**Perkins**, Eli 1839-1910 ScFEYrs
**Perkins**, Elizabeth 1961- IntMPA 92
**Perkins**, Elizabeth Ann 1960- WhoEnt 92
**Perkins**, Floyd 1930- AmMWSc 92
**Perkins**, Floyd Jerry 1924- WhoRel 92, WhoWest 92
**Perkins**, Frances 1880-1965 HanAmWH, RComAH
**Perkins**, Frances 1882-1965 AmPolLe [port], FacFETw
**Perkins**, Frances J. 1919- WhoBlA 92
**Perkins**, Francis Layton 1912- Who 92
**Perkins**, Frank Overton 1938- AmMWSc 92
**Perkins**, Frederic 1828-1899 ScFEYrs
**Perkins**, Frederick Beecher 1828-1899 BenetAL 91
**Perkins**, George 1930- WrDr 92
**Perkins**, George Burton 1930- IntAu&W 91
**Perkins**, George Roberts 1812-1876 BiInAmS
**Perkins**, Gerald Vern, Jr. 1948- WhoMW 92
**Perkins**, Gladys Patricia 1921- WhoBlA 92
**Perkins**, Happy R. 1955- WhoAmL 92
**Perkins**, Harold Jackson 1930- AmMWSc 92
**Perkins**, Harolyn King 1937- AmMWSc 92
**Perkins**, Henry Crawford, Jr 1935- AmMWSc 92
**Perkins**, Henry Frank 1921- AmMWSc 92
**Perkins**, Henry Lee 1958- WhoWest 92
**Perkins**, Henry S. 1833-1914 NewAmDM
**Perkins**, Herbert Asa 1918- AmMWSc 92
**Perkins**, Huel D. 1924- WhoBlA 92
**Perkins**, Irwyn Morse 1920- Who 92
**Perkins**, Jacob 1766-1849 BiInAmS
**Perkins**, James 1911- WrDr 92
**Perkins**, James 1943- AmMWSc 92
**Perkins**, James A. DrAPF 91
**Perkins**, James Alfred 1911- IntWW 91, Who 92
**Perkins**, James Francis 1924- AmMWSc 92
**Perkins**, James Harold 1928- WhoAmL 92
**Perkins**, James O 1940- WhoIns 92
**Perkins**, Janet Sanford 1913- AmMWSc 92
**Perkins**, Jim 1949- WhoAmP 91
**Perkins**, John Gerard, Jr. 1955- WhoFI 92
**Perkins**, John H. 1921- IntWW 91
**Perkins**, John Henry Rowland, II 1934- IntMPA 92
**Perkins**, John Kadri 1959- WhoFI 92
**Perkins**, John M. WhoBlA 92
**Perkins**, John M. 1930- RelLAm 91
**Perkins**, John MacIvor 1935- NewAmDM
**Perkins**, John Phillip 1937- AmMWSc 92
**Perkins**, Karl Arthur, Jr. 1936- WhoEnt 92
**Perkins**, Karon Elaine 1959- WhoAmL 92
**Perkins**, Kenneth 1926- Who 92
**Perkins**, Kenneth L 1924- AmMWSc 92
**Perkins**, Kenneth Roy 1942- AmMWSc 92
**Perkins**, Kenneth Warren 1927- AmMWSc 92
**Perkins**, Larry Howard 1955- WhoRel 92
**Perkins**, Leonard L. 1933- WhoBlA 92
**Perkins**, Lewis Bryant, Jr. WhoBlA 92
**Perkins**, Linda Marie 1950- WhoBlA 92
**Perkins**, Linwood, Jr. 1928- WhoAmL 92
**Perkins**, Louvenia Black 1948- WhoBlA 92
**Perkins**, Lucy Ann WhoBlA 92
**Perkins**, Lucy Fitch 1865-1937 BenetAL 91
**Perkins**, Maxwell 1884-1947 FacFETw
**Perkins**, Maxwell Evarts 1884-1947 BenetAL 91
**Perkins**, Merle Lester 1919- IntAu&W 91
**Perkins**, Michael DrAPF 91
**Perkins**, Michael 1942- IntAu&W 91, WrDr 92
**Perkins**, Mildred Kelley 1908- WhoAmP 91
**Perkins**, Millie 1938- IntMPA 92
**Perkins**, Myla Levy 1939- WhoBlA 92
**Perkins**, Nancy Leeds 1956- WhoAmL 92
**Perkins**, Norris Lynwood, III 1947- WhoMW 92
**Perkins**, Ottis Lawrence 1936- WhoRel 92
**Perkins**, Paul Bouthillier 1961- WhoFI 92
**Perkins**, Peter 1928- TwCPaSc
**Perkins**, Peter 1935- AmMWSc 92
**Perkins**, Phyllis Hartley 1934- WhoWest 92
**Perkins**, Rebecca Daeda 1955- WhoAmP 91
**Perkins**, Richard Scott 1940- AmMWSc 92
**Perkins**, Richard W, Jr 1932- AmMWSc 92
**Perkins**, Robert Austin 1934- WhoFI 92
**Perkins**, Robert E. L. 1925- WhoBlA 92
**Perkins**, Robert Louis 1931- AmMWSc 92
**Perkins**, Robert Martin 1904- WhoMW 92
**Perkins**, Robert Peter 1952- WhoFI 92
**Perkins**, Robert Rex 1940- WhoRel 92
**Perkins**, Robert William 1961- WhoMW 92
**Perkins**, Roger Allan 1943- WhoAmL 92
**Perkins**, Roger Bruce 1935- AmMWSc 92
**Perkins**, Ronald Dee 1935- AmMWSc 92
**Perkins**, Roswell Burchard 1926- WhoAmL 92
**Perkins**, S. Scott 1954- WhoAmL 92
**Perkins**, Sam Bruce 1961- WhoBlA 92
**Perkins**, Samuel 1948- WhoAmL 92
**Perkins**, Samuel Bruce 1961- BlkOlyM
**Perkins**, Shirley M. 1926- WhoRel 92
**Perkins**, Sterrett Theodore 1932- AmMWSc 92
**Perkins**, T.W. DrAPF 91
**Perkins**, Thomas Cole 1933- WhoIns 92
**Perkins**, Thomas James 1932- WhoWest 92
**Perkins**, Thomas K 1932- AmMWSc 92
**Perkins**, Thomas P. 1940- WhoBlA 92
**Perkins**, Thomas Ralph 1931- WhoAmP 91
**Perkins**, Victoria Marie 1942- WhoRel 92
**Perkins**, Walton A, III 1933- AmMWSc 92
**Perkins**, William Clopton 1934- AmMWSc 92
**Perkins**, William Eldredge 1938- AmMWSc 92
**Perkins**, William H., Jr. 1921- WhoMW 92
**Perkins**, William Hardwick 1940- WhoEnt 92
**Perkins**, William Hughes 1923- AmMWSc 92
**Perkins**, William O., Jr. 1926- WhoBlA 92
**Perkins**, William Randolph 1934- AmMWSc 92
**Perkins**, Willis Drummond 1926- AmMWSc 92
**Perkins**, Winston E 1935- WhoIns 92
**Perkins-Carpenter**, Betty Lou 1931- WhoFI 92
**Perkins-Frederick**, Pamela M. DrAPF 91
**Perkinson**, Diana Agnes Zouzelka 1943- WhoFI 92, WhoMW 92
**Perkinson**, Edward Brandon 1940- WhoMW 92
**Perkinson**, Jesse Dean 1914- IntWW 91
**Perko**, F. Michael 1946- WhoMW 92
**Perko**, Lawrence Marion 1936- AmMWSc 92
**Perkoff**, Gerald Thomas 1926- AmMWSc 92, IntWW 91
**Perkovich**, Robert 1951- WhoAmL 92
**Perkowitz**, Sidney 1939- AmMWSc 92
**Perks**, Anthony Manning AmMWSc 92
**Perks**, Clifford 1915- Who 92
**Perks**, Norman William 1932- AmMWSc 92
**Perks**, Roger Ian 1921- WhoRel 92
**Perl**, Edward Roy 1926- AmMWSc 92
**Perl**, Martin Lewis 1927- AmMWSc 92, IntWW 91
**Perl**, Ronald L. 1951- WhoAmL 92
**Perl**, Ruth June 1929- WrDr 92
**Perl**, William R 1906- IntAu&W 91
**Perla**, Randall Michael 1949- WhoAmL 92
**Perlberg**, Deborah DrAPF 91
**Perlberg**, Fred d1991 NewYTBS 91
**Perlberg**, Jules Martin 1931- WhoAmL 92
**Perlberg**, Mark DrAPF 91
**Perlberger**, Martin 1928- WhoEnt 92
**Perle**, Eugene Gabriel 1922- WhoAmL 92, WhoEnt 92
**Perle**, George 1915- NewAmDM, WhoEnt 92
**Perle**, Richard N 1941- WhoAmP 91
**Perlea**, Jonel 1900-1970 NewAmDM
**Perlemuter**, Vlado 1904- IntWW 91
**Perler**, Andrew Mitchell 1940- WhoMW 92
**Perley** BenetAL 91
**Perley**, James E 1939- AmMWSc 92
**Perley**, Merrill E 1915- WhoAmP 91
**Perley**, Peter Ernest 1944- WhoAmP 91
**Perlgut**, Louis E 1915- AmMWSc 92
**Perlich**, Robert Willard 1915- AmMWSc 92
**Perlick**, Nancy Beth 1944- WhoFI 92
**Perlin**, Alan S. 1952- WhoAmL 92
**Perlin**, Arthur Saul 1923- AmMWSc 92
**Perlin**, Gary Laurence 1951- WhoFI 92
**Perlin**, Joel David 1950- WhoWest 92
**Perlin**, John 1944- ConAu 134
**Perlin**, Jordan 1921- WhoFI 92
**Perlin**, Michael Howard AmMWSc 92
**Perlin**, Seymour 1925- AmMWSc 92
**Perlis**, The Raja of 1920- IntWW 91
**Perlis**, Alan Jay 1922- AmMWSc 92
**Perlis**, Irwin Bernard 1925- AmMWSc 92
**Perlis**, Michael Fredrick 1947- WhoAmL 92, WhoFI 92, WhoWest 92
**Perlis**, Michael Steven 1953- WhoEnt 92
**Perlis**, Sam 1913- AmMWSc 92
**Perlman**, Anne S. DrAPF 91
**Perlman**, Barry Stuart 1939- AmMWSc 92
**Perlman**, Daniel Hessel 1935- WhoMW 92
**Perlman**, David 1918- WhoWest 92
**Perlman**, Ely 1913- AmMWSc 92
**Perlman**, Isador d1991 NewYTBS 91
**Perlman**, Isadore 1915- AmMWSc 92, IntWW 91
**Perlman**, Itzhak 1945- FacFETw, IntWW 91, NewAmDM, Who 92, WhoEnt 92A
**Perlman**, John Niels DrAPF 91
**Perlman**, Kato Lenard 1928- AmMWSc 92
**Perlman**, Lawrence 1938- WhoFI 92, WhoMW 92
**Perlman**, Lawrence 1952- WhoRel 92
**Perlman**, Maier 1937- AmMWSc 92
**Perlman**, Matthew Saul 1936- WhoAmL 92
**Perlman**, Michael David 1942- AmMWSc 92
**Perlman**, Morris Leonard 1916- AmMWSc 92
**Perlman**, Philip Stewart 1945- AmMWSc 92
**Perlman**, Rhea WhoEnt 92
**Perlman**, Rhea 1948- IntMPA 92
**Perlman**, Richard 1920- AmMWSc 92
**Perlman**, Richard Brian 1951- WhoAmL 92
**Perlman**, Robert 1938- AmMWSc 92
**Perlman**, Ron 1950- IntMPA 92
**Perlman**, Sandra Lee 1944- WhoEnt 92
**Perlman**, Scott David 1958- WhoAmL 92
**Perlman**, Susan Gail 1950- WhoRel 92
**Perlman**, T 1923- AmMWSc 92
**Perlmuth**, William Alan 1929- WhoAmL 92
**Perlmutt**, Joseph Hertz 1918- AmMWSc 92
**Perlmutter**, Alfred 1914- AmMWSc 92
**Perlmutter**, Alvin H. LesBEnT 92
**Perlmutter**, Alvin Howard 1928- WhoEnt 92
**Perlmutter**, Arnold 1928- AmMWSc 92
**Perlmutter**, Arthur 1930- AmMWSc 92
**Perlmutter**, Daniel D 1931- AmMWSc 92
**Perlmutter**, David M. 1934- IntMPA 92
**Perlmutter**, David Milton 1939- WhoAmL 92
**Perlmutter**, David Stuart 1962- WhoFI 92
**Perlmutter**, Diane F. 1945- WhoFI 92
**Perlmutter**, Donna WhoEnt 92
**Perlmutter**, Frank 1912- AmMWSc 92, WhoFI 92
**Perlmutter**, Howard D 1938- AmMWSc 92
**Perlmutter**, Isaac 1912- AmMWSc 92
**Perlmutter**, Leonard Michael 1925- WhoWest 92
**Perlmutter**, Louis 1934- WhoFI 92
**Perlmutter**, Marion 1948- WhoMW 92
**Perlmutter**, Martin Lee 1947- WhoEnt 92
**Perlmutter**, Milton Manuel 1956- WhoWest 92
**Perlmutter**, Roger M 1952- AmMWSc 92
**Perlmutter**, Sandra Pauline 1952- WhoAmP 91
**Perlo**, H. Golightly 1931- WhoEnt 92
**Perloff**, David Steven 1942- AmMWSc 92
**Perloff**, Jean Marcosson 1942- WhoAmL 92
**Perloff**, Jeffrey Mark 1950- WhoFI 92, WhoWest 92
**Perloff**, Marjorie 1931- WrDr 92
**Perloff**, William H, Jr 1936- AmMWSc 92
**Perlongher**, Nestor 1948- ConSpAP
**Perlongo**, Daniel James 1942- WhoEnt 92
**Perlot**, Enzo 1933- IntWW 91
**Perlov**, Dadie 1929- WhoFI 92
**Perlow**, Gilbert Jerome 1916- AmMWSc 92
**Perlow**, Mina Rea Jones AmMWSc 92
**Perls**, Frederick Solomon 1894?-1970 FacFETw
**Perls**, Laura Posner 1905-1990 FacFETw
**Perlstadt**, Harry 1942- WhoMW 92
**Perlstein**, Jerome Howard 1941- AmMWSc 92
**Perman**, Andre 1957- WhoEnt 92
**Perman**, Gary Wayne 1961- WhoEnt 92
**Perman**, Martey Robert 1939- WhoAmL 92
**Perman**, Norman Wilford 1928- WhoEnt 92
**Perman**, Sherwood 1937- WhoMW 92
**Perman**, Victor 1926- AmMWSc 92
**Permar**, Raymond Thomas 1933- WhoRel 92
**Permut**, David A. IntMPA 92
**Permut**, Steven L. 1950- WhoAmL 92
**Permutt**, Solbert 1925- AmMWSc 92
**Perna**, Frank, Jr. 1938- WhoWest 92
**Perna**, Nicholas Salvatore 1942- WhoFI 92
**Pernacciaro**, Samuel John 1936- WhoMW 92
**Pernecky**, Mark Louis 1961- WhoFI 92, WhoMW 92
**Pernick**, Benjamin J 1931- AmMWSc 92
**Pernow**, Bengt 1924- IntWW 91
**Pero**, Janice Gay 1943- AmMWSc 92
**Pero**, Joseph John 1939- WhoFI 92, WhoIns 92
**Pero**, Michael Andrew 1941- WhoIns 92
**Perocchi**, Joyce Guglielmino 1953- WhoAmL 92
**Perol**, Gilbert 1926- IntWW 91
**Peron**, Anne 1908- IntAu&W 91
**Peron**, Eva 1919-1952 FacFETw [port]
**Peron**, Juan Domingo 1895-1974 FacFETw [port]
**Peron**, Maria Estela IntWW 91
**Perona**, Gerald Frank 1943- WhoMW 92
**Perona**, Joseph James 1930- AmMWSc 92
**Perone**, John Michael 1945- WhoAmP 91
**Perone**, Samuel Patrick 1938- AmMWSc 92
**Peronnet**, Francois R R 1946- AmMWSc 92
**Peronnet**, Gabriel Andre 1919- IntWW 91
**Perot**, H. Ross 1930- WhoFI 92
**Perot**, Phanor L, Jr 1928- AmMWSc 92
**Perot**, Ross 1930- IntWW 91
**Perotin** NewAmDM
**Perotti**, Rose Norma 1930- WhoFI 92, WhoMW 92
**Peroulas**, Maria 1950- WhoAmP 91
**Peroutka**, Joseph Henry, III 1965- WhoAmP 91
**Peroutka**, Stephen Joseph 1954- AmMWSc 92
**Perovich**, Donald Kole 1950- AmMWSc 92
**Perowne**, Benjamin Cubitt 1921- Who 92
**Perowne**, Freya Who 92

**Perozeni**, Ruth Elizabeth Lotz 1966- *WhoMW 92*
**Perozzi**, Edmund Frank 1946- *AmMWSc 92*
**Perpener**, Winifred Uveda 1929- *WhoBlA 92*
**Perper**, Lloyd 1921- *AmMWSc 92*
**Perper**, Robert J 1933- *AmMWSc 92*
**Perpetua and Felicitas** d203 *EncEarC*
**Perpich**, Rudy 1928- *IntWW 91*
**Perpich**, Rudy George 1928- *WhoAmP 91*
**Perr**, Irwin Norman 1928- *AmMWSc 92*
**Perr**, Simon 1962- *TwCPaSc*
**Perrault**, Dominique *IntWW 91*
**Perrault**, Dorothy Ann Jacques 1937- *WhoFI 92*
**Perrault**, Guy 1927- *AmMWSc 92*
**Perrault**, Jacques 1944- *AmMWSc 92*
**Perrault**, Marcel Joseph 1914- *AmMWSc 92*
**Perrault**, Michel 1925- *NewAmDM*
**Perrault**, Pierre 1927- *IntDcF 2-2*
**Perrault**, Raymond Joseph 1926- *IntWW 91*
**Perreau**, Gigi 1941- *IntMPA 92*
**Perreault**, David Alfred 1942- *AmMWSc 92*
**Perreault**, Ellen *DrAPF 91*
**Perreault**, George *DrAPF 91*
**Perreault**, Germain 1916- *IntWW 91*
**Perreault**, John *DrAPF 91*
**Perreault**, Paul Frederick 1929- *WhoFI 92*
**Perrein**, Michele Marie-Claude 1929- *IntWW 91*
**Perrella**, Anthony Joseph 1942- *WhoFI 92*
**Perrella**, Donald J. 1928- *WhoHisp 92*
**Perrello**, Paul Joseph 1957- *WhoEnt 92*
**Perrenod**, Douglas Arthur 1947- *WhoWest 92*
**Perret**, Auguste 1874-1954 *DcTwDes, FacFETw*
**Perret**, Gene Richard 1937- *WhoEnt 92*
**Perret**, George 1910- *AmMWSc 92*
**Perret**, Gloria McKinnon 1929- *WhoAmP 91*
**Perret**, Joseph Aloysius 1929- *WhoWest 92*
**Perret**, Peter James 1941- *WhoEnt 92*
**Perret**, William Riker 1908- *AmMWSc 92*
**Perrett**, Bryan 1934- *IntAu&W 91, WrDr 92*
**Perrett**, Desmond Seymour 1937- *Who 92*
**Perrett**, Jane Pugh 1955- *WhoFI 92*
**Perrett**, John 1906- *Who 92*
**Perrette**, Jean Rene 1931- *WhoFI 92*
**Perretti**, Peter *WhoAmP 91*
**Perri**, Fortunato *WhoAmP 91*
**Perri**, Joseph Mark 1917- *AmMWSc 92*
**Perriam**, Wendy Angela 1940- *IntAu&W 91*
**Perriand**, Charlotte 1903- *DcTwDes*
**Perrich**, Jerry Robert 1947- *WhoMW 92*
**Perrie**, Walter 1949- *IntAu&W 91*
**Perrigo**, Lyle Donovan 1930- *WhoWest 92*
**Perrigo**, Steven Richard 1944- *WhoMW 92*
**Perrill**, Stephen Arthur 1941- *AmMWSc 92*
**Perriman**, Brett 1965- *WhoBlA 92*
**Perrimon**, Vivian Spence 1926- *WhoBlA 92*
**Perrin**, Arnold *DrAPF 91*
**Perrin**, Bill K 1938- *WhoAmP 91*
**Perrin**, Carrol Hollingsworth 1912- *AmMWSc 92*
**Perrin**, Charles John 1940- *Who 92*
**Perrin**, Charles Lee 1938- *AmMWSc 92*
**Perrin**, Chuck J. 1946- *WhoEnt 92*
**Perrin**, David Thomas Perry 1951- *WhoBlA 92*
**Perrin**, Edward Burton 1931- *AmMWSc 92*
**Perrin**, Eugene Victor 1927- *AmMWSc 92*
**Perrin**, Francis Henri Jean Siegfried 1901- *IntWW 91*
**Perrin**, Jac Dean, Jr. 1957- *WhoRel 92*
**Perrin**, James Stuart 1936- *AmMWSc 92*
**Perrin**, Jean Baptiste 1870-1942 *WhoNob 90*
**Perrin**, John Henry 1916- *Who 92*
**Perrin**, John Paul 1943- *WhoMW 92*
**Perrin**, Lesley Davison *WhoEnt 92*
**Perrin**, Michael Warren 1946- *WhoAmL 92*
**Perrin**, Norman Arthur 1930- *Who 92*
**Perrin**, Robert 1925- *WhoFI 92, WhoIns 92*
**Perrin**, Robert Mark 1958- *WhoMW 92*
**Perrin**, Vic *ConTFT 9*
**Perrin**, Victor 1916-1989 *ConTFT 9*
**Perrin**, William Fergus 1938- *AmMWSc 92*
**Perrine**, Frederic Auten Combs 1862-1908 *BiInAmS*
**Perrine**, Henry 1797-1840 *BiInAmS*
**Perrine**, John W 1927- *AmMWSc 92*
**Perrine**, Laurence 1915- *IntAu&W 91, WrDr 92*
**Perrine**, Norman Paul 1961- *WhoMW 92*
**Perrine**, R L 1924- *AmMWSc 92*
**Perrine**, Valerie 1943- *IntMPA 92, WhoEnt 92*
**Perring**, Franklyn Hugh 1927- *Who 92*
**Perring**, John Raymond 1931- *Who 92*
**Perring**, Ralph 1905- *Who 92*
**Perrino**, Betty V 1927- *WhoAmP 91*
**Perrino**, Charles T 1938- *AmMWSc 92*
**Perrins**, Christopher Miles 1935- *Who 92*
**Perris**, David 1929- *Who 92*
**Perris**, John Douglas 1928- *Who 92*
**Perris**, Terrence George 1947- *WhoAmL 92*
**Perritt**, Alexander M 1928- *AmMWSc 92*
**Perritt**, Henry Hardy, Jr. 1944- *WhoFI 92*
**Perron**, Andre R. 1960- *WhoAmL 92*
**Perron**, James Patrick 1955- *WhoAmP 91*
**Perron**, Wendy 1947- *WhoEnt 92*
**Perron**, Yvon G 1925- *AmMWSc 92*
**Perrone**, Hector d1991 *NewYTBS 91 [port]*
**Perrone**, Joao Consani 1922- *IntWW 91*
**Perrone**, Nicholas 1930- *AmMWSc 92*
**Perrone Compagni**, Dino 1897-1950 *BiDExR*
**Perronet**, Jean-David 1708-1794 *BlkwCEP*
**Perros**, Theodore Peter 1922- *AmMWSc 92*
**Perrot**, Jules 1810-1892 *ThHEIm [port]*
**Perrot**, Nicholas 1644-1718? *BenetAL 91*
**Perrott**, David Russell 1942- *WhoWest 92*
**Perrott**, Pamela Rundle 1941- *WhoWest 92*
**Perrotta**, Anthony Joseph 1937- *AmMWSc 92*
**Perrotta**, Anthony Paul 1936- *WhoFI 92*
**Perrotta**, James 1919- *AmMWSc 92*
**Perrotta**, Joseph David 1960- *WhoAmL 92*
**Perrow**, Howard 1923- *Who 92*
**Perrucci**, Michael J 1953- *WhoAmP 91*
**Perrucci**, Robert 1931- *ConAu 34NR*
**Perry** *Who 92*
**Perry**, Baron 1921- *IntWW 91*
**Perry**, Alan Dean 1957- *WhoEnt 92*
**Perry**, Alan Joseph 1930- *Who 92*
**Perry**, Albert Leujay 1947- *WhoFI 92*
**Perry**, Albert Solomon 1915- *AmMWSc 92*
**Perry**, Alexander 1939- *WhoRel 92*
**Perry**, Alexis E. 1944- *WhoBlA 92*
**Perry**, Alfred Eugene 1931- *AmMWSc 92*
**Perry**, Andre 1937- *WhoEnt 92*
**Perry**, Andy 1952- *WhoEnt 92*
**Perry**, Anne 1938- *WrDr 92*
**Perry**, Anthony 1929- *IntMPA 92*
**Perry**, Anthony Frank 1965- *WhoWest 92*
**Perry**, Antoinette Krueger 1954- *WhoWest 92*
**Perry**, Aubrey M. 1937- *WhoBlA 92*
**Perry**, Barney Blair 1953- *WhoEnt 92*
**Perry**, Benjamin 1939- *WhoBlA 92*
**Perry**, Benjamin L., Jr. 1918- *WhoBlA 92*
**Perry**, Beryl Henry, Jr. 1956- *WhoFI 92*
**Perry**, Billy Wayne 1937- *AmMWSc 92*
**Perry**, Blair Lane 1929- *WhoAmL 92*
**Perry**, Bliss 1880-1954 *BenetAL 91*
**Perry**, Bonne Lu 1929- *WhoWest 92*
**Perry**, Brenda L. 1948- *WhoBlA 92*
**Perry**, Carleton Flood 1931- *WhoAmP 91*
**Perry**, Carrie Saxon *WhoAmP 91, WhoBlA 92*
**Perry**, Carrie Saxon 1931- *NotBlAW 92 [port]*
**Perry**, Charles Austin 1928- *WhoWest 92*
**Perry**, Charles Bruce 1903- *Who 92*
**Perry**, Charles Edgar, Jr. 1942- *WhoRel 92*
**Perry**, Charles Lewis 1933- *AmMWSc 92*
**Perry**, Charles Robert, Jr. 1947- *WhoMW 92*
**Perry**, Charles Rufus, Jr 1936- *AmMWSc 92*
**Perry**, Charles S. 1936- *WhoAmL 92*
**Perry**, Charles Wayne 1948- *WhoRel 92*
**Perry**, Charles Wayne 1951- *WhoMW 92*
**Perry**, Charles William 1910- *AmMWSc 92*
**Perry**, Clark William 1936- *AmMWSc 92*
**Perry**, Clive Howe 1936- *AmMWSc 92*
**Perry**, Cynthia Shepard *WhoAmP 91*
**Perry**, Dale Lynn 1947- *AmMWSc 92*
**Perry**, Dan C. 1958- *WhoAmL 92*
**Perry**, Danny Lamar, Sr 1945- *WhoAmP 91*
**Perry**, Darold Lynn 1951- *WhoMW 92*
**Perry**, David *WhoRel 92*
**Perry**, David 1931- *Who 92*
**Perry**, David 1958- *WhoAmP 91*
**Perry**, David Allan 1954- *WhoFI 92*
**Perry**, David Anthony 1938- *AmMWSc 92*
**Perry**, David Carter 1948- *AmMWSc 92*
**Perry**, David Lee 1942- *WhoAmP 91*
**Perry**, David Lewis 1940- *WhoAmL 92, WhoFI 92*
**Perry**, David M 1917- *WhoAmP 91*
**Perry**, David Niles 1940- *WhoWest 92*
**Perry**, David Norman *Who 92*
**Perry**, De Wayne William 1950- *WhoWest 92*
**Perry**, Dennis 1932- *AmMWSc 92*
**Perry**, Dennis Gordon 1942- *AmMWSc 92*
**Perry**, Donald A. 1938- *WhoEnt 92*
**Perry**, Donald Charles 1925- *WhoRel 92*
**Perry**, Donald Cleveland 1940- *WhoAmP 91*
**Perry**, Donald Dunham 1922- *AmMWSc 92*
**Perry**, Donald Lester, II 1958- *WhoWest 92*
**Perry**, Douglas *WhoEnt 92*
**Perry**, Dwight Arnold 1955- *WhoMW 92, WhoRel 92*
**Perry**, E. Eugene 1957- *WhoRel 92*
**Perry**, E. Lynn 1949- *WhoAmL 92*
**Perry**, Earl 1921- *IntMPA 92*
**Perry**, Ed 1946- *WhoAmP 91*
**Perry**, Edith Early 1943- *WhoAmP 91*
**Perry**, Edmond S 1912- *AmMWSc 92*
**Perry**, Edward Belk 1939- *AmMWSc 92*
**Perry**, Edward Gordon, III 1947- *WhoEnt 92*
**Perry**, Edward K. *WhoRel 92*
**Perry**, Edward Mahlon 1928- *AmMWSc 92*
**Perry**, Edward Ted Samuel 1937- *WhoEnt 92*
**Perry**, Eleanor 1915-1981 *ReelWom [port]*
**Perry**, Elizabeth *DrAPF 91*
**Perry**, Emma Bradford *WhoBlA 92*
**Perry**, Erik David 1952- *AmMWSc 92*
**Perry**, Ernest 1908- *TwCPaSc*
**Perry**, Ernest George 1908- *Who 92*
**Perry**, Eston Lee 1936- *WhoMW 92*
**Perry**, Eugene Addison 1940- *WhoRel 92*
**Perry**, Eugene Arthur 1938- *AmMWSc 92*
**Perry**, Eugene Calvin, Jr. 1953- *WhoBlA 92*
**Perry**, Eugene Carleton, Jr 1933- *AmMWSc 92*
**Perry**, Evelyn Reis *WhoFI 92*
**Perry**, Felix Edwin 1942- *WhoAmP 91*
**Perry**, Felton *WhoBlA 92*
**Perry**, Floyde E. *WhoRel 92*
**Perry**, Frances Mary 1907- *Who 92*
**Perry**, Francis J 1918- *WhoAmP 91*
**Perry**, Frank 1930- *ConTFT 9, IntMPA 92, WhoEnt 92*
**Perry**, Frank Anthony 1921- *AmMWSc 92, WhoBlA 92*
**Perry**, Franklin D. *WhoBlA 92*
**Perry**, Fred 1909- *FacFETw*
**Perry**, Fred John 1909- *IntWW 91*
**Perry**, Frederick John 1909- *Who 92*
**Perry**, Garry Alfred 1962- *WhoAmL 92*
**Perry**, George 1935- *WrDr 92*
**Perry**, George 1953- *AmMWSc 92*
**Perry**, George Cox 1935- *IntAu&W 91*
**Perry**, George Henry 1920- *Who 92*
**Perry**, George Lewis 1934- *WhoFI 92*
**Perry**, George Sessions 1910-1956 *BenetAL 91, TwCWW 91*
**Perry**, George Williamson 1926- *WhoAmL 92*
**Perry**, George Wilson 1929- *WhoFI 92*
**Perry**, Georgette *DrAPF 91*
**Perry**, Gerald 1960- *WhoBlA 92*
**Perry**, Gloria Burgess 1936- *WhoMW 92*
**Perry**, Gregory Michael 1948- *WhoAmL 92*
**Perry**, H. William 1941- *WhoRel 92*
**Perry**, Harold 1924- *AmMWSc 92, WhoBlA 92*
**Perry**, Harold A 1917?-1991 *News 92-1*
**Perry**, Harold Otto 1921- *AmMWSc 92*
**Perry**, Harold R. d1991 *NewYTBS 91 [port]*
**Perry**, Harold R. 1916-1991 *CurBio 91N*
**Perry**, Harold Robert 1916-1991 *WhoBlA 92N*
**Perry**, Harold Tyner, Jr 1926- *AmMWSc 92*
**Perry**, Hart d1991 *NewYTBS 91 [port]*
**Perry**, Horace Mitchell, Jr 1923- *AmMWSc 92*
**Perry**, I. Chet 1943- *WhoFI 92*
**Perry**, J Warren 1921- *AmMWSc 92*
**Perry**, Jack Richard 1930- *WhoAmP 91*
**Perry**, Jacquelin 1918- *AmMWSc 92*
**Perry**, James Alfred *AmMWSc 92*
**Perry**, James Benn 1950- *WhoFI 92*
**Perry**, James De Wolf, Jr. 1871-1947 *RelLAm 91*
**Perry**, James Ernest 1923- *AmMWSc 92*
**Perry**, James Gregory 1952- *WhoWest 92*
**Perry**, James Warner 1948- *AmMWSc 92*
**Perry**, Jane Ellen 1958- *WhoRel 92*
**Perry**, Jean B. 1946- *WhoBlA 92*
**Perry**, Jean Louise 1950- *WhoWest 92*
**Perry**, Jerald Isaac, Sr. 1950- *WhoBlA 92*
**Perry**, Jerome John 1929- *AmMWSc 92*
**Perry**, Jerry Eileen *WhoAmP 91*
**Perry**, John *Who 92*
**Perry**, John 1954- *WhoAmP 91*
**Perry**, John Arthur 1921- *AmMWSc 92*
**Perry**, John B. 1945- *WhoBlA 92*
**Perry**, John Buckley 1825-1872 *BiInAmS*
**Perry**, John D *WhoAmP 91*
**Perry**, John E 1924- *AmMWSc 92*
**Perry**, John Francis, Jr 1923- *AmMWSc 92*
**Perry**, John Freeman *Who 92*
**Perry**, John Murray 1925- *AmMWSc 92*
**Perry**, John Neville 1920- *Who 92*
**Perry**, John Richard 1943- *IntWW 91*
**Perry**, John Stephen 1931- *AmMWSc 92*
**Perry**, John Van Buren 1928- *WhoWest 92*
**Perry**, John Vivian, Jr 1924- *AmMWSc 92*
**Perry**, John William 1938- *Who 92*
**Perry**, Joseph Earl, Jr 1917- *AmMWSc 92*
**Perry**, Julia 1924-1979 *NewAmDM, NotBlAW 92*
**Perry**, June Carter 1943- *WhoBlA 92*
**Perry**, June Martin 1947- *WhoBlA 92*
**Perry**, Kenneth W 1936- *AmMWSc 92*
**Perry**, Lansford Wilder 1955- *WhoFI 92*
**Perry**, Lee Charles, Jr. 1955- *WhoBlA 92*
**Perry**, Lee Rowan 1933- *WhoAmL 92, WhoFI 92, WhoWest 92*
**Perry**, Leonard Douglas, Jr. 1952- *WhoBlA 92*
**Perry**, Lilla Cabot 1848-1933 *HanAmWH*
**Perry**, Lloyd Holden 1916- *AmMWSc 92*
**Perry**, Lorin Edward 1914- *AmMWSc 92*
**Perry**, Lowell W. 1931- *WhoBlA 92*
**Perry**, Lowell Wesley, Jr. 1956- *WhoBlA 92*
**Perry**, Malcolm Blythe 1930- *AmMWSc 92*
**Perry**, Margaret 1933- *WhoBlA 92, WrDr 92*
**Perry**, Margaret D 1921- *WhoAmP 91*
**Perry**, Margaret Nutt 1940- *AmMWSc 92*
**Perry**, Marion *DrAPF 91*
**Perry**, Marion Judith Helz 1943- *IntAu&W 91*
**Perry**, Marion Walter 1911- *WhoFI 92*
**Perry**, Marney Dunman, Jr 1926- *WhoAmP 91*
**Perry**, Marsha G 1936- *WhoAmP 91*
**Perry**, Mary Hertzog 1922- *AmMWSc 92*
**Perry**, Mary Jane 1948- *AmMWSc 92*
**Perry**, Matthew Calbraith 1794-1858 *BenetAL 91*
**Perry**, Matthew J., Jr. 1921- *WhoAmL 92*
**Perry**, Michael Charles 1933- *IntAu&W 91, Who 92, WrDr 92*
**Perry**, Michael Clinton 1945- *WhoMW 92*
**Perry**, Michael Dean 1965- *WhoBlA 92*
**Perry**, Michael Harris 1955- *WhoMW 92*
**Perry**, Michael James 1955- *WhoEnt 92*
**Perry**, Michael John 1945- *WhoAmL 92*
**Perry**, Michael Paul 1947- *AmMWSc 92*
**Perry**, Milton d1991 *NewYTBS 91*
**Perry**, Nelson Allen 1937- *AmMWSc 92*
**Perry**, Nora 1831-1896 *BenetAL 91*
**Perry**, Norman *Who 92*
**Perry**, Norman Henry 1944- *Who 92*
**Perry**, Norman Robert 1929- *WhoRel 92*
**Perry**, Oliver Hazard 1785-1819 *BenetAL 91*
**Perry**, Patsy Brewington 1933- *WhoBlA 92*
**Perry**, Paul 1926- *AmMWSc 92*
**Perry**, Paul 1936- *WhoEnt 92*
**Perry**, Paul F. 1932- *WhoRel 92*
**Perry**, Pauline 1931- *Who 92*
**Perry**, Peter George 1923- *Who 92*
**Perry**, Peter M 1941- *AmMWSc 92*
**Perry**, Ralph Barton 1876-1957 *BenetAL 91*
**Perry**, Randolph, Jr 1923- *AmMWSc 92*
**Perry**, Randolph Hugh 1951- *WhoAmL 92*
**Perry**, Randy L 1940- *AmMWSc 92*
**Perry**, Reeves Baldwin 1935- *AmMWSc 92*
**Perry**, Rhoda E *WhoAmP 91*
**Perry**, Richard 1944- *WhoBlA 92*
**Perry**, Richard H. *DrAPF 91*
**Perry**, Richard Lee 1930- *AmMWSc 92, WhoWest 92*
**Perry**, Rick 1950- *WhoAmP 91*
**Perry**, Rickey L. 1949- *WhoRel 92*
**Perry**, Ritchie 1942- *IntAu&W 91*
**Perry**, Robert Cephas 1946- *WhoBlA 92*
**Perry**, Robert Haynes 1933- *WhoRel 92*
**Perry**, Robert Hood, Jr 1928- *AmMWSc 92*
**Perry**, Robert Joseph 1934- *WhoFI 92*
**Perry**, Robert Lee 1932- *WhoBlA 92, WhoMW 92*
**Perry**, Robert Leonard 1941- *AmMWSc 92*
**Perry**, Robert Michael 1931- *WhoWest 92*
**Perry**, Robert Nathaniel, III 1942- *AmMWSc 92*
**Perry**, Robert Palese 1931- *AmMWSc 92, IntWW 91*
**Perry**, Robert Riley 1934- *AmMWSc 92*
**Perry**, Robert W 1921- *AmMWSc 92*
**Perry**, Robin *DrAPF 91*
**Perry**, Roger 1940- *Who 92*
**Perry**, Roland Rick 1958- *WhoHisp 92*
**Perry**, Ronald *WhoEnt 92*
**Perry**, Ronald 1952- *WhoAmL 92*
**Perry**, Rudolph John 1936- *Who 92*
**Perry**, Ruth 1936- *WhoEnt 92*
**Perry**, Samuel Victor 1918- *Who 92*
**Perry**, Seymour Monroe 1921- *AmMWSc 92, IntWW 91*
**Perry**, Sharon Lynn 1952- *WhoRel 92*

**Perry,** Sherryl Rosenbaum 1941- WhoAmL 92
**Perry,** Simon 1943- IntMPA 92
**Perry,** Stephen Clayton 1942- WhoFI 92
**Perry,** Stewart Ronald 1932- WhoAmL 92
**Perry,** Thelma Davis WhoBlA 92
**Perry,** Thomas WrDr 92
**Perry,** Thomas Hobart 1813-1849 BiInAmS
**Perry,** Thomas Lockwood 1916- AmMWSc 92
**Perry,** Thomas Oliver 1925- AmMWSc 92
**Perry,** Thomas Richard 1954- WhoFI 92
**Perry,** Thomas Sergeant 1845-1928 BenetAL 91
**Perry,** Thornton Dudley 1941- WhoAmP 91
**Perry,** Tilden Wayne 1919- AmMWSc 92
**Perry,** Tim 1958- WhoAmP 91
**Perry,** Timothy D. 1965- WhoBlA 92
**Perry,** Timothy Sewell 1947- WhoAmL 92
**Perry,** Troy Deroy 1940- RelLAm 91
**Perry,** Val M WhoIns 92
**Perry,** Vernon G 1921- AmMWSc 92
**Perry,** Vernon P 1927- AmMWSc 92
**Perry,** Wayne D. 1944- WhoBlA 92
**Perry,** William Anthony 1962- WhoBlA 92
**Perry,** William Arthur 1937- Who 92
**Perry,** William Daniel 1944- AmMWSc 92
**Perry,** William E. 1932- WhoBlA 92
**Perry,** William Harold 1952- WhoRel 92
**Perry,** William James 1927- AmMWSc 92
**Perry,** William Joseph 1930- WhoWest 92
**Perry,** William Joseph 1962- WhoMW 92
**Perry,** William Leon 1945- AmMWSc 92
**Perry,** William Merritt, III 1955- WhoFI 92
**Perry,** William Rodwell, III 1959- WhoBlA 92
**Perry,** Yvonne Scruggs 1933- WhoBlA 92
**Perry-Daniel,** Annie Vee 1940- WhoRel 92
**Perry of Southwark,** Baroness 1931- Who 92
**Perry of Walton,** Baron 1921- Who 92
**Perryman,** Charles Richard 1916- AmMWSc 92
**Perryman,** Douglas 1930- Who 92
**Perryman,** Elizabeth Kay 1940- AmMWSc 92
**Perryman,** James Harvey 1918- AmMWSc 92
**Perryman,** John Keith 1935- AmMWSc 92
**Perryman,** Lavonia Lauren WhoBlA 92
**Perryman,** Lee WhoEnt 92
**Perryman,** Margot 1938- TwCPaSc
**Perryman,** Robert 1964- WhoBlA 92
**Persad,** Emmanuel 1935- AmMWSc 92
**Persampieri,** Nicholas Frank, Jr. 1959- WhoAmL 92
**Persans,** Peter D 1953- AmMWSc 92
**Persaud,** Inder 1926- WhoBlA 92
**Persaud,** Trivedi Vidhya Nandan 1940- AmMWSc 92
**Perschbacher,** Debra Bassett 1956- WhoAmL 92
**Perschbacher,** Rex Robert 1946- WhoAmL 92
**Perschetz,** Arthur Driban 1943- WhoAmL 92, WhoIns 92
**Perschetz,** Martin L. 1952- WhoAmL 92
**Perschy,** Maria 1940- IntMPA 92
**Perse,** Saint-John 1887-1975 FacFETw
**Persell,** Dave Matthew 1954- WhoRel 92
**Persell,** Ralph M 1908- AmMWSc 92
**Persell,** William Dailey 1943- WhoRel 92
**Persey,** Robert 1951- TwCPaSc
**Pershan,** Peter Silas 1934- AmMWSc 92
**Pershan,** Richard Henry 1930- WhoAmL 92
**Pershing,** Bruce Lee 1953- WhoMW 92
**Pershing,** J. J. 1860-1948 BenetAL 91
**Pershing,** John J 1860-1948 RComAH
**Pershing,** John Joseph 1860-1948 FacFETw [port]
**Pershing,** Lucille Virginia 1916- WhoAmP 91
**Pershing,** Robert George 1941- WhoMW 92
**Persiani,** Paul J 1921- AmMWSc 92
**Persichetti,** Vincent 1915-1987 FacFETw, NewAmDM
**Persico,** Joseph E. 1930- WrDr 92
**Persico,** Lou 1955- WhoFI 92
**Persico,** Vincent Anthony 1948- WhoAmP 91
**Persinger,** Louis 1887-1966 NewAmDM
**Persip,** Charles Lawrence 1929- WhoEnt 92
**Perske,** Betty Joan 1924- WhoEnt 92
**Perskie,** Steven Philip 1945- WhoAmP 91
**Persky,** Burton 1938- WhoMW 92
**Persky,** George 1938- AmMWSc 92
**Persky,** Harold 1917- AmMWSc 92
**Persky,** Lester 1919- AmMWSc 92
**Persky,** Lester 1927- IntMPA 92, WhoEnt 92
**Persky,** Lisa Jane WhoEnt 92
**Persky,** William Allan 1931- WhoEnt 92
**Persky-Denoff** LesBEnT 92
**Persoff,** Nehemiah 1919- IntMPA 92, WhoEnt 92
**Person,** Chuck Connors 1964- WhoBlA 92, WhoMW 92
**Person,** Clayton Oscar 1922- AmMWSc 92
**Person,** Curtis Standifer, Jr 1934- WhoAmP 91
**Person,** Dawn Renee 1956- WhoBlA 92
**Person,** Donald Ames 1938- AmMWSc 92
**Person,** Earle G. 1928- WhoBlA 92
**Person,** Earle George, Jr 1928- WhoAmP 91
**Person,** Evert Bertil 1914- WhoEnt 92, WhoWest 92
**Person,** James Carl 1936- AmMWSc 92
**Person,** James Stewart, III 1964- WhoWest 92
**Person,** Leslie Robin 1962- WhoBlA 92
**Person,** Paula 1935- WhoMW 92
**Person,** Stanley R 1928- AmMWSc 92
**Person,** Steven John 1944- AmMWSc 92
**Person,** Tom DrAPF 91
**Person,** Waverly J. 1926- WhoBlA 92
**Person,** William Alfred 1945- WhoBlA 92
**Person,** Willis Bagley 1928- AmMWSc 92
**Personeus,** Gordon Rowland 1922- AmMWSc 92
**Personick,** Stewart David 1947- AmMWSc 92
**Persons,** Augustus Archilus 1866-1917 BiInAmS
**Persons,** James Andrew 1948- WhoWest 92
**Persons,** Oscar Newton 1939- WhoAmP 91
**Persons,** W. Ray 1953- WhoAmL 92, WhoBlA 92
**Persoon,** James Richard 1951- WhoMW 92
**Persson,** Goran 1949- IntWW 91
**Persson,** Jorgen 1936- IntWW 91
**Persson,** Phyllis-Ann 1945- WhoRel 92
**Persson,** Sigurd 1914- DcTwDes
**Persson,** Sven Eric 1945- AmMWSc 92
**Persson,** Sverker 1921- AmMWSc 92
**Persson,** Walter Helge 1928- WhoRel 92
**Persson,** William Michael Dermot Who 92
**Pert,** Candace B 1946- AmMWSc 92
**Pert,** Edwin Harry 1933- WhoAmP 91
**Pertel,** Richard 1928- AmMWSc 92
**Perth,** Archbishop of Who 92
**Perth,** Archbishop of d1991 Who 92N
**Perth,** Archbishop of 1937- Who 92
**Perth,** Assistant Bishops of Who 92
**Perth,** Earl of 1907- Who 92
**Perth,** Provost of Who 92
**Perthou,** Alison Chandler 1945- WhoWest 92
**Pertica,** Alexander Jose 1961- AmMWSc 92, WhoWest 92
**Pertini,** Alessandro 1896-1990 FacFETw
**Pertini,** Sandro 1896-1990 AnObit 1990
**Pertschuk,** Michael 1933- WhoAmP 91
**Pertwee,** Jon 1919- IntMPA 92
**Pertwee,** Michael 1916- WrDr 92
**Pertwee,** Michael H R 1916- IntAu&W 91
**Pertwee,** Roland 1885-1963 ScFEYrs
**Peru And Bolivia,** Bishop of 1949- Who 92
**Perumareddi,** Jayarama Reddi 1936- AmMWSc 92
**Perun,** John Joseph, Jr. 1963- WhoFI 92
**Perun,** Thomas John 1937- AmMWSc 92
**Perutz,** Kathrin DrAPF 91
**Perutz,** Kathrin 1939- ConNov 91, IntAu&W 91
**Perutz,** Leo 1884-1957 ScFEYrs
**Perutz,** Max 1914- WrDr 92
**Perutz,** Max Ferdinand 1914- FacFETw, IntWW 91, Who 92, WhoNob 90
**Peruzzo,** Albert Louis 1951- WhoFI 92, WhoMW 92
**Peruzzotti,** George Peter 1935- AmMWSc 92
**Pervin,** William Joseph 1930- AmMWSc 92
**Pervo,** Richard Ivan 1942- WhoRel 92
**Pervukhin,** Mikhail Georg'evich 1904- SovUnBD
**Pervukhin,** Mikhail Georgievich 1904-1978 FacFETw
**Pervyshin,** Erlen Kirikovich 1932- IntWW 91
**Perwin,** Scott Eliot 1955- WhoAmL 92
**Pery** Who 92
**Peryam,** David Roger 1915- WhoMW 92
**Perz,** John Mark 1940- AmMWSc 92
**Perzak,** Frank John 1932- AmMWSc 92
**Perzel,** John Michael 1950- WhoAmP 91
**Perzigian,** Jerry WhoEnt 92
**Pesaran,** Hashem 1946- Who 92
**Pescadero,** Joey ConAu 135
**Pescadero,** Julia ConAu 135
**Pescatore,** Pierre 1919- IntWW 91
**Pesce,** Amadeo J 1938- AmMWSc 92
**Pesce,** Amadeo John 1938- WhoMW 92
**Pesce,** Gabriel Vincent 1924- WhoWest 92
**Pesce,** Gaetano 1939- DcTwDes
**Pesce,** Michael A 1942- AmMWSc 92
**Pesce,** Michael L 1943- WhoAmP 91
**Pesch,** Leroy Allen 1931- WhoFI 92
**Pesch,** Peter 1934- AmMWSc 92
**Pesch,** William Roger 1950- WhoMW 92
**Peschau,** David Fred 1948- WhoEnt 92
**Peschio,** Thomas Dissette 1940- WhoMW 92
**Peschke,** Donald B. 1947- WhoFI 92
**Peschken,** Diether Paul 1931- AmMWSc 92
**Pesci,** Frank Bernard, Sr 1929- WhoAmP 91
**Pesci,** Joe 1943- IntMPA 92, WhoEnt 92
**Pesci,** Timothy Louis 1944- WhoAmP 91
**Pescod,** Mainwaring Bainbridge 1933- Who 92
**Pescow,** Donna 1954- IntMPA 92
**Pesek,** Boris Peter 1926- IntAu&W 91, WhoMW 92, WrDr 92
**Pesek,** John Thomas, Jr 1921- AmMWSc 92
**Pesek,** Joseph Joel 1944- AmMWSc 92
**Pesek,** Libor 1933- IntWW 91, Who 92, WhoEnt 92
**Peselnick,** Louis 1924- AmMWSc 92
**Pesenti,** Antonio 1910- IntWW 91
**Peseroff,** Joyce DrAPF 91
**Pesetsky,** Bette DrAPF 91
**Pesetsky,** Bette 1932- ConAu 133
**Pesetsky,** Irwin 1930- AmMWSc 92
**Peshewa,** Macaki 1941- RelLAm 91
**Peshkin,** Murray 1925- AmMWSc 92
**Peshkin,** Samuel David 1925- WhoAmL 92, WhoFI 92, WhoMW 92
**Pesker,** Nick Leo 1946- WhoEnt 92
**Peskett,** Stan 1937- TwCPaSc
**Peskett,** Stanley Victor 1918- Who 92
**Peskett,** William 1952- ConPo 91, WrDr 92
**Peskin,** Arnold Michael 1944- AmMWSc 92
**Peskin,** Michael Edward 1951- AmMWSc 92
**Peskin,** Myron I. 1927- WhoFI 92
**Peskin,** Richard Leonard 1934- AmMWSc 92
**Peskin,** Richard Martin 1944- Who 92
**Peskoff,** Joel S. 1957- WhoFI 92
**Pesmazoglu,** John Stevens 1918- IntWW 91
**Pesner,** Leon 1921- WhoAmP 91
**Pesner,** Susan M. 1951- WhoAmL 92
**Pesola,** Anja Helena 1947- IntWW 91
**Pesola,** Robert 1949- WhoEnt 92
**Pesola,** William Ernest 1945- WhoFI 92, WhoMW 92
**Pesqueira,** Ralph Raymond WhoHisp 92
**Pesqueira,** Richard E. 1937- WhoHisp 92
**Pessagno,** J. Meric 1933- WhoRel 92
**Pessen,** David W 1925- AmMWSc 92
**Pessen,** Edward 1920- IntAu&W 91, WrDr 92
**Pessen,** Helmut 1921- AmMWSc 92
**Pessia,** Wayne Joseph 1963- WhoRel 92
**Pessl,** Fred, Jr 1932- AmMWSc 92
**Pessoa,** Fernando 1888-1935 FacFETw
**Pessoa,** Michelle Marie 1966- WhoEnt 92
**Pesson,** Lynn L 1927- AmMWSc 92
**Pesta,** Carl Michael 1938- WhoMW 92
**Pesta,** Michael George, IV 1964- WhoEnt 92
**Pestalozzi,** Johann Heinrich 1746-1827 BlkwCEP
**Pestana,** Carlos 1936- AmMWSc 92
**Pestana,** Harold Richard 1931- AmMWSc 92
**Pestell** Who 92
**Pestell,** Catherine Eva 1933- IntWW 91, Who 92
**Pestell,** John Edmund 1930- Who 92
**Pestell,** John Richard 1916- Who 92
**Pester,** Jack Cloyd 1935- WhoFI 92
**Pestka,** Sidney 1936- AmMWSc 92
**Pestl-Ciccolo,** Kris Ann 1963- WhoAmL 92
**Peston** Who 92
**Peston,** Baron 1931- Who 92
**Pestrong,** Raymond 1937- AmMWSc 92
**Pestronk,** Alan 1946- AmMWSc 92
**Pesyna,** Gail Marlane 1948- WhoFI 92
**Petaccia,** Mario A. DrAPF 91
**Petain,** Henri 1856-1951 EncTR 91 [port]
**Petain,** Henri Philippe 1856-1951 FacFETw [port]
**Petaja,** Emil 1915- IntAu&W 91, TwCSFW 91, WrDr 92
**Petajan,** Jack Hougen 1930- AmMWSc 92
**Petak,** George WhoAmP 91
**Petch,** Barry Irvine 1933- Who 92
**Petch,** Howard Earle 1925- AmMWSc 92, WhoWest 92
**Petch,** Norman James 1917- IntWW 91, Who 92
**Petchler,** John William 1956- WhoFI 92
**Petecki,** Bohdan Antoni 1931- IntAu&W 91
**Petelos,** Tony 1953- WhoAmP 91
**Peter** d64? EncEarC [port]
**Peter I** 1672-1725 BlkwCEP
**Peter II** 1715-1730 BlkwCEP
**Peter II** 1923-1970 FacFETw
**Peter III** 1728-1762 BlkwCEP
**Peter,** Archbishop 1926- WhoRel 92
**Peter Chrysologus** 400?-454 EncEarC
**Peter of Alexandria** EncEarC
**Peter of Spain** 1205?-1277 DcLB 115
**Peter,** Paul & Mary FacFETw, NewAmDM
**Peter The Fuller** d488 EncEarC
**Peter the Great** 1672-1725 BlkwCEP
**Peter,** Arnold Philimon 1957- WhoAmL 92, WhoWest 92
**Peter,** Carl J. d1991 NewYTBS 91
**Peter,** Carroll E. 1929- WhoMW 92
**Peter,** Emil, III 1942- WhoFI 92
**Peter,** Emmett DrAPF 91
**Peter,** Hugh 1598-1660 BenetAL 91
**Peter,** James Bernard 1933- AmMWSc 92
**Peter,** Janos 1910- IntWW 91
**Peter,** Laurence 1919-1990 AnObit 1990
**Peter,** Lily IntAu&W 91
**Peter,** Oliver Bernard 1930- WhoWest 92
**Peter,** Phillips Smith 1932- WhoAmL 92, WhoFI 92
**Peter,** Richard Ector 1943- AmMWSc 92
**Peter,** Robert 1805-1894 BiInAmS
**Peter,** Robert Christian 1948- WhoMW 92
**Peter,** Val Joseph 1934- WhoRel 92
**Peter,** Zoltan Antal 1944- WhoEnt 92
**Peterborough,** Bishop of 1925- Who 92
**Peterborough,** Dean of Who 92
**Petercsak,** James Julius 1944- WhoEnt 92
**Peterfreund,** Stuart DrAPF 91
**Peterfreund,** Stuart Samuel 1945- IntAu&W 91
**Petering,** David Harold 1942- AmMWSc 92
**Petering,** Harold George AmMWSc 92
**Peterjohn,** Glenn William 1921- AmMWSc 92
**Peterken,** Laurence Edwin 1931- Who 92
**Peterkiewicz,** Jerzy 1916- ConNov 91, IntAu&W 91, Who 92, WrDr 92
**Peterkin,** George Alexander, Jr. 1927- WhoFI 92
**Peterkin,** Julia 1880-1961 BenetAL 91
**Peterkin,** Neville 1915- Who 92
**Peterkofsky,** Alan 1930- AmMWSc 92
**Peterle,** Tony J 1925- AmMWSc 92
**Peterlin,** Anton 1908- AmMWSc 92
**Peterlin,** Boris Matija 1947- AmMWSc 92
**Peterlin,** Michael Leslie 1945- WhoMW 92, WhoRel 92
**Peterman,** David A 1935- AmMWSc 92
**Peterman,** David Randall 1959- WhoWest 92
**Peterman,** Donna Cole 1947- WhoMW 92
**Peterman,** Keith Eugene 1947- AmMWSc 92
**Peterman,** Leotis 1934- WhoBlA 92
**Peterman,** Peggy M. 1936- WhoBlA 92
**Peterman,** Zell Edwin 1934- AmMWSc 92
**Peternal,** Nancy Farrell 1929- WhoAmP 91
**Peternel,** Joan DrAPF 91
**Peters,** A. G. WhoRel 92
**Peters,** Alan 1929- AmMWSc 92
**Peters,** Alan Winthrop 1937- AmMWSc 92
**Peters,** Alexander Robert 1936- AmMWSc 92
**Peters,** Arthur Gordon Who 92
**Peters,** Aulana Louise 1941- WhoAmL 92, WhoBlA 92
**Peters,** B Frank 1933- AmMWSc 92
**Peters,** Barbara Humbird 1948- WhoWest 92
**Peters,** Barbara M. Stratton 1949- WhoWest 92
**Peters,** Benjamin Justin 1962- WhoEnt 92
**Peters,** Bernadette 1948- ConMus 7 [port], IntMPA 92, WhoEnt 92
**Peters,** Boyd Leon 1951- WhoMW 92
**Peters,** Brian WrDr 92
**Peters,** Brock 1927- IntMPA 92, WhoEnt 92
**Peters,** Brock G. 1927- WhoBlA 92
**Peters,** Bruce Harry 1937- AmMWSc 92
**Peters,** Carl Friedrich 1779-1827 NewAmDM
**Peters,** Carol Ann Dudycha 1938- WhoMW 92
**Peters,** Caroljean Natalie 1931- WhoMW 92
**Peters,** Carolyn J 1948- WhoAmP 91
**Peters,** Charles L., Jr. 1935- WhoBlA 92
**Peters,** Charles Merrell 1953- WhoFI 92
**Peters,** Charles William 1927- AmMWSc 92
**Peters,** Cheryl Olga 1951- WhoIns 92
**Peters,** Christian Henry Frederick 1813-1890 BiInAmS
**Peters,** Christopher Edward 1950- WhoAmL 92
**Peters,** Clarence J 1940- AmMWSc 92
**Peters,** Clay Etha, II 1962- WhoRel 92
**Peters,** Connie 1933- WhoAmP 91
**Peters,** Dale Thompson 1934- AmMWSc 92
**Peters,** David Farr 1958- WhoRel 92

**Peters**, David Keith 1938- *Who 92*
**Peters**, David Louis 1945- *WhoFI 92*
**Peters**, David M 1954- *WhoAmP 91*
**Peters**, David Stewart 1941- *AmMWSc 92*
**Peters**, David Walter 1935- *WhoRel 92*
**Peters**, Denis John 1953- *WhoEnt 92*
**Peters**, Dennis Gail 1937- *AmMWSc 92, WhoMW 92*
**Peters**, Don Clayton 1931- *AmMWSc 92*
**Peters**, Donald Joseph 1959- *WhoFI 92*
**Peters**, Douglas Cameron 1955- *WhoWest 92*
**Peters**, Doyle Buren 1922- *AmMWSc 92*
**Peters**, E 1926- *AmMWSc 92*
**Peters**, Earl 1927- *AmMWSc 92*
**Peters**, Earl Louis 1934- *WhoRel 92*
**Peters**, Edgar Eugene 1952- *WhoFI 92*
**Peters**, Edward Dyer 1849-1917 *BiInAmS*
**Peters**, Edward James 1944- *AmMWSc 92*
**Peters**, Edward Lee 1954- *WhoFI 92*
**Peters**, Edward Tehle 1935- *AmMWSc 92*
**Peters**, Elizabeth *ConAu 36NR, WrDr 92*
**Peters**, Elizabeth Anne 1940- *WhoMW 92*
**Peters**, Ellen Ash *WhoAmP 91*
**Peters**, Ellen Ash 1930- *WhoAmL 92*
**Peters**, Ellis *IntAu&W 91X, IntWW 91, Who 92, WrDr 92*
**Peters**, Elroy John 1922- *AmMWSc 92*
**Peters**, Erskine Alvin 1948- *WhoBlA 92*
**Peters**, Esther Caroline 1952- *AmMWSc 92*
**Peters**, Fenton 1935- *WhoBlA 92*
**Peters**, Frank Albert 1931- *WhoFI 92*
**Peters**, Frank Lewis, Jr. 1930- *WhoEnt 92*
**Peters**, Frederick Whitten 1946- *WhoAmL 92*
**Peters**, Fredus Nelson, IV 1958- *WhoMW 92*
**Peters**, Garry Lowell 1952- *WhoFI 92*
**Peters**, Geoffrey *IntAu&W 91X*
**Peters**, George Alfred 1924- *WhoAmL 92*
**Peters**, George Henry 1934- *Who 92*
**Peters**, Gerald Alan 1943- *AmMWSc 92*
**Peters**, Gerald Joseph 1941- *AmMWSc 92*
**Peters**, Geraldine Joan *AmMWSc 92*
**Peters**, Gordon Benes 1931- *WhoEnt 92*
**Peters**, Henry A 1920- *AmMWSc 92*
**Peters**, Henry Buckland 1916- *AmMWSc 92*
**Peters**, Henry H 1941- *WhoAmP 91*
**Peters**, Henry John 1924- *WhoMW 92*
**Peters**, Herbert David 1948- *WhoAmP 91*
**Peters**, Howard August 1926- *AmMWSc 92*
**Peters**, Howard McDowell 1940- *AmMWSc 92*
**Peters**, Isaak 1826-1911 *RelLAm 91*
**Peters**, J Elbert 1933- *WhoAmP 91*
**Peters**, Jack Richard 1930- *WhoRel 92*
**Peters**, Jack Warren 1916- *AmMWSc 92*
**Peters**, James 1934- *AmMWSc 92*
**Peters**, James Empson 1954- *AmMWSc 92*
**Peters**, James John 1941- *AmMWSc 92*
**Peters**, James Ray 1946- *WhoMW 92*
**Peters**, James Sedalia, II *WhoBlA 92*
**Peters**, Jeanne Elizabeth 1943- *WhoMW 92*
**Peters**, Jeffrey L 1939- *AmMWSc 92*
**Peters**, Jennifer Laura 1954- *WhoEnt 92*
**Peters**, Joan K. *DrAPF 91*
**Peters**, John Basil 1952- *WhoFI 92*
**Peters**, John H. 1946- *WhoEnt 92*
**Peters**, John Henry 1924- *AmMWSc 92*
**Peters**, John Lyon 1920- *WhoAmP 91*
**Peters**, John Murphy 1956- *WhoMW 92*
**Peters**, Johnnie Mae 1929- *WhoAmP 91*
**Peters**, Jon 1947- *IntMPA 92, WhoEnt 92*
**Peters**, Jonathan C. 1946- *IntWW 91*
**Peters**, Joseph John 1907- *AmMWSc 92*
**Peters**, Joyce Eileen 1953- *WhoWest 92*
**Peters**, Justin 1946- *AmMWSc 92*
**Peters**, Kelly Boyte 1958- *WhoRel 92*
**Peters**, Kelly Jean 1940- *WhoEnt 92*
**Peters**, Kenneth Darryl, Sr. 1949- *WhoBlA 92*
**Peters**, Kenneth Jamieson 1923- *Who 92*
**Peters**, Kenneth P 1952- *WhoAmP 91*
**Peters**, Kenneth Reed, Jr. 1947- *WhoMW 92*
**Peters**, Kevin Casey 1952- *WhoAmP 91*
**Peters**, Kevin Scott 1949- *AmMWSc 92*
**Peters**, Lance 1934- *IntAu&W 91*
**Peters**, Lanny Lee 1952- *WhoRel 92*
**Peters**, Larry Albur 1954- *WhoRel 92*
**Peters**, Lee Alan *WhoMW 92*
**Peters**, Lenrie 1932- *ConPo 91, WrDr 92*
**Peters**, Leo Charles 1931- *AmMWSc 92*
**Peters**, Leon, Jr 1923- *AmMWSc 92*
**Peters**, Leroy Lynn 1931- *AmMWSc 92*
**Peters**, LeRoy Richard 1943- *WhoWest 92*
**Peters**, Leslie 1942- *WhoAmL 92*
**Peters**, Lester John 1942- *AmMWSc 92*
**Peters**, Lewis 1932- *AmMWSc 92*
**Peters**, Lori Susan 1958- *WhoFI 92, WhoMW 92*
**Peters**, Lynn Randolph 1925- *AmMWSc 92*
**Peters**, Margot 1933- *WrDr 92*
**Peters**, Margot McCullough 1933- *IntAu&W 91*
**Peters**, Marjorie Young 1928- *WhoAmP 91*
**Peters**, Martin Trevor 1936- *Who 92*
**Peters**, Marvin Arthur 1933- *AmMWSc 92*
**Peters**, Mary Elizabeth 1939- *Who 92*
**Peters**, Maureen 1935- *IntAu&W 91, WrDr 92*
**Peters**, Max S 1920- *AmMWSc 92*
**Peters**, Michael *WhoBlA 92*
**Peters**, Michael Bartley 1943- *WhoMW 92*
**Peters**, Michael Ray 1949- *WhoAmP 91*
**Peters**, Michael Wayne 1952- *WhoRel 92*
**Peters**, Michael Wood 1938- *AmMWSc 92*
**Peters**, Natasha *IntAu&W 91, WrDr 92*
**Peters**, Paul Conrad 1928- *AmMWSc 92*
**Peters**, Penn A 1938- *AmMWSc 92*
**Peters**, Perry 1931- *WhoAmP 91*
**Peters**, Philip Boardman 1935- *AmMWSc 92*
**Peters**, Philip Carl 1938- *AmMWSc 92*
**Peters**, Philip H 1921- *AmMWSc 92*
**Peters**, R. Jonathan 1927- *WhoAmL 92*
**Peters**, Ralph B 1922- *WhoAmP 91*
**Peters**, Ralph Frew 1929- *WhoFI 92*
**Peters**, Ralph I 1947- *AmMWSc 92*
**Peters**, Randall Douglas 1942- *AmMWSc 92*
**Peters**, Raymond Eugene 1933- *WhoFI 92, WhoWest 92*
**Peters**, Raymond Harry 1918- *Who 92*
**Peters**, Raymond Robert 1942- *WhoWest 92*
**Peters**, Richard Morse 1922- *AmMWSc 92*
**Peters**, Richard Stanley 1919- *IntAu&W 91, Who 92, WrDr 92*
**Peters**, Robert *DrAPF 91*
**Peters**, Robert 1924- *WrDr 92*
**Peters**, Robert Allen 1927- *WhoMW 92*
**Peters**, Robert Edward 1940- *AmMWSc 92*
**Peters**, Robert G *WhoAmP 91*
**Peters**, Robert Geoffrey 1940- *Who 92*
**Peters**, Robert Henry 1946- *AmMWSc 92*
**Peters**, Robert L. 1924- *ConPo 91*
**Peters**, Robert Louis 1924- *IntAu&W 91*
**Peters**, Robert Timothy 1946- *WhoAmL 92*
**Peters**, Robert Wayne 1945- *WhoAmL 92*
**Peters**, Robert Wayne 1950- *WhoFI 92, WhoWest 92*
**Peters**, Roberta 1930- *FacFETw, NewAmDM, WhoEnt 92*
**Peters**, Roger Paul 1943- *AmMWSc 92*
**Peters**, Roscoe Hoffman, Jr. 1945- *WhoBlA 92*
**Peters**, Rotimi 1955- *BlkOlyM*
**Peters**, Roy *TwCWW 91*
**Peters**, S. Jeffrey 1924- *WhoFI 92*
**Peters**, Samuel A. 1934- *WhoBlA 92*
**Peters**, Samuel Andrew 1735-1826 *BenetAL 91*
**Peters**, Samuel Anthony 1934- *WhoAmL 92*
**Peters**, Sheila Renee 1959- *WhoBlA 92*
**Peters**, Stanley W 1927- *WhoAmP 91*
**Peters**, Stefan 1909- *AmMWSc 92*
**Peters**, Steven 1948- *WhoFI 92*
**Peters**, Theodore, Jr 1922- *AmMWSc 92*
**Peters**, Theophilus 1921- *Who 92*
**Peters**, Thomas G 1945- *AmMWSc 92*
**Peters**, Thomas J. 1942- *ConAu 135*
**Peters**, Thomas Michael 1937- *AmMWSc 92*
**Peters**, Till Justus Nathan 1934- *AmMWSc 92*
**Peters**, Tom *ConAu 135*
**Peters**, Viola *WhoEnt 92*
**Peters**, Virginia 1924- *WhoEnt 92*
**Peters**, Wallace 1924- *IntWW 91, Who 92*
**Peters**, William 1921- *WhoEnt 92*
**Peters**, William 1923- *Who 92*
**Peters**, William Alfred 1940- *WhoBlA 92*
**Peters**, William C. 1920- *WrDr 92*
**Peters**, William Callier 1920- *AmMWSc 92*
**Peters**, William Frank 1934- *WhoWest 92*
**Peters**, William Lee 1939- *AmMWSc 92*
**Peters**, William Wesley d1991 *NewYTBS 91 [port]*
**Peters**, Winston R. *IntWW 91*
**Petersberger**, Ralph Isaac 1933- *WhoAmL 92*
**Petersdorf**, Robert George 1926- *AmMWSc 92, IntWW 91*
**Petersen**, Allan Ernest 1918- *WhoBlA 92*
**Petersen**, Arthur Everett, Jr. 1949- *WhoBlA 92*
**Petersen**, Arthur Meredith 1942- *WhoWest 92*
**Petersen**, Bent Edvard 1942- *AmMWSc 92*
**Petersen**, Betty L. 1921- *WhoRel 92*
**Petersen**, Bruce H 1937- *AmMWSc 92*
**Petersen**, Bruce Lee 1942- *WhoRel 92*
**Petersen**, Bruce Wallace 1936- *AmMWSc 92*
**Petersen**, Carl Frank 1937- *AmMWSc 92*
**Petersen**, Charlie Frederick 1915- *AmMWSc 92*
**Petersen**, Daniel F 1951- *WhoAmP 91*
**Petersen**, David Lee 1943- *WhoRel 92*
**Petersen**, Dennis Roger *AmMWSc 92*
**Petersen**, Donald *DrAPF 91*
**Petersen**, Donald E 1926- *AmMWSc 92*
**Petersen**, Donald Edward 1958- *WhoAmL 92*
**Petersen**, Donald Eugene 1926- *IntWW 91*
**Petersen**, Donald Felix 1928- *WhoWest 92*
**Petersen**, Donald Francis 1926- *AmMWSc 92*
**Petersen**, Donald H 1934- *AmMWSc 92*
**Petersen**, Donald Ralph 1929- *AmMWSc 92*
**Petersen**, Douglas Arndt 1944- *WhoMW 92*
**Petersen**, Douglas W *WhoAmP 91*
**Petersen**, Edward Leland 1932- *AmMWSc 92*
**Petersen**, Edward S 1921- *AmMWSc 92*
**Petersen**, Edwin L. 1944- *WhoWest 92*
**Petersen**, Eileen Ramona 1937- *WhoBlA 92*
**Petersen**, Einar Olaf 1923- *WhoEnt 92*
**Petersen**, Eugene E 1924- *AmMWSc 92*
**Petersen**, Finn Bo 1951- *WhoWest 92*
**Petersen**, Frederick Adolph 1913- *AmMWSc 92*
**Petersen**, Gary Walter 1939- *AmMWSc 92*
**Petersen**, Gene 1944- *AmMWSc 92*
**Petersen**, George Bouet 1933- *IntWW 91*
**Petersen**, Gerald Lee 1946- *WhoRel 92*
**Petersen**, Gina Kristie 1969- *WhoEnt 92*
**Petersen**, Harold, Jr 1940- *AmMWSc 92*
**Petersen**, Henry E. d1991 *NewYTBS 91 [port]*
**Petersen**, Howard C. 1910- *IntWW 91*
**Petersen**, Howard Edwin 1932- *WhoAmL 92*
**Petersen**, Ingo Hans 1930- *AmMWSc 92*
**Petersen**, Jack 1911-1990 *AnObit 1990*
**Petersen**, James Charles 1928- *WhoAmL 92*
**Petersen**, James L. 1947- *WhoAmL 92*
**Petersen**, Jeffrey 1920- *Who 92*
**Petersen**, Jeffrey Charles 1920- *IntWW 91*
**Petersen**, Jeffrey Lee 1947- *AmMWSc 92*
**Petersen**, Jens 1923- *IntWW 91*
**Petersen**, Johannes B. *Who 92*
**Petersen**, John David 1947- *AmMWSc 92*
**Petersen**, John Robert 1929- *AmMWSc 92*
**Petersen**, Joseph Claine 1925- *AmMWSc 92*
**Petersen**, Karl Endel 1943- *AmMWSc 92*
**Petersen**, Kenneth C 1936- *AmMWSc 92*
**Petersen**, Kim Eberhard 1956- *WhoFI 92*
**Petersen**, Lyndell 1931- *WhoAmP 91*
**Petersen**, Marshall Arthur 1938- *WhoFI 92*
**Petersen**, Maureen Jeanette Miller 1956- *WhoMW 92*
**Petersen**, Melvin William 1936- *WhoFI 92*
**Petersen**, Morris Smith 1933- *AmMWSc 92*
**Petersen**, Nancy Sue 1943- *AmMWSc 92*
**Petersen**, Neal Lennard 1937- *WhoAmL 92*
**Petersen**, Niels Helveg 1939- *IntWW 91*
**Petersen**, Norman Richard, Jr. 1933- *WhoRel 92*
**Petersen**, Norman William 1933- *WhoFI 92*
**Petersen**, Owen Dale 1944- *WhoAmL 92*
**Petersen**, P J 1941- *IntAu&W 91*
**Petersen**, Patricia Ann 1935- *WhoMW 92*
**Petersen**, Patrick John 1966- *WhoEnt 92*
**Petersen**, Paul 1945- *IntMPA 92*
**Petersen**, Quentin Richard 1924- *AmMWSc 92*
**Petersen**, Raymond Carl 1929- *AmMWSc 92*
**Petersen**, Richard Randolph 1940- *AmMWSc 92*
**Petersen**, Robert J 1937- *AmMWSc 92*
**Petersen**, Robert Virgil 1926- *AmMWSc 92*
**Petersen**, Rodney Jay 1963- *WhoMW 92*
**Petersen**, Roger Gene 1924- *AmMWSc 92*
**Petersen**, Roland 1926- *WhoWest 92*
**Petersen**, Ronald Lynn 1945- *WhoEnt 92*
**Petersen**, Stephen D. 1943- *WhoAmL 92*
**Petersen**, Ulrich 1927- *AmMWSc 92*
**Petersen**, Vernon Leroy 1926- *WhoWest 92*
**Petersen**, W Harold 1928- *WhoIns 92*
**Petersen**, W. W. *WhoRel 92*
**Petersen**, Wallace Christian 1943- *AmMWSc 92*
**Petersen**, William 1953- *IntMPA 92*
**Petersen**, William James 1929- *WhoRel 92*
**Petersen**, William Lawrence 1950- *WhoRel 92*
**Petersen**, Wolfgang 1941- *IntMPA 92, WhoEnt 92*
**Petersen-Frey**, Roland 1937- *WhoFI 92*
**Petersham**, Viscount 1945- *Who 92*
**Petersham**, Maud 1889-1971 *ChlLR 24 [port]*
**Petersham**, Maude 1889-1971 *BenetAL 91*
**Petersham**, Miska 1888-1960 *BenetAL 91, ChlLR 24 [port]*
**Petersime**, Martin Alan 1953- *WhoMW 92*
**Petersmeyer**, Charles Wrede 1919- *WhoEnt 92*
**Peterson**, Adaire *WhoIns 92*
**Peterson**, Agnes Marie 1926- *WhoAmP 91*
**Peterson**, Alan Herbert 1932- *AmMWSc 92*
**Peterson**, Alan Herbert 1948- *WhoBlA 92*
**Peterson**, Alan J *WhoAmP 91*
**Peterson**, Alan Reed 1940- *WhoAmP 91*
**Peterson**, Allen Montgomery 1922- *AmMWSc 92*
**Peterson**, Alphonse 1926- *WhoBlA 92*
**Peterson**, Andrea L. 1952- *WhoAmL 92*
**Peterson**, Andrew R 1942- *AmMWSc 92*
**Peterson**, Ann C. *WhoAmL 92*
**Peterson**, Arnold 1914- *AmMWSc 92*
**Peterson**, Arthur Carl 1923- *AmMWSc 92*
**Peterson**, Arthur Edwin 1923- *AmMWSc 92*
**Peterson**, Arthur George 1944- *WhoMW 92*
**Peterson**, Audrey Clinton 1917- *WhoBlA 92*
**Peterson**, Barbara Ann Bennett 1942- *WhoWest 92*
**Peterson**, Barbara Jo 1943- *WhoWest 92*
**Peterson**, Barry Don 1946- *WhoAmL 92*
**Peterson**, Barry Wayne 1942- *AmMWSc 92*
**Peterson**, Benjamin 1942- *WhoBlA 92*
**Peterson**, Betty Ann 1929- *WhoAmP 91*
**Peterson**, Bobbie Vern 1928- *AmMWSc 92*
**Peterson**, Bradley Eugene 1961- *WhoMW 92*
**Peterson**, Bradley Michael 1951- *AmMWSc 92*
**Peterson**, Brooke Alan 1949- *WhoAmL 92, WhoWest 92*
**Peterson**, Bruce Bigelow 1935- *AmMWSc 92*
**Peterson**, Bruce Dwight 1948- *WhoMW 92*
**Peterson**, Bruce Edward 1954- *WhoFI 92*
**Peterson**, Bruce Henry 1918- *WrDr 92*
**Peterson**, Bruce Jon 1945- *AmMWSc 92*
**Peterson**, Carl M. 1914- *WhoBlA 92*
**Peterson**, Carl Roy 1930- *WhoAmL 92*
**Peterson**, Carlos Randall 1947- *WhoRel 92*
**Peterson**, Cary G 1953- *WhoAmP 91*
**Peterson**, Cassandra 1951- *ConTFT 9, WhoEnt 92*
**Peterson**, Cathryn J 1952- *WhoIns 92*
**Peterson**, Cathryn Mary *Who 92*
**Peterson**, Charles E 1914- *WhoAmP 91*
**Peterson**, Charles Eric 1914- *WhoWest 92*
**Peterson**, Charles Fillmore 1920- *AmMWSc 92*
**Peterson**, Charles Gordon 1926- *WhoAmL 92*
**Peterson**, Charles Henry 1946- *AmMWSc 92*
**Peterson**, Charles Jacobs 1819-1887 *BenetAL 91*
**Peterson**, Charles John 1945- *AmMWSc 92, WhoMW 92*
**Peterson**, Charles Leslie 1924- *AmMWSc 92*
**Peterson**, Charles Marquis 1943- *AmMWSc 92*
**Peterson**, Charles Roland 1935- *WhoAmP 91*
**Peterson**, Chase N. 1929- *WhoWest 92*
**Peterson**, Chris Robert 1961- *WhoWest 92*
**Peterson**, Christmas *WrDr 92*
**Peterson**, Clare Gray 1917- *AmMWSc 92*
**Peterson**, Clarence James, Jr 1928- *AmMWSc 92*
**Peterson**, Clarence Josephus 1932- *WhoBlA 92*
**Peterson**, Clinton E 1916- *AmMWSc 92*
**Peterson**, Coleman Hollis 1948- *WhoMW 92*
**Peterson**, Colin Vyvyan 1932- *Who 92*
**Peterson**, Collin C. 1944- *AlmAP 92 [port], WhoMW 92*
**Peterson**, Collin Clark 1944- *WhoAmP 91*
**Peterson**, Connie L. 1946- *WhoAmL 92*
**Peterson**, Craig A 1947- *WhoAmP 91*
**Peterson**, Curtis Morris 1942- *AmMWSc 92*
**Peterson**, Curtis N *WhoAmP 91*
**Peterson**, Cynthia Wyeth 1933- *AmMWSc 92*
**Peterson**, Dallas Odell 1925- *AmMWSc 92*
**Peterson**, Dana Gregg 1947- *WhoWest 92*
**Peterson**, Darryl Ronnie 1943- *AmMWSc 92*
**Peterson**, Darwin Wilson 1938- *AmMWSc 92*
**Peterson**, Daryl George 1950- *WhoWest 92*
**Peterson**, David 1943- *IntWW 91*
**Peterson**, David Allan 1938- *AmMWSc 92*
**Peterson**, David Frederick 1937- *WhoAmP 91*

**Peterson,** David Maurice 1940- *AmMWSc 92*
**Peterson,** David Oscar 1950- *AmMWSc 92*
**Peterson,** David R. 1942- *WhoEnt 92*
**Peterson,** David Robert 1943- *Who 92*
**Peterson,** David Robert 1954- *WhoFI 92*
**Peterson,** David T 1922- *AmMWSc 92*
**Peterson,** David West 1940- *AmMWSc 92*
**Peterson,** Dean Everett 1941- *AmMWSc 92*
**Peterson,** Dean F, Jr 1913- *AmMWSc 92*
**Peterson,** Dean McCormack 1931- *WhoWest 92*
**Peterson,** Delaine Charles 1936- *WhoFI 92*
**Peterson,** Dennis Roy 1949- *WhoMW 92*
**Peterson,** Derek Allen 1961- *WhoWest 92*
**Peterson,** Donald 1956- *ConAu 135*
**Peterson,** Donald Bruce 1931- *AmMWSc 92*
**Peterson,** Donald C *WhoAmP 91*
**Peterson,** Donald Curtis 1931- *WhoFI 92*
**Peterson,** Donald Franklin 1925- *WhoIns 92*
**Peterson,** Donald I 1922- *AmMWSc 92*
**Peterson,** Donald J 1935- *AmMWSc 92*
**Peterson,** Donald Lee 1930- *AmMWSc 92*
**Peterson,** Donald M 1936- *WhoIns 92*
**Peterson,** Donald Matthew 1936- *WhoFI 92*
**Peterson,** Donald Neil 1941- *AmMWSc 92*
**Peterson,** Donald Palmer 1929- *AmMWSc 92*
**Peterson,** Donald Richard 1921- *AmMWSc 92*
**Peterson,** Donald W. 1929- *WhoAmL 92*
**Peterson,** Donald William 1925- *AmMWSc 92, WhoWest 92*
**Peterson,** Donna C 1946- *WhoAmP 91*
**Peterson,** Dorothy 1900?- *NotBlAW 92*
**Peterson,** Dorothy Hawkins 1932- *WhoWest 92*
**Peterson,** Doug 1948- *WhoAmP 91*
**Peterson,** Douglas 1935- *AlmAP 92 [port]*
**Peterson,** Dwight Arthur 1948- *WhoAmP 91*
**Peterson,** Earl Andrew 1940- *AmMWSc 92*
**Peterson,** Edward A. 1943- *WhoEnt 92*
**Peterson,** Edward Charles 1929- *AmMWSc 92*
**Peterson,** Edward Myron 1946- *WhoEnt 92*
**Peterson,** Edward N. 1925- *WrDr 92*
**Peterson,** Edward Norman 1925- *IntAu&W 91*
**Peterson,** Edwin J. 1930- *WhoAmL 92, WhoAmP 91, WhoWest 92*
**Peterson,** Edwin Loose 1915- *WrDr 92*
**Peterson,** Elaine Novotny 1925- *WhoMW 92*
**Peterson,** Elbert Axel 1918- *AmMWSc 92*
**Peterson,** Ellengene Hodges 1940- *AmMWSc 92*
**Peterson,** Elmer 1930- *WrDr 92*
**Peterson,** Elmor Lee 1938- *AmMWSc 92*
**Peterson,** Erik Frank 1951- *WhoFI 92*
**Peterson,** Ernest A 1931- *AmMWSc 92*
**Peterson,** Ernest W 1938- *AmMWSc 92*
**Peterson,** Ernest Wesley 1926- *WhoRel 92*
**Peterson,** Esther Eggertsen 1906- *WhoAmP 91*
**Peterson,** Eugene James 1949- *AmMWSc 92*
**Peterson,** Eugene K. 1920-1985 *WhoBlA 92N*
**Peterson,** Forrest 1922- *FacFETw*
**Peterson,** Francis Carl 1942- *AmMWSc 92*
**Peterson,** Frank Lynn 1941- *AmMWSc 92*
**Peterson,** Franklin Delano 1932- *WhoAmL 92*
**Peterson,** Franklin Paul 1930- *AmMWSc 92*
**Peterson,** Fred 1933- *AmMWSc 92*
**Peterson,** Frederick Forney 1928- *AmMWSc 92*
**Peterson,** Fredric Dahlin 1937- *WhoRel 92*
**Peterson,** Gale Eugene 1944- *WhoMW 92*
**Peterson,** Gary A 1940- *AmMWSc 92*
**Peterson,** Gary Glenn 1953- *WhoEnt 92*
**Peterson,** Gary Lee 1936- *AmMWSc 92*
**Peterson,** Gary Paul 1952- *WhoEnt 92*
**Peterson,** Gary William 1946- *WhoEnt 92*
**Peterson,** Gene Richard 1949- *WhoRel 92*
**Peterson,** Geoff *DrAPF 91*
**Peterson,** George Earl 1934- *AmMWSc 92*
**Peterson,** George Ellsworth, Jr. 1937- *WhoWest 92*
**Peterson,** George Harold 1931- *AmMWSc 92*
**Peterson,** George P 1930- *AmMWSc 92*
**Peterson,** Georgia Bodell *WhoAmP 91*
**Peterson,** Gerald A 1932- *AmMWSc 92*
**Peterson,** Gerald Alvin 1931- *AmMWSc 92*
**Peterson,** Gerald E 1938- *AmMWSc 92*
**Peterson,** Gerald Elroy 1933- *WhoEnt 92*
**Peterson,** Gerald Joseph 1947- *WhoWest 92*
**Peterson,** Gerard M. 1932- *WhoBlA 92*
**Peterson,** Gilbert A. 1935- *WhoRel 92*
**Peterson,** Gilbert Allan 1935- *ConAu 35NR*
**Peterson,** Glenn Walter 1922- *AmMWSc 92*
**Peterson,** Gregory Wayne 1955- *WhoWest 92*
**Peterson,** Harold A 1908- *AmMWSc 92*
**Peterson,** Harold Arthur 1926- *AmMWSc 92*
**Peterson,** Harold LeRoy 1938- *AmMWSc 92*
**Peterson,** Harold LeRoy 1946- *AmMWSc 92*
**Peterson,** Harold Oscar 1909- *AmMWSc 92, WhoMW 92*
**Peterson,** Harry Austin, Sr. 1906- *WhoEnt 92*
**Peterson,** Harry C 1931- *AmMWSc 92*
**Peterson,** Harry Leroy 1940- *WhoWest 92*
**Peterson,** Harry Valdemar 1927- *WhoMW 92*
**Peterson,** Harry W. 1923- *WhoBlA 92*
**Peterson,** Hazel Agnes 1916- *AmMWSc 92*
**Peterson,** Henry 1818-1891 *BenetAL 91*
**Peterson,** Holger Martin 1912- *WhoFI 92*
**Peterson,** Holly Coulter 1954- *WhoMW 92*
**Peterson,** Howard Boyd 1912- *AmMWSc 92*
**Peterson,** Howard Cooper 1939- *WhoAmL 92, WhoFI 92, WhoWest 92*
**Peterson,** Idelle M 1938- *AmMWSc 92*
**Peterson,** Irene Renie 1927- *WhoWest 92*
**Peterson,** Irvin Leslie 1926- *AmMWSc 92*
**Peterson,** Isobel Rose 1911- *WhoAmP 91*
**Peterson,** Jack Edwin 1928- *AmMWSc 92*
**Peterson,** Jack Huston, Jr. 1964- *WhoFI 92*
**Peterson,** Jack Kenneth 1932- *AmMWSc 92*
**Peterson,** Jack Milton 1920- *AmMWSc 92*
**Peterson,** James A 1935- *WhoAmP 91*
**Peterson,** James Algert 1915- *AmMWSc 92, WhoWest 92*
**Peterson,** James Douglas 1948- *AmMWSc 92*
**Peterson,** James Lincoln 1942- *WhoMW 92*
**Peterson,** James Lowell 1942- *AmMWSc 92*
**Peterson,** James Macon 1937- *AmMWSc 92*
**Peterson,** James Oliver 1937- *AmMWSc 92*
**Peterson,** James Paul 1960- *WhoAmL 92*
**Peterson,** James Ray 1924- *AmMWSc 92*
**Peterson,** James Robert 1932- *AmMWSc 92*
**Peterson,** James T *AmMWSc 92*
**Peterson,** Jan Kent 1945- *WhoMW 92*
**Peterson,** Jane Louise 1947- *AmMWSc 92*
**Peterson,** Janet Brooks 1924- *AmMWSc 92*
**Peterson,** Janet Sylvia *AmMWSc 92*
**Peterson,** Jerome *WhoAmP 91*
**Peterson,** Jim *DrAPF 91*
**Peterson,** John 1935- *WhoAmP 91*
**Peterson,** John Booth 1905- *AmMWSc 92*
**Peterson,** John Carl *AmMWSc 92*
**Peterson,** John E 1938- *WhoAmP 91*
**Peterson,** John Edward 1953- *WhoRel 92*
**Peterson,** John Edward, Jr 1921- *AmMWSc 92*
**Peterson,** John Eric 1914- *AmMWSc 92, WhoWest 92*
**Peterson,** John Everett 1937- *WhoRel 92*
**Peterson,** John Ivan 1928- *AmMWSc 92*
**Peterson,** John L 1953- *WhoAmP 91*
**Peterson,** John Leonard 1933- *WhoWest 92*
**Peterson,** John M 1938- *AmMWSc 92*
**Peterson,** John Vernon 1960- *WhoMW 92*
**Peterson,** John Willard 1921- *WhoRel 92*
**Peterson,** Johnny Wayne 1946- *AmMWSc 92*
**Peterson,** Jon L. 1943- *WhoEnt 92*
**Peterson,** Joseph Louis 1929- *AmMWSc 92*
**Peterson,** Joseph Richard 1942- *AmMWSc 92*
**Peterson,** Julian Arnold 1939- *AmMWSc 92*
**Peterson,** Julie 1949- *WhoAmP 91*
**Peterson,** Karen *DrAPF 91*
**Peterson,** Karen 1941- *WhoWest 92*
**Peterson,** Kathy Lynn 1956- *WhoEnt 92*
**Peterson,** Keith *DrAPF 91*
**Peterson,** Ken M. 1946- *WhoAmL 92*
**Peterson,** Kendall Robert 1929- *AmMWSc 92*
**Peterson,** Kenneth Allen, Sr. 1939- *WhoMW 92*
**Peterson,** Kenneth C 1921- *AmMWSc 92*
**Peterson,** Kenneth Curtis, Jr. 1941- *WhoRel 92*
**Peterson,** Kenneth J 1935- *WhoIns 92*
**Peterson,** Kenneth Richard 1946- *WhoRel 92*
**Peterson,** Kevin Bruce 1948- *WhoWest 92*
**Peterson,** Kirk Charles 1949- *WhoEnt 92*
**Peterson,** Kristina Ann 1963- *WhoFI 92*
**Peterson,** Lance George 1940- *AmMWSc 92*
**Peterson,** Larry James 1942- *AmMWSc 92*
**Peterson,** Lauren Michael 1943- *AmMWSc 92*
**Peterson,** Laurence E 1931- *AmMWSc 92*
**Peterson,** Laverne E 1925- *AmMWSc 92*
**Peterson,** Lennart Rudolph 1936- *AmMWSc 92*
**Peterson,** Leona M. 1929- *WhoMW 92*
**Peterson,** Leroy 1930- *WhoWest 92*
**Peterson,** LeRoy DeWayne 1941- *WhoAmP 91*
**Peterson,** Leroy Eric 1917- *AmMWSc 92*
**Peterson,** Leslie Ernest *Who 92*
**Peterson,** Leslie Ernest 1928- *WhoRel 92*
**Peterson,** Levi Savage 1933- *WhoWest 92*
**Peterson,** Lloyd, Jr. 1958- *WhoBlA 92*
**Peterson,** Lorna Ingrid 1956- *WhoBlA 92*
**Peterson,** Lowell 1950- *WhoEnt 92, WhoWest 92*
**Peterson,** Lowell E 1926- *AmMWSc 92*
**Peterson,** Lowell S 1937- *WhoAmP 91*
**Peterson,** Lynn Louise Meister 1941- *AmMWSc 92*
**Peterson,** Lysle Henry 1921- *AmMWSc 92*
**Peterson,** Malcolm Lee 1927- *AmMWSc 92*
**Peterson,** Marcella Tandy *WhoBlA 92*
**Peterson,** Marie Katherine 1942- *WhoRel 92*
**Peterson,** Marion 1923- *WhoAmP 91*
**Peterson,** Mark Alan 1962- *WhoFI 92*
**Peterson,** Mark Michael 1961- *WhoFI 92*
**Peterson,** Martha 1916- *IntWW 91*
**Peterson,** Martin Lee 1956- *WhoAmL 92*
**Peterson,** Martin Lynn 1943- *WhoAmP 91*
**Peterson,** Mary *DrAPF 91*
**Peterson,** Mary Ellis *DrAPF 91*
**Peterson,** Mary Lou 1931- *WhoAmP 91*
**Peterson,** Maureen Laurett *WhoBlA 92*
**Peterson,** Maurice 1952- *WhoBlA 92*
**Peterson,** Maurice Lewellen 1913- *AmMWSc 92*
**Peterson,** Melbert Eugene 1930- *AmMWSc 92*
**Peterson,** Melvin Norman Adolph 1929- *AmMWSc 92*
**Peterson,** Merle Francis 1916- *WhoAmP 91*
**Peterson,** Merrill D. 1921- *WrDr 92*
**Peterson,** Michael Charles 1960- *WhoWest 92*
**Peterson,** Michael Gerald 1952- *WhoMW 92*
**Peterson,** Michael J *WhoAmP 91*
**Peterson,** Michael Lawrance 1951- *WhoWest 92*
**Peterson,** Michelle Monica 1959- *WhoBlA 92*
**Peterson,** Mike 1960- *WhoAmP 91*
**Peterson,** Miller Harrell 1925- *AmMWSc 92*
**Peterson,** Millie M 1944- *WhoAmP 91*
**Peterson,** Monica *WhoEnt 92*
**Peterson,** N Curtis, Jr 1922- *WhoAmP 91*
**Peterson,** Nad A. 1926- *WhoFI 92*
**Peterson,** Nancy 1943- *WhoAmP 91*
**Peterson,** Nancy Ann 1947- *WhoFI 92*
**Peterson,** Nancy Jo 1955- *WhoFI 92*
**Peterson,** Neal Alfred 1929- *AmMWSc 92*
**Peterson,** Norman Cornelius 1929- *AmMWSc 92*
**Peterson,** Norman L 1935- *AmMWSc 92*
**Peterson,** Norris Adrian 1953- *WhoFI 92*
**Peterson,** Oscar 1925- *NewAmDM*
**Peterson,** Oscar Emmanuel 1925- *IntWW 91, Who 92, WhoBlA 92, WhoEnt 92*
**Peterson,** Oscar James, III 1935- *WhoFI 92*
**Peterson,** Osler Leopold 1946- *WhoAmL 92*
**Peterson,** Otis G 1936- *AmMWSc 92*
**Peterson,** Pamela Parrish 1954- *WhoFI 92*
**Peterson,** Patricia Elizabeth 1942- *WhoMW 92*
**Peterson,** Patricia Lynn 1952- *WhoMW 92*
**Peterson,** Paul Ames 1928- *WhoAmL 92*
**Peterson,** Paul Constant 1940- *AmMWSc 92*
**Peterson,** Paul E 1929- *AmMWSc 92*
**Peterson,** Paul E. 1940- *IntWW 91*
**Peterson,** Paul Edward 1935- *WhoWest 92*
**Peterson,** Paul Joseph 1964- *WhoEnt 92*
**Peterson,** Paul W 1925- *AmMWSc 92*
**Peterson,** Pete 1935- *WhoAmP 91*
**Peterson,** Peter Andrew 1925- *AmMWSc 92*
**Peterson,** Peter G. 1926- *IntWW 91, WhoFI 92*
**Peterson,** Philip J. 1955- *WhoFI 92*
**Peterson,** Ralph 1924- *WhoFI 92*
**Peterson,** Ralph Alan 1951- *WhoAmL 92*
**Peterson,** Ralph Edward 1918- *AmMWSc 92*
**Peterson,** Ralph Edward 1932- *WhoRel 92*
**Peterson,** Ralph Henry 1922- *WhoAmL 92*
**Peterson,** Randolph W 1953- *WhoAmP 91*
**Peterson,** Ray E 1938- *WhoAmP 91*
**Peterson,** Raymond Dale August 1930- *AmMWSc 92*
**Peterson,** Raymond Glen 1936- *AmMWSc 92*
**Peterson,** Reider Sverre 1939- *AmMWSc 92*
**Peterson,** Richard 1928- *WhoAmP 91*
**Peterson,** Richard Austin 1932- *WrDr 92*
**Peterson,** Richard Burnett 1949- *AmMWSc 92*
**Peterson,** Richard Carl 1948- *AmMWSc 92, WhoMW 92*
**Peterson,** Richard Carson 1953- *WhoFI 92, WhoMW 92*
**Peterson,** Richard Charles 1931- *AmMWSc 92*
**Peterson,** Richard Edward 1946- *WhoWest 92*
**Peterson,** Richard Elsworth 1921- *AmMWSc 92*
**Peterson,** Richard Elton 1941- *WhoMW 92*
**Peterson,** Richard George 1941- *AmMWSc 92*
**Peterson,** Richard Hermann 1942- *WhoWest 92*
**Peterson,** Richard John 1955- *WhoFI 92*
**Peterson,** Richard S. 1938- *ConAu 133*
**Peterson,** Richard W. 1949- *IntMPA 92*
**Peterson,** Richard Walter 1933- *AmMWSc 92*
**Peterson,** Richard William 1925- *WhoAmL 92*
**Peterson,** Robert *DrAPF 91*
**Peterson,** Robert 1924- *IntAu&W 91*
**Peterson,** Robert Anthony, Jr. 1956- *WhoRel 92*
**Peterson,** Robert Austin 1925- *WhoFI 92*
**Peterson,** Robert Byron *WhoFI 92*
**Peterson,** Robert C 1936- *AmMWSc 92*
**Peterson,** Robert Dean 1948- *WhoMW 92*
**Peterson,** Robert Eugene 1930- *WhoAmP 91*
**Peterson,** Robert H F 1935- *AmMWSc 92*
**Peterson,** Robert Hampton 1922- *AmMWSc 92*
**Peterson,** Robert L. 1932- *WhoMW 92*
**Peterson,** Robert Lawrence 1939- *AmMWSc 92*
**Peterson,** Robert Lee 1930- *AmMWSc 92*
**Peterson,** Robert W 1925- *AmMWSc 92*
**Peterson,** Robert W 1929- *WhoAmP 91*
**Peterson,** Rocky L. 1952- *WhoAmL 92*
**Peterson,** Roger 1928- *WhoEnt 92*
**Peterson,** Roger Eric 1937- *WhoFI 92*
**Peterson,** Roger Marshall 1936- *WhoFI 92*
**Peterson,** Roger Shipp 1931- *AmMWSc 92*
**Peterson,** Roger Tory 1908- *BenetAL 91, IntWW 91*
**Peterson,** Roland Oscar 1932- *WhoFI 92, WhoWest 92*
**Peterson,** Rolf Eugene 1921- *AmMWSc 92*
**Peterson,** Rolf Olin 1949- *AmMWSc 92*
**Peterson,** Ronald A 1937- *AmMWSc 92*
**Peterson,** Ronald Arthur 1920- *WhoWest 92*
**Peterson,** Ronald M 1922- *AmMWSc 92*
**Peterson,** Ronald R. 1948- *WhoAmL 92*
**Peterson,** Roy Jerome 1939- *AmMWSc 92*
**Peterson,** Roy Otto 1916- *WhoWest 92*
**Peterson,** Roy Phillip 1934- *AmMWSc 92*
**Peterson,** Roy Reed 1924- *AmMWSc 92*
**Peterson,** Rudolph A. 1904- *IntWW 91*
**Peterson,** Rudolph Nicholas 1932- *AmMWSc 92*
**Peterson,** Russell Wilbur 1916- *IntWW 91, WhoAmP 91*
**Peterson,** S. Dean 1923- *IntMPA 92*
**Peterson,** Sally Lu 1942- *WhoMW 92*
**Peterson,** Sandra Byrd *WhoMW 92*
**Peterson,** Selmer Wilfred 1917- *AmMWSc 92*
**Peterson,** Sharon Elizabeth 1958- *WhoWest 92*
**Peterson,** Sheri L. Haines 1958- *WhoMW 92*
**Peterson,** Shirley Ann 1935- *WhoAmP 91*
**Peterson,** Shirley D. 1941- *WhoAmL 92*
**Peterson,** Spencer Alan 1940- *AmMWSc 92*
**Peterson,** Spiro 1922- *IntAu&W 91*
**Peterson,** Stanley Lee 1949- *WhoWest 92*
**Peterson,** Stephen Anselm Anoka 1949- *WhoAmP 91*
**Peterson,** Stephen Craig 1940- *AmMWSc 92*
**Peterson,** Stephen Frank 1942- *AmMWSc 92*
**Peterson,** Stephen Lee 1940- *WhoRel 92*
**Peterson,** Steven Lloyd *AmMWSc 92*
**Peterson,** Susan *DrAPF 91*
**Peterson,** Susan Grace 1950- *WhoEnt 92*
**Peterson,** Sushila Jane-Clinton 1952- *WhoBlA 92*
**Peterson,** Thage G. 1933- *IntWW 91*
**Peterson,** Thomas Charles 1955- *WhoRel 92*
**Peterson,** Thomas Emery 1954- *WhoFI 92*

**Peterson**, Thomas Francis 1956- *WhoAmL 92*
**Peterson**, Timothy Lee 1946- *AmMWSc 92*
**Peterson**, Todd Steven 1959- *WhoFI 92*
**Peterson**, Tom Loomis 1932- *WhoAmL 92*
**Peterson**, Vance Tullin 1944- *WhoWest 92*
**Peterson**, Vern Leroy 1934- *AmMWSc 92*
**Peterson**, Victor Lowell 1934- *AmMWSc 92*
**Peterson**, Vincent Zetterberg 1921- *AmMWSc 92*
**Peterson**, W C *WhoAmP 91*
**Peterson**, Wallace C. *WrDr 92*
**Peterson**, Wallace Carroll 1921- *WhoAmP 91*
**Peterson**, Walter 1922- *IntWW 91, WhoAmP 91*
**Peterson**, Walter Fritiof 1920- *WhoRel 92*
**Peterson**, Ward Davis, Jr 1927- *AmMWSc 92*
**Peterson**, Warren Stanley 1927- *AmMWSc 92*
**Peterson**, Wilbur Carroll 1913- *AmMWSc 92*
**Peterson**, William Allen 1934- *WhoAmL 92*
**Peterson**, William Arthur 1950- *WhoMW 92*
**Peterson**, William Donald 1929- *WhoFI 92*
**Peterson**, William E. 1913- *WhoBlA 92*
**Peterson**, William E 1936- *WhoAmP 91*
**Peterson**, William G 1944- *WhoAmP 91*
**Peterson**, William George 1944- *WhoAmL 92*
**Peterson**, William Roger 1927- *AmMWSc 92*
**Peterson**, William T. 1930-1986 *WhoBlA 92N*
**Peterson**, William Wesley 1924- *AmMWSc 92*
**Peterson**, Willie Diamond 1911- *WhoBlA 92*
**Peterson-Falzone**, Sally Jean 1942- *AmMWSc 92*
**Peterson Johnson**, Carlita Lucille 1951- *WhoMW 92*
**Peterson-Kennedy**, Sydney Ellen 1958- *AmMWSc 92*
**Peterson-More**, Diana L. 1950- *WhoWest 92*
**Petersson**, George A 1942- *AmMWSc 92*
**Peterzen**, Elisabet 1938- *IntAu&W 91*
**Petes**, Thomas Douglas 1947- *AmMWSc 92*
**Petesch**, Natalie L.M. *DrAPF 91, IntAu&W 91*
**Petett**, Freddye Webb 1943- *WhoBlA 92*
**Pethel**, James Leroy 1936- *WhoEnt 92*
**Pethel**, Stanley Robert 1950- *WhoEnt 92*
**Petherbridge**, Deanna 1939- *TwCPaSc*
**Petherbridge**, Edward 1936- *Who 92*
**Pethica**, Brian Anthony 1926- *AmMWSc 92*
**Pethick**, Christopher John 1942- *AmMWSc 92*
**Pethick**, Geoffrey Loveston 1907- *Who 92*
**Pethrick**, Richard Arthur 1942- *IntWW 91*
**Pethtel**, Dave 1951- *WhoAmP 91*
**Pethybridge**, Roger William 1934- *WrDr 92*
**Peticolas**, Warner Leland 1929- *AmMWSc 92*
**Petiet**, Thomas Wayne 1943- *WhoEnt 92*
**Petievich**, Gerald 1944- *WrDr 92*
**Petillo**, John Joseph, Jr 1949- *WhoIns 92*
**Petillo**, Phillip J 1945- *AmMWSc 92*
**Petinga**, Charles Michael 1946- *WhoMW 92*
**Petingi**, Roberto 1953- *WhoHisp 92*
**Petioni**, Muriel M. 1914- *WhoBlA 92*
**Petit**, Buddy 1897-1931 *NewAmDM*
**Petit**, Dinshaw Manockjee 1934- *Who 92*
**Petit**, Eugene Pierre *IntWW 91*
**Petit**, Georges 1835?-1900 *ThHEIm*
**Petit**, Jean-Louis 1937- *WhoEnt 92*
**Petit**, Patricia Jean 1935- *WhoRel 92*
**Petit**, Pierre 1922- *IntWW 91*
**Petit**, Roland 1924- *IntWW 91, Who 92*
**Petitan**, Debra Ann Burke 1932- *WhoMW 92*
**Petitmengin**, Jacques 1928- *IntWW 91*
**Petito**, George Daniel 1941- *WhoFI 92*
**Petitt**, Gerald William 1945- *WhoFI 92*
**Petitt**, Gus A 1937- *AmMWSc 92*
**Petitt**, Richard George 1948- *WhoFI 92*
**Petka**, Ed 1943- *WhoAmP 91*
**Petke**, Frederick David 1942- *AmMWSc 92*
**Petkevis**, Edward Raymond 1960- *WhoAmL 92*
**Petkov**, Petko Danev 1942- *IntWW 91*
**Petley**, Roy 1950- *TwCPaSc*
**Petlyura**, Semyon Vasilyevich 1879-1926 *FacFETw*
**Peto**, Henry 1920- *Who 92*
**Peto**, Michael 1938- *Who 92*
**Peto**, Richard 1943- *Who 92*
**Peto**, Rosemary 1916- *TwCPaSc*
**Petra**, Daniel Phillip 1964- *WhoMW 92*
**Petrack**, Barbara Kepes 1927- *AmMWSc 92*
**Petrak**, William Allen *WhoAmP 91*
**Petrakis**, Harry Mark *DrAPF 91*
**Petrakis**, Harry Mark 1923- *ConNov 91, WhoMW 92, WrDr 92*
**Petrakis**, Leonidas 1935- *AmMWSc 92*
**Petrakis**, Nicholas Louis 1922- *AmMWSc 92, WhoWest 92*
**Petrakos**, Chris *DrAPF 91*
**Petrakov**, Nikolai Yakovlevich 1937- *IntWW 91*
**Petrakov**, Nikolay Yakovlevich 1937- *SovUnBD*
**Petrali**, John Patrick 1933- *AmMWSc 92*
**Petranek**, Stephen Lynn 1944- *ConAu 133*
**Petrarca**, Anthony Edward 1929- *AmMWSc 92*
**Petrarca**, David 1962- *WhoEnt 92*
**Petrarca**, Joseph A *WhoAmP 91*
**Petras**, John W. 1940- *WrDr 92*
**Petras**, Michael Luke 1932- *AmMWSc 92*
**Petrasek**, Emil John 1940- *AmMWSc 92*
**Petrasich**, John Moris 1945- *WhoAmL 92*
**Petrassi**, Goffredo 1904- *ConCom 92, IntWW 91, NewAmDM*
**Petrasso**, Richard David 1944- *AmMWSc 92*
**Petre** *Who 92*
**Petre**, Baron 1942- *Who 92*
**Petre**, Donna Marie 1947- *WhoWest 92*
**Petre**, Francis Herbert Loraine 1927- *Who 92*
**Petre**, Zoe 1940- *IntWW 91*
**Petrecca**, Michael Anthony 1960- *WhoAmL 92*
**Petrella**, Ronald Vincent 1935- *AmMWSc 92*
**Petrella**, Vance John 1947- *AmMWSc 92*
**Petrelli**, Joseph Lawrence 1951- *WhoIns 92*
**Petrenko**, Aleksey Vasilevich 1938- *IntWW 91*
**Petrey**, Harry Lee 1901- *WhoIns 92*
**Petri**, Carl Axel Henrik 1929- *IntWW 91*
**Petri**, Egon 1881-1962 *NewAmDM*
**Petri**, Elio 1929-1982 *FacFETw, IntDcF 2-2 [port]*
**Petri**, Leo Henry 1914- *AmMWSc 92*
**Petri**, Michala 1958- *IntWW 91*
**Petri**, Thomas E *WhoAmP 91*
**Petri**, Thomas Everet 1940- *WhoMW 92*
**Petri**, Tom 1940- *AlmAP 92 [port]*
**Petri**, William Henry, III 1938- *AmMWSc 92*
**Petri**, William Hugh 1944- *AmMWSc 92*
**Petric**, Ivo 1931- *ConCom 92, WhoEnt 92*
**Petricciani**, John C 1936- *AmMWSc 92*
**Petrich**, Robert Paul 1941- *AmMWSc 92*
**Petricioli**, Gustavo 1928- *IntWW 91*
**Petrick**, Ernest N 1922- *AmMWSc 92*
**Petricka**, Russell James 1942- *WhoMW 92*
**Petrides**, Frederique Joanne 1903-1983 *NewAmDM*
**Petrie**, Allan Kendrick 1928- *WhoWest 92*
**Petrie**, Bruce Inglis 1926- *WhoAmL 92*
**Petrie**, Daniel 1920- *ConTFT 9, IntMPA 92*
**Petrie**, Donald Archibald 1921- *WhoFI 92*
**Petrie**, Dorothea Grundy *WhoEnt 92*
**Petrie**, George O. *ConTFT 9*
**Petrie**, Harry R. 1926- *WhoBlA 92*
**Petrie**, Joan Caroline 1920- *Who 92*
**Petrie**, John M 1905- *AmMWSc 92*
**Petrie**, Paul *DrAPF 91*
**Petrie**, Paul 1928- *ConPo 91, WrDr 92*
**Petrie**, Paul James 1928- *IntAu&W 91*
**Petrie**, Peter 1932- *IntWW 91, Who 92*
**Petrie**, Rhona *IntAu&W 91X, WrDr 92*
**Petrie**, Robert John 1946- *WhoEnt 92*
**Petrie**, William Leo 1923- *AmMWSc 92*
**Petrie**, William Marshall 1946- *AmMWSc 92*
**Petriello**, Richard P 1942- *AmMWSc 92*
**Petrignani**, Rinaldo 1927- *IntWW 91*
**Petrik**, Michael Thomas 1957- *WhoAmL 92*
**Petrilli**, Giuseppe 1913- *IntWW 91*
**Petrilli**, Joseph R 1942- *WhoAmP 91*
**Petrillo**, Dennis Dale 1954- *WhoRel 92, WhoWest 92*
**Petrillo**, Edward William 1947- *AmMWSc 92*
**Petrillo**, James C. 1892-1984 *NewAmDM*
**Petrin**, Helen Fite 1940- *WhoAmL 92*
**Petrina**, Anthony J. *WhoWest 92*
**Petringenaru**, Adrian 1933- *IntAu&W 91*
**Petrini-Poli**, Vincent Henri 1939- *WhoMW 92*
**Petrinovic**, Ruth Chaves 1931- *WhoEnt 92*
**Petrirena**, Mario J. 1953- *WhoHisp 92*
**Petris**, Nicholas C 1923- *WhoAmP 91*
**Petritsky**, Anatoliy Galaktionovich 1895-1964 *SovUnBD*
**Petro**, Anthony James 1930- *AmMWSc 92*
**Petro**, Anthony Michael 1948- *WhoFI 92*
**Petro**, James Michael 1948- *WhoAmP 91*
**Petro**, Janos 1937- *WhoEnt 92*
**Petro**, John William 1930- *AmMWSc 92*
**Petro**, Nancy Bero 1948- *WhoMW 92*
**Petro**, Nicolai N. 1958- *ConAu 135*
**Petro**, Peter Paul, Jr 1940- *AmMWSc 92*
**Petro**, Thomas Carlton 1962- *WhoRel 92*
**Petrocelli**, Anthony Joseph 1937- *WhoFI 92*
**Petrof**, Robert Charles 1937- *AmMWSc 92*
**Petroff**, John 1941- *WhoFI 92*
**Petroff**, Pierre Marc 1940- *AmMWSc 92*
**Petrokubi**, Marilyn 1951- *WhoEnt 92*
**Petrolati**, Thomas M *WhoAmP 91*
**Petron**, Donald Robert 1946- *WhoWest 92*
**Petrone**, Richard F. 1947- *WhoEnt 92*
**Petrone**, Rocco A 1926- *AmMWSc 92*
**Petrone**, Thomas 1937- *WhoAmP 91*
**Petroni**, Romeo Geno 1929- *WhoAmP 91*
**Petronio**, Marco 1912- *AmMWSc 92*
**Petropoulos**, Constantine Chris 1931- *AmMWSc 92*
**Petros**, Raymond Louis, Jr. 1950- *WhoAmL 92*
**Petrosian**, Suren Martirosovich 1925- *IntWW 91*
**Petrosino**, Giuseppe 1860-1909 *DcAmImH*
**Petroskey**, Belinda Wehner 1951- *WhoAmP 91*
**Petroski**, Alan 1952- *WhoMW 92*
**Petroski**, Catherine *DrAPF 91*
**Petroski**, Catherine 1939- *IntAu&W 91*
**Petroski**, Henry *DrAPF 91*
**Petroski**, Henry 1942- *WrDr 92*
**Petroski**, Henry J 1942- *AmMWSc 92*
**Petrosky**, Anthony *DrAPF 91*
**Petross**, Precious Doris *WhoBlA 92*
**Petrosyan**, Tigran Vartanovich 1929-1984 *SovUnBD*
**Petrosyants**, Andronik Melkonovich 1906- *IntWW 91*
**Petrou**, David Michael 1949- *IntMPA 92*
**Petrou**, Panayiotis Polydorou 1955- *AmMWSc 92*
**Petrouske**, Rosalie Sanara *DrAPF 91*
**Petrov**, Andrey Pavlovich 1930- *SovUnBD*
**Petrov**, Boris Nikolayevich 1930- *IntWW 91*
**Petrov**, Ivan Ivanovich 1920- *SovUnBD*
**Petrov**, Michel *ConAu 134*
**Petrov**, Nicolas 1933- *WhoEnt 92*
**Petrov**, Rem Viktorovich 1930- *IntWW 91*
**Petrov**, Vasiliy Ivanovich 1917- *IntWW 91, SovUnBD*
**Petrov**, Vladimir M. d1991 *NewYTBS 91*
**Petrov**, Vladimir Mikhailovich 1922- *IntWW 91*
**Petrov**, Vladimir Mikhaylovich 1896-1966 *SovUnBD*
**Petrov**, Yuriy Vladimirovich 1932- *IntWW 91*
**Petrov-Bytov**, Pavel Petrovich 1895-1960 *SovUnBD*
**Petrov-Vodkin**, Kuz'ma Sergeevich 1878-1939 *SovUnBD*
**Petrovic**, Louis John 1940- *AmMWSc 92*
**Petrovich**, Fred 1941- *AmMWSc 92*
**Petrovich**, Janice 1946- *WhoHisp 92*
**Petrovichev**, Nikolai Alexandrovich 1918- *IntWW 91*
**Petrovics**, Emil 1930- *IntWW 91*
**Petrovits**, Loty 1937- *IntAu&W 91*
**Petrovsky**, Boris *ConAu 134*
**Petrovsky**, Boris Vasiliyevich 1908- *IntWW 91*
**Petrowski**, Gary E 1941- *AmMWSc 92*
**Petrucci**, Ottaviano 1466-1539 *NewAmDM*
**Petrucci**, Ralph Herbert 1930- *AmMWSc 92*
**Petrucci**, Sergio 1932- *AmMWSc 92*
**Petrucciani**, Michel 1962- *WhoEnt 92*
**Petruccio**, Steven James 1961- *SmATA 67 [port]*
**Petrucelli**, Frank *WhoRel 92*
**Petrucelli**, Lawrence Michael 1932- *AmMWSc 92*
**Petruk**, William 1930- *AmMWSc 92*
**Petruno**, Frank Delano 1932- *WhoFI 92*
**Petrunoff**, Vance T. 1956- *WhoWest 92*
**Petrus Hispanus** 1205?-1277 *DcLB 115*
**Petrus**, Eugene Francis 1947- *WhoMW 92*
**Petrus**, Placidus Sujitno 1951- *WhoFI 92*
**Petrus**, Robert Thomas 1957- *WhoFI 92*
**Petrush**, John Joseph 1942- *WhoAmL 92*
**Petrushevskaya**, Lyudmila 1938- *IntWW 91, SovUnBD*
**Petruska**, John Andrew 1933- *AmMWSc 92*
**Petrusky**, John W. 1935- *WhoFI 92*
**Petruzzi**, Christopher Robert 1951- *WhoFI 92, WhoWest 92*
**Petry**, Ann *DrAPF 91*
**Petry**, Ann 1908- *BenetAL 91, ConNov 91, WhoBlA 92, WrDr 92*
**Petry**, Ann 1911- *NotBlAW 92*
**Petry**, Ann 1912- *AfrAmW*
**Petry**, Heinz 1919- *IntWW 91*
**Petry**, Paul E 1946- *WhoIns 92*
**Petry**, Ray C. 1903- *WhoRel 92*
**Petry**, Robert Franklin 1936- *AmMWSc 92*
**Petry**, Robert Kendrick 1912- *AmMWSc 92*
**Petry**, Stanley Edward 1966- *WhoBlA 92*
**Petry**, Ted Mallory 1938- *WhoMW 92*
**Petryka**, Zbyslaw Jan 1930- *AmMWSc 92*
**Petryshyn**, Walter Volodymyr 1929- *AmMWSc 92*
**Petschek**, Albert George 1928- *AmMWSc 92*
**Petschek**, Harry E 1930- *AmMWSc 92*
**Petschek**, Rolfe George 1954- *AmMWSc 92*
**Petsko**, Gregory Anthony 1948- *AmMWSc 92*
**Pett**, Raymond Austin 1941- *Who 92*
**Pettaway**, Charles, Jr. 1949- *WhoBlA 92*
**Pettee**, William Henry 1838-1904 *BiInAmS*
**Pettegrew**, David Lyman d1914 *BiInAmS*
**Pettegrew**, Raleigh K 1931- *AmMWSc 92*
**Pettengill**, Gordon Hemenway 1926- *AmMWSc 92, IntWW 91*
**Pettengill**, Olive Standish 1924- *AmMWSc 92*
**Petters**, Jon Christopher 1953- *WhoMW 92*
**Petters**, Robert Michael 1950- *AmMWSc 92*
**Pettersen**, Howard Eugene 1922- *AmMWSc 92*
**Pettersen**, James Clark 1932- *AmMWSc 92*
**Pettersen**, Kevin Will 1956- *WhoFI 92*
**Pettersen**, Kjell Will 1927- *WhoFI 92*
**Pettersen**, Mary J *WhoAmP 91*
**Pettersen**, Rena Oldfield *ScFEYrs*
**Pettersen**, Thomas Morgan 1950- *WhoWest 92*
**Petterson**, Donald K. 1930- *IntWW 91*
**Petterson**, Melvyn 1947- *TwCPaSc*
**Petterson**, Robert Carlyle 1923- *AmMWSc 92*
**Petterway**, Jackie Willis *WhoBlA 92*
**Pettes**, Robert Carlton 1922- *WhoMW 92*
**Pettet**, Simon *DrAPF 91*
**Pettett**, Deane H 1920- *WhoIns 92*
**Pettey**, Dix Hayes 1941- *AmMWSc 92*
**Petteys**, D.F. *DrAPF 91*
**Petti**, Edward Charles 1939- *WhoFI 92*
**Pettibone**, Marian Hope 1908- *AmMWSc 92*
**Pettibone**, Peter John 1939- *WhoAmL 92, WhoFI 92*
**Pettiette**, Alison Yvonne 1952- *WhoAmL 92, WhoFI 92*
**Pettifer**, Julian 1935- *IntAu&W 91, Who 92*
**Pettiford**, Betty Irene 1928- *WhoAmP 91*
**Pettiford**, Oscar 1922-1960 *NewAmDM*
**Pettiford**, Quentin H. 1929- *WhoBlA 92*
**Pettiford**, Reuben J., Jr. 1960- *WhoBlA 92*
**Pettiford**, Steven Douglas 1948- *WhoBlA 92*
**Pettigrew**, Anne Stone *WhoAmL 92*
**Pettigrew**, Carl Newton 1964- *WhoFI 92*
**Pettigrew**, Carolyn Landers 1945- *WhoRel 92*
**Pettigrew**, Dana Mary 1951- *WhoEnt 92*
**Pettigrew**, Dennis Alva 1947- *WhoFI 92*
**Pettigrew**, Grady L., Jr. 1943- *WhoBlA 92*
**Pettigrew**, James Eugene, Jr 1945- *AmMWSc 92, WhoMW 92*
**Pettigrew**, John Douglas 1943- *Who 92*
**Pettigrew**, L. Eudora 1928- *NotBlAW 92*
**Pettigrew**, Norman M *AmMWSc 92*
**Pettigrew**, Russell 1920- *Who 92*
**Pettigrew**, Steven Lee 1949- *WhoWest 92*
**Pettigrew**, Thomas Fraser 1931- *WhoWest 92, WrDr 92*
**Pettijohn**, David E 1934- *AmMWSc 92*
**Pettijohn**, Francis John 1904- *AmMWSc 92*
**Pettijohn**, Richard Robert 1946- *AmMWSc 92*
**Pettijohn**, Terry Frank 1948- *AmMWSc 92*
**Pettinato**, Frank Anthony 1921- *AmMWSc 92*
**Pettinella**, Nicholas Anthony 1942- *WhoFI 92*
**Pettinga**, Cornelius Wesley 1921- *AmMWSc 92, WhoFI 92*
**Pettingill**, Olin Sewall, Jr 1907- *AmMWSc 92*
**Pettingill**, William Leroy 1866-1905 *RelLAm 91*
**Pettinotti**, James Walter 1932- *WhoEnt 92*
**Pettis**, Gary George 1958- *WhoBlA 92*
**Pettis**, Joyce Owens 1946- *WhoBlA 92*
**Pettis**, Ronald Eugene 1939- *WhoWest 92*
**Pettis-Roberson**, Shirley McCumber *WhoWest 92*
**Pettit**, Alvin Dwight 1945- *WhoBlA 92*
**Pettit**, Arthur G. 1938-1977 *ConAu 135*
**Pettit**, Christine Marie 1961- *WhoWest 92*
**Pettit**, Daniel 1915- *Who 92*
**Pettit**, David J 1936- *AmMWSc 92*

**Pettit**, David Starling 1942- *WhoRel 92*
**Pettit**, Flora Hunter *AmMWSc 92*
**Pettit**, Frances Marie 1927- *WhoAmP 91*
**Pettit**, Frederick S 1930- *AmMWSc 92*
**Pettit**, George Robert 1929- *AmMWSc 92, WhoWest 92*
**Pettit**, Ghery DeWitt 1926- *WhoWest 92*
**Pettit**, Hugh Boyd, III 1952- *WhoAmP 91*
**Pettit**, James Harvey 1876-1914 *BiInAmS*
**Pettit**, John Whitney 1935- *WhoAmL 92, WhoEnt 92*
**Pettit**, Margaret Esta 1926- *WhoEnt 92*
**Pettit**, Michael *DrAPF 91*
**Pettit**, Nelson M. 1938- *WhoWest 92*
**Pettit**, Peter Acker 1955- *WhoRel 92*
**Pettit**, Ray Howard 1933- *AmMWSc 92*
**Pettit**, Richard Bolton 1944- *AmMWSc 92*
**Pettit**, Robert Eugene 1928- *AmMWSc 92*
**Pettit**, Robert L. 1952- *WhoAmL 92*
**Pettit**, Russell Dean 1941- *AmMWSc 92*
**Pettit**, Stephen John 1959- *WhoRel 92*
**Pettit**, Steven Lane 1949- *WhoEnt 92*
**Pettit**, Tamara 1948- *WhoAmP 91*
**Pettit**, Thomas Henry 1929- *AmMWSc 92*
**Pettit**, Tom *LesBEnT 92*
**Pettit**, Vincent King 1924- *WhoRel 92*
**Pettit**, Wendy Jean 1945- *WhoFI 92*
**Pettit**, William Dutton, Jr. 1949- *WhoFI 92, WhoWest 92*
**Pettit**, William Dutton, Sr. 1920- *WhoFI 92*
**Pettite**, William Clinton 1937- *WhoWest 92*
**Pettiti**, Louis Edmond 1916- *IntWW 91*
**Pettitt**, Bernard Montgomery 1953- *AmMWSc 92*
**Pettitt**, Gordon Charles 1934- *Who 92*
**Pettofrezzo**, Anthony J 1931- *AmMWSc 92*
**Pettress**, Andrew William 1937- *WhoBlA 92*
**Pettry**, David Emory 1935- *AmMWSc 92*
**Pettus**, David 1925- *AmMWSc 92*
**Pettus**, Jolene Denise 1961- *WhoAmL 92*
**Pettus**, William Gower 1925- *AmMWSc 92*
**Pettus-Bellamy**, Brenda Karen 1957- *WhoBlA 92*
**Pettway**, Jo Celeste 1952- *WhoBlA 92*
**Petty**, Barrett Reed 1941- *WhoFI 92*
**Petty**, Bob 1940- *WhoBlA 92*
**Petty**, Bruce Anthony 1938- *WhoBlA 92*
**Petty**, Charles Sutherland 1920- *AmMWSc 92*
**Petty**, Clinton Myers 1923- *AmMWSc 92*
**Petty**, Donald Griffin 1949- *WhoWest 92*
**Petty**, Douglas Cooper, Jr. 1931- *WhoFI 92*
**Petty**, Douglass 1953- *WhoRel 92*
**Petty**, Eric D *WhoAmP 91*
**Petty**, Floyd Ernest 1928- *WhoAmP 91*
**Petty**, H. Michael, Sr. 1961- *WhoRel 92*
**Petty**, Howard Raymond 1954- *AmMWSc 92, WhoMW 92*
**Petty**, John Fitzmaurice 1935- *Who 92*
**Petty**, John Stuart 1949- *WhoRel 92*
**Petty**, Joseph Taggart 1951- *WhoAmP 91*
**Petty**, Kenneth Mark 1944- *WhoMW 92*
**Petty**, Larry Dean 1941- *WhoFI 92*
**Petty**, Leanne 1960- *WhoEnt 92*
**Petty**, Marge 1946- *WhoAmP 91*
**Petty**, Phillip N. 1953- *WhoFI 92*
**Petty**, Rachel Monteith 1943- *WhoBlA 92*
**Petty**, Reginald E. 1935- *WhoBlA 92*
**Petty**, Robert Owen 1933- *AmMWSc 92*
**Petty**, Robert Scott 1947- *WhoAmP 91*
**Petty**, Ronald Franklin 1947- *WhoFI 92*
**Petty**, Ross David 1952- *WhoAmL 92*
**Petty**, Stephen Eugene 1957- *WhoMW 92*
**Petty**, Thomas Lee 1932- *AmMWSc 92*
**Petty**, Thomas Ramsey 1949- *WhoRel 92*
**Petty**, Tom 1950- *CurBio 91 [port]*
**Petty**, Tom 1952- *NewAmDM, WhoEnt 92*
**Petty**, Travis Hubert 1928- *WhoFI 92*
**Petty**, W. H. 1921- *WrDr 92*
**Petty**, Wallace Eugene 1935- *WhoRel 92*
**Petty**, William 1737-1805 *BlkwEAR*
**Petty**, William Calvin, III 1940- *WhoFI 92*
**Petty**, William Clayton 1938- *AmMWSc 92*
**Petty**, William Henry 1921- *Who 92*
**Petty-Fitzmaurice** *Who 92*
**Pettyjohn**, Fritz 1945- *WhoAmP 91*
**Pettyjohn**, J Coy *WhoAmP 91*
**Pettyjohn**, Wayne A 1933- *AmMWSc 92*
**Petuchowski**, Jakob Josef d1991 *NewYTBS 91*
**Petuchowski**, Jakob Josef 1925- *WrDr 92*
**Petura**, John C *AmMWSc 92*
**Petushkova**, Yelena Vladimirovna 1940- *SovUnBD*
**Petuskey**, John Albert 1938- *WhoRel 92*
**Petz**, Martin Xavier 1960- *WhoMW 92*
**Petz**, Thomas Joseph 1930- *WhoMW 92*
**Petzak**, Scott Allen 1963- *WhoEnt 92*
**Petzel**, Florence Eloise 1911- *WhoWest 92*
**Petzke**, Wayne Edward 1947- *WhoMW 92*
**Petzold**, Carol Stoker *WhoAmP 91*
**Petzold**, Edgar 1930- *AmMWSc 92*
**Petzold**, Horst Willy 1923- *WhoWest 92*
**Petzold**, Linda Ruth 1954- *WhoWest 92*
**Petzold**, Robert George 1917- *WhoEnt 92*
**Peugeot**, Patrick 1937- *WhoIns 92*
**Peugeot**, Roland 1926- *IntWW 91*
**Peugh**, Roger Dennis 1943- *WhoRel 92*
**Peukert**, Detlev *ConAu 133*
**Peukert**, Detlev J. K. 1950- *ConAu 133*
**Peura**, Robert Allan 1943- *AmMWSc 92*
**Peurifoy**, Paul Vastine 1927- *AmMWSc 92*
**Peurifoy**, Robert Claude 1951- *WhoRel 92*
**Peurye**, Lloyd Martin 1949- *WhoMW 92*
**Pevear**, Richard *DrAPF 91*
**Pevear**, Roberta Charlotte 1930- *WhoAmP 91*
**Pevec**, Anthony Edward 1925- *WhoRel 92*
**Pevehouse**, Byron C 1927- *AmMWSc 92*
**Peverall**, John *IntMPA 92*
**Peverly**, John Howard 1944- *AmMWSc 92*
**Pevey**, James *ScFEYrs*
**Pevney**, Joseph 1920- *IntMPA 92*
**Pevovar**, Eddy Howard 1953- *WhoEnt 92*
**Pevsner**, Aihud 1925- *AmMWSc 92*
**Pevsner**, Anton 1886-1962 *FacFETw*
**Pevsner**, Nikolaus 1902-1983 *DcTwDes, FacFETw*
**Pevsner**, Stella *SmATA 14AS [port]*
**Pew**, George Thompson, Jr. 1942- *WhoFI 92*
**Pewe**, Troy Lewis 1918- *AmMWSc 92, WhoWest 92*
**Pewett**, James Ward 1949- *WhoAmL 92*
**Pewitt**, Edward Gale 1932- *AmMWSc 92*
**Pews**, Richard Garth 1938- *AmMWSc 92*
**Pewter**, Jim Deviny *WhoEnt 92*
**Pex**, David Allen 1954- *WhoFI 92*
**Pexton**, Catherine Larkin 1936- *WhoAmP 91*
**Peyghambarian**, Nasser 1954- *AmMWSc 92*
**Peynaud**, Emile Jean Pierre 1912- *IntWW 91*
**Peyrefitte**, Alain 1925- *IntWW 91*
**Peyrefitte**, Roger 1907- *IntAu&W 91, IntWW 91, Who 92*
**Peyrelevade**, Jean 1939- *IntWW 91*
**Peyron**, Fredrik 1923- *WhoAmP 91*
**Peyronnin**, Chester A, Jr 1925- *AmMWSc 92*
**Peyronnin**, Joseph Felix, III 1947- *WhoEnt 92*
**Peyrouse**, John Claude, Jr. 1928- *WhoEnt 92*
**Peyser**, John 1916- *IntMPA 92*
**Peyser**, Monique Vaune 1960- *WhoEnt 92*
**Peyser**, Peter A 1921- *WhoAmP 91, WhoFI 92*
**Peyster**, Steven *DrAPF 91*
**Peyton** *Who 92*
**Peyton**, Gordon Pickett 1941- *WhoAmL 92*
**Peyton**, Henry E. *WhoBlA 92*
**Peyton**, Jasper E. 1926- *WhoBlA 92*
**Peyton**, K M *IntAu&W 91X*
**Peyton**, K. M. 1929- *WrDr 92*
**Peyton**, Kathleen Wendy 1929- *IntAu&W 91, Who 92*
**Peyton**, Leonard James 1924- *AmMWSc 92*
**Peyton**, Louise Garvin 1941- *WhoFI 92*
**Peyton**, Malcolm C. *WhoEnt 92*
**Peyton**, Patrick 1909- *WhoRel 92*
**Peyton**, Robert Vance 1946- *WhoEnt 92*
**Peyton**, Ronald Douglas 1946- *WhoFI 92*
**Peyton of Yeovil**, Baron 1919- *IntWW 91, Who 92*
**Pez**, Guido Peter 1941- *AmMWSc 92*
**Pezel**, Johann Christoph 1639-1694 *NewAmDM*
**Pezet**, A Washington 1889- *ScFEYrs*
**Pezolet**, Michel 1946- *AmMWSc 92*
**Pezuela**, Joaquin de la 1761-1830 *HisDSpE*
**Pezuela**, Juan Manuel de la 1810-1875 *HisDSpE*
**Pezza**, Kim Marie 1960- *WhoEnt 92*
**Pezzella**, Paul Michael 1947- *WhoAmP 91*
**Pezzi**, Shelley 1956- *WhoHisp 92*
**Pezzullo**, Ralph 1951- *ConAu 135*
**Pfadt**, Robert E 1915- *AmMWSc 92*
**Pfaeffle**, Walter H. 1940- *WhoFI 92*
**Pfaehler**, Brenda 1939- *WhoAmP 91*
**Pfaelzer**, Mariana R. 1926- *WhoAmL 92*
**Pfaender**, Frederic Karl 1943- *AmMWSc 92*
**Pfaff**, Donald Chesley 1936- *AmMWSc 92*
**Pfaff**, Donald Wells 1939- *AmMWSc 92*
**Pfaff**, Judith 1946- *WorArt 1980*
**Pfaff**, Judy 1946- *IntWW 91*
**Pfaff**, Kevin Carl 1958- *WhoMW 92*
**Pfaff**, Lawrence White 1942- *WhoMW 92*
**Pfaff**, Nancy Watson 1942- *WhoRel 92*
**Pfaff**, Philip James 1947- *WhoWest 92*
**Pfaff**, Robert James 1943- *WhoAmL 92*
**Pfaff**, Terence Randall 1960- *WhoAmP 91*
**Pfaff**, Virginia Carolyn 1935- *WhoEnt 92*
**Pfaff**, William 1928- *WrDr 92*
**Pfaff**, William Wallace 1930- *AmMWSc 92*
**Pfaffenberger**, Gary Samuel 1941- *WhoWest 92*
**Pfaffenberger**, William Elmer 1943- *AmMWSc 92*
**Pfafflin**, James Reid 1930- *AmMWSc 92*
**Pfaffman**, Madge Anna 1939- *AmMWSc 92*
**Pfaffmann**, Carl 1913- *AmMWSc 92, IntWW 91*
**Pfahler**, Gerhard 1897-1976 *EncTR 91*
**Pfahler**, Paul Leighton 1930- *AmMWSc 92*
**Pfahnl**, Arnold 1923- *AmMWSc 92*
**Pfaltz**, Hugo M, Jr 1931- *WhoAmP 91*
**Pfaltzgraff**, John Andrew 1936- *AmMWSc 92*
**Pfaltzgraff**, Mark Andrew 1961- *WhoMW 92*
**Pfalzner**, Paul Michael 1923- *AmMWSc 92*
**Pfander**, William Harvey 1923- *AmMWSc 92*
**Pfanner**, Louise 1955- *SmATA 68 [port]*
**Pfannkuch**, Hans Olaf 1932- *AmMWSc 92*
**Pfatteicher**, Philip Henry 1935- *WhoRel 92*
**Pfau**, Anthony Victor 1960- *WhoEnt 92*
**Pfau**, Charles Julius 1935- *AmMWSc 92*
**Pfau**, Joann Grace 1967- *WhoRel 92*
**Pfautch**, Roy 1936- *WhoAmP 91, WhoRel 92*
**Pfautz**, John Jay 1949- *WhoIns 92*
**Pfeffer**, David H. 1935- *WhoAmL 92*
**Pfeffer**, Janice Marie *AmMWSc 92*
**Pfeffer**, John T 1935- *AmMWSc 92*
**Pfeffer**, Leo 1910- *WhoAmL 92*
**Pfeffer**, Marc Alan *AmMWSc 92*
**Pfeffer**, Paul Edward 1942- *WhoAmP 91*
**Pfeffer**, Philip Elliot 1941- *AmMWSc 92*
**Pfeffer**, Richard Lawrence 1930- *AmMWSc 92*
**Pfeffer**, Robert 1928- *WhoFI 92*
**Pfeffer**, Robert 1935- *AmMWSc 92*
**Pfeffer**, Susan Beth 1948- *IntAu&W 91*
**Pfeffer**, Washek F 1936- *AmMWSc 92*
**Pfeffer von Salomon**, Franz 1888-1968 *EncTR 91*
**Pfefferkorn**, Elmer Roy, Jr 1931- *AmMWSc 92*
**Pfefferkorn**, Hermann Wilhelm 1940- *AmMWSc 92*
**Pfeifer**, Diane Patricia 1950- *WhoEnt 92*
**Pfeifer**, Eugene 1945- *WhoMW 92*
**Pfeifer**, Gerard David 1937- *AmMWSc 92*
**Pfeifer**, James E 1938- *WhoIns 92*
**Pfeifer**, Jean 1934- *WhoFI 92*
**Pfeifer**, Maurice Alvin 1936- *WhoFI 92*
**Pfeifer**, Michael David 1937- *WhoRel 92*
**Pfeifer**, Paul Edward 1942- *WhoAmP 91*
**Pfeifer**, Richard Wallace 1951- *AmMWSc 92*
**Pfeiffer**, Alfred 1932- *IntWW 91*
**Pfeiffer**, Astrid Elizabeth 1934- *WhoFI 92*
**Pfeiffer**, Carl Curt 1908- *AmMWSc 92*
**Pfeiffer**, Carl J 1937- *AmMWSc 92*
**Pfeiffer**, Carroll Athey 1906- *AmMWSc 92*
**Pfeiffer**, Curtis Dudley 1943- *AmMWSc 92*
**Pfeiffer**, Douglas Robert 1946- *AmMWSc 92*
**Pfeiffer**, Egbert Wheeler 1915- *AmMWSc 92*
**Pfeiffer**, Eric A 1935- *AmMWSc 92*
**Pfeiffer**, Ernst Friedrich 1922- *IntWW 91*
**Pfeiffer**, Gerald G. 1939- *WhoWest 92*
**Pfeiffer**, Heinz Gerhard 1920- *AmMWSc 92*
**Pfeiffer**, Jane Cahill *LesBEnT 92*
**Pfeiffer**, Jane Cahill 1932- *WhoEnt 92*
**Pfeiffer**, Loren Neil 1939- *AmMWSc 92*
**Pfeiffer**, Margaret Kolodny 1944- *WhoAmL 92*
**Pfeiffer**, Michelle 1957- *WhoEnt 92*
**Pfeiffer**, Michelle 1958- *IntMPA 92*
**Pfeiffer**, Michelle 1959- *IntWW 91*
**Pfeiffer**, Norman *DcTwDes*
**Pfeiffer**, Paul Edwin 1917- *AmMWSc 92*
**Pfeiffer**, Raymond John 1937- *AmMWSc 92*
**Pfeiffer**, Richard C, Jr 1944- *WhoAmP 91*
**Pfeiffer**, Robert John 1920- *WhoFI 92, WhoWest 92*
**Pfeiffer**, Ross Douglas 1947- *WhoMW 92*
**Pfeiffer**, Sophia Douglass 1918- *WhoAmP 91*
**Pfeiffer**, Steven Eugene 1940- *AmMWSc 92*
**Pfeil**, Bill 1941- *WhoAmP 91*
**Pfeil**, Don Curtis 1923- *WhoFI 92*
**Pfeil**, Fred *DrAPF 91*
**Pfeil**, Fred 1949- *ConAu 133*
**Pfeil**, John D. 1952- *WhoMW 92*
**Pfeil**, William Roger 1940- *WhoMW 92*
**Pfender**, Emil 1925- *AmMWSc 92, WhoMW 92*
**Pfendt**, Henry George 1934- *WhoFI 92*
**Pfening**, Frederic Denver, III 1949- *WhoEnt 92, WhoMW 92*
**Pfennigstorf**, Werner 1934- *WhoAmL 92*
**Pfennigwerth**, Paul Leroy 1929- *AmMWSc 92*
**Pfenninger**, Karl H. 1944- *WhoWest 92*
**Pfeuffer**, Robert John 1925- *WhoEnt 92*
**Pfingston**, Roger *DrAPF 91*
**Pfister**, Arthur *DrAPF 91*
**Pfister**, Charles 1940- *DcTwDes*
**Pfister**, Donald Henry 1945- *AmMWSc 92*
**Pfister**, Edward Joseph 1934- *WhoEnt 92*
**Pfister**, Fred Roger 1946- *WhoMW 92*
**Pfister**, James Joseph 1946- *WhoFI 92, WhoMW 92*
**Pfister**, Karl Anton 1941- *WhoMW 92*
**Pfister**, Philip Carl 1925- *AmMWSc 92*
**Pfister**, Richard Charles 1933- *AmMWSc 92*
**Pfister**, Robert M 1933- *AmMWSc 92*
**Pfitzner**, Hans 1869-1949 *EncTR 91 [port], NewAmDM*
**Pfitzner**, Josef 1901-1945 *EncTR 91*
**Pfitzner**, Kurt Patrick 1958- *WhoWest 92*
**Pfizenmayer**, Frank John 1936- *WhoAmL 92*
**Pfizer**, Charles 1823-1906 *BiInAmS*
**Pflanzer**, Richard Gary 1940- *AmMWSc 92*
**Pflaum**, Melanie Sophia 1909- *IntAu&W 91*
**Pflaum**, Ronald Trenda 1922- *AmMWSc 92*
**Pflaum**, Steven F. 1955- *WhoAmL 92*
**Pfleiderer**, Otto 1904- *IntWW 91*
**Pflibsen**, Kent Paul 1955- *WhoWest 92*
**Pflieger**, William Leo 1932- *AmMWSc 92*
**Pflimlin**, Pierre 1907- *IntWW 91, Who 92*
**Pflueger**, Bruce Edward 1957- *WhoEnt 92*
**Pflug**, Gerald Ralph 1941- *AmMWSc 92*
**Pflug**, Irving John 1923- *AmMWSc 92*
**Pflug**, Raymond John 1919- *WhoWest 92*
**Pfluger**, Clarence Eugene 1930- *AmMWSc 92*
**Pflugfelder**, Hala 1921- *AmMWSc 92*
**Pflugfelder**, Hala O. 1921- *WhoWest 92*
**Pflugradt**, William d1991 *NewYTBS 91*
**Pfluke**, John H 1931- *AmMWSc 92*
**Pflum**, Daniel Lee 1947- *WhoAmL 92*
**Pfnur**, Vinzenz 1937- *WhoRel 92*
**Pfohl**, Ronald John 1937- *AmMWSc 92*
**Pfortmiller**, Sandra Clair 1939- *WhoWest 92*
**Pforzheimer**, Harry, Jr. 1915- *WhoWest 92*
**Pfost**, Don Charles 1929- *WhoEnt 92*
**Pfouts**, Ralph William 1920- *WhoFI 92*
**Pfrang**, Edward Oscar 1929- *AmMWSc 92*
**Pfrimer**, Walter 1881-1968 *BiDExR*
**Pfrogner**, Ray Long 1934- *AmMWSc 92*
**Pfuderer**, Helen A 1939- *AmMWSc 92*
**Pfuehler**, Susan Gullberg 1930- *WhoWest 92*
**Pfund**, Edward Theodore, Jr. 1923- *WhoFI 92, WhoWest 92*
**Pfuntner**, Allan Robert 1946- *WhoWest 92*
**Phadke**, Kalindi *AmMWSc 92*
**Phadke**, Madhav Shridhar 1948- *AmMWSc 92*
**Phaff**, Herman Jan 1913- *AmMWSc 92*
**Phair**, George 1918- *AmMWSc 92*
**Phair**, James Joseph 1939- *WhoIns 92*
**Phair**, John P 1934- *AmMWSc 92*
**Phalen**, Clarence Arthur 1924- *WhoAmP 91*
**Phalen**, James Francis 1945- *WhoFI 92*
**Phalen**, William Edmund 1916- *AmMWSc 92*
**Phalese**, Pierre 1510?-1575? *NewAmDM*
**Phalke**, Dadasaheb 1870-1944 *IntDcF 2-2*
**Pham Van Dong** 1906- *FacFETw, IntWW 91*
**Pham Van Ky** 1916- *IntWW 91*
**Pham**, Kinh Dinh 1956- *WhoWest 92*
**Pham**, Tuan Anh 1954- *WhoFI 92*
**Pham**, Tuan Duc 1938- *AmMWSc 92*
**Pham**, Tuan Quoc 1938- *WhoFI 92*
**Pham-Gia**, Thu 1945- *AmMWSc 92*
**Phan Dinh Khai** 1911- *WhoNob 90*
**Phan**, Chon-Ton 1930- *AmMWSc 92*
**Phan**, Cong Luan 1941- *AmMWSc 92*
**Phan**, Kok-Wee 1939- *AmMWSc 92*
**Phan**, Peter Cho 1943- *WhoRel 92*
**Phan**, Sem Hin 1949- *AmMWSc 92*
**Phan**, Thieu Van 1961- *WhoWest 92*
**Phaneuf**, Ronald Arthur 1947- *AmMWSc 92*
**Phang**, James Ming *AmMWSc 92*
**Phanos**, Titos 1929- *IntWW 91*
**Phansiri**, Betty Jo 1950- *WhoWest 92*
**Phantog** 1939- *IntWW 91*
**Phao Sriyanond** d1960 *FacFETw*
**Pharand**, Donat 1922- *IntWW 91*
**Pharaon**, Ghaith R *NewYTBS 91 [port]*
**Pharaon**, Ghaith Rashad 1940- *IntWW 91*
**Phares**, Alain Joseph 1942- *AmMWSc 92*
**Phares**, Cleveland Kirk 1938- *AmMWSc 92*
**Phares**, Marguerite Linton 1917- *WhoEnt 92*
**Phares**, Russell Eugene, Jr 1937- *AmMWSc 92*

**Pharis,** Richard Persons 1937- *AmMWSc 92*
**Pharis,** William Henry, III 1953- *WhoRel 92*
**Pharo,** Richard Levers 1936- *AmMWSc 92*
**Pharoah,** Peter Oswald Derrick 1934- *Who 92*
**Pharr,** Michael Milton 1940- *WhoFI 92, WhoWest 92*
**Pharr,** Steve Macon 1953- *WhoAmL 92*
**Pharris,** Ann Marie 1950- *WhoEnt 92*
**Pharriss,** Bruce Bailey 1937- *AmMWSc 92, WhoWest 92*
**Phat Huynh Tan** 1913-1989 *FacFETw*
**Phatak,** Sharad Chintaman 1932- *AmMWSc 92*
**Phears,** William D. 1917- *WhoBlA 92*
**Pheasant,** Richard 1920- *AmMWSc 92*
**Pheffer,** Audrey Iris 1941- *WhoAmP 91*
**Pheiffer,** Chester Harry 1921- *AmMWSc 92*
**Phelan,** Andrew James 1923- *Who 92*
**Phelan,** Bernard Q 1949- *WhoAmP 91*
**Phelan,** Carole Mary Ross 1925- *WhoRel 92*
**Phelan,** Earl Walter 1900- *AmMWSc 92*
**Phelan,** Francis 1925- *ConAu 36NR*
**Phelan,** Gary Edward 1960- *WhoAmL 92*
**Phelan,** James Frederick 1917- *AmMWSc 92*
**Phelan,** James Joseph 1937- *AmMWSc 92*
**Phelan,** James P. 1951- *WhoMW 92*
**Phelan,** James Pius X 1951- *ConAu 35NR*
**Phelan,** James W *WhoAmP 91*
**Phelan,** John Joseph, Jr. 1931- *IntWW 91*
**Phelan,** Mary Benedict 1902- *WhoRel 92*
**Phelan,** Mary Kay 1914- *IntAu&W 91, WrDr 92*
**Phelan,** Phyllis White 1951- *WhoMW 92*
**Phelan,** R M 1921- *AmMWSc 92*
**Phelan,** Richard John 1937- *WhoAmL 92, WhoMW 92*
**Phelan,** Robert Gerard 1933- *WhoAmP 91*
**Phelan,** Robert J, Jr 1933- *AmMWSc 92*
**Phelan,** Robin Eric 1945- *WhoAmL 92*
**Phelan,** Sean Patrick 1967- *WhoWest 92*
**Phelan,** Thomas 1925- *WhoRel 92*
**Phelps,** Abel Mix 1851-1902 *BilnAmS*
**Phelps,** Allen Warner 1950- *AmMWSc 92*
**Phelps,** Almira Hart Lincoln 1793-1884 *BilnAmS*
**Phelps,** Anthony John 1922- *Who 92*
**Phelps,** Arthur Van Rensselaer 1923- *AmMWSc 92*
**Phelps,** C. Kermit 1908- *WhoBlA 92*
**Phelps,** C. Ronald 1930- *WhoRel 92*
**Phelps,** Charles Frederick 1934- *Who 92*
**Phelps,** Christopher Prine 1943- *AmMWSc 92*
**Phelps,** Constance Kay 1940- *WhoBlA 92*
**Phelps,** Creighton Halstead 1940- *AmMWSc 92*
**Phelps,** Daniel James 1947- *AmMWSc 92*
**Phelps,** David D 1947- *WhoAmP 91*
**Phelps,** Dean *DrAPF 91*
**Phelps,** Dean G 1934- *AmMWSc 92*
**Phelps,** Dennis Lane 1955- *WhoRel 92*
**Phelps,** Donald Gayton 1929- *WhoBlA 92*
**Phelps,** Douglas Alan 1951- *WhoRel 92*
**Phelps,** Edmund Strother 1933- *IntWW 91*
**Phelps,** Edna Mae 1920- *WhoAmP 91*
**Phelps,** Elizabeth 1815-1852 *BenetAL 91*
**Phelps,** Elizabeth Stuart 1844-1910 *HanAmWH*
**Phelps,** Frederick Martin, III 1933- *AmMWSc 92, WhoMW 92*
**Phelps,** Frederick Martin, IV 1960- *AmMWSc 92*
**Phelps,** George Clayton 1935- *AmMWSc 92*
**Phelps,** Gilbert 1915- *ConNov 91, WrDr 92*
**Phelps,** Gilbert Henry 1915- *IntAu&W 91*
**Phelps,** Harriette Longacre 1936- *AmMWSc 92*
**Phelps,** Harvey W 1922- *WhoAmP 91*
**Phelps,** Harvey William 1922- *WhoWest 92*
**Phelps,** Howard Thomas Henry Middleton 1926- *Who 92*
**Phelps,** J. Alfred 1927- *ConAu 135*
**Phelps,** Jack 1926- *AmMWSc 92*
**Phelps,** James Douglas 1955- *WhoAmP 91*
**Phelps,** James Parkhurst 1924- *AmMWSc 92*
**Phelps,** Justin Andrew 1925- *WhoRel 92*
**Phelps,** Lee Barry 1938- *AmMWSc 92*
**Phelps,** Leonard Thomas Herbert 1917- *Who 92*
**Phelps,** Leroy Nash 1930- *AmMWSc 92*
**Phelps,** Mark Steven 1947- *WhoWest 92*
**Phelps,** Maurice Arthur 1935- *Who 92*
**Phelps,** Michael Edward 1939- *AmMWSc 92*
**Phelps,** Michael Everett Joseph 1947- *WhoWest 92*
**Phelps,** Patricia C 1930- *AmMWSc 92*
**Phelps,** Paulding 1933- *AmMWSc 92*
**Phelps,** Pharo A 1928- *AmMWSc 92*
**Phelps,** Richard William 1946- *WhoFI 92*
**Phelps,** Richard Wintour 1925- *Who 92*
**Phelps,** Robert Frederick, Jr. 1956- *WhoAmL 92*
**Phelps,** Robert Ralph 1926- *AmMWSc 92*
**Phelps,** Robin McCann 1957- *WhoWest 92*
**Phelps,** Ronald P 1947- *AmMWSc 92*
**Phelps,** W Robert *WhoAmP 91*
**Phelps,** William Cunningham 1934- *WhoIns 92*
**Phelps,** William Lyon 1865-1943 *BenetAL 91*
**Phelps,** William Robert 1928- *AmMWSc 92*
**Phelps Brown,** Ernest Henry *Who 92*
**Phelps-Patterson,** Lucy 1931- *WhoBlA 92*
**Phemister,** Robert David 1936- *AmMWSc 92*
**Pheneger,** Stephen Charles 1960- *WhoMW 92*
**Phenicie,** Mark Elihu 1954- *WhoAmP 91*
**Phenix,** Gloria Gayle 1956- *WhoMW 92*
**Phenix,** Philip Henry 1915- *WrDr 92*
**Pherigo,** Lindsey Price 1920- *WhoRel 92*
**Phetteplace,** Thurston Mason 1877-1913 *BilnAmS*
**Phibbs,** Clifford Matthew 1930- *WhoMW 92*
**Phibbs,** Garnett Ersiel 1922- *WhoRel 92*
**Phibbs,** Paul Vester, Jr 1942- *AmMWSc 92*
**Phibbs,** Philip Monford 1931- *WhoWest 92*
**Phibbs,** Roderic H 1930- *AmMWSc 92*
**Phifer,** Forrest Keith 1956- *WhoAmL 92*
**Phifer,** Lyle Hamilton 1927- *AmMWSc 92*
**Phifer,** Ross S 1941- *WhoIns 92*
**Phifer,** Sky D 1954- *WhoAmL 92*
**Philadelphus** *AmPeW*
**Philander,** S. George H. 1942- *WhoBlA 92*
**Philanthropos** *AmPeW*
**Philaret** 1935- *IntWW 91*
**Philaret,** Metropolitan 1903-1985 *RelLAm 91*
**Philaticus** *IntAu&W 91X*
**Philbin,** Daniel Michael 1935- *AmMWSc 92*
**Philbin,** Edward J 1932- *WhoAmP 91*
**Philbin,** Edward James 1932- *WhoAmL 92*
**Philbin,** Jack *LesBEnT 92*
**Philbin,** Jeffrey Stephen 1942- *AmMWSc 92*
**Philbin,** John Arthur 1934- *WhoAmL 92*
**Philbin,** William J. 1907- *Who 92*
**Philbrick,** Ann Mathews 1956- *WhoRel 92*
**Philbrick,** Charles Russell 1940- *AmMWSc 92*
**Philbrick,** Edward D 1936- *WhoAmP 91*
**Philbrick,** Ralph 1934- *AmMWSc 92*
**Philbrick,** Shailer Shaw 1908- *AmMWSc 92*
**Philbrick,** Stephen *DrAPF 91*
**Philby,** H A R 1912-1988 *FacFETw*
**Phile,** Philip d1793 *NewAmDM*
**Phileas** d304? *EncEarC*
**Philenia** *BenetAL 91*
**Philidor,** Francois-Andre-Danican 1726-1795 *NewAmDM*
**Philip** 1639?-1676 *RComAH*
**Philip I** 1478-1516 *HisDSpE*
**Philip II** 1527-1598 *HisDSpE*
**Philip III** 1578-1621 *HisDSpE*
**Philip IV** 1605-1665 *HisDSpE*
**Philip V** 1683-1746 *HisDSpE*
**Philip,** King *BenetAL 91*
**Philip of Side** *EncEarC*
**Philip the Arabian** 204?-249 *EncEarC*
**Philip,** A G Davis 1929- *AmMWSc 92*
**Philip,** Alexander Morrison 1942- *Who 92*
**Philip,** James Peyton, Jr 1930- *WhoAmP 91*
**Philip,** John Robert 1927- *IntWW 91, Who 92*
**Philip,** Peter Joseph 1937- *WhoAmP 91*
**Philip,** Roland Stephen 1938- *WhoMW 92*
**Philip,** William Warren 1926- *WhoFI 92*
**Philip-Bradfield,** Sheilah 1956- *WhoEnt 92*
**Philipp,** Elliot Elias 1915- *WrDr 92*
**Philipp,** Herbert Reynold 1928- *AmMWSc 92*
**Philipp,** Isidor 1863-1958 *NewAmDM*
**Philipp,** Manfred 1945- *AmMWSc 92*
**Philipp,** Perry Fred 1913- *WhoFI 92*
**Philipp,** Ronald E 1932- *AmMWSc 92*
**Philipp,** Thomas J. 1936- *WhoRel 92*
**Philipp,** Walter V 1936- *AmMWSc 92*
**Philippa of Hainault** 1314?-1369 *EncAmaz 91*
**Philippart,** Michel Paul 1935- *AmMWSc 92*
**Philippe de Vitry** *NewAmDM*
**Philippe,** Andre 1926- *IntWW 91*
**Philippe,** Andre J. 1926- *Who 92*
**Philippe,** Beatrice 1948- *WhoFI 92*
**Philippe,** Paulita 1937- *WhoRel 92*
**Philippidis,** Alex 1963- *IntAu&W 91*
**Philippot,** Michel Paul 1925- *NewAmDM*
**Philippou,** Andreas N. 1944- *IntWW 91*
**Philippou,** Andreas Nicolaou 1944- *AmMWSc 92*
**Philipps** *Who 92*
**Philipps,** Edward William 1938- *WhoFI 92*
**Philipps,** Hanning *Who 92*
**Philipps,** Marion 1908- *Who 92*
**Philipps,** Richard Hanning 1904- *Who 92*
**Philips,** Ambrose 1674-1749 *RfGEnL 91*
**Philips,** Barbara *WhoAmP 91*
**Philips,** Billy Ulyses 1946- *AmMWSc 92*
**Philips,** Cyril 1912- *Who 92, WrDr 92*
**Philips,** Cyril Henry 1912- *IntWW 91*
**Philips,** George 1931- *WhoFI 92*
**Philips,** James Davison 1920- *WhoRel 92*
**Philips,** John 1676-1709 *RfGEnL 91*
**Philips,** Judson 1903- *IntAu&W 91*
**Philips,** Judson Christopher 1942- *AmMWSc 92*
**Philips,** Judson Pentecost 1903-1989 *BenetAL 91*
**Philips,** Justin Robin Drew 1948- *Who 92*
**Philips,** Katherine 1631-1664 *RfGEnL 91*
**Philips,** Laura Alma 1957- *AmMWSc 92*
**Philips,** Miklosh 1961- *WhoEnt 92*
**Philips,** Peter 1561-1628 *NewAmDM*
**Philipsborn,** John Timothy 1949- *WhoAmL 92, WhoWest 92*
**Philipsborn,** Randall H. 1952- *WhoWest 92*
**Philipsen,** Judith Lynne Johnson 1942- *AmMWSc 92*
**Philipson,** Garry 1921- *Who 92*
**Philipson,** John Trevor Graham 1948- *Who 92*
**Philipson,** Joseph 1918- *AmMWSc 92, WhoWest 92*
**Philipson,** Lloyd Lewis 1928- *AmMWSc 92*
**Philipson,** Robert James 1916- *IntWW 91, Who 92*
**Philipson,** Robin 1916- *TwCPaSc*
**Philipson-Stow,** Christopher 1920- *Who 92*
**Phillabaum,** Corliss Edwin 1933- *WhoEnt 92*
**Philleo,** Robert Eugene 1923- *AmMWSc 92*
**Philley,** John Calvin 1935- *AmMWSc 92*
**Phillies,** George David Joseph 1947- *AmMWSc 92*
**Phillifent,** John T *TwCSFW 91*
**Phillimore** *Who 92*
**Phillimore,** Baron 1911- *Who 92*
**Phillimore,** John Gore 1908- *Who 92*
**Phillip,** Malcolm Irving 1934- *WhoRel 92*
**Phillip,** Michael John 1929- *WhoBlA 92*
**Phillip,** White, III 1956- *WhoBlA 92*
**Phillippe,** Mary Jane Barker Beaman 1919- *WhoAmP 91*
**Phillips** *ThHEIm, Who 92*
**Phillips,** Baroness *Who 92*
**Phillips,** Acen L. 1935- *WhoBlA 92*
**Phillips,** Adrian Alexander Christian 1940- *Who 92*
**Phillips,** Alan *Who 92*
**Phillips,** Alan Guy 1949- *WhoWest 92*
**Phillips,** Alan LeRoy 1949- *WhoRel 92*
**Phillips,** Alfred Patrick 1927- *WhoRel 92*
**Phillips,** Alfredo 1935- *IntWW 91*
**Phillips,** Allan Robert 1914- *AmMWSc 92*
**Phillips,** Allen Thurman 1938- *AmMWSc 92*
**Phillips,** Alma Bercovitz 1923- *WhoWest 92*
**Phillips,** Almarin 1925- *WhoAmL 92*
**Phillips,** Alvah H 1928- *AmMWSc 92*
**Phillips,** Alvin B 1920- *AmMWSc 92*
**Phillips,** Andre 1959- *BlkOlyM*
**Phillips,** Andrew Bassett 1945- *Who 92*
**Phillips,** Andrew Craig 1922- *WhoAmP 91*
**Phillips,** Andrew Wheeler 1844-1915 *BilnAmS*
**Phillips,** Angela Marie 1947- *WhoWest 92*
**Phillips,** Anna 1936- *WhoWest 92*
**Phillips,** Annabelle W. 1926- *WhoRel 92*
**Phillips,** Anne *Who 92*
**Phillips,** Anne Dinsmore 1935- *WhoEnt 92*
**Phillips,** Anthony Charles Julian 1936- *Who 92*
**Phillips,** Anthony Francis 1937- *WhoAmL 92*
**Phillips,** Anthony George 1943- *AmMWSc 92*
**Phillips,** Arthur d1991 *Who 92N*
**Phillips,** Arthur 1948- *WhoIns 92*
**Phillips,** Arthur Page 1917- *AmMWSc 92*
**Phillips,** Arthur Sol 1948- *WhoFI 92*
**Phillips,** Arthur William, Jr 1915- *AmMWSc 92*
**Phillips,** Aubrey *TwCPaSc*
**Phillips,** Barbara 1936- *WhoBlA 92*
**Phillips,** Barbara Jean 1942- *WhoAmP 91*
**Phillips,** Barnet, IV 1948- *WhoAmL 92*
**Phillips,** Basil Oliphant 1930- *WhoBlA 92*
**Phillips,** Benjamin 1917- *AmMWSc 92*
**Phillips,** Bertha 1940- *WhoBlA 92*
**Phillips,** Bertrand D. 1938- *WhoBlA 92*
**Phillips,** Betty *DrAPF 91*
**Phillips,** Betty Lou *WhoWest 92*
**Phillips,** Beverly Gay 1954- *WhoRel 92*
**Phillips,** Billy Joe 1931- *WhoAmP 91*
**Phillips,** Bobby *WhoAmP 91*
**Phillips,** Bobby Mal 1941- *AmMWSc 92*
**Phillips,** Brent *WhoEnt 92*
**Phillips,** Brian Antony Morley 1942- *AmMWSc 92*
**Phillips,** Brian Ross 1935- *AmMWSc 92*
**Phillips,** Bruce A 1938- *AmMWSc 92*
**Phillips,** Bruce Edwin 1934- *AmMWSc 92*
**Phillips,** Burrill 1907-1988 *NewAmDM*
**Phillips,** C Eugene 1932- *WhoAmP 91*
**Phillips,** Calbert Inglis 1925- *Who 92*
**Phillips,** Calvin L. *WhoRel 92*
**Phillips,** Carleton Jaffrey 1942- *AmMWSc 92*
**Phillips,** Carlton Vernon 1924- *WhoFI 92*
**Phillips,** Carol Fenton 1932- *AmMWSc 92*
**Phillips,** Carol Fox 1939- *WhoFI 92*
**Phillips,** Carter Glasgow 1952- *WhoAmL 92*
**Phillips,** Caryl 1958- *ConNov 91, WrDr 92*
**Phillips,** Chandler Allen 1942- *AmMWSc 92*
**Phillips,** Channing E 1928-1987 *FacFETw*
**Phillips,** Charles Eugene 1933- *WhoAmP 91*
**Phillips,** Charles Franklin, Jr 1934- *WhoAmP 91*
**Phillips,** Charles Garrett 1916- *Who 92*
**Phillips,** Charles Henry 1858-1951 *RelLAm 91*
**Phillips,** Charles W 1920- *AmMWSc 92*
**Phillips,** Chris Allen 1962- *WhoRel 92*
**Phillips,** Christopher Hallowell 1920- *WhoAmP 91*
**Phillips,** Clarence E 1950- *WhoAmP 91*
**Phillips,** Clarence W *WhoAmP 91*
**Phillips,** Colette Alice-Maude 1954- *WhoBlA 92*
**Phillips,** Constance Ann 1941- *WhoBlA 92*
**Phillips,** Cyrus Eastman, IV 1944- *WhoAmL 92*
**Phillips,** D. John *IntMPA 92*
**Phillips,** Daliar Clotille 1965- *WhoEnt 92*
**Phillips,** Daniel P. 1917- *WhoBlA 92*
**Phillips,** Darrell 1956- *WhoWest 92*
**Phillips,** David 1924- *IntWW 91*
**Phillips,** David 1936- *AmMWSc 92*
**Phillips,** David 1939- *IntWW 91, Who 92*
**Phillips,** David Alan 1926- *Who 92*
**Phillips,** David Berry 1940- *AmMWSc 92*
**Phillips,** David Chilton 1924- *Who 92*
**Phillips,** David Colin 1940- *AmMWSc 92*
**Phillips,** David Graham 1867-1911 *BenetAL 91, TwCLC 44 [port]*
**Phillips,** David Lee 1948- *WhoMW 92*
**Phillips,** David Lowell 1929- *AmMWSc 92*
**Phillips,** David Mann 1938- *AmMWSc 92*
**Phillips,** David Richard 1942- *AmMWSc 92*
**Phillips,** David T 1938- *AmMWSc 92*
**Phillips,** David William 1946- *AmMWSc 92*
**Phillips,** Dean H. 1927- *WhoMW 92*
**Phillips,** Deborah F 1953- *WhoAmP 91*
**Phillips,** Dennis *DrAPF 91, WrDr 92*
**Phillips,** Derek L. 1934- *WrDr 92*
**Phillips,** Dewi Zephaniah 1934- *Who 92, WrDr 92*
**Phillips,** Diane Susan 1942- *Who 92*
**Phillips,** Dilcia R. 1949- *WhoBlA 92*
**Phillips,** Don Irwin 1945- *AmMWSc 92*
**Phillips,** Don T 1942- *AmMWSc 92*
**Phillips,** Donald Arthur 1945- *AmMWSc 92*
**Phillips,** Donald David 1926- *AmMWSc 92*
**Phillips,** Donald Herman 1941- *AmMWSc 92*
**Phillips,** Donald John 1930- *IntWW 91, WhoFI 92*
**Phillips,** Donald Kenney 1931- *AmMWSc 92*
**Phillips,** Donald Lewis 1933- *WhoWest 92*
**Phillips,** Donald Lundahl 1952- *AmMWSc 92*
**Phillips,** Donna Rose 1961- *WhoWest 92*
**Phillips,** Dorothy Alease 1924- *WhoRel 92*
**Phillips,** Dorothy Kay 1945- *WhoAmL 92*
**Phillips,** Douglas J 1931- *AmMWSc 92*
**Phillips,** Dwight Edward 1944- *AmMWSc 92*
**Phillips,** E Alan 1937- *AmMWSc 92*
**Phillips,** Earl W. 1917- *WhoBlA 92*
**Phillips,** Earmia Jean 1941- *WhoBlA 92*
**Phillips,** Ed *WhoAmP 91*
**Phillips,** Edward 1926- *AmMWSc 92*
**Phillips,** Edward Alexander 1942- *WhoBlA 92*
**Phillips,** Edward Charles 1944- *WhoMW 92*
**Phillips,** Edward Everett 1927- *WhoFI 92*
**Phillips,** Edward John 1940- *WhoFI 92*
**Phillips,** Edward Martin 1935- *WhoBlA 92*
**Phillips,** Edward Thomas John 1930- *Who 92*
**Phillips,** Edwin Allen 1915- *AmMWSc 92*

Phillips, Edwin William 1904- WhoFI 92
Phillips, Edwin William 1918- Who 92
Phillips, Eldon Franklin 1941- WhoWest 92
Phillips, Ella Mae 1931- WhoAmP 91
Phillips, Elliott Hunter 1919- WhoAmL 92
Phillips, Elwood Hudson 1914- WhoFI 92
Phillips, Eric Lawrance 1909- Who 92
Phillips, Eric McLaren, Jr. 1952- WhoBlA 92
Phillips, Esther Rodlitz 1933- AmMWSc 92
Phillips, Eugenie Elvira 1918- WhoBlA 92
Phillips, F. Allison 1937- WhoBlA 92
Phillips, Fitzgerald 1893-1978 WhoBlA 92N
Phillips, Frances DrAPF 91
Phillips, Francis Clifford 1850-1920 BiInAmS
Phillips, Francis Noriega-Pons 1947- WhoFI 92
Phillips, Frank TwCSFW 91
Phillips, Frank Edward 1930- WhoBlA 92
Phillips, Frank Jay 1881-1911 BiInAmS
Phillips, Fred 1918- Who 92
Phillips, Fred Melville 1954- AmMWSc 92, WhoWest 92
Phillips, Fred Ronald 1940- WhoFI 92
Phillips, Frederick Brian 1946- WhoBlA 92
Phillips, Frederick Falley 1946- WhoMW 92
Phillips, Frederick Stanley 1928- WhoFI 92
Phillips, Gail 1944- WhoAmP 91
Phillips, Gary Wilson 1940- AmMWSc 92
Phillips, Gayle Sarratt 1939- WhoAmP 91
Phillips, Geneva Ficker 1920- WhoWest 92
Phillips, George Douglas 1928- AmMWSc 92
Phillips, George L. 1949- WhoAmL 92
Phillips, George Wygant, Jr 1929- AmMWSc 92
Phillips, Gerald B 1925- AmMWSc 92
Phillips, Gerald C 1922- AmMWSc 92
Phillips, Gerald Hayden 1943- Who 92
Phillips, Gerald M. 1928- WrDr 92
Phillips, Glen Edwin 1933- WhoAmP 91
Phillips, Glenn Owen 1946- WhoBlA 92
Phillips, Grace Briggs 1923- AmMWSc 92
Phillips, Gregory Conrad 1954- AmMWSc 92
Phillips, Guy Frank 1923- AmMWSc 92
Phillips, Harold L. 1955- WhoRel 92
Phillips, Harry 1911- TwCPaSc
Phillips, Harvey 1929- NewAmDM
Phillips, Harvey Gene 1929- WhoEnt 92
Phillips, Hayden Who 92
Phillips, Helen M. 1926- WhoBlA 92
Phillips, Henry 1914- Who 92
Phillips, Henry Wallace 1869-1930 BenetAL 91
Phillips, Herbert A, Jr. 1928- WhoIns 92
Phillips, Horace 1917- IntWW 91, Who 92
Phillips, Hugh Jefferson 1922- AmMWSc 92
Phillips, I. Van Keith 1943- WhoEnt 92
Phillips, Ian 1938- Who 92
Phillips, Irna d1974 LesBEnT 92
Phillips, Jack ConAu 35NR
Phillips, Jack Ewart 1933- WhoAmL 92
Phillips, Jacob Robinson 1929- AmMWSc 92
Phillips, Jacqueline Loehler 1935- WhoAmP 91
Phillips, James A 1919- AmMWSc 92
Phillips, James Allen 1952- WhoRel 92
Phillips, James Arthur 1941- WhoFI 92
Phillips, James Atlee 1915- WrDr 92
Phillips, James Cecil 1954- WhoMW 92
Phillips, James Charles 1933- AmMWSc 92
Phillips, James D, Jr WhoAmP 91
Phillips, James Daniel 1933- WhoAmP 91
Phillips, James Dickson, Jr. 1922- WhoAmL 92
Phillips, James Jackson 1954- WhoAmL 92
Phillips, James Lawrence 1932- WhoBlA 92
Phillips, James M 1934- AmMWSc 92
Phillips, James McJunkin 1929- WhoRel 92
Phillips, James Oscar, III 1944- WhoAmL 92
Phillips, James W 1930- AmMWSc 92
Phillips, James Woodward 1943- AmMWSc 92
Phillips, Jayne Anne DrAPF 91
Phillips, Jayne Anne 1952- BenetAL 91, ConNov 91, IntAu&W 91, WrDr 92
Phillips, Jean Allen 1918- AmMWSc 92
Phillips, Jeffrey Gordon 1952- WhoMW 92
Phillips, Jeremy Patrick Manfred 1941- Who 92
Phillips, Jerry Clyde 1935- AmMWSc 92
Phillips, Jimmy E 1939- WhoIns 92
Phillips, John 1926- Who 92
Phillips, John A. 1949- ConAu 133
Phillips, John Andrew 1951- WhoRel 92
Phillips, John Bomar 1947- WhoAmL 92
Phillips, John C. 1948- WhoAmL 92
Phillips, John David 1942- WhoFI 92
Phillips, John David, Jr. 1947- WhoFI 92
Phillips, John E 1928- WhoAmP 91
Phillips, John Edward 1934- AmMWSc 92
Phillips, John Fleetwood Stewart 1917- Who 92
Phillips, John Francis 1911- Who 92
Phillips, John Howell, Jr 1925- AmMWSc 92
Phillips, John Hunter, Jr 1930- AmMWSc 92
Phillips, John Jason, II 1938- WhoBlA 92
Phillips, John Lawrence, Jr. 1923- WrDr 92
Phillips, John Lynch 1951- AmMWSc 92
Phillips, John M. 1920- WhoBlA 92
Phillips, John Paul 1932- WhoWest 92
Phillips, John Perrow 1925- AmMWSc 92
Phillips, John R 1935- AmMWSc 92
Phillips, John Randall 1940- Who 92
Phillips, John Raymond 1936- WhoAmL 92
Phillips, John Richard 1934- AmMWSc 92, WhoWest 92
Phillips, John S. 1861-1949 BenetAL 91
Phillips, John Spencer 1953- AmMWSc 92
Phillips, John Thomas, II 1954- WhoAmP 91
Phillips, John Walter 1918- WhoMW 92
Phillips, Joseph Brantley, Jr. 1931- WhoAmL 92
Phillips, Joseph C. WhoEnt 92
Phillips, Joseph C. 1962- WhoBlA 92
Phillips, Joseph D 1938- AmMWSc 92
Phillips, Joseph Michael, Jr. 1956- WhoFI 92, WhoMW 92
Phillips, Joshua 1936- WhoMW 92
Phillips, Joy Burcham 1917- AmMWSc 92
Phillips, Julia 1944- IntMPA 92, News 92-1 [port]
Phillips, Julia M 1954- AmMWSc 92
Phillips, June M. J. 1941- WhoBlA 92
Phillips, Karen Borlaug 1956- WhoAmP 91, WhoFI 92
Phillips, Kate Johnson DrAPF 91
Phillips, Keith L 1937- AmMWSc 92
Phillips, Keith Wendall 1946- WhoRel 92, WhoWest 92
Phillips, Kenneth L. 1947- WhoFI 92
Phillips, Kenneth Lloyd 1918- AmMWSc 92
Phillips, Kenneth Peter 1936- WhoMW 92
Phillips, Kevin Emil 1955- WhoAmP 91
Phillips, Lacy Darryl 1963- WhoWest 92
Phillips, Larry 1951- WhoAmP 91
Phillips, Larry Duane 1948- WhoFI 92
Phillips, Larry Edward 1942- WhoAmL 92, WhoFI 92
Phillips, Laurie Gwenn 1959- WhoAmL 92
Phillips, Lawrence Stone 1941- AmMWSc 92
Phillips, Layn R. 1952- WhoAmL 92
Phillips, Lee Revell 1953- AmMWSc 92
Phillips, Lee Trinkle 1918- WhoAmP 91
Phillips, Lee Vern 1930- AmMWSc 92
Phillips, Leo A. 1931- WhoBlA 92
Phillips, Leo Augustus 1931- AmMWSc 92
Phillips, Leo Harold, Jr. 1945- WhoAmL 92, WhoFI 92
Phillips, Leon A 1923- AmMWSc 92
Phillips, Leon Francis 1935- IntWW 91
Phillips, Leroy Daniel 1935- WhoBlA 92
Phillips, Lesley Rebecca 1945- RelLAm 91
Phillips, Leslie 1924- IntMPA 92
Phillips, Lewis 1920- WhoAmP 91
Phillips, Lewis Milton 1921- WhoAmP 91
Phillips, Linda 1947- WhoEnt 92
Phillips, Linda A. Bousfield 1950- WhoMW 92
Phillips, Lloyd Austin 1928- WhoRel 92
Phillips, Lloyd Garrison, Jr. 1941- WhoBlA 92
Phillips, Lou Diamond 1962- IntMPA 92
Phillips, Louis DrAPF 91
Phillips, Louis Christopher 1939- IntAu&W 91
Phillips, Lyle Llewellyn 1923- AmMWSc 92
Phillips, Lyman C. 1939- WhoMW 92
Phillips, M J 1876- ScFEYrs
Phillips, Marisa 1932- Who 92
Phillips, Mark IntAu&W 91X, TwCSFW 91, WrDr 92
Phillips, Mark Anthony Peter 1948- Who 92
Phillips, Marshall 1932- AmMWSc 92
Phillips, Martha Henderson 1942- WhoAmP 91
Phillips, Marvin W 1929- AmMWSc 92
Phillips, Mary McDonough d1991 NewYTBS 91
Phillips, Max 1924- Who 92
Phillips, Mel 1945- WhoAmP 91
Phillips, Melba 1907- AmMWSc 92
Phillips, Melville James 1930- AmMWSc 92
Phillips, Melvin Romine 1921- WhoRel 92
Phillips, Merle H 1928- WhoAmP 91
Phillips, Mervyn John 1930- Who 92
Phillips, Michael IntAu&W 91X
Phillips, Michael 1916- IntMPA 92
Phillips, Michael 1943- IntMPA 92
Phillips, Michael Canavan 1940- AmMWSc 92
Phillips, Michael Ian 1938- AmMWSc 92
Phillips, Michael John 1948- WhoFI 92
Phillips, Michael Joseph DrAPF 91
Phillips, Michael Joseph 1937- IntAu&W 91, WrDr 92
Phillips, Michael Keith 1943- WhoAmP 91
Phillips, Michael Vito 1943- WhoEnt 92
Phillips, Michelle 1944- IntMPA 92
Phillips, Michelle Gilliam 1944- WhoEnt 92
Phillips, Mildred E 1928- AmMWSc 92
Phillips, Monte Leroy 1937- AmMWSc 92
Phillips, Morris Clayton, Jr 1944- WhoAmP 91
Phillips, N Christopher AmMWSc 92
Phillips, Nat, Jr. 1930- WhoRel 92
Phillips, Neville Crompton 1916- Who 92
Phillips, Nicholas 1938- Who 92
Phillips, Nick 1965- WhoEnt 92
Phillips, Nicolas R. Guthrie 1934- WhoFI 92
Phillips, Norman AmMWSc 92
Phillips, Norman David 1931- WhoMW 92
Phillips, Norman Edgar 1928- AmMWSc 92
Phillips, Norman L. 1957- WhoWest 92
Phillips, Olin Ray 1934- WhoAmP 91
Phillips, Owen M 1930- AmMWSc 92
Phillips, Owen Martin 1930- IntWW 91, Who 92
Phillips, Packard E. 1938- WhoAmL 92
Phillips, Pamela Kim 1958- WhoAmL 92, WhoFI 92
Phillips, Patrick Edward 1931- WhoWest 92
Phillips, Patrick Paul 1955- WhoAmL 92
Phillips, Paul WhoEnt 92
Phillips, Paul 1956- WhoAmP 91
Phillips, Paul J 1942- AmMWSc 92
Phillips, Perry Edward 1944- AmMWSc 92
Phillips, Peter 1930- Who 92
Phillips, Peter 1939- TwCPaSc
Phillips, Peter Charles B 1948- AmMWSc 92
Phillips, Philip Kay 1933- WhoFI 92, WhoMW 92
Phillips, Philip Wirth 1958- AmMWSc 92
Phillips, R. A. J. 1922- WrDr 92
Phillips, Ralph Leonard 1925- WhoBlA 92
Phillips, Ralph Saul 1913- AmMWSc 92
Phillips, Ralph W 1918- AmMWSc 92
Phillips, Randall Clinger 1924- WhoRel 92
Phillips, Randy Ernest 1950- WhoAmP 91
Phillips, Reid Lloyd 1952- WhoAmL 92
Phillips, Rex Philip 1913- Who 92
Phillips, Richard Arlan 1933- AmMWSc 92
Phillips, Richard Charles Jonathan 1947- Who 92
Phillips, Richard Dean 1929- AmMWSc 92
Phillips, Richard E, Jr 1936- AmMWSc 92
Phillips, Richard Edward 1930- AmMWSc 92
Phillips, Richard Hart 1922- AmMWSc 92
Phillips, Richard Lang 1934- AmMWSc 92
Phillips, Richard P 1928- AmMWSc 92
Phillips, Robert DrAPF 91
Phillips, Robert d1991 NewYTBS 91
Phillips, Robert 1938- WrDr 92
Phillips, Robert Allan 1937- AmMWSc 92
Phillips, Robert Bass, Jr 1932- AmMWSc 92
Phillips, Robert Edward 1923- AmMWSc 92
Phillips, Robert Francis 1936- WhoIns 92
Phillips, Robert Gibson 1936- AmMWSc 92
Phillips, Robert Hansbury 1924- WhoBlA 92
Phillips, Robert James, Jr. 1955- WhoAmL 92
Phillips, Robert Lee 1938- WhoAmP 91
Phillips, Robert Rhodes AmMWSc 92
Phillips, Robert Schaeffer 1938- WhoEnt 92
Phillips, Robert Thomas 1945- WhoAmP 91
Phillips, Robert Ward 1929- AmMWSc 92
Phillips, Robin 1942- Who 92, WhoWest 92
Phillips, Robin Francis 1940- Who 92
Phillips, Rog 1909-1965 TwCSFW 91
Phillips, Roger 1939- WhoFI 92
Phillips, Roger Guy AmMWSc 92
Phillips, Roger Winston 1942- AmMWSc 92
Phillips, Rohan Hilary AmMWSc 92
Phillips, Romeo Eldridge 1928- WhoBlA 92
Phillips, Ronald Carl 1932- AmMWSc 92
Phillips, Ronald Edward 1929- AmMWSc 92
Phillips, Ronald Frank 1934- WhoAmL 92, WhoWest 92
Phillips, Ronald Lewis 1940- AmMWSc 92
Phillips, Ronald William 1949- Who 92
Phillips, Rondall Van 1945- WhoWest 92
Phillips, Ronnie Jack 1951- WhoFI 92
Phillips, Rosemarye L. 1926- WhoBlA 92
Phillips, Roy G. 1934- WhoBlA 92
Phillips, Royce Wayne 1953- WhoRel 92
Phillips, Rufus 1929- WhoAmP 91
Phillips, Russell Allan 1935- AmMWSc 92
Phillips, Russell C 1923- AmMWSc 92
Phillips, Ruth Brosi 1940- AmMWSc 92
Phillips, S Michael 1940- AmMWSc 92
Phillips, Samuel 1921-1990 AnObit 1990
Phillips, Samuel C 1921- AmMWSc 92
Phillips, Sandra Sammataro WhoWest 92
Phillips, Scott David 1953- WhoFI 92
Phillips, Scott Douglas 1946- WhoFI 92
Phillips, Seth Harold 1951- WhoAmP 91
Phillips, Sian IntWW 91, Who 92
Phillips, Sidney Earl 1955- WhoFI 92
Phillips, Sidney Frederick 1933- AmMWSc 92
Phillips, Spencer Kleckner 1914- WhoMW 92
Phillips, Stephen 1864-1915 RfGEnL 91
Phillips, Stephen Lee 1940- AmMWSc 92
Phillips, Steven J 1948- AmMWSc 92
Phillips, Steven Jones 1929- AmMWSc 92
Phillips, Susan Meredith 1944- WhoAmP 91
Phillips, Sydney William Charles d1991 Who 92N
Phillips, Ted Ray 1948- WhoWest 92
Phillips, Teddy Steve 1917- WhoEnt 92
Phillips, Terence Martyn 1946- AmMWSc 92
Phillips, Terry Lee 1951- WhoAmP 91
Phillips, Terry LeMoine 1938- WhoMW 92
Phillips, Theodore Locke 1933- AmMWSc 92
Phillips, Thomas Edworth, Jr. 1944- WhoFI 92
Phillips, Thomas Gould AmMWSc 92
Phillips, Thomas H. 1942- WhoEnt 92
Phillips, Thomas James 1958- AmMWSc 92
Phillips, Thomas John 1948- WhoMW 92
Phillips, Thomas Joseph 1947- AmMWSc 92
Phillips, Thomas Kent 1947- WhoRel 92
Phillips, Thomas L. 1924- IntWW 91, WhoFI 92
Phillips, Thomas Lee 1947- WhoAmL 92
Phillips, Thomas Leonard 1924- AmMWSc 92
Phillips, Thomas R 1949- WhoAmP 91
Phillips, Thomas Royal 1949- WhoAmL 92
Phillips, Thomas Wade 1943- WhoAmL 92
Phillips, Tina S. 1955- WhoWest 92
Phillips, Tom 1937- IntWW 91, TwCPaSc, Who 92
Phillips, Tom Lee 1931- AmMWSc 92
Phillips, Traci Lynn 1966- WhoFI 92
Phillips, Travis J 1919- AmMWSc 92
Phillips, Vel R. 1924- NotBlAW 92, WhoAmP 91, WhoBlA 92
Phillips, Veril LeRoy 1943- AmMWSc 92
Phillips, Vincent Mallory 1950- WhoAmP 91
Phillips, W. Thomas 1943- WhoBlA 92
Phillips, Walter J WhoAmP 91
Phillips, Ward ConAu 133
Phillips, Warren Henry 1926- IntWW 91, WhoFI 92
Phillips, Wendell 1811-1884 BenetAL 91, RComAH
Phillips, Wendell Francis 1921- AmMWSc 92
Phillips, Wendell H WhoAmP 91
Phillips, Wendell K. d1991 NewYTBS 91
Phillips, Wilburn R. WhoBlA 92
Phillips, Willard L, Jr 1941- WhoAmP 91
Phillips, Willard R. 1950- WhoFI 92
Phillips, William ConAu 35NR, IntWW 91, Who 92
Phillips, William 1906- WrDr 92
Phillips, William A. 1925- WhoAmL 92
Phillips, William Baars 1934- AmMWSc 92
Phillips, William Battle 1857-1918 BiInAmS
Phillips, William Dale 1925- AmMWSc 92
Phillips, William Daniel 1948- AmMWSc 92

**Phillips,** William Ernest John 1929- *AmMWSc 92*
**Phillips,** William Erwin 1947- *WhoAmP 91*
**Phillips,** William George 1929- *AmMWSc 92*
**Phillips,** William H 1918- *AmMWSc 92*
**Phillips,** William K 1936- *WhoIns 92*
**Phillips,** William M 1942- *WhoIns 92*
**Phillips,** William Maurice 1922- *AmMWSc 92*
**Phillips,** William Revell 1929- *AmMWSc 92*
**Phillips,** William Russell, Sr. 1948- *WhoAmL 92*
**Phillips,** Winfred M 1940- *AmMWSc 92*
**Phillips,** Winifred 1882-1958 *TwCPaSc*
**Phillips,** Yorke Peter 1932- *AmMWSc 92*
**Phillips-Garcia,** Gary Lee 1948- *WhoHisp 92*
**Phillips Griffiths,** Allen *Who 92*
**Phillips-Jones,** Linda *WhoWest 92*
**Phillips-Quagliata,** Julia Molyneux 1938- *AmMWSc 92*
**Phillips-Watkins,** Nora Marie 1960- *WhoMW 92*
**Phillips Yount,** Kimberly Jo 1962- *WhoEnt 92*
**Phillipson,** David W. 1942- *WrDr 92*
**Phillipson,** Eliot Asher 1939- *AmMWSc 92*
**Phillipson,** Michael 1940- *ConAu 133*
**Phillipson,** Paul Edgar 1933- *AmMWSc 92*
**Phillis,** John Whitfield 1936- *AmMWSc 92*
**Phillis,** Robert Weston 1945- *IntWW 91, Who 92*
**Phillis,** Yannis A. *DrAPF 91*
**Phillpotts,** Adelaide 1896- *IntAu&W 91, WrDr 92*
**Phillpotts,** Adelaide Eden 1896- *Who 92*
**Phillpotts,** Eden 1862-1960 *ScFEYrs*
**Phills,** Bobby Ray 1945- *AmMWSc 92*
**Philmus,** Robert M. 1943- *WrDr 92*
**Philo of Alexandria** 20?BC-50?AD *EncEarC*
**Philo Pacifus** *AmPeW*
**Philo,** Gordon Charles George 1920- *Who 92*
**Philo,** John Sterner 1948- *AmMWSc 92*
**Philogene,** Bernard J R 1940- *AmMWSc 92*
**Philoon,** Wallace C, Jr 1923- *AmMWSc 92*
**Philostorgius** 368?-439? *EncEarC*
**Philotheos** 1924- *WhoRel 92*
**Philoxenus of Mabbug** 440?-523 *EncEarC*
**Philp,** Hedley James 1943- *WhoWest 92*
**Philp,** Peter 1920- *IntAu&W 91, WrDr 92*
**Philp,** Richard Blain 1934- *AmMWSc 92*
**Philp,** Richard Nilson 1943- *IntAu&W 91*
**Philp,** Richard Paul 1947- *AmMWSc 92*
**Philp,** Robert Herron, Jr 1934- *AmMWSc 92*
**Philpot,** Ford 1917- *WhoRel 92*
**Philpot,** Glyn 1884-1937 *TwCPaSc*
**Philpot,** John Lee 1935- *AmMWSc 92*
**Philpot,** Jonathan David 1956- *WhoEnt 92*
**Philpot,** Oliver Lawrence Spurling 1913- *Who 92*
**Philpot,** Timothy N 1951- *WhoAmP 91*
**Philpot,** William H., Jr. 1957- *WhoAmL 92*
**Philpott,** A.L. d1991 *NewYTBS 91*
**Philpott,** Albert Lee 1919- *WhoAmP 91*
**Philpott,** Charles William 1932- *AmMWSc 92*
**Philpott,** Delbert E 1923- *AmMWSc 92*
**Philpott,** Delbert Eugene 1923- *WhoWest 92*
**Philpott,** James Alvin, Jr. 1947- *WhoAmL 92*
**Philpott,** Jane 1918- *AmMWSc 92*
**Philpott,** John Davis 1931- *WhoAmP 91*
**Philpott,** Larry La Fayette 1937- *WhoEnt 92*
**Philpott,** Lindsey 1948- *WhoWest 92*
**Philpott,** Michael Ronald 1940- *AmMWSc 92*
**Philpott,** Richard John 1936- *AmMWSc 92*
**Philpotts,** Anthony Robert 1938- *AmMWSc 92*
**Philps,** Frank Richard 1914- *Who 92*
**Philps,** Richard 1914- *WrDr 92*
**Phinazee,** Annette L. 1920-1983 *NotBlAW 92*
**Phinizy,** Robert Burchall 1926- *WhoFI 92*
**Phinney,** Bernard Orrin 1917- *AmMWSc 92*
**Phinney,** David Garland 1949- *WhoEnt 92*
**Phinney,** Ernest Emery 1948- *WhoEnt 92*
**Phinney,** Frederick Warren 1922- *WhoRel 92*
**Phinney,** George Jay 1930- *AmMWSc 92*
**Phinney,** Harry Kenyon 1918- *AmMWSc 92*
**Phinney,** Nanette 1945- *AmMWSc 92*
**Phinney,** Ralph E 1928- *AmMWSc 92*
**Phinney,** Robert A 1936- *AmMWSc 92*
**Phinney,** William Charles 1930- *AmMWSc 92*
**Phipps** *Who 92*
**Phipps,** Allen Mayhew 1938- *WhoFI 92*
**Phipps,** Arthur Raymond 1931- *WhoFI 92*
**Phipps,** Charles Howard 1926- *WhoFI 92*
**Phipps,** Christopher Douglas 1959- *WhoAmL 92*
**Phipps,** Colin Barry 1934- *Who 92*
**Phipps,** David Lee 1945- *WhoAmL 92*
**Phipps,** Donald Lee, Jr. 1939- *WhoFI 92*
**Phipps,** Grace May *IntAu&W 91*
**Phipps,** Herbert Edward 1941- *WhoAmP 91*
**Phipps,** James Bird 1934- *AmMWSc 92*
**Phipps,** John B. 1925- *WhoMW 92*
**Phipps,** John Tom 1937- *WhoAmL 92, WhoMW 92*
**Phipps,** Lawrence Henry 1954- *WhoRel 92*
**Phipps,** Leslie William 1930- *Who 92*
**Phipps,** Patrick Michael 1945- *AmMWSc 92*
**Phipps,** Paul Frederick 1921- *WhoMW 92*
**Phipps,** Peter Beverley Powell 1936- *AmMWSc 92*
**Phipps,** Richard L 1935- *AmMWSc 92*
**Phipps,** Roger John *AmMWSc 92*
**Phipps,** Simon Wilton 1921- *Who 92*
**Phipps,** Tony Randell 1953- *WhoEnt 92*
**Phipps,** William 1651-1695 *BenetAL 91*
**Phipps,** William Eugene 1930- *WhoRel 92, WrDr 92*
**Phips,** William 1651-1695 *BenetAL 91*
**Phipson,** Joan *ConAu 36NR*
**Phipson,** Joan 1912- *IntAu&W 91, WrDr 92*
**Phister,** Montgomery, Jr 1926- *AmMWSc 92*
**Phizackerley,** Gerald Robert 1929- *Who 92*
**Phleger,** Charles Frederick 1938- *AmMWSc 92*
**Phleger,** Fred B 1909- *AmMWSc 92*
**Phocas,** George John 1927- *WhoFI 92*
**Phoebus,** Edgar 1941- *WhoIns 92*
**Phoenix,** Charles Henry 1922- *AmMWSc 92*
**Phoenix,** David A 1916- *AmMWSc 92*
**Phoenix,** David Arthur 1958- *WhoEnt 92*
**Phoenix,** Donald R *AmMWSc 92*
**Phoenix,** G. Keith 1946- *WhoAmL 92*
**Phoenix,** John 1823-1861 *BenetAL 91*
**Phoenix,** River 1970- *ConTFT 9, NewYTBS 91 [port]*
**Phoenix,** River 1971- *IntMPA 92*
**Phomvihane,** Kaysone 1920- *IntWW 91*
**Phong,** Duong Hong 1953- *AmMWSc 92*
**Phoofolo,** Monyane Paanya 1946- *IntWW 91*
**Phoolan Devi** *EncAmaz 91*
**Phororo,** Daniel Rakoro 1934- *IntWW 91*
**Photinos,** Panos John 1948- *AmMWSc 92, WhoWest 92*
**Photinus** d376 *EncEarC*
**Photius** 810?-895? *EncEarC*
**Phounsavanh,** Nouhak *IntWW 91*
**Phreaner,** David Gray 1946- *WhoRel 92*
**Phung Thi Chinh** *EncAmaz 91*
**Phung,** Doan Lien 1940- *AmMWSc 92*
**Phyla** *EncAmaz 91*
**Physcoa** *EncAmaz 91*
**Physick,** John Frederick 1923- *Who 92*
**Physick,** Philip Syng 1768-1837 *BiInAmS*
**Phythian,** Brian A 1932- *IntAu&W 91, WrDr 92*
**Pi,** Wen-Yi Shih 1935- *WhoWest 92*
**Pi-Sunyer,** F Xavier 1933- *AmMWSc 92*
**Pi-Sunyer,** Xavier *WhoHisp 92*
**Pia,** Gary Ernest 1951- *WhoFI 92*
**Piacentini,** Ann 1959- *WhoFI 92*
**Piachaud,** David Francois James 1945- *Who 92*
**Piacsek,** Bela Emery 1937- *AmMWSc 92, WhoMW 92*
**Piaf,** Edith 1915-1963 *FacFETw [port], NewAmDM*
**Piaget,** Jean 1896-1980 *FacFETw*
**Piala,** Joseph J 1921- *AmMWSc 92*
**Pialat,** Maurice 1925- *IntDcF 2-2 [port], IntMPA 92*
**Pialet,** Joseph William 1951- *AmMWSc 92*
**Pian,** Carlson Chao-Ping 1945- *AmMWSc 92*
**Pian,** Charles Hsueh Chien 1921- *AmMWSc 92*
**Pian,** Theodore H H 1919- *AmMWSc 92*
**Pianetta,** Piero Antonio 1949- *AmMWSc 92*
**Pianfetti,** John Andrew 1907- *AmMWSc 92*
**Pianka,** Eric R 1939- *AmMWSc 92, WrDr 92*
**Pianka,** Uri 1937- *WhoEnt 92*
**Pianko,** Theodore A. 1955- *WhoAmL 92*
**Piano & Rogers** *DcTwDes*
**Piano,** Renzo 1937- *DcTwDes, IntWW 91*
**Pianotti,** Roland Salvatore 1930- *AmMWSc 92*
**Piantadosi,** Claude 1923- *AmMWSc 92*
**Piantini,** Carlos 1927- *WhoEnt 92*
**Piapot** 1816-1908 *RelLAm 91*
**Piasecki,** Boleslaw 1915-1979 *BiDExR*
**Piasecki,** Bruce *DrAPF 91*
**Piasecki,** Frank Nicholas 1919- *AmMWSc 92*
**Piasecki,** Joseph Kenneth 1946- *WhoMW 92*
**Piasecki,** Leonard R 1923- *AmMWSc 92*
**Piasek,** Joseph Ross 1950- *WhoEnt 92*
**Piassick,** Joel Bernard 1940- *WhoAmL 92*
**Piatak,** David Michael 1936- *AmMWSc 92*
**Piatier,** Andre 1914- *IntWW 91*
**Piatigorsky,** Gregor 1903-1976 *NewAmDM*
**Piatigorsky,** Joram Paul 1940- *AmMWSc 92*
**Piatkowski,** Thomas Frank 1938- *AmMWSc 92*
**Piatt,** David Michael 1954- *WhoMW 92*
**Piatt,** John James 1835-1917 *BenetAL 91*
**Piatt,** Richard C., II 1953- *WhoRel 92*
**Piatt,** Sarah Morgan 1836-1919 *BenetAL 91*
**Piavis,** George Walter 1922- *AmMWSc 92*
**Piazza,** Carl Frank 1945- *WhoAmL 92*
**Piazza,** Duane Eugene 1954- *WhoWest 92*
**Piazza,** Marguerite 1926- *WhoEnt 92*
**Piazzolla,** Astor 1921- *NewAmDM*
**Pibulsonggram,** Nitya 1941- *IntWW 91*
**Pica,** John Anthony, Jr 1952- *WhoAmP 91*
**Picachy,** Lawrence Trevor 1916- *IntWW 91, Who 92, WhoRel 92*
**Picano,** Felice *DrAPF 91*
**Picano,** Felice A. 1944- *WhoEnt 92*
**Picard,** Barbara Leonie 1917- *IntAu&W 91, WrDr 92*
**Picard,** Cecil J 1938- *WhoAmP 91*
**Picard,** Dennis J *AmMWSc 92*
**Picard,** Howard Richard 1939- *WhoFI 92*
**Picard,** Irving H. 1941- *WhoAmL 92*
**Picard,** Jacques Jean 1934- *WhoFI 92*
**Picard,** Laurent 1927- *WhoFI 92*
**Picard,** M Dane 1927- *AmMWSc 92*
**Picard,** Pierre-Olivier *WhoEnt 92*
**Picard,** Rainer Hans 1946- *WhoMW 92*
**Picard,** Richard Henry 1938- *AmMWSc 92*
**Picard,** Robert George 1951- *IntAu&W 91*
**Picard,** Thomas Joseph, Jr. 1933- *WhoFI 92*
**Picardi,** Ferdinand Louis 1930- *WhoAmP 91*
**Picariello,** Pasquale 1959- *WhoAmL 92*
**Picasso,** Pablo 1881-1973 *FacFETw [port]*
**Picasso,** Paloma 1949- *IntWW 91, News 91 [port], WhoHisp 92*
**Piccard,** Auguste 1884-1962 *FacFETw*
**Piccard,** Jacques 1922- *Who 92*
**Piccard,** Jacques Ernest Jean 1922- *IntWW 91*
**Piccarreta,** Michael Louis 1949- *WhoAmL 92*
**Picchione,** Nicholas Everett 1928- *WhoFI 92*
**Picchioni,** Albert Louis 1921- *AmMWSc 92*
**Picciano,** Mary Frances Ann 1946- *AmMWSc 92*
**Piccin,** Marshall Joseph 1929- *WhoMW 92*
**Piccini,** Niccolo 1728-1800 *NewAmDM*
**Piccinini,** Janice A 1945- *WhoAmP 91*
**Piccinini,** Robert M. *WhoFI 92*
**Piccinni,** Niccolo 1728-1800 *BlkwCEP*
**Picciolo,** Grace Lee 1934- *AmMWSc 92*
**Piccione,** Anthony *DrAPF 91*
**Piccione,** John Anthony 1958- *WhoFI 92*
**Piccione,** John William 1947- *WhoFI 92*
**Piccione,** Nancy A. 1948- *WhoEnt 92*
**Piccioni,** Oreste 1915- *AmMWSc 92*
**Picciotti,** Anthony Dean 1962- *WhoAmL 92*
**Picciotto,** Charles Edward 1942- *AmMWSc 92*
**Piccirelli,** Robert Anthony 1930- *AmMWSc 92*
**Picco,** Giandomenico *NewYTBS 91 [port]*
**Picco,** Ronald Charles 1948- *WhoWest 92*
**Picco,** Steven Joseph 1948- *WhoAmL 92*
**Piccola,** Jeffrey Early 1948- *WhoAmP 91*
**Piccoli,** Michel 1925- *IntMPA 92, IntWW 91*
**Piccolini,** Richard John 1933- *AmMWSc 92*
**Piccolo,** Joseph Anthony 1953- *WhoFI 92*
**Piccolo,** Lucio 1903-1969 *DcLB 114 [port], FacFETw*
**Piccone,** Joseph Anthony 1935- *WhoWest 92*
**Picerni,** Paul 1922- *IntMPA 92*
**Picerni,** Paul Horace 1922- *WhoEnt 92*
**Picha,** Kenneth G 1925- *AmMWSc 92*
**Pichal,** Henri Thomas, II 1923- *AmMWSc 92*
**Pichan,** Barbara T. 1960- *WhoAmL 92*
**Pichanick,** Francis Martin 1936- *AmMWSc 92*
**Pichardo,** Nelson Alexander 1958- *WhoHisp 92*
**Piche,** Roland 1938- *TwCPaSc*
**Picher,** Paul J 1914- *WhoAmP 91*
**Pichini,** Roberta D'Onofrio 1947- *WhoAmL 92*
**Pichler,** Joseph A. 1939- *IntWW 91*
**Pichler,** Joseph Anton 1939- *WhoFI 92, WhoMW 92*
**Pichois,** Claude 1925- *IntWW 91*
**Picht,** Hartmut Reinhard 1954- *WhoFI 92*
**Picirilli,** Robert Eugene 1932- *WhoRel 92*
**Pick,** Arthur Joseph, Jr. 1931- *WhoWest 92*
**Pick,** Charles Samuel 1917- *Who 92*
**Pick,** Frank 1878-1941 *DcTwDes*
**Pick,** James Block 1943- *WhoWest 92*
**Pick,** James Raymond 1936- *AmMWSc 92*
**Pick,** John Barclay 1921- *WrDr 92*
**Pick,** Lupu 1886-1931 *IntDcF 2-2*
**Pick,** Ralph Herbert Hans 1957- *WhoAmP 91*
**Pick,** Richard Samuel Burns 1915- *WhoEnt 92*
**Pick,** Robert Orville 1940- *AmMWSc 92*
**Pick,** Roy James 1941- *AmMWSc 92*
**Pick,** W Samuel *WhoAmP 91*
**Pickands,** James, III 1931- *AmMWSc 92*
**Pickar,** David 1948- *AmMWSc 92*
**Pickard,** Albert Marshall 1922- *WhoAmP 91*
**Pickard,** Barbara Gillespie 1936- *AmMWSc 92*
**Pickard,** Bob 1934- *WhoAmP 91*
**Pickard,** Brian Alan 1952- *WhoWest 92*
**Pickard,** Cyril 1917- *Who 92*
**Pickard,** Cyril Stanley 1917- *IntWW 91*
**Pickard,** David Janard 1933- *WhoWest 92*
**Pickard,** David L 1936- *WhoIns 92*
**Pickard,** George Lawson 1913- *AmMWSc 92*
**Pickard,** Howard Brevard 1917- *WhoAmL 92*
**Pickard,** Huia Masters 1909- *Who 92*
**Pickard,** Jerome P. d1991 *NewYTBS 91 [port]*
**Pickard,** John Allan 1940- *WhoAmL 92*
**Pickard,** John Greg 1949- *WhoFI 92*
**Pickard,** John Q. *TwCWW 91*
**Pickard,** Kevin Robert 1951- *WhoMW 92*
**Pickard,** Lee A. 1938- *WhoAmL 92*
**Pickard,** Michael 1932- *Who 92*
**Pickard,** Myrna Rae 1935- *AmMWSc 92*
**Pickard,** Nancy 1945- *WrDr 92*
**Pickard,** Porter Louis, Jr 1922- *AmMWSc 92*
**Pickard,** Scott Streetman 1949- *WhoMW 92*
**Pickard,** Terry Roy 1945- *WhoAmL 92*
**Pickard,** Tom 1946- *ConPo 91, IntAu&W 91, WrDr 92*
**Pickard,** William Frank 1941- *WhoBlA 92*
**Pickard,** William Freeman 1932- *AmMWSc 92*
**Pickard,** William Marshall, Jr. 1920- *WhoRel 92*
**Pickart,** Don Edward 1928- *WhoWest 92*
**Pickart,** Stanley Joseph 1926- *AmMWSc 92*
**Pickavance,** Thomas Gerald 1915- *IntWW 91, Who 92*
**Pickel,** A. W., III 1955- *WhoRel 92*
**Pickel,** Frederick Hugh 1952- *WhoFI 92*
**Pickell,** Charles Norman 1927- *WhoRel 92*
**Pickell,** Timothy Vernon 1952- *WhoAmL 92*
**Pickelmann,** Henry Michael 1947- *WhoRel 92*
**Picken,** Laurence Ernest Rowland 1909- *Who 92*
**Picken,** R. David 1945- *WhoAmL 92, WhoAmP 91*
**Pickens,** Alexander Legrand 1921- *WhoWest 92*
**Pickens,** Andrew 1739-1817 *BlkwEAR*
**Pickens,** Charles Glenn 1936- *AmMWSc 92, WhoMW 92*
**Pickens,** Jo Ann 1950- *IntWW 91*
**Pickens,** Marion Lee 1932- *WhoAmP 91*
**Pickens,** Peter E 1928- *AmMWSc 92*
**Pickens,** Thomas Boone, Jr. 1928- *IntWW 91, WhoFI 92*
**Pickens,** Watie Riley 1926- *WhoEnt 92*
**Pickens,** William 1881-1954 *BenetAL 91*
**Pickens,** William, III 1936- *WhoBlA 92*
**Pickens,** William Garfield 1927- *WhoBlA 92*
**Picker,** David V. 1931- *IntMPA 92*
**Picker,** Eugene D. 1903- *IntMPA 92*
**Picker,** Harvey Shalom 1942- *AmMWSc 92*
**Picker,** Martin 1929- *WrDr 92*
**Picker,** Sidney I., Jr. 1934- *WhoAmL 92*
**Picker,** Tobias 1954- *NewAmDM*
**Pickerill,** Mary Lou 1931- *WhoAmP 91*
**Pickering,** AvaJane 1951- *WhoWest 92*
**Pickering,** Basil Montagu d1878 *DcLB 106*
**Pickering,** Charles 1805-1878 *BiInAmS*
**Pickering,** Charles Denton 1950- *WhoMW 92*

**Pickering**, Charles Willis 1937- *WhoAmP 91*
**Pickering**, Ed Richard 1934- *AmMWSc 92*
**Pickering**, Edward 1912- *Who 92*
**Pickering**, Edward Charles 1846-1919 *BiInAmS*
**Pickering**, Edward Davies 1912- *IntAu&W 91, IntWW 91*
**Pickering**, Eileen Marion *TwCWW 91*
**Pickering**, Errol Neil 1938- *Who 92*
**Pickering**, Frank E *AmMWSc 92*
**Pickering**, Fred 1919- *Who 92*
**Pickering**, George Roscoe, Jr 1912- *WhoAmP 91*
**Pickering**, Gregory Haley 1960- *WhoRel 92*
**Pickering**, Harry J, Sr 1919- *WhoAmP 91*
**Pickering**, Herbert Kitchener 1915- *Who 92*
**Pickering**, Howard W 1935- *AmMWSc 92*
**Pickering**, James Stidger 1948- *WhoEnt 92*
**Pickering**, Jerry L 1942- *AmMWSc 92*
**Pickering**, John 1777-1846 *BenetAL 91*
**Pickering**, John Frederick 1939- *Who 92*
**Pickering**, John Harold 1916- *WhoAmL 92*
**Pickering**, John Robertson 1925- *Who 92*
**Pickering**, Kathleen Cumings 1943- *WhoMW 92*
**Pickering**, Linda Jane 1944- *WhoAmL 92*
**Pickering**, Miles Gilbert 1943- *AmMWSc 92*
**Pickering**, Ranard Jackson 1929- *AmMWSc 92*
**Pickering**, Richard Edward Ingram 1929- *Who 92*
**Pickering**, Richard Joseph 1934- *AmMWSc 92*
**Pickering**, Robert Easton 1934- *IntAu&W 91, WrDr 92*
**Pickering**, Robert Perry 1950- *WhoBlA 92*
**Pickering**, Rose 1947- *WhoEnt 92*
**Pickering**, Thomas G 1940- *AmMWSc 92*
**Pickering**, Thomas Reeve 1931- *IntWW 91, Who 92, WhoAmP 91*
**Pickering**, Timothy 1745-1829 *AmPolLe, BenetAL 91*
**Pickering**, Victoria L 1951- *WhoIns 92*
**Pickering**, W H 1910- *AmMWSc 92*
**Pickering**, William 1796-1854 *DcLB 106 [port]*
**Pickering**, William Hayward 1910- *IntWW 91*
**Pickering**, William Todd 1946- *WhoRel 92*
**Pickern**, Malcolm E. 1955- *WhoRel 92*
**Pickerstein**, Harold James 1946- *WhoAmL 92*
**Pickert**, Robert Walter 1936- *WhoMW 92*
**Pickett**, Albert Dean 1949- *WhoAmL 92*
**Pickett**, Alvin L. 1930- *WhoBlA 92*
**Pickett**, Bill Wayne 1930- *AmMWSc 92*
**Pickett**, Cecil Bruce 1945- *AmMWSc 92*
**Pickett**, Clarence Evan 1884-1965 *AmPeW*
**Pickett**, David *WhoEnt 92*
**Pickett**, David Franklin, Jr. 1936- *WhoWest 92*
**Pickett**, Donald Andrew 1953- *WhoAmL 92*
**Pickett**, Donna A. 1949- *WhoBlA 92*
**Pickett**, Dovie T. 1921- *WhoBlA 92*
**Pickett**, Dovie Theodosia 1921- *WhoAmP 91*
**Pickett**, Edward Ernest 1920- *AmMWSc 92*
**Pickett**, Elizabeth *ReelWom [port]*
**Pickett**, George R 1925- *AmMWSc 92*
**Pickett**, Gloria W. 1937- *WhoMW 92*
**Pickett**, Henry B., Jr. 1938- *WhoBlA 92*
**Pickett**, Herbert McWilliams 1943- *AmMWSc 92*
**Pickett**, Jackson Brittain 1943- *AmMWSc 92*
**Pickett**, James Edward 1954- *AmMWSc 92*
**Pickett**, James M 1937- *AmMWSc 92*
**Pickett**, John Harold 1943- *AmMWSc 92*
**Pickett**, Kathleen Cynthia 1953- *WhoAmL 92*
**Pickett**, Lawrence Kimball 1919- *AmMWSc 92*
**Pickett**, Leroy Kenneth 1937- *AmMWSc 92*
**Pickett**, Michael D. 1947- *WhoWest 92*
**Pickett**, Morris John 1915- *AmMWSc 92*
**Pickett**, Owen 1930- *AlmAP 92 [port]*
**Pickett**, Owen Bradford 1930- *WhoAmP 91*
**Pickett**, Patricia Booth 1931- *AmMWSc 92*
**Pickett**, Raymond Wallace, Jr. 1955- *WhoRel 92*
**Pickett**, Robert C 1928- *WhoIns 92*
**Pickett**, Robert E. 1936- *WhoBlA 92*
**Pickett**, Steward T A 1950- *AmMWSc 92*
**Pickett**, Theodore R., Jr. 1923- *WhoWest 92*
**Pickett**, Thomas 1912- *Who 92*
**Pickett**, Thomas Ernest 1937- *AmMWSc 92*
**Pickett**, Thomas George 1942- *WhoFI 92*
**Pickett**, Thomas William 1957- *WhoFI 92*
**Pickett**, Will Hays, Jr 1955- *WhoAmP 91*
**Pickett**, William Walter 1952- *WhoFI 92*
**Pickett**, Wilson 1941- *NewAmDM, WhoEnt 92*
**Pickett-Heaps**, Jeremy David 1940- *AmMWSc 92*
**Pickford**, David Michael 1926- *Who 92*
**Pickford**, Lillian Mary 1902- *Who 92*
**Pickford**, Mary *Who 92*
**Pickford**, Mary 1893-1979 *FacFETw [port], ReelWom [port]*
**Pickford**, Thomas Michael, Jr. 1958- *WhoAmL 92*
**Pickholtz**, Raymond L 1932- *AmMWSc 92*
**Pickholz**, Jerome Walter 1932- *WhoFI 92*
**Pickholz**, Marvin G. 1942- *WhoAmL 92*
**Pickholz**, Morris 1919- *WhoRel 92*
**Picking**, John 1939- *TwCPaSc*
**Pickle**, J. J. 1913- *AlmAP 92 [port], WhoAmP 91*
**Pickle**, Joseph Wesley, Jr. 1935- *WhoRel 92, WhoWest 92*
**Pickle**, Linda Williams 1948- *AmMWSc 92*
**Pickle**, Ramona Lee 1931- *WhoAmP 91*
**Pickle**, Robert Douglas 1937- *WhoAmL 92*
**Pickles**, James 1925- *Who 92*
**Pickles**, Marlon William 1931- *WhoFI 92*
**Pickman**, Jerome *IntMPA 92*
**Pickman**, Phillip 1938- *WhoWest 92*
**Picknell**, Walter John 1956- *WhoEnt 92*
**Pickover**, Stephen Mark 1957- *WhoEnt 92*
**Pickrell**, John A 1941- *AmMWSc 92*
**Pickrell**, Kenneth LeRoy 1910- *AmMWSc 92*
**Pickrell**, Mark M 1954- *AmMWSc 92*
**Pickslay**, Peter *WhoAmL 92*
**Pickthall**, Marjorie L. C. 1883-1922 *BenetAL 91*
**Pickthorn**, Charles 1927- *Who 92*
**Pickton**, Thomas Emil 1949- *WhoMW 92*
**Pickup**, David Cunliffe 1936- *Who 92*
**Pickup**, David Francis William 1953- *Who 92*
**Pickup**, Ronald Alfred 1940- *Who 92*
**Pickus**, Albert Pierre 1931- *WhoAmL 92*
**Pickwell**, George Vincent 1933- *AmMWSc 92*
**Pickworth**, Wallace Bruce 1946- *AmMWSc 92*
**Pico**, Fernando 1941- *WhoHisp 92*
**Pico**, Guillermo 1915- *AmMWSc 92*
**Pico**, Rafael 1912- *WhoHisp 92*
**Picon**, Hector Tomas, Jr. 1952- *WhoHisp 92*
**Picone**, J Michael 1948- *AmMWSc 92*
**Picone**, John, Jr. 1952- *WhoFI 92*
**Picot**, Jules Jean Charles 1932- *AmMWSc 92*
**Picott**, J. Rupert 1916-1989 *WhoBlA 92N*
**Picotte**, Terri Rosella 1947- *WhoMW 92*
**Picou**, Alphonse *ConAu 34NR*
**Picou**, Alphonse 1878-1961 *NewAmDM*
**Picou**, Jarl Jerome 1963- *WhoEnt 92*
**Picou**, Thomas Maurice 1937- *WhoBlA 92*
**Picraux**, Danice R 1946- *WhoAmP 91*
**Picraux**, Samuel Thomas 1943- *AmMWSc 92*
**Pictet**, Francois-Charles 1929- *Who 92*
**Picton**, Bernard *IntAu&W 91X, WrDr 92*
**Picton**, Harold D 1932- *AmMWSc 92*
**Picton**, Jacob Glyndwr 1912- *Who 92*
**Picton-Turbervill**, Edith 1872-1960 *BiDBrF 2*
**Picus**, Gerald Sherman 1926- *AmMWSc 92*
**Piczak**, John P 1940- *WhoAmP 91*
**Piddington**, Jack Hobart 1910- *IntWW 91*
**Piddington**, Philip Michael 1931- *Who 92*
**Piddock**, James Anthony 1956- *WhoEnt 92*
**Pidgeon**, George Campbell 1872-1971 *RelLAm 91*
**Pidgeon**, John 1926- *Who 92*
**Pidgeon**, Rezin E, Jr *AmMWSc 92*
**Pidgin**, Charles Felton 1844-1923 *BenetAL 91*
**Pidoux**, Edmond 1908- *IntAu&W 91*
**Pie**, James L. J. d1991 *NewYTBS 91*
**Piech**, Ferdinand 1937- *Who 92*
**Piech**, Kenneth Robert *AmMWSc 92*
**Piech**, Margaret Ann 1942- *AmMWSc 92*
**Piechocinski**, Thomas Anthony 1934- *WhoRel 92*
**Piechocki**, Stanislaw Ryszard 1955- *IntAu&W 91*
**Piechota**, Paul Arnold 1957- *WhoMW 92*
**Piechuta**, Michael Paul 1960- *WhoFI 92*
**Pieck**, Wilhelm 1876-1960 *EncTR 91 [port]*
**Pieczenik**, George 1944- *AmMWSc 92*
**Piedmont**, Richard Stuart 1948- *WhoAmL 92*
**Piedra**, Alberto Martinez 1926- *WhoAmP 91*
**Piedra**, Francisco J. *WhoHisp 92*
**Piedra**, Silvia L. 1949- *WhoHisp 92*
**Piedrahita**, Lucas Fernandez de *HisDSpE*
**Piehl**, Donald Herbert 1939- *AmMWSc 92*
**Piehl**, Frank John 1926- *AmMWSc 92*
**Piehler**, Wendell Howard 1936- *WhoEnt 92*
**Piekarski**, Konstanty 1915- *AmMWSc 92*
**Piekarski**, Stan *WhoAmP 91*
**Piekos**, Henry 1926- *WhoAmP 91*
**Piel**, Carolyn F 1918- *AmMWSc 92*
**Piel**, Gerard 1915- *AmMWSc 92, IntAu&W 91, IntWW 91*
**Piel**, Kenneth Martin 1936- *AmMWSc 92*
**Piel**, Reinhard Wilhelm 1956- *WhoEnt 92*
**Piel**, Robert John 1945- *WhoAmP 91*
**Piel**, William Frederick 1941- *AmMWSc 92*
**Pielet**, Howard M 1942- *AmMWSc 92*
**Pielke**, Roger Alvin 1946- *AmMWSc 92*
**Pielmeier**, John 1949- *IntAu&W 91, WrDr 92*
**Pielou**, Evelyn C 1924- *AmMWSc 92*
**Pielou**, William P 1922- *AmMWSc 92*
**Pienaar**, Leon Visser 1936- *AmMWSc 92*
**Pienaar**, Louis Alexander 1926- *IntWW 91*
**Piene**, Otto 1928- *IntWW 91*
**Pieniazek**, Szczepan Aleksander 1913- *IntWW 91*
**Pienkowski**, Jan Michal 1936- *Who 92*
**Pienkowski**, Robert Louis 1932- *AmMWSc 92*
**Pienta**, Norbert J 1952- *AmMWSc 92*
**Pienta**, Roman Joseph 1931- *AmMWSc 92*
**Pieper**, Darold D. 1944- *WhoAmL 92, WhoWest 92*
**Pieper**, David Robert *AmMWSc 92*
**Pieper**, David Robert 1948- *WhoMW 92*
**Pieper**, Edward Charles 1949- *WhoMW 92*
**Pieper**, Ernst 1928- *IntWW 91*
**Pieper**, Franz August Otto 1852-1931 *RelLAm 91*
**Pieper**, George Francis 1926- *AmMWSc 92*
**Pieper**, Heinz Paul 1920- *AmMWSc 92*
**Pieper**, Paul Jay 1954- *WhoMW 92*
**Pieper**, Rex Delane 1934- *AmMWSc 92*
**Pieper**, Richard Edward 1941- *AmMWSc 92*
**Pieper**, Steven Charles 1943- *AmMWSc 92*
**Pieper**, Thomas Allen 1956- *WhoRel 92*
**Piepho**, Robert Walter 1942- *AmMWSc 92*
**Piepho**, Susan Brand 1942- *AmMWSc 92*
**Piepmeier**, Edward Harman 1937- *AmMWSc 92*
**Pier**, Allan Clark 1928- *AmMWSc 92*
**Pier**, Arthur Stanwood 1874-1966 *BenetAL 91*
**Pier**, Gerald Bryan *AmMWSc 92*
**Pier**, Harold William 1935- *AmMWSc 92*
**Pier**, Stanley Morton *AmMWSc 92*
**Pieraccini**, Giovanni 1918- *IntAu&W 91*
**Pierard**, Jean Arthur 1934- *AmMWSc 92*
**Pierard**, Richard V 1934- *IntAu&W 91, WrDr 92*
**Pierard**, Richard Victor 1934- *WhoRel 92*
**Pieras**, Jaime, Jr. 1924- *WhoAmL 92, WhoAmP 91*
**Pierce**, Aaronetta Hamilton 1943- *WhoBlA 92*
**Pierce**, Alan Kraft 1931- *AmMWSc 92*
**Pierce**, Alexander Webster, Jr 1931- *AmMWSc 92*
**Pierce**, Allan Dale 1936- *AmMWSc 92*
**Pierce**, Arleen Cecilia 1939- *AmMWSc 92*
**Pierce**, Arthur Henry 1867-1914 *BiInAmS*
**Pierce**, Barbara Elaine 1928- *WhoEnt 92*
**Pierce**, Bob *WhoAmP 91*
**Pierce**, Bruce John 1938- *WhoWest 92*
**Pierce**, Camden Ballard 1932- *AmMWSc 92*
**Pierce**, Carl William 1939- *AmMWSc 92*
**Pierce**, Carol S 1938- *AmMWSc 92*
**Pierce**, Chester Middlebrook 1927- *AmMWSc 92, WhoBlA 92*
**Pierce**, Clarence Albert, Jr 1928- *WhoAmP 91*
**Pierce**, Cynthia Straker *WhoBlA 92*
**Pierce**, Cyril Marvin 1939- *AmMWSc 92*
**Pierce**, Daniel Marshall 1928- *WhoAmP 91*
**Pierce**, Daniel Thornton 1940- *AmMWSc 92*
**Pierce**, Darrell William 1955- *WhoAmL 92*
**Pierce**, Daryl Eugene 1963- *WhoRel 92*
**Pierce**, David A 1957- *WhoAmP 91*
**Pierce**, David Edward 1953- *WhoAmL 92*
**Pierce**, David L 1947- *WhoAmP 91*
**Pierce**, Deborah Mary *WhoWest 92*
**Pierce**, Delilah W. 1904- *WhoBlA 92*
**Pierce**, Devon Way 1966- *WhoEnt 92*
**Pierce**, Don Frederick 1915- *WhoEnt 92*
**Pierce**, Donald Fay 1930- *WhoAmL 92*
**Pierce**, Donald N 1921- *AmMWSc 92*
**Pierce**, Donna L. 1952- *WhoAmL 92*
**Pierce**, Dorothy Helen *AmMWSc 92*
**Pierce**, Douglas Franklin 1924- *WhoFI 92*
**Pierce**, Earl S. 1942- *WhoBlA 92*
**Pierce**, Edward Allen 1947- *WhoEnt 92*
**Pierce**, Edward Charles 1930- *WhoAmP 91*
**Pierce**, Edward Ronald 1937- *AmMWSc 92*
**Pierce**, Elliot Stearns 1922- *AmMWSc 92*
**Pierce**, Elwood F *ScFEYrs*
**Pierce**, Felix J 1932- *AmMWSc 92*
**Pierce**, Francis Casimir 1924- *WhoFI 92*
**Pierce**, Francis William 1915- *Who 92*
**Pierce**, Frank Powell 1953- *WhoAmL 92*
**Pierce**, Franklin 1804-1869 *AmPolLe [port], BenetAL 91, RComAH*
**Pierce**, Frederick S. *LesBEnT 92*
**Pierce**, Frederick S. 1933- *IntMPA 92*
**Pierce**, Frederick Watson 1903- *WhoBlA 92*
**Pierce**, Frederick Watson, IV 1962- *WhoWest 92*
**Pierce**, G Alvin 1931- *AmMWSc 92*
**Pierce**, George 1941- *WhoAmP 91*
**Pierce**, George Adams 1943- *WhoWest 92*
**Pierce**, Gordon Barry 1925- *AmMWSc 92*
**Pierce**, Gregory W. 1957- *WhoBlA 92*
**Pierce**, Gretchen Natalie 1945- *WhoFI 92*
**Pierce**, Harry Frederick 1941- *AmMWSc 92*
**Pierce**, Hinton Rainer 1927- *WhoAmL 92*
**Pierce**, Hugh Humphrey 1931- *Who 92*
**Pierce**, Jack Robert 1939- *AmMWSc 92*
**Pierce**, Jack Vincent 1919- *AmMWSc 92*
**Pierce**, Jack Warren 1927- *AmMWSc 92*
**Pierce**, James Benjamin 1939- *AmMWSc 92*
**Pierce**, James Blair 1959- *WhoAmL 92*
**Pierce**, James Bruce 1922- *AmMWSc 92*
**Pierce**, James Eric 1940- *WhoRel 92*
**Pierce**, James Franklin 1950- *WhoWest 92*
**Pierce**, James Kenneth 1944- *AmMWSc 92*
**Pierce**, James Otto, II 1937- *AmMWSc 92*
**Pierce**, Jennifer Ember 1943- *WhoEnt 92*
**Pierce**, Jerry Thomas 1943- *WhoAmP 91*
**Pierce**, Joan Joy 1941- *WhoAmP 91*
**Pierce**, Joe E. 1924- *WrDr 92*
**Pierce**, Joe Eugene 1924- *IntAu&W 91, WhoWest 92*
**Pierce**, John d1897 *BiInAmS*
**Pierce**, John Albert 1925- *AmMWSc 92*
**Pierce**, John Charles 1950- *WhoAmP 91*
**Pierce**, John Frank 1920- *AmMWSc 92*
**Pierce**, John Gregory 1942- *AmMWSc 92*
**Pierce**, John Grissim 1920- *AmMWSc 92*
**Pierce**, John R. 1910- *WrDr 92*
**Pierce**, John Richard, Jr. 1964- *WhoFI 92*
**Pierce**, John Robert 1949- *WhoAmL 92*
**Pierce**, John Robinson 1910- *AmMWSc 92, IntWW 91*
**Pierce**, John Thomas 1949- *AmMWSc 92*
**Pierce**, Joseph Leroy 1905-1990 *WhoBlA 92N*
**Pierce**, Josiah, Jr 1861-1902 *BiInAmS*
**Pierce**, Keith Robert 1942- *AmMWSc 92*
**Pierce**, Kenneth Lee 1937- *AmMWSc 92*
**Pierce**, Kenneth Ray 1934- *AmMWSc 92*
**Pierce**, Kevin Michael 1958- *WhoAmL 92*
**Pierce**, Lawrence Warren 1924- *WhoAmL 92, WhoBlA 92*
**Pierce**, Leonard L 1932- *WhoAmP 91*
**Pierce**, Leslie Ryan 1951- *WhoMW 92*
**Pierce**, Lorne 1890-1961 *BenetAL 91*
**Pierce**, Louis 1929- *AmMWSc 92*
**Pierce**, Lynn Gail 1950- *WhoAmL 92*
**Pierce**, Madelene Evans 1904- *AmMWSc 92*
**Pierce**, Marianne Louise 1949- *WhoFI 92*
**Pierce**, Marion Armbruster 1909- *AmMWSc 92*
**Pierce**, Mary Jo 1935- *WhoEnt 92*
**Pierce**, Matthew Lee 1952- *AmMWSc 92*
**Pierce**, Meredith Ann 1958- *IntAu&W 91, SmATA 67 [port], WrDr 92*
**Pierce**, Michael Patrick 1960- *WhoAmL 92, WhoEnt 92*
**Pierce**, Milton J. 1915- *WhoFI 92*
**Pierce**, Morton Allen 1948- *WhoAmL 92*
**Pierce**, Nathaniel Field 1934- *AmMWSc 92*
**Pierce**, Nathaniel W. 1942- *WhoRel 92*
**Pierce**, Newton Barris 1856-1916 *BiInAmS*
**Pierce**, Patricia Jobe 1943- *IntAu&W 91*
**Pierce**, Paul Leslie 1944- *WhoRel 92*
**Pierce**, Percy Everett 1932- *AmMWSc 92*
**Pierce**, Ponchitta A. 1942- *WhoBlA 92*
**Pierce**, Ponchitta Anne 1942- *WhoEnt 92*
**Pierce**, R Dean 1929- *AmMWSc 92*
**Pierce**, Raymond O., Jr. 1931- *WhoBlA 92*
**Pierce**, Reginald James 1909- *Who 92*
**Pierce**, Reuben G. 1926- *WhoBlA 92*
**Pierce**, Richard Austin 1918- *WrDr 92*
**Pierce**, Richard Herbert 1943- *WhoAmP 91*
**Pierce**, Richard Hilton 1935- *WhoAmL 92*
**Pierce**, Richard James, Jr. 1943- *WhoAmL 92*
**Pierce**, Richard Scott 1927- *AmMWSc 92*
**Pierce**, Ricklin Ray 1953- *WhoAmL 92*
**Pierce**, Ricky Charles 1959- *WhoBlA 92*

Pierce, Robert Charles 1947- AmMWSc 92
Pierce, Robert Donald 1936- WhoEnt 92
Pierce, Robert Henry Horace, Jr 1910- AmMWSc 92
Pierce, Robert L. WhoRel 92
Pierce, Robert Lorne WhoFI 92, WhoWest 92
Pierce, Robert Milton 1931- WhoMW 92
Pierce, Robert Wesley 1945- AmMWSc 92
Pierce, Robert Willard 1914-1978 RelLAm 91
Pierce, Robert William 1940- AmMWSc 92, WhoWest 92
Pierce, Roger J 1911- AmMWSc 92
Pierce, Ronald Cecil 1949- AmMWSc 92
Pierce, Roy 1923- WrDr 92
Pierce, Rudolph F. 1942- WhoAmL 92, WhoBlA 92
Pierce, Russell Dale 1938- AmMWSc 92
Pierce, Samuel R, Jr WhoAmP 91
Pierce, Samuel R., Jr. 1922- WhoBlA 92
Pierce, Samuel Riley, Jr. 1922- IntWW 91, WhoFI 92
Pierce, Shancy 1942- WhoEnt 92
Pierce, Shelby Crawford 1932- WhoMW 92
Pierce, Sidney Kendrick 1944- AmMWSc 92
Pierce, Steven D 1949- WhoAmP 91
Pierce, Walter J. 1941- WhoBlA 92
Pierce, Wayne Stanley 1942- AmMWSc 92
Pierce, Webb d1991 NewYTBS 91
Pierce, Webb 1926- NewAmDM
Pierce, William Arthur, Jr 1918- AmMWSc 92
Pierce, William Charles 1945- WhoMW 92
Pierce, William Dallas 1940- WhoBlA 92
Pierce, William G 1904- AmMWSc 92
Pierce, William Gamewell 1904- WhoWest 92
Pierce, William H 1933- AmMWSc 92
Pierce, William James 1921- WhoAmL 92
Pierce, William Joseph 1954- WhoRel 92
Pierce, William R 1915- AmMWSc 92
Pierce, William Schuler 1937- AmMWSc 92
Pierceall, Gregory Micheal 1950- WhoMW 92
Pierceall, Richard Morgan 1953- WhoEnt 92
Piercey, Montford F 1942- AmMWSc 92
Piercy Who 92
Piercy, Baron 1946- Who 92
Piercy, George Robert 1928- AmMWSc 92
Piercy, Gordon Clayton 1944- WhoWest 92
Piercy, Joanna Elizabeth Who 92
Piercy, Marge DrAPF 91
Piercy, Marge 1936- BenetAL 91, ConNov 91, ConPo 91, TwCSFW 91, WrDr 92
Piercy, Penelope Katherine 1916- Who 92
Piergallini, Alfred A. 1946- WhoMW 92
Pierik, David Vincent 1966- WhoWest 92
Pierik, Marilyn Anne 1939- WhoWest 92
Pieringer, Arthur Paul 1924- AmMWSc 92
Pieringer, Ronald Arthur 1935- AmMWSc 92
Pierius EncEarC
Pierlot, Hubert 1883-1963 EncTR 91
Pierlot, Hubert 1883-1964 FacFETw
Pierlot, Pierre 1921- NewAmDM
Pierman, Carol J. DrAPF 91
Piermarini, Gasper J 1933- AmMWSc 92
Pierne, Gabriel 1863-1937 NewAmDM
Pierno, Anthony Robert 1932- WhoAmL 92
Pieroni, Leonard J. 1939- WhoWest 92
Pieroth, Elmar 1934- IntWW 91
Pierotti, John 1911-1987 ConAu 133
Pierotti, John William 1936- WhoAmL 92
Pierotti, Robert Amadeo 1931- AmMWSc 92
Pierpoint, Powell 1922- WhoAmL 92
Pierpoint, Robert LesBEnT 92
Pierpont, Cortlandt Godwin 1942- AmMWSc 92
Pierpont, John 1785-1866 BenetAL 91
Pierrard, John Martin 1928- AmMWSc 92
Pierre, Abbe IntWW 91
Pierre, Abbe 1912- Who 92
Pierre, Andrew J. 1934- IntWW 91
Pierre, Clara 1939- WrDr 92
Pierre, Dallas 1933- WhoBlA 92
Pierre, Donald Arthur 1936- AmMWSc 92, WhoWest 92
Pierre, Gerald P. 1951- WhoBlA 92
Pierre, Jennifer Casey 1953- WhoBlA 92
Pierre, John Maxwell, Jr. 1940- WhoMW 92
Pierre, Leon L 1922- AmMWSc 92
Pierre, Marie-Joseph 1945- WhoRel 92
Pierre, Percy Anthony 1939- WhoBlA 92
Pierre, Robert V 1928- AmMWSc 92
Pierre-Brossolette, Claude 1928- IntWW 91
Pierre-Louis, Constant 1939- WhoBlA 92
Pierrehumbert, Raymond T 1954- AmMWSc 92
Pierret, Alain Marie 1930- IntWW 91
Pierret, Robert Francis 1940- AmMWSc 92
Pierro, Louis John 1931- AmMWSc 92
Pierron, George Joseph, Jr. 1947- WhoAmL 92
Pierrone EncAmaz 91
Piers, Charles Robert Fitzmaurice 1903- Who 92
Piers, Desmond William 1913- Who 92
Piersante, Denise 1954- WhoFI 92, WhoMW 92
Pierschbacher, Mary Lou Reynolds 1937- WhoAmP 91
Pierschbacher, Michael Dean 1951- AmMWSc 92
Pierse, Terence Joseph 1951- WhoFI 92
Piersee, Charles Ralph 1931- WhoRel 92, WhoWest 92
Piersen, William D. 1942- WrDr 92
Pierskalla, William P 1934- AmMWSc 92
Piersma, Bernard J 1938- AmMWSc 92
Piersol, Allan Gerald 1930- AmMWSc 92
Piersol, Lawrence L 1940- WhoAmP 91
Pierson, Al WhoEnt 92
Pierson, Arthur Tappan 1837-1911 RelLAm 91
Pierson, Bernice Frances 1906- AmMWSc 92
Pierson, Beverly Kanda 1944- AmMWSc 92
Pierson, David Renick 1951- WhoAmL 92
Pierson, David W 1926- AmMWSc 92
Pierson, Edgar Franklin 1909- AmMWSc 92
Pierson, Edward Joseph, Jr. 1948- WhoFI 92
Pierson, Edward S 1937- AmMWSc 92
Pierson, Ellery Merwin 1935- AmMWSc 92
Pierson, Frank 1925- IntMPA 92
Pierson, Frank Romer 1925- WhoEnt 92
Pierson, Gary Clinton 1959- WhoAmL 92
Pierson, George Wilson 1904- WrDr 92
Pierson, Herbert Fletcher 1914- WhoEnt 92
Pierson, Jerry D. 1933- WhoMW 92
Pierson, Jim WhoAmP 91
Pierson, Keith Bernard 1949- AmMWSc 92
Pierson, Margaret Rosalind 1941- WhoEnt 92
Pierson, Marty Delbert 1959- WhoMW 92
Pierson, Merle Dean 1942- AmMWSc 92
Pierson, Quinton Ellsworth 1950- WhoFI 92
Pierson, Richard Norris, Jr 1929- AmMWSc 92
Pierson, Robert 1911- WrDr 92
Pierson, Robert David 1935- WhoFI 92
Pierson, Robert Leon 1955- WhoAmL 92
Pierson, Samuel Thomas 1950- WhoFI 92
Pierson, Thomas Charles 1947- AmMWSc 92
Pierson, Thomas Claude 1922- WhoEnt 92
Pierson, Wayne George 1950- WhoFI 92
Pierson, Willard James, Jr 1922- AmMWSc 92
Pierson, William George 1951- WhoAmL 92
Pierson, William Grant 1933- AmMWSc 92
Pierson, William R 1922- AmMWSc 92
Pierson, William R 1930- AmMWSc 92
Pierucci, Mauro 1942- AmMWSc 92
Pierucci, Olga 1926- AmMWSc 92
Pies, Ronald E. 1940- WhoWest 92
Piesco, Nicholas Peter 1946- AmMWSc 92
Pieski, Edwin Thomas 1924- AmMWSc 92
Piet, John H. 1914- WrDr 92
Piet, Steven James 1956- WhoWest 92
Pieters, Carle M 1943- AmMWSc 92
Pieterse, Cosmo 1925?- LiExTwC
Pieterse, Hendrik Johannes Christoffel 1936- WhoRel 92
Pieterse, Zola Budd NewYTBS 91 [port]
Pietersen, William Gerard 1937- WhoFI 92
Pietila, Reima Frans Ilmari 1923- IntWW 91
Pietra, Giuseppe G 1930- AmMWSc 92
Pietra, Italo d1991 NewYTBS 91
Pietraface, William John 1949- AmMWSc 92
Pietrantoni, Joseph George 1938- WhoFI 92
Pietras, Slawomir 1943- WhoEnt 92
Pietri, Charles Edward 1930- AmMWSc 92
Pietri, Pedro Juan DrAPF 91
Pietri, Pedro Juan 1943- WhoHisp 92
Pietro, William Joseph 1956- AmMWSc 92
Pietrofesa, John Joseph 1940- WhoMW 92
Pietrusewsky, Michael, Jr 1944- AmMWSc 92
Pietruski, John Michael, Jr. 1933- IntWW 91
Pietrusza, David 1949- ConAu 135
Pietrusza, Edward Walter 1918- AmMWSc 92
Pietruszka, Gregory James 1958- WhoWest 92
Pietruszka, Michael F. 1956- WhoAmL 92
Pietruszko, Regina 1929- AmMWSc 92
Pietrzak, Daniel M. 1939- WhoRel 92
Pietrzak, Lawrence Michael 1942- AmMWSc 92
Pietrzak, Leonard Walter 1939- WhoFI 92
Pietrzak, Lynn Marie 1958- WhoMW 92
Pietrzyk, Leslie DrAPF 91
Pietsch, Carl Walter 1930- WhoAmP 91
Pietsch, Heinz-Dieter 1944- TwCPaSc
Pietsch, Paul Andrew 1929- AmMWSc 92, WhoMW 92
Pietsch, Theodore Wells 1945- AmMWSc 92
Piette, Lawrence Hector 1932- AmMWSc 92
Piette, Ludovic 1826-1877 ThHEIm
Piettre, Andre 1906- IntWW 91
Pieve, Carlos 1929- WhoHisp 92
Pievsky, Max 1925- WhoAmP 91
Pieyre De Mandiargues, Andre 1909- GuFrLit 1, IntWW 91
Piez, Karl Anton 1924- AmMWSc 92
Pifarre, Juan Jorge 1942- WhoHisp 92
Pifer, Alan DcAmImH
Pifer, Alan 1921- IntWW 91
Pifer, Lewis Arthur 1945- WhoEnt 92
Pifko, Allan Bert 1938- AmMWSc 92
Pigage, Leo C 1913- AmMWSc 92
Pigden, Wallace James 1920- AmMWSc 92
Pigeat, Henri Michel 1939- IntWW 91
Pigford, Thomas H 1922- AmMWSc 92
Piggot, Aaron Snowden 1822-1869 BiInAmS
Piggot, Cameron 1856?-1911 BiInAmS
Piggott, Alan 1923- WrDr 92
Piggott, Donald James 1920- Who 92
Piggott, Francis James Claude 1910- Who 92
Piggott, Lester 1935- FacFETw
Piggott, Lester Keith 1935- IntWW 91, Who 92
Piggott, Michael R 1930- AmMWSc 92
Piggott, Stuart 1910- ConAu 134, IntWW 91, Who 92
Pighills, Joseph 1902-1984 TwCPaSc
Pigiet, Vincent P 1943- AmMWSc 92
Pigman, Jack Richard 1944- WhoAmL 92
Pignanelli, Frank R 1960- WhoAmP 91
Pignataro, Augustus 1943- AmMWSc 92
Pignataro, Louis J 1923- AmMWSc 92
Pignatelli, Debora Becker 1947- WhoAmP 91
Pignatelli, Frank 1946- Who 92
Pigno, Antonia Quintana DrAPF 91
Pignocco, Arthur John 1929- AmMWSc 92
Pignolet, Louis H 1943- AmMWSc 92
Pignon, Edouard 1905- IntWW 91
Pigot, George 1946- Who 92
Pigot, Thomas Herbert 1921- Who 92
Pigott, Berkeley Henry 1925- Who 92
Pigott, Charles McGee 1929- WhoFI 92, WhoWest 92
Pigott, Charles Sedgie 1920- WhoRel 92
Pigott, Christopher Donald 1928- Who 92
Pigott, George M 1928- AmMWSc 92
Pigott, Joe Ned 1925- WhoAmL 92
Pigott, Miles Thomas 1923- AmMWSc 92
Pigott, Richard Lacy 1955- WhoFI 92
Pigott, Robert 1924- WhoAmP 91
Pigott-Brown, William Brian 1941- Who 92
Pigott-Smith, Tim 1946- IntMPA 92, IntWW 91
Pigozzi, Don 1935- AmMWSc 92
Piguet, Michel 1932- NewAmDM
Pih, Hui 1922- AmMWSc 92
Pihir, James Frank 1945- WhoMW 92
Pihl, James Melvin 1943- WhoWest 92
Pihl, Mary Mackenzie 1916- Who 92
Pihl, Robert O 1939- AmMWSc 92
Pihl, Wayne Andrew 1938- WhoMW 92
Pihlajamaki, Veikko Jaako Uolevi 1922- IntWW 91
Piipari, Anna-Liisa 1940- IntWW 91
Piirma, Irja 1920- AmMWSc 92, WhoMW 92
Piirto, Douglas Donald 1948- WhoWest 92
Piirto, Jane DrAPF 91
Pijper, Willem 1894-1947 NewAmDM
Pikaizen, Viktor Aleksandrovich 1933- IntWW 91
Pikal, Michael Jon 1939- AmMWSc 92
Pikarsky, Milton AmMWSc 92
Pike, Baroness 1918- Who 92
Pike, Albert 1809-1891 BenetAL 91
Pike, Arthur Clausen 1939- AmMWSc 92
Pike, Betty Ruth 1938- WhoFI 92
Pike, Carl Stephen 1945- AmMWSc 92
Pike, Charles P 1941- AmMWSc 92
Pike, Charles R IntAu&W 91X, TwCWW 91, WrDr 92
Pike, Christopher SmATA 68
Pike, Donald Wayne 1949- WhoAmP 91
Pike, Edward Roy 1929- Who 92
Pike, Eileen Halsey 1918- AmMWSc 92
Pike, George Harold, Jr. 1933- WhoRel 92
Pike, Gordon E 1942- AmMWSc 92
Pike, J G 1930- AmMWSc 92
Pike, James Albert, Jr. 1913-1969? RelLAm 91
Pike, James Maitland Nicholson 1916- Who 92
Pike, John Nazarian 1929- AmMWSc 92
Pike, John S. IntMPA 92, WhoEnt 92
Pike, Judith Robyn 1959- WhoAmL 92
Pike, Julian M 1930- AmMWSc 92
Pike, Keith Schade 1947- AmMWSc 92
Pike, Larry Samuel 1939- WhoAmL 92
Pike, LeRoy 1928- AmMWSc 92
Pike, Linda Joy 1953- AmMWSc 92
Pike, Loy Dean 1940- AmMWSc 92
Pike, Marilyn Cecile AmMWSc 92
Pike, Mary Eleanor 1940- WhoAmP 91
Pike, Mary Hayden 1824-1908 BenetAL 91
Pike, Michael 1931- Who 92
Pike, Nicholas 1743-1819 BiInAmS
Pike, Nicholas 1818-1905 BiInAmS
Pike, Peter Leslie 1937- Who 92
Pike, Philip 1914- IntWW 91
Pike, Philip Ernest Housden 1914- Who 92
Pike, Ralph Edwin 1915- AmMWSc 92
Pike, Ralph W 1935- AmMWSc 92
Pike, Richard Joseph 1937- AmMWSc 92
Pike, Robert Merrett 1906- AmMWSc 92
Pike, Robert William 1941- WhoAmL 92, WhoFI 92, WhoIns 92
Pike, Ronald Marston 1925- AmMWSc 92
Pike, Roscoe Adams 1925- AmMWSc 92
Pike, Ruth 1931- ConAu 134
Pike, Ruth Lillian 1916- AmMWSc 92
Pike, Sally Jane 1947- WhoEnt 92
Pike, St John Surridge 1909- Who 92
Pike, Stephen Michael 1953- WhoAmL 92
Pike, William 1905- Who 92
Pike, William Abbot d1895 BiInAmS
Pike, William Edward 1929- WhoFI 92
Pike, Zebulon Montgomery 1779-1813 BenetAL 91
Pikelny, Dov Buryl 1933- WhoRel 92
Piker, Joan Francis 1925- WhoEnt 92
Pikler, Charles WhoEnt 92
Pikler, George Maurice 1942- AmMWSc 92
Piklo, Charlene Lorraine 1954- WhoFI 92
Pikoraitis, Dale Edward 1957- WhoMW 92
Pikrallidas, Christ Eftychios 1951- WhoFI 92
Piksanov, Nikolay Kiryakovich 1878-1969 SovUnBD
Pikunas, Justin 1920- IntAu&W 91, WrDr 92
Pikus, Anita 1938- AmMWSc 92
Pikus, David Heller 1955- WhoAmL 92
Pikus, Irwin Mark 1936- AmMWSc 92
Pilachowski, Catherine Anderson 1949- AmMWSc 92
Piland, John Charles 1961- WhoAmL 92
PiLand, Neill Finnes 1943- WhoFI 92
Piland, Richard N. 1944- WhoMW 92
Pilant, Walter L 1931- AmMWSc 92
Pilar, Frank Louis 1927- AmMWSc 92
Pilar, Guillermo Roman 1933- AmMWSc 92
Pilarcik, Kathleen Frances 1960- WhoMW 92
Pilarczyk, Daniel Edward 1934- IntWW 91, WhoMW 92, WhoRel 92
Pilarski, Adam Mark 1948- WhoFI 92
Pilarski, James Philip 1946- WhoMW 92
Pilarski, Laura P. 1926- WrDr 92
Pilarzyk, Thomas James 1949- WhoMW 92
Pilat, Michael Joseph 1938- AmMWSc 92
Pilati, Charles Francis 1945- AmMWSc 92
Pilato, Louis Peter 1944- WhoAmL 92
Pilbrow, Richard 1933- WhoEnt 92
Pilbrow, Richard Hugh 1933- Who 92
Pilcer, Sonia DrAPF 91
Pilch, John Joseph 1936- WhoRel 92
Pilch, Susan Marie 1954- AmMWSc 92
Pilchard, Edwin Ivan 1925- AmMWSc 92
Pilcher, Benjamin Lee 1938- AmMWSc 92
Pilcher, Carl Bernard 1947- AmMWSc 92
Pilcher, Dennis 1906- Who 92
Pilcher, James Brownie 1929- WhoAmL 92, WhoAmP 91
Pilcher, James Eric 1942- AmMWSc 92
Pilcher, Patricia WhoAmP 91
Pilcher, Robin Sturtevant 1902- Who 92
Pilcher, Rosamunde 1924- IntAu&W 91, WrDr 92
Pilcher, Tony 1936- IntMPA 92
Pilcher, Valter Ennis 1925- AmMWSc 92
Pilchik, Ely Emanuel 1913- WhoRel 92
Pilditch, James George Christopher 1929- Who 92
Pilditch, Richard 1926- Who 92
Pile, Frederick 1915- Who 92
Pile, Frederick Alfred 1884-1976 CurBio 91N

**Pile**, John F. 1924- *ConAu 36NR*
**Pile**, Michael David Mc Kenzie 1954- *WhoBlA 92*
**Pile**, Philip H 1946- *AmMWSc 92*
**Pile**, Susan *IntMPA 92*
**Pile**, William 1919- *Who 92*
**Pile**, William Dennis 1919- *IntWW 91*
**Pileggi**, Vincent Joseph 1928- *AmMWSc 92*
**Pilet**, Stanford Christian 1931- *AmMWSc 92*
**Pilger**, Dianna Lynne 1963- *WhoMW 92*
**Pilger**, John Richard 1939- *Who 92*
**Pilger**, Kevin Eugene 1962- *WhoMW 92*
**Pilger**, Rex Herbert, Jr 1948- *AmMWSc 92*
**Pilger**, Richard Christian, Jr 1932- *AmMWSc 92, WhoMW 92*
**Pilgeram**, Laurence Oscar 1924- *AmMWSc 92*
**Pilgrim**, Anne *IntAu&W 91X, WrDr 92*
**Pilgrim**, Cecil Stanley 1932- *Who 92*
**Pilgrim**, Constance Maud Eva 1911- *IntAu&W 91*
**Pilgrim**, Derral *WrDr 92*
**Pilgrim**, Donald 1929- *AmMWSc 92*
**Pilgrim**, Hyman Ira 1925- *AmMWSc 92*
**Pilgrim**, Jessie 1958- *WhoAmP 91*
**Pilgrim**, Walter Edward 1934- *WhoRel 92*
**Pilibosian**, Helene *DrAPF 91*
**Pilie**, Martin Arnaud 1933- *WhoAmL 92*
**Piliniszky**, Janos 1921-1981 *FacFETw*
**Piliponis**, John Andrew 1953- *WhoAmL 92*
**Pilitt**, Patricia Ann 1942- *AmMWSc 92*
**Pilkenton**, Kenneth L. 1943- *WhoRel 92*
**Pilkerton**, A Raymond 1935- *AmMWSc 92*
**Pilkey**, Dav 1966- *SmATA 68 [port]*
**Pilkey**, Orrin H, Jr 1934- *AmMWSc 92*
**Pilkey**, Walter David 1936- *AmMWSc 92*
**Pilkiewicz**, Frank George 1946- *AmMWSc 92*
**Pilkington**, Alastair *Who 92*
**Pilkington**, Antony 1935- *Who 92*
**Pilkington**, Francis 1570?-1638 *NewAmDM*
**Pilkington**, Godfrey *Who 92*
**Pilkington**, Kevin *DrAPF 91*
**Pilkington**, Lawrence Herbert Austin 1911- *Who 92*
**Pilkington**, Lionel Alexander Bethune 1920- *IntWW 91, Who 92*
**Pilkington**, Lou Ann 1924- *AmMWSc 92*
**Pilkington**, Michael John 1937- *Who 92*
**Pilkington**, Peter 1933- *Who 92*
**Pilkington**, Richard Godfrey 1918- *Who 92*
**Pilkington**, Roger Windle 1915- *IntAu&W 91, Who 92, WrDr 92*
**Pilkington**, Theo C 1935- *AmMWSc 92*
**Pilkington**, Thomas Milborne-Swinnerton-1934- *Who 92*
**Pilkis**, Simon J 1942- *AmMWSc 92*
**Pilko**, Robert Michael 1952- *WhoFI 92*
**Pill**, Erastes *ConAu 133*
**Pill**, Jeffrey Maclin 1942- *WhoEnt 92*
**Pill**, Malcolm 1938- *Who 92*
**Pilla**, Anthony Michael 1932- *WhoMW 92, WhoRel 92*
**Pilla**, Arthur Anthony 1936- *AmMWSc 92*
**Pillai**, Padmanabha S 1931- *AmMWSc 92*
**Pillai**, Raghavan 1898- *Who 92*
**Pillai**, Thankappan A K 1950- *AmMWSc 92*
**Pillans**, Charles Palmer, III 1940- *WhoAmL 92*
**Pillar**, Charles Littlefield 1911- *WhoWest 92*
**Pillar**, Kenneth Harold 1924- *Who 92*
**Pillar**, Walter Oscar 1940- *AmMWSc 92*
**Pillar**, William 1924- *Who 92*
**Pillard**, Richard Colestock 1933- *AmMWSc 92*
**Pillay**, Dathathry Trichinopoly Natraj 1931- *AmMWSc 92*
**Pillay**, K K Sivasankara 1935- *AmMWSc 92*
**Piller**, Herbert 1926- *AmMWSc 92*
**Pilli**, Dominick Anthony 1957- *WhoAmL 92, WhoEnt 92*
**Pilliar**, Robert Mathews 1939- *AmMWSc 92*
**Pilling**, Amy Robinson 1960- *WhoEnt 92*
**Pilling**, Ann 1944- *WrDr 92*
**Pilling**, Arnold Remington 1926- *WhoMW 92*
**Pilling**, Christopher 1936- *ConPo 91, IntAu&W 91, WrDr 92*
**Pilling**, George William 1942- *WhoAmL 92*
**Pilling**, James Constantine 1846-1895 *BiInAmS*
**Pilling**, Janet Kavanaugh 1951- *WhoAmL 92*
**Pilling**, Joseph Grant 1945- *Who 92*
**Pilling**, Steve Paul 1958- *WhoFI 92*
**Pilliod**, Charles J., Jr. 1918- *IntWW 91*
**Pillion**, Dennis Joseph 1950- *AmMWSc 92*
**Pillittere**, Joseph Thomas 1932- *WhoAmP 91*
**Pillmore**, Charles Lee 1930- *AmMWSc 92*
**Pilloff**, Herschel Sydney 1940- *AmMWSc 92*
**Pillow**, Vanita J. 1949- *WhoBlA 92*
**Pillsbury**, Dale Ronald 1940- *AmMWSc 92*
**Pillsbury**, Edmund Pennington 1943- *IntWW 91*
**Pillsbury**, George Sturgis 1921- *WhoAmP 91*
**Pillsbury**, Harold C 1922- *AmMWSc 92*
**Pillsbury**, John Elliott 1846-1919 *BiInAmS*
**Pillsbury**, John Henry 1846-1910 *BiInAmS*
**Pillsbury**, Leland Clark 1947- *WhoFI 92*
**Pillsbury**, Parker 1809-1898 *BenetAL 91*
**Pilnyak**, Boris 1894-1937 *FacFETw, SovUnBD*
**Pilo**, Randel Anthony 1958- *WhoFI 92*
**Pilon**, Jean-Guy 1930- *IntAu&W 91, IntWW 91*
**Pilon**, Jean-Guy 1931- *AmMWSc 92*
**Pilong**, Thomas Joseph 1951- *WhoEnt 92*
**Pilot**, Ann Hobson 1943- *WhoBlA 92*
**Pilot**, Christopher H 1953- *AmMWSc 92*
**Pilot**, Douglas Montgomery 1945- *WhoRel 92*
**Pilpel**, Harriet Fleischl d1991 *NewYTBS 91 [port]*
**Pilpel**, Robert H. *DrAPF 91*
**Pilson**, Michael Edward Quinton 1933- *AmMWSc 92*
**Pilson**, Neal *LesBEnT 92*
**Pilson**, Neal Howard 1940- *WhoEnt 92*
**Pilson**, Sidney L. 1948- *WhoFI 92*
**Pilsudski**, Jozef 1867-1935 *EncTR 91 [port], FacFETw*
**Pilsworth**, Edward S *ScFEYrs*
**Piltch**, Martin Stanley 1939- *AmMWSc 92*
**Pilun-Owad**, Chaiyut 1948- *WhoFI 92*
**Pilz**, Clifford G 1921- *AmMWSc 92*
**Pilzer**, Penny Ann 1952- *WhoAmL 92*
**Pimbley**, George Herbert, Jr 1922- *AmMWSc 92*
**Pimbley**, Walter Thornton 1930- *AmMWSc 92*
**Pimblott**, Simon Martin 1962- *AmMWSc 92*
**Pimen**, Patriarch 1910-1990 *AnObit 1990, FacFETw, SovUnBD*
**Pimenov**, Yuriy Ivanovich 1903-1977 *SovUnBD*
**Pimenta**, Simon Ignatius *Who 92*
**Pimenta**, Simon Ignatius 1920- *IntWW 91, WhoRel 92*
**Pimental**, Patricia Ann 1956- *WhoMW 92*
**Pimentel**, David 1925- *AmMWSc 92*
**Pimentel**, George Claude 1922- *AmMWSc 92*
**Pimentel**, Victor *WhoEnt 92*
**Pimlott**, Benjamin John 1945- *Who 92*
**Pimlott**, Steven *ConTFT 9*
**Pimsler**, Stuart 1949- *WhoEnt 92*
**Pin-Mei**, Ignatius Kung Gong 1901- *WhoRel 92*
**Pina**, Eduardo Isidorio 1931- *AmMWSc 92*
**Pina**, Enrique 1936- *AmMWSc 92*
**Pina**, Gary 1956- *WhoHisp 92*
**Pina**, Jorge 1954- *WhoHisp 92*
**Pina**, Matilde Lozano 1946- *WhoHisp 92*
**Pina**, Urbano *WhoHisp 92*
**Pina-Cabral**, Daniel 1924- *WhoRel 92*
**Pina-Cabral**, Daniel de 1924- *Who 92*
**Pina-Rosales**, Gerardo 1948- *WhoHisp 92*
**Pinado**, Alan E. 1931- *WhoBlA 92*
**Pinaeva**, Ludmila Iosifovna 1936- *SovUnBD*
**Pinaire**, Richard A 1949- *WhoAmP 91*
**Pinajian**, John Joseph 1921- *AmMWSc 92*
**Pinanski**, Viola R 1898- *WhoAmP 91*
**Pinar Lopez**, Blas 1918- *BiDExR*
**Pinard**, Raymond R. 1930- *WhoFI 92*
**Pinard**, Yvon 1940- *IntWW 91*
**Pinay**, Antoine 1891- *IntWW 91, Who 92*
**Pincay**, Laffit, Jr. 1946- *WhoHisp 92*
**Pinch**, Harry Louis 1929- *AmMWSc 92*
**Pinch**, John G. 1948- *WhoEnt 92*
**Pinch**, John Michael 1952- *WhoWest 92*
**Pinchak**, Alfred Cyril 1935- *AmMWSc 92*
**Pincham**, Robert Eugene, Sr. 1925- *WhoBlA 92*
**Pincham**, Roger James 1935- *Who 92*
**Pinchasi**, Raphael 1940- *IntWW 91*
**Pinchback**, Pinckney Benton Stewart 1837-1921 *AmPolLe*
**Pinchbeck**, Robert Thomas, Jr. 1959- *WhoFI 92*
**Pincher**, Chapman 1914- *IntAu&W 91, Who 92, WrDr 92*
**Pincher**, H Chapman 1914- *ConAu 34NR*
**Pinchin**, Malcolm Cyril 1933- *Who 92*
**Pinchot**, Ann *WrDr 92*
**Pinchot**, Bronson 1959- *ConTFT 9, IntMPA 92, WhoEnt 92*
**Pinchot**, Gifford 1865-1946 *AmPolLe*
**Pinck**, Robert Lloyd 1920- *AmMWSc 92*
**Pinckaers**, B Hubert 1924- *AmMWSc 92*
**Pinckard**, Mara 1941- *WhoWest 92*
**Pinckard**, Robert Neal 1941- *AmMWSc 92*
**Pinckney**, Andrew Morgan, Jr. 1933- *WhoBlA 92*
**Pinckney**, C. Cotesworth 1939- *WhoAmL 92*
**Pinckney**, Callan 1939- *WhoEnt 92*
**Pinckney**, Charles 1757-1824 *BlkwEAR*
**Pinckney**, Charles Cotesworth 1746-1825 *AmPolLe, BlkwEAR*
**Pinckney**, Edward Lewis 1963- *WhoBlA 92*
**Pinckney**, Eliza Lucas 1722?-1793 *BlkwEAR, HanAmWH, PorAmW*
**Pinckney**, Elizabeth Lucas 1722?-1793 *BiInAmS*
**Pinckney**, James 1942- *WhoBlA 92*
**Pinckney**, Josephine 1895-1957 *BenetAL 91*
**Pinckney**, Lewis, Jr. 1932- *WhoBlA 92*
**Pinckney**, Robert L 1923- *AmMWSc 92*
**Pinckney**, Stanley 1940- *WhoBlA 92*
**Pinckney**, Theodore R. 1901- *WhoBlA 92*
**Pinckney**, Thomas 1750-1828 *AmPolLe*
**Pincock**, Richard Earl 1935- *AmMWSc 92*
**Pincott**, Leslie Rundell 1923- *IntWW 91, Who 92*
**Pincus**, Andrew Lewis 1930- *WhoEnt 92*
**Pincus**, Ann Terry 1937- *WhoEnt 92*
**Pincus**, Edward Kalvin 1931- *WhoAmL 92*
**Pincus**, Edward Ralph 1938- *WhoEnt 92*
**Pincus**, George 1935- *AmMWSc 92*
**Pincus**, Howard Jonah 1922- *AmMWSc 92, WhoWest 92*
**Pincus**, Irving 1918- *AmMWSc 92*
**Pincus**, Jack Howard 1939- *AmMWSc 92*
**Pincus**, Joanne L 1930- *WhoAmP 91*
**Pincus**, Jonathan Henry 1935- *AmMWSc 92*
**Pincus**, Laura 1963- *WhoAmL 92*
**Pincus**, Philip A 1936- *AmMWSc 92*
**Pincus**, Seth Henry 1948- *AmMWSc 92*
**Pincus**, Theodore *AmMWSc 92*
**Pincus**, Theodore Henry 1933- *WhoFI 92*
**Pincus**, Thomas David 1948- *WhoFI 92*
**Pinczuk**, Aron 1939- *AmMWSc 92*
**Pindborg**, Jens Jorgen 1921- *IntWW 91*
**Pindell**, Howardena D. 1943- *WhoBlA 92*
**Pindell**, Terry 1947- *ConAu 133*
**Pinder**, Albert Reginald 1920- *AmMWSc 92*
**Pinder**, Andrew *Who 92*
**Pinder**, Charles 1921- *Who 92*
**Pinder**, Chuck *TwCWW 91*
**Pinder**, Frank E. 1911- *WhoBlA 92*
**Pinder**, George Francis 1942- *AmMWSc 92*
**Pinder**, John Andrew 1947- *Who 92*
**Pinder**, John Edgar, III 1944- *AmMWSc 92*
**Pinder**, Kenneth Lyle 1929- *AmMWSc 92*
**Pinder**, Nelson W. 1932- *WhoBlA 92*
**Pinder**, Wilhelm 1878-1947 *EncTR 91*
**Pindera**, Jerzy Tadeusz 1914- *AmMWSc 92, WhoFI 92*
**Pinderhughes**, Charles Alfred 1919- *WhoBlA 92*
**Pinderski**, Jerome Wilbert, Jr. 1957- *WhoAmL 92*
**Pindling**, Lynden Oscar 1930- *IntWW 91, Who 92*
**Pindok**, Marie Theresa 1941- *AmMWSc 92*
**Pindzola**, Michael Stuart 1948- *AmMWSc 92*
**Pine**, Charles 1943- *WhoFI 92*
**Pine**, Charles Joseph 1951- *WhoWest 92*
**Pine**, Charles Warren 1915- *WhoAmP 91*
**Pine**, James Alexander 1912- *WhoAmP 91*
**Pine**, Jeffrey Barry 1955- *WhoAmL 92*
**Pine**, Jerome 1928- *AmMWSc 92*
**Pine**, John 1690-1756 *BlkwCEP*
**Pine**, Leo 1922- *AmMWSc 92*
**Pine**, Lloyd A 1933- *AmMWSc 92*
**Pine**, Martin J 1927- *AmMWSc 92*
**Pine**, Michael B *AmMWSc 92*
**Pine**, Robert Graham 1946- *WhoFI 92*
**Pine**, Robert S 1918- *WhoAmP 91*
**Pine**, Stanley H 1935- *AmMWSc 92*
**Pine**, Theodor *IntAu&W 91X*
**Pine**, William *WrDr 92*
**Pineau**, Christian 1904- *IntWW 91*
**Pineau**, Christian Paul Francis 1904- *Who 92*
**Pineau**, Edward L 1956- *WhoAmP 91*
**Pineau**, Robert Joseph 1959- *WhoAmL 92*
**Pineau-Valencienne**, Didier 1931- *IntWW 91*
**Pineault**, Serge Rene 1947- *AmMWSc 92*
**Pineda**, Andres, Jr. 1951- *WhoHisp 92, WhoWest 92*
**Pineda**, Antonio Jesus, Jr. 1948- *WhoHisp 92*
**Pineda**, Gilbert 1948- *WhoHisp 92*
**Pineda**, Patricia Salas 1951- *WhoHisp 92*
**Pineda**, Ramon Jose 1959- *WhoHisp 92*
**Pineda y Bascunan**, Francisco Nunez de *HisDSpE*
**Pinedo**, Michael L. *WhoHisp 92*
**Pinedo**, T. Christopher 1960- *WhoAmL 92*
**Pineiro**, Alexander, Sr. 1956- *WhoHisp 92*
**Pineiro**, Enrique *WhoHisp 92*
**Pineiro**, Pedro J. 1942- *WhoHisp 92*
**Pineiro-Montes**, Carlos 1955- *WhoHisp 92*
**Pinel**, Philippe 1745-1826 *BlkwCEP*
**Pineo**, Charles Chipman, III 1947- *WhoWest 92*
**Pinero**, Antonio R. *WhoHisp 92*
**Pinero**, Arthur Wing 1855-1934 *RfGEnL 91*
**Pinero**, Eugenio 1945- *WhoHisp 92*
**Pinero**, Gerald Joseph 1943- *AmMWSc 92*
**Pinero**, Luis Amilcar 1955- *WhoHisp 92*
**Pines**, Alexander 1945- *AmMWSc 92*
**Pines**, Burt 1939- *WhoAmL 92*
**Pines**, David 1924- *AmMWSc 92*
**Pines**, Herman 1902- *AmMWSc 92, WhoMW 92*
**Pines**, Judith Aiello *WhoFI 92*
**Pines**, Kermit L 1916- *AmMWSc 92*
**Pines**, Lois G 1940- *WhoAmP 91*
**Pines**, Paul *DrAPF 91*
**Pines**, Seemon H 1926- *AmMWSc 92*
**Pines**, Susan J *WhoAmP 91*
**Pines**, Wayne Lloyd 1943- *WhoFI 92*
**Ping**, Charles Jackson 1930- *WhoMW 92*
**Pingali**, Keshav Kumar 1957- *AmMWSc 92*
**Pingel**, Carl Raymond 1935- *WhoIns 92*
**Pingel**, John Spencer 1916- *WhoFI 92*
**Pingel**, Klaus G. 1914- *IntWW 91*
**Pingel**, Steven R. 1944- *WhoAmL 92*
**Pingert**, Chris M *WhoAmP 91*
**Pinget**, Robert 1919- *GuFrLit 1, IntAu&W 91, IntWW 91*
**Pingleton**, Susan Kasper 1946- *AmMWSc 92*
**Pingree**, Bruce Douglas 1947- *WhoAmL 92*
**Pings**, Anthony Claude 1951- *WhoFI 92, WhoWest 92*
**Pings**, C J 1929- *AmMWSc 92*
**Pings**, Cornelius John 1929- *WhoWest 92*
**Pinhas**, Stacy 1964- *WhoEnt 92*
**Pinheiro**, Marilyn Lays 1924- *AmMWSc 92*
**Pinheiro Farinha**, Joao de Deus 1919- *IntWW 91*
**Pinhiero de Azevedo**, Jose Baptista 1917-1983 *FacFETw*
**Pinholster**, Garland Folsom *WhoAmP 91*
**Pini**, Giorgio 1899-1987 *BiDExR*
**Pini-Corsi**, Antonio 1858-1918 *NewAmDM*
**Piniella**, Louis Victor 1943- *WhoMW 92*
**Pinilla-Garzon**, Jose Humberto 1932- *WhoHisp 92*
**Pininfarina**, Sergio 1926- *Who 92*
**Pinion**, F. B. 1908- *WrDr 92*
**Pinion**, Francis Bertram 1908- *IntAu&W 91*
**Pinion**, Phillip E 1952- *WhoAmP 91*
**Pink Floyd** *FacFETw, NewAmDM*
**Pink**, David Anthony Herbert 1936- *AmMWSc 92*
**Pink**, Ernest Edwin 1942- *WhoWest 92*
**Pink**, Michael Quentin 1955- *WhoRel 92*
**Pinkard**, Bedford L. 1931- *WhoBlA 92*
**Pinkard**, Deloris Elaine 1944- *WhoBlA 92*
**Pinkard**, Norman Thomas 1941- *WhoBlA 92*
**Pinkas**, Robert Paul 1953- *WhoAmL 92, WhoFI 92*
**Pinkava**, Donald John 1933- *AmMWSc 92*
**Pinkayan**, Subin 1934- *IntWW 91*
**Pinkel**, B 1909- *AmMWSc 92*
**Pinkel**, Donald Paul 1926- *AmMWSc 92*
**Pinkel**, Robert 1946- *AmMWSc 92*
**Pinkelton**, Norma Harris 1927- *WhoBlA 92*
**Pinker**, George 1924- *Who 92*
**Pinker**, George Douglas 1924- *IntWW 91*
**Pinker**, Robert Arthur 1931- *Who 92*
**Pinkerson**, Alan Lee *AmMWSc 92*
**Pinkert**, Ted Charles 1947- *WhoWest 92*
**Pinkerton**, A Alan 1943- *AmMWSc 92*
**Pinkerton**, Albert Duane, II 1942- *WhoAmL 92*
**Pinkerton**, Allan 1819-1884 *BenetAL 91*
**Pinkerton**, Charles Frederick 1940- *WhoAmL 92*
**Pinkerton**, Clayton David 1931- *WhoWest 92*
**Pinkerton**, Edith Charlene 1953- *WhoRel 92*
**Pinkerton**, Frank Henry 1945- *AmMWSc 92*
**Pinkerton**, James Donald 1940- *WhoFI 92*
**Pinkerton**, John Edward 1939- *AmMWSc 92*
**Pinkerton**, John Henry McKnight 1920- *Who 92*
**Pinkerton**, Milo Schoblaska 1953- *WhoMW 92*

**Pinkerton**, Peter Harvey 1934- *AmMWSc 92*
**Pinkerton**, William Ross 1913- *Who 92*
**Pinkett**, Allen Jerome 1964- *WhoBlA 92*
**Pinkett**, Harold Thomas 1914- *WhoBlA 92, WrDr 92*
**Pinkett**, Mary *WhoAmP 91*
**Pinkham**, Chester Allen, III 1936- *AmMWSc 92*
**Pinkham**, Clarkson Wilfred 1919- *WhoWest 92*
**Pinkham**, Daniel 1923- *NewAmDM, WhoEnt 92*
**Pinkham**, Daniel, Jr 1923- *ConCom 92*
**Pinkham**, Daniel Bernard 1958- *WhoEnt 92*
**Pinkham**, George Joseph 1945- *WhoWest 92*
**Pinkham**, Henry Charles 1948- *AmMWSc 92*
**Pinkham**, Richard A. R. *LesBEnT 92*
**Pinkham**, Robin Remick 1944- *WhoFI 92*
**Pinkney**, Alphonso 1930- *WhoBlA 92*
**Pinkney**, Arnold R. 1931- *WhoBlA 92*
**Pinkney**, D. Timothy 1948- *WhoWest 92*
**Pinkney**, Dove Savage 1932- *WhoBlA 92*
**Pinkney**, Edward 1802-1828 *NinCLC 31 [port]*
**Pinkney**, Edward Coote 1802-1828 *BenetAL 91*
**Pinkney**, Jerry 1939- *WhoBlA 92*
**Pinkney**, John Edward 1948- *WhoBlA 92*
**Pinkney**, William D. 1935- *WhoBlA 92*
**Pinkowicz**, Christine Ann 1961- *WhoEnt 92*
**Pinkstaff**, Carlin Adam 1934- *AmMWSc 92*
**Pinkstaff**, Martin LaVaughn 1926- *WhoEnt 92*
**Pinkston**, Earl Roland 1910- *AmMWSc 92*
**Pinkston**, Frank Chapman 1923- *WhoAmP 91*
**Pinkston**, Isabel Hay 1922- *WhoRel 92*
**Pinkston**, John Turner 1915- *AmMWSc 92*
**Pinkston**, John Turner, III 1942- *AmMWSc 92*
**Pinkston**, Margaret Fountain 1919- *AmMWSc 92*
**Pinkston**, Moses Samuel 1923- *WhoBlA 92, WhoRel 92*
**Pinkston**, Richard L., Jr. 1955- *WhoRel 92*
**Pinkston**, William Thomas 1931- *AmMWSc 92*
**Pinkus**, Edward C. 1938- *WhoAmL 92*
**Pinkus**, Hermann 1905- *AmMWSc 92*
**Pinkus**, Jack Leon 1930- *AmMWSc 92*
**Pinkwasser**, D. *WhoRel 92*
**Pinkwater**, Daniel Manus 1941- *TwCSFW 91, WrDr 92*
**Pinkwater**, Manus *WrDr 92*
**Pinn**, Sameul J., Jr. 1935- *WhoBlA 92*
**Pinna**, William Peter 1943- *WhoAmL 92*
**Pinnas**, Jacob Louis 1940- *AmMWSc 92*
**Pinnavaia**, Thomas J 1938- *AmMWSc 92*
**Pinnell**, Charles 1929- *AmMWSc 92*
**Pinnell**, Gary Ray 1951- *WhoFI 92*
**Pinnell**, Richard Tilden 1942- *WhoEnt 92*
**Pinnell**, Robert Peyton 1938- *AmMWSc 92, WhoWest 92*
**Pinner**, David 1940- *WrDr 92*
**Pinner**, David John 1940- *IntAu&W 91*
**Pinner**, Hayim 1925- *Who 92*
**Pinner**, Joma *ConAu 34NR*
**Pinner**, Ruth Margaret *Who 92*
**Pinney**, Constance Forsberg 1942- *WhoWest 92*
**Pinney**, Edmund 1917- *WhoWest 92*
**Pinney**, Edmund Joy 1917- *AmMWSc 92*
**Pinney**, George Bruce 1952- *WhoEnt 92*
**Pinney**, Sidney Dillingham, Jr. 1924- *WhoAmL 92*
**Pinnick**, Harry Thomas 1921- *AmMWSc 92*
**Pinnington**, Eric Henry 1938- *AmMWSc 92*
**Pinnington**, Geoffrey Charles 1919- *IntAu&W 91, Who 92*
**Pinnington**, Roger Adrian 1932- *Who 92*
**Pinnington-Hughes**, John *Who 92*
**Pinninti**, Krishna Rao 1950- *WhoFI 92*
**Pinnix**, John Lawrence 1947- *WhoAmL 92*
**Pinnock**, Harry James 1927- *Who 92*
**Pinnock**, Thomas *DrAPF 91*
**Pinnock**, Trevor 1946- *IntWW 91, NewAmDM, Who 92, WhoEnt 92*
**Pinnola**, Ciro d1946 *DcAmImH*
**Pinnow**, Arno Lee 1941- *WhoWest 92*
**Pinnow**, Kenneth Elmer 1928- *AmMWSc 92*
**Pino**, Anthony John 1948- *WhoFI 92*
**Pino**, Frank, Jr. 1942- *WhoHisp 92*
**Pino**, Haydee C. 1959- *WhoHisp 92*
**Pino**, Joe Oracio 1945- *WhoHisp 92*
**Pino**, John 1931- *WhoAmP 91*
**Pino**, Lewis Nicholas 1924- *AmMWSc 92*
**Pino**, Loe Anne Kimball 1935- *WhoAmL 92*
**Pino**, Michael Thomas 1953- *WhoWest 92*
**Pino**, Richard Edmund 1966- *WhoFI 92*
**Pino**, Richard M 1950- *AmMWSc 92*
**Pinoak**, Justin Willard *WrDr 92*
**Pinochet**, Augusto 1915- *FacFETw [port]*
**Pinochet Ugarte**, Augusto 1915- *IntWW 91*
**Pinola**, Joseph John 1925- *WhoFI 92, WhoWest 92*
**Pinoli**, Burt Arthur 1954- *WhoWest 92*
**Pinschmidt**, Mary Warren 1934- *AmMWSc 92*
**Pinschmidt**, Robert Krantz, Jr 1945- *AmMWSc 92*
**Pinschmidt**, William Conrad, Jr 1926- *AmMWSc 92*
**Pinsent**, Christopher 1922- *Who 92*
**Pinsent**, Roger Philip 1916- *Who 92*
**Pinsker**, Allen 1930- *IntMPA 92*
**Pinsker**, Penny Collias 1942- *WhoEnt 92*
**Pinsker**, Sanford *DrAPF 91*
**Pinsker**, Sanford S. 1941- *WrDr 92*
**Pinski**, David 1872-1959 *LiExTwC*
**Pinski**, Gabriel 1937- *AmMWSc 92*
**Pinsky**, Carl 1928- *AmMWSc 92*
**Pinsky**, Carl Muni 1938- *AmMWSc 92*
**Pinsky**, David Bruce 1962- *WhoEnt 92*
**Pinsky**, Leonard 1935- *AmMWSc 92*
**Pinsky**, Mark A 1940- *AmMWSc 92*
**Pinsky**, Michael S. 1945- *WhoAmL 92*
**Pinsky**, Paul 1950- *WhoAmP 91*
**Pinsky**, Robert *DrAPF 91*
**Pinsky**, Robert 1940- *BenetAL 91, ConPo 91, WrDr 92*
**Pinsky**, Stephen Howard 1944- *WhoRel 92*
**Pinsley**, Edward Allan 1927- *AmMWSc 92*
**Pinson**, Barry 1925- *Who 92*
**Pinson**, David Craig 1954- *WhoRel 92*
**Pinson**, Elliot N 1935- *AmMWSc 92*
**Pinson**, Ellis Rex, Jr 1925- *AmMWSc 92*
**Pinson**, Ernest Alexander *AmMWSc 92*
**Pinson**, James Wesley 1937- *AmMWSc 92*
**Pinson**, Jerry D 1942- *WhoAmP 91*
**Pinson**, John C 1931- *AmMWSc 92*
**Pinson**, Rex, Jr 1925- *AmMWSc 92*
**Pinson**, Robert Lewis 1942- *WhoFI 92*
**Pinson**, Thomas J. 1927- *WhoBlA 92*
**Pinson**, Vada Edward, Jr. 1938- *WhoBlA 92*
**Pinson**, Valerie F. 1930- *WhoBlA 92*
**Pinson**, Valerie Ford 1930- *WhoAmP 91*
**Pinson**, William Hamet, Jr 1919- *AmMWSc 92*
**Pinson**, William M., Jr. 1934- *WrDr 92*
**Pinson**, William Meredith 1934- *WhoRel 92*
**Pinsoneault**, R J 1929- *WhoAmP 91*
**Pinstrup-Andersen**, Per 1939- *WhoFI 92*
**Pint**, Rose Mary *WhoRel 92*
**Pinta**, Wanda Bohan 1918- *WhoWest 92*
**Pintak**, Lawrence Edward 1955- *WhoFI 92*
**Pintar**, Anton James 1940- *WhoAmP 91*
**Pintar**, M Mik 1934- *AmMWSc 92*
**Pintasilgo**, Maria de Lourdes 1930- *IntWW 91*
**Pintauro**, Joseph *DrAPF 91*
**Pinter**, Antonia *Who 92*
**Pinter**, Charles Claude 1932- *AmMWSc 92*
**Pinter**, Ferenc Janos 1961- *WhoMW 92*
**Pinter**, Gabriel George 1925- *AmMWSc 92*
**Pinter**, Harold 1930- *CnDBLB 8 [port], FacFETw, IntAu&W 91, IntMPA 92, IntWW 91, RfGEnL 91, Who 92, WhoEnt 92, WrDr 92*
**Pinter**, Joseph Kalman 1953- *WhoWest 92*
**Pinter**, Paul James, Jr 1946- *AmMWSc 92*
**Pintile**, Lucian *WhoEnt 92*
**Pintner**, James David 1949- *WhoMW 92*
**Pinto**, Frank G 1934- *AmMWSc 92*
**Pinto**, Isaac *BenetAL 91*
**Pinto**, Isaac 1715-1787 *BlkwCEP*
**Pinto**, Jacqueline 1927- *WrDr 92*
**Pinto**, John 1924- *WhoAmP 91, WhoHisp 92*
**Pinto**, John Darwin 1940- *AmMWSc 92*
**Pinto**, John Gilbert 1940- *AmMWSc 92*
**Pinto**, John Marion 1956- *WhoEnt 92*
**Pinto**, John S 1949- *WhoAmP 91*
**Pinto**, Lawrence Henry 1943- *AmMWSc 92*
**Pinto**, Les *WhoHisp 92*
**Pinto Balsemao**, Francisco Jose Pereira 1937- *IntWW 91*
**Pinto Barbosa**, Antonio Manuel 1917- *IntWW 91*
**Pinto Da Silva**, Pedro Goncalves *AmMWSc 92*
**Pinto Diaz**, Francisco Antonio 1775-1858 *HisDSpE*
**Pinza**, Ezio 1892-1957 *FacFETw, NewAmDM*
**Pinzka**, Charles Frederick 1918- *AmMWSc 92*
**Pinzon**, Vicente Yanez 1463?-1514 *HisDSpE*
**Pinzon-Umana**, Eduardo 1931- *WhoHisp 92*
**Pinzow**, Anne Phyllis 1949- *WhoEnt 92*
**Pioch**, Richard Paul 1922- *AmMWSc 92*
**Piomelli**, Sergio 1931- *AmMWSc 92*
**Pion**, Lawrence V 1926- *AmMWSc 92*
**Pionius** d250 *EncEarC*
**Pionke**, Harry Bernhard *AmMWSc 92*
**Piontek**, Heinz 1925- *ConAu 34NR, IntAu&W 91, IntWW 91*
**Piontek**, Mark Clarence 1960- *WhoAmL 92*
**Piontkowski**, Timothy A. 1960- *WhoMW 92*
**Piore**, Emanuel Ruben 1908- *AmMWSc 92, IntWW 91*
**Piore**, Nora 1912- *AmMWSc 92*
**Piorko**, Adam M 1947- *AmMWSc 92*
**Piot**, Peter 1949- *IntWW 91*
**Piotrovsky**, Boris B 1907?-1990 *FacFETw*
**Piotrowicz**, Stephen R 1945- *AmMWSc 92*
**Piotrowski**, Czeslaw Wojciech 1926- *IntWW 91*
**Piotrowski**, George 1942- *AmMWSc 92*
**Piotrowski**, Joseph Martin 1936- *AmMWSc 92*
**Piotrowski**, Zbigniew 1953- *AmMWSc 92*
**Pious**, Donald A 1930- *AmMWSc 92*
**Piovanelli**, Silvano 1924- *IntWW 91, WhoRel 92*
**Piovanetti-Pietri**, J. Enrique 1939- *WhoHisp 92*
**Piozzi**, Hester Lynch *BlkwCEP*
**Pipa**, Rudolph Louis 1930- *AmMWSc 92*
**Pipberger**, Hubert V 1920- *AmMWSc 92*
**Pipe**, Murray A. *WhoRel 92*
**Pipenberg**, Kenneth James 1920- *AmMWSc 92*
**Piper**, Adrian Margaret Smith 1948- *WhoBlA 92*
**Piper**, Annette Cleone 1936- *WhoMW 92*
**Piper**, Bright Harold 1918- *IntWW 91, Who 92*
**Piper**, Carlyle Ashton 1925- *IntWW 91*
**Piper**, Carol Adeline 1924- *WhoMW 92*
**Piper**, David d1990 *NewYTBS 91*
**Piper**, David 1918-1990 *AnObit 1990*
**Piper**, David Towry d1990 *IntWW 91N, Who 92N*
**Piper**, David Zink 1935- *AmMWSc 92*
**Piper**, Douglas Edward 1923- *AmMWSc 92*
**Piper**, Edgar L 1937- *AmMWSc 92*
**Piper**, Edward 1938-1990 *AnObit 1990, TwCPaSc*
**Piper**, Edwin Ford 1871-1939 *BenetAL 91*
**Piper**, Elwood A. 1934- *WhoBlA 92*
**Piper**, Ervin L 1923- *AmMWSc 92*
**Piper**, George Earle 1932- *WhoFI 92*
**Piper**, H Beam 1904-1964 *TwCSFW 91*
**Piper**, James Robert 1933- *AmMWSc 92*
**Piper**, James Underhill 1937- *AmMWSc 92*
**Piper**, Jane d1991 *NewYTBS 91*
**Piper**, John 1903- *TwCPaSc*
**Piper**, John 1934- *AmMWSc 92*
**Piper**, John Anthony 1930- *IntWW 91*
**Piper**, John Egerton Christmas 1903- *IntWW 91, Who 92*
**Piper**, Karen Lynn 1952- *WhoAmL 92*
**Piper**, Klaus 1911- *IntWW 91*
**Piper**, Marceline Hewes 1929- *WhoAmP 91*
**Piper**, Patricia K 1934- *WhoAmP 91*
**Piper**, Paul J. 1935- *WhoBlA 92*
**Piper**, Peter *Who 92*
**Piper**, Richard Carl 1932- *AmMWSc 92*
**Piper**, Robert Paul 1933- *WhoAmL 92*
**Piper**, Roger D 1928- *AmMWSc 92*
**Piper**, Thomas Laurence, III 1941- *WhoFI 92*
**Piper**, Thomas Samuel 1932- *WhoRel 92*
**Piper**, W. Archibald 1935- *WhoBlA 92*
**Piper**, Walter Nelson 1940- *AmMWSc 92*
**Piper**, William Howard 1933- *WhoMW 92*
**Piper**, William Weidman 1925- *AmMWSc 92*
**Piperno**, Elliot 1938- *AmMWSc 92*
**Pipes**, Paul Bruce 1941- *AmMWSc 92*
**Pipes**, Richard 1923- *WrDr 92*
**Pipes**, Robert Byron 1941- *AmMWSc 92*
**Pipes**, Wesley O 1932- *AmMWSc 92*
**Pipes**, William H. *WhoBlA 92*
**Pipher**, Joseph 1949- *WhoEnt 92*
**Pipinich**, Robert E 1935- *WhoAmP 91*
**Pipitone**, Phyllis L. *WhoMW 92*
**Pipkin**, Allen Compere 1931- *AmMWSc 92*
**Pipkin**, Alva 1931- *WhoFI 92, WhoWest 92*
**Pipkin**, Bernard Wallace 1927- *AmMWSc 92*
**Pipkin**, Broughton 1913- *Who 92*
**Pipkin**, Charles Harry Broughton 1913- *IntWW 91*
**Pipkin**, Francis Marion 1925- *AmMWSc 92*
**Pipkin**, H. Wayne 1939- *WhoRel 92*
**Pipkin**, Marvin Grady 1949- *WhoAmL 92*
**Pippard**, Brian 1920- *IntWW 91, Who 92*
**Pippen**, Richard Wayne 1935- *AmMWSc 92*
**Pippen**, Scott 1965- *WhoBlA 92*
**Pippen**, Scottie 1965- *News 92-2 [port], WhoMW 92*
**Pippert**, Raymond Elmer 1938- *AmMWSc 92, WhoMW 92*
**Pippin**, Donald Ferrell 1925- *WhoEnt 92*
**Pique**, Fernando Rafael 1952- *WhoFI 92*
**Piquet**, Nelson 1952- *IntWW 91*
**Piquette**, Jean Conrad 1950- *AmMWSc 92*
**Piraino**, Paul Lynn 1964- *WhoRel 92*
**Pirandello**, Luigi 1867-1936 *FacFETw, WhoNob 90*
**Piranesi**, Giovanni Battista 1720-1778 *BlkwCEP*
**Pirani**, Conrad Levi 1914- *AmMWSc 92*
**Piranian**, George 1914- *AmMWSc 92*
**Piratin**, Philip 1907- *Who 92*
**Pirazzi**, Sylvia M. 1934- *WhoHisp 92*
**Pirch**, James Herman 1937- *AmMWSc 92*
**Pircher**, Leo Joseph 1933- *WhoAmL 92*
**Pire**, Dominique 1910-1969 *WhoNob 90*
**Pire**, Jules 1878-1953 *FacFETw*
**Pirela**, Reynaldo *WhoAmP 91*
**Pirela Figueroa**, Reynaldo *WhoHisp 92*
**Pirelli**, Leopoldo 1925- *IntWW 91, Who 92*
**Pires**, Antonio J 1944- *WhoAmP 91*
**Pires**, Laura J. *WhoBlA 92*
**Pires**, Pedro Verona Rodrigues 1934- *IntWW 91*
**Pires**, Renato Guedes 1961- *AmMWSc 92*
**Pires De Miranda**, Pedro 1928- *IntWW 91*
**Piretti**, Giancarlo 1940- *DcTwDes*
**Pirie**, David 1946- *WrDr 92*
**Pirie**, David Tarbat 1946- *IntAu&W 91*
**Pirie**, Gordon 1918- *Who 92*
**Pirie**, Henry Ward 1922- *Who 92*
**Pirie**, Iain Gordon 1933- *Who 92*
**Pirie**, Madsen 1940- *Who 92*
**Pirie**, Norman Wingate 1907- *Who 92*
**Pirie**, Psyche 1918- *Who 92*
**Pirie**, Robert Burns, Jr 1933- *WhoAmP 91*
**Pirie**, Robert Gordon 1936- *AmMWSc 92*
**Pirie**, Robert S. 1934- *WhoFI 92*
**Pirie**, Walter Ronald 1934- *AmMWSc 92*
**Piringer**, Albert Aloysius, Jr 1921- *AmMWSc 92*
**Piriz-Ballon**, Ramiro 1938- *IntWW 91*
**Pirkle**, Earl C 1922- *AmMWSc 92*
**Pirkle**, Estus Washington 1930- *WhoRel 92*
**Pirkle**, Fredric Lee 1949- *AmMWSc 92*
**Pirkle**, George Emory 1947- *WhoEnt 92*
**Pirkle**, Hubert Chaille 1924- *AmMWSc 92*
**Pirkle**, John Ward 1937- *WhoEnt 92*
**Pirkle**, William Arthur 1945- *AmMWSc 92*
**Pirkle**, William H 1934- *AmMWSc 92*
**Pirl**, Joerg Norbert 1942- *WhoMW 92*
**Pirlot**, Paul 1920- *AmMWSc 92*
**Pirlot De Corbion**, Edmond 1916- *IntWW 91*
**Pirnie**, Ian Hugh 1935- *Who 92*
**Pirnot**, Thomas Leonard 1943- *AmMWSc 92*
**Piro**, Frank 1920-1989 *FacFETw*
**Piro**, Lydia A. 1950- *WhoHisp 92*
**Pirofsky**, Bernard 1926- *AmMWSc 92*
**Pirog**, Richard Stanley 1956- *WhoMW 92*
**Pirolli**, Linda Tarver 1956- *WhoAmL 92*
**Piromgraipakd**, Somchai 1945- *WhoRel 92*
**Pirone**, Louis Anthony 1945- *AmMWSc 92*
**Pirone**, Michelle 1962- *WhoFI 92*
**Pirone**, Thomas Pascal 1936- *AmMWSc 92*
**Pironio**, Eduardo 1920- *IntWW 91, WhoRel 92*
**Pirooz**, Perry Parviz 1928- *AmMWSc 92*
**Pirot**, Alison T Lohans 1949- *IntAu&W 91*
**Piroue**, Pierre Adrien 1931- *AmMWSc 92*
**Pirow**, Oswald 1890-1959 *BiDExR*
**Pirozynski**, Jan 1936- *IntWW 91*
**Pirraglia**, Joseph A 1928- *AmMWSc 92*
**Pirri**, Anthony Nicholas 1943- *AmMWSc 92*
**Pirrie**, David Blair 1938- *Who 92*
**Pirro**, Mark S. 1956- *WhoEnt 92*
**Pirrung**, Michael Craig 1955- *AmMWSc 92*
**Pirsch**, Carol McBride 1936- *WhoAmP 91*
**Pirsig**, Robert M. 1928- *BenetAL 91*
**Pirsson**, Louis Valentine 1860-1919 *BiInAmS*
**Pirtle**, Eugene Claude 1921- *AmMWSc 92*
**Pirtle**, Robert M 1945- *AmMWSc 92*
**Pirtle**, Ronald M. 1954- *WhoBlA 92*
**Pirubhakaran**, Vellupillai 1954- *IntWW 91*
**Pirzada**, Syed Sharifuddin 1923- *IntWW 91, Who 92*
**Pisacane**, Vincent L 1933- *AmMWSc 92*
**Pisacrita**, Marie Seliste 1946- *WhoFI 92*
**Pisani**, Edgard 1918- *IntWW 91, Who 92*
**Pisani**, Joseph R 1929- *WhoAmP 91*
**Pisano**, A. Robert *IntMPA 92*
**Pisano**, A. Robert 1943- *WhoAmL 92*
**Pisano**, Alfonso L 1928- *WhoAmP 91*
**Pisano**, Charles 1960- *WhoFI 92*
**Pisano**, Daniel Joseph, Jr 1946- *AmMWSc 92*

**Pisano**, Joseph Carmen 1941- *AmMWSc 92*
**Pisano**, Judy Belushi 1951- *WhoEnt 92*
**Pisano**, Michael A 1923- *AmMWSc 92*
**Pisano**, Vincent J. 1953- *WhoAmL 92*
**Pisarenko**, Olgierd 1947- *WhoEnt 92*
**Pisaroni**, Benedetta 1793-1872 *NewAmDM*
**Pisarowicz**, James Alexander 1951- *WhoWest 92*
**Pisarzewicz**, Paul Jerome 1948- *WhoMW 92*
**Piscal**, Francis Phillip 1939- *WhoAmL 92*
**Pischel**, Ken Donald 1950- *AmMWSc 92*
**Pischinger**, Franz Felix 1930- *IntWW 91*
**Pischl**, Adolph John 1920- *WhoEnt 92*
**Pisciotta**, Anthony Vito 1921- *AmMWSc 92*
**Pisciotta**, Samuel James 1938- *WhoWest 92*
**Piscitelli**, Joseph 1934- *AmMWSc 92*
**Piscitello**, Antonino 1944- *WhoFI 92*
**Piscitiello**, Anthony Michael 1947- *WhoMW 92*
**Piscopo**, Joe 1951- *IntMPA 92*
**Piscopo**, John E *WhoAmP 91*
**Piscopo**, Joseph Charles 1951- *WhoEnt 92*
**Piscopo**, Rich 1955- *WhoRel 92*
**Piscotty**, John Stanley 1944- *WhoFI 92*
**Piserchia**, Doris 1928- *IntAu&W 91, TwCSFW 91, WrDr 92*
**Piserchio**, Robert J 1934- *AmMWSc 92*
**Pisha**, Susan C 1943- *WhoAmP 91*
**Pishaw**, Karl Joseph 1953- *WhoRel 92*
**Pisier**, Marie-France 1944- *IntMPA 92*
**Pisk**, Paul A. 1893-1990 *NewAmDM*
**Piskin**, Scott Paul 1961- *WhoFI 92*
**Piskor**, Stanislaw 1944- *IntAu&W 91*
**Piskorski**, John Joseph 1955- *WhoAmL 92*
**Piskorski**, Thomas James 1955- *WhoAmL 92*
**Piskotin**, Mikhail Ivanovich 1924- *IntWW 91, SovUnBD*
**Pisner**, Susan Jill 1957- *WhoAmL 92*
**Pisney**, Raymond Frank 1940- *WhoMW 92*
**Pissarro**, Camille 1830-1903 *ThHEIm [port]*
**Pissarro**, Felix 1874-1897 *ThHEIm [port]*
**Pissarro**, Julie 1838-1922 *ThHEIm*
**Pissarro**, Lucien 1863-1944 *ThHEIm [port], TwCPaSc*
**Pissarro**, Orovida Camille 1893-1968 *TwCPaSc*
**Pistella**, Frank Joseph 1951- *WhoAmP 91*
**Pister**, Karl S 1925- *AmMWSc 92*
**Pister**, Karl Stark 1925- *WhoWest 92*
**Pistilli**, John Anthony 1925- *WhoEnt 92*
**Pistner**, Stephen Lawrence 1932- *WhoFI 92*
**Pistole**, Thomas Gordon 1942- *AmMWSc 92*
**Piston**, Walter 1894-1976 *FacFETw, NewAmDM*
**Pistone**, Rick *DrAPF 91*
**Pistono**, Frances Anne 1944- *WhoAmP 91*
**Pistoria**, Paul G 1907- *WhoAmP 91*
**Pistorius**, Vladimir 1951- *IntAu&W 91*
**Piszkiewicz**, Dennis 1941- *AmMWSc 92*
**Pita**, Edward Gerald 1925- *AmMWSc 92*
**Pita**, Francisco Pablo 1944- *WhoHisp 92*
**Pita**, Frank J., Jr. 1957- *WhoHisp 92*
**Pita**, George Louis 1961- *WhoHisp 92*
**Pita**, Juana Rosa 1939- *IntAu&W 91*
**Pita**, Julio C *AmMWSc 92*
**Pitagorsky**, George 1942- *WhoFI 92*
**Pitana** *EncAmaz 91*
**Pitarka**, Bashkim Pamiz 1942- *IntWW 91*
**Pitaro**, Carl D *WhoAmP 91*
**Pitaro**, Vincent L. d1991 *NewYTBS 91*
**Pitas**, Robert E *AmMWSc 92*
**Pitassi**, Robert Albert 1947- *WhoAmL 92*
**Pitblado**, David 1912- *Who 92*
**Pitblado**, David B. 1912- *IntWW 91*
**Pitcairn**, Donald M 1921- *AmMWSc 92*
**Pitcher**, Arthur Everett 1912- *AmMWSc 92*
**Pitcher**, DePuyster Gilbert 1928- *AmMWSc 92*
**Pitcher**, Desmond Henry 1935- *Who 92*
**Pitcher**, Dixon M *WhoAmP 91*
**Pitcher**, Eric John 1946- *AmMWSc 92*
**Pitcher**, Frederick M. A. 1932- *WhoBlA 92*
**Pitcher**, George 1925- *IntAu&W 91, WrDr 92*
**Pitcher**, Griffith Fontaine 1937- *WhoAmL 92*
**Pitcher**, Harvey John 1936- *IntAu&W 91, WrDr 92*
**Pitcher**, Helen Ione 1931- *WhoWest 92*
**Pitcher**, John William 1950- *WhoAmP 91*
**Pitcher**, Max Grow 1935- *WhoFI 92*
**Pitcher**, Moll d1813 *BenetAL 91*
**Pitcher**, Molly 1754-1832 *BenetAL 91, HanAmWH*
**Pitcher**, Oliver *DrAPF 91*
**Pitcher**, Tom Stephen 1926- *AmMWSc 92*
**Pitcher**, Wallace Spencer 1919- *Who 92*
**Pitcher**, Wayne Harold, Jr 1944- *AmMWSc 92*
**Pitcher**, Zina 1797-1872 *BiInAmS*
**Pitchers**, Christopher John 1942- *Who 92*
**Pitchford** *Who 92*
**Pitchford**, Armin Cloyst 1922- *AmMWSc 92*
**Pitchford**, Charles Neville *Who 92*
**Pitchford**, Christopher John 1947- *Who 92*
**Pitchford**, Dean Stanley 1951- *WhoEnt 92*
**Pitchford**, Gerard Spencer 1953- *WhoBlA 92*
**Pitchford**, John Hereward 1904- *Who 92*
**Pitchford**, John W. *Who 92*
**Pitchford**, Kenneth S 1931- *IntAu&W 91*
**Pitchford**, Leanne Carolyn 1950- *AmMWSc 92*
**Pitchforth**, Harry 1917- *Who 92*
**Pitchforth**, R. Vivian 1895-1982 *TwCPaSc*
**Pitcock**, James Allison 1929- *AmMWSc 92*
**Pitcock**, Louis, Jr 1924- *WhoAmP 91*
**Pitegoff**, Peter Robert 1953- *WhoFI 92*
**Pitegoff**, Thomas Michael 1949- *WhoAmL 92*
**Pitelka**, Frank Alois 1916- *AmMWSc 92*
**Pitelka**, Louis Frank 1947- *AmMWSc 92*
**Pitesky**, Isadore 1918- *AmMWSc 92*
**Pitezel**, Frank F 1923- *WhoAmP 91*
**Pitfield**, Michael 1937- *Who 92*
**Pitfield**, Peter Michael 1937- *IntWW 91*
**Pitfield**, Thomas B. 1903- *NewAmDM*
**Pitha**, John Joseph 1920- *AmMWSc 92*
**Pitha**, Josef 1933- *AmMWSc 92*
**Pitha-Rowe**, Paula Marie 1937- *AmMWSc 92*
**Pithart**, Petr 1941- *IntWW 91*
**Pitis**, Marcela Eugenia 1914- *IntWW 91*
**Pitkin**, Anne *DrAPF 91*
**Pitkin**, Charles Alfred 1853?-1916 *BiInAmS*
**Pitkin**, Edward Thaddeus 1930- *AmMWSc 92*
**Pitkin**, Joan 1932- *WhoAmP 91*
**Pitkin**, Kenneth P 1954- *WhoAmP 91*
**Pitkin**, Roy Macbeth 1934- *AmMWSc 92, WhoWest 92*
**Pitkin**, Ruthanne B 1944- *AmMWSc 92*
**Pitkin**, Walter B. 1878-1953 *BenetAL 91*
**Pitkow**, Howard Spencer 1941- *AmMWSc 92*
**Pitlanish**, Mary Lynn 1964- *WhoMW 92*
**Pitler**, Howard Jerome 1952- *WhoMW 92*
**Pitler**, Robert Louis 1940- *WhoAmL 92*
**Pitlick**, Frances Ann 1940- *AmMWSc 92*
**Pitman**, Benn 1822-1910 *BiInAmS*
**Pitman**, Brian Ivor 1931- *IntWW 91, Who 92*
**Pitman**, David Christian 1936- *Who 92*
**Pitman**, Edwin James George 1897- *Who 92*
**Pitman**, James 1901- *IntAu&W 91*
**Pitman**, Jennifer Susan 1946- *Who 92*
**Pitman**, P.V. *TwCPaSc*
**Pitman**, Randy Ernest 1955- *WhoEnt 92*
**Pitner**, Samuel Ellis 1932- *AmMWSc 92*
**Pitney**, Mahlon 1858-1924 *FacFETw*
**Pitney**, Thomas Garry 1943- *WhoFI 92*
**Pitofsky**, Robert 1929- *WhoAmL 92, WhoAmP 91*
**Pitoi**, Sere 1935- *Who 92*
**Pitone**, Louise Katherine 1938- *WhoFI 92*
**Pitoniak**, Gregory E 1954- *WhoAmP 91*
**Pitoniak**, Marc Francis 1951- *WhoFI 92*
**Pitot**, Henry C, III 1930- *AmMWSc 92*
**Pitot**, Henry Clement 1930- *WhoMW 92*
**Pitra**, Frantisek 1932- *IntWW 91*
**Pitrat**, Charles William 1928- *AmMWSc 92*
**Pitre**, Felix 1949- *WhoEnt 92*
**Pitre**, Henry Nolle, Jr 1937- *AmMWSc 92*
**Pitrolo**, James L, Jr 1945- *WhoAmP 91*
**Pitrone**, Jean Maddern 1920- *WrDr 92*
**Pitrone**, Margo Rae 1960- *WhoRel 92*
**Pitt** *Who 92*
**Pitt**, Barrie 1918- *Who 92, WrDr 92*
**Pitt**, Barrie William Edward 1918- *IntAu&W 91*
**Pitt**, Bertram 1932- *AmMWSc 92, WhoMW 92*
**Pitt**, Bruce R 1949- *AmMWSc 92*
**Pitt**, Charles H 1929- *AmMWSc 92*
**Pitt**, Charles Horace 1929- *WhoWest 92*
**Pitt**, Colin Geoffrey 1935- *AmMWSc 92*
**Pitt**, Darryl Maynard 1955- *WhoEnt 92*
**Pitt**, David Charles 1938- *IntAu&W 91, WrDr 92*
**Pitt**, David George 1921- *IntAu&W 91*
**Pitt**, Desmond Gordon 1922- *Who 92*
**Pitt**, Donald Alfred 1926- *AmMWSc 92*
**Pitt**, Gavin Alexander 1915- *WhoFI 92, WhoMW 92*
**Pitt**, George 1938- *WhoAmL 92, WhoFI 92, WhoMW 92*
**Pitt**, George Edward 1916- *Who 92*
**Pitt**, Harry 1914- *Who 92*
**Pitt**, Harry Raymond 1914- *IntWW 91*
**Pitt**, Harvey Lloyd 1945- *WhoAmL 92*
**Pitt**, Jane 1938- *AmMWSc 92*
**Pitt**, Judson Hamilton 1953- *WhoMW 92*
**Pitt**, Loren Dallas 1939- *AmMWSc 92*
**Pitt**, Michael Edward 1949- *Who 92*
**Pitt**, Theophilus Harper, Jr. 1936- *WhoFI 92*
**Pitt**, Ursula 1935- *TwCPaSc*
**Pitt**, William 1708-1778 *BlkwCEP, BlkwEAR*
**Pitt**, William Alexander 1942- *WhoWest 92*
**Pitt**, William Henry 1937- *Who 92*
**Pitt**, Woodrow Wilson, Jr 1935- *AmMWSc 92*
**Pitt-Kethley**, Fiona 1954- *ConPo 91, IntAu&W 91, WrDr 92*
**Pitt of Hampstead**, Baron 1913- *Who 92*
**Pitta**, Susan Margaret 1957- *WhoFI 92*
**Pittam**, Robert Raymond 1919- *Who 92*
**Pittel**, Harvey 1943- *NewAmDM*
**Pittel**, Stuart 1944- *AmMWSc 92*
**Pittelko**, Roger Dean 1932- *WhoMW 92, WhoRel 92*
**Pittendrigh**, Colin Stephenson 1918- *AmMWSc 92, IntWW 91*
**Pittenger**, Arthur O 1936- *AmMWSc 92*
**Pittenger**, Jerry Lee 1947- *WhoMW 92*
**Pittenger**, John Chapman 1930- *WhoAmP 91*
**Pittenger**, Norman 1905- *IntAu&W 91, WrDr 92*
**Pittenger**, Thad Heckle, Jr 1921- *AmMWSc 92*
**Pitter**, Richard Leon 1947- *AmMWSc 92*
**Pitter**, Ruth 1897- *ConPo 91, IntAu&W 91, IntWW 91, Who 92, WrDr 92*
**Pitti**, Donald Robert 1929- *WhoFI 92*
**Pittillo**, Jack Daniel 1938- *AmMWSc 92*
**Pittman**, Audrey Bullock 1916- *WhoBlA 92*
**Pittman**, Charles U, Jr 1939- *AmMWSc 92*
**Pittman**, Chatty Roger *AmMWSc 92*
**Pittman**, Darryl E. 1948- *WhoBlA 92*
**Pittman**, Edward D 1930- *AmMWSc 92*
**Pittman**, Edwin Lloyd 1935- *WhoAmL 92, WhoAmP 91*
**Pittman**, Fred Estes 1932- *AmMWSc 92*
**Pittman**, G F, Jr 1927- *AmMWSc 92*
**Pittman**, Ineva 1934- *WhoBlA 92*
**Pittman**, James A., Jr. 1927- *IntWW 91*
**Pittman**, James Allen, Jr 1927- *AmMWSc 92*
**Pittman**, James Ronald 1925- *WhoBlA 92*
**Pittman**, Kenneth Arthur 1937- *AmMWSc 92*
**Pittman**, Margaret 1901- *AmMWSc 92*
**Pittman**, Marvin B. 1931- *WhoBlA 92*
**Pittman**, Matthew Dale 1969- *WhoRel 92*
**Pittman**, Melvin Amos 1905- *AmMWSc 92*
**Pittman**, Philip McMillan 1941- *WhoMW 92*
**Pittman**, Quentin J 1952- *AmMWSc 92*
**Pittman**, Ray Calvin *AmMWSc 92*
**Pittman**, Rena Arlena 1912- *WhoAmP 91*
**Pittman**, Richard Harding *WhoEnt 92*
**Pittman**, Robert King, Jr. 1957- *WhoWest 92*
**Pittman**, Robert Preston 1940- *AmMWSc 92*
**Pittman**, Robert W. *LesBEnT 92*
**Pittman**, Robert Warren 1953- *WhoEnt 92, WhoFI 92*
**Pittman**, Roland Nathan 1944- *AmMWSc 92*
**Pittman**, Ron Davis 1945- *WhoFI 92*
**Pittman**, Ronald W *WhoAmP 91*
**Pittman**, Sample Noel 1927- *WhoBlA 92*
**Pittman**, Timona Miller 1926- *WhoEnt 92*
**Pittman**, Virgil 1916- *WhoAmL 92*
**Pittman**, William Trullender 1962- *WhoFI 92*
**Pittner**, Kelly Casas 1961- *WhoWest 92*
**Pittock**, Joan 1930- *WrDr 92*
**Pitts**, Andrew Williams, Jr 1931- *WhoAmP 91*
**Pitts**, Barry James Roger 1940- *AmMWSc 92*
**Pitts**, Bernard Ray 1944- *WhoWest 92*
**Pitts**, Brenda S. 1950- *WhoBlA 92*
**Pitts**, Charles W 1933- *AmMWSc 92*
**Pitts**, Cyril 1916- *Who 92*
**Pitts**, Danny Carrol 1950- *WhoRel 92*
**Pitts**, David Eugene 1939- *AmMWSc 92*
**Pitts**, David Ryder 1957- *WhoWest 92*
**Pitts**, Don LeRoy 1928- *WhoEnt 92*
**Pitts**, Donald Franklin 1933- *WhoBlA 92*
**Pitts**, Donald Graves 1926- *AmMWSc 92*
**Pitts**, Donald James 1945- *AmMWSc 92*
**Pitts**, Donald Ross 1929- *AmMWSc 92*
**Pitts**, Dorothy L. 1913- *WhoBlA 92*
**Pitts**, Earl Albert, Sr 1919- *WhoAmP 91*
**Pitts**, Eugene, III 1940- *WhoEnt 92*
**Pitts**, Gary Benjamin 1952- *WhoAmL 92*
**Pitts**, Gerald Nelson 1943- *AmMWSc 92*
**Pitts**, Gregory Philip 1949- *WhoBlA 92*
**Pitts**, Grover Cleveland 1918- *AmMWSc 92*
**Pitts**, Jack Nelson Evangelista 1948- *WhoBlA 92*
**Pitts**, James Donald, Jr. 1938- *WhoBlA 92, WhoMW 92*
**Pitts**, James Ninde, Jr 1921- *AmMWSc 92*
**Pitts**, Joe W., III 1960- *WhoAmL 92, WhoFI 92*
**Pitts**, John Kennedy 1925- *Who 92*
**Pitts**, John Martin 1945- *WhoBlA 92*
**Pitts**, John Roland 1948- *AmMWSc 92*
**Pitts**, Jon T 1948- *AmMWSc 92*
**Pitts**, Joseph R 1939- *WhoAmP 91*
**Pitts**, Lorenzo, Jr. 1946- *WhoBlA 92*
**Pitts**, M. Henry 1916- *WhoBlA 92*
**Pitts**, Malcolm John 1950- *AmMWSc 92*
**Pitts**, Martha Jean 1943- *WhoWest 92*
**Pitts**, Martin 1945- *WhoEnt 92*
**Pitts**, Neal Powell 1953- *WhoAmL 92*
**Pitts**, Noah Odas, Jr 1921- *WhoAmP 91*
**Pitts**, Randolph Marshall 1948- *WhoEnt 92*
**Pitts**, Robert Duane 1932- *WhoRel 92*
**Pitts**, Robert Eugene, Jr. 1948- *WhoMW 92*
**Pitts**, Robert Gary 1945- *AmMWSc 92*
**Pitts**, Ronald James, Sr. 1942- *WhoBlA 92*
**Pitts**, Ruth Eleanor 1939- *WhoEnt 92*
**Pitts**, Terence *WhoAmP 91*
**Pitts**, Thomas Griffin 1935- *AmMWSc 92*
**Pitts**, Vera L. 1931- *WhoBlA 92*
**Pitts**, Wanna Dene 1932- *AmMWSc 92*
**Pitts**, William Clarence 1929- *WhoWest 92*
**Pitts**, William Henry 1914- *WhoBlA 92*
**Pitts**, William Lee, Jr. 1937- *WhoRel 92*
**Pitts Crick**, R. *Who 92*
**Pitts-Tucker**, Robert St John 1909- *Who 92*
**Pittuck**, Douglas 1911- *TwCPaSc*
**Pittz**, Eugene P 1939- *AmMWSc 92*
**Pitzele**, Barnett Sylvain 1942- *WhoMW 92*
**Pitzer**, Kenneth Sanborn 1914- *AmMWSc 92, IntWW 91*
**Pitzer**, Russell Mosher 1938- *AmMWSc 92*
**Pitzner**, Richard William 1946- *WhoAmL 92*
**Pius I** *EncEarC*
**Pius VI** 1717-1799 *BlkwCEP*
**Pius X** 1835-1914 *FacFETw*
**Pius XI** 1857-1939 *EncTR 91 [port], FacFETw*
**Pius XII** 1876-1958 *EncTR 91 [port], FacFETw*
**Piva**, Giulio 1940- *WhoFI 92*
**Pivarnik**, Alfred J *WhoAmP 91*
**Piver**, M Steven 1934- *AmMWSc 92*
**Piver**, Susan Lori 1957- *WhoEnt 92*
**Piveronus**, Peter John, Jr. 1941- *WhoMW 92*
**Pivonka**, William 1930- *AmMWSc 92*
**Pivorun**, Edward Broni 1946- *AmMWSc 92*
**Pivot**, Bernard 1935- *IntAu&W 91, IntWW 91*
**Piwoni**, Marvin Dennis 1947- *AmMWSc 92*
**Piwonka**, Thomas Squire 1937- *AmMWSc 92*
**Pix**, Mary 1666-1720? *BlkwCEP*
**Pix Weston**, John *Who 92*
**Pixerecourt**, Rene de 1773-1844 *GuFrLit 1*
**Pixley**, Alden F 1928- *AmMWSc 92*
**Pixley**, Carl Preston 1942- *AmMWSc 92*
**Pixley**, Emily Chandler 1904- *AmMWSc 92*
**Pixley**, Neville 1905- *Who 92*
**Pixley**, Norman Stewart 1898- *Who 92*
**Piza**, Arthur Luiz de 1928- *IntWW 91*
**Pizam**, Abraham 1937- *WhoFI 92*
**Pizarnik**, Alejandra 1936-1972 *ConSpAP, SpAmWW*
**Pizarro**, Antonio Geraldo 1942- *WhoHisp 92*
**Pizarro**, David 1931- *WhoEnt 92*
**Pizarro**, Francisco 1478-1541 *HisDSpE*
**Pizarro**, Gonzalo 1506-1548 *HisDSpE*
**Pizarro**, Jose *WhoHisp 92*
**Pizarro**, Pedro 1499?-1589 *HisDSpE*
**Pizer**, Elizabeth Hayden 1954- *WhoEnt 92*
**Pizer**, Lewis Ivan 1932- *AmMWSc 92*
**Pizer**, Richard David 1944- *AmMWSc 92*
**Pizer**, Stephen M 1941- *AmMWSc 92*
**Pizer**, Vernon 1918- *WrDr 92*
**Pizey**, Mark 1899- *Who 92*
**Piziak**, Robert 1943- *AmMWSc 92*
**Piziak**, Veronica Kelly 1942- *AmMWSc 92*
**Piziali**, Michael H. 1953- *WhoAmL 92*
**Pizitz**, Jacuelyn Cooper 1941- *WhoWest 92*
**Pizor**, Faith K and Comp, T Allan *ScFEYrs*
**Pizzamiglio**, Albert Theodore *WhoEnt 92*
**Pizzamiglio**, Nancy Alice 1936- *WhoEnt 92*
**Pizzano**, Rudolph 1957- *WhoFI 92*
**Pizzarello**, Donald Joseph 1933- *AmMWSc 92*
**Pizzella**, Anthony Nicola 1957- *WhoFI 92*
**Pizzetti**, Ildebrando 1880-1968 *NewAmDM*
**Pizzey**, Erin Patria Margaret *Who 92*

**Pizzi,** Anthony Charles 1953- *WhoAmP 91*
**Pizzi,** Charles Peter 1950- *WhoFI 92*
**Pizzi,** Donna Lee 1945- *WhoEnt 92*
**Pizzi,** Pier Luigi 1930- *WhoEnt 92*
**Pizzi,** Skip 1954- *WhoEnt 92*
**Pizzica,** Philip Andrew 1945- *AmMWSc 92*
**Pizzimenti,** David Michael 1954- *WhoRel 92*
**Pizzimenti,** John Joseph 1946- *AmMWSc 92*
**Pizzini,** Louis Celeste 1932- *AmMWSc 92*
**Pizzo,** Joseph Francis *AmMWSc 92*
**Pizzo,** Philip A 1944- *AmMWSc 92*
**Pizzo,** Salvatore Vincent 1944- *AmMWSc 92*
**Pizzolato,** Thompson Demetrio 1943- *AmMWSc 92*
**Pizzorno,** Joseph Egidio, Jr. 1947- *WhoWest 92*
**Pizzuti,** Anthony David 1946- *WhoFI 92*
**Pizzuti,** Carolyn Suzanne 1958- *WhoEnt 92*
**Pizzuto,** Emanuelina *WhoEnt 92*
**Pizzuto,** Michael Julian 1943- *WhoEnt 92, WhoMW 92*
**Pizzuto,** William *WhoEnt 92*
**Pjevach,** Michael George 1959- *WhoMW 92*
**Pla,** George L. *WhoHisp 92*
**Pla,** Gwendolyn W 1939- *AmMWSc 92*
**Pla,** Josefina 1909- *SpAmWW*
**Plaa,** Gabriel Leon 1930- *AmMWSc 92*
**Place,** Allen 1955- *WhoAmP 91*
**Place,** Godfrey 1921- *Who 92*
**Place,** Janet Dobbins 1953- *AmMWSc 92*
**Place,** John B. M. 1925- *IntWW 91*
**Place,** Margaret Mikki Lee 1948- *WhoFI 92*
**Place,** Mary Kay *WhoEnt 92*
**Place,** Mary Kay 1947- *IntMPA 92*
**Place,** Ralph L 1936- *AmMWSc 92*
**Place,** Richard Fulton 1942- *WhoAmL 92*
**Place,** Robert Daniel 1941- *AmMWSc 92*
**Place,** Thomas Alan 1938- *AmMWSc 92*
**Place,** Virgil Alan 1924- *AmMWSc 92*
**Placek,** Albert Charles 1950- *WhoMW 92*
**Placeres,** Alfred *WhoHisp 92*
**Placet,** Ronald Vincent 1959- *WhoWest 92*
**Placette,** Adonia Dell 1951- *WhoEnt 92*
**Plache,** Kimberly Marie 1961- *WhoAmP 91*
**Placher,** William Carl 1948- *WhoRel 92*
**Placier,** Philip R. 1933- *WhoAmL 92*
**Placio,** Lee John, Jr. 1934- *WhoAmL 92*
**Placious,** Robert Charles 1923- *AmMWSc 92*
**Placke,** Eric David 1961- *WhoAmL 92*
**Plackman,** Carl 1943- *TwCPaSc*
**Placzek,** Mathew Walter, Jr. 1945- *WhoAmL 92*
**Pladsen,** Clifford James, Jr. 1943- *WhoMW 92*
**Plaeger,** Frederick Joseph, II 1953- *WhoAmL 92*
**Plafker,** George 1929- *AmMWSc 92*
**Plagemann,** Bentz 1913- *IntAu&W 91*
**Plagemann,** Bentz 1913-1991 *ConAu 134*
**Plagemann,** Peter Guenter Wilhelm 1928- *AmMWSc 92*
**Plagens,** Donald John 1937- *WhoMW 92*
**Plagenz,** George Richard 1923- *WhoRel 92*
**Plager,** John Everett 1927- *AmMWSc 92*
**Plager,** S Jay *WhoAmP 91*
**Plager,** S. Jay 1931- *WhoAmL 92*
**Plager,** Steven Paul 1962- *WhoMW 92*
**Plagge,** James Clarence 1911- *AmMWSc 92*
**Plagman,** Linda Marie 1947- *WhoMW 92*
**Plaidy,** Jean *IntAu&W 91X, Who 92, WrDr 92*
**Plain,** Belva *DrAPF 91*
**Plain,** Belva 1918- *IntAu&W 91, WrDr 92*
**Plair,** Norman Vincent 1943- *WhoMW 92*
**Plaisant,** Francois Marcel 1932- *IntWW 91*
**Plaisted,** Robert Leroy 1929- *AmMWSc 92*
**Plaister,** Sydney d1991 *Who 92N*
**Plaistowe,** Ian 1942- *Who 92*
**Plait,** Alan Oscar 1926- *AmMWSc 92*
**Plaja,** Eugenio 1914- *IntWW 91*
**Plakke,** Ronald Keith 1935- *AmMWSc 92*
**Plambeck,** Frank Theodore, Jr. 1931- *WhoEnt 92*
**Plambeck,** James Alan 1938- *AmMWSc 92*
**Plambeck,** Louis, Jr 1912- *AmMWSc 92*
**Plamondon,** Joseph Edward 1941- *AmMWSc 92*
**Plamthottam,** Sebastian S 1951- *AmMWSc 92*
**Plana,** Tony 1953- *ConTFT 9*
**Planas,** Carlos *WhoHisp 92*
**Planata,** Steven Joseph 1955- *WhoEnt 92*
**Planche,** James Robinson 1796-1880 *RfGEnL 91*
**Plancher,** Robert Lawrence 1932- *WhoFI 92*
**Planchon,** Harry Peter, Jr. 1941- *WhoMW 92*
**Planchon,** Roger 1931- *FacFETw, IntWW 91*
**Planck,** Erwin 1893-1945 *EncTR 91*
**Planck,** Max 1858-1947 *EncTR 91 [port]*
**Planck,** Max Karl Ernst Ludwig 1858-1947 *FacFETw, WhoNob 90*
**Plancon,** Pol 1851-1914 *NewAmDM*
**Plane,** Robert Allen 1927- *AmMWSc 92*
**Planeta-Malecka,** Izabela 1930- *IntWW 91*
**Plangere,** Jules L., III 1944- *WhoFI 92*
**Planinc,** Milka, Mrs. 1924- *IntWW 91*
**Planitzer,** Russell E. *WhoFI 92*
**Plank,** Charles Andrews 1928- *AmMWSc 92*
**Plank,** Don Allen 1939- *AmMWSc 92*
**Plank,** Donald Leroy 1937- *AmMWSc 92*
**Plank,** Frank Benjamin, III 1942- *WhoRel 92*
**Plank,** Karl Andrews 1951- *WhoRel 92*
**Plank,** Stephen J 1927- *AmMWSc 92*
**Plank,** William G. 1935- *WhoWest 92*
**Plankey,** Francis William, Jr 1945- *AmMWSc 92*
**Plankis,** Joseph Vitautas 1943- *WhoMW 92*
**Plano,** Jack Charles 1921- *IntAu&W 91, WrDr 92*
**Plano,** Richard James 1929- *AmMWSc 92*
**Planson,** Rollie Joe 1945- *WhoMW 92*
**Plant,** Al O 1930- *WhoAmP 91*
**Plant,** B J 1933- *AmMWSc 92*
**Plant,** Chris 1946- *WhoAmP 91*
**Plant,** David William 1931- *WhoAmL 92*
**Plant,** Mark William 1955- *WhoFI 92*
**Plant,** Mary 1943- *TwCPaSc*
**Plant,** Raymond 1945- *Who 92*
**Plant,** Richard E 1947- *AmMWSc 92*
**Plant,** Robert Anthony 1948- *WhoEnt 92*
**Plant,** William J 1926- *AmMWSc 92*
**Plant,** William James 1944- *AmMWSc 92*
**Planta,** Louis von 1917- *IntWW 91*
**Plante,** David *DrAPF 91*
**Plante,** David 1940- *ConAu 36NR, ConNov 91, IntAu&W 91, LiExTwC, WrDr 92*
**Plante,** Jacques 1929-1986 *FacFETw*
**Plante,** Julian Gerard *WhoMW 92*
**Plante,** Mary Michaelinda 1934- *WhoRel 92*
**Plantey,** Alain 1924- *IntAu&W 91*
**Plantey,** Alain Gilles 1924- *IntWW 91*
**Planting,** Peter John 1937- *WhoWest 92*
**Plantinga,** Alvin *WrDr 92*
**Plantinga,** Alvin 1932- *WhoRel 92*
**Planton,** Stanley Peter, Jr. 1947- *WhoMW 92*
**Plants,** Helen Lester 1925- *AmMWSc 92, WhoMW 92*
**Plantu** 1951- *IntWW 91*
**Planz,** Allen *DrAPF 91*
**Plapinger,** Robert Edwin 1923- *AmMWSc 92*
**Plapp,** Bryce Vernon 1939- *AmMWSc 92*
**Plapp,** Frederick Vaughn 1949- *AmMWSc 92*
**Plapp,** John E 1929- *AmMWSc 92*
**Plascak-Craig,** Faye Dene 1945- *WhoMW 92*
**Plasencia,** Juan de d1590 *HisDSpE*
**Plasencio,** Nellie E. 1925- *WhoHisp 92*
**Plasier,** Leroy J 1942- *WhoAmP 91*
**Plasil,** Franz 1939- *AmMWSc 92*
**Plaskett,** Frederick Joseph 1926- *Who 92*
**Plaskett,** Thomas G. 1943- *WhoFI 92*
**Plaskett,** Thomas George 1943- *IntWW 91*
**Plaskitt,** Piers 1954- *WhoEnt 92*
**Plass,** Gilbert Norman 1920- *AmMWSc 92*
**Plass,** Harold J, Jr 1922- *AmMWSc 92*
**Plassmann,** Elizabeth Hebb 1928- *AmMWSc 92*
**Plassmann,** Eugene Adolph 1921- *AmMWSc 92*
**Plassmeyer,** Norbert Bernard 1938- *WhoAmP 91*
**Plasterer,** George Michael 1951- *WhoRel 92*
**Plastov,** Arkadiy Aleksandrovich 1893-1972 *SovUnBD*
**Plastow,** David 1932- *Who 92*
**Plastow,** David Arnold Stuart 1932- *IntWW 91*
**Plastow,** John Robert 1958- *WhoRel 92*
**Plaszczak,** Roman Thaddeus 1943- *WhoAmL 92*
**Plat,** Richard Vertin 1929- *WhoFI 92*
**Plata,** Armando Luis Carlos 1949- *WhoHisp 92*
**Platau,** Gerard Oscar 1926- *AmMWSc 92*
**Plate,** Charles Alfred 1941- *AmMWSc 92*
**Plate,** Henry 1925- *AmMWSc 92*
**Plate,** Janet Margaret 1943- *AmMWSc 92*
**Plate,** Janet Margaret Dieterle 1943- *WhoMW 92*
**Plate,** Thomas Gordon 1944- *WhoWest 92*
**Plateis,** Marvin Jerome 1931- *WhoFI 92*
**Platek,** Richard Alan 1940- *AmMWSc 92*
**Platek,** S. Frank 1952- *WhoMW 92*
**Platen,** Carl Henrik G:son von 1913- *IntWW 91*
**Plater,** Alan 1935- *WrDr 92*
**Plater,** Alan Frederick 1935- *IntAu&W 91, Who 92*
**Plater,** Emilja 1806-1831 *EncAmaz 91*
**Plater,** Zygmunt Jan Broel 1943- *WhoAmL 92*
**Platford,** Robert Frederick 1933- *AmMWSc 92*
**Plath,** James *DrAPF 91*
**Plath,** Margaret D. 1948- *WhoMW 92*
**Plath,** Scott Richmond 1953- *WhoMW 92*
**Plath,** Sylvia 1932-1963 *BenetAL 91, ConAu 34NR, FacFETw [port], HanAmWH, ModAWWr*
**Platis,** Jim George 1927- *WhoMW 92*
**Platner,** Bronson 1946- *WhoAmP 91*
**Platner,** Edward D 1934- *AmMWSc 92*
**Platner,** Warren 1919- *DcTwDes*
**Platner,** Wesley Stanley 1915- *AmMWSc 92*
**Platnick,** Norman I 1951- *AmMWSc 92*
**Plato** 427?BC-347BC *ScFEYrs*
**Plato** 428BC-346BC *EncEarC*
**Plato** 428?BC-348?BC *CIMLC 8 [port]*
**Plato,** Ann 1820?- *NotBlAW 92*
**Plato,** Chris C 1931- *AmMWSc 92*
**Plato,** Phillip Alexander 1943- *AmMWSc 92*
**Platon,** Metropolitan 1866-1934 *RelLAm 91*
**Platon,** Nicolas 1909- *IntWW 91*
**Platonov,** Sergei Fedorovich 1860-1933 *FacFETw*
**Platonov,** Vladimir Petrovich 1939- *IntWW 91*
**Platos,** Stanley d1991 *NewYTBS 91*
**Platov,** Mariquita *DrAPF 91*
**Platowski,** Andrew C. 1947- *WhoMW 92*
**Platsoucas,** Chris Dimitrios 1951- *AmMWSc 92*
**Platt** *Who 92*
**Platt,** Alan Edward 1936- *AmMWSc 92*
**Platt,** Albert Thomas 1927- *WhoRel 92*
**Platt,** Alexander Hartley 1955- *WhoAmL 92*
**Platt,** Anthony Michael Westlake 1928- *Who 92*
**Platt,** Austin Pickard 1937- *AmMWSc 92*
**Platt,** Charles 1944- *IntAu&W 91, TwCSFW 91, WrDr 92*
**Platt,** Colin 1934- *WrDr 92*
**Platt,** Colin Peter Sherard 1934- *Who 92*
**Platt,** Donald Hewitt 1946- *WhoEnt 92*
**Platt,** Donald R 1923- *WhoAmP 91*
**Platt,** Dwight Rich 1931- *AmMWSc 92*
**Platt,** Eleanor Frances 1938- *Who 92*
**Platt,** Eugene *DrAPF 91*
**Platt,** Eugene 1939- *WrDr 92*
**Platt,** Franklin 1844-1900 *BiInAmS*
**Platt,** Harold Kirby 1942- *WhoAmL 92*
**Platt,** Henry Edmund 1922- *WhoMW 92*
**Platt,** James Earl 1944- *AmMWSc 92*
**Platt,** James Robert 1948- *WhoFI 92, WhoWest 92*
**Platt,** John 1886- *TwCPaSc*
**Platt,** John Rader 1918- *AmMWSc 92*
**Platt,** Jonathan James 1950- *WhoAmL 92*
**Platt,** Joseph Beaven 1915- *AmMWSc 92, WhoWest 92*
**Platt,** Kenneth Allan 1923- *AmMWSc 92, IntWW 91*
**Platt,** Lawrence David 1947- *AmMWSc 92*
**Platt,** Leslie A. 1944- *WhoAmL 92*
**Platt,** Lindsey *Who 92*
**Platt,** Lon Stuart 1952- *WhoAmL 92*
**Platt,** Lucian B 1931- *AmMWSc 92*
**Platt,** Margaret 1931- *Who 92*
**Platt,** Mark E. *WhoEnt 92*
**Platt,** Marvin Stanley *AmMWSc 92*
**Platt,** Milt *IntMPA 92*
**Platt,** Milton M 1921- *AmMWSc 92*
**Platt,** Nicholas 1936- *IntWW 91, WhoAmP 91*
**Platt,** Norman 1920- *Who 92*
**Platt,** Peter 1924- *Who 92*
**Platt,** Peter Godfrey 1937- *WhoAmL 92*
**Platt,** Randall Robert 1952- *WhoEnt 92*
**Platt,** Richard A. *WhoBlA 92*
**Platt,** Robert Swanton, Jr 1925- *AmMWSc 92*
**Platt,** Ronald Dean 1942- *AmMWSc 92*
**Platt,** Stephen 1954- *Who 92*
**Platt,** Stephen Eugene 1945- *WhoAmL 92*
**Platt,** Terence Charles 1936- *Who 92*
**Platt,** Thomas Boyne 1927- *AmMWSc 92*
**Platt,** Thomas Collier 1925- *WhoAmL 92*
**Platt,** Thomas Reid 1949- *AmMWSc 92*
**Platt,** William Henry 1940- *WhoAmL 92*
**Platt,** William James 1893- *Who 92*
**Platt,** William Joshua, III 1942- *AmMWSc 92*
**Platt,** William Rady 1915- *AmMWSc 92*
**Platt,** William Raymond 1951- *WhoWest 92*
**Platt,** Winston Alan 1948- *WhoRel 92*
**Platt Aloia,** Kathryn Ann *AmMWSc 92*
**Platt of Writtle,** Baroness 1923- *Who 92*
**Platten,** Donald C. d1991 *NewYTBS 91 [port]*
**Platten,** Stephen George 1947- *Who 92*
**Platter,** Sanford 1939- *AmMWSc 92*
**Platters,** The *NewAmDM*
**Platthy,** Jeno 1920- *WhoFI 92, WhoMW 92*
**Platthy,** Terrance Lee 1950- *WhoMW 92*
**Plattner,** Karl *IntWW 91N*
**Plattner,** Richard Serber 1952- *WhoAmL 92*
**Platto,** Charles 1945- *WhoAmL 92*
**Platts,** Dennis Robert 1933- *AmMWSc 92*
**Platts,** William Sidney 1928- *AmMWSc 92*
**Platts-Mills,** John Faithful Fortescue 1906- *Who 92*
**Platus,** Daniel Herschel 1932- *AmMWSc 92*
**Platz,** James Ernest 1943- *AmMWSc 92*
**Platz,** Judith Rachel *DrAPF 91*
**Platz,** Matthew S 1951- *AmMWSc 92*
**Platz,** Robert Dole *AmMWSc 92*
**Platzer,** Edward George 1938- *AmMWSc 92*
**Platzer,** Maximilian Franz 1933- *AmMWSc 92*
**Platzer,** William John 1933- *WhoAmL 92*
**Platzker,** Arnold C.G. 1936- *WhoWest 92*
**Platzman,** George William 1920- *AmMWSc 92*
**Platzman,** Philip M 1935- *AmMWSc 92*
**Plaugher,** Michael Jon 1964- *WhoEnt 92*
**Plaush,** Albert Charles *AmMWSc 92*
**Plaut,** Andrew George 1937- *AmMWSc 92*
**Plaut,** Gerhard Wolfgang Eugen 1921- *AmMWSc 92*
**Plaut,** Jonathan Victor 1942- *WhoRel 92*
**Plaut,** Marshall 1944- *AmMWSc 92*
**Plaut,** Roger David 1966- *WhoEnt 92*
**Plaut,** W Gunther 1912- *IntAu&W 91, WrDr 92*
**Plaut,** Walter 1923- *AmMWSc 92*
**Plaut,** Wofl Gunther 1912- *WhoRel 92*
**Plautz,** Donald Melvin 1942- *AmMWSc 92*
**Plautz,** Jolene Marie 1956- *WhoAmP 91*
**Plavec,** Mirek Josef 1925- *AmMWSc 92*
**Plavin,** Richard Jeffrey 1946- *WhoRel 92*
**Plavinsky,** Dmitri 1937- *IntWW 91*
**Plawecki,** David Anthony 1947- *WhoAmP 91*
**Plaxico,** James Samuel 1924- *AmMWSc 92*
**Plaxton,** Cecil Andrew 1902- *Who 92*
**Player,** David Arnott 1927- *Who 92*
**Player,** Denis Sydney 1913- *Who 92*
**Player,** Gary 1935- *IntWW 91, Who 92*
**Player,** Gary Jim 1935- *FacFETw*
**Player,** Mary Anne 1920- *AmMWSc 92, WhoMW 92*
**Player,** Willa B. 1909- *NotBlAW 92 [port], WhoBlA 92*
**Playfair,** Edward 1909- *Who 92*
**Playfair,** Edward Wilder 1909- *IntWW 91*
**Playfair,** Giles 1910- *ConAu 133*
**Playford,** Henry 1657?-1707? *NewAmDM*
**Playford,** John 1623-1686 *NewAmDM*
**Playford,** Jonathan Richard 1940- *Who 92*
**Playter,** Robert Franklin 1934- *AmMWSc 92*
**Plaza,** Sixto 1944- *WhoHisp 92*
**Plaza,** Wayne Frank 1945- *WhoAmL 92*
**Plazak,** Richard A 1937- *WhoIns 92*
**Plazek,** Donald John 1931- *AmMWSc 92*
**Pleas,** John Roland 1938- *WhoBlA 92*
**Pleasant,** Albert E., III 1944- *WhoBlA 92*
**Pleasant,** James Carroll 1936- *AmMWSc 92*
**Pleasant,** James Scott 1943- *WhoAmL 92*
**Pleasant,** Mae Barbee Boone 1919- *WhoBlA 92*
**Pleasant,** Mark Fredrick 1951- *WhoEnt 92*
**Pleasant,** Mary Ellen 1814?-1904 *NotBlAW 92 [port]*
**Pleasant,** Robert Dale 1946- *WhoMW 92*
**Pleasants,** Charles Wrenn 1937- *WhoBlA 92*
**Pleasants,** Elsie W *AmMWSc 92*
**Pleasants,** Henry 1910- *WhoEnt 92, WrDr 92*
**Pleasants,** Julian Randolph 1918- *AmMWSc 92*
**Pleasence,** Donald 1919- *IntMPA 92, IntWW 91, Who 92, WhoEnt 92*
**Pleasure,** David 1938- *AmMWSc 92*
**Pleasure,** Robert Jonathan 1942- *WhoAmL 92*
**Pleban,** Uwe Frederik 1952- *WhoFI 92*
**Plebuch,** Richard Karl 1935- *AmMWSc 92*
**Plechash,** Alexander 1953- *WhoMW 92*
**Pledger,** Richard Alfred 1932- *AmMWSc 92*
**Pledger,** Robert Warren 1944- *WhoFI 92*
**Pledger,** Verline S. 1927- *WhoBlA 92*
**Pleeth,** William 1916- *Who 92*
**Pleggenkuhle,** Lavern Ross 1942- *WhoMW 92*
**Pleijel,** Agneta 1940- *IntAu&W 91*

**Plelmann**, Kenneth Joseph, Jr. 1962- *WhoMW 92*
**Plein**, Elmer Michael 1906- *AmMWSc 92*
**Plein**, Joy Bickmore 1925- *AmMWSc 92*
**Plekhanov**, Georgi Valentinovich 1857-1919 *FacFETw*
**Pleming-Yocum**, Laura Chalker 1913- *WhoRel 92, WhoWest 92*
**Plemmons**, Gerald Thomas 1940- *WhoEnt 92*
**Plemmons**, Robert James 1939- *AmMWSc 92*
**Plemons**, Terry D 1941- *AmMWSc 92*
**Plena**, Jose 1951- *WhoHisp 92*
**Plender**, Richard Owen 1945- *Who 92*
**Plenderleith**, Harold James 1898- *Who 92*
**Plenderleith**, Ian 1943- *Who 92*
**Plenderleith**, Thomas Donald 1921- *Who 92*
**Plendl**, Hans Siegfried 1927- *AmMWSc 92*
**Plenert**, Gerhard Johannes 1948- *WhoFI 92*
**Plenty Coups** 1848-1932 *RelLAm 91*
**Plescia**, Otto John 1921- *AmMWSc 92*
**Plescoff**, Georges 1918- *IntWW 91*
**Pleshette**, Eugene *IntMPA 92*
**Pleshette**, Suzanne *WhoEnt 92*
**Pleshette**, Suzanne 1937- *IntMPA 92*
**Pleskow**, Eric 1924- *IntMPA 92*
**Pleskow**, Eric Roy *WhoEnt 92*
**Pleskow**, Raoul 1931- *NewAmDM, WhoEnt 92*
**Pless**, Irwin Abraham 1925- *AmMWSc 92*
**Pless**, Vera Stepen 1931- *AmMWSc 92*
**Plesset**, Milton Spinoza 1908- *AmMWSc 92*
**Plessis**, Hubert du 1922- *ConCom 92*
**Plessman**, Connie Kay 1950- *WhoMW 92*
**Plessner**, Yakir 1935- *IntWW 91*
**Plessy**, Boake Lucien 1938- *AmMWSc 92*
**Pletcher**, Eldon L. 1922- *ConAu 133*
**Pletcher**, Peggy Jo 1932- *WhoWest 92*
**Pletcher**, Richard H 1935- *AmMWSc 92*
**Pletcher**, Wayne Albert 1942- *AmMWSc 92*
**Pletsch**, Donald James 1912- *AmMWSc 92*
**Plett**, Edelbert Gregory 1939- *AmMWSc 92*
**Plett**, Harvey G. 1933- *WhoRel 92*
**Plett**, Leslie P. 1943- *WhoRel 92*
**Pletta**, Dan Henry 1903- *AmMWSc 92*
**Plettner**, Leo *WhoEnt 92*
**Pletz**, Thomas Gregory 1943- *WhoAmL 92*
**Pleven**, Rene 1901- *IntWW 91*
**Pleven**, Rene Jean 1901- *Who 92*
**Plewa**, Casmere Joseph 1926- *WhoAmP 91*
**Plewa**, John Robert 1945- *WhoAmP 91, WhoMW 92*
**Plewa**, Michael Jacob 1947- *AmMWSc 92*
**Plewes**, Steven Arthur 1954- *WhoFI 92*
**Plexico**, Clark *WhoAmP 91*
**Pleydell-Bouverie** *Who 92*
**Pleyel**, Ignace Joseph 1757-1831 *NewAmDM*
**Pleyer**, Wilhelm 1901-1974 *EncTR 91*
**Pliatzky**, Leo 1919- *IntWW 91, Who 92*
**Plichta**, Thomas Francis 1952- *WhoFI 92*
**Plick et Plock** *ConAu 35NR*
**Plier**, Robert Edwin 1947- *WhoFI 92*
**Plies**, Dennis Bryon 1942- *WhoEnt 92*
**Plievier**, Theodor 1892-1955 *LiExTwC*
**Plimmer**, Jack Reynolds 1927- *AmMWSc 92*
**Plimpton**, George 1927- *WrDr 92*
**Plimpton**, George Ames 1927- *IntWW 91*
**Plimpton**, John Hamilton 1931- *WhoWest 92*
**Plimpton**, Martha 1970- *IntMPA 92*
**Plimpton**, Robert Stanley, Sr. 1925- *WhoWest 92*
**Plimpton**, Rodney F, Jr 1937- *AmMWSc 92*
**Plimpton**, Susan B 1943- *WhoIns 92*
**Pline**, Dale S. 1938- *WhoWest 92*
**Plint**, Colin Arnold 1926- *AmMWSc 92*
**Plinton**, James O., Jr. 1914- *WhoBlA 92*
**Pliny The Younger** 61?-113? *EncEarC*
**Plischke**, Elmer 1914- *WrDr 92*
**Plisetskaya**, Erika Michael 1929- *AmMWSc 92*
**Plisetskaya**, Maiya Mikhailovna 1925- *IntWW 91*
**Plisetskaya**, Maya 1925- *FacFETw*
**Plisetskaya**, Maya Mikhaylovna 1925- *SovUnBD*
**Plishka**, Paul 1941- *NewAmDM*
**Pliskin**, William Aaron 1920- *AmMWSc 92*
**Plitt**, Henry G. 1918- *IntMPA 92, WhoEnt 92*
**Plivier**, Theodor 1892-1955 *LiExTwC*
**Plock**, Richard James 1931- *AmMWSc 92*
**Plocke**, Donald J 1929- *AmMWSc 92*
**Plockinger**, Erwin 1914- *IntWW 91*
**Ploder**, Robert Frank 1942- *WhoFI 92*
**Plodinec**, Matthew John 1946- *AmMWSc 92*
**Ploeser**, Walter Christian 1907- *WhoAmP 91*
**Ploetz**, Alfred 1860-1940 *EncTR 91*
**Plog**, Michael Bellamy 1944- *WhoMW 92*
**Ploger**, Robert Riis 1915- *WhoMW 92*
**Ploiesteanul**, Nifon *WhoRel 92*
**Ploix**, Helene Marie Joseph 1944- *IntWW 91*
**Plomer**, William 1903-1973 *LiExTwC, RfGEnL 91*
**Plomer**, William Charles Franklin 1903-1973 *ConAu 34NR*
**Plomley**, Roy 1914-1985 *FacFETw*
**Plomp**, Teunis 1938- *WhoRel 92*
**Plomski**, Marcella Judy 1946- *WhoMW 92*
**Plona**, Thomas Joseph 1948- *AmMWSc 92*
**Plonkey**, Kenneth Dale 1937- *WhoWest 92*
**Plonsey**, Robert 1924- *AmMWSc 92*
**Plonsker**, Larry 1934- *AmMWSc 92*
**Plonsky**, Andrew Walter 1912- *AmMWSc 92*
**Plonus**, Martin 1933- *AmMWSc 92*
**Ploog**, Holli Ilene 1947- *WhoAmP 91, WhoWest 92*
**Plopper**, Charles George 1944- *AmMWSc 92, WhoWest 92*
**Plosker**, George Raphael 1949- *WhoWest 92*
**Ploth**, David W 1941- *AmMWSc 92*
**Plotinus** 205?-270 *EncEarC*
**Plotka**, Edward Dennis 1938- *AmMWSc 92*
**Plotke**, Frederick 1909- *AmMWSc 92*
**Plotkin**, Albert 1920- *WhoRel 92*
**Plotkin**, Allen 1942- *AmMWSc 92*
**Plotkin**, Dee Keyser 1941- *WhoEnt 92*
**Plotkin**, Eugene Isaak 1932- *AmMWSc 92*
**Plotkin**, Henry H 1927- *AmMWSc 92*
**Plotkin**, Irving Herman 1941- *WhoFI 92*
**Plotkin**, Jacob Manuel 1941- *AmMWSc 92*
**Plotkin**, Manuel D 1923- *WhoAmP 91*
**Plotkin**, Martin 1922- *AmMWSc 92*
**Plotkin**, Paul 1950- *WhoRel 92*
**Plotkin**, Stanley Alan 1932- *AmMWSc 92*
**Plotnick**, Gary David 1941- *AmMWSc 92*
**Plotnick**, Paul William 1947- *WhoAmL 92*
**Plotnicki**, Steven Joel 1954- *WhoEnt 92*
**Plotnikoff**, Nicholas Peter 1927- *AmMWSc 92*
**Plott**, Charles R. 1938- *WhoWest 92*
**Plotz**, Charles M 1921- *AmMWSc 92*
**Plotz**, Paul Hunter 1937- *AmMWSc 92*
**Plotz**, Richard Douglas 1948- *AmMWSc 92*
**Plouffe**, Thomas Louis 1960- *WhoAmL 92*
**Ploughe**, William D 1929- *AmMWSc 92*
**Plourde**, Charles C *WhoAmP 91*
**Plourde**, J Rosaire 1923- *AmMWSc 92*
**Plourde**, Joseph Aurele *Who 92*
**Plourde**, Joseph Aurele 1915- *IntWW 91*
**Plourde**, Ross A. 1956- *WhoAmL 92*
**Plouviez**, Peter William 1931- *Who 92*
**Plovnick**, Mark Stephen 1946- *WhoWest 92*
**Plovnick**, Ross Harris 1942- *AmMWSc 92*
**Plowden** *Who 92*
**Plowden**, Baron 1907- *IntWW 91, Who 92*
**Plowden**, Lady *Who 92*
**Plowden**, Lady 1910- *IntWW 91*
**Plowden**, Alison 1931- *IntAu&W 91, WrDr 92*
**Plowden**, David 1932- *WrDr 92*
**Plowden**, William Julius Lowthian 1935- *Who 92*
**Plowden Roberts**, Hugh Martin 1932- *Who 92*
**Plowman**, Anthony 1905- *Who 92*
**Plowman**, Edward Earl 1931- *WhoRel 92*
**Plowman**, Francis Wilds 1902- *WhoAmP 91*
**Plowman**, Joan Marie 1951- *WhoAmP 91*
**Plowman**, John 1908- *Who 92*
**Plowman**, Margaret Jamison 1937- *WhoWest 92*
**Plowman**, Ronald Dean 1928- *AmMWSc 92*
**Plowman**, Stephanie 1922- *WrDr 92*
**Plowman**, Timothy 1944- *AmMWSc 92*
**Plowright**, David *LesBEnT 92 [port]*
**Plowright**, David Ernest 1930- *IntWW 91, Who 92*
**Plowright**, Joan 1929- *IntMPA 92*
**Plowright**, Joan Ann 1929- *Who 92*
**Plowright**, Joan Anne 1929- *IntWW 91, WhoEnt 92*
**Plowright**, Rosalind Anne 1949- *IntWW 91, Who 92*
**Plowright**, Walter 1923- *Who 92*
**Plows**, William Herbert 1935- *AmMWSc 92*
**Plubell**, Ann Marie 1950- *WhoAmL 92*
**Pluche**, Noel-Antoine 1688-1761 *BlkwCEP*
**Plucknett**, William Kennedy 1916- *AmMWSc 92*
**Pluckrose**, Henry 1931- *IntAu&W 91*
**Plue**, Arnold Frederick 1917- *AmMWSc 92*
**Plueckhahn**, Diana Lynn 1941- *WhoFI 92*
**Plug**, Enrik C. H. A. 1929- *IntWW 91*
**Pluhar**, Zdenek 1913- *IntAu&W 91, IntWW 91*
**Pluimer**, Robert Peter 1941- *WhoRel 92*
**Plum**, Ann Therese 1921- *WhoRel 92*
**Plum**, Bernard Mark 1952- *WhoAmL 92*
**Plum**, Fred 1924- *AmMWSc 92*
**Plum**, Gary Lee 1948- *WhoMW 92*
**Plum**, Jennifer *WrDr 92*
**Plum**, Kenneth Ray 1941- *WhoAmP 91*
**Plum**, Matthias, Jr. 1933- *WhoFI 92*
**Plum**, Patrick *Who 92*
**Plum**, Richard Eugene 1928- *WhoWest 92*
**Plumb** *Who 92*
**Plumb**, Baron 1925- *IntWW 91, Who 92*
**Plumb**, John 1911- *Who 92, WrDr 92*
**Plumb**, John 1927- *TwCPaSc*
**Plumb**, John Alfred 1933- *AmMWSc 92*
**Plumb**, John Harold 1911- *IntAu&W 91, IntWW 91*
**Plumb**, John Laverne 1933- *AmMWSc 92*
**Plumb**, Ralph Edward 1953- *WhoRel 92*
**Plumb**, Robert Charles 1926- *AmMWSc 92*
**Plumb**, Thomas John 1952- *WhoAmP 91*
**Plumb**, William Lansing 1932- *DcTwDes*
**Plumbly**, Derek John 1948- *Who 92*
**Plumbridge**, Robin Allan 1935- *IntWW 91*
**Plume**, John Trevor 1914- *Who 92*
**Plumlee**, Karl Warren 1949- *AmMWSc 92*
**Plumlee**, Millard P, Jr 1921- *AmMWSc 92*
**Plumley**, Jack Martin 1910- *Who 92*
**Plumley**, Peter W. 1928- *WhoMW 92*
**Plumly**, Daniel Harp 1953- *WhoAmL 92*
**Plumly**, Stanley *DrAPF 91*
**Plumly**, Stanley 1930- *BenetAL 91*
**Plumly**, Stanley 1939- *ConPo 91, IntAu&W 91, WrDr 92*
**Plummer** *Who 92*
**Plummer**, Alan 1931- *TwCPaSc*
**Plummer**, Albert J 1908- *AmMWSc 92*
**Plummer**, Amanda 1957- *IntMPA 92, WhoEnt 92*
**Plummer**, Arthur Christopher 1929- *Who 92*
**Plummer**, Ben *IntAu&W 91X, TwCWW 91*
**Plummer**, Benjamin Frank 1936- *AmMWSc 92*
**Plummer**, Bill 1947- *WhoWest 92*
**Plummer**, Brian 1934- *TwCPaSc*
**Plummer**, Charles Carlton 1937- *AmMWSc 92*
**Plummer**, Christopher *Who 92*
**Plummer**, Christopher 1927- *IntMPA 92*
**Plummer**, Christopher 1929- *IntWW 91*
**Plummer**, Daniel C 1927- *WhoIns 92*
**Plummer**, Daniel Clarence, III 1927- *WhoFI 92*
**Plummer**, Desmond 1914- *WrDr 92*
**Plummer**, E Ward 1940- *AmMWSc 92*
**Plummer**, Frederick G 1844?-1913 *BiInAmS*
**Plummer**, Gayther Lynn 1925- *AmMWSc 92*
**Plummer**, Glenn Rodney 1955- *WhoEnt 92*
**Plummer**, Henry Sheppard 1946- *WhoFI 92*
**Plummer**, James Walter 1920- *AmMWSc 92*
**Plummer**, Joel 1933- *WhoAmP 91*
**Plummer**, John Dennis 1943- *WhoRel 92*
**Plummer**, John Thomas 1807-1865 *BiInAmS*
**Plummer**, Jonathan 1761-1819 *BenetAL 91*
**Plummer**, Kenneth Alexander 1928- *WhoMW 92*
**Plummer**, Lawrence H 1940- *WhoAmP 91*
**Plummer**, Leo Heathcote 1923- *Who 92*
**Plummer**, Mark Alan 1936- *AmMWSc 92*
**Plummer**, Matthew W., Sr. 1920- *WhoBlA 92*
**Plummer**, Michael David 1937- *AmMWSc 92*
**Plummer**, Michael Justin 1947- *WhoBlA 92*
**Plummer**, Michael Kenneth 1954- *WhoFI 92*
**Plummer**, Michael V 1945- *AmMWSc 92*
**Plummer**, Milton *WhoBlA 92*
**Plummer**, Nelson W. 1938- *WhoWest 92*
**Plummer**, Ora B. 1940- *WhoBlA 92*
**Plummer**, Otho Raymond 1938- *AmMWSc 92*
**Plummer**, Patricia Lynne Moore *AmMWSc 92*
**Plummer**, Paul James 1946- *WhoFI 92*
**Plummer**, Peter Edward 1919- *Who 92*
**Plummer**, Robin 1931- *TwCPaSc*
**Plummer**, Roger Lawrence 1942- *WhoFI 92, WhoMW 92*
**Plummer**, Stephen Baird 1947- *WhoAmL 92*
**Plummer**, Steven Tsosie 1944- *WhoWest 92*
**Plummer**, Thomas H, Jr 1933- *AmMWSc 92*
**Plummer**, William Allan 1927- *AmMWSc 92*
**Plummer**, William Francis 1947- *WhoWest 92*
**Plummer**, William Torsch 1939- *AmMWSc 92*
**Plummer of St Marylebone**, Baron 1914- *Who 92*
**Plummer-Talley**, Olga Ann 1934- *WhoBlA 92*
**Plump**, Leslie Z. 1934- *WhoAmL 92*
**Plumpp**, Sterling Dominic 1940- *WhoBlA 92*
**Plumpton**, Alan 1926- *Who 92*
**Plumptre** *Who 92*
**Plumstead**, Isobel Mary 1947- *Who 92*
**Plumtree**, A 1936- *AmMWSc 92*
**Plunk**, Robert M 1932- *WhoIns 92*
**Plunket** *Who 92*
**Plunket**, Baron 1925- *Who 92*
**Plunket Greene**, Mary *Who 92*
**Plunkett** *Who 92*
**Plunkett**, James 1920- *ConNov 91, WrDr 92*
**Plunkett**, Jim 1947- *WhoHisp 92*
**Plunkett**, Joseph Charles 1933- *WhoFI 92, WhoWest 92*
**Plunkett**, Maryann 1953- *WhoEnt 92*
**Plunkett**, Michael Stewart 1937- *WhoFI 92*
**Plunkett**, Paul B. 1957- *WhoAmL 92*
**Plunkett**, Paul Edward 1935- *WhoAmL 92*
**Plunkett**, Peter Daniel 1959- *WhoFI 92*
**Plunkett**, Robert 1919- *AmMWSc 92*
**Plunkett**, Robert Lee 1922- *AmMWSc 92*
**Plunkett**, Warren Francis 1920- *WhoIns 92*
**Plunkett**, William Joseph 1921- *Who 92*
**Plunkett**, William Kingsbury 1943- *AmMWSc 92*
**Pluscec**, Josip 1928- *AmMWSc 92*
**Plusquellic**, Donald L 1949- *WhoAmP 91, WhoMW 92*
**Pluth**, Donald John 1936- *AmMWSc 92*
**Pluth**, Joseph John 1943- *AmMWSc 92*
**Plutschow**, Herbert Eugen 1939- *WhoWest 92*
**Plutzer**, Martin David 1944- *AmMWSc 92*
**Pluygers**, Catherine 1955- *WhoEnt 92*
**Pluznik**, Dov Herbert 1935- *AmMWSc 92*
**Plybon**, Benjamin Francis 1930- *AmMWSc 92, WhoMW 92*
**Plybon**, Robert B. 1948- *WhoFI 92*
**Plyler**, Aaron Wesley 1926- *WhoAmP 91*
**Plymale**, Charles E 1935- *AmMWSc 92*
**Plymale**, Donald Lee 1934- *AmMWSc 92*
**Plymale**, Edward Lewis 1914- *AmMWSc 92*
**Plymale**, Harry Hambleton 1928- *AmMWSc 92*
**Plymale**, Steven Frederick 1946- *WhoRel 92*
**Plymat**, William N 1911- *WhoIns 92*
**Plymell**, Charles *DrAPF 91*
**Plymouth**, Archdeacon of *Who 92*
**Plymouth**, Bishop of 1937- *Who 92*
**Plymouth**, Bishop Suffragan of 1939- *Who 92*
**Plymouth**, Earl of 1923- *Who 92*
**Plympton**, George Washington 1827-1907 *BiInAmS*
**Plymyer**, John Robert 1931- *WhoWest 92*
**Plyushch**, Leonid Ivanovich 1939- *SovUnBD*
**Pneuman**, Gerald W 1931- *AmMWSc 92*
**Po**, Henry N 1937- *AmMWSc 92*
**Poag**, Charles N *WhoAmP 91*
**Poag**, Claude Wylie 1937- *AmMWSc 92*
**Poag**, Coleman G 1930- *WhoAmP 91*
**Poage**, George Coleman 1880-1962 *BlkOlyM*
**Poage**, Scott T 1931- *AmMWSc 92*
**Poague**, Leland 1948- *WrDr 92*
**Poague**, Leland Allen 1948- *IntAu&W 91*
**Poananga**, Brian Matauru 1924- *Who 92*
**Poarch**, Sonya Lee Fansler 1941- *WhoWest 92*
**Poate**, John Milo 1940- *AmMWSc 92*
**Poaty-Souchalaty**, Alphonse Mouissou *IntWW 91*
**Pober**, Jordan S *AmMWSc 92*
**Pober**, Kenneth William 1940- *AmMWSc 92*
**Pober**, Zalmon 1939- *AmMWSc 92*
**Pobereskin**, Meyer 1916- *AmMWSc 92*
**Pobereskin**, Stuart 1948- *WhoAmL 92*
**Pobiner**, Bonnie Fay 1959- *AmMWSc 92*
**Pobiner**, Harvey 1927- *AmMWSc 92*
**Pobo**, Kenneth *DrAPF 91*
**Pocahontas** 1595?-1617 *BenetAL 91*
**Pocahontas** 1596?-1617 *PorAmW [port], RComAH*
**Poccia**, Dominic Louis 1945- *AmMWSc 92*
**Pochan**, John Michael 1942- *AmMWSc 92*
**Poche**, Marc B 1934- *WhoAmP 91*
**Pochick**, Francis Edward 1931- *WhoFI 92*
**Pochop**, Larry Otto 1940- *AmMWSc 92*

**Pochron,** Sharon *AmMWSc 92*
**Pocius,** Alphonsus Vytautas 1948- *AmMWSc 92, WhoMW 92*
**Pocker,** Richard James 1954- *WhoAmL 92*
**Pocker,** Yeshayau 1928- *AmMWSc 92, WhoWest 92*
**Pocklington,** Peter H. 1941- *WhoWest 92*
**Pocklington,** Susan Jean 1958- *WhoMW 92*
**Pocknett,** Lawrence W 1934- *WhoIns 92*
**Pocock,** Donald Arthur 1920- *Who 92*
**Pocock,** Gordon James 1933- *Who 92*
**Pocock,** Kenneth Walter 1913- *Who 92*
**Pocock,** Leslie Frederick 1918- *Who 92*
**Pocock,** Robert *TwCWW 91*
**Pocock,** Roger 1865-1941 *ScFEYrs, TwCWW 91*
**Pocock,** Stanley Albert John 1928- *AmMWSc 92*
**Pocock,** Tom *WrDr 92*
**Pocock,** Tom 1925- *IntAu&W 91*
**Pocrass,** Richard Dale 1940- *WhoFI 92*
**Podas,** William M 1916- *AmMWSc 92*
**Podboy,** Alvin Michael, Jr. 1947- *WhoAmL 92, WhoMW 92*
**Podboy,** John Watts 1943- *WhoWest 92*
**Poddar,** Ramendra Kumar 1930- *IntWW 91, Who 92*
**Poddar,** Syamal K 1945- *AmMWSc 92*
**Podell,** Albert N. 1937- *IntMPA 92*
**Podell,** Richard Jay 1943- *WhoAmL 92*
**Podgayev,** Grigoriy Yefimovich 1920- *IntWW 91*
**Podgers,** Alexander Robert 1946- *AmMWSc 92*
**Podgor,** Ellen Sue 1952- *WhoAmL 92*
**Podgorecki,** Adam 1925- *WrDr 92*
**Podgorny,** Nikolay Viktorovich 1903-1983 *SovUnBD*
**Podgorsak,** Ervin B 1943- *AmMWSc 92*
**Podgorski,** Robert Paul 1943- *WhoMW 92*
**Podgorsky,** Arnold Bruce 1951- *WhoAmL 92*
**Podhoretz,** Norman *FacFETw*
**Podhoretz,** Norman 1930- *BenetAL 91, IntWW 91, WhoRel 92, WrDr 92*
**Podhorzer,** Munio *IntMPA 92*
**Podhorzer,** Nathan 1919- *IntMPA 92*
**Podila,** Gopi Krishna 1957- *AmMWSc 92*
**Podio,** Augusto L 1940- *AmMWSc 92*
**Podis,** Eunice Evelyn 1922- *WhoMW 92*
**Podkowinski,** Marian Aleksander 1909- *IntWW 91*
**Podlas,** Thomas Joseph 1940- *AmMWSc 92*
**Podleckis,** Edward Vidas 1956- *AmMWSc 92*
**Podlena,** Frantisek 1940- *IntWW 91*
**Podles,** Eleanor Pauline 1920- *WhoAmP 91*
**Podleski,** Thomas Roger 1934- *AmMWSc 92*
**Podlich,** William F 1944- *WhoIns 92*
**Podlin,** Mark Joseph 1953- *WhoFI 92, WhoMW 92*
**Podmore,** Ian Laing 1933- *Who 92*
**Podolin,** Lee Jacob 1930- *WhoMW 92*
**Podoll,** Lynn Allan 1941- *WhoRel 92*
**Podoloff,** Maurice 1890-1985 *FacFETw*
**Podolsky,** Edward *ScFEYrs*
**Podolsky,** Edward 1902- *ScFEYrs*
**Podolsky,** Richard James 1923- *AmMWSc 92*
**Podopulu,** Soula 1935- *IntAu&W 91*
**Podosek,** Frank A 1941- *AmMWSc 92*
**Podowski,** Michael Zbigniew 1940- *AmMWSc 92*
**Podrabinek,** Aleksandr Pinkhosovich 1953- *SovUnBD*
**Podrebarac,** Eugene George 1929- *AmMWSc 92*
**Podro,** Michael Isaac 1931- *Who 92*
**Podshadley,** Arlon George 1928- *AmMWSc 92*
**Podskalny,** Judith Mary *AmMWSc 92*
**Poduska,** John W, Sr 1937- *AmMWSc 92*
**Poduslo,** Shirley Ellen *AmMWSc 92*
**Podvoysky,** Nicholas Ilich 1880-1948 *FacFETw*
**Podzimek,** Josef 1923- *AmMWSc 92, WhoMW 92*
**Poe,** Anthony John 1929- *AmMWSc 92*
**Poe,** Booker 1936- *WhoBlA 92*
**Poe,** David Russell 1948- *WhoAmL 92*
**Poe,** Donald Patrick 1948- *AmMWSc 92*
**Poe,** Douglas Allan 1942- *WhoAmL 92*
**Poe,** Edgar Allan 1809-1849 *BenetAL 91, RComAH, ScFEYrs*
**Poe,** Harry Lee 1950- *WhoRel 92*
**Poe,** Herbert Watts 1951- *WhoMW 92*
**Poe,** James L. 1950- *WhoRel 92*
**Poe,** Martin 1942- *AmMWSc 92*
**Poe,** Michael Lindsey 1948- *WhoEnt 92*
**Poe,** Reigh Kessen 1949- *WhoAmL 92*
**Poe,** Richard D 1931- *AmMWSc 92*
**Poe,** Robert George, Jr. 1954- *WhoFI 92*
**Poe,** Robert Hilleary 1934- *AmMWSc 92*
**Poe,** Sidney LaMarr 1942- *AmMWSc 92*
**Poe,** Stephen *IntMPA 92*
**Poe,** Steven Dee 1950- *WhoMW 92*
**Poe,** Wellon B 1923- *WhoAmP 91*
**Poe,** William Randall 1955- *WhoWest 92*
**Poedtke,** Carl Henry George, Jr. 1938- *WhoMW 92*
**Poehlein,** Gary Wayne 1936- *AmMWSc 92*
**Poehler,** Theodore O 1935- *AmMWSc 92*
**Poehlman,** John Milton 1910- *AmMWSc 92*
**Poehner,** Raymond Glenn 1923- *WhoFI 92, WhoWest 92*
**Poel,** Robert Herman 1941- *AmMWSc 92*
**Poel,** Russell J 1934- *AmMWSc 92*
**Poellnitz,** Fred Douglas 1944- *WhoBlA 92*
**Poellot,** Luther 1913- *WhoRel 92*
**Poelman,** Ronald Stoddard 1953- *WhoAmL 92*
**Poen,** Monte M. 1930- *WhoWest 92*
**Poenie,** Martin Francis 1951- *AmMWSc 92*
**Poenitz,** Wofgang P 1938- *AmMWSc 92*
**Poensgen,** Gisbert 1923- *IntWW 91*
**Poepoe,** Andrew Keliikuniaupuni 1935- *WhoAmP 91*
**Poeppel,** Roger Brian 1941- *AmMWSc 92*
**Poeppelmeier,** Kenneth Reinhard 1949- *AmMWSc 92, WhoMW 92*
**Poepplein,** Ronald Francis 1950- *WhoAmL 92*
**Poertner,** Lee Anne 1936- *WhoWest 92*
**Poeschel,** Gordon Paul 1942- *AmMWSc 92*
**Poese,** Lester E 1913- *AmMWSc 92*
**Poesnecker,** Gerald E. *WhoRel 92*
**Poet,** Raymond B 1920- *AmMWSc 92*
**Poethig,** Eunice Blanchard 1930- *WhoRel 92*
**Poethig,** Richard Scott 1953- *AmMWSc 92*
**Poetker,** Frances Louise 1912- *WhoFI 92*
**Poett,** Nigel 1907- *Who 92*
**Poettcker,** Henry 1925- *WhoRel 92*
**Poetter,** Bruce E. 1951- *WhoMW 92*
**Poettmann,** Fred H 1919- *AmMWSc 92*
**Poetzsch,** T. Peter 1941- *WhoAmL 92*
**Poff,** Bing C 1936- *WhoAmP 91*
**Poff,** Richard H 1923- *WhoAmP 91*
**Poffenbarger,** Phillip Lynn 1937- *AmMWSc 92*
**Poffenberger,** Virginia 1934- *WhoAmP 91*
**Poganski,** Donald John 1928- *IntAu&W 91, WrDr 92*
**Pogany,** Gilbert Claude 1932- *AmMWSc 92*
**Pogell,** Burton M 1928- *AmMWSc 92*
**Pogemiller,** Lawrence J 1951- *WhoAmP 91*
**Poger,** Ruth 1937- *WhoAmP 91*
**Pogge,** Horst 1926- *WhoFI 92*
**Poggeler,** Otto 1928- *IntWW 91*
**Poggenburg,** John Kenneth, Jr 1935- *AmMWSc 92*
**Poggenedorf,** Richard Jay 1950- *WhoMW 92*
**Poggio,** Andrew John 1941- *AmMWSc 92*
**Poggio,** Gian Franco 1927- *AmMWSc 92*
**Poggione,** P Daniel 1939- *WhoAmP 91*
**Pogo,** A Oscar 1927- *AmMWSc 92*
**Pogo,** Beatriz G T 1932- *AmMWSc 92*
**Pogodin,** Nikolay Fedorovich 1900-1962 *SovUnBD*
**Pogorelich,** Ivo 1958- *IntWW 91*
**Pogorelov,** Aleksey Vasiliyevich 1919- *IntWW 91*
**Pogorski,** Louis August 1922- *AmMWSc 92*
**Pogorzelski,** Henry Andrew 1922- *AmMWSc 92*
**Pogorzelski,** Ronald James 1944- *AmMWSc 92*
**Pogrebin,** Bertrand B. 1934- *WhoAmL 92*
**Pogrebin,** Letty Cottin 1939- *IntAu&W 91, WrDr 92*
**Pogrebnyak,** Yakov Petrovich 1928- *IntWW 91*
**Pogue,** Brent Daryl 1954- *WhoBlA 92*
**Pogue,** Charles Edward, Jr. 1950- *WhoEnt 92*
**Pogue,** D. Eric 1949- *WhoBlA 92*
**Pogue,** Donald Eric 1949- *WhoFI 92*
**Pogue,** Forrest Carlisle 1912- *WrDr 92*
**Pogue,** Frank G., Jr. 1939- *WhoBlA 92*
**Pogue,** John Parker 1925- *AmMWSc 92*
**Pogue,** Lester Clarence 1943- *WhoBlA 92*
**Pogue,** Lloyd Welch 1899- *WhoAmL 92*
**Pogue,** Randall F 1962- *AmMWSc 92*
**Pogue,** Richard Allen 1948- *WhoMW 92*
**Pogue,** Richard Ewert 1930- *AmMWSc 92*
**Pogue,** Richard James 1943- *WhoBlA 92*
**Pogue,** Richard Welch 1928- *WhoAmL 92*
**Pogue,** Samuel Franklin 1919- *WhoMW 92*
**Pogue,** Thomas Franklin 1935- *WhoFI 92, WhoMW 92*
**Pogue,** Welch 1899- *IntWW 91*
**Pogues,** The *ConMus 6 [port]*
**Pogutse,** Oleg Pavlovich 1936- *IntWW 91*
**Pohaha** *EncAmaz 91*
**Poher,** Alain Emile Louis Marie 1909- *IntWW 91*
**Pohjola,** Toivo Topias 1931- *IntWW 91*
**Pohl,** Daniel Martin 1959- *WhoMW 92*
**Pohl,** Douglas George 1944- *AmMWSc 92*
**Pohl,** Frederic 1919- *BenetAL 91*
**Pohl,** Frederik *DrAPF 91*
**Pohl,** Frederik 1919- *ConNov 91, IntAu&W 91, TwCSFW 91, WrDr 92*
**Pohl,** Glyn William 1913- *WhoRel 92*
**Pohl,** James Rudolph *WhoEnt 92*
**Pohl,** John Henning 1944- *WhoWest 92*
**Pohl,** Karl Otto 1929- *IntWW 91, Who 92*
**Pohl,** Kathleen Sharon 1951- *WhoMW 92*
**Pohl,** Lance Rudy *AmMWSc 92*
**Pohl,** Leif Alan 1940- *WhoRel 92*
**Pohl,** Oswald 1892-1951 *EncTR 91 [port]*
**Pohl,** Paul Michael 1948- *WhoAmL 92*
**Pohl,** Richard Walter 1916- *AmMWSc 92*
**Pohl,** Robert O 1929- *AmMWSc 92*
**Pohl,** Victoria Mary 1930- *AmMWSc 92*
**Pohl,** William Francis 1937- *AmMWSc 92*
**Pohlad,** Carl R. *WhoMW 92*
**Pohland,** Albert 1919- *AmMWSc 92*
**Pohland,** Frederick G 1931- *AmMWSc 92*
**Pohland,** Hermann W 1934- *AmMWSc 92*
**Pohle,** Frederick V 1919- *AmMWSc 92*
**Pohler,** Susan J 1955- *WhoAmP 91*
**Pohley,** William John 1949- *WhoMW 92*
**Pohlhaus,** Gaile Margaret 1938- *WhoRel 92*
**Pohlman,** Carlyle George 1931- *WhoMW 92*
**Pohlman,** David Lawrence 1944- *WhoWest 92*
**Pohlman,** Julius 1848-1910 *BiInAmS*
**Pohlman,** Kimberly Kaye 1961- *WhoMW 92*
**Pohlmann,** Hans Peter 1933- *AmMWSc 92*
**Pohlmann,** Juergen Lothar Wolfgang 1934- *AmMWSc 92*
**Pohlmann,** Ken C. 1952- *WhoEnt 92*
**Pohlmann,** Patty Lou 1939- *WhoMW 92*
**Pohlo,** Ross 1931- *AmMWSc 92*
**Pohm,** A V 1927- *AmMWSc 92*
**Pohmer,** Thomas Paul 1952- *WhoFI 92*
**Pohorecky,** Larissa Alexandra 1942- *AmMWSc 92*
**Pohrer,** Jack Edward 1940- *WhoAmP 91*
**Pohrt,** Tom *SmATA 67 [port]*
**Poiani,** Eileen Louise 1943- *AmMWSc 92*
**Poignant,** Raymond 1917- *IntWW 91*
**Poillon,** William Neville *AmMWSc 92*
**Poinar,** George O, Jr 1936- *AmMWSc 92*
**Poincare,** Raymond 1860-1934 *EncTR 91 [port], FacFETw*
**Poincelot,** Raymond Paul, Jr 1944- *AmMWSc 92*
**Poindexter,** Edward Haviland 1930- *AmMWSc 92*
**Poindexter,** Gammiel Gray 1944- *WhoBlA 92*
**Poindexter,** Graham Stuart 1948- *AmMWSc 92*
**Poindexter,** Hildrus A. 1901-1987 *WhoBlA 92N*
**Poindexter,** Jeanne Stove 1936- *AmMWSc 92*
**Poindexter,** John Bruce 1944- *WhoFI 92*
**Poindexter,** John Marlane *IntWW 91*
**Poindexter,** Malcolm P. 1925- *WhoBlA 92*
**Poindexter,** Mark Carey 1951- *WhoEnt 92*
**Poindexter,** Richard Grover 1945- *WhoRel 92*
**Poindexter,** Robert L. 1912- *WhoBlA 92*
**Poindexter,** William Green, IV 1944- *WhoAmP 91*
**Poindexter,** Zeb F. 1929- *WhoBlA 92*
**Poinier,** Porter 1853-1876 *BiInAmS*
**Poinsett,** Alexander C. 1926- *WhoBlA 92*
**Poinsette,** Donald Eugene 1914- *WhoFI 92*
**Pointer Sisters** *NewAmDM*
**Pointer,** James Edgar, Jr 1922- *WhoAmP 91*
**Pointer,** Noel 1956- *WhoBlA 92*
**Pointer,** Richard H. 1944- *WhoBlA 92*
**Pointer,** Richard Hamilton 1944- *AmMWSc 92*
**Pointer,** Sam Clyde, Jr. 1934- *WhoAmL 92*
**Poire,** Jean Gustave 1926- *IntWW 91*
**Poiret,** Jean *IntWW 91*
**Poiret,** Paul 1879-1944 *DcTwDes*
**Poirier,** Anne 1942- *WorArt 1980*
**Poirier,** Carol Sue 1963- *WhoWest 92*
**Poirier,** Charles Philip 1937- *AmMWSc 92*
**Poirier,** Frank Eugene 1940- *AmMWSc 92*
**Poirier,** Gary Raymond 1938- *AmMWSc 92*
**Poirier,** Jacques Charles 1927- *AmMWSc 92*
**Poirier,** John Anthony 1932- *AmMWSc 92, WhoMW 92*
**Poirier,** Kevin 1940- *WhoAmP 91*
**Poirier,** Lionel Albert 1937- *AmMWSc 92*
**Poirier,** Louis 1910- *IntAu&W 91*
**Poirier,** Louis 1918- *AmMWSc 92*
**Poirier,** Miriam Christine Mohrhoff 1940- *AmMWSc 92*
**Poirier,** Patrick 1942- *WorArt 1980*
**Poirier,** Paul N 1948- *WhoAmP 91*
**Poirier,** Philip P. 1920-1979 *ConAu 133*
**Poirier,** Richard 1925- *IntAu&W 91, WrDr 92*
**Poirier,** Richard Oveila 1947- *WhoEnt 92, WhoFI 92, WhoWest 92*
**Poirier,** Robert Victor 1939- *AmMWSc 92*
**Poirier,** Victor L 1941- *AmMWSc 92*
**Poirot,** James Wesley 1931- *WhoFI 92, WhoWest 92*
**Poirot-Delpech,** Bertrand M. A. H. 1929- *IntWW 91*
**Poirrier,** Michael Anthony 1942- *AmMWSc 92*
**Pois,** Joseph 1905- *WhoAmL 92, WhoFI 92*
**Poisner,** Alan Mark 1934- *AmMWSc 92*
**Poitevint,** Alec Loyd, II 1947- *WhoAmP 91*
**Poitier,** Sidney *WhoEnt 92*
**Poitier,** Sidney 1924- *FacFETw, IntWW 91, WhoBlA 92*
**Poitier,** Sidney 1927- *IntMPA 92, Who 92*
**Pojanowski,** Joseph A, III 1948- *WhoAmP 91*
**Pojasek,** Robert B *AmMWSc 92*
**Pojeta,** John, Jr 1935- *AmMWSc 92*
**Poka Laenui** 1946- *WhoAmL 92*
**Pokagon,** Simon, Chief 1830-1899 *BenetAL 91*
**Pokaski,** Daniel Francis 1949- *WhoAmP 91*
**Poker Alice** 1851-1930 *EncAmaz 91*
**Pokorni,** Orysia 1938- *WhoEnt 92, WhoMW 92*
**Pokornowski,** Ronald Felix 1933- *WhoMW 92*
**Pokorny,** Alex Daniel 1918- *AmMWSc 92*
**PoKorny,** Fern Kathryn 1949- *WhoAmP 91*
**Pokorny,** Franklin Albert 1930- *AmMWSc 92*
**Pokorny,** Gerold E 1928- *AmMWSc 92*
**Pokorny,** Joel 1940- *AmMWSc 92*
**Pokorny,** Kathryn Stein 1944- *AmMWSc 92*
**Pokorski,** Robert James 1952- *WhoMW 92*
**Pokoski,** John Leonard 1937- *AmMWSc 92*
**Pokotilow,** Manny David 1938- *WhoAmL 92*
**Pokrant,** Marvin Arthur 1943- *AmMWSc 92*
**Pokras,** Harold Herbert 1918- *AmMWSc 92*
**Pokras,** Sheila Frances Grabelle 1935- *WhoAmP 91*
**Pokrovsky,** Mikhail Nikolaevich 1868-1932 *SovUnBD*
**Pokrovsky,** Valentin *IntWW 91*
**Pol Pot** 1928- *FacFETw, IntWW 91*
**Pol,** Anne 1947- *WhoFI 92*
**Pol,** Louis George 1949- *WhoMW 92*
**Polac,** Michel 1930- *IntWW 91*
**Polach,** Jaroslav G. 1914- *WrDr 92*
**Polach,** Jaroslav Jay George 1914- *WhoFI 92*
**Polachek,** Solomon William 1945- *WhoFI 92*
**Polack,** Joseph A 1920- *AmMWSc 92*
**Polahar,** Andrew Francis 1950- *AmMWSc 92*
**Polak,** Andrew Joseph 1911- *WhoAmP 91*
**Polak,** Arnold 1927- *AmMWSc 92*
**Polak,** Cornelia Julia 1908- *Who 92*
**Polak,** Elijah 1931- *AmMWSc 92*
**Polak,** George 1923- *WhoFI 92*
**Polak,** Jacques Jacobus 1914- *IntWW 91, WhoFI 92*
**Polak,** Joel Allan 1937- *AmMWSc 92*
**Polak,** Julia Margaret 1939- *Who 92*
**Polak,** Vivian Louise 1952- *WhoAmL 92*
**Polak,** Werner L. 1936- *WhoAmL 92*
**Polakoff,** Abe *WhoEnt 92*
**Polakoff,** Keith 1941- *WrDr 92*
**Polakoff,** Keith Ian 1941- *WhoWest 92*
**Polakoski,** Kenneth Leo 1944- *AmMWSc 92*
**Polan,** Carl E 1931- *AmMWSc 92*
**Polan,** Charles M, Jr *WhoAmP 91*
**Polan,** David Jay 1951- *WhoWest 92*
**Polanco,** Richard 1951- *WhoAmP 91*
**Polanco,** Richard G. 1951- *WhoHisp 92*
**Poland,** Alan P 1940- *AmMWSc 92*
**Poland,** Albert 1941- *WhoEnt 92*
**Poland,** Arthur I 1943- *AmMWSc 92*
**Poland,** Dorothy 1937- *IntAu&W 91, WrDr 92*
**Poland,** Edmund Nicholas 1917- *Who 92*
**Poland,** Jack Dean 1930- *AmMWSc 92*
**Poland,** James Leroy 1940- *AmMWSc 92*
**Poland,** John C 1939- *AmMWSc 92*
**Poland,** Joseph Fairfield 1908- *AmMWSc 92*
**Poland,** Karyn Jean Simon 1952- *WhoEnt 92*
**Poland,** Marguerite 1950- *WrDr 92*
**Poland,** Richard Clayton 1947- *WhoAmP 91*
**Poland,** Richard Domville 1914- *Who 92*
**Poland,** Russell E *AmMWSc 92*

**Poland**, Stephen Glen 1939- *WhoMW 92*
**Polaner**, Jerome L 1915- *AmMWSc 92*
**Polani**, Paul Emanuel 1914- *IntWW 91, Who 92*
**Polanski**, Roman 1933- *FacFETw, IntDcF 2-2 [port], IntMPA 92, IntWW 91, WhoEnt 92*
**Polansky**, Marilyn MacArthur *AmMWSc 92*
**Polansky**, Sol 1926- *WhoAmP 91*
**Polanyi**, John Charles 1929- *AmMWSc 92, IntWW 91, Who 92, WhoNob 90*
**Polascik**, Mary Ann 1940- *WhoMW 92*
**Polatnick**, Jerome 1922- *AmMWSc 92*
**Polavarapu**, Prasad Leela *AmMWSc 92*
**Polavieja**, Camilo Garcia de *HisDSpE*
**Polay**, Bruce 1949- *WhoEnt 92*
**Polcyn**, Daniel Stephen 1933- *AmMWSc 92, WhoMW 92*
**Pole** *Who 92*
**Pole**, Jack Richon 1922- *IntAu&W 91, IntWW 91, Who 92, WrDr 92*
**Pole**, Nelson 1941- *WhoMW 92*
**Pole**, Peter Van Notten 1921- *Who 92*
**Polebaum**, Mark Neal 1952- *WhoAmL 92*
**Polednik**, Jindrich 1937- *IntWW 91*
**Poledouris**, Basil *IntMPA 92*
**Polejes**, J D 1934- *AmMWSc 92*
**Polelle**, Michael J. 1938- *WhoAmL 92*
**Polemitou**, Olga Andrea 1950- *WhoFI 92*
**Polen-Dorn**, Linda Frances 1945- *WhoFI 92*
**Polenberg**, Richard 1937- *IntAu&W 91, WrDr 92*
**Polenske**, Karen Rosel 1937- *WhoFI 92*
**Polestak**, Walter John S 1926- *AmMWSc 92*
**Polet**, Herman 1930- *AmMWSc 92*
**Poletti**, Alan Ronald 1937- *IntWW 91*
**Poletti**, Syria 1921- *SpAmWW*
**Poletti**, Ugo 1914- *IntWW 91, WhoRel 92*
**Polevoy**, Boris 1908-1981 *SovUnBD*
**Polevoy**, Nancy Tally 1944- *WhoAmL 92*
**Polgar**, George 1919- *AmMWSc 92*
**Polgar**, Laszlo 1947- *IntWW 91*
**Polgar**, Peter 1936- *WhoWest 92*
**Polge**, Christopher 1926- *Who 92*
**Polge**, Robert J 1928- *AmMWSc 92*
**Polglase**, William James 1917- *AmMWSc 92*
**Polhemus**, John Thomas 1929- *AmMWSc 92*
**Polhemus**, Neil W 1951- *AmMWSc 92*
**Polhill**, John Bowen 1939- *WhoRel 92*
**Poli**, Corrado 1935- *AmMWSc 92*
**Poli**, Rinaldo 1956- *AmMWSc 92*
**Poliak**, Aaron 1925- *AmMWSc 92*
**Poliakoff**, Matthew 1919- *WhoAmP 91*
**Poliakoff**, Stephen *Who 92*
**Poliakoff**, Stephen 1953- *IntAu&W 91, WrDr 92*
**Policansky**, David J 1944- *AmMWSc 92*
**Police** *FacFETw*
**Police**, The *NewAmDM*
**Polich**, Joseph Martin, Jr. 1947- *WhoMW 92*
**Policoff**, Susan Lewis *DrAPF 91*
**Policy**, Vincent Mark 1948- *WhoAmL 92*
**Polier**, Dan A. *IntMPA 92*
**Polier**, Marcy Zalben 1952- *WhoEnt 92*
**Poliferno**, Mario Joseph 1930- *AmMWSc 92*
**Polik**, William Frederick 1960- *AmMWSc 92*
**Polikoff**, Benet, Jr. 1936- *WhoAmL 92*
**Polillo**, Sergio 1917- *IntWW 91*
**Polimeni**, Albert D 1938- *AmMWSc 92*
**Polimeni**, Philip Iniziato 1934- *AmMWSc 92*
**Polin**, Donald 1925- *AmMWSc 92*
**Polin**, Milton Harold 1930- *WhoRel 92*
**Polin**, Raymond 1910- *IntWW 91*
**Poliner**, Robert S 1943- *WhoAmP 91*
**Poling**, Bruce Earl 1944- *AmMWSc 92*
**Poling**, Clyde Edward 1914- *AmMWSc 92*
**Poling**, Craig 1953- *AmMWSc 92*
**Poling**, Daniel Alfred 1884-1968 *RelLAm 91*
**Poling**, George Wesley 1935- *AmMWSc 92*
**Poling**, Harold Arthur 1925- *IntWW 91, WhoFI 92, WhoMW 92*
**Poling**, Kermit William 1941- *WhoRel 92*
**Poling**, Richard Duane 1955- *WhoAmL 92*
**Poling**, Stephen Michael 1946- *AmMWSc 92*
**Poling**, Wayne Allen 1950- *WhoRel 92*
**Polinger**, David Harris 1927- *WhoEnt 92*
**Polinsky**, A. Mitchell 1948- *WhoAmL 92*
**Polinsky**, Janet 1930- *WhoAmP 91*
**Polinsky**, Robert Alexander 1941- *WhoAmP 91*
**Polinsky**, Ronald John 1948- *AmMWSc 92*
**Polinszky**, Karoly 1922- *IntWW 91*
**Polis**, Gary Allan 1946- *AmMWSc 92*
**Polis**, Michael Philip 1943- *AmMWSc 92*
**Polis**, Samuel 1926- *WhoWest 92*
**Polish**, Daniel Friedland 1942- *WhoRel 92*
**Polish**, Jacob d1991 *NewYTBS 91*
**Polish**, John 1917- *WhoAmP 91*
**Polish**, William Matthew 1948- *WhoEnt 92*
**Polisi**, Joseph William 1947- *WhoEnt 92*
**Politan**, Nicholas H. 1935- *WhoAmL 92*
**Polite**, Carlene Hatcher 1932- *WhoBlA 92*
**Polite**, Craig K. 1947- *WhoBlA 92*
**Polite**, Frank *DrAPF 91*
**Polite**, Marie Ann 1954- *WhoBlA 92*
**Polite**, Theron Jerome 1930- *WhoBlA 92*
**Politella**, Dario 1921- *WrDr 92*
**Politis**, Demetrios V. 1960- *WhoMW 92*
**Politis**, Timothy Jude 1944- *WhoFI 92*
**Polito**, Frank Joseph 1952- *WhoEnt 92*
**Polito**, William F. d1991 *NewYTBS 91 [port]*
**Polito**, William Philip 1938- *WhoAmL 92*
**Politte**, Eric Glynn 1960- *WhoFI 92*
**Politte**, Richard Andrew 1958- *WhoMW 92*
**Politz**, Henry A 1932- *WhoAmP 91*
**Politz**, Henry Anthony 1932- *WhoAmL 92*
**Politz**, Nyle Anthony 1953- *WhoAmL 92*
**Politzer**, Hugh David *AmMWSc 92*
**Politzer**, Peter Andrew 1937- *AmMWSc 92*
**Politzer**, S Robert 1929- *WhoAmP 91*
**Polivka**, Brian Edward 1952- *WhoMW 92*
**Polivka**, Raymond Peter 1929- *AmMWSc 92*
**Polivnick**, Paul 1947- *WhoEnt 92*
**Polk**, Anthony Joseph 1941- *WhoBlA 92*
**Polk**, C 1920- *AmMWSc 92*
**Polk**, Carol Fultz 1952- *WhoFI 92*
**Polk**, Charles Carrington 1892-1990 *WhoBlA 92N*
**Polk**, Conrad Joseph 1939- *AmMWSc 92*
**Polk**, David Patrick 1940- *WhoRel 92*
**Polk**, Don 1955- *WhoBlA 92*
**Polk**, Donna Lee 1943- *WhoAmP 91*
**Polk**, Eugene Steven, Sr. 1939- *WhoBlA 92*
**Polk**, Gene-Ann 1926- *WhoBlA 92*
**Polk**, George Douglas 1919- *WhoBlA 92*
**Polk**, Hiram Carey, Jr 1936- *AmMWSc 92*
**Polk**, James K 1795-1849 *RComAH*
**Polk**, James Knox 1795-1849 *AmPolLe [port], BenetAL 91*
**Polk**, John George 1932- *WhoFI 92*
**Polk**, Judith A 1942- *WhoAmP 91*
**Polk**, Lee 1923- *WhoEnt 92*
**Polk**, Lee Thomas 1945- *WhoAmL 92*
**Polk**, Lorna Marie 1948- *WhoBlA 92*
**Polk**, Malcolm Benny 1938- *AmMWSc 92*
**Polk**, Peter Patrick 1936- *WhoMW 92*
**Polk**, Richard A. 1936- *WhoBlA 92*
**Polk**, Robert Forrest 1947- *WhoMW 92*
**Polk**, Robert L. 1928- *WhoBlA 92*
**Polk**, Ron Lamont 1955- *WhoBlA 92*
**Polk**, William C. 1935- *WhoBlA 92*
**Polk**, William Mecklenberg 1844-1918 *BiInAmS*
**Polk**, William Merrill 1935- *WhoAmP 91*
**Polka**, Matthew Merle 1959- *WhoAmL 92*
**Polke**, Sigmar 1941- *WorArt 1980*
**Polking**, John C 1934- *AmMWSc 92*
**Polking**, Kirk 1925- *WrDr 92*
**Polking**, Kirk Dorothy 1925- *WhoMW 92*
**Polkinghorne**, John Charlton 1930- *IntWW 91, Who 92*
**Polkowski**, Delphine Theresa 1930- *WhoMW 92*
**Polkowski**, Lawrence B 1929- *AmMWSc 92*
**Poll**, Edward 1941- *WhoFI 92*
**Poll**, Heinz 1926- *WhoEnt 92, WhoMW 92*
**Poll**, Jacobus Daniel 1930- *AmMWSc 92*
**Poll**, Martin H. *IntMPA 92*
**Poll**, Martin Harvey *WhoEnt 92*
**Pollack**, Alan Myron 1958- *WhoWest 92*
**Pollack**, Andrew Gerard 1958- *WhoFI 92*
**Pollack**, Anita Jean 1946- *Who 92*
**Pollack**, Annette Thieman 1953- *WhoEnt 92*
**Pollack**, Ben 1903-1971 *NewAmDM*
**Pollack**, Bernard Leonard 1920- *AmMWSc 92*
**Pollack**, Bruce Robert 1953- *WhoEnt 92*
**Pollack**, Drue 1947- *WhoEnt 92*
**Pollack**, Edward 1931- *AmMWSc 92*
**Pollack**, Emanuel Davis 1942- *AmMWSc 92, WhoMW 92*
**Pollack**, Gerald A. 1929- *WhoFI 92*
**Pollack**, Gerald H 1940- *AmMWSc 92*
**Pollack**, Gerald Leslie 1933- *AmMWSc 92, WhoMW 92*
**Pollack**, Henry Nathan 1936- *AmMWSc 92*
**Pollack**, Herbert 1905- *AmMWSc 92*
**Pollack**, Ilana 1946- *IntWW 91*
**Pollack**, Irwin W 1927- *AmMWSc 92*
**Pollack**, J Dennis 1931- *AmMWSc 92*
**Pollack**, James Barney 1938- *AmMWSc 92*
**Pollack**, Jane Susan 1945- *WhoAmL 92, WhoEnt 92*
**Pollack**, Jeffrey Lee 1945- *WhoFI 92*
**Pollack**, Jeffrey Miles 1952- *WhoEnt 92*
**Pollack**, Jerome Marvin 1926- *AmMWSc 92*
**Pollack**, Joe 1931- *WhoEnt 92, WhoMW 92*
**Pollack**, Joseph 1939- *WhoFI 92*
**Pollack**, Lana 1942- *WhoAmP 91*
**Pollack**, Louis 1920- *AmMWSc 92*
**Pollack**, Louis Rubin 1919- *AmMWSc 92*
**Pollack**, Maxwell Aaron 1915- *AmMWSc 92*
**Pollack**, Michael Joel 1942- *WhoAmL 92, WhoEnt 92*
**Pollack**, Milton 1906- *WhoAmL 92*
**Pollack**, Rachel *DrAPF 91, TwCSFW 91*
**Pollack**, Ralph Martin 1943- *AmMWSc 92*
**Pollack**, Reginald 1924- *WrDr 92*
**Pollack**, Rhoda-Gale 1937- *WhoEnt 92*
**Pollack**, Richard 1935- *AmMWSc 92*
**Pollack**, Robert 1933- *WhoIns 92*
**Pollack**, Robert Elliot 1940- *AmMWSc 92*
**Pollack**, Robert Leon 1926- *AmMWSc 92*
**Pollack**, Sidney Solomon 1929- *AmMWSc 92*
**Pollack**, Solomon R 1934- *AmMWSc 92*
**Pollack**, Stanley P. 1928- *WhoAmL 92, WhoFI 92*
**Pollack**, Stuart Alan 1951- *WhoRel 92*
**Pollack**, Sydney 1934- *IntDcF 2-2 [port], IntMPA 92, IntWW 91, WhoEnt 92*
**Pollack**, Sylvia Byrne 1940- *AmMWSc 92*
**Pollack**, William 1926- *AmMWSc 92*
**Pollak**, Barth 1928- *AmMWSc 92*
**Pollak**, Edward 1932- *AmMWSc 92*
**Pollak**, Edward Barry 1934- *WhoFI 92*
**Pollak**, Emil John 1947- *AmMWSc 92*
**Pollak**, Fred Hugo 1935- *AmMWSc 92*
**Pollak**, Henry Otto 1927- *AmMWSc 92*
**Pollak**, Jay Mitchell 1937- *WhoAmL 92*
**Pollak**, Jerry Leslie 1929- *WhoFI 92*
**Pollak**, Kurt 1933- *AmMWSc 92*
**Pollak**, Leonard A. 1952- *WhoFI 92*
**Pollak**, Michael 1926- *AmMWSc 92*
**Pollak**, Norman L. 1931- *WhoWest 92*
**Pollak**, Ruth Scheinfeld 1929- *WhoEnt 92*
**Pollak**, Victor Eugene 1926- *AmMWSc 92, WhoMW 92*
**Pollak**, Victor Louis 1930- *AmMWSc 92*
**Pollak**, Viktor A 1917- *AmMWSc 92*
**Pollak**, William Maurice 1950- *WhoAmL 92*
**Pollan**, Carolyn Joan 1937- *WhoAmP 91*
**Pollan**, Stephen Michael 1929- *WhoAmL 92, WhoFI 92*
**Pollan-Cohen**, Shirley B. *DrAPF 91*
**Polland**, Madeleine A 1918- *IntAu&W 91, SmATA 68 [port], WrDr 92*
**Polland**, Rebecca Robbins 1922- *WhoFI 92*
**Polland**, Stephen Max 1939- *WhoMW 92*
**Pollara**, Bernard 1927- *AmMWSc 92*
**Pollard**, Alfonso McInham 1952- *WhoBlA 92*
**Pollard**, Alton Brooks, III 1956- *WhoBlA 92, WhoRel 92*
**Pollard**, Antony John Griffin 1937- *Who 92*
**Pollard**, Arthur 1922- *WrDr 92*
**Pollard**, Arthur Joseph 1956- *AmMWSc 92*
**Pollard**, B Tommy 1941- *WhoAmP 91*
**Pollard**, Barry *Who 92*
**Pollard**, Bernard 1927- *Who 92*
**Pollard**, Brian Ray 1952- *WhoAmL 92*
**Pollard**, Charles 1945- *Who 92*
**Pollard**, Charles Barry 1927- *Who 92*
**Pollard**, Charles Oscar, Jr 1937- *AmMWSc 92*
**Pollard**, Christopher Charles 1957- *Who 92*
**Pollard**, Diane S. 1944- *WhoBlA 92*
**Pollard**, Douglas Frederick William 1940- *AmMWSc 92*
**Pollard**, Edward A. 1831-1872 *BenetAL 91*
**Pollard**, Emily Frances *WhoBlA 92*
**Pollard**, Eric Wilton 1917- *WhoWest 92*
**Pollard**, Eve *Who 92*
**Pollard**, Frances Marguerite 1920- *WhoMW 92*
**Pollard**, Frank Edward 1932- *WhoAmL 92*
**Pollard**, Franklin Dawes 1934- *WhoRel 92*
**Pollard**, Frederick Douglas, Jr 1915- *BlkOlyM*
**Pollard**, Freeman Wallace 1922- *WhoBlA 92*
**Pollard**, Fritz 1894-1986 *FacFETw*
**Pollard**, G B, Jr *WhoAmP 91*
**Pollard**, Harvey Bruce 1943- *AmMWSc 92*
**Pollard**, James Edward 1943- *AmMWSc 92*
**Pollard**, Jeffrey William 1950- *AmMWSc 92*
**Pollard**, John 1914- *IntAu&W 91, WrDr 92*
**Pollard**, John Henry 1933- *AmMWSc 92*
**Pollard**, John Oliver 1937- *WhoAmL 92*
**Pollard**, John Stanley 1922- *IntAu&W 91*
**Pollard**, Joseph Augustine 1924- *WhoFI 92*
**Pollard**, Joseph Warren 1956- *WhoFI 92*
**Pollard**, Kenneth Michael 1952- *WhoWest 92*
**Pollard**, Michael J. 1939- *IntMPA 92*
**Pollard**, Michael Ross 1947- *WhoAmL 92*
**Pollard**, Morris 1916- *AmMWSc 92*
**Pollard**, Muriel Ransom 1953- *WhoBlA 92*
**Pollard**, Odell 1927- *WhoAmP 91*
**Pollard**, Overton Price 1933- *WhoAmL 92*
**Pollard**, Percival 1869-1911 *BenetAL 91*
**Pollard**, Percy Edward, Sr. 1943- *WhoBlA 92*
**Pollard**, Raymond J. 1932- *WhoBlA 92*
**Pollard**, Richard Byrd *AmMWSc 92*
**Pollard**, Richard Frederick David 1941- *Who 92*
**Pollard**, Robert Eugene 1924- *AmMWSc 92*
**Pollard**, Sidney 1925- *Who 92, WrDr 92*
**Pollard**, Terry Wayne 1958- *WhoRel 92*
**Pollard**, Thomas Dean 1942- *AmMWSc 92*
**Pollard**, Thomas Evan 1921- *WrDr 92*
**Pollard**, Timothy David 1959- *WhoEnt 92*
**Pollard**, William Blake 1950- *AmMWSc 92*
**Pollard**, William E. 1915- *WhoBlA 92*
**Pollard**, William Lawrence 1944- *WhoBlA 92*
**Pollari**, Robert William 1925- *WhoAmP 91*
**Pollart**, Dale Flavian 1932- *AmMWSc 92*
**Pollatsek**, Harriet Suzanne 1942- *AmMWSc 92*
**Pollay**, Michael 1931- *AmMWSc 92*
**Pollay**, Richard L. 1932- *WhoMW 92*
**Pollchik**, Allan Lee 1949- *WhoWest 92*
**Pollen**, Arabella Rosalind Hungerford 1961- *IntWW 91*
**Pollen**, John Michael Hungerford 1919- *Who 92*
**Pollen**, Peregrine Michael Hungerford 1931- *Who 92*
**Pollet**, Elizabeth *DrAPF 91*
**Pollet**, Richard *WhoAmL 92*
**Pollet**, Sylvester *DrAPF 91*
**Pollexfen**, Jack 1918- *IntMPA 92*
**Pollexfen**, Muriel *ScFEYrs*
**Polley**, Edward Herman 1923- *AmMWSc 92*
**Polley**, Ernest 1936- *WhoAmP 91*
**Polley**, John Richard 1917- *AmMWSc 92*
**Polley**, Judith Anne 1938- *IntAu&W 91, WrDr 92*
**Polley**, Lowell David 1948- *AmMWSc 92*
**Polley**, Margaret J 1933- *AmMWSc 92*
**Polley**, Max Eugene 1928- *WhoRel 92*
**Polley**, Nora Catharine 1947- *WhoEnt 92*
**Polley**, Richard Donald 1937- *WhoFI 92*
**Polley**, Terry Lee 1947- *WhoAmL 92, WhoWest 92*
**Polley**, William Alphonse 1942- *WhoMW 92*
**Polley**, William Emory 1921- *WhoBlA 92*
**Pollicino**, Joseph Anthony 1939- *WhoFI 92*
**Pollihan**, Thomas Henry 1949- *WhoAmL 92*
**Pollikoff**, Max 1904-1984 *NewAmDM*
**Pollin**, Jack Murph 1922- *AmMWSc 92*
**Pollin**, Pierre Louis 1947- *WhoMW 92*
**Pollin**, William 1922- *AmMWSc 92*
**Pollinger**, William Joshua 1944- *WhoAmL 92*
**Pollington**, Viscount 1959- *Who 92*
**Pollini**, Maurizio 1942- *IntWW 91, NewAmDM*
**Pollis**, Marcia Feldman 1937- *WhoMW 92*
**Pollitt**, David *WhoEnt 92*
**Pollitt**, Ernesto 1938- *WhoWest 92*
**Pollitt**, John 1926- *IntWW 91*
**Pollitt**, Katha *DrAPF 91*
**Pollitt**, Richard Malone, Jr 1952- *WhoAmP 91*
**Pollitzer**, William Sprott 1923- *AmMWSc 92*
**Pollner**, Martin Robert 1934- *WhoAmL 92*
**Pollnow**, Gilbert Frederick 1925- *AmMWSc 92*
**Pollnow**, Jan L *WhoIns 92*
**Pollock** *Who 92*
**Pollock**, Alexander 1944- *Who 92*
**Pollock**, Alexander John 1943- *WhoFI 92*
**Pollock**, Ann H. 1956- *WhoAmL 92*
**Pollock**, Ann Kelly 1959- *WhoAmL 92*
**Pollock**, Bruce McFarland 1926- *AmMWSc 92*
**Pollock**, Channing 1880-1946 *BenetAL 91*
**Pollock**, Charles 1930- *DcTwDes*
**Pollock**, D D 1918- *AmMWSc 92*
**Pollock**, Dale 1950- *IntMPA 92*
**Pollock**, David Jeffrey 1951- *WhoMW 92*
**Pollock**, David John Frederick 1942- *Who 92*
**Pollock**, David Linton d1991 *Who 92N*
**Pollock**, Earl Edward 1928- *WhoAmL 92*
**Pollock**, Edward G 1931- *AmMWSc 92*
**Pollock**, Ellen Clara *Who 92*
**Pollock**, Elliot B. 1959- *WhoEnt 92*
**Pollock**, Frank Lillie 1876- *ScFEYrs*
**Pollock**, Franklin 1926- *AmMWSc 92*
**Pollock**, Fred 1937- *TwCPaSc*
**Pollock**, G Donald 1928- *AmMWSc 92*
**Pollock**, Gene Edward 1934- *WhoMW 92*
**Pollock**, George d1991 *Who 92N*

**Pollock,** George F. 1928- *Who 92*
**Pollock,** George Howard 1923- *AmMWSc 92*
**Pollock,** Giles Montagu- 1928- *Who 92*
**Pollock,** Herbert Chermside 1913- *AmMWSc 92*
**Pollock,** Ian 1950- *TwCPaSc*
**Pollock,** Jackson 1912-1956 *FacFETw, RComAH*
**Pollock,** John Archie 1957- *AmMWSc 92*
**Pollock,** John Charles *WrDr 92*
**Pollock,** John Charles 1923- *IntAu&W 91*
**Pollock,** John Denton 1926- *Who 92*
**Pollock,** John Joseph 1933- *AmMWSc 92*
**Pollock,** John Phleger 1920- *WhoAmL 92, WhoWest 92*
**Pollock,** L W 1918- *AmMWSc 92*
**Pollock,** Lawrence J. *WhoEnt 92*
**Pollock,** Leland Wells 1943- *AmMWSc 92*
**Pollock,** Martin Rivers 1914- *Who 92*
**Pollock,** Michael 1916- *IntWW 91, Who 92*
**Pollock,** Michael L 1936- *AmMWSc 92*
**Pollock,** Neal Jay 1947- *WhoFI 92*
**Pollock,** Paul Edward 1938- *WhoIns 92*
**Pollock,** Peter Brian 1936- *Who 92*
**Pollock,** Richard Edwin 1928- *WhoWest 92*
**Pollock,** Robert Elwood 1936- *AmMWSc 92*
**Pollock,** Robert Michael 1926- *WhoAmP 91*
**Pollock,** Sharon *IntAu&W 91*
**Pollock,** Sharon 1936- *WrDr 92*
**Pollock,** Stephen Becker 1951- *WhoEnt 92*
**Pollock,** Stephen M 1936- *AmMWSc 92*
**Pollock,** Stephen Michael 1936- *WhoMW 92*
**Pollock,** Stewart G 1932- *WhoAmP 91*
**Pollock,** Stewart Glasson 1932- *WhoAmL 92*
**Pollock,** Thomas 1943- *IntMPA 92*
**Pollock,** Thomas P. 1943- *WhoEnt 92, WhoWest 92*
**Pollock,** William H. M. *Who 92*
**Pollock-Ciampi,** Judith A. 1960- *WhoAmL 92*
**Pollok,** Nicholas Lewis, III 1926- *AmMWSc 92*
**Pollycove,** Myron 1921- *AmMWSc 92*
**Polmanski,** Ted Chester 1955- *WhoEnt 92*
**Polmanteer,** Keith Earl 1923- *AmMWSc 92*
**Polmar,** Stephen Holland *AmMWSc 92*
**Polnaszek,** Carl Francis 1945- *AmMWSc 92*
**Polner,** Alex Ray 1957- *WhoEnt 92*
**Polo,** James F. 1950- *WhoHisp 92*
**Polo,** Santiago Ramos 1922- *AmMWSc 92*
**Polome,** Edgar Charles 1920- *WhoRel 92*
**Polomskey,** Harry 1927- *WhoAmP 91*
**Polon,** Linda Beth 1943- *WhoWest 92*
**Polon,** Martin Ishiah 1942- *WhoFI 92*
**Polonia,** Luis Andrew 1964- *WhoHisp 92*
**Polonis,** Douglas Hugh 1928- *AmMWSc 92*
**Polonskaya,** Yelizaveta Grigore'vna 1890-1969 *SovUnBD*
**Polonsky,** Abraham 1910- *IntDcF 2-2, IntMPA 92*
**Polonsky,** Anthony 1940- *IntAu&W 91*
**Polonsky,** Antony 1940- *WrDr 92*
**Polonsky,** Helen 1936- *WhoAmP 91*
**Polonsky,** Ivan Paul 1929- *AmMWSc 92*
**Polonsky,** Vyacheslav Pavlovich 1886-1932 *SovUnBD*
**Polony,** Geza Elemer 1954- *WhoEnt 92*
**Polos,** James 1944- *WhoFI 92*
**Polosa,** Canio 1928- *AmMWSc 92*
**Polotsky,** Hans Jacob 1905- *IntWW 91*
**Poloujadoff,** Michel E 1932- *AmMWSc 92*
**Polovets,** Alexander 1935- *WhoWest 92*
**Polovin,** Vladimir 1880-1957 *TwCPaSc*
**Polow,** Bertram 1918- *WhoAmL 92*
**Polowczyk,** Carl John 1933- *AmMWSc 92*
**Polowy,** Henry 1918- *AmMWSc 92*
**Poloyac,** Michael, II 1952- *WhoAmP 91*
**Polozkov,** Ivan Kuzmich 1935- *IntWW 91, SovUnBD*
**Polozkova,** Lidia Pavlovna 1929- *IntWW 91*
**Polozola,** Frank Joseph 1942- *WhoAmL 92*
**Polsby,** Daniel D. 1945- *WhoAmL 92*
**Polsfuss,** Craig Lyle 1950- *WhoMW 92*
**Polsinelli,** Anthony Renato 1944- *WhoMW 92*
**Polsinelli,** Jerry 1928- *WhoMW 92*
**Polsky,** Alexander Samuel 1951- *WhoAmL 92*
**Polson,** Charles David Allen 1947- *AmMWSc 92*
**Polson,** Donald Allan 1911- *WhoWest 92*
**Polson,** James Bernard 1938- *AmMWSc 92*
**Polson,** Samuel Lewis 1956- *WhoRel 92*
**Polson,** William Jerry 1943- *AmMWSc 92*
**Polster,** James *DrAPF 91*
**Polster,** Stephen James 1953- *WhoRel 92*
**Polstra,** Larry John 1945- *WhoAmL 92*
**Polt,** Sarah Stephens 1926- *AmMWSc 92*
**Poltawska,** Wanda Wiktoria 1921- *IntWW 91*
**Poltimore,** Baron 1957- *Who 92*
**Poltorak,** Andrew Stephen 1938- *AmMWSc 92*
**Poltrack,** David F. *LesBEnT 92, WhoEnt 92*
**Poluhowich,** John Jacob 1939- *AmMWSc 92*
**Polukhina,** Valentina 1936- *ConAu 135*
**Polumbo,** Anthony L 1945- *WhoAmP 91*
**Polunin,** Nicholas *IntWW 91, Who 92*
**Polunin,** Nicholas 1909- *IntAu&W 91, WrDr 92*
**Polunsky,** Steven Michael 1959- *WhoAmP 91*
**Polus,** Judith Ann 1943- *WhoWest 92*
**Polve,** James Herschal 1921- *AmMWSc 92*
**Polvere,** Daniel Michael 1942- *WhoAmL 92*
**Polvinen,** Tuomo Ilmari 1931- *IntWW 91*
**Polwarth,** Baron 1916- *IntWW 91*
**Polwarth,** Lord 1916- *Who 92*
**Polwarth,** Master of 1947- *Who 92*
**Polya,** George 1887-1985 *FacFETw*
**Polya,** John Bela 1914- *WrDr 92*
**Polyakov,** Alexander 1945- *AmMWSc 92*
**Polyakov,** Vasiliy Ivanovich 1913- *IntAu&W 91*
**Polyakov,** Victor Nikolayevich 1915- *IntWW 91*
**Polyakov,** Vladimir Porfiriyevich 1931- *IntWW 91*
**Polyansky,** Anatoliy Trofimovich 1928- *IntWW 91*
**Polyansky,** Dmitriy Stepanovich 1917- *IntWW 91, SovUnBD*
**Polycarp** d156? *EncEarC*
**Polychronakos,** Venetios Alexander 1945- *AmMWSc 92*
**Polychronopoulos,** Constantine Dimitrius 1958- *AmMWSc 92*
**Polycrates** *EncEarC*
**Polydoris,** Nicholas George 1930- *WhoFI 92, WhoMW 92*
**Polydoris,** Steven Nicholas 1954- *WhoEnt 92, WhoMW 92*
**Polye,** William Ronald 1914- *AmMWSc 92*
**Polynesia,** Bishop in 1935- *Who 92*
**Polyniak,** Alan John 1955- *WhoEnt 92*
**Polynice,** Olden 1964- *WhoBlA 92*
**Polyzos,** George Constantine 1959- *WhoWest 92*
**Polyzou,** Wayne Nicholas 1952- *WhoMW 92*
**Polze,** Werner 1931- *IntWW 91*
**Polzer,** Charles William 1930- *WhoWest 92*
**Polzer,** Eckhard Franz 1943- *WhoFI 92*
**Polzer,** Wilfred L 1931- *AmMWSc 92*
**Polzin,** Charles Henry 1954- *WhoAmL 92*
**Polzin,** David Allen 1934- *WhoMW 92*
**Polzin,** David J 1951- *AmMWSc 92*
**Polzin,** John Theodore 1919- *WhoAmL 92*
**Polzin,** Paul Elmer 1943- *WhoFI 92*
**Polzl,** Klara *EncTR 91*
**Poma,** Eugenio 1944- *WhoRel 92*
**Pomare,** Eleo 1937- *WhoBlA 92*
**Pombal,** Sebastiao deCarvalho, marques de 1699-1782 *BlkwCEP*
**Pombo,** Manuel *WhoHisp 92*
**Pomerance,** Bernard 1940- *BenetAL 91, IntAu&W 91, WrDr 92*
**Pomerance,** Carl 1944- *AmMWSc 92*
**Pomerance,** Fay 1912- *TwCPaSc*
**Pomerance,** Herbert S 1917- *AmMWSc 92*
**Pomerance,** Josephine Alma Wertheim 1910-1980 *AmPeW*
**Pomerance,** Philip Lindsay 1956- *WhoAmL 92*
**Pomerance,** Roger Leslie 1951- *WhoFI 92, WhoMW 92*
**Pomerantseva,** Erna Vasil'evna 1899-1980 *SovUnBD*
**Pomerantz,** Edward *DrAPF 91*
**Pomerantz,** Irwin Herman 1934- *AmMWSc 92*
**Pomerantz,** Jerald Michael 1954- *WhoAmL 92*
**Pomerantz,** Lawrence Stewart 1943- *WhoFI 92*
**Pomerantz,** Martin 1939- *AmMWSc 92*
**Pomerantz,** Martin Arthur 1916- *AmMWSc 92*
**Pomerantz,** Marvin Alvin 1930- *WhoAmP 91*
**Pomerantz,** Melvin 1932- *AmMWSc 92*
**Pomerantz,** Seymour Herbert 1928- *AmMWSc 92*
**Pomeranz,** Bruce Herbert 1937- *AmMWSc 92*
**Pomeranz,** Felix 1926- *WhoFI 92*
**Pomeranz,** Janet Bellcourt 1930- *AmMWSc 92*
**Pomeranz,** Jerome Raphael 1930- *WhoMW 92*
**Pomeranz,** Virginia E. 1925?-1986 *ConAu 134*
**Pomeranz,** Yeshajahu 1922- *AmMWSc 92*
**Pomerene,** James Herbert 1920- *AmMWSc 92*
**Pomerening,** James Albert 1929- *AmMWSc 92*
**Pomerleau,** Ovide F 1940- *AmMWSc 92*
**Pomeroy** *Who 92*
**Pomeroy,** Benjamin Sherwood 1911- *AmMWSc 92, WhoAmP 91*
**Pomeroy,** David James 1951- *WhoMW 92*
**Pomeroy,** Duane Franklin 1952- *WhoAmP 91*
**Pomeroy,** Earl 1952- *WhoAmP 91*
**Pomeroy,** Elwaine Franklin 1933- *WhoAmP 91*
**Pomeroy,** Harlan 1923- *WhoAmL 92*
**Pomeroy,** Horace B 1937- *WhoAmP 91*
**Pomeroy,** John S 1929- *AmMWSc 92*
**Pomeroy,** John Seltzer 1929- *WhoWest 92*
**Pomeroy,** Kent Lytle 1935- *WhoWest 92*
**Pomeroy,** Lawrence Richards 1925- *AmMWSc 92*
**Pomeroy,** Ralph *DrAPF 91*
**Pomeroy,** Richard James 1937- *AmMWSc 92*
**Pomeroy,** Robert Corttis 1943- *WhoAmL 92*
**Pomeroy,** Roland Kenneth 1945- *AmMWSc 92*
**Pomeroy,** Theodore Medad 1824-1905 *AmPolLe*
**Pomeroy,** William Curtis *ScFEYrs*
**Pomeroy,** William R. 1952- *WhoFI 92*
**Pomes,** Adrian Francis 1920- *AmMWSc 92*
**Pomfret,** Joan *IntAu&W 91X*
**Pomfret,** John 1667-1702? *RfGEnL 91*
**Pomian,** Ronald J 1957- *AmMWSc 92*
**Pomicino,** Paolo Cirino 1939- *IntWW 91*
**Pomilio,** Anthony Kenneth 1920- *WhoAmL 92*
**Pomilla,** Frank R 1926- *AmMWSc 92*
**Pommer,** Eric Stephen 1951- *WhoAmL 92*
**Pommers,** Leon 1914- *WhoEnt 92*
**Pommersheim,** James Martin 1937- *AmMWSc 92*
**Pommerville,** Jeffrey Carl 1948- *AmMWSc 92, WhoWest 92*
**Pomo,** Roberto Dario 1949- *WhoHisp 92*
**Pomodoro,** Arnaldo 1926- *IntWW 91*
**Pomonis,** James George 1932- *AmMWSc 92*
**Pompadur,** I. Martin *LesBEnT 92*
**Pompadur,** I. Martin 1935- *WhoEnt 92*
**Pompan,** Jack Maurice 1926- *WhoFI 92*
**Pompea,** Stephen M. 1953- *WhoWest 92*
**Pompei,** Gian Franco 1915- *IntWW 91*
**Pompeo,** Jeffrey William 1957- *WhoAmL 92*
**Pompeo,** John Anthony 1934- *WhoEnt 92*
**Pompey,** Charles Spencer 1915- *WhoBlA 92*
**Pompey,** Maurice 1923- *WhoBlA 92*
**Pompey,** Sherman Lee 1930- *WhoFI 92, WhoWest 92*
**Pompian,** Mark Monroe 1953- *WhoEnt 92*
**Pompidou,** Georges 1911-1974 *FacFETw [port]*
**Pompusch,** Anita *WhoRel 92*
**Pomraning,** Gerald C 1936- *AmMWSc 92*
**Pomroy,** Cynthia Jean 1960- *WhoEnt 92*
**Pomus,** Jerome d1991 *NewYTBS 91 [port]*
**Ponaras,** Anthony A 1947- *AmMWSc 92*
**Ponce,** Carlos 1948- *WhoHisp 92*
**Ponce,** Christopher B. *WhoHisp 92*
**Ponce,** Gabriel 1939- *WhoHisp 92*
**Ponce,** Manuel 1882-1948 *NewAmDM*
**Ponce,** Manuel Leon 1945- *WhoHisp 92*
**Ponce,** Merrihelen 1938- *WhoHisp 92*
**Ponce,** Tony 1925- *WhoHisp 92*
**Ponce de Leon,** Alicia *WhoHisp 92*
**Ponce de Leon,** Juan 1460?-1521 *BenetAL 91, HisDSpE*
**Ponce Enrile,** Juan 1924- *IntWW 91*
**Ponceau,** Pierre Etienne Du *BenetAL 91*
**Poncelet,** Christian 1928- *IntWW 91*
**Poncet,** Ducaud Laborde *EncAmaz 91*
**Poncet,** Jean Andre F. *Who 92*
**Poncha,** Rustom Pestonji *AmMWSc 92*
**Ponchielli,** Amilcare 1834-1886 *NewAmDM*
**Poncy,** Charles N 1922- *WhoAmP 91*
**Pond,** Byron O. 1936- *WhoMW 92*
**Pond,** Carole *Who 92*
**Pond,** Daniel James 1949- *WhoWest 92*
**Pond,** David Martin 1942- *AmMWSc 92*
**Pond,** Frederick Eugene 1856-1925 *BenetAL 91*
**Pond,** George Gilbert 1861-1920 *BiInAmS*
**Pond,** George Stephen 1940- *AmMWSc 92*
**Pond,** Grace 1910- *IntAu&W 91, WrDr 92*
**Pond,** Helen Barbara 1924- *WhoEnt 92*
**Pond,** James B. 1838-1903 *BenetAL 91*
**Pond,** Jesse E, Jr 1917- *WhoAmP 91*
**Pond,** Joan *DrAPF 91*
**Pond,** Judson Samuel 1922- *AmMWSc 92*
**Pond,** Norman H. 1938- *WhoWest 92*
**Pond,** Phyllis J 1930- *WhoAmP 91*
**Pond,** Thomas Alexander 1924- *AmMWSc 92*
**Pond,** Wilson Gideon 1930- *AmMWSc 92*
**Ponder,** Billy Wayne 1933- *AmMWSc 92*
**Ponder,** Catherine 1927- *RelLAm 91, WhoRel 92*
**Ponder,** Eunice Wilson 1929- *WhoBlA 92*
**Ponder,** Felix, Jr 1946- *AmMWSc 92*
**Ponder,** Harold Leon 1927- *WhoIns 92*
**Ponder,** Henry 1928- *WhoBlA 92*
**Ponder,** Herman 1928- *AmMWSc 92*
**Ponder,** Jacqueline Arrena 1946- *WhoAmP 91*
**Ponder,** James Alton 1933- *WhoRel 92*
**Ponder,** Patricia *IntAu&W 91X, WrDr 92*
**Ponder,** Randall Scott 1959- *WhoWest 92*
**Ponder,** Reginald Wallace 1937- *WhoRel 92*
**Ponder,** Todd Wesley 1959- *WhoAmL 92*
**Ponder,** Zeno Herbert 1920- *WhoAmP 91*
**Pondillo,** Robert James 1951- *WhoEnt 92*
**Pondrom,** Lee Girard 1933- *AmMWSc 92*
**Poneleit,** Charles Gustav 1940- *AmMWSc 92*
**Ponessa,** Joseph Thomas 1941- *AmMWSc 92*
**Ponet,** James Edward 1946- *WhoRel 92*
**Pong,** Schwe Fang 1936- *AmMWSc 92*
**Pong,** Ting-Chuen 1957- *AmMWSc 92*
**Pong,** William 1927- *AmMWSc 92*
**Ponge,** Francis 1899- *IntAu&W 91*
**Ponge,** Francis 1899-1988 *FacFETw, GuFrLit 1*
**Pongpanit,** Montree 1943- *IntWW 91*
**Pongratz,** Morris Bernard 1942- *AmMWSc 92*
**Poniackek,** Harvey *WhoFI 92*
**Poniatowska,** Elena 1933- *BenetAL 91, DcLB 113 [port], SpAmWW*
**Poniatowski,** Michel Casimir 1922- *IntWW 91*
**Poniatowski,** Stanislaw August 1732-1798 *BlkwCEP*
**Ponicsan,** Darryl *DrAPF 91*
**Ponikvar,** Dale Leon 1949- *WhoAmL 92*
**Poniman,** S. 1926- *IntWW 91*
**Ponitz,** David Henry 1931- *WhoFI 92*
**Ponka,** Lawrence John 1949- *WhoFI 92, WhoMW 92*
**Ponka,** Premysl 1941- *AmMWSc 92*
**Ponnamperuma,** Cyril Andrew 1923- *AmMWSc 92, IntWW 91*
**Ponnapalli,** Ramachandramurty 1933- *AmMWSc 92*
**Ponne,** Nanci Teresa 1958- *WhoFI 92*
**Ponnelle,** Jean-Pierre 1932-1988 *FacFETw*
**Ponomarenko,** Pantaleimon Kondrat'evich 1902-1984 *SovUnBD*
**Ponomarev,** Boris Nikolaevich 1905- *SovUnBD*
**Ponomarev,** Nikolay Afanas'evich 1918- *SovUnBD*
**Ponomarev,** Paul 1944- *AmMWSc 92*
**Ponomareva,** Nina Ivanovna 1929- *SovUnBD*
**Ponomaryov,** Boris Nikolayevich 1905- *IntWW 91*
**Ponoroff,** Lawrence 1953- *WhoAmL 92*
**Pons,** Bernard 1926- *IntWW 91*
**Pons,** Lily 1898-1976 *NewAmDM*
**Pons,** Rafael Francisco 1963- *WhoMW 92*
**Pons,** Stanley *AmMWSc 92*
**Pons,** Victor Manuel, Jr 1935- *WhoAmP 91*
**Pons,** William Francis, Jr. 1948- *WhoEnt 92*
**Pons-Nunez,** Victor Manuel 1935- *WhoAmL 92*
**Ponselle,** Carmela 1892-1977 *NewAmDM*
**Ponselle,** Rosa 1897-1981 *FacFETw, NewAmDM*
**Ponseti,** Ignacio Vives 1914- *AmMWSc 92*
**Ponsonby** *Who 92*
**Ponsonby,** Ashley 1921- *Who 92*
**Ponsonby,** D A 1907- *IntAu&W 91, WrDr 92*
**Ponsonby,** Myles Walter 1924- *Who 92*
**Ponsonby,** Robert Noel 1926- *Who 92*
**Ponsonby of Shulbrede,** Baron 1958- *Who 92*
**Ponsot,** Marie *DrAPF 91*
**Pont,** Marco del 1765-1821 *HisDSpE*
**Pontarelli,** Domenic Joseph 1912- *AmMWSc 92*
**Pontarelli,** Thomas 1949- *WhoIns 92*
**Pontarolo,** Michael Joseph 1947- *WhoAmL 92*
**Pontau,** Arthur E 1951- *AmMWSc 92*
**Ponte,** Joseph G, Jr 1925- *AmMWSc 92*
**Ponte,** Lowell Alton 1946- *WhoHisp 92*
**Pontecorvo,** Bruno Maksimovich 1913- *IntWW 91*
**Pontecorvo,** Gillo 1919- *IntDcF 2-2 [port], IntMPA 92, IntWW 91*
**Pontecorvo,** Giulio 1923- *WhoFI 92*
**Pontecorvo,** Guido 1907- *IntWW 91, Who 92*
**Pontefract,** Archdeacon of *Who 92*

**Pontefract,** Bishop Suffragan of 1922- *Who 92*
**Ponten,** Josef 1883-1940 *EncTR 91 [port]*
**Ponter,** Anthony Barrie 1933- *AmMWSc 92, WhoMW 92*
**Pontes,** Henry A. *WhoHisp 92*
**Ponthenkandath,** Sasidharan 1945- *WhoMW 92*
**Ponthiey,** Adelaide *EncAmaz 91*
**Ponti,** Carlo 1913- *IntMPA 92, IntWW 91*
**Ponti,** Carlo, Signora *Who 92*
**Ponti,** Gio 1891-1979 *DcTwDes*
**Ponti,** Michael 1937- *IntWW 91*
**Ponti-Aldo,** Yusuf Benavil 1927- *WhoHisp 92*
**Pontiac** 1720?-1769 *BenetAL 91, BlkwEAR, RComAH*
**Pontianus** *EncEarC*
**Ponticello,** Gerald S 1939- *AmMWSc 92*
**Ponticello,** Ignazio Salvatore 1939- *AmMWSc 92*
**Pontifex,** David More 1922- *Who 92*
**Pontin,** Frederick William 1906- *Who 92*
**Pontin,** John Graham 1937- *Who 92*
**Pontinen,** Richard Ernest 1933- *AmMWSc 92*
**Pontius,** Dieter J J 1914- *AmMWSc 92*
**Pontius,** Duane Henry 1939- *AmMWSc 92*
**Pontius,** E C 1915- *AmMWSc 92*
**Pontius,** John Samuels 1945- *WhoAmP 91*
**Pontius,** Steven Kent 1945- *AmMWSc 92*
**Pontolillo,** Peter A. *WhoRel 92*
**Ponton,** Richard Edward 1937- *WhoFI 92*
**Pontoppidan,** Henning 1925- *AmMWSc 92*
**Pontoppidan,** Henrik 1857-1943 *FacFETw, WhoNob 90*
**Pontrelli,** Gene J 1933- *AmMWSc 92*
**Ponty,** Jean-Luc 1942- *NewAmDM, WhoEnt 92*
**Ponzi,** Philip Charles 1943- *WhoFI 92*
**Ponziani,** Peter John 1953- *WhoAmL 92*
**Ponzio,** Nicholas Michael *AmMWSc 92*
**Ponzo,** Bruce Joseph 1955- *WhoWest 92*
**Ponzo,** Peter James 1934- *AmMWSc 92*
**Pooch,** Udo Walter 1943- *AmMWSc 92*
**Poochikian,** Guiragos K 1945- *AmMWSc 92*
**Poodry,** Clifton Arthur 1943- *AmMWSc 92*
**Pool,** Adam de Sola 1957- *WhoFI 92*
**Pool,** Dan L *WhoAmP 91*
**Pool,** Edwin Lewis 1921- *AmMWSc 92*
**Pool,** Ithiel de Sola 1917-1984 *FacFETw*
**Pool,** James C T 1937- *AmMWSc 92*
**Pool,** Jeannie Gayle 1951- *WhoWest 92*
**Pool,** Karl Hallman 1939- *AmMWSc 92*
**Pool,** Mark Allen 1953- *WhoWest 92*
**Pool,** Marquita Jones 1945- *WhoBlA 92*
**Pool,** Mary Jane *WhoFI 92*
**Pool,** Monte J 1934- *AmMWSc 92*
**Pool,** Peter Edward 1936- *AmMWSc 92*
**Pool,** Robert Morris 1940- *AmMWSc 92*
**Pool,** Roy Ransom 1934- *AmMWSc 92*
**Pool,** Terry Franklin 1953- *WhoRel 92*
**Pool,** Thomas Burgess 1948- *AmMWSc 92*
**Pool,** Vera C. 1946- *WhoBlA 92*
**Pool,** William Robert 1937- *AmMWSc 92*
**Pool,** Winford H, Jr 1926- *AmMWSc 92*
**Poole** *Who 92*
**Poole,** Baron 1911- *IntWW 91, Who 92*
**Poole,** Alfred Claude, Sr. 1934- *WhoEnt 92*
**Poole,** Andrew E 1935- *AmMWSc 92*
**Poole,** Anthony Cecil James 1927- *Who 92*
**Poole,** Anthony Robin 1939- *AmMWSc 92*
**Poole,** Avril Anne Barker 1934- *Who 92*
**Poole,** Barbara Ann 1935- *WhoWest 92*
**Poole,** Brenda Sharon 1960- *WhoRel 92*
**Poole,** Carolyn Ann 1931- *IntAu&W 91*
**Poole,** Cecil F. *WhoAmL 92, WhoAmP 91*
**Poole,** Cecil F. 1914- *WhoBlA 92*
**Poole,** Charles Patton, Jr 1927- *AmMWSc 92*
**Poole,** Charlie 1892-1931 *NewAmDM*
**Poole,** Colin Frank 1950- *AmMWSc 92*
**Poole,** D. Bruce 1959- *WhoAmL 92, WhoAmP 91*
**Poole,** Darryl Vernon 1946- *WhoFI 92*
**Poole,** David Anthony 1938- *Who 92*
**Poole,** David Arthur Ramsay 1935- *Who 92*
**Poole,** David James 1931- *IntWW 91, Who 92*
**Poole,** Dillard M. 1939- *WhoBlA 92*
**Poole,** Donald Ray 1932- *AmMWSc 92*
**Poole,** Doris Theodore 1923- *AmMWSc 92*
**Poole,** Edward Otto 1931- *WhoRel 92*
**Poole,** Ernest 1880-1950 *BenetAL 91*
**Poole,** Francis *DrAPF 91*
**Poole,** Frank S. 1913- *IntMPA 92*
**Poole,** George 1915- *TwCPaSc*
**Poole,** George Douglas 1942- *AmMWSc 92*
**Poole,** H K 1931- *AmMWSc 92*
**Poole,** Henry 1873-1928 *TwCPaSc*
**Poole,** Henry Joe, Jr. 1957- *WhoWest 92*
**Poole,** Herman 1849-1906 *BiInAmS*
**Poole,** Isobel Anne 1941- *Who 92*
**Poole,** James F. 1936- *WhoBlA 92*
**Poole,** John 1786-1872? *RfGEnL 91*
**Poole,** John Anthony 1932- *AmMWSc 92*
**Poole,** John Terry 1937- *AmMWSc 92*
**Poole,** John William 1931- *AmMWSc 92*
**Poole,** Josephine 1933- *WrDr 92*
**Poole,** Marion L. 1921- *WhoBlA 92*
**Poole,** Phil 1959- *WhoAmP 91*
**Poole,** Philip 1954- *WhoMW 92*
**Poole,** Rachel Irene 1924- *WhoBlA 92*
**Poole,** Richard 1945- *ConAu 135*
**Poole,** Richard John 1929- *Who 92*
**Poole,** Richard Turk, Jr 1931- *AmMWSc 92*
**Poole,** Robert Wayne 1944- *AmMWSc 92*
**Poole,** Romeo *ScFEYrs*
**Poole,** Ronald James 1947- *WhoFI 92*
**Poole,** Ronald John 1936- *AmMWSc 92*
**Poole,** Thomas George 1952- *WhoRel 92*
**Poole,** Thomas H., Sr. *WhoBlA 92*
**Poole,** Tim Kent 1959- *WhoMW 92*
**Poole,** Van B 1935- *WhoAmP 91*
**Poole,** William Daniel 1932- *WhoFI 92*
**Poole,** William Eugene, Jr. 1960- *WhoWest 92*
**Poole,** William Frederick 1821-1894 *BenetAL 91*
**Poole,** William Hope 1927- *AmMWSc 92*
**Poole,** William Kenneth 1939- *AmMWSc 92*
**Poole-Heard,** Blanche Denise 1951- *WhoBlA 92*
**Poole-Wilson,** Philip Alexander 1943- *Who 92*
**Pooler,** Catherine Mary 1954- *WhoAmL 92*
**Pooler,** Francis, Jr 1926- *AmMWSc 92*
**Pooler,** John Preston 1935- *AmMWSc 92*
**Pooley,** Alan Setzler 1938- *AmMWSc 92*
**Pooley,** Beverley John 1934- *WhoAmL 92*
**Pooley,** Derek 1937- *Who 92*
**Pooley,** Frederick Bernard 1916- *Who 92*
**Pooley,** Peter 1936- *Who 92*
**Pooley,** Robin 1936- *Who 92*
**Pooley,** Vanessa 1954- *TwCPaSc*
**Poon,** Bing Toy 1924- *AmMWSc 92*
**Poon,** Calvin P C 1935- *AmMWSc 92*
**Poon,** Chi-Sang *AmMWSc 92*
**Poon,** James C. 1932- *WhoWest 92*
**Poon,** Ting-Chung 1955- *AmMWSc 92*
**Poonawala,** Ismail Kurbanhusein 1937- *WhoWest 92*
**Poonja,** Mohamed 1948- *WhoFI 92, WhoWest 92*
**Poor,** Clarence Alexander 1911- *WhoWest 92*
**Poor,** Harold Vincent 1951- *AmMWSc 92*
**Poor,** James T 1932- *WhoIns 92*
**Poor,** Janet Meakin 1929- *WhoMW 92*
**Poor,** Peter Varnum 1926- *WhoEnt 92*
**Poorbaugh,** Earl Eugene 1934- *WhoFI 92*
**Poore,** Aubrey Bonner 1945- *AmMWSc 92*
**Poore,** Benjamin 1820-1887 *BenetAL 91*
**Poore,** Duncan *Who 92*
**Poore,** Emery Ray Vaughn 1937- *AmMWSc 92*
**Poore,** Herbert Edward 1930- *Who 92*
**Poore,** James Albert, III 1943- *WhoAmL 92*
**Poore,** Jesse H, Jr *AmMWSc 92*
**Poore,** Martin Edward Duncan 1925- *Who 92*
**Poorman,** Lawrence Eugene 1926- *AmMWSc 92, WhoMW 92*
**Poorooshasb,** Hormozd Bahman 1936- *AmMWSc 92*
**Poortvliet,** Marien *SmATA 65*
**Poortvliet,** Rien 1932- *SmATA 65 [port]*
**Poortvliet,** William G 1931- *WhoIns 92*
**Poorvin,** David Walter 1946- *AmMWSc 92*
**Poorvu,** William James 1935- *WhoEnt 92*
**Poos,** George Ireland 1923- *AmMWSc 92*
**Poos,** Jacques F. 1935- *IntWW 91*
**Poot,** Anton 1929- *Who 92*
**Poot,** Marcel 1901- *NewAmDM*
**Pootjes,** Christine Fredricka 1927- *AmMWSc 92*
**Poovaiah,** Bachettira Wthappa 1943- *AmMWSc 92*
**Poovey,** William Arthur 1913- *WhoRel 92, WrDr 92*
**Pop,** Emil 1939- *AmMWSc 92*
**Pop,** Iggy *NewAmDM*
**Pop,** Valeriu Eugen *IntWW 91*
**Pop-Stojanovic,** Zoran Rista 1935- *AmMWSc 92*
**Popa,** Magdalena *WhoEnt 92*
**Popa,** Pretor 1922- *Who 92*
**Popa,** Vasko d1991 *NewYTBS 91*
**Popcorn,** Faith *NewYTBS 91 [port]*
**Pope,** His Holiness the *Who 92*
**Pope,** Addison W. 1926- *WhoBlA 92*
**Pope,** Alexander 1688-1744 *BlkwCEP [port], CnDBLB 2 [port], RfGEnL 91*
**Pope,** Andrew Jackson, Jr. 1913- *WhoAmL 92*
**Pope,** Andrew Lancelot 1912- *Who 92*
**Pope,** Barbara J. 1948- *WhoMW 92*
**Pope,** Barbara L 1945- *AmMWSc 92*
**Pope,** Bernard G 1943- *AmMWSc 92*
**Pope,** Bill Jordan 1922- *AmMWSc 92*
**Pope,** Cathryn Mary 1957- *Who 92*
**Pope,** Charles Edward, II 1931- *AmMWSc 92*
**Pope,** Daniel Loring 1931- *AmMWSc 92*
**Pope,** Daniel Townsend 1913- *AmMWSc 92*
**Pope,** David Bruce 1945- *WhoAmL 92*
**Pope,** David Peter 1939- *AmMWSc 92*
**Pope,** Deborah *DrAPF 91*
**Pope,** Donald Raymond 1934- *WhoWest 92*
**Pope,** Donna 1931- *WhoAmP 91, WhoFI 92*
**Pope,** Douglas Vanstone 1945- *WhoFI 92*
**Pope,** Dudley 1925- *WrDr 92*
**Pope,** Dudley Bernard Egerton 1925- *IntAu&W 91, Who 92*
**Pope,** Durand L. 1946- *WhoEnt 92*
**Pope,** Edward John Andrew 1962- *WhoWest 92*
**Pope,** Ernle *Who 92*
**Pope,** Franklin Leonard 1840-1895 *BiInAmS*
**Pope,** Fred Wallace, Jr. 1941- *WhoAmL 92*
**Pope,** Generoso 1891-1950 *DcAmImH*
**Pope,** Geoffrey George 1934- *Who 92*
**Pope,** Gustavus W *ScFEYrs*
**Pope,** Henry 1922- *WhoBlA 92*
**Pope,** Howard E *WhoIns 92*
**Pope,** Isaac S. 1939- *WhoBlA 92*
**Pope,** Jacqueline S 1931- *WhoAmP 91*
**Pope,** James Arthur 1956- *WhoAmP 91*
**Pope,** James M. 1927- *WhoBlA 92*
**Pope,** Jane LaRue 1929- *WhoWest 92*
**Pope,** Jeremy James Richard 1943- *Who 92*
**Pope,** Jesse Rondo 1932- *WhoMW 92*
**Pope,** John Clifford 1911- *Who 92*
**Pope,** John Ernle 1921- *Who 92*
**Pope,** John Keyler 1931- *AmMWSc 92*
**Pope,** John William 1947- *WhoWest 92*
**Pope,** Joseph *AmMWSc 92*
**Pope,** Joseph 1914- *Who 92*
**Pope,** Joseph N. *WhoBlA 92*
**Pope,** Kerig Rodgers 1935- *WhoEnt 92*
**Pope,** Lance *Who 92*
**Pope,** Larry Debbs 1940- *AmMWSc 92*
**Pope,** Larry Elmer 1941- *AmMWSc 92*
**Pope,** Lester Neal 1946- *IntAu&W 91*
**Pope,** Malcolm H 1941- *AmMWSc 92*
**Pope,** Martin 1918- *AmMWSc 92*
**Pope,** Marvin Hoyle 1916- *WhoRel 92*
**Pope,** Mary Ann Irwin 1932- *WhoEnt 92*
**Pope,** Mary E *AmMWSc 92*
**Pope,** Mary Maude 1916- *WhoBlA 92*
**Pope,** Max Lyndell 1932- *WhoWest 92*
**Pope,** Michael Arthur 1944- *WhoAmL 92*
**Pope,** Michael Donald K. *Who 92*
**Pope,** Michael Thor 1933- *AmMWSc 92*
**Pope,** Mirian Artis 1952- *WhoBlA 92*
**Pope,** Nathan Reinhart 1949- *WhoRel 92*
**Pope,** Nicholas 1949- *TwCPaSc*
**Pope,** Noel Kynaston 1918- *AmMWSc 92*
**Pope,** Paul Sullivan 1933- *WhoEnt 92*
**Pope,** Paul Terrell 1942- *AmMWSc 92*
**Pope,** Peter T. 1934- *WhoFI 92, WhoWest 92*
**Pope,** Randy Darrell 1954- *WhoMW 92*
**Pope,** Ray 1924- *IntAu&W 91*
**Pope,** Richard W 1933- *WhoIns 92*
**Pope,** Robert Glynn 1935- *WhoFI 92*
**Pope,** Robert William 1916- *Who 92*
**Pope,** Ruben Edward, III 1948- *WhoBlA 92*
**Pope,** Susan Lyon *DrAPF 91*
**Pope,** Terence 1941- *TwCPaSc*
**Pope,** Thomas H, III 1946- *WhoAmP 91*
**Pope,** Tim 1957- *WhoAmP 91*
**Pope,** Timothy 1953- *WhoFI 92*
**Pope,** Wendell LaVon 1928- *AmMWSc 92*
**Pope,** William Kenneth 1901- *WhoRel 92*
**Pope,** William L. 1960- *WhoAmL 92*
**Pope,** William Robert 1918- *WhoAmL 92*
**Pope,** William Robert, Jr. 1946- *WhoAmL 92*
**Pope-Hennessy,** John 1913- *Who 92, WrDr 92*
**Pope-Hennessy,** John W 1913- *ConAu 35NR*
**Pope-Hennessy,** John Wyndham 1913- *IntAu&W 91, IntWW 91*
**Popejoy,** Steven Lance 1957- *WhoMW 92*
**Popejoy,** William Dean 1925- *AmMWSc 92*
**Popek,** John George 1945- *WhoFI 92*
**Popel,** Aleksander S 1945- *AmMWSc 92*
**Popelar,** Carl H 1938- *AmMWSc 92*
**Popeleski,** Janet 1952- *WhoEnt 92*
**Popelka,** Larry Deane 1958- *WhoFI 92*
**Popenchenko,** Valeriy Vladimirovich 1937-1975 *SovUnBD*
**Popenoe,** Edwin Alonzo 1853-1913 *BiInAmS*
**Popenoe,** Edwin Alonzo 1922- *AmMWSc 92*
**Popenoe,** Hugh 1929- *AmMWSc 92*
**Poperen,** Jean Maurice 1925- *IntWW 91*
**Popescu,** Dumitru 1928- *IntWW 91*
**Popescu,** Dumitru Radu 1935- *IntWW 91*
**Popescu,** Ioan-Iovitz 1932- *IntWW 91*
**Popham,** Christopher John 1927- *Who 92*
**Popham,** Hugh 1920- *IntAu&W 91, WrDr 92*
**Popham,** Melinda *DrAPF 91*
**Popham,** Mervyn Reddaway 1927- *Who 92*
**Popham,** Richard Allen 1913- *AmMWSc 92*
**Popitz,** Johannes 1884-1945 *EncTR 91 [port]*
**Popjak,** George Joseph 1914- *AmMWSc 92, IntWW 91, Who 92*
**Popkewitz,** Thomas Stanley 1940- *WhoMW 92*
**Popkin,** A H 1913- *AmMWSc 92*
**Popkin,** Alan Joel 1948- *WhoEnt 92*
**Popkin,** Joel 1932- *WhoFI 92*
**Popkin,** Mark Anthony 1929- *WhoEnt 92*
**Popkin,** Michael Kenneth 1943- *AmMWSc 92, WhoMW 92*
**Popko,** Kathleen Marie 1943- *WhoRel 92*
**Popkov,** Viktor Yefimovich 1932-1974 *SovUnBD*
**Poplack,** Kenneth David 1926- *WhoRel 92*
**Poplar,** Carl D. 1943- *WhoAmL 92*
**Poplavsky,** Boris Yulianovich 1903-1935 *LiExTwC*
**Poplawski,** Joseph Walter 1932- *WhoMW 92*
**Poplawsky,** Alex James 1948- *AmMWSc 92*
**Pople,** George Ross 1945- *WhoEnt 92*
**Pople,** John Anthony 1925- *AmMWSc 92, IntWW 91, Who 92*
**Poploff,** Michelle 1956- *ConAu 135, SmATA 67 [port]*
**Poplyk,** Gregory A. 1963- *WhoEnt 92*
**Popoff,** Frank Peter 1935- *IntWW 91, WhoFI 92, WhoMW 92*
**Poponyak,** Raymond William 1951- *WhoFI 92*
**Popov,** Aleksandr Dmitrievich 1892-1961 *SovUnBD*
**Popov,** Alexander Ivan 1921- *AmMWSc 92*
**Popov,** Dmitar *IntWW 91*
**Popov,** Dusko 1912-1981 *FacFETw*
**Popov,** E P 1913- *AmMWSc 92*
**Popov,** Elizabeth M 1915- *WhoAmP 91*
**Popov,** Gavriil Kharitonovich 1936- *IntWW 91, SovUnBD*
**Popov,** Nikolav Ivanovich 1936- *IntWW 91*
**Popov,** Oleg Konstantinovich 1930- *IntWW 91*
**Popov,** Pavel Il'ich 1872-1950 *SovUnBD*
**Popov,** Viktor Ivanovich 1918- *IntWW 91, Who 92*
**Popov,** Vladimir Dmitrievich 1941- *IntWW 91, SovUnBD*
**Popov,** Yevgeniy Pavlovich 1914- *IntWW 91*
**Popova,** Lyubov' Sergeevna 1889-1924 *SovUnBD*
**Popova,** Nina 1922- *WhoEnt 92*
**Popovic,** Nenad D. 1909- *WrDr 92*
**Popovic,** Vojin 1922- *AmMWSc 92*
**Popovic,** Zoran 1941- *AmMWSc 92*
**Popovich,** Frank 1923- *AmMWSc 92*
**Popovich,** Helen Houser 1935- *WhoMW 92*
**Popovich,** M 1917- *AmMWSc 92*
**Popovich,** Pavel 1930- *FacFETw*
**Popovich,** Peter S 1920- *WhoAmP 91*
**Popovich,** Peter Stephen 1920- *WhoAmL 92, WhoMW 92*
**Popovich,** Robert Peter 1939- *AmMWSc 92*
**Popovich,** Steve S. 1932- *WhoWest 92*
**Popovics,** Alexander Joseph 1948- *WhoMW 92*
**Popovics,** Sandor 1921- *AmMWSc 92*
**Popovsky,** Mark Alexandrovich 1922- *LiExTwC*
**Popp,** Bernard F. 1917- *WhoRel 92*
**Popp,** Carl John 1941- *AmMWSc 92*
**Popp,** Frank Donald 1932- *AmMWSc 92, WhoMW 92*
**Popp,** Gerhard 1940- *AmMWSc 92*
**Popp,** James Alan 1945- *AmMWSc 92*
**Popp,** Lucia 1939- *IntWW 91, NewAmDM*
**Popp,** Nathaniel William George 1940- *WhoRel 92*
**Popp,** Phyllis Irene 1957- *WhoMW 92*
**Popp,** Raymond Arthur 1930- *AmMWSc 92*
**Poppa,** Ryal Robert 1933- *WhoFI 92, WhoWest 92*
**Poppe,** Carl Hugo 1936- *AmMWSc 92*
**Poppe,** Frances Winnie Perez 1942- *WhoFI 92*
**Poppe,** Fred C 1923- *ConAu 35NR*
**Poppe,** Leonard Bruce 1959- *WhoRel 92*
**Poppe,** Wassily 1918- *AmMWSc 92*
**Poppelbaum,** Wolfgang Johannes 1924- *AmMWSc 92*
**Poppele,** Richard E 1936- *AmMWSc 92*
**Poppen,** Henry Alvin 1922- *WhoAmP 91*

**Poppendiek,** Heinz Frank 1919- *AmMWSc 92*
**Poppenhagen,** Dennis Joseph 1938- *WhoAmP 91*
**Poppensiek,** George Charles 1918- *AmMWSc 92*
**Popper,** Arthur N 1943- *AmMWSc 92*
**Popper,** Daniel Magnes 1913- *AmMWSc 92*
**Popper,** David 1843-1913 *NewAmDM*
**Popper,** Frank James 1944- *WrDr 92*
**Popper,** Hans 1903-1988 *FacFETw*
**Popper,** Karl 1902- *IntWW 91, Who 92, WrDr 92*
**Popper,** Karl Raimund 1902- *FacFETw*
**Popper,** Pamela Anne 1956- *WhoFI 92*
**Popper,** Robert 1932- *WhoAmL 92*
**Popper,** Robert David 1927- *AmMWSc 92*
**Popper,** Thomas Leslie 1933- *AmMWSc 92*
**Popper,** Walter Lincoln 1920- *WhoFI 92*
**Poppino,** Allen Gerald 1925- *WhoFI 92*
**Poppino,** Kathryn *DrAPF 91*
**Poppino,** Rollie E. 1922- *WrDr 92*
**Poppler,** Doris Swords 1924- *WhoAmL 92*
**Popplewell,** Catharine Margaret 1929- *Who 92*
**Popplewell,** James Malcolm 1942- *AmMWSc 92*
**Popplewell,** Oliver 1927- *Who 92*
**Poppoff,** Ilia George 1924- *AmMWSc 92, WhoWest 92*
**Poppy,** Andrew 1954- *ConCom 92*
**Poppy,** Willard Joseph 1907- *AmMWSc 92*
**Poprick,** Mary Ann 1939- *WhoMW 92*
**Pops,** Horace 1936- *AmMWSc 92*
**Poracky,** Paul Bernard *WhoAmL 92*
**Porakis,** Cally *DrAPF 91*
**Poranski,** Chester F, Jr 1937- *AmMWSc 92*
**Porat,** Ami 1946- *WhoEnt 92*
**Porath,** Jerome Richard 1946- *WhoRel 92*
**Porath,** Jonathan David 1944- *WhoRel 92*
**Porcaro,** Michael Francis 1948- *WhoFI 92, WhoWest 92*
**Porcella,** Arthur David 1918- *WhoAmL 92*
**Porcella,** Donald Burke 1937- *AmMWSc 92*
**Porcelli,** Joseph Vito 1935- *WhoFI 92*
**Porcello,** Jack Samuel 1960- *WhoRel 92*
**Porcello,** Leonard J 1934- *AmMWSc 92*
**Porch,** Douglas 1944- *WrDr 92*
**Porch,** Roger *WhoAmP 91*
**Porch,** William Morgan 1944- *AmMWSc 92*
**Porche,** Verandah *DrAPF 91*
**Porcher,** Francis Peyre 1825-1895 *BiInAmS*
**Porcher,** Michael Somerville 1921- *Who 92*
**Porcher,** Richard Dwight 1939- *AmMWSc 92*
**Porchester,** Lord 1956- *Who 92*
**Porco,** Carmen 1947- *WhoAmP 91*
**Pordum,** Francis J *WhoAmP 91*
**Pore,** Robert Scott 1938- *AmMWSc 92*
**Porebski,** Tadeusz 1931- *IntWW 91*
**Porembka,** David Thomas 1953- *WhoMW 92*
**Poretsky,** Joel A. 1946- *WhoAmL 92*
**Poretz,** Ronald David 1940- *AmMWSc 92*
**Porges,** Arthur 1915- *TwCSFW 91*
**Porges,** K. Shelly 1953- *WhoWest 92*
**Porges,** Michael *DrAPF 91*
**Porges,** Walter Rudolf 1931- *WhoEnt 92*
**Pories,** Walter J 1930- *AmMWSc 92*
**Porile,** Norbert Thomas 1932- *AmMWSc 92*
**Porizkova,** Paulina 1965- *WhoEnt 92*
**Porkolab,** Miklos 1939- *AmMWSc 92*
**Porn,** Ingmar 1935- *WrDr 92*
**Porphyry** 232?-305? *EncEarC*
**Porpora,** Nicola 1686-1768 *NewAmDM*
**Porras,** Martin de 1579- *HisDSpE*
**Porras-Field,** Esperanza 1954- *WhoHisp 92*
**Porrata,** Manuel Francisco, Jr. 1965- *WhoHisp 92*
**Porreca,** David Philip 1942- *WhoWest 92*
**Porreca,** Vincent Joe 1941- *WhoAmP 91*
**Porrero,** Henry, Jr. 1945- *WhoWest 92*
**Porretta,** Louis Paul 1926- *WhoMW 92*
**Porrino,** Peter R 1956- *WhoIns 92*
**Porritt** *Who 92*
**Porritt,** Baron 1900- *IntWW 91, Who 92*
**Porritt,** Jonathon 1950- *IntWW 91, Who 92*
**Porro,** Michael John 1951- *WhoFI 92*
**Porsch,** Denise Keller 1957- *WhoWest 92*
**Porsche,** Ferdinand 1875-1951 *DcTwDes, EncTR 91 [port], FacFETw*
**Porsche,** Jules D 1909- *AmMWSc 92*
**Porsching,** Thomas August 1936- *AmMWSc 92*
**Port,** Curtis DeWitt 1930- *AmMWSc 92, WhoMW 92*
**Port,** Louise A. M. *WhoFI 92*
**Port,** Marc Carey 1955- *WhoWest 92*
**Port,** Robert Stanley 1927- *WhoRel 92*
**Port,** Sidney C 1935- *AmMWSc 92*
**Port Elizabeth,** Bishop of 1929- *Who 92*
**Port Moresby,** Archbishop of 1932- *Who 92*
**Port of Spain,** Archbishop of 1929- *Who 92*
**Porta,** Costanzo 1528-1601 *NewAmDM*
**Porta,** Eduardo Angel 1924- *AmMWSc 92*
**Porta,** Horacio A 1939- *AmMWSc 92*
**Portal** *Who 92*
**Portal,** Ellis *IntAu&W 91X, WrDr 92*
**Portal,** Gilbert Marcel Adrien 1930- *WhoFI 92*
**Portal,** Jonathan 1953- *Who 92*
**Portal,** Magda 1903-1989 *SpAmWW*
**Portal of Hungerford,** Baroness d1990 *Who 92N*
**Portalatin,** Maria 1937- *WhoHisp 92*
**Portales,** Alfredo 1946- *WhoRel 92*
**Portales,** Marco A. *WhoHisp 92*
**Portales,** Ramon, Sr. 1929- *WhoHisp 92*
**Portanier,** Francis 1929- *WhoFI 92*
**Portarlington,** Earl of 1938- *Who 92*
**Porte,** Barbara Ann *DrAPF 91*
**Porte,** Daniel, Jr 1931- *AmMWSc 92*
**Porte,** Michael Sheldon 1932- *WhoMW 92*
**Porte,** Thierry Georges 1957- *WhoFI 92*
**Portee,** Frank, III 1955- *WhoBlA 92*
**Portela,** Denis Charles 1952- *WhoFI 92*
**Portela,** Mary Green 1932- *WhoEnt 92*
**Portela,** Rafael 1947- *WhoHisp 92*
**Portelance,** Vincent Damien 1923- *AmMWSc 92*
**Portelli,** Vincent George 1932- *WhoFI 92*
**Porten,** Anthony Ralph 1947- *Who 92*
**Porten,** Bezalel 1931- *WrDr 92*
**Porten,** Henny 1890-1960 *EncTR 91*
**Porteous,** Christopher 1921- *Who 92*
**Porteous,** Christopher Selwyn 1935- *Who 92*
**Porteous,** James 1926- *Who 92*
**Porteous,** Leslie Crichton 1901- *IntAu&W 91*
**Porteous,** Norman Walker 1898- *Who 92*
**Porteous,** Patrick Anthony 1918- *Who 92*
**Porter** *Who 92*
**Porter,** A Duane 1936- *AmMWSc 92, WhoWest 92*
**Porter,** A.P. 1945- *SmATA 68 [port]*
**Porter,** Alan Leslie 1945- *AmMWSc 92*
**Porter,** Alastair Robert Wilson 1928- *Who 92*
**Porter,** Albert Brown 1864-1909 *BiInAmS*
**Porter,** Albert S. 1930- *WhoBlA 92*
**Porter,** Albert Wright 1923- *WhoWest 92*
**Porter,** Allen Edward 1926- *WhoEnt 92*
**Porter,** Alvin *TwCWW 91*
**Porter,** Andrew 1743-1813 *BiInAmS*
**Porter,** Andrew 1928- *IntWW 91, WrDr 92*
**Porter,** Andrew Peabody 1946- *WhoRel 92*
**Porter,** Arthur 1910- *Who 92*
**Porter,** Arthur L. 1940- *WhoBlA 92*
**Porter,** Arthur T. 1924- *IntWW 91*
**Porter,** Arthur Thomas 1924- *Who 92*
**Porter,** Arthur Woods 1955- *WhoWest 92*
**Porter,** Barry *Who 92*
**Porter,** Barry Alan 1957- *WhoFI 92*
**Porter,** Bern *DrAPF 91*
**Porter,** Bern 1911- *WrDr 92*
**Porter,** Bernard 1941- *IntAu&W 91, WrDr 92*
**Porter,** Bernard Harden 1911- *IntAu&W 91*
**Porter,** Beverly Fearn 1935- *AmMWSc 92*
**Porter,** Bill 1932- *WhoAmP 91*
**Porter,** Blanche Troullier 1933- *WhoBlA 92*
**Porter,** Brian 1928- *IntAu&W 91, WrDr 92*
**Porter,** Burton F 1936- *IntAu&W 91, WrDr 92*
**Porter,** Carol Denise 1948- *WhoBlA 92, WhoEnt 92*
**Porter,** Carson Page 1945- *WhoFI 92*
**Porter,** Charles Burnham 1840-1909 *BiInAmS*
**Porter,** Charles O 1919- *WhoAmP 91*
**Porter,** Charles Raleigh, Jr. 1922- *WhoAmL 92*
**Porter,** Charles Warren 1925- *AmMWSc 92*
**Porter,** Charles William 1939- *WhoBlA 92*
**Porter,** Charlotte 1854-1942 *ScFEYrs*
**Porter,** Charlotte & Clarke, Helen A *ScFEYrs*
**Porter,** Christopher Charles 1965- *WhoEnt 92*
**Porter,** Clarence A 1939- *AmMWSc 92, WhoBlA 92*
**Porter,** Clark Alfred 1925- *AmMWSc 92*
**Porter,** Cloyd Allen 1935- *WhoAmP 91*
**Porter,** Clyde L, Jr 1932- *AmMWSc 92*
**Porter,** Cole 1891-1964 *FacFETw, NewAmDM, RComAH*
**Porter,** Cole 1893-1964 *BenetAL 91*
**Porter,** Curt Culwell 1914- *AmMWSc 92*
**Porter,** Curtiss E. 1939- *WhoBlA 92*
**Porter,** Daniel Morris 1936- *AmMWSc 92*
**Porter,** Darrell Dean 1938- *AmMWSc 92*
**Porter,** David 1780-1843 *BenetAL 91*
**Porter,** David 1941- *AmMWSc 92, WhoEnt 92*
**Porter,** David Brownfield 1906- *Who 92*
**Porter,** David Dixon 1813-1891 *BenetAL 91*
**Porter,** David Dixon 1935- *AmMWSc 92*
**Porter,** David Gray 1953- *WhoEnt 92*
**Porter,** David Hugh 1935- *WhoEnt 92*
**Porter,** David John 1948- *Who 92*
**Porter,** Dean Allen 1939- *WhoMW 92*
**Porter,** Dixie Lee 1931- *WhoFI 92, WhoWest 92*
**Porter,** Don 1912- *IntMPA 92*
**Porter,** Don Cecil, Sr. 1912- *WhoEnt 92*
**Porter,** Donald 1939- *WhoFI 92*
**Porter,** Donald Clayton 1939- *WrDr 92*
**Porter,** Donald James 1921- *WhoAmL 92*
**Porter,** Donald Richard 1944- *WhoMW 92*
**Porter,** Dorothea Noelle Naomi 1927- *Who 92*
**Porter,** Dorothy 1905- *NotBlAW 92*
**Porter,** Dorothy B. 1905- *WhoBlA 92*
**Porter,** Dubose 1953- *WhoAmP 91*
**Porter,** Duncan MacNair 1937- *AmMWSc 92*
**Porter,** E. Melvin 1930- *WhoBlA 92*
**Porter,** Edwin S. *BenetAL 91*
**Porter,** Edwin S. 1869-1941 *IntDcF 2-2*
**Porter,** Eleanor H. 1868-1920 *BenetAL 91*
**Porter,** Eliot 1901-1990 *AnObit 1990, CurBio 91N*
**Porter,** Ellis Nathaniel 1931- *WhoBlA 92*
**Porter,** Emerson Leon 1949- *WhoRel 92*
**Porter,** Eric 1928- *Who 92*
**Porter,** Eric Richard 1928- *IntWW 91*
**Porter,** Ernest R. 1926- *WhoFI 92*
**Porter,** Everette M. 1910- *WhoBlA 92*
**Porter,** Frederic Edwin 1922- *AmMWSc 92*
**Porter,** Frederick J. 1883-1944 *TwCPaSc*
**Porter,** Frederick Stanley, Jr 1926- *AmMWSc 92*
**Porter,** Gary *WhoAmP 91*
**Porter,** Gary Dean 1942- *AmMWSc 92*
**Porter,** Gary Lynn 1959- *WhoFI 92*
**Porter,** Gary Stephan 1952- *WhoRel 92*
**Porter,** Gene Stratton 1863-1924 *BenetAL 91*
**Porter,** Gene T 1956- *WhoAmP 91*
**Porter,** George 1920- *IntAu&W 91, WhoNob 90, WrDr 92*
**Porter,** George A 1931- *AmMWSc 92*
**Porter,** George Barrington 1939- *Who 92*
**Porter,** Gerald Bassett 1926- *AmMWSc 92*
**Porter,** Gerald Joseph 1937- *AmMWSc 92*
**Porter,** Geraldine Ruth 1932- *WhoAmP 91*
**Porter,** Gilbert Harris 1925- *AmMWSc 92*
**Porter,** Gloria Jean 1951- *WhoBlA 92*
**Porter,** Grady J. 1918- *WhoBlA 92*
**Porter,** Gregg Harlan 1958- *WhoEnt 92*
**Porter,** Hal 1911-1984 *RfGEnL 91*
**Porter,** Hardin Kibbe 1917- *AmMWSc 92*
**Porter,** Harry Boone 1923- *WhoRel 92*
**Porter,** Harry Randall 1952- *WhoAmP 91*
**Porter,** Harvey 1931- *WhoFI 92*
**Porter,** Hayden Samuel, Jr 1945- *AmMWSc 92*
**Porter,** Henry Knox, III 1957- *WhoFI 92*
**Porter,** Herschel Donovan 1924- *AmMWSc 92*
**Porter,** Horace 1837-1921 *BenetAL 91*
**Porter,** Howard Charles 1913- *WhoAmP 91*
**Porter,** Ivor Forsyth 1913- *Who 92*
**Porter,** Jack R 1938- *AmMWSc 92*
**Porter,** Jack Ray 1938- *WhoMW 92*
**Porter,** James Albert 1964- *WhoWest 92*
**Porter,** James Armer, Jr 1922- *AmMWSc 92*
**Porter,** James Colegrove 1937- *AmMWSc 92*
**Porter,** James Forrest 1928- *Who 92*
**Porter,** James Franklin *AmMWSc 92*
**Porter,** James H. 1933- *WhoBlA 92*
**Porter,** James Kenneth 1934- *WhoAmL 92*
**Porter,** James Morris 1931- *WhoAmL 92*
**Porter,** James Neil 1931- *WhoFI 92, WhoWest 92*
**Porter,** James W 1946- *AmMWSc 92*
**Porter,** Janet Elaine 1953- *WhoMW 92*
**Porter,** Janice Lee 1953- *SmATA 68*
**Porter,** Jeffrey Alan 1955- *WhoFI 92*
**Porter,** Jessica Gettemy 1956- *WhoAmL 92*
**Porter,** Jim R. *WhoMW 92*
**Porter,** Joe Ashby *DrAPF 91*
**Porter,** John Addison 1822-1866 *BiInAmS*
**Porter,** John Alan 1934- *Who 92*
**Porter,** John Andrew 1916- *Who 92*
**Porter,** John Charles 1925- *AmMWSc 92*
**Porter,** John E 1921- *AmMWSc 92*
**Porter,** John E. 1935- *AlmAP 92 [port]*
**Porter,** John Edward 1935- *WhoAmP 91, WhoMW 92*
**Porter,** John Henry 1950- *WhoBlA 92*
**Porter,** John Hill 1933- *WhoFI 92*
**Porter,** John J 1932- *AmMWSc 92*
**Porter,** John Richard 1932- *WhoBlA 92*
**Porter,** John Robert 1940- *AmMWSc 92*
**Porter,** John Simon H. *Who 92*
**Porter,** John Stephen 1932- *WhoEnt 92*
**Porter,** John T. 1941- *WhoBlA 92*
**Porter,** John Talbot 1825-1910 *BiInAmS*
**Porter,** John W. 1931- *WhoBlA 92*
**Porter,** John Willard 1915- *AmMWSc 92*
**Porter,** John William 1937- *AmMWSc 92*
**Porter,** John Wilson A. 1931- *WhoMW 92*
**Porter,** Johnny Ray 1944- *AmMWSc 92*
**Porter,** Jonathan 1938- *WhoWest 92*
**Porter,** Joseph Ashby 1942- *IntAu&W 91*
**Porter,** Joseph E., III 1946- *WhoBlA 92*
**Porter,** Joshua Roy 1921- *IntAu&W 91, Who 92, WrDr 92*
**Porter,** Joyce 1924-1990 *ConAu 133*
**Porter,** Joyce Klowden 1949- *WhoEnt 92*
**Porter,** Karen Collins 1953- *WhoMW 92*
**Porter,** Karl Hampton 1939- *WhoBlA 92, WhoEnt 92*
**Porter,** Katherine Ann 1951- *WhoMW 92*
**Porter,** Katherine Anne 1890-1980 *BenetAL 91, FacFETw, ModAWWr, TwCWW 91*
**Porter,** Katheryne Adelade 1934- *WhoWest 92*
**Porter,** Keith Roberts 1912- *AmMWSc 92*
**Porter,** Kenneth Raymond 1931- *AmMWSc 92*
**Porter,** Kevin 1950- *WhoBlA 92*
**Porter,** Lana Garner 1943- *WhoFI 92*
**Porter,** Lawrence Delpino 1932- *AmMWSc 92*
**Porter,** Lee 1929- *WhoRel 92*
**Porter,** Lee Albert 1934- *AmMWSc 92*
**Porter,** Leo Earle 1939- *AmMWSc 92*
**Porter,** Leonard Edgar 1934- *AmMWSc 92*
**Porter,** Leslie 1920- *IntWW 91, Who 92*
**Porter,** Lew F 1918- *AmMWSc 92*
**Porter,** Lionel 1943- *WhoBlA 92*
**Porter,** Lynn K 1929- *AmMWSc 92*
**Porter,** Marcellus Clay 1938- *AmMWSc 92*
**Porter,** Marcia C. *WhoEnt 92*
**Porter,** Marguerite Ann 1948- *Who 92*
**Porter,** Melvin Kenneth 1912- *Who 92*
**Porter,** Mia Lachone 1965- *WhoBlA 92*
**Porter,** Michael 1948- *TwCPaSc*
**Porter,** Michael Charles 1953- *WhoBlA 92, WhoMW 92*
**Porter,** Michael E. 1947- *WrDr 92*
**Porter,** Michael LeRoy 1947- *WhoBlA 92*
**Porter,** Michael Pell 1940- *WhoAmL 92, WhoWest 92*
**Porter,** Murray 1909- *Who 92*
**Porter,** Myron Joseph 1948- *WhoRel 92*
**Porter,** Nancy Jean 1930- *WhoRel 92*
**Porter,** Ned Allen 1943- *AmMWSc 92*
**Porter,** Neil Anthony 1930- *IntWW 91*
**Porter,** Nina *WrDr 92*
**Porter,** Noah 1811-1892 *BenetAL 91*
**Porter,** Nora Roxanne 1949- *WhoEnt 92*
**Porter,** Otha L. 1928- *WhoBlA 92*
**Porter,** Owen Archuel 1943- *AmMWSc 92*
**Porter,** Patricia L 1940- *WhoAmP 91*
**Porter,** Patrick A. 1944- *WhoBlA 92*
**Porter,** Paul A. d1975 *LesBEnT 92*
**Porter,** Paul David 1953- *WhoMW 92*
**Porter,** Peter 1929- *ConPo 91, WrDr 92*
**Porter,** Peter Neville Frederick 1929- *IntAu&W 91, IntWW 91, Who 92*
**Porter,** Quincy 1897-1966 *NewAmDM*
**Porter,** Ralph Franklyn 1942- *WhoRel 92*
**Porter,** Raymond P 1930- *AmMWSc 92*
**Porter,** Richard A 1933- *AmMWSc 92*
**Porter,** Richard Arlen 1930- *WhoAmP 91*
**Porter,** Richard D 1944- *AmMWSc 92*
**Porter,** Richard Dee 1923- *AmMWSc 92*
**Porter,** Richard Ernest 1933- *WhoWest 92*
**Porter,** Richard Francis 1928- *AmMWSc 92*
**Porter,** Richard Howard 1942- *WhoAmL 92*
**Porter,** Richard Needham 1932- *AmMWSc 92*
**Porter,** Richard Sylvester 1923- *WhoBlA 92*
**Porter,** Richard W 1913- *AmMWSc 92*
**Porter,** Robert 1932- *IntWW 91, Who 92*
**Porter,** Robert Carl, Jr. 1927- *WhoAmL 92*
**Porter,** Robert George 1924- *Who 92*
**Porter,** Robert H 1952- *WhoAmP 91*
**Porter,** Robert Hugh 1955- *WhoFI 92*
**Porter,** Robert Jerome, Jr. 1949- *WhoFI 92*
**Porter,** Robert Stanley 1924- *Who 92*
**Porter,** Robert Thomas 1949- *WhoEnt 92*
**Porter,** Robert William 1926- *WhoAmL 92*
**Porter,** Robert William 1938- *AmMWSc 92*
**Porter,** Robert Willis 1926- *AmMWSc 92*
**Porter,** Robert Wilson 1923- *Who 92*
**Porter,** Rodney Robert 1917-1985 *WhoNob 90*
**Porter,** Roger Blaine 1946- *WhoAmP 91*
**Porter,** Roger J 1942- *AmMWSc 92*
**Porter,** Roger Stephen 1928- *AmMWSc 92*
**Porter,** Ronald Dean 1945- *AmMWSc 92*
**Porter,** Roy *Who 92*
**Porter,** Samuel Richard 1952- *WhoRel 92*
**Porter,** Sanford Dee 1953- *AmMWSc 92*

**Porter,** Scott 1959- *WhoFI 92*
**Porter,** Scott E. 1924- *WhoBlA 92*
**Porter,** Sheena 1935- *WrDr 92*
**Porter,** Shirley 1930- *Who 92*
**Porter,** Spencer Kellogg 1937- *AmMWSc 92*
**Porter,** Stanley Earl 1956- *WhoRel 92*
**Porter,** Stephen Cummings 1934- *AmMWSc 92*
**Porter,** Stephen Winthrop 1925- *WhoEnt 92*
**Porter,** Steven Harold 1958- *WhoWest 92*
**Porter,** Stuart Williams 1937- *WhoFI 92*
**Porter,** Susan Gift 1948- *WhoRel 92*
**Porter,** Sydney W, Jr 1932- *AmMWSc 92*
**Porter,** Sylvia 1913-1991 *CurBio 91N, News 91*
**Porter,** Sylvia F. 1913-1991 *ConAu 134, NewYTBS 91 [port]*
**Porter,** Terence Lee 1935- *AmMWSc 92*
**Porter,** Terry 1963- *WhoBlA 92*
**Porter,** Thea *Who 92*
**Porter,** Thomas Conrad 1822-1901 *BiInAmS*
**Porter,** Thomas J. 1958- *WhoRel 92*
**Porter,** Thomas Joseph, Jr. 1941- *WhoEnt 92*
**Porter,** Thomas Wayne 1911- *AmMWSc 92*
**Porter,** Timothy L. *DrAPF 91*
**Porter,** Verna Louise 1941- *WhoAmL 92*
**Porter,** Vernon Ray 1935- *AmMWSc 92*
**Porter,** W. L. *WhoRel 92*
**Porter,** Walter 1590?-1659 *NewAmDM*
**Porter,** Walter Stanley 1909- *Who 92*
**Porter,** Walter Thomas, Jr. 1934- *WhoWest 92*
**Porter,** Warren Paul 1939- *AmMWSc 92*
**Porter,** Wilbur Arthur 1941- *AmMWSc 92*
**Porter,** William *WhoEnt 92*
**Porter,** William A *AmMWSc 92*
**Porter,** William E 1925- *WhoAmP 91*
**Porter,** William Frank 1951- *AmMWSc 92*
**Porter,** William Hudson 1940- *AmMWSc 92*
**Porter,** William L 1917- *AmMWSc 92*
**Porter,** William Samuel 1930- *AmMWSc 92*
**Porter,** William Sydney *BenetAL 91, FacFETw*
**Porter,** William Trotter 1809-1858 *BenetAL 91*
**Porter-Barge,** Yvonne 1942- *WhoBlA 92*
**Porter Of Luddenham,** Baron 1920- *IntWW 91, Who 92*
**Portera,** Alan August 1951- *WhoRel 92*
**Porterfield,** Christopher 1937- *WhoEnt 92*
**Porterfield,** Douglas Hunter 1963- *WhoFI 92*
**Porterfield,** Eugene E 1946- *WhoAmP 91*
**Porterfield,** Ira Deward 1920- *AmMWSc 92*
**Porterfield,** James Stuart 1924- *Who 92*
**Porterfield,** Jay G 1921- *AmMWSc 92*
**Porterfield,** Nolan *DrAPF 91*
**Porterfield,** Nolan 1936- *WhoMW 92*
**Porterfield,** RoseAnn Foppiani 1964- *WhoMW 92*
**Porterfield,** Susan Payne 1943- *AmMWSc 92*
**Porterfield,** William Wendell 1936- *AmMWSc 92*
**Portes,** Alejandro 1944- *ConAu 36NR*
**Portes,** Richard David 1941- *IntWW 91, Who 92*
**Porteus,** James Oliver 1929- *AmMWSc 92*
**Porth,** Carol Mattson 1930- *AmMWSc 92*
**Portilla,** Jose Antonio, Jr. 1926- *WhoHisp 92*
**Portillo,** Carol D. 1963- *WhoHisp 92*
**Portillo,** Ernesto *WhoHisp 92*
**Portillo,** Estela *DrAPF 91*
**Portillo,** Febe 1945- *WhoHisp 92*
**Portillo,** Juan 1945- *WhoHisp 92*
**Portillo,** Kimberly Joy 1962- *WhoWest 92*
**Portillo,** Michael Denzil Xavier 1953- *IntWW 91, Who 92*
**Portillo,** Raul M. 1955- *WhoHisp 92*
**Portillo,** Roberto 1942- *WhoHisp 92*
**Portillo Y Diez De Sollano,** Alvaro del 1914- *IntWW 91*
**Portis,** Alan Mark 1926- *AmMWSc 92*
**Portis,** Archie Ray, Jr 1949- *AmMWSc 92*
**Portis,** Charles 1933- *TwCWW 91, WrDr 92*
**Portis,** Charles McColl 1933- *IntAu&W 91*
**Portis,** John L 1943- *AmMWSc 92*
**Portis,** Kattie Harmon 1942- *WhoBlA 92*
**Portisch,** Hugo 1927- *ConAu 36NR*
**Portisch,** Lajos 1937- *IntWW 91*
**Portland,** Earl of 1919- *Who 92*
**Portland,** Paul James 1946- *WhoRel 92*
**Portlock,** Carver A. 1934- *WhoBlA 92*
**Portlock,** David Edward 1944- *AmMWSc 92*
**Portman** *Who 92*
**Portman,** Viscount 1934- *Who 92*
**Portman,** Deborah S 1948- *WhoAmP 91*
**Portman,** Donald James 1922- *AmMWSc 92*
**Portman,** Glenn Arthur 1949- *WhoAmL 92, WhoFI 92*
**Portman,** Oscar William 1924- *AmMWSc 92*
**Portman,** Robert Mason 1959- *WhoAmL 92*
**Portmann,** Glenn Arthur 1931- *AmMWSc 92*
**Portmann,** Walter Oddo 1929- *AmMWSc 92*
**Portner,** Allen 1934- *AmMWSc 92*
**Portney,** Joseph Nathaniel 1927- *WhoWest 92*
**Portnoff,** Michael Rodney 1949- *AmMWSc 92*
**Portnoi,** Henry *WhoEnt 92*
**Portnoy,** Alicia 1955- *LiExTwC*
**Portnoy,** Bernard 1929- *AmMWSc 92*
**Portnoy,** Debbi 1962- *AmMWSc 92*
**Portnoy,** Esther 1945- *AmMWSc 92*
**Portnoy,** Irwin Milton 1930- *WhoAmL 92*
**Portnoy,** Norman Abbye 1944- *AmMWSc 92*
**Portnoy,** Sara S. 1926- *WhoAmL 92*
**Portnoy,** Stephen Lane 1942- *AmMWSc 92*
**Portnoy,** William M 1930- *AmMWSc 92*
**Portobello,** Petronella *WrDr 92*
**Portoghese,** Philip S 1931- *AmMWSc 92*
**Porton,** Gary G. *WhoRel 92*
**Ports,** James Franklin, Jr 1958- *WhoAmP 91*
**Portsmouth,** Archdeacon of *Who 92*
**Portsmouth,** Bishop of 1935- *Who 92*
**Portsmouth,** Bishop of 1936- *Who 92*
**Portsmouth,** Earl of 1954- *Who 92*
**Portsmouth,** Provost of *Who 92*
**Portugais,** Howard L. 1939- *WhoEnt 92*
**Portugalov,** Nikolai S. *NewYTBS 91 [port]*
**Portuges,** Paul C. *DrAPF 91*
**Portuondo,** Jose Francisco 1953- *WhoHisp 92*
**Portway,** Christopher 1923- *IntAu&W 91*
**Portway,** Christopher Thomas *WhoAmP 91*
**Portway,** Douglas 1922- *TwCPaSc*
**Portwood,** Lucile Mitchell 1913- *AmMWSc 92*
**Portz,** Herbert Lester 1921- *AmMWSc 92*
**Porvaznik,** Martin 1947- *AmMWSc 92*
**Pory,** John 1572-1635 *BenetAL 91, BiInAmS*
**Porzel,** Francis Bernard 1913- *AmMWSc 92*
**Porzio,** Michael Anthony 1942- *AmMWSc 92*
**Posada-Angel,** Juan Carlos 1951- *WhoFI 92*
**Posadas Ocampo,** Juan Jesus 1926- *WhoRel 92*
**Posamentier,** Alfred S 1942- *AmMWSc 92*
**Posamentier,** Evelyn *DrAPF 91*
**Posavac,** Emil James 1939- *WhoMW 92*
**Posch,** Fritz 1911- *IntWW 91*
**Posch,** Robert John, Jr. 1950- *WhoAmL 92*
**Poschel,** Bruno Paul Henry 1929- *AmMWSc 92*
**Poschmann,** Andrew William 1939- *WhoFI 92*
**Poscover,** Maury B. 1944- *WhoAmL 92*
**Poseidon,** Pantelis Lee 1955- *WhoFI 92*
**Posen,** Gerald 1935- *AmMWSc 92*
**Posen,** Susan Orzack 1945- *WhoAmL 92*
**Poser,** Hans August Louis 1907- *IntWW 91*
**Poserina,** John J., Jr. 1932- *WhoAmL 92*
**Posey,** Alexander Lawrence 1873-1908 *BenetAL 91*
**Posey,** Bruce Keith 1952- *WhoBlA 92*
**Posey,** C J 1906- *AmMWSc 92*
**Posey,** Daniel Earl 1947- *AmMWSc 92*
**Posey,** Edward W. 1927- *WhoBlA 92*
**Posey,** Eldon Eugene *AmMWSc 92*
**Posey,** Elsa 1938- *WhoEnt 92*
**Posey,** Franz Adrian 1930- *AmMWSc 92*
**Posey,** Irvin L 1955- *WhoAmP 91*
**Posey,** Mark Nichols 1965- *WhoRel 92*
**Posey,** Robert Giles 1947- *AmMWSc 92*
**Posey,** Ronald Anthony 1953- *WhoBlA 92*
**Posey,** William Marvin 1954- *WhoRel 92*
**Posfay,** George 1921- *WhoRel 92*
**Posha,** D. Richard 1951- *WhoMW 92*
**Poshard,** Glenn 1945- *WhoAmP 91, WhoMW 92*
**Poshard,** Glenn W. 1945- *AlmAP 92 [port]*
**Poshusta,** Ronald D 1935- *AmMWSc 92*
**Posibeyev,** Grigoriy Andreyevich 1935- *IntWW 91*
**Poskanzer,** Arthur M 1931- *AmMWSc 92*
**Poskitt,** Trevor John 1934- *Who 92*
**Poskozim,** Paul Stanley 1940- *AmMWSc 92*
**Posler,** Gerry Lynn 1942- *AmMWSc 92*
**Poslusny,** Jerrold Neal 1944- *AmMWSc 92*
**Posluszny,** Usher 1947- *AmMWSc 92*
**Posnak,** Robert Lincoln 1938- *WhoIns 92*
**Posner,** Aaron Sidney 1920- *AmMWSc 92*
**Posner,** Brian Scott 1961- *WhoFI 92*
**Posner,** David S. 1945- *WhoAmL 92*
**Posner,** Edward Charles 1933- *AmMWSc 92, WhoWest 92*
**Posner,** Gary Herbert 1943- *AmMWSc 92*
**Posner,** Gerald Seymour 1927- *AmMWSc 92*
**Posner,** Henry, III 1955- *WhoFI 92*
**Posner,** Herbert Bernard 1930- *AmMWSc 92*
**Posner,** Herbert S 1931- *AmMWSc 92*
**Posner,** Irina *LesBEnT 92*
**Posner,** Jerome B 1932- *AmMWSc 92*
**Posner,** Linda Irene 1939- *WhoEnt 92*
**Posner,** Linda Rosanne 1940- *WhoWest 92*
**Posner,** Louis Joseph 1956- *WhoAmL 92*
**Posner,** Marilyn Hope Ackerman 1946- *WhoEnt 92*
**Posner,** Martin 1935- *AmMWSc 92*
**Posner,** Michael J. 1960- *WhoAmL 92*
**Posner,** Michael Vivian 1931- *IntWW 91, Who 92, WrDr 92*
**Posner,** Morton Jacob 1942- *AmMWSc 92*
**Posner,** Neil Barry 1949- *WhoWest 92*
**Posner,** Philip 1944- *AmMWSc 92*
**Posner,** Rebecca 1929- *Who 92, WrDr 92*
**Posner,** Richard *DrAPF 91*
**Posner,** Richard 1944- *IntAu&W 91, WrDr 92*
**Posner,** Richard A. 1939- *ConAu 135*
**Posner,** Richard Allen 1939- *WhoAmL 92, WhoAmP 91*
**Posner,** Roy Edward 1933- *WhoFI 92*
**Posner,** Victor 1918- *WhoFI 92*
**Posnett,** Richard 1919- *Who 92*
**Posnett,** Richard Neil 1919- *IntWW 91*
**Posnette,** Adrian Frank 1914- *IntWW 91, Who 92*
**Posnick,** Adolph 1926- *WhoFI 92*
**Posokhin,** Mikhail Vasil'evich 1910- *SovUnBD*
**Posokhin,** Mikhail Vasiliyevich 1910- *IntWW 91*
**Pospelov,** Germogen Sergeyevich 1914- *IntWW 91*
**Pospelov,** Petr Nikolaevich 1898-1979 *SovUnBD*
**Pospelov,** Pyotr N 1898-1979 *FacFETw*
**Pospisil,** Leopold Jaroslav 1923- *WrDr 92*
**Poss,** Howard Lionel 1925- *AmMWSc 92*
**Poss,** Janet C *WhoAmP 91*
**Poss,** Richard Leon 1944- *AmMWSc 92, WhoMW 92*
**Poss,** Stanley M 1929- *AmMWSc 92*
**Poss,** Stephen Daniel 1955- *WhoAmL 92, WhoFI 92*
**Possanza,** Genus John 1937- *AmMWSc 92*
**Possehl,** Carl Louis 1945- *WhoRel 92*
**Possemato,** Paul Michael 1933- *WhoWest 92*
**Possidente,** Bernard Philip, Jr 1954- *AmMWSc 92*
**Possin,** George Edward 1941- *AmMWSc 92*
**Possley,** Leroy Henry 1928- *AmMWSc 92*
**Possmayer,** Fred 1939- *AmMWSc 92*
**Post,** Alan 1914- *WhoWest 92*
**Post,** Alda Dzintra 1946- *WhoMW 92*
**Post,** Avery Denison 1924- *WhoRel 92*
**Post,** Benjamin 1911- *AmMWSc 92*
**Post,** Boyd Wallace 1928- *AmMWSc 92*
**Post,** Daniel 1929- *AmMWSc 92*
**Post,** David Alan 1941- *WhoEnt 92*
**Post,** Douglas Manners 1920- *AmMWSc 92*
**Post,** Douglass Edmund 1945- *AmMWSc 92*
**Post,** Elroy Wayne 1943- *AmMWSc 92*
**Post,** Emily 1873-1960 *BenetAL 91*
**Post,** Frederick Just 1929- *AmMWSc 92*
**Post,** Gaines, Jr. 1937- *WhoWest 92*
**Post,** George 1918- *AmMWSc 92*
**Post,** George Edward 1838-1909 *BiInAmS*
**Post,** H. Christian 1945- *WhoBlA 92*
**Post,** Harold L 1924- *WhoAmP 91*
**Post,** Herschel 1939- *IntWW 91, Who 92*
**Post,** Howard William 1896- *AmMWSc 92*
**Post,** Irving Gilbert 1937- *AmMWSc 92*
**Post,** J L 1929- *AmMWSc 92*
**Post,** John E 1926- *AmMWSc 92*
**Post,** Jonathan V *DrAPF 91*
**Post,** Joseph 1913- *AmMWSc 92*
**Post,** Kenneth Graham 1908- *Who 92*
**Post,** Louis Freeland 1849-1928 *DcAmImH*
**Post,** M Dean 1916- *AmMWSc 92*
**Post,** Madison John 1946- *AmMWSc 92*
**Post,** Markie *WhoEnt 92*
**Post,** Markie 1950- *ConTFT 9*
**Post,** Melville Davisson 1871-1930 *BenetAL 91*
**Post,** Mike *WhoEnt 92*
**Post,** Mortimer *IntAu&W 91X*
**Post,** Richard Freeman 1918- *AmMWSc 92*
**Post,** Richard S *AmMWSc 92*
**Post,** Robert Charles 1947- *WhoAmL 92*
**Post,** Robert Elliott 1924- *AmMWSc 92*
**Post,** Robert Lickely 1920- *AmMWSc 92*
**Post,** Robert M 1942- *AmMWSc 92*
**Post,** Roy G 1923- *AmMWSc 92*
**Post,** Russell Lee, Jr 1937- *WhoAmP 91*
**Post,** Ted *IntMPA 92*
**Post,** Wiley 1899-1935 *FacFETw [port]*
**Post,** William Joseph 1950- *WhoWest 92*
**Postal,** Gail A. 1938- *WhoEnt 92*
**Postal,** Steve Jon 1941- *WhoEnt 92*
**Poste,** George Henry 1944- *AmMWSc 92*
**Postel,** Suzan *WhoEnt 92*
**Postel-Vinay,** Andre 1911- *IntWW 91*
**Postelnek,** William 1918- *AmMWSc 92*
**Posten,** Harry Owen 1928- *AmMWSc 92*
**Posten,** William S. 1931- *WhoBlA 92*
**Poster,** Carol *DrAPF 91*
**Poster,** Cyril Dennis 1924- *WrDr 92*
**Poster,** Mark 1941- *IntAu&W 91, WrDr 92*
**Poster,** Steven 1944- *IntMPA 92*
**Poster,** Steven B. 1944- *WhoEnt 92*
**Posteritas** *ScFEYrs*
**Postgate,** John Raymond 1922- *IntWW 91, Who 92*
**Postgate,** Richmond Seymour 1908- *Who 92*
**Postgate,** Stephen 1959- *TwCPaSc*
**Posthuma,** Albert Elwood 1919- *WhoMW 92*
**Posthumus,** Richard Earl 1950- *WhoAmP 91*
**Postic,** Bosko 1931- *AmMWSc 92*
**Postilio,** Tom 1970- *WhoEnt 92*
**Postl,** Anton 1916- *AmMWSc 92*
**Postl,** Karl Anton *BenetAL 91*
**Postle,** Donald Sloan 1922- *AmMWSc 92*
**Postler,** Ermin Joseph 1942- *WhoFI 92*
**Postlethwait,** John Harvey 1944- *AmMWSc 92*
**Postlethwait,** Raymond Woodrow 1913- *AmMWSc 92*
**Postlethwait,** Samuel Noel 1918- *AmMWSc 92*
**Postlethwaite,** Arnold Eugene *AmMWSc 92*
**Postlethwaite,** Kenneth Eugene 1911- *WhoMW 92*
**Postlewait,** Harry Owen 1933- *WhoFI 92*
**Postlewaite,** David Sterling 1941- *WhoMW 92*
**Postlewaite,** Philip Frederick *WhoAmL 92*
**Postma,** Herman 1933- *AmMWSc 92*
**Postma,** Johannes Menne 1935- *ConAu 135*
**Postma,** Steven J. 1947- *WhoWest 92*
**Postman,** Robert Derek 1941- *AmMWSc 92*
**Postmus,** Clarence, Jr 1927- *AmMWSc 92*
**Postnikov,** Stanislav Ivanovich 1928- *IntWW 91*
**Postol,** Sidney S *WhoAmP 91*
**Poston,** Anita Owings 1949- *WhoAmL 92*
**Poston,** Bryan A 1924- *WhoAmP 91*
**Poston,** Carl C., Jr. 1921- *WhoBlA 92*
**Poston,** Ersa Hines 1921- *NotBlAW 92, WhoBlA 92*
**Poston,** Freddie Lee, Jr 1946- *AmMWSc 92*
**Poston,** Hugh Arthur 1929- *AmMWSc 92*
**Poston,** James Richard 1925- *WhoAmP 91*
**Poston,** John Michael 1935- *AmMWSc 92*
**Poston,** John Ware 1937- *AmMWSc 92*
**Poston,** McCracken, Jr 1959- *WhoAmP 91*
**Poston,** Richard Waverly 1914- *WhoMW 92*
**Poston,** Tom 1927- *IntMPA 92, WhoEnt 92*
**Postow,** Elliot 1940- *AmMWSc 92*
**Postyshev,** Pavel Petrovich 1887-1939 *SovUnBD*
**Posvar,** Mildred Miller 1924- *WhoEnt 92*
**Posvic,** Harvey Walter 1921- *AmMWSc 92*
**Poswick,** Charles 1924- *IntWW 91*
**Poswillo,** D E 1927- *AmMWSc 92*
**Poswillo,** David Ernest 1927- *Who 92*
**Posz,** Wayne Thomas 1947- *WhoAmP 91*
**Potac,** Svatopluk 1925- *IntWW 91*
**Potamian,** Brother 1847-1917 *BiInAmS*
**Potamius of Lisbon** d359? *EncEarC*
**Potapenko,** Fyodor Ivanovich 1927- *IntWW 91*
**Potaracke,** Rochelle Mary 1935- *WhoRel 92*
**Potash,** Milton 1924- *AmMWSc 92*
**Potash,** Stephen Jon 1945- *WhoWest 92*
**Potashner,** Steven Jay 1945- *AmMWSc 92*
**Potchen,** E James 1932- *AmMWSc 92*
**Potchen,** Joseph Anton 1931- *WhoIns 92*
**Pote,** Frank Robert, Sr 1919- *WhoIns 92*
**Poteat,** James Donald 1935- *WhoRel 92*
**Poteat,** William Louis 1944- *AmMWSc 92*
**Poteet,** Dwayne Lee 1959- *WhoMW 92*
**Poteet,** Kim Diane 1952- *WhoMW 92*
**Poteet,** Thomas M, Jr 1935- *WhoIns 92*
**Potempa,** Lawrence Albert 1951- *AmMWSc 92*
**Potemra,** Thomas Andrew 1938- *AmMWSc 92*
**Potente,** Eugene, Jr. 1921- *WhoFI 92, WhoMW 92*

**Potenza,** Joseph Anthony 1941- *AmMWSc 92*
**Potenza,** Joseph Michael 1947- *WhoAmL 92*
**Potesta,** Ralph J *WhoAmP 91*
**Poth,** Edgar J 1899- *AmMWSc 92*
**Poth,** Harry Augustus, Jr. 1911- *WhoAmL 92*
**Poth,** James Edward 1933- *AmMWSc 92*
**Poth,** Peter Paul 1929- *WhoFI 92*
**Poth,** Stefan Michael 1933- *WhoFI 92*
**Pothoven,** Marvin Arlo 1946- *AmMWSc 92, WhoMW 92*
**Potila,** Antti 1938- *IntWW 91*
**Potkay,** Stephen 1937- *AmMWSc 92*
**Potkonjak,** Theodore Samuel 1956- *WhoAmL 92*
**Potmesil,** Milam 1926- *AmMWSc 92*
**Potnis,** Vasant Raghunath 1928- *AmMWSc 92*
**Potocki,** Joseph Edmund 1936- *WhoWest 92*
**Potocki,** Kenneth Anthony 1940- *AmMWSc 92*
**Potoczny,** Henry Basil 1944- *AmMWSc 92*
**Potok,** Chaim *DrAPF 91*
**Potok,** Chaim 1929- *BenetAL 91, ConAu 35NR, ConNov 91, WrDr 92*
**Potokar,** Ralph MacNair 1952- *WhoMW 92*
**Potoker,** Edward Martin 1931- *WrDr 92*
**Potrafke,** Earl Mark 1930- *AmMWSc 92*
**Potratz,** Wayne Edward 1942- *WhoMW 92*
**Potrc,** Miran 1938- *IntWW 91*
**Pott,** George F, Jr 1943- *WhoAmP 91*
**Pottakis,** Yannis A. 1939- *IntWW 91*
**Pottasch,** Stuart Robert 1932- *AmMWSc 92*
**Pottenger,** Thomas A *WhoAmP 91*
**Potter,** A. Wayne 1953- *WhoRel 92*
**Potter,** Allan G 1930- *AmMWSc 92*
**Potter,** Allan L 1947- *WhoAmP 91*
**Potter,** Allen Meyers 1924- *Who 92*
**Potter,** Andrew Elwin, Jr 1926- *AmMWSc 92*
**Potter,** Arthur Kingscote 1905- *Who 92*
**Potter,** Beatrix 1866-1943 *FacFETw*
**Potter,** Beverly Ann 1944- *WhoFI 92*
**Potter,** Bridget *LesBEnT 92*
**Potter,** Bridget 1943- *WhoEnt 92*
**Potter,** Calvin 1945- *WhoAmP 91*
**Potter,** Carol *DrAPF 91*
**Potter,** Carol Stewart 1948- *WhoEnt 92*
**Potter,** Charlene Marie 1945- *WhoAmP 91*
**Potter,** Charles Arthur, Jr. 1925- *WhoWest 92*
**Potter,** Charles E. 1916-1979 *ConAu 135*
**Potter,** Charles Francis 1885-1962 *RelLAm 91*
**Potter,** Charles Steel, Jr. 1959- *WhoMW 92*
**Potter,** Clarkson Nott 1928- *WhoFI 92*
**Potter,** David Dickinson 1930- *AmMWSc 92*
**Potter,** David Edward 1937- *AmMWSc 92*
**Potter,** David Eric 1949- *AmMWSc 92*
**Potter,** David Samuel 1925- *AmMWSc 92*
**Potter,** Dennis 1935- *FacFETw, IntAu&W 91, IntMPA 92, IntWW 91, Who 92, WrDr 92*
**Potter,** Donald B 1923- *AmMWSc 92*
**Potter,** Donald Charles 1922- *Who 92*
**Potter,** Donald Irwin 1941- *AmMWSc 92*
**Potter,** Douglas Marion 1945- *AmMWSc 92*
**Potter,** Elizabeth Vaughan 1914- *AmMWSc 92*
**Potter,** Ernest Frank 1923- *Who 92*
**Potter,** Ernest Luther 1940- *WhoAmL 92*
**Potter,** Francis Malcolm 1932- *Who 92*
**Potter,** Frank 1936- *IntWW 91*
**Potter,** Frank Walter, Jr 1942- *AmMWSc 92*
**Potter,** Fred Leon 1948- *WhoIns 92*
**Potter,** George Ernest 1937- *WhoMW 92*
**Potter,** George Harris 1936- *WhoFI 92, WhoMW 92*
**Potter,** George Henry 1932- *AmMWSc 92*
**Potter,** Gerald Lee 1945- *AmMWSc 92*
**Potter,** Gilbert David 1924- *AmMWSc 92*
**Potter,** Hamilton Fish, Jr. 1928- *WhoAmL 92*
**Potter,** Helen Beatrix 1866-1943 *TwCPaSc*
**Potter,** Ian *Who 92*
**Potter,** Jack Arthur 1917- *WhoMW 92*
**Potter,** James Albert 1927- *WhoRel 92*
**Potter,** James D 1944- *AmMWSc 92*
**Potter,** James Gregor 1907- *AmMWSc 92*
**Potter,** James Martin 1941- *AmMWSc 92*
**Potter,** James Vincent 1936- *WhoRel 92*
**Potter,** Jane Huntington 1921- *AmMWSc 92*
**Potter,** Jay Hill *TwCWW 91, WrDr 92*
**Potter,** Jennifer 1949- *WrDr 92*
**Potter,** Jeremy *Who 92*
**Potter,** Jeremy 1922- *IntAu&W 91, WrDr 92*
**Potter,** Jeremy Patrick L. *Who 92*
**Potter,** John 1913- *Who 92*
**Potter,** John Clarkson 1921- *AmMWSc 92*
**Potter,** John Edward 1949- *WhoEnt 92*
**Potter,** John F 1925- *AmMWSc 92*
**Potter,** John Herbert 1928- *Who 92*
**Potter,** John Howell 1954- *WhoWest 92*
**Potter,** John Leith 1923- *AmMWSc 92*
**Potter,** John McEwen 1920- *Who 92*
**Potter,** John William 1918- *WhoAmL 92, WhoMW 92*
**Potter,** Joseph Raymond 1916- *Who 92*
**Potter,** Judith Diggs 1941- *WhoBlA 92*
**Potter,** Kenneth Roy 1919- *WhoRel 92*
**Potter,** Lawrence Merle 1924- *AmMWSc 92*
**Potter,** Lincoln Truslow 1933- *AmMWSc 92*
**Potter,** Loren David 1918- *AmMWSc 92*
**Potter,** Madeleine *IntMPA 92*
**Potter,** Malcolm *Who 92*
**Potter,** Margaret 1926- *IntAu&W 91, WrDr 92*
**Potter,** Mark Howard 1937- *Who 92*
**Potter,** Mary 1900-1981 *TwCPaSc*
**Potter,** Merle C 1936- *AmMWSc 92*
**Potter,** Michael 1924- *AmMWSc 92*
**Potter,** Michael 1951- *TwCPaSc*
**Potter,** Michael John 1969- *WhoEnt 92*
**Potter,** Michael William 1959- *WhoFI 92*
**Potter,** Myrtle Stephens 1958- *WhoBlA 92*
**Potter,** Nancy *DrAPF 91*
**Potter,** Neil H 1938- *AmMWSc 92*
**Potter,** Noel, Jr 1940- *AmMWSc 92*
**Potter,** Noel Marshall 1945- *AmMWSc 92, WhoMW 92*
**Potter,** Norman D 1928- *AmMWSc 92*
**Potter,** Norman N 1926- *AmMWSc 92*
**Potter,** Orlando B 1928- *WhoAmP 91*
**Potter,** Paul 1853-1921 *BenetAL 91*
**Potter,** Paul Edwin 1925- *AmMWSc 92, WhoMW 92*
**Potter,** Philip A. 1921- *DcEcMov*
**Potter,** Philip Alford 1921- *IntWW 91, Who 92*
**Potter,** Ralph Benajah, Jr. 1931- *WhoRel 92*
**Potter,** Ralph Miles 1927- *AmMWSc 92*
**Potter,** Raymond *Who 92*
**Potter,** Raymond 1933- *Who 92*
**Potter,** Richard C 1919- *AmMWSc 92*
**Potter,** Richard Clifford 1946- *WhoAmL 92*
**Potter,** Richard Lyle 1926- *AmMWSc 92*
**Potter,** Richard R 1926- *AmMWSc 92*
**Potter,** Richard Wendell 1932- *WhoEnt 92*
**Potter,** Robert Daniel 1923- *WhoAmL 92*
**Potter,** Robert Joseph 1932- *AmMWSc 92*
**Potter,** Robert L. Andrew 1932- *WhoWest 92*
**Potter,** Roderick H 1938- *WhoAmP 91*
**Potter,** Ronald Jeremy 1922- *Who 92*
**Potter,** Ronald Stanley James 1921- *Who 92*
**Potter,** Rosario H Yap 1928- *AmMWSc 92*
**Potter,** Rosemary *WhoAmP 91*
**Potter,** Suzanne *DrAPF 91*
**Potter,** Tanya Jean 1956- *WhoAmL 92*
**Potter,** Thomas D 1939- *WhoIns 92*
**Potter,** Thomas Eugene 1933- *WhoAmP 91*
**Potter,** Thomas Franklin 1941- *AmMWSc 92*
**Potter,** Tina Elizabeth 1961- *WhoEnt 92*
**Potter,** Trevor Alexander McClurg 1955- *WhoAmL 92*
**Potter,** Van Rensselaer 1911- *AmMWSc 92*
**Potter,** Vincent G. 1928- *WrDr 92*
**Potter,** Wentworth Edwards 1942- *WhoMW 92*
**Potter,** Wilfrid John *Who 92*
**Potter,** William Bartlett 1938- *WhoFI 92*
**Potter,** William Ian 1902- *Who 92*
**Potter,** William James 1948- *WhoFI 92*
**Potter,** Yerda McIntyre 1941- *WhoAmP 91*
**Potterton,** Homan 1946- *Who 92*
**Potthoff,** Richard Frederick 1932- *AmMWSc 92*
**Pottie,** David Laren 1952- *WhoEnt 92*
**Pottier,** Gerald J., Jr. 1946- *WhoWest 92*
**Pottinger,** Albert A. 1928- *WhoBlA 92*
**Pottinger,** William George 1916- *Who 92*
**Pottker,** Janice Marie 1948- *WhoFI 92*
**Pottle,** Christopher 1932- *AmMWSc 92*
**Pottle,** Harry 1925- *IntMPA 92*
**Pottmeyer,** Hermann Josef 1934- *WhoRel 92*
**Pottmeyer,** Judith Ann 1954- *AmMWSc 92*
**Pottorff,** Jo Ann 1936- *WhoAmP 91*
**Pottorff,** William Thomas 1914- *WhoAmP 91*
**Pottorff-Albrecht,** Phyllis Demeter 1942- *WhoRel 92*
**Pottruck,** David S. 1948- *WhoWest 92*
**Potts,** Albert Mintz 1914- *AmMWSc 92*
**Potts,** Annie 1952- *IntMPA 92, WhoEnt 92*
**Potts,** Anthony Vincent 1945- *WhoMW 92*
**Potts,** Archibold 1932- *Who 92*
**Potts,** Archie d1991 *Who 92N*
**Potts,** Barbara J 1932- *WhoAmP 91*
**Potts,** Barbara Joyce 1932- *WhoMW 92*
**Potts,** Barbara Susan 1950- *WhoWest 92*
**Potts,** Byron C 1930- *AmMWSc 92*
**Potts,** Charles *DrAPF 91*
**Potts,** Dennis Walker 1945- *WhoAmL 92*
**Potts,** Donald Cameron 1942- *AmMWSc 92*
**Potts,** Donald Harry 1921- *AmMWSc 92*
**Potts,** Donald Ralph 1930- *WhoRel 92*
**Potts,** Gordon Oliver 1924- *AmMWSc 92*
**Potts,** Harold E. 1921- *WhoBlA 92*
**Potts,** Howard Calvin 1928- *AmMWSc 92*
**Potts,** Humphrey 1931- *Who 92*
**Potts,** Ian 1936- *TwCPaSc*
**Potts,** James Edward 1918- *AmMWSc 92*
**Potts,** Jean 1910- *WrDr 92*
**Potts,** Jeff 1951- *WhoAmP 91*
**Potts,** John Calvin 1906- *AmMWSc 92*
**Potts,** John Earl 1944- *AmMWSc 92*
**Potts,** John Thomas, Jr 1932- *AmMWSc 92*
**Potts,** Kenneth Hampson d1990 *Who 92N*
**Potts,** Kevin T 1928- *AmMWSc 92*
**Potts,** Lawrence Walter 1945- *AmMWSc 92*
**Potts,** Malcolm 1935- *AmMWSc 92*
**Potts,** Mark John *AmMWSc 92*
**Potts,** Melvin Lester 1921- *AmMWSc 92*
**Potts,** Mena E. 1936- *WhoMW 92*
**Potts,** Peter 1935- *Who 92*
**Potts,** Richard 1938- *IntAu&W 91, WrDr 92*
**Potts,** Richard Allen 1940- *AmMWSc 92*
**Potts,** Robert Leslie 1944- *WhoAmL 92*
**Potts,** Robert Paul 1947- *WhoFI 92*
**Potts,** Robin 1944- *Who 92*
**Potts,** Sammie *WhoBlA 92*
**Potts,** Thomas Edmund 1908- *Who 92*
**Potts,** Thomas Lee 1962- *WhoMW 92*
**Potts,** William Rockhill, Jr. 1936- *WhoEnt 92*
**Potts-Williams,** Madge 1955- *WhoMW 92*
**Pottsepp,** L 1929- *AmMWSc 92*
**Potuznik,** Charles Laddy 1947- *WhoAmL 92*
**Potvin,** Alfred Raoul 1942- *AmMWSc 92, WhoMW 92*
**Potvin,** George Albert 1948- *WhoAmP 91*
**Potvin,** Jane B 1935- *WhoAmP 91*
**Potvin,** Pierre 1932- *AmMWSc 92*
**Potwardoski,** Elaine Noel 1957- *WhoEnt 92*
**Potworowski,** Edouard Francois 1940- *AmMWSc 92*
**Potyraj,** Paul Anthony 1960- *AmMWSc 92*
**Potzick,** James Edward 1941- *AmMWSc 92*
**Pou,** Jack Wendell 1923- *AmMWSc 92*
**Pou,** Wendell Morse 1937- *AmMWSc 92*
**Poucher,** John Scott 1945- *AmMWSc 92*
**Poucher,** Mellor Proctor 1929- *AmMWSc 92*
**Poucher,** William B 1948- *AmMWSc 92*
**Pouget,** Marie 1949- *WhoHisp 92*
**Pough,** Frederick Harvey 1906- *AmMWSc 92, WhoWest 92*
**Pough,** Frederick Harvey 1942- *AmMWSc 92*
**Pough,** Richard Hooper 1904- *AmMWSc 92*
**Pough,** W Newton 1921- *WhoAmP 91*
**Pough,** Willie Newton 1921- *WhoAmL 92*
**Pouilloux,** Jean 1917- *IntWW 91*
**Poujade,** Pierre 1920- *IntWW 91*
**Poujade,** Pierre Marie Raymond 1920- *BiDExR*
**Poujade,** Robert 1928- *IntWW 91*
**Poukey,** James W 1940- *AmMWSc 92*
**Poularikas,** Alexander D 1933- *AmMWSc 92*
**Poulenc,** Francis 1899-1963 *FacFETw, NewAmDM*
**Poulet,** Georges M. Joseph 1914- *IntWW 91*
**Poulet,** Robert 1893- *BiDExR*
**Poulides,** Fotis George 1914- *IntWW 91*
**Poulik,** Miroslav Dave 1923- *AmMWSc 92*
**Poulikakos,** Dimos 1955- *AmMWSc 92*
**Poulin,** A., Jr. *DrAPF 91*
**Poulin,** A., Jr. 1938- *ConPo 91, WrDr 92*
**Poulin,** Gabrielle 1929- *IntAu&W 91*
**Poulin,** Joseph Alphonse 1948- *WhoEnt 92*
**Poulin,** Thomas E 1956- *WhoAmP 91*
**Pouliot,** George Stephen 1954- *WhoEnt 92*
**Pouliot,** Roger M 1937- *WhoAmP 91*
**Poulos,** Dennis A 1932- *AmMWSc 92*
**Poulos,** Michael James 1931- *WhoFI 92, WhoIns 92*
**Poulos,** Nicholas A 1926- *AmMWSc 92*
**Poulos,** Spyros 1960- *WhoEnt 92*
**Poulose,** Pathickal K 1939- *AmMWSc 92*
**Poulsen,** Boyd Joseph 1933- *AmMWSc 92*
**Poulsen,** Dennis Robert 1946- *WhoWest 92*
**Poulsen,** Fern Sue 1959- *WhoMW 92*
**Poulsen,** Harold L *WhoAmP 91*
**Poulsen,** Keila Daun 1948- *WhoWest 92*
**Poulsen,** Lawrence Leroy 1933- *AmMWSc 92*
**Poulshock,** Marc Brad 1964- *WhoEnt 92*
**Poulsom,** Robert Colin 1947- *WhoAmL 92*
**Poulson,** Donald Frederick 1910- *AmMWSc 92*
**Poulson,** Gerry 1935- *WhoEnt 92*
**Poulson,** Lance Kuld 1943- *WhoMW 92*
**Poulson,** Richard Edwin 1928- *AmMWSc 92*
**Poulson,** Sandra Louise 1947- *WhoWest 92*
**Poulter,** Brian Henry 1941- *Who 92*
**Poulter,** Charles Dale 1942- *AmMWSc 92*
**Poulter,** Dolores Irma 1941- *AmMWSc 92*
**Poulter,** Howard C 1925- *AmMWSc 92*
**Poulter,** Thomas C 1897-1978 *FacFETw*
**Poultney,** Sherman King 1937- *AmMWSc 92*
**Poultney,** Tony 1938- *TwCPaSc*
**Poulton,** Bruce R 1927- *AmMWSc 92*
**Poulton,** Charles Edgar 1917- *AmMWSc 92*
**Poulton,** Craig Kidd 1951- *WhoFI 92*
**Poulton,** Richard Christopher 1938- *Who 92*
**Poulton,** Yvonne *TwCPaSc*
**Poumele,** Galea'i Peni 1926- *WhoAmP 91*
**Pouncey,** Denys Duncan Rivers 1906- *Who 92*
**Pouncey,** Philip Michael Rivers d1990 *Who 92N*
**Pouncey,** Philip Michael Rivers 1910- *IntWW 91*
**Pound,** Ezra 1885-1972 *BenetAL 91, BiDExR, FacFETw [port], PoeCrit 4 [port], RComAH*
**Pound,** Ezra Loomis 1885-1972 *LiExTwC*
**Pound,** John B. 1946- *WhoAmL 92*
**Pound,** John David 1946- *Who 92*
**Pound,** Keith Salisbury 1933- *Who 92*
**Pound,** Leslie *IntMPA 92*
**Pound,** Louise 1872-1958 *BenetAL 91*
**Pound,** Robert Vivian 1919- *AmMWSc 92, IntWW 91*
**Pound,** Roscoe 1870-1965 *BenetAL 91*
**Pound,** Thomas 1650?-1703 *BiInAmS*
**Pounder,** C. C. H. 1952- *WhoBlA 92*
**Pounder,** Elton Roy 1916- *AmMWSc 92*
**Pounder,** Rafton John d1991 *Who 92N*
**Pounders,** Gregory K. 1960- *WhoRel 92*
**Pounds,** Augustine Wright 1936- *WhoBlA 92*
**Pounds,** Billy Dean 1930- *WhoAmL 92*
**Pounds,** Edgar George Derek 1922- *Who 92*
**Pounds,** Elaine 1946- *WhoBlA 92*
**Pounds,** Elton William 1935- *WhoRel 92*
**Pounds,** Ernest Ray 1947- *WhoAmP 91*
**Pounds,** Kenneth Alwyne 1934- *IntWW 91, Who 92*
**Pounds,** Kenneth Ray 1942- *WhoBlA 92*
**Pounds,** Moses B. 1947- *WhoBlA 92*
**Poundstone,** William N 1925- *AmMWSc 92*
**Poungui,** Ange Edouard *IntWW 91*
**Pounian,** Charles A. 1926- *WhoMW 92*
**Pountain,** Eric 1933- *Who 92*
**Pountain,** Eric John 1933- *IntWW 91*
**Pountney,** David Willoughby 1947- *IntWW 91, Who 92*
**Poupard,** James Arthur 1943- *AmMWSc 92*
**Poupard,** Paul 1930- *IntWW 91, WhoRel 92*
**Pouplier,** Erik 1926- *IntAu&W 91*
**Pour-El,** Akiva 1925- *AmMWSc 92*
**Pour-El,** Marian Boykan *AmMWSc 92, WhoMW 92*
**Pourcho,** Roberta Grace 1934- *AmMWSc 92*
**Pourchot,** Pat *WhoAmP 91*
**Pourciau,** Kerry L. 1951- *WhoBlA 92*
**Poure,** James Allen 1937- *WhoMW 92*
**Pourfarrokh,** Ali *WhoWest 92*
**Pouring,** Andrew A 1932- *AmMWSc 92*
**Pournelle,** Jerry 1933- *IntAu&W 91, TwCSFW 91, WrDr 92*
**Pournelle,** Jerry Eugene 1933- *WhoWest 92*
**Pourtales,** Louis Francois de 1823?-1880 *BiInAmS*
**Pouschine,** John Laurence 1957- *WhoFI 92*
**Pousette,** Lena Marie *WhoEnt 92*
**Poussaint,** Alvin Francis 1934- *AmMWSc 92, WhoBlA 92*
**Poussaint,** Ann Ashmore 1942- *WhoBlA 92*
**Poussaint,** Renee Francine 1944- *NotBlAW 92, WhoBlA 92*
**Poussart,** Denis 1940- *AmMWSc 92*
**Pousseur,** Henri 1929- *ConCom 92, NewAmDM*
**Poust,** Rolland Irvin 1943- *AmMWSc 92*
**Pout,** Harry Wilfrid 1920- *Who 92*

**Poutsiaka,** John William 1925- AmMWSc 92
**Poutsiaka,** William J 1952- WhoIns 92
**Poutsma,** Marvin Lloyd 1937- AmMWSc 92
**Povar,** Morris Leon 1920- AmMWSc 92
**Poveda,** Carlos Manuel, III 1963- WhoHisp 92
**Poveda Burbano,** Alfredo d1990 IntWW 91N
**Poveda Burbano,** Alfredo 1925-1990 FacFETw
**Pover,** Alan John 1933- Who 92
**Poverman,** C.E. DrAPF 91
**Povey,** Ray 1947- TwCPaSc
**Povey,** Thomas George 1920- WhoFI 92
**Povich,** David 1935- WhoAmL 92
**Povinelli,** Louis A 1931- AmMWSc 92
**Povish,** Kenneth Joseph 1924- WhoMW 92, WhoRel 92
**Povlsen,** Shirley 1927- WhoAmP 91
**Povman,** Morton 1931- WhoAmP 91
**Povzhitkov,** Moysey Michael 1928- AmMWSc 92
**Pow,** Tom 1950- ConAu 134
**Powalky,** Karl Rudolph 1817-1881 BiInAmS
**Powanda,** Michael Christopher 1942- AmMWSc 92
**Powar,** William Louis 1946- WhoFI 92
**Powathil,** Joseph 1930- IntWW 91
**Powden,** Carl D 1954- WhoAmP 91
**Powders,** Vernon Neil 1941- AmMWSc 92
**Powditch,** Alan 1912- Who 92
**Powdrill,** Gary Leo 1945- WhoMW 92
**Powe,** B. W. 1955- ConAu 133
**Powe,** Bruce Allen 1925- IntAu&W 91, WrDr 92
**Powe,** Joseph S. 1946- WhoBlA 92
**Powe,** L. A. Scot, Jr. 1943- WhoAmL 92
**Powe,** Ralph Elward 1944- AmMWSc 92
**Powell** Who 92
**Powell,** Adam Clayton 1908-1972 FacFETw [port]
**Powell,** Adam Clayton, III 1946- WhoBlA 92
**Powell,** Adam Clayton, Jr. 1908-1972 AmPolLe, BlkLC [port], RelLAm 91
**Powell,** Adam Clayton, Sr. 1865-1953 RelLAm 91
**Powell,** Addie Scott 1922- WhoBlA 92
**Powell,** Alan 1928- AmMWSc 92
**Powell,** Alan T WhoAmP 91
**Powell,** Albert E 1919- AmMWSc 92
**Powell,** Albert Edgar, Jr. 1950- WhoEnt 92
**Powell,** Albert Edward 1927- Who 92
**Powell,** Alfred WhoBlA 92
**Powell,** Amy Purcell 1933- WhoAmP 91
**Powell,** Amy Tuck 1963- WhoAmP 91
**Powell,** Anthony 1905- CnDBLB 7 [port], ConNov 91, FacFETw, IntAu&W 91, RfGEnL 91, WrDr 92
**Powell,** Anthony Dymoke 1905- IntWW 91, Who 92
**Powell,** Archie James 1950- WhoBlA 92
**Powell,** Arnet L 1915- AmMWSc 92
**Powell,** Arnold Joseph Philip Who 92
**Powell,** Arnold Joseph Philip 1921- IntWW 91
**Powell,** Arthur Barrington 1918- Who 92
**Powell,** Aston Wesley 1909- WhoBlA 92
**Powell,** Benjamin Neff 1941- AmMWSc 92
**Powell,** Bernard Lawrence 1945- AmMWSc 92
**Powell,** Bernice Fletcher 1949- WhoBlA 92
**Powell,** Beverly Jo Taylor 1940- IntAu&W 91
**Powell,** Bobby Earl 1941- AmMWSc 92
**Powell,** Brad Bernell 1933- WhoEnt 92
**Powell,** Brian M 1938- AmMWSc 92
**Powell,** Bruce Allan 1941- AmMWSc 92
**Powell,** Bud 1924-1966 NewAmDM
**Powell,** Burnele Venable 1947- WhoAmL 92
**Powell,** Burwell Frederick 1933- AmMWSc 92
**Powell,** C Clayton 1927- WhoAmP 91, WhoBlA 92
**Powell,** C J WhoAmP 91
**Powell,** Carol Christine 1941- WhoMW 92
**Powell,** Cecil Frank 1903-1969 WhoNob 90
**Powell,** Cedric John 1935- AmMWSc 92
**Powell,** Charles 1941- Who 92
**Powell,** Charles Carleton, Jr 1942- AmMWSc 92
**Powell,** Charles David 1941- IntWW 91
**Powell,** Charles L., Jr. 1931- WhoBlA 92
**Powell,** Charles Lewis 1933- WhoAmP 91
**Powell,** Charles M. d1991 NewYTBS 91
**Powell,** Charles P. 1923- WhoBlA 92
**Powell,** Charles William 1937- WhoRel 92
**Powell,** Christopher Gaylord 1969- WhoEnt 92
**Powell,** Clarence Dean, Jr. 1939- WhoBlA 92
**Powell,** Clayton Jermiah, Jr 1957- WhoAmP 91
**Powell,** Clilan Bethany 1894-1977 WhoBlA 92N
**Powell,** Clinton Cobb 1918- AmMWSc 92
**Powell,** Colin 1937- ConBlB 1 [port]
**Powell,** Colin L WhoAmP 91
**Powell,** Colin L 1937- FacFETw, WhoBlA 92
**Powell,** Colin Luther 1937- IntWW 91, NewYTBS 91 [port], Who 92
**Powell,** Craig 1940- WrDr 92
**Powell,** Craig Steven 1950- WhoAmL 92
**Powell,** Curtis Everett 1961- WhoEnt 92
**Powell,** Dannye Romine DrAPF 91
**Powell,** Darlene Wright 1960- WhoBlA 92
**Powell,** Darrell Lee 1959- WhoBlA 92
**Powell,** David 1914- Who 92
**Powell,** David Clark 1927- WhoWest 92
**Powell,** David Greatorex 1933- WhoFI 92
**Powell,** David L. 1938- WhoBlA 92
**Powell,** David Lee 1936- AmMWSc 92
**Powell,** David Wayne 1957- WhoRel 92
**Powell,** Dawn 1897-1965 BenetAL 91, ConLC 66 [port]
**Powell,** Dennis Duane 1961- WhoRel 92
**Powell,** DeWayne Anthone 1950- WhoMW 92
**Powell,** Dewi Watkin 1920- Who 92
**Powell,** Diane Elaine 1955- WhoAmL 92
**Powell,** Dick d1963 LesBEnT 92
**Powell,** Dilys IntAu&W 91
**Powell,** Dilys 1901- Who 92
**Powell,** Don Watson 1938- AmMWSc 92
**Powell,** Donald Ashmore 1938- AmMWSc 92
**Powell,** Dudley Vincent 1917- WhoBlA 92
**Powell,** Durwood Royce 1951- WhoAmL 92
**Powell,** Earl Dean 1959- WhoRel 92
**Powell,** Edward Gordon 1946- AmMWSc 92
**Powell,** Edward Lee 1941- WhoAmP 91
**Powell,** Edward Lee, I 1958- WhoEnt 92, WhoMW 92
**Powell,** Enid Levinger DrAPF 91
**Powell,** Enoch IntWW 91, Who 92
**Powell,** Enoch 1912- IntAu&W 91, WrDr 92
**Powell,** Enoch 1915- FacFETw
**Powell,** Ernestine Breisch 1906- WhoFI 92, WhoMW 92
**Powell,** Ervin William 1922- AmMWSc 92
**Powell,** Francis Turner 1914- Who 92
**Powell,** Francis X 1929- AmMWSc 92
**Powell,** Frank ScFEYrs
**Powell,** Frank Ludwig, Jr 1952- AmMWSc 92
**Powell,** Fred Earl, III 1930- WhoRel 92
**Powell,** G M, III 1910- AmMWSc 92
**Powell,** Gary Lee 1941- AmMWSc 92
**Powell,** Gayle Lett 1943- WhoBlA 92
**Powell,** Geoffrey Who 92
**Powell,** Geoffrey 1914- WrDr 92
**Powell,** Geoffry Charles Hamilton 1920- Who 92
**Powell,** George Everett, III 1948- WhoFI 92, WhoMW 92
**Powell,** George Everett, Jr. 1926- WhoMW 92
**Powell,** George Louis 1940- AmMWSc 92
**Powell,** George Wythe 1936- AmMWSc 92
**Powell,** Georgette Seabrooke 1916- WhoBlA 92
**Powell,** Gloria J. 1936- WhoBlA 92
**Powell,** Gordon George 1911- WrDr 92
**Powell,** Gordon W 1928- AmMWSc 92
**Powell,** Grady Wilson 1932- WhoBlA 92
**Powell,** Graham Reginald 1935- AmMWSc 92
**Powell,** Gregory DrAPF 91
**Powell,** H. Jefferson 1954- WhoAmL 92
**Powell,** Harold 1932- AmMWSc 92
**Powell,** Harold Grant 1957- WhoRel 92
**Powell,** Harry Allan Rose 1912- Who 92
**Powell,** Harry Douglas 1937- AmMWSc 92
**Powell,** Hazel Nunn 1935- WhoAmP 91
**Powell,** Herbert Marcus d1991 Who 92N
**Powell,** Horace W, Sr WhoAmP 91
**Powell,** Howard B 1933- AmMWSc 92
**Powell,** Hugh N 1922- AmMWSc 92
**Powell,** Jack Edward 1921- AmMWSc 92
**Powell,** James 1942- TwCWW 91, WrDr 92
**Powell,** James Bobbitt 1938- WhoFI 92
**Powell,** James Cleveland 1937- WhoAmL 92
**Powell,** James Dan 1934- WhoWest 92
**Powell,** James Daniel 1934- AmMWSc 92
**Powell,** James Dixie 1938- WhoRel 92
**Powell,** James Henry 1926- AmMWSc 92
**Powell,** James Lawrence 1936- AmMWSc 92, WhoWest 92
**Powell,** James Leon 1957- WhoFI 92
**Powell,** James R, Jr 1932- AmMWSc 92
**Powell,** James Raymond 1937- WhoMW 92
**Powell,** James Richard 1944- WhoRel 92
**Powell,** Jane 1929- IntMPA 92
**Powell,** Jeanette Deloris 1942- WhoMW 92
**Powell,** Jeanne Adele 1933- AmMWSc 92
**Powell,** Jeff 1939- AmMWSc 92
**Powell,** Jerrel B 1930- AmMWSc 92
**Powell,** Jerry Alan 1933- AmMWSc 92
**Powell,** Jerry T. 1933- WhoAmL 92
**Powell,** Jim Wayne 1952- WhoEnt 92
**Powell,** John 1882-1963 NewAmDM
**Powell,** John Alfred 1923- Who 92
**Powell,** John Allen 1947- WhoAmP 91
**Powell,** John Duane 1925- WhoAmP 91
**Powell,** John Enoch 1912- IntWW 91, Who 92
**Powell,** John Frederick 1915- Who 92
**Powell,** John Geoffrey 1928- Who 92
**Powell,** John Leonard 1919- AmMWSc 92
**Powell,** John Lewis 1902- WhoBlA 92
**Powell,** John Lewis 1950- Who 92
**Powell,** John Paul 1950- WhoRel 92
**Powell,** John R WhoAmP 91
**Powell,** John Wesley 1834-1902 BenetAL 91, BiInAmS
**Powell,** John William 1928- WhoAmP 91
**Powell,** Jonathan Leslie 1947- IntWW 91, Who 92
**Powell,** Joseph DrAPF 91
**Powell,** Joseph E 1952- IntAu&W 91
**Powell,** Joseph Hansford 1946- WhoBlA 92
**Powell,** Joseph T. 1923- WhoBlA 92
**Powell,** Juan Herschel 1960- WhoBlA 92
**Powell,** Julia Gertrude 1907- WhoWest 92
**Powell,** Justin Christopher 1943- AmMWSc 92
**Powell,** Keith Peter 1955- WhoWest 92
**Powell,** Kenneth Alasandro 1945- WhoBlA 92
**Powell,** Kenneth Edward 1952- WhoAmL 92
**Powell,** Kenneth Grant 1960- AmMWSc 92
**Powell,** Lane Alan 1955- WhoWest 92
**Powell,** Larson Merrill 1932- WhoFI 92
**Powell,** Lawrie William 1934- Who 92
**Powell,** Leola P. 1932- WhoBlA 92
**Powell,** Leslie Charles 1927- AmMWSc 92
**Powell,** Lewis Earl 1927- WhoMW 92
**Powell,** Lewis F, Jr 1907- WhoAmP 91
**Powell,** Lewis Franklin, Jr 1907- FacFETw, IntWW 91, Who 92, WhoAmL 92
**Powell,** Loyd Earl, Jr 1928- AmMWSc 92
**Powell,** Marvin 1955- WhoBlA 92
**Powell,** Mel 1923- ConCom 92, NewAmDM, WhoWest 92
**Powell,** Melchior Daniel 1935- WhoWest 92
**Powell,** Michael WhoEnt 92
**Powell,** Michael 1905-1990 AnObit 1990, FacFETw, IntDcF 2-2 [port]
**Powell,** Michael, and Emeric Pressburger IntDcF 2-2 [port]
**Powell,** Michael A 1937- AmMWSc 92
**Powell,** Michael Anthony 1963- NewYTBS 91 [port]
**Powell,** Michael Francis 1950- WhoMW 92
**Powell,** Michael James David 1936- IntWW 91, Who 92
**Powell,** Michael Robert 1941- AmMWSc 92
**Powell,** Michael Vance 1946- WhoAmL 92
**Powell,** Mike 1963- BlkOlyM
**Powell,** Miles, Jr. 1926- WhoFI 92
**Powell,** Myrtis H. 1939- WhoBlA 92
**Powell,** Nathaniel Thomas 1928- AmMWSc 92
**Powell,** Neil 1948- ConAu 34NR, ConPo 91, IntAu&W 91, WrDr 92
**Powell,** Nicholas 1935- Who 92
**Powell,** Noble R 1930- AmMWSc 92
**Powell,** Norborne Berkeley 1914- AmMWSc 92
**Powell,** Norman Scott 1934- WhoEnt 92
**Powell,** Padgett DrAPF 91
**Powell,** Padgett 1952- WrDr 92
**Powell,** Pedgett 1952- IntAu&W 91
**Powell,** Peggy Jean 1933- WhoWest 92
**Powell,** Percival Hugh 1912- Who 92
**Powell,** Peter Irwin Augustus 1942- WhoEnt 92
**Powell,** Peter John 1928- WhoRel 92
**Powell,** Philip IntWW 91
**Powell,** Philip 1921- Who 92
**Powell,** Philip Melancthon, Jr. 1941- WhoBlA 92
**Powell,** R B 1920- AmMWSc 92
**Powell,** Ralph Robert 1936- AmMWSc 92
**Powell,** Ramon Jesse 1935- WhoFI 92
**Powell,** Ray WhoAmP 91
**Powell,** Raymond 1928- Who 92
**Powell,** Raymond William 1944- WhoFI 92
**Powell,** Rex Lynn 1942- AmMWSc 92
**Powell,** Richard 1909- Who 92
**Powell,** Richard Anthony 1917- AmMWSc 92
**Powell,** Richard Cinclair 1929- AmMWSc 92, WhoMW 92
**Powell,** Richard Clarence 1943- WhoMW 92
**Powell,** Richard Conger 1939- AmMWSc 92
**Powell,** Richard Duane 1935- WhoWest 92
**Powell,** Richard Grant 1938- AmMWSc 92
**Powell,** Richard James 1931- AmMWSc 92
**Powell,** Richard Maurice 1951- WhoBlA 92
**Powell,** Richard Royle 1909- IntWW 91
**Powell,** Rita 1922- WhoRel 92
**Powell,** Robert 1944- IntWW 91
**Powell,** Robert Delafield 1919- AmMWSc 92
**Powell,** Robert Dominick 1942- WhoFI 92
**Powell,** Robert E. 1919- WhoBlA 92
**Powell,** Robert Ellis 1936- AmMWSc 92
**Powell,** Robert Eugene 1955- WhoMW 92
**Powell,** Robert Everett 1934- WhoRel 92
**Powell,** Robert Lane B. Who 92
**Powell,** Robert Lee 1928- AmMWSc 92
**Powell,** Robert Meaker 1930- WhoBlA 92
**Powell,** Robert W, Jr 1929- AmMWSc 92
**Powell,** Robert Wendell, Jr. 1930- WhoFI 92
**Powell,** Robert William 1909- Who 92
**Powell,** Roberta A. 1952- WhoWest 92
**Powell,** Robin Dale 1934- AmMWSc 92
**Powell,** Robin Thigpen 1958- WhoMW 92
**Powell,** Roderick Anthony 1964- WhoFI 92
**Powell,** Roger d1990 Who 92N
**Powell,** Roger Allen 1949- AmMWSc 92
**Powell,** Roger Gant 1949- WhoFI 92
**Powell,** Ronald Allan 1946- AmMWSc 92
**Powell,** Ronald James 1949- WhoWest 92
**Powell,** Sally Jane Who 92
**Powell,** Sharon Kay 1961- AmMWSc 92
**Powell,** Sharon Lee 1940- WhoFI 92
**Powell,** Shirley DrAPF 91
**Powell,** Smith Thompson, III 1940- AmMWSc 92
**Powell,** Stephen Lee 1958- WhoMW 92
**Powell,** Stephen Walter 1955- WhoAmL 92
**Powell,** Steven Loyd 1954- WhoRel 92
**Powell,** Talmage 1920- IntAu&W 91, WrDr 92
**Powell,** Ted Ferrell 1935- WhoWest 92
**Powell,** Thomas 1809-1887 BenetAL 91
**Powell,** Thomas Francis A. 1925- WhoBlA 92
**Powell,** Thomas Joseph 1967- WhoWest 92
**Powell,** Thomas Mabrey 1942- AmMWSc 92
**Powell,** Thomas Shaw 1946- AmMWSc 92
**Powell,** Tim Who 92
**Powell,** Verne Q. 1879-1968 NewAmDM
**Powell,** Victor George Edward 1929- Who 92
**Powell,** Violet 1912- IntAu&W 91, WrDr 92
**Powell,** Virginia TwCPaSc
**Powell,** Walter, Jr. WhoEnt 92
**Powell,** Walter E 1931- WhoAmP 91
**Powell,** Warren Howard 1934- AmMWSc 92
**Powell,** Watson, Jr 1917- WhoIns 92
**Powell,** Wayne Hugh 1946- WhoBlA 92
**Powell,** Wellington 1959- WhoWest 92
**Powell,** Wendell WhoAmP 91
**Powell,** William 1935- WhoBlA 92
**Powell,** William Albert 1935- WhoFI 92
**Powell,** William Allan 1921- AmMWSc 92
**Powell,** William Arnold, Jr. 1929- WhoFI 92
**Powell,** William J. 1908- WhoBlA 92
**Powell,** William John, Jr 1935- AmMWSc 92
**Powell,** William Morton 1930- AmMWSc 92
**Powell,** William O., Jr. 1934- WhoBlA 92
**Powell,** William Rhys 1948- Who 92
**Powell,** William Roger 1953- WhoRel 92
**Powell,** William St John 1945- AmMWSc 92
**Powell,** Yvonne Macon 1936- WhoBlA 92
**Powell-Cotton,** Christopher 1918- Who 92
**Powell-Jones,** John E. 1925- IntWW 91
**Powell-Jones,** John Ernest 1925- Who 92
**Powell-Smith,** Vincent 1939- IntAu&W 91, WrDr 92
**Powelson,** Elizabeth Eugenie 1924- AmMWSc 92
**Powelson,** John Palen 1920- WhoWest 92, WrDr 92
**Powelson,** Robert Loran 1929- AmMWSc 92
**Powen,** John Thomas 1963- WhoAmL 92
**Power,** Alastair John Cecil 1958- Who 92
**Power,** Brian St Quentin, Mrs. Who 92
**Power,** Caroline 1955- TwCPaSc
**Power,** Cornelius Michael 1913- WhoRel 92
**Power,** Cyril 1872-1951 TwCPaSc
**Power,** Dennis Michael 1941- AmMWSc 92, WhoWest 92
**Power,** Dorothy K 1932- WhoAmP 91

Power, Eugene Barnum 1905- Who 92
Power, F. William 1925- WhoMW 92
Power, Geoffrey 1933- AmMWSc 92
Power, Gordon G 1935- AmMWSc 92
Power, Harry Waldo, III 1945- AmMWSc 92
Power, Jack, Jr. 1945- WhoRel 92
Power, James 1944- TwCPaSc
Power, James Francis 1929- AmMWSc 92
Power, Joan F 1958- AmMWSc 92
Power, John Bruce 1936- WhoAmL 92, WhoFI 92
Power, John G 1932- WhoIns 92
Power, John Paul 1958- WhoAmP 91
Power, Jules 1921- WhoEnt 92
Power, Leonel 1380?-1445 NewAmDM
Power, Marjorie DrAPF 91
Power, Mary Claude WhoRel 92
Power, Mary Susan WhoAmP 91
Power, Michael George 1924- Who 92
Power, Mimi Mary Anne 1955- WhoWest 92
Power, Noel Plunkett 1929- Who 92
Power, Robert Cornelius 1922- WhoBlA 92
Power, Thomas G WhoAmP 91
Power, Victor DrAPF 91
Power, Walter Robert 1924- AmMWSc 92
Power, William Edward 1915- WhoRel 92
Power, William Larkin 1934- WhoRel 92
Powers, Alan Dale 1929- WhoWest 92
Powers, Alexandra Maximillan 1948- WhoEnt 92
Powers, Ann 1946- WhoAmL 92
Powers, Anna Bertha Josephine 1912- WhoAmP 91
Powers, Anne 1913- WrDr 92
Powers, Anthony Richard, Jr. 1942- WhoMW 92
Powers, Arthur B 1928- WhoAmP 91
Powers, Basil L 1932- WhoAmP 91
Powers, Bill 1931- WrDr 92
Powers, Bruce Postell 1940- WhoRel 92
Powers, C.F., Jr. 1923- IntMPA 92
Powers, Charles F. DrAPF 91
Powers, Cynthia Ann Munoz 1963- WhoMW 92
Powers, Dale Robert 1949- AmMWSc 92
Powers, Dana Auburn 1948- AmMWSc 92
Powers, Daniel D 1935- AmMWSc 92
Powers, Darden 1932- AmMWSc 92
Powers, David Leon 1932- WhoWest 92
Powers, David Leusch 1939- AmMWSc 92
Powers, David Richard 1939- WhoMW 92
Powers, David Vincent 1954- WhoWest 92
Powers, Deane Fishburne, Jr. 1955- WhoFI 92
Powers, Dennis A 1938- AmMWSc 92
Powers, Dennis Harley 1938- WhoEnt 92
Powers, Donald Howard, Jr 1930- AmMWSc 92
Powers, Donna Dottley 1960- WhoEnt 92
Powers, Doris Hurt 1927- WhoFI 92
Powers, Dudley 1911- WhoEnt 92
Powers, Edmund Maurice AmMWSc 92
Powers, Edward Alton 1927- WhoRel 92
Powers, Edward Herbert 1942- WhoAmL 92
Powers, Edward James 1936- AmMWSc 92
Powers, Edward Joseph, Jr 1935- AmMWSc 92
Powers, Edward Lawrence 1915- AmMWSc 92
Powers, Edwin Malvin 1915- WhoWest 92
Powers, Eldon Nathaniel 1932- WhoFI 92
Powers, Ernest Michael 1942- WhoMW 92
Powers, Evelyn Joyce WhoEnt 92
Powers, Frank 1941- WhoEnt 92
Powers, Gary James 1945- AmMWSc 92
Powers, Georgia 1933- NotBlAW 92
Powers, Georgia M. WhoBlA 92
Powers, Georgia M 1923- WhoAmP 91
Powers, Gerard E, Jr 1934- WhoAmP 91
Powers, Gregory Robert 1960- WhoEnt 92
Powers, Harry Robert, Jr 1923- AmMWSc 92
Powers, Hurshal George 1933- WhoWest 92
Powers, J Bradley 1937- AmMWSc 92
Powers, J. Edward 1947- WhoEnt 92
Powers, J. F. 1917- BenetAL 91, ConNov 91, IntAu&W 91, WrDr 92
Powers, James B. WhoRel 92
Powers, James Cecil 1937- AmMWSc 92
Powers, James Francis 1938- WhoFI 92
Powers, James J 1936- WhoIns 92
Powers, James Matthew 1943- AmMWSc 92
Powers, Jean D 1930- AmMWSc 92
Powers, JoAnne Patricia 1953- WhoWest 92
Powers, John A 1922-1980 FacFETw
Powers, John A. 1926- IntWW 91
Powers, John Clancey, Jr 1931- AmMWSc 92
Powers, John E 1927- AmMWSc 92
Powers, John G., Jr. 1930- WhoMW 92
Powers, John Joseph 1918- AmMWSc 92
Powers, John Kieran 1947- WhoAmL 92
Powers, John Michael 1946- AmMWSc 92
Powers, John Orin 1922- AmMWSc 92
Powers, John Patrick 1943- AmMWSc 92
Powers, John R. 1945- ConLC 66 [port]
Powers, John Richard, Jr. 1931- WhoMW 92
Powers, Joseph 1931- AmMWSc 92
Powers, Joseph Edward 1949- AmMWSc 92
Powers, Joseph Robert 1948- AmMWSc 92
Powers, K H 1925- AmMWSc 92
Powers, Kathryn Dolores 1929- WhoMW 92
Powers, Kendall Gardner 1930- AmMWSc 92
Powers, L C TwCSFW 91
Powers, Larry James 1944- AmMWSc 92
Powers, Linda Sue 1948- AmMWSc 92
Powers, Lonnie Austin 1945- WhoAmL 92
Powers, Louis John 1912- AmMWSc 92
Powers, M L IntAu&W 91X, WrDr 92
Powers, Mala 1921- IntMPA 92
Powers, Mala 1931- WhoEnt 92
Powers, Mamon, Sr. WhoBlA 92
Powers, Mamon M., Jr. 1948- WhoBlA 92
Powers, Marcelina Venus 1927- AmMWSc 92
Powers, Marcus Eugene 1929- WhoAmL 92, WhoFI 92
Powers, Mark Healey 1954- WhoAmP 91
Powers, Michael Brian 1953- WhoAmL 92
Powers, Michael Jerome 1941- AmMWSc 92
Powers, Nora WrDr 92
Powers, Patricia Lynn 1952- WhoMW 92
Powers, Patricia Stacy WhoAmL 92
Powers, Patrick J. WhoRel 92
Powers, Paul Joseph 1935- WhoFI 92, WhoMW 92
Powers, Paul S 1905- ScFEYrs
Powers, Paul William 1942- WhoAmP 91
Powers, Paullete 1941- WhoFI 92, WhoWest 92
Powers, Pierce William, Jr. 1946- WhoMW 92
Powers, Ray Lloyd 1929- WhoAmP 91
Powers, Richard F., III 1946- WhoFI 92
Powers, Richard James 1940- AmMWSc 92
Powers, Robert D 1933- AmMWSc 92
Powers, Robert Field AmMWSc 92
Powers, Robert M 1942- IntAu&W 91, WrDr 92
Powers, Robert S, Jr 1934- AmMWSc 92
Powers, Robert William 1922- AmMWSc 92
Powers, Runas, Jr. 1938- WhoBlA 92
Powers, Sharon A. 1955- WhoWest 92
Powers, Stefanie 1942- IntMPA 92
Powers, Stefanie 1945- WhoEnt 92
Powers, Stephen 1936- WhoWest 92
Powers, Stephen Lee 1966- WhoMW 92
Powers, Thomas E 1925- AmMWSc 92
Powers, Tim WrDr 92
Powers, Tim 1952- ConAu 134, TwCSFW 91
Powers, Wayne Fuller 1961- WhoEnt 92
Powers, Wendell Holmes 1915- AmMWSc 92
Powers, William Alan 1952- WhoWest 92
Powers, William Allen, III AmMWSc 92
Powers, William Charles, Jr. 1946- WhoAmL 92
Powers, William D WhoAmP 91
Powers, William Francis 1940- AmMWSc 92
Powers, William John 1949- AmMWSc 92
Powers, William Shotwell 1910- WhoAmP 91
Powers, William T. 1926- WrDr 92
Powers, Winston Donald 1930- WhoBlA 92
Powers Lee, Susan Glenn AmMWSc 92
Powerscourt, Viscount 1935- Who 92
Powerscourt, Sheila WrDr 92
Powhatan d1618 BenetAL 91
Powis, Earl of 1925- Who 92
Powis, Alfred 1930- IntWW 91, WhoFI 92
Powis, Constance Gail 1946- WhoAmL 92
Powis, Garth 1946- AmMWSc 92
Powitz, Robert W 1942- AmMWSc 92
Powl, Theodore Guthrie 1943- WhoWest 92
Powledge, Fred 1935- WrDr 92
Powlen, David Michael 1953- WhoMW 92
Powles, Guy 1905- Who 92
Powles, Guy Richardson 1905- IntWW 91
Powles, John G 1936- WhoIns 92
Powles, Percival Mount 1930- AmMWSc 92
Powles, William Earnest 1919- AmMWSc 92
Powless, David Griffin 1953- WhoMW 92
Powless, Kenneth Barnett 1917- WhoAmL 92
Powlett Who 92
Powlett, Philip Frederick d1991 Who 92N
Powley, Edward Harrison, III 1943- WhoEnt 92
Powley, George R 1916- AmMWSc 92
Powley, John Albert 1936- Who 92
Powling, Chris 1943- WrDr 92
Pownall, David 1938- ConNov 91, IntAu&W 91, WrDr 92
Pownall, Frederick M. 1937- WhoAmL 92, WhoFI 92
Pownall, Henry Charles 1927- Who 92
Pownall, Henry Joseph 1942- AmMWSc 92
Pownall, John Harvey 1933- Who 92
Pownall, John Lionel 1929- Who 92
Pownall, Leslie Leigh 1921- Who 92
Pownall, Malcolm Wilmor 1933- AmMWSc 92
Pownall, Melvin Jordan 1923- WhoRel 92
Pownall, Thomas 1722-1805 BenetAL 91, BlkwEAR
Powrie, William Duncan 1926- AmMWSc 92
Powsner, Edward R 1926- AmMWSc 92
Powys Who 92
Powys, J. C. 1872-1963 LiExTwC
Powys, John Cowper 1872-1963 FacFETw, RfGEnL 91
Powys, Llewelyn 1884-1939 FacFETw
Powys, T.F. 1875-1953 FacFETw, RfGEnL 91
Poxon, Jeffrey Allan 1946- WhoFI 92
Poydock, Mary Eymard 1910- AmMWSc 92, WhoRel 92
Poyer, David DrAPF 91
Poyer, Joe 1939- IntAu&W 91, WrDr 92
Poyer, Joe Lee 1931- AmMWSc 92
Poyhonen, Mark 1947- WhoMW 92
Poyner, James Marion 1914- WhoAmL 92
Poyner, Ken DrAPF 91
Poynor, James Madison, Jr. 1931- WhoEnt 92
Poynter, Bill Charles 1935- WhoAmP 91
Poynter, Edward 1836-1919 TwCPaSc
Poynter, James Morrison 1939- WhoWest 92
Poynter, James William 1909- AmMWSc 92
Poynter, John Riddoch 1929- IntWW 91
Poynter, Malcolm 1946- TwCPaSc
Poynter, Margaret 1927- ConAu 36NR
Poynter, Philip A 1942- WhoIns 92
Poynter, Robert Louis 1926- AmMWSc 92
Poynton, Hilton 1905- Who 92
Poynton, Joseph Patrick 1934- AmMWSc 92
Poynton, Orde 1906- Who 92
Poyntz, Samuel Greenfield Who 92
Poyntz, Samuel Greenfield 1926- IntWW 91
Poyo, Gerald E. WhoHisp 92
Poythress, Vern Sheridan 1946- WhoRel 92
Poyton, Herbert Guy 1911- AmMWSc 92
Poyton, Robert Oliver 1944- AmMWSc 92
Poza, Ernesto J. 1950- WhoFI 92
Poza, Margarita 1948- WhoHisp 92
Pozdro, John Walter 1923- WhoEnt 92
Pozela, Juras 1925- IntWW 91
Pozil, Paul L 1938- WhoIns 92
Poziomek, Edward John 1933- AmMWSc 92
Poznanski, Andrew K 1931- AmMWSc 92
Poznansky, Mark Joab 1946- AmMWSc 92
PoZniak, Beata 1963- WhoEnt 92
Pozo, Chano 1915-1948 NewAmDM
Pozo, Santiago 1957- WhoWest 92
Pozo, Susan 1955- WhoFI 92
Pozonsky, Paul Michael 1955- WhoAmL 92
Pozorski, Joseph Michael, Jr. 1957- WhoAmL 92
Pozos, Robert Steven 1942- AmMWSc 92
Pozsgay, Imre 1933- IntWW 91
Pozza, Larry Allen 1957- WhoRel 92
Pozzessere, Heather Graham WrDr 92
Pozzi, Gianantonio 1949- IntAu&W 91
Prabhakar, Bellur Subbanna 1951- AmMWSc 92
Prabhakar, Jagdish Chandra 1925- AmMWSc 92
Prabhakara, Cuddapah 1934- AmMWSc 92
Prabhjot Kaur 1924- IntWW 91
Prabhjot, Kaur 1927- IntAu&W 91
Prabhu, Narahari Umanath 1924- AmMWSc 92
Prabhu, Vasant K 1939- AmMWSc 92
Prabhu, Venkatray G 1930- AmMWSc 92
Prabhu, Vilas Anandrao 1948- AmMWSc 92
Prabhudesai, Mukund M 1942- AmMWSc 92
Prabhupada, Abhay Charan DeBhaktivedanta 1896-1977 RelLAm 91
Prabulos, Joseph J, Jr 1938- AmMWSc 92
Prachar, Daniel A. 1964- WhoMW 92
Prachar, Thomas Patrick 1952- WhoEnt 92
Pracht, Drenda Kay 1952- WhoMW 92
Pracht, Ronald Joe 1951- WhoRel 92
Prachthauser, Don Carl 1951- WhoAmL 92
Pracy, Robert 1921- Who 92
Prada, Alberto Armando 1962- WhoMW 92
Prada, Alfredo Sadi 1934- WhoHisp 92
Prada, Antonio J. 1946- WhoHisp 92
Prada, Michel Andre Jean Edmond 1940- IntWW 91
Praddaude, Hernan Camilo 1932- AmMWSc 92
Pradhan, Trilochan 1929- IntWW 91
Pradier, Henri Joseph Marie 1931- IntWW 91
Prado, Bessie A. 1953- WhoHisp 92
Prado, Cesar, Jr. 1945- WhoHisp 92
Prado, Edward Charles 1947- WhoAmL 92
Prado, Faustino Lucio 1946- WhoHisp 92
Prado, Holly DrAPF 91
Prado, Jesus M. WhoHisp 92
Prado, Luis Antonio 1948- WhoHisp 92
Prado, Maria Esther 1959- WhoHisp 92
Prado, Marta 1951- WhoHisp 92
Prado, Melvin Ralph 1955- WhoHisp 92
Prado Aranguiz, Jorge Jose 1937- IntWW 91
Prado Vallejo, Julio 1924- IntWW 91
Prados, John W 1929- AmMWSc 92
Prados, Ronald Anthony 1946- AmMWSc 92
Prady, Norman 1933- WhoMW 92
Praed, Rosa Caroline Murray-Prior 1851-1935 ScFEYrs
Praed, Winthrop Mackworth 1802-1839 RfGEnL 91
Praeger, Betzabe Maria 1932- WhoMW 92
Praeger, Frederick Amos 1916- IntWW 91
Praeger, Herman Albert, Jr. 1920- WhoMW 92
Praeger, Sandy 1944- WhoAmP 91
Praetorius, H. Rainer 1952- WhoMW 92
Praetorius, Hieronymus 1560-1629 NewAmDM
Praetorius, Michael 1571-1621 NewAmDM
Praeuner, Howard Mylan 1932- WhoMW 92
Prag, Andrew John 1941- Who 92
Prag, Arthur Barry 1938- AmMWSc 92, WhoWest 92
Prag, Derek 1923- Who 92
Prag, John Who 92
Prager, Alice Heinecke 1930- WhoEnt 92
Prager, David 1918- WhoAmP 91
Prager, Denis Jules 1938- AmMWSc 92
Prager, Jan Clement 1934- AmMWSc 92
Prager, Jonas 1938- WhoFI 92
Prager, Julianne Heller 1924- AmMWSc 92
Prager, Martin 1939- AmMWSc 92
Prager, Morton David 1927- AmMWSc 92
Prager, Ronald Steven 1943- WhoAmL 92
Prager, Stephen 1928- AmMWSc 92
Prager, Stewart Charles 1948- AmMWSc 92
Prager, Susan Westerberg 1942- WhoAmL 92
Pragnell, Anthony William 1921- Who 92
Prague, Edith G 1925- WhoAmP 91
Prahl, Joseph Markel 1943- AmMWSc 92
Prahlad, Kadaba V 1926- AmMWSc 92
Prain, Ronald Lindsay d1991 Who 92N
Prain, Ronald Lindsay 1907- IntWW 91
Prairie, Michael L 1950- AmMWSc 92
Prairie, Richard Lane 1934- AmMWSc 92
Prais, Michael Gene AmMWSc 92
Prais, Sigbert Jon 1928- Who 92
Praissman, Melvin 1940- AmMWSc 92
Prak, Mark Jay 1955- WhoAmL 92
Prakasam, Tata B S 1936- AmMWSc 92
Prakash, Anand 1934- AmMWSc 92
Prakash, Louise 1943- AmMWSc 92
Prakash, Satya 1938- AmMWSc 92
Prakash, Shamsher 1933- AmMWSc 92
Prakash, Surya G K 1953- AmMWSc 92
Prakke, Lucas 1938- IntWW 91
Prall, Bruce Randall 1942- AmMWSc 92
Prall, Joan Elaine Heil 1931- WhoEnt 92
Prall, Richard Anning 1956- WhoWest 92
Prall, Stuart E. 1929- WrDr 92
Prall, Stuart Edward 1929- IntAu&W 91
Pramer, David 1923- AmMWSc 92
Pramoedya Ananta Toer 1925- IntWW 91
Pramoedya, Ananta Toer 1925- ConAu 134
Pramoj, Mom Rachawongse Kukrit 1911- IntWW 91
Pramoj, Mom Rachawongse Seni 1905- IntWW 91
Pramuk, Mary Theresa 1967- WhoRel 92
Pran Nath, Pandit 1918- NewAmDM
Prance, Ghillean T 1937- AmMWSc 92
Prance, Ghillean Tolmie 1937- IntWW 91, Who 92
Prandini, Giovanni 1943- IntWW 91

**Prandota,** Miroslaw 1938- *IntAu&W 91*
**Prane,** Joseph W 1923- *AmMWSc 92*
**Prang,** Louis 1824-1909 *BiInAmS*
**Prange,** Arthur Jergen, Jr 1926- *AmMWSc 92*
**Prange,** Henry Davies 1942- *AmMWSc 92*
**Prange,** Paul A. 1953- *WhoEnt 92*
**Prange,** Richard E 1932- *AmMWSc 92*
**Pranger,** Robert 1931- *WrDr 92*
**Pranger,** Robert John 1931- *WhoAmP 91*
**Pranger,** Walter 1934- *AmMWSc 92*
**Prankerd,** Thomas Arthur John 1924- *Who 92*
**Prante,** Franklin C 1947- *WhoAmP 91*
**Prantera,** Amanda 1942- *IntAu&W 91, WrDr 92*
**Prapas Charusathira** *IntWW 91*
**Prapas,** Aristotle G 1922- *AmMWSc 92*
**Pras,** Robert Thomas 1941- *WhoFI 92*
**Prasad,** Ananda S 1928- *AmMWSc 92*
**Prasad,** Arun *AmMWSc 92*
**Prasad,** Ashoka 1955- *IntWW 91*
**Prasad,** Biren 1949- *AmMWSc 92*
**Prasad,** Brij 1942- *WhoFI 92*
**Prasad,** Chandan 1941- *AmMWSc 92*
**Prasad,** Jayasimha Swamy 1948- *WhoWest 92*
**Prasad,** Kailash 1930- *AmMWSc 92*
**Prasad,** Kedar N 1935- *AmMWSc 92*
**Prasad,** Marehalli Gopalan 1950- *AmMWSc 92*
**Prasad,** Naresh 1939- *AmMWSc 92*
**Prasad,** Paras Nath 1946- *AmMWSc 92*
**Prasad,** Raghubir 1936- *AmMWSc 92*
**Prasad,** Rameshwar 1936- *AmMWSc 92*
**Prasad,** Rupi *AmMWSc 92*
**Prasad,** S E *AmMWSc 92*
**Prasad,** Suresh 1937- *AmMWSc 92*
**Prasada,** Krishna 1894- *Who 92*
**Prasanna,** Hullahalli Rangaswamy 1946- *AmMWSc 92*
**Prasanna Kumar,** V K 1956- *AmMWSc 92*
**Prasasvinitchai,** Sudhee 1931- *Who 92*
**Prashad,** Nagindra *AmMWSc 92*
**Prashar,** Paul D 1930- *AmMWSc 92*
**Prashar,** Usha Kumari 1948- *Who 92*
**Prask,** Henry Joseph 1936- *AmMWSc 92*
**Prassel,** Allen William 1922- *WhoAmP 91*
**Prassel,** Frederick Franz 1934- *WhoFI 92*
**Prasuhn,** Alan Lee 1938- *AmMWSc 92*
**Prat,** Jordi, Jr. 1949- *WhoHisp 92*
**Prat Echaurren,** Jorge 1918-1971 *BiDExR*
**Pratchett,** Terry 1948- *IntAu&W 91, TwCSFW 91, WrDr 92*
**Prate,** Alain 1928- *IntWW 91*
**Prater,** Arthur Nickolaus 1909- *AmMWSc 92*
**Prater,** C D 1917- *AmMWSc 92*
**Prater,** Carol Ann 1950- *WhoMW 92*
**Prater,** John D 1917- *AmMWSc 92*
**Prater,** John Edward 1938- *WhoFI 92*
**Prater,** John L. 1939- *WhoRel 92*
**Prater,** John Thomas 1951- *AmMWSc 92*
**Prater,** L. Michael 1954- *WhoEnt 92*
**Prater,** Lawrence Arnold 1917- *WhoRel 92*
**Prater,** Oscar L. *WhoBlA 92*
**Prater,** T A 1920- *AmMWSc 92*
**Prater,** Walter Lloyd 1955- *WhoWest 92*
**Prater,** Willis Richard 1942- *WhoMW 92*
**Prather,** Elbert Charlton 1930- *AmMWSc 92*
**Prather,** Jeffrey Lynn 1941- *WhoBlA 92*
**Prather,** John Gideon 1919- *WhoAmL 92*
**Prather,** Joseph W 1939- *WhoAmP 91*
**Prather,** Kenneth Earl 1933- *WhoAmL 92*
**Prather,** Lenore L 1931- *WhoAmP 91*
**Prather,** Lenore Loving 1931- *WhoAmL 92*
**Prather,** Mary Elizabeth Sturkie 1929- *AmMWSc 92*
**Prather,** Michael John 1947- *AmMWSc 92*
**Prather,** Paul E. 1957- *WhoAmL 92*
**Prather,** Richard 1921- *IntAu&W 91*
**Prather,** Richard Scott 1921- *WrDr 92*
**Prather,** Thomas L., Jr. 1940- *WhoBlA 92*
**Prather,** Thomas Leigh 1936- *AmMWSc 92*
**Pratley,** Alan Sawyer 1933- *Who 92*
**Pratley,** Clive William 1929- *Who 92*
**Pratley,** David Illingworth 1948- *Who 92*
**Pratley,** Gerald *IntMPA 92*
**Pratley,** Gerald Arthur 1923- *IntAu&W 91*
**Pratley,** James Nicholas 1928- *AmMWSc 92*
**Pratney,** Winkie 1944- *IntAu&W 91*
**Pratolini,** Vasco d1991 *IntWW 91N*
**Pratolini,** Vasco 1913- *IntAu&W 91*
**Prator,** Lloyd Eugene 1944- *WhoRel 92*
**Prats,** Christopher Thomas 1941- *WhoHisp 92*
**Prats,** Francisco 1922- *AmMWSc 92*
**Prats,** Jorge J. 1945- *WhoHisp 92*
**Prats,** Michael 1925- *AmMWSc 92*
**Pratt** *Who 92*
**Pratt,** Alexander Thomas 1938- *WhoBlA 92*
**Pratt,** Andrew LeRoy 1959- *WhoRel 92*
**Pratt,** Anthony Malcolm G. *Who 92*
**Pratt,** Arnold Warburton 1920- *AmMWSc 92*
**Pratt,** Arthur Geoffrey 1922- *Who 92*
**Pratt,** Arthur John 1905- *AmMWSc 92*
**Pratt,** Brian 1934- *TwCPaSc*
**Pratt,** Charles 1714?-1794 *BlkwEAR*
**Pratt,** Charles Benton 1930- *AmMWSc 92*
**Pratt,** Charles Dudley, Jr. 1927- *WhoFI 92*
**Pratt,** Charles Walter 1944- *AmMWSc 92*
**Pratt,** Christopher Leslie 1947- *Who 92*
**Pratt,** Dan Edwin 1924- *AmMWSc 92*
**Pratt,** Darrell Bradford 1920- *AmMWSc 92*
**Pratt,** David 1932- *AmMWSc 92*
**Pratt,** David Mariotti 1918- *AmMWSc 92*
**Pratt,** David R 1929- *AmMWSc 92*
**Pratt,** David Terry 1934- *AmMWSc 92*
**Pratt,** David W 1937- *AmMWSc 92*
**Pratt,** Davis 1923-1991 *NewYTBS 91*
**Pratt,** Diane McMahon *AmMWSc 92*
**Pratt,** Donald Oliver 1944- *WhoAmL 92*
**Pratt,** Douglas Charles 1931- *AmMWSc 92*
**Pratt,** E. J. 1882-1964 *BenetAL 91, RfGEnL 91*
**Pratt,** Edmund T., Jr. 1927- *IntWW 91*
**Pratt,** Edmund Taylor, Jr. 1927- *WhoFI 92*
**Pratt,** Elizabeth Ann 1933- *AmMWSc 92*
**Pratt,** Eugene Frank 1946- *WhoFI 92*
**Pratt,** Fletcher 1897-1956 *TwCSFW 91*
**Pratt,** George 1917- *Who 92*
**Pratt,** George Byington, III 1936- *WhoMW 92*
**Pratt,** George C 1928- *WhoAmP 91*
**Pratt,** George Cheney 1928- *WhoAmL 92*
**Pratt,** George Janes, Jr. 1948- *WhoWest 92*
**Pratt,** George L 1926- *AmMWSc 92*
**Pratt,** George Woodman, Jr 1927- *AmMWSc 92*
**Pratt,** Harlan Kelley 1914- *AmMWSc 92*
**Pratt,** Harold Irving 1937- *WhoAmL 92*
**Pratt,** Harry Davis 1915- *AmMWSc 92*
**Pratt,** Henry Brooks 1933- *WhoRel 92*
**Pratt,** Herbert T 1926- *AmMWSc 92*
**Pratt,** Hugh MacDonald 1900- *Who 92*
**Pratt,** Irene A 1924- *WhoAmP 91*
**Pratt,** J. C. 1927- *WhoBlA 92*
**Pratt,** Jack, Jr. 1941- *WhoFI 92*
**Pratt,** Jack E *WhoAmP 91*
**Pratt,** James Norwood 1942- *IntAu&W 91*
**Pratt,** John Christopher 1935- *IntWW 91*
**Pratt,** John Clark 1932- *IntAu&W 91, WhoWest 92, WrDr 92*
**Pratt,** John Francis Isaac 1913- *Who 92*
**Pratt,** John Helm 1910- *WhoAmL 92*
**Pratt,** John Michael 1946- *WhoAmP 91*
**Pratt,** Judith A 1941- *WhoAmP 91*
**Pratt,** Kelly Jane 1957- *WhoEnt 92*
**Pratt,** Kevin Burton 1949- *WhoAmL 92*
**Pratt,** Lawrence D 1942- *WhoAmP 91*
**Pratt,** Lee Herbert 1942- *AmMWSc 92*
**Pratt,** Leighton C 1923- *WhoAmP 91*
**Pratt,** Louis Hill 1937- *WhoBlA 92*
**Pratt,** Mable 1943- *WhoBlA 92*
**Pratt,** Melanie M 1952- *AmMWSc 92*
**Pratt,** Melvin Lemar 1946- *WhoBlA 92*
**Pratt,** Michael John 1933- *Who 92*
**Pratt,** Minnie Bruce *DrAPF 91*
**Pratt,** Neal Edwin 1937- *AmMWSc 92*
**Pratt,** Parker Frost 1918- *AmMWSc 92*
**Pratt,** Paul 1890-1948 *NewAmDM*
**Pratt,** Peter Lynn 1927- *Who 92*
**Pratt,** Philip Chase 1920- *AmMWSc 92*
**Pratt,** Renee *WhoAmP 91*
**Pratt,** Richard Houghton 1934- *AmMWSc 92*
**Pratt,** Richard J 1927- *AmMWSc 92*
**Pratt,** Richard T 1937- *WhoAmP 91*
**Pratt,** Robert Henry 1922- *WhoFI 92*
**Pratt,** Robert Windsor 1950- *WhoAmL 92*
**Pratt,** Ronald Franklin 1948- *WhoWest 92*
**Pratt,** Rosalie Rebollo 1933- *WhoWest 92*
**Pratt,** Ruth Jones 1923- *WhoBlA 92*
**Pratt,** Solomon Althanasius James 1921- *IntWW 91*
**Pratt,** Stephen Turnham 1955- *AmMWSc 92*
**Pratt,** Suzanne Jean 1947- *WhoWest 92*
**Pratt,** Terrence Wendall 1940- *AmMWSc 92*
**Pratt,** Theodore 1901-1969 *BenetAL 91*
**Pratt,** Timothy Jean Geoffrey 1934- *Who 92*
**Pratt,** Vaughan Ronald 1944- *AmMWSc 92, WhoWest 92*
**Pratt,** Walden Penfield 1928- *AmMWSc 92, WhoWest 92*
**Pratt,** Wayne Joseph 1961- *WhoMW 92*
**Pratt,** William Gordon 1954- *WhoIns 92*
**Pratt,** William Henry 1822-1893 *BiInAmS*
**Pratt,** William Winston 1921- *AmMWSc 92*
**Pratt-Thomas,** Harold Rawling 1913- *AmMWSc 92*
**Pratte,** Paul Alfred 1938- *WhoWest 92*
**Prattis,** Lawrence 1926- *WhoBlA 92*
**Prausnitz,** Frederik 1920- *NewAmDM*
**Prausnitz,** John Michael 1928- *AmMWSc 92*
**Pravitz,** Donald Russell 1915- *WhoWest 92*
**Prawel,** Sherwood Peter, Jr 1932- *AmMWSc 92*
**Prawer,** S. S. 1925- *WrDr 92*
**Prawer,** Siegbert Salomon 1925- *IntAu&W 91, IntWW 91, Who 92*
**Prawer Jhabvala,** Ruth *Who 92*
**Prawiro,** Radius 1928- *IntWW 91*
**Praxeas** *EncEarC*
**Pray,** Charles P 1945- *WhoAmP 91*
**Pray,** David W 1942- *WhoIns 92*
**Pray,** Donald Eugene 1932- *WhoAmL 92*
**Pray,** Donald George 1928- *AmMWSc 92*
**Pray,** John Allan 1949- *WhoAmL 92*
**Pray,** Lloyd Charles 1919- *AmMWSc 92*
**Pray,** Ralph Emerson 1926- *AmMWSc 92, WhoWest 92*
**Pray,** Ralph Marble, III 1938- *WhoAmL 92*
**Pray,** Thomas Richard 1923- *AmMWSc 92*
**Prazma,** Jiri *AmMWSc 92*
**Preacher,** Stephen Preston 1949- *WhoWest 92*
**Preate,** Ernest D., Jr. 1940- *WhoAmL 92, WhoAmP 91*
**Prebble,** David Lawrence 1932- *Who 92*
**Prebble,** John 1915- *IntAu&W 91, TwCWW 91, WrDr 92*
**Prebble,** John Edward Curtis 1915- *Who 92*
**Prebble,** Richard William 1948- *IntWW 91*
**Prebisch,** Raul 1901-1986 *FacFETw*
**Prebish,** Charles S. 1944- *WhoRel 92*
**Preble,** Duane 1936- *WhoWest 92*
**Preble,** Olivia Toby 1947- *AmMWSc 92*
**Preble,** Robert Curtis, Jr 1922- *WhoIns 92, WhoMW 92*
**Preblud,** Stephen Robert 1948- *AmMWSc 92*
**Prebluda,** Harry Jacob 1911- *AmMWSc 92*
**Prebula,** Mary Aunita 1953- *WhoAmL 92*
**Precht,** Robert *LesBEnT 92*
**Prechtel-Kluskens,** Claire 1962- *WhoAmL 92*
**Preciado,** Steve Manuel 1954- *WhoHisp 92*
**Preckshot,** G W 1918- *AmMWSc 92*
**Preckwinkle,** Toni *WhoAmP 91*
**Precopio,** Frank Mario 1925- *AmMWSc 92*
**Predecki,** Paul K 1938- *AmMWSc 92*
**Predmore,** Michael P. 1938- *ConAu 34NR*
**Predpall,** Daniel Francis 1946- *WhoFI 92*
**Preece,** Grant 1943- *WhoAmP 91*
**Preece,** Lawrence 1942- *TwCPaSc*
**Preece,** McCoy D. 1954- *WhoWest 92*
**Preece,** Norma 1922- *WhoWest 92*
**Preece,** Patricia 1900-1971 *TwCPaSc*
**Preece,** Sherman Joy, Jr 1923- *AmMWSc 92*
**Preedom,** Barry Mason 1940- *AmMWSc 92*
**Preedy,** John Robert Knowlton 1918- *AmMWSc 92*
**Preer,** Evelyn 1896-1932 *NotBlAW 92*
**Preer,** James Randolph 1944- *AmMWSc 92*
**Preer,** John Randolph, Jr 1918- *AmMWSc 92, IntWW 91*
**Pregaldin,** Anton Joseph 1931- *WhoMW 92*
**Pregerson,** Harry *WhoAmP 91*
**Pregerson,** Harry 1923- *WhoAmL 92*
**Pregger,** Fred Titus 1924- *AmMWSc 92*
**Pregl,** Fritz 1859-1930 *WhoNob 90*
**Pregnall,** William Stuart 1931- *WhoRel 92*
**Preheim,** Lynn Dale 1962- *WhoAmL 92*
**Preheim,** Vern Quincy 1935- *WhoRel 92*
**Prehm,** Dianne Miller 1948- *WhoMW 92*
**Prehm,** John Thomas, Jr. 1922- *WhoMW 92*
**Prehn,** Richmond Talbot 1922- *AmMWSc 92*
**Preikschat,** Ekkehard 1943- *AmMWSc 92*
**Preikschat,** F K 1910- *AmMWSc 92*
**Preis,** Mary Louise *WhoAmP 91*
**Preis,** Reagan L 1928- *WhoIns 92*
**Preiser,** Stanley 1927- *AmMWSc 92*
**Preiskel,** Barbara Scott 1924- *WhoBlA 92*
**Preiskel,** Robert Howard 1922- *WhoAmL 92*
**Preisler,** Harvey D 1941- *AmMWSc 92*
**Preisler,** Joseph J 1919- *AmMWSc 92*
**Preisman,** Albert 1901- *AmMWSc 92*
**Preiss,** Benjamin 1933- *AmMWSc 92*
**Preiss,** Beth 1954- *WhoFI 92*
**Preiss,** Donald Merle 1927- *AmMWSc 92*
**Preiss,** Frederick John 1942- *AmMWSc 92*
**Preiss,** Ivor Louis 1933- *AmMWSc 92*
**Preiss,** Jack 1932- *AmMWSc 92*
**Prejean,** Joe David 1940- *AmMWSc 92*
**Prejean,** Ruby D. 1925- *WhoBlA 92*
**Prekopa,** Andras 1929- *AmMWSc 92*
**Prelas,** Mark Antonio 1953- *AmMWSc 92*
**Prelinger,** Catherine M. d1991 *NewYTBS 91*
**Prell,** George D 1951- *AmMWSc 92*
**Prell,** Warren Lee 1943- *AmMWSc 92*
**Prelli,** F Philip *WhoAmP 91*
**Prelog,** Vladimir 1906- *AmMWSc 92, IntWW 91, Who 92, WhoNob 90*
**Prelow,** Arleigh 1953- *WhoBlA 92*
**Prelutsky,** Jack 1940- *IntAu&W 91, SmATA 66 [port], WrDr 92*
**Prem Tinsulanonda** 1920- *IntWW 91*
**Prem,** F. Herbert, Jr. 1932- *WhoAmL 92*
**Prem,** Konald Arthur 1920- *AmMWSc 92*
**Prem,** Prakash Singh 1926- *IntAu&W 91*
**Prem,** Tinsulanonda 1920- *FacFETw*
**Prem Chand,** D. 1916- *IntWW 91*
**Premachandra,** Bhartur N 1930- *AmMWSc 92*
**Premadasa,** Ranasinghe 1924- *IntWW 91, Who 92*
**Premanand,** Visvanatha 1929- *AmMWSc 92*
**Premasagar,** P. Victor *WhoRel 92*
**Premauer,** Werner 1912- *IntWW 91*
**Premawardhana,** Shanta Devadasa Ellawala 1952- *WhoRel 92*
**Preminger,** Otto 1905-1986 *IntDcF 2-2 [port]*
**Preminger,** Otto 1906?-1986 *ConAu 134, FacFETw*
**Premnath,** Devadasan Nithya 1950- *WhoRel 92*
**Premus,** Robert 1939- *WhoFI 92*
**Premuzic,** Eugene T 1929- *AmMWSc 92*
**Prend,** Joseph 1920- *AmMWSc 92*
**Prender,** Bart *TwCWW 91*
**Prendergast,** Anthony 1931- *Who 92*
**Prendergast,** Brian 1948- *WhoFI 92*
**Prendergast,** Franklin G 1945- *AmMWSc 92*
**Prendergast,** George Aloysius 1933- *WhoFI 92*
**Prendergast,** James Francis 1917- *WhoAmP 91*
**Prendergast,** John 1912- *Who 92*
**Prendergast,** John Joseph 1952- *WhoFI 92*
**Prendergast,** Joseph Thomas, Jr 1945- *WhoAmP 91*
**Prendergast,** Kevin Henry 1929- *AmMWSc 92*
**Prendergast,** Maurice 1859-1924 *FacFETw*
**Prendergast,** Michael Gregory 1958- *WhoAmL 92*
**Prendergast,** Peter 1946- *TwCPaSc*
**Prendergast,** Peter Thomas 1946- *IntWW 91*
**Prendergast,** Richard Halsey 1945- *WhoAmP 91*
**Prendergast,** Robert Anthony 1931- *AmMWSc 92*
**Prendergast,** Robert James Christie V 1941- *Who 92*
**Prendergast,** Simone 1930- *Who 92*
**Prendergast,** Thomas A. 1933- *WhoFI 92*
**Prendergast,** Walter Kieran 1942- *IntWW 91, Who 92*
**Prendergast,** William John 1942- *WhoWest 92*
**Prener,** Robert 1939- *AmMWSc 92*
**Prengle,** H William, Jr 1919- *AmMWSc 92*
**Prenovitz,** Sheldon M. 1950- *WhoFI 92*
**Prensky,** Wolf 1930- *AmMWSc 92*
**Prentice,** Daniel David 1941- *Who 92*
**Prentice,** David 1936- *TwCPaSc*
**Prentice,** Dixon Wright 1919- *WhoAmP 91*
**Prentice,** Eugene Miles, III 1942- *WhoAmL 92, WhoFI 92*
**Prentice,** Geoffrey Allan 1946- *AmMWSc 92*
**Prentice,** George Dennison 1802-1870 *BenetAL 91*
**Prentice,** Jack L 1931- *AmMWSc 92*
**Prentice,** James Douglas 1930- *AmMWSc 92*
**Prentice,** John 1920- *Who 92*
**Prentice,** Margarita *WhoAmP 91*
**Prentice,** Margarita 1931- *WhoHisp 92*
**Prentice,** Neville 1920- *AmMWSc 92*
**Prentice,** Norman Macdonald 1925- *AmMWSc 92*
**Prentice,** Penelope *DrAPF 91*
**Prentice,** Reginald 1923- *Who 92*
**Prentice,** Reginald Ernest 1923- *IntWW 91*
**Prentice,** Robert Craig 1951- *WhoMW 92*
**Prentice,** Ross L 1946- *AmMWSc 92*
**Prentice,** Thomas 1919- *Who 92*
**Prentice,** Wilbert Neil 1923- *AmMWSc 92*
**Prentice,** William 1919- *Who 92*
**Prentice,** Winifred 1910- *Who 92*
**Prentis,** John Brooke, III 1937- *WhoMW 92, WhoRel 92*
**Prentiss,** Albert Nelson 1836-1896 *BiInAmS*
**Prentiss,** C J *WhoAmP 91*
**Prentiss,** Charles Gary 1942- *WhoWest 92*
**Prentiss,** Charles William 1874-1915 *BiInAmS*
**Prentiss,** Daniel Webster 1843-1899 *BiInAmS*
**Prentiss,** Elizabeth Payson 1818-1878 *BenetAL 91*

**Prentiss,** Paula 1939- IntMPA 92
**Prentiss,** Robert Noble, Jr. 1943- WhoFI 92
**Prentiss,** Robert Woodworth 1857-1913 BiInAmS
**Prentiss,** William Case 1924- AmMWSc 92
**Prentke,** Richard Ottesen 1945- WhoAmL 92
**Prenzlow,** Carl Frederick 1930- AmMWSc 92
**Prenzlow,** Elmer John-Charles, Jr. 1929- WhoMW 92, WhoRel 92
**Preobrazhenska,** Ol'ga Iosifovna 1871-1962 SovUnBD
**Preobrazhenskaya,** Ol'ga Ivanovna 1881-1971 SovUnBD
**Preobrazhensky,** Yevgeniy Aleksandrovich 1886-1937 SovUnBD
**Preonas,** George Elias 1943- WhoAmL 92
**Preovolos,** Penelope Athene 1955- WhoAmL 92
**Preparata,** Franco Paolo 1935- AmMWSc 92
**Prepas,** Ellie E 1947- AmMWSc 92
**Prepost,** Richard 1935- AmMWSc 92
**Prerau,** David Stewart AmMWSc 92
**Presas,** Arturo WhoHisp 92
**Presberry,** Iva Viola 1949- WhoMW 92
**Presby,** Herman M 1941- AmMWSc 92
**Presch,** William Frederick 1942- AmMWSc 92
**Prescott,** Albert Benjamin 1832-1905 BiInAmS
**Prescott,** Allie WhoRel 92
**Prescott,** Basil Osborne 1911- AmMWSc 92
**Prescott,** Benjamin 1907- AmMWSc 92
**Prescott,** Caleb IntAu&W 91X, TwCWW 91
**Prescott,** Casey ConAu 133, SmATA 66
**Prescott,** Charles Young 1938- AmMWSc 92
**Prescott,** David Julius 1939- AmMWSc 92
**Prescott,** David Marshall 1926- AmMWSc 92
**Prescott,** Douglas W 1951- WhoAmP 91
**Prescott,** Gerald H 1937- AmMWSc 92
**Prescott,** Gerald Roscoe 1902- WhoEnt 92
**Prescott,** Glenn Carleton, Jr 1923- AmMWSc 92
**Prescott,** Henry Emil, Jr 1936- AmMWSc 92
**Prescott,** J R V 1931- IntAu&W 91, WrDr 92
**Prescott,** Joel Henry 1941- WhoWest 92
**Prescott,** John 1919- TwCWW 91
**Prescott,** John Herbert Dudley 1937- Who 92
**Prescott,** John Hernage 1935- AmMWSc 92
**Prescott,** John Leslie 1938- IntWW 91, Who 92
**Prescott,** John Mack 1921- AmMWSc 92
**Prescott,** Jon Michael 1939- AmMWSc 92
**Prescott,** Jon Riley 1943- WhoWest 92
**Prescott,** Lansing M 1941- AmMWSc 92
**Prescott,** Lansing Mason 1941- WhoMW 92
**Prescott,** Lawrence Malcolm 1934- WhoWest 92
**Prescott,** Mark 1948- Who 92
**Prescott,** Paul Ithel 1931- AmMWSc 92
**Prescott,** Peter George Addington 1924- Who 92
**Prescott,** Peter John 1936- Who 92
**Prescott,** Peter Richard Kyle 1943- Who 92
**Prescott,** Stephen M 1948- AmMWSc 92
**Prescott,** Westby William P. Who 92
**Prescott,** William Bruce 1951- WhoRel 92
**Prescott,** William Hickling 1796-1859 BenetAL 91
**Prescott,** William Warren 1855-1944 AmPeW
**Present,** Jess J WhoAmP 91
**Preses,** Jack Michael 1947- AmMWSc 92
**Preska,** Margaret Louise Robinson 1938- WhoMW 92
**Preskill,** John P 1953- AmMWSc 92
**Presland,** John David 1930- Who 92
**Preslaski,** Michelle Lynn WhoMW 92
**Presle,** Micheline 1922- IntMPA 92
**Presley,** Bobby Joe 1935- AmMWSc 92
**Presley,** Calvin Alonzo 1914- WhoBlA 92
**Presley,** Cecil Travis 1941- AmMWSc 92
**Presley,** Elvis 1935-1977 FacFETw [port], NewAmDM, RComAH
**Presley,** John Moody 1926- WhoMW 92
**Presley,** Oscar Glen 1942- WhoBlA 92
**Presley,** Priscilla 1945- IntMPA 92, WhoEnt 92
**Presley,** Robert B 1924- WhoAmP 91
**Presley,** Robert Buel 1924- WhoWest 92
**Presley,** Stanley Patrick 1951- WhoAmP 91
**Preslock,** James Peter AmMWSc 92
**Presnal,** Billy Charles 1932- WhoAmP 91
**Presnall,** Dean C 1935- AmMWSc 92
**Presnell,** Lacy Martin, III 1951- WhoAmL 92
**Presnell,** Ronald I 1933- AmMWSc 92
**Presnell,** Sharon June 1940- WhoMW 92
**Press,** Barry Harris Jay 1951- WhoWest 92
**Press,** Charles 1922- WhoMW 92
**Press,** Daniel Mark 1964- WhoAmL 92
**Press,** Frank 1924- AmMWSc 92, IntWW 91, WhoAmP 91
**Press,** Harry Cody, Jr. 1931- WhoBlA 92
**Press,** Jeffery Bruce 1947- AmMWSc 92
**Press,** John 1920- WrDr 92
**Press,** John Bryant 1920- IntAu&W 91, Who 92
**Press,** Linda Seghers 1950- AmMWSc 92
**Press,** Lloyd Douglas, Jr. 1950- WhoEnt 92, WhoWest 92
**Press,** Newtol 1930- AmMWSc 92
**Press,** O. Charles 1922- WrDr 92
**Press,** Richard Stern 1939- WhoFI 92
**Press,** S James 1931- AmMWSc 92
**Press,** Samuel Beloff 1936- WhoRel 92
**Press,** Simone Juda DrAPF 91
**Press,** Simone Naomi Juda 1943- IntAu&W 91
**Press,** Skip DrAPF 91
**Press,** Steve 1946- WhoAmP 91
**Press,** Steven Michael 1963- WhoAmL 92
**Press,** Tamara Natanovna 1937- IntWW 91
**Press,** William Henry 1948- AmMWSc 92
**Pressburg,** Bernard S 1918- AmMWSc 92
**Pressburger,** Emeric 1902-1988 FacFETw
**Presser,** Bruce Douglas AmMWSc 92
**Presser,** Cary 1952- AmMWSc 92
**Presser,** Dorothy 1929- WhoAmP 91
**Presser,** Jackie 1926-1988 FacFETw
**Presser,** Leon 1940- AmMWSc 92, WhoHisp 92
**Presser,** Stephen Bruce 1946- WhoAmL 92
**Presser,** Theodore 1848-1925 NewAmDM
**Pressey,** Junius Batten, Jr. 1947- WhoBlA 92
**Pressey,** Paul Matthew 1958- WhoBlA 92
**Pressey,** Russell 1935- AmMWSc 92
**Pressler,** Herman Paul, III 1930- WhoAmL 92, WhoRel 92
**Pressler,** Larry 1942- AlmAP 92 [port], IntWW 91, WhoAmP 91, WhoMW 92
**Pressler,** Philip Bernard 1946- WhoFI 92
**Pressley,** Fred G., Jr. 1953- WhoAmL 92
**Pressley,** James Ray 1946- WhoWest 92
**Pressley,** Ronald James 1951- WhoAmL 92
**Pressley,** Stephen, Jr. 1947- WhoBlA 92
**Pressley,** Ted Kermit 1938- WhoRel 92
**Pressly,** Barbara B 1937- WhoAmP 91
**Pressman,** Ada Irene 1927- AmMWSc 92
**Pressman,** Alan 1941- WhoAmL 92
**Pressman,** Barney d1991 NewYTBS 91 [port]
**Pressman,** Berton Charles 1926- AmMWSc 92
**Pressman,** David 1913- WhoEnt 92
**Pressman,** Edward R. IntMPA 92, WhoEnt 92
**Pressman,** Edward R. 1943- ConTFT 9
**Pressman,** Irwin Samuel 1939- AmMWSc 92
**Pressman,** J. J., Mrs. Who 92
**Pressman,** Jacob 1919- WhoRel 92
**Pressman,** Judy Kolodny 1947- WhoAmL 92
**Pressman,** Lawrence 1939- IntMPA 92
**Pressman,** Michael 1950- IntMPA 92
**Pressman,** Norman Jules 1948- AmMWSc 92
**Pressmann,** John F 1952- WhoAmP 91
**Presson,** Francis Tennery 1925- WhoFI 92
**Presson,** William Carl 1962- WhoFI 92
**Prest,** Victor Kent 1913- AmMWSc 92
**Prest,** William Marchant, Jr 1941- AmMWSc 92
**Prestage,** James J. 1926- WhoBlA 92
**Prestage,** Jewel Limar 1931- WhoAmP 91, WhoBlA 92
**Prestanski,** Harry Thomas 1947- WhoMW 92
**Prestayko,** Archie William 1941- AmMWSc 92
**Prestegard,** Allen Lee 1936- WhoFI 92
**Prestegard,** James Harold 1944- AmMWSc 92
**Prestemon,** Dean R 1934- AmMWSc 92
**Prestia,** Michael Anthony 1931- WhoFI 92
**Prestia,** Shirley Rose 1947- WhoEnt 92
**Prestini,** James 1908- DcTwDes
**Prestipino,** Bart 1922- WhoAmP 91
**Preston** Who 92
**Preston,** Aldon Emory 1960- WhoRel 92
**Preston,** Ann 1813-1872 HanAmWH
**Preston,** Beth Brown DrAPF 91
**Preston,** Beth Brown 1953- IntAu&W 91
**Preston,** Billy 1946- WhoBlA 92, WhoEnt 92
**Preston,** Bruce Marshall 1949- WhoAmL 92
**Preston,** Carey Maddox 1915- WhoBlA 92
**Preston,** Charles George 1940- WhoAmL 92
**Preston,** Colleen Ann 1955- WhoAmL 92
**Preston,** Daniel S. DrAPF 91
**Preston,** Donald 1941- WhoFI 92
**Preston,** Edward Carter 1884-1965 TwCPaSc
**Preston,** Edward Lee 1925- WhoBlA 92
**Preston,** Erasmus Darwin 1851-1906 BiInAmS
**Preston,** Eric Miles AmMWSc 92
**Preston,** Eugene Anthony 1952- WhoBlA 92
**Preston,** F. Leslie 1903- Who 92
**Preston,** Fayrene WrDr 92
**Preston,** Floyd W 1923- AmMWSc 92
**Preston,** Frances E. L. 1840?-1929 NotBlAW 92
**Preston,** Frances W. WhoEnt 92
**Preston,** Frederick Willard 1912- AmMWSc 92
**Preston,** Geoffrey Averill 1924- Who 92
**Preston,** George Nelson 1938- WhoBlA 92
**Preston,** George W, III 1930- AmMWSc 92
**Preston,** Glenn Wetherby 1922- AmMWSc 92
**Preston,** Ian Mathieson Hamilton 1932- Who 92
**Preston,** Ivy 1913- WrDr 92
**Preston,** Ivy Alice Kinross 1913- IntAu&W 91
**Preston,** Jack 1931- AmMWSc 92
**Preston,** James Allen 1955- WhoMW 92
**Preston,** James Benson 1926- AmMWSc 92
**Preston,** James E. 1933- WhoFI 92
**Preston,** James Faulkner, III 1939- AmMWSc 92
**Preston,** James Herman 1951- WhoRel 92
**Preston,** Jeffrey William 1940- Who 92
**Preston,** John Elwood 1941- WhoAmL 92
**Preston,** John O'Driscoll 1950- WhoEnt 92
**Preston,** Joseph, Jr 1947- WhoAmP 91, WhoBlA 92
**Preston,** Joseph Harold 1926- WhoMW 92
**Preston,** Julia Jackson Christian 1887-1991 NewYTBS 91
**Preston,** Keith 1884-1927 BenetAL 91
**Preston,** Keith Foncell 1938- AmMWSc 92
**Preston,** Kelly 1963- IntMPA 92
**Preston,** Kendall, Jr 1927- AmMWSc 92, WhoFI 92
**Preston,** Kenneth 1901- Who 92
**Preston,** Lee 1944- WhoAmP 91
**Preston,** Leonard 1948- WhoBlA 92
**Preston,** Leslie Who 92
**Preston,** Lewis T. 1926- IntWW 91
**Preston,** Lewis Thompson 1926- WhoFI 92
**Preston,** Margaret Junkin 1820-1897 BenetAL 91
**Preston,** Mark 1956- WhoHisp 92
**Preston,** Mark Frederick 1954- WhoMW 92
**Preston,** Melvin Alexander 1921- AmMWSc 92
**Preston,** Michael B. 1933- WhoBlA 92
**Preston,** Michael Richard 1927- Who 92
**Preston,** Myles Park 1927- Who 92
**Preston,** Paul 1946- IntWW 91
**Preston,** Peter 1922- Who 92
**Preston,** Peter John 1938- IntAu&W 91, IntWW 91, Who 92
**Preston,** Ray 1947- WhoAmP 91
**Preston,** Reginald Dawson 1908- IntWW 91, Who 92, WrDr 92
**Preston,** Richard IntAu&W 91X
**Preston,** Richard 1910- WrDr 92
**Preston,** Richard Clark 1933- WhoBlA 92
**Preston,** Richard McCann 1954- WhoFI 92
**Preston,** Richard Swain 1925- AmMWSc 92
**Preston,** Robert Arthur 1944- AmMWSc 92, WhoWest 92
**Preston,** Robert D 1923- WhoIns 92
**Preston,** Robert F 1929- WhoAmP 91
**Preston,** Robert Julian 1942- AmMWSc 92
**Preston,** Robert Leslie 1942- AmMWSc 92
**Preston,** Rodney LeRoy 1931- AmMWSc 92
**Preston,** Ronald 1916- Who 92
**Preston,** Ronald Haydn 1913- Who 92
**Preston,** Seymour Stotler, III 1933- WhoFI 92
**Preston,** Simon 1938- NewAmDM
**Preston,** Simon John 1938- IntWW 91, Who 92
**Preston,** Stephen Boylan 1919- AmMWSc 92
**Preston,** Swanee H. T., Jr. 1924- WhoBlA 92
**Preston,** Thomas Alexander 1927- AmMWSc 92
**Preston,** Timothy William 1935- Who 92
**Preston,** Tobias James 1962- WhoWest 92
**Preston,** Vernon Renell 1969- WhoEnt 92
**Preston,** Walter James 1925- Who 92
**Preston,** William Burton 1937- AmMWSc 92
**Preston,** William Hable 1921- WhoEnt 92
**Preston,** William M 1909- AmMWSc 92
**Preston-Thomas,** Hugh 1923- AmMWSc 92
**Prestopino,** Frank J 1949- WhoIns 92
**Prestridge,** Pamela Adair 1945- WhoAmL 92
**Prestrud,** Stuart H. 1919- WhoWest 92
**Prestt,** Arthur Miller 1925- Who 92
**Prestt,** Ian 1929- Who 92
**Prestwich,** Glenn Downes 1948- AmMWSc 92
**Prestwich,** Kenneth Neal 1949- AmMWSc 92
**Prestwich,** Michael 1943- ConAu 134
**Prestwich,** Michael Charles 1943- Who 92
**Prestwidge,** Kathleen Joyce 1927- AmMWSc 92
**Prestwidge-Bellinger,** Barbara Elizabeth 1945- WhoBlA 92
**Prestwood,** Viscount 1956- Who 92
**Prestwood,** Alvin Tennyson 1929- WhoAmL 92
**Prestwood,** Annie Katherine 1935- AmMWSc 92
**Presutti,** Michael John, Jr. 1962- WhoEnt 92
**Preszler,** Alan Melvin 1939- AmMWSc 92
**Prete,** John Donald 1934- WhoAmP 91
**Pretenders,** The NewAmDM
**Prether,** Jonelle L. 1957- WhoEnt 92
**Preti,** George 1944- AmMWSc 92
**Preti,** Luigi 1914- IntWW 91
**Pretka,** John E 1919- AmMWSc 92
**Pretlow,** Thomas Garrett, II 1939- AmMWSc 92
**Preto,** Francisco Barcelos Rolao 1893-1977 BiDExR
**Pretoria,** Bishop of 1936- Who 92
**Pretre,** Georges 1924- IntWW 91, NewAmDM, WhoEnt 92
**Pretti,** Bradford Joseph 1930- WhoRel 92
**Pretto,** Franklin David 1946- WhoRel 92
**Pretto-Ferro,** Franklin David 1946- WhoHisp 92
**Pretty,** David Walter 1925- WhoIns 92
**Pretty,** Katharine Bridget 1945- Who 92
**Pretty,** Kenneth McAlpine 1929- AmMWSc 92
**Prettyman,** Elijah Barrett, Jr. 1925- WhoAmL 92
**Prettyman,** Keith Arthur 1951- WhoIns 92
**Prettyman,** Quandra 1933- WhoBlA 92
**Pretzer,** C Andrew 1928- AmMWSc 92
**Preuett,** Danny Gene 1959- WhoRel 92
**Preuitt,** James E 1935- WhoAmP 91
**Preul,** Herbert C 1926- AmMWSc 92
**Preus,** Anthony 1936- WhoFI 92
**Preus,** David Walter 1922- WhoRel 92
**Preus,** Jacob Aall Ottesen 1920- RelLAm 91, WhoRel 92
**Preus,** Marilyn Ione 1944- AmMWSc 92
**Preus,** Martin William 1954- AmMWSc 92
**Preus,** Robert David 1924- WhoRel 92
**Preusch,** Charles D 1917- AmMWSc 92
**Preusch,** Peter Charles 1953- AmMWSc 92
**Preuss,** Albert F 1926- AmMWSc 92
**Preuss,** Gregory Edward 1946- WhoFI 92
**Preuss,** Paul 1942- TwCSFW 91, WrDr 92
**Preuss,** Roger Emil 1922- WhoMW 92
**Preuss,** Ronald Stephen 1935- WhoAmL 92, WhoMW 92
**Preuster,** Christopher W. 1942- IntMPA 92
**Prevatt,** Karen Elizabeth 1947- WhoAmL 92
**Prevatt,** Rubert Waldemar 1925- AmMWSc 92
**Prevec,** Ludvik Anthony 1936- AmMWSc 92
**Prevedel,** Frank 1932- WhoAmP 91
**Prevert,** Jacques 1900-1977 FacFETw, GuFrLit 1
**Previant,** David 1910- WhoAmL 92
**Previc,** Edward Paul 1931- AmMWSc 92
**Previn,** Andre 1929- FacFETw, IntMPA 92, NewAmDM, Who 92, WhoEnt 92, WrDr 92
**Previn,** Andre George 1929- IntWW 91
**Previte,** Joseph James 1936- AmMWSc 92
**Prevorsek,** Dusan Ciril 1922- AmMWSc 92
**Prevost Brothers** DcAmImH
**Prevost,** Andre 1934- NewAmDM
**Prevost,** Antoine-Francois 1697-1763 BlkwCEP
**Prevost,** Christopher 1935- Who 92
**Prevost,** Edward James 1941- WhoFI 92
**Prevost,** Jean Herve 1947- AmMWSc 92
**Prevost,** Stephen McCully 1938- WhoFI 92
**Prevost,** Winthrop Warren 1917- WhoEnt 92
**Prevost/Linton,** Charles 1949- WhoEnt 92
**Prevots,** Naima 1935- ConAu 135
**Prewitt,** Al Bert 1907- WhoBlA 92
**Prewitt,** Charles Thompson 1933- AmMWSc 92

**Prewitt**, Judith Martha Shimansky 1935- AmMWSc 92
**Prewitt**, Kenneth 1936- WrDr 92
**Prewitt**, Larry R 1945- AmMWSc 92
**Prewitt**, Lena Voncille Burrell 1932- WhoBlA 92
**Prewitt**, Russell Lawrence, Jr 1943- AmMWSc 92
**Prewitt**, William Chandler 1946- WhoFI 92
**Prewoznik**, Jerome Frank 1934- WhoAmL 92
**Prey**, Hermann 1929- IntWW 91, NewAmDM, Who 92
**Preyer**, Lunsford Richardson 1919- WhoAmP 91
**Preysing**, Konrad, Count von 1880-1950 EncTR 91 [port]
**Preysz**, Louis Robert Fonss, III 1944- WhoFI 92
**Prezant**, Robert Steven 1951- AmMWSc 92
**Prezeau**, Louis E. 1943- WhoBlA 92
**Prezeau**, Maryse 1942- WhoBlA 92
**Prezelin**, Barbara Berntsen 1948- AmMWSc 92
**Prezent**, Isaak Izrailovich 1902-1970? SovUnBD
**Prezihov**, Voranc 1893-1950 LiExTwC
**Preziosi**, Giovanni 1881-1945 BiDExR
**Prezioso**, Roman W 1949- WhoAmP 91
**Prezzolini**, Giuseppe 1882-1982 BiDExR, DcAmImH
**Priano**, Gina Suzanne 1970- WhoEnt 92
**Pribanic**, Victor Hunter 1954- WhoAmL 92
**Pribble**, Mary Jo 1930- AmMWSc 92
**Pribil**, Stephen 1919- AmMWSc 92
**Pribor**, Donald B 1932- AmMWSc 92
**Pribor**, Hugo C 1928- AmMWSc 92
**Pribor**, Jeffrey Douglas 1957- WhoFI 92
**Pribram**, John Karl 1941- AmMWSc 92
**Pribram**, Karl H. WrDr 92
**Pribram**, Karl Harry 1919- AmMWSc 92
**Pribula**, Alan Joseph 1948- AmMWSc 92
**Pribush**, Robert A 1946- AmMWSc 92
**Pribyl**, Joyce Marie 1946- WhoMW 92
**Prica**, Srdja 1905- Who 92
**Price**, A. Yvonne Conn 1930- WhoBlA 92
**Price**, Alan Edwin 1933- WhoAmL 92
**Price**, Alan Roger 1942- AmMWSc 92
**Price**, Alan Thomas 1949- WhoFI 92
**Price**, Albert H. 1922- WhoBlA 92
**Price**, Albert J 1940- WhoAmP 91
**Price**, Alfred Douglas 1947- WhoBlA 92
**Price**, Alfred Lee 1935- WhoAmL 92
**Price**, Alice L. DrAPF 91
**Price**, Alson K 1938- AmMWSc 92
**Price**, Alvin Audis 1917- AmMWSc 92
**Price**, Alvin Helm 1941- WhoRel 92
**Price**, Andrea R. 1959- WhoBlA 92
**Price**, Anthony 1928- IntAu&W 91, Who 92, WrDr 92
**Price**, Antony 1945- IntWW 91
**Price**, Arthur WhoEnt 92
**Price**, Arthur Leolin 1924- Who 92
**Price**, Arthur Richard 1951- WhoFI 92, WhoWest 92
**Price**, Barry Who 92
**Price**, Barry David Keith 1933- Who 92
**Price**, Benjamin Terence 1921- Who 92
**Price**, Bernard Albert 1944- Who 92
**Price**, Bobby Earl 1937- AmMWSc 92
**Price**, Byron Frederick 1936- AmMWSc 92
**Price**, C A 1927- AmMWSc 92
**Price**, Cecil 1915- WrDr 92
**Price**, Cecil Edward 1956- WhoRel 92
**Price**, Cecil Ernest 1921- Who 92
**Price**, Charles 1940- WhoBlA 92
**Price**, Charles Eldridge 1959- WhoWest 92
**Price**, Charles Eugene WhoBlA 92
**Price**, Charles H., II 1931- IntWW 91, Who 92, WhoAmP 91
**Price**, Charles Morton 1926- AmMWSc 92
**Price**, Charles R 1932- AmMWSc 92
**Price**, Charles Rugge- 1936- Who 92
**Price**, Charles Steven 1955- WhoAmL 92
**Price**, Christopher 1932- Who 92
**Price**, Clara Sue WhoAmP 91
**Price**, Dale WhoAmP 91
**Price**, Dale 1924- WhoAmL 92
**Price**, Dan Q 1919- WhoAmP 91
**Price**, Daniel George 1943- WhoMW 92
**Price**, Daniel Martin 1955- WhoAmL 92
**Price**, David Who 92
**Price**, David 1924- Who 92
**Price**, David Alan 1948- AmMWSc 92
**Price**, David B., Jr. 1945- WhoBlA 92
**Price**, David C 1934- AmMWSc 92
**Price**, David Cecil Long 1940- AmMWSc 92
**Price**, David E. 1940- AlmAP 92 [port]
**Price**, David Edgar 1914- AmMWSc 92
**Price**, David Eugene 1940- WhoAmP 91
**Price**, David Lee 1934- WhoBlA 92
**Price**, David Thomas 1943- AmMWSc 92
**Price**, Dennis Joe 1955- WhoRel 92
**Price**, Dolores Holland 1932- WhoAmP 91
**Price**, Dolores Rose 1961- WhoAmP 91
**Price**, Don 1933- WhoEnt 92
**Price**, Don Krasher 1910- IntWW 91
**Price**, Donald Ray 1939- AmMWSc 92
**Price**, Donald Wayne 1961- WhoAmL 92
**Price**, Donna 1913- AmMWSc 92
**Price**, Earnest, Jr. 1919- WhoRel 92
**Price**, Edgar Dayton ScFEYrs
**Price**, Edward Dean 1919- WhoAmL 92, WhoWest 92
**Price**, Edward Hector 1920- AmMWSc 92
**Price**, Edward J, III 1952- WhoAmP 91
**Price**, Edward Reynolds 1933- IntAu&W 91
**Price**, Edward Warren 1920- AmMWSc 92
**Price**, Elizabeth Louise 1934- WhoBlA 92
**Price**, Elton 1933- AmMWSc 92
**Price**, Eric Hardiman Mockford 1931- Who 92
**Price**, Eugene Elona 1958- WhoWest 92
**Price**, Eugenia 1916- IntAu&W 91, RelLAm 91
**Price**, Faye Hughes WhoBlA 92
**Price**, Florence 1888-1953 NotBlAW 92
**Price**, Florence Bea 1888-1953 NewAmDM
**Price**, Florence Beatrice Smith 1888-1953 FacFETw
**Price**, Francis 1950- Who 92
**Price**, Frank LesBEnT 92
**Price**, Frank 1922- Who 92
**Price**, Frank 1930- IntMPA 92, IntWW 91, WhoEnt 92, WhoFI 92, WhoWest 92
**Price**, Frederick Kenneth Cercie 1932- WhoRel 92, WhoWest 92
**Price**, Frederick William 1932- AmMWSc 92
**Price**, Gail Elizabeth 1945- WhoFI 92
**Price**, Gail J. Goodman 1950- WhoWest 92
**Price**, Gail Mary 1935- WhoAmP 91
**Price**, Gareth 1939- Who 92
**Price**, Gary Glen 1945- WhoMW 92
**Price**, Gary Michael 1958- WhoAmL 92
**Price**, Gayl Baader 1949- WhoWest 92
**Price**, Gene Temple 1957- WhoAmL 92
**Price**, Geoffrey Alan Who 92
**Price**, George 1919- Who 92
**Price**, George A 1926- WhoAmP 91
**Price**, George Baker 1929- WhoBlA 92
**Price**, George Cadle 1919- IntWW 91
**Price**, Geraint Who 92
**Price**, Gilbert d1991 NewYTBS 91
**Price**, Gilbert 1942-1991 WhoBlA 92N
**Price**, Glenn Albert 1923- AmMWSc 92
**Price**, Griffith Baley 1905- AmMWSc 92, WhoMW 92
**Price**, Griffith Baley, Jr. 1942- WhoAmL 92
**Price**, H Ryan 1912-1986 FacFETw
**Price**, Harold Anthony 1919- AmMWSc 92
**Price**, Harold James 1943- AmMWSc 92
**Price**, Harold M 1931- AmMWSc 92
**Price**, Harry James 1941- AmMWSc 92
**Price**, Henry Escoe 1947- WhoEnt 92
**Price**, Henry J. 1937- WhoAmL 92
**Price**, Henry Locher 1922- AmMWSc 92
**Price**, Hilary Martin Connop 1912- Who 92
**Price**, Howard Charles 1942- AmMWSc 92, WhoMW 92
**Price**, Howard William 1930- WhoWest 92
**Price**, Hubert, Jr WhoAmP 91
**Price**, Hugh Bernard 1941- WhoBlA 92
**Price**, Hugh Criswell 1939- AmMWSc 92
**Price**, Humphrey Wallace 1954- WhoWest 92
**Price**, I. Edward 1942- WhoFI 92
**Price**, J. P. 1947- WhoRel 92
**Price**, James Clarence 1932- AmMWSc 92
**Price**, James D WhoAmP 91
**Price**, James F 1932- AmMWSc 92
**Price**, James Felix 1947- AmMWSc 92
**Price**, James Franklin 1948- AmMWSc 92
**Price**, James Gordon 1926- AmMWSc 92, IntWW 91
**Price**, James Joseph 1911- WhoAmP 91
**Price**, James Newton 1947- WhoWest 92
**Price**, James Robert 1912- IntWW 91, Who 92
**Price**, James Rogers 1942- WhoBlA 92
**Price**, James Tucker 1955- WhoAmL 92
**Price**, Jay Berry 1915- WhoWest 92
**Price**, Jeannine Alleenica 1949- WhoWest 92
**Price**, Jennifer IntAu&W 91X
**Price**, Joe 1935- WhoWest 92
**Price**, Joel McClendon AmMWSc 92
**Price**, John Alan 1938- Who 92
**Price**, John Aley 1947- WhoAmL 92
**Price**, John Avner 1932- AmMWSc 92
**Price**, John C 1959- AmMWSc 92
**Price**, John Charles 1937- AmMWSc 92
**Price**, John David Ewart 1927- AmMWSc 92
**Price**, John Edward 1942- WhoRel 92
**Price**, John Elwood 1935- WhoBlA 92
**Price**, John Lister Willis 1915- Who 92
**Price**, John Maurice 1922- Who 92
**Price**, John Walter 1930- Who 92
**Price**, John Wheatley WhoRel 92
**Price**, John Wilson 1938- WhoRel 92
**Price**, Jonathan DrAPF 91
**Price**, Jonathan Greenway 1950- AmMWSc 92
**Price**, Joseph Earl 1930- AmMWSc 92, WhoWest 92
**Price**, Joseph Hubbard 1939- WhoAmL 92
**Price**, Joseph L. 1931- WhoBlA 92
**Price**, Joseph Levering 1942- AmMWSc 92
**Price**, Judith 1937- WhoBlA 92
**Price**, Jules Morton 1929- WhoFI 92
**Price**, Julian 1943- WhoFI 92
**Price**, Kathleen McCormick 1932- WhoWest 92
**Price**, Kay 1943- WhoEnt 92
**Price**, Keith Glenn 1941- WhoWest 92
**Price**, Keith Robinson 1930- AmMWSc 92
**Price**, Kenneth Elbert 1926- AmMWSc 92
**Price**, Kenneth Hugh AmMWSc 92
**Price**, Kenneth Michael 1963- WhoFI 92
**Price**, Kent Sparks, Jr 1936- AmMWSc 92
**Price**, Kingsley Blake 1917- WrDr 92
**Price**, Larry H. 1961- WhoEnt 92
**Price**, Lawrence Edward 1943- AmMWSc 92
**Price**, Lawrence Howard 1952- AmMWSc 92
**Price**, Lee 1950- WhoFI 92
**Price**, Leigh 1941- WhoFI 92
**Price**, Leland Fletcher 1951- WhoEnt 92
**Price**, Leolin Who 92
**Price**, Leonard 1933- AmMWSc 92
**Price**, Leonard Russell 1942- WhoAmP 91
**Price**, Leonard Sidney 1922- Who 92
**Price**, Leontyne 1927- ConBlB 1 [port], ConMus 6 [port], FacFETw [port], HanAmWH, IntWW 91, NewAmDM, NotBlAW 92 [port], Who 92, WhoBlA 92, WhoEnt 92
**Price**, Leslie Victor 1920- Who 92
**Price**, Llewelyn Ralph 1912- Who 92
**Price**, Lloyd 1933- NewAmDM
**Price**, Margaret 1941- NewAmDM
**Price**, Margaret Berenice 1941- IntWW 91, Who 92
**Price**, Margaret P WhoAmP 91
**Price**, Margaret Ruth 1956- WhoWest 92
**Price**, Mark Walter 1956- WhoMW 92
**Price**, Marshall Langton 1878-1915 BiInAmS
**Price**, Martin Burton 1928- AmMWSc 92
**Price**, Mary Brent 1931- WhoAmP 91
**Price**, Mary Kathleen 1942- WhoAmL 92
**Price**, Mary Vaughan 1949- AmMWSc 92
**Price**, Maureen G 1951- AmMWSc 92
**Price**, Maurice David 1915- Who 92
**Price**, Megan D 1954- WhoAmP 91
**Price**, Michael Benjamin 1940- WhoMW 92
**Price**, Michael Felipe 1965- WhoFI 92
**Price**, Michael Glendon 1947- AmMWSc 92
**Price**, Michael J. 1950- WhoBlA 92
**Price**, Monroe Edwin 1938- WhoAmL 92
**Price**, Nancy DrAPF 91
**Price**, Nancy P. 1932- WhoEnt 92
**Price**, Nelson 1928- WhoRel 92
**Price**, Norman 1915- Who 92
**Price**, Otis 1943- WhoIns 92
**Price**, Overton Westfeldt 1873-1914 BiInAmS
**Price**, Owen Thomas Williams 1924- WhoFI 92
**Price**, Pamela Anita 1952- WhoBlA 92
**Price**, Paul Arms 1942- AmMWSc 92
**Price**, Paul Buford 1932- IntWW 91, WhoWest 92
**Price**, Paul Buford, Jr 1932- AmMWSc 92
**Price**, Paul L. 1945- WhoAmL 92
**Price**, Paul Sanford 1942- WhoBlA 92
**Price**, Paul W 1932- WhoIns 92
**Price**, Penelope 1950- WhoEnt 92
**Price**, Peter Bryan 1944- Who 92
**Price**, Peter J 1924- AmMWSc 92
**Price**, Peter Michael 1946- AmMWSc 92
**Price**, Peter Nicholas 1942- Who 92
**Price**, Peter Owen 1930- Who 92
**Price**, Peter S. Who 92
**Price**, Peter Wilfrid 1938- AmMWSc 92
**Price**, Phyllis E. DrAPF 91
**Price**, Ralph Who 92
**Price**, Ralph Lorin 1939- AmMWSc 92
**Price**, Ramon B. 1933- WhoBlA 92
**Price**, Ray 1926- WhoEnt 92
**Price**, Ray 1928- NewAmDM
**Price**, Ray Anthony 1957- WhoEnt 92
**Price**, Ray Oscar 1961- WhoMW 92
**Price**, Raymond Alex 1933- AmMWSc 92
**Price**, Reynolds DrAPF 91
**Price**, Reynolds 1933- BenetAL 91, ConNov 91, WrDr 92
**Price**, Richard DrAPF 91, LesBEnT 92, TwCPaSc
**Price**, Richard 1723-1791 BlkwCEP, BlkwEAR
**Price**, Richard Graydon 1933- AmMWSc 92
**Price**, Richard Henry 1943- AmMWSc 92
**Price**, Richard J. WhoMW 92
**Price**, Richard Marcus 1940- AmMWSc 92
**Price**, Richard Michael 1964- WhoAmL 92
**Price**, Richard Taft, Jr. 1954- WhoFI 92
**Price**, Robert IntWW 91, Who 92
**Price**, Robert 1929- AmMWSc 92
**Price**, Robert 1932- WhoEnt 92, WhoFI 92
**Price**, Robert Allen 1934- AmMWSc 92
**Price**, Robert Conrad, II 1958- WhoWest 92
**Price**, Robert Dale 1927- WhoAmP 91
**Price**, Robert E. 1942- WhoWest 92
**Price**, Robert Earle 1936- WhoAmP 91
**Price**, Robert George 1928- Who 92
**Price**, Robert Harold 1949- AmMWSc 92
**Price**, Robert John G. Who 92
**Price**, Robert Lesley 1941- WhoRel 92
**Price**, Robert Stanley 1937- WhoAmL 92
**Price**, Roger 1944- ConAu 35NR, IntAu&W 91, WrDr 92
**Price**, Roger DeForrest 1929- AmMWSc 92
**Price**, Roger Lawrence 1944- WhoAmL 92
**Price**, Roland John Stuart 1961- WhoEnt 92
**Price**, Rollo Edward Crwys 1916- Who 92
**Price**, Ron DrAPF 91
**Price**, Ronald Francis 1926- WrDr 92
**Price**, Ronald James 1933- WhoFI 92
**Price**, Ross Eugene 1907- WhoRel 92
**Price**, Roy Cantrell 1935- WhoRel 92, WhoWest 92
**Price**, Roy Kenneth 1916- Who 92
**Price**, Ruby Jewell Timms WhoBlA 92
**Price**, S. David DrAPF 91
**Price**, Sadie F d1903 BiInAmS
**Price**, Samuel 1923- AmMWSc 92
**Price**, Sandra Jane 1962- WhoFI 92
**Price**, Stanley 1931- IntAu&W 91, WrDr 92
**Price**, Stephen Richie 1955- WhoAmP 91
**Price**, Steven 1937- AmMWSc 92
**Price**, Steven 1962- WhoFI 92
**Price**, Stuart Michael 1967- WhoMW 92
**Price**, Sue Ellen 1948- WhoRel 92
**Price**, Susan 1955- IntAu&W 91, WrDr 92
**Price**, Suzanne D. 1921- WhoBlA 92
**Price**, T Rowe 1898-1983 FacFETw
**Price**, Terence Who 92
**Price**, Terry L. 1953- WhoEnt 92
**Price**, Thomas Allan 1944- WhoMW 92
**Price**, Thomas Daniel, Jr. 1954- WhoAmL 92
**Price**, Thomas Emile 1921- WhoMW 92
**Price**, Thomas Munro 1937- WhoWest 92
**Price**, Thomas R 1934- AmMWSc 92
**Price**, Todd Alan 1957- WhoEnt 92
**Price**, Uvedale 1747-1829 BlkwCEP
**Price**, V.B. DrAPF 91
**Price**, Victor 1930- IntAu&W 91, WrDr 92
**Price**, Vincent 1911- IntMPA 92, IntWW 91
**Price**, Vincent Leonard 1911- WhoEnt 92
**Price**, Virgil 1908- WhoWest 92
**Price**, Vivian William Cecil 1926- Who 92
**Price**, Wallace Walter 1921- WhoBlA 92
**Price**, Walter Bailey 1955- WhoEnt 92
**Price**, Walter Van Vranken 1896- AmMWSc 92
**Price**, Warren WhoAmP 91
**Price**, Warren, III 1943- WhoAmL 92, WhoWest 92
**Price**, Weldon R WhoAmP 91
**Price**, William DrAPF 91
**Price**, William Alrich, Jr 1924- AmMWSc 92
**Price**, William Anthony 1959- WhoMW 92
**Price**, William Charles 1909- Who 92
**Price**, William Charles 1930- AmMWSc 92
**Price**, William Frederick Barry 1925- Who 92
**Price**, William George 1934- Who 92
**Price**, William Geraint 1943- Who 92
**Price**, William John R. Who 92
**Price**, William Melvin 1953- WhoMW 92
**Price**, William S., III 1923- WhoBlA 92
**Price**, William Sloane 1939- WhoFI 92
**Price**, Willis Joseph 1931- WhoWest 92
**Price**, Winford Hugh Protheroe 1926- Who 92
**Price-Bailey**, Janet M. 1961- WhoWest 92
**Price Boday**, Mary Kathryn 1945- WhoEnt 92, WhoWest 92
**Price-Curtis**, William 1944- WhoBlA 92
**Price Evans**, David Alan Who 92
**Price-Sheehy**, Gail Leslie 1957- WhoAmL 92
**Pricer**, Francis Wayne 1935- WhoMW 92
**Pricer**, Wilbur David 1935- AmMWSc 92
**Prichard**, George Edwards 1916- AmMWSc 92
**Prichard**, John David 1948- WhoRel 92
**Prichard**, Katharine Susannah 1883-1969 RfGEnL 91, SmATA 66 [port]
**Prichard**, Mathew Caradoc Thomas 1943- Who 92

**Prichard,** Montague Illtyd d1991 *Who 92N*
**Prichard,** Neal Wayne 1933- *WhoMW 92*
**Prichard,** Peter S. 1944- *WhoFI 92*
**Prichard,** Ray Allen 1941- *WhoWest 92*
**Prichard,** Richard Augustin R. *Who 92*
**Prichard,** Richard Julian Paget 1915- *Who 92*
**Prichard,** Robert Allyn *WhoAmP 91*
**Prichard,** Robert Williams 1923- *AmMWSc 92*
**Prichard-Jones,** John 1913- *Who 92*
**Prickett,** Dave Rowan 1953- *WhoAmL 92*
**Prickett,** David Clinton 1918- *WhoWest 92*
**Prickett,** Gordon Odin 1935- *WhoMW 92*
**Prickett,** Stephen 1939- *Who 92, WrDr 92*
**Prickett,** T. A. 1934- *WhoRel 92*
**Prickett,** Thomas 1913- *Who 92*
**Prickett,** William *WhoIns 92*
**Prickman,** Thomas Bain 1902- *Who 92*
**Prida,** Dolores 1943- *WhoHisp 92*
**Priday,** Christopher Bruton 1926- *Who 92*
**Priddle,** Robert John 1938- *Who 92*
**Priddy,** Arminta Pearl 1955- *WhoMW 92*
**Priddy,** Dottie 1935- *WhoAmP 91*
**Priddy,** Robert Ray 1929- *WhoMW 92*
**Priddy,** Stewart Beauregard 1940- *AmMWSc 92*
**Pride,** Alfred Melville 1897-1988 *FacFETw*
**Pride,** Amelia Perry 1858-1932 *NotBlAW 92*
**Pride,** Armistead Scott 1906-1991 *WhoBlA 92N*
**Pride,** Charley 1938- *WhoBlA 92*
**Pride,** Charley 1939- *WhoEnt 92*
**Pride,** Douglas Elbridge 1942- *AmMWSc 92*
**Pride,** Douglas Spencer 1959- *WhoRel 92*
**Pride,** Hemphill P., II 1936- *WhoBlA 92*
**Pride,** J. Thomas 1940- *WhoBlA 92*
**Pride,** John Bernard 1929- *WrDr 92*
**Pride,** John L. 1940- *WhoBlA 92*
**Pride,** Walter LaVon 1922- *WhoBlA 92*
**Prideaux,** Humphrey 1915- *Who 92*
**Prideaux,** Humphrey Povah Treverbian 1915- *IntWW 91*
**Prideaux,** John 1911- *Who 92*
**Prideaux,** John Denys Charles Anstice 1944- *Who 92*
**Prideaux,** John Francis 1911- *IntWW 91*
**Prideaux,** Julian Humphrey 1942- *Who 92*
**Prideaux,** Walter Arbuthnot 1910- *Who 92*
**Pridgeon,** James Stephen 1948- *WhoWest 92*
**Pridham,** Brian Robert 1934- *Who 92*
**Pridham,** Kenneth Robert Comyn 1922- *Who 92*
**Pridmore-Brown,** David Clifford 1928- *AmMWSc 92*
**Pridnia,** John D *WhoAmP 91*
**Priebe,** Berl E 1918- *WhoAmP 91*
**Prielipp,** Robert Walter 1936- *AmMWSc 92, WhoMW 92*
**Priem,** Windle Beecher 1937- *WhoFI 92*
**Priemer,** Roland 1943- *AmMWSc 92*
**Prien,** Gunther 1908-1941 *EncTR 91 [port]*
**Priene** *EncAmaz 91*
**Prier,** James Eddy 1924- *AmMWSc 92*
**Pries,** Kenneth Karl 1946- *WhoRel 92*
**Pries,** Ralph W. 1919- *IntMPA 92*
**Priesand,** Sally Jane 1946- *WhoRel 92*
**Priesing,** Charles Paul 1929- *AmMWSc 92*
**Priest,** Benny Carman 1959- *WhoAmL 92*
**Priest,** Charles R 1946- *WhoAmP 91*
**Priest,** Christopher 1943- *IntAu&W 91, TwCSFW 91, WrDr 92*
**Priest,** Colin Herbert Dickinson C. *Who 92*
**Priest,** David Gerard 1938- *AmMWSc 92*
**Priest,** George L. 1947- *WhoAmL 92*
**Priest,** Homer Farnum 1916- *AmMWSc 92*
**Priest,** Jean Lane Hirsch 1928- *AmMWSc 92*
**Priest,** John 1931- *WhoEnt 92*
**Priest,** Joseph Roger 1929- *AmMWSc 92*
**Priest,** Margaret 1944- *TwCPaSc*
**Priest,** Marlon L. *WhoBlA 92*
**Priest,** Matthew A 1949- *AmMWSc 92*
**Priest,** Melville S 1912- *AmMWSc 92*
**Priest,** Peter H. 1955- *WhoAmL 92*
**Priest,** Robert Eugene 1926- *AmMWSc 92*
**Priest,** Robert George 1933- *Who 92*
**Priest,** Ruth Emily 1933- *WhoRel 92*
**Priest,** Sharon Devlin 1947- *WhoAmP 91*
**Priester,** Julian Anthony 1935- *WhoBlA 92*
**Priester,** Karl-Heinz 1913-1960 *BiDExR*
**Priester,** Mary 1953- *WhoWest 92*
**Priestland,** Gerald Francis d1991 *Who 92N*
**Priestland,** Gerald Francis 1927- *IntAu&W 91*
**Priestley,** Brian 1946- *IntAu&W 91*
**Priestley,** Carol Lynn 1943- *WhoFI 92, WhoWest 92*
**Priestley,** Charles Henry Brian 1915- *IntWW 91, Who 92*
**Priestley,** Clive 1935- *Who 92*
**Priestley,** J. B. 1894-1984 *CnDBLB 6 [port], FacFETw, RfGEnL 91, TwCSFW 91*
**Priestley,** J. B., Mrs. *Who 92*
**Priestley,** John Christopher 1939- *Who 92*
**Priestley,** Joseph 1733-1804 *BenetAL 91, BiInAmS, BlkwCEP*
**Priestley,** Leslie William 1933- *Who 92*
**Priestley,** Maurice Bertram 1933- *Who 92*
**Priestley,** Philip John 1946- *Who 92*
**Priestley,** Robert Henry 1946- *Who 92*
**Priestman,** Bertram 1868-1951 *TwCPaSc*
**Priestman,** Jane 1930- *Who 92*
**Priestman,** John David 1926- *Who 92*
**Priestman,** Martin 1949- *ConAu 135*
**Priestner,** Edward Bernard 1936- *WhoFI 92*
**Priestner,** Wilton 1934- *TwCPaSc*
**Prieto,** Antonio L. 1965- *WhoHisp 92*
**Prieto,** Argenis Ray 1948- *WhoMW 92*
**Prieto,** Arnaldo da Costa 1930- *IntWW 91*
**Prieto,** Carlos 1937- *WhoEnt 92*
**Prieto,** Claudio R. 1933- *WhoHisp 92*
**Prieto,** Mariana Beeching 1912- *IntAu&W 91*
**Prieto,** Mercy *WhoHisp 92*
**Prieto,** Miguel A. 1943- *WhoHisp 92*
**Prietto,** Mario *WhoHisp 92*
**Prieur,** David John 1942- *AmMWSc 92*
**Prieve,** Dennis Charles 1947- *AmMWSc 92*
**Prieve,** E. Arthur *WhoEnt 92, WhoMW 92*
**Prigent,** Michel 1950- *IntWW 91*
**Prigge,** Liz Maynard 1952- *WhoWest 92*
**Prignano,** Charles Michael 1949- *WhoWest 92*
**Prigodich,** Richard Victor 1951- *AmMWSc 92*
**Prigogine,** Ilya 1917- *AmMWSc 92, FacFETw, IntWW 91, Who 92, WhoNob 90*
**Prigot,** Melvin 1920- *AmMWSc 92*
**Prikry,** Karel Libor 1944- *AmMWSc 92*
**Priley,** Stephen Anthony 1947- *WhoAmP 91*
**Prill,** Arnold L *AmMWSc 92*
**Prillaman,** Roger Lee 1952- *WhoEnt 92*
**Prillaman,** Terry S., Jr. 1959- *WhoAmL 92*
**Prim,** Richard Douglas 1954- *WhoRel 92*
**Prim,** Robert Clay 1921- *AmMWSc 92*
**Prima,** Louis 1911-1978 *FacFETw, NewAmDM*
**Primack,** Joel Robert 1945- *AmMWSc 92*
**Primack,** Leonard 1936- *WhoFI 92*
**Primack,** Marshall Philip 1941- *AmMWSc 92*
**Primack,** Marvin Herbert 1931- *WhoWest 92*
**Primack,** Richard Bart 1950- *AmMWSc 92*
**Primak,** William L 1917- *AmMWSc 92*
**Primakoff,** Paul 1944- *AmMWSc 92*
**Primakov,** Yevgeniy Maksimovich 1929- *IntWW 91, SovUnBD*
**Primarolo,** Dawn 1954- *Who 92*
**Primas,** Barbara Jean 1949- *WhoBlA 92*
**Primas,** Melvin R, Jr 1949- *WhoAmP 91*
**Primasius** *EncEarC*
**Primatesta,** Raul Francisco 1919- *IntWW 91, WhoRel 92*
**Prime,** Benjamin Youngs 1733-1791 *BenetAL 91*
**Prime,** Daniel James 1959- *WhoMW 92*
**Prime,** Derek Arthur d1990 *Who 92N*
**Prime,** Derek James 1931- *WrDr 92*
**Prime,** Frederick 1846-1915 *BiInAmS*
**Prime,** Henry Ashworth 1921- *Who 92*
**Prime,** Kathleen Purcell 1957- *WhoFI 92*
**Prime,** Temple 1832-1903 *BiInAmS*
**Primeau,** Lawrence Steven 1947- *WhoAmP 91*
**Primeaux,** Henry, III 1941- *WhoFI 92*
**Primi,** Don Alexis 1947- *WhoFI 92*
**Primiano,** Frank Paul, Jr 1939- *AmMWSc 92*
**Primm,** Beny Jene 1928- *WhoBlA 92*
**Primo,** Al *LesBEnT 92*
**Primo,** Albert Thomas 1935- *WhoEnt 92*
**Primo,** Marie Nash 1928- *WhoMW 92*
**Primo,** Quintin E., Jr. 1913- *WhoBlA 92*
**Primo,** Quintin Ebenezer, Jr. 1913- *WhoRel 92*
**Primo de Rivera,** Jose Antonio 1903-1936 *EncTR 91 [port], FacFETw*
**Primo de Rivera,** Miguel 1870-1930 *FacFETw*
**Primo de Rivera,** Pilar 1910?-1991 *NewYTBS 91*
**Primo de Rivera Y Saenz De Heredia,** Jose 1903-1936 *BiDExR*
**Primo de Verdad y Ramos,** Francisco 1760-1808 *HisDSpE*
**Primous,** Emma M. 1942- *WhoBlA 92*
**Primps,** William Guthrie 1949- *WhoAmL 92*
**Primrose** *Who 92*
**Primrose,** John Ure 1960- *Who 92*
**Primrose,** William 1903-1982 *FacFETw, NewAmDM*
**Primus,** The *Who 92*
**Primus,** Barry 1938- *IntMPA 92*
**Primus,** Barry, Mrs. *WhoEnt 92*
**Primus,** Bobbie J. 1934- *WhoBlA 92*
**Primus,** Constance Merrill 1931- *WhoEnt 92*
**Primus,** Mary Jane Davis 1924- *WhoMW 92*
**Primus,** Pearl 1919- *NotBlAW 92, WhoBlA 92*
**Primus,** Wendell Eugene 1946- *NewYTBS 91 [port]*
**Prince** 1958- *IntMPA 92, IntWW 91, WhoBlA 92, WhoEnt 92*
**Prince** 1960- *NewAmDM*
**Prince,** A. Cheryl 1945- *WhoBlA 92*
**Prince,** Alan Theodore 1915- *AmMWSc 92*
**Prince,** Alfred M 1928- *AmMWSc 92*
**Prince,** Alison 1931- *WrDr 92*
**Prince,** Andrew Lee 1952- *WhoBlA 92*
**Prince,** Anna L. *WhoEnt 92*
**Prince,** Anthony 1921- *Who 92*
**Prince,** Charles William *AmMWSc 92*
**Prince,** Cheryl Patrice 1956- *WhoBlA 92*
**Prince,** David Allan 1932- *AmMWSc 92*
**Prince,** David Cannon 1950- *WhoAmL 92*
**Prince,** David P. 1954- *WhoEnt 92*
**Prince,** Denver Lee 1932- *AmMWSc 92*
**Prince,** Derek 1915- *ConAu 34NR*
**Prince,** Edgar Oliver 1947- *WhoBlA 92*
**Prince,** Edward 1928- *AmMWSc 92*
**Prince,** Eric D 1946- *AmMWSc 92*
**Prince,** Ernest S. 1942- *WhoBlA 92*
**Prince,** Eugene Augustus 1930- *WhoAmP 91*
**Prince,** F. T. 1912- *ConPo 91, IntAu&W 91, LiExTwC, WrDr 92*
**Prince,** Frank Michael 1946- *WhoAmL 92*
**Prince,** Frank Templeton 1912- *Who 92*
**Prince,** Gregory Antone *AmMWSc 92*
**Prince,** Harold 1928- *FacFETw, IntMPA 92, WhoEnt 92*
**Prince,** Harold Hoopes 1941- *AmMWSc 92*
**Prince,** Harold S. 1928- *IntWW 91*
**Prince,** Harold Smith 1928- *Who 92*
**Prince,** Harry E 1953- *AmMWSc 92*
**Prince,** Herbert N 1929- *AmMWSc 92*
**Prince,** Hugh Anthony 1911- *Who 92*
**Prince,** Jack 1938- *AmMWSc 92*
**Prince,** James T 1920- *AmMWSc 92*
**Prince,** Joan Marie 1954- *WhoBlA 92*
**Prince,** John 1751-1836 *BiInAmS*
**Prince,** John Luther, III 1941- *AmMWSc 92*
**Prince,** Kathleen Corinne 1948- *WhoWest 92*
**Prince,** Kenneth Stephen 1950- *WhoAmL 92*
**Prince,** Larry L. *WhoFI 92*
**Prince,** Lisa Spangler 1961- *WhoFI 92*
**Prince,** Lucy Terry 1730?-1821 *NotBlAW 92*
**Prince,** M David *AmMWSc 92*
**Prince,** Mack J 1919- *AmMWSc 92*
**Prince,** Martin 1937- *WhoFI 92*
**Prince,** Martin Irwin 1937- *AmMWSc 92*
**Prince,** Morton Bronenberg 1924- *AmMWSc 92*
**Prince,** Nancy Gardner 1799- *NotBlAW 92*
**Prince,** Peter Derek 1915- *RelLAm 91*
**Prince,** Richard Everett 1947- *WhoBlA 92*
**Prince,** Richard Hudson 1951- *WhoEnt 92*
**Prince,** Robert Harry 1942- *AmMWSc 92*
**Prince,** Robert Lanston 1954- *WhoAmP 91*
**Prince,** Robert Mason 1914- *WhoFI 92, WhoMW 92*
**Prince,** Robert William, III 1955- *WhoRel 92*
**Prince,** Roger Charles 1950- *AmMWSc 92*
**Prince,** Terry Jamison 1949- *AmMWSc 92*
**Prince,** Thomas 1687-1758 *BenetAL 91*
**Prince,** Warren Victor 1911- *WhoFI 92*
**Prince,** William 1913- *IntMPA 92*
**Prince-Smith,** Richard 1928- *Who 92*
**Princen,** Henricus Mattheus 1937- *AmMWSc 92*
**Princen,** Lambertus Henricus 1930- *AmMWSc 92*
**Principal,** Victoria 1950- *IntAu&W 91, IntMPA 92, WhoEnt 92*
**Principato,** Gregory Onofrio 1956- *WhoAmP 91*
**Principe,** Walter Henry 1922- *WhoRel 92*
**Princz,** Gary 1947- *WhoEnt 92*
**Prindle,** Barclay Ward 1938- *WhoAmP 91*
**Prindle,** Bryce 1909- *AmMWSc 92*
**Prindle,** Hazel W 1924- *WhoAmP 91*
**Prindle,** Mark Dean 1924- *WhoAmP 91*
**Prindle,** Nicholas C. 1959- *WhoEnt 92*
**Prindle,** Richard Alan 1925- *AmMWSc 92*
**Prindle,** Robert William 1950- *WhoWest 92*
**Prindle,** William Roscoe 1926- *AmMWSc 92*
**Prine,** Andrew 1936- *IntMPA 92*
**Prine,** Andrew Lewis 1936- *WhoEnt 92*
**Prine,** Gordon Madison 1928- *AmMWSc 92*
**Prine,** John 1946- *ConMus 7 [port], WhoEnt 92*
**Prineas,** John William 1935- *AmMWSc 92*
**Prineas,** Ronald James 1937- *AmMWSc 92*
**Pring,** Daryl Roger 1942- *AmMWSc 92*
**Pring,** David Andrew Michael d1991 *Who 92N*
**Pring,** Richard Anthony 1938- *Who 92*
**Pring,** Robert Bradford 1951- *WhoFI 92*
**Pring-Mill,** Robert Duguid Forrest 1924- *Who 92*
**Pringle,** Barbara C 1939- *WhoAmP 91*
**Pringle,** Charles 1919- *Who 92*
**Pringle,** Curt L 1959- *WhoAmP 91*
**Pringle,** Cyrus Guernsey 1838-1911 *BiInAmS*
**Pringle,** David 1950- *ConAu 134*
**Pringle,** David Noble 1954- *WhoFI 92*
**Pringle,** Derek Hair 1926- *Who 92*
**Pringle,** Donald Frank McKenzie 1930- *IntWW 91*
**Pringle,** Dorothy Jutton 1919- *AmMWSc 92*
**Pringle,** Edward E 1914- *WhoAmP 91*
**Pringle,** George Overton 1923- *WhoFI 92*
**Pringle,** James Robert Henry 1939- *IntWW 91*
**Pringle,** James Scott 1937- *AmMWSc 92*
**Pringle,** John 1912- *WrDr 92*
**Pringle,** John Martin Douglas 1912- *IntAu&W 91, IntWW 91, Who 92*
**Pringle,** John Quinton 1864-1926 *TwCPaSc*
**Pringle,** Laurence P. 1935- *SmATA 68 [port]*
**Pringle,** Lewis Gordon 1941- *WhoFI 92*
**Pringle,** Margaret Ann 1946- *Who 92*
**Pringle,** Oran A 1923- *AmMWSc 92*
**Pringle,** Robert M 1936- *WhoAmP 91*
**Pringle,** Robert William 1920- *Who 92*
**Pringle,** Roberta F. 1944- *WhoWest 92*
**Pringle,** Ronald Sandy Alexander 1945- *WhoWest 92*
**Pringle,** Steuart 1928- *Who 92*
**Pringle,** Thomas Walker 1957- *WhoFI 92*
**Pringle,** Wallace C, Jr 1941- *AmMWSc 92*
**Pringle-Jones,** Jennifer Suzanne 1946- *IntAu&W 91*
**Prinja,** Anil Kant 1955- *WhoWest 92*
**Prins,** Robert Jack 1932- *WhoEnt 92*
**Prins,** Rudolph 1935- *AmMWSc 92*
**Prinster,** Dan 1962- *WhoAmP 91*
**Printz,** Morton Philip 1936- *AmMWSc 92*
**Prinz,** Dianne Kasnic 1938- *AmMWSc 92*
**Prinz,** Gary A 1938- *AmMWSc 92*
**Prinz,** Joachim 1902-1988 *FacFETw*
**Prinz,** Martin 1931- *AmMWSc 92*
**Prinz,** Patricia N 1942- *AmMWSc 92*
**Prinzi,** Nancy Rae 1948- *WhoMW 92*
**Prinzivalli,** Joseph Anthony, Jr. 1955- *WhoFI 92*
**Priola,** Donald Victor 1938- *AmMWSc 92*
**Prioleau,** Diane Thys 1934- *WhoAmP 91*
**Prioleau,** Peter Sylvester 1949- *WhoBlA 92*
**Prioleau,** Sara Nelliene 1940- *WhoBlA 92*
**Prior** *Who 92*
**Prior,** Baron 1927- *IntWW 91, Who 92*
**Prior,** Allan 1922- *IntAu&W 91, WrDr 92*
**Prior,** Christopher 1912- *Who 92*
**Prior,** David James *AmMWSc 92*
**Prior,** Edwina M 1910- *WhoAmP 91*
**Prior,** Gary L. 1943- *WhoAmL 92*
**Prior,** Jean Cutler 1940- *AmMWSc 92*
**Prior,** John Alan 1913- *AmMWSc 92*
**Prior,** John Thompson 1917- *AmMWSc 92*
**Prior,** Joseph LaFayette 1935- *WhoMW 92*
**Prior,** Kenneth Francis William 1926- *WrDr 92*
**Prior,** Matthew 1664-1721 *BlkwCEP, RfGEnL 91*
**Prior,** Michael Herbert 1939- *AmMWSc 92*
**Prior,** Paul Verdayne 1921- *AmMWSc 92*
**Prior,** Peter James 1919- *Who 92*
**Prior,** Richard Marion 1942- *AmMWSc 92*
**Prior,** Robert L. 1941- *WhoMW 92*
**Prior,** Ronald L 1945- *AmMWSc 92*
**Prior,** William Johnson 1924- *Who 92*
**Prior,** William Martin 1949- *WhoEnt 92*
**Priore,** Roger L 1938- *AmMWSc 92*
**Prioreschi,** Plinio 1930- *AmMWSc 92*
**Pripstein,** Morris 1935- *AmMWSc 92*
**Prisbrey,** Keith A 1945- *AmMWSc 92*
**Priscillian** 340?-387? *EncEarC*
**Prisock,** Kerry Lee 1960- *WhoAmL 92*
**Pristavkin,** Anatoliy Ignatevich 1931- *IntWW 91, SovUnBD*
**Pritchard** *Who 92*
**Pritchard,** Baron 1910- *Who 92*
**Pritchard,** Arthur Alan 1922- *Who 92*
**Pritchard,** Austin Wyatt 1929- *AmMWSc 92*
**Pritchard,** Claudius Hornby, Jr. 1927- *WhoMW 92*

**Pritchard,** Dalton H 1921- *AmMWSc 92*
**Pritchard,** Daron 1954- *WhoBlA 92*
**Pritchard,** David Edward 1941- *AmMWSc 92*
**Pritchard,** David Graham 1945- *AmMWSc 92*
**Pritchard,** David Michael 1954- *WhoEnt 92*
**Pritchard,** Donald William 1922- *AmMWSc 92*
**Pritchard,** Douglas Evan 1947- *WhoEnt 92*
**Pritchard,** Ernest Thackeray 1928- *AmMWSc 92*
**Pritchard,** Evan Thomas 1955- *WhoEnt 92*
**Pritchard,** G Ian 1929- *AmMWSc 92*
**Pritchard,** Glyn O 1931- *AmMWSc 92*
**Pritchard,** Gordon 1939- *AmMWSc 92*
**Pritchard,** Gwynedd Idris 1924- *Who 92*
**Pritchard,** Gwynn *Who 92*
**Pritchard,** Hayden N 1933- *AmMWSc 92*
**Pritchard,** Hugh Wentworth 1903- *Who 92*
**Pritchard,** Huw Owen 1928- *AmMWSc 92*
**Pritchard,** Iorwerth Gwynn 1946- *Who 92*
**Pritchard,** Jack Arthur 1921- *AmMWSc 92*
**Pritchard,** James Edward 1922- *AmMWSc 92*
**Pritchard,** Joel 1925- *WhoWest 92*
**Pritchard,** Joel M 1925- *WhoAmP 91*
**Pritchard,** John 1921-1989 *NewAmDM*
**Pritchard,** John B 1943- *AmMWSc 92*
**Pritchard,** John Michael 1921-1989 *FacFETw*
**Pritchard,** John Paul, Jr 1929- *AmMWSc 92*
**Pritchard,** Kenneth John 1926- *Who 92*
**Pritchard,** Kenneth William 1933- *Who 92*
**Pritchard,** Llewelyn G. 1937- *WhoAmL 92*
**Pritchard,** Lois Ruth Breur 1946- *WhoFI 92*
**Pritchard,** Marion K. Smith *WhoBlA 92*
**Pritchard,** Mary Elizabeth 1946- *WhoMW 92*
**Pritchard,** Mary Hanson 1924- *AmMWSc 92*
**Pritchard,** Melissa *DrAPF 91*
**Pritchard,** Neil 1911- *IntWW 91, Who 92*
**Pritchard,** Norman Henry, II *DrAPF 91*
**Pritchard,** Parmely Herbert 1941- *AmMWSc 92*
**Pritchard,** R John 1945- *IntAu&W 91, WrDr 92*
**Pritchard,** Raymond John 1931- *WhoFI 92*
**Pritchard,** Robert Leslie 1924- *AmMWSc 92*
**Pritchard,** Robert Starling 1929- *WhoEnt 92*
**Pritchard,** Robert Starling, II 1929- *WhoBlA 92*
**Pritchard,** Teresa Noreen 1953- *WhoAmL 92*
**Pritchard,** Thomas Owen 1932- *Who 92*
**Pritchard,** Wenton Maurice 1931- *AmMWSc 92*
**Pritchard,** Wilbur L 1923- *AmMWSc 92*
**Pritchard,** William Baker 1950- *WhoAmP 91*
**Pritchard,** William Grady, Jr 1927- *WhoIns 92*
**Pritchard,** William H. 1932- *DcLB 111 [port], IntAu&W 91, WrDr 92*
**Pritchard,** William Roy 1924- *AmMWSc 92*
**Pritchett,** A G 1928- *WhoAmP 91*
**Pritchett,** Allen Monroe 1949- *WhoMW 92*
**Pritchett,** Bruce Michael, Sr. 1940- *WhoWest 92*
**Pritchett,** Carr Waller 1823-1910 *BiInAmS*
**Pritchett,** David V. 1939- *WhoFI 92*
**Pritchett,** Ervin Garrison 1920- *AmMWSc 92*
**Pritchett,** John Franklyn 1942- *AmMWSc 92*
**Pritchett,** Joseph Allen 1962- *WhoRel 92*
**Pritchett,** Joseph Everett 1948- *WhoMW 92*
**Pritchett,** Kay 1946- *ConAu 135*
**Pritchett,** Lafayette Bow 1934- *WhoAmL 92*
**Pritchett,** Lawrence Forrest 1956- *WhoEnt 92*
**Pritchett,** P W 1928- *AmMWSc 92*
**Pritchett,** Philip Lentner 1944- *AmMWSc 92*
**Pritchett,** Phillip Harold 1958- *WhoFI 92*
**Pritchett,** Randall Floyd 1945- *AmMWSc 92*
**Pritchett,** Ron 1929- *TwCWW 91*
**Pritchett,** Samuel Travis 1938- *WhoIns 92*
**Pritchett,** Thomas Ronald 1925- *AmMWSc 92*
**Pritchett,** V. S. 1900- *ConNov 91, FacFETw, RfGEnL 91, WrDr 92*
**Pritchett,** Victor 1900- *Who 92*
**Pritchett,** Victor Sawdon 1900- *IntAu&W 91, IntWW 91*
**Pritchett,** William Carr 1925- *AmMWSc 92*
**Pritchett,** William Henry 1930- *AmMWSc 92*
**Pritchett,** William Lawrence 1918- *AmMWSc 92*
**Pritham,** Gordon Herman 1907- *AmMWSc 92*
**Pritikin,** Frederick Harry 1942- *WhoMW 92*
**Pritikin,** Marvin E 1922- *WhoIns 92*
**Pritikin,** Nathan 1915-1985 *FacFETw*
**Pritsker,** A Alan B 1933- *AmMWSc 92*
**Pritt,** Charlotte J 1949- *WhoAmP 91*
**Prittie** *Who 92*
**Pritts,** Bradley Arthur, Jr. 1955- *WhoMW 92*
**Pritz,** Alan K *WhoIns 92*
**Pritz,** Michael Burton 1947- *WhoWest 92*
**Pritzker,** Fred Howard 1950- *WhoAmL 92*
**Pritzker,** Jay Arthur 1922- *WhoFI 92, WhoMW 92*
**Pritzker,** Nicholas J. *WhoFI 92*
**Pritzker,** Robert A 1926- *AmMWSc 92*
**Pritzker,** Robert Alan 1926- *WhoFI 92, WhoMW 92*
**Pritzker,** Steven 1939- *WhoEnt 92, WhoWest 92*
**Pritzker,** Thomas Jay 1950- *WhoFI 92, WhoMW 92*
**Pritzlaff,** August H, Jr 1924- *AmMWSc 92*
**Pritzlaff,** John Charles, Jr 1925- *WhoAmP 91*
**Prival,** Michael Joseph 1945- *AmMWSc 92*
**Privateer,** Paul Michael 1946- *ConAu 135*
**Privett,** Caryl Penney 1948- *WhoAmL 92*
**Privett,** Donald F 1955- *WhoIns 92*
**Privette,** Coy Clarence 1933- *WhoAmP 91*
**Privette,** William Edward 1949- *WhoRel 92*
**Privitera,** Carmelo Anthony 1923- *AmMWSc 92*
**Privitera,** Linda Fisher 1946- *WhoRel 92*
**Privitera,** Philip Joseph 1938- *AmMWSc 92*
**Privman,** Vladimir 1955- *AmMWSc 92*
**Privott,** Wilbur Joseph, Jr 1938- *AmMWSc 92*
**Prizer,** Charles J 1924- *AmMWSc 92*
**Prlain,** Pete 1924- *WhoEnt 92*
**Pro,** Philip Martin 1946- *WhoAmL 92, WhoWest 92*
**Proakis,** Anthony George 1940- *AmMWSc 92*
**Proakis,** John George 1935- *AmMWSc 92*
**Proba** *EncEarC*
**Probala,** Andrew Eugene 1908- *WhoMW 92*
**Probasco,** Jeanetta *WhoBlA 92*
**Probasco,** William Lee 1937- *WhoRel 92*
**Prober,** Alexandra Jaworski 1907- *WhoWest 92*
**Prober,** Daniel Ethan 1948- *AmMWSc 92*
**Prober,** Richard 1937- *AmMWSc 92*
**Probert,** David Henry 1938- *Who 92*
**Probert,** Ronald 1934- *Who 92*
**Probine,** Mervyn Charles 1924- *Who 92*
**Probst,** Albert Henry 1912- *AmMWSc 92*
**Probst,** Dorothy Jean 1953- *WhoMW 92*
**Probst,** Gerald William 1922- *AmMWSc 92*
**Probst,** John Elwin 1940- *WhoRel 92*
**Probst,** Raymond R. 1919- *IntWW 91*
**Probst,** Walter Carl, Jr. 1937- *WhoRel 92*
**Probstein,** Ronald F 1928- *AmMWSc 92*
**Proby,** Peter 1911- *Who 92*
**Probyn,** Harold Melsome 1891- *Who 92*
**Procaccini,** Donald J 1939- *AmMWSc 92*
**Procci,** Warren R 1947- *AmMWSc 92*
**Procel,** Guillermo, Jr. 1947- *WhoHisp 92*
**Prochaska,** Bradley Joseph 1955- *WhoAmL 92*
**Prochaska,** Joseph J, Jr. 1951- *WhoIns 92*
**Prochaska,** Robert *DrAPF 91*
**Prochazka,** Svante 1928- *AmMWSc 92*
**Prochazkova,** Iva 1953- *ConAu 135, SmATA 68 [port]*
**Prochnow,** Herbert Victor *IntAu&W 91, IntWW 91*
**Prochnow,** Herbert Victor 1897- *WrDr 92*
**Prochnow,** Herbert Victor, Jr. 1931- *WhoMW 92*
**Prock,** Alfred 1930- *AmMWSc 92*
**Procknow,** Donald Eugene 1923- *AmMWSc 92*
**Prockop,** Darwin J 1929- *AmMWSc 92*
**Prockop,** Leon D 1934- *AmMWSc 92*
**Procktor,** Patrick 1936- *Who 92*
**Proclus of Constantinople** d446 *EncEarC*
**Procope,** Ernesta G. *WhoBlA 92*
**Procope,** Ernesta G. 19--?- *NotBlAW 92 [port]*
**Procope,** John Levy 1925- *WhoBlA 92*
**Procope,** Russell 1908-1981 *NewAmDM*
**Procope,** Ulla 1921-1968 *DcTwDes*
**Procopio,** Joseph Guydon 1940- *WhoAmL 92*
**Procopio,** Michael Joseph 1961- *WhoAmL 92*
**Procopius of Caesarea** 500?-565? *EncEarC*
**Procopius of Gaza** 475?-538? *EncEarC*
**Procter,** Alan Robert 1939- *AmMWSc 92*
**Procter,** Carol Ann 1941- *WhoEnt 92*
**Procter,** Dod 1891-1972 *TwCPaSc*
**Procter,** Ernest 1886-1935 *TwCPaSc*
**Procter,** Harvey Thornton, Jr. 1945- *WhoBlA 92*
**Procter,** John Ernest 1918- *WhoRel 92*
**Procter,** John Robert 1844-1903 *BiInAmS*
**Procter,** Norma 1928- *Who 92*
**Procter,** Robert John Dudley 1935- *Who 92*
**Procter,** Sidney 1925- *Who 92*
**Procter,** William 1817-1874 *BiInAmS*
**Proctor,** Alan Ray 1945- *AmMWSc 92*
**Proctor,** Andrew Stuart 1947- *WhoFI 92*
**Proctor,** Anthony James 1931- *Who 92*
**Proctor,** Barbara Gardner *WhoBlA 92*
**Proctor,** Barbara Gardner 1933- *NotBlAW 92 [port]*
**Proctor,** Charles Darnell 1922- *AmMWSc 92*
**Proctor,** Charles Lafayette 1923- *AmMWSc 92*
**Proctor,** Charles Lafayette, II 1954- *AmMWSc 92*
**Proctor,** Charles Mahan 1917- *AmMWSc 92*
**Proctor,** Clarke Wayne 1942- *AmMWSc 92*
**Proctor,** David George 1928- *AmMWSc 92, WhoMW 92*
**Proctor,** David Ray 1956- *WhoAmL 92*
**Proctor,** David Victor 1930- *Who 92*
**Proctor,** Deborah Suzanne 1951- *WhoEnt 92*
**Proctor,** Dennis Vernon 1954- *WhoRel 92*
**Proctor,** Donald Frederick 1913- *AmMWSc 92*
**Proctor,** Earl D. 1941- *WhoBlA 92*
**Proctor,** Edna Dean 1829-1923 *BenetAL 91*
**Proctor,** Edward Knox 1961- *WhoAmL 92*
**Proctor,** Geo *TwCSFW 91*
**Proctor,** George W. *WrDr 92*
**Proctor,** Grover Belmont, Jr. 1951- *WhoMW 92*
**Proctor,** Harvey *Who 92*
**Proctor,** Ian Douglas Ben 1918- *Who 92*
**Proctor,** Ilene Sandra 1951- *WhoEnt 92*
**Proctor,** Ivan D 1939- *AmMWSc 92*
**Proctor,** J F 1928- *AmMWSc 92*
**Proctor,** James E, Jr *WhoAmP 91*
**Proctor,** James Moody, II 1959- *WhoAmL 92*
**Proctor,** James Roscoe 1938- *WhoAmP 91*
**Proctor,** James Timothy 1946- *WhoAmL 92*
**Proctor,** Jerry Franklin 1932- *AmMWSc 92*
**Proctor,** Jesse Heighton 1908- *Who 92*
**Proctor,** John Thomas Arthur 1940- *AmMWSc 92*
**Proctor,** Julian Warrilow 1942- *AmMWSc 92*
**Proctor,** Keith Harvey 1947- *Who 92*
**Proctor,** Leonard D. 1919- *WhoBlA 92*
**Proctor,** Lister Hill 1938- *WhoAmP 91*
**Proctor,** Nancy Jean 1936- *WhoAmP 91*
**Proctor,** Paul Dean 1918- *AmMWSc 92*
**Proctor,** Richard James 1931- *AmMWSc 92*
**Proctor,** Richard Lee 1944- *WhoAmP 91*
**Proctor,** Roderick 1914- *Who 92*
**Proctor,** Sally *WhoWest 92*
**Proctor,** Samuel D. 1921- *ConAu 133*
**Proctor,** Samuel Dewitt 1921- *WhoBlA 92, WhoRel 92*
**Proctor,** Stanley Irving 1936- *WhoFI 92, WhoMW 92*
**Proctor,** Stanley Irving, Jr 1936- *AmMWSc 92*
**Proctor,** Susan Anthony 1948- *WhoEnt 92*
**Proctor,** Thomas F. Goldsmith 1950- *WhoEnt 92*
**Proctor,** Thomas Gilmer 1933- *AmMWSc 92*
**Proctor,** Thomas H 1842- *ScFEYrs*
**Proctor,** Timothy DeWitt 1949- *WhoBlA 92*
**Proctor,** Vernon Willard 1927- *AmMWSc 92*
**Proctor,** W J, Jr 1925- *AmMWSc 92*
**Proctor,** William Gilbert, Jr. 1941- *WrDr 92*
**Proctor,** William H. 1945- *WhoBlA 92*
**Proctor-Beauchamp,** Christopher Radstock *Who 92*
**Procul Harum** *NewAmDM*
**Prodan,** David 1902- *IntWW 91*
**Prodany,** Nicholas W *AmMWSc 92*
**Prodell,** Albert Gerald 1925- *AmMWSc 92*
**Prodger,** Kim Anne 1956- *WhoWest 92*
**Prody,** Gerry Ann 1952- *AmMWSc 92*
**Proebsting,** Edward Louis, Jr 1926- *AmMWSc 92*
**Proebsting,** William Martin 1951- *AmMWSc 92*
**Proenza,** Luis Mariano 1944- *AmMWSc 92*
**Proescher,** Ward Hornblower 1935- *WhoWest 92*
**Profeit-LeBlanc,** Louise Frances 1951- *WhoRel 92*
**Professor Longhair** 1918-1980 *ConMus 6 [port], NewAmDM*
**Professor X** *IntAu&W 91X*
**Proffer,** Marvin E 1931- *WhoAmP 91*
**Proffit,** David Stephen 1960- *WhoAmL 92*
**Proffit,** William R 1936- *AmMWSc 92*
**Proffitt,** Curtis Ray 1935- *WhoAmP 91*
**Proffitt,** John Matthew Gladney 1948- *WhoEnt 92*
**Proffitt,** John Richard 1930- *WhoFI 92*
**Proffitt,** Max Rowland 1940- *AmMWSc 92*
**Proffitt,** Thomas Jefferson, Jr 1932- *AmMWSc 92*
**Proffitt,** Thurber Dennis, III 1943- *WhoRel 92*
**Profio,** A Edward 1931- *AmMWSc 92*
**Profit,** Kirk A 1952- *WhoAmP 91*
**Profit,** Vera Barbara 1945- *WhoMW 92*
**Profumo,** David *ConNov 91*
**Profumo,** John Dennis 1915- *IntWW 91, Who 92*
**Progelhof,** Richard Carl 1936- *AmMWSc 92*
**Progoff,** Ira 1921- *ConAu 133*
**Prohammer,** Frederick George 1922- *AmMWSc 92*
**Prohaska,** Charles Anton 1920- *AmMWSc 92*
**Prohaska,** Joseph Robert 1945- *AmMWSc 92*
**Prohaska,** Lawrence Charles 1953- *WhoEnt 92*
**Prohofsky,** Earl William 1935- *AmMWSc 92*
**Prohosky,** Donald E. 1930- *WhoWest 92*
**Proicou,** Michael Chris 1963- *WhoWest 92*
**Proietti,** Gary Leo 1952- *WhoRel 92*
**Prokai,** Bela 1937- *AmMWSc 92*
**Prokhanov,** Ivan Stepanovich 1869-1935 *SovUnBD*
**Prokhorov,** Aleksandr Mikhailovich 1916- *IntWW 91*
**Prokhorov,** Alexander Mikhailovich 1916- *Who 92, WhoNob 90*
**Prokhorova,** Violetta *Who 92*
**Prokhovnik,** Simon Jacques 1920- *WrDr 92*
**Prokipcak,** Joseph Michael 1937- *AmMWSc 92*
**Prokocimer,** Karen Joyce 1954- *WhoFI 92*
**Prokof'ev,** Aleksandr Andreevich 1900-1971 *SovUnBD*
**Prokof'ev,** Sergey Sergeevich 1891-1953 *SovUnBD*
**Prokof'ev,** Yuriy Anatol'evich 1939- *SovUnBD*
**Prokof'eva-Bel'govskaya,** Aleksandra A. 1903-1984 *SovUnBD*
**Prokofiev,** Oleg *TwCPaSc*
**Prokofiev,** Serge 1891-1953 *FacFETw, NewAmDM*
**Prokofiev,** Yuri Anatolevich 1939- *IntWW 91*
**Prokop,** Jan Stuart 1934- *AmMWSc 92*
**Prokop,** Michael Joseph 1944- *AmMWSc 92*
**Prokop,** Ruth Timberlake *WhoAmP 91*
**Prokop,** Ruth Timberlake 1939- *WhoAmL 92*
**Prokopoff,** Stephen Stephen 1929- *WhoMW 92*
**Prokopovich,** Feofan 1681-1736 *BlkwCEP*
**Prokosch,** Frederic 1908- *IntAu&W 91*
**Prokosch,** Frederic 1908-1989 *BenetAL 91, FacFETw*
**Prokosch,** Walther d1991 *NewYTBS 91*
**Prokoshkin,** Yuriy Dmitriyevich 1929- *IntWW 91*
**Proksch,** Alfred 1891- *BiDExR*
**Proksch,** Gary J 1944- *AmMWSc 92*
**Prom,** Stephen George 1954- *WhoAmL 92*
**Promboin,** Ronald Lewis 1945- *WhoFI 92*
**Promersberger,** William J 1912- *AmMWSc 92*
**Promisel,** Nathan E 1908- *AmMWSc 92*
**Promislo,** Daniel 1932- *WhoAmL 92*
**Promnitz,** Lawrence Charles 1944- *AmMWSc 92*
**Promyslov,** Vladimir Fedorovich 1908- *IntWW 91*
**Proni,** John Roberto 1942- *AmMWSc 92*
**Pronk,** Johannes Pieter 1940- *IntWW 91*
**Pronko,** Peter Paul 1938- *AmMWSc 92*
**Pronzini,** Bill 1943- *TwCWW 91, WrDr 92*
**Proom,** William Arthur 1916- *Who 92*
**Proops,** Marjorie *Who 92, WrDr 92*
**Proops,** William Robert 1929- *AmMWSc 92*
**Proper,** Stan *DrAPF 91*
**Propes,** Ernest 1909- *AmMWSc 92*

**Propes,** Major Thomas 1957- *WhoRel 92*
**Propes,** Victor Lee 1938- *WhoBlA 92*
**Prophet,** Arthur Shelley 1918- *Who 92*
**Prophet,** Carl Wright 1929- *AmMWSc 92*
**Prophet,** Elizabeth 1890-1960 *NotBlAW 92 [port]*
**Prophet,** Elizabeth Clare 1940- *RelLAm 91*
**Prophet,** John 1931- *Who 92*
**Prophet,** Marcus L. 1918-1973 *RelLAm 91*
**Prophet,** Matthew Waller, Jr. 1930- *WhoWest 92*
**Prophet,** Richard L., Jr. *WhoBlA 92*
**Prophete,** Beaumanoir 1920- *WhoBlA 92*
**Prophit,** Penny Pauline 1939- *Who 92*
**Propp,** Dale Hartley 1935- *WhoWest 92*
**Propp,** Jacob Henry 1941- *AmMWSc 92*
**Propp,** Vladimir Yakovlevich 1895-1970 *SovUnBD*
**Proppe,** Duane W 1945- *AmMWSc 92*
**Propper,** Arthur 1910- *Who 92*
**Propper,** Dan *DrAPF 91*
**Propst,** Catherine Lamb 1946- *AmMWSc 92*
**Propst,** Franklin Moore 1935- *AmMWSc 92*
**Propst,** Howard Benson 1923- *WhoAmP 91*
**Propst,** Kent Wesley 1956- *WhoMW 92*
**Propst,** Michael Truman 1940- *WhoWest 92*
**Propst,** Robert 1921- *DcTwDes*
**Propst,** Robert Bruce 1931- *WhoAmL 92*
**Propst,** Terrell Wayne 1956- *WhoAmP 91*
**Prorok,** Robert F. 1952- *WhoAmL 92*
**Prorokov,** Boris Ivanovich 1911-1972 *SovUnBD*
**Prosch,** Harry 1917- *WrDr 92*
**Proschan,** Frank 1921- *AmMWSc 92*
**Prose,** Francine 1947- *WrDr 92*
**Prose,** Philip H 1916- *AmMWSc 92*
**Prosen,** Harry 1930- *AmMWSc 92*
**Prosen,** Rose Mary *DrAPF 91*
**Prosise,** Amy Schroeder 1913- *WhoMW 92*
**Proskauer,** Eric S 1903- *AmMWSc 92*
**Proske,** Joseph Walter 1936- *AmMWSc 92*
**Proskin,** Arnold W 1938- *WhoAmP 91*
**Proskurin,** Petr Lukich 1928- *IntWW 91*
**Proskurowski,** Wlodzimierz 1936- *AmMWSc 92*
**Prosky,** Leon 1933- *AmMWSc 92*
**Prosky,** Robert 1930- *IntMPA 92*
**Prosky,** Robert Joseph 1930- *WhoEnt 92*
**Prosnitz,** Donald *AmMWSc 92*
**Prosper of Aquitaine** 390?-455? *EncEarC*
**Prosperi,** Louis Anthony 1954- *WhoAmL 92*
**Prosperi,** Robert 1942- *WhoFI 92*
**Pross,** Hugh Frederick 1942- *AmMWSc 92*
**Prosser,** Lord 1934- *Who 92*
**Prosser,** Bruce Reginal, Jr. 1953- *WhoRel 92*
**Prosser,** C. Ladd 1907- *IntWW 91*
**Prosser,** Charles Smith 1860-1916 *BiInAmS*
**Prosser,** Clifford Andrew 1948- *WhoAmL 92*
**Prosser,** Clifford Ladd 1907- *AmMWSc 92*
**Prosser,** Daniel Lee 1951- *WhoMW 92*
**Prosser,** David Thomas, Jr 1942- *WhoAmP 91*
**Prosser,** Elvet John 1932- *Who 92*
**Prosser,** Francis Ware, Jr 1927- *AmMWSc 92*
**Prosser,** Franklin Pierce 1935- *AmMWSc 92*
**Prosser,** Harold Lee *DrAPF 91*
**Prosser,** Harold Lee 1944- *WrDr 92*
**Prosser,** Ian Maurice Gray 1943- *IntWW 91, Who 92*
**Prosser,** John Martin 1932- *WhoWest 92*
**Prosser,** John Robert 1959- *WhoRel 92*
**Prosser,** Margaret Theresa 1937- *Who 92*
**Prosser,** Peter Edward 1946- *WhoRel 92*
**Prosser,** Raymond Frederick 1919- *Who 92*
**Prosser,** Reese Trego 1927- *AmMWSc 92*
**Prosser,** Robert M 1923- *AmMWSc 92*
**Prosser,** Thomas d1870 *BiInAmS*
**Prosser,** Thomas John 1931- *AmMWSc 92*
**Prosser,** William David *Who 92*
**Prost,** Alain Marie Pascal 1955- *IntWW 91*
**Prostak,** Arnold S 1929- *AmMWSc 92*
**Protan,** John 1920- *WhoAmP 91*
**Protas,** Ron *WhoEnt 92*
**Protazanov,** Yakov 1881-1945 *IntDcF 2-2 [port]*
**Protazanov,** Yakov Aleksandrovich 1881-1945 *SovUnBD*
**Protero,** Dodi 1935- *WhoEnt 92*
**Prothero,** Donald Ross 1954- *AmMWSc 92*
**Prothero,** Eric Anderson 1963- *WhoFI 92*
**Prothero,** John W 1932- *AmMWSc 92*
**Protheroe,** Alan Hackford 1934- *IntWW 91, Who 92*
**Protheroe,** William Mansel 1925- *AmMWSc 92*
**Prothro,** Gerald Dennis 1942- *WhoBlA 92*
**Prothro,** Johnnie W 1922- *AmMWSc 92*
**Prothro,** Johnnie Watts 1922- *WhoBlA 92*
**Prothro,** Louise Robinson 1920- *WhoBlA 92*
**Protic,** Emil George 1948- *WhoWest 92*
**Protigal,** Stanley Nathan 1950- *WhoAmL 92*
**Protokowicz,** Stanley Edward, Jr. 1954- *WhoAmL 92*
**Protopapas,** Nakos 1927- *IntWW 91*
**Protopopescu,** Serban Dan 1945- *AmMWSc 92*
**Protopopov,** Oleg Alekseevich *SovUnBD*
**Protopopovs,** the *FacFETw*
**Protovin,** Richard M. d1991 *NewYTBS 91*
**Protter,** Murray Harold 1918- *AmMWSc 92*
**Protter,** Philip Elliott 1949- *AmMWSc 92*
**Protz,** Richard 1934- *AmMWSc 92*
**Protzman,** Grant D 1950- *WhoAmP 91*
**Protzman,** Grant Dale 1950- *WhoWest 92*
**Proud,** Ernest L 1933- *WhoIns 92*
**Proud,** Gary 1943- *WhoAmP 91*
**Proud,** Harold John Granville Ellis 1906- *Who 92*
**Proud,** John 1907- *Who 92*
**Proud,** John Frederick 1942- *WhoWest 92*
**Proud,** Robert Donald 1949- *WhoEnt 92*
**Proudfit,** Carol Marie 1937- *AmMWSc 92, WhoMW 92*
**Proudfit,** Herbert K 1940- *AmMWSc 92*
**Proudfoot,** Bernadette Agnes 1921- *AmMWSc 92*
**Proudfoot,** Bill 1940- *WhoAmP 91*
**Proudfoot,** Bruce *Who 92*
**Proudfoot,** Bruce Falconer 1903- *Who 92*
**Proudfoot,** George Wilfred 1921- *Who 92*
**Proudfoot,** Harry D., Jr. 1916- *WhoFI 92*
**Proudfoot,** Vincent Bruce 1930- *Who 92*
**Proudfoot,** Wayne Lee 1939- *WhoRel 92*
**Proudfoot,** Wilfred *Who 92*
**Proudfoot,** William d1990 *Who 92N*
**Prough,** Russell Allen 1943- *AmMWSc 92*
**Proulx,** Amedee Wilfrid 1932- *WhoRel 92*
**Proulx,** Ernest E 1931- *WhoAmP 91*
**Proulx,** Michael John 1948- *WhoWest 92*
**Proulx,** Norman R 1951- *WhoAmP 91*
**Proulx,** Pierre R 1938- *AmMWSc 92*
**Proulx,** Robert George 1954- *WhoFI 92*
**Proulx,** William John 1963- *WhoEnt 92*
**Proust,** Antonin 1832-1905 *ThHEIm*
**Proust,** Marcel 1871-1922 *FacFETw [port], GuFrLit 1*
**Prout,** Carl Wesley 1941- *WhoWest 92*
**Prout,** Christopher 1942- *Who 92*
**Prout,** Curtis 1915- *AmMWSc 92, IntWW 91*
**Prout,** Franklin Sinclair 1920- *AmMWSc 92*
**Prout,** George Russell, Jr 1924- *AmMWSc 92*
**Prout,** Hiram Augustus 1808-1862 *BiInAmS*
**Prout,** James Harold 1927- *AmMWSc 92*
**Prout,** Margaret Fisher 1875-1963 *TwCPaSc*
**Prout,** Mary Ann 1801-1884 *NotBlAW 92*
**Prout,** Patrick M. 1941- *WhoBlA 92*
**Prout,** Ralph Eugene 1933- *WhoWest 92*
**Prout,** Thaddeus Edmund 1923- *AmMWSc 92*
**Prout,** Timothy 1923- *AmMWSc 92*
**Prouty,** Chilton E 1914- *AmMWSc 92*
**Prouty,** Norman R. 1939- *WhoFI 92*
**Prouty,** Olive 1882-1974 *BenetAL 91*
**Prouty,** Richard Metcalf 1924- *AmMWSc 92*
**Prouve,** Jean 1901- *FacFETw*
**Provan,** James Lyal Clark 1936- *Who 92*
**Provan,** Marie *Who 92*
**Provaznik,** Marie d1991 *NewYTBS 91*
**Provder,** Theodore 1939- *AmMWSc 92*
**Provencal,** Leo A 1928- *WhoAmP 91*
**Provencher,** Gerald Martin 1937- *AmMWSc 92*
**Provencio,** Dolores *WhoHisp 92*
**Provencio,** Jesus Roberto 1925- *AmMWSc 92*
**Provencio,** John H. 1933- *WhoHisp 92*
**Provencio,** Ricardo B. 1947- *WhoHisp 92*
**Provenza,** Dominic Vincent 1917- *AmMWSc 92*
**Provenzale,** Maryellen Kirby 1938- *WhoAmL 92*
**Provenzano,** Ayla Suzan 1963- *WhoMW 92*
**Provenzo,** Eugene 1949- *ConAu 135*
**Proverb,** Robert Joseph 1946- *AmMWSc 92*
**Providence,** Wayne *DrAPF 91*
**Provin,** Cleo Elbert 1948- *WhoAmP 91*
**Province,** Martin Robert 1956- *WhoEnt 92*
**Provine,** Dorothy 1937- *IntMPA 92*
**Provine,** Robert Raymond 1943- *AmMWSc 92*
**Provis,** Dorothy Louise 1926- *WhoMW 92*
**Provorny,** Frederick Alan 1946- *WhoAmL 92*
**Provost,** Caterina F. *DrAPF 91*
**Provost,** Ernest Edmund 1921- *AmMWSc 92*
**Provost,** Gail Levine 1944- *SmATA 65*
**Provost,** Gary 1944- *ConAu 133, SmATA 66*
**Provost,** Gilles R 1945- *WhoAmP 91*
**Provost,** Lloyd 1931- *WhoIns 92*
**Provost,** Marsha Parks 1947- *WhoBlA 92*
**Provost,** Paul E 1915- *WhoAmP 91*
**Provost,** Philip Joseph 1935- *AmMWSc 92*
**Provost,** Ronald Harold 1942- *AmMWSc 92*
**Provost,** Sarah *DrAPF 91*
**Provow,** Jeffrey Steven 1957- *WhoWest 92*
**Provus,** Barbara Lee 1949- *WhoFI 92*
**Prowell,** Gregory Dean 1949- *WhoAmL 92*
**Prowler,** Harley *ConAu 133*
**Prowse,** Albert Richard Graham 1931- *IntWW 91*
**Prowse,** David Charles 1935- *WhoEnt 92*
**Prowse,** Florence Irene *Who 92*
**Prowse,** Juliet 1936- *ConTFT 9*
**Prowse,** Stephen David 1960- *WhoFI 92*
**Prowse,** Stephen James *AmMWSc 92*
**Proxmire,** William 1915- *IntWW 91, WhoAmP 91*
**Proyect,** Martin H. 1932- *WhoWest 92*
**Proysen,** Alf 1914-1970 *ChlLR 24 [port], SmATA 67*
**Prozan,** Lawrence Ira 1961- *WhoFI 92*
**Prozumenshchikova,** Galina Nikolaevna 1948- *SovUnBD*
**Prucha,** John James 1924- *AmMWSc 92*
**Pruckmayr,** Gerfried 1933- *AmMWSc 92*
**Prude,** Walter F., Mrs. *Who 92*
**Pruden,** Suzanne Yvonne 1946- *WhoEnt 92*
**Prudence,** Robert Thomas 1944- *AmMWSc 92*
**Prudencio,** Nelson 1944- *BlkOlyM*
**Prudentius** 348?-405? *EncEarC*
**Pruder,** Gary David 1932- *AmMWSc 92*
**Prud'homme,** Albert Fredric 1952- *WhoFI 92*
**Prud'Homme,** Jacques 1940- *AmMWSc 92*
**Prudhomme,** Nellie Rose 1948- *WhoBlA 92*
**Prudhomme,** Rene-Francois-Armend 1839-1907 *WhoNob 90*
**Prud'homme,** Robert Emery 1946- *AmMWSc 92*
**Prud'Homme,** Robert Krafft 1948- *AmMWSc 92*
**Prudhon,** Rolland A, Jr 1942- *AmMWSc 92*
**Prueitt,** Melvin Lewis 1932- *WhoWest 92*
**Pruess,** Kenneth Paul 1932- *AmMWSc 92*
**Pruess,** Steven Arthur 1944- *AmMWSc 92*
**Pruett,** Charles David *AmMWSc 92*
**Pruett,** Clayton Dunklin 1935- *WhoFI 92*
**Pruett,** Esther D R 1920- *AmMWSc 92*
**Pruett,** Helen Gorham 1919- *WhoMW 92*
**Pruett,** Herbert Eldon 1939- *WhoWest 92*
**Pruett,** Jack Kenneth 1932- *AmMWSc 92*
**Pruett,** Jane McGill 1927- *WhoAmP 91*
**Pruett,** John Robert 1923- *AmMWSc 92*
**Pruett,** Lilian Pibernik-Benyovszky 1930- *WhoEnt 92*
**Pruett,** Patricia Onderdonk 1930- *AmMWSc 92*
**Pruett,** Roy L 1924- *AmMWSc 92*
**Pruett-Jones,** Stephen Glen 1952- *AmMWSc 92*
**Prufer,** Olaf Herbert 1930- *WhoMW 92*
**Prugh,** John Drew 1932- *AmMWSc 92*
**Prugh,** William Byron 1945- *WhoAmL 92*
**Prugovecki,** Eduard 1937- *AmMWSc 92*
**Pruitt,** Albert Wesley 1940- *AmMWSc 92*
**Pruitt,** Alonzo Clemons 1951- *WhoBlA 92*
**Pruitt,** Anne Smith *WhoBlA 92*
**Pruitt,** Basil Arthur, Jr 1930- *AmMWSc 92*
**Pruitt,** Clarence 1925- *WhoEnt 92*
**Pruitt,** Clarence O. 1927- *WhoBlA 92*
**Pruitt,** David Carl, III 1933- *WhoAmP 91*
**Pruitt,** Fred Roderic 1938- *WhoBlA 92*
**Pruitt,** George Albert 1946- *WhoBlA 92*
**Pruitt,** Glyndon C 1928- *WhoAmP 91*
**Pruitt,** Gregory Donald 1951- *WhoBlA 92*
**Pruitt,** Ida 1888-1985 *HanAmWH*
**Pruitt,** Ina 1905- *WhoWest 92*
**Pruitt,** J. Doug 1945- *WhoWest 92*
**Pruitt,** James Boubias 1964- *WhoBlA 92*
**Pruitt,** James Donald 1937- *WhoMW 92*
**Pruitt,** Jay W., Jr. 1959- *WhoFI 92*
**Pruitt,** Jimmy D. 1962- *WhoRel 92*
**Pruitt,** Ken 1957- *WhoAmP 91*
**Pruitt,** Kenneth M 1933- *AmMWSc 92*
**Pruitt,** Mary *WhoAmP 91*
**Pruitt,** Mike 1954- *WhoBlA 92*
**Pruitt,** Nancy Clark 1952- *WhoAmL 92*
**Pruitt,** Nancy L 1953- *AmMWSc 92*
**Pruitt,** Robert Grady, III 1954- *WhoAmL 92*
**Pruitt,** Roger Arthur 1936- *AmMWSc 92*
**Pruitt,** Russell Clyde 1927- *WhoMW 92*
**Pruitt,** Timothy Carol 1956- *WhoRel 92*
**Pruitt,** Wes *WhoAmP 91*
**Pruitt,** William *DrAPF 91*
**Pruitt,** William Charles, Jr. 1926- *WhoRel 92*
**Pruitt,** William Edwin 1934- *AmMWSc 92*
**Pruitt,** William Keith 1964- *WhoRel 92*
**Pruitt,** William O 1922- *IntAu&W 91, WrDr 92*
**Pruitt,** William O, Jr 1922- *AmMWSc 92*
**Prunariu,** Dumitru 1952- *FacFETw*
**Pruneau,** S. Michael 1960- *WhoMW 92*
**Pruning Knife** *ScFEYrs*
**Prunskene,** Kazimera-Danute Prano 1943- *SovUnBD*
**Prunskiene,** Kazimera-Danute 1943- *SovUnBD*
**Prunskiene,** Kazimiera-Danute 1943- *IntWW 91*
**Prunty,** Howard Edward *WhoBlA 92*
**Prunty,** Lyle Delmar 1945- *AmMWSc 92*
**Prunty,** Paul E 1943- *WhoAmP 91*
**Prunty,** Wyatt *DrAPF 91*
**Prupas,** Melvern Irving 1926- *WhoEnt 92, WhoFI 92*
**Prus,** Francis Vincent 1927- *WhoFI 92*
**Prusa,** James Graham 1948- *WhoMW 92*
**Prusaczyk,** Joseph Edward 1944- *AmMWSc 92*
**Prusak,** Maximilian Michael 1943- *WhoAmL 92*
**Prusas,** Zenon C 1921- *AmMWSc 92*
**Prusch,** Robert Daniel 1939- *AmMWSc 92*
**Prusiner,** Stanley Ben 1942- *AmMWSc 92, WhoWest 92*
**Prusinowski,** Julie Ellen 1952- *WhoEnt 92*
**Pruslin,** Fred Howard 1951- *AmMWSc 92*
**Prusoff,** William Herman 1920- *AmMWSc 92*
**Pruss,** Rebecca M 1950- *AmMWSc 92*
**Pruss,** Stanley McQuaide 1943- *AmMWSc 92*
**Pruss,** Thaddeus P 1934- *AmMWSc 92*
**Prussia,** Leland S. 1929- *IntWW 91*
**Prussin,** Jeffrey A. 1943- *WhoFI 92*
**Prussin,** Stanley Gerald 1939- *AmMWSc 92*
**Prussing,** John E 1940- *AmMWSc 92*
**Pruter,** Karl Hugo 1920- *WhoRel 92*
**Pruter,** Karl Hugo Reiling 1920- *RelLAm 91*
**Pruter,** Margaret Franson *WhoMW 92*
**Prutkin,** Lawrence 1935- *AmMWSc 92*
**Prutkov,** Kozma *IntAu&W 91X*
**Prutkovsky,** Semyon 1923- *WhoAmL 92*
**Prutton,** Martin 1934- *WrDr 92*
**Pruzan,** Irene 1949- *WhoEnt 92, WhoMW 92*
**Pruzanski,** Waldemar 1928- *AmMWSc 92*
**Pruzansky,** Jacob Julius 1921- *AmMWSc 92*
**Pruzansky,** Joshua Murdock 1940- *WhoAmL 92*
**Pry,** James William, II 1945- *WhoAmL 92*
**Pry,** Robert Henry 1923- *AmMWSc 92*
**Pryanishnikov,** Dmitriy Nikolaevich 1865-1948 *SovUnBD*
**Prybutok,** Benn *WhoIns 92*
**Prybyla,** Jan 1927- *IntAu&W 91*
**Prybyla,** Jan S. 1927- *WrDr 92*
**Pryce,** Edward L. 1914- *WhoBlA 92*
**Pryce,** George Terry 1934- *IntWW 91, Who 92*
**Pryce,** James Taylor 1936- *Who 92*
**Pryce,** Jonathan 1947- *IntMPA 92, IntWW 91, Who 92, WhoEnt 92*
**Pryce,** Maurice Henry Lecorney 1913- *IntWW 91, Who 92*
**Pryce,** Roy 1928- *Who 92*
**Pryce,** Terry *Who 92*
**Pryce-Jones,** Alan Payan 1908- *IntWW 91, Who 92*
**Pryce-Jones,** David 1936- *WrDr 92*
**Pryce-Jones,** David 1959- *IntAu&W 91*
**Prychodko,** William Wasyl 1922- *AmMWSc 92*
**Pryde,** Arthur Edward 1946- *WhoBlA 92*
**Pryde,** Everett Hilton 1918- *AmMWSc 92*
**Pryde,** James 1866-1941 *TwCPaSc*
**Pryde,** Mabel 1871-1918 *TwCPaSc*
**Pryear,** Doris Armstrong *WhoMW 92*
**Pryer,** John 1929- *Who 92*
**Pryer,** Nancy Kathryn 1959- *AmMWSc 92*
**Pryfogle,** Marion Lee 1944- *WhoRel 92*
**Pryjmak,** Peter Gothart 1949- *WhoFI 92*
**Pryke,** David Dudley 1912- *Who 92*
**Pryke,** Roy Thomas 1940- *Who 92*
**Pryn,** William John 1928- *Who 92*
**Prynne,** J. H. 1936- *ConPo 91, IntAu&W 91, WrDr 92*
**Pryor,** Adel 1918- *WrDr 92*
**Pryor,** Ann G 1941- *WhoAmP 91*
**Pryor,** Arthur John 1939- *Who 92*
**Pryor,** Brian Hugh 1931- *Who 92*
**Pryor,** C Nicholas, Jr 1938- *AmMWSc 92*
**Pryor,** Calvin Caffey 1928- *WhoBlA 92*
**Pryor,** Chester Cornelius, II 1930- *WhoBlA 92*
**Pryor,** David 1934- *AlmAP 92 [port]*
**Pryor,** David Bram 1951- *AmMWSc 92*
**Pryor,** David Hampton 1934- *IntWW 91, WhoAmP 91*

Pryor, Douglas Keith 1944- WhoWest 92
Pryor, Fred Howard 1934- WhoRel 92
Pryor, Frederic L. 1933- WhoFI 92
Pryor, Gordon Roy 1935- AmMWSc 92
Pryor, Hubert 1916- WhoFI 92
Pryor, James D. 1914-1983 WhoBlA 92N
Pryor, Jerry Dennis 1952- WhoFI 92
Pryor, Jill Anne 1963- WhoAmL 92
Pryor, John Pembro 1937- Who 92
Pryor, Joseph Ehrman 1918- AmMWSc 92
Pryor, Julius, Jr. 1924- WhoBlA 92
Pryor, Lillian W. 1917- WhoBlA 92
Pryor, Marilyn Ann Zirk 1936- AmMWSc 92
Pryor, Mark L 1963- WhoAmP 91
Pryor, Michael J 1925- AmMWSc 92
Pryor, Peter Malachia 1926- WhoAmL 92
Pryor, Peter Patrick 1946- WhoWest 92
Pryor, Richard 1940- IntMPA 92, IntWW 91, WhoBlA 92, WhoEnt 92
Pryor, Richard J 1940- AmMWSc 92
Pryor, Robert Charles 1938- Who 92
Pryor, Samuel Frazier, III 1928- WhoAmL 92
Pryor, Shepherd Green, III 1919- WhoAmL 92
Pryor, Shepherd Green, IV 1946- WhoFI 92
Pryor, Tedmund Wylie 1956- WhoFI 92
Pryor, Thomas M. 1912- IntMPA 92
Pryor, Vanessa WrDr 92
Pryor, Wayne Arthur 1928- AmMWSc 92
Pryor, William Austin 1929- AmMWSc 92
Pryor, William C 1932- WhoAmP 91
Prys-Davies Who 92
Prys-Davies, Baron 1923- Who 92
Prys-Jones, A G 1888- IntAu&W 91
Pryse, Fitzgerald Spencer 1880- TwCPaSc
Pryse, James Morgan, Jr. 1859-1942 RelLAm 91
Pryse-Phillips, William Edward Maiben 1937- AmMWSc 92
Prystowsky, Harry 1925- AmMWSc 92
Prystowsky, Seymour 1936- WhoRel 92
Prytherch, Suzanne Martha 1956- WhoEnt 92
Prytz, Anton Frederick Winter Jakhelln 1878-1945 BiDExR
Prywes, Moshe AmMWSc 92
Prywes, Noah S 1925- AmMWSc 92
Przirembel, Christian E G 1942- AmMWSc 92
Przybilla, Carla 1935- WhoRel 92
Przyborski, David Bruce 1952- WhoMW 92
Przybylowicz, Edwin P 1933- AmMWSc 92
Przybylowicz, Edwin Paul 1933- WhoFI 92
Przybylska, Maria 1923- AmMWSc 92
Przybylski, Ronald J 1936- AmMWSc 92
Przybysz, Janusz Anastazy 1926- IntAu&W 91
Przybysz, John Xavier 1950- AmMWSc 92
Przybysz, Kenneth Louis 1947- WhoAmP 91
Przybytek, James Theodore 1945- AmMWSc 92
Przymanowski, Janusz 1922- IntAu&W 91
Przypkowski, Andrzej Jozef 1930- IntAu&W 91
Psalmanazar, George 1679?-1763 BlkwCEP
Psarouthakis, John 1932- AmMWSc 92, WhoFI 92
Pscheidt, Gordon Robert 1928- AmMWSc 92
Pschunder, Ralph J 1920- AmMWSc 92
Pseudo-Dionysius the Areopagite DcLB 115
Psiharis, Nicholas 1915- WhoEnt 92
Psioda, Joseph Adam 1949- AmMWSc 92
Psuty, Norbert Phillip 1937- AmMWSc 92
Pszczolkowski, Diane Margaret 1964- WhoMW 92
Ptacek, Anton D 1933- AmMWSc 92
Ptacek, Donald James 1948- WhoMW 92
Ptacek, William H. WhoWest 92
Ptak, John IntMPA 92
Ptak, Roger Leon 1938- AmMWSc 92
Ptak, Victor Anthony 1932- WhoMW 92
Ptashkin, Barry Irwin 1944- WhoFI 92, WhoMW 92
Ptashne, Mark 1940- AmMWSc 92
Ptashne, Mark Stephen 1940- IntWW 91
Ptasynski, Harry 1926- WhoWest 92
Ptolemy EncEarC
Ptolemy, Claudius 83?-161 NewAmDM
Pu Chaozhu 1929- IntWW 91
Pu Shan 1923- IntWW 91
Pu Ta-Hai 1922- IntWW 91
Pu-yi, Henry 1906-1967 FacFETw
Puapua, Tomasi 1938- IntWW 91
Puar, Mohindar S 1935- AmMWSc 92
Public Enemy News 92-1 [port]
Publicola BenetAL 91
Publius BenetAL 91
Pubols, Benjamin Henry, Jr 1931- AmMWSc 92
Pubols, Lillian Menges 1939- AmMWSc 92
Pubols, Merton Harold 1931- AmMWSc 92
Puccetti, Patricia Irene 1956- WhoRel 92
Pucci, Emilio 1914- DcTwDes, IntWW 91
Pucci, Mark Leonard 1947- WhoEnt 92
Pucci, Paul F 1923- AmMWSc 92
Pucciarelli, Albert John 1950- WhoAmL 92
Puccinelli, Leo John 1921- WhoAmP 91
Puccinelli, Robert A 1937- WhoIns 92
Puccini, Giacomo 1858-1924 FacFETw [port], NewAmDM
Puccio, Bernardo Robert 1944- WhoWest 92
Pucel, David Joseph 1940- WhoMW 92
Pucel, Robert A 1926- AmMWSc 92
Pucheu, Pierre Firmin 1899-1944 BiDExR
Puchtler, Holde 1920- AmMWSc 92
Puchy, James John 1956- WhoRel 92
Puck, Mary Hill 1919- AmMWSc 92
Puck, Theodore Thomas 1916- AmMWSc 92, IntWW 91, WhoWest 92
Puck, Wolfgang NewYTBS 91 [port]
Puckett, Allen Emerson 1919- AmMWSc 92, WhoWest 92
Puckett, Elizabeth Ann 1943- WhoAmL 92
Puckett, Hoyle Brooks 1925- AmMWSc 92
Puckett, Hugh 1929- AmMWSc 92
Puckett, James Philip 1937- WhoAmP 91
Puckett, Kirby 1961- WhoBlA 92, WhoMW 92
Puckett, Lute ConAu 133
Puckett, Paul David 1941- WhoWest 92
Puckett, Richard Edward 1932- WhoWest 92
Puckett, Riley 1894-1946 NewAmDM
Puckett, Robert Hugh 1935- WhoMW 92
Puckett, Russell Elwood 1929- AmMWSc 92
Puckette, Stephen Elliott 1927- AmMWSc 92
Pucknat, John Godfrey 1931- AmMWSc 92
Pucko, Diane Bowles 1940- WhoMW 92
Puckorius, Paul Ronald 1930- AmMWSc 92
Puckrein, Gary Alexander 1949- WhoBlA 92
Pudaite, Rochunga 1928- WhoRel 92
Puddephatt, Andrew Charles 1950- Who 92
Puddephatt, Richard John 1943- AmMWSc 92
Puddington, Ira E 1911- AmMWSc 92
Puddington, Lynn 1956- AmMWSc 92
Pudelkiewicz, Walter Joseph 1923- AmMWSc 92
Pudles, Gary Allen 1962- WhoAmL 92
Pudlin, Dave B 1952- WhoAmP 91
Pudney, Gary Laurence 1934- WhoEnt 92, WhoWest 92
Pudnos, Stanley Herbert 1930- WhoIns 92
Pudovkin, Vsevelod Illarionovitch 1893-1953 FacFETw
Pudovkin, Vsevolod 1893-1953 IntDcF 2-2 [port]
Pudovkin, Vsevolod Illarionovich 1893-1953 SovUnBD
Puechner, Ray DrAPF 91
Puechner, Ray 1935- WrDr 92
Puelicher, John A. 1920- WhoMW 92
Puello, Andres D. 1932- WhoHisp 92
Puente, Antonio Enrique 1952- WhoHisp 92
Puente, Jose Garza 1949- WhoWest 92
Puente, Robert 1958- WhoAmP 91
Puente, Robert R. 1958- WhoHisp 92
Puente, Stephen L. WhoHisp 92
Puente, Teresa Christina 1967- WhoHisp 92
Puente, Tito 1923- FacFETw, WhoHisp 92
Puente, Tito Anthony 1923- WhoEnt 92
Puente, Victor, Sr. WhoHisp 92
Puente, Yolanda 1964- WhoHisp 92
Puente-Duany, Hary P. 1944- WhoHisp 92
Puentes, Arnold 1956- WhoHisp 92
Puentes, Carlos Julian 1958- WhoHisp 92
Puentes, Charles Theodore, Jr. 1933- WhoHisp 92
Puentes, Roberto Santos 1929- WhoHisp 92
Puenzo, Luis 1949- IntWW 91
Pueppke, Steven Glenn 1950- AmMWSc 92
Puerckhauer, Gerhard Wilhelm Richard 1930- AmMWSc 92
Puerner, Paul Raymond 1927- WhoAmL 92
Puerta, Antonio Medina 1956- WhoWest 92
Puesan Khoury, Cesar A. 1938- WhoRel 92
Pueschel, Rudolf Franz 1934- AmMWSc 92
Pueschel, Siegfried M 1931- AmMWSc 92
Puett, J David 1939- AmMWSc 92
Puett, Terry Lee 1943- WhoRel 92
Puette, William J. DrAPF 91
Puetz, William Charles 1950- WhoMW 92
Pueyrredon, Juan Martin de 1777-1850 HisDSpE
Puff, Robert David 1933- AmMWSc 92
Puff, Theresa Ann 1963- WhoMW 92
Puffe, Paul 1953- WhoRel 92
Puffer, John H 1941- AmMWSc 92
Puffer, Merle E. 1915- WhoEnt 92
Puffer, Nancy Placek 1933- WhoWest 92
Puffer, Thomas Ray 1931- WhoAmP 91
Puga, Francisco Javier 1942- WhoHisp 92
Puga, Rafael WhoHisp 92
Pugay, Jeffrey Ibanez 1958- WhoFI 92, WhoWest 92
Pugel, Robert Joseph 1941- WhoAmP 91
Pugh, Alan Virgil 1952- WhoAmP 91
Pugh, Alastair Tarrant 1928- Who 92
Pugh, Andrew Cartwright 1937- Who 92
Pugh, Arthur James 1937- WhoFI 92
Pugh, Barbara Ellen 1945- WhoMW 92
Pugh, Bradley Keith 1960- WhoMW 92
Pugh, C Emmett 1940- WhoAmP 91
Pugh, Charles Edward 1922- Who 92
Pugh, Claud Ervin 1939- AmMWSc 92
Pugh, Clementine A. WhoBlA 92
Pugh, Daniel Wilbert 1945- WhoEnt 92, WhoMW 92
Pugh, David Milton 1929- AmMWSc 92
Pugh, E Neville 1935- AmMWSc 92
Pugh, Emerson William 1929- AmMWSc 92
Pugh, Evan 1828-1864 BiInAmS
Pugh, G. Douglas 1923- WhoBlA 92
Pugh, Harold Valentine 1899- Who 92
Pugh, Helen Pedersen 1934- WhoWest 92
Pugh, Howel Griffith 1933- AmMWSc 92
Pugh, Idwal 1918- Who 92
Pugh, Jean Elizabeth 1928- AmMWSc 92
Pugh, Jeffrey Keith 1957- WhoFI 92
Pugh, Jessie Truman 1923- WhoRel 92
Pugh, John 1945- WhoAmP 91
Pugh, John Arthur 1920- Who 92
Pugh, John E. 1928- WhoRel 92
Pugh, John Stanley 1927- Who 92
Pugh, John W 1923- AmMWSc 92
Pugh, John Wilbur 1912- WrDr 92
Pugh, Keith E., Jr. 1937- WhoAmL 92
Pugh, Kevin WhoEnt 92
Pugh, Kyle Mitchell, Jr. 1937- WhoEnt 92, WhoWest 92
Pugh, Lawrence R. 1933- WhoFI 92
Pugh, Lionel Roger Price 1916- Who 92
Pugh, Marlana Patrice 1952- WhoBlA 92
Pugh, Patterson David Gordon 1920- Who 92
Pugh, Peter David S. Who 92
Pugh, Richard Crawford 1929- WhoWest 92
Pugh, Robert E 1933- AmMWSc 92
Pugh, Robert William, Sr. 1926- WhoBlA 92
Pugh, Roderick W. 1919- WhoBlA 92
Pugh, Roger Courtenay Beckwith 1917- Who 92
Pugh, Russell Oris 1927- WhoEnt 92
Pugh, Sheenagh 1950- ConPo 91, WrDr 92
Pugh, Ted Who 92
Pugh, Thomas Jefferson 1917- WhoBlA 92
Pugh, Thomas W WhoAmP 91
Pugh, Willard Earl 1959- WhoEnt 92
Pugh, William David 1904- Who 92
Pugh, William Wallace 1941- WhoAmL 92
Pugh, William Whitmell Hill 1954- WhoAmL 92
Pugin, Nikolay Andrevevich 1940- IntWW 91
Puglia, Charles David 1941- AmMWSc 92
Puglia, Charles Raymond 1927- AmMWSc 92
Puglielli, Vincent George 1943- AmMWSc 92
Pugliese, Albert 1954- WhoFI 92
Pugliese, Brian Patrick 1960- WhoMW 92
Pugliese, Juan Carlos 1915- IntWW 91
Pugliese, Michael 1927- AmMWSc 92
Pugliese, Robert Francis 1933- WhoAmL 92, WhoFI 92
Puglise, John Michael 1948- WhoMW 92
Puglisi, Angela Aurora 1949- IntAu&W 91
Puglisi, Davide Felice Brett 1963- WhoWest 92
Pugmire, Ronald J 1937- AmMWSc 92
Pugo, Boris Karlovich 1937- IntWW 91, SovUnBD
Pugsley, Alfred Grenvile 1903- IntWW 91, Who 92
Pugsley, David Philip 1944- Who 92
Pugsley, James H 1936- AmMWSc 92
Puhakka, Matti Juhani 1945- IntWW 91
Puhalla, John Edward 1939- AmMWSc 92
Puhk, Heino 1923- WhoMW 92
Puhl, Richard James 1944- AmMWSc 92
Puhr, Stephen Patrick 1959- WhoFI 92
Puhvel, Sirje Madli 1939- AmMWSc 92
Pui, Ching-Hon 1951- AmMWSc 92
Puig, Gilberto, Jr. 1961- WhoHisp 92
Puig, Manuel 1932-1990 AnObit 1990, BenetAL 91, ConLC 65 [port], DcLB 113 [port], FacFETw, LiExTwC
Puig, Nicolas 1952- WhoHisp 92
Puig, Vicente P. WhoHisp 92
Puig De La Bellacasa, Jose Joaquin 1931- Who 92
Puigdollers, Carmen DrAPF 91
Puja, Frigyes 1921- IntWW 91
Pujado, Peter Raymond 1944- WhoMW 92
Pujals, Humberto A., Jr. 1952- WhoHisp 92
Pujo, Maurice 1872-1955 BiDExR
Pujol I Soley, Jordi 1930- IntWW 91
Pukhova, Zoya Pavlovna 1936- IntWW 91, SovUnBD
Pukkila, Patricia Jean 1948- AmMWSc 92
Pulaski, Casimir DcAmImH
Pulaski, Casimir 1747-1779 BlkwEAR
Pulaski, Charles Alexander, Jr. 1941- WhoAmL 92
Pulaski, Mary Ann 1916- WrDr 92
Pulay, George 1923-1981 ConAu 135
Pulay, Peter 1941- AmMWSc 92
Pulcheria 399-453 EncEarC
Pulczinski, Jeanette Gail 1956- WhoAmP 91
Puleo, Joseph Sam 1954- WhoEnt 92
Puleston, Harry Samuel 1917- AmMWSc 92
Pulford, Richard Charles 1944- Who 92
Pulgram, William DcTwDes
Pulham, Peter Rose 1910-1956 TwCPaSc
Pulice, Deano Salvatore 1957- WhoRel 92
Pulido, Miguel A. WhoHisp 92
Pulido, Miguel L 1934- AmMWSc 92
Pulido, Richard 1960- WhoHisp 92
Pulido, Rudolph Valentino, Sr. 1939- WhoHisp 92
Pulido, Victor Ismael 1961- WhoHisp 92
Puligandla, Viswanadham 1938- AmMWSc 92
Pulis, Lee Clark 1948- WhoMW 92
Pulito, Aldo Martin 1920- AmMWSc 92
Pulitzer, Joseph 1847-1911 BenetAL 91, RComAH
Pulitzer, Joseph, Jr. 1913- IntWW 91
Pulkkinen, Gayla Sue 1946- WhoAmP 91
Pullan, Brian Sebastian 1935- Who 92
Pullan, George Thomas 1929- AmMWSc 92
Pullan, Harry 1928- AmMWSc 92
Pullan, John Marshall 1915- Who 92
Pullarkat, Raju Krishnan 1939- AmMWSc 92
Pullee, Ernest Edward 1907- Who 92
Pullee, Margaret 1910- TwCPaSc
Pullein-Thompson, Christine 1930- IntAu&W 91, WrDr 92
Pullein-Thompson, Denis Who 92
Pullein-Thompson, Diana WrDr 92
Pullein-Thompson, Josephine WrDr 92
Pullen, Bailey Price 1940- AmMWSc 92
Pullen, David John 1936- AmMWSc 92
Pullen, Doug 1957- WhoEnt 92
Pullen, Edwin Wesley 1923- AmMWSc 92
Pullen, James Ralph 1936- WhoMW 92
Pullen, Keats A, Jr 1916- AmMWSc 92
Pullen, Kent 1942- WhoAmP 91
Pullen, Kent Edward 1942- WhoWest 92
Pullen, Milton William, Jr 1914- AmMWSc 92
Pullen, Penny Lynne 1947- WhoAmP 91
Pullen, Reginald 1922- Who 92
Pullen, Richard Owen 1944- WhoAmL 92, WhoFI 92
Pullen, Thomas Marion 1919- AmMWSc 92
Pullen-Brown, Stephanie D. 1949- WhoBlA 92
Pullenza-Ortiz, Patricia 1950- WhoWest 92
Pulley, Clyde Wilson 1934- WhoBlA 92
Pulley, Lewis Carl 1954- WhoAmL 92
Pulley, Paul 1936- WhoAmP 91
Pulley, Reginald 1926- WhoBlA 92
Pulley, Trish Bass 1962- WhoRel 92
Pulley, William Paul, Jr. 1936- WhoAmL 92
Pulleyblank, Edwin George 1922- Who 92, WrDr 92
Pulliam, Betty E. 1941- WhoBlA 92
Pulliam, Della Denise 1963- WhoEnt 92
Pulliam, Eugene Smith 1914- WhoFI 92
Pulliam, Francine S. 1937- WhoWest 92
Pulliam, H Ronald 1945- AmMWSc 92
Pulliam, James Augustus 1933- AmMWSc 92
Pulliam, Keshia Knight 1979- WhoEnt 92
Pulliam, Larry Dean 1951- WhoFI 92
Pulliam, Mark Stephen 1955- WhoAmL 92
Pulliam, Martha 1891-1991 NewYTBS 91
Pulliam, Martina Anne WhoRel 92
Pulliam, Norman F 1942- WhoAmP 91
Pulliam, Paul Edison 1912- WhoWest 92
Pulliam, Russell Bleecker 1949- WhoRel 92
Pulliam, Sandra Brandt 1959- WhoFI 92
Pulliam, Stanley Russell 1952- WhoRel 92
Pulliam, Yvonne Antoinette WhoMW 92
Pullig, Tillman R 1922- AmMWSc 92

**Pullin**, Jorge Alfredo 1963- *WhoFI 92*
**Pulling**, Albert Van Siclen 1891-1980 *ConAu 135*
**Pulling**, Edward d1991 *NewYTBS 91*
**Pulling**, Nathaniel H 1920- *AmMWSc 92*
**Pulling**, Pierre *ConAu 135*
**Pulling**, Ronald W *AmMWSc 92*
**Pulling**, Thomas Leffingwell 1939- *WhoFI 92*
**Pullinger**, Alan 1913- *Who 92*
**Pullinger**, John Elphick 1930- *Who 92*
**Pullman**, Bill 1954- *IntMPA 92*
**Pullman**, Ira 1921- *AmMWSc 92*
**Pullman**, Maynard Edward 1927- *AmMWSc 92*
**Pullman**, Norman J 1931- *AmMWSc 92*
**Pullman**, Philip 1946- *SmATA 65 [port]*
**Pullman**, Theodore Neil 1918- *AmMWSc 92*
**Pullukat**, Thomas Joseph 1941- *AmMWSc 92*
**Pulman**, Michael Barraclough 1933- *WrDr 92*
**Pulos**, Arthur J. 1917- *DcTwDes*
**Puls**, Gerd 1927- *WhoEnt 92*
**Puls**, Robert W 1950- *AmMWSc 92*
**Pulse**, Jeffrey Howard 1958- *WhoRel 92*
**Pulsford**, Petronella 1946- *ConAu 133*
**Pulsifer**, Allen Huntington 1937- *AmMWSc 92*
**Pulsifer**, Andrew Rice 1959- *WhoFI 92*
**Pulsifer**, Edgar Darling 1934- *WhoFI 92, WhoMW 92*
**Pulsifer**, Harold Trowbridge 1886-1948 *BenetAL 91*
**Pulsifer**, William Henry 1831-1905 *BiInAmS*
**Puluse**, Donald Anthony 1936- *WhoEnt 92*
**Pulvari**, Charles F 1907- *AmMWSc 92*
**Pulvermacher**, Louis C. 1928- *WhoAmL 92*
**Pulvertaft**, David Martin 1938- *Who 92*
**Pulvertaft**, Lalage 1925- *WrDr 92*
**Pulvirent**, Stuart Marc 1959- *WhoFI 92*
**Pulzer**, Peter George Julius 1929- *Who 92, WrDr 92*
**Puma**, J. *WhoHisp 92*
**Pumacahua**, Mateo Garcia *HisDSpE*
**Pumfrey**, Nicholas Richard 1951- *Who 92*
**Pumo**, Dorothy Ellen 1951- *AmMWSc 92*
**Pump**, Phillip Myron 1947- *WhoRel 92*
**Pumpelly**, Raphael 1837-1923 *BenetAL 91*
**Pumper**, Robert William 1921- *AmMWSc 92*
**Pumphrey**, Gerald Robert 1947- *WhoAmL 92*
**Pumphrey**, Jean *DrAPF 91*
**Pumphrey**, Laurence 1916- *Who 92*
**Pumphrey**, Roger Mack 1947- *WhoRel 92*
**Pun**, Pattle Pak-Toe 1946- *AmMWSc 92*
**Punch**, James Darrell 1936- *AmMWSc 92*
**Punch**, Jerry L *AmMWSc 92*
**Punch**, Sandra Lee 1952- *WhoWest 92*
**Pundeff**, Marin V. 1921- *WrDr 92*
**Punderson**, John Oliver 1918- *AmMWSc 92*
**Pundmann**, Ed John, Jr. 1939- *WhoMW 92*
**Pundsack**, Arnold L 1938- *AmMWSc 92*
**Pundsack**, Frederick Leigh 1925- *AmMWSc 92*
**Pung**, Oscar J 1951- *AmMWSc 92*
**Pungan**, Vasile 1926- *Who 92*
**Pungor**, Erno 1923- *IntWW 91*
**Punj**, Vikram 1957- *WhoFI 92*
**Punjala**, Shiv Shanker 1929- *IntWW 91*
**Punnett**, Hope Handler 1927- *AmMWSc 92*
**Punnett**, Robert Malcolm 1936- *WrDr 92*
**Punnett**, Thomas R 1926- *AmMWSc 92*
**Punt**, Leonard Cornelis 1940- *WhoMW 92*
**Punt**, Terry Lee 1949- *WhoAmP 91*
**Puntenney**, Dee Gregory 1948- *AmMWSc 92*
**Punwani**, Dharam Vir 1942- *AmMWSc 92*
**Punwar**, Jalamsinh K 1923- *AmMWSc 92*
**Punzi**, Debra 1956- *WhoEnt 92*
**Punzi**, Henry Anthony 1958- *WhoHisp 92*
**Puolanne**, Ulla Kaija 1931- *IntWW 91*
**Puopolo**, Rocco Nicholas 1949- *WhoRel 92*
**Pupin**, Michael *DcAmImH*
**Pupin**, Michael I. 1858-1935 *BenetAL 91*
**Pupo**, Jorge I. 1960- *WhoHisp 92*
**Pupo**, Timothy J. 1963- *WhoFI 92*
**Pupo-Mayo**, Gustavo Alberto 1955- *WhoHisp 92*
**Purandare**, Yeshwant K 1934- *AmMWSc 92*
**Purbo**, Onno Widodo 1962- *AmMWSc 92*
**Purboyo**, Arthur 1958- *WhoMW 92*
**Purbrick**, Robert Lamburn 1919- *AmMWSc 92*
**Purce**, Thomas Les 1946- *WhoBlA 92*
**Purcell**, Alexander Holmes 1942- *WhoWest 92*
**Purcell**, Alexander Holmes, III 1942- *AmMWSc 92*
**Purcell**, Amelia Allerton 1953- *WhoFI 92*
**Purcell**, Ann R *WhoAmP 91*
**Purcell**, Benton Allen 1969- *WhoEnt 92*
**Purcell**, Bill 1953- *WhoAmP 91*
**Purcell**, Charles Kipps 1959- *WhoAmL 92, WhoWest 92*
**Purcell**, Denis d1990 *Who 92N*
**Purcell**, Donald 1916- *IntAu&W 91*
**Purcell**, Edward Mills 1912- *AmMWSc 92, Who 92, WhoNob 90*
**Purcell**, Elizabeth Ann 1951- *WhoFI 92*
**Purcell**, Everett Wayne 1924- *AmMWSc 92*
**Purcell**, Fenton Peter 1942- *WhoFI 92*
**Purcell**, Harry 1919- *Who 92*
**Purcell**, Henry 1659-1695 *NewAmDM*
**Purcell**, James Eugene 1936- *AmMWSc 92*
**Purcell**, James Lawrence 1929- *WhoAmL 92*
**Purcell**, Joe *WhoAmP 91*
**Purcell**, John M. 1939- *WhoRel 92*
**Purcell**, John Marshall 1932- *WhoMW 92*
**Purcell**, Joseph Carroll 1921- *AmMWSc 92*
**Purcell**, Keith Frederick 1939- *AmMWSc 92*
**Purcell**, Kenneth 1928- *AmMWSc 92*
**Purcell**, Lee 1953- *WhoEnt 92*
**Purcell**, Martin James 1918- *WhoAmL 92*
**Purcell**, Michael 1923- *Who 92*
**Purcell**, Patrick B. 1943- *IntMPA 92, WhoEnt 92, WhoFI 92*
**Purcell**, Philip James 1943- *WhoFI 92*
**Purcell**, Richard Evan 1952- *WhoEnt 92*
**Purcell**, Richard Fick 1924- *WhoAmL 92*
**Purcell**, Robert Harry 1935- *AmMWSc 92*
**Purcell**, Robert W. d1991 *NewYTBS 91*
**Purcell**, Sally 1944- *ConPo 91, WrDr 92*
**Purcell**, Stuart McLeod, III 1944- *WhoFI 92, WhoWest 92*
**Purcell**, William 1909- *WrDr 92*
**Purcell**, William Ernest 1909- *Who 92*
**Purcell**, William Henry Samuel 1912- *Who 92*
**Purcell**, William Paul 1935- *AmMWSc 92*
**Purcell**, William Paxson, III 1953- *WhoAmL 92*
**Purchas**, Christopher Patrick Brooks 1943- *Who 92*
**Purchas**, Francis 1919- *Who 92*
**Purchas**, Robin Michael 1946- *Who 92*
**Purchas**, Samuel 1575?-1626 *BenetAL 91*
**Purchase**, Earl Ralph 1919- *AmMWSc 92*
**Purchase**, Harvey Graham 1936- *AmMWSc 92*
**Purchase**, Thomas Joseph 1949- *WhoRel 92*
**Purcifull**, Dan Elwood 1935- *AmMWSc 92*
**Purden**, Roma Laurette 1928- *IntAu&W 91, Who 92*
**Purdie**, Henry Augustus 1840-1911 *BiInAmS*
**Purdie**, Neil 1935- *AmMWSc 92*
**Purdom**, Billy Joe 1947- *WhoAmP 91*
**Purdom**, Edmund 1924- *IntMPA 92*
**Purdom**, James Francis Whitehurst 1943- *AmMWSc 92*
**Purdom**, Paul W, Jr 1940- *AmMWSc 92*
**Purdom**, Paul Walton, Jr. 1940- *WhoMW 92*
**Purdom**, R Don 1926- *WhoIns 92*
**Purdom**, Ray Caldwell 1943- *AmMWSc 92*
**Purdom**, Tom 1936- *TwCSFW 91, WrDr 92*
**Purdom**, William Berlin 1934- *AmMWSc 92*
**Purdon**, Corran William Brooke 1921- *Who 92*
**Purdon**, James Ralph, Jr 1933- *AmMWSc 92*
**Purdon**, Kevin Eric 1955- *WhoFI 92*
**Purdue**, Albert Homer 1861-1917 *BiInAmS*
**Purdue**, Jack Olen 1913- *AmMWSc 92*
**Purdue**, Peter 1943- *AmMWSc 92*
**Purdum**, Herbert *TwCWW 91*
**Purdum**, Robert L. 1935- *IntWW 91, WhoFI 92*
**Purdy**, A. W. 1918- *WrDr 92*
**Purdy**, Al 1918- *BenetAL 91, ConPo 91, RfGEnL 91*
**Purdy**, Alan Harris 1923- *AmMWSc 92*
**Purdy**, Carol 1943- *SmATA 66 [port]*
**Purdy**, Charles Michael 1951- *WhoRel 92*
**Purdy**, D C 1929- *AmMWSc 92*
**Purdy**, David Lawrence 1928- *AmMWSc 92*
**Purdy**, Frazier Rodney 1929- *WhoFI 92*
**Purdy**, Gary Rush 1936- *AmMWSc 92*
**Purdy**, J Lawrence 1927- *WhoIns 92*
**Purdy**, James *DrAPF 91, IntAu&W 91*
**Purdy**, James 1923- *BenetAL 91, ConNov 91, IntWW 91, WrDr 92*
**Purdy**, Joseph Donald 1942- *WhoWest 92*
**Purdy**, Laurence Henry 1926- *AmMWSc 92*
**Purdy**, Marlene Ann 1941- *WhoAmP 91*
**Purdy**, Richard Little 1904-1990 *AnObit 1990*
**Purdy**, Robert H 1930- *AmMWSc 92*
**Purdy**, Robert John 1916- *Who 92*
**Purdy**, Sherry Marie 1960- *WhoAmL 92*
**Purdy**, William Crossley 1930- *AmMWSc 92*
**Pure**, Ellen *AmMWSc 92*
**Purens**, Ilmars *DrAPF 91*
**Purfeerst**, Clarence M 1928- *WhoAmP 91*
**Puri**, Ambrogio 1920- *IntWW 91*
**Puri**, Kewal Krishan 1933- *AmMWSc 92*
**Puri**, Narindra Nath 1933- *AmMWSc 92*
**Puri**, Om Parkash 1935- *AmMWSc 92*
**Puri**, Pratap 1938- *AmMWSc 92*
**Puri**, Prem Singh 1936- *AmMWSc 92*
**Puri**, Surendra Kumar 1940- *AmMWSc 92*
**Puri**, Yesh Paul 1929- *AmMWSc 92*
**Purich**, Daniel Lee *AmMWSc 92*
**Purifoy**, John David 1952- *WhoEnt 92*
**Purim**, Flora 1942- *WhoEnt 92*
**Purinton**, Barbara de Boncoeur Allen 1949- *WhoRel 92*
**Purinton**, George Dana 1856-1897 *BiInAmS*
**Purisch**, Steven Donald 1945- *AmMWSc 92*
**Purishkevich**, Vladimir Mitrofanovich 1870-1920 *BiDExR*
**Puritz**, David A *WhoAmP 91*
**Purkerson**, Mabel Louise 1931- *AmMWSc 92*
**Purkey**, Harry R 1934- *WhoAmP 91*
**Purkhiser**, E Dale 1931- *AmMWSc 92*
**Purkis**, Andrew James 1949- *Who 92*
**Purkis**, Ian Edward 1925- *AmMWSc 92*
**Purkiser**, Westlake Taylor 1910- *WhoRel 92*
**Purko**, John 1929- *AmMWSc 92*
**Purl**, Linda 1955- *IntMPA 92*
**Purl**, O Thomas 1924- *AmMWSc 92*
**Purle**, Charles Lambert 1947- *Who 92*
**Purmort**, Francis Walworth, Jr 1930- *WhoIns 92*
**Purnell**, Alton 1911- *WhoBlA 92*
**Purnell**, Carolyn J. 1939- *WhoBlA 92*
**Purnell**, Charles Giles 1921- *WhoAmL 92*
**Purnell**, Dallas Michael 1939- *AmMWSc 92*
**Purnell**, John H. 1941- *WhoFI 92*
**Purnell**, Lee J. 1896- *WhoBlA 92*
**Purnell**, Marshall E. 1950- *WhoBlA 92*
**Purnell**, Nicholas Robert 1944- *Who 92*
**Purnell**, Paul Oliver 1936- *Who 92*
**Puro**, Donald George 1947- *AmMWSc 92*
**Puro**, Michael Steven 1949- *WhoAmP 91*
**Purohit**, Milind Vasant 1957- *AmMWSc 92*
**Purple**, Richard L 1936- *AmMWSc 92*
**Purpura**, Dominick Paul 1927- *AmMWSc 92, IntWW 91*
**Purpura**, Joseph Matthew 1950- *WhoMW 92*
**Purrington**, Edward Cobb 1929- *WhoEnt 92*
**Purrington**, Lynwood N *WhoAmP 91*
**Purrington**, Robert Daniel 1936- *AmMWSc 92*
**Purrington**, Suzanne T 1938- *AmMWSc 92*
**Purry**, Jean Pierre *DcAmImH*
**Pursch**, Susan Marie 1948- *WhoRel 92*
**Pursch**, William Claude 1939- *WhoMW 92*
**Purse**, Hugh Robert Leslie 1940- *Who 92*
**Purseglove**, John William 1912- *Who 92*
**Pursel**, Harold Max, Sr. 1921- *WhoWest 92*
**Pursel**, Jach *RelLAm 91*
**Pursel**, Robert P. 1934- *WhoWest 92*
**Pursel**, Stewart Ephraim 1930- *WhoMW 92*
**Pursel**, Vernon George 1936- *AmMWSc 92*
**Pursell**, Carl D. 1932- *AlmAP 92 [port]*
**Pursell**, Carl D 1933- *WhoAmP 91*
**Pursell**, Carl Duane 1932- *WhoMW 92*
**Pursell**, Cleo Wilburn 1918- *WhoRel 92*
**Pursell**, Lyle Eugene 1926- *AmMWSc 92*
**Pursell**, Mary Helen 1939- *AmMWSc 92*
**Pursell**, Ronald A 1930- *AmMWSc 92*
**Pursell**, William Whitney 1926- *WhoEnt 92*
**Purser**, Donald Joseph 1954- *WhoAmL 92*
**Purser**, Fred O 1931- *AmMWSc 92*
**Purser**, John W. 1942- *WrDr 92*
**Purser**, Keith 1944- *TwCPaSc*
**Purser**, Paul Emil 1918- *AmMWSc 92*
**Purser**, Philip 1925- *WrDr 92*
**Purser**, Philip John 1925- *IntAu&W 91*
**Purser**, Robert Duane 1957- *WhoRel 92*
**Purser**, Sarah 1848-1943 *FacFETw*
**Purses**, Samuel D 1942- *WhoAmP 91*
**Pursey**, Derek Lindsay 1927- *AmMWSc 92*
**Pursglove**, Laurence Albert 1924- *AmMWSc 92*
**Pursh**, Frederick 1774-1820 *BiInAmS*
**Pursifull**, Carmen Maria 1930- *WhoHisp 92*
**Pursinger**, Marvin Gavin 1923- *WhoFI 92*
**Pursley**, George William 1954- *WhoRel 92*
**Pursley**, Michael Bader 1945- *AmMWSc 92*
**Pursley**, Ricky Anthony 1954- *WhoAmL 92*
**Purssell**, Anthony John Richard 1926- *Who 92*
**Purtell**, Dennis Joseph 1940- *WhoFI 92*
**Purtell**, Lawrence Robert 1947- *WhoAmL 92*
**Purtill**, Richard L. 1931- *WrDr 92*
**Purtilo**, David Theodore *AmMWSc 92*
**Purtle**, John Ingram 1923- *WhoAmP 91*
**Purton**, Christopher Roger 1938- *AmMWSc 92*
**Purucker**, Hobart Lorentz Gottfried de 1874-1942 *RelLAm 91*
**Purves**, Dale 1938- *AmMWSc 92*
**Purves**, Daphne 1908- *Who 92*
**Purves**, Elizabeth Mary 1950- *Who 92*
**Purves**, Libby 1950- *IntAu&W 91*
**Purves**, William 1931- *IntWW 91, Who 92*
**Purves**, William Kirkwood 1934- *AmMWSc 92*
**Purviance**, Daniel Joe 1956- *WhoWest 92*
**Purviance**, Farris Converse, III 1952- *WhoAmL 92*
**Purvin**, Robert L. d1991 *NewYTBS 91*
**Purvis**, Archie C., Jr. 1939- *WhoBlA 92, WhoEnt 92*
**Purvis**, Clinton Clifford, III 1954- *WhoRel 92*
**Purvis**, Colbert Thaxton 1920- *AmMWSc 92*
**Purvis**, George Allen 1933- *AmMWSc 92*
**Purvis**, George Frank, Jr 1914- *WhoIns 92*
**Purvis**, Harriet Forten 1810-1909 *NotBlAW 92 [port]*
**Purvis**, Henry R. *Who 92*
**Purvis**, John Anderson 1942- *WhoAmL 92, WhoWest 92*
**Purvis**, John L 1926- *AmMWSc 92*
**Purvis**, John Robert 1938- *Who 92*
**Purvis**, John Thomas 1951- *AmMWSc 92*
**Purvis**, Melvin 1903-1960 *FacFETw*
**Purvis**, Merton Brown 1923- *AmMWSc 92*
**Purvis**, Neville 1936- *Who 92*
**Purvis**, Perrin Hays 1918- *WhoAmP 91*
**Purvis**, Randall W. B. 1957- *WhoAmL 92*
**Purvis**, Ronald Scott 1928- *WhoFI 92*
**Purvis**, Sarah Forten 1811?-1898? *NotBlAW 92*
**Purvis**, Stewart Peter 1947- *Who 92*
**Purvis**, William 1948- *WhoEnt 92*
**Purvis**, William Jesse, Jr. 1956- *WhoRel 92*
**Puryear**, Alvin N. 1937- *WhoBlA 92*
**Puryear**, Bennet 1826-1914 *BiInAmS*
**Puryear**, Boyd Alfred 1945- *WhoBlA 92*
**Puryear**, Byron Nelson 1913- *WhoAmP 91*
**Puryear**, Marion Brooks 1951- *WhoRel 92*
**Puryear**, Martin 1941- *IntWW 91*
**Pusack**, George Williams 1920- *Who 92*
**Pusateri**, Joseph Michael 1939- *WhoRel 92*
**Pusateri**, Lawrence Xavier 1931- *WhoAmL 92, WhoFI 92, WhoMW 92*
**Puscas**, Louis 1915- *WhoRel 92*
**Pusch**, Allen Lewis 1934- *AmMWSc 92*
**Pusch**, Brian Walter 1954- *WhoAmL 92*
**Pusch**, William Gerard 1935- *WhoAmL 92*
**Pusey**, Anne E 1949- *AmMWSc 92*
**Pusey**, Daniel Irvin 1947- *WhoMW 92*
**Pusey**, Nathan Marsh 1907- *IntWW 91, Who 92*
**Pusey**, P Lawrence 1952- *AmMWSc 92*
**Pusey**, William Anderson 1936- *WhoAmL 92*
**Pushic**, David Michael 1953- *WhoEnt 92*
**Pushkar**, Paul 1936- *AmMWSc 92*
**Pushkarev**, Boris S. 1929- *WrDr 92*
**Pushkin**, Aleksandr Ivanovich 1907-1970 *SovUnBD*
**Pusinelli**, Nigel 1919- *Who 92*
**Puskas**, Charles Barto, Jr. 1951- *WhoRel 92*
**Puskas**, Elek 1942- *WhoFI 92*
**Puskas**, Ferenc 1926- *FacFETw*
**Puski**, Gabor 1938- *AmMWSc 92*
**Puskin**, Jerome Sanford 1942- *AmMWSc 92*
**Puslecki**, Edward 1951- *WhoRel 92*
**Puster**, Richard Lee 1940- *AmMWSc 92*
**Pustilnik**, David Daniel 1931- *WhoAmL 92*
**Pustovar**, Paul Thomas 1951- *WhoMW 92*
**Puszkin**, Elena Getner *AmMWSc 92*
**Puszkin**, Saul 1938- *AmMWSc 92*
**Putala**, Eugene Charles 1922- *AmMWSc 92*
**Putatunda**, Susil Kumar 1948- *WhoMW 92*
**Putbrese**, Charles Edward 1931- *WhoEnt 92*
**Puthenpurakal**, Joseph Mathew 1949- *WhoMW 92*
**Puthoff**, Francis Urban 1922- *WhoMW 92*
**Puthoff**, Harold Edward 1936- *AmMWSc 92*
**Putman**, Andree 1925- *DcTwDes*
**Putman**, Carol Jean 1943- *WhoWest 92*
**Putman**, Donald Lee 1944- *AmMWSc 92*

**Putman**, Edison Walker 1916- *AmMWSc 92*
**Putman**, George Wendell 1929- *AmMWSc 92*
**Putman**, James Earl 1952- *WhoMW 92*
**Putman**, Kathleen Harvey 1913- *WhoAmP 91*
**Putman**, Lesley Jane 1961- *WhoMW 92*
**Putman**, Loucile Minnie 1929- *WhoAmP 91*
**Putman**, Michael 1948- *WhoAmL 92*
**Putman**, Thomas Harold 1930- *AmMWSc 92*
**Putnam**, Abbott 1920- *AmMWSc 92*
**Putnam**, Abbott Allen 1920- *WhoMW 92*
**Putnam**, Alan R 1939- *AmMWSc 92*
**Putnam**, Alfred Lunt 1916- *AmMWSc 92*
**Putnam**, Barry J 1954- *WhoAmP 91*
**Putnam**, Bluford Hugh 1950- *WhoFI 92*
**Putnam**, Calvin Richard 1924- *AmMWSc 92*
**Putnam**, Charles E 1941- *AmMWSc 92*
**Putnam**, Frank William 1917- *AmMWSc 92*
**Putnam**, Frederic Ward 1839-1915 *BiInAmS*
**Putnam**, Frederick Warren, Jr. 1917- *WhoRel 92*
**Putnam**, G L 1913- *AmMWSc 92*
**Putnam**, G P 1814-1872 *DcLB 106 [port]*
**Putnam**, George Patrick 1925- *WhoMW 92*
**Putnam**, Glendora M. 1923- *WhoBlA 92*
**Putnam**, Hilary 1926- *IntWW 91, WrDr 92*
**Putnam**, Hugh D 1928- *AmMWSc 92*
**Putnam**, Israel 1718-1790 *BenetAL 91, BlkwEAR*
**Putnam**, J E *WhoAmP 91*
**Putnam**, J. Wesley 1951- *WhoRel 92*
**Putnam**, James Jackson 1846-1918 *BiInAmS*
**Putnam**, Jeremiah L 1939- *AmMWSc 92*
**Putnam**, John *IntAu&W 91X*
**Putnam**, Joseph Duncan 1855-1881 *BiInAmS*
**Putnam**, Leon Joseph 1928- *WhoRel 92*
**Putnam**, Loren Smith 1913- *AmMWSc 92*
**Putnam**, Mary Louise Duncan 1832-1903 *BiInAmS*
**Putnam**, Pamela Kay 1946- *WhoAmL 92*
**Putnam**, Paul A 1930- *AmMWSc 92*
**Putnam**, Richard Johnson 1913- *WhoAmL 92*
**Putnam**, Rosalind 1906-1986 *WhoBlA 92N*
**Putnam**, Samuel 1892-1950 *BenetAL 91*
**Putnam**, Stearns Tyler 1917- *AmMWSc 92*
**Putnam**, Thomas Milton 1945- *AmMWSc 92*
**Putnam**, Thomas Milton, Jr 1922- *AmMWSc 92*
**Putnam**, William Lowell 1924- *WhoWest 92*
**Putnam's**, G.P., Sons *DcLB 106*
**Putney**, Blake Fuqua 1923- *AmMWSc 92*
**Putney**, Floyd Johnson 1910- *AmMWSc 92*
**Putney**, Fred Silver 1881-1918 *BiInAmS*
**Putney**, Gail J. *WrDr 92*
**Putney**, James Wiley, Jr 1946- *AmMWSc 92*
**Putney**, John *WrDr 92*
**Putney**, John A, Jr 1939- *WhoIns 92*
**Putney**, John Alden, Jr. 1939- *WhoFI 92*
**Putney**, Kenneth Alan 1955- *WhoMW 92*
**Putney**, Lacey Edward 1928- *WhoAmP 91*
**Putney**, Mark William 1929- *WhoMW 92*
**Putney**, Mary Engler 1933- *WhoFI 92*
**Putney**, Nancy Hoddinott 1960- *WhoEnt 92*
**Putney**, Paul William 1940- *WhoAmL 92*
**Putney**, Scott David *AmMWSc 92*
**Putriment**, Pauline Titus 1922- *WhoAmP 91*
**Putrino**, Michael 1955- *WhoEnt 92*
**Putt**, B. Keith 1955- *WhoRel 92*
**Putt**, Eric Douglas 1915- *AmMWSc 92*
**Putt**, John Ward 1924- *AmMWSc 92*
**Putt**, Larry Allen 1945- *WhoFI 92*
**Putt**, Robert Allen 1952- *WhoRel 92*
**Puttappa**, Kuvempu 1904- *IntAu&W 91*
**Puttaswamaiah**, Bannikuppe M 1932- *AmMWSc 92*
**Putter**, Irving 1923- *AmMWSc 92*
**Putterman**, Allen Michael 1938- *WhoMW 92*
**Putterman**, David Alan 1958- *WhoEnt 92*
**Putterman**, Gerald Joseph 1937- *AmMWSc 92*
**Putterman**, Seth Jay *AmMWSc 92*
**Puttick**, Richard George 1916- *Who 92*
**Puttler**, Benjamin 1930- *AmMWSc 92*
**Puttlitz**, Donald Herbert 1938- *AmMWSc 92*
**Puttlitz**, Karl Joseph 1941- *AmMWSc 92*
**Puttnam**, David 1941- *IntMPA 92*
**Puttnam**, David Terence 1941- *IntWW 91, Who 92, WhoEnt 92*
**Puttroff**, Stephen Allen 1949- *WhoMW 92*
**Putts**, Gorley 1913- *Who 92*
**Putz**, Francis Edward 1952- *AmMWSc 92*
**Putz**, Gerard Joseph 1943- *AmMWSc 92*
**Putzell**, Edwin Joseph, Jr. 1913- *WhoFI 92*
**Putzig**, Donald Edward 1943- *AmMWSc 92*
**Puvis de Chavannes**, Pierre 1824-1898 *ThHEIm*
**Puxon**, Margaret 1915- *Who 92*
**Puyana**, Rafael 1931- *IntWW 91, NewAmDM*
**Puyau**, Francis A 1928- *AmMWSc 92*
**Puyear**, Donald E 1932- *AmMWSc 92*
**Puysegur**, Jacques-Francois, marquis de 1656-1743 *BlkwCEP*
**Puzantian**, Vahe Ropen 1929- *AmMWSc 92*
**Puzey**, Leonard Uriah *WhoEnt 92*
**Puzinas**, James 1960- *WhoFI 92*
**Puziss**, Milton 1920- *AmMWSc 92*
**Puzo**, Mario *DrAPF 91*
**Puzo**, Mario 1920- *BenetAL 91, ConNov 91, WrDr 92*
**Puzynski**, Stanislaw 1936- *IntWW 91*
**Pyatakov**, Georgiy Leonidovich 1890-1937 *SovUnBD*
**Pyatakov**, Grigory L 1890-1937 *FacFETw*
**Pyatt**, Clyde Dwight 1928- *WhoRel 92*
**Pyatt**, William Allan 1916- *Who 92*
**Pyatt**, William Gorrell 1953- *WhoRel 92*
**Pyavko**, Vladislav Ivanovich 1941- *IntWW 91, SovUnBD*
**Pybrum**, Steven Mark 1951- *WhoWest 92*
**Pyburn**, William F 1927- *AmMWSc 92*
**Pybus**, Rodney 1938- *ConPo 91, IntAu&W 91, WrDr 92*
**Pybus**, William Michael 1923- *Who 92*
**Pye**, David Thomas 1942- *WhoWest 92*
**Pye**, Earl Louis 1926- *AmMWSc 92*
**Pye**, Edgar George 1925- *AmMWSc 92*
**Pye**, Edward Kendall 1938- *AmMWSc 92*
**Pye**, Jack *ConAu 133*
**Pye**, John David 1932- *Who 92*
**Pye**, Lenwood D 1937- *AmMWSc 92*
**Pye**, Michael 1946- *WrDr 92*
**Pye**, Norman 1913- *Who 92*
**Pye**, Orrea F *AmMWSc 92*
**Pye**, William 1938- *TwCPaSc*
**Pye**, William Burns 1938- *IntWW 91*
**Pyfer**, John Frederick, Jr. 1946- *WhoAmL 92*
**Pyfer**, S Clark 1919- *WhoAmP 91*
**Pykare**, Nina *WrDr 92*
**Pyke**, David Alan 1921- *Who 92*
**Pyke**, John Secrest, Jr. 1938- *WhoAmL 92*
**Pyke**, Magnus 1908- *Who 92, WrDr 92*
**Pyke**, Ronald 1931- *AmMWSc 92*
**Pyke**, Thomas Nicholas, Jr 1942- *AmMWSc 92*
**Pyke**, Thomas Richard 1932- *AmMWSc 92*
**Pyke**, Willie Oranda 1930- *WhoBlA 92*
**Pylant**, Carol Sue 1953- *WhoMW 92*
**Pyle**, A. M. 1945- *WrDr 92*
**Pyle**, Barbara *WhoAmP 91*
**Pyle**, Betty June 1938- *WhoAmP 91*
**Pyle**, Betty Lou Iyla Thompson 1923- *WhoAmP 91*
**Pyle**, Cyril Alfred *Who 92*
**Pyle**, Denver 1920- *ConTFT 9*
**Pyle**, Ernie 1900-1945 *BenetAL 91, FacFETw [port]*
**Pyle**, Floyd Haskell 1946- *WhoRel 92*
**Pyle**, Howard 1853-1911 *BenetAL 91*
**Pyle**, Howard, III 1940- *WhoAmP 91, WhoFI 92*
**Pyle**, James Johnston 1914- *AmMWSc 92*
**Pyle**, James L 1938- *AmMWSc 92*
**Pyle**, John Tillman 1935- *AmMWSc 92*
**Pyle**, K Roger 1941- *AmMWSc 92*
**Pyle**, Katharine 1863-1938 *SmATA 66*
**Pyle**, Leonard Duane 1930- *AmMWSc 92*
**Pyle**, Martin Wayne 1959- *WhoRel 92*
**Pyle**, Michael Terry 1938- *WhoIns 92*
**Pyle**, Randy L 1955- *WhoAmP 91*
**Pyle**, Robert Lawrence 1923- *AmMWSc 92*
**Pyle**, Robert Noble 1926- *WhoAmP 91*
**Pyle**, Robert V 1923- *AmMWSc 92*
**Pyle**, Robert Wendell 1908- *AmMWSc 92*
**Pyle**, Robert Wendell, Jr 1936- *AmMWSc 92*
**Pyle**, Russell 1941- *WhoEnt 92*
**Pyle**, Thomas Edward 1941- *AmMWSc 92*
**Pyle**, Walter MacDonald 1921- *WhoAmP 91*
**Pyle**, Walter Robert 1944- *WhoWest 92*
**Pyler**, Richard Ernst 1941- *AmMWSc 92*
**Pyles**, Carol DeLong 1948- *WhoFI 92, WhoMW 92*
**Pyles**, J. A. 1949- *WhoBlA 92*
**Pyles**, John E. 1927- *WhoBlA 92*
**Pyles**, Thomas 1905-1980 *ConAu 133*
**Pyles**, Vern 1919- *WhoAmP 91*
**Pylinski**, Albert, Jr. 1953- *WhoFI 92*
**Pylipow**, Stanley Ross 1936- *WhoFI 92*
**Pym** *Who 92*
**Pym**, Baron 1922- *IntWW 91, Who 92*
**Pym**, Barbara 1913-1980 *ConAu 34NR, FacFETw, RfGEnL 91*
**Pyman**, Lancelot Frank Lee 1910- *Who 92*
**Pynadath**, Thomas I 1929- *AmMWSc 92*
**Pynch**, Larry E. 1956- *WhoFI 92*
**Pynchon**, Thomas *DrAPF 91*
**Pynchon**, Thomas 1937- *BenetAL 91, ConNov 91, FacFETw, IntAu&W 91, IntWW 91, TwCSFW 91, WrDr 92*
**Pyndus**, Philip Richard 1921- *WhoAmP 91*
**Pyne**, Donald Eugene 1929- *WhoRel 92*
**Pyne**, Eben Wright 1917- *WhoFI 92*
**Pyne**, Natasha 1946- *IntWW 91*
**Pyne**, William Richard, Jr. 1949- *WhoEnt 92*
**Pynenburg**, Mary Helen 1956- *WhoWest 92*
**Pynes**, Gene Dale 1933- *AmMWSc 92*
**Pynn**, Kathleen Ann 1950- *WhoMW 92*
**Pynn**, Roger 1945- *AmMWSc 92*
**Pynnonen**, Bruce W 1954- *AmMWSc 92*
**Pynnonen**, Bruce William 1954- *WhoMW 92*
**Pyper**, Gordon R 1924- *AmMWSc 92*
**Pyper**, James William 1934- *AmMWSc 92, WhoWest 92*
**Pyper**, Mark Christopher Spring-Rice 1947- *Who 92*
**Pyrah**, Leslie Norman 1899- *Who 92*
**Pyrce**, Janice Margaret 1951- *WhoMW 92*
**Pyrcioch**, Eugene Joseph 1920- *AmMWSc 92*
**Pyr'ev**, Ivan Aleksandrovich 1901-1968 *SovUnBD*
**Pysh**, Joseph John 1935- *AmMWSc 92*
**Pytches**, David 1931- *Who 92*
**Pytel**, Barbara Anna 1950- *WhoMW 92*
**Pytell**, Robert Henry 1926- *WhoMW 92*
**Pythagoras** 582?BC-500?BC *NewAmDM*
**Pythodoris** *EncAmaz 91*
**Python**, Monty *ConAu 35NR*
**Pytka**, Stephen Milton 1947- *WhoFI 92*
**Pytkowicz**, Ricardo Marcos 1929- *AmMWSc 92*
**Pytlewski**, Louis Lawrence 1932- *AmMWSc 92*
**Pytte**, Agnar 1932- *AmMWSc 92, WhoMW 92*
**Pytte**, Erling 1937- *AmMWSc 92*
**Pyun**, Chong Wha 1930- *AmMWSc 92*
**Pyun**, Matthew Sung Kwan 1937- *WhoAmL 92*

# Q

**Q** *RfGEnL 91*
**Qabbani,** Muhammad Rashid *WhoRel 92*
**Qabbani,** Nizar 1923- *LiExTwC*
**Qaboos Bin Said** 1940- *IntWW 91*
**Qaddafi,** Mu'ammar al- *IntWW 91*
**Qaddafi,** Muammer el- 1942- *FacFETw [port]*
**Qadhafi,** Mu'ammar al- *IntWW 91*
**Qadri,** Syed M Hussain 1942- *AmMWSc 92*
**Qamar,** Nadi Abu 1917- *WhoBlA 92*
**Qaqon** *EncAmaz 91*
**Qasba,** Pradmann K 1938- *AmMWSc 92*
**Qasim,** Syed Reazul 1938- *AmMWSc 92*
**Qasimi,** Saqr bin Muhammad Al 1920- *IntWW 91*
**Qatar,** Emir of *IntWW 91*
**Qaysi,** Riyadh Mehmoud Sami al- 1939- *IntWW 91*
**Qazi,** Khizir Hayat A. 1945- *WhoFI 92*
**Qazi,** Moin 1956- *IntAu&W 91*
**Qazi,** Qutubuddin H 1931- *AmMWSc 92*
**Qazilbash,** Imtiaz Ali 1934- *WhoFI 92*
**Qi Yuanjing** 1929- *IntWW 91*
**Qian Jiazu** 1909- *IntWW 91*
**Qian Lingxi** 1916- *IntWW 91*
**Qian Linzhao** 1906- *IntWW 91*
**Qian Liren** 1925- *IntWW 91*
**Qian Min** *IntWW 91*
**Qian Qichen** 1928- *IntWW 91*
**Qian Renyuan** 1917- *IntWW 91*
**Qian Sanqiang** 1910- *IntWW 91*
**Qian Weichang** 1912- *IntWW 91*
**Qian Xinzhong** 1911- *IntWW 91*
**Qian Xuesen** 1910- *IntWW 91*
**Qian Yongchang** 1933- *IntWW 91*
**Qian Zhengying** 1922- *IntWW 91*
**Qian Zhongshu** 1910- *IntWW 91*
**Qian,** Renyuan 1917- *AmMWSc 92*
**Qiang Xiaochu** *IntWW 91*
**Qiao Guanhua** 1908-1983 *FacFETw*
**Qiao Shi** 1924- *IntWW 91*
**Qiao Shiguang** 1937- *IntWW 91*
**Qiao Xiaoguang** 1918- *IntWW 91*
**Qin Benli** 1917-1991 *NewYTBS 91*
**Qin Chuan** 1919- *IntWW 91*
**Qin Hezhen** 1913- *IntWW 91*
**Qin Jin** 1875-1907 *EncAmaz 91*
**Qin Jiwei** 1914- *IntWW 91*
**Qin Wencai** 1925- *IntWW 91*
**Qin Yingji** 1915- *IntWW 91*
**Qin Zhaoyang** 1916- *IntWW 91*
**Qin Zhongda** 1923- *IntWW 91*
**Qoyawayma,** Polingaysi 1892- *HanAmWH*
**Qu Wu** 1898- *IntWW 91*
**Quaal,** Ward Louis 1919- *WhoEnt 92, WhoFI 92, WhoMW 92*
**Quackenbush,** Carr Lane W 1946- *AmMWSc 92*
**Quackenbush,** Charles W 1954- *WhoAmP 91*
**Quackenbush,** David John 1951- *WhoFI 92*
**Quackenbush,** Forrest Ward 1907- *AmMWSc 92*
**Quackenbush,** Justin Lowe 1929- *WhoAmL 92*
**Quackenbush,** Robert L *WhoAmP 91*
**Quackenbush,** Robert Lee 1943- *AmMWSc 92*
**Quackenbush,** Ronald Vern 1952- *WhoAmP 91*
**Quad,** M. *BenetAL 91*
**Quade,** Charles Richard 1936- *AmMWSc 92*
**Quade,** Dana Edward Anthony 1935- *AmMWSc 92*
**Quade,** David Jon 1954- *WhoMW 92*
**Quade,** Jonathan Dana 1963- *WhoEnt 92*
**Quader,** Ather A. 1941- *WhoMW 92*
**Quader,** Ather Abdul 1941- *AmMWSc 92*
**Quadflieg,** Will 1914- *IntWW 91*
**Quadir,** Kamal Uddin Mohammad 1951- *WhoFI 92*
**Quadir,** Tariq 1953- *AmMWSc 92*
**Quadratus** *EncEarC*
**Quadri,** Fazle Rab 1948- *WhoAmL 92*
**Quadri,** Syed Kaleemullah *AmMWSc 92*
**Quadrio Curzio,** Alberto 1937- *IntWW 91*
**Quadros,** Alyce Jean 1927- *WhoFI 92*
**Quadros,** Janio 1917- *IntWW 91*
**Quadt,** R A 1916- *AmMWSc 92*
**Quagliano,** James Vincent 1915- *AmMWSc 92*
**Quagliano,** Tony *DrAPF 91*
**Quagliato,** Fred C. 1950- *WhoAmL 92*
**Quaid,** Dennis 1954- *IntMPA 92, IntWW 91*
**Quaid,** Randy 1950- *IntMPA 92, WhoEnt 92A*
**Quaife,** Mary Louise *AmMWSc 92*
**Quail,** John Wilson 1936- *AmMWSc 92*
**Quail,** Peter Hugh 1944- *AmMWSc 92*
**Quaile,** James Patrick 1943- *AmMWSc 92*
**Quain,** John Patrick 1944- *WhoMW 92*
**Quaintance,** Robert Forsyth, Jr. 1950- *WhoAmL 92*
**Quainton,** Anthony Cecil Eden 1934- *WhoAmP 91*
**Quaison-Sackey,** Alexander 1924- *IntWW 91*
**Quale,** G. Robina 1931- *WrDr 92*
**Quale,** Gladys Robina 1931- *WhoMW 92*
**Qualley,** Ronald Gene 1946- *WhoRel 92*
**Qualls,** Charles Lee 1964- *WhoRel 92*
**Qualls,** Clifford Ray 1936- *AmMWSc 92*
**Qually,** Robert Lee 1947- *WhoEnt 92, WhoMW 92*
**Qualman,** Gene 1948- *WhoFI 92*
**Qualman,** Roger Robert 1956- *WhoFI 92*
**Qualset,** Calvin Odell 1937- *AmMWSc 92*
**Qualter,** Terence H. 1925- *WrDr 92*
**Quam,** David Lawrence 1942- *AmMWSc 92*
**Quam,** William Porter 1949- *WhoWest 92*
**Quamme,** Gary Arthur 1944- *AmMWSc 92*
**Quamme,** Harvey Allen 1940- *AmMWSc 92*
**Quan Shuren** 1930- *IntWW 91*
**Quan Zhenghuan** 1932- *IntWW 91*
**Quan,** Gordon Jinpoing 1948- *WhoAmL 92*
**Quan,** Lisa Ling 1967- *WhoWest 92*
**Quan,** Stuart F 1949- *AmMWSc 92*
**Quan,** William 1948- *AmMWSc 92*
**Quan,** Xina Shu-Wen 1957- *AmMWSc 92*
**Quander,** Rohulamin 1943- *WhoBlA 92*
**Quandt,** Bernhardt 1903- *IntWW 91*
**Quandt,** Earl Raymond, Jr 1934- *AmMWSc 92*
**Quandt,** Eldor C. 1939- *WhoMW 92*
**Quandt,** Richard 1930- *WrDr 92*
**Quandt,** Richard Emeric 1930- *WhoFI 92*
**Quandt,** William B. 1941- *ConAu 35NR*
**Quandt,** William Bauer 1941- *WrDr 92*
**Quane,** Denis Joseph 1935- *AmMWSc 92*
**Quanquin,** Bruno Jean 1959- *WhoMW 92*
**Quansah-Dankwa,** Juliana Aba 1955- *WhoBlA 92*
**Quanstrom,** Walter Roy 1942- *AmMWSc 92*
**Quant,** Mary 1934- *DcTwDes, FacFETw, IntWW 91, Who 92*
**Quantrill,** Malcolm 1931- *ConAu 35NR, Who 92, WrDr 92*
**Quantrill,** William Ernest 1939- *Who 92*
**Quantz,** Johann Joachim 1697-1773 *NewAmDM*
**Quantz,** John O 1868-1903 *BiInAmS*
**Qu'appelle,** Bishop of 1932- *Who 92*
**Quarles,** Benjamin A. 1904- *WhoBlA 92*
**Quarles,** Carroll Adair, Jr 1938- *AmMWSc 92*
**Quarles,** Francis 1592-1644 *RfGEnL 91*
**Quarles,** George R. 1927- *WhoBlA 92*
**Quarles,** Gilford Godfrey 1909- *AmMWSc 92*
**Quarles,** Herbert DuBois 1929- *WhoBlA 92*
**Quarles,** James Addison 1837-1907 *BiInAmS*
**Quarles,** James Linwood, III 1946- *WhoAmL 92*
**Quarles,** John Monroe 1942- *AmMWSc 92*
**Quarles,** Joseph James 1911- *WhoBlA 92*
**Quarles,** Margo Benita *WhoFI 92*
**Quarles,** Norma *LesBEnT 92*
**Quarles,** Norma 1936- *NotBlAW 92*
**Quarles,** Norma R. 1936- *WhoBlA 92*
**Quarles,** Richard Hudson 1939- *AmMWSc 92*
**Quarles,** Richard Wingfield 1911- *AmMWSc 92*
**Quarles,** Ruth Brett 1914- *WhoBlA 92*
**Quarles,** Steven Princeton 1942- *WhoAmL 92*
**Quarles,** William Daniel 1948- *WhoAmL 92*
**Quarmby,** David Anthony 1941- *Who 92*
**Quaroni,** Andrea 1946- *AmMWSc 92*
**Quarracino,** Antonio 1923- *WhoRel 92*
**Quarrelles,** James Ivan 1926- *WhoBlA 92*
**Quarren Evans,** Kerry 1926- *Who 92*
**Quarrie,** Bruce 1947- *WrDr 92*
**Quarrie,** Donald 1951- *BlkOlyM [port], IntWW 91*
**Quarrington,** Paul 1953- *WrDr 92*
**Quarrington,** Paul 1954?- *ConLC 65 [port]*
**Quarry,** Mary Ann *AmMWSc 92*
**Quarry,** Nick *IntAu&W 91X, WrDr 92*
**Quartano,** Ralph Nicholas 1927- *Who 92*
**Quartararo,** Ignatius Nicholas 1926- *AmMWSc 92*
**Quartermain,** James *IntAu&W 91X, WrDr 92*
**Quarterman,** Elsie 1910- *AmMWSc 92*
**Quartey,** Clement *BlkOlyM*
**Quarton,** William Barlow 1903- *WhoEnt 92*
**Quarve,** Roy Martin 1944- *WhoFI 92*
**Quasha,** George *DrAPF 91*
**Quasha,** William Howard 1912- *WhoFI 92*
**Quasimodo,** Salvatore 1901-1968 *DcLB 114 [port], FacFETw, WhoNob 90*
**Quass,** La Verne Carl 1937- *AmMWSc 92*
**Quass,** Mary Kathryn 1950- *WhoEnt 92*
**Quast,** Jay Charles 1923- *AmMWSc 92*
**Quastel,** D M J 1936- *AmMWSc 92*
**Quastel,** Michael Reuben 1933- *AmMWSc 92*
**Quasten,** Johannes 1900-1987 *EncEarC*
**Quastler,** Shirley L. 1946- *WhoMW 92*
**Quate,** Calvin F 1923- *AmMWSc 92*
**Quatermass,** Martin *ConAu 134*
**Quatrano,** Ralph Stephen 1941- *AmMWSc 92*
**Quatre Etoiles** *ScFEYrs*
**Quatrella,** David Leonard 1955- *WhoAmL 92*
**Quatremere,** Etienne Marc 1782-1857 *BlkwCEP*
**Quatremere deQuincy,** Antoine-Chrysostome 1755-1849 *BlkwCEP*
**Quatrone,** Rich *DrAPF 91*
**Quattlebaum,** Donald Anderson 1953- *WhoFI 92*
**Quattlebaum,** Walter Emmett, Jr. 1922- *WhoFI 92*
**Quattlebum,** Donald Lee 1957- *WhoRel 92*
**Quattro,** Mark Henry 1955- *WhoAmL 92*
**Quattrocchi,** Rocco Anthony 1927- *WhoAmP 91*
**Quattrocci-Racine,** Laura Mae 1964- *WhoMW 92*
**Quattrochi,** Dale Anthony 1950- *AmMWSc 92*
**Quattrociocchi,** Ralph *WhoAmP 91*
**Quattropani,** Steven L 1943- *AmMWSc 92*
**Quattrucci,** Joseph 1925- *WhoAmP 91*
**Quave,** Gerald Joullian, Sr. 1933- *WhoFI 92*
**Quay,** John Ferguson 1932- *AmMWSc 92*
**Quay,** Paul Douglas 1949- *AmMWSc 92*
**Quay,** Paul Michael 1924- *AmMWSc 92, WhoRel 92*
**Quay,** Russell 1922- *TwCPaSc*
**Quay,** Thomas Emery 1934- *WhoAmL 92*
**Quay,** Thomas Lavelle 1914- *AmMWSc 92*
**Quay,** Wilbur Brooks 1927- *AmMWSc 92*
**Quayle,** Anthony 1913-1989 *FacFETw*
**Quayle,** Eric 1921- *ConAu 36NR, WrDr 92*
**Quayle,** J Danforth 1947- *WhoAmP 91*
**Quayle,** James Danforth 1947- *AmPolLe, IntWW 91, Who 92*
**Quayle,** John Clare 1956- *WhoEnt 92, WhoMW 92*
**Quayle,** John Rodney 1926- *Who 92*
**Quayle,** Marilyn 1949- *WhoMW 92*
**Quayle,** Mary Jane Ward *BenetAL 91*
**Quayle,** Thomas David Graham 1936- *Who 92*
**Quaynor,** Thomas Addo 1935- *WhoBlA 92*
**Quazi,** Azizul H 1935- *AmMWSc 92*
**Quddus,** Munir 1959- *WhoFI 92*
**Que,** Lawrence, Jr *AmMWSc 92*
**Que Hee,** Shane Stephen 1946- *AmMWSc 92, WhoWest 92*
**Quebbemann,** Aloysius John 1933- *AmMWSc 92*
**Quebec,** Archbishop of 1912- *Who 92*
**Quebec,** Bishop of 1940- *Who 92*
**Quednau,** Franz Wolfgang 1930- *AmMWSc 92*
**Queen** *ConMus 6 [port]*
**Queen Latifah** 1970?- *ConBlB 1 [port], ConMus 6 [port], News 92-2 [port]*
**Queen,** Daniel 1934- *AmMWSc 92, WhoEnt 92*

**Queen,** Ellery *BenetAL 91, FacFETw*
**Queen,** Michael L 1962- *WhoAmP 91*
**Queen,** Robert Calvin 1912- *WhoBlA 92*
**Queenan,** Charles Joseph, Jr. 1930- *WhoFI 92*
**Queenan,** John T 1933- *AmMWSc 92*
**Queener,** Sherry Fream 1943- *AmMWSc 92*
**Queener,** Stephen Wyatt 1943- *AmMWSc 92*
**Queeney,** Paul Joseph, Jr. 1954- *WhoWest 92*
**Queensberry,** Marquess of 1929- *Who 92*
**Queensland North,** Bishop of 1926- *Who 92*
**Queffelec,** Anne 1948- *IntWW 91*
**Queguiner,** Jean 1921- *Who 92*
**Queiros,** Raquel de 1910- *BenetAL 91*
**Queler,** Eve *IntWW 91, WhoEnt 92*
**Queler,** Eve 1936- *NewAmDM*
**Queller,** Fred 1932- *WhoAmL 92*
**Quellmalz,** Frederick 1912- *WhoMW 92*
**Quellmalz,** Henry 1915- *WhoFI 92*
**Quello,** James H. *LesBEnT 92 [port]*
**Quello,** James H 1914- *WhoAmP 91*
**Quello,** James Henry 1914- *WhoFI 92*
**Quene,** Theo 1930- *IntWW 91*
**Queneau,** Paul E 1911- *AmMWSc 92*
**Queneau,** Raymond 1903-1976 *GuFrLit 1*
**Quenington,** Viscount 1950- *Who 92*
**Quennell,** Joan Mary 1923- *Who 92*
**Quennell,** Peter 1905- *IntWW 91, Who 92, WrDr 92*
**Quenon,** Robert Hagerty 1928- *WhoFI 92*
**Quense,** John Henry 1943- *WhoFI 92*
**Quentin,** George Heinz 1934- *AmMWSc 92*
**Quentin,** Maurice *BlkwCEP*
**Queral,** Luis Emilio 1921- *WhoAmP 91*
**Querejazu Calvo,** Roberto 1913- *Who 92*
**Quereshi,** Mohammed Younus 1929- *WhoMW 92*
**Querfeld,** Charles William 1933- *AmMWSc 92*
**Querinjean,** Pierre Joseph 1942- *AmMWSc 92*
**Querry,** Marvin Richard 1935- *AmMWSc 92*
**Quertermus,** Carl John, Jr 1943- *AmMWSc 92*
**Quesada,** Antonio F 1925- *AmMWSc 92*
**Quesada,** Antonio R. 1948- *WhoHisp 92*
**Quesada,** Antonio Rettschlag 1948- *WhoMW 92*
**Quesada,** Catalina 1944- *WhoHisp 92*
**Quesada,** Violeta 1947- *BlkOlyM*
**Quesenberry,** Charles P 1931- *AmMWSc 92*
**Quesenberry,** James C. 1956- *WhoEnt 92*
**Quesenberry,** Kenneth Hays 1947- *AmMWSc 92*
**Quesenberry,** Robin Elaine 1957- *WhoRel 92*
**Quesnay,** Francois 1694-1774 *BlkwCEP*
**Quesnel,** David John 1950- *AmMWSc 92*
**Quessep,** Giovanni 1939- *ConSpAP*
**Quest,** Erica *WrDr 92*
**Questad,** David Lee 1952- *AmMWSc 92*
**Questel,** Mae 1908- *WhoEnt 92*
**Quester,** Aline Olson 1943- *WhoFI 92*
**Quester,** George 1936- *WrDr 92*
**Quester,** George H. 1936- *ConAu 34NR*
**Questiaux,** Nicole Francoise 1930- *IntWW 91*
**Questrom,** Allen I. 1941- *WhoFI 92, WhoMW 92*
**Quevedo,** Sylvestre Grado 1949- *WhoHisp 92*
**Quevedo,** Walter Cole, Jr 1930- *AmMWSc 92*
**Quezada,** Abel d1991 *NewYTBS 91*
**Quezada,** Abel 1920?-1991 *ConAu 133*
**Quezada,** Leticia *WhoHisp 92*
**Quezada,** Pedro 1943- *WhoAmL 92*
**Quibano,** Jairo Alfonso 1953- *WhoHisp 92*
**Quibell,** Charles Fox 1936- *AmMWSc 92*
**Quick,** Albert Thomas 1939- *WhoAmL 92*
**Quick,** Anthony Oliver Hebert 1924- *Who 92*
**Quick,** Armand J 1894-1978 *FacFETw*
**Quick,** Barbara 1954- *ConAu 133*
**Quick,** Bob 1939- *TwCPaSc*
**Quick,** Charles 1957- *TwCPaSc*
**Quick,** Charles E. 1933- *WhoBlA 92*
**Quick,** Dorothy 1944- *Who 92*
**Quick,** Edward E 1935- *WhoAmP 91*
**Quick,** Edward Raymond 1943- *WhoMW 92*
**Quick,** George Kenneth 1947- *WhoBlA 92*
**Quick,** Herbert 1861-1925 *BenetAL 91, ScFEYrs*
**Quick,** Jack Beaver 1947- *WhoFI 92*
**Quick,** James S 1940- *AmMWSc 92*
**Quick,** Joan B *WhoAmP 91*
**Quick,** Leslie Charles, III 1953- *WhoFI 92*
**Quick,** Mike 1959- *WhoBlA 92*
**Quick,** Norman *WhoRel 92*
**Quick,** Norman 1922- *Who 92*
**Quick,** Perry Day 1945- *WhoFI 92*
**Quick,** R. Edward 1927- *WhoBlA 92*
**Quick,** Thomas Clarkson 1955- *WhoFI 92*
**Quick,** Thomas L 1929- *ConAu 34NR*
**Quick,** William Andrew 1925- *AmMWSc 92*
**Quick,** William Kellon 1933- *WhoRel 92*
**Quick,** William Thomas 1946- *WhoWest 92*
**Quick,** William W. 1943- *WhoMW 92*
**Quicke,** John 1922- *Who 92*
**Quicksall,** David Lawrence 1950- *WhoAmL 92*
**Quicksilver Messenger Service** *NewAmDM*
**Quidd,** David Andrew 1954- *WhoAmL 92, WhoAmP 91*
**Quidde,** Ludwig 1858-1941 *WhoNob 90*
**Quie,** Albert Harold 1923- *WhoAmP 91*
**Quie,** Paul Gerhardt 1925- *AmMWSc 92*
**Quigg,** Chris 1944- *AmMWSc 92*
**Quigg,** Donald James 1916- *WhoAmL 92*
**Quigg,** Philip W. 1920- *ConAu 35NR*
**Quigg,** Richard J 1930- *AmMWSc 92*
**Quigg,** Thomas Lynn 1956- *WhoFI 92*
**Quigless,** Milton Douglas, Jr. 1945- *WhoBlA 92*
**Quigley,** Anthony Leslie Coupland 1946- *Who 92*
**Quigley,** Eamonn Martin 1952- *WhoMW 92*
**Quigley,** Frank Douglas 1928- *AmMWSc 92*
**Quigley,** Gary Joseph 1942- *AmMWSc 92*
**Quigley,** George *Who 92*
**Quigley,** Gerard Paul 1942- *AmMWSc 92*
**Quigley,** Herbert Joseph, Jr 1937- *AmMWSc 92*
**Quigley,** James P 1942- *AmMWSc 92*
**Quigley,** Jerome Harold 1925- *WhoFI 92*
**Quigley,** Johanna Mary *Who 92*
**Quigley,** John Michael 1942- *WhoFI 92*
**Quigley,** Joseph John 1947- *WhoFI 92*
**Quigley,** Martin *DrAPF 91*
**Quigley,** Martin, Jr. 1917- *IntMPA 92*
**Quigley,** Peter 1925- *TwCPaSc*
**Quigley,** Philip J. 1943- *WhoWest 92*
**Quigley,** Robert James 1940- *AmMWSc 92*
**Quigley,** Robert Murvin 1934- *AmMWSc 92*
**Quigley,** Roger A 1934- *WhoIns 92*
**Quigley,** Thomas Harry, Jr. 1942- *WhoRel 92*
**Quigley,** Thomas J. 1923- *WhoAmL 92*
**Quigley,** William George 1929- *Who 92*
**Quigley,** William J. 1951- *ConTFT 9, IntMPA 92*
**Quijada,** Rodrigo 1942- *IntAu&W 91*
**Quijano,** Alfonso 1939- *WhoHisp 92*
**Quijano,** Raul Alberto 1923- *IntWW 91*
**Quijas,** Louis F., Jr. 1951- *WhoHisp 92*
**Quiles,** Paul 1942- *IntWW 91*
**Quiles Rodriguez,** Edwin Rafael 1949- *WhoHisp 92*
**Quilici,** Diana Lynne 1961- *WhoMW 92*
**Quilici,** Joe 1925- *WhoAmP 91*
**Quilico,** Gino 1955- *NewAmDM*
**Quilico,** Louis 1929- *NewAmDM*
**Quill,** John Daniel 1943- *WhoRel 92*
**Quill,** Laurence Larkin 1901- *AmMWSc 92*
**Quill,** Michael Joseph 1905-1966 *DcAmImH*
**Quill,** Monica *ConAu 34NR*
**Quillan,** Eddie 1907-1990 *ConTFT 9*
**Quillen,** Cecil Dyer, Jr. 1937- *WhoAmL 92, WhoFI 92*
**Quillen,** Daniel G 1940- *AmMWSc 92*
**Quillen,** Edmond W, Jr 1953- *AmMWSc 92*
**Quillen,** Ford C 1938- *WhoAmP 91*
**Quillen,** George Robert 1928- *WhoAmP 91*
**Quillen,** James H. 1916- *AlmAP 92 [port]*
**Quillen,** James Henry 1916- *WhoAmP 91*
**Quillen,** Lloyd Douglas 1943- *WhoFI 92*
**Quillen,** R. Clark 1941- *WhoEnt 92*
**Quillen,** William Tatem 1935- *WhoAmL 92*
**Quiller,** Andrew *IntAu&W 91X, WrDr 92*
**Quiller-Couch,** Arthur 1863-1944 *RfGEnL 91*
**Quilley,** Denis 1927- *IntWW 91*
**Quilley,** Denis Clifford 1927- *Who 92*
**Quilliam,** James Peter 1920- *Who 92*
**Quilliam,** Juan Pete 1915- *Who 92*
**Quilliam,** Peter *Who 92*
**Quilliam,** William Reed, Jr. 1929- *WhoAmL 92*
**Quilligan,** James Joseph, Jr 1912- *AmMWSc 92*
**Quillin,** Charles Robert 1938- *AmMWSc 92*
**Quillin,** Margaret E. 1960- *WhoMW 92*
**Quilliot,** Roger 1925- *IntWW 91*
**Quilter,** Anthony 1937- *Who 92*
**Quilter,** Barney 1919- *WhoAmP 91*
**Quilter,** David Tudway 1921- *Who 92*
**Quilter,** Roger 1877-1953 *NewAmDM*
**Quilter,** Roger 1921- *TwCPaSc*
**Quimby,** Fred William 1945- *AmMWSc 92*
**Quimby,** Freeman Henry 1915- *AmMWSc 92*
**Quimby,** George 1913- *WrDr 92*
**Quimby,** George Irving 1913- *ConAu 34NR, WhoWest 92*
**Quimby,** Harriet 1875-1912 *HanAmWH*
**Quimpo,** Rafael Gonzales 1939- *AmMWSc 92*
**Quin** *Who 92*
**Quin,** Dan *BenetAL 91*
**Quin,** Gerald M d1991 *NewYTBS 91*
**Quin,** Joseph Marvin 1947- *WhoFI 92*
**Quin,** Joyce Gwendolen 1944- *Who 92*
**Quin,** Louis DuBose 1928- *AmMWSc 92*
**Quin,** Mary Patricia 1953- *WhoFI 92*
**Quin,** Whayne Sherman 1937- *WhoAmL 92, WhoFI 92*
**Quinan,** Allen *ScFEYrs A*
**Quinan,** James Roger 1921- *AmMWSc 92*
**Quinby,** Isaac Ferdinand 1821-1891 *BiInAmS*
**Quince,** Kevin 1950- *WhoBlA 92*
**Quince,** Peter *IntAu&W 91X, Who 92*
**Quincy,** Edmund *DrAPF 91*
**Quincy,** Edmund 1808-1877 *AmPeW*
**Quincy,** Josiah 1772-1864 *BenetAL 91*
**Quincy,** Josiah Phillips 1829-1910 *BenetAL 91*
**Quincy,** Ronald Lee 1950- *WhoBlA 92*
**Quindlen,** John Joseph 1932- *WhoFI 92*
**Quine,** Stephen Shawn 1945- *WhoEnt 92*
**Quine,** Willard V 1908- *AmMWSc 92, WrDr 92*
**Quine,** Willard Van Orman 1908- *IntAu&W 91, IntWW 91, Who 92*
**Quinlan,** Alan Geoffrey 1933- *Who 92*
**Quinlan,** C. Patrick 1922- *WhoMW 92*
**Quinlan,** Daniel A 1958- *AmMWSc 92*
**Quinlan,** Dennis Charles 1943- *AmMWSc 92*
**Quinlan,** Guy Christian 1939- *WhoAmL 92*
**Quinlan,** Henry 1906- *Who 92*
**Quinlan,** John Edward 1930- *AmMWSc 92*
**Quinlan,** John Michael 1936- *WhoAmL 92*
**Quinlan,** Kathleen 1954- *IntMPA 92, WhoEnt 92*
**Quinlan,** Kenneth Paul 1928- *AmMWSc 92*
**Quinlan,** Michael 1930- *Who 92*
**Quinlan,** Michael J 1938- *WhoIns 92*
**Quinlan,** Timothy John 1958- *WhoWest 92*
**Quinlan,** William Joseph, Jr. 1939- *WhoAmL 92*
**Quinlan,** William Louis 1930- *WhoAmP 91*
**Quinlivan,** William Leslie G 1921- *AmMWSc 92*
**Quinn,** A Peter, Jr 1923- *WhoIns 92*
**Quinn,** Aidan 1959- *IntMPA 92*
**Quinn,** Alexander James 1932- *WhoRel 92*
**Quinn,** Alfred Thomas 1922- *WhoBlA 92*
**Quinn,** Anne Katherine Larson 1966- *WhoMW 92*
**Quinn,** Anthony 1916- *IntMPA 92*
**Quinn,** Anthony Rudolph Oaxaca 1915- *WhoEnt 92, WhoHisp 92*
**Quinn,** Anthony Rudolph Oaxaca 1916- *IntWW 91*
**Quinn,** Arthur Hobson 1875-1960 *BenetAL 91*
**Quinn,** B E 1915- *AmMWSc 92*
**Quinn,** Barry George 1934- *AmMWSc 92*
**Quinn,** Bernetta *DrAPF 91*
**Quinn,** Beverly Wilson 1943- *WhoAmP 91*
**Quinn,** Brian *Who 92*
**Quinn,** Brian 1936- *Who 92*
**Quinn,** C Jack 1929- *AmMWSc 92*
**Quinn,** Cameron Paige 1957- *WhoAmL 92*
**Quinn,** Charles Vincent 1961- *WhoAmL 92*
**Quinn,** Ciaran Patrick 1959- *WhoFI 92*
**Quinn,** Cindy Lee 1949- *WhoWest 92*
**Quinn,** Cosmas Edward 1926- *AmMWSc 92*
**Quinn,** Daniel Joseph 1945- *WhoFI 92*
**Quinn,** David 1909- *WrDr 92*
**Quinn,** David Alfred 1936- *WhoFI 92*
**Quinn,** David Beers 1909- *Who 92*
**Quinn,** David Lee 1938- *AmMWSc 92*
**Quinn,** Dennis Wayne 1947- *AmMWSc 92*
**Quinn,** Diane C. 1942- *WhoBlA 92*
**Quinn,** Doris Marilyn 1923- *WhoAmP 91*
**Quinn,** Dwight Wilson 1917- *WhoAmP 91*
**Quinn,** Edwin John 1927- *AmMWSc 92*
**Quinn,** Elizabeth R. 1944- *WhoFI 92*
**Quinn,** Esther Casier 1922- *ConAu 35NR*
**Quinn,** Francis A. 1921- *WhoRel 92, WhoWest 92*
**Quinn,** Frank Russell *AmMWSc 92*
**Quinn,** Frank S 1946- *AmMWSc 92*
**Quinn,** Galen Warren 1922- *AmMWSc 92*
**Quinn,** George David 1950- *AmMWSc 92*
**Quinn,** Gerald M. d1991 *NewYTBS 91*
**Quinn,** Gerald V. 1952- *WhoEnt 92*
**Quinn,** Gertrude Patricia 1921- *AmMWSc 92*
**Quinn,** Harold Patrick, Jr. 1955- *WhoAmL 92*
**Quinn,** Helen Rhoda 1943- *AmMWSc 92*
**Quinn,** James Aiden O'Brien 1932- *Who 92*
**Quinn,** James Allen 1954- *AmMWSc 92*
**Quinn,** James Amos 1939- *AmMWSc 92*
**Quinn,** James Brian 1928- *ConAu 35NR*
**Quinn,** James Charles Frederick 1919- *Who 92*
**Quinn,** James Gerard 1938- *AmMWSc 92*
**Quinn,** James Joseph 1936- *WhoEnt 92*
**Quinn,** James Maurice 1929- *WhoMW 92*
**Quinn,** James P 1933- *WhoIns 92*
**Quinn,** James Peter, Sr. 1934- *WhoRel 92*
**Quinn,** James Steven Brian 1936- *Who 92*
**Quinn,** James W. 1945- *WhoAmL 92*
**Quinn,** Jane Bryant 1939- *WhoFI 92*
**Quinn,** Jarus William 1930- *AmMWSc 92*
**Quinn,** Jeff 1951- *WhoEnt 92, WhoFI 92*
**Quinn,** John *DrAPF 91*
**Quinn,** John A 1932- *AmMWSc 92*
**Quinn,** John Brian Patrick 1943- *WhoWest 92*
**Quinn,** John Collins 1925- *WhoFI 92*
**Quinn,** John Joseph 1933- *AmMWSc 92*
**Quinn,** John R. 1929- *WhoRel 92, WhoWest 92*
**Quinn,** John Robert 1927- *WhoWest 92*
**Quinn,** John Robert 1948- *WhoAmP 91*
**Quinn,** Joseph *WhoAmP 91*
**Quinn,** Joseph Allan 1942- *WhoEnt 92*
**Quinn,** Joseph R. 1932- *WhoAmL 92, WhoAmP 91, WhoWest 92*
**Quinn,** Julia Marie 1960- *WhoAmL 92*
**Quinn,** Kenneth 1920- *WrDr 92*
**Quinn,** Laura Marie 1933- *WhoAmL 92*
**Quinn,** LeBris Smith 1954- *AmMWSc 92, WhoWest 92*
**Quinn,** Longworth D. 1943-1990 *WhoBlA 92N*
**Quinn,** Loyd Yost 1917- *AmMWSc 92*
**Quinn,** Martin *WrDr 92*
**Quinn,** Martin Vincent 1948- *WhoFI 92*
**Quinn,** Michael Desmond 1936- *WhoFI 92*
**Quinn,** Michael H 1943- *AmMWSc 92*
**Quinn,** Patricia K. *WhoEnt 92*
**Quinn,** Patrick *WhoAmP 91, WhoMW 92*
**Quinn,** Patrick James 1946- *WhoWest 92*
**Quinn,** Patrick William 1955- *WhoAmL 92*
**Quinn,** Peter 1941- *WrDr 92*
**Quinn,** Randy L. 1956- *WhoRel 92*
**Quinn,** Richard Kendall 1957- *WhoMW 92*
**Quinn,** Richard M, Jr 1965- *WhoAmP 91*
**Quinn,** Richard Paul 1942- *AmMWSc 92*
**Quinn,** Robert George 1936- *AmMWSc 92*
**Quinn,** Robert Joseph, Jr 1956- *WhoAmP 91, WhoMW 92*
**Quinn,** Robert M 1941- *AmMWSc 92*
**Quinn,** Rod King 1938- *AmMWSc 92*
**Quinn,** Rodney S 1923- *WhoAmP 91*
**Quinn,** Ruairi 1946- *IntWW 91*
**Quinn,** Seabury 1889-1969 *ScFEYrs*
**Quinn,** Sheila 1920- *Who 92*
**Quinn,** Simon *WrDr 92*
**Quinn,** Stanley J., Jr. 1915- *IntMPA 92*
**Quinn,** Teresa Moss 1952- *WhoAmL 92*
**Quinn,** Thomas Patrick 1930- *AmMWSc 92*
**Quinn,** Timothy Charles, Jr. 1936- *WhoAmL 92*
**Quinn,** Vincent Kevin 1931- *WhoIns 92*
**Quinn,** William A 1928- *WhoIns 92*
**Quinn,** William Chandler 1949- *WhoEnt 92*
**Quinn,** William Halston 1955- *WhoFI 92*
**Quinn,** William Hewes 1918- *AmMWSc 92*
**Quinn,** William John 1911- *IntWW 91*
**Quinn,** Yvonne Susan 1951- *WhoAmL 92*
**Quinnan,** Gerald Vincent, Jr 1947- *AmMWSc 92*
**Quinnen,** Peter John 1945- *Who 92*
**Quinney,** Paul Reed 1924- *AmMWSc 92*
**Quinney,** Richard 1934- *WrDr 92*
**Quinon,** Jose Manuel 1950- *WhoAmL 92*
**Quinones,** Alberto Louis 1956- *WhoHisp 92*
**Quinones,** Carlos Ramon 1951- *WhoFI 92*
**Quinones,** Ferdinand Antonio 1922- *AmMWSc 92*
**Quinones,** Francisco Mariano 1830-1908 *HisDSpE*
**Quinones,** John Manuel 1952- *WhoHisp 92*
**Quinones,** Jose Ramon, Jr. 1950- *WhoHisp 92*
**Quinones,** Louis Edward 1932- *WhoHisp 92*
**Quinones,** Luis Ignacio 1951- *WhoHisp 92*
**Quinones,** Magaly *DrAPF 91*
**Quinones,** Mark A 1931- *AmMWSc 92, WhoHisp 92*
**Quinones,** Samuel 1949- *WhoHisp 92*
**Quinones,** Thomas 1955- *WhoHisp 92*

**Quinones,** Wilfredo 1957- *WhoHisp 92*
**Quinones Amezquita,** Mario Rafael 1933- *IntWW 91*
**Quinones-D'Brassis,** R. Rafael 1937- *WhoWest 92*
**Quinones-Keber,** Eloise *WhoHisp 92*
**Quinones Rivera,** Victor 1948- *WhoHisp 92*
**Quinones-Suarez,** Miguel Angel 1967- *WhoHisp 92*
**Quinot,** Raymond G A 1920- *IntAu&W 91*
**Quinsey,** Vernon Lewis 1944- *AmMWSc 92*
**Quint,** Arnold Harris 1942- *WhoAmL 92*
**Quint,** Hillard Jay 1964- *WhoAmL 92*
**Quintana,** Betty J. 1946- *WhoHisp 92*
**Quintana,** Carlos Narcis 1965- *WhoHisp 92*
**Quintana,** Edward M. *WhoHisp 92*
**Quintana,** Henry, Jr. 1952- *WhoHisp 92*
**Quintana,** Julio C. 1945- *WhoHisp 92*
**Quintana,** Leroy V. *DrAPF 91*
**Quintana,** Leroy V. 1944- *WhoHisp 92*
**Quintana,** Luis Antonio 1960- *WhoHisp 92*
**Quintana,** M. V. 1953- *WhoHisp 92*
**Quintana,** Manuel E. 1947- *WhoHisp 92*
**Quintana,** Ricardo Beckwith, Jr. 1940- *WhoMW 92*
**Quintana,** Ronald Preston 1936- *AmMWSc 92*
**Quintana,** Sammy Joseph 1949- *WhoHisp 92*
**Quintana,** Yamile 1940- *WhoHisp 92*
**Quintana-Diaz,** Julio C. 1945- *WhoHisp 92*
**Quintanilha,** Alexandre Tiedtke 1945- *AmMWSc 92*
**Quintanilla,** Guadalupe C. 1937- *WhoHisp 92*
**Quintanilla,** Michael Ray 1954- *WhoHisp 92*
**Quintano Roo,** Andres 1787-1851 *HisDSpE*
**Quintela,** Abel R. 1946- *WhoHisp 92*
**Quintela,** Richard Gerard 1964- *WhoHisp 92*
**Quinter,** James 1816-1888 *AmPeW*
**Quintero,** Conrad O. 1952- *WhoHisp 92*
**Quintero,** Frank, Jr. 1958- *WhoAmL 92*
**Quintero,** Janneth Ivon 1960- *WhoHisp 92*
**Quintero,** Jess *WhoHisp 92*
**Quintero,** Jesus Marciano 1961- *WhoHisp 92*
**Quintero,** Jose 1924- *WhoEnt 92, WhoHisp 92*
**Quintero,** Orlando A. *WhoHisp 92*
**Quintero,** Ruben 1952- *WhoHisp 92*
**Quintero,** Ruben David 1949- *WhoHisp 92*
**Quintero Arce,** Carlos 1920- *WhoRel 92*
**Quintian,** Andres Rogelio 1920- *WhoFI 92*
**Quintiere,** Gary G. 1944- *WhoAmL 92*
**Quintiere,** James G 1940- *AmMWSc 92*
**Quintilliano,** Luigi *DcAmImH*
**Quinto,** David Walter 1955- *WhoAmL 92*
**Quinto,** Eric Todd 1951- *AmMWSc 92*
**Quinton** *Who 92*
**Quinton,** Baron 1925- *IntWW 91, Who 92*
**Quinton,** Lord 1925- *WrDr 92*
**Quinton,** Arthur Robert 1924- *AmMWSc 92*
**Quinton,** Barbara A. 1941- *WhoBlA 92*
**Quinton,** Dee Arlington 1939- *AmMWSc 92*
**Quinton,** John 1929- *Who 92*
**Quinton,** John Grand 1929- *IntWW 91*
**Quinton,** Jose I. 1881-1925 *NewAmDM*
**Quinton,** Marcelle *TwCPaSc*
**Quinton,** Paul Marquis 1944- *WhoWest 92*
**Quinton-Cox,** Robert 1926- *AmMWSc 92*
**Quintyne,** Irwin Sinclair 1926- *WhoBlA 92*
**Quiocho,** Florante A 1937- *AmMWSc 92*
**Quirarte,** Jacinto 1931- *WhoHisp 92*
**Quirico,** Deborah Lynn *WhoWest 92*
**Quirin,** Albert J 1948- *WhoIns 92*
**Quirin,** Philip J 1940- *WhoIns 92*
**Quiring,** Patti Lee *WhoMW 92*
**Quirk,** Cathleen *DrAPF 91*
**Quirk,** Charles Randolph 1920- *IntWW 91*
**Quirk,** Christopher Sean 1958- *WhoFI 92*
**Quirk,** Desmond John 1929- *IntWW 91*
**Quirk,** James Patrick 1924- *IntWW 91*
**Quirk,** John A 1951- *WhoAmP 91*
**Quirk,** John Stanton S. *Who 92*
**Quirk,** John Thomas 1933- *AmMWSc 92*
**Quirk,** Randolph 1920- *IntAu&W 91, Who 92, WrDr 92*
**Quirk,** Robert Joseph 1931- *WhoAmP 91*
**Quirk,** Roderic P 1941- *AmMWSc 92*
**Quirk,** Rory Fitzjames 1943- *WhoAmL 92*
**Quirke,** Terence Thomas, Jr 1929- *AmMWSc 92*
**Quiroga,** Carmen Lucila 1946- *WhoHisp 92*
**Quiroga,** Dario O. 1941- *WhoHisp 92*
**Quiroga,** Elena *IntAu&W 91, IntWW 91*
**Quiroga,** Francisco Gracia *WhoHisp 92*
**Quiroga,** Horacio 1878-1937 *BenetAL 91*
**Quiroga,** Indalecio Ruiz 1937- *WhoHisp 92*
**Quiroga,** Jorge Humberto 1950- *WhoHisp 92*
**Quiroga,** Jose A. 1959- *WhoHisp 92*
**Quiroga,** Robert *WhoHisp 92*
**Quiroga,** Roger *WhoHisp 92*
**Quiroga,** Vasco de 1470?-1565 *HisDSpE*
**Quiros,** Carlos F 1946- *AmMWSc 92*
**Quiros,** Carlos Francisco 1946- *WhoWest 92*
**Quiroz,** Alfred James 1944- *WhoHisp 92*
**Quiroz,** Jesse M. 1939- *WhoHisp 92*
**Quiroz,** Julie *WhoHisp 92*
**Quiroz,** Martin 1955- *WhoHisp 92*
**Quiroz,** Roderick S 1923- *AmMWSc 92*
**Quisenberry,** Dan Ray 1938- *AmMWSc 92*
**Quisenberry,** John Ascum 1924- *WhoMW 92*
**Quisenberry,** John Bryan 1941- *WhoEnt 92*
**Quisenberry,** Karl Spangler, Jr 1926- *AmMWSc 92*
**Quisenberry,** Nancy Lou 1938- *WhoMW 92*
**Quisenberry,** Richard Keith 1934- *AmMWSc 92*
**Quisenberry,** Robert Max 1956- *WhoWest 92*
**Quisenberry,** Virgil L 1946- *AmMWSc 92*
**Quisenberry,** Walter Brown 1912- *AmMWSc 92*
**Quisling,** Vidkun 1887-1945 *BiDExR, EncTR 91 [port], FacFETw [port]*
**Quismorio,** Francisco P, Jr 1941- *AmMWSc 92, WhoWest 92*
**Quissell,** David Olin 1944- *AmMWSc 92*
**Quist,** Adrian d1991 *NewYTBS 91*
**Quist,** Allen J 1944- *WhoAmP 91*
**Quist,** Arvin Sigvard 1933- *AmMWSc 92*
**Quist,** George Robert 1920- *WhoIns 92*
**Quist,** Gordon Jay 1937- *WhoMW 92*
**Quist,** Jeanette Fitzgerald 1948- *WhoEnt 92*
**Quist,** Peter Jay 1955- *WhoAmL 92*
**Quist,** Raymond Willard 1934- *AmMWSc 92*
**Quist,** William Edward 1935- *AmMWSc 92*
**Quistad,** Gary Bennet 1947- *AmMWSc 92*
**Quistgaard,** Jens 1919- *DcTwDes*
**Quitevis,** Minda Altea 1937- *WhoWest 92*
**Quitman,** Wallace *TwCSFW 91*
**Quitmeyer,** John Mark 1950- *WhoAmL 92*
**Quittner,** Howard 1922- *AmMWSc 92*
**Quitugua,** Antonio Ogo *WhoAmP 91*
**Quitugua,** Franklin Joseph 1933- *WhoAmP 91*
**Quivers,** Eric Stanley 1955- *WhoBlA 92*
**Quivers,** William Wyatt, Sr. 1919- *WhoBlA 92*
**Quock,** Joan Marie 1941- *WhoFI 92, WhoWest 92*
**Quock,** Raymond Mark 1948- *AmMWSc 92*
**Quodvultdeus** d453? *EncEarC*
**Quon,** Check Yuen 1949- *AmMWSc 92*
**Quon,** David Shi Haung 1931- *AmMWSc 92*
**Quraishi,** Abdul Aziz Bin Said Al 1930- *IntWW 91*
**Quraishi,** Mohammed Sayeed 1924- *AmMWSc 92*
**Qureshi,** A H 1932- *AmMWSc 92*
**Qureshi,** Ishtiaq Husain 1903- *IntWW 91*
**Qureshi,** Moeen Ahmad 1930- *IntWW 91*
**Qureshi,** Nilofer 1947- *AmMWSc 92*
**Qutub,** Musa Y 1940- *AmMWSc 92*
**Qutub,** Musa Yacub 1940- *WhoMW 92*
**Quynn,** Richard Grayson 1928- *AmMWSc 92*
**Quyth,** Gabriel *WrDr 92*

# R

**R.R.** *AmPeW*
**Ra,** Sun *NewAmDM*
**Raab,** Frederick Herbert 1946- *AmMWSc 92*
**Raab,** Fredric Joseph 1952- *WhoEnt 92*
**Raab,** George Gregory 1947- *WhoAmP 91*
**Raab,** Harry Frederick, Jr 1926- *AmMWSc 92*
**Raab,** Ira Jerry 1935- *WhoAmL 92*
**Raab,** Jacob Lee 1938- *AmMWSc 92*
**Raab,** Joseph A 1934- *AmMWSc 92*
**Raab,** Lawrence *DrAPF 91*
**Raab,** Madeline Murphy 1945- *WhoBlA 92*
**Raab,** Menachem 1923- *WhoRel 92*
**Raab,** Michael William 1943- *WhoEnt 92*
**Raab,** Paul Richard 1958- *WhoMW 92*
**Raab,** Sheldon 1937- *WhoAmL 92*
**Raab,** Wallace Albert 1921- *AmMWSc 92*
**Raab,** Walter Ferdinand 1924- *WhoFI 92*
**Raab,** Yaron Roni 1964- *WhoEnt 92*
**Raabe,** Herbert P 1909- *AmMWSc 92*
**Raabe,** Paul Richard 1953- *WhoRel 92*
**Raabe,** Peter 1872-1945 *EncTR 91 [port]*
**Raabe,** Robert Donald 1924- *AmMWSc 92*
**Raabe,** William Alan 1953- *WhoMW 92*
**Raad,** Virginia 1925- *WhoEnt 92*
**Raaen,** Vernon F 1918- *AmMWSc 92*
**Raaff,** Anton 1714-1797 *NewAmDM*
**Raaflaub,** Vernon Arthur 1938- *WhoRel 92*
**Raam,** Shanthi 1941- *AmMWSc 92*
**Raamot,** Tonis 1932- *AmMWSc 92*
**Raaphorst,** G Peter *AmMWSc 92*
**Raas,** Daniel Alan 1947- *WhoAmL 92*
**Raasch,** Gilbert O 1903- *AmMWSc 92*
**Raasch,** Lou Reinhart 1944- *AmMWSc 92*
**Raasch,** Maynard Stanley 1915- *AmMWSc 92*
**Raasch,** Randolph Howard 1956- *WhoRel 92*
**Raatikainen,** Kaisa 1928- *IntWW 91*
**Raats,** Jaan 1932- *IntWW 91, SovUnBD*
**Rab,** Paul Alexis 1944- *AmMWSc 92*
**Raba,** Carl Franz, Jr 1937- *AmMWSc 92*
**Rabade,** Jose Manuel 1922- *WhoHisp 92*
**Rabadjija,** Neven 1954- *WhoAmL 92*
**Rabaeus,** Bengt 1917- *IntWW 91*
**Rabago,** Antonio J. 1953- *WhoHisp 92*
**Rabago,** Karl R. 1957- *WhoHisp 92*
**Rabalais,** Francis Cleo 1937- *AmMWSc 92*
**Rabalais,** John Wayne 1944- *AmMWSc 92*
**Raban,** Jonathan 1942- *IntWW 91, Who 92, WrDr 92*
**Raban,** Morton 1940- *AmMWSc 92*
**Rabasa,** Emilio O. 1925- *IntWW 91*
**Rabassa,** Albert Oscar 1936- *WhoHisp 92*
**Rabassa,** Gregory 1922- *IntWW 91, WhoHisp 92, WrDr 92*
**Rabb,** Bruce 1941- *WhoAmL 92, WhoFI 92*
**Rabb,** Ellis 1930- *WhoEnt 92*
**Rabb,** George Bernard 1930- *AmMWSc 92*
**Rabb,** Harriet Schaffer 1941- *WhoAmL 92*
**Rabb,** Maurice F. *WhoBlA 92*
**Rabb,** Maxwell M. 1910- *IntWW 91, WhoAmP 91*
**Rabb,** Robert Lamar 1919- *AmMWSc 92*
**Rabb,** Theodore K. 1937- *WrDr 92*
**Rabban,** David M. 1949- *WhoAmL 92*
**Rabbani,** Ruhiyyih 1910- *WhoRel 92*
**Rabbe,** David Ellsworth 1955- *WhoFI 92*
**Rabbi,** The Chief *Who 92*
**Rabbit,** Guy 1943- *AmMWSc 92*
**Rabbitt,** Edward Thomas 1941- *WhoEnt 92*
**Rabbitt,** Thomas *DrAPF 91*
**Rabbitts,** Terence Howard 1946- *Who 92*
**Rabbula** d435 *EncEarC*
**Rabby,** Pat *DrAPF 91*
**Rabe,** Allen E 1931- *AmMWSc 92*
**Rabe,** Ausma 1926- *AmMWSc 92*
**Rabe,** Berniece 1928- *IntAu&W 91, WrDr 92*
**Rabe,** David 1940- *BenetAL 91, DcLB Y91 [port], WrDr 92*
**Rabe,** David William 1940- *IntMPA 92, WhoEnt 92*
**Rabe,** Edward Frederick 1918- *AmMWSc 92*
**Rabe,** Folke 1935- *ConCom 92*
**Rabe,** Tish Sommers 1951- *WhoEnt 92*
**Rabe,** Virgil William 1930- *WhoRel 92*
**Rabel,** Fredric M 1938- *AmMWSc 92*
**Rabel,** William Huitt 1941- *WhoIns 92*
**Rabemananjara,** Jacques 1913?- *IntWW 91*
**Raben,** Irwin A 1922- *AmMWSc 92*
**Rabenirina,** Remi *WhoRel 92*
**Rabenold,** Kathryn Tuttle 1907- *WhoEnt 92*
**Rabenstein,** Albert Louis 1931- *AmMWSc 92*
**Rabenstein,** Dallas Leroy 1942- *AmMWSc 92*
**Rabenstein,** Manfred 1911- *WhoRel 92*
**Rabenstine,** James Robert 1948- *WhoIns 92*
**Raber,** Douglas John 1942- *AmMWSc 92*
**Raber,** Martin Newman 1947- *AmMWSc 92*
**Rabetafika,** Joseph Albert Blaise 1932- *IntWW 91*
**Rabi,** I. I. 1898-1988 *FacFETw [port]*
**Rabi,** Isidor Isaac 1898-1988 *WhoNob 90*
**Rabideau,** Peter W 1940- *AmMWSc 92*
**Rabideau,** Sherman Webber 1920- *AmMWSc 92*
**Rabie,** Ronald Lee 1946- *AmMWSc 92*
**Rabiger,** Dorothy June 1935- *AmMWSc 92*
**Rabii,** Jamshid 1946- *AmMWSc 92*
**Rabii,** Sohrab 1937- *AmMWSc 92*
**Rabin,** Arthur S. 1948- *WhoEnt 92*
**Rabin,** Brian Robert 1927- *Who 92*
**Rabin,** Bruce S *AmMWSc 92*
**Rabin,** Chaim 1915- *WrDr 92*
**Rabin,** Elijah Zephania 1937- *AmMWSc 92*
**Rabin,** Elliott D. 1953- *WhoWest 92*
**Rabin,** Erwin R 1930- *AmMWSc 92*
**Rabin,** Harvey *AmMWSc 92*
**Rabin,** Herbert 1928- *AmMWSc 92*
**Rabin,** Itzhak 1922- *IntWW 91*
**Rabin,** Jack 1930- *WhoFI 92*
**Rabin,** Jeffrey Mark 1955- *AmMWSc 92*
**Rabin,** Joseph Harry 1927- *WhoFI 92, WhoMW 92*
**Rabin,** Michael 1936-1972 *NewAmDM*
**Rabin,** Michael O 1931- *AmMWSc 92*
**Rabin,** Monroe Stephen Zane 1939- *AmMWSc 92*
**Rabin,** Oskar 1928- *IntWW 91*
**Rabin,** Paul Irwin 1938- *WhoIns 92*
**Rabin,** Robert 1928- *AmMWSc 92*
**Rabin,** Robert L. 1939- *WhoAmL 92*
**Rabin,** Sam 1903- *TwCPaSc*
**Rabin,** Yitzhak 1922- *FacFETw*
**Rabiner,** Lawrence Richard 1943- *AmMWSc 92*
**Rabino,** Isaac 1938- *AmMWSc 92*
**Rabinovich,** Eliezer M 1937- *AmMWSc 92*
**Rabinovich,** Isaak Moyseevich 1894-1961 *SovUnBD*
**Rabinovich,** Sergio Rospigliosi 1928- *AmMWSc 92*
**Rabinovitch,** B S 1919- *AmMWSc 92*
**Rabinovitch,** B. Seymour 1919- *IntWW 91*
**Rabinovitch,** Benton Seymour 1919- *Who 92*
**Rabinovitch,** Celia Mildred 1954- *WhoRel 92*
**Rabinovitch,** Marlene 1946- *AmMWSc 92*
**Rabinovitch,** Max Joel 1929- *WhoFI 92*
**Rabinovitch,** Michel Pinkus 1926- *AmMWSc 92*
**Rabinovitch,** Peter S *AmMWSc 92*
**Rabinovitch,** Sholem 1859-1916 *DcAmImH*
**Rabinovitz,** Abby *WhoEnt 92*
**Rabinovitz,** Jason *IntMPA 92*
**Rabinovitz,** Jason 1921- *WhoEnt 92*
**Rabinovitz,** Marco 1923- *AmMWSc 92*
**Rabinovitz,** Mayer *WhoAmL 92*
**Rabinovitz,** Rubin 1938- *WrDr 92*
**Rabinow,** Jacob 1910- *AmMWSc 92*
**Rabinowicz,** Ernest 1926- *AmMWSc 92*
**Rabinowicz,** Mordka Harry 1919- *WrDr 92*
**Rabinowitch,** Victor 1934- *AmMWSc 92*
**Rabinowitz,** Harry 1916- *IntWW 91, Who 92*
**Rabinowitz,** Israel Nathan 1935- *AmMWSc 92*
**Rabinowitz,** Jack Grant 1927- *AmMWSc 92*
**Rabinowitz,** James Robert 1942- *AmMWSc 92*
**Rabinowitz,** Jay Andrew 1927- *WhoAmL 92, WhoAmP 91, WhoWest 92*
**Rabinowitz,** Jesse C. 1925- *IntWW 91*
**Rabinowitz,** Jesse Charles 1925- *AmMWSc 92*
**Rabinowitz,** Joseph Loshak 1923- *AmMWSc 92*
**Rabinowitz,** Lawrence 1933- *AmMWSc 92*
**Rabinowitz,** Louis 1915- *WhoEnt 92*
**Rabinowitz,** Mario 1936- *AmMWSc 92, WhoWest 92*
**Rabinowitz,** Martin Jay 1931- *WhoAmL 92*
**Rabinowitz,** Marvin 1939- *WhoFI 92*
**Rabinowitz,** Max Eugene 1946- *WhoEnt 92*
**Rabinowitz,** Mayer Elya 1939- *WhoRel 92*
**Rabinowitz,** Paul H 1939- *AmMWSc 92*
**Rabinowitz,** Philip 1926- *AmMWSc 92*
**Rabinowitz,** Ronald 1943- *AmMWSc 92*
**Rabinowitz,** Solomon J. *BenetAL 91*
**Rabinowitz,** Stanley Samuel 1917- *WhoRel 92*
**Rabinowitz,** Wilbur M. 1918- *WhoFI 92*
**Rabins,** Michael J 1932- *AmMWSc 92*
**Rabitz,** Herschel Albert 1944- *AmMWSc 92*
**Rabius,** Sharon Kay 1942- *WhoMW 92*
**Rabjohn,** Norman 1915- *AmMWSc 92*
**Rabkin,** Eric S 1942- *ScFEYrs*
**Rabkin,** Eric S. 1946- *WhoMW 92*
**Rabkin,** Mitchell T 1930- *AmMWSc 92, IntWW 91*
**Rabkin,** Mitchell Thornton 1930- *WhoFI 92*
**Rabl,** Ari 1942- *AmMWSc 92*
**Rabl,** Veronika Ariana 1945- *AmMWSc 92*
**Rabold,** Gary Paul 1939- *AmMWSc 92*
**Rabold,** Robert E H *WhoIns 92*
**Rabolt,** John Francis 1949- *AmMWSc 92*
**Rabon,** Timothy Alan 1954- *WhoFI 92*
**Rabon,** Tom B, Jr 1954- *WhoAmP 91*
**Rabor,** Samuel Abarquez 1944- *WhoMW 92*
**Raborg,** Frederick A., Jr. *DrAPF 91*
**Raborn,** William 1905-1990 *AnObit 1990*
**Rabosky,** Joseph George 1944- *WhoFI 92*
**Rabovsky,** Jean *AmMWSc 92*
**Rabovsky,** Jean 1937- *WhoWest 92*
**Rabow,** Gerald 1928- *WrDr 92*
**Raboy,** Marc 1948- *ConAu 135*
**Raboy,** S. Caesar 1936- *WhoFI 92, WhoIns 92*
**Raboy,** Sol 1920- *AmMWSc 92*
**Rabrich,** Marla Perper 1951- *WhoMW 92*
**Rabson,** Alan S 1926- *AmMWSc 92*
**Rabson,** Gustave 1920- *AmMWSc 92*
**Rabson,** Robert 1926- *AmMWSc 92*
**Rabson,** Thomas A 1932- *AmMWSc 92*
**Rabuck,** Bob *WhoAmP 91*
**Rabuck,** David Glenn *AmMWSc 92*
**Rabuka,** Sitiveni Ligamamada 1948- *IntWW 91*
**Rabukawaqa,** Josua Rasilau 1917- *IntWW 91, Who 92*
**Rabung,** John Russell 1943- *AmMWSc 92*
**Rabussay,** Dietmar Paul 1941- *AmMWSc 92*
**Raby,** Albert 1933-1988 *FacFETw*
**Raby,** Bruce Alan 1930- *AmMWSc 92*
**Raby,** Clyde T. 1934- *WhoBlA 92*
**Raby,** Derek 1927- *WrDr 92*
**Raby,** Stuart 1947- *AmMWSc 92*
**Raby,** Teddy Lee 1928- *WhoRel 92*
**Raby,** Victor Harry d1990 *Who 92N*
**Racca,** Romulus Hugh Bartholomeu 1927- *WhoFI 92*
**Raccah,** Paul M 1933- *AmMWSc 92*
**Race,** Ernest 1913-1963 *DcTwDes*
**Race,** George Justice 1926- *AmMWSc 92*
**Race,** Howard Everett 1918- *WhoAmP 91*
**Race,** Lisa Anne 1961- *WhoWest 92*
**Race,** Reg 1947- *Who 92*
**Race,** Ruth Ann *Who 92*
**Race,** Steve 1921- *Who 92*
**Race,** Stuart Rice 1926- *AmMWSc 92*
**Racette,** George William 1929- *AmMWSc 92*
**Racey,** Thomas James 1952- *AmMWSc 92*
**Rach,** Randolph Carl 1951- *AmMWSc 92*
**Rachal,** Patricia *DrAPF 91*
**Rachel,** Eric Mark 1954- *WhoEnt 92*
**Rachel,** Naomi *DrAPF 91*
**Rachele,** Henry 1929- *AmMWSc 92*
**Rachelle,** Tamar 1959- *WhoEnt 92*
**Racheter,** Donald Paul 1947- *WhoAmP 91, WhoMW 92*
**Rachev,** Svetlozar Todorov 1951- *WhoWest 92*
**Rachford,** Fred *DrAPF 91*
**Rachford,** Henry Herbert, Jr 1925- *AmMWSc 92*
**Rachford,** Thomas Milton 1942- *AmMWSc 92*
**Rachilde** 1860-1953 *FrenWW*
**Rachins,** Alan *WhoEnt 92*

**Rachinski,** Howard Dale 1951- *WhoWest 92*
**Rachinsky,** Joseph W 1946- *WhoIns 92*
**Rachinsky,** Michael Richard 1931- *AmMWSc 92*
**Rachkov,** Albert Ivanovich 1927- *IntWW 91*
**Rachleff,** Owen Spencer 1934- *WhoEnt 92*
**Rachleff,** Peter Jay 1951- *WhoMW 92*
**Rachlin,** Alan Sanders 1942- *WhoAmL 92*
**Rachlin,** Joseph Wolfe 1936- *AmMWSc 92*
**Rachlin,** Nahid *DrAPF 91*
**Rachlin,** Richard S. 1947- *WhoAmL 92*
**Rachlis,** Arnold Israel 1949- *WhoRel 92*
**Rachman,** Stanley Jack 1934- *WrDr 92*
**Rachmaninoff,** Sergei Vasilyevich 1873-1943 *FacFETw [port]*
**Rachmaninov,** Sergei 1873-1943 *NewAmDM*
**Rachmeler,** Martin 1928- *AmMWSc 92, WhoWest 92*
**Racic,** Frank-Josip 1947- *WhoEnt 92*
**Racicot,** Marc 1948- *WhoAmP 91*
**Racicot,** Marc F. 1948- *WhoAmL 92, WhoWest 92*
**Racicot,** Rachel I 1968- *WhoAmP 91*
**Racin,** Bonnie Mae Veronica 1945- *WhoMW 92*
**Racina,** Thom 1946- *WhoEnt 92, WhoWest 92*
**Racine,** Douglas A 1952- *WhoAmP 91*
**Racine,** Jean Claude B. *WhoFI 92*
**Racine,** Michel Louis 1945- *AmMWSc 92*
**Racine,** Norman O 1923- *WhoAmP 91*
**Racine,** Rene 1939- *AmMWSc 92*
**Racine,** Richard Anthony 1953- *WhoEnt 92*
**Raciszewski,** Zbigniew 1922- *AmMWSc 92*
**Rack,** Edward Paul 1931- *AmMWSc 92*
**Rack,** Henry Johann 1942- *AmMWSc 92*
**Rackar,** Richard Mathew 1945- *WhoFI 92*
**Racke,** Kenneth David 1959- *AmMWSc 92*
**Racker,** Efraim d1991 *NewYTBS 91 [port]*
**Racker,** Efraim 1913- *AmMWSc 92, IntWW 91*
**Rackham,** Arthur 1867-1939 *FacFETw, TwCPaSc*
**Rackham,** John 1916-1976 *TwCSFW 91*
**Rackis,** Joseph John 1922- *AmMWSc 92*
**Rackleff,** Owen Spencer 1934- *WhoEnt 92*
**Rackley,** H Wayne 1937- *WhoIns 92*
**Rackley,** Lurma M. 1949- *WhoBlA 92*
**Rackman,** Joseph Robert 1948- *WhoRel 92*
**Rackmil,** Milton R. *IntMPA 92*
**Rackoff,** Jerome S 1946- *AmMWSc 92*
**Rackow,** Eric C *AmMWSc 92*
**Rackow,** Herbert 1917- *AmMWSc 92*
**Racle,** Fred Arnold 1932- *AmMWSc 92*
**Racobs,** Peter E. 1957- *WhoAmL 92*
**Racotta,** Radu Gheorghe 1930- *AmMWSc 92*
**Ractliffe,** Robert Edward George 1943- *WhoFI 92*
**Racunas,** Bernard J 1943- *AmMWSc 92*
**Racusen,** David 1925- *AmMWSc 92*
**Racusen,** Richard Harry 1948- *AmMWSc 92*
**Raczynski,** Edward 1891- *Who 92*
**Rad,** Franz N 1943- *AmMWSc 92*
**Rada,** Alexander 1923- *WhoWest 92*
**Rada,** Heath Kenneth *WhoRel 92*
**Radabaugh,** Dennis Charles 1942- *AmMWSc 92*
**Radabaugh,** Mike *WhoAmL 92*
**Radabaugh,** Robert Eugene 1913- *AmMWSc 92*
**Radaker,** Kevin Paul 1956- *WhoMW 92*
**Radanovics,** Charles 1932- *AmMWSc 92, WhoMW 92*
**Radasky,** David Jacob 1948- *WhoAmL 92*
**Radatz,** Charles Arthur 1943- *WhoEnt 92*
**Radauskas,** Henrikas 1910-1970 *LiExTwC*
**Radavich,** David *DrAPF 91*
**Radavich,** David Allen 1949- *WhoEnt 92*
**Radbill,** John R 1932- *AmMWSc 92*
**Radcliff-Umstead,** Douglas 1944- *WrDr 92*
**Radcliffe,** Alec 1917- *AmMWSc 92*
**Radcliffe,** Ann 1764-1823 *RfGEnL 91*
**Radcliffe,** Anthony Frank 1933- *Who 92*
**Radcliffe,** Aubrey 1941- *WhoBlA 92*
**Radcliffe,** Charles W 1925- *WhoAmP 91*
**Radcliffe,** Dale W 1949- *WhoAmP 91*
**Radcliffe,** Edward B 1936- *AmMWSc 92*
**Radcliffe,** Francis Charles Joseph 1939- *Who 92*
**Radcliffe,** Gerald Eugene 1923- *WhoAmL 92, WhoMW 92*
**Radcliffe,** Hugh John Reginald Joseph 1911- *Who 92*
**Radcliffe,** Percy 1916- *IntWW 91, Who 92*
**Radcliffe,** R Stephen 1945- *WhoIns 92*
**Radcliffe,** Robert James 1940- *WhoRel 92*
**Radcliffe,** S Victor 1927- *AmMWSc 92*
**Radcliffe,** Sebastian Everard 1972- *Who 92*
**Radcliffe,** Timothy Peter Joseph 1945- *Who 92*
**Radcliffe,** William Louis 1958- *WhoAmL 92*
**Radclyffe,** Charles Edward M. *Who 92*
**Radd,** F J 1921- *AmMWSc 92*
**Radda,** George K. 1936- *Who 92*
**Radda,** George Karoly 1936- *IntWW 91*
**Raddall,** Thomas 1903- *BenetAL 91*
**Raddall,** Thomas Head 1903- *ConNov 91, WrDr 92*
**Raddatz,** Leslie 1911- *WhoEnt 92*
**Radde,** Leonard Carl 1935- *WhoRel 92*
**Radden,** James David, Sr 1945- *WhoAmP 91*
**Radden,** Thelma Gibson 1903- *WhoBlA 92*
**Radding,** Andrew 1944- *WhoAmL 92*
**Radding,** Charles Meyer 1930- *AmMWSc 92*
**Radebaugh,** Ray 1939- *AmMWSc 92, WhoWest 92*
**Radecki,** Anthony Eugene 1939- *WhoMW 92*
**Radecki,** Dane Joseph 1950- *WhoRel 92*
**Radek,** Karl Bernardovich 1885-1940? *FacFETw*
**Radek,** Karl Berngardovich 1885-1939 *SovUnBD*
**Radeka,** Veljko 1930- *AmMWSc 92*
**Radel,** Glenn Michael 1957- *WhoEnt 92*
**Radel,** Stanley Robert 1932- *AmMWSc 92*
**Radelfinger,** Frank Gustave 1870?-1904 *BiInAmS*
**Radell,** Sally Anne 1957- *WhoEnt 92*
**Rademacher,** Franz 1906-1973 *EncTR 91*
**Rademacher,** Hollis William 1935- *WhoFI 92*
**Rademacher,** Leo Edward 1926- *AmMWSc 92*
**Rademacher,** Robert Hollis 1962- *WhoMW 92*
**Rademacher,** Robert Paul 1942- *WhoRel 92*
**Rademaker Grunewald,** Augusto Hamann 1905- *IntWW 91*
**Raden,** Louis 1929- *WhoFI 92, WhoMW 92*
**Rader,** Charles Allen 1932- *AmMWSc 92*
**Rader,** Charles Phillip 1935- *AmMWSc 92*
**Rader,** Dick Allen 1940- *WhoRel 92*
**Rader,** Dotson *DrAPF 91*
**Rader,** Douglas Lee 1944- *WhoWest 92*
**Rader,** Elizabeth 1951- *WhoFI 92*
**Rader,** Joan Sperry 1934- *WhoAmP 91*
**Rader,** John L 1927- *WhoAmP 91*
**Rader,** Larry William 1936- *WhoAmL 92*
**Rader,** Louis T 1911- *AmMWSc 92*
**Rader,** Paul Alexander 1934- *WhoRel 92*
**Rader,** Paul Daniel 1879-1938 *RelLAm 91*
**Rader,** Paul MacFarland 1939- *WhoWest 92*
**Rader,** Ralph Wilson 1930- *WhoWest 92*
**Rader,** Randall R 1949- *WhoAmP 91*
**Rader,** Randall Ray 1949- *WhoAmL 92*
**Rader,** Ronald Alan 1951- *AmMWSc 92*
**Rader,** Sharon Zimmerman 1939- *WhoRel 92*
**Rader,** Steven Palmer 1952- *WhoAmP 91*
**Rader,** William Austin 1916- *AmMWSc 92*
**Rader,** William Donald 1929- *WhoMW 92*
**Rader,** William Ernest 1916- *AmMWSc 92*
**Rader,** William Sherman 1921- *WhoAmL 92*
**Radermacher,** Reinhard 1952- *AmMWSc 92*
**Radewagen,** Amata Coleman 1947- *WhoAmP 91*
**Radewagen,** Fred 1944- *WhoAmP 91*
**Radewald,** John Dale 1929- *AmMWSc 92*
**Radey,** Richard Greger 1933- *WhoFI 92*
**Radez,** David Charles 1946- *WhoFI 92*
**Radford,** Alan 1940- *AmMWSc 92*
**Radford,** Albert Ernest 1918- *AmMWSc 92*
**Radford,** Courtenay Arthur Ralegh 1900- *IntWW 91, Who 92*
**Radford,** David Clarke 1954- *AmMWSc 92*
**Radford,** David Eugene 1943- *AmMWSc 92*
**Radford,** Edward Parish 1922- *AmMWSc 92*
**Radford,** Herschel Donald 1911- *AmMWSc 92*
**Radford,** Joseph 1918- *Who 92*
**Radford,** Kenneth Charles 1941- *AmMWSc 92*
**Radford,** Loren E 1928- *AmMWSc 92*
**Radford,** Norman DePue, Jr. 1943- *WhoAmL 92*
**Radford,** Ralegh *Who 92*
**Radford,** Richard F. *DrAPF 91*
**Radford,** Robert Edwin 1921- *Who 92*
**Radford,** Ronald 1916- *Who 92*
**Radford,** Terence 1939- *AmMWSc 92*
**Radforth,** Norman William 1912- *AmMWSc 92*
**Radha,** Sivananda 1911- *ConAu 36NR, WhoRel 92*
**Radha,** Swami Sivananda *ConAu 36NR*
**Radhakrishnamurthy,** Bhandaru 1928- *AmMWSc 92*
**Radhakrishnan,** Chittur Venkitasubhan 1937- *AmMWSc 92*
**Radi,** Essam Radi Abd al-Hamid *IntWW 91*
**Radice,** Barbara *ConAu 133*
**Radice,** Edward Albert 1907- *Who 92*
**Radice,** Frank J. 1949- *WhoEnt 92*
**Radice,** Gary Paul 1952- *AmMWSc 92*
**Radice,** Giles Heneage 1936- *Who 92*
**Radice,** Italo de Lisle 1911- *Who 92*
**Radice,** James Richard 1946- *WhoEnt 92*
**Radick,** Jerry Jack 1935- *WhoEnt 92*
**Radigan,** C. Raymond 1935- *WhoAmL 92*
**Radigan,** Dennis M 1938- *WhoAmP 91*
**Radigan,** J Joseph 1929- *WhoAmP 91*
**Radiguet,** Raymond 1903-1923 *GuFrLit 1*
**Radillo,** Eduardo, Jr. 1928- *WhoHisp 92*
**Radimer,** Kenneth John 1920- *AmMWSc 92*
**Radin,** Charles Lewis 1945- *AmMWSc 92*
**Radin,** Doris *DrAPF 91*
**Radin,** Eric Leon 1934- *AmMWSc 92*
**Radin,** John William 1944- *AmMWSc 92*
**Radin,** Mitchell Ellis 1955- *WhoAmL 92*
**Radin,** Nathan 1919- *AmMWSc 92*
**Radin,** Norman Samuel 1920- *AmMWSc 92*
**Radin,** Paul 1913- *IntMPA 92*
**Radin,** Ruth Yaffe 1938- *WrDr 92*
**Radin,** Shelden Henry 1936- *AmMWSc 92*
**Radinsky,** Joseph Ruben 1936- *WhoRel 92*
**Radio,** Thomas John 1953- *WhoAmL 92*
**Radishchev,** Aleksandr Nikolayevich 1749-1802 *BlkwCEP*
**Radisson,** Pierre Esprit 1636-1710? *BenetAL 91*
**Raditsa,** Bogdan 1904- *LiExTwC*
**Radji,** Parviz Camran 1936- *Who 92*
**Radke,** Dale Lee 1933- *WhoMW 92, WhoRel 92*
**Radke,** Frederick Herbert 1923- *AmMWSc 92*
**Radke,** Jan Rodger 1942- *WhoMW 92*
**Radke,** Lawrence Frederick 1942- *AmMWSc 92*
**Radke,** Rodney Owen 1942- *AmMWSc 92*
**Radke,** William John 1947- *AmMWSc 92*
**Radkowsky,** Alvin 1915- *AmMWSc 92*
**Radler,** Barbara Walsh 1957- *WhoAmL 92*
**Radley,** Eric John 1917- *WrDr 92*
**Radley,** Sheila *IntAu&W 91X, WrDr 92*
**Radley-Smith,** Eric John *Who 92*
**Radloff,** Harold David 1937- *AmMWSc 92*
**Radloff,** Roger James 1940- *AmMWSc 92*
**Radloff,** Ronald Francis 1957- *WhoMW 92*
**Radlov,** Sergey Ernestovich 1892-1958 *SovUnBD*
**Radlove,** Shirley Kagan 1939- *WhoMW 92*
**Radlow,** James *AmMWSc 92*
**Radmacher,** Rebecca Sue 1959- *WhoWest 92*
**Radmer,** Michael John 1945- *WhoAmL 92, WhoMW 92*
**Radner,** Rebecca *DrAPF 91*
**Radner,** Roy 1927- *AmMWSc 92, IntWW 91, WhoFI 92*
**Radnitz,** Alan 1944- *AmMWSc 92*
**Radnitz,** Brad 1930- *WhoEnt 92*
**Radnitz,** Robert B. 1924- *IntMPA 92*
**Radnofsky,** Kenneth *WhoEnt 92*
**Radnor,** Earl of 1927- *Who 92*
**Radnor,** Alan T. 1946- *WhoAmL 92*
**Rado,** George Tibor 1917- *AmMWSc 92*
**Radojevic,** Danilo *WhoEnt 92*
**Radomski,** Jack London 1920- *AmMWSc 92*
**Radomski,** Robyn Lynn 1954- *WhoMW 92*
**Radon,** Jenik Richard 1946- *WhoAmL 92, WhoFI 92*
**Radonovich,** Lewis Joseph 1944- *AmMWSc 92*
**Radosevich,** Lee George 1938- *AmMWSc 92*
**Radoski,** Henry Robert 1936- *AmMWSc 92*
**Radovich,** Donald 1932- *WhoWest 92*
**Radovsky,** Frank Jay 1929- *AmMWSc 92*
**Radovsky,** Vicki Jo 1952- *WhoWest 92*
**Radowitz,** Stuart P. *DrAPF 91*
**Radspinner,** Diana Braiden 1942- *WhoEnt 92*
**Radspinner,** John Asa 1917- *AmMWSc 92*
**Radtke,** Douglas Dean 1938- *AmMWSc 92*
**Radtke,** Gunter 1925- *IntAu&W 91*
**Radtke,** Randall James 1951- *WhoAmP 91*
**Radtke,** Rosetta *DrAPF 91*
**Radtke,** Schrade Fred 1919- *AmMWSc 92*
**Radua,** Maikali *WhoRel 92*
**Raduchel,** William James 1946- *WhoFI 92*
**Radulescu,** Gheorghe 1914- *IntWW 91*
**Raduns,** Kerry Bruce 1956- *WhoWest 92*
**Radwan,** Mohamed Ahmed 1926- *AmMWSc 92*
**Radwanska,** Ewa 1938- *AmMWSc 92*
**Radway,** Laurence Ingram 1919- *WhoAmP 91*
**Radwin,** Howard Martin 1931- *AmMWSc 92*
**Radys,** Arvin Anthony 1942- *WhoWest 92*
**Radys,** Raymond George 1940- *WhoWest 92*
**Radyukevich,** Leonid Vladimirovich 1932- *IntWW 91*
**Radzhabov,** Nazir Radzhabovich 1939- *IntWW 91*
**Radzialowski,** Frederick M 1939- *AmMWSc 92*
**Radzicki,** Michael Joseph 1958- *WhoFI 92*
**Radziemski,** Leon Joseph 1937- *AmMWSc 92*
**Radzik,** Mark Alan 1965- *WhoFI 92*
**Radzikowski,** M St Anthony 1919- *AmMWSc 92*
**Radzinowicz,** Leon 1906- *IntWW 91, Who 92, WrDr 92*
**Radzinsky,** Edvard Stanislavovich 1936- *IntWW 91*
**Radziwill,** Antoni Henryk 1775-1833 *NewAmDM*
**Rae,** Alexander Lindsay 1923- *IntWW 91*
**Rae,** Allan Alexander Sinclair 1925- *Who 92*
**Rae,** Bob 1948- *CurBio 91 [port]*
**Rae,** Charles Robert Angus d1990 *Who 92N*
**Rae,** Henrietta 1859-1928 *TwCPaSc*
**Rae,** Henry Edward Grant 1925- *Who 92*
**Rae,** Hugh C. 1935- *WrDr 92*
**Rae,** Hugh Crauford 1935- *IntAu&W 91*
**Rae,** John 1931- *Who 92*
**Rae,** John 1934- *WhoEnt 92*
**Rae,** John 1942- *Who 92*
**Rae,** John Malcolm 1931- *IntAu&W 91, WrDr 92*
**Rae,** Matthew Sanderson, Jr. 1922- *WhoAmL 92, WhoAmP 91, WhoFI 92, WhoWest 92*
**Rae,** Peter Murdoch MacPhail 1944- *AmMWSc 92*
**Rae,** Robert Keith 1948- *Who 92*
**Rae,** Robert Wright 1914- *Who 92*
**Rae,** Ronald Arthur R. *Who 92*
**Rae,** Stephen 1944- *AmMWSc 92*
**Rae,** Wallace 1914- *Who 92*
**Rae,** William H, Jr 1927- *AmMWSc 92*
**Rae,** William J 1929- *AmMWSc 92*
**Rae-Grant,** Quentin A 1929- *AmMWSc 92*
**Rae Smith,** David Douglas 1919- *Who 92*
**Rae-Venter,** Barbara 1948- *AmMWSc 92*
**Raeburn,** Andrew Harvey 1933- *WhoFI 92*
**Raeburn,** Antonia 1934- *WrDr 92*
**Raeburn,** Boyd 1913-1966 *NewAmDM*
**Raeburn,** David Antony 1927- *Who 92*
**Raeburn,** Digby *Who 92*
**Raeburn,** John Ross 1912- *Who 92*
**Raeburn,** Michael Edward Norman 1954- *Who 92*
**Raeburn,** William Digby 1915- *Who 92*
**Raedeke,** Linda Dismore 1950- *WhoWest 92*
**Raeder,** Erich 1876-1960 *EncTR 91 [port]*
**Raeder,** Myrna Sharon 1947- *WhoAmL 92*
**Raedler,** Dorothy Florence 1917- *WhoEnt 92*
**Raeff,** Marc 1923- *WrDr 92*
**Rael,** Eppie David 1943- *AmMWSc 92*
**Rael,** Henry Sylvester 1928- *WhoWest 92*
**Rael,** Juan Jose 1948- *WhoHisp 92*
**Rael,** Phil 1921- *WhoHisp 92*
**Rael,** Selimo C. 1946- *WhoHisp 92*
**Raemer,** Harold R 1924- *AmMWSc 92*
**Raeschild,** Sheila *DrAPF 91*
**Raese,** John Reeves 1950- *WhoAmP 91*
**Raese,** John Thomas 1930- *AmMWSc 92*
**Raeside,** James Inglis 1926- *AmMWSc 92*
**Raesly,** Barboura Genevieve 1932- *WhoAmL 92*
**Raess,** Beat Urs 1945- *WhoMW 92*
**Raether,** Edward W. 1936- *WhoMW 92*
**Raether,** Manfred 1927- *AmMWSc 92*
**Raetz,** Christian Rudolf Hubert 1946- *AmMWSc 92*
**Raetz,** Greg Christie 1949- *WhoAmP 91*
**Rafael,** Gideon 1913- *IntWW 91, Who 92*
**Rafael,** Ruth Kelson 1929- *WhoWest 92*
**Rafajko,** Robert Richard 1931- *AmMWSc 92, WhoFI 92*
**Rafanelli,** Kenneth R 1937- *AmMWSc 92*
**Rafeedie,** Edward 1929- *WhoAmL 92, WhoWest 92*
**Rafeld,** Frederick James 1940- *WhoMW 92*
**Rafelski,** Johann 1950- *AmMWSc 92, WhoWest 92*
**Rafelson,** Bob 1933- *IntDcF 2-2 [port], IntMPA 92, IntWW 91, WhoEnt 92*
**Rafelson,** Max Emanuel, Jr 1921- *AmMWSc 92, WhoMW 92*
**Raff,** Allan Maurice 1923- *AmMWSc 92*
**Raff,** Daniel Martin Gorodetsky 1951- *WhoFI 92*
**Raff,** Hershel 1953- *AmMWSc 92*
**Raff,** Howard V 1950- *AmMWSc 92*
**Raff,** Joachim 1822-1882 *NewAmDM*
**Raff,** Lionel M 1934- *AmMWSc 92*

**Raff**, Martin Charles 1938- *Who 92*
**Raff**, Martin Jay 1937- *AmMWSc 92*
**Raff**, Morton Spencer 1923- *AmMWSc 92*
**Raff**, Rudolf Albert 1941- *AmMWSc 92*
**Raff**, Samuel J 1920- *AmMWSc 92*
**Raffa**, Dominic C 1918- *WhoAmP 91*
**Raffa**, Joseph *DrAPF 91*
**Raffa**, Kenneth Francis 1950- *WhoMW 92*
**Raffa**, Robert B *AmMWSc 92*
**Raffaelli**, Jean-Francois 1850-1924 *ThHEIm*
**Raffalovich**, George 1880- *ScFEYrs*
**Raffan**, Keith William Twort 1949- *Who 92*
**Raffat**, Donne *LiExTwC*
**Raffauf**, Robert Francis 1916- *AmMWSc 92*
**Raffel**, Burton *DrAPF 91*
**Raffel**, Burton Nathan 1928- *IntAu&W 91*
**Raffel**, Charles Michael 1950- *WhoRel 92*
**Raffel**, Jack I 1930- *AmMWSc 92*
**Raffel**, Sidney 1911- *AmMWSc 92*
**Raffeld**, David *DrAPF 91*
**Raffell**, Donald Howard 1919- *WhoEnt 92*
**Raffelson**, Harold 1920- *AmMWSc 92*
**Raffelson**, Michael 1946- *WhoFI 92*
**Raffenetti**, Richard Charles 1942- *AmMWSc 92*
**Raffensperger**, Edgar M 1926- *AmMWSc 92*
**Raffensperger**, Edward Cowell 1914- *AmMWSc 92*
**Rafferty**, Alexander Fanning, Jr. 1954- *WhoEnt 92*
**Rafferty**, Anne Judith *Who 92*
**Rafferty**, Bob 1964- *WhoAmP 91*
**Rafferty**, Edson Howard 1943- *WhoFI 92*
**Rafferty**, Frances 1922- *IntMPA 92*
**Rafferty**, Frank Thomas 1925- *AmMWSc 92*
**Rafferty**, James Paul 1952- *WhoFI 92*
**Rafferty**, John Knox 1938- *WhoAmP 91*
**Rafferty**, Joseph Anstice *Who 92*
**Rafferty**, Keen Alexander, Jr 1926- *AmMWSc 92*
**Rafferty**, Kevin *IntAu&W 91*
**Rafferty**, Kevin Lawrence 1933- *Who 92*
**Rafferty**, Kevin Robert 1944- *Who 92*
**Rafferty**, Michael William 1961- *WhoFI 92*
**Rafferty**, Nancy S 1930- *AmMWSc 92*
**Rafferty**, Paul Francis 1959- *WhoAmL 92*
**Rafferty**, S. S. 1930- *WrDr 92*
**Raffi** *SmATA 68*
**Raffin**, Deborah 1953- *IntMPA 92, WhoEnt 92*
**Raffini**, James Peter 1941- *WhoMW 92*
**Raffler**, Hans 1930- *WhoIns 92*
**Raffo**, Carlos 1927- *Who 92*
**Rafi**, Mohammed 1944- *IntWW 91*
**Rafinesque**, Constantine Samuel 1783-1840 *BenetAL 91, BiInAmS*
**Rafkin**, Louise *DrAPF 91*
**Rafla**, Sameer 1930- *AmMWSc 92*
**Rafn**, Eleanor Yolanda 1932- *WhoWest 92*
**Rafols**, Jose Antonio 1943- *AmMWSc 92*
**Rafsanjani**, Hojatoleslam Hashemi 1934- *IntWW 91*
**Raft**, George 1895-1980 *FacFETw*
**Raft**, Steven Howard 1960- *WhoWest 92*
**Raftelis**, George Anthony 1947- *WhoFI 92*
**Rafter**, Gale William 1925- *AmMWSc 92*
**Rafter**, George W 1851-1907 *BiInAmS*
**Raftery**, J. Patrick *WhoEnt 92*
**Raftery**, Peter Albert 1929- *IntWW 91, Who 92*
**Raftery**, William John 1916- *WhoRel 92*
**Raftis**, Alkis 1942- *WhoEnt 92*
**Raftopoulos**, Demetrios D 1926- *AmMWSc 92, WhoMW 92*
**Rafuse**, John Laurence 1936- *WhoWest 92*
**Rafuse**, Robert P 1932- *AmMWSc 92*
**Ragab**, Mohamed Mahmoud 1952- *WhoWest 92*
**Ragadio**, Antonio A. 1916- *WhoWest 92*
**Ragaini**, Richard Charles 1942- *AmMWSc 92*
**Ragalis**, John Leonard 1962- *WhoMW 92*
**Ragan**, Barbara Mary 1949- *WhoEnt 92*
**Ragan**, Charles Ellis, III 1944- *AmMWSc 92*
**Ragan**, Charles Ransom 1947- *WhoAmL 92*
**Ragan**, David Michael 1955- *WhoMW 92*
**Ragan**, Donal Mackenzie 1929- *AmMWSc 92*
**Ragan**, Harold J *WhoAmP 91*
**Ragan**, Harvey Albert 1929- *AmMWSc 92*
**Ragan**, Hugh *WhoAmP 91*
**Ragan**, James *DrAPF 91*
**Ragan**, James Francis 1949- *WhoFI 92*
**Ragan**, James Joseph 1944- *WhoEnt 92*
**Ragan**, John Charles 1960- *WhoRel 92*
**Ragan**, Joseph Douglas 1940- *WhoAmP 91*
**Ragan**, Robert Malcolm 1932- *AmMWSc 92*
**Ragan**, Seaborn Bryant Timmons 1929- *WhoFI 92*
**Ragatz**, John Ballard 1940- *WhoWest 92*
**Ragatz**, Thomas George 1934- *WhoAmL 92, WhoMW 92*
**Ragen**, Brian Abel 1958- *WhoMW 92*
**Ragent**, Boris 1924- *AmMWSc 92*
**Ragep**, F Jamil 1950- *AmMWSc 92*
**Rager**, Marianne Margaret 1967- *WhoWest 92*
**Rager**, Richard Scott 1948- *WhoIns 92*
**Ragg**, Theodore David Butler 1919- *Who 92*
**Ragged**, Hyder 1863-1940 *ScFEYrs*
**Raggi**, Reena 1951- *WhoAmL 92*
**Raggio**, Carl W *WhoAmP 91*
**Raggio**, Kenneth Gaylord 1949- *WhoAmL 92*
**Raggio**, William J 1926- *WhoAmP 91*
**Raggio**, William John 1926- *WhoWest 92*
**Raghavachari**, Krishnan 1953- *AmMWSc 92*
**Raghavan**, Pramila *AmMWSc 92*
**Raghavan**, Rajagopal 1943- *AmMWSc 92*
**Raghavan**, Ramaswamy Srinivasa 1937- *AmMWSc 92*
**Raghavan**, Srikant 1950- *WhoMW 92*
**Raghavan**, Srinivasa 1940- *AmMWSc 92*
**Raghavan**, Thirukkannamangai E S 1940- *AmMWSc 92*
**Raghavan**, Valayamghat 1931- *AmMWSc 92, WhoMW 92*
**Ragheb**, Hussein S 1924- *AmMWSc 92*
**Raghuveer**, Mysore R 1957- *AmMWSc 92*
**Raghuvir**, Nuggehalli Narayana 1930- *AmMWSc 92*
**Ragins**, Herzl 1929- *AmMWSc 92*
**Ragins**, Naomi *AmMWSc 92*
**Ragir**, John Arthur 1950- *WhoMW 92*
**Raglan**, Baron 1927- *Who 92*
**Ragland**, Alwine Mulhearn 1913- *WhoAmL 92*
**Ragland**, John Leonard 1931- *AmMWSc 92*
**Ragland**, Kathryn Marie 1948- *WhoEnt 92*
**Ragland**, Michael Steven 1958- *WhoBlA 92*
**Ragland**, Paul C 1936- *AmMWSc 92*
**Ragland**, Robert Allen 1954- *WhoAmL 92*
**Ragland**, Robert Oliver 1931- *IntMPA 92*
**Ragland**, Samuel Connelly 1946- *WhoWest 92*
**Ragland**, Sherman Leon, II 1962- *WhoBlA 92*
**Ragland**, Tommy 1949- *WhoAmP 91*
**Ragland**, William Lauman, III 1934- *AmMWSc 92*
**Ragland**, William McKenzie, Jr. 1960- *WhoAmL 92*
**Ragland**, Wylheme Harold 1946- *WhoBlA 92, WhoRel 92*
**Ragle**, John Linn 1933- *AmMWSc 92*
**Ragle**, Richard Harrison 1923- *AmMWSc 92*
**Ragni**, Gerome d1991 *NewYTBS 91 [port]*
**Ragni**, Gerome 1942-1991 *ConAu 134*
**Ragon**, Michel 1924- *IntAu&W 91, IntWW 91*
**Ragone**, David Vincent 1936- *AmMWSc 92*
**Ragone**, Lourdes Margarita 1939- *WhoHisp 92*
**Ragotzkie**, Robert Austin 1924- *AmMWSc 92*
**Ragozin**, David Lawrence 1941- *AmMWSc 92*
**Ragsdale**, Carl Vandyke 1925- *WhoEnt 92*
**Ragsdale**, Charles Lea Chester 1929- *WhoBlA 92*
**Ragsdale**, David Willard 1952- *AmMWSc 92*
**Ragsdale**, Diane 1952- *WhoAmP 91*
**Ragsdale**, Edward Floyd 1939- *WhoAmP 91*
**Ragsdale**, George Henry d1895 *BiInAmS*
**Ragsdale**, George Robinson 1936- *WhoAmL 92*
**Ragsdale**, Harvey Larimore 1940- *AmMWSc 92*
**Ragsdale**, Kathleen Mary 1964- *WhoWest 92*
**Ragsdale**, Ken 1967- *WhoEnt 92*
**Ragsdale**, Lincoln Johnson 1926- *WhoBlA 92, WhoFI 92*
**Ragsdale**, Nancy Nealy 1938- *AmMWSc 92*
**Ragsdale**, Paul B. 1945- *WhoBlA 92*
**Ragsdale**, Paul Burdett 1945- *WhoAmP 91*
**Ragsdale**, Ronald O 1932- *AmMWSc 92*
**Ragsdell**, Kenneth Martin 1942- *AmMWSc 92*
**Raguse**, Craig Burton-Kirkham 1957- *WhoEnt 92*
**Raha**, Chitta Ranjan 1926- *AmMWSc 92*
**Rahal**, Leo James 1939- *AmMWSc 92*
**Rahal**, Mary G 1946- *WhoIns 92*
**Rahall**, Nick J. 1949- *AlmAP 92 [port]*
**Rahall**, Nick Joe, II 1949- *WhoAmP 91, WhoFI 92*
**Raham**, Richard Gary 1946- *WhoEnt 92*
**Rahaman**, Abdool 1931- *WhoRel 92*
**Rahe**, James Edward 1939- *AmMWSc 92*
**Rahe**, Maurice Hampton 1944- *AmMWSc 92*
**Rahe**, Richard Henry 1936- *AmMWSc 92*
**Raheel**, Mastura 1938- *AmMWSc 92*
**Raher**, Richard Ray 1949- *WhoRel 92*
**Rahfeldt**, Daryl Gene 1947- *WhoRel 92*
**Rahimi**, Mansour 1954- *WhoWest 92*
**Rahimtoola**, Habib Ibrahim d1991 *Who 92N*
**Rahimtoola**, Shahbudin Hooseinally 1931- *AmMWSc 92*
**Rahlmann**, Donald Frederick 1923- *AmMWSc 92*
**Rahm**, David Alan 1941- *WhoAmL 92, WhoFI 92*
**Rahm**, David Charles 1927- *AmMWSc 92*
**Rahm**, Susan Berkman 1943- *WhoAmL 92*
**Rahman**, Abdul 1903-1990 *AnObit 1990, CurBio 91N, FacFETw*
**Rahman**, Abul Khayer Mohammad Matiur 1952- *WhoFI 92*
**Rahman**, Ahmed Assem 1940- *WhoMW 92*
**Rahman**, Hamood-ur 1910- *IntWW 91*
**Rahman**, Janab M. Matiur *IntWW 91*
**Rahman**, Mahdi Abdul 1942- *WhoBlA 92*
**Rahman**, Md Azizur 1941- *AmMWSc 92*
**Rahman**, Mizanur 1932- *AmMWSc 92*
**Rahman**, Mohammad Azizur 1925- *IntWW 91*
**Rahman**, Mujibur 1920-1975 *FacFETw*
**Rahman**, Talat Shahnaz 1948- *AmMWSc 92*
**Rahman**, Tunku Abdul *IntWW 91*
**Rahman**, Yueh Erh 1930- *AmMWSc 92*
**Rahman Khan**, Ataur 1905- *IntWW 91*
**Rahmani**, Cherif 1945- *IntWW 91*
**Rahmat-Samii**, Yahya 1948- *AmMWSc 92*
**Rahmmings**, Keith *DrAPF 91*
**Rahn**, Cynthia Lee 1958- *WhoMW 92*
**Rahn**, Hermann *IntWW 91N*
**Rahn**, Hermann 1912- *AmMWSc 92*
**Rahn**, Joan Elma 1929- *AmMWSc 92*
**Rahn**, John 1944- *WhoEnt 92*
**Rahn**, Kenneth A 1940- *AmMWSc 92*
**Rahn**, Lawrence Joseph 1951- *WhoFI 92*
**Rahn**, Muriel 1911-1961 *NotBlAW 92*
**Rahn**, Perry H 1936- *AmMWSc 92*
**Rahn**, Perry Hendricks 1936- *WhoMW 92*
**Rahn**, Pete Kevin 1954- *WhoAmP 91*
**Rahner**, Karl 1904-1984 *DcEcMov, FacFETw*
**Raho**, George M. *WhoEnt 92*
**Raht**, August Wilhelm 1843-1916 *BiInAmS*
**Rahtjen**, Bruce Donald 1933- *WhoRel 92*
**Rahtz**, Philip Arthur 1921- *Who 92*
**Rahv**, Philip 1908-1973 *BenetAL 91*
**Rahwan**, Ralf George 1941- *AmMWSc 92*
**Rai**, Amarendra Kumar 1952- *AmMWSc 92*
**Rai**, Chander Mohan 1943- *WhoWest 92*
**Rai**, Charanjit 1929- *AmMWSc 92*
**Rai**, Dhanpat 1943- *AmMWSc 92*
**Rai**, Indra Bahadur 1927- *IntAu&W 91*
**Rai**, Iqbal Singh 1936- *AmMWSc 92*
**Rai**, Kanti R 1932- *AmMWSc 92*
**Rai**, Karamjit Singh 1931- *AmMWSc 92*
**Raia**, Joseph S *WhoAmP 91*
**Raible**, Peter Spilman 1929- *WhoRel 92, WhoWest 92*
**Raible**, Robert H 1935- *AmMWSc 92*
**Raibley**, Parvin Rudolph 1926- *WhoMW 92*
**Raica**, Robert 1954- *WhoAmP 91*
**Raich**, Henry 1919- *AmMWSc 92*
**Raich**, John Carl 1937- *AmMWSc 92*
**Raich**, William Judd 1927- *AmMWSc 92*
**Raiche**, Maureen E *WhoAmP 91*
**Raiche**, Robert Edward 1937- *WhoAmP 91*
**Raichel**, Daniel R 1935- *AmMWSc 92*
**Raichle**, Marcus Edward 1937- *AmMWSc 92*
**Raider**, Stanley Irwin 1934- *AmMWSc 92*
**Raidi** 1938- *IntWW 91*
**Raieff**, Josef *WhoEnt 92*
**Raiford**, Morgan B 1912- *AmMWSc 92*
**Raiford**, Ralph Michael 1945- *WhoAmL 92*
**Raiford**, Roger Lee 1942- *WhoBlA 92*
**Raigoza**, Jaime 1937- *WhoHisp 92*
**Raihall**, Denis T 1941- *WhoIns 92*
**Raihn**, Kurt Francis 1962- *WhoWest 92*
**Raijman**, Luisa J 1934- *AmMWSc 92*
**Raikes**, Charles FitzGerald 1930- *WhoAmL 92, WhoFI 92*
**Raikes**, Iwan 1921- *Who 92*
**Raikh**, Zinaida Nikolaevna 1894-1939 *SovUnBD*
**Raikhel**, Natasha V *AmMWSc 92*
**Raikkonen**, Erkki Aleksanteri 1900-1961 *BiDExR*
**Raikow**, Radmila Boruvka 1939- *AmMWSc 92*
**Raikow**, Robert Jay 1939- *AmMWSc 92*
**Railsback**, Steve 1948- *IntMPA 92*
**Railsback**, Tom 1932- *WhoAmP 91*
**Railton**, Mary 1906- *Who 92*
**Railton**, Ruth 1915- *Who 92*
**Railton**, William Scott 1935- *WhoAmL 92*
**Raimi**, Ralph Alexis 1924- *AmMWSc 92*
**Raimi**, Sam 1959- *IntMPA 92*
**Raimo**, Angela Maria 1939- *WhoAmL 92*
**Raimond**, Jean-Bernard 1926- *IntWW 91*
**Raimondi**, Albert Anthony 1925- *AmMWSc 92*
**Raimondi**, Anthony John 1928- *AmMWSc 92*
**Raimondi**, Peter John, III 1955- *WhoFI 92*
**Raimondi**, Pietro 1929- *AmMWSc 92*
**Raimondi**, Ruggero 1941- *IntWW 91, NewAmDM*
**Rain**, Allan Beaton 1940- *WhoMW 92*
**Raina**, Ashok K 1942- *AmMWSc 92*
**Rainal**, Attilio Joseph 1930- *AmMWSc 92*
**Rainbird**, George 1905-1986 *ConAu 133*
**Rainbolt**, David Eugene 1956- *WhoFI 92*
**Rainbolt**, Mary Louise 1925- *AmMWSc 92*
**Rainbow**, Andrew James 1943- *AmMWSc 92*
**Rainbow**, Conrad 1926- *Who 92*
**Rainbow**, Paul Andrew 1955- *WhoRel 92*
**Rainbow-Earhart**, Kathryn Adeline 1921- *WhoBlA 92*
**Raine**, Cedric Stuart 1940- *AmMWSc 92*
**Raine**, Charles Herbert, III 1937- *WhoBlA 92*
**Raine**, Craig 1944- *ConPo 91, WrDr 92*
**Raine**, Craig Anthony 1944- *IntAu&W 91, IntWW 91, Who 92*
**Raine**, Harcourt Neale 1923- *Who 92*
**Raine**, John Stephen 1941- *Who 92*
**Raine**, Kathleen 1908- *ConPo 91, RfGEnL 91, WrDr 92*
**Raine**, Kathleen Jessie 1908- *IntAu&W 91, IntWW 91, Who 92*
**Raine**, Neale *Who 92*
**Raine**, William MacLeod 1871-1954 *BenetAL 91, TwCWW 91*
**Rainer**, Fletcher Young, III 1943- *WhoWest 92*
**Rainer**, Friedrich 1903-1947 *BiDExR*
**Rainer**, John David 1921- *AmMWSc 92*
**Rainer**, Luise *Who 92*
**Rainer**, Norman Barry 1929- *AmMWSc 92*
**Rainer**, Thomas Spratling 1955- *WhoRel 92*
**Rainer**, Yvonne *ReelWom*
**Rainer**, Yvonne 1934- *ConAu 133, IntDcF 2-2*
**Raines**, Arthur *AmMWSc 92*
**Raines**, Brian Edwin 1962- *WhoEnt 92*
**Raines**, Colden Douglas 1915- *WhoBlA 92*
**Raines**, Franklin Delano 1949- *WhoFI 92*
**Raines**, Gary L 1946- *AmMWSc 92*
**Raines**, Helon *DrAPF 91*
**Raines**, James Ray 1937- *WhoRel 92*
**Raines**, Jeremy Keith 1947- *AmMWSc 92*
**Raines**, Jerry Richard 1946- *WhoRel 92*
**Raines**, Richard Clifton 1946- *WhoAmL 92*
**Raines**, Robert Charles 1954- *WhoEnt 92*
**Raines**, Ronald Bruce 1929- *WhoFI 92*
**Raines**, Ronald T 1958- *AmMWSc 92*
**Raines**, Thaddeus Joseph 1918- *AmMWSc 92*
**Raines**, Tim D. 1950- *WhoFI 92*
**Raines**, Timothy 1959- *WhoBlA 92*
**Raines**, Walter R. 1940- *WhoBlA 92*
**Raines**, William C. 1909- *WhoBlA 92*
**Rainey**, Barbara Ann 1949- *WhoWest 92*
**Rainey**, Bessye Coleman 1929- *WhoBlA 92*
**Rainey**, Clifford 1948- *TwCPaSc*
**Rainey**, Donald Glenn 1931- *WhoAmP 91*
**Rainey**, Donald Paul 1940- *AmMWSc 92*
**Rainey**, Ford 1908- *WhoEnt 92*
**Rainey**, Gene Edward 1934- *WrDr 92*
**Rainey**, Gregory Ross 1955- *WhoWest 92*
**Rainey**, Henry Thomas 1860-1934 *AmPolLe*
**Rainey**, Howard H 1927- *WhoAmP 91*
**Rainey**, James Herbert 1953- *WhoAmL 92*
**Rainey**, James Lee, Jr. 1929- *WhoFI 92*
**Rainey**, John Marion, Jr 1942- *AmMWSc 92*
**Rainey**, Larry Curtis 1950- *WhoMW 92*
**Rainey**, Loyd Daniel 1951- *WhoEnt 92*
**Rainey**, Ma 1886-1939 *NewAmDM, NotBlAW 92 [port]*
**Rainey**, Mary Louise 1943- *AmMWSc 92*
**Rainey**, Robert Hamric 1918- *AmMWSc 92*
**Rainey**, Robert Lee 1950- *WhoEnt 92*
**Rainey**, Ron Paul 1946- *WhoEnt 92*
**Rainey**, Sylvia Valentine *WhoBlA 92*
**Rainey**, William Joel 1946- *WhoFI 92*
**Rainger**, Peter 1924- *Who 92*
**Rainier III** 1923- *IntWW 91*
**Rainier**, Priaulx 1903-1986 *NewAmDM*
**Rainiero**, Joseph W. 1939- *WhoRel 92*
**Rainis**, Albert Edward 1941- *AmMWSc 92*
**Rainis**, Andrew 1940- *AmMWSc 92*
**Rainone**, Michael Carmine 1918- *WhoAmL 92*
**Rains**, Albert 1902-1991 *CurBio 91N*
**Rains**, Albert McKinley d1991 *NewYTBS 91 [port]*

**Rains**, Anthony John Harding 1920- *Who 92*
**Rains**, Catherine Burke 1959- *WhoWest 92*
**Rains**, Claude 1889-1967 *FacFETw*
**Rains**, Dale Osborn 1936- *WhoEnt 92*
**Rains**, Darrel 1945- *WhoRel 92*
**Rains**, Donald W 1937- *AmMWSc 92*
**Rains**, George Washington 1817-1898 *BiInAmS*
**Rains**, Harry Hano 1909- *WhoAmL 92*
**Rains**, Henry Thomas 1955- *WhoRel 92*
**Rains**, Horace 1912- *WhoBlA 92*
**Rains**, Jack M 1937- *WhoAmP 91*
**Rains**, Merritt Neal 1943- *WhoAmL 92*
**Rains**, Roger Keranen 1940- *AmMWSc 92*
**Rains**, Theodore Conrad 1925- *AmMWSc 92*
**Rains**, Vance Clifton 1967- *WhoRel 92*
**Rainsford**, Greta M. 1936- *WhoBlA 92*
**Rainsford**, Seymour Grome 1900- *Who 92*
**Raintree**, Diane *DrAPF 91*
**Rainville**, David Paul 1952- *AmMWSc 92*
**Rainwater**, David Luther 1947- *AmMWSc 92*
**Rainwater**, David Neal 1948- *WhoAmL 92*
**Rainwater**, James Carlton 1946- *AmMWSc 92*
**Rainwater**, Janette 1922- *WhoWest 92*
**Rainwater**, John Victor, Jr. 1942- *WhoRel 92*
**Rainwater**, Leo James 1917-1986 *WhoNob 90*
**Rainwater**, Marjorie Akins 1927- *WhoAmP 91*
**Rainwater**, Nathan Randy 1955- *WhoRel 92*
**Rainwater**, Richard E *NewYTBS 91 [port]*
**Rainwater**, Wallace Eugene 1924- *WhoAmP 91*
**Rairden**, John Ruel, III 1930- *AmMWSc 92*
**Rairdin**, Craig Allen 1959- *WhoMW 92*
**Rais**, Abdul J. *Who 92*
**Raisa**, Rosa 1893-1963 *NewAmDM*
**Raisanen**, Heikki Martti 1941- *IntWW 91, WhoRel 92*
**Raisani**, Sardar Ghaus Bakhsh 1924- *IntWW 91*
**Raisbeck**, Barbara 1928- *AmMWSc 92*
**Raisbeck**, Gordon 1925- *AmMWSc 92*
**Raisch**, William A 1928- *WhoAmP 91*
**Raisen**, Elliott 1928- *AmMWSc 92*
**Raish**, Scott Charles 1961- *WhoFI 92*
**Raisian**, John 1949- *WhoFI 92*
**Raisler**, Kenneth Mark 1951- *WhoAmL 92*
**Raisman**, John Michael 1929- *IntWW 91, Who 92*
**Raison**, John Charles Anthony 1926- *Who 92*
**Raison**, Timothy 1929- *Who 92*
**Raisor**, Philip *DrAPF 91*
**Raisovich**, Chris Jane 1958- *WhoMW 92*
**Raisz**, Lawrence Gideon 1925- *AmMWSc 92*
**Raiter**, George L *WhoAmP 91*
**Raithel**, Albert Lawrence, III 1954- *WhoWest 92*
**Raitt**, Alan William 1930- *WrDr 92*
**Raitt**, Bonnie Lynn 1949- *WhoEnt 92*
**Raitt**, Jill 1931- *WhoRel 92*
**Raitt**, Ralph James, Jr 1929- *AmMWSc 92*
**Raitz**, Vladimir Gavrilovich 1922- *Who 92*
**Raizada**, Mohan K 1948- *AmMWSc 92*
**Raizen**, Carol Eileen 1938- *AmMWSc 92*
**Raizen**, Senta Amon 1924- *AmMWSc 92*
**Raiziss**, Sonia *DrAPF 91*
**Raizman**, Paula 1911- *AmMWSc 92*
**Raizman**, Yuliy Yakovlevich 1903- *SovUnBD*
**Raj**, Baldev 1935- *AmMWSc 92*
**Raj**, Harkisan D 1926- *AmMWSc 92*
**Raj**, Kakkadan Nandanath 1924- *IntWW 91, Who 92*
**Raj**, Pradeep 1949- *AmMWSc 92*
**Raj**, Rishi S *AmMWSc 92*
**Raja**, Rajendran 1948- *AmMWSc 92*
**Raja Haji Ahmad**, Aznam 1928- *IntWW 91*
**Rajabi-Asl**, Ali 1963- *WhoWest 92*
**Rajagopal**, Attipat Krishnaswamy 1937- *AmMWSc 92*
**Rajagopal**, K R 1950- *AmMWSc 92*
**Rajagopal**, P K 1936- *AmMWSc 92*
**Rajagopalan**, K V 1930- *AmMWSc 92*
**Rajagopalan**, Parthasarathi 1930- *AmMWSc 92*
**Rajagopalan**, Raj *AmMWSc 92*
**Rajah**, Arumugam Ponnu 1911- *Who 92*
**Rajah**, Nalliah Thillainada 1941- *WhoFI 92*
**Rajan**, M. S. 1920- *WrDr 92*
**Rajan**, Mannaraswamighala Sreeranga 1920- *IntWW 91*
**Rajan**, Periasamy Karivaratha 1942- *AmMWSc 92*
**Rajan**, Thiruchandurai Viswanathan 1945- *AmMWSc 92*
**Rajan**, Tilottama 1951- *WrDr 92*
**Rajani**, Guli R. 1942- *WhoFI 92*
**Rajanna**, Bettaiya *AmMWSc 92*
**Rajaraman**, Srinivasan 1943- *AmMWSc 92*
**Rajaratnam**, N 1934- *AmMWSc 92*
**Rajaratnam**, Sinnathamby 1915- *IntWW 91*
**Rajbansi**, Amichand 1942- *IntWW 91*
**Rajchman**, Jan A 1911- *AmMWSc 92*
**Rajendran**, Vazhaikkurichi M 1952- *AmMWSc 92*
**Rajeshwar**, Krishnan 1949- *AmMWSc 92*
**Rajhathy**, Tibor 1920- *AmMWSc 92*
**Rajk**, Lazlo 1909-1949 *FacFETw*
**Rajlich**, Vaclav Thomas 1939- *AmMWSc 92*
**Rajna**, Thomas 1928- *IntWW 91*
**Rajnak**, Katheryn Edmonds 1937- *AmMWSc 92*
**Rajnak**, Stanley L 1936- *AmMWSc 92*
**Rajneesh**, Bhagwan Shree 1931-1990 *AnObit 1990, FacFETw, RelLAm 91*
**Rajniss**, Ferenc 1893-1946 *BiDExR*
**Rajoppi**, Joanne 1947- *WhoAmP 91*
**Rajsuman**, Rochit 1964- *AmMWSc 92, WhoMW 92*
**Raju**, Anand Penmetsa 1957- *WhoMW 92*
**Raju**, Ivatury Sanyasi 1944- *AmMWSc 92*
**Raju**, Mudundi Ramakrishna 1931- *AmMWSc 92*
**Raju**, Namboori Bhaskara 1943- *AmMWSc 92*
**Raju**, Palanichamy Pillai 1937- *AmMWSc 92*
**Raju**, Poolla Tirupati 1904- *WrDr 92*
**Raju**, Satyanarayana G V 1934- *AmMWSc 92*
**Rak**, Lorraine Karen 1959- *WhoAmL 92*
**Raka**, Eugene Cd 1924- *AmMWSc 92*
**Rakauskas**, Joseph A. *WhoEnt 92, WhoFI 92*
**Rake**, Adrian Vaughan 1934- *AmMWSc 92*
**Raker**, Charles W 1920- *AmMWSc 92*
**Rakes**, Allen Huff 1933- *AmMWSc 92*
**Rakes**, Jerry Max 1932- *AmMWSc 92*
**Rakestraw**, Gregory Allen 1949- *WhoAmL 92*
**Rakestraw**, James William 1936- *AmMWSc 92*
**Rakestraw**, Kyle Damon 1961- *WhoBlA 92*
**Rakestraw**, Priscilla B *WhoAmP 91*
**Rakestraw**, Robert Vincent 1943- *WhoRel 92*
**Rakestraw**, Roy Martin 1942- *AmMWSc 92*
**Rakhimbabaeva**, Zakhra 1923- *IntWW 91*
**Rakhimova**, Ibodat 1922- *IntWW 91*
**Rakhit**, Gopa *AmMWSc 92*
**Rakhit**, Sumanas 1930- *AmMWSc 92*
**Rakhlin**, Natan Grigor'evich 1906-1979 *SovUnBD*
**Rakhmanin**, Oleg Borisovich 1924- *IntWW 91*
**Rakic**, Pasko 1933- *AmMWSc 92*
**Rakita**, Louis *AmMWSc 92*
**Rakita**, Philip Erwin 1944- *AmMWSc 92*
**Rakoczy**, Jacob David 1955- *WhoMW 92*
**Rakoff**, Alvin 1927- *WrDr 92*
**Rakoff**, Alvin 1937- *IntMPA 92*
**Rakoff**, Henry 1924- *AmMWSc 92*
**Rakoff**, Jed Saul 1943- *WhoAmL 92*
**Rakoff**, Todd D. 1946- *WhoAmL 92*
**Rakoff**, Vivian Morris 1928- *AmMWSc 92*
**Rakosi**, Carl *DrAPF 91*
**Rakosi**, Carl 1903- *ConPo 91, WrDr 92*
**Rakosi**, Matyas 1892-1971 *FacFETw*
**Rakosky**, Joseph, Jr 1921- *AmMWSc 92*
**Rakotoarijaona**, Desire 1923- *IntWW 91*
**Rakotoniaina**, Justin 1933- *IntWW 91*
**Rakovsky**, Khristian Georgievich 1873-1941 *SovUnBD*
**Rakovsky**, Khristian Georgyevich 1873-1938 *FacFETw*
**Rakow**, Thomas Charles 1956- *WhoRel 92*
**Rakowski**, Mieczyslaw Franciszek 1926- *IntWW 91*
**Rakowski**, Robert F 1941- *AmMWSc 92*
**Rakowsky**, Frederick William 1928- *AmMWSc 92*
**Rakowsky**, Ronald John 1944- *WhoAmL 92*
**Raksakulthai**, Vinai 1942- *WhoMW 92*
**Raksin**, David 1912- *IntMPA 92, NewAmDM, WhoEnt 92*
**Raksis**, Joseph W 1942- *AmMWSc 92*
**Rakusan**, Karel Josef 1935- *AmMWSc 92*
**Rakutis**, Ruta 1939- *WhoWest 92*
**Rale**, Sebastien 1657?-1724 *BenetAL 91*
**Ralegh**, Walter 1551?-1618 *BenetAL 91*
**Ralegh**, Walter 1552?-1618 *RfGEnL 91*
**Ralegh**, Walter 1554?-1618 *CnDBLB 1 [port]*
**Raleigh**, Allan *ScFEYrs*
**Raleigh**, Cecil Baring 1934- *AmMWSc 92, WhoWest 92*
**Raleigh**, Douglas Overholt 1929- *AmMWSc 92*
**Raleigh**, James 1926- *WhoEnt 92*
**Raleigh**, James Arthur 1938- *AmMWSc 92*
**Raleigh**, Jean Margaret Macdonald C. *Who 92*
**Raleigh**, Richard *ConAu 133*
**Raleigh**, Walter 1551?-1618 *BenetAL 91*
**Raley**, Charles Francis, Jr 1923- *AmMWSc 92*
**Raley**, Cheri Elaine 1951- *WhoWest 92*
**Raley**, John Howard 1916- *AmMWSc 92*
**Raley**, Patti J 1946- *WhoAmP 91*
**Ralite**, Jack 1928- *IntWW 91*
**Rall**, David Platt 1926- *AmMWSc 92, IntWW 91*
**Rall**, Harris Franklin 1870-1964 *RelLAm 91*
**Rall**, J. Edward 1920- *IntWW 91*
**Rall**, Jack Alan 1944- *AmMWSc 92*
**Rall**, Joseph Edward 1920- *AmMWSc 92*
**Rall**, Lloyd L 1916- *AmMWSc 92*
**Rall**, Louis Baker 1930- *AmMWSc 92*
**Rall**, Raymond Wallace 1926- *AmMWSc 92*
**Rall**, Stanley Carlton, Jr 1943- *AmMWSc 92*
**Rall**, Theodore William 1928- *AmMWSc 92*
**Rall**, Waldo 1924- *AmMWSc 92*
**Rall**, Wilfrid 1922- *AmMWSc 92*
**Rall**, William Frederick 1951- *AmMWSc 92*
**Ralley**, Thomas G 1939- *AmMWSc 92*
**Ralli**, Godfrey 1915- *Who 92*
**Ralling**, Christopher 1929- *Who 92*
**Rallis**, George J. 1918- *IntWW 91*
**Rallo**, Douglas 1953- *WhoAmL 92*
**Rallo**, James Gilbert 1942- *WhoFI 92*
**Ralls**, Jack Warner 1920- *AmMWSc 92*
**Ralls**, Katherine Smith 1939- *AmMWSc 92*
**Ralls**, Kenneth M 1938- *AmMWSc 92*
**Ralls**, Michael James 1958- *WhoAmL 92*
**Ralls**, Rawleigh Hazen, III 1932- *WhoAmL 92*
**Ralph**, Alan Edgar 1951- *WhoAmP 91*
**Ralph**, C John 1940- *AmMWSc 92*
**Ralph**, Charles Leland 1929- *AmMWSc 92*
**Ralph**, Colin John 1951- *Who 92*
**Ralph**, David Clinton 1922- *WhoMW 92*
**Ralph**, James 1695?-1762 *BenetAL 91*
**Ralph**, Julian 1853-1903 *BenetAL 91*
**Ralph**, Margaret Nutting 1941- *WhoRel 92*
**Ralph**, Peter 1936- *AmMWSc 92*
**Ralph**, Sheryl Lee 1956- *WhoBlA 92*
**Ralph**, Theodore James 1930- *WhoAmL 92*
**Ralph**, William L 1850-1907 *BiInAmS*
**Ralphs**, Enid Mary 1915- *Who 92*
**Ralphson**, Mary *EncAmaz 91*
**Ralstin**, Richard Lowell 1947- *WhoWest 92*
**Ralston**, Anthony 1930- *AmMWSc 92*
**Ralston**, David Edmund 1954- *WhoAmP 91*
**Ralston**, David Thomas, Jr. 1954- *WhoFI 92*
**Ralston**, Douglas Edmund 1932- *AmMWSc 92*
**Ralston**, Edward J. 1938- *WhoBlA 92*
**Ralston**, Elizabeth Wall 1945- *AmMWSc 92*
**Ralston**, Elreta Melton Alexander 1919- *WhoBlA 92*
**Ralston**, Gilbert Alexander 1912- *WhoWest 92*
**Ralston**, Henry James 1906- *AmMWSc 92*
**Ralston**, Henry James, III 1935- *AmMWSc 92*
**Ralston**, Jackson Harvey 1857-1945 *AmPeW*
**Ralston**, James Vickroy, Jr 1943- *AmMWSc 92*
**Ralston**, Joanne Smoot 1939- *WhoFI 92*
**Ralston**, John Peter 1951- *AmMWSc 92*
**Ralston**, Ken *WhoEnt 92*
**Ralston**, Margarete A 1954- *AmMWSc 92*
**Ralston**, Rachel Walters 1915- *WhoWest 92*
**Ralston**, Richard Hugh 1937- *WhoAmL 92*
**Ralston**, Robert D 1924- *AmMWSc 92*
**Ralston**, Roy Boggs 1917- *WhoFI 92*
**Ralston**, Steven Philip 1954- *WhoFI 92*
**Ralston**, Timothy John 1956- *WhoRel 92*
**Ram**, Budh 1935- *AmMWSc 92*
**Ram**, C Venkata S 1948- *AmMWSc 92*
**Ram**, J Sri 1928- *AmMWSc 92*
**Ram**, Jaglivan 1908-1986 *FacFETw*
**Ram**, Jeffrey L 1945- *AmMWSc 92*
**Ram**, Madhira Dasaradhi 1935- *AmMWSc 92*
**Ram**, Michael 1936- *AmMWSc 92*
**Ram**, Michael Jay 1940- *AmMWSc 92, WhoAmL 92*
**Ram**, Neil Marshall 1952- *AmMWSc 92*
**Ram Dass**, Baba 1931- *RelLAm 91*
**Ram-Mohan**, L Ramdas 1944- *AmMWSc 92*
**Rama IX** 1927- *FacFETw*
**Rama**, Swami 1925- *RelLAm 91*
**Rama**, Zen Master 1950- *RelLAm 91*
**Rama**, Angel 1920?-1983 *LiExTwC*
**Rama**, Carlos M. 1921- *IntWW 91*
**Rama**, John C 1958- *WhoAmP 91*
**Rama Rao**, Nandamuri Taraka 1923- *IntWW 91*
**Rama Rau**, Santha 1923- *IntAu&W 91, IntWW 91, LiExTwC, Who 92*
**Ramachandran**, Chittoor Krishna 1945- *AmMWSc 92*
**Ramachandran**, Gopalasamudram Narayana 1922- *IntWW 91, Who 92*
**Ramachandran**, Janakiraman 1935- *AmMWSc 92*
**Ramachandran**, Muthukrishnan 1943- *AmMWSc 92*
**Ramachandran**, N *AmMWSc 92*
**Ramachandran**, Pallassana N *AmMWSc 92*
**Ramachandran**, Parthasarathi 1921- *IntWW 91*
**Ramachandran**, Subramania 1938- *AmMWSc 92*
**Ramachandran**, Vangipuram S 1929- *AmMWSc 92*
**Ramachandran**, Venkatanarayana D 1934- *AmMWSc 92*
**Ramachandran**, Vilayanur Subramanian 1951- *AmMWSc 92*
**Ramadhani**, John Acland *Who 92*
**Ramadhani**, John Acland 1932- *IntWW 91*
**Ramadhyani**, Satish 1949- *AmMWSc 92*
**Ramaema**, Elias Phisoana 1933- *IntWW 91*
**Ramage**, Colin Stokes 1921- *AmMWSc 92*
**Ramage**, David, Jr. *WhoRel 92*
**Ramage**, Granville 1919- *Who 92*
**Ramage**, Samuel Johnson, II 1957- *WhoEnt 92*
**Ramagopal**, Mudumbi Vijaya 1952- *AmMWSc 92*
**Ramagopal**, Subbanaidu 1941- *AmMWSc 92, WhoWest 92*
**Ramahatra**, Victor 1945- *IntWW 91*
**Ramakar** *WhoEnt 92*
**Ramaker**, David Ellis 1943- *AmMWSc 92*
**Ramakrishan**, S 1949- *AmMWSc 92*
**Ramakrishna**, Sri 1836-1886 *RelLAm 91*
**Ramakrishna**, Kilaparti 1955- *AmMWSc 92*
**Ramakrishnan**, Raghu 1961- *AmMWSc 92*
**Ramakrishnan**, Terizhandur S *AmMWSc 92*
**Ramakrishnan**, Venkataswamy 1929- *AmMWSc 92, WhoFI 92*
**Ramakumar**, Ramachandra Gupta 1936- *AmMWSc 92*
**Ramaley**, James Francis 1941- *AmMWSc 92*
**Ramaley**, Judith Aitken 1941- *AmMWSc 92*
**Ramaley**, Louis 1937- *AmMWSc 92*
**Ramaley**, Robert Folk 1935- *AmMWSc 92*
**Ramalingam**, Mysore Loganathan 1954- *AmMWSc 92*
**Ramalingaswami**, Vulimiri 1921- *IntWW 91*
**Ramamoorthy**, Chittoor V 1926- *AmMWSc 92*
**Ramamoorthy**, Panapakkam A 1949- *AmMWSc 92*
**Ramamurthy**, Amurthur C *AmMWSc 92*
**Ramamurti**, Krishnamurti 1919- *AmMWSc 92*
**Raman**, Aravamudhan 1937- *AmMWSc 92*
**Raman**, Chandrasekhara Venkata 1888-1970 *WhoNob 90*
**Raman**, Subramanian 1938- *AmMWSc 92*
**Raman**, Varadaraja Venkata *AmMWSc 92*
**Ramana Maharshi**, Sri 1879-1950 *RelLAm 91*
**Ramanan**, V R V 1952- *AmMWSc 92*
**Ramanantsoa**, Gabriel 1906- *IntWW 91*
**Ramanathan**, Ganapathiagraharam V *AmMWSc 92*
**Ramanathan**, M *AmMWSc 92*
**Ramanathan**, Muthiah 1936- *WhoFI 92*
**Ramanathan**, Veerabhadran 1944- *AmMWSc 92*
**Ramangkura**, Virabongsa 1943- *IntWW 91*
**Ramani**, Raja Venkat 1938- *AmMWSc 92*
**Ramanujam**, Gopala 1915- *IntWW 91*
**Ramanujam**, V M Sadagopa 1946- *AmMWSc 92*
**Ramanujan**, A.K. *DrAPF 91*
**Ramanujan**, A. K. 1929- *ConPo 91, WrDr 92*
**Ramanujan**, Melapalayam Srinivasan 1931- *AmMWSc 92*
**Ramaphosa**, Matamela Cyril 1953- *IntWW 91*
**Ramaprasad**, Bindi Ramanna 1942- *WhoFI 92*
**Ramaprasad**, K R 1938- *AmMWSc 92*
**Ramasamy**, Savakkattu Muniappan 1942- *WhoWest 92*
**Ramasastry**, Sai Sudarshan 1945- *AmMWSc 92*

Ramaswami, Devabhaktuni 1933- AmMWSc 92, WhoMW 92
Ramaswami, Vaidyanathan 1950- AmMWSc 92
Ramaswamy, H N 1937- AmMWSc 92
Ramaswamy, Kizhanatham V 1935- AmMWSc 92
Ramaswamy, Padmanabhan 1953- WhoWest 92
Ramaswamy, Venkatachalam 1955- AmMWSc 92
Ramat, Charles Samuel 1951- WhoFI 92
Ramaty, Reuven 1937- AmMWSc 92
Ramay, James Charles, Jr. 1951- WhoFI 92
Ramayya, Akunuri V 1938- AmMWSc 92
Ramazzotto, Louis John 1940- AmMWSc 92
Rambahadur Limbu, Captain 1939- Who 92
Rambaut, Paul Christopher 1940- AmMWSc 92
Ramberg, Charles F, Jr AmMWSc 92
Ramberg, Charles Henry 1943- WhoAmP 91
Ramberg, Joanne Anderson 1926- WhoMW 92
Ramberg, Patricia Lynn 1951- WhoMW 92
Ramberg, Steven Eric 1948- AmMWSc 92
Rambert, Charles Jean Julien 1924- IntWW 91
Rambert, Marie 1888-1982 FacFETw
Rambo, Bettye R. 1936- WhoBlA 92
Rambo, G Dan 1928- WhoAmP 91
Rambo, JoAnn Weslie 1953- WhoIns 92
Rambo, John 1944- BlkOlyM
Rambo, Lewis Ray 1943- WhoRel 92
Rambo, Sylvia H. 1936- WhoAmL 92
Rambusch, Viggo Frode Edward 1900- WhoFI 92
Ramdas, Anant Krishna 1930- AmMWSc 92
Rame, David IntAu&W 91X
Rameau, Jean-Philippe 1683-1764 BlkwCEP, NewAmDM
Ramel, Stig 1927- IntWW 91
Ramelson, Baruch 1910- Who 92
Ramer, Bruce 1933- WhoAmL 92, WhoEnt 92, WhoWest 92
Ramer, James LeRoy 1935- WhoFI 92, WhoMW 92
Ramer, Luther Grimm 1908- AmMWSc 92
Ramette, Richard Wales 1927- AmMWSc 92
Ramey, Carl Robert 1941- WhoAmL 92
Ramey, Chester Eugene 1943- AmMWSc 92
Ramey, Daniel Bruce 1949- AmMWSc 92
Ramey, Denny L. 1947- WhoAmL 92, WhoFI 92
Ramey, Drucilla 1946- WhoAmL 92
Ramey, Estelle R 1917- AmMWSc 92
Ramey, Felicenne H. WhoBlA 92
Ramey, Felicenne Houston WhoWest 92
Ramey, George Grover 1938- WhoRel 92
Ramey, H J, Jr 1925- AmMWSc 92
Ramey, Harmon Hobson, Jr 1930- AmMWSc 92
Ramey, John Henry 1926- WhoMW 92
Ramey, John Michael 1958- WhoRel 92
Ramey, John Mulvey 1952- WhoFI 92
Ramey, John Randall 1921- WhoAmP 91
Ramey, Mary Price 1930- WhoAmP 91
Ramey, Melvin Richard 1938- AmMWSc 92
Ramey, Phillip 1939- ConCom 92
Ramey, Robert Lee 1922- AmMWSc 92
Ramey, Roger Lane 1949- WhoEnt 92
Ramey, Roy Richard 1947- AmMWSc 92
Ramey, Russell Kevin 1959- WhoAmL 92
Ramey, Samuel 1942- NewAmDM
Ramey, Steven A 1952- WhoAmP 91
Ramey, Valerie Ann 1959- WhoFI 92
Ramezan, Massood AmMWSc 92
Ramfjord, Sigurd 1911- AmMWSc 92
Ramfors, Bo C. E. 1936- IntWW 91
Ramgoolam, Seewoosagur 1900-1985 FacFETw
Ramig, Robert E 1922- AmMWSc 92
Ramilingam, Subbiah 1935- AmMWSc 92
Ramin, Manfred, Mme Who 92
Ramires, Elaine Grace 1956- WhoEnt 92
Ramirez, Alejandro 1774-1821 HisDSpE
Ramirez, Alfred WhoAmP 91, WhoHisp 92
Ramirez, Alice DrAPF 91
Ramirez, Amelie G. 1951- WhoHisp 92
Ramirez, Antonio, Jr. 1955- WhoHisp 92
Ramirez, Arthur P 1956- AmMWSc 92
Ramirez, Arturo 1947- WhoHisp 92
Ramirez, Arturo J. 1960- WhoHisp 92
Ramirez, Baudelio 1941- WhoHisp 92
Ramirez, Berta C. 1942- WhoHisp 92
Ramirez, Blandina Cardenas WhoHisp 92
Ramirez, Carlos 1957- WhoHisp 92
Ramirez, Carlos A. 1953- WhoHisp 92
Ramirez, Carlos D. 1946- WhoHisp 92
Ramirez, Carlos David 1946- WhoFI 92
Ramirez, Carlos M. 1951- WhoHisp 92
Ramirez, Celso Lopez 1950- WhoHisp 92
Ramirez, Dan WhoHisp 92
Ramirez, David 1959- WhoHisp 92
Ramirez, David Eugene 1952- WhoHisp 92
Ramirez, David M. 1948- WhoHisp 92
Ramirez, Domingo Victor 1932- WhoHisp 92
Ramirez, Donald E. 1943- WhoHisp 92
Ramirez, Donald Edward 1943- AmMWSc 92
Ramirez, Enrique Rene 1930- WhoHisp 92
Ramirez, Ernest E. 1940- WhoHisp 92
Ramirez, Fausto 1923- AmMWSc 92
Ramirez, Filomena R. 1944- WhoHisp 92
Ramirez, Francisco AmMWSc 92
Ramirez, Gene Richard 1942- WhoHisp 92
Ramirez, Gilbert 1921- WhoBlA 92, WhoHisp 92
Ramirez, Gladys 1962- WhoHisp 92
Ramirez, Guillermo 1934- AmMWSc 92, WhoHisp 92
Ramirez, Gus 1953- WhoHisp 92
Ramirez, Hermes 1948- BlkOlyM
Ramirez, Hugo A. 1942- WhoHisp 92
Ramirez, Humberto Rafael 1963- WhoEnt 92
Ramirez, Irene 1962- WhoHisp 92
Ramirez, J Roberto 1941- AmMWSc 92, WhoHisp 92
Ramirez, Jack 1939- WhoAmP 91
Ramirez, Jesse Ralph 1952- WhoMW 92
Ramirez, Joan 1961- WhoHisp 92
Ramirez, Joel Tito 1923- WhoHisp 92
Ramirez, John 1943- WhoHisp 92, WhoWest 92
Ramirez, John Edward 1953- WhoHisp 92
Ramirez, Johnny 1957- WhoHisp 92
Ramirez, Jorge Hernan 1963- WhoHisp 92
Ramirez, Jose Lorenzo 1959- WhoHisp 92
Ramirez, Jose Luis 1936- WhoHisp 92
Ramirez, Jose Luis 1955- WhoWest 92
Ramirez, Jose M. 1955- WhoHisp 92
Ramirez, Jose S., Sr. 1919- WhoHisp 92
Ramirez, Joseph 1937- WhoHisp 92
Ramirez, Juan WhoHisp 92
Ramirez, Juan, Jr. 1945- WhoHisp 92
Ramirez, Juan A. 1961- WhoHisp 92
Ramirez, Julio Jesus 1955- WhoHisp 92
Ramirez, Kevin Michael 1947- WhoHisp 92
Ramirez, Lewis 1942- WhoHisp 92
Ramirez, Luis 1957- WhoHisp 92
Ramirez, Luis Angel 1950- WhoHisp 92
Ramirez, Manuel A. WhoHisp 92
Ramirez, Maria Fiorini 1948- WhoFI 92
Ramirez, Mario E., Jr. WhoHisp 92
Ramirez, Mario Efrain 1926- WhoHisp 92
Ramirez, Mike 1954- WhoHisp 92
Ramirez, Olga 1936- WhoHisp 92
Ramirez, Oscar 1946- WhoHisp 92
Ramirez, Pete Lopez 1949- WhoHisp 92
Ramirez, Rafael 1959- WhoHisp 92
Ramirez, Ralph Henry 1949- WhoMW 92
Ramirez, Raul Anthony 1944- WhoWest 92
Ramirez, Raul Daniel 1952- WhoWest 92
Ramirez, Ricardo 1936- WhoHisp 92, WhoRel 92
Ramirez, Richard 1954- WhoHisp 92
Ramirez, Richard G. 1952- WhoHisp 92
Ramirez, Robert T. 1948- WhoHisp 92
Ramirez, Roberto WhoAmP 91, WhoHisp 92
Ramirez, Rolando Ricardo 1958- WhoHisp 92
Ramirez, Roy Rene-Salvador 1959- WhoHisp 92
Ramirez, Ruben Ramirez 1953- WhoHisp 92
Ramirez, Samuel WhoAmP 91, WhoHisp 92
Ramirez, Sara Estella 1881-1910 HanAmWH
Ramirez, Saul, Jr. WhoHisp 92
Ramirez, Saul N, Jr WhoAmP 91
Ramirez, Selma Angela 1955- WhoHisp 92
Ramirez, Stephen 1957- WhoHisp 92
Ramirez, Steven Adrian 1961- WhoWest 92
Ramirez, Tina WhoHisp 92
Ramirez, Victor E. WhoHisp 92
Ramirez, W Fred 1941- AmMWSc 92
Ramirez, William Earl 1951- WhoWest 92
Ramirez, William Z. 1954- WhoHisp 92
Ramirez-Boulette, Teresa WhoHisp 92
Ramirez-De-Arellano, Diana DrAPF 91
Ramirez-De-Arellano, Diana 1919- IntAu&W 91
Ramirez de Arellano, Diana Teresa C. 1919- WhoHisp 92
Ramirez de Fuenleal, Sebastian d1547 HisDSpE
Ramirez de Velasco, Juan d1597 HisDSpE
Ramirez-Garcia, Mari Carmen 1955- WhoHisp 92
Ramirez Mercado, Sergio 1942- IntWW 91
Ramirez Pantojas, Rosa M. WhoHisp 92
Ramirez Pantojas, Rosin WhoAmP 91
Ramirez-Piscina, Julian 1956- WhoFI 92
Ramirez-Rivera, Jose 1929- WhoHisp 92
Ramirez-Ronda, Carlos Hector 1943- AmMWSc 92, WhoHisp 92
Ramirez Vazquez, Pedro 1919- IntWW 91
Ramirez Vega, Adrian Nelson 1934- WhoHisp 92
Ramis, Guillermo J. 1945- WhoHisp 92
Ramis, Harold 1944- IntMPA 92
Ramis, Harold Allen 1944- WhoEnt 92
Ramiscal, Elmer Febenito 1942- WhoFI 92
Ramjuttun, Dinesh 1946- IntWW 91
Ramke, Bin DrAPF 91
Ramke, Bin 1947- IntAu&W 91
Ramke, Thomas Franklin 1917- AmMWSc 92
Ramler, Edward Otto 1916- AmMWSc 92
Ramler, W J 1921- AmMWSc 92
Ramm, Alexander G 1940- AmMWSc 92, WhoMW 92
Ramm, Dietolf 1942- AmMWSc 92
Ramm, MacDonald 1924- Who 92
Rammer, Irwyn Alden 1928- AmMWSc 92
Ramming, David Wilbur 1946- AmMWSc 92
Ramnefalk, Marien Louise 1941- IntAu&W 91
Ramo, Roberta Cooper 1942- WhoWest 92
Ramo, Simon 1913- AmMWSc 92, IntWW 91, WhoFI 92, WhoWest 92, WrDr 92
Ramo, Virginia M. Smith WhoWest 92
Ramohalli, Kumar Nanjunda Rao 1945- AmMWSc 92
Ramon, Angelo A. 1944- WhoHisp 92
Ramon, Jaime WhoHisp 92
Ramon, Jose-Maria Crispin 1937- WhoHisp 92
Ramon, Leslie ScFEYrs
Ramon, Serafin 1934- AmMWSc 92
Ramon-Moliner, Enrique 1927- AmMWSc 92
Ramon y Cajal, Santiago 1852-1934 WhoNob 90
Ramona, Jan WhoEnt 92
Ramond, Pierre Michel 1943- AmMWSc 92
Ramont, Mark S. 1956- WhoEnt 92
Ramos, Adam R. 1946- WhoHisp 92
Ramos, Adrian 1956- TwCPaSc
Ramos, Albert A. 1927- WhoWest 92
Ramos, Charles Edward 1942- WhoHisp 92
Ramos, David J. WhoHisp 92
Ramos, Domingo 1958- WhoHisp 92
Ramos, Eva WhoHisp 92
Ramos, Fidel 1928- FacFETw, IntWW 91
Ramos, Fred 1959- WhoHisp 92
Ramos, Fred M., Jr. 1949- WhoHisp 92
Ramos, Gene Maurice 1932- WhoBlA 92
Ramos, Graciliano 1892-1953 BenetAL 91
Ramos, Harold Smith 1928- AmMWSc 92
Ramos, Hipolito BlkOlyM
Ramos, J. E., Jr. 1959- WhoHisp 92
Ramos, J. Mario 1956- WhoEnt 92, WhoWest 92
Ramos, Jesus A. WhoHisp 92
Ramos, John Salias 1942- WhoHisp 92
Ramos, Jose S. 1950- WhoHisp 92
Ramos, Joseph Steven 1943- WhoHisp 92
Ramos, Juan Ignacio 1953- AmMWSc 92, WhoHisp 92
Ramos, Kenneth 1956- WhoHisp 92
Ramos, Lillian AmMWSc 92
Ramos, Linda Marie 1961- WhoWest 92
Ramos, Lolinda Daoang 1934- WhoAmP 91
Ramos, Lolita J. 1945- WhoHisp 92
Ramos, Lydia WhoHisp 92
Ramos, Manuel 1951- WhoHisp 92
Ramos, Mario Anthony 1953- WhoHisp 92
Ramos, Mario Manuel 1959- WhoAmL 92
Ramos, Mary Angel 1959- WhoHisp 92
Ramos, Oreste, Jr 1946- WhoAmP 91
Ramos, Philip M. WhoHisp 92
Ramos, Phillip V. 1949- WhoHisp 92
Ramos, Ramon Rolando 1946- WhoHisp 92
Ramos, Raul 1946- WhoHisp 92
Ramos, Raul Antonio 1931- WhoHisp 92
Ramos, Robert Anthony WhoHisp 92
Ramos, Rosa Alicia 1953- WhoHisp 92
Ramos, Tab 1967- WhoHisp 92
Ramos, Valeriano 1958- WhoHisp 92
Ramos, Vivian Eleanor 1946- WhoMW 92
Ramos, William WhoHisp 92
Ramos-Alamo, Sandra WhoHisp 92
Ramos Arizpe, Jose Miguel 1775-1843 HisDSpE
Ramos-Diaz, Oreste WhoHisp 92
Ramos-Escobar, Jose Luis 1950- WhoHisp 92
Ramos-Garcia, Luis A. 1945- WhoHisp 92
Ramos Otero, Manuel 1948- WhoHisp 92
Ramos-Polanco, Bernardo 1946- WhoHisp 92
Ramp, Floyd Lester 1923- AmMWSc 92
Ramp, Marjorie Jean Sumerwell 1924- WhoMW 92
Ramp, Warren Kibby 1939- AmMWSc 92
Rampacek, Carl 1913- AmMWSc 92
Rampacek, Charles M. 1943- WhoFI 92
Rampal, Jean-Pierre 1922- ConMus 6 [port], FacFETw, NewAmDM
Rampal, Jean-Pierre Louis 1922- IntWW 91, Who 92, WhoEnt 92
Rampalli, Sitaram 1944- WhoMW 92
Rampersad, Arnold WrDr 92
Rampersad, Arnold 1941- ConAu 133, DcLB 111 [port], WhoBlA 92
Rampersad, Peggy A. Snellings 1933- WhoMW 92
Ramphal, Shridath Surendranath 1928- IntWW 91, Who 92
Ramphul, Indur 1931- IntWW 91
Ramphul, Indurduth 1931- Who 92
Ramphul, Radha Krishna 1926- IntWW 91
Rampil, Ira Jay 1953- WhoWest 92
Rampino, Michael Robert 1948- AmMWSc 92
Rampling, Anne ConAu 36NR, WrDr 92
Rampling, Charlotte 1946- IntMPA 92, IntWW 91
Rampling, Madeleine 1941- TwCPaSc
Rampone, Alfred Joseph 1925- AmMWSc 92
Rampp, Donald L 1935- AmMWSc 92
Rampton, Calvin Lewellyn 1913- WhoAmP 91
Rampton, Jack 1920- Who 92
Ramrakha, Sushil Sarat 1968- WhoWest 92
Ramras, Mark Bernard 1941- AmMWSc 92
Rams, Armando Ignacio, Jr. 1962- WhoHisp 92
Rams, Dieter 1932- DcTwDes, WhoFI 92
Ramsauer, Kirk Lee 1947- WhoFI 92
Ramsay Who 92
Ramsay, Lord 1948- Who 92
Ramsay, Alexander 1754?-1824 BiInAmS
Ramsay, Alexander William Burnett 1938- Who 92
Ramsay, Allan 1686-1758 BlkwCEP, RfGEnL 91
Ramsay, Allan John 1937- Who 92
Ramsay, Andrew 1686-1743 BlkwCEP
Ramsay, Arlan 1937- AmMWSc 92
Ramsay, Charles Alexander 1936- Who 92
Ramsay, David 1749-1815 BenetAL 91, BlkwEAR
Ramsay, David John 1939- AmMWSc 92
Ramsay, DeVere Maxwell 1925- WhoRel 92
Ramsay, Donald Allan 1922- AmMWSc 92, IntWW 91, Who 92
Ramsay, Eric Guy 1927- WhoWest 92
Ramsay, Gustavus Remak 1937- WhoEnt 92
Ramsay, Henry Thomas 1907- Who 92
Ramsay, Jay 1958- ConAu 135
Ramsay, John Barada 1929- AmMWSc 92, WhoWest 92
Ramsay, John Erwin 1915- WhoAmP 91
Ramsay, John Graham 1931- Who 92
Ramsay, John Martin 1930- AmMWSc 92
Ramsay, Karin Kinsey 1930- WhoRel 92
Ramsay, Kenneth A. WhoRel 92
Ramsay, Margaret 1908-1991 NewYTBS 91
Ramsay, Margaret Ann 1935- WhoAmP 91
Ramsay, Maynard Jack 1914- AmMWSc 92
Ramsay, Nancy Jean 1949- WhoRel 92
Ramsay, Norman James Gemmill 1916- Who 92
Ramsay, Ogden Bertrand 1932- AmMWSc 92
Ramsay, Patricia 1886-1974 TwCPaSc
Ramsay, Patrick George Alexander 1926- Who 92
Ramsay, Richard Alexander McGregor 1949- Who 92
Ramsay, Robert Henry 1925- WhoFI 92, WhoWest 92
Ramsay, Thomas 1907- Who 92
Ramsay, Thomas Anderson 1920- Who 92
Ramsay, William 1852-1916 WhoNob 90
Ramsay, William Charles 1930- AmMWSc 92
Ramsay-Fairfax-Lucy, Edmund J. W. H. C. Who 92
Ramsay Rae, Ronald Arthur 1910- Who 92
Ramsaye, Terry 1885-1954 BenetAL 91
Ramsbotham Who 92
Ramsbotham, David 1934- Who 92
Ramsbotham, Meredith 1943- TwCPaSc
Ramsbotham, Peter 1919- IntWW 91, Who 92
Ramsbury, Area Bishop of 1930- Who 92
Ramsby, Mark Delivan 1947- WhoWest 92
Ramsdale, Dan Jerry 1942- AmMWSc 92

**Ramsdell**, Donald Charles 1938- *AmMWSc 92*
**Ramsdell**, Robert Cole 1920- *AmMWSc 92*
**Ramsden**, E. H. *WrDr 92*
**Ramsden**, Herbert 1927- *Who 92, WrDr 92*
**Ramsden**, Hugh Edwin 1921- *AmMWSc 92*
**Ramsden**, James Edward 1923- *Who 92*
**Ramsden**, John 1950- *Who 92*
**Ramsden**, John Andrew 1947- *WrDr 92*
**Ramsden**, John Michael 1928- *Who 92*
**Ramsden**, Michael *Who 92*
**Ramsden**, Michael 1947- *TwCPaSc*
**Ramsden**, Sally *Who 92*
**Ramseier**, Roger I. 1936- *WhoWest 92*
**Ramsell**, Donald John 1958- *WhoAmL 92*
**Ramseur**, Andre William 1949- *WhoBlA 92*
**Ramseur**, Donald E. 1919- *WhoBlA 92*
**Ramseur**, George Shuford 1926- *AmMWSc 92*
**Ramseur**, Isabelle R. 1906- *WhoBlA 92*
**Ramsey**, Alan T 1938- *AmMWSc 92*
**Ramsey**, Alf 1920- *FacFETw*
**Ramsey**, Alfred 1920- *Who 92*
**Ramsey**, Alma *TwCPaSc*
**Ramsey**, Anne Catherine 1959- *WhoWest 92*
**Ramsey**, Arthur Albert 1940- *AmMWSc 92*
**Ramsey**, Arthur Michael 1904-1988 *DcEcMov, FacFETw*
**Ramsey**, Basil Albert Rowland 1929- *Who 92*
**Ramsey**, Bill 1931- *WhoEnt 92*
**Ramsey**, Bob Newton 1938- *WhoMW 92*
**Ramsey**, Brian Gaines 1937- *AmMWSc 92*
**Ramsey**, Charles Edward, Jr. 1956- *WhoBlA 92*
**Ramsey**, Charlie Banks, Jr. 1965- *WhoRel 92*
**Ramsey**, Claude 1918- *WhoWest 92*
**Ramsey**, Clovis Boyd 1934- *AmMWSc 92*
**Ramsey**, David Selmer 1931- *WhoMW 92*
**Ramsey**, Dero Saunders 1928- *AmMWSc 92*
**Ramsey**, Donna Elaine 1941- *WhoBlA 92*
**Ramsey**, Elizabeth Mapelsden 1906- *AmMWSc 92*
**Ramsey**, Fred Lawrence 1939- *AmMWSc 92*
**Ramsey**, Freeman, Jr. 1943- *WhoBlA 92*
**Ramsey**, Gael Kathleen 1942- *Who 92*
**Ramsey**, Gordon Clark 1941- *WrDr 92*
**Ramsey**, Gwynn W 1931- *AmMWSc 92*
**Ramsey**, Harold Arch 1927- *AmMWSc 92*
**Ramsey**, Henry, Jr. 1934- *WhoBlA 92*
**Ramsey**, Henry Bassette, Jr 1924- *WhoIns 92*
**Ramsey**, J W 1934- *WhoAmP 91*
**Ramsey**, Jackson Eugene 1938- *WhoAmP 91*
**Ramsey**, James H. 1931- *WhoBlA 92*
**Ramsey**, James Marvin 1924- *AmMWSc 92*
**Ramsey**, Jarold *DrAPF 91*
**Ramsey**, Jarold 1937- *WrDr 92*
**Ramsey**, Jed Junior 1925- *AmMWSc 92*
**Ramsey**, Jerie Gail 1937- *WhoMW 92*
**Ramsey**, Jerome Capistrano 1953- *WhoBlA 92*
**Ramsey**, Jerry Dwain 1933- *AmMWSc 92*
**Ramsey**, Jerry Warren 1932- *AmMWSc 92*
**Ramsey**, John Charles 1933- *AmMWSc 92*
**Ramsey**, John Scott 1939- *AmMWSc 92*
**Ramsey**, Kevin Dean 1964- *WhoEnt 92*
**Ramsey**, Laura Critchley 1962- *WhoAmL 92*
**Ramsey**, Lawrence William 1945- *AmMWSc 92*
**Ramsey**, Leland Keith 1952- *WhoWest 92*
**Ramsey**, Leonard Gerald Gwynne d1990 *Who 92N*
**Ramsey**, Liston Bryan 1919- *WhoAmP 91*
**Ramsey**, Lloyd Hamilton 1921- *AmMWSc 92*
**Ramsey**, Maynard, III 1943- *AmMWSc 92*
**Ramsey**, Milton W 1848?-1906 *ScFEYrs*
**Ramsey**, Natalie Therese 1963- *WhoEnt 92*
**Ramsey**, Normal Foster, Jr. 1915- *WhoNob 90*
**Ramsey**, Norman F. 1915- *WrDr 92*
**Ramsey**, Norman Foster 1915- *IntWW 91, Who 92*
**Ramsey**, Norman Foster, Jr 1915- *AmMWSc 92*
**Ramsey**, Norman Park 1922- *WhoAmL 92*
**Ramsey**, Otto Bryant 1909- *WhoBlA 92*
**Ramsey**, P Virginia *WhoAmP 91*
**Ramsey**, Paul *DrAPF 91*
**Ramsey**, Paul 1924- *ConPo 91, WrDr 92*
**Ramsey**, Paul Roger 1945- *AmMWSc 92*
**Ramsey**, Paul W 1919- *AmMWSc 92*
**Ramsey**, Peter Michael 1943- *WhoMW 92*
**Ramsey**, Richard David 1947- *WhoAmP 91*
**Ramsey**, Richard Harold 1936- *AmMWSc 92*
**Ramsey**, Richard Ralph 1940- *WhoAmP 91*
**Ramsey**, Robert Bruce 1944- *AmMWSc 92*
**Ramsey**, Ross LaMar 1937- *WhoWest 92*
**Ramsey**, Shawn Summers 1962- *WhoWest 92*
**Ramsey**, Stephen Douglas 1947- *WhoAmL 92*
**Ramsey**, Tom *WhoAmP 91*
**Ramsey**, Waldo Emerson W. *Who 92*
**Ramsey**, Walter S. *WhoBlA 92*
**Ramsey**, William Crites 1912- *WhoAmP 91*
**Ramsey**, William Dale, Jr. 1936- *WhoFI 92*
**Ramseyer**, J. Mark 1954- *WhoAmL 92*
**Ramseyer**, Joseph Eicher 1869-1944 *RelLAm 91*
**Ramseyer**, Loretta Lynne 1946- *WhoAmL 92*
**Ramshaw**, John David 1944- *AmMWSc 92*
**Ramsley**, Alvin Olsen 1920- *AmMWSc 92*
**Ramson**, Ronald W. *WhoRel 92*
**Ramspott**, Lawrence Dewey 1934- *AmMWSc 92*
**Ramstad**, Jim 1946- *AlmAP 92 [port], WhoAmP 91, WhoMW 92*
**Ramstad**, Paul Ellertson 1918- *AmMWSc 92*
**Ramstein**, William Louis 1950- *WhoWest 92*
**Ramu** 196-?-1985 *FacFETw*
**Ramulu**, Mamidala 1949- *AmMWSc 92*
**Ramundo**, Thomas Joseph, Jr. 1948- *WhoRel 92*
**Ramunno**, Thomas Paul 1952- *WhoMW 92*
**Ramus**, Joseph S 1940- *AmMWSc 92*
**Ramwell**, Peter William *AmMWSc 92*
**Ran**, Shulamit 1949- *NewAmDM, WhoEnt 92, WhoMW 92*
**Rana**, Damodar Shumshere Jung Bahadur 1928- *IntWW 91*
**Rana**, J *IntAu&W 91X, WrDr 92*
**Rana**, Jai Pratap 1937- *IntWW 91*
**Rana**, Mohammad A 1949- *AmMWSc 92*
**Rana**, Mohammed Waheeduz-Zaman 1934- *AmMWSc 92*
**Rana**, Ram S 1928- *AmMWSc 92*
**Ranade**, Madhav Bhaskar 1942- *AmMWSc 92*
**Ranade**, Madhu G. 1953- *WhoMW 92*
**Ranade**, Madhukar G 1953- *AmMWSc 92*
**Ranade**, Vinayak Vasudeo 1938- *AmMWSc 92*
**Ranadive**, Narendranath Santuram 1930- *AmMWSc 92*
**Ranahan**, John Paul 1945- *WhoMW 92*
**Ranalli**, Anthony William 1930- *AmMWSc 92*
**Ranasinghe**, K. A. Parinda 1926- *Who 92*
**Rance**, Anita Michelle 1963- *WhoEnt 92*
**Rance**, Gerald Francis 1927- *IntWW 91, Who 92*
**Rance**, Quentin E. 1935- *WhoWest 92*
**Rance**, Victoria 1959- *TwCPaSc*
**Ranchhodlal**, Chinubhai Madhowlal d1990 *Who 92N*
**Ranchhodlal**, Chinubhai Madhowlal 1929- *Who 92*
**Ranchod**, Bhadra 1944- *IntWW 91*
**Rancitelli**, Louis A. 1939- *WhoMW 92*
**Ranck**, James Byrne, Jr *AmMWSc 92*
**Ranck**, Jody Lee 1964- *WhoFI 92*
**Ranck**, John *LesBEnT 92*
**Ranck**, John Philip 1936- *AmMWSc 92*
**Ranck**, John Stevens 1945- *WhoWest 92*
**Ranck**, Ralph Oliver 1923- *AmMWSc 92*
**Rancourt**, John Herbert 1946- *WhoFI 92*
**Rand**, A. Barry 1945- *WhoBlA 92*
**Rand**, Anne M *WhoAmP 91*
**Rand**, Anthony Eden 1939- *WhoAmP 91*
**Rand**, Arthur Gorham, Jr 1935- *AmMWSc 92*
**Rand**, Austin Stanley 1932- *AmMWSc 92*
**Rand**, Ayn 1905-1982 *BenetAL 91, FacFETw [port], TwCSFW 91*
**Rand**, Brett *IntAu&W 91X, TwCWW 91*
**Rand**, Carolyn 1938- *WhoFI 92*
**Rand**, Harold 1928- *IntMPA 92*
**Rand**, Howard Benjamin 1889- *WhoRel 92*
**Rand**, J. H. *WrDr 92*
**Rand**, James Leland 1935- *AmMWSc 92*
**Rand**, Kenneth Richard, Jr. 1937- *WhoFI 92*
**Rand**, Lawrence Anthony 1942- *WhoFI 92*
**Rand**, Leon 1930- *AmMWSc 92*
**Rand**, Mat *TwCWW 91*
**Rand**, Patricia June 1926- *AmMWSc 92*
**Rand**, Paul 1914- *DcTwDes*
**Rand**, Peter *DrAPF 91*
**Rand**, Peter W 1929- *AmMWSc 92*
**Rand**, Phillip Gordon 1934- *AmMWSc 92*
**Rand**, Richard Peter 1937- *AmMWSc 92*
**Rand**, Rick W 1957- *WhoAmP 91*
**Rand**, Robert Collom 1917- *AmMWSc 92*
**Rand**, Salvatore John 1933- *AmMWSc 92*
**Rand**, Samuel 1953- *WhoFI 92*
**Rand**, Stephen Colby 1949- *AmMWSc 92*
**Rand**, Theodore Dehon 1836-1903 *BiInAmS*
**Rand**, Walter 1919- *WhoAmP 91*
**Rand**, William 1926- *WhoAmL 92*
**Rand**, William Medden 1938- *AmMWSc 92*
**Randa**, James P 1947- *AmMWSc 92*
**Randall**, Alan John 1944- *WhoFI 92, WhoMW 92*
**Randall**, Ann Knight *WhoBlA 92*
**Randall**, Arthur Raymond 1927- *WhoFI 92*
**Randall**, Barbara Ann 1958- *WhoMW 92*
**Randall**, Barbara Feucht 1925- *AmMWSc 92*
**Randall**, Belle *DrAPF 91*
**Randall**, Benjamin F. 1946- *WhoRel 92*
**Randall**, Bill 1932- *WhoAmP 91*
**Randall**, Bob 1937- *WhoEnt 92*
**Randall**, Chandler Corydon 1935- *WhoRel 92*
**Randall**, Charles Addison, Jr 1915- *AmMWSc 92*
**Randall**, Charles Chandler 1913- *AmMWSc 92*
**Randall**, Charles H. 1920- *ConAu 133*
**Randall**, Charles Hamilton 1928- *AmMWSc 92*
**Randall**, Charles McWilliams 1938- *AmMWSc 92*
**Randall**, Charles Richard 1920- *Who 92*
**Randall**, Claire 1919- *WhoBlA 92, WhoRel 92*
**Randall**, Clay *IntAu&W 91X, TwCWW 91*
**Randall**, Clifford W 1936- *AmMWSc 92*
**Randall**, Craig 1957- *WhoFI 92*
**Randall**, Dale B. J. 1929- *WrDr 92*
**Randall**, David Clark 1945- *AmMWSc 92*
**Randall**, David John 1938- *AmMWSc 92*
**Randall**, David Keith 1950- *WhoEnt 92*
**Randall**, Dick J. 1931- *WhoWest 92*
**Randall**, Donald Millard 1926- *WhoAmP 91*
**Randall**, Donald Sexton 1927- *WhoWest 92*
**Randall**, Dudley *DrAPF 91*
**Randall**, Dudley 1914- *BenetAL 91, BlkLC [port], ConPo 91, WrDr 92*
**Randall**, Dudley Felker 1914- *WhoBlA 92*
**Randall**, Edmund Laurence 1920- *Who 92*
**Randall**, Edwin Clarence 1949- *WhoAmP 91*
**Randall**, Eileen Louise 1926- *AmMWSc 92*
**Randall**, Elizabeth 1953- *WhoAmP 91*
**Randall**, Eric A 1946- *AmMWSc 92*
**Randall**, Florence Engel 1917- *WrDr 92*
**Randall**, Francis Ballard 1931- *WrDr 92*
**Randall**, Francis James 1942- *AmMWSc 92*
**Randall**, Gary A. 1953- *WhoEnt 92*
**Randall**, Gary Lee 1943- *WhoAmP 91*
**Randall**, Gerald Jean 1931- *WhoIns 92*
**Randall**, Gyles Wade 1942- *AmMWSc 92*
**Randall**, Henry Thomas 1914- *AmMWSc 92*
**Randall**, Howard M 1936- *AmMWSc 92*
**Randall**, J. K. 1929- *NewAmDM*
**Randall**, J Malcom 1916- *AmMWSc 92*
**Randall**, James Carlton, Jr 1937- *AmMWSc 92*
**Randall**, James Edwin 1924- *AmMWSc 92*
**Randall**, James Grafton 1951- *WhoAmL 92*
**Randall**, James R. 1924- *WhoFI 92*
**Randall**, James Ryder 1839-1908 *BenetAL 91*
**Randall**, Janet *WrDr 92*
**Randall**, Janet Ann 1943- *AmMWSc 92*
**Randall**, Jim Allen 1950- *WhoAmP 91*
**Randall**, John Carl 1949- *WhoMW 92*
**Randall**, John D 1932- *AmMWSc 92*
**Randall**, John Douglas 1942- *AmMWSc 92*
**Randall**, John Ernest 1924- *AmMWSc 92, WhoWest 92*
**Randall**, John Frank 1918- *AmMWSc 92*
**Randall**, John Herman 1871-1946 *AmPeW*
**Randall**, John L. 1933- *WrDr 92*
**Randall**, John Witt 1813-1892 *BiInAmS*
**Randall**, Joseph Lindsay 1932- *AmMWSc 92*
**Randall**, Joshua *TwCWW 91, WrDr 92*
**Randall**, Judith Harriet 1936- *WhoEnt 92*
**Randall**, Julia *DrAPF 91*
**Randall**, Julia 1923- *ConPo 91, WrDr 92*
**Randall**, Kenneth Allan 1932- *WhoAmP 91*
**Randall**, Laura Helen 1950- *WhoRel 92*
**Randall**, Lawrence Kessler, Jr 1938- *AmMWSc 92*
**Randall**, Linda Lea 1946- *AmMWSc 92*
**Randall**, Margaret *DrAPF 91*
**Randall**, Margaret 1936- *ConPo 91, LiExTwC, WrDr 92*
**Randall**, Marta 1948- *TwCSFW 91, WrDr 92*
**Randall**, Mercedes Moritz 1895-1977 *AmPeW*
**Randall**, Michael Bennett 1919- *IntAu&W 91, IntWW 91*
**Randall**, Nicholas John 1948- *WhoWest 92*
**Randall**, Peter 1923- *AmMWSc 92*
**Randall**, Phillip Melvin 1946- *WhoBlA 92*
**Randall**, Queen F. 1935- *WhoBlA 92*
**Randall**, Ralph Edward 1947- *WhoAmL 92*
**Randall**, Raymond Victor 1920- *AmMWSc 92*
**Randall**, Robert *ConAu 36NR, TwCSFW 91, WrDr 92*
**Randall**, Robert Lee 1936- *WhoFI 92*
**Randall**, Robert Quentin 1945- *WhoMW 92*
**Randall**, Robin Hahne Steffanie 1961- *WhoEnt 92*
**Randall**, Rona *WrDr 92*
**Randall**, Rona 1938- *IntAu&W 91*
**Randall**, Samuel Jackson 1828-1890 *AmPolLe*
**Randall**, Stephen F. *IntMPA 92*
**Randall**, Steve 1952- *WhoWest 92*
**Randall**, Steven B. 1944- *WhoFI 92*
**Randall**, Stuart 1938- *Who 92*
**Randall**, Tony *LesBEnT 92*
**Randall**, Tony 1920- *IntMPA 92, WhoEnt 92A*
**Randall**, Walter Clark 1916- *AmMWSc 92*
**Randall**, Willard Sterne 1942- *WrDr 92*
**Randall**, William B. 1921- *WhoFI 92*
**Randall**, William Brian 1951- *WhoMW 92*
**Randall**, William Carl 1941- *AmMWSc 92*
**Randall**, William Clarence 1943- *WhoAmP 91*
**Randall**, William Edward 1920- *Who 92*
**Randall**, William S. 1940- *WhoWest 92*
**Randazzo**, Anthony *WhoEnt 92*
**Randazzo**, Anthony Frank 1941- *AmMWSc 92*
**Randazzo**, Joseph Albert 1942- *WhoWest 92*
**Randazzo**, Vince Joseph 1937- *WhoFI 92*
**Rande**, Jeno 1922- *IntWW 91*
**Randell**, Beverley 1931- *WrDr 92*
**Randell**, Peter Neil 1933- *Who 92*
**Randell**, Richard 1946- *AmMWSc 92*
**Randels**, James Bennett 1931- *AmMWSc 92*
**Randerath**, Kurt 1929- *AmMWSc 92*
**Randerson**, Darryl 1937- *AmMWSc 92*
**Randerson**, Sherman 1935- *AmMWSc 92*
**Randhawa**, Jagir Singh 1922- *AmMWSc 92*
**Randi**, James 1928- *WhoEnt 92, WrDr 92*
**Randic**, Milan 1930- *AmMWSc 92*
**Randic**, Mirjana 1934- *AmMWSc 92*
**Randinitis**, Edward J 1940- *AmMWSc 92*
**Randisi**, Elaine Marie 1926- *WhoWest 92*
**Randisi**, Robert J 1951- *TwCWW 91, WrDr 92*
**Randklev**, Edward Hjalmer 1939- *WhoWest 92*
**Randl**, Mary Anne Eliza 1949- *WhoEnt 92*
**Randle**, Berdine Caronell 1929- *WhoBlA 92*
**Randle**, Carver A. 1942- *WhoBlA 92*
**Randle**, Ellen Eugenia Foster 1948- *WhoEnt 92, WhoWest 92*
**Randle**, Lucious A. 1927- *WhoBlA 92*
**Randle**, Michael Charles 1952- *WhoWest 92*
**Randle**, Philip 1926- *Who 92*
**Randle**, Philip John 1926- *IntWW 91*
**Randle**, Robert James 1923- *AmMWSc 92*
**Randle**, Rodger A 1943- *WhoAmP 91*
**Randle**, William Crawford 1952- *WhoWest 92*
**Randleman**, Thomas Lee 1942- *WhoMW 92*
**Randles**, Chester 1918- *AmMWSc 92*
**Randles**, Ronald Herman 1942- *AmMWSc 92*
**Randlett**, Herbert Eldridge, Jr 1917- *AmMWSc 92*
**Randlett**, James Raymond 1942- *WhoAmP 91*
**Randlev**, Karen *DrAPF 91*
**Randman**, Barry I. 1958- *WhoFI 92*
**Randol**, Burton 1937- *AmMWSc 92*
**Randol**, George Cedric 1930- *WhoWest 92*
**Randol**, Jon Charles 1953- *WhoMW 92*
**Randolf**, Alma Louise 1957- *WhoBlA 92*
**Randolph**, A Philip 1889-1979 *FacFETw [port], RComAH*
**Randolph**, A Raymond 1943- *WhoAmP 91*
**Randolph**, Alan Dean 1934- *AmMWSc 92*
**Randolph**, Amanda 1902?-1967 *NotBlAW 92*
**Randolph**, Arthur Raymond 1943- *WhoAmL 92*
**Randolph**, Asa Philip 1889-1979 *AmPeW*
**Randolph**, Bernard Clyde 1922- *WhoBlA 92*
**Randolph**, Bernard P. 1933- *WhoBlA 92*

**Randolph,** Bruce Bradley 1960- *WhoWest 92*
**Randolph,** Christopher Craven 1956- *WhoAmL 92*
**Randolph,** Daniel Parker 1946- *WhoAmL 92, WhoMW 92*
**Randolph,** David 1914- *WhoEnt 92*
**Randolph,** David E. 1936- *WhoBlA 92*
**Randolph,** Denys 1926- *IntWW 91, Who 92*
**Randolph,** Donald Appleby 1939- *WhoMW 92*
**Randolph,** Edmund 1753-1813 *AmPolLe [port], BenetAL 91, BlkwEAR*
**Randolph,** Edward Gordon, Jr 1942- *WhoAmP 91*
**Randolph,** Elizabeth 1917- *WhoBlA 92*
**Randolph,** Elizabeth 1930- *ConAu 135*
**Randolph,** Francis Fitz, Jr. 1927- *WhoFI 92*
**Randolph,** Isham 1848-1920 *BiInAmS*
**Randolph,** James B. 1923- *WhoBlA 92*
**Randolph,** James Collier 1944- *AmMWSc 92*
**Randolph,** James E 1940- *AmMWSc 92*
**Randolph,** James Harrison, Sr. 1917- *WhoFI 92*
**Randolph,** Jennings 1902- *WhoAmP 91*
**Randolph,** John 1773-1833 *AmPolLe, BenetAL 91*
**Randolph,** John 1915- *WhoEnt 92*
**Randolph,** John Fitz 1904- *AmMWSc 92*
**Randolph,** John Hugh Edward 1913- *Who 92*
**Randolph,** John Louis, Jr. 1953- *WhoAmL 92*
**Randolph,** Judson Graves 1927- *AmMWSc 92*
**Randolph,** Kenneth Norris 1938- *AmMWSc 92*
**Randolph,** Leo 1958- *BlkOlyM*
**Randolph,** Leonard *DrAPF 91*
**Randolph,** Leonard Washington, Jr. 1954- *WhoBlA 92*
**Randolph,** Louis T. 1928- *WhoBlA 92*
**Randolph,** Lynwood Parker 1938- *AmMWSc 92*
**Randolph,** Malcolm Logan 1920- *AmMWSc 92*
**Randolph,** Michael Keith 1946- *WhoAmP 91*
**Randolph,** Michael Richard Spencer 1925- *IntAu&W 91, Who 92*
**Randolph,** Nancy Elizabeth *WhoBlA 92*
**Randolph,** Nathaniel Archer 1858-1887 *BiInAmS*
**Randolph,** Paschal Beverly 1825-1875 *RelLAm 91*
**Randolph,** Paul Herbert 1925- *AmMWSc 92*
**Randolph,** Peyton 1721-1775 *BlkwEAR*
**Randolph,** Philip L 1931- *AmMWSc 92*
**Randolph,** Robert Lee 1926- *WhoBlA 92*
**Randolph,** Robert McGehee 1936- *WhoAmL 92*
**Randolph,** Robert Raymond 1937- *WhoAmL 92*
**Randolph,** Steven 1946- *WhoWest 92*
**Randolph,** Thomas 1605?-1635? *RfGEnL 91*
**Randolph,** Toni Regina 1962- *WhoBlA 92*
**Randolph,** Valerie Robin 1962- *WhoAmL 92*
**Randolph,** Vance 1892- *BenetAL 91*
**Randolph,** Virginia 1870-1958 *NotBlAW 92 [port]*
**Randolph,** Willie Larry, Jr. 1954- *WhoBlA 92*
**Randour,** Paul Alfred 1935- *WhoAmL 92, WhoFI 92*
**Randrup,** Jorgen 1946- *AmMWSc 92*
**Rands,** Bernard 1934- *ConCom 92, NewAmDM*
**Randt,** Clark Thorp 1917- *AmMWSc 92*
**Randt,** Clark Thorp, Jr. 1945- *WhoAmL 92*
**Randy,** Harry Anthony 1945- *AmMWSc 92*
**Ranelagh,** John O'B. *Who 92*
**Ranelli,** John Raymond 1946- *WhoFI 92*
**Raner,** Guy Havard, Jr 1919- *WhoAmP 91*
**Raney,** Bob 1945 *WhoAmP 91*
**Raney,** David Elliot 1951- *WhoMW 92*
**Raney,** George Neal 1922- *AmMWSc 92*
**Raney,** Gloria Juhl 1955- *WhoFI 92*
**Raney,** Harley Gene 1940- *AmMWSc 92*
**Raney,** J P 1931- *AmMWSc 92*
**Raney,** Jimmie W *WhoAmP 91*
**Raney,** Miriam Day 1922- *WhoEnt 92*
**Raney,** Richard Beverly 1906- *AmMWSc 92*
**Raney,** Russell Keith 1937- *AmMWSc 92*
**Raney,** Tucker 1952- *WhoAmL 92*
**Raney,** Wayne 1921- *NewAmDM*
**Raney,** William Perin 1927- *AmMWSc 92*
**Ranftl,** Robert M 1925- *AmMWSc 92*
**Ranftl,** Robert Matthew 1925- *WhoFI 92, WhoWest 92*
**Ranfurly,** Earl of 1929- *Who 92*
**Rang,** Edward Roy 1927- *AmMWSc 92*
**Rang,** Humphrey Peter 1936- *Who 92*
**Ranganathan,** Brahmanpalli N 1945- *AmMWSc 92*
**Ranganayaki,** Rambabu Pothireddy 1942- *AmMWSc 92*
**Range,** Dawn Marie 1966- *WhoFI 92*
**Range,** M. Athalie 1918- *WhoBlA 92*
**Range,** Martha Ann *WhoEnt 92*
**Range,** R Michael 1944- *AmMWSc 92*
**Rangel,** Charles B. 1930- *AlmAP 92 [port], WhoAmP 91, WhoBlA 92*
**Rangel,** Ignacio 1953- *WhoHisp 92*
**Rangel,** Irma 1931- *WhoAmP 91, WhoHisp 92*
**Rangel,** Lyle E. 1943- *WhoHisp 92*
**Rangel,** Robert Edward 1938- *WhoHisp 92*
**Rangel,** Roger Henrique 1958- *WhoHisp 92*
**Rangell,** Sydelle Ray 1931- *WhoEnt 92*
**Ranger,** Douglas 1916- *Who 92*
**Ranger,** Keith Brian 1935- *AmMWSc 92*
**Ranger,** Terence Osborn 1929- *Who 92*
**Rangila,** Nancy Arnevna 1936- *WhoWest 92*
**Rangley,** Olivia *WrDr 92*
**Rango,** Albert 1942- *AmMWSc 92*
**Rangoonwala,** Mohamed Aly 1924- *IntWW 91*
**Ranhand,** Jon M 1939- *AmMWSc 92*
**Ranhotra,** Gurbachan Singh 1935- *AmMWSc 92*
**Rani of Jhansi** *EncAmaz 91*
**Ranieri,** Daniel J 1951- *WhoAmP 91*
**Ranieri,** Lorraide M 1943- *IntAu&W 91*
**Ranieri,** Richard Leo 1943- *AmMWSc 92*
**Ranieri,** Richard Stephen 1959- *WhoAmL 92*
**Ranieri,** Robert A *WhoAmP 91*
**Ranis,** Gustav 1929- *WhoFI 92, WrDr 92*
**Ranish,** Donald Roseman 1943- *WhoWest 92*
**Raniville,** Francis O 1920- *IntAu&W 91*
**Ranjeva,** Raymond 1942- *IntWW 91*
**Rank,** Benjamin 1911- *Who 92*
**Rank,** Benjamin Keith 1911- *IntWW 91*
**Rank,** Bill 1904-1979 *NewAmDM*
**Rank,** Gerald Henry 1940- *AmMWSc 92*
**Rank,** Hugh Donald 1932- *WhoMW 92*
**Rank,** John Thomas 1947- *WhoAmL 92*
**Rank,** Joseph McArthur 1918- *IntWW 91, Who 92*
**Rank,** Otto 1884-1939 *FacFETw*
**Rankeillour,** Baron 1935- *Who 92*
**Rankel,** Lillian Ann *AmMWSc 92*
**Ranken,** J. Thomas 1956- *WhoWest 92*
**Ranken,** William Allison 1928- *AmMWSc 92*
**Ranki,** Dezso 1951- *IntWW 91*
**Ranki,** Gyorgy 1907- *ConCom 92, IntWW 91*
**Rankin,** Alexander Donald 1916- *AmMWSc 92*
**Rankin,** Alfred Marshall, Jr. 1941- *WhoFI 92, WhoMW 92*
**Rankin,** Alick Michael 1935- *IntWW 91, Who 92*
**Rankin,** Andrew 1924- *Who 92*
**Rankin,** Ann 1950- *WhoAmL 92*
**Rankin,** Arthur David 1936- *WhoMW 92*
**Rankin,** Charles I. 1937- *WhoBlA 92*
**Rankin,** Clyde Evan, III 1950- *WhoAmL 92*
**Rankin,** Douglas Whiting 1931- *AmMWSc 92*
**Rankin,** Edgar E. 1914-1981 *WhoBlA 92N*
**Rankin,** Edward Anthony 1940- *WhoBlA 92*
**Rankin,** Edward J 1948- *WhoIns 92*
**Rankin,** Gary Laban 1948- *WhoRel 92*
**Rankin,** Gary O'Neal 1949- *AmMWSc 92*
**Rankin,** Gene Raymond 1940- *WhoAmL 92*
**Rankin,** Helen Cross *WhoWest 92*
**Rankin,** Herbert David 1931- *WrDr 92*
**Rankin,** Ian 1932- *Who 92*
**Rankin,** James Deans 1918- *Who 92*
**Rankin,** James Michael 1949- *WhoMW 92*
**Rankin,** James Patrick 1957- *WhoFI 92*
**Rankin,** James Winton 1943- *WhoAmL 92*
**Rankin,** Jean 1905- *Who 92*
**Rankin,** Jeannette 1880-1973 *AmPolLe, FacFETw, RComAH*
**Rankin,** Jeannette Pickering 1880-1973 *AmPeW, HanAmWH*
**Rankin,** Jeremiah Eames 1828-1924 *BenetAL 91*
**Rankin,** Joanna Marie *AmMWSc 92*
**Rankin,** Joel Sender 1931- *AmMWSc 92*
**Rankin,** John 1923- *AmMWSc 92*
**Rankin,** John Carter 1919- *AmMWSc 92, WhoMW 92*
**Rankin,** John Horsley Grey 1937- *AmMWSc 92*
**Rankin,** Joseph Eugene 1920- *AmMWSc 92*
**Rankin,** K. L. 1898-1991 *CurBio 91N*
**Rankin,** Karl L. d1991 *NewYTBS 91*
**Rankin,** L Helen 1936- *WhoAmP 91*
**Rankin,** Marlene O. 1939- *WhoBlA 92*
**Rankin,** Michael L. *WhoBlA 92*
**Rankin,** Paula *DrAPF 91*
**Rankin,** Robert Alexander 1915- *Who 92*
**Rankin,** Robert Craig McPherson 1937- *Who 92*
**Rankin,** Sidney 1931- *AmMWSc 92*
**Rankin,** William Parkman 1917- *WhoFI 92, WhoWest 92*
**Rankin-Bass** *LesBEnT 92*
**Rankine,** Baxter James 1936- *WhoFI 92*
**Rankine,** Jean Morag 1941- *Who 92*
**Rankine,** John *WrDr 92*
**Rankine,** John 1918- *TwCSFW 91*
**Rankine,** John 1923- *WhoAmP 91*
**Ranking,** Robert Duncan 1915- *Who 92*
**Rankl,** Karl Franz 1898-1968 *NewAmDM*
**Ranly,** Donald Peter 1935- *WhoMW 92*
**Rann,** Emery Louvelle 1914- *WhoBlA 92*
**Rannabargar,** Marvin Ray 1939- *WhoRel 92*
**Rannels,** Donald Eugene, Jr 1946- *AmMWSc 92*
**Ranney,** Brooks 1915- *AmMWSc 92*
**Ranney,** Carleton David 1928- *AmMWSc 92*
**Ranney,** David Francis 1943- *AmMWSc 92*
**Ranney,** Helen M 1920- *AmMWSc 92, IntWW 91*
**Ranney,** J Buckminster 1919- *AmMWSc 92*
**Ranney,** Richard Raymond 1939- *AmMWSc 92*
**Ranney,** Richard William 1944- *WhoMW 92*
**Rannie,** Ian 1915- *Who 92*
**Ranniger,** Leslie Jean 1957- *WhoAmL 92*
**Rannit,** Aleksis 1914-1985 *LiExTwC*
**Ranoa,** Regina Bautista 1961- *WhoWest 92*
**Ranon,** Jose Antonio 1932- *WhoHisp 92*
**Ranov,** Theodor 1910- *AmMWSc 92*
**Ransbottom,** Michael Allen 1958- *WhoMW 92*
**Ransburg,** Frank S. 1943- *WhoBlA 92*
**Ranschburg,** Herbert Josef 1919- *WhoFI 92*
**Ransford,** George Henry 1941- *AmMWSc 92*
**Ransford,** Oliver 1914- *WrDr 92*
**Ransick,** Barry A. 1953- *WhoFI 92*
**Ransil,** Bernard J 1929- *AmMWSc 92*
**Ransleben,** Guido E, Jr 1925- *AmMWSc 92*
**Ransley,** Peter 1931- *IntAu&W 91, WrDr 92*
**Ransmeier,** Denis Sirera 1947- *WhoFI 92*
**Ransohoff,** Joseph 1915- *AmMWSc 92*
**Ransohoff,** Martin *LesBEnT 92*
**Ransohoff,** Martin 1927- *IntMPA 92, WhoEnt 92*
**Ransom,** Bill *DrAPF 91*
**Ransom,** Bill 1945- *IntAu&W 91*
**Ransom,** Bruce Davis 1951- *AmMWSc 92*
**Ransom,** Burnella Jackson 1940- *WhoBlA 92*
**Ransom,** C J 1940- *AmMWSc 92*
**Ransom,** Candice F. 1952- *WrDr 92*
**Ransom,** David P. 1932- *WhoRel 92*
**Ransom,** Dick 1929- *WhoAmP 91*
**Ransom,** Eugene 1927- *WhoEnt 92*
**Ransom,** Gary Elliott 1941- *WhoBlA 92*
**Ransom,** Harry Howe 1922- *WrDr 92*
**Ransom,** J T 1920- *AmMWSc 92*
**Ransom,** Jay Ellis 1914- *WrDr 92*
**Ransom,** Jeremy *WhoEnt 92*
**Ransom,** John Crowe 1888-1974 *BenetAL 91, ConAu 34NR, FacFETw*
**Ransom,** Norman 1923- *WhoBlA 92*
**Ransom,** Preston L. 1936- *WhoBlA 92*
**Ransom,** Preston Lee 1936- *AmMWSc 92*
**Ransom,** Reverdy Cassius 1861-1959 *RelLAm 91*
**Ransom,** Richard E *WhoAmP 91*
**Ransom,** Richard E. 1932- *WhoAmL 92, WhoWest 92*
**Ransom,** Robert Edward, Jr. 1933- *WhoEnt 92*
**Ransom,** Robert Louis 1950- *WhoRel 92*
**Ransom,** Willard Blystone 1916- *WhoBlA 92*
**Ransom,** William Harrison 1938- *WhoAmL 92*
**Ransom,** William Henry Howe 1958- *WhoEnt 92*
**Ransome,** Arthur 1884-1967 *ScFEYrs*
**Ransome,** Ronald Dean 1954- *AmMWSc 92*
**Ranson,** Charles Wesley 1903-1988 *DcEcMov*
**Ranson,** Guy Harvey 1916- *WhoRel 92*
**Ranson,** John S 1929- *WhoAmP 91*
**Ranson,** Nicholas *DrAPF 91*
**Ranson,** Robert David 1942- *WhoFI 92*
**Ranson,** Ronald George, Jr. 1941- *WhoEnt 92*
**Ranson,** Samuel Lee 1923- *WhoAmP 91*
**Ransopher,** Tad D. 1949- *WhoAmL 92*
**Rant,** James William 1936- *Who 92*
**Rant,** William Howard 1945- *AmMWSc 92*
**Ranta,** Donald Eli 1942- *WhoFI 92*
**Ranta Aho,** Martha Helen 1923- *WhoMW 92*
**Rantanen,** Jarmo Heikki Kullervo 1944- *IntWW 91*
**Rantzen,** Esther Louise 1940- *Who 92*
**Ranu,** Harcharan Singh *AmMWSc 92, IntWW 91*
**Ranu,** Rajinder S 1940- *AmMWSc 92*
**Ranum,** Jane 1947- *WhoAmP 91*
**Ranum,** Paul Arthur 1929- *WhoRel 92*
**Ranz,** William E 1922- *AmMWSc 92*
**Ranzahuer,** Guillermo Gonzalez 1928- *WhoRel 92*
**Ranzoni,** Francis Verne 1916- *AmMWSc 92*
**Rao Shoukun** 1915- *IntWW 91*
**Rao Xingli** 1925- *IntWW 91*
**Rao,** Ananda G 1930- *AmMWSc 92*
**Rao,** B Seshagiri 1936- *AmMWSc 92*
**Rao,** Balakrishna Raghavendra 1936- *AmMWSc 92*
**Rao,** Calyampudi Radhakrishna 1920- *IntWW 91, Who 92*
**Rao,** Chalamalasetty Venkateswara 1941- *AmMWSc 92*
**Rao,** Chandra Rajeswar 1914- *IntWW 91*
**Rao,** Chintamani Nagesa Ramachandra 1934- *IntWW 91, Who 92*
**Rao,** Desiraju Bhavanarayana 1936- *AmMWSc 92*
**Rao,** Devulapalli V G L N 1933- *AmMWSc 92*
**Rao,** Gandikota V 1934- *AmMWSc 92*
**Rao,** Girimaji J Sathyanarayana 1934- *AmMWSc 92*
**Rao,** Gopal Subba 1938- *AmMWSc 92*
**Rao,** Gopalakrishna M 1944- *AmMWSc 92*
**Rao,** Gundu Hirisave Rama 1938- *AmMWSc 92*
**Rao,** Helene Tragos 1964- *WhoMW 92*
**Rao,** Jaganmohan Boppana Lakshmi 1936- *AmMWSc 92*
**Rao,** Jalagam Vengala 1922- *IntWW 91*
**Rao,** Jammalamadaka S *AmMWSc 92*
**Rao,** Jonnagadda Nalini Kanth 1937- *AmMWSc 92*
**Rao,** K. Ramkrishna 1932- *WrDr 92*
**Rao,** K V N 1933- *AmMWSc 92*
**Rao,** K. Vaninadha 1957- *WhoMW 92*
**Rao,** Kalipatnapu Narasimha 1937- *AmMWSc 92*
**Rao,** Kandarpa Narahari 1921- *AmMWSc 92*
**Rao,** Koduru V. S. 1940- *WhoBlA 92*
**Rao,** Kona Prabhakara 1916- *IntWW 91*
**Rao,** Krothapalli Ranga 1941- *AmMWSc 92*
**Rao,** M S 1942- *AmMWSc 92*
**Rao,** Malempati Madhusudana 1929- *AmMWSc 92*
**Rao,** Mamidanna S 1931- *AmMWSc 92*
**Rao,** Mentreddi Anandha 1937- *AmMWSc 92*
**Rao,** Mrinalini Chatta *AmMWSc 92*
**Rao,** Nutakki Gouri Sankara 1933- *AmMWSc 92*
**Rao,** P Krishna 1930- *AmMWSc 92*
**Rao,** P. V. Narasimha 1921- *Who 92*
**Rao,** Palakurthi Suresh Chandra 1947- *AmMWSc 92*
**Rao,** Pamulaparti Venkata Narasimha 1921- *NewYTBS 91*
**Rao,** Papineni Seethapathi 1937- *AmMWSc 92*
**Rao,** Pejaver Vishwamber 1935- *AmMWSc 92*
**Rao,** Pemmaraju Narasimha 1928- *AmMWSc 92*
**Rao,** Pemmaraju Venugopala 1932- *AmMWSc 92*
**Rao,** Pemmasani Dharma 1933- *AmMWSc 92*
**Rao,** Poduri S R S 1934- *AmMWSc 92*
**Rao,** Potu Narasimha 1930- *AmMWSc 92*
**Rao,** Prakash 1941- *AmMWSc 92*
**Rao,** R A *AmMWSc 92*
**Rao,** R A 1934- *AmMWSc 92*
**Rao,** Raj G. 1946- *WhoFI 92*
**Rao,** Raja 1908- *ConNov 91, LiExTwC, RfGEnL 91*
**Rao,** Raja 1909- *IntWW 91, WrDr 92*
**Rao,** Ramachandra M R 1931- *AmMWSc 92*
**Rao,** Ramgopal P 1942- *AmMWSc 92*
**Rao,** Salem S 1934- *AmMWSc 92*
**Rao,** Samohineeveesu Trivikrama 1944- *AmMWSc 92*
**Rao,** Shankaranarayana Ramohallinanjunda 1923- *AmMWSc 92*
**Rao,** Sreedhar P 1943- *AmMWSc 92*
**Rao,** Suryanarayana K 1939- *AmMWSc 92*
**Rao,** V Udaya S 1938- *AmMWSc 92*

**Rao,** Valluru Bhavanarayana 1934- AmMWSc 92
**Rao,** Vaman 1933- WhoFI 92
**Rao,** Vasan N 1929- AmMWSc 92
**Rao,** Veldanda Venugopal 1930- AmMWSc 92
**Rao,** Vijay Madan 1950- AmMWSc 92
**Rao,** Vijayendra Kasturi Ranga Varadaraja 1908- IntWW 91
**Rao,** Yalamanchili A K 1943- AmMWSc 92
**Rao,** Yalamanchili Krishna 1941- AmMWSc 92
**Rao,** Yedavalli Shyamsunder 1930- AmMWSc 92
**Raouf,** Abdul 1929- AmMWSc 92
**Raoul,** Alfred 1930- IntWW 91
**Rapa,** Philip John, II 1945- WhoEnt 92
**Rapa,** Stephen Joseph 1958- WhoEnt 92
**Rapaccioli,** Michel Antoine 1934- WhoFI 92
**Rapacz,** Jan 1928- AmMWSc 92
**Rapaczynski,** Andrzej 1947- WhoAmL 92
**Rapai,** Gyula 1923- IntWW 91
**Rapaka,** Rao Sambasiva 1943- AmMWSc 92
**Rapanos,** Judith Ann 1939- WhoAmP 91
**Rapant,** Larry DrAPF 91
**Rapaport,** Carol Jean 1957- WhoFI 92
**Rapaport,** Elliot 1924- AmMWSc 92
**Rapaport,** Felix Theodosius 1929- AmMWSc 92
**Rapaport,** Herman 1947- ConAu 35NR
**Rapaport,** Irving 1925- AmMWSc 92
**Rapaport,** Jacobo 1930- AmMWSc 92
**Rapaport,** Pola Garance 1956- WhoEnt 92
**Rapaport,** Samuel I 1921- AmMWSc 92
**Rapaport,** William Joseph 1946- AmMWSc 92
**Rapeanu,** Valeriu 1931- IntWW 91
**Raper,** Carlene Allen 1925- AmMWSc 92
**Raper,** George d1990 Who 92N
**Raper,** Graham 1932- Who 92
**Raper,** Kenneth Bryan 1908- IntWW 91
**Rapf,** Matthew d1991 LesBEnT 92, NewYTBS 91
**Rapf,** Matthew 1920- IntMPA 92
**Rapf,** Maurice Harry 1914- WhoEnt 92
**Rapfogel,** William Eugene 1955- WhoFI 92
**Raphael** 1943?- CurBio 91 [port]
**Raphael,** Adam Eliot Geoffrey 1938- IntAu&W 91, Who 92
**Raphael,** Bernard Joseph 1935- WhoBlA 92
**Raphael,** Chaim 1908- Who 92, WrDr 92
**Raphael,** Dan DrAPF 91
**Raphael,** David Daiches 1916- Who 92, WrDr 92
**Raphael,** Donna Mary 1958- WhoWest 92
**Raphael,** Farid 1933- IntWW 91
**Raphael,** Frederic 1931- ConNov 91, IntMPA 92, WrDr 92
**Raphael,** Frederic Michael DrAPF 91
**Raphael,** Frederic Michael 1931- IntAu&W 91, IntWW 91, Who 92
**Raphael,** John Patrick 1955- WhoAmP 91
**Raphael,** Lennox DrAPF 91
**Raphael,** Lev 1954- ConAu 134
**Raphael,** Louise Arakelian 1937- AmMWSc 92
**Raphael,** Mark Ross 1952- WhoRel 92
**Raphael,** Martin George 1946- WhoWest 92
**Raphael,** Paul Michel 1963- WhoFI 92
**Raphael,** Phyllis DrAPF 91
**Raphael,** Ralph Alexander 1921- Who 92
**Raphael,** Rick 1919- WrDr 92
**Raphael,** Sally Jessy WhoEnt 92
**Raphael,** Sarah 1960- TwCPaSc
**Raphael,** Stuart I 1938- WhoIns 92
**Raphael,** Thomas 1922- AmMWSc 92
**Raphael,** Timothy John 1929- Who 92
**Raphael,** Wendy TwCPaSc
**Raphaelson,** Joel 1928- WhoMW 92
**Raphaelson,** Samson 1896-1983 BenetAL 91
**Raphel,** David 1925- IntMPA 92
**Raphling,** Sam 1910- NewAmDM
**Raphoe,** Bishop of 1940- Who 92
**Rapier,** Kenny 1936- WhoAmP 91
**Rapier,** Pascal Moran 1914- WhoWest 92
**Rapier,** Wayne WhoEnt 92
**Rapilly,** Yves Georges 1931- IntWW 91
**Rapin,** Isabelle 1927- AmMWSc 92
**Rapin,** John Edward 1958- WhoMW 92
**Rapisardi,** Salvatore C 1941- AmMWSc 92
**Rapke,** Jack WhoEnt 92
**Rapkin,** Joan Teresa Markwood 1944- WhoEnt 92
**Rapkin,** Myron Colman 1938- AmMWSc 92
**Rapoport,** Abraham 1926- AmMWSc 92
**Rapoport,** Alan M. 1942- ConAu 134
**Rapoport,** Anatol 1911- AmMWSc 92
**Rapoport,** Bernard 1917- WhoFI 92, WhoIns 92
**Rapoport,** David E. 1956- WhoAmL 92
**Rapoport,** Henry 1918- AmMWSc 92
**Rapoport,** Iosif Abramovich 1912- IntWW 91
**Rapoport,** Judith Livant 1933- AmMWSc 92
**Rapoport,** Lorence 1919- AmMWSc 92
**Rapoport,** Louis 1942- WrDr 92
**Rapoport,** Miles 1949- WhoAmP 91
**Rapoport,** Natalie 1927- WhoAmP 91
**Rapoport,** Robert Norman 1924- WrDr 92
**Rapoport,** Roger 1946- WrDr 92
**Rapoport,** Stanley I 1932- AmMWSc 92
**Raposo,** Jose Hipolito 1885-1953 BiDExR
**Raposo,** Mario 1929- IntWW 91
**Rapoza,** Robert Augustus 1950- WhoFI 92
**Rapoza,** Tony A. 1919- WhoWest 92
**Rapp,** Christian F. 1933- WhoFI 92
**Rapp,** Donald 1934- AmMWSc 92
**Rapp,** Dorothy Glaves 1943- AmMWSc 92
**Rapp,** Fred 1929- AmMWSc 92
**Rapp,** George 1757-1847 BenetAL 91
**Rapp,** George Robert, Jr 1930- AmMWSc 92
**Rapp,** Gerald Duane 1933- WhoAmL 92, WhoFI 92
**Rapp,** Ilana Beth 1968- WhoEnt 92
**Rapp,** James Allen 1946- WhoFI 92
**Rapp,** Janet Lorraine 1921- WhoMW 92
**Rapp,** John Edward 1936- WhoMW 92
**Rapp,** John P 1934- AmMWSc 92
**Rapp,** Larry P. 1948- WhoFI 92
**Rapp,** Lea Bayers 1946- WhoFI 92
**Rapp,** Paul Ernest 1949- AmMWSc 92
**Rapp,** Paul Winston 1937- WhoEnt 92
**Rapp,** Richard Henry 1937- AmMWSc 92
**Rapp,** Robert 1921- AmMWSc 92
**Rapp,** Robert 1929- AmMWSc 92
**Rapp,** Robert Anthony 1934- AmMWSc 92
**Rapp,** Robert David 1950- WhoAmL 92
**Rapp,** Robert Dietrich 1930- AmMWSc 92
**Rapp,** Stephen John 1949- WhoAmP 91
**Rapp,** Waldean G 1936- AmMWSc 92
**Rapp,** William F. 1918- WhoMW 92
**Rapp,** William Rodger 1936- AmMWSc 92
**Rapp,** William Venable 1939- WhoFI 92
**Rapp,** Wolfgang 1944- WhoFI 92
**Rapp-Svrcek,** Paul S 1955- WhoAmP 91
**Rappaport,** Anna Maria 1940- WhoIns 92
**Rappaport,** Aron M 1904- AmMWSc 92
**Rappaport,** Charles Owen 1950- WhoAmL 92
**Rappaport,** Cyril M. 1921- WhoMW 92
**Rappaport,** David 1907- AmMWSc 92
**Rappaport,** David 1951-1990 ConTFT 9
**Rappaport,** David 1952-1990 AnObit 1990
**Rappaport,** Earle Samuel, Jr. 1935- WhoAmL 92
**Rappaport,** George Lee 1920- WhoEnt 92
**Rappaport,** Harry P 1927- AmMWSc 92
**Rappaport,** Irving 1923- AmMWSc 92
**Rappaport,** James Wyant 1956- WhoFI 92
**Rappaport,** Jerry Marc 1951- WhoEnt 92
**Rappaport,** Lawrence 1928- AmMWSc 92
**Rappaport,** Maurice 1926- AmMWSc 92
**Rappaport,** Raymond, Jr 1922- AmMWSc 92
**Rappaport,** Richard Warren 1948- WhoAmL 92
**Rappaport,** Roy Abraham 1926- WhoRel 92
**Rappaport,** Samuel 1932- WhoAmP 91
**Rappaport,** Sherman Loeb 1930- WhoMW 92
**Rappaport,** Stephen Morris 1948- AmMWSc 92
**Rappaport,** Stephen S 1938- AmMWSc 92
**Rappaport,** Steve 1948- ConAu 134
**Rappeneau,** Jean-Paul 1932- IntWW 91
**Rapper,** Irving 1904- IntMPA 92
**Rapperport,** Eugene J 1930- AmMWSc 92
**Rapping,** Leonard A. d1991 NewYTBS 91
**Rapping,** Leonard Allen 1934- WhoFI 92
**Rappleyea,** Alan Andrew 1961- WhoAmL 92
**Rappleyea,** Clarence D 1933- WhoAmP 91
**Rappoport,** David Steven 1957- ConAu 133
**Rappoport,** Fred 1946- WhoEnt 92
**Rappoport,** Gerald J. 1925- IntMPA 92
**Rapport,** David Joseph 1939- AmMWSc 92
**Rapport,** Joe Rooks 1957- WhoRel 92
**Rapport,** Maurice M 1919- AmMWSc 92
**Rapport,** Richard Louis 1915- WhoMW 92
**Rapson,** Ralph 1914- DcTwDes, IntWW 91
**Rapson,** Richard L. 1937- WhoWest 92, WrDr 92
**Rapuano,** Mary Anne 1934- WhoWest 92
**Rapundalo,** Stephen T 1958- AmMWSc 92
**Raquel,** Edward M. WhoHisp 92
**Rard,** Joseph Antoine 1945- AmMWSc 92
**Rarick,** John Richard 1924- WhoAmP 91
**Raridon,** Richard Jay 1931- AmMWSc 92
**Rarita,** William Roland 1907- AmMWSc 92
**Ras,** Zbigniew Wieslaw 1947- AmMWSc 92
**Rasa,** Ponciano C WhoAmP 91
**Rasaiah,** Jayendran C 1934- AmMWSc 92
**Rasanen,** Eric K 1946- WhoIns 92
**Rasanen,** Eric Konrad 1946- WhoFI 92
**Rasaputram,** Warnasena 1927- IntWW 91
**Rasband,** Ronald A. 1951- WhoWest 92
**Rasband,** S Neil 1939- AmMWSc 92
**Rasberry,** Robert Eugene WhoBlA 92
**Rasberry,** Stanley Dexter 1941- AmMWSc 92
**Rascals,** The NewAmDM
**Rasch,** Ellen M 1927- AmMWSc 92
**Rasch,** Janet Smith 1962- WhoAmL 92
**Rasch,** Otto 1891-1948 EncTR 91
**Rasch,** Richard Guy Carne 1918- Who 92
**Rasch,** Robert 1926- AmMWSc 92
**Rasche,** John Frederick 1936- AmMWSc 92
**Rasche,** Robert Harold 1941- WhoFI 92, WhoMW 92
**Raschke,** Carl Allan 1944- WhoRel 92, WhoWest 92
**Raschko,** Elizabeth Bernadette 1925- WhoWest 92
**Rasco,** Albert 1925- WhoAmP 91
**Rasco,** Barbara A 1957- AmMWSc 92
**Rasco,** Kay Frances 1925- WhoMW 92
**Rascoe,** Burton 1892-1957 BenetAL 91
**Rase,** Howard F 1921- AmMWSc 92
**Rase,** William 1926- WhoEnt 92
**Raseman,** Chad J 1918- AmMWSc 92
**Rasenick,** Mark M 1949- AmMWSc 92
**Rasenick,** Mark Mitchell WhoMW 92
**Raser,** Harold Eugene 1947- WhoRel 92
**Raser,** Lorri Ann 1962- WhoMW 92
**Rasera,** Robert Louis 1939- AmMWSc 92
**Rasero,** Lawrence Joseph, Jr 1938- WhoAmP 91
**Rasey,** Janet Sue 1942- AmMWSc 92
**Rash,** Alan Vance 1931- WhoAmL 92
**Rash,** Fred Howard 1941- AmMWSc 92
**Rash,** Jay Justen 1941- AmMWSc 92
**Rash,** John Edward 1943- AmMWSc 92
**Rash,** Steven Britton 1947- WhoFI 92
**Rashad,** Ahmad 1949- WhoBlA 92
**Rashad,** Phylicia WhoEnt 92
**Rashad,** Phylicia 1948- IntMPA 92, WhoBlA 92
**Rashdall,** Edward 1860-1888 ThHEIm
**Rasheed,** Howard S. 1953- WhoBlA 92
**Rasheed,** Suraiya AmMWSc 92
**Rashford,** John Harvey 1947- WhoBlA 92
**Rashid bin Said al-Maktoum,** Sheikh 1914-1990 AnObit 1990
**Rashid Bin Said Al-Maktum** IntWW 91
**Rashid bin Said al Maktum,** Sheik 1914-1990 FacFETw
**Rashid,** Carl, Jr. 1948- WhoAmL 92
**Rashid,** Mohammad 1915- IntWW 91
**Rashid,** Muhammad H. 1945- WhoMW 92
**Rashid,** Salim 1949- WhoFI 92, WhoMW 92
**Rashid,** Zafar 1950- WhoIns 92
**Rashidov,** Sharaf Rashidovich 1917-1983 SovUnBD
**Rashied,** A. John 1941- WhoBlA 92
**Rashish,** Myer 1924- WhoAmP 91
**Rashkin,** Jay Arthur 1933- AmMWSc 92
**Rashkind,** William Jacobson 1922- AmMWSc 92
**Rashkow,** Ronald 1940- WhoFI 92
**Rashleigh,** Richard 1958- Who 92
**Rashleigh Belcher,** John Who 92
**Rasic,** Janko 1938- WhoFI 92
**Rasile,** Craig Vincent 1961- WhoAmL 92
**Rasin,** Alexander Parks, III 1943- WhoAmL 92
**Rask,** Michael Raymond 1930- WhoFI 92, WhoWest 92
**Rask,** Norman 1933- AmMWSc 92
**Raska,** Karel Frantisek, Jr 1939- AmMWSc 92
**Raskas,** Heschel Joshua 1941- AmMWSc 92
**Raski,** Dewey John 1917- AmMWSc 92
**Raskin,** Abraham Henry 1911- IntAu&W 91
**Raskin,** Barbara 1935- IntAu&W 91
**Raskin,** Betty Lou 1924- AmMWSc 92
**Raskin,** Jane Serene 1955- WhoAmL 92
**Raskin,** Joan 1930- AmMWSc 92
**Raskin,** Judith 1928-1984 NewAmDM
**Raskin,** Neil Hugh 1935- AmMWSc 92
**Raskin,** Victor 1944- WhoMW 92
**Raskind,** Leo Joseph 1919- WhoAmL 92, WhoFI 92
**Raskob,** Anthony William, Jr. 1960- WhoWest 92
**Raskova,** Jana D 1940- AmMWSc 92
**Rasky,** Harry 1928- WhoEnt 92
**Raslear,** Thomas G 1947- AmMWSc 92
**Rasminsky,** Louis 1908- Who 92
**Rasmus,** John Charles 1941- WhoAmL 92
**Rasmusen,** Benjamin Arthur 1926- AmMWSc 92
**Rasmuson,** Brent Jacobsen 1950- WhoWest 92
**Rasmuson,** Elmer Edwin 1909- WhoFI 92, WhoWest 92
**Rasmussen,** A L 1909- WhoAmP 91
**Rasmussen,** Alice Call 1947- WhoMW 92
**Rasmussen,** Anders Fogh 1953- IntWW 91
**Rasmussen,** Arlette Irene AmMWSc 92
**Rasmussen,** Bruce David 1946- WhoAmP 91
**Rasmussen,** Chris Royce 1931- AmMWSc 92
**Rasmussen,** Dale Alan 1952- WhoMW 92
**Rasmussen,** David Irvin 1934- AmMWSc 92
**Rasmussen,** David Tab 1958- AmMWSc 92
**Rasmussen,** Dennis Loy 1940- WhoFI 92
**Rasmussen,** Don Henry 1944- AmMWSc 92
**Rasmussen,** Douglas John 1941- WhoAmL 92
**Rasmussen,** Eric Ashby 1956- WhoWest 92
**Rasmussen,** Evie Webb 1952- WhoFI 92
**Rasmussen,** Harry Paul 1939- AmMWSc 92
**Rasmussen,** Howard 1925- AmMWSc 92
**Rasmussen,** James Michael 1959- WhoMW 92
**Rasmussen,** Janet Elaine 1949- WhoWest 92
**Rasmussen,** Jeffrey Gene 1960- WhoFI 92
**Rasmussen,** Jeri Wharton 1934- WhoAmP 91
**Rasmussen,** Jessie K 1945- WhoAmP 91
**Rasmussen,** Jewell J 1940- AmMWSc 92
**Rasmussen,** John Curtis, Jr 1943- WhoAmP 91
**Rasmussen,** John Oscar, Jr 1926- AmMWSc 92
**Rasmussen,** Jon Hildreth 1938- WhoMW 92
**Rasmussen,** Julie Shimmon 1940- WhoEnt 92
**Rasmussen,** Karl Aage 1947- ConCom 92
**Rasmussen,** Kathleen Goertz 1958- AmMWSc 92
**Rasmussen,** Kathleen Maher 1948- AmMWSc 92
**Rasmussen,** Lenore Ivanna 1939- WhoWest 92
**Rasmussen,** Leo Brown 1941- WhoAmP 91
**Rasmussen,** Lois E Little 1938- AmMWSc 92
**Rasmussen,** Lowell W 1910- AmMWSc 92
**Rasmussen,** Marilyn WhoAmP 91
**Rasmussen,** Marva Jean 1957- WhoEnt 92, WhoRel 92
**Rasmussen,** Maud Truby Christian WhoAmP 91
**Rasmussen,** Maurice L 1935- AmMWSc 92
**Rasmussen,** Mike Joseph 1947- WhoWest 92
**Rasmussen,** Norman Carl 1927- AmMWSc 92, IntWW 91
**Rasmussen,** Paul G 1939- AmMWSc 92
**Rasmussen,** Poul Norregaard 1922- IntWW 91
**Rasmussen,** Raun Jay 1928- WhoFI 92
**Rasmussen,** Reinhold Albert 1936- AmMWSc 92
**Rasmussen,** Richard Robert 1946- WhoAmL 92
**Rasmussen,** Robert A 1933- AmMWSc 92
**Rasmussen,** Robert Dee 1936- WhoFI 92
**Rasmussen,** Roberta A WhoAmP 91
**Rasmussen,** Ronald Dean 1930- WhoAmP 91
**Rasmussen,** Roy 1919- TwCPaSc
**Rasmussen,** Russell Lee AmMWSc 92
**Rasmussen,** Stuart Ricard 1906- WhoWest 92
**Rasmussen,** Theodore Brown 1910- AmMWSc 92
**Rasmussen,** Thomas Val, Jr. 1954- WhoWest 92
**Rasmussen,** Tom 1940- WhoAmP 91
**Rasmussen,** V Philip, Jr 1950- AmMWSc 92
**Rasmussen,** Viggo J. 1915- IntWW 91
**Rasmussen,** William Otto 1942- AmMWSc 92
**Rasmusson,** Donald C 1931- AmMWSc 92
**Rasmusson,** Douglas Dean 1946- AmMWSc 92
**Rasmusson,** Eugene Martin 1929- AmMWSc 92
**Rasmusson,** Gary Henry 1936- AmMWSc 92
**Rasnake,** Marshall Everett 1924- WhoAmP 91
**Rasnake,** Monroe 1942- AmMWSc 92
**Rasolondraibe,** Peri 1947- WhoMW 92, WhoRel 92
**Rasool,** Ali Fareed 1965- WhoEnt 92
**Rasor,** Ned S 1927- AmMWSc 92
**Rasor,** Reba Graham 1926- WhoAmL 92
**Rasoul,** Husam A.A. 1950- WhoMW 92
**Rasovsky,** Yuri 1944- WhoEnt 92
**Rasp,** Ed 1922- WhoEnt 92
**Raspberry,** Salli 1940- IntAu&W 91

**Raspberry,** William 1935- *ConBlB 2 [port]*
**Raspberry,** William J. 1935- *WhoBlA 92*
**Raspe,** Rudolf Erich 1737-1794 *ScFEYrs*
**Rasplicka,** Paul Jay 1956- *WhoFI 92*
**Rasporich,** Anthony Walter 1940- *WhoWest 92*
**Rasputin,** Grigory Yefimovich 1872-1916 *FacFETw*
**Rasputin,** Valentin Grigor'evich 1937- *SovUnBD*
**Rasputin,** Valentin Grigorovich 1937- *IntWW 91*
**Rass,** Rebecca *DrAPF 91*
**Rass,** Rebecca Rivka 1936- *IntAu&W 91*
**Rassadin,** Stanislav Borisovich 1935- *IntWW 91*
**Rassekh,** Nosratollah 1924- *WhoWest 92*
**Rassier,** Donald B. 1929- *WhoWest 92*
**Rassin,** David Keith 1942- *AmMWSc 92*
**Rassmussen,** Jorgen 1931- *DcTwDes*
**Rassulo,** Donna Marie 1951- *WhoEnt 92*
**Rassweiler,** Merrill 1910- *AmMWSc 92*
**Rast,** Howard Eugene, Jr 1934- *AmMWSc 92*
**Rast,** Nicholas 1927- *AmMWSc 92*
**Rast,** Walter, Jr 1944- *AmMWSc 92*
**Rast,** Walter Emil 1930- *WhoMW 92, WhoRel 92*
**Rastall,** Peter 1931- *AmMWSc 92*
**Rastall,** Rodney Lee 1956- *WhoEnt 92*
**Rastani,** Kasra 1959- *AmMWSc 92*
**Rastegar,** Nader Esmail 1953- *WhoFI 92*
**Rastell,** John 1475?-1536 *RfGEnL 91*
**Rastelli,** Philip d1991 *NewYTBS 91*
**Rastkatov,** Alexander 1953- *ConCom 92*
**Rastogi,** Anil Kumar 1942- *WhoMW 92*
**Rastogi,** Prabhat Kumar 1944- *AmMWSc 92*
**Rastogi,** Raghunath Prasad 1926- *IntWW 91*
**Rastogi,** Suresh Chandra 1937- *AmMWSc 92*
**Rasweiler,** John Jacob, IV 1943- *AmMWSc 92*
**Raszka,** Terry Lee 1948- *WhoIns 92*
**Rataiczak,** Raymond D 1944- *WhoMW 92*
**Rataj,** Edward William 1947- *WhoAmL 92*
**Ratajczak,** Helen Vosskuhler 1938- *AmMWSc 92*
**Ratajczak,** Henryk 1932- *IntWW 91*
**Ratanov,** Anatoliy Petrovich 1921- *IntWW 91*
**Ratch,** Jerry *DrAPF 91*
**Ratches,** James Arthur 1942- *AmMWSc 92*
**Ratchford,** Joseph Thomas 1935- *AmMWSc 92*
**Ratchford,** Robert James 1924- *AmMWSc 92*
**Ratchford,** William R 1934- *WhoAmP 91*
**Ratchye,** Boyd Havens 1938- *WhoAmL 92*
**Ratcliff,** Antony Robin Napier 1925- *Who 92*
**Ratcliff,** Blair Norman 1944- *AmMWSc 92*
**Ratcliff,** Bruce Ephlin 1941- *WhoWest 92*
**Ratcliff,** Carter *DrAPF 91*
**Ratcliff,** Carter 1941- *WrDr 92*
**Ratcliff,** Donald Earl 1951- *WhoRel 92*
**Ratcliff,** Gene Austin 1930- *WhoFI 92*
**Ratcliff,** Howard Duane 1950- *WhoRel 92*
**Ratcliff,** John 1914- *TwCPaSc*
**Ratcliff,** John Garrett 1945- *WhoAmL 92*
**Ratcliff,** Keith Frederick 1938- *AmMWSc 92*
**Ratcliff,** Milton, Jr 1944- *AmMWSc 92*
**Ratcliff,** Sam R 1942- *WhoAmP 91*
**Ratcliff,** Sonia 1939- *TwCPaSc*
**Ratcliffe,** Alfonso F. 1928- *WhoBlA 92*
**Ratcliffe,** Andrew 1948- *TwCPaSc*
**Ratcliffe,** Charles Thomas 1938- *AmMWSc 92*
**Ratcliffe,** David N 1949- *WhoIns 92*
**Ratcliffe,** E. Jane 1917- *WrDr 92*
**Ratcliffe,** Eric Hallam *WrDr 92*
**Ratcliffe,** Frederick William 1927- *Who 92*
**Ratcliffe,** Michael 1935- *Who 92*
**Ratcliffe,** Nicholas Morley 1938- *AmMWSc 92*
**Ratcliffe,** Ryan Cooper 1959- *WhoWest 92*
**Ratcliffe,** Stephen *DrAPF 91*
**Ratcliffe,** William 1870-1955 *TwCPaSc*
**Rateaver,** Bargyla 1916- *AmMWSc 92, WhoWest 92*
**Rateb,** Aisha 1928- *IntWW 91*
**Ratekin,** Ned Harry 1929- *WhoMW 92*
**Rates,** Norman M. 1924- *WhoBlA 92*
**Ratford,** David John Edward 1934- *Who 92*
**Rath,** Bhakta Bhusan 1934- *AmMWSc 92*
**Rath,** Charles E 1919- *AmMWSc 92*
**Rath,** Dale E 1942- *WhoAmP 91*
**Rath,** Diane Doehne 1953- *WhoAmP 91*
**Rath,** E J *ScFEYrs*
**Rath,** Ernst vom 1909-1938 *EncTR 91*
**Rath,** Francis Steven 1955- *WhoAmL 92*
**Rath,** George Edward 1913- *WhoRel 92*
**Rath,** Nigam Prasad 1958- *AmMWSc 92*
**Rath,** Sara *DrAPF 91*
**Rath,** Thomas David 1945- *WhoAmP 91*
**Rathaus,** Karol 1895-1954 *NewAmDM*
**Rathbone,** Basil 1892-1967 *FacFETw*
**Rathbone,** John Francis Warre 1909- *Who 92*
**Rathbone,** John Rankin 1933- *Who 92*
**Rathbone,** Julian 1935- *ConAu 34NR, WrDr 92*
**Rathbone,** Norman Stanley 1914- *Who 92*
**Rathbone,** Perry Townsend 1911- *IntWW 91*
**Rathbone,** Tim *Who 92*
**Rathborne,** St. George 1854-1938 *TwCWW 91*
**Rathborne,** St. George Henry 1854-1938 *ScFEYrs*
**Rathbun,** Edwin Roy, Jr 1922- *AmMWSc 92*
**Rathbun,** Gary Lee 1956- *WhoFI 92*
**Rathbun,** Randall Keith 1953- *WhoAmL 92*
**Rathbun,** Richard 1852-1918 *BiInAmS*
**Rathbun,** Ted Allan 1942- *AmMWSc 92*
**Rathbun,** William B 1932- *AmMWSc 92*
**Rathburn,** Carlisle Baxter, Jr 1924- *AmMWSc 92*
**Rathcavan,** Baron 1909- *Who 92*
**Rathcke,** Beverly Jean 1945- *AmMWSc 92*
**Rathcreedan,** Baron 1949- *Who 92*
**Rathdonnell,** Baron 1938- *Who 92*
**Rathe,** Stephen Mark 1949- *WhoEnt 92*
**Rathenau,** Walther 1867-1922 *EncTR 91 [port], FacFETw*
**Rather,** Dan *LesBEnT 92 [port]*
**Rather,** Dan 1931- *IntAu&W 91, IntMPA 92, IntWW 91*
**Rather,** Gordon Smeade, Jr. 1939- *WhoAmL 92*
**Rather,** James B, Jr 1911- *AmMWSc 92*
**Rather,** Jonathan Massey 1960- *WhoFI 92*
**Rather,** Lelland Joseph 1913- *AmMWSc 92*
**Rather,** Shari Anne 1948- *WhoMW 92*
**Rathje,** James Lee 1947- *WhoFI 92*
**Rathjen,** Warren Francis 1929- *AmMWSc 92*
**Rathke,** Frances Gregg 1960- *WhoFI 92*
**Rathke,** Heinrich Karl Martin Hans 1928- *IntWW 91*
**Rathke,** Jerome William 1947- *AmMWSc 92*
**Rathke,** Michael William 1941- *AmMWSc 92*
**Rathkopf,** Daren Anthony 1933- *WhoAmL 92*
**Rathlesberger,** James H 1948- *WhoAmP 91*
**Rathman,** George Henry 1941- *WhoFI 92*
**Rathman,** Thomas Dean 1962- *WhoBlA 92*
**Rathman,** William Ernest 1927- *WhoAmL 92*
**Rathmann,** Carl Erich 1945- *AmMWSc 92*
**Rathmann,** Franz Heinrich 1904- *AmMWSc 92*
**Rathmell,** Lilian 1909- *TwCPaSc*
**Rathmell,** Neil 1947- *WrDr 92*
**Rathmell,** Thomas 1912- *TwCPaSc*
**Rathnam,** Premila 1936- *AmMWSc 92*
**Rathnow,** Hans 1934- *WhoIns 92*
**Rati,** Robert Dean 1939- *WhoFI 92, WhoMW 92*
**Ratia,** Armi 1912-1979 *DcTwDes*
**Ratican,** Peter Jay 1943- *WhoWest 92*
**Ratiner,** Leigh S. 1939- *WhoAmL 92*
**Ratino,** John Manfred 1956- *WhoAmL 92*
**Ratinoff,** Marshall Dale 1949- *WhoFI 92*
**Ratiu,** Ion 1917- *WrDr 92*
**Ratiu,** Tudor Stefan 1950- *WhoWest 92*
**Ratkin,** Annette Levy 1927- *WhoRel 92*
**Ratkowski,** Valerie A. 1954- *WhoMW 92*
**Ratledge,** Colin 1936- *Who 92*
**Ratleff,** Edward 1950- *BlkOlyM*
**Ratliff,** Bill 1936- *WhoAmP 91*
**Ratliff,** Charles Edward, Jr. 1926- *WhoFI 92*
**Ratliff,** Floyd 1919- *AmMWSc 92, IntWW 91*
**Ratliff,** Francis Tenney 1919- *AmMWSc 92*
**Ratliff,** Gerald Lee 1944- *WhoEnt 92*
**Ratliff,** Gerald R 1938- *WhoAmP 91*
**Ratliff,** Jack 1934- *WhoAmL 92*
**Ratliff,** James B 1918- *WhoAmP 91*
**Ratliff,** James Conway 1940- *WhoWest 92*
**Ratliff,** James Oliver 1946- *WhoAmP 91*
**Ratliff,** Joe Samuel 1950- *WhoBlA 92*
**Ratliff,** Leigh Ann 1961- *WhoWest 92*
**Ratliff,** Louis Jackson, Jr 1931- *AmMWSc 92, WhoWest 92*
**Ratliff,** Norman B, Jr 1938- *AmMWSc 92*
**Ratliff,** Patricia A 1933- *WhoAmP 91*
**Ratliff,** Priscilla N 1940- *AmMWSc 92*
**Ratliff,** Robert L 1931- *AmMWSc 92*
**Ratliff,** Ronald D. 1950- *WhoRel 92*
**Ratliff,** Ronald Eugene 1947- *WhoRel 92*
**Ratliff,** Scott 1943- *WhoAmP 91*
**Ratliff,** Thomas James 1955- *WhoWest 92*
**Ratliff,** William Durrah, Jr. 1921- *WhoAmL 92*
**Ratliff,** William Elmore 1937- *WhoWest 92*
**Ratnaswamy,** John Peter 1960- *WhoAmL 92*
**Ratnayake,** Walisundera Mudiyanselage N 1949- *AmMWSc 92*
**Ratner,** Albert 1937- *AmMWSc 92*
**Ratner,** Buddy Dennis 1947- *AmMWSc 92, WhoWest 92*
**Ratner,** David Louis 1931- *WhoFI 92*
**Ratner,** Debra *DrAPF 91*
**Ratner,** Gerald Irving 1949- *IntWW 91, Who 92*
**Ratner,** Harvey *WhoMW 92*
**Ratner,** Kenneth Paul 1958- *WhoFI 92*
**Ratner,** Lawrence Theodore 1923- *AmMWSc 92*
**Ratner,** Lazarus Gershon 1923- *AmMWSc 92*
**Ratner,** Lisa Karen 1953- *WhoEnt 92*
**Ratner,** Lorman 1932- *WrDr 92*
**Ratner,** Marc Leonard 1926- *WhoWest 92*
**Ratner,** Mark A 1942- *AmMWSc 92*
**Ratner,** Michael Ira 1949- *AmMWSc 92*
**Ratner,** Milton D. d1991 *NewYTBS 91*
**Ratner,** Payne Harry, Jr. 1924- *WhoAmL 92*
**Ratner,** Robert 1941- *AmMWSc 92*
**Ratner,** Rochelle *DrAPF 91*
**Ratner,** Rochelle 1948- *IntAu&W 91, WrDr 92*
**Ratner,** Sarah 1903- *AmMWSc 92*
**Ratner,** Sidney 1908- *WhoFI 92*
**Ratner,** Steven Arnold 1954- *WhoEnt 92*
**Ratney,** Ronald Steven 1932- *AmMWSc 92*
**Ratnoff,** Oscar Davis 1916- *AmMWSc 92, IntWW 91, WhoMW 92*
**Ratsiraka,** Didier 1936- *IntWW 91*
**Rattan,** Kuldip S. 1948- *WhoMW 92*
**Rattan,** Kuldip Singh 1948- *AmMWSc 92*
**Rattanakoses,** Mana 1925- *IntWW 91*
**Rattazzi,** Mario Cristiano 1935- *AmMWSc 92*
**Ratte,** Charles A 1927- *AmMWSc 92*
**Ratte,** James C 1925- *AmMWSc 92*
**Rattee,** Donald 1937- *Who 92*
**Rattee,** Michael *DrAPF 91*
**Rattenbury,** Ken 1920- *ConAu 134*
**Ratterree,** John 1956- *WhoAmL 92*
**Ratterree,** Tom 1935- *WhoAmP 91*
**Ratti,** Achille *EncTR 91*
**Ratti,** Jogindar Singh 1935- *AmMWSc 92*
**Ratti,** Ronald Andrew 1948- *WhoFI 92*
**Rattigan,** Terence 1911-1977 *CnDBLB 7 [port], FacFETw, RfGEnL 91*
**Rattle,** Simon 1955- *IntWW 91, NewAmDM, Who 92, WhoEnt 92, WhoWest 92*
**Rattley,** Jessie M. 1929- *WhoBlA 92*
**Rattley,** Jessie Menifield 1929- *WhoAmP 91*
**Rattliff,** Herman W 1926- *WhoAmP 91*
**Rattner,** Barnett Alvin 1950- *AmMWSc 92*
**Rattner,** Jerome Bernard 1945- *AmMWSc 92*
**Rattner,** Steven Lawrence 1952- *WhoFI 92*
**Ratto,** Peter Angelo 1930- *AmMWSc 92*
**Ratton,** Michael Thomas 1961- *WhoAmL 92*
**Rattray,** Alfred Adolphus 1925- *IntWW 91*
**Rattray,** Basil Andrew 1927- *AmMWSc 92*
**Rattray,** David *DrAPF 91*
**Rattray,** Maurice, Jr 1922- *AmMWSc 92*
**Rattray,** Simon *WrDr 92*
**Ratts,** Kenneth Wayne 1932- *AmMWSc 92*
**Ratty,** Frank John, Jr 1923- *AmMWSc 92*
**Ratushinskaia,** Irina 1954- *LiExTwC*
**Ratushinskaya,** Irina 1954- *FacFETw, IntWW 91, LiExTwC*
**Ratushinskaya,** Irina Borisovna 1954- *SovUnBD*
**Ratz,** H C 1927- *AmMWSc 92*
**Ratz,** John Louis 1947- *AmMWSc 92*
**Ratzenberger,** John Dezso 1947- *WhoEnt 92*
**Ratzinger,** Joseph Alois 1927- *IntWW 91, WhoRel 92*
**Ratzlaff,** David Edward 1938- *WhoRel 92*
**Ratzlaff,** Kermit O 1921- *AmMWSc 92*
**Ratzlaff,** Marc Henry 1942- *AmMWSc 92*
**Ratzlaff,** Ruben Menno 1917- *WhoRel 92*
**Ratzlaff,** Stanley Abe 1935- *WhoFI 92*
**Ratzlaff,** Vernon Paul 1925- *WhoWest 92*
**Ratzlaff,** Willis 1926- *AmMWSc 92*
**Rau,** A Ravi Prakash 1945- *AmMWSc 92*
**Rau,** Adolf Wilhelm 1922- *IntWW 91*
**Rau,** Alan Scott 1942- *WhoAmL 92*
**Rau,** Allen H 1958- *AmMWSc 92*
**Rau,** Allen Howard 1958- *WhoMW 92*
**Rau,** Bantwal Ramakrishna 1951- *AmMWSc 92*
**Rau,** Charles 1826-1887 *BiInAmS*
**Rau,** Charles Alfred, Jr 1942- *AmMWSc 92*
**Rau,** Dhanvanthi Rama 1893-1987 *FacFETw*
**Rau,** Eric 1928- *AmMWSc 92*
**Rau,** Gregory Hudson 1948- *AmMWSc 92*
**Rau,** Johannes 1931- *IntWW 91*
**Rau,** Lee Arthur 1940- *WhoAmL 92*
**Rau,** Manfred Ernst 1942- *AmMWSc 92*
**Rau,** R Ronald 1920- *AmMWSc 92*
**Rau,** Richard Raymond 1928- *AmMWSc 92*
**Rau,** Santha Rama *IntWW 91, Who 92*
**Rau,** Weldon Willis 1921- *AmMWSc 92*
**Raub,** Daniel Joseph 1947- *WhoMW 92*
**Raub,** Harry Lyman, III 1919- *AmMWSc 92*
**Raub,** Thomas Jeffrey *AmMWSc 92*
**Raub,** William F 1939- *AmMWSc 92*
**Raub,** William Henry, III 1954- *WhoFI 92*
**Raubal,** Angela 1908-1931 *EncTR 91 [port]*
**Raubenheimer,** George Harding 1923- *IntAu&W 91*
**Rauber,** Lauren A 1946- *AmMWSc 92*
**Rauch,** Carl Thomas, III 1942- *WhoRel 92*
**Rauch,** David L 1951- *WhoAmP 91*
**Rauch,** Donald J 1935- *AmMWSc 92*
**Rauch,** Emil Bruno 1919- *AmMWSc 92*
**Rauch,** Fred D 1931- *AmMWSc 92*
**Rauch,** Gary Clark 1942- *AmMWSc 92*
**Rauch,** Glenn Andrew 1938- *WhoMW 92*
**Rauch,** Harold 1925- *AmMWSc 92*
**Rauch,** Helene Coben *AmMWSc 92*
**Rauch,** Henry William 1942- *AmMWSc 92*
**Rauch,** Herbert Emil 1935- *AmMWSc 92*
**Rauch,** Irmengard 1933- *WrDr 92*
**Rauch,** Jeffrey B. 1945- *WhoMW 92*
**Rauch,** Jeffrey Baron 1945- *AmMWSc 92*
**Rauch,** Lawrence L 1919- *AmMWSc 92*
**Rauch,** Lawrence Lee 1919- *WhoWest 92*
**Rauch,** Marshall Arthur 1923- *WhoAmP 91*
**Rauch,** Paul David 1933- *WhoEnt 92*
**Rauch,** Richard Travis 1955- *AmMWSc 92*
**Rauch,** Sol 1940- *AmMWSc 92*
**Rauch,** Stephen P. 1941- *WhoEnt 92*
**Rauch,** Stewart Emmart, Jr 1921- *AmMWSc 92*
**Rauch,** William Eric 1935- *WhoRel 92*
**Raucher,** Herman 1928- *IntMPA 92, WhoEnt 92, WrDr 92*
**Raucher,** Stanley 1948- *AmMWSc 92*
**Rauchfuss,** Thomas Bigley 1949- *AmMWSc 92*
**Rauchfuss,** Wolfgang 1931- *IntWW 91*
**Raucina,** Thomas Frank 1946- *WhoEnt 92, WhoWest 92*
**Rauckhorst,** William H 1940- *AmMWSc 92*
**Raud,** Valda 1920- *IntAu&W 91*
**Raudkivi,** A. J. 1920- *WrDr 92*
**Raudorf,** Thomas Walter 1943- *AmMWSc 92*
**Raudsepp,** Karl 1908- *WhoRel 92*
**Raue,** Jorg Emil 1936- *WhoWest 92*
**Rauenhorst,** Gerald 1927- *WhoFI 92*
**Rauff,** Edward Allen 1929- *WhoRel 92*
**Rauff,** Walter Herman Julius 1907-1984 *FacFETw*
**Rauff,** Walther 1906-1984 *EncTR 91*
**Raugh,** Stanley Wayne 1948- *WhoAmP 91*
**Raughton,** Jimmie Leonard 1943- *WhoWest 92*
**Rauh,** J. Randall 1947- *WhoWest 92*
**Rauh,** Joseph L, Jr 1911- *WhoAmP 91*
**Rauh,** Robert David, Jr 1943- *AmMWSc 92*
**Rauhut,** Michael McKay 1930- *AmMWSc 92*
**Rauk,** Arvi 1942- *AmMWSc 92*
**Raulet,** David Henri 1954- *AmMWSc 92*
**Raulin,** Roger Albert 1948- *WhoFI 92*
**Raulins,** Nancy Rebecca 1916- *AmMWSc 92*
**Raullerson,** Calvin Henry 1920- *WhoBlA 92*
**Raulston,** James Chester 1940- *AmMWSc 92*
**Raum,** Arnold 1908- *WhoAmL 92*
**Raun,** Arthur Phillip 1934- *AmMWSc 92*
**Raun,** Earle Spangler 1924- *AmMWSc 92*
**Raun,** Ned S 1925- *AmMWSc 92*
**Raup,** David Malcolm 1933- *AmMWSc 92*
**Raup,** Hugh Miller 1901- *AmMWSc 92*
**Raup,** Omer Beaver 1930- *AmMWSc 92*
**Raup,** Philip Martin 1914- *WhoFI 92*
**Raup,** Robert Bruce, Jr 1929- *AmMWSc 92*
**Rausch,** David John 1940- *AmMWSc 92*
**Rausch,** David Leon 1937- *AmMWSc 92*
**Rausch,** Douglas Alfred 1928- *AmMWSc 92*
**Rausch,** Doyle W 1931- *AmMWSc 92*
**Rausch,** Gerald 1938- *AmMWSc 92*
**Rausch,** Gertrude Marie 1940- *WhoRel 92*
**Rausch,** James Peter 1938- *AmMWSc 92*
**Rausch,** Jean-Marie Victor Alphonse 1929- *IntWW 91*
**Rausch,** Jeffrey Lynn 1953- *WhoWest 92*
**Rausch,** Marvin D 1930- *AmMWSc 92*
**Rausch,** Michael W. 1949- *WhoEnt 92*
**Rausch,** Richard L 1935- *WhoAmP 91*

**Rausch**, Robert Lloyd 1921- AmMWSc 92
**Rausch**, Steven K 1955- AmMWSc 92
**Rausch**, Thomas Peter 1941- WhoRel 92
**Rauschenbach**, Henri S WhoAmP 91
**Rauschenberg**, Dale Eugene 1938- WhoEnt 92
**Rauschenberg**, Robert 1925- FacFETw, IntWW 91, News 91 [port]
**Rauschenberger**, Floyd Arthur, III 1954- WhoAmP 91
**Rauschenbusch**, Walter 1861-1918 RelLAm 91
**Rauscher**, Frank Joseph, Jr 1931- AmMWSc 92
**Rauscher**, Grant K 1922- AmMWSc 92
**Rauscher**, Hannah Sarah 1925- WhoAmP 91
**Rauscher**, Tomlinson Gene 1946- AmMWSc 92
**Rauschkolb**, Richard Stephen 1947- WhoWest 92
**Rauschkolb**, Roy Simpson 1933- AmMWSc 92, WhoWest 92
**Rauschning**, Hermann 1887-1982 EncTR 91 [port]
**Rausen**, Aaron Reuben 1930- AmMWSc 92
**Rauser**, Wilfried Ernst 1936- AmMWSc 92
**Raushel**, Frank Michael 1949- AmMWSc 92
**Raushenbush**, Stephen d1991 NewYTBS 91
**Raut**, Kamalakar Balkrishna 1920- AmMWSc 92
**Rautaharju**, Pentti M 1932- AmMWSc 92
**Rautavaara**, Einojuhani 1928- ConCom 92
**Rautenberg**, Robert Frank 1943- WhoFI 92, WhoWest 92
**Rautenberg**, Theodore Herman 1930- AmMWSc 92
**Rautenstrauch**, Carl Peter 1936- AmMWSc 92
**Rautenstraus**, R C 1924- AmMWSc 92
**Rauth**, Andrew Michael 1935- AmMWSc 92
**Rauth**, Joseph Thomas 1955- WhoMW 92
**Rauti**, Giuseppe Umberto 1926- BiDExR
**Rautsola**, Riku Heikki 1954- WhoFI 92
**Ravage**, John William 1937- WhoWest 92
**Raval**, Dilip N 1933- AmMWSc 92
**Ravanel**, Jean 1920- IntWW 91
**Rave**, James A. WhoRel 92
**Rave**, Terence William 1938- AmMWSc 92
**Raveche**, Elizabeth Marie 1950- AmMWSc 92
**Raveche**, Harold Joseph 1943- AmMWSc 92
**Raveed**, Dan 1921- AmMWSc 92
**Raveendran**, Ekarath 1950- AmMWSc 92
**Ravel**, Joanne Macow 1924- AmMWSc 92
**Ravel**, Maurice 1875-1937 FacFETw [port], NewAmDM
**Raveling**, Dennis Graff 1939- AmMWSc 92
**Raveling**, George Henry 1937- WhoBlA 92
**Ravelo**, Daniel F. 1939- WhoHisp 92
**Ravelo**, Robert F. 1947- IntMPA 92
**Raven**, Bertram Herbert 1926- WhoWest 92
**Raven**, Clara 1907- AmMWSc 92
**Raven**, Francis Harvey 1928- AmMWSc 92, WhoMW 92
**Raven**, John Albert 1941- Who 92
**Raven**, John Armstrong 1920- Who 92
**Raven**, Kathleen 1910- Who 92
**Raven**, Larry Joseph 1939- WhoAmP 91
**Raven**, Lyle Jack 1957- WhoMW 92
**Raven**, Patricia Elaine 1943- WhoAmP 91
**Raven**, Peter Bernard AmMWSc 92
**Raven**, Peter Hamilton 1936- AmMWSc 92, IntWW 91
**Raven**, Robert Dunbar 1923- WhoAmL 92
**Raven**, Ronald William 1904- Who 92, WrDr 92
**Raven**, Simon 1927- ConNov 91, IntAu&W 91, Who 92, WrDr 92
**Raven**, Simon Arthur Noel 1927- IntWW 91
**Raven-Hill**, Leonard 1867-1942 TwCPaSc
**Raven-Riemann**, Carolyn Sue 1945- WhoEnt 92
**Raven-Symone** 1985- WhoBlA 92
**Ravenel**, Arthur, Jr. 1927- AlmAP 92 [port], WhoAmP 91
**Ravenel**, Charles Dufort 1938- WhoAmP 91
**Ravenel**, Douglas Conner 1947- AmMWSc 92
**Ravenel**, Edmund 1797-1871 BiInAmS
**Ravenel**, Henry, Jr. 1934- WhoFI 92
**Ravenel**, Henry William 1814-1887 BiInAmS
**Ravenel**, St. Julien 1819-1882 BiInAmS
**Ravenell**, Joseph Phillip 1940- WhoBlA 92
**Ravenell**, Mildred 1944- WhoBlA 92
**Ravenell**, William Hudson 1942- WhoBlA 92
**Ravenhall**, David Geoffrey 1927- AmMWSc 92
**Ravenholt**, Reimert Thorolf 1925- AmMWSc 92
**Ravens**, Karl Friedrich 1927- IntWW 91
**Ravenscroft**, Edward 1643?- RfGEnL 91
**Ravenscroft**, John Robert Parker 1939- Who 92
**Ravenscroft**, Raymond Lockwood 1931- Who 92
**Ravenscroft**, Thomas 1590?-1635? NewAmDM
**Ravensdale**, Baron 1923- IntWW 91, Who 92
**Ravensdale**, Thomas Corney d1990 Who 92N
**Ravensong**, Cindy 1953- RelLAm 91
**Ravensworth**, Baron 1924- Who 92
**Raventos**, Antolin, IV 1925- AmMWSc 92
**Raventos**, George 1939- WhoHisp 92
**Raventos-Suarez**, Carmen Elvira 1947- AmMWSc 92
**Raver**, Leonard 1927- WhoEnt 92
**Ravera**, Camilla 1889-1988 FacFETw
**Raverat**, Gwen 1885-1957 TwCPaSc
**Ravesteyn**, Sybold van 1889- DcTwDes
**Ravetch**, Irving 1920- IntMPA 92
**Ravetz**, Alison 1930- WrDr 92
**Ravichandran**, Ramarathnam WhoFI 92
**Ravicz**, Arthur Eugene 1930- AmMWSc 92
**Ravilious**, Eric 1903-1943 TwCPaSc
**Raville**, Milton E 1921- AmMWSc 92
**Ravin**, Richard Michael 1943- WhoIns 92
**Ravinal**, Rosemary 1954- WhoHisp 92
**Ravindra**, Mysore Vedavyasachar 1939- WhoFI 92
**Ravindra**, Nuggehalli Muthanna 1955- AmMWSc 92
**Ravindra**, Ravi 1939- AmMWSc 92, ConAu 35NR, WhoRel 92
**Ravindran**, Nair Narayanan 1934- AmMWSc 92
**Raviola**, Franco Paolo 1960- WhoWest 92
**Raviola d'Elia**, Giuseppina E 1935- AmMWSc 92
**Ravirosa Wade**, Leandro 1920- IntWW 91
**Ravitch**, Diane 1938- IntWW 91
**Ravitch**, Diane Silvers 1938- NewYTBS 91 [port]
**Ravitch**, Mark Mitchell 1910- AmMWSc 92
**Ravitch**, Norman 1936- WrDr 92
**Ravitsky**, Charles 1917- AmMWSc 92
**Ravitz**, Abe 1927- WrDr 92
**Ravitz**, Gary Jay 1951- WhoAmL 92
**Ravitz**, John WhoAmP 91
**Ravitz**, Leonard J, Jr 1925- AmMWSc 92
**Ravitz**, Marc Emil 1957- WhoFI 92
**Ravitz**, Robert J. 1930- WhoFI 92
**Raviv**, Josef 1934- AmMWSc 92
**Ravkind**, Sidney Lawrance 1936- WhoAmL 92
**Ravnholt**, Eiler Christian 1923- WhoAmP 91
**Raw**, Cecil John Gough 1929- AmMWSc 92
**Rawal**, Kanti M 1940- AmMWSc 92
**Rawal**, Rashmikant U. 1948- WhoWest 92
**Rawat**, Arun Kumar 1945- AmMWSc 92
**Rawat**, Banmali Singh 1947- AmMWSc 92, WhoWest 92
**Rawbone**, Alfred Raymond 1923- Who 92
**Rawcliffe**, Derek Alec 1921- Who 92
**Rawdin**, Grant 1959- WhoAmL 92
**Rawes**, Francis Roderick 1916- Who 92
**Rawiri**, Georges 1932- IntWW 91
**Rawitch**, Allen Barry 1940- AmMWSc 92
**Rawitch**, Robert Joe 1945- ConAu 133
**Rawitscher**, George Heinrich 1928- AmMWSc 92
**Rawitz**, Margaret Jill 1949- WhoAmL 92
**Rawl**, Alfred Victor 1946- WhoAmP 91
**Rawl**, Arthur Julian 1942- WhoFI 92
**Rawl**, Lawrence G. IntWW 91
**Rawl**, Lawrence G. 1928- WhoFI 92
**Rawles**, Edward Hugh 1945- WhoAmL 92, WhoMW 92
**Rawles**, Elizabeth Gibbs 1943- WhoBlA 92
**Rawley**, Alan David 1934- Who 92
**Rawley**, James A. 1916- WrDr 92
**Rawling**, Frank L, Jr 1935- AmMWSc 92
**Rawlings**, Boynton Mott 1935- WhoFI 92
**Rawlings**, Charles Adrian 1936- AmMWSc 92
**Rawlings**, Clarence Alvin 1943- AmMWSc 92
**Rawlings**, Gary Don 1948- AmMWSc 92
**Rawlings**, George Chancellor, Jr 1921- WhoAmP 91
**Rawlings**, Howard P 1937- WhoAmP 91
**Rawlings**, Hunter Ripley, III 1944- WhoMW 92
**Rawlings**, Jerry 1947- IntWW 91
**Rawlings**, John A. 1925- WhoRel 92
**Rawlings**, John Oren 1932- AmMWSc 92
**Rawlings**, Margaret 1906- Who 92
**Rawlings**, Margaret Mary 1955- WhoEnt 92
**Rawlings**, Marilyn Manuela 1956- WhoBlA 92
**Rawlings**, Marjorie Kinnan 1896-1953 BenetAL 91, FacFETw
**Rawlings**, Martha 1942- WhoBlA 92
**Rawlings**, Mary 1936- WhoWest 92
**Rawlings**, Patricia Elizabeth 1939- Who 92
**Rawlings**, Rob Roy 1920- WhoAmP 91
**Rawlings**, Robert Hoag 1924- WhoWest 92
**Rawlings**, Samuel Craig 1938- AmMWSc 92
**Rawlins**, Adrian ConTFT 9
**Rawlins**, C.L. DrAPF 91
**Rawlins**, Colin Guy Champion 1919- Who 92
**Rawlins**, Darsie 1912- TwCPaSc
**Rawlins**, Elizabeth B. 1927- WhoBlA 92
**Rawlins**, Gordon John 1944- Who 92
**Rawlins**, John 1922- Who 92
**Rawlins**, John Stuart Pepys 1922- IntWW 91
**Rawlins**, Michael David 1941- Who 92
**Rawlins**, Nolan Omri 1938- AmMWSc 92
**Rawlins**, Peter Jonathan 1951- IntWW 91, Who 92
**Rawlins**, Sedrick John 1927- WhoBlA 92
**Rawlins**, Stephen Last 1932- AmMWSc 92
**Rawlins**, Susan DrAPF 91
**Rawlins**, Wilson Terry 1949- AmMWSc 92
**Rawlinson** Who 92
**Rawlinson**, Anthony Henry John 1936- Who 92
**Rawlinson**, Charles Frederick Melville 1934- Who 92
**Rawlinson**, David John 1935- AmMWSc 92
**Rawlinson**, Dennis George Fielding 1919- Who 92
**Rawlinson**, John Alan 1940- AmMWSc 92
**Rawlinson**, Stuart Elbert 1950- WhoWest 92
**Rawlinson Of Ewell**, Baron 1919- IntWW 91, Who 92
**Rawls**, Eugenia WhoEnt 92
**Rawls**, Frank Macklin 1952- WhoAmL 92, WhoRel 92
**Rawls**, George H. 1928- WhoBlA 92
**Rawls**, Henry Ralph 1935- AmMWSc 92
**Rawls**, John 1921- IntWW 91, WrDr 92
**Rawls**, John Marvin, Jr 1946- AmMWSc 92
**Rawls**, Lou 1935- NewAmDM
**Rawls**, Lou 1936- WhoBlA 92, WhoEnt 92
**Rawls**, Louis 1905- WhoBlA 92
**Rawls**, Raleigh Richard 1925- WhoBlA 92
**Rawls**, Rodney Alan 1956- WhoBlA 92
**Rawls**, Sol Waite, III 1948- WhoFI 92, WhoMW 92
**Rawls**, William Bryant d1991 NewYTBS 91
**Rawls**, William D., Sr. WhoBlA 92
**Rawls**, William Edgar 1933- AmMWSc 92
**Rawn**, Michael David 1953- WhoMW 92
**Rawn**, William Leete, III 1943- WhoFI 92
**Rawnsley**, Howard Melody 1925- AmMWSc 92
**Rawnsley**, Kenneth 1926- Who 92
**Raworth**, Thomas Moore 1938- IntAu&W 91
**Raworth**, Tom 1938- ConPo 91, WrDr 92
**Rawson**, Christopher Selwyn Priestley 1928- Who 92
**Rawson**, Claude Julien 1935- IntAu&W 91, WrDr 92
**Rawson**, Eric Gordon 1937- AmMWSc 92
**Rawson**, James Rulon Young 1943- AmMWSc 92, WhoMW 92
**Rawson**, Jessica Mary 1943- Who 92
**Rawson**, Kay Thompson 1939- WhoAmP 91
**Rawson**, Kenneth John 1926- Who 92
**Rawson**, Leonard Lee 1954- WhoAmP 91
**Rawson**, Merle R. 1924- IntWW 91
**Rawson**, Michael James 1957- WhoWest 92
**Rawson**, Raymond D 1940- WhoAmP 91
**Rawson**, Richard Ray 1928- AmMWSc 92
**Rawson**, Robert Orrin 1917- AmMWSc 92
**Rawson**, Roger F 1939- WhoAmP 91
**Rawson**, Rulon Wells 1908- AmMWSc 92
**Rawsthorne**, Alan 1905-1971 NewAmDM
**Rawsthorne**, Anthony Robert 1943- Who 92
**Rawsthorne**, John 1936- Who 92
**Ray**, Ajit Kumar 1925- AmMWSc 92
**Ray**, Ajit Nath 1912- IntWW 91, Who 92
**Ray**, Alden E 1931- AmMWSc 92
**Ray**, Aldo 1926-1991 ConTFT 9, NewYTBS 91 [port]
**Ray**, Allen Cobble 1941- AmMWSc 92
**Ray**, Andrew 1948- WhoBlA 92
**Ray**, Apurba Kanti 1943- AmMWSc 92
**Ray**, Arliss Dean 1929- WhoFI 92
**Ray**, Arun Bikas 1935- WhoMW 92
**Ray**, Asit Kumar 1954- AmMWSc 92
**Ray**, Austin H. 1943- WhoBlA 92
**Ray**, Bill 1922- WhoAmP 91
**Ray**, Bradley Stephen 1957- WhoFI 92
**Ray**, Bruce David 1955- WhoWest 92
**Ray**, Carl Kenneth, II 1953- WhoAmL 92
**Ray**, Charles, Jr 1911- AmMWSc 92
**Ray**, Charles Dean 1927- AmMWSc 92
**Ray**, Charles Joseph 1911- WhoMW 92
**Ray**, Charlotte E. 1850-1911 NotBlAW 92
**Ray**, Clarence Thorpe 1916- AmMWSc 92
**Ray**, Clayton Edward 1933- AmMWSc 92
**Ray**, Cread L., Jr. 1931- WhoAmL 92, WhoAmP 91
**Ray**, Cyril 1908- Who 92, WrDr 92
**Ray**, Cyril 1908-1991 ConAu 135
**Ray**, Dale C 1933- AmMWSc 92
**Ray**, Dan Alan 1933- WhoAmP 91, WhoRel 92
**Ray**, Dan S 1937- AmMWSc 92
**Ray**, David DrAPF 91
**Ray**, David 1932- ConPo 91, WrDr 92
**Ray**, David Bruce 1953- WhoBlA 92
**Ray**, David Christian 1961- WhoWest 92
**Ray**, David Eugene 1932- IntAu&W 91
**Ray**, David Lewin 1929- WhoWest 92
**Ray**, David Scott 1930- AmMWSc 92
**Ray**, Dixy Lee 1914- ConAu 134, IntWW 91
**Ray**, Donald Page 1916- WhoFI 92
**Ray**, Dorothy Jean 1919- WrDr 92
**Ray**, Douglas Ellsworth 1947- WhoAmL 92
**Ray**, Earl Elmer 1929- AmMWSc 92
**Ray**, Edward Ernest 1924- Who 92
**Ray**, Edward John 1944- WhoFI 92, WhoMW 92
**Ray**, Eva K 1933- AmMWSc 92
**Ray**, Frank Allen 1949- WhoAmL 92, WhoMW 92
**Ray**, Frank David 1940- WhoMW 92
**Ray**, Frederick Kalb 1944- AmMWSc 92
**Ray**, G Carleton 1928- AmMWSc 92
**Ray**, Gary Alan 1958- WhoMW 92
**Ray**, Gilbert T. 1944- WhoAmL 92, WhoBlA 92
**Ray**, Glen William 1947- WhoMW 92
**Ray**, H. Cordelia 1849?-1916 NotBlAW 92
**Ray**, H. Richard, Jr. 1953- WhoRel 92
**Ray**, Harry Bruce 1953- WhoAmL 92
**Ray**, Howard Eugene 1926- AmMWSc 92
**Ray**, Hugh Massey, Jr. 1943- WhoAmL 92
**Ray**, Jack Harris 1924- WhoFI 92
**Ray**, Jacqueline Walker 1944- WhoBlA 92
**Ray**, James Allen 1931- WhoFI 92
**Ray**, James Alton 1932- AmMWSc 92
**Ray**, James Davis, Jr 1918- AmMWSc 92
**Ray**, James Edward 1922- WhoAmP 91
**Ray**, James P 1944- AmMWSc 92
**Ray**, James R., III 1963- WhoBlA 92
**Ray**, James William, Sr 1939- WhoAmP 91
**Ray**, Jesse Paul 1916- AmMWSc 92
**Ray**, John WhoAmP 91
**Ray**, John Delbert 1930- AmMWSc 92
**Ray**, John Robert 1921- AmMWSc 92
**Ray**, John Robert 1939- AmMWSc 92
**Ray**, John Walker 1936- WhoMW 92
**Ray**, Johnnie 1927-1990 AnObit 1990, NewAmDM
**Ray**, Johnny 1957- WhoBlA 92
**Ray**, Jonathan David 1963- WhoRel 92
**Ray**, Judith Diana 1946- WhoBlA 92
**Ray**, Judy DrAPF 91
**Ray**, Judy 1939- WrDr 92
**Ray**, Judy Self 1946- WhoFI 92
**Ray**, Katherine Melchior 1964- WhoEnt 92
**Ray**, Kelley WhoEnt 92
**Ray**, Leo Eldon 1937- WhoWest 92
**Ray**, Man 1890-1976 DcTwDes, FacFETw
**Ray**, Marianne Yurasko 1934- WhoWest 92
**Ray**, Mario A. 1945- WhoHisp 92
**Ray**, Mary 1932- WrDr 92
**Ray**, Mary E. 1911- WhoBlA 92
**Ray**, Mary Louise Ryan 1954- WhoAmL 92
**Ray**, Mercer Z. 1911- WhoBlA 92
**Ray**, Michael Edwin 1949- WhoAmL 92
**Ray**, Michael Lynn 1965- WhoRel 92
**Ray**, Michael Thomas 1954- WhoIns 92
**Ray**, Moses Alexander 1920- WhoBlA 92
**Ray**, Nicholas 1911-1979 IntDcF 2-2 [port]
**Ray**, Nik E. 1944- WhoWest 92
**Ray**, Oakley S 1931- AmMWSc 92
**Ray**, Paul Dean 1934- AmMWSc 92
**Ray**, Paul Leo 1946- WhoWest 92
**Ray**, Paul R., Jr. 1943- WhoFI 92
**Ray**, Peter Martin 1931- AmMWSc 92
**Ray**, Peter Sawin 1944- AmMWSc 92
**Ray**, Philip Bicknell 1917- Who 92
**Ray**, Prasanta K 1941- AmMWSc 92
**Ray**, Raymond Billy 1943- WhoAmL 92
**Ray**, Richard 1927- WhoAmP 91, WhoBlA 92
**Ray**, Richard Archibald 1936- WhoRel 92
**Ray**, Richard B. 1927- AlmAP 92 [port]
**Ray**, Richard Eugene 1950- WhoMW 92
**Ray**, Richard Rex 1942- WhoBlA 92
**Ray**, Richard Schell 1928- AmMWSc 92
**Ray**, Richard Stanley 1937- WhoWest 92
**Ray**, Robert WhoAmP 91
**Ray**, Robert Allen 1939- AmMWSc 92

**Ray**, Robert D. 1928- *IntWW 91, WhoAmP 91*
**Ray**, Robert Durant 1914- *AmMWSc 92*
**Ray**, Robert Francis 1947- *IntWW 91, Who 92*
**Ray**, Robert H. 1940- *ConAu 135*
**Ray**, Robert J 1935- *IntAu&W 91*
**Ray**, Robin *Who 92*
**Ray**, Roger Dale 1938- *WhoMW 92*
**Ray**, Ronald Dudley 1942- *WhoAmL 92*
**Ray**, Rose Marie 1943- *AmMWSc 92*
**Ray**, Roy L 1939- *WhoAmP 91*
**Ray**, Ruthann 1956- *WhoFI 92*
**Ray**, Sammy Mehedy 1919- *AmMWSc 92*
**Ray**, Sandy Frederick 1898- *WhoBlA 92*
**Ray**, Satyajit 1921- *IntDcF 2-2 [port], IntMPA 92, IntWW 91, Who 92*
**Ray**, Sheila G. 1930- *WrDr 92*
**Ray**, Shreela *DrAPF 91*
**Ray**, Sib Narayan 1921- *WrDr 92*
**Ray**, Siba Prasad 1944- *AmMWSc 92*
**Ray**, Siddhartha Sankar 1920- *IntWW 91*
**Ray**, Susanne Gettings 1938- *WhoMW 92*
**Ray**, Sylvian Richard 1931- *AmMWSc 92*
**Ray**, Verne A 1929- *AmMWSc 92*
**Ray**, W Harmon 1940- *AmMWSc 92*
**Ray**, Walter I., Jr. 1923- *WhoBlA 92*
**Ray**, Walter S *WhoAmP 91*
**Ray**, Wesley *TwCWW 91*
**Ray**, William Benjamin *WhoBlA 92*
**Ray**, William Donald 1943- *WhoWest 92*
**Ray**, William F. 1915- *WhoFI 92*
**Ray**, William J 1945- *AmMWSc 92*
**Ray**, William Jackson, Jr 1932- *AmMWSc 92*
**Ray-Chaudhuri**, Dilip K 1929- *AmMWSc 92*
**Ray-Chaudhuri**, Dwijendra Kumar 1933- *AmMWSc 92*
**Ray-Goins**, Jeanette 1933- *WhoBlA 92*
**Ray-Lynch**, Leopold Augustus 1951- *WhoWest 92*
**Raybon**, Gregory 1961- *AmMWSc 92*
**Raybon**, Irma Julian 1912- *WhoBlA 92*
**Rayborn**, Grayson Hanks 1939- *AmMWSc 92*
**Rayborn**, William Lee 1936- *WhoAmP 91*
**Raybould**, Howard 1946- *TwCPaSc*
**Rayburn**, B B Sixty 1916- *WhoAmP 91*
**Rayburn**, Carole Ann 1938- *WhoRel 92*
**Rayburn**, Gene *IntMPA 92, LesBEnT 92, WhoEnt 92*
**Rayburn**, James Michael 1949- *WhoMW 92*
**Rayburn**, Louis Alfred 1921- *AmMWSc 92*
**Rayburn**, Margaret Shaw 1927- *WhoAmP 91*
**Rayburn**, Marlon Cecil, Jr 1931- *AmMWSc 92*
**Rayburn**, Samuel Taliaferro 1882-1961 *AmPolLe, FacFETw [port]*
**Rayburn**, Stephen R. 1942- *WhoMW 92*
**Rayburn**, Wendell Gilbert 1929- *WhoBlA 92, WhoMW 92*
**Rayburn**, William Reed 1940- *AmMWSc 92*
**Raychaudhuri**, Anilbaran *AmMWSc 92*
**Raychaudhuri**, Kamal Kumar 1947- *AmMWSc 92*
**Raychowdhury**, Pratip Nath 1932- *AmMWSc 92*
**Raycraft**, Stan *TwCSFW 91*
**Raye**, Jimmy *WhoBlA 92*
**Raye**, John 1941- *WhoBlA 92*
**Raye**, Martha *LesBEnT 92*
**Raye**, Martha 1916- *IntMPA 92*
**Raye**, Vance Wallace 1946- *WhoBlA 92*
**Rayer**, Francis G 1921-1981 *TwCSFW 91*
**Rayes**, Ghazi al 1935- *IntWW 91*
**Rayfield**, Denise E. 1955- *WhoBlA 92*
**Rayfield**, Donald 1942- *WrDr 92*
**Rayfield**, Gary Gene 1947- *WhoRel 92*
**Rayfield**, George W 1936- *AmMWSc 92*
**Rayford**, Brenda L. 1940- *WhoBlA 92*
**Rayford**, Floyd Kinnard 1957- *WhoBlA 92*
**Rayford**, Lee Edward 1935- *WhoBlA 92*
**Rayford**, Phillip Leon 1927- *AmMWSc 92, WhoBlA 92*
**Rayford**, Zula M. 1941- *WhoBlA 92*
**Raygorodetsky**, Roman 1929- *LiExTwC*
**Rayher**, Edward *DrAPF 91*
**Raykin**, Arkadiy Isaakovich 1911-1987 *SovUnBD*
**Rayl**, Granville Monroe 1917- *WhoRel 92*
**Rayl**, Harris Ashton 1953- *WhoMW 92*
**Rayl**, John Edward 1947- *WhoMW 92*
**Rayl**, Ruth Corena 1952- *WhoFI 92*
**Rayle**, David Lee 1942- *AmMWSc 92*
**Rayle**, Richard Eugene 1939- *AmMWSc 92*
**Rayleigh**, Baron 1960- *Who 92*
**Rayleigh**, Jane Marie *WhoEnt 92*
**Raylesberg**, Alan Ira 1950- *WhoAmL 92*
**Rayman**, Mohamad Khalil 1938- *AmMWSc 92*
**Raymer**, Elwyn Carlos 1935- *WhoEnt 92*
**Raymer**, Michael Robert 1917- *Who 92*
**Raymon**, Louis 1939- *AmMWSc 92*
**Raymond**, Arthur *WhoAmP 91*
**Raymond**, Arthur Charles 1933- *WhoAmP 91*
**Raymond**, Arthur E 1899- *AmMWSc 92*
**Raymond**, Bobby *WhoAmP 91*
**Raymond**, Burke Munson 1934- *WhoWest 92*
**Raymond**, Charles Forest 1939- *AmMWSc 92*
**Raymond**, Charles Walker, III 1937- *WhoFI 92*
**Raymond**, Clarinda Harriss *DrAPF 91*
**Raymond**, Dale Rodney 1949- *AmMWSc 92*
**Raymond**, David James 1943- *AmMWSc 92*
**Raymond**, David Walker 1945- *WhoAmL 92*
**Raymond**, Derek *WrDr 92*
**Raymond**, Diana Joan 1916- *IntAu&W 91, WrDr 92*
**Raymond**, Ellsworth 1912- *WrDr 92*
**Raymond**, Eugene Thomas 1923- *WhoWest 92*
**Raymond**, Frank 1943- *WhoEnt 92*
**Raymond**, Gene 1908- *IntMPA 92, WhoEnt 92*
**Raymond**, Gerald Patrick 1933- *AmMWSc 92*
**Raymond**, Gerard Anthony 1954- *WhoEnt 92*
**Raymond**, Guy 1911- *WhoEnt 92*
**Raymond**, Henry James, II 1957- *WhoBlA 92*
**Raymond**, Henry Jarvis 1820-1869 *BenetAL 91*
**Raymond**, Howard Lawrence 1929- *AmMWSc 92*
**Raymond**, Jenette Lee 1945- *WhoEnt 92*
**Raymond**, John 1948- *WhoEnt 92*
**Raymond**, John Charles 1948- *AmMWSc 92*
**Raymond**, Judith Ann 1938- *WhoAmP 91*
**Raymond**, Kenneth Norman 1942- *AmMWSc 92*
**Raymond**, Lawrence W 1935- *AmMWSc 92*
**Raymond**, Lee R. 1938- *WhoFI 92*
**Raymond**, Loren Arthur 1943- *AmMWSc 92*
**Raymond**, Louis 1934- *AmMWSc 92*
**Raymond**, Mary *IntAu&W 91X*
**Raymond**, Maurice A 1938- *AmMWSc 92*
**Raymond**, Monica E. *DrAPF 91*
**Raymond**, P T *ScFEYrs*
**Raymond**, Patrick 1924- *WrDr 92*
**Raymond**, Patrick Ernest 1924- *IntAu&W 91*
**Raymond**, Paula 1925- *IntMPA 92*
**Raymond**, Philip Warren 1955- *WhoEnt 92, WhoMW 92*
**Raymond**, Phillip Gregory 1957- *WhoBlA 92*
**Raymond**, Rhoades Robert 1949- *WhoFI 92*
**Raymond**, Richard Carter 1952- *WhoAmL 92*
**Raymond**, Robert Earl 1926- *WhoRel 92*
**Raymond**, Robert Edward 1936- *WhoWest 92*
**Raymond**, Ronald C 1951- *WhoAmP 91*
**Raymond**, Ronald Keith 1961- *WhoEnt 92*
**Raymond**, Rossiter Worthington 1840-1918 *BiInAmS*
**Raymond**, Russell Ernest *WhoAmL 92*
**Raymond**, Samuel 1920- *AmMWSc 92*
**Raymond**, Susan Grant 1943- *WhoWest 92*
**Raymond**, William Francis 1922- *Who 92*
**Raymond**, William Marshall 1934- *WhoFI 92*
**Raymond-Savage**, Anne 1939- *AmMWSc 92*
**Raymonda**, John Warren 1939- *AmMWSc 92*
**Raymos**, Dion Cason 1956- *WhoAmL 92*
**Raymund**, Mahlon 1932- *AmMWSc 92*
**Raynal**, Dudley Jones 1947- *AmMWSc 92*
**Raynal**, Guillaume-Thomas 1713-1796 *BlkwCEP*
**Raynal**, Guillaume Thomas Francois 1713-1796 *BenetAL 91*
**Raynard**, Shirley M 1942- *WhoAmP 91*
**Raynaud**, Jean Guillaume Marie 1925- *IntWW 91*
**Raynaud**, Pierre 1917- *IntWW 91*
**Rayne** *Who 92*
**Rayne**, Baron 1918- *IntWW 91, Who 92*
**Rayne**, Edward 1922- *Who 92*
**Rayne**, John A 1927- *AmMWSc 92*
**Rayne**, Richard Winfred, III 1961- *WhoFI 92*
**Rayner** *Who 92*
**Rayner**, Baron 1926- *IntWW 91, Who 92*
**Rayner**, Anthony George 1944- *WhoWest 92*
**Rayner**, Arno Alfred 1928- *WhoWest 92*
**Rayner**, Brenda Susan 1953- *WhoEnt 92*
**Rayner**, Bryan Roy 1932- *Who 92*
**Rayner**, Claire 1931- *IntAu&W 91, WrDr 92*
**Rayner**, Claire Berenice 1931- *Who 92*
**Rayner**, David Edward 1940- *Who 92*
**Rayner**, Edward John 1936- *Who 92*
**Rayner**, John Desmond 1924- *WrDr 92*
**Rayner**, John Norman 1936- *AmMWSc 92*
**Rayner**, Keith *Who 92*
**Rayner**, Mary 1933- *WrDr 92*
**Rayner**, Mary Yoma 1933- *IntAu&W 91*
**Rayner**, William 1929- *TwCWW 91, WrDr 92*
**Rayner-Canham**, Geoffrey William 1944- *AmMWSc 92*
**Raynes**, Bertram C 1924- *AmMWSc 92*
**Raynes**, Edward Peter 1945- *IntWW 91, Who 92*
**Raynham**, Viscount 1945- *Who 92*
**Raynolds**, David Robert 1928- *WhoWest 92*
**Raynolds**, Peter Webb 1951- *AmMWSc 92*
**Raynolds**, Robert 1902-1964 *BenetAL 91*
**Raynolds**, Stuart 1927- *AmMWSc 92*
**Raynor**, Henry 1917- *WrDr 92*
**Raynor**, Joe B 1923- *WhoAmP 91*
**Raynor**, John Patrick 1923- *WhoMW 92*
**Raynor**, Lynn S. 1940- *IntMPA 92*
**Raynor**, Robert Layton 1954- *WhoRel 92*
**Raynor**, Susanne 1948- *AmMWSc 92*
**Raynor-Gelvin**, Vera *DrAPF 91*
**Raynovich**, George, Jr. 1931- *WhoAmL 92*
**Raynowska**, Bernard J 1925- *WhoAmP 91*
**Raynsford**, Nick *Who 92*
**Raynsford**, Robert Wayne, Jr. 1935- *WhoFI 92*
**Raynsford**, Wyvill Richard Nicolls 1945- *Who 92*
**Rayon**, Paul E., III 1950- *WhoBlA 92*
**Rayport**, Mark 1922- *AmMWSc 92*
**Rayside**, John Stuart 1942- *AmMWSc 92*
**Rayson**, Barbara M *AmMWSc 92*
**Rayson**, John Chandler 1949- *WhoAmP 91*
**Rayudu**, Garimella V S 1936- *AmMWSc 92*
**Rayvid**, Jay 1932- *WhoEnt 92*
**Raz**, Avraham 1945- *AmMWSc 92*
**Raz**, Joseph 1939- *Who 92*
**Razaf**, Andy 1895-1973 *BenetAL 91*
**Razafimahatratra**, Victor 1921- *IntWW 91, WhoRel 92*
**Razafimbahiny**, Jules Alphonse 1922- *IntWW 91*
**Razafindrabe**, Armand 1931- *IntWW 91*
**Razak**, Charles Kenneth 1918- *AmMWSc 92*
**Razak**, Mohamad Najib bin tun Haj Abdul 1954- *IntWW 91*
**Razaleigh Hamzah** 1936?- *IntWW 91*
**Razdan**, Mohan Kishen *AmMWSc 92*
**Razdan**, Raj Kumar 1929- *AmMWSc 92*
**Razgaitis**, Richard A 1944- *AmMWSc 92*
**Razgon**, Lev Emmanuelivich 1908- *SovUnBD*
**Razi**, Kathleen Ann 1950- *WhoMW 92*
**Razia**, Sultana d1240 *EncAmaz 91*
**Raziuddin**, Syed Husaini 1957- *WhoMW 92*
**Razl**, Stanislav 1920- *IntWW 91*
**Razniak**, Stephen L 1934- *AmMWSc 92*
**Razo**, Jose H. 1951- *WhoHisp 92*
**Razonable**, John 1943- *WhoHisp 92*
**Razook**, Richard J. *WhoHisp 92*
**Razouk**, Rashad Elias 1911- *AmMWSc 92*
**Razumovsky**, Georgiy Petrovich 1936- *IntWW 91, SovUnBD*
**Razzall**, Leonard Humphrey 1912- *Who 92*
**Razzano**, Frank Charles 1948- *WhoAmL 92*
**Razzano**, Pasquale Angelo 1943- *WhoAmL 92*
**Razzino**, James Edward 1946- *WhoFI 92*
**Re**, Edward D. 1920- *WhoAmL 92*
**Re**, Richard N 1944- *AmMWSc 92*
**Rea** *Who 92*
**Rea**, Baron 1928- *Who 92*
**Rea**, Betty 1904-1965 *TwCPaSc*
**Rea**, David Kenerson 1942- *AmMWSc 92*
**Rea**, David Richard 1940- *AmMWSc 92*
**Rea**, Donald George 1929- *AmMWSc 92*
**Rea**, Dorothy Callaway 1939- *WhoAmP 91*
**Rea**, Ernest 1945- *Who 92*
**Rea**, George Robert, Jr 1939- *WhoAmP 91*
**Rea**, Jack D 1933- *WhoAmP 91*
**Rea**, James Edmond 1935- *WhoFI 92*
**Rea**, James F 1937- *WhoAmP 91*
**Rea**, James Taylor 1907- *Who 92*
**Rea**, James Thomas 1945- *WhoWest 92*
**Rea**, John Rowland 1933- *Who 92*
**Rea**, Kathryn Pollyanna 1957- *WhoWest 92*
**Rea**, Kenneth Harold 1946- *AmMWSc 92*
**Rea**, Michael J, Jr 1940- *WhoAmP 91*
**Rea**, Natalie B. 1956- *WhoAmL 92*
**Rea**, Robert Hall 1934- *WhoWest 92*
**Rea**, Roger Uhl 1944- *WhoMW 92*
**Rea**, Rupert Lascelles P. *Who 92*
**Rea**, Sharon Wallis 1945- *WhoWest 92*
**Rea**, Susan *DrAPF 91*
**Rea**, Tom *DrAPF 91*
**Rea**, William J. 1920- *WhoAmL 92, WhoWest 92*
**Rea**, William John, Jr. 1953- *WhoAmL 92*
**Rea Price**, John 1937- *Who 92*
**Reach**, Charles H. 1930- *WhoFI 92*
**Reachi**, Santiago 1898- *WhoHisp 92*
**Read**, Miss *Who 92*
**Read**, Miss 1913- *WrDr 92*
**Read**, Alan Ernest Alfred 1926- *Who 92*
**Read**, Albert James 1926- *AmMWSc 92*
**Read**, Allan Alexander *Who 92*
**Read**, Allan Alexander 1923- *WhoRel 92*
**Read**, Anthony 1935- *IntAu&W 91, WrDr 92*
**Read**, Antony *Who 92*
**Read**, Arthur Martin, II 1946- *WhoAmP 91*
**Read**, Brian 1927- *WrDr 92*
**Read**, Charles 1918- *Who 92*
**Read**, Charles Arthur 1919- *WhoAmL 92*
**Read**, Charles H 1918- *AmMWSc 92*
**Read**, D E 1924- *AmMWSc 92*
**Read**, Dale T 1946- *WhoAmP 91*
**Read**, Daniel 1757-1836 *NewAmDM*
**Read**, David 1910- *WrDr 92*
**Read**, David Hadley 1921- *AmMWSc 92*
**Read**, David Haxton Carswell 1910- *Who 92, WhoRel 92*
**Read**, David John 1939- *Who 92*
**Read**, David Thomas 1947- *AmMWSc 92*
**Read**, Donald 1930- *WrDr 92*
**Read**, Donald William 1914- *WhoEnt 92*
**Read**, Elfreida 1920- *WrDr 92*
**Read**, Floyd M 1924- *AmMWSc 92*
**Read**, Frank Henry 1934- *Who 92*
**Read**, Frank Thompson 1938- *WhoAmL 92*
**Read**, Gardner 1913- *NewAmDM, WrDr 92*
**Read**, George Wesley 1934- *AmMWSc 92*
**Read**, Harold Thomas 1938- *WhoFI 92*
**Read**, Harrison Andrew 1950- *WhoRel 92*
**Read**, Harry 1924- *Who 92*
**Read**, Herbert 1893-1968 *DcTwDes, RfGEnL 91*
**Read**, Herbert Edward 1893-1968 *FacFETw*
**Read**, Imelda Mary 1939- *Who 92*
**Read**, Jan 1917- *WrDr 92*
**Read**, Joel *WhoFI 92, WhoRel 92*
**Read**, John Antony 1913- *Who 92*
**Read**, John Emms 1918- *IntWW 91, Who 92*
**Read**, John Frederick 1940- *AmMWSc 92*
**Read**, John Hamilton 1924- *AmMWSc 92*
**Read**, John Leslie 1935- *Who 92*
**Read**, Leonard Ernest 1925- *Who 92*
**Read**, Lionel Frank 1929- *Who 92*
**Read**, Margaret Helen d1991 *Who 92N*
**Read**, Marsha H *AmMWSc 92*
**Read**, Marvin, Jr. 1936- *WhoRel 92*
**Read**, Mary 1692?-1721 *EncAmaz 91*
**Read**, Matthew Canfield 1823-1902 *BiInAmS*
**Read**, Mel *Who 92*
**Read**, Melinda Ruth Boucher 1957- *WhoRel 92*
**Read**, Merrill Stafford 1928- *AmMWSc 92*
**Read**, Miss *IntAu&W 91X*
**Read**, Motte Alston 1872-1920 *BiInAmS*
**Read**, Opie 1852-1939 *BenetAL 91*
**Read**, Paul Eugene 1937- *AmMWSc 92*
**Read**, Philip Lloyd 1932- *AmMWSc 92*
**Read**, Piers Paul 1941- *ConNov 91, IntAu&W 91, IntWW 91, Who 92, WrDr 92*
**Read**, Raymond Charles 1924- *AmMWSc 92*
**Read**, Robert E 1933- *AmMWSc 92*
**Read**, Robert G 1918- *AmMWSc 92*
**Read**, Robert H 1928- *AmMWSc 92*
**Read**, Robert Logan 1938- *WhoWest 92*
**Read**, Robert P, Jr 1946- *WhoAmP 91*
**Read**, Robert Richard 1929- *AmMWSc 92*
**Read**, Ronald Cedric 1924- *AmMWSc 92*
**Read**, Simon 1949- *TwCPaSc*
**Read**, Sylvia Joan *WrDr 92*
**Read**, Thomas Buchanan 1822-1872 *BenetAL 91*
**Read**, Thomas Thornton 1943- *AmMWSc 92*
**Read**, Virginia Hall 1937- *AmMWSc 92*
**Read**, William Brooks 1926- *WhoAmP 91*
**Read**, William F 1915- *AmMWSc 92*
**Read**, William George 1921- *AmMWSc 92*
**Read-Connole**, Elizabeth Lee 1952- *AmMWSc 92*
**Readdy**, Arthur F, Jr 1928- *AmMWSc 92*
**Reade**, Brian Anthony 1940- *Who 92*
**Reade**, Charles 1814-1884 *RfGEnL 91*
**Reade**, Chris Evans 1966- *WhoEnt 92*
**Reade**, Claire Elizabeth 1952- *WhoAmL 92*
**Reade**, Clyde Nixon 1906- *Who 92*
**Reade**, Hamish *WrDr 92*
**Reade**, Maxwell Ossian 1916- *AmMWSc 92*
**Reade**, Philip *ScFEYrs*

**Reade**, Robert Mellor 1940- *WhoFI 92, WhoWest 92*
**Reader**, Dennis J. *DrAPF 91*
**Reader**, George Gordon 1919- *AmMWSc 92*
**Reader**, James Dale 1937- *WhoFI 92*
**Reader**, Joseph 1934- *AmMWSc 92*
**Reader**, Wayne Truman 1939- *AmMWSc 92*
**Reader Harris**, Diana 1912- *Who 92*
**Readett**, Anne Leslie 1961- *WhoMW 92*
**Readey**, Dennis W 1937- *AmMWSc 92*
**Readhead**, Carol Winifred 1947- *AmMWSc 92*
**Reading**, Area Bishop of 1930- *Who 92*
**Reading**, Marquess of 1942- *Who 92*
**Reading**, Anthony John 1933- *AmMWSc 92*
**Reading**, Bertice d1991 *NewYTBS 91*
**Reading**, James Bruce 1943- *WhoAmL 92*
**Reading**, James Cardon 1937- *AmMWSc 92*
**Reading**, John Frank 1939- *AmMWSc 92*
**Reading**, Kathleen Anne 1962- *WhoMW 92*
**Reading**, Peter 1946- *ConPo 91, IntAu&W 91, WrDr 92*
**Reading**, Rogers W 1934- *AmMWSc 92*
**Readinger**, David M 1935- *WhoAmP 91*
**Readnour**, Jerry Michael 1940- *AmMWSc 92*
**Readwin**, Edgar Seeley 1915- *Who 92*
**Ready**, Elizabeth M 1953- *WhoAmP 91*
**Ready**, George Banks 1957- *WhoAmP 91*
**Ready**, Jack Wesley 1943- *WhoRel 92*
**Ready**, John Fetsch 1932- *AmMWSc 92*
**Ready**, Leah Henriquez 1947- *WhoHisp 92*
**Reagan**, Brad Rock 1959- *WhoAmL 92*
**Reagan**, Daryl David 1925- *AmMWSc 92*
**Reagan**, Gary Don 1941- *WhoAmL 92, WhoWest 92*
**Reagan**, Harry Edwin, III 1940- *WhoAmL 92*
**Reagan**, James Oliver 1945- *AmMWSc 92*
**Reagan**, James W 1918- *AmMWSc 92*
**Reagan**, Janet Thompson 1945- *WhoWest 92*
**Reagan**, John Albert 1941- *AmMWSc 92*
**Reagan**, Michael Joseph 1954- *WhoAmL 92*
**Reagan**, Nancy Davis 1923- *IntWW 91, WhoWest 92, WrDr 92*
**Reagan**, Patricia Ann *ConAu 134*
**Reagan**, Ronald *LesBEnT 92*
**Reagan**, Ronald 1911- *BenetAL 91, IntMPA 92, RComAH, Who 92*
**Reagan**, Ronald Wilson 1911- *AmPolLe [port], FacFETw [port], IntWW 91, WhoAmP 91, WhoWest 92*
**Reagan**, Stevan Ray 1956- *WhoEnt 92*
**Reagan**, Thomas Eugene 1947- *AmMWSc 92*
**Reagan**, William Joseph 1943- *AmMWSc 92*
**Reagan**, William Ralph 1935- *WhoFI 92*
**Reagon**, Bernice J. 1942- *NotBlAW 92 [port]*
**Reagon**, Bernice Johnson 1942- *WhoBlA 92*
**Reagor**, John Charles 1938- *AmMWSc 92*
**Real**, Cathleen Clare 1934- *WhoRel 92*
**Real**, Charles Edward 1943- *WhoMW 92*
**Real**, Frank Joseph 1933- *WhoMW 92*
**Real**, Leslie Allan 1950- *AmMWSc 92*
**Real**, Manuel Lawrence 1924- *WhoAmL 92, WhoWest 92*
**Reale**, Salvatore Joseph 1933- *WhoFI 92*
**Realf**, Richard 1834-1878 *BenetAL 91*
**Realmuto**, Anthony John 1961- *WhoEnt 92*
**Reals**, William Joseph 1920- *AmMWSc 92*
**Reals**, Willis Braithwaite 1925- *WhoFI 92*
**Ream**, Bernard Claude 1939- *AmMWSc 92*
**Ream**, Lloyd Walter, Jr 1953- *AmMWSc 92*
**Ream**, Robert R 1936- *WhoAmP 91*
**Reamer**, Shirley Jean 1935- *WhoRel 92*
**Reames**, Cheryl Wallace 1945- *WhoRel 92*
**Reames**, Donald Vernon 1936- *AmMWSc 92*
**Reames**, Jeffrey Alan 1949- *WhoMW 92*
**Reames**, Timothy Paul 1935- *WhoAmL 92, WhoFI 92*
**Reams**, Bernard Dinsmore, Jr. 1943- *WhoAmL 92, WhoFI 92, WhoMW 92*
**Reams**, Lee Thomas 1934- *WhoWest 92*
**Reams**, Max Warren 1938- *AmMWSc 92*
**Reams**, Michael Thomas 1966- *WhoEnt 92*
**Reams**, Willie Mathews, Jr 1930- *AmMWSc 92*
**Reams-Whitmire**, Vernetta Maria 1930- *WhoBlA 92*
**Reamy**, Tom 1935-1977 *TwCSFW 91*
**Reaney**, Gilbert 1924- *WhoEnt 92*
**Reaney**, James 1926- *BenetAL 91, ConPo 91, RfGEnL 91, WrDr 92*
**Reaney**, James Crerar 1926- *ConAu 15AS [port]*
**Reap**, James B. 1930- *WhoAmL 92*
**Reap**, James John 1948- *AmMWSc 92*
**Reap**, Mary Margaret 1941- *WhoRel 92*
**Reapsome**, James Willis 1928- *WhoRel 92*
**Rearden**, Carole Ann 1946- *AmMWSc 92, WhoWest 92*
**Rearden**, Sara B. *WhoBlA 92*
**Reardon**, Andrew Fitzpatrick 1945- *WhoFI 92*
**Reardon**, Anna Joyce 1910- *AmMWSc 92*
**Reardon**, Barry *IntMPA 92*
**Reardon**, Bernard M. G. 1913- *WrDr 92*
**Reardon**, Bill *WhoAmP 91*
**Reardon**, Craig 1953- *WhoWest 92*
**Reardon**, D. Barry *WhoEnt 92*
**Reardon**, Daniel Francis 1932- *WhoRel 92*
**Reardon**, Dennis J. 1944- *WrDr 92*
**Reardon**, Edward Joseph, Jr 1943- *AmMWSc 92*
**Reardon**, Frank Emond 1953- *WhoAmL 92*
**Reardon**, Frederick H 1932- *AmMWSc 92*
**Reardon**, John 1930-1987 *NewAmDM*
**Reardon**, John Joseph 1921- *AmMWSc 92*
**Reardon**, John Patrick 1933- *Who 92*
**Reardon**, Joseph Daniel 1944- *AmMWSc 92*
**Reardon**, Joseph Edward 1938- *AmMWSc 92*
**Reardon**, Joseph Patrick 1940- *AmMWSc 92*
**Reardon**, Judy E 1958- *WhoAmP 91*
**Reardon**, Mark William 1956- *WhoAmL 92*
**Reardon**, Martin Alan 1932- *Who 92*
**Reardon**, Patrick Austin 1950- *WhoAmL 92*
**Reardon**, Robert Joseph 1928- *WhoFI 92*
**Reardon**, Terrence James 1950- *WhoAmP 91*
**Reardon**, Thomas Webster, Jr. 1959- *WhoAmL 92*
**Reardon**, William J 1941- *WhoAmP 91*
**Reardon-Smith**, William *Who 92*
**Rearick**, David F 1932- *AmMWSc 92*
**Rearick**, Thomas Charles 1953- *WhoFI 92*
**Reas**, Keith Scott 1951- *WhoWest 92*
**Reasenberg**, Robert David 1942- *AmMWSc 92*
**Reaser**, Donald Frederick 1931- *AmMWSc 92*
**Reaser**, Richard Lee 1932- *WhoWest 92*
**Reaser**, Vernon Neal, Jr. 1942- *WhoAmL 92*
**Reason**, Cyril 1931- *TwCPaSc*
**Reason**, Joseph Henry 1905- *WhoBlA 92*
**Reason**, Rex 1928- *IntMPA 92*
**Reasoner**, Carroll Jane 1951- *WhoAmL 92*
**Reasoner**, Harry d1991 *LesBEnT 92 [port]*
**Reasoner**, Harry 1923-1991 *ConAu 135, CurBio 91N, NewYTBS 91 [port], News 92-1*
**Reasoner**, Harry Max 1939- *WhoAmL 92*
**Reasoner**, James M 1953- *TwCWW 91*
**Reasoner**, John W 1940- *AmMWSc 92*
**Reasoner**, Stephen M. 1944- *WhoAmL 92*
**Reasoner**, Willis Irl, III 1951- *WhoAmL 92*
**Reasons**, Kent M 1940- *AmMWSc 92*
**Reasor**, Mark Jae 1945- *AmMWSc 92*
**Reath**, George, Jr. 1939- *WhoAmL 92, WhoFI 92*
**Reaugh**, Jack Logan, Jr. 1944- *WhoRel 92*
**Reaume**, David Michael 1941- *WhoFI 92*
**Reaven**, Eve P 1928- *AmMWSc 92*
**Reaver**, J. Russell 1915- *WrDr 92*
**Reaves**, Benjamin Franklin 1932- *WhoBlA 92*
**Reaves**, Charles 1956- *WhoFI 92*
**Reaves**, Craig Charles 1952- *WhoAmL 92*
**Reaves**, Darryl 1960- *WhoAmP 91*
**Reaves**, E. Fredericka M. 1938- *WhoBlA 92*
**Reaves**, Franklin Carlwell 1942- *WhoBlA 92*
**Reaves**, Gibson 1923- *AmMWSc 92, WhoWest 92*
**Reaves**, Ginevera N. 1925- *WhoBlA 92*
**Reaves**, Harry Lee 1927- *AmMWSc 92*
**Reaves**, Henry L 1919- *WhoAmP 91*
**Reaves**, J. Michael *WrDr 92*
**Reaves**, Jefferson, Sr 1925- *WhoAmP 91*
**Reaves**, Kenneth Martin 1954- *WhoRel 92*
**Reaves**, Michael *TwCSFW 91, WrDr 92*
**Reaves**, Richard Wright 1914- *WhoMW 92*
**Reaves-Phillips**, Sandra *ConTFT 9*
**Reavey-Cantwell**, Nelson Henry 1926- *AmMWSc 92*
**Reavill**, David William 1948- *WhoWest 92*
**Reavis**, Charles Stephen 1945- *WhoEnt 92*
**Reavis**, Dick J. 1945- *ConAu 133*
**Reavis**, Herbert M., Jr. 1956- *WhoRel 92*
**Reavis**, John William, Jr. 1935- *WhoBlA 92*
**Reavis**, Lincoln 1933- *WhoAmL 92*
**Reavis**, Robert Arthur 1949- *WhoWest 92*
**Reavis**, Theodore Edward 1937- *WhoWest 92*
**Reavley**, Thomas Morrow 1921- *WhoAmL 92, WhoAmP 91*
**Reay**, Lord 1937- *Who 92*
**Reay**, Master of 1965- *Who 92*
**Reay**, Alan *Who 92*
**Reay**, David William 1940- *Who 92*
**Reay**, Hubert Alan 1925- *Who 92*
**Reay**, John 1947- *TwCPaSc*
**Reay**, John R 1934- *AmMWSc 92*
**Reay**, John Sinclair Shewan 1932- *Who 92*
**Reay**, William Edwin 1954- *WhoFI 92*
**Reazin**, George Harvey, Jr 1928- *AmMWSc 92*
**Reba**, Richard Charney 1932- *AmMWSc 92*
**Rebach**, Steve 1942- *AmMWSc 92*
**Reback**, Joyce Ellen 1948- *WhoAmL 92*
**Reback**, Richard Neal 1954- *WhoAmL 92*
**Rebane**, Hans *DcAmImH*
**Rebane**, John T. 1946- *WhoAmL 92*
**Rebatet**, Lucien 1903-1972 *BiDExR*
**Rebbeck**, Denis 1914- *IntWW 91, Who 92*
**Rebbeck**, Lester James, Jr. 1929- *WhoMW 92*
**Rebbi**, Claudio 1943- *AmMWSc 92*
**Rebe**, Bernd Werner 1939- *IntWW 91*
**Rebec**, George Vincent 1949- *AmMWSc 92*
**Rebeck**, David Paul 1950- *WhoRel 92*
**Rebek**, Julius, Jr 1944- *AmMWSc 92*
**Rebel**, Adam *TwCWW 91*
**Rebel**, William J 1934- *AmMWSc 92*
**Rebele**, Anthony P. *WhoHisp 92*
**Rebelein**, Paul Richard 1938- *WhoAmP 91, WhoMW 92*
**Rebell**, Walter 1951- *WhoRel 92*
**Rebello-Lopez**, Francisco *WhoAmL 92*
**Rebelo De Sousa**, Baltasar 1922- *IntWW 91*
**Rebenfeld**, Ludwig 1928- *AmMWSc 92*
**Reber**, Clark L 1937- *WhoAmP 91*
**Reber**, David James 1944- *WhoAmL 92*
**Reber**, Elwood Frank 1919- *AmMWSc 92*
**Reber**, Glenn B 1952- *WhoAmP 91*
**Reber**, James Paul 1947- *WhoFI 92*
**Reber**, Jane C *WhoAmP 91*
**Reber**, Jerry D 1939- *AmMWSc 92*
**Reber**, Raymond Andrew 1942- *AmMWSc 92*
**Reber**, Robert D, Jr 1947- *WhoAmP 91*
**Reber**, Sidney Craft, Jr. 1918- *WhoRel 92*
**Rebers**, Paul Armand 1923- *AmMWSc 92*
**Rebert**, M. Charles 1920- *WrDr 92*
**Rebeyrolle**, Paul 1926- *IntWW 91*
**Rebhuhn**, Deborah 1946- *AmMWSc 92*
**Rebhun**, Lionel Israel 1926- *AmMWSc 92*
**Rebick**, Charles 1944- *AmMWSc 92*
**Rebikov**, Vladimir 1866-1920 *NewAmDM*
**Rebillot**, Chris Conrad 1952- *WhoFI 92*
**Reble**, John H. 1887- *RelLAm 91*
**Rebling**, Eberhard 1911- *IntWW 91*
**Rebman**, Kenneth Ralph 1940- *AmMWSc 92*
**Rebocho Vaz**, Camilo Augusto de Miranda 1920- *IntWW 91*
**Rebolledo**, Tey Diana 1937- *WhoHisp 92*
**Rebollo-Lopez**, Francisco *WhoAmP 91*
**Rebora**, Clemente 1885-1957 *DcLB 114 [port]*
**Reboredo**, Pedro *WhoHisp 92*
**Rebori**, Robert Louis 1935- *WhoFI 92*
**Rebouche**, Charles Joseph 1948- *AmMWSc 92*
**Reboul**, Theo Todd, III 1922- *AmMWSc 92*
**Rebstock**, Irma Dell 1927- *WhoAmP 91*
**Rebstock**, Theodore Lynn 1925- *AmMWSc 92*
**Rebuck**, Ernest C 1944- *AmMWSc 92*
**Rebuck**, John Walter 1914- *AmMWSc 92*
**Rebuffe-Scrive**, Marielle Francoise *AmMWSc 92*
**Recabo**, Jaime Miguel 1950- *WhoAmL 92*
**Recant**, Lillian 1922- *AmMWSc 92*
**Recchion**, Eugene Laverne 1918- *WhoFI 92*
**Rech**, Richard Howard 1928- *AmMWSc 92*
**Rechard**, Ottis William 1924- *AmMWSc 92*
**Rechard**, Paul A 1927- *AmMWSc 92*
**Rechard**, Paul Albert 1927- *WhoFI 92*
**Rechcigl**, Miloslav, Jr 1930- *AmMWSc 92*
**Reche**, Otto Carl 1879-1966 *EncTR 91*
**Recheis**, Kathe 1928- *IntAu&W 91*
**Rechenberg**, Basil William 1928- *WhoRel 92*
**Rechendorff**, Torben 1937- *IntWW 91*
**Rechnitz**, Garry Arthur 1936- *AmMWSc 92*
**Rechnitzer**, Andreas Buchwald 1924- *AmMWSc 92*
**Recht**, Howard Leonard 1927- *AmMWSc 92*
**Recht**, Ray 1947- *WhoEnt 92*
**Rechtien**, James Joseph 1938- *WhoMW 92*
**Rechtien**, Richard Douglas 1933- *AmMWSc 92*
**Rechtin**, Eberhardt 1926- *AmMWSc 92, WhoWest 92*
**Rechtin**, Michael David 1944- *AmMWSc 92*
**Rechtman**, Cynthia 1946- *WhoRel 92*
**Rechtschaffen**, Allan 1927- *AmMWSc 92*
**Rechy**, John *DrAPF 91*
**Rechy**, John 1934- *BenetAL 91, ConNov 91, WrDr 92*
**Rechy**, John Francisco *WhoHisp 92*
**Reck**, Andrew Joseph 1927- *IntAu&W 91, WrDr 92*
**Reck**, Carleen *WhoRel 92*
**Reck**, Gene Paul 1937- *AmMWSc 92*
**Reck**, Joel Marvin 1941- *WhoAmL 92*
**Reck**, Richard Alan 1949- *WhoFI 92*
**Reck**, Ruth Annette *AmMWSc 92*
**Reck**, Waldo Emerson 1903- *WhoMW 92*
**Reck-Malleczewen**, Friedrich 1884-1945 *EncTR 91*
**Reckard**, Edgar Carpenter, Jr. 1919- *WhoRel 92*
**Reckase**, Mark Daniel 1944- *AmMWSc 92*
**Reckdahl**, Joan Marie 1936- *WhoAmP 91*
**Reckel**, Rudolph P 1934- *AmMWSc 92*
**Reckhow**, Kenneth Howland 1948- *AmMWSc 92*
**Reckhow**, Warren Addison 1921- *AmMWSc 92*
**Reckitt**, Basil Norman 1905- *IntWW 91, Who 92*
**Reckman**, Robert Frederick 1922- *WhoAmP 91*
**Recknagel**, Richard Otto 1916- *AmMWSc 92*
**Reckner**, David M. 1962- *WhoEnt 92*
**Recktenwald**, Fred William 1946- *WhoMW 92*
**Recktenwald**, Gerald William 1929- *AmMWSc 92*
**Recktenwald**, Horst Claus d1990 *IntWW 91N*
**Recktenwald**, James A., Jr. 1953- *WhoMW 92*
**Record**, Alice B 1921- *WhoAmP 91*
**Record**, Lincoln Fredrick 1939- *WhoMW 92*
**Record**, M Thomas, Jr 1942- *AmMWSc 92*
**Record**, Richard Thomas 1939- *WhoEnt 92*
**Record**, Rush Hamil 1917- *WhoAmL 92*
**Records**, Raymond Edwin 1930- *AmMWSc 92*
**Recsei**, Andrew A 1902- *AmMWSc 92*
**Recsei**, Paul Andor 1945- *AmMWSc 92*
**Rectenwald**, Gary Michael 1949- *WhoFI 92*
**Rector**, Alwin H. 1915- *WhoMW 92*
**Rector**, Bruce Johnson 1953- *WhoFI 92*
**Rector**, Charles Willson 1926- *AmMWSc 92*
**Rector**, David Richard 1951- *WhoMW 92*
**Rector**, Floyd Clinton, Jr 1929- *AmMWSc 92*
**Rector**, John Michael 1943- *WhoAmL 92*
**Rector**, Lee Tate 1927- *WhoAmP 91*
**Rector**, Liam *DrAPF 91*
**Rector**, Mark Edward 1961- *WhoAmL 92*
**Rector**, Nancy Lamp 1953- *WhoAmP 91*
**Rector**, Richard Robert 1925- *WhoEnt 92*
**Rector**, Robert Rush 1947- *WhoEnt 92*
**Rector**, Shirley *WhoAmP 91*
**Rector**, Susan Darnell 1959- *WhoAmL 92, WhoMW 92*
**Rector**, William Gordon 1922- *WhoAmP 91*
**Red Hot Chili Peppers**, The *ConMus 7 [port]*
**Red Jacket** *BenetAL 91*
**Red Maiden**, The *EncAmaz 91*
**Red Virgin**, The *EncAmaz 91*
**Reda**, David Neil 1947- *WhoAmL 92*
**Redaelli Spreafico**, Enrico 1911- *IntWW 91*
**Redal**, Rueben H. *WhoRel 92*
**Redalen**, Elton R *WhoAmP 91*
**Redalieu**, Elliot 1939- *AmMWSc 92*
**Redbeard** 1953- *WhoEnt 92*
**Redbone**, Leon *WhoEnt 92*
**Redburn**, Dianna Ammons 1943- *AmMWSc 92*
**Redcliff**, Robert Wayne 1959- *WhoAmL 92*
**Redd**, Aaron Hershall 1928- *WhoRel 92*
**Redd**, Albert Carter, Sr. 1917- *WhoBlA 92*
**Redd**, Charles Hardy 1936- *WhoAmP 91*
**Redd**, George N. 1903-1989 *WhoBlA 92N*
**Redd**, John Packard 1930- *WhoAmP 91*
**Redd**, M. Paul, Sr. 1928- *WhoBlA 92*
**Redd**, Orial Anne 1924- *WhoBlA 92*
**Redd**, Thomasina A. 1941- *WhoBlA 92*
**Redd**, William L. 1950- *WhoBlA 92*
**Reddan**, John R 1939- *AmMWSc 92*
**Reddan**, William Gerald 1927- *AmMWSc 92*
**Reddaway**, Brian *Who 92*
**Reddaway**, George Frank Norman 1918- *Who 92*
**Reddaway**, Jean 1923- *TwCPaSc*
**Reddaway**, Norman *Who 92*
**Reddaway**, Peter 1939- *WrDr 92*

**Reddaway**, William Brian 1913- IntWW 91, Who 92, WrDr 92
**Reddell**, Donald Lee 1937- AmMWSc 92
**Redden**, Barry 1960- WhoBlA 92
**Redden**, Camille J. 1930- WhoBlA 92
**Redden**, Gene Vernard 1947- WhoWest 92
**Redden**, Harral Arthur, Jr. 1936- WhoFI 92
**Redden**, Jack A 1926- AmMWSc 92
**Redden**, James Anthony 1929- WhoAmL 92, WhoAmP 91, WhoWest 92
**Redden**, Nigel A. 1950- WhoEnt 92
**Redden**, Patricia Ann 1941- AmMWSc 92
**Redden**, W. Glenn 1950- WhoFI 92, WhoWest 92
**Redder**, Thomas Joseph WhoAmP 91
**Reddersen**, Brad Rawson 1952- WhoFI 92
**Reddick**, Alzo Jackson 1937- WhoAmP 91, WhoBlA 92
**Reddick**, Bradford Beverly 1954- AmMWSc 92
**Reddick**, Johnnie Ervin 1935- WhoRel 92
**Reddick**, Linda H. 1916- WhoBlA 92
**Reddick**, Peter 1924- TwCPaSc
**Reddick**, Thomas J., Jr. 1919- WhoBlA 92
**Reddick-Mitchum**, Rhoda Anne 1937- AmMWSc 92
**Reddien**, Charles Henry, Jr. 1944- WhoAmL 92, WhoWest 92
**Reddig**, Walter Eduard 1936- WhoMW 92
**Reddin**, Keith 1956?- ConLC 67 [port]
**Redding**, David A. 1923- WrDr 92
**Redding**, Foster Kinyon 1929- AmMWSc 92
**Redding**, Frank L, Jr WhoAmP 91
**Redding**, J Saunders 1906-1988 FacFETw
**Redding**, J. Saunders 1907-1988 BenetAL 91
**Redding**, Joann Gentry WhoMW 92
**Redding**, Joseph Stafford 1921- AmMWSc 92
**Redding**, Kenneth 1959- WhoMW 92
**Redding**, Louis L. WhoBlA 92
**Redding**, Mary Lou WhoRel 92
**Redding**, Otis 1941-1967 FacFETw, NewAmDM
**Redding**, Richard William 1923- AmMWSc 92
**Redding**, Rogers Walker 1942- AmMWSc 92
**Reddington**, Joseph 1947- WhoMW 92
**Reddington**, Michael 1932- Who 92
**Reddington**, Michael 1946- WhoFI 92
**Reddish**, Mitchell Glenn 1953- WhoRel 92
**Reddish**, Paul Sigman 1910- AmMWSc 92
**Reddish**, Robert Lee 1919- AmMWSc 92
**Reddish**, Vincent Cartledge 1926- Who 92
**Reddoch**, Allan Harvey 1931- AmMWSc 92
**Reddoch**, John B. 1956- WhoAmL 92
**Reddog** 1954- WhoEnt 92
**Reddy**, Bandaru Sivarama 1932- AmMWSc 92
**Reddy**, Churku Mohan 1942- AmMWSc 92
**Reddy**, Gade Subbarami 1935- AmMWSc 92
**Reddy**, Gunda AmMWSc 92
**Reddy**, Helen 1942- IntMPA 92
**Reddy**, Helen Maxine 1941- WhoEnt 92
**Reddy**, Janardan K 1938- AmMWSc 92
**Reddy**, Junuthula N 1945- AmMWSc 92
**Reddy**, Kalluru Jayarami 1953- AmMWSc 92
**Reddy**, Kapuluru Chandrasekhara 1942- AmMWSc 92
**Reddy**, Kasu Brahmananda 1909- IntWW 91
**Reddy**, Marri Channa 1919- IntWW 91
**Reddy**, Michael Bernard 1954- WhoAmL 92
**Reddy**, Mohan Muthireval 1942- AmMWSc 92
**Reddy**, Murali Kalakoti 1958- WhoFI 92
**Reddy**, Nagendranath K. 1937- WhoWest 92
**Reddy**, Narender Pabbathi 1947- AmMWSc 92
**Reddy**, Neelam Sanjiva 1913- IntWW 91
**Reddy**, Nuka Venkatarami 1950- WhoFI 92
**Reddy**, Padala Vykuntha 1946- AmMWSc 92
**Reddy**, Parvathareddy Balarami 1942- AmMWSc 92
**Reddy**, Paul W. 1940- WhoFI 92
**Reddy**, Raj 1937- AmMWSc 92
**Reddy**, Ram Kadiri 1949- WhoWest 92
**Reddy**, RamaKrishna Pashuvula 1936- AmMWSc 92
**Reddy**, Reginald James 1934- AmMWSc 92
**Reddy**, Robert Jackson 1937- WhoAmP 91
**Reddy**, Sanjiva 1913- Who 92
**Reddy**, Satti Paddi 1932- AmMWSc 92
**Reddy**, Sudhakar M 1938- AmMWSc 92
**Reddy**, Thomas Bradley 1933- AmMWSc 92
**Reddy**, Tirumuru Varada 1941- WhoMW 92
**Reddy**, Venkat N 1922- AmMWSc 92
**Reddy**, William L 1938- AmMWSc 92
**Rede**, George Henry 1952- WhoHisp 92
**Redefer**, Jeff Alan 1955- WhoEnt 92
**Redei**, Gyorgy Pal 1921- AmMWSc 92
**Redeker**, Allan Grant 1924- AmMWSc 92
**Redelsperger**, Kenneth 1940- WhoAmP 91
**Redemann**, Eric John 1952- WhoWest 92
**Redenius**, Montie Mac 1939- WhoMW 92
**Redente**, Edward Francis 1951- AmMWSc 92, WhoWest 92
**Reder**, Anthony Thomas 1952- WhoMW 92
**Reder**, Friedrich H 1919- AmMWSc 92
**Reder**, Walter d1991 NewYTBS 91
**Reder**, Walter 1915- EncTR 91
**Redesdale**, Baron d1991 Who 92N
**Redesdale**, Baron 1967- Who 92
**Redetzki**, Helmut M 1921- AmMWSc 92
**Redfearn**, Paul Leslie, Jr 1926- AmMWSc 92
**Redfern**, David 1947- TwCPaSc
**Redfern**, John D. 1936- WhoFI 92
**Redfern**, John Joseph, III 1939- WhoFI 92
**Redfern**, June 1951- TwCPaSc
**Redfern**, Philip 1922- Who 92
**Redfern**, Richard Robert 1951- WhoFI 92, WhoMW 92
**Redfern**, Robert Earl 1929- AmMWSc 92
**Redfern**, Robert Seth 1933- WhoAmP 91
**Redfield**, Alfred Guillou 1929- AmMWSc 92
**Redfield**, David 1925- AmMWSc 92
**Redfield**, Holland L, Jr 1943- WhoAmP 91
**Redfield**, John A 1933- AmMWSc 92
**Redfield**, John Howard 1815-1895 BiInAmS
**Redfield**, Liza 1930- WhoEnt 92
**Redfield**, Lynn 1944- WhoWest 92
**Redfield**, Rosemary Jeanne 1948- AmMWSc 92
**Redfield**, William C 1789-1857 BiInAmS
**Redfield**, William David 1915- AmMWSc 92
**Redford**, Charles Robert 1937- Who 92
**Redford**, Donald Kirkman 1919- Who 92
**Redford**, John W B 1928- AmMWSc 92
**Redford**, Robert Who 92
**Redford**, Robert 1937- FacFETw, IntMPA 92, IntWW 91, WhoEnt 92
**Redgate**, Edward Stewart 1925- AmMWSc 92
**Redgrave**, Corin 1939- IntMPA 92
**Redgrave**, Lynn FacFETw
**Redgrave**, Lynn 1943- IntMPA 92, IntWW 91, Who 92, WhoEnt 92
**Redgrave**, Michael 1908-1985 FacFETw
**Redgrave**, Rachel Who 92
**Redgrave**, Roy Michael Frederick 1925- Who 92
**Redgrave**, Vanessa 1937- FacFETw, IntMPA 92, IntWW 91, Who 92, WhoEnt 92
**Redgrove**, Peter 1932- ConPo 91, WrDr 92
**Redgrove**, Peter William 1932- IntAu&W 91, IntWW 91, Who 92
**Redgwick**, Hubert Arthur 1906- WhoFI 92
**Redhead**, Brian 1929- Who 92
**Redhead**, Michael Logan Gonne 1929- Who 92
**Redhead**, Paul Aveling 1924- AmMWSc 92
**Redhead**, Scott Alan 1950- AmMWSc 92
**Redheffer**, Raymond Moos 1921- AmMWSc 92
**Redi**, Martha Harper AmMWSc 92
**Redi**, Olav 1938- AmMWSc 92
**Redican**, Kerry John 1950- WhoFI 92
**Redick**, Mark Lankford 1954- AmMWSc 92
**Redick**, Thomas Ferguson 1921- AmMWSc 92
**Redig**, Paul Robert 1949- WhoMW 92
**Rediger**, Alvin LeRoy 1918- WhoMW 92
**Rediger**, Richard Kim 1950- WhoAmL 92
**Rediker**, Robert Harmon 1924- AmMWSc 92
**Redin**, Robert Daniel 1928 AmMWSc 92
**Redinbo**, G Robert 1939- AmMWSc 92
**Reding**, Leo J WhoAmP 91
**Reding**, Nicholas Lee 1934- WhoFI 92, WhoMW 92
**Redinger**, James Collins 1937- WhoMW 92
**Redinger**, Richard Norman 1938- AmMWSc 92
**Redington**, Charles Bahr 1942- AmMWSc 92
**Redington**, James Duggan 1945- WhoRel 92
**Redington**, Patrick Edward 1946- WhoRel 92
**Redington**, Richard Lee 1933- AmMWSc 92
**Redington**, Rowland Wells 1924- AmMWSc 92
**Redisch**, Walter 1898- AmMWSc 92
**Redish**, Edward Frederick 1942- AmMWSc 92
**Redish**, Janice Copen 1941- AmMWSc 92
**Redish**, Kenneth Adair 1926- AmMWSc 92
**Redish**, Martin Harris 1945- WhoAmL 92
**Redleaf**, Diane Lynn 1954- WhoAmL 92
**Redlich**, Donald Harold 1929- WhoEnt 92
**Redlich**, Fredrick Carl 1910- AmMWSc 92
**Redlich**, Marc 1946- WhoAmL 92
**Redlich**, Martin George 1928- AmMWSc 92
**Redlich**, Norman 1925- WhoAmL 92
**Redlich**, Robert Walter 1928- AmMWSc 92
**Redlin**, Rolland W 1920- WhoAmP 91
**Redlinger**, Leonard Maurice 1922- AmMWSc 92
**Redlinger**, Samuel Edward 1949- WhoMW 92
**Redman**, Ben Ray 1896-1961 BenetAL 91
**Redman**, Charles E 1943- WhoAmP 91
**Redman**, Charles Edwin 1931- AmMWSc 92
**Redman**, Clarence Owen 1942- WhoAmL 92
**Redman**, Colvin Manuel 1935- AmMWSc 92
**Redman**, Denis Arthur Kay 1910- Who 92
**Redman**, Don 1900-1964 NewAmDM
**Redman**, Donald Roger 1936- AmMWSc 92
**Redman**, James W. 1915- WhoBlA 92
**Redman**, John B. 1914- IntWW 91
**Redman**, Joseph IntAu&W 91X
**Redman**, Karleen Krepps 1954- WhoWest 92
**Redman**, Kenneth 1906- AmMWSc 92
**Redman**, Lister Appleton 1933- WrDr 92
**Redman**, Mabel ScFEYrs
**Redman**, Maurice 1922- Who 92
**Redman**, Richard Elson 1938- WhoAmP 91, WhoMW 92
**Redman**, Robert Shelton 1935- AmMWSc 92
**Redman**, Scott Thomas 1957- WhoAmL 92
**Redman**, Sydney 1914- Who 92
**Redman**, William Charles 1923- AmMWSc 92
**Redman**, William W, Jr 1933- WhoAmP 91
**Redman-Johnson**, Chloe Louise 1942- WhoFI 92
**Redmann**, Robert Emanuel 1941- AmMWSc 92
**Redmayne**, Barbara WrDr 92
**Redmayne**, Clive 1927- Who 92
**Redmayne**, Nicholas 1938- Who 92
**Redmer**, Alfred Willy, Jr 1956- WhoAmP 91
**Redmon**, Ann Louise 1925- WhoBlA 92
**Redmon**, Bob Glen 1931- WhoWest 92
**Redmon**, Harry Smith, Jr. 1934- WhoAmL 92
**Redmon**, John King 1920- AmMWSc 92, WhoFI 92
**Redmon**, Michael James 1941- AmMWSc 92
**Redmon**, William E. 1940- WhoRel 92
**Redmond**, Billy Lee 1942- AmMWSc 92
**Redmond**, Donald Eugene, Jr 1939- AmMWSc 92
**Redmond**, Donald Michael 1948- AmMWSc 92, WhoMW 92
**Redmond**, Donald Paul 1932- WhoMW 92
**Redmond**, Douglas Rollen 1918- AmMWSc 92
**Redmond**, Edward Crosby 1921- WhoAmL 92
**Redmond**, Eugene B. DrAPF 91
**Redmond**, Eugene B. 1937- WhoBlA 92
**Redmond**, Gerald 1934- WrDr 92
**Redmond**, James 1918- Who 92
**Redmond**, James Ronald 1928- AmMWSc 92
**Redmond**, Jane Smith 1948- WhoBlA 92
**Redmond**, John Durham 1948- WhoFI 92
**Redmond**, John Peter 1925- AmMWSc 92
**Redmond**, Kelly Thomas 1952- WhoWest 92
**Redmond**, Martin 1937- Who 92
**Redmond**, Peter John 1929- AmMWSc 92
**Redmond**, Richard Anthony 1947- WhoAmL 92
**Redmond**, Robert 1934- WhoAmL 92
**Redmond**, Robert F 1927- AmMWSc 92
**Redmond**, Robert Spencer 1919- Who 92
**Redmond**, Scott Douglas 1954- WhoWest 92
**Redmond**, Thomas Paul 1954- WhoRel 92
**Redmond**, Virgil Blair 1928- WhoRel 92
**Redmond**, William A 1908- WhoAmP 91
**Redmont**, Bernard LesBEnT 92
**Redmont**, Jane Carol 1952- WhoRel 92
**Redmore**, Derek 1938- AmMWSc 92
**Redmount**, Melvin B 1926- AmMWSc 92
**Redner**, Sidney 1951- AmMWSc 92
**Redo**, Maria E 1925- WhoAmP 91
**Redo**, Martha Maria 1960- WhoAmL 92
**Redo**, Saverio Frank 1920- AmMWSc 92
**Redon**, Leonard Eugene 1951- WhoBlA 92
**Redondo**, Antonio 1948- AmMWSc 92, WhoWest 92
**Redondo**, Jose A. WhoHisp 92
**Redondo-Churchward**, Irene 1942- WhoHisp 92
**Redondo de Feldman**, Susana WhoHisp 92
**Redondo Ortega**, Onesimo 1905-1936 BiDExR
**Redpath**, Anne 1895-1965 TwCPaSc
**Redpath**, James 1833-1891 BenetAL 91
**Redpath**, John Sloneker, Jr. WhoEnt 92
**Redpath**, John Thomas 1915- Who 92
**Redrick**, Virginia Pendleton 1945- WhoBlA 92
**Redshaw**, Peggy Ann 1948- AmMWSc 92
**Redshaw**, Peter Robert Gransden 1942- Who 92
**Redshaw**, Seymour Cunningham 1906- Who 92
**Redshaw**, Thomas Dillon DrAPF 91
**Redstone**, Edward S. 1928- IntMPA 92
**Redstone**, Sumner Murray 1923- IntMPA 92, WhoAmL 92, WhoEnt 92, WhoFI 92
**Redus**, Gary Eugene 1956- WhoBlA 92
**Redwine**, Edward David 1947- WhoAmP 91
**Redwine**, R. Kevin 1958- WhoAmL 92
**Redwine**, Robert Page 1947- AmMWSc 92
**Redwood**, John 1951- WrDr 92
**Redwood**, John Alan 1951- Who 92
**Redwood**, Peter 1937- Who 92
**Redwood**, R G 1936- AmMWSc 92
**Ree**, Alexius Taikyue 1902- AmMWSc 92
**Ree**, Buren Russel 1943- AmMWSc 92
**Ree**, Francis H 1936- AmMWSc 92
**Ree**, William O 1913- AmMWSc 92
**Reeber**, Robert Richard 1937- AmMWSc 92
**Reeburgh**, William Scott 1940- AmMWSc 92
**Reece**, Avalon B. 1927- WhoBlA 92
**Reece**, Beth Pauley 1945- WhoMW 92
**Reece**, Byron 1917-1958 BenetAL 91
**Reece**, Charles 1927- Who 92
**Reece**, Donald J. WhoRel 92
**Reece**, Edward Vans Paynter 1936- Who 92
**Reece**, Eric Elliott 1909- IntWW 91
**Reece**, Gordon 1930- IntWW 91
**Reece**, James Gordon 1930- Who 92
**Reece**, Joe Wilson 1935- AmMWSc 92
**Reece**, Judith Fleur 1941- WhoAmP 91
**Reece**, Marshall Philip 1954- WhoMW 92
**Reece**, Marynell D 1920- WhoAmP 91
**Reece**, Max G. 1931- WhoRel 92
**Reece**, Paynter Who 92
**Reece**, Richard Terrance 1935- WhoRel 92
**Reece**, Robert Denton 1939- WhoRel 92
**Reece**, Robert Watson 1925- WhoAmL 92
**Reece**, Sterling Richard 1933- WhoFI 92
**Reece**, Steve Duane 1955- WhoMW 92
**Reece**, Steven 1947- WhoBlA 92
**Reece**, Wayne 1957- WhoAmP 91
**Reeck**, Darrell 1939- WhoRel 92
**Reeck**, Gerald Russell 1945- AmMWSc 92
**Reed**, A Thomas 1946- AmMWSc 92
**Reed**, Addison W. 1929- WhoBlA 92
**Reed**, Adolphus Redolph 1912- WhoBlA 92
**Reed**, Adrian Faragher 1906- AmMWSc 92
**Reed**, Adrian Harbottle 1921- Who 92
**Reed**, Alan Barry 1940- WhoAmP 91
**Reed**, Alec Edward 1934- Who 92
**Reed**, Alfonzo 1938- WhoBlA 92
**Reed**, Alfred 1921- NewAmDM, WhoEnt 92
**Reed**, Allan Hubert 1941- AmMWSc 92
**Reed**, Allen Ralph 1959- WhoAmL 92
**Reed**, Allene Wallace WhoBlA 92
**Reed**, Andre Darnell 1964- WhoBlA 92
**Reed**, April Anne 1930- Who 92
**Reed**, Barry St George Austin 1931- Who 92
**Reed**, Beatrice M. 1916- WhoBlA 92
**Reed**, Betty Lou 1927- WhoAmP 91
**Reed**, Brent C AmMWSc 92
**Reed**, Brian Edward 1955- WhoAmL 92
**Reed**, Bruce Loring 1934- AmMWSc 92
**Reed**, Burness Jean 1930- WhoAmP 91
**Reed**, C. Robert 1944- WhoFI 92
**Reed**, Carol 1906-1976 FacFETw, IntDcF 2-2 [port]
**Reed**, Charles Allen 1912- AmMWSc 92
**Reed**, Charles Bass 1941- IntWW 91
**Reed**, Charles E 1913- AmMWSc 92
**Reed**, Charles E 1922- AmMWSc 92
**Reed**, Charles Gordon 1935- WhoAmL 92
**Reed**, Charles Ray 1944- WhoAmP 91
**Reed**, Charlotte 1948- WhoMW 92
**Reed**, Christine Emerson 1944- WhoAmP 91
**Reed**, Christopher Alan 1947- AmMWSc 92
**Reed**, Clarence Hammit, III 1957- WhoBlA 92

**Reed,** Clarke Thomas 1928- *WhoAmP 91*
**Reed,** Coke S 1940- *AmMWSc 92*
**Reed,** Cordell 1938- *WhoBlA 92*
**Reed,** Cynthia Kay 1952- *WhoRel 92*
**Reed,** Daisy Frye *WhoBlA 92*
**Reed,** Dale Hardy 1930- *AmMWSc 92*
**Reed,** Dallas John 1929- *WhoWest 92*
**Reed,** Daniel A 1957- *AmMWSc 92*
**Reed,** David 1945- *Who 92*
**Reed,** David 1949- *WhoBlA 92*
**Reed,** David Benson 1927- *WhoRel 92*
**Reed,** David George 1945- *WhoWest 92*
**Reed,** David LaRue 1949- *WhoRel 92*
**Reed,** David Scudder 1931- *WhoIns 92*
**Reed,** David William 1952- *AmMWSc 92*
**Reed,** Denis William 1917-1979 *TwCPaSc*
**Reed,** Dennis James 1946- *WhoWest 92*
**Reed,** Derryl L. *WhoBlA 92*
**Reed,** Diane Gray 1945- *WhoFI 92*
**Reed,** Dolores M 1932- *WhoAmP 91*
**Reed,** Don Wayne 1940- *WhoRel 92*
**Reed,** Donal J 1924- *AmMWSc 92*
**Reed,** Donald Blackhall 1915- *WhoAmP 91*
**Reed,** Donald James 1930- *AmMWSc 92*
**Reed,** Donald Lewis 1940- *WhoRel 92*
**Reed,** Douglas Byron 1946- *WhoFI 92*
**Reed,** Douglas F. 1949- *WhoFI 92*
**Reed,** Dwayme Milton 1933- *WhoWest 92*
**Reed,** Dwayne Milton 1933- *AmMWSc 92*
**Reed,** Dwight Thomas 1955- *WhoWest 92*
**Reed,** Eddie 1945- *WhoBlA 92*
**Reed,** Edward Brandt 1920- *AmMWSc 92*
**Reed,** Edward Cornelius, Jr. 1924- *WhoAmL 92*
**Reed,** Edward John 1913- *Who 92*
**Reed,** Eliot *WrDr 92*
**Reed,** Elizabeth Liggett 1895-1978 *ConAu 133*
**Reed,** Elizabeth Wagner 1912- *AmMWSc 92*
**Reed,** Ellen Elizabeth 1940- *AmMWSc 92, WhoMW 92*
**Reed,** Esther De Berdt 1746-1780 *BlkwEAR*
**Reed,** Eugene D 1919- *AmMWSc 92*
**Reed,** Eva M d1901 *BiInAmS*
**Reed,** Evangeline Thomas 1930- *WhoEnt 92*
**Reed,** F Everett 1914- *AmMWSc 92*
**Reed,** Falani W *WhoAmP 91*
**Reed,** Farie Mae 1931- *WhoAmP 91*
**Reed,** Florine 1905- *WhoBlA 92*
**Reed,** Floyd T. 1915- *WhoBlA 92*
**Reed,** Frank Engelhart 1935- *WhoFI 92*
**Reed,** Frank Fremont, II 1928- *WhoWest 92*
**Reed,** Frank Metcalf 1912- *WhoFI 92, WhoWest 92*
**Reed,** Fred DeWitt, Jr 1937- *AmMWSc 92*
**Reed,** Gary W *WhoAmP 91*
**Reed,** Gavin Barras 1934- *Who 92*
**Reed,** George Farrell 1922- *AmMWSc 92*
**Reed,** George Ford, Jr. 1946- *WhoFI 92, WhoWest 92*
**Reed,** George Franklin 1935- *WhoIns 92*
**Reed,** George Henry 1942- *AmMWSc 92*
**Reed,** George Rowland 1955- *WhoFI 92*
**Reed,** George W, Jr 1920- *AmMWSc 92*
**Reed,** Gerald 1913- *AmMWSc 92*
**Reed,** Gerald Wilfred 1945- *WhoMW 92*
**Reed,** Geraldine Sumner 1917- *WhoAmP 91*
**Reed,** Gerard Alexander 1941- *WhoRel 92, WhoWest 92*
**Reed,** Gordon Wies 1899- *WhoAmP 91*
**Reed,** Gregory J. 1948- *WhoBlA 92*
**Reed,** H. Owen 1910- *WrDr 92*
**Reed,** Harrison Merrick, Jr. 1898-19--? *ConAu 134*
**Reed,** Harry Wendel 1933- *WhoWest 92*
**Reed,** Hazell *AmMWSc 92*
**Reed,** Helen Bernice 1917- *WhoWest 92*
**Reed,** Henry 1914-1986 *FacFETw*
**Reed,** Horace Beecher 1923- *AmMWSc 92*
**Reed,** Howard Douglas 1951- *WhoEnt 92*
**Reed,** Irving Stoy 1923- *AmMWSc 92*
**Reed,** Ishmael *DrAPF 91*
**Reed,** Ishmael 1938- *AfrAmW, BenetAL 91, BlkLC [port], ConNov 91, ConPo 91, TwCWW 91, WrDr 92*
**Reed,** Ishmael Scott 1938- *IntWW 91, WhoBlA 92, WhoWest 92*
**Reed,** Jack Wilson 1923- *AmMWSc 92*
**Reed,** James 1922- *WrDr 92*
**Reed,** James 1935- *WhoBlA 92*
**Reed,** James Anthony 1939- *WhoWest 92*
**Reed,** James Everette 1944- *WhoRel 92*
**Reed,** James M. 1933- *WhoFI 92*
**Reed,** James Robert, Jr 1940- *AmMWSc 92*
**Reed,** James Stalford 1938- *AmMWSc 92*
**Reed,** James W. 1935- *WhoBlA 92*
**Reed,** Jane Barbara *IntAu&W 91, Who 92*
**Reed,** Jane Garson 1948- *WhoMW 92*
**Reed,** Jasper Percell 1929- *WhoBlA 92*
**Reed,** Jeremy 1951- *ConPo 91, WrDr 92*
**Reed,** Jerry 1937- *WhoEnt 92*
**Reed,** Joann 1939- *WhoBlA 92*
**Reed,** Joe Louis 1938- *WhoAmP 91, WhoBlA 92*
**Reed,** Joel 1942- *AmMWSc 92*
**Reed,** Joel Leston 1951- *WhoFI 92*
**Reed,** John *SourALJ*
**Reed,** John 1887-1920 *BenetAL 91, FacFETw, RComAH*
**Reed,** John Calvin, Jr 1930- *AmMWSc 92*
**Reed,** John F. 1949- *AlmAP 92 [port]*
**Reed,** John Francis 1949- *WhoAmP 91*
**Reed,** John Frederick 1911- *AmMWSc 92*
**Reed,** John H, III 1949- *WhoAmP 91*
**Reed,** John Hathaway 1921- *WhoAmP 91*
**Reed,** John J R 1932- *AmMWSc 92*
**Reed,** John Langdale 1931- *Who 92*
**Reed,** John Oren 1856-1916 *BiInAmS*
**Reed,** John R. *DrAPF 91*
**Reed,** John Shedd 1917- *IntWW 91*
**Reed,** John Shepard 1939- *WhoFI 92*
**Reed,** John Silas 1887-1920 *LiExTwC*
**Reed,** John W. 1918- *WhoAmL 92*
**Reed,** Joseph 1741-1785 *BlkwEAR*
**Reed,** Joseph 1920- *AmMWSc 92*
**Reed,** Joseph 1944- *AmMWSc 92*
**Reed,** Joseph Raymond 1930- *AmMWSc 92*
**Reed,** Joseph V, Jr 1937- *WhoAmP 91*
**Reed,** Joseph Verner 1937- *IntWW 91*
**Reed,** Joseph W. 1932- *WrDr 92*
**Reed,** Juta Kuttis *AmMWSc 92*
**Reed,** Karlen J. 1958- *WhoAmL 92*
**Reed,** Kathleen Rand 1947- *WhoBlA 92*
**Reed,** Kathryn Ellen 1952- *WhoMW 92*
**Reed,** Keith Allen 1939- *WhoAmL 92*
**Reed,** Kenneth Paul 1937- *AmMWSc 92*
**Reed,** Kevin Francis 1948- *WhoAmL 92*
**Reed,** Kit *ConAu 36NR, DrAPF 91, WhoEnt 92*
**Reed,** Kit 1932- *WrDr 92*
**Reed,** Kit 1954- *TwCSFW 91*
**Reed,** Lambert S., II 1937- *WhoBlA 92*
**Reed,** Larita D. 1960- *WhoBlA 92*
**Reed,** Larry Allen 1948- *WhoEnt 92*
**Reed,** Larry S. *WhoMW 92*
**Reed,** Laurance Douglas 1937- *Who 92*
**Reed,** Laurence Wilcox 1942- *WhoMW 92*
**Reed,** Leon Samuel 1949- *WhoFI 92*
**Reed,** Leslie Edwin 1925- *Who 92*
**Reed,** Lester James 1925- *AmMWSc 92*
**Reed,** Lester W 1917- *AmMWSc 92*
**Reed,** Liki, II 1954- *WhoAmP 91*
**Reed,** Lloyd H. 1922- *WhoBlA 92*
**Reed,** Lola N. 1923- *WhoBlA 92*
**Reed,** Lou 1942- *IntWW 91, NewAmDM, WhoEnt 92*
**Reed,** Lowell A., Jr. 1930- *WhoAmL 92*
**Reed,** M. N. 1905-19--? *ConAu 134*
**Reed,** Margaret Anne *WhoEnt 92*
**Reed,** Marilyn L. 1950- *WhoFI 92*
**Reed,** Marion Guy 1931- *AmMWSc 92*
**Reed,** Mark Arthur 1955- *AmMWSc 92*
**Reed,** Mary Betz 1954- *WhoMW 92*
**Reed,** Mary Lou *WhoAmP 91*
**Reed,** Maurice L. 1924- *WhoBlA 92*
**Reed,** Melvin 1933- *WhoRel 92*
**Reed,** Melvin LeRoy 1929- *AmMWSc 92*
**Reed,** Michael Charles 1942- *AmMWSc 92*
**Reed,** Michael George 1956- *WhoMW 92*
**Reed,** Michael H. 1949- *WhoBlA 92*
**Reed,** Michael Haywood 1949- *WhoAmL 92*
**Reed,** Michael Kamin 1962- *WhoRel 92*
**Reed,** Myrtle 1874-1911 *BenetAL 91*
**Reed,** Nathaniel Pryor 1933- *WhoAmP 91*
**Reed,** Nell Donnelly 1889-1991 *NewYTBS 91*
**Reed,** Nelson Addington 1926- *WhoMW 92*
**Reed,** Nigel 1913- *Who 92*
**Reed,** Norman Bruce 1949- *WhoWest 92*
**Reed,** Norman D 1935- *AmMWSc 92*
**Reed,** Nuu'alii M E *WhoAmP 91*
**Reed,** Oliver *Who 92*
**Reed,** Oliver 1938- *IntMPA 92, IntWW 91, WhoEnt 92*
**Reed,** Pamela 1949- *WhoEnt 92*
**Reed,** Pamela 1953- *IntMPA 92*
**Reed,** Pat 1946- *WhoAmP 91*
**Reed,** Peter N. *WhoHisp 92*
**Reed,** Peter William 1939- *AmMWSc 92*
**Reed,** Philip Chandler 1952- *WhoEnt 92*
**Reed,** R M 1906- *AmMWSc 92*
**Reed,** Randall R 1921- *AmMWSc 92*
**Reed,** Ray Paul 1927- *WhoWest 92*
**Reed,** Raymond Edgar 1922- *AmMWSc 92*
**Reed,** Rebecca S. 1964- *WhoWest 92*
**Reed,** Rex 1938- *WhoEnt 92, WrDr 92*
**Reed,** Richard Jay 1928- *AmMWSc 92*
**Reed,** Richard John 1922- *AmMWSc 92, IntWW 91*
**Reed,** Richard P 1934- *AmMWSc 92*
**Reed,** Rick 1947- *WhoAmP 91*
**Reed,** Robert 1932- *IntMPA 92*
**Reed,** Robert 1956- *TwCSFW 91*
**Reed,** Robert Alan 1942- *WhoAmL 92*
**Reed,** Robert Dixon, Sr. 1927- *WhoFI 92*
**Reed,** Robert George, III 1927- *WhoFI 92, WhoWest 92*
**Reed,** Robert Marshall 1941- *AmMWSc 92*
**Reed,** Robert Michael 1957- *WhoWest 92*
**Reed,** Robert Oliver 1938- *Who 92*
**Reed,** Robert Phillip 1952- *WhoAmL 92*
**Reed,** Robert Willard 1941- *AmMWSc 92*
**Reed,** Roberta Gable 1945- *AmMWSc 92*
**Reed,** Rodney J. 1932- *WhoBlA 92*
**Reed,** Ronald David 1945- *WhoRel 92*
**Reed,** Ronald Keith 1932- *AmMWSc 92*
**Reed,** Rosemary 1948- *WhoEnt 92*
**Reed,** Rowena 1901-1988 *DcTwDes*
**Reed,** Russell, Jr 1922- *AmMWSc 92*
**Reed,** Ruth Elizabeth 1946- *AmMWSc 92*
**Reed,** Sam Glen 1946- *WhoAmP 91*
**Reed,** Sam Sumner 1941- *WhoAmP 91*
**Reed,** Sampson 1800-1880 *BenetAL 91*
**Reed,** Scott Warren 1949- *WhoFI 92*
**Reed,** Sheila A. 1958- *WhoBlA 92*
**Reed,** Sherman Kennedy 1919- *AmMWSc 92*
**Reed,** Simon *IntAu&W 91X*
**Reed,** Stanley 1884-1980 *FacFETw*
**Reed,** Stanley 1911- *WrDr 92*
**Reed,** Stanley William 1911- *Who 92*
**Reed,** Stephen 1801?-1877 *BiInAmS*
**Reed,** Stephen Dillon 1951- *WhoEnt 92*
**Reed,** Stephen Russell 1949- *WhoAmP 91*
**Reed,** Stuart Arthur 1930- *AmMWSc 92*
**Reed,** T. J. 1937- *WrDr 92*
**Reed,** Ted Brooks 1923- *WhoAmP 91*
**Reed,** Terence James 1937- *Who 92*
**Reed,** Terry Eugene 1945- *AmMWSc 92, WhoMW 92*
**Reed,** Theodore H 1922- *AmMWSc 92*
**Reed,** Theresa Greene 1923- *WhoBlA 92*
**Reed,** Thomas Binnington 1926- *AmMWSc 92*
**Reed,** Thomas Brackett 1839-1902 *AmPolLe*
**Reed,** Thomas Care 1934- *IntWW 91*
**Reed,** Thomas Edward 1923- *AmMWSc 92*
**Reed,** Thomas Francis 1957- *WhoFI 92*
**Reed,** Thomas Freeman 1937- *AmMWSc 92*
**Reed,** Thomas J. 1927- *WhoBlA 92*
**Reed,** Thomas James 1940- *WhoAmL 92*
**Reed,** Thomas Thornton 1902- *Who 92, WrDr 92*
**Reed,** Tony Norman 1951- *WhoMW 92*
**Reed,** Vincent Emory 1928- *WhoBlA 92*
**Reed,** W. Franklin 1946- *WhoAmL 92*
**Reed,** Walter 1851-1902 *BiInAmS, FacFETw*
**Reed,** Warren Douglas 1938- *AmMWSc 92*
**Reed,** Wilbur R. 1936- *WhoBlA 92*
**Reed,** William *AmMWSc 92*
**Reed,** William Alfred 1936- *AmMWSc 92*
**Reed,** William Doyle 1897- *AmMWSc 92*
**Reed,** William Edward 1914- *AmMWSc 92*
**Reed,** William F *WhoAmP 91*
**Reed,** William Harlow 1848-1915 *BiInAmS*
**Reed,** William J 1946- *AmMWSc 92*
**Reed,** William LaForest 1912- *WhoRel 92*
**Reed,** William Robert 1922- *AmMWSc 92*
**Reed,** Willis 1942- *WhoBlA 92*
**Reed-Hill,** Robert E 1913- *AmMWSc 92*
**Reed-Miller,** Rosemary E. 1939- *WhoBlA 92*
**Reed-Purvis,** Henry 1928- *Who 92*
**Reede,** Fred Allan, Jr. 1956- *WhoFI 92*
**Reede,** James William, Jr. 1952- *WhoBlA 92*
**Reeder,** Carolyn 1937- *ConAu 135, SmATA 66*
**Reeder,** Charles Edgar 1927- *AmMWSc 92*
**Reeder,** Christopher Andrew 1957- *WhoMW 92*
**Reeder,** Clifton Lee 1918- *WhoMW 92*
**Reeder,** Clyde 1924- *AmMWSc 92*
**Reeder,** David Franklin 1951- *WhoRel 92*
**Reeder,** Dennis Harry 1946- *WhoEnt 92*
**Reeder,** Don David 1935- *AmMWSc 92*
**Reeder,** F. Robert 1943- *WhoAmL 92*
**Reeder,** Hubert 1948- *IntAu&W 91*
**Reeder,** John 1949- *Who 92*
**Reeder,** John Hamilton 1944- *AmMWSc 92*
**Reeder,** John P., Jr. 1937- *WhoRel 92*
**Reeder,** John Raymond 1914- *AmMWSc 92*
**Reeder,** Michael Thomas 1961- *WhoMW 92*
**Reeder,** Odette Kehne 1930- *WhoAmP 91*
**Reeder,** Paul Lorenz 1936- *AmMWSc 92*
**Reeder,** Ray R 1943- *AmMWSc 92*
**Reeder,** Robert Harry 1930- *WhoAmL 92, WhoMW 92*
**Reeder,** Ronald Howard 1939- *AmMWSc 92*
**Reeder,** Samuel Kenneth 1938- *WhoWest 92*
**Reeder,** Thomas Allen 1946- *WhoEnt 92*
**Reeder,** William Glase 1929- *AmMWSc 92*
**Reeder,** Willie R., Jr. 1923-1984 *WhoBlA 92N*
**Reeds,** Lloyd George 1917- *AmMWSc 92*
**Reedstrom,** Ernest Lisle 1928- *WhoMW 92*
**Reedy,** George E. 1917- *WrDr 92*
**Reedy,** George Edward 1917- *IntAu&W 91, IntWW 91, WhoMW 92*
**Reedy,** John J 1927- *WhoAmP 91*
**Reedy,** John Joseph 1927- *AmMWSc 92*
**Reedy,** Michael K 1934- *AmMWSc 92*
**Reedy,** Norris John 1934- *Who 92*
**Reedy,** Robert Challenger 1942- *AmMWSc 92*
**Reedy,** William Joseph, Jr. 1940- *WhoMW 92*
**Reedy,** William Marion 1862-1920 *BenetAL 91*
**Reeg,** Kurtis Bradford 1954- *WhoAmL 92*
**Reeher,** James Irwin 1948- *WhoRel 92*
**Reeke,** George Norman, Jr 1943- *AmMWSc 92*
**Reeker,** Larry Henry 1943- *AmMWSc 92*
**Reekie,** Henry Enfield 1907- *Who 92*
**Reekie,** Howard James 1949- *WhoEnt 92*
**Reel,** Jerry Royce 1938- *AmMWSc 92*
**Reeman,** Douglas 1924- *WrDr 92*
**Reeman,** Douglas Edward 1924- *IntAu&W 91*
**Reemtsma,** Keith 1925- *AmMWSc 92*
**Reen,** Terry Peter 1951- *WhoMW 92*
**Reenstra,** Arthur Leonard 1936- *AmMWSc 92*
**Reents,** Sue *WhoAmP 91*
**Reents,** William David, Jr 1954- *AmMWSc 92*
**Reep,** Robert Gregg 1954- *WhoAmP 91*
**Rees** *Who 92*
**Rees,** Baron 1926- *Who 92*
**Rees,** Albert Lloyd George 1916- *IntWW 91*
**Rees,** Alfred William 1925- *WhoRel 92*
**Rees,** Allan W 1933- *AmMWSc 92*
**Rees,** Alun Hywel 1928- *AmMWSc 92*
**Rees,** Anthony John David 1943- *Who 92*
**Rees,** Arthur Morgan 1912- *Who 92*
**Rees,** Barbara 1934- *WrDr 92*
**Rees,** Barbara Elizabeth 1934- *IntAu&W 91*
**Rees,** Brian 1929- *ConAu 133, Who 92*
**Rees,** Brinley Roderick 1919- *Who 92*
**Rees,** Charles Sparks 1940- *AmMWSc 92*
**Rees,** Charles Wayne 1927- *IntWW 91, Who 92*
**Rees,** Charles William Stanley 1907- *Who 92*
**Rees,** David 1918- *Who 92*
**Rees,** David 1936- *WrDr 92*
**Rees,** David Allan 1936- *IntWW 91, Who 92*
**Rees,** Earl Douglas 1928- *AmMWSc 92*
**Rees,** Eberhard F M 1908- *AmMWSc 92*
**Rees,** Elaine 1940- *WhoFI 92*
**Rees,** Ennis *DrAPF 91*
**Rees,** Erica Sue 1956- *WhoMW 92*
**Rees,** Florence Gwendolen 1906- *Who 92*
**Rees,** Frank William, Jr. 1943- *WhoFI 92*
**Rees,** Garnet d1990 *Who 92N*
**Rees,** Gomer *DrAPF 91*
**Rees,** Grover Joseph, III 1951- *WhoAmL 92*
**Rees,** Gwendolen *Who 92*
**Rees,** Harland 1909- *Who 92*
**Rees,** Haydn *Who 92*
**Rees,** Henry 1916- *WrDr 92*
**Rees,** Horace Benner, Jr 1926- *AmMWSc 92*
**Rees,** Hubert 1923- *IntWW 91, Who 92*
**Rees,** Hugh *Who 92*
**Rees,** Hugh Francis E. *Who 92*
**Rees,** Ioan Bowen 1929- *WrDr 92*
**Rees,** Ivor *Who 92*
**Rees,** Joan 1927- *WrDr 92*
**Rees,** John 1948- *AmMWSc 92*
**Rees,** John Bromfield Gay 1912-1965 *TwCPaSc*
**Rees,** John Charles 1949- *Who 92*
**Rees,** John David 1932- *AmMWSc 92*
**Rees,** John Edward Hugh 1928- *Who 92*
**Rees,** John Ivor *Who 92*
**Rees,** John Krom 1851-1907 *BiInAmS*
**Rees,** John Owen 1923- *WhoMW 92*
**Rees,** John Robert 1930- *AmMWSc 92*
**Rees,** John Samuel 1931- *Who 92*
**Rees,** Lane Charles 1951- *WhoFI 92, WhoWest 92*
**Rees,** Lesley Howard 1942- *Who 92*
**Rees,** Leslie 1905- *WrDr 92*
**Rees,** Leslie Lloyd 1919- *Who 92*
**Rees,** Linford *Who 92*
**Rees,** Llewellyn *Who 92*
**Rees,** Manfred Hugh 1926- *AmMWSc 92*
**Rees,** Marian *LesBEnT 92*
**Rees,** Martin J 1942- *AmMWSc 92*
**Rees,** Martin John 1942- *IntWW 91, Who 92*
**Rees,** Merlyn 1920- *IntWW 91, Who 92*
**Rees,** Meuric *Who 92*
**Rees,** Michael *Who 92*
**Rees,** Michael Joseph 1954- *WhoMW 92*
**Rees,** Mina S 1902- *AmMWSc 92*
**Rees,** Owen 1934- *Who 92*
**Rees,** Paul Klein 1902- *AmMWSc 92*
**Rees,** Paul Stomberg 1900- *WrDr 92*
**Rees,** Paul Stromberg 1900- *WhoRel 92*

**Rees**, Peter Magnall 1921- Who 92
**Rees**, Peter Wynne 1948- Who 92
**Rees**, Philip 1941- Who 92
**Rees**, Ray 1943- Who 92
**Rees**, Raymond F. 1944- WhoWest 92
**Rees**, Rees Bynon 1915- AmMWSc 92
**Rees**, Richard 1900-1970 TwCPaSc
**Rees**, Richard Ellis Meuric 1924- Who 92
**Rees**, Richard John William 1917- Who 92
**Rees**, Richard Michael 1935- Who 92
**Rees**, Roberts M 1920- AmMWSc 92
**Rees**, Robin Lee 1962- WhoEnt 92
**Rees**, Roger 1944- IntMPA 92, WhoEnt 92
**Rees**, Rolf Stephen 1960- AmMWSc 92
**Rees**, Seth Cook 1854-1933 RelLAm 91
**Rees**, Stanley Who 92
**Rees**, Stephen J 1947- WhoAmP 91
**Rees**, Thomas Charles 1939- AmMWSc 92
**Rees**, Thomas L 1939- WhoAmP 91
**Rees**, Thomas M 1925- WhoAmP 91
**Rees**, Thomas Morgan Haydn 1915- Who 92
**Rees**, Tom 1947- WhoAmP 91
**Rees**, Walter Llewellyn 1901- Who 92
**Rees**, William Howard Guest 1928- Who 92
**Rees**, William Hurst 1917- Who 92
**Rees**, William James 1922- AmMWSc 92
**Rees**, William Linford 1914- Who 92, WrDr 92
**Rees**, William Smith, Jr 1959- AmMWSc 92
**Rees**, William Wendell 1933- AmMWSc 92
**Rees-Davies**, William Rupert 1916- Who 92
**Rees-Jones**, Geoffrey Rippon 1914- Who 92
**Rees-Mogg** Who 92
**Rees-Mogg**, Baron 1928- Who 92
**Rees-Mogg**, Lord 1928- IntWW 91
**Rees-Mogg**, William 1928- IntAu&W 91
**Rees-Williams** Who 92
**Reese**, Albert Moore WhoWest 92
**Reese**, Alferd George 1934- WhoMW 92
**Reese**, Andy Clare 1942- AmMWSc 92
**Reese**, Bob L 1929- WhoAmP 91
**Reese**, Boyd Turner, Jr. 1945- WhoRel 92
**Reese**, Bruce Alan 1923- AmMWSc 92
**Reese**, Cecil Everett 1921- AmMWSc 92
**Reese**, Colin Bernard 1930- IntWW 91, Who 92
**Reese**, Colin Edward 1950- Who 92
**Reese**, Curtis Williford 1887-1961 RelLAm 91
**Reese**, Daniel G 1927- WhoAmP 91
**Reese**, David 1961- WhoAmL 92
**Reese**, Della 1931- WhoBlA 92, WhoEnt 92
**Reese**, Douglas Evans 1963- WhoWest 92
**Reese**, Elwyn Thomas 1912- AmMWSc 92
**Reese**, Ernst S 1931- AmMWSc 92
**Reese**, Floyd Ernest 1917- AmMWSc 92
**Reese**, Frederick D. 1929- WhoBlA 92
**Reese**, Gary Fuller 1938- WhoWest 92
**Reese**, Glenn G WhoAmP 91
**Reese**, Gregory Lamarr 1949- WhoBlA 92
**Reese**, Herschel Henry 1935- WhoMW 92
**Reese**, Howard Fred 1947- WhoFI 92, WhoMW 92
**Reese**, Jacob 1825-1907 BiInAmS
**Reese**, Jim E. 1912-1976 ConAu 134
**Reese**, Jim L 1958- WhoAmP 91
**Reese**, John 1910-1981 TwCWW 91
**Reese**, John Mansel 1906- Who 92
**Reese**, John Terence 1913- Who 92
**Reese**, Joseph Hammond, Jr. 1928- WhoFI 92
**Reese**, Kenneth Wendell 1930- WhoFI 92
**Reese**, Kerry David 1953- WhoRel 92
**Reese**, Lizette Woodworth 1856-1935 BenetAL 91
**Reese**, Lymon C 1917- AmMWSc 92
**Reese**, Mamie Bynes WhoBlA 92
**Reese**, Mansel Who 92
**Reese**, Martha Grace 1953- WhoRel 92
**Reese**, Matthew Anderson 1927- WhoAmP 91
**Reese**, Melissa Proffitt 1960- WhoAmL 92
**Reese**, Michael Paul 1959- WhoRel 92
**Reese**, Millard Griffin, Jr 1931- AmMWSc 92
**Reese**, Milous J. WhoBlA 92
**Reese**, Mona Lyn 1951- WhoEnt 92
**Reese**, Paul WhoAmP 91
**Reese**, Richard Frank 1945- WhoMW 92
**Reese**, Robert J 1947- WhoAmP 91
**Reese**, Robert Jenkins 1947- WhoAmL 92, WhoWest 92
**Reese**, Robert Trafton 1942- AmMWSc 92, WhoWest 92
**Reese**, Ronald Malcolm 1938- AmMWSc 92
**Reese**, Roy Charles 1949- WhoRel 92
**Reese**, Steven Paul 1960- WhoEnt 92
**Reese**, Stuart Harry 1955- WhoFI 92
**Reese**, Ted M. 1959- WhoMW 92
**Reese**, Thomas A. 1949- WhoMW 92
**Reese**, Thomas Sargent 1935- AmMWSc 92
**Reese**, Viola Kathryn 1953- WhoBlA 92
**Reese**, Weldon Harold 1927- AmMWSc 92
**Reese**, William 1937- AmMWSc 92
**Reese**, William Albert, III 1932- WhoWest 92
**Reese**, William Dean 1928- AmMWSc 92
**Reese**, William George 1917- AmMWSc 92
**Reese**, William Harry 1947- WhoFI 92
**Reese**, William Willis 1940- WhoFI 92
**Reeser**, Donald M. 1931- WhoRel 92
**Reeser**, Jan E. 1948- WhoRel 92
**Reeser**, Jeannie G. WhoHisp 92
**Reeser**, Jeannie G 1943- WhoAmP 91
**Reeser**, Robert Duane 1931- WhoWest 92
**Reesman**, Arthur Lee 1933- AmMWSc 92
**Reesman**, James Robert, Jr. 1963- WhoEnt 92
**Reesman**, William Richard 1940- WhoWest 92
**Reesor**, John Elgin 1920- AmMWSc 92
**Reethof**, Gerhard 1922- AmMWSc 92
**Reetz**, Clement Ryan 1962- WhoAmL 92
**Reetz**, Harold Frank, Jr 1948- AmMWSc 92
**Reeve**, Anthony 1938- IntWW 91, Who 92
**Reeve**, Arthur B. 1880-1936 BenetAL 91, ScFEYrs
**Reeve**, Aubrey C 1937- AmMWSc 92
**Reeve**, Catharine J. 1941- WhoMW 92
**Reeve**, Charles Trevor 1915- Who 92
**Reeve**, Christopher 1952- IntMPA 92, IntWW 91, WhoEnt 92
**Reeve**, Clara 1729-1807 RfGEnL 91
**Reeve**, David William 1955- WhoWest 92
**Reeve**, Ernest Basil 1912- AmMWSc 92
**Reeve**, F. D. DrAPF 91
**Reeve**, F. D. 1928- ConPo 91, IntAu&W 91, WrDr 92
**Reeve**, James Ernest 1926- Who 92
**Reeve**, Joel IntAu&W 91X
**Reeve**, John 1936- AmMWSc 92
**Reeve**, John 1944- Who 92
**Reeve**, Marian E 1920- AmMWSc 92
**Reeve**, Marjorie Frances Who 92
**Reeve**, Michael David 1943- IntWW 91, Who 92
**Reeve**, Peter 1934- AmMWSc 92
**Reeve**, Robin Martin 1934- Who 92
**Reeve**, Ronald C 1920- AmMWSc 92
**Reeve**, Suzanne Elizabeth 1942- Who 92
**Reeve**, Trevor Who 92
**Reever**, Richard Eugene AmMWSc 92
**Reeverts**, Donald John 1937- WhoWest 92
**Reeves**, Alan M. WhoBlA 92
**Reeves**, Alexis Scott 1949- WhoBlA 92
**Reeves**, Andrew Louis 1924- AmMWSc 92
**Reeves**, Barbara Ann 1949- WhoAmL 92
**Reeves**, Barry L 1935- AmMWSc 92
**Reeves**, C C, Jr 1930- AmMWSc 92
**Reeves**, Carla Marianne 1949- WhoWest 92
**Reeves**, Christopher Reginald 1936- IntWW 91, Who 92
**Reeves**, Dale Leslie 1936- AmMWSc 92
**Reeves**, Daniel Edward 1944- WhoWest 92
**Reeves**, Daniel Morton 1948- WhoWest 92
**Reeves**, Donald Buster 1945- WhoRel 92
**Reeves**, Donald St John 1934- Who 92
**Reeves**, Edmond Morden 1934- AmMWSc 92
**Reeves**, Emery Irving 1929- WhoWest 92
**Reeves**, Fontaine Brent, Jr 1939- AmMWSc 92
**Reeves**, Frances Cowart 1919- WhoAmP 91
**Reeves**, Garland Phillip 1944- WhoEnt 92
**Reeves**, Geoffrey D 1961- AmMWSc 92
**Reeves**, George Paul 1918- WhoRel 92
**Reeves**, Gordon Who 92
**Reeves**, Helen May 1945- Who 92
**Reeves**, Henry Courtland 1933- AmMWSc 92
**Reeves**, Homer Eugene 1928- AmMWSc 92
**Reeves**, James Blanchette 1924- AmMWSc 92
**Reeves**, James Doyle 1927- WhoAmP 91
**Reeves**, Jerry John 1943- AmMWSc 92
**Reeves**, Jim 1923-1964 NewAmDM
**Reeves**, John Paul 1942- AmMWSc 92
**Reeves**, John Raymond 1957- WhoAmP 91
**Reeves**, John T 1928- AmMWSc 92
**Reeves**, Julius Lee 1961- WhoBlA 92
**Reeves**, Keanu 1964- IntMPA 92, News 92-1 [port]
**Reeves**, Keanu 1965- ConTFT 9
**Reeves**, Larry Alan 1952- WhoRel 92
**Reeves**, Leeann Moore 1947- WhoWest 92
**Reeves**, Leonard Wallace 1930- AmMWSc 92
**Reeves**, Louise 1944- WhoBlA 92
**Reeves**, Marjorie E. 1905- WrDr 92
**Reeves**, Marjorie Ethel 1905- IntWW 91, Who 92
**Reeves**, Martha Rose 1941- WhoBlA 92
**Reeves**, Michael 1944-1969 IntDcF 2-2
**Reeves**, Michael S. 1935- WhoBlA 92
**Reeves**, Michael Stanley 1935- WhoFI 92
**Reeves**, Nigel Barrie Reginald 1939- Who 92
**Reeves**, Patricia Houts 1947- IntAu&W 91
**Reeves**, Paul Alfred 1932- IntWW 91, Who 92
**Reeves**, Peggy 1941- WhoAmP 91
**Reeves**, Perry Clayton 1942- AmMWSc 92
**Reeves**, Philip Thomas Langford 1931- Who 92
**Reeves**, Polly R WhoAmP 91
**Reeves**, R C 1948- AmMWSc 92
**Reeves**, Raymond 1943- AmMWSc 92
**Reeves**, Richard Edwin 1912- AmMWSc 92
**Reeves**, Robert Blake 1930- AmMWSc 92
**Reeves**, Robert Donald 1942- AmMWSc 92
**Reeves**, Robert Estill 1942- WhoAmP 91
**Reeves**, Robert Grant 1960- WhoEnt 92
**Reeves**, Robert Grier 1920- AmMWSc 92
**Reeves**, Robert R 1930- AmMWSc 92
**Reeves**, Robert William 1939- AmMWSc 92
**Reeves**, Roger Allan 1960- WhoFI 92, WhoMW 92
**Reeves**, Roger Marcel 1934- AmMWSc 92
**Reeves**, Roy Franklin 1922- AmMWSc 92
**Reeves**, Sandra Lee 1942- WhoAmP 91
**Reeves**, Sheri Kazue 1965- WhoEnt 92
**Reeves**, Steve 1926- IntMPA 92
**Reeves**, T Joseph 1923- AmMWSc 92
**Reeves**, Thomas C. 1936- WrDr 92
**Reeves**, Thomas William, Jr. 1953- WhoEnt 92
**Reeves**, Trish DrAPF 91
**Reeves**, W Preston 1935- AmMWSc 92
**Reeves**, William Boyd 1932- WhoAmL 92
**Reeves**, William Carlisle 1916- AmMWSc 92
**Reeves**, William Desmond 1937- Who 92
**Reeves**, William Gordon 1938- Who 92
**Reeves**, William Pember 1857-1932 RfGEnL 91
**Reeves**, Willie Lloyd, Jr. 1949- WhoBlA 92
**Reeves**, Wilson Alvin 1919- AmMWSc 92
**Reffell**, Derek 1928- Who 92
**Reffell**, Derek Roy 1928- IntWW 91
**Reffes**, Howard Allen 1928- AmMWSc 92
**Reffner**, John A 1935- AmMWSc 92
**Refior**, Everett Lee 1919- WhoAmP 91
**Refojo**, Miguel Fernandez 1928- AmMWSc 92
**Refshauge**, William 1913- Who 92
**Refshauge**, William Dudley 1913- IntWW 91
**Refsland**, Gary Arlan 1944- WhoWest 92
**Reft**, Chester Stanley 1944- AmMWSc 92
**Regal**, Dorothea Weir 1946- WhoAmL 92
**Regal**, Jean Frances AmMWSc 92
**Regal**, Philip Joe 1939- AmMWSc 92
**Regalado**, Jose Marcelino, Jr. 1961- WhoHisp 92
**Regalbuto**, Joe WhoEnt 92
**Regan**, Agnes Gertrude 1869-1943 RelLAm 91
**Regan**, Ann Ellen 1962- WhoWest 92
**Regan**, Ann Kennedy 1923- WhoAmP 91
**Regan**, Brad IntAu&W 91X
**Regan**, Charles Daniel 1936- WhoWest 92
**Regan**, Charles Maurice 1925- Who 92
**Regan**, Colleen A. 1949- WhoFI 92
**Regan**, Dennis Martin 1937- WhoRel 92
**Regan**, Donald H. 1944- WhoAmL 92
**Regan**, Donald T 1918- WhoAmP 91
**Regan**, Donald Thomas 1918- IntWW 91, Who 92
**Regan**, Edward V WhoAmP 91
**Regan**, Edward Van Buren 1930- WhoFI 92
**Regan**, Francis 1903- AmMWSc 92, WhoMW 92
**Regan**, Francisco Antonio 1941- WhoRel 92
**Regan**, Gerald Augustine 1929- IntWW 91, Who 92
**Regan**, Gerald Thomas 1931- AmMWSc 92
**Regan**, Glen Barrie 1946- WhoWest 92
**Regan**, Harold James 1943- WhoFI 92
**Regan**, James Dale 1931- AmMWSc 92
**Regan**, Jennifer DrAPF 91
**Regan**, John B 1934- WhoAmP 91
**Regan**, John Bernard Jack 1934- WhoWest 92
**Regan**, John Denniss 1943- WhoWest 92
**Regan**, Lenore Worth 1935- WhoFI 92
**Regan**, Michael Gibson 1956- WhoRel 92
**Regan**, Michael Patrick 1941- WhoAmL 92
**Regan**, Patrick John 1938- WhoRel 92
**Regan**, Ray WhoAmP 91
**Regan**, Raymond John 1934- WhoWest 92
**Regan**, Raymond Wesley 1943- AmMWSc 92
**Regan**, Robert Martin 1930- WhoAmP 91
**Regan**, Robert P 1936- WhoAmP 91
**Regan**, Stephen Daniel 1947- WhoMW 92
**Regan**, Sylvia 1908- WhoEnt 92
**Regan**, Thomas Hartin 1925- AmMWSc 92
**Regan**, Thomas M 1941- AmMWSc 92
**Regan**, Timothy Joseph 1924- AmMWSc 92
**Regan**, Tom WhoRel 92
**Regan**, William Joseph, Jr. 1946- WhoFI 92, WhoIns 92
**Regardie**, Francis Israel 1907-1985 RelLAm 91
**Regehr**, Duncan WhoEnt 92
**Regelbrugge**, Roger Rafael 1930- WhoFI 92
**Regele**, Michael Bruce 1952- WhoRel 92, WhoWest 92
**Regelson**, William 1925- AmMWSc 92
**Regen**, David Marvin 1934- AmMWSc 92
**Regenbrecht**, D E 1924- AmMWSc 92
**Regener**, Victor H 1913- AmMWSc 92
**Regenstein**, Joe Mac 1943- AmMWSc 92
**Regenstreif**, Herbert 1935- WhoAmL 92, WhoFI 92
**Regenstreif**, S. Peter 1936- WrDr 92
**Reger**, Bill 1942- WhoAmP 91
**Reger**, Bonnie Jane 1940- AmMWSc 92
**Reger**, Daniel Lewis 1945- AmMWSc 92
**Reger**, James Frederick 1924- AmMWSc 92
**Reger**, Max 1873-1916 NewAmDM
**Reger**, Richard David 1939- AmMWSc 92
**Reges**, Marie Stephen 1915- WhoRel 92
**Regester**, Michael 1947- IntWW 91
**Regezi**, Joseph Alberts 1943- AmMWSc 92
**Reggans**, John B., III 1956- WhoBlA 92
**Reggiani**, Renee 1925- ConAu 36NR
**Reggiani**, Serge 1922- IntWW 91
**Reggie**, Doris Boustany 1930- WhoAmP 91
**Reggie**, Ed Michael 1952- WhoFI 92
**Reggio**, Vito Anthony 1929- WhoMW 92
**Regier**, Gail DrAPF 91
**Regier**, Henry Abraham 1930- AmMWSc 92
**Regier**, Jon Louis 1922- WhoRel 92
**Regier**, Lloyd Wesley 1928- AmMWSc 92
**Regier**, Norman Willard 1940- WhoWest 92
**Regina**, Archbishop of 1930- Who 92
**Reginald**, R 1948- ScFEYrs
**Reginald**, R and Menville, Douglas ScFEYrs
**Reginald**, Robert 1948- IntAu&W 91
**Reginato**, Robert Joseph 1935- WhoWest 92
**Regis**, John 1966- IntWW 91
**Regis**, Mario Enrique 1946- WhoWest 92
**Register**, Charles Leon, Sr. 1959- WhoRel 92
**Register**, Cheryl 1945- IntAu&W 91
**Register**, Jasper C. 1937- WhoBlA 92
**Register**, Milton Dean 1951- WhoRel 92
**Register**, Richard Alan 1963- AmMWSc 92
**Register**, Ulma Doyle 1920- AmMWSc 92
**Regler**, Gustav 1898-1963 LiExTwC
**Regna**, Peter P 1909- AmMWSc 92
**Regnart**, Jacob 1540?-1599 NewAmDM
**Regnell**, Barbara Caramella 1935- WhoEnt 92, WhoMW 92
**Regner**, David Joseph 1931- WhoAmP 91
**Regner**, John LaVerne 1946- AmMWSc 92
**Regner**, Sidney Lawrence 1903- WhoRel 92
**Regnery**, David Cook 1918- AmMWSc 92
**Regnier**, Charles 1914- IntWW 91
**Regnier**, Francois Jean 1933- WhoFI 92
**Regnier**, Frederick Eugene 1938- AmMWSc 92
**Regnier**, Rex Walter 1938- WhoEnt 92
**Regnier**, Richard Olin 1929- WhoAmP 91
**Rego**, George Browne 1934- IntWW 91
**Rego**, Lawrence WhoHisp 92
**Rego**, Paula 1935- IntWW 91, TwCPaSc, Who 92, WorArt 1980
**Rego**, Vernon J AmMWSc 92
**Rego**, Vernon Joseph 1956- WhoHisp 92
**Regoli**, Domenico 1933- AmMWSc 92
**Regoli**, John W WhoAmP 91
**Regueiferos**, Enrique 1948- BlkOlyM
**Regueiro**, Maria Cristina 1947- WhoHisp 92
**Reguero**, Edward Anthony 1960- WhoFI 92, WhoWest 92
**Reguero**, M. A. 1918- WhoHisp 92
**Reguero**, Melodie Huber 1956- WhoFI 92, WhoWest 92
**Regula**, Ralph 1924- WhoMW 92
**Regula**, Ralph S. 1924- AlmAP 92 [port], WhoAmP 91
**Regulski**, Jerzy 1924- IntWW 91
**Regulski**, Thomas Walter 1943- AmMWSc 92
**Regunathan**, Perialwar 1940- AmMWSc 92
**Reh**, Jeffrey Keith 1959- WhoAmL 92
**Reh**, Thomas Andrew 1955- AmMWSc 92
**Reh**, Thomas Edward 1943- WhoMW 92

**Reha,** Rose Krivisky 1920- *WhoMW 92*
**Rehagen,** Bart Alan 1964- *WhoMW 92*
**Rehak,** Matthew Joseph 1929- *AmMWSc 92*
**Rehak,** Pavel 1945- *AmMWSc 92*
**Rehak,** Thomas Frank 1952- *WhoWest 92*
**Rehart,** Burton Schyler 1934- *WhoWest 92*
**Rehbein,** Edna Aguirre 1955- *WhoHisp 92*
**Rehbein,** Edward Andrew 1947- *WhoFI 92, WhoRel 92*
**Rehberg,** Chessie Elmer 1911- *AmMWSc 92*
**Rehberg,** Dennis R 1955- *WhoAmP 91*
**Rehbock,** Richard Alexander 1946- *WhoAmL 92*
**Rehder,** Harald Alfred 1907- *AmMWSc 92*
**Rehder,** Kai 1928- *AmMWSc 92*
**Reher,** Raymond Agudo 1948- *WhoFI 92*
**Rehfeld,** Jens Frederik 1941- *IntWW 91*
**Rehfeld,** R. Rex 1926- *WhoFI 92*
**Rehfield,** David Michael 1942- *AmMWSc 92*
**Rehfield,** Lawrence Wilmer 1938- *AmMWSc 92*
**Rehfuss,** Mary 1927- *AmMWSc 92*
**Rehkopf,** Charles Frederick 1908- *WhoRel 92*
**Rehkugler,** Gerald E 1935- *AmMWSc 92*
**Rehlander,** Monte D 1939- *WhoAmP 91*
**Rehm,** Allan Stanley 1936- *AmMWSc 92*
**Rehm,** Diana Aed 1936- *WhoEnt 92*
**Rehm,** George W 1941- *AmMWSc 92*
**Rehm,** Gerald S 1927- *WhoAmP 91*
**Rehm,** Jack Daniel 1932- *WhoMW 92*
**Rehm,** John Bartram 1930- *WhoAmL 92*
**Rehm,** John Edwin 1924- *WhoMW 92*
**Rehm,** Lynn P 1941- *AmMWSc 92*
**Rehm,** Ronald George 1938- *AmMWSc 92*
**Rehm,** Thomas R 1929- *AmMWSc 92*
**Rehm,** Wolfgang 1929- *WhoEnt 92*
**Rehme,** Robert G. 1935- *IntMPA 92*
**Rehn,** George Ralph 1948- *WhoFI 92*
**Rehn,** Lynn Eduard 1945- *AmMWSc 92*
**Rehn,** Victor Leonard 1927- *AmMWSc 92*
**Rehnquist,** William 1924- *RComAH*
**Rehnquist,** William H 1924- *FacFETw, IntWW 91, Who 92*
**Rehnquist,** William Hubbs 1924- *AmPolLe, WhoAmL 92, WhoAmP 91*
**Rehor,** David George 1939- *WhoFI 92*
**Rehor,** Jean Helen 1926- *WhoMW 92*
**Rehr,** John Jacob 1945- *AmMWSc 92*
**Rehrer,** Ruth 1932- *WhoEnt 92*
**Rehrmann,** Eileen Mary 1944- *WhoAmP 91*
**Rehwaldt,** Charles A 1925- *AmMWSc 92*
**Rehwaldt,** Timothy Jon 1958- *WhoRel 92*
**Rehwoldt,** Robert E 1935- *AmMWSc 92*
**Reiach,** Alan 1910- *Who 92*
**Reibel,** Kurt 1926- *AmMWSc 92*
**Reibel-Shinfeld,** Diane Karen *AmMWSc 92*
**Reiber,** Gregory Duane 1955- *WhoWest 92*
**Reibman,** Jeanette Fichman 1915- *WhoAmP 91*
**Reibman,** Nathan Lewis 1911- *WhoAmL 92*
**Reibstein,** Regina *DrAPF 91*
**Reice,** Seth Robert 1947- *AmMWSc 92*
**Reich,** Allan J. 1948- *WhoAmL 92*
**Reich,** Brian M 1927- *AmMWSc 92*
**Reich,** Bruce P 1956- *WhoIns 92*
**Reich,** Charles 1942- *AmMWSc 92*
**Reich,** Charles William 1930- *AmMWSc 92*
**Reich,** Claude Virgil 1921- *AmMWSc 92*
**Reich,** Daniel 1941- *AmMWSc 92*
**Reich,** Donald Arthur 1929- *AmMWSc 92*
**Reich,** Edgar 1927- *AmMWSc 92*
**Reich,** Ellen *DrAPF 91*
**Reich,** Eunice Thelma 1947- *WhoFI 92*
**Reich,** Ferenc 1930- *WhoEnt 92*
**Reich,** George Arthur 1933- *AmMWSc 92*
**Reich,** Hans Jurgen 1943- *AmMWSc 92*
**Reich,** Herbert Joseph 1900- *AmMWSc 92*
**Reich,** Ieva Lazdins 1942- *AmMWSc 92*
**Reich,** Ismar M 1924- *AmMWSc 92*
**Reich,** Jack E 1910- *WhoIns 92*
**Reich,** Jack Egan 1910- *WhoFI 92*
**Reich,** James Harry 1950- *AmMWSc 92*
**Reich,** John Theodore d1988 *IntWW 91N*
**Reich,** Larry Sam 1946- *WhoAmL 92*
**Reich,** Lawrence Allan 1937- *WhoAmL 92*
**Reich,** Leo 1924- *AmMWSc 92*
**Reich,** Lilly 1885-1947 *DcTwDes*
**Reich,** Mark Carlton 1964- *WhoRel 92*
**Reich,** Marvin Fred 1947- *AmMWSc 92*
**Reich,** Melvin 1932- *AmMWSc 92*
**Reich,** Michael 1945- *WhoFI 92*
**Reich,** Murray H 1922- *AmMWSc 92*
**Reich,** Nathaniel Edwin 1907- *AmMWSc 92*
**Reich,** Otto J 1945- *WhoAmP 91*
**Reich,** Pauline Carole 1946- *WhoAmL 92, WhoFI 92*
**Reich,** Peter Gordon 1926- *Who 92*
**Reich,** Reinhold 1935- *WhoMW 92*
**Reich,** Richard 1904- *IntAu&W 91*
**Reich,** Richard Allen 1962- *WhoFI 92*
**Reich,** Richard Joseph 1956- *WhoAmL 92*
**Reich,** Seymour David 1933- *WhoRel 92*
**Reich,** Simeon 1948- *AmMWSc 92, WhoWest 92*
**Reich,** Stephen Jay 1955- *WhoFI 92*
**Reich,** Steve 1936- *ConCom 92, IntWW 91, NewAmDM, WhoEnt 92*
**Reich,** Steven Frederick 1961- *WhoAmL 92*
**Reich,** Vernon Henry 1939- *AmMWSc 92*
**Reich,** Wilhelm 1897-1957 *FacFETw*
**Reich,** William Phillips 1944- *WhoMW 92*
**Reich-Ranicki,** Marcel 1920- *IntWW 91*
**Reicha,** Antonin 1770-1836 *NewAmDM*
**Reicha,** Josef 1752-1795 *NewAmDM*
**Reichard,** David Wark 1948- *WhoWest 92*
**Reichard,** Grant Wesley 1938- *AmMWSc 92*
**Reichard,** H F 1920- *AmMWSc 92*
**Reichard,** Ronnal Paul 1950- *AmMWSc 92*
**Reichard,** Sherwood Marshall 1928- *AmMWSc 92*
**Reichard-Zamora,** Hector 1910- *WhoHisp 92*
**Reichardt,** Carl E. 1931- *WhoWest 92*
**Reichardt,** Glenn Richard 1951- *WhoAmL 92*
**Reichardt,** Johann Friedrich 1752-1814 *NewAmDM*
**Reichardt,** John Field 1948- *WhoAmP 91*
**Reichardt,** John William 1940- *AmMWSc 92*
**Reichardt,** Louise 1779-1826 *NewAmDM*
**Reichardt,** Robert Heinrich 1927- *IntWW 91*
**Reichart,** Charles Valerian 1910- *AmMWSc 92*
**Reichart,** Walter A. 1903- *WrDr 92*
**Reichartz,** W. Dan 1946- *WhoWest 92*
**Reichbach,** Naomi Estelle 1934- *WhoWest 92*
**Reichberg,** Samuel Bringeissen 1946- *AmMWSc 92*
**Reiche,** Ludwig P 1919- *AmMWSc 92*
**Reiche,** Marvin Gary 1949- *WhoWest 92*
**Reichek,** Jesse 1916- *WhoWest 92*
**Reichek,** Joshua A.S. 1952- *WhoEnt 92*
**Reichel,** Aaron Israel 1950- *WhoAmL 92*
**Reichel,** Philip Lee 1946- *WhoWest 92*
**Reichel,** William Louis 1927- *AmMWSc 92*
**Reichelderfer,** Charles Franklin 1937- *AmMWSc 92*
**Reichelderfer,** Thomas Elmer 1916- *AmMWSc 92*
**Reichelt,** Ferdinand Herbert 1941- *WhoMW 92*
**Reichenau,** Walter von 1884-1942 *EncTR 91 [port]*
**Reichenbach,** Bruce 1943- *WrDr 92*
**Reichenbach,** Bruce Robert 1943- *IntAu&W 91*
**Reichenbach,** George Sheridan 1929- *AmMWSc 92*
**Reichenbach,** Thomas 1947- *WhoWest 92*
**Reichenbacher,** Paul H 1940- *AmMWSc 92*
**Reichenbecher,** Vernon Edgar, Jr 1948- *AmMWSc 92*
**Reichenstein,** William Robert 1952- *WhoFI 92*
**Reicher,** Robert Jay 1956- *WhoEnt 92*
**Reicher,** Seth Adam 1964- *WhoFI 92*
**Reichert,** Gilles Bernard Marc 1966- *WhoEnt 92*
**Reichert,** Jack Frank 1930- *WhoFI 92, WhoMW 92*
**Reichert,** John Douglas 1938- *AmMWSc 92*
**Reichert,** Jonathan F 1931- *AmMWSc 92*
**Reichert,** Leo E, Jr 1932- *AmMWSc 92*
**Reichert,** Linda Marie 1952- *WhoEnt 92*
**Reiches,** Nancy A 1949- *AmMWSc 92*
**Reichgott,** Ember D 1953- *WhoAmP 91*
**Reichgott,** Michael Joel 1940- *AmMWSc 92*
**Reichl,** Mary Thomas 1928- *WhoMW 92, WhoRel 92*
**Reichle,** Alfred Douglas 1920- *AmMWSc 92*
**Reichle,** David Edward 1938- *AmMWSc 92*
**Reichle,** Frederick Adolph 1935- *AmMWSc 92*
**Reichle,** Walter Thomas 1928- *AmMWSc 92*
**Reichler,** Robert Jay 1937- *AmMWSc 92*
**Reichlin,** Louise 1941- *WhoEnt 92, WhoWest 92*
**Reichlin,** Morris 1934- *AmMWSc 92*
**Reichlin,** Seymour 1924- *AmMWSc 92*
**Reichman,** Fredrick Thomas 1925- *WhoWest 92*
**Reichman,** James Berry 1960- *WhoAmL 92*
**Reichman,** Jerome H. 1936- *WhoAmL 92*
**Reichman,** Omer James 1947- *AmMWSc 92*
**Reichman,** Sandor 1941- *AmMWSc 92*
**Reichmanis,** Elsa 1953- *AmMWSc 92*
**Reichmann,** Albert *WhoFI 92*
**Reichmann,** Manfred Eliezer 1925- *AmMWSc 92*
**Reichmann,** Paul *WhoFI 92*
**Reichmann,** Paul 1930- *IntWW 91*
**Reichmann,** Paul 1931?- *CurBio 91 [port]*
**Reichmann,** Richard Sherman, Jr. 1944- *WhoMW 92*
**Reichner,** Henry Falkner 1960- *WhoAmL 92*
**Reichsman,** Ann B. 1951- *WhoMW 92*
**Reichsman,** Franz Karl 1913- *AmMWSc 92*
**Reichstein,** Tadeus 1897- *IntWW 91, Who 92, WhoNob 90*
**Reichstetter,** Arthur Charles 1946- *WhoFI 92*
**Reichter,** Arlo Ray 1947- *WhoRel 92*
**Reichwein,** Adolf 1898-1944 *EncTR 91 [port]*
**Reicin,** Ronald Ian 1942- *WhoAmL 92, WhoMW 92*
**Reickert,** Erick Arthur 1935- *WhoFI 92, WhoMW 92*
**Reid,** Adrienne Wilder 1955- *WhoIns 92*
**Reid,** Alan Clifford 1961- *WhoWest 92*
**Reid,** Alan Forrest 1931- *IntWW 91*
**Reid,** Alastair 1926- *ConPo 91, WrDr 92*
**Reid,** Albert Leggat 1934- *WhoEnt 92*
**Reid,** Alexander 1932- *Who 92*
**Reid,** Allen Francis 1917- *AmMWSc 92*
**Reid,** Andrew H. 1940- *WrDr 92*
**Reid,** Andrew Milton 1929- *Who 92*
**Reid,** Ann Schafer 1963- *WhoEnt 92*
**Reid,** Antonio *WhoEnt 92*
**Reid,** Archibald, IV 1930- *AmMWSc 92*
**Reid,** Archibald Cameron 1915- *Who 92*
**Reid,** B. L. 1918-1990 *ConAu 133, DcLB 111 [port]*
**Reid,** Barbara *DrAPF 91*
**Reid,** Barbara Ellen 1953- *WhoRel 92*
**Reid,** Barry Jonathan 1957- *WhoFI 92, WhoWest 92*
**Reid,** Baxter Ellis, Jr. 1943- *WhoMW 92*
**Reid,** Belmont Mervyn 1927- *WhoFI 92, WhoWest 92*
**Reid,** Benjamin F. 1937- *WhoBlA 92*
**Reid,** Benjamin Franklin 1937- *WhoRel 92*
**Reid,** Beryl 1920- *IntMPA 92, Who 92*
**Reid,** Bobby Leroy 1929- *AmMWSc 92*
**Reid,** Brian Robert 1938- *AmMWSc 92*
**Reid,** Bruce Eugene 1950- *WhoEnt 92, WhoWest 92*
**Reid,** Bryan S, III 1951- *WhoIns 92*
**Reid,** Charles E. *WhoBlA 92*
**Reid,** Charles Feder 1933- *AmMWSc 92*
**Reid,** Charles H. 1934- *WhoBlA 92*
**Reid,** Charles L. 1927- *WrDr 92*
**Reid,** Charles Phillip Patrick 1940- *AmMWSc 92*
**Reid,** Charlotte T. *LesBEnT 92*
**Reid,** Christopher 1949- *ConPo 91, IntAu&W 91, WrDr 92*
**Reid,** Clarice D *AmMWSc 92*
**Reid,** Clarice Wills 1931- *WhoBlA 92*
**Reid,** Clyde Henderson, Jr. 1928- *WrDr 92*
**Reid,** David Boswell 1805-1863 *BiInAmS*
**Reid,** David Corey 1945- *WhoMW 92*
**Reid,** David Mayne 1940- *AmMWSc 92*
**Reid,** David Paul 1954- *WhoAmL 92, WhoAmP 91*
**Reid,** Dixie Lee 1942- *WhoWest 92*
**Reid,** Donald David *WhoEnt 92*
**Reid,** Donald Eugene 1930- *AmMWSc 92*
**Reid,** Donald House 1935- *AmMWSc 92*
**Reid,** Donald J 1938- *AmMWSc 92*
**Reid,** Donald Michele 1958- *WhoRel 92*
**Reid,** Donald Sidney 1945- *WhoEnt 92*
**Reid,** Donna Joyce 1954- *WhoEnt 92*
**Reid,** Dorothy Davenport 1895-1977 *ReelWom [port]*
**Reid,** Dougal Gordon 1925- *Who 92*
**Reid,** Douglas Foster 1953- *WhoFI 92*
**Reid,** Douglas William John 1934- *Who 92*
**Reid,** Edith C. *WhoBlA 92*
**Reid,** Edward Snover 1930- *WhoAmL 92*
**Reid,** Ellis Edmund, III 1934- *WhoBlA 92*
**Reid,** Eric William 1952- *WhoBlA 92*
**Reid,** Escott Meredith 1905- *IntWW 91*
**Reid,** Evans Burton 1913- *AmMWSc 92*
**Reid,** F Joseph 1930- *AmMWSc 92*
**Reid,** F. Theodore, Jr. 1929- *WhoBlA 92*
**Reid,** Forrest 1875-1947 *RfGEnL 91*
**Reid,** Frances *WhoEnt 92*
**Reid,** Frances Evelyn Kroll 1944- *WhoEnt 92*
**Reid,** Frances Marion Pugh 1910- *WhoWest 92*
**Reid,** Frances P. 1910- *WrDr 92*
**Reid,** Gary Badger 1956- *WhoEnt 92*
**Reid,** George Bernard, Jr. 1948- *WhoAmL 92*
**Reid,** George Kell 1918- *AmMWSc 92*
**Reid,** George Newlands 1939- *Who 92*
**Reid,** George Oswald 1903- *Who 92*
**Reid,** George Ranald Macfarlane d1991 *Who 92N*
**Reid,** George Thomson Henderson d1990 *Who 92N*
**Reid,** George W 1917- *AmMWSc 92*
**Reid,** Geraldine Wold 1944- *WhoMW 92*
**Reid,** Goldie Hartshorn 1913- *WhoBlA 92*
**Reid,** Graham Livingstone 1937- *Who 92*
**Reid,** H F, Jr 1917- *AmMWSc 92*
**Reid,** Harold Martin 1928- *Who 92*
**Reid,** Harold W 1916- *WhoAmP 91*
**Reid,** Harry 1939- *AlmAP 92 [port], IntWW 91, WhoAmP 91, WhoWest 92*
**Reid,** Hay Bruce, Jr 1939- *AmMWSc 92*
**Reid,** Henrietta *WrDr 92*
**Reid,** Herbert O., Sr. d1991 *NewYTBS 91*
**Reid,** Hugh 1933- *Who 92*
**Reid,** Iain 1942- *Who 92*
**Reid,** Ian Andrew 1943- *AmMWSc 92*
**Reid,** Ian George 1921- *Who 92*
**Reid,** Inez Smith 1937- *WhoBlA 92*
**Reid,** Ivo *Who 92*
**Reid,** J Frederick 1927- *WhoIns 92*
**Reid,** J R 1968- *BlkOlyM, WhoBlA 92*
**Reid,** Jack Richard 1947- *AmMWSc 92*
**Reid,** James 1921- *Who 92*
**Reid,** James B 1935- *WhoAmP 91*
**Reid,** James Cutler 1918- *AmMWSc 92*
**Reid,** James Dolan 1930- *AmMWSc 92*
**Reid,** James Douglas 1819?-1901 *BiInAmS*
**Reid,** James Edward 1951- *WhoAmL 92*
**Reid,** James L 1844-1910 *BiInAmS*
**Reid,** James M. 1953- *WhoRel 92*
**Reid,** James Robert 1943- *Who 92*
**Reid,** James Sims, Jr. 1926- *WhoFI 92, WhoMW 92*
**Reid,** Janie Ellen 1950- *WhoBlA 92*
**Reid,** Jeff Goodwyn, Jr 1951- *WhoAmP 91*
**Reid,** Joel Otto 1936- *WhoBlA 92*
**Reid,** John 1910- *WrDr 92*
**Reid,** John 1947- *Who 92*
**Reid,** John Boyd 1929- *Who 92*
**Reid,** John Daniel 1924- *WhoBlA 92*
**Reid,** John David 1909- *AmMWSc 92*
**Reid,** John James Andrew 1925- *Who 92*
**Reid,** John Kelman Sutherland 1910- *Who 92*
**Reid,** John Low 1943- *Who 92*
**Reid,** John Mitchell 1926- *AmMWSc 92*
**Reid,** John P. 1930- *WrDr 92*
**Reid,** John Phillip 1930- *WhoAmL 92*
**Reid,** John Reynolds, Jr 1933- *AmMWSc 92*
**Reid,** John Robert 1928- *Who 92*
**Reid,** John Robson 1925- *Who 92*
**Reid,** John Spence 1942- *WhoAmP 91*
**Reid,** Joseph Lee 1923- *AmMWSc 92*
**Reid,** Juanin A. *WhoHisp 92*
**Reid,** Karl Nevelle, Jr 1934- *AmMWSc 92*
**Reid,** Kate 1930- *IntMPA 92*
**Reid,** Kenneth Brooks 1943- *AmMWSc 92*
**Reid,** Kenneth Edward 1940- *WhoMW 92*
**Reid,** Langhorne, III 1950- *WhoFI 92*
**Reid,** Lawrence Charles 1948- *WhoIns 92*
**Reid,** Lealaifuaneva Peter E 1932- *WhoAmP 91*
**Reid,** Leslie 1919- *Who 92*
**Reid,** Leslie Bancroft 1934- *WhoBlA 92*
**Reid,** Lloyd Duff 1942- *AmMWSc 92*
**Reid,** Lois Jean 1937- *AmMWSc 92*
**Reid,** Lola Cynthia McAdams 1945- *AmMWSc 92*
**Reid,** Loren 1905- *WrDr 92*
**Reid,** Lyle *WhoAmP 91*
**Reid,** Lynne McArthur 1923- *Who 92*
**Reid,** Malcolm Herbert Marcus 1927- *Who 92*
**Reid,** Martin *Who 92*
**Reid,** Martin 1928- *IntWW 91*
**Reid,** Maude K. *WhoBlA 92*
**Reid,** Max Fisher 1944- *WhoEnt 92*
**Reid,** Mayne 1818-1883 *BenetAL 91*
**Reid,** Megan Beth 1954- *WhoWest 92*
**Reid,** Meta Mayne *WrDr 92*
**Reid,** Michael Baron 1952- *AmMWSc 92*
**Reid,** Michael Edward 1950- *WhoWest 92*
**Reid,** Michael J 1954- *WhoAmP 91*
**Reid,** Michaela Ann 1933- *IntAu&W 91*
**Reid,** Miles Alvin 1931- *WhoBlA 92*
**Reid,** Milton A. 1930- *WhoBlA 92*
**Reid,** Nanci Glick 1941- *WhoFI 92*
**Reid,** Norman 1915- *TwCPaSc, Who 92*
**Reid,** Norman R 1933- *WhoIns 92*
**Reid,** Norman Robert 1915- *IntWW 91*
**Reid,** Ogden Rogers 1925- *IntWW 91, WhoAmP 91*
**Reid,** Oswald Hutton 1951- *WhoBlA 92*
**Reid,** Parlane John 1937- *AmMWSc 92*
**Reid,** Pat 1910-1990 *AnObit 1990*
**Reid,** Percy Fergus Ivo 1911- *Who 92*
**Reid,** Peter Daer 1925- *Who 92*
**Reid,** Philip *IntAu&W 91X, Who 92*
**Reid,** Philip Dean 1937- *AmMWSc 92*
**Reid,** Preston Harding 1923- *AmMWSc 92*
**Reid,** Ralph R 1934- *AmMWSc 92*
**Reid,** Ralph Waldo Emerson 1915- *WhoFI 92*
**Reid,** Randall *DrAPF 91*
**Reid,** Randall Clyde 1931- *WhoWest 92*
**Reid,** Richard *WhoRel 92*
**Reid,** Richard Alan 1938- *WhoWest 92*
**Reid,** Richard J 1932- *AmMWSc 92*

**Reid**, Robert 1921- Who 92
**Reid**, Robert 1933-1990 AnObit 1990
**Reid**, Robert 1955- WhoBlA 92
**Reid**, Robert Basil 1921- IntWW 91
**Reid**, Robert C 1924- AmMWSc 92
**Reid**, Robert Daniel 1914-1980 WhoBlA 92N
**Reid**, Robert Dennis 1924- WhoBlA 92
**Reid**, Robert Edward 1903- WhoBlA 92
**Reid**, Robert Lelon 1942- AmMWSc 92
**Reid**, Robert Leslie AmMWSc 92
**Reid**, Robert Leslie 1951- AmMWSc 92
**Reid**, Robert Osborne 1921- AmMWSc 92
**Reid**, Robert Paul 1934- Who 92
**Reid**, Robert Philip 1933- WhoAmP 91
**Reid**, Roberto Elliott 1930- WhoBlA 92
**Reid**, Roderick Vincent, Jr 1932- AmMWSc 92
**Reid**, Rolland Ramsay 1926- AmMWSc 92
**Reid**, Ronald G. 1964- WhoEnt 92
**Reid**, Ronda Eunese 1955- WhoBlA 92
**Reid**, Rosemary K 1933- WhoAmP 91
**Reid**, Rubin J. WhoBlA 92
**Reid**, Rufus Lamar 1944- WhoEnt 92
**Reid**, Russell Martin 1941- AmMWSc 92
**Reid**, Selwyn Charles 1944- WhoBlA 92
**Reid**, Seona Elizabeth 1950- Who 92
**Reid**, Sidney George 1923- AmMWSc 92
**Reid**, Sina M. 1944- WhoBlA 92
**Reid**, Spencer 1952- WhoWest 92
**Reid**, Stanley Lyle 1930- AmMWSc 92
**Reid**, Ted Warren 1939- AmMWSc 92
**Reid**, Thomas 1710-1796 BlkwCEP
**Reid**, Thomas Fenton 1932- WhoRel 92
**Reid**, Thomas S 1911- AmMWSc 92
**Reid**, Tim 1944- WhoBlA 92
**Reid**, Timothy 1936- WhoFI 92
**Reid**, Timothy Escott 1936- IntWW 91
**Reid**, Vernon H. 1904- WhoBlA 92
**Reid**, Vic 1913- RfGEnL 91, WrDr 92
**Reid**, Vic 1913-1987 ConNov 91
**Reid**, Victor Stafford 1913- IntAu&W 91
**Reid**, Whitelaw 1837-1912 BenetAL 91
**Reid**, Whitelaw 1913- Who 92
**Reid**, Wilfred 1923- WhoBlA 92
**Reid**, Willard Malcolm 1910- AmMWSc 92
**Reid**, William 1921- Who 92
**Reid**, William 1926- Who 92
**Reid**, William Alexander 1943- WhoRel 92
**Reid**, William Bradley 1920- AmMWSc 92
**Reid**, William Gordon 1943- Who 92
**Reid**, William Harper 1933- AmMWSc 92
**Reid**, William Hill 1926- AmMWSc 92
**Reid**, William James 1927- AmMWSc 92
**Reid**, William John 1945- AmMWSc 92
**Reid**, William Kennedy 1931- Who 92
**Reid**, William Macpherson 1938- Who 92
**Reid**, William Michael 1954- WhoFI 92
**Reid**, William Shaw 1938- AmMWSc 92
**Reid**, William Stanford 1913- IntWW 91
**Reid**, William T 1907- AmMWSc 92
**Reid**, Yolanda A. 1954- WhoHisp 92
**Reid Banks**, Lynne Who 92
**Reid Banks**, Lynne 1929- ChlLR 24 [port], WrDr 92
**Reid-Bookhart**, Patricia Ann 1950- WhoBlA 92
**Reid Cabral**, Donald J. 1923- IntWW 91
**Reid-King**, Richard Douglass 1962- WhoRel 92
**Reida**, Larry 1935- WhoAmP 91
**Reidelbach**, Michael Joseph, Sr. 1946- WhoMW 92
**Reidenbach**, William John 1930- WhoFI 92
**Reidenberg**, Marcus Milton 1934- AmMWSc 92
**Reider**, George M, Jr 1940- WhoIns 92
**Reider**, Harry Robert 1940- WhoWest 92
**Reider**, Malcolm John 1914- AmMWSc 92
**Reider**, Paul Joseph 1951- AmMWSc 92
**Reider**, Richard Gary 1941- AmMWSc 92
**Reidhaven**, Viscount 1963- Who 92
**Reidies**, Arno H 1925- AmMWSc 92
**Reidinger**, Russell Frederick, Jr 1945- AmMWSc 92
**Reidlinger**, Anthony A 1926- AmMWSc 92
**Reidy**, Carolyn Kroll 1949- IntWW 91
**Reidy**, Daniel Abell 1959- WhoEnt 92
**Reidy**, Frank J 1914- WhoAmP 91
**Reidy**, Gerald Patrick 1929- WhoFI 92
**Reidy**, James Joseph 1936- AmMWSc 92
**Reidy**, Joseph Patrick Irwin d1991 Who 92N
**Reidy**, Michael J WhoAmP 91
**Reidy**, Richard F 1935- WhoIns 92
**Reidy**, Richard Robert 1947- WhoWest 92
**Reierson**, Gary B. 1948- ConAu 36NR
**Reierson**, Gary Bruce 1948- WhoRel 92
**Reierson**, James 1941- AmMWSc 92
**Reif**, Arnold E 1924- AmMWSc 92
**Reif**, Charles Braddock 1912- AmMWSc 92
**Reif**, David Adams 1946- WhoAmP 91
**Reif**, Donald John 1931- AmMWSc 92
**Reif**, Eric Peter 1942- WhoAmL 92
**Reif**, Frederick 1927- AmMWSc 92
**Reif**, John H 1951- AmMWSc 92
**Reif**, John Steven 1940- WhoWest 92
**Reif**, Joseph Anthony 1921- WhoAmL 92
**Reif**, L Rafael 1950- AmMWSc 92
**Reif**, Louis Raymond 1923- WhoFI 92
**Reif**, Van Dale 1947- AmMWSc 92
**Reif-Lehrer**, Liane 1934- AmMWSc 92
**Reifenberg**, Gerald H 1931- AmMWSc 92
**Reifenheiser**, Thomas V. 1935- WhoFI 92
**Reifenrath**, Dorothy Ann 1922- WhoMW 92
**Reifenrath**, William Gerald 1947- AmMWSc 92
**Reiff**, A.E. DrAPF 91
**Reiff**, Arthur Frederick 1936- WhoAmP 91
**Reiff**, Glenn Austin 1923- AmMWSc 92
**Reiff**, Harry Elmer 1924- AmMWSc 92
**Reiff**, Lee Herbert 1929- WhoRel 92
**Reiff**, Patricia Hofer 1950- AmMWSc 92
**Reiff**, Robert 1918-1982 ConAu 135
**Reiff**, Robert L. DrAPF 91
**Reiff**, Theodore Curtis 1942- WhoFI 92, WhoWest 92
**Reiff**, Thomas Mark 1958- WhoEnt 92
**Reiff**, William Michael 1942- AmMWSc 92
**Reiffel**, Leonard 1927- AmMWSc 92, WhoFI 92
**Reiffen**, Barney 1927- AmMWSc 92
**Reiffenstein**, Rhoderic John 1938- AmMWSc 92
**Reifler**, Clifford Bruce 1931- AmMWSc 92
**Reifler**, Samuel DrAPF 91
**Reifschneider**, Walter 1926- AmMWSc 92
**Reifsnider**, Kenneth Leonard 1940- AmMWSc 92
**Reifsnyder**, William Edward 1924- AmMWSc 92
**Reig**, June 1933- IntAu&W 91
**Reig**, June Wilson 1933- WhoEnt 92
**Reigate**, Archdeacon of Who 92
**Reigate**, Baron 1905- Who 92
**Reigel**, Earl William 1935- AmMWSc 92
**Reigeluth**, Charles Morgan 1946- WhoMW 92
**Reighard**, Patton Breon 1949- WhoEnt 92
**Reigstad**, Ruth Elaine 1923- WhoRel 92
**Reiher**, Frederick Bernard Carl 1945- Who 92
**Reiher**, Harold Frederick 1927- AmMWSc 92
**Reikofski**, Mary Therese 1949- WhoEnt 92
**Reil**, Krin Marie 1962- WhoWest 92
**Reile**, Louis 1925- WrDr 92
**Reiley**, Steven Edward 1960- WhoWest 92
**Reiley**, Thomas Noel 1938- WhoFI 92
**Reiley**, Thomas Phillip 1950- WhoFI 92
**Reiling**, Cecilia Powers 1926- WhoRel 92
**Reiling**, Gilbert Henry 1928- AmMWSc 92
**Reilly**, Baron d1990 Who 92N
**Reilly**, Lord 1912-1990 AnObit 1990
**Reilly**, Anne Kathleen 1954- WhoAmL 92
**Reilly**, Bernard Edward 1935- AmMWSc 92
**Reilly**, Charles Austin 1916- AmMWSc 92
**Reilly**, Charles Bernard 1929- AmMWSc 92
**Reilly**, Charles Conrad 1940- AmMWSc 92
**Reilly**, Charles E., Jr. 1928- IntMPA 92
**Reilly**, Charles James 1950- WhoAmL 92
**Reilly**, Charles Nelson 1931- IntMPA 92, WhoEnt 92
**Reilly**, Christopher Aloysius, Jr 1942- AmMWSc 92
**Reilly**, Christopher F AmMWSc 92
**Reilly**, Conor Desmond 1952- WhoAmL 92
**Reilly**, Daniel Patrick 1928- WhoRel 92
**Reilly**, D'Arcy Patrick 1909- Who 92
**Reilly**, Edward Arthur 1943- WhoAmL 92
**Reilly**, Edward Francis, Jr 1937- WhoAmP 91, WhoMW 92
**Reilly**, Edwin David, Jr 1932- AmMWSc 92
**Reilly**, Emmett B 1920- AmMWSc 92
**Reilly**, Esther Huntington 1917- WhoWest 92
**Reilly**, Eugene Patrick 1939- AmMWSc 92
**Reilly**, Francis X. 1916- WhoAmL 92
**Reilly**, Frank Daniel 1949- AmMWSc 92
**Reilly**, Hilda Christine 1920- AmMWSc 92
**Reilly**, Hugh Thomas 1925- AmMWSc 92
**Reilly**, Jad DrAPF 91
**Reilly**, James Anthony 1941- WhoMW 92
**Reilly**, James Patrick 1933- AmMWSc 92
**Reilly**, James Patrick 1937- AmMWSc 92
**Reilly**, James Patrick 1950- AmMWSc 92
**Reilly**, James Richard 1945- WhoAmP 91
**Reilly**, James William 1935- AmMWSc 92
**Reilly**, Jeremy 1934- Who 92
**Reilly**, John Bernard 1947- WhoAmL 92
**Reilly**, Joseph F 1915- AmMWSc 92
**Reilly**, Joy Harriman 1942- WhoMW 92
**Reilly**, Kevin Denis 1937- AmMWSc 92
**Reilly**, Kevin Francis 1955- WhoFI 92
**Reilly**, Kevin P 1928- WhoAmP 91
**Reilly**, Margaret Anne 1937- AmMWSc 92
**Reilly**, Marguerite 1919- AmMWSc 92
**Reilly**, Maryanne Claire 1959- WhoFI 92
**Reilly**, Maureen Anne 1956- WhoAmP 91
**Reilly**, Michael Atlee 1948- WhoFI 92
**Reilly**, Michael George 1949- WhoWest 92
**Reilly**, Michael Gerard 1957- WhoAmL 92
**Reilly**, Michael Hunt 1939- AmMWSc 92
**Reilly**, Nancy DrAPF 91
**Reilly**, Nina-Marie 1954- WhoEnt 92
**Reilly**, Noel M.P. d1991 NewYTBS 91
**Reilly**, Noel Marcus Prowse d1991 Who 92N
**Reilly**, Norman Raymund 1940- AmMWSc 92
**Reilly**, Park McKnight 1920- AmMWSc 92
**Reilly**, Patrick Who 92
**Reilly**, Patrick 1909- IntWW 91
**Reilly**, Patrick John 1925- WhoFI 92, WhoWest 92
**Reilly**, Paul 1912- DcTwDes
**Reilly**, Paul Cameron 1948- WhoEnt 92
**Reilly**, Peter C. 1907- WhoFI 92, WhoMW 92
**Reilly**, Peter John 1938- AmMWSc 92
**Reilly**, Richard Anthony 1935- WhoFI 92
**Reilly**, Richard J 1930- AmMWSc 92
**Reilly**, Robert Frederick 1952- WhoFI 92, WhoMW 92
**Reilly**, Robert Rowen 1938- WhoMW 92
**Reilly**, Robert Thomas 1922- WhoMW 92, WrDr 92
**Reilly**, Robin 1928- WrDr 92
**Reilly**, Sean 1961- WhoAmP 91
**Reilly**, Sidney 1874-1925 FacFETw
**Reilly**, Thomas Augustine 1943- WhoRel 92
**Reilly**, Thomas E AmMWSc 92
**Reilly**, Thomas Edward, Jr. 1959- WhoAmL 92
**Reilly**, Vincent Francis 1958- WhoAmL 92
**Reilly**, William Francis 1938- WhoFI 92
**Reilly**, William Kane 1940- WhoAmP 91
**Reilly**, William Thomas 1949- WhoAmL 92
**Reily**, William Singer 1924- AmMWSc 92
**Reim**, Robert E AmMWSc 92
**Reim**, Ruthann 1943- WhoWest 92
**Reiman**, Donald Henry 1934- Who 92
**Reimann**, Aribert 1936- ConCom 92, NewAmDM
**Reimann**, Bernhard Erwin Ferdinand 1922- AmMWSc 92, WhoWest 92
**Reimann**, Erwin M 1942- AmMWSc 92
**Reimann**, Hans 1930- AmMWSc 92
**Reimann**, Hobart Ansteth 1897- AmMWSc 92
**Reimann**, Ronald Hill, Jr. 1963- WhoWest 92
**Reimarus**, Hermann Samuel 1694-1768 BlkwCEP
**Reimche**, Sarah Curran 1917- IntAu&W 91
**Reimer**, Bennett 1932- WhoEnt 92
**Reimer**, Charles Blaisdell 1921- AmMWSc 92
**Reimer**, Chris Russel 1949- WhoWest 92
**Reimer**, Dennis D 1940- AmMWSc 92
**Reimer**, Diedrich 1925- AmMWSc 92
**Reimer**, Elmer Isaac 1922- WhoRel 92
**Reimer**, Glenda Faith 1950- WhoAmP 91
**Reimer**, Rollin 1939- WhoAmP 91
**Reimers**, Thomas John AmMWSc 92
**Reimnitz**, Elroi 1948- WhoRel 92
**Reimold**, Robert J 1941- AmMWSc 92
**Reimschussel**, Ernest F 1917- AmMWSc 92
**Rein**, Alan James 1948- AmMWSc 92
**Rein**, Arnold Robert 1928- WhoMW 92
**Rein**, Diane Carla AmMWSc 92
**Rein**, James Earl 1923- AmMWSc 92
**Rein**, Martin L 1915- WhoIns 92
**Rein**, Robert 1928- AmMWSc 92
**Rein**, Robert G, Jr 1940- AmMWSc 92
**Rein**, Stanley M. 1946- WhoAmL 92
**Reina**, Nicholas Joseph 1948- WhoHisp 92
**Reinagle**, Alexander 1756-1809 NewAmDM
**Reinard**, Roy 1954- WhoAmP 91
**Reinauer**, Richard 1926- IntMPA 92
**Reinberg**, Alan R 1931- AmMWSc 92
**Reinberg**, Deborah IntMPA 92
**Reinbergs**, Ernests 1920- AmMWSc 92
**Reinbold**, George W 1919- AmMWSc 92
**Reinbold**, Grace Ann 1941- WhoEnt 92, WhoFI 92
**Reinbold**, James S. DrAPF 91
**Reinbold**, Leo 1933- WhoAmP 91
**Reinbold**, Paul Earl 1943- AmMWSc 92
**Reince**, Martha Mary 1962- WhoWest 92
**Reinders**, Victor A 1906- AmMWSc 92
**Reineccius**, Gary 1944- AmMWSc 92
**Reineck**, Gay Beste DrAPF 91
**Reinecke**, Carl 1824-1910 NewAmDM
**Reinecke**, Ed 1924- WhoAmP 91
**Reinecke**, Jean Otis 1909- DcTwDes
**Reinecke**, Manfred Gordon 1935- AmMWSc 92
**Reinecke**, Robert Dale 1929- AmMWSc 92
**Reinecke**, Thomas Leonard 1945- AmMWSc 92
**Reinecke**, William Gerald 1935- AmMWSc 92
**Reinecker**, Herbert 1914- EncTR 91
**Reineke**, Charles Everett 1938- AmMWSc 92
**Reineke**, Martha Jane 1954- WhoRel 92
**Reinemund**, John Adam 1919- AmMWSc 92
**Reiner**, Albey M 1941- AmMWSc 92
**Reiner**, Carl LesBEnT 92
**Reiner**, Carl 1922- FacFETw, WhoEnt 92
**Reiner**, Carl 1923- IntMPA 92
**Reiner**, Charles Brailove 1920- AmMWSc 92
**Reiner**, Fritz 1888-1963 FacFETw, NewAmDM
**Reiner**, Ira 1936- WhoAmL 92
**Reiner**, Irma Moses 1922- AmMWSc 92, WhoMW 92
**Reiner**, James Anthony 1958- WhoMW 92
**Reiner**, John Maximilian 1912- AmMWSc 92
**Reiner**, Leopold 1911- AmMWSc 92
**Reiner**, Manny d1974 LesBEnT 92
**Reiner**, Peter Alan 1953- WhoMW 92
**Reiner**, Rob LesBEnT 92, WhoEnt 92
**Reiner**, Rob 1945- IntMPA 92, IntWW 91
**Reiner**, Rob 1947- News 91 [port]
**Reiner**, Samuel Theodore 1933- WhoAmL 92
**Reiner**, Sidney d1991 NewYTBS 91
**Reiner**, Yvette M. 1936- WhoMW 92
**Reiners**, Al WhoEnt 92
**Reiners**, Gernot H. 1942- WhoFI 92
**Reiners**, William A 1937- AmMWSc 92
**Reiners**, William Joseph 1923- Who 92
**Reinert**, Heinrich 1920- IntWW 91
**Reinert**, James A 1944- AmMWSc 92
**Reinert**, Pamela Ann 1952- WhoMW 92
**Reinert**, Richard Allyn 1935- AmMWSc 92
**Reinert**, Ronald WhoAmP 91
**Reinerth**, Hans 1900- EncTR 91
**Reinertsen**, Norman 1934- WhoFI 92
**Reinertson**, James Wayne 1927- WhoMW 92
**Reines**, Alvin Jay 1926- WhoRel 92
**Reines**, Bernard Jacob 1907- WhoEnt 92
**Reines**, Daniel AmMWSc 92
**Reines**, Frederick 1918- AmMWSc 92, IntWW 91
**Reiness**, Gary 1945- AmMWSc 92
**Reinfeld**, Stuart Glenn 1959- WhoAmL 92
**Reinfurt**, Donald William 1938- AmMWSc 92
**Reinganum**, Victor 1907- TwCPaSc
**Reingold**, Edward Martin 1945- AmMWSc 92, WhoMW 92
**Reingold**, Haim 1910- AmMWSc 92, WhoMW 92
**Reingold**, Irving 1921- AmMWSc 92
**Reingold**, Iver David 1949- AmMWSc 92
**Reingold**, Paul D. 1951- WhoAmL 92
**Reinhard**, Bryant Louis 1949- WhoWest 92
**Reinhard**, Edward Humphrey 1913- AmMWSc 92
**Reinhard**, James Richard 1929- WhoAmL 92
**Reinhard**, Jean Beryl 1915- WhoWest 92
**Reinhard**, John Frederick 1908- AmMWSc 92
**Reinhard**, John Frederick, Jr 1951- AmMWSc 92
**Reinhard**, Karl R 1916- AmMWSc 92
**Reinhard**, Norman Arthur 1939- WhoMW 92
**Reinhardt**, Ad 1913-1967 FacFETw
**Reinhardt**, Burt LesBEnT 92
**Reinhardt**, Burt 1920- WhoEnt 92
**Reinhardt**, Charles Francis 1933- AmMWSc 92
**Reinhardt**, Django 1910-1953 ConMus 7 [port], NewAmDM
**Reinhardt**, Donald Joseph 1938- AmMWSc 92
**Reinhardt**, Fritz 1895-1969? EncTR 91 [port]
**Reinhardt**, Gottfried 1911- IntMPA 92
**Reinhardt**, Howard Earl 1927- AmMWSc 92
**Reinhardt**, John Edward 1920- IntWW 91, WhoAmP 91, WhoBlA 92
**Reinhardt**, Jon David 1943- WhoAmP 91
**Reinhardt**, Juergen 1946- AmMWSc 92
**Reinhardt**, Karl David 1954- WhoMW 92
**Reinhardt**, Madge DrAPF 91
**Reinhardt**, Max 1873-1943 EncTR 91 [port], FacFETw
**Reinhardt**, Max 1915- IntWW 91, Who 92
**Reinhardt**, Richard Alan 1922- AmMWSc 92
**Reinhardt**, Richard R 1934- WhoAmP 91
**Reinhardt**, Robert Milton 1927- AmMWSc 92
**Reinhardt**, Stephen WhoAmP 91
**Reinhardt**, Stephen Roy 1931- WhoAmL 92
**Reinhardt**, Susan Elizabeth WhoMW 92
**Reinhardt**, Walter Albert 1931- AmMWSc 92

**Reinhardt**, William Nelson 1939- *AmMWSc 92*
**Reinhardt**, William Parker 1942- *AmMWSc 92*
**Reinhart**, Bruce Lloyd 1930- *AmMWSc 92*
**Reinhart**, Charles Franklin 1946- *WhoEnt 92*
**Reinhart**, Dietrich Thomas 1949- *WhoMW 92*
**Reinhart**, Gregory Duncan 1951- *AmMWSc 92*
**Reinhart**, John Belvin 1917- *AmMWSc 92*
**Reinhart**, Mark Jeffrey 1955- *WhoWest 92*
**Reinhart**, Michael P 1952- *AmMWSc 92*
**Reinhart**, Richard D 1929- *AmMWSc 92*
**Reinhart**, Richard John 1951- *WhoEnt 92*
**Reinhart**, Robert Rountree, Jr. 1947- *WhoAmL 92*
**Reinhart**, Roy Herbert 1919- *AmMWSc 92*
**Reinhart**, Stanley E, Jr 1928- *AmMWSc 92*
**Reinhart**, Steven 1953- *WhoWest 92*
**Reinhart**, Terry Eugene 1949- *WhoFI 92*
**Reinheimer**, John David 1920- *AmMWSc 92*
**Reinheimer**, Julian 1925- *AmMWSc 92*
**Reinhold**, Allen Kurt 1936- *WhoWest 92*
**Reinhold**, Hans Ansgar 1897-1968 *DcAmImH*
**Reinhold**, Judge *WhoEnt 92*
**Reinhold**, Judge 1956- *IntMPA 92*
**Reinhold**, Robert 1941- *ConAu 133*
**Reinhold**, Toni 1954- *WhoEnt 92*
**Reinhold**, Vernon Nye 1931- *AmMWSc 92*
**Reinig**, James William 1954- *AmMWSc 92*
**Reinig**, William Charles 1924- *AmMWSc 92*
**Reiniger**, Douglas Haigh 1948- *WhoAmL 92*
**Reiniger**, Lotte 1899-1981 *ReelWom [port]*
**Reining**, Priscilla Copeland 1923- *AmMWSc 92*
**Reininger**, Edward Joseph 1929- *AmMWSc 92*
**Reininger**, Paul Michael 1961- *WhoFI 92*
**Reinisch**, Nancy Rae 1953- *WhoWest 92*
**Reinke**, Andrew John 1962- *WhoMW 92*
**Reinke**, David Albert 1933- *AmMWSc 92*
**Reinke**, John Henry 1915- *WhoMW 92*
**Reinke**, Lester Allen 1946- *AmMWSc 92*
**Reinke**, Stefan Michael 1958- *WhoAmL 92*
**Reinke**, William Andrew 1928- *AmMWSc 92*
**Reinke**, William John 1930- *WhoAmL 92*
**Reinking**, Ann H. 1950- *WhoEnt 92*
**Reinking**, Larry Norman *AmMWSc 92*
**Reinking**, Mark Kent 1959- *WhoMW 92*
**Reinmuth**, Oscar McNaughton 1927- *AmMWSc 92*
**Reinmuth**, William Henry 1932- *AmMWSc 92*
**Reino**, Fernando 1929- *IntWW 91*
**Reinoehl**, Dennis Ray 1948- *WhoFI 92*
**Reinoehl**, Richard Louis 1944- *WhoMW 92*
**Reins**, Ralph Erich 1940- *WhoFI 92*
**Reinsborough**, Vincent Conrad 1935- *AmMWSc 92*
**Reinsch**, J. Leonard d1991 *LesBEnT 92*
**Reinsch**, James L. d1991 *NewYTBS 91 [port]*
**Reinsch**, Paul Samuel 1869-1923 *AmPeW*
**Reinsch**, William Alan 1946- *WhoAmP 91*
**Reinschmidt**, Kenneth F 1938- *AmMWSc 92*
**Reinschmidt**, Michael Anthony 1961- *WhoFI 92*
**Reinsdorf**, Jerry Michael 1936- *WhoFI 92, WhoMW 92*
**Reinsel**, Gregory Charles 1948- *AmMWSc 92*
**Reinshagen**, Gerlind 1926- *IntWW 91*
**Reinsma**, Harold Lawrence 1928- *WhoMW 92*
**Reinstein**, Alan Lee 1928- *WhoAmL 92*
**Reinstein**, Henry Allen 1922- *WhoWest 92*
**Reinstein**, Lawrence Elliot 1945- *AmMWSc 92*
**Reinstein**, William George 1939- *WhoAmP 91*
**Reinthaller**, Anton 1895-1959 *BiDExR*
**Reintjes**, J Francis 1912- *AmMWSc 92*
**Reintjes**, John Francis, Jr 1945- *AmMWSc 92*
**Reintjes**, Marten 1932- *AmMWSc 92*
**Reintsema**, Robert Arnold 1937- *WhoAmP 91*
**Reinus**, William R. 1953- *WhoMW 92*
**Reiplinger**, John Edward 1942- *WhoEnt 92, WhoFI 92, WhoMW 92*
**Reis**, Arthur Henry, Jr 1946- *AmMWSc 92*
**Reis**, Donald J 1931- *AmMWSc 92*
**Reis**, Frank Henry 1936- *WhoFI 92*
**Reis**, Harold F. 1916- *WhoAmL 92*
**Reis**, Irvin L 1926- *AmMWSc 92*
**Reis**, Jean Stevenson 1914- *WhoWest 92*
**Reis**, Patrick Raymond 1948- *WhoWest 92*
**Reis**, Paul G 1925- *AmMWSc 92*
**Reis**, Walter Joseph 1918- *AmMWSc 92*
**Reisa**, James Joseph, Jr 1941- *AmMWSc 92*
**Reisberg**, Boris Elliott 1935- *AmMWSc 92*
**Reisberg**, Joseph 1921- *AmMWSc 92*
**Reisberg**, Leon Elton 1949- *WhoWest 92*
**Reisberg**, Richard S. 1941- *WhoEnt 92*
**Reisbig**, Ronald Luther 1938- *AmMWSc 92*
**Reisch**, Bruce Irving 1955- *AmMWSc 92*
**Reisch**, Harold Franklin 1920- *WhoAmP 91*
**Reisch**, Kenneth William 1929- *AmMWSc 92*
**Reischauer**, Edwin 1910-1990 *AnObit 1990*
**Reischauer**, Edwin Oldfather d1990 *IntWW 91N*
**Reische**, Alan Lawrence 1939- *WhoAmL 92*
**Reischman**, Charles J. 1955- *WhoRel 92*
**Reischman**, Michael Mack 1942- *AmMWSc 92*
**Reischman**, Placidus George 1926- *AmMWSc 92*
**Reisel**, Robert Benedict 1925- *AmMWSc 92*
**Reisel**, Vladimir 1919- *IntAu&W 91*
**Reisen**, Milton R. *WhoRel 92*
**Reisen**, William Kenneth 1946- *AmMWSc 92*
**Reisenauer**, Hubert Michael 1920- *AmMWSc 92*
**Reisenbach**, Sanford E. *IntMPA 92*
**Reisenberg**, Nadia 1904-1983 *NewAmDM*
**Reiser**, Castle O 1912- *AmMWSc 92*
**Reiser**, David Richard 1959- *WhoFI 92*
**Reiser**, H Joseph 1946- *AmMWSc 92*
**Reiser**, Morton Francis 1919- *AmMWSc 92*
**Reiser**, Paul 1957- *IntMPA 92*
**Reiser**, Peter Jacob 1953- *AmMWSc 92*
**Reiser**, Raymond 1906- *AmMWSc 92*
**Reiser**, Sheldon 1930- *AmMWSc 92*
**Reisert**, Charles Edward, Jr. 1941- *WhoMW 92*
**Reisert**, Patricia 1937- *AmMWSc 92*
**Reisfeld**, Ralph Alfred 1926- *AmMWSc 92*
**Reish**, Donald James 1924- *AmMWSc 92*
**Reising**, Richard F 1934- *AmMWSc 92*
**Reisinger**, George Lambert 1930- *WhoFI 92, WhoWest 92*
**Reisinger**, Joseph G 1929- *AmMWSc 92*
**Reiskin**, Allan B 1936- *AmMWSc 92*
**Reiskind**, Jonathan 1940- *AmMWSc 92*
**Reisler**, Donald Laurence 1941- *AmMWSc 92*
**Reisler**, Hanna 1943- *AmMWSc 92*
**Reisler**, Helen Barbara 1933- *WhoFI 92*
**Reisman**, Abraham Joseph 1925- *AmMWSc 92*
**Reisman**, Arnold 1927- *AmMWSc 92*
**Reisman**, Arnold 1934- *AmMWSc 92*
**Reisman**, Bernard 1926- *WhoRel 92*
**Reisman**, David 1909- *FacFETw*
**Reisman**, David S. 1958- *WhoAmL 92*
**Reisman**, Elias 1926- *AmMWSc 92*
**Reisman**, Harold Bernard 1935- *AmMWSc 92*
**Reisman**, Howard Maurice 1937- *AmMWSc 92*
**Reisman**, Jane *WhoEnt 92*
**Reisman**, Otto 1928- *AmMWSc 92*
**Reisman**, Stanley S 1941- *AmMWSc 92*
**Reisman**, William M. 1939- *WhoAmL 92*
**Reismann**, Herbert 1926- *AmMWSc 92*
**Reisner**, Allen *IntMPA 92*
**Reisner**, Barbara *DrAPF 91*
**Reisner**, Edward John 1947- *WhoAmL 92*
**Reisner**, Gerald Seymour 1926- *AmMWSc 92*
**Reisner**, Phyllis 1934- *WhoFI 92, WhoWest 92*
**Reisner**, Robert George 1921-1974 *ConAu 135*
**Reisner**, Ronald M 1929- *AmMWSc 92*
**Reiss**, Alvin 1932- *WhoEnt 92*
**Reiss**, Alvin Herbert 1930- *WhoEnt 92*
**Reiss**, Barbara Eve *DrAPF 91*
**Reiss**, Carol S 1950- *AmMWSc 92*
**Reiss**, Dale Anne 1947- *WhoFI 92*
**Reiss**, Diana 1948- *AmMWSc 92*
**Reiss**, Elaine Serlin 1940- *WhoFI 92*
**Reiss**, Eric 1924- *AmMWSc 92*
**Reiss**, Errol 1942- *AmMWSc 92*
**Reiss**, George R. 1903- *WhoMW 92*
**Reiss**, Gertrude *DrAPF 91*
**Reiss**, Howard 1922- *AmMWSc 92, IntWW 91*
**Reiss**, Howard R 1929- *AmMWSc 92*
**Reiss**, Ira Leonard 1925- *WrDr 92*
**Reiss**, James *DrAPF 91*
**Reiss**, Jeffrey *LesBEnT 92*
**Reiss**, Jeffrey C. 1942- *IntMPA 92*
**Reiss**, Jerome Lee 1928- *WhoMW 92*
**Reiss**, John Barlow 1939- *WhoAmL 92*
**Reiss**, John C. 1922- *WhoRel 92*
**Reiss**, John Henry 1918- *Who 92*
**Reiss**, Keith Westcott 1945- *AmMWSc 92*
**Reiss**, Kenneth William 1959- *WhoFI 92, WhoMW 92*
**Reiss**, Mayo *ScFEYrs*
**Reiss**, Oscar Kully 1921- *AmMWSc 92*
**Reiss**, Rhoda 1943- *WhoAmP 91*
**Reiss**, Robert Cornell 1932- *WhoIns 92*
**Reiss**, Ronn 1932- *WhoWest 92*
**Reiss**, Seth Michael 1952- *WhoAmL 92*
**Reiss**, Steven Alan 1951- *WhoAmL 92*
**Reiss**, Stuart A. 1921- *IntMPA 92*
**Reiss**, Timothy James 1942- *IntWW 91*
**Reiss**, William Dean 1937- *AmMWSc 92*
**Reisse**, Robert Alan 1946- *AmMWSc 92*
**Reissig**, Magdalena 1923- *AmMWSc 92*
**Reissman**, Maurice L. *WhoFI 92*
**Reissmann**, Thomas Lincoln 1920- *AmMWSc 92*
**Reissner**, Eric 1913- *AmMWSc 92*
**Reist**, Elmer Joseph 1930- *AmMWSc 92*
**Reist**, Parker Cramer 1933- *AmMWSc 92*
**Reist**, William Henry 1951- *WhoRel 92*
**Reistad**, Gordon Mackenze 1944- *AmMWSc 92*
**Reister**, David B 1942- *AmMWSc 92*
**Reister**, Lawrence Arnold 1926- *WhoFI 92*
**Reister**, Raymond Alex 1929- *WhoAmL 92, WhoMW 92*
**Reiswig**, Henry Michael 1936- *AmMWSc 92*
**Reiswig**, Jon Albert, II 1959- *WhoWest 92*
**Reiswig**, Kay B *WhoAmP 91*
**Reiswig**, Robert D 1929- *AmMWSc 92*
**Reisz**, Howard Frederick, Jr. 1939- *WhoRel 92*
**Reisz**, Karel 1926- *IntDcF 2-2 [port], IntMPA 92, IntWW 91, Who 92*
**Reit**, Barry 1942- *AmMWSc 92*
**Reit**, Ernest Marvin I 1932- *AmMWSc 92*
**Reitan**, Daniel Kinseth 1921- *AmMWSc 92*
**Reitan**, Harold Theodore 1928- *WhoWest 92*
**Reitan**, Paul Hartman 1928- *AmMWSc 92*
**Reitan**, Phillip Jennings 1929- *AmMWSc 92*
**Reitan**, Ralph Meldahl 1922- *AmMWSc 92*
**Reitemeier**, George 1931- *WhoWest 92*
**Reitemeier**, Joseph Richard 1954- *WhoMW 92*
**Reitemeier**, Richard Joseph 1923- *AmMWSc 92*
**Reiten**, Chester *WhoAmP 91*
**Reiten**, Eivind 1953- *IntWW 91*
**Reiten**, Richard 1941- *WhoWest 92*
**Reitenour**, Steven Lynn 1956- *WhoMW 92*
**Reiter**, Allen Gary 1950- *WhoAmL 92*
**Reiter**, Douglas Marc 1953- *WhoWest 92*
**Reiter**, Elmar Rudolf 1928- *AmMWSc 92*
**Reiter**, Glenn Mitchell 1951- *WhoAmL 92*
**Reiter**, Harold Braun 1942- *AmMWSc 92*
**Reiter**, Janusz 1952- *IntWW 91*
**Reiter**, Joseph Henry 1929- *WhoAmL 92*
**Reiter**, Marshall Allan 1942- *AmMWSc 92*
**Reiter**, Nathan I, Jr 1917- *WhoAmP 91*
**Reiter**, Raymond 1939- *AmMWSc 92*
**Reiter**, Richard Lawrence 1947- *WhoEnt 92*
**Reiter**, Robert Edward 1943- *WhoFI 92*
**Reiter**, Russel Joseph 1936- *AmMWSc 92*
**Reiter**, Stanley 1925- *AmMWSc 92*
**Reiter**, Thomas *DrAPF 91*
**Reiter**, Thomas John 1955- *WhoAmL 92*
**Reiter**, William Frederick, Jr 1938- *AmMWSc 92*
**Reith**, Barony of *Who 92*
**Reith**, Christopher John 1928- *Who 92*
**Reith**, Douglas 1919- *Who 92*
**Reith**, John C.W. d1968 *LesBEnT 92 [port]*
**Reith**, Louis John 1939- *WhoRel 92*
**Reith**, Maarten E A 1946- *AmMWSc 92*
**Reith**, Martin 1935- *Who 92*
**Reith**, Peter 1950- *IntWW 91*
**Reithel**, Robert James 1917- *WhoWest 92*
**Reitler**, William Robert 1954- *WhoEnt 92*
**Reitman**, Ivan 1946- *IntMPA 92, WhoEnt 92*
**Reitman**, Mitchell H. 1958- *WhoFI 92*
**Reitman**, Robert Stanley 1933- *WhoFI 92*
**Reitmeister**, Noel William 1938- *WhoFI 92*
**Reitmeyer**, William L 1928- *AmMWSc 92*
**Reitnour**, Clarence Melvin 1933- *AmMWSc 92*
**Reitsch**, Hanna 1912-1979 *EncTR 91 [port], FacFETw*
**Reitsema**, Robert Harold 1920- *AmMWSc 92*
**Reitter**, Rose *DrAPF 91*
**Reitz**, Allen Bernard 1956- *AmMWSc 92*
**Reitz**, Curtis Randall *WhoAmL 92*
**Reitz**, Del *DrAPF 91*
**Reitz**, Henry Matthew 1922- *WhoMW 92*
**Reitz**, Herman J 1916- *AmMWSc 92*
**Reitz**, John Marsteller 1925- *WhoMW 92*
**Reitz**, John Richard 1923- *AmMWSc 92*
**Reitz**, Joseph Anthony 1952- *WhoFI 92*
**Reitz**, Richard Elmer 1938- *AmMWSc 92, WhoWest 92*
**Reitz**, Richard Henry 1940- *AmMWSc 92*
**Reitz**, Robert Alan 1926- *AmMWSc 92*
**Reitz**, Robert Rex 1943- *AmMWSc 92*
**Reitz**, Ronald Charles 1939- *AmMWSc 92*
**Reitzel**, Robert 1849-1898 *BenetAL 91*
**Reitzell**, Hans Ulrich *WhoRel 92*
**Reivich**, Martin 1933- *AmMWSc 92*
**Reizenstein**, Franz 1911-1968 *NewAmDM*
**Reizer**, Jonathan 1940- *AmMWSc 92, WhoWest 92*
**Rejai**, Mostafa 1931- *WrDr 92*
**Rejali**, Abbas Mostafavi 1921- *AmMWSc 92*
**Rejent**, Marian Magdalen 1920- *WhoMW 92*
**Rejment**, Wladyslaw Stanislaw 1867-1925 *WhoNob 90*
**Rejto**, Peter A 1934- *AmMWSc 92*
**Rekai**, Catherine Kati 1921- *IntAu&W 91*
**Rekasius**, Zenonas V 1928- *AmMWSc 92*
**Reker**, Arthur William 1955- *WhoEnt 92*
**Rekers**, Robert George 1920- *AmMWSc 92*
**Reklaitis**, Gintaras Victor 1942- *AmMWSc 92*
**Reklau**, Tecla Sund *WhoRel 92*
**Rekoff**, M G, Jr 1929- *AmMWSc 92*
**Rekola**, Esko Johannes 1919- *IntWW 91*
**Rekowski**, John Joseph 1951- *WhoAmP 91*
**Rekunkov**, Aleksandr Mikhailovich 1920- *IntWW 91*
**Reldan**, Robert Ronald 1942- *WhoFI 92*
**Relias**, John Alexis 1946- *WhoMW 92*
**Relin**, Leonard 1936- *WhoAmL 92*
**Relkin**, Parris Craig 1954- *WhoEnt 92*
**Rell**, M Jodi *WhoAmP 91*
**Rella**, Anthony Joseph 1934- *WhoAmL 92*
**Relle**, Attila Tibor 1959- *WhoMW 92*
**Relle**, Ferenc Matyas 1922- *WhoMW 92*
**Rellie**, Alastair James Carl Euan 1935- *Who 92*
**Relly**, Gavin Walter Hamilton 1926- *IntWW 91, Who 92*
**Relman**, Arnold Seymour 1923- *AmMWSc 92*
**Relph**, Kaye B 1918- *WhoAmP 91*
**Relph**, Michael *IntMPA 92, IntWW 91*
**Relph**, Michael Leighton George *Who 92*
**Relph**, Simon 1940- *IntMPA 92*
**Relph**, Simon George Michael 1940- *Who 92*
**Relson**, Harry 1920- *WhoFI 92*
**Relton**, Stanley 1923- *Who 92*
**Relue**, Josie Ann 1962- *WhoFI 92*
**Relyea**, Douglas Irving 1930- *AmMWSc 92*
**Relyea**, John Franklin 1947- *AmMWSc 92*
**Relyea**, Kenneth George 1941- *AmMWSc 92*
**Relyea**, Paul Emery 1947- *WhoEnt 92*
**Relyea**, Robert E. 1930- *IntMPA 92*
**Relyea**, Robert Gordon 1917- *WhoWest 92*
**Remacle**, Rosemary 1942- *WhoWest 92*
**Remar**, James 1953- *IntMPA 92*
**Remar**, Joseph Francis 1938- *AmMWSc 92*
**Remar**, Robert Boyle 1948- *WhoAmL 92*
**Remarque**, Erich Maria 1898-1970 *BenetAL 91, EncTR 91 [port], FacFETw, LiExTwC*
**Rembar**, Charles 1915- *WrDr 92*
**Rembe**, Toni 1936- *WhoAmL 92*
**Rembert**, David Hopkins, Jr 1937- *AmMWSc 92*
**Rembert**, Emma White *WhoBlA 92*
**Rembert**, Sanco K. *WhoRel 92*
**Rembusch**, Trueman T. 1909- *IntMPA 92*
**Remec**, Miha 1928- *IntAu&W 91*
**Remedios**, Alberto Telisforo 1935- *IntWW 91, Who 92*
**Remedios**, E C 1941- *AmMWSc 92*
**Remelius**, Roger Martin 1948- *WhoEnt 92*
**Remeneski**, Shirley Rodriguez 1938- *WhoHisp 92*
**Remenyi**, Ede 1828-1898 *NewAmDM*
**Remenyik**, Carl John 1927- *AmMWSc 92*
**Remer**, Donald Sherwood 1943- *AmMWSc 92*
**Remer**, Otto-Ernst 1912- *BiDExR, EncTR 91 [port]*
**Remers**, William Alan 1932- *AmMWSc 92*
**Remesal**, Antonio de 1570- *HisDSpE*
**Remey**, Charles Mason 1874-1974 *RelLAm 91*
**Remez**, Aharon 1919- *Who 92*
**Remick**, Barbara R 1938- *WhoAmP 91*
**Remick**, Forrest J 1931- *AmMWSc 92*
**Remick**, Lee d1991 *LesBEnT 92, NewYTBS 91 [port]*
**Remick**, Lee 1935- *IntWW 91*
**Remick**, Lee 1935-1991 *CurBio 91N*
**Remick**, Lee 1936?-1991 *News 92-1*
**Remick**, Lloyd Zane 1938- *WhoEnt 92*
**Remick**, Oscar Eugene 1932- *WhoRel 92*
**Remick**, Robert Harold 1947- *WhoRel 92*
**Remillard**, Stephen Philip *AmMWSc 92*

**ReMine**, William Hervey 1918- *AmMWSc 92*
**Reminger**, Richard Thomas 1931- *WhoAmL 92, WhoMW 92*
**Remington**, C R, Jr 1924- *AmMWSc 92*
**Remington**, Charles Lee 1922- *AmMWSc 92*
**Remington**, Clinton O, III 1945- *WhoAmP 91*
**Remington**, Deborah Williams 1935- *IntWW 91*
**Remington**, Delwin Woolley 1950- *WhoWest 92*
**Remington**, Frederic 1861-1909 *BenetAL 91*
**Remington**, Frederic S 1861-1909 *TwCWW 91*
**Remington**, Jack Samuel 1931- *AmMWSc 92*
**Remington**, Joseph Price 1847-1918 *BiInAmS*
**Remington**, Lloyd Dean 1919- *AmMWSc 92*
**Remington**, Mark *IntAu&W 91X, TwCWW 91*
**Remington**, Mary 1920- *TwCPaSc*
**Remington**, Richard Delleraine 1931- *AmMWSc 92*
**Remington**, Tad Walter 1962- *WhoWest 92*
**Remington**, Thomas Timbrook 1943- *WhoAmL 92*
**Remington**, Walter Bruce, II 1950- *WhoFI 92*
**Remington**, William Roscoe 1918- *AmMWSc 92*
**Remizov**, A. *ConAu 133*
**Remizov**, A. M. *ConAu 133*
**Remizov**, Aleksei 1877-1957 *ConAu 133*
**Remizov**, Alexei Mikhailovich 1877-1957 *FacFETw*
**Remizov**, Alexei Mikhaylovich 1877-1957 *LiExTwC*
**Remler**, Edward A 1934- *AmMWSc 92*
**Remley**, Marlin Eugene 1921- *AmMWSc 92*
**Remme**, John Marlen 1935- *WhoEnt 92*
**Remmel**, Randall James 1949- *AmMWSc 92*
**Remmel**, Ronald Sylvester 1943- *AmMWSc 92*
**Remmelink**, Jan 1922- *IntWW 91*
**Remmenga**, D Elaine 1932- *WhoAmP 91*
**Remmenga**, Elmer Edwin 1927- *AmMWSc 92*
**Remmers**, Marvin Henry 1935- *WhoRel 92*
**Remmers**, R Wiley 1916- *WhoAmP 91*
**Remmert**, Pete 1934- *WhoAmP 91*
**Remnant** *Who 92*
**Remnant**, Baron 1930- *Who 92*
**Remo**, John Lucien 1941- *AmMWSc 92*
**Remo**, John William 1936- *WhoMW 92*
**Remold**, Heinz G 1937- *AmMWSc 92*
**Remole**, Arnulf 1928- *AmMWSc 92*
**Remond**, Sarah P. 1826-1894 *NotBlAW 92 [port]*
**Remondini**, David Joseph 1931- *AmMWSc 92*
**Remondini**, Walter Lino 1960- *WhoFI 92*
**Remont**, Roy 1929- *WhoRel 92*
**Rempel**, Arthur Gustav 1910- *AmMWSc 92*
**Rempel**, Garry Llewellyn 1944- *AmMWSc 92*
**Rempel**, Herman G 1902- *AmMWSc 92*
**Rempel**, William Ewert 1921- *AmMWSc 92*
**Rempfer**, Gertrude Fleming 1912- *AmMWSc 92*
**Rempfer**, Robert Weir 1914- *AmMWSc 92*
**Remple**, Timothy Kirk 1955- *WhoWest 92*
**Rempp**, Patricia Yvonne 1935- *WhoWest 92*
**Remsberg**, Ellis Edward 1943- *AmMWSc 92*
**Remsberg**, Louis Philip, Jr 1933- *AmMWSc 92*
**Remsen**, Bert 1925- *IntMPA 92, WhoEnt 92*
**Remsen**, Charles C, III 1937- *AmMWSc 92*
**Remsen**, James Vanderbeek, Jr 1949- *AmMWSc 92*
**Remson**, Anthony Terence 1952- *WhoBlA 92*
**Remson**, Irwin 1923- *AmMWSc 92*
**Remus**, Eugene *WhoBlA 92*
**Remy**, Colonel *FacFETw*
**Remy**, Charles Nicholas 1924- *AmMWSc 92*
**Remy**, David Carroll 1929- *AmMWSc 92*
**Remy**, Pierre-Jean 1937- *IntAu&W 91, IntWW 91*
**Remy**, Ray *WhoFI 92, WhoWest 92*
**Remy**, Robert E 1952- *WhoIns 92*
**Ren Jianxin** 1925- *IntWW 91*
**Ren Meie** *IntWW 91*
**Ren Rong** 1917- *IntWW 91*
**Ren Wuzhi** 1929- *IntWW 91*
**Ren Zhibin** *IntWW 91*
**Ren Zhongyi** 1914- *IntWW 91*
**Ren**, Peter 1948- *AmMWSc 92*
**Ren**, Shang-Fen *AmMWSc 92*
**Ren**, Shang Yuan 1940- *AmMWSc 92*
**Renac**, Mike 1920- *WhoMW 92*
**Renals**, Stanley 1923- *Who 92*
**Renan**, Ernest 1823-1892 *GuFrLit 1*
**Renan**, Sergio 1933- *WhoEnt 92*
**Renard**, Jules 1864-1910 *GuFrLit 1*
**Renard**, Kenneth G 1934- *AmMWSc 92*
**Renard**, Maurice 1875-1939 *ScFEYrs, TwCSFW 91A*
**Renard**, Maurice and Jean, Albert *ScFEYrs*
**Renard**, Paul Steven 1934- *WhoMW 92*
**Renard**, Robert Joseph 1923- *AmMWSc 92*
**Renard**, Ronald Lee 1949- *WhoWest 92*
**Renardy**, Michael 1955- *AmMWSc 92*
**Renardy**, Yuriko 1955- *AmMWSc 92*
**Renaud**, Bernadette 1945- *ConAu 134, SmATA 66 [port]*
**Renaud**, Dennis L 1942- *WhoAmP 91*
**Renaud**, Jacques 1943- *IntAu&W 91*
**Renaud**, Leo P *AmMWSc 92*
**Renaud**, Madeleine 1900- *IntWW 91*
**Renaud**, Madeleine 1903- *Who 92*
**Renaud**, Ronald N 1959- *WhoAmP 91*
**Renaud**, Serge 1927- *AmMWSc 92*
**Renauer**, Albin 1959- *ConAu 133*
**Renault**, Gilbert 1904-1984 *FacFETw*
**Renault**, Jacques Roland 1933- *AmMWSc 92*
**Renault**, Louis 1843-1918 *WhoNob 90*
**Renault**, Mary 1905-1983 *FacFETw, RfGEnL 91*
**Renault**, Rick *ConAu 35NR*
**Rencehausen**, Linda Mary 1950- *WhoWest 92*
**Rench**, Richard E 1941- *WhoAmP 91*
**Renchard**, William S. 1908- *IntWW 91*
**Renchard**, William Shryock 1908- *WhoFI 92*
**Rencher**, Alvin C 1934- *AmMWSc 92*
**Rencricca**, Nicholas John 1941- *AmMWSc 92*
**Renda**, Francis Joseph 1939- *AmMWSc 92*
**Rendall**, Peter Godfrey 1909- *Who 92*
**Rendall**, Ted Seator 1933- *WhoRel 92*
**Rende**, Karen Ann 1947- *WhoWest 92*
**Rendel**, Betty J *WhoAmP 91*
**Rendell**, David H 1935- *AmMWSc 92*
**Rendell**, Joan *WrDr 92*
**Rendell**, Ruth 1930- *ConNov 91, IntAu&W 91, IntWW 91, WrDr 92*
**Rendell**, Ruth Barbara 1930- *Who 92*
**Rendell**, William 1908- *Who 92*
**Render**, Arlene 1943- *WhoBlA 92*
**Render**, Sylvia Lyons 1913- *WhoBlA 92N*
**Render**, William H. 1950- *WhoBlA 92*
**Rendig**, Victor Vernon 1919- *AmMWSc 92*
**Rendina**, George 1923- *AmMWSc 92*
**Rendine**, Robert J *WhoAmP 91*
**Rendl-Marcus**, Mildred 1928- *WhoFI 92*
**Rendle**, Michael Russel 1931- *IntWW 91, Who 92*
**Rendle**, Peter Critchfield 1919- *Who 92*
**Rendle-Short**, John 1919- *WrDr 92*
**Rendleman**, Danny *DrAPF 91*
**Rendlen**, Albert L *WhoAmP 91*
**Rendlen**, Albert Lewis 1922- *WhoAmL 92, WhoMW 92*
**Rendlen**, Charles Earnest, III 1950- *WhoAmP 91*
**Rendlen**, Charles Earnest, Jr 1919- *WhoAmP 91*
**Rendlesham**, Baron 1915- *Who 92*
**Rendon**, Armando B *DrAPF 91*
**Rendon**, Armando B. 1939- *WhoHisp 92, WrDr 92*
**Rendon**, Florencio H. 1950- *WhoHisp 92*
**Rendon**, Josefina Muniz 1949- *WhoHisp 92*
**Rendon**, Juan Jose, Sr. 1945- *WhoHisp 92*
**Rendon**, Ruth Marie 1961- *WhoHisp 92*
**Rendon**, Sally *WhoHisp 92*
**Rendon**, Uriel 1960- *WhoHisp 92*
**Rendon-Herrero**, Oswald 1937- *WhoHisp 92*
**Rendtorff**, Robert Carlisle 1915- *AmMWSc 92*
**Rendu**, Jean-Michel Marie 1944- *WhoWest 92*
**Rene**, Albert 1935- *IntWW 91, Who 92*
**Rene**, Louis 1918- *IntWW 91*
**Reneau**, Daniel Dugan, Jr 1940- *AmMWSc 92*
**Reneau**, John 1927- *AmMWSc 92*
**Reneau**, Raymond B, Jr 1941- *AmMWSc 92*
**Renee de Bourbon** *EncAmaz 91*
**Renegar**, George Elmo 1921- *WhoRel 92*
**Reneke**, James Allen 1937- *AmMWSc 92*
**Reneker**, Darrell Hyson 1929- *AmMWSc 92, WhoMW 92*
**Renetzky**, Alvin 1940- *WhoWest 92*
**Reney**, Everett R 1914- *WhoAmP 91*
**Renfield**, Richard Lee 1932- *WrDr 92*
**Renfrew** *Who 92*
**Renfrew**, Andrew Colin 1937- *IntWW 91*
**Renfrew**, Charles Byron 1928- *WhoAmL 92*
**Renfrew**, Charles McDonald 1929- *Who 92*
**Renfrew**, Colin 1937- *WrDr 92*
**Renfrew**, Edgar Earl 1915- *AmMWSc 92*
**Renfrew**, Glen McGarvie 1928- *Who 92*
**Renfrew**, Malcolm MacKenzie 1910- *AmMWSc 92*
**Renfrew**, Robert Morrison 1938- *AmMWSc 92*
**Renfrew of Kaimsthorn**, Baron 1937- *Who 92*
**Renfrey**, Lionel Edward William 1916- *Who 92*
**Renfro**, Donald William 1931- *WhoWest 92*
**Renfro**, J Larry *AmMWSc 92*
**Renfro**, Mel 1941- *WhoBlA 92*
**Renfro**, Michael Dean 1957- *WhoMW 92*
**Renfro**, Raymond Zafar Hannan 1952- *WhoFI 92*
**Renfro**, Sally *DrAPF 91*
**Renfro**, Steven L. 1964- *WhoWest 92*
**Renfro**, William Charles 1930- *AmMWSc 92*
**Renfro**, William Leonard 1945- *WhoAmL 92*
**Renfroe**, Earl W. 1907- *WhoBlA 92*
**Renfroe**, Harris Burt 1936- *AmMWSc 92*
**Renfroe**, Iona Antoinette 1953- *WhoBlA 92*
**Renfrow**, Edward 1940- *WhoAmP 91*
**Rengan**, Krishnaswamy 1937- *AmMWSc 92*
**Rengarajan**, Sembiam Rajagopal 1948- *WhoWest 92*
**Renger**, Annemarie 1919- *IntWW 91*
**Renger**, James Dietrich 1940- *WhoFI 92*
**Rengstorff**, George W P 1920- *AmMWSc 92*
**Renich**, Paul William 1919- *AmMWSc 92*
**Renick**, James C. 1948- *WhoBlA 92*
**Renick**, Kyle 1948- *WhoEnt 92*
**Renick**, Ralph d1991 *NewYTBS 91*
**Renick**, William Jackson 1953- *WhoAmP 91*
**Renier**, Elizabeth *IntAu&W 91X*
**Renier**, Elizabeth 1916- *WrDr 92*
**Renier**, James J. 1930- *WhoFI 92, WhoMW 92*
**Renis**, Harold E 1930- *AmMWSc 92*
**Renk**, Kristin Yates 1959- *WhoFI 92*
**Renka**, Robert Joseph 1947- *AmMWSc 92*
**Renke**, John K 1946- *WhoAmP 91*
**Renke**, Marian 1930- *IntWW 91*
**Renken**, Duane Allen 1932- *WhoMW 92*
**Renken**, James Howard 1935- *AmMWSc 92*
**Renken**, Robert 1922- *WhoAmP 91*
**Renkey**, Edmund Joseph, Jr 1940- *AmMWSc 92*
**Renkin**, Eugene Marshall 1926- *AmMWSc 92*
**Renn**, Donald Walter 1932- *AmMWSc 92*
**Renn**, Kurt Daniel 1964- *WhoFI 92*
**Renn**, Ludwig 1889-1979 *EncTR 91 [port]*
**Renna**, John P 1920- *WhoAmP 91*
**Rennat**, Harry O 1922- *AmMWSc 92*
**Renne**, David Smith 1943- *AmMWSc 92*
**Renne**, Janice Lynn 1952- *WhoWest 92*
**Renne**, Louise Hornbeck 1937- *WhoAmP 91*
**Renne**, Merlin Moulthrop 1945- *WhoAmP 91*
**Rennebohm**, J. Fred 1927- *WhoRel 92*
**Renneke**, David Richard 1940- *AmMWSc 92*
**Renneke**, Earl Wallace 1928- *WhoAmP 91*
**Rennell**, Baron 1935- *Who 92*
**Rennels**, Christopher David 1957- *WhoWest 92*
**Rennels**, Marion G 1928- *WhoIns 92*
**Rennels**, Marshall L 1939- *AmMWSc 92*
**Renner**, Bruce *DrAPF 91*
**Renner**, Clarence E. 1922- *WhoAmL 92, WhoMW 92*
**Renner**, Daniel Segismundo 1953- *WhoWest 92*
**Renner**, Darwin S 1910- *AmMWSc 92*
**Renner**, George R 1946- *WhoAmP 91*
**Renner**, George Richard *WhoWest 92*
**Renner**, Gerard W 1921- *AmMWSc 92*
**Renner**, John Wilson 1924- *AmMWSc 92*
**Renner**, Karl 1870-1950 *EncTR 91*
**Renner**, Paul 1878-1956 *DcTwDes*
**Renner**, Robert George 1923- *WhoAmL 92*
**Renner**, Ruth 1925- *AmMWSc 92*
**Renner**, Terrence Alan 1947- *AmMWSc 92*
**Renner-Tana**, Patti *DrAPF 91*
**Rennerfeldt**, Earl R 1938- *WhoAmP 91*
**Rennert**, Charles Joseph 1962- *WhoAmL 92*
**Rennert**, Joseph 1919- *AmMWSc 92*
**Rennert**, Owen M 1938- *AmMWSc 92*
**Rennert**, Richard Scott 1956- *ConAu 135, SmATA 67*
**Rennert**, Wolfgang 1922- *IntWW 91*
**Rennhard**, Hans Heinrich 1928- *AmMWSc 92*
**Rennick**, Barbara Ruth 1919- *AmMWSc 92*
**Rennick**, Kyme Elizabeth Wall 1953- *WhoAmL 92*
**Rennie**, Alexander Allan 1917- *Who 92*
**Rennie**, Archibald Louden 1924- *Who 92*
**Rennie**, Basil Cameron 1920- *WrDr 92*
**Rennie**, Carol Ann 1939- *WhoIns 92*
**Rennie**, Donald Andrews 1922- *AmMWSc 92*
**Rennie**, Donald Wesley 1925- *AmMWSc 92*
**Rennie**, Edward Peter 1936- *WhoFI 92*
**Rennie**, James Clarence 1926- *AmMWSc 92*
**Rennie**, James Douglas Milne 1931- *Who 92*
**Rennie**, John Chalmers 1907- *Who 92*
**Rennie**, John Shaw 1917- *Who 92*
**Rennie**, John Vernon Lockhart 1903- *IntWW 91*
**Rennie**, Kevin F 1958- *WhoAmP 91*
**Rennie**, Paul Steven 1946- *AmMWSc 92*
**Rennie**, Richard George 1958- *WhoEnt 92*
**Rennie**, Robert Alvin 1917- *WhoFI 92*
**Rennie**, Robert John 1949- *AmMWSc 92*
**Rennie**, Thomas Howard 1943- *AmMWSc 92*
**Rennilson**, Justin J 1926- *AmMWSc 92*
**Reno**, Barbara Morrison 1946- *WhoAmP 91*
**Reno**, Clint *TwCWW 91*
**Reno**, Don 1927-1984 *NewAmDM*
**Reno**, Frederick Edmund 1939- *AmMWSc 92*
**Reno**, Harley W 1939- *AmMWSc 92*
**Reno**, Jack H. 1935- *WhoEnt 92*
**Reno**, James *WhoFI 92*
**Reno**, Mark *TwCWW 91*
**Reno**, Martin 1936- *WhoMW 92*
**Reno**, Martin A 1936- *AmMWSc 92*
**Reno**, Ottie Wayne 1929- *WhoAmL 92, WhoMW 92*
**Reno**, Robert Charles 1943- *AmMWSc 92*
**Reno**, Robert H 1917- *WhoIns 92*
**Reno**, Roger 1924- *WhoAmL 92*
**Reno**, Russell Ronald, Jr. 1933- *WhoAmL 92*
**Reno**, Stephen Jerome 1944- *WhoRel 92*
**Renoir family** *ThHEIm*
**Renoir**, Edmond 1849-1943? *ThHEIm [port]*
**Renoir**, Jean 1894-1979 *FacFETw [port], IntDcF 2-2 [port]*
**Renoir**, Pierre-Auguste 1841-1919 *ThHEIm [port]*
**Renoll**, Elmo Smith 1922- *AmMWSc 92*
**Renoll**, Mary Wilhelmine 1906- *AmMWSc 92*
**Renouf**, Francis 1918- *Who 92*
**Renovica**, Milanko 1928- *IntWW 91*
**Renowden**, Charles Raymond 1923- *Who 92*
**Renowden**, Glyndwr Rhys 1929- *Who 92*
**Renquist**, Thomas Arn 1947- *WhoRel 92*
**Renschler**, Clifford Lyle 1955- *AmMWSc 92*
**Rense**, William A 1914- *AmMWSc 92*
**Rensel**, Dennis James 1950- *WhoWest 92*
**Rensenbrink**, Don 1932- *WhoAmP 91*
**Renshaw**, Georgie Gordon 1927- *WhoRel 92*
**Renshaw**, Maurice 1912- *Who 92*
**Renshaw**, Samuel 1892-1981 *ConAu 133*
**Rensi**, Edward Henry 1944- *WhoFI 92*
**Rensin**, Hy d1991 *NewYTBS 91*
**Rensink**, Marvin Edward 1939- *AmMWSc 92*
**Rensink**, Wilmer 1933- *WhoAmP 91*
**Renson**, Jean Felix 1930- *WhoWest 92*
**Rensselaer** *BiInAmS*
**Renstrom**, Darrell George 1931- *WhoAmP 91*
**Rentchnick**, Pierre 1923- *IntWW 91*
**Renteln**, Theodor Adrian von 1897-1946 *EncTR 91 [port]*
**Renter**, Lois Irene Hutson 1929- *WhoMW 92*
**Renteria**, Deborah Maria 1952- *WhoHisp 92*
**Renteria**, Esther *WhoHisp 92*
**Renteria**, Hermelinda 1960- *WhoHisp 92*
**Renteria**, Jess L. 1943- *WhoHisp 92*
**Renteria**, Joe R. 1931- *WhoHisp 92*
**Renteria**, Joseph *WhoHisp 92*
**Renthal**, Robert David 1945- *AmMWSc 92*
**Rentie**, Frieda 1932- *WhoBlA 92*
**Rentmeester**, Kenneth R 1931- *AmMWSc 92*
**Rentmeester**, Kenneth Richard 1931- *WhoMW 92*
**Rentner**, James David 1940- *WhoFI 92*
**Renton** *Who 92*
**Renton**, Baron 1908- *Who 92*
**Renton**, Gordon Pearson 1928- *Who 92*
**Renton**, Helen Ferguson 1931- *Who 92*

**Renton**, John Johnston 1934- *AmMWSc 92*
**Renton**, Kenneth William 1944- *AmMWSc 92*
**Renton**, Ronald Timothy 1932- *Who 92*
**Renton**, Timothy 1932- *IntWW 91*
**Rentsch**, Joan Rae 1959- *WhoMW 92*
**Rentschler**, Alvin Eugene 1940- *WhoFI 92, WhoMW 92*
**Rentschler**, Frederick Brant 1939- *IntWW 91, WhoFI 92*
**Rentschler**, Jack G *WhoAmP 91*
**Rentschler**, James Malone 1933- *WhoAmP 91*
**Rentschler**, William Henry 1925- *WhoMW 92*
**Rentz**, David Charles 1942- *AmMWSc 92*
**Rentz**, Willie Derrell 1942- *WhoRel 92*
**Rentzel**, Delos Wilson d1991 *NewYTBS 91 [port]*
**Rentzepis**, Peter 1934- *IntWW 91*
**Rentzepis**, Peter M 1934- *AmMWSc 92*
**Renuart**, Adhemar William 1931- *AmMWSc 92*
**Renvall**, Johan *WhoEnt 92*
**Renwick** *Who 92*
**Renwick**, Baron 1935- *Who 92*
**Renwick**, Edward Sabine 1823-1912 *BiInAmS*
**Renwick**, Fred Blackwell 1930- *WrDr 92*
**Renwick**, J Alan A 1936- *AmMWSc 92*
**Renwick**, James, Sr 1792-1863 *BiInAmS*
**Renwick**, James Harrison 1926- *Who 92*
**Renwick**, Joyce *DrAPF 91*
**Renwick**, Lucille Christine 1965- *WhoBlA 92*
**Renwick**, Richard Eustace 1938- *Who 92*
**Renwick**, Robin 1937- *Who 92*
**Renwick**, Robin William 1937- *IntWW 91*
**Renz**, Jeffrey Thomas 1949- *WhoAmL 92*
**Renzema**, Theodore Samuel 1912- *AmMWSc 92*
**Renzetti**, Attilio D, Jr 1920- *AmMWSc 92*
**Renzetti**, Nicholas A 1914- *AmMWSc 92*
**Renzi**, Alfred Arthur 1925- *AmMWSc 92*
**Renzi**, Paul *WhoEnt 92*
**Renzy**, Bernard Thomas, III 1937- *WhoAmL 92*
**REO Speedwagon** *NewAmDM*
**Reott**, Raymond Thomas 1955- *WhoAmL 92*
**Repa**, Brian Stephen 1942- *AmMWSc 92*
**Repak**, Arthur Jack 1940- *AmMWSc 92*
**Repak**, Michael Joseph 1957- *WhoAmL 92*
**Repaske**, Roy 1925- *AmMWSc 92*
**Repasky**, Larry Joseph, Jr. 1955- *WhoEnt 92*
**Repeck**, Sally Anne 1956- *WhoMW 92*
**Repetti**, James Randolph 1953- *WhoAmL 92*
**Repicci**, Francis C 1944- *WhoAmP 91*
**Repine**, John E 1944- *AmMWSc 92*
**Repine**, Robert R 1948- *WhoAmP 91*
**Repka**, Benjamin C 1927- *AmMWSc 92*
**Repka**, Joan Ann 1948- *WhoRel 92*
**Repko**, Wayne William 1940- *AmMWSc 92*
**Replacements**, The *ConMus 7 [port]*
**Replansky**, Naomi *DrAPF 91*
**Replansky**, Naomi 1918- *IntAu&W 91*
**Replin**, Stephen David 1947- *WhoFI 92*
**Replogle**, Clyde R 1935- *AmMWSc 92*
**Replogle**, David Robert 1931- *WhoFI 92*
**Replogle**, John A 1934- *AmMWSc 92*
**Replogle**, John Asher 1937- *WhoWest 92*
**Replogle**, Lanny Lee 1934- *AmMWSc 92*
**Replogle**, Robert Lee 1931- *AmMWSc 92*
**Repoli**, Michael Gerald 1948- *WhoIns 92*
**Reporter**, Minocher C 1928- *AmMWSc 92*
**Reporter**, Shapoor 1921- *Who 92*
**Repp**, Ed Earl 1900-1979 *TwCWW 91*
**Repp**, Glenn, IV 1931- *WhoAmP 91*
**Repp**, John *DrAPF 91*
**Repp**, Richard Cooper 1936- *Who 92*
**Reppa**, Jerome J 1925- *WhoAmP 91*
**Repper**, Charles John 1934- *AmMWSc 92*
**Repper**, George Robert 1954- *WhoAmL 92*
**Repperger**, Daniel William 1942- *AmMWSc 92*
**Reppert**, Steve Marion 1946- *AmMWSc 92*
**Repplier**, Agnes 1855-1950 *BenetAL 91*
**Reppond**, Kermit Dale 1945- *AmMWSc 92*
**Reppucci**, Nicholas Dickon 1941- *AmMWSc 92*
**Reppy**, John David 1931- *AmMWSc 92*
**Reps**, David Nathan 1926- *WhoFI 92*
**Reps**, John W. 1921- *WrDr 92*
**Repsher**, Lawrence Harvey 1939- *WhoWest 92*
**Repton**, Bishop Suffragan of 1936- *Who 92*
**Requa**, Joseph Earl 1938- *AmMWSc 92*
**Requarth**, William H 1913- *AmMWSc 92*
**Requat**, R Earl 1938- *WhoAmP 91*
**Reque**, Paul Gerhard 1907- *AmMWSc 92*
**Requicha**, Aristides A G 1939- *AmMWSc 92, WhoWest 92*
**Rerick**, Mark Newton 1934- *AmMWSc 92*
**Rericka**, Catherine E. 1963- *WhoFI 92*
**Resch**, George Michael 1940- *AmMWSc 92*
**Resch**, Helmuth 1933- *AmMWSc 92*
**Resch**, Joseph Anthony 1914- *AmMWSc 92*
**Resch**, Tracy William 1949- *WhoAmL 92*
**Rescher**, Nicholas 1928- *AmMWSc 92*
**Rescia**, Richard R. 1930- *WhoEnt 92*
**Rescigno**, Aldo 1924- *AmMWSc 92*
**Rescigno**, Thomas Nicola 1947- *AmMWSc 92*
**Resconich**, Emil Carl 1923- *AmMWSc 92*
**Resconich**, Samuel 1933- *AmMWSc 92*
**Rescorla**, Robert A 1940- *AmMWSc 92*
**Resek**, Robert William 1935- *WhoMW 92*
**Resen**, W. Patrick 1946- *WhoWest 92*
**Resendez**, Arnoldo Horacio 1953- *WhoHisp 92*
**Resendez**, Ruben Antonio 1967- *WhoHisp 92*
**Resh**, James *WhoRel 92*
**Reshetilov**, Vladimir Ivanovich 1937- *IntWW 91*
**Reshetnev**, Mikhail Fedorovich 1924- *IntWW 91*
**Reshetnikov**, Fedor Grigorevich 1919- *IntWW 91*
**Reshetnikov**, Fedor Pavlovich 1906- *SovUnBD*
**Reshkin**, Mark 1933- *AmMWSc 92*
**Reshotko**, Eli 1930- *AmMWSc 92*
**Reshtia**, Sayed Qassem 1913- *IntWW 91*
**Resig**, Janice Anne 1950- *WhoMW 92*
**Resing**, Henry Anton 1933- *AmMWSc 92*
**Reskey**, Patricia Anne 1952- *WhoFI 92*
**Reskin**, Charles Max 1944- *WhoMW 92*
**Reskind**, John *ConAu 35NR*
**Resko**, John A 1932- *AmMWSc 92*
**Resler**, E L, Jr 1925- *AmMWSc 92*
**Resler**, Roger A. 1964- *WhoRel 92*
**Resmer**, Mark Anthony 1954- *WhoWest 92*
**Resmini**, Ronald Joseph 1942- *WhoAmL 92*
**Resnais**, Alain 1922- *FacFETw, IntDcF 2-2 [port], IntMPA 92, IntWW 91, Who 92*
**Resnekov**, Leon 1928- *AmMWSc 92, WhoMW 92*
**Resnick**, Alice Robie 1939- *WhoAmL 92, WhoAmP 91, WhoMW 92*
**Resnick**, Charles A 1939- *AmMWSc 92*
**Resnick**, Cindy L 1949- *WhoAmP 91*
**Resnick**, David Bruce 1954- *WhoFI 92*
**Resnick**, Evan Scott 1954- *WhoEnt 92*
**Resnick**, Jack d1991 *NewYTBS 91 [port]*
**Resnick**, Joel B 1935- *AmMWSc 92*
**Resnick**, Joel H. *IntMPA 92*
**Resnick**, Kenneth 1934- *WhoEnt 92*
**Resnick**, Lazer 1938- *AmMWSc 92*
**Resnick**, Martin I 1943- *AmMWSc 92, WhoMW 92*
**Resnick**, Mike 1942- *TwCSFW 91, WrDr 92*
**Resnick**, Oscar 1924- *AmMWSc 92*
**Resnick**, Patricia 1953- *ConAu 135*
**Resnick**, Paul R 1934- *AmMWSc 92*
**Resnick**, Phillip Stanley 1944- *WhoAmL 92*
**Resnick**, Robert 1923- *AmMWSc 92*
**Resnick**, Sidney I 1945- *AmMWSc 92*
**Resnick**, Sol Donald 1918- *AmMWSc 92, WhoWest 92*
**Resnick**, Stephanie 1959- *WhoAmL 92*
**Resnick**, Stewart Allen 1936- *WhoWest 92*
**Resnicoff**, Ethel 1947- *WhoEnt 92*
**Resnicow**, Herbert 1921- *WrDr 92*
**Resnicow**, Norman Jakob 1947- *WhoAmL 92*
**Resnik**, David Alan 1956- *WhoFI 92*
**Resnik**, Frank Edward 1928- *AmMWSc 92, WhoFI 92*
**Resnik**, Harvey Lewis Paul 1930- *AmMWSc 92*
**Resnik**, Judith 1949-1986 *FacFETw*
**Resnik**, Regina 1922- *NewAmDM*
**Resnik**, Regina 1924- *IntWW 91, WhoEnt 92A*
**Resnik**, Robert Alan 1924- *AmMWSc 92*
**Resnik**, Robert Kenneth 1936- *AmMWSc 92*
**Resnikoff**, George Joseph 1915- *AmMWSc 92*
**Resnikoff**, Howard L 1937- *AmMWSc 92*
**Resnikova**, Eva 1951- *WhoEnt 92*
**Reso**, Anthony 1931- *AmMWSc 92*
**Reso**, Anthony 1934- *WhoFI 92*
**Reso**, Sidney Joseph 1935- *Who 92, WhoFI 92*
**Resor**, Pamela P 1942- *WhoAmP 91*
**Respess**, James Walter 1926- *WhoAmL 92*
**Respighi**, Ottorino 1879-1936 *FacFETw, NewAmDM*
**Ress**, Charles William 1933- *WhoMW 92*
**Ress**, Lisa *DrAPF 91*
**Ress**, Rudyard Joseph 1950- *AmMWSc 92*
**Ress**, William J 1940- *WhoAmP 91*
**Resseguie**, James Lynn 1945- *WhoRel 92*
**Ressler**, Charlotte 1924- *AmMWSc 92*
**Ressler**, Neil William 1939- *AmMWSc 92*
**Ressler**, Newton 1923- *AmMWSc 92*
**Rest**, Ann H 1942- *WhoAmP 91*
**Rest**, David 1917- *AmMWSc 92*
**Rest**, Friedrich Otto 1913- *WhoRel 92*
**Rest**, Richard Franklin *AmMWSc 92*
**Restaino**, Alfred Joseph 1931- *AmMWSc 92*
**Restaino**, Frederick A 1934- *AmMWSc 92*
**Restak**, Richard M. 1942- *WrDr 92*
**Restak**, Richard Martin 1942- *IntAu&W 91*
**Restani**, Jane A. 1948- *WhoAmL 92*
**Restemeyer**, William Edward 1916- *AmMWSc 92*
**Rester**, Alfred Carl, Jr 1940- *AmMWSc 92*
**Rester**, David Hampton 1934- *AmMWSc 92*
**Rester**, George G. 1923- *WhoEnt 92, WhoWest 92*
**Restieaux**, Cyril Edward 1910- *Who 92*
**Restino**, Janet *DrAPF 91*
**Restivo**, James John, Jr. 1946- *WhoAmL 92*
**Restivo**, Raymond M. 1934- *WhoFI 92*
**Restle**, Frank 1927-1982? *ConAu 133*
**Resto**, Jose 1921- *WhoHisp 92*
**Reston**, James 1909- *IntAu&W 91, IntWW 91, WrDr 92*
**Restorff**, James Brian 1949- *AmMWSc 92*
**Restrepo**, Carlos Armando 1950- *WhoHisp 92*
**Restrepo**, George Anthony, Jr. 1933- *WhoHisp 92*
**Restrepo**, Jose Manuel 1781-1863 *HisDSpE*
**Restrepo**, Richard J. 1923- *WhoHisp 92*
**Restrepo**, Rodrigo Alvaro 1930- *AmMWSc 92*
**Restrepo-Londono**, Andres 1942- *Who 92*
**Reswick**, James Bigelow 1922- *AmMWSc 92, IntWW 91*
**Retallack**, Gregory John 1951- *AmMWSc 92, WhoWest 92*
**Retallack**, Joan *DrAPF 91*
**Retallick**, William Bennett 1925- *AmMWSc 92*
**Retamoza**, Rudy A. 1941- *WhoHisp 92*
**Retchless**, Mary Hellon 1934- *WhoAmP 91*
**Retcofsky**, Herbert L 1935- *AmMWSc 92*
**Retelle**, John Powers, Jr 1946- *AmMWSc 92*
**Reth**, Theresa Annette 1955- *WhoAmL 92*
**Rethberg**, Elisabeth 1894-1976 *NewAmDM*
**Retherford**, Charles V. 1927- *WhoAmL 92*
**Retherford**, James Ronald 1937- *AmMWSc 92*
**Rethore**, Bernard Gabriel 1941- *WhoFI 92, WhoWest 92*
**Rethwisch**, David Gerard 1959- *AmMWSc 92, WhoMW 92*
**Reti**, Ingrid *DrAPF 91*
**Retief**, Daniel Hugo 1922- *AmMWSc 92*
**Retif**, Thomas Newton 1942- *WhoEnt 92*
**Retif de la Bretonne**, Nicolas-Edme 1734-1806 *BlkwCEP*
**Retnakaran**, Arthur 1934- *AmMWSc 92*
**Retore**, Guy 1924- *IntWW 91*
**Retsema**, James Allan 1942- *AmMWSc 92*
**Rettaliata**, Antonia P 1944- *WhoAmP 91*
**Rettaliata**, John B. d1991 *NewYTBS 91*
**Rettaliata**, John Theodore 1911- *AmMWSc 92*
**Rettedal**, Arne 1926- *IntWW 91*
**Rettel**, Jean 1925- *IntWW 91*
**Rettenmeyer**, Carl William 1931- *AmMWSc 92*
**Rettenmier**, Carl Wayne 1952- *AmMWSc 92*
**Retter**, James Robert 1925- *WhoFI 92*
**Retter**, Steven Lyle 1952- *WhoMW 92*
**Rettie**, Philip 1926- *Who 92*
**Rettig**, Frannie M. 1947- *WhoBlA 92*
**Rettig**, James Melvin 1943- *WhoAmL 92*
**Rettig**, Michael Franklin 1962- *WhoAmL 92*
**Rettig**, Tom 1941- *IntMPA 92*
**Rettori**, Ovidio 1934- *AmMWSc 92*
**Rettura**, Joseph 1953- *WhoEnt 92*
**Retz**, Madame de *EncAmaz 91*
**Retz**, Konrad Charles 1952- *AmMWSc 92*
**Retzer**, Elmer 1931- *WhoAmP 91*
**Retzer**, Jeanine 1938- *WhoRel 92*
**Retzer**, Kenneth Albert 1933- *AmMWSc 92*
**Retzer**, Mary Jane 1931- *WhoRel 92*
**Retzer**, Michael L *WhoAmP 91*
**Retzlaff**, Ernest 1918- *AmMWSc 92*
**Retzloff**, David George 1939- *AmMWSc 92*
**Reu**, Johann Michael 1869-1943 *RelLAm 91*
**Reuben**, Carola C. *WhoHisp 92*
**Reuben**, David 1933- *WrDr 92*
**Reuben**, Don Harold 1928- *WhoAmL 92, WhoMW 92*
**Reuben**, Jacob 1910- *WhoAmL 92*
**Reuben**, Jacques 1936- *AmMWSc 92*
**Reuben**, John Philip 1930- *AmMWSc 92*
**Reuben**, Lawrence Mark 1948- *WhoAmL 92*
**Reuben**, Lucy Jeanette 1949- *WhoBlA 92, WhoFI 92*
**Reuben**, Richard N 1920- *AmMWSc 92*
**Reuben**, Roberta C 1936- *AmMWSc 92*
**Reuben**, Susan Lynn 1948- *WhoFI 92*
**Reubens**, Paul *ConTFT 9*
**Reuber**, Grant Louis 1927- *IntWW 91, WrDr 92*
**Reuber**, Melvin D 1930- *AmMWSc 92*
**Reubke**, Julius 1834-1858 *NewAmDM*
**Reucroft**, Philip J 1935- *AmMWSc 92*
**Reucroft**, Stephen 1943- *AmMWSc 92*
**Reudink**, Douglas O 1939- *AmMWSc 92*
**Reukauf**, Robert Barnes 1953- *WhoAmP 91*
**Reuland**, Donald John 1937- *AmMWSc 92*
**Reuland**, Raymond *WhoAmP 91*
**Reuland**, Robert John 1935- *AmMWSc 92*
**Reum**, James Michael 1946- *WhoAmL 92*
**Reum**, W. Robert 1942- *WhoFI 92*
**Reuning**, Richard Henry 1941- *AmMWSc 92*
**Reupke**, Michael 1936- *Who 92*
**Reupke**, William Albert 1940- *AmMWSc 92*
**Reusch**, Donald Carl 1956- *WhoRel 92*
**Reusch**, William Henry 1931- *AmMWSc 92*
**Reuschlein**, Earl Vincent 1921- *WhoMW 92*
**Reuse**, Ronald 1946- *WhoFI 92, WhoMW 92*
**Reuss**, Carl Frederick 1915- *WhoRel 92*
**Reuss**, Henry S 1912- *WhoAmP 91*
**Reuss**, Priscilla A. 1946- *WhoFI 92*
**Reuss**, Robert L 1942- *AmMWSc 92*
**Reuss**, Ronald Merl 1933- *AmMWSc 92*
**Reuss von Plauen**, Heinrich XXVI 1942- *WhoRel 92*
**Reusser**, Fritz 1928- *AmMWSc 92*
**Reussner**, George Henry 1918- *AmMWSc 92*
**Reuszer**, Herbert William 1903- *AmMWSc 92*
**Reut**, Anatoliy Antonovich 1928- *IntWW 91*
**Reuter**, Bjarne 1950- *SmATA 68 [port]*
**Reuter**, Edzard 1928- *IntWW 91, Who 92*
**Reuter**, Gerald Louis 1934- *AmMWSc 92*
**Reuter**, Gerd Edzard Harry 1921- *Who 92*
**Reuter**, Harald 1934- *AmMWSc 92*
**Reuter**, Jeanette Miller 1921- *WhoMW 92*
**Reuter**, Paul d1990 *IntWW 91N*
**Reuter**, Robert A 1928- *AmMWSc 92*
**Reuter**, Robert Carl, Jr 1939- *AmMWSc 92*
**Reuter**, Rocky James 1956- *WhoMW 92*
**Reuter**, Rolf Friedrich 1926- *WhoEnt 92*
**Reuter**, Stewart R 1934- *AmMWSc 92*
**Reuter**, Wilhad 1930- *AmMWSc 92*
**Reuter**, William L 1934- *AmMWSc 92*
**Reutersward**, Carl Fredrik 1934- *IntWW 91*
**Reuther**, David Louis 1946- *IntAu&W 91*
**Reuther**, Terry Lee 1944- *WhoAmP 91*
**Reuther**, Theodore Carl, Jr 1933- *AmMWSc 92*
**Reuther**, Walter 1907-1970 *FacFETw*
**Reuther**, Walter 1911- *AmMWSc 92, WhoWest 92*
**Reutiman**, Robert William, Jr. 1944- *WhoAmL 92*
**Reutlinger**, Barbara *WhoEnt 92*
**Reutov**, Olyeg Aleksandrovich 1920- *IntWW 91*
**Reutter**, Hermann 1900-1985 *NewAmDM*
**Reutzel**, Barry Lane 1951- *WhoAmP 91*
**Reuwee**, Alvin Daniel 1943- *WhoMW 92*
**Reuwer**, Joseph Francis, Jr 1931- *AmMWSc 92*
**Revans**, Reginald William 1907- *Who 92*
**Revard**, Stella Hill Purce 1933- *WhoMW 92*
**Revay**, Andrew W, Jr 1933- *AmMWSc 92*
**Reveal**, Ernest Ira, III 1948- *WhoAmL 92*
**Reveal**, James L 1941- *AmMWSc 92*
**Revel**, Bernard 1885-1940 *DcAmImH, RelLAm 91*
**Revel**, Gary Neal 1949- *WhoEnt 92, WhoFI 92*
**Revel**, Harry 1905-1958 *NewAmDM*
**Revel**, Jean-Francois 1924- *IntWW 91*
**Revel**, Jean Paul 1930- *AmMWSc 92*
**Revel**, Ricky Joe 1956- *WhoEnt 92*
**Revelante**, Noelia 1942- *AmMWSc 92*
**Reveles**, Robert A. 1932- *WhoHisp 92*
**Reveley**, Edith 1930- *WrDr 92*
**Revell**, Anthony Leslie 1935- *Who 92*
**Revell**, Donald *DrAPF 91*
**Revell**, Dorothy Evangeline Tompkins 1911- *WhoMW 92*
**Revell**, Fleming Hewitt, Jr. 1849-1931 *RelLAm 91*
**Revell**, James D 1929- *AmMWSc 92*
**Revell**, John Harold 1906- *WhoWest 92*

**Revell**, John Robert Stephen 1920- WrDr 92
**Revell**, Patsy Roberts 1928- WhoAmP 91
**ReVelle**, Charles S 1938- AmMWSc 92
**Revelle**, Randy 1941- WhoAmP 91
**Revelle**, Robert, Sr. 1947- WhoBlA 92
**Revelle**, Roger 1909- AmMWSc 92, IntWW 91
**Revelle**, Roger 1909-1991 CurBio 91N, NewYTBS 91 [port]
**Revelli**, Clare 1952- WhoEnt 92
**Revelos**, Constantine Nicholas 1938- WhoMW 92
**Revels**, Hiram Rhoades 1822-1901 AmPolLe [port], RelLAm 91
**Revelstoke**, Baron 1911- Who 92
**Revely**, William 1941- WhoBlA 92, WhoRel 92
**Revenaugh**, Justin Scott 1962- WhoWest 92
**Revenko**, Grigoriy Ivanovich 1936- IntWW 91, SovUnBD
**Revens**, John Cosgrove, Jr 1947- WhoAmP 91
**Reventlow**, Christian Ditlev 1748-1827 BlkwCEP
**Reventlow**, Ernst, Count von 1869-1943 EncTR 91
**Reventlow**, Ernst Christian E, Graf zu 1869-1943 BiDExR
**Reverand**, Cedric Dwight, II 1941- WhoWest 92
**Revercomb**, George Hughes 1929- WhoAmL 92
**Revercomb**, Horace Austin, III 1948- WhoAmL 92
**Reverdin**, Olivier 1913- IntWW 91, Who 92
**Reverdy**, Michele 1943- ConCom 92
**Reverdy**, Pierre 1889-1960 FacFETw, GuFrLit 1
**Revere**, Anne 1903-1990 AnObit 1990
**Revere**, Paul 1735-1818 BenetAL 91, BlkwEAR, RComAH
**Revesz**, Akos George 1927- AmMWSc 92
**Revesz**, Bruce Julius 1938- WhoEnt 92
**Revesz**, George 1923- AmMWSc 92
**Revesz**, Marie B. 1952- WhoRel 92
**Revesz**, Zsolt 1950- AmMWSc 92
**Revett**, Nicholas 1720-1804 BlkwCEP
**Revetta**, Frank Alexander 1928- AmMWSc 92
**Revill**, Clive 1930- IntMPA 92
**Revilla**, Carmen WhoHisp 92
**Revilla Beltran**, Vincenne Maria 1952- WhoHisp 92
**Revillagigedo**, Conde de 1740-1799 HisDSpE
**Revillard**, Jean-Pierre Remy 1938- AmMWSc 92
**Revis**, Nathaniel W. 1939- WhoBlA 92
**Revoile**, Sally Gates AmMWSc 92
**Revollo Bravo**, Mario 1919- IntWW 91, WhoRel 92
**Revolta**, Johnny d1991 NewYTBS 91
**Revson**, James d1991 NewYTBS 91
**Revuelta**, Pedro DrAPF 91
**Revueltas**, Jose 1914-1976 FacFETw
**Revueltas**, Silvestre 1899-1940 NewAmDM
**Revzen**, Joel WhoEnt 92
**Revzin**, Alvin Morton 1926- AmMWSc 92
**Revzin**, Arnold 1943- AmMWSc 92
**Rew**, William Edmund 1923- WhoFI 92
**Rewald**, John 1912- WrDr 92
**Rewbotham**, Fraser Dickson 1941- WhoFI 92
**Rewcastle**, Neill Barry 1931- AmMWSc 92
**Rewoldt**, Gregory 1948- AmMWSc 92
**Rex**, Christopher Davis 1951- WhoEnt 92
**Rex**, Frances Lillian 1911- WhoAmP 91
**Rex**, George Abraham 1845-1895 BiInAmS
**Rex**, John Arderne 1925- Who 92, WrDr 92
**Rex**, Lonnie Royce 1928- WhoRel 92
**Rex**, Robert 1909- Who 92
**Rex**, Robert Walter AmMWSc 92
**Rexach Benitez**, Roberto 1929- WhoAmP 91, WhoHisp 92
**Rexed**, Bror A. 1914- IntWW 91
**Rexer**, Joachim 1928- AmMWSc 92
**Rexford**, Dean R 1915- AmMWSc 92
**Rexford**, Eben E. 1848-1916 BenetAL 91
**Rexing**, David Joseph 1950- WhoWest 92
**Rexroad**, Caird Eugene, Jr 1947- AmMWSc 92
**Rexroad**, Carl Buckner 1925- AmMWSc 92
**Rexroth**, Kenneth 1905-1982 BenetAL 91, ConAu 34NR, FacFETw
**Rey**, Alberto Enrique 1960- WhoHisp 92
**Rey**, Anthony M. d1991 NewYTBS 91 [port]
**Rey**, Antonio B. 1940- WhoHisp 92
**Rey**, Bret TwCWW 91, WrDr 92
**Rey**, Carlos Raul 1959- WhoFI 92
**Rey**, Charles Albert 1934- AmMWSc 92
**Rey**, Daniel WhoHisp 92
**Rey**, Fernando 1912- IntWW 91
**Rey**, Fernando 1917- IntMPA 92
**Rey**, Frank, Jr. 1932- WhoHisp 92
**Rey**, Jesus WhoHisp 92
**Rey**, John A. 1942- WhoHisp 92
**Rey**, Juan Carlos 1957- WhoWest 92
**Rey**, Margret 1906- WrDr 92
**Rey**, Margret E 1906- IntAu&W 91
**Rey**, William K 1925- AmMWSc 92
**Rey-Tejerina**, Arsenio 1938- WhoHisp 92
**Reycraft**, George Dewey 1924- WhoAmL 92
**Reyer**, Randall William 1917- AmMWSc 92
**Reyero**, Cristina 1949- AmMWSc 92
**Reyes**, Adriel 1970- WhoRel 92
**Reyes**, Albert L. 1958- WhoHisp 92
**Reyes**, Alfonso 1889-1959 BenetAL 91, FacFETw
**Reyes**, Andre WhoEnt 92
**Reyes**, Andres Arenas 1931- AmMWSc 92
**Reyes**, Andres Jesus 1943- WhoRel 92
**Reyes**, Antonio 1939- WhoHisp 92
**Reyes**, Aurora C. 1938- WhoHisp 92
**Reyes**, Ben WhoHisp 92
**Reyes**, Ben T WhoAmP 91
**Reyes**, Benjamin 1952- WhoHisp 92
**Reyes**, Benjamin Cerdon 1930- WhoEnt 92
**Reyes**, Carlos DrAPF 91
**Reyes**, Carlos 1935- IntAu&W 91
**Reyes**, Cecille Lizzette 1962- WhoHisp 92
**Reyes**, Christopher Michael 1956- WhoWest 92
**Reyes**, Cynthia Paula 1960- WhoHisp 92
**Reyes**, David Alfred 1951- WhoWest 92
**Reyes**, David Edward 1947- WhoHisp 92
**Reyes**, Delia WhoHisp 92
**Reyes**, Eduardo 1965- WhoHisp 92
**Reyes**, Edward 1944- WhoHisp 92
**Reyes**, Emilio Alejandro 1959- WhoHisp 92
**Reyes**, Eugene Fernando, III 1942- WhoHisp 92
**Reyes**, Frank WhoHisp 92
**Reyes**, Frank Rodriguez 1934- WhoHisp 92
**Reyes**, Guillermo Agusto 1963- WhoHisp 92
**Reyes**, Harold E. 1954- WhoHisp 92
**Reyes**, Henry G 1929- WhoAmP 91
**Reyes**, Janie 1940- WhoAmP 91
**Reyes**, Jesse G. 1952- WhoHisp 92
**Reyes**, Jorge A. 1949- WhoHisp 92
**Reyes**, Jose Antonio 1940- WhoRel 92
**Reyes**, Jose Israel 1941- WhoHisp 92
**Reyes**, Jose N., Jr. 1955- WhoHisp 92
**Reyes**, Juan Sablan WhoAmP 91
**Reyes**, Leopoldo Guadalupe 1940- WhoHisp 92
**Reyes**, Lico 1946- WhoHisp 92
**Reyes**, Lillian Jenny 1955- WhoAmL 92
**Reyes**, Lonnie C. 1942- WhoRel 92
**Reyes**, Luis WhoHisp 92
**Reyes**, Manuel, Jr. 1929- WhoHisp 92
**Reyes**, Manuel A. WhoHisp 92
**Reyes**, Marco Antonio 1955- WhoHisp 92
**Reyes**, Narciso G. 1914- IntWW 91, Who 92
**Reyes**, Oscar J. 1936- WhoHisp 92
**Reyes**, Philip 1936- AmMWSc 92
**Reyes**, Raymond T. WhoHisp 92
**Reyes**, Richard Ellis 1951- WhoHisp 92
**Reyes**, Richard R. 1954- WhoHisp 92
**Reyes**, Robert WhoHisp 92
**Reyes**, Rodrigo Berenguer De Los 1924- WhoIns 92
**Reyes**, Rogelio 1931- WhoHisp 92
**Reyes**, Sarah Lorraine 1961- WhoHisp 92
**Reyes**, Tony 1942- WhoHisp 92
**Reyes**, Victor E 1959- AmMWSc 92
**Reyes**, Victor Ioannis 1959- WhoAmL 92
**Reyes**, Victor M. F. 1931- WhoHisp 92
**Reyes**, Vinicio H. 1934- WhoHisp 92
**Reyes**, Zoila 1920- AmMWSc 92
**Reyes-Baez**, Gloria E. 1946- WhoHisp 92
**Reyes de Ruiz**, Neris B. WhoHisp 92
**Reyes-Guerra**, Antonio, Jr. 1919- WhoHisp 92
**Reyes-Guerra**, David Richard 1933- WhoHisp 92
**Reyes-Kopack**, Laura WhoHisp 92
**Reyhner**, Theodore Alison 1940- AmMWSc 92
**Reyhner**, Theodore O 1915- AmMWSc 92
**Reyles**, Carlos 1868-1938 BenetAL 91
**Reyman**, Pamela Carolyn 1959- WhoEnt 92
**Reymond**, Patricia Ann 1935- WhoMW 92
**Reymont**, Wladyslaw 1868-1924 FacFETw
**Reymont**, Wladyslaw Stanislaw 1867-1925 WhoNob 90
**Reyna**, Carlos Fernando 1942- WhoHisp 92
**Reyna**, Felipe 1945- WhoHisp 92
**Reyna**, Jimmie Valdenebro 1952- WhoAmL 92
**Reyna**, Jose R. 1941- WhoHisp 92
**Reyna**, Luis Guillermo 1956- AmMWSc 92
**Reyna**, R. Michael 1964- WhoHisp 92
**Reyna**, Ralph WhoHisp 92
**Reyna**, Valerie F. 1955- WhoHisp 92
**Reyna**, Valerie Frances 1955- WhoWest 92
**Reynafarje**, Baltazar AmMWSc 92
**Reynaga**, Jesse Richard 1951- WhoHisp 92
**Reynal**, Thomas Douglas 1957- WhoFI 92
**Reynales**, Barbara Wallace 1927- WhoWest 92
**Reynales**, Carlos H. 1922- WhoWest 92
**Reynard**, Alan Mark 1932- AmMWSc 92
**Reynard**, Kennard Anthony 1939- AmMWSc 92
**Reynard**, Muriel Joyce 1945- WhoAmL 92
**Reynardus**, Jorge E. 1944- WhoHisp 92
**Reynaud**, Paul 1878-1966 EncTR 91 [port], FacFETw
**Reynen**, Debra Marie 1964- WhoMW 92
**Reyner**, William Stanley, Jr. 1945- WhoAmL 92
**Reynes**, Stephen Alan 1946- WhoAmP 91
**Reynhout**, James Kenneth 1942- AmMWSc 92
**Reynik**, Robert John 1932- AmMWSc 92
**Reynold**, Frederic 1936- Who 92
**Reynolds**, A.H. DrAPF 91
**Reynolds**, A. William 1933- WhoFI 92, WhoMW 92
**Reynolds**, Alan 1926- TwCPaSc, Who 92
**Reynolds**, Alan Anthony 1942- WhoFI 92
**Reynolds**, Albert 1932- Who 92
**Reynolds**, Albert 1935- IntWW 91
**Reynolds**, Albert Keith 1914- AmMWSc 92
**Reynolds**, Alva-Inez 1933- WhoFI 92
**Reynolds**, Andrew Buchanan 1939- WhoBlA 92
**Reynolds**, Anna 1936- IntWW 91
**Reynolds**, Arthur Graham 1914- Who 92
**Reynolds**, Audrey Lucile WhoBlA 92
**Reynolds**, Barbara 1914- Who 92
**Reynolds**, Barbara A. WhoBlA 92
**Reynolds**, Barrie 1932- WrDr 92
**Reynolds**, Bernard Robert 1915- TwCPaSc
**Reynolds**, Bradford Charles 1948- WhoFI 92
**Reynolds**, Brian Edgar 1936- AmMWSc 92
**Reynolds**, Bruce C 1948- WhoAmP 91
**Reynolds**, Bruce G 1937- AmMWSc 92
**Reynolds**, Bruce Howard 1935- WhoBlA 92
**Reynolds**, Burt 1936- IntMPA 92, IntWW 91, WhoEnt 92
**Reynolds**, C Leslie 1858?-1913 BiInAmS
**Reynolds**, Catherine Cox 1928- WhoAmP 91
**Reynolds**, Charles WhoAmP 91
**Reynolds**, Charles Albert 1923- AmMWSc 92
**Reynolds**, Charles C 1927- AmMWSc 92
**Reynolds**, Charles F 1947- AmMWSc 92
**Reynolds**, Charles McKinley, Jr. 1937- WhoBlA 92
**Reynolds**, Charles Patrick 1952- WhoWest 92
**Reynolds**, Charles William 1917- AmMWSc 92
**Reynolds**, Christina Leah Collier 1957- WhoMW 92
**Reynolds**, Christopher John 1947- WhoAmL 92
**Reynolds**, Clark Winton 1934- WhoFI 92
**Reynolds**, Clarke WhoEnt 92
**Reynolds**, Claude Lewis, Jr 1948- AmMWSc 92
**Reynolds**, Clay DrAPF 91
**Reynolds**, Clay 1949- TwCWW 91
**Reynolds**, Daniel Steven WhoAmL 92
**Reynolds**, David B 1949- AmMWSc 92
**Reynolds**, David George 1933- AmMWSc 92
**Reynolds**, David James 1924- Who 92
**Reynolds**, David Parham 1915- IntWW 91, WhoFI 92
**Reynolds**, David Robert WhoIns 92
**Reynolds**, David Stephen 1932- AmMWSc 92
**Reynolds**, Debbie 1932- IntMPA 92
**Reynolds**, Dennis William 1946- WhoMW 92
**Reynolds**, Dick WhoAmP 91
**Reynolds**, Don Rupert 1938- AmMWSc 92
**Reynolds**, Don William 1926- WhoFI 92
**Reynolds**, Donald C 1920- AmMWSc 92
**Reynolds**, Donald Dean 1921- WhoWest 92
**Reynolds**, Donald Kelly 1919- AmMWSc 92
**Reynolds**, Dorothy L 1928- WhoAmP 91
**Reynolds**, Edward 1942- WhoBlA 92
**Reynolds**, Edwin 1831-1909 BiInAmS
**Reynolds**, Elbert Brunner, Jr 1924- AmMWSc 92
**Reynolds**, Elmer Robert 1846-1907 BiInAmS
**Reynolds**, Eric Vincent 1904- Who 92
**Reynolds**, Eva Mary Barbara Who 92
**Reynolds**, Francis E. DrAPF 91
**Reynolds**, Francis Martin Baillie 1932- Who 92
**Reynolds**, Frank d1983 LesBEnT 92
**Reynolds**, Frank 1876-1953 TwCPaSc
**Reynolds**, Frank Arrowsmith 1916- Who 92
**Reynolds**, Frank Everett 1930- WhoRel 92
**Reynolds**, Frank Miller 1921- WhoRel 92
**Reynolds**, Gary W. 1948- WhoRel 92
**Reynolds**, Gary Wayne 1957- WhoEnt 92
**Reynolds**, Gene LesBEnT 92
**Reynolds**, Gene 1925- WhoEnt 92
**Reynolds**, George Lazenby, Jr. 1927- WhoRel 92
**Reynolds**, George Thomas 1917- AmMWSc 92
**Reynolds**, George Warren 1916- AmMWSc 92
**Reynolds**, George William, Jr 1928- AmMWSc 92
**Reynolds**, Gerald Alfred John 1942- WhoEnt 92
**Reynolds**, Gillian 1935- Who 92
**Reynolds**, Glenn Harlan 1960- WhoAmL 92
**Reynolds**, Glenn Myron 1936- AmMWSc 92
**Reynolds**, Graham Who 92
**Reynolds**, Graham 1914- IntAu&W 91, WrDr 92
**Reynolds**, Grant 1908- WhoBlA 92
**Reynolds**, Guy Edwin K. Who 92
**Reynolds**, Harold Truman 1918- AmMWSc 92
**Reynolds**, Harry 1964- BlkOlyM
**Reynolds**, Harry Aaron, Jr 1928- AmMWSc 92
**Reynolds**, Harry G. 1915- WhoBlA 92
**Reynolds**, Harry Lincoln 1925- AmMWSc 92
**Reynolds**, Harry Weatherly, Jr. 1946- WhoFI 92
**Reynolds**, Helen Elizabeth 1925- WhoFI 92
**Reynolds**, Herbert McGaughey 1942- AmMWSc 92
**Reynolds**, Howard ScFEYrs
**Reynolds**, Ida Manning 1946- WhoBlA 92
**Reynolds**, Jack 1929- AmMWSc 92
**Reynolds**, Jack Raymond 1916- Who 92
**Reynolds**, Jack W. 1923- WhoFI 92, WhoMW 92
**Reynolds**, Jacqueline Ann 1930- AmMWSc 92
**Reynolds**, James 1908- Who 92
**Reynolds**, James Blair 1939- AmMWSc 92
**Reynolds**, James F. 1914- WhoBlA 92
**Reynolds**, James Harold 1945- AmMWSc 92
**Reynolds**, James Van 1946- WhoBlA 92, WhoEnt 92
**Reynolds**, Jason Matthew 1948- WhoWest 92
**Reynolds**, Jefferson Wayne 1926- AmMWSc 92
**Reynolds**, Jeremiah N. 1799?-1858 BenetAL 91
**Reynolds**, Jerry 1962- WhoBlA 92
**Reynolds**, Jerry Owen 1944- WhoWest 92
**Reynolds**, Jody Philippe 1962- WhoEnt 92
**Reynolds**, John WrDr 92
**Reynolds**, John 1788-1865 BenetAL 91
**Reynolds**, John Allen 1955- WhoAmL 92
**Reynolds**, John C 1935- AmMWSc 92
**Reynolds**, John Curby 1948- WhoWest 92
**Reynolds**, John Dick 1921- AmMWSc 92
**Reynolds**, John Douglas 1942- WhoWest 92
**Reynolds**, John Elliott, III 1952- AmMWSc 92
**Reynolds**, John F. 1951- WhoFI 92
**Reynolds**, John Francis 1921- WhoMW 92
**Reynolds**, John Hamilton 1923- AmMWSc 92, IntWW 91
**Reynolds**, John Horace 1937- AmMWSc 92
**Reynolds**, John Hughes, IV 1940- AmMWSc 92
**Reynolds**, John Keith 1919- AmMWSc 92
**Reynolds**, John M. 1954- WhoEnt 92
**Reynolds**, John Murray 1901- ScFEYrs
**Reynolds**, John T. LesBEnT 92
**Reynolds**, John Terrence 1937- AmMWSc 92
**Reynolds**, John Theodore 1925- AmMWSc 92
**Reynolds**, John W. 1921- WhoAmL 92, WhoMW 92
**Reynolds**, John Weston 1930- AmMWSc 92
**Reynolds**, John Z 1940- AmMWSc 92
**Reynolds**, Jonathan Randolph 1942- WhoEnt 92
**Reynolds**, Joseph 1935- AmMWSc 92
**Reynolds**, Joseph Charles 1930- WhoAmP 91
**Reynolds**, Joseph Hurley 1946- WhoAmL 92

**Reynolds,** Joseph Jones 1822-1899 *BiInAmS*
**Reynolds,** Joseph Melvin 1924- *AmMWSc 92*
**Reynolds,** Joshua 1723-1792 *BlkwCEP*
**Reynolds,** Joshua Paul 1906- *AmMWSc 92*
**Reynolds,** Joyce Maire 1918- *IntWW 91, Who 92*
**Reynolds,** Judy Taylor 1947- *WhoFI 92*
**Reynolds,** Julian A *WhoAmP 91*
**Reynolds,** June M 1925- *WhoAmP 91*
**Reynolds,** Karen Jeanne 1940- *WhoEnt 92*
**Reynolds,** Katherine Anne 1962- *WhoMW 92*
**Reynolds,** Keith Ronald 1943- *IntAu&W 91*
**Reynolds,** Kevin A 1963- *AmMWSc 92*
**Reynolds,** Kimberley 1955- *ConAu 135*
**Reynolds,** Larry Owen 1940- *AmMWSc 92*
**Reynolds,** Larry T. 1938- *ConAu 134*
**Reynolds,** Leighton Durham 1930- *Who 92*
**Reynolds,** Leo Thomas 1945- *WhoFI 92*
**Reynolds,** Leslie Boush, Jr 1923- *AmMWSc 92*
**Reynolds,** Lewis Dayton 1937- *WhoRel 92*
**Reynolds,** Lloyd 1910- *WrDr 92*
**Reynolds,** Mack 1917-1983 *TwCSFW 91*
**Reynolds,** Madge *WrDr 92*
**Reynolds,** Marion Rudolph, Jr 1945- *AmMWSc 92*
**Reynolds,** Marjorie 1921- *IntMPA 92*
**Reynolds,** Marjorie Lavers 1931- *AmMWSc 92*
**Reynolds,** Mark A. 1953- *WhoMW 92*
**Reynolds,** Mark William 1937- *WhoMW 92*
**Reynolds,** Martin L *WhoAmP 91*
**Reynolds,** Martin Richard Finch 1943- *Who 92*
**Reynolds,** Michael David 1954- *AmMWSc 92*
**Reynolds,** Michael Emanuel 1931- *Who 92*
**Reynolds,** Michael Frank 1930- *Who 92*
**Reynolds,** Micheal John 1958- *WhoFI 92*
**Reynolds,** Milton L. 1924- *WhoBlA 92*
**Reynolds,** Moira Davison 1915- *WhoMW 92*
**Reynolds,** Nancy Remick 1938- *WhoEnt 92*
**Reynolds,** Nanette Lee 1946- *WhoBlA 92*
**Reynolds,** Orland Bruce 1922- *AmMWSc 92*
**Reynolds,** Orr Esrey 1920- *AmMWSc 92*
**Reynolds,** Pamela Christine Schrom 1945- *IntAu&W 91*
**Reynolds,** Pamela Terese 1963- *WhoBlA 92*
**Reynolds,** Patricia Ann 1946- *WhoRel 92*
**Reynolds,** Patrick 1948- *WhoWest 92*
**Reynolds,** Patrick Allen 1957- *WhoMW 92*
**Reynolds,** Paul George 1922- *WhoFI 92*
**Reynolds,** Paul V. *WhoRel 92*
**Reynolds,** Peter 1929- *Who 92*
**Reynolds,** Peter Herbert 1940- *AmMWSc 92*
**Reynolds,** Peter James 1949- *AmMWSc 92*
**Reynolds,** Peter William John 1929- *IntWW 91*
**Reynolds,** Philip Alan 1920- *Who 92, WrDr 92*
**Reynolds,** R. J. 1960- *WhoBlA 92*
**Reynolds,** Ray Thomas 1933- *AmMWSc 92*
**Reynolds,** Raymond 1923- *WhoMW 92*
**Reynolds,** Richard Alan 1938- *AmMWSc 92*
**Reynolds,** Richard Clyde 1929- *AmMWSc 92*
**Reynolds,** Richard Henry 1913- *WhoWest 92*
**Reynolds,** Richard Johnson 1925- *AmMWSc 92*
**Reynolds,** Richard Louis 1953- *WhoAmL 92*
**Reynolds,** Richard Paulsen 1946- *WhoWest 92*
**Reynolds,** Richard Samuel, III 1934- *WhoAmP 91*
**Reynolds,** Richard Truman 1942- *AmMWSc 92*
**Reynolds,** Ricky Scott 1965- *WhoBlA 92*
**Reynolds,** Robert Alan 1949- *WhoFI 92*
**Reynolds,** Robert Coltart, Jr 1927- *AmMWSc 92*
**Reynolds,** Robert D 1944- *AmMWSc 92*
**Reynolds,** Robert David 1943- *AmMWSc 92*
**Reynolds,** Robert Eugene 1934- *AmMWSc 92*
**Reynolds,** Robert Harrison 1913- *WhoFI 92, WhoWest 92*
**Reynolds,** Robert Hugh 1937- *WhoMW 92*
**Reynolds,** Robert Joel 1944- *WhoFI 92*
**Reynolds,** Robert Leonard, Jr 1930- *WhoAmP 91*
**Reynolds,** Robert Lester 1917- *WhoRel 92*
**Reynolds,** Robert Louis 1939- *WhoFI 92*
**Reynolds,** Robert N 1922- *AmMWSc 92*
**Reynolds,** Robert Ware 1942- *AmMWSc 92*
**Reynolds,** Robert Williams 1927- *AmMWSc 92*
**Reynolds,** Roger 1934- *ConCom 92, NewAmDM*
**Reynolds,** Roger Lee 1934- *WhoEnt 92*
**Reynolds,** Roger Smith 1943- *AmMWSc 92*
**Reynolds,** Rolland C 1925- *AmMWSc 92*
**Reynolds,** Ronald J 1943- *AmMWSc 92*
**Reynolds,** Rosalie Dean 1926- *AmMWSc 92, WhoMW 92*
**Reynolds,** Russell Joseph 1941- *WhoAmP 91*
**Reynolds,** Russell Seaman, Jr. 1931- *WhoFI 92*
**Reynolds,** Ruth 1915- *TwCPaSc*
**Reynolds,** Sallie Blackburn 1940- *WhoMW 92*
**Reynolds,** Samuel D, Jr 1931- *AmMWSc 92*
**Reynolds,** Sheldon 1923- *IntMPA 92*
**Reynolds,** Stephen Edward 1916- *AmMWSc 92*
**Reynolds,** Stephen Philip 1948- *WhoWest 92*
**Reynolds,** Steve 1920- *WhoAmP 91*
**Reynolds,** Stuart 1907- *IntMPA 92*
**Reynolds,** Susan Elizabeth 1950- *WhoFI 92*
**Reynolds,** Suzanne 1959- *WhoWest 92*
**Reynolds,** Sydney 1939- *IntAu&W 91*
**Reynolds,** Telfer Barkley 1921- *AmMWSc 92*
**Reynolds,** Thomas Bernard 1940- *WhoWest 92*
**Reynolds,** Thomas De Witt 1929- *AmMWSc 92*
**Reynolds,** Thomas M *WhoAmP 91*
**Reynolds,** Thomas Morgan 1943- *WhoFI 92*
**Reynolds,** Thomas P. 1952- *WhoFI 92*
**Reynolds,** Thomas Upton, II 1954- *WhoAmP 91*
**Reynolds,** Tim *DrAPF 91*
**Reynolds,** Tom Davidson 1929- *AmMWSc 92*
**Reynolds,** Vernon H 1926- *AmMWSc 92*
**Reynolds,** Viola J. 1925- *WhoBlA 92*
**Reynolds,** W Ann 1937- *NewYTBS 91 [port]*
**Reynolds,** W. Ronnie 1939- *WhoRel 92*
**Reynolds,** Warren Lind 1920- *AmMWSc 92, WhoMW 92*
**Reynolds,** Wayne McFall 1947- *WhoWest 92*
**Reynolds,** William Bradford 1942- *WhoAmP 91*
**Reynolds,** William Craig 1933- *AmMWSc 92, WhoWest 92*
**Reynolds,** William Francis 1930- *AmMWSc 92*
**Reynolds,** William J. 1956- *WrDr 92*
**Reynolds,** William Jensen 1920- *WhoRel 92*
**Reynolds,** William Leroy 1945- *WhoAmL 92*
**Reynolds,** William MacKenzie, Jr. 1921- *WhoAmL 92*
**Reynolds,** William Oliver 1915- *Who 92*
**Reynolds,** William Roger 1929- *AmMWSc 92*
**Reynolds,** William Roscoe 1942- *WhoAmL 92, WhoAmP 91*
**Reynolds,** William Walter 1925- *AmMWSc 92*
**Reynolds,** Wynetka Ann King 1937- *AmMWSc 92*
**Reynolds-Hunt,** Kathleen Ann 1947- *WhoWest 92*
**Reynolds-Stephens,** William 1862-1943 *TwCPaSc*
**Reynolds-Warnhoff,** Patricia 1933- *AmMWSc 92*
**Reynoldson,** W Ward 1920- *WhoAmP 91*
**Reynosa,** Leo *WhoHisp 92*
**Reynoso,** Cruz 1931- *WhoHisp 92*
**Reynoso,** Gustavo D 1932- *AmMWSc 92*
**Reynoso,** Jose *WhoHisp 92*
**Reynoso,** Jose S. 1953- *WhoHisp 92*
**Reyntiens,** Nicholas Patrick 1925- *Who 92*
**Reynvaan,** Michael Thomas 1953- *WhoAmL 92*
**Reyor,** Rose Ann 1919- *WhoAmP 91*
**Reyzen,** Mark Osipovich 1895-1970? *SovUnBD*
**Reza,** Fazlollah M 1915- *AmMWSc 92*
**Reza,** Jesus *WhoHisp 92*
**Reza,** Veronica Cristina 1962- *WhoHisp 92*
**Rezac,** Don M 1940- *WhoAmP 91*
**Rezac,** Pamela Jean 1947- *WhoMW 92*
**Rezac,** Stephan Robert 1953- *WhoWest 92*
**Rezach,** Brian Daniel 1957- *WhoFI 92*
**Rezak,** Michael 1948- *AmMWSc 92*
**Rezak,** Richard 1920- *AmMWSc 92*
**Rezanka,** Ivan 1931- *AmMWSc 92*
**Rezek,** Geoffrey Robert 1941- *AmMWSc 92*
**Rezek,** Ivan Emil 1914- *WhoAmP 91*
**Rezendes,** Dennis 1929- *WhoWest 92*
**Rezits,** Joseph 1925- *WrDr 92*
**Rezmerski,** John Calvin *DrAPF 91*
**Rezneck,** Daniel Albert 1935- *WhoAmL 92*
**Rezner,** Barbara Ann 1955- *WhoAmL 92*
**Reznicek,** Anton Albert 1950- *AmMWSc 92*
**Reznick,** Bruce Arie 1953- *AmMWSc 92, WhoMW 92*
**Reznick,** Scott Matthew 1946- *WhoFI 92*
**Reznik,** Andrew Albert 1942- *WhoAmL 92*
**Reznikoff,** Charles 1894-1976 *BenetAL 91*
**Reznikoff,** William Stanton 1941- *AmMWSc 92*
**Rezzonico,** Renzo 1929- *WhoFI 92*
**Rhadamanthus** *AmPeW*
**Rhallys,** George J. *IntWW 91*
**Rhamy,** Robert Keith 1927- *AmMWSc 92*
**Rhea,** Alexander Dodson, III 1919- *IntWW 91, Who 92*
**Rhea,** Ann Crawford 1940- *WhoWest 92*
**Rhea,** Edward Buford, Jr. 1934- *WhoMW 92*
**Rhea,** Jerry Dwaine 1950- *WhoFI 92*
**Rhea,** Michael 1946- *WhoBlA 92*
**Rhea,** Mildred Louise 1911- *WhoWest 92*
**Rhead,** William James 1946- *AmMWSc 92*
**Rheault,** Lillian I 1919- *WhoAmP 91*
**Rhee,** Choon Jai 1935- *AmMWSc 92*
**Rhee,** G-Yull 1939- *AmMWSc 92*
**Rhee,** Haewun 1937- *AmMWSc 92*
**Rhee,** Jay Jea-yong 1937- *AmMWSc 92*
**Rhee,** Moon-Jhong 1935- *AmMWSc 92*
**Rhee,** Seong Kwan 1936- *AmMWSc 92*
**Rhee,** Sue Goo 1943- *AmMWSc 92*
**Rhee,** Susan Byungsook 1937- *WhoMW 92*
**Rhee,** Syngman *DcAmImH*
**Rhee,** Syngman 1875-1965 *FacFETw*
**Rhee,** Tong-Chin 1936- *WhoMW 92*
**Rhee,** Yang Ho 1943- *WhoMW 92*
**Rhees,** Raymond Charles 1914- *AmMWSc 92*
**Rhees,** Reuben Ward 1941- *AmMWSc 92*
**Rhees,** William Jones 1830-1907 *BiInAmS*
**Rheims,** Maurice 1910- *IntWW 91*
**Rhein,** John Hancock Willing, III 1931- *WhoFI 92*
**Rhein,** Robert Alden 1933- *AmMWSc 92*
**Rhein,** Timothy J. 1941- *WhoWest 92*
**Rheinberger,** Joseph 1839-1901 *NewAmDM*
**Rheinboldt,** Werner Carl 1927- *AmMWSc 92*
**Rheingold,** Arnold L 1940- *AmMWSc 92*
**Rheinheimer,** Kurt *DrAPF 91*
**Rheinlander,** Harold F 1919- *AmMWSc 92*
**Rheins,** Lawrence A 1955- *AmMWSc 92*
**Rheins,** Melvin S 1920- *AmMWSc 92*
**Rheinstein,** John 1930- *AmMWSc 92*
**Rheinstein,** Peter Howard 1943- *AmMWSc 92, WhoAmL 92*
**Rheinwald,** James George 1948- *AmMWSc 92*
**Rhem,** Anthony Jaren 1960- *WhoFI 92*
**Rhemtulla,** Akbar Hussein 1939- *AmMWSc 92*
**Rhetta,** Helen L. *WhoBlA 92*
**Rhim,** Johng Sik 1930- *AmMWSc 92*
**Rhim,** Won-Kyu 1937- *AmMWSc 92*
**Rhind,** David William 1943- *Who 92*
**Rhind,** J Christopher 1934- *WhoIns 92*
**Rhind,** James Thomas 1922- *WhoAmL 92*
**Rhine,** Joseph B 1895-1980 *FacFETw*
**Rhine,** Larry 1912- *WhoEnt 92*
**Rhinehart,** June Acie 1934- *WhoBlA 92*
**Rhinehart,** Luke 1932- *WhoEnt 92*
**Rhinehart,** Richard Scott 1956- *WhoAmL 92*
**Rhinehart,** Robert Russell, II 1946- *AmMWSc 92*
**Rhinehart,** Shelby Aaron 1927- *WhoAmP 91*
**Rhinehart,** Susan Oneacre 1938- *WrDr 92*
**Rhinehart,** Vernon Morel 1935- *WhoBlA 92*
**Rhinelander,** John Bassett 1933- *WhoAmL 92, WhoAmP 91*
**Rhines,** Frederick N 1907- *AmMWSc 92*
**Rhines,** Jesse Algeron 1948- *WhoBlA 92*
**Rhines,** Marie Louise *WhoEnt 92*
**Rhines,** Peter Broomell 1942- *AmMWSc 92, IntWW 91*
**Rhinesmith,** Herbert Silas 1907- *AmMWSc 92*
**Rho,** George Ilhyon 1960- *WhoFI 92*
**Rho,** Jinnque 1938- *AmMWSc 92*
**Rho,** Joon H 1922- *AmMWSc 92*
**Rhoad,** Thomas Nathaniel 1923- *WhoAmP 91*
**Rhoades,** Billy E. 1928- *WhoMW 92*
**Rhoades,** Billy Eugene 1928- *AmMWSc 92*
**Rhoades,** Everett Ronald 1931- *AmMWSc 92*
**Rhoades,** Gary Daniel 1957- *WhoFI 92*
**Rhoades,** Geoffrey 1898- *TwCPaSc*
**Rhoades,** Harlan Leon 1928- *AmMWSc 92*
**Rhoades,** James David 1937- *AmMWSc 92*
**Rhoades,** James J 1941- *WhoAmP 91*
**Rhoades,** James Lawrence 1933- *AmMWSc 92*
**Rhoades,** John Skylstead, Sr. 1925- *WhoAmL 92, WhoWest 92*
**Rhoades,** Jon Allen 1937- *WhoIns 92*
**Rhoades,** Kathryn Ann 1960- *WhoRel 92*
**Rhoades,** Marcus Morton 1903- *AmMWSc 92*
**Rhoades,** Richard G 1938- *AmMWSc 92*
**Rhoades,** Rodney A 1939- *AmMWSc 92*
**Rhoades,** Rodney Allen 1939- *WhoMW 92*
**Rhoades,** Samuel Thomas 1946- *WhoBlA 92*
**Rhoades-Ingvaldsen,** Catherine Ann 1962- *WhoFI 92*
**Rhoads,** Allen R 1941- *AmMWSc 92*
**Rhoads,** Dean A 1935- *WhoAmP 91*
**Rhoads,** Dean Allan 1935- *WhoWest 92*
**Rhoads,** Donald Cave 1938- *AmMWSc 92*
**Rhoads,** Frederick Milton 1936- *AmMWSc 92*
**Rhoads,** George Grant 1940- *AmMWSc 92*
**Rhoads,** James Berton 1928- *IntWW 91*
**Rhoads,** James E. 1828-1895 *AmPeW*
**Rhoads,** John McFarlane 1919- *AmMWSc 92*
**Rhoads,** Jonathan Evans 1907- *AmMWSc 92*
**Rhoads,** Karroll G 1948- *WhoAmP 91*
**Rhoads,** Kathryn Lynn 1948- *WhoEnt 92*
**Rhoads,** Mark Quentin 1946- *WhoAmP 91*
**Rhoads,** Nancy Glenn 1957- *WhoAmL 92*
**Rhoads,** Patricia Mary 1953- *WhoFI 92*
**Rhoads,** Paul Spottswood 1898- *AmMWSc 92*
**Rhoads,** Robert E 1944- *AmMWSc 92*
**Rhoads,** Robert K. 1954- *WhoAmL 92*
**Rhoads,** Sara Jane 1920- *AmMWSc 92*
**Rhoads,** William Denham 1934- *AmMWSc 92*
**Rhodas,** Virginia *IntAu&W 91*
**Rhode,** Deborah Lynn 1952- *WhoAmL 92*
**Rhode,** Edward A, Jr 1926- *AmMWSc 92*
**Rhode,** Edward Albert 1926- *WhoWest 92*
**Rhode,** Kenneth George 1909- *WhoIns 92*
**Rhode,** Paul Gerald 1953- *WhoRel 92*
**Rhode,** Solon Lafayette, III 1938- *AmMWSc 92*
**Rhode,** William Stanley 1941- *AmMWSc 92*
**Rhodeman,** Clare M. 1932- *WhoBlA 92*
**Rhoden,** Eric 1964- *WhoEnt 92*
**Rhoden,** George Vincent 1926- *BlkOlyM*
**Rhoden,** Grady Lamar 1937- *WhoAmP 91*
**Rhoden,** Rebecca Jane 1942- *WhoMW 92*
**Rhoden,** Richard Allan 1930- *AmMWSc 92, WhoBlA 92*
**Rhodes,** Alan Charles 1951- *WhoRel 92*
**Rhodes,** Alice Graham 1941- *WhoAmL 92*
**Rhodes,** Alice M. 1951- *WhoAmL 92*
**Rhodes,** Allen Franklin 1924- *AmMWSc 92*
**Rhodes,** Andrew James 1911- *AmMWSc 92*
**Rhodes,** Anne L. 1935- *WhoBlA 92*
**Rhodes,** Anne Lou 1935- *WhoWest 92*
**Rhodes,** Anthony 1916- *IntAu&W 91, WrDr 92*
**Rhodes,** Ashby Marshall 1923- *AmMWSc 92*
**Rhodes,** Basil 1915- *Who 92*
**Rhodes,** Bernard Joseph 1956- *WhoAmL 92*
**Rhodes,** Bessie M. L. 1935- *WhoBlA 92*
**Rhodes,** Betty Jane 1921- *WhoEnt 92*
**Rhodes,** Buck Austin 1935- *AmMWSc 92*
**Rhodes,** C. Adrienne 1961- *WhoBlA 92*
**Rhodes,** Cecil d1990 *Who 92N*
**Rhodes,** Cecil John 1853-1902 *BenetAL 91*
**Rhodes,** Charles Kirkham 1939- *AmMWSc 92*
**Rhodes,** Chester Dusty 1921- *WhoAmP 91*
**Rhodes,** Christene Ford 1926- *WhoAmP 91*
**Rhodes,** Cynthia 1956- *IntMPA 92*
**Rhodes,** Dallas D 1947- *AmMWSc 92*
**Rhodes,** David 1917- *WhoEnt 92*
**Rhodes,** David R 1936- *AmMWSc 92*
**Rhodes,** Donald Frederick 1932- *AmMWSc 92*
**Rhodes,** Donald R 1923- *AmMWSc 92*
**Rhodes,** Duplain *WhoBlA 92*
**Rhodes,** E 1938- *AmMWSc 92*
**Rhodes,** Edward 1943- *WhoBlA 92*
**Rhodes,** Edward Joseph, Jr 1946- *AmMWSc 92*
**Rhodes,** Edward Thomas, Sr. 1933- *WhoBlA 92*
**Rhodes,** Eric Foster 1927- *WhoFI 92*
**Rhodes,** Eugene Manlove 1869-1934 *BenetAL 91, TwCWW 91*
**Rhodes,** Frank 1950- *WhoAmP 91*
**Rhodes,** Frank E *WhoAmP 91*
**Rhodes,** Frank Harold Trevor 1926- *AmMWSc 92, IntWW 91*

**Rhodes**, George Harold Lancashire 1916- Who 92
**Rhodes**, Gordon Ellsworth 1927- WhoIns 92
**Rhodes**, H Henry ScFEYrs
**Rhodes**, Harold 1910- NewAmDM
**Rhodes**, Helen Mary 1921- WhoMW 92
**Rhodes**, Horace Gibson 1927- WhoAmL 92
**Rhodes**, Ian Burton 1941- AmMWSc 92
**Rhodes**, Jacob Lester 1922- AmMWSc 92
**Rhodes**, Jacqueline Yvonne 1949- WhoMW 92
**Rhodes**, James Allen 1909- WhoAmP 91
**Rhodes**, James B 1928- AmMWSc 92
**Rhodes**, James Ford 1848-1927 BenetAL 91
**Rhodes**, James Kendall 1937- WhoEnt 92
**Rhodes**, James Lamar, Jr. 1948- WhoWest 92
**Rhodes**, Jeanne WhoBlA 92
**Rhodes**, John Andrew 1949- Who 92
**Rhodes**, John Christopher Douglas 1946- Who 92
**Rhodes**, John David 1925- WhoAmL 92
**Rhodes**, John Ivor McKinnon 1914- Who 92
**Rhodes**, John J 1916- WhoAmP 91
**Rhodes**, John J., III 1943- AlmAP 92 [port], WhoWest 92
**Rhodes**, John Jacob 1916- IntWW 91, WhoAmL 92
**Rhodes**, John Lewis 1937- AmMWSc 92
**Rhodes**, John Marshell 1926- AmMWSc 92
**Rhodes**, Joseph, Jr. 1947- WhoBlA 92
**Rhodes**, Judith Carol 1949- AmMWSc 92
**Rhodes**, Kenneth Earle 1960- WhoEnt 92
**Rhodes**, Kent d1991 NewYTBS 91 [port]
**Rhodes**, Kent Bertis 1958- WhoWest 92
**Rhodes**, Landon Harrison 1947- AmMWSc 92
**Rhodes**, Leland TwCWW 91
**Rhodes**, Lelia G. WhoBlA 92
**Rhodes**, Marion 1907- Who 92
**Rhodes**, Mary WhoAmP 91
**Rhodes**, Mike Kevin 1959- WhoMW 92
**Rhodes**, Mitchell Lee 1940- AmMWSc 92
**Rhodes**, Paula R. 1949- WhoBlA 92
**Rhodes**, Paula Renette 1949- WhoAmL 92
**Rhodes**, Peregrine 1925- Who 92
**Rhodes**, Peter John 1940- Who 92
**Rhodes**, Philip 1922- IntAu&W 91, Who 92, WrDr 92
**Rhodes**, Ray 1950- WhoBlA 92
**Rhodes**, Reginald Paul 1918- Who 92
**Rhodes**, Richard DrAPF 91
**Rhodes**, Richard 1937- IntAu&W 91, WrDr 92
**Rhodes**, Richard Ayer, II 1922- AmMWSc 92
**Rhodes**, Richard David Walton 1942- Who 92
**Rhodes**, Richard L. 1937- IntWW 91
**Rhodes**, Richard Leiter, Jr. 1934- WhoMW 92
**Rhodes**, Rick 1951- WhoEnt 92
**Rhodes**, Robert Allen 1941- AmMWSc 92
**Rhodes**, Robert Carl 1936- AmMWSc 92
**Rhodes**, Robert Charles 1926- WhoMW 92
**Rhodes**, Robert Elliott 1945- Who 92
**Rhodes**, Robert Shaw 1936- AmMWSc 92, WhoBlA 92
**Rhodes**, Rondell H 1918- AmMWSc 92
**Rhodes**, Russell G 1939- AmMWSc 92
**Rhodes**, Samuel 1941- WhoEnt 92
**Rhodes**, Samuel Thomas 1944- WhoAmP 91
**Rhodes**, Stephen Michael 1949- WhoFI 92
**Rhodes**, Thomas W. 1946- WhoAmL 92
**Rhodes**, Timothy Earl 1957- WhoAmL 92
**Rhodes**, Victoria Elizabeth 1957- WhoEnt 92
**Rhodes**, Wanda E 1916- WhoAmP 91
**Rhodes**, William Clifford 1932- AmMWSc 92
**Rhodes**, William Harker 1925- AmMWSc 92
**Rhodes**, William Henry 1822-1876 ScFEYrs
**Rhodes**, William Holman 1935- AmMWSc 92
**Rhodes**, William Reginald 1935- WhoFI 92
**Rhodes**, William Terrill 1943- AmMWSc 92
**Rhodes**, Yorke Edward 1936- AmMWSc 92
**Rhodes**, Zandra 1940- IntWW 91
**Rhodes**, Zandra Lindsey 1940- Who 92
**Rhodes James**, Robert 1933- Who 92
**Rhodin**, Johannes A G 1922- AmMWSc 92
**Rhodin**, Thor Nathaniel, Jr 1920- AmMWSc 92
**Rhodine**, Charles Norman 1931- AmMWSc 92
**Rhodogune** EncAmaz 91
**Rhody**, Ronald Edward 1932- WhoFI 92
**Rhoe**, Kenneth Roland 1926- WhoRel 92
**Rhomberg**, Rudolf Robert 1922- WhoFI 92
**Rhone**, Richard Wallace 1946- WhoAmP 91
**Rhone**, Steven A. 1953- WhoFI 92
**Rhone**, Sylvia 1952- ConBlB 2 [port]
**Rhone**, Sylvia M. 1952- WhoBlA 92
**Rhone**, Trevor D. 1940- WrDr 92
**Rhone**, Trevor Dave 1940- IntAu&W 91
**Rhorer**, William Garrett 1913- WhoFI 92
**Rhoten**, William Blocher 1943- AmMWSc 92
**Rhoton**, Albert Loren, Jr 1932- AmMWSc 92
**Rhoy**, Nicholas Alan 1938- WhoWest 92
**Rhue**, Judith Williams WhoMW 92
**Rhue**, Morton WrDr 92
**Rhule**, Homer A 1921- WhoIns 92
**Rhum**, Susan Caroline 1932- WhoAmP 91
**Rhykerd**, Charles Loren 1929- AmMWSc 92
**Rhymes**, Beverly Guyton 1931- WhoRel 92
**Rhymes**, Douglas Alfred 1914- Who 92, WrDr 92
**Rhyne**, A Leonard 1934- AmMWSc 92
**Rhyne**, Charles S. 1912- WrDr 92
**Rhyne**, Charles Sylvanus 1912- WhoAmL 92, WhoFI 92
**Rhyne**, James Jennings 1938- AmMWSc 92
**Rhyne**, Johnathan L, Jr 1955- WhoAmP 91
**Rhyne**, Katherine Lynn 1955- WhoAmL 92
**Rhyne**, Nancy 1926- ConAu 133, SmATA 66
**Rhyne**, Robert Glenn, Jr. 1944- WhoFI 92
**Rhyne**, Sidney White 1931- WhoAmL 92
**Rhyne**, Theodore Lauer 1944- WhoMW 92
**Rhyne**, Thomas Crowell 1942- AmMWSc 92
**Rhyne**, V Thomas 1942- AmMWSc 92
**Rhyner**, Charles R 1940- AmMWSc 92
**Rhynsburger**, Robert Whitman 1925- AmMWSc 92
**Rhys** Who 92
**Rhys**, Jean 1890-1979 CnDBLB 7 [port], ConAu 35NR, FacFETw, LiExTwC, RfGEnL 91
**Rhys**, Jean 1894-1979 BenetAL 91
**Rhys**, Keidrych 1915- IntAu&W 91
**Rhys-Davies**, John IntMPA 92
**Rhys Jones**, Griffith 1953- Who 92
**Rhys Williams**, Gareth 1961- Who 92
**Riabouchinska**, Tatiana 1916- Who 92
**Riach**, Douglas Alexander 1919- WhoWest 92
**Riahi**, Daniel Nourollah 1943- AmMWSc 92
**Rial**, Carol 1963- WhoHisp 92
**Rian**, Edwin Harold 1900- WhoRel 92
**Riasanovsky**, Nicholas V. 1923- WrDr 92
**Riaz**, M 1925- AmMWSc 92
**Ribak**, Charles Eric 1950- AmMWSc 92, WhoWest 92
**Ribalow**, M.Z. DrAPF 91
**Riban**, David Michael 1936- AmMWSc 92
**Ribar**, Dixie Lee 1938- WhoMW 92
**Ribarits**, John Martin 1960- WhoAmL 92
**Ribas**, Ivan Gene 1947- WhoHisp 92
**Ribaudo**, Tony 1941- WhoAmP 91
**Ribault**, Jean 1520?-1565 BenetAL 91
**Ribaut**, Jean 1520?-1565 BenetAL 91
**Ribbans**, Geoffrey Wilfrid 1927- Who 92
**Ribbe**, Paul Hubert 1935- AmMWSc 92
**Ribbens**, William B 1937- AmMWSc 92
**Ribbentrop**, Joachim von 1893-1946 BiDExR, EncTR 91 [port], FacFETw [port]
**Ribbins**, Gertrude 1924- WhoBlA 92
**Ribble**, Dale Raymond 1952- WhoRel 92
**Ribble**, Terry Lee 1950- WhoRel 92
**Ribbs**, William Theodore, Jr. 1956- WhoBlA 92
**Ribbs**, Willy T. 1956- ConBlB 2 [port]
**Ribe**, Fred Linden 1924- AmMWSc 92
**Ribe**, M L 1919- AmMWSc 92
**Ribeiro**, Antonio 1928- IntWW 91, WhoRel 92
**Ribeiro**, Aquilino 1885-1963 LiExTwC
**Ribeiro**, Frank Henry 1949- WhoFI 92
**Ribeiro**, João Ubaldo 1940- BenetAL 91
**Ribeiro**, Joao Ubaldo 1941- ConLC 67 [port]
**Ribeiro**, Joao Ubaldo Osorio Pimentel 1941- IntWW 91
**Ribelin**, William Eugene 1924- AmMWSc 92
**Ribellia**, Patrick A 1947- WhoAmP 91
**Ribenboim**, Paulo 1928- AmMWSc 92
**Ribera**, Gilbert Joseph 1936- WhoHisp 92
**Ribera**, John E. 1944- WhoHisp 92
**Ribera**, Perafan de 1492-1577 HisDSpE
**Riberholdt**, Gunnar 1933- IntWW 91
**Ribero**, Michael A. 1956- WhoHisp 92
**Ribes**, Luis 1940- AmMWSc 92
**Ribes**, Pierre Raoul Martial 1919- IntWW 91
**Ribi**, Edgar 1920- AmMWSc 92
**Ribicic**, Mitja 1919- IntWW 91
**Ribicoff**, Abraham A. 1910- IntWW 91, WhoAmP 91
**Rible**, Morton 1938- WhoFI 92, WhoMW 92
**Riblet**, Gordon Potter 1943- AmMWSc 92
**Riblet**, Henry B 1911- AmMWSc 92
**Riblet**, Leslie Alfred 1941- AmMWSc 92
**Riblet**, Roy Johnson 1942- AmMWSc 92
**Ribman**, Ronald 1932- WrDr 92
**Ribman**, Ronald Burt 1932- WhoEnt 92
**Ribner**, Herbert Spencer 1913- AmMWSc 92
**Ribnik**, Thelma Naoma 1934- WhoWest 92
**Riboud**, Antoine Amedee Paul 1918- IntWW 91
**Ricanek**, Carolyn Wright 1939- WhoBlA 92
**Ricard**, Charles 1922- IntAu&W 91
**Ricard**, John H. 1940- WhoBlA 92, WhoRel 92
**Ricard**, Ronny Joseph 1951- WhoAmP 91
**Ricardez**, Mario L. 1929- WhoHisp 92
**Ricardi**, Leon J 1924- AmMWSc 92
**Ricardi**, Leon Joseph 1924- WhoWest 92
**Ricardo**, David 1772-1823 BlkwCEP, DcLB 107 [port]
**Ricardo-Campbell**, Rita 1920- WhoHisp 92, WhoWest 92
**Ricards**, Harold Andrew, Jr. 1917- WhoFI 92
**Ricards**, Philip Clayton 1944- WhoRel 92
**Ricaurte**, Antonio de 1786-1814 HisDSpE
**Ricca**, Paul Joseph 1939- AmMWSc 92
**Ricca**, Thomas A. 1947- WhoAmL 92
**Ricca**, Vincent Thomas 1935- AmMWSc 92
**Riccardi**, Lori 1964- WhoFI 92
**Riccards**, Michael P 1944- IntAu&W 91
**Ricchiuti**, Paul B 1925- IntAu&W 91
**Ricci**, Benjamin 1923- AmMWSc 92
**Ricci**, Brian Francis 1957- WhoMW 92
**Ricci**, Enzo 1925- AmMWSc 92
**Ricci**, Giovanni Mario 1929- WhoFI 92
**Ricci**, John Ettore 1907- AmMWSc 92
**Ricci**, John Silvio, Jr 1940- AmMWSc 92
**Ricci**, Joseph Anthony 1962- WhoAmL 92
**Ricci**, Nina 1883-1970 DcTwDes
**Ricci**, Renato 1896-1956 BiDExR
**Ricci**, Robert Ronald 1945- WhoFI 92
**Ricci**, Ruggiero 1918- IntWW 91, NewAmDM, WhoEnt 92
**Ricciardelli**, Carl F 1931- WhoIns 92
**Ricciardelli**, Peter A. 1954- WhoWest 92
**Ricciardi**, Lawrence R. WhoAmL 92
**Ricciardi**, Robert Paul 1946- AmMWSc 92
**Ricciarelli**, Katia 1946- WhoEnt 92
**Riccio**, Jerome Michael 1955- WhoFI 92
**Riccio**, Joyce Ann 1952- WhoAmL 92
**Riccio**, Thomas Patrick 1955- WhoEnt 92
**Riccitelli**, Bruce Robert 1948- WhoEnt 92
**Ricciuti**, Florence Christine 1944- AmMWSc 92
**Ricciuti**, Renato Edmund 1916- WhoAmP 91
**Ricco**, Raymond Joseph 1948- WhoWest 92
**Riccoboni**, Marie Jeanne 1713-1792 FrenWW
**Riccoboni**, Marie-Jeanne Laboras de M. 1713-1792 BlkwCEP
**Riccobono**, Paul Xavier 1939- AmMWSc 92
**Rice** Who 92
**Rice**, Alice Hegan 1870-1942 BenetAL 91
**Rice**, Allen Troy 1962- WhoBlA 92
**Rice**, Anne DrAPF 91
**Rice**, Anne 1941- BenetAL 91, ConAu 36NR, CurBio 91 [port], WrDr 92
**Rice**, Anne Estelle 1879-1959 TwCPaSc
**Rice**, Barbara Lynn 1955- WhoEnt 92
**Rice**, Barbara Pollak 1937- WhoWest 92
**Rice**, Barbara Slyder 1937- AmMWSc 92
**Rice**, Benjamin Manson, Jr. 1930- WhoFI 92
**Rice**, Bernard 1914- AmMWSc 92
**Rice**, Brian John 1963- WhoMW 92
**Rice**, Brian Keith 193?- WrDr 92
**Rice**, C. Duncan 1942- WrDr 92
**Rice**, Cale Young 1872-1943 BenetAL 91
**Rice**, Charles 1841-1901 BiInAmS
**Rice**, Charles Dale 1934- WhoMW 92
**Rice**, Charles E WhoAmP 91
**Rice**, Charles Edward 1932- AmMWSc 92
**Rice**, Charles Howard 1925- WhoAmP 91
**Rice**, Charles Lane 1945- WhoWest 92
**Rice**, Charles Merton 1925- AmMWSc 92
**Rice**, Charles Moen, III 1952- AmMWSc 92
**Rice**, Christine E AmMWSc 92
**Rice**, Clifford Paul 1940- AmMWSc 92
**Rice**, Condoleezza 1954- WhoBlA 92
**Rice**, Constance Williams 1945- WhoBlA 92
**Rice**, Cora Lee 1926- WhoBlA 92
**Rice**, Dale Howard 1943- WhoWest 92
**Rice**, Dale Warren 1930- AmMWSc 92
**Rice**, Dale Wilson 1932- AmMWSc 92
**Rice**, Darrel Alan 1947- WhoAmL 92
**Rice**, David E 1933- AmMWSc 92
**Rice**, David Eugene, Jr. 1916- WhoBlA 92
**Rice**, David Gordon 1942- WhoWest 92
**Rice**, David L. DrAPF 91
**Rice**, David Lee 1929- WhoMW 92
**Rice**, Deckie M 1924- WhoAmP 91
**Rice**, Dennis George 1927- Who 92
**Rice**, Dennis Keith 1939- AmMWSc 92
**Rice**, Desmond 1924- Who 92
**Rice**, Devereux Dunlap 1952- WhoWest 92
**Rice**, Don DrAPF 91
**Rice**, Donald B 1939- WhoAmP 91
**Rice**, Donald L. 1938- WrDr 92
**Rice**, Dorothy P. 1922- IntWW 91
**Rice**, Dorothy Pechman 1922- AmMWSc 92
**Rice**, Douglas Edward 1962- WhoMW 92
**Rice**, Edward A. 1929- WhoBlA 92
**Rice**, Edward Everett 1848-1924 NewAmDM
**Rice**, Edward William 1911- WhoWest 92
**Rice**, Elmer 1892-1967 BenetAL 91, FacFETw, ScFEYrs
**Rice**, Elroy Leon 1917- AmMWSc 92
**Rice**, Emmett J WhoAmP 91, WhoBlA 92
**Rice**, Eugene Ward 1949- WhoMW 92
**Rice**, Ferill Jeane 1926- WhoMW 92
**Rice**, Frank J 1924- AmMWSc 92
**Rice**, Fred 1926- WhoBlA 92
**Rice**, Frederick Anders Hudson 1917- AmMWSc 92
**Rice**, Frederick Colton 1938- WhoWest 92
**Rice**, Gary Rex 1945- WhoAmL 92
**Rice**, George Lawrence, III 1951- WhoAmL 92
**Rice**, George Staples 1849-1920 BiInAmS
**Rice**, Glen A. 1967- WhoBlA 92
**Rice**, Gordon Kenneth 1927- Who 92
**Rice**, Grantland 1880-1954 BenetAL 91
**Rice**, Greg d1991 NewYTBS 91
**Rice**, Gregory 1916-1991 CurBio 91N
**Rice**, Gregory Joseph 1954- WhoAmL 92
**Rice**, H. Craig 1945- WhoRel 92, WhoWest 92
**Rice**, H. Robert WhoFI 92
**Rice**, Harold Leon 1941- WhoAmP 91
**Rice**, Harry E ScFEYrs
**Rice**, Haynes 1932- WhoBlA 92
**Rice**, Helen Steiner 1900?-1981 ConAu 133
**Rice**, J. Andrew 1953- WhoFI 92
**Rice**, Jack 1925- WhoAmP 91
**Rice**, Jack Morris 1948- AmMWSc 92
**Rice**, James Briggs, Jr. 1940- WhoAmL 92
**Rice**, James Cyrus 1950- WhoMW 92
**Rice**, James I 1925- WhoAmP 91
**Rice**, James K 1923- AmMWSc 92
**Rice**, James Kinsey 1941- AmMWSc 92
**Rice**, James Leonard 1944- WhoRel 92
**Rice**, James R 1940- AmMWSc 92
**Rice**, James Thomas 1933- AmMWSc 92
**Rice**, Jerry J. 1959- WhoEnt 92
**Rice**, Jerry L. 1954- WhoRel 92
**Rice**, Jerry Lee 1962- WhoBlA 92, WhoWest 92
**Rice**, Jerry Mercer 1940- AmMWSc 92
**Rice**, Jim 1953- WhoBlA 92
**Rice**, Jim 1957- WhoAmP 91
**Rice**, John Edward 1927- WhoAmL 92
**Rice**, John Joseph 1939- WhoFI 92
**Rice**, John Minot 1833-1901 BiInAmS
**Rice**, John Reynolds 1946- WhoFI 92
**Rice**, John Richard 1895-1980 RelLAm 91
**Rice**, John Rischard 1934- AmMWSc 92
**Rice**, John T 1931- AmMWSc 92
**Rice**, John Tate 1948- WhoAmL 92
**Rice**, John W WhoAmP 91
**Rice**, Joseph David 1942- WhoAmP 91
**Rice**, Joseph Lee, III 1932- WhoFI 92
**Rice**, Joseph M 1857-1934 DcAmImH
**Rice**, Julian Casavant 1924- WhoAmL 92, WhoWest 92
**Rice**, Kenner Cralle 1940- AmMWSc 92
**Rice**, Kenneth Lloyd 1937- WhoFI 92, WhoMW 92
**Rice**, Larry Dean 1953- WhoAmP 91
**Rice**, Linda Johnson 1958- WhoBlA 92
**Rice**, Lois Dickson 1933- WhoBlA 92
**Rice**, Louise Allen 1940- WhoBlA 92
**Rice**, Lyle K 1905- WhoAmP 91
**Rice**, Marilyn Louise 1946- WhoMW 92
**Rice**, Marion McBurney 1923- AmMWSc 92
**Rice**, Mary Esther 1926- AmMWSc 92
**Rice**, Maurice Ainsworth 1936- WhoFI 92, WhoMW 92
**Rice**, Max McGee 1928- WhoRel 92
**Rice**, Melanie Ailene 1957- WhoEnt 92
**Rice**, Michael John 1940- AmMWSc 92
**Rice**, Michael Lee 1963- WhoMW 92
**Rice**, Michael Lewis 1943- WhoWest 92
**Rice**, Mitchell F. 1948- WhoBlA 92
**Rice**, Nancy Reed 1940- AmMWSc 92
**Rice**, Nelson, Sr 1932- WhoAmP 91
**Rice**, Norman WhoAmP 91
**Rice**, Norman 1943- WhoWest 92

**Rice**, Norman Blann 1943- *WhoBlA 92*
**Rice**, Norman Molesworth 1939- *AmMWSc 92*
**Rice**, Otis K. 1919- *WrDr 92*
**Rice**, Otis LaVerne 1922- *WhoFI 92, WhoMW 92*
**Rice**, Pamela Ann 1956- *WhoBlA 92*
**Rice**, Patricia Ann 1946- *WhoWest 92*
**Rice**, Patrick James 1965- *WhoMW 92*
**Rice**, Paul *DrAPF 91*
**Rice**, Paul Jackson 1938- *WhoAmL 92*
**Rice**, Paul LaVerne 1906- *AmMWSc 92*
**Rice**, Peter 1939- *AmMWSc 92*
**Rice**, Peter Anthony Morrish 1928- *Who 92*
**Rice**, Peter D. *Who 92*
**Rice**, Peter Milton 1937- *AmMWSc 92*
**Rice**, Philip A 1936- *AmMWSc 92*
**Rice**, R. Michael 1948- *WhoFI 92*
**Rice**, Ramona Gail 1950- *WhoMW 92*
**Rice**, Randall Glenn 1918- *AmMWSc 92*
**Rice**, Randolf James 1947- *WhoAmL 92*
**Rice**, Richard Campbell 1933- *WhoMW 92*
**Rice**, Richard Eugene 1943- *AmMWSc 92*
**Rice**, Richard Leland 1943- *WhoFI 92*
**Rice**, Richard W 1931- *AmMWSc 92*
**Rice**, Rick Blackburn 1954- *WhoFI 92*
**Rice**, Rip G 1924- *AmMWSc 92*
**Rice**, Robert Arnot 1911- *AmMWSc 92*
**Rice**, Robert C. 1923- *WhoBlA 92*
**Rice**, Robert Collin 1959- *WhoAmL 92*
**Rice**, Robert Hafling 1944- *AmMWSc 92*
**Rice**, Robert Vernon 1924- *AmMWSc 92*
**Rice**, Rodney Vincent 1957- *WhoEnt 92*
**Rice**, Roger Douglas 1921- *WhoEnt 92*
**Rice**, Ronald L 1945- *WhoAmP 91*
**Rice**, Roy Warren 1934- *AmMWSc 92*
**Rice**, Ruby Lee 1929- *WhoRel 92*
**Rice**, Sally 1949- *WhoAmP 91*
**Rice**, Sandra Diane 1964- *WhoWest 92*
**Rice**, Sheila 1947- *WhoAmP 91*
**Rice**, Shirley J 1929- *WhoAmP 91*
**Rice**, Stan *DrAPF 91*
**Rice**, Stan 1942- *ConAu 36NR*
**Rice**, Stanley Alan 1947- *AmMWSc 92*
**Rice**, Stanley Donald 1945- *AmMWSc 92*
**Rice**, Stephen Landon 1941- *AmMWSc 92*
**Rice**, Stephen Manfred 1959- *WhoWest 92*
**Rice**, Steven Dale 1947- *WhoWest 92*
**Rice**, Stuart Alan 1932- *AmMWSc 92, IntWW 91*
**Rice**, Susie Leon 1922- *WhoBlA 92*
**Rice**, T.D. *BenetAL 91*
**Rice**, Theodore Roosevelt 1919- *AmMWSc 92*
**Rice**, Thomas B 1946- *AmMWSc 92*
**Rice**, Thomas Charles 1956- *WhoAmL 92*
**Rice**, Thomas Dartmouth 1808-1860 *NewAmDM*
**Rice**, Thomas E P, Jr 1923- *WhoAmP 91*
**Rice**, Thomas Maurice 1939- *AmMWSc 92*
**Rice**, Thomas R. 1945- *WhoWest 92*
**Rice**, Tim 1944- *FacFETw*
**Rice**, Tim Miles Bindon 1944- *IntWW 91*
**Rice**, Timothy Miles Bindon 1944- *Who 92*
**Rice**, V Thomas 1920- *WhoAmP 91*
**Rice**, Verdine D 1918- *WhoAmP 91*
**Rice**, Victor Albert 1941- *IntWW 91, WhoFI 92*
**Rice**, Virgil Thomas 1920- *WhoAmL 92*
**Rice**, Virginia *WhoAmP 91*
**Rice**, W B 1918- *AmMWSc 92*
**Rice**, W R 1924- *WhoAmP 91*
**Rice**, Wallace William 1936- *WhoWest 92*
**Rice**, Walter Herbert 1937- *WhoAmL 92, WhoMW 92*
**Rice**, Walter Wilburn 1918- *AmMWSc 92*
**Rice**, Warren 1925- *AmMWSc 92*
**Rice**, Wendell Alfred 1939- *AmMWSc 92*
**Rice**, William Abbott 1912- *AmMWSc 92*
**Rice**, William E. 1933- *WhoBlA 92*
**Rice**, William James 1927- *AmMWSc 92*
**Rice**, William Phipps 1944- *WhoFI 92*
**Rice**, Winston Edward 1946- *WhoAmL 92*
**Rice-Oxley**, James Keith 1920- *Who 92*
**Rice-Young**, Amy Lucetta 1952- *WhoEnt 92*
**Rich**, Abby M 1950- *AmMWSc 92*
**Rich**, Adrienne *DrAPF 91*
**Rich**, Adrienne 1929- *BenetAL 91, ConPo 91, FacFETw, HanAmWH, IntWW 91, ModAWWr, WhoWest 92, WrDr 92*
**Rich**, Alan 1924- *WhoEnt 92*
**Rich**, Alexander 1924- *AmMWSc 92, IntWW 91*
**Rich**, Alfred 1856-1921 *TwCPaSc*
**Rich**, Andrew Paterson 1954- *WhoMW 92*
**Rich**, Arthur 1937- *AmMWSc 92*
**Rich**, Arthur Gilbert 1936- *AmMWSc 92*
**Rich**, Avery Edmund 1915- *AmMWSc 92*
**Rich**, Barbara *ConAu 36NR*
**Rich**, Barnaby 1542-1617 *RfGEnL 91*
**Rich**, Ben Arthur 1947- *WhoAmL 92, WhoWest 92*
**Rich**, Ben R 1925- *AmMWSc 92*
**Rich**, Ben Robert 1925- *WhoFI 92*
**Rich**, Bennett M. 1909-1984 *ConAu 134*
**Rich**, Bernard 1917-1987 *FacFETw*
**Rich**, Berni 1929- *WhoMW 92*
**Rich**, Beverly Eileen 1950- *WhoAmP 91*
**Rich**, Brian Darryl 1962- *WhoAmL 92*
**Rich**, Bruce Allan 1939- *WhoAmL 92*
**Rich**, Buddy 1917-1987 *NewAmDM*
**Rich**, Charles Allan 1932- *WhoEnt 92*
**Rich**, Charles Clayton 1922- *AmMWSc 92*
**Rich**, Charlie 1932- *NewAmDM*
**Rich**, Clayton 1924- *AmMWSc 92, IntWW 91*
**Rich**, Daniel Alan 1950- *WhoFI 92*
**Rich**, Daniel Hulbert 1942- *AmMWSc 92*
**Rich**, David Allen *WhoMW 92*
**Rich**, David Lowell 1920- *IntMPA 92, WhoEnt 92*
**Rich**, Donald L *WhoAmP 91*
**Rich**, Earl Robert 1925- *AmMWSc 92*
**Rich**, Elaine Sommers 1926- *IntAu&W 91, WhoRel 92, WrDr 92*
**Rich**, Elizabeth Gamsky 1958- *WhoAmL 92*
**Rich**, Elizabeth Grace 1928- *WhoAmP 91*
**Rich**, Elliot 1919- *AmMWSc 92*
**Rich**, Eric 1921- *WhoFI 92*
**Rich**, Frances Luther 1910- *WhoWest 92*
**Rich**, Frank Hart 1949- *IntAu&W 91, WhoEnt 92*
**Rich**, Frank Hart, Jr. 1949- *IntWW 91*
**Rich**, Gareth Edward 1961- *WhoWest 92*
**Rich**, George Sunderland 1948- *WhoFI 92*
**Rich**, Giles S *WhoAmP 91*
**Rich**, Giles Sutherland 1904- *WhoAmL 92*
**Rich**, Glenn Eugene 1949- *WhoAmP 91*
**Rich**, H Thompson 1893- *ScFEYrs*
**Rich**, Harry E. 1940- *WhoFI 92*
**Rich**, Harry Louis 1917- *AmMWSc 92*
**Rich**, J. Dennis 1945- *WhoEnt 92, WhoMW 92*
**Rich**, J. Peter 1953- *WhoAmL 92*
**Rich**, James Arthur 1950- *WhoEnt 92*
**Rich**, James Edward 1951- *WhoAmP 91*
**Rich**, Jeffrey A 1945- *WhoAmP 91*
**Rich**, Jerry Lynn 1951- *WhoRel 92*
**Rich**, Jimmy Ray 1950- *AmMWSc 92*
**Rich**, John *IntMPA 92, LesBEnT 92*
**Rich**, John 1925- *WhoEnt 92*
**Rich**, John Charles 1937- *AmMWSc 92*
**Rich**, John Rowland 1928- *IntWW 91, Who 92*
**Rich**, Joseph Anthony 1916- *AmMWSc 92*
**Rich**, Joseph Ash 1943- *WhoWest 92*
**Rich**, Joseph William 1937- *AmMWSc 92*
**Rich**, Judith Margaret 1940- *WhoEnt 92*
**Rich**, Kenneth C 1943- *AmMWSc 92*
**Rich**, Kenneth Eugene 1943- *AmMWSc 92*
**Rich**, Kerry *WhoAmP 91*
**Rich**, Lee *LesBEnT 92*
**Rich**, Lee 1926- *IntMPA 92*
**Rich**, Leonard G 1925- *AmMWSc 92*
**Rich**, Linvil G 1921- *AmMWSc 92*
**Rich**, Louise Dickinson d1991 *NewYTBS 91*
**Rich**, Louise Dickinson 1903- *BenetAL 91*
**Rich**, Louise Dickinson 1903-1991 *ConAu 134, CurBio 91N, SmATA 67*
**Rich**, Luise D d1991 *NewYTBS 91*
**Rich**, Mark 1932- *AmMWSc 92*
**Rich**, Marvin A 1931- *AmMWSc 92*
**Rich**, Marvin R 1947- *AmMWSc 92*
**Rich**, Matty *NewYTBS 91*
**Rich**, Matty 1972- *WhoBlA 92*
**Rich**, Michael 1940- *AmMWSc 92*
**Rich**, Michael Anthony 1931- *Who 92*
**Rich**, Michael Joseph 1945- *WhoAmL 92*
**Rich**, Michael Samuel 1933- *Who 92*
**Rich**, Nigel Mervyn Sutherland 1945- *Who 92*
**Rich**, Paul B 1950- *IntAu&W 91*
**Rich**, Peter Hamilton 1939- *AmMWSc 92*
**Rich**, Raymond Thomas 1899-1959 *AmPeW*
**Rich**, Richard *BenetAL 91*
**Rich**, Richard Douglas 1936- *AmMWSc 92*
**Rich**, Robert Bruce 1949- *WhoAmL 92*
**Rich**, Robert E., Sr. *WhoFI 92*
**Rich**, Robert G, Jr 1930- *WhoAmP 91*
**Rich**, Robert Graham, Jr. 1930- *IntWW 91*
**Rich**, Robert Peter 1919- *AmMWSc 92*
**Rich**, Robert Regier 1941- *AmMWSc 92*
**Rich**, Robert Stephen 1938- *WhoAmL 92, WhoWest 92*
**Rich**, Rolla Ross 1945- *WhoWest 92*
**Rich**, Ronald Lee 1927- *AmMWSc 92*
**Rich**, Royal Allen 1934- *AmMWSc 92*
**Rich**, Ruthanne 1941- *WhoEnt 92*
**Rich**, S. Judith *WhoMW 92*
**Rich**, Saul 1917- *AmMWSc 92*
**Rich**, Shirley 1922- *WhoEnt 92*
**Rich**, Stanley C. 1920- *WhoBlA 92*
**Rich**, Susan Marie Solliday 1941- *AmMWSc 92*
**Rich**, Terrell L 1939- *AmMWSc 92*
**Rich**, Therese Ann 1948- *WhoRel 92*
**Rich**, Thomas Blaise 1951- *WhoRel 92*
**Rich**, Thomas Hewitt 1941- *AmMWSc 92*
**Rich**, Travis Dean 1940- *AmMWSc 92*
**Rich**, Walter George 1946- *WhoFI 92*
**Rich**, Wayne Schermerhorn 1912- *WhoAmP 91*
**Rich**, Wilbur C. 1939- *WhoBlA 92*
**Richard** *Who 92*
**Richard**, Baron 1932- *IntWW 91, Who 92*
**Richard**, Adrienne 1921- *WrDr 92*
**Richard**, Alexander *WhoAmP 91*
**Richard**, Alfred Joseph 1928- *AmMWSc 92*
**Richard**, Allen Joseph 1947- *WhoAmP 91*
**Richard**, Alvin J. 1932- *WhoBlA 92*
**Richard**, Anita Louise 1951- *WhoWest 92*
**Richard**, Arlene Castain 1955- *WhoBlA 92*
**Richard**, B. Loynd *WhoMW 92*
**Richard**, Barry Scott 1942- *WhoAmP 91*
**Richard**, Benjamin H 1929- *AmMWSc 92*
**Richard**, Carla Jean 1944- *WhoMW 92*
**Richard**, Christian Remi 1941- *IntWW 91*
**Richard**, Christopher Alan 1951- *AmMWSc 92*
**Richard**, Christopher Marc 1949- *WhoWest 92*
**Richard**, Claude 1932- *AmMWSc 92*
**Richard**, Claude 1944- *AmMWSc 92*
**Richard**, Cliff 1940- *IntMPA 92, IntWW 91, Who 92, WrDr 92*
**Richard**, David Allan 1945- *WhoFI 92*
**Richard**, Earl Joseph 1940- *WhoRel 92*
**Richard**, Ellen 1957- *WhoEnt 92*
**Richard**, Floyd Anthony 1952- *WhoBlA 92*
**Richard**, Frederick Hugh 1938- *WhoFI 92*
**Richard**, Henri-Claude 1944- *WhoBlA 92*
**Richard**, Holly Beth 1957- *WhoEnt 92*
**Richard**, Howard 1921- *WhoAmL 92*
**Richard**, James L. 1917- *WhoBlA 92*
**Richard**, Janice Muriel 1945- *WhoMW 92*
**Richard**, Jean Barthelemy 1921- *IntWW 91*
**Richard**, Jean-Paul 1936- *AmMWSc 92*
**Richard**, Jefferson 1946- *WhoEnt 92*
**Richard**, John L 1938- *AmMWSc 92*
**Richard**, John P *AmMWSc 92*
**Richard**, Joseph Henri Maurice 1921- *FacFETw*
**Richard**, Mae *WhoEnt 92*
**Richard**, Mark M. 1939- *WhoAmL 92*
**Richard**, Marthe 1889-1982 *FacFETw*
**Richard**, Patrick 1938- *AmMWSc 92*
**Richard**, Pierre Joseph Herve 1946- *AmMWSc 92*
**Richard**, R. Paul 1950- *WhoBlA 92*
**Richard**, Ralph Michael 1930- *AmMWSc 92*
**Richard**, Ralph Zachary *WhoEnt 92*
**Richard**, Richard Ray 1927- *AmMWSc 92*
**Richard**, Robert Carter 1938- *WhoWest 92*
**Richard**, Robert H 1927- *AmMWSc 92*
**Richard**, Robert John 1947- *WhoWest 92*
**Richard**, Robert Leo 1945- *WhoEnt 92*
**Richard**, Sandra Clayton *WhoFI 92*
**Richard**, Susan *WrDr 92*
**Richard**, Terry Gordon 1945- *AmMWSc 92*
**Richard**, William Ralph, Jr 1922- *AmMWSc 92*
**Richardello**, Ronald Anthony 1943- *WhoEnt 92*
**Richards** *Who 92*
**Richards**, A M 1926- *AmMWSc 92*
**Richards**, Adrian F 1929- *AmMWSc 92*
**Richards**, Albert 1919-1945 *TwCPaSc*
**Richards**, Albert Glenn 1909- *AmMWSc 92*
**Richards**, Albert Gustav 1917- *AmMWSc 92*
**Richards**, Alun *Who 92*
**Richards**, Alun 1929- *IntAu&W 91*
**Richards**, Ann 1933- *CurBio 91 [port], News 91 [port]*
**Richards**, Ann W. 1933- *AlmAP 92 [port]*
**Richards**, Ann Willis 1933- *IntWW 91, WhoAmP 91*
**Richards**, Archibald Banks 1911- *Who 92*
**Richards**, Arthur A. 1924- *WhoBlA 92*
**Richards**, Arthur Cyril 1921- *Who 92*
**Richards**, Arthur L. 1907- *IntWW 91*
**Richards**, Beah *IntMPA 92, WhoBlA 92*
**Richards**, Beah 1926- *NotBlAW 92 [port]*
**Richards**, Bertrand *Who 92*
**Richards**, Beth Ann 1951- *WhoRel 92*
**Richards**, Bradley James 1958- *WhoAmL 92*
**Richards**, Brenda Sharlene 1955- *WhoMW 92*
**Richards**, Brian Henry 1938- *Who 92*
**Richards**, Brian Mansel 1932- *Who 92*
**Richards**, Brooks *Who 92*
**Richards**, Bruce S. 1955- *WhoWest 92*
**Richards**, Bruce Stephen 1944- *WhoMW 92*
**Richards**, Burt 1930- *WhoEnt 92*
**Richards**, Carmeleete A. 1948- *WhoFI 92*
**Richards**, Catherine Margaret 1940- *Who 92*
**Richards**, Ceri 1903-1971 *TwCPaSc*
**Richards**, Charles Anthony Langdon 1911- *Who 92*
**Richards**, Charles Brinckerhoff 1833-1919 *BiInAmS*
**Richards**, Charles Davis 1920- *AmMWSc 92*
**Richards**, Charles Jack 1937- *WhoRel 92*
**Richards**, Charles Napier *ScFEYrs*
**Richards**, Charles Norman 1942- *AmMWSc 92*
**Richards**, ChrisAnn 1958- *WhoMW 92*
**Richards**, Christine-Louise 1910- *WhoEnt 92, WrDr 92*
**Richards**, Christos 1957- *WhoWest 92*
**Richards**, Clare *WrDr 92*
**Richards**, Clyde Rich 1921- *AmMWSc 92*
**Richards**, Cyndi *DrAPF 91*
**Richards**, Cynthia Ann 1959- *WhoMW 92*
**Richards**, Dale Owen 1927- *AmMWSc 92*
**Richards**, Daniel Wells 1928- *WhoMW 92*
**Richards**, David A. J. 1944- *WhoAmL 92*
**Richards**, David Alan 1945- *WhoAmL 92*
**Richards**, David Gordon 1928- *Who 92*
**Richards**, David Thomas 1950- *WhoEnt 92*
**Richards**, DeLeon Marie 1976- *WhoBlA 92*
**Richards**, Denis 1910- *IntAu&W 91*
**Richards**, Denis Edward 1923- *Who 92*
**Richards**, Denis George 1910- *Who 92, WrDr 92*
**Richards**, Dick 1936- *IntMPA 92*
**Richards**, Dickinson Woodruff 1895-1973 *WhoNob 90*
**Richards**, Donald Crawford 1932- *WhoFI 92*
**Richards**, E. Grant *DcLB 112*
**Richards**, Earl Frederick 1923- *AmMWSc 92*
**Richards**, Edmund A 1935- *AmMWSc 92*
**Richards**, Edmund Bertrand 1913- *Who 92*
**Richards**, Edward *TwCSFW 91*
**Richards**, Edward A. 1930- *WhoBlA 92*
**Richards**, Edward Trenton d1991 *Who 92N*
**Richards**, Edward Trenton 1908- *IntWW 91*
**Richards**, Elfyn John 1914- *Who 92*
**Richards**, Ellen Henrietta Swallow 1842-1911 *BiInAmS*
**Richards**, Elvige Cassard 1956- *WhoAmL 92*
**Richards**, Eugene Lamb 1838-1912 *BiInAmS*
**Richards**, Evelyn E 1927- *WhoAmP 91*
**Richards**, F Paul 1946- *AmMWSc 92*
**Richards**, Fannie M. 1840-1922 *NotBlAW 92*
**Richards**, Frances 1903- *TwCPaSc*
**Richards**, Francis Asbury 1917- *AmMWSc 92*
**Richards**, Francis Brooks 1918- *Who 92*
**Richards**, Francis Neville *Who 92*
**Richards**, Francis Russell 1944- *AmMWSc 92*
**Richards**, Frank Frederick 1928- *AmMWSc 92*
**Richards**, Frederic Middlebrook 1925- *AmMWSc 92, IntWW 91*
**Richards**, Frederick *WhoAmP 91*
**Richards**, Frederick, II 1938- *AmMWSc 92*
**Richards**, Frederick Francis, Jr. 1936- *WhoFI 92*
**Richards**, Gary Paul 1950- *AmMWSc 92*
**Richards**, Geoffrey Norman 1927- *AmMWSc 92*
**Richards**, George A. d1951 *LesBEnT 92*
**Richards**, George Patrick 1948- *WhoWest 92*
**Richards**, Gerald Thomas 1933- *WhoAmL 92, WhoWest 92*
**Richards**, Gloria Delise 1940- *IntAu&W 91*
**Richards**, Gordon 1904-1986 *FacFETw*
**Richards**, Grant 1872-1948 *DcLB 112 [port]*
**Richards**, Graydon Edward 1933- *AmMWSc 92*
**Richards**, Gwynfryn 1902- *Who 92*
**Richards**, Harold F 1894- *ScFEYrs*
**Richards**, Harold Rex 1926- *AmMWSc 92*
**Richards**, Henry *TwCSFW 91*
**Richards**, Herbert East 1919- *WhoRel 92, WhoWest 92*
**Richards**, Hilda 1936- *WhoBlA 92*
**Richards**, Hubert John 1921- *IntAu&W 91*
**Richards**, Hugh Taylor 1918- *AmMWSc 92*
**Richards**, I A 1893-1979 *ConAu 34NR, FacFETw, RfGEnL 91*
**Richards**, Isaac Vivian 1952- *Who 92*
**Richards**, Isaac Vivian Alexander 1952- *IntWW 91*
**Richards**, Jack Lester 1940- *AmMWSc 92*
**Richards**, James 1907- *IntAu&W 91*
**Richards**, James Alan 1913- *Who 92*
**Richards**, James Austin, Jr 1916- *AmMWSc 92*
**Richards**, James Frederick 1927- *AmMWSc 92*
**Richards**, James L 1946- *AmMWSc 92*

**Richards,** James Maude 1907- *Who 92, WrDr 92*
**Richards,** James R 1933- *WhoAmP 91*
**Richards,** James William 1921- *WhoWest 92*
**Richards,** Janet Radcliffe 1944- *ConAu 133*
**Richards,** Jerry Lee 1939- *WhoRel 92*
**Richards,** Jess 1943- *WhoEnt 92*
**Richards,** Joanne S 1945- *AmMWSc 92*
**Richards,** Jody 1938- *WhoAmP 91*
**Richards,** Joe Bryan 1929- *WhoAmL 92*
**Richards,** John 1927- *IntWW 91*
**Richards,** John 1933- *Who 92*
**Richards,** John Arthur 1918- *Who 92*
**Richards,** John Charles Chisholm 1927- *Who 92*
**Richards,** John Deacon 1931- *Who 92*
**Richards,** John Hall 1930- *AmMWSc 92*
**Richards,** John Harold 1950- *WhoAmP 91*
**Richards,** John M. 1937- *WhoWest 92*
**Richards,** John Wheeler 1936- *WhoFI 92*
**Richards,** Johnetta Gladys 1950- *WhoBlA 92*
**Richards,** Jonathan Ian 1936- *AmMWSc 92*
**Richards,** Joseph Dudley 1917- *AmMWSc 92*
**Richards,** Katherine Mary 1941- *WhoWest 92*
**Richards,** Keith 1943- *IntWW 91, WhoEnt 92*
**Richards,** Kenneth Edwin 1917- *WhoWest 92*
**Richards,** Kenneth Julian 1932- *AmMWSc 92*
**Richards,** Kent Harold 1939- *WhoRel 92, WhoWest 92*
**Richards,** L Willard 1932- *AmMWSc 92*
**Richards,** LaClaire Lissetta Jones *WhoMW 92*
**Richards,** Laura Elizabeth 1850-1943 *BenetAL 91*
**Richards,** LaVerne W. 1947- *WhoBlA 92*
**Richards,** Leon 1945- *WhoBlA 92*
**Richards,** Leonard Martin 1935- *WhoFI 92*
**Richards,** Lloyd 1923?- *ConBlB 2 [port]*
**Richards,** Lloyd G. *WhoBlA 92*
**Richards,** Lloyd George *WhoEnt 92*
**Richards,** Lorenzo Adolph 1904- *AmMWSc 92*
**Richards,** Loretta Theresa 1929- *WhoBlA 92*
**Richards,** Lysander Salmon 1835-1926 *ScFEYrs*
**Richards,** Malcolm Cecil 1947- *WhoMW 92*
**Richards,** Marilee *DrAPF 91*
**Richards,** Mark 1922- *WrDr 92*
**Richards,** Mark George 1955- *WhoMW 92*
**Richards,** Mark P *AmMWSc 92*
**Richards,** Marta Alison 1952- *WhoAmL 92, WhoFI 92*
**Richards,** Marvin Sherrill 1922- *AmMWSc 92*
**Richards,** Melanie *DrAPF 91*
**Richards,** Michael 1915- *Who 92*
**Richards,** Michael Anthony 1926- *Who 92*
**Richards,** Michael Howard 1945- *WhoMW 92*
**Richards,** Morris Dick 1939- *WhoWest 92*
**Richards,** Nancy Jill Schanfald 1961- *WhoEnt 92*
**Richards,** Norman Blanchard 1924- *WhoAmL 92*
**Richards,** Norval Richard 1916- *AmMWSc 92*
**Richards,** Oliver Christopher 1933- *AmMWSc 92*
**Richards,** Patti Rutland 1960- *WhoEnt 92*
**Richards,** Paul *IntAu&W 91X*
**Richards,** Paul 1949- *TwCPaSc*
**Richards,** Paul A. 1927- *WhoAmL 92, WhoWest 92*
**Richards,** Paul Bland 1924- *AmMWSc 92*
**Richards,** Paul Granston 1943- *AmMWSc 92*
**Richards,** Paul Linford 1934- *AmMWSc 92*
**Richards,** Perry Samuel 1953- *WhoRel 92*
**Richards,** Peter 1936- *Who 92*
**Richards,** Peter Michael 1934- *AmMWSc 92*
**Richards,** Philip Raymond 1958- *WhoAmL 92*
**Richards,** R Ronald 1937- *AmMWSc 92*
**Richards,** Reuben Francis 1929- *WhoFI 92*
**Richards,** Rex 1922- *Who 92*
**Richards,** Rex Edward 1922- *IntWW 91*
**Richards,** Richard 1932- *WhoAmP 91*
**Richards,** Richard Alun 1920- *Who 92*
**Richards,** Richard Davison 1927- *AmMWSc 92*
**Richards,** Richard Earl 1934- *AmMWSc 92*
**Richards,** Richard Jean *WhoMW 92*
**Richards,** Richard Meredyth 1920- *Who 92*
**Richards,** Robert Charles 1939- *WhoFI 92*
**Richards,** Roberta Lynne 1945- *AmMWSc 92*
**Richards,** Roger Thomas 1942- *AmMWSc 92*
**Richards,** Ronald Charles William 1923- *IntAu&W 91*
**Richards,** Ronald Edwin 1908- *Who 92*
**Richards,** Ronald Gene 1952- *WhoMW 92*
**Richards,** Roosevelt 1933- *WhoBlA 92*
**Richards,** Russell J. 1947- *WhoFI 92*
**Richards,** Sandra Lee 1946- *WhoBlA 92*
**Richards,** Stanley Harold 1922- *WhoFI 92*
**Richards,** Stephens 1935- *WhoRel 92*
**Richards,** Steven Paul 1947- *WhoRel 92*
**Richards,** Susan 1948- *ConAu 135*
**Richards,** Suzanne V. 1927- *WhoAmL 92*
**Richards,** Terri Linn 1954- *WhoMW 92*
**Richards,** Theodore William 1868-1928 *WhoNob 90*
**Richards,** Thomas H. 1942- *WhoAmL 92*
**Richards,** Thomas L 1942- *AmMWSc 92*
**Richards,** Victor 1918- *AmMWSc 92*
**Richards,** Vincent Philip Haslewood 1933- *WhoWest 92*
**Richards,** Viv 1952- *FacFETw*
**Richards,** Vivian *Who 92*
**Richards,** Wade Joseph 1941- *WhoWest 92*
**Richards,** Walter Bruce 1941- *AmMWSc 92, WhoMW 92*
**Richards,** Wesley Jon 1942- *WhoEnt 92*
**Richards,** William Alexander, III 1958- *WhoEnt 92*
**Richards,** William Earl 1921- *WhoBlA 92*
**Richards,** William George 1920- *WhoFI 92*
**Richards,** William James 1947- *WhoAmL 92*
**Richards,** William Joseph 1936- *AmMWSc 92*
**Richards,** William Leslie 1916- *IntAu&W 91*
**Richards,** William Reese 1938- *AmMWSc 92*
**Richards,** William Sidney 1910- *WhoAmP 91*
**Richards,** Winn L 1928- *WhoAmP 91*
**Richards,** Winston Ashton *AmMWSc 92*
**Richards,** Winston Ashton 1935- *WhoBlA 92*
**Richards-Alexander,** Billie J. *WhoBlA 92*
**Richards-Maldonado,** Judy 1954- *WhoHisp 92*
**Richards-Stower,** Nancy Ann 1951- *WhoAmP 91*
**Richardson** *Who 92*
**Richardson,** Baron 1910- *IntWW 91, Who 92, WrDr 92*
**Richardson,** Alan 1923- *WrDr 92*
**Richardson,** Albert Dion 1946- *WhoBlA 92*
**Richardson,** Albert Edward 1929- *AmMWSc 92*
**Richardson,** Alfred, Jr 1932- *AmMWSc 92*
**Richardson,** Alfred Lloyd 1927- *WhoBlA 92*
**Richardson,** Allan Charles Barbour 1932- *AmMWSc 92*
**Richardson,** Allyn 1918- *AmMWSc 92*
**Richardson,** Anne *WrDr 92*
**Richardson,** Anne Strickland 1956- *WhoEnt 92*
**Richardson,** Anthony *Who 92*
**Richardson,** Anthony 1950- *Who 92*
**Richardson,** Anthony W. 1957- *WhoBlA 92*
**Richardson,** Arlan Gilbert 1942- *AmMWSc 92*
**Richardson,** Arleta 1923- *ConAu 36NR*
**Richardson,** Arthur Bertholin Larsen 1935- *WhoWest 92*
**Richardson,** Arthur Jerold 1938- *AmMWSc 92*
**Richardson,** Arthur Leslie 1910- *WhoWest 92*
**Richardson,** Arthur Wilhelm 1963- *WhoWest 92*
**Richardson,** Avis June 1931- *WhoRel 92*
**Richardson,** Barbara Connell 1947- *WhoMW 92*
**Richardson,** Ben T *WhoAmP 91*
**Richardson,** Betty 1935- *WhoMW 92*
**Richardson,** Betty Hansen 1953- *WhoAmP 91*
**Richardson,** Bill 1947- *AlmAP 92 [port], WhoAmP 91, WhoHisp 92*
**Richardson,** Billy 1936- *AmMWSc 92*
**Richardson,** Bob 1945- *WhoAmP 91*
**Richardson,** Bobbie L 1926- *AmMWSc 92*
**Richardson,** Bobby Harold 1944- *WhoAmP 91*
**Richardson,** Bonham C. 1939- *ConAu 135*
**Richardson,** Campbell 1930- *WhoAmL 92*
**Richardson,** Carl Colley, Jr. 1941- *WhoFI 92*
**Richardson,** Carolyn Jane 1943- *WhoWest 92*
**Richardson,** Charles *Who 92*
**Richardson,** Charles Bonner 1959- *AmMWSc 92*
**Richardson,** Charles Clifton 1935- *AmMWSc 92*
**Richardson,** Charles Francis 1851-1913 *BenetAL 91*
**Richardson,** Charles Phillip 1933- *WhoMW 92*
**Richardson,** Charles Raymond 1934- *WhoRel 92*
**Richardson,** Charles Ronald 1949- *WhoBlA 92*
**Richardson,** Charles T. 1947- *WhoAmL 92*
**Richardson,** Charles Walter Philipps 1905- *Who 92*
**Richardson,** Chris Paul 1957- *WhoWest 92*
**Richardson,** Clarence Robert 1931- *AmMWSc 92*
**Richardson,** Clarence Wade 1942- *AmMWSc 92*
**Richardson,** Clint Dewitt 1956- *WhoBlA 92*
**Richardson,** Clyta Faith 1915- *WhoRel 92*
**Richardson,** Cordell 1946- *WhoBlA 92*
**Richardson,** Curtis John 1944- *AmMWSc 92*
**Richardson,** Dana Roland 1945- *WhoFI 92*
**Richardson,** Daniel Ray 1939- *AmMWSc 92*
**Richardson,** David 1928- *Who 92*
**Richardson,** David 1942- *WrDr 92*
**Richardson,** David Bacon 1916- *WhoFI 92*
**Richardson,** David John 1943- *WhoEnt 92*
**Richardson,** David Louis 1948- *AmMWSc 92*
**Richardson,** David Neal 1939- *WhoFI 92*
**Richardson,** David P, Jr 1948- *WhoAmP 91*
**Richardson,** David Preston, Jr. 1948- *WhoBlA 92*
**Richardson,** David W 1925- *AmMWSc 92*
**Richardson,** David William 1932- *Who 92*
**Richardson,** Deane W. 1930- *DcTwDes*
**Richardson,** Deanna Ruth 1956- *WhoMW 92*
**Richardson,** Delroy M. 1938- *WhoBlA 92*
**Richardson,** Dennis Michael 1949- *WhoAmL 92*
**Richardson,** DeRutha Gardner 1941- *WhoBlA 92*
**Richardson,** Diane *WhoEnt 92*
**Richardson,** Diane 1951- *WhoWest 92*
**Richardson,** Don *WhoEnt 92*
**Richardson,** Don Orland 1934- *AmMWSc 92*
**Richardson,** Donald Charles 1937- *WhoFI 92*
**Richardson,** Donald Edward 1931- *AmMWSc 92*
**Richardson,** Donald Porter 1932- *WhoMW 92*
**Richardson,** Dorothy 1873-1957 *RfGEnL 91*
**Richardson,** Dorothy Hood 1943- *WhoRel 92*
**Richardson,** Dorothy Miller 1873-1957 *FacFETw*
**Richardson,** Douglas Fielding 1929- *WhoAmL 92, WhoFI 92*
**Richardson,** Earl Stanford 1943- *WhoBlA 92*
**Richardson,** Edward Allen 1936- *WhoRel 92*
**Richardson,** Edward Henderson, Jr 1911- *AmMWSc 92*
**Richardson,** Egerton 1912- *Who 92*
**Richardson,** Eleanor Elizabeth 1948- *WhoFI 92*
**Richardson,** Eleanor L *WhoAmP 91*
**Richardson,** Elisha R. 1931- *WhoBlA 92*
**Richardson,** Elisha Roscoe 1931- *AmMWSc 92*
**Richardson,** Elliot Lee 1920- *IntWW 91, Who 92, WhoAmL 92*
**Richardson,** Emilie White *WhoFI 92*
**Richardson,** Eric *Who 92*
**Richardson,** Eric Harvey 1927- *AmMWSc 92*
**Richardson,** Ernest A. 1925- *WhoBlA 92*
**Richardson,** Evelyn D *WhoAmP 91*
**Richardson,** Everett V 1924- *AmMWSc 92*
**Richardson,** F C 1936- *AmMWSc 92, WhoBlA 92*
**Richardson,** Frances Marian 1922- *AmMWSc 92*
**Richardson,** Frank 1950- *WhoBlA 92*
**Richardson,** Frank Craig, Jr. 1952- *WhoAmL 92*
**Richardson,** Frank H. 1933- *IntWW 91, WhoFI 92*
**Richardson,** Frank McLean 1904- *Who 92, WrDr 92*
**Richardson,** Fred L 1942- *WhoAmP 91*
**Richardson,** Frederick S 1939- *AmMWSc 92*
**Richardson,** Gary Haight 1931- *AmMWSc 92*
**Richardson,** Gary Joe 1945- *WhoRel 92*
**Richardson,** Gary Lee 1947- *WhoAmP 91*
**Richardson,** Geoffrey Alan 1936- *WrDr 92*
**Richardson,** George Barclay 1924- *IntWW 91, Who 92, WrDr 92*
**Richardson,** George C. 1929- *WhoBlA 92*
**Richardson,** George Peter 1935- *WhoRel 92*
**Richardson,** George S 1921- *AmMWSc 92*
**Richardson,** George Taylor 1924- *IntWW 91, Who 92*
**Richardson,** Gerald Clemen 1937- *WhoFI 92*
**Richardson,** Gerald Laverne 1928- *AmMWSc 92*
**Richardson,** Gerald Michael 1953- *WhoAmL 92*
**Richardson,** Gilda Faye 1926- *WhoBlA 92*
**Richardson,** Gladwell 1904-1980 *TwCWW 91*
**Richardson,** Gloria 1922- *NotBlAW 92*
**Richardson,** Gloster V. 1941- *WhoBlA 92*
**Richardson,** Gordon Banning 1937- *WhoAmP 91*
**Richardson,** Gordon Dalyell 1917- *IntWW 91*
**Richardson,** Graham 1949- *IntWW 91*
**Richardson,** Graham Edmund 1913- *Who 92*
**Richardson,** Graham McGavock 1912- *AmMWSc 92*
**Richardson,** Grant Lee 1919- *AmMWSc 92*
**Richardson,** H L 1927- *WhoAmP 91*
**Richardson,** Hal 1951- *WhoEnt 92*
**Richardson,** Harold 1938- *AmMWSc 92*
**Richardson,** Harold Edward 1922- *WhoBlA 92*
**Richardson,** Harry W. 1938- *WrDr 92*
**Richardson,** Henry Anthony 1925- *Who 92*
**Richardson,** Henry Handel 1870-1946 *LiExTwC, RfGEnL 91*
**Richardson,** Henry J., III 1941- *WhoBlA 92*
**Richardson,** Henry Russell 1938- *AmMWSc 92*
**Richardson,** Herbert D 1950- *WhoAmP 91*
**Richardson,** Herbert Heath 1930- *AmMWSc 92*
**Richardson,** Horace Vincent 1913- *Who 92*
**Richardson,** Hugh Edward 1905- *Who 92*
**Richardson,** Ian William 1934- *IntWW 91, Who 92*
**Richardson,** Irvin Whaley 1934- *AmMWSc 92*
**Richardson,** Ivor 1930- *Who 92*
**Richardson,** J Mark 1954- *AmMWSc 92*
**Richardson,** J Steven 1943- *AmMWSc 92*
**Richardson,** Jack *WhoAmP 91*
**Richardson,** Jack 1935- *WrDr 92*
**Richardson,** Jack C. 1934- *BenetAL 91*
**Richardson,** James *DrAPF 91*
**Richardson,** James Albert 1915- *AmMWSc 92*
**Richardson,** James Allen 1948- *WhoMW 92*
**Richardson,** James Armstrong 1922- *Who 92*
**Richardson,** James Claude 1946- *WhoRel 92*
**Richardson,** James Elijah 1960- *WhoEnt 92*
**Richardson,** James F *WhoAmP 91*
**Richardson,** James Fairgrieve 1940- *WhoIns 92*
**Richardson,** James John 1941- *Who 92*
**Richardson,** James M 1940- *WhoAmP 91*
**Richardson,** James Philip 1951- *WhoFI 92*
**Richardson,** James T 1928- *AmMWSc 92*
**Richardson,** James Troy 1941- *WhoRel 92, WhoWest 92*
**Richardson,** James Wyman 1930- *AmMWSc 92, WhoMW 92*
**Richardson,** Jamie Irene 1952- *WhoAmL 92*
**Richardson,** Jane S 1941- *AmMWSc 92*
**Richardson,** Jasper E 1922- *AmMWSc 92*
**Richardson,** Jay 1957- *WhoAmL 92*
**Richardson,** Jay Wilson, Jr 1940- *AmMWSc 92*
**Richardson,** Jeffery Howard 1948- *AmMWSc 92*
**Richardson,** Jennifer Jane Goode 1951- *WhoEnt 92*
**Richardson,** Jennifer Roberts 1960- *WhoRel 92*
**Richardson,** Jillian 1965- *BlkOlyM*
**Richardson,** Joanna *IntAu&W 91, IntWW 91, Who 92, WrDr 92*
**Richardson,** Joely 1958- *IntWW 91*
**Richardson,** Joely 1965- *IntMPA 92*
**Richardson,** John 1796-1852 *BenetAL 91*
**Richardson,** John Carroll 1932- *WhoAmL 92*
**Richardson,** John David Benbow 1919- *Who 92*
**Richardson,** John Edmon 1942- *WhoWest 92*
**Richardson,** John Eric 1905- *Who 92*
**Richardson,** John Eric 1916- *Who 92*

**Richardson,** John Farquhar d1991 *Who 92N*
**Richardson,** John Flint 1906- *Who 92*
**Richardson,** John Francis 1934- *Who 92*
**Richardson,** John Francis 1952- *WhoFI 92*
**Richardson,** John Jacob 1940- *WhoRel 92*
**Richardson,** John L 1935- *AmMWSc 92*
**Richardson,** John MacLaren, Jr. 1942- *WhoRel 92*
**Richardson,** John Marshall 1921- *AmMWSc 92*
**Richardson,** John Mead 1918- *AmMWSc 92*
**Richardson,** John Paul 1938- *AmMWSc 92, WhoMW 92*
**Richardson,** John Reginald 1912- *AmMWSc 92*
**Richardson,** John Stephen 1950- *Who 92*
**Richardson,** John Vinson, Jr. 1949- *WhoWest 92*
**Richardson,** Johnny L. 1952- *WhoBlA 92*
**Richardson,** Jonathan L 1935- *AmMWSc 92*
**Richardson,** Joseph 1940- *WhoBlA 92*
**Richardson,** Joseph Ablett, Jr. 1928- *WhoAmL 92, WhoFI 92*
**Richardson,** Joseph Gerald 1923- *AmMWSc 92*
**Richardson,** Joseph John, Sr. 1930- *WhoMW 92, WhoRel 92*
**Richardson,** Josephine *Who 92*
**Richardson,** Julia Rankin 1946- *WhoAmL 92*
**Richardson,** Julieanna Lynn 1954- *WhoFI 92*
**Richardson,** K. Scott 1951- *WhoFI 92*
**Richardson,** Kathleen Harris 1948- *WhoAmL 92*
**Richardson,** Kathleen Margaret 1938- *Who 92*
**Richardson,** Kathleen Schueller 1938- *AmMWSc 92*
**Richardson,** Keith Edward 1947- *WhoWest 92*
**Richardson,** Keith Erwin 1928- *AmMWSc 92*
**Richardson,** Kenneth 1956- *WhoEnt 92*
**Richardson,** Kenneth Albert 1926- *Who 92*
**Richardson,** Kenneth Augustus 1939- *Who 92*
**Richardson,** Kenneth John 1946- *WhoFI 92*
**Richardson,** Kermit W 1929- *WhoAmP 91*
**Richardson,** Lacy Franklin 1937- *WhoBlA 92*
**Richardson,** Lavon Preston 1925- *AmMWSc 92*
**Richardson,** Lawrence 1923- *WhoAmP 91*
**Richardson,** Lee S 1929- *AmMWSc 92*
**Richardson,** Leo 1931- *WhoBlA 92*
**Richardson,** Leonard Frederick 1944- *AmMWSc 92*
**Richardson,** Linda Waters 1946- *WhoBlA 92*
**Richardson,** Linford Lawson 1941- *WhoWest 92*
**Richardson,** Lionel Earl d1990 *Who 92N*
**Richardson,** Louis M. 1927- *WhoBlA 92*
**Richardson,** Luns C. 1928- *WhoBlA 92*
**Richardson,** Lynford M 1932- *WhoIns 92*
**Richardson,** Mabel Lowe 1896- *WhoAmP 91*
**Richardson,** Madison Franklin 1943- *WhoBlA 92*
**Richardson,** Margaret Milner 1943- *WhoAmL 92*
**Richardson,** Marianne Briggs 1942- *WhoRel 92*
**Richardson,** Mark Denton 1953- *WhoEnt 92*
**Richardson,** Mark Lee 1952- *WhoAmP 91*
**Richardson,** Mary Elizabeth 1916- *WhoWest 92*
**Richardson,** Mary Elizabeth 1927- *AmMWSc 92*
**Richardson,** Mary Frances 1941- *AmMWSc 92*
**Richardson,** Mary Margaret 1932- *WhoBlA 92*
**Richardson,** Mary Raleigh 1888?- *BiDBrF 2*
**Richardson,** Matthew Statisfield 1972- *WhoBlA 92*
**Richardson,** Mattie Lou 1924- *WhoAmP 91*
**Richardson,** Maurice Howe 1851-1912 *BiInAmS*
**Richardson,** Melvin M 1928- *WhoAmP 91*
**Richardson,** Michael 1925- *Who 92*
**Richardson,** Michael Lewellyn 1950- *AmMWSc 92*
**Richardson,** Michael Oborne 1908- *Who 92*
**Richardson,** Midge Turk 1930- *IntAu&W 91, WrDr 92*
**Richardson,** Mike Calvin 1961- *WhoBlA 92*
**Richardson,** Mildred Tourtillott 1907- *WhoMW 92*
**Richardson,** Miles 1932- *WrDr 92*
**Richardson,** Miranda 1958- *IntMPA 92, Who 92*
**Richardson,** Myrtle H 1907- *WhoAmP 91*
**Richardson,** Natasha 1963- *IntMPA 92*
**Richardson,** Natasha Jane 1963- *Who 92, WhoEnt 92*
**Richardson,** Neal A 1926- *AmMWSc 92*
**Richardson,** Nola Mae 1936- *WhoBlA 92*
**Richardson,** Nolan 1941- *WhoBlA 92*
**Richardson,** Odis Gene 1940- *WhoBlA 92*
**Richardson,** Owen Willans 1879-1959 *WhoNob 90*
**Richardson,** Pamela Lee 1961- *WhoMW 92*
**Richardson,** Patrick James 1947- *WhoFI 92*
**Richardson,** Patrick William 1925- *WhoAmL 92*
**Richardson,** Paul Alan 1961- *WhoWest 92*
**Richardson,** Paul E. L. 1957- *WhoBlA 92*
**Richardson,** Paul Ernest 1934- *AmMWSc 92*
**Richardson,** Paul Noel 1925- *AmMWSc 92*
**Richardson,** Paul Ralph 1932- *WhoEnt 92*
**Richardson,** Paul W 1916- *WhoAmP 91*
**Richardson,** Paula Anne Drake 1951- *WhoAmP 91*
**Richardson,** Peter Damian 1935- *AmMWSc 92, IntWW 91, Who 92*
**Richardson,** Philip Livermore 1940- *AmMWSc 92*
**Richardson,** Pooh 1966- *WhoBlA 92*
**Richardson,** Ralph 1902-1983 *FacFETw*
**Richardson,** Ralph H. 1935- *WhoBlA 92*
**Richardson,** Ralph Herman 1935- *WhoMW 92*
**Richardson,** Ralph J 1941- *AmMWSc 92*
**Richardson,** Randall Miller 1948- *AmMWSc 92*
**Richardson,** Ray *WhoAmP 91*
**Richardson,** Rayman Paul 1939- *AmMWSc 92*
**Richardson,** Raymond C 1929- *AmMWSc 92*
**Richardson,** Rhonda Karen 1956- *WhoBlA 92*
**Richardson,** Richard Colby, Jr. 1933- *WhoWest 92*
**Richardson,** Richard Harvey 1938- *AmMWSc 92*
**Richardson,** Richard Judson 1935- *WrDr 92*
**Richardson,** Richard Laurel 1926- *AmMWSc 92*
**Richardson,** Robert 1806-1876 *AmPeW*
**Richardson,** Robert Augustus 1912- *Who 92*
**Richardson,** Robert Coleman 1937- *AmMWSc 92*
**Richardson,** Robert Edward 1955- *WhoMW 92*
**Richardson,** Robert Esplin 1924- *AmMWSc 92*
**Richardson,** Robert Eugene 1941- *WhoBlA 92*
**Richardson,** Robert Francis 1929- *Who 92*
**Richardson,** Robert Galloway 1926- *WrDr 92*
**Richardson,** Robert John 1942- *WhoEnt 92*
**Richardson,** Robert Lloyd 1929- *AmMWSc 92*
**Richardson,** Robert Louis 1922- *AmMWSc 92*
**Richardson,** Robert S *TwCSFW 91*
**Richardson,** Robert William 1904- *WhoFI 92*
**Richardson,** Robert William 1910- *WhoWest 92*
**Richardson,** Robert William 1935- *AmMWSc 92*
**Richardson,** Roger Gerald 1953- *WhoBlA 92*
**Richardson,** Roger Glynn 1949- *WhoAmP 91*
**Richardson,** Ronald Frederick 1913- *Who 92*
**Richardson,** Rory Fleming 1953- *WhoWest 92*
**Richardson,** Roy 1931- *WhoFI 92*
**Richardson,** Rudy James 1945- *AmMWSc 92, WhoMW 92*
**Richardson,** Rupert Florence, Mrs. 1930- *WhoBlA 92*
**Richardson,** Russell McClellan 1952- *WhoRel 92*
**Richardson,** Ruth *IntWW 91*
**Richardson,** Ruth Margaret 1950- *Who 92*
**Richardson,** Sally K 1933- *WhoAmP 91*
**Richardson,** Sam Scruton 1919- *Who 92*
**Richardson,** Samuel 1689-1761 *BlkwCEP, CnDBLB 2 [port], RfGEnL 91*
**Richardson,** Samuel Carlyle 1946- *WhoMW 92*
**Richardson,** Scovel 1912- *WhoBlA 92*
**Richardson,** Sheila J. 1948- *WhoWest 92*
**Richardson,** Simon Alaisdair S. *Who 92*
**Richardson,** Stephen H 1932- *AmMWSc 92*
**Richardson,** Steven Scott 1959- *WhoFI 92*
**Richardson,** Stewart Lee, Jr 1940- *WhoAmP 91*
**Richardson,** Susan D 1962- *AmMWSc 92*
**Richardson,** Suzann 1939- *WhoAmP 91*
**Richardson,** Terry Lee 1939- *WhoMW 92*
**Richardson,** Thomas 1931- *AmMWSc 92*
**Richardson,** Thomas Andrew 1955- *WhoFI 92*
**Richardson,** Thomas Anthony 1922- *Who 92*
**Richardson,** Thomas Hampton 1941- *WhoMW 92*
**Richardson,** Thomas Legh 1941- *Who 92*
**Richardson,** Thomas Sturgis, Jr. 1952- *WhoWest 92*
**Richardson,** Thomas Wilson 1940- *WhoWest 92*
**Richardson,** Timothy 1942- *WhoBlA 92*
**Richardson,** Tom 1948- *WhoEnt 92*
**Richardson,** Tony *Who 92*
**Richardson,** Tony 1928- *FacFETw, IntDcF 2-2 [port], IntMPA 92, IntWW 91, Who 92, WhoEnt 92*
**Richardson,** Tony 1928-1991 *NewYTBS 91 [port]*
**Richardson,** Verlin Homer 1930- *AmMWSc 92*
**Richardson,** Wallace Lloyd 1927- *AmMWSc 92*
**Richardson,** Walter P. 1907- *WhoBlA 92*
**Richardson,** Wayne Michael 1948- *WhoBlA 92*
**Richardson,** Willard Earl 1924- *WhoEnt 92*
**Richardson,** William *Who 92*
**Richardson,** William 1916- *Who 92*
**Richardson,** William Allen, Jr 1932- *WhoAmP 91*
**Richardson,** William Blaine 1947- *WhoWest 92*
**Richardson,** William C 1940- *AmMWSc 92*
**Richardson,** William Chase 1940- *IntWW 91*
**Richardson,** William Eli 1933- *WhoMW 92*
**Richardson,** William Eric 1915- *Who 92*
**Richardson,** William Harry 1931- *AmMWSc 92*
**Richardson,** William J. 1933- *WhoBlA 92*
**Richardson,** William Winfree, III 1939- *WhoAmL 92*
**Richardson,** Woody 1919- *WhoEnt 92*
**Richardson-Bunbury,** Michael *Who 92*
**Richardson Gonzales,** James H. *WhoHisp 92*
**Richardson Of Duntisbourne,** Baron 1915- *IntWW 91, Who 92*
**Richart,** Douglas Stephen 1931- *WhoFI 92*
**Richart,** F E, Jr 1918- *AmMWSc 92*
**Richart,** Ralph M 1933- *AmMWSc 92*
**Richarz,** Werner Gunter 1948- *AmMWSc 92*
**Richason,** Benjamin Franklin, Jr 1922- *AmMWSc 92*
**Richason,** George R, Jr 1916- *AmMWSc 92*
**Richberg,** Carl George 1928- *AmMWSc 92*
**Richberg,** Donald Randall 1881-1960 *FacFETw*
**Richburg,** Billy Keith 1946- *WhoFI 92*
**Richdale,** David Allen 1937- *WhoAmL 92*
**Riche,** Alan *IntMPA 92*
**Riche,** Beau Aaron 1967- *WhoRel 92*
**Riche,** Pierre 1921- *IntWW 91*
**Richelson,** Elliott 1943- *AmMWSc 92*
**Richens,** Muriel Whittaker *WhoWest 92*
**Richer,** Claude-Lise 1928- *AmMWSc 92*
**Richer,** Harvey Brian 1944- *AmMWSc 92*
**Richer,** Jean-Claude 1933- *AmMWSc 92*
**Richer,** Stephen Bruce 1946- *WhoAmP 91*
**Richer,** Yvon 1943- *IntWW 91*
**Richerson,** Hal Bates 1929- *AmMWSc 92*
**Richerson,** Jim Vernon 1943- *AmMWSc 92*
**Richerson,** John Henry 1926- *WhoRel 92*
**Richerson,** Peter James 1943- *AmMWSc 92*
**Richerson,** Stephen Wayne 1951- *WhoRel 92*
**Richert,** Anton Stuart 1935- *AmMWSc 92*
**Richert,** John Louis 1931- *WhoAmL 92*
**Richert,** Nancy Dembeck 1945- *AmMWSc 92*
**Richert,** Paul 1948- *WhoAmL 92*
**Riches,** David William Henry 1955- *AmMWSc 92*
**Riches,** Derek 1912- *Who 92*
**Riches,** Ian 1908- *Who 92*
**Riches,** Kenneth 1908- *Who 92*
**Riches,** Kenneth William 1962- *WhoWest 92*
**Riches,** Leonard W. *WhoRel 92*
**Riches,** Lizzie 1950- *TwCPaSc*
**Riches,** Pierre Pietro 1927- *WhoRel 92*
**Riches,** Wesley William 1914- *AmMWSc 92*
**Richesin,** Charles Ross 1962- *WhoFI 92*
**Richeson,** Cena Golder *DrAPF 91*
**Richeson,** Cena Golder 1941- *IntAu&W 91*
**Richeson,** Cyndi *DrAPF 91*
**Richeson,** Hugh Anthony, Jr. 1947- *WhoAmL 92*
**Richet,** Charles Robert 1850-1935 *WhoNob 90*
**Richetti,** John J. 1938- *WrDr 92*
**Richey,** Bruce Radford 1951- *WhoMW 92*
**Richey,** Charles Robert 1923- *WhoAmL 92*
**Richey,** Clarence B 1910- *AmMWSc 92*
**Richey,** Everett Eldon 1923- *WhoRel 92, WhoWest 92*
**Richey,** Herman Glenn, Jr 1932- *AmMWSc 92*
**Richey,** Leland John 1961- *WhoEnt 92*
**Richey,** Rodney L. 1955- *WhoFI 92*
**Richey,** Willis Dale 1930- *AmMWSc 92*
**Richgels,** Robert William 1944- *WhoMW 92*
**Richichi,** Joseph 1946- *WhoAmL 92*
**Richie,** Donald 1924- *WrDr 92*
**Richie,** Donald Steiner 1924- *IntAu&W 91*
**Richie,** John Peter, Jr 1956- *AmMWSc 92*
**Richie,** Leroy C. 1941- *WhoAmL 92, WhoBlA 92*
**Richie,** Lionel 1950- *NewAmDM*
**Richie,** Lionel B., Jr. 1949- *WhoEnt 92*
**Richie,** Lionel Brockman, Jr. 1950- *WhoBlA 92*
**Richie,** Sharon Ivey 1949- *WhoBlA 92*
**Richie,** Winston Henry 1925- *WhoBlA 92*
**Richier,** Germaine 1904-1959 *FacFETw*
**Richilde** *EncAmaz 91*
**Richings,** Lewis David George 1920- *Who 92*
**Richins,** Barry Lane 1941- *WhoWest 92*
**Richkind,** Melvyn 1939- *WhoWest 92*
**Richland,** Diane Linda 1957- *WhoAmL 92*
**Richler,** Mordecai 1931- *BenetAL 91, ConNov 91, FacFETw, IntAu&W 91, IntWW 91, LiExTwC, RfGEnL 91, Who 92, WrDr 92*
**Richley,** E A 1928- *AmMWSc 92*
**Richley,** Robert Douglas 1944- *WhoFI 92*
**Richlin,** Jack 1933- *AmMWSc 92*
**Richman,** Alex 1929- *AmMWSc 92*
**Richman,** Anthony E. 1941- *WhoFI 92, WhoWest 92*
**Richman,** Arthur 1886-1944 *BenetAL 91*
**Richman,** David Bruce 1942- *WhoWest 92*
**Richman,** David M 1932- *AmMWSc 92*
**Richman,** David Paul 1943- *AmMWSc 92*
**Richman,** Debbie Ann 1956- *WhoEnt 92*
**Richman,** Donald 1922- *AmMWSc 92*
**Richman,** Elliot *DrAPF 91*
**Richman,** Frances Bragan *DrAPF 91*
**Richman,** Frances Sharpe 1947- *WhoEnt 92*
**Richman,** Isaac 1932- *AmMWSc 92*
**Richman,** Jarrell 1929- *WhoWest 92*
**Richman,** Joan F. 1939- *WhoEnt 92*
**Richman,** John Emmett 1951- *WhoMW 92*
**Richman,** John Marshall 1927- *WhoFI 92, WhoMW 92*
**Richman,** Julia 1855-1912 *DcAmImH*
**Richman,** Justin Lewis 1925- *AmMWSc 92*
**Richman,** Kathleen Jacob 1957- *WhoAmP 91*
**Richman,** Lawrence I. 1954- *WhoAmL 92*
**Richman,** Marc H 1936- *AmMWSc 92*
**Richman,** Marvin Jordan 1939- *WhoFI 92, WhoWest 92*
**Richman,** Monroe Franklin 1927- *WhoFI 92*
**Richman,** Paul 1942- *WhoFI 92*
**Richman,** Paul Jeffrey 1961- *WhoAmL 92*
**Richman,** Peter Mark 1927- *IntMPA 92, WhoEnt 92*
**Richman,** Robert Michael 1950- *AmMWSc 92*
**Richman,** Roger H 1929- *AmMWSc 92*
**Richman,** Stella 1922- *Who 92*
**Richman,** Stephen I. 1933- *WhoAmL 92*
**Richman,** Sumner 1929- *AmMWSc 92*
**Richman,** Susan Lynn 1957- *WhoMW 92*
**Richman,** Theodore Charles 1951- *WhoAmL 92*
**Richmond,** Archdeacon of *Who 92*
**Richmond,** Duke of 1929- *Who 92*
**Richmond,** Alan 1919- *Who 92*
**Richmond,** Andrew John 1931- *Who 92*
**Richmond,** Anthony Henry 1925- *WrDr 92*
**Richmond,** Arthur Dean 1944- *AmMWSc 92*
**Richmond,** Charles William 1938- *AmMWSc 92*
**Richmond,** Chester Robert 1929- *AmMWSc 92*
**Richmond,** Claude Harry 1935- *WhoWest 92*
**Richmond,** Clifford 1914- *Who 92*
**Richmond,** Cora Lodencia Veronica Scott 1840-1923 *RelLAm 91*
**Richmond,** David William 1964- *WhoFI 92*

**Richmond**, Delores Ruth 1951- *WhoBlA 92*
**Richmond**, Donald J 1943- *WhoAmP 91*
**Richmond**, F M 1922- *AmMWSc 92*
**Richmond**, Francis Henry Arthur *Who 92*
**Richmond**, Frederick W 1923- *WhoAmP 91*
**Richmond**, Gail Levin 1946- *WhoAmL 92*
**Richmond**, Gerald Martin 1914- *AmMWSc 92, WhoWest 92*
**Richmond**, Harold O. 1938- *WhoBlA 92*
**Richmond**, Herbert Bernard 1920- *WhoAmL 92*
**Richmond**, Hugh Macrae 1932- *WhoEnt 92, WrDr 92*
**Richmond**, Isabelle Louise *AmMWSc 92*
**Richmond**, J H 1922- *AmMWSc 92*
**Richmond**, James Kenneth 1920- *AmMWSc 92*
**Richmond**, James M 1941- *AmMWSc 92*
**Richmond**, James Matthew 1941- *WhoMW 92*
**Richmond**, Joanne Sue 1958- *WhoRel 92*
**Richmond**, John 1907- *WhoAmL 92*
**Richmond**, John 1924- *Who 92*
**Richmond**, John 1926- *Who 92*
**Richmond**, John Christopher Blake d1990 *IntWW 91N*
**Richmond**, John Melvyn 1939- *WhoFI 92*
**Richmond**, John William 1955- *WhoEnt 92*
**Richmond**, Jon 1957- *WhoAmL 92*
**Richmond**, Jonas Edward 1929- *AmMWSc 92, WhoWest 92*
**Richmond**, Jonathan Young 1941- *AmMWSc 92*
**Richmond**, Joyce Cortright 1947- *WhoFI 92*
**Richmond**, Julius B. 1916- *IntWW 91*
**Richmond**, Julius Benjamin 1916- *AmMWSc 92*
**Richmond**, LaVerne Ann 1935- *WhoAmP 91*
**Richmond**, Leigh *TwCSFW 91, WrDr 92*
**Richmond**, Lester Anderson 1944- *WhoFI 92*
**Richmond**, Lindell Bruce 1929- *WhoAmP 91*
**Richmond**, LuEllen Josephine 1950- *WhoAmP 91*
**Richmond**, Mark 1931- *Who 92*
**Richmond**, Mark Henry 1931- *IntWW 91*
**Richmond**, Martha Ellis 1941- *AmMWSc 92*
**Richmond**, Marvin Henry 1951- *WhoWest 92*
**Richmond**, Mary E 1861-1928 *DcAmImH*
**Richmond**, Mary Ellen 1861-1928 *HanAmWH*
**Richmond**, Michael Lloyd 1945- *WhoAmL 92*
**Richmond**, Milo Eugene 1939- *AmMWSc 92*
**Richmond**, Mitch 1965- *BlkOlyM, WhoBlA 92*
**Richmond**, Myrian Patricia 1942- *WhoBlA 92*
**Richmond**, Norris L. 1931- *WhoBlA 92*
**Richmond**, Oliffe 1919-1977 *TwCPaSc*
**Richmond**, Patricia Ann 1947- *AmMWSc 92*
**Richmond**, Peter 1943- *Who 92*
**Richmond**, Richard Thomas 1933- *WhoEnt 92, WhoMW 92*
**Richmond**, Robert Chaffee 1943- *AmMWSc 92*
**Richmond**, Robert H 1954- *AmMWSc 92*
**Richmond**, Robert P. 1914- *WrDr 92*
**Richmond**, Robert Stephen 1958- *WhoEnt 92*
**Richmond**, Robin 1951- *TwCPaSc*
**Richmond**, Rocsan *WhoEnt 92*
**Richmond**, Rodney Welch 1940- *WhoBlA 92*
**Richmond**, Roe 1910- *TwCWW 91*
**Richmond**, Roger C. 1945- *WhoAmL 92*
**Richmond**, Rollin Charles 1944- *AmMWSc 92*
**Richmond**, Samuel Bernard 1919- *WhoFI 92*
**Richmond**, Steve *DrAPF 91*
**Richmond**, Ted 1912- *IntMPA 92*
**Richmond**, Thomas G 1957- *AmMWSc 92*
**Richmond**, Tyronza R. 1940- *WhoBlA 92*
**Richmond**, Virginia Elizabeth 1947- *WhoFI 92*
**Richmond**, Walt 1922-1977 *TwCSFW 91*
**Richmond**, William Blake 1842-1921 *TwCPaSc*
**Richmond**, William D 1925- *AmMWSc 92*
**Richmond**, William Patrick 1932- *WhoAmL 92*
**Richmond-Sell**, Adrianne 1944- *WhoEnt 92*
**Richnell**, Donovan Thomas 1911- *Who 92*
**Richstone**, Douglas Orange 1949- *AmMWSc 92*
**Richstone**, Robert Edward 1949- *WhoEnt 92*
**Richtarich**, Thomas Philip 1952- *WhoAmP 91*
**Richter**, Anne 1939- *IntAu&W 91*
**Richter**, Bruce Edward 1954- *WhoWest 92*
**Richter**, Burton 1931- *AmMWSc 92, FacFETw, IntWW 91, Who 92, WhoNob 90, WhoWest 92*
**Richter**, Conrad 1890-1968 *BenetAL 91, TwCWW 91*
**Richter**, Curt Paul 1894- *AmMWSc 92*
**Richter**, Curt Paul 1894-1988 *FacFETw*
**Richter**, Don 1930- *WhoAmP 91*
**Richter**, Donald 1930- *AmMWSc 92*
**Richter**, Donald Paul 1924- *WhoAmL 92*
**Richter**, Dorothy Anne 1948- *AmMWSc 92*
**Richter**, Edward Eugene 1919- *AmMWSc 92*
**Richter**, Erwin 1934- *AmMWSc 92*
**Richter**, Eugen 1839-1896 *ScFEYrs*
**Richter**, G Paul 1937- *AmMWSc 92*
**Richter**, George Neal 1930- *AmMWSc 92*
**Richter**, Gerhard 1932- *IntWW 91, WorArt 1980*
**Richter**, Goetz Wilfried 1922- *AmMWSc 92*
**Richter**, Hans 1843-1916 *NewAmDM*
**Richter**, Hans 1888-1976 *FacFETw, IntDcF 2-2 [port]*
**Richter**, Hans Peter 1925- *IntAu&W 91*
**Richter**, Hans Werner 1908- *IntAu&W 91, IntWW 91*
**Richter**, Harold Gene 1925- *AmMWSc 92*
**Richter**, Harvena 1919- *WrDr 92*
**Richter**, Helen Wilkinson *AmMWSc 92*
**Richter**, Herbert Peter 1939- *AmMWSc 92*
**Richter**, Horst-Eberhard 1923- *IntWW 91*
**Richter**, Ira George Rik 1939- *WhoWest 92*
**Richter**, James Edward 1949- *WhoRel 92*
**Richter**, Joel Edward 1949- *AmMWSc 92*
**Richter**, John Lewis 1933- *AmMWSc 92*
**Richter**, Judith Anne 1942- *AmMWSc 92, WhoMW 92*
**Richter**, Karl 1926-1981 *FacFETw, NewAmDM*
**Richter**, Kenneth Irving 1921- *WhoEnt 92*
**Richter**, M. Zach 1958- *WhoEnt 92*
**Richter**, Mary Kaye 1945- *WhoMW 92*
**Richter**, Maxwell 1933- *AmMWSc 92*
**Richter**, Raymond C 1918- *AmMWSc 92*
**Richter**, Reinhard Hans 1937- *AmMWSc 92*
**Richter**, Richard Wayne 1946- *WhoAmP 91*
**Richter**, Robert 1929- *WhoEnt 92*
**Richter**, Robert Lawrence 1934- *WhoRel 92*
**Richter**, Robert Welch 1933- *WhoFI 92*
**Richter**, Roy 1956- *AmMWSc 92*
**Richter**, Stephen L 1942- *AmMWSc 92*
**Richter**, Sviatoslav 1914- *FacFETw*
**Richter**, Sviatoslav 1915- *Who 92*
**Richter**, Svyatoslav 1915- *NewAmDM*
**Richter**, Svyatoslav Teofilovich 1915- *SovUnBD*
**Richter**, Svyatoslav Theofilovich 1915- *IntWW 91*
**Richter**, Thomas A 1938- *AmMWSc 92*
**Richter**, Tobin Marais 1944- *WhoAmL 92*
**Richter**, W.D. 1945- *IntMPA 92, WhoEnt 92*
**Richter**, Ward Robert 1930- *AmMWSc 92*
**Richter**, Wayne H 1936- *AmMWSc 92*
**Richter Prada**, Pedro *IntWW 91*
**Richters**, Arnis 1928- *AmMWSc 92*
**Richthofen**, Manfred, Baron von 1892-1918 *FacFETw [port]*
**Richthofen**, Wolfram, Baron von 1895-1945 *EncTR 91 [port]*
**Richtol**, Herbert H 1932- *AmMWSc 92*
**Richwine**, John Robert 1940- *WhoMW 92*
**Rick**, Charles Madeira, Jr 1915- *AmMWSc 92, IntWW 91*
**Rick**, Christian E 1913- *AmMWSc 92*
**Rick**, Paul David *AmMWSc 92*
**Rickaby**, David A *AmMWSc 92*
**Rickard**, Cole *TwCWW 91, WrDr 92*
**Rickard**, Corwin Lloyd 1926- *AmMWSc 92*
**Rickard**, David Leon 1928- *WhoAmP 91*
**Rickard**, Eugene Clark 1943- *AmMWSc 92, WhoMW 92*
**Rickard**, James Alexander 1926- *AmMWSc 92*
**Rickard**, James Joseph 1940- *AmMWSc 92*
**Rickard**, John Hellyar 1940- *Who 92*
**Rickard**, John Terrell 1947- *AmMWSc 92*
**Rickard**, Lawrence Vroman 1926- *AmMWSc 92*
**Rickard**, Lee J 1949- *AmMWSc 92*
**Rickard**, Peter 1922- *Who 92*
**Rickard**, Ruth David 1926- *WhoMW 92*
**Rickard**, William Howard, Jr 1926- *AmMWSc 92*
**Rickards**, Barrie 1938- *Who 92*
**Rickards**, Leonard Myron 1927- *WhoFI 92*
**Rickart**, Charles Earl 1913- *AmMWSc 92*
**Rickborn**, Bruce Frederick 1935- *AmMWSc 92*
**Ricke**, P. Scott 1948- *WhoWest 92*
**Rickels**, Karl 1924- *AmMWSc 92*
**Rickenbacker**, Edward Vernon 1890-1973 *FacFETw [port]*
**Rickenbacker**, Harry Lee 1943- *WhoAmP 91*
**Rickenberg**, Howard V 1922- *AmMWSc 92*
**Ricker**, George F 1930- *WhoAmP 91*
**Ricker**, Joanne Danette 1965- *WhoWest 92*
**Ricker**, Neil Lawrence 1948- *AmMWSc 92*
**Ricker**, Richard Edmond 1952- *AmMWSc 92*
**Ricker**, Richard W 1914- *AmMWSc 92*
**Rickerby**, Joseph d1850 *DcLB 106*
**Rickert**, David A 1940- *AmMWSc 92*
**Rickert**, Douglas Edward 1946- *AmMWSc 92*
**Rickert**, Edwin Weimer 1914- *WhoFI 92*
**Rickert**, Florence Evelyn 1914- *WhoAmP 91*
**Rickert**, John F. *IntMPA 92*
**Rickert**, John Franklin 1924- *WhoEnt 92*
**Rickert**, Neil William 1939- *AmMWSc 92*
**Rickert**, Russell Kenneth 1926- *AmMWSc 92*
**Rickets**, Reginald Anthony Scott 1929- *Who 92*
**Ricketson**, Daniel 1813-1898 *BenetAL 91*
**Ricketson**, Edward D, Jr *WhoAmP 91*
**Rickett**, Denis Hubert Fletcher 1907- *IntWW 91, Who 92*
**Rickett**, Frederic Lawrence 1939- *AmMWSc 92*
**Rickett**, Gene 1931- *WhoRel 92*
**Rickett**, Peter John 1923- *WhoEnt 92*
**Rickett**, Raymond 1927- *Who 92*
**Rickett**, William Francis Sebastian 1953- *Who 92*
**Ricketts**, Abdy Henry Gough 1905- *Who 92*
**Ricketts**, Alexander *ScFEYrs*
**Ricketts**, Anne Theresa 1919- *Who 92*
**Ricketts**, Charles 1866-1931 *TwCPaSc*
**Ricketts**, David William 1935- *WhoBlA 92*
**Ricketts**, Gary Eugene 1935- *AmMWSc 92*
**Ricketts**, Howard Taylor 1871-1910 *BiInAmS*
**Ricketts**, John Adrian 1924- *AmMWSc 92*
**Ricketts**, Liese L 1920- *WhoAmP 91*
**Ricketts**, Mac Linscott 1930- *WhoRel 92*
**Ricketts**, Marijane G. *DrAPF 91*
**Ricketts**, Michael Rodney 1923- *Who 92*
**Ricketts**, Pierre De Peyster 1848?-1918 *BiInAmS*
**Ricketts**, Ralph Robert 1902- *WrDr 92*
**Ricketts**, Robert 1917- *Who 92*
**Ricketts**, Ronald N. 1943- *WhoAmL 92*
**Ricketts**, Theresa *Who 92*
**Ricketts**, Thomas Roland 1931- *WhoFI 92, WhoMW 92*
**Ricketts**, Timothy D. 1958- *WhoMW 92*
**Rickey**, Branch 1881-1965 *FacFETw, RComAH*
**Rickey**, Douglas Keith 1957- *WhoAmP 91*
**Rickey**, Frank Atkinson, Jr 1938- *AmMWSc 92*
**Rickey**, George 1907- *FacFETw*
**Rickey**, June Evelyn Million 1923- *WhoWest 92*
**Rickey**, Martin Eugene 1927- *AmMWSc 92*
**Rickey**, Ronald Thomas 1940- *WhoAmP 91*
**Rickford**, John R 1949- *IntAu&W 91*
**Rickford**, Jonathan Braithwaite Keevil 1944- *Who 92*
**Rickheit**, Alan 1939- *WhoAmP 91*
**Ricklefs**, Robert Eric 1943- *AmMWSc 92*
**Rickles**, Don 1926- *IntMPA 92*
**Rickles**, Donald Jay 1926- *WhoEnt 92*
**Rickles**, Frederick R 1942- *AmMWSc 92*
**Rickles**, Norman Harold 1920- *AmMWSc 92*
**Rickley**, David Arthur 1956- *WhoWest 92*
**Ricklin**, Saul 1919- *AmMWSc 92*
**Rickman**, Alan *IntMPA 92*
**Rickman**, Claude Roger 1917- *WhoRel 92*
**Rickman**, Geoffrey Edwin 1932- *Who 92*
**Rickman**, Hans Peter 1918- *WrDr 92*
**Rickman**, Herbert Paul 1931- *WhoAmP 91*
**Rickman**, Lewis Daniel, Sr. 1900- *WhoBlA 92*
**Rickman**, Michael Raymond 1962- *WhoAmL 92, WhoMW 92*
**Rickman**, Ray 1948- *WhoAmP 91, WhoBlA 92*
**Rickman**, Ronald Wayne 1940- *AmMWSc 92*
**Rickman**, Tom 1940- *WhoEnt 92*
**Rickman**, Wayne Lee 1957- *WhoFI 92*
**Rickover**, Hyman George 1900-1986 *FacFETw*
**Ricks**, Albert William 1900- *WhoBlA 92*
**Ricks**, Beverly Lee 1928- *AmMWSc 92*
**Ricks**, Christopher 1933- *WrDr 92*
**Ricks**, Christopher Bruce 1933- *IntWW 91, Who 92*
**Ricks**, Daniel Mark 1951- *WhoAmL 92*
**Ricks**, David Trulock 1936- *Who 92*
**Ricks**, Don Frank 1929- *WhoWest 92*
**Ricks**, George R. 1924- *WhoBlA 92*
**Ricks**, John 1910- *Who 92*
**Ricks**, John Paul 1955- *WhoFI 92*
**Ricks**, Mark G 1924- *WhoAmP 91, WhoWest 92*
**Ricks**, Robert Michael 1950- *WhoWest 92*
**Ricks**, Robert Neville 1942- *Who 92*
**Ricksecker**, Ralph E 1912- *AmMWSc 92*
**Rickson**, Gary Ames 1942- *WhoBlA 92*
**Rickter**, Donald Oscar 1931- *AmMWSc 92*
**Rickus**, Gwenneth Margaret 1925- *Who 92*
**Rickword**, Edgell 1898-1982 *ConAu 36NR, RfGEnL 91*
**Ricla**, Conde de 1720-1780 *HisDSpE*
**Rico**, Francisco 1942- *IntWW 91*
**Rico**, Joseph John 1954- *WhoHisp 92*
**Rico**, Julie 1957- *WhoHisp 92*
**Rico**, Neil *DrAPF 91*
**Ricord**, Louis Chester 1951- *AmMWSc 92*
**Ricordi**, Giovanni 1785-1853 *NewAmDM*
**Ricotta**, Anthony Vincent 1932- *WhoFI 92*
**Ridd**, John William Gregory 1931- *Who 92*
**Riddagh**, Robert W 1914- *WhoAmP 91*
**Riddel**, Joseph Neill 1931- *WrDr 92*
**Riddell**, J L 1807-1867 *ScFEYrs*
**Riddell**, Jacqueline Anne 1965- *WhoFI 92*
**Riddell**, James 1933- *AmMWSc 92*
**Riddell**, John *BenetAL 91*
**Riddell**, John 1934- *Who 92*
**Riddell**, John Evans 1913- *AmMWSc 92*
**Riddell**, John Leonard 1807-1865 *BiInAmS*
**Riddell**, Robert F 1902-1984 *FacFETw*
**Riddell**, Robert James, Jr 1923- *AmMWSc 92, WhoWest 92*
**Riddell-Webster**, John Alexander 1921- *Who 92*
**Riddelsdell**, Mildred 1913- *Who 92*
**Ridder**, Daniel Hickey 1922- *WhoWest 92*
**Ridder**, Mary Jane d1991 *NewYTBS 91*
**Ridder**, Ruthe B 1929- *WhoAmP 91*
**Ridder**, Victor L., Jr. d1991 *NewYTBS 91*
**Ridderbusch**, Karl 1932- *NewAmDM*
**Riddick**, Douglas Smith 1942- *WhoFI 92*
**Riddick**, Eugene E. 1938- *WhoBlA 92*
**Riddick**, Frank Adams, Jr 1929- *AmMWSc 92, IntWW 91*
**Riddick**, Graham Edward Galloway 1955- *Who 92*
**Riddick**, John Allen 1903- *AmMWSc 92*
**Riddick**, Louise K. 1917- *WhoBlA 92*
**Riddick**, Steven Earl 1951- *BlkOlyM*
**Riddiford**, Lynn Moorhead 1936- *AmMWSc 92, WhoWest 92*
**Riddle**, Bedford Neal 1899- *WhoBlA 92*
**Riddle**, Charles A 1955- *WhoAmP 91*
**Riddle**, Charles Addison, III 1955- *WhoAmL 92*
**Riddle**, Clarine Nardi *WhoAmP 91*
**Riddle**, Donald Lee 1945- *AmMWSc 92*
**Riddle**, Earl Waldo 1920- *WhoRel 92*
**Riddle**, George Herbert Needham 1940- *AmMWSc 92*
**Riddle**, Hugh Joseph 1912- *Who 92*
**Riddle**, Kay Williams 1933- *WhoAmP 91*
**Riddle**, Lawrence H 1954- *AmMWSc 92*
**Riddle**, Matthew Casey 1938- *WhoWest 92*
**Riddle**, Maxwell 1907- *WhoMW 92*
**Riddle**, Nelson 1921-1985 *FacFETw, NewAmDM*
**Riddle**, Sturgis Lee 1909- *WhoRel 92*
**Riddle**, Wayne Allen 1945- *AmMWSc 92*
**Riddoch**, Hilda Johnson 1923- *WhoWest 92*
**Riddoch**, John Haddow d1991 *Who 92N*
**Ride**, Sally 1951- *FacFETw, IntWW 91*
**Ride**, W. D. L. 1926- *WrDr 92*
**Rideal**, Liz 1954- *TwCPaSc*
**Ridener**, Fred Louis, Jr 1944- *AmMWSc 92*
**Ridenhour**, Carlton *WhoEnt 92*
**Ridenhour**, Richard Lewis 1932- *AmMWSc 92*
**Ridenour**, Allen Clyde 1947- *WhoRel 92*
**Ridenour**, David Allen 1962- *WhoFI 92*
**Ridenour**, John Marvin 1930- *WhoEnt 92*
**Ridenour**, Marcella V 1945- *AmMWSc 92*
**Rideout**, Darryl *DrAPF 91*
**Rideout**, Donald Eric 1942- *AmMWSc 92*
**Rideout**, Douglas Warren 1939- *WhoEnt 92*
**Rideout**, Harry Freeman 1942- *WhoAmP 91*
**Rideout**, Janet Litster 1939- *AmMWSc 92*
**Rideout**, Patricia Irene 1931- *WhoEnt 92*
**Rideout**, Richard Scott 1950- *WhoAmL 92*
**Rideout**, Roger William 1935- *Who 92*
**Rideout**, Sheldon P 1927- *AmMWSc 92*
**Rideout**, Vincent C 1924- *AmMWSc 92*
**Rider**, Agatha Ann 1919- *AmMWSc 92*
**Rider**, Benjamin Franklin 1921- *AmMWSc 92*
**Rider**, Brent Taylor 1942- *WhoFI 92*
**Rider**, Brett *TwCWW 91*

**Rider**, Brian Clayton 1948- WhoAmL 92
**Rider**, Debra Alice 1965- WhoRel 92
**Rider**, Don Keith 1918- AmMWSc 92
**Rider**, Fremont 1885-1962 ScFEYrs
**Rider**, Gregory Ashford 1949- WhoFI 92
**Rider**, Harry Durbin 1905- WhoAmP 91
**Rider**, Joseph Alfred 1921- AmMWSc 92
**Rider**, Marilyn Ann 1941- WhoFI 92
**Rider**, Paul Edward, Sr 1940- AmMWSc 92
**Rider**, Robert Farrington 1928- WhoFI 92
**Rider**, Ronald Edward 1945- AmMWSc 92
**Rider**, Rowland Vance 1915- AmMWSc 92
**Ridesatthedoor**, Darnell Elaine 1952- WhoEnt 92
**Ridge**, Anthony Hubert 1913- IntWW 91, Who 92
**Ridge**, David A WhoAmP 91
**Ridge**, Douglas Poll 1944- AmMWSc 92
**Ridge**, John Charles 1955- AmMWSc 92
**Ridge**, John Drew 1909- AmMWSc 92
**Ridge**, John R. 1827-1867 BenetAL 91
**Ridge**, Lola 1883-1941 BenetAL 91
**Ridge**, Martin 1923- WhoWest 92
**Ridge**, Sterling WhoAmP 91
**Ridge**, Thomas J 1945- WhoAmP 91
**Ridge**, Tom 1945- AlmAP 92 [port]
**Ridgel**, Gus Tolver 1926- WhoBlA 92
**Ridgers**, John Nalton Sharpe 1910- Who 92
**Ridges-Horton**, Lee Esther 1951- WhoBlA 92
**Ridgeway**, Bill Tom 1927- AmMWSc 92, WhoBlA 92
**Ridgeway**, Jason WrDr 92
**Ridgeway**, John Michael 1959- WhoEnt 92
**Ridgeway**, L Don 1948- WhoAmP 91
**Ridgeway**, Patricia Flynn 1952- WhoRel 92
**Ridgeway**, William C. 1942- WhoBlA 92
**Ridgewell**, John 1937- TwCPaSc
**Ridgley**, Thomas Brennan 1940- WhoAmL 92
**Ridgway**, Audubon Whelock 1877-1901 BilnAmS
**Ridgway**, Charles B. 1930- WhoRel 92
**Ridgway**, David NewYTBS 91 [port]
**Ridgway**, David Wenzel 1904- WhoEnt 92, WhoWest 92
**Ridgway**, Ellis Branson 1939- AmMWSc 92
**Ridgway**, George Junior 1922- AmMWSc 92
**Ridgway**, Helen Jane 1937- AmMWSc 92
**Ridgway**, James Stratman 1936- AmMWSc 92
**Ridgway**, Jason IntAu&W 91X
**Ridgway**, John 1938- WrDr 92
**Ridgway**, Judith Anne 1939- IntAu&W 91
**Ridgway**, Matthew B. 1895- IntWW 91
**Ridgway**, Matthew Bunker 1895- FacFETw, Who 92
**Ridgway**, Paul Campbell 1951- WhoEnt 92
**Ridgway**, Randal Alan 1955- WhoMW 92
**Ridgway**, Richard L 1935- AmMWSc 92
**Ridgway**, Robert Worrell 1939- AmMWSc 92
**Ridgway**, Rozanne L WhoAmP 91
**Ridgway**, Sam H 1936- AmMWSc 92
**Ridgway**, Stuart L 1922- AmMWSc 92
**Ridgway**, William C, III 1936- AmMWSc 92
**Ridha**, R A 1937- AmMWSc 92
**Ridilla**, Andrea Jayne 1956- WhoEnt 92
**Riding**, Laura ConAu 135
**Riding**, Laura d1991 NewYTBS 91
**Riding**, Laura 1901- BenetAL 91, ConPo 91, IntWW 91, WrDr 92
**Ridinger**, Bradley Bryan 1964- WhoFI 92
**Ridings**, C Leslie, Jr 1926- WhoAmP 91
**Ridings**, Gus Ray 1918- AmMWSc 92
**Ridington**, Robin 1939- WrDr 92
**Ridl**, Jack DrAPF 91
**Ridland**, John M. DrAPF 91
**Ridland**, John Murray 1933- WhoWest 92
**Ridlen**, Judith Elaine 1948- WhoRel 92
**Ridlen**, Julian 1940- WhoAmP 91
**Ridlen**, Samuel Franklin 1916- AmMWSc 92, WhoMW 92
**Ridler**, Anne 1912- ConPo 91, IntAu&W 91, Who 92, WrDr 92
**Ridler**, Vivian Hughes 1913- Who 92
**Ridley** Who 92
**Ridley**, Viscount 1925- Who 92
**Ridley**, Adam 1942- Who 92
**Ridley**, Alfred Denis 1948- WhoBlA 92
**Ridley**, Betty Who 92
**Ridley**, Betty Ann 1926- WhoRel 92
**Ridley**, Charles Robert 1948- WhoBlA 92
**Ridley**, Daniel Carlyle 1953- WhoRel 92
**Ridley**, Edward Alexander Keane 1904- Who 92
**Ridley**, Esther Joanne 1924- AmMWSc 92
**Ridley**, Florida Ruffin 1861-1943 NotBlAW 92
**Ridley**, Francis ScFEYrs
**Ridley**, Frederick Fernand 1928- Who 92
**Ridley**, Gary John 1951- WhoRel 92
**Ridley**, Gordon 1921- Who 92
**Ridley**, Harold Who 92
**Ridley**, Harry Joseph 1923- WhoBlA 92
**Ridley**, Hubert Dale 1966- WhoRel 92
**Ridley**, J Dorsey 1953- WhoAmP 91
**Ridley**, Jane Margaret 1949- WhoEnt 92
**Ridley**, Jasper 1920- WrDr 92
**Ridley**, Jasper Godwin 1920- IntAu&W 91, Who 92
**Ridley**, Laurence Howard, II 1937- WhoEnt 92
**Ridley**, Mark 1956- ConAu 133
**Ridley**, May Alice WhoBlA 92
**Ridley**, Michael Who 92
**Ridley**, Michael Kershaw 1937- Who 92
**Ridley**, Mildred Betty 1909- Who 92
**Ridley**, Nicholas 1929- IntWW 91, Who 92
**Ridley**, Nicholas Harold 1906- Who 92
**Ridley**, Paula Frances Cooper 1944- Who 92
**Ridley**, Peter Tone 1936- AmMWSc 92
**Ridley**, Philip Waller 1921- Who 92
**Ridley**, Robert Henderson 1911- WhoRel 92
**Ridley**, Robert Michael 1947- Who 92
**Ridley**, Sidney 1902- Who 92
**Ridley**, Tony Melville 1933- Who 92
**Ridley**, Vinton T 1928- WhoAmP 91
**Ridley**, William Terence Colborne 1915- Who 92
**Ridley-Thomas**, Roger 1939- Who 92
**Ridley-Tree**, Paul Herbert 1916- WhoWest 92
**Ridolfo**, Anthony Sylvester 1918- AmMWSc 92
**Ridout**, Godfrey 1918- NewAmDM
**Ridout**, Ronald 1916- IntAu&W 91, WrDr 92
**Ridpath**, Ian 1947- IntAu&W 91
**Ridpath**, John Clark 1840-1900 BenetAL 91
**Ridruejo**, Dionisio 1912-1975 DcLB 108 [port]
**Ridruejo Jimenez**, Dionisio 1912-1975 BiDExR
**Ridsdale**, Julian 1915- Who 92
**Ridsdale**, Victoire Evelyn Patricia 1921- Who 92
**Rie**, John E 1944- AmMWSc 92
**Rie**, Lucie 1902- Who 92
**Riebe**, Cynthia Morris 1946- WhoWest 92
**Riebel**, Alan Chester 1927- WhoAmP 91
**Rieber-Mohn**, Georg Fredrik 1945- IntWW 91
**Riebeseh1**, E. Allan 1938- WhoAmL 92, WhoFI 92
**Riebesell**, John F 1948- AmMWSc 92
**Riebling**, Tia Melissa 1964- WhoEnt 92
**Riebman**, Leon 1920- AmMWSc 92
**Riechel**, Thomas Leslie 1950- AmMWSc 92
**Riechers**, Donald Frank 1925- WhoRel 92
**Riechers**, Inez Richardson 1926- WhoAmP 91
**Riechert**, Susan Elise 1945- AmMWSc 92
**Rieck**, Carole Ann 1937- WhoRel 92
**Rieck**, Charles Lange 1939- WhoAmL 92
**Rieck**, H G 1922- AmMWSc 92
**Rieck**, James Nelson 1939- AmMWSc 92
**Rieck**, Norman Wilbur 1923- AmMWSc 92
**Rieck**, Stephen Charles 1949- WhoAmP 91
**Rieck**, Thomas Booth 1951- WhoFI 92
**Rieck-Coffey**, Kristine Julie 1942- WhoFI 92, WhoMW 92
**Riecke**, Edgar Erick 1944- AmMWSc 92
**Riecker**, Margaret Ann 1933- WhoAmP 91
**Riecker**, Robert E 1936- AmMWSc 92
**Rieckhoff**, Klaus E 1928- AmMWSc 92
**Rieddle**, Christian L. 1957- WhoFI 92
**Riede**, Ronald Frederick, Jr. 1957- WhoMW 92
**Riedel**, Bernard Edward 1919- AmMWSc 92
**Riedel**, David Robert 1946- WhoMW 92
**Riedel**, Eberhard Karl 1939- AmMWSc 92
**Riedel**, Ernest Paul 1931- AmMWSc 92
**Riedel**, Gerhardt Frederick 1951- AmMWSc 92
**Riedel**, Harley E., II 1949- WhoAmL 92
**Riedel**, Paul Schreiter 1911- WhoFI 92
**Riedel**, Richard A. 1922- WhoWest 92
**Riedel**, Richard Anthony 1922- AmMWSc 92
**Riedel**, Richard Frank 1951- WhoEnt 92
**Riedel**, Walter Robert 1945- WhoRel 92
**Riedel**, William Rex 1927- AmMWSc 92
**Rieder**, Conly LeRoy 1950- AmMWSc 92
**Rieder**, James Thomas 1947- WhoEnt 92
**Rieder**, Ronald Frederic 1933- AmMWSc 92
**Rieder**, Ronald Frederick 1932- WhoWest 92
**Rieder**, Ronald Olrich 1942- AmMWSc 92
**Rieder**, Sidney Victor 1921- AmMWSc 92
**Rieder**, William G 1934- AmMWSc 92
**Rieder**, William Gary 1934- WhoMW 92
**Riederer-Henderson**, Mary Ann 1943- AmMWSc 92
**Rieders**, Fredric 1922- AmMWSc 92
**Riedesel**, Carl Clement 1910- AmMWSc 92
**Riedesel**, Frederika Charlotte Louise von 1746-1808 BlkwEAR
**Riedesel**, Friederike C. L., Baroness von 1746-1808 BenetAL 91
**Riedesel**, Marvin LeRoy 1925- AmMWSc 92
**Riedhammer**, Thomas M AmMWSc 92
**Riedinger**, Leo Louis 1944- AmMWSc 92
**Riedl**, H Raymond 1935- AmMWSc 92
**Riedl**, John Orth, Jr 1937- AmMWSc 92
**Riedl**, Rose Marie 1940- WhoRel 92
**Riedlbauch**, Vaclav 1947- IntWW 91
**Riedman**, James Robert 1959- WhoFI 92
**Riedman**, Richard M 1933- AmMWSc 92
**Riedo**, Paul Alphonse 1953- WhoEnt 92
**Riefe**, Alan 1925- WrDr 92
**Riefe**, Barbara WrDr 92
**Riefenstahl**, Leni 1902- EncTR 91 [port], FacFETw, IntDcF 2-2 [port], IntWW 91, ReelWom [port], WhoEnt 92
**Rieff**, Philip 1922- WrDr 92
**Rieffel**, Marc A 1937- AmMWSc 92
**Riefler**, Donald Brown 1927- WhoFI 92
**Riegel**, Byron 1906-1975 FacFETw
**Riegel**, Byron William 1938- WhoWest 92
**Riegel**, Garland Tavner 1914- AmMWSc 92
**Riegel**, Ilse Leers 1916- AmMWSc 92
**Riegel**, Jeffrey Allen 1965- WhoEnt 92
**Riegel**, John Kent 1938- WhoAmL 92
**Riegel**, Kenneth 1938- WhoEnt 92
**Riegel**, Kurt Wetherhold 1939- AmMWSc 92
**Riegel**, Robert H. WhoRel 92
**Riegels**, Guy Anthony 1945- WhoFI 92
**Rieger**, Anne Lloyd 1935- AmMWSc 92
**Rieger**, Elaine June 1937- WhoWest 92
**Rieger**, Homer 1933- WhoAmP 91
**Rieger**, Martin Max 1920- AmMWSc 92
**Rieger**, Mitchell Sheridan 1922- WhoAmL 92, WhoMW 92
**Rieger**, Philip Henri 1935- AmMWSc 92
**Rieger**, Samuel 1921- AmMWSc 92
**Rieger**, Steven Arthur 1952- WhoAmP 91
**Rieger**, William W 1922- WhoAmP 91
**Riegert**, Paul William 1923- AmMWSc 92
**Riegert**, Peter 1947- IntMPA 92
**Riegert**, Robert Adolf 1923- WhoAmL 92
**Riegger**, Otto K 1935- AmMWSc 92
**Riegger**, Wallingford 1885-1961 NewAmDM
**Riegle**, Donald W., Jr. 1938- AlmAP 92 [port], IntWW 91, WhoAmP 91
**Riegle**, Donald Wayne, Jr. 1938- WhoMW 92
**Riegle**, Gail Daniel 1935- AmMWSc 92
**Riegler**, Alan Martin 1946- WhoFI 92
**Riegler**, Josef 1938- IntWW 91
**Riegner**, Gerhart M. 1911- IntWW 91
**Riegner**, Gerhart Moritz 1911- WhoRel 92
**Riegsecker**, Marvin D 1937- WhoAmP 91
**Riehl**, Curtis Alan 1963- WhoEnt 92
**Riehl**, Emil Joseph WhoAmP 91
**Riehl**, Herbert 1915- AmMWSc 92
**Riehl**, James Patrick 1948- AmMWSc 92
**Riehl**, Jerry A 1933- AmMWSc 92
**Riehl**, Mary Agatha 1921- AmMWSc 92
**Riehl**, Robert Michael 1951- AmMWSc 92
**Riehl**, Walter 1881-1953 BiDExR
**Riehle**, Helen 1950- WhoAmP 91
**Riehle**, Robert Arthur, Jr 1947- AmMWSc 92
**Riehle**, Theodore Martin, III 1947- WhoAmP 91
**Riehm**, Carl Richard 1935- AmMWSc 92
**Riehm**, John P 1935- AmMWSc 92
**Rieke**, Carol Anger 1908- AmMWSc 92
**Rieke**, Garl Kalman 1942- AmMWSc 92
**Rieke**, George Henry 1943- AmMWSc 92
**Rieke**, Herman Henry, III 1937- AmMWSc 92
**Rieke**, James Kirk 1924- AmMWSc 92
**Rieke**, Marcia Jean 1951- AmMWSc 92
**Rieke**, Paul Eugene 1934- AmMWSc 92
**Rieke**, Reuben Dennis 1939- AmMWSc 92
**Rieke**, Richard Davis 1935- WhoWest 92
**Rieke**, William Oliver 1931- AmMWSc 92
**Riekels**, Jerald Wayne 1932- AmMWSc 92
**Riekert**, Louis Albert 1935- WhoFI 92
**Riel**, Gordon Kienzle 1934- AmMWSc 92
**Riel**, Louis David 1844-1885 RelLAm 91
**Riel**, Pauline Skinner 1923- WhoAmP 91
**Riel**, Rene Rosaire 1923- AmMWSc 92
**Riel**, Ruth Ellen 1957- WhoRel 92
**Riel**, Steven DrAPF 91
**Riemann**, Hans 1920- AmMWSc 92
**Riemann**, James Michael 1940- AmMWSc 92
**Riemann**, John G 1928- AmMWSc 92
**Riemenschneider**, Albert 1878-1950 NewAmDM
**Riemenschneider**, Albert Louis 1936- AmMWSc 92
**Riemenschneider**, Dan LaVerne 1952- WhoMW 92, WhoRel 92
**Riemenschneider**, Paul Arthur 1920- AmMWSc 92
**Riemenschneider**, Sherman Delbert 1943- AmMWSc 92
**Riemer**, Donald Neil 1934- AmMWSc 92
**Riemer**, Paul 1924- AmMWSc 92
**Riemer**, Robert Kirk AmMWSc 92
**Riemer**, Robert Lee 1951- AmMWSc 92
**Riemer**, Ruby DrAPF 91
**Riemer-Rubenstein**, Delilah 1910- AmMWSc 92
**Riemerschmidt**, Richard 1868-1957 DcTwDes
**Riemersma**, H 1928- AmMWSc 92
**Rienacker**, Gunther 1904- IntWW 91
**Riendeau**, Russell Joseph 1958- WhoFI 92
**Rienecker**, Peter Raymond 1960- WhoEnt 92
**Rienhardt**, Rolf 1903- EncTR 91
**Rienow**, Robert 1909-1989 ConAu 36NR
**Rienzi**, Thomas Matthew Michael 1919- WhoWest 92
**Rier**, John Paul, Jr. 1925- WhoBlA 92
**Ries**, Carole Elizabeth 1940- WhoEnt 92
**Ries**, Edward Richard 1918- AmMWSc 92, WhoFI 92
**Ries**, Ferdinand 1784-1838 NewAmDM
**Ries**, Herman Elkan, Jr 1911- AmMWSc 92
**Ries**, Mary Martha 1959- WhoAmL 92
**Ries**, Michelle Lucille 1962- WhoMW 92
**Ries**, Richard Ralph 1935- AmMWSc 92
**Ries**, Ronald Edward 1944- AmMWSc 92
**Ries**, Stanley K 1927- AmMWSc 92
**Ries**, Stephen Michael 1944- AmMWSc 92
**Ries**, Thomas G WhoAmP 91
**Ries**, Thomas Michael 1957- WhoEnt 92
**Riescher**, Ronald A. 1941- WhoFI 92
**Riesco**, German 1941- IntWW 91, Who 92
**Riese**, Arthur Carl 1955- WhoWest 92
**Riese**, Jane 1945- WhoEnt 92
**Riese**, Russell L 1923- AmMWSc 92
**Riese**, Walter Charles Rusty 1951- AmMWSc 92
**Rieselbach**, Richard Edgar 1933- AmMWSc 92
**Riesen**, Austin Herbert 1913- AmMWSc 92
**Riesen**, John William 1941- AmMWSc 92
**Riesenberg**, Felix 1879-1939 BenetAL 91
**Riesenberger**, John Richard 1948- WhoMW 92
**Riesenburger**, Patricia Jeffries 1961- WhoAmL 92
**Riesenfeld**, Peter William 1945- AmMWSc 92
**Riesenfeld**, Richard F 1944- AmMWSc 92
**Riesenfeld**, Stefan Conrad 1948- WhoFI 92
**Riesenhuber**, Heinz Friedrich 1935- IntWW 91
**Rieser**, Joseph A., Jr. 1947- WhoAmL 92
**Rieser**, Leonard M 1922- AmMWSc 92
**Rieser**, Michael Lee 1954- WhoRel 92
**Riesgo**, Armando WhoHisp 92
**Rieske**, John Samuel 1923- AmMWSc 92
**Riesman**, David 1909- ConAu 34NR, WrDr 92
**Riesman**, David, Jr. 1909- BenetAL 91
**Riess**, Karlem 1913- AmMWSc 92
**Riess**, Ronald Dean 1940- AmMWSc 92
**Riesz**, Peter 1926- AmMWSc 92
**Riethmiller**, David W. 1951- WhoEnt 92
**Riethof**, Thomas Robert 1927- AmMWSc 92
**Rieti**, Vittorio 1898- ConCom 92, NewAmDM
**Rietveld**, Gerrit T. 1888-1964 DcTwDes
**Rietveld**, Gerrit Thomas 1888-1964 FacFETw
**Rietveld**, Willis James 1942- AmMWSc 92
**Rietz**, Edward Gustave 1911- AmMWSc 92
**Rieuf**, Glenn Allen, Jr. 1952- WhoEnt 92
**Riew**, Changkiu Keith 1928- WhoMW 92
**Riewald**, Jacobus Gerhardus 1910- IntAu&W 91
**Riewald**, Paul Gordon 1941- AmMWSc 92
**Rifai**, Ahmed K. 1934- WhoMW 92
**Rifa'i**, Zaid al- 1936- IntWW 91
**Rifas**, Leonard 1946- AmMWSc 92
**Rifbjerg**, Klaus 1931- IntAu&W 91, IntWW 91
**Rife**, Anita 1946- WhoBlA 92
**Rife**, David Cecil 1901- AmMWSc 92
**Rife**, Jack 1943- WhoAmP 91
**Rife**, Jean WhoEnt 92
**Rife**, Jerry Lee 1945- WhoWest 92
**Rife**, Sarah Jane WhoFI 92
**Rife**, William C 1933- AmMWSc 92
**Rifenburgh**, Richard Philip 1932- WhoFI 92, WhoWest 92
**Riffe**, John Vernon 1951- WhoWest 92
**Riffe**, Vernal G., Jr. WhoMW 92
**Riffe**, Vernal G, Jr 1925- WhoAmP 91
**Riffee**, William Harvey 1944- AmMWSc 92
**Riffel**, Jerome Dean 1941- WhoAmL 92
**Riffel**, Norman D 1938- WhoAmP 91

Riffenburgh, Robert Harry 1931- *AmMWSc 92*
Riffer, Richard 1939- *AmMWSc 92*
Riffey, Meribeth M 1924- *AmMWSc 92*
Riffle, Jerry William 1934- *AmMWSc 92*
Riffle, Kenneth H 1945- *WhoAmP 91*
Rifino, Carl Biaggio 1938- *AmMWSc 92*
Rifkin, Arthur *DrAPF 91*
Rifkin, Arthur 1937- *AmMWSc 92*
Rifkin, Barry Richard 1940- *AmMWSc 92*
Rifkin, Erik 1940- *AmMWSc 92*
Rifkin, Glenn Howard 1953- *WhoFI 92*
Rifkin, Harmon 1942- *IntMPA 92*
Rifkin, Jeremy 1945- *WrDr 92*
Rifkin, Joshua 1944- *IntWW 91, NewAmDM, WhoEnt 92*
Rifkin, Julian 1915- *IntMPA 92*
Rifkin, Julie Kaye *WhoAmP 91*
Rifkin, Larry Scott 1956- *WhoAmL 92*
Rifkin, Lawrence Brian *WhoEnt 92*
Rifkin, Monroe M. *LesBEnT 92*
Rifkin, Richard S. 1957- *WhoMW 92*
Rifkin, Shepard *DrAPF 91*
Rifkin, Shepard 1918- *IntAu&W 91, TwCWW 91, WrDr 92*
Rifkind, Arleen B 1938- *AmMWSc 92*
Rifkind, Basil M 1934- *AmMWSc 92*
Rifkind, David 1929- *AmMWSc 92*
Rifkind, Joseph Moses 1940- *AmMWSc 92*
Rifkind, Malcolm 1946- *Who 92*
Rifkind, Malcolm Leslie 1946- *IntWW 91*
Rifkind, Richard A 1930- *AmMWSc 92*
Rifkind, Robert Singer 1936- *WhoAmL 92*
Rifman, Eileen Nissenbaum 1944- *WhoEnt 92*
Riford, Lloyd Steve, Jr 1924- *WhoAmP 91*
Rigamonti, Robert 1950- *WhoEnt 92*
Riganati, John Philip 1944- *AmMWSc 92*
Rigas, Anthony L 1931- *AmMWSc 92*
Rigas, Demetrios A 1921- *AmMWSc 92*
Rigas, Harriett B 1934- *AmMWSc 92*
Rigassio, James Louis 1923- *AmMWSc 92*
Rigattieri, Lisa 1953- *WhoIns 92*
Rigatto, Henrique 1937- *AmMWSc 92*
Rigau, Marco Antonio, Jr 1946- *WhoAmP 91*
Rigaud, Michel Jean 1939- *AmMWSc 92*
Rigby, Barry Gordon 1954- *WhoWest 92*
Rigby, Bryan 1933- *Who 92*
Rigby, Charlotte Edith 1940- *AmMWSc 92*
Rigby, Donald W 1929- *AmMWSc 92*
Rigby, E B 1930- *AmMWSc 92*
Rigby, Edward H. 1943- *WhoBlA 92*
Rigby, F Lloyd 1918- *AmMWSc 92*
Rigby, Fred Durnford 1914- *AmMWSc 92*
Rigby, Harold Ainsworth 1879-1938 *TwCPaSc*
Rigby, Hugh John 1914- *Who 92*
Rigby, J Keith 1926- *AmMWSc 92*
Rigby, Jean Prescott *IntWW 91, Who 92*
Rigby, John *Who 92*
Rigby, Kenneth 1925- *WhoAmL 92*
Rigby, Malcolm 1909- *AmMWSc 92*
Rigby, Norman Leslie 1920- *Who 92*
Rigby, Paul Herbert 1924- *AmMWSc 92*
Rigby, Perry G 1932- *AmMWSc 92*
Rigby, Peter William Jack 1947- *Who 92*
Rigby, Reginald Francis 1919- *Who 92*
Rigby, T. H. 1925- *ConAu 36NR*
Rigden, Geoffrey 1943- *TwCPaSc*
Rigden, John Saxby 1934- *AmMWSc 92*
Rigdon, Glenn Joseph 1950- *WhoMW 92*
Rigdon, Orville Wayne 1932- *AmMWSc 92*
Rigdon, Raymond Harrison 1905- *AmMWSc 92*
Rigdon, Richard Levi 1945- *WhoAmP 91*
Rigdon, Robert David 1942- *AmMWSc 92*
Rigdon, Ronald Milton 1937- *WhoFI 92, WhoMW 92*
Rigdon, V. Bruce 1936- *WhoRel 92*
Rigel, William Malcolm 1926- *WhoRel 92*
Riger, Martin 1910- *WhoAmL 92*
Rigert, David 1951- *SovUnBD*
Rigert, James Aloysius 1935- *AmMWSc 92*
Rigg, Diana 1938- *IntMPA 92, IntWW 91, Who 92, WhoEnt 92*
Riggi, Stephen Joseph 1937- *AmMWSc 92*
Riggins, John *NewYTBS 91 [port]*
Riggins, Lester 1928- *WhoBlA 92*
Riggins, Ronald Stewart 1956- *WhoFI 92*
Riggins, Thomas Hart 1951- *WhoFI 92*
Riggio, Donald Joseph 1926- *WhoEnt 92*
Riggio, Nicholas Jospeh, Sr. 1930- *WhoAmL 92*
Riggle, Everett C 1932- *AmMWSc 92*
Riggle, J W 1924- *AmMWSc 92*
Riggle, John H 1926- *AmMWSc 92*
Riggle, Timothy A 1940- *AmMWSc 92*
Riggleman, James Dale 1933- *AmMWSc 92*
Riggs, Anna Claire 1944- *WhoFI 92, WhoMW 92*
Riggs, Arthur Dale 1939- *AmMWSc 92*
Riggs, Arthur Jordy 1916- *WhoAmL 92*
Riggs, Austen Fox, II 1924- *AmMWSc 92*
Riggs, Benjamin C 1914- *AmMWSc 92*
Riggs, Bobby 1918- *FacFETw*
Riggs, Byron Lawrence 1931- *AmMWSc 92*
Riggs, Carl Daniel 1920- *AmMWSc 92*
Riggs, Charles Lathan 1923- *AmMWSc 92*
Riggs, Charles Lee 1946- *AmMWSc 92*
Riggs, Conrad Albert 1963- *WhoAmL 92*
Riggs, Dale 1930- *WhoAmP 91*
Riggs, David 1941- *ConAu 133*
Riggs, David Lynn 1943- *WhoFI 92*
Riggs, David Ramsey 1941- *WhoWest 92*
Riggs, Dixon L 1924- *AmMWSc 92*
Riggs, Donald Eugene 1942- *WhoMW 92*
Riggs, Elizabeth A. 1942- *WhoBlA 92*
Riggs, Enrique A. 1943- *WhoBlA 92*
Riggs, Frank 1950- *AlmAP 92 [port], WhoWest 92*
Riggs, Frank D 1950- *WhoAmP 91*
Riggs, Gerald Antonio 1960- *WhoBlA 92*
Riggs, Hammond Greenwald, Jr 1931- *AmMWSc 92*
Riggs, Harry L. 1914- *WhoBlA 92*
Riggs, Henry Earle 1935- *WhoWest 92*
Riggs, James Arthur 1936- *WhoFI 92*
Riggs, James W, Jr 1914- *AmMWSc 92*
Riggs, John Arthur 1946- *WhoAmP 91*
Riggs, John L 1926- *AmMWSc 92*
Riggs, John Paul 1934- *WhoMW 92*
Riggs, John T., II 1947- *WhoRel 92*
Riggs, Karl A, Jr 1929- *AmMWSc 92*
Riggs, Karl Alton, Jr. 1929- *WhoFI 92*
Riggs, Lorrin Andrews 1912- *AmMWSc 92, IntWW 91*
Riggs, Louis William 1922- *AmMWSc 92*
Riggs, Lynn 1899-1954 *BenetAL 91*
Riggs, Mary Kathryn 1935- *WhoFI 92*
Riggs, Melvin David 1937- *WhoAmP 91*
Riggs, Olen Lonnie, Jr 1925- *AmMWSc 92*
Riggs, Philip Shaefer 1906- *AmMWSc 92*
Riggs, Richard 1938- *AmMWSc 92*
Riggs, Robert D 1932- *AmMWSc 92*
Riggs, Robert E. 1927- *WrDr 92*
Riggs, Robert Edwon 1927- *WhoWest 92*
Riggs, Robert Wayne 1956- *WhoEnt 92*
Riggs, Roderick D 1931- *AmMWSc 92*
Riggs, Roderick Douglas 1931- *WhoAmP 91*
Riggs, Ronald M. 1949- *WhoFI 92*
Riggs, Schultz 1941- *AmMWSc 92*
Riggs, Stanley R 1938- *AmMWSc 92*
Riggs, Stephen R. 1812-1883 *BenetAL 91*
Riggs, Steven Ray 1959- *WhoAmP 91*
Riggs, Stuart 1928- *AmMWSc 92*
Riggs, Thomas Rowland 1921- *AmMWSc 92*
Riggs, Victoria G 1956- *AmMWSc 92*
Riggs, Warren Elwood 1927- *WhoAmP 91*
Riggs, Xen Michael 1959- *WhoEnt 92*
Riggsby, Ernest Duward 1925- *AmMWSc 92*
Riggsby, William Stuart 1936- *AmMWSc 92*
Righetti, Robert Silvio 1949- *WhoRel 92*
Righi-Lambertini, Egano 1906- *IntWW 91, WhoRel 92*
Righteous Brothers *NewAmDM*
Righter, Walter Cameron 1923- *WhoRel 92*
Righthand, Vera Fay 1930- *AmMWSc 92*
Rightmire, G. Philip 1942- *ConAu 135*
Rightmire, George Philip 1942- *AmMWSc 92*
Rightmire, Robert 1931- *AmMWSc 92*
Rights, Graham Henry 1935- *WhoRel 92*
Rightsel, Wilton Adair 1921- *AmMWSc 92*
Rigler, A Kellam 1929- *AmMWSc 92*
Rigler, Neil Edward 1908- *AmMWSc 92*
Rigney, Carl Jennings 1925- *AmMWSc 92*
Rigney, David Arthur 1938- *AmMWSc 92, WhoMW 92*
Rigney, David Roth 1950- *AmMWSc 92*
Rigney, Harlan 1933- *WhoAmP 91*
Rigney, Howard Ernest 1922- *Who 92*
Rigney, James Arthur 1931- *AmMWSc 92*
Rigney, John Shannon 1945- *WhoFI 92*
Rigney, Mary Margaret 1926- *AmMWSc 92*
Rigole, William Morrise 1951- *WhoWest 92*
Rigolosi, Vincent Paul 1932- *WhoAmP 91*
Rigoni, Orlando 1917- *IntAu&W 91*
Rigor, Benjamin Morales, Sr 1936- *AmMWSc 92*
Rigor, Bradley Glenn 1955- *WhoAmL 92*
Rigout, Marcel 1928- *IntWW 91*
Rigrod, William W 1913- *AmMWSc 92*
Rigsbee, David *DrAPF 91*
Rigsbee, William Alton 1926- *WhoIns 92*
Rigsby, Billy *WhoAmP 91*
Rigsby, Esther Martin *WhoBlA 92*
Rigsby, George Pierce 1915- *AmMWSc 92*
Rigsby, Howard 1909-1975 *TwCWW 91*
Rigsby, John Newton 1946- *WhoEnt 92, WhoFI 92*
Rigsby, Larry Wayne 1950- *WhoWest 92*
Rigual, Antonio Ramon 1946- *WhoHisp 92*
Riha, William E, Jr 1943- *AmMWSc 92*
Rihani, Amin *DcAmImH*
Rihani, Sarmad Albert 1954- *WhoMW 92*
Rihbang, Abraham Mitrie *DcAmImH*
Riherd, John Arthur 1946- *WhoAmL 92*
Rihm, Alexander, Jr 1916- *AmMWSc 92*
Rihm, Paul Charles 1953- *WhoFI 92*
Rihm, Wolfgang 1952- *ConCom 92, NewAmDM*
Riikola, Michael Edward 1951- *WhoAmL 92*
Riis, Jacob 1849-1914 *FacFETw*
Riis, Jacob A *SourALJ*
Riis, Jacob A. 1849-1914 *BenetAL 91*
Riis, Jacob August 1849-1914 *DcAmImH*
Riis, Povl 1925- *IntWW 91*
Riisager, Knudage 1897-1974 *NewAmDM*
Rijke, Arie Marie 1934- *AmMWSc 92*
Rijken, Hedy L 1958- *WhoAmP 91*
Rijken, Max 1920- *WhoAmP 91*
Rijo, Jose 1965- *WhoHisp 92*
Rijo, Jose Antonio 1965- *WhoBlA 92*
Rikanovic, Svetozar 1938- *Who 92*
Rikans, Lora Elizabeth 1940- *AmMWSc 92*
Rike, Greg 1951- *WhoEnt 92*
Rike, Paul Miller 1913- *AmMWSc 92*
Riker, Donald Allen 1958- *WhoRel 92*
Riker, Donald Kay 1945- *AmMWSc 92*
Riker, Joseph Thaddeus, III 1940- *WhoWest 92*
Riker, Walter Franklyn, Jr 1916- *AmMWSc 92*
Riker, William H. 1920- *IntWW 91*
Riker, William Kay 1925- *AmMWSc 92*
Riker, William Wolle 1951- *WhoEnt 92*
Rikhoff, Jean *DrAPF 91*
Rikhter, Svyatoslav Teofilovich 1915- *SovUnBD*
Rikihisa, Yasuko *AmMWSc 92*
Rikki *ConAu 34NR*
Rikli, Arthur Eugene 1917- *WhoFI 92*
Rikli, Donald Carl 1927- *WhoAmL 92*
Riklis, Meshulam 1923- *IntWW 91, WhoFI 92*
Rikmenspoel, Robert 1930- *AmMWSc 92*
Rikon, Michael 1945- *WhoAmL 92*
Rikoski, Richard A. 1941- *WhoFI 92*
Rikoski, Richard Anthony 1941- *AmMWSc 92, WhoMW 92*
Rikvold, Per Arne 1948- *AmMWSc 92*
Rila, Charles Clinton 1928- *AmMWSc 92*
Rile, Joanne Clarissa 1934- *WhoEnt 92*
Riles, James Byrum 1938- *AmMWSc 92*
Riles, Wilson Camanza 1917- *WhoAmP 91, WhoBlA 92, WhoWest 92*
Riley, Anne Rutledge 1963- *WhoAmL 92*
Riley, Arch Wilson, Jr. 1957- *WhoAmL 92*
Riley, Avis Monica 1953- *WhoBlA 92*
Riley, B. Gresham 1938- *WhoWest 92*
Riley, Benjamin Kneeland 1957- *WhoAmL 92*
Riley, Bernard Jerome 1928- *AmMWSc 92*
Riley, Bridget 1931- *IntWW 91, TwCPaSc*
Riley, Bridget Louise 1931- *Who 92*
Riley, C Ronald 1938- *WhoIns 92*
Riley, Carole A. *WhoRel 92*
Riley, Carroll L. 1923- *WrDr 92*
Riley, Catherine I 1947- *WhoAmP 91*
Riley, Charles Homer 1932- *WhoRel 92*
Riley, Charles Logan Rex 1946- *WhoWest 92*
Riley, Charles Marshall 1920- *AmMWSc 92*
Riley, Charles Valentine 1843-1895 *BilnAmS*
Riley, Charles Victor 1921- *AmMWSc 92*
Riley, Charles Wilbur, Sr. 1950- *WhoBlA 92*
Riley, Christopher John 1947- *Who 92*
Riley, Claude Frank, Jr 1922- *AmMWSc 92*
Riley, Clayton 1935- *WhoBlA 92*
Riley, Clyde 1939- *AmMWSc 92*
Riley, Dan 1946- *ConAu 135*
Riley, Danny Arthur 1944- *AmMWSc 92*
Riley, David 1942- *AmMWSc 92*
Riley, David Everett, Jr. 1959- *WhoMW 92*
Riley, David Waegar 1921- *AmMWSc 92*
Riley, Dennis Lawrence 1945- *WhoAmP 91*
Riley, Dennis Patrick 1947- *AmMWSc 92*
Riley, Derrell Wayne 1951- *WhoWest 92*
Riley, Dick 1946- *WrDr 92*
Riley, Donald Ray 1947- *AmMWSc 92*
Riley, Doris J 1929- *WhoAmP 91*
Riley, Dorothy B 1925- *WhoAmP 91*
Riley, Dorothy Comstock 1924- *WhoAmL 92, WhoMW 92*
Riley, Dorothy Comstock 1941- *WhoAmP 91*
Riley, Edgar Francis, Jr 1914- *AmMWSc 92*
Riley, Edward Calverley 1923- *WrDr 92*
Riley, Emile Edward 1934- *WhoBlA 92*
Riley, Eve Montgomery 1955- *WhoBlA 92*
Riley, Frances L 1928- *WhoAmP 91*
Riley, Gene Alden 1930- *AmMWSc 92*
Riley, Gerald Wayne 1950- *WhoWest 92*
Riley, Glenn Pleasants 1960- *WhoBlA 92*
Riley, Harold 1934- *TwCPaSc*
Riley, Harold Eugene 1928- *WhoFI 92, WhoIns 92*
Riley, Harold Eugene, Jr. 1943- *WhoMW 92*
Riley, Harold John, Jr. 1940- *WhoFI 92*
Riley, Harris D, Jr 1925- *AmMWSc 92*
Riley, Herbert James 1925- *WhoWest 92*
Riley, Howard Francis, Jr. 1942- *WhoAmL 92*
Riley, Jack 1935- *WhoEnt 92*
Riley, Jacqueline Ann 1935- *WhoWest 92*
Riley, James A 1937- *AmMWSc 92*
Riley, James C. 1943- *ConAu 133*
Riley, James Daniel 1920- *AmMWSc 92*
Riley, James F. 1912-1985 *ConAu 134*
Riley, James L. *WhoHisp 92*
Riley, James N 1943- *WhoAmP 91*
Riley, James Whitcomb 1849-1916 *BenetAL 91*
Riley, Jeannie Carolyn 1945- *WhoEnt 92*
Riley, Jocelyn *DrAPF 91*
Riley, Jocelyn Carol 1949- *IntAu&W 91*
Riley, John 1940- *WhoEnt 92, WhoWest 92*
Riley, John David 1933- *WhoRel 92*
Riley, John F 1943- *WhoIns 92*
Riley, John Francis 1927- *WhoWest 92*
Riley, John Francis, III 1955- *WhoWest 92*
Riley, John Graham 1945- *WhoFI 92*
Riley, John M *WhoAmP 91*
Riley, John Paul 1927- *AmMWSc 92*
Riley, John Robert 1954- *WhoRel 92*
Riley, John Roland Christopher 1925- *Who 92*
Riley, John Thomas 1942- *AmMWSc 92*
Riley, Joseph James 1939- *WhoMW 92*
Riley, Joseph Patrick, Jr 1943- *WhoAmP 91*
Riley, Judith Merkle 1942- *ConAu 35NR*
Riley, Karl 1955- *WhoWest 92*
Riley, Kathleen Ann 1945- *WhoFI 92*
Riley, Ken *WhoAmP 91*
Riley, Kenneth Gene 1935- *WhoWest 92*
Riley, Kenneth Gene 1959- *WhoRel 92*
Riley, Kenneth J. 1947- *WhoBlA 92*
Riley, Kenneth Lloyd 1941- *AmMWSc 92*
Riley, Kenneth Loyd, Jr. 1957- *WhoRel 92*
Riley, Kevin Thomas 1943- *WhoIns 92*
Riley, Larry *WhoBlA 92*
Riley, Lawrence Joseph 1914- *WhoRel 92*
Riley, Lee Hunter, Jr 1932- *AmMWSc 92*
Riley, Lewis R 1935- *WhoAmP 91*
Riley, Linda Marie 1953- *WhoRel 92*
Riley, Madeleine 1933- *WrDr 92*
Riley, Mark Anthony 1959- *AmMWSc 92*
Riley, Matilda White 1911- *WomSoc*
Riley, Matthew Howard, Jr *WhoAmP 91*
Riley, Meg Amelia 1955- *WhoRel 92*
Riley, Michael D. *DrAPF 91*
Riley, Michael Hylan 1951- *WhoAmL 92*
Riley, Michael Robert 1938- *WhoMW 92*
Riley, Michael Verity 1933- *AmMWSc 92*
Riley, Michael Waltermier 1946- *AmMWSc 92*
Riley, Michelle Patricia 1959- *WhoFI 92*
Riley, Mike *WhoAmP 91*
Riley, Mikel Ralph 1955- *WhoMW 92*
Riley, Monica 1926- *AmMWSc 92*
Riley, N Allen 1915- *AmMWSc 92*
Riley, Negail R. 1930- *WhoBlA 92*
Riley, Patricia Lee 1952- *WhoWest 92*
Riley, Patrick Eugene 1949- *AmMWSc 92*
Riley, Paul 1944- *TwCPaSc*
Riley, Paul J *WhoAmP 91*
Riley, Perry Eugene 1950- *WhoRel 92*
Riley, Peter Julian 1933- *AmMWSc 92*
Riley, Ralph 1924- *IntWW 91, Who 92*
Riley, Randall Alan 1949- *WhoRel 92*
Riley, Raymond Edward 1947- *WhoMW 92*
Riley, Reed Farrar 1927- *AmMWSc 92*
Riley, Richard 1950- *TwCPaSc*
Riley, Richard Fowble 1917- *AmMWSc 92*
Riley, Richard King 1936- *AmMWSc 92*
Riley, Richard Lord 1911- *AmMWSc 92*
Riley, Richard Wilson 1933- *WhoAmL 92, WhoAmP 91*
Riley, Richard Wilson 1935- *IntWW 91*
Riley, Robert Annan, III 1955- *WhoFI 92*
Riley, Robert C 1928- *AmMWSc 92*
Riley, Robert Gene 1946- *AmMWSc 92*
Riley, Robert Lee 1935- *AmMWSc 92*
Riley, Rosetta Margueritte 1940- *WhoBlA 92*
Riley, Sarah Anne 1946- *WhoFI 92*
Riley, Stephen James 1943- *AmMWSc 92*
Riley, Steven Edwin, Jr. 1953- *WhoAmL 92*
Riley, Sumpter Marion, Jr. 1903- *WhoBlA 92*
Riley, Terry 1935- *NewAmDM, WhoEnt 92*
Riley, Terry Mitchell 1935- *IntWW 91*
Riley, Thomas Joseph 1943- *WhoMW 92*
Riley, Thomas Joseph 1944- *WhoAmL 92*
Riley, Thomas N 1939- *AmMWSc 92*
Riley, Timothy Crocker 1946- *WhoAmP 91*

**Riley,** Timothy Michael 1954- *WhoFI 92*
**Riley,** Victor J., Jr. 1931- *WhoFI 92*
**Riley,** Wayne Joseph 1959- *WhoBlA 92*
**Riley,** William A 1924- *WhoAmP 91*
**Riley,** William Bell 1861-1947 *RelLAm 91*
**Riley,** William F 1925- *AmMWSc 92*
**Riley,** William Jay 1947- *WhoAmL 92*
**Riley,** William Robert 1922- *AmMWSc 92*
**Riley,** William Scott 1940- *WhoBlA 92*
**Riley,** Woodbridge 1869-1933 *BenetAL 91*
**Riley-Scott,** Barbara P. 1928- *WhoBlA 92*
**Riley-Smith,** Jonathan Simon Christopher 1938- *Who 92*
**Rilke,** Rainer Maria 1875-1926 *FacFETw, LiExTwC*
**Rill,** James Franklin 1933- *WhoAmL 92, WhoFI 92*
**Rill,** Randolph Lynn 1944- *AmMWSc 92*
**Rillema,** James Alan 1942- *AmMWSc 92*
**Rilling,** Hans Christopher 1933- *AmMWSc 92*
**Rilling,** Helmuth 1933- *IntWW 91, NewAmDM, WhoEnt 92*
**Rillings,** James H 1942- *AmMWSc 92*
**Rim,** Dock Sang 1928- *AmMWSc 92*
**Rim,** Kwan 1934- *AmMWSc 92*
**Rim,** Yong Sung 1935- *AmMWSc 92*
**Rimai,** Donald Saul 1949- *AmMWSc 92*
**Rimai,** Lajos 1930- *AmMWSc 92*
**Riman,** Josef 1925- *IntWW 91*
**Rimbach,** Evangeline Lois 1932- *WhoEnt 92, WhoMW 92*
**Rimbaud,** Arthur 1854-1891 *GuFrLit 1, PoeCrit 3 [port]*
**Rimbault,** Geoffrey Acworth 1908- *Who 92*
**Rimbey,** Peter Raymond 1947- *AmMWSc 92*
**Rimer,** Colin Percy Farquharson 1944- *Who 92*
**Rimerman,** Ira Stephen 1938- *WhoFI 92*
**Rimerman,** Morton Walter 1929- *WhoFI 92*
**Rimerman,** Thomas W. 1934- *WhoFI 92*
**Rimes,** William John 1918- *AmMWSc 92*
**Rimington,** Claude 1902- *IntWW 91, Who 92*
**Rimington,** John David 1935- *Who 92*
**Rimland,** David 1944- *AmMWSc 92*
**Rimland,** Edward Mark 1963- *WhoFI 92*
**Rimm,** Alfred A 1934- *AmMWSc 92*
**Rimmer,** Frederick William 1914- *Who 92*
**Rimmer,** Harry 1890-1955 *RelLAm 91*
**Rimmer,** William 1816-1879 *BenetAL 91*
**Rimmington,** Edith 1902- *TwCPaSc*
**Rimmington,** Eric 1926- *TwCPaSc*
**Rimmington,** Gerald Thorneycroft 1930- *WrDr 92*
**Rimoin,** David 1936- *AmMWSc 92*
**Rimrott,** F P J 1927- *AmMWSc 92*
**Rimsky-Korsakov,** Nikolai 1844-1908 *NewAmDM*
**Rimsza,** Skip *WhoAmP 91*
**Rin-Tin-Tin** d1932 *FacFETw*
**Rinaldi,** Donald M *WhoAmP 91*
**Rinaldi,** Keith Stephen 1952- *WhoAmL 92*
**Rinaldi,** Leonard Daniel 1924- *AmMWSc 92*
**Rinaldi,** Nicholas M. *DrAPF 91*
**Rinaldi,** Nicholas Michael 1934- *IntAu&W 91*
**Rinaldi,** Ophelia Sandoval 1933- *WhoHisp 92*
**Rinaldo,** Charles R *AmMWSc 92*
**Rinaldo,** Jeffrey Allen 1955- *WhoWest 92*
**Rinaldo,** Matthew J. 1931- *AlmAP 92 [port]*
**Rinaldo,** Matthew John 1931- *WhoAmP 91*
**Rinard,** Gilbert Allen 1939- *AmMWSc 92*
**Rinard,** Jack Coleman 1936- *WhoAmL 92*
**Rinas,** Ernie Emil 1955- *WhoRel 92*
**Rinchik,** Eugene M 1957- *AmMWSc 92*
**Rinchin,** Lodongiin 1929- *IntWW 91*
**Rincon,** Dale Timothy *WhoWest 92*
**Rincu,** Ion *WhoRel 92*
**Rind,** David Harold 1948- *AmMWSc 92*
**Rind,** Sherry *DrAPF 91*
**Rinde,** Erik Arthur 1965- *WhoWest 92*
**Rinden,** David Lee 1941- *WhoRel 92*
**Rinderer,** Thomas Earl 1943- *AmMWSc 92*
**Rinderknecht,** Heinrich 1913- *AmMWSc 92*
**Rindfleisch,** Norval *DrAPF 91*
**Rindfusz,** Robert Dale 1946- *WhoWest 92*
**Rindlaub,** Jean Wade d1991 *NewYTBS 91 [port]*
**Rindlaub,** John Wade 1934- *WhoEnt 92*
**Rindler,** Wolfgang 1924- *AmMWSc 92*
**Rindone,** Guy E 1922- *AmMWSc 92*
**Rine,** David C 1941- *AmMWSc 92*
**Rinehart,** Charles R. 1947- *WhoFI 92, WhoWest 92*
**Rinehart,** Dana G *WhoAmP 91*
**Rinehart,** Dana Gillman 1946- *WhoMW 92*
**Rinehart,** Darlene Meinert 1939- *WhoMW 92*
**Rinehart,** Dennis Oliver 1946- *WhoRel 92*
**Rinehart,** Edgar A 1928- *AmMWSc 92*
**Rinehart,** Frank Palmer 1944- *AmMWSc 92*
**Rinehart,** Jay Kent 1940- *AmMWSc 92*
**Rinehart,** Joetta Feezor 1933- *WhoRel 92*
**Rinehart,** John Sargent 1915- *AmMWSc 92*
**Rinehart,** Kathryn Ann 1948- *WhoMW 92*
**Rinehart,** Kenneth Lloyd 1929- *AmMWSc 92*
**Rinehart,** Mary Roberts 1876-1958 *BenetAL 91*
**Rinehart,** Nita *WhoAmP 91*
**Rinehart,** Renee Lorraine 1962- *WhoWest 92*
**Rinehart,** Robert R 1932- *AmMWSc 92*
**Rinehart,** Walter Arley 1936- *AmMWSc 92, WhoMW 92*
**Rinehart,** Wilbur Allan 1930- *AmMWSc 92*
**Riner,** James William 1936- *WhoAmL 92*
**Riner,** John William 1924- *AmMWSc 92*
**Riner,** Ronald Nathan 1949- *WhoFI 92*
**Riner,** Tom 1946- *WhoAmP 91*
**Rines,** Howard Wayne 1942- *AmMWSc 92*
**Rines,** John Randolph 1947- *WhoFI 92, WhoMW 92*
**Rinfret,** Gabriel-Edouard 1905- *Who 92*
**Ring,** Carolyn Louise 1926- *WhoAmP 91*
**Ring,** Dennis Randall 1952- *AmMWSc 92*
**Ring,** Douglas *IntAu&W 91X, WrDr 92*
**Ring,** Herbert Everett 1925- *WhoFI 92, WhoMW 92*
**Ring,** James 1927- *Who 92*
**Ring,** James Edward Patrick 1940- *WhoFI 92*
**Ring,** James George 1938- *AmMWSc 92, WhoMW 92*
**Ring,** James Walter 1929- *AmMWSc 92*
**Ring,** Jamie Childs 1939- *WhoWest 92*
**Ring,** Jennifer *WhoAmP 91*
**Ring,** John Robert 1915- *AmMWSc 92*
**Ring,** Leonard M. 1923- *WhoAmL 92, WhoMW 92*
**Ring,** Lindsay 1914- *Who 92*
**Ring,** Lindsay Roberts 1914- *IntWW 91*
**Ring,** Michael Wilson 1943- *WhoAmL 92*
**Ring,** Morey Abraham 1932- *AmMWSc 92*
**Ring,** Paul Joseph 1928- *AmMWSc 92*
**Ring,** Richard Alexander 1938- *AmMWSc 92*
**Ring,** Robert E 1922- *AmMWSc 92*
**Ring,** Robert John 1943- *WhoEnt 92*
**Ring,** Rodney Everett 1927- *WhoRel 92*
**Ring,** Ronald Herman 1938- *WhoAmL 92*
**Ring,** William Ellis 1949- *WhoEnt 92*
**Ring,** Wolfhard 1930- *IntWW 91*
**Ringadoo,** Veerasamy 1920- *IntWW 91, Who 92*
**Ringbom,** Sixten 1935- *IntWW 91*
**Ringeisen,** Richard Delose 1944- *AmMWSc 92*
**Ringel,** Alfredo 1952- *WhoEnt 92*
**Ringel,** Dean 1947- *WhoAmL 92*
**Ringel,** Deborah Taper 1957- *WhoEnt 92*
**Ringel,** Fred Morton 1929- *WhoAmL 92*
**Ringel,** Harvey Norman 1903- *WhoEnt 92, WhoMW 92*
**Ringel,** Robert Lewis 1937- *WhoMW 92*
**Ringel,** Samuel Morris 1924- *AmMWSc 92*
**Ringel,** Steven Adam 1962- *AmMWSc 92*
**Ringen,** Catherine Oleson 1943- *WhoMW 92*
**Ringen,** Sonja Gay 1953- *WhoWest 92*
**Ringen,** Stein 1945- *Who 92*
**Ringenberg,** Lawrence Albert 1915- *AmMWSc 92*
**Ringenberg,** William Carey 1939- *WhoMW 92, WhoRel 92*
**Ringer,** David P *AmMWSc 92*
**Ringer,** Eugene 1937- *WhoRel 92*
**Ringer,** James Milton 1943- *WhoAmL 92*
**Ringer,** Larry Joel 1937- *AmMWSc 92*
**Ringer,** Robert J. 1938- *WrDr 92*
**Ringer,** Robert Kosel 1929- *AmMWSc 92*
**Ringert,** William F 1932- *WhoAmP 91*
**Ringerwole,** Joan Mae 1943- *WhoMW 92*
**Ringger,** Michael G. 1952- *WhoFI 92*
**Ringgold,** Faith 1930- *WhoBlA 92, WorArt 1980 [port]*
**Ringham,** Gary Lewis 1941- *AmMWSc 92*
**Ringhofer,** William Michael 1945- *WhoIns 92*
**Ringle,** Brett Adelbert 1951- *WhoAmL 92*
**Ringle,** David Allan 1924- *AmMWSc 92*
**Ringle,** John Clayton 1935- *AmMWSc 92*
**Ringleben,** Joachim 1945- *WhoRel 92*
**Ringlee,** Robert J 1926- *AmMWSc 92*
**Ringler,** Daniel Howard 1941- *AmMWSc 92*
**Ringler,** Ira 1928- *AmMWSc 92*
**Ringler,** Neil Harrison 1945- *AmMWSc 92*
**Ringler,** Robert L 1922- *AmMWSc 92*
**Ringler,** Stanley Arthur 1941- *WhoRel 92*
**Ringo,** George Roy 1917- *AmMWSc 92*
**Ringo,** James Lewis 1951- *AmMWSc 92*
**Ringo,** John Alan 1941- *AmMWSc 92*
**Ringo,** John Moyer 1943- *AmMWSc 92*
**Ringo,** Johnny *TwCWW 91*
**Ringoen,** Richard Miller 1926- *WhoFI 92, WhoMW 92*
**Ringold,** Anthony F. 1931- *WhoAmL 92*
**Ringold,** Clay *TwCWW 91, WrDr 92*
**Ringold,** David Allan 1956- *WhoAmL 92*
**Ringold,** Francine *DrAPF 91*
**Ringrose,** John Robert 1932- *Who 92*
**Rings,** Randall Eugene 1962- *WhoAmL 92*
**Rings,** Roy Wilson 1916- *AmMWSc 92*
**Ringsdorf,** Warren Marshall, Jr 1930- *AmMWSc 92*
**Ringstad,** Constance Cates 1958- *WhoAmL 92*
**Ringstad,** John Gordon, Jr. 1957- *WhoEnt 92*
**Ringuette,** David Aaron 1958- *WhoWest 92*
**Ringwald,** Donald C. 1917-1987 *ConAu 36NR*
**Ringwald,** Molly 1968- *IntMPA 92, WhoEnt 92*
**Ringwalt,** Richard Alexander 1937- *WhoWest 92*
**Ringwood,** Alfred Edward 1930- *IntWW 91, Who 92*
**Ringwood,** Gwen Pharis 1910- *BenetAL 91*
**Rinhart,** Floyd 1915- *WrDr 92*
**Rinhart,** Marion 1916- *WrDr 92*
**Rini,** Frank John 1952- *AmMWSc 92*
**Rink,** George 1942- *AmMWSc 92*
**Rink,** Jeffrey Eugene 1955- *WhoEnt 92*
**Rink,** Margaret Joan *Who 92*
**Rink,** Oliver Albert 1947- *WhoWest 92*
**Rink,** Richard Donald 1941- *AmMWSc 92*
**Rinke,** Stephen Gerard 1961- *WhoEnt 92*
**Rinkel,** Ralph Chris 1911- *WhoFI 92*
**Rinkema,** Lynn Ellen *AmMWSc 92*
**Rinker,** Charles Washington, Jr 1940- *WhoAmP 91*
**Rinker,** Craig Wayne 1945- *WhoRel 92*
**Rinker,** Earl A, III 1935- *WhoAmP 91*
**Rinker,** George Albert, Jr 1945- *AmMWSc 92*
**Rinker,** George Clark 1922- *AmMWSc 92*
**Rinker,** Robert G 1929- *AmMWSc 92*
**Rinkewich,** Mindy *DrAPF 91*
**Rinks,** Randy *WhoAmP 91*
**Rinne,** John Norman 1944- *AmMWSc 92*
**Rinne,** Mark Douglas 1952- *WhoWest 92*
**Rinne,** Robert W 1932- *AmMWSc 92*
**Rinne,** Vernon Wilmer 1925- *AmMWSc 92*
**Rinnemaki,** William Allen 1951- *WhoAmP 91*
**Rinsch,** Charles Emil 1932- *WhoWest 92*
**Rinsch,** Maryann Elizabeth 1939- *WhoWest 92*
**Rinse,** Jacobus 1900- *AmMWSc 92*
**Rinser,** Luise 1911- *IntWW 91*
**Rinsky,** Joel Charles 1938- *WhoAmL 92, WhoFI 92*
**Rinsky,** Judith Lynn 1941- *WhoFI 92*
**Rinsland,** Roland D. 1933- *WhoBlA 92*
**Rinsler,** Dennis 1947- *WhoEnt 92*
**Rinsley,** Donald Brendan 1928- *AmMWSc 92*
**Rintala,** William Thayer 1938- *WhoAmL 92*
**Rintelen,** Anton 1876-1946 *BiDExR, EncTR 91*
**Rintelmann,** Richard Frederick 1928- *WhoMW 92*
**Rintels,** David W. *LesBEnT 92*
**Rintool,** Katherine 1890-1970 *TwCPaSc*
**Rintzler,** Marius Adrian 1932- *IntWW 91*
**Rinzel,** John Matthew 1944- *AmMWSc 92*
**Rinzler,** Carol Ann 1937- *ConAu 135*
**Rinzler,** Carol Eisen 1941-1990 *ConAu 133*
**Rinzler,** Kenneth 1955- *WhoAmP 91*
**Rinzler,** Paul Emmet 1953- *WhoWest 92*
**Rio,** Donald C 1957- *AmMWSc 92*
**Rio,** Maria Esther 1936- *AmMWSc 92*
**Rio,** Sheldon T 1927- *AmMWSc 92*
**Rioch,** David McKenzie 1900- *AmMWSc 92*
**Riojas,** Ana 1932- *WhoHisp 92*
**Riopel,** James L 1934- *AmMWSc 92*
**Riopelle,** Arthur J 1920- *AmMWSc 92*
**Riopelle,** Jean Paul 1923- *FacFETw, IntWW 91*
**Riordan,** Barrett Joseph 1940- *WhoFI 92*
**Riordan,** Bill d1991 *NewYTBS 91 [port]*
**Riordan,** Carol Campbell 1946- *WhoEnt 92*
**Riordan,** James 1936- *WrDr 92*
**Riordan,** James F 1934- *AmMWSc 92*
**Riordan,** James Louis 1949- *WhoEnt 92*
**Riordan,** James Quentin 1927- *WhoFI 92*
**Riordan,** James R 1949- *WhoAmP 91*
**Riordan,** John Francis 1936- *WhoFI 92, WhoMW 92*
**Riordan,** John Richard 1943- *AmMWSc 92*
**Riordan,** Kevin Michael 1958- *WhoMW 92*
**Riordan,** Michael Davitt 1921- *AmMWSc 92*
**Riordan,** Michael Joseph 1959- *WhoFI 92*
**Riordan,** Patrick Michael 1949- *WhoWest 92*
**Riordan,** Robert Vincent 1946- *WhoMW 92*
**Riordan,** William F 1941- *WhoAmP 91, WhoWest 92*
**Riordon,** J Spruce 1936- *AmMWSc 92*
**Riordon,** Michael 1944- *ConAu 133*
**Rios,** Alberto 1952- *ConAu 34NR*
**Rios,** Alberto Alvaro *DrAPF 91*
**Rios,** Alberto Alvaro 1952- *WhoHisp 92, WhoWest 92*
**Rios,** Armando C., Jr. 1958- *WhoHisp 92*
**Rios,** Benjamin Bejarano 1931- *WhoHisp 92*
**Rios,** Bret Shay 1951- *WhoEnt 92*
**Rios,** Deborah Charmayne 1954- *WhoRel 92*
**Rios,** Dolores Garcia 1964- *WhoHisp 92*
**Rios,** Evelyn Deerwester 1916- *WhoFI 92*
**Rios,** Francisco Gonzalez, Jr. 1950- *WhoHisp 92*
**Rios,** Freddy *WhoHisp 92*
**Rios,** Gilberto Ernesto 1951- *WhoHisp 92*
**Rios,** Irma Garcia 1938- *WhoHisp 92*
**Rios,** Joe 1957- *WhoHisp 92*
**Rios,** Jorge C. 1953- *WhoHisp 92*
**Rios,** Joseph A. 1941- *WhoHisp 92*
**Rios,** Joseph Leon Guerrero 1928- *WhoAmP 91*
**Rios,** Juan 1914- *IntAu&W 91, IntWW 91*
**Rios,** Miguel 1941- *WhoFI 92*
**Rios,** Miguel, Jr. 1941- *WhoHisp 92*
**Rios,** Oscar *WhoHisp 92*
**Rios,** Pedro Agustin 1938- *AmMWSc 92*
**Rios,** Peter D 1949- *WhoAmP 91, WhoHisp 92*
**Rios,** Rolando Guillermo 1940- *WhoEnt 92*
**Rios,** Ronald 1957- *WhoHisp 92*
**Rios,** Sylvia C. 1940- *WhoHisp 92*
**Rios-Bustamante,** Antonio 1948- *WhoHisp 92*
**Rios de Betancourt,** Ethel 1926- *WhoHisp 92*
**Rios Montt,** Efrain 1927- *IntWW 91*
**Rios Olivares,** Eddy O. 1942- *WhoHisp 92*
**Rios-Rodriguez,** Rafael 1956- *WhoHisp 92*
**Riotte,** Jules Charles Emile 1901- *WhoWest 92*
**Rioux,** Claude 1953- *AmMWSc 92*
**Rioux,** Robert Lester 1927- *AmMWSc 92*
**Rioux,** Roland A *WhoAmP 91*
**Ripa Di Meana,** Carlo 1929- *IntWW 91, Who 92*
**Riparbelli,** Carlo 1910- *AmMWSc 92*
**Riphenburg,** Carol Jean 1945- *WhoMW 92*
**Ripin,** Barrett Howard 1942- *AmMWSc 92*
**Ripinsky-Naxon,** Michael 1944- *WhoWest 92*
**Ripka,** William Charles 1939- *AmMWSc 92*
**Ripley,** Alvin *TwCWW 91*
**Ripley,** Brian David 1952- *Who 92*
**Ripley,** Bruce Jay 1958- *WhoFI 92*
**Ripley,** Dennis L 1938- *AmMWSc 92*
**Ripley,** Dillon *Who 92*
**Ripley,** Dillon 1913- *Who 92*
**Ripley,** Earle Allison 1933- *AmMWSc 92, WhoWest 92*
**Ripley,** Elmer Horton 1891-1982 *FacFETw*
**Ripley,** George 1802-1880 *BenetAL 91*
**Ripley,** Hilda L. 1942- *WhoHisp 92*
**Ripley,** Hugh 1916- *Who 92*
**Ripley,** Jack *IntAu&W 91X, WrDr 92*
**Ripley,** Jeffrey Kim 1955- *WhoEnt 92*
**Ripley,** Leoso A 1922- *WhoAmP 91*
**Ripley,** Mike 1952- *IntAu&W 91*
**Ripley,** Randall Butler 1938- *WrDr 92*
**Ripley,** Robert Clarence 1940- *AmMWSc 92*
**Ripley,** Robert L. 1893-1949 *BenetAL 91*
**Ripley,** S. Dillon 1913- *IntWW 91*
**Ripley,** Sidney Dillon, II 1913- *AmMWSc 92*
**Ripley,** Stuart McKinnon 1930- *WhoWest 92*
**Ripley,** Sydney William Leonard d1991 *Who 92N*
**Ripley,** Thomas H 1927- *AmMWSc 92*
**Ripley,** William Ellis 1917- *AmMWSc 92*
**Ripling,** E J 1921- *AmMWSc 92*
**Ripmeester,** John Adrian 1944- *AmMWSc 92*
**Ripoll,** Carlos 1922- *LiExTwC*
**Ripoll,** Edward Conrad 1924- *WhoAmP 91*
**Ripon,** Bishop of 1931- *Who 92*
**Ripon,** Dean of *Who 92*
**Ripp,** William Robert 1924- *WhoAmP 91*
**Rippa,** Vincent Raymond *WhoAmP 91*
**Rippe,** William Jay 1942- *WhoMW 92*
**Rippel,** Julius A. d1990 *NewYTBS 91*
**Rippen,** Alvin Leonard 1917- *AmMWSc 92*
**Rippen,** Thomas Edward 1953- *AmMWSc 92*
**Rippengal,** Derek 1928- *Who 92*
**Ripper,** Rita Jo 1950- *WhoWest 92*

**Ripperger,** Eugene Arman 1914- *AmMWSc 92*
**Rippey,** Clayton 1923- *WhoWest 92*
**Rippie,** Edward Grant 1931- *AmMWSc 92*
**Rippin,** Andrew Lawrence 1950- *WhoRel 92*
**Ripple,** Kenneth F *WhoAmP 91*
**Ripple,** Kenneth Frances 1943- *WhoAmL 92, WhoMW 92*
**Ripple,** Richard Carl 1934- *WhoAmL 92*
**Ripple,** William John 1952- *AmMWSc 92, WhoWest 92*
**Rippley,** La Vern J. 1935- *WrDr 92*
**Ripplinger,** George Raymond, Jr. 1945- *WhoAmL 92*
**Ripplinger,** Gregg Thomas 1963- *WhoEnt 92*
**Rippon** *Who 92*
**Rippon,** Angela *LesBEnT 92*
**Rippon,** Angela 1944- *IntAu&W 91, IntWW 91*
**Rippon,** John Willard 1932- *AmMWSc 92*
**Rippon,** Peter 1950- *TwCPaSc*
**Rippon,** Thomas Richard 1946- *WhoAmP 91*
**Rippon Of Hexham,** Baron 1924- *IntWW 91, Who 92*
**Rippons,** Cleveland L. 1954- *WhoFI 92*
**Ripps,** Harris 1927- *AmMWSc 92*
**Rippy,** Rodney Allen 1968- *WhoBlA 92*
**Rips,** E M 1921- *AmMWSc 92*
**Rips,** Lance Jeffrey 1947- *WhoMW 92*
**Ripy,** Sara Louise 1924- *AmMWSc 92*
**Riq** *ConAu 135, SmATA 66*
**Ririe,** Craig Martin 1943- *WhoWest 92*
**Ririe,** David 1922- *AmMWSc 92*
**Ririe,** Thomas Robert 1964- *WhoFI 92*
**Ris,** Hans 1914- *AmMWSc 92, IntWW 91*
**Ris,** William Krakow 1915- *WhoAmL 92*
**Risany,** Dennis Joseph 1945- *WhoFI 92, WhoMW 92*
**Risberg,** Robert Lawrence, Sr. 1935- *WhoFI 92*
**Risbrook,** Arthur Timothy 1929- *WhoBlA 92*
**Risbud,** Subhash Hanamant 1947- *AmMWSc 92*
**Risby,** Edward Louis 1933- *AmMWSc 92*
**Risby,** Terence Humphrey 1947- *AmMWSc 92*
**Risch,** James E 1943- *WhoAmP 91*
**Risch,** Stephen John 1950- *AmMWSc 92*
**Rischar,** Anne Mary 1937- *WhoRel 92*
**Rischbieter,** Karlos 1927- *IntWW 91*
**Rischel,** Jorgen 1934- *IntWW 91*
**Rischin,** Moses 1925- *WhoWest 92, WrDr 92*
**Rischiotto,** Ann Marie 1957- *WhoWest 92*
**Rischitelli,** Donald Gary 1961- *WhoWest 92*
**Risdon,** Michael Paul 1946- *WhoMW 92*
**Risdon,** Thomas Joseph 1939- *AmMWSc 92*
**Rise,** John Ernest 1954- *WhoWest 92*
**Riseberg,** Leslie Allen 1943- *AmMWSc 92*
**Risebrough,** Doug 1954- *WhoWest 92*
**Riseley-Prichard,** Richard Augustin 1925- *Who 92*
**Riseman,** Edward M 1942- *AmMWSc 92*
**Risen,** Mary Jane 1953- *WhoMW 92*
**Risen,** William Maurice, Jr 1940- *AmMWSc 92*
**Risenhoover,** Ted M 1934- *WhoAmP 91*
**Risenhoover,** Terry Jack, II 1965- *WhoFI 92*
**Riser,** Mary Elizabeth 1945- *AmMWSc 92*
**Riser,** Nathan Wendell 1920- *AmMWSc 92*
**Rish,** Seymour A. 1921- *WhoFI 92*
**Rishbeth,** John d1991 *Who 92N*
**Rishbeth,** John 1918- *IntWW 91*
**Rishel,** Mary Ann Malinchak *DrAPF 91*
**Rishel,** Raymond Warren 1930- *AmMWSc 92*
**Rishel,** Richard Clinton 1943- *WhoFI 92*
**Rishell,** William Arthur 1940- *AmMWSc 92*
**Risher,** John R., Jr. 1938- *WhoBlA 92*
**Risher,** Paul David 1935- *WhoFI 92*
**Rishtya,** Kassim *IntWW 91*
**Rishwain,** Mark Benjamin 1961- *WhoAmL 92*
**Risi,** Dino 1917- *IntDcF 2-2 [port]*
**Risica,** Loretta Cash 1930- *WhoFI 92*
**Rising,** Edward James 1926- *AmMWSc 92*
**Rising,** James David 1942- *AmMWSc 92*
**Rising,** Richard Linn 1920- *WhoRel 92*
**Rising,** Willard Bradley 1839-1910 *BiInAmS*
**Risinger,** Gerald E 1933- *AmMWSc 92*
**Risius,** Marvin Leroy 1931- *AmMWSc 92*
**Risk,** Douglas James 1941- *Who 92*
**Risk,** Michael John 1940- *AmMWSc 92*
**Risk,** Thomas 1922- *Who 92*
**Risk,** Thomas Neilson 1922- *IntWW 91*
**Risk,** William Symington 1909- *Who 92*
**Riskas,** Harry James 1920- *WhoWest 92*
**Riskas,** Mike 1934- *WhoWest 92*
**Riske,** William Kenneth 1949- *WhoEnt 92*
**Riskin,** Adrian Boreas 1963- *WhoWest 92*
**Riskin,** Jules 1926- *AmMWSc 92*
**Risley,** Gregory Byron 1949- *WhoMW 92*
**Risley,** John Stetler 1942- *AmMWSc 92*
**Risley,** Kathryn Hanford 1954- *WhoEnt 92*
**Risley,** Michael Samuel *AmMWSc 92*
**Risley,** Samuel Doty 1845-1920 *BiInAmS*
**Rislove,** David Joel 1940- *AmMWSc 92*
**Risner,** Paul Edward 1957- *WhoAmL 92*
**Risnes,** Marilyn Louise Neitzert 1935- *WhoMW 92*
**Risness,** Eric John 1927- *Who 92*
**Risom,** Jens 1916- *DcTwDes*
**Rison,** Andre Previn 1967- *WhoBlA 92*
**Rison,** Faye Rison 1942- *WhoBlA 92*
**Riss,** Robert Bailey 1927- *WhoFI 92*
**Riss,** Walter 1925- *AmMWSc 92*
**Rissanen,** Jorma Johannes 1932- *AmMWSc 92*
**Risse,** Guenter Bernhard 1932- *AmMWSc 92*
**Risse,** Klaus H. 1929- *WhoFI 92*
**Risseeuw,** John Lewis 1945- *WhoWest 92*
**Risser,** Arthur Crane, Jr 1938- *AmMWSc 92*
**Risser,** Fred A 1927- *WhoAmP 91, WhoMW 92*
**Risser,** Jonathan 1869-1917 *BiInAmS*
**Risser,** Paul Gillan 1939- *AmMWSc 92*
**Rissien,** Edward L. *IntMPA 92*
**Rissler,** Jane Francina 1946- *AmMWSc 92*
**Rissner,** Danton 1940- *IntMPA 92*
**Risso,** Harry Francis 1929- *WhoHisp 92*
**Risso,** Patricia Ann *WhoWest 92*
**Risson,** Robert Joseph Henry 1901- *Who 92*
**Rist,** Henry D 1926- *WhoAmP 91*
**Rist,** John Michael 1936- *Who 92*
**Rist,** Seward 1943- *WhoBlA 92*
**Rist,** Susan E. *WhoBlA 92*
**Ristau,** Kenneth Eugene, Jr. 1939- *WhoAmL 92*
**Ristau,** Mark Moody 1944- *WhoAmL 92*
**Riste,** Olav 1933- *IntWW 91, WrDr 92*
**Ristenbatt,** Marlin P 1928- *AmMWSc 92*
**Ristenpart,** Karl 1900-1967 *NewAmDM*
**Ristey,** William J 1938- *AmMWSc 92*
**Ristic,** Miodrag 1918- *AmMWSc 92*
**Ristic,** Velimir Mihailo 1936- *AmMWSc 92*
**Ristikivi,** Karl 1912-1977 *LiExTwC*
**Ristow,** Bruce W 1940- *AmMWSc 92*
**Ristow,** Bruno 1940- *WhoWest 92*
**Ristow,** Walter W. 1908- *WrDr 92*
**Ristroph,** John Heard 1946- *AmMWSc 92*
**Ristuccia,** Matthew Paul 1952- *WhoRel 92*
**Ristvet,** Byron Leo 1947- *AmMWSc 92*
**Riswadkar,** Ashutosh Vishnu 1947- *WhoMW 92*
**Ritblat,** John Henry 1935- *IntWW 91, Who 92*
**Ritcey,** Gordon M 1930- *AmMWSc 92*
**Ritch,** Robert 1944- *AmMWSc 92*
**Ritcheson,** Charles Ray 1925- *Who 92*
**Ritchey,** James Salem 1950- *WhoFI 92*
**Ritchey,** John Michael 1940- *AmMWSc 92*
**Ritchey,** Kenneth Dale 1944- *AmMWSc 92*
**Ritchey,** Mercedes B. 1919- *WhoBlA 92*
**Ritchey,** Michael Lee 1956- *WhoAmL 92*
**Ritchey,** Patrick William 1949- *WhoAmL 92*
**Ritchey,** Paul Andrew 1950- *WhoMW 92*
**Ritchey,** Samuel Donley, Jr. 1933- *WhoWest 92*
**Ritchey,** Sanford Jewell 1930- *AmMWSc 92*
**Ritchey,** William Michael 1925- *AmMWSc 92*
**Ritchie** *Who 92*
**Ritchie,** Adam Burke 1939- *AmMWSc 92*
**Ritchie,** Albert 1939- *WhoAmL 92*
**Ritchie,** Albert Edgar 1916- *Who 92*
**Ritchie,** Alexander Charles 1921- *AmMWSc 92*
**Ritchie,** Alexander James Otway 1928- *Who 92*
**Ritchie,** Anthony Elliot 1915- *Who 92*
**Ritchie,** Austin E 1918- *AmMWSc 92*
**Ritchie,** Betty Caraway 1929- *AmMWSc 92*
**Ritchie,** Brenda Rachel 1927- *AmMWSc 92*
**Ritchie,** Buzz 1947- *WhoAmP 91*
**Ritchie,** Calvin Donald 1930- *AmMWSc 92*
**Ritchie,** Candace Kay 1961- *WhoMW 92*
**Ritchie,** Cedric E. 1927- *IntWW 91*
**Ritchie,** Cedric Elmer 1927- *WhoFI 92*
**Ritchie,** Charles Stewart Almon 1906- *Who 92*
**Ritchie,** Daniel L. *LesBEnT 92*
**Ritchie,** Daniel Lee 1931- *WhoWest 92*
**Ritchie,** David Malcolm 1950- *AmMWSc 92*
**Ritchie,** David Robert 1948- *Who 92*
**Ritchie,** David Wayne 1961- *WhoMW 92*
**Ritchie,** Douglas Malcolm 1941- *Who 92*
**Ritchie,** Edwin 1921- *ConAu 35NR*
**Ritchie,** Elisavietta *DrAPF 91*
**Ritchie,** Eric Robert David 1942- *WhoWest 92*
**Ritchie,** Ernest LeRoy 1953- *WhoWest 92*
**Ritchie,** Evelyn *DrAPF 91*
**Ritchie,** Garry Harlan 1938- *WhoEnt 92*
**Ritchie,** Gary Alan 1941- *AmMWSc 92*
**Ritchie,** George Stephen 1914- *Who 92*
**Ritchie,** Gisela Fuhrmann *WhoMW 92*
**Ritchie,** Harlan 1935- *AmMWSc 92*
**Ritchie,** Horace David 1920- *Who 92*
**Ritchie,** Ian Carl 1947- *Who 92*
**Ritchie,** J. Murdoch 1925- *IntWW 91*
**Ritchie,** James Cunningham 1929- *AmMWSc 92*
**Ritchie,** James Edward Thomson d1991 *Who 92N*
**Ritchie,** James Martin 1917- *IntWW 91, Who 92*
**Ritchie,** James Walter 1920- *Who 92*
**Ritchie,** Jean 1922- *NewAmDM*
**Ritchie,** Jerry Carlyle 1937- *AmMWSc 92*
**Ritchie,** Joe 1949- *WhoBlA 92*
**Ritchie,** Joe T 1937- *AmMWSc 92*
**Ritchie,** John Bennett 1924- *WhoWest 92*
**Ritchie,** John Hindle 1937- *Who 92*
**Ritchie,** Joseph Murdoch 1925- *AmMWSc 92, Who 92*
**Ritchie,** Kenneth Gordon 1921- *Who 92*
**Ritchie,** Kim 1936- *AmMWSc 92*
**Ritchie,** Louise Reid 1951- *WhoBlA 92*
**Ritchie,** Malcolm Luther 1920- *WhoMW 92*
**Ritchie,** Margaret Claire 1937- *Who 92*
**Ritchie,** Martin *Who 92*
**Ritchie,** Michael 1938- *IntMPA 92*
**Ritchie,** Michael Brunswick 1938- *WhoEnt 92*
**Ritchie,** Paul S. 1951- *WhoAmL 92*
**Ritchie,** Richard Lee 1946- *WhoFI 92*
**Ritchie,** Robert Blackwood 1937- *Who 92*
**Ritchie,** Robert Oliver 1948- *AmMWSc 92, WhoWest 92*
**Ritchie,** Robert Wells 1935- *AmMWSc 92*
**Ritchie,** Rufus Haynes 1924- *AmMWSc 92*
**Ritchie,** Shirley Anne 1940- *Who 92*
**Ritchie,** Stanley 1935- *NewAmDM*
**Ritchie,** Stephen G 1954- *AmMWSc 92*
**Ritchie,** Thomas Russell 1946- *WhoMW 92*
**Ritchie,** Wallace Parks, Jr 1935- *AmMWSc 92*
**Ritchie,** William Paul 1946- *WhoAmL 92*
**Ritchie,** William Sidney 1953- *WhoMW 92*
**Ritchie,** Wyman 1929- *WhoRel 92*
**Ritchie of Dundee,** Baron 1919- *Who 92*
**Ritenour,** Elston Russell 1953- *WhoMW 92*
**Ritenour,** Gary Lee 1938- *AmMWSc 92*
**Ritenour,** Lee 1952- *ConMus 7 [port]*
**Riter,** Charles L. 1941- *WhoAmL 92*
**Riter,** George Monroe 1957- *WhoAmL 92*
**Riter,** John Randolph, Jr 1933- *AmMWSc 92*
**Riter,** Stephen 1940- *AmMWSc 92*
**Ritger,** Richard August 1938- *WhoMW 92*
**Rithauddeen Al-Haj Bin Tengku Ismail,** A. 1932- *IntWW 91*
**Ritland,** Richard Martin 1925- *AmMWSc 92*
**Ritman,** Barbara Ellen 1946- *WhoWest 92*
**Ritorto,** Rocco John 1949- *WhoFI 92*
**Ritrosi,** Joseph Arthur 1957- *WhoMW 92*
**Ritschel,** James Allan 1930- *WhoFI 92, WhoMW 92*
**Ritschel,** Wolfgang Adolf 1933- *AmMWSc 92, WhoMW 92*
**Ritsko,** John James 1945- *AmMWSc 92*
**Ritson,** David Mark 1924- *AmMWSc 92*
**Ritsos,** Giannes *ConAu 133*
**Ritsos,** Yannis 1909- *LiExTwC*
**Ritsos,** Yannis 1909-1990 *AnObit 1990, ConAu 133, FacFETw*
**Ritt,** James Anthony 1931- *WhoMW 92*
**Ritt,** Martin d1990 *IntWW 91N*
**Ritt,** Martin 1902-1990 *IntDcF 2-2 [port]*
**Ritt,** Martin 1914-1990 *AnObit 1990, ConTFT 9, FacFETw*
**Ritt,** Martin 1920-1990 *CurBio 91N*
**Ritt,** Paul Edward, Jr 1928- *AmMWSc 92*
**Ritt,** Robert King 1924- *AmMWSc 92*
**Ritt,** Roger M. 1950- *WhoAmL 92*
**Rittberg,** Eric Joseph 1962- *WhoAmP 91*
**Rittelmeyer,** Louis Frederick, Jr 1924- *AmMWSc 92*
**Rittenbach,** Gail Sylvia 1948- *WhoWest 92*
**Rittenbaugh,** Cheryl K 1946- *AmMWSc 92*
**Rittenberg,** Alan 1938- *AmMWSc 92*
**Rittenberg,** Leon Hirsch, Jr. 1934- *WhoAmL 92*
**Rittenberg,** Marc A. 1945- *WhoWest 92*
**Rittenberg,** Mark Alan 1963- *WhoMW 92*
**Rittenberg,** Marvin Barry 1931- *AmMWSc 92*
**Rittenberg,** Sydney Charles 1914- *AmMWSc 92*
**Rittenbury,** Max Sanford 1928- *AmMWSc 92*
**Rittenhouse,** Bruce Dean 1951- *WhoFI 92*
**Rittenhouse,** Carl Harris 1922- *WhoWest 92*
**Rittenhouse,** David 1732-1796 *BiInAmS, BlkwEAR*
**Rittenhouse,** Diana Angela 1939- *WhoAmP 91*
**Rittenhouse,** Harry George 1942- *AmMWSc 92*
**Rittenhouse,** Jessie B. 1869-1948 *BenetAL 91*
**Rittenhouse,** Larry Ronald *AmMWSc 92*
**Rittenhouse,** Shirley Bash 1928- *WhoMW 92*
**Rittenhouse,** Susan E 1945- *AmMWSc 92*
**Rittenhouse,** William Henry 1922- *WhoRel 92*
**Ritter,** A 1923- *AmMWSc 92*
**Ritter,** Alfred Francis, Jr. 1946- *WhoFI 92*
**Ritter,** Ann L. 1933- *WhoAmL 92, WhoFI 92*
**Ritter,** August *WhoAmP 91*
**Ritter,** Bruce 1927- *WhoRel 92*
**Ritter,** Carl A 1932- *AmMWSc 92*
**Ritter,** Dale Franklin 1932- *AmMWSc 92*
**Ritter,** Dale William 1919- *WhoWest 92*
**Ritter,** Daniel Benjamin 1937- *WhoFI 92*
**Ritter,** David Allen 1954- *WhoMW 92*
**Ritter,** Deborah Bradford 1953- *WhoAmL 92*
**Ritter,** Don 1940- *AlmAP 92 [port]*
**Ritter,** Donald Lawrence 1940- *WhoAmP 91*
**Ritter,** E Gene 1928- *AmMWSc 92*
**Ritter,** Edmond Jean 1915- *AmMWSc 92*
**Ritter,** Edward S 1954- *WhoIns 92*
**Ritter,** Enloe Thomas 1939- *AmMWSc 92*
**Ritter,** Frances Raymond 1840-1890 *HanAmWH*
**Ritter,** Garry Lee 1949- *AmMWSc 92*
**Ritter,** Gerhard 1888-1967 *EncTR 91*
**Ritter,** Gerhard A. 1929- *IntWW 91*
**Ritter,** Gerhard X 1936- *AmMWSc 92*
**Ritter,** Guy Franklin 1933- *WhoFI 92*
**Ritter,** Hartien Sharp 1918- *AmMWSc 92*
**Ritter,** Hedda F 1945- *WhoIns 92*
**Ritter,** Hope Thomas Martin, Jr 1919- *AmMWSc 92*
**Ritter,** Howard Lowell 1946- *WhoEnt 92*
**Ritter,** Hubert August 1924- *AmMWSc 92*
**Ritter,** James Carroll 1935- *AmMWSc 92*
**Ritter,** James William 1942- *WhoFI 92*
**Ritter,** Jeffrey B. 1954- *WhoAmL 92*
**Ritter,** Jerry E. 1935- *WhoFI 92*
**Ritter,** John *LesBEnT 92*
**Ritter,** John 1948- *IntMPA 92*
**Ritter,** John Earl, Jr 1939- *AmMWSc 92*
**Ritter,** Johnathan Southworth 1948- *WhoEnt 92*
**Ritter,** Jorge Eduardo 1950- *IntWW 91*
**Ritter,** Joseph Elmer 1892-1967 *RelLAm 91*
**Ritter,** Joseph John *AmMWSc 92*
**Ritter,** Joseph M 1950- *WhoIns 92*
**Ritter,** Karen A 1953- *WhoAmP 91*
**Ritter,** Karl 1888-1977 *EncTR 91 [port]*
**Ritter,** Karla Schwensen 1950- *AmMWSc 92*
**Ritter,** Margaret Jean 1925- *WhoAmP 91*
**Ritter,** Mark Alfred 1948- *AmMWSc 92*
**Ritter,** Miriam Virginia 1957- *WhoAmP 91*
**Ritter,** Nadine Marie 1958- *AmMWSc 92*
**Ritter,** Norman L. 1934- *WhoFI 92*
**Ritter,** Norman Richard 1929- *WhoFI 92*
**Ritter,** Preston Peck Otto 1941- *AmMWSc 92*
**Ritter,** R Brown 1921- *AmMWSc 92*
**Ritter,** Rick Ronald 1947- *WhoWest 92*
**Ritter,** Robert Joseph 1925- *WhoAmL 92, WhoFI 92*
**Ritter,** Rogers C 1929- *AmMWSc 92*
**Ritter,** Russell Joseph 1932- *WhoWest 92*
**Ritter,** Tex 1905-1974 *NewAmDM*
**Ritter,** Thomas D *WhoAmP 91*
**Ritter,** Thomas J. 1922- *WhoBlA 92*
**Ritter,** Walter Adolf 1932- *WhoRel 92*
**Ritter,** Walter Paul 1929- *AmMWSc 92*
**Ritter,** William Francis McKnight 1846?-1917 *BiInAmS*
**Ritter,** William Frederick 1942- *AmMWSc 92*
**Ritterhoff,** Robert J 1910- *AmMWSc 92*
**Ritterman,** Murray B 1914- *AmMWSc 92*
**Ritterson,** Albert L 1924- *AmMWSc 92*
**Rittgers,** Charles Henry 1951- *WhoAmL 92*
**Rittinger,** Carolyne June 1942- *WhoMW 92*
**Rittman,** Frank Sears 1960- *WhoEnt 92*
**Rittmann,** Bruce Edward 1950- *AmMWSc 92*
**Rittmer,** Sheldon L 1928- *WhoAmP 91*
**Rittner,** Edmund Sidney 1919- *AmMWSc 92*
**Rittner,** Luke Philip Hardwick 1947- *IntWW 91, Who 92*

**Ritts**, Herb 1954?- *News 92-2 [port]*
**Ritts**, Roy Ellot, Jr 1929- *AmMWSc 92*
**Ritts**, William Henry, III 1943- *WhoMW 92*
**Rittschof**, Daniel 1946- *AmMWSc 92*
**Ritvo**, Edward R 1930- *AmMWSc 92*
**Ritvo**, Harriet 1946- *WrDr 92*
**Ritvo**, Lucille B 1920- *WhoAmP 91*
**Ritz**, David 1943- *WhoEnt 92*
**Ritz**, Dianne Patricia 1947- *WhoMW 92*
**Ritz**, Kenneth Francis 1935- *WhoAmL 92*
**Ritz**, Victor Henry 1934- *AmMWSc 92*
**Ritz-Gold**, Caroline Joyce *AmMWSc 92*
**Ritzen**, Jo 1945- *IntWW 91*
**Ritzenberg**, Jeremy 1959- *WhoAmL 92*
**Ritzert**, Roger William 1936- *AmMWSc 92*
**Ritzi**, Earl Michael 1946- *AmMWSc 92*
**Ritzka**, Timothy Joseph 1959- *WhoAmL 92*
**Ritzman**, Robert L 1932- *AmMWSc 92*
**Ritzman**, Thomas A 1914- *AmMWSc 92*
**Ritzmann**, Leonard W 1921- *AmMWSc 92*
**Ritzmann**, Ronald Fred 1943- *AmMWSc 92*
**Ritzo**, Eugene 1919- *WhoAmP 91*
**Riva**, John F 1929- *AmMWSc 92*
**Riva**, Joseph Peter, Jr 1935- *AmMWSc 92*
**Riva-Aguero**, Jose de 1783-1858 *HisDSpE*
**Riva-Aguero Y Osma**, Jose de la 1885-1944 *BiDExR*
**Riva Saleta**, Luis Octavio 1949- *WhoHisp 92*
**Rivadavia**, Bernardino 1780-1845 *HisDSpE*
**Rivadeneira**, Luis E. 1937- *WhoHisp 92*
**Rivard**, David *DrAPF 91*
**Rivard**, Jerome G 1932- *AmMWSc 92*
**Rivard**, Steven A. 1963- *WhoFI 92*
**Rivarol**, Antoine de 1753-1801 *BlkwCEP*
**Rivas**, Daniel E. 1945- *WhoHisp 92*
**Rivas**, David 1953- *WhoHisp 92*
**Rivas**, Edgar J. 1933- *WhoHisp 92*
**Rivas**, Eneida 1957- *WhoHisp 92*
**Rivas**, Fernando *WhoHisp 92*
**Rivas**, Henry Vasquez, Sr. 1952- *WhoHisp 92*
**Rivas**, John Edward 1961- *WhoMW 92*
**Rivas**, Joseph M. 1951- *WhoHisp 92*
**Rivas**, Marian Lucy 1943- *AmMWSc 92*
**Rivas**, Martin, Sr. *WhoHisp 92*
**Rivas**, Mercedes 1931- *WhoHisp 92*
**Rivas**, Milagros 1955- *WhoHisp 92*
**Rivas**, Robert *WhoRel 92*
**Rivas**, Ronald K. 1958- *WhoHisp 92*
**Rivas**, Wilfredo Jose 1949- *WhoHisp 92*
**Rivas-Mijares**, Gustavo 1922- *IntWW 91*
**Rive**, Kenneth 1919- *IntMPA 92*
**Rive**, Richard 1931-1989 *LiExTwC*
**Rivela**, Louis John 1942- *AmMWSc 92*
**Riveland**, A R 1923- *AmMWSc 92*
**Rivello**, Robert Matthew 1921- *AmMWSc 92*
**Rivenbark**, Rembert Reginald 1912- *WhoFI 92*
**Riveness**, Phillip J 1947- *WhoAmP 91*
**Rivenson**, Abraham S 1926- *AmMWSc 92*
**River**, Gregory Nathan 1954- *WhoFI 92*
**Rivera**, Alvin D. *WhoHisp 92*
**Rivera**, Americo, Jr 1928- *AmMWSc 92, WhoHisp 92*
**Rivera**, Anastacio S. *WhoHisp 92*
**Rivera**, Angel Miguel 1955- *WhoHisp 92*
**Rivera**, Antonio T *WhoIns 92*
**Rivera**, Armando Remonte 1940- *WhoWest 92*
**Rivera**, Aurelio *WhoHisp 92*
**Rivera**, Carlos 1955- *WhoHisp 92*
**Rivera**, Chita 1933- *IntMPA 92, WhoHisp 92*
**Rivera**, Craig Alan 1954- *WhoFI 92*
**Rivera**, Daniel Carlos 1931- *WhoIns 92*
**Rivera**, Diana Huizar 1953- *WhoHisp 92*
**Rivera**, Diego 1886-1957 *FacFETw, ModArCr 2 [port]*
**Rivera**, Don *WhoHisp 92*
**Rivera**, Eddy 1938- *WhoBlA 92*
**Rivera**, Edgardo 1953- *WhoHisp 92*
**Rivera**, Edward *DrAPF 91, WhoHisp 92*
**Rivera**, Edwin 1948- *WhoHisp 92*
**Rivera**, Edwin A. 1946- *WhoHisp 92*
**Rivera**, Eladio A., Jr. *WhoHisp 92*
**Rivera**, Ernairis *DrAPF 91*
**Rivera**, Evangelina 1953- *WhoHisp 92*
**Rivera**, Evelyn Margaret 1929- *AmMWSc 92, WhoMW 92*
**Rivera**, Evelyn Socias 1959- *WhoHisp 92*
**Rivera**, Ezequiel Ramirez 1942- *AmMWSc 92, WhoHisp 92*
**Rivera**, Fanny 1953- *WhoHisp 92*
**Rivera**, Frank E., Sr. 1928- *WhoHisp 92*
**Rivera**, George 1955- *WhoHisp 92*
**Rivera**, Geraldo *LesBEnT 92 [port]*
**Rivera**, Geraldo 1943- *IntMPA 92, WhoEnt 92*
**Rivera**, Geraldo Miguel 1943- *WhoHisp 92*
**Rivera**, Hector 1951- *WhoHisp 92*
**Rivera**, Hector A. 1943- *WhoHisp 92*
**Rivera**, Hector L. *WhoHisp 92*
**Rivera**, Henry Michael 1946- *WhoAmP 91, WhoHisp 92*
**Rivera**, Jaime *WhoHisp 92*
**Rivera**, Jennifer Anntoinette 1956- *WhoHisp 92*
**Rivera**, Jerry M 1946- *WhoAmP 91*
**Rivera**, John 1945- *WhoHisp 92*
**Rivera**, John A. 1954- *WhoHisp 92*
**Rivera**, John David 1948- *WhoHisp 92*
**Rivera**, Jon Lawrence 1960- *WhoEnt 92*
**Rivera**, Jose 1938- *WhoAmP 91, WhoHisp 92*
**Rivera**, Jose Eustacio 1889-1928 *BenetAL 91*
**Rivera**, Jose Fructosa 1784?-1854 *HisDSpE*
**Rivera**, Jose J. 1951- *WhoHisp 92*
**Rivera**, Jose Luis 1946- *WhoHisp 92*
**Rivera**, Juan 1953- *WhoHisp 92*
**Rivera**, Juan B., II 1940- *WhoHisp 92*
**Rivera**, Juan M. 1944- *WhoHisp 92*
**Rivera**, Juan Manuel 1943- *WhoHisp 92*
**Rivera**, Julia E. 1949- *WhoHisp 92*
**Rivera**, Laura E. 1945- *WhoHisp 92*
**Rivera**, Lloyd David 1947- *WhoHisp 92*
**Rivera**, Louis Reyes *DrAPF 91*
**Rivera**, Louis Reyes 1945- *WhoHisp 92*
**Rivera**, Lucia 1938- *WhoHisp 92*
**Rivera**, Lucy 1937- *WhoHisp 92*
**Rivera**, Luis 1964- *WhoHisp 92*
**Rivera**, Luis Eduardo 1940- *WhoHisp 92*
**Rivera**, Luis Ernesto 1950- *WhoHisp 92*
**Rivera**, Luis J. 1953- *WhoHisp 92*
**Rivera**, Marcelina 1962- *WhoHisp 92*
**Rivera**, Marco Antonio 1945- *WhoHisp 92*
**Rivera**, Mario Angel 1941- *WhoHisp 92*
**Rivera**, Martin Garcia 1963- *WhoHisp 92*
**Rivera**, Mary Lou 1950- *WhoMW 92*
**Rivera**, Mercedes A. 1954- *WhoHisp 92*
**Rivera**, Migdalia Vazquez 1961- *WhoHisp 92*
**Rivera**, Miquela C. 1954- *WhoHisp 92*
**Rivera**, Nancy J. 1964- *WhoHisp 92*
**Rivera**, Oscar R. 1956- *WhoAmL 92*
**Rivera**, Oswald 1944- *WhoHisp 92*
**Rivera**, Peter Angel 1933- *WhoHisp 92*
**Rivera**, Rafael *WhoHisp 92*
**Rivera**, Rafael J. 1940- *WhoHisp 92*
**Rivera**, Rafael Rene 1950- *WhoHisp 92*
**Rivera**, Ramon Luis 1929- *WhoAmP 91, WhoHisp 92*
**Rivera**, Raul 1930- *WhoHisp 92*
**Rivera**, Ray *WhoHisp 92*
**Rivera**, Rhonda Rae 1938- *WhoAmL 92*
**Rivera**, Richard E. 1947- *WhoFI 92, WhoHisp 92*
**Rivera**, Robert A. 1940- *WhoHisp 92*
**Rivera**, Roberto 1953- *WhoHisp 92*
**Rivera**, Roland Gilbert 1938- *WhoAmP 91*
**Rivera**, Ron *WhoHisp 92*
**Rivera**, Rosa M. 1950- *WhoHisp 92*
**Rivera**, Salvador *WhoHisp 92*
**Rivera**, Sandra Lynn 1955- *WhoHisp 92*
**Rivera**, Theodore Basiliso 1955- *WhoHisp 92*
**Rivera**, Thomas D. 1928- *WhoHisp 92*
**Rivera**, Tomas 1935-1984 *BenetAL 91, TwCWW 91*
**Rivera**, Tony A. 1944- *WhoHisp 92*
**Rivera**, Victor Manuel 1916- *WhoHisp 92, WhoRel 92, WhoWest 92*
**Rivera**, Vincent 1950- *WhoHisp 92*
**Rivera**, Walter 1955- *WhoAmL 92, WhoHisp 92*
**Rivera**, William Henry 1931- *AmMWSc 92*
**Rivera**, William McLeod 1934- *WhoHisp 92*
**Rivera-Alequin**, Ulpiano H. 1938- *WhoHisp 92*
**Rivera-Alvarez**, Miguel-Angel 1952- *WhoHisp 92*
**Rivera Bigas**, Juan 1929- *WhoHisp 92*
**Rivera-Brenes**, Luis 1916- *WhoAmP 91*
**Rivera-Calimlim**, Leonor *AmMWSc 92*
**Rivera-Carlo**, Roberto 1955- *WhoHisp 92*
**Rivera-Colon**, Angel Antonio 1947- *WhoHisp 92*
**Rivera-Cruz**, Hector 1950- *WhoAmP 91, WhoHisp 92*
**Rivera Domenech**, Angel L. 1940- *WhoHisp 92*
**Rivera-Garcia**, Ignacio 1914- *WhoHisp 92*
**Rivera-Izcoa**, Carmen 1928- *WhoHisp 92*
**Rivera-Lopez**, Angel 1944- *WhoHisp 92*
**Rivera-Matos**, Noelia 1949- *WhoHisp 92*
**Rivera-Mazziotta**, Coralina 1959- *WhoAmL 92*
**Rivera-Morales**, Roberto 1953- *WhoHisp 92*
**Rivera Ortiz**, Gilberto 1932- *WhoAmP 91, WhoHisp 92*
**Rivera Ortiz**, Juan *WhoAmP 91*
**Rivera-Pagan**, Carmen A. 1923- *WhoHisp 92*
**Rivera Perez**, Efrain E. *WhoHisp 92*
**Rivera Ramirez**, Alba 1947- *WhoAmP 91*
**Rivera-Ramos**, Efren 1947- *WhoHisp 92*
**Rivera-Rivera**, Felix A. 1948- *WhoHisp 92*
**Rivera-Rodas**, Hernan 1940- *WhoHisp 92*
**Rivera-Viera**, Diana T. 1949- *WhoHisp 92*
**Rivera y Damas**, Arturo *WhoRel 92*
**Riverdale**, Baron 1901- *Who 92*
**Riverin**, Bruno 1941- *WhoFI 92*
**Riverina**, Bishop of 1927- *Who 92*
**Riverman**, Rylla Claire 1955- *WhoWest 92*
**Rivero**, Ana Margarita 1960- *WhoHisp 92*
**Rivero**, Andres *DrAPF 91*
**Rivero**, Andres 1936- *WhoHisp 92*
**Rivero**, Eliana S. 1940- *WhoHisp 92*
**Rivero**, Emilio Adolfo 1947- *WhoHisp 92*
**Rivero**, Hector M. *WhoHisp 92*
**Rivero**, Jorge *WhoEnt 92*
**Rivero**, Juan A. 1923- *WhoHisp 92*
**Rivero**, Juan Arturo 1923- *AmMWSc 92*
**Rivero**, Julio B. 1929- *WhoRel 92*
**Rivero**, Marilyn Elaine Keith 1942- *WhoAmP 91*
**Rivero**, Marita Joy 1943- *WhoBlA 92*
**Rivero**, Mauricio Agustin 1947- *WhoWest 92*
**Rivers**, Alfred J. 1925- *WhoBlA 92*
**Rivers**, Ann *DrAPF 91*
**Rivers**, Cheryl P *WhoAmP 91*
**Rivers**, Clarence Joseph 1931- *WhoBlA 92*
**Rivers**, David Buchanan 1937- *WhoRel 92*
**Rivers**, David Eugene 1943- *WhoBlA 92*
**Rivers**, David Lawrence 1944- *WhoBlA 92*
**Rivers**, Denovious Adolphus 1928- *WhoBlA 92*
**Rivers**, Donald Lee 1943- *WhoMW 92*
**Rivers**, Dorothy 1933- *WhoBlA 92*
**Rivers**, Douglas Bernard 1951- *AmMWSc 92*
**Rivers**, Gary C. 1951- *WhoBlA 92*
**Rivers**, Glenn Anton 1961- *WhoBlA 92*
**Rivers**, Griffin Harold 1939- *WhoBlA 92*
**Rivers**, Helene 1916- *WhoWest 92*
**Rivers**, Horace William 1941- *WhoRel 92*
**Rivers**, J.W. *DrAPF 91*
**Rivers**, Jerry Margaret 1929- *AmMWSc 92*
**Rivers**, Jessie Markert 1949- *AmMWSc 92*
**Rivers**, Joan *LesBEnT 92*
**Rivers**, Joan 1933- *IntMPA 92, WhoEnt 92, WrDr 92*
**Rivers**, Joan 1935- *IntAu&W 91*
**Rivers**, John James 1824-1913 *BiInAmS*
**Rivers**, John R. 1946- *WhoWest 92*
**Rivers**, Johnny 1942- *WhoBlA 92*
**Rivers**, Johnny 1949- *WhoBlA 92*
**Rivers**, Larry 1923- *IntWW 91*
**Rivers**, Len *WhoBlA 92*
**Rivers**, Leslie Susan 1951- *WhoMW 92*
**Rivers**, Louis 1922- *WhoBlA 92*
**Rivers**, Marie Bie 1928- *WhoEnt 92*
**Rivers**, Mickey 1948- *WhoBlA 92*
**Rivers**, Paul Michael 1944- *AmMWSc 92*
**Rivers**, Philip R 1948- *WhoAmP 91*
**Rivers**, Richard Davis 1934- *WhoAmL 92*
**Rivers**, Richard Robinson 1942- *WhoAmL 92*
**Rivers**, Robert Joseph, Jr. 1931- *WhoBlA 92*
**Rivers**, Sam 1930- *NewAmDM*
**Rivers**, Shane 1941- *WhoRel 92*
**Rivers**, Thomas Milton 1888-1962 *FacFETw*
**Rivers**, Valerie L. 1952- *WhoBlA 92*
**Rivers**, Vernon Frederick 1933- *WhoBlA 92*
**Rivers**, William J 1936- *AmMWSc 92*
**Riverso**, Renato M. 1934- *WhoFI 92*
**Rives**, Amelie *BenetAL 91*
**Rives**, Janet McMillan 1944- *WhoMW 92*
**Rives**, John Edgar 1933- *AmMWSc 92*
**Rives**, Stanley Gene 1930- *WhoMW 92*
**Rives**, Sterling Edwards, Jr 1921- *WhoAmP 91*
**Rives**, Thomas Nelson 1946- *WhoRel 92*
**Rives**, William Legrande 1940- *WhoFI 92*
**Rivest**, Brian Roger 1950- *AmMWSc 92*
**Rivest**, Ronald L *AmMWSc 92*
**Rivet**, Albert Lionel Frederick 1915- *IntAu&W 91, IntWW 91, Who 92, WrDr 92*
**Rivet**, Diana Wittmer 1931- *WhoAmL 92, WhoFI 92*
**Rivett**, Geoffrey Christopher 1932- *Who 92*
**Rivett**, Robert Wyman 1921- *AmMWSc 92*
**Rivett**, Rohan 1917-1977 *ConAu 135*
**Rivett-Carnac**, Miles James 1933- *Who 92*
**Rivett-Carnac**, Nicholas 1927- *Who 92*
**Rivett-Drake**, Jean 1909- *Who 92*
**Rivette**, Jacques 1928- *IntDcF 2-2, IntWW 91*
**Rivetti**, Henry Conrad 1924- *AmMWSc 92*
**Rivie**, Daniel Juan 1964- *WhoHisp 92*
**Rivier**, Catherine L 1943- *AmMWSc 92*
**Rivier**, Jean E F 1941- *AmMWSc 92*
**Rivier**, Joaquin 1937- *WhoHisp 92*
**Rivier**, Nicolas Yves 1941- *AmMWSc 92*
**Riviere**, Briton 1840-1920 *TwCPaSc*
**Riviere**, Christopher Henry 1956- *WhoAmL 92*
**Riviere**, George Robert 1943- *AmMWSc 92*
**Riviere**, Georges 1855-1943 *ThHEIm*
**Riviere**, Jim Edmond 1953- *AmMWSc 92*
**Rivin**, Donald 1934- *AmMWSc 92*
**Rivkin**, David Wolfe 1955- *WhoAmL 92*
**Rivkin**, Donald Herschel 1924- *WhoAmL 92*
**Rivkin**, Dyann S. *WhoEnt 92*
**Rivkin**, Ellis 1918- *WrDr 92*
**Rivkin**, Goldie Waxman 1936- *WhoFI 92*
**Rivkin**, Israel 1938- *AmMWSc 92*
**Rivkin**, J.F. *DrAPF 91*
**Rivkin**, Maxcy 1937- *AmMWSc 92*
**Rivkin**, Richard Bob 1949- *AmMWSc 92*
**Rivlin**, Alice Mitchell 1931- *HanAmWH, WhoFI 92*
**Rivlin**, Catherine Amy 1957- *WhoAmL 92*
**Rivlin**, Geoffrey 1940- *Who 92*
**Rivlin**, Harry N. d1991 *NewYTBS 91 [port]*
**Rivlin**, Moshe 1925- *IntWW 91*
**Rivlin**, Richard S 1934- *AmMWSc 92*
**Rivlin**, Ronald Samuel 1915- *AmMWSc 92*
**Rivlin**, Theodore J 1926- *AmMWSc 92*
**Rivoyre**, Christine Berthe Claude D. de 1921- *IntAu&W 91, IntWW 91*
**Rix**, Bernard Anthony 1944- *Who 92*
**Rix**, Brian 1924- *Who 92*
**Rix**, John 1917- *Who 92*
**Rix**, Linda Christine 1959- *WhoMW 92*
**Rix**, Luther 1942- *WhoEnt 92*
**Rix**, Robert 1953- *WhoAmL 92*
**Rix**, Timothy John 1934- *IntWW 91, Who 92*
**Rixmann**, Drix 1950- *WhoEnt 92*
**Rixon**, Bob *DrAPF 91*
**Rixon**, James Michael 1945- *WhoFI 92*
**Rixon**, Raymond Harwood 1926- *AmMWSc 92*
**Riza**, Alper Ali 1948- *Who 92*
**Rizack**, Martin A 1926- *AmMWSc 92*
**Rizai**, Matthew M. 1956- *WhoMW 92*
**Rizai**, Matthew Metin 1956- *WhoFI 92*
**Rizal**, Jose 1861-1896 *HisDSpE*
**Rizk**, Waheeb 1921- *Who 92*
**Rizkalla**, Sami H 1945- *AmMWSc 92*
**Rizki**, Tahir Mirza 1924- *AmMWSc 92, WhoMW 92*
**Riznyk**, Stefano Thomas 1958- *WhoAmL 92*
**Rizo**, Marco 1916- *WhoHisp 92*
**Rizor**, Amelia Margaret 1963- *WhoRel 92*
**Rizpah** *EncAmaz 91*
**Rizvi**, Iftikhar Husain 1936- *IntAu&W 91*
**Rizvi**, Jacqueline 1944- *TwCPaSc*
**Rizvi**, Syed Qalab Abbas 1945- *WhoMW 92*
**Rizvi**, Tanzeem R. 1949- *WhoWest 92*
**Rizza**, Paul Frederick 1938- *AmMWSc 92*
**Rizzello**, Michael Gaspard 1926- *Who 92*
**Rizzi**, George Peter 1937- *AmMWSc 92*
**Rizzi**, Joseph Vito 1949- *WhoFI 92*
**Rizzo**, Anthony Augustine 1928- *AmMWSc 92*
**Rizzo**, Donald Charles 1945- *AmMWSc 92*
**Rizzo**, Francis 1936- *WhoEnt 92*
**Rizzo**, Frank 1920-1991 *News 92-1*
**Rizzo**, Frank L. 1920-1991 *CurBio 91N, NewYTBS 91 [port]*
**Rizzo**, Henry C *WhoAmP 91*
**Rizzo**, James M 1938- *WhoIns 92*
**Rizzo**, Jeffrey Jerome 1954- *WhoEnt 92*
**Rizzo**, Joseph L 1942- *WhoIns 92*
**Rizzo**, Michael James 1958- *WhoMW 92*
**Rizzo**, Peter Jacob 1940- *AmMWSc 92*
**Rizzo**, Richard David 1944- *WhoFI 92*
**Rizzo**, Ronald Stephen 1941- *WhoAmL 92*
**Rizzo**, Thomas Gerard 1955- *AmMWSc 92*
**Rizzoli**, Angelo 1943- *IntWW 91*
**Rizzotto**, Kathleen Marie 1959- *WhoWest 92*
**Rizzuto**, Alan John 1951- *WhoWest 92*
**Rizzuto**, Anthony B 1930- *AmMWSc 92*
**Rizzuto**, Carmela Rita 1942- *WhoWest 92*
**Rizzuto**, Helen Morrissey *DrAPF 91*
**Rizzuto**, Jim 1945- *WhoAmP 91*
**Rizzuto**, Sharida 1948- *IntAu&W 91*
**Ro Jai-Bong** *IntWW 91*
**Ro-Choi**, Tae Suk 1937- *AmMWSc 92*
**Roa**, Dorie Correces 1952- *WhoRel 92*
**Roa Bastos**, Augusto 1917- *BenetAL 91, DcLB 113 [port], IntWW 91, LiExTwC*
**Roa-Kouri**, Raul 1936- *IntWW 91*
**Roach**, Ann Dominic *WhoRel 92*
**Roach**, Archibald Wilson Kilbourne 1920- *AmMWSc 92*
**Roach**, Arvid Edward, II 1951- *WhoAmL 92*
**Roach**, Christine Marie 1954- *WhoAmL 92*
**Roach**, Dale Anthony 1945- *WhoMW 92*
**Roach**, David Michael 1939- *AmMWSc 92*
**Roach**, Deloris 1944- *WhoBlA 92*
**Roach**, Don 1936- *AmMWSc 92*
**Roach**, Donald Vincent 1932- *AmMWSc 92*
**Roach**, Donald Wycoff 1934- *WhoMW 92*
**Roach**, Edgar Mayo, Jr. 1948- *WhoAmL 92*
**Roach**, Francis Aubra 1935- *AmMWSc 92*
**Roach**, Gray Francis 1933- *Who 92*

Roach, Hal, Jr. IntMPA 92
Roach, Hildred Elizabeth 1937- WhoBlA 92
Roach, J Robert 1913- AmMWSc 92
Roach, John D. C. 1943- WhoFI 92, WhoWest 92
Roach, John Faunce 1912- AmMWSc 92
Roach, John Robert 1921- WhoMW 92, WhoRel 92
Roach, John Vinson, II 1938- WhoFI 92
Roach, Jon Chris 1963- WhoMW 92
Roach, Jon Gilbert 1944- WhoAmL 92
Roach, Lee 1937- WhoBlA 92
Roach, Lonnie Calvin 1951- WhoAmP 91
Roach, Margot Ruth 1934- AmMWSc 92
Roach, Max 1924- WhoBlA 92
Roach, Max 1925- NewAmDM
Roach, Maxwell Lemuel 1924- IntWW 91, WhoEnt 92
Roach, Pamela Jean 1948- WhoAmP 91
Roach, Peter John 1948- AmMWSc 92
Roach, Randy 1951- WhoAmP 91
Roach, Richard Russel 1934- WhoRel 92
Roach, Robert Corwine, Jr. 1956- WhoWest 92
Roach, Robert Michael, Jr. 1955- WhoAmL 92
Roach, Russ 1947- WhoAmP 91
Roach, Steven Arthur 1961- WhoAmL 92
Roach, Thomas Adair 1929- WhoAmP 91
Roach, Thomas Bankson 1938- WhoWest 92
Roach, Thomas Henry, II 1959- WhoMW 92
Roach, William D 1931- WhoAmP 91
Roach, William Kenney 1942- AmMWSc 92
Roach, William Russell 1940- WhoFI 92
Roache, Lewie Calvin 1925- AmMWSc 92
Roache, Patrick Michael, Jr. 1946- WhoFI 92
Roaden, Kenneth Bobby 1962- WhoMW 92
Roades, John Leslie 1951- WhoAmP 91
Roadhouse, Wilbur M. 1951- WhoAmL 92
Roads, Christopher Herbert 1934- Who 92
Roads, Curtis Bryant 1951- WhoEnt 92
Roads, John Owen 1950- AmMWSc 92
Roads, Peter George 1917- Who 92
Roadstrum, William H 1915- AmMWSc 92
Roaf, Clifton G. 1941- WhoBlA 92
Roake, William Earl 1919- AmMWSc 92
Roales, Robert R 1944- AmMWSc 92, WhoMW 92
Roalsvig, Jan Per 1928- AmMWSc 92
Roan, Forrest Calvin, Jr. 1944- WhoAmL 92
Roan, Tattie Mae Williams 1928- WhoFI 92
Roan, Tom d1958 TwCWW 91
Roan, Vernon P 1935- AmMWSc 92
Roane, Curtis Woodard 1921- AmMWSc 92
Roane, David James, Jr. 1960- WhoFI 92
Roane, Glenwood P. 1930- WhoBlA 92
Roane, Martha Kotila 1921- AmMWSc 92
Roane, Philip Ransom, Jr 1927- AmMWSc 92, WhoBlA 92
Roantree, Robert Joseph 1924- AmMWSc 92
Roark, Bruce 1920- AmMWSc 92
Roark, Dallas M. 1931- WrDr 92
Roark, Denis Darel 1943- WhoWest 92
Roark, Garland TwCWW 91
Roark, Garland 1904-1985 BenetAL 91
Roark, Helen Wills 1905- Who 92
Roark, James E 1945- WhoAmP 91
Roark, James L 1943- AmMWSc 92
Roark, Terry P 1938- AmMWSc 92
Roark, Terry Paul 1938- WhoWest 92
Roath, William Wesley 1934- AmMWSc 92
Roazen, Paul 1936- WrDr 92
Rob, Charles G 1913- AmMWSc 92
Rob, Charles Granville 1913- Who 92
Robach, Roger J WhoAmP 91
Robach, Roger J. d1991 NewYTBS 91
Roback, Selwyn 1924- AmMWSc 92
Robak, Jennie 1932- WhoAmP 91
Robakidse, Grigol 1884-1962 LiExTwC
Robana, Abderrahman 1938- WhoFI 92
Robard, Jackson ConAu 35NR
Robards, Jason 1922- IntMPA 92
Robards, Jason Nelson, Jr. 1922- IntWW 91, WhoEnt 92
Robards, Sam IntMPA 92
Robards, Sam 1962?- ConTFT 9
Robards, Thomas Frederick 1946- WhoFI 92
Robarts, Anthony Julian 1937- Who 92
Robarts, Basil 1915- Who 92
Robarts, Eric Kirkby 1908- Who 92
Robarts, Julian Who 92
Robator, Charles Richard 1937- WhoEnt 92
Robaugh, David Allan 1954- AmMWSc 92
Robayashi, Koji 1907- IntWW 91
Robb, Brian 1913- TwCPaSc
Robb, Carole 1943- TwCPaSc
Robb, Charles S. 1939- AlmAP 92 [port], WhoAmP 91
Robb, Charles Spittal 1939- IntWW 91
Robb, Dean Allan 1924- WhoAmL 92
Robb, Dean Allen, Sr. 1924- WhoMW 92
Robb, Ernest Willard 1931- AmMWSc 92
Robb, Floyd Owen 1946- WhoEnt 92
Robb, Frank Belfield 1913- WhoAmL 92
Robb, Jacqueline Denise 1963- WhoMW 92
Robb, James Arthur 1938- AmMWSc 92
Robb, James Christie 1924- Who 92
Robb, James Harding 1920- WrDr 92
Robb, John 1932- IntWW 91
Robb, John Anthony, Jr. 1947- WhoAmL 92
Robb, John S. BenetAL 91
Robb, John Weddell 1936- Who 92
Robb, John Wesley 1919- WhoRel 92
Robb, Michael S WhoIns 92
Robb, Patrick K. 1955- WhoAmL 92
Robb, Richard A 1942- AmMWSc 92
Robb, Richard John 1950- AmMWSc 92
Robb, Robert Clifton, Jr 1945- WhoAmP 91
Robb, Scott Hall 1944- WhoAmL 92
Robb, Thomas Bradley 1932- WhoRel 92
Robb, Thomas Wilbern 1953- AmMWSc 92
Robb, Tom 1933- TwCPaSc
Robb, Walter L 1928- AmMWSc 92
Robb, Walter Lee 1928- WhoFI 92
Robbat, Albert, Jr 1954- AmMWSc 92
Robbe, Joan Eda 1946- WhoAmP 91
Robbe-Grillet, Alain 1922- FacFETw, GuFrLit 1, IntAu&W 91, IntWW 91, Who 92
Robbelen, Gerhard Paul Karl 1929- IntWW 91
Robben, Stan Joseph 1966- WhoMW 92
Robbers, James Earl 1934- AmMWSc 92
Robberson, Donald Lewis 1941- AmMWSc 92
Robbie, Seymour LesBEnT 92
Robbin, Joel W 1941- AmMWSc 92
Robbins, Alan 1943- WhoAmP 91
Robbins, Alan Ira 1953- WhoAmL 92
Robbins, Alfred S. 1925- WhoBlA 92
Robbins, Allen Bishop 1930- AmMWSc 92
Robbins, Andrew Joseph 1910- WhoRel 92
Robbins, April Ruth AmMWSc 92
Robbins, Barbara Ann 1956- WhoMW 92
Robbins, Bryan Thomas, Jr. 1957- WhoRel 92
Robbins, Chandler Seymour 1918- AmMWSc 92
Robbins, Channing WhoEnt 92
Robbins, Charles Dudley, III 1943- WhoWest 92
Robbins, Clarence Ralph 1938- AmMWSc 92
Robbins, Clyde W 1926- WhoAmP 91
Robbins, Conrad W. 1921- WhoWest 92
Robbins, D Hurley 1937- AmMWSc 92
Robbins, Dale Alan 1953- WhoRel 92
Robbins, Darryl Andrew 1945- WhoMW 92
Robbins, David Alvin 1947- AmMWSc 92
Robbins, David Arthur 1944- WhoEnt 92
Robbins, David Edward 1949- WhoAmL 92
Robbins, David O 1943- AmMWSc 92
Robbins, David Overly 1943- WhoMW 92
Robbins, Deborah Ruth 1960- WhoRel 92
Robbins, Donald Eugene 1937- AmMWSc 92
Robbins, Donald Michael 1935- WhoAmL 92
Robbins, Doren DrAPF 91
Robbins, Edith Schultz 1941- AmMWSc 92
Robbins, Eleanora Iberall 1942- AmMWSc 92
Robbins, Ernest Aleck 1926- AmMWSc 92
Robbins, Frank Edward 1924- WhoAmL 92
Robbins, Frederick C. 1916- Who 92
Robbins, Frederick Chapman 1916- AmMWSc 92, IntWW 91, WhoMW 92, WhoNob 90
Robbins, Fredrick Chapman 1916- FacFETw
Robbins, Gary 1940- WhoAmP 91
Robbins, Gary D WhoAmP 91
Robbins, Gerald Henry 1931- WhoEnt 92, WhoMW 92
Robbins, Gordon Daniel 1940- AmMWSc 92
Robbins, Gregory Alan 1965- WhoRel 92
Robbins, Gregory Allen 1952- WhoRel 92
Robbins, Harold Who 92
Robbins, Harold 1912- IntAu&W 91, WrDr 92
Robbins, Harold 1916- BenetAL 91, FacFETw, IntWW 91
Robbins, Harvey Arnold 1922- WhoFI 92
Robbins, Helen 1949- TwCPaSc
Robbins, Herbert Ellis 1915- AmMWSc 92, IntWW 91
Robbins, Herman C. 1928- WhoBlA 92
Robbins, Honey-Miam 1930- WhoFI 92
Robbins, Jack Howard 1957- WhoWest 92
Robbins, Jackie Wayne Darmon 1940- AmMWSc 92
Robbins, Jacob 1922- AmMWSc 92
Robbins, James Clifford AmMWSc 92
Robbins, James Edward 1931- WhoWest 92
Robbins, James Tate 1945- WhoFI 92
Robbins, James Watson 1801-1879 BiInAmS
Robbins, Jane Marla 1943- ConAu 134
Robbins, Jay Howard 1934- AmMWSc 92
Robbins, Jerome 1918- FacFETw, IntWW 91, RComAH, Who 92, WhoEnt 92
Robbins, Jerome David 1953- WhoMW 92
Robbins, Jo Ann 1932- WhoRel 92
Robbins, John Alan 1938- AmMWSc 92
Robbins, John B 1932- AmMWSc 92
Robbins, John Edward 1935- AmMWSc 92
Robbins, John Michael, Jr. 1947- WhoFI 92
Robbins, Kathleen Marie 1949- WhoEnt 92
Robbins, Kay WrDr 92
Robbins, Keith Gilbert 1940- IntWW 91, Who 92
Robbins, Kelly F. 1959- WhoAmL 92
Robbins, Kelly Roy AmMWSc 92
Robbins, Kenneth Carl 1917- AmMWSc 92
Robbins, Kenneth Randall 1944- WhoEnt 92
Robbins, Kevin F. 1958- WhoBlA 92
Robbins, L H ScFEYrs
Robbins, Lafo Elizabeth 1963- WhoMW 92
Robbins, Lanny Arnold 1940- AmMWSc 92
Robbins, Leonard 1955- WhoBlA 92
Robbins, Leonard Gilbert 1945- AmMWSc 92
Robbins, Leonard H. 1877-1947 BenetAL 91
Robbins, Lionel Charles 1898-1984 FacFETw
Robbins, Louise Marie 1928- AmMWSc 92
Robbins, Marion LeRon 1941- AmMWSc 92
Robbins, Martin DrAPF 91
Robbins, Marty 1925-1982 NewAmDM
Robbins, Matthew IntMPA 92
Robbins, Matthew Ruehl 1950- WhoAmL 92
Robbins, Michael Who 92
Robbins, Michael Alan 1956- WhoAmL 92
Robbins, Millard D. 1919- WhoBlA 92
Robbins, Murray 1931- AmMWSc 92
Robbins, Naomi Bograd 1937- AmMWSc 92
Robbins, Neville 1938- WhoWest 92
Robbins, Norman 1935- AmMWSc 92
Robbins, Norman Nelson 1919- WhoAmL 92
Robbins, Orem O 1915- WhoIns 92
Robbins, Paul Edward 1928- AmMWSc 92
Robbins, Paul R 1930- ConAu 35NR
Robbins, Peter Norman 1955- WhoWest 92
Robbins, Philip Jerome 1940- WhoMW 92
Robbins, Phillips Wesley 1930- AmMWSc 92
Robbins, R W 1920- AmMWSc 92
Robbins, Ralph Compton 1921- AmMWSc 92
Robbins, Ralph Robert 1938- AmMWSc 92
Robbins, Randy J. WhoEnt 92
Robbins, Ray Charles 1920- WhoFI 92
Robbins, Raymond Frank Michael 1928- Who 92
Robbins, Richard DrAPF 91
Robbins, Richard 1927- TwCPaSc
Robbins, Richard 1940- IntMPA 92
Robbins, Richard J AmMWSc 92
Robbins, Richard Michael 1915- Who 92
Robbins, Robert 1918- AmMWSc 92
Robbins, Robert Dennis 1944- WhoAmP 91
Robbins, Robert J. 1924- WhoBlA 92
Robbins, Robert John 1944- AmMWSc 92
Robbins, Robert Kanner 1947- AmMWSc 92
Robbins, Robert Marvin 1924- WhoMW 92
Robbins, Robert Raymond 1946- AmMWSc 92
Robbins, Roy M. 1904-1981 ConAu 36NR
Robbins, Sanford Lee 1949- WhoEnt 92
Robbins, Sara Ellen 1952- WhoAmL 92
Robbins, Sheryl DrAPF 91
Robbins, Sidney Martin 1912- WhoFI 92
Robbins, Stanley L 1915- AmMWSc 92
Robbins, Stephen WhoAmP 91
Robbins, Stephen Douglas 1959- WhoFI 92
Robbins, Stuart DrAPF 91
Robbins, Thomas Landau 1943- WhoRel 92
Robbins, Tim 1958- IntMPA 92
Robbins, Tod 1888-1949 ScFEYrs
Robbins, Tom 1936- BenetAL 91, ConNov 91, IntWW 91, WrDr 92
Robbins, Vernon Earl 1921- WhoAmL 92
Robbins, Vernon Kay 1939- WhoRel 92
Robbins, Virginia Ann 1936- WhoAmP 91
Robbins, Warren 1923- WhoBlA 92
Robbins, Wayne Brian 1951- AmMWSc 92
Robbins, William Curtis, Jr. 1948- WhoEnt 92
Robbins, William Perry 1941- AmMWSc 92
Robbins, William Randolph 1912- WhoRel 92
Robbins-Roth, Cynthia H. 1953- WhoWest 92
Robblee, Alexander 1919- AmMWSc 92
Robboy, Susan Hintz 1949- WhoEnt 92
Robe, Edward Scott 1936- WhoAmL 92
Robe, Thurlow Richard 1934- AmMWSc 92
Robeck, Cecil Melvin, Jr. 1945- WhoWest 92
Robeck, Gordon G 1923- AmMWSc 92
Robek, Mary Frances 1927- WhoMW 92
Robel, Gregory Frank 1955- AmMWSc 92
Robel, Robert Joseph 1933- AmMWSc 92, WhoMW 92
Robel, Ruth Ann 1937- WhoAmP 91
Robel, Stephen B 1923- AmMWSc 92
Robelot, Milton Paul 1909- WhoRel 92
Robens Who 92
Robens, Jane Florence 1931- AmMWSc 92
Robens Of Woldingham, Baron 1910- IntWW 91, Who 92
Robens Of Woldingham, Lord 1910- WrDr 92
Robenson, James Melford 1941- WhoWest 92
Roberge, Andree Groleau 1938- AmMWSc 92
Roberge, Fernand Adrien 1935- AmMWSc 92
Roberge, Guy 1915- Who 92
Roberge, James Kerr 1938- AmMWSc 92
Roberge, M Sheila WhoAmP 91
Roberge, Marcien Romeo 1934- AmMWSc 92
Roberson, Alidean Slate 1927- WhoAmP 91
Roberson, Charles Ed DrAPF 91
Roberson, Dalton Anthony 1937- WhoBlA 92
Roberson, Earl 1931- WhoBlA 92
Roberson, Edward Lee 1935- AmMWSc 92
Roberson, F. Alexis H. 1942- WhoBlA 92
Roberson, Fred O., Jr. 1947- WhoFI 92
Roberson, Gary WhoBlA 92
Roberson, Ginger Calhoun 1947- WhoWest 92
Roberson, Gloria Grant WhoBlA 92
Roberson, Herman Ellis 1934- AmMWSc 92
Roberson, Irvin 1935- BlkOlyM
Roberson, John A 1925- AmMWSc 92
Roberson, Lawrence R. 1946- WhoBlA 92
Roberson, Linda 1947- WhoAmL 92
Roberson, Lizzie 1860-1945 RelLAm 91
Roberson, Lynn Marie 1951- WhoAmL 92
Roberson, Nathan Russell 1930- AmMWSc 92
Roberson, Robert Errol 1923- AmMWSc 92
Roberson, Robert H 1928- AmMWSc 92
Roberson, Robert Stephen 1942- WhoFI 92
Roberson, Sandra Short 1950- WhoBlA 92
Roberson, Steven Henry 1949- WhoMW 92
Roberson, Ward Bryce 1939- AmMWSc 92
Robert, Adrian WrDr 92
Robert, Andre 1926- AmMWSc 92
Robert, Holly Miriam 1954- WhoFI 92
Robert, Hubert 1733-1808 BlkwCEP
Robert, Jacques Frederic 1928- IntWW 91
Robert, Kearny Quinn, Jr 1943- AmMWSc 92
Robert, Lionel TwCSFW 91, WrDr 92
Robert, Patricia Harrison 1939- IntMPA 92
Robert, Scott Matthew 1962- WhoWest 92
Robert, Stephen 1940- WhoFI 92
Robert, Suzanne 1957- AmMWSc 92
Robert, William Henry, III 1945- WhoAmP 91
Robert-Houdin 1805-1871 ScFEYrs B
Roberti, David A 1939- WhoAmP 91
Roberti, Mario Andrew 1935- WhoAmL 92, WhoFI 92
Robertiello, Richard C. 1923- WrDr 92
Robertin, Hector 1932- WhoWest 92
Roberto, Holden IntWW 91
Roberto, James Blair 1946- AmMWSc 92

**Robertory,** Robert Joseph 1938- *WhoAmL 92*
**Roberts** *Who 92*
**Roberts,** A S, Jr 1935- *AmMWSc 92*
**Roberts,** A Wayne 1934- *AmMWSc 92*
**Roberts,** Adam *Who 92*
**Roberts,** Adam 1940- *WrDr 92*
**Roberts,** Alan Silverman 1939- *WhoWest 92*
**Roberts,** Albert 1908- *Who 92*
**Roberts,** Albert 1911- *Who 92*
**Roberts,** Alfred Lloyd 1942- *WhoBlA 92*
**Roberts,** Alfred Nathan 1917- *AmMWSc 92*
**Roberts,** Allan Deverell 1950- *Who 92*
**Roberts,** Allen Earl 1917- *WhoEnt 92*
**Roberts,** Alwyn 1933- *Who 92*
**Roberts,** Andrew 1963- *ConAu 135*
**Roberts,** Andrew Lyle 1938- *Who 92*
**Roberts,** Angus Thomas 1913- *Who 92*
**Roberts,** Anita Bauer 1942- *AmMWSc 92*
**Roberts,** Ann *Who 92*
**Roberts,** Ann F. *WhoBlA 92*
**Roberts,** Anthony Harris 1943- *WhoWest 92*
**Roberts,** Anthony John 1944- *Who 92*
**Roberts,** Archibald Edward 1915- *WhoWest 92*
**Roberts,** Arthur 1912- *AmMWSc 92*
**Roberts,** Arthur Loten 1906- *Who 92*
**Roberts,** Arthur Owen 1923- *WhoRel 92*
**Roberts,** Audrey Nadine 1935- *AmMWSc 92*
**Roberts,** Augustine Bruce 1932- *WhoRel 92*
**Roberts,** B. K. 1907- *WhoAmL 92*
**Roberts,** Barbara 1936- *AlmAP 92 [port], IntWW 91, WhoAmP 91, WhoWest 92*
**Roberts,** Barbara Haig *Who 92*
**Roberts,** Barbara Lea 1951- *WhoAmP 91*
**Roberts,** Benjamin Charles 1917- *Who 92, WrDr 92*
**Roberts,** Benjamin Titus 1823-1893 *RelLAm 91*
**Roberts,** Benny Lloyd 1942- *WhoAmL 92*
**Roberts,** Bernard 1933- *IntWW 91*
**Roberts,** Bert 1928- *TwCPaSc*
**Roberts,** Bert C., Jr. 1942- *WhoFI 92*
**Roberts,** Bertie 1919- *Who 92*
**Roberts,** Betty B 1932- *WhoAmP 91*
**Roberts,** Beverly Randolph 1948- *WhoMW 92*
**Roberts,** Blanche Elizabeth 1955- *WhoBlA 92*
**Roberts,** Bobby L. 1938- *WhoBlA 92*
**Roberts,** Bradley Lee 1946- *AmMWSc 92*
**Roberts,** Brian 1930- *IntAu&W 91, WrDr 92*
**Roberts,** Brian Charles 1958- *WhoFI 92*
**Roberts,** Brian Michael 1957- *WhoAmL 92*
**Roberts,** Brian Richard 1906- *IntAu&W 91*
**Roberts,** Brian Stanley 1936- *Who 92*
**Roberts,** Brigham Henry 1857-1933 *BenetAL 91, RelLAm 91*
**Roberts,** Bruce R 1933- *AmMWSc 92*
**Roberts,** Bryan Clieve 1923- *Who 92*
**Roberts,** Bryan Wilson 1938- *AmMWSc 92*
**Roberts,** Bryndis Wynette 1957- *WhoBlA 92*
**Roberts,** Brynley Francis 1931- *Who 92*
**Roberts,** Burnell R. 1927- *IntWW 91*
**Roberts,** Burnell Richard 1927- *WhoFI 92, WhoMW 92*
**Roberts,** Burton Bennett 1922- *WhoAmL 92*
**Roberts,** C. Kenneth 1930- *WhoAmL 92*
**Roberts,** C Patrick 1936- *WhoAmP 91*
**Roberts,** C Sheldon 1926- *AmMWSc 92*
**Roberts,** Calvin 1945- *WhoFI 92*
**Roberts,** Carlisle, Jr. 1955- *WhoAmL 92*
**Roberts,** Carlyle Jones 1928- *AmMWSc 92*
**Roberts,** Carmel Montgomery 1928- *AmMWSc 92*
**Roberts,** Carter Dale 1944- *WhoIns 92*
**Roberts,** Catherine 1917- *WrDr 92*
**Roberts,** Catherine Harrison 1958- *AmMWSc 92*
**Roberts,** Cedric Kenelm 1918- *Who 92*
**Roberts,** Chalmers 1910- *WrDr 92*
**Roberts,** Chalmers McGeagh 1910- *IntWW 91*
**Roberts,** Charles A, Jr 1925- *AmMWSc 92*
**Roberts,** Charles Brockway 1918- *AmMWSc 92*
**Roberts,** Charles G. D. 1860-1943 *BenetAL 91, RfGEnL 91*
**Roberts,** Charles Joseph 1953- *WhoAmP 91*
**Roberts,** Charles L. 1943- *WhoBlA 92*
**Roberts,** Charles Morgan 1932- *WhoWest 92*
**Roberts,** Charles Patrick 1936- *WhoMW 92*
**Roberts,** Charles Sheldon 1937- *AmMWSc 92*
**Roberts,** Charles W., Jr. 1962- *WhoHisp 92*
**Roberts,** Charlotte Fitch 1859-1917 *BiInAmS*
**Roberts,** Cheryl Dornita Lynn 1958- *WhoBlA 92*
**Roberts,** Chester Arthur 1948- *WhoAmP 91*
**Roberts,** Chris Alan 1948- *WhoEnt 92*
**Roberts,** Christopher William 1937- *Who 92*
**Roberts,** Clare A. 1953- *WhoMW 92*
**Roberts,** Clarence Richard 1926- *AmMWSc 92*
**Roberts,** Cokie *LesBEnT 92*
**Roberts,** Cornelius Sheldon 1926- *WhoWest 92*
**Roberts,** Curtis *IntMPA 92*
**Roberts,** Curtis Bush 1933- *WhoIns 92*
**Roberts,** Dan *TwCWW 91, WrDr 92*
**Roberts,** Daniel Altman 1922- *AmMWSc 92*
**Roberts,** Danny Kent 1952- *WhoRel 92*
**Roberts,** Darrell Lynn 1939- *AmMWSc 92*
**Roberts,** Darryl 1944- *WhoAmP 91*
**Roberts,** David Allen 1954- *WhoMW 92*
**Roberts,** David Arthur 1924-1987 *ConAu 134*
**Roberts,** David Caron 1944- *WhoFI 92*
**Roberts,** David Craig 1948- *AmMWSc 92*
**Roberts,** David Duncan 1954- *AmMWSc 92*
**Roberts,** David Earl 1923- *WhoAmP 91*
**Roberts,** David Ewart 1921- *Who 92*
**Roberts,** David Francis 1941- *Who 92*
**Roberts,** David Gerald 1951- *WhoEnt 92*
**Roberts,** David Glendenning 1928- *WhoAmL 92, WhoAmP 91*
**Roberts,** David Gwilym 1925- *Who 92*
**Roberts,** David Hall 1947- *AmMWSc 92*
**Roberts,** David John 1919- *Who 92*
**Roberts,** David Michael 1931- *Who 92*
**Roberts,** David Stone 1943- *WhoRel 92*
**Roberts,** David Wilfred Alan 1921- *AmMWSc 92*
**Roberts,** Dawn C 1941- *WhoAmP 91*
**Roberts,** Dean Winn, Jr 1945- *AmMWSc 92*
**Roberts,** Debra J 1954- *WhoIns 92*
**Roberts,** Delbert E., Jr. 1947- *WhoRel 92*
**Roberts,** Denis Edwin 1917- *Who 92*
**Roberts,** Denise *WhoEnt 92*
**Roberts,** Dennis Carl 1948- *WhoWest 92*
**Roberts,** Dennis Charles 1952- *WhoEnt 92*
**Roberts,** Dennis William 1943- *WhoWest 92*
**Roberts,** Denys 1923- *Who 92, WrDr 92*
**Roberts,** Denys Tudor Emil 1923- *IntWW 91*
**Roberts,** Derek 1947- *TwCPaSc*
**Roberts,** Derek Franklyn 1942- *Who 92*
**Roberts,** Derek Harry 1931- *WrDr 92*
**Roberts,** Derek Harry 1932- *IntWW 91, Who 92*
**Roberts,** DeWayne 1927- *AmMWSc 92*
**Roberts,** Donald Albert 1935- *WhoFI 92*
**Roberts,** Donald Duane 1929- *AmMWSc 92, WhoAmP 91*
**Roberts,** Donald Eugene 1942- *WhoRel 92*
**Roberts,** Donald Lee 1929- *WhoBlA 92*
**Roberts,** Donald Ray 1929- *AmMWSc 92*
**Roberts,** Donald Ray 1942- *AmMWSc 92*
**Roberts,** Donald Wilson 1933- *AmMWSc 92*
**Roberts,** Doris 1930- *WhoEnt 92*
**Roberts,** Doris Emma 1915- *AmMWSc 92*
**Roberts,** Douglas B. *WhoMW 92*
**Roberts,** Durward Thomas, Jr 1942- *AmMWSc 92, WhoMW 92*
**Roberts,** Dwight Loren 1949- *WhoWest 92*
**Roberts,** E. F. 1930- *WhoAmL 92*
**Roberts,** Earl C 1921- *AmMWSc 92*
**Roberts,** Earl John 1913- *AmMWSc 92*
**Roberts,** Earlene *WhoAmP 91*
**Roberts,** Edgar 1946- *WhoBlA 92*
**Roberts,** Edgar D 1931- *AmMWSc 92*
**Roberts,** Edward A. 1950- *WhoBlA 92*
**Roberts,** Edward Adam 1940- *Who 92*
**Roberts,** Edward Baer 1935- *WhoFI 92*
**Roberts,** Edward Calhoun 1937- *WhoAmL 92, WhoAmP 91*
**Roberts,** Edward Eric 1911- *Who 92*
**Roberts,** Edward Fergus Sidney 1901- *Who 92*
**Roberts,** Edward James Keymer 1908- *Who 92*
**Roberts,** Edwin 1941- *BlkOlyM*
**Roberts,** Edwin Kirk 1922- *AmMWSc 92*
**Roberts,** Eileen Doris Frahm 1933- *WhoEnt 92*
**Roberts,** Eirlys Rhiwen Cadwaladr 1911- *IntAu&W 91, Who 92*
**Roberts,** Elizabeth Madox 1881-1941 *FacFETw, TwCWW 91*
**Roberts,** Elizabeth Madox 1886-1941 *BenetAL 91*
**Roberts,** Ella S. 1927- *WhoBlA 92*
**Roberts,** Emrys d1990 *Who 92N*
**Roberts,** Enoch G 1940- *WhoIns 92*
**Roberts,** Eric 1914- *WrDr 92*
**Roberts,** Eric 1956- *IntMPA 92, WhoEnt 92*
**Roberts,** Eric Matthias 1914- *Who 92*
**Roberts,** Eric Stenius 1952- *WhoWest 92*
**Roberts,** Eric Wayne 1963- *WhoFI 92*
**Roberts,** Ernest Alfred Cecil 1912- *Who 92*
**Roberts,** Eugene 1920- *AmMWSc 92*
**Roberts,** Eugene Edward 1945- *WhoRel 92*
**Roberts,** Eve *WhoEnt 92*
**Roberts,** Evelyn Hoard 1920- *WhoBlA 92*
**Roberts,** Floyd Edward, Jr 1934- *AmMWSc 92*
**Roberts,** Francis Donald 1938- *AmMWSc 92*
**Roberts,** Francis Stone 1944- *WhoFI 92*
**Roberts,** Frank 1907- *Who 92*
**Roberts,** Frank 1915- *WhoWest 92*
**Roberts,** Frank Kenyon 1907- *IntWW 91*
**Roberts,** Frank Livezey 1915- *WhoAmP 91*
**Roberts,** Franklin Lewis 1934- *AmMWSc 92*
**Roberts,** Fred Stephen 1943- *AmMWSc 92*
**Roberts,** Fred T 1941- *WhoIns 92*
**Roberts,** Freddy Lee 1941- *AmMWSc 92*
**Roberts,** Gareth Gwyn 1940- *Who 92*
**Roberts,** Gary David 1957- *WhoFI 92*
**Roberts,** Gary Raymond 1948- *WhoAmL 92, WhoEnt 92*
**Roberts,** Gemma 1929- *WhoHisp 92*
**Roberts,** Gene *WhoAmP 91*
**Roberts,** Geoffrey Frank Ingleson 1926- *Who 92*
**Roberts,** Geoffrey Newland 1906- *Who 92*
**Roberts,** Geoffrey P. H. *Who 92*
**Roberts,** George *DrAPF 91*
**Roberts,** George A 1919- *AmMWSc 92, IntWW 91*
**Roberts,** George Adam 1919- *WhoFI 92, WhoWest 92*
**Roberts,** George Arnott 1930- *Who 92*
**Roberts,** George Christopher 1936- *WhoFI 92, WhoWest 92*
**Roberts,** George E 1926- *AmMWSc 92*
**Roberts,** George Harrison 1944- *WhoIns 92*
**Roberts,** George P 1937- *AmMWSc 92*
**Roberts,** George Philip 1906- *Who 92*
**Roberts,** George Preston, Jr. 1947- *WhoAmL 92*
**Roberts,** George R. *WhoFI 92*
**Roberts,** George W 1938- *AmMWSc 92*
**Roberts,** Gerry Rea 1940- *WhoEnt 92*
**Roberts,** Gilbert 1934- *Who 92*
**Roberts,** Gillian *DrAPF 91*
**Roberts,** Gillian Frances 1944- *Who 92*
**Roberts,** Glenn Dale 1943- *AmMWSc 92*
**Roberts,** Glyn Caerwyn 1940- *WhoMW 92*
**Roberts,** Gordon 1921- *Who 92*
**Roberts,** Grady H., Jr. 1940- *WhoBlA 92*
**Roberts,** Grant *ConAu 35NR*
**Roberts,** Granville Oral 1918- *WhoRel 92*
**Roberts,** Gwilym *Who 92*
**Roberts,** Gwilym Edffrwd 1928- *Who 92*
**Roberts,** Harlan William, III 1931- *WhoBlA 92*
**Roberts,** Harold R 1930- *AmMWSc 92*
**Roberts,** Harry Heil 1940- *AmMWSc 92*
**Roberts,** Harry Morris, Jr. 1938- *WhoAmL 92, WhoFI 92*
**Roberts,** Harry Vivian 1923- *AmMWSc 92*
**Roberts,** Helen Hamilton 1952- *WhoMW 92*
**Roberts,** Helen Starr 1933- *WhoEnt 92*
**Roberts,** Henry Reginald 1916- *WhoIns 92*
**Roberts,** Herbert Joel 1954- *WhoEnt 92*
**Roberts,** Herbert John 1919- *Who 92*
**Roberts,** Herman 1924- *WhoBlA 92*
**Roberts,** Hermese E. 1913- *WhoBlA 92*
**Roberts,** Howard C 1910- *AmMWSc 92*
**Roberts,** Howard Radclyffe 1906- *AmMWSc 92*
**Roberts,** Hugh Eifion Pritchard 1927- *Who 92*
**Roberts,** Hugh Martin P. *Who 92*
**Roberts,** I. M. *WrDr 92*
**Roberts,** Ian White 1927- *Who 92*
**Roberts,** Ieuan Wyn 1930- *Who 92*
**Roberts,** Iolo Francis 1925- *WrDr 92*
**Roberts,** Irene 1925- *IntAu&W 91, WrDr 92*
**Roberts,** Irene C. *WhoFI 92*
**Roberts,** Irving 1915- *AmMWSc 92*
**Roberts,** Ivor *WrDr 92*
**Roberts,** Ivor Anthony 1946- *Who 92*
**Roberts,** J Kent 1922- *AmMWSc 92*
**Roberts,** J.R. *TwCWW 91, WrDr 92*
**Roberts,** J T Adrian 1944- *AmMWSc 92*
**Roberts,** J W *ScFEYrs*
**Roberts,** J. William 1942- *WhoAmL 92*
**Roberts,** Jack Earl 1928- *WhoAmP 91*
**Roberts,** Jacqueline Johnson 1944- *WhoAmP 91, WhoBlA 92*
**Roberts,** James Allen 1934- *AmMWSc 92*
**Roberts,** James Alvin 1950- *WhoMW 92*
**Roberts,** James C, Jr 1926- *AmMWSc 92*
**Roberts,** James Carl 1953- *WhoFI 92*
**Roberts,** James D. 1927- *WrDr 92*
**Roberts,** James E. 1903- *WhoBlA 92*
**Roberts,** James Ernest 1943- *WhoEnt 92*
**Roberts,** James Ernest, Sr 1924- *AmMWSc 92*
**Roberts,** James H 1932- *WhoAmP 91*
**Roberts,** James Hall *WrDr 92*
**Roberts,** James Hazelton 1925- *WhoAmP 91*
**Roberts,** James Herbert 1915- *AmMWSc 92*
**Roberts,** James J 1947- *IntAu&W 91*
**Roberts,** James Joseph 1947- *WhoEnt 92*
**Roberts,** James L. 1942- *WhoFI 92*
**Roberts,** James Lamar, Jr 1945- *WhoAmP 91*
**Roberts,** James Lewis 1951- *AmMWSc 92*
**Roberts,** James M 1941- *AmMWSc 92*
**Roberts,** James McGregor 1923- *WhoWest 92*
**Roberts,** James Norman 1943- *WhoFI 92*
**Roberts,** James Owen 1930- *WhoFI 92*
**Roberts,** James Richard 1937- *AmMWSc 92*
**Roberts,** James T. L. 1954- *WhoBlA 92*
**Roberts,** James Thomas 1965- *WhoAmP 91*
**Roberts,** James William 1928- *WhoAmP 91*
**Roberts,** Jamie E. 1956- *WhoEnt 92*
**Roberts,** Jane *Who 92*
**Roberts,** Jane 1929-1984 *RelLAm 91*
**Roberts,** Jane Carolyn 1932- *AmMWSc 92*
**Roberts,** Janet *DrAPF 91*
**Roberts,** Janice L. 1959- *WhoBlA 92*
**Roberts,** Jay 1927- *AmMWSc 92*
**Roberts,** Jean Reed 1939- *WhoAmL 92*
**Roberts,** Jeffery David 1943- *WhoFI 92*
**Roberts,** Jeffrey W. 1946- *WhoAmL 92*
**Roberts,** Jeffrey Warren 1944- *AmMWSc 92*
**Roberts,** Jeremy Michael Graham 1941- *Who 92*
**Roberts,** Jerry Allan 1931- *AmMWSc 92*
**Roberts,** Jim 1938- *WhoAmP 91*
**Roberts,** Joan Ellen 1944- *WhoEnt 92*
**Roberts,** Joan Howard d1990 *Who 92N*
**Roberts,** Joan Ila 1935- *WrDr 92*
**Roberts,** Joan Marie 1932- *AmMWSc 92*
**Roberts,** Joel Laurence 1940- *AmMWSc 92*
**Roberts,** John *IntAu&W 91X, TwCWW 91, Who 92*
**Roberts,** John Alden 1955- *WhoAmL 92*
**Roberts,** John Alexander, Jr. 1937- *WhoMW 92*
**Roberts,** John Anthony 1928- *Who 92*
**Roberts,** John Arthur 1917- *Who 92*
**Roberts,** John B. 1912- *WhoBlA 92*
**Roberts,** John Burnham 1913- *AmMWSc 92*
**Roberts,** John Charles 1940- *WhoAmL 92*
**Roberts,** John Charles Quentin 1933- *Who 92*
**Roberts,** John Chester 1947- *WhoFI 92*
**Roberts,** John Clarke 1951- *WhoFI 92, WhoWest 92*
**Roberts,** John D 1918- *AmMWSc 92, IntWW 91, WhoWest 92*
**Roberts,** John Derham 1942- *WhoAmL 92*
**Roberts,** John Edwin 1920- *AmMWSc 92*
**Roberts,** John England 1922- *AmMWSc 92*
**Roberts,** John Eric 1907- *Who 92*
**Roberts,** John Frederick 1913- *Who 92*
**Roberts,** John Fredrick 1928- *AmMWSc 92*
**Roberts,** John Glover, Jr. 1955- *WhoAmL 92*
**Roberts,** John Harvey Polmear 1935- *Who 92*
**Roberts,** John Henderson 1906- *AmMWSc 92*
**Roberts,** John Herbert 1933- *Who 92*
**Roberts,** John Joseph 1922- *WhoFI 92, WhoIns 92*
**Roberts,** John Kenneth, Jr 1936- *WhoIns 92*
**Roberts,** John Laing 1939- *Who 92*
**Roberts,** John Lewis 1922- *AmMWSc 92*
**Roberts,** John Lewis 1928- *Who 92*
**Roberts,** John M. 1916- *IntWW 91*
**Roberts,** John Melville 1931- *AmMWSc 92*
**Roberts,** John Morris 1928- *IntAu&W 91, IntWW 91, Who 92, WrDr 92*
**Roberts,** John Oliver 1924- *Who 92*
**Roberts,** John Peter Lee 1930- *WhoEnt 92*
**Roberts,** John Stephen 1937- *AmMWSc 92*
**Roberts,** Jon Manfred 1948- *WhoWest 92*
**Roberts,** Joseph Buffington 1923- *AmMWSc 92*
**Roberts,** Joseph J 1952- *WhoAmP 91*
**Roberts,** Joseph Linton 1929- *AmMWSc 92*
**Roberts,** Julia 1967- *ConTFT 9, CurBio 91 [port], IntMPA 92, IntWW 91, News 91 [port], -91-3 [port], WhoEnt 92*
**Roberts,** Julia Baldwin 1953- *WhoWest 92*
**Roberts,** Julian *Who 92*
**Roberts,** Julian Lee, Jr 1935- *AmMWSc 92*

**Roberts,** Karl Vernon 1958- WhoWest 92
**Roberts,** Kathryn Dolliver 1942- WhoAmP 91
**Roberts,** Kay George 1950- WhoBlA 92
**Roberts,** Keith 1935- IntAu&W 91, TwCSFW 91, WrDr 92
**Roberts,** Keith 1958- TwCPaSc
**Roberts,** Keith Edward, Sr. 1928- WhoAmL 92, WhoMW 92
**Roberts,** Kenneth 1885-1957 BenetAL 91
**Roberts,** Kenneth David 1931- AmMWSc 92
**Roberts,** Kevin 1940- IntAu&W 91, WrDr 92
**Roberts,** Kevin Thomas 1957- WhoAmL 92
**Roberts,** Kim DrAPF 91
**Roberts,** Larry 1940- WhoFI 92, WhoWest 92
**Roberts,** Larry D 1946- WhoAmP 91
**Roberts,** Larry Michael 1957- WhoAmL 92
**Roberts,** Larry Paul 1950- WhoEnt 92
**Roberts,** Larry Spurgeon 1935- AmMWSc 92
**Roberts,** Lawrence G 1937- AmMWSc 92
**Roberts,** Lawrence Lee 1947- IntAu&W 91
**Roberts,** Lee Knight 1949- AmMWSc 92
**Roberts,** Leigh M 1925- AmMWSc 92
**Roberts,** Len DrAPF 91
**Roberts,** Leonard 1929- AmMWSc 92
**Roberts,** Leonard H. 1949- WhoFI 92
**Roberts,** Leonidas Howard 1921- AmMWSc 92
**Roberts,** Leslie Gordon 1941- AmMWSc 92
**Roberts,** Lewis Edward John 1922- IntWW 91, Who 92
**Roberts,** Lewis H WhoIns 92
**Roberts,** Lillian WhoAmP 91
**Roberts,** Lillian 1928- WhoBlA 92
**Roberts,** Linda A. 1959- WhoRel 92
**Roberts,** Liona Russell, Jr. 1928- WhoWest 92
**Roberts,** Lionel IntAu&W 91X
**Roberts,** Lonnie 1937- WhoAmP 91
**Roberts,** Lorin Watson 1923- AmMWSc 92, WhoWest 92
**Roberts,** Lorraine Marie 1930- WhoBlA 92
**Roberts,** Louis Douglas 1918- AmMWSc 92
**Roberts,** Louis Reed 1923- AmMWSc 92
**Roberts,** Louis W 1913- AmMWSc 92
**Roberts,** Louis Wright 1913- WhoBlA 92
**Roberts,** Luckey 1887-1968 NewAmDM
**Roberts,** Lyman Jackson AmMWSc 92
**Roberts,** Malcolm Blair 1936- WhoAmP 91
**Roberts,** Marcus 1964- ConMus 6 [port]
**Roberts,** Marcus Rees 1951- TwCPaSc
**Roberts,** Margie Lee Stewart 1927- WhoAmP 91
**Roberts,** Marie Dyer 1943- WhoWest 92
**Roberts,** Mark 1921- WhoEnt 92
**Roberts,** Mark Owen 1911- WhoIns 92
**Roberts,** Mark Scott 1951- WhoAmL 92
**Roberts,** Markley 1930- WhoFI 92
**Roberts,** Martin 1920- AmMWSc 92
**Roberts,** Mary Fedarko 1947- AmMWSc 92
**Roberts,** Mary Linda 1944- WhoAmP 91
**Roberts,** Maurice Aaron 1910- WhoAmL 92
**Roberts,** Mervin Francis 1922- AmMWSc 92
**Roberts,** Michael 1908- IntWW 91, Who 92, WrDr 92
**Roberts,** Michael Foster 1943- AmMWSc 92
**Roberts,** Michael James 1936- WhoAmL 92
**Roberts,** Michael Joseph 1942- WhoWest 92
**Roberts,** Michael Lawrence 1939- WhoWest 92
**Roberts,** Michael V. 1948- WhoBlA 92
**Roberts,** Michael Victor 1948- WhoAmP 91
**Roberts,** Michael William 1949- WhoAmL 92
**Roberts,** Mike 1944- WhoEnt 92
**Roberts,** Morton Spitz 1926- AmMWSc 92
**Roberts,** Nancy Correll 1924- WrDr 92
**Roberts,** Narlie 1931- WhoBlA 92
**Roberts,** Nathan McCain 1962- WhoAmL 92
**Roberts,** Nora 1950- WrDr 92
**Roberts,** Norbert Joseph 1916- AmMWSc 92
**Roberts,** Norman Frank 1931- WhoWest 92
**Roberts,** Norman Hailstone 1922- AmMWSc 92
**Roberts,** Norman John 1959- WhoMW 92
**Roberts,** Norman Leslie 1935- WhoAmL 92, WhoFI 92
**Roberts,** Norman Stafford 1926- Who 92
**Roberts,** Oral 1918- RelLAm 91, WhoRel 92
**Roberts,** Owen J 1875-1955 FacFETw
**Roberts,** Owen Josephus 1875-1955 AmPeW, AmPolLe
**Roberts,** Owen W WhoAmP 91
**Roberts,** P Elaine 1944- AmMWSc 92
**Roberts,** Pamela Martha 1949- WhoEnt 92
**Roberts,** Paquita Hudson 1938- WhoBlA 92
**Roberts,** Pat 1936- AlmAP 92 [port]
**Roberts,** Patricia 1955- BlkOlyM
**Roberts,** Patrick John 1942- Who 92
**Roberts,** Patrick Kent 1948- WhoMW 92
**Roberts,** Paul Alfred 1931- AmMWSc 92
**Roberts,** Paul Craig 1939- WhoAmP 91
**Roberts,** Paul Harry 1929- AmMWSc 92, IntWW 91, Who 92
**Roberts,** Paul Osborne, Jr 1933- AmMWSc 92
**Roberts,** Paula WrDr 92
**Roberts,** Percy Charles 1920- Who 92
**Roberts,** Pernell WhoEnt 92
**Roberts,** Pernell 1930- IntMPA 92
**Roberts,** Perry TwCPaSc
**Roberts,** Peter DrAPF 91
**Roberts,** Peter A. 1951- WhoFI 92
**Roberts,** Peter Morse 1955- AmMWSc 92
**Roberts,** Peter S 1937- WhoIns 92
**Roberts,** Philip Who 92
**Roberts,** Philip Bedlington 1921- Who 92
**Roberts,** Philip Davies 1938- WrDr 92
**Roberts,** Philip J. 1948- WhoWest 92
**Roberts,** Philip Lee 1953- WhoRel 92
**Roberts,** Phyllida Katharine S. Who 92
**Roberts,** Priscilla Jane 1949- Who 92
**Roberts,** R Michael AmMWSc 92
**Roberts,** R. Philip 1950- WhoRel 92
**Roberts,** Ralph 1915- AmMWSc 92
**Roberts,** Ralph Jackson 1911- AmMWSc 92
**Roberts,** Ralph Joel 1920- WhoEnt 92, WhoFI 92
**Roberts,** Randy 1951- ConAu 134
**Roberts,** Ray 1913- WhoAmP 91
**Roberts,** Raymond Harcourt 1931- Who 92
**Roberts,** Raymond Rohrer 1958- WhoRel 92
**Roberts,** Reginald Francis 1923- AmMWSc 92
**Roberts,** Rhonda WhoAmP 91
**Roberts,** Richard 1911-1980 FacFETw
**Roberts,** Richard 1931- Who 92
**Roberts,** Richard 1938- AmMWSc 92
**Roberts,** Richard A 1935- AmMWSc 92
**Roberts,** Richard B 1933- AmMWSc 92
**Roberts,** Richard Calvin 1925- AmMWSc 92
**Roberts,** Richard David 1938- WhoMW 92
**Roberts,** Richard Douglas 1916- Who 92
**Roberts,** Richard Frederick Anthony 1932- IntWW 91, Who 92
**Roberts,** Richard Harris 1924- AmMWSc 92
**Roberts,** Richard James 1922- WhoFI 92
**Roberts,** Richard John 1943- AmMWSc 92
**Roberts,** Richard Julian 1930- Who 92
**Roberts,** Richard Norman 1930- AmMWSc 92
**Roberts,** Richard Owen 1931- WhoRel 92
**Roberts,** Richard W 1921- AmMWSc 92
**Roberts,** Robert, III 1930- WhoAmL 92
**Roberts,** Robert Abram 1923- AmMWSc 92
**Roberts,** Robert Cantwell 1935- WhoWest 92
**Roberts,** Robert Evan 1912- Who 92
**Roberts,** Robert Richard, III 1944- WhoIns 92
**Roberts,** Robert Russell 1931- AmMWSc 92
**Roberts,** Robert Thaddeus, Jr. 1952- WhoAmL 92, WhoFI 92
**Roberts,** Robert William 1923- AmMWSc 92
**Roberts,** Robin Wendell 1959- WhoFI 92
**Roberts,** Roger L. 1927- WhoWest 92
**Roberts,** Ronald C 1936- AmMWSc 92
**Roberts,** Ronald Eldridge 1942- WhoRel 92
**Roberts,** Ronald Frederick 1944- AmMWSc 92
**Roberts,** Ronald John 1941- Who 92
**Roberts,** Ronnie Spencer 1943- AmMWSc 92
**Roberts,** Rosalee Ann 1943- WhoMW 92
**Roberts,** Rosemary DrAPF 91
**Roberts,** Roy 1927- WhoMW 92
**Roberts,** Roy Ernest James 1928- IntWW 91, Who 92
**Roberts,** Roy J. 1940- WhoBlA 92
**Roberts,** Roy Ronald 1945- WhoRel 92
**Roberts,** Roy S. WhoBlA 92
**Roberts,** Royston Murphy 1918- AmMWSc 92
**Roberts,** Sally WrDr 92
**Roberts,** Sally-Ann 1953- WhoBlA 92
**Roberts,** Samuel 1948- Who 92
**Roberts,** Samuel Kelton 1944- WhoBlA 92
**Roberts,** Samuel Smith 1936- WhoEnt 92
**Roberts,** Sandra Brown 1939- WhoFI 92
**Roberts,** Sanford B 1934- AmMWSc 92
**Roberts,** Selyf 1912- IntAu&W 91
**Roberts,** Seymour M. 1934- WhoFI 92
**Roberts,** Sheila DrAPF 91
**Roberts,** Sheila 1942- LiExTwC
**Roberts,** Shelagh 1924- Who 92
**Roberts,** Shepherd 1932- AmMWSc 92
**Roberts,** Sidney Who 92
**Roberts,** Sidney 1918- AmMWSc 92
**Roberts,** Simon 1946- TwCPaSc
**Roberts,** Stanley Leroy 1962- WhoRel 92
**Roberts,** Stephen 1915- Who 92
**Roberts,** Stephen 1938- IntMPA 92
**Roberts,** Stephen D 1942- AmMWSc 92
**Roberts,** Stephen Pritchard 1949- Who 92
**Roberts,** Stephen Wandless 1939- WhoAmL 92, WhoAmP 91
**Roberts,** Stephen Winston 1941- AmMWSc 92
**Roberts,** Steve 1941- WhoEnt 92
**Roberts,** Steve W. 1947- WhoMW 92
**Roberts,** Steven C 1952- WhoAmP 91, WhoBlA 92
**Roberts,** Steven C. 1961- WhoFI 92
**Roberts,** Steven K 1952?- News 92-1 [port]
**Roberts,** Susan Jean 1958- AmMWSc 92
**Roberts,** Talmadge 1931- WhoBlA 92
**Roberts,** Ted Blake 1952- WhoAmP 91
**Roberts,** Terrence James 1941- WhoBlA 92
**Roberts,** Theodore Goodrich 1877-1953 BenetAL 91
**Roberts,** Theodore Harris 1929- WhoFI 92, WhoMW 92
**Roberts,** Theodore S 1926- AmMWSc 92
**Roberts,** Thomas Arnold d1990 Who 92N
**Roberts,** Thomas D 1935- AmMWSc 92
**Roberts,** Thomas David 1938- AmMWSc 92
**Roberts,** Thomas George 1929- AmMWSc 92
**Roberts,** Thomas Glasdir 1918- AmMWSc 92
**Roberts,** Thomas Hunt 1961- WhoAmL 92
**Roberts,** Thomas Keith 1947- WhoRel 92
**Roberts,** Thomas L 1932- AmMWSc 92, WhoBlA 92
**Roberts,** Thomas Leroy 1942- WhoAmL 92
**Roberts,** Thomas M AmMWSc 92
**Roberts,** Thomas Michael 1952- WhoAmP 91
**Roberts,** Thomas Raymond 1947- WhoAmL 92
**Roberts,** Thomas Somerville 1911- Who 92
**Roberts,** Timothy Paul 1951- WhoEnt 92
**Roberts,** Timothy R 1954- AmMWSc 92
**Roberts,** Tommy Ed 1940- WhoAmP 91
**Roberts,** Tony 1939- IntMPA 92, WhoEnt 92
**Roberts,** Trev WrDr 92
**Roberts,** Verne Louis 1939- AmMWSc 92
**Roberts,** Vicki Michele 1959- WhoEnt 92
**Roberts,** Virgil Dean 1922- WhoAmP 91
**Roberts,** Virgil Patrick 1947- WhoBlA 92, WhoEnt 92, WhoFI 92
**Roberts,** W. Adolphe 1886- BenetAL 91
**Roberts,** W Neil 1931- AmMWSc 92
**Roberts,** Wagner WrDr 92
**Roberts,** Walden Kay 1934- AmMWSc 92
**Roberts,** Walter 1915-1990 AnObit 1990
**Roberts,** Walter Herbert B 1915- AmMWSc 92
**Roberts,** Walter Lenn 1962- WhoAmP 91
**Roberts,** Walter Orr 1915- AmMWSc 92
**Roberts,** Warren Wilcox 1926- AmMWSc 92
**Roberts,** Wayne TwCWW 91
**Roberts,** Wendell Lee 1938- AmMWSc 92
**Roberts,** Wesley A. 1938- WhoBlA 92, WhoRel 92
**Roberts,** Wilbur Eugene 1942- WhoMW 92
**Roberts,** Wilfrid Hubert Wace d1991 Who 92N
**Roberts,** Will TwCPaSc
**Roberts,** Willard Lewis 1904- AmMWSc 92
**Roberts,** William IntMPA 92
**Roberts,** William 1895-1980 TwCPaSc
**Roberts,** William 1936- Who 92
**Roberts,** William, Jr. 1942- WhoAmL 92
**Roberts,** William C AmMWSc 92
**Roberts,** William Dan 1952- WhoMW 92
**Roberts,** William Frank 1937- WhoFI 92
**Roberts,** William Hugh 1917- WhoAmP 91
**Roberts,** William John 1918- AmMWSc 92
**Roberts,** William John 1920- WhoFI 92
**Roberts,** William Kenneth 1928- AmMWSc 92
**Roberts,** William Thomas 1944- WhoRel 92
**Roberts,** William Woodruff, Jr 1942- AmMWSc 92
**Roberts,** Willo David 1928- IntAu&W 91
**Roberts,** Willo Davis 1928- WrDr 92
**Roberts,** Wilmoth Fitzgerald 1934- WhoBlA 92
**Roberts,** Wyn Who 92
**Roberts,** Y Carol 1941- WhoAmP 91
**Roberts-DeGennaro,** Maria 1947- WhoWest 92
**Roberts-Jones,** Ivor 1913- IntWW 91, TwCPaSc, Who 92
**Roberts-Marcus,** Helen Miriam 1943- AmMWSc 92
**Roberts-Pichette,** Patricia Ruth 1930- AmMWSc 92
**Roberts-West,** George Arthur Alston- Who 92
**Robertsen,** John Alan 1926- AmMWSc 92
**Robertshaw,** Joseph Earl 1934- AmMWSc 92
**Robertson** Who 92
**Robertson,** Lord 1912- Who 92
**Robertson,** A F 1912- AmMWSc 92
**Robertson,** Abel Alfred Lazzarini, Jr 1926- AmMWSc 92
**Robertson,** Agnes DrAPF 91
**Robertson,** Alan 1920- Who 92
**Robertson,** Alan D. 1958- WhoBlA 92
**Robertson,** Alan Robert 1940- AmMWSc 92
**Robertson,** Alan S 1941- WhoAmP 91
**Robertson,** Alex F 1932- AmMWSc 92
**Robertson,** Alexander 1927-1978 TwCPaSc
**Robertson,** Alexander, IV 1959- WhoAmL 92
**Robertson,** Alexander Allen 1919- AmMWSc 92
**Robertson,** Alexander John 1930- WhoAmL 92
**Robertson,** Alvin Cyrrale 1962- BlkOlyM, WhoBlA 92, WhoMW 92
**Robertson,** Andre Levett 1957- WhoBlA 92
**Robertson,** Andrew 1921-1986 ConAu 134
**Robertson,** Andrew 1936- AmMWSc 92
**Robertson,** Ann Eliza Worcester 1826-1905 RelLAm 91
**Robertson,** Anne Strachan Who 92
**Robertson,** Archibald Thomas 1863-1934 RelLAm 91
**Robertson,** Baldwin 1934- AmMWSc 92
**Robertson,** Barbara 1945- TwCPaSc
**Robertson,** Barbara Anne 1931- IntAu&W 91, WrDr 92
**Robertson,** Benjamin W. 1931- WhoBlA 92
**Robertson,** Beverly Ellis 1939- AmMWSc 92
**Robertson,** Bobby Ken 1938- AmMWSc 92
**Robertson,** Brian James 1951- WhoMW 92
**Robertson,** Brian Paul DrAPF 91
**Robertson,** Bryan Charles Francis 1925- Who 92
**Robertson,** Charles 1940- Who 92
**Robertson,** Charles Alfred Stuart 1933- WhoRel 92
**Robertson,** Charles Martin 1911- Who 92
**Robertson,** Charles Robert Suttie 1920- Who 92
**Robertson,** Charles William, Jr 1943- AmMWSc 92
**Robertson,** Cliff 1925- IntMPA 92, WhoEnt 92
**Robertson,** Clyde Henry 1929- AmMWSc 92
**Robertson,** Dale 1923- IntMPA 92
**Robertson,** Dale 1954- WhoAmP 91
**Robertson,** Dale LyMoine 1923- WhoEnt 92
**Robertson,** Dale Norman 1925- AmMWSc 92
**Robertson,** Dale Wayne 1954- WhoRel 92
**Robertson,** Daniel Carlton 1951- WhoWest 92
**Robertson,** Daphne Jean Black 1937- Who 92
**Robertson,** David 1947- AmMWSc 92
**Robertson,** David Arthur 1948- WhoMW 92
**Robertson,** David Byres 1960- WhoAmP 91
**Robertson,** David C 1942- AmMWSc 92
**Robertson,** David G C 1941- AmMWSc 92
**Robertson,** David Lars Manwaring 1917- Who 92
**Robertson,** David Murray 1932- AmMWSc 92
**Robertson,** David Wayne 1955- AmMWSc 92, WhoMW 92
**Robertson,** David Werner 1955- WhoAmP 91
**Robertson,** Dawn Smith 1960- WhoBlA 92, WhoMW 92
**Robertson,** Denise 1933- IntAu&W 91
**Robertson,** Don B. 1942- WhoEnt 92
**Robertson,** Don G. 1951- WhoEnt 92
**Robertson,** Donald 1910- AmMWSc 92
**Robertson,** Donald B 1931- WhoAmP 91
**Robertson,** Donald Buchanan 1932- Who 92
**Robertson,** Donald Claus 1940- AmMWSc 92

**Robertson,** Donald Edwin 1929- *AmMWSc 92*
**Robertson,** Donald Eric 1934- *WhoRel 92*
**Robertson,** Donald Hubert 1934- *AmMWSc 92*
**Robertson,** Donald Irwin 1922- *WhoEnt 92*
**Robertson,** Donald Sage 1921- *AmMWSc 92, WhoMW 92*
**Robertson,** Dougal 1924-1991 *ConAu 135*
**Robertson,** Douglas Frederick 1946- *WhoMW 92*
**Robertson,** Douglas James 1955- *WhoRel 92*
**Robertson,** Douglas Reed 1938- *AmMWSc 92*
**Robertson,** Douglas Scott 1945- *AmMWSc 92*
**Robertson,** Douglas Welby 1924- *AmMWSc 92*
**Robertson,** Douglas William 1898- *Who 92*
**Robertson,** Eck 1887-1975 *NewAmDM*
**Robertson,** Edward D 1930- *WhoAmP 91*
**Robertson,** Edward D., Jr. 1952- *WhoAmL 92, WhoAmP 91, WhoMW 92*
**Robertson,** Edward L 1944- *AmMWSc 92*
**Robertson,** Edward Neil 1950- *WhoMW 92*
**Robertson,** Edwin David 1946- *WhoAmL 92, WhoFI 92*
**Robertson,** Edwin Oscar 1923- *WhoFI 92*
**Robertson,** Ellis *ConAu 36NR*
**Robertson,** Elspeth *WrDr 92*
**Robertson,** Eric 1887-1941 *TwCPaSc*
**Robertson,** Ernest Garland 1931- *WhoRel 92*
**Robertson,** Eugene Corley 1915- *AmMWSc 92*
**Robertson,** Evelyn Crawford, Jr. 1941- *WhoBlA 92*
**Robertson,** Florence Winkler 1945- *WhoMW 92*
**Robertson,** Forbes 1915- *AmMWSc 92*
**Robertson,** Francis Calder F. *Who 92*
**Robertson,** Frank C. 1890-1969 *BenetAL 91, TwCWW 91*
**Robertson,** Frederick John 1931- *AmMWSc 92*
**Robertson,** Frederick Noel 1935- *AmMWSc 92*
**Robertson,** G Philip 1953- *AmMWSc 92*
**Robertson,** Gary Jerome 1938- *WhoMW 92*
**Robertson,** Geoffrey Ronald 1946- *Who 92*
**Robertson,** George Beryl, Jr. 1943- *WhoFI 92*
**Robertson,** George David 1956- *WhoAmL 92*
**Robertson,** George Gordon 1916- *AmMWSc 92*
**Robertson,** George Harcourt 1943- *AmMWSc 92*
**Robertson,** George Islay Macneill 1946- *Who 92*
**Robertson,** George Leven 1921- *AmMWSc 92*
**Robertson,** George Louis 1947- *WhoFI 92*
**Robertson,** Gertrude 1924- *WhoBlA 92*
**Robertson,** Glenn D, Jr 1924- *AmMWSc 92*
**Robertson,** Gordon Perry 1958- *WhoAmL 92*
**Robertson,** Graeme Alan 1945- *Who 92*
**Robertson,** Graham 1866-1948 *TwCPaSc*
**Robertson,** H Thomas, II *AmMWSc 92*
**Robertson,** Hamish 1931- *Who 92*
**Robertson,** Harold Rocke 1912- *Who 92*
**Robertson,** Harry S 1921- *AmMWSc 92*
**Robertson,** Henry 1848-1930 *TwCPaSc*
**Robertson,** Herbert Chapman, Jr. 1928- *WhoFI 92*
**Robertson,** Horace Bascomb, Jr. 1923- *WhoAmL 92*
**Robertson,** Howard W. *DrAPF 91*
**Robertson,** Hugh Duff 1957- *WhoAmL 92, WhoEnt 92*
**Robertson,** Hugh Elburn 1919- *AmMWSc 92*
**Robertson,** Hugh Mereth 1955- *AmMWSc 92*
**Robertson,** Iain Samuel 1945- *IntWW 91, Who 92*
**Robertson,** Ian 1949- *TwCPaSc*
**Robertson,** Ian George William 1922- *Who 92*
**Robertson,** Ian Macbeth 1918- *Who 92*
**Robertson,** Ian Macdonald *Who 92*
**Robertson,** J A L 1925- *AmMWSc 92*
**Robertson,** Jack M 1937- *AmMWSc 92*
**Robertson,** Jacqueline Lee 1947- *AmMWSc 92*
**Robertson,** James d1991 *Who 92N*
**Robertson,** James 1839-1902 *RelLAm 91*
**Robertson,** James 1931- *TwCPaSc*
**Robertson,** James 1938- *WhoAmL 92*
**Robertson,** James Aldred 1931- *AmMWSc 92*
**Robertson,** James Alexander 1931- *AmMWSc 92*
**Robertson,** James Alexander Rowland 1910- *Who 92*
**Robertson,** James Allen 1948- *WhoAmL 92, WhoFI 92, WhoWest 92*
**Robertson,** James B. 1940- *WhoBlA 92*
**Robertson,** James Byron 1937- *AmMWSc 92, WhoWest 92*
**Robertson,** James Colvert 1932- *WhoFI 92*
**Robertson,** James David 1922- *AmMWSc 92*
**Robertson,** James Douglas 1948- *AmMWSc 92*
**Robertson,** James Downie 1931- *Who 92*
**Robertson,** James E 1924- *AmMWSc 92*
**Robertson,** James Edward 1931- *WhoMW 92*
**Robertson,** James Geddes 1910- *Who 92*
**Robertson,** James I 1930- *IntAu&W 91*
**Robertson,** James I., Jr. 1930- *WrDr 92*
**Robertson,** James L. 1940- *WhoAmL 92*
**Robertson,** James Lawton 1940- *WhoAmP 91*
**Robertson,** James Magruder 1943- *AmMWSc 92*
**Robertson,** James McDonald 1940- *AmMWSc 92*
**Robertson,** James Sean, III 1950- *WhoAmL 92*
**Robertson,** James Smith 1917- *Who 92*
**Robertson,** James Sydnor 1920- *AmMWSc 92*
**Robertson,** James Taylor, Jr 1923- *WhoAmP 91*
**Robertson,** James Thomas 1931- *AmMWSc 92*
**Robertson,** Janet 1935- *SmATA 68 [port]*
**Robertson,** Jean 1928- *Who 92*
**Robertson,** Jeffrey Ray 1957- *WhoMW 92*
**Robertson,** Jerold C 1933- *AmMWSc 92*
**Robertson,** Jerry Earl 1932- *AmMWSc 92, WhoFI 92*
**Robertson,** Jerry L 1933- *AmMWSc 92*
**Robertson,** John A. 1943- *WhoAmL 92*
**Robertson,** John Anderson 1931- *WhoAmP 91*
**Robertson,** John Bernard 1936- *WhoAmL 92*
**Robertson,** John Bernard 1940- *WhoMW 92*
**Robertson,** John Carnegie 1917- *Who 92*
**Robertson,** John Connell 1931- *AmMWSc 92*
**Robertson,** John David 1952- *WhoEnt 92*
**Robertson,** John David 1960- *AmMWSc 92*
**Robertson,** John David H. *Who 92*
**Robertson,** John Gilbert 1932- *WhoBlA 92*
**Robertson,** John Harvey 1941- *AmMWSc 92*
**Robertson,** John Keith 1926- *Who 92*
**Robertson,** John S. Jack 1949- *WhoWest 92*
**Robertson,** John Windeler 1934- *Who 92*
**Robertson,** Jon 1942- *WhoEnt 92*
**Robertson,** Jon H. 1942- *WhoBlA 92*
**Robertson,** Joseph David 1944- *WhoAmL 92*
**Robertson,** Joseph Edmond 1918- *WhoFI 92, WhoMW 92*
**Robertson,** Joseph Henry 1906- *AmMWSc 92*
**Robertson,** Julia Ann *Who 92*
**Robertson,** Karen A. *WhoBlA 92*
**Robertson,** Karen Lee 1955- *WhoWest 92*
**Robertson,** Keith 1914- *WrDr 92*
**Robertson,** Keith 1914-1991 *ConAu 135*
**Robertson,** Keith Carlton d1991 *NewYTBS 91*
**Robertson,** Kenneth Ray 1941- *AmMWSc 92*
**Robertson,** Kirk *DrAPF 91*
**Robertson,** Kristin Elizabeth 1955- *WhoWest 92*
**Robertson,** Lawrence Marshall, Jr. 1932- *WhoWest 92*
**Robertson,** Leon H. 1934- *WhoFI 92*
**Robertson,** Leslie Earl 1928- *AmMWSc 92*
**Robertson,** Lewis 1922- *IntWW 91, Who 92*
**Robertson,** Linda Lou 1940- *WhoAmL 92*
**Robertson,** Linwood Righter 1940- *WhoFI 92*
**Robertson,** Lyle Purmal 1933- *AmMWSc 92*
**Robertson,** Lynn E. 1921- *WhoBlA 92*
**Robertson,** Lynn Shelby, Jr 1916- *AmMWSc 92*
**Robertson,** Lynne Nannen 1936- *WhoMW 92*
**Robertson,** Malcolm Slingsby 1906- *AmMWSc 92*
**Robertson,** Marian 1921- *WrDr 92*
**Robertson,** Marian Ella 1920- *WhoWest 92*
**Robertson,** Martin Wesley, Jr. 1962- *WhoRel 92*
**Robertson,** Mary Elsie *DrAPF 91*
**Robertson,** Melvina 1934- *WhoMW 92*
**Robertson,** Merton M 1924- *AmMWSc 92*
**Robertson,** Michael Brian 1948- *WhoFI 92*
**Robertson,** Michael James 1950- *WhoMW 92*
**Robertson,** Michael S 1935- *WhoAmP 91*
**Robertson,** Milton James 1927- *WhoMW 92*
**Robertson,** Morgan 1861-1915 *BenetAL 91, ScFEYrs*
**Robertson,** Nancy 1909- *Who 92*
**Robertson,** Nat Clifton 1919- *AmMWSc 92*
**Robertson,** Nathan Arthur 1946- *WhoWest 92*
**Robertson,** Noel Farnie 1923- *Who 92*
**Robertson,** Norman Robert Ean 1931- *Who 92*
**Robertson,** Oscar 1938- *FacFETw*
**Robertson,** Oscar Palmer 1938- *BlkOlyM, WhoBlA 92, WhoFI 92*
**Robertson,** Pat 1930- *RelLAm 91, WhoRel 92*
**Robertson,** Patrick Allan Pearson 1913- *Who 92*
**Robertson,** Paul *WhoRel 92*
**Robertson,** Paul Joseph 1946- *WhoAmP 91*
**Robertson,** Peter Arthur 1928- *WhoEnt 92*
**Robertson,** Peter James 1947- *WhoWest 92*
**Robertson,** Philip Alan 1938- *AmMWSc 92*
**Robertson,** Philip Scott 1943- *WhoAmP 91*
**Robertson,** Philip W 1934- *WhoAmP 91*
**Robertson,** Piedad F. *WhoHisp 92*
**Robertson,** Quincy L. 1934- *WhoBlA 92*
**Robertson,** Quindonell S. *WhoBlA 92*
**Robertson,** R. Bruce *WhoFI 92*
**Robertson,** Raleigh John 1942- *AmMWSc 92*
**Robertson,** Ralph Byron 1943- *WhoAmL 92*
**Robertson,** Randal McGavock 1911- *AmMWSc 92*
**Robertson,** Raymond E 1940- *AmMWSc 92*
**Robertson,** Reuben Buck, III 1939- *WhoAmP 91*
**Robertson,** Richard Boyd 1936- *WhoAmP 91*
**Robertson,** Richard Earl 1933- *AmMWSc 92*
**Robertson,** Richard Ross 1914- *Who 92*
**Robertson,** Richard Stuart 1942- *WhoFI 92*
**Robertson,** Richard Thomas 1945- *AmMWSc 92*
**Robertson,** Robert 1909- *Who 92*
**Robertson,** Robert 1934- *AmMWSc 92*
**Robertson,** Robert Alexander 1922- *Who 92*
**Robertson,** Robert Gordon 1917- *IntWW 91*
**Robertson,** Robert Graham Hamish 1943- *AmMWSc 92*
**Robertson,** Robert Henry 1929- *Who 92*
**Robertson,** Robert James 1943- *AmMWSc 92*
**Robertson,** Robert L 1925- *AmMWSc 92*
**Robertson,** Robert T. *WhoWest 92*
**Robertson,** Ronald Foote d1991 *Who 92N*
**Robertson,** Ronald Wade *WhoAmP 91*
**Robertson,** Ross *Who 92*
**Robertson,** Ross Elmore 1915- *AmMWSc 92*
**Robertson,** Rutherford 1913- *Who 92*
**Robertson,** Rutherford Ness 1913- *IntWW 91*
**Robertson,** Sara Jene 1934- *WhoAmP 91*
**Robertson,** Scott Harrison 1945- *AmMWSc 92*
**Robertson,** Sidney Park 1914- *Who 92*
**Robertson,** Stella M *AmMWSc 92*
**Robertson,** Stephen *SmATA 66*
**Robertson,** Stephen Lee 1949- *WhoEnt 92*
**Robertson,** Stewart *WhoEnt 92*
**Robertson,** Stuart Donald Treadgold 1935- *AmMWSc 92*
**Robertson,** T M 1922- *AmMWSc 92*
**Robertson,** Ted Z *WhoAmP 91*
**Robertson,** Thomas N 1931- *AmMWSc 92*
**Robertson,** Tim 1937- *AmMWSc 92*
**Robertson,** Timothy Joel 1937- *WhoMW 92*
**Robertson,** Toby *Who 92*
**Robertson,** Toby 1928- *ConTFT 9*
**Robertson,** Tom 1829-1871 *RfGEnL 91*
**Robertson,** Tom Grayson 1939- *WhoEnt 92*
**Robertson,** Vernon Colin 1922- *Who 92*
**Robertson,** W D 1913- *AmMWSc 92*
**Robertson,** Walter Volley 1931- *AmMWSc 92*
**Robertson,** Wilbert Joseph, Jr 1928- *AmMWSc 92*
**Robertson,** William 1721-1793 *BenetAL 91, BlkwCEP*
**Robertson,** William, IV 1943- *AmMWSc 92*
**Robertson,** William Bruce 1923- *Who 92*
**Robertson,** William Charles 1950- *WhoFI 92*
**Robertson,** William Duncan 1922- *Who 92*
**Robertson,** William G 1929- *AmMWSc 92*
**Robertson,** William Hugh, Jr. 1952- *WhoRel 92*
**Robertson,** William O 1925- *AmMWSc 92*
**Robertson,** William P. *DrAPF 91*
**Robertson,** William Richard 1941- *WhoFI 92, WhoMW 92*
**Robertson,** William Van Bogaert 1914- *AmMWSc 92*
**Robertson of Brackla,** Ian Argyll 1913- *Who 92*
**Robertson of Oakridge,** Baron 1930- *Who 92*
**Robertstad,** Gordon Wesley 1923- *AmMWSc 92*
**Robeson,** Eslanda Goode 1896-1965 *CurBio 91N, NotBlAW 92 [port]*
**Robeson,** Kenneth *TwCSFW 91, WrDr 92*
**Robeson,** Paul 1898-1976 *BenetAL 91, ConBlB 2 [port], FacFETw [port], NewAmDM, RComAH*
**Robespierre,** Maximilien-Marie-Isidore 1758-1794 *BlkwCEP*
**Robey,** Douglas John Brett 1914- *Who 92*
**Robey,** Frank A *AmMWSc 92*
**Robey,** Pamela Gehron 1952- *AmMWSc 92*
**Robey,** Roger Lewis 1946- *AmMWSc 92*
**Robey,** Stephen John 1936- *WhoFI 92*
**Robey,** Susanna Horton 1937- *WhoMW 92*
**Robfogel,** Susan Salitan 1943- *WhoAmL 92*
**Robichaud,** Louis J. *DcAmImH*
**Robichaud,** Louis Joseph 1925- *IntWW 91*
**Robichaux,** Jolyn H. 1928- *WhoBlA 92*
**Robidoux,** Phillip Henri 1958- *WhoWest 92*
**Robie,** Clarence W. *WhoBlA 92*
**Robie,** Joan Hake *WhoRel 92*
**Robie,** Norman William 1942- *AmMWSc 92*
**Robie,** Richard Allen 1928- *AmMWSc 92*
**Robie,** Ronald Boyd 1937- *WhoAmL 92, WhoWest 92*
**Robie,** Thomas 1688?-1729 *BiInAmS*
**Robie,** William Randolph 1944- *WhoAmL 92*
**Robillard,** Edmond 1917- *WhoRel 92*
**Robillard,** Florence 1926- *WhoAmP 91*
**Robillard,** Geoffrey 1923- *AmMWSc 92*
**Robillard,** Kim L. 1955- *WhoEnt 92*
**Robilliard,** Gordon Allan 1943- *AmMWSc 92*
**Robin,** Alan Jay 1950- *WhoAmL 92*
**Robin,** Allen Maurice 1934- *AmMWSc 92*
**Robin,** Arthur de Quetteville 1929- *WrDr 92*
**Robin,** Burton Howard 1926- *AmMWSc 92*
**Robin,** Craig Stewart 1956- *WhoWest 92*
**Robin,** Dany 1927- *IntMPA 92*
**Robin,** Eugene Debs 1919- *AmMWSc 92*
**Robin,** Gabriel Marie Louis 1929- *IntWW 91*
**Robin,** Gordon de Quetteville 1921- *Who 92*
**Robin,** Ian 1909- *Who 92*
**Robin,** Jerome 1933- *WhoFI 92*
**Robin,** Michael 1919- *AmMWSc 92*
**Robin,** Natalie Louise 1921- *WhoEnt 92*
**Robin,** Theodore Tydings, Jr. 1939- *WhoAmL 92*
**Robiner,** Donald Maxwell 1935- *WhoAmL 92, WhoMW 92*
**Robinet,** Harriette Gillem 1931- *WhoBlA 92*
**Robinett,** Stephen 1941- *TwCSFW 91, WrDr 92*
**Robinette,** Charles Dennis 1935- *AmMWSc 92*
**Robinette,** Earl Lawrence 1935- *WhoMW 92*
**Robinette,** Hillary, Jr 1913- *AmMWSc 92*
**Robinette,** Martin Smith 1939- *AmMWSc 92*
**Robinovitch,** Murray R 1939- *AmMWSc 92*
**Robinow,** Carl Franz 1909- *AmMWSc 92*
**Robinow,** Meinhard 1909- *AmMWSc 92*
**Robinowitz,** Joe Reece 1950- *WhoEnt 92*
**Robins,** Brian 1928- *TwCPaSc*
**Robins,** Charles Richard 1928- *AmMWSc 92*
**Robins,** Corinne *DrAPF 91*
**Robins,** Drew Bingham 1946- *WhoWest 92*
**Robins,** Edwin Claiborne, Sr. 1910- *WhoFI 92*
**Robins,** Eli 1921- *AmMWSc 92*
**Robins,** Elizabeth *BenetAL 91*
**Robins,** Elizabeth 1865?-1952 *BenetAL 91*
**Robins,** Frank B 1924- *WhoAmP 91*
**Robins,** Jack 1919- *AmMWSc 92*
**Robins,** Janis 1925- *AmMWSc 92*
**Robins,** Larry Wayne 1959- *WhoRel 92*
**Robins,** Lawrence Arthur 1949- *WhoAmL 92*

**Robins**, Lee Nelken 1922- *IntWW 91*
**Robins**, Leonard Edward 1921- *Who 92*
**Robins**, Malcolm Owen 1918- *Who 92*
**Robins**, Marjorie McCarthy 1914- *WhoMW 92*
**Robins**, Michael H. 1941- *ConAu 133*
**Robins**, Michael Harry 1948- *WhoMW 92*
**Robins**, Milton Franklin 1922- *WhoRel 92*
**Robins**, Morris Joseph 1939- *AmMWSc 92*
**Robins**, Natalie *DrAPF 91*
**Robins**, Norman Alan 1934- *AmMWSc 92*
**Robins**, Patricia *IntAu&W 91X, WrDr 92*
**Robins**, Ralph 1932- *Who 92*
**Robins**, Richard Dean 1942- *AmMWSc 92*
**Robins**, Robert Henry 1921- *IntWW 91, Who 92, WrDr 92*
**Robins**, Roland Kenith 1926- *AmMWSc 92*
**Robins**, William Edward Charles 1924- *Who 92*
**Robinson** *Who 92*
**Robinson**, A. M. Lewin 1916- *WrDr 92*
**Robinson**, A R 1921- *AmMWSc 92*
**Robinson**, Adelbert Carl 1926- *WhoAmL 92, WhoFI 92*
**Robinson**, Adeline Black 1915- *WhoBlA 92*
**Robinson**, Alan Brent 1946- *WhoAmL 92*
**Robinson**, Alan Hadley 1934- *WhoWest 92*
**Robinson**, Alastair *Who 92*
**Robinson**, Albert 1915- *Who 92*
**Robinson**, Albert 1947-1974 *BlkOlyM*
**Robinson**, Albert Arnold 1937- *WhoBlA 92*
**Robinson**, Albert Dean 1939- *AmMWSc 92*
**Robinson**, Albert Edward Phineas 1915- *IntWW 91*
**Robinson**, Albert Lee 1938- *WhoAmP 91*
**Robinson**, Albert M. *WhoBlA 92*
**Robinson**, Alcurtis *WhoBlA 92*
**Robinson**, Alcurtis 1940- *WhoIns 92*
**Robinson**, Alexander Jacob 1920- *WhoMW 92*
**Robinson**, Alfred Green 1928- *AmMWSc 92*
**Robinson**, Alfreda P. 1932- *WhoBlA 92*
**Robinson**, Alice Jean McDonnell 1922- *WhoEnt 92*
**Robinson**, Alix Ida 1937- *AmMWSc 92*
**Robinson**, Allan Richard 1932- *AmMWSc 92*
**Robinson**, Alvin J. 1936- *WhoBlA 92*
**Robinson**, Alwyn Arnold 1929- *Who 92*
**Robinson**, Anastasia 1692?-1755 *NewAmDM*
**Robinson**, Andrew 1939- *WhoBlA 92*
**Robinson**, Andrew Jordt 1942- *WhoEnt 92*
**Robinson**, Angela Yvonne 1956- *WhoBlA 92*
**Robinson**, Ann 1937- *Who 92*
**Robinson**, Ann Garrett 1934- *WhoBlA 92*
**Robinson**, Ann Loftin 1944- *WhoFI 92*
**Robinson**, Annettmarie 1940- *WhoWest 92*
**Robinson**, Annie Erskine 1874-1925 *BiDBrF 2*
**Robinson**, Anthony *DrAPF 91*
**Robinson**, Arnie, Jr 1948- *BlkOlyM*
**Robinson**, Arnold 1929- *WhoWest 92*
**Robinson**, Arthur 1914- *AmMWSc 92*
**Robinson**, Arthur Alexander 1924- *Who 92*
**Robinson**, Arthur B 1942- *AmMWSc 92*
**Robinson**, Arthur Geoffrey 1917- *Who 92*
**Robinson**, Arthur Grant 1916- *AmMWSc 92*
**Robinson**, Arthur Napoleon Raymond 1926- *IntWW 91, Who 92*
**Robinson**, Arthur R 1929- *AmMWSc 92*
**Robinson**, Arthur Robin 1943- *AmMWSc 92*
**Robinson**, Arthur S 1925- *AmMWSc 92*
**Robinson**, Aubrey Eugene, Jr. 1922- *WhoAmL 92, WhoBlA 92*
**Robinson**, Austin *Who 92*
**Robinson**, Barbara 1928- *TwCPaSc*
**Robinson**, Barbara Aitken 1928- *WhoRel 92*
**Robinson**, Barbara Jean 1954- *WhoBlA 92*
**Robinson**, Barbara Paul 1941- *WhoAmL 92*
**Robinson**, Barry Lane 1943- *WhoBlA 92*
**Robinson**, Basil William 1912- *IntWW 91, Who 92, WrDr 92*
**Robinson**, Beatrice Letterman 1941- *AmMWSc 92*
**Robinson**, Benjamin Ellison, III 1963- *WhoBlA 92*
**Robinson**, Benjamin Harton 1934- *WhoAmP 91*
**Robinson**, Benjamin Pierce 1947- *WhoEnt 92*
**Robinson**, Bernard Leo 1924- *WhoAmL 92, WhoFI 92, WhoWest 92*
**Robinson**, Berol 1924- *AmMWSc 92*
**Robinson**, Beverly Jean 1957- *WhoBlA 92*
**Robinson**, Bill *Who 92*
**Robinson**, Bill 1878-1949 *FacFETw, NewAmDM*
**Robinson**, Bill, Jr. 1943- *WhoBlA 92*
**Robinson**, Bob 1951- *TwCPaSc*
**Robinson**, Brenda Evette 1956- *WhoBlA 92*
**Robinson**, Brenda M. *WhoBlA 92*
**Robinson**, Brian Howard 1944- *AmMWSc 92*
**Robinson**, Brian Lewis 1936- *Who 92*
**Robinson**, Brooks 1937- *FacFETw*
**Robinson**, Bruce 1912- *Who 92*
**Robinson**, Bruce 1946- *IntMPA 92*
**Robinson**, Bruce B 1933- *AmMWSc 92*
**Robinson**, Bryant, Sr. *WhoRel 92*
**Robinson**, C N 1928- *WhoAmP 91*
**Robinson**, C Paul 1941- *AmMWSc 92*
**Robinson**, Cal 1951- *WhoMW 92*
**Robinson**, Calvin Stanford 1920- *WhoAmL 92*
**Robinson**, Campbell William 1933- *AmMWSc 92*
**Robinson**, Carl 1958- *TwCPaSc*
**Robinson**, Carl Cornell 1946- *WhoBlA 92*
**Robinson**, Carl Dayton 1942- *WhoBlA 92*
**Robinson**, Carl Terrell 1947- *WhoEnt 92*
**Robinson**, Carol Evonne 1959- *WhoBlA 92*
**Robinson**, Carol W. 1953- *WhoBlA 92*
**Robinson**, Carole Ann 1935- *WhoFI 92*
**Robinson**, Carrie C. 1912- *WhoBlA 92*
**Robinson**, Cas 1935- *WhoAmP 91*
**Robinson**, Casey Perry 1932- *AmMWSc 92*
**Robinson**, Catherine 1904- *WhoBlA 92*
**Robinson**, Cecelia Ann 1948- *WhoBlA 92*
**Robinson**, Cecil Howard 1928- *AmMWSc 92*
**Robinson**, Cecilia Yvonne 1966- *WhoWest 92*
**Robinson**, Charles 1818-1894 *BenetAL 91*
**Robinson**, Charles 1940- *WhoBlA 92*
**Robinson**, Charles Albert 1921- *AmMWSc 92*
**Robinson**, Charles Alvin 1941- *WhoEnt 92*
**Robinson**, Charles Budd, Jr 1871-1913 *BiInAmS*
**Robinson**, Charles C 1932- *AmMWSc 92*
**Robinson**, Charles Clifton 1937- *WhoIns 92*
**Robinson**, Charles Dee 1932- *AmMWSc 92*
**Robinson**, Charles E. 1926- *WhoBlA 92*
**Robinson**, Charles E. 1933- *WhoWest 92*
**Robinson**, Charles Edwards 1939- *WhoAmP 91*
**Robinson**, Charles Frederic 1942- *WhoAmL 92*
**Robinson**, Charles J 1947- *AmMWSc 92*
**Robinson**, Charles James 1958- *WhoFI 92*
**Robinson**, Charles James, Jr. 1951- *WhoMW 92*
**Robinson**, Charles Nelson 1928- *AmMWSc 92*
**Robinson**, Charles Sherwood 1920- *WhoWest 92*
**Robinson**, Charles Wesley 1919- *WhoWest 92*
**Robinson**, Charlotte L. 1924- *WhoBlA 92*
**Robinson**, Christopher John 1936- *Who 92*
**Robinson**, Christopher Philipse 1938- *Who 92*
**Robinson**, Chuck Frank 1956- *WhoMW 92*
**Robinson**, Clare *Who 92*
**Robinson**, Clarence B 1911- *WhoAmP 91, WhoBlA 92*
**Robinson**, Clarence G. 1920- *WhoBlA 92*
**Robinson**, Clark 1943- *AmMWSc 92*
**Robinson**, Clark Shove, Jr 1917- *AmMWSc 92*
**Robinson**, Clark Zachary 1961- *WhoWest 92*
**Robinson**, Clayton David 1955- *WhoRel 92*
**Robinson**, Cleveland L. 1914- *WhoBlA 92*
**Robinson**, Cliff Trent 1960- *WhoBlA 92*
**Robinson**, Clifton Eugene Bancroft 1926- *Who 92*
**Robinson**, Cloyd Erwin 1938- *WhoAmP 91*
**Robinson**, Coleman Townsend 1838-1872 *BiInAmS*
**Robinson**, Curtis 1934- *AmMWSc 92, WhoBlA 92*
**Robinson**, Curtis L. 1958- *WhoBlA 92*
**Robinson**, D M 1907- *AmMWSc 92*
**Robinson**, Daniel Alfred 1932- *AmMWSc 92*
**Robinson**, Daniel Arley 1928- *WhoWest 92*
**Robinson**, Daniel Lee 1923- *WhoBlA 92*
**Robinson**, Daniel Owen 1918- *AmMWSc 92*
**Robinson**, Daphne McCaskey 1912- *WhoBlA 92*
**Robinson**, David 1929- *AmMWSc 92*
**Robinson**, David 1965- *BlkOlyM*
**Robinson**, David Adair 1925- *AmMWSc 92*
**Robinson**, David Bancroft 1924- *AmMWSc 92*
**Robinson**, David Duncan 1943- *Who 92*
**Robinson**, David Howard 1948- *WhoAmL 92*
**Robinson**, David Joseph 1937- *WhoMW 92*
**Robinson**, David Julien 1930- *IntAu&W 91, Who 92*
**Robinson**, David Lee 1943- *AmMWSc 92*
**Robinson**, David Mason 1932- *AmMWSc 92*
**Robinson**, David Maurice 1965- *WhoBlA 92*
**Robinson**, David Nelson 1933- *AmMWSc 92*
**Robinson**, David Ray 1963- *WhoEnt 92*
**Robinson**, David Roger 1951- *WhoWest 92*
**Robinson**, David Weaver 1914- *AmMWSc 92*
**Robinson**, David Zav 1927- *AmMWSc 92*
**Robinson**, Davis Rowland 1940- *WhoAmL 92*
**Robinson**, Dean 1946- *ConAu 36NR*
**Robinson**, Dean Michael 1942- *WhoAmL 92*
**Robinson**, Dean Wentworth 1929- *AmMWSc 92*
**Robinson**, Deanna Adell 1945- *WhoBlA 92*
**Robinson**, Denauvo M. 1949- *WhoBlA 92*
**Robinson**, Derek 1932- *Who 92, WrDr 92*
**Robinson**, Derek Anthony 1942- *Who 92*
**Robinson**, Derek John Scott 1938- *AmMWSc 92*
**Robinson**, Donald d1991 *NewYTBS 91*
**Robinson**, Donald 1913-1991 *ConAu 135*
**Robinson**, Donald Alonzo 1920- *AmMWSc 92*
**Robinson**, Donald Fay 1905- *WhoRel 92*
**Robinson**, Donald Keith 1932- *AmMWSc 92*
**Robinson**, Donald Lee 1929- *WhoRel 92*
**Robinson**, Donald Lee 1930- *WhoBlA 92*
**Robinson**, Donald Louis 1936- *WhoAmP 91*
**Robinson**, Donald Nellis 1933- *AmMWSc 92*
**Robinson**, Donald Peter 1928- *WhoEnt 92, WhoMW 92*
**Robinson**, Donald Stetson 1928- *AmMWSc 92*
**Robinson**, Donald W, Jr 1921- *AmMWSc 92*
**Robinson**, Donald Wilford 1928- *AmMWSc 92*
**Robinson**, Donald William Bradley *Who 92*
**Robinson**, Donald William Bradley 1922- *IntWW 91*
**Robinson**, Dorlos 1935- *WhoAmP 91*
**Robinson**, Douglas George 1943- *WhoAmL 92*
**Robinson**, Douglas Walter 1934- *AmMWSc 92*
**Robinson**, Duncan *Who 92*
**Robinson**, E Arthur, Jr *AmMWSc 92*
**Robinson**, Earl d1991 *NewYTBS 91*
**Robinson**, Earl 1910- *NewAmDM*
**Robinson**, Earl 1910-1991 *ConAu 135, News 92-1*
**Robinson**, Eddie 1919- *WhoBlA 92*
**Robinson**, Edgar Allen 1933- *WhoFI 92*
**Robinson**, Edith 1924- *WhoBlA 92*
**Robinson**, Edsel F. 1928- *WhoBlA 92*
**Robinson**, Edward A *ScFEYrs*
**Robinson**, Edward A. 1935- *WhoBlA 92*
**Robinson**, Edward A and Wall, George A *ScFEYrs*
**Robinson**, Edward Allen 1949- *WhoFI 92*
**Robinson**, Edward Ashton 1949- *WhoBlA 92*
**Robinson**, Edward Austin 1897- *IntWW 91, Who 92*
**Robinson**, Edward G 1893-1973 *FacFETw*
**Robinson**, Edward J 1936- *AmMWSc 92*
**Robinson**, Edward Joseph 1940- *WhoFI 92*
**Robinson**, Edward Kay *ScFEYrs*
**Robinson**, Edward Lee 1933- *AmMWSc 92*
**Robinson**, Edward Lewis 1945- *AmMWSc 92*
**Robinson**, Edward T., III 1932- *WhoAmL 92*
**Robinson**, Edwin Allin 1907- *AmMWSc 92*
**Robinson**, Edwin Arlington 1869-1935 *BenetAL 91, ConAu 133, FacFETw*
**Robinson**, Edwin Hollis 1942- *AmMWSc 92*
**Robinson**, Edwin James, Jr 1916- *AmMWSc 92*
**Robinson**, Edwin Meade *BenetAL 91*
**Robinson**, Edwin S 1935- *AmMWSc 92*
**Robinson**, Effie *WhoBlA 92*
**Robinson**, Ella S. 1943- *WhoBlA 92*
**Robinson**, Ellen-Ann 1950- *WhoAmP 91*
**Robinson**, Emyre Barrios 1926- *WhoHisp 92*
**Robinson**, Enders Anthony 1930- *AmMWSc 92*
**Robinson**, Eric B. 1961- *WhoBlA 92*
**Robinson**, Eric Embleton 1927- *Who 92*
**Robinson**, Ernest Preston, Sr. 1947- *WhoBlA 92*
**Robinson**, Eunice Primus 1935- *WhoBlA 92*
**Robinson**, Farrel Richard 1927- *AmMWSc 92, WhoMW 92*
**Robinson**, Faye 1943- *NewAmDM*
**Robinson**, Fisher J. 1929- *WhoBlA 92*
**Robinson**, Fisher Joseph 1929- *WhoRel 92*
**Robinson**, Florence Claire Crim 1932- *WhoEnt 92*
**Robinson**, Florine Samantha 1935- *WhoFI 92*
**Robinson**, Floyd A. 1936- *WhoBlA 92*
**Robinson**, Francis Alastair 1937- *Who 92*
**Robinson**, Francis E 1909- *WhoAmP 91*
**Robinson**, Frank 1935- *FacFETw, WhoBlA 92*
**Robinson**, Frank B. 1886-1948 *RelLAm 91*
**Robinson**, Frank Bennett 1914- *WhoMW 92*
**Robinson**, Frank Ernest 1930- *AmMWSc 92*
**Robinson**, Frank J. 1939- *WhoBlA 92*
**Robinson**, Frank M 1926- *TwCSFW 91, WrDr 92*
**Robinson**, Frank Robert 1938- *WhoEnt 92, WhoWest 92*
**Robinson**, Frank W 1926- *WhoIns 92*
**Robinson**, Frank William 1937- *WhoRel 92*
**Robinson**, Franklin Clement 1852-1910 *BiInAmS*
**Robinson**, Fred Miller 1942- *WhoEnt 92*
**Robinson**, Frederick *ScFEYrs*
**Robinson**, Frederick Byron 1855-1910 *BiInAmS*
**Robinson**, Frederick Cayley 1862-1927 *TwCPaSc*
**Robinson**, G. Bruce 1907- *WhoBlA 92*
**Robinson**, Garry Lewin 1951- *WhoEnt 92*
**Robinson**, Gary Dale 1938- *WhoWest 92*
**Robinson**, Gary O. 1935- *WhoBlA 92*
**Robinson**, Gay Elizabeth Clara 1933- *WhoRel 92*
**Robinson**, Gene Conrad 1928- *AmMWSc 92*
**Robinson**, Genevieve 1940- *WhoBlA 92*
**Robinson**, Geoffrey *TwCPaSc, Who 92*
**Robinson**, Geoffrey 1938- *Who 92*
**Robinson**, George Ali 1939- *WhoBlA 92*
**Robinson**, George David 1913- *AmMWSc 92*
**Robinson**, George Edward, Jr 1916- *AmMWSc 92*
**Robinson**, George L. *WhoBlA 92*
**Robinson**, George McKinsey 1947- *WhoRel 92*
**Robinson**, George S 1945- *WhoAmP 91*
**Robinson**, George Waller 1941- *AmMWSc 92*
**Robinson**, George Wilse 1924- *AmMWSc 92*
**Robinson**, Gerald Arthur 1929- *AmMWSc 92*
**Robinson**, Gerald Garland 1933- *AmMWSc 92*
**Robinson**, Gershon Duvall 1918- *AmMWSc 92*
**Robinson**, Gertrude Edith 1923- *AmMWSc 92*
**Robinson**, Gertrude Rivers 1927- *WhoBlA 92*
**Robinson**, Gilbert A 1928- *WhoAmP 91*
**Robinson**, Gilbert C 1919- *AmMWSc 92*
**Robinson**, Gilbert de Beauregard 1906- *AmMWSc 92, WrDr 92*
**Robinson**, Gill Doncelia 1948- *WhoBlA 92*
**Robinson**, Glen Moore, III 1943- *AmMWSc 92*
**Robinson**, Glen O. *LesBEnT 92*
**Robinson**, Glen O. 1936- *WhoAmL 92*
**Robinson**, Glenn Hugh 1912- *AmMWSc 92*
**Robinson**, Gordon Heath 1931- *AmMWSc 92*
**Robinson**, Gregory Robert 1955- *WhoMW 92*
**Robinson**, Gregory Scott 1962- *WhoFI 92*
**Robinson**, Grover C, III *WhoAmP 91*
**Robinson**, Guner Suzek 1937- *AmMWSc 92*
**Robinson**, H James 1949- *WhoAmP 91*
**Robinson**, Haddon William 1931- *WhoRel 92*
**Robinson**, Hamilton Burrows Greaves 1910- *AmMWSc 92*
**Robinson**, Harold Barrett 1922- *WhoRel 92*
**Robinson**, Harold Ernest 1932- *AmMWSc 92*
**Robinson**, Harold Frank 1918- *AmMWSc 92*
**Robinson**, Harold George Robert 1924- *Who 92*
**Robinson**, Harold Leonard 1947- *WhoRel 92*
**Robinson**, Harriet Burlingame Lewis *WhoAmP 91*
**Robinson**, Harriet Hanson 1825-1911 *HanAmWH*
**Robinson**, Harriet Jane Hanson 1825-1911 *BenetAL 91*
**Robinson**, Harry 1925- *AmMWSc 92*
**Robinson**, Harry G., III 1942- *WhoBlA 92*

**Robinson,** Harry Granville, III 1942- *WhoFI 92*
**Robinson,** Harry Perry 1859-1930 *ScFEYrs*
**Robinson,** Henrietta 1919- *WhoAmP 91*
**Robinson,** Henry 1936- *WhoBlA 92*
**Robinson,** Henry Crabb 1775-1867 *DcLB 107 [port]*
**Robinson,** Henry Morton 1898-1961 *BenetAL 91*
**Robinson,** Henry William 1924- *AmMWSc 92*
**Robinson,** Herbert A. 1927- *WhoBlA 92*
**Robinson,** Herbert Fisk 1924- *WhoWest 92*
**Robinson,** Herbert William 1914- *WhoFI 92, WhoWest 92*
**Robinson,** Herk 1940- *WhoMW 92*
**Robinson,** Holly 1965- *WhoBlA 92*
**Robinson,** Horatio Nelson 1806-1867 *BiInAmS*
**Robinson,** Howard Addison 1909- *AmMWSc 92*
**Robinson,** Hubbell d1974 *LesBEnT 92*
**Robinson,** Hubert Nelson 1909- *WhoBlA 92*
**Robinson,** Hugh Gettys 1928- *AmMWSc 92*
**Robinson,** Hugh Granville 1932- *WhoBlA 92*
**Robinson,** Ian 1934- *IntAu&W 91*
**Robinson,** Ida LaFosse 1934- *WhoRel 92*
**Robinson,** Ira Charles 1940- *WhoBlA 92*
**Robinson,** Irwin Jay 1928- *WhoAmL 92, WhoFI 92*
**Robinson,** Isaiah E. 1924- *WhoBlA 92*
**Robinson,** Ivor 1923- *AmMWSc 92*
**Robinson,** J. Cordell 1940- *WhoHisp 92*
**Robinson,** J. Kenneth 1932- *WhoRel 92*
**Robinson,** J. Lewis 1918- *WrDr 92*
**Robinson,** J Mack 1923- *WhoIns 92*
**Robinson,** J Michael 1943- *AmMWSc 92*
**Robinson,** Jack, Jr. 1942- *WhoBlA 92*
**Robinson,** Jack Albert 1930- *WhoFI 92, WhoMW 92*
**Robinson,** Jack E. *WhoBlA 92*
**Robinson,** Jack Errol, III 1960- *WhoFI 92*
**Robinson,** Jack Fay 1914- *WhoMW 92, WhoRel 92*
**Robinson,** Jack Landy 1940- *AmMWSc 92*
**Robinson,** Jackie 1919-1972 *FacFETw [port], RComAH*
**Robinson,** Jacqueline J. *WhoBlA 92*
**Robinson,** Jacqui 1935- *WhoBlA 92*
**Robinson,** James *WhoEnt 92*
**Robinson,** James Arthur 1949- *WhoIns 92*
**Robinson,** James Burnell 1944- *WhoMW 92, WhoRel 92*
**Robinson,** James D., III 1935- *IntWW 91*
**Robinson,** James Dixon, III 1935- *WhoFI 92*
**Robinson,** James Edward 1943- *WhoBlA 92*
**Robinson,** James Edward 1954- *WhoRel 92*
**Robinson,** James Ford, Jr. 1955- *WhoEnt 92*
**Robinson,** James Harvey 1863-1936 *BenetAL 91*
**Robinson,** James Kenneth 1943- *WhoAmL 92*
**Robinson,** James L. 1940- *WhoBlA 92*
**Robinson,** James Lawrence 1942- *AmMWSc 92, WhoMW 92*
**Robinson,** James McOmber 1920- *AmMWSc 92*
**Robinson,** James Richard 1942- *WhoAmL 92*
**Robinson,** James Vance 1943- *AmMWSc 92*
**Robinson,** James Walker 1930- *WhoAmP 91*
**Robinson,** James Waymond 1926- *WhoBlA 92*
**Robinson,** James William 1923- *AmMWSc 92*
**Robinson,** James William 1938- *AmMWSc 92*
**Robinson,** Jancis Mary 1950- *IntAu&W 91, Who 92*
**Robinson,** Jane Alexander 1931- *WhoBlA 92*
**Robinson,** Janice Marie 1943- *WhoRel 92*
**Robinson,** Janice Sheryl 1952- *WhoAmL 92*
**Robinson,** Jason Guy 1934- *WhoBlA 92*
**Robinson,** Jayne G. 1912- *WhoBlA 92*
**Robinson,** Jeems Anton 1933- *WhoMW 92*
**Robinson,** Jeremy *DrAPF 91*
**Robinson,** Jerome David 1941- *AmMWSc 92*
**Robinson,** Jerome Lawrence 1922- *WhoFI 92*
**Robinson,** Jerome Stancil 1924- *WhoRel 92*
**Robinson,** Jerry Allen 1939- *AmMWSc 92*
**Robinson,** Jerry H. 1932- *WhoAmL 92, WhoFI 92*
**Robinson,** Jesse Lee 1912- *WhoBlA 92*
**Robinson,** Jill *DrAPF 91*
**Robinson,** Jim C. 1943- *WhoBlA 92*
**Robinson,** Joan 1903-1983 *FacFETw*
**Robinson,** John *DrAPF 91*
**Robinson,** John 1704-1766 *BlkwEAR*
**Robinson,** John 1922- *AmMWSc 92*
**Robinson,** John 1943- *Who 92*
**Robinson,** John Alexander 1935- *WhoWest 92*
**Robinson,** John Armstrong 1925- *Who 92*
**Robinson,** John Bowers, Jr. 1946- *WhoFI 92*
**Robinson,** John Dennis 1953- *WhoWest 92*
**Robinson,** John E. 1942- *WhoBlA 92*
**Robinson,** John E, Jr 1924- *AmMWSc 92*
**Robinson,** John F. 1944- *WhoBlA 92*
**Robinson,** John H. 1934- *WhoRel 92*
**Robinson,** John Hamilton 1927- *WhoFI 92*
**Robinson,** John Henry 1955- *WhoAmP 91*
**Robinson,** John L. 1930- *WhoBlA 92*
**Robinson,** John Mark 1948- *WhoEnt 92*
**Robinson,** John Mitchell *AmMWSc 92*
**Robinson,** John Murrell 1945- *AmMWSc 92*
**Robinson,** John Paul 1939- *AmMWSc 92*
**Robinson,** John Price 1927- *AmMWSc 92*
**Robinson,** Johnathan Prather 1953- *WhoBlA 92*
**Robinson,** Jonathan N. 1922- *WhoBlA 92*
**Robinson,** Jontyle Theresa 1947- *WhoBlA 92*
**Robinson,** Joseph 1927- *Who 92*
**Robinson,** Joseph 1940- *WhoBlA 92*
**Robinson,** Joseph Dewey 1928- *AmMWSc 92*
**Robinson,** Joseph Douglass 1934- *AmMWSc 92*
**Robinson,** Joseph Edward 1925- *AmMWSc 92*
**Robinson,** Joseph Robert 1939- *AmMWSc 92, WhoMW 92*
**Robinson,** Joseph Taylor 1872-1937 *FacFETw*
**Robinson,** Julia Bowman 1919-1985 *HanAmWH*
**Robinson,** Karen Denise 1956- *WhoBlA 92*
**Robinson,** Kathleen Marian 1911- *Who 92*
**Robinson,** Kathleen Moore 1954- *WhoAmL 92*
**Robinson,** Kayne 1943- *WhoAmP 91*
**Robinson,** Keith *Who 92*
**Robinson,** Keith 1955- *WhoEnt 92*
**Robinson,** Kenneth 1911- *IntWW 91, Who 92*
**Robinson,** Kenneth 1947- *WhoBlA 92*
**Robinson,** Kenneth Ernest 1914- *IntWW 91, Who 92*
**Robinson,** Kenneth Eugene 1947- *WhoBlA 92*
**Robinson,** Kenneth Patrick 1933- *WhoAmL 92*
**Robinson,** Kenneth Robert 1921- *AmMWSc 92*
**Robinson,** Kenneth Warren 1946- *WhoWest 92*
**Robinson,** Kent 1924- *AmMWSc 92*
**Robinson,** Kenthedo 1954- *WhoEnt 92*
**Robinson,** Kerry Brent 1958- *WhoRel 92*
**Robinson,** Kim Stanley 1952- *IntAu&W 91, TwCSFW 91, WrDr 92*
**Robinson,** Kitty 1921- *WhoBlA 92*
**Robinson,** Larry *WhoAmP 91, WhoBlA 92*
**Robinson,** Larry Robert 1936- *WhoFI 92, WhoIns 92*
**Robinson,** Lauren Danielle 1964- *WhoBlA 92*
**Robinson,** Lawrence B. 1919- *WhoBlA 92*
**Robinson,** Lawrence Baylor 1919- *AmMWSc 92*
**Robinson,** Lawrence D. 1942- *WhoBlA 92*
**Robinson,** Learthon Steven 1925- *WhoBlA 92*
**Robinson,** Lee Fisher 1923- *Who 92*
**Robinson,** Lee Harris 1939- *WhoAmL 92*
**Robinson,** Lennox 1886-1958 *FacFETw, RfGEnL 91*
**Robinson,** Leonard H, Jr 1943- *WhoAmP 91*
**Robinson,** Leonard Harrison, Jr. 1943- *WhoBlA 92*
**Robinson,** Leonard Keith 1920- *Who 92*
**Robinson,** Leonard Wallace *DrAPF 91*
**Robinson,** Lewis Howe 1930- *AmMWSc 92*
**Robinson,** Lillian S. *DrAPF 91*
**Robinson,** Linda Gosden 1953- *WhoFI 92*
**Robinson,** Linda Parent 1943- *WhoAmP 91*
**Robinson,** Lloyd *ConAu 36NR, Who 92*
**Robinson,** Lloyd Burdette 1929- *AmMWSc 92*
**Robinson,** Lois Hart 1927- *WhoMW 92*
**Robinson,** Lou *DrAPF 91*
**Robinson,** Louie, Jr. 1926- *WhoBlA 92*
**Robinson,** Louis 1926- *AmMWSc 92*
**Robinson,** Louise Ann 1956- *WhoEnt 92*
**Robinson,** Lowell Warren 1949- *WhoFI 92*
**Robinson,** Luther D. 1922- *WhoBlA 92*
**Robinson,** M John 1938- *AmMWSc 92*
**Robinson,** Manuel 1931- *WhoBlA 92*
**Robinson,** Marcus 1912- *Who 92*
**Robinson,** Margaret A. *DrAPF 91*
**Robinson,** Margaret Chisolm 1930- *AmMWSc 92*
**Robinson,** Margaret King 1906- *WhoAmP 91*
**Robinson,** Marguerite S. 1935- *WrDr 92*
**Robinson,** Marilyn Patricia 1946- *WhoBlA 92*
**Robinson,** Marilynne 1943- *ConNov 91, WrDr 92*
**Robinson,** Mark Bryan 1960- *WhoRel 92*
**Robinson,** Mark Leighton 1927- *WhoFI 92, WhoWest 92*
**Robinson,** Mark Noel Foster 1946- *Who 92*
**Robinson,** Mark Tabor 1926- *AmMWSc 92*
**Robinson,** Mars Ray 1956- *WhoRel 92*
**Robinson,** Martha Dolores 1956- *WhoBlA 92*
**Robinson,** Martin Alvin 1930- *AmMWSc 92*
**Robinson,** Mary 1944- *CurBio 91 [port], IntWW 91, Who 92*
**Robinson,** Mary Elizabeth 1946- *WhoBlA 92*
**Robinson,** Matilda Turner 1951- *WhoBlA 92*
**Robinson,** Matthew 1914- *BlkOlyM*
**Robinson,** Maude Eloise 1927- *WhoBlA 92*
**Robinson,** Maurice C. 1932- *WhoBlA 92*
**Robinson,** Max d1988 *LesBEnT 92*
**Robinson,** Max 1939-1988 *WhoBlA 92N*
**Robinson,** Melinda Zuppann 1954- *WhoFI 92*
**Robinson,** Melvin P. 1935- *WhoBlA 92*
**Robinson,** Merton Arnold 1925- *AmMWSc 92*
**Robinson,** Michael David 1953- *WhoBlA 92*
**Robinson,** Michael Francis 1954- *WhoFI 92*
**Robinson,** Michael Hill 1929- *AmMWSc 92*
**Robinson,** Michael K 1951- *AmMWSc 92*
**Robinson,** Michael Maurice Jeffries 1927- *Who 92*
**Robinson,** Mildred Wigfall 1944- *WhoAmL 92*
**Robinson,** Milton Bernidine 1913- *WhoBlA 92, WhoRel 92*
**Robinson,** Milton J. 1935- *WhoBlA 92*
**Robinson,** Minnie Lenetha *WhoMW 92*
**Robinson,** Moureen Ann *Who 92*
**Robinson,** Muriel F. Cox 1927- *WhoBlA 92*
**Robinson,** Myron 1928- *AmMWSc 92*
**Robinson,** Myron Frederick 1943- *WhoBlA 92*
**Robinson,** Myrtle Tonne 1929- *AmMWSc 92*
**Robinson,** Nancy Anne 1940- *WhoRel 92*
**Robinson,** Nancy Drue 1930- *WhoRel 92*
**Robinson,** Nathaniel 1951- *WhoBlA 92*
**Robinson,** Neal Clark 1942- *AmMWSc 92*
**Robinson,** Neil 1929- *Who 92*
**Robinson,** Neil Cibley, Jr. 1942- *WhoAmL 92*
**Robinson,** Niall B. L. *Who 92*
**Robinson,** Nina 1943- *WhoBlA 92*
**Robinson,** Noah R. *WhoBlA 92*
**Robinson,** Norman Edward 1942- *AmMWSc 92*
**Robinson,** Norman R. 1909- *WhoBlA 92*
**Robinson,** Norman T., Jr. 1918- *WhoBlA 92*
**Robinson,** Oliver John 1908- *Who 92*
**Robinson,** Ollie Ama 1924- *WhoAmP 91*
**Robinson,** Oswald Horsley 1926- *Who 92*
**Robinson,** Otis Bernard 1961- *WhoRel 92*
**Robinson,** Otis Hall 1835-1912 *BiInAmS*
**Robinson,** Patrick William 1943- *Who 92*
**Robinson,** Paul E. 1940- *WhoEnt 92*
**Robinson,** Paul Randall 1937- *WhoAmP 91*
**Robinson,** Paul Ronald 1950- *AmMWSc 92*
**Robinson,** Pete *WhoAmP 91*
**Robinson,** Peter 1922- *Who 92*
**Robinson,** Peter 1932- *AmMWSc 92, WhoWest 92*
**Robinson,** Peter 1953- *WhoAmL 92*
**Robinson,** Peter Clark 1938- *WhoFI 92*
**Robinson,** Peter Damian 1926- *Who 92*
**Robinson,** Peter David 1948- *IntWW 91, Who 92*
**Robinson,** Peter Eliot 1950- *WhoMW 92*
**Robinson,** Peter John 1944- *AmMWSc 92*
**Robinson,** Peter Lee, Jr. 1922- *WhoBlA 92*
**Robinson,** Peter Michael 1947- *Who 92*
**Robinson,** Phil Alden 1950- *WhoEnt 92*
**Robinson,** Philip 1949- *Who 92*
**Robinson,** Philip Ely d1920 *BiInAmS*
**Robinson,** Philip Henry 1926- *Who 92*
**Robinson,** Philip Stewart 1847-1902 *ScFEYrs*
**Robinson,** Phyllis 1946- *WhoAmP 91*
**Robinson,** Phyllis Lester 1946- *WhoAmL 92*
**Robinson,** Press L 1937- *AmMWSc 92*
**Robinson,** Prezell Russell 1922- *WhoBlA 92*
**Robinson,** R. David 1941- *WhoBlA 92*
**Robinson,** Ralph M 1926- *AmMWSc 92*
**Robinson,** Randall *NewYTBS 91 [port]*
**Robinson,** Randall Bruce 1946- *WhoEnt 92*
**Robinson,** Randall S. *WhoBlA 92*
**Robinson,** Randall S. 1939- *WhoBlA 92*
**Robinson,** Raphael Mitchel 1911- *AmMWSc 92, WhoWest 92*
**Robinson,** Raymond *IntWW 91, Who 92*
**Robinson,** Raymond Edwin 1932- *WhoEnt 92*
**Robinson,** Raymond Francis 1914- *AmMWSc 92*
**Robinson,** Renault A. 1942- *WhoBlA 92*
**Robinson,** Rex Julian 1904- *AmMWSc 92*
**Robinson,** Richard Alan 1942- *AmMWSc 92*
**Robinson,** Richard Allen, Jr. 1936- *WhoWest 92*
**Robinson,** Richard C 1937- *AmMWSc 92*
**Robinson,** Richard Carleton, Jr 1927- *AmMWSc 92*
**Robinson,** Richard Clark 1940- *WhoFI 92*
**Robinson,** Richard Dunlop 1921- *WhoFI 92*
**Robinson,** Richard Edmund 1936- *WhoWest 92*
**Robinson,** Richard Gary 1931- *WhoFI 92*
**Robinson,** Richard Lee 1957- *WhoAmL 92*
**Robinson,** Richard Russell 1925- *WhoAmL 92*
**Robinson,** Richard Warren 1930- *AmMWSc 92*
**Robinson,** Rick Lee 1952- *WhoWest 92*
**Robinson,** Rob 1955- *WhoFI 92, WhoMW 92*
**Robinson,** Robb 1922- *WhoAmP 91*
**Robinson,** Robert 1886-1975 *WhoNob 90*
**Robinson,** Robert 1927- *WrDr 92*
**Robinson,** Robert Armstrong 1925- *WhoFI 92, WhoIns 92*
**Robinson,** Robert Blacque 1927- *WhoWest 92*
**Robinson,** Robert E *WhoAmP 91*
**Robinson,** Robert Earl 1927- *AmMWSc 92*
**Robinson,** Robert Edward 1947- *WhoAmP 91*
**Robinson,** Robert Eugene 1927- *AmMWSc 92*
**Robinson,** Robert George 1920- *AmMWSc 92*
**Robinson,** Robert George 1937- *AmMWSc 92*
**Robinson,** Robert Henry 1927- *IntAu&W 91, Who 92*
**Robinson,** Robert James 1935- *WhoMW 92*
**Robinson,** Robert L. 1936- *WhoFI 92*
**Robinson,** Robert L, Jr 1937- *AmMWSc 92*
**Robinson,** Robert Leo 1926- *AmMWSc 92*
**Robinson,** Robert Love, Jr. 1961- *WhoBlA 92*
**Robinson,** Robert W 1941- *AmMWSc 92*
**Robinson,** Roger 1940- *WhoBlA 92*
**Robinson,** Roger James 1932- *Who 92*
**Robinson,** Roland 1912- *ConPo 91, IntAu&W 91, WrDr 92*
**Robinson,** Ronald Alan 1952- *WhoWest 92*
**Robinson,** Ronald C 1930- *WhoAmP 91*
**Robinson,** Ronald Edward 1920- *Who 92*
**Robinson,** Ronald Guilfred 1955- *WhoRel 92*
**Robinson,** Ronald James 1946- *WhoFI 92*
**Robinson,** Ronald Michael 1942- *WhoFI 92*
**Robinson,** Ronnie W. 1942- *WhoBlA 92*
**Robinson,** Roosevelt V. *WhoBlA 92*
**Robinson,** Rosalyn Karen 1946- *WhoBlA 92*
**Robinson,** Roscoe, Jr. 1928- *WhoBlA 92*
**Robinson,** Roscoe Ross 1929- *AmMWSc 92*
**Robinson,** Rose Miles 1939- *WhoBlA 92*
**Robinson,** Ross Utley 1928- *AmMWSc 92*
**Robinson,** Rowland Evans 1833-1900 *BenetAL 91*
**Robinson,** Roxana *WrDr 92*
**Robinson,** Roxana Barry 1946- *IntAu&W 91*
**Robinson,** Roy Garland, Jr 1921- *AmMWSc 92*
**Robinson,** Rubye Doris 1942-1967 *NotBlAW 92*
**Robinson,** Rubye Doris Smith 1942-1967 *FacFETw*
**Robinson,** Rumeal James 1966- *WhoBlA 92*
**Robinson,** Russel Gordon 1957- *WhoAmL 92*
**Robinson,** Russell Lee 1931- *AmMWSc 92*
**Robinson,** Ruth 1949- *WhoBlA 92*
**Robinson,** Ruth M 1921- *WhoAmP 91*
**Robinson,** S. Benton 1928- *WhoBlA 92*
**Robinson,** S. Yolanda 1946- *WhoBlA 92, WhoMW 92*
**Robinson,** Sally S. 1933- *WhoMW 92*
**Robinson,** Samuel 1935- *WhoBlA 92*

**Roche,** Lidia Alicia 1939- *AmMWSc 92*
**Roche,** Marcel 1920- *IntWW 91*
**Roche,** Marilyn M 1939- *WhoAmP 91*
**Roche,** Patrick James 1942- *WhoAmL 92*
**Roche,** Patrick William 1948- *WhoMW 92*
**Roche,** Paul 1916- *ConPo 91*
**Roche,** Paul 1928- *IntAu&W 91, WrDr 92*
**Roche,** Peter Bouton 1945- *WhoFI 92*
**Roche,** Robert Paul 1937- *WhoAmL 92*
**Roche,** Rodney Sylvester 1934- *AmMWSc 92*
**Roche,** Thomas Edward 1944- *AmMWSc 92*
**Roche,** Thomas Gabriel 1909- *Who 92*
**Roche,** Thomas Stephen 1946- *AmMWSc 92*
**Rochee,** Arthur Stewart, Sr. 1933- *WhoHisp 92*
**Rochefort,** Christiane 1917- *FrenWW*
**Rochefort,** John S 1924- *AmMWSc 92*
**Rochefort,** Joseph Guy 1929- *AmMWSc 92*
**Rochefoucalt,** Mademoiselle de la *EncAmaz 91*
**Rocheleau,** Robert *AmMWSc 92*
**Rochelle,** Jay Cooper 1938- *WhoRel 92*
**Rochelle,** Robert Thomas 1945- *WhoAmP 91*
**Rochelle,** Robert W 1923- *AmMWSc 92*
**Rochen,** Donald Michael 1943- *WhoMW 92*
**Rocher,** Guy 1924- *IntWW 91*
**Rocherolle,** Eugenie Katherine 1936- *WhoEnt 92*
**Rochester,** Archdeacon of *Who 92*
**Rochester,** Baron 1916- *Who 92*
**Rochester,** Bishop of 1935- *Who 92*
**Rochester,** Dean of *Who 92*
**Rochester,** Earl of 1647-1680 *RfGEnL 91*
**Rochester,** Anna 1880-1966 *AmPeW*
**Rochester,** Dudley Fortescue 1928- *AmMWSc 92*
**Rochester,** Eugene Wallace 1943- *AmMWSc 92*
**Rochester,** George Dixon 1908- *IntWW 91, Who 92*
**Rochester,** Mattilyn Talford 1941- *WhoAmP 91*
**Rochester,** Michael Grant 1932- *AmMWSc 92*
**Rochet,** Waldeck 1905-1983 *FacFETw*
**Rocheta,** Manuel Farrajota 1906- *Who 92*
**Rochette,** Craig Richard 1959- *WhoWest 92*
**Rochford,** Joseph Patrick 1935- *WhoAmP 91*
**Rochin,** Refugio Ismael 1941- *WhoFI 92*
**Rochin-Rodriguez,** Refugio Ismael 1941- *WhoHisp 92*
**Rochkind,** Louis Philipp 1948- *WhoAmL 92*
**Rochlin,** Doris *DrAPF 91*
**Rochlin,** Irma *WhoAmP 91*
**Rochlin,** Phillip 1923- *AmMWSc 92*
**Rochlin,** Robert Sumner 1922- *AmMWSc 92*
**Rochling,** Hermann 1872-1955 *EncTR 91 [port]*
**Rochlis,** Jeffrey Aaron 1945- *WhoWest 92*
**Rochon,** Jean 1938- *IntWW 91*
**Rochovansky,** Olga Maria *AmMWSc 92*
**Rochow,** Eugene George 1909- *AmMWSc 92*
**Rochow,** Theodore George 1907- *AmMWSc 92*
**Rochow,** William Frantz 1927- *AmMWSc 92*
**Rochwarger,** Leonard *WhoAmP 91*
**Rock,** Arthur 1926- *WhoFI 92*
**Rock,** Barrett Nelson 1942- *AmMWSc 92*
**Rock,** Barry Lee 1958- *WhoEnt 92*
**Rock,** Chet A 1944- *AmMWSc 92*
**Rock,** Clinton Andrew, Jr. 1915- *WhoRel 92*
**Rock,** Elizabeth Jane 1924- *AmMWSc 92*
**Rock,** Gail Ann 1940- *AmMWSc 92*
**Rock,** George Calvert 1934- *AmMWSc 92*
**Rock,** James *ScFEYrs*
**Rock,** Michael Keith 1951- *AmMWSc 92*
**Rock,** Miles 1840-1901 *BilnAmS*
**Rock,** Paul Bernard 1945- *AmMWSc 92*
**Rock,** Paul Elliot 1943- *Who 92*
**Rock,** Peter Alfred 1939- *AmMWSc 92*
**Rock,** Philip Joseph 1937- *WhoAmP 91*
**Rock,** Phillip Joseph 1937- *WhoMW 92*
**Rock,** R Rand, II 1949- *WhoAmP 91*
**Rock,** Richard R 1924- *WhoAmP 91*
**Rock,** Terry Garth 1955- *WhoFI 92*
**Rock,** William Booth 1947- *WhoEnt 92*
**Rock,** William Konstantin 1923- *WhoMW 92*
**Rock-Bailey,** Jinni *WhoBlA 92*
**Rockafellar,** Ralph Tyrrell 1935- *AmMWSc 92*
**Rockaway,** John D, Jr 1938- *AmMWSc 92*
**Rockburne,** Dorothea *IntWW 91*
**Rockburne,** Dorothea 1934- *WorArt 1980*
**Rockcastle,** Verne Norton 1920- *AmMWSc 92*
**Rocke,** Basil 1904-1966 *TwCPaSc*
**Rocke,** David M 1946- *AmMWSc 92*
**Rocke,** John Roy Mansfield 1918- *Who 92*
**Rocke,** Randall Richard 1949- *WhoEnt 92*
**Rockefeller,** David 1915- *FacFETw, IntWW 91, Who 92, WhoFI 92*
**Rockefeller,** Edwin Shaffer 1927- *WhoAmL 92*
**Rockefeller,** James S. 1902- *IntWW 91*
**Rockefeller,** James Stillman 1902- *Who 92*
**Rockefeller,** Jeannette Edris 1918- *WhoWest 92*
**Rockefeller,** John D 1839-1937 *RComAH*
**Rockefeller,** John D., III 1906-1978 *FacFETw*
**Rockefeller,** John D., IV *NewYTBS 91 [port]*
**Rockefeller,** John D., IV 1937- *AlmAP 92 [port]*
**Rockefeller,** John Davison, IV 1937- *IntWW 91, WhoAmP 91*
**Rockefeller,** John Davison, Jr 1874-1960 *FacFETw*
**Rockefeller,** Laurance Spelman 1910- *IntWW 91, Who 92*
**Rockefeller,** Laurence 1910- *FacFETw*
**Rockefeller,** Martha Baird 1895-1971 *NewAmDM*
**Rockefeller,** Nelson Aldrich 1908-1979 *AmPolLe, FacFETw [port]*
**Rockefeller,** Sharon Percy *LesBEnT 92*
**Rockefeller,** Sharon Percy 1944- *WhoAmP 91*
**Rockefeller,** Winthrop 1912-1973 *FacFETw*
**Rockemann,** David Douglas 1954- *WhoMW 92*
**Rockenstein,** William J 1949- *WhoIns 92*
**Rocker,** Tracy Quinton 1966- *WhoBlA 92*
**Rockermann,** Catherine Thompson 1961- *WhoAmL 92*
**Rockett,** D. Joe 1942- *WhoAmL 92*
**Rockett,** Damon Emerson 1938- *WhoBlA 92*
**Rockett,** John A 1922- *AmMWSc 92*
**Rockett,** Thomas John 1934- *AmMWSc 92*
**Rockett,** William Henry 1946- *WhoEnt 92*
**Rockette,** Howard Earl, Jr 1944- *AmMWSc 92*
**Rockey,** Dawn 1961- *WhoAmP 91, WhoMW 92*
**Rockey,** Jay *WhoFI 92*
**Rockey,** John Henry 1931- *AmMWSc 92*
**Rockfern,** Danielle *WrDr 92*
**Rockhampton,** Bishop of 1935- *Who 92*
**Rockhill,** Jack Kerrigan 1930- *WhoFI 92*
**Rockhill,** Theron D 1937- *AmMWSc 92*
**Rockhill,** William Woodville 1854-1914 *BilnAmS*
**Rockhold,** Lois M *WhoAmP 91*
**Rockhold,** Robin William 1951- *AmMWSc 92*
**Rockingham,** John 1911-1987 *FacFETw*
**Rocklage,** Mary Roch 1935- *WhoMW 92, WhoRel 92*
**Rocklage,** Norma, Sr. 1933- *WhoRel 92*
**Rockland,** Louis B 1919- *AmMWSc 92*
**Rockland,** Michael Aaron 1935- *WrDr 92*
**Rocklen,** Kathy Hellenbrand 1951- *WhoAmL 92, WhoFI 92*
**Rockler,** Walter James 1920- *WhoAmL 92*
**Rockley,** Baron 1934- *IntWW 91, Who 92*
**Rockley,** L. E. 1916- *WrDr 92*
**Rocklin,** Albert Louis 1921- *AmMWSc 92*
**Rocklin,** David Samuel 1931- *Who 92*
**Rocklin,** Isadore J 1907- *AmMWSc 92, WhoFI 92*
**Rocklin,** Ross E *AmMWSc 92*
**Rocklin,** Roy David 1953- *AmMWSc 92*
**Rocklynne,** Ross 1913-1988 *TwCSFW 91*
**Rockmore,** Ronald Marshall 1930- *AmMWSc 92*
**Rockne,** Knute 1888-1931 *FacFETw [port]*
**Rockne,** Sue Lorentzen 1934- *WhoAmP 91*
**Rockoff,** Maxine Lieberman 1938- *AmMWSc 92*
**Rockoff,** Seymour David 1931- *AmMWSc 92*
**Rockower,** Edward Brandt 1943- *AmMWSc 92*
**Rockowitz,** Noah Ezra 1949- *WhoAmL 92*
**Rocks,** James Engel 1939- *WhoMW 92*
**Rocks,** Judith Ann 1939- *WhoEnt 92*
**Rocks,** Lawrence 1933- *AmMWSc 92*
**Rocks,** Michael Joseph 1947- *WhoAmP 91*
**Rockstad,** Howard Kent 1935- *AmMWSc 92*
**Rockstein,** Morris 1916- *AmMWSc 92*
**Rockstroh,** Dennis John 1942- *WhoWest 92*
**Rockstroh,** Lenna M 1924- *WhoAmP 91*
**Rockstroh,** Todd Jay 1956- *AmMWSc 92*
**Rockstrom,** Albert Raymond 1917- *WhoWest 92*
**Rockwell,** Alfred Perkins 1834-1903 *BilnAmS*
**Rockwell,** Anne 1934- *WrDr 92*
**Rockwell,** Bruce Allen 1943- *WhoRel 92*
**Rockwell,** David Alan 1945- *AmMWSc 92*
**Rockwell,** Dennis Michael 1961- *WhoMW 92*
**Rockwell,** Don Arthur 1938- *WhoWest 92*
**Rockwell,** Donald O 1942- *AmMWSc 92*
**Rockwell,** Elizabeth Adams 1928- *WhoAmP 91*
**Rockwell,** Elizabeth Dennis 1921- *WhoFI 92*
**Rockwell,** Elizabeth Goode 1920- *WhoEnt 92*
**Rockwell,** George Lincoln 1918-1967 *BiDExR*
**Rockwell,** Hays Hamilton 1936- *WhoRel 92*
**Rockwell,** John 1940- *IntAu&W 91*
**Rockwell,** Julius, Jr 1918- *AmMWSc 92*
**Rockwell,** Kenneth H 1936- *AmMWSc 92*
**Rockwell,** Levon Irvin 1924- *WhoAmP 91*
**Rockwell,** Norman 1894-1978 *BenetAL 91*
**Rockwell,** Norman Perceval 1894-1978 *FacFETw*
**Rockwell,** Robert Franklin 1946- *AmMWSc 92*
**Rockwell,** Robert Goode 1922- *WhoWest 92*
**Rockwell,** Robert Lawrence 1935- *AmMWSc 92*
**Rockwell,** Sara Campbell 1943- *AmMWSc 92*
**Rockwell,** Steven Wayne 1954- *WhoMW 92*
**Rockwell,** Theodore 1922- *AmMWSc 92*
**Rockwell,** Thomas 1933- *WrDr 92*
**Rockwell,** Thomas H 1929- *AmMWSc 92*
**Rockwood,** Bruce Lindsley 1946- *WhoAmL 92*
**Rockwood,** Charles Greene, Jr 1843-1913 *BilnAmS*
**Rockwood,** Franklin Alexander 1936- *WhoFI 92*
**Rockwood,** Linda Lee 1950- *WhoAmL 92*
**Rockwood,** Roy *ScFEYrs, SmATA 67*
**Rockwood,** Stephen Dell 1943- *AmMWSc 92*
**Rockwood,** William Philip 1930- *AmMWSc 92*
**Rocque,** Vincent Joseph 1945- *WhoAmL 92*
**Rocz,** Ronald Noble Steven 1945- *WhoEnt 92*
**Rod,** David Lawrence 1938- *AmMWSc 92*
**Rod,** Janice Marie 1955- *WhoRel 92*
**Rodabaugh,** David Joseph 1938- *AmMWSc 92, WhoWest 92*
**Rodahl,** Kaare 1917- *AmMWSc 92, WrDr 92*
**Rodan,** Gideon Alfred 1934- *AmMWSc 92*
**Rodan,** Mendi 1929- *WhoEnt 92*
**Rodari,** Gianni 1920-1980 *ChlLR 24 [port]*
**Rodarte,** Joseph Robert 1938- *AmMWSc 92, WhoHisp 92*
**Rodbard,** David 1941- *AmMWSc 92*
**Rodbell,** Martin 1925- *AmMWSc 92*
**Rodchenko,** Aleksandr Mikhailovich 1891-1956 *FacFETw*
**Rodchenko,** Aleksandr Mikhaylovich 1891-1956 *SovUnBD*
**Rodd** *Who 92*
**Rodd,** John 1905- *WrDr 92*
**Rodd,** Marcia 1940- *WhoEnt 92*
**Rodda,** Bruce Edward 1942- *AmMWSc 92*
**Rodda,** Errol David 1928- *AmMWSc 92*
**Rodda,** James Erwin 1934- *WhoRel 92*
**Rodda,** Luca 1960- *WhoFI 92*
**Rodda,** Peter Ulisse 1929- *AmMWSc 92*
**Rodda,** Richard Earl 1945- *WhoEnt 92*
**Rodda,** Terrence 1944- *WhoEnt 92*
**Roddam,** Franc *WhoEnt 92*
**Roddam,** Franc 1946- *IntMPA 92*
**Roddan,** Gilbert McMicking d1990 *Who 92N*
**Roddan,** Ray Gene 1947- *WhoMW 92*
**Rodden,** Dennis John 1953- *WhoMW 92*
**Rodden,** Robert Morris 1922- *AmMWSc 92*
**Roddenberry,** Eugene Wesley 1921-1991 *ConAu 135, NewYTBS 91 [port]*
**Roddenberry,** Gene *ConAu 135*
**Roddenberry,** Gene d1991 *LesBEnT 92*
**Roddenberry,** Gene 1921- *IntMPA 92*
**Roddenberry,** Gene 1921-1991 *News 92-2*
**Roddewig,** Richard John 1948- *WhoMW 92*
**Roddey,** John Gardiner Richards 1937- *WhoFI 92*
**Roddick,** Alan 1937- *WrDr 92*
**Roddick,** Anita Lucia 1942- *IntWW 91*
**Roddick,** David Bruce 1948- *WhoWest 92*
**Roddick,** James Archibald 1925- *AmMWSc 92*
**Roddick,** John William, Jr 1926- *AmMWSc 92*
**Roddick,** Winston 1940- *Who 92*
**Roddie,** Ian Campbell 1928- *IntWW 91, Who 92*
**Roddis,** Louis H., Jr. d1991 *NewYTBS 91*
**Roddis,** Louis Harry, Jr 1918- *AmMWSc 92, IntWW 91*
**Roddis,** Richard Stiles Law 1930- *WhoIns 92*
**Roddis,** Winifred Mary Kim *AmMWSc 92*
**Roddy,** David John 1932- *AmMWSc 92*
**Roddy,** Howard W. 1950- *WhoBlA 92*
**Roddy,** Lee 1921- *WrDr 92*
**Roddy,** Martin Thomas 1946- *AmMWSc 92*
**Rode,** Daniel Leon 1942- *AmMWSc 92*
**Rode,** Ebbe 1910- *IntWW 91*
**Rode,** Helle 1954- *WhoAmL 92*
**Rode,** James Dean 1948- *WhoFI 92, WhoMW 92*
**Rode,** Jonathan Pace 1948- *AmMWSc 92*
**Rode,** Larry Jon 1960- *WhoAmP 91*
**Rode,** Mary Wilbur 1942- *WhoMW 92*
**Rodeback,** George Wayne 1921- *AmMWSc 92*
**Rodeck,** Charles Henry 1944- *Who 92*
**Rodeck,** Willard Martin 1929- *WhoMW 92*
**Rodee,** Bernard Leslie 1958- *WhoMW 92*
**Rodefer,** Stephen 1940- *ConPo 91, IntAu&W 91, WrDr 92*
**Rodeiro,** Jose Manuel 1949- *WhoHisp 92*
**Rodela,** Leo E 1932- *WhoAmP 91*
**Rodell,** Charles Franklin 1942- *AmMWSc 92*
**Rodell,** Michael Byron 1932- *AmMWSc 92*
**Rodell,** Timothy Clarke 1951- *WhoWest 92*
**Rodeman,** Frederick Ernest 1938- *WhoMW 92*
**Rodeman,** Richard Dean 1953- *WhoAmL 92*
**Rodemeyer,** Stephen A 1940- *AmMWSc 92*
**Rodems,** James D 1926- *AmMWSc 92*
**Roden,** Earl of 1909- *Who 92*
**Roden,** Gunnar Ivo 1928- *AmMWSc 92*
**Roden,** Johanna Wahl 1928- *WhoWest 92*
**Rodenberger,** Charles Alvard 1926- *AmMWSc 92*
**Rodenburg,** Clifton Glenn 1949- *WhoAmL 92*
**Rodenhauser,** Paul 1937- *WhoMW 92*
**Rodenhuis,** David Roy 1936- *AmMWSc 92*
**Rodenstock,** Rudolf 1917- *IntWW 91*
**Roder,** Hans Martin 1930- *AmMWSc 92*
**Roderick,** Caerwyn Eifion 1927- *Who 92*
**Roderick,** Charles Edward Morys 1910- *Who 92*
**Roderick,** Charles Elmer 1931- *WhoFI 92*
**Roderick,** David Milton 1924- *IntWW 91*
**Roderick,** Gerald John 1924- *WhoAmP 91*
**Roderick,** Gilbert Leroy 1933- *AmMWSc 92*
**Roderick,** John R 1926- *WhoAmP 91*
**Roderick,** Thomas Huston 1930- *AmMWSc 92*
**Roderick,** William Rodney 1933- *AmMWSc 92*
**Roderuck,** Charlotte Elizabeth 1919- *AmMWSc 92*
**Roderus,** Frank 1942- *TwCWW 91, WrDr 92*
**Rodes,** John Edward 1923- *WrDr 92*
**Rodes,** Robert Emmet, Jr. 1927- *WhoAmL 92*
**Rodeschin,** Beverly T 1936- *WhoAmP 91*
**Rodesiler,** Paul Frederick 1941- *AmMWSc 92*
**Rodewald,** James Michael 1942- *WhoMW 92*
**Rodewald,** Lynn B 1939- *AmMWSc 92*
**Rodewald,** Paul Gerhard, Jr 1936- *AmMWSc 92*
**Rodewald,** Richard David 1944- *AmMWSc 92*
**Rodey,** Glenn Eugene 1936- *AmMWSc 92*
**Rodey,** Patrick Michael 1943- *WhoAmP 91, WhoWest 92*
**Rodez,** Andrew LaMarr 1931- *WhoBlA 92*
**Rodger,** Alan Ferguson 1944- *Who 92*
**Rodger,** Allan George 1902- *Who 92*
**Rodger,** George William Adam 1908- *IntWW 91*
**Rodger,** Patrick Campbell 1920- *Who 92*
**Rodger,** Stanley Joseph 1940- *IntWW 91*
**Rodger,** William Glendinning d1990 *Who 92N*
**Rodgers,** Alan Shortridge 1931- *AmMWSc 92*
**Rodgers,** Alice Lynn 1942- *WhoFI 92*
**Rodgers,** Andrew Piers 1944- *Who 92*
**Rodgers,** Anthony Recarido, Sr. 1951- *WhoBlA 92*
**Rodgers,** Aubrey 1929- *AmMWSc 92*
**Rodgers,** Augustus 1945- *WhoBlA 92*
**Rodgers,** Barbara Lorraine 1946- *WhoBlA 92*
**Rodgers,** Barbara Noel 1912- *Who 92*
**Rodgers,** Beverly 1954- *WhoAmP 91*
**Rodgers,** Billy Russell 1936- *AmMWSc 92*
**Rodgers,** Bradley Moreland 1942- *AmMWSc 92*
**Rodgers,** Buck 1938- *WhoWest 92*
**Rodgers,** Carolyn M. *DrAPF 91, IntAu&W 91, WrDr 92*
**Rodgers,** Carolyn M. 1945- *ConPo 91*

**Rodgers,** Carolyn Marie 1943- *WhoBlA 92*
**Rodgers,** Charles 1941- *WhoBlA 92*
**Rodgers,** Charles H 1932- *AmMWSc 92*
**Rodgers,** David Marlie 1945- *WhoRel 92*
**Rodgers,** Debbie Dee 1955- *WhoMW 92*
**Rodgers,** Del 1960- *WhoBlA 92*
**Rodgers,** Earl Gilbert 1921- *AmMWSc 92*
**Rodgers,** Edward 1927- *WhoBlA 92*
**Rodgers,** Edward J 1923- *AmMWSc 92*
**Rodgers,** Frank Gerald 1946- *AmMWSc 92*
**Rodgers,** Franklin C. 1931- *ConAu 133*
**Rodgers,** Frederic Barker 1940- *WhoAmL 92, WhoWest 92*
**Rodgers,** G Philip 1928- *WhoAmP 91*
**Rodgers,** George 1925- *Who 92*
**Rodgers,** Glen Ernest 1944- *AmMWSc 92*
**Rodgers,** Guy William, Jr. 1935- *WhoBlA 92*
**Rodgers,** Harold William 1907- *Who 92*
**Rodgers,** Horace J. 1925- *WhoBlA 92*
**Rodgers,** James Earl 1943- *AmMWSc 92*
**Rodgers,** James Edward 1938- *AmMWSc 92*
**Rodgers,** James R. 1947- *WhoBlA 92*
**Rodgers,** Jerome Thomas 1943- *WhoFI 92*
**Rodgers,** Jim *WhoMW 92*
**Rodgers,** Jimmie 1897-1933 *NewAmDM*
**Rodgers,** Joan 1956- *IntWW 91*
**Rodgers,** Joe 1933- *IntWW 91*
**Rodgers,** Joe M 1933- *WhoAmP 91*
**Rodgers,** John 1812-1882 *BiInAmS*
**Rodgers,** John 1906- *Who 92, WrDr 92*
**Rodgers,** John 1914- *AmMWSc 92, IntWW 91*
**Rodgers,** John Anthony, III 1938- *WhoFI 92*
**Rodgers,** John Barclay, Jr 1933- *AmMWSc 92*
**Rodgers,** John Hunter 1944- *WhoAmL 92*
**Rodgers,** John James 1930- *AmMWSc 92*
**Rodgers,** John M 1928- *WhoAmP 91*
**Rodgers,** Johnathan *LesBEnT 92*
**Rodgers,** Johnathan 1946- *WhoEnt 92, WhoMW 92*
**Rodgers,** Johnathan A. 1946- *WhoBlA 92*
**Rodgers,** Joseph James, Jr. 1939- *WhoBlA 92*
**Rodgers,** Kyle L. 1958- *WhoRel 92*
**Rodgers,** Lawrence Rodney, Sr 1920- *AmMWSc 92*
**Rodgers,** Louis Dean 1930- *WhoMW 92*
**Rodgers,** Mary 1931- *IntAu&W 91, NewAmDM, WhoEnt 92, WrDr 92*
**Rodgers,** Michael A J 1936- *AmMWSc 92*
**Rodgers,** Napoleon *WhoBlA 92*
**Rodgers,** Nelson Earl 1915- *AmMWSc 92*
**Rodgers,** Patricia Elaine Joan *IntWW 91*
**Rodgers,** Patricia Elaine Joan 1948- *Who 92*
**Rodgers,** Paul Baxter, III 1952- *WhoAmL 92*
**Rodgers,** Pepper *ConAu 133*
**Rodgers,** Piers *Who 92*
**Rodgers,** Ralph Emerson 1954- *WhoAmL 92*
**Rodgers,** Raymond Gene 1936- *WhoWest 92*
**Rodgers,** Richard 1902-1979 *BenetAL 91, FacFETw, NewAmDM*
**Rodgers,** Richard Michael 1945- *AmMWSc 92*
**Rodgers,** Robert Albert 1957- *WhoEnt 92*
**Rodgers,** Robert Stanleigh 1945- *AmMWSc 92*
**Rodgers,** Rod Audrian 1937- *WhoBlA 92*
**Rodgers,** Sarah *DrAPF 91*
**Rodgers,** Sarah Jane 1927- *WhoAmP 91*
**Rodgers,** Sheridan Joseph 1929- *AmMWSc 92*
**Rodgers,** Shirlaw Johnston *TwCWW 91*
**Rodgers,** Shirley Marie 1948- *WhoBlA 92*
**Rodgers,** W.R. 1909-1969 *RfGEnL 91*
**Rodgers,** Warren Lee 1950- *WhoAmP 91*
**Rodgers,** William 1928- *FacFETw*
**Rodgers,** William M., Jr. 1941- *WhoBlA 92*
**Rodgers,** William Thomas 1928- *IntWW 91, Who 92*
**Rodgman,** Alan 1924- *AmMWSc 92*
**Rodia,** Jacob Stephen 1923- *AmMWSc 92*
**Rodiani,** Onorata d1472 *EncAmaz 91*
**Rodibaugh,** Robert Kurtz 1916- *WhoAmL 92*
**Rodieck,** Robert William 1937- *AmMWSc 92*
**Rodier,** Michael Xavier 1959- *WhoFI 92*
**Rodig,** Oscar Rudolf 1929- *AmMWSc 92*
**Rodiger,** W. Gregory, III 1959- *WhoFI 92*
**Rodimer,** Frank Joseph 1927- *WhoRel 92*
**Rodin,** Alvin E 1926- *AmMWSc 92*
**Rodin,** Burton 1933- *AmMWSc 92*
**Rodin,** Ervin Y 1932- *AmMWSc 92*
**Rodin,** Judith 1944- *AmMWSc 92, IntWW 91*
**Rodin,** Martha Kinscher 1929- *AmMWSc 92*
**Rodin,** Yury Leo 1936- *WhoMW 92*
**Rodin-Novak,** Sheila Karen 1947- *WhoEnt 92*
**Rodine,** Robert Henry 1929- *AmMWSc 92*
**Rodini,** Benjamin Thomas, Jr 1947- *AmMWSc 92*
**Rodino,** Peter Wallace, Jr. 1909- *IntWW 91, WhoAmP 91*
**Rodino,** Vincent Louis 1929- *WhoFI 92*
**Rodio,** Stephen Albert 1957- *WhoAmL 92*
**Rodionov,** Aleksey Alekseyevich 1922- *IntWW 91*
**Rodisch,** Robert Joseph 1919- *WhoRel 92*
**Roditi,** Edouard 1910- *ConAu 14AS [port], ConPo 91, WrDr 92*
**Rodkey,** Frederick Lee 1919- *AmMWSc 92*
**Rodkey,** Frederick Stanley, Jr. 1930- *WhoAmL 92, WhoMW 92*
**Rodkey,** Leo Scott 1941- *AmMWSc 92*
**Rodkiewicz,** Czeslaw Mateusz *AmMWSc 92*
**Rodkin,** Henry Hollison 1935- *WhoMW 92*
**Rodman,** Alpine Clarence 1952- *WhoFI 92, WhoWest 92*
**Rodman,** Charles William 1928- *AmMWSc 92*
**Rodman,** Dale A. 1940- *WhoMW 92*
**Rodman,** David Lawrence 1956- *WhoFI 92*
**Rodman,** Dennis 1961?- *News 91 [port], -91-3 [port]*
**Rodman,** Dennis Keith 1961- *WhoBlA 92*
**Rodman,** Ellen Rena 1940- *WhoEnt 92*
**Rodman,** Eric *ConAu 36NR*
**Rodman,** George Robinson 1948- *WhoEnt 92*
**Rodman,** Harvey Meyer 1940- *AmMWSc 92*
**Rodman,** Howard A. *ConLC 65 [port]*
**Rodman,** Howard Andrew 1950- *WhoEnt 92*
**Rodman,** James Purcell 1926- *AmMWSc 92, WhoMW 92*
**Rodman,** John Gray 1951- *WhoEnt 92*
**Rodman,** Lawrence Bernard 1949- *WhoAmL 92*
**Rodman,** Maia *DrAPF 91*
**Rodman,** Morton Joseph 1918- *AmMWSc 92*
**Rodman,** Nathaniel Fulford, Jr 1926- *AmMWSc 92*
**Rodman,** Selden 1909- *BenetAL 91*
**Rodman,** Sue Arlene 1951- *WhoFI 92, WhoWest 92*
**Rodman,** Toby C 1918- *AmMWSc 92*
**Rodman,** William Louis 1858-1916 *BiInAmS*
**Rodne,** Kjell John 1948- *WhoMW 92*
**Rodney** *Who 92*
**Rodney,** Baron 1920- *Who 92*
**Rodney,** David Ross 1919- *AmMWSc 92*
**Rodney,** Earl 1933- *WhoFI 92*
**Rodney,** Earnest Abram 1917- *AmMWSc 92*
**Rodney,** Janet *DrAPF 91*
**Rodney,** Karl Basil 1940- *WhoBlA 92*
**Rodney,** Martin Hurtus 1909- *WhoBlA 92*
**Rodney,** William 1923- *WrDr 92*
**Rodney,** William Stanley 1926- *AmMWSc 92*
**Rodnina,** Irina 1953- *FacFETw*
**Rodnina,** Irina Konstantinovna 1949- *SovUnBD*
**Rodning,** Charles Bernard 1943- *AmMWSc 92*
**Rodolff,** Dale Ward 1938- *WhoFI 92*
**Rodolfo,** Kelvin S 1936- *AmMWSc 92*
**Rodos,** Joseph Jerry 1933- *WhoMW 92*
**Rodosovich,** Peter 1959- *WhoAmP 91*
**Rodov,** Semen Abramovich 1893-1968 *SovUnBD*
**Rodovich,** Andrew Paul 1948- *WhoAmL 92*
**Rodowskas,** Christopher A, Jr 1939- *AmMWSc 92*
**Rodowsky,** Lawrence F *WhoAmP 91*
**Rodowsky,** Lawrence Francis 1930- *WhoAmL 92*
**Rodrick,** Gary Eugene 1943- *AmMWSc 92*
**Rodrick,** Mary Lofy *AmMWSc 92*
**Rodricks,** Daniel J. 1954- *ConAu 133*
**Rodricks,** Joseph Victor 1938- *AmMWSc 92*
**Rodrigo,** Joaquin 1901- *FacFETw, NewAmDM*
**Rodrigo,** Russell Godfrey *AmMWSc 92*
**Rodrigo,** Thomas James 1950- *WhoHisp 92*
**Rodrigue,** Christine M. 1952- *WhoWest 92*
**Rodrigue,** George Pierre 1931- *AmMWSc 92*
**Rodrigues,** Alberto 1911- *Who 92*
**Rodrigues,** Alfred Benjamin Kameeiamoku 1947- *WhoWest 92*
**Rodrigues,** Antonio S. *WhoHisp 92*
**Rodrigues,** David M. 1945- *WhoHisp 92*
**Rodrigues,** Mark 1948- *WhoWest 92*
**Rodrigues,** Merlyn M 1938- *AmMWSc 92*
**Rodriguez,** Abel Tomas, Sr. 1942- *WhoHisp 92*
**Rodriguez,** Adna Rosa 1934- *WhoHisp 92*
**Rodriguez,** Albert Ray 1960- *WhoHisp 92*
**Rodriguez,** Albert S. 1933- *WhoHisp 92*
**Rodriguez,** Alberto F 1945- *WhoIns 92*
**Rodriguez,** Alberto M. 1942- *WhoHisp 92*
**Rodriguez,** Aleida *DrAPF 91*
**Rodriguez,** Alex *WhoHisp 92*
**Rodriguez,** Alfonso Camarillo 1938- *WhoHisp 92*
**Rodriguez,** Alfredo *WhoHisp 92*
**Rodriguez,** Alma Delia 1965- *WhoHisp 92*
**Rodriguez,** Alonzo T. *WhoHisp 92*
**Rodriguez,** Amador *WhoHisp 92*
**Rodriguez,** Ana Milagros 1949- *WhoHisp 92*
**Rodriguez,** Andres 1923- *CurBio 91 [port]*
**Rodriguez,** Andres 1924- *IntWW 91*
**Rodriguez,** Andres F 1929- *AmMWSc 92, WhoHisp 92*
**Rodriguez,** Andres Fraga 1929- *WhoWest 92*
**Rodriguez,** Angel Alfredo 1941- *WhoHisp 92*
**Rodriguez,** Angel Edgardo 1949- *WhoHisp 92*
**Rodriguez,** Angel R. 1934- *WhoHisp 92*
**Rodriguez,** Antonio David 1957- *WhoHisp 92*
**Rodriguez,** Argelia Velez 1936- *AmMWSc 92*
**Rodriguez,** Ariel A. 1947- *WhoHisp 92*
**Rodriguez,** Armando M. 1921- *WhoHisp 92*
**Rodriguez,** Armando Osorio 1929- *WhoHisp 92*
**Rodriguez,** Art A. 1958- *WhoHisp 92*
**Rodriguez,** Augusto 1954- *AmMWSc 92, WhoHisp 92*
**Rodriguez,** Aurelio 1947- *WhoHisp 92*
**Rodriguez,** Aurora 1940- *WhoHisp 92*
**Rodriguez,** Bartolo G. *WhoHisp 92*
**Rodriguez,** Beatriz *WhoEnt 92*
**Rodriguez,** Beatriz 1951- *WhoHisp 92*
**Rodriguez,** Belgica 1941- *WhoHisp 92*
**Rodriguez,** Ben *WhoHisp 92*
**Rodriguez,** Benjamin 1938- *WhoHisp 92*
**Rodriguez,** Benjamin, Jr. 1943- *WhoHisp 92*
**Rodriguez,** Carlos Augusto 1954- *WhoAmL 92*
**Rodriguez,** Carlos Eduardo 1941- *AmMWSc 92, WhoHisp 92*
**Rodriguez,** Carlos J. 1941- *WhoHisp 92*
**Rodriguez,** Carmen M. 1950- *WhoHisp 92*
**Rodriguez,** Carmen N. 1957- *WhoHisp 92*
**Rodriguez,** Cesar 1945- *WhoHisp 92*
**Rodriguez,** Charles 1942- *WhoHisp 92*
**Rodriguez,** Charles 1947- *WhoHisp 92*
**Rodriguez,** Charles F 1938- *AmMWSc 92, WhoHisp 92*
**Rodriguez,** Chi Chi 1935- *WhoHisp 92*
**Rodriguez,** Cipriano Facundo 1907- *WhoHisp 92*
**Rodriguez,** Ciro D 1946- *WhoAmP 91, WhoHisp 92*
**Rodriguez,** Clara Elsie 1944- *WhoHisp 92*
**Rodriguez,** Daniel 1965- *WhoHisp 92*
**Rodriguez,** Daniel B. 1962- *WhoAmL 92*
**Rodriguez,** Daniel R. *WhoHisp 92*
**Rodriguez,** Danny Fajardo 1949- *WhoHisp 92*
**Rodriguez,** David Arthur 1946- *WhoHisp 92*
**Rodriguez,** Dennis Milton 1943- *AmMWSc 92*
**Rodriguez,** Desiderio, Sr. 1942- *WhoHisp 92*
**Rodriguez,** Domingo 1939- *WhoHisp 92*
**Rodriguez,** Domingo Antonio *WhoHisp 92*
**Rodriguez,** Doris L. 1927- *WhoBlA 92*
**Rodriguez,** Douglas Luis *BlkOlyM*
**Rodriguez,** Edmundo 1935- *WhoHisp 92*
**Rodriguez,** Eduardo 1957- *WhoHisp 92*
**Rodriguez,** Eduardo Ariel 1955- *WhoAmL 92, WhoHisp 92*
**Rodriguez,** Eduardo L. 1944- *WhoHisp 92*
**Rodriguez,** Eladio Rafael 1937- *WhoHisp 92*
**Rodriguez,** Eli Monserrate 1946- *WhoHisp 92*
**Rodriguez,** Elias *WhoHisp 92*
**Rodriguez,** Eliott 1956- *WhoHisp 92*
**Rodriguez,** Elisa 1936- *WhoHisp 92*
**Rodriguez,** Elizabeth 1953- *WhoHisp 92*
**Rodriguez,** Elmer Arturo 1934- *WhoHisp 92*
**Rodriguez,** Eloy 1947- *WhoHisp 92, WhoWest 92*
**Rodriguez,** Emma Jean 1944- *WhoHisp 92*
**Rodriguez,** Eriberto G. 1928- *WhoHisp 92*
**Rodriguez,** Ernesto Angelo 1947- *WhoHisp 92*
**Rodriguez,** Ernesto Jesus 1954- *WhoHisp 92*
**Rodriguez,** Eugene 1933- *AmMWSc 92*
**Rodriguez,** Eugene 1940- *WhoHisp 92*
**Rodriguez,** Eva I. 1948- *WhoHisp 92*
**Rodriguez,** Federico G. 1939- *WhoHisp 92*
**Rodriguez,** Felipe, Jr. *WhoHisp 92*
**Rodriguez,** Felipe N. *WhoHisp 92*
**Rodriguez,** Ferdinand 1928- *AmMWSc 92, WhoHisp 92*
**Rodriguez,** Florence Ann 1954- *WhoHisp 92*
**Rodriguez,** Francisco 1959- *WhoHisp 92*
**Rodriguez,** Francisco 1966- *WhoHisp 92*
**Rodriguez,** Frank John 1920- *WhoAmP 91*
**Rodriguez,** Fred 1949- *WhoHisp 92*
**Rodriguez,** Frederick Marshall 1938- *WhoHisp 92*
**Rodriguez,** Galindo 1955- *WhoHisp 92*
**Rodriguez,** Gilbert 1941- *WhoHisp 92*
**Rodriguez,** Gilberto 1929- *AmMWSc 92*
**Rodriguez,** Gilda Ena 1952- *WhoAmL 92*
**Rodriguez,** Gloria G. 1948- *WhoHisp 92, WhoRel 92*
**Rodriguez,** Gregorio 1946- *WhoHisp 92*
**Rodriguez,** Guillermo 1956- *WhoHisp 92*
**Rodriguez,** Guillermo, Jr. 1968- *WhoHisp 92*
**Rodriguez,** Guisella 1959- *WhoHisp 92*
**Rodriguez,** Gustavo Adolfo 1949- *WhoHisp 92*
**Rodriguez,** Harold Vernon 1932- *AmMWSc 92*
**Rodriguez,** Hector Manuel 1949- *WhoAmL 92*
**Rodriguez,** Hector Philip 1956- *WhoHisp 92*
**Rodriguez,** Hector R. 1938- *WhoHisp 92*
**Rodriguez,** Henry, Jr. 1955- *WhoHisp 92*
**Rodriguez,** Heriberto, III 1958- *WhoHisp 92*
**Rodriguez,** Hiram *WhoHisp 92*
**Rodriguez,** Homer *WhoHisp 92*
**Rodriguez,** Hugo A. 1950- *WhoHisp 92*
**Rodriguez,** Humberto 1931- *WhoHisp 92*
**Rodriguez,** Isabel Lorraine *WhoHisp 92*
**Rodriguez,** Israel I. 1937- *WhoHisp 92*
**Rodriguez,** Jacinto 1932- *AmMWSc 92, WhoHisp 92*
**Rodriguez,** Jacqueline Caridad 1967- *WhoHisp 92*
**Rodriguez,** James 1956- *WhoHisp 92*
**Rodriguez,** James J. 1946- *WhoAmL 92*
**Rodriguez,** Jerry Wayne 1938- *WhoMW 92*
**Rodriguez,** Jesse 1942- *WhoHisp 92*
**Rodriguez,** Jesus Gene 1952- *WhoHisp 92*
**Rodriguez,** Jesus Jorge 1946- *WhoHisp 92*
**Rodriguez,** Jesus Rafael 1960- *WhoHisp 92*
**Rodriguez,** Jesus Ybarra 1945- *WhoHisp 92*
**Rodriguez,** Joaquin 1934- *AmMWSc 92*
**Rodriguez,** Joe D. 1943- *WhoHisp 92*
**Rodriguez,** John 1958- *WhoHisp 92*
**Rodriguez,** John C., Jr. 1930- *WhoHisp 92*
**Rodriguez,** John H. *WhoHisp 92*
**Rodriguez,** John Perez 1959- *WhoHisp 92*
**Rodriguez,** Johnny *WhoHisp 92*
**Rodriguez,** Johnny 1952- *WhoHisp 92*
**Rodriguez,** Jorge 1950- *WhoHisp 92*
**Rodriguez,** Jorge 1956- *WhoHisp 92*
**Rodriguez,** Jorge Luis 1940- *AmMWSc 92*
**Rodriguez,** Jorge Luis 1944- *WhoHisp 92*
**Rodriguez,** Jorge Luis 1957- *WhoHisp 92*
**Rodriguez,** Jose 1949- *WhoHisp 92*
**Rodriguez,** Jose Cayetano 1761-1823 *HisDSpE*
**Rodriguez,** Jose Enrique 1933- *AmMWSc 92, WhoHisp 92*
**Rodriguez,** Jose G. 1945- *WhoHisp 92*
**Rodriguez,** Jose Guillermo 1956- *WhoAmP 91*
**Rodriguez,** Jose Luis *WhoHisp 92*
**Rodriguez,** Jose R. 1959- *WhoHisp 92*
**Rodriguez,** Joseph H. *WhoHisp 92*
**Rodriguez,** Joseph H. 1930- *WhoAmL 92*
**Rodriguez,** Joseph Lawerence 1952- *WhoHisp 92*
**Rodriguez,** Joyce Katherine 1963- *WhoEnt 92*
**Rodriguez,** Juan Alfonso 1941- *WhoHisp 92*
**Rodriguez,** Juan Antonio, Jr. 1946- *WhoHisp 92*
**Rodriguez,** Juan G. 1920- *WhoHisp 92*
**Rodriguez,** Juan Guadalupe 1920- *AmMWSc 92*
**Rodriguez,** Juan J. 1951- *WhoHisp 92*
**Rodriguez,** Juan Manuel 1771-1843 *HisDSpE*
**Rodriguez,** Juan Manuel 1957- *WhoFI 92*
**Rodriguez,** Juan N. 1948- *WhoHisp 92*
**Rodriguez,** Judith 1936- *ConPo 91, WrDr 92*
**Rodriguez,** Julia Garced 1929- *WhoHisp 92*
**Rodriguez,** Julian Saenz 1938- *WhoHisp 92*
**Rodriguez,** Julio 1935- *WhoHisp 92*
**Rodriguez,** Kenneth Leigh 1959- *WhoHisp 92*
**Rodriguez,** Kyrsis Raquel 1948- *WhoHisp 92*
**Rodriguez,** Leonard 1944- *WhoWest 92*
**Rodriguez,** Leonardo 1938- *WhoHisp 92*
**Rodriguez,** Lina S. 1949- *WhoHisp 92*

**Rodriguez**, Lorraine Ditzler 1920- *AmMWSc 92*
**Rodriguez**, Louis J. 1933- *WhoHisp 92*
**Rodriguez**, Luis 1944- *WhoHisp 92*
**Rodriguez**, Luis F 1947- *AmMWSc 92*
**Rodriguez**, Luis Francisco 1953- *WhoHisp 92*
**Rodriguez**, Lula *WhoHisp 92*
**Rodriguez**, Lynne Roxanne 1954- *WhoBlA 92*
**Rodriguez**, Manuel *WhoHisp 92*
**Rodriguez**, Manuel H. 1930- *WhoHisp 92*
**Rodriguez**, Manuel J. 1935- *WhoHisp 92*
**Rodriguez**, Marcos *WhoHisp 92*
**Rodriguez**, Maria Carla 1954- *WhoHisp 92*
**Rodriguez**, Maria del Pilar *WhoHisp 92*
**Rodriguez**, Maria Martinez 1945- *WhoHisp 92*
**Rodriguez**, Maria Teresa 1953- *WhoHisp 92*
**Rodriguez**, Marie R. 1961- *WhoHisp 92*
**Rodriguez**, Mario J. 1932- *WhoHisp 92*
**Rodriguez**, Mark Gregory 1957- *WhoHisp 92*
**Rodriguez**, Matt L. 1936- *WhoHisp 92*
**Rodriguez**, Meriemil 1940- *WhoHisp 92*
**Rodriguez**, Michael Reynaldo 1957- *WhoHisp 92*
**Rodriguez**, Miguel *WhoHisp 92*
**Rodriguez**, Miguel 1931- *WhoRel 92*
**Rodriguez**, Miguel E., Jr. 1934- *WhoHisp 92*
**Rodriguez**, Mike Angel 1957- *WhoHisp 92*
**Rodriguez**, Milagros 1947- *WhoHisp 92*
**Rodriguez**, Milton A. 1951- *WhoHisp 92*
**Rodriguez**, Moises 1958- *WhoRel 92*
**Rodriguez**, Nancy E. 1953- *WhoHisp 92*
**Rodriguez**, Nicolas 1897-1940 *BiDExR*
**Rodriguez**, Nilda Ocasio de 1943- *WhoHisp 92*
**Rodriguez**, Norma Kristine 1966- *WhoHisp 92*
**Rodriguez**, Pablo 1955- *WhoHisp 92*
**Rodriguez**, Pascual *WhoHisp 92*
**Rodriguez**, Patricia Ann 1958- *WhoHisp 92*
**Rodriguez**, Paul *WhoHisp 92*
**Rodriguez**, Paul E. 1956- *WhoHisp 92*
**Rodriguez**, Paul Henry 1937- *WhoHisp 92*
**Rodriguez**, Paul Lopez 1939- *WhoHisp 92*
**Rodriguez**, Paul R. *WhoHisp 92*
**Rodriguez**, Pedro *WhoHisp 92*
**Rodriguez**, Peter 1926- *WhoHisp 92*
**Rodriguez**, Peter Ernest 1950- *WhoHisp 92*
**Rodriguez**, Placido 1940- *WhoRel 92*
**Rodriguez**, Plinio A. 1942- *WhoHisp 92*
**Rodriguez**, Rafael *BlkOlyM*
**Rodriguez**, Ralph *WhoHisp 92*
**Rodriguez**, Ramon *WhoHisp 92*
**Rodriguez**, Ramon 1921- *WhoHisp 92*
**Rodriguez**, Ramon J. 1950- *WhoHisp 92*
**Rodriguez**, Ramon Joe 1934- *WhoHisp 92*
**Rodriguez**, Raul G. 1952- *WhoHisp 92*
**Rodriguez**, Ray 1951- *WhoEnt 92*
**Rodriguez**, Ray Cortez 1929- *WhoHisp 92*
**Rodriguez**, Raymond *WhoEnt 92*
**Rodriguez**, Raymond Mendoza 1924- *WhoHisp 92*
**Rodriguez**, Rene Mauricio 1946- *WhoHisp 92*
**Rodriguez**, Rene R., Jr. 1962- *WhoHisp 92*
**Rodriguez**, Renee Gonzalez *WhoHisp 92*
**Rodriguez**, Reynaldo, Jr. 1944- *WhoRel 92*
**Rodriguez**, Rich 1963- *WhoHisp 92*
**Rodriguez**, Richard Antonio 1942- *WhoHisp 92*
**Rodriguez**, Richard Fajardo 1945- *WhoHisp 92*
**Rodriguez**, Richard Garcia 1958- *WhoWest 92*
**Rodriguez**, Rick 1954- *WhoHisp 92*
**Rodriguez**, Rita D. 1956- *WhoHisp 92*
**Rodriguez**, Rita M. 1942- *WhoHisp 92*
**Rodriguez**, Robert A. 1946- *WhoHisp 92*
**Rodriguez**, Robert H. *WhoHisp 92*
**Rodriguez**, Robert J. 1962- *WhoHisp 92*
**Rodriguez**, Robert Xavier 1946- *NewAmDM*
**Rodriguez**, Roberta Ann 1957- *WhoHisp 92*
**Rodriguez**, Roberto R. 1942- *WhoHisp 92*
**Rodriguez**, Rocio A. 1952- *WhoHisp 92*
**Rodriguez**, Rocio del Pilar *AmMWSc 92*
**Rodriguez**, Rodd *WhoHisp 92*
**Rodriguez**, Rodney Tapanes 1946- *WhoHisp 92*
**Rodriguez**, Rodri Josefina 1955- *WhoHisp 92*
**Rodriguez**, Rolando Damian 1957- *WhoHisp 92*
**Rodriguez**, Roman 1951- *WhoWest 92*
**Rodriguez**, Ronald 1954- *WhoHisp 92*
**Rodriguez**, Rosa M. 1955- *WhoHisp 92*
**Rodriguez**, Rosario 1969- *WhoHisp 92*
**Rodriguez**, Ruben *WhoHisp 92*
**Rodriguez**, Rudy, Jr. *WhoHisp 92*
**Rodriguez**, Russell A. 1957- *WhoHisp 92*
**Rodriguez**, Sebastian James 1936- *WhoHisp 92*
**Rodriguez**, Sergio 1930- *AmMWSc 92, WhoHisp 92*
**Rodriguez**, Simon Yldefonso 1928- *WhoHisp 92*
**Rodriguez**, Sylvan Robert, Jr. 1948- *WhoHisp 92*
**Rodriguez**, Sylvia B. 1947- *WhoHisp 92*
**Rodriguez**, Sylvia G 1941- *WhoAmP 91*
**Rodriguez**, Teresa *WhoHisp 92*
**Rodriguez**, Thomas Richard 1947- *WhoHisp 92*
**Rodriguez**, Tony *WhoHisp 92*
**Rodriguez**, Valerio Sierra 1922- *WhoHisp 92*
**Rodriguez**, Vicente *WhoHisp 92*
**Rodriguez**, Victor *WhoAmP 91, WhoHisp 92*
**Rodriguez**, Victor David 1942- *WhoHisp 92*
**Rodriguez**, Vincent Angel 1921- *WhoHisp 92*
**Rodriguez**, Walter Enrique 1948- *WhoHisp 92*
**Rodriguez**, Ward Arthur 1948- *WhoHisp 92*
**Rodriguez**, William Robert *DrAPF 91*
**Rodriguez**, Yolanda *WhoHisp 92*
**Rodriguez-Borges**, Carlina 1952- *WhoHisp 92*
**Rodriguez Cabrillo**, Juan *HisDSpE*
**Rodriguez-Camilloni**, Humberto Leonardo 1945- *WhoHisp 92*
**Rodriguez Campomanes**, Pedro 1723-1803 *HisDSpE*
**Rodriguez Campos**, Orestes 1927- *IntWW 91*
**Rodriguez-Cintron**, William 1959- *WhoHisp 92*
**Rodriguez Colon**, Charles Anthony 1954- *WhoAmP 91*
**Rodriguez de Francia**, Jose Gaspar *HisDSpE*
**Rodriguez-del Valle**, Nuri 1945- *WhoHisp 92*
**Rodriguez De Yurre**, Prudencio 1941- *WhoHisp 92*
**Rodriguez-Diaz**, Juan E. 1941- *WhoAmL 92*
**Rodriguez-Erdmann**, Franz 1935- *WhoHisp 92*
**Rodriguez-Florido**, Jorge Julio 1943- *WhoHisp 92*
**Rodriguez Fonseca**, Juan de *HisDSpE*
**Rodriguez Freile**, Juan 1566-1638 *HisDSpE*
**Rodriguez-Garcia**, Frank 1934- *WhoAmP 91*
**Rodriguez Graf**, Barbara Ann 1956- *WhoHisp 92*
**Rodriguez Hernandez**, Aurea E. 1948- *WhoHisp 92*
**Rodriguez-Holguin**, Jeanette 1954- *WhoHisp 92*
**Rodriguez-Howard**, Mayra *WhoHisp 92*
**Rodriguez Kimbell**, Silvya *WhoHisp 92*
**Rodriguez Lara**, Guillermo 1923- *IntWW 91*
**Rodriguez-Leal**, Jose Maria 1923-1991 *WhoHisp 92N*
**Rodriguez-Luis**, Julio 1937- *WhoHisp 92*
**Rodriguez-Mendoza**, Amalia 1946- *WhoHisp 92*
**Rodriguez Negron**, Enrique *WhoAmP 91, WhoHisp 92*
**Rodriguez-O**, Jaime E. 1940- *WhoHisp 92*
**Rodriguez-Orellana**, Manuel 1948- *WhoAmL 92*
**Rodriguez-Pagan**, Juan Antonio 1942- *WhoHisp 92*
**Rodriguez-Parada**, Jose Manuel 1953- *AmMWSc 92*
**Rodriguez-Peralta**, Carmen Laura 1956- *WhoHisp 92*
**Rodriguez-Perez**, Hilda D. 1939- *WhoHisp 92*
**Rodriguez Remeneski**, Shirley 1938- *WhoAmP 91*
**Rodriguez-Rivera**, Angel Luis 1947- *WhoFI 92*
**Rodriguez Roche**, Jose Antonio 1955- *WhoHisp 92*
**Rodriguez Rodriguez**, Carlos Rafael 1913- *IntWW 91*
**Rodriguez-Roque**, Victor Bernabe 1935- *WhoHisp 92*
**Rodriguez-Sardinas**, Orlando 1938- *WhoHisp 92*
**Rodriguez-Schieman**, Hildegarde *WhoHisp 92*
**Rodriguez-Sierra**, Jorge F 1945- *AmMWSc 92*
**Rodriguez-Sierra**, Jorge Fernando 1945- *WhoHisp 92*
**Rodriguez-Sosa**, Sergio A. 1947- *WhoHisp 92*
**Rodriguez Suarez**, Roberto 1923- *WhoHisp 92*
**Rodriguez Zorrilla**, Jose Santiago 1752-1832 *HisDSpE*
**Rodriquez**, Dolores *EncAmaz 91*
**Rodriquez**, Mildred Shepherd 1923- *AmMWSc 92*
**Rodstol**, David Ronald 1949- *WhoWest 92*
**Rodulfo**, Lillie M. 1947- *WhoHisp 92*
**Rodway**, Allan Edwin 1919- *WrDr 92*
**Rodwell**, Daniel Alfred Hunter 1936- *Who 92*
**Rodwell**, John Dennis 1946- *AmMWSc 92*
**Rodwell**, Victor William 1929- *AmMWSc 92*
**Rodwin**, Lloyd 1919- *WrDr 92*
**Rodysill**, Jerome Otto 1929- *WhoFI 92*
**Rodzianko**, Paul 1945- *WhoFI 92*
**Rodzinski**, Artur 1892-1958 *NewAmDM*
**Rodzinski**, Richard 1945- *WhoEnt 92*
**Rodzyanko**, Michael Vladimirovich 1859-1924 *FacFETw*
**Roe**, Anthony Maitland 1929- *Who 92*
**Roe**, Arnold 1925- *AmMWSc 92*
**Roe**, Audrey R. 1946- *WhoBlA 92*
**Roe**, Benson Bertheau 1918- *AmMWSc 92, WhoWest 92*
**Roe**, Bruce Allan 1942- *AmMWSc 92*
**Roe**, Byron Paul 1934- *AmMWSc 92, WhoMW 92*
**Roe**, Charles Richard 1940- *WhoEnt 92*
**Roe**, Clifford Ashley, Jr. 1942- *WhoAmL 92*
**Roe**, Daphne A 1923- *AmMWSc 92*
**Roe**, David Christopher 1948- *AmMWSc 92*
**Roe**, David Kelmer 1933- *AmMWSc 92*
**Roe**, Derek Arthur 1937- *WrDr 92*
**Roe**, E. P. 1838-1888 *BenetAL 91*
**Roe**, Earl DeForest 1918- *WhoRel 92*
**Roe**, Ernest 1920- *WrDr 92*
**Roe**, Geoffrey Eric 1944- *Who 92*
**Roe**, Glenn Dana 1931- *AmMWSc 92*
**Roe**, James Maurice, Jr 1942- *AmMWSc 92*
**Roe**, Jerry D 1936- *WhoAmP 91*
**Roe**, John William 1961- *WhoAmL 92*
**Roe**, Keith *WhoAmP 91*
**Roe**, Kenneth A 1916- *AmMWSc 92*
**Roe**, Kenneth Andrew d1991 *NewYTBS 91*
**Roe**, Kenneth Keith 1945- *WhoFI 92*
**Roe**, Marion Audrey 1936- *Who 92*
**Roe**, Mark J. 1951- *WhoAmL 92*
**Roe**, Pamela 1942- *AmMWSc 92*
**Roe**, Peter Hugh O'Neil 1934- *AmMWSc 92*
**Roe**, Raigh 1922- *Who 92*
**Roe**, Rex 1925- *Who 92*
**Roe**, Robert A. 1924- *AlmAP 92 [port], WhoAmP 91*
**Roe**, Robert A 1954- *WhoAmP 91*
**Roe**, Ryong-Joon 1929- *AmMWSc 92*
**Roe**, Shirley Ann 1942- *WhoMW 92*
**Roe**, William Gordon *Who 92*
**Roe**, William P 1923- *AmMWSc 92*
**Roebber**, John Leonard 1931- *AmMWSc 92*
**Roeber**, Eugene Franz 1867-1917 *BiInAmS*
**Roebling**, John Augustus 1806-1869 *BiInAmS*
**Roebling**, Mary Gindhart *WhoFI 92*
**Roebuck**, Derek 1935- *WrDr 92*
**Roebuck**, Elmo D 1934- *WhoAmP 91*
**Roebuck**, Gerard Francis 1953- *WhoBlA 92*
**Roebuck**, Isaac Field 1930- *AmMWSc 92*
**Roebuck**, James Randolph, Jr 1945- *WhoAmP 91, WhoBlA 92*
**Roebuck**, John Clifford 1950- *WhoAmL 92*
**Roebuck**, Joseph Chester 1946- *WhoFI 92*
**Roebuck**, Roy Delville 1929- *Who 92*
**Roebuck-Hoard**, Marcia Veronica 1950- *WhoBlA 92*
**Roeck**, Thomas J., Jr. 1944- *WhoFI 92*
**Roecker**, Robert Maar 1922- *AmMWSc 92*
**Roecker**, William Alan 1942- *IntAu&W 91*
**Roedder**, Edwin Woods 1919- *AmMWSc 92*
**Roedder**, William Chapman, Jr. 1946- *WhoAmL 92*
**Roedel**, George Frederick 1916- *AmMWSc 92*
**Roedel**, Paul Robert 1927- *WhoFI 92*
**Roeder**, Anthony David 1949- *WhoMW 92*
**Roeder**, Charles William 1942- *AmMWSc 92, WhoWest 92*
**Roeder**, David Lowell 1939- *WhoMW 92*
**Roeder**, David William 1939- *AmMWSc 92*
**Roeder**, Edward A 1939- *AmMWSc 92*
**Roeder**, Lois M 1932- *AmMWSc 92*
**Roeder**, Martin 1925- *AmMWSc 92*
**Roeder**, Michael Lee 1950- *WhoAmL 92*
**Roeder**, Peter Ludwig 1932- *AmMWSc 92*
**Roeder**, Ralph 1890- *ScFEYrs*
**Roeder**, Richard Anthony 1951- *WhoWest 92*
**Roeder**, Robert Charles 1937- *AmMWSc 92*
**Roeder**, Robert Gayle 1942- *AmMWSc 92*
**Roeder**, Stephen Bernhard Walter 1939- *AmMWSc 92, WhoWest 92*
**Roederer**, Juan Gualterio 1929- *AmMWSc 92*
**Roederer**, Mario 1963- *AmMWSc 92*
**Roeding**, Richard Louis 1930- *WhoAmP 91*
**Roeg**, Nicolas 1928- *IntDcF 2-2 [port], IntMPA 92*
**Roeg**, Nicolas Jack 1928- *IntWW 91, Who 92, WhoEnt 92*
**Roeger**, Anton, III 1935- *AmMWSc 92*
**Roehl**, Perry Owen 1925- *AmMWSc 92*
**Roehl**, Richard *WhoAmP 91*
**Roehm**, Edward Charles 1946- *WhoFI 92*
**Roehm**, Ernst 1887-1934 *FacFETw*
**Roehm**, James R 1948- *WhoIns 92*
**Roehrick**, John *WhoAmP 91*
**Roehrick**, William 1912- *WhoEnt 92*
**Roehrig**, Catharine H. 1949- *ConAu 134, SmATA 67*
**Roehrig**, Frederick Karl 1942- *AmMWSc 92*
**Roehrig**, Gerald Ralph 1941- *AmMWSc 92*
**Roehrig**, Jimmy Richard 1949- *AmMWSc 92*
**Roehrig**, Karla Louise 1946- *AmMWSc 92*
**Roehrs**, Robert Christian 1931- *WhoWest 92*
**Roel**, Edmundo Lorenzo 1917- *WhoHisp 92*
**Roel**, Lawrence Edmund 1949- *AmMWSc 92*
**Roelfs**, Alan Paul 1936- *AmMWSc 92, WhoMW 92*
**Roelke**, Ada Ellen 1928- *WhoWest 92*
**Roelke**, Donald Ray 1949- *WhoMW 92*
**Roell**, C. J., Mrs. 1955- *WhoFI 92*
**Roellig**, Harold Frederick 1930- *AmMWSc 92*
**Roellig**, Leonard Oscar 1927- *AmMWSc 92*
**Roelofs**, Terry Dean 1942- *AmMWSc 92*
**Roelofs**, Thomas Harwood 1937- *AmMWSc 92*
**Roelofs**, Wendell L 1938- *AmMWSc 92*
**Roels**, Edwin Dale 1934- *WhoRel 92*
**Roels**, Oswald A 1921- *AmMWSc 92*
**Roeltgen**, Kenneth W. *WhoRel 92*
**Roem**, Mohammad 1908- *IntWW 91*
**Roemer**, Buddy 1943- *AlmAP 92 [port], News 91 [port], WhoAmP 91*
**Roemer**, Charles Elson, III 1943- *IntWW 91*
**Roemer**, Elizabeth 1929- *AmMWSc 92*
**Roemer**, Ernest Albin, Jr 1931- *WhoAmP 91*
**Roemer**, Ferdinand 1818-1891 *BiInAmS*
**Roemer**, John Alan 1949- *WhoFI 92*
**Roemer**, John E. 1945- *WhoWest 92*
**Roemer**, Louis Edward 1934- *AmMWSc 92*
**Roemer**, Milton Irwin 1916- *AmMWSc 92*
**Roemer**, Richard Arthur 1939- *AmMWSc 92*
**Roemer**, Rita Lakshmi 1956- *WhoMW 92*
**Roemer**, Tim *WhoAmP 91*
**Roemer**, Tim 1956- *AlmAP 92 [port], WhoMW 92*
**Roemer**, William Frederick 1933- *WhoFI 92*
**Roemerman**, Steven Dane 1951- *WhoFI 92*
**Roemerman**, William Henry 1953- *WhoAmL 92*
**Roemmele**, Brian Karl 1961- *WhoFI 92, WhoWest 92*
**Roenbaugh**, Susan *WhoAmP 91*
**Roenfeldt**, Roger David 1938- *WhoIns 92*
**Roenigk**, William J 1929- *AmMWSc 92*
**Roentgen**, Wilhelm Conrad 1845-1923 *WhoNob 90*
**Roepe**, Paul David 1960- *AmMWSc 92*
**Roeper**, Richard Allen 1938- *WhoMW 92*
**Roepke**, Harlan Hugh 1930- *AmMWSc 92*
**Roepke**, Raymond Rollin 1911- *AmMWSc 92*
**Roer**, Robert David 1952- *AmMWSc 92*
**Roerich**, Nicholas Konstantin 1874-1947 *FacFETw*
**Roerich**, Nicolas Konstantinovitch 1874-1947 *RelLAm 91*
**Roericht**, Nick 1932- *DcTwDes*
**Roerig**, David L *AmMWSc 92*
**Roerig**, Sandra Charlene *AmMWSc 92*
**Roes**, Nicholas A. 1952- *WhoFI 92*
**Roesberry**, Dennis Dwayne 1945- *WhoWest 92*
**Roesch**, Robert Eugene 1951- *WhoMW 92*
**Roesch**, Warren Dale 1945- *WhoWest 92*
**Roesch**, William Carl 1923- *AmMWSc 92*
**Roesel**, Catherine Elizabeth 1920- *AmMWSc 92*
**Roeseler**, William G. 1943- *WhoWest 92*
**Roeseler**, Wolfgang Guenther Joachim 1925- *WhoFI 92*
**Roeser**, Kirk George 1943- *WhoIns 92*
**Roeser**, Ronald O. 1950- *WhoAmL 92*
**Roeser**, Ross Joseph 1942- *AmMWSc 92*

**Roesijadi**, Guritno 1948- AmMWSc 92
**Roesing**, Timothy George 1947- AmMWSc 92
**Roeske**, Arlys Mae 1934- WhoEnt 92
**Roeske**, Paulette DrAPF 91
**Roeske**, Roger William 1927- AmMWSc 92
**Roesky**, Herbert W. 1935- IntWW 91
**Roesler**, Frederick Lewis 1934- AmMWSc 92
**Roesler**, John Reed 1954- WhoAmL 92
**Roesler**, Joseph Frank 1930- AmMWSc 92
**Roesler**, Max A. 1933- WhoFI 92
**Roesler**, Richard Frederick 1958- WhoWest 92
**Roesler**, Robert Cabaniss 1944- WhoAmL 92
**Roesmer**, Josef 1928- AmMWSc 92
**Roesner**, Larry A AmMWSc 92
**Roesner**, Larry August 1941- WhoFI 92
**Roess**, William B 1938- AmMWSc 92
**Roesser**, Jean Wolberg 1930- WhoAmP 91
**Roesser**, Mary Carol 1959- WhoWest 92
**Roessle**, Heinz F. WhoFI 92
**Roessler**, Barton 1932- AmMWSc 92
**Roessler**, Charles Ervin 1934- AmMWSc 92
**Roessler**, David Martyn 1940- AmMWSc 92, WhoMW 92
**Roessler**, Martin A 1939- AmMWSc 92
**Roessler**, P. Dee 1941- WhoAmL 92
**Roessler**, Robert L 1921- AmMWSc 92
**Roessler**, Ronald James 1939- WhoAmL 92
**Roessmann**, Uros 1925- AmMWSc 92
**Roessner**, Gilbert George 1918- WhoFI 92
**Roessner**, Michaela TwCSFW 91
**Roest**, Aryan Ingomar 1925- AmMWSc 92
**Roestam**, Soepardjo 1926- IntWW 91
**Roeth**, Frederick Warren 1941- AmMWSc 92
**Roethe**, James Norton 1942- WhoAmL 92
**Roethel**, David Albert Hill 1926- AmMWSc 92
**Roethke**, Theodore 1908-1963 BenetAL 91, FacFETw
**Roethlisberger**, Eric M. 1934- IntWW 91
**Roetling**, Paul G 1933- AmMWSc 92
**Roetman**, Ernest Levane 1936- AmMWSc 92
**Roetman**, Robb Alan 1969- WhoEnt 92
**Roettger**, Dorye 1932- WhoEnt 92
**Roettger**, Norman Charles, Jr. 1930- WhoAmL 92
**Roettgers**, David John 1957- WhoAmL 92
**Roetzel**, Danny Nile 1952- WhoAmL 92
**Roeves**, Maurice 1937- IntMPA 92
**Rofe**, Barbara Dale 1946- WhoFI 92
**Rofes**, Eric Edward 1954- WrDr 92
**Roff**, Alan Lee 1936- WhoAmL 92
**Roff**, Derek Michael 1932- Who 92
**Roff**, John Hugh, Jr. 1931- WhoFI 92
**Roffers**, Mary 1953- WhoAmP 91
**Roffey**, Harry Norman 1911- Who 92
**Roffey**, Robert Cameron, Jr 1935- WhoIns 92
**Roffler-Tarlov**, Suzanne K 1938- AmMWSc 92
**Roffman**, Frederick S. 1945- WhoEnt 92
**Roffman**, Howard WhoEnt 92
**Roffman**, Richard Henry 1913- WhoEnt 92
**Roffman**, Rosaly DeMaios DrAPF 91
**Roffman**, Steven 1944- AmMWSc 92
**Roffol-Dobies**, Pamela Anne 1951- WhoFI 92
**Roffwarg**, Howard Philip 1932- AmMWSc 92
**Rog**, Francis S. 1930- WhoRel 92
**Rog-Swiostek**, Mieczyslaw Jan 1919- IntWW 91
**Rogado**, Armando Laguador 1944- WhoMW 92
**Rogalla**, Steve Leon 1953- WhoAmP 91
**Rogalski**, Carol Jean 1937- WhoMW 92
**Rogalski-Wilk**, Adrian Alice 1953- AmMWSc 92
**Rogaly**, Joseph 1935- WrDr 92
**Rogan**, Eleanor Groeniger 1942- AmMWSc 92
**Rogan**, John 1928- Who 92
**Rogan**, John B 1930- AmMWSc 92
**Rogan**, Mary Lou 1956- WhoAmP 91
**Rogan**, Robert William WhoFI 92
**Rogan**, Walter J 1949- AmMWSc 92
**Rogat**, Dorothy Shiff 1913- WhoFI 92
**Rogatz**, Peter 1926- AmMWSc 92
**Rogaway**, Betty Jane 1921- WhoWest 92
**Rogawski**, Michael Andrew 1952- AmMWSc 92
**Roge**, Pascal 1951- IntWW 91
**Roge**, Paul E. WhoAmL 92
**Roge**, Ronald William 1947- WhoFI 92
**Rogeberg**, Thomas Edward 1943- WhoEnt 92, WhoRel 92
**Rogel**, Todd Stephen 1952- WhoAmL 92
**Rogell**, Irma Rose WhoEnt 92
**Rogell**, Ronald Marc 1969- WhoEnt 92
**Rogenski**, Marion M 1926- WhoAmP 91
**Roger Of Taize** 1915- IntWW 91
**Roger**, Douglas 1964- WhoWest 92
**Roger**, Kent M. 1955- WhoAmL 92
**Roger**, Noelle 1874-1953 ScFEYrs
**Roger**, William Alexander 1947- AmMWSc 92
**Roger-Ducasse**, Jean 1873-1954 NewAmDM
**Roger-Henrichsen**, Gudmund 1907- IntAu&W 91
**Rogerio**, JoAnn 1967- WhoHisp 92
**Rogero**, Leroy Harry, Jr. 1946- WhoFI 92
**Rogers**, Adrian Pierce 1931- WhoRel 92
**Rogers**, Adrianne Ellefson 1933- AmMWSc 92
**Rogers**, Al 1926- WhoEnt 92
**Rogers**, Alan Barde 1918- AmMWSc 92
**Rogers**, Alan Ernest Exel 1941- AmMWSc 92
**Rogers**, Alan Francis Bright 1907- Who 92
**Rogers**, Alfred R. 1931- WhoBlA 92
**Rogers**, Allan Ralph 1932- Who 92
**Rogers**, Allen Eugene 1922- WhoEnt 92
**Rogers**, Alvin Lee 1929- AmMWSc 92
**Rogers**, Andrew J, Jr 1944- WhoAmP 91
**Rogers**, Arthur Curtis 1856-1917 BiInAmS
**Rogers**, Arthur Rex 1931- WhoWest 92
**Rogers**, Aurelia Spencer 1834-1922 RelLAm 91
**Rogers**, Barbara Ann 1941- WhoWest 92
**Rogers**, Barbara Radcliffe 1939- WhoAmP 91
**Rogers**, Benjamin 1911- IntWW 91
**Rogers**, Benjamin D, Jr 1919- WhoAmP 91
**Rogers**, Bernard 1893-1968 NewAmDM
**Rogers**, Bernard Rousseau 1944- WhoBlA 92
**Rogers**, Bernard William 1921- IntWW 91, Who 92
**Rogers**, Bertha DrAPF 91
**Rogers**, Bessie Story ScFEYrs
**Rogers**, Bethany 1967- WhoFI 92
**Rogers**, Beverly Jane 1943- AmMWSc 92
**Rogers**, Bradley Barney 1957- WhoWest 92
**Rogers**, Brian Douglas 1950- WhoAmP 91
**Rogers**, Brian Frederick 1923- Who 92
**Rogers**, Bruce DrAPF 91
**Rogers**, Bruce Allen 1961- WhoAmL 92
**Rogers**, Bruce G 1925- AmMWSc 92
**Rogers**, Bruce Joseph 1924- AmMWSc 92
**Rogers**, Bryan Allen 1925- WhoFI 92, WhoMW 92
**Rogers**, C Ambrose 1920- Who 92
**Rogers**, C B, Jr 1929- WhoIns 92
**Rogers**, Carl Edward d1991 NewYTBS 91
**Rogers**, Carl Ernest 1938- WhoRel 92
**Rogers**, Carl Lindbergh Bernard 1928- IntWW 91
**Rogers**, Carl R 1902-1987 FacFETw
**Rogers**, Carleton Carson, Jr. 1935- WhoFI 92
**Rogers**, Carson 1924- WhoAmP 91
**Rogers**, Charles 1904- IntMPA 92
**Rogers**, Charles 1930- TwCPaSc
**Rogers**, Charles C 1931- AmMWSc 92
**Rogers**, Charles Calvin 1929-1990 WhoBlA 92N
**Rogers**, Charles D. 1935- WhoBlA 92
**Rogers**, Charles Edwin 1929- AmMWSc 92, WhoMW 92
**Rogers**, Charles Graham 1929- AmMWSc 92
**Rogers**, Charlie Ellic 1938- AmMWSc 92
**Rogers**, Chester Benjamin 1939- WhoAmP 91
**Rogers**, Chloe 1918- WhoAmP 91
**Rogers**, Christine Marie 1958- WhoRel 92
**Rogers**, Christopher Bruce 1958- WhoWest 92
**Rogers**, Christopher David 1956- WhoEnt 92
**Rogers**, Claude 1907-1979 TwCPaSc
**Rogers**, Claude Marvin 1919- AmMWSc 92
**Rogers**, Claude Ronn 1949- WhoMW 92
**Rogers**, Claudette J 1939- WhoAmP 91
**Rogers**, Craig Alan 1959- WhoFI 92
**Rogers**, Dan Loren 1944- WhoMW 92
**Rogers**, Daryl DrAPF 91
**Rogers**, David Andrews 1959- WhoEnt 92
**Rogers**, David Arthur 1921- Who 92
**Rogers**, David Bryan 1929- Who 92
**Rogers**, David Elliott 1926- AmMWSc 92
**Rogers**, David Franklin 1957- WhoMW 92
**Rogers**, David Freeman 1937- AmMWSc 92
**Rogers**, David Hale 1918- WhoWest 92
**Rogers**, David Jeffrey 1966- WhoEnt 92
**Rogers**, David John 1960- WhoAmL 92
**Rogers**, David Peter 1957- AmMWSc 92
**Rogers**, David Rodney 1949- WhoAmL 92
**Rogers**, David T, Jr 1935- AmMWSc 92
**Rogers**, David William 1959- WhoBlA 92
**Rogers**, David William Oliver 1945- AmMWSc 92
**Rogers**, Decatur WhoBlA 92
**Rogers**, Del Marie DrAPF 91
**Rogers**, Dennis Lee 1953- WhoWest 92
**Rogers**, Dexter 1921- AmMWSc 92
**Rogers**, Diana Lynn WhoEnt 92
**Rogers**, Dianna WhoBlA 92
**Rogers**, Don 1928- WhoAmP 91
**Rogers**, Donald B 1936- AmMWSc 92
**Rogers**, Donald Eugene 1932- AmMWSc 92
**Rogers**, Donald Richard 1932- AmMWSc 92
**Rogers**, Donald Warren 1932- AmMWSc 92
**Rogers**, Donna Whitaker 1960- WhoBlA 92
**Rogers**, Douglas Herbert 1926- AmMWSc 92
**Rogers**, Dwane Leslie 1943- WhoWest 92
**Rogers**, Earline S WhoAmP 91
**Rogers**, Earline S. 1934- WhoBlA 92
**Rogers**, Edmund Pendleton, III 1941- WhoAmL 92
**Rogers**, Edward LesBEnT 92
**Rogers**, Edward 1909- Who 92
**Rogers**, Edward 1911- TwCPaSc
**Rogers**, Edward Samuel 1933- WhoFI 92
**Rogers**, Edwin Henry 1936- AmMWSc 92
**Rogers**, Elijah Baby 1939- WhoBlA 92
**Rogers**, Elliot Folger d1895 BiInAmS
**Rogers**, Emery Herman 1921- AmMWSc 92
**Rogers**, Eric Malcolm 1902- AmMWSc 92
**Rogers**, Eric William Evan 1925- Who 92
**Rogers**, Ethel Tench 1914- WhoEnt 92
**Rogers**, Eugene WhoAmP 91
**Rogers**, Fairman 1833-1900 BiInAmS
**Rogers**, Felix John 1947- WhoMW 92
**Rogers**, Floyd TwCWW 91, WrDr 92
**Rogers**, Frances Arlene 1923- AmMWSc 92, WhoMW 92
**Rogers**, Frank WhoAmP 91
**Rogers**, Frank 1920- Who 92
**Rogers**, Frank Hugh 1960- WhoMW 92
**Rogers**, Franklin Robert 1921- WrDr 92
**Rogers**, Fred 1928- IntMPA 92
**Rogers**, Fred Baker 1926- AmMWSc 92
**Rogers**, Fred Eugene 1933- WhoMW 92
**Rogers**, Fred McFeely 1928- WhoEnt 92
**Rogers**, Freddie Clyde 1922- WhoBlA 92
**Rogers**, Gail Christiansen 1953- WhoWest 92
**Rogers**, Gardner Spencer 1926- WhoFI 92
**Rogers**, Garry Lee 1950- WhoRel 92
**Rogers**, Gary Allen 1945- AmMWSc 92
**Rogers**, George 1935- WhoAmP 91, WhoBlA 92
**Rogers**, George, III 1947- WhoBlA 92, WhoMW 92
**Rogers**, George Ernest 1927- IntWW 91
**Rogers**, George Theodore 1919- Who 92
**Rogers**, George William 1917- WrDr 92
**Rogers**, George Winters, Jr WhoAmP 91
**Rogers**, Gerald Stanley 1928- AmMWSc 92
**Rogers**, Gifford Eugene 1920- AmMWSc 92
**Rogers**, Ginger 1911- FacFETw, IntMPA 92, IntWW 91, WhoEnt 92
**Rogers**, H C, Jr 1923- AmMWSc 92
**Rogers**, H. Dennis 1948- WhoAmL 92
**Rogers**, Harold D. 1937- AlmAP 92 [port]
**Rogers**, Harold Dallas 1937- WhoAmP 91
**Rogers**, Harold E., Jr. 1930- WhoAmL 92
**Rogers**, Harry Eugene, III 1959- WhoEnt 92
**Rogers**, Hartley, Jr 1926- AmMWSc 92
**Rogers**, Harvey Wilbur 1945- AmMWSc 92
**Rogers**, Helen Evelyn Wahrgren 1924- WhoWest 92
**Rogers**, Henry Augustus 1918- Who 92
**Rogers**, Henry C. 1914- IntMPA 92
**Rogers**, Henry Darwin 1808-1866 BiInAmS
**Rogers**, Herbert F. 1925- WhoFI 92
**Rogers**, Horace Elton 1902- AmMWSc 92
**Rogers**, Howard 1946- TwCPaSc
**Rogers**, Howard Gardner 1915- AmMWSc 92
**Rogers**, Howard H 1926- AmMWSc 92
**Rogers**, Howard Paul 1932- WhoWest 92
**Rogers**, Howard Samuel 1921- WhoWest 92
**Rogers**, Howard Topping 1908- AmMWSc 92
**Rogers**, Howell Wade 1943- AmMWSc 92, WhoMW 92
**Rogers**, Hubert Augustus 1887-1976 RelLAm 91
**Rogers**, Hugh Charles Innes d1991 Who 92N
**Rogers**, Hugo H, Jr 1947- AmMWSc 92
**Rogers**, Ingrid 1951- IntAu&W 91
**Rogers**, Isabel Wood 1924- WhoRel 92
**Rogers**, J Jean 1943- WhoAmP 91
**Rogers**, J Robert 1940- WhoAmP 91
**Rogers**, J Stanley 1939- WhoAmP 91
**Rogers**, Jack David 1937- AmMWSc 92
**Rogers**, Jack Wyndall, Jr 1943- AmMWSc 92
**Rogers**, Jalane DrAPF 91
**Rogers**, James Albert 1940- AmMWSc 92
**Rogers**, James Albert 1944- WhoAmL 92
**Rogers**, James Barry 1933- WhoEnt 92
**Rogers**, James Beeland, Jr. 1942- WhoFI 92
**Rogers**, James Blythe 1802-1852 BiInAmS
**Rogers**, James Devitt 1929- WhoAmL 92
**Rogers**, James Edwin 1929- AmMWSc 92
**Rogers**, James Eugene, Jr. 1947- WhoFI 92, WhoMW 92
**Rogers**, James Franklin 1952- WhoAmL 92
**Rogers**, James H. WhoRel 92
**Rogers**, James Joseph 1942- AmMWSc 92
**Rogers**, James Samuel 1934- AmMWSc 92
**Rogers**, James Stewart 1932- AmMWSc 92
**Rogers**, James Ted, Jr 1942- AmMWSc 92
**Rogers**, James Terence 1926- AmMWSc 92
**Rogers**, James Thomas 1941- WhoAmL 92
**Rogers**, James Virgil, Jr 1922- AmMWSc 92
**Rogers**, Jane Rosalind 1952- IntAu&W 91
**Rogers**, Janet L. 1950- WhoMW 92
**Rogers**, Jannea Suzanne 1962- WhoAmL 92
**Rogers**, Jay Lee 1962- WhoFI 92
**Rogers**, Jerry Dale 1954- AmMWSc 92, WhoMW 92
**Rogers**, Jerry James 1943- WhoRel 92
**Rogers**, Jesse Thomas 1957- WhoFI 92
**Rogers**, Jesse Wallace 1941- AmMWSc 92
**Rogers**, Jimmy Deryl 1951- WhoRel 92
**Rogers**, Jimmy Roger 1938- WhoRel 92
**Rogers**, Joan Marian 1920- IntAu&W 91
**Rogers**, John 1648-1721 BenetAL 91
**Rogers**, John 1949- IntWW 91
**Rogers**, John Christopher 1962- WhoRel 92
**Rogers**, John D 1940- WhoAmP 91
**Rogers**, John Ernest 1947- AmMWSc 92
**Rogers**, John Francis William 1956- WhoAmP 91
**Rogers**, John Gilbert, Jr 1941- AmMWSc 92
**Rogers**, John I, III 1937- WhoAmP 91
**Rogers**, John James William 1930- AmMWSc 92
**Rogers**, John Kevin 1949- WhoRel 92
**Rogers**, John Michael 1935- Who 92
**Rogers**, John Michael Thomas 1938- Who 92
**Rogers**, John Robson 1928- Who 92
**Rogers**, John Samuel 1944- WhoRel 92
**Rogers**, John T. WhoAmL 92
**Rogers**, John W. 1918- WhoBlA 92
**Rogers**, John W, Jr WhoAmP 91, WhoFI 92
**Rogers**, John Willis 1929- Who 92
**Rogers**, Jonathan 1928- WhoAmP 91
**Rogers**, Joseph Edward 1951- WhoAmL 92
**Rogers**, Joseph Wood 1937- AmMWSc 92
**Rogers**, Judith W. WhoAmL 92, WhoAmP 91
**Rogers**, Justin Towner, Jr. 1929- WhoFI 92, WhoMW 92
**Rogers**, Katharine M. 1932- WrDr 92
**Rogers**, Katherine D 1955- WhoAmP 91
**Rogers**, Keith WrDr 92
**Rogers**, Kenneth Cannicott 1929- AmMWSc 92
**Rogers**, Kenneth D 1921- AmMWSc 92
**Rogers**, Kenneth Ray 1938- WhoEnt 92
**Rogers**, Kenneth Scipio 1935- AmMWSc 92
**Rogers**, Kenny 1938- IntMPA 92
**Rogers**, Kenny 1941- NewAmDM
**Rogers**, Larry 1961- WhoRel 92
**Rogers**, Larry James 1934- WhoAmP 91
**Rogers**, Lawrence F. 1937- WhoBlA 92
**Rogers**, Lawrence H., II 1921- IntMPA 92, WhoEnt 92
**Rogers**, Lebbeus Harding 1847-1932 ScFEYrs
**Rogers**, Lee Edward 1937- AmMWSc 92
**Rogers**, Lee Jasper 1955- WhoAmL 92, WhoFI 92
**Rogers**, Leo Joseph, Jr. 1936- WhoFI 92
**Rogers**, Lewis Henry 1910- AmMWSc 92
**Rogers**, Linda 1944- IntAu&W 91
**Rogers**, Linwood Arthur 1917- WhoAmP 91
**Rogers**, Lloyd Sloan 1914- AmMWSc 92
**Rogers**, Lockhart Burgess 1917- AmMWSc 92
**Rogers**, Lonnie Lee 1916- WhoAmP 91
**Rogers**, Lorene Lane 1914- AmMWSc 92
**Rogers**, Lynn Leroy 1939- AmMWSc 92
**Rogers**, Malcolm Austin 1948- Who 92
**Rogers**, Marc Francis 1957- WhoWest 92
**Rogers**, Marion Alan 1936- AmMWSc 92
**Rogers**, Mark Charles AmMWSc 92
**Rogers**, Marlin Norbert 1923- AmMWSc 92
**Rogers**, Martin 1951- TwCPaSc
**Rogers**, Martin Hartley Guy 1925- IntWW 91, Who 92

**Rogers,** Martin John Wyndham 1931- *Who 92*
**Rogers,** Mary Anne Henley 1856-1937 *BiDBrF 2*
**Rogers,** Matthew R. 1961- *WhoAmL 92*
**Rogers,** Maurice Arthur Thorold 1911- *Who 92*
**Rogers,** Mayrine D 1925- *WhoAmP 91*
**Rogers,** Melinda Jane 1964- *WhoWest 92*
**Rogers,** Melvin F. 1931- *WhoFI 92*
**Rogers,** Michael *DrAPF 91, Who 92*
**Rogers,** Michael Alan 1950- *WhoWest 92*
**Rogers,** Michael Charles 1949- *WhoBlA 92*
**Rogers,** Michael David 1954- *WhoMW 92*
**Rogers,** Michael Holmes 1949- *WhoWest 92*
**Rogers,** Michael Joseph 1944- *AmMWSc 92*
**Rogers,** Michael Thomas 1941- *WhoFI 92*
**Rogers,** Mick *IntAu&W 91X*
**Rogers,** Millard Foster, Jr. 1932- *WhoMW 92*
**Rogers,** Milton Bardstown 1939- *WhoWest 92*
**Rogers,** Mimi 1956- *IntMPA 92*
**Rogers,** Morris Ralph 1924- *AmMWSc 92*
**Rogers,** Murray Rowland Fletcher d1991 *Who 92N*
**Rogers,** Myrtle Beatrice 1925- *WhoAmP 91*
**Rogers,** N. Stewart 1930- *WhoFI 92*
**Rogers,** Nancy Hardin 1948- *WhoAmL 92*
**Rogers,** Nelson Burton 1927- *WhoRel 92*
**Rogers,** Nelson K 1928- *AmMWSc 92*
**Rogers,** Nigel 1935- *NewAmDM*
**Rogers,** Nigel David 1935- *Who 92*
**Rogers,** Nolan Ray 1931- *WhoAmP 91*
**Rogers,** Norman 1931- *WhoBlA 92*
**Rogers,** Norman Charles 1916- *Who 92*
**Rogers,** Norman Ernest, Jr. 1951- *WhoAmL 92*
**Rogers,** Oscar Allan, Jr. 1928- *WhoBlA 92*
**Rogers,** Owen Maurice 1930- *AmMWSc 92*
**Rogers,** P. E., Mrs. *Who 92*
**Rogers,** Palmer, Jr 1927- *AmMWSc 92*
**Rogers,** Pamela 1927- *WrDr 92*
**Rogers,** Parry *Who 92*
**Rogers,** Pat *TwCSFW 91*
**Rogers,** Pat 1938- *IntAu&W 91, WrDr 92*
**Rogers,** Patricia Louise 1926- *WhoWest 92*
**Rogers,** Patrick Kerr 1776-1828 *BiInAmS*
**Rogers,** Patti Ann 1965- *WhoMW 92*
**Rogers,** Pattiann *DrAPF 91*
**Rogers,** Paul 1917- *IntWW 91, Who 92*
**Rogers,** Paul A'Court 1939- *WhoFI 92*
**Rogers,** Paul Grant 1921- *WhoAmP 91*
**Rogers,** Paul Scott 1949- *WhoAmP 91*
**Rogers,** Paul W. 1926- *WhoMW 92*
**Rogers,** Peaches Eleanor 1933- *WhoAmP 91*
**Rogers,** Peggy J. 1951- *WhoBlA 92*
**Rogers,** Percival Hallewell 1912- *Who 92*
**Rogers,** Peter 1916- *IntMPA 92*
**Rogers,** Peter 1933- *TwCPaSc*
**Rogers,** Peter Brian 1941- *Who 92*
**Rogers,** Peter H 1945- *AmMWSc 92*
**Rogers,** Peter Norman 1938- *WhoFI 92*
**Rogers,** Phil H 1924- *AmMWSc 92*
**Rogers,** Philip 1908- *Who 92*
**Rogers,** Philip Virgilius 1907- *AmMWSc 92*
**Rogers,** Quinton Ray 1936- *AmMWSc 92*
**Rogers,** Ralph B. 1909- *WhoFI 92*
**Rogers,** Ralph D. *LesBEnT 92*
**Rogers,** Ralph Loucks 1922- *AmMWSc 92*
**Rogers,** Raymond N 1927- *AmMWSc 92*
**Rogers,** Rebecca *ScFEYrs*
**Rogers,** Rex Martin 1952- *WhoRel 92*
**Rogers,** Richard 1933- *DcTwDes, Who 92*
**Rogers,** Richard Adams 1930- *WhoAmP 91*
**Rogers,** Richard Brewer 1944- *AmMWSc 92*
**Rogers,** Richard C 1953- *AmMWSc 92*
**Rogers,** Richard Dean 1921- *WhoAmL 92, WhoMW 92*
**Rogers,** Richard George 1933- *IntWW 91*
**Rogers,** Richard Gregory 1955- *WhoMW 92, WhoWest 92*
**Rogers,** Richard Hilton 1935- *WhoFI 92*
**Rogers,** Richard Hunter 1939- *WhoAmL 92*
**Rogers,** Richard Michael 1944- *WhoAmL 92*
**Rogers,** Richard Raymond 1943- *WhoFI 92*
**Rogers,** Richard Wayne 1943- *WhoIns 92*
**Rogers,** Rick Alan 1953- *WhoFI 92*
**Rogers,** Robert 1731-1795 *BenetAL 91*
**Rogers,** Robert Cameron 1862-1912 *BenetAL 91*
**Rogers,** Robert Empie 1813-1884 *BiInAmS*
**Rogers,** Robert Grant 1938- *WhoRel 92*
**Rogers,** Robert H, Jr 1928- *WhoAmP 91*
**Rogers,** Robert Larry 1942- *AmMWSc 92*
**Rogers,** Robert M *AmMWSc 92*
**Rogers,** Robert N 1933- *AmMWSc 92*
**Rogers,** Robert Reed 1929- *WhoWest 92*
**Rogers,** Robert Stan 1953- *WhoEnt 92*
**Rogers,** Robert W 1912- *IntAu&W 91*
**Rogers,** Robert Wayne 1938- *AmMWSc 92*
**Rogers,** Robin Don 1957- *AmMWSc 92*
**Rogers,** Roddy R 1934- *AmMWSc 92*
**Rogers,** Rodney Albert 1926- *AmMWSc 92*
**Rogers,** Ronald D 1918- *WhoIns 92*
**Rogers,** Rosemary 1932- *IntAu&W 91, WrDr 92*
**Rogers,** Roy 1911- *FacFETw, IntMPA 92, NewAmDM*
**Rogers,** Samuel 1763-1855 *RfGEnL 91*
**Rogers,** Samuel John 1934- *AmMWSc 92*
**Rogers,** Sandra Louise 1947- *WhoAmP 91*
**Rogers,** Scott Bailey 1955- *WhoRel 92*
**Rogers,** Senta S 1923- *AmMWSc 92*
**Rogers,** Sharyn Gail 1948- *WhoAmL 92*
**Rogers,** Shorty 1924- *NewAmDM*
**Rogers,** Sidney Mills, III 1957- *WhoAmL 92*
**Rogers,** Spencer Lee 1905- *AmMWSc 92*
**Rogers,** Stanfield 1919- *AmMWSc 92*
**Rogers,** Stanley 1934- *WhoAmP 91*
**Rogers,** Stanley William, Jr. 1956- *WhoFI 92*
**Rogers,** Stearns Walter 1934- *AmMWSc 92*
**Rogers,** Steffen Harold 1941- *AmMWSc 92*
**Rogers,** Stewart Evan 1936- *WhoEnt 92*
**Rogers,** Susan Florence *WhoEnt 92*
**Rogers,** Susan Rae Knoef 1948- *WhoAmL 92*
**Rogers,** Terence Arthur 1924- *AmMWSc 92*
**Rogers,** Terrell Randolph 1952- *WhoRel 92*
**Rogers,** Theodore Courtney 1934- *WhoFI 92*
**Rogers,** Thomas 1927- *WrDr 92*
**Rogers,** Thomas Brent 1962- *WhoRel 92*
**Rogers,** Thomas Charles 1924- *WhoAmP 91*
**Rogers,** Thomas Edward 1912- *Who 92*
**Rogers,** Thomas Edwin 1917- *AmMWSc 92*
**Rogers,** Thomas F 1923- *AmMWSc 92*
**Rogers,** Thomas Gordon Parry 1924- *Who 92*
**Rogers,** Thomas Hardin 1932- *AmMWSc 92, WhoWest 92*
**Rogers,** Thomas S. *LesBEnT 92 [port]*
**Rogers,** Thomas Sydney 1954- *WhoAmL 92*
**Rogers,** Timmie *WhoBlA 92*
**Rogers,** Timothy Folk 1947- *WhoAmP 91*
**Rogers,** Timothy Revelle 1960- *WhoAmP 91*
**Rogers,** Tony *DrAPF 91*
**Rogers,** Tyler Stewart 1895-1967 *ConAu 134*
**Rogers,** Vern Child 1941- *AmMWSc 92*
**Rogers,** Verneida Elizabeth 1939- *WhoAmP 91*
**Rogers,** Victor W. 1962- *WhoHisp 92*
**Rogers,** Waid 1927- *AmMWSc 92*
**Rogers,** Walter E 1908- *WhoAmP 91*
**Rogers,** Walter Russell 1945- *AmMWSc 92*
**Rogers,** Wayne 1933- *IntMPA 92*
**Rogers,** Werner 1941- *WhoAmP 91*
**Rogers,** Will 1879-1935 *BenetAL 91, FacFETw*
**Rogers,** Will, Jr. 1912- *IntMPA 92*
**Rogers,** Willard L 1917- *AmMWSc 92*
**Rogers,** William 1919- *WrDr 92*
**Rogers,** William Alan 1921- *AmMWSc 92*
**Rogers,** William Augustus 1832-1898 *BiInAmS*
**Rogers,** William Barton 1804-1882 *BiInAmS*
**Rogers,** William Cordell 1943- *WhoFI 92, WhoWest 92*
**Rogers,** William Dale 1945- *WhoRel 92*
**Rogers,** William Dill 1927- *WhoAmL 92*
**Rogers,** William Edwin 1936- *AmMWSc 92*
**Rogers,** William F, III 1916- *WhoAmP 91*
**Rogers,** William Fenna, Jr. 1912- *WhoFI 92*
**Rogers,** William Irvine 1927- *AmMWSc 92*
**Rogers,** William Leslie 1934- *AmMWSc 92*
**Rogers,** William P. 1913- *IntWW 91*
**Rogers,** William Pierce 1913- *AmPolLe, Who 92*
**Rogers,** William Richard, Jr 1929- *WhoAmP 91*
**Rogers,** William Sherman 1951- *WhoAmL 92*
**Rogers,** William Shields, Jr. 1943- *WhoWest 92*
**Rogers,** Wilmer Alexander 1933- *AmMWSc 92*
**Rogers-Bell,** Mamie Lee 1954- *WhoBlA 92*
**Rogers-Grundy,** Ethel W. 1938- *WhoBlA 92*
**Rogers-Lomax,** Alice Faye 1950- *WhoBlA 92*
**Rogers-Martin,** Timothy Lawrence 1958- *WhoRel 92*
**Rogers-Wollman,** Maja Deon 1963- *WhoEnt 92*
**Rogerson,** Alan Thomas 1943- *WrDr 92*
**Rogerson,** Allen Collingwood 1940- *AmMWSc 92*
**Rogerson,** Anita Andres 1937- *WhoEnt 92*
**Rogerson,** Asa Benjamin 1939- *AmMWSc 92*
**Rogerson,** Barry *Who 92*
**Rogerson,** James William 1962- *WhoMW 92*
**Rogerson,** John Bernard, Jr 1922- *AmMWSc 92*
**Rogerson,** John Edward 1920- *WhoMW 92*
**Rogerson,** Nicolas 1943- *Who 92*
**Rogerson,** Peter Freeman 1944- *AmMWSc 92*
**Rogerson,** Robert James 1943- *AmMWSc 92*
**Rogerson,** Susan *Who 92*
**Rogerson,** Thomas Dean 1946- *AmMWSc 92*
**Roget,** Cristiane 1955- *WhoEnt 92*
**Rogg,** Lionel 1936- *NewAmDM, Who 92*
**Rogg,** Oskar G *WhoAmP 91*
**Rogg,** Sanford G. 1917-1976 *ConAu 134*
**Rogge,** Dwaine William 1938- *WhoFI 92*
**Rogge,** Joel Jay 1934- *WhoRel 92*
**Rogge,** Richard Daniel 1926- *WhoWest 92*
**Rogge,** Thomas Ray 1935- *AmMWSc 92, WhoMW 92*
**Roggeman,** Willem Maurits 1935- *IntAu&W 91*
**Roggenbuck,** Robert Raymond 1945- *WhoMW 92*
**Roggenkamp,** Paul Leonard 1927- *AmMWSc 92*
**Roggero,** Miguel Mike Leonardo 1962- *WhoWest 92*
**Roggiano,** Alfredo Angel 1919- *WhoHisp 92*
**Rogic,** Milorad Mihailo 1931- *AmMWSc 92*
**Rogin,** Gilbert *DrAPF 91*
**Roginski,** Robert Theodore 1961- *WhoMW 92*
**Rogler,** John Charles 1927- *AmMWSc 92*
**Rogler,** Lloyd H. 1930- *WhoHisp 92*
**Rogler,** Lloyd Henry 1930- *WrDr 92*
**Rogna,** Lawrence G. 1946- *WhoFI 92*
**Rogness,** Peter *WhoRel 92*
**Rognier,** Philip Andre 1943- *WhoWest 92*
**Rognlie,** Dale Murray 1933- *AmMWSc 92*
**Rognlien,** Thomas Dale 1945- *AmMWSc 92*
**Rognoni,** Virginio 1924- *IntWW 91*
**Rognrud,** Gordon Allen 1956- *WhoWest 92*
**Rogocki,** Jozefa 1957- *TwCPaSc*
**Rogoff,** Gerald Lee 1939- *AmMWSc 92*
**Rogoff,** Ilan 1943- *IntWW 91*
**Rogoff,** Jay *DrAPF 91*
**Rogoff,** Joseph Bernard 1908- *AmMWSc 92*
**Rogoff,** Kenneth S. 1953- *WhoFI 92*
**Rogoff,** Lynn *WhoEnt 92*
**Rogoff,** Martin Harold 1926- *AmMWSc 92*
**Rogoff,** William Milton 1916- *AmMWSc 92*
**Rogol,** Alan David 1941- *AmMWSc 92*
**Rogolsky,** Marvin 1939- *AmMWSc 92*
**Rogosa,** George Leon 1924- *AmMWSc 92*
**Rogovin,** Mitchell 1930- *WhoAmP 91*
**Rogow,** Arnold A. 1924- *WrDr 92*
**Rogow,** Zack *DrAPF 91*
**Rogowski,** A R 1905- *AmMWSc 92*
**Rogowski,** Robert Stephen 1938- *AmMWSc 92*
**Rogowsky,** Martin Lawrence 1948- *WhoAmP 91*
**Rogstad,** Mark Roland 1957- *WhoWest 92*
**Roguska-Kyts,** Jadwiga 1932- *AmMWSc 92*
**Roh Tae Woo** 1932- *FacFETw, IntWW 91*
**Roh,** Raymond Vincent 1932- *WhoRel 92*
**Roh,** Tae Woo 1932- *Who 92*
**Roha,** Max Eugene 1923- *AmMWSc 92*
**Rohach,** Alfred F 1934- *AmMWSc 92*
**Rohadfox,** Ronald Otto 1935- *WhoBlA 92*
**Rohan,** Paul E 1943- *AmMWSc 92*
**Rohan,** Robert J *WhoAmP 91*
**Rohan,** Sue *WhoAmP 91*
**Rohan-Vargas,** Fred 1949- *WhoHisp 92*
**Rohatgi,** Pradeep Kumar 1943- *AmMWSc 92*
**Rohatgi,** Upendra Singh 1949- *AmMWSc 92*
**Rohatgi,** Vijay 1939- *AmMWSc 92*
**Rohatyn,** Felix George 1928- *WhoFI 92*
**Rohde,** Charles Raymond 1922- *AmMWSc 92*
**Rohde,** Florence Virginia 1918- *AmMWSc 92*
**Rohde,** Gil C, Jr 1948- *WhoIns 92*
**Rohde,** Gilbert 1894-1944 *DcTwDes, FacFETw*
**Rohde,** Helmut 1925- *IntWW 91*
**Rohde,** James Vincent 1939- *WhoFI 92, WhoWest 92*
**Rohde,** Johan 1856-1935 *DcTwDes*
**Rohde,** Richard Allen 1929- *AmMWSc 92*
**Rohde,** Richard Whitney 1940- *AmMWSc 92*
**Rohde,** Steve Mark 1946- *AmMWSc 92*
**Rohde,** Suzanne Louise 1963- *AmMWSc 92*
**Rohe,** George Henry 1851-1899 *BiInAmS*
**Roheim,** Paul Samuel 1925- *AmMWSc 92*
**Rohen,** Edward 1931- *IntAu&W 91*
**Rohen,** Jane Frances 1928- *WhoRel 92*
**Rohila,** Pritam Kumar 1935- *WhoWest 92*
**Rohl,** Arthur N 1930- *AmMWSc 92*
**Rohla,** Dru Allen 1954- *WhoEnt 92*
**Rohlf,** F James 1936- *AmMWSc 92*
**Rohlf,** Marvin Euguene 1927- *AmMWSc 92*
**Rohlf,** Robert Michael 1946- *WhoEnt 92*
**Rohlfing,** Duane L 1933- *AmMWSc 92*
**Rohlfing,** Frederick W 1928- *WhoAmP 91*
**Rohlfing,** Martin Henry 1932- *WhoRel 92*
**Rohlfing,** Paul Deadrick 1963- *WhoMW 92*
**Rohlfing,** Stephen Roy 1936- *AmMWSc 92*
**Rohlfing,** Timothy B. 1959- *WhoRel 92*
**Rohlfs,** Carl W. 1951- *WhoRel 92*
**Rohlfs,** Charles, Mrs. *BenetAL 91*
**Rohlfs,** Christian 1849-1938 *FacFETw*
**Rohlig,** Harald Ernst 1926- *WhoEnt 92*
**Rohm,** C E Tapie, Jr 1947- *AmMWSc 92*
**Rohm,** Charles E 1935- *WhoIns 92*
**Rohm,** Ernst 1887-1934 *BiDExR, EncTR 91 [port]*
**Rohm,** Robert Allan 1949- *WhoRel 92*
**Rohman,** Michael 1925- *AmMWSc 92*
**Rohmer,** Eric 1920- *FacFETw, IntDcF 2-2, IntMPA 92, IntWW 91, Who 92, WhoEnt 92*
**Rohmer,** Richard 1924- *TwCSFW 91, WrDr 92*
**Rohmer,** Sax 1883-1959 *FacFETw, ScFEYrs*
**Rohn,** Elizabeth Janda 1931- *WhoAmP 91*
**Rohn,** Gordon Frederick 1939- *WhoRel 92, WhoWest 92*
**Rohn,** Robert Jones 1918- *AmMWSc 92*
**Rohner,** Georges 1907- *IntWW 91*
**Rohner,** Ralph John 1938- *WhoAmL 92*
**Rohner,** Ronald P. 1935- *WrDr 92*
**Rohner,** Thomas John 1936- *AmMWSc 92*
**Roholt,** Oliver A, Jr 1916- *AmMWSc 92*
**Rohovsky,** Michael William 1937- *AmMWSc 92*
**Rohr,** Brian P 1947- *WhoIns 92*
**Rohr,** David M 1947- *AmMWSc 92*
**Rohr,** James Edward 1948- *WhoFI 92*
**Rohr,** Leonard Carl 1921- *WhoBlA 92*
**Rohr,** Richard David 1926- *WhoAmL 92*
**Rohr,** Robert Charles 1922- *AmMWSc 92*
**Rohr,** Stephen Phillip 1941- *WhoMW 92*
**Rohrabacher,** Dana 1947- *AlmAP 92 [port], WhoWest 92*
**Rohrabacher,** Dana Tyrone 1947- *WhoAmP 91*
**Rohrbach,** Clayton John, III 1944- *WhoFI 92*
**Rohrbach,** Eric John 1951- *WhoAmP 91*
**Rohrbach,** Kenneth G 1940- *AmMWSc 92*
**Rohrbach,** Larry 1946- *WhoAmP 91*
**Rohrbach,** Michael Steven *AmMWSc 92*
**Rohrbach,** Peter Alpaugh 1953- *WhoAmL 92*
**Rohrbach,** Peter Thomas 1926- *IntAu&W 91, WrDr 92*
**Rohrbach,** Roger P 1942- *AmMWSc 92*
**Rohrbach,** William 1943- *WhoAmP 91*
**Rohrbacher,** Paul David 1950- *WhoRel 92*
**Rohrback,** Michael David 1954- *WhoWest 92*
**Rohrbaugh,** Richard Leander 1936- *WhoRel 92*
**Rohrberg,** Roderick George 1925- *WhoWest 92*
**Rohrbough,** Keith James 1949- *WhoAmL 92, WhoWest 92*
**Rohrbough,** Linda Jandecka 1947- *WhoMW 92*
**Rohrbough,** Malcolm Justin 1932- *WrDr 92*
**Rohren,** Brenda Marie Anderson 1959- *WhoMW 92*
**Rohrer,** Douglas C 1942- *AmMWSc 92*
**Rohrer,** Grace Jemison 1924- *WhoAmP 91*
**Rohrer,** Heinrich 1933- *AmMWSc 92, IntWW 91, Who 92, WhoNob 90*
**Rohrer,** James William *AmMWSc 92*
**Rohrer,** Reed Beaver 1954- *WhoAmL 92*
**Rohrer,** Richard Carl, Jr. 1946- *WhoFI 92*
**Rohrer,** Robert Harry 1918- *AmMWSc 92*
**Rohrer,** Ronald A *AmMWSc 92*
**Rohrer,** Susan Earley 1955- *WhoEnt 92*
**Rohrer,** Wesley M, Jr 1921- *AmMWSc 92*
**Rohrig,** Ignatius A 1910- *AmMWSc 92*

**Rohrig**, Norman 1944- *AmMWSc 92*
**Rohringer**, Roland 1929- *AmMWSc 92*
**Rohrkemper**, Paul H. *WhoFI 92*
**Rohrl**, Helmut 1927- *AmMWSc 92*
**Rohrlich**, Fritz 1921- *AmMWSc 92*
**Rohrman**, Douglass Frederick 1941- *WhoAmL 92, WhoFI 92*
**Rohrmann**, Charles A 1911- *AmMWSc 92*
**Rohrs**, Barbara Mason 1946- *WhoRel 92*
**Rohrs**, Harold Clark 1940- *AmMWSc 92*
**Rohrs**, John Theodore, III 1955- *WhoAmL 92*
**Rohrs**, Karl 1910- *IntWW 91*
**Rohrs**, Roger C. 1946- *WhoEnt 92*
**Rohrschneider**, Larry Ray 1944- *AmMWSc 92*
**Rohsenow**, Warren M 1921- *AmMWSc 92*
**Rohwedder**, William Kenneth 1932- *AmMWSc 92*
**Rohweder**, Dwayne A 1926- *AmMWSc 92*
**Rohweder**, James Edward 1964- *WhoMW 92*
**Rohwer**, Bruce Steven 1951- *WhoAmP 91*
**Rohwer**, Robert G 1920- *AmMWSc 92*
**Rohy**, David Alan 1940- *AmMWSc 92*
**Roia**, Frank Costa, Jr 1936- *AmMWSc 92*
**Roig**, J. Adalberto, Jr. *WhoHisp 92*
**Roig**, J. Adalberto, Sr. *WhoHisp 92*
**Roijen**, Jan Herman Van d1991 *Who 92N*
**Roin**, Howard James 1953- *WhoAmL 92*
**Roiphe**, Ann *DrAPF 91*
**Roiphe**, Anne Richardson 1935- *WrDr 92*
**Roisler**, Glenn Harvey 1952- *WhoFI 92*
**Roisman**, Emily Neisloss 1959- *WhoAmL 92*
**Roisman**, Peter Scott 1960- *WhoEnt 92*
**Roistacher**, Seymour Lester 1922- *AmMWSc 92*
**Roiter**, Eric D. 1948- *WhoAmL 92*
**Roith**, Oscar 1927- *Who 92*
**Roitman**, Howard Alan 1948- *WhoAmL 92*
**Roitman**, James Nathaniel 1941- *AmMWSc 92*
**Roitman**, Judy 1945- *AmMWSc 92*
**Roitman**, Peter 1949- *AmMWSc 92*
**Roitt**, Ivan Maurice 1927- *Who 92*
**Roitz**, Edward J 1955- *WhoAmP 91*
**Roiz**, Myriam 1938- *WhoWest 92*
**Roizin**, Leon d1991 *NewYTBS 91*
**Roizin**, Leon 1912- *AmMWSc 92*
**Roizman**, Bernard 1929- *AmMWSc 92, IntWW 91*
**Roizman**, Owen 1936- *IntMPA 92*
**Rojas**, Cookie 1939- *WhoHisp 92*
**Rojas**, Francisco Jose 1944- *IntWW 91*
**Rojas**, Gonzalo 1917- *ConSpAP*
**Rojas**, Guillermo 1938- *WhoHisp 92*
**Rojas**, Luis Diaz 1964- *WhoHisp 92*
**Rojas**, Luis E 1953- *WhoAmP 91, WhoHisp 92*
**Rojas**, Manuel 1896-1973 *BenetAL 91*
**Rojas**, Manuel Joseph 1948- *WhoHisp 92*
**Rojas**, Mel 1966- *WhoHisp 92*
**Rojas**, Paul 1912- *WhoHisp 92*
**Rojas**, Ricardo *BlkOlyM*
**Rojas**, Richard Raimond 1931- *AmMWSc 92*
**Rojas**, Robert R. 1927- *WhoHisp 92*
**Rojas**, Roland Samuel 1932- *WhoAmP 91*
**Rojas**, Ronald S. 1952- *WhoFI 92*
**Rojas De Moreno Diaz**, Maria Eugenia 1934- *IntWW 91*
**Rojas-Lombardi**, Felipe d1991 *NewYTBS 91 [port], WhoHisp 92N*
**Rojas Mena**, Luis 1917- *WhoRel 92*
**Rojiani**, Kamal B 1948- *AmMWSc 92*
**Rojo**, Alfonso 1921- *AmMWSc 92*
**Rojo**, Jerry Neil 1935- *WhoEnt 92*
**Rojo**, Luis Angel 1934- *IntWW 91*
**Rokach**, Joshua 1935- *AmMWSc 92*
**Rokeach**, Luis Alberto 1951- *AmMWSc 92*
**Rokeby**, Thomas R C 1921- *AmMWSc 92*
**Roker**, Roxie *WhoBlA 92*
**Rokes**, Willis Park 1926- *WhoIns 92*
**Rokison**, Kenneth Stuart 1937- *Who 92*
**Rokitka**, Mary Anne *AmMWSc 92*
**Rokk**, Marika 1913- *EncTR 91 [port]*
**Rokke**, Mona 1940- *IntWW 91*
**Rokni**, Mohammad Ali 1958- *AmMWSc 92*
**Rokop**, Donald J 1939- *AmMWSc 92*
**Rokoske**, Thomas Leo 1939- *AmMWSc 92*
**Rokossovsky**, Konstantin Konstantinovich 1896-1968 *FacFETw, SovUnBD*
**Rokowsky**, Morris d1991 *NewYTBS 91*
**Rokus**, Josef Wilhelm 1942- *WhoFI 92*
**Rol**, Pieter Klaas 1927- *AmMWSc 92*
**Rola-Pleszczynski**, Marek 1947- *AmMWSc 92*
**Rolan**, Phidalia Lynn 1961- *WhoWest 92*
**Roland**, Alex 1944- *AmMWSc 92*
**Roland**, Benautrice, Jr. 1945- *WhoBlA 92*
**Roland**, Billy Ray 1926- *WhoFI 92*
**Roland**, Brian Dale 1950- *WhoEnt 92*
**Roland**, Charles Gordon 1933- *AmMWSc 92*
**Roland**, Clarence Herrel 1933- *WhoRel 92*
**Roland**, David Alfred, Sr 1943- *AmMWSc 92*
**Roland**, David Leonard 1948- *WhoEnt 92, WhoFI 92*
**Roland**, Dennis Michael 1949- *AmMWSc 92*
**Roland**, Emmerett Wilbur 1931- *WhoRel 92*
**Roland**, Gilbert 1905- *IntMPA 92, WhoHisp 92*
**Roland**, John Wanner 1950- *WhoAmL 92*
**Roland**, Johnny E. 1943- *WhoBlA 92*
**Roland**, Judi D *WhoAmP 91*
**Roland**, Nicholas *Who 92*
**Roland**, Richard Ralph 1952- *WhoAmL 92*
**Roland**, Robert 1919- *WhoEnt 92*
**Roland**, Thomas Matthew 1960- *WhoEnt 92*
**Roland de La Platiere**, Jeanne-Marie 1754-1793 *BlkwCEP*
**Roland de la Platiere**, Marie Jeanne P. 1754-1793 *FrenWW*
**Roland-King**, Francine Charla *WhoEnt 92*
**Roland Smith**, Gordon 1931- *WrDr 92*
**Rolandis**, Nicos A. 1934- *IntWW 91*
**Rolando**, William Arthur *WhoAmP 91*
**Rolark**, Calvin W. 1927- *WhoBlA 92*
**Rolark**, M. Wilhelmina *WhoBlA 92*
**Rolark**, Wilhelmina J *WhoAmP 91*
**Rold**, John W 1927- *AmMWSc 92*
**Roldan**, Amadeo 1900-1939 *NewAmDM*
**Roldan**, Charles Robert 1940- *WhoHisp 92*
**Roldan**, Luis Gonzalez 1925- *AmMWSc 92*
**Roldan**, Nancy *WhoHisp 92*
**Rolde**, Neil Richard 1931- *WhoAmP 91*
**Rolett**, Ellis Lawrence 1930- *AmMWSc 92*
**Roletta**, Richard Peter 1939- *WhoWest 92*
**Rolewicz**, Robert John 1954- *WhoMW 92*
**Roley**, Sutton Wilson 1925- *WhoEnt 92*
**Rolf**, Clyde Norman 1937- *AmMWSc 92*
**Rolf**, Frederick 1926- *WhoEnt 92*
**Rolf**, Howard Leroy 1928- *AmMWSc 92*
**Rolf**, Lester Leo, Jr 1940- *AmMWSc 92*
**Rolf**, Percy Henry 1915- *Who 92*
**Rolf**, Richard L 1935- *AmMWSc 92*
**Rolfe**, Cynthia Elaine 1953- *WhoFI 92*
**Rolfe**, Frederick 1860-1913 *LiExTwC, RfGEnL 91*
**Rolfe**, Frederick William 1860-1913 *ScFEYrs*
**Rolfe**, Gary Lavelle 1946- *AmMWSc 92*
**Rolfe**, Henry Cuthbert Norris 1908- *Who 92*
**Rolfe**, Hume B. *Who 92*
**Rolfe**, John 1585-1622 *BenetAL 91*
**Rolfe**, John 1927- *AmMWSc 92*
**Rolfe**, Marianne Teresa N. *Who 92*
**Rolfe**, Michael N. 1937- *WhoFI 92, WhoMW 92*
**Rolfe**, Nigel 1950- *TwCPaSc*
**Rolfe**, Rial Dewitt 1952- *AmMWSc 92*
**Rolfe**, Ronald Stuart 1945- *WhoAmL 92*
**Rolfe**, Stanley Theodore 1934- *AmMWSc 92*
**Rolfe**, William David Ian 1936- *Who 92*
**Rolfe Johnson**, Anthony 1940- *IntWW 91*
**Rolfs**, Edward C *WhoAmP 91*
**Rolfs**, Thomas John 1922- *WhoMW 92*
**Rolicki**, Janusz Andrzej 1938- *IntAu&W 91*
**Rolin**, Judi M. 1946- *WhoEnt 92*
**Rolison**, Jay P, Jr 1929- *WhoAmP 91*
**Roll** *Who 92*
**Roll**, Barbara Honeyman 1910- *WhoWest 92*
**Roll**, Barbara Honeyman Heath 1910- *AmMWSc 92*
**Roll**, Charles Weissert 1928- *WhoAmP 91*
**Roll**, David Byron 1940- *AmMWSc 92*
**Roll**, David E 1948- *AmMWSc 92*
**Roll**, Donna *WhoEnt 92*
**Roll**, Frederic 1921- *AmMWSc 92*
**Roll**, James 1912- *Who 92*
**Roll**, James Robert 1958- *AmMWSc 92*
**Roll**, John Donald 1912- *AmMWSc 92*
**Roll**, Paul M *AmMWSc 92*
**Roll**, Peter Guy 1933- *AmMWSc 92*
**Roll Of Ipsden**, Baron 1907- *IntWW 91, Who 92, WrDr 92*
**Rolland**, Alvin Eugene 1930- *WhoAmP 91*
**Rolland**, Dale Everett 1955- *WhoRel 92*
**Rolland**, Ian McKenzie *WhoIns 92*
**Rolland**, Ian McKenzie 1933- *WhoFI 92, WhoMW 92*
**Rolland**, Lawrence Anderson Lyon 1937- *Who 92*
**Rolland**, Lucien G. 1916- *WhoFI 92*
**Rolland**, Marjorie 1951- *WhoMW 92*
**Rolland**, Michael Jackson 1943- *WhoFI 92*
**Rolland**, Romain 1866-1944 *FacFETw, GuFrLit 1, WhoNob 90*
**Rolland**, William Woody 1931- *AmMWSc 92*
**Rollason**, Grace Saunders 1919- *AmMWSc 92*
**Rollason**, Herbert Duncan 1917- *AmMWSc 92*
**Rolle**, Albert Eustace 1935- *WhoBlA 92*
**Rolle**, Andrew 1922- *WrDr 92*
**Rolle**, Esther *IntMPA 92, WhoBlA 92, WhoEnt 92*
**Rolle**, F Robert 1939- *AmMWSc 92*
**Rolle**, Kurt Christian 1938- *WhoMW 92*
**Rolle**, Myra Moss 1937- *WhoWest 92*
**Rolle**, Richard 1300?-1349 *RfGEnL 91*
**Rollefson**, Aimar Andre 1940- *AmMWSc 92*
**Rollefson**, Ragnar 1906- *AmMWSc 92*
**Rollefson**, Richard Carl 1948- *WhoEnt 92*
**Rollefson**, Robert John 1941- *AmMWSc 92*
**Rollenhagen**, Douglas Lyle 1953- *WhoMW 92*
**Roller**, David Charles 1937- *WhoMW 92*
**Roller**, Douglas Charles 1961- *WhoRel 92*
**Roller**, Duane Henry DuBose 1920- *AmMWSc 92*
**Roller**, Herbert Alfred 1927- *AmMWSc 92*
**Roller**, Jeanne Keeney 1948- *WhoMW 92*
**Roller**, John Herschel 1949- *WhoRel 92*
**Roller**, Michael Harris 1922- *AmMWSc 92*
**Roller**, Peter Paul 1940- *AmMWSc 92*
**Roller**, Susan Lorrayne 1954- *WhoWest 92*
**Roller**, Thomas Benjamin 1950- *WhoFI 92*
**Roller**, Warren L 1929- *AmMWSc 92*
**Roller**, Wolfgang 1929- *IntWW 91*
**Rolleston**, Francis Stopford 1940- *AmMWSc 92*
**Rolley**, Alan W. 1933- *WhoFI 92, WhoMW 92*
**Rolley**, Daryl Taylor 1967- *WhoFI 92*
**Rollhaus**, Philip Edward, Jr. 1934- *WhoFI 92*
**Rollier**, Francois 1915- *IntWW 91*
**Rollin**, Roger B. 1930- *WrDr 92*
**Rolling Stones** *FacFETw, NewAmDM*
**Rollinger**, Charles N 1934- *AmMWSc 92*
**Rollino**, John 1944- *AmMWSc 92*
**Rollins**, Avon William, Sr. 1941- *WhoBlA 92*
**Rollins**, Charlemae 1897-1979 *HanAmWH*
**Rollins**, Charlemae Hill 1897-1979 *NotBlAW 92 [port]*
**Rollins**, Daryl Thomas 1950- *WhoFI 92*
**Rollins**, Ethel Eugenia 1932- *WhoBlA 92*
**Rollins**, Frank West 1860-1915 *ScFEYrs*
**Rollins**, Harold Bert 1939- *AmMWSc 92*
**Rollins**, Howard 1950- *IntMPA 92*
**Rollins**, Howard A, Jr 1927- *AmMWSc 92*
**Rollins**, Howard E., Jr. 1951- *WhoBlA 92*
**Rollins**, Howard Ellsworth, Jr. 1950- *WhoEnt 92*
**Rollins**, Jack 1914- *IntMPA 92*
**Rollins**, James Herrell 1944- *WhoAmL 92*
**Rollins**, James Richard 1939- *WhoWest 92*
**Rollins**, Lee Owen 1938- *WhoBlA 92*
**Rollins**, Linda 1941- *WhoAmP 91*
**Rollins**, Orville Woodrow 1923- *AmMWSc 92*
**Rollins**, Philip Ashton 1869-1950 *BenetAL 91*
**Rollins**, Reed Clark 1911- *AmMWSc 92, IntWW 91*
**Rollins**, Richard Albert 1927- *WhoBlA 92*
**Rollins**, Robert *ScFEYrs*
**Rollins**, Roger William 1939- *AmMWSc 92, WhoMW 92*
**Rollins**, Ronald Roy 1930- *AmMWSc 92*
**Rollins**, Sonny 1929- *NewAmDM*
**Rollins**, Sonny 1930- *ConMus 7 [port], WhoBlA 92, WhoEnt 92*
**Rollins**, Wade Cuthbert 1912- *AmMWSc 92*
**Rollins**, Walter 1922- *WhoAmP 91*
**Rollins**, Walter Theodore 1930- *WhoBlA 92*
**Rollins**, Wayne 1955- *WhoBlA 92*
**Rollins**, Wayne Gilbert 1929- *WrDr 92*
**Rollins-Page**, Earl Arthur 1940- *AmMWSc 92*
**Rollinson**, Mark 1935- *WhoAmL 92*
**Rollison**, David Ray 1944- *WhoWest 92*
**Rollison**, John A, III 1950- *WhoAmP 91*
**Rollman**, Gary Bernard 1941- *AmMWSc 92*
**Rollmann**, Louis Deane 1939- *AmMWSc 92*
**Rollo** *Who 92*
**Rollo**, Lord 1915- *Who 92*
**Rollo**, Master of 1943- *Who 92*
**Rollo**, Frank David 1939- *AmMWSc 92, WhoFI 92*
**Rollo**, Ian McIntosh 1926- *AmMWSc 92*
**Rollo**, Vera Foster 1924- *WrDr 92*
**Rollock**, Barbara T. *WhoBlA 92*
**Rollosson**, George William 1923- *AmMWSc 92*
**Rolls**, Eric Charles 1923- *IntAu&W 91, WrDr 92*
**Rolls**, John Marland, Jr. 1937- *WhoAmL 92*
**Rollwitz**, William Lloyd 1922- *AmMWSc 92*
**Rolnick**, Neil Burton 1947- *WhoEnt 92*
**Rolnick**, William Barnett 1936- *AmMWSc 92, WhoMW 92*
**Rolnicki**, Thomas Edward 1949- *WhoMW 92*
**Rolo**, Cyril Felix 1918- *Who 92*
**Roloff**, Marston Val 1943- *AmMWSc 92*
**Roloff**, Michael 1937- *IntAu&W 91*
**Roloff**, ReBecca Koenig 1954- *WhoIns 92*
**Roloff**, Thomas Paul 1965- *WhoFI 92*
**Rolofson**, George Lawrence 1938- *AmMWSc 92*
**Rolon**, Jose 1883-1945 *NewAmDM*
**Rolon Marrero**, Andres 1944- *WhoAmP 91*
**Rolontz**, Lee Alison 1962- *WhoEnt 92*
**Rolontz**, Robert 1920- *WhoEnt 92*
**Rolph**, C. H. 1901- *Who 92, WrDr 92*
**Rolph**, Cecil Hewitt 1901- *IntAu&W 91*
**Rolph**, David Paul 1933- *WhoEnt 92*
**Rolph**, Glenn Douglas 1947- *WhoEnt 92*
**Rolphe**, Ben Richard, Jr. 1932- *WhoWest 92*
**Rolshoven**, Hubertus *IntWW 91N*
**Rolston**, Charles Hopkins 1927- *AmMWSc 92*
**Rolston**, Dennis Eugene 1943- *AmMWSc 92*
**Rolston**, Holmes, III 1932- *WhoRel 92, WhoWest 92*
**Rolston**, Kenneth Vijaykumar Isaac 1951- *AmMWSc 92*
**Rolston**, Lawrence H 1922- *AmMWSc 92*
**Rolston**, Stephen Garry 1962- *WhoRel 92*
**Rolt**, David 1915- *TwCPaSc*
**Rolvaag**, Karl F. 1913-1990 *CurBio 91N*
**Rolvaag**, O.E. 1876-1931 *TwCWW 91*
**Rolvaag**, Ole E. 1876-1931 *DcAmImH*
**Rolvaag**, Ole Edvart 1876-1931 *BenetAL 91, FacFETw*
**Rolwing**, Raymond H 1931- *AmMWSc 92*
**Rom**, Joseph William 1928- *WhoWest 92*
**Rom**, Roy Curt 1922- *AmMWSc 92*
**Rom**, Zohar Ayal 1965- *WhoEnt 92*
**Roma**, Patrick 1949- *WhoAmP 91*
**Romack**, Frank Eldon 1924- *AmMWSc 92*
**Romadin**, Nikolay Mikhaylovich 1903- *SovUnBD*
**Romagnani**, Sergio 1939- *AmMWSc 92*
**Romagnoli**, Robert Joseph 1931- *AmMWSc 92*
**Romagosa**, Elmo Lawrence 1924- *WhoRel 92*
**Romaguera**, Enrique 1942- *WhoMW 92*
**Romahi**, Seif al-Wady al- 1938- *IntWW 91*
**Romain**, Roderick Jessel Anidjar 1916- *Who 92*
**Romaine**, Elaine *DrAPF 91*
**Romaine**, Henry S 1933- *WhoIns 92*
**Romaine**, Henry Simmons 1933- *WhoFI 92*
**Romaine**, Paul 1905-1986 *FacFETw*
**Romains**, Jules 1885-1972 *ConAu 34NR, FacFETw, GuFrLit 1*
**Roman**, Agustin A. 1928- *WhoRel 92*
**Roman**, Alfred Victor 1940- *WhoEnt 92*
**Roman**, Andy, Jr. 1965- *WhoHisp 92*
**Roman**, Angel Luis 1950- *WhoAmP 91*
**Roman**, Angelo, Jr. 1954- *WhoEnt 92, WhoHisp 92*
**Roman**, Ann 1945- *AmMWSc 92*
**Roman**, Bernard John 1940- *AmMWSc 92*
**Roman**, Chester John 1924- *WhoRel 92*
**Roman**, Chris Leonard 1966- *WhoHisp 92*
**Roman**, Erasmo Tanon, Jr. 1932- *WhoHisp 92*
**Roman**, Gilbert 1940- *WhoHisp 92*
**Roman**, Gloria Belle 1941- *WhoRel 92*
**Roman**, Gustavo Campos 1946- *AmMWSc 92*
**Roman**, Harold 1926- *WhoFI 92*
**Roman**, Herschel Lewis 1914- *AmMWSc 92*
**Roman**, Jesse 1931- *AmMWSc 92*
**Roman**, John Charles 1920- *WhoMW 92*
**Roman**, Laura M 1955- *AmMWSc 92*
**Roman**, Lawrence *WhoEnt 92*
**Roman**, Lawrence 1921- *IntMPA 92*
**Roman**, Nancy Grace 1925- *AmMWSc 92*
**Roman**, Paul 1925- *AmMWSc 92*
**Roman**, Petre 1946- *IntWW 91*
**Roman**, Richard J 1951- *AmMWSc 92*
**Roman**, Roberto 1940- *WhoHisp 92*
**Roman**, Roy M. *WhoHisp 92*
**Roman**, Ruth 1924- *IntMPA 92*
**Roman**, Spencer Myles 1949- *WhoIns 92*
**Roman**, Stanford A, Jr 1942- *AmMWSc 92*
**Roman**, Susan 1939- *WhoMW 92*
**Roman-Arroyo**, Belinda 1962- *WhoHisp 92*
**Roman-Barber**, Helen 1946- *WhoFI 92*
**Romanek**, James Joseph 1951- *WhoAmL 92*
**Romanelli**, Carmin 1957- *WhoEnt 92*
**Romanelli**, Peter Nicholas 1948- *WhoWest 92*
**Romanenko**, Yuri 1944- *FacFETw*
**Romanes**, George John 1916- *Who 92*
**Romani**, Barbara Ann 1961- *WhoAmL 92*
**Romani**, David Alan 1957- *WhoAmL 92*
**Romani**, Roger Joseph 1919- *AmMWSc 92*

**Romaniak,** Stanislaw Antoni 1948- *IntAu&W 91*
**Romaniello,** Charlotte *DrAPF 91*
**Romanik,** Jerzy 1931- *IntWW 91*
**Romankiw,** Lubomyr Taras 1931- *AmMWSc 92*
**Romanko,** Richard Robert 1925- *AmMWSc 92*
**Romanko,** Stephen Joseph, Jr. 1968- *WhoEnt 92*
**Romano,** Albert 1927- *AmMWSc 92*
**Romano,** Andrea 1955- *WhoWest 92*
**Romano,** Antonio Harold 1929- *AmMWSc 92*
**Romano,** Benito 1949- *WhoAmL 92*
**Romano,** Brenda J. 1958- *WhoEnt 92*
**Romano,** Clifford Samuel 1951- *WhoWest 92*
**Romano,** Ennio 1925- *WhoWest 92*
**Romano,** Irene Marion 1950- *WhoAmP 91*
**Romano,** Jack d1991 *NewYTBS 91*
**Romano,** John 1908- *AmMWSc 92, IntWW 91*
**Romano,** John 1948- *ConAu 133*
**Romano,** John A 1923- *WhoAmP 91*
**Romano,** Louis 1921- *WrDr 92*
**Romano,** Mark Anthony 1958- *WhoFI 92*
**Romano,** Paula Josephine 1940- *AmMWSc 92*
**Romano,** Robert Scheman 1942- *WhoFI 92*
**Romano,** Roberta 1952- *WhoAmL 92*
**Romano,** Salvatore James 1941- *AmMWSc 92*
**Romano,** Sergio 1929- *IntWW 91*
**Romano,** Xavier Eduardo 1960- *WhoHisp 92*
**Romano-V.,** Octavio I. 1932- *WhoHisp 92*
**Romanoff,** Elijah Bravman 1913- *AmMWSc 92*
**Romanoff,** Marjorie Reinwald 1923- *WhoMW 92*
**Romanoff,** Stanley M., Jr. 1948- *WhoMW 92*
**Romanos Melodos** 485?-560? *EncEarC*
**Romanos,** Nabil Elias 1965- *WhoWest 92*
**Romanov,** Grigoriy Vasil'evich 1923- *SovUnBD*
**Romanov,** Grigoriy Vasilyevich 1923- *IntWW 91*
**Romanov,** Panteleymon Sergeyevich 1884-1938 *FacFETw*
**Romanovicz,** Dwight Keith 1948- *AmMWSc 92*
**Romanow,** Louise Rozak 1950- *AmMWSc 92*
**Romanow,** Marina 1955- *WhoFI 92*
**Romanow,** Richard Brian 1953- *WhoAmP 91*
**Romanow,** Roy John *WhoWest 92*
**Romanowski,** Christopher Andrew 1953- *AmMWSc 92*
**Romanowski,** Curtis James 1954- *WhoMW 92*
**Romanowski,** Kenneth 1952- *WhoFI 92*
**Romanowski,** Robert David 1931- *AmMWSc 92*
**Romanowski,** Thomas Andrew 1925- *AmMWSc 92*
**Romans,** Ann 1929- *WhoBlA 92*
**Romans,** Bernard 1720?-1784? *BenetAL 91, BiInAmS*
**Romans,** James Bond 1914- *AmMWSc 92*
**Romans,** John Richard 1933- *AmMWSc 92*
**Romans,** John Thomas 1933- *WhoFI 92*
**Romans,** Pat *WhoAmP 91*
**Romans,** Robert Charles 1937- *AmMWSc 92*
**Romans,** Robert Gordon 1909- *AmMWSc 92*
**Romans-Hess,** Alice Yvonne 1947- *AmMWSc 92*
**Romansky,** Monroe James 1911- *AmMWSc 92*
**Romanuk,** Fred W. 1944- *WhoWest 92*
**Romanus,** Richard 1943- *WhoEnt 92*
**Romanus,** Sven Einar 1906- *IntWW 91*
**Romanyak,** James Andrew 1944- *WhoAmL 92*
**Romary,** John Kirk 1934- *AmMWSc 92*
**Romashin,** Anatoliy Vladimirovich 1931- *IntWW 91*
**Romashov,** Boris Sergeevich 1896-1958 *SovUnBD*
**Romay,** Fulgencia 1944- *BlkOlyM*
**Rombach,** Hans Dieter 1953- *AmMWSc 92*
**Rombach,** Michiel Christiaan 1955- *WhoWest 92*
**Rombauer,** Marjorie Lorraine 1927- *WhoAmL 92, WhoWest 92*
**Rombeau,** John Lee 1939- *AmMWSc 92*
**Romberg,** Sigmund 1887-1951 *FacFETw, NewAmDM*
**Romberger,** John Albert 1925- *AmMWSc 92*
**Romberger,** Karl Arthur 1934- *AmMWSc 92*
**Romberger,** Samuel B 1939- *AmMWSc 92*
**Rombough,** Bartlett B. 1924- *WhoFI 92, WhoWest 92*
**Rombs,** Vincent Joseph 1918- *WhoFI 92, WhoMW 92*
**Rome,** Anthony *IntAu&W 91X, WrDr 92*
**Rome,** Carol Ann 1945- *WhoRel 92*
**Rome,** Donald Lee 1929- *WhoAmL 92, WhoFI 92*
**Rome,** Doris Spector 1926- *AmMWSc 92*
**Rome,** Harold 1908- *NewAmDM*
**Rome,** Harold Jacob 1908- *WhoEnt 92*
**Rome,** James Alan 1942- *AmMWSc 92*
**Rome,** Leonard H 1949- *AmMWSc 92*
**Rome,** Marcus *DrAPF 91*
**Rome,** Margaret *WrDr 92*
**Rome,** Martin 1925- *AmMWSc 92*
**Rome,** Morton Eugene 1913- *WhoAmL 92*
**Rome,** Tony *IntAu&W 91X*
**Romeo,** John 1952- *WhoEnt 92*
**Romeo,** John Thomas 1940- *AmMWSc 92*
**Romeo,** Neola Fern 1914- *WhoAmP 91*
**Romeo,** Peter John 1942- *WhoAmL 92*
**Romeo,** Tony 1956- *AmMWSc 92*
**Romer,** Alfred 1906- *AmMWSc 92*
**Romer,** Carl William 1904- *WhoRel 92*
**Romer,** I Carl, Jr 1931- *AmMWSc 92*
**Romer,** John 1941- *WrDr 92*
**Romer,** Josef 1892-1944 *EncTR 91 [port]*
**Romer,** Mark Lemon Robert 1927- *Who 92*
**Romer,** Paul Michael 1955- *WhoFI 92*
**Romer,** Robert Horton 1931- *AmMWSc 92*
**Romer,** Roy 1928- *AlmAP 92 [port]*
**Romer,** Roy R. 1928- *IntWW 91, WhoAmP 91, WhoWest 92*
**Romeril,** John 1945- *WrDr 92*
**Romero,** Alberto C. 1950- *WhoHisp 92*
**Romero,** Alejandro F 1937- *AmMWSc 92*
**Romero,** Cesar 1907- *IntMPA 92, WhoHisp 92*
**Romero,** Claude Gilbert 1936- *WhoRel 92*
**Romero,** Daniel H. 1928- *WhoHisp 92*
**Romero,** Ed L. *WhoHisp 92*
**Romero,** Ed L 1934- *WhoAmP 91*
**Romero,** Edgardo 1957- *WhoHisp 92*
**Romero,** Elmer 1956- *WhoHisp 92*
**Romero,** Elvio 1926- *ConSpAP*
**Romero,** Emilio Felipe 1946- *WhoHisp 92*
**Romero,** Enrique A. 1947- *WhoRel 92*
**Romero,** Esteban Enos 1951- *WhoHisp 92*
**Romero,** Filiberto Martimiano 1934- *WhoHisp 92*
**Romero,** Frank 1943- *WhoHisp 92*
**Romero,** Freddie Joseph 1956- *WhoAmL 92*
**Romero,** Frederick 1947- *WhoWest 92*
**Romero,** Frederick Armand 1948- *WhoAmL 92*
**Romero,** Georg L. 1954- *WhoHisp 92*
**Romero,** George A. 1940- *IntDcF 2-2 [port], IntMPA 92*
**Romero,** Gilbert E. *WhoHisp 92*
**Romero,** Gilbert E 1955- *WhoAmP 91*
**Romero,** Henry, Jr. 1946- *WhoHisp 92*
**Romero,** Irene *WhoHisp 92*
**Romero,** Jacob B 1932- *AmMWSc 92*
**Romero,** Joe *WhoHisp 92*
**Romero,** Juan Carlos 1937- *AmMWSc 92, WhoHisp 92*
**Romero,** Kenneth Phillip 1960- *WhoHisp 92*
**Romero,** Leo *DrAPF 91*
**Romero,** Leo 1950- *WhoHisp 92*
**Romero,** Leon A. 1951- *WhoHisp 92*
**Romero,** Leota V. 1921- *WhoHisp 92*
**Romero,** Lucille Bernadette 1955- *WhoHisp 92*
**Romero,** Martin E. *WhoHisp 92*
**Romero,** Miguel 1949- *WhoEnt 92*
**Romero,** Orlando Arturo 1945- *WhoHisp 92*
**Romero,** Oscar 1917-1980 *FacFETw*
**Romero,** Paul Anthony, Sr. 1961- *WhoHisp 92*
**Romero,** Paulo Armando 1943- *WhoHisp 92*
**Romero,** Pepe 1944- *IntWW 91*
**Romero,** Phil Andrew 1949- *WhoHisp 92*
**Romero,** Philip James 1953- *WhoHisp 92*
**Romero,** Raymond G. 1954- *WhoHisp 92*
**Romero,** Richard Joseph 1955- *WhoHisp 92*
**Romero,** Thomas Arthur 1939- *WhoAmP 91*
**Romero,** Tino 1935- *WhoHisp 92*
**Romero-Barcelo,** Carlos Antonio 1932- *IntWW 91, WhoAmP 91, WhoHisp 92*
**Romero-Font,** Luis Guillermo 1952- *WhoFI 92*
**Romero Herrera,** Carlos 1941- *IntWW 91*
**Romero Kolbeck,** Gustavo 1923- *IntWW 91*
**Romero Mena,** Carlos Humberto *IntWW 91*
**Romero-Sierra,** Cesar Aurelio 1931- *AmMWSc 92*
**Romero Y Galdames,** Oscar Arnulfo 1917-1980 *DcEcMov*
**Romes,** Charles Michael 1954- *WhoBlA 92*
**Romesberg,** Floyd Eugene 1927- *AmMWSc 92*
**Romeu,** Andres Avelino 1952- *WhoMW 92*
**Romeu,** Jorge Luis *DrAPF 91*
**Romey,** William Dowden 1930- *AmMWSc 92*
**Romich,** Barry A. 1945- *WhoFI 92*
**Romick,** Gerald J 1932- *AmMWSc 92*
**Romig,** Alton Dale, Jr 1953- *AmMWSc 92*
**Romig,** Edgar Dutcher 1921- *WhoRel 92*
**Romig,** Phillip Richardson 1938- *AmMWSc 92*
**Romig,** Robert P 1936- *AmMWSc 92*
**Romig,** Robert William McClelland 1929- *AmMWSc 92*
**Romig,** William D 1914- *AmMWSc 92*
**Romig,** William Robert 1926- *AmMWSc 92*
**Romilly,** Jean-Edme 1739-1779 *BlkwCEP*
**Romine,** Charles Everett, Jr 1936- *WhoAmP 91*
**Romine,** Robert Lee 1930- *WhoEnt 92*
**Rominger,** Anna Sue 1947- *WhoAmL 92*
**Rominger,** Carl Ludwig 1820-1907 *BiInAmS*
**Rominger,** James Corridon 1920- *WhoAmP 91*
**Rominger,** James McDonald 1928- *AmMWSc 92*
**Rominger,** Susan E. Hofacre 1957- *WhoMW 92*
**Romino,** Dominick Joseph 1911- *WhoAmP 91*
**Romita,** Pier Luigi 1924- *IntWW 91*
**Romiti,** Cesare 1923- *IntWW 91*
**Romito,** Edmund D. 1926- *WhoMW 92*
**Romjue,** Nickell *DrAPF 91*
**Romley,** Martin *WhoEnt 92*
**Romley,** Richard M. 1949- *WhoAmL 92*
**Romm,** Judah Leonard 1946- *WhoRel 92*
**Romm,** Mikhail Il'ich 1901-1971 *SovUnBD*
**Rommel,** Erwin 1891-1944 *EncTR 91 [port], FacFETw [port]*
**Rommel,** Marjorie Ann 1933- *AmMWSc 92*
**Rommel,** Timothy Martin 1959- *WhoFI 92*
**Romney,** Earl of 1910- *Who 92*
**Romney,** Carl Fredrick 1924- *AmMWSc 92*
**Romney,** Edgar O. 1943- *WhoBlA 92*
**Romney,** Evan M 1925- *AmMWSc 92*
**Romney,** Joseph Barnard 1935- *WhoRel 92, WhoWest 92*
**Romney,** Richard Bruce 1942- *WhoAmL 92*
**Romney,** Richard Miles 1952- *WhoWest 92*
**Romney,** Seymour L 1917- *AmMWSc 92*
**Romney,** Steve *IntAu&W 91X, TwCWW 91*
**Romney-Brown,** Cheryl *DrAPF 91*
**Romo,** Eloise R. 1948- *WhoHisp 92*
**Romo,** John B. 1946- *WhoHisp 92*
**Romo,** Jose Leon 1930- *WhoHisp 92, WhoRel 92*
**Romo,** Oscar I. 1929- *WhoHisp 92*
**Romo,** Paul J. 1936- *WhoHisp 92*
**Romo,** Ric 1958- *WhoHisp 92*
**Romo,** Ricardo 1943- *WhoHisp 92*
**Romo,** Rolando 1947- *WhoHisp 92*
**Romo,** William Joseph 1934- *AmMWSc 92*
**Romo Gutierrez,** Fernando 1915- *WhoRel 92*
**Romoff,** Joyce Weizer 1954- *WhoAmL 92*
**Romoser,** Bruce Allen 1936- *WhoRel 92*
**Romoser,** Sally Beth 1958- *WhoWest 92*
**Romoser,** William Sherburne 1940- *AmMWSc 92, WhoMW 92*
**Romovacek,** George R 1923- *AmMWSc 92*
**Romp,** Walter Gary 1944- *WhoMW 92*
**Rompe,** Robert 1905- *IntWW 91*
**Rompis,** Robert James 1951- *WhoFI 92*
**Romrell,** Lynn John 1944- *AmMWSc 92*
**Romsdahl,** Marvin Magnus 1930- *AmMWSc 92*
**Romsey,** Lord 1947- *Who 92*
**Romsos,** Dale Richard 1941- *AmMWSc 92*
**Romtvedt,** David *DrAPF 91*
**Romtvedt,** David William 1950- *IntAu&W 91*
**Romualdez,** Eduardo Z. 1909- *IntWW 91*
**Romualdi,** James P 1929- *AmMWSc 92*
**Romualdi,** Pino Nettuno 1913-1988 *BiDExR*
**Romulo,** Carlos P 1899-1985 *FacFETw*
**Romun,** Isak *DrAPF 91*
**Rona,** Donna C *AmMWSc 92*
**Rona,** George 1924- *AmMWSc 92*
**Rona,** Mehmet 1939- *AmMWSc 92*
**Rona,** Peter Arnold 1934- *AmMWSc 92*
**Ronald,** Allan Ross 1938- *AmMWSc 92*
**Ronald,** Bruce Pender 1939- *AmMWSc 92*
**Ronald,** Edith *Who 92*
**Ronald,** Keith 1928- *AmMWSc 92*
**Ronald,** Robert Charles 1944- *AmMWSc 92*
**Ronald,** Thomas Iain 1933- *WhoFI 92*
**Ronaldshay,** Earl of 1965- *Who 92*
**Ronan,** Alfred Gregory 1947- *WhoAmP 91*
**Ronan,** Colin Alistair 1920- *WrDr 92*
**Ronan,** Helen *DrAPF 91*
**Ronan,** James Joseph 1961- *WhoAmL 92*
**Ronan,** John J. *DrAPF 91*
**Ronan,** Michael Thomas 1949- *AmMWSc 92*
**Ronan,** Patrick 1940- *WhoAmL 92*
**Ronan,** R. Scott 1947- *WhoAmL 92*
**Ronan,** Rhonda 1947- *WhoEnt 92*
**Ronan,** Richard *DrAPF 91*
**Ronan,** Sean G. 1924- *IntWW 91*
**Ronan,** William John 1912- *WhoFI 92*
**Ronat,** Arthur Walter 1928- *WhoWest 92*
**Ronay,** Egon *IntAu&W 91, IntWW 91, Who 92*
**Ronay,** Emma 1961- *TwCPaSc*
**Ronbeck,** Sissel 1950- *IntWW 91*
**Ronca,** Luciano Bruno 1935- *AmMWSc 92*
**Ronca,** Michael Vincent 1953- *WhoFI 92*
**Ronca,** William E., III 1962- *WhoHisp 92*
**Roncadori,** Ronald Wayne 1935- *AmMWSc 92*
**Roncalio,** Ceil *WhoAmP 91*
**Roncalli,** Angelo Giuseppe *ConAu 134*
**Roncallo,** Angelo D 1927- *WhoAmP 91*
**Ronco,** Frank, Jr 1926- *AmMWSc 92*
**Ronda,** James P. 1943- *ConAu 134*
**Rondeau,** Clement Robert 1928- *WhoFI 92*
**Rondeau,** Doris Jean 1941- *WhoFI 92, WhoWest 92*
**Rondeau,** Jose 1773-1844 *HisDSpE*
**Rondeau,** Patrick John 1959- *WhoAmL 92*
**Rondelli,** Lucio 1924- *IntWW 91*
**Rondepierre,** Edmond F 1930- *WhoIns 92*
**Rondepierre,** Edmond Francois 1930- *WhoAmL 92*
**Rondestvedt,** Christian Scriver, Jr 1923- *AmMWSc 92*
**Rondinelli,** Dennis August 1943- *WhoFI 92*
**Rondini,** Adele 1921- *IntAu&W 91*
**Rondon,** Edania Cecilia 1960- *WhoAmL 92*
**Rondon,** Fernando E 1936- *WhoAmP 91*
**Rondon,** Salomon *WhoAmP 91*
**Rondon-Tollens,** Salomon *WhoHisp 92*
**Ronel,** Samuel Hanan *AmMWSc 92*
**Ronell,** Avital 1956- *ConAu 133*
**Ronemus,** Michael Baylor 1955- *WhoAmL 92*
**Ronemus,** Thor Gladden 1930- *WhoAmL 92*
**Ronen,** David 1946- *WhoMW 92*
**Roner,** Kent Harry 1948- *WhoWest 92*
**Roness,** Ronald Ralph 1943- *WhoRel 92*
**Roney,** John Harvey 1932- *WhoAmL 92, WhoWest 92*
**Roney,** Michele Marie 1964- *WhoMW 92*
**Roney,** Paul H. 1921- *WhoAmL 92*
**Roney,** Raymond G. 1941- *WhoBlA 92*
**Roney,** Robert K 1922- *AmMWSc 92*
**Roney,** Wallace 1960- *WhoEnt 92*
**Rong Gaotang** 1912- *IntWW 91*
**Rong Yiren** 1916- *IntWW 91*
**Rongone,** Edward Laurel 1926- *AmMWSc 92*
**Rongstad,** Orrin James 1931- *AmMWSc 92*
**Ronhovde,** Virginia S 1909- *WhoAmP 91*
**Ronick,** Peter Craig 1955- *WhoEnt 92*
**Roningen,** Vernon Oley 1939- *WhoFI 92*
**Ronis,** Deri Joy 1951- *WhoRel 92*
**Ronis,** Max Lee 1930- *AmMWSc 92*
**Ronkin,** Bruce Edward 1957- *WhoEnt 92*
**Ronkin,** R R 1919- *AmMWSc 92*
**Ronn,** Avigdor Meir 1938- *AmMWSc 92*
**Ronn,** Ehud Israel 1950- *WhoFI 92*
**Ronne,** Finn 1899-1980 *FacFETw*
**Ronneburger,** Uwe 1920- *IntWW 91*
**Ronner,** Amy Debra 1953- *WhoAmL 92*
**Ronningen,** Reginald Martin 1947- *AmMWSc 92*
**Ronningen,** Thomas Spooner 1918- *AmMWSc 92*
**Ronnow,** Helge *WhoRel 92*
**Rono,** Peter 1967- *BlkOlyM*
**Ronquillo,** Allan Louis 1941- *WhoFI 92*
**Ronquillo,** Marcos G. 1953- *WhoHisp 92*
**Ronquillo,** Pablo Javier 1932- *WhoHisp 92*
**Ronsen,** Bruce 1945- *WhoMW 92*
**Ronsheim,** Sally B. 1917?-1990 *ConAu 133*
**Ronsisvalle,** Daniel 1936- *WhoRel 92*
**Ronsley,** Joseph 1931- *WrDr 92*
**Ronsman,** Wayne John 1938- *WhoWest 92*
**Ronson,** Gerald Maurice 1939- *IntWW 91, Who 92*
**Ronson,** Mark *ConAu 34NR*
**Ronson,** Raoul R. 1931- *WhoEnt 92, WhoFI 92*
**Ronstadt,** Linda 1946- *ConTFT 9, NewAmDM*
**Ronstadt,** Linda Marie 1946- *FacFETw, WhoEnt 92, WhoHisp 92*
**Ronstadt,** Peter 1942- *WhoWest 92*
**Rontgen,** Wilhelm Conrad 1845-1923 *FacFETw*
**Rony,** Peter R 1939- *AmMWSc 92*

**Ronyak**, Dawn Simonson 1932- *WhoMW 92*
**Ronzio**, Robert A 1938- *AmMWSc 92*
**Ronzio**, Robert Anthony 1938- *WhoWest 92*
**Roobol**, Norman R 1934- *AmMWSc 92*
**Rood**, Don D 1930- *WhoIns 92*
**Rood**, Johannes Joseph Van 1926- *IntWW 91*
**Rood**, Joseph Lloyd 1922- *AmMWSc 92*
**Rood**, Kathleen Cecilia 1967- *WhoEnt 92*
**Rood**, Ogden Nicholas 1831-1902 *BiInAmS*
**Rood**, Robert Thomas 1942- *AmMWSc 92*
**Roodenko**, Igal d1991 *NewYTBS 91*
**Roodkowsky**, Alice May 1921- *WhoAmP 91*
**Roodman**, Stanford Trent 1939- *AmMWSc 92*
**Roof**, Betty Sams 1926- *AmMWSc 92*
**Roof**, Deborah Ann 1948- *WhoWest 92*
**Roof**, Jack Glyndon 1913- *AmMWSc 92*
**Roof**, Katharine Metcalf *ScFEYrs*
**Roof**, Raymond Bradley, Jr 1929- *AmMWSc 92*
**Rook**, Alan 1909- *ConPo 91*
**Rook**, Douglas Brian 1946- *WhoEnt 92*
**Rook**, Harry Lorenz 1940- *AmMWSc 92*
**Rook**, Peter Francis Grosvenor 1949- *Who 92*
**Rook**, Timothy Earl 1949- *WhoMW 92*
**Rook**, Tony 1932- *WrDr 92*
**Rooke**, Constance 1942- *IntAu&W 91*
**Rooke**, Daphne 1914- *ConNov 91, WrDr 92*
**Rooke**, Daphne Marie 1914- *Who 92*
**Rooke**, Denis 1924- *Who 92*
**Rooke**, Denis Eric 1924- *IntWW 91*
**Rooke**, Giles Hugh 1930- *Who 92*
**Rooke**, James Smith 1916- *Who 92*
**Rooke**, Leon *DrAPF 91*
**Rooke**, Leon 1934- *IntAu&W 91, WrDr 92*
**Rooke**, Noel 1881-1953 *TwCPaSc*
**Rooke**, Thomas Matthew 1842-1942 *TwCPaSc*
**Rooke**, Vera Margaret 1924- *Who 92*
**Rooker**, Jeffrey William 1941- *Who 92*
**Rooker**, LeRoy S 1947- *WhoAmP 91*
**Rooker**, Michael *IntMPA 92*
**Rooker**, Michael 1955?- *ConTFT 9*
**Rooker**, Paul George 1943- *WhoFI 92*
**Rooks**, Charles Shelby 1924- *WhoBlA 92, WhoRel 92*
**Rooks**, Eleanor Knee 1927- *WhoAmP 91*
**Rooks**, H Corbyn 1910- *AmMWSc 92*
**Rooks**, James Orville 1922- *WhoAmP 91*
**Rooks**, Wendell Hofma, II 1931- *AmMWSc 92*
**Rooley**, Anthony 1944- *Who 92*
**Room**, Abram Matveevich 1894-1976 *SovUnBD*
**Room**, Adrian Richard West 1933- *IntAu&W 91*
**Room**, David Benjamin 1964- *WhoWest 92*
**Room**, Robin Gerald Walden 1939- *AmMWSc 92*
**Roome**, Oliver McCrea 1921- *Who 92*
**Roomful of Blues** *ConMus 7 [port]*
**Roon**, Robert Jack 1943- *AmMWSc 92*
**Rooney**, Andrew A. 1919- *IntMPA 92, WrDr 92*
**Rooney**, Andy *LesBEnT 92 [port]*
**Rooney**, Denis Michael Hall 1919- *IntWW 91, Who 92*
**Rooney**, E. Ashley *WhoRel 92*
**Rooney**, Francis Xavier 1927- *IntWW 91*
**Rooney**, George Willard 1915- *WhoAmL 92*
**Rooney**, J Patrick 1927- *WhoIns 92*
**Rooney**, James Arthur 1943- *AmMWSc 92*
**Rooney**, James Byron *WhoAmL 92*
**Rooney**, James F 1935- *WhoAmP 91*
**Rooney**, John E 1939- *WhoAmP 91*
**Rooney**, John Edward 1942- *WhoFI 92*
**Rooney**, John Joseph 1915- *WhoAmL 92, WhoAmP 91*
**Rooney**, John Lossin 1940- *WhoWest 92*
**Rooney**, John Philip 1932- *WhoAmL 92, WhoMW 92*
**Rooney**, Kathleen Dixon 1949- *WhoFI 92*
**Rooney**, Kevin D 1944- *WhoAmP 91*
**Rooney**, Lawrence Frederick 1926- *AmMWSc 92*
**Rooney**, Lloyd William 1939- *AmMWSc 92*
**Rooney**, Lucy 1926- *ConAu 135*
**Rooney**, Matthew A. 1949- *WhoAmL 92*
**Rooney**, Michael J. 1941- *WhoFI 92*
**Rooney**, Michael James 1947- *WhoAmL 92, WhoMW 92*
**Rooney**, Michael John 1944- *Who 92*
**Rooney**, Mick 1944- *TwCPaSc*
**Rooney**, Mickey 1920- *IntMPA 92, WhoEnt 92*
**Rooney**, Mickey 1922- *FacFETw*
**Rooney**, Patrick Michael 1958- *WhoFI 92*
**Rooney**, Paul George 1925- *AmMWSc 92*
**Rooney**, Peter John 1950- *WhoEnt 92*
**Rooney**, Phillip Bernard 1944- *WhoFI 92, WhoMW 92*
**Rooney**, Seamus Augustine 1943- *AmMWSc 92*
**Rooney**, Susan Kay 1946- *WhoFI 92*
**Rooney**, Terence Henry 1950- *Who 92*
**Rooney**, Thomas Peter 1932- *AmMWSc 92*
**Rooney**, Tom 1922- *WhoEnt 92*
**Rooney**, Victor Martin 1937- *AmMWSc 92*
**Roop**, Connie 1951- *WrDr 92*
**Roop**, Eugene Frederic 1942- *WhoMW 92, WhoRel 92*
**Roop**, Jack J 1933- *WhoAmP 91*
**Roop**, Joseph McLeod 1941- *WhoWest 92*
**Roop**, Peter 1951- *WrDr 92*
**Roop**, Richard Allan 1955- *AmMWSc 92*
**Roop**, Robert Dickinson 1949- *AmMWSc 92*
**Roope**, Bruce Edward 1952- *WhoAmP 91*
**Roorda**, Ervin Glen 1938- *WhoRel 92*
**Roorda**, John 1939- *AmMWSc 92*
**Roorda**, Walter John 1930- *WhoAmP 91*
**Roos**, Albert 1914- *AmMWSc 92*
**Roos**, C William 1927- *AmMWSc 92*
**Roos**, Casper 1925- *WhoEnt 92*
**Roos**, Charles Edwin 1927- *AmMWSc 92*
**Roos**, David Bernard 1928- *WhoWest 92*
**Roos**, Fred 1934- *IntMPA 92*
**Roos**, Frederick Ried 1934- *WhoEnt 92*
**Roos**, Frederick William 1940- *AmMWSc 92*
**Roos**, Henry 1921- *AmMWSc 92*
**Roos**, John Francis 1932- *AmMWSc 92*
**Roos**, Jorgen 1922- *IntDcF 2-2 [port]*
**Roos**, Kelley *WrDr 92*
**Roos**, Leo 1937- *AmMWSc 92*
**Roos**, Michael 1945- *WhoAmP 91*
**Roos**, Murphe *WrDr 92*
**Roos**, Nestor Robert 1925- *WhoWest 92*
**Roos**, Noralou P. 1942- *WrDr 92*
**Roos**, Philip G 1938- *AmMWSc 92*
**Roos**, Randy *WhoEnt 92*
**Roos**, Raymond Philip 1944- *AmMWSc 92*
**Roos**, Thomas Bloom 1930- *AmMWSc 92*
**Roos**, William 1911- *WrDr 92*
**Roosa**, Daniel Bennett St. John 1838-1908 *BiInAmS*
**Roosa**, Jan Bertorotta 1937- *WhoMW 92*
**Roosa**, Robert Andrew 1925- *AmMWSc 92*
**Roosa**, Robert V. 1918- *IntWW 91*
**Roose-Evans**, James 1927- *ConAu 35NR, SmATA 65 [port], WrDr 92*
**Roose-Evans**, James Humphrey 1927- *IntAu&W 91, Who 92*
**Roosenraad**, Cris Thomas 1941- *AmMWSc 92*
**Roosenschoon**, Hans 1952- *ConCom 92*
**Roosevelt**, Anna Eleanor 1884-1962 *AmPolLe*
**Roosevelt**, C V S 1915- *AmMWSc 92*
**Roosevelt**, Eleanor 1884-1962 *AmPeW, BenetAL 91, FacFETw [port], HanAmWH, PorAmW [port], RComAH*
**Roosevelt**, Elliott 1910-1990 *AnObit 1990, CurBio 91N*
**Roosevelt**, Franklin D. 1882-1945 *BenetAL 91, RComAH*
**Roosevelt**, Franklin Delano 1882-1945 *AmPolLe [port], EncTR 91 [port], FacFETw [port]*
**Roosevelt**, James 1907-1991 *ConAu 135, CurBio 91N, NewYTBS 91 [port]*
**Roosevelt**, James, Jr. 1945- *WhoAmL 92, WhoAmP 91*
**Roosevelt**, Joseph Willard 1918- *WhoEnt 92*
**Roosevelt**, Kermit 1889-1943 *BenetAL 91*
**Roosevelt**, Mark 1955- *WhoAmP 91*
**Roosevelt**, Oliver Wolcott, II 1927- *WhoEnt 92*
**Roosevelt**, Robert Barnwell 1829-1906 *BiInAmS*
**Roosevelt**, Selwa 1929- *ConAu 134*
**Roosevelt**, Theodore 1858-1919 *AmPolLe [port], BenetAL 91, BiInAmS, DcAmImH, FacFETw [port], RComAH, WhoNob 90*
**Roosevelt**, Theodore, IV 1942- *WhoFI 92*
**Roosta**, Ramin 1953- *WhoWest 92*
**Root**, Alan Charles 1925- *WhoFI 92*
**Root**, Allen William 1933- *AmMWSc 92*
**Root**, Charles Arthur 1938- *AmMWSc 92*
**Root**, Charles Joseph, Jr. 1940- *WhoWest 92*
**Root**, David Harley 1937- *AmMWSc 92*
**Root**, David Hugh 1959- *WhoFI 92*
**Root**, Deane Leslie 1947- *WhoEnt 92*
**Root**, Edwin W 1840?-1870 *BiInAmS*
**Root**, Elihu 1845-1880 *BiInAmS*
**Root**, Elihu 1845-1937 *AmPeW, AmPolLe, FacFETw, WhoNob 90*
**Root**, Elizabeth Jean 1931- *AmMWSc 92*
**Root**, George Frederick 1820-1895 *BenetAL 91, NewAmDM, RelLAm 91*
**Root**, Harlan D 1926- *AmMWSc 92*
**Root**, Henry James 1941- *WhoEnt 92*
**Root**, Howard Eugene 1926- *Who 92*
**Root**, John David 1940- *WhoRel 92*
**Root**, John Walter 1935- *AmMWSc 92*
**Root**, Judith *DrAPF 91*
**Root**, L Eugene 1910- *AmMWSc 92*
**Root**, Larry Donald 1936- *WhoFI 92*
**Root**, Mary Ann 1960- *WhoAmL 92*
**Root**, Mary Avery 1918- *AmMWSc 92*
**Root**, Michael John 1951- *WhoRel 92*
**Root**, Oren 1803?-1885 *BiInAmS*
**Root**, Oren 1838-1907 *BiInAmS*
**Root**, Paul John 1929- *AmMWSc 92*
**Root**, Phyllis 1949- *WrDr 92*
**Root**, Richard Bruce 1936- *AmMWSc 92*
**Root**, Richard Kay *AmMWSc 92*
**Root**, Samuel I 1930- *AmMWSc 92*
**Root**, Wells 1900- *IntMPA 92*
**Root**, William Dixon 1951- *WhoWest 92*
**Root**, William L 1919- *AmMWSc 92*
**Root**, William Pitt *DrAPF 91*
**Root**, William Pitt 1941- *ConPo 91, IntAu&W 91, WrDr 92*
**Root-Bernstein**, Robert Scott 1953- *AmMWSc 92*
**Rootare**, Hillar Muidar 1928- *AmMWSc 92*
**Roote**, Tom Stafford, Jr. 1934- *WhoRel 92*
**Rootenberg**, Jacob 1936- *AmMWSc 92*
**Rootes** *Who 92*
**Rootes**, Baron 1917- *IntWW 91, Who 92*
**Roothaan**, Clemens Carel Johannes 1918- *AmMWSc 92*
**Rootham**, William L. 1923- *WhoFI 92*
**Roots**, Betty Ida *AmMWSc 92*
**Roots**, Ernest Frederick 1923- *AmMWSc 92*
**Roots**, Guy Robert Godfrey 1946- *Who 92*
**Roots**, Paul John 1929- *Who 92*
**Roots**, Peter Charles 1921- *WhoFI 92*
**Roovers**, J 1937- *AmMWSc 92*
**Roozen**, Kenneth James 1943- *AmMWSc 92*
**Roozen**, Mary Louise 1921- *WhoMW 92*
**Roozen**, Peter Kip 1958- *WhoRel 92*
**Ropchan**, Jim R. 1950- *WhoWest 92*
**Roper** *Who 92*
**Roper**, Bill Lee 1937- *WhoRel 92*
**Roper**, Bobby L. *WhoBlA 92*
**Roper**, Clinton Marcus 1921- *Who 92*
**Roper**, Clyde Forrest Eugene 1937- *AmMWSc 92*
**Roper**, David 1954- *IntAu&W 91*
**Roper**, Edward Warren 1858-1898 *BiInAmS*
**Roper**, Geoffrey 1942- *TwCPaSc*
**Roper**, Gerald C 1933- *AmMWSc 92*
**Roper**, Glade F. 1953- *WhoAmL 92*
**Roper**, Grace Trott 1925- *WhoBlA 92*
**Roper**, Harry Joseph 1940- *WhoAmL 92*
**Roper**, John Charles Abercromby 1915- *Who 92*
**Roper**, John Dee 1935- *WhoRel 92*
**Roper**, John Francis Hodgess 1935- *Who 92*
**Roper**, L David 1935- *AmMWSc 92*
**Roper**, L V Sam 1931- *WhoAmP 91*
**Roper**, Larry Lester 1948- *WhoRel 92*
**Roper**, Laura Wood 1911- *WrDr 92*
**Roper**, Maryann 1949- *AmMWSc 92*
**Roper**, Michael 1932- *Who 92*
**Roper**, Patricia Anderson 1945- *WhoBlA 92*
**Roper**, Paul Duane 1951- *WhoRel 92*
**Roper**, Paul James 1939- *AmMWSc 92*
**Roper**, Richard Walter 1945- *WhoBlA 92*
**Roper**, Robert 1928- *AmMWSc 92*
**Roper**, Robert Burnell 1921- *Who 92*
**Roper**, Robert Edward 1916- *WhoAmP 91*
**Roper**, Robert George 1933- *AmMWSc 92*
**Roper**, Stephen David 1945- *AmMWSc 92, WhoWest 92*
**Roper**, Stephen Robert 1962- *WhoRel 92*
**Roper**, Walter William 1945- *WhoWest 92*
**Roper**, Warren Richard 1938- *IntWW 91, Who 92*
**Roper**, William L 1948- *AmMWSc 92*
**Roper-Curzon** *Who 92*
**Roper-Jackson**, Renee *DrAPF 91*
**Ropes**, John Warren 1927- *AmMWSc 92*
**Ropner**, David *Who 92*
**Ropner**, John 1937- *Who 92*
**Ropner**, John Raymond 1903- *Who 92*
**Ropner**, Robert Douglas 1921- *Who 92*
**Ropner**, William Guy David 1924- *Who 92*
**Ropp**, Gordon L 1933- *WhoAmP 91*
**Ropp**, Gus Anderson 1918- *AmMWSc 92*
**Ropp**, John Willson 1962- *WhoFI 92*
**Ropp**, Richard C 1927- *AmMWSc 92*
**Ropp**, Walter Shade 1922- *AmMWSc 92*
**Roque**, Francis Xavier 1928- *WhoRel 92*
**Roque**, Margarita *WhoHisp 92*
**Roque**, Roberto Dizon 1929- *WhoMW 92*
**Roque**, Ruben 1957- *WhoHisp 92*
**Roquelaure**, A. N. *ConAu 36NR, WrDr 92*
**Roquemaurel**, Ithier de 1914- *IntWW 91*
**Roquemore**, Leroy 1935- *AmMWSc 92*
**Roques**, Alban Joseph 1941- *AmMWSc 92*
**Roques**, John 1938- *Who 92*
**Roquitte**, Bimal C 1931- *AmMWSc 92*
**Rorabacher**, David Bruce 1935- *AmMWSc 92*
**Roraback**, Thomas Joseph 1943- *WhoIns 92*
**Rorabaugh**, Donald T 1944- *AmMWSc 92*
**Rorabaugh**, Joan 1928- *WhoAmP 91*
**Rore**, Cipriano da 1515?-1565 *NewAmDM*
**Rorem**, C Rufus 1894-1988 *FacFETw*
**Rorem**, Ned 1923- *ConCom 92, NewAmDM*
**Rorem**, Sharon Kay 1955- *WhoEnt 92*
**Rorer**, David Cooke 1937- *AmMWSc 92*
**Rorer**, John Whiteley 1930- *WhoFI 92*
**Rorie**, Charles David, Sr. 1936- *WhoMW 92*
**Rorie**, Roger L 1947- *WhoAmP 91*
**Rorig**, Kurt Joachim 1920- *AmMWSc 92*
**Rorimer**, Louis 1947- *WhoAmL 92*
**Roripaugh**, Robert 1930- *TwCWW 91, WrDr 92*
**Rork**, Allen Wright 1944- *WhoIns 92*
**Rork**, Eugene Wallace 1940- *AmMWSc 92*
**Rork**, Gerald Stephen 1947- *AmMWSc 92*
**Rork**, Robert Terry 1939- *WhoFI 92*
**Rorke**, John 1923- *Who 92*
**Rorke**, Lucy Balian 1929- *AmMWSc 92*
**Rorres**, Chris 1941- *AmMWSc 92*
**Rorschach**, Harold Emil, Jr 1926- *AmMWSc 92*
**Rorstad**, Otto Peder 1947- *AmMWSc 92*
**Rorty**, Amelie Oskenberg 1932- *WrDr 92*
**Rorty**, Richard McKay 1931- *IntWW 91, WrDr 92*
**Ros**, Enrique Jorge 1927- *IntWW 91*
**Ros-Lehtinan**, Ileana Carmen 1952- *WhoAmP 91*
**Ros-Lehtinen**, Ileana 1952- *AlmAP 92 [port], WhoHisp 92*
**Rosa**, Casimir Joseph 1933- *AmMWSc 92*
**Rosa**, Eugene John 1937- *AmMWSc 92*
**Rosa**, Fredric David 1946- *WhoFI 92, WhoWest 92*
**Rosa**, Joao Guimaraes 1908-1967 *DcLB 113 [port]*
**Rosa**, Josephine 1929- *WhoHisp 92*
**Rosa**, Margarita 1953- *WhoHisp 92*
**Rosa**, Marta T. 1957- *WhoHisp 92*
**Rosa**, Nestor 1936- *AmMWSc 92*
**Rosa**, Paul James, Jr 1927- *WhoAmP 91*
**Rosa**, Richard John 1927- *AmMWSc 92*
**Rosa**, Rose Nelida 1939- *WhoHisp 92*
**Rosa**, William 1948- *WhoHisp 92*
**Rosa-Gonzalez**, Ferdinand 1940- *WhoHisp 92*
**Rosa Guzman**, Antonio *WhoAmP 91, WhoHisp 92*
**Rosa Ocasio**, Joaquin *WhoAmP 91*
**Rosado**, Caleb 1942- *WhoHisp 92*
**Rosado**, David *WhoAmP 91, WhoHisp 92*
**Rosado**, John Allen 1936- *AmMWSc 92*
**Rosado**, Jose Francisco 1948- *WhoHisp 92*
**Rosado**, Julio Rosado, Jr. 1942- *WhoHisp 92*
**Rosado**, Nytza I. 1962- *WhoHisp 92*
**Rosado**, Peggy Moran 1946- *WhoEnt 92*
**Rosado**, Raul *WhoHisp 92*
**Rosado**, Wanda I. 1962- *WhoHisp 92*
**Rosado**, Wilfredo 1961- *WhoHisp 92*
**Rosado-Linera**, Ramon Arturo 1963- *WhoHisp 92*
**Rosado Mendez**, Emilio 1911- *WhoHisp 92*
**Rosado-Vila**, Luis, II 1931- *WhoHisp 92*
**Rosaldo**, Renato Ignacio, Jr. 1941- *WhoHisp 92*
**Rosales**, Javier Alberto 1965- *WhoHisp 92*
**Rosales**, John Albert 1956- *WhoHisp 92*
**Rosales**, Marco 1913- *WhoEnt 92*
**Rosales**, Maria E. 1961- *WhoHisp 92*
**Rosales**, Miguel 1943- *WhoHisp 92*
**Rosales**, Sylvia 1917- *WhoEnt 92*
**Rosales-Sharp**, Maria Consolacion 1927- *AmMWSc 92*
**Rosan**, Alan Mark 1948- *AmMWSc 92*
**Rosan**, Burton 1928- *AmMWSc 92*
**Rosand**, David 1938- *WrDr 92*
**Rosander**, Arlyn Custer 1903- *WhoWest 92*
**Rosane**, Edwin L 1936- *WhoIns 92*
**Rosano**, Henri Louis 1924- *AmMWSc 92*
**Rosano**, Thomas Gerard 1948- *AmMWSc 92*
**Rosapepe**, James C 1951- *WhoAmP 91*
**Rosar**, Madeleine E 1955- *AmMWSc 92*
**Rosar**, Virginia Wiley 1926- *WhoFI 92*
**Rosario**, Anna G. 1953- *WhoHisp 92*
**Rosario**, Carlos *WhoHisp 92*
**Rosario**, Darlene 1964- *WhoHisp 92*
**Rosario**, Edgardo N 1957- *WhoAmP 91, WhoHisp 92*
**Rosario**, Efrain d1991 *WhoHisp 92N*
**Rosario**, Lourdes M. 1961- *WhoHisp 92*
**Rosario**, Robert 1951- *WhoHisp 92*
**Rosario**, Victor 1966- *WhoHisp 92*
**Rosario**, William 1951- *WhoHisp 92*
**Rosario Collazo**, Francisco 1931- *WhoHisp 92*
**Rosario-Garcia**, Efrain 1938- *WhoHisp 92*

**Rosario Rodriguez,** Jose Angel 1946- *WhoHisp 92*
**Rosas,** Cesar *WhoHisp 92*
**Rosas,** Joan Xicota 1958- *WhoFI 92*
**Rosas,** Jose Leopold 1944- *WhoHisp 92*
**Rosas,** Juan Manuel de 1793-1877 *HisDSpE*
**Rosas,** Laura 1957- *WhoHisp 92*
**Rosas,** Leo 1944- *WhoHisp 92*
**Rosas,** Lou Michael 1956- *WhoHisp 92*
**Rosas,** Maurice O. 1944- *WhoHisp 92*
**Rosas,** Roberto Garcia, Jr. 1957- *WhoHisp 92*
**Rosas,** Salvador Miguel 1950- *WhoHisp 92*
**Rosas de Oquendo,** Mateo 1559?-1621? *HisDSpE*
**Rosas Vega,** Gabriel 1939- *IntWW 91*
**Rosasco,** William Sebastian, III 1929- *WhoAmP 91*
**Rosati,** Joseph 1789-1843 *DcAmImH*
**Rosati,** Robert Louis 1942- *AmMWSc 92*
**Rosato,** Frank Joseph 1925- *AmMWSc 92*
**Rosauer,** Elmer Augustine 1930- *AmMWSc 92*
**Rosazza,** John N 1940- *AmMWSc 92*
**Rosazza,** Peter Anthony 1935- *WhoRel 92*
**Rosbaud,** Hans 1895-1962 *NewAmDM*
**Rosberg,** David William 1919- *AmMWSc 92*
**Rosberg,** Rose *DrAPF 91*
**Rosberg,** Rose 1916- *WrDr 92*
**Rosberg,** Zvi 1947- *AmMWSc 92*
**Rosborg,** James Theodore 1950- *WhoMW 92*
**Rosborough,** Bradley James 1958- *WhoWest 92*
**Rosborough,** John Paul 1930- *AmMWSc 92*
**Rosborough,** Michael John 1948- *WhoAmL 92*
**Rosch,** Jean 1915- *IntWW 91*
**Rosch,** John Thomas 1939- *WhoAmL 92*
**Roscher,** David Moore 1937- *AmMWSc 92*
**Roscher,** Marina L. *DrAPF 91*
**Roscher,** Nina Matheny 1938- *AmMWSc 92*
**Roschlau,** Walter Hans Ernest 1924- *AmMWSc 92*
**Rosco,** Jerry 1950- *IntAu&W 91*
**Roscoe,** Bruce Kraig 1950- *WhoMW 92*
**Roscoe,** Charles *TwCWW 91*
**Roscoe,** Charles William 1924- *AmMWSc 92*
**Roscoe,** Daniel Evan 1967- *WhoMW 92*
**Roscoe,** Gareth 1948- *Who 92*
**Roscoe,** Henry George 1930- *AmMWSc 92*
**Roscoe,** John Miner 1943- *AmMWSc 92*
**Roscoe,** John Stanley, Jr 1922- *AmMWSc 92*
**Roscoe,** Robert Bell 1906- *Who 92*
**Roscoe,** Theodore 1906- *ScFEYrs*
**Roscoe,** Wilma J. 1938- *WhoBlA 92*
**Roscopf,** Charles Buford 1928- *WhoAmL 92*
**Rose of Cimmaron** *EncAmaz 91*
**Rose,** Aaron 1920- *AmMWSc 92*
**Rose,** Al 1916- *WrDr 92*
**Rose,** Alan Douglas 1945- *WhoAmL 92*
**Rose,** Albert 1910- *AmMWSc 92*
**Rose,** Albert Schoenburg, Jr. 1945- *WhoAmL 92*
**Rose,** Alec d1991 *NewYTBS 91*
**Rose,** Alec Richard d1991 *Who 92N*
**Rose,** Alex 1946- *IntMPA 92*
**Rose,** Alvin W. 1916- *WhoBlA 92*
**Rose,** Andrew *Who 92*
**Rose,** Andrew John 1965- *WhoFI 92*
**Rose,** Aquila 1696?-1723 *BenetAL 91*
**Rose,** Arthur 1921- *WhoBlA 92*
**Rose,** Arthur James *Who 92*
**Rose,** Arthur L 1932- *AmMWSc 92*
**Rose,** Arthur William 1931- *AmMWSc 92*
**Rose,** Aubert Verner, Jr. 1926- *WhoRel 92*
**Rose,** Axl *WhoEnt 92*
**Rose,** Axl 1962?- *News 92-1 [port]*
**Rose,** Barbara Blanchard 1927- *WhoMW 92*
**Rose,** Barry 1923- *Who 92*
**Rose,** Barry Michael 1934- *Who 92*
**Rose,** Benjamin Lacy 1914- *WhoRel 92*
**Rose,** Bernard Peter 1957- *WhoFI 92*
**Rose,** Bernard William George 1916- *Who 92*
**Rose,** Bessie L. 1958- *WhoBlA 92*
**Rose,** Billy 1899-1966 *FacFETw*
**Rose,** Birgit 1943- *AmMWSc 92*
**Rose,** Bolivar Boykin 1949- *WhoAmL 92*
**Rose,** Bram 1907- *AmMWSc 92, IntWW 91*
**Rose,** Brian 1930- *Who 92*
**Rose,** Brian Andrew 1951- *WhoMW 92*
**Rose,** Carl E 1914- *WhoAmP 91*
**Rose,** Carl Martin, Jr 1936- *AmMWSc 92*
**Rose,** Caroline Baer 1913-1975 *WomSoc*
**Rose,** Charles, III 1939- *WhoAmP 91*
**Rose,** Charles Buckley 1938- *AmMWSc 92*
**Rose,** Charles Frederick 1926- *Who 92*
**Rose,** Charles Ray 1942- *WhoEnt 92*
**Rose,** Charles William 1940- *AmMWSc 92*
**Rose,** Charlie *LesBEnT 92*
**Rose,** Charlie 1939- *AlmAP 92 [port]*
**Rose,** Chester Arthur 1941- *WhoFI 92*
**Rose,** Christine Brooke *Who 92*
**Rose,** Christopher 1937- *Who 92*
**Rose,** Claire *DrAPF 91*
**Rose,** Clifford *Who 92*
**Rose,** Clive 1921- *IntWW 91, Who 92*
**Rose,** Colin 1945- *TwCPaSc*
**Rose,** Daniel 1929- *WhoFI 92*
**Rose,** Daniel Asa *DrAPF 91*
**Rose,** David 1910-1990 *AnObit 1990*
**Rose,** David 1921- *AmMWSc 92*
**Rose,** David Allan 1937- *WhoFI 92*
**Rose,** David Edward 1924- *Who 92*
**Rose,** David Louis 1942- *WhoAmL 92*
**Rose,** David William 1930- *WhoWest 92*
**Rose,** Dennis Norman 1948- *WhoFI 92*
**Rose,** Diane Marie 1961- *WhoFI 92*
**Rose,** Donald Clayton 1920- *AmMWSc 92*
**Rose,** Donald Glenn 1922- *WhoWest 92*
**Rose,** Donald Henry Gair 1926- *Who 92*
**Rose,** Douglas Raymond 1942- *WhoRel 92*
**Rose,** Earl Alexander 1946- *WhoEnt 92*
**Rose,** Earl Forrest 1926- *AmMWSc 92, WhoAmL 92*
**Rose,** Elinor K. 1920- *WrDr 92*
**Rose,** Eliot Joseph Benn 1909- *IntWW 91, Who 92, WrDr 92*
**Rose,** Elizabeth *WhoEnt 92*
**Rose,** Elizabeth 1933- *SmATA 68*
**Rose,** Elizabeth M. *WhoFI 92*
**Rose,** Emma 1962- *TwCPaSc*
**Rose,** Ernst 1932- *WhoMW 92*
**Rose,** Evans, Jr 1932- *WhoAmP 91*
**Rose,** Evelyn 1925- *WrDr 92*
**Rose,** Francis 1909-1979 *TwCPaSc*
**Rose,** Francis L 1935- *AmMWSc 92*
**Rose,** Francois Jean-Baptiste Hubert de 1910- *IntWW 91*
**Rose,** Frank Anthony 1920-1991 *NewYTBS 91 [port]*
**Rose,** Frank Clifford 1926- *Who 92*
**Rose,** Frank Edward 1927- *AmMWSc 92, WhoMW 92*
**Rose,** Fred 1897-1954 *NewAmDM*
**Rose,** Gary Lee 1950- *WhoAmP 91*
**Rose,** Gary Michael 1957- *WhoRel 92*
**Rose,** Gene Fuerst 1918- *AmMWSc 92*
**Rose,** Geoffrey Arthur 1926- *Who 92*
**Rose,** George David 1939- *AmMWSc 92*
**Rose,** George G 1922- *AmMWSc 92*
**Rose,** Gerald 1935- *SmATA 68*
**Rose,** Gerald Gershon 1921- *Who 92*
**Rose,** Gordon Wilson 1924- *AmMWSc 92*
**Rose,** Graham John 1928- *Who 92*
**Rose,** Gregory Mancel 1953- *WhoWest 92*
**Rose,** Harold Bertram 1923- *Who 92*
**Rose,** Harold Wayne 1940- *AmMWSc 92*
**Rose,** Harvey Arnold 1947- *AmMWSc 92*
**Rose,** Herbert G 1930- *AmMWSc 92*
**Rose,** Herbert Herman 1929- *WhoRel 92*
**Rose,** Hieromonk Seraphim 1934-1982 *RelLAm 91*
**Rose,** Howard Francis, Jr. 1934- *WhoFI 92*
**Rose,** Hugh Michael 1940- *Who 92*
**Rose,** Ian 1957- *WhoAmL 92*
**Rose,** Ira Marvin 1921- *AmMWSc 92*
**Rose,** Irwin Allan 1926- *AmMWSc 92*
**Rose,** Israel Harold 1917- *AmMWSc 92*
**Rose,** Jack 1911- *IntMPA 92*
**Rose,** Jack 1917- *Who 92*
**Rose,** Jacobus 1957- *WhoEnt 92*
**Rose,** James *Who 92*
**Rose,** James A *AmMWSc 92*
**Rose,** James C *AmMWSc 92*
**Rose,** James David 1942- *AmMWSc 92*
**Rose,** James Stephenson 1926- *AmMWSc 92*
**Rose,** James Turner 1935- *WhoFI 92*
**Rose,** Janet 1947- *WhoAmP 91*
**Rose,** Jeffrey David 1931- *Who 92*
**Rose,** Jennifer Joan 1951- *WhoAmL 92*
**Rose,** Jerzy Edwin 1909- *AmMWSc 92*
**Rose,** Jim *Who 92, WhoAmP 91*
**Rose,** Joel *DrAPF 91*
**Rose,** Joel Steven 1948- *IntAu&W 91*
**Rose,** John A 1940- *WhoAmP 91*
**Rose,** John Charles 1924- *AmMWSc 92*
**Rose,** John Creighton 1922- *AmMWSc 92*
**Rose,** John Raymond 1934- *Who 92*
**Rose,** John Theodore 1934- *WhoAmP 91*
**Rose,** John Thomas 1943- *WhoFI 92*
**Rose,** Jonathan Chapman 1941- *WhoAmL 92, WhoAmP 91*
**Rose,** Joseph Hugh 1934- *WhoRel 92*
**Rose,** Joseph J 1925- *WhoIns 92*
**Rose,** Joseph Lawrence 1942- *AmMWSc 92*
**Rose,** Joyce A. *DrAPF 91*
**Rose,** Joyce Dora Hester 1929- *Who 92*
**Rose,** Judy Sizemore 1939- *WhoFI 92*
**Rose,** Julian 1947- *Who 92*
**Rose,** Kate 1948- *TwCPaSc*
**Rose,** Kathleen Blount 1908- *WhoAmP 91*
**Rose,** Kathleen Mary 1945- *AmMWSc 92*
**Rose,** Kenneth 1924- *WrDr 92*
**Rose,** Kenneth 1935- *AmMWSc 92*
**Rose,** Kenneth David 1949- *AmMWSc 92*
**Rose,** Kenneth Dwight 1912- *WhoMW 92*
**Rose,** Kenneth E 1915- *AmMWSc 92*
**Rose,** Kenneth Vivian 1924- *IntAu&W 91, Who 92*
**Rose,** Lawrence W *TwCSFW 91*
**Rose,** Lee H. 1955- *WhoEnt 92*
**Rose,** Leonard 1918-1984 *NewAmDM*
**Rose,** Leonard Eugene 1924- *WhoMW 92*
**Rose,** Lois Lynn Hall 1951- *WhoMW 92*
**Rose,** Louis Ward 1951- *WhoAmL 92*
**Rose,** Lynne *DrAPF 91*
**Rose,** Martin Engelbert 1947- *WhoRel 92*
**Rose,** Mary R 1956- *WhoAmP 91*
**Rose,** Michael 1937- *ConAu 133*
**Rose,** Michael Allen 1956- *WhoRel 92*
**Rose,** Michael Leonard 1952- *WhoEnt 92*
**Rose,** Michael Robertson 1955- *AmMWSc 92*
**Rose,** Michael Thomas 1947- *WhoAmP 91*
**Rose,** Milton Edward 1925- *AmMWSc 92*
**Rose,** Mitchell 1951- *AmMWSc 92*
**Rose,** Nathan Howard 1952- *WhoRel 92*
**Rose,** Nicholas John 1924- *AmMWSc 92*
**Rose,** Noel Richard 1927- *AmMWSc 92*
**Rose,** Norman 1923- *WhoAmL 92*
**Rose,** Norman Anthony 1934- *WrDr 92*
**Rose,** Norman Carl 1929- *AmMWSc 92*
**Rose,** Paul 1935- *Who 92, WrDr 92*
**Rose,** Paul Edward 1947- *WhoFI 92, WhoMW 92*
**Rose,** Pete 1938- *WhoFI 92*
**Rose,** Pete 1941- *News 91 [port]*
**Rose,** Pete 1942- *FacFETw*
**Rose,** Peter Henry 1925- *AmMWSc 92*
**Rose,** Peter I. 1933- *WrDr 92*
**Rose,** Peter R 1935- *AmMWSc 92*
**Rose,** Philip I 1939- *AmMWSc 92*
**Rose,** Phyllis *ConAu 36NR*
**Rose,** Phyllis 1942- *ConAu 135, WrDr 92*
**Rose,** Rachelle Sylvia 1946- *WhoBlA 92*
**Rose,** Raymond E. 1926- *WhoBlA 92*
**Rose,** Raymond Edward 1926- *AmMWSc 92*
**Rose,** Raymond Wesley, Jr 1941- *AmMWSc 92*
**Rose,** Reginald *LesBEnT 92*
**Rose,** Reginald 1920- *WhoEnt 92*
**Rose,** Reginald 1921- *IntMPA 92*
**Rose,** Reva 1936- *WhoEnt 92*
**Rose,** Richard 1933- *IntAu&W 91, IntWW 91, Who 92, WrDr 92*
**Rose,** Richard Alfred 1952- *WhoEnt 92*
**Rose,** Richard Carroll 1940- *AmMWSc 92*
**Rose,** Richard Loomis 1936- *WhoAmL 92*
**Rose,** Richard Scott 1959- *WhoWest 92*
**Rose,** Robert Arthur 1931- *WhoAmL 92*
**Rose,** Robert E. 1939- *WhoAmL 92, WhoWest 92*
**Rose,** Robert Edgar 1939- *WhoAmP 91*
**Rose,** Robert Gordon 1943- *WhoAmL 92*
**Rose,** Robert John 1930- *WhoRel 92*
**Rose,** Robert Joseph, Sr. 1954- *WhoAmL 92*
**Rose,** Robert Leon 1920- *AmMWSc 92, WhoWest 92*
**Rose,** Robert M 1937- *AmMWSc 92*
**Rose,** Robert Neal 1951- *WhoFI 92*
**Rose,** Robert R., Jr. 1915- *WhoWest 92*
**Rose,** Roger 1958- *WhoEnt 92*
**Rose,** Ronald Noble Steven 1945- *WhoEnt 92*
**Rose,** Rose 1946- *TwCPaSc*
**Rose,** Rubye Blevins *WhoEnt 92*
**Rose,** Seth David 1948- *AmMWSc 92*
**Rose,** Sharon Kay 1942- *WhoMW 92*
**Rose,** Shelvie 1936- *WhoBlA 92*
**Rose,** Stanley Jay 1918- *WhoFI 92*
**Rose,** Stephen *IntMPA 92*
**Rose,** Stephen B 1927- *WhoIns 92*
**Rose,** Stuart 1911- *Who 92*
**Rose,** Stuart Alan 1942- *AmMWSc 92*
**Rose,** Susan A. Schultz 1911- *WhoRel 92*
**Rose,** Susan Marie 1950- *WhoMW 92*
**Rose,** T. T. *WhoRel 92*
**Rose,** Terry W 1942- *WhoAmP 91*
**Rose,** Terry William 1942- *WhoAmL 92*
**Rose,** Tim 1953- *TwCPaSc*
**Rose,** Timothy Laurence 1941- *AmMWSc 92*
**Rose,** Vincent C 1930- *AmMWSc 92*
**Rose,** Walter Deane 1920- *AmMWSc 92*
**Rose,** Wayne Burl 1932- *AmMWSc 92*
**Rose,** Wendy *DrAPF 91*
**Rose,** Wilfred Andrew 1916- *Who 92*
**Rose,** Will 1889-1977 *ConAu 134*
**Rose,** William 1919- *WhoMW 92*
**Rose,** William B 1929- *WhoAmP 91*
**Rose,** William Dake 1928- *AmMWSc 92*
**Rose,** William Ingersoll 1944- *WhoMW 92*
**Rose,** William Ingersoll, Jr 1944- *AmMWSc 92*
**Rose,** William K 1935- *AmMWSc 92*
**Rose,** William Shepard, Jr. 1948- *WhoAmL 92*
**Rose,** Zelda B *AmMWSc 92*
**Rose-Ackerman,** Susan 1942- *WhoAmL 92, WhoFI 92*
**Rose-Heim,** William Bentley 1955- *WhoRel 92*
**Rose/Smith,** Al Israel *DrAPF 91*
**Roseau,** Maurice Edmond Adolphe 1925- *IntWW 91*
**Roseberry,** John L 1936- *AmMWSc 92*
**Rosebery,** Earl of 1929- *Who 92*
**Rosebery,** Dean Arlo 1919- *AmMWSc 92*
**Rosebery,** Richard Jay 1935- *WhoFI 92*
**Roseboom,** Eugene Holloway, Jr 1926- *AmMWSc 92*
**Roseborough,** Teresa Wynn 1958- *WhoAmL 92*
**Rosebrough,** Walter M., Jr. 1954- *WhoFI 92*
**Rosebush,** Judson George 1947- *WhoEnt 92*
**Rosecrance,** Richard 1930- *WrDr 92*
**Rosecrans,** John A 1935- *AmMWSc 92*
**Rosedale,** Peter Klaus 1931- *WhoAmP 91*
**Rosefielde,** Steven Shelley 1942- *WhoFI 92*
**Rosegay,** Avery 1929- *AmMWSc 92*
**Rosehart,** Robert George 1943- *AmMWSc 92*
**Rosehill,** Lord 1954- *Who 92*
**Rosehnal,** Mary Ann 1943- *WhoWest 92*
**Roseingrave,** Thomas 1688-1766 *NewAmDM*
**Rosekopf,** Thomas Arthur 1958- *WhoRel 92*
**Roseland,** Craig R 1949- *AmMWSc 92*
**Rosell,** Antoinette Fraser 1926- *WhoAmP 91*
**Rosell,** Barry Scott 1964- *WhoMW 92*
**Rosell,** Sharon Lynn 1948- *WhoWest 92*
**Roselle,** David 1939- *IntWW 91*
**Roselle,** David Paul 1939- *AmMWSc 92*
**Roselli,** Charles Eugene 1952- *AmMWSc 92*
**Roselli,** Francesco 1961- *WhoAmL 92*
**Roselli,** Richard Joseph 1954- *WhoAmL 92*
**Roselli,** Robert J 1947- *AmMWSc 92*
**Rosellini,** Albert D 1910- *WhoAmP 91*
**Roseman,** Arnold S 1930- *AmMWSc 92*
**Roseman,** Carey Schwartz 1955- *WhoAmL 92*
**Roseman,** Charles Sanford 1945- *WhoAmL 92*
**Roseman,** Jack 1931- *WhoFI 92*
**Roseman,** Jennifer Eileen 1952- *WhoBlA 92*
**Roseman,** Joseph Jacob 1935- *AmMWSc 92*
**Roseman,** Kenneth David 1939- *WrDr 92*
**Roseman,** Robert Drew 1947- *WhoAmL 92*
**Roseman,** Ronald Ariah 1933- *WhoEnt 92*
**Roseman,** Saul 1921- *AmMWSc 92, IntWW 91*
**Roseman,** Theodore Jonas 1941- *AmMWSc 92*
**Rosemark,** Peter Jay 1955- *AmMWSc 92*
**Rosemberg,** Eugenia *AmMWSc 92*
**Rosemeyer,** Jon Michael 1954- *WhoAmL 92*
**Rosemond,** George P 1910- *AmMWSc 92*
**Rosemond,** John H. 1917- *WhoBlA 92*
**Rosemond,** John Henry 1917- *WhoAmP 91*
**Rosemond,** Lemuel Menefield 1920- *WhoBlA 92*
**Rosemond,** Manning Wyllard, Jr. 1918- *WhoBlA 92*
**Rosemond,** Philip Saltonstall 1955- *WhoEnt 92*
**Rosemont,** David Anthony 1956- *WhoWest 92*
**Rosemont,** Norman *LesBEnT 92*
**Rosemont,** Norman 1924- *WhoEnt 92*
**Rosen,** Alan 1927- *AmMWSc 92*
**Rosen,** Albert 1924- *IntWW 91*
**Rosen,** Albert Leonard 1924- *WhoWest 92*
**Rosen,** Arthur Leonard 1934- *AmMWSc 92*
**Rosen,** Arthur Zelig 1920- *AmMWSc 92*
**Rosen,** Avram Abbot 1915- *WhoRel 92*
**Rosen,** Barry Howard 1942- *WhoMW 92*
**Rosen,** Barry Philip 1944- *AmMWSc 92*
**Rosen,** Bernard 1930- *AmMWSc 92*
**Rosen,** Bruce Irwin 1952- *AmMWSc 92*
**Rosen,** C A 1917- *AmMWSc 92*
**Rosen,** Carol Zwick *AmMWSc 92*
**Rosen,** Charles 1927- *IntWW 91, NewAmDM, Who 92*
**Rosen,** Charles Henry 1930- *WhoEnt 92, WhoWest 92*
**Rosen,** Cheryl Hope 1963- *WhoEnt 92*
**Rosen,** David 1921- *AmMWSc 92*
**Rosen,** David A 1926- *AmMWSc 92*
**Rosen,** David Allen 1955- *WhoWest 92*
**Rosen,** David Moses 1912- *WhoRel 92*
**Rosen,** Dianne L *AmMWSc 92*
**Rosen,** Eden Ruth 1951- *WhoEnt 92*
**Rosen,** Edward M 1930- *AmMWSc 92*
**Rosen,** Eve Cutler 1952- *WhoAmL 92, WhoIns 92*
**Rosen,** Frank *TwCPaSc*
**Rosen,** Fred Saul 1930- *AmMWSc 92*

**Rosen**, George DrAPF 91
**Rosen**, George M. 1936- WhoWest 92
**Rosen**, Gerald DrAPF 91
**Rosen**, Gerald 1938- WrDr 92
**Rosen**, Gerald Harris 1933- AmMWSc 92
**Rosen**, Gerald M AmMWSc 92
**Rosen**, Haiim B. 1922- IntWW 91
**Rosen**, Harold A 1926- AmMWSc 92
**Rosen**, Harry Mark 1946- AmMWSc 92
**Rosen**, Harvey Sheldon 1949- WhoFI 92
**Rosen**, Henry 1946- AmMWSc 92
**Rosen**, Howard 1914- WhoFI 92
**Rosen**, Howard 1939- AmMWSc 92
**Rosen**, Howard Neal 1942- AmMWSc 92
**Rosen**, Howard Robert 1960- WhoAmL 92
**Rosen**, Irving 1924- AmMWSc 92
**Rosen**, Irwin Gary 1954- AmMWSc 92
**Rosen**, Ismond 1924- TwCPaSc
**Rosen**, Jacqueline I. 1952- WhoEnt 92
**Rosen**, James Carl 1949- AmMWSc 92
**Rosen**, James Martin 1939- AmMWSc 92
**Rosen**, Jeff 1955- WhoAmP 91
**Rosen**, Jeffrey Adam 1958- WhoAmL 92
**Rosen**, Jeffrey J. 1949- WhoAmL 92
**Rosen**, Jeffrey Kenneth 1941- AmMWSc 92
**Rosen**, Jeffrey Mark 1945- AmMWSc 92
**Rosen**, Jeremy 1942- Who 92
**Rosen**, John Friesner 1935- AmMWSc 92
**Rosen**, Johnny 1944- WhoEnt 92
**Rosen**, Joseph David 1935- AmMWSc 92
**Rosen**, Joshua Philip 1956- WhoAmL 92
**Rosen**, Judah Ben 1922- AmMWSc 92, WhoMW 92
**Rosen**, Kathy Meryl Strauss 1956- WhoEnt 92
**Rosen**, Kenneth DrAPF 91
**Rosen**, Kenneth M. d1976 LesBEnT 92
**Rosen**, Kenneth Roy 1950- WhoIns 92
**Rosen**, Kenneth T. 1948- WhoFI 92
**Rosen**, Lawrence Richard 1936- WhoEnt 92
**Rosen**, Leon 1926- AmMWSc 92
**Rosen**, Leonard Craig 1936- AmMWSc 92
**Rosen**, Lester L 1924- WhoAmP 91
**Rosen**, Louis 1918- AmMWSc 92
**Rosen**, Marc Allen 1958- AmMWSc 92
**Rosen**, Mark Arnold 1951- WhoAmL 92
**Rosen**, Martin Jack 1931- WhoWest 92
**Rosen**, Marvin 1927- AmMWSc 92
**Rosen**, Marvin Jerold 1929- WhoWest 92
**Rosen**, Michael 1927- Who 92
**Rosen**, Michael 1946- WrDr 92
**Rosen**, Michael Boris 1940- WhoAmL 92
**Rosen**, Michael Howard 1943- WhoFI 92
**Rosen**, Michael Ira 1938- AmMWSc 92
**Rosen**, Michael James 1949- WhoAmL 92
**Rosen**, Michael Wayne 1946- IntAu&W 91
**Rosen**, Milton Jacques 1920- AmMWSc 92
**Rosen**, Milton W 1915- AmMWSc 92
**Rosen**, Milton William 1915- IntWW 91
**Rosen**, Moishe 1932- RelLAm 91, WhoRel 92, WhoWest 92
**Rosen**, Mordecai David 1951- AmMWSc 92
**Rosen**, Mortimer Gilbert 1931- AmMWSc 92
**Rosen**, Myor 1917- WhoEnt 92
**Rosen**, Nathan 1909- AmMWSc 92
**Rosen**, Nathaniel Kent 1948- WhoEnt 92
**Rosen**, Neil Steven 1953- WhoAmL 92
**Rosen**, Norma DrAPF 91
**Rosen**, Norman Charles 1941- AmMWSc 92
**Rosen**, Norman Edward 1938- WhoFI 92
**Rosen**, Ora Mendelsohn 1935- AmMWSc 92
**Rosen**, Paul 1928- AmMWSc 92
**Rosen**, Perry 1930- AmMWSc 92
**Rosen**, Peter 1943- WhoEnt 92
**Rosen**, Philip 1922- AmMWSc 92
**Rosen**, Rae Dichter 1947- WhoFI 92
**Rosen**, Ralph J 1919- WhoAmP 91
**Rosen**, Richard 1949- WrDr 92
**Rosen**, Richard Andrew 1953- WhoAmL 92
**Rosen**, Richard David 1948- AmMWSc 92
**Rosen**, Richard Lewis 1943- WhoAmL 92
**Rosen**, Richard M. d1991 NewYTBS 91
**Rosen**, Robert 1934- AmMWSc 92
**Rosen**, Robert Arnold 1936- WhoFI 92
**Rosen**, Robert L. 1937- IntMPA 92
**Rosen**, Sam 1920- WrDr 92
**Rosen**, Samuel 1923- AmMWSc 92, WhoMW 92
**Rosen**, Sanford Edward 1920- WhoRel 92
**Rosen**, Sanford Jay 1937- WhoAmL 92, WhoWest 92
**Rosen**, Saul 1922- AmMWSc 92
**Rosen**, Saul W 1928- AmMWSc 92
**Rosen**, Seth Lloyd 1956- WhoAmL 92
**Rosen**, Seymour 1935- AmMWSc 92
**Rosen**, Sherman David 1930- WhoMW 92
**Rosen**, Sherwin 1938- WhoFI 92, WhoMW 92
**Rosen**, Sidney 1916- AmMWSc 92, WrDr 92
**Rosen**, Sidney Marvin 1939- WhoAmL 92
**Rosen**, Simon Peter 1933- AmMWSc 92
**Rosen**, Sol 1932- AmMWSc 92
**Rosen**, Stanley Howard 1929- WrDr 92
**Rosen**, Stephen 1934- AmMWSc 92
**Rosen**, Stephen L 1937- AmMWSc 92
**Rosen**, Steven Charles 1953- WhoEnt 92
**Rosen**, Steven David 1943- AmMWSc 92
**Rosen**, Steven K. 1961- WhoEnt 92
**Rosen**, Steven Terry 1952- AmMWSc 92
**Rosen**, Sylvia DrAPF 91
**Rosen**, William Edward 1927- AmMWSc 92
**Rosen**, William Edward 1951- WhoFI 92
**Rosen**, William G 1921- AmMWSc 92
**Rosen**, William M 1941- AmMWSc 92
**Rosen**, William Warren 1936- WhoAmL 92
**Rosenak**, Charles B. 1927- ConAu 134
**Rosenak**, Chuck ConAu 134
**Rosenak**, Jan 1930- ConAu 134
**Rosenau**, Anita H. 1923- WhoEnt 92
**Rosenau**, Fred W 1922- WhoAmP 91
**Rosenau**, John 1943- AmMWSc 92
**Rosenau**, Werner 1929- AmMWSc 92
**Rosenau**, William Allison 1926- AmMWSc 92
**Rosenay**, Charles F. 1962- WhoEnt 92, WhoFI 92
**Rosenbach**, A. S. W. 1876-1952 BenetAL 91
**Rosenbaum**, David Mark 1935- AmMWSc 92
**Rosenbaum**, E C WhoAmP 91
**Rosenbaum**, Eugene Joseph 1907- AmMWSc 92
**Rosenbaum**, Fred J 1937- AmMWSc 92
**Rosenbaum**, Fred Jerome 1937- WhoMW 92
**Rosenbaum**, H S 1932- AmMWSc 92
**Rosenbaum**, Harold Dennis 1921- AmMWSc 92
**Rosenbaum**, I Alfred 1920- WhoAmP 91
**Rosenbaum**, Ira Joel 1941- AmMWSc 92
**Rosenbaum**, Irving Joseph 1921- WhoRel 92
**Rosenbaum**, Jacob I. 1927- WhoAmL 92
**Rosenbaum**, James Edward 1943- WhoMW 92
**Rosenbaum**, James Michael 1944- WhoAmL 92
**Rosenbaum**, Jean 1927- WhoWest 92
**Rosenbaum**, Joel L 1933- AmMWSc 92
**Rosenbaum**, Joseph Hans 1925- AmMWSc 92
**Rosenbaum**, Joseph Irving 1947- WhoAmL 92
**Rosenbaum**, Lisa Lenchner 1955- WhoMW 92
**Rosenbaum**, Lois Omenn 1950- WhoAmL 92
**Rosenbaum**, Manuel 1929- AmMWSc 92
**Rosenbaum**, Marcos 1935- AmMWSc 92
**Rosenbaum**, Martin M 1923- WhoIns 92
**Rosenbaum**, Martin Michael 1923- WhoAmL 92
**Rosenbaum**, Paul Leonard 1937- WhoFI 92
**Rosenbaum**, Richard Merrill 1931- WhoAmP 91
**Rosenbaum**, Robert Abraham 1915- AmMWSc 92
**Rosenbaum**, Stanley Ned 1939- WhoRel 92
**Rosenbaum**, Victor WhoEnt 92
**Rosenberg**, Aaron E 1937- AmMWSc 92
**Rosenberg**, Abraham 1924- AmMWSc 92
**Rosenberg**, Alan Stewart 1930- WhoAmL 92
**Rosenberg**, Alburt M 1927- AmMWSc 92
**Rosenberg**, Alex 1926- AmMWSc 92
**Rosenberg**, Alexander F 1927- AmMWSc 92
**Rosenberg**, Alfred 1893-1946 BiDExR, EncTR 91 [port]
**Rosenberg**, Alicia Gabriela 1961- WhoAmL 92
**Rosenberg**, Allan 1938- AmMWSc 92
**Rosenberg**, Andreas 1924- AmMWSc 92
**Rosenberg**, Andrew Lloyd 1950- WhoEnt 92
**Rosenberg**, Arnold Leonard 1941- AmMWSc 92
**Rosenberg**, Arnold Morry 1934- AmMWSc 92
**Rosenberg**, Auria Eleanor WhoAmP 91
**Rosenberg**, Barr Marvin 1942- WhoFI 92
**Rosenberg**, Bernard 1928- WhoAmL 92
**Rosenberg**, Bruce Alan 1934- IntAu&W 91, WrDr 92
**Rosenberg**, Burton M. WhoFI 92
**Rosenberg**, Carol Weiss 1944- WhoEnt 92
**Rosenberg**, Charles E 1936- AmMWSc 92
**Rosenberg**, Claude N., Jr. 1928- WrDr 92
**Rosenberg**, Dale Henry 1927- WhoMW 92
**Rosenberg**, Dale Norman 1928- WhoMW 92
**Rosenberg**, Dan Yale 1922- AmMWSc 92, WhoWest 92
**Rosenberg**, David DrAPF 91, WhoAmL 92
**Rosenberg**, David 1946- WhoAmL 92
**Rosenberg**, David Michael 1943- AmMWSc 92
**Rosenberg**, Dennis Melville Leo 1921- AmMWSc 92
**Rosenberg**, Diane Lynne 1945- WhoAmL 92
**Rosenberg**, Donald Martin 1933- WhoFI 92
**Rosenberg**, Edith E 1928- AmMWSc 92
**Rosenberg**, Eli Ira 1943- AmMWSc 92
**Rosenberg**, Ellen Small 1950- WhoMW 92
**Rosenberg**, Ethel Greenglass 1915-1953 HanAmWH
**Rosenberg**, Eva 1953- WhoWest 92
**Rosenberg**, Frank P. 1913- IntMPA 92
**Rosenberg**, Fred A 1932- AmMWSc 92
**Rosenberg**, Frederic D. 1945- WhoEnt 92
**Rosenberg**, Gary 1959- AmMWSc 92
**Rosenberg**, Gary David 1944- AmMWSc 92, WhoMW 92
**Rosenberg**, Gary Marc 1950- WhoAmL 92
**Rosenberg**, George WhoFI 92
**Rosenberg**, George Stanley 1930- WrDr 92
**Rosenberg**, Gerald Alan 1944- WhoAmL 92
**Rosenberg**, Gilbert Mortimer 1922- AmMWSc 92
**Rosenberg**, Grant E. IntMPA 92
**Rosenberg**, Harold 1906-1978 FacFETw
**Rosenberg**, Harry 1940- AmMWSc 92
**Rosenberg**, Henri 1950- WhoRel 92
**Rosenberg**, Henry 1941- AmMWSc 92
**Rosenberg**, Henry A., Jr. 1929- WhoFI 92
**Rosenberg**, Henry Mark 1914- AmMWSc 92
**Rosenberg**, Herbert Irving 1939- AmMWSc 92
**Rosenberg**, Herman 1920- AmMWSc 92
**Rosenberg**, Hilding 1892-1985 NewAmDM
**Rosenberg**, Howard Alan 1927- WhoWest 92
**Rosenberg**, Howard Anthony 1942- WhoWest 92
**Rosenberg**, Howard C 1947- AmMWSc 92
**Rosenberg**, Howard Charles 1947- WhoMW 92
**Rosenberg**, Ira Edward 1941- AmMWSc 92
**Rosenberg**, Irene Vera 1936- WhoEnt 92
**Rosenberg**, Irwin Harold 1935- AmMWSc 92
**Rosenberg**, Isaac 1890-1918 FacFETw, RfGEnL 91, TwCPaSc
**Rosenberg**, Isadore Nathan 1919- AmMWSc 92
**Rosenberg**, Ivo George 1934- AmMWSc 92
**Rosenberg**, J. Mitchell 1906- WrDr 92
**Rosenberg**, James Michael 1940- WhoFI 92
**Rosenberg**, Jay Arthur 1939- WhoAmL 92
**Rosenberg**, Jerome Laib 1921- AmMWSc 92
**Rosenberg**, Jerry C 1929- AmMWSc 92
**Rosenberg**, Joel Barry 1942- WhoFI 92
**Rosenberg**, John d1991 LesBEnT 92
**Rosenberg**, John D. 1929- WrDr 92
**Rosenberg**, John K. 1945- WhoAmL 92
**Rosenberg**, Jonathan Micah 1951- AmMWSc 92
**Rosenberg**, Joseph 1917- WhoEnt 92
**Rosenberg**, Joseph 1926- AmMWSc 92
**Rosenberg**, Karen Krisher 1959- WhoAmL 92
**Rosenberg**, Kenneth Ira 1947- WhoAmL 92
**Rosenberg**, L.M. DrAPF 91
**Rosenberg**, Lawson Lawrence 1920- AmMWSc 92
**Rosenberg**, Lee Evan 1952- WhoFI 92
**Rosenberg**, Leon Emanuel 1933- AmMWSc 92
**Rosenberg**, Leon T 1928- AmMWSc 92
**Rosenberg**, Leonard 1931- AmMWSc 92
**Rosenberg**, Liz DrAPF 91
**Rosenberg**, Manuel 1930- WhoFI 92
**Rosenberg**, Mark 1948- IntMPA 92
**Rosenberg**, Marshal E. 1936- WhoFI 92
**Rosenberg**, Martin 1946- AmMWSc 92
**Rosenberg**, Marvin WrDr 92
**Rosenberg**, Marvin 1906- WhoAmP 91
**Rosenberg**, Marvin J 1931- AmMWSc 92
**Rosenberg**, Maurice 1919- WhoAmL 92
**Rosenberg**, Michael 1937- WhoAmL 92
**Rosenberg**, Morris 1922- WrDr 92
**Rosenberg**, Murray David 1925- AmMWSc 92
**Rosenberg**, Murray David 1940- AmMWSc 92
**Rosenberg**, Nathan 1927- WhoFI 92
**Rosenberg**, Norman J 1930- AmMWSc 92
**Rosenberg**, Norman Lewis 1942- WhoMW 92
**Rosenberg**, Paul 1910- AmMWSc 92
**Rosenberg**, Peter David 1942- WhoAmL 92
**Rosenberg**, Philip 1931- AmMWSc 92
**Rosenberg**, Pierre Max 1936- IntWW 91
**Rosenberg**, Ralph 1949- WhoAmP 91
**Rosenberg**, Reinhardt M 1912- AmMWSc 92
**Rosenberg**, Richard Carl 1943- AmMWSc 92
**Rosenberg**, Richard K. 1942- IntMPA 92
**Rosenberg**, Richard M. NewYTBS 91 [port]
**Rosenberg**, Richard Martin 1933- AmMWSc 92
**Rosenberg**, Richard Morris 1930- IntWW 91, Who 92, WhoFI 92, WhoWest 92
**Rosenberg**, Richard Stuart 1939- AmMWSc 92
**Rosenberg**, Rick IntMPA 92, LesBEnT 92
**Rosenberg**, Robert 1930- AmMWSc 92
**Rosenberg**, Robert Charles 1945- AmMWSc 92
**Rosenberg**, Robert D AmMWSc 92
**Rosenberg**, Robert Jay 1947- WhoAmL 92
**Rosenberg**, Robert Melvin 1926- AmMWSc 92
**Rosenberg**, Roger Ellis 1943- WhoWest 92
**Rosenberg**, Ronald C 1937- AmMWSc 92
**Rosenberg**, Roy A. 1930- WhoRel 92
**Rosenberg**, Ruth Helen Borsuk 1935- WhoAmL 92
**Rosenberg**, Samuel 1949- WhoFI 92
**Rosenberg**, Samuel I 1950- WhoAmP 91
**Rosenberg**, Sanders David 1926- AmMWSc 92
**Rosenberg**, Saul Allen 1927- AmMWSc 92
**Rosenberg**, Saul H AmMWSc 92
**Rosenberg**, Saul Howard 1957- AmMWSc 92, WhoMW 92
**Rosenberg**, Sheli Zysman 1942- WhoAmL 92, WhoFI 92
**Rosenberg**, Stanley C WhoAmP 91
**Rosenberg**, Stephen Francis 1949- WhoFI 92
**Rosenberg**, Steven A 1940- AmMWSc 92, CurBio 91 [port]
**Rosenberg**, Steven Loren 1941- AmMWSc 92
**Rosenberg**, Stuart 1927- IntMPA 92, WhoEnt 92
**Rosenberg**, Stuart A 1947- AmMWSc 92
**Rosenberg**, Sydney J. 1914- WhoWest 92
**Rosenberg**, Theodore Jay 1937- AmMWSc 92
**Rosenberg**, Warren L 1954- AmMWSc 92
**Rosenberg**, Wolfgang 1915- WrDr 92
**Rosenberger**, Albert Thomas 1950- AmMWSc 92
**Rosenberger**, Alfred L 1949- AmMWSc 92
**Rosenberger**, Beryl Guy 1935- WhoRel 92
**Rosenberger**, Dale Brian 1954- WhoRel 92
**Rosenberger**, Dianna Joy WhoFI 92
**Rosenberger**, Francis Coleman DrAPF 91
**Rosenberger**, Franz 1933- AmMWSc 92
**Rosenberger**, Glen Moyer 1941- WhoRel 92
**Rosenberger**, John Knox 1942- AmMWSc 92
**Rosenberger**, Walter Emerson 1918- WhoEnt 92
**Rosenberry**, Katharine 1943- WhoAmL 92
**Rosenberry**, Terrone Lee 1943- AmMWSc 92
**Rosenblatt**, Adylin Isabelle 1926- WhoWest 92
**Rosenblatt**, Arthur ConAu 134
**Rosenblatt**, Arthur S. 1938- ConAu 134, SmATA 68
**Rosenblatt**, Charles Steven 1952- AmMWSc 92
**Rosenblatt**, Cy Hart 1954- WhoAmP 91
**Rosenblatt**, Daniel Bernard 1956- AmMWSc 92
**Rosenblatt**, David 1919- AmMWSc 92
**Rosenblatt**, David Hirsch 1927- AmMWSc 92
**Rosenblatt**, David Sidney 1946- AmMWSc 92
**Rosenblatt**, Eddie 1934- WhoEnt 92
**Rosenblatt**, Gerd Matthew 1933- AmMWSc 92
**Rosenblatt**, Joan Raup 1926- AmMWSc 92
**Rosenblatt**, Joe 1933- ConPo 91
**Rosenblatt**, Joseph 1933- WrDr 92
**Rosenblatt**, Judah Isser 1931- AmMWSc 92
**Rosenblatt**, Karin Ann 1954- AmMWSc 92
**Rosenblatt**, Louis 1928- WhoEnt 92
**Rosenblatt**, Michael 1947- AmMWSc 92
**Rosenblatt**, Murray 1926- AmMWSc 92, WhoWest 92
**Rosenblatt**, Paul Gerhardt 1928- WhoAmL 92
**Rosenblatt**, Peter Ronald 1933- WhoAmP 91
**Rosenblatt**, Richard Bruce 1954- WhoAmL 92
**Rosenblatt**, Richard Heinrich 1930- AmMWSc 92
**Rosenblatt**, Roger 1940- ConAu 34NR
**Rosenblatt**, Roger Alan 1945- AmMWSc 92

**Rosenblith,** Eric *WhoEnt 92*
**Rosenblith,** Walter Alter 1913- *AmMWSc 92, IntWW 91*
**Rosenblitt,** Alice *DrAPF 91*
**Rosenbloom,** Alfred A, Jr 1921- *AmMWSc 92*
**Rosenbloom,** Arlan Lee 1934- *AmMWSc 92*
**Rosenbloom,** Aviva Kligfeld 1947- *WhoRel 92*
**Rosenbloom,** Daniel 1930- *WhoFI 92*
**Rosenbloom,** Jerry Samuel 1939- *WhoIns 92*
**Rosenbloom,** Joel 1935- *AmMWSc 92*
**Rosenbloom,** Joseph R. 1928- *WrDr 92*
**Rosenbloom,** Lewis Stanley 1953- *WhoAmL 92*
**Rosenbloom,** Noah H. 1915- *WrDr 92*
**Rosenbloom,** Noah Hayyim 1915- *WhoRel 92*
**Rosenbloom,** Noah Schanfield 1924- *WhoAmL 92*
**Rosenbloom,** Norma Frisch 1925- *WhoAmL 92, WhoAmP 91*
**Rosenbloom,** Paul Charles 1920- *AmMWSc 92*
**Rosenblum,** Annette Tannenholz 1942- *AmMWSc 92*
**Rosenblum,** Arthur H 1909- *AmMWSc 92*
**Rosenblum,** Bruce 1926- *AmMWSc 92*
**Rosenblum,** Carla Nadine 1937- *WhoWest 92*
**Rosenblum,** Charles 1905- *AmMWSc 92*
**Rosenblum,** Edward G. 1944- *WhoAmL 92*
**Rosenblum,** Eugene David 1920- *AmMWSc 92*
**Rosenblum,** Freeman N. 1937- *WhoMW 92*
**Rosenblum,** Harold 1918- *AmMWSc 92*
**Rosenblum,** Howard Edwin 1928- *AmMWSc 92*
**Rosenblum,** Irwin Yale 1942- *AmMWSc 92*
**Rosenblum,** John William 1944- *WhoFI 92*
**Rosenblum,** Lawrence Jay 1944- *AmMWSc 92*
**Rosenblum,** Leonard Allen 1936- *AmMWSc 92*
**Rosenblum,** Lya Dym 1926- *WhoMW 92*
**Rosenblum,** Martin Jack *DrAPF 91*
**Rosenblum,** Martin Jack 1946- *IntAu&W 91*
**Rosenblum,** Martin Jacob 1928- *AmMWSc 92*
**Rosenblum,** Marvin 1926- *AmMWSc 92*
**Rosenblum,** Matthew Jay 1954- *WhoAmL 92*
**Rosenblum,** Myron 1925- *AmMWSc 92*
**Rosenblum,** Myron 1933- *WhoEnt 92*
**Rosenblum,** Nancy L. 1947- *ConAu 133*
**Rosenblum,** Peter 1941- *WhoEnt 92*
**Rosenblum,** Richard Mark 1950- *WhoWest 92*
**Rosenblum,** Robert *WhoEnt 92*
**Rosenblum,** Robert 1927- *Who 92, WrDr 92*
**Rosenblum,** Sam 1923- *AmMWSc 92*
**Rosenblum,** Stephen Saul 1942- *AmMWSc 92*
**Rosenblum,** Stewart Irwin *WhoEnt 92*
**Rosenblum,** Victor Gregory 1925- *WhoAmL 92*
**Rosenblum,** William I 1935- *AmMWSc 92*
**Rosenblum,** William M *AmMWSc 92*
**Rosenbluth,** Jack 1930- *AmMWSc 92*
**Rosenbluth,** Marion Helen 1928- *WhoMW 92*
**Rosenbluth,** Marshall N 1927- *AmMWSc 92*
**Rosenbluth,** Sidney Alan 1933- *AmMWSc 92*
**Rosenboom,** David 1947- *NewAmDM*
**Rosenbrock,** Howard Harry 1920- *IntWW 91, Who 92*
**Rosenbrook,** William, Jr 1938- *AmMWSc 92*
**Rosenburg,** Dale Weaver 1927- *AmMWSc 92*
**Rosencrans,** Howard Aaron 1961- *WhoFI 92*
**Rosencrans,** Steven I 1938- *AmMWSc 92*
**Rosencrantz,** James R 1914- *WhoAmP 91*
**Rosencrantz,** Lawrence 1945- *WhoFI 92*
**Rosencwaig,** Allan 1941- *AmMWSc 92*
**Rosendahl,** Bruce Ray 1946- *AmMWSc 92*
**Rosendahl,** Gottfried R 1911- *AmMWSc 92*
**Rosendale,** George William 1933- *WhoFI 92*
**Rosendale,** Roger John 1928- *WhoMW 92*
**Rosende Subiabre,** Hugo 1916- *IntWW 91*
**Rosendin,** Raymond J. 1929- *WhoHisp 92*
**Rosene,** Linda Roberts 1938- *WhoFI 92*
**Rosene,** Walter, Jr 1912- *AmMWSc 92*
**Rosener,** James David 1955- *WhoAmL 92*
**Rosenfeld,** Albert Hyman 1920- *IntAu&W 91*
**Rosenfeld,** Alfred John 1922- *Who 92*
**Rosenfeld,** Arthur H 1926- *AmMWSc 92*
**Rosenfeld,** Arthur H. 1930- *WhoAmL 92, WhoFI 92*
**Rosenfeld,** Azriel 1931- *AmMWSc 92*
**Rosenfeld,** Beverly Rita 1936- *WhoFI 92*
**Rosenfeld,** Carl 1944- *AmMWSc 92*
**Rosenfeld,** Charles Richard 1941- *AmMWSc 92*
**Rosenfeld,** Daniel David 1933- *AmMWSc 92*
**Rosenfeld,** Eric R. *NewYTBS 91*
**Rosenfeld,** Ervin 1934- *WhoEnt 92*
**Rosenfeld,** Frederick Harvey 1937- *WhoAmL 92*
**Rosenfeld,** George 1919- *AmMWSc 92*
**Rosenfeld,** Harry Leonard 1955- *WhoRel 92*
**Rosenfeld,** Irwin Ira 1951- *WhoWest 92*
**Rosenfeld,** Isadore 1926- *AmMWSc 92*
**Rosenfeld,** Jack Lee 1935- *AmMWSc 92*
**Rosenfeld,** Jayn Frances 1938- *WhoEnt 92*
**Rosenfeld,** Jennifer Wilcoxen 1960- *WhoAmL 92*
**Rosenfeld,** Jerold Charles 1943- *AmMWSc 92*
**Rosenfeld,** Joel 1957- *WhoMW 92*
**Rosenfeld,** John L 1920- *AmMWSc 92*
**Rosenfeld,** Leonard M 1938- *AmMWSc 92*
**Rosenfeld,** Leonard Sidney 1913- *AmMWSc 92*
**Rosenfeld,** Louis 1925- *AmMWSc 92*
**Rosenfeld,** Mark Allan d1991 *NewYTBS 91*
**Rosenfeld,** Martin 1932- *WhoFI 92, WhoWest 92*
**Rosenfeld,** Martin Herbert 1926- *AmMWSc 92*
**Rosenfeld,** Martin Jerome 1944- *WhoAmL 92, WhoMW 92*
**Rosenfeld,** Melvin 1934- *AmMWSc 92*
**Rosenfeld,** Melvin Arthur 1918- *AmMWSc 92*
**Rosenfeld,** Mitchell Allan 1928- *WhoAmP 91*
**Rosenfeld,** Mitchell Barry 1957- *WhoAmL 92*
**Rosenfeld,** Monroe H. *BenetAL 91*
**Rosenfeld,** Morris 1862-1923 *BenetAL 91*
**Rosenfeld,** Nancy *WhoAmL 92*
**Rosenfeld,** Norman Samuel 1934- *AmMWSc 92*
**Rosenfeld,** Paul 1890-1946 *BenetAL 91*
**Rosenfeld,** Robert Charles 1949- *WhoAmL 92*
**Rosenfeld,** Robert L 1937- *AmMWSc 92*
**Rosenfeld,** Robert Samson 1921- *AmMWSc 92*
**Rosenfeld,** Ron Gershon 1946- *AmMWSc 92*
**Rosenfeld,** Scott Michael 1958- *WhoAmL 92*
**Rosenfeld,** Sheldon 1921- *AmMWSc 92*
**Rosenfeld,** Stephen I 1939- *AmMWSc 92*
**Rosenfeld,** Steven Ira 1949- *WhoEnt 92*
**Rosenfeld,** Stuart Michael 1948- *AmMWSc 92*
**Rosenfeld,** Warren Steven 1955- *WhoAmL 92*
**Rosenfeld,** William *DrAPF 91*
**Rosenfelder,** Alfred S 1916- *WhoIns 92*
**Rosenfeldt,** Stuart Alan 1955- *WhoAmL 92*
**Rosenfelt,** Frank E. 1921- *IntMPA 92*
**Rosenfelt,** Frank Edward 1921- *IntWW 91*
**Rosenfield,** Alan R 1931- *AmMWSc 92*
**Rosenfield,** Arthur Ted 1942- *AmMWSc 92*
**Rosenfield,** Daniel 1932- *AmMWSc 92*
**Rosenfield,** Gary Charles 1955- *WhoWest 92*
**Rosenfield,** Israel 1939- *WrDr 92*
**Rosenfield,** James H. *LesBEnT 92 [port]*
**Rosenfield,** James Steven 1962- *WhoWest 92*
**Rosenfield,** Joan Samour 1939- *AmMWSc 92*
**Rosenfield,** Jonas, Jr. 1915- *IntMPA 92*
**Rosenfield,** Mark Jay 1948- *WhoAmL 92*
**Rosenfield,** Richard Ernest 1915- *AmMWSc 92*
**Rosenfield,** Robert Lee 1934- *AmMWSc 92, WhoMW 92*
**Rosenfield,** Sharon Manette Doner 1950- *WhoRel 92*
**Rosengard,** Andrew Brian 1958- *WhoEnt 92*
**Rosengard,** Herbert H. 1927- *WhoMW 92*
**Rosengreen,** Theodore E 1937- *AmMWSc 92*
**Rosengren,** Jack Whitehead 1926- *AmMWSc 92*
**Rosengren,** John 1928- *AmMWSc 92*
**Rosengren,** William R. 1934- *WhoAmL 92, WhoFI 92*
**Rosenhaft,** Ann Williams 1926- *WhoAmP 91*
**Rosenhan,** A Kirk 1940- *AmMWSc 92*
**Rosenheim,** D E 1926- *AmMWSc 92*
**Rosenheim,** Daniel Edward 1949- *WhoWest 92*
**Rosenhein,** Laurence David 1951- *WhoMW 92*
**Rosenhoffer,** Chris 1913- *WhoMW 92*
**Rosenholtz,** Ira N 1945- *AmMWSc 92*
**Rosenhouse,** Howard 1939- *WhoAmL 92*
**Rosenhouse,** Irwin *WhoEnt 92*
**Rosenkilde,** Carl Edward 1937- *AmMWSc 92*
**Rosenkoetter,** Gerald Edwin 1927- *WhoFI 92, WhoMW 92*
**Rosenkrantz,** Barbara G 1923- *AmMWSc 92*
**Rosenkrantz,** Daniel J 1943- *AmMWSc 92*
**Rosenkrantz,** Harris 1922- *AmMWSc 92*
**Rosenkrantz,** Jacob Alvin 1914- *AmMWSc 92*
**Rosenkrantz,** Linda *DrAPF 91*
**Rosenkrantz,** Marcy Ellen 1948- *AmMWSc 92*
**Rosenkranz,** Eugen Emil 1931- *AmMWSc 92*
**Rosenkranz,** Herbert S 1933- *AmMWSc 92*
**Rosenkranz,** Philip William 1945- *AmMWSc 92*
**Rosenkranz,** Stanley William 1933- *WhoAmL 92*
**Rosenlicht,** Maxwell 1924- *AmMWSc 92*
**Rosenlicht,** Maxwell Alexander 1924- *WhoWest 92*
**Rosenman,** Daniel 1930- *WhoFI 92*
**Rosenman,** Dorothy d1991 *NewYTBS 91*
**Rosenman,** Dorothy 1900-1991 *CurBio 91N*
**Rosenman,** Howard *IntMPA 92*
**Rosenman,** Irwin David 1923- *AmMWSc 92*
**Rosenman,** John B. *DrAPF 91*
**Rosenman,** Leonard 1924- *ConTFT 9, IntMPA 92*
**Rosenman,** Ray Harold 1920- *AmMWSc 92*
**Rosenmann,** Edward A 1940- *AmMWSc 92*
**Rosenn,** Harold 1917- *WhoAmL 92, WhoFI 92*
**Rosenn,** Max 1910- *WhoAmL 92*
**Rosenne,** Meir 1931- *IntWW 91*
**Rosenne,** Shabtai 1917- *IntWW 91*
**Rosenow,** Edward Carl, Jr 1909- *AmMWSc 92*
**Rosenow,** John Edward 1949- *WhoFI 92, WhoMW 92*
**Rosenow,** Sheryl Lynn 1958- *WhoAmL 92*
**Rosenquist,** Bruce David 1934- *AmMWSc 92*
**Rosenquist,** Edward P 1938- *AmMWSc 92*
**Rosenquist,** Glenn Carl 1931- *AmMWSc 92*
**Rosenquist,** Grace Link *AmMWSc 92*
**Rosenquit,** Bernard d1991 *NewYTBS 91*
**Rosensaft,** Lester Jay 1958- *WhoAmL 92*
**Rosensaft,** Menachem Z. 1948- *WrDr 92*
**Rosensaft,** Menachem Zwi 1948- *WhoAmL 92*
**Rosenshein,** Joseph Samuel 1929- *AmMWSc 92*
**Rosenshein,** Neil Abbot 1947- *WhoEnt 92*
**Rosenshine,** Allen Gilbert 1939- *WhoFI 92*
**Rosenshine,** Matthew *AmMWSc 92*
**Rosenson,** Lawrence 1931- *AmMWSc 92*
**Rosenspire,** Allen Jay 1949- *AmMWSc 92*
**Rosenstark,** Sol 1936- *AmMWSc 92*
**Rosensteel,** George T 1947- *AmMWSc 92*
**Rosenstein,** A B 1920- *AmMWSc 92*
**Rosenstein,** Alan Herbert 1936- *AmMWSc 92*
**Rosenstein,** Allen Bertram 1920- *WhoWest 92*
**Rosenstein,** Barry Sheldon 1951- *AmMWSc 92*
**Rosenstein,** David 1943- *WhoFI 92*
**Rosenstein,** George Morris, Jr 1937- *AmMWSc 92*
**Rosenstein,** Gertrude *IntMPA 92*
**Rosenstein,** Ira *DrAPF 91*
**Rosenstein,** Joseph Geoffrey 1941- *AmMWSc 92*
**Rosenstein,** Laurence S 1941- *AmMWSc 92*
**Rosenstein,** Nils Rosen von 1706-1773 *BlkwCEP*
**Rosenstein,** Nils Rosen von 1752-1824 *BlkwCEP*
**Rosenstein,** Robert 1933- *AmMWSc 92*
**Rosenstein,** Robert Bryce 1954- *WhoAmL 92*
**Rosenstein,** Robert William 1944- *AmMWSc 92*
**Rosenstein,** Samuel M. 1909- *WhoAmL 92*
**Rosenstein,** Sheldon William 1927- *AmMWSc 92*
**Rosenstock,** Elliot David 1932- *WhoRel 92*
**Rosenstock,** Herbert Bernhard 1924- *AmMWSc 92*
**Rosenstock,** Jack I. *WhoFI 92*
**Rosenstock,** Lawrence M 1943- *WhoAmP 91*
**Rosenstock,** Paul Daniel 1935- *AmMWSc 92*
**Rosenstraus,** Maurice Jay 1951- *AmMWSc 92*
**Rosenstreich,** David Leon 1942- *AmMWSc 92*
**Rosensweig,** Jacob 1930- *AmMWSc 92*
**Rosensweig,** Norton S 1935- *AmMWSc 92*
**Rosensweig,** Ronald E 1932- *AmMWSc 92*
**Rosental,** Ruben *WhoHisp 92*
**Rosenthal,** Abby Jane *DrAPF 91*
**Rosenthal,** Abraham Michael 1922- *IntWW 91*
**Rosenthal,** Alan David 1949- *WhoAmL 92*
**Rosenthal,** Albert Jay 1928- *WhoFI 92*
**Rosenthal,** Alex 1914- *AmMWSc 92*
**Rosenthal,** Alexander E 1912- *WhoIns 92*
**Rosenthal,** Allan Lawrence 1948- *AmMWSc 92*
**Rosenthal,** Arnold H. 1933- *WhoEnt 92*
**Rosenthal,** Arnold Joseph 1922- *AmMWSc 92*
**Rosenthal,** Arthur Frederick 1931- *AmMWSc 92*
**Rosenthal,** Barbara *DrAPF 91*
**Rosenthal,** Bernard G. 1922- *WrDr 92*
**Rosenthal,** Bob *DrAPF 91*
**Rosenthal,** Bud 1934- *IntMPA 92*
**Rosenthal,** Carole *DrAPF 91*
**Rosenthal,** David H. *DrAPF 91*
**Rosenthal,** David Harry 1965- *WhoFI 92, WhoMW 92*
**Rosenthal,** David Michael 1961- *WhoEnt 92*
**Rosenthal,** Donald 1926- *AmMWSc 92*
**Rosenthal,** Donald B. 1937- *WrDr 92*
**Rosenthal,** Donald Hackett 1953- *WhoFI 92*
**Rosenthal,** Earl Edgar 1921- *WhoMW 92*
**Rosenthal,** Edward d1991 *NewYTBS 91 [port]*
**Rosenthal,** Edward Leonard 1948- *WhoMW 92*
**Rosenthal,** Edward William 1950- *WhoEnt 92*
**Rosenthal,** Elise Beverly 1946- *WhoWest 92*
**Rosenthal,** Emily M. d1991 *NewYTBS 91*
**Rosenthal,** Erwin 1904- *WrDr 92*
**Rosenthal,** Erwin Isak Jacob d1991 *Who 92N*
**Rosenthal,** F 1925- *AmMWSc 92*
**Rosenthal,** Frank Vernon 1908- *WhoIns 92*
**Rosenthal,** Fred 1931- *AmMWSc 92*
**Rosenthal,** Fritz 1911- *AmMWSc 92*
**Rosenthal,** Gerald A 1939- *AmMWSc 92*
**Rosenthal,** Gerson Max, Jr 1922- *AmMWSc 92*
**Rosenthal,** Halina d1991 *NewYTBS 91 [port]*
**Rosenthal,** Harold Leslie 1922- *AmMWSc 92, WhoMW 92*
**Rosenthal,** Henry Bernard 1917- *AmMWSc 92*
**Rosenthal,** Herbert Marshall *WhoAmL 92*
**Rosenthal,** Herschel 1918- *WhoAmP 91*
**Rosenthal,** Howard 1924- *AmMWSc 92*
**Rosenthal,** Howard Gary *WhoMW 92*
**Rosenthal,** Ira Maurice 1920- *AmMWSc 92*
**Rosenthal,** J William 1922- *AmMWSc 92*
**Rosenthal,** Jack Morris 1931- *IntAu&W 91, Who 92*
**Rosenthal,** James Edward 1942- *WhoIns 92*
**Rosenthal,** Jean 1923- *IntWW 91*
**Rosenthal,** Jeffrey 1953- *AmMWSc 92*
**Rosenthal,** Joel 1946- *WhoAmP 91*
**Rosenthal,** John David 1950- *WhoWest 92*
**Rosenthal,** John William 1945- *AmMWSc 92*
**Rosenthal,** Judith Wolder 1945- *AmMWSc 92*
**Rosenthal,** Kenneth Lee 1950- *AmMWSc 92*
**Rosenthal,** Kenneth Steven 1951- *WhoMW 92*
**Rosenthal,** Lee 1937- *AmMWSc 92*
**Rosenthal,** Leonard Jason 1942- *AmMWSc 92*
**Rosenthal,** Liliana Hermosilla 1943- *WhoHisp 92*
**Rosenthal,** Lois C 1946- *AmMWSc 92*
**Rosenthal,** Louis Aaron 1922- *AmMWSc 92*
**Rosenthal,** M.L. *DrAPF 91*
**Rosenthal,** M. L. 1917- *ConPo 91, WrDr 92*
**Rosenthal,** Manuel 1904- *NewAmDM*
**Rosenthal,** Marc Ian 1959- *WhoEnt 92*
**Rosenthal,** Marshall 1940- *WhoMW 92*
**Rosenthal,** Maureen Diane *Who 92*
**Rosenthal,** Michael Bruce 1955- *WhoAmL 92*
**Rosenthal,** Michael David 1943- *AmMWSc 92*
**Rosenthal,** Michael R 1939- *AmMWSc 92*
**Rosenthal,** Milton Frederick 1913- *WhoFI 92*
**Rosenthal,** Miriam Dick *AmMWSc 92*

**Rosenthal**, Moriz 1862-1946 *NewAmDM*
**Rosenthal**, Morton Manueu 1931- *WhoRel 92*
**Rosenthal**, Murray Alan 1954- *WhoMW 92*
**Rosenthal**, Murray Wilford 1926- *AmMWSc 92*
**Rosenthal**, Murray William 1918- *AmMWSc 92*
**Rosenthal**, Myron *AmMWSc 92*
**Rosenthal**, Nathan Raymond 1925- *AmMWSc 92*
**Rosenthal**, Norman Leon 1944- *Who 92*
**Rosenthal**, Paul Edmond 1951- *WhoAmL 92*
**Rosenthal**, Paul M. 1954- *WhoEnt 92*
**Rosenthal**, Peter 1941- *AmMWSc 92*
**Rosenthal**, Peter M. 1950- *WhoAmL 92*, *WhoEnt 92*
**Rosenthal**, Philip 1916- *IntWW 91*
**Rosenthal**, Philip 1949- *WhoWest 92*
**Rosenthal**, Philip David 1963- *WhoWest 92*
**Rosenthal**, Phillip 1948- *WhoEnt 92*
**Rosenthal**, Rachel 1926- *WhoEnt 92*
**Rosenthal**, Richard Alan 1936- *AmMWSc 92*
**Rosenthal**, Rick 1949- *IntMPA 92*
**Rosenthal**, Robert E. 1945- *WhoBlA 92*
**Rosenthal**, Robert Joseph 1956- *WhoMW 92*
**Rosenthal**, Robert M. 1936- *IntMPA 92*
**Rosenthal**, Robert Sylvestre 1940- *WhoMW 92*
**Rosenthal**, Rudolph 1923- *AmMWSc 92*
**Rosenthal**, Saul Haskell 1936- *AmMWSc 92*
**Rosenthal**, Saul W 1918- *AmMWSc 92*
**Rosenthal**, Sol 1934- *WhoAmL 92*, *WhoEnt 92*
**Rosenthal**, Sol Roy *AmMWSc 92*
**Rosenthal**, Stanley Arthur 1926- *AmMWSc 92*
**Rosenthal**, Stanley Lawrence 1929- *AmMWSc 92*
**Rosenthal**, Steven Siegmund 1949- *WhoAmL 92*
**Rosenthal**, Stuart Allan 1948- *WhoAmL 92*
**Rosenthal**, Theodore Bernard 1914- *AmMWSc 92*
**Rosenthal**, Thomas Gabriel 1935- *IntWW 91*, *Who 92*
**Rosenthal**, Thomas Gerald 1938- *WhoMW 92*
**Rosenthal**, Tomme Neil 1926- *WhoFI 92*
**Rosenthal**, William J. 1920- *WhoAmL 92*
**Rosenthal**, William S 1925- *AmMWSc 92*
**Rosenthale**, Marvin E 1933- *AmMWSc 92*
**Rosenwald**, Gary W 1941- *AmMWSc 92*
**Rosenwald**, John *DrAPF 91*
**Rosenwasser**, Lanny Jeffery *AmMWSc 92*
**Rosenzweig**, Barney *LesBEnT 92*
**Rosenzweig**, Barney 1937- *IntMPA 92*
**Rosenzweig**, Carl 1946- *AmMWSc 92*
**Rosenzweig**, Charles Leonard 1952- *WhoAmL 92*
**Rosenzweig**, David 1940- *WhoWest 92*
**Rosenzweig**, David Yates 1933- *AmMWSc 92*
**Rosenzweig**, Geri *DrAPF 91*
**Rosenzweig**, Harry 1907- *WhoAmP 91*
**Rosenzweig**, Mark Richard 1922- *AmMWSc 92*, *IntWW 91*, *WhoWest 92*
**Rosenzweig**, Michael Leo 1941- *AmMWSc 92*
**Rosenzweig**, Norman 1924- *AmMWSc 92*, *WhoMW 92*
**Rosenzweig**, Oscar John 1922- *WhoMW 92*
**Rosenzweig**, Paul Samuel 1959- *WhoAmL 92*
**Rosenzweig**, Peggy A 1936- *WhoAmP 91*
**Rosenzweig**, Phyllis *DrAPF 91*
**Rosenzweig**, Richard Stuart 1935- *WhoEnt 92*
**Rosenzweig**, Roy 1950- *ConAu 35NR*
**Rosenzweig**, Saul 1907- *WhoMW 92*
**Rosenzweig**, Walter 1927- *AmMWSc 92*
**Rosenzweig**, William David 1946- *AmMWSc 92*
**Rosenzweig-Diaz**, Roberto de 1924- *IntWW 91*
**Rosequist**, David Kay 1954- *WhoAmL 92*
**Rosett**, Ann Doyle 1955- *WhoRel 92*
**Rosett**, Arthur Irwin 1934- *WhoAmL 92*, *WhoWest 92*
**Rosett**, Marianna *WhoEnt 92*
**Rosette**, Fabian R. 1948- *WhoHisp 92*
**Rosevear**, John William 1927- *AmMWSc 92*
**Roseveare**, Robert William 1924- *Who 92*
**Rosewarn**, John 1940- *Who 92*
**Rosewater**, Frank 1856- *ScFEYrs*
**Rosewell**, Edward Joseph 1928- *WhoAmP 91*
**Roshal'**, Grigoriy L'vovich 1899-1983 *SovUnBD*
**Roshal**, Jay Yehudie 1922- *AmMWSc 92*
**Roshel**, John Albert, Jr. 1941- *WhoMW 92*
**Roshell**, Marvin J 1932- *WhoAmP 91*
**Roshko**, Alexana *AmMWSc 92*
**Roshko**, Anatol 1923- *AmMWSc 92*
**Rosholt**, Michael 1920- *IntWW 91*
**Roshon**, George Kenneth 1942- *WhoFI 92*
**Roshwalb**, Irving 1924- *AmMWSc 92*
**Roshwald**, Mordecai 1921- *TwCSFW 91*, *WrDr 92*
**Roshwald**, Mordecai M. *DrAPF 91*
**Rosi**, David 1932- *AmMWSc 92*
**Rosi**, Francesco 1922- *IntDcF 2-2*, *IntMPA 92*, *IntWW 91*
**Rosi**, Fred 1921- *AmMWSc 92*
**Rosi**, Philip Rinaldo 1938- *WhoAmL 92*
**Rosich**, Rayner Karl 1940- *WhoWest 92*
**Rosicky**, Bohumir 1922- *IntWW 91*
**Rosier**, David Lewis 1937- *WhoFI 92*
**Rosier**, Frederick 1915- *Who 92*
**Rosier**, James 1575?-1635 *BenetAL 91*
**Rosier**, Ronald Crosby 1943- *AmMWSc 92*
**Rosier**, Stanley Bruce 1928- *Who 92*
**Rosillo**, Salvador Edmundo 1936- *WhoHisp 92*
**Rosin**, James 1946- *WhoEnt 92*
**Rosin**, Morris 1924- *WhoFI 92*
**Rosin**, Robert Fisher 1936- *AmMWSc 92*
**Rosin**, Walter L. *WhoRel 92*
**Rosinek**, Jeffrey 1941- *WhoAmL 92*
**Rosing**, Richard 1955- *WhoEnt 92*
**Rosing**, Wayne C 1947- *AmMWSc 92*
**Rosing-Schow**, Niels 1954- *ConCom 92*
**Rosinger**, Eva L J 1941- *AmMWSc 92*
**Rosinger**, Herbert Eugene 1942- *AmMWSc 92*
**Rosini**, James Edward 1953- *WhoAmL 92*
**Rosinski**, Jan 1917- *AmMWSc 92*
**Rosinski**, Joanne *AmMWSc 92*
**Rosinski**, Michael A 1962- *AmMWSc 92*
**Rosiny**, Frank Richard 1940- *WhoAmL 92*
**Roska**, Fred James 1954- *AmMWSc 92*
**Roskam**, Alan Dee 1945- *WhoFI 92*
**Roskam**, Jan 1930- *AmMWSc 92*
**Roskamp**, Gordon Keith 1950- *AmMWSc 92*
**Roskamp**, Karl Wilhelm 1923- *WhoFI 92*, *WhoMW 92*, *WrDr 92*
**Roskell**, John Smith 1913- *Who 92*
**Roskens**, Ronald W *WhoAmP 91*
**Roskes**, Gerald J 1943- *AmMWSc 92*
**Roskies**, Ethel 1933- *AmMWSc 92*
**Roskies**, Ralph Zvi 1940- *AmMWSc 92*
**Roskill** *Who 92*
**Roskill**, Baron 1911- *IntWW 91*, *Who 92*
**Roskill**, Ashton Wentworth d1991 *Who 92N*
**Roskill**, Mark Wentworth 1933- *WrDr 92*
**Roskill**, Oliver Wentworth 1906- *Who 92*
**Roskin**, Lewis Ross 1920- *WhoEnt 92*
**Rosko**, Michael Daniel 1949- *WhoFI 92*
**Roskoff**, Allen N 1950- *WhoAmP 91*
**Roskos**, Roland R 1940- *AmMWSc 92*
**Roskoski**, Joann Pearl 1947- *AmMWSc 92*
**Roskoski**, Robert, Jr 1939- *AmMWSc 92*
**Rosky**, Burton Seymour 1927- *WhoAmL 92*, *WhoWest 92*
**Rosky**, Theodore Samuel 1937- *WhoFI 92*
**Roslavets**, Nikolay Andreevich 1881-1944 *SovUnBD*
**Rosler**, Lawrence 1934- *AmMWSc 92*
**Rosler**, Martha *DrAPF 91*
**Rosler**, Richard S 1937- *AmMWSc 92*
**Rosling**, Derek Norman 1930- *Who 92*
**Rosling**, Peter Edward 1929- *Who 92*
**Roslinski**, Lawrence Michael 1942- *AmMWSc 92*
**Roslycky**, Eugene Bohdan 1927- *AmMWSc 92*
**Rosman**, Howard 1929- *AmMWSc 92*
**Rosman**, Steven Michael 1956- *WhoRel 92*
**Rosmarin**, Philip Craig 1947- *WhoWest 92*
**Rosmini**, Gary David 1952- *WhoFI 92*, *WhoWest 92*
**Rosnack**, Richard John 1959- *WhoFI 92*
**Rosner**, Anthony Leopold 1943- *AmMWSc 92*
**Rosner**, Bernat 1932- *WhoFI 92*
**Rosner**, Daniel E 1933- *AmMWSc 92*
**Rosner**, Daniel Eric 1958- *WhoAmL 92*
**Rosner**, David *DrAPF 91*
**Rosner**, Fred 1935- *AmMWSc 92*
**Rosner**, Ira Neil 1959- *WhoAmL 92*
**Rosner**, Jonathan Lincoln 1941- *AmMWSc 92*, *WhoMW 92*
**Rosner**, Judah Leon 1939- *AmMWSc 92*
**Rosner**, Marsha R 1950- *AmMWSc 92*
**Rosner**, Paul 1935- *WhoEnt 92*
**Rosner**, Rick 1941- *WhoEnt 92*
**Rosner**, Robert 1947- *AmMWSc 92*, *WhoMW 92*
**Rosner**, Robert Allan 1956- *WhoWest 92*
**Rosner**, Seth 1931- *WhoAmL 92*
**Rosner**, Sheldon David 1941- *AmMWSc 92*
**Rosner**, William 1933- *AmMWSc 92*
**Rosness**, Betty June 1924- *WhoFI 92*
**Rosny**, J H aine 1856-1940 *ScFEYrs*
**Rosochacki**, Daniel *DrAPF 91*
**Rosoff**, Betty 1920- *AmMWSc 92*
**Rosoff**, Morton 1922- *AmMWSc 92*
**Rosoff**, William A. 1943- *WhoAmL 92*, *WhoFI 92*
**Rosolino**, Frank 1926-1978 *NewAmDM*
**Rosolowski**, Joseph Henry 1930- *AmMWSc 92*
**Rosoman**, Leonard 1913- *TwCPaSc*
**Rosoman**, Leonard Henry 1913- *IntWW 91*, *Who 92*
**Rosomoff**, Hubert Lawrence 1927- *AmMWSc 92*
**Rosow**, I. Peter 1937- *WhoFI 92*
**Rosow**, Jerome Morris 1919- *WhoAmP 91*
**Rosow**, Stuart L. 1950- *WhoAmL 92*
**Rosowski**, Robert Bernard 1940- *WhoFI 92*
**Rosowsky**, Andre 1936- *AmMWSc 92*
**Rospigliosi** *Who 92*
**Ross** *Who 92*
**Ross**, Lord 1927- *Who 92*
**Ross**, Adrian E. 1912- *WhoFI 92*
**Ross**, Alan 1922- *ConPo 91*, *IntAu&W 91*, *Who 92*, *WrDr 92*
**Ross**, Alan 1926- *AmMWSc 92*
**Ross**, Alberta B 1928- *AmMWSc 92*
**Ross**, Alex R 1919- *AmMWSc 92*
**Ross**, Alexander 1783-1856 *BenetAL 91*
**Ross**, Alexander 1907- *Who 92*
**Ross**, Alexander 1920- *AmMWSc 92*
**Ross**, Alfred William d1991 *Who 92N*
**Ross**, Allan Anderson 1939- *WhoEnt 92*
**Ross**, Alonzo Harvey 1950- *AmMWSc 92*
**Ross**, Alta Catharine 1947- *AmMWSc 92*
**Ross**, Alvin 1922- *WhoWest 92*
**Ross**, Andre Louis Henry 1922- *IntWW 91*
**Ross**, Andrew Christian 1931- *Who 92*
**Ross**, Angus 1911- *WrDr 92*
**Ross**, Angus 1927- *WrDr 92*
**Ross**, Anthony Roger 1953- *WhoBlA 92*
**Ross**, Archibald 1911- *Who 92*
**Ross**, Archibald David Manisty 1911- *IntWW 91*
**Ross**, Arnold J. 1938- *WhoAmL 92*
**Ross**, Arthur Leonard 1924- *AmMWSc 92*
**Ross**, Audrey 1938- *WhoEnt 92*
**Ross**, Audrey Ann 1960- *WhoAmL 92*
**Ross**, Barnaby *BenetAL 91*
**Ross**, Barry 1944- *WhoEnt 92*
**Ross**, Barry A. 1954- *WhoRel 92*
**Ross**, Barry Lowell 1938- *WhoRel 92*
**Ross**, Bernard 1934- *AmMWSc 92*
**Ross**, Bernd 1924- *AmMWSc 92*
**Ross**, Betsy 1752-1836 *BlkwEAR*
**Ross**, Betty Grace 1931- *WhoFI 92*
**Ross**, Bradford 1912- *WhoAmL 92*
**Ross**, Bradley Alfred 1952- *AmMWSc 92*
**Ross**, Brian 1948- *IntAu&W 91*
**Ross**, Bruce Brian 1944- *AmMWSc 92*
**Ross**, Byron Warren 1920- *WhoRel 92*
**Ross**, Carol Joyce Waller 1942- *WhoMW 92*
**Ross**, Carson 1946- *WhoAmP 91*
**Ross**, Catherine *IntAu&W 91X*, *WrDr 92*
**Ross**, Catherine Laverne 1948- *WhoBlA 92*
**Ross**, Charles 1918- *WhoBlA 92*
**Ross**, Charles 1924- *TwCPaSc*
**Ross**, Charles Alexander 1933- *AmMWSc 92*
**Ross**, Charles Burton 1934- *AmMWSc 92*
**Ross**, Charles C. 1914- *WhoBlA 92*
**Ross**, Charles Johnson 1922- *WhoMW 92*
**Ross**, Charles R, Jr 1956- *WhoAmP 91*
**Ross**, Chester Wheeler 1922- *WhoMW 92*, *WhoRel 92*
**Ross**, Christopher Theodore William 1925- *WhoAmL 92*
**Ross**, Christopher Wade Stelyan 1943- *WhoAmP 91*
**Ross**, Clarissa *WrDr 92*
**Ross**, Claud Richard 1924- *IntWW 91*, *Who 92*
**Ross**, Claude G 1917- *WhoAmP 91*
**Ross**, Clay Campbell, Jr 1936- *AmMWSc 92*
**Ross**, Cleon Walter 1934- *AmMWSc 92*
**Ross**, Coleman DeVane 1943- *WhoFI 92*
**Ross**, Curlee 1929- *WhoBlA 92*
**Ross**, D. Scott 1950- *WhoFI 92*
**Ross**, Dana *WrDr 92*
**Ross**, Daniel Delano 1940- *WhoFI 92*
**Ross**, Daniel I *WhoAmP 91*
**Ross**, Daniel Manuel 1918- *WhoFI 92*
**Ross**, David *DrAPF 91*
**Ross**, David 1941- *TwCPaSc*
**Ross**, David A. *NewYTBS 91 [port]*
**Ross**, David A 1936- *AmMWSc 92*
**Ross**, David Bryan 1953- *WhoEnt 92*
**Ross**, David Charles 1956- *WhoEnt 92*, *WhoMW 92*
**Ross**, David Michael 1948- *WhoEnt 92*
**Ross**, David Samuel 1937- *AmMWSc 92*
**Ross**, David Stanley 1947- *AmMWSc 92*
**Ross**, David W. 1960- *WhoAmL 92*
**Ross**, David Ward 1937- *AmMWSc 92*
**Ross**, Debra Benita 1956- *WhoFI 92*, *WhoMW 92*
**Ross**, Dennis Kent 1942- *AmMWSc 92*, *WhoMW 92*
**Ross**, Diana 1944- *FacFETw*, *IntMPA 92*, *IntWW 91*, *NewAmDM*, *NotBlAW 92 [port]*, *WhoBlA 92*, *WhoEnt 92*
**Ross**, Don Carl 1927- *WhoIns 92*
**Ross**, Don R 1941- *WhoAmP 91*
**Ross**, Donald, Jr. 1941- *WhoMW 92*
**Ross**, Donald Clarence 1924- *AmMWSc 92*
**Ross**, Donald Edward 1930- *WhoFI 92*
**Ross**, Donald Edward 1937- *WhoEnt 92*
**Ross**, Donald Hugh 1949- *WhoMW 92*
**Ross**, Donald Joseph 1928- *AmMWSc 92*
**Ross**, Donald K 1925- *AmMWSc 92*
**Ross**, Donald Keith 1925- *WhoFI 92*
**Ross**, Donald Lewis 1936- *AmMWSc 92*
**Ross**, Donald MacArthur *Who 92*
**Ross**, Donald MacArthur 1927- *IntWW 91*
**Ross**, Donald Morris 1923- *AmMWSc 92*
**Ross**, Donald Murray 1914- *AmMWSc 92*
**Ross**, Donald Nixon 1922- *Who 92*
**Ross**, Donald Roe 1922- *WhoAmL 92*, *WhoAmP 91*, *WhoMW 92*
**Ross**, Doris A. 1923- *WhoBlA 92*
**Ross**, Doris Laune 1926- *AmMWSc 92*
**Ross**, Douglas Allen 1937- *WhoMW 92*
**Ross**, Douglas H. *WhoRel 92*
**Ross**, Douglas Taylor 1929- *AmMWSc 92*
**Ross**, Duncan Alexander 1928- *Who 92*
**Ross**, E R 1937- *WhoIns 92*
**Ross**, Edna Genevieve 1916- *WhoAmP 91*
**Ross**, Edward 1937- *WhoBlA 92*, *WhoMW 92*
**Ross**, Edward A 1866-1951 *DcAmImH*
**Ross**, Edward W. *WhoFI 92*
**Ross**, Edward William, Jr 1925- *AmMWSc 92*
**Ross**, Eldon Wayne 1934- *AmMWSc 92*
**Ross**, Elliott M 1949- *AmMWSc 92*
**Ross**, Elmer Pearl *WhoAmP 91*
**Ross**, Ernest 1920- *AmMWSc 92*
**Ross**, Ernest 1942- *Who 92*
**Ross**, Eulalie Steinmetz 1910-1975 *ConAu 134*
**Ross**, Frank 1904-1990 *ConTFT 9*
**Ross**, Frank Howard, III 1946- *WhoMW 92*
**Ross**, Frank Kenneth 1943- *WhoBlA 92*
**Ross**, Fred *DrAPF 91*
**Ross**, Fred Michael 1921- *AmMWSc 92*
**Ross**, Frederick Keith 1942- *AmMWSc 92*
**Ross**, Gary Earl *DrAPF 91*
**Ross**, George Campbell 1900- *Who 92*
**Ross**, George E. 1933- *WhoRel 92*
**Ross**, Gerald Elliott 1941- *WhoAmL 92*
**Ross**, Gerald Fred 1930- *AmMWSc 92*
**Ross**, German Reed *WhoRel 92*
**Ross**, Gilbert John 1947- *WhoMW 92*
**Ross**, Gilbert Stuart 1930- *AmMWSc 92*
**Ross**, Glenn Evan 1958- *WhoFI 92*
**Ross**, Glynn 1914- *WhoEnt 92*, *WhoWest 92*
**Ross**, Gordon 1930- *AmMWSc 92*
**Ross**, Griff Terry, Sr 1920- *AmMWSc 92*
**Ross**, Harley Harris 1935- *AmMWSc 92*
**Ross**, Harold *BenetAL 91*, *FacFETw*
**Ross**, Harry Scott 1960- *WhoAmP 91*
**Ross**, Harvey Mayer 1927- *WhoFI 92*
**Ross**, Helaine *IntAu&W 91X*, *WrDr 92*
**Ross**, Helaine Swerdloff 1949- *WhoEnt 92*
**Ross**, Henry d1991 *NewYTBS 91*
**Ross**, Henry A. *WhoRel 92*
**Ross**, Henry Schuyler d1902 *BiInAmS*
**Ross**, Herbert 1927- *IntMPA 92*
**Ross**, Herbert David 1927- *WhoEnt 92*
**Ross**, Hope Snider 1910- *WhoAmP 91*
**Ross**, Howard Persing 1935- *AmMWSc 92*, *WhoWest 92*
**Ross**, Howard Philip 1939- *WhoAmL 92*, *WhoFI 92*
**Ross**, Hugh 1898-1990 *NewAmDM*
**Ross**, Hugh Courtney 1923- *AmMWSc 92*, *WhoWest 92*
**Ross**, Hugh Norman 1945- *WhoRel 92*
**Ross**, I Louise 1928- *WhoAmP 91*
**Ross**, Ian Gordon 1926- *IntWW 91*
**Ross**, Ian Kenneth 1930- *AmMWSc 92*
**Ross**, Ian M 1927- *AmMWSc 92*
**Ross**, Ian Munro 1927- *IntWW 91*, *WhoFI 92*
**Ross**, Ira Joseph 1933- *AmMWSc 92*
**Ross**, Irvine E 1908- *AmMWSc 92*
**Ross**, James 1913- *Who 92*
**Ross**, James Alexander 1911- *Who 92*
**Ross**, James E 1921- *WhoAmP 91*
**Ross**, James Edward 1959- *WhoEnt 92*
**Ross**, James H. 1938- *WhoFI 92*, *WhoMW 92*
**Ross**, James Neil, Jr 1940- *AmMWSc 92*
**Ross**, James Robert 1923- *WhoAmP 91*
**Ross**, James Robert 1934- *WhoRel 92*
**Ross**, James Ulric 1941- *WhoAmL 92*
**Ross**, James William 1928- *AmMWSc 92*
**Ross**, James Yeiser 1961- *WhoAmL 92*
**Ross**, Janet 1914- *WhoWest 92*
**Ross**, Jean Marie 1942- *WhoAmP 91*
**Ross**, Jeffrey 1943- *AmMWSc 92*

**Ross,** Jeffrey Kenneth *WhoAmL 92*
**Ross,** Jeffrey Steven 1947- *WhoEnt 92*
**Ross,** Jerrold 1935- *WhoEnt 92*
**Ross,** Jim Buck 1917- *WhoAmP 91*
**Ross,** JoAnn *WhoRel 92*
**Ross,** Joanne A. 1929- *WhoBlA 92*
**Ross,** John 1926- *AmMWSc 92, WhoWest 92*
**Ross,** John, Jr 1928- *AmMWSc 92*
**Ross,** John B 1939- *AmMWSc 92*
**Ross,** John Brandon Alexander 1947- *AmMWSc 92*
**Ross,** John Edward 1929- *AmMWSc 92*
**Ross,** John Gordon 1951- *WhoEnt 92*
**Ross,** John J. *WhoAmL 92*
**Ross,** John MacDonald 1908- *WhoRel 92*
**Ross,** John Paul 1927- *AmMWSc 92*
**Ross,** Jonathan *WrDr 92*
**Ross,** Joseph C 1927- *AmMWSc 92*
**Ross,** Joseph E. 1940- *WhoMW 92*
**Ross,** Joseph Foster 1910- *WhoWest 92*
**Ross,** Joseph Hansbro 1925- *AmMWSc 92*
**Ross,** Joseph Lanny 1940- *WhoRel 92*
**Ross,** Joy Belle 1910- *WhoBlA 92*
**Ross,** June Rosa Pitt 1931- *AmMWSc 92*
**Ross,** Katharine 1943- *IntMPA 92, WhoEnt 92*
**Ross,** Kathleen Anne 1941- *WhoWest 92*
**Ross,** Keith 1927- *Who 92*
**Ross,** Keith Alan 1952- *AmMWSc 92*
**Ross,** Kenneth 1941- *IntMPA 92*
**Ross,** Kenneth Allen 1936- *AmMWSc 92*
**Ross,** Kerry Lynn 1960- *WhoWest 92*
**Ross,** Kevin Arnold 1955- *WhoBlA 92*
**Ross,** Kristine Marie 1962- *WhoHisp 92*
**Ross,** Lanson Clifford, Jr. 1936- *WhoWest 92*
**Ross,** Lawrence James 1929- *AmMWSc 92*
**Ross,** Leonard 1908- *WhoEnt 92*
**Ross,** Leonard Lester 1927- *AmMWSc 92*
**Ross,** Leonard Q. *BenetAL 91, IntAu&W 91X, Who 92, WrDr 92*
**Ross,** Lesa Moore 1959- *WhoFI 92*
**Ross,** Lewis Nathan d1991 *Who 92N*
**Ross,** Lewis Nathan 1911- *IntWW 91*
**Ross,** Lillian *SourALJ*
**Ross,** Louis 1912- *AmMWSc 92*
**Ross,** Louis Robert 1932- *WhoMW 92*
**Ross,** Lowell William 1932- *WhoAmP 91*
**Ross,** Lynne Fischer 1944- *AmMWSc 92*
**Ross,** Malcolm *IntAu&W 91X, WrDr 92*
**Ross,** Malcolm 1929- *AmMWSc 92*
**Ross,** Malcolm Keir 1910- *Who 92*
**Ross,** Marc Hansen 1928- *AmMWSc 92*
**Ross,** Maria Elena 1945- *WhoHisp 92*
**Ross,** Marilyn *WrDr 92*
**Ross,** Marilyn Ann 1939- *WhoWest 92*
**Ross,** Marion *WhoEnt 92*
**Ross,** Mark Samuel 1957- *WhoAmL 92*
**Ross,** Mark Stephen 1957- *WhoRel 92*
**Ross,** Mark Steven 1946- *WhoAmL 92*
**Ross,** Martin *RfGEnL 91*
**Ross,** Martin Russell 1922- *AmMWSc 92*
**Ross,** Marvin 1931- *AmMWSc 92*
**Ross,** Marvin Franklin 1951- *AmMWSc 92*
**Ross,** Mary Adelaide Eden 1896- *IntAu&W 91*
**Ross,** Mary Harvey 1925- *AmMWSc 92*
**Ross,** Mary Olivia *WhoBlA 92*
**Ross,** Matthew 1953- *WhoAmL 92*
**Ross,** Maurice James 1908- *Who 92*
**Ross,** Merrill Arthur, Jr 1935- *AmMWSc 92*
**Ross,** Michael d1985 *LesBEnT 92*
**Ross,** Michael Aaron 1941- *WhoAmL 92*
**Ross,** Michael Frederick 1950- *WhoAmL 92, WhoFI 92*
**Ross,** Michael H 1930- *AmMWSc 92*
**Ross,** Michael Neil 1952- *WhoMW 92*
**Ross,** Michael Ralph 1947- *AmMWSc 92*
**Ross,** Mike 1961- *WhoAmP 91*
**Ross,** Molly Owings 1954- *WhoWest 92*
**Ross,** Monte 1932- *AmMWSc 92*
**Ross,** Murray George 1910- *WrDr 92*
**Ross,** Myron Donald 1909- *WhoFI 92*
**Ross,** Myron Jay 1942- *AmMWSc 92*
**Ross,** N. Rodney 1957- *WhoBlA 92*
**Ross,** Neil 1944- *WhoFI 92*
**Ross,** Nell Triplett 1922- *WhoFI 92*
**Ross,** Nicholas, Mrs. *Who 92*
**Ross,** Norman Keith 1943- *WhoFI 92*
**Ross,** Norman Stilliard 1919- *Who 92*
**Ross,** Norton Morris 1925- *AmMWSc 92*
**Ross,** Otho Bescent, III 1951- *WhoAmL 92*
**Ross,** Pamela Jean 1944- *WhoRel 92*
**Ross,** Patrick Conroy 1929- *WhoFI 92*
**Ross,** Patrick George 1948- *WhoAmL 92*
**Ross,** Philip 1926- *AmMWSc 92*
**Ross,** Philip Norman, Jr 1943- *AmMWSc 92*
**Ross,** Phyllis Harrison 1936- *WhoBlA 92*
**Ross,** Ralph M. 1936- *WhoBlA 92*
**Ross,** Randolph Ernest 1955- *WhoFI 92*
**Ross,** Regina D. 1948- *WhoBlA 92*
**Ross,** Reuben James, Jr 1918- *AmMWSc 92*
**Ross,** Rhoda Helen 1934- *WhoFI 92*
**Ross,** Richard *IntWW 91, Who 92*
**Ross,** Richard 1935- *Who 92*
**Ross,** Richard 1937- *WhoFI 92*
**Ross,** Richard C 1927- *WhoAmP 91*
**Ross,** Richard Francis 1935- *AmMWSc 92, WhoMW 92*
**Ross,** Richard Harris 1958- *WhoFI 92*
**Ross,** Richard Henry 1916- *AmMWSc 92*
**Ross,** Richard Henry, Jr 1946- *AmMWSc 92*
**Ross,** Richard Manning 1946- *WhoAmL 92*
**Ross,** Richard Starr 1924- *AmMWSc 92*
**Ross,** Richard Wayne 1953- *WhoAmL 92*
**Ross,** Robert 1912- *Who 92*
**Ross,** Robert Anderson 1931- *AmMWSc 92*
**Ross,** Robert Edgar 1948- *AmMWSc 92*
**Ross,** Robert Edward 1937- *AmMWSc 92*
**Ross,** Robert Evan 1947- *WhoMW 92*
**Ross,** Robert Gordon 1922- *AmMWSc 92*
**Ross,** Robert Grierson, II 1950- *WhoFI 92*
**Ross,** Robert Jeremy 1939- *Who 92*
**Ross,** Robert Leon 1936- *WhoRel 92*
**Ross,** Robert P. 1934- *WhoBlA 92*
**Ross,** Robert Resolved, Jr. 1947- *WhoFI 92*
**Ross,** Robert Simon 1920- *WhoMW 92*
**Ross,** Robert Talman 1940- *AmMWSc 92*
**Ross,** Roderick Alexander 1926- *AmMWSc 92*
**Ross,** Roger Scott 1946- *WhoAmL 92*
**Ross,** Ronald 1857-1932 *WhoNob 90*
**Ross,** Ronald Douglas 1920- *Who 92*
**Ross,** Ronald Rickard 1931- *AmMWSc 92*
**Ross,** Roseanna Gaye 1949- *WhoMW 92*
**Ross,** Russell 1929- *AmMWSc 92, WhoWest 92*
**Ross,** Ruth Elizabeth 1947- *WhoWest 92*
**Ross,** Sam 1912- *WhoEnt 92, WrDr 92*
**Ross,** Sam Jones, Jr 1931- *AmMWSc 92*
**Ross,** Scott *WhoRel 92*
**Ross,** Scott 1939- *WhoEnt 92*
**Ross,** Scott Alan 1951- *WhoEnt 92*
**Ross,** Shepley Littlefield 1927- *AmMWSc 92*
**Ross,** Sidney 1926- *AmMWSc 92*
**Ross,** Sidney David 1918- *AmMWSc 92*
**Ross,** Sinclair 1908- *BenetAL 91, ConNov 91, FacFETw, IntAu&W 91, RfGEnL 91, TwCWW 91, WrDr 92*
**Ross,** Sophie *Who 92*
**Ross,** Stanford G. 1931- *WhoAmL 92*
**Ross,** Stanley Edmond 1962- *WhoMW 92*
**Ross,** Stanley Elijah 1922- *AmMWSc 92*
**Ross,** Stanley Ralph 1940- *WhoEnt 92*
**Ross,** Stephen Charles 1957- *WhoMW 92*
**Ross,** Stephen T 1931- *AmMWSc 92*
**Ross,** Stephen Thomas 1944- *AmMWSc 92*
**Ross,** Steven *LesBEnT 92*
**Ross,** Steven Charles 1947- *WhoWest 92*
**Ross,** Steven David 1950- *WhoAmL 92*
**Ross,** Steven J. 1927- *IntMPA 92, IntWW 91, WhoFI 92*
**Ross,** Steven William 1946- *WhoRel 92*
**Ross,** Stuart 1949- *TwCPaSc*
**Ross,** Stuart Robert 1942- *WhoEnt 92*
**Ross,** Stuart Thom 1923- *AmMWSc 92*
**Ross,** Susan Julia 1943- *WhoAmL 92*
**Ross,** Susan Linda *WhoAmL 92*
**Ross,** Sydney 1915- *AmMWSc 92*
**Ross,** Terence William 1935- *WhoWest 92*
**Ross,** Terrence *DrAPF 91*
**Ross,** Theodore William 1935- *AmMWSc 92*
**Ross,** Theophil Walter 1948- *WhoEnt 92*
**Ross,** Thomas Edward 1942- *AmMWSc 92*
**Ross,** Thomas McCallum 1931- *WhoFI 92*
**Ross,** Timothy David M. *Who 92*
**Ross,** Timothy Jack 1949- *AmMWSc 92*
**Ross,** Tom Leonard 1952- *WhoEnt 92*
**Ross,** Tom M. 1933- *WhoWest 92*
**Ross,** Tony 1938- *ConAu 35NR, SmATA 65 [port], WrDr 92*
**Ross,** Victor 1919- *Who 92*
**Ross,** Victor, Mrs. *WhoRel 92*
**Ross,** Victor Julius 1935- *WhoWest 92*
**Ross,** W E D 1912- *TwCWW 91*
**Ross,** W. W. E. 1894-1966 *BenetAL 91*
**Ross,** Walter Hugh Malcolm 1943- *Who 92*
**Ross,** Wayne Anthony 1943- *WhoAmL 92*
**Ross,** Wilbur Louis, Jr. 1937- *WhoFI 92*
**Ross,** Willard H 1930- *WhoAmP 91*
**Ross,** William 1912- *WrDr 92*
**Ross,** William 1936- *Who 92*
**Ross,** William Alexander Jackson 1937- *WhoBlA 92*
**Ross,** William D 1917- *AmMWSc 92*
**Ross,** William Daniel 1917- *WhoFI 92*
**Ross,** William Donald 1913- *AmMWSc 92*
**Ross,** William J 1930- *AmMWSc 92*
**Ross,** William Jarboe 1930- *WhoAmL 92*
**Ross,** William Mackie 1922- *Who 92*
**Ross,** William Max 1925- *AmMWSc 92*
**Ross,** William Michael 1945- *AmMWSc 92*
**Ross,** William Warfield 1926- *WhoAmL 92*
**Ross,** Winston A. 1941- *WhoBlA 92*
**Ross,** Zola 1912-1989 *TwCWW 91*
**Ross-Audley,** Cheryl Yvonne 1950- *WhoBlA 92*
**Ross-Bryant,** Lynn 1944- *WhoRel 92*
**Ross-Jacobs,** Ruth Ann 1934- *WhoFI 92*
**Ross-Macdonald,** Malcolm 1932- *WrDr 92*
**Ross-Macdonald,** Malcolm John 1932- *IntAu&W 91*
**Ross-Munro,** Colin William Gordon 1928- *Who 92*
**Ross of Newport,** Baron 1926- *Who 92*
**Ross Russell,** Graham 1933- *Who 92*
**Ross Talbot,** Sylvia *WhoRel 92*
**Rossa,** Robert Frank 1942- *AmMWSc 92*
**Rossabi,** Morris 1941- *WrDr 92*
**Rossall,** Richard Edward 1926- *AmMWSc 92*
**Rossan,** Richard Norman 1928- *AmMWSc 92*
**Rossano,** August Thomas 1916- *AmMWSc 92*
**Rossant,** Janet 1950- *AmMWSc 92*
**Rossardi,** Orlando 1938- *WhoHisp 92*
**Rossbach,** Edmund 1914- *DcTwDes*
**Rossbach,** Gerhard 1893-1967 *EncTR 91 [port]*
**Rossbacher,** Lisa Ann 1952- *AmMWSc 92*
**Rossberg,** Sara 1952- *TwCPaSc*
**Rossby,** Hans Thomas 1937- *AmMWSc 92*
**Rosse,** Earl of 1936- *Who 92*
**Rosse,** Cornelius 1938- *AmMWSc 92*
**Rosse,** Ian *WrDr 92*
**Rosse,** Irving Collins 1859?-1901 *BiInAmS*
**Rosse,** Wendell Franklyn 1933- *AmMWSc 92*
**Rossel,** Guillermo Leonardo 1945- *WhoHisp 92*
**Rossel,** Seymour 1945- *WrDr 92*
**Rossell,** Deac 1944- *WhoEnt 92*
**Rossellini,** Isabella 1952- *IntMPA 92, IntWW 91*
**Rossellini,** Roberto 1906- *FacFETw*
**Rossellini,** Roberto 1906-1977 *IntDcF 2-2 [port]*
**Rossen,** Joel N 1927- *AmMWSc 92*
**Rossen,** John 1910- *WhoMW 92*
**Rossen,** Jordan 1934- *WhoAmL 92*
**Rossen,** Robert 1908-1966 *IntDcF 2-2 [port]*
**Rossen,** Roger Downey 1935- *AmMWSc 92*
**Rossenbach,** Marc Merlin 1957- *WhoRel 92*
**Rosser,** Barbara Ann Allen 1952- *WhoEnt 92*
**Rosser,** J. Allyn *DrAPF 91*
**Rosser,** James M. 1939- *WhoBlA 92*
**Rosser,** James Milton 1939- *WhoWest 92*
**Rosser,** John 1931- *TwCPaSc*
**Rosser,** John Barkley 1907- *AmMWSc 92*
**Rosser,** Malcolm Edward, IV 1955- *WhoAmL 92*
**Rosser,** Melvyn 1926- *Who 92*
**Rosser,** Pearl 1935- *WhoBlA 92*
**Rosser,** Rachel Mary *Who 92*
**Rosser,** Richard Andrew 1944- *Who 92*
**Rosser,** Samuel Blanton 1934- *WhoBlA 92*
**Rosseter,** Philip 1567?-1623 *NewAmDM*
**Rosseter,** Thomas Arthur 1935- *WhoMW 92*
**Rossetti,** Christina 1830-1894 *RfGEnL 91*
**Rossetti,** Dante Gabriel 1828-1882 *CnDBLB 4 [port], RfGEnL 91*
**Rossetti,** Louis Michael 1948- *AmMWSc 92*
**Rossetti,** Paul P 1923- *WhoIns 92*
**Rossetti,** Robert John 1947- *WhoFI 92*
**Rossetto,** Louis, Sr. d1991 *NewYTBS 91*
**Rossettos,** John N 1932- *AmMWSc 92*
**Rossey,** John W., Jr. 1943- *WhoWest 92*
**Rossi,** Adolfo 1857-1921 *DcAmImH*
**Rossi,** Agnelo 1913- *IntWW 91, WhoRel 92*
**Rossi,** Aldo 1931- *DcTwDes, IntWW 91*
**Rossi,** Alice S. 1922- *WomSoc*
**Rossi,** Amadeo Joseph 1954- *WhoWest 92*
**Rossi,** Bruno B 1905- *AmMWSc 92, IntWW 91*
**Rossi,** Cesare 1887-1967 *BiDExR*
**Rossi,** Dominick F., Jr. 1941- *WhoFI 92*
**Rossi,** Edward P 1934- *AmMWSc 92*
**Rossi,** Ennio Claudio 1931- *AmMWSc 92*
**Rossi,** Faust F. 1932- *WhoAmL 92*
**Rossi,** Frank Arthur 1937- *WhoFI 92*
**Rossi,** George Victor 1929- *AmMWSc 92*
**Rossi,** Gustavo Alberto 1942- *WhoHisp 92*
**Rossi,** Guy Anthony 1952- *WhoWest 92*
**Rossi,** Harald Herman 1917- *AmMWSc 92*
**Rossi,** Hugh 1927- *Who 92*
**Rossi,** Hugo 1935- *AmMWSc 92*
**Rossi,** Irving d1991 *NewYTBS 91*
**Rossi,** John Joseph 1946- *AmMWSc 92*
**Rossi,** Joseph Anthony 1955- *WhoEnt 92*
**Rossi,** Lee *DrAPF 91*
**Rossi,** Luigi 1598-1653 *NewAmDM*
**Rossi,** Luis Heber 1948- *WhoHisp 92*
**Rossi,** Marcianus F *ScFEYrs*
**Rossi,** Mario 1958- *TwCPaSc*
**Rossi,** Michael Anthony 1955- *WhoAmL 92*
**Rossi,** Michelangelo 1602-1656 *NewAmDM*
**Rossi,** Miriam 1952- *AmMWSc 92*
**Rossi,** Nicholas Peter 1927- *AmMWSc 92*
**Rossi,** Opilio 1910- *WhoRel 92*
**Rossi,** Philip Joseph 1943- *WhoRel 92*
**Rossi,** Raymond Ernest 1953- *WhoAmL 92, WhoMW 92*
**Rossi,** Robert Daniel 1950- *AmMWSc 92*
**Rossi,** Robert John 1928- *WhoFI 92*
**Rossi,** Robert Joseph 1942- *WhoRel 92*
**Rossi,** Salamone 1570?-1628? *NewAmDM*
**Rossi,** Thomas J 1946- *WhoAmP 91*
**Rossi,** Walter T. *WhoWest 92*
**Rossi,** William Matthew 1954- *WhoAmL 92*
**Rossi-Lemeni,** Niccola 1920-1991 *NewAmDM*
**Rossi-Lemeni,** Nicola d1991 *NewYTBS 91*
**Rossides,** Eugene Telemachus 1927- *WhoAmL 92, WhoAmP 91*
**Rossier,** Alain B 1930- *AmMWSc 92*
**Rossignol,** Philippe Albert 1950- *AmMWSc 92*
**Rossin,** A David 1931- *AmMWSc 92*
**Rossin,** P C 1923- *AmMWSc 92*
**Rossing,** Thomas D 1929- *AmMWSc 92*
**Rossington,** David Ralph 1932- *AmMWSc 92*
**Rossini,** Frederick Anthony 1939- *AmMWSc 92*
**Rossini,** Frederick Dominic 1899- *AmMWSc 92, IntWW 91*
**Rossini,** Gioacchino 1792-1868 *NewAmDM*
**Rossinot,** Andre 1939- *IntWW 91*
**Rossio,** Jeffrey L 1947- *AmMWSc 92*
**Rossio,** Richard Dominic 1933- *WhoMW 92*
**Rossiter,** Anthony 1926- *TwCPaSc*
**Rossiter,** Bryant William 1931- *AmMWSc 92*
**Rossiter,** Charles *DrAPF 91*
**Rossiter,** Clare *ConAu 135*
**Rossiter,** Francis 1931- *Who 92*
**Rossiter,** John 1916- *IntAu&W 91, WrDr 92*
**Rossiter,** Michael Anthony 1935- *WhoAmP 91*
**Rossiter,** Robert E. 1946- *WhoMW 92*
**Rossiter,** Robert Francis, Jr. 1956- *WhoMW 92*
**Rossiter,** Sarah *DrAPF 91*
**Rossitto,** Conrad 1926- *AmMWSc 92*
**Rossky,** Peter Jacob 1950- *AmMWSc 92*
**Rossler,** Fritz 1912- *BiDExR*
**Rossler,** Willis Kenneth, Jr. 1946- *WhoFI 92*
**Rossley,** Paul R 1938- *WhoIns 92*
**Rosslyn,** Earl of 1958- *Who 92*
**Rossman,** Amy Yarnell 1946- *AmMWSc 92*
**Rossman,** Charles Raymond 1938- *ConAu 34NR*
**Rossman,** Cynthia Ann 1956- *WhoFI 92*
**Rossman,** Douglas Athon 1936- *AmMWSc 92*
**Rossman,** Elmer Chris 1919- *AmMWSc 92*
**Rossman,** George Robert 1944- *AmMWSc 92*
**Rossman,** Isadore 1913- *AmMWSc 92*
**Rossman,** Richard Alan 1939- *WhoAmL 92*
**Rossman,** Toby Gale 1942- *AmMWSc 92*
**Rossmann,** Charles Boris 1945- *WhoMW 92*
**Rossmann,** Jack Eugene 1936- *WhoMW 92*
**Rossmann,** Michael G 1930- *AmMWSc 92*
**Rossmann,** Michael Louis 1954- *WhoRel 92*
**Rossmann,** Tatiana 1944- *WhoMW 92*
**Rossmiller,** John David 1935- *AmMWSc 92*
**Rossmiller,** Richard Allen 1928- *WhoMW 92*
**Rossmoore,** Harold W 1925- *AmMWSc 92*
**Rossmore,** Baron 1931- *Who 92*
**Rossnagel,** Brian Gordon 1952- *AmMWSc 92*
**Rossner,** Judith *DrAPF 91*
**Rossner,** Judith 1935- *BenetAL 91, ConNov 91, IntAu&W 91, WrDr 92*
**Rossner,** Lawrence Franklin 1938- *AmMWSc 92*
**Rosso,** Christine Hehmeyer 1947- *WhoAmL 92*
**Rosso,** Lewis T. 1911- *IntMPA 92*
**Rosso,** Louis T. 1933- *WhoWest 92*
**Rosso,** Pedro 1941- *AmMWSc 92*
**Rossol,** Frederick Carl 1933- *AmMWSc 92*
**Rossomando,** Edward Frederick 1939- *AmMWSc 92*
**Rosson,** H F 1929- *AmMWSc 92*
**Rosson,** Peggy 1935- *WhoAmP 91*
**Rosson,** Reinhardt Arthur 1949- *AmMWSc 92*
**Rosson,** Renal B. 1919- *WhoAmL 92*

**Rossoni**, Edmondo 1884-1965 *BiDExR*
**Rossotti**, Charles Ossola 1941- *WhoFI 92*
**Rossovich**, Rick 1957- *IntMPA 92*
**Rossow**, Peter William 1948- *AmMWSc 92*
**Rossow**, Vernon J 1926- *AmMWSc 92*
**Rosswall**, Thomas 1941- *Who 92*
**Rost**, Ernest Stephan 1934- *AmMWSc 92*
**Rost**, Peter Lewis 1930- *Who 92*
**Rost**, Thomas Lowell 1941- *AmMWSc 92*
**Rost**, William Joseph 1926- *AmMWSc 92*
**Rost Van Tonningen**, Meinoud Marinus 1894-1945 *BiDExR*
**Rosta**, Endre 1909- *IntWW 91*
**Rostal**, Max d1991 *Who 92N*
**Rostamian**, Rouben 1949- *AmMWSc 92*
**Rosten**, Irwin *LesBEnT 92*
**Rosten**, Irwin 1924- *WhoEnt 92*
**Rosten**, Keith Alan 1956- *WhoWest 92*
**Rosten**, Leo 1908- *ConNov 91, WrDr 92*
**Rosten**, Leo C 1908- *IntAu&W 91, Who 92*
**Rosten**, Leo Calvin 1908- *BenetAL 91, WhoEnt 92*
**Rosten**, Norman *DrAPF 91*
**Rosten**, Norman 1914- *BenetAL 91*
**Rostenbach**, Royal E 1912- *AmMWSc 92*
**Rostenkowski**, Dan 1928- *AlmAP 92 [port], IntWW 91, WhoAmP 91, WhoMW 92*
**Roster**, Michael 1945- *WhoAmL 92*
**Rostker**, Skipper 1919- *WhoAmP 91*
**Rostoker**, Gordon 1940- *AmMWSc 92*
**Rostoker**, Norman 1925- *AmMWSc 92*
**Rostoker**, William 1924- *AmMWSc 92*
**Rostomian**, Stepan 1956- *ConCom 92*
**Roston**, Murray 1928- *IntAu&W 91, WrDr 92*
**Roston**, Ruth *DrAPF 91*
**Rostov**, Stefan *WrDr 92*
**Rostow**, Eugene V. 1913- *WrDr 92*
**Rostow**, Eugene Victor 1913- *IntWW 91, Who 92*
**Rostow**, Walt W. 1916- *WrDr 92*
**Rostow**, Walt Whitman 1916- *AmPolLe, IntWW 91, Who 92, WhoAmP 91*
**Rostron**, Frank d1991 *Who 92N*
**Rostropovich**, Mstislav 1927- *FacFETw [port], NewAmDM, Who 92*
**Rostropovich**, Mstislav Leopoldovich 1927- *IntWW 91, SovUnBD, WhoEnt 92*
**Rostvold**, Gerhard Norman 1919- *WhoFI 92, WhoWest 92*
**Rostworowski**, Marek 1921- *IntWW 91*
**Rosuck**, Jordan I. *WhoFI 92*
**Rosvall**, Charles Richard 1948- *WhoWest 92*
**Roswaenge**, Helge 1897-1972 *NewAmDM*
**Roswell**, David Frederick 1942- *AmMWSc 92*
**Roszak**, Joe Gerard 1958- *WhoWest 92*
**Roszak**, Theodore 1907-1981 *FacFETw*
**Roszel**, Jeffie Fisher 1926- *AmMWSc 92*
**Roszell**, Douglas King 1941- *WhoWest 92*
**Roszkowski**, Adolph Peter 1928- *AmMWSc 92*
**Roszkowski**, Janusz 1928- *IntAu&W 91, IntWW 91*
**Roszkowski**, Stanley Julian 1923- *WhoAmL 92*
**Roszman**, Larry Joe 1944- *AmMWSc 92*
**Rosztoczy**, Ferenc Erno 1932- *WhoFI 92*
**Rota**, Bertram 1903-1966 *DcLB Y91 [port]*
**Rota**, Gian-Carlo 1932- *AmMWSc 92, IntWW 91*
**Rota**, Nino 1911-1979 *FacFETw, NewAmDM*
**Rotan**, Constance S. 1935- *WhoBlA 92*
**Rotan**, Constance Smith 1935- *WhoAmL 92*
**Rotar**, Peter P 1929- *AmMWSc 92*
**Rotariu**, George Julian 1917- *AmMWSc 92*
**Rotatori**, Peter, Jr 1935- *WhoAmP 91*
**Rotbart**, Harley Aaron 1953- *WhoWest 92*
**Rotbart**, Heidi Lee 1957- *WhoWest 92*
**Rotberg**, Eugene Harvey 1930- *IntWW 91, WhoFI 92*
**Rotblat**, Joseph 1908- *IntAu&W 91, IntWW 91, Who 92, WrDr 92*
**Rotch**, Abbott Lawrence 1861-1912 *BiInAmS*
**Rotch**, Peter Boylston 1941- *WhoAmL 92*
**Rotch**, Thomas Morgan 1849-1914 *BiInAmS*
**Rotchford**, Patricia Kathleen 1945- *WhoFI 92, WhoMW 92*
**Rotcop**, J. Kenneth 1934- *WhoEnt 92*
**Rote**, Neal Stewart 1946- *WhoMW 92*
**Rotella**, Alexis *DrAPF 91*
**Rotella**, Elyce Jean 1946- *WhoFI 92*
**Rotella**, Mimmo 1918- *IntWW 91*
**Rotelli**, Delbert Leroy 1934- *WhoAmP 91*
**Rotello**, Michael Victor 1952- *WhoAmP 91*
**Rotem**, Chava Eve 1928- *AmMWSc 92*
**Rotenberg**, A Daniel 1934- *AmMWSc 92*
**Rotenberg**, Don Harris 1934- *AmMWSc 92*
**Rotenberg**, Gregg M. 1966- *WhoFI 92*
**Rotenberg**, Jon Fred 1947- *WhoAmP 91*
**Rotenberg**, Joseph Isaac 1949- *WhoFI 92*
**Rotenberg**, Keith Saul 1950- *AmMWSc 92*
**Rotenberg**, Manuel 1930- *AmMWSc 92*
**Rotenberg**, Marc Steven 1960- *WhoAmL 92*
**Rotenberg**, Mark Benjamin 1954- *WhoAmL 92*
**Rotenberg**, Maurice 1914- *WhoFI 92*
**Rotenberg**, Rena Elsa 1935- *WhoRel 92*
**Rotenberg**, Robert Louis 1949- *WhoMW 92*
**Rotenberg**, Sheldon 1917- *WhoEnt 92*
**Rotenberry**, John Thomas *AmMWSc 92*
**Rotenstreich**, Jon Wallace 1943- *WhoFI 92*
**Rotenstreich**, Nathan 1914- *IntWW 91*
**Rotermund**, Albert J, Jr 1940- *AmMWSc 92*
**Roters**, Eberhard 1929- *IntWW 91*
**Rotgin**, Helaine K 1915- *WhoAmP 91*
**Roth**, Alfred 1879-1948 *BiDExR*
**Roth**, Allan Charles 1946- *AmMWSc 92*
**Roth**, Allan Robert 1931- *WhoFI 92*
**Roth**, Alvin Eliot 1951- *WhoFI 92*
**Roth**, Andrew 1919- *IntAu&W 91, Who 92, WrDr 92*
**Roth**, Ariel A 1927- *AmMWSc 92*
**Roth**, Arthur J. *DrAPF 91*
**Roth**, Arthur Jason 1949- *AmMWSc 92*
**Roth**, Audrey 1915- *WhoAmP 91*
**Roth**, Barbara 1916- *AmMWSc 92*
**Roth**, Beatrice *DrAPF 91*
**Roth**, Ben G 1942- *AmMWSc 92*
**Roth**, Benjamin 1909- *AmMWSc 92*
**Roth**, Bernard 1933- *AmMWSc 92*
**Roth**, Bobby *IntMPA 92*
**Roth**, Charles 1939- *AmMWSc 92*
**Roth**, Charles Barron 1942- *AmMWSc 92*
**Roth**, Connie Rae 1961- *WhoMW 92*
**Roth**, Daniel 1920- *AmMWSc 92*
**Roth**, Daniel James 1931- *WhoMW 92*
**Roth**, David Albert 1962- *WhoWest 92*
**Roth**, David John 1940- *WhoMW 92*
**Roth**, Dewey *DrAPF 91*
**Roth**, Donald Alfred 1918- *AmMWSc 92*
**Roth**, Doyle Jack Key 1958- *WhoRel 92*
**Roth**, Duane Alvin 1957- *WhoRel 92*
**Roth**, Eldon Sherwood 1929- *AmMWSc 92*
**Roth**, Eleanor *DrAPF 91*
**Roth**, Elisabeth Dietlind Wilma 1947- *WhoRel 92*
**Roth**, Elliott Jay 1957- *WhoMW 92*
**Roth**, Eugene 1935- *WhoAmL 92*
**Roth**, Frank Albert 1958- *WhoAmL 92*
**Roth**, George Stanley 1946- *AmMWSc 92*
**Roth**, Gerald Irwin 1931- *WhoAmP 91*
**Roth**, Gerald J 1941- *AmMWSc 92*
**Roth**, Hadden Wing 1930- *WhoAmL 92*
**Roth**, Harold 1931- *AmMWSc 92*
**Roth**, Harold Philmore 1915- *AmMWSc 92*
**Roth**, Harrison 1931- *WhoFI 92*
**Roth**, Heinz Dieter 1936- *AmMWSc 92*
**Roth**, Henry 1906?- *BenetAL 91, ConNov 91, WrDr 92*
**Roth**, Henry H. *DrAPF 91*
**Roth**, Herbert Richard 1928- *WhoEnt 92*
**Roth**, Howard 1925- *AmMWSc 92*
**Roth**, Irma Doris Brubaker 1914- *WhoAmP 91*
**Roth**, Irving Leroy 1926- *WhoAmP 91*
**Roth**, Ivan Lambert 1928- *AmMWSc 92*
**Roth**, J Reece 1937- *AmMWSc 92*
**Roth**, Jack A 1945- *AmMWSc 92*
**Roth**, Jack Joseph 1920- *WhoMW 92*
**Roth**, James *WhoAmP 91*
**Roth**, James A 1951- *AmMWSc 92*
**Roth**, James Frank 1925- *AmMWSc 92*
**Roth**, James Luther Aumont 1917- *AmMWSc 92*
**Roth**, Jane Richards 1935- *WhoAmL 92*
**Roth**, Jay Sanford 1919- *AmMWSc 92*
**Roth**, Jerome A 1940- *AmMWSc 92*
**Roth**, Jerome Allan 1943- *AmMWSc 92*
**Roth**, Jesse 1934- *AmMWSc 92*
**Roth**, Joe 1948- *IntMPA 92, WhoEnt 92, WhoFI 92*
**Roth**, Joel G. 1929- *WhoAmL 92*
**Roth**, John Austin 1934- *AmMWSc 92*
**Roth**, John L, Jr 1949- *AmMWSc 92*
**Roth**, John Paul 1922- *AmMWSc 92*
**Roth**, John R 1939- *AmMWSc 92*
**Roth**, Jonathan Nicholas 1938- *AmMWSc 92*
**Roth**, Joseph 1894-1939 *LiExTwC*
**Roth**, Joseph 1948- *WhoWest 92*
**Roth**, June 1926- *WrDr 92*
**Roth**, Kent Alan 1952- *WhoAmP 91*
**Roth**, Klaus Friedrich 1925- *IntWW 91, Who 92*
**Roth**, Lane 1943- *WhoEnt 92*
**Roth**, Laura Maurer 1930- *AmMWSc 92*
**Roth**, Lawrence Frederick, Jr. 1948- *WhoEnt 92*
**Roth**, Lawrence Max 1936- *AmMWSc 92*
**Roth**, Lawrence O 1928- *AmMWSc 92*
**Roth**, Lewis Franklin 1914- *AmMWSc 92*
**Roth**, Linwood Evans 1929- *AmMWSc 92*
**Roth**, M. Augustine 1926- *WhoMW 92*
**Roth**, Margarete Marie *WhoMW 92*
**Roth**, Marie M 1926- *AmMWSc 92*
**Roth**, Mark A 1957- *AmMWSc 92*
**Roth**, Mark Andrew 1956- *WhoFI 92*
**Roth**, Mark Edward 1954- *WhoAmL 92*
**Roth**, Marlen Deanne Vilas 1949- *WhoAmP 91*
**Roth**, Martin 1917- *IntWW 91, Who 92*
**Roth**, Martin 1924- *ConAu 134*
**Roth**, Marty *ConAu 134*
**Roth**, Michael 1931- *WhoAmL 92*
**Roth**, Michael William 1952- *AmMWSc 92*
**Roth**, Moira 1933- *WhoWest 92*
**Roth**, Nelson Eugene 1949- *WhoAmL 92*
**Roth**, Niles 1925- *AmMWSc 92*
**Roth**, Norman Gilbert 1924- *AmMWSc 92, WhoMW 92*
**Roth**, Paul A. 1930- *IntMPA 92*
**Roth**, Paul Frederick 1932- *AmMWSc 92*
**Roth**, Peter Hans 1942- *AmMWSc 92*
**Roth**, Philip *DrAPF 91*
**Roth**, Philip 1933- *BenetAL 91, ConAu 36NR, ConLC 66 [port], ConNov 91, CurBio 91 [port], FacFETw, IntAu&W 91, IntWW 91, Who 92, WrDr 92*
**Roth**, Phillip Joseph 1920- *WhoAmL 92*
**Roth**, Phillip Joseph 1959- *WhoEnt 92*
**Roth**, Rande K 1954- *WhoAmP 91*
**Roth**, Raymond Edward 1918- *AmMWSc 92*
**Roth**, Rene Romain 1928- *AmMWSc 92*
**Roth**, Richard A. 1943- *IntMPA 92*
**Roth**, Richard Alan 1958- *WhoEnt 92*
**Roth**, Richard C. 1937- *WhoFI 92*
**Roth**, Richard Francis 1938- *AmMWSc 92*
**Roth**, Richard J 1941- *WhoIns 92*
**Roth**, Richard J, Jr 1942- *WhoIns 92*
**Roth**, Richard James, Sr 1919- *WhoIns 92*
**Roth**, Richard Lee 1931- *WhoAmP 91*
**Roth**, Richard Lewis 1936- *AmMWSc 92*
**Roth**, Richard Stefan 1947- *WhoWest 92*
**Roth**, Rise Beth 1960- *WhoRel 92*
**Roth**, Robert Andrew, Jr 1946- *AmMWSc 92*
**Roth**, Robert Charles 1945- *WhoAmL 92*
**Roth**, Robert Earl 1925- *AmMWSc 92*
**Roth**, Robert Earl 1937- *AmMWSc 92*
**Roth**, Robert Henry, Jr 1939- *AmMWSc 92*
**Roth**, Robert Joseph 1920- *WrDr 92*
**Roth**, Robert Mark 1943- *AmMWSc 92*
**Roth**, Robert Paul 1919- *WhoRel 92*
**Roth**, Robert S 1926- *AmMWSc 92*
**Roth**, Robert Steele 1930- *AmMWSc 92*
**Roth**, Rodney J 1927- *AmMWSc 92*
**Roth**, Roland Ray 1943- *AmMWSc 92*
**Roth**, Ronald John 1947- *AmMWSc 92*
**Roth**, Ronald Stewart 1948- *WhoRel 92*
**Roth**, Roy William 1929- *AmMWSc 92*
**Roth**, Sanford Harold 1934- *WhoWest 92*
**Roth**, Sanford Irwin 1932- *AmMWSc 92, WhoMW 92*
**Roth**, Sheldon H 1943- *AmMWSc 92*
**Roth**, Shirley H *AmMWSc 92*
**Roth**, Sol 1927- *WhoRel 92*
**Roth**, Stephen 1942- *AmMWSc 92*
**Roth**, Stephen Benno 1954- *WhoEnt 92*
**Roth**, Stephen Eliot 1962- *WhoEnt 92*
**Roth**, Stephen Evans 1960- *WhoAmL 92*
**Roth**, Thomas Allan 1937- *AmMWSc 92*
**Roth**, Thomas Frederic 1932- *AmMWSc 92*
**Roth**, Toby 1938- *AlmAP 92 [port], WhoAmP 91, WhoMW 92*
**Roth**, Walter 1922- *AmMWSc 92*
**Roth**, Walter 1929- *WhoAmL 92*
**Roth**, Walter John 1939- *AmMWSc 92*
**Roth**, Wilfred 1922- *AmMWSc 92*
**Roth**, William George 1938- *IntWW 91*
**Roth**, William V., Jr. 1921- *AlmAP 92 [port], IntWW 91*
**Roth**, William Victor, Jr 1921- *WhoAmP 91*
**Roth Pollvogt**, Nancy Ann 1963- *WhoMW 92*
**Rotha**, Paul 1907-1984 *IntDcF 2-2 [port]*
**Rothauge**, Charles Harry 1919- *AmMWSc 92*
**Rothaus**, Barry 1936- *WhoWest 92*
**Rothaus**, Oscar Seymour 1927- *AmMWSc 92*
**Rothbard**, Michael 1946- *WhoEnt 92*
**Rothbart**, Herbert Lawrence 1937- *AmMWSc 92*
**Rothbart**, Lenny Mars 1952- *WhoEnt 92*
**Rothberg**, Gerald Morris 1931- *AmMWSc 92*
**Rothberg**, Joseph Eli 1935- *AmMWSc 92*
**Rothberg**, Lewis Josiah 1956- *AmMWSc 92*
**Rothberg**, Simon 1921- *AmMWSc 92*
**Rothberger**, Joseph Meyer 1937- *WhoRel 92*
**Rothblat**, George H 1935- *AmMWSc 92*
**Rothblatt**, Daniel Morris 1958- *WhoRel 92*
**Rothchild**, Irving 1913- *AmMWSc 92*
**Rothchild**, Robert 1946- *AmMWSc 92*
**Rothdeutsch**, Ken 1943- *WhoEnt 92*
**Rothe**, Carl Frederick 1929- *AmMWSc 92*
**Rothe**, Erhard William 1931- *AmMWSc 92*
**Rothe**, Herbert 1928- *WhoEnt 92*
**Rothe**, Jean-Pierre-Edmond d1991 *IntWW 91N*
**Rothe**, Karolyn Regina 1947- *AmMWSc 92*
**Rothe-Barneson**, June Emma 1931- *WhoRel 92*
**Rotheim**, Minna B 1933- *AmMWSc 92*
**Rothell**, George Edwin 1930- *IntWW 91*
**Rothenbacher**, Hansjakob 1928- *AmMWSc 92*
**Rothenberg**, Alan I. 1939- *WhoWest 92*
**Rothenberg**, Alan S 1951- *AmMWSc 92*
**Rothenberg**, Albert 1930- *AmMWSc 92*
**Rothenberg**, Betty Lynne 1946- *WhoEnt 92*
**Rothenberg**, Elliot Calvin 1939- *WhoAmP 91, WhoFI 92, WhoMW 92*
**Rothenberg**, Frederick M. 1942- *WhoAmL 92, WhoFI 92*
**Rothenberg**, Gilbert Steven 1951- *WhoAmL 92*
**Rothenberg**, Harvey David 1937- *WhoWest 92*
**Rothenberg**, Herbert Carl 1919- *AmMWSc 92*
**Rothenberg**, Jerome *DrAPF 91*
**Rothenberg**, Jerome 1931- *ConPo 91, IntAu&W 91, WrDr 92*
**Rothenberg**, Jerome 1935- *BenetAL 91*
**Rothenberg**, Lawrence Neil 1940- *AmMWSc 92*
**Rothenberg**, Mortimer Abraham 1920- *AmMWSc 92*
**Rothenberg**, Peter Jay 1941- *WhoAmL 92*
**Rothenberg**, Robert Edward 1908- *WrDr 92*
**Rothenberg**, Ronald Isaac *AmMWSc 92*
**Rothenberg**, Russell Allen 1958- *WhoWest 92*
**Rothenberg**, Sheldon Philip 1929- *AmMWSc 92*
**Rothenberg**, Stephen 1941- *AmMWSc 92*
**Rothenberg**, Susan 1945- *IntWW 91, WorArt 1980 [port]*
**Rothenberger**, Anneliese 1926- *IntWW 91*
**Rothenberger**, Curt Ferdinand 1896-1959 *EncTR 91*
**Rothenberger**, Jack Renninger 1930- *WhoRel 92*
**Rothenberger**, Victor Conrad Immanuel 1923- *WhoRel 92*
**Rothenberger**, William 1922- *WhoAmP 91*
**Rothenbuhler**, Walter Christopher 1920- *AmMWSc 92*
**Rothenbury**, Raymand Albert 1937- *AmMWSc 92*
**Rothenstein**, John 1901- *Who 92, WrDr 92*
**Rothenstein**, John Knewstub Maurice 1901- *IntAu&W 91, IntWW 91*
**Rothenstein**, Michael 1908- *IntWW 91, TwCPaSc, Who 92*
**Rothenstein**, William 1872-1945 *TwCPaSc*
**Rother**, Ana 1931- *AmMWSc 92*
**Rother**, Konrad Frank 1927- *WhoMW 92*
**Rother**, Reinhold Friedrich Wilhelm 1843-1889 *BiInAmS*
**Rotherham**, Jean 1922- *AmMWSc 92*
**Rotherham**, John Kevitt 1910- *Who 92*
**Rotherham**, Leonard 1913- *IntWW 91, Who 92*
**Rothermel**, Fred Allen 1940- *WhoRel 92*
**Rothermel**, Joseph Jackson 1918- *AmMWSc 92*
**Rothermel**, Richard Allan 1950- *WhoAmL 92*
**Rothermel**, Samuel Royden 1957- *WhoWest 92*
**Rothermere**, Viscount 1925- *IntWW 91, Who 92*
**Rotherwick**, Baron 1912- *Who 92*
**Rothery**, Richard Jon 1945- *WhoEnt 92*
**Rothes**, Earl of 1932- *Who 92*
**Rothfeld**, Leonard B 1933- *AmMWSc 92*
**Rothfelder**, Maureen Kehoe 1960- *WhoAmL 92*
**Rothfield**, Lawrence I 1927- *AmMWSc 92*
**Rothfield**, Naomi Fox 1929- *AmMWSc 92*
**Rothfus**, Jeffrey Cleveland 1953- *WhoEnt 92*
**Rothfus**, John Arden 1932- *AmMWSc 92*
**Rothfus**, Robert R 1919- *AmMWSc 92*
**Rothfuss**, Earl Levering 1952- *WhoEnt 92*
**Rothfuss**, Franklin Edward, Jr. 1946- *WhoRel 92*
**Rothfuss**, Nan H 1943- *WhoAmP 91*
**Rothgarn**, Mildred 1935- *WhoMW 92*
**Rothgeb**, John Martin, Jr. 1949- *WhoMW 92*
**Rothgeb**, Marion Russ 1936- *WhoMW 92*
**Rothhammer**, Craig Robert 1954- *WhoWest 92*
**Rothhaus**, Finlay C 1957- *WhoAmP 91*
**Rothko**, Mark 1903-1970 *FacFETw*
**Rothkopf**, David Jochanan 1955- *WhoFI 92*

**Rothkopf**, Michael H 1939- AmMWSc 92
**Rothkopf**, Rhoda Caren WhoFI 92
**Rothkrug**, Leonard Filreis 1928- WhoAmL 92
**Rothleder**, Stephen David 1937- AmMWSc 92
**Rothlisberger**, Hazel Marie 1911- AmMWSc 92
**Rothman**, Adam Alan 1960- WhoFI 92
**Rothman**, Alan Bernard 1927- AmMWSc 92
**Rothman**, Alan Michael 1943- AmMWSc 92
**Rothman**, Albert J 1924- AmMWSc 92
**Rothman**, Alvin Harvey 1930- AmMWSc 92
**Rothman**, Arthur I 1938- AmMWSc 92
**Rothman**, Bernard 1932- WhoAmL 92, WhoFI 92
**Rothman**, Chuck DrAPF 91
**Rothman**, Claire Lynda 1928- WhoEnt 92
**Rothman**, David Bill 1952- WhoAmL 92
**Rothman**, David J. WrDr 92
**Rothman**, Francoise 1923- AmMWSc 92
**Rothman**, Frank 1926- IntMPA 92, WhoAmL 92, WhoEnt 92, WhoFI 92
**Rothman**, Frank George 1930- AmMWSc 92
**Rothman**, George Lovell 1954- WhoEnt 92
**Rothman**, Herbert B 1924- AmMWSc 92
**Rothman**, Howard Barry 1938- AmMWSc 92
**Rothman**, Howard Joel 1945- WhoAmL 92
**Rothman**, James Edward 1950- AmMWSc 92
**Rothman**, Joel 1938- WrDr 92
**Rothman**, Judith IntAu&W 91X, WrDr 92
**Rothman**, Julius Lawrence 1920- WhoWest 92
**Rothman**, Karen May 1950- WhoEnt 92
**Rothman**, Kenneth J 1935- WhoAmP 91
**Rothman**, Laurence Sidney 1940- AmMWSc 92
**Rothman**, Marie Henderson WhoAmL 92
**Rothman**, Martha D 1938- WhoAmP 91
**Rothman**, Martin 1946- WhoFI 92
**Rothman**, Michael David 1942- WhoAmP 91
**Rothman**, Milton A 1919- AmMWSc 92
**Rothman**, Neal Jules 1928- AmMWSc 92
**Rothman**, Paul George 1923- AmMWSc 92
**Rothman**, Philip A. 1958- WhoFI 92
**Rothman**, Richard Harrison 1936- AmMWSc 92
**Rothman**, Robert Aaron 1931- WhoRel 92
**Rothman**, Robert J. 1954- WhoFI 92
**Rothman**, Sam 1920- AmMWSc 92
**Rothman**, Sara Weinstein 1929- AmMWSc 92
**Rothman**, Stephanie ReelWom
**Rothman**, Stephanie 1936- WhoEnt 92
**Rothman**, Stephen Sutton 1935- AmMWSc 92
**Rothman**, Steven J 1927- AmMWSc 92
**Rothman**, Steven John 1927- WhoMW 92
**Rothman**, Stewart Neil 1930- WhoWest 92
**Rothman**, Sydney 1897- Who 92
**Rothman**, Thomas E. 1954- IntMPA 92
**Rothman**, Thomas Edgar 1954- WhoEnt 92
**Rothman**, William 1959- WhoFI 92
**Rothman-Denes**, Lucia B 1943- AmMWSc 92
**Rothmeier**, Steven George 1946- WhoFI 92, WhoMW 92
**Rothmer**, Dorothy TwCPaSc
**Rothmuller**, Marko WhoEnt 92
**Rothnie**, Alan 1920- Who 92
**Rothrock**, George Moore 1919- AmMWSc 92
**Rothrock**, Jan Campbell 1935- WhoFI 92
**Rothrock**, John William 1920- AmMWSc 92
**Rothrock**, Larry R 1940- AmMWSc 92
**Rothrock**, Paul E 1948- AmMWSc 92
**Rothrock**, Thomas Stephenson 1928- AmMWSc 92
**Rothschild** Who 92
**Rothschild**, Baron 1936- IntWW 91, Who 92
**Rothschild**, Lord 1910-1990 AnObit 1990, FacFETw
**Rothschild**, Amalie Randolph 1945- WhoEnt 92
**Rothschild**, Brian James 1934- AmMWSc 92
**Rothschild**, Bruce Lee 1941- AmMWSc 92
**Rothschild**, David 1941- AmMWSc 92
**Rothschild**, Donald Phillip 1927- WhoAmL 92
**Rothschild**, Edmund Leopold de 1916- IntWW 91, Who 92
**Rothschild**, Elie Robert de 1917- IntWW 91
**Rothschild**, Emma 1948- Who 92
**Rothschild**, Evelyn De 1931- Who 92
**Rothschild**, Frank Peter 1961- WhoFI 92
**Rothschild**, Gilbert Robert 1915- AmMWSc 92
**Rothschild**, Guy De 1909- Who 92
**Rothschild**, Guy Edouard Alphonse Paul de 1909- IntWW 91
**Rothschild**, Henry 1932- AmMWSc 92
**Rothschild**, Herbert 1921- WhoFI 92
**Rothschild**, John David 1945- WhoAmL 92
**Rothschild**, Joseph 1931- WrDr 92
**Rothschild**, Kenneth J 1948- AmMWSc 92
**Rothschild**, Kenneth Richard 1946- WhoAmL 92
**Rothschild**, Kurt William 1914- WrDr 92
**Rothschild**, Leopold David De 1927- Who 92
**Rothschild**, Loren Robert 1938- WhoWest 92
**Rothschild**, Marcus Adolphus 1924- AmMWSc 92
**Rothschild**, Michael 1942- WhoWest 92
**Rothschild**, Michael Lee 1952- WhoWest 92
**Rothschild**, Miriam Louisa 1908- Who 92
**Rothschild**, Mitchel Ernest 1955- WhoEnt 92
**Rothschild**, Paul Warren 1918- WhoAmL 92
**Rothschild**, Richard Eiseman 1943- AmMWSc 92
**Rothschild**, Richard Luke 1955- WhoEnt 92
**Rothschild**, Robert 1911- IntWW 91, Who 92
**Rothschild**, Sigmund 1917-1991 NewYTBS 91
**Rothschild**, Steven James 1944- WhoAmL 92
**Rothschild**, Walter Gustav 1924- AmMWSc 92
**Rothstein**, Aser 1918- AmMWSc 92
**Rothstein**, Barbara Jacobs 1939- WhoAmL 92, WhoWest 92
**Rothstein**, Barry Steven 1953- WhoWest 92
**Rothstein**, Charlotte M 1924- WhoAmP 91
**Rothstein**, Cy 1934- WhoWest 92
**Rothstein**, Deborah 1956- WhoFI 92
**Rothstein**, Edwin C 1933- AmMWSc 92
**Rothstein**, Esther Ruth WhoAmL 92
**Rothstein**, Gerald Alan 1941- WhoFI 92
**Rothstein**, Howard 1935- AmMWSc 92
**Rothstein**, Jerome 1918- AmMWSc 92
**Rothstein**, Lewis Robert 1920- AmMWSc 92
**Rothstein**, Mark Alan 1949- WhoAmL 92
**Rothstein**, Morton 1922- AmMWSc 92
**Rothstein**, Morton 1926- WhoWest 92
**Rothstein**, Robert 1925- AmMWSc 92
**Rothstein**, Robert Alan 1946- WhoAmL 92
**Rothstein**, Robert Richard 1944- WhoAmL 92
**Rothstein**, Rodney Joel 1947- AmMWSc 92
**Rothstein**, Samuel 1917- AmMWSc 92
**Rothstein**, Samuel 1921- WrDr 92
**Rothstein**, Saul 1920- Who 92
**Rothwarf**, Allen 1935- AmMWSc 92
**Rothwarf**, Frederick 1930- AmMWSc 92
**Rothwax**, Harold J. 1930- WhoAmL 92
**Rothweiler**, Paul R. 1931- WrDr 92
**Rothwell**, Evelyn 1911- NewAmDM
**Rothwell**, Frederick Mirvan 1923- AmMWSc 92
**Rothwell**, Geoffrey Scott 1953- WhoFI 92
**Rothwell**, Gideon Franklin, IV 1928- WhoFI 92
**Rothwell**, Kenneth Sprague 1921- WrDr 92
**Rothwell**, Margaret Irene 1938- Who 92
**Rothwell**, Norman Vincent 1924- AmMWSc 92
**Rothwell**, Paul L 1938- AmMWSc 92
**Rothwell**, R. Clinton 1945- WhoEnt 92
**Rothwell**, Richard Pennefather 1836-1901 BiInAmS
**Rothwell**, Robert Alan 1939- WhoWest 92
**Rothwell**, Sheila Gwendoline 1935- Who 92
**Rothwell**, Victor Howard 1945- WrDr 92
**Rothwell**, William Stanley 1924- AmMWSc 92
**Roti**, Fred B 1920- WhoAmP 91
**Roti**, Thomas David 1945- WhoAmL 92
**Roti Roti**, Joseph Lee 1943- AmMWSc 92
**Rotimi**, Emmanuel Gladstone Ola 1938- IntAu&W 91
**Rotimi**, Ola 1938- ConBlB 1 [port], WrDr 92
**Rotkin**, Isadore David 1921- AmMWSc 92
**Rotkin**, Michael Eric 1945- WhoWest 92
**Rotman**, Arthur 1926- WhoRel 92
**Rotman**, Boris 1924- AmMWSc 92
**Rotman**, David Aaron 1945- WhoAmL 92
**Rotman**, Douglas Allen 1942- WhoWest 92
**Rotman**, Harold H AmMWSc 92
**Rotman**, Joseph Jonah 1934- AmMWSc 92
**Rotman**, Leslie 1954- WhoEnt 92
**Rotman**, Marvin Z 1933- AmMWSc 92
**Rotman**, Walter 1922- AmMWSc 92
**Rotmistrov**, Pavel Alekseevich 1901-1982 SovUnBD
**Rotnicki**, Richard Michael 1962- WhoMW 92
**Rotondi**, Dorothy A 1958- WhoAmP 91
**Rotondi**, Samuel 1946- WhoAmP 91
**Rotsler**, William 1926- TwCSFW 91, WrDr 92
**Rott**, Nicholas 1917- AmMWSc 92
**Rottas**, Ray 1927- WhoAmP 91, WhoWest 92
**Rotte**, Joanna 1944- WhoEnt 92
**Rottenberg**, Hagai 1936- AmMWSc 92
**Rottenberg**, Herman 1916- WhoEnt 92
**Rotter**, Hans 1932- WhoRel 92
**Rotter**, Jerome Israel 1949- AmMWSc 92
**Rotter**, Paul Talbott 1918- WhoFI 92
**Rottink**, Bruce Allan 1947- AmMWSc 92
**Rottler**, Terry Robert 1951- WhoAmP 91
**Rottman**, Fritz M 1937- AmMWSc 92
**Rottman**, Gary James 1944- AmMWSc 92
**Rottmann**, Warren Leonard 1943- AmMWSc 92
**Rottschaefer**, William Andrew 1933- WhoRel 92, WhoWest 92
**Rotty**, Ralph M 1923- AmMWSc 92
**Rotunda**, Donald Theodore 1945- WhoFI 92
**Rotunda**, Ronald Daniel 1945- WhoAmL 92
**Rotunno**, Giuseppe IntMPA 92
**Rotz**, Anna Overcash 1940- WhoAmP 91
**Rotz**, Christopher Alan 1948- AmMWSc 92
**Rotzell**, Willett Enos 1871-1913 BiInAmS
**Rouard**, Pierre d1989 IntWW 91N
**Rouart**, Henri 1833-1912 ThHEIm
**Roub**, Bryan Roger 1941- WhoFI 92
**Roubal**, Ronald Keith 1935- AmMWSc 92
**Roubal**, William Theodore 1930- AmMWSc 92, WhoWest 92
**Roubenoff**, Ronenn AmMWSc 92
**Roubey**, Lester Walter 1915- WhoRel 92
**Roubicek**, Rudolf V 1918- AmMWSc 92
**Roubik**, David Ward 1951- AmMWSc 92
**Roubos**, Gary Lynn 1936- WhoFI 92
**Rouch**, David Lee 1957- WhoMW 92
**Rouch**, Jean 1917- IntDcF 2-2 [port], IntWW 91
**Rouda**, Kaira Sturdivant WhoMW 92
**Roudane**, Charles 1927- WhoFI 92
**Roudebush**, Richard L 1918- WhoAmP 91
**Roudy**, Yvette 1929- IntWW 91
**Roudybush**, Alexandra 1911- IntAu&W 91
**Roudybush**, Franklin 1906- WhoFI 92
**Roueche**, Berton DrAPF 91
**Roueche**, Berton 1911- BenetAL 91, WrDr 92
**Rouf**, Mohammed Abdur 1933- AmMWSc 92
**Roufa**, Donald Jay 1943- AmMWSc 92
**Rouffa**, Albert Stanley 1919- AmMWSc 92
**Rougeau**, Weldon Joseph 1942- WhoMW 92
**Rough**, David S. 1933- WhoFI 92
**Rough**, Gaylord Earl 1924- AmMWSc 92
**Roughgarden**, Jonathan David 1946- AmMWSc 92
**Roughley**, Peter James 1947- AmMWSc 92
**Roughton**, Philip Hugh 1949- WhoRel 92
**Roughton**, William Lemuel, Jr. 1947- WhoAmL 92
**Rougier**, Charles Jeremy 1933- Who 92
**Rougier**, Richard George 1932- Who 92
**Rougraff**, Maurice E 1926- WhoIns 92
**Rougvie**, Malcolm Arnold 1928- AmMWSc 92
**Rouhana**, Stephen William 1956- WhoMW 92
**Rouhana**, William Joseph, Jr. 1952- WhoEnt 92
**Rouillard**, Zelda Jeanne 1929- WhoWest 92
**Rouillon**, Fernand 1920- IntWW 91
**Rouilly**, Jean 1943- IntWW 91
**Rouin**, Carole Christine 1939- WhoAmL 92
**Roukema**, Marge 1929- AlmAP 92 [port], WhoAmP 91
**Roukes**, Michael L 1953- AmMWSc 92
**Roulac**, Stephen E. 1945- WhoFI 92
**Rouleau**, Joseph-Alfred 1929- IntWW 91
**Rouleau**, Mark Louis 1956- WhoFI 92
**Rouleau**, Wilfred T 1929- AmMWSc 92
**Roulhac**, Edgar Edwin 1946- WhoBlA 92
**Roulhac**, Joseph D. 1916- WhoBlA 92
**Roulhac**, Nellie Gordon 1924- WhoBlA 92
**Roulhac**, Roy L. 1943- WhoBlA 92
**Roulier**, Caroline Ann 1938- WhoMW 92
**Roulier**, John Arthur 1941- AmMWSc 92
**Roullard**, Geoffrey Dee 1952- WhoAmL 92
**Roulston**, David J 1936- AmMWSc 92
**Roulston**, Donald 1937- WhoAmP 91
**Roulston**, John Frank Clement 1941- WhoRel 92
**Roulston**, Thomas Mervyn 1920- AmMWSc 92
**Roumain**, Jacques 1907-1944 BlkLC [port]
**Roumajon**, Yves Pierre Jean 1914- IntWW 91
**Round**, G F 1932- AmMWSc 92
**Round**, Nicholas Grenville 1938- Who 92
**Roundell**, Henry J. 1947- WhoFI 92
**Roundfield**, Danny Thomas 1953- WhoBlA 92
**Rounds**, Bruce C 1928- WhoAmP 91
**Rounds**, Burton Ward 1924- AmMWSc 92
**Rounds**, Donald Edwin 1926- AmMWSc 92
**Rounds**, Fred G 1925- AmMWSc 92
**Rounds**, Glen 1906- BenetAL 91, WrDr 92
**Rounds**, Michael WhoAmP 91
**Rounds**, Richard Clifford 1943- AmMWSc 92
**Rounds**, Virgil 1928- WhoAmP 91
**Roundtree**, Eugene V. N. 1927- WhoBlA 92
**Roundtree**, Nicholas John 1956- WhoBlA 92
**Roundtree**, Richard 1942- IntMPA 92, WhoBlA 92, WhoEnt 92
**Rounick**, Jack A. 1935- WhoFI 92
**Rounsaville**, Bruce J 1949- AmMWSc 92
**Rounsaville**, Lucious Brown, Jr. 1954- WhoBlA 92
**Rounseville**, Robert 1914-1974 NewAmDM
**Rounsley**, Robert R 1931- AmMWSc 92
**Rountree**, Asa 1927- WhoAmL 92
**Rountree**, Ella Jackson 1936- WhoBlA 92
**Rountree**, Herbert Horton 1921- WhoAmP 91
**Rountree**, Janet 1937- AmMWSc 92
**Rountree**, Louise M. 1921- WhoBlA 92
**Rountree**, Owen TwCWW 91, WrDr 92
**Rountree**, Peter Charles Robert 1936- Who 92
**Rountree**, Robert Benjamin 1924- WhoFI 92
**Rountree**, Ruthann Louise 1950- WhoWest 92
**Rountree**, Thomas J. 1927- WrDr 92
**Rountree**, William Clifford 1941- WhoAmP 91
**Rountree**, William M 1917- WhoAmP 91
**Roupe**, James Paul 1957- WhoFI 92
**Roupp**, Albert Allen 1930- WhoMW 92
**Rouquette**, Adrien Emmanuel 1813-1887 BenetAL 91
**Rouquette**, Francis Marion, Jr 1942- AmMWSc 92
**Rouquette**, Francois Dominique 1810-1890 BenetAL 91
**Roura**, Andres 1937- WhoHisp 92
**Rourke**, Arlene Carol 1944- WhoFI 92
**Rourke**, Arthur W 1942- AmMWSc 92
**Rourke**, Constance M. 1885-1941 BenetAL 91
**Rourke**, Gary William 1946- WhoFI 92
**Rourke**, James TwCWW 91
**Rourke**, Michael James 1934- WhoFI 92
**Rourke**, Mickey WhoEnt 92
**Rourke**, Mickey 1953?- CurBio 91 [port]
**Rourke**, Mickey 1955- IntWW 91
**Rourke**, Mickey 1956- IntMPA 92
**Rourke**, Russell Arthur 1931- WhoAmP 91
**Rourke**, Susan F 1954- WhoAmP 91
**Rous** Who 92
**Rous**, Lady EncAmaz 91
**Rous**, Francis Peyton 1879-1970 WhoNob 90
**Rous**, Stephen N 1931- AmMWSc 92
**Rous**, William Edward 1939- Who 92
**Rousakis**, John Paul 1929- WhoAmP 91
**Rouse**, Anthony 1911- Who 92
**Rouse**, Barry Tyrrell 1942- AmMWSc 92
**Rouse**, Bishop Claude, Jr. 1948- WhoBlA 92
**Rouse**, Carl Albert 1926- AmMWSc 92
**Rouse**, Charlie 1924-1988 NewAmDM
**Rouse**, Christopher 1949- NewAmDM
**Rouse**, Christopher Chapman, III 1949- WhoEnt 92
**Rouse**, Dala Evelyn 1944- WhoWest 92
**Rouse**, Dana Jeane 1945- WhoEnt 92
**Rouse**, David B 1949- AmMWSc 92
**Rouse**, Donald E. 1932- WhoBlA 92
**Rouse**, E. Clive 1901- Who 92
**Rouse**, Elaine Burdett 1915- WhoAmP 91
**Rouse**, Gene Gordon, Sr. 1923- WhoBlA 92
**Rouse**, George Elverton 1934- AmMWSc 92
**Rouse**, Glenn Everett 1928- AmMWSc 92
**Rouse**, Gregory Stanley 1954- WhoFI 92
**Rouse**, Hunter 1906- AmMWSc 92
**Rouse**, Irene DrAPF 91
**Rouse**, Irving 1913- IntWW 91, WrDr 92
**Rouse**, Jacqueline Anne 1950- WhoBlA 92
**Rouse**, John Wilson, Jr 1937- AmMWSc 92, WhoFI 92
**Rouse**, Lawrence James, Jr 1942- AmMWSc 92
**Rouse**, LeGrand A., II 1933- WhoAmL 92
**Rouse**, Parke Shepherd, Jr. 1915- WrDr 92
**Rouse**, Richard James 1954- WhoAmP 91
**Rouse**, Robert Arthur 1943- AmMWSc 92
**Rouse**, Robert Hunter 1940- WhoAmP 91
**Rouse**, Robert S 1930- AmMWSc 92

**Rouse,** Roy Dennis 1920- AmMWSc 92
**Rouse,** Susan Kingsnorth 1943- WhoEnt 92
**Rouse,** Terrie 1952- WhoBlA 92
**Rouse,** Thomas C 1934- AmMWSc 92
**Rouse,** William Bradford 1947- AmMWSc 92
**Rouse,** William Merriam 1884-1937 ScFEYrs
**Rousek,** Edwin J 1917- AmMWSc 92
**Rousek,** Melvin Dean 1933- WhoMW 92
**Rousell,** Don Herbert 1931- AmMWSc 92
**Rouselle,** William C. 1946- WhoEnt 92
**Roush,** Allan Herbert 1918- AmMWSc 92
**Roush,** Fred William 1947- AmMWSc 92
**Roush,** George Jonathan 1937- WhoFI 92, WhoWest 92
**Roush,** J Edward 1920- WhoAmP 91
**Roush,** Lawrence William 1951- WhoFI 92
**Roush,** Marvin Leroy 1934- AmMWSc 92
**Roush,** Matt 1959- WhoEnt 92
**Roush,** Nancy Schmidt 1951- WhoAmL 92
**Roush,** William Burdette 1945- AmMWSc 92
**Roushar,** Victor Thomas 1937- WhoAmL 92
**Rouslin,** William 1938- AmMWSc 92
**Rouson,** Lee 1962- WhoBlA 92
**Rousopoulos,** Deno 1950- WhoMW 92
**Rousou,** J A AmMWSc 92
**Rouss,** Ruth 1914- WhoFI 92
**Roussakis,** Nicolas 1934- WhoEnt 92
**Rousse,** Georges 1947- WorArt 1980
**Rousseau,** Cecil Clyde 1938- AmMWSc 92
**Rousseau,** Conrad Ernest, Jr. 1937- WhoFI 92
**Rousseau,** Denis Lawrence 1940- AmMWSc 92
**Rousseau,** Eugene Ellsworth 1932- WhoEnt 92
**Rousseau,** George S 1941- IntAu&W 91, WrDr 92
**Rousseau,** Jean-Jacques 1712-1778 BlkwCEP, NewAmDM
**Rousseau,** Lucien G, Jr 1945- WhoAmP 91
**Rousseau,** Mark Owen 1940- WhoMW 92
**Rousseau,** Paul Emile 1929- Who 92
**Rousseau,** Pierre 1725-1785 BlkwCEP
**Rousseau,** Richard Wilfred 1924- WhoRel 92
**Rousseau,** Robert G 1950- WhoAmP 91
**Rousseau,** Ronald William 1943- AmMWSc 92
**Rousseau,** Theodore 1812-1867 ThHEIm
**Rousseau,** Viateur 1914- AmMWSc 92
**Rousseau,** Victor 1879-1960 ScFEYrs, TwCSFW 91
**Roussel,** Albert 1869-1937 FacFETw, NewAmDM
**Roussel,** Claude 1919- IntWW 91
**Roussel,** John S 1921- AmMWSc 92
**Roussel,** Joseph Donald 1929- AmMWSc 92
**Roussel,** Lyon 1923- Who 92
**Roussel,** Raymond 1877-1933 GuFrLit 1
**Roussel,** Robert Walter 1916- WhoAmL 92
**Roussel,** Theodore 1847-1926 TwCPaSc
**Rousselet,** Andre Claude Lucien 1922- IntWW 91
**Roussell,** Norman 1934- WhoBlA 92
**Rousselle,** Regis 1948- IntWW 91
**Rousselot,** David Rex 1956- WhoFI 92
**Rousselot,** John Harbin 1927- WhoAmP 91
**Rousselot,** Peter Frese 1942- WhoAmL 92
**Rousselot,** Philippe IntMPA 92
**Rousset,** Alain WhoFI 92
**Roussey,** Robert Stanley 1935- WhoMW 92
**Roussin,** Robert Warren 1939- AmMWSc 92
**Roussos,** Constantine 1947- AmMWSc 92
**Roussos,** Stavros G. 1918- Who 92
**Roussos,** Stephen Bernard 1960- WhoRel 92
**Roustan,** Yvon Dominique 1944- WhoAmL 92
**Rout,** Owen Howard 1930- Who 92
**Routbort,** Jules Lazar 1937- AmMWSc 92
**Routh,** Donald Kent 1937- AmMWSc 92
**Routh,** Donald Thomas 1936- Who 92
**Routh,** Donna Morrison 1943- WhoWest 92
**Routh,** Francis John 1927- WrDr 92
**Routh,** John William 1957- WhoAmL 92
**Routh,** Joseph Isaac 1910- AmMWSc 92
**Routhier,** Maurice 1913- WhoAmP 91
**Routien,** John Broderick 1913- AmMWSc 92
**Routledge and Kegan Paul** DcLB 106
**Routledge and Warne** DcLB 106
**Routledge,** Alan 1919- Who 92
**Routledge,** George 1812-1888 DcLB 106
**Routledge,** George, and Sons DcLB 106
**Routledge,** Patricia 1929- Who 92
**Routledge,** Richard Donovan 1948- AmMWSc 92
**Routley,** Douglas George 1929- AmMWSc 92
**Routly,** Paul McRae 1926- AmMWSc 92
**Routson,** Clell Dennis 1946- WhoFI 92
**Routson,** Ronald C 1933- AmMWSc 92
**Routson,** Samuel John 1949- WhoAmP 91
**Routt,** Thomas H. 1930-1991 WhoBlA 92N
**Routte-Gomez,** Eneid G. 1944- WhoBlA 92
**Routtenberg,** Aryeh 1939- AmMWSc 92
**Rouverol,** Jean 1916- WhoEnt 92
**Rouviere,** Philibert 1809-1865 ThHEIm
**Rouvray,** Dennis Henry 1938- AmMWSc 92
**Roux,** Abraham Johannes Andries 1914- IntWW 91
**Roux,** Ambroise Marie Casimir 1921- IntWW 91
**Roux,** Bernard Georges Marie 1934- IntWW 91
**Roux,** David Gerhardus 1920- IntWW 91
**Roux,** Jacques 1907- IntWW 91
**Roux,** Jean-Louis 1923- IntWW 91, WhoEnt 92
**Roux,** John DrAPF 91
**Roux,** Kenneth H 1948- AmMWSc 92
**Roux,** Michel Andre 1941- Who 92
**Roux,** Stanley Joseph 1942- AmMWSc 92
**Roux,** Vincent J. 1937- WhoBlA 92
**Rouxel,** Jean 1935- IntWW 91
**Rouze,** Jeffrey Alan 1952- WhoMW 92
**Rovainen,** Carl 1939- AmMWSc 92
**Rove,** Frances Ann 1960- WhoAmL 92
**Rove,** Karl Christian 1950- WhoAmP 91
**Rovelli,** Carlo 1956- AmMWSc 92
**Rovelstad,** Gordon Henry 1921- AmMWSc 92
**Rovelstad,** Randolph Andrew 1920- AmMWSc 92
**Rover,** Carl 1889-1942 EncTR 91 [port]
**Rover,** Constance Mary 1910- WrDr 92
**Rovera,** Giovanni 1940- AmMWSc 92
**Rovere,** Richard 1915-1979 BenetAL 91
**Roverud,** Eleanor 1912- WhoMW 92
**Rovetto,** Michael Julien 1943- AmMWSc 92
**Rovick,** Allen Asher 1928- AmMWSc 92
**Rovin,** Ronald 1942- WhoMW 92
**Rovine,** Arthur William 1937- WhoAmL 92
**Rovira,** Joachim Jack 1945- WhoHisp 92
**Rovira,** Lois Ann 1937- WhoAmP 91
**Rovira,** Luis D 1923- WhoAmP 91
**Rovira,** Luis Dario 1923- WhoAmL 92, WhoWest 92
**Rovira,** Maritza WhoHisp 92
**Rovira,** Martino Francisco 1940- WhoHisp 92
**Rovit,** Earl DrAPF 91
**Rovit,** Earl 1927- WrDr 92
**Rovit,** Richard Lee 1924- AmMWSc 92
**Rovner,** Arkady DrAPF 91
**Rovner,** David Patrick Ryan 1952- WhoAmL 92
**Rovner,** David Richard 1930- AmMWSc 92
**Rovner,** Gerald Conrad 1942- WhoAmL 92
**Rovner,** Ilana Kara Diamond 1938- WhoAmL 92, WhoMW 92
**Rovner,** Jerome Sylvan 1940- AmMWSc 92
**Rovnyak,** George Charles 1941- AmMWSc 92
**Rovnyak,** James L 1939- AmMWSc 92
**Row,** Clark 1934- AmMWSc 92
**Row,** John Alfred 1905- Who 92
**Row,** Peter L. WhoEnt 92
**Row,** Philip John d1990 Who 92N
**Row,** Thomas Henry 1935- AmMWSc 92
**Rowallan,** Baron 1919- Who 92
**Rowan and Martin** LesBEnT 92
**Rowan,** Albert T. 1927- WhoBlA 92
**Rowan,** Albert Theodore 1927- WhoRel 92
**Rowan,** Andrew Summers BenetAL 91
**Rowan,** Carl T. 1925- ConBlB 1 [port], FacFETw
**Rowan,** Carl Thomas 1925- Who 92, WhoBlA 92
**Rowan,** Danielle IntMPA 92
**Rowan,** Deirdre WrDr 92
**Rowan,** Dighton Francis 1914- AmMWSc 92
**Rowan,** Hester IntAu&W 91X, WrDr 92
**Rowan,** Jo WhoEnt 92
**Rowan,** John Patrick 1945- WhoAmP 91
**Rowan,** Katherine Ellen 1954- WhoMW 92
**Rowan,** Keith Patterson 1934- WhoWest 92
**Rowan,** M.M. 1943- TwCWW 91, WrDr 92
**Rowan,** Nancy Gordon 1946- AmMWSc 92
**Rowan,** Patricia Adrienne Who 92
**Rowan,** Ronald Thomas 1941- WhoAmL 92
**Rowan-Legg,** Allan Aubrey 1912- Who 92
**Rowand,** Will H 1908- AmMWSc 92
**Rowark,** Maureen 1933- WhoMW 92
**Rowat,** Donald C. 1921- WrDr 92
**Rowberry,** David Joseph 1953- WhoWest 92
**Rowbotham,** David 1924- ConPo 91, WrDr 92
**Rowbotham,** David Harold 1924- IntAu&W 91
**Rowbotham,** Sheila 1943- WrDr 92
**Rowcroft,** Charles 1795?-1856 ScFEYrs
**Rowden,** Alphro John 1906- WhoRel 92
**Rowden,** Marcus Aubrey 1928- WhoAmL 92
**Rowden,** Mark Allen 1957- WhoRel 92
**Rowe,** Adrian Harold Redfern 1925- Who 92
**Rowe,** Albert P 1934- WhoAmP 91, WhoBlA 92
**Rowe,** Allan Duncan 1951- WhoFI 92
**Rowe,** Allen McGhee, Jr 1932- AmMWSc 92
**Rowe,** Andrew 1935- Who 92
**Rowe,** Anne E 1944- WhoAmP 91
**Rowe,** Anne Prine 1927- AmMWSc 92
**Rowe,** Arthur W 1931- AmMWSc 92
**Rowe,** Bonnie Gordon 1922- WhoEnt 92
**Rowe,** Brian H 1931- AmMWSc 92
**Rowe,** Bridget 1950- Who 92
**Rowe,** Carl Osborn 1944- WhoWest 92
**Rowe,** Carleton Norwood 1928- AmMWSc 92
**Rowe,** Charles David 1939- AmMWSc 92
**Rowe,** Christa F. 1959- WhoBlA 92
**Rowe,** Colon Harvey, Jr 1939- WhoAmP 91
**Rowe,** David John 1936- AmMWSc 92
**Rowe,** David Winfield 1954- WhoAmL 92
**Rowe,** Douglas Henry 1938- WhoEnt 92
**Rowe,** Edward C 1933- AmMWSc 92
**Rowe,** Edward John 1910- AmMWSc 92
**Rowe,** Elizabeth 1674-1737 BlkwCEP
**Rowe,** Elizabeth Snow 1943- AmMWSc 92
**Rowe,** Ellen Betts 1951- WhoFI 92
**Rowe,** Englebert L 1925- AmMWSc 92
**Rowe,** Frank Devon, Jr. 1951- WhoFI 92
**Rowe,** Gail Stuart 1936- WhoWest 92
**Rowe,** George G 1921- AmMWSc 92
**Rowe,** H E 1927- AmMWSc 92
**Rowe,** Harris 1923- WhoAmP 91
**Rowe,** Harvey John 1936- WhoMW 92
**Rowe,** Helen Who 92
**Rowe,** Henry 1916- Who 92
**Rowe,** Henry Theodore, Jr. 1932- WhoEnt 92
**Rowe,** Herman F. W. 1943- WhoEnt 92
**Rowe,** Irving 1913- AmMWSc 92
**Rowe,** James H 1909-1984 FacFETw
**Rowe,** James Jefferson 1950- WhoAmP 91
**Rowe,** James Lincoln 1917- AmMWSc 92
**Rowe,** Jasper C. 1945- WhoBlA 92
**Rowe,** Jay Elwood 1947- AmMWSc 92
**Rowe,** Jeremy 1928- Who 92
**Rowe,** Jeremy Stephen 1952- WhoEnt 92
**Rowe,** Jimmy L. 1932- WhoBlA 92
**Rowe,** John Carlos 1945- ConAu 36NR
**Rowe,** John Edward 1941- AmMWSc 92
**Rowe,** John James 1944- AmMWSc 92
**Rowe,** John Jermyn 1936- Who 92
**Rowe,** John L. 1914-1975? ConAu 135
**Rowe,** John Michael 1939- AmMWSc 92
**Rowe,** John Stanley 1918- AmMWSc 92
**Rowe,** John W AmMWSc 92
**Rowe,** John Westel 1924- AmMWSc 92
**Rowe,** John William 1945- WhoFI 92
**Rowe,** Joseph E 1927- AmMWSc 92
**Rowe,** Kathryn Llewellyn 1958- WhoEnt 92
**Rowe,** Kenneth Eugene 1934- AmMWSc 92
**Rowe,** Larry Linwell 1948- WhoAmL 92
**Rowe,** Lawrence A 1948- AmMWSc 92
**Rowe,** Lee Allen 1936- WhoWest 92
**Rowe,** Mae Irene 1927- WhoMW 92
**Rowe,** Marieli Dorothy WhoMW 92
**Rowe,** Marilyn Johnson 1954- WhoBlA 92
**Rowe,** Mark J 1943- AmMWSc 92
**Rowe,** Marvin W 1937- AmMWSc 92
**Rowe,** Mary Budd 1925- AmMWSc 92
**Rowe,** Mary Sue 1940- WhoWest 92
**Rowe,** Nansi Irene 1940- WhoBlA 92
**Rowe,** Nathaniel H 1931- AmMWSc 92
**Rowe,** Nicholas 1674?-1718 RfGEnL 91
**Rowe,** Norbert Edward 1898- Who 92
**Rowe,** Norman Lester d1991 Who 92N
**Rowe,** Norman Wayne 1948- WhoMW 92
**Rowe,** Owen John Tressider 1922- Who 92
**Rowe,** Pamela Sue 1953- WhoMW 92
**Rowe,** Patrick Barton 1939- Who 92
**Rowe,** Paul E 1927- AmMWSc 92
**Rowe,** Peter Noel 1919- Who 92
**Rowe,** Peter Wentworth 1935- WhoAmL 92
**Rowe,** Peter Whitmill 1928- Who 92
**Rowe,** Randall Charles 1945- AmMWSc 92
**Rowe,** Raymond Grant 1941- AmMWSc 92
**Rowe,** Reginald Emeric 1949- WhoMW 92
**Rowe,** Richard Brian 1933- Who 92
**Rowe,** Richard Burton 1872?-1902 BiInAmS
**Rowe,** Richard Holmes 1937- WhoAmL 92
**Rowe,** Richard J 1930- AmMWSc 92
**Rowe,** Richard L. 1926- WhoBlA 92
**Rowe,** Robb Wendal 1939- WhoFI 92
**Rowe,** Robert Hetsley 1929- WhoFI 92, WhoIns 92, WhoWest 92
**Rowe,** Robert Lester 1942- WhoMW 92
**Rowe,** Robert S 1920- AmMWSc 92
**Rowe,** Robert Stewart 1920- Who 92
**Rowe,** Ronald Kerry 1951- AmMWSc 92
**Rowe,** Roy 1905- IntMPA 92
**Rowe,** Roy Ernest 1929- Who 92
**Rowe,** Stephen Christian WhoRel 92
**Rowe,** Temple Scott 1956- WhoWest 92
**Rowe,** Thomas Dudley 1910- AmMWSc 92
**Rowe,** Thomas Dudley, Jr. 1942- WhoAmL 92
**Rowe,** Timothy Adams 1951- WhoEnt 92
**Rowe,** Todd Kevin 1960- WhoMW 92
**Rowe,** Verald Keith 1914- AmMWSc 92
**Rowe,** Vernon Dodds 1944- AmMWSc 92
**Rowe,** William Bruce 1935- AmMWSc 92
**Rowe,** William David 1930- AmMWSc 92
**Rowe,** William Kenneth 1944- WhoWest 92
**Rowe,** William Leon 1915- WhoBlA 92
**Rowe,** William Leonard 1931- WhoRel 92
**Rowe-Ham,** David 1935- IntWW 91, Who 92
**Rowe-Maas,** Betty Lu 1925- WhoFI 92, WhoWest 92
**Rowekamp,** Barry Lewis 1955- WhoWest 92
**Rowekamp,** Leonard G. 1952- WhoAmL 92
**Rowell,** Albert John 1929- AmMWSc 92
**Rowell,** Charles Frederick 1935- AmMWSc 92
**Rowell,** Charles H. DrAPF 91
**Rowell,** Chester Morrison, Jr 1925- AmMWSc 92
**Rowell,** Douglas Geoffrey 1943- WrDr 92
**Rowell,** Edward Leonidas 1928- WhoAmP 91
**Rowell,** Edward Morgan 1931- WhoAmP 91
**Rowell,** Eldrige Bates 1952- WhoRel 92
**Rowell,** George 1923- WrDr 92
**Rowell,** Harry Brown, Jr. 1941- WhoFI 92
**Rowell,** James Victor 1939- WhoAmP 91
**Rowell,** John 1916- Who 92
**Rowell,** John Bartlett 1918- AmMWSc 92
**Rowell,** John Martin 1935- AmMWSc 92, Who 92
**Rowell,** Loring B 1930- AmMWSc 92
**Rowell,** Neal Pope 1926- AmMWSc 92
**Rowell,** Peter Putnam 1946- AmMWSc 92
**Rowell,** Robert Lee 1932- AmMWSc 92
**Rowen,** Burt 1921- AmMWSc 92
**Rowen,** Herbert H. 1916- WrDr 92
**Rowen,** Marshall WhoWest 92
**Rowen,** William H 1918- AmMWSc 92
**Rowett,** Diane L. 1961- WhoWest 92
**Rowett,** Helen 1915- WrDr 92
**Rowey,** Alan Michael 1949- WhoEnt 92
**Rowin,** Gerald L 1937- AmMWSc 92
**Rowinski,** Alexander 1931- IntAu&W 91
**Rowinski,** Francis C. WhoRel 92
**Rowland,** Alex Thomas 1931- AmMWSc 92
**Rowland,** Arthur Ray 1930- WrDr 92
**Rowland,** Beverly Jean 1948- WhoMW 92
**Rowland,** Christopher Charles 1947- Who 92
**Rowland,** David Who 92
**Rowland,** David 1924- DcTwDes
**Rowland,** David Lawrence 1950- AmMWSc 92, WhoMW 92
**Rowland,** David Powys 1917- Who 92
**Rowland,** Dennis Herbert 1946- WhoWest 92
**Rowland,** Donald S 1928- TwCWW 91
**Rowland,** F Sherwood 1927- AmMWSc 92
**Rowland,** Frank R. 1964- WhoRel 92
**Rowland,** Frank Sherwood 1927- IntWW 91
**Rowland,** Harry Manning, Jr. 1957- WhoRel 92
**Rowland,** Henry Augustus 1848-1901 BiInAmS
**Rowland,** Henry C 1874-1933 ScFEYrs
**Rowland,** Herbert Grimley 1905- Who 92
**Rowland,** Herbert Leslie 1925- WhoFI 92
**Rowland,** Iris WrDr 92
**Rowland,** Ivan W 1910- AmMWSc 92
**Rowland,** J. R. 1925- ConPo 91, WrDr 92
**Rowland,** J. Roy 1926- AlmAP 92 [port]
**Rowland,** James 1922- Who 92
**Rowland,** James Anthony 1922- IntWW 91
**Rowland,** James Brian 1946- WhoMW 92
**Rowland,** James H. 1909- WhoBlA 92
**Rowland,** James Norman 1934- WhoWest 92
**Rowland,** James Richard 1940- AmMWSc 92
**Rowland,** James Roy, Jr 1926- WhoAmP 91
**Rowland,** Jan Reagan 1944- WhoEnt 92

Rowland, Jay Alan 1946- WhoAmL 92
Rowland, John Andrew 1959- WhoRel 92
Rowland, John David 1933- Who 92
Rowland, John Grosvenor 1957- WhoAmP 91
Rowland, John H 1934- AmMWSc 92
Rowland, John Russell 1925- IntWW 91
Rowland, Landon Hill 1937- WhoFI 92, WhoMW 92
Rowland, Lenton O, Jr 1943- AmMWSc 92
Rowland, Leon Floyd 1945- WhoBlA 92
Rowland, Lewis Phillip 1925- AmMWSc 92
Rowland, Neil Edward 1947- AmMWSc 92
Rowland, Neil Wilson 1919- AmMWSc 92
Rowland, Peter Kenneth 1938- IntAu&W 91, WrDr 92
Rowland, Richard Howell 1944- WhoEnt 92
Rowland, Richard Lloyd 1929- AmMWSc 92
Rowland, Robert Edmund 1923- AmMWSc 92
Rowland, Robert Todd 1922- Who 92
Rowland, Roland W. 1917- IntWW 91
Rowland, Roy IntMPA 92
Rowland, Ruth Gailey 1922- WhoWest 92
Rowland, Sattley Clark 1938- AmMWSc 92
Rowland, Stanley Paul 1916- AmMWSc 92
Rowland, Susan Blake 1946- WhoWest 92
Rowland, Theodore Justin 1927- AmMWSc 92, WhoMW 92
Rowland, Timothy Lee 1949- WhoWest 92
Rowland, Vernon 1922- AmMWSc 92
Rowland, Walter Francis 1931- AmMWSc 92
Rowland, William Fredrick Rick 1934- WhoRel 92
Rowland, William Joseph 1943- AmMWSc 92
Rowland, William L 1946- WhoIns 92
Rowland-Entwistle, Theodore 1925- IntAu&W 91
Rowlands, Alexander Eric 1948- WhoRel 92
Rowlands, David 1947- Who 92
Rowlands, David T, Jr 1930- AmMWSc 92
Rowlands, Edward 1940- Who 92
Rowlands, Gena 1936- IntMPA 92, WhoEnt 92
Rowlands, John Alan 1945- AmMWSc 92
Rowlands, John Henry Lewis 1947- Who 92
Rowlands, John Kendall 1931- Who 92
Rowlands, John Martin 1925- Who 92
Rowlands, John Samuel 1915- Who 92
Rowlands, Maldwyn Jones 1918- Who 92
Rowlands, Martin Who 92
Rowlands, Martyn Omar 1923- Who 92
Rowlands, R O 1914- AmMWSc 92
Rowlands, Robert Edward 1936- AmMWSc 92
Rowlandson, Mary BenetAL 91
Rowlenson, Richard Charles 1949- WhoFI 92
Rowles, Arlene Beverly 1935- WhoMW 92
Rowles, Charles Scott 1953- WhoWest 92
Rowles, James George 1918- WhoEnt 92, WhoWest 92
Rowles, Stacy Amanda 1955- WhoEnt 92
Rowlett, George 1941- TwCPaSc
Rowlett, Roger Scott 1955- AmMWSc 92
Rowlett, Russell Johnston, III 1945- AmMWSc 92
Rowlett, Russell Johnston, Jr 1920- AmMWSc 92
Rowley, Ames Dorrance ConAu 133
Rowley, Beverley Davies 1941- WhoFI 92
Rowley, Charles 1926- Who 92
Rowley, Daniel Agnew 1954- WhoAmL 92
Rowley, David Alton 1940- AmMWSc 92
Rowley, Donald Adams 1923- AmMWSc 92
Rowley, Durwood B 1929- AmMWSc 92
Rowley, Evelyn Fish 1927- WhoAmP 91
Rowley, Frederick Allan 1922- Who 92
Rowley, Geoffrey Herbert 1935- WhoFI 92
Rowley, Geoffrey William 1926- Who 92
Rowley, George Richard 1923- AmMWSc 92
Rowley, Janet D 1925- AmMWSc 92
Rowley, John Charles 1919- Who 92
Rowley, John H. 1917- IntMPA 92
Rowley, John Vincent d'Alessio 1907- Who 92
Rowley, Joshua Francis 1920- Who 92
Rowley, Peter 1918- Who 92
Rowley, Peter DeWitt 1942- AmMWSc 92, WhoWest 92
Rowley, Peter Templeton 1929- AmMWSc 92
Rowley, Richard L 1951- AmMWSc 92
Rowley, Robert Deane, Jr. 1941- WhoRel 92
Rowley, Rodney Ray 1934- AmMWSc 92
Rowley, Wayne A 1933- AmMWSc 92
Rowley, Wayne Allred 1933- WhoMW 92
Rowley, William 1585?-1626 RfGEnL 91
Rowley, William Dean 1939- WhoWest 92
Rowley-Conwy Who 92
Rowley Hill, George Alfred Who 92
Rowling, Wallace 1927- Who 92
Rowling, Wallace Edward 1927- IntWW 91
Rowlinson, John Shipley 1926- IntWW 91, Who 92
Rownd, Robert Harvey 1937- AmMWSc 92
Rowney, John Adalbert 1945- WhoIns 92
Rowning, John 1701?-1771 BlkwCEP
Rowntree, Derek 1936- WrDr 92
Rowntree, Kenneth 1915- TwCPaSc
Rowntree, Norman Andrew Forster d1991 Who 92N
Rowntree, Norman Andrew Forster 1912- IntWW 91
Rowntree, Robert Fredric 1930- AmMWSc 92
Rowntree Clifford, Paul Who 92
Rowny, Edward Leon 1917- IntWW 91, WhoAmP 91
Rowoth, Olin Arthur 1921- AmMWSc 92
Rowse, A. L. 1903- ConPo 91, WrDr 92
Rowse, Alfred Leslie 1903- IntAu&W 91, IntWW 91, Who 92
Rowsell, Edmund Lionel P. Who 92
Rowsell, Harry Cecil 1921- AmMWSc 92
Rowsey, Sharon Easthom 1962- WhoAmL 92
Rowson, John Anthony 1930- Who 92
Rowson, Susanna 1762-1824 BenetAL 91
Rowton, Richard Lee 1928- AmMWSc 92
Rowzee, E R 1908- AmMWSc 92
Roxana EncAmaz 91
Roxana d311BC EncAmaz 91
Roxas, Savina DrAPF 91
Roxbee Cox Who 92
Roxborough, Mildred 1927- WhoBlA 92
Roxburgh, Iain Edge 1943- Who 92
Roxburgh, Ian Walter 1939- Who 92
Roxburgh, James William 1921- Who 92
Roxburgh, John 1919- Who 92
Roxburghe, Duke of 1954- Who 92
Roxby, Robert 1940- AmMWSc 92
Roxin, Emilio O 1922- AmMWSc 92
Roy, Alexander 1937- WhoEnt 92
Roy, Americus Melvin 1929- WhoBlA 92
Roy, Andrew Donald 1920- Who 92
Roy, Ann Lee 1936- WhoAmP 91
Roy, Archie E. 1924- WrDr 92
Roy, Arthur Douglas 1925- Who 92
Roy, Arun K 1938- AmMWSc 92
Roy, Asim 1948- WhoFI 92
Roy, Bill, Jr WhoAmP 91
Roy, Bimal 1909-1966 IntDcF 2-2 [port]
Roy, Catherine Elizabeth 1948- WhoWest 92
Roy, Charles Edward 1917- WhoRel 92
Roy, Claude 1915- IntWW 91
Roy, Claude Charles 1928- AmMWSc 92
Roy, David C 1937- AmMWSc 92
Roy, David P. 1951- WhoFI 92
Roy, Della M 1926- AmMWSc 92
Roy, Dev Kumar 1951- AmMWSc 92
Roy, Dipak 1946- AmMWSc 92
Roy, Donald H 1936- AmMWSc 92
Roy, Elsijane Trimble 1916- WhoAmL 92
Roy, Emile Joseph 1920- WhoAmP 91
Roy, Gabriel D 1939- AmMWSc 92
Roy, Gabriel L 1938- AmMWSc 92
Roy, Gabrielle 1909-1983 BenetAL 91
Roy, Gregor Andrew 1929- WhoEnt 92
Roy, Guy 1939- AmMWSc 92
Roy, Harold Edward 1921- WhoFI 92, WhoWest 92
Roy, Harry 1943- AmMWSc 92
Roy, Ian 1912- Who 92
Roy, James 1922- WrDr 92
Roy, James De Wall 1940- WhoFI 92
Roy, James Stapleton 1935- WhoAmP 91
Roy, Jasper K. WhoBlA 92
Roy, Jean-Claude 1927- AmMWSc 92
Roy, Jessie H. 1895-1986 WhoBlA 92N
Roy, Joe Eddie, Sr. d1988 WhoBlA 92N
Roy, Jules 1907- IntWW 91
Roy, Kevin Brian 1959- WhoRel 92
Roy, Klaus George 1924- NewAmDM
Roy, M S 1946- AmMWSc 92
Roy, Marie Lessard 1944- AmMWSc 92
Roy, Maurice 1905-1985 FacFETw, RelLAm 91
Roy, Melinda WhoEnt 92
Roy, Paul Emile, Jr. 1942- WhoFI 92, WhoMW 92
Roy, Paul-H 1924- AmMWSc 92
Roy, Pradip Kumar 1943- AmMWSc 92
Roy, Prodyot 1935- AmMWSc 92
Roy, Rabindra 1939- AmMWSc 92
Roy, Radha Raman 1921- AmMWSc 92
Roy, Rajarshi 1954- AmMWSc 92
Roy, Ralph Lord 1928- WhoRel 92
Roy, Ram Babu 1933- AmMWSc 92, WhoWest 92
Roy, Raman K 1947- AmMWSc 92
Roy, Ramendra Prasad 1942- WhoWest 92
Roy, Raymond 1919- WhoRel 92, WhoWest 92
Roy, Raymond Albert, Jr. 1954- WhoWest 92
Roy, Richard James 1944- WhoAmL 92
Roy, Rob 1933- AmMWSc 92
Roy, Robert Francis 1930- AmMWSc 92
Roy, Robert Michael McGregor 1942- AmMWSc 92
Roy, Robert Russell 1957- WhoMW 92
Roy, Robin 1946- ConAu 36NR
Roy, Roger P 1940- WhoAmP 91
Roy, Rustum 1924- AmMWSc 92
Roy, Sheila 1948- Who 92
Roy, Thomas Clayton, III 1949- WhoRel 92
Roy, Tom 1958- WhoEnt 92
Roy, Welton J., Jr. 1939- WhoBlA 92
Roy, William Arthur 1948- AmMWSc 92
Roy, William R 1926- AmMWSc 92
Roy, William Robert 1926- WhoAmP 91
Roy-Burman, Pradip 1938- AmMWSc 92, WhoWest 92
Royal, Princess 1950- IntWW 91, Who 92R
Royal, A Richard 1939- WhoAmP 91
Royal, Bertrand ScFEYrs
Royal, C. Charles, Sr. WhoBlA 92
Royal, Dan TwCWW 91, WrDr 92
Royal, Dan Stephen 1961- WhoWest 92
Royal, Daniel Charles, Jr. 1943- WhoEnt 92
Royal, George Calvin, Jr 1921- AmMWSc 92
Royal, Henry Duval 1948- AmMWSc 92
Royal, James E. 1941- WhoBlA 92
Royal, John F. d1978 LesBEnT 92
Royal, Richard DrAPF 91
Royal, Richard M 1935- WhoIns 92
Royal, Rosamund WrDr 92
Royal, William Henry 1924- WhoMW 92
Royal-Gordon, John Donald 1955- WhoWest 92
Royall, Anne Newport 1769-1854 BenetAL 91
Royall, Bob Lee 1956- WhoRel 92
Royall, Kenneth Claiborne, Jr 1918- WhoAmP 91
Royall, Richard Miles 1939- AmMWSc 92
Royall, Vanessa ConAu 34NR
Royals, Edwin Earl 1919- AmMWSc 92
Roybal, Dolores E. 1953- WhoHisp 92
Roybal, Edward R. 1916- AlmAP 92 [port], WhoAmP 91, WhoHisp 92, WhoWest 92
Roybal-Allard, Lucille 1941- WhoAmP 91, WhoHisp 92
Royce, Barrie Saunders Hart 1933- AmMWSc 92
Royce, David Nowill 1920- Who 92
Royce, Edward R 1951- WhoAmP 91
Royce, Frederick Henry 1934- WhoAmP 91
Royce, George James 1938- AmMWSc 92
Royce, James E 1914- ConAu 34NR, WrDr 92
Royce, James Emmet 1914- WhoRel 92
Royce, John 1944- Who 92
Royce, Josiah 1855-1916 AmPeW, BenetAL 91, BiInAmS, FacFETw
Royce, Kenneth 1920- IntAu&W 91, WrDr 92
Royce, Paul C 1928- AmMWSc 92
Royce, William Calvin, III 1948- WhoEnt 92
Royce, William Francis 1916- AmMWSc 92
Roychoudhuri, Chandrasekhar 1942- AmMWSc 92, WhoFI 92
Royden, Christopher 1937- Who 92
Royden, Halsey Lawrence 1928- AmMWSc 92
Royds, John Caress 1920- Who 92
Royds, Mabel 1874-1941 TwCPaSc
Roye, Monica R. Hargrove 1955- WhoBlA 92
Royer, Bill 1929- WhoAmP 91
Royer, Charles Theodore 1939- WhoAmP 91, WhoWest 92
Royer, David Lee 1950- WhoIns 92
Royer, Dennis Jack 1941- AmMWSc 92
Royer, Donald Jack 1928- AmMWSc 92
Royer, Fanchon 1902- ReelWom [port]
Royer, Garfield Paul 1942- AmMWSc 92
Royer, Jean 1920- IntWW 91
Royer, Richard Adrian 1951- WhoMW 92
Royer, Theodore Henry 1936- WhoAmP 91
Royer, Thomas Clark 1941- AmMWSc 92
Royer, Thomas Jerry 1943- WhoFI 92
Royko, Mike 1922- WrDr 92
Royko, Mike 1932- WhoMW 92
Roysksund, Conrad 1931- WhoMW 92
Roylance, Pamela Jean 1952- WhoEnt 92
Royle Who 92
Royle, David 1947- TwCPaSc
Royle, Edwin Milton 1862-1942 BenetAL 91
Royle, Guinevere Eve 1960- WhoMW 92
Royle, Herbert F. 1870-1958 TwCPaSc
Royle, Stanley 1888-1961 TwCPaSc
Royle, Timothy Lancelot Fanshawe 1931- Who 92
Royo Sanchez, Aristides 1940- IntWW 91
Roys, Chester Crosby 1912- AmMWSc 92
Roys, Paul Allen 1926- AmMWSc 92
Royse, Daniel Joseph 1950- AmMWSc 92
Royster, Darryl 1954- WhoMW 92
Royster, Don M., Sr. 1944- WhoBlA 92
Royster, George Durward, Jr. 1941- WhoAmL 92
Royster, Julia Doswell 1951- AmMWSc 92
Royster, L H 1936- AmMWSc 92
Royster, Robert WhoRel 92
Royster, Roger Lee 1949- AmMWSc 92
Royster, Vermont 1914- WrDr 92
Royster, Vermont Connecticut 1914- IntAu&W 91, IntWW 91
Royster, Vivian Hall 1951- WhoBlA 92
Royster, Wimberly Calvin 1925- AmMWSc 92
Royston, James Howard 1948- WhoRel 92
Royston, Lloyd Leonard WhoBlA 92
Royston, Richard John 1931- AmMWSc 92
Royt, Paulette Anne 1945- AmMWSc 92
Roytburd, Victor 1945- AmMWSc 92
Rozanov, Evgeny Grigorevich 1925- IntWW 91
Rozanski, Edward Casimir 1915- WhoMW 92
Rozanski, George 1912- AmMWSc 92
Rozanski, Stanley Howard 1952- WhoAmL 92
Rozario, Michael Who 92
Rozas, Carlos Luis 1944- WhoHisp 92
Rozbruch, Michael Andrew 1955- WhoFI 92
Rozdilsky, Bohdan 1916- AmMWSc 92
Roze, Uldis 1938- AmMWSc 92
Rozeboom, Lloyd Eugene 1908- AmMWSc 92
Rozee, Kenneth Roy 1931- AmMWSc 92
Rozel, Samuel Joseph 1935- WhoAmL 92, WhoFI 92
Rozell, Herbert 1931- WhoAmP 91
Rozell, Joseph Gerard 1959- WhoMW 92
Rozell, William Barclay 1943- WhoAmL 92
Rozelle, Ralph B 1932- AmMWSc 92
Rozema, Edward Ralph 1945- AmMWSc 92
Rozema, Patricia ReelWom
Rozen, Jerome George, Jr 1928- AmMWSc 92
Rozenberg, Helen S. 1954- WhoAmL 92
Rozenberg, J E 1922- AmMWSc 92
Rozenberg, Michael Albert 1949- WhoIns 92
Rozendal, David Bernard 1937- AmMWSc 92
Rozendale, David S. 1934- WhoFI 92
Rozenel', Natal'ya Aleksandrovna 1902-1965 SovUnBD
Rozes, Simone 1920- IntWW 91
Rozewicz, Tadeusz 1921- ConAu 36NR, IntWW 91
Rozgonyi, George A 1937- AmMWSc 92
Rozhdestvensky, Gennadi Nikolaevich 1931- Who 92, WhoEnt 92
Rozhdestvensky, Gennadiy Nikolaevich 1931- SovUnBD
Rozhdestvensky, Gennadiy Nikolayevich 1931- IntWW 91
Rozhdestvensky, Gennady 1931- NewAmDM
Rozhdestvensky, Robert Ivanovich 1932- IntAu&W 91, IntWW 91, SovUnBD
Rozhin, Jurij 1931- AmMWSc 92, WhoMW 92
Rozier, Carolyn K 1944- AmMWSc 92
Rozier, Gilbert Donald 1940- WhoBlA 92
Rozier, Mike 1961- WhoBlA 92
Rozimir, Felix Yakovliewich 1936- LiExTwC
Roziner, Feliks Yakovlevich 1936- LiExTwC
Rozman, Joseph John, Jr. 1944- WhoMW 92
Rozmiarek, Harry 1939- AmMWSc 92
Rozmiarek, Mildred Irene 1917- WhoAmP 91
Rozov, Viktor Sergeevich 1913- IntWW 91
Rozovsky, Mark 1937- IntWW 91
Rozran, Jack Louis 1939- WhoMW 92
Rozsa, Kevin Mitchell 1963- WhoMW 92
Rozsa, Miklos 1907- IntMPA 92, IntWW 91, NewAmDM, WhoEnt 92
Rozsnyai, Balazs 1929- AmMWSc 92
Rozycki, Paul Andrew 1944- WhoMW 92
Rozzell, Bobby Leon 1956- WhoRel 92
Rozzell, Scott Ellis 1949- WhoAmL 92
Rozzell, Thomas Clifton 1937- AmMWSc 92
Rozzi, Tullio 1941- AmMWSc 92
Ru Xin 1932- IntWW 91
Ru Zhijuan 1925- IntWW 91
Ru, Zhi-juan 1925- IntAu&W 91
Rua, Milton Juan 1946- WhoAmP 91
Ruan Bosheng 1912- IntWW 91

**Ruan Chongwu** 1933- *IntWW 91*
**Ruane**, J Michael *WhoAmP 91*
**Ruane**, Joseph Edward 1929- *WhoIns 92*
**Ruano**, Jose *WhoHisp 92*
**Ruano**, William J. 1908- *WhoAmL 92*
**Ruark**, Gibbons *DrAPF 91*
**Ruark**, Mary Lynn 1948- *WhoAmP 91*
**Ruark**, Robert 1915-1965 *BenetAL 91*
**Rubach**, Peggy 1947- *WhoAmP 91, WhoWest 92*
**Rubanyi**, Gabor Michael 1947- *AmMWSc 92*
**Rubas**, Vytautas 1931- *WhoMW 92*
**Rubash**, Norman Joseph 1932- *WhoFI 92*
**Rubatzky**, Vincent E 1932- *AmMWSc 92*
**Rubayi**, Salah 1942- *WhoWest 92*
**Rubb**, Peggy-Grace Plourd 1931- *WhoEnt 92*
**Rubbert**, Paul Edward 1937- *AmMWSc 92*
**Rubbia**, Carlo 1934- *AmMWSc 92, IntWW 91, Who 92, WhoNob 90*
**Rubbra**, Edmund 1901-1986 *FacFETw, NewAmDM*
**Rubega**, Robert A 1927- *AmMWSc 92*
**Rubel**, Edwin W 1942- *AmMWSc 92*
**Rubel**, Howard Alan 1956- *WhoFI 92*
**Rubel**, James L. *TwCWW 91*
**Rubel**, Joan Gertrude 1950- *WhoEnt 92*
**Rubel**, Lee Albert 1928- *AmMWSc 92*
**Rubel**, Mark Burrill 1958- *WhoEnt 92*
**Rubeli**, Paul E. 1943- *WhoWest 92*
**Rubello**, David Jerome 1935- *WhoMW 92*
**Ruben**, Aaron d1987 *LesBEnT 92*
**Ruben**, Alan Miles 1931- *WhoAmL 92*
**Ruben**, Audrey H. *WhoAmL 92*
**Ruben**, Gary A. 1924- *WhoMW 92*
**Ruben**, Ida Gass 1929- *WhoAmP 91*
**Ruben**, John Alex 1947- *AmMWSc 92*
**Ruben**, Joseph 1951- *ConTFT 9, IntMPA 92*
**Ruben**, Laurens Norman 1927- *AmMWSc 92*
**Ruben**, Morris P 1919- *AmMWSc 92*
**Ruben**, Peter N. 1960- *WhoEnt 92*
**Ruben**, Regina Lansing 1950- *AmMWSc 92*
**Ruben**, Robert Joel 1933- *AmMWSc 92*
**Ruben**, Vitaliy Petrovich 1914- *IntWW 91*
**Rubendall**, Ben Dale 1941- *WhoMW 92*
**Rubenfeld**, Lester A 1940- *AmMWSc 92*
**Rubenfeld**, Stephen Alan 1948- *WhoMW 92*
**Rubenis**, Juris Y. 1925- *IntWW 91*
**Rubens**, Bernice 1928- *ConNov 91, WrDr 92*
**Rubens**, Bernice Ruth 1928- *IntAu&W 91, IntWW 91, Who 92*
**Rubens**, Brad A. 1961- *WhoEnt 92*
**Rubens**, Sidney Michel 1910- *AmMWSc 92*
**Rubenson**, Daniel Leon 1953- *WhoFI 92*
**Rubenson**, J G 1920- *AmMWSc 92*
**Rubenstein**, Abraham Daniel 1907- *AmMWSc 92*
**Rubenstein**, Alan 1955- *WhoFI 92*
**Rubenstein**, Albert d1991 *NewYTBS 91*
**Rubenstein**, Albert Harold 1923- *AmMWSc 92*
**Rubenstein**, Albert Marvin 1918- *AmMWSc 92*
**Rubenstein**, Arthur Harold 1937- *AmMWSc 92, WhoMW 92*
**Rubenstein**, Benjamin 1932- *WhoAmL 92*
**Rubenstein**, Bernard 1937- *WhoEnt 92*
**Rubenstein**, Bonnie Sue 1961- *WhoMW 92*
**Rubenstein**, Carol *DrAPF 91*
**Rubenstein**, David Paul 1944- *WhoEnt 92*
**Rubenstein**, Edward 1924- *AmMWSc 92, IntWW 91*
**Rubenstein**, Eric Davis 1952- *WhoMW 92*
**Rubenstein**, Gerda 1931- *TwCPaSc*
**Rubenstein**, Gregory Curtis 1950- *WhoMW 92*
**Rubenstein**, Howard S 1931- *AmMWSc 92*
**Rubenstein**, Irwin 1931- *AmMWSc 92*
**Rubenstein**, Jacob Samuel 1949- *WhoRel 92*
**Rubenstein**, James Michael 1944- *WhoFI 92*
**Rubenstein**, Jeffrey Carl 1942- *WhoAmL 92*
**Rubenstein**, Jerome Max 1927- *WhoAmL 92*
**Rubenstein**, Joshua Seth 1954- *WhoAmL 92*
**Rubenstein**, Lee Aaron 1956- *WhoEnt 92*
**Rubenstein**, Leonard Samuel 1918- *WhoWest 92*
**Rubenstein**, Paul Max 1939- *WhoEnt 92*
**Rubenstein**, Raeanne *WhoEnt 92*
**Rubenstein**, Richard 1953- *WhoAmL 92*
**Rubenstein**, Richard E. 1938- *WrDr 92*
**Rubenstein**, Richard L 1924- *IntAu&W 91*
**Rubenstein**, Richard Lowell 1924- *WhoRel 92, WrDr 92*
**Rubenstein**, Richard Wright 1944- *WhoAmL 92*
**Rubenstein**, William Louis 1956- *WhoEnt 92*
**Rubenthaler**, Gordon Lawrence 1932- *AmMWSc 92*
**Ruber**, Ernest 1934- *AmMWSc 92*
**Ruberg**, Robert E. 1927- *WhoAmL 92*
**Ruberg**, Robert Lionel 1941- *WhoMW 92*
**Rubery**, Daniel Joseph 1940- *WhoMW 92*
**Rubery**, Eileen Doris 1943- *Who 92*
**Rubey**, John Alfred 1951- *WhoEnt 92*
**Rubiano-Groot**, Alfonso 1921- *WhoHisp 92*
**Rubik**, Erno 1944- *IntWW 91*
**Rubiks**, Alfreds 1935- *SovUnBD A*
**Rubiks**, Alfreds Petrovich 1935- *IntWW 91*
**Rubin**, Alan 1923- *AmMWSc 92*
**Rubin**, Alan 1938- *AmMWSc 92*
**Rubin**, Alan A 1926- *AmMWSc 92*
**Rubin**, Alan Barry 1941- *AmMWSc 92*
**Rubin**, Alan J 1934- *AmMWSc 92, WhoMW 92*
**Rubin**, Albert Louis 1927- *AmMWSc 92*
**Rubin**, Allan Avrom 1916- *WhoAmL 92*
**Rubin**, Allen Gershon 1930- *AmMWSc 92*
**Rubin**, Alvin B. d1991 *NewYTBS 91*
**Rubin**, Anne Loughran 1955- *WhoAmL 92*
**Rubin**, Arthur I 1927- *AmMWSc 92*
**Rubin**, Barney 1924- *AmMWSc 92*
**Rubin**, Barry 1950- *WrDr 92*
**Rubin**, Barry Alan 1945- *WhoRel 92*
**Rubin**, Benjamin Arnold 1917- *AmMWSc 92*
**Rubin**, Bernard 1919- *AmMWSc 92*
**Rubin**, Blake Douglas 1955- *WhoAmL 92*
**Rubin**, Bruce Alan 1951- *WhoAmL 92*
**Rubin**, Bruce Joel 1942- *AmMWSc 92*
**Rubin**, Burton Jay 1946- *WhoAmL 92*
**Rubin**, Byron Herbert 1943- *AmMWSc 92*
**Rubin**, Carl Bernard 1920- *WhoAmL 92*
**Rubin**, Charles Alexis 1953- *WhoFI 92*
**Rubin**, Charles Donald 1958- *WhoAmL 92*
**Rubin**, Charles Stuart 1943- *AmMWSc 92*
**Rubin**, Cyrus E 1921- *AmMWSc 92*
**Rubin**, Daniel Lee 1955- *WhoWest 92*
**Rubin**, David Charles 1943- *AmMWSc 92*
**Rubin**, David Joel 1957- *WhoAmL 92*
**Rubin**, Deborah Carol 1956- *WhoEnt 92*
**Rubin**, Diana Kwiatkowski *DrAPF 91*
**Rubin**, Donald Bruce 1943- *AmMWSc 92*
**Rubin**, Donald Howard 1948- *AmMWSc 92*
**Rubin**, Donald Joel 1945- *WhoEnt 92*
**Rubin**, Donald L. 1923- *WhoFI 92*
**Rubin**, Edward S 1941- *AmMWSc 92*
**Rubin**, Emanuel 1928- *AmMWSc 92*
**Rubin**, Erwin Leonard 1933- *WhoAmL 92, WhoEnt 92*
**Rubin**, G A 1926- *AmMWSc 92*
**Rubin**, Gail Bonita 1962- *WhoAmL 92*
**Rubin**, Gary Allan 1946- *WhoEnt 92*
**Rubin**, Gary Lee 1950- *WhoAmL 92*
**Rubin**, George R 1931- *WhoAmP 91*
**Rubin**, Gerald M 1950- *AmMWSc 92*
**Rubin**, Gerald Mayer 1950- *WhoWest 92*
**Rubin**, Harry 1926- *AmMWSc 92*
**Rubin**, Harry 1960- *WhoAmL 92*
**Rubin**, Harry Meyer 1952- *WhoEnt 92*
**Rubin**, Harvey Louis 1914- *AmMWSc 92*
**Rubin**, Henry Park 1943- *WhoEnt 92*
**Rubin**, Herbert 1918- *WhoAmL 92*
**Rubin**, Herbert 1923- *AmMWSc 92*
**Rubin**, Herbert 1930- *AmMWSc 92*
**Rubin**, Herman 1926- *AmMWSc 92*
**Rubin**, Howard Arnold 1940- *AmMWSc 92*
**Rubin**, Hyman 1913- *WhoAmP 91*
**Rubin**, Ina Tanya 1946- *WhoWest 92*
**Rubin**, Isaac D 1931- *AmMWSc 92*
**Rubin**, Izhak 1942- *AmMWSc 92*
**Rubin**, Jacob 1919- *AmMWSc 92*
**Rubin**, Janet Elaine 1950- *WhoEnt 92*
**Rubin**, Jean *DrAPF 91*
**Rubin**, Jean E 1926- *AmMWSc 92*
**Rubin**, Jeffrey Charles 1946- *WhoFI 92*
**Rubin**, Jeffrey Wayne 1950- *WhoAmL 92*
**Rubin**, Jerome Sanford 1925- *WhoAmL 92, WhoFI 92*
**Rubin**, Jerry 1938- *FacFETw*
**Rubin**, Joanne Leslie 1950- *WhoMW 92*
**Rubin**, Joel David 1959- *WhoWest 92*
**Rubin**, Joel E 1928- *AmMWSc 92*
**Rubin**, Joel Harvey 1945- *WhoMW 92*
**Rubin**, John Michael 1956- *WhoWest 92*
**Rubin**, Juan E. 1944- *WhoFI 92*
**Rubin**, Karl C 1956- *AmMWSc 92*
**Rubin**, Kelly Andrea 1965- *WhoEnt 92*
**Rubin**, Kenneth 1928- *AmMWSc 92*
**Rubin**, Kenneth A. 1954- *WhoFI 92*
**Rubin**, Kenneth Allen 1947- *WhoAmL 92*
**Rubin**, Kenneth Warnell 1920- *Who 92*
**Rubin**, Kerry L. 1956- *WhoFI 92*
**Rubin**, Larry *DrAPF 91*
**Rubin**, Larry 1930- *WrDr 92*
**Rubin**, Larry Bruce 1958- *WhoMW 92*
**Rubin**, Larry Jerome 1930- *IntAu&W 91*
**Rubin**, Lawrence G 1925- *AmMWSc 92*
**Rubin**, Lawrence Ira 1945- *WhoWest 92*
**Rubin**, Leon E 1921- *AmMWSc 92*
**Rubin**, Leon Julius 1913- *AmMWSc 92*
**Rubin**, Leonard Roy 1939- *AmMWSc 92*
**Rubin**, Leonard Sidney 1922- *AmMWSc 92*
**Rubin**, Louis 1922- *AmMWSc 92*
**Rubin**, Louis Decimus, Jr. 1923- *IntWW 91*
**Rubin**, Mark *DrAPF 91*
**Rubin**, Mark Richard 1944- *WhoMW 92*
**Rubin**, Martin Israel 1915- *AmMWSc 92*
**Rubin**, Martin N. 1928- *WhoFI 92*
**Rubin**, Maryiln Bernice *AmMWSc 92*
**Rubin**, Max 1916- *AmMWSc 92*
**Rubin**, Melissa Seide 1963- *WhoAmL 92*
**Rubin**, Melvin Lynne 1932- *AmMWSc 92*
**Rubin**, Meyer 1924- *AmMWSc 92*
**Rubin**, Michael Howard 1962- *WhoWest 92*
**Rubin**, Milton D 1914- *AmMWSc 92*
**Rubin**, Mitchell Irving 1902- *AmMWSc 92*
**Rubin**, Morton Harold 1938- *AmMWSc 92*
**Rubin**, Morton Joseph 1917- *AmMWSc 92*
**Rubin**, Nathan 1912- *AmMWSc 92*
**Rubin**, Ofie Tuchman *WhoAmL 92*
**Rubin**, Paul David 1955- *WhoEnt 92*
**Rubin**, Paul Harold 1942- *WhoFI 92*
**Rubin**, Peggy Miller 1953- *WhoFI 92*
**Rubin**, Randolph Adam 1953- *WhoEnt 92*
**Rubin**, Richard Allan 1942- *WhoAmL 92*
**Rubin**, Richard Lee 1946- *AmMWSc 92*
**Rubin**, Richard Mark 1937- *AmMWSc 92*
**Rubin**, Rick 1963- *WhoEnt 92*
**Rubin**, Rivka Leah Jacobs 1952- *IntAu&W 91*
**Rubin**, Robert Edward 1938- *WhoFI 92*
**Rubin**, Robert Howard 1941- *AmMWSc 92*
**Rubin**, Robert Jay 1932- *AmMWSc 92*
**Rubin**, Robert Joseph 1946- *WhoAmP 91*
**Rubin**, Robert Joshua 1926- *AmMWSc 92*
**Rubin**, Robert Samuel 1954- *WhoAmL 92*
**Rubin**, Robert Terry 1936- *AmMWSc 92*
**Rubin**, Ronald Philip 1933- *AmMWSc 92*
**Rubin**, Rose Luttan 1917- *WhoAmL 92*
**Rubin**, Rose Mohr 1939- *WhoFI 92*
**Rubin**, S. Smelka 1925- *WhoRel 92*
**Rubin**, Samuel H 1916- *AmMWSc 92*
**Rubin**, Samuel Harry 1924- *WhoAmP 91*
**Rubin**, Saul H 1923- *AmMWSc 92*
**Rubin**, Saul Howard 1912- *AmMWSc 92*
**Rubin**, Seymour Jeffrey 1914- *WhoFI 92*
**Rubin**, Sheldon 1932- *AmMWSc 92*
**Rubin**, Stan Sanvel *DrAPF 91*
**Rubin**, Stanley 1917- *IntMPA 92*
**Rubin**, Stanley 1928- *WrDr 92*
**Rubin**, Stanley Creamer 1917- *WhoEnt 92*
**Rubin**, Stanley G 1938- *AmMWSc 92*
**Rubin**, Stanley Gerald 1938- *WhoMW 92*
**Rubin**, Stephen 1938-1991 *NewYTBS 91*
**Rubin**, Stephen Edward 1941- *WhoFI 92*
**Rubin**, Theodore I. 1923- *WrDr 92*
**Rubin**, Tod Douglas 1958- *WhoFI 92*
**Rubin**, Vera Cooper 1928- *AmMWSc 92, IntWW 91*
**Rubin**, Walter 1933- *AmMWSc 92*
**Rubin**, William 1927- *IntWW 91*
**Rubin**, William David 1953- *WhoAmP 91*
**Rubin**, Wladyslaw d1990 *IntWW 91N*
**Rubin-Tilles**, Max Abraham 1922- *WhoRel 92*
**Rubinfeld**, Daniel Lee 1945- *WhoAmL 92*
**Rubinger**, Richard 1943- *WhoMW 92*
**Rubini**, Giovanni-Battista 1795-1854 *NewAmDM*
**Rubini**, Michel 1942- *WhoEnt 92*
**Rubink**, William Louis 1947- *AmMWSc 92*
**Rubino**, Andrew M 1922- *AmMWSc 92*
**Rubino**, Frank *DrAPF 91*
**Rubino**, Michael Joseph 1947- *WhoAmL 92*
**Rubino**, Theodore Salvatore A 1911- *WhoAmP 91*
**Rubino**, Victor Joseph 1940- *WhoFI 92*
**Rubino**, Vincent Charles 1970- *WhoEnt 92*
**Rubinoff**, Ira 1938- *AmMWSc 92*
**Rubinoff**, Lionel 1930- *WrDr 92*
**Rubinoff**, Morris 1917- *AmMWSc 92*
**Rubinoff**, Roberta Wolff 1939- *AmMWSc 92*
**Rubinovitz**, Robert Neal 1962- *WhoFI 92*
**Rubinovitz**, Samuel 1929- *WhoFI 92*
**Rubinowitz**, Leonard S. 1943- *WhoAmL 92*
**Rubins**, Jack 1931- *Who 92*
**Rubins**, Roy Selwyn 1935- *AmMWSc 92*
**Rubinson**, Judith Faye 1952- *AmMWSc 92*
**Rubinson**, Kalman 1941- *AmMWSc 92*
**Rubinson**, Kenneth A 1944- *AmMWSc 92*
**Rubinstein**, Alan Jay *WhoAmL 92*
**Rubinstein**, Alice Beryl 1940- *WhoEnt 92*
**Rubinstein**, Amnon 1931- *IntWW 91*
**Rubinstein**, Anton 1829-1894 *NewAmDM*
**Rubinstein**, Arthur 1887-1982 *FacFETw [port]*
**Rubinstein**, Artur 1887-1982 *NewAmDM*
**Rubinstein**, Asher A 1947- *AmMWSc 92*
**Rubinstein**, Cara 1962- *WhoAmL 92*
**Rubinstein**, Charles B 1933- *AmMWSc 92*
**Rubinstein**, David A. 1946- *WhoMW 92*
**Rubinstein**, Eduardo Hector 1931- *AmMWSc 92*
**Rubinstein**, Frederic Armand 1931- *WhoAmL 92*
**Rubinstein**, Gillian 1942- *SmATA 68 [port], WrDr 92*
**Rubinstein**, Harry 1930- *AmMWSc 92*
**Rubinstein**, Helge 1929- *ConAu 134*
**Rubinstein**, Hilary 1926- *WrDr 92*
**Rubinstein**, Hilary Harold 1926- *IntAu&W 91, Who 92*
**Rubinstein**, Howard 1945- *WhoFI 92*
**Rubinstein**, John 1946- *IntMPA 92*
**Rubinstein**, John Arthur 1946- *WhoEnt 92*
**Rubinstein**, Karen *WhoRel 92*
**Rubinstein**, Lawrence Victor 1946- *AmMWSc 92*
**Rubinstein**, Lucien Jules 1924- *AmMWSc 92*
**Rubinstein**, Lydia 1936- *AmMWSc 92*
**Rubinstein**, Mark 1935- *AmMWSc 92*
**Rubinstein**, Michael Bernard 1920- *Who 92*
**Rubinstein**, Moshe Fajwel 1930- *AmMWSc 92*
**Rubinstein**, Nicolai 1911- *Who 92*
**Rubinstein**, Richard P. 1947- *IntMPA 92*
**Rubinstein**, Richard Paul 1947- *WhoEnt 92*
**Rubinstein**, Roy 1936- *AmMWSc 92*
**Rubinstein**, Susan Lee Goldring 1959- *WhoAmL 92*
**Rubinton**, Peter Don 1936- *WhoAmL 92*
**Rubio**, Jesus Ramiro 1952- *WhoHisp 92*
**Rubio**, Lorenzo Sifuentes 1952- *WhoHisp 92*
**Rubio**, Rafael 1928- *AmMWSc 92*
**Rubio**, Ralph *WhoHisp 92*
**Rubio**, Suzanne Sarah *WhoEnt 92*
**Rubio**, Tammy *WhoHisp 92*
**Rubio-Boitel**, Fernando Fabian 1945- *WhoHisp 92*
**Rubiralta**, Manuel *WhoHisp 92*
**Rubis**, David Daniel 1924- *AmMWSc 92*
**Rubis**, Leon Joseph 1952- *WhoFI 92*
**Ruble**, Ann 1953- *WhoRel 92, WhoWest 92*
**Ruble**, Bernard Roy 1923- *WhoMW 92*
**Ruble**, Randall Tucker 1932- *WhoRel 92*
**Rublee**, Dale Allan 1951- *WhoMW 92*
**Rublee**, Parke Alstan 1949- *AmMWSc 92*
**Rubloff**, Burton 1912- *WhoMW 92*
**Rubloff**, Gary W 1944- *AmMWSc 92*
**Rubner**, Ben 1921- *Who 92*
**Rubnitz**, Myron Ethan 1924- *AmMWSc 92, WhoMW 92*
**Rubottom**, Carole Marie 1944- *WhoEnt 92*
**Rubottom**, Don 1956- *WhoAmP 91*
**Rubottom**, George M 1940- *AmMWSc 92*
**Rubottom**, Roy Richard, Jr. 1912- *IntWW 91*
**Rubright**, Ellen M. 1964- *WhoAmL 92*
**Rubright**, James Alfred 1946- *WhoAmL 92*
**Rubtsov**, Nikolay Fyodorovich 1931- *IntWW 91*
**Rubtsov**, Nikolay Mikhaylovich 1936-1971 *SovUnBD*
**Ruby**, Charles Andrew 1951- *WhoEnt 92*
**Ruby**, Charles Leroy 1900- *WhoAmL 92, WhoWest 92*
**Ruby**, Charles Silvers 1940- *WhoFI 92*
**Ruby**, Edward George 1949- *AmMWSc 92*
**Ruby**, Harry 1895-1974 *NewAmDM*
**Ruby**, Jack 1911-1967 *FacFETw [port]*
**Ruby**, John L 1912- *AmMWSc 92*
**Ruby**, John Robert 1935- *AmMWSc 92*
**Ruby**, Kathryn *DrAPF 91*
**Ruby**, Lawrence 1925- *AmMWSc 92, WhoWest 92*
**Ruby**, Michael Gordon 1940- *AmMWSc 92*
**Ruby**, Philip Randolph 1925- *AmMWSc 92*
**Ruby**, Robert H. *WrDr 92*
**Ruby**, Ronald Henry 1932- *AmMWSc 92*
**Ruby**, Stanley 1920- *AmMWSc 92*
**Ruby**, Stanley L. 1937- *WhoAmL 92*
**Rubython**, Eric Gerald 1921- *Who 92*
**Ruch**, Richard Hurley 1930 *WhoFI 92, WhoMW 92*
**Ruch**, Richard Julius 1932- *AmMWSc 92*
**Ruch**, Rodney R 1933- *AmMWSc 92*
**Ruch**, Sandra Joy 1938- *WhoEnt 92*
**Ruchelman**, Leonard I. 1933- *WrDr 92*
**Ruchin**, Cecile Ann 1936- *WhoEnt 92*
**Ruchkin**, Daniel S 1935- *AmMWSc 92*
**Ruchman**, Isaac 1909- *AmMWSc 92*
**Ruchti**, Randal Charles 1946- *AmMWSc 92*
**Rucinska**, Ewa J *AmMWSc 92*
**Rucinski**, Robert D. 1943- *WhoWest 92*
**Ruck**, Andrew J 1930- *WhoIns 92*
**Ruck**, Bertha 1878-1978 *ScFEYrs*
**Ruck**, Peter Frederick C. *Who 92*
**Ruck Keene**, John Robert 1917- *Who 92*
**Ruckdaschel**, Jay Ronald 1933- *WhoMW 92*
**Ruckebusch**, Guy Bernard 1949- *AmMWSc 92*

**Ruckelshaus**, John C, III 1959- *WhoAmP 91*
**Ruckelshaus**, William Doyle 1932- *IntWW 91, WhoAmP 91*
**Ruckenstein**, Eli 1925- *AmMWSc 92*
**Rucker**, Arthur Nevil d1991 *Who 92N*
**Rucker**, Clinton Allen 1945- *WhoEnt 92*
**Rucker**, Daniel Edward 1956- *WhoWest 92*
**Rucker**, Dean 1955- *WhoAmP 91*
**Rucker**, Douglas Pendleton, Jr. 1945- *WhoAmL 92*
**Rucker**, Everett Maxwell 1954- *WhoMW 92*
**Rucker**, James Bivin 1935- *AmMWSc 92*
**Rucker**, Jeffrey Hamilton 1942- *Who 92*
**Rucker**, Jerry D *WhoAmP 91*
**Rucker**, John R 1915- *WhoAmP 91*
**Rucker**, Kenneth Lee 1937- *WhoMW 92*
**Rucker**, Nannie George *WhoAmP 91*
**Rucker**, Nannie George 1914- *WhoBlA 92*
**Rucker**, Reginald J. 1947- *WhoBlA 92*
**Rucker**, Retanio Anthony Joseph 1959- *WhoAmL 92*
**Rucker**, Richard Sim 1947- *WhoMW 92*
**Rucker**, Robert Blain 1941- *AmMWSc 92*
**Rucker**, Robert D., Jr. *WhoBlA 92*
**Rucker**, Robert Louis, Jr. 1947- *WhoBlA 92*
**Rucker**, Rudy 1946- *TwCSFW 91, WrDr 92*
**Rucker**, Thomas Douglas 1926- *WhoWest 92*
**Ruckerbauer**, Gerda Margareta 1926- *AmMWSc 92*
**Ruckers** *NewAmDM*
**Ruckert**, Ann Johns 1945- *WhoEnt 92*
**Ruckle**, William Henry 1936- *AmMWSc 92*
**Rucklidge**, John Christopher 1938- *AmMWSc 92*
**Ruckman**, Jo Ann 1938- *WhoWest 92*
**Ruckman**, Stanley Neal 1939- *WhoWest 92*
**Rucknagel**, Donald Louis 1928- *AmMWSc 92*
**Rucks**, Alfred J. 1935- *WhoBlA 92*
**Rud**, Richard Wayne 1932- *WhoAmP 91*
**Ruda**, Howard 1932- *WhoFI 92*
**Ruda**, Jose Maria 1924- *IntWW 91*
**Rudakov**, Konstantin Ivanovich 1891-1949 *SovUnBD*
**Rudat**, Martin August 1952- *AmMWSc 92*
**Rudavsky**, Alexander Bohdan 1925- *AmMWSc 92*
**Rudavsky**, Dahlia C. 1951- *WhoAmL 92*
**Rudaz**, Serge 1954- *AmMWSc 92*
**Rudbach**, Jon Anthony 1937- *AmMWSc 92, WhoWest 92*
**Rudberg**, Joe Arthur 1947- *WhoFI 92*
**Rudd**, Amanda S. 1923- *WhoBlA 92*
**Rudd**, D F 1935- *AmMWSc 92*
**Rudd**, DeForest Porter 1923- *AmMWSc 92*
**Rudd**, Delaney 1962- *WhoBlA 92*
**Rudd**, Eldon *WhoAmP 91, WhoWest 92*
**Rudd**, Hughes *LesBEnT 92*
**Rudd**, Hurley W 1927- *WhoAmP 91*
**Rudd**, Hynda L. 1936- *WhoWest 92*
**Rudd**, James M. 1916- *WhoBlA 92*
**Rudd**, Jimmy Dean 1943- *WhoAmP 91*
**Rudd**, Leo Slaton 1924- *WhoRel 92*
**Rudd**, Margaret *WrDr 92*
**Rudd**, Millard Eugene 1927- *AmMWSc 92*
**Rudd**, Nigel 1946- *Who 92*
**Rudd**, Noreen L 1940- *AmMWSc 92*
**Rudd**, Norman Julian Peter Joseph 1943- *Who 92*
**Rudd**, Orville Lee, II 1922- *WhoFI 92*
**Rudd**, Paul Ryan 1940- *WhoEnt 92*
**Rudd**, Robert L 1921- *AmMWSc 92*
**Rudd**, Robert Michael 1939- *WhoEnt 92*
**Rudd**, Steele 1868-1935 *RfGEnL 91*
**Rudd**, Velva Elaine 1910- *AmMWSc 92*
**Rudd**, Walter Greyson 1943- *AmMWSc 92*
**Rudd**, Willie Lesslie 1944- *WhoBlA 92*
**Rudd-Jones**, Derek 1924- *Who 92*
**Rudd-Moore**, Dorothy 1940- *WhoBlA 92*
**Ruddat**, Manfred 1932- *AmMWSc 92*
**Ruddell**, Alanna 1956- *AmMWSc 92*
**Ruddell**, Gary Ronald 1948- *WhoFI 92*
**Rudden**, Bernard 1933- *Who 92*
**Rudden**, Eileen Marie 1950- *WhoFI 92*
**Rudden**, James 1911- *Who 92*
**Rudder**, Brian L 1944- *WhoIns 92*
**Ruddick**, J. Perry 1936- *WhoFI 92*
**Ruddick**, James John 1923- *AmMWSc 92*
**Ruddick**, Keith 1939- *AmMWSc 92*
**Ruddick**, Steve 1954- *WhoAmP 91*
**Ruddle**, Francis Hugh 1929- *AmMWSc 92, IntWW 91*
**Ruddle**, Nancy Hartman 1940- *AmMWSc 92*
**Ruddock**, Joan Mary 1943- *IntWW 91, Who 92*
**Ruddon**, Raymond Walter, Jr 1936- *AmMWSc 92*
**Rudduck**, Barbara Jene 1942- *WhoFI 92*
**Ruddy**, Albert S. 1934- *ConTFT 9, IntMPA 92*
**Ruddy**, Anna C d1946 *DcAmImH*
**Ruddy**, Arlo Wayne 1915- *AmMWSc 92*
**Ruddy**, Frank S. 1937- *WhoAmL 92*
**Ruddy**, Frank Stephen 1937- *WhoAmP 91*
**Rude**, Alfred Lyman 1958- *WhoAmP 91*
**Rude**, Brian David 1955- *WhoAmP 91, WhoMW 92*
**Rude**, George Frederic Elliot 1910- *IntWW 91*
**Rude**, George Frederick Elliot 1910- *Who 92*
**Rude**, Paul A 1930- *AmMWSc 92*
**Rude**, Theodore Alfred 1925- *AmMWSc 92*
**Rudee**, Mervyn Lea 1935- *AmMWSc 92*
**Rudel**, Hans-Ulrich 1916-1982 *BiDExR, EncTR 91 [port], FacFETw*
**Rudel**, Julius 1921- *NewAmDM, WhoEnt 92*
**Rudel**, Lawrence L 1941- *AmMWSc 92*
**Rudell**, Michael I. 1943- *WhoEnt 92*
**Ruden**, Morton Robert 1937- *WhoAmL 92*
**Ruden**, Violet Howard *WhoRel 92*
**Rudenberg**, Frank Hermann 1927- *AmMWSc 92*
**Rudenberg**, H Gunther 1920- *AmMWSc 92*
**Rudenko**, Yuri Nikolayevitch 1931- *IntWW 91*
**Rudenstine**, Neil Leon 1935- *IntWW 91, NewYTBS 91 [port], Who 92*
**Ruder**, Brian 1954- *WhoFI 92*
**Ruder**, David S 1929- *WhoAmP 91*
**Ruder**, Diane G. 1941- *WhoMW 92*
**Ruder**, Lois Jean Rodriguez 1951- *WhoHisp 92*
**Ruder**, Phillip 1939- *WhoEnt 92*
**Ruder**, William 1921- *WhoFI 92*
**Ruderman**, Irving Warren 1920- *AmMWSc 92*
**Ruderman**, Joan V *AmMWSc 92*
**Ruderman**, Malvin Avram 1927- *AmMWSc 92*
**Ruderman**, Ronald 1943- *WhoFI 92*
**Ruders**, Poul 1949- *ConCom 92*
**Rudershausen**, Charles Gerald 1928- *AmMWSc 92*
**Rudesill**, James Turner 1923- *AmMWSc 92*
**Rudge**, Alan Walter 1937- *Who 92*
**Rudge**, William Edwin 1939- *AmMWSc 92*
**Rudgers**, Anthony Joseph 1938- *AmMWSc 92*
**Rudholm**, Sten 1918- *IntWW 91*
**Rudiakov**, Michael 1934- *WhoEnt 92*
**Rudicel**, Chandler Clifton 1905- *WhoAmP 91*
**Rudie**, Evelyn *IntMPA 92, WhoEnt 92*
**Rudin**, Alfred 1924- *AmMWSc 92*
**Rudin**, Andrew C. 1943- *WhoRel 92*
**Rudin**, Anne 1924- *WhoAmP 91*
**Rudin**, Anne Noto 1924- *WhoWest 92*
**Rudin**, Arnold James 1934- *WhoRel 92*
**Rudin**, Bernard D 1927- *AmMWSc 92*
**Rudin**, Ernst 1874-1952 *EncTR 91*
**Rudin**, Jenny 1928- *WhoWest 92*
**Rudin**, Mary Ellen 1924- *AmMWSc 92*
**Rudin**, Scott 1958- *IntMPA 92*
**Rudin**, Tomi Richard Perrott 1934- *Who 92*
**Rudin**, Walter 1921- *AmMWSc 92*
**Ruding**, H. O. 1939- *IntWW 91*
**Rudinger**, George 1911- *AmMWSc 92*
**Rudinger**, Joel *DrAPF 91*
**Rudini** 1929- *IntWW 91*
**Rudins**, Leonids 1928- *WhoFI 92*
**Rudinsky**, Norma Leigh 1928- *WhoWest 92*
**Rudisha**, Daniel Matesi 1946- *BlkOlyM*
**Rudisill**, Abra *WhoEnt 92*
**Rudisill**, Carl Sidney 1929- *AmMWSc 92*
**Rudisill**, Cecil Wayne 1937- *WhoEnt 92*
**Rudisill**, D.P. 1902-1978 *ConAu 135*
**Rudisill**, Richard 1932- *WhoWest 92*
**Rudisill**, Robert Mack, Jr. 1945- *WhoAmL 92*
**Rudkin**, David 1936- *Who 92, WrDr 92*
**Rudkin**, George Thomas 1917- *AmMWSc 92*
**Rudkin**, James David 1936- *IntAu&W 91*
**Rudkin**, Walter Charles 1922- *Who 92*
**Rudko**, Doris *WhoEnt 92*
**Rudko**, Robert I 1942- *AmMWSc 92*
**Rudland**, Margaret Florence 1945- *Who 92*
**Rudlin**, David Alan 1947- *WhoAmL 92*
**Rudloe**, Jack 1943- *WrDr 92*
**Rudloff**, Hans-Jorg 1940- *Who 92*
**Rudloff**, William Joseph 1941- *WhoAmL 92*
**Rudman**, Albert J 1928- *AmMWSc 92*
**Rudman**, Daniel 1927- *AmMWSc 92*
**Rudman**, Edward Irving 1937- *WhoFI 92*
**Rudman**, Jeffrey B. 1948- *WhoAmL 92*
**Rudman**, Mark *DrAPF 91*
**Rudman**, Michael Edward 1939- *Who 92*
**Rudman**, Peter S 1929- *AmMWSc 92*
**Rudman**, Reuben 1937- *AmMWSc 92*
**Rudman**, Solomon Kal 1930- *WhoEnt 92*
**Rudman**, Warren B. 1930- *AlmAP 92 [port], WhoAmP 91*
**Rudman**, Warren Bruce 1930- *IntWW 91*
**Rudmose**, H Wayne 1915- *AmMWSc 92*
**Rudner**, Rivka 1935- *AmMWSc 92*
**Rudner**, Sara 1944- *WhoEnt 92*
**Rudnev**, Konstantin Nikolaevich 1911-1980 *SovUnBD*
**Rudney**, Harry 1918- *AmMWSc 92*
**Rudnick**, Alan A. *WhoAmL 92*
**Rudnick**, Albert 1922- *AmMWSc 92*
**Rudnick**, Gary 1946- *AmMWSc 92*
**Rudnick**, Irene K 1929- *WhoAmP 91*
**Rudnick**, Isadore 1917- *AmMWSc 92*
**Rudnick**, Joseph Alan 1944- *AmMWSc 92*
**Rudnick**, Lawrence 1949- *AmMWSc 92*
**Rudnick**, Linda Janet 1950- *WhoAmL 92*
**Rudnick**, Marvin Jack 1948- *WhoAmL 92*
**Rudnick**, Michael Dennis 1945- *AmMWSc 92*
**Rudnick**, Rebecca Sophie 1952- *WhoAmL 92*
**Rudnick**, Robert Alan 1948- *WhoAmL 92*
**Rudnick**, Stanley J 1937- *AmMWSc 92*
**Rudnickas**, Albert Joseph 1961- *WhoFI 92*
**Rudnicki**, Adolf d1990 *IntWW 91N*
**Rudnicki**, Steven Abramo 1959- *WhoFI 92*
**Rudnicki**, Zbigniew 1928- *IntWW 91*
**Rudnik**, Raphael *DrAPF 91*
**Rudnycka**, Inka *WhoEnt 92*
**Rudnyk**, Marian E 1960- *AmMWSc 92*
**Rudnytsky**, Roman Victor 1942- *WhoEnt 92*
**Rudo**, Frieda Galindo 1923- *AmMWSc 92*
**Rudoe**, Wulf 1916- *Who 92*
**Rudofsky**, Bernard 1905- *DcTwDes*
**Rudolf**, Anthony 1942- *ConPo 91, WrDr 92*
**Rudolf**, Jacob P *WhoAmP 91*
**Rudolf**, Leslie E 1927- *AmMWSc 92*
**Rudolf**, Max 1902- *NewAmDM, WhoEnt 92*
**Rudolf**, Paul Otto 1906- *AmMWSc 92*
**Rudolph**, Abraham Morris 1924- *AmMWSc 92*
**Rudolph**, Alan 1943- *IntMPA 92*
**Rudolph**, Alan 1948- *IntDcF 2-2 [port]*
**Rudolph**, Arnold Jack 1918- *AmMWSc 92*
**Rudolph**, Catherine Ann 1952- *WhoMW 92*
**Rudolph**, Emanuel David 1927- *AmMWSc 92, WhoMW 92*
**Rudolph**, Frederick 1920- *IntWW 91*
**Rudolph**, Frederick Byron 1944- *AmMWSc 92*
**Rudolph**, Gilbert Lawrence 1946- *WhoAmL 92*
**Rudolph**, Guilford George 1918- *AmMWSc 92*
**Rudolph**, Jeffrey Stewart 1942- *AmMWSc 92*
**Rudolph**, Lee *DrAPF 91*
**Rudolph**, Lee 1948- *AmMWSc 92, IntAu&W 91*
**Rudolph**, Luther Day 1930- *AmMWSc 92*
**Rudolph**, Mark Edward 1921- *WhoRel 92*
**Rudolph**, Paul Marvin 1918- *IntWW 91*
**Rudolph**, Philip S 1912- *AmMWSc 92*
**Rudolph**, Ray Ronald 1927- *AmMWSc 92*
**Rudolph**, Raymond Neil 1946- *AmMWSc 92*
**Rudolph**, Richard 1948- *WhoFI 92*
**Rudolph**, Ronald Alvin 1949- *WhoWest 92*
**Rudolph**, Sara Sally Jane 1943- *WhoMW 92*
**Rudolph**, Stephen Bert 1953- *WhoEnt 92*
**Rudolph**, Thomas Keith 1961- *WhoWest 92*
**Rudolph**, Walter Paul 1937- *WhoWest 92*
**Rudolph**, William Brown 1938- *AmMWSc 92*
**Rudolph**, Wilma 1940- *FacFETw, NotBlAW 92 [port], WhoBlA 92*
**Rudolph**, Wilma Glodean 1940- *BlkOlyM [port]*
**Rudomin**, Esther *SmATA 68, WrDr 92*
**Rudowski**, Witold Janusz 1918- *IntWW 91*
**Rudoy**, Peter Winston 1952- *WhoEnt 92*
**Rudrananda**, Swami 1928-1973 *RelLAm 91*
**Rudrum**, Alan 1932- *ConAu 36NR, WrDr 92*
**Rudvalis**, Arunas 1945- *AmMWSc 92*
**Rudy**, Bernardo 1948- *AmMWSc 92*
**Rudy**, C Guy 1936- *WhoAmP 91*
**Rudy**, Clifford R 1943- *AmMWSc 92*
**Rudy**, Cynthia Jo 1958- *WhoEnt 92*
**Rudy**, David Robert 1934- *WhoMW 92*
**Rudy**, Dorothy *DrAPF 91*
**Rudy**, Elmer Clyde 1931- *WhoAmL 92*
**Rudy**, Lester Howard 1918- *AmMWSc 92*
**Rudy**, Paul Passmore, Jr 1933- *AmMWSc 92*
**Rudy**, Richard L 1921- *AmMWSc 92*
**Rudy**, Ruth Corman 1938- *WhoAmP 91*
**Rudy**, Thomas James 1948- *WhoWest 92*
**Rudy**, Thomas Philip 1924- *AmMWSc 92*
**Rudy**, Willis 1920- *WrDr 92*
**Rudy**, Yoram 1946- *AmMWSc 92, WhoMW 92*
**Rudzik**, Allan D 1934- *AmMWSc 92*
**Rudzinska**, Maria Anna *AmMWSc 92*
**Rudzinski**, Kenneth William 1947- *WhoFI 92*
**Rudzinski**, Witold 1913- *IntWW 91*
**Rudzinski**, Zbigniew 1935- *ConCom 92*
**Rudzki**, Robert A. 1953- *WhoFI 92*
**Rudzutak**, Yan Ernestovich 1887-1938 *SovUnBD*
**Rue**, Edward Evans 1924- *AmMWSc 92*
**Rue**, James Sandvik 1929- *AmMWSc 92*
**Rue**, Leonard Lee, III 1926- *WrDr 92*
**Rue**, Rolland R 1935- *AmMWSc 92*
**Rue**, Rosemary 1928- *Who 92*
**Ruebe**, Bambi Lynn 1957- *WhoWest 92*
**Ruebel**, Jeffrey Clay 1955- *WhoAmL 92*
**Ruebner**, Boris Henry 1923- *AmMWSc 92, WhoWest 92*
**Rueckert**, Roland R 1931- *AmMWSc 92*
**Rued**, Dave *WhoAmP 91*
**Rued**, Royden Dale 1926- *WhoAmP 91*
**Rueda**, Alfonso 1940- *WhoWest 92*
**Ruedeman**, Candace Fenimore 1947- *WhoWest 92*
**Rueden**, Henry Anthony 1949- *WhoMW 92*
**Ruedenberg**, Klaus 1920- *AmMWSc 92*
**Ruedisili**, Lon Chester 1939- *AmMWSc 92*
**Ruef**, John Samuel 1927- *WhoRel 92, WrDr 92*
**Ruefer**, Michael Alvin 1958- *WhoMW 92*
**Rueff**, Margaret Lillian 1922- *WhoAmP 91*
**Ruefle**, Mary *DrAPF 91*
**Ruegamer**, William Raymond 1922- *AmMWSc 92*
**Rueger**, Daniel Scott 1957- *WhoMW 92*
**Rueger**, Lauren J 1921- *AmMWSc 92*
**Ruegg**, Stephen Lawrence 1959- *WhoWest 92*
**Ruegg**, Walter Joseph 1920- *WhoRel 92*
**Ruegger**, Philip Theophil, III 1949- *WhoAmL 92*
**Ruegsegger**, Donald Ray, Jr 1942- *AmMWSc 92, WhoMW 92*
**Ruegsegger**, Harvey Alcid 1935- *WhoRel 92*
**Ruehl**, Mercedes *ConTFT 9, IntMPA 92*
**Ruehle**, John Leonard 1931- *AmMWSc 92*
**Ruehli**, Albert Emil 1937- *AmMWSc 92*
**Ruehlmann**, Virginia Juergens 1924- *WhoMW 92*
**Ruel**, Maurice M J 1937- *AmMWSc 92*
**Ruelas**, Abraham Antonio 1952- *WhoHisp 92*
**Ruelius**, Hans Winfried 1915- *AmMWSc 92*
**Ruelke**, Otto Charles 1923- *AmMWSc 92*
**Ruell**, Patrick *IntAu&W 91, WrDr 92*
**Ruelle**, David Pierre 1935- *IntWW 91*
**Ruenitz**, Peter Carmichael 1943- *AmMWSc 92*
**Rueppel**, Melvin Leslie 1945- *AmMWSc 92*
**Ruesch**, Jurgen 1909- *AmMWSc 92*
**Ruesga**, Eugenio Perez 1930- *WhoEnt 92*
**Ruesink**, Albert William 1940- *AmMWSc 92, WhoMW 92*
**Ruess**, Thomas J. 1950- *WhoWest 92*
**Ruether**, Rosemary Radford 1936- *HanAmWH, IntWW 91, WhoRel 92, WrDr 92*
**Ruetman**, Sven Helmuth 1927- *AmMWSc 92*
**Ruetz**, Gerhard G. 1937- *WhoEnt 92*
**Rueve**, Charles Richard 1918- *AmMWSc 92*
**Ruf**, Harold William, Jr. 1934- *WhoAmL 92, WhoMW 92*
**Ruf**, Ludwig 1898-1936 *EncTR 91*
**Ruf**, Robert Henry, Jr 1932- *AmMWSc 92*
**Rufe**, Stephen Craig 1956- *WhoMW 92*
**Rufenach**, Clifford L 1936- *AmMWSc 92*
**Rufenacht**, Richard Frank 1957- *WhoMW 92*
**Rufener**, JoAnn Kathleen 1934- *WhoMW 92*
**Ruff**, Arthur William, Jr 1930- *AmMWSc 92*
**Ruff**, Charles F. C. 1939- *WhoAmL 92*
**Ruff**, Dureen Anne 1931- *WhoMW 92*
**Ruff**, George Antony 1941- *AmMWSc 92*
**Ruff**, George Edward 1941- *WhoMW 92*
**Ruff**, George Elson 1928- *AmMWSc 92*
**Ruff**, Howard J. *ConAu 36NR*
**Ruff**, Irwin S 1932- *AmMWSc 92*
**Ruff**, Jamie Carless 1962- *WhoBlA 92*
**Ruff**, John K 1932- *AmMWSc 92*
**Ruff**, Joseph W. 1939- *WhoAmL 92*
**Ruff**, Michael A. 1964- *WhoEnt 92*
**Ruff**, Michael David 1941- *AmMWSc 92*
**Ruff**, Robert LaVerne 1939- *AmMWSc 92*
**Ruff**, Robert Louis 1950- *WhoMW 92*
**Ruff**, Ronald Armin 1941- *WhoAmP 91*
**Ruff**, Todd Michael 1966- *WhoWest 92*
**Ruff**, William Willis 1914- *Who 92*
**Ruffa**, Anthony Richard 1933- *AmMWSc 92*
**Ruffalo**, Alan Michael 1943- *WhoWest 92*
**Ruffcorn**, Kevin Edward 1951- *WhoRel 92*
**Ruffelle**, Frances 1966- *ConTFT 9*

**Ruffer**, David G 1937- *AmMWSc 92*
**Ruffian** 1972-1975 *FacFETw*
**Ruffin**, Benjamin S. 1941- *WhoBlA 92*
**Ruffin**, Craige 1902- *WhoFI 92*
**Ruffin**, David 1941-1991 *ConMus 6 [port], NewYTBS 91 [port], News 91, WhoBlA 92N*
**Ruffin**, Edmund 1794-1865 *BiInAmS*
**Ruffin**, Herbert 1940- *WhoBlA 92*
**Ruffin**, James E. 1937- *WhoBlA 92*
**Ruffin**, Janice E. 1942- *WhoBlA 92*
**Ruffin**, John 1943- *WhoBlA 92*
**Ruffin**, John H., Jr. 1934- *WhoBlA 92*
**Ruffin**, John Walter, Jr. 1941- *WhoBlA 92*
**Ruffin**, Josephine St. Pierre 1842-1924 *HanAmWH, NotBlAW 92 [port]*
**Ruffin**, Paul *DrAPF 91*
**Ruffin**, Richard D. 1924- *WhoBlA 92*
**Ruffin**, Roy J. 1938- *WhoFI 92*
**Ruffin**, Spaulding Merrick 1923- *AmMWSc 92*
**Ruffine**, Richard S 1928- *AmMWSc 92*
**Ruffing**, Charles 1904-1986 *FacFETw*
**Ruffini**, Attilio 1924- *IntWW 91*
**Ruffini**, Eugene Romano 1931- *WhoEnt 92*
**Ruffini**, Richard John 1954- *WhoMW 92*
**Ruffins**, Reynolds 1930- *WhoBlA 92*
**Ruffle**, John Frederick 1937- *WhoFI 92*
**Ruffle**, Mary *Who 92*
**Ruffner**, Charles Louis 1936- *WhoAmL 92*
**Ruffner**, Frederick G., Jr. 1926- *WhoFI 92*
**Ruffner**, James Alan 1930- *AmMWSc 92*
**Ruffner**, Ray P. 1946- *WhoBlA 92*
**Ruffner**, William Henry 1824-1908 *BiInAmS*
**Ruffo**, Titta 1877-1953 *NewAmDM*
**Ruffolo**, Edward A. 1963- *WhoMW 92*
**Ruffolo**, Giorgio 1926- *IntWW 91*
**Ruffolo**, John Joseph, Jr 1942- *AmMWSc 92*
**Ruffolo**, Lisa M. *DrAPF 91*
**Ruffolo**, Robert Richard, Jr 1950- *AmMWSc 92*
**Ruffus**, Stephen *DrAPF 91*
**Rufinus of Aquileia** 345?-410 *EncEarC*
**Ruflin**, Paul Leroy 1954- *WhoMW 92*
**Rufner**, Richard Kevin 1947- *WhoAmL 92*
**Rufo**, Gregory John 1954- *WhoAmL 92*
**Rufolo**, Anthony Michael 1948- *WhoFI 92, WhoWest 92*
**Ruga**, Elliott 1955- *WhoEnt 92*
**Rugambwa**, Laurean *Who 92*
**Rugambwa**, Laurean 1912- *IntWW 91, WhoRel 92*
**Rugarli**, Giampaolo 1932- *IntWW 91*
**Rugby**, Baron 1951- *Who 92*
**Ruge**, Donald Louis 1963- *WhoMW 92*
**Ruge**, Michael Helmuth 1962- *WhoMW 92*
**Ruge**, Thomas R. 1949- *WhoAmL 92*
**Rugen**, Lloyd Leonard 1917- *WhoMW 92*
**Rugenstein**, Robert Wayne 1921- *WhoWest 92*
**Ruger**, Peter H. 1941- *WhoAmL 92*
**Ruger**, William Batterman 1916- *WhoFI 92*
**Rugeroni**, Ian *WhoFI 92*
**Rugg**, Dean Sprague 1923- *WhoMW 92*
**Rugge**, Henry F 1936- *AmMWSc 92*
**Rugge**, Hugo R 1935- *AmMWSc 92*
**Rugge-Price**, Charles Keith Napier *Who 92*
**Ruggeri**, Robert Edward 1952- *WhoAmL 92*
**Ruggeri**, Zaverio Marcello 1945- *AmMWSc 92, WhoWest 92*
**Ruggerio**, Dominick J 1948- *WhoAmP 91*
**Ruggero**, Mario Alfredo 1943- *AmMWSc 92*
**Ruggieri**, Helen *DrAPF 91*
**Ruggieri**, John Giovanni Francesco 1965- *WhoAmL 92*
**Ruggieri**, Michael Raymond 1954- *AmMWSc 92*
**Ruggieri**, Pasquale 1933- *WhoFI 92*
**Ruggiero**, Alessandro Gabriele 1940- *AmMWSc 92*
**Ruggiero**, Anthony William 1941- *WhoFI 92*
**Ruggiero**, Charles Howard 1947- *WhoEnt 92, WhoMW 92*
**Ruggiero**, David A 1949- *AmMWSc 92*
**Ruggiero**, Joseph A 1943- *WhoAmP 91*
**Ruggiero**, Matthew John 1932- *WhoEnt 92*
**Ruggiero**, Renato 1930- *IntWW 91*
**Ruggiero**, Richard S 1944- *WhoAmP 91*
**Ruggill**, Solomon P. 1906- *WhoWest 92*
**Ruggles**, Carl 1876-1971 *FacFETw*
**Ruggles**, Carl Sprague 1876-1971 *NewAmDM*
**Ruggles**, Daniel 1810-1897 *BiInAmS*
**Ruggles**, Eugene *DrAPF 91*
**Ruggles**, Ivan Dale 1927- *AmMWSc 92*
**Ruggles-Brise**, Guy Edward 1914- *Who 92*
**Ruggles-Brise**, John Archibald 1908- *Who 92*
**Rugh**, William A 1936- *WhoAmP 91*
**Rugh**, Wilson J, II 1944- *AmMWSc 92*
**Rugheimer**, Norman MacGregor 1930- *AmMWSc 92*
**Rugnetta**, Joseph Francis, Jr 1957- *WhoIns 92*
**Rugo**, Marieve *DrAPF 91*
**Rugo**, Steven Alfred 1953- *WhoMW 92*
**Rugoff**, Edward Nathaniel 1955- *WhoEnt 92*
**Rugolo**, Pete 1915- *IntMPA 92, NewAmDM*
**Ruh**, Edwin 1924- *AmMWSc 92*
**Ruh**, H. John 1955- *WhoMW 92*
**Ruh**, Mary Frances 1941- *AmMWSc 92*
**Ruh**, Richard David 1949- *WhoMW 92*
**Ruh**, Robert 1930- *AmMWSc 92*
**Ruhe**, Carl Henry William 1915- *AmMWSc 92*
**Ruhe**, David Sieger 1914- *WhoRel 92*
**Ruhe**, Robert Victory 1918- *AmMWSc 92*
**Ruhe**, Volker 1942- *IntWW 91*
**Ruhen**, Olaf 1911- *WrDr 92*
**Ruhfus**, Jurgen 1930- *IntWW 91, Who 92*
**Ruhl**, Harold L. 1944- *WhoFI 92*
**Ruhl**, Kenneth James 1948- *WhoAmP 91*
**Ruhl**, Roland Luther 1942- *AmMWSc 92*
**Ruhlin**, Peggy Miller 1949- *WhoMW 92*
**Ruhlin**, Richard P 1936- *WhoAmP 91*
**Ruhling**, Robert Otto 1942- *AmMWSc 92*
**Ruhlman**, Terrell Louis 1926- *WhoWest 92*
**Ruhlmann**, Emile-Jacques 1869-1933 *DcTwDes*
**Ruhm**, Thomas Francis 1935- *WhoAmL 92, WhoFI 92*
**Ruhmann**, Heinz 1902- *EncTR 91 [port]*
**Ruhmann Wennhold**, Ann Gertrude 1932- *AmMWSc 92*
**Ruhmkorff**, Betty M 1933- *WhoAmP 91*
**Ruhnau**, Heinz 1929- *IntWW 91, Who 92*
**Ruhnke**, Lothar Hasso 1931- *AmMWSc 92*
**Rui Xingwen** 1927- *IntWW 91*
**Ruibal**, Rodolfo 1927- *AmMWSc 92*
**Ruibal**, Salvador 1953- *WhoHisp 92*
**Ruijgh**, Cornelis Jord 1930- *IntWW 91*
**Ruina**, J P 1923- *AmMWSc 92*
**Ruini**, Camillo 1931- *WhoRel 92*
**Ruis**, Thomas Paul 1947- *WhoEnt 92*
**Ruisi**, Christopher S 1949- *WhoIns 92*
**Ruitenberg**, Elis Joost 1937- *IntWW 91*
**Ruiz**, Andrew Michael 1941- *WhoHisp 92*
**Ruiz**, Anthony *WhoHisp 92*
**Ruiz**, Armando 1957- *WhoAmP 91, WhoHisp 92*
**Ruiz**, Bernardo 1953- *IntAu&W 91*
**Ruiz**, Brunilda 1936- *WhoEnt 92*
**Ruiz**, Carl P 1934- *AmMWSc 92*
**Ruiz**, Darlene Elizabeth *WhoHisp 92*
**Ruiz**, Dolores M. 1958- *WhoHisp 92*
**Ruiz**, Edward F. *WhoHisp 92*
**Ruiz**, Emilio 1944- *WhoHisp 92*
**Ruiz**, Emilio Alfaro 1957- *WhoHisp 92*
**Ruiz**, Francisco 1960- *WhoHisp 92*
**Ruiz**, Frederick R. 1943- *WhoHisp 92*
**Ruiz**, George *WhoHisp 92*
**Ruiz**, Gilbert *WhoHisp 92*
**Ruiz**, Gregory Lopez 1959- *WhoHisp 92*
**Ruiz**, Henry 1936- *WhoHisp 92*
**Ruiz**, Hildebrando 1945- *WhoHisp 92*
**Ruiz**, Hilton 1952- *WhoHisp 92*
**Ruiz**, J. Anthony 1946- *WhoHisp 92*
**Ruiz**, J. Edgar *WhoHisp 92*
**Ruiz**, Jerry Joseph 1955- *WhoAmL 92*
**Ruiz**, Jesus, Jr. 1939- *WhoHisp 92*
**Ruiz**, Joaquin 1951- *WhoHisp 92*
**Ruiz**, Jose 1925- *WhoRel 92*
**Ruiz**, Jose Cheito *WhoHisp 92*
**Ruiz**, Jose Garcia 1947- *WhoWest 92*
**Ruiz**, Jose Luis *WhoHisp 92*
**Ruiz**, Leo Bayani 1948- *WhoEnt 92*
**Ruiz**, Leticia 1957- *WhoHisp 92*
**Ruiz**, Lisbeth J. 1949- *WhoHisp 92*
**Ruiz**, Maria Cristina 1952- *WhoHisp 92*
**Ruiz**, Mark Louie, Jr. 1935- *WhoHisp 92*
**Ruiz**, Martha Ce 1956- *WhoHisp 92*
**Ruiz**, Norberto 1954- *WhoHisp 92*
**Ruiz**, Pedro 1936- *WhoHisp 92*
**Ruiz**, Peter Virgil, II 1951- *WhoHisp 92*
**Ruiz**, Ramon Eduardo 1921- *WhoHisp 92*
**Ruiz**, Raul 1941- *IntDcF 2-2*
**Ruiz**, Reynaldo 1940- *WhoHisp 92*
**Ruiz**, Richard A. 1950- *WhoHisp 92*
**Ruiz**, Richard S. 1932- *WhoHisp 92*
**Ruiz**, Robert J. 1949- *WhoHisp 92*
**Ruiz**, Roberto 1925- *WhoHisp 92*
**Ruiz**, Roberto C. *WhoHisp 92*
**Ruiz**, Rosemary L. *WhoHisp 92*
**Ruiz**, Ruby R. 1949- *WhoHisp 92*
**Ruiz**, Ruth Alicia 1956- *WhoHisp 92*
**Ruiz**, Sergio 1954- *WhoHisp 92*
**Ruiz**, Sharon Kay 1945- *WhoFI 92*
**Ruiz**, Vicki L. 1955- *WhoHisp 92*
**Ruiz**, Vicki Lynn 1955- *WhoWest 92*
**Ruiz**, Wallace David 1951- *WhoHisp 92*
**Ruiz**, William C. 1944- *WhoHisp 92*
**Ruiz-Contreras**, Anita *WhoHisp 92*
**Ruiz de Alarcon y Mendoza**, Juan 1580-1639 *HisDSpE*
**Ruiz De Alda Y Miquelez**, Julio 1897-1936 *BiDExR*
**Ruiz de Apodaca**, Juan 1767-1835 *HisDSpE*
**Ruiz-De-Conde**, Justina 1909- *WhoHisp 92*
**Ruiz de Montoya**, Antonio 1583-1653 *HisDSpE*
**Ruiz-Fornells**, Enrique 1925- *ConAu 36NR*
**Ruiz-Fornells**, Enrique S. 1925- *WhoHisp 92*
**Ruiz-Isley**, Griselda A. 1942- *WhoHisp 92*
**Ruiz-Julia**, Angela M. 1940- *WhoHisp 92*
**Ruiz-Petrich**, Elena 1933- *AmMWSc 92*
**Ruiz Soler**, Antonio 1921- *Who 92*
**Ruiz-Valera**, Phoebe Lucile 1950- *WhoHisp 92*
**Rukashaza**, Oswald 1950- *IntWW 91*
**Rukavina**, Norman Andrew 1937- *AmMWSc 92*
**Rukavina**, Peter Paul 1954- *WhoMW 92*
**Rukavina**, Tom 1950- *WhoAmP 91*
**Rukeyser**, Louis 1933- *ConAu 36NR*
**Rukeyser**, Louis Richard 1933- *IntWW 91, WhoFI 92*
**Rukeyser**, M. S., Jr. 1931- *WhoFI 92*
**Rukeyser**, Muriel 1913- *BenetAL 91*
**Rukeyser**, Muriel 1913-1980 *HanAmWH*
**Rukeyser**, William S 1939- *IntAu&W 91*
**Rukhin**, Andrew Leo 1946- *AmMWSc 92*
**Ruknudin**, Abdul Majeed 1952- *AmMWSc 92*
**Ruland**, Richard 1932- *ConAu 36NR*
**Ruland**, Vernon Joseph 1931- *WhoRel 92*
**Rulau**, H Darlene 1929- *WhoAmP 91*
**Rulau**, Russell 1926- *WhoAmP 91, WhoMW 92*
**Rule**, Allyn H 1934- *AmMWSc 92*
**Rule**, Brian Francis *Who 92*
**Rule**, Charles Frederick 1955- *WhoAmL 92*
**Rule**, Chris Allen 1958- *WhoAmL 92*
**Rule**, Daniel Rhodes 1940- *WhoEnt 92*
**Rule**, David Charles 1937- *Who 92*
**Rule**, Elton H. d1990 *LesBEnT 92 [port]*
**Rule**, Elton Hoert 1916-1990 *FacFETw*
**Rule**, Jane 1931- *BenetAL 91, ConNov 91, IntAu&W 91, WrDr 92*
**Rule**, Janice 1931- *IntMPA 92*
**Rule**, Margaret Helen 1928- *Who 92*
**Rule-Hoffman**, Richard Carl 1947- *WhoMW 92*
**Ruley**, Stanley Eugene 1934- *WhoWest 92*
**Rulf**, Benjamin 1934- *AmMWSc 92*
**Rulfo**, Juan 1918-1986 *BenetAL 91, DcLB 113 [port]*
**Rulfs**, Charles Leslie 1920- *AmMWSc 92*
**Ruliffson**, Willard Sloan 1918- *AmMWSc 92*
**Rulifson**, Johns Frederick 1941- *AmMWSc 92*
**Rulifson**, Paul John 1958- *WhoWest 92*
**Rulifson**, Roger Allen 1951- *AmMWSc 92*
**Rullan**, Pilar M. 1941- *WhoHisp 92*
**Rulli**, Carmen Joseph 1925- *WhoEnt 92*
**Rullman**, Carl W, Sr *WhoAmP 91*
**Rulon**, Elizabeth Ann 1955- *WhoAmP 91*
**Rulon**, Philip Reed 1934- *WhoWest 92, WrDr 92*
**Rulon**, Richard M 1922- *AmMWSc 92*
**Rulon**, Russell Ross 1936- *AmMWSc 92*
**Rumage**, Randall 1960- *WhoEnt 92*
**Rumage**, Sarah Agnes 1956- *WhoAmL 92*
**Rumaker**, Michael *DrAPF 91*
**Rumaker**, Michael 1932- *ConNov 91, WrDr 92*
**Ruman**, Saul I. 1925- *WhoAmL 92*
**Rumbach**, William Ervin 1934- *AmMWSc 92*
**Rumbarger**, Charles D *WhoIns 92*
**Rumbarger**, John H 1925- *AmMWSc 92*
**Rumbaugh**, Melvin Dale 1929- *AmMWSc 92*
**Rumbaut**, Julio Vincent 1952- *WhoHisp 92*
**Rumbaut**, Luis *WhoHisp 92*
**Rumbelow**, Arthur Anthony 1943- *Who 92*
**Rumbelow**, Martin 1937- *Who 92*
**Rumble**, Douglas, III 1942- *AmMWSc 92*
**Rumble**, Edmund Taylor, III 1942- *AmMWSc 92*
**Rumble**, John Bertram 1928- *Who 92*
**Rumble**, Peter William 1929- *Who 92*
**Rumbold**, Algernon *Who 92*
**Rumbold**, Angela 1932- *Who 92*
**Rumbold**, Henry 1947- *Who 92*
**Rumbold**, Horace Algernon 1906- *Who 92*
**Rumbold**, Jack 1920- *Who 92*
**Rumbough**, Roy Albert, Jr. 1955- *WhoFI 92, WhoMW 92*
**Rumburg**, Charles Buddy 1931- *AmMWSc 92*
**Rumelhart**, David Everett 1942- *WhoWest 92*
**Rumely**, John Hamilton 1926- *AmMWSc 92*
**Rumens**, Carol 1944- *ConPo 91, WrDr 92*
**Rumens**, Carol Ann 1944- *IntAu&W 91*
**Rumer**, Ralph R, Jr 1931- *AmMWSc 92*
**Rumfeldt**, Robert Clark 1936- *AmMWSc 92*
**Rumfelt**, Donna Rainey 1953- *WhoFI 92*
**Rumfield**, Valerie Lynn 1966- *WhoMW 92*
**Rumford**, Count *BenetAL 91, BiInAmS*
**Rummage**, Frederick Charles 1931- *WhoAmP 91*
**Rummel**, Edgar Ferrand 1929- *WhoAmL 92*
**Rummel**, Robert Edwin 1911- *AmMWSc 92*
**Rummel**, Robert Wiland 1915- *AmMWSc 92*
**Rummel**, S. Michael 1951- *WhoMW 92*
**Rummens**, F H A 1933- *AmMWSc 92*
**Rummerfield**, Philip Sheridan 1922- *WhoWest 92*
**Rummery**, Terrance Edward 1937- *AmMWSc 92*
**Rumor**, Mariano 1915-1990 *FacFETw*
**Rumpel**, Max Leonard 1936- *AmMWSc 92*
**Rumpf**, John L 1921- *AmMWSc 92*
**Rumpf**, R J 1916- *AmMWSc 92*
**Rumph**, Annie Alridge 1917- *WhoBlA 92*
**Rumph**, Arnold 1929- *WhoRel 92*
**Rumpler**, Edmund 1872-1940 *DcTwDes*
**Rumscheidt**, H. Martin 1935- *ConAu 36NR*
**Rumscheidt**, Hans-Martin 1935- *WhoRel 92*
**Rumsey**, James 1743-1792 *BiInAmS*
**Rumsey**, R. Douglas 1918- *WhoFI 92*
**Rumsey**, Theron S 1939- *AmMWSc 92*
**Rumsey**, Victor Henry 1919- *AmMWSc 92*
**Rumsey**, William LeRoy 1951- *AmMWSc 92*
**Rumsfeld**, Donald 1932- *WhoAmP 91*
**Rumsfeld**, Donald H. 1932- *IntWW 91, WhoFI 92*
**Rumyantsev**, Aleksey Matveyevich 1905- *IntWW 91*
**Runacres**, Eric Arthur 1916- *Who 92*
**Runbeck**, Linda C 1946- *WhoAmP 91*
**Runcie** *Who 92*
**Runcie**, Baron 1921- *IntWW 91, Who 92*
**Runcie**, John Fryer 1942- *WhoMW 92*
**Runcie**, Robert 1921- *FacFETw*
**Runcie**, Robert Alexander Kennedy 1921- *WhoRel 92*
**Runciman** *Who 92*
**Runciman**, Lex *DrAPF 91*
**Runciman**, Steven 1903- *IntWW 91, Who 92, WrDr 92*
**Runciman**, Walter 1870-1949 *EncTR 91*
**Runciman of Doxford**, Viscount 1934- *Who 92*
**Runck**, Roger John 1912- *WhoMW 92*
**Runco**, Paul D 1957- *AmMWSc 92*
**Runco**, William Joseph 1957- *WhoAmL 92, WhoAmP 91*
**Runcorn**, Keith 1922- *Who 92*
**Runcorn**, Stanley Keith 1922- *IntWW 91*
**Rund**, Douglas Andrew 1945- *WhoMW 92*
**Rund**, Hanno *AmMWSc 92*
**Rund**, John Valentine 1938- *AmMWSc 92*
**Runde**, James A. 1946- *WhoFI 92*
**Runde**, Michael C. 1944- *WhoAmL 92*
**Runde**, Stephen John 1952- *WhoMW 92*
**Rundel**, Philip Wilson 1943- *AmMWSc 92*
**Rundel**, Robert Dean 1940- *AmMWSc 92*
**Rundell**, Clark Ace 1938- *AmMWSc 92*
**Rundell**, Harold Lee 1922- *AmMWSc 92*
**Rundell**, Kelly Jean 1960- *WhoAmL 92*
**Rundell**, Mary Kathleen 1946- *AmMWSc 92*
**Rundell**, Thomas Gardner 1945- *WhoAmL 92*
**Rundgren**, Todd 1948- *WhoEnt 92*
**Rundio**, Louis Michael, Jr. 1943- *WhoAmL 92*
**Rundle**, Anne *IntAu&W 91*
**Rundle**, Christopher John Spencer 1938- *Who 92*
**Rundle**, John Louis 1930- *Who 92*
**Rundle**, Juliet Walker 1938- *WhoAmP 91*
**Rundle**, Katherine Fernandez 1951- *WhoHisp 92*
**Rundles**, James Isaiah 1920- *WhoBlA 92*
**Rundles**, Ralph Wayne 1911- *AmMWSc 92*
**Rundlett**, Ellsworth Turner, III 1946- *WhoAmL 92*
**Rundo**, John 1925- *AmMWSc 92*
**Rundquist**, Howard Irving 1929- *WhoFI 92*
**Rundquist**, Larry A. 1947- *WhoWest 92*
**Rundstedt**, Gerd von 1875-1953 *EncTR 91 [port]*
**Rundstedt**, Karl Rudolf Gerd von 1875-1953 *FacFETw*
**Rundstrom**, James Arthur 1941- *WhoMW 92*
**Runeckles**, Victor Charles 1930- *AmMWSc 92*
**Runes**, Richard Norton 1944- *WhoAmL 92*
**Runey**, Gerald Luther 1938- *AmMWSc 92*
**Runfola**, Ross Thomas 1943- *WhoAmL 92*

**Rung,** Donald Charles, Jr 1932- *AmMWSc 92*
**Runge,** Carlisle Ford 1953- *WhoFI 92*
**Runge,** Donald Edward 1938- *WhoMW 92*
**Runge,** Edward C A 1933- *AmMWSc 92*
**Runge,** John Steven 1951- *WhoFI 92*
**Runge,** Richard John 1921- *AmMWSc 92*
**Runge,** Solveig G 1941- *WhoAmP 91*
**Runge,** Thomas Marschall 1924- *AmMWSc 92*
**Runger,** Donald R. 1936- *WhoFI 92*
**Runia,** Klaas 1926- *WhoRel 92*
**Runice,** Robert E. 1929- *WhoWest 92*
**Runion,** Howell Irwin 1933- *AmMWSc 92*
**Runjic,** Andjelko 1938- *IntWW 91*
**Runk,** Benjamin Franklin Dewees 1906- *AmMWSc 92*
**Runk,** Lee Hammond 1940- *WhoFI 92*
**Runke,** Sidney Morris 1911- *AmMWSc 92*
**Runkel,** Richard A 1932- *AmMWSc 92*
**Runkle,** James Reade 1951- *AmMWSc 92, WhoMW 92*
**Runkle,** John Daniel 1822-1902 *BiInAmS*
**Runkle,** Linda Rae 1950- *WhoAmL 92*
**Runkles,** Jack Ralph 1922- *AmMWSc 92*
**Runnalls,** Nelva Earline Gross 1930- *AmMWSc 92*
**Runnalls,** O John C 1924- *AmMWSc 92*
**Runnells,** Clive 1926- *WhoFI 92*
**Runnells,** Donald DeMar 1936- *AmMWSc 92, WhoWest 92*
**Runnels,** Bernice 1925- *WhoBlA 92*
**Runnels,** Jerry Spencer 1940- *WhoIns 92*
**Runnels,** John Hugh 1935- *AmMWSc 92*
**Runnels,** Judith Cotton 1935- *WhoAmP 91*
**Runnels,** Lynn Kelli 1938- *AmMWSc 92*
**Runnels,** Robert Clayton 1935- *AmMWSc 92*
**Runnels,** Sidney Marion 1948- *WhoAmP 91*
**Runnels,** Susan Lum 1947- *WhoAmL 92*
**Runner,** George Cyril, Jr. 1952- *WhoRel 92*
**Runner,** Jeffrey Scott 1961- *WhoWest 92*
**Runner,** Meredith Noftzger 1914- *AmMWSc 92*
**Running Eagle** *EncAmaz 91*
**Running,** Andrew Richard 1957- *WhoAmL 92*
**Running,** Leona Glidden 1916- *WhoRel 92*
**Running,** Richard V 1946- *WhoAmP 91*
**Runnion,** Daniel Thomas 1949- *WhoIns 92*
**Runnion,** Howard J., Jr. 1930- *WhoFI 92*
**Runnion,** Kenneth N. 1950- *WhoWest 92*
**Runnion-Bareford,** David George 1947- *WhoRel 92*
**Runquist,** Olaf A 1931- *AmMWSc 92*
**Runstadler,** Peter William, Jr 1934- *AmMWSc 92*
**Runswick,** Daryl 1946- *ConCom 92*
**Runyan,** Cynthia Mildred 1951- *WhoRel 92*
**Runyan,** David Todd 1932- *WhoMW 92*
**Runyan,** John Stephen 1938- *WhoFI 92*
**Runyan,** John William, Jr 1924- *AmMWSc 92*
**Runyan,** Michael Henry 1947- *WhoAmL 92*
**Runyan,** S H *WhoAmP 91*
**Runyan,** Thora J 1931- *AmMWSc 92*
**Runyan,** Timothy Jack 1941- *WhoMW 92*
**Runyan,** William E. 1945- *WhoWest 92*
**Runyan,** William Scottie 1931- *AmMWSc 92*
**Runyon,** Damon *SourALJ*
**Runyon,** Damon 1884-1946 *BenetAL 91, FacFETw*
**Runyon,** Guy Eric 1945- *WhoFI 92*
**Runyon,** Marvin Travis 1924- *WhoFI 92*
**Runyon,** Rita Juliet 1954- *WhoFI 92*
**Runyon,** Sandy 1948- *WhoAmP 91*
**Runyon,** Theodore Hubert, Jr. 1930- *WhoRel 92*
**Runzo,** Joseph John 1948- *WhoRel 92*
**Ruocchio,** Patricia Jeanne 1958- *IntAu&W 91*
**Ruof,** Clarence Herman 1919- *AmMWSc 92*
**Ruof,** Richard Alan 1932- *WhoRel 92*
**Ruoff,** Arthur Louis 1930- *AmMWSc 92*
**Ruoff,** Theodore Burton Fox d1990 *Who 92N*
**Ruoff,** William 1940- *AmMWSc 92*
**Ruona,** Arthur Ernest 1920- *WhoMW 92*
**Ruona,** Wayne Archibald 1914- *WhoAmP 91*
**Ruotsala,** Albert P 1926- *AmMWSc 92*
**Ruotsala,** James Alfred 1934- *WhoWest 92*
**Rupaal,** Ajit S 1933- *AmMWSc 92*
**Rupe,** Marvin Neal 1963- *WhoMW 92*
**Rupel,** Lawrence Michael 1948- *WhoRel 92*
**Rupert,** Anthony Edward 1916- *IntWW 91*
**Rupert,** Claud Stanley 1919- *AmMWSc 92*
**Rupert,** David Andrew 1940- *WhoRel 92, WhoWest 92*
**Rupert,** Donald William 1946- *WhoAmL 92*
**Rupert,** Dorothy 1926- *WhoAmP 91*
**Rupert,** Earlene Atchison 1921- *AmMWSc 92*
**Rupert,** Gerald Bruce 1930- *AmMWSc 92*
**Rupert,** Hoover 1917- *WhoRel 92*
**Rupert,** John Paul 1946- *AmMWSc 92*
**Rupert,** Richard Albert 1947- *WhoEnt 92*
**Rupert,** Timothy Newton 1966- *WhoRel 92*
**Rupert's Land,** Archbishop of 1928- *Who 92*
**Rupf,** John Albert, Jr 1939- *AmMWSc 92*
**Rupia,** Paul Milyango 1938- *IntWW 91*
**Rupich,** Martin Walter 1952- *AmMWSc 92*
**Rupley,** John Allen 1933- *AmMWSc 92*
**Rupley,** Theodore J 1939- *WhoIns 92*
**Rupnik,** Karen Laurene 1962- *WhoFI 92*
**Rupnik,** Wayne Raymond 1954- *WhoFI 92*
**Ruport,** Scott Hendricks 1949- *WhoAmL 92, WhoMW 92*
**Rupp,** Daniel Gabriel 1936- *WhoFI 92*
**Rupp,** David Carroll 1935- *WhoRel 92*
**Rupp,** Galen Lee 1943- *WhoMW 92*
**Rupp,** George Erik 1942- *WhoRel 92*
**Rupp,** James H 1918- *WhoAmP 91*
**Rupp,** James M. 1935- *WhoEnt 92, WhoFI 92, WhoMW 92*
**Rupp,** Jean Louise 1945- *WhoWest 92*
**Rupp,** John Jay 1940- *AmMWSc 92*
**Rupp,** Lawrence James 1932- *WhoIns 92*
**Rupp,** Lee 1938- *WhoAmP 91*
**Rupp,** Ralph Russell 1929- *AmMWSc 92*
**Rupp,** Richard H. 1934- *WrDr 92*
**Rupp,** W Dean 1938- *AmMWSc 92*
**Rupp,** Walter H 1909- *AmMWSc 92*
**Ruppe,** Loret Miller 1936- *WhoAmP 91*
**Ruppel,** David John 1962- *WhoMW 92*
**Ruppel,** Earl George 1932- *AmMWSc 92*
**Ruppel,** Edward Thompson 1925- *AmMWSc 92*
**Ruppel,** Robert Frank 1925- *AmMWSc 92*
**Ruppel,** Thomas Conrad 1930- *AmMWSc 92*
**Ruppelt,** Ronna Faith *WhoAmL 92*
**Ruppenthal,** Karl M. 1917- *WrDr 92*
**Ruppert,** Chester *TwCSFW 91*
**Ruppert,** David *AmMWSc 92*
**Ruppert,** James *DrAPF 91*
**Ruppert,** Rupert Earl 1943- *WhoAmL 92, WhoAmP 91*
**Rupprecht,** Elizabeth 1932- *WhoMW 92*
**Rupprecht,** Kevin Robert 1955- *AmMWSc 92*
**Ruprecht,** Mary Margaret 1934- *WhoAmP 91*
**Ruprecht,** Thomas G 1941- *WhoIns 92*
**Rupwate,** D. D. *WhoRel 92*
**Rus Hordorwich,** Nancy Anne 1947- *WhoMW 92*
**Rusack,** Robert Claflin 1926- *WhoRel 92*
**Rusakov,** Konstantin Viktorovich 1909-1986 *SovUnBD*
**Rusay,** Ronald Joseph 1945- *AmMWSc 92*
**Rusbridge,** Brian John 1922- *Who 92*
**Rusbridger,** James 1928- *ConAu 134*
**Rusby,** Cameron 1926- *Who 92*
**Ruscello,** Dennis Michael 1947- *AmMWSc 92*
**Rusch,** Donald Harold 1938- *AmMWSc 92*
**Rusch,** Frederick Albert 1938- *WhoRel 92*
**Rusch,** Jonathan Jay 1952- *WhoAmL 92*
**Rusch,** Michael Milton 1952- *WhoFI 92*
**Rusch,** Robert D. *WhoEnt 92*
**Rusch,** Thomas William 1946- *WhoMW 92*
**Rusch,** Wilbert H, Sr 1913- *AmMWSc 92*
**Rusch,** William Graham 1937- *WhoRel 92*
**Ruscha,** Edward 1937- *WorArt 1980 [port]*
**Ruscha,** Edward Joseph 1937- *IntWW 91*
**Ruschak,** Kenneth John 1949- *AmMWSc 92*
**Rusche,** Brian *WhoRel 92*
**Rusche,** Kimberle Dawn 1966- *WhoWest 92*
**Ruschell,** Stephen Matthew 1949- *WhoAmL 92*
**Ruschenberger,** William Samuel Waithman 1807-1895 *BiInAmS*
**Ruscher,** Paul H 1955- *AmMWSc 92*
**Ruschi,** Augusto 1916-1986 *FacFETw*
**Ruschmeyer,** Orlando R 1925- *AmMWSc 92*
**Rusconi,** Louis Joseph 1926- *WhoWest 92*
**Ruse,** Gary Alan 1946- *IntAu&W 91*
**Ruse,** Paul W, Jr 1943- *WhoAmP 91*
**Rusek,** Andrzej 1939- *WhoMW 92*
**Rusen,** Paul D 1935- *WhoAmP 91*
**Ruser,** Kevin L. 1953- *WhoAmL 92*
**Rush,** Aiken P, Jr 1939- *WhoIns 92*
**Rush,** Alvin *LesBEnT 92*
**Rush,** Alvin 1926- *WhoEnt 92*
**Rush,** Barbara *IntMPA 92*
**Rush,** Barbara 1930- *WhoEnt 92*
**Rush,** Benjamin 1745-1813 *BenetAL 91, BlkwEAR, HanAmWH*
**Rush,** Benjamin 1746-1813 *AmPolLe [port], BiInAmS*
**Rush,** Benjamin Franklin, Jr 1924- *AmMWSc 92*
**Rush,** Bob Roy 1942- *WhoRel 92*
**Rush,** Bobby 1946- *WhoAmP 91*
**Rush,** Brian Paul 1958- *WhoAmP 91*
**Rush,** Cecil Archer 1917- *AmMWSc 92*
**Rush,** Charles Kenneth 1921- *AmMWSc 92*
**Rush,** Charles Merle 1942- *AmMWSc 92*
**Rush,** Christopher 1944- *WrDr 92*
**Rush,** Chuck 1953- *WhoEnt 92*
**Rush,** David A. 1940- *WhoEnt 92*
**Rush,** David Eugene 1943- *AmMWSc 92*
**Rush,** Domenica Marie 1937- *WhoWest 92*
**Rush,** Fletcher Grey, Jr. 1917- *WhoAmL 92*
**Rush,** Francis Roberts *Who 92*
**Rush,** Frank E, Jr 1921- *AmMWSc 92*
**Rush,** Gary Alfred 1935- *WhoWest 92*
**Rush,** Gary Robert 1954- *WhoMW 92*
**Rush,** Herman *LesBEnT 92*
**Rush,** Herman 1929- *IntMPA 92*
**Rush,** Herman E. 1929- *WhoEnt 92, WhoWest 92*
**Rush,** Hugh D 1926- *WhoAmP 91*
**Rush,** James 1786-1869 *BenetAL 91, BiInAmS*
**Rush,** James E 1935- *AmMWSc 92*
**Rush,** Jean Cochran 1933- *WhoMW 92*
**Rush,** John Edwin, Jr 1937- *AmMWSc 92*
**Rush,** John Joseph 1936- *AmMWSc 92*
**Rush,** Kenneth 1910- *IntWW 91, WhoAmP 91*
**Rush,** Kent Rodney 1938- *AmMWSc 92*
**Rush,** Kip John 1964- *WhoRel 92*
**Rush,** Loren 1935- *NewAmDM*
**Rush,** Norman 1933- *IntAu&W 91*
**Rush,** Otis 1934- *NewAmDM*
**Rush,** Philip 1908- *WrDr 92*
**Rush,** Richard 1930- *IntMPA 92*
**Rush,** Richard Marion 1928- *AmMWSc 92*
**Rush,** Richard William 1921- *AmMWSc 92*
**Rush,** Robert B. *WhoFI 92*
**Rush,** Sonya C. 1959- *WhoBlA 92*
**Rush,** Stanley 1920- *AmMWSc 92*
**Rush,** William 1919- *WhoAmP 91*
**Rush,** William Edward 1942- *WhoRel 92*
**Rush,** William Harvey 1941- *WhoMW 92*
**Rush,** William John 1934- *WhoAmL 92*
**Rushbrooke,** G. Stanley 1915- *Who 92*
**Rushbury,** Henry 1889-1968 *TwCPaSc*
**Rushdie,** Salman *NewYTBS 91 [port]*
**Rushdie,** Salman 1947- *ConNov 91, FacFETw, IntAu&W 91, IntWW 91, LiExTwC, RfGEnL 91, Who 92, WhoRel 92, WrDr 92*
**Rushdy,** Ahmed 1924- *IntWW 91*
**Rushen,** Patrice *WhoBlA 92*
**Rusher,** Derwood H., II 1954- *WhoAmL 92*
**Rusher,** William Allen 1923- *WrDr 92*
**Rushford,** Antony Redfern *Who 92*
**Rushford,** Eloise Johnson *WhoMW 92*
**Rushforth,** Craig Knewel 1937- *AmMWSc 92*
**Rushforth,** Norman B 1932- *AmMWSc 92*
**Rushforth,** Samuel Roberts 1945- *AmMWSc 92*
**Rushing,** Allen Joseph 1944- *AmMWSc 92*
**Rushing,** Byron 1942- *WhoAmP 91*
**Rushing,** Byron D. 1942- *WhoBlA 92*
**Rushing,** Frank C 1906- *AmMWSc 92*
**Rushing,** George A. *WhoBlA 92*
**Rushing,** Jane Gilmore 1925- *TwCWW 91, WrDr 92*
**Rushing,** Janet LaRene 1958- *WhoAmL 92*
**Rushing,** Jimmy 1903-1972 *NewAmDM*
**Rushing,** Rayburn Lewis 1922- *WhoRel 92*
**Rushing,** Roy Eugene 1943- *WhoFI 92*
**Rushing,** Thomas Benny 1941- *AmMWSc 92*
**Rushmer,** Robert F. 1914- *ConAu 134*
**Rushmer,** Robert Frazer 1914- *AmMWSc 92*
**Rushnell,** Squire D. *LesBEnT 92*
**Rushnell,** Squire Derrick 1938- *WhoEnt 92*
**Rushton,** Allan Crockett 1939- *WhoAmP 91*
**Rushton,** Brian Mandel 1933- *AmMWSc 92*
**Rushton,** David W. 1945- *WhoEnt 92*
**Rushton,** George 1868-1948 *TwCPaSc*
**Rushton,** Ian Lawton 1931- *Who 92*
**Rushton,** Priscilla Strickland 1942- *AmMWSc 92*
**Rushton,** Robert Archie 1943- *WhoAmP 91*
**Rushton,** William 1937- *IntAu&W 91, WrDr 92*
**Rushton,** William George 1937- *Who 92*
**Rushton,** William James, III 1929- *WhoIns 92*
**Rushworth,** Derek 1920- *Who 92*
**Rushworth,** Robert 1924- *FacFETw*
**Rusila** *EncAmaz 91*
**Rusinek,** Michal 1904- *IntAu&W 91, IntWW 91*
**Rusinko,** Frank, Jr 1930- *AmMWSc 92, WhoMW 92*
**Rusinko,** Susan 1922- *ConAu 133*
**Rusk,** Carroll Gay, Jr. 1951- *WhoAmL 92*
**Rusk,** David Patrick 1940- *WhoAmP 91*
**Rusk,** Dean 1909- *AmPolLe, FacFETw, IntWW 91, Who 92*
**Rusk,** Howard Archibald 1901-1989 *FacFETw*
**Rusk,** Michael James 1959- *WhoMW 92*
**Rusk,** Ralph L. 1888-1962 *BenetAL 91*
**Rusk,** Robert F *WhoAmP 91*
**Ruska,** Ernst 1906-1988 *FacFETw, WhoNob 90*
**Ruskai,** Mary Beth 1944- *AmMWSc 92*
**Ruskan,** Ronald Jan 1951- *WhoAmP 91*
**Ruske,** David John 1963- *WhoMW 92*
**Ruskin,** Andrea B. 1960- *WhoEnt 92*
**Ruskin,** Arnold M 1937- *AmMWSc 92*
**Ruskin,** Asa Paul 1929- *AmMWSc 92*
**Ruskin,** Coby *LesBEnT 92*
**Ruskin,** John 1819-1900 *CnDBLB 4 [port], RfGEnL 91*
**Ruskin,** Joseph Richard 1924- *WhoEnt 92*
**Ruskin,** Mary Kathy 1953- *WhoEnt 92*
**Ruskin,** Morris 1962- *WhoEnt 92*
**Ruskin,** Richard A 1924- *AmMWSc 92*
**Ruskin,** Robert Edward 1916- *AmMWSc 92*
**Rusla** *EncAmaz 91*
**Rusling,** James Francis 1946- *AmMWSc 92*
**Rusnak,** Michael 1921- *WhoRel 92*
**Rusoff,** Irving Isadore 1915- *AmMWSc 92*
**Rusoff,** Louis Leon 1910- *AmMWSc 92*
**Russ,** Albert J 1929- *WhoAmP 91*
**Russ,** Charles Paul, III 1944- *WhoAmL 92*
**Russ,** Charles Roger 1937- *AmMWSc 92*
**Russ,** Daniel Christopher 1961- *WhoFI 92, WhoWest 92*
**Russ,** David Perry 1945- *AmMWSc 92*
**Russ,** Edmond Vincent, Jr. 1944- *WhoMW 92*
**Russ,** Gerald A 1936- *AmMWSc 92*
**Russ,** Guston Price, III 1946- *AmMWSc 92*
**Russ,** James Stewart 1940- *AmMWSc 92*
**Russ,** Jay Edmond 1950- *WhoAmL 92*
**Russ,** Joanna 1937- *BenetAL 91, ConNov 91, TwCSFW 91, WrDr 92*
**Russ,** Joseph, IV 1936- *WhoAmP 91*
**Russ,** Lawrence *DrAPF 91*
**Russ,** Stanley 1930- *WhoAmP 91*
**Russ,** William 1951?- *ConTFT 9*
**Russ Spaar,** Lisa *DrAPF 91*
**Russaw,** Joyce Belynda 1952- *WhoMW 92*
**Russe,** Conrad Thomas Campbell 1954- *WhoFI 92*
**Russek,** Arnold 1926- *AmMWSc 92*
**Russek,** Trula Wells 1921- *WhoAmP 91*
**Russek-Cohen,** Estelle 1951- *AmMWSc 92*
**Russel,** Darrell Arden 1921- *AmMWSc 92*
**Russel,** Marjorie Ellen 1944- *AmMWSc 92*
**Russel,** William Bailey 1945- *AmMWSc 92*
**Russell** *Who 92*
**Russell,** Earl 1937- *Who 92*
**Russell Sage** *DcAmImH*
**Russell,** Alan James 1962- *AmMWSc 92*
**Russell,** Alan K 1937- *ScFEYrs*
**Russell,** Alan Keith 1932- *Who 92*
**Russell,** Alastair Muir 1949- *Who 92*
**Russell,** Albert Muir Galloway 1925- *Who 92*
**Russell,** Alexander 1880-1953 *NewAmDM*
**Russell,** Alexander William 1938- *Who 92*
**Russell,** Allan Melvin 1930- *AmMWSc 92*
**Russell,** Allen Stevenson 1915- *AmMWSc 92*
**Russell,** Andrew Milo 1948- *WhoEnt 92*
**Russell,** Angela Veta 1943- *WhoAmP 91*
**Russell,** Anna 1911- *NewAmDM, Who 92*
**Russell,** Anthony John *Who 92*
**Russell,** Anthony Patrick 1947- *AmMWSc 92*
**Russell,** Archibald 1904- *Who 92*
**Russell,** Archibald Edward 1904- *IntWW 91*
**Russell,** Armand King 1932- *WhoEnt 92*
**Russell,** Arthur Colin 1906- *Who 92*
**Russell,** August Wayne 1942- *WhoBlA 92*
**Russell,** B Don 1948- *AmMWSc 92*
**Russell,** Barbara Winifred 1910- *Who 92*
**Russell,** Bert 1956- *WhoAmP 91*
**Russell,** Bertram *ScFEYrs*
**Russell,** Bertrand A 1872-1970 *FacFETw [port]*
**Russell,** Bertrand Arthur William 1872-1970 *WhoNob 90*
**Russell,** Beverly A. *DrAPF 91*
**Russell,** Beverly A. 1947- *WhoBlA 92*
**Russell,** Beverly Carradine, Jr 1947- *WhoAmP 91*
**Russell,** Bill 1934- *FacFETw, WhoBlA 92*
**Russell,** Bradley Scott 1963- *WhoAmL 92*
**Russell,** Brian Fitzgerald 1904- *Who 92, WrDr 92*
**Russell,** Bruce 1946- *TwCPaSc*
**Russell,** Campy 1952- *WhoBlA 92*
**Russell,** Carol Ann 1943- *WhoFI 92, WhoWest 92*

**Russell**, CarolAnn *DrAPF 91*
**Russell**, Carolyn *WhoAmP 91*
**Russell**, Catherine Marie 1910- *AmMWSc 92*
**Russell**, Cazzie 1944- *WhoBlA 92*
**Russell**, Cecil Anthony Francis 1921- *Who 92*
**Russell**, Charles Addison 1921- *AmMWSc 92*
**Russell**, Charles Allyn 1920- *WhoRel 92*
**Russell**, Charles Bradley 1940- *AmMWSc 92*
**Russell**, Charles Clayton 1937- *AmMWSc 92*
**Russell**, Charles Edward *DcAmImH*
**Russell**, Charles Edward 1860-1941 *BenetAL 91*
**Russell**, Charles Ian 1918- *Who 92*
**Russell**, Charles M 1865-1926 *TwCWW 91*
**Russell**, Charles S 1926- *WhoAmP 91*
**Russell**, Charles Stevens 1926- *WhoAmL 92*
**Russell**, Charles Stevens, Jr. 1957- *WhoAmL 92*
**Russell**, Charles Taze 1852-1916 *RelLAm 91*
**Russell**, Charles Wayman 1938- *WhoRel 92*
**Russell**, Charlie L. 1932- *WhoBlA 92*
**Russell**, Charlotte Sananes 1927- *AmMWSc 92*
**Russell**, Christopher *Who 92*
**Russell**, Christopher Thomas 1943- *AmMWSc 92*
**Russell**, Chuck *IntMPA 92*
**Russell**, Clifford Springer 1938- *WhoFI 92*
**Russell**, Conrad 1937- *WrDr 92*
**Russell**, Dale A 1937- *AmMWSc 92*
**Russell**, Dan M., Jr. 1913- *WhoAmL 92*
**Russell**, Dana 1949- *WhoWest 92*
**Russell**, David A 1935- *AmMWSc 92*
**Russell**, David Hamilton *Who 92*
**Russell**, David L 1939- *AmMWSc 92*
**Russell**, David L. 1942- *WhoAmL 92*
**Russell**, David Lee 1956- *WhoWest 92*
**Russell**, David Paul 1941- *WhoAmL 92*
**Russell**, David Sturrock W. *Who 92*
**Russell**, David Syme 1916- *Who 92, WrDr 92*
**Russell**, David Williams 1945- *WhoAmL 92, WhoFI 92, WhoMW 92*
**Russell**, Dennis C 1927- *AmMWSc 92*
**Russell**, Dian Bishop 1952- *WhoBlA 92*
**Russell**, Diana E H 1938- *ConAu 34NR*
**Russell**, Diane Haddock 1935- *AmMWSc 92*
**Russell**, Donald Andrew Frank Moore 1920- *Who 92*
**Russell**, Donald Glenn 1931- *AmMWSc 92*
**Russell**, Donald Lee 1946- *WhoRel 92*
**Russell**, Donald Stuart 1906- *IntWW 91, WhoAmL 92, WhoAmP 91*
**Russell**, Donald W 1951- *WhoIns 92*
**Russell**, Dora 1894-1986 *BiDBrF 2*
**Russell**, Doris Mae 1926- *WhoAmP 91*
**Russell**, Dorothy Delores 1950- *WhoBlA 92*
**Russell**, Douglas Stewart 1916- *AmMWSc 92*
**Russell**, Edmund Louis, III 1951- *WhoWest 92*
**Russell**, Edward Augustine 1916- *Who 92*
**Russell**, Edward Thomas 1941- *WhoFI 92*
**Russell**, Edward Walter 1904- *Who 92*
**Russell**, Edwin Ernest 1942- *WhoMW 92*
**Russell**, Edwin John Cumming 1939- *Who 92*
**Russell**, Edwin R. 1913- *WhoBlA 92*
**Russell**, Eileen Alison *Who 92*
**Russell**, Elizabeth Ann 1955- *WhoEnt 92*
**Russell**, Elizabeth Shull 1913- *AmMWSc 92*
**Russell**, Eric Frank 1905-1978 *TwCSFW 91*
**Russell**, Ernest 1933- *WhoBlA 92*
**Russell**, Ernest Everett 1923- *AmMWSc 92*
**Russell**, Evelyn 1912- *Who 92*
**Russell**, Findlay Ewing 1919- *AmMWSc 92, WhoWest 92*
**Russell**, Fox *ScFEYrs*
**Russell**, Francia 1938- *WhoEnt 92, WhoWest 92*
**Russell**, Francis 1910- *IntAu&W 91*
**Russell**, Francis Mark 1927- *Who 92*
**Russell**, Frank *DrAPF 91*
**Russell**, Frank 1868-1903 *BiInAmS*
**Russell**, Franklin 1926- *WrDr 92*
**Russell**, Franklin Taylor 1936- *WhoAmL 92*
**Russell**, Frederick A 1915- *AmMWSc 92*
**Russell**, Gary E. 1950- *WhoMW 92, WhoRel 92*
**Russell**, Gay Martin 1933- *WhoEnt 92, WhoWest 92*
**Russell**, George 1923- *NewAmDM*
**Russell**, George 1935- *IntWW 91, Who 92*
**Russell**, George A 1921- *AmMWSc 92*
**Russell**, George A. 1923- *WhoBlA 92*
**Russell**, George Albert 1936- *AmMWSc 92*
**Russell**, George Allen 1923- *WhoEnt 92*
**Russell**, George Alton, Jr. *WhoBlA 92*
**Russell**, George Austin, Jr. 1948- *WhoRel 92*
**Russell**, George H. 1945- *WhoFI 92*
**Russell**, George K 1937- *AmMWSc 92*
**Russell**, George Michael 1908- *Who 92*
**Russell**, George William 1867-1935 *CnDBLB 5 [port], RfGEnL 91*
**Russell**, Gerald Charles 1942- *WhoAmL 92*
**Russell**, Gerald Francis Morris 1928- *Who 92*
**Russell**, Gerald Frederick 1944- *AmMWSc 92*
**Russell**, Gerald Vincent 1946- *WhoWest 92*
**Russell**, Glen Allan 1925- *AmMWSc 92*
**Russell**, Glenn C 1921- *AmMWSc 92*
**Russell**, Glenn Vinton 1922- *AmMWSc 92*
**Russell**, Gordon 1892-1980 *DcTwDes*
**Russell**, Graham R. *Who 92*
**Russell**, Grant E 1916- *AmMWSc 92*
**Russell**, Harold Ian Lyle 1934- *Who 92*
**Russell**, Harold LeRoy 1934- *WhoFI 92*
**Russell**, Harriet Anne 1941- *WhoAmP 91*
**Russell**, Harriet Shaw 1952- *WhoMW 92*
**Russell**, Harvey Clarence 1918- *WhoBlA 92*
**Russell**, Helen Ross 1915- *WrDr 92*
**Russell**, Henry 1812-1900 *NewAmDM*
**Russell**, Henry Franklin 1940- *AmMWSc 92*
**Russell**, Henry George 1941- *AmMWSc 92*
**Russell**, Henry Phillip, Jr 1916- *WhoAmP 91*
**Russell**, Herman Jerome 1930- *WhoBlA 92, WhoFI 92*
**Russell**, Hilary *DrAPF 91*
**Russell**, Howard Lewis *DrAPF 91*
**Russell**, Ian John 1943- *Who 92*
**Russell**, Irwin 1853-1879 *BenetAL 91*
**Russell**, Israel Cook 1852-1906 *BiInAmS*
**Russell**, James *WrDr 92*
**Russell**, James 1928- *AmMWSc 92*
**Russell**, James A, Jr 1917- *AmMWSc 92, WhoBlA 92*
**Russell**, James Austin 1952- *WhoWest 92*
**Russell**, James Christopher 1938- *AmMWSc 92*
**Russell**, James Donald Murray 1934- *WhoMW 92*
**Russell**, James E 1940- *AmMWSc 92*
**Russell**, James Edward 1931- *AmMWSc 92*
**Russell**, James Francis Buchanan 1924- *Who 92*
**Russell**, James Knox 1919- *Who 92*
**Russell**, James Madison, III 1940- *AmMWSc 92*
**Russell**, James Michael 1960- *WhoAmL 92*
**Russell**, James N, Jr 1907- *AmMWSc 92*
**Russell**, James Paul 1945- *WhoFI 92*
**Russell**, James Sargent 1903- *IntWW 91*
**Russell**, James T 1944- *AmMWSc 92*
**Russell**, James Torrance 1931- *AmMWSc 92*
**Russell**, Jane 1921- *ConTFT 9, IntMPA 92*
**Russell**, Jay Alan 1957- *WhoEnt 92*
**Russell**, Jay D. 1950- *WhoFI 92*
**Russell**, Jeffrey Burton 1934- *WrDr 92*
**Russell**, Jeremy 1935- *WrDr 92*
**Russell**, Jim *WhoAmP 91*
**Russell**, Joel W 1939- *AmMWSc 92*
**Russell**, John *TwCWW 91*
**Russell**, John 1885-1956 *BenetAL 91*
**Russell**, John 1919- *ConAu 34NR, IntAu&W 91, IntWW 91, Who 92, WrDr 92*
**Russell**, John Albert 1913- *AmMWSc 92*
**Russell**, John Alvin 1934- *AmMWSc 92*
**Russell**, John Blair 1929- *AmMWSc 92*
**Russell**, John Davidson 1946- *WhoAmP 91*
**Russell**, John Drinker 1911- *WhoAmL 92*
**Russell**, John George 1941- *AmMWSc 92*
**Russell**, John Harry 1926- *Who 92*
**Russell**, John Henry 1919- *AmMWSc 92*
**Russell**, John Joseph, Jr. 1957- *WhoRel 92*
**Russell**, John Lawson 1917- *Who 92*
**Russell**, John Leonard 1906- *IntAu&W 91, WrDr 92*
**Russell**, John Lewis 1808-1873 *BiInAmS*
**Russell**, John Lynn, Jr 1930- *AmMWSc 92*
**Russell**, John McCandless *AmMWSc 92*
**Russell**, John Peterson, Jr. 1947- *WhoBlA 92*
**Russell**, John Richardson 1951- *WhoAmP 91*
**Russell**, John Thomas 1931- *WhoAmP 91*
**Russell**, John W 1923- *WhoAmP 91*
**Russell**, Joseph D. 1914- *WhoBlA 92*
**Russell**, Joseph J. 1934- *WhoBlA 92*
**Russell**, Joseph Louis 1936- *AmMWSc 92*
**Russell**, Joseph Michael 1947- *WhoAmL 92*
**Russell**, Karen Drury 1954- *WhoAmL 92*
**Russell**, Kay A. 1954- *WhoBlA 92*
**Russell**, Keith A. *WhoRel 92*
**Russell**, Keith Bradley 1956- *WhoBlA 92*
**Russell**, Keith Palmer, Jr. 1945- *WhoFI 92, WhoWest 92*
**Russell**, Ken 1927- *IntDcF 2-2 [port], IntMPA 92, IntWW 91, Who 92, WhoEnt 92*
**Russell**, Kenneth Calvin 1936- *AmMWSc 92*
**Russell**, Kenneth Edwin 1924- *AmMWSc 92*
**Russell**, Kenneth Homer 1933- *AmMWSc 92*
**Russell**, Kenneth Victor 1929- *WrDr 92*
**Russell**, Kurt 1951- *IntMPA 92*
**Russell**, Kurt Von Vogel 1951- *WhoEnt 92*
**Russell**, Leon W. 1949- *WhoBlA 92*
**Russell**, Leonard, Mrs. *Who 92*
**Russell**, Leonard Alonzo 1949- *WhoBlA 92*
**Russell**, Leonard Nelson 1922- *AmMWSc 92*
**Russell**, Lewis Keith 1931- *AmMWSc 92*
**Russell**, Liane Brauch 1923- *AmMWSc 92*
**Russell**, Lillian 1861-1922 *DcAmImH, NewAmDM*
**Russell**, Linus Eli 1848-1917 *BiInAmS*
**Russell**, Lloyd A 1921- *WhoAmP 91*
**Russell**, Loris Shano 1904- *AmMWSc 92*
**Russell**, Louise 1931- *WhoWest 92*
**Russell**, Mark *Who 92*
**Russell**, Mark 1932- *ConMus 6 [port], WhoEnt 92*
**Russell**, Marlou 1956- *WhoWest 92*
**Russell**, Martin 1934- *WrDr 92*
**Russell**, Martin Guthrie 1914- *Who 92*
**Russell**, Martin James 1934- *IntAu&W 91*
**Russell**, Marvin W 1927- *AmMWSc 92*
**Russell**, Mary Patricia 1942- *WhoMW 92*
**Russell**, Maurice V. 1923- *WhoBlA 92*
**Russell**, Michael James 1958- *WhoAmL 92, WhoFI 92*
**Russell**, Michael John 1954- *WhoAmL 92*
**Russell**, Michael W 1944- *AmMWSc 92*
**Russell**, Morley Egerton 1929- *AmMWSc 92*
**Russell**, Muir *Who 92*
**Russell**, Nancy Jeanne 1938- *AmMWSc 92*
**Russell**, Nathaniel S. 1930- *WhoBlA 92*
**Russell**, Newton R 1927- *WhoAmP 91*
**Russell**, Newton Requa 1927- *WhoWest 92*
**Russell**, Nipsey 1924- *WhoBlA 92*
**Russell**, Norma C 1937- *WhoAmP 91*
**Russell**, Norman 1945- *WhoRel 92*
**Russell**, Norman H. *DrAPF 91*
**Russell**, Norman H. 1921- *WrDr 92*
**Russell**, O. Ruth 1897-1979 *ConAu 133*
**Russell**, Osborne 1814-1865? *BenetAL 91*
**Russell**, Patricia A. 1943- *WhoEnt 92*
**Russell**, Patricia T 1931- *WhoAmP 91*
**Russell**, Patrick *Who 92*
**Russell**, Patrick James 1959- *WhoRel 92, WhoWest 92*
**Russell**, Paul d1991 *NewYTBS 91*
**Russell**, Paul 1956- *ConAu 133*
**Russell**, Paul E 1924- *AmMWSc 92*
**Russell**, Paul Edgar 1924- *WhoWest 92*
**Russell**, Paul Snowden 1925- *AmMWSc 92*
**Russell**, Paul Telford 1935- *AmMWSc 92*
**Russell**, Pee Wee 1906-1969 *NewAmDM*
**Russell**, Peggy Taylor 1927- *WhoEnt 92*
**Russell**, Percy J 1926- *AmMWSc 92*
**Russell**, Peter 1921- *ConPo 91, WrDr 92*
**Russell**, Peter Byrom 1918- *AmMWSc 92*
**Russell**, Peter Edward Lionel Russell 1913- *Who 92*
**Russell**, Peter James 1947- *AmMWSc 92*
**Russell**, Philip Boyd 1944- *AmMWSc 92*
**Russell**, Philip King 1932- *AmMWSc 92*
**Russell**, Philip Welsford Richmond 1919- *IntWW 91, Who 92*
**Russell**, R. Stephen *DrAPF 91*
**Russell**, Ralph Timothy 1948- *WhoIns 92*
**Russell**, Ray *DrAPF 91*
**Russell**, Ray 1924- *IntAu&W 91, WrDr 92*
**Russell**, Raymond Alvin 1917- *AmMWSc 92*
**Russell**, Raymond Francis, Jr. 1953- *WhoMW 92*
**Russell**, Richard Bruce 1949- *WhoWest 92*
**Russell**, Richard Dana 1906- *AmMWSc 92*
**Russell**, Richard Doncaster 1929- *AmMWSc 92*
**Russell**, Richard Lawson 1940- *AmMWSc 92*
**Russell**, Richard Olney, Jr 1932- *AmMWSc 92*
**Russell**, Robert Alan 1949- *WhoFI 92*
**Russell**, Robert Christopher Hamlyn 1921- *Who 92*
**Russell**, Robert Elson, Sr 1941- *WhoAmP 91*
**Russell**, Robert John 1938- *AmMWSc 92*
**Russell**, Robert John 1946- *WhoRel 92*
**Russell**, Robert Joseph 1933- *WhoFI 92*
**Russell**, Robert Lee 1927- *AmMWSc 92*
**Russell**, Robert Leonard 1916- *WhoFI 92*
**Russell**, Robert Lloyd 1941- *WhoFI 92*
**Russell**, Robert M 1941- *AmMWSc 92*
**Russell**, Robert M. 1943- *WhoRel 92*
**Russell**, Robert Mark 1929- *Who 92*
**Russell**, Robert Raymond 1920- *AmMWSc 92*
**Russell**, Robert W 1924- *ConAu 34NR*
**Russell**, Robert Weldon, III 1946- *WhoAmP 91*
**Russell**, Roger 1938- *WhoAmP 91*
**Russell**, Roger Wolcott 1914- *Who 92*
**Russell**, Ronald 1924- *WrDr 92*
**Russell**, Ronald Christopher 1940- *Who 92*
**Russell**, Ross 1909- *ConAu 34NR*
**Russell**, Ross F 1919- *AmMWSc 92*
**Russell**, Roy *IntAu&W 91*
**Russell**, Roy 1918- *WrDr 92*
**Russell**, Rudolf Rosenfeld 1925- *Who 92*
**Russell**, Russell George 1942- *WhoMW 92*
**Russell**, Ruth Lois 1928- *AmMWSc 92*
**Russell**, Sam W 1945- *WhoAmP 91*
**Russell**, Samuel Lee 1948- *WhoAmL 92*
**Russell**, Sandra *DrAPF 91*
**Russell**, Scott D 1952- *AmMWSc 92*
**Russell**, Shane *IntAu&W 91X, TwCWW 91*
**Russell**, Sharman Apt *DrAPF 91*
**Russell**, Sharon May 1944- *AmMWSc 92*
**Russell**, Spencer 1923- *Who 92*
**Russell**, Spencer Thomas 1923- *IntWW 91*
**Russell**, Stephen Mims 1931- *AmMWSc 92*
**Russell**, Stephen Speh 1943- *WhoAmL 92*
**Russell**, Steven Turner 1950- *WhoAmL 92*
**Russell**, Stuart Jonathan 1962- *AmMWSc 92*
**Russell**, Sue Ellen 1959- *WhoAmL 92*
**Russell**, T L 1930- *AmMWSc 92*
**Russell**, T W Fraser 1934- *AmMWSc 92*
**Russell**, Terence Francis 1931- *Who 92*
**Russell**, Terrance K 1954- *WhoIns 92*
**Russell**, Terrence R 1940- *AmMWSc 92*
**Russell**, Theresa 1957- *IntMPA 92*
**Russell**, Thomas 1920- *Who 92*
**Russell**, Thomas Arthur 1953- *WhoWest 92*
**Russell**, Thomas Edward 1942- *AmMWSc 92*
**Russell**, Thomas Frank 1924- *WhoFI 92*
**Russell**, Thomas H 1853?-1916 *BiInAmS*
**Russell**, Thomas J, Jr 1931- *AmMWSc 92*
**Russell**, Thomas Patrick 1926- *Who 92*
**Russell**, Thomas Paul 1952- *AmMWSc 92*
**Russell**, Thomas S 1922- *WhoAmP 91*
**Russell**, Thomas Solon 1922- *AmMWSc 92*
**Russell**, Thomas Webb 1940- *AmMWSc 92*
**Russell**, Timothy *DrAPF 91, WhoEnt 92*
**Russell**, Tomas Morgan 1934- *WhoAmL 92, WhoIns 92*
**Russell**, Virginia Ann 1925- *AmMWSc 92*
**Russell**, W. H. 1820-1907 *BenetAL 91*
**Russell**, W. M. S. 1925- *WrDr 92*
**Russell**, Wallace Clayton, Jr 1928- *WhoAmP 91*
**Russell**, Wesley L. 1938- *WhoBlA 92*
**Russell**, Wilbert Ambrick 1922- *AmMWSc 92*
**Russell**, Wilbert C. 1926- *WhoBlA 92*
**Russell**, William *DrAPF 91*
**Russell**, William Arthur, Jr 1947- *WhoAmP 91*
**Russell**, William Charles 1955- *AmMWSc 92*
**Russell**, William Dean 1938- *WhoAmP 91*
**Russell**, William Fenton 1934- *BlkOlyM [port]*
**Russell**, William Fletcher, III 1950- *WhoEnt 92*
**Russell**, William Folsom 1963- *WhoRel 92*
**Russell**, William L. 1910- *IntWW 91*
**Russell**, William Lawson 1910- *AmMWSc 92*
**Russell**, William Martin 1947- *IntAu&W 91, IntWW 91, Who 92*
**Russell**, William Robert 1913- *Who 92*
**Russell**, William T 1920- *AmMWSc 92*
**Russell**, Willy 1947- *ConTFT 9, WrDr 92*
**Russell-Davis**, John Darelan 1912- *Who 92*
**Russell of Liverpool**, Baron 1952- *Who 92*
**Russell Taylor**, Elisabeth 1930- *ConAu 34NR, WrDr 92*
**Russell Vick**, Arnold Oughtred *Who 92*
**Russen**, David *ScFEYrs*
**Russen**, Eric Justin 1974- *WhoEnt 92*
**Russen**, Lynn Noelle Schuette 1970- *WhoEnt 92*
**Russen**, Robert L. 1946- *WhoEnt 92*
**Russer**, Maximilian F. 1939- *WhoRel 92*
**Russert**, Timothy J. *LesBEnT 92*
**Russert-Given**, Jan Lynne 1949- *WhoFI 92*
**Russett**, Bruce Martin 1935- *WrDr 92*
**Russett**, Cynthia Eagle 1937- *WrDr 92*

**Russey,** William Edward 1939- *AmMWSc 92*
**Russfield,** Agnes Burt 1917- *AmMWSc 92*
**Russi,** Gary Dean 1946- *AmMWSc 92*
**Russi,** Simon 1911- *AmMWSc 92*
**Russick,** Bertram Warren 1921- *WhoMW 92*
**Russin,** Darius Giles 1953- *WhoMW 92*
**Russin,** Nicholas Charles 1922- *AmMWSc 92*
**Russki,** Nicholas 1854-1918 *FacFETw*
**Russman,** Richard 1947- *WhoAmP 91*
**Russo,** Albert *DrAPF 91*
**Russo,** Albert 1943- *IntAu&W 91*
**Russo,** Alvin Leon 1924- *WhoWest 92*
**Russo,** Anne P. *DrAPF 91*
**Russo,** Anthony E 1926- *WhoAmP 91*
**Russo,** Anthony Gennaro 1962- *WhoFI 92*
**Russo,** Anthony Joseph 1953- *WhoFI 92*
**Russo,** Anthony R 1937- *AmMWSc 92*
**Russo,** David C *WhoAmP 91*
**Russo,** Dennis Charles 1950- *AmMWSc 92*
**Russo,** Diane Lucille 1961- *WhoRel 92*
**Russo,** Donna Marie 1963- *WhoAmL 92*
**Russo,** Edwin Price 1938- *AmMWSc 92*
**Russo,** Emanuel Joseph 1934- *AmMWSc 92*
**Russo,** Gene C 1935- *WhoAmP 91*
**Russo,** John A, Jr 1933- *AmMWSc 92*
**Russo,** John Francis 1933- *WhoAmP 91*
**Russo,** John Peter 1943- *WhoEnt 92*
**Russo,** Jose 1942- *AmMWSc 92, WhoMW 92*
**Russo,** Joseph Martin 1949- *AmMWSc 92*
**Russo,** Joyce Chasse 1938- *WhoRel 92*
**Russo,** Kathie Regan *WhoAmP 91*
**Russo,** Laura 1943- *WhoWest 92*
**Russo,** Marius Thomas 1922- *WhoAmP 91*
**Russo,** Martin A. 1944- *AlmAP 92 [port], WhoMW 92*
**Russo,** Marty 1944- *WhoAmP 91*
**Russo,** Michael Eugene 1939- *AmMWSc 92*
**Russo,** Michael John 1960- *WhoMW 92*
**Russo,** Nancy Felipe 1943- *WhoHisp 92*
**Russo,** Ralph P 1952- *AmMWSc 92*
**Russo,** Raymond Joseph 1944- *AmMWSc 92*
**Russo,** Richard 1949- *ConAu 133*
**Russo,** Richard Donald 1952- *WhoAmL 92*
**Russo,** Richard F 1927- *AmMWSc 92*
**Russo,** Robert Joseph 1955- *WhoRel 92*
**Russo,** Robert Vernon 1958- *WhoWest 92*
**Russo,** Ronald John 1949- *WhoAmL 92*
**Russo,** Roy Lawrence 1935- *AmMWSc 92*
**Russo,** Roy R. 1936- *WhoAmL 92*
**Russo,** Salvatore Franklin 1938- *AmMWSc 92, WhoWest 92*
**Russo,** Thomas Anthony 1943- *WhoAmL 92*
**Russo,** Thomas Joseph 1936- *AmMWSc 92*
**Russo,** Vincent Barney 1944- *WhoEnt 92*
**Russo,** Vincent Joseph 1950- *WhoWest 92*
**Russo,** William 1928- *NewAmDM, WhoEnt 92*
**Russo Jervolino,** Rosa 1936- *IntWW 91*
**Russock,** Howard Israel 1947- *AmMWSc 92*
**Russolo,** Luigi 1885-1947 *NewAmDM*
**Russon,** David 1944- *Who 92*
**Russu,** Irina Maria 1948- *AmMWSc 92*
**Rust,** Bernhard 1883-1945 *BiDExR, EncTR 91 [port]*
**Rust,** Charles Chapin 1935- *AmMWSc 92*
**Rust,** David Maurice 1939- *AmMWSc 92*
**Rust,** Edward B, Jr 1950- *WhoIns 92*
**Rust,** Edward Barry, Jr. 1950- *WhoFI 92, WhoMW 92*
**Rust,** Friedrich Wilhelm 1739-1796 *NewAmDM*
**Rust,** James H. 1940- *WhoRel 92*
**Rust,** James Harold 1936- *AmMWSc 92*
**Rust,** Josef 1907- *IntWW 91*
**Rust,** Joseph C. 1941- *WhoWest 92*
**Rust,** Joseph William 1925- *AmMWSc 92*
**Rust,** Kurt 1942- *WhoAmL 92*
**Rust,** Larry Duwayne 1947- *WhoRel 92*
**Rust,** Lawrence Wayne, Jr 1937- *AmMWSc 92*
**Rust,** Libby Karen 1951- *WhoWest 92*
**Rust,** Michael Keith 1948- *AmMWSc 92*
**Rust,** Nancy S 1928- *WhoAmP 91*
**Rust,** Nicholas Cregg 1946- *WhoWest 92*
**Rust,** Patricia Joan 1958- *WhoEnt 92*
**Rust,** Philip Frederick 1947- *AmMWSc 92*
**Rust,** Richard Henry 1921- *AmMWSc 92*
**Rust,** Richard W 1942- *AmMWSc 92*
**Rust,** Robert E. 1928- *WhoMW 92*
**Rust,** Robert Warren 1928- *WhoAmL 92, WhoFI 92*
**Rust,** S. Murray, III 1939- *WhoFI 92*
**Rust,** Stephen Carl 1952- *WhoRel 92*
**Rust,** Steven Ronald *AmMWSc 92*
**Rust,** Thomas Joseph 1948- *WhoRel 92*
**Rust,** Velma Irene 1914- *AmMWSc 92*
**Rust,** Walter David 1944- *AmMWSc 92*
**Rust,** William P 1826?-1891 *BiInAmS*
**Rustad,** Douglas Scott 1940- *AmMWSc 92*
**Rustad,** Gerald 1944- *WhoAmP 91*
**Rustagi,** Jagdish S 1923- *AmMWSc 92*
**Rustagi,** Krishna Prasad 1932- *AmMWSc 92*
**Rustagi,** Narendra Kumar 1953- *WhoFI 92*
**Rustam,** Mardi Ahmed 1932- *WhoEnt 92, WhoFI 92*
**Rustand,** Jon Arthur 1963- *WhoEnt 92*
**Rustay,** George Allen 1944- *WhoAmL 92*
**Rusted,** Ian Edwin L H 1921- *AmMWSc 92*
**Rusten,** Elmer Mathew 1902- *WhoMW 92*
**Rusterholz,** Barbara Lomas 1945- *WhoMW 92*
**Rusterholz,** Heinrich Rainer 1934- *WhoRel 92*
**Rustgi,** Moti Lal 1929- *AmMWSc 92*
**Rustgi,** Om Prakash 1931- *AmMWSc 92*
**Rustigian,** Robert 1915- *AmMWSc 92*
**Rustin,** Bayard 1910-1987 *AmPeW, FacFETw*
**Rustin,** Jean 1928- *IntWW 91*
**Rustioni,** Aldo 1941- *AmMWSc 92*
**Ruston,** Henry 1929- *AmMWSc 92*
**Ruston,** John Harry Gerald *Who 92*
**Rustvold,** Katherine Jo 1950- *WhoWest 92*
**Rusy,** Ben F 1927- *AmMWSc 92*
**Ruta,** Suzanne *DrAPF 91*
**Rutan,** Elbert L 1943- *AmMWSc 92*
**Rutan,** Richard Glenn 1938- *WhoWest 92*
**Rutberg,** Arthur Sidney 1956- *WhoRel 92*
**Rutberg,** Fredric D. 1945- *WhoAmL 92*
**Rutenberg,** Aaron Charles 1923- *AmMWSc 92*
**Rutenberg,** Morton Wolf 1921- *AmMWSc 92*
**Rutenberg-Rosenberg,** Sharon Leslie 1951- *WhoMW 92*
**Rutford,** Robert Hoxie 1933- *AmMWSc 92*
**Rutger,** John Neil 1934- *AmMWSc 92*
**Rutgers,** Jay G 1924- *AmMWSc 92*
**Rutgers,** Katharine Phillips 1910- *WhoEnt 92*
**Ruth** *EncEarC*
**Ruth,** Babe 1895-1948 *RComAH*
**Ruth,** Byron E 1931- *AmMWSc 92*
**Ruth,** George Herman 1895-1948 *FacFETw [port]*
**Ruth,** James Allan 1946- *AmMWSc 92*
**Ruth,** John Moore 1924- *AmMWSc 92*
**Ruth,** John Nicholas 1934- *WhoAmL 92*
**Ruth,** Lloyd Dee 1947- *WhoFI 92*
**Ruth,** Marsha Diane 1950- *WhoFI 92*
**Ruth,** Martha Cruz *WhoAmP 91*
**Ruth,** Peter McCord 1949- *WhoEnt 92*
**Ruth,** Rodney 1934- *WhoEnt 92*
**Ruth,** Royal Francis 1925- *AmMWSc 92*
**Ruthchild,** Geraldine Quietlake *WhoFI 92*
**Rutherford,** Andrew 1929- *Who 92*
**Rutherford,** Charles 1939- *AmMWSc 92*
**Rutherford,** Clara Beryl 1912- *WhoAmP 91*
**Rutherford,** Derek Thomas Jones 1930- *Who 92*
**Rutherford,** Edward Arnold 1945- *WhoRel 92*
**Rutherford,** Ernest 1871-1937 *FacFETw, WhoNob 90*
**Rutherford,** Gordon Malcolm 1939- *Who 92*
**Rutherford,** Harold Phillip, III 1951- *WhoBlA 92*
**Rutherford,** Herman Graham 1908- *Who 92*
**Rutherford,** Jack Dow 1933- *IntWW 91, WhoMW 92*
**Rutherford,** James Charles 1946- *AmMWSc 92*
**Rutherford,** James L 1950- *WhoAmP 91*
**Rutherford,** James William 1925- *WhoAmP 91*
**Rutherford,** Joel Steven 1959- *WhoRel 92*
**Rutherford,** John 1695-1779 *BlkwCEP*
**Rutherford,** John Garvey 1942- *AmMWSc 92*
**Rutherford,** John L 1924- *AmMWSc 92*
**Rutherford,** Joseph Franklin 1869-1942 *RelLAm 91*
**Rutherford,** Kenneth Gerald 1924- *AmMWSc 92*
**Rutherford,** Leigh Ann Allen 1953- *WhoAmL 92*
**Rutherford,** Malcolm *Who 92*
**Rutherford,** Malcolm John 1939- *AmMWSc 92*
**Rutherford,** Mark 1831-1913 *RfGEnL 91*
**Rutherford,** Michael *DrAPF 91*
**Rutherford,** Paul Harding 1938- *AmMWSc 92*
**Rutherford,** Reid 1952- *WhoFI 92*
**Rutherford,** Robert Lee 1958- *WhoMW 92*
**Rutherford,** Thomas 1924- *Who 92*
**Rutherford,** Thomas Truxtun 1947- *WhoAmP 91*
**Rutherford,** Thomas Truxtun, II 1947- *WhoWest 92*
**Rutherford,** Van Dean 1929- *WhoFI 92*
**Rutherford,** William Drake 1939- *WhoAmP 91*
**Rutherford,** William Fain, Jr. 1953- *WhoAmL 92*
**Rutherford,** William M 1929- *AmMWSc 92*
**Rutherfurd,** Lewis Morris 1816-1892 *BiInAmS*
**Rutherglen,** George A. 1949- *WhoAmL 92*
**Rutherston,** Albert 1881-1953 *TwCPaSc*
**Ruthizer,** Theodore 1948- *WhoAmL 92*
**Ruthman,** Thomas Robert 1933- *WhoFI 92, WhoMW 92*
**Ruthnaswamy,** Elizabeth Kuanghu *Who 92*
**Ruthven** *Who 92*
**Ruthven,** Douglas M 1938- *AmMWSc 92*
**Ruthven,** Kenneth Knowles 1936- *IntWW 91*
**Ruthven of Canberra,** Viscount 1964- *Who 92*
**Rutishauser,** Urs Stephen 1946- *AmMWSc 92*
**Rutkiewicz,** Ignacy 1929- *IntWW 91*
**Rutkin,** Philip 1933- *AmMWSc 92*
**Rutkoff,** Alan Stuart 1952- *WhoAmL 92*
**Rutkowski,** Antoni 1920- *IntWW 91*
**Rutkowski,** James Anthony 1942- *WhoAmP 91*
**Rutkowski,** Lawrence 1953- *WhoAmP 91*
**Rutkowski,** Thaddeus *DrAPF 91*
**Rutland,** Duke of 1919- *Who 92*
**Rutland,** Fairy Davenport 1943- *WhoAmL 92*
**Rutland,** George Patrick 1932- *WhoFI 92*
**Rutland,** Helen Marie 1939- *WhoAmP 91*
**Rutland,** Leon W 1919- *AmMWSc 92*
**Rutland,** Robert Larry 1947- *WhoIns 92*
**Rutland,** William G. 1918- *WhoBlA 92*
**Rutledge,** Archibald 1883-1973 *BenetAL 91*
**Rutledge,** Betty Louise 1937- *WhoRel 92*
**Rutledge,** Carl Thomas 1944- *AmMWSc 92*
**Rutledge,** Charles O 1937- *AmMWSc 92*
**Rutledge,** Charles Ozwin 1937- *WhoMW 92*
**Rutledge,** Daniel Patrick 1945- *WhoMW 92*
**Rutledge,** Delbert Leroy 1925- *AmMWSc 92*
**Rutledge,** Dorothy Stallworth 1930- *AmMWSc 92*
**Rutledge,** Edward 1749-1800 *BlkwEAR*
**Rutledge,** Essie Manuel 1934- *WhoBlA 92*
**Rutledge,** Felix N 1917- *AmMWSc 92*
**Rutledge,** Gene Preston 1925- *AmMWSc 92*
**Rutledge,** Harley Dean 1926- *AmMWSc 92*
**Rutledge,** Ivan Cate 1915- *WhoAmL 92*
**Rutledge,** Jackie Joe 1941- *AmMWSc 92*
**Rutledge,** James Luther 1937- *AmMWSc 92*
**Rutledge,** Jennifer M. 1951- *WhoBlA 92*
**Rutledge,** Jerry Eugene 1936- *WhoIns 92*
**Rutledge,** John 1739-1800 *AmPolLe, BlkwEAR*
**Rutledge,** John Francis 1925- *WhoAmL 92*
**Rutledge,** John L. 1938- *WhoFI 92*
**Rutledge,** Joseph Dela 1928- *AmMWSc 92*
**Rutledge,** Joseph Robert 1952- *WhoEnt 92*
**Rutledge,** Kevin Joseph 1960- *WhoEnt 92*
**Rutledge,** Lester T 1924- *AmMWSc 92*
**Rutledge,** Lewis James 1924- *AmMWSc 92*
**Rutledge,** Michael James 1956- *WhoMW 92*
**Rutledge,** Paul Edmund, III 1953- *WhoIns 92*
**Rutledge,** Philip J. 1925- *WhoBlA 92*
**Rutledge,** Phyllis J 1932- *WhoAmP 91*
**Rutledge,** Robert B 1935- *AmMWSc 92*
**Rutledge,** Robert L 1930- *AmMWSc 92*
**Rutledge,** Roger Keith 1946- *WhoAmL 92*
**Rutledge,** Thomas Alexander 1947- *WhoAmL 92*
**Rutledge,** Thomas Franklin 1921- *AmMWSc 92*
**Rutledge,** W. Bradford 1942- *WhoWest 92*
**Rutledge,** Wiley B 1894-1949 *FacFETw*
**Rutledge,** William Lyman 1952- *WhoBlA 92*
**Rutledge,** William P. 1942- *WhoWest 92*
**Rutledge,** Wyman Coe 1924- *AmMWSc 92*
**Rutman,** Darrett Bruce 1929- *WrDr 92*
**Rutman,** Robert Jesse 1919- *AmMWSc 92*
**Rutner,** Emile 1921- *AmMWSc 92*
**Rutowski,** Ronald Lee 1949- *AmMWSc 92*
**Rutsala,** Vern *DrAPF 91*
**Rutsala,** Vern 1934- *ConPo 91, IntAu&W 91*
**Rutsala,** Vern A. 1934- *WhoWest 92, WrDr 92*
**Rutschky,** Charles William 1923- *AmMWSc 92*
**Rutschow,** Robert Frederick 1931- *WhoAmL 92*
**Rutsky,** Lester *DrAPF 91*
**Rutstein,** Alexander 1929- *WhoMW 92*
**Rutstein,** David W. 1944- *WhoAmL 92, WhoFI 92*
**Rutstein,** Martin S 1940- *AmMWSc 92*
**Rutstein,** Sheldon 1934- *WhoFI 92*
**Rutt,** Cecil Richard 1925- *IntWW 91, Who 92*
**Rutt,** Harry Weaver 1948- *WhoRel 92*
**Rutt,** Susan Elizabeth 1948- *WhoAmP 91*
**Rutt,** Wilmer Mellinger 1934- *WhoMW 92*
**Ruttan,** Susan *WhoEnt 92*
**Ruttan,** Vernon W 1924- *AmMWSc 92*
**Ruttan,** Vernon Wesley 1924- *WhoMW 92*
**Ruttenberg,** Alison Lee 1959- *WhoAmL 92*
**Ruttenberg,** David Paul 1963- *WhoEnt 92*
**Ruttenberg,** Herbert David 1930- *AmMWSc 92*
**Ruttenberg,** Stanley 1926- *AmMWSc 92*
**Ruttencutter,** Brian Boyle 1953- *WhoFI 92*
**Rutter,** Arthur John 1917- *Who 92*
**Rutter,** Cloudsley 1867-1903 *BiInAmS*
**Rutter,** Deborah Frances 1956- *WhoEnt 92*
**Rutter,** Edgar A, Jr 1937- *AmMWSc 92*
**Rutter,** Frank 1876-1937 *ThHEIm*
**Rutter,** Frank 1918- *Who 92*
**Rutter,** Henry Alouis, Jr 1922- *AmMWSc 92*
**Rutter,** John Cleverdon 1919- *Who 92*
**Rutter,** John Milford 1945- *IntWW 91, Who 92*
**Rutter,** Koann Sue 1953- *WhoMW 92*
**Rutter,** Marshall Anthony 1931- *WhoAmL 92*
**Rutter,** Michael 1933- *WrDr 92*
**Rutter,** Michael L *AmMWSc 92*
**Rutter,** Michael Llewellyn 1933- *IntAu&W 91, IntWW 91, Who 92*
**Rutter,** Nathaniel Westlund 1932- *AmMWSc 92*
**Rutter,** Norman Colpoy Simpson 1909- *Who 92*
**Rutter,** Owen 1899-1944 *ScFEYrs*
**Rutter,** Thomas Bell 1935- *WhoAmL 92*
**Rutter,** Trevor John 1934- *Who 92*
**Rutter,** William J 1928- *AmMWSc 92*
**Ruttimann,** Urs E 1938- *AmMWSc 92*
**Ruttinger,** George David 1948- *WhoAmL 92*
**Ruttle,** Henry Samuel 1906- *Who 92*
**Ruttmann,** Walter 1887-1941 *IntDcF 2-2 [port]*
**Rutz,** Lenard O 1924- *AmMWSc 92*
**Rutz,** Richard Frederick 1919- *AmMWSc 92*
**Rutzen,** Arthur Cooper, Jr. 1947- *WhoFI 92*
**Ruud,** Clayton Olaf 1934- *AmMWSc 92*
**Ruus,** E 1917- *AmMWSc 92*
**Ruusuvuori,** Aarno Emil 1925- *IntWW 91*
**Ruuytel,** Arnold Fyodorovich 1928- *IntWW 91*
**Ruvalcaba,** Rogelio H A 1934- *AmMWSc 92*
**Ruvalcaba-Flores,** Rosemary 1959- *WhoHisp 92*
**Ruvalds,** John 1940- *AmMWSc 92*
**Ruvolo,** James 1948- *WhoAmP 91*
**Ruwart,** David Peter *WhoAmL 92*
**Ruwart,** Mary Jean 1949- *AmMWSc 92*
**Ruwe,** Dean Melvin 1938- *WhoFI 92*
**Ruwe,** Robert P. 1941- *WhoAmL 92*
**Ruwe,** William David 1953- *AmMWSc 92*
**Ruwet,** Joseph N 1917- *WhoAmP 91*
**Ruwitch,** Robert Simon 1914- *WhoFI 92*
**Ruwwe,** William Otto 1930- *WhoMW 92*
**Rux,** Bruce MacKenzie 1946- *WhoRel 92*
**Ruxin,** Paul Theodore 1943- *WhoAmL 92*
**Ruxton,** George Frederick 1820-1848 *BenetAL 91*
**Ruyan,** Jerry Lee 1946- *WhoMW 92*
**Ruybalid,** Louis Arthur 1925- *WhoWest 92*
**Ruyle,** Kim Ernest 1953- *WhoMW 92*
**Ruyle,** William Vance 1920- *AmMWSc 92*
**Ruz,** Helen *EncAmaz 91*
**Ruza,** Steven Barry 1962- *WhoAmL 92*
**Ruzbasan,** Anthony 1947- *WhoMW 92*
**Ruze,** John 1916- *AmMWSc 92*
**Ruzicka,** Francis Frederick, Jr 1917- *AmMWSc 92*
**Ruzicka,** Leopold Stephen 1887-1976 *WhoNob 90*
**Ruzicka,** Mary Helen 1945- *WhoEnt 92*
**Ruzow,** Daniel Arthur 1951- *WhoAmL 92*
**Rwabwogo,** Leo *BlkOlyM*
**Ryabinkina,** Yelena Lvovna 1941- *IntWW 91*
**Ryabov,** Yakov Petrovich 1928- *IntWW 91*
**Ryal,** David Lowell 1953- *WhoWest 92*
**Ryal,** Dick 1945- *WhoEnt 92*
**Ryall,** Alan S, Jr 1931- *AmMWSc 92*
**Ryals,** George Lynwood, Jr 1941- *AmMWSc 92*
**Ryan,** Abram Joseph 1838-1886 *BenetAL 91*
**Ryan,** Adrian 1920- *TwCPaSc*
**Ryan,** Agnes 1878-1954 *AmPeW*
**Ryan,** Agnes C. 1928- *WhoBlA 92*
**Ryan,** Alan 1940- *WrDr 92*
**Ryan,** Alan James 1940- *IntWW 91, Who 92*

**Ryan**, Allan James 1915- *AmMWSc 92*
**Ryan**, Amy Elizabeth 1963- *WhoFI 92*
**Ryan**, Anne Webster 1927- *AmMWSc 92*
**Ryan**, Arnold W 1951- *WhoAmP 91*
**Ryan**, Arthur Frederick 1942- *WhoFI 92*
**Ryan**, Arthur N. *IntMPA 92*
**Ryan**, Arthur Norman 1938- *WhoEnt 92, WhoWest 92*
**Ryan**, Bill Chatten 1928- *AmMWSc 92*
**Ryan**, Carl Ray 1938- *AmMWSc 92*
**Ryan**, Carol Crawford 1936- *WhoMW 92*
**Ryan**, Cathrine Smith 1930- *WhoWest 92*
**Ryan**, Cecil Benjamin 1916- *AmMWSc 92*
**Ryan**, Charles Barbour 1950- *WhoFI 92*
**Ryan**, Charles Edward 1940- *WhoFI 92*
**Ryan**, Charles Edward, Jr 1938- *AmMWSc 92*
**Ryan**, Charles F 1941- *AmMWSc 92*
**Ryan**, Charles J, Jr 1936- *WhoAmP 91*
**Ryan**, Christopher Nigel 1929- *Who 92*
**Ryan**, Christopher Paul 1955- *WhoAmL 92*
**Ryan**, Christopher Paul 1959- *WhoAmL 92*
**Ryan**, Clarence Augustine, Jr 1931- *AmMWSc 92, WhoWest 92*
**Ryan**, Clarence E, Jr *AmMWSc 92*
**Ryan**, Corinne Marie 1947- *WhoMW 92*
**Ryan**, Daberath 1946- *WhoWest 92*
**Ryan**, Dale Scott 1947- *AmMWSc 92*
**Ryan**, Dana Lynn 1955- *WhoAmL 92*
**Ryan**, Daniel Joseph 1961- *WhoIns 92*
**Ryan**, Daniel Leo 1930- *WhoMW 92, WhoRel 92*
**Ryan**, Daniel Nolan 1930- *WhoFI 92*
**Ryan**, Dave *AmMWSc 92*
**Ryan**, David George 1937- *AmMWSc 92*
**Ryan**, Denis Edgar 1928- *Who 92*
**Ryan**, Derek 1954- *Who 92*
**Ryan**, Donald Edwin 1935- *AmMWSc 92*
**Ryan**, Donald F 1930- *AmMWSc 92*
**Ryan**, Donald Patrick 1930- *WhoMW 92*
**Ryan**, Douglas Earl 1922- *AmMWSc 92*
**Ryan**, Edward J., Jr. 1953- *WhoWest 92*
**Ryan**, Edward L 1939- *WhoAmP 91*
**Ryan**, Edward McNeill 1920- *AmMWSc 92*
**Ryan**, Edward Patrick 1946- *WhoFI 92*
**Ryan**, Edward W. 1932- *WhoFI 92*
**Ryan**, Edwin *WhoAmL 92*
**Ryan**, Finley Leroy, Jr 1933- *WhoAmP 91*
**Ryan**, Fran *ConTFT 9*
**Ryan**, Frank 1931- *IntWW 91*
**Ryan**, Frederick Joseph, Jr. 1955- *WhoWest 92*
**Ryan**, Frederick Merk 1932- *AmMWSc 92*
**Ryan**, George Francis 1956- *WhoFI 92*
**Ryan**, George Frisbie 1921- *AmMWSc 92*
**Ryan**, George H 1934- *WhoAmP 91*
**Ryan**, George H., Sr. 1934- *WhoMW 92*
**Ryan**, George William 1939- *WhoMW 92*
**Ryan**, Gerard Charles 1931- *Who 92*
**Ryan**, Harold L. 1923- *WhoAmL 92, WhoWest 92*
**Ryan**, Herbert 1921- *WhoAmP 91*
**Ryan**, Herbert Joseph 1931- *WhoRel 92*
**Ryan**, Hewson A. d1991 *NewYTBS 91*
**Ryan**, Howard Chris 1916- *WhoAmP 91*
**Ryan**, J. Harold d1961 *LesBEnT 92*
**Ryan**, J. Richard 1929- *WhoAmL 92*
**Ryan**, Jack d1991 *NewYTBS 91*
**Ryan**, Jack 1925- *WhoMW 92*
**Ryan**, Jack A 1929- *AmMWSc 92*
**Ryan**, Jack Lewis 1933- *AmMWSc 92*
**Ryan**, James Anthony 1943- *AmMWSc 92*
**Ryan**, James Edward 1935- *WhoMW 92*
**Ryan**, James Frederick 1928- *WhoAmL 92*
**Ryan**, James Harry 1943- *WhoWest 92*
**Ryan**, James Herbert 1931- *WhoFI 92*
**Ryan**, James L *WhoAmP 91*
**Ryan**, James Leo 1932- *WhoAmL 92, WhoMW 92*
**Ryan**, James M 1932- *AmMWSc 92*
**Ryan**, James Michael 1947- *AmMWSc 92*
**Ryan**, James Patrick 1947- *AmMWSc 92*
**Ryan**, James Smith 1931- *WhoRel 92*
**Ryan**, James Walter 1935- *AmMWSc 92*
**Ryan**, Jane G 1940- *WhoAmP 91*
**Ryan**, Janice E. *WhoRel 92*
**Ryan**, Jean Ann 1950- *WhoEnt 92*
**Ryan**, Jerry David 1956- *WhoWest 92*
**Ryan**, Jerry Lee 1961- *WhoMW 92*
**Ryan**, John 1921- *WrDr 92*
**Ryan**, John 1925- *WrDr 92*
**Ryan**, John 1940- *Who 92*
**Ryan**, John Augustine 1869-1945 *AmPeW, RelLAm 91*
**Ryan**, John Barry 1933- *WhoRel 92*
**Ryan**, John Bruce 1944- *WhoFI 92*
**Ryan**, John C 1941- *WhoAmP 91*
**Ryan**, John Clemens 1959- *WhoFI 92*
**Ryan**, John Donald 1921- *AmMWSc 92*
**Ryan**, John E, Jr 1939- *WhoIns 92*
**Ryan**, John Edward 1941- *WhoWest 92*
**Ryan**, John F 1935- *AmMWSc 92*
**Ryan**, John Francis, Jr. 1944- *WhoFI 92*
**Ryan**, John Gerald Christopher 1921- *IntAu&W 91*
**Ryan**, John M. 1926- *WhoMW 92*
**Ryan**, John Michael 1962- *WhoAmL 92*
**Ryan**, John P. 1938- *IntMPA 92*
**Ryan**, John Peter 1921- *AmMWSc 92*
**Ryan**, John Thomas 1916- *WhoMW 92*
**Ryan**, John Thomas, III 1943- *WhoFI 92*
**Ryan**, John Thomas, Jr. 1912- *WhoFI 92*
**Ryan**, John William 1926- *AmMWSc 92*
**Ryan**, Jon Michael 1943- *AmMWSc 92*
**Ryan**, Joseph Benjamin 1954- *WhoFI 92*
**Ryan**, Joseph J *WhoAmP 91*
**Ryan**, Joseph Thomas 1913- *WhoRel 92*
**Ryan**, Joseph W., Jr. 1948- *WhoAmL 92*
**Ryan**, Julian Gilbert 1913- *AmMWSc 92*
**Ryan**, Julie Ann 1959- *WhoMW 92*
**Ryan**, Kathleen Marie 1937- *WhoRel 92*
**Ryan**, Kay *DrAPF 91*
**Ryan**, Kenneth John 1926- *AmMWSc 92*
**Ryan**, Kevin Durwood 1961- *WhoWest 92*
**Ryan**, Kevin M 1939- *WhoIns 92*
**Ryan**, Kevin Matthew 1939- *WhoFI 92*
**Ryan**, Laurence *Who 92*
**Ryan**, Lehan Jerome 1935- *WhoAmL 92*
**Ryan**, Leo Vincent 1927- *WhoFI 92, WhoMW 92*
**Ryan**, Leonard Eames 1930- *WhoAmL 92*
**Ryan**, Linda Marie 1955- *WhoMW 92*
**Ryan**, Liz 1959- *WhoEnt 92*
**Ryan**, Louis Farthing 1947- *WhoAmL 92, WhoFI 92*
**Ryan**, Marah Ellis 1866-1934 *TwCWW 91*
**Ryan**, Margaret *DrAPF 91*
**Ryan**, Margaret Mary 1925- *WhoAmP 91*
**Ryan**, Mark Douglas 1952- *WhoEnt 92*
**Ryan**, Mark Xavier 1963- *WhoAmL 92*
**Ryan**, Marsha Ann 1947- *WhoBlA 92*
**Ryan**, Mary Elizabeth *DrAPF 91*
**Ryan**, Mary Gene 1953- *WhoWest 92*
**Ryan**, Mary Nell H. 1956- *WhoMW 92*
**Ryan**, Mary P. 1945- *ConAu 134*
**Ryan**, Matthew J 1932- *WhoAmP 91*
**Ryan**, Meg 1961- *IntMPA 92, IntWW 91*
**Ryan**, Meg 1963- *ConTFT 9*
**Ryan**, Michael *DrAPF 91*
**Ryan**, Michael 1946- *ConLC 65 [port]*
**Ryan**, Michael Clifford 1948- *WhoAmL 92*
**Ryan**, Michael Cole 1951- *WhoMW 92*
**Ryan**, Michael Edmond 1938- *WhoFI 92*
**Ryan**, Michael Edward 1952- *WhoEnt 92*
**Ryan**, Michael J 1947- *WhoIns 92*
**Ryan**, Michael James, IV 1958- *WhoMW 92*
**Ryan**, Michael Jay 1951- *WhoMW 92*
**Ryan**, Michael Lee 1951- *WhoAmL 92*
**Ryan**, Michael Louis 1945- *WhoFI 92, WhoWest 92*
**Ryan**, Michael T 1925- *AmMWSc 92*
**Ryan**, Mike, II 1951- *WhoFI 92, WhoMW 92*
**Ryan**, Mitchell 1928- *IntMPA 92*
**Ryan**, Nancy M 1938- *IntAu&W 91*
**Ryan**, Nigel *LesBEnT 92, Who 92*
**Ryan**, Nolan 1947- *FacFETw*
**Ryan**, Norman W 1919- *AmMWSc 92*
**Ryan**, Patricia Ann 1931- *WhoRel 92*
**Ryan**, Patricia Maria 1962- *WhoEnt 92*
**Ryan**, Patricia Marie 1960- *WhoFI 92*
**Ryan**, Patrick Daniel 1944- *WhoRel 92*
**Ryan**, Patrick G. 1937- *WhoFI 92, WhoIns 92*
**Ryan**, Patrick J. 1938- *WhoFI 92*
**Ryan**, Patrick Walter 1933- *AmMWSc 92*
**Ryan**, Paul 1955- *TwCPaSc*
**Ryan**, Peter Allen 1923- *IntWW 91, WrDr 92*
**Ryan**, Peter M. 1948- *WhoFI 92*
**Ryan**, Peter Michael 1943- *AmMWSc 92*
**Ryan**, Rachel *WrDr 92*
**Ryan**, Randel Edward, Jr. 1940- *WhoWest 92*
**Ryan**, Reade Haines, Jr. 1937- *WhoAmL 92*
**Ryan**, Richard Alexander 1925- *AmMWSc 92*
**Ryan**, Richard Patrick 1938- *AmMWSc 92*
**Ryan**, Richie 1929- *IntWW 91*
**Ryan**, Rob Paul 1955- *WhoEnt 92*
**Ryan**, Robert Collins 1953- *WhoAmL 92, WhoMW 92*
**Ryan**, Robert Davis 1941- *WhoAmL 92*
**Ryan**, Robert Dean 1933- *AmMWSc 92*
**Ryan**, Robert F 1922- *AmMWSc 92*
**Ryan**, Robert J 1927- *AmMWSc 92*
**Ryan**, Robert J, Jr 1939- *WhoAmP 91*
**Ryan**, Robert Pat 1925- *AmMWSc 92*
**Ryan**, Robert Reynolds 1936- *AmMWSc 92*
**Ryan**, Robert Stone 1928- *WhoAmL 92*
**Ryan**, Robert Thomas 1947- *WhoAmP 91*
**Ryan**, Roger Baker 1932- *AmMWSc 92*
**Ryan**, Rosemary 1939- *WhoFI 92*
**Ryan**, Sheena Ross 1944- *WhoFI 92*
**Ryan**, Sheila Morag Clark *Who 92*
**Ryan**, Simeon P 1922- *AmMWSc 92*
**Ryan**, Steven J 1953- *WhoAmP 91*
**Ryan**, Stewart Richard 1942- *AmMWSc 92*
**Ryan**, Susan Maree 1942- *IntWW 91*
**Ryan**, Terry 1922- *WhoEnt 92*
**Ryan**, Tex *TwCWW 91*
**Ryan**, Thomas 1929- *TwCPaSc*
**Ryan**, Thomas A. *WhoRel 92*
**Ryan**, Thomas Anthony 1936- *Who 92*
**Ryan**, Thomas Arthur, Jr 1940- *AmMWSc 92*
**Ryan**, Thomas John 1943- *AmMWSc 92*
**Ryan**, Thomas Michael 1958- *WhoMW 92*
**Ryan**, Thomas P, Jr 1929- *WhoAmP 91*
**Ryan**, Thomas Patrick 1946- *WhoRel 92*
**Ryan**, Thomas Smyth 1943- *WhoMW 92*
**Ryan**, Thomas Timothy, Jr. 1945- *WhoAmL 92*
**Ryan**, Thomas William 1953- *WhoAmL 92*
**Ryan**, Thomas Wilton 1946- *AmMWSc 92*
**Ryan**, Tim *LesBEnT 92*
**Ryan**, Timothy J. 1945- *WhoFI 92*
**Ryan**, Todd Michael 1947- *WhoFI 92*
**Ryan**, Una Scully 1941- *AmMWSc 92*
**Ryan**, Veronica 1956- *TwCPaSc*
**Ryan**, Victor Albert 1920- *AmMWSc 92*
**Ryan**, Vince 1947- *WhoAmP 91*
**Ryan**, Wayne L 1927- *AmMWSc 92*
**Ryan**, William 1948- *WrDr 92*
**Ryan**, William A 1919- *WhoAmP 91*
**Ryan**, William B F 1939- *AmMWSc 92*
**Ryan**, William Clark 1951- *WhoAmL 92*
**Ryan**, William Francis 1925- *WhoRel 92*
**Ryan**, William Frank 1924- *WhoFI 92, WhoMW 92*
**Ryan**, William George 1951- *AmMWSc 92*
**Ryan**, William Joseph 1932- *WhoEnt 92, WhoFI 92*
**Ryan**, William Joseph 1949- *WhoAmP 91*
**Ryan**, William Murray 1922- *WhoAmP 91*
**Ryan-Amundson**, Kristine *WhoMW 92*
**Ryan-White**, Jewell 1943- *WhoBlA 92*
**Ryangina**, Serafima Vasil'evna 1891-1955 *SovUnBD*
**Ryant**, Bradley Erven 1935- *WhoRel 92*
**Ryant**, Charles J, Jr 1920- *AmMWSc 92*
**Ryason**, Porter Raymond 1929- *AmMWSc 92*
**Ryazanov**, David Borisovich 1870-1938 *SovUnBD*
**Ryazanov**, Eldar 1927- *IntWW 91*
**Ryazanov**, El'dar Aleksandrovich 1927- *SovUnBD*
**Ryazhsky**, Georgiy Georgievich 1895-1952 *SovUnBD*
**Ryba**, Earle Richard 1934- *AmMWSc 92*
**Ryback**, Ralph Simon 1940- *AmMWSc 92*
**Rybak**, Michael D 1951- *WhoAmP 91*
**Rybak**, William C 1921- *WhoAmP 91*
**Rybakov**, Aleksei Mironovich 1925- *IntWW 91*
**Rybakov**, Anatoli 1911- *ConAu 135, IntAu&W 91*
**Rybakov**, Anatoliy Naumovich 1911- *IntWW 91, SovUnBD*
**Rybarczyk**, Robert L 1938- *WhoAmP 91*
**Rybczynski**, Tadeusz Mieczyslaw 1923- *Who 92*
**Rybczynski**, Witold 1943- *WrDr 92*
**Rybicka**, Zofia 1920- *IntAu&W 91*
**Rybicki**, Irvin W. 1924- *DcTwDes*
**Rybolt**, John E. *WhoRel 92*
**Rybolt**, Robert Marsh 1913- *WhoAmL 92*
**Rybot**, Doris *WrDr 92*
**Ryburn**, Hubert James 1897- *Who 92*
**Ryce**, Donald Theodore 1943- *WhoAmL 92*
**Rycheck**, Mark Rule 1937- *AmMWSc 92*
**Rycheck**, Russell Rule 1932- *AmMWSc 92*
**Rychecky**, Helen Rose 1922- *WhoMW 92*
**Rychlak**, Joseph F. 1928- *WrDr 92*
**Rychlak**, Joseph Frank 1928- *WhoMW 92*
**Rychlak**, Ronald Joseph 1957- *WhoAmL 92*
**Rychlewski**, Jan 1934- *IntWW 91*
**Rychter-Danczyk**, Veronica Ann 1957- *WhoMW 92*
**Ryckman**, DeVere Wellington 1924- *AmMWSc 92*
**Ryckman**, Louise 1946- *WhoAmP 91*
**Ryckman**, Raymond Edward 1917- *AmMWSc 92*
**Ryckmans**, Pierre 1935- *IntWW 91*
**Rycroft**, Charles 1914- *WrDr 92*
**Rycroft**, Donald C 1938- *WhoIns 92*
**Rycroft**, Hedley Brian 1918- *IntWW 91*
**Rycroft**, Richard Newton 1918- *Who 92*
**Rydalch**, Ann 1935- *WhoAmP 91*
**Rydbeck**, Olof 1913- *IntWW 91, Who 92*
**Rydder**, Niels Leegaard 1952- *WhoWest 92*
**Rydell**, Catherine M 1950- *WhoAmP 91*
**Rydell**, Charlene B *WhoAmP 91*
**Rydell**, Chris *ConTFT 9*
**Rydell**, Christopher *ConTFT 9*
**Rydell**, Forbes *WrDr 92*
**Rydell**, Mark *WhoEnt 92A*
**Rydell**, Mark 1934- *IntMPA 92*
**Rydell**, Roger Paul 1955- *WhoMW 92*
**Rydell**, Sheila Veronica 1964- *WhoEnt 92*
**Rydell**, Wendell *WrDr 92*
**Rydell**, Wendy 1927- *WrDr 92*
**Ryden**, Ernest Edwin, Jr. 1931- *WhoRel 92*
**Ryden**, Fred Ward 1919- *AmMWSc 92*
**Ryden**, Hope *WrDr 92*
**Ryden**, Kenneth 1917- *Who 92*
**Ryder** *Who 92*
**Ryder**, Arthur John 1913- *WrDr 92*
**Ryder**, D F 1919- *AmMWSc 92*
**Ryder**, David James 1938- *WhoMW 92*
**Ryder**, Edward Alexander 1931- *Who 92*
**Ryder**, Edward Jonas 1929- *AmMWSc 92*
**Ryder**, Eric Charles 1915- *Who 92*
**Ryder**, Gail Ruth 1948- *WhoWest 92*
**Ryder**, Georgia Atkins 1924- *WhoBlA 92*
**Ryder**, Hal 1950- *WhoWest 92*
**Ryder**, Herboth Strother 1928- *WhoAmL 92*
**Ryder**, Joanne 1946- *ConAu 133, SmATA 65 [port]*
**Ryder**, John Adam 1852-1895 *BiInAmS*
**Ryder**, John Douglass 1907- *AmMWSc 92*
**Ryder**, John Louis *WhoAmP 91*
**Ryder**, Jonathan *IntAu&W 91X, WrDr 92*
**Ryder**, Kenneth, Jr 1940- *WhoAmP 91*
**Ryder**, Kenneth William, Jr 1945- *AmMWSc 92*
**Ryder**, Lois Juanita 1931- *WhoWest 92*
**Ryder**, M. L. 1927- *WrDr 92*
**Ryder**, Mahler B. 1937- *WhoBlA 92*
**Ryder**, Mark Ernest 1958- *WhoFI 92*
**Ryder**, Oliver A 1946- *AmMWSc 92*
**Ryder**, Oliver Allison 1946- *WhoWest 92*
**Ryder**, Peter 1942- *Who 92*
**Ryder**, Peter Hugh Dudley 1913- *Who 92*
**Ryder**, Raymond Teele 1957- *WhoEnt 92*
**Ryder**, Richard Andrew 1949- *Who 92*
**Ryder**, Richard Armitage 1931- *AmMWSc 92*
**Ryder**, Richard Daniel 1944- *AmMWSc 92*
**Ryder**, Richard Hood Jack Dudley 1940- *Who 92*
**Ryder**, Robert E D 1907-1986 *FacFETw*
**Ryder**, Robert J 1931- *AmMWSc 92*
**Ryder**, Robert Thomas 1941- *AmMWSc 92*
**Ryder**, Ronald Arch 1928- *AmMWSc 92*
**Ryder**, Sandra Smith 1949- *WhoFI 92*
**Ryder**, Sarah *DrAPF 91*
**Ryder**, Sophie 1963- *TwCPaSc*
**Ryder**, Thom *WrDr 92*
**Ryder**, Thomas Gerard 1932- *WhoAmL 92*
**Ryder**, Tom 1949- *WhoAmP 91*
**Ryder**, Winona 1971- *IntMPA 92, News 91 [port]*
**Ryder Of Eaton Hastings**, Baron 1916- *IntWW 91, Who 92*
**Ryder Of Warsaw**, Baroness 1923- *IntWW 91, Who 92*
**Rydholm**, Ralph Williams 1937- *WhoEnt 92, WhoFI 92*
**Rydill**, Louis Joseph 1922- *Who 92*
**Rydin**, Bo 1932- *IntWW 91*
**Rydon**, Norman d1991 *Who 92N*
**Rydz**, John S 1925- *AmMWSc 92*
**Rydz-Smigly**, Edward 1886-1941 *EncTR 91 [port]*
**Rydzel**, James A. 1946- *WhoAmL 92*
**Rye**, C. Richard 1935- *IntWW 91*
**Rye**, Danny Michael 1946- *AmMWSc 92*
**Rye**, David Blake 1943- *WhoAmP 91*
**Rye**, Karl Erik 1952- *WhoFI 92*
**Rye**, Robert O 1938- *AmMWSc 92*
**Ryeburn**, David 1935- *AmMWSc 92*
**Ryel**, Lawrence Atwell 1930- *AmMWSc 92*
**Ryer**, Michael Edward 1959- *WhoRel 92*
**Ryerson**, Adolphus Egerton 1803-1882 *RelLAm 91*
**Ryerson**, Alice J. *DrAPF 91*
**Ryerson**, Fairy Electa 1914- *WhoWest 92*
**Ryerson**, George Douglas 1934- *AmMWSc 92, WhoMW 92*
**Ryerson**, Joseph L 1918- *AmMWSc 92*
**Ryerson**, Paul Sommer 1946- *WhoAmL 92*
**Ryerson**, Timothy Dale 1952- *WhoEnt 92*
**Ryerson**, Victor David 1947- *WhoAmL 92*
**Ryerson**, W. Newton 1902- *WhoFI 92*
**Ryff**, John V 1932- *AmMWSc 92*
**Ryga**, George 1932- *BenetAL 91*
**Ryge**, Gunnar 1916- *AmMWSc 92*
**Rygiel**, Alexander John, Sr. 1937- *WhoFI 92*
**Rygiewicz**, Paul Thaddeus 1952- *WhoWest 92*
**Ryherd**, Larry Earl 1940- *WhoIns 92, WhoMW 92*
**Rykbost**, Kenneth Albert 1941- *AmMWSc 92*
**Ryken**, Leland 1942- *WhoMW 92, WrDr 92*
**Ryker**, Lee Chester 1940- *AmMWSc 92*
**Ryker**, Norman J., Jr. 1926- *WhoFI 92, WhoMW 92*
**Rykiel**, Sonia 1930- *DcTwDes, IntWW 91*
**Rykov**, Aleksey Ivanovich 1881-1938 *SovUnBD*
**Rykov**, Alexei Ivanovich 1881-1938 *FacFETw*
**Rykov**, Vasily Nazarovich 1918- *IntWW 91*
**Rykwert**, Joseph 1926- *Who 92, WrDr 92*
**Ryland**, Adolphine Mary 1903-1983 *TwCPaSc*
**Ryland**, David Ronald 1945- *WhoAmL 92*
**Ryland**, John 1900- *Who 92*

**Ryland,** Ralph Benjamin, Jr. 1953- *WhoEnt 92*
**Ryland,** Timothy Richard Godfrey F 1938- *Who 92*
**Ryland,** William Hugh 1934- *WhoFI 92*
**Rylander,** Henry Grady, Jr 1921- *AmMWSc 92*
**Rylander,** Michael Kent 1935- *AmMWSc 92*
**Rylander,** Robert Allan 1947- *WhoWest 92*
**Rylands,** George Humphrey Wolferstan 1902- *Who 92*
**Rylant,** Cynthia 1954- *SmATA 13AS [port], WrDr 92*
**Ryle,** Anthony 1927- *WrDr 92*
**Ryle,** Edward Joseph 1930- *WhoRel 92*
**Ryle,** Kenneth Sherriff 1912- *Who 92*
**Ryle,** Martin 1918-1984 *ConAu 133, WhoNob 90*
**Ryle,** Michael 1927- *ConAu 133*
**Ryle,** Michael Thomas 1927- *Who 92*
**Ryles,** Nancy 1937- *WhoAmP 91*
**Ryles,** Scott Allen 1959- *WhoFI 92*
**Ryles,** Tim *WhoAmP 91*
**Ryles,** Tim 1941- *WhoIns 92*
**Rylov,** Arkadiy Aleksandrovich 1870-1939 *SovUnBD*
**Rymal,** Kenneth Stuart 1922- *AmMWSc 92*
**Ryman,** Geoff *TwCSFW 91*
**Ryman,** Geoff 1951- *ConAu 134*
**Ryman,** John 1930- *Who 92*
**Ryman,** Robert 1930- *WorArt 1980 [port]*
**Rymar,** Julian W. 1919- *WhoFI 92, WhoMW 92*
**Rymer,** Judith Marquis 1940- *WhoWest 92*
**Rymer,** Pamela Ann 1941- *WhoAmL 92, WhoAmP 91*
**Rymer,** Richard A. 1939- *WhoMW 92*
**Rymer,** S. Brad, III 1953- *WhoFI 92*
**Rymer,** Thomas Arrington 1925- *WhoAmP 91*
**Rymer,** William Zev 1939- *AmMWSc 92*
**Rymer-Jones,** John Murray 1897- *Who 92*
**Rymon,** Larry Maring 1934- *AmMWSc 92*
**Rynasiewicz,** Joseph 1917- *AmMWSc 92*
**Rynbrandt,** Donald Jay 1940- *AmMWSc 92*
**Rynd,** James Arthur 1942- *AmMWSc 92*
**Rynd,** Richard *WhoAmP 91*
**Ryndin,** Vadim Fedorovich 1902-1974 *SovUnBD*
**Rynear,** Nina Cox 1916- *WhoWest 92*
**Rynearson,** Earl 1938- *WhoRel 92*
**Rynearson,** Rodney Richard 1935- *WhoMW 92, WhoRel 92*
**Rynecki,** Steven Bernard 1944- *WhoAmL 92*
**Rynew,** Arden Nicholas 1943- *WhoEnt 92*
**Ryniker,** Bruce Walter Durland 1940- *WhoWest 92*
**Ryniker,** Roy Stephen 1957- *WhoFI 92*
**Rynkiewicz,** Walter Paul 1930- *WhoAmL 92*
**Rynn,** Nathan 1923- *AmMWSc 92*
**Rynne,** Etienne Andrew 1932- *IntWW 91*
**Rynning,** Ole 1809-1838 *BenetAL 91*
**Ryntz,** Rose A 1957- *AmMWSc 92*
**Ryntz,** Rose Ann 1957- *WhoMW 92*
**Ryom,** Peter 1937- *NewAmDM*
**Ryon,** Allen Dale 1920- *AmMWSc 92*
**Rypdal,** Terje 1947- *ConCom 92*
**Rypka,** Eugene Weston 1925- *AmMWSc 92, WhoWest 92*
**Ryrie,** William 1928- *Who 92*
**Ryrie,** William Sinclair 1928- *IntWW 91, WhoFI 92*
**Rys,** John Lawrence 1937- *WhoAmL 92*
**Rys-Rozsevac,** Jan 1901-1946 *BiDExR*
**Rysanek,** Leonie 1926- *IntWW 91, NewAmDM, WhoEnt 92*
**Ryschkewitsch,** George Eugene 1929- *AmMWSc 92*
**Ryser,** Fred A, Jr 1920- *AmMWSc 92*
**Ryser,** Hugues Jean-Paul 1926- *AmMWSc 92*
**Ryskamp,** Carroll Joseph 1930- *WhoFI 92*
**Ryskamp,** Kenneth Lee 1932- *WhoAmL 92*
**Ryskind,** Morris 1895-1985 *FacFETw*
**Ryssdal,** Rolv Einar 1914- *IntWW 91*
**Ryste,** Ruth Anlaug 1932- *IntWW 91*
**Rystephanick,** Raymond Gary 1940- *AmMWSc 92*
**Rysz,** Anthony M. *WhoRel 92*
**Rytand,** David A 1909- *AmMWSc 92*
**Rytkheu,** Yuriy Sergeyevich 1930- *IntAu&W 91, IntWW 91*
**Rytting,** Joseph Howard 1942- *AmMWSc 92*
**Ryu,** Jisoo Vinsky 1941- *AmMWSc 92*
**Ryugo,** Kay 1920- *AmMWSc 92*
**Ryun,** James Ronald 1947- *FacFETw*
**Ryutin,** Martem'yan Nikitich 1890-1937 *SovUnBD*
**Ryuytel',** Arnol'd Feodorovich 1928- *SovUnBD*
**Rywkin,** Michael 1925- *WhoFI 92*
**Ryzhkov,** Nikolai Ivanovich 1929- *IntWW 91*
**Ryzhkov,** Nikolay Ivanovich 1929- *SovUnBD*
**Ryzlak,** Maria Teresa 1938- *AmMWSc 92*
**Ryznar,** Caroline Lucille 1950- *WhoEnt 92*
**Rzad,** Stefan Jacek 1938- *AmMWSc 92*
**Rzeminski,** Peter Joseph 1947- *WhoFI 92, WhoMW 92*
**Rzepecki,** Mark Stanley 1963- *WhoMW 92*
**Rzeszotarski,** Waclaw Janusz 1936- *AmMWSc 92*
**Rzewnicki,** Janet 1953- *WhoAmP 91*
**Rzewski,** Frederic 1938- *ConCom 92, NewAmDM*
**Rzheshevsky,** Aleksandr Georgievich 1903-1967 *SovUnBD*
**Rzhevsky,** Vladimir Vasilevich 1919- *IntWW 91*

# S

**S**, Elizabeth Von *IntAu&W 91X*
**S.**, Svend Otto *SmATA 67*
**S.L.C.** *ConAu 135*
**S. Millan**, Natacha *WhoHisp 92*
**S.S.** *ConAu 36NR*
**Sa**, Angelo Calmon de 1935- *IntWW 91*
**Saacke**, Richard George 1931- *AmMWSc 92*
**Saad**, Joseph Kanan 1948- *WhoWest 92*
**Saada**, Adel Selim 1934- *AmMWSc 92*
**Saadian**, Javid 1953- *WhoFI 92*
**Saady**, Marlow 1953- *WhoEnt 92*
**Saal**, Frank Edward 1947- *WhoMW 92*
**Saal**, Jennifer *WrDr 92*
**Saal**, Jocelyn *WrDr 92*
**Saalfeld**, Fred Eric 1935- *AmMWSc 92*
**Saalfeld**, Richard L. 1944- *WhoFI 92*
**Saaock**, Eileen F 1927- *IntAu&W 91*
**Saar**, Betye 1926- *NotBlAW 92*
**Saar**, Betye I. 1926- *WhoBlA 92*
**Saar**, Frederick Arthur 1946- *WhoWest 92*
**Saari**, Albin Toivo 1930- *WhoWest 92*
**Saari**, Donald Gene 1940- *AmMWSc 92, WhoMW 92*
**Saari**, Eugene E 1936- *AmMWSc 92*
**Saari**, Jack Theodore 1943- *AmMWSc 92*
**Saari**, Kathryn Celeste 1948- *WhoMW 92*
**Saari**, Walfred Spencer 1932- *AmMWSc 92*
**Saari-Nordhaus**, Raaidah 1962- *WhoMW 92*
**Saariaho**, Kaija 1952- *ConCom 92*
**Saarinen**, Aarne 1913- *IntWW 91*
**Saarinen**, Eero 1910-1961 *DcTwDes, FacFETw, ModArCr 2 [port]*
**Saarinen**, Eliel 1873-1950 *DcTwDes, FacFETw*
**Saarinen**, Louise Gessellius 1879-1968 *DcTwDes*
**Saarlas**, Maido 1930- *AmMWSc 92*
**Saask**, Aapo 1943- *WhoFI 92*
**Saatchi**, Charles 1943- *IntWW 91, Who 92, WhoFI 92*
**Saatchi**, Maurice 1946- *IntWW 91, Who 92, WhoFI 92*
**Saaty**, Thomas L 1926- *AmMWSc 92*
**Saaty**, Thomas Lorie 1926- *WhoFI 92*
**Saavedra**, Charles James 1941- *WhoFI 92*
**Saavedra**, Edgardo 1963- *WhoHisp 92*
**Saavedra**, Henry *WhoAmP 91, WhoHisp 92*
**Saavedra**, Juan M 1941- *AmMWSc 92, WhoHisp 92*
**Saavedra**, Kiki *WhoHisp 92*
**Saavedra**, Kleber 1945- *WhoHisp 92*
**Saavedra**, Leonel Orlando 1950- *WhoHisp 92*
**Saavedra**, Louis 1933- *WhoHisp 92*
**Saavedra**, Louis E *WhoAmP 91*
**Saavedra**, Louis F 1933- *WhoWest 92*
**Saavedra**, Richard 1954- *WhoHisp 92*
**Saavedra**, Ro 1952- *WhoWest 92*
**Saavedra Ceron**, Alvaro de *HisDSpE*
**Saavedra Guzman**, Antonio de 1570- *HisDSpE*
**Saavedra Lamas**, Carlos 1878-1959 *WhoNob 90*
**Saba** 439-532 *EncEarC*
**Saba**, Elias 1932- *IntWW 91*
**Saba**, George Peter, II 1940- *AmMWSc 92*
**Saba**, Hanna 1909- *IntWW 91*
**Saba**, Joseph Philip 1947- *WhoAmL 92*
**Saba**, Shoichi 1919- *AmMWSc 92, IntWW 91*
**Saba**, Thomas Maron 1941- *AmMWSc 92*
**Saba**, Umberto 1883-1957 *DcLB 114 [port], FacFETw*
**Saba**, William George 1932- *AmMWSc 92*
**Sabacky**, M Jerome 1939- *AmMWSc 92*
**Sabadell**, Alberto Jose 1929- *AmMWSc 92*
**Sabadell**, Stewart August 1962- *WhoFI 92*
**Sabah**, Ali Khalifa al- 1945- *IntWW 91*
**Sabah**, Jaber al-Ahmad al-Jaber al- 1928- *IntWW 91*
**Sabah**, Jaber al-Ali al-Salem al- 1926- *IntWW 91*
**Sabah**, Saad al-Abdullah al-Salem al- 1930- *IntWW 91*
**Sabah**, Sabah al-Ahmad al-Jaber al- 1929- *IntWW 91*
**Sabah**, Salim al-Sabah al-Salim al- 1937- *IntWW 91*
**Sabah**, Saud Nasir al- 1944- *IntWW 91*
**Saban**, Haim *LesBEnT 92*
**Sabas**, John Robert Ione 1947- *WhoWest 92*
**Sabastian**, Archimandrite 1863-1940 *RelLAm 91*
**Sabata**, Victor de *NewAmDM*
**Sabatell**, Henry P. 1937- *WhoFI 92*
**Sabatelli**, John Raymond 1946- *WhoRel 92*
**Sabatelli**, Philip Michael 1937- *WhoMW 92*
**Sabates**, Felix N. *WhoHisp 92*
**Sabath**, Kenneth Michael 1956- *WhoAmL 92*
**Sabath**, Leon David 1930- *AmMWSc 92*
**Sabatier**, Jose Manuel 1943- *WhoHisp 92*
**Sabatier**, Paul 1854-1941 *WhoNob 90*
**Sabatier**, Robert 1923- *IntAu&W 91, IntWW 91*
**Sabatini**, David Domingo 1931- *AmMWSc 92*
**Sabatini**, Gabriela 1970- *IntWW 91*
**Sabatini**, John A 1945- *WhoAmP 91*
**Sabatini**, Lawrence 1930- *WhoRel 92, WhoWest 92*
**Sabatini**, Lawrence John 1919- *Who 92*
**Sabatini**, Robert N 1936- *WhoAmP 91*
**Sabatini**, Steven Thomas 1951- *WhoFI 92*
**Sabato**, Ernesto 1911- *BenetAL 91, IntWW 91*
**Sabato**, George Frank 1947- *WhoWest 92*
**Sabato**, Jorge Federico 1938- *IntWW 91*
**Sabattani**, Aurelio 1912- *IntWW 91, WhoRel 92*
**Sabau**, Carmen Sybile 1933- *WhoMW 92*
**Sabbadini**, Edris Rinaldo 1930- *AmMWSc 92*
**Sabbagh**, Harold A 1937- *AmMWSc 92*
**Sabbagh**, Harold Abraham 1937- *WhoMW 92*
**Sabbagh**, Hussein Rashid al- 1938- *IntWW 91*
**Sabbaghian**, Mehdy 1935- *AmMWSc 92*
**Sabbah**, Hassan i *ConAu 133*
**Sabbah**, Michael *WhoRel 92*
**Sabbah**, Michel 1933- *IntWW 91*
**Sabban**, Esther Louise 1948- *AmMWSc 92*
**Sabbath**, David Jonathan 1958- *WhoEnt 92*
**Sabben-Clare**, Ernest E. 1910- *Who 92*
**Sabben-Clare**, James Paley 1941- *Who 92*
**Sabbert-Muck**, Judith Kay 1952- *WhoMW 92*
**Sabe**, Quien *TwCSFW 91*
**Sabel**, Clara Ann 1932- *AmMWSc 92*
**Sabella**, Joseph Edward 1942- *WhoFI 92*
**Sabelli**, Hector C 1937- *AmMWSc 92*
**Sabelli**, Hector Carlos 1937- *WhoMW 92*
**Sabelli**, Nora Hojvat 1936- *AmMWSc 92*
**Sabelli**, Veronica 1956- *WhoAmL 92*
**Sabellius** *EncEarC*
**Saber**, Aaron Jaan 1946- *AmMWSc 92*
**Saberhagen**, Bret *NewYTBS 91 [port]*
**Saberhagen**, Fred 1930- *TwCSFW 91, WrDr 92*
**Saberhagen**, Fred Thomas 1930- *IntAu&W 91*
**Sabers**, Richard Wayne 1938- *WhoAmL 92, WhoAmP 91, WhoMW 92*
**Sabersky**, Rolf H 1920- *AmMWSc 92*
**Sabes**, William Ruben 1931- *AmMWSc 92*
**Sabesin**, Seymour Marshall 1932- *AmMWSc 92*
**Sabet**, Hormoz 1936- *WhoFI 92*
**Sabet**, Tawfik Younis 1926- *AmMWSc 92*
**Sabetta**, Stephen Arduino 1959- *WhoFI 92*
**Sabey**, Burns Roy 1928- *AmMWSc 92*
**Sabey**, David Randall 1952- *WhoAmL 92*
**Sabey**, John Louis 1925- *WhoWest 92*
**Sabharwal**, Chaman Lal 1937- *AmMWSc 92*
**Sabharwal**, Kulbir 1943- *AmMWSc 92*
**Sabharwal**, Pritam Singh 1937- *AmMWSc 92*
**Sabharwal**, Ranjit Singh 1925- *AmMWSc 92, WhoWest 92*
**Sabhavasu**, Pramual 1927- *IntWW 91*
**Sabia**, Raffaele 1933- *AmMWSc 92*
**Sabian**, Michael Arthur 1942- *WhoAmL 92*
**Sabiani**, Simon Pierre 1888-1956 *BiDExR*
**Sabicas** 1917-1990 *AnObit 1990*
**Sabidussi**, Gert Otto 1929- *AmMWSc 92*
**Sabik**, Joseph Andrew 1943- *WhoMW 92*
**Sabin**, Albert 1906- *FacFETw [port], Who 92*
**Sabin**, Albert B 1906- *AmMWSc 92, IntWW 91*
**Sabin**, Edwin L 1870-1952 *ScFEYrs*
**Sabin**, Gregory Mark 1960- *WhoWest 92*
**Sabin**, Howard Westcott 1916- *Who 92*
**Sabin**, Jack Charles 1921- *WhoFI 92, WhoWest 92*
**Sabin**, John Rogers 1940- *AmMWSc 92*
**Sabin**, Joseph 1821-1881 *BenetAL 91*
**Sabin**, Mark *TwCWW 91*
**Sabin**, Neal Fredric 1956- *WhoEnt 92*
**Sabin**, Paul Robert 1943- *Who 92*
**Sabin**, Thomas Daniel 1936- *AmMWSc 92*
**Sabin**, W John 1941- *WhoAmP 91*
**Sabina** *EncEarC*
**Sabina**, Leslie Robert 1928- *AmMWSc 92*
**Sabine**, Charles Pruden 1941- *WhoWest 92*
**Sabine**, Lorenzo 1803-1877 *BenetAL 91*
**Sabine**, Neville Warde 1910- *Who 92*
**Sabine**, Peter Aubrey 1924- *Who 92*
**Sabine**, Randall Travis 1948- *WhoAmP 91*
**Sabine**, Wallace Clement Ware 1868-1919 *BiInAmS*
**Sabine**, William Henry Waldo 1903- *IntAu&W 91, WrDr 92*
**Sabines**, Jaime 1926- *ConSpAP*
**Sabines**, Luis 1917- *WhoHisp 92*
**Sabins**, Floyd F 1931- *AmMWSc 92*
**Sabinson**, Harvey Barnett 1924- *WhoEnt 92, WhoFI 92*
**Sabinson**, Lee d1991 *NewYTBS 91*
**Sabinson**, Mara Beth 1946- *WhoEnt 92*
**Sabirova**, Malika Abdurakhmanovna 1942- *IntWW 91*
**Sabisky**, Edward Stephen 1932- *AmMWSc 92*
**Sabiston**, Charles Barker, Jr 1933- *AmMWSc 92*
**Sabiston**, David Coston, Jr 1924- *AmMWSc 92, IntWW 91*
**Sablan**, Benigno M *WhoAmP 91*
**Sablan**, David Castro *WhoAmP 91*
**Sablan**, Gregorio C *WhoAmP 91*
**Sablan**, Jesus Rosario *WhoAmP 91*
**Sablan**, Manuel Cabrera *WhoAmP 91*
**Sablan**, Vicente Masga 1948- *WhoAmP 91*
**Sablatash**, Mike 1935- *AmMWSc 92*
**Sable**, Barbara Kinsey 1927- *WhoEnt 92*
**Sable**, Edward George 1924- *AmMWSc 92*
**Sable**, Henry Zodoc 1918- *AmMWSc 92*
**Sable**, Martin Howard 1924- *IntAu&W 91, WrDr 92*
**Sablik**, Martin J 1939- *AmMWSc 92*
**Sabloff**, Steven E. 1947- *WhoWest 92*
**Sabnis**, Anant Govind 1944- *AmMWSc 92*
**Sabnis**, Gajanan Mahadeo 1941- *AmMWSc 92*
**Sabnis**, Suman T 1935- *AmMWSc 92*
**Sabo**, Alvin Owen 1943- *WhoAmL 92*
**Sabo**, Julius Jay 1921- *AmMWSc 92*
**Sabo**, Martin Olav 1938- *AlmAP 92 [port], WhoAmP 91, WhoMW 92*
**Sabo**, Ronald William 1944- *WhoAmL 92*
**Saboeiro**, Gregory Roy 1961- *WhoMW 92*
**Sabol**, George Paul 1939- *AmMWSc 92*
**Sabol**, Lori Stein 1957- *WhoAmL 92*
**Sabol**, Steven Layne 1944- *AmMWSc 92*
**Sabolcik**, Gene 1951- *WhoFI 92*
**Sabota**, Francis Robert 1919- *WhoAmP 91*
**Saboungi**, Marie-Louise Jean 1948- *AmMWSc 92*
**Sabouret**, Yves Marie Georges 1936- *IntWW 91*
**Sabourin**, Clemonce 1910- *WhoBlA 92*
**Sabourin**, Josanne Rizzo 1952- *WhoMW 92*
**Sabourin**, Louis 1935- *IntWW 91*
**Sabourin**, Thomas Donald 1951- *AmMWSc 92*
**Sabourn**, Robert Joseph Edmond 1926- *AmMWSc 92*
**Sabre**, Dirk *IntAu&W 91X, WrDr 92*
**Sabree**, Clarice Salaam 1949- *WhoBlA 92*
**Sabreen**, Richard Paul 1946- *WhoEnt 92*
**Sabri**, Ali 1920- *IntWW 91*
**Sabrosky**, Curtis Williams 1910- *AmMWSc 92*
**Sabry**, Aly d1991 *NewYTBS 91 [port]*
**Sabry**, Ismail 1952- *AmMWSc 92*
**Sabry**, Zakaria I 1932- *AmMWSc 92*
**Sabsai**, Pinkhos Vladimirovich 1893-1980 *SovUnBD*
**Sabshin**, Melvin 1925- *AmMWSc 92*
**Sabuco**, Alice Marie 1953- *WhoMW 92*
**Sabuco**, Valentino 1949- *WhoFI 92*
**Saburov**, Maksim Zakharovich 1900- *FacFETw, SovUnBD*
**Saby**, John Sanford 1921- *AmMWSc 92*
**Sacajawea** 1788?-1884 *BenetAL 91*

**Sacasas**, Rene 1947- *WhoAmL 92*
**Saccany**, Catherine Dorothy 1951- *WhoMW 92*
**Sacco and Vanzetti** *FacFETw*
**Sacco and Vanzetti** d1927 *DcAmImH*
**Sacco**, Anthony G 1944- *AmMWSc 92*
**Sacco**, Bruno 1934- *DcTwDes*
**Sacco**, James A 1935- *WhoAmP 91*
**Sacco**, Louis Joseph, Jr 1924- *AmMWSc 92*
**Sacco**, Nicola 1891-1927 *DcAmImH*
**Saccoman**, Frank 1931- *AmMWSc 92*
**Saccoman**, John Joseph 1939- *AmMWSc 92*
**Saccomandi**, Vito 1939- *IntWW 91*
**Sacerdote**, Peter M. 1937- *WhoFI 92*
**Sachan**, Dileep Singh 1938- *AmMWSc 92*
**Sachar**, Emily 1958- *ConAu 135*
**Sacharow**, Stanley 1935- *WhoFI 92*
**Sachdev**, Goverdhan Pal 1941- *AmMWSc 92*
**Sachdev**, Neena Kaur 1959- *WhoFI 92*
**Sachdev**, Sham L 1937- *AmMWSc 92*
**Sachdev**, Subir 1961- *AmMWSc 92*
**Sachdev**, Suresh 1954- *AmMWSc 92*
**Sachdeva**, Baldev Krishan 1939- *AmMWSc 92*
**Sacher**, Alex 1922- *AmMWSc 92*
**Sacher**, Edward 1934- *AmMWSc 92*
**Sacher**, Paul 1906- *IntWW 91, NewAmDM*
**Sacher**, Robert Francis 1947- *AmMWSc 92*
**Sacher**, Steven Jay 1942- *WhoAmL 92*
**Sacher-Masoch**, Leopold von 1836?-1895 *NinCLC 31 [port]*
**Sachetta**, Joseph 1958- *WhoFI 92*
**Sachleben**, Richard Alan 1956- *AmMWSc 92*
**Sachs**, Alice *WhoAmP 91*
**Sachs**, Allan Maxwell 1921- *AmMWSc 92*
**Sachs**, Andrew 1930- *ConTFT 9*
**Sachs**, Arieh 1932- *IntAu&W 91*
**Sachs**, Benjamin David 1936- *AmMWSc 92*
**Sachs**, David 1933- *AmMWSc 92*
**Sachs**, David Howard 1942- *AmMWSc 92*
**Sachs**, Edward Max, Jr. 1946- *WhoMW 92*
**Sachs**, Elizabeth-Ann *DrAPF 91*
**Sachs**, Frederick 1941- *AmMWSc 92*
**Sachs**, Frederick Lee 1938- *AmMWSc 92*
**Sachs**, George 1936- *AmMWSc 92*
**Sachs**, Hans 1494-1576 *NewAmDM*
**Sachs**, Harvey Maurice 1944- *AmMWSc 92*
**Sachs**, Herbert K 1919- *AmMWSc 92*
**Sachs**, Howard Frederic 1925- *WhoAmL 92, WhoMW 92*
**Sachs**, Howard George 1943- *AmMWSc 92*
**Sachs**, Jerome Michael 1914- *WhoMW 92*
**Sachs**, John Richard 1934- *AmMWSc 92*
**Sachs**, Judith 1947- *WrDr 92*
**Sachs**, Leonard 1909-1990 *AnObit 1990*
**Sachs**, Leonie Nelly 1891-1970 *WhoNob 90*
**Sachs**, Leroy 1917- *WhoMW 92*
**Sachs**, Lester Marvin 1927- *AmMWSc 92*
**Sachs**, Lloyd Robert 1950- *WhoEnt 92*
**Sachs**, Marilyn 1927- *IntAu&W 91, SmATA 68 [port], WrDr 92*
**Sachs**, Marjorie Bell 1926- *WhoMW 92*
**Sachs**, Martin William 1937- *AmMWSc 92*
**Sachs**, Marvin Leonard 1926- *AmMWSc 92*
**Sachs**, Mendel 1927- *AmMWSc 92, IntAu&W 91, WrDr 92*
**Sachs**, Michael Alexander Geddes 1932- *Who 92*
**Sachs**, Michael David 1961- *WhoEnt 92*
**Sachs**, Murray 1924- *IntAu&W 91, WrDr 92*
**Sachs**, Murray B *AmMWSc 92*
**Sachs**, Nelly 1891-1970 *LiExTwC*
**Sachs**, Nelly 1891-1971 *FacFETw*
**Sachs**, Patricia S. *WhoFI 92*
**Sachs**, Peter Griggs 1939- *WhoFI 92*
**Sachs**, Peter Sandor 1947- *WhoAmL 92*
**Sachs**, Rainer Kurt 1932- *AmMWSc 92*
**Sachs**, Robert Green 1916- *AmMWSc 92, IntWW 91*
**Sachs**, Robert H. 1939- *WhoAmL 92*
**Sachs**, Roy M 1930- *AmMWSc 92*
**Sachs**, Samuel, II 1935- *WhoMW 92*
**Sachs**, Sidney Stanley 1916- *WhoAmL 92*
**Sachs**, Stephen H 1934- *WhoAmP 91*
**Sachs**, Steven Warren 1947- *WhoIns 92*
**Sachs**, Theodore Bernard 1868-1916 *BiInAmS*
**Sachs**, Thomas Dudley 1925- *AmMWSc 92*
**Sachs**, William 1942- *WhoEnt 92*
**Sachs**, William Lewis 1947- *WhoRel 92*
**Sachse**, Wolfgang H 1942- *AmMWSc 92*
**Sachtleben**, Clyde Clinton 1936- *AmMWSc 92*
**Sachtler**, Wolfgang Max Hugo 1924- *AmMWSc 92*
**Sacino**, D F 1930- *WhoIns 92*
**Sack**, Daniel Edward 1962- *WhoRel 92*
**Sack**, E A, Jr 1930- *AmMWSc 92*
**Sack**, Edgar Albert 1930- *WhoFI 92*
**Sack**, Fred David 1947- *AmMWSc 92*
**Sack**, George H, Jr 1943- *AmMWSc 92*
**Sack**, James McDonald, Jr. 1948- *WhoEnt 92, WhoMW 92*
**Sack**, John 1930- *WhoEnt 92*
**Sack**, Richard Bradley 1935- *AmMWSc 92*
**Sack**, Robert A 1944- *AmMWSc 92*
**Sack**, Robert David 1939- *WhoAmL 92*
**Sack**, Ronald Leslie 1935- *AmMWSc 92*
**Sack**, Sylvan Hanan 1932- *WhoAmL 92*
**Sack**, Wolfgang Otto 1928- *AmMWSc 92*
**Sackeim**, Harold A 1951- *AmMWSc 92*
**Sackett**, Gary Gordon 1940- *WhoAmL 92*
**Sackett**, Glenn Charles 1951- *WhoRel 92*
**Sackett**, Hugh F. 1930- *WhoFI 92*
**Sackett**, Lee Alan 1962- *WhoMW 92*
**Sackett**, W T, Jr 1921- *AmMWSc 92*
**Sackett**, William Malcolm 1930- *AmMWSc 92*
**Sackheim**, William *LesBEnT 92*
**Sackheim**, William B. 1919- *IntMPA 92*
**Sackin**, Richard A. 1946- *WhoFI 92*
**Sackin**, Stanley Owen 1936- *WhoFI 92*
**Sacklen**, Per *WhoEnt 92*
**Sackler**, Arthur Brian 1950- *WhoAmL 92*
**Sackler**, Howard 1929-1982 *BenetAL 91*
**Sackler**, Lori R. 1951- *WhoFI 92*
**Sackley**, Gary David 1950- *WhoAmP 91*
**Sackman**, Barbara Mae 1931- *WhoAmP 91*
**Sackman**, George Lawrence 1933- *AmMWSc 92*
**Sackman**, Jerome L 1929- *AmMWSc 92*
**Sackmann**, I Juliana 1942- *AmMWSc 92*
**Sackmann**, Robert Carl 1932- *WhoRel 92*
**Sackmann**, Thomas Fredrick 1952- *WhoFI 92*
**Sackner**, Marvin Arthur 1932- *AmMWSc 92*
**Sacks**, Albert M. d1991 *NewYTBS 91*
**Sacks**, Bernard Ross 1939- *WhoAmL 92*
**Sacks**, Clifford Eugene 1953- *AmMWSc 92*
**Sacks**, David Arnold 1940- *WhoAmL 92*
**Sacks**, David B 1950- *AmMWSc 92*
**Sacks**, David G. 1924- *WhoFI 92*
**Sacks**, David G 1950- *WhoAmP 91*
**Sacks**, Gerald Enoch 1933- *AmMWSc 92*
**Sacks**, Ira Stephen 1948- *WhoAmL 92*
**Sacks**, Jerome 1931- *AmMWSc 92*
**Sacks**, Jonathan 1943- *AmMWSc 92*
**Sacks**, Jonathan 1948- *IntWW 91*
**Sacks**, Jonathan Henry 1948- *Who 92*
**Sacks**, Lawrence Edgar 1920- *AmMWSc 92*
**Sacks**, Lawrence J 1928- *AmMWSc 92*
**Sacks**, Martin 1924- *AmMWSc 92*
**Sacks**, Martin Edward 1943- *AmMWSc 92*
**Sacks**, Oliver *NewYTBS 91 [port]*
**Sacks**, Oliver 1933- *ConLC 67 [port], WrDr 92*
**Sacks**, Oliver Wolf 1933- *IntWW 91*
**Sacks**, Peter *DrAPF 91*
**Sacks**, Samuel 1908- *IntMPA 92, WhoEnt 92*
**Sacks**, William 1924- *AmMWSc 92*
**Sacks**, William 1926- *AmMWSc 92*
**Sacksteder**, Richard Carl 1928- *AmMWSc 92*
**Sacksteder**, Thomas M. 1950- *WhoMW 92*
**Sackston**, Waldemar E 1918- *AmMWSc 92*
**Sackton**, Frank Joseph 1912- *WhoWest 92*
**Sacktor**, Bertram 1922- *AmMWSc 92*
**Sackville** *Who 92*
**Sackville**, Baron 1913- *Who 92*
**Sackville**, Charles *RfGEnL 91*
**Sackville**, Thomas 1536-1608 *RfGEnL 91*
**Sackville**, Thomas Geoffrey 1950- *Who 92*
**Sackville-West** *Who 92*
**Sackville-West**, Vita 1892-1962 *FacFETw*
**Sackwood**, Mark 1926- *Who 92*
**Saco**, Beverly Marie 1963- *WhoFI 92*
**Saco**, Jose Antonio 1797-1879 *HisDSpE*
**Sacon**, Kiyoshi Kinoshita 1931- *WhoRel 92*
**Sacopulos**, Peter John 1963- *WhoAmL 92*
**Sadagopan**, Varadachari *AmMWSc 92*
**Sadana**, Ajit 1947- *AmMWSc 92*
**Sadana**, Yoginder Nath 1931- *AmMWSc 92*
**Sadanaga**, Kiyoshi 1920- *AmMWSc 92*
**Sadanaga**, Ryoichi 1920- *IntWW 91*
**Sadat**, Anwar el- 1918-1981 *FacFETw [port]*
**Sadava**, David Eric 1946- *AmMWSc 92, WhoWest 92*
**Sadd**, John Roswell 1933- *WhoMW 92*
**Saddam Hussein** 1937- *IntWW 91*
**Saddlemyer**, Ann 1932- *IntAu&W 91, WrDr 92*
**Saddler**, Allen 1923- *IntAu&W 91, WrDr 92*
**Saddler**, Donald Edward 1920- *WhoEnt 92*
**Saddler**, K Allen *IntAu&W 91X*
**Saddler**, Roderick 1965- *WhoBlA 92*
**Saddler**, William E. 1915- *WhoBlA 92*
**Saddock**, Harry G. 1929- *WhoFI 92*
**Sade**, Donatien-Alphonse-F., marquis de 1740-1814 *BlkwCEP*
**Sade**, Norman G. 1934- *WhoAmL 92*
**Sadeck**, Lorraine Jeanne 1949- *WhoRel 92*
**Sadee**, Wolfgang 1942- *AmMWSc 92*
**Sadeghi**, Ali 1955- *WhoWest 92*
**Sadeghi**, Nasser 1934- *WhoWest 92*
**Sadeh**, Pinhas 1929- *ConAu 34NR*
**Sadeh**, Willy Zeev 1932- *AmMWSc 92*
**Sadek**, George 1928- *WhoEnt 92*
**Sadek**, Salah Eldine 1920- *WhoMW 92*
**Sadeque**, Shahwar 1942- *Who 92*
**Sader**, Carol H 1935- *WhoAmP 91*
**Sader**, Neil Steven 1958- *WhoMW 92*
**Sader**, Robert Mayo 1948- *WhoAmL 92, WhoAmP 91*
**Sadie the Goat** *EncAmaz 91*
**Sadie**, Stanley 1930- *IntAu&W 91, Who 92, WrDr 92*
**Sadie**, Stanley John 1930- *IntWW 91*
**Sadik**, Farid 1934- *AmMWSc 92*
**Sadik**, Nafis 1929- *IntWW 91*
**Sadilek**, Vladimir 1933- *WhoFI 92, WhoWest 92*
**Sadiq** 1950- *TwCPaSc*
**Sadjadi**, Firooz Ahmadi *AmMWSc 92*
**Sadjadi**, Shirley 1964- *WhoAmL 92*
**Sadleir**, William Kent 1954- *WhoAmP 91*
**Sadler**, Al 1936- *WhoAmP 91*
**Sadler**, Amy 1924- *TwCWW 91, WrDr 92*
**Sadler**, Arthur Graham 1925- *AmMWSc 92*
**Sadler**, Barry 1941-1989 *FacFETw*
**Sadler**, Charles Robinson, Jr 1950- *AmMWSc 92, WhoWest 92*
**Sadler**, David Gary 1939- *WhoFI 92*
**Sadler**, Dick 1928- *WhoAmP 91*
**Sadler**, G W 1925- *AmMWSc 92*
**Sadler**, Geoffrey Willis 1943- *WrDr 92*
**Sadler**, George D 1952- *AmMWSc 92*
**Sadler**, Ivan 1950- *WhoRel 92*
**Sadler**, J Evan 1951- *AmMWSc 92*
**Sadler**, James Bertram 1911- *WhoMW 92*
**Sadler**, James C 1920- *AmMWSc 92*
**Sadler**, Jeff *WrDr 92*
**Sadler**, Jeff 1943- *TwCWW 91*
**Sadler**, Jerry Martin *DrAPF 91*
**Sadler**, Joan 1927- *Who 92*
**Sadler**, John Stephen 1930- *Who 92*
**Sadler**, Kenneth Marvin 1949- *WhoBlA 92*
**Sadler**, Louis Ray 1937- *WhoAmP 91, WhoWest 92*
**Sadler**, Luther Fuller, Jr. 1942- *WhoAmL 92*
**Sadler**, Mark *IntAu&W 91X, WrDr 92*
**Sadler**, Michael Ervin 1948- *AmMWSc 92*
**Sadler**, Monroe Scharff 1920- *AmMWSc 92*
**Sadler**, Paul 1955- *WhoAmP 91*
**Sadler**, Roy H 1929- *WhoAmP 91*
**Sadler**, Stanley Gene 1938- *AmMWSc 92*
**Sadler**, Thomas William 1949- *AmMWSc 92*
**Sadler**, Wilbert L. *WhoBlA 92*
**Sadler**, William Alan, Jr. 1931- *WhoWest 92*
**Sadler**, William Otho 1903- *AmMWSc 92*
**Sadli**, Mohammad 1922- *IntWW 91*
**Sadlock**, Richard Alan 1961- *WhoAmL 92*
**Sadock**, Benjamin 1933- *AmMWSc 92*
**Sadock**, Virginia A 1938- *AmMWSc 92*
**Sadoff**, Ahren J 1936- *AmMWSc 92*
**Sadoff**, Harold Lloyd 1924- *AmMWSc 92*
**Sadoff**, Ira *DrAPF 91*
**Sadosky**, Thomas Lee 1939- *AmMWSc 92*
**Sadoulet**, Bernard 1944- *AmMWSc 92, IntWW 91*
**Sadove**, A. Robert 1921- *IntWW 91*
**Sadoway**, Donald Robert 1950- *AmMWSc 92*
**Sadowski**, Chester M 1936- *AmMWSc 92*
**Sadowski**, George 1950- *WhoWest 92*
**Sadowski**, Ivan J 1960- *AmMWSc 92*
**Sadowski**, Wieslaw 1922- *IntWW 91*
**Sadowski**, William Edward 1944- *WhoAmL 92, WhoAmP 91*
**Sadowski**, William F. *WhoFI 92*
**Sadowsky**, Edward L 1929- *WhoAmP 91*
**Sadowsky**, John 1949- *AmMWSc 92*
**Sadoyama**, Nancy Artis 1947- *WhoWest 92*
**Sadruddin**, Moe 1943- *WhoFI 92, WhoWest 92*
**Sadtler**, Philip 1909- *AmMWSc 92*
**Sadun**, Alberto Carlo 1955- *AmMWSc 92*
**Sadun**, Alfredo Arrigo 1950- *WhoWest 92*
**Sadurski**, Edward Alan 1949- *AmMWSc 92*
**Sae**, Andy S W 1941- *AmMWSc 92*
**Saebo**, Magne 1929- *IntWW 91*
**Saeboe**, Magne 1929- *WhoRel 92*
**Saeda**, Scott Thomas 1964- *WhoAmL 92*
**Saegebarth**, Klaus Arthur 1929- *AmMWSc 92*
**Saeger**, Victor William 1933- *AmMWSc 92*
**Saeger**, William Bresler 1951- *WhoFI 92*
**Saeks**, Allen Irving 1932- *WhoAmL 92*
**Saeks**, Richard E 1941- *AmMWSc 92*
**Saelens**, David Arthur 1943- *AmMWSc 92*
**Saemala**, Francis Joseph 1944- *IntWW 91*
**Saeman**, W C 1914- *AmMWSc 92*
**Saemann**, Jesse C, Jr 1921- *AmMWSc 92*
**Saenger**, Bruce W 1943- *WhoIns 92*
**Saenger**, Bruce Walter 1943- *WhoFI 92*
**Saenger**, Eugene L 1917- *AmMWSc 92*
**Saenz**, Albert William 1923- *AmMWSc 92*
**Saenz**, Alonzo A. 1940- *WhoHisp 92*
**Saenz**, Benito, Jr 1944- *WhoAmP 91*
**Saenz**, David R. *WhoHisp 92*
**Saenz**, Diana Eloise 1949- *WhoHisp 92*
**Saenz**, Gilbert 1941- *WhoHisp 92*
**Saenz**, Gracie *WhoHisp 92*
**Saenz**, Jacinto 1940- *WhoHisp 92*
**Saenz**, Jaime 1921-1986 *ConSpAP*
**Saenz**, Jose Carlos 1938- *WhoHisp 92*
**Saenz**, Jose Maria 179-?-1834 *HisDSpE*
**Saenz**, Manuela 1793-1856 *HisDSpE*
**Saenz**, Marc B. 1950- *WhoHisp 92*
**Saenz**, Michael 1925- *WhoHisp 92*
**Saenz**, P. Alex 1950- *WhoHisp 92*
**Saenz**, Ramiro 1935- *WhoHisp 92*
**Saenz**, Reynaldo V 1940- *AmMWSc 92*
**Saenz**, Richard J. 1954- *WhoHisp 92*
**Saenz**, Robert 1938- *WhoHisp 92*
**Saenz**, Rogelio 1958- *WhoHisp 92*
**Saenz De Cosculluela**, Javier 1944- *IntWW 91*
**Saeta**, Philip Max 1931- *WhoAmL 92*
**Saether**, Ole Anton 1936- *AmMWSc 92*
**Saettler**, Alfred William 1940- *AmMWSc 92*
**Saeva**, Franklin Donald 1938- *AmMWSc 92*
**Saeverud**, Harald 1897- *ConCom 92*
**Saevre**, Phyllis Schrader 1935- *WhoMW 92*
**Saez**, Juan Carlos 1956- *AmMWSc 92*
**Saez**, Pedro Justo *WhoHisp 92*
**Saf**, John Carl 1964- *WhoFI 92*
**Safai**, Bijan *AmMWSc 92*
**Safanie**, Alvin H 1924- *AmMWSc 92*
**Safar**, Peter 1924- *AmMWSc 92*
**Safdari**, Yahya Bhai 1930- *AmMWSc 92*
**Safdie**, Moshe 1938- *IntAu&W 91, IntWW 91, WrDr 92*
**Safdy**, Max Errol 1941- *AmMWSc 92*
**Safe**, Kenneth Shaw, Jr. 1929- *WhoFI 92*
**Safe**, Stephen Harvey 1940- *AmMWSc 92*
**Safer**, Brian 1942- *AmMWSc 92*
**Safer**, Morley *LesBEnT 92 [port]*
**Safer**, Morley 1931- *IntMPA 92, WrDr 92*
**Saferite**, Linda Lee 1947- *WhoWest 92*
**Saferstein**, Lowell G 1940- *AmMWSc 92*
**Saferstein**, Richard 1941- *AmMWSc 92*
**Safewright**, Deniece Rogers 1960- *WhoAmL 92*
**Saff**, Edward Barry 1944- *AmMWSc 92*
**Saffar**, Salman Mohamed al- 1931- *IntWW 91*
**Saffeir**, Harvey J 1929- *WhoIns 92*
**Saffeir**, Harvey Joseph 1929- *WhoFI 92*
**Saffel**, E. Frank 1923- *WhoBlA 92*
**Saffels**, Dale Emerson 1921- *WhoAmL 92, WhoMW 92*
**Saffer**, Alfred 1918- *AmMWSc 92*
**Saffer**, Charles Martin, Jr 1914- *AmMWSc 92*
**Saffer**, Henry Walker 1935- *AmMWSc 92*
**Saffer**, Judith Mack 1942- *WhoEnt 92*
**Safferman**, Robert S 1932- *AmMWSc 92*
**Saffin**, John 1626?-1710 *BenetAL 91*
**Saffioti**, Carol Lee *DrAPF 91*
**Saffiotti**, Umberto 1928- *AmMWSc 92*
**Saffir**, Arthur Joel 1941- *AmMWSc 92*
**Saffle**, M. W. 1923- *IntMPA 92*
**Saffle**, Michael Benton 1946- *WhoEnt 92*
**Saffman**, Philip Geoffrey 1931- *AmMWSc 92, Who 92*
**Saffo**, Mary Beth 1948- *AmMWSc 92*
**Saffold**, Oscar E. 1941- *WhoBlA 92*
**Safford**, James Merrill 1822-1907 *BiInAmS*
**Safford**, Joan Bainbridge 1936- *WhoAmL 92*
**Safford**, Lawrence Oliver 1938- *AmMWSc 92*
**Safford**, Richard Whiley 1924- *AmMWSc 92*
**Safford**, Robert O 1934- *WhoIns 92*
**Safford**, Truman Henry 1836-1901 *BiInAmS*
**Saffran**, Bernard 1936- *WhoFI 92*
**Saffran**, Judith 1923- *AmMWSc 92*
**Saffran**, Murray 1924- *AmMWSc 92*
**Saffren**, Melvin Michael 1929- *AmMWSc 92*
**Safi**, Deborah Cavazos 1953- *WhoAmL 92*
**Safir**, Andrew Jeffrey 1948- *WhoFI 92*
**Safir**, Natalie *DrAPF 91*
**Safir**, Peter Oliver 1945- *WhoAmL 92*
**Safir**, Sidney 1923- *IntMPA 92*
**Safir**, Sidney Robert 1916- *AmMWSc 92*
**Safire**, William 1929- *IntAu&W 91, IntWW 91, WhoAmP 91, WrDr 92*

**Safko**, John Loren 1938- AmMWSc 92
**Safley**, Lawson McKinney, Jr 1950- AmMWSc 92
**Safley**, R Z 1946- WhoAmP 91
**Safonov**, Michael G 1948- AmMWSc 92
**Safran**, Claire 1930- IntAu&W 91
**Safran**, Edward Myron 1937- WhoFI 92
**Safran**, Hubert Mayer 1930- WhoAmL 92
**Safran**, Perry Renfrow 1950- WhoAmL 92
**Safran**, Samuel A 1951- AmMWSc 92
**Safranek**, Stephen Joseph 1960- WhoAmL 92
**SaFranko**, Mark Peter 1950- WhoEnt 92
**Safranyik**, Laszlo 1938- AmMWSc 92
**Safron**, Sanford Alan 1941- AmMWSc 92
**Safronchuk**, Vasiliy Stepanovich 1925- IntWW 91
**Safsel**, Joseph Solomon 1932- WhoRel 92
**Sagadin**, Meridee J. 1955- WhoFI 92
**Sagal**, Katie WhoEnt 92A
**Sagal**, Matthew Warren 1936- AmMWSc 92
**Sagale**, Taligalu WhoAmP 91
**Sagall**, Solomon LesBEnT 92
**Sagalow**, Ty Rone 1958- WhoAmL 92
**Sagalyn**, Lynne B. 1947- ConAu 134
**Sagalyn**, Paul Leon 1921- AmMWSc 92
**Sagalyn**, Rita C 1924- AmMWSc 92
**Sagami**, Kim WhoEnt 92
**Sagan**, Carl 1934- AmMWSc 92, ConAu 36NR, FacFETw, WrDr 92
**Sagan**, Carl Edward 1934- IntWW 91
**Sagan**, Francoise 1935- FacFETw, FrenWW, GuFrLit 1, IntWW 91, Who 92
**Sagan**, Gene Hill d1991 NewYTBS 91
**Sagan**, Hans 1928- AmMWSc 92
**Sagan**, John 1921- WhoFI 92, WhoMW 92
**Sagan**, Leon Francis 1941- AmMWSc 92
**Sagan**, Leonard A 1928- AmMWSc 92
**Sagan**, Leontine 1889-1974 ReelWom [port]
**Sagan**, Miriam DrAPF 91
**Sagana** EncAmaz 91
**Sagansky**, Jeff LesBEnT 92, WhoEnt 92
**Sagansky**, Jeff 1953- IntMPA 92
**Sagar**, William Clayton 1929- AmMWSc 92
**Sagaral**, Erasmo G 1936- AmMWSc 92
**Sagarin**, James Leon 1951- WhoMW 92, WhoRel 92
**Sagarra**, Eda 1933- IntWW 91
**Sagatelian**, Alexander Andreevich 1959- WhoWest 92
**Sagatelyan**, Mikhail 1927- IntWW 91
**Sagawa**, Kiichi 1926- AmMWSc 92
**Sagawa**, Shirley Sachi 1961- WhoAmL 92
**Sagawa**, Yoneo 1926- AmMWSc 92, WhoWest 92
**Sagdeev**, Roald Zinnurovich 1932- IntWW 91, SovUnBD
**Sagdeyev**, Roald 1933- FacFETw
**Sage**, Andrew Patrick 1933- AmMWSc 92
**Sage**, Gloria W 1936- AmMWSc 92
**Sage**, Harvey J 1933- AmMWSc 92
**Sage**, Helene E 1946- AmMWSc 92
**Sage**, Howard DrAPF 91
**Sage**, Jay Peter 1943- AmMWSc 92
**Sage**, Joseph D 1931- AmMWSc 92
**Sage**, Joseph Francois 1935- WhoEnt 92
**Sage**, Larry Guy 1946- WhoAmL 92
**Sage**, Lorna 1943- Who 92, WrDr 92
**Sage**, Martin 1935- AmMWSc 92
**Sage**, Martin Lee 1935- AmMWSc 92
**Sage**, Nathaniel McLean, Jr 1918- AmMWSc 92
**Sage**, Norman Douglas 1942- WhoMW 92
**Sage**, Orrin Grant, Jr 1946- AmMWSc 92
**Sage**, Roderick Duncan 1926- WhoWest 92
**Sage**, Ronald P, Jr 1962- WhoAmP 91
**Sagebrecht**, Marianne 1945- IntMPA 92
**Sagel**, Jim DrAPF 91
**Sager**, Allan Henry 1934- WhoRel 92
**Sager**, Alvin Douglas 1939- WhoRel 92
**Sager**, Clifford J 1916- AmMWSc 92
**Sager**, Craig A., Sr. 1944- WhoRel 92
**Sager**, Donald Allen 1930- WhoIns 92
**Sager**, Donald Jack 1938- WhoMW 92
**Sager**, Earl Vincent 1945- AmMWSc 92
**Sager**, John Clutton 1942- AmMWSc 92
**Sager**, John William 1946- WhoAmL 92
**Sager**, Jonathan Ward 1954- WhoAmL 92
**Sager**, Lawrence Gene 1941- WhoAmL 92
**Sager**, Pamela H. 1961- WhoAmL 92
**Sager**, Ray Stuart 1942- AmMWSc 92
**Sager**, Ronald E 1947- AmMWSc 92
**Sager**, Ruth 1918- AmMWSc 92
**Sager**, Steven T 1953- WhoAmP 91
**Sager**, Steven Travis 1957- WhoAmL 92
**Sager**, Theresa Louise 1955- WhoMW 92
**Sager**, Thomas William AmMWSc 92
**Sager**, William Frederick 1918- AmMWSc 92
**Sagerman**, Robert H 1930- AmMWSc 92
**Sagers**, David L. 1956- WhoFI 92
**Sagers**, Richard Douglas 1928- AmMWSc 92
**Sagers**, Rudolph, Jr. 1955- WhoBlA 92
**Sagert**, Norman Henry 1936- AmMWSc 92
**Saget**, Bob WhoEnt 92
**Saget**, Louis Joseph Edouard 1915- IntWW 91
**Sagett**, Jan Jeffrey 1943- WhoAmL 92
**Saggers**, Geoffrey WhoIns 92
**Saggese**, Alfred E, Jr 1946- WhoAmP 91
**Saggese**, Anthony James, Jr. 1949- WhoAmL 92
**Saggiomo**, Andrew Joseph 1931- AmMWSc 92
**Saggs**, Henry 1920- WrDr 92
**Saggs**, Henry William Frederick 1920- IntAu&W 91
**Sagi**, Charles J 1935- AmMWSc 92
**Sagi**, Charles Joseph 1935- WhoMW 92
**Sagic**, Djordje DcAmImH
**Sagik**, Bernard Phillip 1925- AmMWSc 92
**Saginaw**, Rose Blas 1926- WhoFI 92
**Sagiuchi**, Toshiyuki 1950- WhoFI 92
**Sagle**, Arthur A AmMWSc 92
**Saglik**, Aysel 1938- WhoMW 92
**Saglio**, Jean-Francois 1936- IntWW 91
**Sagman**, Gail 1957- TwCPaSc
**Sago**, Paul Edward 1931- WhoRel 92
**Sagraves**, Barbara Darling 1935- WhoAmP 91
**Sagstetter**, Karen DrAPF 91
**Sah**, Chih-Han 1934- AmMWSc 92
**Sah**, Chih-Tang 1932- AmMWSc 92
**Sah**, Raaj Kumar 1952- WhoFI 92
**Saha**, Anil 1930- AmMWSc 92
**Saha**, Bijay S AmMWSc 92
**Saha**, Gopal Bandhu 1938- AmMWSc 92, WhoMW 92
**Saha**, Jadu Gopal 1931- AmMWSc 92
**Saha**, Pamela S 1951- AmMWSc 92
**Saha**, Subrata 1942- AmMWSc 92
**Sahade**, Jorge 1915- IntWW 91
**Sahadi**, Robert J. WhoFI 92
**Sahagun**, Bernardino de 1499?-1590? HisDSpE
**Sahagun**, Carlos 1938- DcLB 108 [port]
**Sahagun de la Parra**, Jose de Jesus 1922- WhoRel 92
**Sahai**, Yogeshwar 1945- WhoMW 92
**Sahakian**, William S. 1921- WrDr 92
**Sahara**, Robert Fumio 1942- WhoWest 92
**Sahas**, Daniel John 1940- WhoRel 92
**Sahasrabuddhe**, Chintaman Gopal 1936- AmMWSc 92
**Sahasrabudhe**, Madhu R 1925- AmMWSc 92
**Sahatjian**, Ronald Alexander 1942- AmMWSc 92
**Sahay**, A Chittaranjan 1925- IntAu&W 91
**Sahbari**, Javad Jabbari 1944- AmMWSc 92
**Sahgal**, Nayantara 1927- ConNov 91, IntAu&W 91, IntWW 91, WrDr 92
**Sahgal**, Ranjit 1951- WhoFI 92
**Sahid**, Joseph Robert 1944- WhoAmL 92
**Sahin**, Hayati 1956- WhoFI 92
**Sahinen**, Winston Martin 1931- AmMWSc 92
**Sahl**, Michael 1934- NewAmDM
**Sahl**, Mort 1927- FacFETw
**Sahl**, Mort Lyon 1927- IntWW 91
**Sahl**, Morton Lyon 1927- WhoEnt 92
**Sahlein**, Don 1924- WhoEnt 92
**Sahli**, Brenda Payne 1942- AmMWSc 92
**Sahli**, Muhammad S 1935- AmMWSc 92
**Sahlin**, Mauritz 1935- IntWW 91
**Sahlin**, Mona 1957- IntWW 91
**Sahlins**, Marshall ConAu 133
**Sahlins**, Marshall 1930- IntAu&W 91, WrDr 92
**Sahlins**, Marshall D. 1930- ConAu 133
**Sahlman**, Alexander Bruce 1948- WhoEnt 92
**Sahm**, Heinrich 1877-1939 EncTR 91
**Sahney**, Vinod K 1942- AmMWSc 92
**Sahni**, Sartaj Kumar 1949- AmMWSc 92
**Sahni**, Viraht 1944- AmMWSc 92
**Sahota**, Gurcharn Singh 1940- WhoFI 92
**Sahu**, Saura Chandra 1944- AmMWSc 92
**Sahyoun**, Naji Elias 1949- AmMWSc 92
**Sahyun**, Melville R.V. 1940- WhoMW 92
**Sahyun**, Melville Richard Valde 1940- AmMWSc 92
**Sai Baba** 1856-1918 RelLAm 91
**Sai Baba**, Sathya 1926- RelLAm 91
**Sai-Halasz**, George Anthony 1943- AmMWSc 92
**Saia**, David Joseph 1904- WhoAmP 91
**Saia**, Vincent Joseph 1958- WhoFI 92
**Saibel**, Edward 1903- AmMWSc 92
**Saibou**, Ali IntWW 91
**Said**, Ali 1927- IntWW 91
**Said**, Clifford Everett 1937- WhoMW 92
**Said**, Edward W. 1935- IntWW 91, LiExTwC, WrDr 92
**Said**, Faisal bin Ali al- 1927- IntWW 91
**Said**, Hakim Mohammed 1920- IntWW 91
**Said**, Hamid M. 1954- WhoWest 92
**Said**, Rushdi 1920- AmMWSc 92
**Said**, Sami I 1928- AmMWSc 92
**Saidak**, Walter John 1930- AmMWSc 92
**Saide**, Judith Dana 1944- AmMWSc 92
**Saidel**, Gerald Maxwell 1938- AmMWSc 92
**Saidel**, Leo James 1916- AmMWSc 92
**Saidenberg**, Daniel 1906- WhoEnt 92
**Saiduddin**, Syed 1938- AmMWSc 92
**Saied**, Faisal 1951- AmMWSc 92
**Saied**, James Guy 1915- WhoEnt 92
**Saier**, Milton H, Jr 1941- AmMWSc 92
**Saier**, Oskar 1932- IntWW 91
**Saif**, Abdulla Hassan 1945- IntWW 91
**Saif**, Linda Jean 1947- AmMWSc 92
**Saif**, Yehia M 1934- AmMWSc 92
**Saif Al-Islam**, Mohamed al-Badr 1927- IntWW 91
**Saifer**, Mark Gary Pierce 1938- AmMWSc 92
**Saiff**, Edward Ira 1942- AmMWSc 92
**Saifudin** IntWW 91
**Saigal**, Sunil 1957- AmMWSc 92
**Saigh**, Nassir M. Al- 1942- IntWW 91
**Saigo**, Roy Hirofumi 1940- AmMWSc 92
**Saiki**, Jessica DrAPF 91
**Saiki**, Patricia 1930- WhoAmP 91, WhoFI 92, WhoWest 92
**Saikin**, Valeriy Timofeyevich 1937- IntWW 91
**Saikley**, Gilbert Haven 1948- WhoAmL 92
**Sail**, Lawrence 1942- ConPo 91, WrDr 92
**Saila Ould Abeida Ould Ahmed** 1920- HisDSpE
**Saila**, Saul Bernhard 1924- AmMWSc 92
**Sailer**, Henry Powers 1929- WhoAmL 92
**Saili Faasootauloa**, Tuaopepe Falesa P. 1936- IntWW 91
**Sailor**, Samuel 1922- AmMWSc 92
**Sailor**, Vance Lewis 1920- AmMWSc 92
**Sailors**, Jan Dee 1949- WhoRel 92
**Saiman**, Martin S. 1932- WhoAmL 92
**Sain**, Dan D 1935- WhoAmP 91
**Sain**, Michael K 1937- AmMWSc 92
**Sain**, Michael Kent 1937- WhoMW 92
**Sainani**, Ram Hariram 1925- WhoFI 92
**Sainburg**, Richard B. 1924- WhoFI 92
**Sainer**, Arthur 1924- WrDr 92
**Sainer**, Leonard 1909- IntWW 91, Who 92
**Saines**, Emily Gerson 1964- WhoEnt 92
**Saines**, Marvin 1942- WhoWest 92
**Saini**, B. S. 1930- WrDr 92
**Saini**, Balwant Singh 1930- IntAu&W 91
**Saini**, Girdhari Lal 1931- AmMWSc 92
**Saini**, Gulshan Rai 1924- WhoFI 92
**Saini**, Ravinder Kumar 1946- AmMWSc 92
**Sainju**, Mohan Man 1941- IntWW 91
**Sainsbury** Who 92
**Sainsbury**, Baron 1902- IntWW 91, Who 92
**Sainsbury**, David John 1940- IntWW 91, Who 92
**Sainsbury**, Edward Hardwicke 1912- Who 92
**Sainsbury**, Maurice Joseph 1927- IntAu&W 91, WrDr 92
**Sainsbury**, Richard Eric d1991 Who 92N
**Sainsbury**, Robert 1906- Who 92
**Sainsbury**, Robert Stephen 1943- AmMWSc 92
**Sainsbury**, Roger Frederick Who 92
**Sainsbury**, Timothy Alan Davan 1932- Who 92
**Sainsbury Of Preston Candover**, Baron 1927- IntWW 91, Who 92
**Sainsbury of Preston Candover**, Lady Who 92
**Saint Just** 1866-1944 WhoNob 90
**St. Paul** 1964- WhoEnt 92
**Saint**, Andrew 1946- WrDr 92
**Saint**, Andrew John 1946- IntAu&W 91
**Saint**, Assotto DrAPF 91
**Saint**, Dora Jessie 1913- IntAu&W 91, Who 92
**Saint**, Eva Marie 1924- IntMPA 92, WhoEnt 92
**Saint**, James Giles, Jr. 1913- WhoRel 92
**St Albans**, Archdeacon of Who 92
**St Albans**, Bishop of 1929- Who 92
**St Albans**, Dean of Who 92
**St Albans**, Duke of 1939- Who 92
**St Aldwyn**, Earl 1912- Who 92
**St. Amand**, Michael David 1964- WhoAmL 92
**St Amand**, Pierre 1920- AmMWSc 92
**St Amand**, Wilbrod 1927- AmMWSc 92
**St Andrews**, Earl of 1962- Who 92
**St. Andrews**, B.A. DrAPF 91
**St. Andrews**, Barbara WhoRel 92
**St Andrews And Edinburgh**, Archbishop of 1938- Who 92
**St Andrews And Edinburgh**, Bishop of Who 92
**St Andrews Dunkeld & Dunblane**, Bishop of 1925- Who 92
**St Andrews Dunkeld & Dunblane**, Dean of Who 92
**St Angelo**, Allen Joseph 1932- AmMWSc 92
**Saint-Antoine**, Jude 1930- WhoRel 92
**St. Antoine**, Theodore Joseph 1929- WhoAmL 92
**Saint-Arnaud**, Raymond 1935- AmMWSc 92
**St Arnaud**, Roland Joseph AmMWSc 92
**St Asaph**, Bishop of 1934- Who 92
**St Asaph**, Dean of Who 92
**St Aubin De Teran**, Lisa 1953- IntAu&W 91
**St. Aubin de Teran**, Lisa Gioconda 1953- IntWW 91
**St Aubyn** Who 92
**St Aubyn**, Arscott M. Who 92
**St Aubyn**, Giles 1925- IntAu&W 91, WrDr 92
**St Aubyn**, Rod WhoAmP 91
**St Aubyn**, Thomas Edward 1923- Who 92
**Saint-Balmont**, Madame de EncAmaz 91
**St Boniface**, Archbishop of 1926- Who 92
**St Clair** Who 92
**St Clair**, Anne King 1947- AmMWSc 92
**St Clair**, Annetta Elaine 1938- WhoAmP 91
**St. Clair**, Arthur 1736-1818 BenetAL 91, BlkwEAR
**St. Clair**, Carl WhoEnt 92, WhoWest 92
**St. Clair**, Don E. 1958- WhoMW 92
**St. Clair**, Frank Creel 1936- WhoEnt 92
**St. Clair**, Harry Neil 1952- WhoEnt 92
**St. Clair**, Howard Barry 1945- WhoRel 92
**St. Clair**, James Draper 1920- WhoAmL 92
**St. Clair**, Jo Ellen 1963- WhoEnt 92
**St. Clair**, John Gilbert 1945- WhoAmL 92
**St Clair**, Malcolm Archibald James 1927- Who 92
**St Clair**, Margaret 1911- IntAu&W 91, TwCSFW 91, WrDr 92
**St Clair**, Mary Beth Genter 1962- AmMWSc 92
**St. Clair**, Philip DrAPF 91
**St Clair**, Richard William 1940- AmMWSc 92
**St Clair**, Sylvia 1917- WhoEnt 92
**St Clair**, Terry Lee 1943- AmMWSc 92
**St. Clair**, Thomas McBryar 1935- WhoFI 92
**St Clair**, William 1937- IntAu&W 91, WrDr 92
**St Clair**, William Linn 1937- Who 92
**St Clair-Erskine** Who 92
**St Clair-Ford**, Aubrey d1991 Who 92N
**St Clair-Ford**, James Anson 1952- Who 92
**St. Claire**, Erin WrDr 92
**St. Claire**, Frank Arthur 1949- WhoAmL 92
**Saint Claire**, Marian WhoEnt 92
**St Cloud**, Alden DrAPF 91
**St Crispian**, Crispin de IntAu&W 91X
**St. Cyr**, John Albert, II 1949- WhoWest 92
**St Cyr**, Napoleon 1924- IntAu&W 91
**St Cyres**, Viscount 1957- Who 92
**St Davids**, Archdeacon of Who 92
**St Davids**, Bishop of 1926- Who 92
**St Davids**, Dean of Who 92
**St Davids**, Viscount d1991 Who 92N
**St Davids**, Viscount 1939- Who 92
**St Dawn**, Grace Galasso IntAu&W 91
**St. Denis**, Ruth 1879-1968 FacFETw
**St. Dennis**, Jerry A. 1942- WhoFI 92, WhoWest 92
**Saint-Denys-Garneau**, Hector 1912-1943 BenetAL 91
**Saint-Donat**, Bernard Jacques 1946- WhoFI 92
**Saint-Eden**, Dennis IntAu&W 91X
**St Edmundsbury**, Provost of Who 92
**St Edmundsbury And Ipswich**, Bishop of 1931- Who 92
**Saint-Erne**, Nicholas John de 1958- WhoWest 92
**Saint-Evremond**, Charles M., seigneur de 1613-1703 BlkwCEP
**Saint-Exupery**, Antoine de 1900-1943 FacFETw
**Saint-Exupery**, Antoine de 1900-1944 GuFrLit 1, LiExTwC
**Saint-Gaudens**, Augustus 1848-1907 BenetAL 91
**St George**, George 1908- Who 92
**St. George**, Harry ScFEYrs, TwCWW 91
**St. George**, Judith 1931- Au&Arts 7 [port], IntAu&W 91, WrDr 92
**St. George**, Noel ConAu 134
**Saint-Georges**, Joseph Boulogne 1739?-1799 NewAmDM
**St Germain**, Fernand Joseph 1928- WhoAmP 91
**St. Germain**, Gregory ConAu 35NR
**Saint-Germain**, Michelle Ann 1947- WhoWest 92
**St. Germain**, Sheryl DrAPF 91
**St Germaine**, Shirley Ann 1935- WhoAmP 91
**St Germans**, Bishop Suffragan of 1938- Who 92
**St Germans**, Earl of 1941- Who 92
**St Giraud** IntAu&W 91X
**St Helena**, Bishop of 1929- Who 92

St Helens, Baron 1945- Who 92
Saint Jacques, Alfred Joseph 1956- IntAu&W 91
Saint-Jacques, Bernard 1928- WhoWest 92
St Jacques, Raymond 1930-1990 AnObit 1990, ConTFT 9, FacFETw, WhoBlA 92N
Saint-Jacques, Robert G 1941- AmMWSc 92
Saint James, Andrew WrDr 92
St. James, Brian Renard 1958- WhoAmL 92
St. James, Nicholas 1948- WhoWest 92
Saint James, Susan 1946- IntMPA 92, WhoEnt 92
St-Jean, Guy 1941- AmMWSc 92
St Jean, James R 1952- WhoAmP 91
St Jean, Joseph, Jr 1923- AmMWSc 92
St John Who 92
Saint-John Perse 1887-1975 GuFrLit 1, LiExTwC, WhoNob 90
Saint John, Austin WhoEnt 92
St. John, Bernard 1931- IntWW 91
St John, Bill 1932- AmMWSc 92
St. John, Bill Dean 1931- WhoFI 92
St. John, Bruce 1923- ConPo 91, IntAu&W 91, WrDr 92
St. John, Caitlin 1951- WhoEnt 92
St. John, Charles Virgil 1922- WhoMW 92
St John, Daniel Shelton 1923- AmMWSc 92
St. John, David DrAPF 91, IntAu&W 91X, WrDr 92
St John, Douglas Francis 1938- AmMWSc 92
St John, Fraze Lee 1939- AmMWSc 92
St John, Harold 1892- AmMWSc 92
St. John, Hector BenetAL 91
St. John, Henry Sewell, Jr. 1938- WhoFI 92
St. John, Jill 1940- IntMPA 92, WhoEnt 92
St. John, John Pierce 1833-1916 AmPolLe
St John, Judith Brook 1940- AmMWSc 92
St John, Leonie IntAu&W 91X
St. John, Michelle 1967- WhoEnt 92
St John, Nicole IntAu&W 91, WrDr 92
St John, Oliver Beauchamp 1922- Who 92
St John, Patricia Mary 1919- IntAu&W 91, WrDr 92
St John, Peter Alan 1941- AmMWSc 92
St John, Philip IntAu&W 91X, TwCSFW 91, WrDr 92
St John, Philip Alan 1924- AmMWSc 92
St. John, Primus DrAPF 91
St. John, Primus 1939- WhoBlA 92
St John, Ralph C 1942- AmMWSc 92
St John, Robert 1902- IntAu&W 91, WrDr 92
St John, Robert Mahard 1927- AmMWSc 92
St John, Roger Ellis Tudor 1911- Who 92
St. John, Ronald Alan 1959- WhoFI 92
St. John, Ronald Ray 1956- WhoAmL 92
St. John, Seymour 1912- WhoRel 92
St John, Walter McCoy 1944- AmMWSc 92
St. John De La Salle Eno, Brian Peter G. 1948- WhoEnt 92
St John of Bletso, Baron 1957- Who 92
St. John of Fawsey, Baron 1929- WrDr 92
St. John Of Fawsley, Baron 1929- IntWW 91, Who 92
St John Parker, Michael 1941- Who 92
St John-Stevas Who 92
St John-Stevas, Norman 1929- IntAu&W 91
St John Wilson, Colin Alexander Who 92
St John's, Archbishop of 1924- Who 92
St. Johns, Richard R. 1929- IntMPA 92
St Johnston, Colin David 1934- Who 92
St Johnston, Kerry 1931- Who 92
St. Joseph, John Kenneth Sinclair 1912- IntWW 91, Who 92
Saint-Lambert, Jean-Francois de 1717-1803 BlkwCEP
St. Landau, Norman 1925- WhoAmL 92
St. Laurent, Louis Stephen 1882-1973 FacFETw
Saint-Laurent, Richard E. 1933- WhoFI 92
Saint Laurent, Yves 1936- DcTwDes, FacFETw, IntWW 91, Who 92
St Lawrence, Joseph Thomas 1913- WhoAmP 91
St Lawrence, Patricia 1922- AmMWSc 92
St Leger Who 92
St Levan, Baron 1919- Who 92
St Louis, Robert Vincent 1932- AmMWSc 92
Saint-Marcoux, Micheline Coulombe 1938-1985 NewAmDM
St. Martin, Althea Rose 1950- WhoWest 92
St Mary, Donald Frank 1940- AmMWSc 92
St. Mary, Joseph Jerome 1941- WhoBlA 92
St Maurice, Jean-Pierre 1949- AmMWSc 92
St. Mawr, Erin DrAPF 91
St. Omer, Garth ConNov 91, IntAu&W 91, WrDr 92
St. Omer, Vincent V. E. 1934- WhoBlA 92
St Omer, Vincent Victor 1934- AmMWSc 92
St-Onge, Denis Alderic 1929- AmMWSc 92
St Onge, G H AmMWSc 92
St. Onge, Hubert Jules 1946- WhoMW 92
St. Onge, Kevin John 1957- WhoEnt 92
St Onge, Vivian 1959- WhoAmP 91
St. Ores, John William 1949- WhoMW 92
St Oswald, Baron 1919- Who 92
St. Paul, Sterner TwCSFW 91
St Paul's, Dean of Who 92
St-Pierre, Claude 1932- AmMWSc 92
St. Pierre, Connie 1957- WhoEnt 92
St. Pierre, Edward 1952- WhoEnt 92
St Pierre, George R 1930- AmMWSc 92
St-Pierre, Jacques 1920- AmMWSc 92
Saint-Pierre, Jann Maddalena 1950- WhoWest 92
St Pierre, Jean Claude 1942- AmMWSc 92
St. Pierre, Jean Severs 1949- WhoFI 92
St Pierre, Leon Edward 1924- AmMWSc 92
Saint-Pierre, Michael Robert 1947- WhoFI 92
St Pierre, P D S 1925- AmMWSc 92
St. Pierre, Richard W. 1940- WhoWest 92
St Pierre, Ronald Leslie 1938- AmMWSc 92
St. Pierre, Suzanne Alida 1936- WhoEnt 92
St Pierre, Thomas 1932- AmMWSc 92
St Raymond, James V 1957- WhoAmP 91
Saint-Saens, Camille 1835-1921 NewAmDM
Saint-Veltri, Joseph 1944- WhoAmL 92
St. Ville, Thomas Joseph 1953- WhoAmL 92
St Vincent, Viscount 1905- Who 92
St. Vincent, Paul WrDr 92
St Vincent Ferreri, Marquis of Who 92
Sainte-Beuve, Charles-Augustin 1804-1869 GuFrLit 1
Sainte-Johnn, Don 1949- WhoBlA 92
Sainte-Marie, Buffy 1941- NewAmDM
Sainte-Marie, Guy 1928- AmMWSc 92
Saintonge, Rolland A. A. C. de Who 92
Sainty, John Christopher 1934- Who 92
Sainz Nothnangel, Jose 1907- BiDExR
Sainz Rodriguez, Pedro 1897-1986 BiDExR
Saire, Rebecca 1963- ConTFT 9
Saito, Eishiro 1911- IntWW 91
Saito, Eizaburo IntWW 91
Saito, Frank Kiyoji 1945- WhoWest 92
Saito, Juro 1940- IntWW 91
Saito, Kathleen Keiko 1955- WhoWest 92
Saito, Kunikichi 1909- IntWW 91
Saito, Nobufusa 1916- IntWW 91
Saito, Shigeyoshi 1918- IntWW 91
Saito, Takuma 1932- AmMWSc 92
Saito, Theodore T 1942- AmMWSc 92, WhoWest 92
Saito, Yoshimi 1942- WhoEnt 92
Saitoti, George IntWW 91
Sajadah, Vishwanath IntWW 91
Sajak, Pat LesBEnT 92
Sajak, Pat 1946- IntMPA 92
Sajak, Pat 1947- WhoEnt 92
Sajben, Miklos 1931- AmMWSc 92
Sajko, Brian Paul 1962- WhoMW 92
Sak, Joseph 1939- AmMWSc 92
Sakagawa, Gary Toshio AmMWSc 92
Sakaguchi, Dianne Koster 1946- AmMWSc 92
Sakai, Allen Hiroshi 1954- WhoAmL 92
Sakai, Ann K 1951- AmMWSc 92
Sakai, Katsuo 1942- WhoFI 92
Sakai, Peter A. 1954- WhoAmL 92
Sakai, Shoichiro 1928- AmMWSc 92
Sakai, Shota 1921- WhoAmP 91
Sakai, Ted Tetsuo 1945- AmMWSc 92
Sakai, William Shigeru 1942- AmMWSc 92
Sakaino, Kozo 1938- WhoWest 92
Sakakini, Joseph, Jr 1932- AmMWSc 92
Sakakura, Arthur Yoshikazu 1928- AmMWSc 92
Sakalauskas, Michael L. 1951- WhoWest 92
Sakalauskas, Vitautas Vladovich IntWW 91
Sakalauskas, Vitautas Vladovich 1933- SovUnBD
Sakalowsky, Peter Paul, Jr 1942- AmMWSc 92
Sakami, Warwick 1916- AmMWSc 92
Sakamoto, Clarence M 1931- AmMWSc 92
Sakamoto, Misoji 1923- IntWW 91
Sakamoto, Russell J 1944- WhoAmP 91
Sakamoto, Tomokazu 1917- IntWW 91
Sakamoto, Yoshikazu 1927- ConAu 133
Sakanashi, Mark Takeshi 1952- WhoFI 92
Sakano, Theodore K 1938- AmMWSc 92
Sakata, Michita 1916- IntWW 91
Sakayimbo, Cibulenu Robert 1946- WhoRel 92
Sakellarios, Alekos d1991 NewYTBS 91
Sakellariou, Haris 1923- IntAu&W 91
Saker, James Robert 1945- WhoMW 92
Sakhare, Vishwa M 1932- AmMWSc 92
Sakharnov, S. ConAu 133, SmATA 65 [port]
Sakharnov, Svyatoslav 1923- ConAu 133, SmATA 65 [port]
Sakharov, Andrei Dmitrievich 1921-1989 FacFETw [port]
Sakharov, Andrei Dmitriyevich 1921-1989 WhoNob 90
Sakharov, Andrey Dmitrievich 1921-1989 SovUnBD
Sakhnovsky, Alexander Alexandrovitch 1926- AmMWSc 92
Sakhnyuk, Ivan Ivanovich IntWW 91
Saki 1870-1916 FacFETw, RfGEnL 91, ScFEYrs
Sakier, George 1893-1965 DcTwDes
Sakievich, Mark John 1956- WhoAmP 91
Sakita, Bunji 1930- AmMWSc 92
Sakitt, Barbara AmMWSc 92
Sakitt, Mark 1938- AmMWSc 92
Sakkal, Mamoun 1950- WhoWest 92
Sakmar, Ismail Aydin 1925- AmMWSc 92
Sako, Kumao 1924- AmMWSc 92
Sako, Yoshio 1918- AmMWSc 92
Sakoda, William John 1951- AmMWSc 92
Sakol, Jeannie 1928- IntAu&W 91, WrDr 92
Sakowicz, Adrian Walter 1958- WhoMW 92
Sakraida, Michael G. 1959- WhoFI 92
Sakren, Jared 1950- WhoEnt 92
Sakrisson, Richard E. WhoRel 92
Saks, Arnold 1931- WhoEnt 92
Saks, Arnold Arnie 1950- WhoEnt 92
Saks, Gene IntWW 91
Saks, Gene 1921- ConTFT 9, IntMPA 92
Saks, Howard Jerome 1930- WhoWest 92
Saks, Michael Jay 1947- WhoMW 92
Saks, Norman Martin 1929- AmMWSc 92
Saksena, Vishnu P 1934- AmMWSc 92
Sakshaug, Eugene C 1923- AmMWSc 92
Sakulich, John Albert 1941- WhoMW 92
Sakura, John David 1936- AmMWSc 92
Sakurai, Toshio 1945- AmMWSc 92
Sakurai, Yoshifumi 1921- AmMWSc 92
Sakurauchi, Yoshio 1912- IntWW 91
Sakzewski, Albert d1991 Who 92N
Sala, Antonio 1935- WhoHisp 92
Sala, George Augustus 1828-1895 BenetAL 91
Sala, George Augustus 1828-1896 ScFEYrs
Sala, Harold James 1937- WhoRel 92
Sala, Marius 1932- IntWW 91
Salaam, Abdul 1929- WhoBlA 92
Salaam, Kalamu ya DrAPF 91
Salaam, Kalamu ya 1947- IntAu&W 91
Salaam, Salim A. 1922- IntWW 91
Salabert, Maria Teresa 1948- WhoHisp 92
Salabounis, Manuel 1935- WhoMW 92
Salacrou, Armand 1899-1989 GuFrLit 1
Saladin, Jurg X 1929- AmMWSc 92
Saladin, Kenneth S 1949- AmMWSc 92
Saladino, John 1939- DcTwDes
Saladrigas, Carlos Augusto 1948- WhoHisp 92
Salaff, Frederick J. 1945- WhoEnt 92
Salafia, W Ronald 1938- AmMWSc 92
Salafsky, Bernard P 1935- AmMWSc 92
Salah, Abdullah A. 1922- IntWW 91
Salah, Joseph E 1944- AmMWSc 92
Salah An Shiwei, Imam Al-Hadji WhoRel 92
Salahub, Dennis Russell 1946- AmMWSc 92
Salaita, George Nicola 1931- WhoWest 92
Salakhitdinov, Makhmud 1933- IntWW 91
Salam, Abdus 1926- AmMWSc 92, FacFETw, IntWW 91, Who 92, WhoNob 90
Salam, Debera Jean 1957- WhoFI 92
Salam, Fathi M A AmMWSc 92
Salam, Saeb 1905- IntWW 91
Salam al-Khalidi, Anbara 1897-1986 FacFETw
Salama, Clement Andre Tewfik 1938- AmMWSc 92
Salama, Guy 1947- AmMWSc 92
Salama, Kamel 1932- AmMWSc 92
Salaman, Myer Head 1902- Who 92
Salame, Edmund 1926- WhoWest 92
Salamo, Gregory Joseph 1944- AmMWSc 92
Salamon, Ed 1948- WhoEnt 92
Salamon, Ivan Istvan 1918- AmMWSc 92
Salamon, Kenneth J AmMWSc 92
Salamon, Miklos Dezso Gyorgy 1933- WhoWest 92
Salamon, Myron B 1939- AmMWSc 92
Salamon, Renay 1948- WhoFI 92
Salamon, Richard Joseph 1932- AmMWSc 92
Salamone, John M 1947- WhoAmP 91
Salamone, Joseph C 1939- AmMWSc 92
Salamone, Ottavio 1930- IntWW 91
Salamun, Betty A. 1951- WhoEnt 92
Salamun, Peter Joseph 1919- AmMWSc 92
Salan, Raoul 1899-1984 FacFETw
Salanave, Leon Edward 1917- AmMWSc 92
Saland, Linda C 1942- AmMWSc 92
Saland, Linda Carol 1942- WhoWest 92
Saland, Stephen M 1943- WhoAmP 91
Salaneck, William R 1941- AmMWSc 92
Salani EncAmaz 91
Salanitre, Ernest 1915- AmMWSc 92
Salanki, Janos 1929- IntWW 91
Salans, Lester Barry 1936- AmMWSc 92
Salant, Abner Samuel 1930- AmMWSc 92
Salant, Richard Frank 1941- AmMWSc 92
Salant, Richard S. LesBEnT 92
Salant, Richard S. 1914- IntMPA 92
Salardino, Michael George 1949- WhoAmP 91
Salari, Hassan 1953- AmMWSc 92
Salars, Mark Alan 1961- WhoFI 92
Salas, Alan R. 1956- WhoHisp 92
Salas, Alejandro WhoHisp 92
Salas, Didio B. 1919- WhoHisp 92
Salas, Floyd DrAPF 91
Salas, Floyd Francis 1931- WhoHisp 92
Salas, Francisco Jose WhoHisp 92
Salas, Guillermo, Jr. WhoHisp 92
Salas, Gumecindo 1941- WhoHisp 92
Salas, J. Gustavo WhoHisp 92
Salas, Marcos 1944- WhoHisp 92
Salas, Margaret Laurence 1922- Who 92
Salas, Marilyn Sue 1943- WhoWest 92
Salas, Mary Carmen 1937- WhoRel 92
Salas, Max E. 1953- WhoHisp 92
Salas, Melodi L WhoAmP 91
Salas, Pedro Jose I 1954- AmMWSc 92
Salas, Peter 1965- WhoHisp 92
Salas, Raul Ramiro 1953- WhoRel 92
Salas-Quintana, Salvador 1955- AmMWSc 92
Salasin, Sal DrAPF 91
Salati, Octavio M 1914- AmMWSc 92
Salatiello, Thomas B 1945- WhoAmP 91
Salatino, Jim 1949- WhoAmP 91
Salatino, William J. 1956- WhoMW 92
Salatka, Charles DcAmImH
Salatka, Charles Alexander 1918- WhoRel 92
Salaym Bint Malhan EncAmaz 91
Salaz, Mike 1946- WhoAmP 91
Salaz, Mike D. 1946- WhoHisp 92
Salazar, Alberto 1958- WhoHisp 92
Salazar, Aldemar Martinez WhoRel 92
Salazar, Antoinio de Oliveira 1889-1970 BiDExR
Salazar, Antonio de Oliveira 1889-1970 EncTR 91 [port], FacFETw
Salazar, Arturo 1958- WhoRel 92
Salazar, Carmen 1940- WhoHisp 92
Salazar, Cleo 1938- WhoHisp 92
Salazar, Daniel Reynolds 1942- WhoWest 92
Salazar, David Henry 1942- WhoHisp 92
Salazar, David R. S. WhoHisp 92
Salazar, Diego 1945- WhoHisp 92
Salazar, Dolores M. 1945- WhoHisp 92
Salazar, Domingo de 1512-1594 HisDSpE
Salazar, Edward 1944- WhoHisp 92
Salazar, Eliseo M., Jr. 1957- WhoHisp 92
Salazar, Frank WhoEnt 92
Salazar, Fred James, Jr. 1942- WhoHisp 92
Salazar, Gertrude 1936- WhoHisp 92
Salazar, Guadalupe 1944- WhoHisp 92
Salazar, Helen Aquila 1944- WhoHisp 92
Salazar, Hernando 1931- AmMWSc 92
Salazar, I. C. WhoHisp 92
Salazar, Kenneth Vincent 1948- WhoHisp 92
Salazar, Luis Adolfo 1944- WhoHisp 92, WhoWest 92
Salazar, Luis Garcia 1956- WhoHisp 92
Salazar, Lupe Maria 1927- WhoHisp 92
Salazar, Maximiliano Wilfredo 1929- WhoHisp 92
Salazar, Michael B. WhoHisp 92
Salazar, Michael E., Sr. 1956- WhoHisp 92
Salazar, Michael Joseph 1931- WhoWest 92
Salazar, Miriam Larios 1962- WhoHisp 92
Salazar, Nick L WhoAmP 91, WhoHisp 92
Salazar, Rachel DrAPF 91
Salazar, Rachel 1954- WrDr 92
Salazar, Ramiro S. 1954- WhoHisp 92
Salazar, Raymond Anthony 1947- WhoHisp 92
Salazar, Rogelio Gil, Jr. 1962- WhoFI 92
Salazar, Rudy 1941- WhoHisp 92
Salazar, Steve 1965- WhoHisp 92
Salazar, Theresa A. 1955- WhoHisp 92
Salazar, Tony 1959- WhoHisp 92
Salazar, Tony Michael 1952- WhoHisp 92

**Salazar**, Victor M. *WhoHisp 92*
**Salazar-Carrillo**, Jorge 1938- *WhoFI 92, WhoHisp 92*
**Salazar Lopez**, Jose 1910- *IntWW 91, WhoRel 92*
**Salazar Manrique**, Roberto 1936- *IntWW 91*
**Salazar Navarro**, Hernando 1931- *WhoHisp 92*
**Salazar y Espinosa**, Juan de 1508-1560 *HisDSpE*
**Salber**, Eva Juliet 1916- *AmMWSc 92*
**Salberg**, Jeffrey David 1952- *WhoAmL 92*
**Salbu**, Steven Russell 1957- *WhoAmL 92*
**Salce**, Ludwig 1934- *AmMWSc 92*
**Salcedo**, Ernesto 1931- *IntAu&W 91*
**Salcedo**, Herman Francisco 1958- *WhoHisp 92*
**Salcedo**, Jesse Garcia 1948- *WhoEnt 92*
**Salcedo**, Jose Jesus 1960- *WhoHisp 92*
**Salcedo-Bastardo**, Jose Luis 1926- *IntWW 91*
**Salch**, Richard K 1940- *AmMWSc 92*
**Salch**, Steven Charles 1943- *WhoAmL 92*
**Salcher**, Herbert 1929- *IntWW 91*
**Salchert**, Brian *DrAPF 91*
**Salchow**, Gordon Robert 1940- *WhoMW 92*
**Salcido**, Pablo *WhoHisp 92*
**Salcido**, Silvia Astorga *WhoHisp 92*
**Salcito**, Daniel R 1940- *WhoAmP 91*
**Salcman**, Michael 1946- *AmMWSc 92*
**Salcudean**, Martha Eva 1934- *AmMWSc 92, WhoWest 92*
**Saldamando**, Alex *WhoHisp 92*
**Saldana**, Alfonso Manuel 1960- *WhoAmL 92*
**Saldana**, Andrew Joe 1950- *WhoHisp 92*
**Saldana**, Fred, Jr. *WhoHisp 92*
**Saldana**, Johnny 1954- *WhoHisp 92*
**Saldana**, Jose M. *WhoHisp 92*
**Saldana**, Mariana *WhoHisp 92*
**Saldana**, Santiago A., Jr. 1949- *WhoHisp 92*
**Saldana**, Theresa 1955- *WhoHisp 92*
**Saldana-Luna**, Pura 1944- *WhoHisp 92*
**Saldanha**, Leila Genevieve 1955- *AmMWSc 92*
**Saldarini**, Giovanni 1924- *WhoRel 92*
**Saldarini**, Ronald John 1939- *AmMWSc 92*
**Saldarriaga**, Alexander 1960- *WhoFI 92*
**Saldate**, Macario, IV 1941- *WhoHisp 92*
**Saldich**, Robert Joseph 1933- *WhoFI 92, WhoWest 92*
**Saldick**, Jerome 1921- *AmMWSc 92*
**Saldin**, Thomas R. 1946- *WhoAmL 92*
**Saldinger**, Scott Wayne 1968- *WhoEnt 92*
**Saldivar**, Jose D. 1955- *WhoHisp 92*
**Saldivar**, Ramon 1949- *WhoHisp 92*
**Sale**, Chic 1885-1936 *BenetAL 91*
**Sale**, George Edgar 1941- *WhoWest 92*
**Sale**, Kirkpatrick 1937- *ConLC 68 [port], IntAu&W 91, WrDr 92*
**Sale**, Peter Francis 1941- *AmMWSc 92*
**Sale**, Richard 1911- *IntAu&W 91, IntMPA 92, WrDr 92*
**Sale**, Tom S. 1942- *WhoFI 92*
**Saleeb**, Fouad Zaki 1934- *AmMWSc 92*
**Saleeby**, Edward Eli 1927- *WhoAmP 91*
**Saleeby**, Jason Brian 1948- *AmMWSc 92*
**Saleem**, M. *WhoMW 92*
**Saleh**, Adel Abdel Moneim 1942- *AmMWSc 92*
**Saleh**, Ali Abdullah 1942?- *IntWW 91*
**Saleh**, Bahaa E A 1944- *AmMWSc 92*
**Saleh**, David John 1953- *WhoAmL 92*
**Saleh**, Dennis *DrAPF 91*
**Saleh**, Farida Yousry 1939- *AmMWSc 92*
**Saleh**, Rachmat 1930- *IntWW 91*
**Saleh**, Wasfy Seleman 1932- *AmMWSc 92*
**Saleh Houssain**, Ahmed 1956- *BlkOlyM*
**Salehi**, Habib 1935- *AmMWSc 92*
**Salehkhou**, Ghassem 1941- *IntWW 91*
**Salek**, Mustapha Ould *IntWW 91*
**Salem**, Daniel Laurent Manuel 1925- *Who 92*
**Salem**, Donna Jean 1951- *WhoAmL 92*
**Salem**, Edward Murray 1959- *WhoMW 92*
**Salem**, Elie 1930- *IntWW 91*
**Salem**, George Richard 1953- *WhoAmP 91*
**Salem**, Harry 1929- *AmMWSc 92*
**Salem**, John F. 1956- *WhoEnt 92*
**Salem**, Norman, Jr 1950- *AmMWSc 92*
**Salem**, Richard Joseph 1947- *WhoAmL 92*
**Salem**, Semaan Ibrahim 1927- *AmMWSc 92*
**Salemi**, Joseph S. *DrAPF 91*
**Salemi**, Marie Anne 1927- *WhoAmP 91*
**Salemme**, Robert Michael 1943- *AmMWSc 92*
**Salenger**, Lucy Lee 1938- *WhoEnt 92*
**Salentine**, Thomas James 1939- *WhoFI 92*
**Saler**, John Rudofker 1958- *WhoAmP 91*
**Salerni**, Oreste Leroy 1934- *AmMWSc 92*
**Salerno**, Alphonse 1923- *AmMWSc 92*
**Salerno**, Frederic V. 1943- *WhoFI 92*
**Salerno**, James Gene 1950- *WhoAmL 92*
**Salerno**, John Charles 1949- *AmMWSc 92*
**Salerno**, Joseph Michael 1917- *WhoWest 92*
**Salerno**, Louis Joseph 1949- *AmMWSc 92*
**Salerno**, Mary J 1923- *WhoAmP 91*
**Salerno**, Ronald Anthony 1942- *AmMWSc 92*
**Salerno**, Salvatore *DrAPF 91*
**Salerno-Sonnenberg**, Nadja 1961- *WhoEnt 92*
**Sales**, A. R. 1948- *WhoFI 92*
**Sales**, Brian Craig 1947- *AmMWSc 92*
**Sales**, David Joseph 1961- *WhoAmL 92*
**Sales**, Eugenio de Araujo 1920- *WhoRel 92*
**Sales**, James Bohus 1934- *WhoAmL 92, WhoFI 92*
**Sales**, John Keith 1934- *AmMWSc 92*
**Sales**, Michael 1928- *WhoIns 92*
**Sales**, Richard Owen 1948- *WhoBlA 92*
**Sales**, Soupy *LesBEnT 92*
**Sales**, Walter R 1927- *WhoAmP 91*
**Sales**, William Henry d1991 *Who 92N*
**Salesky**, Charles H d1991 *NewYTBS 91*
**Salesky**, William Jeffrey 1957- *WhoWest 92*
**Salet**, Francis 1909- *IntWW 91*
**Saletan**, Leonard Timothy 1915- *AmMWSc 92*
**Saleuddin**, Abu S 1937- *AmMWSc 92*
**Salfi**, Dominick J 1937- *WhoAmP 91*
**Salford**, Bishop of 1938- *Who 92*
**Salgado**, Annivar 1954- *WhoHisp 92*
**Salgado**, Ernesto D 1923- *AmMWSc 92*
**Salgado**, Jose Francisco 1949- *WhoHisp 92*
**Salgado**, Juan, III 1956- *WhoHisp 92*
**Salgado**, Lissette *WhoEnt 92*
**Salgado**, Luis J. 1953- *WhoHisp 92*
**Salgado**, Maria Antonia 1933- *WhoHisp 92*
**Salgado**, Mario A. 1959- *WhoHisp 92*
**Salgado**, Merennagr Ranji Pemsiri 1929- *WhoFI 92*
**Salgado**, Plinio 1895-1975 *BiDExR*
**Salgado**, R. Anthony 1962- *WhoAmL 92*
**Salgado**, Sebastiao 1944- *NewYTBS 91 [port]*
**Salganicoff**, Leon 1924- *AmMWSc 92*
**Salgueiro**, Carmen Escude *WhoEnt 92*
**Salguero**, Ricardo Arturo 1954- *WhoFI 92*
**Salhanick**, Hilton Aaron 1924- *AmMWSc 92*
**Salhany**, James Mitchell 1947- *AmMWSc 92*
**Salhany**, Lucie *LesBEnT 92 [port]*
**Sali**, William T *WhoAmP 91*
**Saliba**, Alfred J 1930- *WhoAmP 91*
**Saliba**, John A. 1937- *ConAu 35NR*
**Saliba**, John Albert 1937- *WhoMW 92, WhoRel 92*
**Saliba**, John H 1938- *WhoIns 92*
**Saliba**, Philip E. 1931- *WhoRel 92*
**Salibello**, Salvatore Joseph 1936- *WhoAmL 92*
**Salicio**, Jose Luis 1954- *WhoHisp 92*
**Salieri**, Antonio 1750-1825 *NewAmDM*
**Salig**, Ronald James 1950- *WhoFI 92*
**Saligman**, Harvey 1938- *WhoFI 92*
**Salignac**, Francois de *BlkwCEP*
**Salih**, Tayeb 1927- *LiExTwC*
**Salihi**, Jalal T 1925- *AmMWSc 92*
**Salik**, Julian Oswald 1909- *AmMWSc 92*
**Salim**, Salim Ahmed 1942- *IntWW 91*
**Salimei**, Marcello 1927- *IntWW 91*
**Salimeno**, George Robert 1931- *WhoAmP 91*
**Salimov**, Akil Umurzakovich 1928- *IntWW 91*
**Salin**, Marvin Leonard 1946- *AmMWSc 92*
**Salin**, William Nathan 1931- *WhoFI 92*
**Salinas**, Carlos 1948- *News 92-1 [port]*
**Salinas**, David 1932- *AmMWSc 92, WhoWest 92*
**Salinas**, Emma *WhoHisp 92*
**Salinas**, Fernando A 1939- *AmMWSc 92*
**Salinas**, Harry Roger 1949- *WhoHisp 92*
**Salinas**, Homer *WhoHisp 92*
**Salinas**, Joseph A. 1955- *WhoEnt 92*
**Salinas**, Leonardo 1933- *WhoHisp 92*
**Salinas**, Lorina *WhoHisp 92*
**Salinas**, Louis Omar *DrAPF 91*
**Salinas**, Luciano, Jr 1950 *WhoHisp 92*
**Salinas**, Luis 1965- *WhoHisp 92*
**Salinas**, Luis Omar 1937- *WhoHisp 92*
**Salinas**, Lupe 1948- *WhoHisp 92*
**Salinas**, Maria Elena *WhoHisp 92*
**Salinas**, Noe 1924- *WhoHisp 92*
**Salinas**, Norberto *WhoHisp 92*
**Salinas**, Oscar 1951- *WhoHisp 92*
**Salinas**, Pedro 1891-1951 *LiExTwC*
**Salinas**, Raul Francisco 1960- *WhoAmL 92*
**Salinas**, Raul G. 1946- *WhoHisp 92*
**Salinas**, Ricardo 1961- *WhoHisp 92*
**Salinas**, Ruben Longino 1954- *WhoHisp 92*
**Salinas**, Rudy 1953- *WhoHisp 92*
**Salinas**, Sharon Anne 1961- *WhoAmL 92*
**Salinas**, Simon 1955- *WhoHisp 92, WhoWest 92*
**Salinas De Gortari**, Carlos 1948- *IntWW 91*
**Salinas-Ender**, Elma T. *WhoHisp 92*
**Salinas Izaguirre**, Abel 1930- *IntWW 91*
**Salinas Izaguirre**, Saul F. 1932- *WhoHisp 92*
**Salinas-Norman**, Bobbi *WhoHisp 92*
**Salinas y Cordoba**, Buenaventura de 1592-1653 *HisDSpE*
**Saling**, Gerald L *WhoAmP 91*
**Salingaros**, Nikos Angelos 1952- *AmMWSc 92*
**Salinger**, Gerhard Ludwig 1934- *AmMWSc 92*
**Salinger**, Herman 1905- *IntAu&W 91*
**Salinger**, J.D. *DrAPF 91*
**Salinger**, J D 1916- *FacFETw*
**Salinger**, J. D. 1919- *BenetAL 91, ConNov 91, IntAu&W 91, IntWW 91, SmATA 67 [port], WrDr 92*
**Salinger**, Jerome David 1919- *Who 92*
**Salinger**, Michael Alvin 1956- *WhoFI 92*
**Salinger**, Pierre *LesBEnT 92*
**Salinger**, Pierre 1925- *Who 92, WrDr 92*
**Salinger**, Pierre Emil George 1925- *IntWW 91*
**Salinger**, Rudolf Michael 1936- *AmMWSc 92*
**Salinger**, Sidney Bernerd, Jr. 1933- *WhoFI 92*
**Salinger**, Wendy *DrAPF 91*
**Saliola**, Frances 1921- *WhoFI 92*
**Salis**, Andrew E 1915- *AmMWSc 92*
**Salis**, Jean Rodolphe de 1901- *IntWW 91*
**Salis**, Steven Anthony 1961- *WhoEnt 92*
**Salisbury**, Bishop of 1928- *Who 92*
**Salisbury**, Dean of *Who 92*
**Salisbury**, Marquess of 1916- *Who 92*
**Salisbury**, Alicia Laing 1939- *WhoAmP 91*
**Salisbury**, Darryl Alan 1943- *WhoMW 92*
**Salisbury**, David Francis 1947- *WhoWest 92*
**Salisbury**, Deale B *WhoAmP 91*
**Salisbury**, Frank B 1926- *IntAu&W 91, WrDr 92*
**Salisbury**, Frank Boyer 1926- *AmMWSc 92*
**Salisbury**, Frank Pressley 1930- *WhoEnt 92*
**Salisbury**, Glenn Wade 1910- *AmMWSc 92*
**Salisbury**, Harrison E. 1908- *BenetAL 91, ConAu 15AS [port], WrDr 92*
**Salisbury**, Harrison Evans 1908- *IntAu&W 91, IntWW 91, Who 92*
**Salisbury**, James Henry 1823-1905 *BiInAmS*
**Salisbury**, Jeffrey L 1950- *AmMWSc 92*
**Salisbury**, Jenny Olivia 1959- *WhoMW 92*
**Salisbury**, John *IntAu&W 91X, Who 92, WrDr 92*
**Salisbury**, John Francis 1930- *WhoAmL 92*
**Salisbury**, John William, Jr 1933- *AmMWSc 92*
**Salisbury**, Joyce E. 1944- *ConAu 135*
**Salisbury**, Matthew Harold 1943- *AmMWSc 92*
**Salisbury**, Neil Elliot 1928- *AmMWSc 92*
**Salisbury**, Ralph *DrAPF 91*
**Salisbury**, Robert G *WhoAmP 91*
**Salisbury**, Robert H 1930- *IntAu&W 91, WrDr 92*
**Salisbury**, Stanley R 1932- *AmMWSc 92*
**Salisbury**, Stephen Matthew 1931- *IntAu&W 91*
**Salisbury**, Wayne 1941- *WhoAmP 91*
**Salisbury**, William 1875- *ScFEYrs*
**Salisch**, Wynn Jay 1951- *WhoEnt 92*
**Salisse**, John Joseph 1926- *Who 92*
**Saliterman**, Richard Arlen 1946- *WhoAmL 92, WhoFI 92, WhoMW 92*
**Salivar**, Charles Joseph 1923- *AmMWSc 92*
**Salk**, Darrell John 1947- *AmMWSc 92*
**Salk**, Jonas 1914- *FacFETw [port], RComAH*
**Salk**, Jonas Edward 1914- *AmMWSc 92, IntWW 91, Who 92, WhoWest 92*
**Salk**, Martha Scheer 1945- *AmMWSc 92*
**Salk**, Sung-Ho Suck 1939- *AmMWSc 92*
**Salkey**, Andrew 1928- *ConNov 91, IntAu&W 91, LiExTwC, WrDr 92*
**Salkin**, David 1906- *AmMWSc 92, WhoWest 92*
**Salkin**, Ira Fred 1941- *AmMWSc 92*
**Salkind**, Alexander *IntWW 91*
**Salkind**, Alexander 1921- *IntMPA 92, WhoEnt 92*
**Salkind**, Alvin J 1927- *AmMWSc 92*
**Salkind**, Ilya 1947- *IntWW 91*
**Salkind**, Ilya 1948- *IntMPA 92*
**Salkind**, Michael Jay 1938- *AmMWSc 92, WhoMW 92*
**Salkoff**, Lawrence Benjamin 1944- *AmMWSc 92*
**Salkow**, Sidney 1911- *IntMPA 92*
**Sall**, Frank M 1937- *WhoAmP 91*
**Sall**, Theodore 1927- *AmMWSc 92*
**Sallaberry**, Fernando R. 1965- *WhoEnt 92*
**Sallada**, Roland A 1917- *WhoAmP 91*
**Sallade**, George Wahr 1922- *WhoAmP 91*
**Sallah**, Majeed Jim 1920- *WhoFI 92*
**Sallah**, Ousman Ahmadou 1938- *IntWW 91*
**Sallal**, Abdullah as- 1917- *IntWW 91*
**Sallam**, Mohamed Abdulaziz 1933- *IntWW 91*
**Sallavanti**, Robert Armando 1942- *AmMWSc 92*
**Sallay**, Stephen 1920- *AmMWSc 92*
**Sallay**, Tibor 1922- *WhoAmL 92*
**Salle**, David 1952- *IntWW 91, WorArt 1980 [port]*
**Sallee**, Don *WhoAmP 91*
**Sallee**, G Thomas 1940- *AmMWSc 92*
**Sallee**, Verney Lee 1942- *AmMWSc 92*
**Sallee**, Wesley William 1951- *WhoWest 92*
**Sallen**, Ira Bruce 1954- *WhoFI 92*
**Sallen**, Marvin Seymour 1930- *WhoMW 92*
**Saller**, Charles Frederick 1950- *AmMWSc 92*
**Salles**, Jaime Carlos 1930- *WhoHisp 92*
**Salles-Cunha**, Sergio Xavier 1947- *WhoWest 92*
**Sallet**, Dirse Wilkis 1936- *AmMWSc 92*
**Salley**, George Henry, III 1954- *WhoAmL 92*
**Salley**, John Jones 1926- *AmMWSc 92*
**Salley**, John Jones, Jr 1954- *AmMWSc 92*
**Salley**, John Thomas 1964- *WhoBlA 92*
**Sallinen**, Aulis 1935- *ConCom 92, NewAmDM*
**Sallinen**, Aulis Heikki 1935- *IntWW 91*
**Sallinger**, David Carl 1953- *WhoEnt 92*
**Sallinger**, Rudolf 1916- *IntWW 91*
**Sallis**, James 1944- *TwCSFW 91, WrDr 92*
**Sallis**, John C. 1938- *WrDr 92*
**Sallman**, Bennett 1917- *AmMWSc 92*
**Sallos**, Joseph 1931- *AmMWSc 92*
**Salman Ibn Abdul Aziz**, Prince 1936- *IntWW 91*
**Salman**, Carlos 1932- *WhoAmP 91*
**Salman**, Salah 1936- *IntWW 91*
**Salmanov**, Grigory Ivanovich 1922- *IntWW 91*
**Salmanov**, Vadim Nikolaevich 1912-1978 *SovUnBD*
**Salmassy**, Omar K 1925- *AmMWSc 92*
**Salmen**, Robert Lee 1940- *WhoFI 92*
**Salmenhaara**, Erkki 1941- *ConCom 92*
**Salmeron**, Fernando 1925- *IntWW 91*
**Salmi**, Ellablanche *DrAPF 91*
**Salmi**, Ernest William 1922- *AmMWSc 92*
**Salmiala**, Bruno Aleksandr 1890-1981 *BiDExR*
**Salmoiraghi**, Gian Carlo 1924- *AmMWSc 92*
**Salmon** *Who 92*
**Salmon**, Baron 1903- *IntWW 91, Who 92*
**Salmon**, Andre 1881-1969 *GuFrLit 1*
**Salmon**, Bradley Guy 1969- *WhoMW 92*
**Salmon**, Brian Lawson 1917- *IntWW 91, Who 92*
**Salmon**, Charles G 1930- *AmMWSc 92*
**Salmon**, Daniel Elmer 1850-1914 *BiInAmS*
**Salmon**, Edward Dickinson 1944- *AmMWSc 92*
**Salmon**, Edward H *WhoAmP 91*
**Salmon**, Edward Togo 1905- *IntAu&W 91*
**Salmon**, Eli J 1928- *AmMWSc 92*
**Salmon**, Finnis Larry 1938- *WhoAmL 92*
**Salmon**, J. Warren 1947- *WhoMW 92*
**Salmon**, James Henry 1932- *AmMWSc 92*
**Salmon**, Jaslin Uriah 1942- *WhoBlA 92*
**Salmon**, John 1925- *WrDr 92*
**Salmon**, John Tenison 1910- *IntWW 91*
**Salmon**, Lee William 1938- *WhoFI 92*
**Salmon**, Maria Virginia 1954- *WhoHisp 92*
**Salmon**, Matt 1936- *WhoAmP 91*
**Salmon**, Merlyn Leigh 1924- *WhoWest 92*
**Salmon**, Michael 1938- *AmMWSc 92*
**Salmon**, Nancy *Who 92*
**Salmon**, Oliver Norton 1917- *AmMWSc 92*
**Salmon**, Peter Alexander 1929- *AmMWSc 92*
**Salmon**, Raymond Edward 1931- *AmMWSc 92*
**Salmon**, Robert 1918- *IntWW 91*
**Salmon**, Stuart Clive 1952- *WhoMW 92*
**Salmon**, Tabitha 1955- *TwCPaSc*
**Salmon**, Thomas David 1916- *Who 92*
**Salmon**, Thomas Noel Desmond Cornwall 1913- *Who 92*
**Salmon**, Vincent 1912- *AmMWSc 92*
**Salmon**, William Alexander 1910- *Who 92*
**Salmon Campbell**, Joan Mitchell 1938- *WhoBlA 92*
**Salmond**, Alexander Elliot Anderson 1954- *Who 92*
**Salmond**, Felix 1888-1952 *NewAmDM*
**Salmond**, William Glover 1941- *AmMWSc 92*

**Salmons,** John Robert 1932- *AmMWSc 92*
**Salmonson,** Jessica Amanda 1950- *ConAu 36NR, TwCSFW 91*
**Salnave,** George Michael 1949- *WhoRel 92*
**Salo,** Ann Sexton D. 1947- *WhoAmL 92*
**Salo,** Ernest Olavi 1919- *AmMWSc 92*
**Salo,** Tera Lea 1960- *WhoWest 92*
**Salo,** Wilmar Lawrence 1937- *AmMWSc 92*
**Salolainen,** Pertti Edvard 1940- *IntWW 91*
**Salom,** Donald Eric 1955- *WhoAmL 92*
**Salom,** Philip 1950- *ConPo 91, IntAu&W 91*
**Salom,** Roberto 1944- *WhoFI 92*
**Saloma-Orozco,** Abraham Eduardo 1941- *WhoFI 92*
**Saloman,** Edward Barry 1940- *AmMWSc 92*
**Salome** 1954- *WorArt 1980*
**Salomon,** Alex K. 1959- *WhoFI 92*
**Salomon,** Darrell Joseph 1939- *WhoAmL 92*
**Salomon,** Erich 1886-1944 *FacFETw*
**Salomon,** Ernst Friedrich Karl von 1902-1972 *BiDExR*
**Salomon,** Ernst von 1902-1972 *EncTR 91 [port]*
**Salomon,** Henry, Jr. d1957 *LesBEnT 92*
**Salomon,** Janet Lynn Nowicki 1953- *WhoEnt 92*
**Salomon,** Johann Peter 1745-1815 *NewAmDM*
**Salomon,** Lothar L 1921- *AmMWSc 92*
**Salomon,** Mark 1935- *AmMWSc 92*
**Salomon,** Mikael *IntMPA 92*
**Salomon,** Richard Adley 1953- *WhoAmL 92*
**Salomon,** Richard Geoffrey 1948- *WhoWest 92*
**Salomon,** Richard Marc 1953- *WhoMW 92*
**Salomon,** Robert Ephriam 1933- *AmMWSc 92*
**Salomon,** Roger Blaine 1928- *WhoMW 92*
**Salomon,** Salomon Maury 1924- *WhoFI 92*
**Salomon,** Servin *WhoHisp 92*
**Salomone,** William Gerald 1948- *WhoAmL 92*
**Salomons,** Jean-Pierre 1911- *IntWW 91*
**Salomonson,** Vincent Victor 1937- *AmMWSc 92*
**Salonek,** Eugene William, Jr. 1957- *WhoRel 92*
**Salonen,** Esa-Pekka 1958- *IntWW 91, NewAmDM, WhoEnt 92, WhoWest 92*
**Saloner,** Garth 1955- *WhoFI 92*
**Salonia,** Antonio Francisco 1927- *IntWW 91*
**Salony,** John, III 1947- *WhoFI 92*
**Salony,** Jon R. 1946- *WhoFI 92*
**Saloom,** Eugene George 1934- *WhoAmP 91*
**Saloom,** Kaliste Joseph, Jr. 1918- *WhoAmL 92*
**Salop,** Archdeacon of *Who 92*
**Salot,** Stuart Edwin 1937- *AmMWSc 92*
**Salotto,** Anthony W 1936- *AmMWSc 92*
**Saloutos,** Theodore 1910-1980 *DcAmImH*
**Salovey,** Ronald 1932- *AmMWSc 92*
**Salowitz,** Stewart Irving 1954- *WhoEnt 92*
**Salpeter,** Edwin E. 1924- *IntWW 91*
**Salpeter,** Edwin Ernest 1924- *AmMWSc 92*
**Salpeter,** Miriam Mirl 1929- *AmMWSc 92*
**Salsbury,** Jason Melvin 1920- *AmMWSc 92*
**Salsbury,** Robert Lawrence 1916- *AmMWSc 92*
**Salsbury,** Roberta Maurano 1946- *WhoEnt 92*
**Salsbury,** Roland S, Jr *WhoAmP 91*
**Salsbury,** Stephen 1931- *WrDr 92*
**Salser,** Winston Albert 1939- *AmMWSc 92*
**Salsig,** Doyen 1923- *WhoWest 92*
**Salsig,** William Winter, Jr 1919- *AmMWSc 92*
**Salsman,** Berney, III 1958- *WhoRel 92*
**Salsman,** Richard Michael 1959- *WhoFI 92*
**Salsman,** Robert Thomas 1937- *WhoMW 92*
**Salstein,** David A *AmMWSc 92*
**Salstrom,** John Stuart 1945- *AmMWSc 92*
**Salt,** Alfred Lewis 1927- *WhoRel 92*
**Salt,** Anthony Houlton d1991 *Who 92N*
**Salt,** Dale L 1924- *AmMWSc 92*
**Salt,** George 1903- *IntWW 91, Who 92*
**Salt,** George William 1919- *AmMWSc 92*
**Salt,** James Frederick Thomas George 1940- *Who 92*
**Salt,** Patrick 1932- *Who 92*
**Salt,** Thomas Michael 1946- *Who 92*
**Salt,** Walter Raymond 1905- *AmMWSc 92*
**Salt-N-Pepa** *ConMus 6 [port]*
**Salta,** Steven Anthony 1955- *WhoWest 92*
**Saltarelli,** Michael A. 1933- *WhoRel 92*
**Salter,** Cedric *WrDr 92*
**Salter,** Edwin Carroll 1927- *WhoMW 92*
**Salter,** Hans J. 1896- *IntMPA 92*
**Salter,** Harry Charles 1918- *Who 92*
**Salter,** Hugh 1921- *WhoAmP 91*
**Salter,** Ian George 1943- *Who 92*
**Salter,** James *DrAPF 91*
**Salter,** James 1925- *BenetAL 91*
**Salter,** Joe R 1943- *WhoAmP 91*
**Salter,** John Rotherham 1932- *IntWW 91*
**Salter,** Kwame S. 1946- *WhoBlA 92*
**Salter,** Lewis Spencer 1926- *AmMWSc 92*
**Salter,** Lionel 1914- *IntAu&W 91*
**Salter,** Lionel Paul 1914- *IntWW 91*
**Salter,** Mary D *IntAu&W 91X, WrDr 92*
**Salter,** Mary Jo *DrAPF 91*
**Salter,** Mary Jo 1954- *WrDr 92*
**Salter,** P. C. 1953- *WhoEnt 92*
**Salter,** Patrick Morris, Jr. 1952- *WhoWest 92*
**Salter,** Phyllis Jean 1959- *WhoMW 92*
**Salter,** Robert Bruce 1924- *AmMWSc 92*
**Salter,** Robert Munkhenk, Jr 1920- *AmMWSc 92*
**Salter,** Roger Franklin 1940- *WhoBlA 92*
**Salter,** Vance Edwin 1948- *WhoAmL 92*
**Salter Ainsworth,** Mary D *IntAu&W 91X*
**Salthe,** Stanley Norman 1930- *AmMWSc 92*
**Salthouse,** Edward Charles 1935- *Who 92*
**Salthouse,** Leonard 1927- *Who 92*
**Saltiel,** Alan Robert 1953- *AmMWSc 92*
**Saltiel,** Jack 1938- *AmMWSc 92*
**Saltman,** Benjamin *DrAPF 91*
**Saltman,** David J 1951- *AmMWSc 92*
**Saltman,** Judith 1947- *IntAu&W 91*
**Saltman,** Paul David 1928- *AmMWSc 92*
**Saltman,** Roy G 1932- *AmMWSc 92*
**Saltman,** Sheldon Arthur 1933- *WhoEnt 92, WhoWest 92*
**Saltman,** William Mose 1917- *AmMWSc 92*
**Saltmarsh,** Robert E. 1931- *WhoMW 92*
**Saltmarsh,** Sara Elizabeth 1956- *WhoAmL 92*
**Saltmarsh,** Sherman W, Jr 1929- *WhoAmP 91*
**Saltnes,** John Norman 1955- *WhoWest 92*
**Salton,** Albin 1916- *WhoFI 92*
**Salton,** Gerard 1927- *AmMWSc 92*
**Salton,** Milton Robert James 1921- *AmMWSc 92, Who 92*
**Saltonstall,** Clarence William, Jr 1925- *AmMWSc 92*
**Saltonstall,** George West 1944- *WhoFI 92*
**Saltonstall,** William Lawrence 1927- *WhoAmP 91*
**Saltoun,** Lady 1930- *Who 92*
**Saltoun,** Andre Meir 1929- *WhoAmL 92*
**Saltsburg,** Howard Mortimer 1928- *AmMWSc 92*
**Saltsman,** Donald L 1933- *WhoAmP 91*
**Saltus,** Edgar 1855-1921 *BenetAL 91*
**Saltveit,** Mikal Endre, Jr 1944- *AmMWSc 92*
**Saltykov,** Aleksey 1934- *IntWW 91*
**Saltz,** Daniel 1932- *AmMWSc 92, WhoWest 92*
**Saltz,** Joel Haskin 1956- *AmMWSc 92*
**Saltz,** Ralph 1948- *WhoAmL 92*
**Saltzberg,** Bernard 1919- *AmMWSc 92*
**Saltzberg,** Burton R 1933- *AmMWSc 92*
**Saltzberg,** Theodore 1927- *AmMWSc 92*
**Saltzburg,** Mary Esther 1939- *WhoAmL 92*
**Saltzburg,** Stephen Allan 1945- *WhoAmL 92*
**Saltzer,** Charles 1918- *AmMWSc 92*
**Saltzer,** Jerome H 1939- *AmMWSc 92*
**Saltzman,** Barry 1931- *AmMWSc 92*
**Saltzman,** Barry 1961- *WhoEnt 92, WhoMW 92*
**Saltzman,** Bernard Edwin 1918- *AmMWSc 92, WhoMW 92*
**Saltzman,** Bernard William 1930- *WhoMW 92*
**Saltzman,** Charles Eskridge 1903- *IntWW 91, Who 92*
**Saltzman,** Harry 1915- *IntMPA 92*
**Saltzman,** Herbert A 1928- *AmMWSc 92*
**Saltzman,** Herbert Royce 1928- *WhoEnt 92*
**Saltzman,** Irene Cameron 1927- *WhoFI 92*
**Saltzman,** Joseph 1939- *WhoEnt 92*
**Saltzman,** Martin D 1941- *AmMWSc 92*
**Saltzman,** Max 1917- *AmMWSc 92*
**Saltzman,** Philip 1928- *WhoEnt 92*
**Saltzman,** Richard Brett 1956- *WhoFI 92*
**Saltzman,** Robert Michael 1954- *WhoAmL 92*
**Saltzman,** Robert Paul 1942- *WhoIns 92*
**Saltzman,** Rosalie Cohen 1937- *WhoMW 92*
**Saltzman,** Sheldon R. 1930- *WhoFI 92*
**Saltzman,** Steven Allen 1953- *WhoEnt 92*
**Salu,** Yehuda 1941- *AmMWSc 92*
**Saludes-Casado,** Esperanza 1934- *WhoHisp 92*
**Saluja,** Jagdish Kumar 1934- *AmMWSc 92*
**Saluja,** Preet Pal Singh *AmMWSc 92*
**Salunkhe,** Dattajeerao K 1925- *AmMWSc 92*
**Salusbury-Trelawny,** J. B. *Who 92*
**Salutsky,** Murrell Leon 1923- *AmMWSc 92*
**Salva,** Antonio 1944- *WhoHisp 92*
**Salva,** Stanley John 1938- *WhoMW 92*
**Salvador,** Fernando 1950- *WhoHisp 92*
**Salvador,** Michael John 1950- *WhoEnt 92*
**Salvador,** Patricia Luisa 1956- *WhoHisp 92*
**Salvador,** Richard Anthony 1927- *AmMWSc 92*
**Salvador,** Romano Leonard 1928- *AmMWSc 92*
**Salvador,** Sal 1925- *WhoEnt 92*
**Salvador Gilij,** Felipe *HisDSpE*
**Salvadori,** Antonio 1941- *AmMWSc 92*
**Salvadori,** M G 1907- *AmMWSc 92*
**Salvadori,** Max William 1908- *IntAu&W 91, WrDr 92*
**Salvadori,** Tedfilo Alexander 1899- *WhoFI 92*
**Salvaggio,** John Edmond 1933- *AmMWSc 92*
**Salvagno,** William Robert, Jr. 1947- *WhoFI 92, WhoWest 92*
**Salvan,** Jacques Leon 1898- *IntAu&W 91, WrDr 92*
**Salvati,** Anthony V. 1944- *WhoFI 92*
**Salvatici,** Nilo 1922- *IntWW 91*
**Salvatierra,** Estella 1961- *WhoAmL 92*
**Salvatierra,** Juan Maria 1644-1717 *HisDSpE*
**Salvatierra,** Richard C. 1920- *WhoHisp 92*
**Salvator,** Joseph Michael 1958- *WhoFI 92*
**Salvatore,** Frank A 1922- *WhoAmP 91*
**Salvatore,** Paul A. 1959- *WhoAmL 92*
**Salvatore,** Richard John 1950- *WhoEnt 92, WhoFI 92*
**Salvatori,** Steven Michael 1954- *WhoWest 92*
**Salvay,** Craig L. 1951- *WhoFI 92*
**Salvendy,** Gavriel 1938- *AmMWSc 92*
**Salverson,** Carol Ann 1944- *WhoWest 92*
**Salvesen,** Bonnie Forbes 1944- *WhoMW 92*
**Salvesen,** Robert H 1924- *AmMWSc 92*
**Salveter,** Sharon Caroline 1949- *AmMWSc 92*
**Salveter,** Theodore Clifton, III 1936- *WhoAmL 92*
**Salvetti,** Carlo 1918- *IntWW 91*
**Salvi,** Richard J 1946- *AmMWSc 92*
**Salvian of Marseilles** 400?-480? *EncEarC*
**Salvidge,** Paul 1946- *Who 92*
**Salvin,** Jeffrey Peter 1943- *WhoFI 92*
**Salvin,** Samuel Bernard 1915- *AmMWSc 92*
**Salvo,** Joseph J 1958- *AmMWSc 92*
**Salvucci,** John T. 1953- *WhoAmL 92*
**Salwen,** Harold 1928- *AmMWSc 92*
**Salwen,** Martin J 1931- *AmMWSc 92*
**Salwin,** Arthur Elliott 1948- *AmMWSc 92*
**Salwin,** Harold 1915- *AmMWSc 92*
**Salyer,** Darnell 1930- *AmMWSc 92*
**Salyer,** Jerry Lee 1936- *WhoAmL 92*
**Salyer,** Kevin Duff 1954- *WhoFI 92*
**Salyer,** Stephen Lee 1950- *WhoEnt 92, WhoFI 92, WhoMW 92*
**Salyers,** Abigail Ann *AmMWSc 92*
**Salykov,** Kakimbek Salykovich 1932- *IntWW 91, SovUnBD*
**Salz,** Anthony Michael Vaughan 1950- *WhoFI 92*
**Salzano,** Francis J 1933- *AmMWSc 92*
**Salzano,** Francisco Mauro 1928- *AmMWSc 92*
**Salzarulo,** Leonard Michael 1927- *AmMWSc 92*
**Salzberg,** Bernard 1907- *AmMWSc 92*
**Salzberg,** Betty 1944- *AmMWSc 92*
**Salzberg,** Brian Matthew 1942- *AmMWSc 92*
**Salzberg,** David Aaron 1920- *AmMWSc 92*
**Salzberg,** Hugh William 1921- *AmMWSc 92*
**Salzbrenner,** Richard John 1948- *AmMWSc 92*
**Salzburg,** Joseph S. 1917- *IntMPA 92*
**Salzedo,** Carlos 1885-1961 *NewAmDM*
**Salzenstein,** Marvin A 1929- *AmMWSc 92*
**Salzer,** Jim 1942- *WhoEnt 92*
**Salzer,** John M 1917- *AmMWSc 92*
**Salzer,** Louis William 1918- *WhoMW 92*
**Salzinger,** Kurt 1929- *ConAu 134*
**Salzler,** Daniel M. 1950- *WhoFI 92*
**Salzman,** Anthony David 1950- *WhoFI 92*
**Salzman,** Barnett Seymour 1939- *WhoEnt 92*
**Salzman,** Edwin William 1928- *AmMWSc 92*
**Salzman,** Eric 1933- *NewAmDM*
**Salzman,** Gary Clyde 1942- *AmMWSc 92*
**Salzman,** Gary Scott 1963- *WhoAmL 92*
**Salzman,** George 1925- *AmMWSc 92*
**Salzman,** Herbert d1990 *IntWW 91N*
**Salzman,** Leon 1915- *AmMWSc 92*
**Salzman,** Marilyn Jean 1939- *WhoAmL 92*
**Salzman,** Norman Post 1926- *AmMWSc 92*
**Salzman,** Pnina 1923- *IntWW 91*
**Salzman,** Richard William 1958- *WhoWest 92*
**Salzman,** Stanley d1991 *NewYTBS 91*
**Salzman,** Stanley P. 1931- *WhoAmL 92*
**Salzman,** Steven Kerry 1952- *AmMWSc 92*
**Salzman,** William Ronald 1936- *AmMWSc 92*
**Salzmann,** Zdenek 1925- *ConAu 36NR*
**Salzweder,** Larry Altus 1944- *WhoMW 92*
**Sam Slick** *BenetAL 91*
**Sam,** David 1933- *WhoAmL 92, WhoWest 92*
**Sam,** Joseph 1923- *AmMWSc 92*
**Sama,** Robert F. 1931- *WhoAmL 92*
**Sama,** Vincent Anthony 1957- *WhoAmL 92, WhoEnt 92*
**Samaan,** Naguib A 1925- *AmMWSc 92*
**Samad,** Jack Lee 1952- *WhoEnt 92*
**Samad,** Shahrir Abdul 1949- *IntWW 91*
**Samagh,** Bakhshish Singh 1938- *AmMWSc 92*
**Samalin,** Edwin 1935- *WhoAmL 92*
**Samanen,** James Martin 1947- *AmMWSc 92*
**Samaniego,** Pamela Susan 1952- *WhoWest 92*
**Samaniego,** Ricardo Arturo 1949- *WhoHisp 92*
**Samaniego,** Robert P. 1952- *WhoHisp 92*
**Samaniego Barriga,** Manuel 1930- *WhoRel 92*
**Samano,** Juan 1753-1820 *HisDSpE*
**Samanowitz,** Ronald Arthur 1944- *WhoAmL 92*
**Samara,** George Albert 1936- *AmMWSc 92*
**Samara,** Noah Azmi 1956- *WhoBlA 92*
**Samarakis,** Antonis 1919- *ConAu 36NR, IntAu&W 91, IntWW 91*
**Samarakoon,** Neville Dunbar Mirahawatte 1919- *Who 92*
**Samaranch,** Juan Antonio 1920- *Who 92*
**Samaranch Torello,** Juan Antonio 1920- *IntWW 91*
**Samarapungavan,** Subrahmanyan 1928- *IntWW 91*
**Samaras,** Andonis 1951- *IntWW 91*
**Samaras,** Lucas 1936- *WorArt 1980 [port]*
**Samaras,** Mary Stenning 1928- *WhoWest 92*
**Samaras,** Nicholas *DrAPF 91*
**Samardich,** Gordon Robert 1927- *WhoFI 92*
**Samardich,** Val 1928- *WhoWest 92*
**Samaroff,** Olga 1882-1948 *FacFETw, NewAmDM*
**Samaroo,** Winston R 1934- *AmMWSc 92*
**Samartha,** Stanley Jedidiah 1920- *DcEcMov*
**Samartini,** James Rogers 1935- *WhoFI 92*
**Samay,** Z. Lance 1944- *WhoAmL 92*
**Samberson,** C Gene 1934- *WhoAmP 91*
**Sambol,** Edward Nicholas 1963- *WhoFI 92*
**Sambol,** Paul Brian 1955- *WhoEnt 92*
**Samborski,** Daniel James 1921- *AmMWSc 92*
**Samboy,** Harold Edward 1934- *WhoFI 92*
**Sambrook,** A. J. 1931- *WrDr 92*
**Sambrook,** Arthur James 1931- *IntAu&W 91*
**Sambrook,** Gordon Hartley 1930- *Who 92*
**Sambrook,** Joseph Frank 1939- *Who 92*
**Sambrot,** William Anthony 1920- *IntAu&W 91*
**Sambursky,** Shmuel d1990 *IntWW 91N*
**Samejima,** Fumiko 1930- *AmMWSc 92*
**Samek,** Edward Lasker 1936- *WhoFI 92*
**Samel,** Jeffrey 1952- *WhoAmL 92*
**Samelson,** Charles Frederick 1917- *WhoMW 92*
**Samelson,** Hans 1916- *AmMWSc 92*
**Samelson,** Lawrence Elliot 1951- *AmMWSc 92*
**Samelson,** William 1928- *IntAu&W 91, WrDr 92*
**Sames,** Richard William 1928- *AmMWSc 92*
**Samet,** Andrew Benjamin 1941- *WhoAmL 92, WhoFI 92*
**Samet,** Marc Krane 1950- *WhoWest 92*
**Samet,** Philip 1922- *AmMWSc 92*
**Samet,** Seymour 1919- *WhoRel 92*
**Sameth,** Jack R. 1926- *WhoEnt 92*
**Samfield,** Max 1918- *AmMWSc 92*
**Sami,** Sedat 1928- *AmMWSc 92*
**Saminsky,** Lazare 1882-1959 *NewAmDM*
**Saminsky,** Robert L. 1947- *WhoAmL 92*
**Samios,** Nicholas Peter 1932- *AmMWSc 92, IntWW 91*
**Samir,** Uri 1930- *AmMWSc 92*
**Samis,** Harvey Voorhees, Jr 1931- *AmMWSc 92*
**Samish,** Adrian d1976 *LesBEnT 92*
**Samitier,** Ricardo 1956- *WhoHisp 92*
**Samitz,** M H 1909- *AmMWSc 92*

**Samkange,** Tommie Marie 1932- *WhoBlA 92*
**Samlan,** Arnold D. 1955- *WhoRel 92*
**Samloff,** I Michael 1932- *AmMWSc 92*
**Sammak,** Emil George 1927- *AmMWSc 92*
**Sammak,** Paul J 1956- *AmMWSc 92*
**Samman,** Peter Derrick 1914- *Who 92*
**Sammartini,** Giovanni Battista 1700?-1775 *BlkwCEP*
**Sammartini,** Giovanni Battista 1701-1775 *NewAmDM*
**Sammartini,** Giuseppe 1695-1750 *NewAmDM*
**Sammelwitz,** Paul H 1933- *AmMWSc 92*
**Sammet,** Jean E 1928- *AmMWSc 92*
**Sammet,** Rolf 1920- *IntWW 91*
**Sammis,** Theodore Wallace 1943- *WhoWest 92*
**Sammons,** David G. 1938- *WhoRel 92*
**Sammons,** David James 1946- *AmMWSc 92*
**Sammons,** Elaine D. *WhoFI 92*
**Sammons,** James Harris 1927- *AmMWSc 92*
**Sammons,** Ronald C 1943- *WhoIns 92*
**Sammons,** William Henley 1929- *WhoRel 92*
**Samms,** Emma 1960- *WhoEnt 92*
**Samms,** Michael Dean 1956- *WhoMW 92*
**Samn,** Sherwood 1941- *AmMWSc 92*
**Samnick,** Norman Kenneth 1940- *WhoAmL 92*
**Samoff,** Joel 1943- *WhoWest 92*
**Samoilov,** David Samuilovich 1920- *SovUnBD*
**Samoilov,** Sergey Michael 1925- *AmMWSc 92*
**Samoilov,** Vladimir Yakovlevich 1924- *IntWW 91*
**Samoilova,** Konkordiya Nikolaevna 1876-1921 *SovUnBD*
**Samoilova,** Tatyana Yevgeniyevna 1934- *IntWW 91*
**Samois,** Mme. de *EncAmaz 91*
**Samokhvalov,** Aleksandr Nikolaevich 1894-1971 *SovUnBD*
**Samole,** Myron Michael 1943- *WhoAmL 92*
**Samollow,** Paul B 1948- *AmMWSc 92*
**Samols,** David R 1945- *AmMWSc 92*
**Samora,** Joanne *WhoHisp 92*
**Samora,** Joseph E, Jr 1955- *WhoAmP 91, WhoHisp 92*
**Samora,** Julian 1920- *WhoHisp 92*
**Samorajski,** Thaddeus 1923- *AmMWSc 92*
**Samors,** Neal S. 1943- *WhoFI 92, WhoMW 92*
**Samosud,** Samuil Abramovich 1884-1964 *SovUnBD*
**Samoszuk,** Michael Konstantine 1953- *WhoWest 92*
**Samowitz,** Lee Allan 1953- *WhoAmP 91*
**Samp,** Edward Joseph, Jr. 1918- *WhoAmL 92*
**Sampedro,** Jose Luis 1917- *IntWW 91*
**Sampedro,** Yvette Yrma 1966- *WhoWest 92*
**Samper,** Armando 1920- *IntWW 91*
**Samper,** J. Phillip 1934- *WhoHisp 92*
**Samper,** Joseph Phillip 1934- *WhoFI 92*
**Samphan,** Khieu *IntWW 91*
**Sampias,** Ernest Joseph 1951- *WhoMW 92*
**Sampier,** Jack Martel 1939- *WhoRel 92*
**Samplaski,** Terry Lee 1958- *WhoRel 92*
**Sample,** Dorothy E 1911- *WhoAmP 91*
**Sample,** Herbert Allan 1961- *WhoBlA 92*
**Sample,** Howard H 1938- *AmMWSc 92*
**Sample,** James Halverson 1914- *AmMWSc 92*
**Sample,** John Thomas 1927- *AmMWSc 92*
**Sample,** Joseph Scanlon 1923- *WhoEnt 92*
**Sample,** Marvin Edward 1928- *WhoWest 92*
**Sample,** Matthew Jon 1954- *WhoMW 92*
**Sample,** Paul E 1928- *AmMWSc 92*
**Sample,** Steven Browning 1940- *AmMWSc 92, WhoWest 92*
**Sample,** Thomas Earl, Jr 1924- *AmMWSc 92*
**Sample,** William Amos 1955- *WhoBlA 92*
**Samples,** Benjamin Norris 1935- *WhoBlA 92*
**Samples,** Brian Joseph 1950- *WhoAmP 91*
**Samples,** Iris Lynette 1948- *WhoMW 92*
**Samples,** Jared Lanier 1965- *WhoBlA 92*
**Samples,** John Wayne 1950- *WhoMW 92*
**Samples,** Reginald McCartney 1918- *Who 92*
**Samples,** William R 1931- *AmMWSc 92*
**Sampley,** Marilyn Yvonne *AmMWSc 92*
**Sampliner,** Linda Hodes 1945- *WhoWest 92*
**Sampliner,** Thomas A. 1946- *WhoAmL 92*
**Sampolinski,** Anthony Thomas 1926- *WhoMW 92*
**Sampras,** Pete 1971- *NewYTBS 91 [port]*
**Sampson,** Albert Richard 1938- *WhoBlA 92*
**Sampson,** Anthony 1926- *IntWW 91, Who 92, WrDr 92*
**Sampson,** Anthony Terrell Seward 1926- *IntAu&W 91*
**Sampson,** Bryan Dirk *WhoWest 92*
**Sampson,** Calvin Coolidge 1928- *AmMWSc 92, WhoBlA 92*
**Sampson,** Carol Ann 1942- *WhoWest 92*
**Sampson,** Charles Berlin 1939- *AmMWSc 92*
**Sampson,** Colin 1929- *Who 92*
**Sampson,** David Ashmore *AmMWSc 92*
**Sampson,** Deborah 1760-1799 *EncAmaz 91*
**Sampson,** Deborah 1760-1827 *HanAmWH, NotBlAW 92*
**Sampson,** Dexter Reid 1930- *AmMWSc 92*
**Sampson,** Donald Ross 1932- *WhoAmL 92*
**Sampson,** Dorothy Vermelle 1919- *WhoBlA 92*
**Sampson,** Douglas Howard 1925- *AmMWSc 92*
**Sampson,** Edith S. 1901-1979 *NotBlAW 92 [port]*
**Sampson,** Edward E 1934- *IntAu&W 91, WrDr 92*
**Sampson,** Edward Joseph, Jr. 1942- *WhoEnt 92*
**Sampson,** Elizabeth Jill 1950- *WhoWest 92*
**Sampson,** Emma Speed 1868-1947 *ConAu 135, SmATA 68 [port]*
**Sampson,** Francis Asbury 1842-1918 *BiInAmS*
**Sampson,** Franklin Delano 1947- *WhoRel 92*
**Sampson,** Geoffrey 1944- *IntAu&W 91, WrDr 92*
**Sampson,** George Lewis 1925- *WhoEnt 92*
**Sampson,** Henry T 1934- *AmMWSc 92*
**Sampson,** Henry Thomas 1934- *WhoBlA 92*
**Sampson,** Herschel Wayne 1944- *AmMWSc 92*
**Sampson,** J. Frank 1928- *WhoWest 92*
**Sampson,** John J. 1935- *WhoAmL 92*
**Sampson,** John Laurence 1929- *AmMWSc 92*
**Sampson,** Joseph Harold 1925- *AmMWSc 92*
**Sampson,** Kelvin *WhoBlA 92*
**Sampson,** Leonard E. 1918- *IntMPA 92*
**Sampson,** Marva W. 1936- *WhoBlA 92*
**Sampson,** Michael J. 1944- *WhoWest 92*
**Sampson,** Patsy Hallock 1932- *WhoMW 92*
**Sampson,** Paul 1959- *AmMWSc 92*
**Sampson,** Phyllis Marie 1928- *AmMWSc 92*
**Sampson,** Ralph 1960- *WhoBlA 92*
**Sampson,** Richard Arnim 1927- *WhoWest 92*
**Sampson,** Richard Thomas 1944- *WhoAmL 92*
**Sampson,** Richard Thomas 1963- *WhoEnt 92*
**Sampson,** Robert R. 1924- *WhoBlA 92*
**Sampson,** Ronald Alvin 1933- *WhoBlA 92*
**Sampson,** Ronald N 1930- *AmMWSc 92*
**Sampson,** Ronald Victor 1918- *IntAu&W 91, WrDr 92*
**Sampson,** Sanford Robert 1937- *AmMWSc 92*
**Sampson,** William B 1934- *AmMWSc 92*
**Sampson,** William Roth 1946- *WhoMW 92*
**Sampson,** William Thomas 1840-1902 *BiInAmS*
**Sampugna,** Joseph 1931- *AmMWSc 92*
**Samra,** Nicholas James 1944- *WhoRel 92*
**Sams,** Bruce Jones, Jr 1928- *AmMWSc 92*
**Sams,** Burnett Henry, III 1931- *AmMWSc 92*
**Sams,** Carl Earnest 1951- *AmMWSc 92*
**Sams,** Dallas C *WhoAmP 91*
**Sams,** David Marcelle 1968- *WhoRel 92*
**Sams,** David Ronald 1958- *WhoEnt 92*
**Sams,** Emmett Sprinkle 1920- *AmMWSc 92*
**Sams,** Eric 1926- *IntAu&W 91, WrDr 92*
**Sams,** Eristus *WhoBlA 92*
**Sams,** Francis John Bradley 1963- *WhoFI 92*
**Sams,** John Robert, Jr 1936- *AmMWSc 92*
**Sams,** John Roland 1922- *WhoRel 92*
**Sams,** Larry Marshall *DrAPF 91*
**Sams,** Lewis Calhoun, Jr 1928- *AmMWSc 92*
**Sams,** Richard Alvin 1946- *AmMWSc 92*
**Sams,** Robert Alan 1945- *WhoAmL 92*
**Sams,** Wiley Mitchell, Jr 1933- *AmMWSc 92*
**Samsell,** Lewis Patrick 1943- *WhoWest 92*
**Samsi** *EncAmaz 91*
**Samson,** Anthony Donald 1933- *WhoAmL 92*
**Samson,** Charles Harold 1924- *AmMWSc 92*
**Samson,** Fred Burton 1940- *AmMWSc 92*
**Samson,** Frederick Eugene, Jr 1918- *AmMWSc 92*
**Samson,** Gary David 1948- *WhoAmL 92*
**Samson,** Jack *ConAu 134*
**Samson,** James Alexander Ross 1928- *AmMWSc 92*
**Samson,** John G. 1922- *ConAu 134*
**Samson,** Richard Eilerts 1944- *WhoAmL 92*
**Samson,** Sten 1916- *AmMWSc 92*
**Samson,** Willis Kendrick 1947- *AmMWSc 92*
**Samsonov,** Alexander Vasilyevich 1859-1914 *FacFETw*
**Samsonowicz,** Henryk 1930- *IntWW 91*
**Samsova,** Galina 1937- *Who 92*
**Samstad,** LaVonne Carrol *WhoAmP 91*
**Samter,** Max 1908- *AmMWSc 92*
**Samudlo,** Jeffrey Bryan 1966- *WhoWest 92*
**Samuel** *EncEarC, Who 92*
**Samuel,** Bishop 1920-1981 *DcEcMov*
**Samuel,** Viscount 1922- *Who 92*
**Samuel,** Adrian Christopher Ian 1915- *Who 92*
**Samuel,** Albert 1937- *AmMWSc 92*
**Samuel,** Aryeh Hermann 1924- *AmMWSc 92*
**Samuel,** Athanasius Yeshue 1907- *WhoRel 92*
**Samuel,** Charles Edward 1945- *AmMWSc 92*
**Samuel,** David Evan 1940- *AmMWSc 92*
**Samuel,** Edmund William 1924- *AmMWSc 92*
**Samuel,** Frederick E. 1924- *WhoBlA 92*
**Samuel,** Gerhard 1924- *NewAmDM, WhoEnt 92*
**Samuel,** Howard David 1924- *WhoAmP 91*
**Samuel,** Irene d1991 *NewYTBS 91*
**Samuel,** Irene 1915-1991 *ConAu 134*
**Samuel,** James Ray 1952- *WhoRel 92*
**Samuel,** Jay Morris 1946- *AmMWSc 92*
**Samuel,** John 1944- *Who 92*
**Samuel,** Juan Milton Romero 1960- *WhoHisp 92*
**Samuel,** Kenneth Landon 1961- *WhoRel 92*
**Samuel,** Lois S. 1925- *WhoBlA 92*
**Samuel,** Mark Aaron 1944- *AmMWSc 92*
**Samuel,** Maurice 1895-1972 *BenetAL 91*
**Samuel,** Michael Dean 1950- *WhoMW 92*
**Samuel,** Minor Booker 1904- *WhoBlA 92*
**Samuel,** Ralph David 1945- *WhoAmL 92*
**Samuel,** Raphael 1946- *WhoAmL 92*
**Samuel,** Reuben 1942- *WhoAmL 92*
**Samuel,** Richard Christopher 1933- *Who 92*
**Samuel,** Robert Thompson 1944- *WhoMW 92*
**Samuel,** Subramanian Johnson 1958- *WhoRel 92*
**Samuel,** Thayil Koshy 1944- *WhoMW 92*
**Samuel,** William Morris 1940- *AmMWSc 92*
**Samuel-Cahn,** Ester 1933- *AmMWSc 92*
**Samuelian,** Mark George 1963- *WhoFI 92*
**Samuels** *Who 92*
**Samuels,** Abram 1920- *IntMPA 92*
**Samuels,** Annette Jacqueline 1935- *WhoBlA 92*
**Samuels,** Arthur Seymour 1925- *AmMWSc 92*
**Samuels,** Barbara Ann 1949- *WhoWest 92*
**Samuels,** Charlotte 1948- *WhoBlA 92*
**Samuels,** Cynthia K. 1946- *ConAu 135*
**Samuels,** Cynthia Kalish 1946- *WhoEnt 92*
**Samuels,** Dorothy Jane 1951- *WhoAmP 91*
**Samuels,** Edward Augustus 1836-1908 *BiInAmS*
**Samuels,** Ernest 1903- *DcLB 111 [port], WrDr 92*
**Samuels,** Everett Paul 1958- *WhoBlA 92*
**Samuels,** James E. 1928- *WhoBlA 92*
**Samuels,** Janet Lee 1953- *WhoAmL 92*
**Samuels,** Joe A. *WhoRel 92*
**Samuels,** John Edward Anthony 1940- *Who 92*
**Samuels,** Lawrence Keith 1951- *WhoWest 92*
**Samuels,** Leslie Eugene 1929- *WhoBlA 92, WhoFI 92*
**Samuels,** Marcia L. 1937- *WhoBlA 92*
**Samuels,** Martin E 1918- *AmMWSc 92*
**Samuels,** Michael Anthony 1939- *WhoAmP 91*
**Samuels,** Michael Louis 1920- *Who 92*
**Samuels,** Myra Lee 1940- *AmMWSc 92*
**Samuels,** Olive Constance 1926- *WhoBlA 92*
**Samuels,** Richard Mel 1943- *WhoEnt 92*
**Samuels,** Robert 1918- *AmMWSc 92*
**Samuels,** Robert Bireley 1940- *AmMWSc 92*
**Samuels,** Robert J. 1938- *WhoBlA 92*
**Samuels,** Robert Joel 1931- *AmMWSc 92*
**Samuels,** Robert Lynn 1930- *AmMWSc 92*
**Samuels,** Ron *WhoEnt 92*
**Samuels,** Ronald S. 1941- *WhoBlA 92*
**Samuels,** Seymour, Jr. 1912- *WhoAmL 92*
**Samuels,** Sondra Lanell 1951- *WhoMW 92*
**Samuels,** Stanley 1929- *AmMWSc 92*
**Samuels,** Stephen H. 1949- *WhoEnt 92*
**Samuels,** Susan Jill 1957- *WhoAmL 92*
**Samuels,** Sy 1931- *WhoEnt 92*
**Samuels,** Thomas William 1934- *WhoRel 92*
**Samuels,** Walter Gerald 1903- *WhoEnt 92*
**Samuels,** Warren J 1933- *IntAu&W 91, WrDr 92*
**Samuels,** Warren Joseph 1933- *WhoAmL 92, WhoFI 92*
**Samuels,** Wilfred D. 1947- *WhoBlA 92*
**Samuelsen,** Roy 1933- *WhoEnt 92*
**Samuelson,** Barbara Shalita 1943- *WhoFI 92*
**Samuelson,** Bengt Ingemar 1934- *AmMWSc 92, IntWW 91*
**Samuelson,** Charles R 1927- *AmMWSc 92*
**Samuelson,** David W. 1924- *IntMPA 92*
**Samuelson,** Derrick William 1929- *WhoAmL 92*
**Samuelson,** Don Arthur 1948- *AmMWSc 92*
**Samuelson,** Donald B 1932- *WhoAmP 91*
**Samuelson,** Donald James 1940- *AmMWSc 92*
**Samuelson,** Ellen Banman *WhoAmP 91*
**Samuelson,** Emma 1960- *WhoEnt 92*
**Samuelson,** H Vaughn 1938- *AmMWSc 92*
**Samuelson,** John T. 1946- *WhoMW 92*
**Samuelson,** Kenneth Lee 1946- *WhoAmL 92, WhoFI 92*
**Samuelson,** Michael 1917- *Who 92*
**Samuelson,** Norbert M. 1936- *WhoRel 92*
**Samuelson,** Paul A. 1915- *Who 92*
**Samuelson,** Paul Anthony 1915- *IntAu&W 91, IntWW 91, WhoFI 92, WhoNob 90, WrDr 92*
**Samuelson,** Peter George Wylie 1951- *IntMPA 92*
**Samuelson,** Robert *WhoAmP 91*
**Samuelson,** Robert Donald 1929- *WhoFI 92*
**Samuelson,** Sydney 1925- *IntMPA 92*
**Samuelson,** Sydney Wylie 1925- *Who 92*
**Samuelson,** Timothy Paul 1951- *WhoMW 92*
**Samuelsson,** Bengt Ingemar 1934- *Who 92, WhoNob 90*
**Samuelu,** Tel II *WhoRel 92*
**Samulon,** Henry A 1915- *AmMWSc 92*
**Samulski,** Edward Thaddeus 1943- *AmMWSc 92*
**Samworth,** David Chetwode 1935- *Who 92*
**Samworth,** Eleanor A 1936- *AmMWSc 92*
**Samy Vellu,** S. 1936- *IntWW 91*
**San,** Nguyen Duy 1932- *WhoMW 92*
**Sanabor,** Louis John 1920- *AmMWSc 92*
**Sanabria,** Harry Louis 1962- *WhoHisp 92*
**Sanabria,** Jane Elizabeth 1962- *WhoFI 92*
**Sanabria,** Luis Angel 1950- *WhoHisp 92*
**Sanabria,** Tomas V. 1953- *WhoHisp 92*
**Sanadi,** D Rao 1920- *AmMWSc 92*
**San Agustin,** Joe Taitano 1930- *WhoAmP 91, WhoWest 92*
**San Antonio,** James Patrick 1925- *AmMWSc 92*
**San Antonio Mendoza,** Oscar 1945- *WhoAmP 91*
**Sanapia** 1895-1979 *RelLAm 91*
**Sanasarian,** Harout O 1929- *WhoAmP 91*
**Sanathanan,** C K 1936- *AmMWSc 92*
**Sanathanan,** Lalitha P 1943- *AmMWSc 92*
**Sanazaro,** Paul Joseph 1922- *AmMWSc 92*
**Sanbar,** Moshe 1926- *IntWW 91*
**Sanberg,** Paul Ronald 1955- *AmMWSc 92*
**Sanborn,** Albert Francis 1913- *AmMWSc 92*
**Sanborn,** Allen Webber 1942- *WhoFI 92*
**Sanborn,** Arthur B 1945- *WhoAmP 91*
**Sanborn,** Charles E 1919- *AmMWSc 92*
**Sanborn,** Dorothy Chappell 1920- *WhoWest 92*
**Sanborn,** Francis Gregory 1838-1884 *BiInAmS*
**Sanborn,** Frank George 1946- *WhoWest 92*
**Sanborn,** Franklin Benjamin 1831-1917 *BenetAL 91*
**Sanborn,** Hugh Wiedman 1939- *WhoRel 92*
**Sanborn,** I B 1932- *AmMWSc 92*
**Sanborn,** Margaret 1915- *IntAu&W 91, WrDr 92*
**Sanborn,** Mark Robert 1946- *AmMWSc 92*
**Sanborn,** Robert B. 1929- *WhoFI 92*
**Sanborn,** Robert Burns 1929- *WhoIns 92*
**Sanborn,** Russell Hobart 1930- *AmMWSc 92*
**Sanborn,** Todd Frank 1958- *WhoMW 92*
**Sanborn,** Warren Gordon 1932- *WhoWest 92*
**Sanborne,** Paul Michael 1950- *AmMWSc 92*
**Sancar,** Aziz *AmMWSc 92*
**Sancar,** Gwendolyn Boles 1949- *AmMWSc 92*
**Sances,** Anthony, Jr 1932- *AmMWSc 92*

**Sancetta,** Constance Antonina 1949- *AmMWSc 92*
**Sanches Perez,** Elias *WhoHisp 92*
**Sanchez,** Adolfo Erik 1935- *WhoHisp 92*
**Sanchez,** Alba 1957- *WhoHisp 92*
**Sanchez,** Albert 1936- *AmMWSc 92, WhoHisp 92*
**Sanchez,** Alex A. *WhoHisp 92*
**Sanchez,** Anna Sinohui 1958- *WhoHisp 92*
**Sanchez,** Antonio L. 1954- *WhoHisp 92*
**Sanchez,** Antonio M. 1932- *WhoHisp 92*
**Sanchez,** Antonio R., Sr. 1916-1992 *WhoHisp 92N*
**Sanchez,** Arlene Michelle 1966- *WhoHisp 92*
**Sanchez,** Armand J. 1933- *WhoHisp 92*
**Sanchez,** Arthur Ronald 1948- *WhoHisp 92*
**Sanchez,** Arturo E. 1949- *WhoHisp 92*
**Sanchez,** Beatrice Rivas 1941- *WhoMW 92*
**Sanchez,** Carlos Antonio 1960- *WhoHisp 92*
**Sanchez,** Cecilia *WhoHisp 92*
**Sanchez,** Christina J. 1963- *WhoHisp 92*
**Sanchez,** Claudio *WhoHisp 92*
**Sanchez,** Cynthia J. 1962- *WhoHisp 92*
**Sanchez,** Daniel J. 1964- *WhoHisp 92*
**Sanchez,** Daniel R. 1936- *WhoHisp 92*
**Sanchez,** David *WhoHisp 92*
**Sanchez,** David A 1933- *AmMWSc 92*
**Sanchez,** David Alan 1933- *WhoHisp 92*
**Sanchez,** David Mario 1942- *WhoHisp 92*
**Sanchez,** Dolores *WhoHisp 92*
**Sanchez,** Don *WhoHisp 92*
**Sanchez,** Dorothy L. 1938- *WhoHisp 92*
**Sanchez,** Edith 1956- *WhoHisp 92*
**Sanchez,** Edwin 1955- *WhoHisp 92*
**Sanchez,** Efrain 1949- *WhoHisp 92*
**Sanchez,** Elba I. 1947- *WhoHisp 92*
**Sanchez,** Eleazar *WhoHisp 92*
**Sanchez,** Elena Ruiz 1940- *WhoAmP 91*
**Sanchez,** Emma Dejillo 1947- *WhoWest 92*
**Sanchez,** Enrique 1932- *WhoHisp 92*
**Sanchez,** Ernest *WhoHisp 92*
**Sanchez,** F. H. 1925- *WhoHisp 92*
**Sanchez,** Fameliza 1940- *WhoHisp 92*
**Sanchez,** Fausto H. 1953- *WhoHisp 92*
**Sanchez,** Federico A. 1935- *WhoHisp 92*
**Sanchez,** Felix 1951- *WhoHisp 92*
**Sanchez,** Fernando Victor 1953- *WhoHisp 92*
**Sanchez,** Florencio 1875-1910 *BenetAL 91, LiExTwC*
**Sanchez,** Frank John 1959- *WhoAmL 92*
**Sanchez,** Gabriel *WhoHisp 92*
**Sanchez,** George L. 1933- *WhoHisp 92*
**Sanchez,** Gilbert 1938- *WhoHisp 92, WhoWest 92*
**Sanchez,** Gilbert Anthony 1930- *WhoHisp 92*
**Sanchez,** Gilbert John 1941- *WhoHisp 92*
**Sanchez,** Gonzalo Jose 1932- *WhoHisp 92*
**Sanchez,** Henry Orlando 1937- *WhoHisp 92*
**Sanchez,** Humberto G. 1947- *WhoHisp 92*
**Sanchez,** Ignacio Roberto 1965- *WhoHisp 92*
**Sanchez,** Irma Ann 1961- *WhoHisp 92*
**Sanchez,** Isaac C. 1941- *WhoHisp 92*
**Sanchez,** Isaac Cornelius 1941- *AmMWSc 92*
**Sanchez,** Israel, Jr. 1963- *WhoHisp 92*
**Sanchez,** James *WhoHisp 92*
**Sanchez,** Javier A. 1960- *WhoHisp 92*
**Sanchez,** Jerry 1945- *WhoHisp 92*
**Sanchez,** Jesus M. 1944- *WhoHisp 92*
**Sanchez,** Jesus Ramirez 1950- *WhoHisp 92*
**Sanchez,** Jesusa 1955- *WhoAmP 91*
**Sanchez,** Joe M. 1933- *WhoHisp 92*
**Sanchez,** John Charles 1950- *WhoHisp 92*
**Sanchez,** Jonathan *WhoHisp 92*
**Sanchez,** Jorge Luis 1956- *WhoHisp 92*
**Sanchez,** Jose 1936- *AmMWSc 92*
**Sanchez,** Jose B., Sr. 1940- *WhoHisp 92*
**Sanchez,** Jose Enrique 1960- *WhoHisp 92*
**Sanchez,** Jose Luis 1952- *WhoHisp 92*
**Sanchez,** Jose Luis 1955- *WhoHisp 92*
**Sanchez,** Jose M. 1943- *WhoHisp 92*
**Sanchez,** Jose Ramon 1951- *WhoHisp 92*
**Sanchez,** Jose T. 1920- *WhoRel 92*
**Sanchez,** Joseph S. 1949- *WhoHisp 92*
**Sanchez,** Juan Francisco 1928- *WhoHisp 92*
**Sanchez,** Juan-Manuel 1955- *WhoHisp 92*
**Sanchez,** Juan Ramon, Jr. 1965- *WhoRel 92*
**Sanchez,** Julian 1941- *WhoHisp 92*
**Sanchez,** Julian Claudio 1938- *WhoHisp 92*
**Sanchez,** Kathleen 1957- *WhoHisp 92*
**Sanchez,** Leonard R. 1942- *WhoHisp 92*
**Sanchez,** Leonedes Monarrize 1951- *WhoFI 92, WhoWest 92*
**Sanchez,** Leveo V. 1930- *WhoHisp 92*
**Sanchez,** Lorenzo 1943- *WhoHisp 92, WhoWest 92*
**Sanchez,** Louis H. 1961- *WhoHisp 92*
**Sanchez,** Louis Patrick 1955- *WhoAmL 92*
**Sanchez,** Luis 1924- *WhoAmP 91, WhoHisp 92*
**Sanchez,** Luis Alberto 1900- *IntWW 91*
**Sanchez,** Luis Humberto 1951- *WhoHisp 92*
**Sanchez,** Luis Rafael 1936- *WhoHisp 92*
**Sanchez,** Lyssil R. 1947- *WhoHisp 92*
**Sanchez,** Manuel 1947- *WhoHisp 92*
**Sanchez,** Manuel Tamayo, Jr. 1949- *WhoHisp 92*
**Sanchez,** Marcos B. 1956- *WhoHisp 92*
**Sanchez,** Mario Ernesto 1947- *WhoHisp 92*
**Sanchez,** Marisabel 1963- *WhoHisp 92*
**Sanchez,** Marla Rena 1956- *WhoHisp 92, WhoWest 92*
**Sanchez,** Marta *WhoEnt 92, WhoHisp 92*
**Sanchez,** Martha Alicia 1944- *WhoHisp 92*
**Sanchez,** Mary B. 1930- *WhoHisp 92*
**Sanchez,** Michael T. 1961- *WhoHisp 92*
**Sanchez,** Miguel Angel, Sr. 1933- *WhoHisp 92*
**Sanchez,** Miguel R. 1950- *WhoHisp 92*
**Sanchez,** Nelson *WhoHisp 92*
**Sanchez,** Norma R. 1939- *WhoHisp 92*
**Sanchez,** Osmundo, Jr. 1939- *WhoFI 92*
**Sanchez,** Patricia Irene *WhoHisp 92*
**Sanchez,** Paul 1964- *WhoRel 92*
**Sanchez,** Pedro Antonio 1940- *AmMWSc 92, WhoHisp 92*
**Sanchez,** Philip A. 1963- *WhoHisp 92*
**Sanchez,** Phillip Victor 1929- *WhoAmP 91, WhoFI 92, WhoHisp 92*
**Sanchez,** Poncho 1951- *WhoHisp 92*
**Sanchez,** Porfirio 1932- *WhoHisp 92*
**Sanchez,** Rafael 1938- *WhoHisp 92*
**Sanchez,** Rafael C. 1919- *WhoHisp 92*
**Sanchez,** Ramiro 1948- *WhoHisp 92*
**Sanchez,** Ramon Antonio 1947- *WhoHisp 92*
**Sanchez,** Ray A. 1940- *WhoHisp 92*
**Sanchez,** Ray F. 1927- *WhoHisp 92*
**Sanchez,** Raymond G 1941- *WhoAmP 91, WhoHisp 92, WhoWest 92*
**Sanchez,** Raymond John 1944- *WhoHisp 92*
**Sanchez,** Raymond L. 1964- *WhoHisp 92*
**Sanchez,** Ricardo *DrAPF 91*
**Sanchez,** Ricardo 1941- *WhoHisp 92*
**Sanchez,** Richard Ray 1946- *WhoAmP 91, WhoHisp 92*
**Sanchez,** Rick *WhoHisp 92*
**Sanchez,** Rick Dante 1940- *WhoHisp 92*
**Sanchez,** Robert *WhoHisp 92*
**Sanchez,** Robert A 1938- *AmMWSc 92*
**Sanchez,** Robert Alfred 1938- *WhoHisp 92*
**Sanchez,** Robert Charles 1956- *WhoHisp 92*
**Sanchez,** Robert F. 1934- *WhoHisp 92*
**Sanchez,** Robert Fortune 1934- *WhoRel 92, WhoWest 92*
**Sanchez,** Robert Francis 1938- *WhoHisp 92*
**Sanchez,** Robert Michael 1947- *WhoAmL 92*
**Sanchez,** Robert Mungerro 1953- *WhoHisp 92*
**Sanchez,** Roberto G. 1922- *WhoHisp 92*
**Sanchez,** Roberto Luis 1957- *WhoHisp 92*
**Sanchez,** Roberto R. 1948- *WhoHisp 92*
**Sanchez,** Rodolfo Balli *WhoHisp 92*
**Sanchez,** Rosaura 1941- *WhoHisp 92*
**Sanchez,** Ross C. *WhoHisp 92*
**Sanchez,** Roxanne 1968- *WhoHisp 92*
**Sanchez,** Rozier Edmond 1931- *WhoHisp 92*
**Sanchez,** Ruben Dario 1943- *WhoRel 92, WhoWest 92*
**Sanchez,** Ruthanne Geralyn 1958- *WhoAmL 92*
**Sanchez,** Sergio Arturo 1950- *WhoHisp 92*
**Sanchez,** Shiree 1957- *WhoHisp 92*
**Sanchez,** Sonia *DrAPF 91*
**Sanchez,** Sonia 1934- *BenetAL 91, BlkLC [port], ConPo 91, NotBlAW 92, WrDr 92*
**Sanchez,** Sonia Benita 1934- *IntAu&W 91, WhoBlA 92*
**Sanchez,** Stella Villarreal 1959- *WhoHisp 92*
**Sanchez,** Sylvia Bertha 1928- *WhoHisp 92*
**Sanchez,** Thomas *DrAPF 91*
**Sanchez,** Thomas 1944- *WhoHisp 92*
**Sanchez,** Trinidad, Jr. *WhoHisp 92*
**Sanchez,** Victoria E. 1954- *WhoHisp 92*
**Sanchez,** Victoria Wagner 1934- *WhoWest 92*
**Sanchez,** Vivian Eugenia 1963- *WhoHisp 92*
**Sanchez,** Walter A. 1958- *WhoHisp 92*
**Sanchez,** William Q. 1951- *WhoHisp 92*
**Sanchez,** Yolanda *WhoHisp 92*
**Sanchez Albornos,** Claudio 1904-1985 *LiExTwC*
**Sanchez Asiain,** Andre Angel 1929- *IntWW 91*
**Sanchez-Boudy,** Jose 1927- *LiExTwC*
**Sanchez-Boudy,** Jose 1928- *WhoHisp 92*
**Sanchez-Carlo,** Maria 1952- *WhoHisp 92*
**Sanchez Carrion,** Luis 1787-1825 *HisDSpE*
**Sanchez de Badajoz,** Hernan 1489- *HisDSpE*
**Sanchez de Sandoval,** Oma Erlinda 1939- *WhoHisp 92*
**Sanchez Ferreri,** Franco Tulio 1909- *WhoHisp 92*
**Sanchez-Garcia,** Janie 1951- *WhoHisp 92*
**Sanchez-Grey Alba,** Esther 1931- *WhoHisp 92*
**Sanchez-H.,** Jose 1951- *WhoHisp 92, WhoWest 92*
**Sanchez Hernandez,** Fidel 1917- *IntWW 91*
**Sanchez Korrol,** Virginia *WhoHisp 92*
**Sanchez-Longo,** Luis P. 1925- *WhoHisp 92*
**Sanchez-Lugo,** Fermin A. 1947- *WhoHisp 92*
**Sanchez-Manjon,** Andres B. 1943- *WhoHisp 92*
**Sanchez Mazas,** Rafael 1894-1966 *BiDExR*
**Sanchez-Owens,** Yvette Anita 1960- *WhoHisp 92*
**Sanchez Pelaez,** Juan 1922- *ConSpAP*
**Sanchez-Robayna,** Andres 1952- *IntAu&W 91*
**Sanchez-Scott,** Milcha *WhoHisp 92*
**Sanchez-Sinencio,** Edgar 1944- *WhoHisp 92*
**Sanchez-Troche,** Luis Fernando 1961- *WhoHisp 92*
**Sanchez-Vilella,** Roberto 1913- *IntWW 91, WhoAmP 91*
**Sanchez-Way,** Ruth Dolores 1940- *WhoHisp 92*
**Sanchidrian,** Maria Del Carmen 1954- *WhoFI 92*
**Sanchini,** Dominick J 1926- *AmMWSc 92*
**Sancho,** Robert *WhoHisp 92*
**Sancho-Rof,** Juan 1940- *IntWW 91*
**Sancier,** Kenneth Martin 1920- *AmMWSc 92*
**Sancilio,** Lawrence F 1932- *AmMWSc 92*
**San Clemente,** Charles Leonard 1914- *AmMWSc 92*
**Sanctuary,** Bryan Clifford 1945- *AmMWSc 92*
**Sanctuary,** Gerald Philip 1930- *Who 92*
**Sand,** George 1804-1876 *FrenWW, GuFrLit 1*
**Sand,** Ivan *WhoAmP 91*
**Sand,** Leonard B 1922- *AmMWSc 92*
**Sand,** Leonard B. 1928- *WhoAmL 92*
**Sand,** Ralph E 1921- *AmMWSc 92*
**Sand,** Ulf 1938- *IntWW 91*
**Sanda,** Dominique 1951- *IntMPA 92*
**Sandage,** Allan Rex 1926- *AmMWSc 92, IntWW 91*
**Sandage,** Elizabeth Anthea 1930- *WhoMW 92*
**Sandall,** Orville Cecil 1939- *AmMWSc 92*
**Sandalow,** Terrance 1934- *WhoAmL 92*
**Sandars,** Christopher Thomas 1942- *Who 92*
**Sandars,** Nancy Katharine 1914- *Who 92*
**Sandars,** Patrick George Henry 1935- *Who 92*
**Sandbach,** Charlie Bernard 1933- *WhoFI 92*
**Sandbach,** Francis Henry d1991 *Who 92N*
**Sandbach,** Francis Henry 1903-1991 *ConAu 135*
**Sandbach,** George Thomas 1946- *WhoAmP 91*
**Sandback,** Patricia Rae 1937- *WhoEnt 92*
**Sandback,** William Arthur 1945- *WhoAmL 92*
**Sandbank,** Charles Peter 1931- *Who 92*
**Sandbank,** Henry 1932- *WhoEnt 92*
**Sandbank,** Viette *DrAPF 91*
**Sandberg,** Ann Linnea *AmMWSc 92*
**Sandberg,** Avery Aba 1921- *AmMWSc 92*
**Sandberg,** Carl Lorens 1922- *AmMWSc 92*
**Sandberg,** Christopher Knoll 1952- *WhoAmL 92*
**Sandberg,** David Gill 1950- *WhoFI 92*
**Sandberg,** Eugene Carl 1924- *AmMWSc 92*
**Sandberg,** Gary Allen 1962- *WhoRel 92*
**Sandberg,** I W 1934- *AmMWSc 92*
**Sandberg,** Jane Carla 1965- *WhoWest 92*
**Sandberg,** Jay Howard 1957- *WhoMW 92*
**Sandberg,** Kathy 1964- *WhoMW 92*
**Sandberg,** Michael 1927- *Who 92*
**Sandberg,** Michael Graham Ruddock 1927- *IntWW 91*
**Sandberg,** Philip A 1937- *AmMWSc 92*
**Sandberg,** Robert Gustave 1939- *AmMWSc 92*
**Sandberg,** Ryne 1959- *WhoMW 92*
**Sandberg,** Wayne L *WhoAmP 91*
**Sandblom,** Philip 1903- *IntWW 91*
**Sandborn,** Virgil A 1928- *AmMWSc 92*
**Sandbrook,** K. R. J. 1943- *ConAu 36NR*
**Sandburg,** Carl 1878-1967 *BenetAL 91, ConAu 35NR, FacFETw [port]*
**Sandburg,** Charles *ConAu 35NR*
**Sandburg,** Charles A. *ConAu 35NR*
**Sandburg,** Helga *IntAu&W 91*
**Sandburg,** Helga 1918- *WrDr 92*
**Sandby,** Paul 1725-1809 *BlkwCEP*
**Sande,** Barbara 1939- *WhoFI 92, WhoWest 92*
**Sande,** Ronald Dean 1942- *AmMWSc 92*
**Sandeen,** Ernest *DrAPF 91*
**Sandefer,** George Larry 1950- *WhoAmL 92*
**Sandefer,** Ira Lee 1944- *WhoRel 92*
**Sandefur,** J David 1952- *WhoAmP 91*
**Sandefur,** Kermit Lorain 1925- *AmMWSc 92*
**Sandefur,** Robert David 1959- *WhoRel 92*
**Sandefur,** Thomas Edwin, Jr. 1939- *WhoFI 92*
**Sandel,** Bill Roy 1945- *AmMWSc 92*
**Sandel,** Jerry Wayne 1942- *WhoAmP 91*
**Sandel,** Vernon Ralph 1933- *AmMWSc 92*
**Sandell,** Lionel Samuel 1945- *AmMWSc 92*
**Sandell,** Terry 1948- *Who 92*
**Sandell,** Tom Johan Ludvig 1936- *IntAu&W 91*
**Sandelson,** Neville Devonshire 1923- *Who 92*
**Sandeman,** Margot 1922- *TwCPaSc*
**Sandeman,** Robert 1718-1771 *BenetAL 91*
**Sander,** Alfred Dick 1925- *WhoWest 92*
**Sander,** C Maureen 1933- *AmMWSc 92*
**Sander,** Cynthia Neomi 1939- *WhoMW 92*
**Sander,** Donald Henry 1933- *AmMWSc 92*
**Sander,** Duane E 1938- *AmMWSc 92*
**Sander,** Ellen Jane 1949- *WhoWest 92*
**Sander,** Eugene George 1935- *AmMWSc 92*
**Sander,** Frank Ernest Arnold 1927- *WhoAmL 92*
**Sander,** Gary Edward 1947- *AmMWSc 92*
**Sander,** Ivan Lee 1928- *AmMWSc 92*
**Sander,** Leonard Michael 1941- *AmMWSc 92*
**Sander,** Linda Dian 1947- *AmMWSc 92*
**Sander,** Louis Frank 1933- *AmMWSc 92*
**Sander,** Louis W 1918- *AmMWSc 92*
**Sander,** Michael Arthur 1941- *IntWW 91*
**Sander,** Richard H. 1956- *WhoAmL 92*
**Sander,** Susan Berry 1953- *WhoWest 92*
**Sander,** Thomas Harvey 1961- *WhoAmL 92*
**Sander,** William August, III 1942- *AmMWSc 92*
**Sanderfer,** Paul Otis 1937- *AmMWSc 92*
**Sanderfoot,** Stephen John 1961- *WhoMW 92*
**Sanderford,** Howard 1935- *WhoAmP 91*
**Sanderford,** John Roy, III 1954- *WhoAmL 92*
**Sanderford,** Richard Hurst 1958- *WhoEnt 92*
**Sanderlin,** George 1915- *WrDr 92*
**Sanderlin,** James B. 1929- *WhoBlA 92*
**Sanderlin,** Owenita 1916- *WrDr 92*
**Sanderling,** Kurt 1912- *IntWW 91, NewAmDM*
**Sanders,** Andrew William, Jr. 1948- *WhoRel 92*
**Sanders,** Archie, Jr. 1937- *WhoBlA 92*
**Sanders,** Arthur Hardie 1924- *WhoEnt 92*
**Sanders,** Augusta Swann 1932- *WhoBlA 92, WhoWest 92*
**Sanders,** Barbara A. *WhoBlA 92*
**Sanders,** Barbara A 1947- *AmMWSc 92*
**Sanders,** Barefoot 1925- *WhoAmL 92*
**Sanders,** Barry *NewYTBS 91 [port]*
**Sanders,** Barry 1968- *ConBlB 1 [port], News 92-1 [port], WhoBlA 92*
**Sanders,** Barry Clayton 1960- *WhoEnt 92*
**Sanders,** Benjamin Elbert 1918- *AmMWSc 92*
**Sanders,** Bernard 1941- *AlmAP 92 [port], CurBio 91 [port], WhoAmP 91*
**Sanders,** Bernie *NewYTBS 91 [port]*
**Sanders,** Bernie 1941?- *News 91 [port]*
**Sanders,** Bobby Gene 1932- *AmMWSc 92*
**Sanders,** Bobby Lee 1935- *AmMWSc 92*
**Sanders,** Brenda Marie 1951- *AmMWSc 92*
**Sanders,** Brett *TwCWW 91, WrDr 92*
**Sanders,** Brice Sidney 1930- *WhoRel 92*
**Sanders,** Bryce Martin, Jr. 1955- *WhoFI 92*
**Sanders,** Carl Edward 1925- *WhoAmP 91*
**Sanders,** Carl Julian 1912- *WhoRel 92*
**Sanders,** Cecil Mallon, Jr. 1961- *WhoRel 92*
**Sanders,** Charles *TwCWW 91*
**Sanders,** Charles Addison 1932- *AmMWSc 92*
**Sanders,** Charles F 1921- *WhoAmP 91*
**Sanders,** Charles F, Jr 1931- *AmMWSc 92*
**Sanders,** Charles Irvine 1936- *AmMWSc 92*
**Sanders,** Charles Leonard 1932-1990 *WhoBlA 92N*

Sanders, Charles Leonard, Jr 1938- *AmMWSc 92*
Sanders, Charles Lionel 1936- *WhoBlA 92*
Sanders, Charlie Eugene 1933- *WhoFI 92*
Sanders, Cheryl Dee 1958- *WhoWest 92*
Sanders, Christine Culp 1948- *AmMWSc 92*
Sanders, Christopher Cavania d1991 *Who 92N*
Sanders, Cyril Woods 1912- *Who 92*
Sanders, Darryl Paul 1936- *AmMWSc 92*
Sanders, David 1926- *IntAu&W 91, WrDr 92*
Sanders, David Clyde 1946- *WhoWest 92*
Sanders, Debra Faye 1952- *IntAu&W 91*
Sanders, Deion Luwynn 1967- *WhoBlA 92*
Sanders, Delbert 1931- *WhoBlA 92*
Sanders, Donald Neil 1927- *IntWW 91, Who 92*
Sanders, Dori 1935- *WhoBlA 92*
Sanders, Douglas Charles 1942- *AmMWSc 92*
Sanders, E C 1920- *WhoAmP 91*
Sanders, Ed *DrAPF 91*
Sanders, Ed 1939- *ConPo 91, IntAu&W 91, WrDr 92*
Sanders, Ed Parish 1937- *Who 92*
Sanders, Edwin Perry Bartley 1940- *WhoAmL 92*
Sanders, Ella J. 1947- *WhoBlA 92*
Sanders, Ernest Levonde 1955- *WhoRel 92*
Sanders, Esther Jeannette 1926- *WhoWest 92*
Sanders, F Kingsley *AmMWSc 92*
Sanders, Frank 1919- *WhoAmP 91*
Sanders, Frank Clarence, Jr 1940- *AmMWSc 92*
Sanders, Franklin D 1935- *WhoIns 92*
Sanders, Frederick 1923- *AmMWSc 92*
Sanders, Gary Glenn 1944- *WhoFI 92, WhoMW 92*
Sanders, Gary Hilton 1946- *AmMWSc 92*
Sanders, George Elwood 1946- *WhoMW 92*
Sanders, George L. 1942- *WhoBlA 92*
Sanders, Gerald Hollie 1924- *WhoMW 92*
Sanders, Gerald Martin 1947- *WhoRel 92*
Sanders, Gilbert Lee 1946- *WhoRel 92*
Sanders, Glenn Carlos 1949- *WhoBlA 92*
Sanders, Grant L 1934- *WhoAmP 91*
Sanders, Gwendolyn W. 1937- *WhoBlA 92*
Sanders, Hank 1942- *WhoAmP 91, WhoBlA 92*
Sanders, Harold Arthur 1919- *WhoRel 92*
Sanders, Harvey David 1925- *AmMWSc 92*
Sanders, Hayes Edward 1930-1954 *BlkOlyM [port]*
Sanders, Henry Marshall 1928- *WhoAmP 91*
Sanders, Hobart C. 1929- *WhoBlA 92*
Sanders, Howard L 1921- *AmMWSc 92*
Sanders, Isaac Warren 1948- *WhoBlA 92*
Sanders, J Lyell, Jr 1924- *AmMWSc 92*
Sanders, Jack Thomas 1935- *WhoRel 92*
Sanders, Jacquelyn Seevak 1931- *WhoMW 92*
Sanders, James Alvin 1927- *WhoRel 92, WhoWest 92*
Sanders, James Dean 1956- *WhoMW 92*
Sanders, James Edward 1911- *IntAu&W 91, WrDr 92*
Sanders, James Grady 1951- *AmMWSc 92*
Sanders, James Vincent 1932- *AmMWSc 92*
Sanders, James William 1929- *WhoBlA 92*
Sanders, Jay Olcutt 1953- *WhoEnt 92*
Sanders, Jay W 1924- *AmMWSc 92*
Sanders, John Arnold 1939- *WhoAmP 91*
Sanders, John Clarke *WhoRel 92*
Sanders, John Claytor 1914- *AmMWSc 92*
Sanders, John D 1938- *AmMWSc 92*
Sanders, John Derek 1933- *Who 92*
Sanders, John Essington 1926- *AmMWSc 92*
Sanders, John Leslie Yorath 1929- *Who 92*
Sanders, John Moncrief 1936- *WhoAmL 92*
Sanders, John P, Sr 1926- *AmMWSc 92*
Sanders, John Reynolds M. *Who 92*
Sanders, John Theodore 1941- *WhoAmP 91*
Sanders, Joseph Stanley 1942- *WhoBlA 92*
Sanders, Kate Emily Tyrrell *Who 92*
Sanders, Keith R. 1939- *WhoMW 92*
Sanders, Kenton M 1950- *AmMWSc 92*
Sanders, L. Everett 1929- *WhoMW 92*
Sanders, Larry Joe 1938- *WhoAmP 91*
Sanders, Laura Green 1942- *WhoBlA 92*
Sanders, Lawrence 1920- *IntAu&W 91, WrDr 92*
Sanders, Lewis A. *WhoFI 92*
Sanders, Lina 1937- *WhoBlA 92*
Sanders, Lou Helen 1951- *WhoBlA 92*
Sanders, Louis Lee 1929- *AmMWSc 92*
Sanders, Marilyn Magdanz 1942- *AmMWSc 92*
Sanders, Marion Andrew 1955- *WhoFI 92*
Sanders, Marlene *LesBEnT 92*
Sanders, Marlene 1931- *WhoEnt 92*
Sanders, Martha Frances *WhoEnt 92*
Sanders, Martin E 1954- *AmMWSc 92*
Sanders, Marvin Cecil 1934- *WhoRel 92*
Sanders, Mary Elizabeth 1917- *AmMWSc 92*
Sanders, Mavis *WhoRel 92*
Sanders, Michael Anthony 1960- *WhoBlA 92*
Sanders, Michael Ray Edward 1946- *WhoAmL 92*
Sanders, Nicholas John 1946- *Who 92*
Sanders, Oliver Paul 1924- *AmMWSc 92*
Sanders, Ottys E 1903- *AmMWSc 92*
Sanders, Paul F 1927- *WhoAmP 91*
Sanders, Paul Hampton 1909- *WhoAmL 92*
Sanders, Peter 1938- *WrDr 92*
Sanders, Peter 1940- *TwCPaSc*
Sanders, Peter Basil 1938- *IntAu&W 91, Who 92*
Sanders, Phyllis Aden 1919- *WhoEnt 92*
Sanders, Phyllis May 1922- *WhoEnt 92*
Sanders, Raymond Adrian 1932- *Who 92*
Sanders, Raymond Thomas 1923- *AmMWSc 92*
Sanders, Rhonda Sheree 1956- *WhoBlA 92*
Sanders, Richard A, Jr 1963- *WhoAmP 91*
Sanders, Richard B 1945- *WhoAmP 91*
Sanders, Richard James 1916- *WhoMW 92*
Sanders, Richard Kinard 1940- *WhoEnt 92*
Sanders, Richard Pat 1943- *AmMWSc 92*
Sanders, Ricky Wayne 1962- *WhoBlA 92*
Sanders, Rober LaFayette 1952- *WhoBlA 92*
Sanders, Robert 1925- *Who 92*
Sanders, Robert B 1938- *AmMWSc 92, WhoBlA 92, WhoWest 92*
Sanders, Robert Charles 1942- *AmMWSc 92*
Sanders, Robert L. 1906-1974 *NewAmDM*
Sanders, Roberta Sue 1958- *WhoMW 92*
Sanders, Roger Benedict 1940- *Who 92*
Sanders, Ronald d1991 *NewYTBS 91 [port]*
Sanders, Ronald 1932-1991 *ConAu 133*
Sanders, Ronald 1948- *IntWW 91, Who 92*
Sanders, Ronald L 1946- *WhoAmP 91*
Sanders, Ronald L 1947- *AmMWSc 92*
Sanders, Sally Ruth 1952- *WhoBlA 92*
Sanders, Samuel *WhoEnt 92*
Sanders, Samuel 1937- *NewAmDM*
Sanders, Samuel Marshall, Jr 1928- *AmMWSc 92*
Sanders, Scott Patrick *DrAPF 91*
Sanders, Scott Russell *DrAPF 91*
Sanders, Scott Russell 1945- *ConAu 35NR*
Sanders, Sherry Christine 1950- *WhoRel 92*
Sanders, Stephanie Ann 1954- *WhoMW 92*
Sanders, Stephen Craig 1959- *WhoWest 92*
Sanders, Steve *WhoEnt 92*
Sanders, Steven 1951- *WhoAmP 91*
Sanders, Steven LeRoy 1959- *WhoBlA 92*
Sanders, T H, Jr 1943- *AmMWSc 92*
Sanders, Teressa Irene 1951- *WhoFI 92*
Sanders, Terrell C., Jr. *WhoRel 92*
Sanders, Terry Barrett 1931- *IntMPA 92, WhoEnt 92*
Sanders, Thelma d1989 *WhoBlA 92N*
Sanders, Theodore Michael, Jr 1927- *AmMWSc 92*
Sanders, Theodore Roland, Jr. 1954- *WhoFI 92*
Sanders, Timothy D 1935- *AmMWSc 92*
Sanders, Victoria Lynn *WhoBlA 92*
Sanders, W Eugene, Jr 1934- *AmMWSc 92*
Sanders, W Thomas 1933- *AmMWSc 92*
Sanders, W W, Jr 1933- *AmMWSc 92*
Sanders, Walter *DrAPF 91*
Sanders, Walter Jeremiah, III 1936- *WhoWest 92*
Sanders, Walter L 1937- *AmMWSc 92*
Sanders, Walter MacDonald, III 1930- *AmMWSc 92*
Sanders, Wayne R, 1947- *WhoFI 92*
Sanders, Wendell Rowan 1933- *WhoBlA 92*
Sanders, Wesley, Jr. 1933- *WhoBlA 92*
Sanders, Wilfred Leroy, Jr 1935- *WhoAmP 91*
Sanders, William Albert 1933- *AmMWSc 92*
Sanders, William Eugene 1933- *WhoFI 92*
Sanders, William Eugene, Jr. 1934- *WhoMW 92*
Sanders, William Evan 1919- *WhoRel 92*
Sanders, William George 1936- *Who 92*
Sanders, William Mac 1919- *WhoBlA 92*
Sanders, William Mack 1926- *AmMWSc 92*
Sanders, Winston P *ConAu 34NR*
Sanders, Woodrow Mac 1943- *WhoBlA 92*
Sanders-Bush, Elaine 1940- *AmMWSc 92*
Sanders-Loehr, Joann 1942- *AmMWSc 92*
Sanders-West, Selma D. 1953- *WhoBlA 92*
Sanderson *Who 92*
Sanderson, Allen *WhoAmP 91*
Sanderson, Arthur Clark 1946- *AmMWSc 92*
Sanderson, Benjamin S 1922- *AmMWSc 92*
Sanderson, Brian Keith 1960- *WhoRel 92*
Sanderson, Bryan *Who 92*
Sanderson, Charles Denis 1934- *Who 92*
Sanderson, Christopher 1939- *TwCPaSc*
Sanderson, Christopher Derek 1948- *WhoEnt 92*
Sanderson, David Alan 1951- *WhoMW 92*
Sanderson, David R. 1933- *WhoWest 92*
Sanderson, Debby P 1941- *WhoAmP 91*
Sanderson, Dennis Carl 1935- *WhoEnt 92*
Sanderson, Donald Eugene 1926- *AmMWSc 92, WhoMW 92*
Sanderson, Douglas Jay 1953- *WhoAmL 92*
Sanderson, Edwin S 1920- *AmMWSc 92*
Sanderson, Floyd Denton 1941- *WhoWest 92*
Sanderson, Frank Philip Bryan 1910- *Who 92*
Sanderson, Gary Warner 1934- *AmMWSc 92*
Sanderson, George Albert 1926- *AmMWSc 92*
Sanderson, George Rutherford 1919- *Who 92*
Sanderson, Glen Charles 1923- *AmMWSc 92*
Sanderson, Henry Preston 1925- *AmMWSc 92*
Sanderson, Irma 1912- *ConAu 135, SmATA 66 [port]*
Sanderson, James George 1949- *AmMWSc 92*
Sanderson, John 1783-1844 *BenetAL 91*
Sanderson, Judson 1921- *AmMWSc 92*
Sanderson, Keith Fred 1932- *Who 92*
Sanderson, Kenneth Chapman 1933- *AmMWSc 92*
Sanderson, Kenneth Edwin 1934- *AmMWSc 92*
Sanderson, Margaret Love *ConAu 135, SmATA 68*
Sanderson, Marie Elizabeth 1921- *AmMWSc 92*
Sanderson, Peter Oliver 1929- *Who 92*
Sanderson, Randy Chris 1954- *WhoBlA 92*
Sanderson, Richard Blodgett 1935- *AmMWSc 92*
Sanderson, Richard James 1933- *AmMWSc 92*
Sanderson, Robert Thomas 1912- *AmMWSc 92*
Sanderson, Ron Eugene 1939- *WhoRel 92*
Sanderson, Roy *Who 92*
Sanderson, Roy 1931- *Who 92*
Sanderson, Stanley Ray 1950- *WhoRel 92*
Sanderson, Stewart F 1924- *IntAu&W 91, WrDr 92*
Sanderson, Tessa *IntWW 91*
Sanderson, Tessa 1956- *BlkOlyM*
Sanderson, William H. 1917- *WhoFI 92*
Sanderson, William Roy 1907- *Who 92*
Sanderson of Ayot, Baron *Who 92*
Sanderson of Bowden, Baron 1933- *Who 92*
Sandes, Flora 1876-1956 *EncAmaz 91*
Sandford, Baron 1920- *Who 92*
Sandford, Arthur 1941- *Who 92*
Sandford, Cedric Thomas 1924- *Who 92*
Sandford, Frank Weston 1862-1948 *RelLAm 91*
Sandford, Gordon Thomas 1929- *WhoEnt 92*
Sandford, Herbert Henry 1916- *Who 92*
Sandford, Jeremy *IntAu&W 91, Who 92*
Sandford, Jeremy 1934- *WrDr 92*
Sandford, John Loren 1929- *ConAu 36NR, WhoRel 92*
Sandford, Kenneth Leslie 1915- *Who 92*
Sandford, Maxwell Tenbrook, II 1944- *AmMWSc 92*
Sandford, Paul Gordon 1961- *WhoFI 92*
Sandford, Paula 1931- *ConAu 36NR*
Sandford, Sara Piper 1958- *WhoAmL 92*
Sandford, Sefton Ronald 1925- *Who 92*
Sandford Smith, Richard Henry 1909- *Who 92*
Sandham, Herbert James 1932- *AmMWSc 92*
Sandhu, Harbhajan Singh 1932- *AmMWSc 92*
Sandhu, Hargurpal Singh 1936- *WhoWest 92*
Sandhu, Mohammad Akram 1936- *AmMWSc 92*
Sandhu, Ranbir Singh 1928- *AmMWSc 92, WhoMW 92*
Sandhu, Shingara Singh 1932- *AmMWSc 92*
Sandhurst, Baron 1920- *Who 92*
Sandhusen, John Eric 1958- *WhoMW 92*
Sandidge, Kanita Durice 1947- *WhoBlA 92, WhoFI 92*
Sandifar, Michael Eugene 1945- *WhoMW 92*
Sandifer, James Roy 1945- *AmMWSc 92*
Sandifer, James Stephen 1948- *WhoRel 92*
Sandifer, Jawn A. 1919- *WhoBlA 92*
Sandifer, Mark M. 1956- *WhoRel 92*
Sandifer, Myron Guy, Jr 1922- *AmMWSc 92*
Sandifer, Paul Alan 1947- *AmMWSc 92*
Sandifer, Ronda Margaret 1954- *AmMWSc 92*
Sandifer, Samuel Hope 1916- *AmMWSc 92*
Sandiford, Cedric d1991 *NewYTBS 91 [port]*
Sandiford, Erskine 1937- *Who 92*
Sandiford, Lloyd Erskine 1937- *IntWW 91*
Sandifur, Cantwell Paul 1903- *WhoIns 92*
Sandilands *Who 92*
Sandilands, Francis 1913- *Who 92*
Sandilands, Francis Edwin Prescott 1913- *IntWW 91*
Sandin, Thomas Robert 1939- *AmMWSc 92*
Sandine, William Ewald 1928- *AmMWSc 92*
Sandino, Augusto Cesar 1893-1934 *FacFETw*
Sandison, Alexander 1943- *Who 92*
Sanditz, Theodore Bert 1946- *WhoMW 92*
Sandle, Floyd Leslie 1913- *WhoBlA 92*
Sandle, Michael 1936- *TwCPaSc*
Sandle, Michael Leonard 1936- *IntWW 91, Who 92*
Sandler, Albert Nathan 1930- *WhoMW 92*
Sandler, Barry 1947- *WhoEnt 92*
Sandler, Benjamin 1957- *WhoHisp 92*
Sandler, Harold 1929- *AmMWSc 92*
Sandler, Herbert M. 1931- *WhoFI 92, WhoWest 92*
Sandler, Irving 1925- *WrDr 92*
Sandler, Jenny *WhoEnt 92*
Sandler, Joan D. 1934- *WhoBlA 92*
Sandler, Joseph Bernard 1937- *WhoRel 92*
Sandler, Laurence Marvin 1929- *AmMWSc 92*
Sandler, Marion Osher 1930- *WhoFI 92, WhoWest 92*
Sandler, Melvin 1937- *AmMWSc 92*
Sandler, Merton 1926- *Who 92, WrDr 92*
Sandler, Paul Mark 1945- *WhoAmL 92*
Sandler, Philip Stanley 1943- *WhoFI 92*
Sandler, Richard Jay 1947- *WhoAmL 92*
Sandler, Rivka Black 1918- *AmMWSc 92*
Sandler, Robert B. *WhoFI 92*
Sandler, Robert Michael 1942- *WhoFI 92*
Sandler, Robert Stephen 1930- *WhoFI 92*
Sandler, Samuel 1921- *AmMWSc 92*
Sandler, Samuel 1926- *WhoMW 92*
Sandler, Sheldon Samuel 1932- *AmMWSc 92*
Sandler, Stanley I 1940- *AmMWSc 92*
Sandler, Stuart Mitchell 1961- *WhoWest 92*
Sandler, Todd Michael 1946- *WhoFI 92, WhoMW 92*
Sandlin, Billy Joe 1927- *AmMWSc 92*
Sandlin, Marlon Joe 1953- *WhoWest 92*
Sandlin, S. Z. 1949- *WhoRel 92*
Sandlin, Sherry *WhoAmP 91*
Sandlin, Steven Monroe 1935- *WhoWest 92*
Sandlin, Tim *DrAPF 91*
Sandlin, Tim 1950- *IntAu&W 91*
Sandman, James Joseph 1951- *WhoAmL 92*
Sandman, Peter 1945- *WrDr 92*
Sandman, Peter Mark 1945- *IntAu&W 91*
Sandman, Rodney Paul 1967- *WhoMW 92*
Sandmann, William Henry 1928- *AmMWSc 92*
Sandmeier, Henry Armin 1920- *AmMWSc 92*
Sandmeier, Ruedi Beat 1945- *WhoWest 92*
Sandmeyer, Esther E 1929- *AmMWSc 92*
Sandmo, Agnar 1938- *IntWW 91*
Sandmore, Donald Robert 1960- *WhoMW 92*
Sandner, John Francis 1941- *WhoFI 92*
Sandness, William John 1948- *WhoAmP 91*
Sando, Arthur R. *LesBEnT 92*
Sando, Ephriam 1934- *WhoWest 92*
Sando, Julianne J 1952- *AmMWSc 92*
Sando, Kenneth Martin 1941- *AmMWSc 92*
Sando, William Jasper 1927- *AmMWSc 92*
Sandok, Paul Louis 1943- *AmMWSc 92*
Sandon, Viscount 1951- *Who 92*
Sandon, J.D. *TwCWW 91, WrDr 92*
Sandor, Anna *WhoEnt 92*
Sandor, Ellen Ruth 1942- *WhoMW 92*
Sandor, George N 1912- *AmMWSc 92*
Sandor, Gyorgy *WhoEnt 92A*
Sandor, Gyorgy 1912- *NewAmDM*
Sandor, Richard Laurence 1941- *WhoFI 92*

Sandor, Thomas 1924- AmMWSc 92
Sandor-Jimenez, Yolanda 1955- WhoHisp 92
Sandos, Michael Steven 1951- WhoHisp 92
Sandos, Tim WhoHisp 92
Sandoungout, Marcel 1927- IntWW 91
Sandoval, Alicia Catherine 1943- WhoHisp 92
Sandoval, Alphonso J. 1923- WhoHisp 92
Sandoval, Andrew M. 1952- WhoHisp 92
Sandoval, Antonio Martinez 1941- WhoHisp 92
Sandoval, Arturo 1949- IntWW 91
Sandoval, Chris 1949- WhoHisp 92
Sandoval, Dolores S. 1937- WhoBlA 92
Sandoval, Don 1966- WhoHisp 92
Sandoval, Donald A 1935- WhoAmP 91, WhoHisp 92
Sandoval, Edward C WhoAmP 91, WhoHisp 92
Sandoval, Edward P. 1960- WhoHisp 92
Sandoval, Ernie 1948- WhoHisp 92
Sandoval, Howard Kenneth 1931- AmMWSc 92, WhoHisp 92
Sandoval, Joe G. 1937- WhoHisp 92
Sandoval, Joseph WhoHisp 92
Sandoval, Marcelo Alex 1960- WhoHisp 92
Sandoval, Mary Jane 1951- WhoHisp 92
Sandoval, Miguel WhoHisp 92
Sandoval, Moises 1930- WhoHisp 92, WhoRel 92
Sandoval, Olivia Medina 1946- WhoHisp 92
Sandoval, R. Christoph 1949- WhoHisp 92
Sandoval, Raul M. 1957- WhoHisp 92
Sandoval, Rik 1952- WhoEnt 92, WhoWest 92
Sandoval, Roberto DrAPF 91
Sandoval, Rodolpho 1942- WhoHisp 92
Sandoval, Rudolph 1929- WhoHisp 92
Sandoval-Beene, Mercedes 1949- WhoHisp 92
Sandow, Bruce Arnold 1945- AmMWSc 92
Sandow, Dean Todd 1958- WhoAmL 92
Sandow, Greg 1943- WhoEnt 92
Sandowski, Norma Jewell 1940- WhoMW 92
Sandoz, G Ellis 1931- IntAu&W 91, WrDr 92
Sandoz, George 1921- AmMWSc 92
Sandoz, Mari 1896-1966 HanAmWH, TwCWW 91
Sandoz, Mari 1901-1966 BenetAL 91
Sandoz, William Charles 1928- WhoAmL 92
Sandquist, Elroy C, Jr 1922- WhoAmP 91
Sandquist, Gary Marlin 1936- AmMWSc 92, WhoWest 92
Sandquist, Ronda Lee 1950- WhoAmL 92
Sandquist, Theodore Richard 1947- WhoRel 92
Sandra, Alexander AmMWSc 92
Sandrapaty, Ramachandra Rao 1942- AmMWSc 92
Sandre, Didier 1946- IntWW 91
Sandri, Joseph Mario 1929- AmMWSc 92
Sandrich, Jay LesBEnT 92
Sandrich, Jay 1932- IntMPA 92
Sandrich, Jay H. 1932- WhoEnt 92
Sandrick, James Francis 1943- WhoMW 92
Sandridge, Robert Lee 1932- AmMWSc 92
Sandrik, James Leslie 1938- AmMWSc 92
Sandroff, Ronni DrAPF 91
Sandrok, Richard William 1943- WhoAmL 92
Sands, A P, III 1945- WhoAmP 91
Sands, Charles Douglas 1964- WhoRel 92
Sands, Daniel Lee 1947- WhoFI 92
Sands, Darry Gene 1947- WhoAmL 92
Sands, David Chandler 1941- AmMWSc 92
Sands, David Henry 1962- WhoAmL 92
Sands, Don William 1926- WhoFI 92
Sands, Donald Edgar 1929- AmMWSc 92
Sands, Douglas Bruce 1934- WhoBlA 92
Sands, Elaine S 1940- AmMWSc 92
Sands, Ethel 1873-1962 TwCPaSc
Sands, George Dewey 1919- AmMWSc 92
Sands, George Harry 1951- WhoFI 92
Sands, George M. 1942- WhoBlA 92
Sands, Henry W. 1933- WhoBlA 92
Sands, Howard 1942- AmMWSc 92
Sands, Jack 1947- WhoAmP 91
Sands, James Keith Marshall 1952- WhoAmL 92
Sands, Jeffrey Alan 1948- AmMWSc 92
Sands, Julian 1958- IntMPA 92
Sands, Martin IntAu&W 91X, WrDr 92
Sands, Mary Alice 1941- WhoBlA 92
Sands, Matthew 1919- AmMWSc 92
Sands, Randall Lee 1962- WhoRel 92
Sands, Richard Dayton 1929- AmMWSc 92
Sands, Richard Hamilton 1929- AmMWSc 92
Sands, Robert C. 1799-1832 BenetAL 91
Sands, Robert-John H 1954- WhoIns 92
Sands, Roger Blakemore 1942- Who 92
Sands, Rosetta F. WhoBlA 92
Sands, Russell Bertram 1940- WhoWest 92
Sands, Russell Lee 1940- WhoFI 92
Sands, Seymour 1918- AmMWSc 92
Sands, Sharon Louise 1944- WhoWest 92
Sands, Tommy 1937- IntMPA 92
Sands, Velma Ahda WhoAmL 92
Sands, William Arthur 1953- WhoWest 92
Sandson, John Ivan 1927- AmMWSc 92
Sandstead, Harold Hilton 1932- AmMWSc 92
Sandsted, Roger France 1918- AmMWSc 92
Sandstrom, Alice Wilhelmina 1914- WhoFI 92
Sandstrom, Boden C. 1945- WhoEnt 92
Sandstrom, Dale Vernon 1950- WhoAmL 92, WhoAmP 91, WhoMW 92
Sandstrom, Donald James 1937- AmMWSc 92
Sandstrom, Donald Richard 1940- AmMWSc 92
Sandstrom, Gustave Frank, Jr. 1943- WhoAmL 92
Sandstrom, Jan 1954- ConCom 92
Sandstrom, Joanne Wulf 1938- WhoWest 92
Sandstrom, John Carl 1963- WhoMW 92
Sandstrom, Mark Rand 1954- WhoRel 92
Sandstrom, Mark Roy 1942- WhoAmL 92
Sandstrom, Robert Edward 1946- WhoWest 92
Sandstrom, Wayne Mark 1927- AmMWSc 92
Sandt, Henry Uriah, Jr. 1951- WhoFI 92
Sandu, Constantine 1943- WhoMW 92
Sanduleak, Nicholas 1933- AmMWSc 92
Sandura, Wilson Runyararo 1941- IntWW 91
Sandus, Oscar 1924- AmMWSc 92
Sandusky, Harold William 1949- AmMWSc 92
Sandusky, John Thomas, Jr 1934- WhoAmP 91
Sandved, Arthur Olav 1931- IntWW 91
Sandven, Lars Arild 1945- WhoWest 92
Sandver, Jean Hart 1950- WhoFI 92, WhoMW 92
Sandvig, Robert L 1923- AmMWSc 92
Sandvik, Peter Olaf 1927- AmMWSc 92
Sandweiss, Jack 1930- AmMWSc 92
Sandwich, Earl of Who 92
Sandwich, Reuben DrAPF 91
Sandwith, Colin John 1936- AmMWSc 92
Sandy, D. Brent 1947- WhoRel 92
Sandy, Stephen DrAPF 91
Sandy, Stephen 1934- ConPo 91, IntAu&W 91, WrDr 92
Sandy, William Haskell 1929- WhoFI 92
Sandys, Baron 1931- Who 92
Sandys, Elspeth Somerville 1940- IntAu&W 91
Sandys, George 1578-1644 BenetAL 91
Sandys, Julian George Winston 1936- Who 92
Sandza, Joseph Gerard 1917- AmMWSc 92
Sanecki, Kay Naylor WrDr 92
Sanejouand, Jean Michel 1934- IntWW 91
Sanem, Michael L. 1942- WhoWest 92
Saner, Reg DrAPF 91
Saner, Reg 1931- ConPo 91, WrDr 92
Saner, Reginald Anthony 1931- IntAu&W 91
Saner, Robert Morton Who 92
Sanes, Joshua Richard 1949- AmMWSc 92
Saneto, Russell Patrick 1950- WhoWest 92
Sanetti, Stephen Louis 1949- WhoAmL 92
Saneyev, Viktor 1945- IntWW 91
Saneyev, Viktor Danilovich 1945- SovUnBD
San Felippo, Ronald Steven 1946- WhoMW 92
Sanfield, Steve DrAPF 91
Sanfilip, Thomas DrAPF 91
Sanfilippo, Jon Walter 1950- WhoMW 92
San Filippo, Joseph, Jr 1944- AmMWSc 92
Sanfilippo, Robert 1950- WhoWest 92
Sanford, Allan Robert 1927- AmMWSc 92, WhoWest 92
Sanford, Annette DrAPF 91
Sanford, Barbara Ann 1941- AmMWSc 92
Sanford, Barbara Hendrick 1927- AmMWSc 92
Sanford, Bruce William 1945- WhoAmL 92, WhoEnt 92
Sanford, Charles 1905- IntMPA 92
Sanford, Charles Steadman, Jr. 1936- IntWW 91, WhoFI 92
Sanford, Christy Sheffield DrAPF 91
Sanford, Don Alberne 1926- WhoMW 92
Sanford, E W d1918 BiInAmS
Sanford, Edward Richard 1928- AmMWSc 92
Sanford, Edward T 1865-1930 FacFETw
Sanford, Elias Benjamin 1843-1932 RelLAm 91
Sanford, George Robert 1927- WhoWest 92
Sanford, Geraldine A.J. DrAPF 91
Sanford, Isabel 1917- IntMPA 92
Sanford, Isabel G. 1917- WhoBlA 92
Sanford, Isabel Gwendolyn WhoEnt 92
Sanford, James R 1933- AmMWSc 92
Sanford, Jay Philip 1928- AmMWSc 92
Sanford, Karl John 1947- AmMWSc 92
Sanford, Katherine Koontz 1915- AmMWSc 92
Sanford, Kathleen Diane 1952- WhoWest 92
Sanford, Kendall Thaine 1943- WhoAmL 92
Sanford, L G 1930- AmMWSc 92
Sanford, Leonard Jacob 1833-1896 BiInAmS
Sanford, Loretta Love 1951- WhoBlA 92
Sanford, Malcolm Thomas 1942- AmMWSc 92
Sanford, Mark 1953- WhoBlA 92
Sanford, Michael David 1945- WhoFI 92
Sanford, Michael Durham 1951- WhoFI 92
Sanford, Paul Everett 1917- AmMWSc 92
Sanford, Richard Frederick 1950- AmMWSc 92
Sanford, Richard Selden AmMWSc 92
Sanford, Robert Alois 1922- AmMWSc 92
Sanford, Ron 1939- WhoWest 92
Sanford, Ruth Eileen 1925- WhoMW 92
Sanford, Suzanne Langford 1951- WhoAmL 92
Sanford, Terry 1917- AlmAP 92 [port], IntWW 91, WhoAmL 92, WhoAmP 91
Sanford, Thomas Bayes 1940- AmMWSc 92
Sanford, Timothy Bryce 1953- WhoEnt 92
Sanford, Wallace Gordon 1923- AmMWSc 92
Sanford, Walter Scott 1956- WhoWest 92
Sanford, Willard C 1932- WhoIns 92
San Francisco, Kevin DrAPF 91
Sang Ye LiExTwC
Sang, Barry Ray 1951- WhoRel 92
Sang, Julius 1948- BlkOlyM
Sangare, August WhoRel 92
Sangare, N'Faly 1933- IntWW 91
Sanger, Alan Rodney 1943- AmMWSc 92
Sanger, Charles Robert 1860-1912 BiInAmS
Sanger, Clyde 1928- ConAu 36NR
Sanger, David John 1947- IntWW 91
Sanger, Eleanor 1929- WhoEnt 92, WhoWest 92
Sanger, Frederick 1918- AmMWSc 92, FacFETw, IntWW 91, Who 92, WhoNob 90
Sanger, Gail 1945- WhoAmL 92
Sanger, Gregory Marshall 1946- AmMWSc 92
Sanger, Herbert Shelton, Jr. 1936- WhoAmL 92
Sanger, Jean M 1941- AmMWSc 92
Sanger, John Morton 1943- WhoAmL 92
Sanger, Jon Edward 1939- AmMWSc 92, WhoMW 92
Sanger, Jonathan WhoEnt 92
Sanger, Joseph William 1941- AmMWSc 92
Sanger, Margaret 1879-1966 RComAH
Sanger, Margaret 1883-1966 BenetAL 91, FacFETw
Sanger, Margaret Louise 1879-1966 HanAmWH
Sanger, Marjory Bartlett 1920- IntAu&W 91, WrDr 92
Sanger, Ruth Ann 1918- IntWW 91, Who 92
Sanger, Warren Glenn 1945- AmMWSc 92
Sanger, William W. d1894 DcAmImH
San Giacomo, Laura IntMPA 92
Sangiovanni-Vincentelli, Alberto Luigi 1947- AmMWSc 92, WhoWest 92
Sangirardi, Margaret Diane 1946- WhoWest 92
Sangmeister, George E. 1931- AlmAP 92 [port]
Sangmeister, George Edward 1931- WhoAmP 91, WhoMW 92
Sangren, Ward Conrad 1923- AmMWSc 92
Sangrey, Dwight A 1940- AmMWSc 92
Sangster, Charles 1822-1893 BenetAL 91
Sangster, Jimmy 1927- IntMPA 92
Sangster, John Laing 1922- Who 92
Sangster, Margaret E. 1838-1912 BenetAL 91
Sangster, Raymond Charles 1928- AmMWSc 92
Sangster, Robert Edmund 1936- Who 92
Sangster, Verley Gene 1933- WhoRel 92
Sangster, William M 1925- AmMWSc 92
Sanguineti, Edoardo 1930- IntWW 91
Sanguinetti, Eugene Frank 1917- WhoWest 92
Sanguinetti, Julio Maria 1936- IntWW 91
Sanguinetty, Jorge A. 1937- WhoHisp 92
Sanhueza, Hernan 1935- WhoFI 92
Sani, Brahma Porinchu 1937- AmMWSc 92
Sani, Robert L 1935- AmMWSc 92
Saniee, Iraj 1956- AmMWSc 92
Sanig, Jane 1960- WhoEnt 92
Sanjana, Espi 1944- WhoFI 92
Sanjare, August WhoRel 92
Sanjian, Avedis K 1921- IntAu&W 91, WrDr 92
Sanjines, Jorge 1936- IntDcF 2-2
San Jose, George L. 1956- WhoHisp 92
San Jose de Betancur, Pedro de 1627-1667 HisDSpE
San Juan, Manuel, Jr 1920- WhoIns 92
Sanjurjo, Carmen Hilda 1952- WhoHisp 92
Sank, David Abraham 1962- WhoFI 92
Sank, Diane 1927- AmMWSc 92
Sank, Victor J 1944- AmMWSc 92
Sankar, D V Siva 1927- AmMWSc 92
Sankar, Seshadri AmMWSc 92
Sankar, Subramanian Vaidya 1959- WhoWest 92
Sankar, Suryanarayan G 1942- AmMWSc 92
Sankar, Thiagas Sriram 1940- AmMWSc 92
Sankbeil, William Alan 1946- WhoAmL 92
Sanker, Donald J 1960- WhoAmP 91
Sankey, Guy Richard 1944- Who 92
Sankey, Ira D. 1840-1908 RelLAm 91
Sankey, Ira David BenetAL 91
Sankey, John Anthony 1930- IntWW 91, Who 92
Sankey, Vernon Louis 1949- Who 92
Sankoff, David 1942- AmMWSc 92
Sankovitz, James Leo 1934- WhoMW 92
Sankovitz, Richard John 1958- WhoAmL 92
Sanks, Charles Randolph, Jr. 1928- WhoRel 92
Sanks, Robert Leland 1916- WhoWest 92
San Mames, Juan J. 1947- WhoHisp 92
Sanmann, Everett Eugene 1937- AmMWSc 92
Sanmartin, Aimee C. 1960- WhoHisp 92
San Martin, Jose de 1778-1850 BenetAL 91, HisDSpE
San Martin, Tomas de 1482-1554 HisDSpE
San Miguel, Pedro Luis 1954- WhoHisp 92
Sann, Klaus Heinrich 1919- AmMWSc 92
Sanneh, Lamin WhoRel 92
Sannella, Joseph L 1933- AmMWSc 92
Sanner, George Elwood 1929- WhoFI 92
Sanner, John Harper 1931- AmMWSc 92, WhoMW 92
Sanner, Monty Ray 1953- WhoWest 92
Sanner, Robert Charles 1945- WhoWest 92
Sanner, Royce N 1931- WhoIns 92
Sanner, Royce Norman 1931- WhoAmL 92
Sannerud, Robert Alan 1954- WhoMW 92
Sannes, Felix Rudolph 1940- AmMWSc 92
Sannes, Philip Loren 1948- AmMWSc 92
San Nicolas, Henry Deleon WhoAmP 91
Sannuti, Peddapullaiah 1941- AmMWSc 92
Sannwald, William Walter 1940- WhoWest 92
Sanny, Charles Gordon 1947- AmMWSc 92
Sano, James David 1954- WhoWest 92
Sano, Kenjiro 1920- IntWW 91
Sano, Roy I. WhoRel 92, WhoWest 92
Sanocki, Edward John, Jr. 1950- WhoAmL 92
Sanoff, Henry 1934- AmMWSc 92
San Pedro, Enrique 1926- WhoRel 92
San Pietro, Anthony 1922- AmMWSc 92
Sanregret, Catherine Ann 1965- WhoWest 92
San Roman, Jose Alfredo Perez 1931-1989 FacFETw
Sansbury, Cyril Kenneth 1905- IntWW 91
Sansbury, Kenneth 1905- Who 92
Sansevero, Michael, Jr 1952- WhoAmP 91
Sansevieri, Daniel Frederick 1946- WhoFI 92
Sansing, Norman Glenn 1932- AmMWSc 92
Sanslone, William Robert 1931- AmMWSc 92
Sansolo, Jack 1943- WhoFI 92
Sansom, Andrew William 1937- Who 92
Sansom, Arthur B. 1920-1991 ConAu 134
Sansom, Dixie Newton 1948- WhoAmP 91
Sansom, Lester A. IntMPA 92
Sansom, Matt R. 1950- WhoWest 92
Sansom, Peter 1958- ConAu 133
Sansom, Richard E 1933- AmMWSc 92
Sansom, William 1912-1976 RfGEnL 91

**Sanson,** William Hendrix 1926- *WhoAmP 91*
**Sansone,** Eric Brandfon 1939- *AmMWSc 92*
**Sansone,** Frances Marie 1931- *AmMWSc 92*
**Sansone,** Francis Joseph 1951- *AmMWSc 92*
**Sansone,** Fred J 1934- *AmMWSc 92*
**Sansone,** Fredrick Rawls 1952- *WhoEnt 92*
**Sansone,** Rocco Carl 1950- *WhoIns 92*
**Sansonetti,** S John 1914- *AmMWSc 92*
**Sansores,** Albert N., Jr. 1950- *WhoHisp 92*
**Sansoucie,** Larry Allen 1951- *WhoRel 92*
**San Soucie,** Robert Louis 1927- *AmMWSc 92*
**Sansoucy,** Andre A. 1957- *WhoAmL 92*
**Sanstead,** Wayne Godfrey 1935- *WhoAmP 91*
**Sansweet,** Stephen Jay 1945- *WhoWest 92*
**Sant,** John Talbot 1932- *WhoAmL 92, WhoFI 92*
**Sant,** John Talbot, Jr. 1960- *WhoAmL 92*
**Sant,** Lorry 1937- *IntWW 91*
**Sant,** Raymond S 1937- *WhoAmP 91*
**Sant,** Thomas Robert 1943- *WhoAmL 92*
**Santa Rosa de Lima** 1586-1617 *HisDSpE*
**Santa,** Jon R. 1946- *WhoMW 92*
**Santa Ana,** Antonio Lopez de 1795-1876 *BenetAL 91*
**Santa Anna,** Antonio Lopez de 1795-1876 *BenetAL 91*
**Santa Aponte,** Jesus *WhoHisp 92*
**Santa Croce,** Anthony Arthur 1947- *WhoEnt 92*
**Santa Cruz,** Allan *WhoAmP 91*
**Santa Cruz,** Ivan 1930- *WhoHisp 92*
**Santa Cruz,** Victor Rafael Andres d1990 *Who 92N*
**Santa Cruz y Calahumana,** Andres de 1792-1865 *HisDSpE*
**Santa Cruz y Espejo,** Francisco Eugenio 1747-1795 *HisDSpE*
**Santa Maria,** Philip Joseph, III 1945- *WhoAmL 92*
**Santa Maria,** Zeke Polanco 1942- *WhoHisp 92*
**Santacana-Nuet,** Francisco 1931- *AmMWSc 92*
**SantaCroce,** John Paul 1959- *WhoFI 92*
**Santaella,** Irma 1924- *WhoHisp 92*
**Santaliz,** Pedro *DrAPF 91*
**Santamaria,** Henry, Jr. 1948- *WhoHisp 92*
**Santamaria,** Jaime 1911- *WhoHisp 92*
**Santamaria,** Vito William 1948- *AmMWSc 92*
**Santamarina,** Juan Carlos 1958- *WhoHisp 92*
**Sant'Ambrogio,** Giuseppe 1931- *AmMWSc 92*
**Santamour,** Frank Shalvey, Jr 1932- *AmMWSc 92*
**Santana,** Ana V. 1963- *WhoHisp 92*
**Santana,** Andres 1968- *WhoHisp 92*
**Santana,** Anthony *WhoHisp 92*
**Santana,** Carlos 1947- *NewAmDM, WhoEnt 92, WhoHisp 92*
**Santana,** Carlota *WhoHisp 92*
**Santana,** Elida *WhoHisp 92*
**Santana,** Jorge Armando 1944- *WhoHisp 92*
**Santana,** Juan Jose 1942- *WhoHisp 92*
**Santana,** Marie 1951- *WhoHisp 92*
**Santana,** Pepe 1942- *WhoHisp 92*
**Santana,** Rafael Francisco 1958- *WhoHisp 92*
**Santana,** Victor Manuel, Jr. 1962- *WhoHisp 92*
**Santana-Alvarez,** Luis F. 1943- *WhoHisp 92*
**Santander,** Francisco de 1792-1840 *HisDSpE*
**Santander,** Teresa 1925- *IntWW 91*
**Santangelo,** Joseph G. 1930- *WhoFI 92*
**Santangelo,** Mario Vincent 1931- *WhoMW 92*
**Santangelo,** Richard Ellis 1960- *WhoEnt 92*
**Santangelo,** Stephen John 1956- *WhoMW 92*
**Santaniello,** Angelo G *WhoAmP 91*
**Santaniello,** Angelo Gary 1924- *WhoAmL 92*
**Santaniello,** Joseph M. *WhoAmL 92*
**Santaniello,** Vincent James, Jr. 1932- *WhoAmL 92*
**Santapau,** Manny 1949- *WhoHisp 92*
**Santare,** Michael Harold 1959- *AmMWSc 92*
**Santarella,** Roy Theodore 1953- *WhoFI 92*
**Santarlasci,** Robert Ardo 1962- *WhoEnt 92*
**Santayana,** George 1863-1952 *BenetAL 91, FacFETw, LiExTwC*
**Sante,** Daniel P 1919- *AmMWSc 92*
**Santee,** Dale William 1953- *WhoWest 92*
**Santee,** Richard Ellis, Jr. 1951- *WhoAmL 92*
**Santee,** Ross 1888- *BenetAL 91*
**Santee,** Ross 1888-1965 *TwCWW 91*
**Santee,** Walt *TwCWW 91*
**Santeiro,** Luis 1947- *WhoHisp 92*
**Sant'Elia,** Antonio *DcTwDes*
**Santell,** Marie 1936- *WhoEnt 92*
**Santell,** Roberta 1937- *WhoAmP 91*
**Santelle,** Patricia Booth 1960- *WhoAmL 92*
**Santelli,** Claude Jean Xavier 1923- *IntWW 91*
**Santelmann,** Paul William 1926- *AmMWSc 92*
**Santen,** Ann Hortenstine 1938- *WhoEnt 92, WhoMW 92*
**Santen,** Richard J 1939- *AmMWSc 92*
**Santer,** Jacques 1937- *IntWW 91*
**Santer,** James Owen 1931- *AmMWSc 92*
**Santer,** Mark *Who 92*
**Santer,** Mark 1936- *IntWW 91*
**Santer,** Melvin 1926- *AmMWSc 92*
**Santer,** Richard Arthur 1937- *WhoMW 92*
**Santerre,** Robert Frank 1940- *AmMWSc 92*
**Santez,** David Lewis *WhoAmL 92*
**Santi,** Daniel V 1942- *AmMWSc 92*
**Santiago,** Aida Esther 1957- *WhoHisp 92*
**Santiago,** Alex *WhoAmP 91*
**Santiago,** Alfredo 1953- *WhoHisp 92*
**Santiago,** Americo *WhoHisp 92*
**Santiago,** Americo L *WhoAmP 91*
**Santiago,** Benito 1965- *WhoHisp 92*
**Santiago,** Bonnie 1966- *WhoHisp 92*
**Santiago,** Carlos Manuel 1961- *WhoFI 92*
**Santiago,** Dawn Teresa 1959- *WhoWest 92*
**Santiago,** Edgardo G. 1949- *WhoHisp 92*
**Santiago,** George 1929- *WhoHisp 92*
**Santiago,** George L. 1958- *WhoHisp 92*
**Santiago,** Gloria B. *WhoHisp 92*
**Santiago,** Isaura Santiago 1946- *WhoHisp 92*
**Santiago,** Ismael *WhoHisp 92*
**Santiago,** Jaime A. *WhoHisp 92*
**Santiago,** James Severo 1944- *WhoHisp 92*
**Santiago,** Jorge *WhoHisp 92*
**Santiago,** Julio Victor 1942- *AmMWSc 92, WhoHisp 92*
**Santiago,** Lorina Yvonne 1966- *WhoHisp 92*
**Santiago,** Luz M. 1948- *WhoHisp 92*
**Santiago,** Mayra C. 1952- *WhoHisp 92*
**Santiago,** Miguel A *WhoAmP 91, WhoHisp 92*
**Santiago,** Miguel de 1625-1706 *HisDSpE*
**Santiago,** Milly 1954- *WhoHisp 92*
**Santiago,** Noel Rivera 1961- *WhoHisp 92*
**Santiago,** Noemi 1953- *AmMWSc 92*
**Santiago,** Ramon 1948- *WhoHisp 92*
**Santiago,** Roberto 1953- *WhoHisp 92*
**Santiago,** Roberto 1963- *WhoBlA 92, WhoHisp 92*
**Santiago,** Rosa Emilia 1935- *WhoHisp 92*
**Santiago,** Saundra 1957- *WhoHisp 92*
**Santiago,** Teresa *WhoHisp 92*
**Santiago-Aviles,** Jorge Juan 1944- *WhoHisp 92*
**Santiago-Delphin,** Eduardo A. 1941- *WhoHisp 92*
**Santiago Garcia,** Presby 1941- *WhoAmP 91, WhoHisp 92*
**Santiago Gonez,** Rafael 1955- *WhoHisp 92*
**Santiago-Melendez,** Miguel 1930- *AmMWSc 92*
**Santiago-Negron,** Salvador 1942- *WhoHisp 92*
**Santiago Vega,** Rosa J. 1938- *WhoHisp 92*
**Santiago y Leon Garabito,** Juan de 1641-1694 *HisDSpE*
**Santidrian,** Santiago 1950- *AmMWSc 92*
**Santiesteban,** Humberto 1934- *WhoHisp 92*
**Santiesteban,** Humberto Tati 1934- *WhoAmP 91*
**Santiful,** Luthur L. *WhoBlA 92*
**Santillan,** Antonio 1936- *WhoFI 92, WhoHisp 92, WhoWest 92*
**Santillan,** Fernando de d1575 *HisDSpE*
**Santillan,** Jose Leopoldo 1957- *WhoFI 92*
**Santillanes,** Janet 1951- *WhoAmL 92*
**Santillano,** Sergio Raul 1951- *WhoHisp 92*
**Santilli,** Alcide 1914- *WhoWest 92*
**Santilli,** Arthur A 1929- *AmMWSc 92*
**Santilli,** Paul David 1946- *WhoAmP 91*
**Santillo,** Carl John 1949- *WhoIns 92*
**Santini,** Danilo John 1945- *WhoMW 92*
**Santini,** James David 1937- *WhoAmP 91*
**Santini,** Rosemarie *DrAPF 91*
**Santisteban,** Carlos *WhoHisp 92*
**Santisteban,** George Anthony 1918- *AmMWSc 92*
**Santmyer,** Helen H. *DrAPF 91*
**Santmyer,** Helen Hooven 1895- *BenetAL 91*
**Santmyer,** Helen Hooven 1895-1986 *FacFETw*
**Santner,** Joseph Frank 1919- *AmMWSc 92*
**Santner,** Thomas Joseph 1947- *AmMWSc 92*
**Santo,** Akiko 1942- *IntWW 91*
**Santo,** Gerald S 1944- *AmMWSc 92*
**Santo,** Ronald Joseph 1940- *WhoAmL 92*
**Santo Pietro,** Vincent Albert 1957- *WhoWest 92*
**Santola,** Daniel Ralph 1949- *WhoAmL 92*
**Santoli,** Joseph Ralph 1957- *WhoAmL 92*
**Santomenna,** Robert Charles 1934- *WhoAmL 92*
**Santomero,** Anthony M. 1946- *WhoFI 92*
**Santomieri,** David M 1945- *WhoIns 92*
**Santona,** Gloria 1950- *WhoHisp 92*
**Santopietro,** Albert Robert 1948- *WhoAmL 92, WhoFI 92*
**Santopietro,** Joseph J 1950- *WhoAmP 91*
**Santor,** Ken *WhoAmP 91*
**Santora,** Kathleen Curry 1958- *WhoAmL 92*
**Santora,** Norman Julian 1935- *AmMWSc 92*
**Santoro,** Alex 1936- *WhoFI 92, WhoMW 92*
**Santoro,** Alfonso L 1939- *WhoAmP 91*
**Santoro,** Ferrucio Fontes 1952- *AmMWSc 92*
**Santoro,** Gene *WhoEnt 92*
**Santoro,** Thomas 1928- *AmMWSc 92*
**Santorsola,** Guido 1904- *ConCom 92*
**Santorsola di Bari Bruno,** Guido 1904- *ConCom 92*
**Santorum,** Richard John 1958- *WhoAmP 91*
**Santorum,** Rick 1958- *AlmAP 92 [port]*
**Santos,** Alfred 1940- *WhoAmP 91*
**Santos,** Bienvenido N. *DrAPF 91*
**Santos,** Corentino Virgilio 1946- *IntWW 91*
**Santos,** Edward Dominic 1943- *WhoHisp 92*
**Santos,** Eugene 1941- *AmMWSc 92*
**Santos,** Francisco Rivera 1930- *WhoAmP 91*
**Santos,** George Wesley 1928- *AmMWSc 92*
**Santos,** Henry J. 1927- *WhoBlA 92*
**Santos,** Hubert J. 1944- *WhoAmL 92*
**Santos,** Joe 1931- *WhoHisp 92*
**Santos,** Jose A. 1950- *WhoHisp 92*
**Santos,** Julian F. 1936- *WhoHisp 92*
**Santos,** Lizette 1955- *WhoHisp 92*
**Santos,** Mathies Joseph 1948- *WhoBlA 92*
**Santos,** Miriam 1956- *WhoFI 92, WhoHisp 92*
**Santos,** Ramon 1941- *ConCom 92*
**Santos,** Reydel 1954- *WhoEnt 92, WhoHisp 92*
**Santos,** Rogelio R. 1943- *WhoHisp 92*
**Santos,** Ruben M. *WhoHisp 92*
**Santos,** Rudy Rodriguez 1959- *WhoHisp 92*
**Santos,** Tina 1949- *WhoEnt 92*
**Santos,** Turibio 1943- *WhoEnt 92*
**Santos-Alborna,** Gipsy 1965- *WhoHisp 92*
**Santos-Buch,** Charles A 1932- *AmMWSc 92*
**Santos Costa,** Fernando 1899-1982 *BiDExR*
**Santos Lopez,** Wilfredo *WhoAmP 91, WhoHisp 92*
**Santos-Martinez,** Jesus 1924- *AmMWSc 92*
**Santovenia,** Nelson Gil 1961- *WhoHisp 92*
**Santry,** Arthur J., Jr. 1918- *IntWW 91*
**Santry,** Barbara Lea 1948- *WhoFI 92, WhoMW 92*
**Santulli,** Thomas V 1915- *AmMWSc 92*
**Santuyo,** Ricardo Taytay 1931- *WhoRel 92, WhoWest 92*
**Santy,** Jeanne-Lois Marschall 1931- *WhoAmP 91*
**Sanui,** Hisashi 1924- *AmMWSc 92*
**San Vincenzo Ferreri,** Marquis of 1911- *Who 92*
**Sanwal,** Bishnu Dat *AmMWSc 92*
**Sanwick,** James Arthur 1951- *WhoWest 92*
**Sanyal,** Ranjan Reiji 1953- *WhoAmL 92*
**Sanyer,** Necmi 1919- *AmMWSc 92*
**San Yu,** U. 1919- *IntWW 91*
**Sanz,** Adolph Nunez 1951- *WhoHisp 92*
**Sanz,** Eleutherio Llorente 1926- *WhoHisp 92*
**Sanz,** Ernesto F. 1933- *WhoHisp 92*
**Sanz,** Luis E. 1943- *WhoHisp 92*
**Sanz,** Olga E. 1924- *WhoHisp 92*
**Sanzenbacher,** Roger Dean 1951- *WhoMW 92*
**Sanzone,** George 1934- *AmMWSc 92*
**SaoBento,** Antonio, Jr *WhoAmP 91*
**Saouma,** Edouard 1926- *IntWW 91, Who 92*
**Sapakie,** Sidney Freidin 1945- *AmMWSc 92, WhoMW 92*
**Sapan,** Joshua *LesBEnT 92*
**Sapareto,** Stephen Alan 1949- *WhoWest 92*
**Sapega,** A E 1925- *AmMWSc 92*
**Sapenter,** Debra 1952- *BlkOlyM*
**Saper,** Clifford B 1952- *AmMWSc 92*
**Saper,** Mark A 1954- *AmMWSc 92*
**Sapers,** Gerald M 1935- *AmMWSc 92*
**Saperstein,** Alvin Martin 1930- *AmMWSc 92, WhoMW 92*
**Saperstein,** David 1937- *IntMPA 92*
**Saperstein,** David Dorn 1946- *AmMWSc 92*
**Saperstein,** Harold Irving 1910- *WhoRel 92*
**Saperstein,** Henry G 1918- *IntMPA 92*
**Saperstein,** Lee W 1943- *AmMWSc 92*
**Saperstein,** Marc Eli 1944- *WhoRel 92*
**Saperstein,** Sidney 1923- *AmMWSc 92, WhoWest 92*
**Saphier,** David 1957- *AmMWSc 92*
**Saphier,** Peter 1940- *IntMPA 92*
**Sapia,** Yvonne 1946- *IntAu&W 91*
**Sapico,** Francisco L 1940- *AmMWSc 92*
**Sapiens,** Alexander 1946- *WhoHisp 92*
**Sapienza,** Al 1956- *WhoWest 92*
**Sapienza,** Maurice 1915- *WhoAmL 92*
**Sapino,** Chester, Jr 1941- *AmMWSc 92*
**Sapinsley,** Elbert Lee 1927- *WhoRel 92*
**Sapinsley,** Lila Manfield 1922- *WhoAmP 91*
**Sapir,** Daniel Gustave 1935- *AmMWSc 92*
**Sapir,** Edward 1884-1939 *BenetAL 91*
**Sapirie,** S R 1909- *AmMWSc 92*
**Sapirie,** Samuel Ralph d1991 *NewYTBS 91*
**Sapiro,** Jerome, Jr. 1942- *WhoAmL 92*
**Sapiro,** Virginia 1951- *IntAu&W 91*
**Sapirstein,** Jonathan Robert 1951- *AmMWSc 92*
**Sapoch,** John Crim, Jr. 1937- *WhoWest 92*
**Sapolsky,** Asher Isadore 1909- *AmMWSc 92*
**Saponara,** Arthur G 1936- *AmMWSc 92*
**Saporoschenko,** Mykola 1924- *AmMWSc 92*
**Saporta,** Jack 1927- *WhoMW 92*
**Saporta,** Marc 1923- *IntWW 91*
**Saporta,** Samuel 1946- *AmMWSc 92*
**Saporta,** Steven Samuel 1954- *WhoEnt 92*
**Saposnik,** Alan Ross 1953- *WhoMW 92*
**Sapp,** Carl Robert 1914- *WhoRel 92*
**Sapp,** Donald Gene 1927- *WhoRel 92, WhoWest 92*
**Sapp,** James Winston 1932- *WhoWest 92*
**Sapp,** Jo *DrAPF 91*
**Sapp,** Neil Carleton 1939- *WhoFI 92*
**Sapp,** Richard Cassell 1928- *AmMWSc 92*
**Sapp,** Walter J 1934- *AmMWSc 92*
**Sapp,** Walter William 1930- *WhoAmL 92, WhoFI 92*
**Sapp-Yarwood,** Debra 1959- *WhoEnt 92*
**Sappell,** Joel 1953- *ConAu 133*
**Sappenfield,** Diane Hastings 1940- *WhoFI 92*
**Sappenfield,** Robert W 1924- *AmMWSc 92*
**Sappenfield,** William Paul 1923- *AmMWSc 92*
**Sapper** 1888-1937 *ScFEYrs, TwCLC 44 [port]*
**Sapper,** Alan Louis Geoffrey 1931- *Who 92*
**Sapper,** Eugene Herbert 1929- *WhoHisp 92*
**Sapper,** Richard 1932- *DcTwDes*
**Sapphire** *DrAPF 91*
**Sappho** *EncAmaz 91*
**Sapra,** Val T 1942- *AmMWSc 92*
**Sapru,** Hreday N *AmMWSc 92*
**Sapsowitz,** Marna Helene 1959- *WhoRel 92*
**Sapsowitz,** Sidney H. 1936- *WhoFI 92, WhoWest 92*
**Sar,** Madhabananda 1933- *AmMWSc 92*
**Sara,** Mia 1968- *ConTFT 9, IntMPA 92*
**Sara,** Raymond Vincent 1927- *AmMWSc 92*
**Sarabasa,** Albert Gonzalez, Jr. 1952- *WhoHisp 92*
**Sarabhai,** Mrinalini 1935- *IntWW 91*
**Sarabia,** Horace 1938- *WhoHisp 92*
**Sarabia,** Louis 1942- *WhoHisp 92*
**Sarac,** Roger *IntAu&W 91X*
**Saraceno,** Anthony Joseph 1933- *AmMWSc 92*
**Sarachek,** Alvin 1927- *AmMWSc 92*
**Sarachik,** Edward S 1941- *AmMWSc 92*
**Sarachik,** Myriam Paula 1933- *AmMWSc 92*
**Sarachik,** Philip E 1931- *AmMWSc 92*
**Saracino,** Daniel Harrison 1947- *AmMWSc 92*
**Sarada,** Thyagaraja 1929- *AmMWSc 92*
**Saraf,** Ashok 1943- *WhoWest 92*
**Saraf,** Dilip Govind 1942- *WhoWest 92*
**Saraf,** Yousuf Ibrahim *WhoRel 92*
**Sarafian,** Richard C. 1935- *IntMPA 92*
**Saragat,** Giuseppe 1898-1988 *FacFETw*
**Sarah,** Duchess of York *ConAu 135, SmATA 66*
**Sarah,** Robert *WhoRel 92*
**Saraiva Guerreiro,** Ramiro Elysio *IntWW 91*
**Sarajcic,** Ivo 1915- *Who 92*
**Sarakwash,** Michael 1925- *AmMWSc 92*

**Saralegui,** Cristina Maria 1948- *WhoHisp 92*
**Saran,** Chitaranjan 1939- *AmMWSc 92*
**Saran,** Deo 1955- *WhoFI 92*
**Sarandan,** Lydia Mary 1938- *WhoRel 92*
**Sarandon,** Chris 1942- *IntMPA 92, WhoEnt 92*
**Sarandon,** Susan 1946- *IntMPA 92*
**Sarandon,** Susan Abigail 1946- *WhoEnt 92*
**Saranow,** Mitchell Harris 1945- *WhoMW 92*
**Sarantakis,** Dimitrios 1936- *AmMWSc 92*
**Sarantes,** Nicholas George 1960- *WhoWest 92*
**Sarantites,** Demetrios George 1933- *AmMWSc 92*
**Sarapata,** Susan Lee 1950- *WhoMW 92*
**Sarasate,** Pablo de 1844-1908 *NewAmDM*
**Sarasate y Navascuez,** Pablo de 1844-1908 *NewAmDM*
**Sarasin,** Alfred Emanuel 1922- *IntWW 91*
**Sarasin,** Arsa 1936- *IntWW 91*
**Sarasin,** Jennifer *WrDr 92*
**Sarasin,** Pote 1907- *IntWW 91*
**Sarasin,** Ronald A 1934- *WhoAmP 91*
**Sarasin,** Warren G 1943- *WhoAmP 91*
**Sarasohn,** Ira J *WhoIns 92*
**Sarason,** Donald Erik 1933- *AmMWSc 92*
**Sarason,** Leonard 1925- *AmMWSc 92*
**Sarason,** Richard Samuel 1948- *WhoRel 92*
**Sarati,** Carmen M. 1931- *WhoHisp 92*
**Sarauskas,** R. George 1945- *WhoRel 92*
**Saravanamuttoo,** Herbert Ian H 1933- *AmMWSc 92*
**Saravia,** Nancy G *AmMWSc 92*
**Saravis,** Calvin 1930- *AmMWSc 92*
**Saravo,** Anne Cobble 1938- *WhoWest 92*
**Sarazen,** Gene 1902- *FacFETw*
**Sarazen,** Jeffrey Michael 1962- *WhoMW 92*
**Sarazen,** Richard Allen 1933- *WhoFI 92*
**Sarazin,** Craig L 1950- *AmMWSc 92*
**Sarbach,** Donald Victor 1911- *AmMWSc 92*
**Sarban** d1989 *TwCSFW 91*
**Sarbanes,** Paul S. 1933- *AlmAP 92 [port]*
**Sarbanes,** Paul Spyros 1933- *IntWW 91, WhoAmP 91*
**Sarber,** Glenn Scott 1929- *WhoMW 92*
**Sarber,** Raymond William 1916- *AmMWSc 92*
**Sarchet,** Bernard Reginald 1917- *AmMWSc 92*
**Sarchet-Waller,** Paul Robert 1947- *WhoRel 92*
**Sarchi,** Bernard 1943- *WhoMW 92*
**Sarcione,** Edward James 1925- *AmMWSc 92*
**Sarcone,** Blaise 1955- *WhoFI 92*
**Sard,** George *WhoFI 92*
**Sard,** Richard 1941- *AmMWSc 92*
**Sard,** Robert Daniel 1915- *AmMWSc 92*
**Sardanis,** Andreas Sotiris 1931- *IntWW 91*
**Sardella,** Dennis Joseph 1941- *AmMWSc 92*
**Sardesai,** Vishwanath M 1932- *AmMWSc 92*
**Sardinas,** August A 1922- *AmMWSc 92*
**Sardinas,** Jose Ramon 1934- *WhoWest 92*
**Sardinas,** Joseph Louis 1919- *AmMWSc 92*
**Sardinha,** Antonio 1888-1925 *BiDExR*
**Sardisco,** John Baptist 1934- *AmMWSc 92*
**Sardou,** Joseph-Marie *WhoRel 92*
**Sardou,** Victorien 1831-1908 *GuFrLit 1*
**Sarduy,** Severo 1937- *BenetAL 91, DcLB 113 [port], LiExTwC*
**Sarei,** Alexis Holyweek 1934- *IntWW 91, Who 92*
**Sarell,** Richard Iwan Alexander 1909- *Who 92*
**Sarell,** Roderick 1913- *Who 92*
**Sarellano,** Luis Humberto 1947- *WhoHisp 92*
**Sarem,** Amir M Sam 1930- *AmMWSc 92*
**Sarett,** Herbert Paul 1916- *AmMWSc 92*
**Sarett,** Lew 1888-1954 *BenetAL 91*
**Sarett,** Lewis Hastings 1917- *AmMWSc 92*
**Sarf,** Peter F. 1922- *WhoFI 92*
**Sarfatti,** Gino *DcTwDes*
**Sarfatti,** Jack 1939- *AmMWSc 92*
**Sarff,** Donohue Ray 1928- *WhoRel 92*
**Sargan,** John Denis 1924- *IntWW 91, Who 92*
**Sargant,** Edmund 1906- *Who 92*
**Sargant,** Naomi Ellen *Who 92*
**Sargant Florence,** Mary 1857-1954 *BiDBrF 2*
**Sarge,** Theodore William 1918- *AmMWSc 92*
**Sargeant,** Epes Winthrop 1872-1938 *ScFEYrs*
**Sargeant,** Frank Charles Douglas 1917- *Who 92*
**Sargeant,** Frank Pilkington *Who 92*
**Sargeant,** Gary 1939- *TwCPaSc*
**Sargeant,** Peter Barry 1936- *AmMWSc 92*
**Sargeant,** Phillip Lester 1954- *WhoEnt 92*
**Sargeaunt,** Henry Anthony 1907- *Who 92*
**Sargent,** Alvin *IntMPA 92*
**Sargent,** Anneila Isabel *AmMWSc 92*
**Sargent,** Bernice Weldon 1906- *AmMWSc 92*
**Sargent,** Charles 1913- *AmMWSc 92*
**Sargent,** Charles Jackson 1929- *WhoRel 92*
**Sargent,** Charles Lee 1937- *WhoFI 92, WhoMW 92*
**Sargent,** David Fisher 1945- *AmMWSc 92*
**Sargent,** Diana Rhea 1939- *WhoWest 92*
**Sargent,** Dick *Who 92*
**Sargent,** Dick 1933- *IntMPA 92*
**Sargent,** E.N. *DrAPF 91*
**Sargent,** Epes 1813-1880 *BenetAL 91*
**Sargent,** Frank Dorrance 1935- *AmMWSc 92*
**Sargent,** Frederick Peter 1940- *AmMWSc 92*
**Sargent,** Gordon Alfred 1938- *AmMWSc 92*
**Sargent,** Harry Tompkins 1947- *WhoWest 92*
**Sargent,** Howard Harrop, III 1936- *AmMWSc 92*
**Sargent,** James Cunningham 1916- *WhoAmL 92*
**Sargent,** Jesse Irene 1852-1932 *HanAmWH*
**Sargent,** John Richard 1925- *Who 92*
**Sargent,** John Singer 1856-1925 *FacFETw, RComAH, ThHEIm, TwCPaSc*
**Sargent,** John Turner 1924- *IntWW 91*
**Sargent,** Joseph 1925- *IntMPA 92*
**Sargent,** Kenneth Albert 1932- *AmMWSc 92*
**Sargent,** Lucius Manlius 1786-1867 *BenetAL 91*
**Sargent,** Lyman T. 1940- *WrDr 92*
**Sargent,** Lyman Tower 1940- *IntAu&W 91*
**Sargent,** Malcolm 1895-1967 *FacFETw, NewAmDM*
**Sargent,** Malcolm Lee 1937- *AmMWSc 92*
**Sargent,** Margaret Holland 1927- *WhoEnt 92*
**Sargent,** Murray, III 1941- *AmMWSc 92*
**Sargent,** Pamela *DrAPF 91*
**Sargent,** Pamela 1948- *IntAu&W 91, TwCSFW 91, WrDr 92*
**Sargent,** Robert *DrAPF 91*
**Sargent,** Robert George 1937- *AmMWSc 92*
**Sargent,** Roger Gary 1939- *AmMWSc 92*
**Sargent,** Roger N 1928- *AmMWSc 92*
**Sargent,** Roger William Herbert 1926- *Who 92*
**Sargent,** Theodore David 1936- *AmMWSc 92*
**Sargent,** Thornton William, III 1928- *AmMWSc 92*
**Sargent,** Wallace Leslie William 1935- *AmMWSc 92, IntWW 91, Who 92, WhoWest 92*
**Sargent,** William Quirk 1945- *AmMWSc 92*
**Sargent,** Winthrop 1753-1820 *BiInAmS*
**Sargent,** Winthrop 1825-1870 *BenetAL 91*
**Sargentich,** Lewis D. 1944- *WhoAmL 92*
**Sargentini,** Neil Joseph *AmMWSc 92*
**Sarges,** Reinhard 1935- *AmMWSc 92*
**Sargeson,** Alan McLeod 1930- *IntWW 91, Who 92*
**Sargeson,** Frank 1903-1982 *RfGEnL 91*
**Sarginson,** Edward William 1919- *Who 92*
**Sargon,** Simon A. 1938- *WhoEnt 92, WhoRel 92*
**Sarhan,** Fathey 1945- *AmMWSc 92*
**Sari,** James William 1942- *AmMWSc 92*
**Sari,** Seppo Olavi 1945- *WhoWest 92*
**Sariaslani,** Sima *AmMWSc 92*
**Saric,** William Samuel 1940- *AmMWSc 92*
**Sarich,** Vincent M 1934- *AmMWSc 92*
**Saricks,** Ambrose 1915- *IntAu&W 91, WrDr 92*
**Sarid,** Dror 1938- *AmMWSc 92*
**Saridis,** George N 1931- *AmMWSc 92*
**Sarikas,** Philip Charles 1960- *WhoWest 92*
**Sarikas,** Robert Henry 1923- *WhoFI 92*
**Sarin,** Prem S *AmMWSc 92*
**Sarjeant,** Peter Thomson 1929- *AmMWSc 92*
**Sarjeant,** Walter James 1944- *AmMWSc 92*
**Sarjeant,** William Antony Swithin 1935- *AmMWSc 92*
**Sark,** Seigneur of *Who 92*
**Sarka** *EncAmaz 91*
**Sarkanen,** Kyosti Vilho 1921- *AmMWSc 92*
**Sarkar,** Anil Kumar 1912- *IntAu&W 91, WrDr 92*
**Sarkar,** Bibudhendra 1935- *AmMWSc 92*
**Sarkar,** Fazlul Hoque 1952- *AmMWSc 92*
**Sarkar,** Kamalaksha 1947- *AmMWSc 92*
**Sarkar,** Nilima 1935- *AmMWSc 92*
**Sarkar,** Nitis 1938- *AmMWSc 92*
**Sarkar,** Satyapriya 1934- *AmMWSc 92*
**Sarkaria,** Gurmukh S 1925- *AmMWSc 92*
**Sarkes,** Louis A 1925- *AmMWSc 92*
**Sarkesian,** Sam Charles 1927- *WhoMW 92*
**Sarkis,** Elias 1924-1985 *FacFETw*
**Sarkisian,** Alan Herbert 1955- *WhoAmL 92*
**Sarkisian,** Cherilyn 1946- *WhoEnt 92*
**Sarkisian,** Jack Reuben 1928- *WhoWest 92*
**Sarkisian,** Sos Artashesovich 1929- *IntWW 91*
**Sarkisov,** Babken Yesayevich 1913- *IntWW 91*
**Sarkisov,** Pavel Jebraelovich 1932- *IntWW 91*
**Sarko,** Anatole 1930- *AmMWSc 92*
**Sarko,** Lynn Lincoln 1956- *WhoAmL 92*
**Sarles,** F William *ScFEYrs*
**Sarles,** F Williams 1931- *AmMWSc 92*
**Sarles,** Lynn Redmon 1930- *AmMWSc 92*
**Sarley,** John G. 1954- *WhoWest 92*
**Sarlo,** George Stephen 1938- *WhoFI 92*
**Sarlos,** Istvan 1921- *IntWW 91*
**Sarlow,** Michael-Tyler Curtis 1952- *WhoEnt 92*
**Sarlui,** Ed 1925- *IntMPA 92*
**Sarma,** Atul C 1939- *AmMWSc 92*
**Sarma,** Dittakavi S R 1936- *AmMWSc 92*
**Sarma,** Padman S 1931- *AmMWSc 92*
**Sarma,** Raghupathy 1937- *AmMWSc 92*
**Sarma,** Ramaswamy Harihara 1939- *AmMWSc 92*
**Sarmazian,** Yessayi *WhoRel 92*
**Sarmiento,** Domingo Faustino 1811-1888 *BenetAL 91*
**Sarmiento,** Gustavo Sanchez 1947- *AmMWSc 92*
**Sarmiento,** Jorge Louis 1946- *AmMWSc 92*
**Sarmiento,** Luis Carlos, Jr. 1961- *WhoHisp 92*
**Sarmiento,** Rafael Apolinar 1937- *AmMWSc 92*
**Sarmiento,** Shirley Jean 1946- *WhoBlA 92*
**Sarmiento De Biscotti,** Luz Socorro 1954- *WhoHisp 92*
**Sarmiento de Gamboa,** Pedro 1530?-1591 *HisDSpE*
**Sarmientos,** Victoriano *BlkOlyM*
**Sarna,** John J 1935- *WhoAmP 91*
**Sarna,** John Paul 1963- *WhoFI 92*
**Sarna,** Jonathan D 1955- *IntAu&W 91, WrDr 92*
**Sarna,** Nahum M. 1923- *WrDr 92*
**Sarna,** Nahum Mattathias 1923- *IntAu&W 91, WhoRel 92*
**Sarna,** Sushil K 1942- *AmMWSc 92*
**Sarna-Wojcicki,** Andrei M 1937- *AmMWSc 92*
**Sarnat,** Marshall 1929- *IntAu&W 91, WrDr 92*
**Sarner,** Richard Alan 1955- *WhoAmL 92*
**Sarner,** Stanley Frederick 1931- *AmMWSc 92*
**Sarneski,** Joseph Edward 1944- *AmMWSc 92*
**Sarney,** Jose 1930- *IntWW 91*
**Sarngadharan,** Mangalasseril G *AmMWSc 92*
**Sarni,** Vincent Anthony 1928- *WhoFI 92*
**Sarno,** Ronald Anthony 1941- *WrDr 92*
**Sarno,** Terese M. 1947- *WhoEnt 92*
**Sarnoff,** David d1971 *LesBEnT 92*
**Sarnoff,** David 1891-1971 *FacFETw*
**Sarnoff,** Dorothy *IntAu&W 91, WhoFI 92, WrDr 92*
**Sarnoff,** Irving 1922- *IntAu&W 91, WrDr 92*
**Sarnoff,** Jill Robin 1954- *WhoAmL 92*
**Sarnoff,** Robert W. *LesBEnT 92*
**Sarnoff,** Robert W. 1918- *IntMPA 92*
**Sarnoff,** Thomas W. *LesBEnT 92*
**Sarnoff,** Thomas W. 1927- *IntMPA 92*
**Sarnoff,** Thomas Warren 1927- *WhoEnt 92*
**Saroff,** Harry Arthur 1914- *AmMWSc 92*
**Sarofim,** Adel Fares 1934- *AmMWSc 92*
**Sarokin,** H. Lee 1928- *WhoAmL 92*
**Saroop,** Narindar 1929- *Who 92*
**Sarosy,** Anne Zvara 1923- *WhoMW 92*
**Saroyan,** Aram 1943- *ConPo 91, IntAu&W 91, WrDr 92*
**Saroyan,** William 1908-1981 *BenetAL 91, FacFETw*
**Sarpalius,** Bill 1948- *AlmAP 92 [port], WhoAmP 91*
**Sarpaneva,** Timo Tapani 1926- *IntWW 91*
**Sarpeneva,** Timo 1926- *DcTwDes*
**Sarphie,** Theodore G 1944- *AmMWSc 92*
**Sarpkaya,** Turgut 1928- *AmMWSc 92*
**Sarpong,** Peter Kwasi 1933- *WhoRel 92*
**Sarr,** Samuel Jonathan Okikiola 1921- *IntWW 91*
**Sarracino,** Cooney 1933- *WhoHisp 92*
**Sarram,** Mehdi 1942- *AmMWSc 92*
**Sarras,** Michael P, Jr *AmMWSc 92*
**Sarraute,** Nathalie 1900- *FacFETw, FrenWW, GuFrLit 1, IntAu&W 91, IntWW 91, LiExTwC, Who 92*
**Sarrazin,** Albertine 1937-1967 *FrenWW*
**Sarrazin,** Michael 1940- *IntMPA 92, WhoEnt 92*
**Sarre,** Claude-Alain 1928- *IntWW 91*
**Sarre,** Massamba 1935- *IntWW 91*
**Sarreals,** E. Don 1931- *WhoBlA 92*
**Sarri,** Samuel 1957- *WhoFI 92*
**Sarrif,** Awni M 1942- *AmMWSc 92*
**Sarris,** Andrew George 1928- *WhoEnt 92*
**Sarry,** Christine 1946- *WhoEnt 92*
**Sarson,** John Christopher 1935- *WhoEnt 92*
**Sarsten,** Gunnar Edward 1937- *WhoFI 92*
**Sartain,** James Edward 1941- *WhoAmL 92*
**Sartain,** Jerry Burton 1945- *AmMWSc 92*
**Sartain,** Shirley Luray 1947- *WhoMW 92*
**Sartell,** Jack A 1924- *AmMWSc 92*
**Sarther,** Lynette Kay 1947- *WhoMW 92*
**Sartin,** Austin Albert 1936- *AmMWSc 92*
**Sartin,** Johnny Nelson, Jr. 1960- *WhoBlA 92*
**Sarto,** Gloria Elizabeth 1929- *WhoWest 92*
**Sarton,** May *DrAPF 91*
**Sarton,** May 1912- *BenetAL 91, ConAu 34NR, ConNov 91, ConPo 91, IntAu&W 91, WrDr 92*
**Sartor,** Albin Francis, Jr 1919- *AmMWSc 92*
**Sartor,** Anthony 1943- *AmMWSc 92*
**Sartore,** John Thornton 1946- *WhoAmL 92*
**Sartorelli,** Alan Clayton 1931- *AmMWSc 92*
**Sartori,** Eva Maria *IntAu&W 91*
**Sartori,** Leo 1929- *AmMWSc 92, WhoMW 92*
**Sartoris,** David John 1955- *AmMWSc 92*
**Sartoris,** Nelson Edward 1941- *AmMWSc 92*
**Sartorius,** Norman 1935- *IntWW 91*
**Sartre,** Jean-Paul 1905-1980 *FacFETw, GuFrLit 1*
**Sartre,** Jean-Paul Charles Aymard 1905-1980 *WhoNob 90*
**Sartwell,** Henry Parker 1792-1867 *BiInAmS*
**Sartwell,** Philip Earl 1908- *AmMWSc 92*
**Sarty,** Peter Griffing 1933- *WhoAmP 91*
**Sartzetakis,** Christos A. 1929- *IntWW 91*
**Sarum,** Archdeacon of *Who 92*
**Sarver,** Barbara Joan 1940- *WhoAmP 91*
**Sarver,** Emory William 1942- *AmMWSc 92*
**Sarvey,** John Michael 1946- *AmMWSc 92*
**Sarwar,** Ghulam 1943- *AmMWSc 92*
**Sarwate,** Dilip Vishwanath 1945- *AmMWSc 92*
**Sarwer-Foner,** Gerald 1924- *AmMWSc 92*
**Sarwer-Foner,** Gerald Jacob 1924- *WhoMW 92*
**Sarwinski,** Raymond Edmund 1936- *AmMWSc 92*
**Sary Ieng** *IntWW 91*
**Saryan,** Leon Aram 1948- *AmMWSc 92*
**Sar'yan,** Martiros Sergeevich 1880-1972 *SovUnBD*
**Sasa'e,** Pagofie 1911- *WhoAmP 91*
**Sasaki,** Clarence Takashi 1941- *AmMWSc 92*
**Sasaki,** Gordon Hiroshi 1942- *AmMWSc 92*
**Sasaki,** Hidetada 1941- *AmMWSc 92*
**Sasaki,** Kyozan Joshu 1907- *RelLAm 91*
**Sasaki,** Man 1926- *IntWW 91*
**Sasaki,** Ruth Fuller Everett 1893-1967 *RelLAm 91*
**Sasaki,** Shigetsu 1882-1945 *RelLAm 91*
**Sasaki,** Tatsuo 1944- *WhoEnt 92*
**Sasaki,** Y. Tito 1938- *WhoWest 92*
**Sasaki,** Yoshi Kazu 1927- *AmMWSc 92*
**Sasamori,** Takashi 1930- *AmMWSc 92*
**Sasaraye** *EncAmaz 91*
**Sasdi,** George P. 1934- *WhoFI 92*
**Sasenick,** Joseph Anthony 1940- *WhoFI 92*
**Sashihara,** Thomas F 1929- *AmMWSc 92*
**Sashin,** Donald 1937- *AmMWSc 92*
**Sashital,** Sanat Ramanath *AmMWSc 92*
**Sasiela,** Richard 1940- *AmMWSc 92*
**Sasin,** Richard 1922- *AmMWSc 92*
**Saskatchewan,** Bishop of 1941- *Who 92*
**Saskatoon,** Bishop of 1933- *Who 92*
**Saski,** Witold 1909- *AmMWSc 92*
**Saslaw,** Leonard David 1927- *AmMWSc 92*
**Saslaw,** Richard Lawrence 1940- *WhoAmP 91*
**Saslow,** Helen *DrAPF 91*
**Saslow,** Michael George 1937- *WhoAmP 91*
**Saslow,** Wayne Mark 1942- *AmMWSc 92*
**Sasman,** Robert T 1923- *AmMWSc 92*
**Sasmor,** Daniel Joseph 1921- *AmMWSc 92*
**Sasner,** John Joseph, Jr 1936- *AmMWSc 92*
**Sason,** Sixten 1912-1969 *DcTwDes*
**Sass,** Daniel B 1919- *AmMWSc 92*
**Sass,** Heinz *AmMWSc 92*

**Sass**, James Robertus 1945- *WhoFI 92, WhoWest 92*
**Sass**, John Harvey 1937- *AmMWSc 92*
**Sass**, Louis Carl 1910- *AmMWSc 92*
**Sass**, Neil David 1951- *WhoMW 92*
**Sass**, Neil Leslie 1944- *AmMWSc 92*
**Sass**, Ronald L 1932- *AmMWSc 92*
**Sass**, Stephen L 1940- *AmMWSc 92*
**Sassa**, Shigeru 1935- *AmMWSc 92*
**Sassaman**, Anne Phillips 1944- *AmMWSc 92*
**Sassaman**, Clay Alan 1948- *AmMWSc 92*
**Sasscer**, Donald S 1929- *AmMWSc 92*
**Sasse**, Edward Alexander 1938- *AmMWSc 92*
**Sassen**, Saskia 1947- *WhoHisp 92*
**Sassen-Dauphinais**, Margurite Therese 1926- *WhoAmP 91*
**Sassenrath**, Ethelda Norberg 1921- *AmMWSc 92*
**Sasser**, Charles W. 1942- *WrDr 92*
**Sasser**, James R. 1936- *AlmAP 92 [port]*
**Sasser**, James Ralph 1936- *IntWW 91, WhoAmP 91*
**Sasser**, Jonathan Drew 1956- *WhoAmL 92*
**Sasser**, Joseph Neal 1921- *AmMWSc 92*
**Sasser**, Lyle Blaine 1939- *AmMWSc 92*
**Sasser**, Thomas Lynn 1946- *WhoRel 92*
**Sasser**, William David 1962- *WhoFI 92*
**Sasser**, William Gray 1927- *WhoEnt 92*
**Sassi**, Gino J 1922- *WhoAmP 91*
**Sassmannshausen**, Gunther 1930- *IntWW 91*
**Sasso**, Eleanor Catherine 1934- *WhoAmP 91*
**Sasso**, Laurence J., Jr. *DrAPF 91*
**Sasso**, Roberto A. 1954- *WhoHisp 92*
**Sasso**, Sandy 1947- *WhoRel 92*
**Sasson**, Albert A. 1941- *WhoMW 92*
**Sasson**, Michel 1935- *WhoEnt 92*
**Sassoon**, Andre Gabriel 1936- *WhoAmL 92*
**Sassoon**, David 1932- *IntWW 91*
**Sassoon**, Humphrey Frederick 1920- *AmMWSc 92*
**Sassoon**, Siegfried 1886-1967 *ConAu 36NR, FacFETw, RfGEnL 91*
**Sassoon**, Timothy John Frederick 1957- *WhoEnt 92*
**Sassoon**, Vidal 1928- *IntWW 91, WhoWest 92*
**Sassou-Nguesso**, Denis 1943- *IntWW 91*
**Sassower**, Harvey L. 1945- *IntMPA 92*
**Sastre**, Antonio 1950- *AmMWSc 92*
**Sastri**, Suri A 1939- *AmMWSc 92*
**Sastry**, Bhamidipaty Venkata Rama 1927- *AmMWSc 92*
**Sastry**, Shankara M L 1946- *AmMWSc 92*
**Sastry**, Vankamamidi Vrn 1940- *AmMWSc 92*
**Sasyniuk**, Betty Irene 1942- *AmMWSc 92*
**Satanowski**, Robert 1918- *IntWW 91*
**Satarawala**, Kershasp Tehmurasp 1916- *IntWW 91*
**Satariano**, Harry John 1950- *WhoMW 92*
**Satas**, Donatas 1929- *AmMWSc 92*
**Satchell**, Edward William John 1916- *Who 92*
**Satchell**, Elizabeth *WhoBlA 92*
**Satchell**, Ernest R. 1941- *WhoBlA 92*
**Satchell**, Robert Bennett 1951- *WhoAmL 92*
**Satcher**, David 1941- *AmMWSc 92, WhoBlA 92*
**Satcher**, Robert Lee, Sr. 1937- *WhoBlA 92*
**Satchidananda**, Swami 1914- *RelLAm 91*
**Satchler**, George Raymond 1926- *AmMWSc 92*
**Satchmo** *NewAmDM*
**Satchwell**, Eric 1926- *TwCPaSc*
**Satchwill**, Charles N. 1947- *WhoMW 92*
**Sater**, Analya *WhoHisp 92*
**Sater**, Terry Michael 1947- *WhoMW 92*
**Sater**, Vernon E 1935- *AmMWSc 92*
**Sateren**, Terry 1943- *WhoEnt 92*
**Sathe**, Sharad Somnath 1940- *AmMWSc 92*
**Sathe**, Shridhar Krishna 1950- *AmMWSc 92*
**Sathe**, Vasant P. 1925- *IntWW 91*
**Sather**, Bryant Thomas 1935- *AmMWSc 92*
**Sather**, Duane Paul 1933- *AmMWSc 92*
**Sather**, Glen Cameron 1943- *WhoWest 92*
**Sather**, Glenn A 1928- *AmMWSc 92*
**Sather**, J Henry 1921- *AmMWSc 92*
**Sather**, Larry Douglas 1950- *WhoAmL 92*
**Sather**, Linda 1950- *WhoMW 92*
**Sather**, Norman F 1936- *AmMWSc 92*
**Satherly**, Arthur 1889-1986 *FacFETw*
**Sathoff**, H John 1931- *AmMWSc 92*
**Satiacum**, Robert d1991 *NewYTBS 91*
**Satian**, Sarkis 1938- *WhoFI 92*
**Satie**, Erik 1866-1925 *FacFETw, NewAmDM*
**Satine**, Barry Roy 1951- *WhoAmL 92*
**Satinoff**, Evelyn *AmMWSc 92*
**Satinsky**, Barnett 1947- *WhoAmL 92*
**Satir**, Birgit H 1934- *AmMWSc 92*
**Satir**, Peter 1936- *AmMWSc 92*
**Satir**, Virginia 1914-1989 *HanAmWH*
**Satkiewicz**, Frank George 1927- *AmMWSc 92*
**Sato**, Daihachiro 1932- *AmMWSc 92*
**Sato**, Eisaku 1901-1975 *FacFETw, WhoNob 90*
**Sato**, Eunice N 1921- *WhoAmP 91*
**Sato**, Frank Saburo 1929- *WhoAmP 91*
**Sato**, Gentei 1926- *AmMWSc 92*
**Sato**, Gordon Hisashi 1927- *AmMWSc 92*
**Sato**, Hiroshi 1918- *AmMWSc 92*
**Sato**, Irving Shigeo 1933- *WhoWest 92*
**Sato**, Isao 1934- *IntAu&W 91*
**Sato**, Isao 1949-1990 *ConTFT 9*
**Sato**, Makiko 1947- *AmMWSc 92*
**Sato**, Mamoru 1937- *WhoWest 92*
**Sato**, Masahiko *AmMWSc 92*
**Sato**, Megumu 1924- *IntWW 91*
**Sato**, Michael Kei 1958- *WhoWest 92*
**Sato**, Moriyoshi 1922- *IntWW 91*
**Sato**, Motoaki 1929- *AmMWSc 92*
**Sato**, Norie 1949- *WhoWest 92*
**Sato**, Paul Hisashi *AmMWSc 92*
**Sato**, Robert Jay 1955- *WhoEnt 92*
**Sato**, Shozo 1933- *WhoMW 92*
**Sato**, Takashi 1927- *IntWW 91*
**Satoh**, Paul Shigemi 1936- *AmMWSc 92*
**Satoh**, Somei 1947- *ConCom 92*
**Satow**, Derek Graham 1923- *Who 92*
**Satowaki**, Joseph Asajiro 1904- *IntWW 91, WhoRel 92*
**Satpathy**, Nandini 1931- *IntWW 91*
**Satprem** 1923- *ConAu 35NR*
**Satran**, Richard 1928- *AmMWSc 92*
**Satre**, Philip Glen 1949- *WhoFI 92, WhoWest 92*
**Satre**, Rodrick Iverson 1951- *WhoWest 92*
**Satrom**, Joseph A *WhoAmP 91*
**Sats**, Natal'ya Il'inichna 1903- *SovUnBD*
**Sattar**, Syed Abdus 1938- *AmMWSc 92*
**Satten**, Robert A 1922- *AmMWSc 92*
**Satten**, Robert Arnold 1922- *WhoWest 92*
**Satter**, Larry Dean 1937- *AmMWSc 92*
**Satter**, Marlene Y *DrAPF 91*
**Satter**, Raymond Nathan 1948- *WhoAmL 92*
**Satter**, Ruth 1923- *AmMWSc 92*
**Satterfield**, Ben *DrAPF 91*
**Satterfield**, Charles N 1921- *AmMWSc 92*
**Satterfield**, David E, III 1920- *WhoAmP 91*
**Satterfield**, Floyd 1945- *WhoBlA 92*
**Satterfield**, Shelby D 1945- *WhoAmP 91*
**Satterfield**, Suzan 1958- *WhoEnt 92*
**Satterlee**, James Donald 1948- *AmMWSc 92*
**Satterlee**, Lowell Duggan 1943- *AmMWSc 92*
**Satterlee**, Peter Hamilton 1946- *WhoEnt 92*
**Satterlee**, Terry Jean 1948- *WhoAmL 92*
**Satterlund**, Donald Robert 1928- *AmMWSc 92*
**Satterly**, Gilbert T 1929- *AmMWSc 92*
**Satterthwaite**, Cameron B 1920- *AmMWSc 92*
**Satterthwaite**, Franklin Eves 1914- *AmMWSc 92*
**Satterthwaite**, Helen Foster 1928- *WhoAmP 91*
**Satterthwaite**, John Richard *Who 92*
**Satterthwaite**, John Richard 1925- *WhoRel 92*
**Satterthwaite**, Richard George 1920- *Who 92*
**Satterwhite**, Donald Thomas 1953- *WhoRel 92*
**Satterwhite**, Frank Joseph 1942- *WhoBlA 92*
**Satterwhite**, John H. 1913- *WhoBlA 92*
**Satterwhite**, Ramon S 1940- *AmMWSc 92*
**Satterwhite**, Rodney Wayne 1942- *WhoAmL 92*
**Satterwhite**, Terry Frank 1946- *WhoWest 92*
**Satterwhite**, William T. 1933- *WhoAmL 92*
**Sattes**, Frederick Lyle 1943- *WhoAmP 91*
**Sattin**, Albert 1931- *AmMWSc 92*
**Sattinger**, David H 1940- *AmMWSc 92*
**Sattinger**, Irvin J 1912- *AmMWSc 92*
**Sattinger**, Michael Jack 1943- *WhoFI 92*
**Sattizahn**, James Edward, Jr 1920- *AmMWSc 92*
**Sattler**, Allan R 1932- *AmMWSc 92*
**Sattler**, Carol Ann 1946- *AmMWSc 92*
**Sattler**, David John 1947- *WhoWest 92*
**Sattler**, Frank A 1920- *AmMWSc 92*
**Sattler**, Helen Roney 1921- *ChlLR 24 [port]*
**Sattler**, Joseph Peter 1940- *AmMWSc 92*
**Sattler**, Robert E 1925- *AmMWSc 92*
**Sattler**, Robert James 1948- *WhoAmP 91*
**Sattler**, Rolf 1936- *AmMWSc 92*
**Sattsangi**, Prem Das 1939- *AmMWSc 92*
**Sattur**, Theodore W 1920- *AmMWSc 92*
**Satuloff**, Barth 1945- *WhoFI 92*
**Saturen**, Ben B. 1948- *WhoWest 92*
**Saturninus** *EncEarC*
**Saturno**, Antony Fidelas 1931- *AmMWSc 92*
**Satya**, Akella V S 1939- *AmMWSc 92*
**Satya-Prakash**, K L 1947- *AmMWSc 92*
**Satyanarayana**, Motupalli 1928- *AmMWSc 92*
**Satyanarayanan**, Mahadev 1953- *AmMWSc 92*
**Satz**, Helmut T G 1936- *AmMWSc 92*
**Satz**, Phyllis Robyne Sdoia 1935- *WhoEnt 92*
**Satz**, Ronald Norman 1944- *WhoMW 92*
**Satz**, Ronald Wayne 1951- *AmMWSc 92, WhoFI 92*
**Sauberlich**, Howerde Edwin 1919- *AmMWSc 92*
**Sauceda**, Dora 1953- *WhoHisp 92*
**Sauceda**, F. Carolina 1962- *WhoHisp 92*
**Sauceda**, Richard 1965- *WhoHisp 92*
**Saucedo**, Jose Guadalupe *WhoRel 92*
**Saucedo**, Manuel V. *WhoHisp 92*
**Saucedo**, Marcelino 1935- *WhoHisp 92*
**Saucedo**, Robert 1932- *WhoHisp 92*
**Saucedo**, Roberto A. 1959- *WhoHisp 92*
**Saucedo**, Tom 1932- *WhoHisp 92*
**Sauceman**, Teddy Carroll 1940- *WhoRel 92*
**Saucier**, Edward Alvin 1956- *WhoRel 92*
**Saucier**, Roger Thomas 1935- *AmMWSc 92*
**Saucier**, Walter Joseph 1921- *AmMWSc 92*
**Sauckel**, Fritz 1894-1945 *EncTR 91 [port]*
**Sauckel**, Fritz Ernst Christoph 1894-1946 *BiDExR*
**Saud Al-Faisal**, Prince 1941- *IntWW 91*
**Saudek**, Christopher D 1941- *AmMWSc 92*
**Saudek**, Robert *LesBEnT 92*
**Saudek**, Robert 1911- *WhoEnt 92*
**Sauder**, Daniel Nathan 1949- *AmMWSc 92*
**Sauder**, John Waggoner 1955- *WhoFI 92*
**Sauder**, William Conrad 1934- *AmMWSc 92*
**Saudi Arabia**, King Of *IntWW 91*
**Sauer**, Charles William 1919- *AmMWSc 92*
**Sauer**, David Bruce 1939- *AmMWSc 92*
**Sauer**, Dennis Theodore 1944- *AmMWSc 92*
**Sauer**, Douglas W 1957- *WhoAmP 91*
**Sauer**, Emil von 1862-1942 *NewAmDM*
**Sauer**, Gordon C. 1921- *WrDr 92*
**Sauer**, Harold John 1953- *WhoMW 92*
**Sauer**, Harry John, Jr 1935- *AmMWSc 92, WhoMW 92*
**Sauer**, Helmut Wilhelm 1936- *AmMWSc 92*
**Sauer**, Herbert H 1929- *AmMWSc 92*
**Sauer**, James Edward, Jr. 1934- *WhoWest 92*
**Sauer**, Jane Gottlieb 1937- *WhoEnt 92*
**Sauer**, John A 1912- *AmMWSc 92*
**Sauer**, John Robert 1936- *AmMWSc 92*
**Sauer**, Jon Robert 1940- *AmMWSc 92*
**Sauer**, Jonathan Deininger 1918- *AmMWSc 92*
**Sauer**, Kenneth 1931- *AmMWSc 92*
**Sauer**, Leonard A 1929- *AmMWSc 92*
**Sauer**, Michael R 1942- *WhoIns 92*
**Sauer**, Myran Charles, Jr 1933- *AmMWSc 92*
**Sauer**, Peter William 1946- *AmMWSc 92*
**Sauer**, Richard John 1939- *AmMWSc 92*
**Sauer**, Robert C. *WhoRel 92*
**Sauer**, Robert Louis 1925- *WhoFI 92*
**Sauer**, Robert William 1941- *WhoMW 92*
**Sauerbrey**, Ellen R 1937- *WhoAmP 91*
**Sauerbruch**, Ferdinand 1875-1951 *EncTR 91 [port]*
**Sauerbrunn**, Robert Dewey 1922- *AmMWSc 92*
**Sauerland**, Eberhardt Karl 1933- *AmMWSc 92*
**Sauerlander**, Willibald 1924- *IntWW 91*
**Sauers**, Richard Frank 1939- *AmMWSc 92*
**Sauers**, Ronald Raymond 1932- *AmMWSc 92*
**Sauerwald**, Frank William 1947- *WhoEnt 92*
**Sauey**, William R 1927- *WhoAmP 91*
**Saufferer**, William Charles *WhoMW 92*
**Saugman**, Per Gotfred 1925- *Who 92*
**Saugrain De Vigni**, Antoine Francois 1763-1820 *BiInAmS*
**Sauguet**, Henri 1901-1989 *FacFETw, NewAmDM*
**Saukerson**, Eleanor *WhoAmP 91*
**Saukkonen**, Juhani 1937- *IntWW 91*
**Saul**, B. Francis, II 1932- *WhoFI 92*
**Saul**, Barbara Ann 1940- *WhoMW 92*
**Saul**, Bradley Scott 1960- *WhoEnt 92, WhoFI 92, WhoMW 92*
**Saul**, Bruno Eduardovich 1932- *IntWW 91*
**Saul**, Eduard 1929- *IntWW 91*
**Saul**, Frank Charles 1910- *WhoAmP 91*
**Saul**, Frank Philip 1930- *AmMWSc 92*
**Saul**, Franklin Robert 1929- *WhoFI 92*
**Saul**, George Brandon *DrAPF 91*
**Saul**, George Brandon, II 1928- *AmMWSc 92*
**Saul**, Irving Isaac 1929- *WhoAmL 92*
**Saul**, John Ralston 1947- *ConAu 133*
**Saul**, Julie Mather 1941- *AmMWSc 92*
**Saul**, Kenneth Louis 1923- *WhoFI 92*
**Saul**, Leon Joseph 1901- *AmMWSc 92*
**Saul**, Lou Ella Rankin 1927- *AmMWSc 92*
**Saul**, Mahir 1951- *WhoMW 92*
**Saul**, Oscar *IntMPA 92*
**Saul**, Oscar 1912- *WhoEnt 92*
**Saul**, Ralph Southey 1922- *IntWW 91, WhoFI 92*
**Saul**, Roger Stephen 1948- *WhoRel 92, WhoWest 92*
**Saul**, Samuel Berrick 1924- *Who 92*
**Saul**, William Edward 1934- *AmMWSc 92*
**Saull**, Keith Michael 1927- *Who 92*
**Saulnier**, Jean-Michel 1930- *IntWW 91*
**Sauls**, Don *WhoRel 92*
**Sauls**, Frederick Inabinette 1934- *WhoWest 92*
**Sauls**, Roger *DrAPF 91*
**Saulsberry**, Guy O. 1900- *WhoBlA 92*
**Saulter**, Gilbert John 1936- *WhoBlA 92*
**Saulter**, Paul Reginald 1935- *Who 92*
**Saumarez** *Who 92*
**Saunders and Otley** *DcLB 106*
**Saunders**, Albert Edward 1919- *Who 92*
**Saunders**, Alexander Hall 1941- *WhoFI 92*
**Saunders**, Andrew Downing 1931- *Who 92*
**Saunders**, Angela Gill 1951- *WhoRel 92*
**Saunders**, Ann Loreille 1930- *IntAu&W 91, WrDr 92*
**Saunders**, Anne 1955- *TwCPaSc*
**Saunders**, Antoinette Mercier 1947- *WhoMW 92*
**Saunders**, Arlene 1935- *WhoEnt 92*
**Saunders**, B David 1944- *AmMWSc 92*
**Saunders**, Barbara Ann 1950- *WhoBlA 92*
**Saunders**, Basil 1925- *Who 92*
**Saunders**, Burt A 1949- *AmMWSc 92*
**Saunders**, C. M. 1918- *WrDr 92*
**Saunders**, C M 1929- *WhoIns 92*
**Saunders**, Calvin Carlton 1950- *WhoAmL 92*
**Saunders**, Charles Baskerville, Jr 1928- *WhoAmP 91*
**Saunders**, Christopher John 1940- *Who 92*
**Saunders**, Christopher Thomas 1907- *Who 92*
**Saunders**, Cicely 1918- *Who 92*
**Saunders**, David 1936- *TwCPaSc*
**Saunders**, David John 1943- *Who 92*
**Saunders**, David John 1956- *WhoEnt 92*
**Saunders**, David Livingston 1939- *WhoAmL 92*
**Saunders**, David Martin St George 1930- *Who 92*
**Saunders**, David William 1936- *Who 92*
**Saunders**, Derek William 1925- *Who 92*
**Saunders**, Donald Frederick 1924- *AmMWSc 92*
**Saunders**, Donald Roy 1940- *AmMWSc 92*
**Saunders**, Doris 1921- *NotBlAW 92*
**Saunders**, Doris E. 1921- *WhoBlA 92*
**Saunders**, Edward A 1925- *AmMWSc 92*
**Saunders**, Edward Howard 1926- *WhoBlA 92*
**Saunders**, Elijah 1934- *WhoBlA 92*
**Saunders**, Elizabeth A. 1948- *WhoBlA 92*
**Saunders**, Ernest Walter 1935- *IntWW 91, Who 92*
**Saunders**, Ethel 1944- *WhoAmP 91*
**Saunders**, Frank Austin 1940- *AmMWSc 92*
**Saunders**, Frank Henry 1934- *WhoWest 92*
**Saunders**, Frank Linwood 1926- *AmMWSc 92*
**Saunders**, Frank Wendell 1922- *AmMWSc 92*
**Saunders**, Fred Michael *AmMWSc 92*
**Saunders**, George Cherdron 1940- *AmMWSc 92*
**Saunders**, George Lawton, Jr. 1931- *WhoAmL 92, WhoFI 92, WhoMW 92*
**Saunders**, Geraldine *DrAPF 91*
**Saunders**, Grady Franklin 1938- *AmMWSc 92*
**Saunders**, Harold H 1930- *WhoAmP 91*
**Saunders**, Helen 1885-1963 *TwCPaSc*
**Saunders**, Herbert Eugene 1940- *WhoRel 92*
**Saunders**, Howard N 1920- *WhoAmP 91*
**Saunders**, Jack *DrAPF 91*
**Saunders**, Jack Palmer 1915- *AmMWSc 92*
**Saunders**, James 1924- *WhoWest 92*
**Saunders**, James 1925- *IntAu&W 91, Who 92*
**Saunders**, James A. 1925- *WrDr 92*
**Saunders**, James Allen 1949- *AmMWSc 92*
**Saunders**, James Charles 1941- *AmMWSc 92*
**Saunders**, James Dale 1950- *WhoRel 92*

**Saunders,** James Harwood 1948- *WhoWest 92*
**Saunders,** James Henry 1923- *AmMWSc 92*
**Saunders,** James Henry 1948- *WhoMW 92*
**Saunders,** James Robert 1931- *AmMWSc 92*
**Saunders,** James Warren 1919- *WhoBlA 92*
**Saunders,** Jean 1932- *WrDr 92*
**Saunders,** Jeffrey John 1943- *AmMWSc 92*
**Saunders,** John *TwCWW 91*
**Saunders,** John 1917- *Who 92*
**Saunders,** John 1943- *WhoAmP 91*
**Saunders,** John Anthony Holt 1917- *IntWW 91*
**Saunders,** John Edward, III 1945- *WhoBlA 92*
**Saunders,** John Henry Boulton 1949- *Who 92*
**Saunders,** John Warren, Jr 1919- *AmMWSc 92*
**Saunders,** Joseph Arthur 1926- *WhoFI 92*
**Saunders,** Joseph Francis 1927- *AmMWSc 92*
**Saunders,** Joseph Lloyd 1935- *AmMWSc 92*
**Saunders,** Keith Alan 1953- *WhoEnt 92*
**Saunders,** Kenneth 1920- *Who 92*
**Saunders,** Kenneth Herbert 1915- *Who 92*
**Saunders,** Kenneth Paul 1948- *WhoBlA 92*
**Saunders,** Kim David 1945- *AmMWSc 92*
**Saunders,** Kurt Martin 1961- *WhoAmL 92*
**Saunders,** Larry 1939- *WhoAmP 91*
**Saunders,** Laurel Barnes 1926- *WhoWest 92*
**Saunders,** Leon Z 1919- *AmMWSc 92*
**Saunders,** Leslie DeWitt 1930- *WhoRel 92*
**Saunders,** Lonna Jeanne *WhoAmL 92, WhoMW 92*
**Saunders,** Lorna D. *DrAPF 91*
**Saunders,** Louisa Ann 1961- *IntAu&W 91*
**Saunders,** Mack *TwCWW 91*
**Saunders,** Mark A. 1946- *WhoAmL 92*
**Saunders,** Martin 1931- *AmMWSc 92*
**Saunders,** Martin Johnston 1949- *WhoAmL 92*
**Saunders,** Mary Alice 1938- *WhoBlA 92*
**Saunders,** Mauderie Hancock 1929- *WhoBlA 92*
**Saunders,** Melissa Lamb 1960- *WhoAmL 92*
**Saunders,** Meredith Roy 1930- *WhoBlA 92*
**Saunders,** Michael Lawrence 1944- *Who 92*
**Saunders,** Monroe Randolph, Jr. 1948- *WhoRel 92*
**Saunders,** Morton Jefferson 1925- *AmMWSc 92*
**Saunders,** N Leslie 1936- *WhoAmP 91*
**Saunders,** Nelson W 1949- *WhoAmP 91*
**Saunders,** Owen 1904- *IntWW 91, Who 92, WrDr 92*
**Saunders,** Paul Christopher 1941- *WhoAmL 92*
**Saunders,** Peter 1911- *Who 92*
**Saunders,** Peter 1950- *ConAu 36NR*
**Saunders,** Peter Gordon 1940- *Who 92*
**Saunders,** Peter Reginald 1928- *AmMWSc 92*
**Saunders,** Phyllis S. 1942- *WhoFI 92*
**Saunders,** Priscilla Prince 1938- *AmMWSc 92*
**Saunders,** Raymond 1933- *Who 92*
**Saunders,** Raymond Jennings 1934- *WhoBlA 92*
**Saunders,** Richard *BenetAL 91*
**Saunders,** Richard 1937- *Who 92*
**Saunders,** Richard L de C H 1908- *AmMWSc 92*
**Saunders,** Richard Lee 1928- *AmMWSc 92*
**Saunders,** Robert Edward 1959- *WhoBlA 92*
**Saunders,** Robert M 1915- *AmMWSc 92*
**Saunders,** Robert M 1945- *WhoAmP 91*
**Saunders,** Robert Mallough 1915- *WhoWest 92*
**Saunders,** Robert Montgomery 1939- *AmMWSc 92*
**Saunders,** Robert Norman 1938- *AmMWSc 92*
**Saunders,** Robert Samuel 1951- *WhoFI 92*
**Saunders,** Robert Walter 1959- *WhoAmL 92, WhoFI 92*
**Saunders,** Robert William, Sr. 1921- *WhoBlA 92*
**Saunders,** Ron 1954- *WhoAmP 91*
**Saunders,** Ronald Stephen 1940- *AmMWSc 92, WhoWest 92*
**Saunders,** Sally Love *DrAPF 91*
**Saunders,** Sally Love 1940- *WhoWest 92*
**Saunders,** Sam Cundiff 1931- *AmMWSc 92*
**Saunders,** Shelley Rae 1950- *AmMWSc 92*
**Saunders,** Stanley 1927- *WhoEnt 92*
**Saunders,** Stuart John 1931- *IntWW 91*
**Saunders,** Terry Rose 1942- *WhoAmL 92*
**Saunders,** Theodore D. 1912- *WhoBlA 92*
**Saunders,** Thomas William 1938- *WhoEnt 92*
**Saunders,** Vincent E., III 1954- *WhoBlA 92*
**Saunders,** Virginia Fox 1938- *AmMWSc 92*
**Saunders,** Wes *WrDr 92*
**Saunders,** Wilfred Leonard 1920- *Who 92*
**Saunders,** William 1822-1900 *BiInAmS*
**Saunders,** William 1923- *IntMPA 92*
**Saunders,** William Arthur 1930- *WhoFI 92*
**Saunders,** William Bruce 1942- *AmMWSc 92*
**Saunders,** William Burnett 1895- *WhoBlA 92*
**Saunders,** William Clinton 1945- *WhoRel 92*
**Saunders,** William H 1920- *AmMWSc 92*
**Saunders,** William Hundley, Jr 1926- *AmMWSc 92*
**Saunders,** William Joseph 1924- *WhoBlA 92*
**Saunders-Henderson,** Martha M. 1924- *WhoBlA 92*
**Saunders Watson,** Michael 1934- *Who 92*
**Saunier-Seite,** Alice Louise 1925- *IntWW 91*
**Sauntry,** Susan Schaefer 1943- *WhoAmL 92*
**Saupe,** Alfred 1925- *AmMWSc 92*
**Saur,** Klaus Gerhard 1941- *IntWW 91*
**Saura,** Carlos 1932- *IntDcF 2-2, IntMPA 92, IntWW 91*
**Saurborn,** Henry Lee, Jr. 1961- *WhoAmL 92*
**Sauret,** Emile 1852-1920 *NewAmDM*
**Saurman,** George E 1926- *WhoAmP 91*
**Sauro,** Joan *DrAPF 91*
**Sauro,** Joseph Pio 1927- *AmMWSc 92*
**Sause,** H William 1920- *AmMWSc 92, WhoMW 92*
**Sausedo,** Ann Elizabeth 1929- *WhoWest 92*
**Sausedo,** Patricia *WhoHisp 92*
**Sausedo,** Robert A. *WhoHisp 92*
**Sausen,** George Neil 1927- *AmMWSc 92*
**Sausen,** John Higdon 1919- *WhoWest 92*
**Sauser-Hall,** Frederic 1887-1961 *ConAu 36NR*
**Saussure,** Horace Benedicte de 1740-1799 *BlkwCEP*
**Sausville,** Joseph Winston 1918- *AmMWSc 92*
**Saute,** Robert E 1929- *AmMWSc 92*
**Saute,** Robert Emile 1929- *WhoWest 92*
**Sauter,** Eddie 1914-1981 *NewAmDM*
**Sauter,** Eric 1948- *WrDr 92*
**Sauter,** Frederick Joseph 1943- *AmMWSc 92*
**Sauter,** John V. 1941- *WhoFI 92*
**Sauter,** L. Scott 1962- *WhoMW 92*
**Sauter,** Leilani *DrAPF 91*
**Sauter,** Van Gordon *LesBEnT 92 [port]*
**Sauter,** Van Gordon 1935- *WhoEnt 92A*
**Sautet,** Claude 1924- *IntDcF 2-2 [port]*
**Sauthoff,** Ned Robert 1949- *AmMWSc 92*
**Sautter,** Chester A 1933- *AmMWSc 92*
**Sautter,** Christian 1940- *IntWW 91*
**Sautter,** Jay Howard 1912- *AmMWSc 92*
**Sautter,** Jeannie 1930- *WhoAmP 91*
**Sautter,** R. Craig *DrAPF 91*
**Sautter,** Terry Glen 1953- *WhoEnt 92*
**Sauvage,** Lester Rosaire 1926- *AmMWSc 92*
**Sauvage,** Michael 1948- *WhoWest 92*
**Sauvagnargues,** Jean Victor 1915- *IntWW 91, Who 92*
**Sauvain,** Philip Arthur 1933- *IntAu&W 91, WrDr 92*
**Sauvan,** Henri Leon 1923- *IntWW 91*
**Sauve,** Jeanne 1922- *Who 92*
**Sauve,** Jeanne 1926- *IntWW 91*
**Sauve,** Opal Pittman 1934- *WhoAmP 91*
**Sauvy,** Alfred d1990 *IntWW 91N*
**Sauzier,** Guy 1910- *Who 92*
**Sauzo,** Richard *WhoHisp 92*
**Sava,** George 1903- *IntAu&W 91, Who 92, WrDr 92*
**Savadove,** Gary Michael 1957- *WhoMW 92*
**Savage,** Alan *WrDr 92*
**Savage,** Albert B 1912- *AmMWSc 92*
**Savage,** Albert Walter 1898- *Who 92*
**Savage,** Archie Bernard, Jr. 1929- *WhoBlA 92*
**Savage,** Augusta 1892-1962 *NotBlAW 92 [port]*
**Savage,** Augustus A 1925- *WhoAmP 91, WhoBlA 92*
**Savage,** Barry J. 1941- *WhoWest 92*
**Savage,** Blair DeWillis 1941- *AmMWSc 92*
**Savage,** Blake *SmATA 65*
**Savage,** C MacLean *ScFEYrs*
**Savage,** Carl Richard, Jr 1942- *AmMWSc 92*
**Savage,** Charles 1918- *AmMWSc 92*
**Savage,** Charles Francis 1906- *AmMWSc 92*
**Savage,** Charles William 1933- *WhoAmP 91*
**Savage,** David 1929- *IntMPA 92*
**Savage,** Dennis James 1925- *WhoBlA 92*
**Savage,** Dennis Jeffrey 1942- *AmMWSc 92*
**Savage,** Donald Elvin 1917- *AmMWSc 92*
**Savage,** Dwayne Cecil 1934- *AmMWSc 92*
**Savage,** E Lynn *AmMWSc 92*
**Savage,** E. Scott 1947- *WhoAmL 92*
**Savage,** Earl John 1931- *AmMWSc 92*
**Savage,** Edward W., Jr. 1933- *WhoBlA 92*
**Savage,** Eldon P 1926- *AmMWSc 92*
**Savage,** Elmer N *WhoAmP 91*
**Savage,** Ernest 1912- *Who 92*
**Savage,** Ernest 1918- *IntAu&W 91, WrDr 92*
**Savage,** Frank 1938- *WhoBlA 92*
**Savage,** Frank X. *WhoRel 92*
**Savage,** Fred 1976- *IntMPA 92*
**Savage,** George Roland 1929- *AmMWSc 92*
**Savage,** Godfrey H 1927- *AmMWSc 92*
**Savage,** Gretchen Susan 1934- *WhoFI 92*
**Savage,** Gus 1925- *AlmAP 92 [port], WhoBlA 92, WhoMW 92*
**Savage,** Henry W. 1859-1927 *NewAmDM*
**Savage,** Horace Christopher 1941- *WhoBlA 92*
**Savage,** I Richard 1925- *AmMWSc 92*
**Savage,** Ian 1960- *WhoFI 92, WhoMW 92*
**Savage,** James Cathey, III 1947- *WhoAmL 92*
**Savage,** James Edward, Jr. 1941- *WhoBlA 92*
**Savage,** James S., III 1956- *WhoAmL 92*
**Savage,** James Wilbur 1905-1989 *RelLAm 91*
**Savage,** Jane Ramsdell 1925- *AmMWSc 92*
**Savage,** Jay Mathers 1928- *AmMWSc 92*
**Savage,** Jimmie Euel 1920- *AmMWSc 92*
**Savage,** John 1949- *IntMPA 92*
**Savage,** John 1950- *WhoEnt 92*
**Savage,** John Edmund 1939- *AmMWSc 92*
**Savage,** John Edward 1907- *AmMWSc 92*
**Savage,** John Lawrence 1936- *WhoWest 92*
**Savage,** John Paul 1946- *WhoMW 92*
**Savage,** John S 1905- *WhoAmP 91*
**Savage,** John T 1925- *WhoAmP 91*
**Savage,** John William 1951- *WhoAmL 92*
**Savage,** Juanita *ScFEYrs*
**Savage,** Kay Webb 1942- *WhoFI 92*
**Savage,** Kent Allen 1961- *WhoFI 92*
**Savage,** Les, Jr. 1922-1958 *TwCWW 91*
**Savage,** Martha Frances Walden 1940- *WhoAmP 91*
**Savage,** Michael 1941- *AmMWSc 92*
**Savage,** Michael Joseph 1872-1940 *FacFETw*
**Savage,** Nevin William 1928- *AmMWSc 92*
**Savage,** Norman Michael 1936- *AmMWSc 92*
**Savage,** Peter 1942- *AmMWSc 92*
**Savage,** Philip Henry 1868-1899 *BenetAL 91*
**Savage,** Richard 1697?-1743 *RfGEnL 91*
**Savage,** Robert Charles 1937- *WhoAmP 91*
**Savage,** Robert E 1932- *AmMWSc 92*
**Savage,** Russell Wayne 1963- *WhoRel 92*
**Savage,** Steven Paul 1950- *AmMWSc 92*
**Savage,** Stuart B 1932- *AmMWSc 92*
**Savage,** Terry Richard 1930- *WhoWest 92*
**Savage,** Thomas 1915- *BenetAL 91, ConAu 15AS [port], IntAu&W 91, TwCWW 91*
**Savage,** Thomas 1948- *IntAu&W 91*
**Savage,** Thomas Hixon 1928- *Who 92*
**Savage,** Thomas Staughton 1804-1880 *BiInAmS*
**Savage,** Thomas Yates 1956- *WhoAmL 92*
**Savage,** Timothy *ScFEYrs*
**Savage,** Tom *DrAPF 91*
**Savage,** Vernon Thomas 1945- *WhoBlA 92*
**Savage,** Wendy Diane 1935- *Who 92*
**Savage,** William Arthur *WhoBlA 92*
**Savage,** William Earl 1918- *WhoRel 92*
**Savage,** William F 1923- *AmMWSc 92*
**Savage,** William Ralph 1926- *AmMWSc 92*
**Savage,** William Zuger 1942- *AmMWSc 92*
**Savageau,** Michael Antonio 1940- *AmMWSc 92*
**Savago,** Peter J 1930- *WhoAmP 91*
**Savaiano,** Dennis Alan 1953- *AmMWSc 92*
**Savala,** Leonard *WhoHisp 92*
**Savalas,** Telly 1924- *IntMPA 92*
**Savalas,** Telly 1926- *IntWW 91*
**Savalas,** Telly Aristoteles 1926- *WhoEnt 92*
**Savan,** Milton 1920- *AmMWSc 92*
**Savant,** Edward H. 1943- *WhoFI 92*
**Savard,** Francis Gerald Kenneth 1918- *AmMWSc 92*
**Savard,** Jean Yves 1935- *AmMWSc 92*
**Savarese,** Fernando, Signora *Who 92*
**Savaria,** Louis A *WhoAmP 91*
**Savariego,** Samuel *WhoHisp 92*
**Savarimuthu,** John Gurubatham 1925- *IntWW 91, WhoRel 92*
**Savarius,** Vincent *LiExTwC*
**Savary,** Alain 1918-1988 *FacFETw*
**Savary,** Jerome 1942- *IntWW 91*
**Savary-Ogden,** Geraldine 1929- *WhoFI 92*
**Savas,** Emanuel S 1931- *WhoAmP 91*
**Savas,** Jonathan Andrew 1962- *WhoFI 92*
**Savchenko,** Alla *WhoEnt 92*
**Savchenko,** Arkadiy Markovich 1936- *IntWW 91*
**Savchenko,** Igor' Andreevich 1906-1950 *SovUnBD*
**Savedoff,** Lydia Goodman 1920- *AmMWSc 92*
**Savedoff,** Malcolm Paul 1928- *AmMWSc 92*
**Savedra,** Jo Ann 1960- *WhoHisp 92*
**Savedra,** Ruben 1932- *WhoHisp 92*
**Saveleva,** Lyudmila 1942- *IntWW 91*
**Savelkoul,** Donald Charles 1917- *WhoAmL 92*
**Savelle,** Jerry Junior 1946- *WhoRel 92*
**Savereide,** Thomas J 1932- *AmMWSc 92*
**Savernake,** Viscount 1982- *Who 92*
**Savery,** Clyde William 1935- *AmMWSc 92*
**Savery,** Constance Winifred 1897- *IntAu&W 91, WrDr 92*
**Savery,** Daniel James 1956- *WhoFI 92*
**Savery,** Harry P 1920- *AmMWSc 92*
**Savery,** Henry 1791-1842 *RfGEnL 91*
**Savesky,** Robert Stuart 1940- *WhoFI 92*
**Savia,** Alfred *WhoMW 92*
**Saviano,** Bernadette 1948- *WhoRel 92*
**Saviano,** Dennis Michael 1955- *WhoFI 92*
**Savic,** Michael I 1929- *AmMWSc 92*
**Savic,** Pavel 1909- *IntWW 91*
**Savic,** Sally *DrAPF 91*
**Savic,** Stanley D 1938- *AmMWSc 92*
**Savickas,** David Francis 1940- *AmMWSc 92*
**Savickas,** Frank David 1935- *WhoAmP 91*
**Savicky,** Randolph Philip 1953- *WhoEnt 92*
**Savides,** Michael Chris 1955- *WhoMW 92*
**Savidge,** Jeffrey Lee 1952- *AmMWSc 92*
**Savigne,** Jesus *BlkOlyM*
**Savile** *Who 92*
**Savile,** Baron 1919- *Who 92*
**Savile,** Douglas Barton Osborne 1909- *AmMWSc 92*
**Savile,** Frank *ScFEYrs*
**Savile,** James 1926- *Who 92*
**Savill,** David Malcolm 1930- *Who 92*
**Savill,** Kenneth Edward 1906- *Who 92*
**Saville,** Clive Howard 1943- *Who 92*
**Saville,** D A 1933- *AmMWSc 92*
**Saville,** John 1916- *Who 92*
**Saville,** John Fleming 1939- *WhoRel 92*
**Saville,** Ken *DrAPF 91*
**Saville,** Mark 1936- *Who 92*
**Saville,** Thorndike, Jr 1925- *AmMWSc 92*
**Saville,** Victor 1897-1979 *IntDcF 2-2 [port]*
**Savimbi,** Jonas 1934- *ConBlB 2 [port], FacFETw, IntWW 91*
**Savin,** Anatoliy Ivanovich 1920- *IntWW 91*
**Savin,** Ronald Richard 1926- *WhoFI 92*
**Savin,** Samuel Marvin 1940- *AmMWSc 92*
**Savina,** Iya 1936- *IntWW 91*
**Savine,** Christopher Mark 1958- *WhoFI 92*
**Savinelli,** Emilio A 1930- *AmMWSc 92*
**Saving,** Thomas Robert 1933- *WhoFI 92*
**Savinkin,** Nikolai Ivanovich 1913- *IntWW 91*
**Savino,** Beatriz *WhoHisp 92*
**Savino,** Felix 1955- *WhoMW 92*
**Savino,** William M. 1949- *WhoAmL 92*
**Savit,** Carl Hertz 1922- *AmMWSc 92*
**Savit,** Diana Marjorie 1952- *WhoAmL 92*
**Savit,** Joseph 1921- *AmMWSc 92*
**Savit,** Robert Steven 1947- *AmMWSc 92*
**Savitch,** Jessica d1983 *LesBEnT 92*
**Savitch,** Walter John 1943- *AmMWSc 92*
**Savitskaya,** Svetlana 1948- *FacFETw*
**Savitsky,** Daniel 1921- *AmMWSc 92*
**Savitsky,** Dennis William 1957- *WhoFI 92*
**Savitsky,** George Boris 1925- *AmMWSc 92*
**Savitsky,** Mikhail Andreevich 1922- *SovUnBD*
**Savitt,** Lynne *DrAPF 91*
**Savitt,** Sam *IntAu&W 91, WrDr 92*
**Savitt,** Susan Schenkel 1943- *WhoAmL 92*
**Savitz,** David Alan 1954- *AmMWSc 92*
**Savitz,** Jan 1941- *AmMWSc 92*
**Savitz,** Maxine Lazarus 1937- *AmMWSc 92*
**Savitz,** Samuel J. 1936- *WhoFI 92*
**Savitzky,** Abraham 1919- *AmMWSc 92*
**Savitzky,** Alan Howard 1950- *AmMWSc 92*
**Savitzky,** Martin F. 1951- *WhoAmL 92*

**Savkar**, Sudhir Dattatraya 1939- *AmMWSc 92*
**Savoca**, Carmen Salvatore 1924- *WhoEnt 92*
**Savocchio**, Joyce *WhoAmP 91*
**Savoia**, Joseph Michael 1952- *WhoFI 92*
**Savoie**, Rodrigue 1936- *AmMWSc 92*
**Savol**, Andrej Martin 1940- *AmMWSc 92*
**Savona**, Michael Richard 1947- *WhoWest 92*
**Savory**, Hubert Newman 1911- *Who 92*
**Savory**, John 1936- *AmMWSc 92*
**Savory**, Leonard E 1920- *AmMWSc 92*
**Savory**, Mark 1943- *WhoFI 92*
**Savory**, Teo *IntAu&W 91, WrDr 92*
**Savos**, Milton George 1927- *AmMWSc 92*
**Savostyuk**, Oleg Mikhaylovich 1927- *SovUnBD*
**Savours**, Dale Norman C. *Who 92*
**Savoy**, Douglas Eugene 1927- *IntAu&W 91, WhoRel 92*
**Savoy**, Guy 1953- *IntWW 91*
**Savoy**, James Cunningham 1930- *WhoWest 92*
**Savoy**, Suzanne Marie 1946- *WhoMW 92*
**Savoyka**, Lydia Ulana d1991 *NewYTBS 91 [port]*
**Savrin**, Louis 1927- *WhoAmL 92*
**Savrun**, Ender 1953- *AmMWSc 92, WhoWest 92*
**Savva**, Savely L. 1932- *WhoWest 92*
**Savvas**, Minas *DrAPF 91*
**Saw Maung** *IntWW 91*
**Saw Maung** 1928- *FacFETw*
**Sawabini**, Nabil George 1951- *WhoFI 92*
**Sawade**, Fritz *EncTR 91*
**Sawallisch**, Wolfgang 1923- *IntWW 91, NewAmDM, WhoEnt 92*
**Sawamura**, Michael Akira 1958- *WhoAmL 92*
**Sawan**, Mahmoud Edwin 1950- *AmMWSc 92*
**Sawan**, Samuel Paul 1950- *AmMWSc 92*
**Saward**, Ernest Welton 1914- *AmMWSc 92*
**Saward**, Michael John 1932- *Who 92*
**Sawardeker**, Jawahar Sazro 1937- *AmMWSc 92*
**Sawaszkiewicz**, Jacek Adam 1947- *IntAu&W 91*
**Sawatari**, Takeo 1939- *AmMWSc 92*
**Sawatzky**, Erich 1934- *AmMWSc 92*
**Sawatzky**, Leonard *WhoRel 92*
**Sawaya**, Michael George 1949- *WhoWest 92*
**Sawchuk**, Alexander Andrew 1945- *AmMWSc 92*
**Sawchuk**, Ronald John 1940- *AmMWSc 92*
**Sawchuk**, Terrance Gordon 1929-1970 *FacFETw*
**Sawdey**, Richard Marshall 1943- *WhoAmL 92*
**Sawdy**, Peter Bryan 1931- *IntWW 91, Who 92*
**Sawelson**, Mel 1929- *IntMPA 92*
**Sawer**, David 1961- *ConCom 92*
**Sawers**, David Richard Hall 1931- *Who 92*
**Sawers**, James Richard, Jr 1940- *AmMWSc 92*
**Sawers**, Larry B. 1942- *WhoFI 92*
**Sawhill**, Roy Bond 1922- *AmMWSc 92*
**Sawhney**, Vipen Kumar *AmMWSc 92*
**Sawicka**, Barbara Danuta *AmMWSc 92*
**Sawicka**, Magda *TwCPaSc*
**Sawicki**, Florence Berniece 1942- *WhoMW 92*
**Sawicki**, John Edward 1944- *AmMWSc 92*
**Sawicki**, Joseph, Jr 1954- *WhoAmP 91*
**Sawicki**, Marianne 1950- *ConAu 36NR, WhoRel 92*
**Sawicki**, Roman Mieczyslaw d1990 *IntWW 91N*
**Sawicki**, Stanley George 1942- *AmMWSc 92*
**Sawicki**, Thomas 1945- *WhoFI 92*
**Sawin**, Clark Timothy 1934- *AmMWSc 92*
**Sawin**, Steven P 1944- *AmMWSc 92*
**Sawinski**, Vincent John 1925- *AmMWSc 92*
**Sawitsky**, Arthur 1916- *AmMWSc 92*
**Sawko**, Felicjan 1937- *Who 92*
**Saworotnow**, Parfeny Pavolich 1924- *AmMWSc 92*
**Sawoski**, John Robert 1962- *WhoWest 92*
**Sawtell**, Jeff 1946- *TwCPaSc*
**Sawtelle**, Roger Allan 1940- *WhoRel 92*
**Sawtelle**, Susan Denise 1952- *WhoAmL 92*
**Sawtrelle**, William Carter *TwCSFW 91*
**Sawutz**, David G 1954- *AmMWSc 92*
**Sawyer**, Alfred M. 1934- *WhoBlA 92*
**Sawyer**, Alfred P 1919- *WhoAmP 91*
**Sawyer**, Amos 1945- *ConBlB 2 [port]*
**Sawyer**, Anthony Charles 1939- *Who 92*
**Sawyer**, Baldwin 1922- *AmMWSc 92*
**Sawyer**, Barbara Jo 1948- *WhoAmP 91*
**Sawyer**, Broadus Eugene 1921- *WhoBlA 92*
**Sawyer**, C Glenn 1922- *AmMWSc 92*
**Sawyer**, Cameron Friedel 1958- *WhoAmL 92*
**Sawyer**, Charles Henry 1915- *AmMWSc 92, IntWW 91*
**Sawyer**, Christopher Glenn 1950- *WhoAmL 92*
**Sawyer**, Constance B 1926- *AmMWSc 92*
**Sawyer**, David Erickson 1927- *AmMWSc 92*
**Sawyer**, David Neal 1940- *WhoFI 92*
**Sawyer**, David W 1910- *AmMWSc 92*
**Sawyer**, David Wendell 1944- *WhoEnt 92*
**Sawyer**, Diane *LesBEnT 92 [port]*
**Sawyer**, Diane 1945- *IntMPA 92*
**Sawyer**, Diane Marie 1962- *WhoWest 92*
**Sawyer**, Don 1947- *ConAu 133*
**Sawyer**, Donald C 1936- *AmMWSc 92*
**Sawyer**, Donald Turner, Jr 1931- *AmMWSc 92*
**Sawyer**, Ed 1926- *WhoAmP 91*
**Sawyer**, Edwin Forrest 1849- *BiInAmS*
**Sawyer**, Eugene, Jr 1934- *WhoAmP 91*
**Sawyer**, F Grant 1918- *WhoAmP 91*
**Sawyer**, Forrest *LesBEnT 92*
**Sawyer**, Forrest Lamar 1932- *WhoAmP 91*
**Sawyer**, Frank S *WhoAmP 91*
**Sawyer**, Frederick George 1918- *AmMWSc 92*
**Sawyer**, Frederick Miles 1924- *AmMWSc 92*
**Sawyer**, George Alanson 1922- *AmMWSc 92*
**Sawyer**, George Edward 1919- *WhoBlA 92*
**Sawyer**, Grant 1918- *WhoAmL 92*
**Sawyer**, Harold S 1920- *WhoAmP 91*
**Sawyer**, Harris Eastman 1868-1911 *BiInAmS*
**Sawyer**, James W 1933- *AmMWSc 92*
**Sawyer**, Jane Orrock 1944- *AmMWSc 92*
**Sawyer**, Jeffrey Wayne 1968- *WhoRel 92*
**Sawyer**, John 1919- *IntAu&W 91, WrDr 92*
**Sawyer**, John Orvel, Jr 1939- *AmMWSc 92*
**Sawyer**, John Stanley 1916- *IntWW 91, Who 92*
**Sawyer**, John Wesley 1917- *AmMWSc 92*
**Sawyer**, Kenneth J 1945- *WhoAmP 91*
**Sawyer**, Lucien Avila 1924- *WhoRel 92*
**Sawyer**, Lynwood *DrAPF 91*
**Sawyer**, Michael E. 1953- *WhoMW 92*
**Sawyer**, Michael Thomas 1958- *WhoAmP 91*
**Sawyer**, Michael Tom 1958- *WhoHisp 92*
**Sawyer**, Nancy 1924- *IntAu&W 91, WrDr 92*
**Sawyer**, Paul Simon 1920- *WhoMW 92*
**Sawyer**, Paul Thompson 1940- *AmMWSc 92*
**Sawyer**, Philip Glen 1948- *WhoWest 92*
**Sawyer**, Philip Nicholas 1925- *AmMWSc 92*
**Sawyer**, Phyllis Rose 1923- *WhoAmP 91*
**Sawyer**, Ralph Stanley 1921- *AmMWSc 92*
**Sawyer**, Raymond Connell 1943- *WhoEnt 92*
**Sawyer**, Raymond Eton 1946- *WhoRel 92, WhoWest 92*
**Sawyer**, Raymond Francis 1932- *AmMWSc 92*
**Sawyer**, Raymond Lee, Jr. 1935- *WhoFI 92*
**Sawyer**, Raymond Terry 1943- *WhoAmL 92*
**Sawyer**, Richard Trevor 1948- *AmMWSc 92*
**Sawyer**, Robert Fennell 1935- *AmMWSc 92*
**Sawyer**, Robert Noel 1946- *WhoIns 92*
**Sawyer**, Roger 1931- *WrDr 92*
**Sawyer**, Roger Holmes 1942- *AmMWSc 92*
**Sawyer**, Roger Martyn 1931- *IntAu&W 91*
**Sawyer**, Russell E., Jr. 1936- *WhoMW 92*
**Sawyer**, Sally 1931- *WhoEnt 92*
**Sawyer**, Sherri Roberson 1952- *WhoEnt 92*
**Sawyer**, Stanley Arthur 1940- *AmMWSc 92, WhoMW 92*
**Sawyer**, Stephen Gilbert 1953- *WhoAmP 91*
**Sawyer**, Thomas Arthur 1946- *WhoWest 92*
**Sawyer**, Thomas C 1945- *WhoAmP 91, WhoMW 92*
**Sawyer**, Thomas Edgar 1932- *WhoFI 92, WhoWest 92*
**Sawyer**, Thomas Ervin 1944- *WhoMW 92*
**Sawyer**, Thomas William 1933- *WhoWest 92*
**Sawyer**, Timothy Ray 1962- *WhoRel 92*
**Sawyer**, Tom 1945- *AlmAP 92 [port]*
**Sawyer**, Waldron Tom 1949- *WhoFI 92*
**Sawyer**, Walter Bryan 1959- *WhoFI 92*
**Sawyer**, Wendell *WhoAmP 91*
**Sawyer**, Wilbur Henderson 1921- *AmMWSc 92*
**Sawyer**, William Curtis 1933- *WhoFI 92*
**Sawyer**, William D 1929- *AmMWSc 92*
**Sawyer**, William Gregory 1954- *WhoBlA 92*
**Sawyer-Laucanno**, Christopher 1951- *ConAu 36NR*
**Sawyer-Lucanno**, Christopher 1951- *WrDr 92*
**Sawyers**, John Lazelle 1925- *AmMWSc 92*
**Sawyers**, Kenneth Norman 1936- *AmMWSc 92*
**Sawyier**, Michael Tod 1948- *WhoAmL 92*
**Sax**, Adolphe 1814-1894 *NewAmDM*
**Sax**, Boria *DrAPF 91*
**Sax**, Herbert 1929- *WhoFI 92, WhoWest 92*
**Sax**, Joseph L 1936- *IntAu&W 91, WrDr 92*
**Sax**, Karl Jolivette 1918- *AmMWSc 92*
**Sax**, Martin *AmMWSc 92*
**Sax**, Mary Randolph 1925- *WhoMW 92*
**Sax**, Nathan Samuel 1958- *WhoFI 92*
**Sax**, Robert James 1938- *WhoFI 92*
**Sax**, Robert Louis 1928- *AmMWSc 92*
**Sax**, Sylvan Maurice 1923- *AmMWSc 92*
**Saxbe**, William B 1916- *WhoAmP 91*
**Saxe**, Adrian Anthony 1943- *WhoWest 92*
**Saxe**, Deborah Crandall 1949- *WhoAmL 92*
**Saxe**, Harry Charles 1920- *AmMWSc 92*
**Saxe**, John Godfrey 1816-1887 *BenetAL 91*
**Saxe**, Jon Sheldon 1936- *WhoAmL 92*
**Saxe**, Leonard 1947- *AmMWSc 92*
**Saxe**, Stanley Richard 1932- *AmMWSc 92*
**Saxena**, Amol 1962- *WhoWest 92*
**Saxena**, Brij B 1930- *AmMWSc 92*
**Saxena**, Narendra K 1936- *AmMWSc 92, WhoWest 92*
**Saxena**, Satish Chandra 1934- *AmMWSc 92*
**Saxena**, Subhash C *AmMWSc 92*
**Saxena**, Surendra K *AmMWSc 92*
**Saxena**, Surrendra Kumar 1926- *IntWW 91*
**Saxena**, Umesh *AmMWSc 92*
**Saxena**, Vinod Kumar 1944- *AmMWSc 92*
**Saxena**, Virendra S. 1936- *WhoMW 92*
**Saxer**, Craig Sandford 1947- *WhoFI 92*
**Saxinger**, W Carl 1941- *AmMWSc 92*
**Saxon**, Alex *WrDr 92*
**Saxon**, Antonia *WrDr 92*
**Saxon**, Bill *ConAu 35NR*
**Saxon**, David Stephen 1920- *AmMWSc 92, Who 92*
**Saxon**, James Glenn 1941- *AmMWSc 92*
**Saxon**, John 1936- *IntMPA 92*
**Saxon**, John David 1950- *WhoAmL 92*
**Saxon**, Lyle 1891-1946 *BenetAL 91*
**Saxon**, Randall Lee 1947- *WhoRel 92*
**Saxon**, Richard 1905- *TwCSFW 91*
**Saxon**, Robert 1924- *AmMWSc 92*
**Saxon**, Spencer David 1927- *WhoEnt 92*
**Saxonhouse**, Gary Roger 1943- *WhoFI 92, WhoMW 92*
**Saxowsky**, David Milton 1954- *WhoAmL 92*
**Saxton**, Colin 1927- *TwCPaSc*
**Saxton**, H. James 1943- *AlmAP 92 [port], WhoAmP 91*
**Saxton**, Harry James 1939- *AmMWSc 92*
**Saxton**, Joseph 1799-1873 *BiInAmS*
**Saxton**, Josephine 1935- *TwCSFW 91, WrDr 92*
**Saxton**, Josephine Mary 1935- *IntAu&W 91*
**Saxton**, Judith *WrDr 92*
**Saxton**, Keith E 1937- *AmMWSc 92*
**Saxton**, Robert 1953- *ConCom 92*
**Saxton**, Robert Louis Alfred 1953- *Who 92*
**Saxton**, William Reginald 1928- *AmMWSc 92*
**Say**, Calvin Kwai Yen 1952- *WhoAmP 91*
**Say**, James Kenneth 1954- *WhoAmL 92*
**Say**, Lucy Way Sistare 1801-1886 *BiInAmS*
**Say**, Marlys Mortensen 1924- *WhoMW 92*
**Say**, Richard David 1914- *IntWW 91, Who 92*
**Say**, Thomas 1787-1834 *BenetAL 91, BiInAmS*
**Sayala**, Chhaya 1950- *AmMWSc 92*
**Sayala**, Dasharatham 1943- *AmMWSc 92*
**Sayan**, Doug *WhoAmP 91*
**Sayano**, Reizo Ray 1937- *WhoWest 92*
**Sayanov**, Vissarion Mikhaylovich 1903-1959 *SovUnBD*
**Sayao**, Bidu 1902- *NewAmDM*
**Sayari**, Hamad Saud al- 1941- *IntWW 91*
**Sayavedra**, Leo *WhoHisp 92*
**Sayce**, Roy Beavan 1920- *Who 92*
**Saydun**, Victor H. 1931- *WhoWest 92*
**Saye And Sele**, Baron 1920- *Who 92*
**Sayed**, As-Sayed Ali As- 1927- *IntWW 91*
**Sayed**, Gamal As 1918- *IntWW 91*
**Sayed**, Mostafa Amr El- 1933- *IntWW 91*
**Sayeed**, Akram 1935- *Who 92*
**Sayeed**, Jonathan 1948- *Who 92*
**Sayeed**, Mohammed Mahmood 1937- *AmMWSc 92*
**Sayeg**, Joseph A 1925- *AmMWSc 92*
**Sayegh**, Fayez S 1927- *AmMWSc 92*
**Sayegh**, Joseph Frieh 1928- *AmMWSc 92*
**Sayeki**, Hidemitsu 1933- *AmMWSc 92*
**Sayer**, Frank Edward, Jr 1918- *WhoAmP 91*
**Sayer**, Guy Mowbray 1924- *Who 92*
**Sayer**, Jane M 1942- *AmMWSc 92*
**Sayer**, John Raymond Keer 1931- *Who 92*
**Sayer**, John Samuel 1917- *AmMWSc 92*
**Sayer**, Michael 1935- *AmMWSc 92*
**Sayer**, Paul 1955- *WrDr 92*
**Sayer**, Royce Orlando 1941- *AmMWSc 92*
**Sayers**, Bruce McArthur 1928- *Who 92*
**Sayers**, Chera Lee 1959- *WhoFI 92*
**Sayers**, Dale Edward 1943- *AmMWSc 92*
**Sayers**, Dorothy L. 1893-1957 *CnDBLB 6 [port], FacFETw, RfGEnL 91*
**Sayers**, Earl Roger 1936- *AmMWSc 92*
**Sayers**, Eric Colin d1991 *Who 92N*
**Sayers**, Gale E. 1943- *WhoBlA 92*
**Sayers**, George 1914- *AmMWSc 92*
**Sayers**, James 1912- *Who 92*
**Sayers**, Janet 1945- *ConAu 134*
**Sayers**, Matthew Herbert Patrick 1908- *Who 92*
**Sayers**, Michael Patrick 1940- *Who 92*
**Sayers**, Valerie *DrAPF 91*
**Sayers**, Valerie 1952- *ConAu 134*
**Sayetta**, Thomas C 1937- *AmMWSc 92*
**Sayette**, Howard L. 1936- *WhoEnt 92*
**Saygun**, Ahmet Adnan d1991 *NewYTBS 91*
**Sayka**, Anthony 1957- *WhoWest 92*
**Saykanic**, John Vincent 1958- *WhoAmL 92*
**Sayle**, William, II 1941- *AmMWSc 92*
**Sayler**, Gene *WhoAmP 91*
**Sayler**, H L 1863-1913 *ScFEYrs*
**Sayler**, Henry B, Jr 1921- *WhoAmP 91*
**Sayler**, J William 1935- *WhoIns 92*
**Sayler**, John George 1940- *WhoMW 92*
**Sayles**, David Cyril 1917- *AmMWSc 92*
**Sayles**, Edward Thomas 1952- *WhoEnt 92*
**Sayles**, Everett Duane 1903- *AmMWSc 92*
**Sayles**, Frederick Livermore 1940- *AmMWSc 92*
**Sayles**, George Osborne 1901- *IntWW 91, Who 92*
**Sayles**, Guy Gaines 1957- *WhoRel 92*
**Sayles**, John 1950- *IntDcF 2-2 [port], IntMPA 92, WrDr 92*
**Sayles**, John Thomas 1950- *IntWW 91, WhoEnt 92*
**Sayles**, Richard Alan 1949- *WhoAmL 92*
**Sayles**, Ronald Lyle 1936- *WhoMW 92*
**Saylor**, Charles Horace 1950- *WhoAmL 92*
**Saylor**, Dennis Elwood 1933- *WhoRel 92, WhoWest 92*
**Saylor**, J. Galen 1902- *WrDr 92*
**Saylor**, John Galen 1902- *IntAu&W 91*
**Saylor**, John Thomas 1931- *WhoAmP 91*
**Saylor**, LeRoy C 1931- *AmMWSc 92*
**Saylor**, Mary Carol-Lenn 1941- *WhoFI 92*
**Saylor**, Paul Edward 1939- *AmMWSc 92*
**Saylor**, Stanley Raymond 1916- *WhoAmP 91*
**Sayne**, V. Lynn 1955- *WhoRel 92*
**Saynor**, John 1930- *Who 92*
**Sayre**, Clifford M, Jr 1930- *AmMWSc 92*
**Sayre**, Daniel Humphrey 1956- *WhoFI 92*
**Sayre**, David 1924- *AmMWSc 92*
**Sayre**, David Matthew 1964- *WhoWest 92*
**Sayre**, Edward Charles 1923- *WhoWest 92*
**Sayre**, Edward Vale 1919- *AmMWSc 92*
**Sayre**, Francis Bowes, Jr. 1915- *WhoRel 92*
**Sayre**, Francis Warren 1924- *AmMWSc 92*
**Sayre**, Geneva 1911- *AmMWSc 92*
**Sayre**, Greg 1957- *WhoAmP 91*
**Sayre**, Herbert Armistead 1866-1916 *BiInAmS*
**Sayre**, James Leroy 1946- *WhoAmL 92*
**Sayre**, John Marshall 1921- *WhoAmL 92, WhoWest 92*
**Sayre**, John Nevin 1884-1977 *AmPeW*
**Sayre**, Kathleen Pope 1950- *WhoIns 92*
**Sayre**, Lewis Albert 1820-1900 *BiInAmS*
**Sayre**, Richard Martin 1928- *AmMWSc 92*
**Sayre**, Robert Marion 1924- *WhoAmP 91*
**Sayre**, Robert Newton 1932- *AmMWSc 92*
**Sayre**, William Whitaker 1927- *AmMWSc 92*
**Sayres**, Alden R 1932- *AmMWSc 92*
**Saz**, Arthur Kenneth 1917- *AmMWSc 92*
**Saz**, Howard Jay 1923- *AmMWSc 92, WhoMW 92*
**Sazama**, Kathleen 1941- *AmMWSc 92*
**Sazer**, Gary Neil 1946- *WhoAmL 92, WhoFI 92*
**Sazonov**, Sergei Dmitriyevich 1861-1927 *FacFETw*
**Sbar**, Marc Lewis 1944- *AmMWSc 92*
**Sbarbaro**, Camillo 1888-1967 *DcLB 114 [port]*
**Sbarbaro**, John Anthony 1936- *WhoWest 92*
**Sbarra**, Anthony J 1922- *AmMWSc 92*

**Sbragia**, Gary W. 1941- *WhoFI 92, WhoWest 92*
**Scacchi**, Greta *IntWW 91*
**Scacchi**, Greta 1960- *IntMPA 92*
**Scaccia**, Angelo M *WhoAmP 91*
**Scaccia**, Carl 1946- *AmMWSc 92*
**Scace**, William Buell 1905- *WhoFI 92*
**Scadding**, John Guyett 1907- *Who 92*
**Scadron**, Michael David 1938- *AmMWSc 92*
**Scadron**, Robert Brian 1941- *WhoMW 92*
**Scafe**, Donald William 1937- *AmMWSc 92*
**Scafe**, Lincoln Robert, Jr. 1922- *WhoWest 92*
**Scafetta**, Joseph, Jr. 1947- *WhoAmL 92*
**Scafidi**, Michelangelo 1960- *WhoAmL 92, WhoWest 92*
**Scafuto**, Michael Joseph 1950- *WhoEnt 92*
**Scaggs**, Boz 1944- *NewAmDM, WhoEnt 92*
**Scaggs**, Edward W. 1932- *WhoBlA 92*
**Scaglione**, Aldo 1925- *IntAu&W 91, WrDr 92*
**Scaglione**, Ann *DrAPF 91*
**Scaglione**, Cecil Frank 1934- *WhoWest 92*
**Scaglione**, Edward Jerry 1944- *WhoRel 92*
**Scaglione**, Paul Anthony 1947- *WhoRel 92*
**Scaglione**, Peter Robert 1925- *AmMWSc 92*
**Scagnelli**, John Mark 1951- *WhoAmL 92*
**Scagnetti**, Jack James 1924- *WhoEnt 92*
**Scaife**, Brendan 1928- *IntWW 91*
**Scaife**, Charles Walter John 1938- *AmMWSc 92*
**Scaino**, Donald A 1932- *WhoIns 92*
**Scala**, Alfred Anthony 1936- *AmMWSc 92*
**Scala**, E 1922- *AmMWSc 92*
**Scala**, James 1934- *AmMWSc 92*
**Scala**, John Richard 1958- *AmMWSc 92*
**Scala**, Luciano Carlo 1923- *AmMWSc 92*
**Scala**, Robert Andrew 1931- *AmMWSc 92*
**Scala**, Sinclaire M 1929- *AmMWSc 92*
**Scala**, Sinclaire Maximilian 1929- *WhoFI 92*
**Scalabrini**, John Baptist 1839-1905 *DcAmImH*
**Scalapino**, Douglas J 1933- *AmMWSc 92*
**Scalapino**, Leslie *DrAPF 91*
**Scalapino**, Leslie 1947- *ConPo 91, WrDr 92*
**Scalapino**, Robert Anthony 1919- *IntAu&W 91, WrDr 92*
**Scalberg**, Daniel Allen 1952- *WhoWest 92*
**Scalera**, Michael Jose 1933- *WhoHisp 92*
**Scales**, Alice Marie 1941- *WhoBlA 92*
**Scales**, Brenda Claudette 1954- *WhoAmL 92*
**Scales**, Claude Moreland, III 1946- *WhoAmL 92*
**Scales**, Erwin Carlvet 1949- *WhoBlA 92*
**Scales**, John Alan 1957- *AmMWSc 92*
**Scales**, John Tracey 1920- *IntWW 91, Who 92*
**Scales**, Luther Damon, Jr. 1919- *WhoAmL 92*
**Scales**, Manderline Elizabeth 1927- *WhoBlA 92*
**Scales**, Melvin Julius, Jr. 1954- *WhoMW 92*
**Scales**, Patricia Bowles 1939- *WhoBlA 92*
**Scales**, Prunella *Who 92*
**Scales**, Prunella Margaret Rumney West *IntWW 91*
**Scales**, Richard Lewis 1928- *WhoMW 92*
**Scales**, Robert L. 1931- *WhoBlA 92*
**Scales**, Stanley R 1923- *AmMWSc 92*
**Scales**, Terence 1932- *TwCPaSc*
**Scales**, William H 1925- *WhoIns 92*
**Scales**, William Webb 1932- *AmMWSc 92*
**Scales-Trent**, Judy 1940- *WhoBlA 92*
**Scalet**, Charles George 1942- *AmMWSc 92*
**Scaletta**, Helen Marguerite 1927- *WhoMW 92*
**Scaletta**, Phillip Jasper 1925- *WhoAmL 92*
**Scaletta**, Phillip Ralph 1949- *WhoAmL 92*
**Scalettar**, Richard 1921- *AmMWSc 92*
**Scaletti**, Joseph Victor 1926- *AmMWSc 92*
**Scaletty**, Richard Paul 1952- *WhoAmL 92*
**Scalfari**, Eugenio 1924- *IntWW 91*
**Scalfaro**, Oscar Luigi 1918- *IntWW 91*
**Scalfarotto**, Robert Emil 1920- *AmMWSc 92*
**Scali**, John *LesBEnT 92*
**Scali**, John Alfred 1918- *IntAu&W 91*
**Scali**, Sam *WhoFI 92*
**Scalia**, Antonin 1936- *AmPolLe, FacFETw, IntWW 91, Who 92, WhoAmL 92, WhoAmP 91*
**Scalia**, Frank 1939- *AmMWSc 92*
**Scalia**, Toni 1939- *ConAu 133*
**Scalici**, Daniel Michael 1955- *WhoMW 92*
**Scaling**, G Wilson, II 1938- *WhoAmP 91*
**Scalish**, Frank Anthony 1940- *WhoFI 92, WhoMW 92*
**Scallan**, Anthony Michael 1936- *AmMWSc 92*
**Scallen**, Stephen Burns 1932- *WhoAmL 92*
**Scallen**, Terence 1935- *AmMWSc 92*
**Scallen**, Thomas Kaine 1925- *WhoEnt 92*
**Scallet**, Barrett Lerner 1916- *AmMWSc 92*
**Scalora**, Frank Salvatore 1927- *AmMWSc 92*
**Scalzi**, Francis Vincent 1933- *AmMWSc 92*
**Scalzi**, John Baptist 1915- *AmMWSc 92*
**Scamardo**, Salvatore Antonio 1962- *WhoEnt 92*
**Scamehorn**, John Robert, Jr. 1932- *WhoRel 92*
**Scamehorn**, Richard Guy 1942- *AmMWSc 92*
**Scammacca**, Nat *DrAPF 91*
**Scamman**, Walter Douglas, Jr 1941- *WhoAmP 91*
**Scammell**, William 1939- *ConPo 91, WrDr 92*
**Scammon**, Charles M 1825-1911 *BiInAmS*
**Scammon**, Richard M. 1915- *IntWW 91, WrDr 92*
**Scammon**, Richard Montgomery 1915- *IntAu&W 91, WhoAmP 91*
**Scanagatti**, Louise *EncAmaz 91*
**Scandalios**, George N. *WhoFI 92*
**Scandalios**, John George 1934- *AmMWSc 92*
**Scandrett**, John Harvey 1933- *AmMWSc 92*
**Scandura**, Joseph M 1932- *AmMWSc 92*
**Scanes**, Colin G 1947- *AmMWSc 92*
**Scanio**, Charles John Vincent 1940- *AmMWSc 92*
**Scanlan**, Arthur Brian 1907- *WrDr 92*
**Scanlan**, Brian James 1962- *WhoFI 92*
**Scanlan**, David M 1956- *WhoAmP 91*
**Scanlan**, Dorothy *Who 92*
**Scanlan**, J A, Jr 1917- *AmMWSc 92*
**Scanlan**, John D *WhoAmP 91*
**Scanlan**, John Oliver 1937- *IntWW 91*
**Scanlan**, Mary Ellen 1942- *AmMWSc 92*
**Scanlan**, Michael 1931- *WhoRel 92*
**Scanlan**, Richard Anthony 1937- *AmMWSc 92*
**Scanlan**, Robert Harris 1914- *AmMWSc 92*
**Scanlan**, Thomas Joseph 1945- *WhoRel 92*
**Scanlan**, Thomas Michael 1941- *WhoMW 92*
**Scanland**, Dennis Lawrence 1947- *WhoRel 92*
**Scanley**, Clyde Stephen 1921- *AmMWSc 92*
**Scanlin**, Cynthia *WhoAmP 91*
**Scanlin**, Steven Fox 1945- *WhoAmP 91*
**Scanlon** *Who 92*
**Scanlon**, Baron 1913- *IntWW 91, Who 92*
**Scanlon**, Charles Harris 1937- *AmMWSc 92*
**Scanlon**, Claire 1962- *TwCPaSc*
**Scanlon**, Eugene F 1924- *WhoAmP 91*
**Scanlon**, Jack M 1942- *AmMWSc 92*
**Scanlon**, John Earl 1925- *AmMWSc 92*
**Scanlon**, Joseph 1930- *WhoAmP 91*
**Scanlon**, Laurie Ann 1961- *WhoMW 92*
**Scanlon**, Michael Joseph 1937- *WhoRel 92*
**Scanlon**, Patrick Francis 1941- *AmMWSc 92*
**Scanlon**, Patrick Michael 1940- *WhoAmL 92*
**Scanlon**, Peter Redmond 1931- *WhoFI 92*
**Scanlon**, Robert Stephen 1952- *WhoEnt 92*
**Scanlon**, Shaun James 1939- *WhoFI 92*
**Scanlon**, Ted G. 1951- *WhoWest 92*
**Scanlon**, Terence J 1931- *WhoAmP 91*
**Scannell**, Elnora Mary 1908- *WhoRel 92*
**Scannell**, James J d1915 *BiInAmS*
**Scannell**, James Parnell 1931- *AmMWSc 92*
**Scannell**, Robert E. 1939- *WhoAmL 92*
**Scannell**, Thomas John 1954- *WhoMW 92*
**Scannell**, Vernon 1922- *ConPo 91, IntAu&W 91, IntWW 91, Who 92, WrDr 92*
**Scannell**, William Edward 1934- *WhoFI 92, WhoWest 92*
**Scannello**, Patrick C 1936- *WhoAmP 91*
**Scano**, Paul Francis 1949- *WhoAmL 92*
**Scanu**, Angelo M 1924- *AmMWSc 92*
**Scapanski**, Marilyn Jean 1935- *WhoAmP 91*
**Scapino**, Robert Peter 1936- *AmMWSc 92*
**Scarabelli**, Michele *WhoEnt 92*
**Scaramuzzi**, Franco 1926- *IntWW 91*
**Scarani**, Mary-Lou 1928- *WhoAmP 91*
**Scarascia-Mugnozza**, Carlo 1920- *IntWW 91, Who 92*
**Scarboro**, James Eckford 1941- *WhoAmL 92*
**Scarborough**, Charles Davis 1941- *WhoAmP 91*
**Scarborough**, Charles S. 1933- *WhoBlA 92*
**Scarborough**, Charles Spurgeon 1933- *AmMWSc 92*
**Scarborough**, Curtiss Clinton 1935- *WhoMW 92*
**Scarborough**, Dorothy 1877-1935 *TwCWW 91*
**Scarborough**, Elizabeth 1947- *TwCSFW 91*
**Scarborough**, Ernest N 1922- *AmMWSc 92*
**Scarborough**, Gene Allen 1940- *AmMWSc 92*
**Scarborough**, Harold E 1897- *ScFEYrs*
**Scarborough**, Hazel Whidden 1922- *WhoAmP 91*
**Scarborough**, Joe 1938- *TwCPaSc*
**Scarborough**, John Sargeant 1935- *WhoFI 92*
**Scarborough**, Jon Dale 1935- *WhoAmP 91*
**Scarborough**, Lee Rutland 1870-1945 *RelLAm 91*
**Scarborough**, Mark Sheldon 1957- *WhoAmP 91*
**Scarborough**, Robert Allen 1946- *WhoEnt 92*
**Scarborough**, Tony *WhoWest 92*
**Scarborough**, William Kauffman 1933- *IntAu&W 91, WrDr 92*
**Scarborough**, Yancey Wilcox, Jr 1922- *WhoIns 92*
**Scarbrough**, Earl of 1932- *Who 92*
**Scarbrough**, Ernest Earl 1947- *WhoFI 92*
**Scarbrough**, Ernest Wade, Jr. 1955- *WhoEnt 92*
**Scarbrough**, George Addison *DrAPF 91*
**Scarbrough**, William Franklin 1940- *WhoRel 92*
**Scarcelli**, Vincent F 1914- *WhoAmP 91*
**Scardera**, Michael 1935- *AmMWSc 92*
**Scardino**, Albert James 1948- *IntAu&W 91*
**Scardino**, Don *IntMPA 92, WhoEnt 92*
**Scarf**, Herbert Eli 1930- *IntWW 91, WhoFI 92*
**Scarf**, Maggie 1932- *IntAu&W 91, WrDr 92*
**Scarfe**, Alan John 1946- *WhoEnt 92*
**Scarfe**, Colin David 1940- *AmMWSc 92*
**Scarfe**, Gerald 1936- *Who 92*
**Scarfe**, Gerald A. 1936- *IntWW 91*
**Scarfe**, Herbert 1920- *TwCPaSc*
**Scarfe**, Jane *Who 92*
**Scarfe**, Wendy 1933- *WrDr 92*
**Scarfe**, Wendy Elizabeth 1933- *IntAu&W 91*
**Scarff**, Edward L. 1930- *WhoWest 92*
**Scarff**, Hope Ann Dyall 1952- *WhoMW 92*
**Scarfone**, Leonard Michael 1929- *AmMWSc 92*
**Scargill**, Arthur 1938- *FacFETw, IntWW 91, Who 92*
**Scargill**, David Ian 1935- *IntAu&W 91, WrDr 92*
**Scargle**, Jeffrey D 1941- *AmMWSc 92*
**Scariano**, Anthony 1918- *WhoAmL 92*
**Scaringe**, Raymond Peter 1950- *AmMWSc 92*
**Scaringe**, Robert P *AmMWSc 92*
**Scarl**, Donald B 1935- *AmMWSc 92*
**Scarlata**, Charles Francis 1941- *WhoAmL 92*
**Scarlatti**, Alessandro 1660-1725 *NewAmDM*
**Scarlatti**, Domenico 1685-1757 *NewAmDM*
**Scarlett** *Who 92*
**Scarlett**, Floyd M 1906- *WhoAmP 91*
**Scarlett**, James Harvey Anglin 1924- *Who 92*
**Scarlett**, John Leopold Campbell 1916- *Who 92*
**Scarlett**, P. Lynn 1949- *WhoWest 92*
**Scarlott**, Sherree Doneice 1957- *WhoRel 92*
**Scarman** *Who 92*
**Scarman**, Baron 1911- *IntWW 91, Who 92*
**Scarminach**, Charles Anthony 1944- *WhoAmL 92*
**Scarne**, Paul Thomas 1947- *WhoWest 92*
**Scaros**, Constantine E. 1945- *WhoFI 92*
**Scarpa**, Anthony F. *WhoFI 92*
**Scarpa**, Antonio 1942- *AmMWSc 92*
**Scarpa**, Carlo 1906-1978 *DcTwDes*
**Scarpa**, Frank James 1962- *WhoEnt 92*
**Scarpa**, Tobia 1935- *DcTwDes*
**Scarpace**, Philip J 1948- *AmMWSc 92*
**Scarpalezos**, Spyros-Constantin 1912- *IntWW 91*
**Scarpelli**, Dante Giovanni 1927- *AmMWSc 92*
**Scarpelli**, Emile Michael 1931- *AmMWSc 92*
**Scarpelli**, Nicholas Joseph 1964- *WhoAmL 92*
**Scarpetti**, Lee *WhoAmP 91*
**Scarpino**, Guy G *WhoAmP 91*
**Scarpino**, Pasquale Valentine 1932- *AmMWSc 92*
**Scarpone**, A John 1931- *AmMWSc 92*
**Scarr**, Marshal A. 1956- *WhoAmL 92*
**Scarr**, Sandra 1936- *IntAu&W 91*
**Scarratt**, David Johnson 1935- *AmMWSc 92*
**Scarritt**, Richard Winn 1938- *WhoMW 92*
**Scarrott**, Michael *IntAu&W 91X*
**Scarry**, Donald Michael 1941- *WhoFI 92*
**Scarry**, Mary 1934- *WhoFI 92*
**Scarry**, Richard 1919- *IntAu&W 91, WrDr 92*
**Scarsdale**, Viscount 1924- *Who 92*
**Scaruffi**, Betty May *WhoWest 92*
**Scaruffi**, Piero 1955- *WhoFI 92*
**Scarvie**, Walter Bernard 1934- *WhoRel 92*
**Scarwid**, Diana *IntMPA 92*
**Scatchard**, John Percival 1910- *Who 92*
**Scatena**, Lorraine Borba 1924- *WhoFI 92, WhoWest 92*
**Scates**, Lucille Marie Sherrod 1914-1977 *RelLAm 91*
**Scates**, Maxine *DrAPF 91*
**Scates**, Robert Malcolm 1917- *WhoAmP 91*
**Scathach** *EncAmaz 91*
**Scatigna**, Louis Gene 1960- *WhoFI 92*
**Scatliff**, James Howard 1927- *AmMWSc 92*
**Scatterday**, James Ware 1935- *AmMWSc 92*
**Scattergood**, Edgar Morris 1936- *AmMWSc 92*
**Scattergood**, Leslie Wayne 1914- *AmMWSc 92*
**Scattergood**, Ronald O 1937- *AmMWSc 92*
**Scattergood**, Thomas W *AmMWSc 92*
**Scattolini**, Lynn Bertman 1948- *WhoFI 92*
**Scavia**, Donald *AmMWSc 92*
**Scavo**, Frank James 1959- *WhoWest 92*
**Scavone**, Daniel James 1957- *WhoEnt 92*
**Scavone**, Sam John 1926- *WhoEnt 92*
**Scavotto**, David Anthony 1953- *WhoMW 92*
**Scavuzzo**, Rudolph J, Jr 1934- *AmMWSc 92*
**Scelba**, Anthony 1947- *WhoEnt 92*
**Scelba**, Mario 1901- *IntWW 91*
**Scelsi**, Giacinto 1905-1989 *NewAmDM*
**Scelsi**, Joseph S 1915- *WhoAmP 91*
**Sceper**, Duane Harold 1946- *WhoAmL 92*
**Scerni**, Fred 1948- *WhoAmP 91*
**Scerpella**, Marino *WhoHisp 92*
**Schaab**, Arnold J. 1939- *WhoAmL 92*
**Schaad**, H. Ronald *WhoMW 92*
**Schaad**, Lawrence Joseph 1930- *AmMWSc 92*
**Schaad**, Norman W 1940- *AmMWSc 92*
**Schaaf**, Geoffrey Charles 1946- *WhoEnt 92*
**Schaaf**, James Lewis 1932- *WhoMW 92, WhoRel 92*
**Schaaf**, John Urban 1955- *WhoMW 92*
**Schaaf**, Milton A 1911- *WhoAmP 91*
**Schaaf**, Norman George 1936- *AmMWSc 92*
**Schaaf**, Richard *DrAPF 91*
**Schaaf**, Robert E 1935- *WhoIns 92*
**Schaaf**, Robert Lester 1929- *AmMWSc 92*
**Schaaf**, Thomas Ken 1943- *AmMWSc 92*
**Schaaf**, William Edward 1938- *AmMWSc 92*
**Schaafsma**, Curtis Forrest 1938- *WhoWest 92*
**Schaal**, Barbara Anna 1947- *AmMWSc 92*
**Schaal**, Herbert Rudolf 1940- *WhoWest 92*
**Schaalman**, Herman Ezra 1916- *WhoRel 92*
**Schaap**, A Paul 1945- *AmMWSc 92*
**Schaap**, James Calvin *DrAPF 91*
**Schaap**, Luke Anthony 1931- *AmMWSc 92*
**Schaap**, Ward Beecher 1923- *AmMWSc 92*
**Schabacker**, Robert Bailey 1922- *WhoFI 92*
**Schabarum**, Peter F. 1929- *WhoHisp 92*
**Schabel**, Hans Georg 1942- *WhoMW 92*
**Schaber**, Douglas Craig 1950- *WhoWest 92*
**Schaber**, Gerald Gene 1938- *AmMWSc 92*
**Schaber**, Gordon Duane 1927- *WhoAmL 92*
**Schaberg**, John Irvin 1955- *WhoAmL 92*
**Schabes**, Alan Elliot 1957- *WhoAmL 92*
**Schabow**, John William 1937- *WhoWest 92*
**Schabram**, Hans 1928- *IntWW 91*
**Schach**, Rolland Sterling 1946- *WhoMW 92*
**Schach**, Stephen Ronald 1947- *AmMWSc 92*
**Schach von Wittenau**, Manfred 1930- *AmMWSc 92*
**Schacher**, Gordon Everett 1935- *AmMWSc 92*
**Schacher**, John Fredrick 1928- *AmMWSc 92*
**Schacher**, Mario A. 1947- *WhoHisp 92*
**Schachleiter**, Albanus 1861-1937 *EncTR 91*
**Schachman**, Howard Kapnek 1918- *AmMWSc 92, IntWW 91*
**Schachner**, Bruno 1911- *WhoAmL 92*
**Schachner**, Nat 1895-1955 *TwCSFW 91*
**Schachner**, Robert Wahl 1940- *WhoEnt 92*
**Schacht**, Henry Brewer 1934- *IntWW 91, WhoFI 92, WhoMW 92*
**Schacht**, Hjalmar 1877-1970 *EncTR 91 [port], FacFETw*

Schacht, Hjalmar Horace Greeley 1877-1970 *BiDExR*
Schacht, Jochen 1939- *AmMWSc 92*
Schacht, Jochen Heinrich 1939- *WhoMW 92*
Schacht, Lee Eastman 1930- *AmMWSc 92*
Schacht, Linda Joan 1944- *WhoEnt 92*
Schacht, Richard 1941- *WrDr 92*
Schacht, Ronald Stuart 1932- *WhoAmL 92*
Schacht, William Eugene 1941- *WhoWest 92*
Schachte, Henry M. d1991 *NewYTBS 91 [port]*
Schachtele, Charles Francis 1942- *AmMWSc 92*
Schachter, David 1927- *AmMWSc 92*
Schachter, E Neil 1943- *AmMWSc 92*
Schachter, Esther Roditti 1933- *WhoFI 92*
Schachter, Frances Fuchs d1991 *NewYTBS 91*
Schachter, Gustav 1926- *WhoFI 92*
Schachter, H 1933- *AmMWSc 92*
Schachter, Hindy Lauer *DrAPF 91*
Schachter, Joseph 1925- *AmMWSc 92*
Schachter, Julius 1936- *AmMWSc 92*
Schachter, Marvin 1924- *WhoAmP 91*
Schachter, Melville 1920- *AmMWSc 92*
Schachter, Michael Ben 1941- *AmMWSc 92*
Schachter, Oscar 1915- *WhoFI 92*
Schachter, Rozalie 1946- *AmMWSc 92*
Schachter, Sandy Rochelle *DrAPF 91*
Schachter-Shalomi, Zalman 1924- *RelLAm 91*
Schack, Arthur Martin 1945- *WhoAmL 92*
Schack, Carl J 1936- *AmMWSc 92*
Schackmann, Randy B. 1953- *WhoRel 92*
Schacter, Bernice Zeldin 1943- *AmMWSc 92*
Schacter, Brent Allan 1942- *AmMWSc 92*
Schacter, David Martin 1941- *WhoAmL 92*
Schacter, Ira Jason 1960- *WhoAmL 92*
Schacter, Jacob Joseph 1950- *WhoRel 92*
Schad, Gerhard Adam 1928- *AmMWSc 92*
Schad, James L. 1917- *WhoRel 92*
Schad, Theodore George, Jr. 1927- *WhoFI 92*
Schad, Theodore M 1918- *AmMWSc 92*
Schade, George Henry 1936- *WhoWest 92*
Schade, Henry A 1900- *AmMWSc 92*
Schade, Malcolm Robert 1950- *WhoAmL 92*
Schader, Harry W., III 1956- *WhoWest 92*
Schadewaldt, Hans 1923- *IntWW 91*
Schadle, William James 1932- *WhoAmL 92*
Schadler, Daniel Leo 1948- *AmMWSc 92*
Schadler, Harvey W 1931- *AmMWSc 92*
Schadler, Robert A 1947- *WhoAmP 91*
Schadt, Frank Leonard, III 1947- *AmMWSc 92*
Schadt, James C *AmMWSc 92*
Schadt, Randall James 1960- *AmMWSc 92*
Schaeberle, Robert M. 1923- *IntWW 91*
Schaechter, Moselio 1928- *AmMWSc 92*
Schaedle, Michail 1927- *AmMWSc 92*
Schaedler, Russell William 1927- *AmMWSc 92*
Schaef, Anne Wilson 1934- *WrDr 92*
Schaefer, A. Russell 1944- *WhoWest 92*
Schaefer, Albert Russell 1944- *AmMWSc 92*
Schaefer, Albrecht 1885-1950 *LiExTwC*
Schaefer, Arnold Edward 1917- *AmMWSc 92*
Schaefer, C. Barry 1939- *WhoFI 92*
Schaefer, Carl *IntMPA 92*
Schaefer, Carl Edred 1945- *WhoMW 92*
Schaefer, Carl Francis 1941- *AmMWSc 92*
Schaefer, Carl W, II 1934- *AmMWSc 92*
Schaefer, Charles Andrew 1958- *WhoWest 92*
Schaefer, Charles Herbert 1935- *AmMWSc 92*
Schaefer, Charles Parks 1950- *WhoMW 92*
Schaefer, Dale Wesley 1941- *AmMWSc 92*
Schaefer, Dan 1936- *AlmAP 92 [port]*
Schaefer, Dan L 1936- *WhoAmP 91*, *WhoWest 92*
Schaefer, Daniel M 1951- *AmMWSc 92*
Schaefer, David Arnold 1948- *WhoAmL 92*
Schaefer, David Edwin 1959- *WhoMW 92*
Schaefer, Donald John 1932- *AmMWSc 92*
Schaefer, Ernst J 1945- *AmMWSc 92*
Schaefer, Francis T 1913- *AmMWSc 92*
Schaefer, Frank William, III 1942- *AmMWSc 92*, *WhoMW 92*
Schaefer, Frederic Charles 1917- *AmMWSc 92*
Schaefer, Frederick John 1953- *WhoWest 92*
Schaefer, Frederick Vail 1949- *AmMWSc 92*
Schaefer, George 1913- *AmMWSc 92*
Schaefer, George 1920- *IntMPA 92*
Schaefer, George Anthony 1928- *IntWW 91*
Schaefer, George L. *LesBEnT 92*
Schaefer, George Louis 1920- *WhoEnt 92*, *WhoWest 92*
Schaefer, Gerald J 1944- *AmMWSc 92*
Schaefer, Harry George 1936- *WhoFI 92*, *WhoWest 92*
Schaefer, Helene Geraldine 1948- *WhoMW 92*
Schaefer, Henry Frederick, III 1944- *AmMWSc 92*
Schaefer, Howard G 1945- *WhoAmP 91*
Schaefer, Inge 1939- *WhoAmP 91*
Schaefer, Jack 1907-1991 *ConAu 133*, *NewYTBS 91*, *SmATA 65*, *-66 [port]*, *TwCWW 91*
Schaefer, Jacob Franklin 1938- *AmMWSc 92*
Schaefer, Jacob W 1919- *AmMWSc 92*
Schaefer, Jame 1940- *WhoAmP 91*
Schaefer, Jimmie Wayne, Jr. 1951- *WhoMW 92*
Schaefer, John A 1927- *WhoAmP 91*
Schaefer, John Paul 1934- *WhoFI 92*
Schaefer, Joseph Albert 1940- *AmMWSc 92*
Schaefer, Joseph Thomas 1943- *AmMWSc 92*, *WhoMW 92*
Schaefer, Karen Lee 1957- *WhoAmL 92*
Schaefer, Leslye Rhonda 1951- *WhoEnt 92*
Schaefer, Michael 1938- *WhoEnt 92*
Schaefer, Michael Anthony 1949- *WhoRel 92*
Schaefer, Michael P 1946- *WhoAmP 91*
Schaefer, Patricia 1930- *WhoEnt 92*, *WhoMW 92*
Schaefer, Paul Theodore 1930- *AmMWSc 92*
Schaefer, Peter James 1965- *WhoFI 92*
Schaefer, Philip Aaron 1941- *WhoAmP 91*
Schaefer, Philip William 1935- *AmMWSc 92*
Schaefer, Richard Gary 1952- *WhoRel 92*
Schaefer, Robert E 1936- *WhoAmP 91*
Schaefer, Robert Earl 1932- *WhoWest 92*
Schaefer, Robert J 1939- *AmMWSc 92*
Schaefer, Robert Stephen 1934- *WhoMW 92*
Schaefer, Robert William 1927- *AmMWSc 92*
Schaefer, Scott R. 1959- *WhoEnt 92*
Schaefer, Seth Clarence 1923- *AmMWSc 92*
Schaefer, Steven Lambert 1954- *WhoEnt 92*
Schaefer, Susan Gene *WhoEnt 92*
Schaefer, Ted *DrAPF 91*
Schaefer, Theodore Peter 1933- *AmMWSc 92*
Schaefer, Wilbur Carls 1925- *AmMWSc 92*
Schaefer, William D. 1928- *ConAu 134*
Schaefer, William Donald 1921- *AlmAP 92 [port]*, *IntWW 91*, *WhoAmP 91*
Schaefer, William G. 1941- *WhoAmL 92*
Schaefer, William Palzer 1931- *AmMWSc 92*
Schaefers, George Albert 1929- *AmMWSc 92*
Schaefers, Wolfgang Friedrich Wilhelm 1930- *IntWW 91*
Schaeffer, Arthur Clyde 1928- *WhoEnt 92*
Schaeffer, Barbara Hamilton 1926- *WhoFI 92*
Schaeffer, Bobb 1913- *AmMWSc 92*
Schaeffer, Boguslaw 1929- *IntAu&W 91*, *IntWW 91*
Schaeffer, Bud Stanley 1927- *WhoWest 92*
Schaeffer, Charles David 1948- *AmMWSc 92*
Schaeffer, David George 1942- *AmMWSc 92*
Schaeffer, David Joseph 1943- *AmMWSc 92*
Schaeffer, Francis August 1912-1984 *FacFETw*, *RelLAm 91*
Schaeffer, Gary N. 1948- *WhoWest 92*
Schaeffer, Gene Thomas 1932- *AmMWSc 92*
Schaeffer, George Christian 1815-1873 *BiInAmS*
Schaeffer, Glen 1948- *WhoAmL 92*
Schaeffer, Glenn William 1953- *WhoFI 92*
Schaeffer, Harold F 1899- *AmMWSc 92*
Schaeffer, Howard John 1927- *AmMWSc 92*
Schaeffer, James Robert 1933- *AmMWSc 92*
Schaeffer, John A. *WhoEnt 92*
Schaeffer, John Frederick *AmMWSc 92*
Schaeffer, Lee Allen 1943- *AmMWSc 92*
Schaeffer, Louis Henry, Jr. 1946- *WhoEnt 92*
Schaeffer, Morris 1907- *AmMWSc 92*
Schaeffer, Peter Viktor 1949- *WhoFI 92*
Schaeffer, Phillip Scott 1955- *WhoFI 92*
Schaeffer, Pierre 1910- *IntWW 91*, *NewAmDM*
Schaeffer, Richard Charles 1952- *WhoRel 92*
Schaeffer, Riley 1927- *AmMWSc 92*
Schaeffer, Robert L, Jr 1917- *AmMWSc 92*
Schaeffer, Ronald Lee 1939- *WhoEnt 92*
Schaeffer, Susan Fromberg *DrAPF 91*
Schaeffer, Susan Fromberg 1941- *ConNov 91*, *WrDr 92*
Schaeffer, Warren Ira 1938- *AmMWSc 92*
Schaeffer, William Dwight 1921- *AmMWSc 92*
Schaefgen, John Raymond 1918- *AmMWSc 92*
Schaefgen, Philip P. 1958- *WhoFI 92*
Schaefgen, Susan Marie 1952- *WhoAmL 92*
Schaeneman, Lewis G., Jr. 1930- *WhoFI 92*
Schaenen, Lee Joel 1925- *WhoEnt 92*
Schaeperkoetter, Jeff W 1949- *WhoAmP 91*
Schaer, Jonathan 1929- *AmMWSc 92*
Schaerf, Carlo 1935- *ConAu 133*
Schaerf, Henry Maximilian 1907- *AmMWSc 92*
Schaetzel, John Robert 1917- *IntWW 91*
Schaetzle, Walter J 1934- *AmMWSc 92*
Schafer, Barry William 1963- *WhoMW 92*
Schafer, Carl Walter 1936- *WhoFI 92*
Schafer, David Edward 1931- *AmMWSc 92*
Schafer, Edward Albert, Jr. 1939- *WhoMW 92*
Schafer, Edward Hetzel 1913- *IntAu&W 91*
Schafer, Gary Lee 1938- *WhoAmP 91*
Schafer, Glenn S 1949- *WhoIns 92*
Schafer, H Erle 1938- *WhoAmP 91*
Schafer, Irwin Arnold 1928- *AmMWSc 92*
Schafer, James A 1939- *AmMWSc 92*
Schafer, James Arthur 1941- *AmMWSc 92*
Schafer, James Kettler 1965- *WhoFI 92*
Schafer, Jerry Sanford 1934- *WhoEnt 92*, *WhoFI 92*, *WhoWest 92*
Schafer, John Francis 1921- *AmMWSc 92*
Schafer, John William, Jr 1937- *AmMWSc 92*
Schafer, Joleen Marie 1966- *WhoWest 92*
Schafer, Karen Lee 1940- *WhoAmP 91*
Schafer, Lee Glenn 1946- *WhoRel 92*
Schafer, Lothar 1939- *AmMWSc 92*
Schafer, Martin *IntMPA 92*
Schafer, Mary Angeline 1960- *WhoEnt 92*
Schafer, Mary Louise 1915- *AmMWSc 92*
Schafer, Natalie d1991 *NewYTBS 91*
Schafer, Peter 1943- *WhoRel 92*
Schafer, R Murray 1933- *ConCom 92*, *NewAmDM*
Schafer, Randall Arthur, Sr. 1959- *WhoEnt 92*
Schafer, Richard Donald 1918- *AmMWSc 92*
Schafer, Robert Louis 1937- *AmMWSc 92*
Schafer, Rollie R 1942- *AmMWSc 92*
Schafer, Ronald W 1938- *AmMWSc 92*
Schafer, Thomas Anton 1918- *WhoRel 92*
Schafer, Wilhelm 1868-1952 *EncTR 91 [port]*
Schafer, William Harry 1936- *WhoMW 92*
Schaff, Adam 1913- *IntWW 91*
Schaff, John Franklin 1931- *AmMWSc 92*
Schaff, Michael Frederick 1957- *WhoAmL 92*
Schaff, Paula Kay 1945- *WhoFI 92*
Schaff, Philip 1819-1893 *RelLAm 91*
Schaff, Phillip 1819-1893 *EncEarC*
Schaffel, Gerson Samuel 1918- *AmMWSc 92*
Schaffel, Larry Sigmond 1933- *WhoMW 92*
Schaffel, Robert 1944- *IntMPA 92*
Schaffer, Arnold Martin 1942- *AmMWSc 92*
Schaffer, Barbara Noyes 1947- *AmMWSc 92*
Schaffer, Boguslaw 1929- *NewAmDM*
Schaffer, Charles 1838-1903 *BiInAmS*
Schaffer, Clark Norman 1967- *WhoEnt 92*
Schaffer, David Edwin 1929- *WhoFI 92*
Schaffer, Erwin Lambert 1936- *AmMWSc 92*
Schaffer, Erwin Michael 1922- *AmMWSc 92*
Schaffer, Frederick Leland 1921- *AmMWSc 92*
Schaffer, George John 1907- *WhoAmL 92*, *WhoMW 92*
Schaffer, Gregory Lynn 1943- *WhoWest 92*
Schaffer, Harwood David 1944- *WhoMW 92*, *WhoRel 92*
Schaffer, Henry Elkin 1938- *AmMWSc 92*
Schaffer, Howard B *WhoAmP 91*
Schaffer, Jack Raymond 1942- *WhoAmP 91*
Schaffer, Joel Lance 1945- *WhoWest 92*
Schaffer, Juan Jorge 1930- *AmMWSc 92*
Schaffer, Marvin Baker 1926- *WhoWest 92*
Schaffer, Priscilla Ann 1941- *AmMWSc 92*
Schaffer, Robert 1920- *AmMWSc 92*
Schaffer, Robert Warren 1962- *WhoAmP 91*, *WhoWest 92*
Schaffer, Sheldon Arthur 1943- *AmMWSc 92*
Schaffer, Stephen Ward 1944- *AmMWSc 92*
Schaffer, Theodore Richard 1932- *WhoRel 92*
Schaffer, William Morris 1945- *AmMWSc 92*
Schaffer-Bough, Tamara Lou 1959- *WhoEnt 92*
Schaffner, Carl Paul 1928- *AmMWSc 92*
Schaffner, Fenton 1920- *AmMWSc 92*
Schaffner, Franklin *LesBEnT 92*
Schaffner, Franklin 1920-1989 *FacFETw*
Schaffner, Franklin J. 1920-1989 *IntDcF 2-2*
Schaffner, Gerald 1927- *AmMWSc 92*
Schaffner, Jakob 1875-1944 *BiDExR*
Schaffner, John Albert 1937- *WhoMW 92*
Schaffner, Joseph Clarence 1930- *AmMWSc 92*
Schaffner, Nicholas d1991 *NewYTBS 91*
Schaffner, Nicholas 1953-1991 *ConAu 135*
Schaffner, Philip Mackenzie 1934- *WhoFI 92*
Schaffner, Robert M 1915- *AmMWSc 92*
Schaffner, Robert Mark 1964- *WhoMW 92*
Schaffner, William Robert 1936- *AmMWSc 92*
Schaffran, Charles Brad 1950- *WhoAmL 92*
Schaffrath, Robert Eben 1922- *AmMWSc 92*
Schaffstein, Friedrich 1905- *IntWW 91*
Schafft, Harry Arthur 1932- *AmMWSc 92*
Schaffter, Ernest Merill James 1922- *Who 92*
Schafrath, Richard P 1937- *WhoAmP 91*
Schafrick, Frederick Craig 1948- *WhoAmL 92*
Schagrin, Elihu 1918- *WhoRel 92*
Schahrer, Karen Diane 1965- *WhoMW 92*
Schaiberger, George Elmer 1928- *AmMWSc 92*
Schaible, Grace Berg *WhoAmP 91*
Schaible, Michael 1940- *DcTwDes*
Schaible, Robert Hilton 1931- *AmMWSc 92*
Schaich, Karen Marie 1947- *AmMWSc 92*
Schaich, William Lee 1944- *AmMWSc 92*
Schaider, Cynthia Denise 1957- *WhoWest 92*
Schaie, K Warner 1928- *ConAu 34NR*
Schain, Eliot *DrAPF 91*
Schairer, G S 1913- *AmMWSc 92*
Schairer, George Swift 1913- *IntWW 91*
Schairer, Robert S 1915- *AmMWSc 92*
Schaive, James Moreko, Jr. 1933- *WhoRel 92*
Schake, Lowell Martin 1939- *AmMWSc 92*
Schakowsky, Janice D 1944- *WhoAmP 91*
Schalcosky, S. Richard 1947- *WhoFI 92*
Schaleger, Larry L 1934- *AmMWSc 92*
Schales, Otto 1910- *AmMWSc 92*
Schalge, Alvin Laverne 1930- *AmMWSc 92*
Schalk, Adolph F 1923- *IntAu&W 91*
Schalk, Eugene Norbert 1932- *WhoFI 92*
Schalk, James Maximillian 1932- *AmMWSc 92*
Schalk, Marshall 1907- *AmMWSc 92*
Schalk, Terry LeRoy 1943- *AmMWSc 92*
Schall, Celia May 1925- *WhoMW 92*
Schall, Elwyn DeLaurel 1918- *AmMWSc 92*
Schall, Joseph Julian 1946- *AmMWSc 92*
Schall, Lawrence Delano 1940- *WhoFI 92*
Schall, Roy Franklin, Jr 1939- *AmMWSc 92*
Schall Holberg, Britta 1941- *IntWW 91*
Schalla, Charence August 1918- *AmMWSc 92*
Schallenberg, Elmer Edward 1929- *AmMWSc 92*
Schallenkamp, Kay 1949- *WhoMW 92*
Schaller, Charles William 1920- *AmMWSc 92*
Schaller, Daryl Richard 1943- *AmMWSc 92*, *WhoFI 92*
Schaller, Edward James 1939- *AmMWSc 92*
Schaller, Francois 1920- *IntWW 91*
Schaller, George B. 1933- *WrDr 92*
Schaller, George Beals 1933- *IntWW 91*
Schaller, Joanne Frances 1943- *WhoWest 92*
Schaller, Robin Edward 1937- *AmMWSc 92*
Schallert, Donovan H 1924- *WhoIns 92*

**Schallert**, Edwin Glenn 1952- *WhoAmL 92*
**Schallert**, James Britton 1948- *WhoIns 92*
**Schallert**, Thomas Anthony 1952- *WhoWest 92*
**Schallert**, William Francis 1927- *AmMWSc 92*
**Schallert**, William Joseph 1922- *WhoEnt 92*
**Schalles**, Robert R 1935- *AmMWSc 92*
**Schallhorn**, Charles H 1944- *AmMWSc 92*
**Schalliol**, Thomas Edgar 1951- *WhoMW 92*
**Schalliol**, Willis Lee 1919- *AmMWSc 92*
**Schally**, Andrew Victor 1926- *AmMWSc 92, IntWW 91, Who 92, WhoNob 90*
**Schalon**, Charles Lawrence 1941- *WhoMW 92*
**Schama**, Simon 1945- *CurBio 91 [port], IntAu&W 91, WrDr 92*
**Schama**, Simon Michael 1945- *IntWW 91*
**Schambach**, Robert W. 1926- *RelLAm 91*
**Schamberg**, Richard 1920- *AmMWSc 92*
**Schamberger**, Robert Dean 1948- *AmMWSc 92*
**Schambra**, Philip Ellis 1934- *AmMWSc 92*
**Schamp**, Homer Ward, Jr 1923- *AmMWSc 92*
**Schanbacher**, Floyd Leon 1941- *AmMWSc 92*
**Schanback**, Jeffrey 1946- *WhoAmL 92*
**Schanberg**, Saul M 1933- *AmMWSc 92*
**Schanberg**, Sydney H 1934- *IntAu&W 91*
**Schanberg**, Sydney Hillel 1934- *IntWW 91*
**Schanck**, Francis R. d1991 *NewYTBS 91*
**Schanck**, John Stillwell 1817-1898 *BiInAmS*
**Schanda**, Joseph, Sr 1930- *WhoAmP 91*
**Schander**, Edwin 1942- *WhoWest 92*
**Schander**, Mary Lea 1947- *WhoWest 92*
**Schanefelt**, Robert Von 1942- *AmMWSc 92*
**Schanerman**, Richard L. 1954- *WhoAmL 92*
**Schanes**, Steven Eli 1924- *WhoFI 92*
**Schanfield**, Moses Samuel 1944- *AmMWSc 92*
**Schank**, Stanley Cox 1932- *AmMWSc 92*
**Schanker**, Jacob Z *AmMWSc 92*
**Schanker**, Neil Bruce 1956- *WhoMW 92*
**Schankman**, Alan Robert 1947- *WhoWest 92*
**Schankman**, Steven Frank 1948- *WhoEnt 92*
**Schanne**, Otto F 1932- *AmMWSc 92*
**Schano**, Edward Arthur 1918- *AmMWSc 92*
**Schanstra**, Carla Ross 1954- *WhoMW 92*
**Schantz**, Edward Joseph 1908- *AmMWSc 92*
**Schantz**, Herbert Felix 1930- *WhoFI 92*
**Schantz**, Peter Mullineaux 1939- *AmMWSc 92*
**Schanuel**, Stephen Hoel 1933- *AmMWSc 92*
**Schanzel**, Dean J 1942- *WhoAmP 91*
**Schanzer**, Kenneth David 1945- *WhoEnt 92*
**Schanzer**, Wolfgang 1924- *WhoEnt 92*
**Schap**, Evelyn K. 1949- *WhoMW 92*
**Schapansky**, Elwood Jay 1938- *WhoWest 92*
**Schaper**, Laurence Teis 1936- *AmMWSc 92*
**Schapera**, Isaac 1905- *Who 92*
**Schapery**, Richard Allan 1935- *AmMWSc 92*
**Schapira**, Morey Rael 1949- *WhoWest 92*
**Schapiro**, Harriette Charlotte 1935- *AmMWSc 92*
**Schapiro**, Herb 1929- *WhoEnt 92*
**Schapiro**, Isabel Margaret *Who 92*
**Schapiro**, Jerome Bentley 1930- *WhoFI 92*
**Schapiro**, Meyer 1904- *FacFETw, IntAu&W 91, Who 92, WrDr 92*
**Schapiro**, Morris A. 1903- *WhoFI 92*
**Schappell**, Frederick George 1938- *AmMWSc 92*
**Schappert**, Gottfried T 1934- *AmMWSc 92*
**Schapsmeier**, Edward Lewis 1927- *IntAu&W 91, WrDr 92*
**Schapsmeier**, Frederick H 1927- *IntAu&W 91, WrDr 92*
**Schar**, Raymond Dewitt 1923- *AmMWSc 92*
**Schar**, Stephen L. 1945- *WhoAmL 92*
**Scharansky**, Natan 1948- *IntWW 91*
**Scharber**, Samuel Robert, Jr 1933- *AmMWSc 92*
**Scharbert**, Josef 1919- *WhoRel 92*
**Scharenberg**, Rolf Paul 1927- *AmMWSc 92*
**Scharer**, John Edward 1939- *AmMWSc 92*
**Scharf**, Aaron 1922- *WrDr 92*
**Scharf**, Arthur Alfred 1927- *AmMWSc 92*
**Scharf**, Bertram 1931- *AmMWSc 92*
**Scharf**, Greg Roark 1948- *WhoRel 92*
**Scharf**, Robert Lee 1920- *WhoAmL 92*
**Scharf**, Walter 1929- *AmMWSc 92*
**Scharfenberg**, Doris Ann 1917- *WhoEnt 92*
**Scharfenberg**, Joachim 1927- *WhoRel 92*
**Scharfetter**, D L 1934- *AmMWSc 92*
**Scharff**, David Parker 1923- *WhoWest 92*
**Scharff**, Edward E. 1946- *WrDr 92*
**Scharff**, Joseph Laurent 1935- *WhoAmL 92*
**Scharff**, Matthew Daniel 1932- *AmMWSc 92*
**Scharff**, Robert L., Jr. 1943- *WhoMW 92*
**Scharff**, Thomas G 1923- *AmMWSc 92*
**Scharfstein**, Lawrence Robert 1927- *AmMWSc 92*
**Scharlatt**, Harold 1947- *WhoFI 92*
**Scharlemann**, Herbert Karl 1927- *WhoRel 92*
**Scharlemann**, Robert Paul 1929- *WhoRel 92*
**Scharn**, Herman Otto Friedrich 1911- *AmMWSc 92*
**Scharnau**, Ralph William 1935- *WhoMW 92*
**Scharnhorst**, Kurt Peter 1936- *AmMWSc 92*
**Scharoff**, Steven Russell 1946- *WhoAmL 92*
**Scharon**, John Vincent, Jr. 1953- *WhoAmL 92*
**Scharp**, Anders 1934- *IntWW 91, WhoFI 92, WhoMW 92*
**Scharpen**, LeRoy Henry 1935- *AmMWSc 92*
**Scharper**, Stephen Bede 1960- *WhoRel 92*
**Scharpf**, Lewis George, Jr 1940- *AmMWSc 92*
**Scharpf**, Robert F 1931- *AmMWSc 92*
**Scharpf**, William George 1925- *AmMWSc 92*
**Scharr**, Jack Barrett 1943- *WhoMW 92*
**Scharrer**, Berta Vogel 1906- *AmMWSc 92, IntWW 91*
**Schartner**, Albert Lyman 1931- *WhoRel 92*
**Scharton**, Terry Don 1939- *AmMWSc 92*
**Scharver**, Jeffrey Douglas 1947- *AmMWSc 92*
**Scharwenka**, Xaver 1850-1924 *NewAmDM*
**Schary**, Dore 1905-1980 *BenetAL 91, FacFETw*
**Schat**, Peter 1935- *ConCom 92*
**Schatell**, Brian *SmATA 66*
**Schatman**, Jill B. 1957- *WhoAmL 92*
**Schatten**, Gerald Phillip 1949- *AmMWSc 92*
**Schatten**, Heide 1946- *AmMWSc 92*
**Schatten**, Kenneth Howard 1944- *AmMWSc 92*
**Schattenburg**, Mark Lee 1956- *AmMWSc 92*
**Schattner**, Robert I 1925- *AmMWSc 92*
**Schattschneider**, David Allen 1939- *WhoRel 92*
**Schattschneider**, Doris Jean 1939- *AmMWSc 92*
**Schatz**, Barbara A. 1948- *WhoAmL 92*
**Schatz**, Dale Errol 1936- *WhoRel 92*
**Schatz**, Edward Gary 1929- *WhoFI 92*
**Schatz**, Edward R 1921- *AmMWSc 92*
**Schatz**, Franklin Scott 1963- *WhoEnt 92*
**Schatz**, George Chappell 1949- *AmMWSc 92*
**Schatz**, Gottfried 1936- *IntWW 91*
**Schatz**, Irwin Jacob 1931- *AmMWSc 92*
**Schatz**, Joseph Arthur 1924- *AmMWSc 92*
**Schatz**, Louis Bordon 1954- *WhoAmL 92*
**Schatz**, Michael A *WhoAmP 91*
**Schatz**, Mona Claire Struhsaker 1950- *WhoWest 92*
**Schatz**, Paul Namon 1928- *AmMWSc 92*
**Schatz**, Philip Ransom 1957- *WhoAmL 92*
**Schatz**, Robert Keith 1927- *WhoWest 92*
**Schatzberg**, Jerry 1927- *IntMPA 92*
**Schatzberg**, Jerry Ned 1927- *WhoEnt 92*
**Schatzki**, Erich d1991 *NewYTBS 91*
**Schatzki**, George 1933- *WhoAmL 92*
**Schatzki**, Thomas Ferdinant 1927- *AmMWSc 92*
**Schatzlein**, Frank Charles 1929- *AmMWSc 92*
**Schatzman**, Arnold Dennis 1938- *WhoAmL 92*
**Schatzman**, Bard Irwin 1950- *WhoMW 92*
**Schatzman**, Evry 1920- *IntWW 91*
**Schatzmann**, Siegfried Samuel 1941- *WhoRel 92*
**Schau**, June Zellers 1948- *WhoAmL 92*
**Schaub**, Clarence Robert 1932- *WhoAmL 92*
**Schaub**, Harry Carl 1929- *WhoAmL 92*
**Schaub**, James H 1925- *AmMWSc 92*
**Schaub**, Marilyn McNamara 1928- *WhoRel 92*
**Schaub**, Raymond Thomas 1933- *WhoRel 92*
**Schaub**, Robert Erhard, Jr. 1939- *WhoMW 92*
**Schaub**, Robert George 1947- *AmMWSc 92*
**Schaub**, Sherwood Anhder, Jr. 1942- *WhoFI 92*
**Schaub**, Stephen Alexander 1940- *AmMWSc 92*
**Schaubel**, Howard James 1916- *WhoMW 92*
**Schaubert**, Daniel Harold 1947- *AmMWSc 92*
**Schauble**, J Herman 1932- *AmMWSc 92*
**Schauble**, Wolfgang 1942- *IntWW 91*
**Schauenberg**, Susan Kay 1945- *WhoMW 92*
**Schauer**, Al Richard 1935- *WhoMW 92*
**Schauer**, Frederick Franklin 1946- *WhoAmL 92*
**Schauer**, John Joseph 1936- *AmMWSc 92*
**Schauer**, Louis Frank 1928- *WhoAmL 92*
**Schauer**, Paul Daniel 1944- *WhoAmP 91*
**Schauer**, Randall Charles 1956- *WhoAmL 92*
**Schauer**, Richard C 1937- *AmMWSc 92*
**Schauer**, Thomas Alfred 1927- *WhoFI 92, WhoMW 92*
**Schauer**, Tone Terjesen 1941- *WhoAmL 92*
**Schauf**, Charles Lawrence 1943- *AmMWSc 92*
**Schauf**, Debara K 1948- *WhoAmP 91*
**Schauf**, Frederick John 1952- *WhoAmL 92*
**Schauf**, Lawrence E. *WhoAmL 92*
**Schauf**, Susan Marie 1951- *WhoAmL 92*
**Schauf**, Victoria 1943- *AmMWSc 92*
**Schaufele**, Roger Donald 1928- *AmMWSc 92*
**Schaufele**, Ronald A 1930- *AmMWSc 92*
**Schaufele**, William Everett, Jr 1923- *WhoAmP 91*
**Schauffert**, Arthur Richard, Jr. 1951- *WhoFI 92*
**Schauffler**, Robert Haven 1879-1964 *BenetAL 91*
**Schaufuss**, Peter 1949- *FacFETw*
**Schaufuss**, Peter 1950- *IntWW 91, Who 92, WhoEnt 92*
**Schaumann**, Rolf 1941- *AmMWSc 92*
**Schaumberg**, Gene David 1939- *AmMWSc 92*
**Schaumberger**, Norman 1929- *AmMWSc 92*
**Schaumburg**, Frank David 1938- *AmMWSc 92*
**Schaumburg**, Herbert Howard 1932- *AmMWSc 92*
**Schaunaman**, Craig *WhoAmP 91*
**Schaus**, Magilla 1951- *WhoEnt 92*
**Schauwecker**, Harry E. 1928- *WhoWest 92*
**Schauwecker**, Margaret Liddie 1934- *WhoFI 92*
**Schawinsky**, Xanti 1904- *DcTwDes*
**Schawlow**, Arthur Leonard 1921- *AmMWSc 92, IntWW 91, Who 92, WhoNob 90, WhoWest 92*
**Schay**, Geza 1934- *AmMWSc 92*
**Schayer**, Richard William 1915- *AmMWSc 92*
**Schea**, Henry Emile, III 1952- *WhoWest 92*
**Scheaffer**, John E 1916- *WhoAmP 91*
**Scheaffer**, Richard Lewis 1940- *AmMWSc 92*
**Schear**, Anthony Dean 1966- *WhoWest 92*
**Schear**, Neal Eugene 1956- *WhoMW 92*
**Schearer**, Karin Johanna 1960- *WhoWest 92*
**Schearer**, Laird D 1931- *AmMWSc 92*
**Schearer**, Sherwood Bruce 1942- *AmMWSc 92*
**Schearer**, William Richard 1935- *AmMWSc 92*
**Scheb**, John Malcolm 1926- *WhoAmL 92*
**Scheb**, Nancy Marie 1947- *WhoRel 92*
**Schebera**, Richard Louis 1937- *WhoRel 92*
**Schechner**, Paul Sheridan 1958- *WhoFI 92*
**Schechner**, Richard 1934- *WhoEnt 92*
**Schechter**, Alan Neil 1939- *AmMWSc 92*
**Schechter**, Allen Edward 1935- *WhoMW 92*
**Schechter**, Clifford 1958- *WhoFI 92*
**Schechter**, Daniel 1931- *AmMWSc 92*
**Schechter**, David Alan 1939- *WhoAmL 92*
**Schechter**, Donald Robert 1946- *WhoAmL 92*
**Schechter**, Geraldine Poppa 1938- *AmMWSc 92*
**Schechter**, Joel 1947- *WhoEnt 92*
**Schechter**, Joel Ernest 1939- *AmMWSc 92*
**Schechter**, Joseph M 1938- *AmMWSc 92*
**Schechter**, Marshall David 1921- *AmMWSc 92*
**Schechter**, Martin 1930- *AmMWSc 92, WhoWest 92*
**Schechter**, Martin David 1945- *AmMWSc 92*
**Schechter**, Michael Gene 1946- *WhoMW 92*
**Schechter**, Milton Seymour 1915- *AmMWSc 92*
**Schechter**, Murray 1935- *AmMWSc 92*
**Schechter**, Nisson 1940- *AmMWSc 92*
**Schechter**, Paul J. 1939- *WhoMW 92*
**Schechter**, Robert Ben 1956- *WhoEnt 92*
**Schechter**, Robert Samuel 1929- *AmMWSc 92*
**Schechter**, Ruth Lisa *IntAu&W 91*
**Schechter**, Ruth Lisa 1927- *WrDr 92*
**Schechter**, Solomon 1850?-1915 *RelLAm 91*
**Schechter**, Steven C. 1966- *WhoEnt 92*
**Schechter**, Sue 1952- *WhoAmP 91*
**Schechterman**, Lawrence 1943- *WhoAmL 92*
**Schechtman**, Barry H 1943- *AmMWSc 92*
**Scheck**, Dennis Randall 1951- *WhoRel 92*
**Scheck**, Frank Foetisch 1923- *WhoAmL 92*
**Scheckler**, Stephen Edward 1944- *AmMWSc 92*
**Scheckter**, Jody David 1950- *IntWW 91*
**Schecter**, Amy 1953- *WhoEnt 92*
**Schecter**, Arnold Joel 1934- *AmMWSc 92*
**Schecter**, Larry 1920- *AmMWSc 92*
**Schecter**, Mary Virginia 1909- *WhoAmP 91*
**Schecter**, Richard Lawrence 1948- *WhoFI 92*
**Schecter**, Sheldon Dale 1926- *WhoAmP 91*
**Schecter**, William H. *WhoMW 92*
**Schectman**, Richard Milton 1932- *AmMWSc 92, WhoMW 92*
**Schectman**, Stephen Barry 1947- *WhoFI 92*
**Schedl**, Harold Paul 1920- *AmMWSc 92*
**Schedler**, Gilbert *DrAPF 91*
**Schedler**, Gilbert Walter 1935- *WhoRel 92*
**Schedler**, Norbert Oscar 1933- *WhoRel 92*
**Schedvin**, Carl Boris 1936- *WrDr 92*
**Scheeder**, Louis William 1946- *WhoEnt 92*
**Scheel**, Carl Alfred 1923- *AmMWSc 92*
**Scheel**, Gustav Adolf 1907-1979 *EncTR 91 [port]*
**Scheel**, Konrad Wolfgang 1932- *AmMWSc 92*
**Scheel**, Mark *DrAPF 91*
**Scheel**, Nivard 1925- *AmMWSc 92*
**Scheel**, Terril Grace 1960- *WhoMW 92*
**Scheel**, Walter 1919- *IntWW 91, Who 92*
**Scheele**, George F 1935- *AmMWSc 92*
**Scheele**, Leonard Andrew 1907- *AmMWSc 92*
**Scheele**, Robert Blain 1940- *AmMWSc 92*
**Scheele**, Roy *DrAPF 91*
**Scheele**, Roy 1942- *WrDr 92*
**Scheeline**, Alexander 1952- *AmMWSc 92, WhoMW 92*
**Scheer**, Alfred C 1926- *AmMWSc 92*
**Scheer**, Bradley Titus 1914- *AmMWSc 92*
**Scheer**, Donald Jordan 1934- *AmMWSc 92*
**Scheer**, Francois 1934- *IntWW 91*
**Scheer**, Janet Kathy 1947- *WhoMW 92*
**Scheer**, Joel Martin 1950- *WhoAmL 92*
**Scheer**, Julian Weisel 1926- *WhoFI 92*
**Scheer**, Milton David 1922- *AmMWSc 92*
**Scheer**, Scott A. 1950- *WhoRel 92*
**Scheer**, Verlin Harold 1949- *WhoIns 92*
**Scheerens**, Joseph Dean 1942- *WhoMW 92*
**Scheerer**, Anne Elizabeth 1924- *AmMWSc 92*
**Scheets**, Lawrence Joseph, III 1954- *WhoRel 92*
**Scheetz**, George Henry 1952- *WhoMW 92*
**Scheetz**, Howard A 1927- *AmMWSc 92*
**Scheetz**, JoEllen *WhoRel 92*
**Scheetz**, Terry R 1941- *WhoAmP 91*
**Schefer**, Robert Wilfred 1946- *AmMWSc 92*
**Scheff**, Benson H 1931- *AmMWSc 92*
**Scheff**, Gerald David 1956- *WhoMW 92*
**Scheff**, Hyman M. 1929- *WhoFI 92*
**Scheffauer**, Herman George 1878-1927 *ScFEYrs*
**Scheffel**, John Frederic 1937- *WhoAmL 92*
**Scheffer**, John R 1939- *AmMWSc 92*
**Scheffer**, Jules Emile 1924- *WhoEnt 92*
**Scheffer**, Robert Paul 1920- *AmMWSc 92*
**Scheffer**, Theodore Comstock 1904- *AmMWSc 92*
**Scheffer**, Victor B 1906- *AmMWSc 92, IntAu&W 91, WrDr 92*
**Scheffler**, Gary Dennis 1949- *WhoMW 92*
**Scheffler**, Immo Erich 1940- *AmMWSc 92*
**Scheffler**, Israel 1923- *IntWW 91*
**Scheffler**, Lewis Francis 1928- *WhoMW 92, WhoRel 92*
**Scheffler**, Stuart Jay 1950- *WhoAmL 92*
**Scheffman**, David Theodore 1943- *WhoFI 92*
**Schefft**, Bruce K. 1952- *WhoMW 92*
**Scheflin**, Alan Walter 1942- *WhoAmL 92*
**Scheflin**, Larry Steven 1946- *WhoEnt 92*
**Schehr**, Curtis Lorin 1958- *WhoAmL 92*
**Schehr**, Frank Edward 1947- *WhoMW 92*
**Schei**, Kenneth George 1940- *WhoWest 92*

**Scheib**, Richard, Jr 1914- *AmMWSc 92*
**Scheibe**, Erhard A. K. 1927- *IntWW 91*
**Scheibe**, Jeffrey Richard 1957- *WhoRel 92*
**Scheibe**, Johann Adolph 1708-1776 *NewAmDM*
**Scheibe**, Murray 1932- *AmMWSc 92*
**Scheibe**, Paul Otto 1934- *AmMWSc 92*
**Scheibel**, Arnold Bernard 1923- *AmMWSc 92*
**Scheibel**, Edward G 1917- *AmMWSc 92*
**Scheibel**, James *WhoAmP 91*
**Scheibel**, Jim 1947- *WhoMW 92*
**Scheibel**, Leonard William 1938- *AmMWSc 92*
**Scheiber**, David Hitz 1931- *AmMWSc 92*
**Scheiber**, Donald Joseph 1932- *AmMWSc 92*
**Scheiber**, Harry N 1935- *IntAu&W 91, WhoAmL 92, WhoWest 92, WrDr 92*
**Scheibl**, Jerome A 1930- *WhoIns 92*
**Scheible**, Wayne G. 1938- *WhoFI 92*
**Scheibner**, Rudolph A 1926- *AmMWSc 92*
**Scheich**, John F. 1942- *WhoAmL 92*
**Scheid**, Cheryl Russell 1948- *AmMWSc 92*
**Scheid**, Francis 1920- *AmMWSc 92*
**Scheid**, Harold E 1922- *AmMWSc 92*
**Scheid**, John Stephen 1955- *WhoMW 92*
**Scheid**, Linda J *WhoAmP 91*
**Scheid**, Stephan Andreas 1941- *AmMWSc 92*
**Scheide**, Richard Gilson 1929- *WhoFI 92*
**Scheidel**, Theodore C, Jr 1944- *WhoAmP 91*
**Scheidemann**, Philipp 1865-1939 *EncTR 91 [port], FacFETw*
**Scheidenhelm**, Richard Joy 1942- *WhoMW 92*
**Scheider**, Roy 1932- *IntMPA 92, IntWW 91*
**Scheider**, Roy Richard 1935- *WhoEnt 92*
**Scheider**, Walt 1930- *WhoAmP 91*
**Scheider**, Wilhelm 1928- *IntWW 91*
**Scheidt**, Francis Matthew 1922- *AmMWSc 92*
**Scheidt**, Lois Ann 1959- *WhoMW 92*
**Scheidt**, Samuel 1587-1654 *NewAmDM*
**Scheidt**, Virgil D 1928- *WhoAmP 91*
**Scheidt**, Walter Robert 1942- *AmMWSc 92*
**Scheie**, Carl Edward 1938- *AmMWSc 92*
**Scheie**, Harold Glendon 1909- *AmMWSc 92*
**Scheie**, Paul Olaf 1933- *AmMWSc 92*
**Scheier**, Michael 1943- *ConAu 36NR*
**Scheifly**, John Edward 1925- *WhoAmL 92*
**Scheig**, Robert L 1931- *AmMWSc 92*
**Scheiman**, Jody Gordon 1953- *WhoMW 92*
**Schein**, Arnold Harold 1916- *AmMWSc 92*
**Schein**, Boris M 1938- *AmMWSc 92*
**Schein**, Daniel Bradley 1959- *WhoAmL 92*
**Schein**, Eugenie *WhoEnt 92*
**Schein**, Hugh F. 1946- *WhoMW 92*
**Schein**, Jerome Daniel 1923- *AmMWSc 92*
**Schein**, Johann Hermann 1586-1630 *NewAmDM*
**Schein**, Lawrence Brian 1944- *AmMWSc 92*
**Schein**, Lorraine *DrAPF 91*
**Schein**, Martin Warren 1925- *AmMWSc 92*
**Schein**, Philip Samuel 1939- *AmMWSc 92*
**Schein**, Richard David 1927- *AmMWSc 92*
**Scheinbaum**, David 1951- *WhoWest 92*
**Scheinberg**, Barry Mark 1948- *WhoAmL 92*
**Scheinberg**, Eliyahu 1934- *AmMWSc 92*
**Scheinberg**, Israel Herbert 1919- *AmMWSc 92*
**Scheinberg**, Peritz 1920- *AmMWSc 92*
**Scheinberg**, Sam Louis 1922- *AmMWSc 92*
**Scheinberg**, Steven Eliot 1952- *WhoFI 92*
**Scheindlin**, Stanley 1926- *AmMWSc 92*
**Scheiner**, Bernard James 1938- *AmMWSc 92*
**Scheiner**, Donald M 1932- *AmMWSc 92*
**Scheiner**, Elliot Ray 1947- *WhoEnt 92*
**Scheiner**, Karen R. 1954- *WhoAmL 92*
**Scheiner**, Peter 1935- *AmMWSc 92*
**Scheiner**, Richard Lloyd 1953- *WhoFI 92*
**Scheiner**, Steve 1951- *AmMWSc 92*
**Scheineson**, Irwin Bruce 1955- *WhoFI 92*
**Scheinholtz**, Leonard Louis 1927- *WhoAmL 92*
**Scheinkman**, Alan David 1950- *WhoAmL 92*
**Scheinok**, Perry Aaron 1931- *AmMWSc 92*
**Scheirer**, Daniel Charles 1946- *AmMWSc 92*
**Scheirer**, James E 1943- *AmMWSc 92*
**Scheiring**, Joseph Frank 1945- *AmMWSc 92*
**Scheirman**, David William 1952- *WhoEnt 92*
**Scheiter**, B Joseph Paul 1935- *AmMWSc 92*
**Scheive**, Annette Marie 1953- *WhoMW 92*
**Schekel**, Kurt Anthony 1943- *AmMWSc 92*
**Schekman**, Randy W 1948- *AmMWSc 92*
**Schelar**, Virginia M. 1924- *WhoFI 92, WhoWest 92*
**Schelar**, Virginia Mae 1924- *AmMWSc 92*
**Schelberg**, Arthur Daniel 1921- *AmMWSc 92*
**Scheld**, Robert William 1920- *WhoIns 92*
**Scheld**, William Michael 1947- *AmMWSc 92*
**Scheldorf**, Jay J 1932- *AmMWSc 92*
**Scheldrup**, John M 1934- *WhoAmP 91*
**Scheler**, Brad Eric 1953- *WhoAmL 92*
**Scheler**, Werner 1923- *IntWW 91*
**Schell**, Allan Carter 1934- *AmMWSc 92*
**Schell**, Anne McCall 1942- *AmMWSc 92*
**Schell**, Farrel Loy 1931- *WhoWest 92*
**Schell**, Fred Martin 1943- *AmMWSc 92*
**Schell**, George W 1921- *AmMWSc 92*
**Schell**, Jessie *DrAPF 91*
**Schell**, Jonathan 1943- *WrDr 92*
**Schell**, Jonathan Edward 1943- *IntAu&W 91*
**Schell**, Joseph Francis 1928- *AmMWSc 92*
**Schell**, Joseph Otis 1914- *WhoRel 92*
**Schell**, Jozef Stephaan 1935- *IntWW 91*
**Schell**, Lois M 1943- *WhoAmP 91*
**Schell**, Maria 1926- *IntMPA 92*
**Schell**, Maximilian 1930- *IntMPA 92, IntWW 91, WhoEnt 92*
**Schell**, Orville 1940- *WrDr 92*
**Schell**, Orville Hickok 1940- *IntAu&W 91*
**Schell**, Richard A. 1950- *WhoAmL 92*
**Schell**, Robert Aloysius 1938- *WhoWest 92*
**Schell**, Robert Ray 1937- *AmMWSc 92*
**Schell**, Steven Donald 1956- *WhoMW 92*
**Schell**, Stewart Claude 1912- *AmMWSc 92*
**Schell**, Susan Elaine 1953- *WhoAmL 92*
**Schell**, William John 1940- *AmMWSc 92*
**Schell**, William R 1932- *AmMWSc 92*
**Schellberg**, Marta Glee 1948- *WhoRel 92*
**Schellberg**, Ruth Mildred 1912- *WhoMW 92*
**Schelle**, Johann 1648-1701 *NewAmDM*
**Schellenberg**, James A. 1932- *WrDr 92*
**Schellenberg**, James Arthur 1932- *IntAu&W 91*
**Schellenberg**, Karl A 1931- *AmMWSc 92*
**Schellenberg**, Paul Jacob 1942- *AmMWSc 92*
**Schellenberg**, Walter 1910-1952 *BiDExR, EncTR 91 [port]*
**Scheller**, Erin Linn 1942- *WhoWest 92*
**Scheller**, Sanford Gregory 1931- *WhoWest 92*
**Scheller**, W A 1929- *AmMWSc 92*
**Schellhorn**, Edward H *WhoAmP 91*
**Schellinck**, Marie 1771-1859 *EncAmaz 91*
**Schelling**, Ernest 1876-1939 *NewAmDM*
**Schelling**, Friedrich Wilhelm Eugen E von 1906- *IntWW 91*
**Schelling**, Friedrich Wilhelm Joseph von 1775-1854 *BlkwCEP*
**Schelling**, Gerald Thomas 1941- *AmMWSc 92*
**Schelling**, Gunther F. K. 1923- *IntWW 91*
**Schelling**, Thomas C. 1921- *WrDr 92*
**Schelling**, Thomas Crombie 1921- *IntAu&W 91, IntWW 91, WhoFI 92*
**Schelling**, Tim A. 1950- *WhoRel 92*
**Schellman**, James *WhoRel 92*
**Schellman**, John Anthony 1924- *AmMWSc 92*
**Schellow**, Erich 1915- *IntWW 91*
**Schellpeper**, Stan 1934- *WhoAmP 91*
**Schelly**, Zoltan Andrew 1938- *AmMWSc 92*
**Schelp**, Richard Herbert 1936- *AmMWSc 92*
**Schelper**, Robert Lawrence 1948- *AmMWSc 92*
**Schelske**, Claire L 1932- *AmMWSc 92*
**Scheltema**, Rudolf S 1926- *AmMWSc 92*
**Scheltgen**, Elmer 1930- *AmMWSc 92*
**Scheman**, Andrew Joseph 1953- *WhoMW 92*
**Schemann**, Ludwig 1852-1938 *EncTR 91*
**Schembechler**, Bo 1929- *WhoMW 92*
**Schember**, Daniel McCrea 1949- *WhoAmL 92*
**Schembri**, Carmelo 1922- *Who 92*
**Schemenauer**, Robert 1934- *WhoAmP 91*
**Schemenauer**, Robert Stuart 1946- *AmMWSc 92*
**Schemm**, Charles Edward 1947- *AmMWSc 92*
**Schemm**, Hans 1891-1935 *EncTR 91 [port]*
**Schemmel**, Rachel A 1929- *AmMWSc 92*
**Schemmel**, Rachel Anne 1929- *WhoMW 92*
**Schemnitz**, Sanford David 1930- *AmMWSc 92*
**Schempp**, Ellory *AmMWSc 92*
**Schemske**, Douglas William 1948- *AmMWSc 92*
**Schena**, Francesco Paolo 1940- *AmMWSc 92*
**Schenberg**, Ivan Irl 1939- *WhoAmP 91*
**Schenck**, A. William, III 1943- *WhoFI 92*
**Schenck**, Alan Earl 1946- *WhoMW 92*
**Schenck**, Andrew Craig 1941- *WhoEnt 92*
**Schenck**, Aubrey 1908- *IntMPA 92*
**Schenck**, Charles Carroll 1871-1914 *BiInAmS*
**Schenck**, Frederick A. 1928- *WhoBlA 92*
**Schenck**, Harry Allen 1938- *AmMWSc 92*
**Schenck**, Henry Paul 1929- *WhoFI 92*
**Schenck**, Hilbert 1926- *TwCSFW 91, WrDr 92*
**Schenck**, Hilbert Van Nydeck, Jr 1926- *AmMWSc 92*
**Schenck**, Jay Ruffner 1915- *AmMWSc 92*
**Schenck**, John Frederic 1939- *AmMWSc 92*
**Schenck**, John Phillip 1933- *WhoMW 92*
**Schenck**, Mary Lyon 1964- *WhoEnt 92*
**Schenck**, Michael U. R. von 1931- *IntWW 91*
**Schenck**, Norman Carl 1928- *AmMWSc 92*
**Schenck**, Paul Haim 1958- *WhoRel 92*
**Schenck**, Robert Leonard 1958- *WhoRel 92*
**Schencman**, Mario Eduardo 1938- *WhoEnt 92*
**Schendel**, Winfried George 1931- *WhoWest 92*
**Scheneman**, Mark Allan 1948- *WhoRel 92*
**Schengrund**, Cara-Lynne 1941- *AmMWSc 92*
**Schenk**, Christopher John 1962- *WhoFI 92*
**Schenk**, Deborah H. 1947- *WhoAmL 92*
**Schenk**, Eric A *AmMWSc 92*
**Schenk**, H L, Jr 1929- *AmMWSc 92*
**Schenk**, Johann 1753-1836 *NewAmDM*
**Schenk**, John Albright 1924- *AmMWSc 92*
**Schenk**, Joseph Anthony 1949- *WhoMW 92*
**Schenk**, Joyce 1937- *IntAu&W 91*
**Schenk**, Paul Edward 1937- *AmMWSc 92*
**Schenk**, Ray Merlin 1946- *WhoWest 92*
**Schenk**, Richard Charles 1951- *WhoRel 92*
**Schenk**, Robert Joseph 1962- *WhoMW 92*
**Schenk**, Roy Urban 1929- *AmMWSc 92*
**Schenk**, Worthington G, Jr 1922- *AmMWSc 92*
**Schenkar**, Joan 1946- *ConAu 133*
**Schenkein**, William Edward 1963- *WhoWest 92*
**Schenkel**, Barbara Ann 1951- *WhoRel 92*
**Schenkel**, Chris *LesBEnT 92*
**Schenkel**, John Alan 1934- *WhoMW 92*
**Schenkel**, Robert H 1944- *AmMWSc 92*
**Schenkelberg**, David Charles 1948- *WhoFI 92*
**Schenken**, Jerald R 1933- *AmMWSc 92, WhoAmP 91*
**Schenkenberg**, Paul Wayne 1953- *WhoMW 92*
**Schenkenberg**, Thomas 1943- *AmMWSc 92*
**Schenker**, Dona 1947- *ConAu 135, SmATA 68 [port]*
**Schenker**, Eric 1931- *WhoFI 92*
**Schenker**, Heinrich 1868-1935 *NewAmDM*
**Schenker**, Henry Hans 1926- *AmMWSc 92*
**Schenker**, Joseph G. 1933- *IntWW 91*
**Schenker**, Marc Benet 1947- *WhoWest 92*
**Schenker**, Steven 1929- *AmMWSc 92*
**Schenkkan**, Dirk McKenzie 1949- *WhoAmL 92*
**Schenkkan**, Pieter Meade 1947- *WhoAmL 92*
**Schenkler**, Bernard 1948- *WhoAmL 92*
**Schenkman**, John Boris 1936- *AmMWSc 92*
**Schennum**, Wayne Edward 1949- *AmMWSc 92*
**Schenter**, Robert Earl 1937- *AmMWSc 92*
**Schenz**, Anne Filer 1945- *AmMWSc 92, WhoMW 92*
**Schenz**, Timothy William 1946- *AmMWSc 92, WhoMW 92*
**Schepartz**, Abner Irwin 1922- *AmMWSc 92*
**Schepartz**, Bernard 1918- *AmMWSc 92*
**Schepartz**, Saul Alexander 1929- *AmMWSc 92*
**Schepeler**, Jeanine Marie 1957- *WhoMW 92*
**Schepers**, Donald Herbert 1951- *WhoMW 92, WhoRel 92*
**Schepers**, Marlyn Glenn 1933- *WhoAmP 91*
**Schepisi**, Fred 1939- *IntDcF 2-2 [port], IntMPA 92*
**Schepisi**, Frederic Alan 1939- *IntAu&W 91, IntWW 91*
**Schepler**, Kenneth Lee 1949- *AmMWSc 92, WhoMW 92*
**Schepp**, George Phillip, Jr. 1955- *WhoWest 92*
**Scheppers**, Gerald J 1933- *AmMWSc 92*
**Scher**, Allen Myron 1921- *AmMWSc 92*
**Scher**, Charles D 1939- *AmMWSc 92*
**Scher**, Herbert Benson 1937- *AmMWSc 92*
**Scher**, Irving 1933- *WhoAmL 92*
**Scher**, Maryonda E 1931- *AmMWSc 92*
**Scher**, Paul Lawrence 1934- *WhoMW 92*
**Scher**, Robert Sander 1934- *AmMWSc 92*
**Scher**, William *AmMWSc 92*
**Scheraga**, Harold A. 1921- *IntWW 91*
**Scheraga**, Harold Abraham 1921- *AmMWSc 92*
**Scheraga**, Joel Dov 1955- *WhoFI 92*
**Scherb**, Frank 1930- *AmMWSc 92*
**Scherba**, Gerald Marron 1927- *AmMWSc 92*
**Scherbakov**, Vladimir Ivanovich 1949- *IntWW 91*
**Scherbarth**, Ray Edwin 1941- *WhoRel 92*
**Scherbenske**, M James 1937- *AmMWSc 92*
**Scherber**, Kit Catherine 1947- *WhoAmP 91*
**Scherberg**, Neal Harvey 1939- *AmMWSc 92*
**Scherberger**, Karen Jean 1962- *WhoFI 92*
**Scherch**, Richard Otto 1926- *WhoRel 92*
**Scherchen**, Hermann 1891-1966 *FacFETw, NewAmDM*
**Scherchen**, Tona 1938- *ConCom 92*
**Schereck**, William John 1913- *WhoMW 92*
**Scherer**, Alfredo Vicente 1903- *IntWW 91, WhoRel 92*
**Scherer**, Anita 1938- *WhoMW 92*
**Scherer**, Carol Louise 1943- *WhoAmP 91*
**Scherer**, Christopher Howard 1965- *WhoEnt 92*
**Scherer**, Frederic Michael 1932- *WhoFI 92*
**Scherer**, George Allen 1907- *AmMWSc 92*
**Scherer**, George Walter 1949- *AmMWSc 92*
**Scherer**, Gregg Charles 1948- *WhoMW 92*
**Scherer**, Harold Nicholas, Jr 1929- *AmMWSc 92*
**Scherer**, Jacques 1912- *Who 92*
**Scherer**, James R 1931- *AmMWSc 92*
**Scherer**, John Robert 1950- *WhoFI 92*
**Scherer**, Kirby Vaughn, Jr 1936- *AmMWSc 92*
**Scherer**, Maurice 1920- *WhoEnt 92*
**Scherer**, Paul 1892-1969 *ConAu 134*
**Scherer**, Paul Joseph 1933- *Who 92*
**Scherer**, Peter Julian 1937- *IntWW 91*
**Scherer**, Peter William 1942- *AmMWSc 92*
**Scherer**, Randy Lynn 1956- *WhoMW 92*
**Scherer**, Ray *LesBEnT 92*
**Scherer**, Robert C 1931- *AmMWSc 92*
**Scherer**, Ronald Callaway 1945- *AmMWSc 92, WhoEnt 92, WhoWest 92*
**Scherer**, Scott *WhoAmP 91*
**Scherer**, Victor Richard 1940- *WhoMW 92*
**Scherfig**, Jan W 1936- *AmMWSc 92*
**Scherger**, Dale Albert 1949- *AmMWSc 92*
**Scherger**, Joseph E. 1950- *WhoWest 92*
**Scherich**, Erwin Thomas 1918- *WhoFI 92, WhoWest 92*
**Scherick**, Edgar J. *LesBEnT 92*
**Scherick**, Edgar J. 1924- *IntMPA 92*
**Scherk**, Peter 1910- *AmMWSc 92*
**Scherkenbach**, Frank Everett 1963- *WhoAmL 92*
**Scherlag**, Benjamin J 1932- *AmMWSc 92*
**Scherle**, William J 1923- *WhoAmP 91*
**Scherler**, Burl Mark 1950- *WhoAmP 91*
**Scherman**, Paul H. *WhoRel 92*
**Scherman**, Thomas 1917-1979 *NewAmDM*
**Schermer**, Eugene DeWayne 1934- *AmMWSc 92*
**Schermer**, J. Leonard 1917- *WhoAmL 92*
**Schermer**, Judith Kahn 1949- *WhoAmL 92*
**Schermer**, Robert Ira 1934- *AmMWSc 92*
**Schermerhorn**, John W 1920- *AmMWSc 92*
**Schermerhorn**, Kenneth 1929- *NewAmDM*
**Schermerhorn**, Kenneth Dewitt 1929- *WhoEnt 92*
**Schermerhorn**, Richard E 1927- *WhoAmP 91*
**Schermerhorn**, Scott Benjamin 1960- *WhoFI 92*
**Schermers**, Henry G. 1928- *IntWW 91*
**Schermers**, Henry Gerhard 1928- *Who 92*
**Schernitzki**, Paul Thomas 1951- *WhoMW 92*
**Scherpereel**, Donald E 1937- *AmMWSc 92*
**Scherr**, Allan L 1940- *AmMWSc 92*
**Scherr**, Charles W 1926- *AmMWSc 92*
**Scherr**, David DeLano 1934- *AmMWSc 92*
**Scherr**, George Harry 1920- *AmMWSc 92, WhoMW 92*
**Scherr**, Harry, III 1944- *WhoFI 92*

**Scherr**, Lawrence 1928- *AmMWSc 92*
**Scherr**, Stephen Arthur 1938- *WhoAmP 91*
**Scherrer**, Joseph Henry 1931- *AmMWSc 92*
**Scherrer**, Rene 1932- *AmMWSc 92*
**Scherrer**, Robert Allan 1932- *AmMWSc 92*
**Scherrer-Bylund**, Paul 1900- *IntWW 91*
**Schertz**, Cletus E 1930- *AmMWSc 92*
**Schertz**, Keith Francis 1927- *AmMWSc 92*
**Schertz**, Mary Helen 1949- *WhoRel 92*
**Schervish**, Mark John 1953- *AmMWSc 92*
**Schery**, Stephen Dale 1945- *AmMWSc 92*
**Scherz**, James Phillip 1937- *AmMWSc 92*
**Scherzer**, Joel *DrAPF 91*
**Schetky**, L M 1922- *AmMWSc 92*
**Schettler**, Paul Davis, Jr 1937- *AmMWSc 92*
**Schetz**, Joseph A 1936- *AmMWSc 92*
**Schetzen**, Martin 1928- *AmMWSc 92*
**Schetzina**, Jan Frederick 1940- *AmMWSc 92*
**Scheu**, Leonard 1904- *WhoWest 92*
**Scheuble**, Philip Arthur, Jr. 1919- *WhoMW 92*
**Scheuch**, Don Ralph 1918- *AmMWSc 92*
**Scheuch**, Erwin K. 1928- *IntWW 91*
**Scheuchenzuber**, H Joseph 1944- *AmMWSc 92*
**Scheuer**, Ernest Martin 1930- *AmMWSc 92*
**Scheuer**, James 1931- *AmMWSc 92*
**Scheuer**, James H. 1920- *AlmAP 92 [port]*, *WhoAmP 91*
**Scheuer**, Paul Josef 1915- *AmMWSc 92*
**Scheuer**, Roger J. 1951- *WhoWest 92*
**Scheuer-Suevel**, Markay Lynn 1959- *WhoRel 92*
**Scheuerle**, Angela Elizabeth 1962- *WhoMW 92*
**Scheuerle**, Paul Norman 1926- *WhoEnt 92*
**Scheufele**, Brian Karl 1958- *WhoWest 92*
**Scheuing**, Richard A 1927- *AmMWSc 92*
**Scheuring**, Garry Joseph 1939- *WhoFI 92*
**Scheusner**, Dale Lee 1944- *AmMWSc 92*, *WhoMW 92*
**Scheuzger**, Thomas Peter 1960- *WhoEnt 92*
**Scheve**, Bernard Joseph 1945- *AmMWSc 92*
**Scheve**, Larry Gerard 1950- *AmMWSc 92*
**Scheve**, May E 1964- *WhoAmP 91*
**Schevill**, James *DrAPF 91*
**Schevill**, James 1920- *ConPo 91*, *IntAu&W 91*, *IntWW 91*, *WrDr 92*
**Scheving**, Lawrence Einar 1920- *AmMWSc 92*
**Schewe**, Phillip 1950- *WhoEnt 92*
**Schewe**, Phillip Frank 1950- *AmMWSc 92*
**Schewel**, Elliot Sidney 1924- *WhoAmP 91*
**Schexnayder**, Brian Edward 1953- *WhoEnt 92*
**Schexnayder**, Charlotte Tillar 1923- *WhoAmP 91*
**Schexnayder**, Mary Anne 1948- *AmMWSc 92*
**Schexnayder**, Thomas Florent 1933- *WhoAmP 91*
**Schexnider**, Alvin J. 1945- *WhoBlA 92*
**Schey**, Harry Moritz 1930- *AmMWSc 92*
**Schey**, John Anthony 1922- *AmMWSc 92*
**Scheyer**, Daniel 1928- *WhoAmL 92*
**Schiaffino**, Silvio Stephen 1927- *AmMWSc 92*
**Schiager**, Keith Jerome 1930- *AmMWSc 92*
**Schiapo**, Bambino *WhoAmP 91*
**Schiappa**, Michael Paul 1964- *WhoMW 92*
**Schiavelli**, Melvyn David 1942- *AmMWSc 92*
**Schiavinato**, Giuseppe 1915- *IntWW 91*
**Schiavo**, Pasco Louis 1937- *WhoAmL 92*
**Schiavone**, James 1917- *IntMPA 92*
**Schiavone**, Richard Gerard 1953- *WhoEnt 92*
**Schiazza**, Guido Domenic 1930- *WhoFI 92*
**Schibanoff**, Harry Andrew 1947- *WhoFI 92*
**Schick**, Albert John *WhoIns 92*
**Schick**, Dorothy Wasserman 1930- *WhoAmP 91*
**Schick**, Elliot *WhoFI 92*
**Schick**, Elliot 1924- *IntMPA 92*
**Schick**, Harry Leon 1927- *WhoFI 92*
**Schick**, James Baldwin McDonald 1940- *WhoMW 92*
**Schick**, Jerome David 1938- *AmMWSc 92*
**Schick**, Kenneth Leonard 1930- *AmMWSc 92*
**Schick**, Lee Henry 1935- *AmMWSc 92*
**Schick**, Lloyd Alan 1945- *AmMWSc 92*
**Schick**, Martin J 1918- *AmMWSc 92*
**Schick**, Michael 1939- *AmMWSc 92*
**Schick**, Paul Kenneth 1932- *AmMWSc 92*
**Schick**, Robert Michael 1954- *WhoAmL 92*
**Schick**, Thomas Edward 1941- *WhoFI 92*
**Schickedantz**, Paul David 1931- *AmMWSc 92*
**Schickel**, Carol Rubinstein d1991 *NewYTBS 91*
**Schickel**, Richard 1933- *ConAu 34NR*, *IntAu&W 91*, *IntWW 91*, *WhoEnt 92*, *WrDr 92*
**Schickele**, Peter 1935- *NewAmDM*, *WhoEnt 92*
**Schicklgruber** *EncTR 91*
**Schieber**, Sylvester Joseph 1946- *WhoFI 92*
**Schiebler**, Gerold Ludwig 1928- *AmMWSc 92*
**Schiebout**, Judith Ann 1946- *AmMWSc 92*
**Schieder**, Joseph Eugene 1908- *WhoRel 92*
**Schiefelbein**, Kenneth Roland 1943- *WhoAmP 91*
**Schiefer**, Alicia C. 1958- *WhoHisp 92*
**Schieferstein**, George Jacob 1942- *AmMWSc 92*
**Schieferstein**, Robert Harold 1931- *AmMWSc 92*
**Schieffelin**, Thomas Lawrence 1936- *WhoFI 92*
**Schieffer**, Bob *IntWW 91*, *LesBEnT 92*
**Schieffer**, Rudolf 1947- *IntWW 91*
**Schiel**, John Michael 1937- *WhoWest 92*
**Schiele**, Charles Burtrum 1942- *WhoMW 92*
**Schiele**, Egon 1890-1918 *FacFETw*
**Schiele**, James Edwin 1929- *WhoFI 92*
**Schiele**, Paul Ellsworth, Jr. 1924- *WhoWest 92*
**Schielke**, Hugo Josef Hans 1938- *WhoFI 92*
**Schiell**, Charles Randall 1952- *WhoWest 92*
**Schiemann**, Konrad Hermann Theodor 1937- *Who 92*
**Schienle**, Jan Hoops 1945- *AmMWSc 92*
**Schierman**, Louis W 1926- *AmMWSc 92*
**Schiermeyer**, Ruth Corry 1938- *WhoAmP 91*
**Schierse**, Paul J. 1928- *WhoRel 92*
**Schiesler**, Mary Antoinette 1934- *WhoBlA 92*
**Schiesler**, Robert Alan 1949- *WhoRel 92*
**Schiess**, Betty Bone 1923- *WhoRel 92*
**Schiess**, Ulrich John 1949- *WhoWest 92*
**Schiesser**, Robert H 1937- *AmMWSc 92*
**Schiesser**, W E 1934- *AmMWSc 92*
**Schiessl**, Carl John 1959- *WhoAmP 91*
**Schiessl**, Daniel Mark 1959- *WhoRel 92*
**Schiessl**, H W 1924- *AmMWSc 92*
**Schiesswohl**, Cynthia Rae Schlegel 1955- *WhoAmL 92*
**Schieve**, William 1929- *AmMWSc 92*
**Schiewetz**, D B 1927- *AmMWSc 92*
**Schifano**, Larry E 1949- *WhoAmP 91*
**Schiferl**, David *AmMWSc 92*
**Schiff**, Andras 1953- *IntWW 91*, *Who 92*
**Schiff**, Anshel J 1936- *AmMWSc 92*
**Schiff**, April 1957- *WhoAmL 92*
**Schiff**, Charles *WhoEnt 92*
**Schiff**, Dobbie G. *WhoEnt 92*
**Schiff**, Emile Louis Constant 1918- *IntWW 91*
**Schiff**, Eric Allan 1950- *AmMWSc 92*
**Schiff**, Gary Stuart 1947- *WhoRel 92*
**Schiff**, Gilbert Martin 1931- *AmMWSc 92*
**Schiff**, Gunther Hans 1927- *WhoAmL 92*
**Schiff**, Harold Irvin 1923- *AmMWSc 92*
**Schiff**, Harris *DrAPF 91*
**Schiff**, Harry 1922- *AmMWSc 92*
**Schiff**, Jacob H 1847-1920 *DcAmImH*
**Schiff**, Jayne Nemerow 1945- *WhoFI 92*
**Schiff**, Jerome A 1931- *AmMWSc 92*
**Schiff**, Joel D 1943- *AmMWSc 92*
**Schiff**, John Jefferson 1916- *WhoIns 92*, *WhoMW 92*
**Schiff**, John Jefferson, Jr. 1916- *WhoFI 92*
**Schiff**, Kenneth Edmund 1963- *WhoFI 92*
**Schiff**, Laurie 1960- *WhoEnt 92*
**Schiff**, Leon 1901- *AmMWSc 92*
**Schiff**, Leonard Norman 1938- *AmMWSc 92*
**Schiff**, Marlene Sandler *WhoFI 92*
**Schiff**, Martha May 1924- *WhoAmP 91*
**Schiff**, Marvin Evan 1937- *WhoAmL 92*
**Schiff**, Molly Jeanette 1927- *WhoMW 92*
**Schiff**, Paul L, Jr 1940- *AmMWSc 92*
**Schiff**, Sidney 1929- *AmMWSc 92*
**Schiff**, Stefan Otto 1930- *AmMWSc 92*
**Schiff**, Stephen *WhoEnt 92*
**Schiff**, Steven H. 1947- *AlmAP 92 [port]*
**Schiff**, Steven Harvey 1947- *WhoWest 92*
**Schiff**, Steven Howard 1947- *WhoAmP 91*
**Schiff**, Zina Leah 1953- *WhoEnt 92*
**Schiffbauer**, William G. 1954- *WhoAmL 92*, *WhoAmP 91*
**Schiffel**, Suzanne Driscoll 1946- *WhoMW 92*
**Schiffeler**, John William 1940- *WhoWest 92*
**Schiffer**, Daniel L. *WhoFI 92*
**Schiffer**, Ira Jeffrey 1951- *WhoRel 92*
**Schiffer**, John Paul 1930- *AmMWSc 92*
**Schiffer**, Lois Jane 1945- *WhoAmL 92*
**Schiffer**, Marianne Tsuk 1935- *AmMWSc 92*
**Schiffer**, Menahem Max 1911- *AmMWSc 92*, *IntWW 91*
**Schiffer**, Michael Brian 1947- *WhoWest 92*
**Schifferman**, Reed Philip 1955- *WhoAmL 92*
**Schiffmacher**, E R 1924- *AmMWSc 92*
**Schiffman**, Daniel 1932- *WhoAmL 92*
**Schiffman**, Gerald *AmMWSc 92*
**Schiffman**, Jack Henry 1921- *WhoEnt 92*
**Schiffman**, Louis F 1927- *AmMWSc 92*, *WhoFI 92*
**Schiffman**, Robert A 1945- *AmMWSc 92*
**Schiffman**, Robert L 1923- *AmMWSc 92*
**Schiffman**, Sandra 1937- *AmMWSc 92*
**Schiffman**, Stephan 1946- *WhoFI 92*
**Schiffman**, Susan S 1940- *AmMWSc 92*
**Schiffmann**, Elliot 1927- *AmMWSc 92*
**Schiffmann**, Robert F 1935- *AmMWSc 92*
**Schiffner**, Charles Robert 1948- *WhoWest 92*
**Schiffner**, Joan Lessing 1944- *WhoWest 92*
**Schiffres**, Irwin Jacob 1930- *WhoAmL 92*
**Schiffrin**, Andre 1935- *IntWW 91*
**Schiffrin**, Ernesto Luis 1946- *AmMWSc 92*
**Schiffrin**, Michael Edward 1946- *WhoAmL 92*
**Schiffrin**, Milton Julius 1914- *AmMWSc 92*, *WhoWest 92*
**Schifreen**, Richard Steven 1952- *AmMWSc 92*
**Schifrin**, Lalo 1932- *IntMPA 92*, *NewAmDM*, *WhoEnt 92*
**Schiftan**, Hans 1899-1941 *EncTR 91*
**Schifter**, Richard 1923- *WhoAmP 91*
**Schifter**, Richard Paul 1953- *WhoAmL 92*
**Schikaneder**, Emanuel 1751-1812 *NewAmDM*
**Schilb**, Theodore Paul 1933- *AmMWSc 92*
**Schilbrack**, Karen Gail 1949- *WhoWest 92*
**Schild**, Albert 1920- *AmMWSc 92*
**Schild**, Geoffrey Christopher 1935- *Who 92*
**Schild**, Rudolph Ernest 1940- *AmMWSc 92*
**Schildberg**, Yvonne Marie 1927- *WhoAmP 91*
**Schildcrout**, Michael 1943- *AmMWSc 92*
**Schildcrout**, Steven Michael 1943- *AmMWSc 92*, *WhoMW 92*
**Schildhause**, Sol *LesBEnT 92*
**Schildkraut**, Carl Louis 1937- *AmMWSc 92*
**Schildkraut**, Joseph Jacob 1934- *AmMWSc 92*
**Schildwachter**, Stephen, Jr. 1962- *WhoMW 92*
**Schile**, Richard Douglas 1931- *AmMWSc 92*
**Schilffarth**, Richard Allen 1931- *WhoAmP 91*
**Schilhab**, Sian Rose 1963- *WhoAmL 92*
**Schilit**, Diane Lipson 1956- *WhoRel 92*
**Schilke**, Charles Noel 1955- *WhoAmL 92*
**Schilke**, Joan Mossong 1943- *WhoMW 92*
**Schillaci**, Mario Edward 1940- *AmMWSc 92*
**Schiller**, Alfred George 1918- *AmMWSc 92*
**Schiller**, Arthur James 1954- *WhoAmL 92*, *WhoMW 92*
**Schiller**, Arthur Michael 1930- *WhoAmL 92*
**Schiller**, Carol Masters 1940- *AmMWSc 92*
**Schiller**, Donald Charles 1942- *WhoAmL 92*
**Schiller**, Fred 1924- *IntMPA 92*
**Schiller**, Friedrich 1940- *WhoMW 92*
**Schiller**, Friedrich von 1759-1805 *BlkwCEP*
**Schiller**, Ginnell Mary 1955- *WhoMW 92*
**Schiller**, Howard Barry 1949- *WhoAmL 92*
**Schiller**, James Joseph 1933- *WhoAmL 92*, *WhoAmP 91*
**Schiller**, Jerry A. 1932- *WhoFI 92*
**Schiller**, Johannes August 1923- *WhoRel 92*, *WhoWest 92*
**Schiller**, John Joseph 1935- *AmMWSc 92*
**Schiller**, Karl 1911- *IntWW 91*, *Who 92*
**Schiller**, Lawrence J. 1936- *IntMPA 92*
**Schiller**, Lawrence Julian 1936- *WhoEnt 92*
**Schiller**, Neal Leander 1949- *AmMWSc 92*
**Schiller**, Paul Omar 1950- *WhoWest 92*
**Schiller**, Peter Wilhelm 1942- *AmMWSc 92*
**Schiller**, Ralph 1926- *AmMWSc 92*
**Schiller**, Robert Achille 1918- *WhoEnt 92*
**Schiller**, William R 1937- *AmMWSc 92*
**Schilletter**, Julian Claude 1901- *AmMWSc 92*
**Schilling**, Allan Edward 1935- *WhoFI 92*
**Schilling**, Charles H 1918- *AmMWSc 92*
**Schilling**, Curtis Louis, Jr 1940- *AmMWSc 92*
**Schilling**, Dean William 1944- *WhoWest 92*
**Schilling**, Deborah Jan 1951- *WhoFI 92*
**Schilling**, Don Russell 1951- *WhoMW 92*
**Schilling**, Edward Eugene 1953- *AmMWSc 92*
**Schilling**, Edward George 1931- *AmMWSc 92*, *WhoFI 92*
**Schilling**, Franklin Charles, Jr. 1958- *WhoFI 92*
**Schilling**, Frederick Augustus, Jr. 1931- *WhoWest 92*
**Schilling**, Friedrich, Jr. 1934- *WhoRel 92*
**Schilling**, Gerd 1939- *AmMWSc 92*
**Schilling**, Herbert Glen 1929- *WhoRel 92*
**Schilling**, James Michael 1957- *WhoEnt 92*
**Schilling**, Janet Naomi 1939- *WhoMW 92*
**Schilling**, John Albert 1917- *AmMWSc 92*
**Schilling**, John H 1927- *AmMWSc 92*
**Schilling**, Katherine Lee Tracy 1925- *WhoMW 92*
**Schilling**, Linda Kaye 1948- *WhoRel 92*
**Schilling**, Mary Elizabeth 1942- *WhoMW 92*
**Schilling**, Mona Lee C. 1941- *WhoHisp 92*
**Schilling**, Prentiss Edwin 1941- *AmMWSc 92*
**Schilling**, Richard James 1933- *WhoWest 92*
**Schilling**, Richard Selwyn Francis 1911- *Who 92*
**Schilling**, Robert Frederick 1919- *AmMWSc 92*
**Schilling**, Stephen William 1946- *WhoAmP 91*
**Schilling**, Sylvester Paul 1904- *WhoRel 92*
**Schilling**, William Frederick 1942- *AmMWSc 92*
**Schillinger**, Edwin Joseph 1923- *AmMWSc 92*
**Schillinger**, John Andrew, Jr 1938- *AmMWSc 92*
**Schillinger**, Joseph 1895-1943 *NewAmDM*
**Schillinger**, Will D. 1959- *WhoEnt 92*
**Schilpp**, Paul A. 1897- *WrDr 92*
**Schilpp**, Paul Arthur 1897- *IntAu&W 91*, *IntWW 91*
**Schilsky**, Eric 1898-1974 *TwCPaSc*
**Schilson**, Robert E 1927- *AmMWSc 92*
**Schilt**, Alfred Ayars 1927- *AmMWSc 92*
**Schiltz**, Hugo 1927- *IntWW 91*
**Schily**, Otto 1932- *IntWW 91*
**Schima**, Francis Joseph 1935- *AmMWSc 92*
**Schimberg**, Armand Bruce 1927- *WhoAmL 92*
**Schimberni**, Mario 1923- *IntWW 91*
**Schimek**, DiAnna Ruth 1940- *WhoAmP 91*
**Schimek**, Robert Alfred 1926- *AmMWSc 92*
**Schimel**, Richard E. 1954- *WhoAmL 92*
**Schimelpfenig**, Clarence William 1930- *AmMWSc 92*
**Schimert**, George 1918- *AmMWSc 92*
**Schimitschek**, Erhard Josef 1931- *AmMWSc 92*
**Schimke**, Dennis J *WhoAmP 91*
**Schimke**, Robert T 1932- *AmMWSc 92*
**Schimmel**, Elihu Myron 1929- *AmMWSc 92*
**Schimmel**, Herbert 1909- *AmMWSc 92*
**Schimmel**, Karl Francis 1936- *AmMWSc 92*
**Schimmel**, Paul Reinhard 1940- *AmMWSc 92*
**Schimmel**, Walter Paul *AmMWSc 92*
**Schimmel**, William Michael 1946- *WhoEnt 92*
**Schimmer**, Bernard Paul 1941- *AmMWSc 92*
**Schimmerling**, Walter 1937- *AmMWSc 92*
**Schimminger**, Robin 1947- *WhoAmP 91*
**Schimpf**, David Jeffrey 1948- *AmMWSc 92*
**Schimpf**, Helen K. 1930- *WhoRel 92*
**Schimpff**, Jill Wagner 1945- *ConAu 135*
**Schin**, Kissu *AmMWSc 92*
**Schinagle**, Erich F 1932- *AmMWSc 92*
**Schindel**, Donald Marvin 1932- *WhoAmL 92*
**Schindel**, Roger H. 1942- *WhoRel 92*
**Schindel**, Ulrich 1935- *IntWW 91*
**Schindelman**, Joseph 1923- *SmATA 67*
**Schindewolf**, Douglas Joseph 1960- *WhoFI 92*
**Schindler**, Abbott Michael 1950- *WhoWest 92*
**Schindler**, Albert Isadore 1927- *AmMWSc 92*
**Schindler**, Alexander Moshe 1925- *IntWW 91*, *WhoRel 92*
**Schindler**, Alma 1879-1964 *FacFETw*
**Schindler**, Catherine 1929- *WhoEnt 92*
**Schindler**, Charles Alvin 1924- *AmMWSc 92*

**Schlotterbeck**, Julius Otto 1865-1917 *BiInAmS*
**Schlotterer**, William Lee 1955- *WhoMW 92*
**Schlotthauer**, John Carl 1930- *AmMWSc 92*
**Schlottmann**, Pedro U J 1947- *AmMWSc 92*
**Schlough**, James Sherwyn 1931- *AmMWSc 92*
**Schlozer**, August Ludwig von 1735-1809 *BlkwCEP*
**Schlub**, Robert Louis 1951- *AmMWSc 92*
**Schlub**, Teresa Rae 1946- *WhoRel 92*
**Schluederberg**, Ann Elizabeth Snider 1929- *AmMWSc 92*
**Schlueter**, Charles *WhoEnt 92*
**Schlueter**, David Arnold 1946- *WhoAmL 92*
**Schlueter**, Donald Jerome 1931- *AmMWSc 92*
**Schlueter**, Donald Paul 1927- *AmMWSc 92*
**Schlueter**, Edgar Albert 1918- *AmMWSc 92*
**Schlueter**, Irene Selma 1912- *WhoAmP 91*
**Schlueter**, Linda Lee 1947- *WhoAmL 92*
**Schlueter**, Michael Andreas 1945- *AmMWSc 92*
**Schlueter**, Michael Anthony 1959- *WhoAmL 92*
**Schlueter**, Robert J 1929- *AmMWSc 92*
**Schlueter**, Stan 1945- *WhoAmP 91*
**Schlumberger**, Jean 1907-1987 *FacFETw*
**Schlumbohm**, Peter 1896-1962 *DcTwDes*
**Schlumpf**, Dennis Lynn 1941- *WhoAmP 91*
**Schlumpf**, Leon 1925- *IntWW 91*
**Schlusselberg**, Martin 1936- *IntMPA 92*
**Schluter**, Michael 1945- *AmMWSc 92*
**Schluter**, Peter Mueller 1933- *WhoFI 92*
**Schluter**, Poul Holmskov 1929- *IntWW 91*
**Schluter**, Robert Arvel 1924- *AmMWSc 92*
**Schluter**, William E 1927- *WhoAmP 91*
**Schlutter**, Lois Cochrane 1953- *WhoMW 92*
**Schmaedecke**, William Louis 1936- *WhoAmL 92*
**Schmaier**, Alvin Harold 1949- *AmMWSc 92*
**Schmalbeck**, Richard Louis 1947- *WhoAmL 92*
**Schmalberger**, Donald C 1926- *AmMWSc 92*
**Schmale**, Arthur H, Jr 1924- *AmMWSc 92*
**Schmalenbach**, Werner 1920- *IntWW 91*
**Schmalenberger**, Jerry Lew 1934- *WhoRel 92, WhoWest 92*
**Schmalensee**, Richard Lee 1944- *WhoFI 92*
**Schmalfeld**, Robert George 1930- *WhoFI 92*
**Schmalle**, Joral *WhoEnt 92*
**Schmalstieg**, Frank Crawford 1940- *AmMWSc 92*
**Schmaltz**, Lawrence Gerard 1957- *WhoFI 92*
**Schmaltz**, Lloyd John 1929- *AmMWSc 92*
**Schmaltz**, Roy Edgar, Jr. 1937- *WhoWest 92*
**Schmalz**, Alfred Chandler 1924- *AmMWSc 92*
**Schmalz**, Gregory David 1952- *WhoWest 92*
**Schmalz**, Philip Frederick 1941- *AmMWSc 92*
**Schmalz**, Robert Fowler 1929- *AmMWSc 92*
**Schmalz**, Thomas G 1948- *AmMWSc 92*
**Schmalzer**, David Keith 1942- *AmMWSc 92*
**Schmandt**, Henry J 1918- *IntAu&W 91, WrDr 92*
**Schmandt**, Jurgen 1929- *WhoFI 92*
**Schmars**, William Thomas 1938- *AmMWSc 92*
**Schmauk**, Theodore Emanuel 1860-1920 *RelLAm 91*
**Schmaus**, Anton 1910-1934 *EncTR 91*
**Schmaus**, Michael 1897- *EncTR 91, IntWW 91*
**Schmechel**, Warren P. 1927- *WhoWest 92*
**Schmeckenbecher**, Arnold F 1920- *AmMWSc 92*
**Schmedding**, Vickie Lynn 1956- *WhoWest 92*
**Schmedtje**, John Frederick 1919- *AmMWSc 92*
**Schmee**, Josef 1945- *AmMWSc 92*
**Schmeelcke**, Robert Carl 1942- *WhoRel 92*
**Schmeelk**, John Frank 1939- *AmMWSc 92*
**Schmeer**, Arline Catherine 1929- *AmMWSc 92*
**Schmehl**, Carl, Jr. 1960- *WhoEnt 92*
**Schmehl**, Michael Robert 1956- *WhoWest 92*
**Schmehl**, Willard Reed 1918- *AmMWSc 92*
**Schmeiser**, Bruce Wayne 1947- *WhoMW 92*
**Schmeiser**, Douglas A 1934- *IntAu&W 91, WrDr 92*
**Schmeisser**, Gerhard, Jr 1926- *AmMWSc 92*
**Schmeits**, Alan Joe 1948- *WhoAmL 92*
**Schmelck**, Robert Marie Jean-Pierre d1990 *IntWW 91N*
**Schmeling**, Helen Margaret 1951- *WhoWest 92*
**Schmeling**, Max 1905- *EncTR 91 [port], FacFETw*
**Schmeling**, Sheila Kay 1949- *AmMWSc 92*
**Schmelkin**, Benjamin 1910- *WhoFI 92*
**Schmell**, Eli David 1950- *AmMWSc 92*
**Schmeller**, Helmut John 1932- *WhoMW 92*
**Schmelling**, Stephen Gordon 1940- *AmMWSc 92*
**Schmeltz**, Irwin 1932- *AmMWSc 92*
**Schmeltz**, William Frederick 1924- *WhoMW 92*
**Schmelz**, Brenda Lea 1958- *WhoAmL 92*
**Schmelz**, Damian Vincent 1932- *AmMWSc 92*
**Schmelzel**, John Edwin 1964- *WhoWest 92*
**Schmelzenbach**, Terry Lee 1954- *WhoMW 92, WhoRel 92*
**Schmelzer**, W. K. Norbert 1921- *IntWW 91*
**Schmemann**, Alexander 1921-1983 *DcEcMov, RelLAm 91*
**Schmenner**, Roger William 1947- *WhoFI 92, WhoMW 92*
**Schmerl**, James H 1940- *AmMWSc 92*
**Schmerling**, Erwin Robert 1929- *AmMWSc 92*
**Schmerr**, Mary Jo F 1945- *AmMWSc 92*
**Schmertmann**, John H 1928- *AmMWSc 92*
**Schmertz**, Herbert *LesBEnT 92*
**Schmertz**, Ida F. S. *WhoFI 92*
**Schmett**, Kim D 1952- *WhoAmP 91*
**Schmett**, Roy Henry 1947- *WhoFI 92*
**Schmetzer**, Alan David 1946- *WhoMW 92*
**Schmickel**, Roy David 1936- *AmMWSc 92*
**Schmid**, Carl William *AmMWSc 92*
**Schmid**, Craig Nicholas 1959- *WhoAmL 92*
**Schmid**, David Milton 1915- *WhoFI 92*
**Schmid**, Frank Richard 1924- *AmMWSc 92*
**Schmid**, Franz Anton 1922- *AmMWSc 92*
**Schmid**, George Edward 1932- *WhoAmP 91*
**Schmid**, George Henry 1931- *AmMWSc 92*
**Schmid**, Gerhard Martin 1929- *AmMWSc 92*
**Schmid**, Hans Heinrich 1937- *WhoRel 92*
**Schmid**, Harald Heinrich Otto 1935- *AmMWSc 92*
**Schmid**, Horst A. *WhoWest 92*
**Schmid**, Jack Robert 1924- *AmMWSc 92*
**Schmid**, John 1926- *ConAu 133*
**Schmid**, John Carolus 1920- *AmMWSc 92*
**Schmid**, John E. 1935- *WhoFI 92*
**Schmid**, John Ullrich 1939- *WhoAmL 92*
**Schmid**, Karl 1920- *AmMWSc 92*
**Schmid**, Lawrence Alfred 1928- *AmMWSc 92*
**Schmid**, Loren Clark 1931- *AmMWSc 92*
**Schmid**, Peter 1927- *AmMWSc 92, WhoWest 92*
**Schmid**, Richard Jay 1929- *WhoIns 92*
**Schmid**, Roman G 1928- *WhoIns 92*
**Schmid**, Rudi 1922- *AmMWSc 92, IntWW 91, WhoWest 92*
**Schmid**, Rudolf 1942- *WhoWest 92*
**Schmid**, Walter Egid 1933- *AmMWSc 92*
**Schmid**, Werner E 1927- *AmMWSc 92*
**Schmid**, Wilfried 1943- *AmMWSc 92*
**Schmid**, William Dale 1937- *AmMWSc 92*
**Schmid**, Wolfgang P. 1929- *IntWW 91*
**Schmid-Schoenbein**, Geert W 1948- *AmMWSc 92*
**Schmidhauser**, John Richard 1922- *WhoAmP 91*
**Schmidhuber**, Guillermo 1943- *IntAu&W 91*
**Schmidhuber**, Peter M. 1931- *IntWW 91, Who 92*
**Schmidle**, Claude Joseph 1920- *AmMWSc 92*
**Schmidle**, Mae S *WhoAmP 91*
**Schmidlin**, Albertus Ernest 1917- *AmMWSc 92*
**Schmidlin**, Frederick W 1925- *AmMWSc 92*
**Schmidlin**, Thomas William 1954- *WhoMW 92*
**Schmidly**, David James 1943- *AmMWSc 92*
**Schmidman**, Jo Ann 1948- *IntAu&W 91*
**Schmidt**, Alan 1946- *WhoFI 92*
**Schmidt**, Alan Frederick 1925- *AmMWSc 92, WhoWest 92*
**Schmidt**, Alan J. 1927- *WhoMW 92*
**Schmidt**, Albert Daniel 1925- *WhoMW 92*
**Schmidt**, Alexander M. d1991 *NewYTBS 91 [port]*
**Schmidt**, Alexander Mackay 1930- *AmMWSc 92*
**Schmidt**, Alfred Otto 1906- *AmMWSc 92*
**Schmidt**, Allen Roy 1948- *WhoWest 92*
**Schmidt**, Annie M.G. 1911- *ConAu 135, SmATA 67 [port]*
**Schmidt**, Anthony John 1927- *AmMWSc 92, WhoMW 92*
**Schmidt**, Arthur Gerard 1944- *AmMWSc 92*
**Schmidt**, Arthur Irwin 1927- *WhoMW 92*
**Schmidt**, Arthur Louis 1927- *WhoAmP 91*
**Schmidt**, Barbara A *AmMWSc 92*
**Schmidt**, Barnet Michael 1958- *AmMWSc 92*
**Schmidt**, Benno C., Jr. 1942- *IntWW 91*
**Schmidt**, Benno Charles, Jr. 1942- *Who 92, WrDr 92*
**Schmidt**, Berlie Louis 1932- *AmMWSc 92*
**Schmidt**, Bruno 1942- *AmMWSc 92*
**Schmidt**, Byron Winfield 1925- *WhoEnt 92*
**Schmidt**, Carl Walter 1925- *WhoIns 92*
**Schmidt**, Charles Edward 1951- *WhoAmL 92*
**Schmidt**, Charles William 1942- *AmMWSc 92*
**Schmidt**, Charles Wilson 1928- *WhoFI 92*
**Schmidt**, Chauncey Everett 1931- *IntWW 91, WhoFI 92*
**Schmidt**, Christopher Eric 1950- *WhoAmL 92*
**Schmidt**, Chuck 1947- *WhoMW 92*
**Schmidt**, Claude Henri 1924- *AmMWSc 92*
**Schmidt**, Claudia Lynn 1947- *WhoWest 92*
**Schmidt**, Clifford LeRoy 1926- *AmMWSc 92*
**Schmidt**, Connie Lu 1949- *WhoWest 92*
**Schmidt**, Conrad Baxter 1941- *WhoMW 92*
**Schmidt**, Dale Anthony 1952- *WhoEnt 92*
**Schmidt**, Daniel Edward, IV 1946- *WhoAmL 92, WhoIns 92*
**Schmidt**, Daniel Joseph 1954- *WhoEnt 92, WhoMW 92*
**Schmidt**, Daniel W. 1942- *NewAmDM*
**Schmidt**, Daryl Dean 1944- *WhoRel 92*
**Schmidt**, David Joseph 1950- *WhoMW 92*
**Schmidt**, David Kelso 1943- *AmMWSc 92, WhoWest 92*
**Schmidt**, Deborah Sue 1953- *WhoWest 92*
**Schmidt**, Dennis Earl 1940- *AmMWSc 92*
**Schmidt**, Dianne Hope 1948- *WhoAmP 91*
**Schmidt**, Donald Arthur 1922- *AmMWSc 92*
**Schmidt**, Donald Dean 1942- *AmMWSc 92*
**Schmidt**, Donald Henry 1935- *AmMWSc 92*
**Schmidt**, Donald L 1930- *AmMWSc 92*
**Schmidt**, Donald L 1931- *AmMWSc 92*
**Schmidt**, Douglas John 1952- *WhoRel 92*
**Schmidt**, Douglas Michael 1950- *WhoAmL 92*
**Schmidt**, Douglas Wocher 1942- *WhoEnt 92*
**Schmidt**, Dwight Lyman 1926- *AmMWSc 92*
**Schmidt**, Earl William 1936- *WhoAmP 91*
**Schmidt**, Eckart W 1935- *AmMWSc 92*
**Schmidt**, Edmund Joseph, III 1958- *WhoAmL 92*
**Schmidt**, Edward Craig 1947- *WhoAmL 92*
**Schmidt**, Edward George 1942- *AmMWSc 92*
**Schmidt**, Edward Matthews 1933- *AmMWSc 92*
**Schmidt**, Eric *DrAPF 91*
**Schmidt**, Eugene Edward 1929- *WhoRel 92*
**Schmidt**, Francis Henry 1941- *AmMWSc 92*
**Schmidt**, Frank W 1929- *AmMWSc 92*
**Schmidt**, Fred Henry 1915- *AmMWSc 92*
**Schmidt**, Frederick Allen 1930- *AmMWSc 92*
**Schmidt**, Frederick D 1932- *WhoAmP 91*
**Schmidt**, Frederick Roland 1936- *WhoAmP 91*
**Schmidt**, Friedrich August 1837-1928 *RelLAm 91*
**Schmidt**, Gary J 1947- *WhoAmP 91*
**Schmidt**, Gary L 1942- *WhoAmP 91*
**Schmidt**, George 1926- *AmMWSc 92*
**Schmidt**, George Thomas *AmMWSc 92*
**Schmidt**, Gerald D 1934- *AmMWSc 92*
**Schmidt**, Gerhard 1919- *IntWW 91*
**Schmidt**, Gerhard 1924- *IntWW 91*
**Schmidt**, Gilbert Carl 1921- *AmMWSc 92*
**Schmidt**, Glen Henry 1931- *AmMWSc 92*
**Schmidt**, Glenn Roy 1943- *AmMWSc 92*
**Schmidt**, Grant Jacob 1948- *WhoWest 92*
**Schmidt**, Gregory Alan 1956- *WhoMW 92*
**Schmidt**, Gregory Wayne 1947- *AmMWSc 92*
**Schmidt**, Guido 1901-1957 *EncTR 91*
**Schmidt**, Gunter 1913- *WhoMW 92*
**Schmidt**, Harold Frank, Jr. 1960- *WhoFI 92*
**Schmidt**, Hartland H 1929- *AmMWSc 92*
**Schmidt**, Harvey 1929- *NewAmDM*
**Schmidt**, Harvey John, Jr 1941- *AmMWSc 92*
**Schmidt**, Heidi Eva 1963- *WhoEnt 92*
**Schmidt**, Helmut 1918- *FacFETw, IntWW 91*
**Schmidt**, Helmut 1928- *AmMWSc 92*
**Schmidt**, Helmut H. W. 1918- *Who 92*
**Schmidt**, Herb Frederick 1930- *WhoRel 92*
**Schmidt**, Howard Jerome 1955- *WhoAmP 91*
**Schmidt**, Jack Russell 1926- *AmMWSc 92*
**Schmidt**, James Craig 1927- *WhoFI 92*
**Schmidt**, Jane Ann 1951- *AmMWSc 92*
**Schmidt**, Jean M 1938- *AmMWSc 92*
**Schmidt**, Jerome P 1928- *AmMWSc 92*
**Schmidt**, John Allen 1940- *AmMWSc 92*
**Schmidt**, John Edward, III 1960- *WhoAmL 92*
**Schmidt**, John Lancaster 1943- *AmMWSc 92*
**Schmidt**, John Louis 1933- *WhoRel 92*
**Schmidt**, John Lynn 1947- *WhoRel 92*
**Schmidt**, John P 1933- *AmMWSc 92*
**Schmidt**, John Richard 1924- *WhoAmP 91*
**Schmidt**, John Richard 1929- *AmMWSc 92*
**Schmidt**, John Thomas 1947- *WhoAmL 92*
**Schmidt**, John Thomas 1949- *AmMWSc 92*
**Schmidt**, John Wesley 1917- *AmMWSc 92*
**Schmidt**, Joost 1893-1948 *DcTwDes*
**Schmidt**, Joseph David 1937- *WhoWest 92*
**Schmidt**, Joseph F. 1955- *WhoMW 92*
**Schmidt**, Joseph W. 1946- *WhoAmL 92, WhoFI 92*
**Schmidt**, June Laurel 1941- *WhoMW 92, WhoRel 92*
**Schmidt**, Justin Orvel 1947- *AmMWSc 92*
**Schmidt**, Karen 1945- *WhoAmP 91*
**Schmidt**, Kari Suzanne 1957- *WhoAmL 92*
**Schmidt**, Kimberly Elizabeth 1958- *WhoEnt 92*
**Schmidt**, Klaus H 1928- *AmMWSc 92*
**Schmidt**, Kurt F 1926- *AmMWSc 92*
**Schmidt**, Lail William, Jr. 1936- *WhoAmL 92, WhoWest 92*
**Schmidt**, Lanny D 1938- *AmMWSc 92*
**Schmidt**, Leigh Eric 1961- *ConAu 133*
**Schmidt**, Leon Herbert 1909- *AmMWSc 92*
**Schmidt**, Liselotte Martha 1933- *WhoEnt 92*
**Schmidt**, Maarten 1929- *AmMWSc 92, IntWW 91*
**Schmidt**, Mark Robert 1956- *WhoMW 92*
**Schmidt**, Mark Thomas 1958- *AmMWSc 92*
**Schmidt**, Marlene *ConAu 133*
**Schmidt**, Mary Sylvia 1937- *WhoRel 92*
**Schmidt**, Michael 1947- *ConPo 91, IntAu&W 91, WrDr 92*
**Schmidt**, Michael R. 1947- *WhoFI 92*
**Schmidt**, Mike 1949- *FacFETw*
**Schmidt**, Norbert Otto 1925- *AmMWSc 92*
**Schmidt**, Ole *WhoEnt 92*
**Schmidt**, Ole 1928- *IntWW 91*
**Schmidt**, P S 1941- *AmMWSc 92*
**Schmidt**, Parbury Pollen 1939- *AmMWSc 92*
**Schmidt**, Patrick Lee 1956- *WhoAmL 92*
**Schmidt**, Paul Gardner 1944- *AmMWSc 92*
**Schmidt**, Paul J 1943- *AmMWSc 92*
**Schmidt**, Paul Joseph 1925- *AmMWSc 92*
**Schmidt**, Paul Otto 1899-1970 *EncTR 91 [port]*
**Schmidt**, Paul Woodward 1926- *AmMWSc 92*
**Schmidt**, Peter 1927- *WhoFI 92*
**Schmidt**, Raymond 1944- *WhoAmP 91*
**Schmidt**, Raymond LeRoy 1942- *AmMWSc 92*
**Schmidt**, Reese Boise 1913- *AmMWSc 92*
**Schmidt**, Richard 1925- *AmMWSc 92*
**Schmidt**, Richard Alan 1943- *WhoMW 92*
**Schmidt**, Richard Arthur 1935- *AmMWSc 92*
**Schmidt**, Richard Edward 1931- *AmMWSc 92*
**Schmidt**, Richard Marlen 1946- *WhoAmP 91*
**Schmidt**, Richard Marten, Jr. 1924- *WhoAmL 92*
**Schmidt**, Richard R *WhoAmP 91*
**Schmidt**, Richard Ralph 1944- *AmMWSc 92*
**Schmidt**, Robert *LesBEnT 92*
**Schmidt**, Robert 1927- *AmMWSc 92*
**Schmidt**, Robert Frederick 1949- *WhoMW 92*
**Schmidt**, Robert Gordon 1924- *AmMWSc 92*
**Schmidt**, Robert John 1956- *WhoWest 92*

**Schmidt**, Robert Neil 1954- *WhoEnt 92*
**Schmidt**, Robert Reinhart 1933- *AmMWSc 92*
**Schmidt**, Robert Sherwood 1928- *AmMWSc 92*
**Schmidt**, Robert W 1926- *AmMWSc 92*
**Schmidt**, Robert W 1930- *AmMWSc 92*
**Schmidt**, Roberta Jeanne 1928- *WhoRel 92*
**Schmidt**, Robin Adair 1930- *WhoMW 92*
**Schmidt**, Roger Paul 1944- *AmMWSc 92*
**Schmidt**, Ronald G 1937- *WhoAmP 91*
**Schmidt**, Ronald Grover 1931- *AmMWSc 92*
**Schmidt**, Ronn 1959- *WhoEnt 92*
**Schmidt**, Rudolph David 1928- *WhoWest 92*
**Schmidt**, Russel Alan, II 1953- *WhoMW 92*
**Schmidt**, Ruth A M 1916- *AmMWSc 92*
**Schmidt**, Sally Jo 1954- *WhoMW 92*
**Schmidt**, Samuel 1950- *WhoHisp 92*
**Schmidt**, Stanley 1944- *TwCSFW 91, WrDr 92*
**Schmidt**, Stanley Albert 1944- *IntAu&W 91*
**Schmidt**, Stephen 1932- *WhoEnt 92*
**Schmidt**, Stephen Arthur 1960- *WhoFI 92*
**Schmidt**, Stephen C. 1945- *WhoFI 92*
**Schmidt**, Stephen Paul *AmMWSc 92*
**Schmidt**, Stephen Paul 1947- *AmMWSc 92*
**Schmidt**, Steven James 1947- *WhoRel 92*
**Schmidt**, Steven Paul *AmMWSc 92*
**Schmidt**, Ted 1957- *WhoEnt 92*
**Schmidt**, Ted A. 1952- *WhoAmL 92*
**Schmidt**, Terry Lane 1943- *WhoWest 92*
**Schmidt**, Thomas Frank 1944- *WhoFI 92, WhoWest 92*
**Schmidt**, Thomas John 1946- *AmMWSc 92*
**Schmidt**, Thomas William 1938- *AmMWSc 92*
**Schmidt**, Tom *DrAPF 91*
**Schmidt**, Victor A 1936- *AmMWSc 92*
**Schmidt**, Victor Hugo 1930- *AmMWSc 92*
**Schmidt**, Volkmar 1932- *AmMWSc 92*
**Schmidt**, W. Carleen 1938- *WhoRel 92*
**Schmidt**, W. Robert *WhoRel 92*
**Schmidt**, Waldemar Adrian *AmMWSc 92*
**Schmidt**, Walter Allan 1948- *WhoRel 92*
**Schmidt**, Walter E. 1936- *WhoAmL 92*
**Schmidt**, Walter Harold 1935- *AmMWSc 92*
**Schmidt**, Wayne Elmer 1927- *WhoRel 92*
**Schmidt**, Wayne Walter 1941- *WhoAmL 92, WhoMW 92*
**Schmidt**, Wendy Sue 1959- *WhoFI 92*
**Schmidt**, Werner H 1914- *AmMWSc 92*
**Schmidt**, Werner P. 1932- *IntWW 91*
**Schmidt**, William Alexander 1947- *WhoAmL 92*
**Schmidt**, William C. 1940- *WhoWest 92*
**Schmidt**, William Charles, Jr. 1939- *WhoRel 92*
**Schmidt**, William Edward 1920- *AmMWSc 92*
**Schmidt**, William Joseph 1946- *WhoMW 92*
**Schmidt**, Wolf 1937- *IntMPA 92*
**Schmidt**, Wolfgang M 1933- *AmMWSc 92*
**Schmidt**, Wyman Carl 1929- *AmMWSc 92*
**Schmidt-Clausen**, Kurt Hermann 1920- *IntWW 91*
**Schmidt-Isserstedt**, Hans 1900-1973 *NewAmDM*
**Schmidt-Koenig**, Klaus 1930- *AmMWSc 92*
**Schmidt-Nielsen**, Bodil Mimi 1918- *AmMWSc 92*
**Schmidt-Nielsen**, Knut 1915- *AmMWSc 92, IntAu&W 91, IntWW 91, WrDr 92*
**Schmidt-Rohr**, Ulrich 1926- *IntWW 91*
**Schmidt-Rottluff**, Karl 1884-1976 *EncTR 91, FacFETw*
**Schmidtbauer**, Laddie A. *WhoFI 92*
**Schmidtberger**, Patrick Lee 1964- *WhoMW 92*
**Schmidtchen**, Rowland H 1920- *WhoAmP 91*
**Schmidtke**, Jon Robert 1943- *AmMWSc 92*
**Schmidtke**, R A 1925- *AmMWSc 92*
**Schmidtmann**, Lucie Ann 1963- *WhoFI 92*
**Schmiechen**, Peter M. *WhoRel 92*
**Schmied**, Wieland 1929- *IntWW 91*
**Schmiedel**, Robert Edward 1953- *WhoMW 92*
**Schmieder**, Carl 1938- *WhoFI 92, WhoWest 92*
**Schmieder**, Robert W 1941- *AmMWSc 92*
**Schmieder**, Wolfgang 1901- *NewAmDM*
**Schmiedeshoff**, Frederick William 1925- *AmMWSc 92*
**Schmiedeshoff**, George M 1955- *AmMWSc 92*
**Schmieg**, Glenn Melwood 1938- *AmMWSc 92*
**Schmiege**, Robert 1941- *WhoFI 92, WhoMW 92*
**Schmiege**, Sandra Kay 1953- *WhoMW 92*
**Schmiegel**, Walter Werner 1941- *AmMWSc 92*
**Schmiel**, David Gerhard 1931- *WhoRel 92*
**Schmincke**, George Thomas 1923- *WhoAmP 91*
**Schminke**, Dennis Richard 1952- *WhoFI 92*
**Schmir**, Gaston L 1933- *AmMWSc 92*
**Schmisseur**, Wilson Edward 1942- *AmMWSc 92*
**Schmit**, Herman H 1939- *WhoIns 92*
**Schmit**, Joseph Lawrence 1933- *AmMWSc 92*
**Schmit**, Kenneth William 1935- *WhoFI 92*
**Schmit**, Loran 1929- *WhoAmP 91*
**Schmit**, Lucien A, Jr 1928- *AmMWSc 92*
**Schmitendorf**, William E 1941- *AmMWSc 92*
**Schmitt**, C L 1912- *WhoAmP 91*
**Schmitt**, Carl 1888-1985 *BiDExR, EncTR 91 [port]*
**Schmitt**, Carveth Joseph Rodney 1934- *WhoFI 92, WhoWest 92*
**Schmitt**, Charles Rudolph 1920- *AmMWSc 92*
**Schmitt**, Cooper Davis 1859-1910 *BiInAmS*
**Schmitt**, Donald Peter 1941- *AmMWSc 92*
**Schmitt**, Edward E. 1926- *WhoAmL 92*
**Schmitt**, Erich 1928- *AmMWSc 92*
**Schmitt**, Florent 1870-1958 *NewAmDM*
**Schmitt**, Francis Otto 1903- *AmMWSc 92, IntWW 91*
**Schmitt**, Frank Joseph, III 1939- *WhoRel 92*
**Schmitt**, George Frederick, Jr 1939- *AmMWSc 92*
**Schmitt**, George Joseph 1928- *AmMWSc 92*
**Schmitt**, Gladys 1909-1972 *BenetAL 91*
**Schmitt**, Glenn Ralph 1961- *WhoAmL 92*
**Schmitt**, Harold William 1928- *AmMWSc 92*
**Schmitt**, Harrison 1935- *FacFETw*
**Schmitt**, Harrison H. 1935- *IntWW 91*
**Schmitt**, Harrison Hagan 1935- *WhoAmP 91*
**Schmitt**, Howard Stanley 1933- *WhoRel 92*
**Schmitt**, Johanna 1953- *AmMWSc 92*
**Schmitt**, John Arvid, Jr 1925- *AmMWSc 92*
**Schmitt**, John Jacob 1938- *WhoRel 92*
**Schmitt**, John Leigh 1941- *AmMWSc 92, WhoMW 92*
**Schmitt**, Joseph Lawrence, Jr 1941- *AmMWSc 92*
**Schmitt**, Joseph Michael 1930- *AmMWSc 92*
**Schmitt**, Joseph W 1939- *WhoIns 92*
**Schmitt**, Klaus 1940- *AmMWSc 92*
**Schmitt**, Kurt 1886-1950 *EncTR 91*
**Schmitt**, Lisa Marie 1963- *WhoWest 92*
**Schmitt**, Mark F. 1923- *WhoRel 92*
**Schmitt**, Mark James 1950- *WhoMW 92*
**Schmitt**, Marshall John 1959- *WhoAmL 92*
**Schmitt**, Neil Martin 1940- *AmMWSc 92*
**Schmitt**, Otto Herbert 1913- *AmMWSc 92*
**Schmitt**, Paul Justin 1945- *WhoMW 92*
**Schmitt**, Paul Milton 1931- *WhoMW 92*
**Schmitt**, Peter *DrAPF 91*
**Schmitt**, Ralph George 1944- *WhoFI 92*
**Schmitt**, Raymond W, Jr 1950- *AmMWSc 92*
**Schmitt**, Richard George 1948- *WhoWest 92*
**Schmitt**, Robert Ferdinand 1934- *WhoAmL 92*
**Schmitt**, Roland Walter 1923- *AmMWSc 92, WhoFI 92*
**Schmitt**, Roman A 1925- *AmMWSc 92*
**Schmitt**, Roman Augustine 1925- *WhoWest 92*
**Schmitt**, Thomas Richard 1964- *WhoRel 92*
**Schmitt**, Wolfgang Rudolph 1944- *WhoFI 92, WhoMW 92*
**Schmitter**, Ruth Elizabeth *AmMWSc 92*
**Schmitthenner**, August Fredrick 1926- *AmMWSc 92*
**Schmitthoff**, Clive Macmillan d1990 *Who 92N*
**Schmitthoff**, Clive Macmillan 1903- *IntAu&W 91, WrDr 92*
**Schmittinger**, John Joseph 1941- *WhoAmL 92*
**Schmitz**, Charles Bernard 1951- *WhoAmL 92*
**Schmitz**, Charles Edison 1919- *WhoRel 92*
**Schmitz**, Dennis *DrAPF 91*
**Schmitz**, Dennis 1937- *ConPo 91, WrDr 92*
**Schmitz**, Dennis Mathew 1937- *WhoWest 92*
**Schmitz**, Edward Henry 1929- *WhoFI 92*
**Schmitz**, Edward James 1950- *WhoFI 92*
**Schmitz**, Eugene Gerard 1929- *WhoFI 92*
**Schmitz**, Eugene H 1934- *AmMWSc 92*
**Schmitz**, Francis John 1932- *AmMWSc 92*
**Schmitz**, George William 1919- *AmMWSc 92*
**Schmitz**, Geraldine *DrAPF 91*
**Schmitz**, Harold Gregory 1943- *AmMWSc 92*
**Schmitz**, Henry 1917- *AmMWSc 92*
**Schmitz**, James H 1911- *TwCSFW 91*
**Schmitz**, John Albert 1940- *AmMWSc 92*
**Schmitz**, John G 1930- *WhoAmP 91*
**Schmitz**, Kenneth Stanley 1943- *AmMWSc 92*
**Schmitz**, Norbert Lewis 1921- *AmMWSc 92*
**Schmitz**, Robert Joseph 1921- *WhoAmP 91*
**Schmitz**, Robert L 1914- *AmMWSc 92*
**Schmitz**, Roger A 1934- *AmMWSc 92*
**Schmitz**, Stephen Louis 1953- *WhoMW 92*
**Schmitz**, Steven Joseph 1947- *WhoWest 92*
**Schmitz**, Thomas John 1941- *WhoFI 92, WhoMW 92*
**Schmitz**, Vincent Herman 1946- *WhoWest 92*
**Schmitz**, William Joseph, Jr 1937- *AmMWSc 92*
**Schmitz**, William Robert 1924- *AmMWSc 92*
**Schmitz**, Wolfgang 1923- *IntWW 91*
**Schmitzer**, Edward Paul 1960- *WhoFI 92*
**Schmoeller**, David 1947- *IntMPA 92*
**Schmoke**, Kurt 1949- *ConBIB 1 [port]*
**Schmoke**, Kurt L 1949- *WhoAmP 91*
**Schmoke**, Kurt Lidell *WhoBIA 92*
**Schmoke**, Leroy Joseph, III 1944- *WhoFI 92*
**Schmokel**, Wolfe W. 1933- *WrDr 92*
**Schmokel**, Wolfe William 1933- *IntAu&W 91*
**Schmoldt**, Hans Edward 1921- *WhoFI 92*
**Schmolka**, Leo Louis 1939- *WhoAmL 92*
**Schmoll**, Harry F., Jr. 1939- *WhoAmL 92*
**Schmolle**, Stella 1908- *TwCPaSc*
**Schmookler**, Andrew Bard 1946- *ConAu 135*
**Schmucker**, Douglas Lees 1944- *AmMWSc 92*
**Schmucker**, Ruby Elvy Ladrach 1923- *WhoMW 92*
**Schmucker**, Samuel Simon 1799-1873 *DcAmImH*
**Schmuckler**, Joseph S 1927- *AmMWSc 92*
**Schmude**, Jurgen 1936- *IntWW 91*
**Schmude**, Keith E 1934- *AmMWSc 92*
**Schmugge**, Thomas Joseph 1937- *AmMWSc 92*
**Schmuhl**, Robert 1948- *ConAu 135*
**Schmuhl**, Robert Philip 1948- *WhoMW 92*
**Schmukler**, Martin L. 1940- *WhoAmL 92*
**Schmukler**, Seymour 1925- *AmMWSc 92*
**Schmulbach**, Charles David 1929- *AmMWSc 92*
**Schmulbach**, James C 1931- *AmMWSc 92*
**Schmults**, Edward C 1931- *WhoAmP 91*
**Schmults**, Edward Charles 1931- *WhoAmL 92, WhoFI 92*
**Schmundt**, Rudolf 1896-1944 *EncTR 91*
**Schmunk**, Philip Paul 1954- *WhoRel 92*
**Schmutte**, Stephen James 1944- *WhoMW 92*
**Schmutz**, Arthur Walter 1921- *WhoWest 92*
**Schmutz**, Ervin Marcell 1915- *AmMWSc 92*
**Schmutz**, John F. *WhoAmL 92*
**Schmutz**, John Francis 1947- *WhoAmL 92*
**Schmutz**, Josef Konrad 1950- *AmMWSc 92*
**Schmutz**, Ray S 1918- *WhoAmP 91*
**Schnaar**, Ronald Lee 1950- *AmMWSc 92*
**Schnaare**, Roger L 1938- *AmMWSc 92*
**Schnaars**, Richard Thomas 1957- *WhoMW 92*
**Schnabel**, Artur 1882-1951 *FacFETw, NewAmDM*
**Schnabel**, George Joseph 1916- *AmMWSc 92*
**Schnabel**, Julian 1951- *IntWW 91, WorArt 1980 [port]*
**Schnabel**, Karl Ulrich 1909- *WhoEnt 92*
**Schnabel**, Robert B 1950- *AmMWSc 92*
**Schnabel**, Stefan Artur 1912- *WhoEnt 92*
**Schnabel**, Truman Gross, Jr 1919- *AmMWSc 92*
**Schnabel**, William John 1910- *WhoMW 92*
**Schnabl**, Frank Joseph 1927- *WhoAmP 91*
**Schnable**, George Luther 1927- *AmMWSc 92*
**Schnably**, Richard Lynn 1955- *WhoEnt 92*
**Schnack**, Gayle Hemingway Jepson 1926- *WhoWest 92*
**Schnack**, Harold Clifford 1918- *WhoFI 92, WhoWest 92*
**Schnack**, Larry G 1937- *AmMWSc 92*
**Schnack**, Larry Gene 1937- *WhoMW 92*
**Schnacke**, Robert Howard 1913- *WhoAmL 92, WhoWest 92*
**Schnackenberg**, Gjertrud 1953- *ConPo 91*
**Schnackenberg**, Joyce A. 1903- *WhoMW 92*
**Schnaible**, H W 1925- *AmMWSc 92*
**Schnall**, Flora 1935- *WhoAmL 92*
**Schnaper**, Harold Warren 1923- *AmMWSc 92*
**Schnapf**, Abraham 1921- *AmMWSc 92*
**Schnapp**, Roger Herbert 1946- *WhoAmL 92, WhoFI 92, WhoWest 92*
**Schnappinger**, Melvin Gerhardt, Jr 1942- *AmMWSc 92*
**Schnare**, Paul Stewart 1936- *AmMWSc 92*
**Schnathorst**, William Charles 1929- *AmMWSc 92*
**Schnatter**, Charles W. 1962- *WhoAmL 92*
**Schnatterly**, Michael Dean 1955- *WhoRel 92*
**Schnatterly**, Stephen Eugene 1938- *AmMWSc 92*
**Schnautz**, William Arthur 1938- *WhoFI 92*
**Schnebel**, Dieter 1930- *ConCom 92*
**Schneberger**, Joseph 1959- *WhoFI 92*
**Schnebly**, Francis David 1926- *WhoWest 92*
**Schnebly**, Lindsay Paul 1961- *WhoEnt 92*
**Schneck**, Gerald Robert 1948- *WhoMW 92*
**Schneck**, Larry 1926- *AmMWSc 92*
**Schneck**, Paul Bennett 1945- *AmMWSc 92*
**Schneck**, William LeRoy 1919- *WhoEnt 92*
**Schneckenburger**, Karen Lynne 1949- *WhoFI 92*
**Schnee**, David Mark 1961- *WhoMW 92*
**Schnee**, Joel Louis 1935- *WhoEnt 92*
**Schneebaum**, Tobias *DrAPF 91*
**Schneebaum**, Tobias 1921- *WrDr 92*
**Schneebaum**, Tobias 1922- *IntAu&W 91*
**Schneeberger**, Eveline E 1934- *AmMWSc 92*
**Schneeberger**, R. Louis 1954- *WhoMW 92*
**Schneeman**, Barbara Olds 1948- *AmMWSc 92*
**Schneeman**, Peter *DrAPF 91*
**Schneemann**, Carolee *DrAPF 91*
**Schneemann**, Carolee 1939- *WorArt 1980 [port]*
**Schneemelcher**, Wilhelm 1914- *IntWW 91, WhoRel 92*
**Schneemeyer**, Lynn F *AmMWSc 92*
**Schneer**, Cecil Jack 1923- *AmMWSc 92*
**Schneer**, Charles H. 1920- *IntMPA 92*
**Schneerson**, Menachem Mendel 1902- *RelLAm 91*
**Schneid**, Edward Joseph 1940- *AmMWSc 92*
**Schneidau**, John Donald, Jr 1913- *AmMWSc 92*
**Schneideman**, Robert Ivan 1926- *WhoEnt 92*
**Schneider**, Aaron *DrAPF 91*
**Schneider**, Adam Louis 1956- *WhoFI 92*
**Schneider**, Alan *LesBEnT 92*
**Schneider**, Alan 1917-1984 *FacFETw*
**Schneider**, Alan M 1925- *AmMWSc 92*
**Schneider**, Alexander 1908- *NewAmDM*
**Schneider**, Alfred 1926- *AmMWSc 92*
**Schneider**, Alfred Marcel 1925- *AmMWSc 92*
**Schneider**, Alfred R. *LesBEnT 92*
**Schneider**, Allan Frank 1926- *AmMWSc 92*
**Schneider**, Allan Stanford 1940- *AmMWSc 92*
**Schneider**, Arthur Lee 1939- *AmMWSc 92*
**Schneider**, Arthur Paul 1930- *WhoEnt 92*
**Schneider**, Arthur Sanford 1929- *AmMWSc 92, WhoMW 92*
**Schneider**, B. V. H. 1927- *WrDr 92*
**Schneider**, Barbara G *AmMWSc 92*
**Schneider**, Barry Charles 1943- *WhoAmL 92, WhoWest 92*
**Schneider**, Barry Evan 1953- *WhoFI 92*
**Schneider**, Barry I 1940- *AmMWSc 92*
**Schneider**, Bart *DrAPF 91*
**Schneider**, Ben Ross, Jr. 1920- *WrDr 92*
**Schneider**, Bernard Arnold 1944- *AmMWSc 92*
**Schneider**, Beverly Belle 1934- *WhoAmL 92*
**Schneider**, Bruce Alton 1941- *AmMWSc 92*
**Schneider**, Bruce E 1950- *AmMWSc 92*
**Schneider**, Bruce Solomon 1942- *AmMWSc 92*
**Schneider**, C Leon *WhoIns 92*
**Schneider**, Calvin 1924- *WhoWest 92*
**Schneider**, Carl Edward 1948- *WhoAmL 92*
**Schneider**, Carl Stanley 1942- *AmMWSc 92*
**Schneider**, Carl W. 1932- *WhoAmL 92*
**Schneider**, Charles L 1913- *AmMWSc 92*
**Schneider**, Claudine Cmarada 1947- *WhoAmP 91*

**Schneider**, Craig William 1948- *AmMWSc 92*
**Schneider**, David Edwin 1937- *AmMWSc 92*
**Schneider**, David Miller 1937- *WhoAmL 92*
**Schneider**, David R. 1960- *WhoFI 92*
**Schneider**, David T 1922- *WhoAmP 91*
**Schneider**, Delwin Byron 1926- *WhoRel 92*
**Schneider**, Dennis Eugene 1957- *WhoFI 92*
**Schneider**, Dennis Ray 1940- *WhoRel 92*
**Schneider**, Dennis Ray 1952- *AmMWSc 92*
**Schneider**, Dick *IntMPA 92*
**Schneider**, Dieter 1935- *IntWW 91*
**Schneider**, Donald 1923- *WhoEnt 92*
**Schneider**, Donald Leonard 1941- *AmMWSc 92*
**Schneider**, Donald Louis 1919- *AmMWSc 92*
**Schneider**, Donna Marie 1956- *WhoFI 92*
**Schneider**, E Gayle 1946- *AmMWSc 92*
**Schneider**, Earl Gary 1933- *WhoAmL 92*
**Schneider**, Edmond J 1946- *IntAu&W 91*
**Schneider**, Edward Greyer 1941- *AmMWSc 92*
**Schneider**, Edward Lee 1947- *AmMWSc 92*
**Schneider**, Edward Lewis 1940- *AmMWSc 92, WhoWest 92*
**Schneider**, Edward Martin 1922- *WhoMW 92*
**Schneider**, Edwin Kahn 1948- *AmMWSc 92*
**Schneider**, Elizabeth 1943- *ConAu 36NR*
**Schneider**, Elizabeth Lynn *DrAPF 91*
**Schneider**, Ellen Shiffrin 1943- *WhoAmL 92*
**Schneider**, Eric Davis 1940- *AmMWSc 92*
**Schneider**, Eric Gene 1949- *WhoEnt 92*
**Schneider**, Eric John 1958- *WhoFI 92*
**Schneider**, Eric West 1952- *AmMWSc 92, WhoMW 92*
**Schneider**, Frank L 1906- *AmMWSc 92*
**Schneider**, Fred Barry 1953- *AmMWSc 92*
**Schneider**, Frederick Howard 1938- *AmMWSc 92*
**Schneider**, G Michael 1945- *AmMWSc 92*
**Schneider**, Gary 1934- *AmMWSc 92*
**Schneider**, Gary Bruce 1947- *WhoMW 92*
**Schneider**, George Ronald 1932- *AmMWSc 92*
**Schneider**, Gerald Edward 1940- *AmMWSc 92*
**Schneider**, Greta Sara 1954- *WhoFI 92*
**Schneider**, Gustavo Francisco 1960- *WhoHisp 92*
**Schneider**, Hans 1927- *AmMWSc 92*
**Schneider**, Harold Lawrence 1942- *WhoAmL 92*
**Schneider**, Harold Norman 1950- *WhoWest 92*
**Schneider**, Harold O 1930- *AmMWSc 92*
**Schneider**, Harold William 1943- *AmMWSc 92*
**Schneider**, Heinz Hermann Gustav 1911- *WhoFI 92*
**Schneider**, Helen Leslie *WhoEnt 92*
**Schneider**, Henry 1915- *AmMWSc 92*
**Schneider**, Henry 1933- *AmMWSc 92*
**Schneider**, Henry Joseph 1920- *AmMWSc 92*
**Schneider**, Henry Peter 1912- *AmMWSc 92*
**Schneider**, Herb William 1931- *WhoMW 92*
**Schneider**, Hope MacAndrew *WhoFI 92*
**Schneider**, Howard 1935- *WhoAmL 92*
**Schneider**, Howard Albert 1912- *AmMWSc 92*
**Schneider**, Howard Barry 1955- *WhoWest 92*
**Schneider**, Hubert George, III 1958- *WhoWest 92*
**Schneider**, Hubert H 1926- *AmMWSc 92*
**Schneider**, Imogene Pauline 1934- *AmMWSc 92*
**Schneider**, Irwin 1932- *AmMWSc 92*
**Schneider**, Jacob David 1946- *AmMWSc 92*
**Schneider**, James Gordon 1925- *WhoAmP 91*
**Schneider**, James Roy 1934- *AmMWSc 92*
**Schneider**, Jerry Allan 1937- *WhoWest 92*
**Schneider**, Joan Wagner 1951- *WhoMW 92*
**Schneider**, John 1954- *IntMPA 92*
**Schneider**, John A. *LesBEnT 92*
**Schneider**, John A. 1926- *IntMPA 92*
**Schneider**, John Arthur 1940- *AmMWSc 92*
**Schneider**, John Christopher 1956- *WhoMW 92*
**Schneider**, John Durbin 1937- *WhoAmP 91*
**Schneider**, John H 1931- *AmMWSc 92*
**Schneider**, John Matthew 1935- *AmMWSc 92*
**Schneider**, John Randall 1949- *WhoFI 92*
**Schneider**, John T 1945- *WhoAmP 91*
**Schneider**, Joseph 1918- *AmMWSc 92*
**Schneider**, Jurg Adolf 1920- *AmMWSc 92*
**Schneider**, Jurgen 1936- *WhoEnt 92*
**Schneider**, Karen Bush 1951- *WhoAmL 92*
**Schneider**, Kathryn Claire 1953- *AmMWSc 92*
**Schneider**, Kathryn Sue 1947- *WhoWest 92*
**Schneider**, Kenneth John 1926- *AmMWSc 92*
**Schneider**, Kenneth Robert 1956- *WhoEnt 92*
**Schneider**, Kent Edward 1945- *WhoEnt 92*
**Schneider**, Kim Nan 1956- *WhoMW 92*
**Schneider**, Lancelot Raymond A. *Who 92*
**Schneider**, Laurence Gordon 1956- *WhoFI 92*
**Schneider**, Lawrence Alan 1949- *WhoAmL 92*
**Schneider**, Lawrence Kruse 1936- *AmMWSc 92*
**Schneider**, Laz Levkoff 1939- *WhoAmL 92*
**Schneider**, Linda Leigh 1957- *WhoMW 92*
**Schneider**, Lloyd Rhynehart 1949- *WhoAmL 92*
**Schneider**, Lon S *AmMWSc 92*
**Schneider**, Louis James 1924- *WhoMW 92*
**Schneider**, Louis King 1934- *WhoRel 92*
**Schneider**, Louise Romero de Martinez 1943- *WhoWest 92*
**Schneider**, Marc H *AmMWSc 92*
**Schneider**, Mark David 1954- *WhoAmL 92*
**Schneider**, Marlin Dale 1942- *WhoAmP 91*
**Schneider**, Martin V 1930- *AmMWSc 92*
**Schneider**, Marvin Walter 1936- *WhoFI 92*
**Schneider**, Mary Willis 1925- *WhoMW 92*
**Schneider**, Matthew Roger 1948- *WhoAmL 92*
**Schneider**, Maxyne Dorothy 1942- *AmMWSc 92*
**Schneider**, Meier *WhoWest 92*
**Schneider**, Meier 1915- *AmMWSc 92*
**Schneider**, Michael Allen 1966- *WhoRel 92*
**Schneider**, Michael Charles 1929- *AmMWSc 92*
**Schneider**, Michael J 1938- *AmMWSc 92*
**Schneider**, Michael Louis 1954- *WhoAmL 92*
**Schneider**, Morris Henry 1923- *AmMWSc 92*
**Schneider**, Nina *DrAPF 91*
**Schneider**, Norman Richard 1943- *AmMWSc 92*
**Schneider**, Oscar 1927- *IntWW 91*
**Schneider**, Pam Horvitz 1951- *WhoAmL 92*
**Schneider**, Pat *DrAPF 91*
**Schneider**, Paul 1897-1939 *EncTR 91 [port]*
**Schneider**, Paul 1934- *AmMWSc 92*
**Schneider**, Paul L 1954- *WhoIns 92*
**Schneider**, Penny Lois 1954- *WhoAmL 92*
**Schneider**, Peter Raymond 1939- *WhoFI 92*
**Schneider**, Philip Allen David 1938- *AmMWSc 92*
**Schneider**, Phillip William, Jr 1944- *AmMWSc 92*
**Schneider**, Ralph Jacob 1922- *AmMWSc 92*
**Schneider**, Richard 1954- *WhoMW 92*
**Schneider**, Richard Clarence 1927- *WhoWest 92*
**Schneider**, Richard J 1936- *WhoAmP 91*
**Schneider**, Richard Louis 1950- *WhoMW 92*
**Schneider**, Richard Theodore 1927- *AmMWSc 92*
**Schneider**, Robert 1921- *AmMWSc 92*
**Schneider**, Robert Fournier 1933- *AmMWSc 92*
**Schneider**, Robert Jerome 1947- *WhoAmL 92*
**Schneider**, Robert Julius 1939- *AmMWSc 92*
**Schneider**, Robert W 1925- *AmMWSc 92*
**Schneider**, Robert W. 1933- *WrDr 92*
**Schneider**, Robert William 1933- *WhoMW 92*
**Schneider**, Ronald E 1928- *AmMWSc 92*
**Schneider**, Rose G 1908- *AmMWSc 92*
**Schneider**, Roy *DrAPF 91*
**Schneider**, Sandra Lee 1944- *AmMWSc 92*
**Schneider**, Sanford 1937- *WhoWest 92*
**Schneider**, Sascha 1946- *WhoEnt 92*
**Schneider**, Sol 1924- *AmMWSc 92*
**Schneider**, Stanley Dale 1921- *WhoRel 92*
**Schneider**, Stephen Henry 1945- *AmMWSc 92*
**Schneider**, Stephen Mark 1965- *WhoFI 92*
**Schneider**, Steven Philip 1960- *WhoMW 92*
**Schneider**, Theodore Frank 1934- *WhoRel 92*
**Schneider**, Thomas J 1948- *WhoAmP 91*
**Schneider**, Thomas Richard 1945- *WhoRel 92*
**Schneider**, Thomas Vernon 1945- *WhoMW 92*
**Schneider**, Walter Carl 1919- *AmMWSc 92*
**Schneider**, William, Jr 1941- *WhoAmP 91*
**Schneider**, William C 1923- *AmMWSc 92*
**Schneider**, William Charles 1940- *AmMWSc 92*
**Schneider**, William George 1915- *AmMWSc 92, IntWW 91, Who 92*
**Schneider**, William James 1939- *WhoFI 92*
**Schneider**, William Paul 1921- *AmMWSc 92*
**Schneider**, Willys Hope 1952- *WhoAmL 92*
**Schneider**, Wolfgang Johann 1949- *AmMWSc 92*
**Schneider**, Wolfgang W 1935- *AmMWSc 92*
**Schneider-Maunoury**, Michel 1931- *WhoFI 92*
**Schneiderat**, Catherine A 1942- *WhoAmP 91*
**Schneiderhan**, Wolfgang 1915- *IntWW 91*
**Schneiderhan**, Wolfgang, Frau *Who 92*
**Schneiderman**, Howard Allen 1927- *AmMWSc 92*
**Schneiderman**, Jill Stephanie 1959- *AmMWSc 92*
**Schneiderman**, L.J. *DrAPF 91*
**Schneiderman**, Lawrence J 1932- *AmMWSc 92*
**Schneiderman**, Martin Howard 1941- *AmMWSc 92*
**Schneiderman**, Marvin Arthur 1918- *AmMWSc 92*
**Schneiderman**, Neil 1937- *AmMWSc 92*
**Schneiderman**, Rose 1882-1972 *DcAmImH, FacFETw, HanAmWH, PorAmW [port]*
**Schneiderman**, William 1949- *WhoWest 92*
**Schneiderman**, William V 1905-1985 *FacFETw*
**Schneiders**, Lolita 1931- *WhoAmP 91*
**Schneiders**, Sandra Marie 1936- *WhoRel 92, WhoWest 92*
**Schneiderwent**, Myron Otto 1935- *AmMWSc 92*
**Schneidkraut**, Marlowe J 1954- *AmMWSc 92*
**Schneidre**, P. *DrAPF 91*
**Schneier**, Arthur 1930- *WhoRel 92*
**Schneier**, Frederick 1927- *IntMPA 92*
**Schneir**, Michael Lewis 1937- *AmMWSc 92*
**Schneir**, Steven Richard 1955- *WhoMW 92*
**Schneirsohn**, Eric E 1926- *WhoAmP 91*
**Schneiter**, George Malan 1931- *WhoWest 92*
**Schneiweiss**, Jeannette W 1920- *AmMWSc 92*
**Schnek**, M. Georges *WhoRel 92*
**Schnekloth**, Hugo 1923- *WhoAmP 91*
**Schnell**, Gary Dean 1942- *AmMWSc 92*
**Schnell**, Gene Wheeler 1924- *AmMWSc 92, WhoMW 92*
**Schnell**, Jay Heist 1932- *AmMWSc 92*
**Schnell**, Jerome Vincent 1934- *AmMWSc 92*
**Schnell**, Joseph *WhoEnt 92*
**Schnell**, Lonnie D. 1949- *WhoFI 92*
**Schnell**, Paul Thomas 1953- *WhoAmL 92*
**Schnell**, Robert Craig 1942- *AmMWSc 92*
**Schnell**, Roger Thomas 1936- *WhoWest 92*
**Schnelle**, Eberhardt *DcTwDes*
**Schnelle**, K B, Jr 1930- *AmMWSc 92*
**Schnelle**, Richard Max 1937- *WhoRel 92*
**Schnelle**, Wolfgang *DcTwDes*
**Schneller**, Carney Joe 1941- *WhoMW 92*
**Schneller**, Eugene S 1943- *AmMWSc 92, WhoWest 92*
**Schneller**, George Charles 1921- *WhoMW 92*
**Schneller**, Richard Francis 1922- *WhoAmP 91*
**Schneller**, Robert John 1950- *WhoFI 92*
**Schneller**, Stewart Wright 1942- *AmMWSc 92*
**Schnepfe**, Marian Moeller 1923- *AmMWSc 92*
**Schnepp**, Otto 1925- *AmMWSc 92*
**Schneps**, Jack 1929- *AmMWSc 92*
**Schner**, Joseph George 1942- *WhoRel 92*
**Schnettler**, Richard Anselm 1937- *AmMWSc 92*
**Schneyer**, Charlotte A 1923- *AmMWSc 92*
**Schnick**, Rosalie Arlene 1942- *WhoMW 92*
**Schniederjans**, Marc James 1950- *AmMWSc 92*
**Schnieders**, Edmund Francis, Jr. 1935- *WhoWest 92*
**Schnier**, David Christian 1942- *WhoFI 92, WhoMW 92*
**Schniewind**, Arno Peter 1929- *AmMWSc 92*
**Schnirman**, Alan Joel 1945- *WhoAmL 92*
**Schnitger** *NewAmDM*
**Schnitger**, Arp 1648-1719 *NewAmDM*
**Schnitke**, Al'fred Garrievich 1934- *SovUnBD*
**Schnitker**, Detmar 1937- *AmMWSc 92*
**Schnitker**, Jurgen H 1958- *AmMWSc 92*
**Schnittke**, Alfred 1934- *ConCom 92, IntWW 91, Who 92*
**Schnittke**, Al'fred Garrievich 1934- *SovUnBD*
**Schnittman**, Michael Stuart 1944- *WhoAmL 92*
**Schnitzer**, Arlene Director 1929- *WhoWest 92*
**Schnitzer**, Bertram 1929- *AmMWSc 92*
**Schnitzer**, Gary Allen 1942- *WhoWest 92*
**Schnitzer**, Howard J 1934- *AmMWSc 92*
**Schnitzer**, Jan Eugeneusz 1957- *AmMWSc 92*
**Schnitzer**, Jeshaia 1918- *WhoRel 92*
**Schnitzer**, Martin C. 1925- *ConAu 134*
**Schnitzer**, Morris 1922- *AmMWSc 92*
**Schnitzer**, Moshe 1921- *IntWW 91*
**Schnitzer**, Robert Allen 1950- *WhoEnt 92*
**Schnitzer**, Robert C. 1906- *WhoEnt 92*
**Schnitzlein**, Harold Norman 1927- *AmMWSc 92*
**Schnitzler**, Arthur 1862-1931 *FacFETw*
**Schnitzler**, Ronald Michael 1939- *AmMWSc 92*
**Schnizer**, Arthur Wallace 1923- *AmMWSc 92*
**Schnobrich**, Roger William 1929- *WhoAmL 92, WhoEnt 92*
**Schnobrich**, William Courtney 1930- *AmMWSc 92*
**Schnoebelen**, William James 1949- *WhoRel 92*
**Schnoes**, Heinrich Konstantin 1939- *AmMWSc 92*
**Schnoes**, James Thomas 1959- *WhoFI 92*
**Schnoll**, Howard Manuel 1935- *WhoFI 92*
**Schnonbaum**, Eduard 1923- *AmMWSc 92*
**Schnoor**, Jerald L 1950- *AmMWSc 92*
**Schnopper**, Herbert William 1933- *AmMWSc 92*
**Schnuck**, Craig 1948- *WhoFI 92, WhoMW 92*
**Schnuck**, Terry Edward 1952- *WhoMW 92*
**Schnucker**, Robert Victor 1932- *WhoRel 92*
**Schnur**, Joel Martin *WhoFI 92*
**Schnur**, Joel Martin 1945- *AmMWSc 92*
**Schnur**, Robert Arnold 1938- *WhoAmL 92, WhoMW 92*
**Schnur**, Rodney Caughren 1945- *AmMWSc 92*
**Schnur**, Sidney 1910- *AmMWSc 92*
**Schnurr**, Richard Allen 1955- *WhoAmL 92*
**Schnurre**, Wolfdietrich 1920- *IntAu&W 91*
**Schnurrenberger**, Paul Robert 1929- *AmMWSc 92*
**Schnyder**, Felix 1910- *Who 92*
**Schober**, Charles Coleman 1924- *AmMWSc 92*
**Schober**, Edward Alfred 1948- *WhoEnt 92*
**Schober**, Glenn E 1938- *AmMWSc 92*
**Schober**, John C 1951- *WhoAmP 91*
**Schobert**, Harold Harris 1943- *AmMWSc 92*
**Schobert**, Michael John 1965- *WhoMW 92*
**Schoby**, Barney 1940- *WhoAmP 91*
**Schoby**, Robert Milton, Jr. 1958- *WhoMW 92*
**Schoch**, Clarissa Anthony 1935- *WhoEnt 92*
**Schoch**, Daniel Anthony 1948- *AmMWSc 92, WhoMW 92*
**Schoch**, David Edmund 1920- *WhoRel 92*
**Schoch**, David Henry 1947- *WhoFI 92*
**Schochet**, Claude Lewis 1944- *AmMWSc 92, WhoMW 92*
**Schochet**, Melvin Leo 1924- *AmMWSc 92*
**Schochet**, Sydney Sigfried, Jr 1937- *AmMWSc 92*
**Schochor**, Jonathan 1946- *WhoAmL 92*
**Schock**, Robert Norman 1939- *AmMWSc 92*
**Schockemoehl**, Gwen Moses 1945- *WhoAmL 92*
**Schockemohle**, Alwin 1937- *IntWW 91*
**Schocken**, Gershom Gustav d1990 *IntWW 91N*
**Schocken**, Joseph L. 1946- *WhoFI 92*
**Schodrof**, Donald Henry 1942- *WhoMW 92*
**Schodt**, Kathleen Patricia 1950- *AmMWSc 92*
**Schoeberle**, Daniel F 1931- *AmMWSc 92*
**Schoech**, Charles Frederick 1949- *WhoAmL 92*

**Schoeck**, Clyde C 1939- *WhoIns 92*
**Schoeck**, Othmar 1886-1957 *NewAmDM*
**Schoeck**, V Jean 1923- *WhoAmP 91*
**Schoedinger**, David Stanton 1942- *WhoMW 92*
**Schoedsack**, Ernest B. 1893-1979 *IntDcF 2-2*
**Schoefer**, Ernest A 1908- *AmMWSc 92*
**Schoeffler**, Bryan 1957- *WhoRel 92*
**Schoeffling**, Michael *IntMPA 92*
**Schoelch**, Lawrence Francis 1953- *WhoAmL 92*
**Schoeld**, Constance Jerrine 1935- *WhoMW 92*
**Schoeller**, Francois 1934- *IntWW 91*
**Schoeller**, Franz Joachim Philipp 1926- *IntWW 91*
**Schoeller**, Thomas Harry 1955- *WhoEnt 92*
**Schoellkopf**, Joseph John, Jr. 1948- *WhoAmL 92*
**Schoellmann**, Guenther 1928- *AmMWSc 92*
**Schoemann**, Rudolph Robert 1930- *WhoAmL 92*
**Schoemehl**, Vincent C, Jr 1946- *WhoAmP 91*
**Schoemperlen**, Clarence Benjamin 1913- *AmMWSc 92*
**Schoemperlen**, Diane 1954- *ConAu 133*
**Schoen**, Arthur Boyer, Jr. 1953- *WhoFI 92*
**Schoen**, Barbara 1924- *IntAu&W 91*
**Schoen**, Charles Judd 1943- *WhoFI 92, WhoMW 92*
**Schoen**, Donald Charles 1953- *WhoMW 92*
**Schoen**, Frederick J 1946- *AmMWSc 92*
**Schoen**, Herbert M 1928- *AmMWSc 92*
**Schoen**, John Warren 1947- *AmMWSc 92*
**Schoen**, Kenneth 1932- *AmMWSc 92*
**Schoen**, Kurt L 1927- *AmMWSc 92*
**Schoen**, Max H 1922- *AmMWSc 92*
**Schoen**, Max Howard 1922- *IntWW 91*
**Schoen**, Rem *WhoFI 92*
**Schoen**, Richard Isaac 1927- *AmMWSc 92*
**Schoen**, Richard M 1950- *AmMWSc 92*
**Schoen**, Robert 1930- *AmMWSc 92*
**Schoen**, Rodric Bruce 1934- *WhoAmL 92*
**Schoen**, Stevan Jay 1944- *WhoAmL 92*
**Schoenbach**, Sol Israel 1915- *WhoEnt 92*
**Schoenbeck**, Paul John 1959- *WhoMW 92*
**Schoenberg**, Arnold 1874-1951 *FacFETw [port], NewAmDM*
**Schoenberg**, Bruce Stuart 1942- *AmMWSc 92*
**Schoenberg**, Daniel Robert 1949- *AmMWSc 92*
**Schoenberg**, Jeffrey M 1959- *WhoAmP 91*
**Schoenberg**, Leonard Norman 1940- *AmMWSc 92*
**Schoenberg**, Mark 1943- *AmMWSc 92*
**Schoenberg**, Mark George 1947- *WhoAmP 91*
**Schoenberg**, Theodore 1939- *AmMWSc 92*
**Schoenberger**, Charlotte Sally 1917- *WhoAmP 91*
**Schoenberger**, Edward Henry 1942- *WhoMW 92*
**Schoenberger**, James A 1919- *AmMWSc 92*
**Schoenberger**, Maralyn Morton 1929- *WhoAmP 91*
**Schoenberger**, Michael 1940- *AmMWSc 92*
**Schoenberger**, Nancy *DrAPF 91*
**Schoenberger**, Nancy 1950- *IntAu&W 91*
**Schoenberger**, Robert J 1938- *AmMWSc 92*
**Schoenblum**, Jeffrey A. 1948- *WhoAmL 92*
**Schoenborn**, Benno P 1936- *AmMWSc 92*
**Schoenborn**, Roger Lee 1948- *WhoRel 92*
**Schoenbrun**, David d1988 *LesBEnT 92*
**Schoenbrun**, David 1915- *IntAu&W 91*
**Schoenbrun**, Michael Paul 1938- *WhoFI 92*
**Schoenbrunn**, Erwin F 1921- *AmMWSc 92*
**Schoendoerffer**, Pierre 1928- *IntWW 91*
**Schoendorf**, Judson Raymond 1942- *WhoWest 92*
**Schoendorf**, Walter John 1927- *WhoFI 92*
**Schoendorf**, William H 1936- *AmMWSc 92*
**Schoene**, Kathleen Snyder 1953- *WhoAmL 92, WhoFI 92, WhoMW 92*
**Schoene**, Norberta Wachter 1943- *AmMWSc 92*
**Schoene**, Robert B 1946- *AmMWSc 92*
**Schoeneberg**, Debra Sue 1953- *WhoEnt 92*
**Schoeneberg**, Wayne Thomas 1946- *WhoAmL 92*
**Schoeneck**, David Lee 1946- *WhoFI 92*
**Schoenecker**, Warren Kroy 1930- *WhoRel 92*
**Schoener**, Eugene Paul 1943- *AmMWSc 92*
**Schoener**, Gary Richard 1944- *WhoMW 92*
**Schoener**, Thomas William 1943- *AmMWSc 92*
**Schoeneweiss**, Donald F 1929- *AmMWSc 92*
**Schoenfein**, Robert A. 1937- *WhoFI 92*
**Schoenfeld**, Alan Henry 1947- *AmMWSc 92*
**Schoenfeld**, Barbara Braun 1953- *WhoAmL 92*
**Schoenfeld**, Cy 1939- *AmMWSc 92*
**Schoenfeld**, David Alan 1945- *AmMWSc 92*
**Schoenfeld**, Hanns-Martin Walter 1928- *WhoFI 92*
**Schoenfeld**, Jerry 1951- *WhoAmP 91*
**Schoenfeld**, Lawrence Jon 1945- *WhoWest 92*
**Schoenfeld**, Lawrence Steven 1941- *AmMWSc 92*
**Schoenfeld**, Lester 1916- *IntMPA 92*
**Schoenfeld**, Maxwell Philip 1936- *IntAu&W 91, WrDr 92*
**Schoenfeld**, Michael P. 1935- *WhoAmL 92*
**Schoenfeld**, Myron Royal 1928- *WhoFI 92*
**Schoenfeld**, Robert George 1926- *AmMWSc 92*
**Schoenfeld**, Robert Louis 1920- *AmMWSc 92*
**Schoenfeld**, Ronald Irwin *AmMWSc 92*
**Schoenfeld**, Scott Reid 1936- *WhoAmL 92*
**Schoenfeld**, Theodore Mark 1907- *AmMWSc 92*
**Schoenfeldt**, Heidi Ann 1965- *WhoEnt 92*
**Schoenfeldt**, Stephanie *DrAPF 91*
**Schoenfield**, Leslie Jack 1932- *AmMWSc 92*
**Schoengarth**, Robert Scott 1949- *WhoWest 92*
**Schoenhals**, Robert James 1933- *AmMWSc 92*
**Schoenhard**, William Charles, Jr. 1949- *WhoFI 92, WhoMW 92*
**Schoenherr**, John 1935- *SmATA 66 [port], SmATA 13AS [port]*
**Schoenherr**, Richard Anthony 1935- *IntAu&W 91, WrDr 92*
**Schoenherr**, Roman Uhrich 1934- *AmMWSc 92*
**Schoenherr**, Walter Joseph 1920- *WhoRel 92*
**Schoenholz**, Walter Kurt 1923- *AmMWSc 92*
**Schoenig**, Vincent Werner 1964- *WhoFI 92*
**Schoenike**, Roland Ernest 1925- *AmMWSc 92*
**Schoening**, John Wolfgang 1937- *WhoFI 92*
**Schoenly**, Kenneth George 1956- *AmMWSc 92*
**Schoenoff**, Arthur William 1930- *WhoEnt 92, WhoMW 92*
**Schoenrock**, Tracy Allen 1960- *WhoMW 92*
**Schoenstadt**, Arthur Loring 1942- *AmMWSc 92*
**Schoenstein**, Joseph Roy 1957- *WhoMW 92*
**Schoenwald**, Larry Wayne *WhoAmP 91*
**Schoenwald**, Maurice Louis 1920- *WhoFI 92*
**Schoenwetter**, James 1935- *AmMWSc 92*
**Schoenwolf**, Gary Charles 1949- *AmMWSc 92*
**Schoep**, Arthur Paul 1920- *WhoEnt 92*
**Schoepfer**, Arthur E 1931- *AmMWSc 92*
**Schoepfer**, Virginia B 1934- *IntAu&W 91*
**Schoepfle**, Gordon Marcus 1915- *AmMWSc 92*
**Schoephoerster**, Lorin Keith 1923- *WhoIns 92, WhoMW 92*
**Schoepke**, Hollis George 1929- *AmMWSc 92*
**Schoepp**, Mark Leonard 1954- *WhoRel 92*
**Schoeppel**, Cynthia Louise *WhoMW 92*
**Schoeps**, Karl Heinz Joachim 1935- *WhoMW 92*
**Schoeser**, Mary 1950- *ConAu 133*
**Schoessler**, John Paul 1942- *AmMWSc 92*
**Schoettger**, Richard A 1932- *AmMWSc 92*
**Schoettger**, Theodore Leo 1920- *WhoWest 92*
**Schoettinger**, Douglas Bruce 1952- *WhoAmL 92*
**Schoettle**, Frederick John 1939- *WhoMW 92*
**Schoettler**, Gail Sinton 1943- *WhoAmP 91, WhoWest 92*
**Schoettler**, James Anthony, Jr. 1956- *WhoAmL 92*
**Schoettler**, R. William 1936- *WhoAmL 92*
**Schofer**, Gordon Keith 1936- *WhoMW 92*
**Schoff**, Paul J. 1958- *WhoAmL 92*
**Schoffer**, Nicolas 1912- *IntWW 91*
**Schoffstall**, Allen M 1939- *AmMWSc 92*
**Schoffstall**, Phil *WhoMW 92*
**Schoffstoll**, Pat Anne 1954- *WhoEnt 92*
**Schofield**, Alfred 1913- *Who 92*
**Schofield**, Alfred Taylor 1846-1929 *ScFEYrs*
**Schofield**, Andrew Noel 1930- *Who 92*
**Schofield**, Anthony Wayne 1949- *WhoAmL 92*
**Schofield**, Bertram 1896- *Who 92*
**Schofield**, Calvin Onderdonk, Jr. 1933- *WhoRel 92*
**Schofield**, Derek 1928- *AmMWSc 92*
**Schofield**, Edmund Acton, Jr 1938- *AmMWSc 92*
**Schofield**, George H. 1929- *WhoFI 92*
**Schofield**, Grace Florence 1925- *Who 92*
**Schofield**, Jack H 1923- *WhoAmP 91*
**Schofield**, Jack Lund 1923- *WhoAmP 91*
**Schofield**, James Roy 1923- *AmMWSc 92*
**Schofield**, James W 1931- *WhoAmP 91*
**Schofield**, John-David Mercer 1938- *WhoRel 92, WhoWest 92*
**Schofield**, John Dean *WhoEnt 92*
**Schofield**, John McAllister 1831-1906 *BiInAmS*
**Schofield**, Michael 1919- *IntAu&W 91, WrDr 92*
**Schofield**, Paul *IntAu&W 91X, WrDr 92*
**Schofield**, Richard Alan 1924- *AmMWSc 92*
**Schofield**, Robert Edwin 1923- *AmMWSc 92*
**Schofield**, Roger Snowden 1937- *Who 92*
**Schofield**, S Gene 1947- *WhoIns 92*
**Schofield**, Sylvia Anne *WrDr 92*
**Schofield**, Sylvia Anne 1918- *IntAu&W 91*
**Schofield**, W. B. 1927- *ConAu 134*
**Schofield**, Wilfred Borden 1927- *AmMWSc 92*
**Schofield**, William 1921- *AmMWSc 92*
**Schofield**, William Greenough 1909- *IntAu&W 91*
**Schofield**, Wyvonna L. 1943- *WhoWest 92*
**Schoger**, Harry George, Jr. 1937- *WhoMW 92*
**Schohl**, Joanna Elizabeth 1954- *WhoMW 92*
**Schoknecht**, Jean Donze *AmMWSc 92*
**Scholar**, Eric M 1939- *AmMWSc 92*
**Scholar**, Michael Charles 1942- *Who 92*
**Scholberg**, Harold Milton 1910- *AmMWSc 92*
**Scholder**, Fritz 1937- *WorArt 1980 [port]*
**Scholderer**, Otto 1834-1902 *ThHEIm*
**Scholefield**, A. T. *ConAu 34NR, SmATA 66 [port]*
**Scholefield**, Alan 1931- *ConAu 34NR, IntAu&W 91, SmATA 66 [port], WrDr 92*
**Scholefield**, Charles Edward 1902- *Who 92*
**Scholer**, Charles Frey 1934- *AmMWSc 92*
**Scholer**, David Milton 1938- *WhoRel 92*
**Scholer**, Randal J. 1956- *WhoAmL 92*
**Scholer**, Sue 1936- *WhoAmP 91*
**Scholes**, Alwyn Denton 1910- *Who 92*
**Scholes**, Charles Patterson 1942- *AmMWSc 92*
**Scholes**, Gordon Glen Denton 1931- *IntWW 91, Who 92*
**Scholes**, Hubert 1921- *Who 92*
**Scholes**, Mary Elizabeth 1924- *Who 92*
**Scholes**, Myron S. 1941- *WhoAmL 92*
**Scholes**, Norman W 1930- *AmMWSc 92*
**Scholes**, Rodney James 1945- *Who 92*
**Scholes**, Samuel Ray, Jr *AmMWSc 92*
**Scholey**, Arthur 1932- *IntAu&W 91, WrDr 92*
**Scholey**, David 1935- *Who 92*
**Scholey**, David Gerald 1935- *IntWW 91*
**Scholey**, Robert 1921- *IntWW 91, Who 92*
**Scholfield**, Charles Rexel 1914- *AmMWSc 92*
**Scholl**, Allan Henry 1935- *WhoWest 92*
**Scholl**, Daniel John 1949- *WhoFI 92*
**Scholl**, David Carl 1956- *WhoIns 92*
**Scholl**, Dennis Michael 1949- *WhoAmP 91*
**Scholl**, Eric Francis 1955- *WhoEnt 92*
**Scholl**, Fenton Thomas, Jr. 1950- *WhoRel 92*
**Scholl**, Gunther 1909- *IntWW 91*
**Scholl**, Hans 1918-1943 *EncTR 91 [port]*
**Scholl**, James Francis 1957- *AmMWSc 92*
**Scholl**, Joan Bernadette 1960- *WhoMW 92*
**Scholl**, Julie Ann 1960- *WhoWest 92*
**Scholl**, Marija Strojnik *AmMWSc 92*
**Scholl**, Philip Jon 1945- *AmMWSc 92*
**Scholl**, Sophie 1921-1943 *EncTR 91 [port]*
**Schollander**, Wendell Leslie, Jr. 1943- *WhoAmL 92*
**Schollenberger**, Charles David 1952- *WhoMW 92*
**Schollenberger**, Charles Sundy 1922- *AmMWSc 92*
**Scholler**, Jean 1919- *AmMWSc 92*
**Scholler**, Thomas Peter 1937- *WhoMW 92*
**Schollkopf**, Ulrich 1927- *IntWW 91*
**Scholnick**, Frank 1925- *AmMWSc 92*
**Scholnick**, Michael *DrAPF 91*
**Scholnick**, Steven Bruce 1955- *AmMWSc 92*
**Scholsky**, Martin Joseph 1930- *WhoRel 92*
**Scholte**, Cassandra 1933- *WhoAmP 91*
**Scholte**, H. P. *DcAmImH*
**Scholten**, Eugene Alvin 1928- *WhoMW 92*
**Scholten**, Paul David 1949- *AmMWSc 92*
**Scholten**, Willem 1927- *IntWW 91*
**Scholtens**, James 1920- *Who 92*
**Scholtens**, Jean Ann 1949- *WhoFI 92*
**Scholtens**, Robert George 1929- *AmMWSc 92*
**Scholtes**, Elizabeth Frances 1962- *WhoRel 92*
**Scholtes**, Wayne Henry 1917- *AmMWSc 92*
**Scholtz**, Amber Erna 1948- *WhoAmP 91*
**Scholtz**, Robert A 1936- *AmMWSc 92*
**Scholtz**, Robert Arno 1936- *WhoWest 92*
**Scholtz-Klink**, Gertrud 1902- *EncAmaz 91, EncTR 91 [port]*
**Scholz**, Brandon 1955- *WhoAmP 91, WhoMW 92*
**Scholz**, Charles Adam 1926- *WhoAmL 92*
**Scholz**, Christopher Henry 1943- *AmMWSc 92*
**Scholz**, Dan Robert 1920- *AmMWSc 92*
**Scholz**, Earl Walter 1925- *AmMWSc 92*
**Scholz**, Jackson 1897-1986 *FacFETw*
**Scholz**, Jane 1948- *WhoMW 92*
**Scholz**, John Joseph, Jr 1926- *AmMWSc 92*
**Scholz**, Lawrence Charles 1933- *AmMWSc 92*
**Scholz**, Mary Edith 1958- *WhoMW 92*
**Scholz**, Paul Drummond 1936- *AmMWSc 92*
**Scholz**, Richard W 1942- *AmMWSc 92*
**Scholz**, Robert George 1930- *AmMWSc 92*
**Scholz**, Rupert 1937- *IntWW 91, Who 92*
**Scholz**, Uwe 1958- *WhoEnt 92*
**Scholz**, Wilfried 1936- *AmMWSc 92*
**Schomaker**, Verner 1914- *AmMWSc 92*
**Schoman**, Charles M, Jr 1924- *AmMWSc 92*
**Schomburger**, John Lee 1961- *WhoAmL 92*
**Schomer**, Donald Lee 1946- *AmMWSc 92*
**Schomer**, Howard 1915- *WhoRel 92*
**Schommer**, Shirley 1928- *WhoAmP 91*
**Schommer**, Trudy Marie 1937- *WhoRel 92*
**Schon** *Who 92*
**Schon**, Baron 1912- *IntWW 91, Who 92*
**Schon**, Alan Wallace 1946- *WhoWest 92*
**Schon**, Isabel 1940- *WhoHisp 92*
**Schon**, Jeffrey V. 1952- *WhoEnt 92*
**Schonbeck**, Niels Daniel 1945- *AmMWSc 92*
**Schonberg**, Harold C 1915- *IntAu&W 91, IntWW 91, WrDr 92*
**Schonberg**, Harold Charles 1915- *WhoEnt 92*
**Schonberg**, Herman 1922- *WhoFI 92*
**Schonberg**, Ina Valborg 1960- *WhoFI 92*
**Schonberg**, Russell George 1926- *AmMWSc 92*
**Schonberg**, Steven Ephraim 1942- *WhoAmL 92*
**Schonbrun**, Adam *DrAPF 91*
**Schonbrunn**, Agnes 1948- *AmMWSc 92*
**Schone**, Albrecht 1925- *IntWW 91*
**Schone**, Harlan Eugene 1932- *AmMWSc 92*
**Schonebeck**, Eugen 1936- *WorArt 1980*
**Schonerer**, Georg, Ritter von 1842-1921 *BiDExR, EncTR 91 [port]*
**Schonewald-Cox**, Christine Micheline *AmMWSc 92*
**Schoney**, Lazarus 1838-1914 *BiInAmS*
**Schonfeld**, Edward 1930- *AmMWSc 92*
**Schonfeld**, Fabian 1923- *WhoRel 92*
**Schonfeld**, Gustav 1934- *AmMWSc 92*
**Schonfeld**, Hyman Kolman 1919- *AmMWSc 92*
**Schonfeld**, Norman J. 1934- *IntMPA 92*
**Schonfeld**, Reese *LesBEnT 92*
**Schonfeld**, Steven Emanuel 1947- *AmMWSc 92*
**Schonfeld**, Victoria E. 1950- *WhoAmL 92*
**Schonhoff**, Robert Lee 1919- *WhoFI 92, WhoRel 92*
**Schonhoff**, Thomas Arthur 1947- *AmMWSc 92*
**Schonhorn**, Harold 1928- *AmMWSc 92*
**Schonhorst**, Melvin Herman 1919- *AmMWSc 92*
**Schoning**, Robert Whitney 1923- *AmMWSc 92*
**Schonstedt**, Erick O 1917- *AmMWSc 92*
**Schonwalder**, Christopher O 1943- *AmMWSc 92*
**Schonzeler**, Hans-Hubert 1925- *IntWW 91*
**Schoof**, Leslie Earl 1951- *WhoEnt 92*
**Schoofs**, Gerald Joseph 1954- *WhoMW 92*
**Schoolar**, Joseph Clayton 1928- *AmMWSc 92*
**Schoolcraft**, Alan L 1952- *WhoAmP 91*
**Schoolcraft**, Donald *WhoAmP 91*
**Schoolcraft**, Henry Rowe 1793-1864 *BenetAL 91, BiInAmS*
**Schooler**, James Morse, Jr. 1936- *WhoBlA 92*
**Schooler**, Lionel Mark 1946- *WhoAmL 92*
**Schooley**, Arthur Thomas 1932- *AmMWSc 92*

**Schooley**, Caroline Naus 1932- *AmMWSc 92*
**Schooley**, David Allan 1943- *AmMWSc 92, WhoWest 92*
**Schooley**, Dolores Harter 1905- *WhoEnt 92*
**Schooley**, James Frederick 1931- *AmMWSc 92*
**Schooley**, Jennifer Lynn 1957- *WhoRel 92*
**Schooley**, John C 1928- *AmMWSc 92*
**Schooley**, John Heilman 1943- *WhoEnt 92*
**Schooley**, Kenneth Ralph 1943- *WhoFI 92*
**Schooley**, Robert T 1949- *AmMWSc 92*
**Schooley**, Warren Calvin 1923- *WhoRel 92*
**Schoolman**, Harold M 1924- *AmMWSc 92*
**Schools**, Charles Hughlette 1929- *WhoFI 92*
**Schoon**, David Jacob 1943- *AmMWSc 92*
**Schoon**, Eugene A. 1952- *WhoAmL 92*
**Schoon**, John Edward 1929- *WhoAmP 91*
**Schoon**, Nelson Roy 1954- *WhoRel 92*
**Schoon**, Richard F 1931- *WhoAmP 91*
**Schoon**, Susan Wylie 1948- *WhoFI 92*
**Schoone**, Raymond Lawrence 1931- *WhoRel 92*
**Schoonen**, Anthony Arthur 1961- *WhoEnt 92*
**Schoonhoven**, Ray James 1921- *WhoAmL 92, WhoMW 92*
**Schoonmaker**, George Russell 1916- *AmMWSc 92*
**Schoonmaker**, L Craig 1944- *WhoAmP 91*
**Schoonmaker**, Richard Clinton 1930- *AmMWSc 92*
**Schoonmaker**, Samuel Vail, III 1935- *WhoAmL 92*
**Schoonmaker**, Thelma *ReelWom*
**Schoonmaker**, Thelma 1945- *ConTFT 9*
**Schoonmaker**, William J., III 1921- *WhoAmL 92*
**Schoonover**, Amy Jo *DrAPF 91*
**Schoonover**, Amy Jo 1937- *IntAu&W 91*
**Schoonover**, Melvin Eugene 1926- *WhoRel 92*
**Schoonover**, Randy 1953- *WhoAmP 91*
**Schoonover**, Ruthann Komarek 1951- *WhoAmP 91*
**Schoonover**, Shirley W. *DrAPF 91*
**Schoonover**, Terrance Vance 1951- *WhoMW 92*
**Schoop**, Ernest R. 1936- *WhoHisp 92*
**Schoor**, Michael Mercier 1942- *WhoAmL 92*
**Schoor**, W Peter 1936- *AmMWSc 92*
**Schopf**, J. William 1941- *ConAu 133*
**Schopf**, James William 1941- *AmMWSc 92*
**Schopf**, Johann David 1752-1800 *BiInAmS*
**Schopf**, Thomas Joseph Morton 1939- *AmMWSc 92*
**Schopf**, William Grant 1948- *WhoAmL 92*
**Schopler**, Harry A 1926- *AmMWSc 92*
**Schopp**, John David 1927- *AmMWSc 92*
**Schopp**, Robert Thomas 1923- *AmMWSc 92*
**Schopp**, Steven Edward 1944- *WhoEnt 92*
**Schoppa**, Elroy 1922- *WhoFI 92, WhoWest 92*
**Schoppa**, R. Keith 1943- *WhoMW 92*
**Schopper**, Herwig Franz 1924- *AmMWSc 92, IntWW 91*
**Schopper**, Herwig Franz 1928- *Who 92*
**Schoppmann**, Kenneth Philip 1964- *WhoFI 92*
**Schor**, Edward Neil 1947- *WhoAmL 92*
**Schor**, Joseph Martin 1929- *AmMWSc 92*
**Schor**, Laurence 1942- *WhoAmL 92*
**Schor**, Lynda *DrAPF 91*
**Schor**, Norberto Aaron 1929- *AmMWSc 92*
**Schor**, Robert 1929- *AmMWSc 92*
**Schor**, Sandra 1932?-1990 *ConLC 65 [port]*
**Schor**, Stanley 1922- *AmMWSc 92*
**Schora**, Barbra Ann 1957- *WhoWest 92*
**Schorb**, E.M. *DrAPF 91*
**Schore**, Neil Eric 1948- *AmMWSc 92*
**Schorer**, Calvin E 1919- *AmMWSc 92*
**Schorer**, Mark 1908-1977 *BenetAL 91*
**Schorgl**, Thomas Barry 1950- *WhoEnt 92, WhoMW 92*
**Schori**, Richard M 1938- *AmMWSc 92*
**Schork**, Michael Anthony 1936- *AmMWSc 92*
**Schorle**, Bernard Joseph, Jr. 1960- *WhoMW 92*
**Schorling**, William Harrison 1949- *WhoAmL 92*
**Schorm**, Evald 1931-1988 *IntDcF 2-2 [port]*
**Schornack**, Gary Raymond 1941- *WhoMW 92*
**Schornack**, John James 1930- *WhoFI 92*
**Schorner**, Ferdinand 1892-1973 *EncTR 91 [port]*
**Schornhorst**, Eric Jay 1960- *WhoFI 92*
**Schornick**, Lynn Barry 1950- *WhoEnt 92*
**Schorno**, Karl Stanley 1939- *AmMWSc 92*
**Schorr**, Alan Edward 1945- *WhoWest 92*
**Schorr**, Arny 1946- *WhoEnt 92*
**Schorr**, Daniel *LesBEnT 92*
**Schorr**, Daniel 1916- *IntMPA 92*
**Schorr**, Eleanor D *WhoAmP 91*
**Schorr**, Friedrich 1888-1953 *NewAmDM*
**Schorr**, Harvey Charles 1943- *WhoFI 92*
**Schorr**, Herbert 1936- *AmMWSc 92*
**Schorr**, Lisbeth Bamberger 1931- *AmMWSc 92*
**Schorr**, Mark 1953- *WrDr 92*
**Schorr**, Mark Scott 1953- *WhoEnt 92*
**Schorr**, Martin Mark 1923- *WhoWest 92*
**Schorr**, Marvin G. 1925- *WhoFI 92*
**Schorr**, Marvin Gerald 1925- *AmMWSc 92*
**Schorr**, Ralph Hartman 1958- *WhoMW 92*
**Schorsch**, Ismar 1935- *WhoRel 92*
**Schory**, Earl A, II 1950- *WhoAmP 91*
**Schory**, Karen Renee 1953- *WhoMW 92*
**Schorzman**, Mark Hewit 1937- *WhoWest 92*
**Schotanus**, Eugene Leroy 1937- *WhoFI 92*
**Schotanus**, Merle William 1931- *WhoAmP 91*
**Schotland**, Richard Morton 1927- *AmMWSc 92*
**Schott**, Arthur Carl Victor 1814-1875 *BiInAmS*
**Schott**, Bernhard 1748-1809 *NewAmDM*
**Schott**, Charles Anthony 1826-1901 *BiInAmS*
**Schott**, Charles George 1951- *WhoAmL 92*
**Schott**, Clifford Joseph 1926- *WhoAmL 92*
**Schott**, Frederick W 1919- *AmMWSc 92*
**Schott**, Garry Lee 1931- *AmMWSc 92*
**Schott**, George E. 1936- *WhoFI 92*
**Schott**, Hans 1922- *AmMWSc 92*
**Schott**, Jeffrey Howard 1947- *AmMWSc 92*
**Schott**, Louis Ried 1949- *WhoWest 92*
**Schott**, Marge 1928- *WhoMW 92*
**Schott**, Mary Alice 1965- *WhoMW 92*
**Schott**, Penelope Scambly *DrAPF 91*
**Schott**, Penelope Scambly 1942- *WrDr 92*
**Schott**, Rudiger 1927- *IntWW 91*
**Schott**, Stephen Harold 1961- *WhoMW 92*
**Schotte**, Jan 1928- *IntWW 91*
**Schotte**, William 1927- *AmMWSc 92*
**Schottel**, Janet L *AmMWSc 92*
**Schottelius**, Byron Arthur 1922- *AmMWSc 92*
**Schottelius**, Dorothy Dickey 1927- *AmMWSc 92*
**Schottelkotte**, Albert Joseph 1927- *WhoEnt 92, WhoMW 92*
**Schottenfeld**, Barbara *ConAu 134*
**Schottenheimer**, Martin Edward 1943- *WhoMW 92*
**Schottenstein**, Jerome M. 1926- *WhoFI 92*
**Schottenstein**, Saul 1924- *WhoFI 92*
**Schotter**, Richard Daniel 1917- *WhoRel 92*
**Schotter**, Roni *DrAPF 91*
**Schottlander**, Dan Edmund 1951- *WhoWest 92*
**Schottmiller**, John Charles 1930- *AmMWSc 92*
**Schottstaedt**, William Walter 1917- *AmMWSc 92*
**Schotz**, Benno 1891-1984 *TwCPaSc*
**Schotz**, Larry 1949- *AmMWSc 92*
**Schotz**, Michael C 1928- *AmMWSc 92*
**Schotzko**, Judith Gilbert 1938- *WhoAmP 91*
**Schoulties**, Calvin Lee 1943- *AmMWSc 92*
**Schoultz**, Solveig von 1907- *IntAu&W 91*
**Schoultz**, Ture William 1940- *AmMWSc 92*
**Schoumacher**, David *LesBEnT 92*
**Schouvaloff**, Alexander 1934- *Who 92*
**Schover**, Leslie Ruth 1952- *WhoMW 92*
**Schow**, Terry D. 1948- *WhoWest 92*
**Schowalter**, Ellen Lefferts 1937- *WhoFI 92*
**Schowalter**, Toni Lee 1948- *WhoEnt 92*
**Schowalter**, William Raymond 1929- *AmMWSc 92*
**Schowen**, Richard Lyle 1934- *AmMWSc 92*
**Schowengerdt**, Franklin Dean 1936- *AmMWSc 92*
**Schowengerdt**, Louis W. *WhoRel 92*
**Schowengerdt**, Robert Alan 1946- *AmMWSc 92*
**Schrack**, Roald Amundsen 1926- *AmMWSc 92*
**Schrade**, Rolande Maxwell Young *WhoEnt 92*
**Schrader**, Alfred Eugene 1953- *WhoAmL 92*
**Schrader**, Barry Walter 1945- *WhoEnt 92*
**Schrader**, Bruce John 1954- *WhoMW 92*
**Schrader**, David 1952- *WhoAmP 91*
**Schrader**, David Alan 1954- *WhoRel 92*
**Schrader**, David Hawley 1925- *AmMWSc 92*
**Schrader**, David Martin 1932- *AmMWSc 92*
**Schrader**, Donald Lee 1946- *WhoAmP 91, WhoWest 92*
**Schrader**, Dorothy Marie 1938- *WhoAmL 92*
**Schrader**, Dorothy Virginia 1921- *AmMWSc 92*
**Schrader**, George Frederick 1920- *AmMWSc 92*
**Schrader**, Henry Carl 1918- *WhoFI 92*
**Schrader**, Keith William 1938- *AmMWSc 92*
**Schrader**, Lawrence Edwin 1941- *AmMWSc 92*
**Schrader**, Lee Frederick 1933- *WhoMW 92*
**Schrader**, Lynn Ann 1964- *WhoMW 92*
**Schrader**, Paul 1946- *IntDcF 2-2 [port], IntMPA 92*
**Schrader**, Paul Joseph 1946- *IntWW 91, WhoEnt 92*
**Schrader**, R J 1918- *AmMWSc 92*
**Schrader**, Robert J. 1918- *WhoFI 92*
**Schrader**, Thomas F. 1950- *WhoFI 92*
**Schrader**, William Thurber 1943- *AmMWSc 92*
**Schradie**, Joseph 1933- *AmMWSc 92*
**Schradieck**, Henry 1846-1918 *NewAmDM*
**Schrady**, David Alan 1939- *AmMWSc 92*
**Schraeder**, James Jay 1949- *WhoMW 92*
**Schraer**, Harald 1920- *AmMWSc 92*
**Schraer**, Rosemary 1924- *AmMWSc 92*
**Schraer**, Rosemary S. J. 1924- *WhoWest 92*
**Schrag**, Calvin Orville 1950- *WhoMW 92, WhoRel 92*
**Schrag**, Crystal Blythe 1965- *WhoFI 92*
**Schrag**, Delbert J. 1921- *WhoRel 92*
**Schrag**, John L 1937- *AmMWSc 92*
**Schrag**, Peter 1931- *IntAu&W 91, WrDr 92*
**Schrag**, Philip Gordon 1943- *WhoAmL 92*
**Schrag**, Robert L 1924- *AmMWSc 92*
**Schrag**, Ronald Karl 1946- *WhoMW 92*
**Schrag**, William Henry 1953- *WhoAmL 92*
**Schrage**, F Eugene 1934- *AmMWSc 92*
**Schrage**, Robert W 1925- *AmMWSc 92*
**Schrage**, Samuel 1920- *AmMWSc 92*
**Schrager**, Gary 1941- *WhoEnt 92*
**Schrager**, Mindy Rae 1958- *WhoFI 92*
**Schram**, Albert-George *WhoEnt 92*
**Schram**, Alfred C 1930- *AmMWSc 92*
**Schram**, Armin 1929- *IntWW 91*
**Schram**, Eugene P 1934- *AmMWSc 92*
**Schram**, Frederick R 1943- *AmMWSc 92*
**Schram**, Henry B. *WhoFI 92*
**Schram**, Peninnah *DrAPF 91*
**Schram**, Spencer Lee 1951- *WhoAmP 91*
**Schram**, Stuart Reynolds 1924- *Who 92*
**Schramek**, Bradley Walter 1960- *WhoMW 92*
**Schramek**, Eric von *Who 92*
**Schramek**, Lynn Beth Gottlieb 1956- *WhoMW 92*
**Schramek**, Tomas 1944- *WhoEnt 92*
**Schramel**, Robert Joseph 1924- *AmMWSc 92*
**Schramm**, Albert *WhoAmP 91*
**Schramm**, Bernard Charles, Jr. 1928- *WhoFI 92*
**Schramm**, Carl J 1946- *WhoIns 92*
**Schramm**, Darrell G.H. *DrAPF 91*
**Schramm**, David N 1945- *AmMWSc 92, ConAu 135*
**Schramm**, John Gilbert 1951- *AmMWSc 92*
**Schramm**, Lee Clyde 1934- *AmMWSc 92*
**Schramm**, Martin William, Jr 1927- *AmMWSc 92*
**Schramm**, Mary Arthur 1932- *AmMWSc 92*
**Schramm**, Paul Howard 1933- *WhoAmL 92*
**Schramm**, Raymond Eugene 1941- *AmMWSc 92, WhoWest 92*
**Schramm**, Richard *DrAPF 91*
**Schramm**, Richard Martin 1940- *WhoMW 92*
**Schramm**, Robert Frederick 1942- *AmMWSc 92*
**Schramm**, Robert William 1934- *AmMWSc 92*
**Schramm**, Vern Lee 1941- *AmMWSc 92*
**Schramm**, Werner 1926- *IntAu&W 91*
**Schramm**, Wilbur 1907- *BenetAL 91*
**Schrank**, Auline Raymond 1915- *AmMWSc 92*
**Schrank**, Glen Edward 1926- *AmMWSc 92*
**Schrank**, Gordon Dabney 1948- *AmMWSc 92*
**Schrank**, Holly L. 1941- *WhoMW 92*
**Schrank**, Jeffrey 1944- *IntAu&W 91, WrDr 92*
**Schrank**, Joseph Anthony 1951- *WhoFI 92*
**Schrank**, Ralf Gerd 1949- *IntWW 91*
**Schrank**, Raymond Edward, II 1944- *WhoAmL 92*
**Schrankel**, Kenneth Reinhold 1945- *AmMWSc 92*
**Schraut**, Kenneth Charles 1913- *AmMWSc 92*
**Schrauzer**, Gerhard N 1932- *AmMWSc 92*
**Schray**, Keith James 1943- *AmMWSc 92*
**Schreader**, Gregory James 1955- *WhoIns 92*
**Schreck**, Alan Edward 1951- *WhoRel 92*
**Schreck**, Carl Bernhard 1944- *AmMWSc 92*
**Schreck**, Charles Edward 1965- *WhoMW 92*
**Schreck**, David Allen 1952- *WhoWest 92*
**Schreck**, James O 1937- *AmMWSc 92*
**Schreck**, Robert A., Jr. 1952- *WhoAmL 92*
**Schreckenberg**, Mary Gervasia 1916- *AmMWSc 92*
**Schreckenberger**, Paul Charles 1947- *WhoMW 92*
**Schreckengast**, William Owen 1926- *WhoAmL 92*
**Schreibels**, William J 1929- *AmMWSc 92*
**Schreiber** *Who 92*
**Schreiber**, Aaron Morris 1927- *WhoAmL 92*
**Schreiber**, Alan D 1942- *AmMWSc 92*
**Schreiber**, Alan Hickman 1944- *WhoAmL 92*
**Schreiber**, Andrew 1918- *WhoWest 92*
**Schreiber**, Averil Elspeth 1933- *WhoMW 92*
**Schreiber**, Avery Lawrence 1935- *WhoEnt 92*
**Schreiber**, B Charlotte 1931- *AmMWSc 92*
**Schreiber**, Bertram Manuel 1940- *WhoMW 92*
**Schreiber**, David Laurence 1941- *AmMWSc 92*
**Schreiber**, David Seyfarth 1936- *AmMWSc 92*
**Schreiber**, Edward d1991 *NewYTBS 91*
**Schreiber**, Edward 1930- *AmMWSc 92*
**Schreiber**, Edward 1943- *WhoWest 92*
**Schreiber**, Eric Christian 1921- *AmMWSc 92*
**Schreiber**, Everett Charles, Jr. 1953- *WhoWest 92*
**Schreiber**, Gaby d1991 *Who 92N*
**Schreiber**, Hans 1944- *AmMWSc 92*
**Schreiber**, Harry, Jr. 1934- *WhoFI 92*
**Schreiber**, Henry Dale 1948- *AmMWSc 92*
**Schreiber**, Henry Peter 1926- *AmMWSc 92*
**Schreiber**, Hermann 1920- *ConAu 36NR*
**Schreiber**, Hermann O L 1920- *IntAu&W 91*
**Schreiber**, Jan *DrAPF 91*
**Schreiber**, Jeffrey Lee 1952- *WhoMW 92*
**Schreiber**, Johannes 1927- *WhoRel 92*
**Schreiber**, Joseph Frederick, Jr 1925- *AmMWSc 92*
**Schreiber**, Kurt Clark 1922- *AmMWSc 92*
**Schreiber**, Kurt Gilbert 1946- *WhoAmL 92*
**Schreiber**, Larry L 1949- *WhoIns 92*
**Schreiber**, Lawrence 1931- *AmMWSc 92*
**Schreiber**, Lola *WhoAmP 91*
**Schreiber**, Marvin Mandel 1925- *AmMWSc 92, WhoMW 92*
**Schreiber**, Melvyn Hirsh 1931- *AmMWSc 92*
**Schreiber**, Otto William 1922- *WhoFI 92, WhoWest 92*
**Schreiber**, Paul J 1940- *AmMWSc 92*
**Schreiber**, Paul Thomas 1954- *WhoMW 92*
**Schreiber**, Richard William 1917- *AmMWSc 92*
**Schreiber**, Robert Alan 1940- *AmMWSc 92*
**Schreiber**, Ron *DrAPF 91*
**Schreiber**, Scott Bernard 1948- *WhoAmL 92*
**Schreiber**, Sidney S 1921- *AmMWSc 92*
**Schreiber**, Steven L. 1942- *WhoEnt 92*
**Schreiber**, Thomas Paul 1924- *AmMWSc 92*
**Schreiber**, William F 1925- *AmMWSc 92*
**Schreiber**, William H 1941- *WhoAmP 91*
**Schreiber**, William Lewis 1943- *AmMWSc 92*
**Schreiber**, Zal 1951- *WhoEnt 92*
**Schreibman**, Martin Paul 1935- *AmMWSc 92*
**Schreibman**, Susan *DrAPF 91*
**Schreider**, Bruce David 1946- *AmMWSc 92*
**Schreier**, Ethan Joshua 1943- *AmMWSc 92*
**Schreier**, Hanspeter 1941- *AmMWSc 92*
**Schreier**, Harold *WhoAmP 91*
**Schreier**, Peter 1935- *IntWW 91, WhoEnt 92*
**Schreier**, Thomas Stephen, Jr. 1962- *WhoFI 92*
**Schreiner**, Albert William 1926- *AmMWSc 92*

**Schreiner**, Anton Franz 1937- *AmMWSc 92*
**Schreiner**, Ceinwen Ann 1943- *AmMWSc 92*
**Schreiner**, Erik Andrew 1935- *AmMWSc 92*
**Schreiner**, Felix 1931- *AmMWSc 92*
**Schreiner**, George E 1922- *AmMWSc 92*
**Schreiner**, Heinz Rupert 1930- *AmMWSc 92*
**Schreiner**, L D, Jr 1932- *WhoAmP 91*
**Schreiner**, Olive 1855-1920 *LiExTwC, RfGEnL 91*
**Schreiner**, Philip Allen 1943- *AmMWSc 92*
**Schreiner**, Robert Nicolas, Jr 1935- *AmMWSc 92*
**Schreiner**, Samuel 1921- *WrDr 92*
**Schreiner**, Samuel Agnew, Jr 1921- *IntAu&W 91*
**Schreiter**, David Charles 1953- *WhoMW 92*
**Schreiter**, Robert John 1947- *WhoRel 92*
**Schreiweis**, Donald Otto 1941- *AmMWSc 92*
**Schreker**, Franz 1878-1934 *NewAmDM*
**Schremp**, Edward Jay 1912- *AmMWSc 92*
**Schremp**, Faith Maryanne 1921- *WhoEnt 92*
**Schremp**, Frederic William 1916- *AmMWSc 92*
**Schrempf**, David William Bill 1942- *WhoWest 92*
**Schrempp**, Warren C. 1919- *WhoAmL 92*
**Schrems**, Delbert 1941- *WhoAmP 91*
**Schrenk**, Edward L 1940- *WhoIns 92*
**Schrenk**, George L 1937- *AmMWSc 92*
**Schrenk**, George Louis 1937- *WhoFI 92*
**Schrenk**, Walter John 1933- *AmMWSc 92*
**Schrenk**, William George 1910- *AmMWSc 92*
**Schrette**, Roland Donald 1929- *WhoAmP 91*
**Schreuder**, Gerard Fritz 1937- *AmMWSc 92*
**Schreurs**, Jan W H 1932- *AmMWSc 92*
**Schreyer**, Edward Richard 1935- *IntWW 91, Who 92*
**Schreyer**, James Marlin 1915- *AmMWSc 92*
**Schreyer**, Manfred Richard 1957- *WhoFI 92*
**Schreyer**, Ralph Courtenay 1919- *AmMWSc 92*
**Schreyer**, William Allen 1928- *IntWW 91, WhoFI 92*
**Schriber**, Jonathan David 1951- *WhoEnt 92*
**Schriber**, Stanley Owen 1940- *AmMWSc 92*
**Schriber**, Thomas J 1935- *AmMWSc 92*
**Schriber-Kruse**, Craig Norman 1955- *WhoWest 92*
**Schricker**, Robert Lee 1928- *AmMWSc 92*
**Schrieber**, Paul Louis 1949- *WhoRel 92*
**Schrieffer**, John Robert 1931- *AmMWSc 92, IntWW 91, Who 92, WhoNob 90, WhoWest 92*
**Schriempf**, John Thomas 1934- *AmMWSc 92*
**Schrier**, Denis J 1955- *AmMWSc 92*
**Schrier**, Elliot 1925- *WhoFI 92*
**Schrier**, Eugene Edwin 1934- *AmMWSc 92*
**Schrier**, John C. 1956- *WhoAmL 92*
**Schrier**, Melvin Henry 1927- *AmMWSc 92*
**Schrier**, Robert William 1936- *AmMWSc 92*
**Schrier**, Stanley Leonard 1929- *AmMWSc 92*
**Schriesheim**, Alan 1930- *AmMWSc 92*
**Schriever**, Bernard Adolf 1910- *AmMWSc 92*
**Schriever**, Fred Martin 1930- *WhoFI 92*
**Schriever**, Richard L 1940- *AmMWSc 92*
**Schriftman**, Ross F 1952- *WhoAmP 91*
**Schripsema**, Wesley D. 1941- *WhoMW 92*
**Schriro**, George R 1921- *AmMWSc 92*
**Schrob**, Amy Sharon 1961- *WhoEnt 92*
**Schrock**, Barbara Jean 1952- *WhoWest 92*
**Schrock**, Gould Frederick 1936- *AmMWSc 92*
**Schrock**, Paul Melvin 1935- *WhoRel 92*
**Schrock**, Richard Royce 1945- *AmMWSc 92*
**Schrock**, Virgil E 1926- *AmMWSc 92*
**Schroder**, Barry Charles 1955- *WhoMW 92*
**Schroder**, David John 1941- *AmMWSc 92*
**Schroder**, Dieter K 1935- *AmMWSc 92*
**Schroder**, Dieter Karl 1935- *WhoWest 92*
**Schroder**, Ernest Melville 1901- *Who 92*
**Schroder**, Ernst Augustus 1915- *IntWW 91*
**Schroder**, Gene David 1944- *AmMWSc 92*
**Schroder**, Gerhard 1921- *IntWW 91*
**Schroder**, Jack Spalding 1917- *AmMWSc 92*
**Schroder**, Jack Spalding, Jr. 1948- *WhoAmL 92*
**Schroder**, Klaus 1928- *AmMWSc 92*
**Schroder**, Kurt, Baron von 1889-1966 *EncTR 91*
**Schroder**, Nathaniel Lee 1956- *WhoRel 92*
**Schroder**, Rick 1970- *IntMPA 92*
**Schroder**, Ricky 1970- *WhoEnt 92*
**Schroder**, Vincent Nils 1920- *AmMWSc 92*
**Schroder**, Werner Hermann 1914- *IntWW 91*
**Schroder**, Wolf-Udo 1942- *AmMWSc 92*
**Schroder-Devrient**, Wilhelmine 1804-1860 *NewAmDM*
**Schrodinger**, Erwin 1887-1961 *FacFETw, WhoNob 90*
**Schrodt**, James Thomas 1937- *AmMWSc 92*
**Schrodt**, Paul Raymond 1938- *WhoRel 92*
**Schrodt**, Verle N 1933- *AmMWSc 92*
**Schroeder**, Aaron Harold 1926- *WhoEnt 92*
**Schroeder**, Alan 1961- *ConAu 133, SmATA 66*
**Schroeder**, Alfred C 1915- *AmMWSc 92*
**Schroeder**, Alice Louise 1941- *AmMWSc 92*
**Schroeder**, Allen C 1941- *AmMWSc 92*
**Schroeder**, Andreas 1946- *WrDr 92*
**Schroeder**, Andreas Peter 1946- *IntAu&W 91*
**Schroeder**, Anita Gayle *AmMWSc 92*
**Schroeder**, Arnold Leon 1935- *WhoWest 92*
**Schroeder**, Barbet 1941- *ConTFT 9, IntMPA 92, IntWW 91*
**Schroeder**, Bruce Edward 1945- *WhoAmL 92*
**Schroeder**, Charles Edgar 1935- *WhoFI 92, WhoMW 92*
**Schroeder**, Christopher H. 1948- *WhoAmL 92*
**Schroeder**, Clinton Alan 1930- *WhoAmL 92*
**Schroeder**, Clinton Paul 1929- *WhoRel 92*
**Schroeder**, Daniel John 1933- *AmMWSc 92*
**Schroeder**, David Harold 1940- *WhoFI 92, WhoMW 92*
**Schroeder**, David Henry 1940- *AmMWSc 92*
**Schroeder**, David J Dean 1942- *AmMWSc 92*
**Schroeder**, Dolores Margaret 1937- *AmMWSc 92*
**Schroeder**, Don David 1945- *WhoEnt 92*
**Schroeder**, Douglas Robert 1943- *WhoWest 92*
**Schroeder**, Duane David 1940- *AmMWSc 92, WhoWest 92*
**Schroeder**, Frank, Jr 1927- *AmMWSc 92*
**Schroeder**, Fred Erich Harald 1932- *WhoMW 92*
**Schroeder**, Fred F 1943- *WhoAmP 91*
**Schroeder**, Frederick John 1947- *WhoFI 92*
**Schroeder**, Frederick John, Jr. 1934- *WhoMW 92*
**Schroeder**, Friedhelm 1947- *AmMWSc 92*
**Schroeder**, Gary *DrAPF 91*
**Schroeder**, Gene 1915-1975 *NewAmDM*
**Schroeder**, George Michael 1957- *WhoAmL 92*
**Schroeder**, Glenn Burnett 1927- *WhoWest 92*
**Schroeder**, Glenn C. 1953- *WhoAmL 92*
**Schroeder**, Hansjuergen Alfred 1926- *AmMWSc 92*
**Schroeder**, Hartmut Richard 1942- *AmMWSc 92*
**Schroeder**, Henry William 1928- *WhoMW 92*
**Schroeder**, Herbert August 1930- *AmMWSc 92*
**Schroeder**, Herman Elbert 1915- *AmMWSc 92*
**Schroeder**, James White 1936- *WhoAmL 92*
**Schroeder**, John 1938- *AmMWSc 92*
**Schroeder**, John Edward 1924- *WhoEnt 92*
**Schroeder**, John Nicholas 1942- *WhoAmP 91*
**Schroeder**, John Richard 1951- *WhoAmP 91*
**Schroeder**, John Speer 1937- *AmMWSc 92*
**Schroeder**, Juel Pierre 1920- *AmMWSc 92*
**Schroeder**, Larry Lee 1938- *WhoMW 92*
**Schroeder**, Lauren Alfred 1937- *AmMWSc 92*
**Schroeder**, Laverne W 1933- *WhoAmP 91*
**Schroeder**, Lee S 1938- *AmMWSc 92*
**Schroeder**, Leila Obier 1925- *WhoAmL 92*
**Schroeder**, Leon William 1921- *AmMWSc 92*
**Schroeder**, LeRoy William 1943- *AmMWSc 92*
**Schroeder**, Luella Ruth 1922- *WhoAmP 91*
**Schroeder**, Manfred Robert 1926- *AmMWSc 92, IntWW 91*
**Schroeder**, Mark Edwin 1946- *AmMWSc 92*
**Schroeder**, Mark Gerard 1957- *WhoAmP 91*
**Schroeder**, Mark William 1961- *WhoEnt 92*
**Schroeder**, Mary *WhoAmP 91*
**Schroeder**, Mary Esther 1947- *WhoWest 92*
**Schroeder**, Mary M *WhoAmP 91*
**Schroeder**, Mary Murphy 1940- *WhoAmL 92, WhoWest 92*
**Schroeder**, Melissa Ann 1953- *WhoAmP 91*
**Schroeder**, Melvin Carroll 1917- *AmMWSc 92*
**Schroeder**, Michael Allan 1938- *AmMWSc 92*
**Schroeder**, Norman John, II 1949- *WhoMW 92*
**Schroeder**, Patricia 1940- *AlmAP 92 [port], WhoAmP 91*
**Schroeder**, Patricia Scott 1940- *WhoWest 92*
**Schroeder**, Paul Clemens 1938- *AmMWSc 92*
**Schroeder**, Paul W. 1927- *IntWW 91*
**Schroeder**, Paul Walter 1927- *WhoMW 92*
**Schroeder**, Peter A 1928- *AmMWSc 92*
**Schroeder**, Philip 1937- *WhoRel 92*
**Schroeder**, Raymond Ernest 1949- *WhoEnt 92*
**Schroeder**, Rebecca Lynn 1954- *WhoMW 92*
**Schroeder**, Reginald 1855-1920 *ScFEYrs*
**Schroeder**, Rita Molthen 1922- *WhoWest 92*
**Schroeder**, Robert Anthony 1912- *WhoAmL 92, WhoFI 92*
**Schroeder**, Robert Samuel 1943- *AmMWSc 92*
**Schroeder**, Roy Philip 1929- *WhoMW 92, WhoRel 92*
**Schroeder**, Rudolph Alrud 1923- *AmMWSc 92*
**Schroeder**, Sandra *DrAPF 91*
**Schroeder**, Steven A 1939- *AmMWSc 92*
**Schroeder**, Steven Alfred 1939- *IntWW 91*
**Schroeder**, Terri Lea 1955- *WhoMW 92*
**Schroeder**, Thomas Dean 1939- *AmMWSc 92*
**Schroeder**, W Carroll 1906- *AmMWSc 92*
**Schroeder**, Walter Adolph 1917- *AmMWSc 92*
**Schroeder**, Walter Albert 1934- *AmMWSc 92*
**Schroeder**, Walter Allen 1954- *WhoFI 92*
**Schroeder**, Walter G 1927- *WhoAmP 91*
**Schroeder**, Warren Lee 1939- *AmMWSc 92*
**Schroeder**, Wayne Harold 1944- *WhoMW 92*
**Schroeder**, William, Jr 1927- *AmMWSc 92*
**Schroeder**, William Gilbert 1911- *WhoAmP 91*
**Schroeder**, William Henry 1944- *AmMWSc 92*
**Schroeder**, William R, Jr 1944- *WhoAmP 91*
**Schroeder**, William Robert 1941- *WhoEnt 92, WhoWest 92*
**Schroeder**, William Widick 1928- *WhoMW 92, WhoRel 92*
**Schroedter**, Gregory James 1946- *WhoAmL 92*
**Schroeer**, Dietrich 1938- *AmMWSc 92*
**Schroeer**, Juergen Max 1933- *AmMWSc 92*
**Schroeher**, Bruce Charles 1940- *WhoIns 92*
**Schroen**, Walter 1930- *AmMWSc 92*
**Schroepfer**, George John, Jr 1932- *AmMWSc 92*
**Schroeppel**, John Earl 1938- *WhoRel 92*
**Schroeppel**, Steven Frank 1949- *WhoMW 92*
**Schroer**, Bernard J 1941- *AmMWSc 92*
**Schroer**, Edmund Armin 1928- *WhoFI 92, WhoMW 92*
**Schroer**, Gene Eldon 1927- *WhoAmL 92*
**Schroer**, Michael Edward 1957- *WhoFI 92*
**Schroer**, Richard Allen 1944- *AmMWSc 92*
**Schroeter**, Gilbert Loren 1936- *AmMWSc 92*
**Schroeter**, Louis C. 1929- *WhoFI 92, WrDr 92*
**Schroeter**, Louis Clarence 1929- *IntAu&W 91*
**Schroeter**, Siegfried Hermann 1934- *AmMWSc 92*
**Schroeter**, Werner 1945- *IntDcF 2-2*
**Schrof**, William Ernst John 1931- *AmMWSc 92*
**Schroff**, Peter David 1926- *AmMWSc 92*
**Schrogie**, John Joseph 1935- *AmMWSc 92*
**Schrohenloher**, Ralph Edward 1933- *AmMWSc 92*
**Schroll**, Gene E 1928- *AmMWSc 92*
**Schroll**, James Robert 1953- *WhoAmP 91*
**Schroll**, Roy Craig 1956- *WhoFI 92*
**Schrolucke**, Marvin Elmer 1930- *WhoRel 92*
**Schrom**, Edward Joseph 1911- *WhoAmP 91*
**Schrom**, Elizabeth Ann 1941- *WhoMW 92*
**Schron**, Robert John 1945- *WhoMW 92*
**Schropfer**, David Waldron 1939- *WhoFI 92*
**Schropp**, James Howard 1943- *WhoAmL 92*
**Schrote**, John E 1936- *WhoAmP 91*
**Schroter**, Stanislaw Gustaw 1917- *AmMWSc 92*
**Schroth**, Milton Neil 1933- *AmMWSc 92*
**Schroth**, Peter William 1946- *WhoAmL 92, WhoFI 92*
**Schrott**, Helmut Gunther 1937- *AmMWSc 92*
**Schrott**, Janet Ann 1941- *WhoMW 92*
**Schrott**, Norman 1938- *WhoMW 92*
**Schrouf**, Myron H 1936- *WhoAmP 91*
**Schroy**, Jerry M 1939- *AmMWSc 92*
**Schruben**, Johanna Stenzel *AmMWSc 92*
**Schruben**, John H 1926- *AmMWSc 92*
**Schrum**, Mary Irene Knoller 1926- *AmMWSc 92*
**Schrum**, Robert Wallace 1930- *AmMWSc 92*
**Schrum**, Ruth Anna 1923- *WhoAmP 91*
**Schrumpf**, Barry James 1943- *AmMWSc 92*
**Schrumpf**, Robyn Lynn 1959- *WhoWest 92*
**Schrunk**, Ivancica Dvorzak 1948- *WhoMW 92*
**Schrutt**, Norman *WhoEnt 92*
**Schryer**, Norman Loren 1943- *AmMWSc 92*
**Schryver**, Bruce John 1944- *WhoWest 92*
**Schryver**, Herbert Francis 1927- *AmMWSc 92*
**Schryver**, Raymond Ernst 1933- *WhoAmL 92*
**Schteingart**, David E 1930- *AmMWSc 92*
**Schteingart**, David Eduardo 1930- *WhoMW 92*
**Schuback**, Philip 1925- *AmMWSc 92*
**Schubauer**, Galen B *AmMWSc 92*
**Schubb**, Kenneth David 1951- *WhoAmL 92*
**Schubel**, Jerry Robert 1936- *AmMWSc 92*
**Schubel**, Max 1932- *WhoEnt 92*
**Schubeler**, Dale Peter 1942- *WhoMW 92*
**Schuber**, William P 1947- *WhoAmP 91*
**Schubert**, Barbara Schuele 1939- *WhoEnt 92*
**Schubert**, Bernard Laurence *WhoEnt 92*
**Schubert**, Bernice Giduz 1913- *AmMWSc 92*
**Schubert**, Blake H. 1939- *WhoFI 92*
**Schubert**, Cedric F 1935- *AmMWSc 92*
**Schubert**, Daniel Sven Paul 1935- *AmMWSc 92*
**Schubert**, David Crawford 1925- *AmMWSc 92*
**Schubert**, Edmund F, Jr 1936- *WhoIns 92*
**Schubert**, Edward Thomas 1927- *AmMWSc 92*
**Schubert**, Ernst 1813-1873 *BiInAmS*
**Schubert**, Franz 1797-1828 *NewAmDM*
**Schubert**, Gerald 1939- *AmMWSc 92*
**Schubert**, Jack *AmMWSc 92*
**Schubert**, John Rockwell 1925- *AmMWSc 92*
**Schubert**, Karel Ralph 1949- *AmMWSc 92*
**Schubert**, Martin William 1935- *WhoFI 92*
**Schubert**, Michael John 1946- *WhoAmL 92*
**Schubert**, Myra Jean 1938- *WhoEnt 92*
**Schubert**, Nancy Ellen 1945- *WhoFI 92, WhoMW 92*
**Schubert**, Ralph Martin 1955- *WhoMW 92*
**Schubert**, Richard F. 1936- *IntWW 91*
**Schubert**, Richard W. 1951- *WhoWest 92*
**Schubert**, Robert William, Jr. 1952- *WhoMW 92*
**Schubert**, Rudolf 1940- *AmMWSc 92*
**Schubert**, Sydney 1928- *Who 92*
**Schubert**, Walter L 1942- *AmMWSc 92*
**Schubert**, William Henry 1944- *WhoMW 92*
**Schubert**, William K 1926- *AmMWSc 92*
**Schubert**, William Kuenneth 1926- *WhoMW 92*
**Schubert**, Wolfgang Manfred 1920- *AmMWSc 92*
**Schubring**, Norman W 1924- *AmMWSc 92*
**Schubring**, Norman William 1924- *WhoMW 92*
**Schucany**, William Roger 1940- *AmMWSc 92*
**Schucher**, Reuben 1922- *AmMWSc 92*
**Schuck**, Carl Joseph 1915- *WhoAmL 92*
**Schuck**, Ernest F 1919- *WhoAmP 91*
**Schuck**, Frederick James 1955- *WhoAmL 92*

**Schuck,** James Michael 1934- AmMWSc 92
**Schuck,** John 1940- IntMPA 92
**Schuck,** Marjorie Massey 1921- WhoFI 92
**Schuck,** Michael Joseph 1953- WhoRel 92
**Schuck,** Peter H 1940- WhoAmP 91
**Schuck,** William 1951- WhoAmP 91
**Schucker,** Gerald D 1936- AmMWSc 92
**Schucker,** Robert Charles 1945- AmMWSc 92
**Schuder,** Donald Lloyd 1922- AmMWSc 92
**Schuder,** John Claude 1922- AmMWSc 92
**Schudson,** Charles Benjamin 1950- WhoAmL 92
**Schudt,** Alicia Marie WhoEnt 92
**Schue,** John R 1932- AmMWSc 92
**Schue,** John Richard 1932- WhoMW 92
**Schueffner,** Dale Willard 1947- WhoIns 92
**Schuel,** Herbert 1935- AmMWSc 92
**Schuele,** Donald Edward 1934- AmMWSc 92
**Schuele,** William John 1923- AmMWSc 92
**Schuelein,** William M 1927- WhoAmP 91
**Schueler,** Bruno Otto Gottfried 1932- AmMWSc 92
**Schueler,** Donald G 1940- AmMWSc 92
**Schueler,** George Frederick 1944- WhoWest 92
**Schueler,** Paul Edgar 1945- AmMWSc 92
**Schuellein,** Robert Joseph 1920- AmMWSc 92
**Schueller,** Anthony L. 1950- WhoRel 92
**Schueller,** Thomas George 1936- WhoAmL 92
**Schueneman,** Arthur Lattz 1943- WhoMW 92
**Schueneman,** Warren Walter 1937- WhoMW 92
**Schuenke,** Donald J 1929- WhoIns 92
**Schuenke,** Donald John 1929- WhoFI 92, WhoMW 92
**Schuenke,** Jeffrey Allen 1956- WhoWest 92
**Schueppert,** George Louis 1938- WhoFI 92
**Schuerch,** Conrad 1918- AmMWSc 92
**Schuering,** Leo Herman, Jr. 1942- WhoAmL 92
**Schuerman,** Douglas Keith 1948- WhoFI 92
**Schuerman,** Norbert Joel 1934- WhoMW 92
**Schuerman,** William Charles 1946- WhoMW 92
**Schuermann,** Allen Clark, Jr 1943- AmMWSc 92
**Schuessel,** Wolfgang 1945- IntWW 91
**Schuessler,** Carlos Francis 1906- AmMWSc 92
**Schuessler,** Hans A 1933- AmMWSc 92
**Schuessler Fiorenza,** Elisabeth 1938- WhoRel 92
**Schuett,** Opal I 1913- WhoAmP 91
**Schuette,** Bill 1953- WhoAmP 91
**Schuette,** Keith Edward 1955- WhoAmP 91
**Schuette,** Michael 1937- WhoAmL 92
**Schuette,** Oswald Francis, Jr 1921- AmMWSc 92
**Schuettinger,** Robert 1936- WrDr 92
**Schuettpelz,** Diane Jean 1958- WhoMW 92
**Schuetz,** Allen W 1936- AmMWSc 92
**Schuetz,** John Michael 1947- WhoWest 92
**Schuetz,** Steven Edward 1959- WhoFI 92
**Schuetze,** Charles Francis 1955- WhoAmL 92
**Schuetzle,** Dennis 1942- AmMWSc 92
**Schuff,** Karen Elizabeth 1937- IntAu&W 91
**Schuffenecker,** Emile 1854-1912 ThHEIm
**Schufle,** Joseph Albert 1917- AmMWSc 92
**Schug,** Gerald Francis 1943- WhoMW 92
**Schug,** John Charles 1936- AmMWSc 92
**Schug,** Kenneth 1924- AmMWSc 92
**Schug,** Kenneth Robert 1924- WhoMW 92
**Schugar,** Harvey 1936- AmMWSc 92
**Schuh,** Frank J AmMWSc 92
**Schuh,** G. Edward 1930- WrDr 92
**Schuh,** George Edward 1930- IntAu&W 91, WhoFI 92
**Schuh,** James Donald 1928- AmMWSc 92
**Schuh,** Joseph Edward 1914- AmMWSc 92
**Schuh,** Merlyn Duane 1945- AmMWSc 92
**Schuh,** Randall Tobias 1943- AmMWSc 92
**Schuhmann,** R, Jr 1914- AmMWSc 92
**Schuhmann,** Robert Ewald 1924- AmMWSc 92
**Schuhmann,** Walter 1898- EncTR 91 [port]
**Schuiling,** John Thys 1912- WhoMW 92
**Schuit,** Kenneth Edward 1942- AmMWSc 92
**Schuit,** Steven Reiner 1942- WhoAmL 92
**Schukken,** Folkert 1935- WhoFI 92
**Schuknecht,** Harold Frederick 1917- AmMWSc 92
**Schul,** Bill D 1928- IntAu&W 91
**Schul,** Bill Dean 1928- WhoMW 92
**Schulberg,** Budd DrAPF 91
**Schulberg,** Budd 1914- BenetAL 91, ConNov 91, IntWW 91, WrDr 92
**Schulberg,** Budd Wilson 1914- IntMPA 92
**Schulberg,** Jay William 1939- WhoFI 92
**Schulberg,** Robin Elise 1950- WhoAmL 92
**Schulberg,** Stuart d1979 LesBEnT 92
**Schuldiner,** Sigmund 1913- AmMWSc 92
**Schuldt,** Everett Arthur 1938- WhoMW 92
**Schuldt,** Marcus Dale 1930- AmMWSc 92
**Schuldt,** Spencer Burt 1930- AmMWSc 92
**Schulenberg,** John William 1930- AmMWSc 92
**Schulenburg,** Friedrich B., Count von der 1865-1939 EncTR 91
**Schulenburg,** Friedrich W., Count von der 1875-1944 EncTR 91 [port]
**Schulenburg,** Fritz-Dietlof, Count VonDer 1902-1944 EncTR 91 [port]
**Schuler,** Alan Norman 1949- AmMWSc 92
**Schuler,** Alison Kay 1948- WhoAmL 92
**Schuler,** Dennis Paul 1941- WhoAmL 92
**Schuler,** George Albert 1933- AmMWSc 92
**Schuler,** Jack William 1940- WhoFI 92
**Schuler,** Jere W 1934- WhoAmP 91
**Schuler,** John Hamilton 1926- WhoAmP 91
**Schuler,** Martin N 1921- AmMWSc 92
**Schuler,** Mathias John 1918- AmMWSc 92
**Schuler,** Michael Harold 1940- WhoWest 92
**Schuler,** Michael Lewis 1953- WhoWest 92
**Schuler,** Mildred Elizabeth 1922- WhoAmP 91
**Schuler,** Paul 1931- WhoAmP 91
**Schuler,** Richard Joseph 1920- WhoMW 92, WhoRel 92
**Schuler,** Robert Eugene 1945- WhoMW 92
**Schuler,** Robert Frederick 1907- AmMWSc 92
**Schuler,** Robert Hugo 1926- AmMWSc 92, WhoMW 92
**Schuler,** Robert Jordan 1939- IntAu&W 91
**Schuler,** Ronald Theodore 1940- AmMWSc 92
**Schuler,** Rudolph William 1919- AmMWSc 92
**Schuler,** Ruth May Wildes 1933- IntAu&W 91
**Schuler,** Ruth Wildes DrAPF 91
**Schuler,** Victor Joseph 1933- AmMWSc 92
**Schulert,** Arthur Robert 1922- AmMWSc 92
**Schulhof,** Michael Peter 1942- WhoEnt 92, WhoFI 92
**Schulhofer,** Stephen Joseph 1942- WhoAmL 92
**Schulian,** John 1945- WhoEnt 92
**Schulke,** Herbert Ardis, Jr 1923- AmMWSc 92
**Schulke,** James Darrell 1932- AmMWSc 92
**Schulkin,** Morris 1919- AmMWSc 92
**Schulkind,** Andy WhoAmP 91
**Schull,** William Jackson 1922- AmMWSc 92
**Schuller,** Gunther 1925- ConCom 92, IntAu&W 91, IntWW 91, NewAmDM, WrDr 92
**Schuller,** Gunther Alexander 1925- WhoEnt 92, WhoWest 92
**Schuller,** Ivan Kohn 1946- AmMWSc 92
**Schuller,** Robert LesBEnT 92
**Schuller,** Robert Anthony 1954- WhoRel 92
**Schuller,** Robert H 1926- IntAu&W 91, WrDr 92
**Schuller,** Robert Harold 1926- RelLAm 91, WhoRel 92, WhoWest 92
**Schullery,** Stephen Edmund 1943- AmMWSc 92
**Schulman,** Alan Michael 1946- WhoMW 92
**Schulman,** Charles K. 1956- WhoMW 92
**Schulman,** Elizabeth Weiner 1950- WhoWest 92
**Schulman,** Grace DrAPF 91
**Schulman,** Harold 1930- AmMWSc 92
**Schulman,** Helen DrAPF 91
**Schulman,** Herbert Michael 1932- AmMWSc 92
**Schulman,** Howard 1949- AmMWSc 92
**Schulman,** Irving 1922- AmMWSc 92
**Schulman,** J Neil 1953- IntAu&W 91
**Schulman,** James Herbert 1915- AmMWSc 92
**Schulman,** Jerome Lewis 1925- AmMWSc 92
**Schulman,** Jerome M 1938- AmMWSc 92
**Schulman,** John A. IntMPA 92
**Schulman,** Joseph Daniel 1941- AmMWSc 92
**Schulman,** LaDonne Heaton 1936- AmMWSc 92
**Schulman,** Lawrence S 1941- AmMWSc 92
**Schulman,** Marc Stuart 1955- WhoFI 92
**Schulman,** Mark Allen 1945- WhoFI 92
**Schulman,** Marvin 1927- AmMWSc 92
**Schulman,** Marvin David 1939- AmMWSc 92
**Schulman,** Mary 1910- IntAu&W 91
**Schulman,** Michael David 1951- WhoFI 92
**Schulman,** Paul Martin 1940- WhoFI 92
**Schulman,** Paul Richard 1947- WhoWest 92
**Schulman,** Robert Ivan 1946- WhoFI 92
**Schulman,** Sarah DrAPF 91
**Schulman,** Seymour 1926- WhoWest 92
**Schulman,** Sidney 1923- AmMWSc 92
**Schulman,** Stephen Gregory 1940- AmMWSc 92
**Schulman,** Steven Gary 1951- WhoAmL 92
**Schulman,** Susan Linda 1945- WhoEnt 92
**Schulman,** Sydney T. 1938- WhoHisp 92
**Schulman,** Tammy Beth 1960- WhoMW 92
**Schulman,** Tom WhoEnt 92
**Schulman,** Tom 1951?- ConAu 133
**Schulmann,** Horst 1933- IntWW 91
**Schulner,** Lawrence Mayer 1938- WhoWest 92
**Schulsinger,** Michael Alan 1952- WhoMW 92
**Schulson,** Erland Maxwell 1941- AmMWSc 92
**Schult,** Dain Leslie 1954- WhoEnt 92, WhoFI 92
**Schult,** Roy Louis 1934- AmMWSc 92, WhoMW 92
**Schult,** Thomas Peter 1954- WhoAmL 92
**Schulte,** Alfons F AmMWSc 92
**Schulte,** Anthony Joseph 1954- WhoMW 92
**Schulte,** Carol Olivieri 1946- WhoEnt 92
**Schulte,** Daniel Herman 1929- AmMWSc 92
**Schulte,** Edward Delavan Nelson 1877-1920 BiInAmS
**Schulte,** Francis B. 1926- WhoRel 92
**Schulte,** Harry Frank 1914- AmMWSc 92
**Schulte,** Harry John, Jr 1925- AmMWSc 92
**Schulte,** Henry Gustave 1920- WhoWest 92
**Schulte,** Jack 1949- WhoFI 92
**Schulte,** Jeffrey Lewis 1949- WhoAmL 92
**Schulte,** Karl Joseph 1871-1941 EncTR 91
**Schulte,** Kathaleen B. 1951- WhoAmL 92
**Schulte,** Mary Ann 1953- WhoFI 92
**Schulte,** Rainer DrAPF 91
**Schulte,** Robert Lawrence 1945- AmMWSc 92
**Schulte,** Rose M. WhoMW 92
**Schulte,** William D. WhoFI 92
**Schulte,** William Hobart, III 1962- WhoWest 92
**Schulte,** William John, Jr 1928- AmMWSc 92
**Schulten,** Cay Gerhard af 1938- IntWW 91
**Schulten,** William Scott 1951- WhoAmL 92
**Schultenover,** David George 1938- WhoRel 92
**Schulter,** Eugene C 1948- WhoAmP 91
**Schulter-Ellis,** Frances Pierce 1923- AmMWSc 92
**Schultes,** Richard Evans 1915- AmMWSc 92, IntWW 91
**Schultheis,** James J 1932- AmMWSc 92
**Schultheis,** Michael James 1932- WhoRel 92
**Schultheis,** Ralph W. 1938- WhoWest 92
**Schultheiss,** Peter M 1924- AmMWSc 92
**Schultz,** Albert Barry 1933- AmMWSc 92
**Schultz,** Alvin Leroy 1921- AmMWSc 92
**Schultz,** Andrew 1960- ConCom 92
**Schultz,** Andrew, Jr 1913- AmMWSc 92
**Schultz,** Arnold Max 1920- AmMWSc 92
**Schultz,** Arthur George 1942- AmMWSc 92
**Schultz,** Arthur Jay 1947- AmMWSc 92
**Schultz,** Arthur Leland 1921- WhoRel 92
**Schultz,** Arthur LeRoy 1928- WhoMW 92, WhoRel 92
**Schultz,** Barbara LesBEnT 92
**Schultz,** Barbara Marie 1943- WhoFI 92, WhoMW 92
**Schultz,** Barry Don 1953- WhoMW 92
**Schultz,** Blanche Beatrice 1920- AmMWSc 92
**Schultz,** Bruce Allan Who 92
**Schultz,** Callan Lee 1966- WhoMW 92
**Schultz,** Carl 1930- WhoRel 92
**Schultz,** Carl Bruce 1956- WhoAmL 92
**Schultz,** Caroline Reel 1936- WhoWest 92
**Schultz,** Charles Edward 1951- WhoMW 92
**Schultz,** Charles L 1928- WhoIns 92
**Schultz,** Cramer William 1926- AmMWSc 92
**Schultz,** Dale W 1953- WhoAmP 91
**Schultz,** David Harold 1942- AmMWSc 92
**Schultz,** Dodi 1930- ConAu 36NR
**Schultz,** Donald Gene 1928- AmMWSc 92
**Schultz,** Donald Paul 1930- AmMWSc 92
**Schultz,** Donald Raymond 1918- AmMWSc 92
**Schultz,** Donna Cole 1937- RelLAm 91
**Schultz,** Duane Robert 1934- AmMWSc 92
**Schultz,** Dutch 1902-1935 FacFETw
**Schultz,** Dwight ConTFT 9
**Schultz,** Edward 1940- AmMWSc 92
**Schultz,** Edward Fred 1947- WhoFI 92
**Schultz,** Edwin Robert 1927- AmMWSc 92
**Schultz,** Eileen Hedy WhoEnt 92
**Schultz,** Emily Celestia 1907- WhoMW 92
**Schultz,** Erich Richard William 1930- WhoRel 92
**Schultz,** Everett Hoyle, Jr 1927- AmMWSc 92
**Schultz,** Frank 1953- WhoMW 92
**Schultz,** Franklin Alfred 1941- AmMWSc 92
**Schultz,** Fred Henry, Jr 1909- AmMWSc 92
**Schultz,** Frederick H. C. 1921- WhoMW 92
**Schultz,** Frederick Herman Carl 1921- AmMWSc 92
**Schultz,** Frederick John 1929- AmMWSc 92
**Schultz,** Gary David 1953- WhoWest 92
**Schultz,** George Adam 1932- AmMWSc 92
**Schultz,** George Edward 1921- WhoFI 92
**Schultz,** Gerald A. 1934- WhoEnt 92, WhoMW 92
**Schultz,** Gerald Edward 1936- AmMWSc 92
**Schultz,** Gerald Ernest 1941- WhoFI 92
**Schultz,** Gilbert Allan 1944- AmMWSc 92
**Schultz,** Gordon R 1945- WhoAmP 91
**Schultz,** Gustav Hobart 1935- WhoRel 92, WhoWest 92
**Schultz,** Harry Pershing 1918- AmMWSc 92
**Schultz,** Harry Wayne 1930- AmMWSc 92
**Schultz,** Herbert Victor, Jr. 1935- WhoEnt 92
**Schultz,** Hilbert Kenneth 1935- AmMWSc 92
**Schultz,** Hyman 1931- AmMWSc 92
**Schultz,** Irwin 1929- AmMWSc 92
**Schultz,** J S 1933- AmMWSc 92
**Schultz,** Jack C 1947- AmMWSc 92
**Schultz,** Jackson L. 1924- WhoFI 92
**Schultz,** James 1947- WhoMW 92
**Schultz,** James Edward 1939- AmMWSc 92
**Schultz,** Jane Schwartz 1932- AmMWSc 92
**Schultz,** Jay Ward 1937- AmMWSc 92
**Schultz,** Jerold M 1935- AmMWSc 92
**Schultz,** John DrAPF 91
**Schultz,** John Clifford 1951- WhoEnt 92
**Schultz,** John E 1936- AmMWSc 92
**Schultz,** John Lawrence 1932- AmMWSc 92
**Schultz,** John Russell 1908- AmMWSc 92
**Schultz,** John Wilfred 1931- AmMWSc 92
**Schultz,** Jon Franklin 1960- WhoMW 92
**Schultz,** Jon S. 1941- WhoAmL 92
**Schultz,** Jonas 1935- AmMWSc 92
**Schultz,** Joseph Penn 1928- WhoRel 92
**Schultz,** Ken A 1937- WhoAmP 91
**Schultz,** Kurt Lee 1946- WhoAmL 92
**Schultz,** Lane D 1944- AmMWSc 92
**Schultz,** Laurence S. 1940- WhoAmL 92
**Schultz,** Leo d1991 Who 92N
**Schultz,** Leslie Brown 1936- WhoWest 92
**Schultz,** Linda Dalquest 1947- AmMWSc 92
**Schultz,** Lorenz Myron, Jr. 1937- WhoRel 92
**Schultz,** Loris Henry 1919- AmMWSc 92
**Schultz,** Louis Edwin 1931- WhoFI 92, WhoMW 92
**Schultz,** Louis Michael 1944- WhoFI 92
**Schultz,** Louis W 1927- WhoAmP 91
**Schultz,** Louis William 1927- WhoAmL 92, WhoMW 92
**Schultz,** Marie Evelyn 1929- WhoRel 92
**Schultz,** Marilyn Frances 1944- WhoAmP 91
**Schultz,** Martin C 1926- AmMWSc 92
**Schultz,** Martin H 1940- AmMWSc 92
**Schultz,** Michael 1938- IntMPA 92, WhoBIA 92
**Schultz,** Myron Gilbert 1935- AmMWSc 92
**Schultz,** Paul Thomas 1962- WhoFI 92, WhoMW 92
**Schultz,** Peter Berthold 1946- AmMWSc 92
**Schultz,** Peter Frank 1940- AmMWSc 92
**Schultz,** Peter G. WhoWest 92
**Schultz,** Peter Hewlett 1944- AmMWSc 92
**Schultz,** Philip DrAPF 91
**Schultz,** Phyllis W 1925- AmMWSc 92
**Schultz,** R Jack 1929- AmMWSc 92
**Schultz,** Ray Karl 1937- AmMWSc 92
**Schultz,** Reinhard Edward 1943- AmMWSc 92

**Schultz**, Richard 1926- *DcTwDes*
**Schultz**, Richard Allen 1939- *WhoAmL 92*
**Schultz**, Richard Martin 1954- *WhoFI 92*
**Schultz**, Richard Michael 1942- *AmMWSc 92*
**Schultz**, Richard Michael 1949- *WhoMW 92*
**Schultz**, Richard Morris 1949- *AmMWSc 92*
**Schultz**, Richard Otto 1930- *AmMWSc 92*
**Schultz**, Robert Bernard 1947- *WhoWest 92*
**Schultz**, Robert Dale 1951- *WhoMW 92*
**Schultz**, Robert George 1933- *AmMWSc 92*
**Schultz**, Robert J. 1930- *WhoFI 92, WhoMW 92*
**Schultz**, Robert John 1944- *AmMWSc 92*
**Schultz**, Robert John 1945- *WhoRel 92*
**Schultz**, Robert Kenneth 1947- *WhoRel 92*
**Schultz**, Robert Lowell 1930- *AmMWSc 92*
**Schultz**, Robert Vernon 1936- *WhoFI 92, WhoMW 92*
**Schultz**, Robert William 1938- *WhoFI 92*
**Schultz**, Rodney Brian 1946- *AmMWSc 92*
**Schultz**, Ronald David 1944- *AmMWSc 92*
**Schultz**, Ronald Edward 1942- *WhoAmL 92*
**Schultz**, Ronald G 1931- *AmMWSc 92*
**Schultz**, Ronald Lee 1938- *WhoFI 92*
**Schultz**, Russ Allen 1947- *WhoEnt 92*
**Schultz**, Russell Thomas *AmMWSc 92*
**Schultz**, Samuel J 1914- *IntAu&W 91, WrDr 92*
**Schultz**, Samuel Jacob 1914- *WhoRel 92*
**Schultz**, Scott Thomas 1957- *WhoAmP 91*
**Schultz**, Shari Lynn 1960- *WhoEnt 92*
**Schultz**, Sheldon 1933- *AmMWSc 92*
**Schultz**, Shelly Irene 1953- *WhoFI 92*
**Schultz**, Stanley George 1931- *AmMWSc 92*
**Schultz**, Stephen John 1943- *WhoAmL 92*
**Schultz**, Steven Alan 1953- *WhoIns 92*
**Schultz**, Steven Allen 1941- *WhoAmL 92*
**Schultz**, Steven Lewellyn 1959- *WhoFI 92*
**Schultz**, Steven Michael 1954- *WhoWest 92*
**Schultz**, T. Paul 1940- *WhoFI 92*
**Schultz**, Terry Allen 1946- *WhoFI 92, WhoMW 92*
**Schultz**, Terry Wayne 1946- *AmMWSc 92*
**Schultz**, Theodore David 1929- *AmMWSc 92*
**Schultz**, Theodore John 1922- *AmMWSc 92*
**Schultz**, Theodore W 1902- *IntAu&W 91, IntWW 91, Who 92, WrDr 92*
**Schultz**, Theodore William 1902- *WhoFI 92, WhoMW 92, WhoNob 90*
**Schultz**, Thomas J 1941- *AmMWSc 92*
**Schultz**, Vernon Frederick 1941- *WhoMW 92*
**Schultz**, Vincent 1922- *AmMWSc 92*
**Schultz**, Waldemar Herbert 1921- *WhoAmP 91*
**Schultz**, Walter Thomas 1941- *WhoMW 92*
**Schultz**, Warren Robert 1949- *WhoMW 92*
**Schultz**, Warren Walter 1941- *AmMWSc 92*
**Schultz**, Wesley Edward 1927- *WhoMW 92*
**Schultz**, William C 1927- *AmMWSc 92*
**Schultz**, William Clinton 1937- *AmMWSc 92*
**Schultze**, Bunny 1866-1939 *BenetAL 91*
**Schultze**, Charles L 1924- *AmMWSc 92*
**Schultze**, Charles Louis 1924- *IntWW 91*
**Schultze**, Ernst Eugene 1944- *WhoWest 92*
**Schultze**, Hans-Peter 1937- *AmMWSc 92*
**Schultze**, Lothar Walter 1920- *AmMWSc 92*
**Schultze**, Norbert 1911- *EncTR 91*
**Schultze**, Walther 1894-1979 *EncTR 91 [port]*
**Schultze-Naumburg**, Paul 1869-1949 *EncTR 91 [port]*
**Schulweis**, Harold Maurice 1925- *WhoRel 92*
**Schulz**, Ann Carol 1941- *WhoAmL 92*
**Schulz**, Arthur R 1925- *AmMWSc 92*
**Schulz**, Bradley Nicholas 1959- *WhoAmL 92*
**Schulz**, Charles 1922- *IntAu&W 91, WrDr 92*
**Schulz**, Charles Emil *AmMWSc 92*
**Schulz**, Charles M. *LesBEnT 92*
**Schulz**, Charles Monroe 1922- *IntWW 91, WhoEnt 92*
**Schulz**, Dale Metherd 1918- *AmMWSc 92*
**Schulz**, David Alan 1952- *WhoAmL 92*
**Schulz**, David Arthur 1934- *AmMWSc 92*
**Schulz**, Donald Norman 1943- *AmMWSc 92*
**Schulz**, Helmut Wilhelm 1912- *AmMWSc 92*
**Schulz**, James L. 1946- *WhoMW 92*
**Schulz**, Jan Ivan 1946- *AmMWSc 92*
**Schulz**, Jeanette 1919- *AmMWSc 92*
**Schulz**, Johann Christoph Friedrich 1920- *AmMWSc 92*
**Schulz**, John C 1955- *AmMWSc 92*
**Schulz**, John Hampshire 1934- *AmMWSc 92*
**Schulz**, John Theodore 1929- *AmMWSc 92*
**Schulz**, Karlo Francis 1917- *AmMWSc 92*
**Schulz**, Leslie Olmstead *AmMWSc 92*
**Schulz**, Marcia Ralston 1951- *WhoEnt 92*
**Schulz**, Max Frederick 1923- *IntAu&W 91, WrDr 92*
**Schulz**, Michael 1943- *AmMWSc 92*
**Schulz**, Otto G 1930- *WhoIns 92*
**Schulz**, Otto George 1930- *WhoFI 92*
**Schulz**, Paul C 1927- *WhoAmP 91*
**Schulz**, Peter 1930- *IntWW 91*
**Schulz**, Rainer Walter 1942- *WhoFI 92, WhoWest 92*
**Schulz**, Ralph Richard 1928- *WhoFI 92*
**Schulz**, Riccardo 1954- *WhoEnt 92*
**Schulz**, Richard A., Jr. 1951- *WhoMW 92*
**Schulz**, Richard Burkart 1920- *AmMWSc 92*
**Schulz**, Robert Branden 1957- *WhoFI 92*
**Schulz**, Robert J 1927- *AmMWSc 92*
**Schulz**, Wallace Wendell 1926- *AmMWSc 92*
**Schulz**, Walter Kurt 1940- *WhoFI 92*
**Schulz**, William 1935- *AmMWSc 92*
**Schulz**, William Frederick 1949- *WhoRel 92*
**Schulz**, William Robert 1952- *WhoAmL 92*
**Schulze**, Eric William 1952- *WhoAmL 92*
**Schulze**, Erwin Emil 1925- *WhoFI 92, WhoMW 92*
**Schulze**, Franz 1927- *WrDr 92*
**Schulze**, Gene Edward 1959- *AmMWSc 92*
**Schulze**, Horst *WhoFI 92*
**Schulze**, Irene Theresa 1929- *AmMWSc 92*
**Schulze**, Karl Ludwig 1911- *AmMWSc 92*
**Schulze**, Kenneth *DrAPF 91*
**Schulze**, Kenneth Willard 1951- *IntAu&W 91*
**Schulze**, LeRoy James 1944- *WhoMW 92*
**Schulze**, Mark Howard 1950- *WhoMW 92*
**Schulze**, Mark Levon 1958- *WhoEnt 92*
**Schulze**, Michael John 1962- *WhoEnt 92*
**Schulze**, Richard T. 1929- *AlmAP 92 [port], WhoAmP 91*
**Schulze**, Richard Wilfred 1937- *WhoFI 92*
**Schulze**, Rudolph 1918- *IntWW 91*
**Schulze**, Tascha Jon 1950- *WhoEnt 92, WhoWest 92*
**Schulze**, Walter Arthur 1943- *AmMWSc 92*
**Schulze**, William Eugene 1934- *AmMWSc 92*
**Schulze-Boysen**, Harro 1909-1942 *EncTR 91 [port]*
**Schum**, Randolph Edgar 1948- *WhoAmL 92*
**Schumacher**, Berthold Walter 1921- *AmMWSc 92*
**Schumacher**, Brockman 1924- *WhoBlA 92*
**Schumacher**, Carl Joseph, Jr. 1926- *WhoAmL 92*
**Schumacher**, Clifford Rodney 1929- *AmMWSc 92*
**Schumacher**, Dietmar 1942- *AmMWSc 92*
**Schumacher**, Ernst Friedrich 1911-1977 *ConAu 34NR*
**Schumacher**, Eugene 1925- *WhoWest 92*
**Schumacher**, Frederick John 1939- *WhoRel 92*
**Schumacher**, Frederick Richmond 1930- *WhoFI 92*
**Schumacher**, Gary Michael 1943- *WhoMW 92*
**Schumacher**, Gebhard Friederich B 1924- *AmMWSc 92*
**Schumacher**, George Adam 1912- *AmMWSc 92*
**Schumacher**, George John 1924- *AmMWSc 92*
**Schumacher**, H Ralph, Jr 1933- *AmMWSc 92*
**Schumacher**, Ignatius 1928- *AmMWSc 92*
**Schumacher**, Joel 1939- *ConTFT 9, IntMPA 92, WhoEnt 92*
**Schumacher**, Jon Lee 1937- *WhoAmL 92*
**Schumacher**, Joseph Charles 1911- *AmMWSc 92*
**Schumacher**, Joseph Nicholas 1928- *AmMWSc 92*
**Schumacher**, Kathleen Miles 1954- *WhoMW 92*
**Schumacher**, Kurt 1895-1952 *EncTR 91 [port]*
**Schumacher**, Martha Jean 1954- *WhoEnt 92*
**Schumacher**, Max Barney 1932- *WhoEnt 92*
**Schumacher**, Paul 1951- *WhoAmP 91*
**Schumacher**, Paul Maynard 1951- *WhoAmL 92*
**Schumacher**, Richard 1955- *WhoFI 92*
**Schumacher**, Richard William 1946- *AmMWSc 92*
**Schumacher**, Robert Alan 1923- *IntWW 91*
**Schumacher**, Robert E 1918- *AmMWSc 92*
**Schumacher**, Robert Thornton 1930- *AmMWSc 92*
**Schumacher**, Roy Joseph 1942- *AmMWSc 92*
**Schumacher**, Stephen Joseph 1942- *WhoAmL 92*
**Schumacher**, Weldon David 1936- *WhoWest 92*
**Schumacher**, William John 1936- *AmMWSc 92*
**Schumack**, Joan Maria 1953- *WhoMW 92*
**Schumaker**, Dale Ray 1961- *WhoEnt 92*
**Schumaker**, John Abraham 1925- *AmMWSc 92*
**Schumaker**, Larry L 1939- *AmMWSc 92*
**Schumaker**, Robert Louis 1920- *AmMWSc 92*
**Schumaker**, Verne Norman 1929- *AmMWSc 92*
**Schuman**, Beatrice *DrAPF 91*
**Schuman**, Clifford Richard 1913- *WhoAmL 92*
**Schuman**, Edward L. 1916- *IntMPA 92*
**Schuman**, Frederick Lewis 1904-1981 *ConAu 135*
**Schuman**, Gerald E 1944- *AmMWSc 92*
**Schuman**, Leonard Michael 1913- *AmMWSc 92*
**Schuman**, Mary Anne 1922- *WhoRel 92*
**Schuman**, Perry Lee 1930- *WhoAmP 91*
**Schuman**, Robert Lee 1954- *WhoAmP 91*
**Schuman**, Robert Paul 1919- *AmMWSc 92*
**Schuman**, Stanley Harold 1925- *AmMWSc 92*
**Schuman**, William 1910- *ConCom 92, FacFETw, NewAmDM*
**Schuman**, William Howard 1910- *IntWW 91*
**Schuman**, William John, Jr 1930- *AmMWSc 92*
**Schuman**, William Paul 1954- *WhoAmL 92*
**Schumann**, Clara 1819-1896 *NewAmDM*
**Schumann**, Edward Lewis 1923- *AmMWSc 92*
**Schumann**, Elisabeth 1885-1952 *FacFETw*
**Schumann**, Elisabeth 1888-1952 *NewAmDM*
**Schumann**, Florence Ford d1991 *NewYTBS 91*
**Schumann**, Gerhard 1911- *EncTR 91 [port]*
**Schumann**, Maurice 1911- *IntWW 91, Who 92*
**Schumann**, Merritt J 1928- *WhoAmP 91*
**Schumann**, Robert 1810-1856 *NewAmDM*
**Schumann**, Scott Eric 1958- *WhoEnt 92*
**Schumann**, Thomas Gerald 1937- *AmMWSc 92*
**Schumann**, Thomas Herbert 1932- *WhoMW 92*
**Schumann**, William Henry, III 1950- *WhoMW 92*
**Schumann**, William Robert 1942- *WhoIns 92*
**Schumann-Heink**, Ernestine 1861-1936 *FacFETw, NewAmDM*
**Schumer**, Charles E. 1950- *AlmAP 92 [port], WhoAmP 91*
**Schumer**, Charles Ellis 1950- *NewYTBS 91 [port]*
**Schumer**, Douglas B 1951- *AmMWSc 92*
**Schumer**, William 1926- *AmMWSc 92*
**Schumm**, Brooke, Jr 1931- *AmMWSc 92, WhoFI 92*
**Schumm**, Dorothy Elaine 1943- *AmMWSc 92*
**Schumm**, Stanley Alfred 1927- *AmMWSc 92*
**Schumsky**, Stanley 1932- *WhoFI 92*
**Schunder**, Mary Cothran 1931- *AmMWSc 92*
**Schuneman**, Calvin W 1926- *WhoAmP 91*
**Schunk**, Eric Henry 1955- *WhoAmL 92*
**Schunk**, Robert Walter *AmMWSc 92*
**Schunn**, Robert Allen 1936- *AmMWSc 92*
**Schupf**, Nicole 1943- *AmMWSc 92*
**Schupp**, Guy 1933- *AmMWSc 92*
**Schupp**, Keith Lowell 1953- *WhoMW 92*
**Schupp**, Orion Edwin, III 1932- *AmMWSc 92*
**Schupp**, Paul Eugene 1937- *AmMWSc 92*
**Schupp**, Ronald Irving 1951- *WhoMW 92, WhoRel 92*
**Schupp**, Tara Lynn 1961- *WhoEnt 92*
**Schuppanzigh**, Ignaz 1776-1830 *NewAmDM*
**Schur**, Gerald 1935- *WhoAmL 92*
**Schur**, Peter Henry 1933- *AmMWSc 92*
**Schur**, Susan D 1940- *WhoAmP 91*
**Schurgin**, William Price 1956- *WhoAmL 92*
**Schurig**, John Eberhard 1945- *AmMWSc 92*
**Schurke**, Paul David 1955- *WhoMW 92*
**Schurle**, Arlo Willard 1943- *AmMWSc 92*
**Schurle**, Robert Ray 1936- *WhoWest 92*
**Schurman**, Dennis Wayne 1947- *WhoAmP 91*
**Schurman**, Donald Glenn 1933- *WhoFI 92*
**Schurman**, Glenn August 1922- *AmMWSc 92*
**Schurman**, Wesley James 1912- *WhoIns 92*
**Schurmann**, Gerard 1924?- *ConCom 92*
**Schurmann**, Leo 1917- *IntWW 91*
**Schurmeier**, Harris McIntosh 1924- *AmMWSc 92*
**Schurr**, Avital 1941- *AmMWSc 92*
**Schurr**, Garmond Gaylord 1918- *AmMWSc 92, WhoMW 92*
**Schurr**, James R 1942- *WhoIns 92*
**Schurr**, John Michael 1937- *AmMWSc 92*
**Schurr**, Karl M 1932- *AmMWSc 92*
**Schurrer**, Augusta 1925- *AmMWSc 92*
**Schurter**, Dennis Dean 1942- *WhoRel 92*
**Schurtman**, William 1932- *WhoAmL 92*
**Schurz**, Carl 1829-1906 *AmPolLe, BenetAL 91, DcAmImH*
**Schurz**, Franklin Dunn, Jr. 1931- *WhoEnt 92, WhoFI 92*
**Schuschnigg**, Kurt 1897-1977 *EncTR 91 [port]*
**Schuschnigg**, Kurt von 1897-1977 *FacFETw*
**Schusky**, Ernest L 1931- *IntAu&W 91, WrDr 92*
**Schussler**, Robert Gibson 1950- *WhoMW 92*
**Schusteff**, David Joseph 1948- *WhoMW 92*
**Schustek**, George W, Jr 1915- *AmMWSc 92*
**Schuster**, Allan D. *WhoFI 92, WhoIns 92*
**Schuster**, Charles Roberts, Jr 1930- *AmMWSc 92*
**Schuster**, David Israel 1935- *AmMWSc 92*
**Schuster**, David J 1947- *AmMWSc 92*
**Schuster**, David John 1953- *WhoMW 92*
**Schuster**, E. Elaine 1936- *WhoAmL 92*
**Schuster**, Eugene F 1941- *AmMWSc 92*
**Schuster**, Felix James 1913- *Who 92*
**Schuster**, Frederick Lee 1934- *AmMWSc 92*
**Schuster**, Gary Benjamin 1946- *AmMWSc 92*
**Schuster**, George Sheah 1940- *AmMWSc 92*
**Schuster**, Hal Jan 1955- *WhoWest 92*
**Schuster**, Hans-Gunter 1918- *IntWW 91*
**Schuster**, Ingeborg I M 1937- *AmMWSc 92*
**Schuster**, Jack Herman 1937- *WhoWest 92*
**Schuster**, James *Who 92*
**Schuster**, James J 1935- *AmMWSc 92*
**Schuster**, James Leo 1912- *Who 92*
**Schuster**, Jeanne M. 1963- *WhoAmL 92*
**Schuster**, Joseph L 1932- *AmMWSc 92*
**Schuster**, Michael Frank 1929- *AmMWSc 92*
**Schuster**, Philip Frederick, II 1945- *WhoAmL 92, WhoFI 92, WhoWest 92*
**Schuster**, Richard Charles 1954- *WhoMW 92*
**Schuster**, Robert Lee 1927- *AmMWSc 92*
**Schuster**, Robert Parks 1945- *WhoAmL 92, WhoWest 92*
**Schuster**, Rudolf Mathias 1921- *AmMWSc 92*
**Schuster**, Sanford Lee 1938- *AmMWSc 92*
**Schuster**, Seymour 1926- *AmMWSc 92, WhoMW 92*
**Schuster**, Todd Mervyn 1933- *AmMWSc 92*
**Schuster**, Vincent Aloysius 1934- *WhoMW 92*
**Schuster**, William John 1948- *AmMWSc 92*
**Schuster-Craig**, John 1949- *WhoEnt 92*
**Schusterman**, Ronald Jay 1932- *AmMWSc 92*
**Schut**, Herman A 1943- *AmMWSc 92*
**Schut**, Robert N 1932- *AmMWSc 92*
**Schutrumpf**, Eckart Ernst 1939- *WhoWest 92*
**Schutt**, Dale W 1938- *AmMWSc 92*
**Schutt**, Leonard D 1926- *WhoIns 92*
**Schutt**, Michael Paul 1962- *WhoAmL 92*
**Schutt**, Paul Frederick 1932- *AmMWSc 92*
**Schutta**, James Thomas 1944- *AmMWSc 92*
**Schutte**, A H 1907- *AmMWSc 92*
**Schutte**, Giles W. 1931- *WhoFI 92*
**Schutte**, Henry John 1925- *WhoFI 92*
**Schutte**, Paula Marion 1941- *WhoFI 92*
**Schutte**, Richard David 1954- *WhoFI 92*
**Schutte**, William Calvin 1941- *AmMWSc 92*
**Schutter**, David John 1945- *WhoMW 92*
**Schutz**, Andrea Louise 1948- *WhoBlA 92*
**Schutz**, Bernard Frederick 1946- *AmMWSc 92*

**Schutz**, Bob Ewald 1940- *AmMWSc 92*
**Schutz**, Donald Frank 1934- *AmMWSc 92*
**Schutz**, Heinrich 1585-1672 *NewAmDM*
**Schutz**, John Adolph 1919- *WhoWest 92*
**Schutz**, John Howard 1933- *WhoRel 92*
**Schutz**, Klaus 1926- *IntWW 91*
**Schutz**, Paul 1910- *IntWW 91*
**Schutz**, Ronald Eugene 1950- *WhoFI 92*
**Schutz**, Wallace J. 1908- *ConAu 135*
**Schutz**, Wilfred M 1930- *AmMWSc 92*
**Schutz**, Will 1925- *WrDr 92*
**Schutz**, William C 1925- *IntAu&W 91*
**Schutz-Marsauche**, Roger 1915- *DcEcMov*
**Schutzbach**, John Stephen 1941- *AmMWSc 92*
**Schutzeichel**, Rudolf 1927- *IntWW 91*
**Schutzenhofer**, Luke A 1939- *AmMWSc 92*
**Schutzman**, Elias 1925- *AmMWSc 92*
**Schutzman**, Leonard 1946- *WhoFI 92*
**Schutzman**, Steven *DrAPF 91*
**Schuur**, Diane *WhoEnt 92*
**Schuur**, Diane 1954?- *ConMus 6 [port]*
**Schuur**, Jerry D 1936- *AmMWSc 92*
**Schuur**, Robert George 1931- *WhoAmL 92*
**Schuurmann**, Frederick James 1940- *AmMWSc 92*
**Schuurmans**, David Meinte 1928- *AmMWSc 92*
**Schuurmans**, Hendrik J L 1928- *AmMWSc 92*
**Schuyler**, Alfred Ernest 1935- *AmMWSc 92*
**Schuyler**, Daniel Merrick 1912- *WhoAmL 92, WhoMW 92*
**Schuyler**, Doris E. *DrAPF 91*
**Schuyler**, James *DrAPF 91*
**Schuyler**, James 1923- *ConPo 91*
**Schuyler**, James 1923-1991 *BenetAL 91, NewYTBS 91 [port]*
**Schuyler**, James Marcus 1923- *IntAu&W 91*
**Schuyler**, James Marcus 1923-1991 *ConAu 134*
**Schuyler**, Keith C 1919- *IntAu&W 91*
**Schuyler**, Louisa Lee 1837-1926 *DcAmImH*
**Schuyler**, Philip John 1733-1804 *BlkwEAR*
**Schuyler**, Philippa 1931-1967 *NotBlAW 92 [port]*
**Schuyler**, Philippa Duke 1931-1967 *NewAmDM*
**Schuyler**, Rob Rene 1932- *WhoAmL 92*
**Schuyler**, Robert Len 1936- *WhoFI 92*
**Schuytema**, Eunice Chambers 1929- *AmMWSc 92*
**Schuyten**, John 1914- *AmMWSc 92*
**Schvey**, Henry I. 1948- *ConAu 133*
**Schwab**, Alexander 1887-1943 *EncTR 91*
**Schwab**, Alice Mae Gwilliam 1938- *WhoWest 92*
**Schwab**, Anne Corcoran *WhoEnt 92*
**Schwab**, Arthur William 1917- *AmMWSc 92*
**Schwab**, Bernard 1926- *AmMWSc 92*
**Schwab**, Bruce B. 1929- *WhoEnt 92*
**Schwab**, Carol Ann 1953- *WhoAmL 92*
**Schwab**, Charles R. *WhoFI 92, WhoWest 92*
**Schwab**, David *WhoAmP 91*
**Schwab**, Eleanor Anne 1931- *WhoAmP 91*
**Schwab**, Ernest Roe 1950- *AmMWSc 92*
**Schwab**, Frederic Lyon 1940- *AmMWSc 92*
**Schwab**, Frederick Charles 1937- *AmMWSc 92*
**Schwab**, Gary Michael 1950- *WhoMW 92*
**Schwab**, Gary Steven 1956- *WhoAmL 92*
**Schwab**, Glenn O 1919- *AmMWSc 92*
**Schwab**, Harold Lee 1932- *WhoAmL 92*
**Schwab**, Helmut 1929- *AmMWSc 92*
**Schwab**, Howard Joel 1943- *WhoAmL 92*
**Schwab**, John Harris 1927- *AmMWSc 92*
**Schwab**, John J 1923- *AmMWSc 92*
**Schwab**, John Joseph 1923- *IntWW 91*
**Schwab**, Linda Sue 1951- *AmMWSc 92*
**Schwab**, Michael 1939- *AmMWSc 92*
**Schwab**, Michael Edward 1958- *WhoEnt 92*
**Schwab**, Robert G 1932- *AmMWSc 92*
**Schwab**, Sheldon *WhoEnt 92*
**Schwab**, Shelly *IntMPA 92, LesBEnT 92*
**Schwab**, Stewart Jon 1954- *WhoAmL 92*
**Schwab**, Susan Carol 1955- *WhoAmP 91*
**Schwab**, Terrance Walter 1940- *WhoAmL 92*
**Schwab**, Thomas Edgard 1958- *WhoAmL 92*
**Schwab**, Thomas Joe 1927- *WhoAmL 92*
**Schwab**, Walter Edwin 1941- *AmMWSc 92*
**Schwabe**, Arthur David 1924- *AmMWSc 92*
**Schwabe**, Calvin Walter 1927- *AmMWSc 92*
**Schwabe**, Christian 1930- *AmMWSc 92*
**Schwabe**, George Blaine, III 1947- *WhoAmL 92*
**Schwabe**, John Bennett, II 1946- *WhoAmL 92*
**Schwabe**, Peter Alexander, Jr. 1935- *WhoWest 92*
**Schwabe**, Randolph 1885-1948 *TwCPaSc*
**Schwaber**, Jerrold 1947- *AmMWSc 92*
**Schwadron**, Harley Lawrence 1942- *WhoFI 92*
**Schwager**, David E 1963- *WhoAmP 91*
**Schwager**, George Willard 1911- *WhoFI 92*
**Schwager**, John Louis 1948- *WhoFI 92*
**Schwager**, Thomas Edward 1951- *WhoFI 92*
**Schwagmeyer**, Roger Glenn 1942- *WhoMW 92*
**Schwaighofer**, Joseph 1924- *AmMWSc 92*
**Schwalb**, Marvin N 1941- *AmMWSc 92*
**Schwalb Lopez Aldana**, Fernando 1916- *IntWW 91*
**Schwalbe**, Alan Lewis 1954- *WhoAmL 92*
**Schwalbe**, Larry Allen 1945- *AmMWSc 92*
**Schwall**, Donald V 1931- *AmMWSc 92*
**Schwall**, Richard Joseph 1949- *AmMWSc 92*
**Schwall**, Robert E 1947- *AmMWSc 92*
**Schwallie**, Daniel Phillip 1955- *WhoFI 92*
**Schwallie**, Robert Cornelius 1941- *WhoFI 92*
**Schwalm**, Fritz Ekkehardt 1936- *AmMWSc 92*
**Schwalm**, Mizuho K 1940- *AmMWSc 92*
**Schwalm**, William A 1947- *AmMWSc 92*
**Schwam**, Marvin Albert 1942- *WhoEnt 92*
**Schwamb**, Donald Frederick 1952- *WhoFI 92*
**Schwamb**, Ludwig 1890-1945 *EncTR 91*
**Schwambach**, Stephen R. 1948- *WhoRel 92*
**Schwan**, Gesine Marianne 1943- *IntWW 91*
**Schwan**, Herman Paul 1915- *AmMWSc 92*
**Schwan**, Judith A 1925- *AmMWSc 92*
**Schwan**, Theodore Carl 1918- *AmMWSc 92*
**Schwan**, Thomas James 1934- *AmMWSc 92*
**Schwandt**, Peter 1939- *AmMWSc 92*
**Schwandt**, Stephen 1947- *IntAu&W 91*
**Schwaneke**, Edward Eugene 1940- *WhoAmP 91*
**Schwaninger**, Thomas Tyler 1957- *WhoWest 92*
**Schwank**, Johannes Walter 1950- *WhoMW 92*
**Schwann**, William Joseph 1913- *WhoEnt 92*
**Schwantes**, Carlos Arnaldo 1945- *WhoWest 92*
**Schwantner**, Joseph 1943- *NewAmDM*
**Schwanz**, Keith Duane 1954- *WhoRel 92*
**Schwanz**, Thomas Lee 1957- *WhoAmL 92*
**Schwarcz**, David Richard 1963- *WhoWest 92*
**Schwarcz**, Ervin H 1924- *AmMWSc 92*
**Schwarcz**, Henry Philip 1933- *AmMWSc 92*
**Schwarcz**, Roy Nicholas 1947- *WhoRel 92*
**Schwarcz**, Steven Lance 1949- *WhoAmL 92*
**Schwark**, August Carl 1948- *WhoMW 92*
**Schwark**, Howard Edward 1917- *WhoMW 92*
**Schwark**, Wayne Stanley 1942- *AmMWSc 92*
**Schwarm**, Richard P *WhoAmP 91*
**Schwarting**, Arthur Ernest 1917- *AmMWSc 92*
**Schwarting**, Gerald Allen 1946- *AmMWSc 92*
**Schwartz**, A Truman 1934- *AmMWSc 92*
**Schwartz**, Aaron Robert 1926- *WhoAmP 91*
**Schwartz**, Abraham 1943- *AmMWSc 92*
**Schwartz**, Alan David 1950- *WhoFI 92*
**Schwartz**, Alan Lee 1941- *AmMWSc 92*
**Schwartz**, Alan Paul 1949- *WhoFI 92*
**Schwartz**, Alan William 1935- *AmMWSc 92*
**Schwartz**, Albert 1923- *AmMWSc 92*
**Schwartz**, Albert B 1922- *AmMWSc 92*
**Schwartz**, Allan James 1939- *AmMWSc 92*
**Schwartz**, Allen Edward 1959- *WhoRel 92*
**Schwartz**, Allen Marvin 1932- *WhoEnt 92*
**Schwartz**, Allyson Y 1948- *WhoAmP 91*
**Schwartz**, Amy 1954- *ChlLR 25 [port]*
**Schwartz**, Anthony 1940- *AmMWSc 92*
**Schwartz**, Anthony Max 1908- *AmMWSc 92*
**Schwartz**, Arnold 1929- *AmMWSc 92*
**Schwartz**, Arnold Edward 1935- *AmMWSc 92*
**Schwartz**, Arthur 1900-1984 *NewAmDM*
**Schwartz**, Arthur 1956- *WhoMW 92*
**Schwartz**, Arthur Gerald 1941- *AmMWSc 92*
**Schwartz**, Arthur Harold 1936- *AmMWSc 92*
**Schwartz**, Arthur Leonard 1941- *WhoFI 92*
**Schwartz**, Arthur Solomon 1924- *WhoWest 92*
**Schwartz**, Barbara Sachs 1925- *WhoAmP 91*
**Schwartz**, Barry Dov 1940- *WhoRel 92*
**Schwartz**, Barry Fredric 1949- *WhoAmL 92*
**Schwartz**, Barry Steven 1950- *WhoAmL 92*
**Schwartz**, Benjamin L 1926- *AmMWSc 92*
**Schwartz**, Bernard *IntMPA 92*
**Schwartz**, Bernard 1923- *WhoAmL 92*
**Schwartz**, Bernard 1927- *AmMWSc 92*
**Schwartz**, Bertram 1924- *AmMWSc 92*
**Schwartz**, Beverly Major 1939- *WhoMW 92*
**Schwartz**, Bradford S 1952- *AmMWSc 92*
**Schwartz**, Brian B 1938- *AmMWSc 92*
**Schwartz**, Brian Jay 1963- *WhoFI 92*
**Schwartz**, Carol Halpert 1939- *WhoFI 92*
**Schwartz**, Carol Levitt 1944- *WhoAmP 91*
**Schwartz**, Charles, Jr. 1922- *WhoAmL 92*
**Schwartz**, Charles D. 1948- *WhoEnt 92*
**Schwartz**, Charles Leon 1931- *AmMWSc 92*
**Schwartz**, Charles Leonard 1957- *WhoEnt 92*
**Schwartz**, Charles Walter 1953- *WhoAmL 92*
**Schwartz**, Colin John 1931- *AmMWSc 92*
**Schwartz**, Corinne O'Hare 1929- *WhoFI 92*
**Schwartz**, Dale Marvin 1942- *WhoAmL 92*
**Schwartz**, Daniel Alan 1942- *AmMWSc 92*
**Schwartz**, Daniel Evan 1952- *AmMWSc 92*
**Schwartz**, Daniel M 1913- *AmMWSc 92*
**Schwartz**, Darrell Michael 1958- *WhoFI 92*
**Schwartz**, David C 1939- *WhoAmP 91*
**Schwartz**, David Jeffrey 1950- *WhoFI 92*
**Schwartz**, David Lee 1964- *WhoAmL 92*
**Schwartz**, David Marcus 1949- *WhoEnt 92*
**Schwartz**, David Nathaniel 1956- *WhoFI 92*
**Schwartz**, Delmore 1913-1966 *BenetAL 91, ConAu 35NR, FacFETw*
**Schwartz**, Donald 1927- *AmMWSc 92*
**Schwartz**, Donald Alan 1926- *AmMWSc 92*
**Schwartz**, Donald Glenn 1940- *WhoEnt 92*
**Schwartz**, Donald Lee 1948- *WhoAmL 92*
**Schwartz**, Doris R *AmMWSc 92*
**Schwartz**, Drew 1919- *AmMWSc 92*
**Schwartz**, Edith Richmond *AmMWSc 92*
**Schwartz**, Edna Barbara 1909- *WhoAmP 91*
**Schwartz**, Edward 1932- *AmMWSc 92*
**Schwartz**, Edward Richard 1934- *WhoAmL 92*
**Schwartz**, Eleanor Brantley 1937- *WhoMW 92*
**Schwartz**, Eli 1921- *ConAu 34NR, IntAu&W 91, WhoFI 92, WrDr 92*
**Schwartz**, Elias 1935- *AmMWSc 92*
**Schwartz**, Elliott 1936- *ConCom 92, NewAmDM*
**Schwartz**, Elliott S 1936- *IntAu&W 91, WrDr 92*
**Schwartz**, Elliott Shelling 1936- *WhoEnt 92*
**Schwartz**, Elmer G 1927- *AmMWSc 92*
**Schwartz**, Emanuel Elliot 1923- *AmMWSc 92*
**Schwartz**, Ernest 1924- *AmMWSc 92*
**Schwartz**, Estar Alma 1950- *WhoAmL 92*
**Schwartz**, Ferdinand Murray 1922- *WhoAmL 92*
**Schwartz**, Frank Joseph 1929- *AmMWSc 92*
**Schwartz**, Gary T. 1940- *WhoAmL 92*
**Schwartz**, George Edwin 1924- *WhoFI 92, WhoWest 92*
**Schwartz**, George X 1915- *WhoAmP 91*
**Schwartz**, Gerald Peter 1938- *AmMWSc 92*
**Schwartz**, Geraldine Cogin 1923- *AmMWSc 92*
**Schwartz**, Harold Daniel 1926- *WhoFI 92*
**Schwartz**, Harold Leon 1933- *AmMWSc 92*
**Schwartz**, Harold Philip 1936- *WhoFI 92*
**Schwartz**, Harry K 1934- *WhoAmP 91*
**Schwartz**, Harry Kane 1934- *WhoAmL 92*
**Schwartz**, Harvey 1941- *WhoAmL 92*
**Schwartz**, Heinz 1924- *AmMWSc 92*
**Schwartz**, Helen Joyce 1943- *WhoMW 92*
**Schwartz**, Henry C C 1956- *WhoAmP 91*
**Schwartz**, Henry Gerard, Jr 1938- *AmMWSc 92*
**Schwartz**, Herbert 1925- *AmMWSc 92*
**Schwartz**, Herbert C 1926- *AmMWSc 92*
**Schwartz**, Herbert Frederick 1935- *WhoAmL 92*
**Schwartz**, Herbert Mark 1948- *AmMWSc 92*
**Schwartz**, Hilda G. *WhoAmL 92*
**Schwartz**, Howard *DrAPF 91*
**Schwartz**, Howard Edwin 1944- *WhoAmP 91*
**Schwartz**, Howard Julius 1936- *AmMWSc 92*
**Schwartz**, Howard L. 1947- *WhoAmL 92*
**Schwartz**, Howard Wyn 1951- *WhoFI 92, WhoMW 92*
**Schwartz**, Ilsa Roslow 1941- *AmMWSc 92*
**Schwartz**, Ira 1947- *AmMWSc 92*
**Schwartz**, Ira A 1915- *AmMWSc 92*
**Schwartz**, Irving Leon 1918- *AmMWSc 92*
**Schwartz**, Irving Lloyd *WhoMW 92*
**Schwartz**, Irving Robert 1923- *AmMWSc 92*
**Schwartz**, Ivan Carey 1962- *WhoEnt 92*
**Schwartz**, J. 1953- *WhoEnt 92*
**Schwartz**, Jack 1931- *AmMWSc 92*
**Schwartz**, Jacob T. 1930- *IntWW 91*
**Schwartz**, Jacob Theodore 1930- *AmMWSc 92*
**Schwartz**, James Evan 1956- *WhoAmL 92*
**Schwartz**, James F 1929- *AmMWSc 92*
**Schwartz**, James Michael 1946- *WhoAmL 92*
**Schwartz**, James Peter 1919- *WhoFI 92*
**Schwartz**, James William 1927- *AmMWSc 92*
**Schwartz**, Jay Allan 1961- *WhoFI 92*
**Schwartz**, Jay W 1934- *AmMWSc 92*
**Schwartz**, Jeff 1955- *WhoEnt 92*
**Schwartz**, Jeffrey *DrAPF 91*
**Schwartz**, Jeffrey 1945- *AmMWSc 92*
**Schwartz**, Jeffrey H 1948- *AmMWSc 92*
**Schwartz**, Jeffrey Joel 1954- *WhoEnt 92*
**Schwartz**, Jeffrey Lee 1943- *AmMWSc 92*
**Schwartz**, Jeffrey Scott 1959- *WhoAmL 92*
**Schwartz**, Jennifer Sue 1966- *WhoEnt 92*
**Schwartz**, Jerome Lawrence 1938- *AmMWSc 92*
**Schwartz**, Jerome Merrill 1952- *WhoAmL 92*
**Schwartz**, Jerome T *WhoAmP 91*
**Schwartz**, Jessica *AmMWSc 92*
**Schwartz**, Joan Poyner 1943- *AmMWSc 92*
**Schwartz**, Joel Barry 1950- *WhoMW 92*
**Schwartz**, Joel L. *DrAPF 91*
**Schwartz**, John Andrew 1952- *WhoWest 92*
**Schwartz**, John C 1947- *WhoIns 92*
**Schwartz**, John Charles 1939- *WhoWest 92*
**Schwartz**, John Gordon 1943- *WhoAmL 92*
**Schwartz**, John H *AmMWSc 92*
**Schwartz**, John Leonard 1946- *WhoWest 92*
**Schwartz**, John Robert 1944- *WhoAmL 92*
**Schwartz**, John T 1926- *AmMWSc 92*
**Schwartz**, Jonathan Ranon 1964- *WhoFI 92*
**Schwartz**, Joseph 1925- *WhoMW 92, WrDr 92*
**Schwartz**, Joseph Barry 1941- *AmMWSc 92*
**Schwartz**, Joseph Robert 1919- *AmMWSc 92*
**Schwartz**, Judah Leon 1934- *AmMWSc 92*
**Schwartz**, Kenneth Bernard 1954- *WhoAmL 92*
**Schwartz**, Kenneth Ernst 1922- *WhoEnt 92, WhoFI 92*
**Schwartz**, Kessel 1920- *WrDr 92*
**Schwartz**, Kimberly Ann 1959- *WhoWest 92*
**Schwartz**, Larry L 1935- *AmMWSc 92*
**Schwartz**, Laure Ann 1961- *WhoRel 92*
**Schwartz**, Laurent 1915- *IntWW 91*
**Schwartz**, Lawrence B 1949- *AmMWSc 92*
**Schwartz**, Lawrence Elliot 1935- *WhoFI 92, WhoMW 92*
**Schwartz**, Leander Joseph 1932- *AmMWSc 92*
**Schwartz**, Lee Alan 1955- *WhoAmL 92*
**Schwartz**, Leland Dwight 1925- *AmMWSc 92*
**Schwartz**, Leon Joseph 1943- *AmMWSc 92*
**Schwartz**, Leonard H 1932- *AmMWSc 92*
**Schwartz**, Leonard Jay 1943- *WhoAmL 92*
**Schwartz**, Leonard William 1943- *AmMWSc 92*
**Schwartz**, Leslie R. 1915- *IntMPA 92*
**Schwartz**, Lillian Feldman 1927- *WhoEnt 92*
**Schwartz**, Linda Barrett 1955- *WhoAmP 91*
**Schwartz**, Lloyd *DrAPF 91*
**Schwartz**, Lloyd 1941- *WhoEnt 92*
**Schwartz**, Louis 1940- *WhoWest 92*
**Schwartz**, Louis B 1913- *IntAu&W 91*
**Schwartz**, Louis Brown 1913- *WrDr 92*
**Schwartz**, Lowell Melvin 1934- *AmMWSc 92*
**Schwartz**, Lyle H 1936- *AmMWSc 92*
**Schwartz**, Lynne Sharon *DrAPF 91*

**Schwartz,** Lynne Sharon 1939- IntAu&W 91, WrDr 92
**Schwartz,** M A 1920- AmMWSc 92
**Schwartz,** Marc Alan 1962- WhoAmL 92
**Schwartz,** Marian DrAPF 91
**Schwartz,** Marshall Zane 1945- AmMWSc 92
**Schwartz,** Martin 1925- AmMWSc 92
**Schwartz,** Martin Alan 1940- AmMWSc 92
**Schwartz,** Martin Alexander 1954- AmMWSc 92
**Schwartz,** Martin Lerner 1945- WhoWest 92
**Schwartz,** Marvin 1922- WhoAmL 92
**Schwartz,** Maurice Edward 1939- AmMWSc 92
**Schwartz,** Maurice Leo 1925- AmMWSc 92
**Schwartz,** Maxime 1940- IntWW 91
**Schwartz,** Melvin 1932- AmMWSc 92, Who 92, WhoNob 90
**Schwartz,** Melvin J 1928- AmMWSc 92
**Schwartz,** Michael 1937- WhoMW 92
**Schwartz,** Michael Averill 1930- AmMWSc 92
**Schwartz,** Michael B. 1938- WhoMW 92
**Schwartz,** Michael H 1959- AmMWSc 92
**Schwartz,** Michael Hal 1958- WhoAmL 92
**Schwartz,** Michael Muni 1943- AmMWSc 92
**Schwartz,** Michael Robinson 1940- WhoMW 92
**Schwartz,** Mildred Anne 1932- IntAu&W 91, WrDr 92
**Schwartz,** Milton Lewis 1920- WhoAmL 92, WhoWest 92
**Schwartz,** Mischa 1926- AmMWSc 92
**Schwartz,** Modest Euphemia 1915- WhoWest 92
**Schwartz,** Morton Allen 1928- AmMWSc 92
**Schwartz,** Morton Donald 1936- AmMWSc 92
**Schwartz,** Morton K 1925- AmMWSc 92
**Schwartz,** Murray Louis 1920- WhoAmL 92
**Schwartz,** Murray Merle 1931- WhoAmL 92
**Schwartz,** Nan Louise 1953- WhoEnt 92
**Schwartz,** Nancy WhoAmP 91
**Schwartz,** Natalie Levy 1938- WhoEnt 92
**Schwartz,** Neena Betty 1926- AmMWSc 92
**Schwartz,** Neil D 1942- WhoIns 92
**Schwartz,** Newton 1925- AmMWSc 92
**Schwartz,** Norman Martin 1935- AmMWSc 92
**Schwartz,** Patricia Roth DrAPF 91
**Schwartz,** Paul 1948- AmMWSc 92
**Schwartz,** Paul Henry, Jr 1936- AmMWSc 92
**Schwartz,** Paul Marc WhoMW 92
**Schwartz,** Paul Michael 1959- WhoAmL 92, WhoFI 92
**Schwartz,** Pauline Mary 1947- AmMWSc 92
**Schwartz,** Peter Larry 1940- AmMWSc 92
**Schwartz,** Philip Charles 1925- WhoFI 92
**Schwartz,** Philip Lawrence 1964- WhoEnt 92
**Schwartz,** Phyllis Judy 1955- WhoEnt 92
**Schwartz,** Ralph Jerome 1919- AmMWSc 92, WhoMW 92
**Schwartz,** Ramon, Jr 1925- WhoAmP 91
**Schwartz,** Renee Gerstler 1933- WhoAmL 92
**Schwartz,** Rhoda DrAPF 91
**Schwartz,** Richard 1936- WhoFI 92
**Schwartz,** Richard Allen 1945- WhoFI 92
**Schwartz,** Richard Dean 1941- AmMWSc 92
**Schwartz,** Richard F 1922- AmMWSc 92
**Schwartz,** Richard Isadore 1951- WhoEnt 92
**Schwartz,** Richard John 1935- AmMWSc 92
**Schwartz,** Robert 1922- AmMWSc 92
**Schwartz,** Robert Bernard 1929- AmMWSc 92
**Schwartz,** Robert D. 1945- WhoMW 92
**Schwartz,** Robert David 1941- AmMWSc 92
**Schwartz,** Robert George 1928- IntWW 91, WhoFI 92, WhoIns 92
**Schwartz,** Robert H. 1948- WhoAmL 92
**Schwartz,** Robert Herman 1934- WhoMW 92
**Schwartz,** Robert Jay 1946- WhoFI 92
**Schwartz,** Robert John 1942- AmMWSc 92
**Schwartz,** Robert Lewis 1948- WhoAmL 92
**Schwartz,** Robert Nelson 1940- AmMWSc 92
**Schwartz,** Robert Saul 1942- AmMWSc 92
**Schwartz,** Robert Stewart 1928- AmMWSc 92
**Schwartz,** Robert William 1944- WhoFI 92
**Schwartz,** Roger Alan 1945- WhoAmL 92
**Schwartz,** Ronald Barry 1955- WhoAmL 92
**Schwartz,** Roy Richard 1943- WhoFI 92
**Schwartz,** Russell 1949- WhoEnt 92
**Schwartz,** Ruth 1924- AmMWSc 92
**Schwartz,** Samuel 1916- AmMWSc 92
**Schwartz,** Samuel Meyer 1929- AmMWSc 92
**Schwartz,** Sandra E 1945- WhoAmP 91
**Schwartz,** Sanford Bernard 1925- AmMWSc 92
**Schwartz,** Seymour I 1928- AmMWSc 92
**Schwartz,** Sheila DrAPF 91
**Schwartz,** Sheila 1936- IntAu&W 91
**Schwartz,** Sheila R. WrDr 92
**Schwartz,** Sheldon 1954- WhoEnt 92
**Schwartz,** Sheldon E 1919- AmMWSc 92
**Schwartz,** Sherwood LesBEnT 92
**Schwartz,** Shirley Eckwall 1935- WhoFI 92, WhoMW 92
**Schwartz,** Simon 1947- WhoRel 92
**Schwartz,** Sorell Lee 1937- AmMWSc 92
**Schwartz,** Stanley Allen 1941- AmMWSc 92, WhoMW 92
**Schwartz,** Stephan Andrew 1942- WhoFI 92
**Schwartz,** Stephen Alfred 1948- WhoFI 92
**Schwartz,** Stephen Blair 1934- WhoFI 92
**Schwartz,** Stephen Eugene 1941- AmMWSc 92
**Schwartz,** Stephen Jay 1947- WhoAmL 92
**Schwartz,** Stephen Lawrence 1948- WhoEnt 92
**Schwartz,** Stephen Mark 1942- AmMWSc 92
**Schwartz,** Steven DrAPF 91
**Schwartz,** Steven Gary 1954- WhoAmL 92
**Schwartz,** Steven Otto 1911- AmMWSc 92
**Schwartz,** Steven Richard 1960- WhoMW 92
**Schwartz,** Stuart Carl 1939- AmMWSc 92
**Schwartz,** Stuart Dawson 1960- WhoFI 92
**Schwartz,** Susan 1959- WhoAmP 91
**Schwartz,** Susan Christine 1949- WhoRel 92
**Schwartz,** Susan Martha 1949- IntAu&W 91
**Schwartz,** Theodore Benoni 1918- AmMWSc 92
**Schwartz,** Thomas Alan 1951- AmMWSc 92
**Schwartz,** Tobias Louis 1928- AmMWSc 92
**Schwartz,** Walter A. LesBEnT 92
**Schwartz,** William 1933- WhoAmL 92
**Schwartz,** William Benjamin 1922- AmMWSc 92
**Schwartz,** William Bernstein, Jr 1921- WhoAmP 91
**Schwartz,** William Jeffrey 1957- WhoMW 92
**Schwartz,** William Joseph 1950- AmMWSc 92
**Schwartz,** William Lewis 1931- AmMWSc 92
**Schwartzbach,** Steven Donald 1947- AmMWSc 92
**Schwartzbart,** Harry 1923- AmMWSc 92
**Schwartzbaum,** David Mark 1961- WhoAmL 92
**Schwartzberg,** Harvey Jay 1928- WhoFI 92
**Schwartzberg,** Henry G 1925- AmMWSc 92
**Schwartzberg,** Hugh Joel 1933- WhoAmL 92, WhoFI 92
**Schwartzberg,** Martin M. 1935- WhoFI 92
**Schwartzel,** Charles Boone 1950- WhoAmL 92
**Schwartzel,** Joseph Charles 1947- WhoEnt 92
**Schwartzenberg,** Roger-Gerard 1943- IntWW 91
**Schwartzentruber,** Daniel Charles 1956- WhoMW 92
**Schwartzhoff,** James Paul 1937- WhoMW 92
**Schwartzkopf,** Edward 1919- WhoAmP 91, WhoMW 92
**Schwartzman,** Andrew Jay LesBEnT 92
**Schwartzman,** Arnold Martin 1936- WhoWest 92
**Schwartzman,** David 1924- WhoFI 92
**Schwartzman,** Herbert Daniel 1933- WhoAmL 92
**Schwartzman,** Jack 1912- WhoAmL 92, WhoFI 92
**Schwartzman,** James Charles 1945- WhoAmL 92
**Schwartzman,** Joseph David 1947- AmMWSc 92
**Schwartzman,** Leon 1931- AmMWSc 92
**Schwartzman,** Robert M 1926- AmMWSc 92
**Schwartzman,** Sylvan David 1913- WhoRel 92
**Schwartzott,** Paul Richard 1946- WhoIns 92
**Schwary,** Richard Joseph 1944- WhoWest 92
**Schwary,** Ronald L. 1944- IntMPA 92
**Schwary,** Ronald Louis 1944- WhoEnt 92
**Schwarz,** Antoine 1943- IntWW 91
**Schwarz,** Anton 1927- AmMWSc 92
**Schwarz,** Cindy Beth 1958- AmMWSc 92
**Schwarz,** Daniel Tracy 1938- WhoEnt 92
**Schwarz,** Dietrich Walter Friedrich 1939- AmMWSc 92
**Schwarz,** Eckhard C A 1930- AmMWSc 92
**Schwarz,** Frank 1924- AmMWSc 92
**Schwarz,** Franz Xaver 1875-1947 EncTR 91 [port]
**Schwarz,** Frederick August Otto, Jr. 1935- WhoAmL 92
**Schwarz,** Gerard 1947- IntWW 91, NewAmDM
**Schwarz,** Gerard Ralph 1947- WhoEnt 92, WhoWest 92
**Schwarz,** H. Marshall 1936- WhoFI 92
**Schwarz,** Hans 1939- WhoRel 92
**Schwarz,** Hans Jakob 1925- AmMWSc 92
**Schwarz,** Harold A 1928- AmMWSc 92
**Schwarz,** Henry G 1928- IntAu&W 91, WrDr 92
**Schwarz,** John 1937- WhoAmP 91
**Schwarz,** John Henry 1941- AmMWSc 92
**Schwarz,** John J.H. 1937- WhoMW 92
**Schwarz,** John Robert 1944- AmMWSc 92
**Schwarz,** John Samuel Paul 1932- AmMWSc 92
**Schwarz,** Jordan Abraham 1937- WhoMW 92
**Schwarz,** Joseph Richard 1954- WhoWest 92
**Schwarz,** Josephine Lindeman 1908- WhoEnt 92
**Schwarz,** Joyce Ann 1946- WhoEnt 92
**Schwarz,** Karen Anne 1957- WhoRel 92
**Schwarz,** Klaus W 1938- AmMWSc 92
**Schwarz,** Leroy Bernard 1941- WhoMW 92
**Schwarz,** Liese O'Halloran 1963- ConAu 133
**Schwarz,** Louis Jay 1946- WhoFI 92
**Schwarz,** Marvin 1929- AmMWSc 92
**Schwarz,** Maurice Jacob 1939- AmMWSc 92
**Schwarz,** May Louise 1945- WhoEnt 92
**Schwarz,** Melvin A. 1950- WhoAmL 92
**Schwarz,** Meyer 1924- AmMWSc 92
**Schwarz,** Michael 1952- WhoAmL 92, WhoWest 92
**Schwarz,** Otto 1919- WhoWest 92
**Schwarz,** Otto John 1942- AmMWSc 92
**Schwarz,** Ralph J 1922- AmMWSc 92
**Schwarz,** Ricardo 1942- AmMWSc 92
**Schwarz,** Richard Howard 1931- AmMWSc 92
**Schwarz,** Rudolf 1905- IntWW 91, Who 92
**Schwarz,** Scott J. 1955- WhoAmL 92
**Schwarz,** Sidney Howard 1953- WhoRel 92
**Schwarz,** Sigmund D 1928- AmMWSc 92
**Schwarz,** Stefan 1914- IntWW 91
**Schwarz,** Steven E 1939- AmMWSc 92
**Schwarz,** William Merlin, Jr 1934- AmMWSc 92
**Schwarz-Bart,** Andre 1928- Who 92
**Schwarz-Schilling,** Christian 1930- IntWW 91
**Schwarze,** Robert Francis 1949- WhoMW 92
**Schwarzenberger,** Georg 1908- IntAu&W 91, Who 92, WrDr 92
**Schwarzenegger,** Arnold 1947- CurBio 91 [port], IntMPA 92, News 91 [port]
**Schwarzenegger,** Arnold Alois 1947- IntWW 91, WhoEnt 92
**Schwarzentraub,** Elizabeth Keith 1949- WhoRel 92
**Schwarzer,** Carl G 1917- AmMWSc 92
**Schwarzer,** Theresa Flynn 1940- AmMWSc 92
**Schwarzer,** William W 1925- WhoAmL 92, WhoWest 92
**Schwarzkopf,** Elisabeth 1915- FacFETw, IntWW 91, NewAmDM, Who 92
**Schwarzkopf,** H. Norman 1934- CurBio 91 [port], FacFETw [port], IntWW 91, NewYTBS 91 [port], Who 92
**Schwarzkopf,** Norman 1934- News 91 [port], -91-3 [port]
**Schwarzkopf,** Peter B 1931- WhoAmP 91
**Schwarzman,** Stephen Allen 1947- WhoFI 92
**Schwarzman,** William Edward 1929- WhoFI 92
**Schwarzrock,** Shirley Pratt 1914- WhoMW 92
**Schwarzschild,** Arthur Zeiger 1930- AmMWSc 92
**Schwarzschild,** Martin 1912- AmMWSc 92, IntWW 91
**Schwarzwalder,** Alan Michael 1943- WhoMW 92
**Schwarzwalder,** John Carl 1917- WhoEnt 92
**Schwass,** Gary L. 1945- WhoFI 92
**Schwassman,** Horst Otto 1922- AmMWSc 92
**Schwatka,** Frederick 1849-1892 BiInAmS
**Schwebach,** Thomas Robert 1955- WhoMW 92
**Schwebel,** Richard Albert 1942- WhoMW 92
**Schwebel,** Solomon Lawrence 1916- AmMWSc 92
**Schwebel,** Stephen M. 1929- IntWW 91
**Schweber,** Silvan Samuel 1928- AmMWSc 92
**Schwed,** Peter Gregory 1952- WhoAmL 92
**Schweda,** Robert Frank 1952- WhoAmL 92
**Schwee,** Leonard Joseph 1936- AmMWSc 92
**Schwegman,** John Edwin 1936- WhoMW 92
**Schwegmann,** Jack Carl 1925- AmMWSc 92
**Schweich,** Anderson M. 1923- WhoBlA 92
**Schweickert,** Richard Allan 1946- AmMWSc 92
**Schweiger,** Anthony Walter 1941- WhoFI 92
**Schweiger,** Debra Jean 1953- WhoMW 92
**Schweiger,** James W 1929- AmMWSc 92
**Schweiger,** Marvin I 1923- AmMWSc 92
**Schweigert,** Bernard Sylvester 1921- AmMWSc 92
**Schweigert,** Lynette Aileen 1949- WhoWest 92
**Schweighardt,** Frank Kenneth 1944- AmMWSc 92
**Schweikart,** Larry 1951- ConAu 134
**Schweiker,** George Christian 1924- AmMWSc 92
**Schweiker,** Jerry W 1931- AmMWSc 92
**Schweiker,** John Steven 1950- WhoAmP 91
**Schweiker,** Richard Schultz 1926- IntWW 91, WhoAmP 91, WhoIns 92
**Schweiker,** William 1953- WhoRel 92
**Schweikert,** Daniel George 1937- AmMWSc 92
**Schweikert,** David WhoAmP 91
**Schweikert,** Emile Alfred 1939- AmMWSc 92
**Schweikert,** Norman Carl 1937- WhoEnt 92
**Schweikher,** Paul 1903- IntWW 91
**Schweinhagen,** Rupert William 1929- WhoMW 92
**Schweinhart,** Richard Alexander 1949- WhoFI 92
**Schweinhaut,** Margaret Collins 1904- WhoAmP 91
**Schweinitz,** Emil Alexander De 1864?-1904 BiInAmS
**Schweinitz,** Lewis David Von 1780-1834 BiInAmS
**Schweinitz,** Wolfgang von 1953- ConCom 92
**Schweinler,** Harold Constantine 1922- AmMWSc 92
**Schweinsberg,** Allen Ross 1942- AmMWSc 92
**Schweiss,** John Francis 1925- AmMWSc 92
**Schweisthal,** Michael Robert 1936- AmMWSc 92
**Schweitzer,** Albert 1875-1965 FacFETw [port], NewAmDM, WhoNob 90
**Schweitzer,** Arthur 1905- IntAu&W 91, WrDr 92
**Schweitzer,** Carl Earle 1914- AmMWSc 92
**Schweitzer,** Donald Gerald 1930- AmMWSc 92
**Schweitzer,** Ed A 1944- WhoAmP 91
**Schweitzer,** Edmund Oscar, III 1947- AmMWSc 92
**Schweitzer,** George Gerard Peter 1953- WhoWest 92
**Schweitzer,** George Keene 1924- AmMWSc 92
**Schweitzer,** Hans 1901- EncTR 91 [port]
**Schweitzer,** Hugo 1861-1917 BiInAmS
**Schweitzer,** Jeffrey Stewart 1946- AmMWSc 92
**Schweitzer,** John William 1941- AmMWSc 92
**Schweitzer,** Leah DrAPF 91
**Schweitzer,** Leland Ray 1941- AmMWSc 92
**Schweitzer,** Louis 1942- IntWW 91
**Schweitzer,** Marilyn Jane 1944- WhoFI 92, WhoMW 92
**Schweitzer,** Mark Glenn 1957- AmMWSc 92
**Schweitzer,** Melvin L 1944- WhoAmP 91
**Schweitzer,** Miguel 1940- Who 92
**Schweitzer,** Paul 1840-1911 BiInAmS
**Schweitzer,** Paul Jerome 1941- AmMWSc 92

**Schweitzer**, Pierre-Paul 1912- *IntWW 91, Who 92*
**Schweitzer**, Raymond D. 1936- *WhoWest 92*
**Schweitzer**, Robert L *WhoAmP 91*
**Schweitzer**, Sharon Marie 1961- *WhoAmL 92*
**Schweitzer Walters**, Miguel 1940- *IntWW 91*
**Schweizer**, Albert Edward 1943- *AmMWSc 92*
**Schweizer**, Berthold 1929- *AmMWSc 92*
**Schweizer**, Edward E 1933- *AmMWSc 92*
**Schweizer**, Edward Ernest 1928- *AmMWSc 92*
**Schweizer**, Felix 1927- *AmMWSc 92*
**Schweizer**, Francois 1942- *AmMWSc 92*
**Schweizer**, Malvina 1906- *AmMWSc 92*
**Schweizer**, Martin Paul *AmMWSc 92*
**Schwelb**, Frank Ernest 1932- *WhoAmL 92, WhoAmP 91*
**Schwelb**, Otto 1931- *AmMWSc 92*
**Schwelitz**, Faye Dorothy 1931- *AmMWSc 92*
**Schweller**, Donald George 1930- *WhoAmL 92*
**Schwendeman**, Joseph Raymond, Jr 1930- *AmMWSc 92*
**Schwendeman**, Richard Henry 1929- *AmMWSc 92*
**Schwendemann**, Steven Clark 1963- *WhoAmL 92*
**Schwendiman**, Gary 1940- *WhoFI 92*
**Schwendiman**, John Leo 1909- *AmMWSc 92*
**Schwendinger**, Gary Van 1945- *WhoMW 92*
**Schwenk**, Allen John 1947- *WhoMW 92*
**Schwenk**, Edwin Miller 1923- *WhoAmP 91*
**Schwenk**, Fred Walter 1938- *AmMWSc 92*
**Schwenk**, Kenneth Raymond 1937- *WhoFI 92*
**Schwenk-Berman**, Laura Leacock 1956- *WhoEnt 92*
**Schwenke**, Karen Ann 1961- *WhoMW 92*
**Schwenker**, J E 1928- *AmMWSc 92*
**Schwenker**, Robert Frederick, Jr 1920- *AmMWSc 92*
**Schwenkfeld Von Ossig**, Caspar 1489-1561 *DcAmImH*
**Schwenn**, Edwin George 1928- *WhoMW 92*
**Schwensfeir**, Robert James, Jr 1934- *AmMWSc 92*
**Schwenterly**, Stanley William, III 1945- *AmMWSc 92*
**Schwenz**, Richard William 1955- *AmMWSc 92*
**Schwenzer**, Gerhard *WhoRel 92*
**Schweppe**, Earl Justin 1927- *AmMWSc 92*
**Schweppe**, John S 1917- *AmMWSc 92*
**Schweppe**, Joseph L 1921- *AmMWSc 92*
**Schweppe**, Marla Karen 1950- *WhoEnt 92*
**Schwer**, Joseph Francis 1936- *AmMWSc 92*
**Schwerdt**, Carlton Everett 1917- *AmMWSc 92*
**Schwerdtfeger**, Charles Frederick 1934- *AmMWSc 92*
**Schwerdtfeger**, Cindy Kay 1963- *WhoRel 92*
**Schwerdtner**, Frederick Howard 1949- *WhoMW 92*
**Schwerer**, Frederick Carl 1941- *AmMWSc 92*
**Schweri**, Margaret Mary 1946- *AmMWSc 92*
**Schwerin**, Charles Henry 1915- *WhoFI 92*
**Schwerin**, Daniel William 1963- *WhoRel 92*
**Schwerin**, Doris *DrAPF 91*
**Schwerin**, Jules Victor 1919- *WhoEnt 92*
**Schwerin von Krosigk**, Johann, Count von 1887-1977 *EncTR 91 [port]*
**Schwerin vonSchwanenfeld**, Ulrich-Wilhelm 1902-1944 *EncTR 91 [port]*
**Schwering**, Felix 1930- *AmMWSc 92*
**Schwerner**, Armand *DrAPF 91*
**Schwerner**, Armand 1927- *ConPo 91, WrDr 92*
**Schwerner**, Nathan H. d1991 *NewYTBS 91*
**Schwert**, Donald Peters 1949- *AmMWSc 92*
**Schwert**, George William 1919- *AmMWSc 92*
**Schwert**, George William, III 1950- *WhoFI 92*
**Schwertsik**, Kurt 1935- *ConCom 92*
**Schwertz**, Joseph S., Jr. 1956- *WhoAmL 92*
**Schwery**, Henri 1932- *WhoRel 92*
**Schwerzel**, Robert Edward 1943- *AmMWSc 92*
**Schwerzler**, Dennis David 1944- *AmMWSc 92*
**Schwethelm**, A C 1931- *WhoAmP 91*
**Schwetman**, Herbert Dewitt 1911- *AmMWSc 92*
**Schwettman**, Harry Alan 1936- *AmMWSc 92*
**Schwetz**, Bernard Anthony 1940- *AmMWSc 92*
**Schwichtenberg**, Daryl Robert 1929- *WhoFI 92, WhoWest 92*
**Schwichtenberg**, Willis Robert 1946- *WhoRel 92*
**Schwiderski**, Ernst Walter 1924- *AmMWSc 92*
**Schwiebert**, Mark William 1950- *WhoAmL 92, WhoAmP 91*
**Schwieder**, Dorothy Ann 1933- *WhoMW 92*
**Schwieger**, Susan Margaret 1951- *WhoMW 92*
**Schwier**, Chris Edward 1956- *AmMWSc 92*
**Schwier**, Priscilla Lamb Guyton 1939- *WhoFI 92*
**Schwiesow**, Ronald Lee 1940- *AmMWSc 92*
**Schwimmer**, Rosika 1877-1948 *AmPeW*
**Schwimmer**, Sigmund 1917- *AmMWSc 92*
**Schwimmer**, Walter d1989 *LesBEnT 92*
**Schwinck**, Ilse 1923- *AmMWSc 92*
**Schwind**, David Ralph 1954- *WhoEnt 92*
**Schwind**, Michael Angelo 1924- *WhoAmL 92*
**Schwindeman**, James Anthony 1955- *AmMWSc 92*
**Schwinden**, Ted 1925- *IntWW 91, WhoAmP 91, WhoWest 92*
**Schwing**, Frank *WhoHisp 92*
**Schwing**, Franklin Burton 1956- *AmMWSc 92*
**Schwing**, Gregory Wayne 1946- *AmMWSc 92*
**Schwing**, Richard C 1934- *AmMWSc 92*
**Schwinger**, Julian 1918- *Who 92, WhoWest 92, WrDr 92*
**Schwinger**, Julian Seymour 1918- *AmMWSc 92, IntWW 91, WhoNob 90*
**Schwinn**, David Ronald 1944- *WhoMW 92*
**Schwintzer**, Christa Rose *AmMWSc 92*
**Schwirzke**, Fred 1927- *AmMWSc 92*
**Schwister**, Jay Edward 1962- *WhoFI 92*
**Schwitters**, Kurt 1887-1948 *DcTwDes, FacFETw*
**Schwitters**, Roy Frederick 1944- *AmMWSc 92*
**Schwob**, Marcel 1867-1905 *GuFrLit 1*
**Schwochow**, Alan Arthur 1953- *WhoRel 92*
**Schwoebel**, Richard Lynn 1931- *AmMWSc 92*
**Schwoerer**, F 1922- *AmMWSc 92*
**Schwope**, Mary Kathryn 1917- *WhoAmP 91*
**Schwortz**, Barrie Marshall 1946- *WhoWest 92*
**Schwyn**, Charles Edward 1932- *WhoWest 92*
**Schwyzer**, Robert 1920- *IntWW 91*
**Schy**, Albert Abe 1920- *AmMWSc 92*
**Schye**, Ted 1948- *WhoAmP 91*
**Schygulla**, Hanna 1943- *IntMPA 92, IntWW 91*
**Schyve**, Paul Milton 1944- *AmMWSc 92*
**Sciabica**, Vincent Samuel 1959- *WhoFI 92*
**Scialdone**, John Joseph 1926- *AmMWSc 92*
**Sciama**, Dennis 1926- *WrDr 92*
**Sciama**, Dennis William 1926- *IntWW 91, Who 92*
**Sciamanda**, Robert Joseph 1931- *AmMWSc 92*
**Sciame**, Donald Richard 1945- *WhoWest 92*
**Sciammarella**, Caesar August 1926- *AmMWSc 92*
**Sciammas**, Jacques Daniel 1956- *WhoFI 92*
**Scianna**, Cosimo 1941- *WhoEnt 92*
**Sciano**, Debra Marie 1958- *WhoAmL 92*
**Sciara**, Frank John 1928- *WhoMW 92*
**Sciarini**, Louis J 1915- *AmMWSc 92*
**Sciarra**, Daniel 1918- *AmMWSc 92*
**Sciarra**, John J 1927- *AmMWSc 92*
**Sciarra**, John J 1932- *AmMWSc 92*
**Sciarra**, Patrick Anthony *WhoMW 92*
**Sciarrino**, Salvatore 1947- *ConCom 92*
**Sciarrone**, Bartley John 1926- *AmMWSc 92*
**Sciascia**, Leonardo 1921-1989 *ConAu 35NR, FacFETw*
**Scibelli**, Anthony M *WhoAmP 91*
**Scibilia**, Philip Chester 1940- *WhoFI 92*
**Scibona**, Nicholas Joseph 1951- *WhoMW 92*
**Scibor-Marchocki**, Romuald Ireneus 1926- *WhoWest 92*
**Scicchitano**, Carmine David 1962- *WhoEnt 92, WhoFI 92*
**Scicli**, Alfonso Guillermo *AmMWSc 92*
**Scidmore**, Allan K 1927- *AmMWSc 92, WhoMW 92*
**Scidmore**, Wright H 1925- *AmMWSc 92*
**Scieszka**, Jon 1954- *ConAu 135, SmATA 68*
**Scifres**, Charles Joel 1941- *AmMWSc 92*
**Scifres**, Donald Ray 1946- *AmMWSc 92*
**Scigliano**, J Michael 1941- *AmMWSc 92*
**Scimone**, Claudio 1934- *WhoEnt 92*
**Scimone**, Diana Elizabeth 1950- *WhoRel 92*
**Scinta**, James 1952- *AmMWSc 92*
**Sciocchetti**, Paul Vincent 1961- *WhoAmL 92*
**Sciolaro**, Charles Michael 1958- *WhoWest 92*
**Sciore**, Edward 1955- *AmMWSc 92*
**Sciorra**, Annabella 1964- *IntMPA 92*
**Sciortino**, John 1959- *WhoAmL 92*
**Sciortino**, Michael Arthur 1949- *WhoAmL 92*
**Scipio**, L Albert, II 1922- *AmMWSc 92*
**Scipio**, Laurence Harold 1942- *WhoBlA 92*
**Scipione**, Richard Stephen 1937- *WhoAmL 92*
**Scirica**, Anthony J *WhoAmP 91*
**Scirica**, Anthony Joseph 1940- *WhoAmL 92*
**Scisson**, Sidney Eugene 1917- *AmMWSc 92*
**Scitovsky**, Anne A 1915- *AmMWSc 92, IntWW 91*
**Scitovsky**, Tibor 1910- *IntWW 91*
**Sciuchetti**, Leo A 1913- *AmMWSc 92*
**Sciulli**, Frank J 1938- *AmMWSc 92*
**Sciulli**, Frederick Rocco 1955- *WhoAmL 92*
**Sciulli**, Paul William 1947- *AmMWSc 92*
**Sciumbato**, Gabriel Lon 1945- *AmMWSc 92*
**Sclair**, M. David 1938- *WhoWest 92*
**Sclar**, Charles Bertram 1925- *AmMWSc 92*
**Sclar**, Nathan 1920- *AmMWSc 92*
**Sclater**, John G. 1940- *IntWW 91*
**Sclater**, John George 1940- *AmMWSc 92, Who 92*
**Sclater**, John Richard 1940- *Who 92*
**Sclater-Booth** *Who 92*
**Sclove**, Stanley Louis 1940- *AmMWSc 92, WhoMW 92*
**Scoates**, Harry William, Jr. 1920- *WhoRel 92*
**Scoates**, Wesley Marvin 1938- *WhoFI 92*
**Scobee**, Francis R 1939-1986 *FacFETw*
**Scobey**, Ellis Hurlbut 1911- *AmMWSc 92*
**Scobey**, James Ralph 1922- *WhoRel 92*
**Scobey**, Robert P 1938- *AmMWSc 92*
**Scobie**, Gavin 1940- *TwCPaSc*
**Scobie**, Ian Alexander 1957- *WhoEnt 92*
**Scobie**, Ilka *DrAPF 91*
**Scobie**, Kenneth Charles 1938- *Who 92*
**Scobie**, Stephen 1943- *BenetAL 91*
**Scoble**, Arthur William John *Who 92*
**Scoble**, Christopher Lawrence 1943- *Who 92*
**Scoby**, Donald Ray 1931- *AmMWSc 92*
**Scoby**, Gloria *WhoFI 92, WhoMW 92*
**Scocca**, John Joseph 1940- *AmMWSc 92*
**Scocozza**, Matthew Vincent 1948- *WhoAmP 91*
**Scofield**, David Willson 1957- *WhoAmL 92*
**Scofield**, Dillon Foster 1943- *AmMWSc 92*
**Scofield**, Gordon L 1925- *AmMWSc 92*
**Scofield**, Herbert Temple 1909- *AmMWSc 92*
**Scofield**, James Howard 1933- *AmMWSc 92*
**Scofield**, John 1951- *ConMus 7 [port], FacFETw*
**Scofield**, Jonathan *WrDr 92*
**Scofield**, Julie Melissa 1958- *WhoAmP 91*
**Scofield**, Paul 1922- *IntMPA 92, IntWW 91, Who 92*
**Scofield**, Robert Vincent, II 1954- *WhoRel 92*
**Scofield**, Sandra K 1947- *WhoAmP 91*
**Scofield**, Todd Carver 1956- *WhoFI 92*
**Scoggin**, Blainard Elmo 1915- *WhoRel 92*
**Scoggin**, James F, Jr 1921- *AmMWSc 92*
**Scoggin**, Van Rogers 1912- *WhoWest 92*
**Scoggins**, James R 1931- *AmMWSc 92*
**Scoggins**, Richard Todd 1949- *WhoRel 92*
**Scoggins**, Robert Conroy 1935- *WhoRel 92*
**Scogin**, Edward C 1921- *WhoAmP 91*
**Scogin**, Ron Lynn 1941- *AmMWSc 92*
**Scogland**, William Lee 1949- *WhoAmL 92*
**Scognamiglio**, Carlo 1944- *IntWW 91*
**Scola**, Daniel Anthony 1929- *AmMWSc 92*
**Scola**, Ettore 1931- *IntDcF 2-2 [port], IntMPA 92, IntWW 91*
**Scola**, Ralph Joseph 1943- *WhoAmL 92*
**Scolaro**, Bernadette 1958- *WhoMW 92*
**Scolaro**, Reginald Joseph 1939- *AmMWSc 92*
**Scolaro**, Vincent 1958- *WhoAmL 92*
**Scoles**, Graham John *AmMWSc 92*
**Scoliere**, Michael Edward 1961- *WhoAmL 92*
**Scollan**, Joseph C. 1942- *WhoAmL 92*
**Scollard**, Clinton 1860-1932 *BenetAL 91*
**Scollard**, David Michael 1947- *AmMWSc 92*
**Scollard**, Jeannette Reddish *WhoWest 92*
**Scollard**, Robert Joseph 1908- *WhoRel 92*
**Scolman**, Theodore Thomas 1926- *AmMWSc 92*
**Scolnick**, Edward M 1940- *AmMWSc 92*
**Scolnik**, Louis *WhoAmP 91*
**Scolnik**, Robert N. 1944- *WhoFI 92*
**Scommegna**, Antonio 1931- *AmMWSc 92*
**Sconiers**, Daryl Anthony 1958- *WhoBlA 92*
**Sconiers**, M. L. *WhoRel 92*
**Sconyers**, Jeff 1935- *WhoFI 92*
**Scoon**, Paul 1935- *IntWW 91, Who 92*
**Scoones**, Reginald 1900- *Who 92*
**Scooros**, Constantine 1947- *WhoEnt 92*
**Scopatz**, Mary Porpiglia 1934- *WhoWest 92*
**Scopatz**, Stephen David 1957- *WhoMW 92*
**Scopaz**, John Matthew 1948- *WhoFI 92*
**Scopel**, Rand Elio 1957- *WhoAmL 92*
**Scoper**, Vincent Gradie, Jr 1933- *WhoAmP 91*
**Scopes**, Leonard Arthur 1912- *Who 92*
**Scopinich-Buhler**, Jill Lorie 1945- *WhoFI 92*
**Scopino**, Tony d1991 *NewYTBS 91*
**Scopp**, Irwin Walter 1909- *AmMWSc 92*
**Scora**, Rainer Walter 1928- *AmMWSc 92, WhoWest 92*
**Scoratow**, Martin Murray 1948- *WhoAmL 92*
**Scorca**, Marc Azzolini 1957- *WhoEnt 92, WhoMW 92*
**Scordelis**, Alexander Costicas 1923- *AmMWSc 92*
**Scordilis**, Stylianos Panagiotis 1948- *AmMWSc 92*
**Scorer**, Philip Segar 1916- *Who 92*
**Scornik**, Juan Carlos *AmMWSc 92*
**Scorsese**, Martin 1942- *BenetAL 91, FacFETw, IntDcF 2-2 [port], IntMPA 92, IntWW 91, Who 92, WhoEnt 92*
**Scorsine**, John Magnus 1957- *WhoWest 92*
**Scorsone**, Ernesto 1952- *WhoAmP 91*
**Scorsone**, Francesco G 1920- *AmMWSc 92*
**Scortia**, Thomas N 1926-1976 *TwCSFW 91*
**Scorza**, Carlo 1897- *BiDExR*
**Scorza**, Sylvio Joseph 1923- *WhoRel 92*
**Scot**, Chesman *TwCSFW 91*
**Scot**, George *BenetAL 91*
**Scotford**, David Matteson 1921- *AmMWSc 92*
**Scotford**, John Edward 1939- *Who 92*
**Scothorne**, Raymond John 1920- *Who 92*
**Scotland**, James 1917-1983 *ConAu 36NR*
**Scotland**, Jay *WrDr 92*
**Scoto**, Renata 1935- *FacFETw*
**Scotson**, John L. 1928-1980 *ConAu 134*
**Scott** *Who 92*
**Scott**, A C 1909- *IntAu&W 91*
**Scott**, A. Timothy 1952- *WhoAmL 92*
**Scott**, Ada Louise 1957- *WhoMW 92*
**Scott**, Alan Fulton, Jr. 1945- *WhoAmL 92*
**Scott**, Alan James 1934- *Who 92*
**Scott**, Alan Ray 1960- *WhoRel 92*
**Scott**, Alastair Ian 1928- *AmMWSc 92, IntWW 91, Who 92*
**Scott**, Albert Duncan 1921- *AmMWSc 92*
**Scott**, Albert J *WhoAmP 91, WhoBlA 92*
**Scott**, Albert Nelson 1916- *WhoBlA 92*
**Scott**, Alex 1923- *WhoAmP 91*
**Scott**, Alexander 1920- *IntAu&W 91, WrDr 92*
**Scott**, Alexander Brian 1933- *IntWW 91*
**Scott**, Alexander Whiteford 1904- *Who 92*
**Scott**, Alfred J. 1913- *WhoBlA 92*
**Scott**, Alfred James 1913- *WhoRel 92*
**Scott**, Alice H. *WhoBlA 92*
**Scott**, Allen 1948- *AmMWSc 92*
**Scott**, Alwyn C 1931- *AmMWSc 92*
**Scott**, Amoret 1930- *WrDr 92*
**Scott**, Amy Annette Holloway 1916- *WhoMW 92*
**Scott**, Andrea Kay 1948- *WhoMW 92*
**Scott**, Andrew 1928- *WhoAmL 92, WhoFI 92*
**Scott**, Andrew Edington 1919- *AmMWSc 92*
**Scott**, Anna Marie Porter Wall 1925- *WhoMW 92*
**Scott**, Anna Wall *WhoAmP 91*
**Scott**, Anthony 1937- *Who 92*
**Scott**, Anthony Douglas 1933- *Who 92*
**Scott**, Arthur Bishop 1938- *WhoBlA 92*
**Scott**, Arthur Finley 1907- *IntAu&W 91, WrDr 92*
**Scott**, Arthur Floyd 1944- *AmMWSc 92*
**Scott**, Aundrea Arthur 1942- *WhoBlA 92*
**Scott**, Basil Y. 1925- *WhoBlA 92*
**Scott**, Becky Beckwith 1947- *WhoBlA 92*

Scott, Benjamin 1929- WhoBlA 92
Scott, Bernard Brandon 1941- WhoRel 92
Scott, Bernice Green 1945- WhoAmP 91
Scott, Beverly Angela 1951- WhoBlA 92
Scott, Bill 1923- IntAu&W 91, WrDr 92
Scott, Bill 1935- TwCPaSc
Scott, Bill 1949- WhoFI 92
Scott, Billy Paul 1943- WhoMW 92
Scott, Blakely Nelson 1948- WhoRel 92
Scott, Bobby Kenneth 1933- WhoAmP 91
Scott, Bobby Randolph AmMWSc 92
Scott, Boyd Franklin 1911- WhoAmP 91
Scott, Bradley Sterling 1948- WhoFI 92
Scott, Brian Edward 1936- WhoIns 92
Scott, Brien 1964- WhoEnt 92
Scott, Brough Who 92
Scott, Bruce Albert 1940- AmMWSc 92
Scott, Bruce L 1932- AmMWSc 92
Scott, Buck 1929- WhoAmP 91
Scott, Byron Antom 1961- WhoBlA 92
Scott, C. Douglas 1952- WhoRel 92
Scott, C. Waldo 1916- WhoBlA 92
Scott, Cal TwCWW 91
Scott, Campbell ConTFT 9
Scott, Campbell 1962- IntMPA 92
Scott, Carl McDonald, III 1954- WhoEnt 92
Scott, Carolynne DrAPF 91
Scott, Carstella H. 1928- WhoBlA 92
Scott, Catherine Margaret Mary Who 92
Scott, Charles Covert 1909- AmMWSc 92
Scott, Charles D 1929- AmMWSc 92
Scott, Charles E. 1940- WhoBlA 92
Scott, Charles E. 1949- WhoBlA 92
Scott, Charles Edward 1929- AmMWSc 92
Scott, Charles Frederick 1942- WhoAmL 92
Scott, Charles Hilary d1991 Who 92N
Scott, Charles James 1929- AmMWSc 92
Scott, Charles K 1945- WhoAmP 91
Scott, Charles Kennard 1945- WhoWest 92
Scott, Charles Peter 1917- Who 92
Scott, Charles S 1932- WhoIns 92
Scott, Charles S., Sr. 1932-1989 FacFETw
Scott, Charles Thomas 1948- BlkOlyM
Scott, Charley 1923- AmMWSc 92
Scott, Charlotte Hanley 1925- WhoBlA 92
Scott, Christopher 1930- IntAu&W 91, WrDr 92
Scott, Clifford Alva 1908- WhoBlA 92
Scott, Clifford Haley 1937- WhoMW 92
Scott, Clifford Ray 1930- WhoEnt 92
Scott, Clifford Ray 1963- WhoWest 92
Scott, Clifton H 1937- WhoAmP 91
Scott, Colin 1941- TwCPaSc
Scott, Colin John Fraser Who 92
Scott, Connie Lou 1943- WhoAmP 91
Scott, Constance Susan 1954- WhoWest 92
Scott, Cornealious Socrates, Sr. 1909- WhoBlA 92
Scott, Cornelius Adolphus 1908- WhoBlA 92
Scott, D Beck 1931- WhoAmP 91
Scott, Dale Monroe 1925- WhoRel 92
Scott, Dale Phillip 1955- WhoRel 92
Scott, Dan Dryden 1928- AmMWSc 92
Scott, Dana S 1932- AmMWSc 92
Scott, Dana Stewart 1932- Who 92
Scott, Darrell Ellis 1965- WhoMW 92
Scott, David Who 92, WhoAmP 91
Scott, David 1916- Who 92
Scott, David 1919- Who 92
Scott, David 1924- Who 92
Scott, David 1945- TwCPaSc
Scott, David Andrew 1948- WhoAmL 92
Scott, David Aubrey 1919- IntAu&W 91, IntWW 91
Scott, David Bytovetzski 1919- AmMWSc 92
Scott, David Evans 1938- AmMWSc 92
Scott, David Frederick 1940- AmMWSc 92
Scott, David Gidley 1924- Who 92
Scott, David Irvin 1947- WhoWest 92
Scott, David Janvier d1991 NewYTBS 91
Scott, David Knight 1940- AmMWSc 92, WhoMW 92
Scott, David L. 1920- WrDr 92
Scott, David Maxwell 1920- AmMWSc 92
Scott, David Robert Main 1921- AmMWSc 92
Scott, David Rodick 1938- WhoAmL 92
Scott, David Vaughan 1942- WhoAmL 92
Scott, David Walter 1947- WrDr 92
Scott, David William 1943- AmMWSc 92
Scott, Deborah Ann 1953- WhoBlA 92
Scott, Debra Kay 1953- WhoAmP 91
Scott, Delbert Lee WhoAmP 91
Scott, Dennis d1991 NewYTBS 91
Scott, Dennis 1952- WhoEnt 92
Scott, Dennis C. 1939- ConPo 91
Scott, Dennis Eugene 1968- WhoBlA 92
Scott, Don 1925- AmMWSc 92
Scott, Donald Who 92
Scott, Donald, Jr 1909- AmMWSc 92
Scott, Donald Albert 1917- AmMWSc 92
Scott, Donald Charles 1920- AmMWSc 92
Scott, Donald Fletcher 1930- IntAu&W 91, WrDr 92
Scott, Donald Howard 1934- AmMWSc 92
Scott, Donald L. 1938- WhoBlA 92
Scott, Donald Michael 1943- WhoWest 92
Scott, Donald Ray 1934- AmMWSc 92
Scott, Donald S 1922- AmMWSc 92
Scott, Donna WhoAmP 91
Scott, Donna Marie 1955- WhoEnt 92
Scott, Donnell 1947- WhoBlA 92
Scott, Douglas d1990 Who 92N
Scott, Douglas Alan 1951- WhoAmL 92
Scott, Douglas Frederick Schumacher 1910- Who 92
Scott, Douglas Gordon 1949- WhoRel 92
Scott, Douglas Keith 1941- Who 92
Scott, Dred 1795?-1858 BenetAL 91
Scott, Duncan Campbell 1862-1947 BenetAL 91, RfGEnL 91
Scott, Duncan MacDonald 1947- WhoEnt 92
Scott, Dwight Baker McNair 1907- AmMWSc 92
Scott, Earle Stanley 1922- AmMWSc 92
Scott, Edward, Jr 1928- WhoAmP 91
Scott, Edward Joseph 1913- AmMWSc 92
Scott, Edward McM Who 92
Scott, Edward Philip 1937- WhoAmP 91
Scott, Edward Robert Dalton 1947- AmMWSc 92
Scott, Edward W 1909- AmMWSc 92
Scott, Edward Walter Who 92
Scott, Edward Walter 1919- DcEcMov, IntWW 91
Scott, Eion George 1931- AmMWSc 92
Scott, Elaine Anderson 1957- WhoFI 92
Scott, Elizabeth Leonard 1917- AmMWSc 92
Scott, Eloise Hale 1932- WhoAmP 91
Scott, Elsie L. WhoBlA 92
Scott, Eric 1945- TwCPaSc
Scott, Eric James Young 1924- AmMWSc 92
Scott, Errico B. 1961- WhoEnt 92
Scott, Esme 1932- Who 92
Scott, Esther Mae 1893-1979 NotBlAW 92
Scott, Eva 1926- WhoAmP 91
Scott, Evelyn 1893-1963 BenetAL 91
Scott, F. Brantley d1991 NewYTBS 91 [port]
Scott, F. R. 1899-1985 BenetAL 91, RfGEnL 91
Scott, Forrest Lindsey 1941- WhoAmL 92
Scott, Francis Reginald 1899-1985 FacFETw
Scott, Frank Alexander, Jr. 1951- WhoFI 92
Scott, Franklin D 1901- IntAu&W 91, WrDr 92
Scott, Franklin Robert 1922- AmMWSc 92
Scott, Fraser Wallace 1946- AmMWSc 92
Scott, Fred William 1915- WhoAmP 91
Scott, Freddie, Jr. 1955- WhoWest 92
Scott, Frederick Arthur 1925- AmMWSc 92
Scott, Fredric Winthrop 1935- AmMWSc 92
Scott, G Firth ScFEYrs
Scott, G. Judson, Jr. 1945- WhoAmL 92
Scott, Garey Baxter 1942- WhoRel 92
Scott, Garland Elmo, Jr 1938- AmMWSc 92
Scott, Gary Lee 1934- WhoAmP 91
Scott, Gary LeRoy 1954- WhoFI 92
Scott, Gary Walter 1943- AmMWSc 92
Scott, Gavin 1950- WrDr 92
Scott, Gene E 1929- AmMWSc 92
Scott, George 1925- IntAu&W 91
Scott, George Barclay d1990 Who 92N
Scott, George C. 1927- IntMPA 92, IntWW 91
Scott, George Campbell 1927- WhoEnt 92
Scott, George Clifford 1926- AmMWSc 92
Scott, George Edmond 1924- WhoWest 92
Scott, George Matthew 1922- WhoAmP 91
Scott, George Prescott 1921- AmMWSc 92
Scott, George Taylor 1914- AmMWSc 92
Scott, George William 1917- AmMWSc 92
Scott, George William 1937- WhoAmP 91
Scott, Gerald William 1931- AmMWSc 92
Scott, Gilbert H. 1946- WhoBlA 92
Scott, Gloria 1938- NotBlAW 92 [port]
Scott, Gloria Dean Randle 1938- WhoBlA 92
Scott, Gordon 1927- IntMPA 92
Scott, Graham Alexander 1927- Who 92
Scott, Grover TwCWW 91
Scott, Hal S. 1943- WhoAmL 92
Scott, Hardiman Who 92
Scott, Harold George 1925- AmMWSc 92
Scott, Harold Russell, Jr. 1935- WhoBlA 92
Scott, Hattie Bell 1945- WhoBlA 92
Scott, Hazel 1920-1981 FacFETw, NotBlAW 92
Scott, Helen S. 1949- WhoAmL 92
Scott, Henry Lawrence 1908- WhoEnt 92
Scott, Henry William, Jr 1916- AmMWSc 92
Scott, Herbert DrAPF 91
Scott, Herbert Andrew 1924- AmMWSc 92
Scott, Hosie L. 1943- WhoBlA 92
Scott, Howard Allen 1926- AmMWSc 92
Scott, Howard Winfield, Jr. 1935- WhoFI 92
Scott, Hubert Donovan 1944- AmMWSc 92
Scott, Hubert R. 1919- WhoBlA 92
Scott, Hugh 1900- WhoAmP 91
Scott, Hugh, III 1949- WhoMW 92
Scott, Hugh B. 1949- WhoBlA 92
Scott, Hugh J. 1933- WhoBlA 92
Scott, Hugh Lawrence, Jr 1944- AmMWSc 92
Scott, Hugh Logan, III 1940- AmMWSc 92
Scott, I. B. 1930- WhoFI 92
Scott, Ian 1940- TwCPaSc
Scott, Ian Dixon 1909- IntWW 91, Who 92
Scott, Ian Richard 1940- Who 92
Scott, Irene Feagin 1912- WhoAmL 92
Scott, J. Brian 1963- WhoMW 92
Scott, J.C. IntMPA 92
Scott, J D AmMWSc 92
Scott, J. Irving Elias 1901-1981 WhoBlA 92N
Scott, J L 1929- AmMWSc 92
Scott, Jack Denton SmATA 14AS [port]
Scott, Jack Hardiman Who 92
Scott, Jacob Reginald 1938- WhoBlA 92
Scott, James 1885-1938 NewAmDM
Scott, James A 1942- WhoAmP 91
Scott, James Alan 1943- AmMWSc 92
Scott, James Alexander 1931- Who 92
Scott, James Alexander 1940- Who 92
Scott, James Archibald 1932- Who 92
Scott, James Brown 1866-1943 AmPeW
Scott, James C 1934- WhoAmP 91
Scott, James C. 1936- WrDr 92
Scott, James Edward 1937- WhoMW 92
Scott, James F., Sr. 1903- WhoBlA 92
Scott, James Floyd 1942- AmMWSc 92
Scott, James Henry 1930- AmMWSc 92
Scott, James Henry 1942- WhoBlA 92
Scott, James Hunter, Jr. 1945- WhoFI 92
Scott, James J 1928- AmMWSc 92
Scott, James Julius 1934- WhoRel 92
Scott, James M 1934- WhoIns 92
Scott, James M 1938- WhoAmP 91
Scott, James Michael 1941- AmMWSc 92
Scott, James Steel 1924- Who 92
Scott, James Walter 1924- Who 92
Scott, Jane IntAu&W 91X, WrDr 92
Scott, Jane Catherine Beecher 1948- WhoMW 92
Scott, Janey WrDr 92
Scott, Jaunita Simons 1936- AmMWSc 92
Scott, Jay 1949- ConAu 133, IntAu&W 91, WhoEnt 92
Scott, Jean Sampson 1925- WhoBlA 92
Scott, Jeffery Warren 1959- WhoRel 92
Scott, Jeffrey Glenn 1946- WhoFI 92
Scott, Jerry Don 1936- WhoFI 92
Scott, Jo Ryman 1929- WhoEnt 92
Scott, John Who 92
Scott, John 1730-1783 RfGEnL 91
Scott, John A. 1948- ConAu 135, ConPo 91, WrDr 92
Scott, John Anthony 1916- WrDr 92
Scott, John B 1944- WhoIns 92
Scott, John Brough 1942- Who 92
Scott, John Campbell 1949- AmMWSc 92
Scott, John Delmoth 1944- AmMWSc 92
Scott, John E WhoAmP 91
Scott, John E, Jr 1927- AmMWSc 92
Scott, John F 1950- WhoAmP 91
Scott, John Francis 1944- AmMWSc 92, WhoWest 92
Scott, John Fraser 1928- IntWW 91, Who 92
Scott, John Frederick WhoAmP 91
Scott, John Gavin 1956- Who 92
Scott, John Hamilton 1936- Who 92
Scott, John Irving E. d1981 ConAu 133
Scott, John James 1924- Who 92
Scott, John Joseph 1950- WhoAmL 92, WhoFI 92, WhoMW 92
Scott, John Marshall William 1930- AmMWSc 92
Scott, John P. 1907- WhoBlA 92
Scott, John Paul 1909- AmMWSc 92
Scott, John Peter 1949- IntAu&W 91
Scott, John Reed 1869- ScFEYrs
Scott, John Roland 1937- WhoAmL 92, WhoFI 92
Scott, John Russell 1951- WhoAmL 92
Scott, John Sherman 1937- WhoBlA 92
Scott, John Stanley 1929- AmMWSc 92
Scott, John T. 1940- WhoBlA 92
Scott, John W 1919- AmMWSc 92
Scott, John Warner 1948- AmMWSc 92
Scott, John Watts, Jr 1938- AmMWSc 92
Scott, John William 1935- WhoFI 92
Scott, John Wyeth 1947- WhoAmP 91
Scott, Jonathan L. 1930- IntWW 91
Scott, Jonathan LaVon 1930- WhoFI 92, WhoWest 92
Scott, Jonathan M. 1952- WhoWest 92
Scott, Joseph Hurlong 1934- AmMWSc 92
Scott, Joseph Lee 1943- AmMWSc 92
Scott, Joseph Mitchell, Jr. 1946- WhoAmL 92
Scott, Joseph Walter 1935- WhoBlA 92
Scott, Joseph Wayne 1959- WhoFI 92
Scott, Juanita Simons 1936- WhoBlA 92
Scott, Judith Sugg 1945- WhoBlA 92
Scott, Julius S., Jr. 1925- WhoBlA 92
Scott, June Rothman 1940- AmMWSc 92
Scott, Justin M. 1957- WhoFI 92
Scott, Karen Christine 1957- AmMWSc 92
Scott, Kathleen 1878-1947 TwCPaSc
Scott, Ken d1991 NewYTBS 91 [port]
Scott, Kenneth 1931- Who 92
Scott, Kenneth C. 1940- WhoMW 92
Scott, Kenneth Daniel WhoAmP 91
Scott, Kenneth Edmund 1903- WhoAmP 91
Scott, Kenneth Elsner 1926- AmMWSc 92
Scott, Kenneth Eugene 1928- WhoAmL 92
Scott, Kenneth Farish 1918- Who 92
Scott, Kenneth Richard 1934- AmMWSc 92, WhoBlA 92
Scott, Kenneth Walter 1925- AmMWSc 92
Scott, Kerrigan Davis 1941- WhoFI 92
Scott, Kevin 1952- TwCPaSc
Scott, Kevin Dale 1966- WhoEnt 92
Scott, Kevin M 1935- AmMWSc 92
Scott, Koni Kim 1942- WhoEnt 92
Scott, L Max 1934- AmMWSc 92
Scott, Larry B. 1961- WhoBlA 92
Scott, Larry Marcus 1945- WhoWest 92
Scott, Laurence Disraeli WhoAmL 92
Scott, Lawrence Tressler 1944- AmMWSc 92
Scott, Lawrence Vernon 1917- AmMWSc 92
Scott, Lawrence William 1924- AmMWSc 92
Scott, Lee Allen, Sr. 1940- WhoFI 92
Scott, Lee Hansen 1926- WhoFI 92
Scott, Leland Latham 1919- AmMWSc 92
Scott, Leon Leroy 1941- WhoBlA 92
Scott, Leonard Lamar 1924- WhoBlA 92
Scott, Leonard Lewy, Jr 1942- AmMWSc 92
Scott, Leonard Stephen 1949- WhoBlA 92
Scott, Levan Ralph 1915- WhoBlA 92
Scott, Lewis Nathanel 1938- WhoBlA 92
Scott, Linus Albert 1923- AmMWSc 92
Scott, Linzy, Jr. 1934- WhoBlA 92
Scott, Lorinda Kay 1964- WhoRel 92
Scott, Lucy Lee 1955- WhoEnt 92
Scott, M. P. Mick 1941- WhoWest 92
Scott, Mack Tommie 1931- AmMWSc 92
Scott, Margaret 1922- Who 92
Scott, Margaret Simon 1934- WhoFI 92
Scott, Mariette Arguimbau WhoHisp 92
Scott, Marilyn Franko WhoMW 92
Scott, Marion B 1912- AmMWSc 92
Scott, Mark Andrew 1949- WhoRel 92
Scott, Mark Edward 1953- WhoAmL 92
Scott, Mark Edward 1955- WhoFI 92
Scott, Martha 1916- IntMPA 92
Scott, Martha Gene 1935- WhoAmP 91
Scott, Martha Richter 1941- AmMWSc 92
Scott, Marvin Bailey 1944- WhoBlA 92
Scott, Marvin Wade 1936- AmMWSc 92
Scott, Marvin Wayne 1952- WhoBlA 92
Scott, Mary Helen 1958- WhoFI 92
Scott, Mary Jean 1931- AmMWSc 92
Scott, Mary Shy WhoBlA 92
Scott, Matthew P 1953- AmMWSc 92
Scott, Maurice FitzGerald 1924- Who 92
Scott, Meckinley 1935- AmMWSc 92
Scott, Melissa Elaine 1960- IntAu&W 91
Scott, Melvina Brooks 1948- WhoBlA 92
Scott, Merilla McCurry 1957- WhoWest 92
Scott, Michael 1923- IntWW 91, Who 92
Scott, Michael 1954- TwCPaSc
Scott, Michael David 1953- WhoAmL 92
Scott, Michael Dean 1957- WhoRel 92
Scott, Michael Dennis 1945- WhoAmL 92, WhoWest 92
Scott, Michael Frederick 1911- Who 92
Scott, Michael John 1932- Who 92
Scott, Michael LeRoy 1949- WhoMW 92
Scott, Michael Timothy 1951- WhoAmL 92
Scott, Michele Catherine 1954- WhoRel 92
Scott, Mildred Hope 1926- WhoMW 92
Scott, Milton Leonard 1915- AmMWSc 92
Scott, Mona Vaughn WhoBlA 92
Scott, Morris Douglas 1945- WhoWest 92
Scott, Morris Lee 1927- WhoAmP 91
Scott, Nancy DrAPF 91
Scott, Natalie Anderson 1906- BenetAL 91
Scott, Nathan A, Jr 1925- IntAu&W 91, WhoBlA 92, WrDr 92
Scott, Nathan Alexander, Jr. 1925- WhoRel 92
Scott, Nathan Tyler 1957- WhoRel 92
Scott, Nellie Chavarria 1956- WhoHisp 92
Scott, Nicholas 1933- Who 92
Scott, Nigel L. 1940- WhoBlA 92
Scott, Norford TwCWW 91
Scott, Norma Joyce 1928- WhoAmP 91
Scott, Norman Jackson, Jr 1934- AmMWSc 92, WhoWest 92
Scott, Norman R 1918- AmMWSc 92

**Scott,** Norman Roy 1936- *AmMWSc 92*
**Scott,** Oliver 1922- *Who 92*
**Scott,** Oliver Lester Schreiner 1919- *Who 92*
**Scott,** Olof Henderson, Jr. 1942- *WhoRel 92*
**Scott,** Osborne E. 1916- *WhoBlA 92*
**Scott,** Otis 1919- *WhoBlA 92*
**Scott,** Otis L. 1941- *WhoBlA 92*
**Scott,** Pamela 1937- *TwCPaSc*
**Scott,** Patricia *WhoAmP 91*
**Scott,** Patrick 1921- *TwCPaSc*
**Scott,** Paul *WhoRel 92*
**Scott,** Paul 1920-1978 *LiExTwC, RfGEnL 91*
**Scott,** Paul Brunson 1937- *AmMWSc 92*
**Scott,** Paul G 1947- *AmMWSc 92*
**Scott,** Paul Henderson 1920- *Who 92*
**Scott,** Paul W. 1958- *WhoFI 92*
**Scott,** Peggy B. 1951- *WhoFI 92*
**Scott,** Percy d1991 *Who 92N*
**Scott,** Peter *Who 92*
**Scott,** Peter 1935- *IntWW 91*
**Scott,** Peter 1946- *WrDr 92*
**Scott,** Peter Bryan 1947- *WhoAmL 92, WhoWest 92*
**Scott,** Peter Carlton 1940- *AmMWSc 92*
**Scott,** Peter Dale 1929- *WhoWest 92*
**Scott,** Peter Denys John 1935- *Who 92*
**Scott,** Peter Douglas 1942- *AmMWSc 92*
**Scott,** Peter Hamilton 1936- *AmMWSc 92*
**Scott,** Peter Hardiman 1920- *Who 92*
**Scott,** Peter John 1948- *AmMWSc 92*
**Scott,** Peter Leslie 1933- *AmMWSc 92*
**Scott,** Peter Markham 1909-1989 *FacFETw*
**Scott,** Peter Michael 1938- *AmMWSc 92*
**Scott,** Philip John 1931- *Who 92*
**Scott,** Portia Alexandria 1946- *WhoBlA 92*
**Scott,** R. J. *WhoMW 92*
**Scott,** R. Lee 1943- *WhoBlA 92*
**Scott,** Rachel Loraine 1954- *WhoBlA 92*
**Scott,** Ralph Asa, Jr 1930- *AmMWSc 92*
**Scott,** Ralph Carmen 1921- *AmMWSc 92*
**Scott,** Ralph Mason 1921- *AmMWSc 92*
**Scott,** Randall Wayne 1945- *WhoAmL 92*
**Scott,** Ray Vernon, Jr. 1950- *WhoFI 92*
**Scott,** Raymond Gerald 1916- *WhoMW 92*
**Scott,** Raymond Peter William 1924- *AmMWSc 92*
**Scott,** Rebecca *WhoEnt 92*
**Scott,** Rebecca Andrews 1939- *WhoMW 92*
**Scott,** Richard *ConAu 135, SmATA 67*
**Scott,** Richard Anthony 1936- *AmMWSc 92*
**Scott,** Richard Baker 1928- *WhoRel 92*
**Scott,** Richard Eley 1945- *WhoAmP 91, WhoBlA 92*
**Scott,** Richard John Dinwoodie 1939- *Who 92*
**Scott,** Richard Lynn 1941- *WhoMW 92*
**Scott,** Richard Philippe 1932- *WhoFI 92*
**Scott,** Richard Rashleigh Folliott 1934- *Who 92*
**Scott,** Richard Royce 1933- *AmMWSc 92*
**Scott,** Richard Thomas 1939- *WhoWest 92*
**Scott,** Richard Walter 1941- *AmMWSc 92*
**Scott,** Ricky Lynn 1958- *WhoRel 92*
**Scott,** Ridley *IntWW 91*
**Scott,** Ridley 1939- *ConTFT 9, CurBio 91 [port], IntDcF 2-2 [port], IntMPA 92, WhoEnt 92*
**Scott,** Robert d1991 *Who 92N*
**Scott,** Robert 1913- *Who 92*
**Scott,** Robert Allen 1953- *AmMWSc 92*
**Scott,** Robert Allyn 1939- *WhoFI 92*
**Scott,** Robert Blackburn 1937- *AmMWSc 92*
**Scott,** Robert Blackburn, Jr *AmMWSc 92*
**Scott,** Robert Bradley 1933- *AmMWSc 92*
**Scott,** Robert Cortez 1947- *WhoAmP 91, WhoBlA 92*
**Scott,** Robert E. 1944- *WhoAmL 92*
**Scott,** Robert Edmond Gabriel 1920- *Who 92*
**Scott,** Robert Edward 1922- *AmMWSc 92*
**Scott,** Robert Edward, Jr. 1945- *WhoAmL 92*
**Scott,** Robert Ellis 1921- *WhoEnt 92*
**Scott,** Robert Eugene 1941- *AmMWSc 92*
**Scott,** Robert Eugene 1954- *WhoWest 92*
**Scott,** Robert F 1868-1912 *FacFETw [port]*
**Scott,** Robert Foster 1925- *AmMWSc 92*
**Scott,** Robert Gene 1951- *WhoAmL 92*
**Scott,** Robert Gray 1960- *WhoFI 92*
**Scott,** Robert Hal 1930- *WhoRel 92*
**Scott,** Robert J 1949- *WhoAmP 91*
**Scott,** Robert Kent 1936- *WhoAmL 92, WhoFI 92*
**Scott,** Robert L. 1935- *WhoBlA 92*
**Scott,** Robert Lane 1922- *AmMWSc 92*
**Scott,** Robert Neal 1941- *AmMWSc 92*
**Scott,** Robert Nelson 1933- *AmMWSc 92*
**Scott,** Robert W 1936- *AmMWSc 92*
**Scott,** Roberta Field 1940- *WhoWest 92*
**Scott,** Robin *Who 92*
**Scott,** Roger Duncan 1943- *WhoEnt 92*
**Scott,** Roland B. 1909- *WhoBlA 92*
**Scott,** Roland Boyd 1909- *AmMWSc 92*
**Scott,** Ronald 1927- *IntWW 91, Who 92*
**Scott,** Ronald Charles 1948- *WhoAmL 92*
**Scott,** Ronald E 1921- *AmMWSc 92*
**Scott,** Ronald F 1929- *AmMWSc 92*
**Scott,** Ronald McLean 1933- *AmMWSc 92*
**Scott,** Roy Albert, III 1934- *AmMWSc 92*
**Scott,** Roy Vernon 1927- *IntAu&W 91, WrDr 92*
**Scott,** Russell Kenneth 1949- *WhoAmL 92*
**Scott,** Ruth 1934- *WhoBlA 92*
**Scott,** Samuel 1946- *WhoBlA 92*
**Scott,** Sarah 1723-1795 *BlkwCEP*
**Scott,** Sheryl Ann 1949- *AmMWSc 92*
**Scott,** Sidney William 1942- *WhoMW 92*
**Scott,** Spencer W 1939- *WhoAmP 91*
**Scott,** Stanley DeForest 1926- *WhoFI 92*
**Scott,** Stanley S 1933- *WhoAmP 91, WhoBlA 92*
**Scott,** Stanley VanAken 1943- *WhoWest 92*
**Scott,** Stephany Sarita 1959- *WhoFI 92*
**Scott,** Stephen Wayne 1948- *WhoAmL 92*
**Scott,** Steven Donald 1941- *AmMWSc 92*
**Scott,** Steven Michael 1952- *WhoFI 92*
**Scott,** Stewart Melvin 1926- *AmMWSc 92*
**Scott,** T. T. *WhoRel 92*
**Scott,** Terence Charles Stuart M. *Who 92*
**Scott,** Theodore R. 1924- *WhoAmL 92, WhoMW 92*
**Scott,** Thomas *WhoAmP 91*
**Scott,** Thomas A 1930- *AmMWSc 92*
**Scott,** Thomas Clevenger 1936- *WhoAmL 92*
**Scott,** Thomas E 1943- *WhoAmP 91*
**Scott,** Thomas Emerson, Jr. 1948- *WhoAmL 92*
**Scott,** Thomas Frederick McNair 1901- *Who 92*
**Scott,** Thomas Jackson 1924- *WhoAmP 91*
**Scott,** Thomas James 1920- *WhoFI 92*
**Scott,** Thomas Jefferson, Jr. 1943- *WhoAmL 92*
**Scott,** Thomas Ryals 1940- *WhoAmP 91*
**Scott,** Thomas Walter 1929- *AmMWSc 92*
**Scott,** Thora *Who 92*
**Scott,** Tim 1937- *TwCPaSc, WorArt 1980*
**Scott,** Timothy 1937- *IntWW 91*
**Scott,** Timothy Dean 1964- *WhoRel 92*
**Scott,** Timothy Van 1942- *WhoBlA 92*
**Scott,** Tom 1918- *ConPo 91, IntAu&W 91, WrDr 92*
**Scott,** Tom E 1933- *AmMWSc 92*
**Scott,** Tom Keck 1931- *AmMWSc 92*
**Scott,** Tony *IntMPA 92, WhoEnt 92*
**Scott,** Tony 1932- *NewAmDM*
**Scott,** Tony 1944- *IntWW 91*
**Scott,** Ulric Carl 1932- *WhoAmP 91*
**Scott,** Van 1921- *WhoAmP 91*
**Scott,** Verne H 1924- *AmMWSc 92*
**Scott,** Vernell Izora 1948- *WhoAmL 92*
**Scott,** Veronica J. 1946- *WhoBlA 92*
**Scott,** Virginia *DrAPF 91*
**Scott,** W. Milo 1917- *WhoMW 92*
**Scott,** W. Richard 1932- *IntWW 91*
**Scott,** W Richard 1939- *AmMWSc 92*
**Scott,** Waldron 1929- *WhoRel 92*
**Scott,** Walter 1771-1832 *CnDBLB 3 [port], DcLB 107 [port], RfGEnL 91*
**Scott,** Walter 1826-1910 *DcLB 112*
**Scott,** Walter 1918- *Who 92*
**Scott,** Walter, Jr. 1931- *WhoFI 92, WhoMW 92*
**Scott,** Walter Alvin 1943- *AmMWSc 92*
**Scott,** Walter D. *LesBEnT 92*
**Scott,** Walter Decker 1915- *WhoEnt 92*
**Scott,** Walter Neil 1935- *AmMWSc 92*
**Scott,** Warwick *WrDr 92*
**Scott,** Werner Ferdinand 1957- *WhoBlA 92*
**Scott,** Wesley E. 1925- *WhoBlA 92*
**Scott,** Wesley Perry 1944- *WhoFI 92*
**Scott,** Whitney *DrAPF 91*
**Scott,** Willard *LesBEnT 92 [port]*
**Scott,** Willard Alvin 1930- *WhoWest 92*
**Scott,** Willard Franklin 1925- *WhoEnt 92*
**Scott,** Willard Philip 1909- *WhoAmL 92*
**Scott,** William 1913-1989 *TwCPaSc*
**Scott,** William Addison, III 1940- *AmMWSc 92*
**Scott,** William Alexander, Jr. 1943- *WhoAmL 92*
**Scott,** William Arthur, III 1949- *WhoWest 92*
**Scott,** William Bell 1811-1890 *RfGEnL 91*
**Scott,** William Beverley 1917- *AmMWSc 92*
**Scott,** William Clifford Munro 1903- *Who 92*
**Scott,** William Coryell 1920- *WhoWest 92*
**Scott,** William D 1931- *AmMWSc 92*
**Scott,** William David 1921- *Who 92*
**Scott,** William Donald 1903- *Who 92*
**Scott,** William Dow 1937- *WhoAmP 91*
**Scott,** William Earl Dodge 1852-1910 *BiInAmS*
**Scott,** William Edd 1944- *WhoBlA 92*
**Scott,** William Edward 1947- *AmMWSc 92*
**Scott,** William Edward 1953- *WhoFI 92, WhoWest 92*
**Scott,** William Edwin 1918- *AmMWSc 92*
**Scott,** William Floyd 1936- *WhoFI 92*
**Scott,** William Fred 1953- *WhoEnt 92*
**Scott,** William G. *Who 92*
**Scott,** William James, Jr 1937- *AmMWSc 92*
**Scott,** William L 1915- *WhoAmP 91*
**Scott,** William Lawrence 1935- *WhoFI 92*
**Scott,** William Paul 1928- *WhoAmL 92, WhoMW 92*
**Scott,** William Raymond 1919- *AmMWSc 92*
**Scott,** William Richard 1944- *WhoMW 92*
**Scott,** William Taussig 1916- *AmMWSc 92*
**Scott,** William Wallace 1913- *AmMWSc 92*
**Scott,** William Wallace 1920- *AmMWSc 92*
**Scott,** William Wootton 1930- *Who 92*
**Scott,** Wilson L 1909-1983 *ConAu 34NR*
**Scott,** Windie Olivia *WhoBlA 92*
**Scott,** Windie Olivia 1952- *WhoAmL 92*
**Scott,** Winfield 1786-1866 *AmPolLe, BenetAL 91*
**Scott,** Winfield Germain 1854-1919 *BiInAmS*
**Scott,** Winfield James 1933- *WhoFI 92, WhoMW 92*
**Scott,** Winfield Townley 1910-1968 *BenetAL 91*
**Scott,** Yolanda Madden 1946- *WhoBlA 92*
**Scott-Barrett,** David 1922- *Who 92*
**Scott-Bowden,** Logan 1920- *Who 92*
**Scott-Elliot,** Aydua Helen 1909- *Who 92*
**Scott Elliot,** James 1902- *Who 92*
**Scott-Ellis** *Who 92*
**Scott-Heron,** Gil 1949- *WhoBlA 92*
**Scott-Hopkins,** James 1921- *Who 92*
**Scott-Jackson,** Lisa Odessa 1960- *WhoBlA 92*
**Scott-James,** Anne Eleanor 1913- *Who 92*
**Scott-Johnson,** Roberta Virginia *WhoBlA 92*
**Scott-Joynt,** Michael Charles *Who 92*
**Scott-Malden,** Charles Peter 1918- *Who 92*
**Scott-Malden,** David 1919- *Who 92*
**Scott-Malden,** Peter *Who 92*
**Scott-Martin,** Stephen A. 1952- *WhoEnt 92*
**Scott-Miller,** Ronald 1904- *Who 92*
**Scott-Moncrieff,** William 1922- *Who 92*
**Scott Nichols,** Dora Hoeflich 1927- *WhoAmP 91*
**Scott Peck,** M 1936- *IntAu&W 91*
**Scott-Smith,** Catherine Mary 1912- *Who 92*
**Scott Tanner,** Amoret 1930- *IntAu&W 91*
**Scott-Thomas,** Kristin *IntMPA 92*
**Scott-Ware,** Barbara Ann 1955- *WhoBlA 92*
**Scott Whyte,** Stuart *Who 92*
**Scott-Williams,** Stephanie 1947- *WhoAmP 91*
**Scott Wright,** Margaret 1923- *Who 92*
**Scotten,** H F *ScFEYrs*
**Scotter,** George Wilby 1933- *AmMWSc 92*
**Scotti,** Antonio 1866-1936 *NewAmDM*
**Scotti,** Christopher Michael 1953- *WhoAmL 92*
**Scotti,** Michael John, Jr. 1938- *WhoFI 92*
**Scotti,** R. A. 1946- *WrDr 92*
**Scotto,** Renata 1934- *NewAmDM*
**Scotto,** Renata 1935- *IntWW 91, WhoEnt 92*
**Scoular,** Robert Frank 1942- *WhoAmL 92*
**Scouller,** Alan 1929- *Who 92*
**Scourby,** Alexander d1985 *LesBEnT 92*
**Scourfield,** Edward Grismond Beaumont D. *Who 92*
**Scouten,** Arthur H 1910- *IntAu&W 91*
**Scouten,** Charles George 1940- *AmMWSc 92*
**Scouten,** William Henry 1942- *AmMWSc 92*
**Scovel,** Al 1939- *WhoAmP 91*
**Scovel,** Myra *DrAPF 91*
**Scovell,** E. J. 1907- *ConPo 91, IntAu&W 91, WrDr 92*
**Scovell,** Josiah Thomas 1841-1915 *BiInAmS*
**Scovell,** Melville Amasa 1855-1912 *BiInAmS*
**Scovell,** William M. 1944- *WhoMW 92*
**Scovell,** William Martin 1944- *AmMWSc 92*
**Scovil,** Larry Emery 1950- *WhoRel 92*
**Scovill,** John Paul 1948- *AmMWSc 92*
**Scovill,** Robert Allen 1960- *WhoEnt 92*
**Scovill,** William Albert 1940- *AmMWSc 92*
**Scoville,** George Richard 1954- *WhoMW 92*
**Scoville,** Herbert, Jr 1915-1985 *FacFETw*
**Scoville,** James Griffin 1940- *IntAu&W 91, WhoMW 92, WrDr 92*
**Scoville,** Laurence McConway, Jr. 1936- *WhoAmL 92*
**Scoville,** Richard Arthur 1935- *AmMWSc 92*
**Scoville,** Vernon Eugene, III 1953- *WhoAmP 91*
**Scow,** Kate Marie 1951- *AmMWSc 92*
**Scow,** Robert Oliver 1920- *AmMWSc 92*
**Scowcroft,** Brent 1925- *IntWW 91, WhoAmP 91*
**Scowcroft,** Jerome Chilwell 1947- *WhoAmL 92*
**Scowcroft,** John Arthur 1954- *WhoFI 92*
**Scowen,** Eric 1910- *Who 92*
**Scozzie,** James Anthony 1943- *AmMWSc 92*
**Scraba,** Douglas G 1940- *AmMWSc 92*
**Scranage,** Clarence, Jr. 1955- *WhoBlA 92*
**Scranton,** Bruce Edward 1946- *AmMWSc 92*
**Scranton,** Mary Isabelle 1950- *AmMWSc 92*
**Scranton,** William Warren 1917- *IntWW 91, WhoAmP 91*
**Scrase-Dickins,** Mark Frederick Hakon 1936- *Who 92*
**Screech,** M. A. 1926- *WrDr 92*
**Screech,** Michael Andrew 1926- *IntWW 91, Who 92*
**Screen,** Pat 1943- *WhoAmP 91*
**Screpetis,** Dennis 1930- *WhoFI 92*
**Scriabin,** Alexander 1872-1915 *NewAmDM*
**Scriabin,** Alexander Nikolayevich 1872-1915 *FacFETw*
**Scriabine,** Alexander 1926- *AmMWSc 92*
**Scribe,** Eugene 1791-1861 *GuFrLit 1*
**Scribner,** Arthur Gerald, Jr. 1955- *WhoBlA 92*
**Scribner,** Belding Hibbard 1921- *AmMWSc 92*
**Scribner,** Charles, Jr. 1921- *IntWW 91*
**Scribner,** David d1991 *NewYTBS 91*
**Scribner,** Dorothy Nesbitt 1938- *WhoWest 92*
**Scribner,** Fred Clark, Jr 1908- *WhoAmP 91, WhoFI 92*
**Scribner,** John David 1941- *AmMWSc 92*
**Scribner,** Sylvia 1923- *ConAu 133*
**Scribner,** William Joseph 1939- *WhoEnt 92*
**Scriggins,** Larry Palmer 1936- *WhoAmL 92*
**Scrignar,** Chester Bruno 1934- *AmMWSc 92*
**Scrimenti,** Thomas J 1960- *WhoAmP 91*
**Scrimgeour,** G.J. *DrAPF 91*
**Scrimgeour,** James R. *DrAPF 91*
**Scrimgeour,** Kenneth Gray 1934- *AmMWSc 92*
**Scrimshaw,** Frank Herbert 1917- *Who 92*
**Scrimshaw,** Nevin Stewart 1918- *AmMWSc 92, IntWW 91*
**Scripp,** Lawrence *WhoEnt 92*
**Scripps,** Charles Edward 1920- *IntWW 91, WhoFI 92, WhoMW 92*
**Script,** Dee *DrAPF 91*
**Scripter,** Frank C. 1918- *WhoFI 92, WhoMW 92*
**Scritsmier,** Jerome Lorenzo 1925- *WhoFI 92, WhoWest 92*
**Scriven,** L E 1931- *AmMWSc 92*
**Scriven,** Wilton Maxwell 1924- *Who 92*
**Scrivener,** Anthony Frank Bertram 1935- *Who 92*
**Scrivener,** Christiane 1925- *IntWW 91, Who 92*
**Scrivener,** Ronald Stratford 1919- *Who 92*
**Scrivenor,** Thomas 1908- *Who 92*
**Scriver,** Charles Robert 1930- *AmMWSc 92*
**Scrivner,** Barbara E. 1931- *WhoEnt 92*
**Scrivner,** Gary Neil 1951- *WhoFI 92*
**Scrivner,** Thomas William 1948- *WhoAmL 92*
**Scroggie,** Alan Ure Reith 1912- *Who 92*
**Scroggie,** Lucy E 1935- *AmMWSc 92*
**Scroggins,** Daryl *DrAPF 91*
**Scroggs,** James Edward 1926- *AmMWSc 92*
**Scruby,** H. David, Jr. 1954- *WhoFI 92*
**Scruby,** Ronald Victor 1919- *Who 92*
**Scruggs,** Allie W. 1927- *WhoBlA 92*
**Scruggs,** Barbara Lee 1932- *WhoAmP 91*
**Scruggs,** Booker T., II 1942- *WhoBlA 92*
**Scruggs,** Cleorah J. 1948- *WhoBlA 92*
**Scruggs,** Donald O 1939- *WhoIns 92*
**Scruggs,** Earl *NewAmDM*
**Scruggs,** Earl Eugene 1924- *WhoEnt 92*
**Scruggs,** Edwin Noel, Jr. 1953- *WhoEnt 92*
**Scruggs,** Jack G 1930- *AmMWSc 92*
**Scruggs,** Larry Glen 1943- *WhoWest 92*
**Scruggs,** Otey Matthew 1929- *WhoBlA 92*
**Scruggs,** Paul C 1937- *WhoAmP 91*
**Scruggs,** Roger Patrick 1945- *WhoEnt 92*
**Scruggs,** Sylvia Ann 1951- *WhoBlA 92*
**Scrutchions,** Benjamin 1926- *WhoBlA 92*
**Scruton,** Roger 1944- *IntWW 91, WrDr 92*
**Scruton,** Roger V 1944- *IntAu&W 91*
**Scruton,** Roger Vernon 1944- *Who 92*
**Scrutton,** Hugh d1991 *Who 92N*

**Scrymgeour** *Who 92*
**Scrymgeour**, Lord 1982- *Who 92*
**Scrymsour**, Ella M 1888- *ScFEYrs*
**Scudamore**, Harold Hunter 1915- *AmMWSc 92*
**Scudamore**, Peter 1958- *IntWW 91*
**Scudamore**, Peter Michael 1958- *Who 92*
**Scudday**, James Franklin 1929- *AmMWSc 92*
**Scudder**, Antoinette 1898-1958 *BenetAL 91*
**Scudder**, Geoffrey George Edgar 1934- *AmMWSc 92*
**Scudder**, Harvey Israel 1919- *AmMWSc 92*
**Scudder**, Henry J, III 1935- *AmMWSc 92*
**Scudder**, Horace E. 1838-1902 *BenetAL 91*
**Scudder**, Jack David 1947- *AmMWSc 92*
**Scudder**, Jack Howard 1919- *WhoWest 92*
**Scudder**, Jeffrey Eric 1962- *AmMWSc 92*
**Scudder**, Robert 1926- *WhoRel 92*
**Scudder**, Samuel Hubbard 1837-1911 *BiInAmS*
**Scudder**, Theodore Townsend, III 1939- *WhoMW 92*
**Scudder**, Vida Dutton 1861-1954 *HanAmWH*
**Scudder**, Walter Tredwell 1920- *AmMWSc 92*
**Scudery**, Madeleine de 1607-1701 *FrenWW*
**Scull**, David Lee 1943- *WhoAmP 91*
**Scull**, Marie-Louise Walter 1943- *WhoEnt 92*
**Scullard**, Geoffrey Layton 1922- *Who 92*
**Sculley**, David W. 1946- *WhoFI 92*
**Sculley**, John 1939- *IntWW 91*, *WhoFI 92*, *WhoWest 92*
**Scullin**, Frederick James, Jr. 1939- *WhoAmL 92*
**Scully**, Charles Francis 1950- *WhoFI 92*
**Scully**, Charles Gilbert 1925- *WhoEnt 92*
**Scully**, Crispian Michael 1945- *Who 92*
**Scully**, Dennis Allen, Jr. 1967- *WhoFI 92*
**Scully**, Erik Paul 1949- *AmMWSc 92*
**Scully**, Erik Vincent 1957- *WhoAmL 92*
**Scully**, Frank E, Jr 1947- *AmMWSc 92*
**Scully**, Gerald William 1941- *WhoFI 92*
**Scully**, James *DrAPF 91*
**Scully**, James 1937- *ConPo 91*, *IntAu&W 91*, *WrDr 92*
**Scully**, Joe 1926- *IntMPA 92*
**Scully**, John Carroll 1932- *WhoFI 92*
**Scully**, Marlan Orvil 1939- *AmMWSc 92*
**Scully**, Robert Edward 1921- *AmMWSc 92*
**Scully**, Roger Tehan 1948- *WhoAmL 92*, *WhoFI 92*
**Scully**, Samuel Edward 1942- *WhoWest 92*
**Scully**, Sean Paul 1945- *IntWW 91*
**Scully**, Susannah Keith 1921- *WhoAmP 91*
**Scully**, Timothy Richard 1954- *WhoMW 92*, *WhoRel 92*
**Scully**, Vin *LesBEnT 92*
**Scully**, Vincent 1920- *WrDr 92*
**Scully**, William James, Jr 1939- *WhoAmP 91*
**Sculthorpe**, Peter 1929- *ConCom 92*
**Sculthorpe**, Peter Joshua 1929- *IntWW 91*
**Scupham**, John Peter 1933- *IntAu&W 91*
**Scupham**, Peter 1933- *ConPo 91*, *WrDr 92*
**Scurfield**, Margaret 1954- *WhoWest 92*
**Scuro**, Joseph E., Jr. 1948- *WhoAmL 92*
**Scurr**, Cyril Frederick 1920- *Who 92*
**Scurry**, Fred L. 1942- *WhoBlA 92*
**Scurry**, Murphy Townsend 1933- *AmMWSc 92*
**Scuse**, Dennis George 1921- *Who 92*
**Scuseria**, Gustavo Enrique 1956- *AmMWSc 92*
**Scutt**, Robin Hugh 1920- *Who 92*
**Sczudlo**, Paul Allan 1955- *WhoAmL 92*
**Sczudlo**, Raymond Stanley 1948- *WhoAmL 92*
**Seabaugh**, Pyrtle W 1935- *AmMWSc 92*
**Seaberg**, Arthur W 1926- *WhoAmP 91*
**Seabiscuit** 1933-1947 *FacFETw*
**Seablom**, Sara Irene 1947- *WhoRel 92*
**Seabloom**, Robert W 1932- *AmMWSc 92*
**Seabolt**, James Davidson 1956- *WhoFI 92*
**Seaborg**, Glenn 1912- *IntAu&W 91*, *WrDr 92*
**Seaborg**, Glenn T 1912- *FacFETw*, *IntWW 91*
**Seaborg**, Glenn Theodore 1912- *AmMWSc 92*, *Who 92*, *WhoNob 90*, *WhoWest 92*
**Seaborn**, Adam *ScFEYrs*
**Seaborn**, James Byrd 1932- *AmMWSc 92*
**Seaborn**, Joseph William, Jr. 1954- *WhoRel 92*
**Seaborn**, Robert Lowder 1911- *Who 92*
**Seabright**, Clarence Arthur 1913- *WhoMW 92*
**Seabright**, John *TwCSFW 91*
**Seabright**, Russell Frederick 1934- *WhoRel 92*
**Seabrook**, Bradley M. 1928- *WhoRel 92*
**Seabrook**, Bradley Maurice 1928- *WhoBlA 92*
**Seabrook**, Geoffrey Leonard 1909- *Who 92*
**Seabrook**, Graeme 1939- *Who 92*
**Seabrook**, Jeremy 1939- *IntAu&W 91*, *WrDr 92*
**Seabrook**, John Guilds, Jr. 1946- *WhoRel 92*
**Seabrook**, Lawrence 1951- *WhoAmP 91*
**Seabrook**, Lemuel, III 1952- *WhoBlA 92*
**Seabrook**, Robert Childs 1919- *WhoIns 92*
**Seabrook**, Robert John 1941- *Who 92*
**Seabrook**, William 1886-1945 *BenetAL 91*
**Seabrook**, William Davidson 1935- *AmMWSc 92*
**Seabrooke**, Elliott 1886-1950 *TwCPaSc*
**Seabrooke**, George Alfred 1923- *Who 92*
**Seabrooke**, Joseph William, Jr. 1947- *WhoFI 92*
**Seabrooks-Edwards**, Marilyn S. 1955- *WhoBlA 92*
**Seaburg**, Curtis Irving, II 1965- *WhoRel 92*
**Seabury**, George John 1844-1909 *BiInAmS*
**Seabury**, Paul 1923- *IntAu&W 91*, *WrDr 92*
**Seabury**, Roberta 1942- *WhoEnt 92*
**Seabury**, Samuel 1729-1796 *BenetAL 91*, *BlkwEAR*
**Seaby**, Wilfred Arthur 1910- *Who 92*
**Seacrist**, Rudy 1925- *WhoAmP 91*
**Seader**, J D 1927- *AmMWSc 92*
**Seader**, Paul Alan 1947- *WhoAmL 92*
**Seadler**, Einar Austin 1957- *WhoFI 92*
**Seadler**, Stephen Edward 1926- *WhoFI 92*
**Seafield**, Earl of 1939- *Who 92*
**Seaforth**, A Nelson *ScFEYrs A*
**Seaga**, Edward Philip George 1930- *IntWW 91*, *Who 92*
**Seagal**, Steven 1951- *IntMPA 92*
**Seagears**, Margaret Jacqueline 1927- *WhoBlA 92*
**Seager** *Who 92*
**Seager**, Allen 1906-1968 *BenetAL 91*
**Seager**, Donald Alfred 1947- *WhoMW 92*
**Seager**, Harry 1931- *TwCPaSc*
**Seager**, Ralph W. *DrAPF 91*
**Seager**, Ralph William 1911- *IntAu&W 91*, *WrDr 92*
**Seager**, Ronald Frank 1918- *Who 92*
**Seager**, Spencer Lawrence 1935- *AmMWSc 92*
**Seagle**, Edgar Franklin 1924- *AmMWSc 92*
**Seagle**, Stan R *AmMWSc 92*
**Seago**, Edward 1910-1974 *TwCPaSc*
**Seagondollar**, Lewis Worth 1920- *AmMWSc 92*
**Seagram**, Norman Meredith 1934- *WhoFI 92*
**Seagrave**, JeanClare 1954- *WhoWest 92*
**Seagrave**, John Dorrington 1926- *AmMWSc 92*
**Seagrave**, Richard C 1935- *AmMWSc 92*
**Seagrave**, Sterling 1937- *ConAu 135*
**Seagraves**, Richard Ward, Jr. 1956- *WhoMW 92*
**Seagroatt**, Conrad *Who 92*
**Seagrove**, Jenny *IntMPA 92*
**Seagull**, Elizabeth Ann 1947- *WhoMW 92*
**Seal**, Barry Herbert 1937- *Who 92*
**Seal**, Basil *IntAu&W 91X*
**Seal**, Gregory Morris 1948- *WhoMW 92*
**Seal**, John Charles 1950- *WhoAmP 91*
**Seal**, John S., Jr. 1944- *WhoFI 92*
**Seal**, Michael 1930- *WhoFI 92*
**Seal**, Richard Godfrey 1935- *Who 92*
**Seal**, Thomas David 1957- *WhoAmL 92*
**Sealander**, John Arthur, Jr 1917- *AmMWSc 92*
**Seale**, Bob 1941- *WhoAmP 91*
**Seale**, Bobby 1936- *WhoBlA 92*
**Seale**, Bobby 1937- *FacFETw*
**Seale**, Dianne B 1945- *AmMWSc 92*
**Seale**, Douglas 1913- *Who 92*
**Seale**, Jan Epton *DrAPF 91*
**Seale**, John Clement 1942- *WhoEnt 92*
**Seale**, John Henry 1921- *Who 92*
**Seale**, Marvin Ernest 1922- *AmMWSc 92*
**Seale**, Petie Zenaide Alma Trigg *WhoEnt 92*
**Seale**, Raymond Ulric 1934- *AmMWSc 92*
**Seale**, Robert Arthur, Jr. 1942- *WhoAmL 92*
**Seale**, Robert L 1928- *AmMWSc 92*
**Seale**, Robert L. 1941- *WhoWest 92*
**Seale**, Robert Lewis 1928- *WhoWest 92*
**Seale**, Robert McMillan 1938- *WhoWest 92*
**Seale**, Robert Mills 1942- *WhoAmP 91*
**Seale**, Samuel Ricardo 1962- *WhoBlA 92*
**Seale**, William 1939- *WrDr 92*
**Seales**, Charles Augustus 1952- *BlkOlyM*
**Seales**, Peter Clinton *Who 92*
**Sealey**, Charles Sumner 1844- *ScFEYrs*
**Sealey**, Leonard 1923- *WrDr 92*
**Sealey**, Leonard George William 1923- *IntAu&W 91*
**Sealey**, Peter S. 1940- *IntMPA 92*
**Seall**, Stephen Albert 1940- *WhoAmL 92*
**Sealls**, Alan Ray *WhoBlA 92*
**Seals**, Connie C. 1931- *WhoBlA 92*
**Seals**, George E. 1942- *WhoBlA 92*
**Seals**, Gerald 1953- *WhoBlA 92*
**Seals**, Jonathan Roger *AmMWSc 92*
**Seals**, Maxine *WhoBlA 92*
**Seals**, R. Grant 1932- *WhoBlA 92*
**Seals**, Rupert Grant 1932- *AmMWSc 92*
**Sealsfield**, Charles 1793-1864 *BenetAL 91*
**Sealts**, Merton M, Jr 1915- *IntAu&W 91*, *WrDr 92*
**Sealy**, Albert H 1917- *WhoAmP 91*
**Sealy**, Joan R. 1942- *WhoBlA 92*
**Sealy**, Tom 1909- *WhoAmL 92*
**Sealy**, Vernol St. Clair *WhoRel 92*
**Seaman**, Augusta Huiell 1879-1950 *BenetAL 91*
**Seaman**, Charles Wilson 1946- *WhoAmL 92*
**Seaman**, Christopher 1942- *IntWW 91*, *Who 92*
**Seaman**, Dick *Who 92*
**Seaman**, Edna 1932- *AmMWSc 92*
**Seaman**, Elizabeth Cochrane 1867-1922 *BenetAL 91*
**Seaman**, Gerald Roberts 1934- *WrDr 92*
**Seaman**, Gilbert Frederick 1912- *Who 92*
**Seaman**, Gregory G 1938- *AmMWSc 92*
**Seaman**, Janet Arlene 1946- *WhoAmP 91*
**Seaman**, John Gates 1919- *WhoAmL 92*
**Seaman**, John Thorsen, Jr. 1926- *WhoFI 92*
**Seaman**, Keith 1920- *Who 92*
**Seaman**, Keith Douglas 1920- *IntWW 91*
**Seaman**, Larry Allen 1948- *WhoEnt 92*
**Seaman**, Lynn 1933- *AmMWSc 92*
**Seaman**, Millard Thomas 1957- *WhoMW 92*
**Seaman**, Peggy Jean 1949- *WhoAmL 92*
**Seaman**, Reginald Jaspar 1923- *Who 92*
**Seaman**, Richard Norman 1949- *WhoAmL 92*
**Seaman**, Ronald L 1947- *AmMWSc 92*
**Seaman**, Sylvia Sybil 1900- *IntAu&W 91*
**Seaman**, Sylvia Sybil 1910- *WrDr 92*
**Seaman**, William A. *WhoRel 92*
**Seaman**, William B 1917- *AmMWSc 92*
**Seaman**, William E 1942- *AmMWSc 92*
**Seaman**, William Henry 1837-1910 *BiInAmS*
**Seaman**, William Lloyd 1934- *AmMWSc 92*
**Seamans**, David A 1927- *AmMWSc 92*
**Seamans**, R C, Jr 1918- *AmMWSc 92*
**Seamans**, Robert Channing, Jr. 1918- *IntWW 91*, *WhoAmP 91*
**Seamans**, William 1925- *WhoEnt 92*
**Seamark** *ScFEYrs*
**Seammen**, Diana Jill 1948- *Who 92*
**Seamon**, David 1948- *WhoMW 92*
**Seamon**, Hollis Rowan *DrAPF 91*
**Seamon**, Kenneth Bruce *AmMWSc 92*
**Seamon**, Robert Edward 1939- *AmMWSc 92*
**Seanor**, Donald A 1936- *AmMWSc 92*
**Seapy**, Dave Glenn 1956- *AmMWSc 92*
**Seaquist**, Don Timothy 1948- *WhoFI 92*
**Seaquist**, Ernest Raymond 1938- *AmMWSc 92*
**Sear**, Frank 1944- *IntAu&W 91*
**Sear**, Michael 1956- *WhoFI 92*
**Sear**, Morey Leonard 1929- *WhoAmL 92*
**Sear**, Robert J 1936- *WhoIns 92*
**Sear**, Walter Edmond 1930- *WhoEnt 92*
**Searby**, Daniel MacLeod 1934- *WhoFI 92*
**Searby**, Philip James 1924- *Who 92*
**Searby**, Richard Henry 1931- *Who 92*
**Searcy**, A W 1925- *AmMWSc 92*
**Searcy**, Charles Jackson 1935- *AmMWSc 92*
**Searcy**, Dennis Grant 1942- *AmMWSc 92*
**Searcy**, James Wendell 1940- *WhoAmP 91*
**Searcy**, Mary Glenn 1925- *WhoAmP 91*
**Searcy**, Michael John 1954- *WhoFI 92*
**Searcy**, Sue Billik 1956- *WhoMW 92*
**Searcy**, Thomas George 1948- *WhoMW 92*
**Searcy**, William Nelson 1942- *WhoAmL 92*
**Seare**, Nicholas *IntAu&W 91X*, *WrDr 92*
**Searight**, Patricia Adelaide *WhoEnt 92*, *WhoWest 92*
**Searight**, Thomas Kay 1929- *AmMWSc 92*
**Searing**, James Edward 1952- *WhoFI 92*
**Searle**, Arthur 1837-1920 *BiInAmS*
**Searle**, Campbell L 1926- *AmMWSc 92*
**Searle**, Elizabeth *DrAPF 91*
**Searle**, George Mary 1839-1918 *BiInAmS*
**Searle**, Gordon Wentworth 1920- *AmMWSc 92*
**Searle**, Graham William 1937- *WrDr 92*
**Searle**, Helen Woodward 1946- *WhoRel 92*
**Searle**, Humphrey 1915-1982 *NewAmDM*
**Searle**, John 1932- *IntWW 91*
**Searle**, John R. 1932- *WrDr 92*
**Searle**, John Randolph 1947- *AmMWSc 92*
**Searle**, Malcolm Walter St Leger 1900- *Who 92*
**Searle**, Norma Zizmer 1925- *AmMWSc 92*
**Searle**, Peter 1941- *Who 92*
**Searle**, Rodney N 1920- *WhoAmP 91*
**Searle**, Roger 1936- *AmMWSc 92*
**Searle**, Ronald 1920- *FacFETw*, *IntAu&W 91*, *IntWW 91*, *TwCPaSc*, *WrDr 92*
**Searle**, Ronald William Fordham 1920- *Who 92*
**Searle**, Shayle Robert 1928- *AmMWSc 92*
**Searle**, Willard F, Jr 1924- *AmMWSc 92*
**Searles**, Arthur Langley 1920- *AmMWSc 92*
**Searles**, Baird 1934- *WrDr 92*
**Searles**, Charles R. 1937- *WhoBlA 92*
**Searles**, Jerry Lee *WhoEnt 92*, *WhoFI 92*, *WhoMW 92*
**Searles**, Lynn Marie 1949- *WhoMW 92*
**Searles**, Richard Brownlee 1936- *AmMWSc 92*
**Searles**, Scott, Jr 1920- *AmMWSc 92*, *WhoMW 92*
**Searles**, Stanley N, Sr 1919- *WhoAmP 91*
**Searls**, Craig Allen 1954- *AmMWSc 92*
**Searls**, Eileen Haughey 1925- *WhoAmL 92*
**Searls**, Hank 1922- *TwCSFW 91*, *WrDr 92*
**Searls**, Hank H 1922- *IntAu&W 91*
**Searls**, James Collier 1926- *AmMWSc 92*
**Searls**, Robert L 1931- *AmMWSc 92*
**Searns**, Robert Michael 1946- *WhoWest 92*
**Sears**, Alan Edward 1951- *WhoWest 92*
**Sears**, Arthur Gerard 1957- *WhoEnt 92*
**Sears**, Bertram E. 1930- *WhoBlA 92*
**Sears**, Charles Edward 1911- *AmMWSc 92*
**Sears**, Curtis Thornton, Jr 1938- *AmMWSc 92*
**Sears**, David Alan 1931- *AmMWSc 92*
**Sears**, David O. 1935- *WrDr 92*
**Sears**, David O'Keefe 1935- *IntAu&W 91*
**Sears**, Derek William George 1948- *AmMWSc 92*
**Sears**, Don Walter 1921- *WhoAmL 92*
**Sears**, Donald A. *DrAPF 91*
**Sears**, Donald Richard 1928- *AmMWSc 92*
**Sears**, Duane William 1946- *AmMWSc 92*
**Sears**, Edmund Hamilton 1937- *WhoFI 92*
**Sears**, Ernest Robert 1910- *AmMWSc 92*, *IntWW 91*
**Sears**, George Ames 1926- *WhoAmL 92*
**Sears**, Harold Frederick 1947- *AmMWSc 92*
**Sears**, Isaac 1730-1786 *BlkwEAR*
**Sears**, J Kern 1920- *AmMWSc 92*
**Sears**, Jack Wood 1918- *AmMWSc 92*
**Sears**, John 1944- *WhoAmP 91*
**Sears**, John Patrick 1940- *WhoAmP 91*
**Sears**, John T 1938- *AmMWSc 92*
**Sears**, John Winthrop 1930- *WhoAmL 92*, *WhoAmP 91*
**Sears**, Karl David 1941- *AmMWSc 92*
**Sears**, Leo A 1927- *AmMWSc 92*
**Sears**, Lowell Edward 1951- *WhoWest 92*
**Sears**, Markham Karli 1946- *AmMWSc 92*
**Sears**, Marvin Lloyd 1928- *AmMWSc 92*
**Sears**, Michael M. 1947- *WhoMW 92*
**Sears**, Mildred Bradley 1933- *AmMWSc 92*
**Sears**, Pauline Snedden 1908- *WomPsyc*
**Sears**, Peter *DrAPF 91*
**Sears**, Raymond Arthur William 1933- *Who 92*
**Sears**, Raymond Eric John 1934- *AmMWSc 92*
**Sears**, Raymond Warrick, Jr 1935- *AmMWSc 92*
**Sears**, Richard Langley 1931- *AmMWSc 92*
**Sears**, Richard W, Jr 1942- *WhoIns 92*
**Sears**, Robert Eugene 1921- *WhoWest 92*
**Sears**, Robert F, Jr 1941- *AmMWSc 92*
**Sears**, Ross A. 1931- *WhoAmL 92*
**Sears**, Steven Lee 1957- *WhoEnt 92*, *WhoWest 92*
**Sears**, Timothy Stephen 1945- *AmMWSc 92*
**Sears**, Varley Fullerton 1937- *AmMWSc 92*
**Sears**, William Bernard 1911- *WhoRel 92*
**Sears**, William R 1913- *AmMWSc 92*
**Sears**, William R 1928- *WhoAmP 91*
**Sears-Collins**, Leah Jeanette 1955- *WhoBlA 92*
**Searson**, William Edward, III 1942- *WhoAmL 92*
**Seary**, Lawrence Anthony 1951- *WhoEnt 92*
**Sease**, John William 1920- *AmMWSc 92*
**Sease**, Robert Dwight, Jr. 1949- *WhoMW 92*
**Seastone**, Brian Arthur 1957- *WhoWest 92*
**Seastrand**, Andrea *WhoAmP 91*
**Seastrand**, James Kent 1929- *WhoAmP 91*
**Seaton**, Colin Robert 1928- *Who 92*

**Seaton**, Edward Lee 1943- *WhoMW 92*
**Seaton**, Esta *DrAPF 91*
**Seaton**, George Leland 1901- *WhoMW 92*
**Seaton**, Henry Eliason 1869-1893 *BiInAmS*
**Seaton**, Jacob Alif 1931- *AmMWSc 92*
**Seaton**, Jean Robarts 1931- *WhoMW 92*
**Seaton**, Maureen *DrAPF 91*
**Seaton**, Michael David 1950- *WhoWest 92*
**Seaton**, Michael John 1923- *IntWW 91, Who 92*
**Seaton**, Peter *DrAPF 91*
**Seaton**, Shirley Smith *WhoBlA 92*
**Seaton**, Vaughn Allen 1928- *AmMWSc 92*
**Seaton**, W. B. 1925- *WhoFI 92, WhoWest 92*
**Seaton**, William Hafford 1924- *AmMWSc 92*
**Seator**, Lynette *DrAPF 91*
**Seats**, Dolores 1928- *IntAu&W 91*
**Seats**, Peggy Chisolm 1951- *WhoFI 92*
**Seattle Slew** 1974- *FacFETw*
**Seatz**, Lloyd Frank 1919- *AmMWSc 92*
**Seaver**, Bryan Rondeau 1956- *WhoWest 92*
**Seaver**, Cynthia Lou 1955- *WhoMW 92*
**Seaver**, James Everett 1918- *WhoMW 92*
**Seaver**, Jay Webber 1855-1915 *BiInAmS*
**Seaver**, Ronald Edward 1937- *WhoMW 92*
**Seaver**, Sally S 1946- *AmMWSc 92*
**Seavers**, Clarence W. 1919- *WhoBlA 92*
**Seavey**, Harrison Stedman, Jr 1952- *WhoAmP 91*
**Seavey**, Marden Homer, Jr 1929- *AmMWSc 92*
**Seavy**, Mary Ethel Ingle 1910- *WhoMW 92*
**Seawall**, Karen Ann 1957- *WhoAmL 92*
**Seaward**, Colin Hugh 1926- *Who 92*
**Seawell**, Buie 1937- *WhoAmP 91*
**Seawell**, Donald Ray 1912- *WhoWest 92*
**Seawell**, William Thomas 1918- *IntWW 91*
**Seawright**, Jack Arlyn 1941- *AmMWSc 92*
**Seay**, Frank H. 1938- *WhoAmL 92*
**Seay**, Frederick Newsome 1963- *WhoRel 92*
**Seay**, Glenn Emmett 1926- *AmMWSc 92*
**Seay**, James *DrAPF 91*
**Seay**, James L. 1939- *WrDr 92*
**Seay**, Joseph Carlton, III 1949- *WhoRel 92*
**Seay**, Lorraine King 1926- *WhoBlA 92*
**Seay**, Norman R. 1932- *WhoBlA 92*
**Seay**, Patrick H 1920- *AmMWSc 92*
**Seay**, Suzanne 1942- *WhoFI 92*
**Seay**, Thomas Nash 1932- *AmMWSc 92*
**Seay**, Thomas Patrick 1941- *WhoFI 92*
**Sebag-Montefiore**, Harold Henry 1924- *Who 92*
**Sebald**, Anthony Vincent *AmMWSc 92*
**Sebald**, Charles William, Jr. 1947- *WhoFI 92*
**Seban**, Ralph A 1917- *AmMWSc 92*
**Seban**, Robert R. 1948- *WhoWest 92*
**Sebastian** d303? *EncEarC*
**Sebastian**, Anthony 1938- *AmMWSc 92*
**Sebastian**, Franklin W 1920- *AmMWSc 92*
**Sebastian**, James Albert 1945- *WhoMW 92*
**Sebastian**, John Edward 1956- *WhoAmP 91*
**Sebastian**, John Francis 1939- *AmMWSc 92*
**Sebastian**, Lee *ConAu 36NR, WrDr 92*
**Sebastian**, Leslie Paul 1923- *AmMWSc 92*
**Sebastian**, Margaret *WrDr 92*
**Sebastian**, Michael James 1930- *WhoFI 92*
**Sebastian**, Peter *WhoAmP 91*
**Sebastian**, Richard Lee 1942- *AmMWSc 92*
**Sebastian**, Shirley Jean 1941- *WhoEnt 92*
**Sebastian**, Stuart d1991 *NewYTBS 91*
**Sebastian**, Tim 1952- *WrDr 92*
**Sebastian**, Timothy 1952- *Who 92*
**Sebastiani**, Donald August *WhoWest 92*
**Sebba**, Felix 1912- *AmMWSc 92*
**Sebby**, Jan Morris 1939- *WhoAmL 92*
**Sebby**, Steven Dale 1957- *WhoFI 92, WhoMW 92*
**Sebek**, Joseph John 1950- *WhoMW 92*
**Sebek**, Oldrich Karel 1919- *AmMWSc 92*
**Sebela**, Vicki Dawn 1964- *WhoFI 92, WhoMW 92*
**Sebelius**, Kathleen Gilligan 1948- *WhoAmP 91*
**Sebell**, Tellervo Maria 1915- *WhoEnt 92, WhoMW 92*
**Sebens**, Raymond Willard 1925- *WhoAmP 91*
**Sebeok**, Thomas A. 1920- *WrDr 92*
**Seberg**, Jean 1939-1979 *FacFETw*
**Sebert**, John Arthur, Jr. 1942- *WhoAmL 92*
**Sebesan**, Dennis John 1947- *WhoRel 92*
**Sebesky**, Gerald John 1941- *WhoEnt 92*
**Sebesta**, Charles Frederick 1914- *AmMWSc 92*
**Sebesta**, Leonard Bruce 1946- *WhoWest 92*
**Sebestyen**, Istvan 1947- *WhoFI 92*
**Sebestyen**, Ouida 1924- *Au&Arts 8 [port], IntAu&W 91, WrDr 92*
**Sebetic**, Paul Gerard 1964- *WhoFI 92*
**Sebetich**, Michael J 1943- *AmMWSc 92*
**Sebhatu**, Mesgun 1946- *WhoBlA 92*
**Sebo**, Stephen Andrew 1934- *AmMWSc 92*
**Sebok**, Gyorgy 1922- *WhoEnt 92*
**Sebok**, Richard Frank 1938- *WhoWest 92*
**Sebora**, David Howard 1916- *WhoMW 92*
**Seborg**, Dale Edward 1941- *AmMWSc 92*
**Sebottendorff**, Rudolf von 1875-1945 *BiDExR*
**Sebranek**, Joseph George 1948- *AmMWSc 92*
**Sebree**, Bruce Randall 1956- *AmMWSc 92*
**Sebright**, Peter Giles Vivian 1953- *Who 92*
**Sebring**, Richard *WhoEnt 92*
**Secchia**, Peter Finley 1937- *WhoAmP 91*
**Secco**, Anthony Silvio 1956- *AmMWSc 92*
**Secco**, Etalo Anthony 1928- *AmMWSc 92*
**Seccomb**, John 1708-1792 *BenetAL 91*
**Seccombe** *Who 92*
**Seccombe**, Baroness 1930- *Who 92*
**Seccombe**, Hugh Digorie 1917- *Who 92*
**Seccombe**, Vernon 1928- *Who 92*
**Sechler**, Dale Truman 1926- *AmMWSc 92*
**Sechrest**, Edward Amacker 1931- *WhoBlA 92*
**Sechrist**, Chalmers Franklin, Jr 1930- *AmMWSc 92*
**Sechrist**, John William 1942- *AmMWSc 92*
**Sechrist**, Lynne Luan 1941- *AmMWSc 92*
**Sechrist**, Sterling George 1919- *WhoAmP 91*
**Sechzer**, Jeri Altneu 1930- *AmMWSc 92*
**Sechzer**, Philip Haim 1914- *AmMWSc 92*
**Secia**, Clifford John 1936- *WhoEnt 92*
**Seciniaz**, Laurent 1938- *WhoFI 92, WhoWest 92*
**Seckel**, Carol Ann 1949- *WhoRel 92*
**Seckel**, Gunter Rudolf 1923- *AmMWSc 92*
**Secker**, Martin 1882-1978 *DcLB 112 [port]*
**Secker**, Martin, and Warburg Limited *DcLB 112*
**Seckinger**, Emilia Posada *WhoHisp 92*
**Seckinger**, James Herbert 1942- *WhoAmL 92*
**Seckler**, Bernard David 1925- *AmMWSc 92*
**Secombe**, Harry 1921- *IntMPA 92, Who 92*
**Secomski**, Kazimierz 1910- *IntWW 91*
**Secondari**, Helen Jean Rogers *WhoEnt 92*
**Secondari**, John H. d1975 *LesBEnT 92*
**Secondat**, Charles-Louis de 1689-1755 *BlkwEAR*
**Seconde**, Reginald 1922- *Who 92*
**Secor**, Donald Terry, Jr 1934- *AmMWSc 92*
**Secor**, Gary Lee 1947- *WhoFI 92, WhoMW 92*
**Secor**, Jack Behrent 1923- *AmMWSc 92*
**Secor**, Lella Faye *AmPeW*
**Secor**, Richard Eugene 1930- *WhoMW 92*
**Secor**, Robert M 1932- *AmMWSc 92*
**Secord**, Robert N 1920- *AmMWSc 92*
**Secord**, Robert P *WhoAmP 91*
**Secoy**, Diane Marie 1938- *AmMWSc 92*
**Secrest**, Bruce Gill 1936- *AmMWSc 92*
**Secrest**, Donald H 1932- *AmMWSc 92*
**Secrest**, Everett Leigh 1928- *AmMWSc 92*
**Secrest**, James Seaton, Sr. 1930- *WhoAmL 92*
**Secrest**, Joe 1946- *WhoAmP 91*
**Secrest**, Maurice Allan 1945- *WhoWest 92*
**Secrest**, Patricia *WhoAmP 91*
**Secrest**, Ronald Dean 1951- *WhoAmL 92*
**Secrest**, Stephen Frederick 1947- *WhoMW 92*
**Secret**, Philip E. *WhoBlA 92*
**Secretan**, Lance Hilary Kenyon 1939- *Who 92*
**Secretariat** 1970-1989 *FacFETw [port]*
**Secrist**, John Adair, III 1947- *AmMWSc 92*
**Secter**, David Irving 1943- *WhoEnt 92*
**Sectzer**, Jose Cesar 1949- *WhoHisp 92*
**Sectzer**, Joseph Cesar 1949- *WhoFI 92*
**Secular**, Sidney 1940- *WhoFI 92*
**Secundus** *EncEarC*
**Secundus** d612 *EncEarC*
**Secundy**, Marian Gray 1938- *WhoBlA 92*
**Seda**, Jose Omar 1954- *WhoHisp 92*
**Seda**, Peter Eugene 1946- *WhoWest 92*
**Seda**, Wilfredo *WhoHisp 92*
**Sedaghat**, Ali Mohamad 1946- *WhoFI 92*
**Sedaka**, Neil 1939- *NewAmDM, WhoEnt 92*
**Sedar**, Albert William 1922- *AmMWSc 92*
**Sedares**, James L. 1956- *WhoEnt 92*
**Sedares**, Lorna Wood 1956- *WhoEnt 92*
**Sedat**, John William 1942- *AmMWSc 92*
**Sedberry**, J Hamilton 1863- *ScFEYrs*
**Sedberry**, Joseph E, Jr 1925- *AmMWSc 92*
**Sedcole**, Cecil Frazer 1927- *IntWW 91, Who 92*
**Seddon**, John d1991 *Who 92N*
**Seddon**, Richard 1915- *TwCPaSc*
**Seddon**, Richard Harding 1915- *Who 92*
**Sedelmaier**, J. J. 1956- *WhoEnt 92*
**Sedelmaier**, John Josef 1933- *WhoEnt 92*
**Sedelow**, Sally Yeates 1931- *AmMWSc 92*
**Sedelow**, Walter Alfred, Jr 1928- *AmMWSc 92, WhoWest 92*
**Sedeno**, Eugene Raymond 1952- *WhoWest 92*
**Sedensky**, James Andrew 1936- *AmMWSc 92*
**Seder**, Allen Michael 1953- *WhoEnt 92*
**Sederbaum**, Arthur David 1944- *WhoAmL 92*
**Sederberg**, Arelo 1931- *IntAu&W 91, WrDr 92*
**Sederburg**, William Albert 1947- *WhoAmP 91*
**Sederstrom**, Karen Ann 1959- *WhoAmL 92*
**Sedgeley**, Carlton Stanley 1939- *WhoEnt 92*
**Sedgeley**, Peter 1930- *TwCPaSc*
**Sedgemore**, Brian Charles John 1937- *Who 92*
**Sedges**, John *AmPeW, ConAu 34NR*
**Sedgman**, Francis Arthur 1927- *Who 92*
**Sedgwick**, A. R. M., Mrs. *Who 92*
**Sedgwick**, Anne Douglas 1873-1935 *BenetAL 91*
**Sedgwick**, Catherine Maria 1789-1867 *BenetAL 91*
**Sedgwick**, Fred 1945- *ConPo 91, WrDr 92*
**Sedgwick**, Frederica M. 1932- *WhoAmL 92*
**Sedgwick**, Harold Bend 1908- *WhoRel 92*
**Sedgwick**, James L 1939- *WhoIns 92*
**Sedgwick**, John Anthony 1950- *WhoAmL 92*
**Sedgwick**, Peter Norman 1943- *Who 92*
**Sedgwick**, Robert T 1933- *AmMWSc 92*
**Sedgwick**, Susan 1789?-1867 *BenetAL 91*
**Sedgwick**, Theodore 1746-1813 *AmPolLe, BlkwEAR*
**Sedgwick**, Timothy Foster 1946- *WhoRel 92*
**Sedillo**, James Joseph 1947- *WhoHisp 92*
**Sedillo**, Pablo 1935- *WhoHisp 92*
**Sedinger**, Kathy Jo 1953- *WhoRel 92*
**Sedita**, Salvador Joseph 1935- *WhoMW 92*
**Sedki**, Atef 1930- *IntWW 91*
**Sedky**, Cherif 1943- *WhoAmL 92*
**Sedlacek**, Evelyn Ann 1919- *WhoMW 92*
**Sedlacek**, Karel Victor 1957- *WhoEnt 92*
**Sedlacek**, William Adam 1936- *AmMWSc 92*
**Sedlack**, Robert Joseph 1935- *WhoFI 92*
**Sedlak**, John Andrew 1934- *AmMWSc 92*
**Sedlak**, Richard 1944- *WhoMW 92*
**Sedler**, Robert Allen 1935- *WhoAmL 92, WhoMW 92*
**Sedlet**, Jacob 1922- *AmMWSc 92*
**Sedley**, Charles 1639?-1701 *RfGEnL 91*
**Sedley**, Stephen John 1939- *Who 92*
**Sedlock**, Joy 1958- *WhoWest 92*
**Sedmak**, Nancy Jean 1951- *WhoAmL 92*
**Sedman**, Yale S 1929- *AmMWSc 92*
**Sedney**, Jules 1922- *IntWW 91*
**Sedney**, R 1927- *AmMWSc 92*
**Sedo**, Kathryn Jennette 1950- *WhoAmL 92*
**Sedor**, Edward Andrew 1939- *AmMWSc 92*
**Sedov**, Leonid I. 1907- *Who 92*
**Sedov**, Leonid Ivanovich 1907- *IntWW 91*
**Sedra**, Adel S 1943- *AmMWSc 92*
**Sedransk**, Joseph Henry 1938- *AmMWSc 92*
**Sedriks**, Aristide John 1938- *AmMWSc 92*
**Sedulius** *EncEarC*
**Sedway**, Lynn Massel 1941- *WhoFI 92*
**Sedwick**, Frank 1924- *WrDr 92*
**Sedykh**, Yuriy 1955- *IntWW 91, SovUnBD*
**See**, Alan Jeffery 1959- *WhoFI 92*
**See**, Carolyn *DrAPF 91*
**See**, Carolyn 1934- *IntAu&W 91, WrDr 92*
**See**, Clyde M, Jr 1941- *WhoAmP 91*
**See**, Gary N 1934- *WhoIns 92*
**See**, Karen Mason 1952- *WhoMW 92*
**See**, Letha Annette 1930- *WhoBlA 92*
**See**, Robert Fleming, Jr. 1942- *WhoAmL 92*
**See**, Ruth Douglas 1910- *ConAu 35NR*
**See**, William Mitchel 1952- *WhoMW 92*
**Seear** *Who 92*
**Seear**, Baroness 1913- *IntWW 91, Who 92*
**Seeba**, Hinrich Claassen 1940- *WhoWest 92*
**Seebach**, David Allen 1951- *WhoMW 92*
**Seebach**, Howard Godfrey 1930- *WhoWest 92*
**Seebach**, J Arthur, Jr 1938- *AmMWSc 92, WhoMW 92*
**Seebart**, George E 1928- *WhoIns 92*
**Seebass**, Alfred Richard, III 1936- *AmMWSc 92, WhoWest 92*
**Seeber**, Brian Richard 1954- *WhoAmL 92*
**Seebert**, Kathleen Anne 1949- *WhoFI 92, WhoMW 92*
**Seebohm**, Baron d1990 *IntWW 91N, Who 92N*
**Seebohm**, Lord 1909-1990 *AnObit 1990*
**Seebohm**, Paul Minor 1916- *AmMWSc 92*
**Seeburger**, George Harold 1935- *AmMWSc 92*
**Seeckt**, Hans von 1866-1936 *EncTR 91 [port], FacFETw*
**Seed**, Cecile Eugenie 1930- *IntAu&W 91*
**Seed**, Harry Bolton 1922- *AmMWSc 92*
**Seed**, Jenny 1930- *WrDr 92*
**Seed**, John Richard 1937- *AmMWSc 92*
**Seed**, Randolph William 1933- *AmMWSc 92*
**Seed**, Thomas Michael 1945- *AmMWSc 92, WhoMW 92*
**Seeder**, Richard Owen 1947- *WhoMW 92*
**Seedorf**, Donna Lynn 1953- *WhoRel 92*
**Seeds**, Dale Stimmel 1918- *WhoWest 92*
**Seeds**, Michael August 1942- *AmMWSc 92*
**Seeds**, Nicholas Warren 1942- *AmMWSc 92*
**Seefehlner**, Egon Hugo 1912- *IntWW 91*
**Seefelder**, Matthias 1920- *IntWW 91*
**Seefeldt**, Vern Dennis *AmMWSc 92*
**Seefeldt**, Waldemar Bernhard 1925- *AmMWSc 92*
**Seefried**, Irmgard 1919-1988 *FacFETw, NewAmDM*
**Seefurth**, Randall N 1941- *AmMWSc 92*
**Seegal**, Richard Field 1945- *AmMWSc 92*
**Seegall**, Manfred Ismar Ludwig 1929- *WhoWest 92*
**Seegar**, Kenneth Michael 1961- *WhoRel 92*
**Seeger**, Alan 1888-1916 *BenetAL 91, FacFETw*
**Seeger**, Andrew Philip 1964- *WhoMW 92*
**Seeger**, Anthony 1945- *WhoEnt 92*
**Seeger**, Charles 1886-1979 *NewAmDM*
**Seeger**, Charles L 1886-1979 *FacFETw*
**Seeger**, Charles Ronald 1931- *AmMWSc 92*
**Seeger**, Christopher Clark 1943- *WhoAmP 91*
**Seeger**, Edward Bethel 1945- *WhoRel 92*
**Seeger**, Edwin Howard 1930- *WhoAmL 92*
**Seeger**, Emily Ann 1947- *WhoRel 92*
**Seeger**, Leinaala Robinson 1944- *WhoAmL 92*
**Seeger**, Michael 1933- *WhoEnt 92*
**Seeger**, Pete 1919- *FacFETw, NewAmDM, WhoEnt 92*
**Seeger**, Philip Anthony 1937- *AmMWSc 92*
**Seeger**, Raymond John 1906- *AmMWSc 92*
**Seeger**, Robert Charles 1940- *AmMWSc 92*
**Seeger**, Ruth Crawford *NewAmDM*
**Seegers**, George Edwin 1942- *WhoFI 92*
**Seegers**, Walter Henry 1910- *AmMWSc 92*
**Seegert**, William Irwin 1951- *WhoFI 92*
**Seegmiller**, David W 1934- *AmMWSc 92*
**Seegmiller**, Jarvis Edwin 1920- *AmMWSc 92*
**Seegmiller**, Robert Earl 1943- *AmMWSc 92*
**Seehausen**, Richard Ferdinand 1925- *WhoMW 92*
**Seeherman**, Julian 1929- *WhoFI 92*
**Seehra**, Mohindar Singh 1940- *AmMWSc 92*
**Seeiso**, Constantine Bereng *IntWW 91*
**Seeiso**, Morena Mathealira 1943- *IntWW 91*
**Seel**, Derek 1932- *Who 92*
**Seel**, Robert Edward 1924- *WhoRel 92*
**Seeland**, David Arthur 1936- *AmMWSc 92*
**Seelbach**, Charles William 1923- *AmMWSc 92*
**Seelenfreund**, Alan 1936- *WhoFI 92, WhoWest 92*
**Seeler**, Elizabeth Alice 1941- *WhoFI 92*
**Seeler**, Robert S. *WhoFI 92*
**Seelert**, Robert L. 1942- *WhoFI 92*
**Seeley**, David William 1944- *WhoRel 92*
**Seeley**, Eric Eugene 1966- *WhoWest 92*
**Seeley**, Gilbert Stewart 1938- *WhoEnt 92, WhoWest 92*
**Seeley**, John George 1915- *AmMWSc 92*
**Seeley**, Kimberley Ann 1960- *WhoMW 92*
**Seeley**, Robert 1936- *AmMWSc 92*
**Seeley**, Robert D 1923- *AmMWSc 92*
**Seeley**, Robert T 1932- *AmMWSc 92*
**Seeley**, Rod R 1945- *AmMWSc 92*
**Seeley**, Roderick Eli 1946- *WhoWest 92*
**Seeley**, Schuyler Drannan 1939- *AmMWSc 92*
**Seeley**, Thomas Dyer 1952- *AmMWSc 92*
**Seeley**, William Parker, Jr. 1937- *WhoAmL 92*
**Seelig**, Jakob Williams 1937- *AmMWSc 92*
**Seelke**, Ralph Walter 1951- *AmMWSc 92*
**Seely** *Who 92*

**Seely**, Gilbert Randall 1929- *AmMWSc 92*
**Seely**, Henry Martyn 1828-1917 *BiInAmS*
**Seely**, J Rodman 1927- *AmMWSc 92*
**Seely**, James Ervin 1954- *AmMWSc 92, WhoMW 92*
**Seely**, Justus Frandsen 1941- *AmMWSc 92*
**Seely**, Michael Wayne 1945- *WhoFI 92*
**Seely**, Nancy Diane 1950- *WhoFI 92*
**Seely**, Nigel 1923- *Who 92*
**Seely**, Robert Eugene 1941- *WhoFI 92*
**Seely**, Robert Fleming 1944- *WhoAmL 92, WhoMW 92*
**Seely**, Samuel 1909- *AmMWSc 92*
**Seelye**, John 1931- *TwCWW 91, WrDr 92*
**Seelye**, John Douglas 1931- *IntAu&W 91*
**Seelye**, Ned H. *WhoHisp 92*
**Seelye**, Sarah Emma *EncAmaz 91*
**Seelye**, Talcott Williams 1922- *IntWW 91*
**Seeman**, Barry Stuart 1962- *WhoFI 92*
**Seeman**, Mary Violette 1935- *AmMWSc 92*
**Seeman**, Nadrian Charles 1945- *AmMWSc 92*
**Seeman**, Philip 1934- *AmMWSc 92*
**Seemann**, Charles Henry, Jr. 1946- *WhoEnt 92*
**Seemann**, Ernest Albright 1929- *WhoAmL 92*
**Seemuth**, David Paul 1956- *WhoRel 92*
**Seeney**, Charles Earl 1943- *AmMWSc 92*
**Seeney**, Leslie Elon Sidney 1922- *Who 92*
**Seeney**, Noel Conway 1926- *Who 92*
**Seerden**, Robert Jennings 1932- *WhoAmL 92*
**Seerley**, Robert Wayne 1930- *AmMWSc 92*
**Seerveld**, Calvin George 1930- *WhoRel 92*
**Seery**, Daniel J 1933- *AmMWSc 92*
**Seery**, Janet *DrAPF 91*
**Seery**, Thomas Francis 1945- *WhoAmP 91*
**Seery**, Virginia Lee 1934- *AmMWSc 92*
**Seese**, June Akers 1935- *ConAu 134*
**Seese**, Thomas M, Jr *WhoAmP 91*
**Seese**, William Shober 1932- *AmMWSc 92*
**Seestern** *ScFEYrs*
**Seethaler**, Myra Knight 1925-1990 *WhoWest 92*
**Seethaler**, William Charles 1937- *WhoFI 92, WhoWest 92*
**Seetharam**, Ramnath 1952- *AmMWSc 92*
**Seeto**, Ling 1933- *Who 92*
**Seetoo**, Amy Dah Sun 1946- *WhoMW 92*
**Seevak**, Sheldon 1929- *WhoFI 92*
**Seevers**, Bradley Jay 1964- *WhoRel 92*
**Seevers**, Charles Junior 1925- *WhoMW 92*
**Seevers**, Delmar Oswell 1919- *AmMWSc 92*
**Seevers**, Gary Leonard 1937- *WhoAmP 91*
**Seevers**, Robert Edward 1935- *AmMWSc 92*
**Seewald**, Elsbeth M. 1927- *WhoMW 92*
**Seeyave**, Rene 1935- *Who 92*
**Sefali**, Michael Malefetsane 1939- *IntWW 91*
**Sefcik**, John Karol 1922- *WhoRel 92*
**Seferiades**, Giorgos Stylianou 1900-1971 *ConAu 36NR*
**Seferiadis**, Yorgos 1900-1971 *WhoNob 90*
**Seferian**, Edward 1931- *WhoEnt 92, WhoWest 92*
**Seferian**, Mark Christopher 1957- *WhoWest 92*
**Seferis**, George *ConAu 36NR*
**Seferis**, George 1900-1971 *FacFETw*
**Seferis**, Giorgos 1900-1971 *WhoNob 90*
**Seff**, Karl 1938- *AmMWSc 92*
**Seff**, Leslie S. 1950- *WhoFI 92*
**Seff**, Philip 1923- *AmMWSc 92*
**Seff**, Richard 1927- *WhoEnt 92*
**Seffl**, Raymond James 1927- *AmMWSc 92*
**Seftenberg**, Stephen Longfellow 1935- *WhoAmL 92*
**Sefton** *Who 92*
**Sefton**, Bobby Ray 1932- *WhoFI 92*
**Sefton**, Catherine *ConAu 34NR, IntAu&W 91X, WrDr 92*
**Sefton of Garston**, Baron 1915- *Who 92*
**Seftor**, Richard Edward Barnet 1952- *WhoWest 92*
**Sega**, Gary Andrew 1941- *AmMWSc 92*
**Segal**, Alan Franklin 1945- *WhoRel 92*
**Segal**, Alan H 1921- *AmMWSc 92*
**Segal**, Alex *LesBEnT 92*
**Segal**, Alexander 1934- *AmMWSc 92*
**Segal**, Alvin 1929- *AmMWSc 92*
**Segal**, Arthur Cherny 1938- *AmMWSc 92*
**Segal**, Bernard 1936- *AmMWSc 92*
**Segal**, Bernard Gerard 1907- *WhoAmL 92*
**Segal**, Bernard L 1929- *AmMWSc 92*
**Segal**, Bernard L. 1930- *WhoAmL 92*
**Segal**, Bernice G 1929- *AmMWSc 92*
**Segal**, Burton Irwin 1943- *WhoFI 92*
**Segal**, David Miller *AmMWSc 92*
**Segal**, David S 1942- *AmMWSc 92*
**Segal**, Earl 1923- *AmMWSc 92*
**Segal**, Edith *DrAPF 91*
**Segal**, Erich 1937- *ConAu 36NR, IntAu&W 91, Who 92, WrDr 92*
**Segal**, Francine 1954- *WhoEnt 92*
**Segal**, George 1924- *FacFETw*
**Segal**, George 1934- *IntMPA 92, IntWW 91, WhoEnt 92*
**Segal**, Gerald A 1934- *AmMWSc 92*
**Segal**, Gloria M 1928- *WhoAmP 91*
**Segal**, Gordon I. 1938- *WhoMW 92*
**Segal**, Graeme Bryce 1941- *Who 92*
**Segal**, Harold Henry 1918- *WhoEnt 92*
**Segal**, Harold Jacob 1941- *AmMWSc 92*
**Segal**, Harold Lewis 1924- *AmMWSc 92*
**Segal**, Harriet 1931- *WrDr 92*
**Segal**, Irving Ezra 1918- *AmMWSc 92, IntWW 91*
**Segal**, Jack 1934- *AmMWSc 92*
**Segal**, Joel Michael 1933- *WhoFI 92*
**Segal**, Jonathan L. 1952- *WhoEnt 92*
**Segal**, Judah Benzion 1912- *IntWW 91, Who 92*
**Segal**, Lore *DrAPF 91*
**Segal**, Lore 1928- *IntAu&W 91, LiExTwC, SmATA 66 [port], WrDr 92*
**Segal**, Lynne 1943- *ConAu 133*
**Segal**, Mark 1935- *AmMWSc 92*
**Segal**, Martin Eli 1916- *WhoEnt 92*
**Segal**, Maurice 1921- *IntMPA 92*
**Segal**, Michael John 1937- *Who 92*
**Segal**, Moshe 1934- *AmMWSc 92*
**Segal**, Robert G d1991 *NewYTBS 91*
**Segal**, Robert Martin 1935- *WhoAmL 92*
**Segal**, Ronald 1932- *WrDr 92*
**Segal**, Ronald Ian 1947- *WhoAmL 92*
**Segal**, Ronald Michael 1932- *IntAu&W 91, IntWW 91*
**Segal**, Rosalind A 1958- *AmMWSc 92*
**Segal**, S. S. 1919- *WrDr 92*
**Segal**, Sanford Leonard 1937- *AmMWSc 92*
**Segal**, Stanley Solomon 1919- *IntAu&W 91*
**Segal**, Stanton 1927- *AmMWSc 92*
**Segal**, Steven Paul 1943- *WhoWest 92*
**Segal**, Susan Ann 1962- *WhoMW 92*
**Segal**, Tali Joan 1961- *WhoAmL 92*
**Segal**, Uri 1944- *IntWW 91*
**Segal**, William 1922- *AmMWSc 92*
**Segall**, Benjamin 1925- *AmMWSc 92*
**Segall**, Harold Nathan 1897- *AmMWSc 92*
**Segall**, James Arnold 1956- *WhoAmL 92*
**Segall**, Mark M. 1948- *WhoWest 92*
**Segall**, Paul Edward 1942- *AmMWSc 92*
**Segall**, Pearl Bloch *DrAPF 91*
**Segall**, Stanley 1930- *AmMWSc 92*
**Segall**, Stephen Barrett 1942- *AmMWSc 92*
**Segall**, Steven A. 1953- *WhoAmL 92*
**Segall-Anable**, Linda Ann 1947- *WhoEnt 92*
**Segar**, Geoffrey 1926- *WhoAmL 92*
**Segar**, William Elias 1923- *AmMWSc 92*
**Segarra**, Jose Enrique 1945- *WhoHisp 92*
**Segarra**, Joseph M 1922- *AmMWSc 92*
**Segarra**, Margarita 1941- *WhoHisp 92*
**Segarra**, Ninfa 1950- *WhoHisp 92*
**Segarra**, Pedro, Jr. 1957- *WhoHisp 92*
**Segarra-Garcia**, Rafael Ivan 1952- *WhoHisp 92*
**Segars**, John Kelvin 1935- *WhoRel 92*
**Segatto**, Bernard Gordon, III 1960- *WhoEnt 92*
**Segatto**, Peter Richard 1928- *AmMWSc 92*
**Sege**, Thomas Davis 1926- *WhoFI 92, WhoWest 92*
**Segebarth**, Larry Scott 1966- *WhoMW 92*
**Segel**, Irwin Harvey 1935- *AmMWSc 92*
**Segel**, J. Norman 1939- *WhoFI 92*
**Segel**, Joseph M. 1931- *WhoFI 92*
**Segel**, Karen Lynn Joseph 1947- *WhoWest 92*
**Segel**, Kenneth Ian 1942- *WhoRel 92*
**Segel**, L 1922- *AmMWSc 92*
**Segel**, Lee Aaron 1932- *AmMWSc 92*
**Segel**, Leonard 1922- *WhoMW 92*
**Segel**, Ralph E 1928- *AmMWSc 92*
**Segel**, Robert G. d1991 *NewYTBS 91*
**Segel**, Scott Jonathon 1962- *WhoAmL 92*
**Segel**, Stanley Lewis 1932- *AmMWSc 92*
**Segelbaum**, Charles Jacob 1939- *WhoRel 92*
**Segelken**, John Maurice 1948- *AmMWSc 92*
**Segelken**, Warren George 1926- *AmMWSc 92*
**Segelman**, Alvin Burton 1931- *AmMWSc 92*
**Segelman**, Florence H 1941- *AmMWSc 92*
**Segelstein**, Irwin B. *LesBEnT 92*
**Seger**, Bob 1945- *NewAmDM, WhoEnt 92*
**Seger**, Martha Romayne 1932- *WhoFI 92*
**Seger**, Roberta 1932- *WhoAmP 91*
**Seger**, Warren Richard 1936- *WhoMW 92, WhoRel 92*
**Segerblom**, Richard *WhoAmP 91*
**Segermark**, Howard S 1941- *WhoAmP 91*
**Segers**, Richard George 1928- *AmMWSc 92*
**Segerstam**, Leif 1944- *ConCom 92*
**Segerstam**, Leif Selim 1944- *WhoEnt 92*
**Segerstedt**, Torgny 1908- *IntWW 91*
**Segerstrom**, Kenneth 1909- *AmMWSc 92*
**Segerstrom**, Paul Stephen 1957- *WhoFI 92, WhoMW 92*
**Segger**, Martin Joseph 1946- *WhoWest 92*
**Seggerman**, Henry Mather 1953- *WhoEnt 92*
**Seghers**, Anna 1900-1983 *LiExTwC*
**Seghers**, Benoni Hendrik 1944- *AmMWSc 92*
**Seghers**, Charles John 1839-1886 *RelLAm 91*
**Seghers**, Pierre 1906- *IntAu&W 91*
**Seginski**, William Enoch 1933- *WhoWest 92*
**Seglias**, Edward 1957- *WhoAmL 92*
**Seglie**, Ernest Augustus 1945- *AmMWSc 92*
**Seglund**, Bruce Richard 1950- *WhoAmL 92*
**Seglund**, James Arnold 1923- *AmMWSc 92*
**Segner**, Edmund Peter, III 1953- *WhoFI 92*
**Segner**, Edmund Peter, Jr 1928- *AmMWSc 92*
**Sego**, Charles Thomas 1955- *WhoEnt 92*
**Sego**, David Charles 1955- *WhoFI 92*
**Sego**, Robert F 1933- *WhoAmP 91*
**Segovia**, Andres 1893-1987 *ConMus 6 [port], FacFETw [port], NewAmDM*
**Segovia**, Antonio 1932- *AmMWSc 92*
**Segovia**, Fernando F. 1948- *WhoHisp 92*
**Segovia**, Jorge 1934- *AmMWSc 92*
**Segovia**, Tomas 1927- *ConSpAP*
**Segraves**, Daniel Lee 1946- *WhoRel 92*
**Segre**, Diego 1922- *AmMWSc 92*
**Segre**, Emilio 1905- *IntAu&W 91*
**Segre**, Emilio Gino 1905- *AmMWSc 92*
**Segre**, Emilio Gino 1905-1989 *WhoNob 90*
**Segre**, Gino C 1938- *AmMWSc 92*
**Segre**, Greta Eubank 1932- *WhoBlA 92*
**Segre**, Mariangela Bertani 1927- *AmMWSc 92*
**Segree**, E. Ramone 1949- *WhoBlA 92*
**Segrest**, Jere Palmer 1940- *AmMWSc 92*
**Segretti**, Marguerite Cecelia 1912- *WhoAmP 91*
**Segrist**, Allen Edward 1931- *WhoMW 92*
**Seguela**, Jacques Louis 1934- *IntWW 91*
**Seguin**, Jerome Joseph 1924- *AmMWSc 92*
**Seguin**, Louis-Roch 1920- *AmMWSc 92*
**Seguin**, Maurice Krisholm 1937- *AmMWSc 92*
**Seguin**, Nicole 1946- *WhoEnt 92*
**Seguin**, Philippe Daniel Alain 1943- *IntWW 91*
**Seguin**, Ward Raymond 1942- *AmMWSc 92*
**Segun**, Mabel D. 1930- *WrDr 92*
**Segundo**, Jose Pedro 1922- *AmMWSc 92*
**Segundo**, Leslie Paul 1953- *WhoWest 92*
**Segur**, Sophie Rostopchine, Comtesse de 1799-1874 *FrenWW*
**Segura**, Denise A. *WhoHisp 92*
**Segura**, Dolores Suarez 1946- *WhoHisp 92*
**Segura**, Gonzalo, Jr 1919- *AmMWSc 92*
**Segura**, Perry 1929- *WhoAmP 91*
**Seguy**, Georges 1927- *IntWW 91*
**Seh-Dong-Hong-Beh** *EncAmaz 91*
**Sehe**, Charles Theodore 1923- *AmMWSc 92*
**Seheult**, Malcolm McDonald Richardson 1949- *WhoAmL 92*
**Sehgal**, Amar Nath 1922- *IntWW 91*
**Sehgal**, Lakshman R 1942- *AmMWSc 92*
**Sehgal**, Om Parkash 1932- *AmMWSc 92*
**Sehgal**, Pravinkumar B 1949- *AmMWSc 92*
**Sehgal**, Prem P 1934- *AmMWSc 92*
**Sehgal**, Surendra N 1932- *AmMWSc 92*
**Sehgal**, Surinder K 1938- *AmMWSc 92*
**Sehler**, Tom *WrDr 92*
**Sehmel**, George Albert 1932- *AmMWSc 92*
**Sehn**, Marvin Daniel 1951- *WhoMW 92*
**Sehon**, Alec 1924- *AmMWSc 92*
**Sehring**, Jonathan Dewey 1956- *WhoEnt 92*
**Seib**, David Henry 1943- *AmMWSc 92*
**Seib**, Edmund John, III 1950- *WhoMW 92*
**Seib**, Karl Edward, Jr. 1944- *WhoAmL 92*
**Seib**, Paul A 1936- *AmMWSc 92*
**Seibel**, Brad Hankinson 1960- *WhoFI 92*
**Seibel**, David Brian 1961- *WhoMW 92*
**Seibel**, Erwin *AmMWSc 92*
**Seibel**, Erwin 1942- *WhoWest 92*
**Seibel**, Frederick Truman 1941- *AmMWSc 92*
**Seibel**, Hugo Rudolf 1937- *AmMWSc 92*
**Seibel**, Robert Franklin 1946- *WhoAmL 92*
**Seibel**, Stuart Dale 1942- *WhoEnt 92*
**Seibel**, Werner 1943- *AmMWSc 92*
**Seibels**, George G, Jr *WhoAmP 91*
**Seiber**, James N 1940- *AmMWSc 92*
**Seiber**, Matyas 1905-1960 *NewAmDM*
**Seiberlich**, Robert Eugene 1960- *WhoEnt 92*
**Seiberling**, John F 1918- *WhoAmP 91*
**Seiberling**, John Frederick 1918- *WhoAmL 92*
**Seibert**, Ann 1934- *WhoAmP 91*
**Seibert**, Donald Vincent 1923- *IntWW 91*
**Seibert**, Florence B d1991 *NewYTBS 91*
**Seibert**, Florence B 1897- *AmMWSc 92*
**Seibert**, Florence B. 1897-1991 *CurBio 91N*
**Seibert**, J A 1953- *AmMWSc 92*
**Seibert**, John F 1951- *WhoIns 92*
**Seibert**, Mary Angelice 1922- *WhoRel 92*
**Seibert**, Michael 1944- *AmMWSc 92*
**Seibert-McCauley**, Mary F. 1930- *WhoBlA 92*
**Seibold**, Carol Duke 1943- *AmMWSc 92*
**Seibold**, Eugen 1918- *IntWW 91*
**Seicol**, Samuel Robert 1951- *WhoRel 92*
**Seid**, Eva 1950- *WhoEnt 92*
**Seid**, Gerald P. 1937- *WhoAmL 92*
**Seidah**, Nabil George 1949- *AmMWSc 92*
**Seide**, Leonard Myron 1929- *WhoFI 92*
**Seide**, Paul 1926- *AmMWSc 92*
**Seidehamel**, Richard Joseph 1940- *AmMWSc 92*
**Seidel**, Andrea Mantell 1947- *WhoEnt 92*
**Seidel**, Arthur Harris 1923- *WhoAmL 92*
**Seidel**, Barry S 1932- *AmMWSc 92*
**Seidel**, Eugene Maurice *WhoWest 92*
**Seidel**, Frederick *DrAPF 91*
**Seidel**, Frederick 1936- *ConPo 91, WrDr 92*
**Seidel**, George Elias, Jr 1943- *AmMWSc 92*
**Seidel**, George Joseph 1932- *IntAu&W 91, WrDr 92*
**Seidel**, George Merle 1930- *AmMWSc 92*
**Seidel**, Gerhard Edward 1917- *WhoAmL 92*
**Seidel**, Henry Murray 1922- *AmMWSc 92*
**Seidel**, Ina 1885-1974 *EncTR 91 [port]*
**Seidel**, Joan Broude 1933- *WhoFI 92*
**Seidel**, John C. *WhoBlA 92*
**Seidel**, John Charles 1933- *AmMWSc 92*
**Seidel**, Kathleen Gilles *WrDr 92*
**Seidel**, Kathleen Gilles 1951- *IntAu&W 91*
**Seidel**, Michael Edward 1945- *AmMWSc 92*
**Seidel**, Neil Douglas 1946- *WhoWest 92*
**Seidel**, Robert Wayne 1945- *WhoWest 92*
**Seidel**, Roger Ray 1958- *WhoMW 92*
**Seidel**, Selvyn 1942- *WhoAmL 92, WhoFI 92*
**Seidel**, Thomas Allen 1934- *WhoAmP 91*
**Seidel**, Thomas Edward 1935- *AmMWSc 92*
**Seidel-Debrick**, Carolyn Sue 1956- *WhoFI 92*
**Seidell**, Barbara Castens 1957- *AmMWSc 92*
**Seidelman**, Arthur Allan *IntMPA 92, WhoEnt 92*
**Seidelman**, Susan *ReelWom*
**Seidelman**, Susan 1952- *IntMPA 92, IntWW 91, WhoEnt 92*
**Seidelman**, Susan 1953- *IntDcF 2-2 [port]*
**Seidelmann**, Paul Kenneth 1937- *AmMWSc 92*
**Seideman**, Walter E 1933- *AmMWSc 92*
**Seiden**, David 1946- *AmMWSc 92*
**Seiden**, Henry 1928- *WhoFI 92*
**Seiden**, Hy 1915- *AmMWSc 92*
**Seiden**, Lewis S 1934- *AmMWSc 92*
**Seiden**, Philip Edward 1934- *AmMWSc 92*
**Seiden**, Steven Arnold 1936- *WhoFI 92*
**Seiden**, Steven Jay 1960- *WhoAmL 92*
**Seidenberg**, Abraham 1916- *AmMWSc 92*
**Seidenberg**, Mark *WhoBlA 92*
**Seidenberg**, Sidney A. 1925- *WhoEnt 92*
**Seidenfaden**, Erik 1910- *IntWW 91*
**Seidenfaden**, Gunnar 1908- *IntWW 91*
**Seidenfeld**, Andrew William 1962- *WhoEnt 92*
**Seidenfeld**, Glenn Kenneth, Jr. 1944- *WhoAmL 92*
**Seidenfeld**, Jerome 1945- *AmMWSc 92*
**Seidensticker**, Robert B. 1929- *WhoFI 92*
**Seidensticker**, Wayde Porter 1938- *WhoEnt 92*
**Seider**, Warren David 1941- *AmMWSc 92*
**Seiders**, Victor Mann 1931- *AmMWSc 92*
**Seidl**, Anton 1850-1898 *NewAmDM*
**Seidl**, Bernard 1952- *WhoMW 92*
**Seidl**, Bryce 1946- *WhoAmP 91*
**Seidl**, Frederick Gabriel Paul 1918- *AmMWSc 92*
**Seidl**, John Michael 1939- *WhoFI 92, WhoWest 92*
**Seidl**, Milos 1923- *AmMWSc 92*
**Seidler**, Ann 1925- *IntAu&W 91, WrDr 92*
**Seidler**, Bernard Alan 1946- *WhoAmL 92*
**Seidler**, Harry 1923- *IntWW 91, WrDr 92*
**Seidler**, Ramon John 1941- *AmMWSc 92*
**Seidler**, Rosemary Joan 1939- *AmMWSc 92*
**Seidler**, Tor 1952- *WrDr 92*
**Seidlits**, Curtis L, Jr 1953- *WhoAmP 91*

**Seidman**, David N 1938- AmMWSc 92
**Seidman**, David Nathaniel 1938- WhoMW 92
**Seidman**, Hugh DrAPF 91
**Seidman**, Hugh 1940- ConAu 35NR, ConPo 91, IntAu&W 91, WrDr 92
**Seidman**, Irving 1930- AmMWSc 92
**Seidman**, Jonathan G 1950- AmMWSc 92
**Seidman**, L William WhoAmP 91
**Seidman**, L. William 1921- IntWW 91
**Seidman**, Lewis William 1921- WhoFI 92
**Seidman**, Martin 1921- AmMWSc 92
**Seidman**, Matthew Sanford 1934- WhoWest 92
**Seidman**, Mitchell Bob 1960- WhoAmL 92
**Seidman**, Paul Joseph 1948- WhoAmL 92
**Seidman**, Robert J. DrAPF 91
**Seidman**, Robert Jerome 1941- WhoEnt 92
**Seidman**, Stephen Benjamin 1944- AmMWSc 92
**Seidman**, Thomas Israel 1935- AmMWSc 92
**Seidman**, Vanessa Rae 1964- WhoEnt 92
**Seidov**, Hassan 1932- IntWW 91
**Seielstad**, George A 1937- AmMWSc 92
**Seif**, Robert Dale 1927- AmMWSc 92
**Seifen**, Ernst 1930- AmMWSc 92
**Seifer**, Arnold David 1940- AmMWSc 92
**Seiferle**, Rebecca DrAPF 91
**Seifert**, Carl A 1938- WhoAmP 91
**Seifert**, George 1921- AmMWSc 92
**Seifert**, George 1940- WhoWest 92
**Seifert**, Jaroslav 1901-1986 FacFETw, WhoNob 90
**Seifert**, Josef 1942- AmMWSc 92
**Seifert**, Karl E 1934- AmMWSc 92, WhoMW 92
**Seifert**, Laurence C AmMWSc 92
**Seifert**, Luke Michael 1957- WhoAmL 92
**Seifert**, Ralph Louis 1943- AmMWSc 92
**Seifert**, Robin 1910- IntWW 91, Who 92
**Seifert**, Stephen Wayne 1957- WhoAmL 92
**Seifert**, Thomas Lloyd 1940- WhoAmL 92
**Seifert**, Timothy Michael 1951- WhoMW 92
**Seifert**, Walter William WhoMW 92
**Seifert**, William Edgar, Jr 1948- AmMWSc 92
**Seifert**, William Norman 1952- WhoRel 92
**Seifert**, William W 1920- AmMWSc 92
**Seiff**, Alvin 1922- AmMWSc 92
**Seiffert**, Stephen Lockhart 1942- AmMWSc 92
**Seifman**, Eli 1936- IntAu&W 91, WrDr 92
**Seifried**, Adele Susan Corbin 1947- AmMWSc 92
**Seifried**, Harold Edwin 1946- AmMWSc 92
**Seifried**, Roger Christian 1941- WhoMW 92
**Seifter**, Eli 1919- AmMWSc 92
**Seifter**, Harvey 1954- WhoWest 92
**Seifter**, Sam 1916- AmMWSc 92
**Seifullina**, Lidiya Yakovlevna 1889-1954 SovUnBD
**Seigel**, Arnold E 1923- AmMWSc 92
**Seigel**, James LeRoy 1935- WhoMW 92
**Seigel**, Jan Kearney 1947- WhoAmL 92
**Seigel**, Richard Allyn 1954- AmMWSc 92
**Seigel**, Robert Alan 1938- WhoRel 92
**Seigel**, Stuart Evan 1933- WhoAmL 92
**Seiger**, Harvey N 1924- AmMWSc 92
**Seiger**, Marvin Barr 1926- AmMWSc 92, WhoMW 92
**Seigfreid**, James T., Jr. 1957- WhoAmL 92
**Seigfreid**, Mark Welling 1958- WhoWest 92
**Seigle**, John William 1929- WhoFI 92
**Seigle**, L L 1917- AmMWSc 92
**Seigler**, David Stanley 1940- AmMWSc 92
**Seigler**, Hilliard Foster 1934- AmMWSc 92
**Seigner**, Louis d1991 IntWW 91N
**Seignoret**, Clarence 1919- IntWW 91, Who 92
**Seignoret**, Eustace Edward 1925- Who 92
**Seignoret**, Eustace Edward 1935- IntWW 91
**Seikel**, Lewis Andrew, III 1958- WhoFI 92
**Seikel**, Mark Timothy 1950- WhoAmP 91
**Seikel**, Oliver Edward 1937- WhoAmL 92
**Seiken**, Arnold 1928- AmMWSc 92
**Seil**, Fredrick John 1933- AmMWSc 92
**Seiler**, Barry DrAPF 91
**Seiler**, Charlotte Woody 1915- WhoMW 92
**Seiler**, David George 1940- AmMWSc 92
**Seiler**, Fritz A 1931- AmMWSc 92
**Seiler**, George J 1941- WhoIns 92
**Seiler**, Gerald Joseph 1949- AmMWSc 92
**Seiler**, Steven Wing 1950- AmMWSc 92
**Seiler**, Timothy Lee 1946- WhoMW 92
**Seiler**, Wallace Urban 1914- WhoMW 92
**Seilhamer**, Ray A. WhoRel 92
**Seilheimer**, David A. 1949- WhoRel 92
**Seilheimer**, Jack Arthur 1935- AmMWSc 92
**Seiling**, Alfred William 1936- AmMWSc 92
**Seim**, Henry Jerome 1919- AmMWSc 92
**Seimas**, John Stephen 1943- WhoEnt 92
**Seince**, Emmanuel 1948- WhoEnt 92
**Seiner**, Jerome Allan 1932- AmMWSc 92
**Seiner**, John Milton 1944- AmMWSc 92
**Seinfeld**, Jerry 1955- WhoEnt 92
**Seinfeld**, John H 1942- AmMWSc 92
**Seinsheimer**, J F, Jr 1913- WhoIns 92
**Seinsheimer**, Joseph Fellman, III 1940- WhoIns 92
**Seinuk**, Ysrael A. 1931- WhoHisp 92
**Seip**, Anne-Lise 1933- IntWW 91
**Seip**, Heige Lunde 1919- IntAu&W 91
**Seip**, Theodore Lorenzo 1842-1903 RelLAm 91
**Seipel**, John Howard 1925- AmMWSc 92
**Seiple**, James Eugene, Jr. 1953- WhoMW 92
**Seipp**, Walter 1925- IntWW 91, Who 92
**Seireg**, Ali A 1927- AmMWSc 92
**Seiss**, Joseph Augustus 1823-1904 RelLAm 91
**Seitchik**, Jerold Alan 1935- AmMWSc 92
**Seitel**, Fraser Paul 1946- WhoFI 92
**Seitelman**, Leon Harold 1940- AmMWSc 92
**Seiters**, Rudolf 1937- IntWW 91
**Seith**, Alex Robert 1934- WhoAmL 92, WhoAmP 91
**Seith**, Thomas Karl 1927- WhoRel 92
**Seitsinger**, Anita 1919- WhoAmP 91
**Seitz**, Anna W 1941- AmMWSc 92
**Seitz**, Collins Jacques 1914- WhoAmL 92
**Seitz**, Craig 1952- WhoEnt 92
**Seitz**, Daniel Bruce 1943- WhoAmL 92
**Seitz**, Don Carlos 1862-1935 BenetAL 91
**Seitz**, Eugene W 1935- AmMWSc 92
**Seitz**, Florian Charles 1926- WhoMW 92
**Seitz**, Frederick 1911- AmMWSc 92, IntWW 91
**Seitz**, Gary M 1943- AmMWSc 92
**Seitz**, Harold A. 1938- WhoMW 92
**Seitz**, John E 1930- WhoAmP 91
**Seitz**, Karen De Raffele 1959- WhoFI 92
**Seitz**, Lane Richard 1946- WhoRel 92
**Seitz**, Larry Max 1940- AmMWSc 92
**Seitz**, Melvin Christian, Jr. 1939- WhoMW 92
**Seitz**, Raymond G 1940- WhoAmP 91
**Seitz**, Raymond G. H. 1940- IntWW 91
**Seitz**, Raymond George Hardenbergh 1940- Who 92
**Seitz**, S Stanley 1923- AmMWSc 92
**Seitz**, Shawn Eliot 1955- WhoRel 92
**Seitz**, Stephen Richard 1944- WhoRel 92
**Seitz**, Thomas J. 1941- WhoMW 92
**Seitz**, Wendell L 1934- AmMWSc 92
**Seitz**, Wesley Donald 1940- AmMWSc 92
**Seitz**, William Rudolf 1943- AmMWSc 92
**Seivers**, David WhoAmP 91
**Sejnowski**, Terrence Joseph 1947- WhoWest 92
**Seka**, Wolf 1939- AmMWSc 92
**Sekalski**, Jozef 1904-1972 TwCPaSc
**Sekanina**, Karl 1926- IntWW 91
**Sekanina**, Zdenek 1936- AmMWSc 92
**Sekaxsu Petakwonexnajunkis** 1950- ConAu 133
**Sekayumptewa**, Loren 1950- WhoWest 92
**Sekellick**, Margaret Jean 1943- AmMWSc 92
**Sekerka**, Ivan 1927- AmMWSc 92
**Sekerka**, Robert Floyd 1937- AmMWSc 92
**Sekers**, David Nicholas Oliver 1943- Who 92
**Sekhar**, Chandra 1942- WhoMW 92
**Sekhon**, Devinder Singh 1944- WhoWest 92
**Sekhon**, Jasmeet M. 1937- WhoMW 92
**Sekhon**, Sant Singh 1931- AmMWSc 92
**Sekhonyana**, Evaristus Rets'elisitsoe 1937- IntWW 91
**Seki**, Hajime 1929- AmMWSc 92
**Seki**, Hozen d1991 NewYTBS 91
**Seki**, Ryoichi 1940- AmMWSc 92
**Sekiguchi**, Yoshi 1931- WhoEnt 92
**Sekimoto**, Tadahiro 1926- AmMWSc 92
**Sekine**, Masao 1912- IntWW 91
**Sekine**, Yasuji 1931- AmMWSc 92
**Sekiya**, Gerald Yoshinori 1942- WhoAmL 92, WhoWest 92
**Sekiya**, Katsutsugu 1938- IntWW 91
**Sekler**, Eduard F. 1920- WrDr 92
**Seko**, Masataka 1923- IntWW 91
**Sekula**, Bernard Charles 1951- AmMWSc 92
**Sekula**, Ireneusz 1943- IntWW 91
**Sekula**, Stanley Ted 1927- AmMWSc 92
**Sekuler**, Robert W 1939- AmMWSc 92
**Sekulovich**, Malden 1916- WhoEnt 92
**Sekutowski**, Dennis G 1948- AmMWSc 92
**Sekyi**, Henry Van Hien 1928- IntWW 91, Who 92
**Sela** EncAmaz 91
**Sela**, Michael 1924- IntWW 91
**Selame**, Elinor 1936- WhoFI 92
**Selander**, Richard Brent 1927- AmMWSc 92
**Selander**, Robert Keith 1927- AmMWSc 92
**Selangor**, the Sultan of 1926- IntWW 91
**Selassie**, Cynthia R 1951- AmMWSc 92
**Selberg**, Atle 1917- AmMWSc 92
**Selberg**, Ingrid 1950- SmATA 68
**Selberherr**, Siegfried 1955- WhoFI 92
**Selbin**, Joel 1931- AmMWSc 92
**Selbo**, Jule Britt 1954- WhoEnt 92
**Selbo**, Ray Gordon 1940- WhoMW 92
**Selborne**, Earl 1940- IntWW 91
**Selborne**, Earl of 1940- Who 92
**Selbourne**, David 1937- IntAu&W 91, WrDr 92
**Selby**, Bishop Suffragan of 1938- Who 92
**Selby**, Viscount 1942- Who 92
**Selby**, Barbara Kenaga 1942- WhoMW 92
**Selby**, Cora Norwood 1920- WhoBlA 92
**Selby**, Curt TwCSFW 91
**Selby**, David 1941- IntMPA 92
**Selby**, Diane Ray Miller 1940- WhoMW 92
**Selby**, Elliott WrDr 92
**Selby**, Frederick Peter 1938- WhoFI 92
**Selby**, Henry M 1918- AmMWSc 92
**Selby**, Hubert, Jr. 1928- BenetAL 91, ConNov 91, WhoEnt 92, WrDr 92
**Selby**, Jerome M. 1948- WhoWest 92
**Selby**, Kenneth 1914- Who 92
**Selby**, Myra Consetta 1955- WhoAmL 92
**Selby**, Paul Bruce 1945- AmMWSc 92
**Selby**, Peter Stephen Maurice Who 92
**Selby**, Philip 1948- IntWW 91
**Selby**, Ralph Irving 1930- WhoBlA 92
**Selby**, Ralph Walford 1915- Who 92
**Selby**, Richard Lee 1956- WhoWest 92
**Selby**, Robert Irwin 1943- WhoMW 92
**Selby**, William 1738?-1798 NewAmDM
**Selby**, William Halford 1902- Who 92
**Selby Wright**, Ronald Who 92
**Selby Wright**, Ronald 1908- WhoRel 92
**Selcer**, David Mark 1943- WhoAmL 92
**Selcer**, Kenneth Edward 1952- WhoEnt 92
**Selck**, Hillard Fred, Jr 1926- WhoAmP 91
**Selden**, Bernice DrAPF 91
**Selden**, Dudley Byrd 1911- AmMWSc 92
**Selden**, George 1915- AmMWSc 92
**Selden**, George 1929- IntAu&W 91
**Selden**, Raman 1937-1991 ConAu 134
**Selden**, Robert Wentworth 1936- AmMWSc 92
**Selden**, Stephen James 1944- WhoAmL 92
**Selders**, Craig Stephen 1953- WhoWest 92
**Selders**, John Leigh 1963- WhoEnt 92
**Seldes**, George 1890- BenetAL 91, IntAu&W 91, WrDr 92
**Seldes**, Gilbert 1893-1970 BenetAL 91
**Seldes**, Marian WhoEnt 92
**Seldin**, Donald Wayne 1920- AmMWSc 92, IntWW 91
**Seldin**, Emanuel Judah 1927- AmMWSc 92
**Seldin**, Jonathan Paul 1942- AmMWSc 92
**Seldin**, Mabel Alice 1909- WhoWest 92
**Seldin**, Maury 1931- ConAu 34NR
**Seldon**, Arthur 1916- Who 92
**Seldon Truss**, Leslie 1892- IntAu&W 91
**Seldte**, Franz 1882-1947 BiDExR, EncTR 91 [port]
**Sele**, Baraka 1950- WhoEnt 92
**Selecman**, Charles E. 1928- IntWW 91
**Selegue**, John Paul 1952- AmMWSc 92
**Selene of Egypt** EncAmaz 91
**Seles**, Monica 1973- IntWW 91
**Seles**, Monica 1974?- News 91 [port], -91-3 [port]
**Selesnick**, Rose Goodman 1926- WhoWest 92
**Seleznev**, Gennadiy Nikolaevich 1947- IntWW 91, SovUnBD
**Self**, Colin 1941- TwCPaSc
**Self**, Colin Ernest 1941- IntWW 91
**Self**, Frank Wesley 1949- WhoBlA 92
**Self**, Glendon Danna 1938- AmMWSc 92
**Self**, Hazzle Layfette 1920- AmMWSc 92
**Self**, Hugh Michael 1921- Who 92
**Self**, Jon Adrian 1967- WhoRel 92
**Self**, L. Douglas 1945- WhoRel 92
**Self**, Lawrence 1924- TwCPaSc
**Self**, Margaret Cabell 1902- IntAu&W 91
**Self**, Nancy Grissom 1929- WhoRel 92
**Self**, Peter John Otter 1919- Who 92
**Self**, Sarah Mabel 1924- WhoAmP 91
**Self**, Stephen 1946- AmMWSc 92
**Self**, William LesBEnT 92
**Self**, William 1921- IntMPA 92
**Self**, William Edwin 1921- WhoEnt 92
**Self**, William Lee 1932- WhoRel 92
**Self-Made Man**, A ScFEYrs
**Selfman**, Florence WhoEnt 92
**Selfridge**, Barbara DrAPF 91
**Selfridge**, George Dever 1924- WhoMW 92
**Selfridge**, Harry Gordon 1864-1947 FacFETw
**Selfridge**, Ralph Gordon 1927- AmMWSc 92
**Selfridge**, Richard Jay, Jr. 1949- WhoAmL 92
**Selfridge**, Thomas E 1882-1908 BiInAmS
**Selgas**, Alfred Michael 1943- WhoHisp 92
**Selgas**, James W. 1943- WhoHisp 92
**Selgrade**, James Francis 1946- AmMWSc 92
**Selig**, Alan Dee 1952- WhoRel 92
**Selig**, Allan H. 1934- WhoMW 92
**Selig**, Ernest Theodore 1933- AmMWSc 92
**Selig**, Oury Levy 1924- WhoFI 92
**Selig**, Robert Livingstone 1932- WhoMW 92
**Selig**, Robert William 1910- IntMPA 92
**Selig**, Walter S 1924- AmMWSc 92
**Seliga**, Thomas A 1937- AmMWSc 92
**Seliger**, Howard Harold 1924- AmMWSc 92
**Seliger**, William George 1922- AmMWSc 92
**Seligman**, Barnard 1923- WhoFI 92
**Seligman**, Brad Stuart 1951- WhoAmL 92
**Seligman**, Bruce R. 1943- WhoFI 92
**Seligman**, Delores Felice WhoAmL 92
**Seligman**, George Benham 1927- AmMWSc 92
**Seligman**, Henry 1909- IntWW 91, Who 92
**Seligman**, Jason Scott 1968- WhoWest 92
**Seligman**, Joel 1950- WhoAmL 92
**Seligman**, Madron Who 92
**Seligman**, Peter 1913- Who 92
**Seligman**, Richard Madron 1918- Who 92
**Seligman**, Robert Bernard 1924- AmMWSc 92
**Seligman**, Selig J. d1969 LesBEnT 92
**Seligman**, Stephen Jacob 1931- AmMWSc 92
**Seligman**, Thomas Knowles 1944- WhoWest 92
**Seligmann**, Bruce Edward AmMWSc 92
**Seligson**, David 1916- AmMWSc 92
**Seligson**, Frances Hess 1949- AmMWSc 92
**Seligy**, Verner Leslie 1940- AmMWSc 92
**Selik**, Joel Gary 1958- WhoAmL 92
**Selika**, Marie 1849?-1937 NewAmDM
**Selikoff**, Irving John 1915- AmMWSc 92
**Selim**, Mostafa Ahmed 1935- AmMWSc 92
**Selin**, Ivan 1937- AmMWSc 92
**Seling**, Theodore Victor 1928- AmMWSc 92, WhoWest 92
**Selinger**, Neil Lewis 1953- WhoAmL 92
**Selinger**, Patricia Griffiths 1949- AmMWSc 92, WhoWest 92
**Selinsky**, Barry Steven 1958- AmMWSc 92
**Selinsky**, Deloris DrAPF 91
**Selke**, Charles Richard 1947- WhoFI 92
**Selke**, William A 1922- AmMWSc 92
**Selker**, Milton Leonard 1915- AmMWSc 92
**Selkirk**, Earl of 1906- IntWW 91, Who 92
**Selkirk**, James Kirkwood 1938- AmMWSc 92
**Selkregg**, Lidia Lippi 1920- WhoAmP 91
**Selkurt**, Ewald Erdman 1914- AmMWSc 92
**Sell**, Alan Philip Frederick 1935- WhoRel 92
**Sell**, Clifford Albert 1927- WhoMW 92
**Sell**, George Roger 1937- AmMWSc 92
**Sell**, Jack M. 1954- WhoEnt 92
**Sell**, James Terrance 1943- WhoMW 92
**Sell**, Jeffrey Alan 1952- AmMWSc 92
**Sell**, Jerry Lee 1931- AmMWSc 92
**Sell**, John Edward 1941- AmMWSc 92
**Sell**, Kenneth W 1931- AmMWSc 92
**Sell**, Mary Lou 1943- WhoHisp 92
**Sell**, Nancy Jean 1945- AmMWSc 92
**Sell**, Robert Emerson 1929- WhoWest 92
**Sell**, Sarah H Wood 1913- AmMWSc 92
**Sell**, Stewart 1935- AmMWSc 92
**Sell**, Vernon Harold 1933- WhoMW 92
**Sell**, William Edward 1923- WhoAmL 92
**Sell**, William Harry 1934- WhoFI 92
**Sella**, Edward Geoffrey 1958- WhoFI 92
**Sella**, George John, Jr. 1928- IntWW 91, WhoFI 92
**Sella**, Zvi Elyahu 1946- WhoFI 92
**Sellaeg**, Wenche Frogn 1937- IntWW 91
**Sellar**, George L 1929- WhoAmP 91
**Sellards**, Lyle Durkin 1929- WhoRel 92
**Sellars**, Derek 1935- TwCPaSc
**Sellars**, Harold Gerard 1953- WhoBlA 92
**Sellars**, James Allen 1958- WhoEnt 92, WhoMW 92
**Sellars**, John Emory 1949- WhoMW 92
**Sellars**, John Ernest 1936- Who 92
**Sellars**, John R 1925- AmMWSc 92
**Sellars**, Peter 1957- IntWW 91, WhoEnt 92
**Sellars**, Terry 1934- TwCPaSc
**Sellars**, Tony Dewayne 1954- WhoEnt 92
**Sellas**, James Thomas 1924- AmMWSc 92
**Selle**, James Edward 1931- AmMWSc 92
**Selle**, Wilbur A 1902- AmMWSc 92
**Sellecca**, Connie 1955- IntMPA 92

**Selleck**, David Jesse 1927- *WhoRel 92*
**Selleck**, George Wilbur 1924- *AmMWSc 92*
**Selleck**, Tom 1945- *IntMPA 92, IntWW 91, WhoEnt 92*
**Selleneit**, P Lloyd *WhoAmP 91*
**Seller**, Gregory Erol 1953- *WhoWest 92*
**Sellers**, Alexandra *WrDr 92*
**Sellers**, Alfred Mayer 1924- *AmMWSc 92*
**Sellers**, Alvin Ferner 1917- *AmMWSc 92*
**Sellers**, Alvin Louis 1916- *AmMWSc 92*
**Sellers**, Barry Curtis 1952- *WhoRel 92*
**Sellers**, Basil Alfred 1935- *Who 92*
**Sellers**, Bettie M. *DrAPF 91*
**Sellers**, Cletus Miller, Jr 1944- *AmMWSc 92*
**Sellers**, Coleman 1827-1907 *BiInAmS*
**Sellers**, Dale 1944- *WhoEnt 92*
**Sellers**, David C. 1964- *WhoMW 92*
**Sellers**, Donald Roscoe 1946- *AmMWSc 92*
**Sellers**, Douglas Edwin 1931- *AmMWSc 92*
**Sellers**, Edward Alexander 1916- *AmMWSc 92*
**Sellers**, Edward Moncrieff 1941- *AmMWSc 92*
**Sellers**, Elizabeth Ann 1949- *WhoEnt 92*
**Sellers**, Emory Robinson 1948- *WhoFI 92*
**Sellers**, Ernest E 1925- *AmMWSc 92*
**Sellers**, Francis Bachman 1930- *AmMWSc 92*
**Sellers**, Frank Jamieson 1928- *AmMWSc 92*
**Sellers**, Franklin H. *WhoRel 92*
**Sellers**, Geoffrey Bernard 1947- *Who 92*
**Sellers**, Gregory Jude 1947- *WhoFI 92, WhoMW 92*
**Sellers**, Isaiah 1802?-1864 *BenetAL 91*
**Sellers**, Jesse W. 1961- *WhoRel 92*
**Sellers**, John William 1916- *AmMWSc 92*
**Sellers**, L. Gene 1953- *WhoAmL 92*
**Sellers**, Lawrence Edward, Jr. 1954- *WhoAmL 92*
**Sellers**, Margaret Regular 1935- *WhoMW 92*
**Sellers**, Norman William Malin 1919- *Who 92*
**Sellers**, Pamela Heflin 1953- *WhoAmL 92*
**Sellers**, Peter 1925-1980 *FacFETw*
**Sellers**, Peter Hoadley 1930- *AmMWSc 92*
**Sellers**, Philip Edward 1937- *Who 92*
**Sellers**, Robert Firth 1924- *Who 92*
**Sellers**, Theresa Ann 1954- *WhoBlA 92*
**Sellers**, Thomas F, Jr 1927- *AmMWSc 92*
**Sellers**, Thomas J. 1911- *WhoBlA 92*
**Sellers**, Walter G. 1925- *WhoBlA 92*
**Sellers**, William 1824-1905 *BiInAmS*
**Sellert**, Wolfgang 1935- *IntWW 91*
**Sellew**, Philip Harl 1953- *WhoRel 92*
**Sellgren**, Kristen 1955- *AmMWSc 92*
**Sellick**, John F 1934- *WhoIns 92*
**Sellick**, Phyllis 1911- *IntWW 91*
**Sellie**, John Martin 1927- *WhoAmP 91*
**Sellier**, Robert Hugh 1933- *Who 92*
**Sellin**, Eric 1933- *IntAu&W 91, WrDr 92*
**Sellin**, H A 1905- *AmMWSc 92*
**Sellin**, Ivan Armand 1939- *AmMWSc 92*
**Sellinger**, Otto Zivko 1929- *AmMWSc 92*
**Sellings**, Arthur 1921-1968 *TwCSFW 91*
**Sellins**, Fannie 1870-1919 *HanAmWH*
**Sellman**, Hunton D 1900- *IntAu&W 91, WrDr 92*
**Sellman**, Roger Raymond 1915- *IntAu&W 91, WrDr 92*
**Sellmer**, George Park 1918- *AmMWSc 92*
**Sellmyer**, David Julian 1938- *AmMWSc 92, WhoMW 92*
**Sellner**, Gustav Rudolf *IntWW 91N*
**Sellner**, Kevin Gregory 1949- *AmMWSc 92*
**Sello**, Allen Ralph 1939- *WhoFI 92*
**Sellors**, Patrick John Holmes 1934- *Who 92*
**Sells**, Arnold Abraham 1926- *WhoEnt 92*
**Sells**, Boake Anthony 1937- *WhoFI 92, WhoMW 92*
**Sells**, Bruce Howard 1930- *AmMWSc 92*
**Sells**, David 1918- *Who 92*
**Sells**, Gary Donnell 1932- *AmMWSc 92*
**Sells**, Harold Robert 1917- *WhoFI 92*
**Sells**, Jackson S 1920- *AmMWSc 92*
**Sells**, Jean Thurber 1940- *AmMWSc 92*
**Sells**, Luther Ray 1936- *WhoRel 92*
**Sells**, Mamie Earl *WhoBlA 92*
**Sells**, Robert Lee 1925- *AmMWSc 92*
**Sellschop**, Jacques Pierre Friedrich 1930- *IntWW 91*
**Sellstedt**, John H 1940- *AmMWSc 92*
**Selly**, Joseph P. d1991 *NewYTBS 91*
**Selly**, Susan *Who 92*
**Selman**, Alan L 1941- *AmMWSc 92*
**Selman**, Bruce R *AmMWSc 92*
**Selman**, Cengiz 1961- *WhoFI 92*
**Selman**, Charles Melvin 1937- *AmMWSc 92*
**Selman**, Helen *WhoAmP 91*
**Selman**, Kelly 1942- *AmMWSc 92*
**Selman**, Michael Gary 1946- *WhoFI 92*
**Selman**, Murray 1926- *WhoFI 92*
**Selman**, Robyn *DrAPF 91*
**Selman**, Roland Wooten, III 1941- *WhoAmL 92*
**Selmanoff**, Michael Kidd 1949- *AmMWSc 92*
**Selmark**, George *IntAu&W 91X*
**Selmer**, Knut S. 1924- *IntWW 91*
**Selnick**, Thomas Conrad 1957- *WhoMW 92, WhoRel 92*
**Selous**, Percy S d1900 *BiInAmS*
**Selove**, Walter 1921- *AmMWSc 92*
**Selover**, David Duden 1948- *WhoFI 92*
**Selover**, James Carroll 1929- *AmMWSc 92*
**Selover**, Theodore Britton, Jr 1931- *AmMWSc 92, WhoMW 92*
**Selsdon**, Baron 1937- *Who 92*
**Selser**, Gregorio d1991 *NewYTBS 91*
**Selsky**, Melvyn Ira 1933- *AmMWSc 92*
**Selsor**, Jonathan 1958- *WhoAmP 91*
**Selstad**, Ronald Wayne 1944- *WhoWest 92*
**Selter**, Gerald A 1940- *AmMWSc 92*
**Seltin**, Richard James 1927- *AmMWSc 92*
**Seltmann**, Heinz 1924- *AmMWSc 92*
**Seltser**, Raymond 1923- *AmMWSc 92*
**Seltz**, Herbert Arnold 1927- *WhoEnt 92*
**Seltzberg**, Berton 1942- *WhoFI 92*
**Seltzer**, Benjamin 1945- *AmMWSc 92*
**Seltzer**, Brian Paul 1955- *WhoAmL 92*
**Seltzer**, Carl Coleman 1908- *AmMWSc 92*
**Seltzer**, Charles Alden 1875-1942 *TwCWW 91*
**Seltzer**, David 1920?- *ConTFT 9*
**Seltzer**, David 1940- *IntMPA 92*
**Seltzer**, Edward 1911- *AmMWSc 92*
**Seltzer**, Frank, III 1950- *WhoEnt 92*
**Seltzer**, H Jack 1922- *WhoAmP 91*
**Seltzer**, James Edward 1936- *AmMWSc 92*
**Seltzer**, Jeffrey Lloyd 1956- *WhoAmL 92, WhoFI 92*
**Seltzer**, Jo Louise 1942- *AmMWSc 92*
**Seltzer**, Joanne *DrAPF 91*
**Seltzer**, Joanne 1929- *IntAu&W 91*
**Seltzer**, Leo 1910- *WhoEnt 92*
**Seltzer**, Leon F 1940- *IntAu&W 91, WrDr 92*
**Seltzer**, Martin S 1937- *AmMWSc 92*
**Seltzer**, Raymond 1935- *AmMWSc 92*
**Seltzer**, Richard *DrAPF 91*
**Seltzer**, Richard C. 1943- *WhoAmL 92*
**Seltzer**, Roger 1937- *IntMPA 92*
**Seltzer**, Samuel 1914- *AmMWSc 92*
**Seltzer**, Stanley 1925- *AmMWSc 92*
**Seltzer**, Stanley 1930- *AmMWSc 92*
**Seltzer**, Walter 1914- *IntMPA 92*
**Selund**, Robert B 1907- *AmMWSc 92*
**Selvadurai**, A P S 1942- *AmMWSc 92*
**Selvadurai**, P. *WhoRel 92*
**Selvage**, Anthony Keith 1939- *WhoEnt 92*
**Selvage**, Paul Anthony 1957- *WhoMW 92*
**Selvakumar**, Chettypalayam Ramanathan 1950- *AmMWSc 92*
**Selvaratnam**, Viswanathan 1934- *IntWW 91*
**Selvera**, Norma Brito 1947- *WhoHisp 92*
**Selverston**, Allen Israel 1936- *AmMWSc 92*
**Selverstone**, Jane Elizabeth 1956- *AmMWSc 92*
**Selvey**, Roy Martin 1914- *WhoMW 92*
**Selvidge**, Harner 1910- *AmMWSc 92*
**Selvidge**, Thomas Ray 1957- *WhoEnt 92*
**Selvin**, Joel 1950- *ConAu 133*
**Selvin**, Nancy 1943- *WhoWest 92*
**Sel'vinsky**, Il'ya L'vovich 1899-1968 *SovUnBD*
**Selvon**, Sam 1923- *ConNov 91, LiExTwC, RfGEnL 91*
**Selvon**, Samuel 1923- *BenetAL 91, WrDr 92*
**Selvon**, Samuel Dickson 1923- *Who 92*
**Selvy**, Barbara 1938- *WhoEnt 92*
**Selway**, John 1938- *TwCPaSc*
**Selwitz**, Charles Myron 1927- *AmMWSc 92*
**Selwitz**, Gary Lewis 1940- *WhoEnt 92*
**Selwood**, Alexis Fuerbringer 1943- *WhoWest 92*
**Selwood**, Cordelia 1920- *TwCPaSc*
**Selwood**, David Henry Deering 1934- *Who 92*
**Selwood**, Pierce Taylor 1939- *WhoAmL 92, WhoFI 92*
**Selwyn**, Francis 1935- *WrDr 92*
**Selwyn**, John Sidney Augustus 1908- *Who 92*
**Selwyn**, Philip Alan 1945- *AmMWSc 92*
**Selya**, Bruce Marshall 1934- *WhoAmL 92, WhoAmP 91*
**Selya**, Roger Mark 1942- *WhoFI 92*
**Selye**, Hans 1907-1982 *FacFETw*
**Selz**, Bernard 1940- *WhoFI 92*
**Selz**, Peter 1919- *WrDr 92*
**Selz**, Peter Howard 1919- *WhoWest 92*
**Selz**, Thalia *DrAPF 91*
**Selzer**, Arthur 1911- *AmMWSc 92*
**Selzer**, David Owen 1951- *WhoMW 92, WhoRel 92*
**Selzer**, Jack Raymond 1943- *WhoAmL 92*
**Selzer**, Melvin Lawrence 1925- *AmMWSc 92*
**Selznick**, David O 1902-1965 *FacFETw*
**Selznick**, Irene 1907-1990 *AnObit 1990*
**Selznick**, Stephen Andrew 1941- *WhoFI 92*
**Sem**, Larry Elmer 1949- *WhoEnt 92*
**Semaan**, Khalil I. H. 1920- *WrDr 92*
**Seman**, Dennis Lloyd 1954- *WhoMW 92*
**Seman**, Gabriel 1925- *AmMWSc 92*
**Seman**, George William 1940- *AmMWSc 92*
**Semancik**, Joseph Francis 1929- *WhoRel 92*
**Semancik**, Joseph Stephen 1938- *AmMWSc 92*
**Semanik**, Anthony James 1942- *WhoMW 92*
**Semans**, Truman Thomas 1926- *WhoFI 92*
**Semansky**, Chris *DrAPF 91*
**Semark**, Philip Norman 1945- *WhoEnt 92*
**Semashko**, Nikolay Aleksandrovich 1874-1949 *SovUnBD*
**Semb**, Sharon Lynn 1957- *WhoFI 92*
**Semba**, Kazue 1949- *AmMWSc 92*
**Sembene**, Ousmane 1923- *IntDcF 2-2 [port]*
**Sembler**, Charles W, II 1965- *WhoAmP 91*
**Sembler**, Melvin F 1930- *WhoAmP 91*
**Sembrich**, Marcella 1858-1935 *NewAmDM*
**Semchyshyn**, Stefan 1940- *ConAu 134*
**Semedo**, Inacio, Jr. 1944- *IntWW 91*
**Semega-Janneh**, Bocar Ousman 1910- *IntWW 91, Who 92*
**Semegen**, Patrick William 1946- *WhoAmL 92*
**Semel**, Martin Ira 1934- *WhoAmL 92*
**Semel**, Maurie 1923- *AmMWSc 92*
**Semel**, Sylvia *DrAPF 91*
**Semel**, Terry 1943- *IntMPA 92, WhoWest 92*
**Semeluk**, George Peter 1924- *AmMWSc 92*
**Semenchuk**, Anatole K. *WhoEnt 92*
**Semeniuk**, Fred Theodor 1915- *AmMWSc 92*
**Semenov** *IntWW 91*
**Semenov**, Julian *ConAu 35NR*
**Semenov**, Nikolai Nikolaevich 1896-1986 *WhoNob 90*
**Semenov**, Nikolay Nikolaevich 1896- *SovUnBD*
**Semenov**, Yulian *ConAu 35NR*
**Semenova**, Galina Vladimirovna 1937- *SovUnBD A*
**Semenova**, Lyudmila Nikolaevna 1899- *SovUnBD*
**Semenovich**, Joseph *DrAPF 91*
**Semensi**, Joseph John 1923- *WhoAmP 91*
**Semento**, Lawrence James 1952- *WhoAmL 92*
**Semenuk**, Nick Sarden 1937- *AmMWSc 92*
**Semenyaka**, Lyudmila Ivanova 1952- *IntWW 91*
**Semerjian**, Hratch G 1943- *AmMWSc 92*
**Semichastny**, Vladimir Yefimovich 1924- *IntWW 91*
**Semichastnyy**, Vladimir Yefimovich 1924- *SovUnBD*
**Seminerio**, Anthony S 1935- *WhoAmP 91*
**Seminetta**, Joseph Thomas 1964- *WhoFI 92*
**Semiramis** *EncAmaz 91*
**Semizorova**, Nina Lvovna 1956- *IntWW 91*
**Semken**, Holmes Alford, Jr 1935- *AmMWSc 92*
**Semken**, John Douglas 1921- *Who 92*
**Semkow**, Jerzy 1928- *IntWW 91, NewAmDM*
**Semler**, Charles Edward 1940- *AmMWSc 92*
**Semler**, Dean *WhoEnt 92*
**Semler**, Dean Russell 1929- *WhoFI 92*
**Semler**, Jerry D. 1937- *WhoFI 92, WhoIns 92, WhoMW 92*
**Semler**, Johann Salomo 1725-1791 *BlkwCEP*
**Semlyen**, Adam 1923- *AmMWSc 92*
**Semmel**, Paul W 1939- *WhoAmP 91*
**Semmelhack**, Martin F 1941- *AmMWSc 92*
**Semmence**, Adrian Murdoch 1926- *Who 92*
**Semmence**, John 1930- *TwCPaSc*
**Semmer**, Robert Clement 1961- *WhoWest 92*
**Semmes**, Raphael 1809-1877 *BenetAL 91*
**Semmes**, Sally Peterson *WhoEnt 92*
**Semmes**, Stephen William 1962- *AmMWSc 92*
**Semmler**, Clement William 1914- *IntAu&W 91, WrDr 92*
**Semmler**, Willi 1942- *WhoFI 92*
**Semmlow**, John Leonard 1942- *AmMWSc 92*
**Semon**, Mark David 1950- *AmMWSc 92*
**Semon**, Roger 1949- *WhoEnt 92*
**Semon**, Waldo Lonsbury 1898- *AmMWSc 92*
**Semon**, Warren Lloyd 1921- *AmMWSc 92*
**Semones**, G. David 1961- *WhoRel 92*
**Semonian**, Robert Alexander 1939- *WhoAmP 91*
**Semonin**, Richard Gerard 1930- *AmMWSc 92, WhoMW 92*
**Semore**, Mary Margie 1920- *WhoFI 92*
**Semos**, Chris Victor 1936- *WhoAmP 91*
**Sempe**, Abel 1912- *IntWW 91*
**Semper**, Colin 1938- *Who 92*
**Sempill** *Who 92*
**Sempill**, Lady 1920- *Who 92*
**Sempill**, Master of 1949- *Who 92*
**Semple**, Andrew Best 1912- *Who 92*
**Semple**, Andrew Greenlees 1934- *Who 92*
**Semple**, Cecil Snowdon 1917- *WhoFI 92*
**Semple**, Goldie 1952- *WhoEnt 92*
**Semple**, Ian Chalmers 1928- *WhoRel 92*
**Semple**, James William 1943- *WhoAmL 92*
**Semple**, John Laughlin 1940- *Who 92*
**Semple**, Lloyd Ashby 1939- *WhoAmL 92*
**Semple**, Lorenzo, Jr. *IntMPA 92*
**Semple**, Pat *TwCPaSc*
**Semple**, Stephen John Greenhill 1926- *Who 92*
**Semple**, T Darrington, Jr 1926- *WhoIns 92*
**Semple**, William David Crowe 1933- *Who 92*
**Semprini** 1908-1990 *AnObit 1990*
**Sempronia** *EncAmaz 91*
**Semprun**, Jorge *IntWW 91*
**Semprun**, Jorge 1920?- *LiExTwC*
**Semrau**, Konrad 1919- *AmMWSc 92*
**Semrod**, T. Joseph 1936- *WhoFI 92*
**Semtner**, Albert Julius, Jr 1941- *AmMWSc 92*
**Semtner**, Paul Joseph 1945- *AmMWSc 92*
**Semura**, Jack Sadatoshi 1941- *AmMWSc 92*
**Semyakina**, Ludmila Ivanovna 1952- *IntWW 91*
**Semyonov**, Julian *ConAu 35NR*
**Semyonov**, Julian 1932- *IntWW 91*
**Semyonov**, Viktor Vladimirovich 1937- *IntWW 91*
**Semyonov**, Vladilen Grigorevich 1932- *IntWW 91*
**Semyonov**, Vladimir Semyonovich 1911- *IntWW 91*
**Semyonov**, Yulian *ConAu 35NR*
**Semyonova**, Galina Vladimirovna 1937- *IntWW 91*
**Sen**, Amar Kumar 1927- *AmMWSc 92*
**Sen**, Amartya K. 1933- *WrDr 92*
**Sen**, Amartya Kumar 1933- *IntWW 91, Who 92*
**Sen**, Amiya K 1930- *AmMWSc 92*
**Sen**, Ashish Kumar 1942- *WhoMW 92*
**Sen**, Bachoo *IntMPA 92*
**Sen**, Buddhadev 1923- *AmMWSc 92*
**Sen**, Colleen Taylor 1944- *WhoMW 92*
**Sen**, Dipak Kumar 1936- *AmMWSc 92*
**Sen**, Emma *Who 92*
**Sen**, Ganes C 1945- *AmMWSc 92*
**Sen**, Mihir 1947- *AmMWSc 92*
**Sen**, Mrinal 1923- *IntDcF 2-2, IntWW 91*
**Sen**, Pabitra Narayan 1944- *AmMWSc 92*
**Sen**, Pranab Kumar 1937- *AmMWSc 92*
**Sen**, Samar 1914- *IntWW 91*
**Sen**, Samar R. 1916- *IntWW 91*
**Sen**, Satyendra Nath 1909- *IntWW 91, Who 92*
**Sen**, Shri Binay Ranjan 1898- *Who 92*
**Sen**, Tapas K 1933- *AmMWSc 92*
**Sen**, Ujjal 1957- *AmMWSc 92*
**Sen Gupta**, Barun Kumar 1931- *AmMWSc 92*
**Sen Gupta**, Ratan 1947- *WhoWest 92*
**Sena**, Estevan S. 1945- *WhoHisp 92*
**Sena**, Glenda Mary Ann 1964- *WhoHisp 92*
**Sena**, Michael Timothy 1956- *WhoEnt 92*
**Senagore**, Anthony J 1958- *AmMWSc 92*
**Senanayake**, Maithripala 1916 *IntWW 91*
**Senancour**, Etienne Pivert de 1770-1846 *GuFrLit 1*
**Senapati**, Nagabhusan 1945- *WhoMW 92*
**Senard**, Jacques 1919- *IntWW 91*
**Senarens**, Luis P 1865-1939 *TwCSFW 91*
**Senarens**, Luis Philip 1863-1939 *BenetAL 91*
**Senatore**, Ford Fortunato 1953- *AmMWSc 92*
**Senay**, Leo Charles, Jr 1927- *AmMWSc 92*
**Senbet**, Lemma W. 1946- *WhoBlA 92*
**Sencak**, John Lee 1957- *WhoFI 92*
**Sencenbaugh**, Joseph Neil 1951- *WhoEnt 92*
**Sencer**, David Judson 1924- *AmMWSc 92*
**Senciall**, Ian Robert 1938- *AmMWSc 92*
**Sencindiver**, John Coe 1948- *AmMWSc 92*
**Senda**, Mototaka 1954- *AmMWSc 92*
**Sendaba**, S. M. *WhoBlA 92*

**Sendak,** Maurice 1928- *BenetAL 91, FacFETw, WrDr 92*
**Sendak,** Maurice Bernard 1928- *IntAu&W 91, IntWW 91, Who 92, WhoEnt 92*
**Sendak,** Theodore Lorraine 1918- *WhoAmP 91*
**Sendall,** Bernard Charles 1913- *Who 92*
**Sendars,** Peggy 1946- *WhoEnt 92*
**Sendek,** Leonard John 1950- *WhoMW 92*
**Sendek,** Martin James 1960- *WhoAmL 92*
**Sendelbach,** Anton G 1924- *AmMWSc 92*
**Sender,** Ramon 1901-1982 *LiExTwC*
**Sender,** Stuart D. 1955- *WhoAmL 92*
**Senderens,** Alain 1939- *IntWW 91*
**Senders,** John W 1920- *AmMWSc 92*
**Sendic,** Raul 1924-1989 *FacFETw*
**Sendlein,** Lyle V A 1933- *AmMWSc 92*
**Sendor,** Benjamin Burton 1953- *WhoAmL 92*
**Sendov,** Blagovest Hristov 1932- *IntWW 91*
**Sendrey,** Albert 1921- *IntMPA 92*
**Sendroy,** Julius, Jr 1900- *AmMWSc 92*
**Senear,** Allen Eugene 1919- *AmMWSc 92*
**Seneca The Younger** 4?BC-65AD *EncEarC*
**Seneca,** Arlena E. 1919- *WhoBlA 92*
**Seneca,** Harry 1909- *AmMWSc 92*
**Seneca,** Joe *IntMPA 92*
**Senecal,** Gerard 1929- *AmMWSc 92*
**Senecal,** Vance E 1921- *AmMWSc 92*
**Senechal,** Alice R. 1955- *WhoAmL 92*
**Senechal,** Lester John 1934- *AmMWSc 92*
**Senechal,** Marjorie Lee 1939- *AmMWSc 92*
**Senechalle,** David Albert 1940- *AmMWSc 92*
**Senegal,** Charles 1930- *WhoBlA 92*
**Senegal,** Phyllis J. 1930- *WhoBlA 92*
**Seneker,** Stanley A. *WhoFI 92, WhoMW 92*
**Senensieb,** Norbert Louis 1930- *WhoWest 92*
**Sener,** Erdogan Mehmet 1946- *WhoMW 92*
**Sener,** Robert N H 1933- *WhoIns 92*
**Senese,** Donald Joseph 1942- *WhoAmP 91*
**Senese,** Thomas Joseph 1932- *WhoFI 92*
**Senesh,** Hannah 1921-1944 *EncAmaz 91*
**Senesino** 1680?-1755? *NewAmDM*
**Senfl,** Ludwig 1486?-1543 *NewAmDM*
**Senft,** Alfred Walter 1924- *AmMWSc 92*
**Senft,** James Ronald *WhoMW 92*
**Senft,** John Franklin 1933- *AmMWSc 92, WhoMW 92*
**Senft,** Joseph Philip 1936- *AmMWSc 92*
**Senft,** Mason George 1942- *WhoEnt 92*
**Senft,** Nadin *TwCPaSc*
**Senftle,** Frank Edward 1921- *AmMWSc 92*
**Senftleber,** Fred Carl 1948- *AmMWSc 92*
**Seng,** Ann Frances 1936- *WhoMW 92*
**Seng,** Michael Paul 1942- *WhoAmL 92*
**Senga,** Robert Maundu 1947- *WhoWest 92*
**Sengar,** Dharmendra Pal Singh 1941- *AmMWSc 92*
**Sengbusch,** Howard George 1917- *AmMWSc 92*
**Senge,** George H 1937- *AmMWSc 92*
**Sengel,** Randal Alan 1948- *AmMWSc 92*
**Sengelaub,** Mary Maurita 1918- *WhoMW 92, WhoRel 92*
**Senger,** Clyde Merle 1929- *AmMWSc 92*
**Sengers,** Jan V 1931- *AmMWSc 92*
**Sengers,** Johanna M H Levelt 1929- *AmMWSc 92*
**Senghaas,** Dieter 1940- *IntWW 91*
**Senghor,** Leopold Sedar 1906- *BlkLC [port], FacFETw, GuFrLit 1, IntAu&W 91, IntWW 91, LiExTwC*
**Sengpiehl,** Paul Marvin 1937- *WhoMW 92*
**Sengstacke,** John H. 1912- *WhoBlA 92*
**Sengstacke,** John Herman Henry 1912- *WhoFI 92, WhoMW 92*
**Sengstacke,** Whittier Alexander, Sr. 1916- *WhoBlA 92*
**Sengupta,** Arjun K. 1937- *IntWW 91*
**Sengupta,** Bhaskar 1944- *AmMWSc 92*
**Sengupta,** Dipak L 1931- *AmMWSc 92*
**Sengupta,** Gautam 1945- *AmMWSc 92*
**Sengupta,** Jati Kumar 1934- *WhoFI 92*
**Sengupta,** Sailes Kumar 1935- *AmMWSc 92*
**Sengupta,** Sumedha 1943- *AmMWSc 92*
**Senhauser,** Donald Albert 1927- *AmMWSc 92*
**Senich,** Donald 1929- *AmMWSc 92*
**Senieur,** Jude Richard 1918- *WhoRel 92*
**Senior,** Alan Gordon 1928- *Who 92*
**Senior,** Boris 1923- *AmMWSc 92*
**Senior,** Bryan 1935- *TwCPaSc*
**Senior,** Donald Paul 1940- *WhoRel 92*
**Senior,** Edward 1902- *Who 92*
**Senior,** Gordon *Who 92*
**Senior,** John Brian 1936- *AmMWSc 92*
**Senior,** John Robert 1927- *AmMWSc 92*
**Senior,** Michael 1940- *WrDr 92*
**Senior,** Olive Edith 1934- *Who 92*
**Senior,** Richard John Lane 1940- *WhoFI 92*
**Senior,** Thomas Bryan Alexander 1928- *AmMWSc 92*
**Senitzer,** David 1944- *AmMWSc 92*
**Senitzky,** Benjamin 1926- *AmMWSc 92*
**Senitzky,** Israel Ralph 1920- *AmMWSc 92*
**Senkbeil,** Harold Leigh 1945- *WhoRel 92*
**Senkler,** George Henry, Jr 1945- *AmMWSc 92*
**Senkowski,** Bernard Zigmund 1927- *AmMWSc 92*
**Senkus,** Murray 1914- *AmMWSc 92*
**Senn,** Alfred Erich 1932- *ConAu 134*
**Senn,** Frank Colvin 1943- *WhoRel 92*
**Senn,** Milton J E 1902- *AmMWSc 92*
**Senn,** Nicholas 1844-1908 *BiInAmS*
**Senn,** Peter Richard 1923- *WhoFI 92*
**Senn,** Robert Franklin 1945- *WhoFI 92*
**Senn,** Taze Leonard 1917- *AmMWSc 92*
**Senna,** Ayrton 1960- *IntWW 91, News 91 [port]*
**Senne,** Joseph Harold, Jr 1919- *AmMWSc 92*
**Senne,** William Ralph 1946- *WhoAmP 91*
**Sennello,** Lawrence Thomas 1937- *AmMWSc 92*
**Senner,** Robert William 1912- *WhoMW 92*
**Sennet,** Charles Joseph 1952- *WhoEnt 92*
**Sennett,** George Burritt 1840-1900 *BiInAmS*
**Sennett,** Henry Herbert, Jr. 1945- *WhoEnt 92*
**Sennett,** John *DrAPF 91*
**Sennett,** Mack 1880-1960 *FacFETw, IntDcF 2-2 [port]*
**Sennett,** Mack 1884-1960 *BenetAL 91*
**Sennett,** Richard 1943- *IntAu&W 91, WrDr 92*
**Sennett,** William C. 1930- *WhoAmL 92*
**Senning,** Ake 1915- *IntWW 91*
**Sennott,** John Stephen 1946- *WhoMW 92*
**Senoff,** Caesar V 1939- *AmMWSc 92*
**Senogles,** Susan Elizabeth *AmMWSc 92*
**Senour,** Maria Nieto 1943- *WhoHisp 92*
**Senoussi,** Badreddine 1933- *Who 92*
**Senozan,** Nail Mehmet 1936- *AmMWSc 92*
**Senquiz,** William 1957-1990 *WhoHisp 92N*
**Sensabaugh,** Mary Elizabeth 1939- *WhoFI 92*
**Sensel,** Charles Werner 1932- *WhoRel 92*
**Senseman,** David Michael 1948- *AmMWSc 92*
**Sensenbrenner,** F. James, Jr. 1943- *AlmAP 92 [port]*
**Sensenbrenner,** F Joseph, Jr 1948- *WhoAmP 91*
**Sensenbrenner,** Frank James, Jr 1943- *WhoAmP 91, WhoFI 92, WhoMW 92*
**Sensenbrenner,** Kenneth Clark 1948- *WhoMW 92*
**Senseney,** Edgar Moore 1856?-1916 *BiInAmS*
**Senseney,** James Denny 1947- *WhoEnt 92*
**Sensenich,** Ila Jeanne 1939- *WhoAmL 92*
**Senseny,** Paul Edward 1950- *AmMWSc 92*
**Sensi** 1907- *Who 92*
**Sensi,** Giuseppe Maria 1907- *IntWW 91*
**Sensi,** Guiseppe Maria 1907- *WhoRel 92*
**Sensiper,** S 1919- *AmMWSc 92*
**Sentelle,** David B 1943- *WhoAmP 91*
**Sentelle,** David Bryan 1943- *WhoAmL 92*
**Sentenn,** Walter Louis, Jr. 1943- *WhoAmL 92*
**Senteno,** Alfonso 1941- *WhoAmP 91*
**Senter,** Lyonel Thomas, Jr. 1933- *WhoAmL 92*
**Senter,** Meredith S., Jr. 1953- *WhoAmL 92, WhoEnt 92*
**Senter,** Merilyn P 1935- *WhoAmP 91*
**Senter,** Roger Campbell 1932- *WhoFI 92*
**Senter,** Thomas Paul 1946- *WhoWest 92*
**Senter,** William Joseph 1921- *WhoFI 92*
**Senter,** William Robert, III 1935- *WhoRel 92*
**Senterfit,** Laurence Benfred 1929- *AmMWSc 92*
**Senti,** Frederic R 1913- *AmMWSc 92*
**Sentilles,** F Dennis, Jr 1941- *AmMWSc 92*
**Sentman,** Davis Daniel 1945- *AmMWSc 92*
**Sentman,** Lee H, III 1937- *AmMWSc 92*
**Senton,** Robert Edmond 1962- *WhoAmL 92*
**Senturia,** Ben Harlan 1910- *AmMWSc 92*
**Senturia,** Jerome B 1938- *AmMWSc 92*
**Senturia,** Stephen David 1940- *AmMWSc 92*
**Senturia,** Todd Alexander 1965- *WhoFI 92*
**Senty,** Carol Lynne 1935- *WhoAmL 92*
**Sentz,** James Curtis 1927- *AmMWSc 92*
**Senum,** Gunnar Ivar 1948- *AmMWSc 92*
**Senungetuk,** Vivian Ruth 1948- *WhoWest 92*
**Senus,** Walter Joseph 1946- *AmMWSc 92*
**Senyk,** George 1926- *AmMWSc 92*
**Senzaki,** Nyogen 1876-1958 *RelLAm 91*
**Senzel,** Alan Joseph 1945- *AmMWSc 92*
**Senzel,** Martin Lee 1944- *WhoAmL 92*
**Seo,** Eddie Tatsu 1935- *AmMWSc 92*
**Seo,** Stanley Toshio 1928- *AmMWSc 92*
**Seoane,** Robert 1958- *WhoEnt 92*
**Seon,** Ben Kuk 1936- *AmMWSc 92*
**Seon,** Gerald Hamilton 1899-1989 *WhoBlA 92N*
**Seow,** Yit Kin 1955- *IntWW 91*
**Sepahpur,** Hayedeh Christina 1958- *WhoFI 92*
**Sepamla,** Sipho 1932- *ConPo 91, WrDr 92*
**Sepeda,** Esther S. 1938- *WhoHisp 92*
**Sepenuk,** Norman 1933- *WhoAmL 92*
**Seperich,** George Joseph 1944- *AmMWSc 92*
**Sepheriades,** Georgios *ConAu 36NR*
**Sepinwall,** Jerry 1940- *AmMWSc 92*
**Sepkoski,** J J, Jr 1948- *AmMWSc 92*
**Sepkoski,** Joseph John 1921- *AmMWSc 92*
**Sepmeyer,** L W 1910- *AmMWSc 92*
**Seppala,** Katherine Seaman 1919- *WhoMW 92*
**Seppala,** Lynn G 1946- *AmMWSc 92*
**Seppala,** Richard Rafael 1905- *IntWW 91*
**Seppala-Holtzman,** David N 1950- *AmMWSc 92*
**Seppi,** Edward Joseph 1930- *AmMWSc 92, WhoWest 92*
**Sepsy,** Charles Frank 1924- *AmMWSc 92*
**Sept,** Clinton LeRoy 1921- *WhoWest 92*
**Septar,** Yacub Mehmet *WhoRel 92*
**Septimius Severus** 145?-211 *EncEarC*
**Sepucha,** Robert Charles 1943- *AmMWSc 92*
**Sepulveda,** Bernardo 1941- *IntWW 91, Who 92*
**Sepulveda,** Carmen M. 1949- *WhoHisp 92*
**Sepulveda,** John Ulises 1954- *WhoHisp 92*
**Sepulveda,** Miguel A. 1955- *WhoHisp 92*
**Sepulveda,** Roberto F. 1947- *WhoHisp 92*
**Sepulveda,** Salvador Antonio 1936- *WhoHisp 92*
**Sepulveda,** Sharon *WhoHisp 92*
**Sepulveda-Bailey,** Jamie Alice 1945- *WhoHisp 92*
**Sepulveda Ruiz-Velasco,** Jose Trinidad 1921- *WhoRel 92*
**Sequeira,** Joel August Louis 1947- *AmMWSc 92*
**Sequeira,** John Edward 1940- *WhoRel 92*
**Sequeira,** John Henry 1949- *WhoFI 92*
**Sequeira,** Luis 1927- *AmMWSc 92, IntWW 91*
**Sequens,** Jiri 1922- *IntWW 91*
**Sequin,** Carlo Heinrich 1941- *AmMWSc 92*
**Sequoya** 1770?-1843 *BenetAL 91*
**Ser,** Randy Jay 1954- *WhoEnt 92*
**Sera,** Enrique Jose 1950- *WhoHisp 92*
**Sera,** Natalie Alderman 1948- *WhoWest 92*
**Serad,** George A 1939- *AmMWSc 92*
**Serafetinides,** Eustace A 1930- *AmMWSc 92*
**Serafimovich,** Aleksandr Serafimovich 1863-1949 *SovUnBD*
**Serafin,** David *Who 92, WrDr 92*
**Serafin,** Frank G 1935- *AmMWSc 92*
**Serafin,** Robert Joseph 1936- *AmMWSc 92*
**Serafin,** Russell Bauer 1948- *WhoAmL 92*
**Serafin,** Tullio 1878-1968 *NewAmDM*
**Serafini,** Angela 1913- *AmMWSc 92*
**Serafini,** Dom 1949- *WhoEnt 92*
**Serafini,** Frank Anthony 1945- *WhoAmP 91*
**Serafini,** Victor Renato 1934- *WhoWest 92*
**Serafy,** D Keith 1947- *AmMWSc 92*
**Seraile,** Janette 1945- *WhoBlA 92*
**Seralnick,** Mark 1954- *WhoMW 92*
**Seraphim** 1913- *IntWW 91*
**Seraphim,** Peter Heinz 1902- *EncTR 91*
**Seraphin,** Bernhard Otto 1923- *AmMWSc 92*
**Seraphin,** Oliver 1943- *IntWW 91*
**Serapion of Thmuis** d362? *EncEarC*
**Serat,** William Felkner 1929- *AmMWSc 92*
**Serban,** Daniel Edward 1957- *WhoAmL 92*
**Serbaroli,** Francis J. 1952- *WhoAmL 92*
**Serbein,** Oscar Nicholas 1919- *WhoWest 92*
**Serber,** Robert 1909- *AmMWSc 92*
**Serbia,** George William 1928- *AmMWSc 92*
**Serbin,** Ivan Dmitrievich 1910-1981 *SovUnBD*
**Serbin,** Lisa Alexandra 1946- *AmMWSc 92*
**Serbin,** Richard Martin 1947- *WhoAmL 92*
**Serby,** John Edward 1902- *Who 92*
**Sercarz,** Eli 1934- *AmMWSc 92*
**Serchuk,** Peter *DrAPF 91*
**Serdarevich,** Bogdan 1921- *AmMWSc 92*
**Serdengecti,** Sedat 1927- *AmMWSc 92*
**Serduke,** Franklin James David 1942- *AmMWSc 92*
**Sere,** Jouko Emil Markus 1927- *IntWW 91*
**Serebrier,** Jose 1938- *IntWW 91, NewAmDM, WhoEnt 92*
**Serebrovsky,** Aleksandr Pavlovich 1884-1938 *SovUnBD*
**Serebrovsky,** Aleksandr Sergeevich 1892-1948 *SovUnBD*
**Serebryakov,** Leonid Petrovich 1890-1937 *SovUnBD*
**Serebryanyi,** Iosif Aleksandrovich 1907-1979 *SovUnBD*
**Sereda,** Robert Emanuel, II 1954- *WhoWest 92*
**Serels,** M. Mitchell 1948- *WhoRel 92*
**Serene,** David Calvin 1953- *WhoAmL 92*
**Serene,** Jan Walden 1952- *WhoAmL 92*
**Serene,** Joseph William 1947- *AmMWSc 92*
**Seres,** William 1930- *WhoAmP 91*
**Serfas,** Richard Thomas 1952- *WhoWest 92*
**Serfling,** Robert Joseph 1939- *AmMWSc 92*
**Serfozo,** Richard Frank 1939- *AmMWSc 92*
**Serge,** Victor 1890-1947 *LiExTwC*
**Sergeant,** Carra Susan 1953- *WhoBlA 92*
**Sergeant,** David Ernest 1927- *AmMWSc 92*
**Sergeant,** Emma 1959- *TwCPaSc*
**Sergeant,** Hildegarde 1941- *WhoRel 92*
**Sergeant,** John 1937- *TwCPaSc*
**Sergeant,** Patrick 1924- *Who 92*
**Sergeev,** Konstantin Mikhaylovich 1910- *SovUnBD*
**Sergeev,** Sergey Nikolaevich 1875-1958 *SovUnBD*
**Sergeev-Tsensky,** Sergey Nikolaevich 1875-1958 *SovUnBD*
**Sergent,** Bernard 1946- *ConAu 133*
**Sergent,** Ernest, Jr. 1943- *WhoBlA 92*
**Sergent,** Robert Lawrence 1930- *WhoAmP 91*
**Sergent,** Stanley H. 1941- *WhoAmL 92*
**Sergey,** Patriarch 1867-1944 *SovUnBD*
**Sergeyev,** Yevgeniy Mikhailovich 1914- *IntWW 91*
**Sergio,** Lisa 1905-1989 *FacFETw*
**Sergovich,** Frederick Raymond 1933- *AmMWSc 92*
**Serianni,** Anthony Stephan 1953- *AmMWSc 92*
**Series,** Emile *Who 92*
**Series,** George William 1920- *Who 92*
**Series,** Joseph Michel Emile 1918- *Who 92*
**Serif,** George Samuel 1928- *AmMWSc 92*
**Seriff,** Aaron Jay 1924- *AmMWSc 92*
**Seriki,** Olusola Oluyemisi 1958- *WhoBlA 92*
**Serin,** Judith *DrAPF 91*
**Serio,** Dianna Lee 1961- *WhoWest 92*
**Serio,** Gregory Vincent 1961- *WhoAmL 92*
**Serio,** Kathryn Beth 1957- *WhoEnt 92*
**Serjeant,** Graham Roger 1938- *IntWW 91, Who 92*
**Serjeant,** Richard *WrDr 92*
**Serjeant,** Robert Bertram 1915- *IntWW 91, Who 92*
**Serjeant,** William Ronald 1921- *Who 92*
**Serkes,** Kenneth Dean 1926- *AmMWSc 92*
**Serkey,** Stephen J 1945- *WhoIns 92*
**Serkin,** Peter 1947- *NewAmDM, WhoEnt 92*
**Serkin,** Peter Adolf 1947- *IntWW 91*
**Serkin,** Rudolf d1991 *Who 92N*
**Serkin,** Rudolf 1903-1991 *CurBio 91N, FacFETw, IntWW 91, -91N, NewAmDM, NewYTBS 91 [port], News 92-1*
**Serle,** Alan Geoffrey 1922- *IntAu&W 91*
**Serle,** Geoffrey 1922- *IntWW 91, WrDr 92*
**Serlin,** Irving 1923- *AmMWSc 92*
**Serlin,** Oscar 1917- *AmMWSc 92*
**Serling,** Robert J 1918- *IntAu&W 91, WrDr 92*
**Serling,** Rod *FacFETw*
**Serling,** Rod d1975 *LesBEnT 92*
**Serling,** Rod 1924-1975 *BenetAL 91, TwCSFW 91*
**Serly,** Tibor 1901-1978 *NewAmDM*
**Serman,** Ilya Zakharovich 1913- *IntWW 91*
**Sermisy,** Claudin de 1490?-1562 *NewAmDM*
**Sermolins,** Maris Andris 1944- *AmMWSc 92*
**Sermon,** Roger Thomas, Jr. 1918- *WhoMW 92*
**Sermon,** Thomas Richard 1947- *Who 92*
**Serna,** David C. 1953- *WhoAmL 92*
**Serna,** Enrique Gonzalo 1946- *WhoHisp 92*
**Serna,** Eric 1949- *WhoHisp 92*
**Serna,** Eric Peter 1949- *WhoAmP 91*
**Serna,** Joe, Jr. *WhoHisp 92*
**Serna,** Jose de la *HisDSpE*

**Serna**, Maria Elena 1941- *WhoHisp 92*
**Serna**, Patricio M. *WhoHisp 92*
**Serna**, Raquel Casiano 1929- *WhoHisp 92*
**Sernas**, Jacques 1925- *IntMPA 92*
**Sernas**, Valentinas A 1938- *AmMWSc 92*
**Sernau**, Stephanie W. 1961- *WhoAmL 92*
**Serne**, Roger Jeffrey 1946- *AmMWSc 92*
**Sernett**, Richard Patrick 1938- *WhoAmL 92, WhoFI 92, WhoMW 92*
**Sernine**, Daniel 1955- *TwCSFW 91A*
**Sernka**, Thomas John 1941- *AmMWSc 92*
**Serocki**, Kazimierz 1922-1981 *NewAmDM*
**Serocky**, William Howard 1936- *WhoMW 92*
**Seroka**, Anna M. 1947- *WhoWest 92*
**Seron**, Richard Zaven 1926- *WhoAmP 91*
**Serota** *Who 92*
**Serota**, Baroness 1919- *Who 92*
**Serota**, Daniel 1945- *Who 92*
**Serota**, Irving 1931- *WhoAmL 92*
**Serota**, Nicholas Andrew 1946- *IntWW 91, Who 92*
**Serota**, Susan Perlstadt 1945- *WhoAmL 92*
**Serote**, Mongane Wally 1944- *ConPo 91, LiExTwC, WrDr 92*
**Serotta**, Gerald 1946- *WhoRel 92*
**Serov**, Vladimir Aleksandrovich 1910-1968 *SovUnBD*
**Serovy**, George K 1926- *AmMWSc 92*
**Serow**, William John 1946- *WhoFI 92*
**Serpe**, Ralph B. 1914- *IntMPA 92*
**Serpell**, David Radford 1911- *Who 92*
**Serpico**, Dominick 1953- *WhoEnt 92*
**Serr**, Frederick E 1952- *AmMWSc 92*
**Serra**, Carlos *WhoHisp 92*
**Serra**, David 1932- *WhoHisp 92*
**Serra**, Emanuel G *WhoAmP 91*
**Serra**, Enrique 1944- *WhoHisp 92*
**Serra**, Junipero 1713-1784 *HisDSpE, RComAH*
**Serra**, Kenneth Emilio 1933- *WhoHisp 92*
**Serra**, Miguel Jose 1713-1784 *BenetAL 91*
**Serra**, Narcis 1943- *IntWW 91*
**Serra**, Paul Charles 1957- *WhoEnt 92*
**Serra**, Richard 1939- *IntWW 91, WorArt 1980 [port]*
**Serra Ramoneda**, Antoni 1933- *IntWW 91*
**Serraglio**, Mario 1965- *WhoMW 92*
**Serraillier**, Ian 1912- *IntAu&W 91, WrDr 92*
**Serrani**, Thom 1947- *WhoAmP 91*
**Serrano**, Alberto Carlos 1931- *WhoHisp 92*
**Serrano**, Basilio, Jr. 1948- *WhoHisp 92*
**Serrano**, Gustavo 1933- *WhoHisp 92*
**Serrano**, Jack 1938- *WhoHisp 92*
**Serrano**, Jose E. 1943- *AlmAP 92 [port], WhoAmP 91*
**Serrano**, Jose E. 1945- *WhoHisp 92*
**Serrano**, Jose Mariano 1788-1852 *HisDSpE*
**Serrano**, Joseph F. 1951- *WhoHisp 92*
**Serrano**, Juan 1934- *WhoWest 92*
**Serrano**, Lynnette Maritza 1964- *WhoHisp 92*
**Serrano**, Maria Christina 1954- *WhoHisp 92*
**Serrano**, Mario E., Jr. 1942- *WhoHisp 92*
**Serrano**, Nestor *WhoHisp 92*
**Serrano**, Nina *DrAPF 91*
**Serrano**, Pedro, Jr. 1953- *WhoHisp 92*
**Serrano**, Sergio Enrique 1953- *WhoHisp 92*
**Serrano**, Stephanie *WhoHisp 92*
**Serrano Caldera**, Alejandro *IntWW 91*
**Serrano Elias**, Jorge *IntWW 91*
**Serrano-Garcia**, Irma 1948- *WhoHisp 92*
**Serrano Suner**, Ramon 1901- *BiDExR*
**Serrata**, Lidia 1947- *WhoAmL 92, WhoHisp 92*
**Serrate**, Israel James 1936- *WhoHisp 92*
**Serrato**, Michael A. 1934- *WhoHisp 92*
**Serrato**, Thomas R. 1955- *WhoHisp 92*
**Serrato-Combe**, Antonio 1945- *WhoHisp 92*
**Serre**, Jean-Pierre 1926- *IntWW 91*
**Serreau**, Coline *IntWW 91*
**Serrette**, Cathy Hollenberg 1954- *WhoAmL 92*
**Serrin**, James B 1926- *AmMWSc 92, IntWW 91*
**Serrin**, James Burton 1926- *WhoMW 92*
**Serritella**, James Anthony 1942- *WhoAmL 92*
**Sersen**, Howard Harry 1929- *WhoFI 92*
**Sersland**, Claudia Jane 1956- *WhoWest 92*
**Serstock**, Doris Shay 1926- *WhoMW 92*
**Serth**, Robert William 1941- *AmMWSc 92*
**Sertner**, Robert Mark 1955- *WhoEnt 92, WhoWest 92*
**Sertoli**, Giandomenico 1922- *IntWW 91*
**Serumgard**, Katharine Aspray 1946- *WhoMW 92*
**SerVaas**, Margaret Ann 1952- *WhoWest 92*
**Servadio**, Gaia 1938- *WrDr 92*
**Servadio**, Gaia Cecilia 1938- *IntAu&W 91*
**Servadio**, Gildo Joseph 1929- *AmMWSc 92*
**Servais**, Ronald Albert 1942- *AmMWSc 92, WhoMW 92*
**Servaites**, Jerome Casimer 1944- *AmMWSc 92*
**Servan-Schreiber**, Jean-Claude 1918- *IntWW 91*
**Servan-Schreiber**, Jean-Jacques 1924- *IntWW 91, Who 92*
**Servando**, Fray *HisDSpE*
**Servatius**, Bernhard 1932- *IntWW 91*
**Servay**, Kenneth John 1953- *WhoAmL 92*
**Serve**, Munson Paul 1939- *AmMWSc 92*
**Serventy**, Vincent Noel *WrDr 92*
**Server**, Greg 1939- *WhoAmP 91*
**Serverian**, Aram 1932- *WhoAmL 92*
**Servi**, I S 1922- *AmMWSc 92*
**Servi**, Leslie D 1955- *AmMWSc 92*
**Service**, Alastair Stanley Douglas 1933- *Who 92*
**Service**, Louisa Anne *Who 92*
**Service**, Robert 1874-1958 *RfGEnL 91*
**Service**, Robert W. 1874-1958 *BenetAL 91, ScFEYrs*
**Service**, Robert William 1874-1958 *FacFETw*
**Service**, Russell Newton 1913- *WhoBlA 92*
**Service**, William Corr 1901- *WhoWest 92*
**Servick**, Susan Kaye 1958- *WhoAmL 92*
**Servidio**, Robbin Carriero 1963- *WhoFI 92*
**Servinski**, Sarah Jane Jeroue 1944- *WhoMW 92*
**Servis**, Kenneth L 1939- *AmMWSc 92*
**Servis**, Robert Eugene 1941- *AmMWSc 92*
**Serviss**, Garrett P. 1851-1929 *BenetAL 91, ScFEYrs, TwCSFW 91*
**Servodidio**, Pat Anthony 1937- *WhoEnt 92, WhoFI 92*
**Servolini**, Luigi 1906- *IntWW 91*
**Servos**, Kurt 1928- *AmMWSc 92*
**Serway**, Raymond A 1936- *AmMWSc 92*
**Serwer**, Philip 1942- *AmMWSc 92*
**Serwy**, Robert Anthony 1950- *WhoMW 92*
**Seshachari**, Neila C. 1934- *WhoWest 92*
**Seshadri**, Conjeevaram Srirangachari 1932- *Who 92*
**Seshadri**, Kalkunte S 1924- *AmMWSc 92*
**Seshadri**, Sengadu Rangaswamy 1928- *AmMWSc 92*
**Seshadri**, Vanamamalai 1928- *AmMWSc 92*
**Seshu**, Lilly Hannah 1925- *AmMWSc 92*
**Seslowsky**, Harvey Michael 1942- *WhoEnt 92, WhoFI 92*
**Sesonske**, Alexander 1921- *AmMWSc 92*
**Sessa**, David Joseph 1938- *AmMWSc 92*
**Sessa**, Donna Benza 1947- *WhoEnt 92*
**Sessa**, Grazia L *AmMWSc 92*
**Sessford**, George Minshull *Who 92*
**Sessing**, Trevor W. 1943- *WhoBlA 92*
**Session**, John Joe 1928- *AmMWSc 92*
**Session**, Johnny Frank 1949- *WhoBlA 92*
**Sessions**, Clark W. 1939- *WhoAmL 92*
**Sessions**, David McKey 1952- *WhoMW 92*
**Sessions**, James Scott 1936- *WhoRel 92*
**Sessions**, Jefferson Beauregard, III 1946- *WhoAmL 92*
**Sessions**, John 1953- *Who 92*
**Sessions**, John O *WhoAmP 91*
**Sessions**, John Turner, Jr 1922- *AmMWSc 92*
**Sessions**, Roger 1896-1985 *FacFETw, NewAmDM*
**Sessions**, William Lad 1943- *WhoRel 92*
**Sessions**, William S. 1930- *IntWW 91, WhoAmP 91*
**Sessions**, William Steele 1930- *WhoAmL 92*
**Sessle**, Barry John 1941- *AmMWSc 92*
**Sessler**, Albert Louis, Jr. 1925- *WhoAmL 92*
**Sessler**, Andrew M 1928- *AmMWSc 92*
**Sessler**, Andrew Marienhoff 1928- *WhoWest 92*
**Sessler**, Gerhard Martin 1931- *AmMWSc 92*
**Sessler**, John Charles 1932- *AmMWSc 92*
**Sessler**, John George 1920- *AmMWSc 92*
**Sessoms**, Frank Eugene 1947- *WhoBlA 92*
**Sessum**, Robert Lee 1943- *WhoRel 92*
**Sestanj**, Kazimir 1927- *AmMWSc 92*
**Sestina**, John E. 1942- *WhoFI 92, WhoMW 92*
**Sestini**, Benedict 1816-1890 *BiInAmS*
**Sestini**, Virgil Andrew 1936- *WhoWest 92*
**Sestric**, Anthony James 1940- *WhoAmL 92, WhoMW 92*
**Setapen**, James Anthony 1948- *WhoEnt 92*
**Setch**, Terry 1936- *IntWW 91, TwCPaSc*
**Setchell**, David Lloyd 1937- *IntWW 91*
**Setchell**, John Stanford, Jr 1942- *AmMWSc 92*
**Setchell**, Marcus Edward 1943- *Who 92*
**Setchko**, Edward Stephen 1926- *WhoRel 92, WhoWest 92*
**Setelik**, James Joseph, Jr. 1952- *WhoRel 92*
**Seter**, Mordecai 1910- *IntWW 91*
**Seteroff**, Sviatoslav Steve 1937- *WhoWest 92*
**Seth**, Brij B 1938- *AmMWSc 92*
**Seth**, Kamal Kishore 1933- *AmMWSc 92*
**Seth**, Rajinder Singh 1937- *AmMWSc 92*
**Seth**, Sharad Chandra 1942- *AmMWSc 92*
**Seth**, Vikram *DrAPF 91*
**Seth**, Vikram 1952- *ConPo 91, WrDr 92*
**Sethares**, George C 1930- *AmMWSc 92*
**Sethares**, James C 1928- *AmMWSc 92*
**Sether**, John Albert 1941- *WhoMW 92*
**Sether**, Lowell Albert 1931- *AmMWSc 92*
**Sethi**, Dhanwant S 1937- *AmMWSc 92*
**Sethi**, Harindar Singh 1933- *WhoWest 92*
**Sethi**, Ishwar Krishan 1948- *AmMWSc 92*
**Sethi**, Jitender K 1939- *AmMWSc 92*
**Sethi**, Narendra Kumar 1935- *WrDr 92*
**Sethi**, Prakash Chandra 1920- *IntWW 91*
**Sethi**, Robbie Clipper *DrAPF 91*
**Sethi**, Shyam Sunder 1942- *WhoFI 92*
**Sethian**, John Dasho 1950- *AmMWSc 92*
**Sethna**, M. J. 1911- *WrDr 92*
**Sethna**, Minocher Jehangirji 1911- *IntAu&W 91*
**Sethna**, Patarasp R 1923- *AmMWSc 92*
**Sethness**, Charles Henry, Jr. 1910- *WhoFI 92*
**Sethness**, Charles Olin 1941- *IntWW 91, WhoFI 92*
**Sethuraman**, Jayaram 1937- *AmMWSc 92*
**Sethuraman**, S 1939- *AmMWSc 92*
**Sethy**, Vimala Hiralal *AmMWSc 92*
**Setian**, Leo 1930- *AmMWSc 92*
**Setian**, Nerses Mikail 1918- *WhoRel 92*
**Setlalekgosi**, Boniface Tshosa *WhoRel 92*
**Setler**, Paulette Elizabeth 1938- *AmMWSc 92*
**Setlich-Drozda**, Kimberly Kay 1956- *WhoFI 92, WhoMW 92*
**Setliff**, Edson Carmack 1941- *AmMWSc 92*
**Setliff**, Frank Lamar 1938- *AmMWSc 92*
**Setliffe**, Andrew Benton, Jr. 1922- *WhoRel 92*
**Setlin**, Alan John 1933- *WhoWest 92*
**Setlow**, Jane Kellock 1919- *AmMWSc 92*
**Setlow**, Peter 1944- *AmMWSc 92*
**Setlow**, Richard Burton 1921- *AmMWSc 92*
**Setlow**, Valerie Petit 1950- *AmMWSc 92*
**Setlowe**, Richard Henry 1933- *WhoEnt 92*
**Seto**, Belinda P L 1948- *AmMWSc 92*
**Seto**, Frank 1925- *AmMWSc 92*
**Seto**, Jane Mei-Chun 1927- *AmMWSc 92*
**Seto**, Joseph Tobey 1924- *AmMWSc 92*
**Seton**, Lady *Who 92*
**Seton**, Anya *IntAu&W 91*
**Seton**, Anya d1990 *Who 92N*
**Seton**, Anya 1904-1990 *AnObit 1990, ConAu 133, CurBio 91N, SmATA 66*
**Seton**, Anya 1916-1990 *BenetAL 91, FacFETw*
**Seton**, Elizabeth Ann 1774-1821 *HanAmWH*
**Seton**, Ernest Thompson 1860-1946 *BenetAL 91*
**Seton**, Iain 1942- *Who 92*
**Seton**, Robert 1926- *Who 92*
**Setrakian**, Berge 1949- *WhoAmL 92*
**Setrakian**, Robert Halg 1962- *WhoFI 92*
**Setser**, Carole Sue 1940- *AmMWSc 92*
**Setser**, Donald W 1935- *AmMWSc 92*
**Setshogo**, Boithoko Moonwa 1941- *Who 92*
**Sette**, Pietro 1915- *IntWW 91*
**Sette Camara**, Jose 1920- *IntWW 91*
**Setterberg**, Gary Richard 1955- *WhoMW 92*
**Settergren**, Carl David 1935- *AmMWSc 92*
**Setterlund**, Jack Edward 1947- *WhoAmL 92*
**Setters**, Daniel E. 1944- *WhoFI 92*
**Setterstrom**, Carl A 1915- *AmMWSc 92*
**Settgast**, Leland G. 1939- *WhoRel 92*
**Settlage**, Arthur Craig 1942- *WhoRel 92*
**Settle**, Bill 1937- *WhoAmP 91*
**Settle**, Edwin Theodore 1901- *WhoRel 92*
**Settle**, Elkanah 1648-1724 *RfGEnL 91*
**Settle**, Frank Alexander, Jr 1937- *AmMWSc 92*
**Settle**, John R. 1965- *WhoBlA 92*
**Settle**, Marvin B., Jr. 1948- *WhoRel 92*
**Settle**, Mary Lee *DrAPF 91*
**Settle**, Mary Lee 1918- *WrDr 92*
**Settle**, Richard Gregg 1949- *AmMWSc 92*
**Settle**, Wilbur Jewell *AmMWSc 92*
**Settle**, William Sydnor 1933- *WhoAmL 92*
**Settlemire**, Carl Thomas 1937- *AmMWSc 92*
**Settlemyer**, Kenneth Theodore 1935- *AmMWSc 92*
**Settler**, Eugene Brian 1936- *WhoEnt 92*
**Settles**, Carl E. 1948- *WhoBlA 92*
**Settles**, F Stan 1938- *AmMWSc 92*
**Settles**, Gary Stuart 1949- *AmMWSc 92*
**Settles**, Harry Emerson 1940- *AmMWSc 92*
**Settles**, Ronald Dean 1938- *AmMWSc 92*
**Settles**, Rosetta Hayes 1920- *WhoBlA 92*
**Settles**, Thomas Edward 1951- *WhoAmL 92, WhoAmP 91*
**Settles**, Trudy Y. 1946- *WhoBlA 92*
**Setton**, Ruth Knafo *DrAPF 91*
**Settoon**, Patrick Delano 1934- *AmMWSc 92*
**Settoon**, William Alden, Jr. 1949- *WhoFI 92*
**Setzepfandt**, Alvin O H, II 1924- *WhoAmP 91*
**Setzer**, Johnsie Julia 1924- *WhoAmP 91*
**Setzer**, Joseph 1950- *WhoRel 92*
**Setzer**, Kirk *WhoMW 92, WhoRel 92*
**Setzler**, Edward Allan 1933- *WhoAmL 92*
**Setzler**, Nikki G 1945- *WhoAmP 91*
**Setzler**, William Edward 1926- *WhoFI 92*
**Setzler-Hamilton**, Eileen Marie 1943- *AmMWSc 92*
**Seubold**, Frank Henry, Jr 1922- *AmMWSc 92*
**Seufert**, Wolf D 1935- *AmMWSc 92*
**Seufzer**, Paul Richard 1921- *AmMWSc 92*
**Seugling**, Earl William, Jr 1933- *AmMWSc 92*
**Seum**, Dan 1940- *WhoAmP 91*
**Seung**, Albert Si-Ngai 1951- *WhoRel 92*
**Seung**, Thomas Kaehao 1930- *ConAu 36NR*
**Seurat**, Georges 1859-1891 *ThHEIm*
**Seus**, Edward J 1935- *AmMWSc 92*
**Seuss**, Dr. *ConAu 135, SmATA 67*
**Seuss**, Dr. 1904- *BenetAL 91, FacFETw, WrDr 92*
**Seva'aetasi**, Suitupu *WhoAmP 91*
**Sevacherian**, Vahram 1942- *AmMWSc 92*
**Sevall**, Jack Sanders 1946- *AmMWSc 92*
**Sevareid**, Arnold Eric 1912- *IntWW 91*
**Sevareid**, Eric *LesBEnT 92*
**Sevareid**, Eric 1912- *FacFETw, IntMPA 92*
**Sevareid**, Peter 1940- *WhoAmL 92*
**Sevario**, Joseph A, III 1944- *WhoAmP 91*
**Sevcik**, Otakar 1852-1934 *NewAmDM*
**Sevcik**, Vernon William 1953- *WhoMW 92*
**Sevem**, James C. 1948- *WhoFI 92*
**Seven**, Johnny Anthony 1931- *WhoEnt 92*
**Seven**, Marilyn 1947- *WhoEnt 92*
**Sevenair**, John P 1943- *AmMWSc 92*
**Sevenants**, Michael R 1938- *AmMWSc 92*
**Seveney**, Gardner F *WhoAmP 91*
**Sever**, David Michael 1948- *AmMWSc 92, WhoMW 92*
**Sever**, John 1943- *Who 92*
**Sever**, John Louis 1932- *AmMWSc 92*
**Severance**, Charles M 1939- *WhoAmP 91*
**Severance**, Harold Gail 1933- *WhoMW 92*
**Severcool**, Shirley Jean 1930- *WhoAmP 91*
**Severe**, John Thomas 1951- *WhoAmL 92*
**Severian of Gabala** d408? *EncEarC*
**Severin**, Adrian *IntWW 91*
**Severin**, Charles Hilarion 1896- *AmMWSc 92*
**Severin**, Charles Matthew 1948- *AmMWSc 92*
**Severin**, Dorothy Virginia Sherman 1942- *Who 92*
**Severin**, Giles Timothy 1940- *IntAu&W 91*
**Severin**, Matthew Joseph 1933- *AmMWSc 92*
**Severin**, Timothy 1940- *IntWW 91, Who 92, WrDr 92*
**Severing**, Carl 1875-1952 *EncTR 91 [port]*
**Severinghaus**, Charles William 1916- *AmMWSc 92*
**Severinghaus**, John Wendell 1922- *AmMWSc 92*
**Severini**, Gino 1883-1966 *FacFETw*
**Severino**, Donna Marie 1958- *WhoAmL 92*
**Severino**, Elizabeth Forrest 1945- *WhoFI 92*
**Severino**, John C. *IntMPA 92, LesBEnT 92*
**Severino**, Robert Anthony 1954- *WhoWest 92*
**Severinsen**, Doc 1927- *NewAmDM, WhoEnt 92*
**Severinsky**, Alexander Jacob 1944- *WhoFI 92*
**Severinus** d482 *EncEarC*
**Severn**, Bill *ConAu 36NR*
**Severn**, Charles B 1939- *AmMWSc 92*
**Severn**, David *Who 92, WrDr 92*
**Severn**, Donald *WrDr 92*
**Severn**, Roy Thomas 1929- *Who 92*
**Severn**, William Irving 1914- *ConAu 36NR*
**Severne**, John 1925- *Who 92*
**Severns**, James George 1929- *WhoEnt 92*
**Severns**, Joan Zagar 1929- *WhoAmP 91*
**Severns**, Matthew Lincoln 1952- *AmMWSc 92*
**Severns**, Penny L 1952- *WhoAmP 91*
**Severns**, Scott Richard 1950- *WhoAmL 92*
**Severo**, Patrick Scott 1959- *WhoWest 92*
**Severs**, Charles A., III 1942- *WhoAmL 92*
**Severs**, Walter Bruce 1938- *AmMWSc 92*

**Severs,** William 1932- *WhoEnt 92*
**Seversike,** Leverne K 1936- *AmMWSc 92*
**Severson,** Arlen Raynold 1939- *AmMWSc 92, WhoMW 92*
**Severson,** B O d1918 *BiInAmS*
**Severson,** David Lester *AmMWSc 92*
**Severson,** Don R. 1934- *WhoWest 92*
**Severson,** Donald E 1919- *AmMWSc 92*
**Severson,** Elmer D 1922- *WhoAmP 91*
**Severson,** Glen Arthur 1949- *WhoMW 92*
**Severson,** Herbert H 1944- *AmMWSc 92*
**Severson,** John Robert 1955- *WhoFI 92*
**Severson,** Keith Edward 1936- *AmMWSc 92*
**Severson,** Michael Rollin 1954- *WhoEnt 92*
**Severson,** Paul Thomas 1928- *WhoEnt 92*
**Severson,** Roland George 1924- *AmMWSc 92*
**Severson,** Ronald Charles 1945- *AmMWSc 92*
**Severtsov,** Aleksey Nikolaevich 1866-1936 *SovUnBD*
**Severud,** Fred N 1899- *AmMWSc 92*
**Severus of Antioch** 465?-538 *EncEarC*
**Severy,** Bruce W. *DrAPF 91*
**Sevey,** Robert Warren 1927- *WhoWest 92*
**Sevian,** Walter Andrew 1940- *AmMWSc 92*
**Sevick,** George Lawrence 1948- *WhoMW 92*
**Sevier,** Ernest Youle 1932- *WhoAmL 92*
**Sevier,** Francis Aloysius Charles 1924- *WhoAmL 92*
**Sevigne,** Marquise de 1626-1696 *FrenWW*
**Sevik,** Maurice 1923- *AmMWSc 92*
**Sevilla,** Carlos A. 1935- *WhoWest 92*
**Sevilla,** Carlos Arthur 1935- *WhoHisp 92*
**Sevilla,** Dennis 1958- *WhoHisp 92*
**Sevilla,** Michael Douglas 1942- *AmMWSc 92*
**Sevillano,** Trinidad 1968- *WhoEnt 92*
**Sevillian,** Clarence Marvin 1945- *WhoBlA 92*
**Sevin,** E 1928- *AmMWSc 92*
**Sevoian,** Martin 1919- *AmMWSc 92*
**Sevon,** William David, III 1933- *AmMWSc 92*
**Sevy,** Roger Warren 1923- *AmMWSc 92*
**Sewal,** Charlotte 1947- *WhoAmP 91*
**Sewalk,** Kathleen M. *DrAPF 91*
**Sewall,** Barbara Jean *IntMPA 92*
**Sewall,** Jonathan 1729-1796 *BenetAL 91*
**Sewall,** Jonathan Mitchell 1748-1808 *BenetAL 91*
**Sewall,** Loyall F 1934- *WhoAmP 91*
**Sewall,** May Eliza Wright 1844-1920 *AmPeW*
**Sewall,** Richard B. 1908- *DcLB 111 [port]*
**Sewall,** Samuel 1652-1730 *BenetAL 91*
**Sewall,** Stephen 1734-1804 *BiInAmS*
**Seward,** Anna 1742-1809 *RfGEnL 91*
**Seward,** Ardina Marie *WhoEnt 92*
**Seward,** Frederick Downing 1931- *AmMWSc 92*
**Seward,** George Chester 1910- *IntWW 91, WhoAmL 92, WhoFI 92*
**Seward,** Guy William 1916- *Who 92*
**Seward,** James Joseph 1951- *WhoAmL 92*
**Seward,** James L *WhoAmP 91*
**Seward,** Jeffrey James 1953- *WhoMW 92*
**Seward,** John E, Jr 1943- *WhoIns 92*
**Seward,** John Edward, Jr. 1943- *WhoFI 92, WhoMW 92*
**Seward,** John Wesley, Jr. 1948- *WhoFI 92*
**Seward,** Mark Douglass 1959- *WhoMW 92*
**Seward,** Roland Quincy, Sr 1917- *WhoAmP 91*
**Seward,** Russell G 1920- *WhoAmP 91*
**Seward,** Steven Le Mar 1946- *WhoMW 92*
**Seward,** Thomas Philip, III 1939- *AmMWSc 92*
**Seward,** William Davis 1938- *AmMWSc 92*
**Seward,** William H 1801-1872 *RComAH*
**Seward,** William Henry 1801-1872 *AmPolLe [port], BenetAL 91*
**Seward,** William Richard 1922- *Who 92*
**Sewart,** Alan 1928- *IntAu&W 91*
**Sewell,** Allan 1915- *Who 92*
**Sewell,** Beverly Jean 1942- *WhoFI 92*
**Sewell,** Brocard 1912- *IntAu&W 91, WrDr 92*
**Sewell,** Charles Robertson 1927- *WhoWest 92*
**Sewell,** Curtis, Jr 1924- *AmMWSc 92*
**Sewell,** Duane Campbell 1918- *AmMWSc 92, WhoWest 92*
**Sewell,** Edward C. 1946- *WhoBlA 92*
**Sewell,** Elisha G. 1849-1924 *RelLAm 91*
**Sewell,** Elizabeth *DrAPF 91*
**Sewell,** Frank Anderson, Jr 1934- *AmMWSc 92*
**Sewell,** Homer B 1920- *AmMWSc 92*
**Sewell,** Isiah Obediah 1938- *WhoBlA 92*
**Sewell,** James Thomas 1942- *WhoRel 92*
**Sewell,** Joe 1898-1990 *FacFETw*
**Sewell,** John I 1933- *AmMWSc 92*
**Sewell,** Joyce Carolyn 1930- *WhoAmP 91*
**Sewell,** Kenneth Glenn 1933- *AmMWSc 92*
**Sewell,** Luther Joseph 1936- *WhoBlA 92*
**Sewell,** Phyllis Shapiro 1930- *WhoFI 92, WhoMW 92*
**Sewell,** Ralph Byron 1940- *WhoFI 92*
**Sewell,** Raymond F 1923- *AmMWSc 92*
**Sewell,** Richard Huston 1946- *WhoBlA 92*
**Sewell,** Sandra Serrano *WhoHisp 92*
**Sewell,** Stephen 1953- *WrDr 92*
**Sewell,** Steven Edward 1963- *WhoBlA 92*
**Sewell,** Thomas Robert McKie 1921- *Who 92*
**Sewell,** Timothy Patrick T. *Who 92*
**Sewell,** William 1909- *WrDr 92*
**Sewell,** William Thomas, Sr. 1934- *WhoMW 92*
**Sewell,** Winifred 1917- *AmMWSc 92*
**Sewright,** Charles William, Jr. 1946- *WhoFI 92*
**Sex Pistols** *NewAmDM*
**Sexauer,** Bradley Lester 1951- *WhoFI 92*
**Sexsmith,** David Randal 1933- *AmMWSc 92*
**Sexsmith,** Frederick Hamilton 1929- *AmMWSc 92*
**Sexsmith,** Robert G 1938- *AmMWSc 92*
**Sexson,** Lynda 1942- *WhoRel 92*
**Sexton,** Alan William 1925- *AmMWSc 92*
**Sexton,** Anne 1928-1974 *BenetAL 91, ConAu 36NR, FacFETw, ModAWWr*
**Sexton,** Clarence D, Jr 1927- *WhoAmP 91*
**Sexton,** David Farrington 1943- *WhoAmL 92, WhoFI 92*
**Sexton,** Donald Lee 1932- *WhoFI 92*
**Sexton,** Edwin T., Jr. 1923-1983 *WhoBlA 92N*
**Sexton,** James Dean 1942- *WhoWest 92*
**Sexton,** John Edward 1942- *WhoAmL 92*
**Sexton,** Ken 1949- *AmMWSc 92*
**Sexton,** Landon C 1941- *WhoAmP 91*
**Sexton,** Larry Wayne 1959- *WhoMW 92*
**Sexton,** Linda Gray 1953- *ConAu 36NR, WrDr 92*
**Sexton,** Michael 1923- *Who 92*
**Sexton,** Michael Bernard 1958- *WhoAmL 92*
**Sexton,** Owen J 1926- *AmMWSc 92*
**Sexton,** Richard *WhoRel 92*
**Sexton,** Thomas F. *DrAPF 91*
**Sexton,** Thomas John 1942- *AmMWSc 92*
**Sexton,** Timothy J. 1940- *WhoMW 92*
**Sexton,** Virginia Staudt 1916- *WomPsyc, WrDr 92*
**Sexton,** Wendell P. *DrAPF 91*
**Sexton,** William C. 1928- *ConAu 133*
**Sexton,** William Frank, Jr. 1947- *WhoMW 92*
**Sextro,** Richard George 1944- *AmMWSc 92*
**Seya,** Tsukasa 1950- *AmMWSc 92*
**Seyb,** Leslie Philip 1915- *AmMWSc 92*
**Seybert,** Adam 1773-1825 *BiInAmS*
**Seybert,** Barry Michael 1956- *WhoEnt 92*
**Seybert,** David Wayne 1950- *AmMWSc 92*
**Seybert,** Henry 1801-1883 *BiInAmS*
**Seybold,** Paul Grant 1937- *AmMWSc 92*
**Seybold,** Virginia Susan 1951- *AmMWSc 92*
**Seybolt,** Peter J 1934- *ConAu 35NR*
**Seybou,** Ali *IntWW 91*
**Seychelles,** Bishop of *Who 92*
**Seydel,** Frank David 1944- *AmMWSc 92*
**Seydel,** Robert E 1942- *AmMWSc 92*
**Seydlitz-Kurzbach,** Walther von 1888-1976 *EncTR 91 [port]*
**Seydou,** Amadou 1928- *IntWW 91*
**Seydou,** Traore 1927- *IntWW 91*
**Seye,** Abdoulaye 1934- *BlkOlyM*
**Seyer,** Jerome Michael 1937- *AmMWSc 92*
**Seyersted,** Finn 1915- *IntWW 91*
**Seyersted,** Per *WrDr 92*
**Seyersted,** Per 1921- *IntAu&W 91*
**Seyfert,** Carl K, Jr 1938- *AmMWSc 92*
**Seyfert,** Howard Bentley, Jr. 1918- *WhoWest 92*
**Seyferth,** Dietmar 1929- *AmMWSc 92*
**Seyferth,** Harold Homer 1922- *WhoWest 92*
**Seyfried,** Thomas Neil 1946- *AmMWSc 92*
**Seyler,** Athene 1889-1990 *AnObit 1990*
**Seyler,** Charles Eugene 1948- *AmMWSc 92*
**Seyler,** Richard G 1933- *AmMWSc 92*
**Seyler,** William C. 1921- *WhoFI 92*
**Seymour** *Who 92*
**Seymour,** Lord 1982- *Who 92*
**Seymour,** A. Barry 1942- *WhoMW 92*
**Seymour,** Alan 1927- *WrDr 92*
**Seymour,** Allyn H 1913- *AmMWSc 92*
**Seymour,** Brian Richard 1944- *AmMWSc 92*
**Seymour,** Cynthia Maria 1933- *WhoBlA 92*
**Seymour,** Dan 1915- *IntMPA 92*
**Seymour,** David Maurice 1952- *WhoRel 92*
**Seymour,** Francis 1928- *Who 92*
**Seymour,** Gerald 1933- *WhoFI 92*
**Seymour,** Gerald 1941- *WrDr 92*
**Seymour,** Harlan Francis 1950- *WhoFI 92*
**Seymour,** Horatio 1810-1886 *AmPolLe*
**Seymour,** Jane 1951- *IntMPA 92, WhoEnt 92*
**Seymour,** Jeffrey Alan 1950- *WhoFI 92, WhoWest 92*
**Seymour,** John 1937- *AlmAP 92 [port], WhoAmP 91*
**Seymour,** John F. 1937- *WhoWest 92*
**Seymour,** Keith Goldin 1922- *AmMWSc 92*
**Seymour,** Laurence Darryl 1935- *WhoBlA 92*
**Seymour,** Lynn 1939- *IntWW 91, Who 92*
**Seymour,** Mary Frances 1948- *WhoAmL 92*
**Seymour,** Mary Powell 1922- *WhoAmP 91*
**Seymour,** Michael Culme- 1909- *Who 92*
**Seymour,** Michael Dennis 1950- *AmMWSc 92*
**Seymour,** Miranda 1948- *WrDr 92*
**Seymour,** Philip Merritt 1945- *WhoRel 92*
**Seymour,** Raymond B 1912- *AmMWSc 92*
**Seymour,** Richard Deming 1955- *WhoMW 92*
**Seymour,** Richard Jones 1929- *AmMWSc 92*
**Seymour,** Richard William 1950- *Who 92*
**Seymour,** Robert F. 1926- *WhoBlA 92*
**Seymour,** Roland Lee 1939- *AmMWSc 92*
**Seymour,** Stanley 1951- *WhoBlA 92*
**Seymour,** Stephanie K *WhoAmP 91*
**Seymour,** Stephanie Kulp 1940- *WhoAmL 92*
**Seymour,** William Joseph 1870-1922 *RelLAm 91*
**Seymour-Harris,** Barbara Laverne 1953- *WhoAmL 92*
**Seymour-Smith,** Martin 1928- *ConPo 91, IntAu&W 91, WrDr 92*
**Seynes,** Philippe de 1910- *IntWW 91*
**Seypidin Aze** 1916- *IntWW 91*
**Seyrig,** Delphine 1932-1990 *AnObit 1990*
**Seyrig,** Delphine Claire Beltiane d1990 *IntWW 91N*
**Seys-Llewellyn,** John Desmond 1912- *Who 92*
**Seyss-Inquart,** Arthur 1892-1946 *BiDExR, EncTR 91 [port], FacFETw*
**Sfaellou,** Calliope 1912- *IntAu&W 91*
**Sfar,** Rachid 1933- *IntWW 91*
**Sfasciotti,** Mary L. 1941- *WhoAmL 92*
**Sfat,** Michael R 1921- *AmMWSc 92*
**Sfekas,** Constantine James 1953- *WhoAmL 92*
**Sfekas,** Stephen James 1947- *WhoAmL 92*
**Sferra,** Pasquale Richard 1927- *AmMWSc 92*
**Sferrazza,** Peter J 1945- *WhoAmP 91*
**Sferrazza,** Peter Joseph 1945- *WhoWest 92*
**Sfikas,** Peter Michael 1937- *WhoAmL 92*
**Sforza,** Caterina 1463-1509 *EncAmaz 91*
**Sforza,** Christierna d1590 *EncAmaz 91*
**Sforza,** Pasquale M 1941- *AmMWSc 92*
**Sforzini,** Richard Henry 1924- *AmMWSc 92*
**Sforzo,** Robert Joseph 1947- *WhoFI 92*
**Sfraga-Panza,** Georgene Angela 1950- *WhoFI 92*
**Sganga,** John B. 1931- *WhoFI 92*
**Sgorlon,** Carlo Pietro Antonio 1930- *IntWW 91*
**Sgoutas,** Demetrios Spiros 1929- *AmMWSc 92*
**Sgro,** Gregory P. 1961- *WhoAmL 92*
**Sgro,** J A 1937- *AmMWSc 92*
**Sha,** William T 1928- *AmMWSc 92*
**Shaaban,** Farouk Ahmed Mohamed 1937- *WhoMW 92*
**Shaad,** Dorothy Jean 1909- *AmMWSc 92*
**Sha'afi,** Ramadan Issa 1938- *AmMWSc 92*
**Shaak,** Graig Dennis 1942- *AmMWSc 92*
**Shaali,** Mohammad Bin Hussain Al- 1950- *IntWW 91*
**Shaath,** Nadim Ali 1945- *AmMWSc 92*
**Shabana,** Ahmed Abdelraouf *AmMWSc 92*
**Shabanov,** Vitaly Mikhailovich 1923- *IntWW 91*
**Shabanowitz,** Harry 1918- *AmMWSc 92*
**Shabaz,** John C. 1931- *WhoAmL 92*
**Shabazz,** Abdulalim 1927- *AmMWSc 92*
**Shabazz,** Kaleem 1947- *WhoBlA 92*
**Shabel,** Barrie Steven 1938- *AmMWSc 92*
**Shabel,** Dennis Joseph 1944- *WhoMW 92*
**Shaber,** David *IntMPA 92*
**Shabica,** Anthony Charles, Jr 1915- *AmMWSc 92*
**Shabica,** Charles Wright 1943- *AmMWSc 92*
**Shachgiliadin,** Vagan Vaganovich 1935- *IntWW 91*
**Shachner,** Harold 1920- *WhoEnt 92*
**Shack,** Roland Vincent 1927- *AmMWSc 92*
**Shack,** William A. 1923- *WhoBlA 92*
**Shack,** William Alfred 1923- *IntWW 91*
**Shack,** William Edward, Jr. 1943- *WhoBlA 92*
**Shack,** William John 1943- *AmMWSc 92*
**Shackelford,** Charles L 1918- *AmMWSc 92*
**Shackelford,** Donald Bruce 1932- *WhoMW 92*
**Shackelford,** Ernest Dabney 1926- *AmMWSc 92*
**Shackelford,** George Franklin 1939- *WhoBlA 92*
**Shackelford,** Ginger Carole Gunn 1946- *WhoAmP 91*
**Shackelford,** Gordon Lee, Jr. 1948- *WhoWest 92*
**Shackelford,** James Floyd 1944- *AmMWSc 92*
**Shackelford,** John Hilary, Jr. 1939- *WhoFI 92*
**Shackelford,** Lawrence Frazier 1933- *WhoAmP 91*
**Shackelford,** Lottie H. 1941- *WhoBlA 92*
**Shackelford,** Lottie Holt 1941- *WhoAmP 91*
**Shackelford,** Robert G 1936- *AmMWSc 92*
**Shackelford,** Sandi 1950- *WhoEnt 92*
**Shackelford,** Scott Addison 1944- *AmMWSc 92*
**Shackelford,** Ted 1946- *WhoEnt 92*
**Shackelford,** Thekla Reese 1934- *WhoMW 92*
**Shackelford,** Walter McDonald 1945- *AmMWSc 92*
**Shackelford,** Wendell Chandler 1939- *WhoWest 92*
**Shackelford,** William G., Jr. 1950- *WhoBlA 92*
**Shackett,** Maryl *DrAPF 91*
**Shackett,** Ralph E 1940- *WhoAmP 91*
**Shackle,** Christopher 1942- *Who 92*
**Shackle,** Dale Richard 1941- *AmMWSc 92*
**Shackle,** George Lennox Sharman 1903- *Who 92, WrDr 92*
**Shackleford,** John Murphy 1929- *AmMWSc 92*
**Shackleford,** William Alton, Sr. 1947- *WhoRel 92*
**Shackleford,** William Lewis 1937- *WhoWest 92*
**Shackleton** *Who 92*
**Shackleton,** Baron 1911- *IntWW 91, Who 92*
**Shackleton,** Lord 1911- *WrDr 92*
**Shackleton,** Elizabeth 1951- *TwCPaSc*
**Shackleton,** Ernest Henry 1874-1922 *FacFETw*
**Shackleton,** Frederick Gerald 1922- *WhoWest 92*
**Shackleton,** Judith *TwCPaSc*
**Shackleton,** Keith Hope 1923- *Who 92*
**Shackleton,** Mary Jane 1934- *WhoMW 92*
**Shackleton,** Nicholas John 1937- *Who 92*
**Shackleton,** Peter 1933- *TwCPaSc*
**Shackleton,** Polly *WhoAmP 91*
**Shackleton,** Robert Millner 1909- *IntWW 91, Who 92*
**Shackleton,** William 1872-1933 *TwCPaSc*
**Shackleton Bailey,** D. R. *Who 92*
**Shacklett,** Robert Lee 1926- *AmMWSc 92*
**Shacklette,** Lawrence Wayne 1945- *AmMWSc 92*
**Shackley,** Douglas John 1938- *WhoFI 92*
**Shacklock,** Constance 1913- *Who 92*
**Shacochis,** Bob *DrAPF 91*
**Shacter,** David Mervyn 1941- *WhoAmL 92, WhoWest 92*
**Shad,** John S R 1923- *WhoAmP 91*
**Shadbolt,** Maurice 1932- *ConNov 91, RfGEnL 91, WrDr 92*
**Shadd,** Mary Ann 1823-1893 *HanAmWH, NotBlAW 92 [port]*
**Shaddock,** Stephen Gorham 1959- *WhoFI 92*
**Shadduck,** James Edward 1959- *WhoAmL 92*
**Shadduck,** John Allen 1939- *AmMWSc 92*
**Shaddy,** James Henry 1938- *AmMWSc 92*
**Shade,** Barbara J. 1933- *WhoBlA 92*
**Shade,** Elwood B 1913- *AmMWSc 92*
**Shade,** Joyce Elizabeth 1953- *AmMWSc 92*
**Shade,** Marvin 1948- *WhoMW 92*
**Shade,** Michael William 1954- *WhoFI 92*
**Shade,** Oscar D. 1931- *WhoBlA 92*
**Shade,** Ray W 1927- *AmMWSc 92*
**Shade,** Robert Eugene *AmMWSc 92*
**Shader,** Leslie Elwin 1935- *AmMWSc 92*
**Shader,** Richard Irwin 1935- *AmMWSc 92*
**Shadi,** Dorothy Clarke 1908- *WhoWest 92*
**Shadoan,** William Lewis 1931- *WhoAmL 92*
**Shadomy,** Smith 1931- *AmMWSc 92*
**Shadowen,** Herbert Edwin 1926- *AmMWSc 92*
**Shadr,** Ivan Dmitrievich 1887-1941 *SovUnBD*
**Shadrawy,** Bernard Francis, Jr. 1948- *WhoAmL 92*
**Shadroui,** Beshara John 1939- *WhoMW 92*

**Shadur,** Milton I. 1924- *WhoAmL 92*
**Shadwell,** Thomas 1640?-1692 *RfGEnL 91*
**Shaefer,** Mark Steven 1957- *WhoMW 92*
**Shaeffer,** Charlie Willard, Jr. 1938- *WhoWest 92*
**Shaeffer,** David Leon 1959- *WhoRel 92*
**Shaeffer,** Joseph Robert 1935- *AmMWSc 92*
**Shaeffer,** Laurie *WhoRel 92*
**Shaeffer,** W A 1867-1946 *FacFETw*
**Shaeiwitz,** Joseph Alan 1952- *AmMWSc 92*
**Shaer,** Ali Hassan ash- 1927- *IntWW 91*
**Shaer,** Elias Hanna 1941- *AmMWSc 92*
**Shaer,** Norman Robert 1937- *AmMWSc 92*
**Shaevel,** Morton Leonard 1936- *AmMWSc 92*
**Shaevsky,** Mark 1935- *WhoAmL 92*
**Shafaat,** Syed Tariq 1953- *WhoWest 92*
**Shafai,** Lotfollah 1941- *AmMWSc 92*
**Shafarevich,** Igor Rostislavovich 1923- *IntWW 91*
**Shafei,** Hussein Mahmoud El- 1918- *IntWW 91*
**Shafer,** A William 1927- *AmMWSc 92*
**Shafer,** Berman Joseph 1927- *WhoMW 92*
**Shafer,** Byron Edwin 1947- *Who 92*
**Shafer,** D. Michael 1953- *ConAu 134*
**Shafer,** Eric Christopher 1950- *WhoRel 92*
**Shafer,** Ernst Smith 1943- *WhoAmP 91*
**Shafer,** Gary Richard 1946- *WhoFI 92*
**Shafer,** James Albert 1924- *WhoWest 92*
**Shafer,** Jeffrey Todd 1959- *WhoFI 92*
**Shafer,** John Milton 1951- *WhoFI 92*
**Shafer,** Jules Alan 1937- *AmMWSc 92*
**Shafer,** M W 1928- *AmMWSc 92*
**Shafer,** Neil 1933- *WrDr 92*
**Shafer,** Norman Rick 1946- *WhoFI 92*
**Shafer,** Patterson 1953- *WhoEnt 92*
**Shafer,** Paul Richard 1923- *AmMWSc 92*
**Shafer,** Raymond Philip 1917- *WhoAmP 91*
**Shafer,** Richard Howard 1944- *AmMWSc 92*
**Shafer,** Robert 1925- *WrDr 92*
**Shafer,** Robert E 1936- *AmMWSc 92*
**Shafer,** Robert Eugene 1936- *WhoWest 92*
**Shafer,** Roberta W. Crow 1950- *WhoFI 92*
**Shafer,** Sharon Guertin 1943- *WhoEnt 92*
**Shafer,** Sheldon Jay 1948- *AmMWSc 92*
**Shafer,** Stephen Joel 1939- *AmMWSc 92*
**Shafer,** Stephen Quentin 1944- *AmMWSc 92*
**Shafer,** Steven Ray 1956- *AmMWSc 92*
**Shafer,** Thomas Howard 1948- *AmMWSc 92*
**Shafer,** W Sue 1941- *AmMWSc 92*
**Shafer,** Wayne L. 1950- *WhoRel 92*
**Shafer,** William Gene 1923- *AmMWSc 92*
**Shafer,** William Lewis, Jr. 1933- *WhoRel 92*
**Shaff,** Beverly Gerard 1925- *WhoWest 92*
**Shaffar,** Scott William 1962- *AmMWSc 92*
**Shaffe,** David Bruce 1950- *WhoAmP 91*
**Shaffer,** Anna *Who 92*
**Shaffer,** Anthony 1926- *WrDr 92*
**Shaffer,** Bernard W 1924- *AmMWSc 92*
**Shaffer,** Boyd Jensen 1925- *WhoWest 92*
**Shaffer,** Charles Franklin 1940- *AmMWSc 92*
**Shaffer,** Charles Henry, Jr 1913- *AmMWSc 92*
**Shaffer,** Charles V 1922- *AmMWSc 92*
**Shaffer,** Dale Eugene 1929- *WrDr 92*
**Shaffer,** Dale Lester 1920- *WhoAmP 91*
**Shaffer,** David 1936- *AmMWSc 92*
**Shaffer,** David Alan 1954- *WhoRel 92*
**Shaffer,** David Bruce 1946- *AmMWSc 92*
**Shaffer,** David H. 1942- *WhoFI 92*
**Shaffer,** David James 1958- *WhoAmL 92*
**Shaffer,** Dewey Lee 1952- *WhoRel 92*
**Shaffer,** Donald 1928- *WhoAmP 91*
**Shaffer,** Dorothy Browne 1923- *AmMWSc 92*
**Shaffer,** Douglas Howerth 1928- *AmMWSc 92*
**Shaffer,** Douglas L. *WhoRel 92*
**Shaffer,** Ellen Kate 1904- *WhoWest 92*
**Shaffer,** Frances Annette 1946- *WhoRel 92*
**Shaffer,** Gail S 1948- *WhoAmP 91*
**Shaffer,** Gary 1935- *WhoEnt 92*
**Shaffer,** Gary Morris 1940- *WhoWest 92*
**Shaffer,** Harry G. 1919- *WrDr 92*
**Shaffer,** Harry Gard, Jr. 1932- *WhoEnt 92, WhoMW 92*
**Shaffer,** Harry Leonard 1933- *AmMWSc 92*
**Shaffer,** Heidi Jo 1956- *WhoWest 92*
**Shaffer,** Jacquelin Bruning 1950- *AmMWSc 92*
**Shaffer,** Jay Charles 1938- *AmMWSc 92*
**Shaffer,** Jerome Arthur 1929- *WrDr 92*
**Shaffer,** John Clifford 1938- *AmMWSc 92*
**Shaffer,** John Jay 1937- *WhoRel 92*
**Shaffer,** Jonathan David 1964- *WhoAmL 92*
**Shaffer,** Judith 1945- *WhoMW 92*
**Shaffer,** Lawrence Bruce 1937- *AmMWSc 92*
**Shaffer,** Louis Richard 1928- *AmMWSc 92*
**Shaffer,** Martin 1950- *WhoAmP 91*
**Shaffer,** Mary Louise 1927- *WhoWest 92*
**Shaffer,** Michael L. 1945- *WhoFI 92*
**Shaffer,** Morris Frank 1910- *AmMWSc 92*
**Shaffer,** Nelson Ross 1948- *AmMWSc 92, WhoMW 92*
**Shaffer,** Patricia M. 1928- *WhoWest 92*
**Shaffer,** Patricia Marie 1928- *AmMWSc 92*
**Shaffer,** Paul 1949- *WhoEnt 92*
**Shaffer,** Paul M. 1942- *WhoRel 92*
**Shaffer,** Peter 1926- *CnDBLB 8 [port], IntAu&W 91, RfGEnL 91, WrDr 92*
**Shaffer,** Peter Levin 1926- *FacFETw, IntWW 91, Who 92*
**Shaffer,** Ray 1932- *WhoAmP 91*
**Shaffer,** Richard James 1931- *WhoAmL 92, WhoFI 92*
**Shaffer,** Richard Jerry, Jr. 1959- *WhoRel 92*
**Shaffer,** Richard Paul 1949- *WhoFI 92*
**Shaffer,** Robert Lynn 1929- *AmMWSc 92*
**Shaffer,** Roberta Ivy 1953- *WhoAmL 92*
**Shaffer,** Roger Lee 1947- *WhoAmP 91*
**Shaffer,** Russell Allen 1933- *AmMWSc 92*
**Shaffer,** Sherrill Lynn 1952- *WhoFI 92*
**Shaffer,** Stephen Carroll 1955- *WhoAmP 91*
**Shaffer,** Thomas Albert 1933- *WhoWest 92*
**Shaffer,** Thomas Hillard *AmMWSc 92*
**Shaffer,** Tim 1945- *WhoAmP 91*
**Shaffer,** Wave H 1909- *AmMWSc 92*
**Shaffer,** Wayne Alan 1954- *WhoAmL 92*
**Shaffer,** Willie Fred, III 1965- *WhoMW 92*
**Shaffert,** Kurt 1929- *WhoAmL 92*
**Shaffner,** Richard Owen 1938- *AmMWSc 92*
**Shaffner-Slade,** Claire Russell 1932- *WhoEnt 92*
**Shaffrey,** Ina Theresa 1911- *WhoAmP 91*
**Shafi,** Mohammad 1937- *AmMWSc 92*
**Shafie,** Mohammed Ghazali 1922- *IntWW 91*
**Shafii-Mousavi,** Morteza 1948- *WhoMW 92*
**Shafiq,** Mohammad Musa 1924- *IntWW 91*
**Shafiq,** Saiyid Ahmad 1929- *AmMWSc 92*
**Shafiroff,** Benjamin Gladstone 1906- *WhoFI 92*
**Shafit-Zagardo,** Bridget 1952- *AmMWSc 92*
**Shafner,** Matthew 1935- *WhoAmL 92*
**Shafner,** R.L. *DrAPF 91*
**Shafner,** Samuel Mark 1953- *WhoAmL 92*
**Shafran,** Daniil Borisovich 1923- *SovUnBD*
**Shafran,** Joseph Mark 1945- *WhoMW 92*
**Shafritz,** David Andrew 1940- *AmMWSc 92*
**Shafroth,** Stephen Morrison 1926- *AmMWSc 92*
**Shafroth,** Will d1991 *NewYTBS 91*
**Shaft,** Grant H 1962- *WhoAmP 91*
**Shaftan,** Gerald Wittes 1926- *AmMWSc 92*
**Shaftesbury,** Earl of 1938- *Who 92*
**Shaftesbury,** Anthony A. Cooper, Earl of 1671-1713 *BlkwCEP*
**Shaftman,** David Harry 1924- *AmMWSc 92*
**Shafto,** Robert Austin 1935- *WhoFI 92*
**Shafton,** Robert M. 1931- *WhoAmL 92*
**Shagal,** Mark Zakharovich *SovUnBD*
**Shagam,** Jerome Ira 1944- *WhoAmL 92*
**Shagam,** Marvin Huckel-Berri *WhoWest 92*
**Shagan,** Steve 1927- *IntMPA 92, WrDr 92*
**Shagari,** Alhaji Shehu Usman Aliu 1925- *IntWW 91*
**Shagari,** Shehu Usman Aliyu 1925- *Who 92*
**Shagass,** Charles 1920- *AmMWSc 92*
**Shaginyan,** Marietta Sergeevna 1888-1982 *SovUnBD*
**Shagory,** George Endicott 1936- *WhoFI 92*
**Shah,** Amritlal Jivraj 1941- *WhoFI 92*
**Shah,** Anil Manubhai 1952- *WhoFI 92*
**Shah,** Ashok Chandulal 1939- *AmMWSc 92*
**Shah,** Atul A 1940- *AmMWSc 92*
**Shah,** Babubhai Vadilal 1935- *AmMWSc 92*
**Shah,** Bhagwan G 1924- *AmMWSc 92*
**Shah,** Bhupendra K 1935- *AmMWSc 92*
**Shah,** Bhupendra Umedchand 1938- *AmMWSc 92*
**Shah,** Dharmishtha V *AmMWSc 92*
**Shah,** Dhiraj Nanchand 1940- *WhoMW 92*
**Shah,** Dinesh Ochhavlal 1938- *AmMWSc 92*
**Shah,** Eddy 1944- *IntWW 91*
**Shah,** Ghulam M 1937- *AmMWSc 92*
**Shah,** Girish Popatlal 1942- *WhoWest 92*
**Shah,** Hamish V 1953- *AmMWSc 92*
**Shah,** Haresh C 1937- *AmMWSc 92*
**Shah,** Hasmukh N 1934- *AmMWSc 92*
**Shah,** Hemendra Kumar 1945- *WhoFI 92*
**Shah,** Idries 1924- *IntAu&W 91, WrDr 92*
**Shah,** Ishwarlal D 1935- *AmMWSc 92*
**Shah,** Jagdeep C 1942- *AmMWSc 92*
**Shah,** Kanti L 1935- *AmMWSc 92*
**Shah,** Keerti V 1928- *AmMWSc 92*
**Shah,** Manesh J 1932- *AmMWSc 92*
**Shah,** Mihr Jahanian 1952- *WhoMW 92*
**Shah,** Mirza Mohammed 1941- *AmMWSc 92*
**Shah,** Pradeep L 1944- *AmMWSc 92*
**Shah,** Prakash C. 1953- *WhoMW 92*
**Shah,** Ramesh Keshavlal 1941- *AmMWSc 92*
**Shah,** Ramesh Trikamlal 1934- *AmMWSc 92*
**Shah,** Rasesh Harshadray 1954- *WhoFI 92*
**Shah,** Ravi Jivanlal 1941- *WhoWest 92*
**Shah,** Shantilal Nathubhai 1930- *AmMWSc 92*
**Shah,** Sheila 1945- *AmMWSc 92*
**Shah,** Shirish 1942- *AmMWSc 92*
**Shah,** Shirish A 1938- *AmMWSc 92*
**Shah,** Surendra P 1936- *AmMWSc 92*
**Shah,** Swarupchand Mohanlal 1905- *AmMWSc 92*
**Shaha,** Rishikesh 1925- *IntWW 91*
**Shahabuddeen,** Mohamed 1931- *IntWW 91*
**Shahabuddin,** Syed 1939- *AmMWSc 92*
**Shahal,** Moshe 1934- *IntWW 91*
**Shahan,** Norman Dean 1934- *WhoFI 92*
**Shahane,** Vasant A. 1923- *WrDr 92*
**Shahani,** Khem Motumal 1923- *AmMWSc 92*
**Shahar,** David 1926- *IntWW 91*
**Shahbender,** R A 1924- *AmMWSc 92*
**Shaheen,** Donald G 1930- *AmMWSc 92*
**Shaheen,** Jeanne 1947- *WhoAmP 91*
**Shaheen,** Michael Edmund, Jr. 1940- *WhoAmL 92*
**Shaheen,** Naseeb 1931- *ConAu 34NR*
**Shahi,** Agha 1920- *IntWW 91*
**Shahida,** Shahriar 1958- *WhoFI 92*
**Shahidi,** Fereidoon 1951- *AmMWSc 92*
**Shahidi,** Freydoon 1947- *AmMWSc 92, WhoMW 92*
**Shahidi,** Nasrollah Thomas 1926- *AmMWSc 92*
**Shahin,** Jamal Khalil 1931- *AmMWSc 92*
**Shahin,** Michael M 1932- *AmMWSc 92*
**Shahine,** Youssef *IntDcF 2-2*
**Shahinian,** Dean Vahan 1953- *WhoRel 92*
**Shahn,** Ben 1898-1969 *FacFETw*
**Shahn,** Ezra 1933- *AmMWSc 92*
**Shahon,** Susan Valerie 1948- *WhoMW 92*
**Shahrik,** H Arto 1923- *AmMWSc 92*
**Shahrokhi,** Firouz 1938- *AmMWSc 92*
**Shahrooz,** Bahram M. 1958- *WhoMW 92*
**Shahruz,** Shahram Mojaddad 1955- *WhoWest 92*
**Shaia,** Harry 1930- *WhoAmL 92*
**Shaievitz,** Sidney 1935- *WhoAmL 92*
**Shaik,** Fatima *DrAPF 91*
**Shaikh,** A Fattah 1937- *AmMWSc 92*
**Shaikh,** Zahir Ahmad 1945- *AmMWSc 92*
**Shaikun,** Michael Gary 1942- *WhoAmL 92*
**Shaiman,** Marc 1959- *WhoEnt 92*
**Shain,** Albert Leopold 1942- *AmMWSc 92*
**Shain,** Irving 1926- *AmMWSc 92*
**Shain,** Kenneth Stephen 1952- *WhoFI 92*
**Shain,** Merle 1935- *IntAu&W 91*
**Shain,** Sydney A 1940- *AmMWSc 92*
**Shain,** William Arthur 1931- *AmMWSc 92*
**Shainin,** Dorian 1914- *AmMWSc 92*
**Shainis,** Murray Joseph 1926- *WhoFI 92*
**Shainman,** Irwin 1921- *WhoEnt 92*
**Shainoff,** John Rieden 1930- *AmMWSc 92*
**Shair,** David Ira 1921- *WhoFI 92*
**Shair,** Fredrick H 1936- *AmMWSc 92*
**Shair,** Robert C 1925- *AmMWSc 92*
**Shairp,** Thomas *ScFEYrs*
**Shaka,** Athan James 1958- *AmMWSc 92*
**Shakaa,** Riyadh al 1941- *IntWW 91*
**Shakarian,** Demos 1913- *RelLAm 91*
**Shakarian,** Stephen Demos 1947- *WhoRel 92*
**Shakarjian,** Michael Peter 1955- *AmMWSc 92*
**Shake,** Roy Eugene 1932- *AmMWSc 92*
**Shaked,** Shaul 1933- *IntWW 91*
**Shakely,** John Bower 1940- *WhoWest 92*
**Shaker,** Mitchell Francis 1922- *WhoAmP 91*
**Shaker,** Mohamed Ibrahim 1933- *IntWW 91, Who 92*
**Shaker,** Sharif Zaid ibn 1934- *IntWW 91*
**Shakerley,** Geoffrey 1932- *Who 92*
**Shakeshaft,** Robin 1947- *AmMWSc 92*
**Shakespeare,** Frank 1925- *IntWW 91, WhoAmP 91*
**Shakespeare,** Frank J. *LesBEnT 92*
**Shakespeare,** John William Richmond 1930- *Who 92*
**Shakespeare,** Nicholas William Richmond 1957- *Who 92*
**Shakespeare,** William 1564-1616 *CnDBLB 1 [port], RfGEnL 91*
**Shakespeare,** William 1927- *Who 92*
**Shakhashiri,** Bassam Zekin 1939- *AmMWSc 92*
**Shakhlin,** Boris Sergeevich 1932- *SovUnBD*
**Shakhnazarov,** Georgiy Khosroevich 1924- *IntWW 91, SovUnBD*
**Shakhovskaya,** Eugenie M. *EncAmaz 91*
**Shaki,** Avner Hai 1928- *IntWW 91*
**Shakin,** Carl M 1934- *AmMWSc 92*
**Shakir,** Adib Akmal 1953- *WhoBlA 92*
**Shakirov,** Midkhat Zakirovich 1916- *SovUnBD*
**Shakkar,** Karim Ebrahim al- 1945- *IntWW 91*
**Shaklan,** Allen Yale 1945- *WhoEnt 92*
**Shaklee,** James Brooker 1945- *AmMWSc 92*
**Shakley,** Larry Eugene 1949- *WhoWest 92*
**Shakoor,** Adam Adib 1947- *WhoBlA 92*
**Shakoor,** Waheedah Aqueelah 1950- *WhoBlA 92*
**Shakow,** David J. 1945- *WhoAmL 92*
**Shaku,** Soyen 1859-1919 *RelLAm 91*
**Shakun,** Wallace 1934- *AmMWSc 92*
**Shalaby,** Shalaby W 1938- *AmMWSc 92*
**Shalaev,** Stepan Alekseevich 1929- *SovUnBD*
**Shalala,** Donna 1941- *CurBio 91 [port]*
**Shalala,** Donna Edna 1941- *IntWW 91, WhoMW 92*
**Shalala,** Philip D. 1937- *WhoFI 92*
**Shalamov,** Varlam 1907-1982 *FacFETw*
**Shalamov,** Varlam Tikhonovich 1907-1982 *SovUnBD*
**Shalaway,** Scott D 1952- *AmMWSc 92*
**Shalayev,** Stepan Alekseevich 1929- *IntWW 91*
**Shale,** David 1932- *AmMWSc 92*
**Shalek,** Robert James 1922- *AmMWSc 92*
**Shaler,** Amos J 1917- *AmMWSc 92*
**Shaler,** Nathaniel Southgate 1841-1906 *BiInAmS*
**Shales,** Thomas William 1948- *WhoEnt 92*
**Shales,** Tom *LesBEnT 92*
**Shalette,** Michael Alan 1935- *WhoFI 92*
**Shalhoob,** Margaret Page 1952- *WhoAmL 92*
**Shalhoub,** Robert M. W. 1952- *WhoAmL 92*
**Shalhoup,** Judy Lynn 1940- *WhoFI 92*
**Shalit,** Gene *LesBEnT 92*
**Shalit,** Gene 1932- *IntMPA 92*
**Shalit,** Harold 1919- *AmMWSc 92*
**Shalita,** Alan Remi 1936- *AmMWSc 92*
**Shallcrass,** John James 1922- *WrDr 92*
**Shallcross,** Frank V 1932- *AmMWSc 92*
**Shallcross,** Helen Clanahan 1913- *WhoWest 92*
**Shallenberger,** Robert Sands 1926- *AmMWSc 92*
**Shallenburger,** Tim *WhoAmP 91*
**Shaller,** David Allyn 1939- *WhoAmL 92*
**Shaller,** Walter Stanley 1918- *WhoAmL 92*
**Shallon,** David 1950- *WhoEnt 92*
**Shallow,** Robert *IntAu&W 91X, WrDr 92*
**Shalloway,** David Irwin 1948- *AmMWSc 92*
**Shalowitz,** Erwin Emmanuel 1924- *AmMWSc 92*
**Shalowitz,** Howard A. 1961- *WhoAmL 92*
**Shalton,** Lonnie Joseph 1941- *WhoAmP 91, WhoMW 92*
**Shalucha,** Barbara 1915- *AmMWSc 92*
**Shalvoy,** James Alan 1951- *WhoWest 92*
**Shalvoy,** Richard Barry 1949- *AmMWSc 92*
**Shalwitz,** Howard 1952- *WhoEnt 92*
**Shalyapin** *NewAmDM*
**Shalyapin,** Fedor Ivanovich 1873-1938 *SovUnBD*
**Sham,** Lu Jeu 1938- *AmMWSc 92*
**Shamah,** Moshe S. 1937- *WhoRel 92*
**Shaman,** Jeffrey M. 1941- *WhoAmL 92*
**Shaman,** Paul 1939- *AmMWSc 92*
**Shamansky,** Robert Norton 1927- *WhoAmP 91*
**Shamansky,** Sherry Lee 1943- *WhoWest 92*
**Shamapani,** Enock 1952- *WhoRel 92*
**Shamas,** James E. 1934- *WhoWest 92*
**Shamash,** Yacov A 1950- *AmMWSc 92*
**Shamask,** Ronaldus 1945- *IntWW 91*
**Shambaugh,** George E, III 1931- *AmMWSc 92*
**Shambaugh,** George Elmer, III 1931- *WhoMW 92*
**Shambaugh,** George Franklin 1928- *AmMWSc 92*
**Shambaugh,** Joan D. *DrAPF 91*
**Shambaugh,** Stephen Ward 1920- *WhoAmL 92, WhoWest 92*
**Shambelan,** Charles 1930- *AmMWSc 92*
**Shamberger,** James M 1940- *WhoIns 92*

**Shamberger,** Raymond J 1934- *AmMWSc 92*
**Shamblin,** A Kent 1935- *WhoIns 92*
**Shamblin,** Arnold Kent 1935- *WhoFI 92*
**Shamblin,** Broaddus Wade 1964- *WhoMW 92, WhoRel 92*
**Shamblin,** Darrell Ray 1927- *WhoRel 92*
**Shamblin,** James E 1932- *AmMWSc 92*
**Shambo,** James Alan 1950- *WhoFI 92*
**Shambroom,** William David 1949- *AmMWSc 92*
**Shamburger,** John Herbert 1925- *AmMWSc 92*
**Shamburger,** Sally C 1953- *WhoIns 92*
**Shamel,** Bonnie Marie 1950- *WhoMW 92*
**Shames,** David Marshall 1939- *AmMWSc 92*
**Shames,** Erica Leslie 1958- *WhoEnt 92*
**Shames,** Ervin Richard 1940- *WhoFI 92*
**Shames,** Irving H 1923- *AmMWSc 92*
**Shames,** William H. d1991 *NewYTBS 91*
**Shamess,** Nancy Lee 1956- *WhoWest 92*
**Shamgar,** Meir 1925- *IntWW 91*
**Shamie,** Raymond 1921- *WhoAmP 91*
**Shamir,** Adi 1952- *AmMWSc 92*
**Shamir,** Moshe 1921- *IntAu&W 91*
**Shamir,** Shimon 1933- *IntWW 91*
**Shamir,** Yitzhak 1915- *FacFETw [port], IntWW 91*
**Shamis,** Edward Anthony, Jr. 1949- *WhoAmL 92*
**Shamis,** Sidney S 1920- *AmMWSc 92*
**Shamma,** Maurice 1926- *AmMWSc 92*
**Shamoian,** Charles Anthony 1931- *AmMWSc 92*
**Shamon,** Paul 1963- *WhoAmP 91*
**Shamoo,** Adil E 1941- *AmMWSc 92*
**Shamos,** Michael Ian 1947- *AmMWSc 92*
**Shamos,** Morris Herbert 1917- *AmMWSc 92*
**Shamoun,** Simon Francis 1946- *AmMWSc 92*
**Shams-Ud Doha,** Aminur Rahman 1929- *Who 92*
**Shamshin,** Vasily Alexandrovich 1926- *IntWW 91*
**Shamsie,** Jalal 1930- *AmMWSc 92*
**Shamsuddin,** Abulkalam Mohammad 1948- *AmMWSc 92*
**Shamwell,** Joe 1944- *WhoBlA 92*
**Shamwell,** Ronald L. 1942- *WhoBlA 92*
**Shan,** Robert Kuocheng 1927- *AmMWSc 92*
**Shan,** Weijian 1953- *WhoFI 92*
**Shanaberg,** Peter Howard 1947- *WhoEnt 92*
**Shanafelt,** Nancy Sue 1947- *WhoWest 92*
**Shanafield,** Harold Arthur 1912- *WhoMW 92*
**Shanahan,** Edmond Michael 1926- *WhoFI 92*
**Shanahan,** Eileen 1924- *WhoAmP 91*
**Shanahan,** James Leo 1939- *WhoFI 92*
**Shanahan,** James P 1933- *WhoIns 92*
**Shanahan,** Marie Julie 1958- *WhoAmL 92*
**Shanahan,** Michael George 1940- *WhoWest 92*
**Shanahan,** Patrick 1931- *AmMWSc 92*
**Shanahan,** Thomas M. 1934- *WhoAmL 92, WhoMW 92*
**Shananhan,** Thomas 1934- *WhoAmP 91*
**Shanaphy,** Edward John 1938- *WhoEnt 92*
**Shanard,** George H 1926- *WhoAmP 91*
**Shanard,** George Harris 1926- *WhoMW 92*
**Shanard,** Marjorie Burns 1913- *WhoAmP 91*
**Shanas,** Ethel 1914- *WhoMW 92, WomSoc*
**Shanaver,** Alice Raynesford 1942- *WhoMW 92*
**Shanberge,** Jacob N 1922- *AmMWSc 92*
**Shand,** Bruce Middleton Hope 1917- *Who 92*
**Shand,** David Hubert Warner 1921- *Who 92*
**Shand,** John Alexander Ogilvie 1942- *Who 92*
**Shand,** Julian Bonham, Jr 1937- *AmMWSc 92*
**Shand,** Michael Lee 1946- *AmMWSc 92*
**Shandling,** Garry 1949- *ConTFT 9*
**Shandor,** Bohdan Donald 1952- *WhoAmL 92*
**Shands,** Franklin M., Sr. 1920- *WhoBlA 92*
**Shands,** Henry Lee 1935- *AmMWSc 92*
**Shands,** Jack L. 1943- *WhoWest 92*
**Shands,** Joseph Walter, Jr 1930- *AmMWSc 92*
**Shane,** Bart *TwCWW 91*
**Shane,** Bob 1934- *WhoEnt 92*
**Shane,** Charles N., Jr. 1936- *WhoAmL 92*
**Shane,** Cindy Lee 1959- *WhoWest 92*
**Shane,** Deborah Lynne 1950- *WhoEnt 92*
**Shane,** Flame-Fortune 1967- *WhoEnt 92*
**Shane,** Harold D 1936- *AmMWSc 92*
**Shane,** Harold Gray 1914- *WhoMW 92*
**Shane,** Jeffrey N. 1941- *WhoFI 92*
**Shane,** John *IntAu&W 91X, TwCWW 91, WrDr 92*
**Shane,** John Denis 1952- *AmMWSc 92*
**Shane,** John Richard 1936- *AmMWSc 92*
**Shane,** Joseph Lawrence 1935- *WhoFI 92*
**Shane,** Mark *IntAu&W 91X, TwCWW 91*
**Shane,** Martin *IntAu&W 91X*
**Shane,** Presson S 1920- *AmMWSc 92*
**Shane,** Rhondo *IntAu&W 91X, TwCWW 91*
**Shane,** Rick 1953- *WhoEnt 92*
**Shane,** Rita *WhoEnt 92*
**Shane,** Robert S 1910- *AmMWSc 92*
**Shane,** Samuel Jacob 1916- *AmMWSc 92*
**Shane,** Steve *TwCWW 91*
**Shane,** Susan Ann 1948- *WhoEnt 92*
**Shane,** Victor *IntAu&W 91X*
**Shanebrook,** J Richard 1938- *AmMWSc 92*
**Shanefield,** Daniel J 1930- *AmMWSc 92*
**Shaner,** David Wayne 1953- *WhoRel 92*
**Shaner,** Gregory Ellis 1942- *AmMWSc 92*
**Shaner,** John Wesley 1942- *AmMWSc 92*
**Shaner,** Richard C. *DrAPF 91*
**Shanes,** Eric 1944- *ConAu 134*
**Shanes,** Kendall Keith 1942- *WhoMW 92*
**Shanet,** Howard 1918- *NewAmDM*
**Shaneyfelt,** Duane L 1934- *AmMWSc 92*
**Shaneyfelt,** Ricky Dean 1959- *WhoMW 92*
**Shanfeldt,** Rachel Dwares 1960- *WhoAmL 92*
**Shanfield,** Henry 1923- *AmMWSc 92*
**Shang,** Ruby *WhoEnt 92*
**Shange,** Ntozake *DrAPF 91, WrDr 92*
**Shange,** Ntozake 1948- *AfrAmW, BenetAL 91, BlkLC [port], ConPo 91, NotBlAW 92, WhoBlA 92*
**Shange,** Ntozake 1949- *HanAmWH*
**Shango,** Shaka Aku *DrAPF 91*
**Shangraw,** Ralph F 1930- *AmMWSc 92*
**Shanholtz,** Vernon Odell 1935- *AmMWSc 92*
**Shanholtzer,** Wesley Lee 1938- *AmMWSc 92*
**Shank,** Brenda Mae Buckhold 1939- *AmMWSc 92*
**Shank,** Charles Philip 1941- *AmMWSc 92*
**Shank,** Charles Vernon 1943- *AmMWSc 92, WhoWest 92*
**Shank,** Dale *DrAPF 91*
**Shank,** Fred R 1940- *AmMWSc 92*
**Shank,** George Deane 1940- *AmMWSc 92*
**Shank,** Harold 1950- *WhoRel 92*
**Shank,** Herbert S 1927- *AmMWSc 92*
**Shank,** Kenneth Earl 1929- *WhoFI 92*
**Shank,** Kenneth Eugene 1949- *AmMWSc 92*
**Shank,** Lowell William 1939- *AmMWSc 92*
**Shank,** Margarethe Erdahl 1910- *WrDr 92*
**Shank,** Maurice E 1921- *AmMWSc 92*
**Shank,** Peter R 1946- *AmMWSc 92*
**Shank,** Richard Eugene 1932- *WhoAmP 91*
**Shank,** Richard Paul 1941- *AmMWSc 92*
**Shank,** Robert Ely 1914- *AmMWSc 92*
**Shank,** Russell 1925- *WhoWest 92*
**Shank,** Suzanne Adams 1946- *WhoAmL 92*
**Shank,** Theodore 1929- *WrDr 92*
**Shank,** William O. 1924- *WhoAmL 92*
**Shankar,** Hari 1930- *AmMWSc 92*
**Shankar,** Ramamurti 1947- *AmMWSc 92*
**Shankar,** Ramsewak *IntWW 91*
**Shankar,** Ravi 1920- *FacFETw, IntWW 91, NewAmDM, Who 92*
**Shankar,** Uday 1902-1977 *FacFETw*
**Shankaranand,** B. 1925- *IntWW 91*
**Shankardass,** Raghuvansh Kumar P. 1930- *IntWW 91*
**Shankel,** Delbert Merrill 1927- *AmMWSc 92*
**Shankel,** Jack Eugene 1932- *WhoRel 92*
**Shanker,** Albert 1928- *WhoAmP 91*
**Shanker,** P. Shiv 1929- *IntWW 91*
**Shankland,** Charles 1942- *WhoFI 92*
**Shankland,** Daniel Leslie 1924- *AmMWSc 92*
**Shankland,** Peter Macfarlane 1901- *WrDr 92*
**Shankland,** Rodney Veeder 1904- *AmMWSc 92*
**Shankle,** Robert Jack 1923- *AmMWSc 92*
**Shanklin,** James Robert, Jr 1941- *AmMWSc 92*
**Shanklin,** Milton D 1924- *AmMWSc 92*
**Shanks,** Ann Zane *WhoEnt 92*
**Shanks,** Bob *LesBEnT 92*
**Shanks,** Carl Harmon, Jr 1932- *AmMWSc 92*
**Shanks,** Duncan 1937- *TwCPaSc*
**Shanks,** Duncan Faichney 1937- *Who 92*
**Shanks,** Edward 1892-1953 *ScFEYrs*
**Shanks,** Ernest Pattison 1911- *Who 92*
**Shanks,** Frances Ann 1934- *WhoEnt 92*
**Shanks,** Hershel 1930- *WhoAmL 92, WhoRel 92*
**Shanks,** Ian Alexander 1948- *IntWW 91, Who 92*
**Shanks,** James A. 1912- *WhoBlA 92*
**Shanks,** James Bates 1917- *AmMWSc 92*
**Shanks,** James Clements, Jr 1921- *AmMWSc 92*
**Shanks,** Joyce Lakey 1930- *WhoMW 92*
**Shanks,** Margaret McCloskey 1953- *WhoAmL 92*
**Shanks,** Richard Joseph 1957- *WhoFI 92*
**Shanks,** Robert Bruce 1950- *WhoAmL 92*
**Shanks,** Robert H. 1932- *WhoEnt 92*
**Shanks,** Roger D 1951- *AmMWSc 92, WhoMW 92*
**Shanks,** Susan Jane *AmMWSc 92*
**Shanks,** Wayne C, III 1947- *AmMWSc 92*
**Shanks,** Wilhelmina Byrd 1951- *WhoBlA 92*
**Shanks,** William Coleman, Jr. 1917- *WhoBlA 92*
**Shankweiler,** Carl David 1946- *WhoRel 92*
**Shanley,** Bernard Michael 1903- *WhoAmP 91*
**Shanley,** Helen *DrAPF 91*
**Shanley,** John Patrick 1950- *ConAu 133, ConTFT 9, IntMPA 92*
**Shanline,** Rix Donald 1926- *WhoMW 92*
**Shanman,** James Alan 1942- *WhoAmL 92*
**Shanmugam,** Keelnatham Thirunavukkarasu 1941- *AmMWSc 92*
**Shanmugan,** K Sam 1943- *AmMWSc 92*
**Shannon,** Earl of 1924- *Who 92*
**Shannon,** Barry Thomas 1952- *AmMWSc 92*
**Shannon,** Charles 1863-1937 *TwCPaSc*
**Shannon,** Charles E *WhoAmP 91*
**Shannon,** Claude Elwood 1916- *AmMWSc 92, IntWW 91*
**Shannon,** Daniel William 1934- *WhoMW 92*
**Shannon,** David Thomas 1933- *WhoBlA 92*
**Shannon,** David William Francis 1941- *Who 92*
**Shannon,** Del 1939-1990 *AnObit 1990, FacFETw*
**Shannon,** Dell *IntAu&W 91X*
**Shannon,** Donald Sutherlin 1935- *WhoMW 92*
**Shannon,** Doris 1924- *IntAu&W 91, WrDr 92*
**Shannon,** Edfred L., Jr. 1926- *WhoWest 92*
**Shannon,** Edward Leo 1939- *WhoMW 92*
**Shannon,** Ella Walton 1933- *WhoMW 92*
**Shannon,** Frederick Dale 1931- *AmMWSc 92*
**Shannon,** George A. 1918- *WhoBlA 92*
**Shannon,** Gerry Eugene 1954- *WhoFI 92*
**Shannon,** Iris R *AmMWSc 92*
**Shannon,** Jack Corum 1935- *AmMWSc 92*
**Shannon,** Jack Dee 1943- *AmMWSc 92*
**Shannon,** James Augustine 1904- *AmMWSc 92, IntWW 91*
**Shannon,** James Jebusa 1862-1923 *TwCPaSc*
**Shannon,** James Michael 1952- *WhoAmP 91*
**Shannon,** Jeanne *DrAPF 91*
**Shannon,** Jerry A, Jr 1924- *AmMWSc 92*
**Shannon,** Joe, Jr. 1940- *WhoAmL 92*
**Shannon,** John A. 1950- *WhoAmL 92*
**Shannon,** John Kingsley *DrAPF 91*
**Shannon,** John Sanford 1931- *WhoAmL 92, WhoFI 92*
**Shannon,** John William 1933- *WhoBlA 92*
**Shannon,** Joseph Thomas, Jr. 1949- *WhoAmL 92*
**Shannon,** Larry J 1937- *AmMWSc 92*
**Shannon,** Leland Marion 1927- *AmMWSc 92*
**Shannon,** Malcolm Lloyd, Jr. 1946- *WhoAmL 92*
**Shannon,** Marian L. H. 1922- *WhoBlA 92*
**Shannon,** Martha Alberter 1958- *WhoFI 92*
**Shannon,** Marylin Linfoot 1941- *WhoAmP 91*
**Shannon,** Michael Edward 1936- *WhoFI 92*
**Shannon,** Michael Scott 1947- *WhoEnt 92*
**Shannon,** Odessa M. 1928- *WhoBlA 92*
**Shannon,** Odessa McKenzie 1928- *WhoAmP 91*
**Shannon,** Richard John 1949- *WhoWest 92*
**Shannon,** Richard Stoll, III 1943- *WhoWest 92*
**Shannon,** Richard Thomas 1931- *IntWW 91*
**Shannon,** Robert Day 1935- *AmMWSc 92*
**Shannon,** Robert F. 1920- *WhoBlA 92*
**Shannon,** Robert Rennie 1932- *AmMWSc 92, WhoWest 92*
**Shannon,** Russell Delbert 1938- *WhoFI 92*
**Shannon,** Shad 1955- *WhoWest 92*
**Shannon,** Spencer Sweet, Jr 1927- *AmMWSc 92*
**Shannon,** Stanton 1928- *AmMWSc 92*
**Shannon,** Steve *TwCWW 91, WrDr 92*
**Shannon,** Sylvester Lorenzo 1933- *WhoBlA 92*
**Shannon,** Wilburn Allen, Jr 1941- *AmMWSc 92*
**Shannon,** William Michael 1940- *AmMWSc 92*
**Shannon,** William Norman, III 1937- *WhoFI 92, WhoMW 92*
**Shanok,** Larry Frank 1947- *WhoFI 92*
**Shanor,** Clarence Richard 1924- *WhoRel 92, WhoWest 92*
**Shanor,** Leland 1914- *AmMWSc 92*
**Shanosky,** Leo Charles 1930- *WhoIns 92*
**Shanov,** Elizabeth 1953- *WhoEnt 92*
**Shansby,** John Gary 1937- *WhoFI 92*
**Shansky,** Michael Steven 1943- *AmMWSc 92*
**Shantaram,** Rajagopal 1939- *AmMWSc 92*
**Shantaram,** V. 1901- *IntWW 91*
**Shanteau,** Robert Marshall 1947- *AmMWSc 92*
**Shanthikumar,** Jeyaveerasingam George 1950- *AmMWSc 92*
**Shanti,** Ragheed Najeeb 1957- *WhoFI 92*
**Shanzer,** Stefan 1924- *AmMWSc 92*
**Shao Dadi** 1938- *IntWW 91*
**Shao Yanxiang** 1933- *IntWW 91*
**Shao,** Gang 1953- *WhoFI 92*
**Shapar,** Howard Kamber 1923- *IntWW 91*
**Shapard,** Robert *DrAPF 91*
**Shapcott,** Jo 1958- *ConAu 135*
**Shapcott,** Sidney Edward 1920- *Who 92*
**Shapcott,** Thomas W. 1935- *ConPo 91, WrDr 92*
**Shaper,** Christopher Thorne 1955- *WhoFI 92*
**Shaper,** Gerald 1927- *Who 92*
**Shapere,** Dudley 1928- *AmMWSc 92*
**Shapero,** Donald Campbell 1942- *AmMWSc 92*
**Shapero,** Harold 1920- *ConCom 92, NewAmDM*
**Shapero,** Harris Joel 1930- *WhoWest 92*
**Shapero,** Neal Eric 1958- *WhoAmL 92*
**Shapey,** Ralph 1921- *ConCom 92, NewAmDM, WhoEnt 92*
**Shaphren,** Susanne *DrAPF 91*
**Shapira,** David S. 1942- *WhoFI 92*
**Shapira,** Raymond 1928- *AmMWSc 92*
**Shapira,** Yaacov 1938- *AmMWSc 92*
**Shapiro,** Alan Elihu 1942- *AmMWSc 92*
**Shapiro,** Alan Isaiah 1951- *WhoWest 92*
**Shapiro,** Alec William 1952- *WhoEnt 92*
**Shapiro,** Aleena Rieger *WhoAmL 92*
**Shapiro,** Alvin 1930- *AmMWSc 92*
**Shapiro,** Alvin Philip 1920- *AmMWSc 92*
**Shapiro,** Anatole Morris 1923- *AmMWSc 92*
**Shapiro,** Arnold *LesBEnT 92*
**Shapiro,** Arthur Maurice 1946- *AmMWSc 92*
**Shapiro,** Ascher H 1916- *AmMWSc 92, IntWW 91*
**Shapiro,** Avraham 1918- *WhoRel 92*
**Shapiro,** Barry 1942- *WhoFI 92, WhoWest 92*
**Shapiro,** Benjamin Louis 1943- *WhoAmL 92*
**Shapiro,** Bennett Michaels 1939- *AmMWSc 92*
**Shapiro,** Bernard 1925- *AmMWSc 92*
**Shapiro,** Bernard Lyon 1932- *AmMWSc 92*
**Shapiro,** Bert Irwin 1941- *AmMWSc 92*
**Shapiro,** Burton Leonard 1934- *AmMWSc 92*
**Shapiro,** Caren Knight 1945- *AmMWSc 92*
**Shapiro,** Carl 1955- *WhoFI 92*
**Shapiro,** Chaim 1931- *WhoRel 92*
**Shapiro,** Charles Saul 1936- *AmMWSc 92*
**Shapiro,** Dan 1910- *WhoEnt 92*
**Shapiro,** David *DrAPF 91*
**Shapiro,** David 1924- *AmMWSc 92*
**Shapiro,** David 1947- *ConPo 91, WrDr 92*
**Shapiro,** David 1954- *WhoIns 92, WhoMW 92*
**Shapiro,** David B *WhoAmP 91*
**Shapiro,** David Jordon 1946- *AmMWSc 92*
**Shapiro,** David L. 1936- *WhoAmL 92*
**Shapiro,** David Louis 1932- *WhoAmL 92*
**Shapiro,** David M 1929- *AmMWSc 92*
**Shapiro,** Donald M 1935- *AmMWSc 92*
**Shapiro,** Douglas York 1941- *AmMWSc 92*
**Shapiro,** Edward K Edik *AmMWSc 92*
**Shapiro,** Edwin Henry 1938- *WhoAmL 92*
**Shapiro,** Edwin Seymour 1928- *AmMWSc 92*
**Shapiro,** Eli 1916- *IntWW 91, WhoFI 92, WrDr 92*
**Shapiro,** Ellen Goldberg 1942- *WhoEnt 92*
**Shapiro,** Erin Patria Margaret 1939- *Who 92*
**Shapiro,** Esther *LesBEnT 92*
**Shapiro,** Eugene 1944- *AmMWSc 92*
**Shapiro,** Eve *WhoEnt 92*
**Shapiro,** Everett Hale 1927- *WhoAmL 92*
**Shapiro,** Florence *WhoAmP 91*
**Shapiro,** Fred Richard 1954- *WhoAmL 92*
**Shapiro,** Gary Michael 1941- *WhoMW 92*

**Shapiro,** George Howard 1936- *WhoAmL 92*
**Shapiro,** George M. 1919- *WhoAmL 92, WhoFI 92*
**Shapiro,** Gilbert 1934- *AmMWSc 92*
**Shapiro,** Gregg *DrAPF 91*
**Shapiro,** Hadassah Ruth 1924- *WhoAmL 92*
**Shapiro,** Harold David 1927- *WhoMW 92*
**Shapiro,** Harold Tafler 1935- *IntWW 91*
**Shapiro,** Harold Tafler 1936- *Who 92*
**Shapiro,** Harry 1902-1990 *AnObit 1990*
**Shapiro,** Harry Lionel 1902- *AmMWSc 92*
**Shapiro,** Harry S. *DrAPF 91*
**Shapiro,** Harvey *DrAPF 91, WhoEnt 92*
**Shapiro,** Harvey 1924- *ConAu 34NR, ConPo 91, IntAu&W 91, WrDr 92*
**Shapiro,** Henry d1991 *NewYTBS 91*
**Shapiro,** Herbert 1907- *AmMWSc 92*
**Shapiro,** Herbert 1929- *WrDr 92*
**Shapiro,** Herman Simon 1929- *AmMWSc 92*
**Shapiro,** Howard Alan 1932- *WhoAmL 92*
**Shapiro,** Howard Maurice 1941- *AmMWSc 92*
**Shapiro,** Irving 1932- *AmMWSc 92*
**Shapiro,** Irving Meyer 1937- *AmMWSc 92*
**Shapiro,** Irving S. 1916- *IntWW 91*
**Shapiro,** Irwin I. 1929- *IntWW 91*
**Shapiro,** Irwin Ira 1929- *AmMWSc 92*
**Shapiro,** Irwin Louis 1932- *AmMWSc 92*
**Shapiro,** Isaac 1931- *WhoAmL 92*
**Shapiro,** Isadore 1916- *WhoFI 92, WhoWest 92*
**Shapiro,** Ivan 1928- *WhoAmL 92*
**Shapiro,** Jack Sol 1941- *AmMWSc 92*
**Shapiro,** Jacob *IntMPA 92*
**Shapiro,** Jacob 1925- *AmMWSc 92*
**Shapiro,** James Alan 1943- *AmMWSc 92*
**Shapiro,** Jan A. 1949- *WhoEnt 92*
**Shapiro,** Jeffrey Howard 1946- *AmMWSc 92*
**Shapiro,** Jeffrey Paul 1950- *AmMWSc 92*
**Shapiro,** Jerald Steven 1943- *WhoFI 92*
**Shapiro,** Jerome Lee 1932- *WhoWest 92*
**Shapiro,** Jesse Marshall 1929- *AmMWSc 92*
**Shapiro,** Joan *DrAPF 91*
**Shapiro,** Joan Dovima 1961- *WhoEnt 92*
**Shapiro,** Joan Isabelle 1943- *WhoMW 92*
**Shapiro,** Joe *WhoAmL 92*
**Shapiro,** Joel 1934- *WhoEnt 92*
**Shapiro,** Joel 1941- *IntWW 91, WorArt 1980 [port]*
**Shapiro,** Joel Alan 1942- *AmMWSc 92*
**Shapiro,** Joseph 1929- *AmMWSc 92*
**Shapiro,** Julia Clare 1937- *WhoMW 92*
**Shapiro,** Karl *DrAPF 91*
**Shapiro,** Karl 1913- *BenetAL 91, ConAu 36NR, ConPo 91, IntAu&W 91, WrDr 92*
**Shapiro,** Karl Jay 1913- *IntWW 91*
**Shapiro,** Ken 1943- *IntMPA 92*
**Shapiro,** Kenneth L 1936- *WhoAmP 91*
**Shapiro,** Larry Jay 1946- *AmMWSc 92*
**Shapiro,** Laurence David 1941- *WhoEnt 92*
**Shapiro,** Lee Tobey 1943- *AmMWSc 92*
**Shapiro,** Leo J. 1921- *WhoMW 92*
**Shapiro,** Leonard David 1943- *AmMWSc 92*
**Shapiro,** Linda Jo 1941- *WhoEnt 92*
**Shapiro,** Lori Rae 1964- *WhoAmL 92*
**Shapiro,** Lorne 1912- *AmMWSc 92*
**Shapiro,** Louis d1991 *NewYTBS 91*
**Shapiro,** Louis Oren 1948- *WhoFI 92*
**Shapiro,** Lucille 1940- *AmMWSc 92*
**Shapiro,** Mark Howard 1940- *AmMWSc 92*
**Shapiro,** Marshall 1929- *WhoMW 92*
**Shapiro,** Martin 1933- *WhoAmL 92*
**Shapiro,** Martin 1937- *AmMWSc 92*
**Shapiro,** Marvin Lincoln 1923- *WhoEnt 92*
**Shapiro,** Marvin S 1936- *WhoAmP 91*
**Shapiro,** Marvin Seymour 1936- *WhoAmL 92*
**Shapiro,** Maurice A 1917- *AmMWSc 92*
**Shapiro,** Maurice Mandel 1915- *AmMWSc 92*
**Shapiro,** Max Andrew 1917- *WhoRel 92*
**Shapiro,** Mel 1935- *WhoEnt 92*
**Shapiro,** Milton S 1913- *WhoAmP 91*
**Shapiro,** Morris 1920- *WhoRel 92*
**Shapiro,** Myra *DrAPF 91*
**Shapiro,** Nancy Ann *WhoEnt 92*
**Shapiro,** Nathan 1924- *AmMWSc 92*
**Shapiro,** Nelson Hirsh 1928- *WhoAmL 92*
**Shapiro,** Nina Beth 1948- *WhoFI 92*
**Shapiro,** Norma Sondra Levy 1928- *WhoAmL 92*
**Shapiro,** Paul Jonathon 1952- *AmMWSc 92*
**Shapiro,** Paul Robert 1953- *AmMWSc 92*
**Shapiro,** Philip 1923- *AmMWSc 92*
**Shapiro,** Ralph 1922- *AmMWSc 92*
**Shapiro,** Rami M. 1951- *WhoRel 92*
**Shapiro,** Raymond E 1927- *AmMWSc 92*
**Shapiro,** Richard Charles 1936- *WhoMW 92*
**Shapiro,** Richard Scott 1958- *WhoAmL 92*
**Shapiro,** Richard Stanley 1925- *WhoWest 92*
**Shapiro,** Robert 1935- *AmMWSc 92*
**Shapiro,** Robert Alan 1946- *WhoFI 92*
**Shapiro,** Robert Allen 1930- *AmMWSc 92*
**Shapiro,** Robert Donald 1942- *WhoMW 92*
**Shapiro,** Robert Frank 1934- *WhoFI 92*
**Shapiro,** Robert Howard 1935- *AmMWSc 92*
**Shapiro,** Robert M. 1945- *WhoFI 92*
**Shapiro,** Robert W. 1938- *IntMPA 92*
**Shapiro,** Romie 1909- *WhoFI 92*
**Shapiro,** Ronald Maurice 1943- *WhoAmL 92*
**Shapiro,** Rubin 1924- *AmMWSc 92*
**Shapiro,** Sam 1914- *AmMWSc 92*
**Shapiro,** Samuel David 1927- *WhoAmP 91*
**Shapiro,** Samuel S 1930- *AmMWSc 92*
**Shapiro,** Sandor Solomon 1933- *AmMWSc 92*
**Shapiro,** Sandra 1944- *WhoAmL 92*
**Shapiro,** Seymour 1924- *AmMWSc 92*
**Shapiro,** Sidney 1931- *AmMWSc 92*
**Shapiro,** Stanley 1925- *WrDr 92*
**Shapiro,** Stanley 1937- *AmMWSc 92*
**Shapiro,** Stanley Kallick 1923- *AmMWSc 92*
**Shapiro,** Stanley Seymour 1940- *AmMWSc 92*
**Shapiro,** Stephen D 1941- *AmMWSc 92*
**Shapiro,** Stephen Michael 1941- *AmMWSc 92*
**Shapiro,** Stewart 1937- *AmMWSc 92*
**Shapiro,** Stuart 1952- *AmMWSc 92*
**Shapiro,** Stuart Charles 1944- *AmMWSc 92*
**Shapiro,** Stuart Louis 1947- *AmMWSc 92*
**Shapiro,** Susan Janine 1951- *WhoMW 92*
**Shapiro,** Tad Steven 1955- *WhoAmL 92*
**Shapiro,** Victor Lenard 1924- *AmMWSc 92*
**Shapiro,** Warren Barry 1941- *AmMWSc 92*
**Shapiro,** William 1927- *AmMWSc 92*
**Shapiro,** Zalman Mordecai 1920- *AmMWSc 92*
**Shapland,** Peter Charles 1923- *Who 92*
**Shapland,** William 1912- *Who 92*
**Shapleigh,** Waldron 1848-1901 *BiInAmS*
**Shapleigh,** Warren McKinney 1920- *IntWW 91*
**Shapley,** Harlow 1885-1972 *FacFETw*
**Shapley,** James Louis 1920- *AmMWSc 92*
**Shapley,** John Roger 1946- *AmMWSc 92*
**Shapley,** Lloyd Stowell 1923- *AmMWSc 92, IntWW 91, WhoWest 92*
**Shapley,** Robert M 1944- *AmMWSc 92*
**Shapo,** Marshall Schambelan 1936- *WhoAmL 92*
**Shapo,** Ronald Allan 1941- *WhoAmL 92*
**Shaporin,** Yuri 1887-1966 *NewAmDM*
**Shaporin,** Yuriy Aleksandrovich 1887-1966 *SovUnBD*
**Shaposhnikov,** Boris Mikhaylovich 1882-1945 *SovUnBD*
**Shapp,** Milton J 1912- *WhoAmP 91*
**Shappirio,** David Gordon 1930- *AmMWSc 92*
**Shappiro,** Herbert *TwCWW 91*
**Shapton,** William Robert 1941- *AmMWSc 92*
**Shar,** Albert O 1944- *AmMWSc 92*
**Shar,** Leonard E 1948- *AmMWSc 92*
**Shara,** Michael M 1949- *AmMWSc 92*
**Sharaff,** Irene 1910- *IntMPA 92*
**Sharah,** Abul 1937- *WhoFI 92*
**Sharan,** Shailendra Kishore 1947- *AmMWSc 92*
**Sharapov,** Viktor Vasilevich 1931- *IntWW 91*
**Sharari,** Hisham 1939- *IntWW 91*
**Sharat Chandra,** G.S. *DrAPF 91*
**Sharat Chandra,** G. S. 1938- *WrDr 92*
**Sharawy,** Mohamed 1941- *AmMWSc 92*
**Sharayev,** Leonid Gavriilovich 1935- *IntWW 91*
**Sharbaf,** Mehrdad Sepehri 1959- *WhoWest 92*
**Sharbaugh,** Amandus Harry 1919- *AmMWSc 92*
**Sharber,** James Randall 1941- *AmMWSc 92*
**Sharber,** Jerry W 1946- *WhoAmP 91*
**Sharbo,** Walter Johnson 1923- *WhoMW 92*
**Sharboneau,** Lorna Rosina 1935- *WhoEnt 92*
**Share,** Don *DrAPF 91*
**Share,** Gerald Harvey 1940- *AmMWSc 92*
**Share,** Leonard 1927- *AmMWSc 92*
**Share,** Michael *IntMPA 92*
**Share,** Norman N 1930- *AmMWSc 92*
**Share,** Richard Hudson 1938- *WhoAmL 92*
**Share,** William Fremont 1926- *WhoMW 92*
**Shareck,** Helen Marie 1930- *WhoWest 92*
**Sharer,** Archibald Wilson 1919- *AmMWSc 92*
**Sharer,** Cyrus J 1922- *AmMWSc 92*
**Shares,** Milton Charles 1931- *WhoEnt 92*
**Sharett,** Alan Richard 1943- *WhoAmL 92*
**Sharett,** Deirdre *DrAPF 91*
**Sharf,** Donald Jack 1927- *AmMWSc 92*
**Sharfman,** Herbert 1909- *WhoAmL 92*
**Sharfman,** Jerome Elliott 1937- *WhoAmL 92*
**Sharfman,** Robert Jay 1936- *WhoAmL 92, WhoMW 92*
**Shargel,** Leon David 1941- *AmMWSc 92*
**Shargool,** Peter Douglas 1935- *AmMWSc 92*
**Shariat,** Hormoz 1955- *WhoWest 92*
**Shariatzadeh,** Vahid 1950- *WhoFI 92*
**Sharick,** Merle Dayton, Jr. 1946- *WhoFI 92*
**Sharif,** M. Nawaz 1942- *ConAu 36NR*
**Sharif,** Nawaz 1949- *IntWW 91*
**Sharif,** Omar 1932- *IntMPA 92, IntWW 91, WhoEnt 92*
**Sharif,** Said Mujtaba 1948- *WhoAmL 92*
**Sharif-Emami,** Jafar 1910- *IntWW 91*
**Shariff,** Asghar J. 1941- *WhoWest 92*
**Shariff,** Ismail 1937- *WhoMW 92*
**Shariffe,** Hussein 1937- *TwCPaSc*
**Sharir,** Abraham 1932- *IntWW 91*
**Sharir,** Yacov 1940- *WhoEnt 92*
**Sharits,** Paul Jeffrey 1943- *WhoEnt 92*
**Sharitz,** Rebecca Reyburn 1944- *AmMWSc 92*
**Sharkansky,** Ira 1938- *WrDr 92*
**Sharkawi,** Mahmoud 1935- *AmMWSc 92*
**Sharkey,** Christine Ann 1951- *WhoWest 92*
**Sharkey,** Colum John 1931- *Who 92*
**Sharkey,** Edward Michael 1946- *WhoAmL 92*
**Sharkey,** Jack 1931- *IntAu&W 91, TwCSFW 91, WrDr 92*
**Sharkey,** John Bernard 1940- *AmMWSc 92*
**Sharkey,** Joseph T. d1991 *NewYTBS 91 [port]*
**Sharkey,** Lee *DrAPF 91*
**Sharkey,** Margaret Mary *AmMWSc 92*
**Sharkey,** Michael John 1958- *WhoAmL 92*
**Sharkey,** Michael Joseph 1953- *AmMWSc 92*
**Sharkey,** Paul William 1945- *WhoRel 92*
**Sharkey,** Ray 1952- *IntMPA 92*
**Sharkey,** Richard David 1957- *WhoWest 92*
**Sharkey,** Robert J. 1944- *WhoWest 92*
**Sharkey,** Robert James 1951- *WhoAmL 92*
**Sharkey,** Thomas D 1953- *AmMWSc 92*
**Sharkey,** Vincent Joseph 1944- *WhoAmL 92*
**Sharkey,** William Henry 1916- *AmMWSc 92*
**Sharkoff,** Eugene Gibb 1925- *AmMWSc 92*
**Sharland,** Edward John 1937- *Who 92*
**Sharland,** John 1937- *IntWW 91*
**Sharlip,** William *DcAmImH*
**Sharlow,** John Francis 1941- *AmMWSc 92*
**Sharma,** Anthony Francis 1937- *WhoRel 92*
**Sharma,** Arjun D 1953- *AmMWSc 92, WhoWest 92*
**Sharma,** Arun Kumar 1924- *IntWW 91*
**Sharma,** Brahma Dutta 1947- *AmMWSc 92*
**Sharma,** Dinesh C 1938- *AmMWSc 92*
**Sharma,** Ghanshyam D 1931- *AmMWSc 92*
**Sharma,** Gopal Chandra 1932- *AmMWSc 92*
**Sharma,** Gopal Krishan 1937- *AmMWSc 92*
**Sharma,** Govind C 1944- *AmMWSc 92*
**Sharma,** Hari M 1938- *AmMWSc 92*
**Sharma,** Jagadish 1923- *AmMWSc 92*
**Sharma,** Jagdev Mittra 1941- *AmMWSc 92*
**Sharma,** Krishna Dayal 1931- *IntWW 91*
**Sharma,** Madan Lal 1934- *AmMWSc 92*
**Sharma,** Mangalore Gokulanand 1927- *AmMWSc 92*
**Sharma,** Minoti *AmMWSc 92*
**Sharma,** Moheswar *AmMWSc 92*
**Sharma,** Neeraj Kumar 1965- *WhoMW 92*
**Sharma,** Opendra K 1941- *AmMWSc 92*
**Sharma,** Prem Lal 1940- *WhoMW 92*
**Sharma,** Raghubir Prasad 1940- *AmMWSc 92*
**Sharma,** Ram Ashrey 1943- *AmMWSc 92*
**Sharma,** Ram Autar 1927- *AmMWSc 92*
**Sharma,** Ram Ratan 1936- *AmMWSc 92*
**Sharma,** Ramesh C 1931- *AmMWSc 92*
**Sharma,** Rameshwar Kumar 1935- *AmMWSc 92*
**Sharma,** Ran S 1937- *AmMWSc 92*
**Sharma,** Sansar C 1938- *AmMWSc 92*
**Sharma,** Santosh Devraj 1934- *AmMWSc 92*
**Sharma,** Satish 1941- *WhoWest 92*
**Sharma,** Shanker Dayal 1918- *IntWW 91, Who 92*
**Sharma,** Shri C 1945- *AmMWSc 92, WhoMW 92*
**Sharma,** Somesh Datt *AmMWSc 92*
**Sharma,** Surendra Prasad 1943- *WhoWest 92*
**Sharma,** Suresh C 1945- *AmMWSc 92*
**Sharma,** Sushil 1956- *WhoFI 92*
**Sharma,** Udhishtra Deva 1928- *AmMWSc 92*
**Sharma,** Usha Kumari *Who 92*
**Sharma,** Vin Kumar 1945- *WhoMW 92*
**Sharma,** Vishnu Datt 1921- *Who 92*
**Sharma,** Wende Louise 1957- *WhoFI 92*
**Sharman,** Peter William 1924- *Who 92*
**Sharman,** William 1926- *WhoWest 92*
**Sharmat,** Marjorie Weinman 1928- *IntAu&W 91, WrDr 92*
**Sharnik,** John *LesBEnT 92*
**Sharnoff,** Mark 1935- *AmMWSc 92*
**Sharoev,** Ioakim Georgevich 1930- *IntWW 91*
**Sharoff,** Janis Valaskovic 1952- *WhoWest 92*
**Sharon,** Lois & Bram *ConMus 6 [port]*
**Sharon,** Ariel 1928- *FacFETw, IntWW 91*
**Sharon,** Michael Harold 1958- *WhoAmL 92*
**Sharon,** Nehama 1929- *AmMWSc 92*
**Sharon,** Reva *DrAPF 91*
**Sharon,** Timothy Michael 1948- *WhoWest 92*
**Sharon,** Yitzhak Yaakov 1936- *AmMWSc 92*
**Sharot,** Stephen 1943- *WrDr 92*
**Sharoubim,** Kamel Fahim 1934- *WhoEnt 92*
**Sharp** *Who 92*
**Sharp,** A C, Jr 1932- *AmMWSc 92*
**Sharp,** A G 1923- *AmMWSc 92*
**Sharp,** Aaron John 1904- *AmMWSc 92*
**Sharp,** Adrian 1951- *Who 92*
**Sharp,** Alan *IntMPA 92*
**Sharp,** Alastair George 1911- *Who 92*
**Sharp,** Allan Rhinehart 1925- *WhoRel 92*
**Sharp,** Allan Roy 1946- *AmMWSc 92*
**Sharp,** Allen 1932- *WhoAmL 92, WhoMW 92*
**Sharp,** Angus *Who 92*
**Sharp,** Archie Bernard 1931- *WhoEnt 92*
**Sharp,** Benjamin 1858-1915 *BiInAmS*
**Sharp,** Bert M 1933- *WhoAmP 91*
**Sharp,** Charles Louis 1951- *WhoBlA 92*
**Sharp,** Clay LaValle 1940- *WhoFI 92*
**Sharp,** Clifford Henry 1922- *WrDr 92*
**Sharp,** Dale Eugene 1953- *WhoMW 92*
**Sharp,** David Burton 1957- *WhoEnt 92*
**Sharp,** David Howland 1938- *AmMWSc 92*
**Sharp,** David Lee 1952- *WhoWest 92*
**Sharp,** Dennis 1933- *WrDr 92*
**Sharp,** Derek Joseph 1925- *Who 92*
**Sharp,** Dexter Brian 1919- *AmMWSc 92*
**Sharp,** Don 1921- *IntMPA 92*
**Sharp,** Doreen Maud 1920- *WrDr 92*
**Sharp,** Doris Fuller 1924- *WhoAmP 91*
**Sharp,** Dorothea 1874-1955 *TwCPaSc*
**Sharp,** Douglas Rice 1949- *WhoRel 92*
**Sharp,** Duane Carl 1938- *WhoWest 92*
**Sharp,** Edward A 1920- *AmMWSc 92*
**Sharp,** Eugene Lester 1926- *AmMWSc 92*
**Sharp,** George 1919- *Who 92*
**Sharp,** George Baldwin 1941- *WhoFI 92*
**Sharp,** George G. 1874-1960 *DcTwDes, FacFETw*
**Sharp,** George Richard 1934- *WhoMW 92*
**Sharp,** Gerald Duane 1933- *AmMWSc 92*
**Sharp,** Granville Maynard 1906- *Who 92*
**Sharp,** Henry, Jr 1923- *AmMWSc 92*
**Sharp,** Homer Franklin, Jr 1936- *AmMWSc 92*
**Sharp,** Homer Glen 1927- *WhoMW 92*
**Sharp,** Hugh T 1929- *AmMWSc 92*
**Sharp,** J. Anthony 1946- *WhoBlA 92*
**Sharp,** James A, Jr 1933- *WhoAmP 91*
**Sharp,** James Alfred 1933- *WhoBlA 92*
**Sharp,** James Franklin 1938- *WhoFI 92*
**Sharp,** James H 1934- *AmMWSc 92*
**Sharp,** James Jack 1939- *AmMWSc 92*
**Sharp,** Jane Ellyn 1934- *WhoFI 92, WhoWest 92*
**Sharp,** Jane Price 1919- *WhoAmP 91*
**Sharp,** Jean Marie 1945- *WhoBlA 92*
**Sharp,** John 1927- *Who 92*
**Sharp,** John Anderson 1944- *WhoAmP 91*
**Sharp,** John Buckner 1920- *AmMWSc 92*
**Sharp,** John Graham 1946- *AmMWSc 92*
**Sharp,** John M. Cartwright 1918- *Who 92*
**Sharp,** John Malcolm, Jr 1944- *AmMWSc 92*
**Sharp,** John Mark 1958- *WhoEnt 92*
**Sharp,** John Roland 1949- *AmMWSc 92*
**Sharp,** John Spencer 1950- *WhoAmP 91*
**Sharp,** John T 1924- *AmMWSc 92*

Sharp, John Turner 1927- AmMWSc 92
Sharp, Jonathan Hawley 1943- AmMWSc 92
Sharp, Joseph Cecil 1934- AmMWSc 92
Sharp, Katharine Lucinda 1865-1914 HanAmWH
Sharp, Kenneth 1926- Who 92
Sharp, Kenneth George 1943- AmMWSc 92
Sharp, Larry D. 1944- WhoAmL 92
Sharp, Lawrence J. 1929- WhoWest 92
Sharp, Lawrence N., Jr. 1959- WhoBlA 92
Sharp, Lee Ajax 1922- AmMWSc 92
Sharp, Leslie 1936- Who 92
Sharp, Louis James, IV 1944- AmMWSc 92
Sharp, Mainwaring Cato Ensor d1990 Who 92N
Sharp, Margery d1991 IntWW 91N, Who 92N
Sharp, Margery 1905-1991 ConAu 134, SmATA 67
Sharp, Max Alan 1948- WhoMW 92
Sharp, Merrill Kim 1941- WhoFI 92
Sharp, Michael Cartwright Who 92
Sharp, Michael Dale 1952- WhoRel 92
Sharp, Michael Keith WhoWest 92
Sharp, Milton Reginald 1909- Who 92
Sharp, Mitchell 1911- IntWW 91
Sharp, Mitchell William 1911- Who 92
Sharp, Nancy 1909- TwCPaSc
Sharp, Nancy Douglas 1932- WhoMW 92
Sharp, Nikki Annette WhoAmP 91
Sharp, Pamela Ann 1950- WhoWest 92
Sharp, Patty Ann 1946- WhoAmP 91
Sharp, Peggy Agostino 1950- WhoWest 92
Sharp, Philip R. 1942- AlmAP 92 [port], WhoAmP 91, WhoMW 92
Sharp, Phillip Allen 1944- AmMWSc 92, IntWW 91
Sharp, Rex Arthur 1960- WhoAmL 92
Sharp, Richard 1915- Who 92
Sharp, Richard Dana 1930- AmMWSc 92
Sharp, Richard L. 1947- WhoFI 92
Sharp, Richard Lee 1935- AmMWSc 92
Sharp, Robert Charles 1907- Who 92
Sharp, Robert Charles 1936- WhoFI 92
Sharp, Robert Phillip 1911- AmMWSc 92, IntWW 91
Sharp, Robert Richard 1941- AmMWSc 92
Sharp, Robert Weimer 1917- WhoAmL 92
Sharp, Ronald Alan 1945- WhoMW 92
Sharp, Saundra DrAPF 91, ReelWom [port]
Sharp, Saundra 1942- WhoBlA 92
Sharp, Stephen A 1947- WhoAmP 91
Sharp, Stephen R 1944- WhoAmP 91
Sharp, Susie Marshall 1907- WhoAmP 91
Sharp, Terry Earl 1935- AmMWSc 92
Sharp, Thomas 1931- Who 92
Sharp, Thomas B 1940- WhoAmP 91
Sharp, Thomas Joseph 1944- AmMWSc 92
Sharp, Tom DrAPF 91
Sharp, William 1855-1905 RfGEnL 91
Sharp, William Broom Alexander 1942- AmMWSc 92
Sharp, William Charles 1953- WhoWest 92
Sharp, William Edward, III 1940- AmMWSc 92
Sharp, William Harold Angus 1915- Who 92
Sharp, William Johnstone 1926- Who 92
Sharp, William R 1936- AmMWSc 92
Sharp, William Russell 1939- WhoWest 92
Sharp, William Wheeler 1923- WhoFI 92
Sharp of Grimsdyke, Baron 1916- Who 92
Sharpe, Anthony 1961- BlkOlyM
Sharpe, Audrey Howell 1938- WhoBlA 92
Sharpe, Brian Sidney 1927- Who 92
Sharpe, Calvin William 1945- WhoAmL 92, WhoBlA 92
Sharpe, Charles Bruce 1926- AmMWSc 92
Sharpe, Charles Norval, Jr 1927- WhoIns 92
Sharpe, Charles Ray 1938- WhoAmP 91
Sharpe, Charles Richard 1925- WhoFI 92
Sharpe, Charles William 1881-1955 TwCPaSc
Sharpe, Cornelia Lynn WhoEnt 92
Sharpe, David James 1930- WhoAmL 92
Sharpe, David McCurry 1938- AmMWSc 92
Sharpe, David Thomas 1946- Who 92
Sharpe, Gary Dale 1941- WhoAmP 91
Sharpe, Grant William 1925- AmMWSc 92
Sharpe, James Shelby 1940- WhoAmL 92
Sharpe, Jean Elizabeth WhoAmL 92
Sharpe, John 1921- Who 92
Sharpe, John Edward 1948- WhoWest 92
Sharpe, John Herbert S. Who 92
Sharpe, Jon TwCWW 91, WrDr 92
Sharpe, Kevin Michael 1949- IntWW 91
Sharpe, Lawrence 1930- AmMWSc 92
Sharpe, Louis Haughton 1927- AmMWSc 92
Sharpe, Louis Kerre 1944- WhoFI 92
Sharpe, Michael John 1941- AmMWSc 92
Sharpe, Peter DrAPF 91
Sharpe, Reginald 1898- Who 92
Sharpe, Richard Samuel 1930- WhoFI 92
Sharpe, Robert F., Sr. 1926- WhoFI 92
Sharpe, Robert John 1948- WhoRel 92
Sharpe, Roger Stanley 1941- AmMWSc 92
Sharpe, Roland Leonard 1923- AmMWSc 92, WhoWest 92
Sharpe, Ronald M. 1940- WhoBlA 92
Sharpe, Thomas R 1944- AmMWSc 92
Sharpe, Thomas Ridley 1928- IntAu&W 91, Who 92
Sharpe, Tom 1928- ConNov 91, IntWW 91, WrDr 92
Sharpe, V. Renee 1953- WhoBlA 92
Sharpe, William 1923- Who 92
Sharpe, William D 1927- AmMWSc 92
Sharpe, William F. 1934- WhoNob 90, WrDr 92
Sharpe, William Forsyth 1934- Who 92, WhoFI 92, WhoWest 92
Sharpe, William James 1908- Who 92
Sharpe, William Joseph, Jr 1952- WhoAmP 91
Sharpe, William Norman, Jr 1938- AmMWSc 92
Sharpe, William R, Jr 1928- WhoAmP 91
Sharples Who 92
Sharples, Baroness 1923- Who 92
Sharples, Douglas Paul 1945- WhoEnt 92
Sharples, Florence Elizabeth 1931- Who 92
Sharples, Frances Ellen 1950- AmMWSc 92
Sharples, George Carroll 1918- AmMWSc 92
Sharples, Judith Carolyn 1944- WhoEnt 92
Sharples, Thomas Davy 1916- WhoWest 92
Sharples, Thomas Davy, Jr. 1951- WhoEnt 92
Sharpless, George Robert AmMWSc 92
Sharpless, Jacob Ricky 1957- WhoAmL 92
Sharpless, K Barry 1941- AmMWSc 92
Sharpless, Nansie Sue 1932- AmMWSc 92
Sharpless, Seth Kinman 1925- AmMWSc 92
Sharpless, Stewart Lane 1926- AmMWSc 92
Sharpless, Thomas Kite 1939- AmMWSc 92
Sharpley, Robert Caldwell 1946- AmMWSc 92
Sharpley, Roger Ernest Dion 1928- Who 92
Sharpp, Nancy Charlene WhoBlA 92
Sharpton, Al NewYTBS 91 [port]
Sharpton, Al 1954- News 91 [port]
Sharpton, Thomas 1949- WhoWest 92
Sharrah, Paul Chester 1914- AmMWSc 92
Sharrard, Richard Forrest 1959- WhoAmL 92
Sharrard, Thomas Earl 1947- WhoEnt 92
Sharratt, Leo TwCPaSc
Sharrett, A Richey 1937- AmMWSc 92
Sharrette, Bill 1947- WhoEnt 92
Sharrieff, Osman Ibn 1935- WhoBlA 92
Sharrock, Roger 1919-1991? ConAu 133
Sharrock, Roger Ian d1990 Who 92N
Sharrow, Leonard 1915- WhoEnt 92
Sharrow, Susan O'Hott AmMWSc 92
Sharswood, William 1836-1905 BiInAmS
Shartle, Keith WhoEnt 92
Shartle, Stanley Musgrave 1922- WhoFI 92
Sharts, Clay Marcus 1931- AmMWSc 92
Sharts, John Edwin, III 1948- WhoAmL 92
Sharum, Bernard Joseph 1944- WhoFI 92
Shasha, Dennis E AmMWSc 92
Shashaani, Avideh WhoFI 92
Shashidhara, Nagalapur Sastry 1940- AmMWSc 92
Shashoua, Victor E 1929- AmMWSc 92
Shasteen, Donald Eugene 1928- WhoAmP 91
Shastri, Lal Bahadur 1904-1966 FacFETw
Shastri, Veerabhaskar Natarajan 1961- WhoEnt 92
Shastry, B Sriram 1950- AmMWSc 92
Shatalin, Stanislav Sergeevich 1934- SovUnBD
Shatalin, Stanislav Sergeyevich 1934- IntWW 91
Shatkin, Aaron Jeffrey 1934- AmMWSc 92, IntWW 91
Shatkin, Allan Paul 1946- WhoAmP 91
Shatkus, Leonard Joseph, Jr. 1955- WhoRel 92
Shatla, Mohamed Nagui 1939- IntWW 91
Shatner, William LesBEnT 92 [port]
Shatner, William 1931- IntMPA 92, IntWW 91, WhoEnt 92
Shatney, Clayton Henry 1943- WhoWest 92
Shatrov, Mikhail Filippovich 1932- IntWW 91, SovUnBD
Shattes, Walter John 1924- AmMWSc 92
Shatto, Gloria McDermith 1931- WhoFI 92
Shattock, David John 1936- Who 92
Shattock, Francis Mario Mackenzie 1922- IntWW 91
Shattock, Gordon 1928- Who 92
Shattock, John Swithun Harvey 1907- Who 92
Shattuck, Alfred John 1954- WhoWest 92
Shattuck, Cathie Ann 1945- WhoAmL 92
Shattuck, Curtis G 1907- WhoIns 92
Shattuck, Howard Francis, Jr. 1920- WhoAmL 92
Shattuck, Lemuel 1793-1859 BiInAmS
Shattuck, Lydia White 1822-1889 BiInAmS
Shattuck, Peter Hamilton 1935- WhoWest 92
Shattuck, Ralph Edward 1929- WhoWest 92
Shattuck, Roger 1923- WrDr 92
Shattuck, Roger W. DrAPF 91
Shattuck, Ruth M 1920- WhoAmP 91
Shattuck, Samuel Walker 1841-1915 BiInAmS
Shattuck, Scott Harlan 1960- WhoEnt 92
Shattuck, Thomas Wayne 1950- AmMWSc 92
Shattuck, William Pitt 1922- WhoAmL 92
Shatz, David Vernon 1954- WhoWest 92
Shatz, Sanford 1959- WhoAmL 92
Shatz, Stephen S 1937- AmMWSc 92
Shau, Hungyi 1952- WhoWest 92
Shaub, Walter M 1947- AmMWSc 92
Shaud, Grant WhoEnt 92
Shaudys, Edgar T 1928- AmMWSc 92
Shaughnessy Who 92
Shaughnessy, Baron 1922- Who 92
Shaughnessy, Alfred 1916- ConAu 134
Shaughnessy, John L 1930- WhoAmP 91
Shaughnessy, Marie Kaneko 1924- WhoFI 92
Shaughnessy, Michael John, Jr. 1951- WhoEnt 92
Shaughnessy, Thomas Patrick 1942- AmMWSc 92
Shaughnessy, Timothy Thomas 1957- WhoAmP 91
Shaul, Frank TwCWW 91
Shaulis, Nelson Jacob 1913- AmMWSc 92
Shaull, Richard 1919- WhoRel 92
Shauro, Vasiliy Filimonovich 1912- IntWW 91
Shave, Kenneth George 1908- Who 92
Shave, Terry 1952- TwCPaSc
Shavell, Steven 1946- WhoAmL 92
Shavelson, Melville 1917- IntAu&W 91, IntMPA 92, WhoEnt 92
Shaver, Alan Garnet 1946- AmMWSc 92
Shaver, Craig H, III 1956- WhoAmP 91
Shaver, Evelyn Louise 1931- AmMWSc 92
Shaver, Gaius Robert 1949- AmMWSc 92
Shaver, Helen 1951- IntMPA 92
Shaver, James L, Jr 1927- WhoAmP 91
Shaver, Kenneth John 1925- AmMWSc 92
Shaver, Kimberly Ann 1959- WhoMW 92
Shaver, Leslie Robert 1947- WhoAmP 91
Shaver, Richard S 1907-1975 TwCSFW 91
Shaver, Robert Harold 1922- AmMWSc 92
Shaver, Roy Allen 1931- AmMWSc 92, WhoMW 92
Shavers, Charlie 1917-1971 NewAmDM
Shavitt, Isaiah 1925- AmMWSc 92
Shavor, Robert Peter 1938- WhoAmP 91
Shaw Who 92
Shaw Yu-Ming 1938- IntWW 91
Shaw, A J 1920- AmMWSc 92
Shaw, Adele Marie d1937 DcAmImH
Shaw, Alan Bosworth 1922- AmMWSc 92
Shaw, Alice J. 1856-1918 NewAmDM
Shaw, Alvia A. 1915- WhoBlA 92
Shaw, Andrew H. 1954- WhoAmL 92
Shaw, Andrew Michael 1959- WhoEnt 92
Shaw, Angus Robertson, III 1932- WhoRel 92
Shaw, Ann 1921- WhoBlA 92
Shaw, Anna Howard 1847-1919 BenetAL 91, HanAmWH, RelLAm 91
Shaw, Anthony John 1930- Who 92
Shaw, Archie R WhoAmP 91
Shaw, Ardyth M. 1941- WhoBlA 92
Shaw, Arthur Daniel, Jr. 1929- WhoFI 92
Shaw, Artie 1910- FacFETw, WhoEnt 92
Shaw, Artie 1910-1990 NewAmDM
Shaw, Barbara Ramsay AmMWSc 92
Shaw, Barry Who 92
Shaw, Barry N. 1940- WhoAmL 92
Shaw, Benjamin Shurtleff 1827-1893 BiInAmS
Shaw, Bernard LesBEnT 92 [port]
Shaw, Bernard 1856-1950 CnDBLB 6 [port], RfGEnL 91
Shaw, Bernard 1940- ConBlB 2 [port], WhoBlA 92
Shaw, Bernard Leslie 1930- IntWW 91, Who 92
Shaw, Bob 1931- TwCSFW 91, WrDr 92
Shaw, Booker Thomas 1951- WhoBlA 92
Shaw, Brenda Roberts 1956- AmMWSc 92
Shaw, Brian IntAu&W 91X, TwCSFW 91, WrDr 92
Shaw, Brian 1933- Who 92
Shaw, Brian K. 1966- WhoBlA 92
Shaw, Bryan TwCSFW 91
Shaw, Bynum DrAPF 91
Shaw, Bynum G. 1923- WrDr 92
Shaw, Bynum Gillette 1923- IntAu&W 91
Shaw, C Frank, III 1944- AmMWSc 92
Shaw, Charles A. 1944- WhoAmL 92, WhoBlA 92
Shaw, Charles Alden 1925- AmMWSc 92, WhoWest 92
Shaw, Charles Barry 1923- Who 92
Shaw, Charles Bergman, Jr 1927- AmMWSc 92
Shaw, Charles Gardner 1917- AmMWSc 92
Shaw, Charles Gardner, III 1948- AmMWSc 92
Shaw, Charles Hugh 1875-1910 BiInAmS
Shaw, Charles Rusanda 1914- WhoMW 92
Shaw, Charles Thurstan 1914- Who 92
Shaw, Charles Timothy 1934- Who 92
Shaw, Cheng-Mei 1926- AmMWSc 92
Shaw, Clifford Dean 1943- WhoRel 92
Shaw, Colin Don 1928- Who 92
Shaw, Curtis E. 1944- WhoBlA 92
Shaw, Curtis Mitchell 1944- WhoBlA 92
Shaw, Daniel Gerald 1957- WhoRel 92
Shaw, Danny Wayne 1947- WhoMW 92
Shaw, David 1936- Who 92
Shaw, David 1952- TwCPaSc
Shaw, David Aitken 1924- Who 92
Shaw, David Allen 1959- WhoWest 92
Shaw, David Anthony 1948- WhoAmL 92
Shaw, David Bruce 1950- WhoAmL 92
Shaw, David Elliot 1951- AmMWSc 92, WhoFI 92
Shaw, David George 1945- AmMWSc 92
Shaw, David Harold 1941- AmMWSc 92
Shaw, David Lawrence 1950- Who 92
Shaw, David Lyle 1943- WhoWest 92
Shaw, David Paul 1950- WhoFI 92
Shaw, David T 1938- AmMWSc 92, WrDr 92
Shaw, Debora 1950- WhoMW 92
Shaw, Denis Martin 1923- AmMWSc 92
Shaw, Denise 1949- WhoBlA 92
Shaw, Dennis 1936- Who 92
Shaw, Dennis Frederick 1924- Who 92
Shaw, Dennis Lee 1955- WhoMW 92
Shaw, Derek Humphrey 1937- AmMWSc 92
Shaw, Don W 1937- AmMWSc 92
Shaw, Donald Hardy 1922- WhoMW 92
Shaw, Doris 1921- WhoFI 92
Shaw, Douglas William David 1928- Who 92
Shaw, Duncan 1925- Who 92
Shaw, E. Clay, Jr. 1939- AlmAP 92 [port]
Shaw, Edgar Albert George 1921- AmMWSc 92
Shaw, Edward Irwin 1927- AmMWSc 92
Shaw, Edward Richard 1850-1903 BiInAmS
Shaw, Edward Stuart 1939- WhoEnt 92
Shaw, Edwin Lawrence 1938- WhoRel 92, WhoWest 92
Shaw, Elden K 1934- AmMWSc 92
Shaw, Elizabeth Orr 1923- WhoAmL 92
Shaw, Elliott Nathan 1920- AmMWSc 92
Shaw, Ellsworth 1920- AmMWSc 92
Shaw, Eloise Laird 1929- WhoAmP 91
Shaw, Elwood R 1918- AmMWSc 92
Shaw, Emil Gilbert 1922- AmMWSc 92
Shaw, Eugene 1925- AmMWSc 92
Shaw, Eugene Clay, Jr 1939- WhoAmP 91
Shaw, Eunice Elizabeth 1934- WhoRel 92
Shaw, Felicity 1918- IntAu&W 91
Shaw, Ferdinand 1933- WhoBlA 92
Shaw, Fiona ConTFT 9
Shaw, Frederic John 1920- WhoWest 92
Shaw, Frederick B. 1935-1980 WhoBlA 92N
Shaw, Frederick Carleton 1937- AmMWSc 92
Shaw, Gavin Brown 1919- Who 92
Shaw, Gaylord Edward 1939- AmMWSc 92
Shaw, Geoffrey Norman 1926- Who 92
Shaw, Geoffrey Peter 1944- Who 92
Shaw, George, II 1959- AmMWSc 92
Shaw, George Anthony Theodore d1990 Who 92N
Shaw, George Bernard 1856-1950 BiDBrF 2, FacFETw [port], ScFEYrs, WhoNob 90
Shaw, George Jerry, Jr. 1940- WhoAmL 92
Shaw, George Neville B. Who 92
Shaw, George William 1924- WhoAmL 92
Shaw, Giles Who 92
Shaw, Glenn Edmond 1938- AmMWSc 92
Shaw, Gordon Lionel 1932- AmMWSc 92

**Shaw**, Harold 1923- *WhoEnt 92*
**Shaw**, Harry, Jr 1927- *AmMWSc 92*
**Shaw**, Harry Alexander, III 1937- *WhoFI 92, WhoMW 92*
**Shaw**, Helen Lester Anderson 1936- *AmMWSc 92*
**Shaw**, Henry 1800-1889 *BiInAmS*
**Shaw**, Henry 1934- *AmMWSc 92*
**Shaw**, Henry I., Jr. 1926- *WrDr 92*
**Shaw**, Henry W. *BenetAL 91*
**Shaw**, Herbert John *AmMWSc 92*
**Shaw**, Herbert Richard 1930- *AmMWSc 92*
**Shaw**, Irene *WrDr 92*
**Shaw**, Irwin 1913-1984 *BenetAL 91, FacFETw*
**Shaw**, Jack Parks 1941- *WhoMW 92*
**Shaw**, James 1939- *WhoMW 92*
**Shaw**, James Gee, III 1948- *WhoFI 92*
**Shaw**, James Harlan 1946- *AmMWSc 92*
**Shaw**, James Headon 1918- *AmMWSc 92*
**Shaw**, James John Sutherland 1912- *Who 92*
**Shaw**, James Renfrew 1930- *WhoEnt 92*
**Shaw**, James Scott 1942- *AmMWSc 92*
**Shaw**, James William 1940- *WhoRel 92, WhoWest 92*
**Shaw**, Jane E 1939- *AmMWSc 92*
**Shaw**, Janet Beeler *DrAPF 91*
**Shaw**, Janet Lynn *WhoEnt 92*
**Shaw**, Jerome Fielding 1955- *WhoEnt 92*
**Shaw**, Jo Edward, Jr. 1934- *WhoAmL 92*
**Shaw**, Joan *DrAPF 91*
**Shaw**, John *DrAPF 91, WhoWest 92*
**Shaw**, John Askew 1946- *AmMWSc 92*
**Shaw**, John Byam 1872-1919 *TwCPaSc*
**Shaw**, John Calman 1932- *Who 92*
**Shaw**, John Campbell 1949- *Who 92*
**Shaw**, John Firth 1948- *WhoWest 92*
**Shaw**, John Frederick 1936- *Who 92*
**Shaw**, John Giles 1931- *Who 92*
**Shaw**, John H 1925- *AmMWSc 92*
**Shaw**, John Malach 1931- *WhoAmL 92*
**Shaw**, John Michael 1914- *Who 92*
**Shaw**, John Michael Robert B. *Who 92*
**Shaw**, John Thomas 1925- *AmMWSc 92*
**Shaw**, Joseph Minard 1925- *WhoRel 92*
**Shaw**, Joseph P d1895 *BiInAmS*
**Shaw**, Joseph Thomas 1919- *WhoMW 92*
**Shaw**, Julius Fennell 1942- *WhoBlA 92*
**Shaw**, Kenneth Alan 1939- *WhoMW 92*
**Shaw**, Kenneth C 1932- *AmMWSc 92*
**Shaw**, Kenneth Noel Francis 1919- *AmMWSc 92*
**Shaw**, Kim Donald 1955- *WhoAmL 92*
**Shaw**, L. Edward, Jr. 1944- *WhoAmL 92*
**Shaw**, Larry Don 1953- *WhoAmP 91*
**Shaw**, Lawrance Neil 1934- *AmMWSc 92*
**Shaw**, Leander J *WhoAmP 91*
**Shaw**, Leander J., Jr. 1930- *WhoBlA 92*
**Shaw**, Leander Jerry, Jr. 1930- *WhoAmL 92*
**Shaw**, Lee Charles 1913- *WhoAmL 92*
**Shaw**, Leonard G 1934- *AmMWSc 92*
**Shaw**, Leonard Ray 1957- *WhoRel 92*
**Shaw**, Leslie M J 1941- *AmMWSc 92*
**Shaw**, Linda *WhoAmP 91, WhoWest 92*
**Shaw**, M P 1936- *AmMWSc 92*
**Shaw**, Margaret 1940- *SmATA 68 [port]*
**Shaw**, Margaret Ann 1933- *AmMWSc 92*
**Shaw**, Margery Wayne 1923- *AmMWSc 92*
**Shaw**, Mario William 1929- *WhoBlA 92*
**Shaw**, Mark Howard 1944- *WhoRel 92, WhoWest 92*
**Shaw**, Mark Robert 1945- *Who 92*
**Shaw**, Mary Louise 1928- *WhoBlA 92*
**Shaw**, Mary M 1943- *AmMWSc 92*
**Shaw**, Mary Michal 1933- *Who 92*
**Shaw**, Maurice Kenneth 1939- *WhoFI 92*
**Shaw**, Max S. *Who 92*
**Shaw**, Maxine *DrAPF 91*
**Shaw**, Melvin B. 1940- *WhoBlA 92*
**Shaw**, Melvin Robert 1948- *WhoMW 92*
**Shaw**, Michael 1924- *AmMWSc 92*
**Shaw**, Michael Allan 1940- *WhoFI 92*
**Shaw**, Michael Dennis 1949- *WhoBlA 92*
**Shaw**, Michael Hearne 1940- *WhoMW 92*
**Shaw**, Michael Hewitt 1935- *Who 92*
**Shaw**, Michael Norman 1920- *Who 92*
**Shaw**, Mike *WhoAmP 91*
**Shaw**, Mike 1943- *WhoAmP 91*
**Shaw**, Milton C 1915- *AmMWSc 92*
**Shaw**, Montgomery Throop 1943- *AmMWSc 92*
**Shaw**, Murray 1908- *ConAu 134*
**Shaw**, Nancy H. 1942- *WhoBlA 92*
**Shaw**, Neil McGowan 1929- *IntWW 91, Who 92, WhoFI 92*
**Shaw**, Neville B. *Who 92*
**Shaw**, Nolan Gail 1929- *AmMWSc 92*
**Shaw**, Pat *WhoEnt 92*
**Shaw**, Patrick 1933- *WhoMW 92*
**Shaw**, Paul Dale 1931- *AmMWSc 92, WhoMW 92*
**Shaw**, Paul Jefferson 1954- *WhoEnt 92*
**Shaw**, Pauline Agassiz 1841-1917 *DcAmImH*
**Shaw**, Peggy Nahas 1958- *WhoRel 92*
**Shaw**, Peter Jack 1924- *Who 92*
**Shaw**, Peter Mark 1955- *WhoFI 92*
**Shaw**, Peter Robert 1956- *AmMWSc 92*
**Shaw**, Philip Eugene 1934- *AmMWSc 92*
**Shaw**, Ralph Arthur 1930- *AmMWSc 92*
**Shaw**, Ralph Edward 1938- *WhoMW 92*
**Shaw**, Randall F 1931- *WhoAmP 91*
**Shaw**, Randy Lee 1945- *WhoMW 92*
**Shaw**, Richard *DrAPF 91*
**Shaw**, Richard David 1938- *WhoFI 92, WhoMW 92*
**Shaw**, Richard Francis 1952- *AmMWSc 92*
**Shaw**, Richard Franklin 1924- *AmMWSc 92*
**Shaw**, Richard Gordon 1943- *WhoBlA 92*
**Shaw**, Richard Gregg 1929- *AmMWSc 92*
**Shaw**, Richard John 1939- *AmMWSc 92*
**Shaw**, Richard John Gildroy 1936- *WhoFI 92*
**Shaw**, Richard Joshua 1923- *AmMWSc 92*
**Shaw**, Richard Melvin 1947- *WhoFI 92*
**Shaw**, Richard P 1933- *AmMWSc 92*
**Shaw**, Robert 1916- *NewAmDM*
**Shaw**, Robert 1925- *Who 92*
**Shaw**, Robert 1931- *IntAu&W 91*
**Shaw**, Robert 1937- *WhoAmP 91*
**Shaw**, Robert Bernard 1934- *WhoAmL 92*
**Shaw**, Robert Blaine 1949- *AmMWSc 92*
**Shaw**, Robert Dawson 1930- *WhoMW 92*
**Shaw**, Robert E. 1931- *WhoFI 92*
**Shaw**, Robert Eugene 1933- *WhoRel 92*
**Shaw**, Robert F *WhoAmP 91*
**Shaw**, Robert Fletcher 1910- *AmMWSc 92*
**Shaw**, Robert G 1924- *WhoAmP 91*
**Shaw**, Robert Harold 1919- *AmMWSc 92*
**Shaw**, Robert Harold 1955- *WhoAmL 92*
**Shaw**, Robert Jennings 1929- *WhoAmP 91*
**Shaw**, Robert Lawson 1916- *WhoEnt 92*
**Shaw**, Robert Macdonald 1912- *Who 92*
**Shaw**, Robert R 1939- *AmMWSc 92*
**Shaw**, Robert Reeves 1936- *AmMWSc 92*
**Shaw**, Robert Wayne 1947- *AmMWSc 92*
**Shaw**, Robert Wayne 1949- *AmMWSc 92*
**Shaw**, Robert William, Jr 1941- *AmMWSc 92, WhoFI 92*
**Shaw**, Rodney 1937- *AmMWSc 92*
**Shaw**, Roger Walz 1934- *AmMWSc 92*
**Shaw**, Ronald Andrew 1958- *WhoEnt 92*
**Shaw**, Ronnie Glen 1958- *IntAu&W 91*
**Shaw**, Ross Franklin 1930- *WhoWest 92*
**Shaw**, Roy 1918- *Who 92*
**Shaw**, Roy Edwin 1925- *Who 92*
**Shaw**, Run Run 1907- *IntWW 91, Who 92*
**Shaw**, Russell B. 1935- *WrDr 92*
**Shaw**, Sally Ann 1959- *WhoWest 92*
**Shaw**, Spencer 1946- *AmMWSc 92*
**Shaw**, Spencer Gilbert 1916- *WhoBlA 92*
**Shaw**, Stan 1952- *WhoBlA 92*
**Shaw**, Stanford Jay 1930- *WrDr 92*
**Shaw**, Stanley Miner 1935- *AmMWSc 92, WhoMW 92*
**Shaw**, Stephen 1948- *AmMWSc 92*
**Shaw**, Steven Andrew 1946- *WhoAmL 92*
**Shaw**, Susan 1938- *TwCPaSc*
**Shaw**, Susan Maxine 1960- *WhoRel 92, WhoWest 92*
**Shaw**, Sydney Herbert 1903- *Who 92*
**Shaw**, Talbert Oscall 1928- *WhoBlA 92*
**Shaw**, Thomas 1843-1919? *BiInAmS*
**Shaw**, Thurstan *Who 92*
**Shaw**, Thurstan 1914- *WrDr 92*
**Shaw**, Vance Patrick 1960- *WhoFI 92*
**Shaw**, Vernon Reed 1937- *AmMWSc 92*
**Shaw**, W J *ScFEYrs*
**Shaw**, Walter Norman 1923- *AmMWSc 92*
**Shaw**, Warren A 1925- *AmMWSc 92*
**Shaw**, Warren Cleaton 1922- *AmMWSc 92*
**Shaw**, Wayne Eugene 1932- *WhoMW 92*
**Shaw**, Wilfrid Garside 1929- *AmMWSc 92*
**Shaw**, William 1937- *WhoAmP 91*
**Shaw**, William Jay 1962- *WhoWest 92*
**Shaw**, William S 1924- *AmMWSc 92*
**Shaw**, William V. 1933- *Who 92*
**Shaw**, William Wesley 1946- *AmMWSc 92*
**Shaw**, Willie G. 1942- *WhoBlA 92*
**Shaw**, Woody 1944-1989 *NewAmDM*
**Shaw**, Woody Herman 1944-1989 *WhoBlA 92N*
**Shaw-Gibson**, Eunice Morrell 1948- *WhoRel 92, WhoWest 92*
**Shaw-Jackson**, Harold Nicholas 1942- *WhoFI 92*
**Shaw-Johnson**, Beverly *DrAPF 91*
**Shaw-Stewart**, Houston 1931- *Who 92*
**Shawa**, Lol Mohammed 1939- *IntWW 91*
**Shawcroft**, Roy Wayne 1938- *AmMWSc 92*
**Shawcross** *Who 92*
**Shawcross**, Baron 1902- *IntWW 91, Who 92*
**Shawcross**, John T. 1924- *WrDr 92*
**Shawcross**, William 1946- *WrDr 92*
**Shawcross**, William Edgerton 1934- *AmMWSc 92*
**Shawe**, Daniel Reeves 1925- *AmMWSc 92*
**Shawe-Taylor**, Desmond 1907- *IntWW 91, Who 92*
**Shawfield**, John Edgar 1940- *WhoFI 92*
**Shawgo**, Barry James 1964- *WhoMW 92*
**Shawkey**, Deborah Ann 1949- *WhoWest 92*
**Shawl**, Stephen Jacobs 1943- *AmMWSc 92*
**Shawley**, John Franklin 1921- *WhoAmP 91*
**Shawn**, Edwin Myers 1891-1972 *FacFETw*
**Shawn**, Frank S *TwCSFW 91, WrDr 92*
**Shawn**, Wallace 1943- *IntMPA 92, WrDr 92*
**Shawn**, William 1907- *IntWW 91*
**Shawnee**, Laura Ann 1953- *WhoBlA 92*
**Shawstad**, Raymond Vernon 1931- *WhoFI 92, WhoWest 92*
**Shawver**, David John 1947- *WhoWest 92*
**Shawver**, Debra Ann 1953- *WhoWest 92*
**Shawver**, Iona Richmond 1939- *WhoMW 92*
**Shawyer**, Bruce L R 1937- *AmMWSc 92*
**Shay**, Edward Norman 1929- *WhoAmL 92*
**Shay**, Frank 1888-1954 *BenetAL 91*
**Shay**, Gene 1935- *WhoEnt 92*
**Shay**, Jerry William 1945- *AmMWSc 92*
**Shay**, Joseph Leo 1942- *AmMWSc 92*
**Shay**, Michael Patrick 1950- *WhoAmL 92*
**Shay**, Peter Yungching 1934- *WhoWest 92*
**Shay**, Philipp Wendell 1914- *WhoFI 92*
**Shay**, Robert Michael 1936- *WhoFI 92*
**Shay**, Roshani Cari 1942- *WhoWest 92*
**Shay**, Thomas W. 1947- *WhoMW 92*
**Shay**, Tim *DrAPF 91*
**Shaye**, Robert 1939- *IntMPA 92*
**Shaye**, Robert Kenneth 1939- *WhoEnt 92*
**Shayegani**, Mehdi 1926- *AmMWSc 92*
**Shaykewich**, Carl Francis 1941- *AmMWSc 92*
**Shaykin**, Leonard P. 1943- *WhoFI 92*
**Shayne**, Bob 1945- *WhoEnt 92*
**Shayne**, Neil T 1932- *WhoAmP 91*
**Shayne**, Robert *IntMPA 92*
**Shays**, Christopher 1945- *AlmAP 92 [port], WhoAmP 91*
**Shays**, Daniel *BenetAL 91*
**Shazly**, Saad Mohamed el-Husseiny el- 1922- *IntWW 91*
**Shchadov**, Mikhail Ivanovich 1927- *IntWW 91*
**Shcharansky**, Anatoliy Borisovich 1948- *SovUnBD*
**Shcharansky**, Anatoly *IntWW 91*
**Shcharansky**, Anatoly 1948- *FacFETw*
**Shchedrin**, Rodion 1932- *ConCom 92, NewAmDM*
**Shchedrin**, Rodion Konstantinovich 1932- *IntWW 91, SovUnBD*
**Shchelokov**, Nikolay Anisimovich 1910-1984 *SovUnBD*
**Shcherbakov**, Aleksandr Sergeevich 1901-1945 *SovUnBD*
**Shcherbatov**, Mikhail Mikhailovich 1733-1790 *BlkwCEP*
**Shcherbina**, Boris Yevdokinovich 1919- *IntWW 91*
**Shcherbitsky**, Vladimir Vasil'evich 1918-1990 *SovUnBD*
**Shcherbitsky**, Vladimir Vasilievich 1918-1990 *FacFETw*
**Shchetinsky**, Alexander 1960- *ConCom 92*
**Shchipachev**, Stepan Petrovich 1899-1980 *SovUnBD*
**Shchukin**, Boris Vasil'evich 1894-1939 *SovUnBD*
**Shchukin**, Sergei 1851-1936 *ThHEIm*
**Shchuko**, Vladimir Alekseevich 1878-1939 *SovUnBD*
**Shchusev**, Aleksey Viktorovich 1873-1949 *SovUnBD*
**Shcolnik**, Robert Milton 1938- *WhoWest 92*
**She** *EncAmaz 91*
**She**, Chiao-Yao 1936- *AmMWSc 92*
**Shea**, Ann Marie 1939- *WhoEnt 92*
**Shea**, Cheryl Lilley 1953- *WhoEnt 92*
**Shea**, Cornelius *TwCWW 91*
**Shea**, Cornelius 1863-192-? *ScFEYrs*
**Shea**, Daniel Francis 1937- *AmMWSc 92*
**Shea**, David M *WhoAmP 91*
**Shea**, David Michael 1922- *WhoAmL 92*
**Shea**, Dennis Gerard 1962- *WhoFI 92*
**Shea**, Donald F 1925- *WhoAmP 91*
**Shea**, Donald Francis 1925- *WhoAmL 92*
**Shea**, Francis Raymond 1913- *WhoRel 92*
**Shea**, Fredericka Palmer 1940- *AmMWSc 92*
**Shea**, George P, Jr 1938- *WhoIns 92*
**Shea**, Gwyn Clarkston 1937- *WhoAmP 91*
**Shea**, J Michael 1942- *WhoAmP 91*
**Shea**, Jack *LesBEnT 92*
**Shea**, Jack 1928- *WhoEnt 92*
**Shea**, James D 1919- *WhoAmP 91*
**Shea**, James H 1932- *AmMWSc 92*
**Shea**, James S 1925- *WhoAmP 91*
**Shea**, James William 1936- *WhoAmL 92*
**Shea**, Jeremy Charles 1937- *WhoAmL 92*
**Shea**, Joan Karozos 1959- *WhoMW 92*
**Shea**, John 1949- *IntMPA 92*
**Shea**, John Dawson Gilmary 1824-1892 *BenetAL 91*
**Shea**, John Dwane 1939- *WhoWest 92*
**Shea**, John Edward 1943- *WhoFI 92*
**Shea**, John Francis 1928- *WhoIns 92*
**Shea**, John Francis, Jr. 1928- *WhoAmL 92*
**Shea**, John J. 1938- *WhoMW 92*
**Shea**, John Raymond Michael, Jr 1938- *AmMWSc 92*
**Shea**, Joseph F 1926- *AmMWSc 92*
**Shea**, Joseph Francis 1926- *IntWW 91*
**Shea**, Kevin A. 1956- *WhoMW 92*
**Shea**, LaDonna Reiner 1948- *WhoWest 92*
**Shea**, Michael Alan 1946- *WhoWest 92*
**Shea**, Michael Francis 1933- *AmMWSc 92*
**Shea**, Michael Joseph 1939- *AmMWSc 92*
**Shea**, Michael Sinclair MacAuslan 1938- *Who 92*
**Shea**, Patrick 1948- *WhoAmP 91*
**Shea**, Philip Joseph 1921- *AmMWSc 92*
**Shea**, Richard David 1919- *WhoRel 92*
**Shea**, Richard Franklin 1903- *AmMWSc 92*
**Shea**, Robert Stanton 1928- *WhoFI 92*
**Shea**, Stephen Michael 1926- *AmMWSc 92*
**Shea**, Terrence W 1941- *WhoIns 92*
**Shea**, Theodore William 1960- *WhoWest 92*
**Shea**, Thomas Joseph 1950- *WhoAmP 91*
**Shea**, Timothy Edward 1898- *AmMWSc 92*
**Shea**, Timothy Guy 1939- *AmMWSc 92*
**Shea**, Virginia Erin 1964- *WhoEnt 92*
**Shea**, William A. 1907-1991 *CurBio 91N, NewYTBS 91 [port]*
**Sheafer**, Peter Wenrich 1819-1891 *BiInAmS*
**Sheaff**, Donald J. 1925- *IntMPA 92*
**Sheaffer**, Louis 1912- *IntAu&W 91, WrDr 92*
**Sheaffer**, M.P.A. *DrAPF 91*
**Sheaffer**, Richard Allen 1950- *WhoWest 92*
**Sheagren**, John Newcomb *AmMWSc 92*
**Sheahan**, John 1923- *WrDr 92*
**Sheahan**, Michael F 1944- *WhoAmP 91*
**Sheahan**, Robert Emmett 1942- *WhoAmL 92*
**Shealy**, Clyde Norman 1932- *AmMWSc 92*
**Shealy**, David Lee 1944- *AmMWSc 92*
**Shealy**, Harry Everett, Jr 1942- *AmMWSc 92*
**Shealy**, Otis Lester 1923- *AmMWSc 92*
**Shealy**, Rod R 1953- *WhoAmP 91*
**Shealy**, Ryan C 1923- *WhoAmP 91*
**Shealy**, William Ross 1925- *WhoRel 92*
**Shealy**, William W 1934- *WhoIns 92*
**Shealy**, Y Fulmer 1923- *AmMWSc 92*
**Shean**, Jeannette Mary 1923- *WhoRel 92*
**Shean**, Timothy Joseph 1945- *WhoFI 92*
**Shear**, Barry d1979 *LesBEnT 92*
**Shear**, Charles L 1953- *AmMWSc 92*
**Shear**, Charles Robert 1942- *AmMWSc 92*
**Shear**, Cornelius Barrett 1912- *AmMWSc 92*
**Shear**, David Ben 1938- *AmMWSc 92*
**Shear**, Kenneth 1945- *WhoAmL 92*
**Shear**, Leroy 1933- *AmMWSc 92*
**Shear**, S Sue 1918- *WhoAmP 91*
**Shear**, William Albert 1942- *AmMWSc 92*
**Shearar**, Jeremy Brown 1931- *IntWW 91*
**Sheard**, John Leo 1924- *AmMWSc 92*
**Sheard**, Michael Henry 1927- *AmMWSc 92*
**Sheard**, Norma Voorhees *DrAPF 91*
**Shearer**, Carolyn Juanita 1944- *WhoWest 92*
**Shearer**, Charles M 1931- *AmMWSc 92*
**Shearer**, Dean Howard 1956- *WhoRel 92*
**Shearer**, Duncan Allan 1920- *AmMWSc 92*
**Shearer**, Edmund Cook 1942- *AmMWSc 92*
**Shearer**, Greg Otis 1947- *AmMWSc 92, WhoMW 92*
**Shearer**, Harry 1943- *IntMPA 92*
**Shearer**, Harry Julius 1943- *WhoEnt 92*
**Shearer**, Hugh 1926- *WhoAmL 92*
**Shearer**, Hugh Lawson 1923- *IntWW 91, Who 92*
**Shearer**, Ian Hamilton *Who 92*
**Shearer**, J Lowen 1921- *AmMWSc 92*
**Shearer**, Janet Sutherland *Who 92*
**Shearer**, John 1926- *Who 92*
**Shearer**, Joy Brampton 1953- *WhoAmL 92*
**Shearer**, Karen Marie *WhoEnt 92*
**Shearer**, Magnus MacDonald 1924- *Who 92*
**Shearer**, Marcia Cathrine 1933- *AmMWSc 92*
**Shearer**, Marian Peck 1949- *WhoRel 92*
**Shearer**, Mark Smith 1952- *WhoAmP 91*
**Shearer**, Moira 1926- *Who 92*
**Shearer**, P. Scott 1948- *WhoMW 92*
**Shearer**, Raymond Charles 1935- *AmMWSc 92*
**Shearer**, Sergio 1939- *WhoHisp 92*
**Shearer**, Thomas Hamilton 1923- *Who 92*
**Shearer**, Thomas Robert 1942- *AmMWSc 92*

**Shearer,** William McCague 1926- *AmMWSc 92*
**Shearer,** William Thomas 1937- *AmMWSc 92*
**Sheares,** Reuben A., II 1933- *WhoBlA 92*
**Shearin,** Kimberly Maria 1964- *WhoBlA 92*
**Shearin,** Morris Lee 1940- *WhoRel 92*
**Shearin,** Nancy Louise 1938- *AmMWSc 92*
**Shearing,** George Albert 1919- *NewAmDM, WhoEnt 92*
**Shearlock,** David John 1932- *Who 92*
**Shearman,** Donald Norman 1926- *Who 92*
**Shearman,** John 1931- *WrDr 92*
**Shearman,** John Kinder Gowran 1931- *IntWW 91, Who 92*
**Shearn,** Allen David 1942- *AmMWSc 92*
**Shearn,** Martin Alvin 1923- *AmMWSc 92*
**Sheasley,** William David 1946- *AmMWSc 92*
**Sheats,** George Frederic 1927- *AmMWSc 92*
**Sheats,** John Eugene 1939- *AmMWSc 92*
**Shebalin,** Vissarion Yakovlevich 1902-1963 *NewAmDM, SovUnBD*
**Shebbeare,** Thomas Andrew 1952- *Who 92*
**Shebell,** Thomas Frank, Jr. 1936- *WhoAmL 92*
**Sheble,** Earl, Jr. 1931- *WhoFI 92*
**Sheble,** Walter Franklin 1926- *WhoAmL 92*
**Sheboldaev,** Boris Petrovich 1895-1937 *SovUnBD*
**Shebs,** Stanley Todd 1960- *WhoWest 92*
**Shechmeister,** Isaac Leo 1913- *AmMWSc 92*
**Shechter,** Harold 1921- *AmMWSc 92*
**Shechter,** Leon 1912- *AmMWSc 92*
**Shechter,** Steven Ben 1949- *WhoMW 92*
**Shechter,** Yaakov 1934- *AmMWSc 92*
**Sheck,** Laurie *DrAPF 91*
**Sheckley,** Robert 1928- *IntAu&W 91, TwCSFW 91, WrDr 92*
**Shecter,** Ben *WrDr 92*
**Shecter,** Felice Nadine 1935- *WhoMW 92*
**Shectman,** Robin *DrAPF 91*
**Shecut,** John Linnaeus Edward Whitridge 1770-1836 *BiInAmS*
**Shedarowich,** Kenneth Scott 1961- *WhoWest 92*
**Shedd,** A. Glenroy 1939- *WhoRel 92*
**Shedd,** Ben Alvin 1947- *WhoEnt 92*
**Shedd,** Charles Fort 1947- *WhoEnt 92*
**Shedd,** Donald Pomroy 1922- *AmMWSc 92*
**Shedd,** Hudson Paul 1926- *WhoRel 92*
**Shedenhelm,** William Rex Charles 1924- *WhoWest 92*
**Shedlarski,** Joseph George, Jr 1939- *AmMWSc 92*
**Shedler,** Gerald Stuart 1939- *AmMWSc 92*
**Shedlock,** Kaye M 1951- *AmMWSc 92*
**Shedrick,** Carl F 1920- *AmMWSc 92*
**Shedrick,** Mary Bernice 1940- *WhoAmP 91*
**Sheean,** Carol A. 1941- *WhoWest 92*
**Sheean,** Vincent 1899-1975 *BenetAL 91*
**Sheed and Ward Limited** *DcLB 112*
**Sheed,** Francis Joseph 1897-1981 *FacFETw*
**Sheed,** Wilfred *FacFETw*
**Sheed,** Wilfred 1930- *BenetAL 91*
**Sheed,** Wilfrid *DrAPF 91*
**Sheed,** Wilfrid 1930- *ConNov 91, LiExTwC, WrDr 92*
**Sheed,** Wilfrid John Joseph 1930- *IntAu&W 91, IntWW 91*
**Sheedy,** Ally 1962- *IntMPA 92, WhoEnt 92*
**Sheedy,** Joseph E 1942- *WhoAmP 91*
**Sheehan,** Albert Vincent 1936- *Who 92*
**Sheehan,** August, Jr 1917- *WhoAmP 91*
**Sheehan,** Bernard Stephen 1935- *AmMWSc 92*
**Sheehan,** Daniel Eugene 1917- *WhoRel 92*
**Sheehan,** Daniel Michael 1944- *AmMWSc 92*
**Sheehan,** Deborah Ann 1953- *WhoEnt 92*
**Sheehan,** Dennis William 1934- *WhoAmL 92, WhoFI 92, WhoMW 92*
**Sheehan,** Desmond 1931- *AmMWSc 92*
**Sheehan,** Gerald Joseph 1944- *WhoIns 92*
**Sheehan,** James Patrick 1942- *WhoFI 92*
**Sheehan,** John Clark 1915- *AmMWSc 92, IntWW 91*
**Sheehan,** John Francis 1906- *AmMWSc 92*
**Sheehan,** John Patrick 1952- *WhoMW 92*
**Sheehan,** Lawrence James 1932- *WhoWest 92*
**Sheehan,** Lorraine M 1937- *WhoAmP 91*
**Sheehan,** Martin J 1957- *WhoAmP 91*
**Sheehan,** Michael Gilbert 1952- *WhoMW 92*
**Sheehan,** Michael Jarboe 1939- *WhoRel 92*
**Sheehan,** Monica Mary 1955- *WhoFI 92*
**Sheehan,** Neil 1936- *IntAu&W 91, WrDr 92*
**Sheehan,** Patricia Ann 1956- *WhoAmL 92*
**Sheehan,** Perley Poore 1875-1943 *ScFEYrs*
**Sheehan,** Perley Poore & Davis, Robert H *ScFEYrs*
**Sheehan,** Robert Duffy 1955- *WhoMW 92*
**Sheehan,** Robert James, II 1937- *WhoFI 92*
**Sheehan,** Rosemary 1938- *WhoAmL 92*
**Sheehan,** Susan 1937- *IntAu&W 91, WrDr 92*
**Sheehan,** Thomas Francis 1929- *WhoAmL 92*
**Sheehan,** Thomas Francis, Jr. 1958- *WhoEnt 92*
**Sheehan,** Thomas Henry, Jr. 1935- *WhoWest 92*
**Sheehan,** Thomas John 1924- *AmMWSc 92*
**Sheehan,** Timothy James 1950- *WhoMW 92*
**Sheehan,** Timothy P 1909- *WhoAmP 91*
**Sheehan,** Tom F. *DrAPF 91*
**Sheehan,** William *LesBEnT 92*
**Sheehan,** William C 1925- *AmMWSc 92*
**Sheehan,** William Francis 1926- *AmMWSc 92*
**Sheehan,** William Harold 1928- *WhoAmL 92*
**Sheehan,** William Joseph 1944- *WhoFI 92*
**Sheehe,** Paul Robert 1925- *AmMWSc 92*
**Sheehy,** Gail *WrDr 92*
**Sheehy,** Helen 1948- *ConAu 133*
**Sheehy,** Howard Sherman, Jr. 1934- *WhoRel 92*
**Sheehy,** John C 1918- *WhoAmP 91*
**Sheehy,** Patrick 1930- *IntWW 91, Who 92*
**Sheehy,** Paul J *WhoAmP 91*
**Sheehy,** Robert Francis 1950- *WhoFI 92*
**Sheehy,** Terence Joseph 1918- *Who 92*
**Sheehy,** Thomas Daniel 1946- *WhoFI 92*
**Sheehy,** Thomas W 1921- *AmMWSc 92*
**Sheeler,** Charles 1883-1965 *DcTwDes, FacFETw*
**Sheeler,** John B 1921- *AmMWSc 92*
**Sheeler,** Mark 1923- *IntMPA 92*
**Sheeley,** Eugene C 1933- *AmMWSc 92*
**Sheeley,** Rachel Evelyn 1966- *WhoMW 92*
**Sheeley,** Richard Moats 1934- *AmMWSc 92*
**Sheely,** W F 1931- *AmMWSc 92*
**Sheen,** Albert A. 1920- *WhoBlA 92*
**Sheen,** Barry 1918- *Who 92*
**Sheen,** Charlie *IntWW 91*
**Sheen,** Charlie 1966- *IntMPA 92, WhoHisp 92*
**Sheen,** Fulton 1895-1979 *FacFETw*
**Sheen,** Fulton J. d1979 *LesBEnT 92*
**Sheen,** Fulton John 1895-1976 *RelLAm 91*
**Sheen,** Martin 1940- *IntMPA 92, IntWW 91, WhoEnt 92, WhoHisp 92*
**Sheen,** Portia Yunn-ling 1919- *WhoWest 92*
**Sheen,** Shuh-Ji 1931- *AmMWSc 92*
**Sheepshanks,** Mary Ryott 1872-1958 *BiDBrF 2*
**Sheer,** M Lana 1945- *AmMWSc 92*
**Sheeran,** Michael John Leo 1940- *WhoRel 92*
**Sheeran,** Patrick Jerome 1942- *AmMWSc 92*
**Sheeran,** Stanley Robert 1916- *AmMWSc 92*
**Sheeran,** William James 1938- *WhoFI 92*
**Sheeran-Emory,** Kathleen Mary 1948- *WhoFI 92*
**Sheerer,** Judy B *WhoAmP 91*
**Sheerin,** Gary Asher 1938- *WhoAmP 91*
**Sheerin,** John Declan 1932- *Who 92*
**Sheerman,** Barry John 1940- *Who 92*
**Sheers,** William Sadler 1948- *AmMWSc 92*
**Sheets,** Allen Frederick 1951- *WhoEnt 92*
**Sheets,** Dolores Santos 1937- *WhoRel 92*
**Sheets,** Donald Guy 1922- *AmMWSc 92*
**Sheets,** George Henkle 1915- *AmMWSc 92*
**Sheets,** Hal Edward 1950- *WhoAmL 92*
**Sheets,** Herman E 1908- *AmMWSc 92*
**Sheets,** James Andrew 1935- *WhoAmP 91*
**Sheets,** Jeffrey Lynn 1949- *WhoMW 92*
**Sheets,** John Wesley, Jr. 1953- *WhoWest 92*
**Sheets,** Kent Jeffrey 1954- *WhoMW 92*
**Sheets,** Maurice Lee 1959- *WhoMW 92*
**Sheets,** Michael Jay 1930- *WhoFI 92*
**Sheets,** Ralph Waldo 1935- *AmMWSc 92*
**Sheets,** Raymond Franklin 1914- *AmMWSc 92*
**Sheets,** Robert Chester 1937- *AmMWSc 92*
**Sheets,** Susan Eileen 1961- *WhoMW 92*
**Sheets,** Thomas Jackson 1926- *AmMWSc 92*
**Sheets,** Van Alan 1953- *WhoAmP 91*
**Sheetz,** David P 1926- *AmMWSc 92*
**Sheetz,** Ernest Austin 1929- *WhoMW 92*
**Sheetz,** Michael Patrick 1946- *AmMWSc 92*
**Sheetz,** Ralph Albert 1908- *WhoAmL 92, WhoFI 92*
**Sheetz,** William Dean 1951- *WhoAmL 92*
**Shefcik,** Kenneth S 1947- *WhoIns 92*
**Shefer,** Joshua 1924- *AmMWSc 92*
**Shefer,** Sarah 1926- *AmMWSc 92*
**Sheff,** Robert 1945- *ConCom 92*
**Sheffer,** Albert L 1929- *AmMWSc 92*
**Sheffer,** Brent Alan 1957- *WhoMW 92*
**Sheffer,** Craig *IntMPA 92*
**Sheffer,** Howard Eugene 1918- *AmMWSc 92*
**Sheffer,** John B, II 1948- *WhoAmP 91*
**Sheffer,** Richard Douglas 1942- *AmMWSc 92*
**Sheffet,** Mary Jane Frances 1946- *WhoMW 92*
**Sheffey,** Fred C. 1928- *WhoBlA 92*
**Sheffey,** Ruthe G. *WhoBlA 92*
**Sheffi,** Yosef *AmMWSc 92*
**Sheffield,** Archdeacon of *Who 92*
**Sheffield,** Baron *Who 92*
**Sheffield,** Bishop of 1930- *Who 92*
**Sheffield,** Provost of *Who 92*
**Sheffield,** Charles *IntAu&W 91, TwCSFW 91, WrDr 92*
**Sheffield,** Elizabeth Baker 1926- *WhoMW 92*
**Sheffield,** Gary Antonian 1968- *WhoBlA 92*
**Sheffield,** Harley George 1932- *AmMWSc 92*
**Sheffield,** Horace L., Jr. 1916- *WhoBlA 92*
**Sheffield,** Joel Benson 1942- *AmMWSc 92*
**Sheffield,** John 1931- *IntMPA 92*
**Sheffield,** John 1936- *AmMWSc 92*
**Sheffield,** John Julian Lionel George 1938- *Who 92*
**Sheffield,** John Vincent 1913- *Who 92*
**Sheffield,** L Thomas 1928- *AmMWSc 92*
**Sheffield,** Larry L 1958- *WhoAmP 91*
**Sheffield,** Leslie Floyd 1925- *WhoMW 92*
**Sheffield,** Reginald 1946- *Who 92*
**Sheffield,** Richard Lee 1950- *AmMWSc 92*
**Sheffield,** Roy Dexter 1922- *AmMWSc 92*
**Sheffield,** Scott Allen 1961- *WhoFI 92*
**Sheffield,** Walter Jervis 1946- *WhoAmL 92*
**Sheffield,** William Jennings 1928- *WhoAmP 91, WhoWest 92*
**Sheffield,** William Johnson 1919- *AmMWSc 92*
**Sheffler,** George Justus 1944- *WhoWest 92*
**Sheffy,** Ben Edward 1920- *AmMWSc 92*
**Shefner,** Evelyn *DrAPF 91*
**Shefner,** Vadim Sergeevich 1915- *SovUnBD*
**Shefrin,** Harold Marvin 1948- *WhoFI 92*
**Shefrin,** Paul 1947- *WhoEnt 92*
**Sheft,** Irving 1919- *AmMWSc 92*
**Sheft,** Mark David 1953- *WhoMW 92*
**Sheft,** Peter Ian 1956- *WhoAmL 92*
**Sheftall,** Willis B., Jr. 1943- *WhoBlA 92*
**Sheftel,** Harry B. *DrAPF 91*
**Sheftel,** Roger Terry 1941- *WhoFI 92*
**Shefter,** Bert 1904- *IntMPA 92*
**Shefter,** Eli 1936- *AmMWSc 92*
**Sheftman,** Howard Stephen 1949- *WhoAmL 92*
**Shefton,** Brian Benjamin 1919- *Who 92*
**Shegal',** Grigoriy Mikhaylovich 1889-1956 *SovUnBD*
**Shegog,** Eric Marshall 1937- *Who 92*
**Sheh,** Robert Bardhyl 1939- *WhoFI 92*
**Shehadi,** William Henry 1906- *AmMWSc 92*
**Shehadie,** Nicholas 1926- *Who 92*
**Shehan,** Lawrence Joseph 1898-1984 *RelLAm 91*
**Shehan,** Patrick Vincent 1942- *WhoEnt 92*
**Shehee,** Virginia Kilpatrick *WhoAmP 91*
**Sheheen,** Robert J 1943- *WhoAmP 91*
**Shehu,** Mehmet 1913-1981 *FacFETw*
**Sheibley,** Fred Easly 1906- *AmMWSc 92*
**Sheid,** Bertrum 1937- *AmMWSc 92*
**Sheikh,** Kazim 1936- *AmMWSc 92*
**Sheikh,** Maqsood Ahmed 1947- *WhoFI 92*
**Sheikh,** Tanveer Ahmed 1949- *WhoFI 92*
**Sheil,** Donald Edward 1938- *WhoAmL 92*
**Sheil,** John 1938- *Who 92*
**Sheils,** Denis Francis 1961- *WhoAmL 92*
**Sheiman,** Ronald Lee 1948- *WhoAmL 92, WhoFI 92*
**Sheiman,** Stuart Melvyn 1942- *WhoAmL 92*
**Shein,** Eugene Milton 1922- *WhoWest 92*
**Sheinaus,** Harold 1918- *AmMWSc 92*
**Sheinberg,** Sidney Jay 1935- *IntMPA 92, WhoEnt 92, WhoFI 92, WhoWest 92*
**Sheiness,** Diana Kay 1947- *AmMWSc 92*
**Sheinfeld,** David 1906- *WhoEnt 92*
**Sheinfeld,** Myron M. 1930- *WhoAmL 92*
**Sheingold,** Abraham 1917- *AmMWSc 92*
**Sheingorn,** Mark Elliot 1944- *AmMWSc 92*
**Sheinin,** Eric Benjamin 1943- *AmMWSc 92*
**Sheinin,** Rose 1930- *AmMWSc 92*
**Sheinson,** Ronald Swiren 1942- *AmMWSc 92*
**Shekelle,** Richard Barten 1933- *AmMWSc 92*
**Shekore,** Mark John 1941- *WhoMW 92*
**Shekter,** William Bernard 1928- *WhoWest 92*
**Shelanski,** Michael L 1941- *AmMWSc 92*
**Shelanski,** Vivien Brodkin 1942- *WhoAmL 92*
**Shelbourne,** Cecily *IntAu&W 91X, WrDr 92*
**Shelbourne,** Philip 1924- *IntWW 91, Who 92*
**Shelburne** *BlkwEAR*
**Shelburne,** Earl of 1941- *Who 92*
**Shelburne,** John Daniel 1943- *AmMWSc 92*
**Shelby,** Bill Hudson 1925- *WhoAmP 91*
**Shelby,** Carolyn June 1949- *WhoEnt 92*
**Shelby,** Cole *TwCWW 91*
**Shelby,** David T. *WhoMW 92*
**Shelby,** Douglas Francis 1954- *WhoFI 92*
**Shelby,** Graham *IntAu&W 91*
**Shelby,** Graham 1940- *WrDr 92*
**Shelby,** James Elbert 1943- *AmMWSc 92*
**Shelby,** James Stanford 1934- *WhoFI 92*
**Shelby,** Jerome 1930- *WhoAmL 92, WhoFI 92*
**Shelby,** Nicholas L 1933- *WhoAmP 91*
**Shelby,** Reginald W. 1920- *WhoBlA 92*
**Shelby,** Reginald W. 1948- *WhoBlA 92*
**Shelby,** Richard C. 1934- *AlmAP 92 [port]*
**Shelby,** Richard Craig 1934- *IntWW 91, WhoAmP 91*
**Shelby,** Richard David 1946- *WhoAmP 91*
**Shelby,** Robert McKinnon 1950- *AmMWSc 92*
**Shelby,** Roselle Price 1929- *WhoAmP 91*
**Shelby,** T H 1910- *AmMWSc 92*
**Shelby,** Thomas Stanley 1958- *WhoWest 92*
**Shelby,** William Alan 1958- *WhoRel 92*
**Shelden,** Arthur H *WhoAmP 91*
**Shelden,** Harold Raymond, II 1942- *AmMWSc 92*
**Shelden,** Robert Merten 1938- *AmMWSc 92*
**Sheldon,** Alice Hastings Bradley 1915?-1987 *ConAu 34NR*
**Sheldon,** Andrew Lee 1938- *AmMWSc 92*
**Sheldon,** Ann *SmATA 67*
**Sheldon,** Bernard 1924- *Who 92*
**Sheldon,** Charles M. 1857-1946 *BenetAL 91*
**Sheldon,** Charles Monroe 1857-1946 *RelLAm 91*
**Sheldon,** Clifford George 1942- *WhoMW 92*
**Sheldon,** David *IntMPA 92, WhoEnt 92*
**Sheldon,** Douglas George 1959- *WhoEnt 92*
**Sheldon,** Drusilla Cochran 1924- *WhoAmP 91*
**Sheldon,** Edward Brewster 1856-1946 *BenetAL 91*
**Sheldon,** Eleanor Bernert 1920- *AmMWSc 92*
**Sheldon,** Eli Howard 1937- *WhoRel 92*
**Sheldon,** Eric 1930- *AmMWSc 92*
**Sheldon,** Frances Dorothy Gigante 1949- *WhoFI 92*
**Sheldon,** Gary 1953- *WhoEnt 92*
**Sheldon,** George H 1947- *WhoAmP 91*
**Sheldon,** Gervase *Who 92*
**Sheldon,** Gilbert Ignatius 1926- *WhoRel 92*
**Sheldon,** Harold 1918- *Who 92*
**Sheldon,** Huntington 1930- *AmMWSc 92*
**Sheldon,** James *IntMPA 92, WhoEnt 92*
**Sheldon,** John *IntAu&W 91X*
**Sheldon,** John, Mrs. 1911- *WhoFI 92*
**Sheldon,** John Denby 1941- *Who 92*
**Sheldon,** John Gervase 1913- *Who 92*
**Sheldon,** John William 1933- *AmMWSc 92*
**Sheldon,** Joseph Kenneth 1943- *AmMWSc 92*
**Sheldon,** Kenny 1923- *WhoEnt 92*
**Sheldon,** Kirk Roy 1958- *WhoFI 92*
**Sheldon,** L. Philip, Jr. *WhoRel 92*
**Sheldon,** Lee *IntAu&W 91X, WrDr 92*
**Sheldon,** Mark Hebberton 1931- *Who 92*
**Sheldon,** Mark Scott 1959- *WhoWest 92*
**Sheldon,** Michael Richard 1949- *WhoAmL 92*
**Sheldon,** Nancy Way 1944- *WhoFI 92*
**Sheldon,** Norman E 1936- *WhoAmP 91*
**Sheldon,** Raccoona *ConAu 34NR*
**Sheldon,** Ralph Edward 1883-1918 *BiInAmS*
**Sheldon,** Richard P 1923- *AmMWSc 92*
**Sheldon,** Robert 1923- *Who 92*
**Sheldon,** Ronald Douglas 1944- *WhoEnt 92*
**Sheldon,** Roy *DcTwDes, IntAu&W 91X, WrDr 92*
**Sheldon,** Samuel 1862-1920 *BiInAmS*
**Sheldon,** Scott *ConAu 35NR*

**Sheldon,** Sidney 1917- *IntAu&W 91, IntMPA 92, IntWW 91, WhoEnt 92, WrDr 92*
**Sheldon,** Terry Lynn 1937- *WhoRel 92*
**Sheldon,** Timothy M 1947- *WhoAmP 91*
**Sheldon,** Vern Edwin 1930- *WhoAmL 92*
**Sheldon,** Victor Lawrence 1921- *AmMWSc 92*
**Sheldon,** William A. *WhoRel 92*
**Sheldon,** William Douglas 1941- *WhoIns 92*
**Sheldon,** William Robert 1927- *AmMWSc 92*
**Sheldrake,** Raymond, Jr 1923- *AmMWSc 92*
**Sheldrick,** George Michael 1942- *IntWW 91*
**Sheldrick,** Peter 1936- *AmMWSc 92*
**Shelef,** Leora Aya *AmMWSc 92*
**Shelef,** Mordecai 1931- *AmMWSc 92*
**Shelepin,** Aleksandr Nikolaevich 1918- *SovUnBD*
**Shelepin,** Alexander Nikolayevich 1918- *FacFETw*
**Sheleski,** Stanley John 1931- *WhoFI 92*
**Shelesnyak,** Moses Chiam 1909- *AmMWSc 92*
**Shelest,** Petr Yefimovich 1908- *SovUnBD*
**Sheley,** Dale 1953- *WhoRel 92*
**Sheley,** Lucille Renn 1915- *WhoAmP 91*
**Shelford,** Cornelius William 1908- *Who 92*
**Sheline,** Glenn Elmer 1918- *AmMWSc 92*
**Sheline,** Raymond Kay 1922- *AmMWSc 92*
**Shelkin,** Barry David 1928- *AmMWSc 92*
**Shelkov,** Vladimir Andreevich 1896-1980 *SovUnBD*
**Shell,** Art *WhoWest 92*
**Shell,** Art 1946- *ConBlB 1 [port], WhoBlA 92*
**Shell,** Donald Lewis 1924- *AmMWSc 92*
**Shell,** Donnie 1952- *WhoBlA 92*
**Shell,** Eddie Wayne 1930- *AmMWSc 92*
**Shell,** Francis Joseph 1922- *AmMWSc 92*
**Shell,** James Randal 1962- *WhoFI 92*
**Shell,** John Weldon 1925- *AmMWSc 92*
**Shell,** Juanita 1940- *WhoBlA 92*
**Shell,** Karl 1938- *WhoFI 92*
**Shell,** Louis Calvin 1925- *WhoAmL 92*
**Shell,** Mary Katherine 1927- *WhoAmP 91*
**Shell,** Owen G., Jr. 1936- *WhoFI 92*
**Shell,** Robert J. 1930- *WhoFI 92*
**Shell,** Theodore A. *WhoBlA 92*
**Shell,** William H. 1910- *WhoBlA 92*
**Shellabarger,** Claire J 1924- *AmMWSc 92*
**Shellabarger,** Samuel 1888-1954 *BenetAL 91*
**Shellard,** Michael Francis Linton 1937- *Who 92*
**Shellenbarger,** Michael Ellsworth 1937- *WhoWest 92*
**Shellenbarger,** Robert Martin 1936- *AmMWSc 92*
**Shellenberger,** Carl H 1935- *AmMWSc 92*
**Shellenberger,** Donald J 1928- *AmMWSc 92*
**Shellenberger,** John Alfred 1900- *AmMWSc 92*
**Shellenberger,** Melvin Kent 1936- *AmMWSc 92*
**Shellenberger,** Paul Robert 1935- *AmMWSc 92*
**Shellenberger,** Thomas E 1932- *AmMWSc 92*
**Shellene,** Jean Mary 1921- *WhoAmP 91*
**Sheller,** Patrick Michael 1961- *WhoAmL 92*
**Shelley,** Alan John 1931- *Who 92*
**Shelley,** Austin L 1922- *AmMWSc 92*
**Shelley,** Carole Augusta 1939- *WhoEnt 92*
**Shelley,** Charles William Evans 1912- *Who 92*
**Shelley,** Dan 1949- *WhoAmP 91*
**Shelley,** Edward George 1933- *AmMWSc 92*
**Shelley,** Edwin F 1921- *AmMWSc 92*
**Shelley,** Howard Gordon 1950- *IntWW 91, Who 92*
**Shelley,** James Edward 1932 *Who 92*
**Shelley,** James LaMar 1915- *WhoAmL 92*
**Shelley,** John *TwCPaSc*
**Shelley,** John 1943- *Who 92*
**Shelley,** John Fletcher 1943- *WhoAmL 92*
**Shelley,** John L 1907- *TwCWW 91*
**Shelley,** Marlin Carl 1948- *WhoWest 92*
**Shelley,** Marshall Bruce 1953- *WhoRel 92*
**Shelley,** Martha A *DrAPF 91*
**Shelley,** Mary 1797-1851 *RfGEnL 91, TwCSFW 91*
**Shelley,** Mary Godwin 1797-1851 *ScFEYrs*
**Shelley,** Mary Wollstonecraft 1797-1851 *CnDBLB 3 [port], DcLB 110 [port]*
**Shelley,** Michael 1951- *WhoRel 92*
**Shelley,** Norman 1903-1980 *FacFETw*
**Shelley,** Pat *DrAPF 91*
**Shelley,** Paula Diane 1953- *WhoEnt 92*
**Shelley,** Percy Bysshe 1792-1822 *CnDBLB 3 [port], DcLB 110 [port], RfGEnL 91*
**Shelley,** Rebecca 1887-1984 *AmPeW*
**Shelley,** Robert J 1941- *WhoAmP 91*
**Shelley,** Rulon Gene 1924- *IntWW 91*
**Shelley,** Savilla May 1953- *WhoWest 92*
**Shelley,** Susanne Mary 1928- *WhoAmL 92*
**Shelley,** Thelma 1920- *WhoEnt 92*
**Shelley,** Ursula 1906- *Who 92*
**Shelley,** Walter Brown 1917- *AmMWSc 92*
**Shelley,** William J 1922- *AmMWSc 92*
**Shellhamer,** Dale Francis 1942- *AmMWSc 92*
**Shellhamer,** Robert Howard 1925- *AmMWSc 92*
**Shellhammer,** Howard Stephen 1935- *AmMWSc 92*
**Shellman,** Lee Charles 1937- *WhoAmP 91*
**Shellock,** Frank G 1954- *AmMWSc 92*
**Shellow,** James Myers 1926- *WhoAmL 92*
**Shelly,** Andrew B. 1834-1913 *RelLAm 91*
**Shelly,** Dennis C 1955- *AmMWSc 92*
**Shelly,** Franklin Jeff 1942- *WhoFI 92, WhoWest 92*
**Shelly,** James H 1932- *AmMWSc 92*
**Shelly,** John Richard 1949- *AmMWSc 92*
**Shelly,** Lisa Maureen 1955- *WhoFI 92*
**Shelly,** Michael Bruce 1929- *WhoEnt 92*
**Shelly,** Timothy Scott 1960- *WhoAmL 92*
**Shelnutt,** Dumas Broughton 1955- *WhoRel 92*
**Shelnutt,** Eve *DrAPF 91*
**Shelnutt,** Eve 1941- *ConAu 14AS [port]*
**Shelnutt,** Robert Curtis 1928- *WhoFI 92*
**Shelokov,** Alexis 1919- *AmMWSc 92*
**Shelor,** Earl Dean 1926- *WhoAmP 91*
**Shelow,** Hy Rubin Doved 1961- *WhoAmL 92*
**Shelp,** Earl Edward 1947- *WhoRel 92*
**Shelp,** Ronald Kent 1941- *WhoFI 92*
**Shelson,** W 1922- *AmMWSc 92*
**Shelton,** Charles Bascom, III 1941- *WhoFI 92*
**Shelton,** Charles E. 1945- *WhoBlA 92*
**Shelton,** Charlita Lucille 1958- *WhoWest 92*
**Shelton,** Cora R. 1925- *WhoBlA 92*
**Shelton,** Cynthia Lee 1957- *WhoWest 92*
**Shelton,** Damon Charles 1922- *AmMWSc 92, WhoMW 92*
**Shelton,** David Everett 1943- *WhoFI 92*
**Shelton,** Dorothy Diehl Rees 1935- *WhoAmL 92*
**Shelton,** Edward E. 1946- *WhoBlA 92*
**Shelton,** Emma 1920- *AmMWSc 92*
**Shelton,** Frank Harvey 1924- *AmMWSc 92*
**Shelton,** Frederick Laine 1962- *WhoWest 92*
**Shelton,** Frederick William 1815-1881 *BenetAL 91*
**Shelton,** George Calvin 1923- *AmMWSc 92*
**Shelton,** Harold 1913- *TwCPaSc*
**Shelton,** Harold Tillman 1941- *WhoBlA 92*
**Shelton,** Harvey William 1936- *WhoBlA 92*
**Shelton,** James Churchill *AmMWSc 92*
**Shelton,** James Douglas 1939- *WhoFI 92*
**Shelton,** James Edward 1929- *AmMWSc 92*
**Shelton,** James Poe 1941- *WhoEnt 92*
**Shelton,** James Reid 1911- *AmMWSc 92, WhoMW 92*
**Shelton,** Jewell Vennerrie 1928- *WhoBlA 92*
**Shelton,** Joanna Reed 1951- *WhoFI 92*
**Shelton,** Joel Edward 1928- *WhoWest 92*
**Shelton,** John 1923- *TwCPaSc*
**Shelton,** John C 1937- *AmMWSc 92*
**Shelton,** John W. 1958- *WhoBlA 92*
**Shelton,** John Wayne 1928- *AmMWSc 92*
**Shelton,** Katherine W. 1943- *WhoEnt 92*
**Shelton,** Keith Ray 1941- *AmMWSc 92*
**Shelton,** Lee Raymond 1927- *WhoBlA 92*
**Shelton,** Leonard Agee 1911- *WhoAmL 92*
**Shelton,** Louis Austin 1927- *WhoRel 92*
**Shelton,** Malcolm Wendell 1919- *WhoRel 92*
**Shelton,** Mark L. 1958- *ConAu 135*
**Shelton,** Michael Patrick 1953- *WhoRel 92*
**Shelton,** Muriel Moore 1921- *WhoRel 92*
**Shelton,** O L 1946- *WhoAmP 91, WhoBlA 92*
**Shelton,** Reid Leroy 1924- *WhoEnt 92*
**Shelton,** Reuben Anderson 1954- *WhoBlA 92*
**Shelton,** Richard *DrAPF 91*
**Shelton,** Richard 1933- *ConPo 91, WrDr 92*
**Shelton,** Robert Charles 1934- *WhoWest 92*
**Shelton,** Robert Loren 1934- *WhoMW 92, WhoRel 92*
**Shelton,** Robert Neal 1948- *AmMWSc 92*
**Shelton,** Robert Ryan 1952- *WhoRel 92*
**Shelton,** Robert Warren 1943- *WhoFI 92*
**Shelton,** Robert Wayne 1923- *AmMWSc 92*
**Shelton,** Ron 1945- *ConTFT 9, IntMPA 92*
**Shelton,** Ronald M 1931- *AmMWSc 92*
**Shelton,** Roosevelt Orinthal 1953- *WhoEnt 92*
**Shelton,** Roy Cresswell, Jr. 1941- *WhoBlA 92*
**Shelton,** S. McDowell 1929- *RelLAm 91, WhoBlA 92*
**Shelton,** Sarah Jackson 1956- *WhoRel 92*
**Shelton,** Sarah V 1919- *WhoAmP 91*
**Shelton,** Shirley Megan 1934- *Who 92*
**Shelton,** Sloane 1934- *WhoEnt 92*
**Shelton,** Thomas Alfred 1951- *WhoRel 92*
**Shelton,** Ulysses 1917- *WhoBlA 92*
**Shelton,** Vern R 1938- *WhoIns 92*
**Shelton,** Wanda Carol 1956- *WhoWest 92*
**Shelton,** Wayne Vernon 1932- *WhoFI 92*
**Shelton,** Wilford Neil 1935- *AmMWSc 92*
**Shelton,** William 1929- *Who 92*
**Shelton,** William C. 1942- *WhoRel 92*
**Shelton,** William Chastain 1916- *WhoFI 92*
**Shelton,** William E. 1944- *IntWW 91*
**Shelton,** William Everett 1944- *WhoMW 92*
**Shelton,** William Lee 1939- *AmMWSc 92*
**Shelton-Colby,** Sally 1944- *WhoAmP 91*
**Sheltra,** Carl F *WhoAmP 91*
**Sheltra,** Nancy J 1948- *WhoAmP 91*
**Shelupsky,** David I 1937- *AmMWSc 92*
**Shelver,** William H 1934- *AmMWSc 92*
**Shema,** Virginia King 1957- *WhoAmL 92*
**Shemanchuk,** Joseph Alexander 1927- *AmMWSc 92*
**Shemano,** Irving 1928- *AmMWSc 92*
**Shemansky,** Donald Eugene 1936- *AmMWSc 92*
**Shemchuk,** Charles John, Jr 1945- *WhoAmP 91*
**Shemdin,** Omar H 1939- *AmMWSc 92*
**Shemel,** Sidney 1913- *WhoEnt 92*
**Shemely,** Charles Louis 1938- *WhoFI 92*
**Shemenski,** Robert Martin 1938- *AmMWSc 92*
**Shemer,** Jack Evvard 1940- *AmMWSc 92, WhoWest 92*
**Shemie,** Bonnie 1949- *ConAu 133*
**Shemilt,** Elaine 1954- *TwCPaSc*
**Shemilt,** L W 1919- *AmMWSc 92*
**Shemin,** David d1991 *NewYTBS 91*
**Shemin,** David 1911- *AmMWSc 92, IntWW 91*
**Shemitz,** Ellen Jean 1961- *WhoAmL 92*
**Shemonsky,** Natalie Kaplin 1934- *WhoAmL 92*
**Shemyakin,** Mikhail Mikhaylovich 1908-1970 *SovUnBD*
**Shemyakin,** Yevgeniy Ivanovich 1929- *IntWW 91*
**Shen Congwen** 1902-1988 *FacFETw*
**Shen Dali** 1938- *IntWW 91*
**Shen Daren** 1928- *IntWW 91*
**Shen Jian** 1915- *IntWW 91*
**Shen Tong** 1968- *ConAu 135*
**Shen Tu** 1919- *IntWW 91*
**Shen Yinluo** 1920- *IntWW 91*
**Shen Yun-ying** 1624-1661 *EncAmaz 91*
**Shen Zulun** 1931- *IntWW 91*
**Shen,** Benjamin Ching-chun 1938- *WhoWest 92*
**Shen,** Benjamin Shih-Ping 1931- *AmMWSc 92*
**Shen,** Catherine 1947- *WhoWest 92*
**Shen,** Che-Kun James 1949- *AmMWSc 92*
**Shen,** Chi-Neng 1917- *AmMWSc 92*
**Shen,** Chih-Kang 1932- *AmMWSc 92*
**Shen,** Chin-Wen 1924- *AmMWSc 92*
**Shen,** Chung Yi 1937- *AmMWSc 92*
**Shen,** Chung Yu 1921- *AmMWSc 92*
**Shen,** Colin Yunkang *AmMWSc 92*
**Shen,** D W C 1920- *AmMWSc 92*
**Shen,** Hao-Ming 1933- *AmMWSc 92*
**Shen,** Hsieh Wen 1931- *AmMWSc 92*
**Shen,** James C. H. 1909- *IntWW 91*
**Shen,** Jun 1959- *WhoWest 92*
**Shen,** Kelvin Kei-Wei 1941- *AmMWSc 92*
**Shen,** Lester Sheng-wei 1955- *AmMWSc 92, WhoMW 92*
**Shen,** Liang Chi 1939- *AmMWSc 92*
**Shen,** Linus Liang-nene 1941- *AmMWSc 92*
**Shen,** Mason Ming-Sun 1945- *WhoWest 92*
**Shen,** Mei-Chang 1931- *AmMWSc 92*
**Shen,** Nelson Mu-Ching 1946- *WhoWest 92*
**Shen,** Nien-Tsu *AmMWSc 92*
**Shen,** Peter Ko-Chun 1938- *AmMWSc 92*
**Shen,** S F 1921- *AmMWSc 92*
**Shen,** Samuel Yi-Wen 1919- *AmMWSc 92*
**Shen,** Sheldon Shih-Ta 1947- *AmMWSc 92*
**Shen,** Sin-Yan 1949- *AmMWSc 92, WhoEnt 92, WhoMW 92*
**Shen,** Tek-Ming *AmMWSc 92*
**Shen,** Thomas T 1926- *AmMWSc 92*
**Shen,** Tsung Ying 1924- *AmMWSc 92*
**Shen,** Vincent Y *AmMWSc 92*
**Shen,** Wei-Chiang 1942- *AmMWSc 92*
**Shen,** Wu-Mian 1942- *AmMWSc 92*
**Shen,** Yuan-Shou 1921- *AmMWSc 92*
**Shen,** Yuen-Ron 1935- *AmMWSc 92*
**Shen,** Yvonne Feng 1942- *AmMWSc 92*
**Shenaut,** John Frederick 1916- *WhoEnt 92*
**Shendrikar,** Arun D 1938- *AmMWSc 92*
**Shenefelt,** Ray Eldon 1933- *AmMWSc 92*
**Shenefelt,** Roy David 1909- *AmMWSc 92*
**Shenefield,** John Hale 1939- *WhoAmL 92, WhoAmP 91*
**Sheneman,** Jack Marshall 1927- *AmMWSc 92*
**Shenfield,** Barbara *Who 92*
**Sheng,** Helen Kong 1955- *WhoFI 92*
**Sheng,** Hwai-Ping 1943- *AmMWSc 92*
**Sheng,** Jack Tse-liang 1929- *WhoAmL 92*
**Sheng,** Ping 1946- *AmMWSc 92*
**Sheng,** Yea-Yi Peter 1946- *AmMWSc 92*
**Shengelaya,** Eldar Nikolayevich 1933- *IntWW 91*
**Shengelaya,** Georgiy Nikolayevich 1937- *IntWW 91*
**Shengelaya,** Nikolay Mikhaylovich 1903-1943 *SovUnBD*
**Shenin,** Oleg Semenovich 1937- *SovUnBD A*
**Shenin,** Oleg Semyonovich 1937- *IntWW 91*
**Shenitzer,** Abe 1921- *AmMWSc 92*
**Shenk,** Howard Fred 1939- *WhoFI 92*
**Shenk,** John Henry 1939- *WhoFI 92*
**Shenk,** John Stoner 1933- *AmMWSc 92*
**Shenk,** Richard Lawrence 1940- *WhoMW 92*
**Shenk,** William E 1906- *AmMWSc 92*
**Shenkarow,** Barry *WhoMW 92*
**Shenkel,** Claude W, Jr 1919- *AmMWSc 92*
**Shenker,** Arden Earl 1938- *WhoAmL 92, WhoWest 92*
**Shenker,** Israel 1925- *IntAu&W 91, WrDr 92*
**Shenker,** Joseph C. 1956- *WhoAmL 92*
**Shenker,** Martin 1928- *AmMWSc 92*
**Shenker,** Scott Joseph 1956- *AmMWSc 92*
**Shenkin,** Henry A 1915- *AmMWSc 92*
**Shenkman,** David Michel 1948- *WhoAmL 92*
**Shenkman,** Mark Ronald 1943- *WhoFI 92*
**Shenkman,** Michael David 1955- *WhoAmL 92*
**Shennan,** Joseph Hugh 1933- *IntWW 91, WrDr 92*
**Shenoi,** Belle Anantha 1929- *AmMWSc 92*
**Shenolikar,** Ashok Kumar *AmMWSc 92*
**Shenosky,** Larry Joe 1958- *WhoEnt 92*
**Shenouda III,** Anba 1923- *IntWW 91*
**Shenouda,** Anba, III 1923- *WhoRel 92*
**Shenoute of Atripe** d450? *EncEarC*
**Shenoy,** Gopal K *AmMWSc 92*
**Shenson,** Walter *IntMPA 92*
**Shenstone,** William 1714-1763 *RfGEnL 91*
**Shenton,** Clive 1946- *Who 92*
**Shenton,** James 1925- *WrDr 92*
**Shep,** Robert Lee 1933- *WhoWest 92*
**Shepanski,** John Francis 1954- *AmMWSc 92*
**Shepard,** Alan 1923- *FacFETw*
**Shepard,** Alan B., Jr. 1923- *IntWW 91*
**Shepard,** Benjamin Henry Jesse Francis *BenetAL 91*
**Shepard,** Beverly Renee 1959- *WhoBlA 92*
**Shepard,** Buford Merle 1942- *AmMWSc 92*
**Shepard,** Charles Upham 1804-1886 *BiInAmS*
**Shepard,** Charles Upham, Jr. 1842-1915 *BiInAmS*
**Shepard,** Charles Virgil 1940- *WhoFI 92*
**Shepard,** Clifford Bishop, III 1959- *WhoAmL 92*
**Shepard,** David C 1929- *AmMWSc 92*
**Shepard,** E.H. 1879-1976 *TwCPaSc*
**Shepard,** Earl Alden 1932- *WhoFI 92, WhoWest 92*
**Shepard,** Edwin Reed 1917- *AmMWSc 92*
**Shepard,** Geoffrey Carroll 1944- *WhoAmL 92*
**Shepard,** George Leo 1947- *WhoFI 92*
**Shepard,** Giles Richard Carless 1937- *Who 92*
**Shepard,** Gregory Mark 1955- *WhoIns 92*
**Shepard,** Harvey Kenneth 1938- *AmMWSc 92*
**Shepard,** Hilary Sue 1959- *WhoEnt 92*
**Shepard,** Huey Percy 1936- *WhoBlA 92*
**Shepard,** Ivan Albert 1925- *WhoMW 92*
**Shepard,** J Neal, Jr 1947- *WhoAmP 91*
**Shepard,** James F 1941- *AmMWSc 92*
**Shepard,** James Henry 1850-1918 *BiInAmS*
**Shepard,** Jeffrey G. 1954- *WhoFI 92*
**Shepard,** Joan *WhoBlA 92*
**Shepard,** Joseph William 1922- *AmMWSc 92*
**Shepard,** Kenneth LeRoy 1937- *AmMWSc 92*

Shepard, Kenneth Wayne 1941- *AmMWSc 92*
Shepard, Kyle Mark 1963- *WhoFI 92, WhoWest 92*
Shepard, Leslie Alan 1917- *WrDr 92*
Shepard, Linda Irene 1945- *WhoBlA 92*
Shepard, Lois Burke 1938- *WhoAmP 91*
Shepard, Lucius *TwCSFW 91, WrDr 92*
Shepard, Margo Ann 1957- *WhoFI 92*
Shepard, Marion L 1937- *AmMWSc 92*
Shepard, Martin 1934- *WrDr 92*
Shepard, Maurice Charles 1916- *AmMWSc 92*
Shepard, Neil *DrAPF 91*
Shepard, Odell 1884-1967 *BenetAL 91*
Shepard, Paul Fenton 1942- *AmMWSc 92*
Shepard, R. Bruce 1950- *WhoWest 92*
Shepard, Randall Terry 1946- *WhoAmL 92, WhoAmP 91, WhoMW 92*
Shepard, Ray A. 1940- *WhoBlA 92*
Shepard, Richard Hance 1922- *AmMWSc 92*
Shepard, Richmond 1929- *WrDr 92*
Shepard, Robert Alford 1945- *WhoEnt 92*
Shepard, Robert Andrews 1923- *AmMWSc 92*
Shepard, Robert Carlton 1933- *WhoWest 92*
Shepard, Robert M. 1932- *WhoFI 92*
Shepard, Robert Stanley 1927- *AmMWSc 92*
Shepard, Roger N 1929- *AmMWSc 92*
Shepard, Roger Newland 1929- *IntWW 91*
Shepard, Sam 1943- *BenetAL 91, FacFETw, IntAu&W 91, IntMPA 92, IntWW 91, LiExTwC, WhoEnt 92, WrDr 92*
Shepard, Samuel, Jr. 1907- *WhoBlA 92*
Shepard, Stephen Benjamin 1939- *WhoFI 92*
Shepard, Stephen John Richard 1947- *WhoAmP 91*
Shepard, Thomas 1605-1649 *BenetAL 91*
Shepard, Thomas H 1923- *AmMWSc 92*
Shepard, Tracy Morgan 1957- *WhoIns 92*
Shepard, William A d1895 *BiInAmS*
Shepard, William Albert 1920- *WhoAmL 92*
Shepard, William Francis, III 1948- *WhoWest 92*
Shepardson, John U 1920- *AmMWSc 92*
Shephard, Carol Lynn 1950- *WhoAmL 92*
Shephard, David W., Sr. 1958- *WhoWest 92*
Shephard, George Clifford 1915- *Who 92*
Shephard, Gillian Patricia 1940- *Who 92*
Shephard, Harold Montague 1918- *Who 92*
Shephard, Harvey *LesBEnT 92*
Shephard, Roy Jesse 1929- *AmMWSc 92, WrDr 92*
Shephard, Rupert 1909- *TwCPaSc*
Shephard, William Danks 1933- *AmMWSc 92*
Shepheard, Joseph Kenneth 1908- *Who 92*
Shepheard, Peter 1913- *Who 92*
Shepheard, Peter Faulkner 1913- *IntWW 91*
Shepherd *Who 92*
Shepherd, Baron 1918- *IntWW 91, Who 92*
Shepherd, Alan Arthur 1927- *Who 92*
Shepherd, Albert Pitt, Jr 1943- *AmMWSc 92*
Shepherd, Allen *DrAPF 91*
Shepherd, Anthony Michael 1958- *WhoEnt 92*
Shepherd, Archie 1922- *Who 92*
Shepherd, Arthur 1880-1958 *NewAmDM*
Shepherd, Benjamin A. 1941- *WhoBlA 92*
Shepherd, Benjamin Arthur 1941- *AmMWSc 92*
Shepherd, Berisford 1917- *WhoBlA 92*
Shepherd, Charles Clinton 1929- *WhoFI 92*
Shepherd, Charles Melville *ScFEYrs*
Shepherd, Charles William Haimes 1917- *Who 92*
Shepherd, Clark W 1933- *WhoIns 92*
Shepherd, Colin 1938- *Who 92*
Shepherd, Cybill 1950- *IntMPA 92, WhoEnt 92*
Shepherd, D G 1912- *AmMWSc 92*
Shepherd, David *Who 92*
Shepherd, David 1931- *TwCPaSc*
Shepherd, David 1944- *TwCPaSc*
Shepherd, David Preston 1940- *AmMWSc 92*
Shepherd, Elmira 1959- *WhoBlA 92*
Shepherd, Elsbeth Weichsel 1952- *WhoMW 92*
Shepherd, Eric William 1913- *Who 92*
Shepherd, Forrest 1800-1888 *BiInAmS*
Shepherd, Freeman Daniel, Jr 1936- *AmMWSc 92*
Shepherd, Gene R. *WhoRel 92*
Shepherd, Geoffrey Thomas 1922- *Who 92*
Shepherd, George Anthony 1931- *Who 92*
Shepherd, George Buell, Jr. 1943- *WhoAmL 92*
Shepherd, George Garrett, Jr. 1941- *WhoMW 92*
Shepherd, George W. 1926- *WrDr 92*
Shepherd, Gilbert B. 1937- *WhoWest 92*
Shepherd, Gordon Greeley 1931- *AmMWSc 92*
Shepherd, Gordon Murray 1933- *AmMWSc 92*
Shepherd, Greta Dandridge 1930- *WhoBlA 92*
Shepherd, Harvey Lawrence 1939- *WhoRel 92*
Shepherd, Horne 1909- *TwCPaSc*
Shepherd, Hurley Sidney 1950- *AmMWSc 92*
Shepherd, J Frank 1932- *WhoAmP 91*
Shepherd, James E 1910- *AmMWSc 92*
Shepherd, James Rodney 1935- *Who 92*
Shepherd, Jay Cee 1953- *WhoRel 92*
Shepherd, Jimmie George 1923- *AmMWSc 92*
Shepherd, John *NewAmDM*
Shepherd, John Alan 1943- *Who 92*
Shepherd, John Barrie 1935- *WhoRel 92*
Shepherd, John Calvin 1925- *WhoAmL 92*
Shepherd, John Dodson 1920- *Who 92*
Shepherd, John Frederic 1954- *WhoAmL 92*
Shepherd, John Michael 1955- *WhoAmL 92*
Shepherd, John Patrick George 1937- *AmMWSc 92*
Shepherd, John R. Roy 1929- *WhoWest 92*
Shepherd, John Thompson 1919- *AmMWSc 92, WhoMW 92*
Shepherd, John William 1960- *WhoEnt 92*
Shepherd, Joseph Emmett 1953- *AmMWSc 92*
Shepherd, Julian Granville 1942- *AmMWSc 92*
Shepherd, Karen 1940- *WhoAmP 91*
Shepherd, Lemuel 1896-1990 *AnObit 1990*
Shepherd, Lemuel Cornick, Jr 1896-1990 *FacFETw*
Shepherd, Linda A 1959- *WhoIns 92*
Shepherd, Linda Jean 1949- *AmMWSc 92*
Shepherd, Lynn Ann *WhoFI 92*
Shepherd, Malcolm Thomas 1952- *WhoBlA 92*
Shepherd, Marian E. 1947- *WhoBlA 92*
Shepherd, Mark, Jr 1923- *AmMWSc 92*
Shepherd, Mark Richard 1953- *WhoAmL 92*
Shepherd, Mary Anne 1950- *WhoMW 92*
Shepherd, Michael *IntAu&W 91X, WrDr 92*
Shepherd, Michael Edward 1958- *WhoEnt 92*
Shepherd, Pamela *DrAPF 91*
Shepherd, Peter 1916- *Who 92*
Shepherd, R. F. 1926- *WhoRel 92, WhoWest 92*
Shepherd, Raymond Edward 1941- *AmMWSc 92*
Shepherd, Raymond Lee 1926- *AmMWSc 92*
Shepherd, Rex E 1945- *AmMWSc 92*
Shepherd, Richard 1927- *IntMPA 92*
Shepherd, Richard Carl 1945- *WhoMW 92*
Shepherd, Richard Charles Scrimgeour 1942- *Who 92*
Shepherd, Richard David 1931- *Who 92*
Shepherd, Robert 1932- *WhoBlA 92*
Shepherd, Robert James 1930- *AmMWSc 92*
Shepherd, Robert Patrick 1955- *WhoAmL 92*
Shepherd, Robin 1933- *AmMWSc 92*
Shepherd, Ronald Francis *Who 92*
Shepherd, Roosevelt Eugene 1933- *WhoBlA 92*
Shepherd, Saundra Dianne 1945- *WhoBlA 92*
Shepherd, Stewart Robert 1948- *WhoAmL 92*
Shepherd, Thomas Irvin 1953- *WhoWest 92*
Shepherd, Veronika Y. 1947- *WhoBlA 92*
Shepherd, Victoria Elizabeth 1954- *WhoRel 92*
Shepherd, Virginia L *AmMWSc 92*
Shepherd, W G 1911- *AmMWSc 92*
Shepherd, Walton 1947- *WhoAmP 91*
Shepherd, William C. 1939- *WhoWest 92*
Shepherd, William Henry, Jr. 1957- *WhoRel 92*
Shepherd, William Lloyd 1915- *AmMWSc 92*
Shepherd, William Stanley 1918- *Who 92*
Shepherdson, John Cedric 1926- *Who 92*
Shepilov, Dmitriy Trofimovich 1905- *SovUnBD*
Shepitko, Larisa 1938-1979 *SovUnBD*
Shepler, John Edward 1950- *WhoEnt 92, WhoMW 92*
Shepley, Carol Ferring 1949- *WhoMW 92*
Shepley, Lawrence Charles 1939- *AmMWSc 92*
Shepp, Allan 1928- *AmMWSc 92*
Shepp, Archie 1937- *NewAmDM*
Shepp, Archie Vernon 1934- *WhoBlA 92*
Shepp, Lawrence Alan 1936- *AmMWSc 92*
Sheppard, Alan Jonathan 1927- *AmMWSc 92*
Sheppard, Albert Parker 1936- *AmMWSc 92*
Sheppard, Allen 1932- *Who 92, WhoFI 92*
Sheppard, Allen John George 1932- *IntWW 91*
Sheppard, Asher R 1943- *AmMWSc 92*
Sheppard, Berton Scott 1936- *WhoAmL 92*
Sheppard, Chester Stephen 1927- *AmMWSc 92*
Sheppard, Clive 1930- *TwCPaSc*
Sheppard, Dalton, Jr 1936- *WhoAmP 91*
Sheppard, Darrell Keith 1965- *WhoRel 92*
Sheppard, David 1929- *IntAu&W 91*
Sheppard, David E 1938- *AmMWSc 92*
Sheppard, David Stuart *Who 92*
Sheppard, David Stuart 1929- *IntWW 91, WrDr 92*
Sheppard, David W 1927- *AmMWSc 92*
Sheppard, Dean 1949- *AmMWSc 92*
Sheppard, Donald M 1937- *AmMWSc 92*
Sheppard, Emory Lamar 1942- *AmMWSc 92*
Sheppard, Erwin 1921- *AmMWSc 92*
Sheppard, Francis Henry Wollaston 1921- *Who 92*
Sheppard, Herbert 1922- *AmMWSc 92*
Sheppard, Howard Reece 1926- *WhoFI 92*
Sheppard, John 1515?-1560? *NewAmDM*
Sheppard, John Clarence 1923- *AmMWSc 92*
Sheppard, John Richard 1944- *AmMWSc 92*
Sheppard, Keith George 1949- *AmMWSc 92*
Sheppard, Louis Clarke 1933- *AmMWSc 92, WhoFI 92*
Sheppard, Matthew Patrick 1951- *WhoFI 92*
Sheppard, Maurice 1947- *TwCPaSc*
Sheppard, Maurice Raymond 1947- *Who 92*
Sheppard, Mervyn Cecil Ffranck 1905- *Who 92*
Sheppard, Michael Avery 1960- *WhoAmP 91*
Sheppard, Moses Maurice 1928- *AmMWSc 92*
Sheppard, Norman 1921- *Who 92*
Sheppard, Norman F, Jr *AmMWSc 92*
Sheppard, Phillip Alton 1942- *WhoAmL 92*
Sheppard, Richard A 1930- *AmMWSc 92*
Sheppard, Roger Floyd 1945- *AmMWSc 92*
Sheppard, Ronald John 1939- *AmMWSc 92, WhoBlA 92*
Sheppard, Shirley Anne 1914- *WhoAmP 91*
Sheppard, Stephen *TwCPaSc*
Sheppard, Steven 1954- *BlkOlyM*
Sheppard, Stevenson Royrayson 1945- *WhoBlA 92*
Sheppard, Thomas Richard 1934- *WhoAmL 92*
Sheppard, Walter Lee, Jr 1911- *AmMWSc 92*
Sheppard, William J 1937- *WhoIns 92*
Sheppard, William James 1931- *AmMWSc 92*
Sheppard, William Vernon 1941- *WhoFI 92*
Sheppard-Gray, Evelyn R. 1958- *WhoWest 92*
Sheppard Moore, Ella 1851-1914 *NotBlAW 92 [port]*
Shepperd, Alfred 1925- *Who 92*
Shepperd, Alfred Joseph 1925- *IntWW 91*
Shepperd, James Douglass 1932- *WhoAmP 91*
Shepperd, Thomas Eugene 1941- *WhoFI 92*
Shepperd, Wayne Delbert 1947- *AmMWSc 92*
Shepperson, George Albert 1922- *Who 92*
Shepperson, Jacqueline Ruth 1935- *AmMWSc 92*
Shepperson, Patricia 1929- *TwCPaSc*
Shepperson, Wilbur 1919- *WrDr 92*
Shepperson, Wilbur Stanley 1919- *WhoWest 92*
Shepphard, Charles B 1949- *WhoAmP 91*
Shepphard, Charles Bernard 1949- *WhoBlA 92*
Shepro, David 1924- *AmMWSc 92*
Shepro, Richard W. 1953- *WhoAmL 92*
Sheps, Cecil George 1913- *AmMWSc 92, IntWW 91*
Sher, Alvin Harvey 1941- *AmMWSc 92*
Sher, Antony 1949- *IntWW 91, Who 92*
Sher, Arden 1933- *AmMWSc 92*
Sher, Barry Nostradamus 1949- *WhoFI 92*
Sher, Byron 1928- *WhoAmP 91*
Sher, Byron D. 1928- *WhoAmL 92*
Sher, Daniel 1943- *WhoEnt 92*
Sher, Irving Harold 1924- *AmMWSc 92*
Sher, Joanna Hollenberg 1933- *AmMWSc 92*
Sher, Louis K. 1914- *IntMPA 92*
Sher, Michael Lee 1938- *WhoAmL 92*
Sher, Patricia R 1931- *WhoAmP 91*
Sher, Paul Phillip 1939- *AmMWSc 92*
Sher, Richard B 1939- *AmMWSc 92*
Sher, Rose *DrAPF 91*
Sher, Rudolph 1923- *AmMWSc 92*
Sher, Samuel Julius 1941- *Who 92*
Sher, Steven *DrAPF 91*
Sher, Victor Herman 1947- *Who 92*
Shera, E Brooks 1935- *AmMWSc 92*
Shera, Joyce Ann 1944- *WhoFI 92*
Sherak, Thomas 1945- *IntMPA 92*
Sherald, Allen Franklin 1942- *AmMWSc 92*
Sherar, J William 1930- *WhoIns 92*
Sheraton, Mimi 1926- *IntAu&W 91*
Sheraton, Neil *WrDr 92*
Sheratsky, Rodney E. 1933- *WrDr 92*
Sherbeck, L Adair 1922- *AmMWSc 92*
Sherbert, Donald R 1935- *AmMWSc 92*
Sherbert, Donald Ray 1935- *WhoMW 92*
Sherbin, Jan *WhoEnt 92*
Sherblom, Anne P 1949- *AmMWSc 92*
Sherbon, John Walter 1933- *AmMWSc 92*
Sherborne, Archdeacon of *Who 92*
Sherborne, Area Bishop of 1935- *Who 92*
Sherbourne, Archibald Norbert 1929- *AmMWSc 92*
Sherbourne, Stephen Ashley 1945- *Who 92*
Sherbrooke, Archbishop of 1920- *Who 92*
Sherburne, Donald W. 1929- *WrDr 92*
Sherburne, James Auril 1941- *AmMWSc 92*
Sherburne, John L 1923- *WhoAmP 91*
Sherby, Kathleen Reilly 1947- *WhoAmL 92, WhoMW 92*
Sherby, Oleg D 1925- *AmMWSc 92*
Sherck, Charles Keith 1922- *AmMWSc 92*
Sherck, Philip E. 1931- *WhoEnt 92*
Sherden, David J 1940- *AmMWSc 92*
Shere, Charles 1935- *NewAmDM*
Sherebrin, Marvin Harold 1937- *AmMWSc 92*
Sheremet, Konstantin Filippovich 1923- *SovUnBD*
Sherer, Austin Renslow 1947- *WhoWest 92*
Sherer, Frank Audemars, Jr. 1947- *WhoAmL 92*
Sherer, Glenn Keith 1943- *AmMWSc 92, WhoMW 92*
Sherer, James Pressly 1939- *AmMWSc 92*
Sherer, Samuel Ayers 1944- *WhoAmL 92*
Sherer, Trace Jeffrey 1963- *WhoAmL 92*
Sheresky, Norman M. 1928- *WhoAmL 92*
Sherf, Arden Frederick 1916- *AmMWSc 92*
Sherf, Harriet N. 1934- *WhoWest 92*
Sherfesee, John 1948- *WhoWest 92*
Sherfey, Geraldine Richards 1929- *WhoMW 92*
Sherfield, Baron 1904- *IntWW 91, Who 92*
Shergalis, William Anthony 1941- *AmMWSc 92*
Shergold, Harold Edward 1936- *WhoIns 92*
Shergold, Harold Taplin 1915- *Who 92*
Sheridan, Cecil Majella 1911- *Who 92*
Sheridan, Christopher Julian 1943- *Who 92*
Sheridan, Claire Eileen 1954- *WhoEnt 92*
Sheridan, Daniel Joseph 1961- *WhoAmL 92*
Sheridan, Daniel Patrick 1946- *WhoRel 92*
Sheridan, Douglas Maynard 1921- *AmMWSc 92*
Sheridan, Frank *ScFEYrs*
Sheridan, George Edward 1915- *WhoWest 92*
Sheridan, Jane *WrDr 92*
Sheridan, Jim 1949- *ConTFT 9*
Sheridan, John Francis 1949- *AmMWSc 92*
Sheridan, John Joseph, III 1945- *AmMWSc 92*
Sheridan, John Patrick, Jr. 1942- *WhoAmL 92*
Sheridan, John Roger 1933- *AmMWSc 92*
Sheridan, Judson Dean 1940- *AmMWSc 92*
Sheridan, Lawrence A 1919- *WhoAmP 91*
Sheridan, Lionel Astor 1927- *Who 92, WrDr 92*
Sheridan, Mark Alexander 1958- *AmMWSc 92*
Sheridan, Michael E *WhoAmP 91*
Sheridan, Michael Francis 1940- *AmMWSc 92*
Sheridan, Michael N 1937- *AmMWSc 92*
Sheridan, Patrick Michael 1940- *WhoFI 92*
Sheridan, Peter 1927- *Who 92*

**Sheridan**, Peter Sterling 1944- *AmMWSc 92*
**Sheridan**, Philip Henry 1831-1888 *BenetAL 91*
**Sheridan**, Philip Henry 1950- *AmMWSc 92*
**Sheridan**, Richard Bert 1918- *WhoMW 92*
**Sheridan**, Richard Brinsley 1751-1816 *BlkwCEP, CnDBLB 2 [port], DramC 1 [port], RfGEnL 91*
**Sheridan**, Richard Collins 1929- *AmMWSc 92*
**Sheridan**, Richard P 1939- *AmMWSc 92*
**Sheridan**, Robert E 1940- *AmMWSc 92*
**Sheridan**, Roderick Gerald 1921- *Who 92*
**Sheridan**, Sally Anne *WhoAmP 91*
**Sheridan**, Thomas 1719-1788 *BlkwCEP*
**Sheridan**, Thomas 1938- *IntAu&W 91, WrDr 92*
**Sheridan**, Thomas Brown 1929- *AmMWSc 92*
**Sheridan**, Walter Thomas 1938- *WhoAmL 92*
**Sheridan**, William 1930- *AmMWSc 92*
**Sheridan**, William Cockburn Russell 1917- *WhoRel 92*
**Sheridan**, William Francis 1936- *AmMWSc 92*
**Sheridan**, William Michael 1956- *WhoFI 92*
**Sheridan-Castellano**, Ardell L. 1943- *WhoEnt 92*
**Sheridon**, Nicholas Keith 1935- *AmMWSc 92*
**Sherif**, Carolyn Wood 1922-1982 *WomPsyc*
**Sheriff**, Kenneth Wayne 1942- *WhoMW 92*
**Sheriff**, Leonard S. d1991 *NewYTBS 91*
**Sheriff**, Robert Edward 1922- *AmMWSc 92*
**Sheriff**, Stephen Meyer 1944- *WhoFI 92*
**Sherin**, Edwin 1930- *WhoEnt 92*
**Sheringham**, George 1884-1937 *TwCPaSc*
**Sherins**, Richard J 1937- *AmMWSc 92*
**Sherk**, Douglas Martyn 1956- *WhoWest 92*
**Sherk**, Frank Arthur 1932- *AmMWSc 92*
**Sherk**, George William 1949- *WhoAmL 92*
**Sherk**, Warren Arthur 1916- *WhoFI 92, WhoWest 92*
**Sherlaw Johnson**, Robert 1932- *ConCom 92, WrDr 92*
**Sherlin**, Clay Harvey 1947- *WhoRel 92*
**Sherlock**, Alexander 1922- *IntWW 91, Who 92*
**Sherlock**, David Christopher 1943- *Who 92*
**Sherlock**, Edward Barry 1932- *Who 92*
**Sherlock**, Emmanell Phillips 1914- *WhoWest 92*
**Sherlock**, John Michael 1926- *WhoRel 92*
**Sherlock**, Marjorie 1879-1973 *TwCPaSc*
**Sherlock**, Michael *LesBEnT 92*
**Sherlock**, Paul V 1930- *WhoAmP 91*
**Sherlock**, Philip 1902- *Who 92*
**Sherlock**, Sheila 1918- *Who 92*
**Sherlock**, Thomas 1678-1761 *BlkwCEP*
**Sherma**, Joseph A 1934- *AmMWSc 92*
**Sherman**, Adria Rothman 1950- *AmMWSc 92*
**Sherman**, Albert Herman 1921- *AmMWSc 92*
**Sherman**, Alfred 1919- *IntWW 91, Who 92*
**Sherman**, Alfred Isaac 1920- *AmMWSc 92*
**Sherman**, Anthony Michael 1940- *AmMWSc 92*
**Sherman**, Arlene 1947- *WhoEnt 92*
**Sherman**, Arnold 1932- *WrDr 92*
**Sherman**, Arthur 1931- *AmMWSc 92*
**Sherman**, Barbara J. 1944- *WhoBlA 92*
**Sherman**, Barnet 1958- *WhoFI 92*
**Sherman**, Beatrice Ettinger 1919- *WhoFI 92*
**Sherman**, Bradford Winslow 1934- *WhoAmP 91*
**Sherman**, Burton Stuart 1930- *AmMWSc 92*
**Sherman**, Byron Wesley 1935- *AmMWSc 92*
**Sherman**, Carol *DrAPF 91*
**Sherman**, Charles Edwin 1934- *WhoEnt 92*
**Sherman**, Charles Henry 1928- *AmMWSc 92*
**Sherman**, Charles Philip 1943- *WhoRel 92*
**Sherman**, Cindy 1954- *IntWW 91, WorArt 1980 [port]*
**Sherman**, D R 1935- *AmMWSc 92*
**Sherman**, David Matthew 1959- *WhoWest 92*
**Sherman**, David Michael 1956- *AmMWSc 92*
**Sherman**, David Robert 1952- *WhoAmL 92*
**Sherman**, Deming Eliot 1943- *WhoAmL 92*
**Sherman**, Donald R. 1930- *WhoFI 92*
**Sherman**, Dorothy Helen 1905- *AmMWSc 92*
**Sherman**, Douglas Richard 1950- *WhoRel 92*
**Sherman**, Edward 1919- *AmMWSc 92*
**Sherman**, Edward Forrester 1945- *WhoBlA 92*
**Sherman**, Edward Francis 1937- *WhoAmL 92*
**Sherman**, Eileen Bluestone 1951- *IntAu&W 91*
**Sherman**, Elaine C. 1938- *WhoMW 92*
**Sherman**, Eric 1947- *WhoEnt 92, WhoWest 92*
**Sherman**, Ethel Cromwell 1906- *WhoMW 92*
**Sherman**, Eugene Jay 1935- *WhoFI 92*
**Sherman**, Frances Adams 1934- *WhoWest 92*
**Sherman**, Francis George Harry 1924- *WhoMW 92*
**Sherman**, Francis Henry 1918- *WhoAmP 91*
**Sherman**, Frank 1916- *IntWW 91*
**Sherman**, Frank Asbury 1841-1915 *BiInAmS*
**Sherman**, Frank Dempster 1860-1916 *BenetAL 91*
**Sherman**, Frank R. 1931- *WhoAmL 92*
**Sherman**, Frank William 1946- *WhoMW 92*
**Sherman**, Fred 1932- *AmMWSc 92*
**Sherman**, Frederick George 1915- *AmMWSc 92*
**Sherman**, Frederick Hood 1947- *WhoAmL 92*
**Sherman**, Frederick S 1928- *AmMWSc 92*
**Sherman**, Gary Edward 1949- *WhoAmL 92*
**Sherman**, Gary Joseph 1941- *AmMWSc 92*
**Sherman**, George d1991 *NewYTBS 91*
**Sherman**, George Charles 1938- *AmMWSc 92*
**Sherman**, Gerald Philip 1940- *AmMWSc 92*
**Sherman**, Glenn Terry 1954- *WhoAmL 92*
**Sherman**, Gordon R 1928- *AmMWSc 92*
**Sherman**, Guy 1958- *WhoEnt 92*
**Sherman**, H Duane 1932- *WhoIns 92*
**Sherman**, Harold 1921- *AmMWSc 92*
**Sherman**, Harry Logan 1927- *AmMWSc 92*
**Sherman**, Helen Wilson 1913- *WhoWest 92*
**Sherman**, Herbert 1920- *AmMWSc 92*
**Sherman**, Howard D. 1961- *WhoFI 92*
**Sherman**, Hunter B. 1943- *WhoRel 92*
**Sherman**, Ian Matthew 1953- *WhoAmL 92*
**Sherman**, Ingrid 1919- *WrDr 92*
**Sherman**, Irwin William 1933- *AmMWSc 92*
**Sherman**, Isaac 1935- *WhoAmL 92*
**Sherman**, James H 1936- *AmMWSc 92*
**Sherman**, James Schoolcraft 1855-1912 *AmPolLe*
**Sherman**, Jeffrey Barry 1948- *WhoFI 92*
**Sherman**, Jerome Kalman 1925- *AmMWSc 92*
**Sherman**, Joe *DrAPF 91*
**Sherman**, John *DrAPF 91*
**Sherman**, John 1613-1685 *BiInAmS*
**Sherman**, John 1823-1900 *AmPolLe [port]*
**Sherman**, John Edwin 1922- *AmMWSc 92*
**Sherman**, John Foord 1919- *AmMWSc 92*
**Sherman**, John Walter 1945- *AmMWSc 92*
**Sherman**, Jory *DrAPF 91*
**Sherman**, Joseph Allen 1929- *WhoAmL 92*
**Sherman**, Joseph E 1919- *AmMWSc 92*
**Sherman**, Joseph Howard 1923- *WhoRel 92*
**Sherman**, Joseph M 1926- *WhoAmP 91*
**Sherman**, Judith Dorothy 1942- *WhoEnt 92*
**Sherman**, Kenneth 1932- *AmMWSc 92*
**Sherman**, L R 1890- *ScFEYrs*
**Sherman**, Larry Ray 1934- *AmMWSc 92*
**Sherman**, Laurence A 1935- *AmMWSc 92*
**Sherman**, Lawrence Francis 1949- *WhoFI 92*
**Sherman**, Lester Ivan 1936- *WhoAmL 92*
**Sherman**, Linda Arlene 1950- *AmMWSc 92*
**Sherman**, Louis *Who 92*
**Sherman**, Louis Allen 1943- *AmMWSc 92*
**Sherman**, Lynn *ConAu 135*
**Sherman**, Malcolm J 1939- *AmMWSc 92*
**Sherman**, Marcus Harvey 1917- *WhoBlA 92*
**Sherman**, Marion Kyle *WhoAmP 91*
**Sherman**, Mark A. 1924- *WhoMW 92*
**Sherman**, Martin 1920- *AmMWSc 92*
**Sherman**, Martin 1938- *WrDr 92*
**Sherman**, Mary Kennedy 1919- *WhoFI 92*
**Sherman**, Merry Rubin 1940- *AmMWSc 92*
**Sherman**, Michael *TwCSFW 91*
**Sherman**, Michael Ian 1944- *AmMWSc 92*
**Sherman**, Michele 1945- *ConAu 36NR*
**Sherman**, Michele C. 1963- *WhoAmL 92*
**Sherman**, Mildred Mozelle 1932- *WhoEnt 92*
**Sherman**, Nancy *DrAPF 91*
**Sherman**, Nancy Ann 1952- *WhoEnt 92*
**Sherman**, Norman K 1935- *AmMWSc 92*
**Sherman**, Oddie Lee *WhoBlA 92*
**Sherman**, Patrick 1928- *WhoWest 92*
**Sherman**, Patsy O'Connell 1930- *AmMWSc 92*
**Sherman**, Paul Dwight, Jr 1942- *AmMWSc 92*
**Sherman**, Paul Willard 1949- *AmMWSc 92*
**Sherman**, Pearl Olsen 1906- *WhoEnt 92*
**Sherman**, Peter Michael *TwCSFW 91*
**Sherman**, Philip Martin 1930- *AmMWSc 92*
**Sherman**, Ray Scott 1939- *WhoRel 92, WhoWest 92*
**Sherman**, Richard B 1929- *IntAu&W 91, WrDr 92*
**Sherman**, Richard John 1950- *WhoMW 92*
**Sherman**, Richard M. 1928- *IntMPA 92*
**Sherman**, Richard S. *WhoEnt 92*
**Sherman**, Robert 1950- *WhoEnt 92, WhoWest 92*
**Sherman**, Robert B. 1925- *IntMPA 92*
**Sherman**, Robert Bernard 1925- *WhoEnt 92, WhoWest 92*
**Sherman**, Robert George 1942- *AmMWSc 92*
**Sherman**, Robert Howard 1929- *AmMWSc 92*
**Sherman**, Robert James 1940- *AmMWSc 92*
**Sherman**, Robert M. *IntMPA 92*
**Sherman**, Roger *WrDr 92*
**Sherman**, Roger 1721-1793 *AmPolLe, BlkwEAR*
**Sherman**, Roger 1930- *WhoFI 92*
**Sherman**, Roger Talbot 1923- *AmMWSc 92*
**Sherman**, Ronald 1941- *AmMWSc 92*
**Sherman**, Russell 1930- *NewAmDM*
**Sherman**, Samuel M. *IntMPA 92*
**Sherman**, Samuel Murray 1944- *AmMWSc 92*
**Sherman**, Scott *WhoEnt 92*
**Sherman**, Scott Bradley 1954- *WhoFI 92*
**Sherman**, Signe Lidfeldt 1913- *WhoFI 92*
**Sherman**, Steve 1938- *WrDr 92*
**Sherman**, Steven Ryan 1950- *WhoFI 92*
**Sherman**, Steven William 1949- *WhoEnt 92*
**Sherman**, Stuart Holmes 1955- *WhoEnt 92*
**Sherman**, Stuart P. 1881-1926 *BenetAL 91*
**Sherman**, Susan *DrAPF 91*
**Sherman**, Theodore A. 1901-1981 *ConAu 134*
**Sherman**, Thomas Fairchild 1934- *AmMWSc 92*
**Sherman**, Thomas Lawrence 1937- *AmMWSc 92*
**Sherman**, Thomas Oakley 1939- *AmMWSc 92*
**Sherman**, Thomas Oscar, Jr. 1948- *WhoBlA 92*
**Sherman**, Tim *WhoAmP 91*
**Sherman**, Vincent 1906- *IntMPA 92*
**Sherman**, Walter Dean 1926- *WhoMW 92*
**Sherman**, Walter Philip 1952- *WhoMW 92, WhoRel 92*
**Sherman**, Warren V 1937- *AmMWSc 92*
**Sherman**, Wayne Bush 1940- *AmMWSc 92*
**Sherman**, William *DrAPF 91*
**Sherman**, William Delano 1942- *WhoAmL 92*
**Sherman**, William Farrar 1937- *WhoAmP 91*
**Sherman**, William Reese 1928- *AmMWSc 92*
**Sherman**, William T. 1820-1891 *BenetAL 91*
**Sherman**, William Tecumseh 1820-1891 *RComAH*
**Sherman**, Zachary 1922- *AmMWSc 92*
**Sherman**, Zelda Charlotte 1924- *WhoWest 92*
**Sherman-Simpson**, Barbara J. 1944- *WhoBlA 92*
**Shero**, John Paul, III 1947- *WhoRel 92*
**Sherockman**, Andrew Antolcik 1913 *AmMWSc 92*
**Sherotsky**, Priscilla Colleen 1943- *WhoWest 92*
**Sherouse**, Alvis 1943- *WhoEnt 92*
**Sherow**, Don Carl 1949- *WhoBlA 92*
**Sherr**, Allan Ellis 1926- *AmMWSc 92*
**Sherr**, Barry Frederick 1944- *AmMWSc 92*
**Sherr**, Evelyn Brown 1946- *AmMWSc 92*
**Sherr**, Morris Max 1930- *WhoAmL 92*
**Sherr**, Rubby 1913- *AmMWSc 92*
**Sherr**, Stanley I 1934- *AmMWSc 92*
**Sherrard**, Joseph Holmes 1942- *AmMWSc 92*
**Sherrard**, Michael David 1928- *Who 92*
**Sherrard**, Raymond Henry 1944- *WhoWest 92*
**Sherred**, T L 1915-1985 *TwCSFW 91*
**Sherrell**, Charles 1936- *WhoHisp 92*
**Sherrell**, Charles Ronald, II 1936- *WhoBlA 92*
**Sherrell**, Lynn Margaret 1940- *WhoAmL 92*
**Sherren**, Anne Terry 1936- *AmMWSc 92, WhoMW 92*
**Sherren**, Leslie Ann Forrester 1958- *WhoAmL 92*
**Sherrer**, Gary L 1948- *WhoAmP 91*
**Sherrer**, Robert E 1923- *AmMWSc 92*
**Sherrick**, Carl Edwin 1924- *AmMWSc 92*
**Sherrick**, Joseph C 1917- *AmMWSc 92*
**Sherriff**, R C 1896-1975 *FacFETw, RfGEnL 91*
**Sherriffs**, Ronald Everett 1934- *WhoEnt 92*
**Sherrill**, Bette Cecile Benham 1944- *AmMWSc 92*
**Sherrill**, Carlyle 1953- *WhoAmP 91*
**Sherrill**, Clarence Ardell James 1924- *WhoEnt 92*
**Sherrill**, H. Virgil 1920- *WhoMW 92*
**Sherrill**, Henry Knox 1890-1980 *RelLAm 91*
**Sherrill**, J C 1917- *AmMWSc 92*
**Sherrill**, Joseph Cyril 1917- *WhoMW 92*
**Sherrill**, Lewis Joseph 1882-1957 *RelLAm 91*
**Sherrill**, Max Douglas 1930- *AmMWSc 92*
**Sherrill**, Robert Sommerville 1954- *WhoFI 92*
**Sherrill**, Thomas Boykin, III 1930- *WhoMW 92*
**Sherrill**, Tom 1946- *WhoAmP 91*
**Sherrill**, Vanita Lytle 1945- *WhoBlA 92*
**Sherrill**, William Henry 1932- *WhoBlA 92*
**Sherrill**, William Manning 1936- *AmMWSc 92*
**Sherrin**, Edward George 1931- *IntAu&W 91, IntWW 91*
**Sherrin**, Ned 1931- *IntMPA 92, Who 92, WrDr 92*
**Sherrington**, Charles Scott 1857-1952 *WhoNob 90*
**Sherrington**, David 1941- *Who 92*
**Sherris**, John C 1921- *AmMWSc 92*
**Sherritt**, George M 1927- *WhoIns 92*
**Sherritt**, Grant Wilson 1923- *AmMWSc 92*
**Sherrod**, Charles M. 1937- *WhoBlA 92*
**Sherrod**, Charles Melvin 1937- *WhoAmP 91*
**Sherrod**, Ezra Cornell 1950- *WhoBlA 92*
**Sherrod**, Hilton Byron 1949- *WhoFI 92*
**Sherrod**, Lloyd B 1931- *AmMWSc 92*
**Sherrod**, R Allen *WhoAmP 91*
**Sherrod**, Robert Lee 1909- *IntWW 91*
**Sherrod**, Theodore Roosevelt 1915- *AmMWSc 92*
**Sherron**, Jim K, Jr 1931- *WhoAmP 91*
**Sherry**, Allan Dean 1945- *AmMWSc 92*
**Sherry**, Clifford Joseph 1943- *AmMWSc 92*
**Sherry**, Dale Alfred 1930- *WhoRel 92*
**Sherry**, Daniel Milton 1940- *WhoEnt 92*
**Sherry**, Edwin J 1933- *AmMWSc 92*
**Sherry**, Fred 1948- *NewAmDM*
**Sherry**, Howard S 1930- *AmMWSc 92*
**Sherry**, James *DrAPF 91*
**Sherry**, John Ernest Horwath 1932- *WhoFI 92*
**Sherry**, John M 1913- *AmMWSc 92*
**Sherry**, Kathleen Susan 1954- *WhoWest 92*
**Sherry**, Norman 1925- *ConAu 34NR, WrDr 92*
**Sherry**, Norman 1935- *IntAu&W 91, Who 92*
**Sherry**, Paul Henry 1933- *WhoMW 92, WhoRel 92*
**Sherry**, Peter Burum 1925- *AmMWSc 92*
**Sherry**, Priscilla Mae *WhoEnt 92*
**Sherry**, Sol 1916- *AmMWSc 92*
**Sherry**, Sylvia *IntAu&W 91, WrDr 92*
**Sherry**, Sylvia 1932- *ConAu 34NR*
**Sherry**, Vincent, Mrs. *Who 92*
**Shersby**, Michael 1933- *Who 92*
**Shershin**, Anthony Connors 1939- *AmMWSc 92*
**Sherstad**, Samuel G. 1947 *WhoFI 92*
**Sherston-Baker**, Robert 1951- *Who 92*
**Shertzer**, Howard Grant 1945- *AmMWSc 92*
**Shertzer**, Leonard Eugene 1929- *WhoRel 92*
**Shervais**, John Walter 1948- *AmMWSc 92*
**Sherval**, David Robert 1933- *Who 92*
**Shervey**, Paul Douglas 1941- *WhoMW 92*
**Shervington**, E. Walter 1906- *WhoBlA 92*
**Sherwin**, Allan Leonard 1932- *AmMWSc 92*
**Sherwin**, Byron Lee 1946- *WhoMW 92, WhoRel 92*
**Sherwin**, James Terry 1933- *WhoFI 92*
**Sherwin**, Judith Johnson 1936- *ConAu 34NR, ConPo 91, WrDr 92*
**Sherwin**, Judith Margo 1940- *WhoMW 92*
**Sherwin**, Martin Barry 1938- *AmMWSc 92*

**Sherwin,** Paul Frederick 1954- *WhoMW 92*
**Sherwin,** Russell P 1924- *AmMWSc 92*
**Sherwin-White,** Adrian Nicholas 1911- *Who 92*
**Sherwood,** Bishop Suffragan of 1940- *Who 92*
**Sherwood,** A Gilbert 1930- *AmMWSc 92*
**Sherwood,** Albert E 1930- *AmMWSc 92*
**Sherwood,** Allen Joseph 1909- *WhoAmL 92, WhoWest 92*
**Sherwood,** Arthur Lawrence 1943- *WhoAmL 92*
**Sherwood,** Arthur Morley 1939- *WhoAmL 92*
**Sherwood,** Arthur Robert 1936- *AmMWSc 92*
**Sherwood,** Bobby 1914-1981 *FacFETw*
**Sherwood,** Bruce Arne 1938- *AmMWSc 92*
**Sherwood,** David J. 1922- *IntWW 91*
**Sherwood,** David William 1943- *WhoIns 92*
**Sherwood,** Devon Fredrick 1943- *WhoAmL 92*
**Sherwood,** Hugh C. 1928- *WrDr 92*
**Sherwood,** Jack Robert 1931- *WhoWest 92*
**Sherwood,** James Blair 1933- *Who 92*
**Sherwood,** Jeffry Rand 1950- *WhoFI 92*
**Sherwood,** Jesse Eugene 1922- *AmMWSc 92*
**Sherwood,** John H. 1913- *WrDr 92*
**Sherwood,** John L 1952- *AmMWSc 92*
**Sherwood,** John Martin 1936- *WhoRel 92*
**Sherwood,** Lawrence Leighton 1954- *WhoWest 92*
**Sherwood,** Louis 1941- *Who 92*
**Sherwood,** Louis Maier 1937- *AmMWSc 92*
**Sherwood,** Madeleine 1922- *IntMPA 92*
**Sherwood,** Madeleine Thornton 1922- *WhoEnt 92*
**Sherwood,** Madisen 1917- *WhoRel 92*
**Sherwood,** Morgan Bronson 1929- *WrDr 92*
**Sherwood,** Nelson *TwCSFW 91*
**Sherwood,** O. Peter 1945- *WhoBlA 92*
**Sherwood,** Philip Karl 1943- *WhoMW 92*
**Sherwood,** Richard Edwin 1928- *WhoAmL 92*
**Sherwood,** Robert Antony 1923- *Who 92*
**Sherwood,** Robert E. 1896-1955 *BenetAL 91, FacFETw*
**Sherwood,** Robert Petersen 1932- *WhoWest 92*
**Sherwood,** Robert Tinsley 1929- *AmMWSc 92*
**Sherwood,** Sharon Dee 1944- *WhoWest 92*
**Sherwood,** Thomas 1934- *Who 92*
**Sherwood,** Trent Ray 1966- *WhoRel 92*
**Sherwood,** Valerie *WrDr 92*
**Sherwood,** Wallace Walter 1944- *WhoBlA 92*
**Sherwood,** William Cullen 1932- *AmMWSc 92*
**Sherwood-Pike,** Martha Allen 1948- *AmMWSc 92*
**Sheryll,** Richard Perry 1956- *AmMWSc 92*
**Sherzan,** Gary 1944- *WhoAmP 91*
**Sherzer,** Harvey Gerald 1944- *WhoAmL 92*
**Shesgreen,** Sean Nicholas 1939- *WhoMW 92*
**Sheshtawy,** Adel A 1940- *AmMWSc 92*
**Sheskin,** Theodore Jerome 1940- *AmMWSc 92*
**Shessler,** Thomas Andrew 1958- *WhoMW 92*
**Shestack,** Jerome Joseph 1925- *WhoAmL 92*
**Shestakov,** Aleksei Ilyich 1949- *AmMWSc 92*
**Shestakova,** Tatyana 1957- *IntWW 91*
**Shestokas,** Jill Barbara 1955- *WhoMW 92*
**Shestopal,** Dawn Angela *Who 92*
**Shestov,** Led 1866-1938 *FacFETw*
**Sheth,** Atul C 1941- *AmMWSc 92*
**Sheth,** Bhogilal 1931- *AmMWSc 92*
**Sheth,** Ketankumar K 1959- *AmMWSc 92*
**Sheth,** Pranlal 1924- *Who 92*
**Shetland,** Llric 1947- *TwCPaSc*
**Shetlar,** David John 1946- *AmMWSc 92*
**Shetlar,** Martin David 1938- *AmMWSc 92*
**Shetlar,** Marvin Roy 1918- *AmMWSc 92*
**Shetler,** Antoinette *AmMWSc 92*
**Shetler,** Stanwyn Gerald 1933- *AmMWSc 92*
**Shettel,** Don Landis, Jr. 1949- *WhoWest 92*
**Shetterly,** Donivan Max 1946- *AmMWSc 92*
**Shettle,** Eric Payson 1943- *AmMWSc 92*
**Shettler,** Walter Robert, Jr. 1950- *WhoRel 92*
**Shetty,** Mulki Radhakrishna 1940- *WhoMW 92*
**Shetzline,** David *DrAPF 91*
**Sheumack,** Colin Davies *Who 92*
**Shevach,** Ethan Menahem 1943- *AmMWSc 92*
**Shevack,** Hilda N 1934- *AmMWSc 92*
**Shevack,** Hilda Natalie *WhoFI 92*
**Shevardnadze,** Eduard 1928- *FacFETw*
**Shevardnadze,** Eduard Amvrosievich 1928- *SovUnBD*
**Shevardnadze,** Eduard Amvrosiyevich 1928- *IntWW 91, Who 92*
**Shevchenko,** Aleksandr Vasil'evich 1882-1948 *SovUnBD*
**Shevchenko,** Arkadiy Nikolayevich 1930- *IntWW 91*
**Shevchenko,** Valentina Semenovna 1935- *SovUnBD*
**Shevchenko,** Valentina Semionovna 1935- *IntWW 91*
**Shevchenko,** Vladimir Pavlovich 1941- *IntWW 91*
**Shevel,** Wilbert Lee 1932- *AmMWSc 92*
**Sheveleva,** Yekaterina 1916- *IntWW 91*
**Sheviak,** Charles John 1947- *AmMWSc 92*
**Shevick,** Steven Karl 1956- *WhoAmP 91*
**Shevin,** David *DrAPF 91*
**Shevin,** Robert Lewis 1934- *WhoAmL 92*
**Shevitz,** Mark H. 1955- *WhoMW 92*
**Shevlin,** Philip Bernard 1939- *AmMWSc 92*
**Shew,** Delbert Craig 1940- *AmMWSc 92*
**Shew,** Rose Jean 1952- *WhoMW 92*
**Shewan,** William 1914- *AmMWSc 92*
**Sheward,** Richard S. 1944- *WhoAmL 92*
**Shewbridge,** Deborah Kay 1963- *WhoEnt 92*
**Shewchuk,** Robert John 1950- *WhoEnt 92*
**Shewchun,** John 1938- *AmMWSc 92*
**Shewen,** Patricia Ellen 1949- *AmMWSc 92*
**Shewmake,** Janice Marie 1946- *WhoAmP 91*
**Shewmaker,** James Edward 1922- *AmMWSc 92*
**Shewmon,** Paul G 1930- *AmMWSc 92*
**Shewry,** Peter Robert 1948- *Who 92*
**Sheynis,** Viktor Leonidovich 1931- *IntWW 91, SovUnBD*
**Shi Liming** 1939- *IntWW 91*
**Shi Lu** 1919- *IntWW 91*
**Shi,** Charlie Y. *WhoWest 92*
**Shi,** J. Stephen 1949- *WhoAmL 92*
**Shi,** Yun Yuan 1932- *AmMWSc 92*
**Shiach,** Gordon Iain Wilson 1935- *Who 92*
**Shiao,** Daniel Da-Fong 1937- *AmMWSc 92*
**Shiau,** Yih-Fu 1942- *AmMWSc 92*
**Shibaev,** Aleksey Ivanovich 1915- *IntWW 91*
**Shibata,** Edward Isamu 1942- *AmMWSc 92*
**Shibata,** George Eishin 1938- *WhoRel 92*
**Shibata,** Shoji 1927- *AmMWSc 92*
**Shibib,** M Ayman 1953- *AmMWSc 92*
**Shibko,** Samuel Isaac 1927- *AmMWSc 92*
**Shibles,** Richard Marwood 1933- *AmMWSc 92*
**Shibles,** Warren 1933- *WrDr 92*
**Shibles,** Warren Alton 1933- *WhoMW 92*
**Shibley,** Arnold P 1933- *WhoAmP 91*
**Shibley,** Gail *WhoAmP 91*
**Shibley,** John Luke 1919- *AmMWSc 92*
**Shibley,** Raymond Nadeem 1925- *WhoAmL 92*
**Shibli,** Mohammed Abdullah 1952- *WhoFI 92*
**Shibutani,** Tamotsu 1920- *IntAu&W 91, WrDr 92*
**Shichi,** Hitoshi 1932- *AmMWSc 92*
**Shichman,** D 1928- *AmMWSc 92*
**Shichor,** David 1933- *WhoWest 92*
**Shick,** Bradley Ullin 1956- *WhoFI 92*
**Shick,** Philip E 1918- *AmMWSc 92*
**Shickich,** Joseph Emil, Jr. 1953- *WhoAmL 92*
**Shickle,** Paul Eugene 1927- *WhoWest 92*
**Shickluna,** John C 1923- *AmMWSc 92*
**Shicoff,** Stuart Dennis 1947- *WhoWest 92*
**Shida,** Mitsuzo 1935- *AmMWSc 92*
**Shide,** Don L *WhoAmP 91*
**Shideler,** Gerald Lee 1938- *AmMWSc 92*
**Shideler,** Isabel Betts 1905- *WhoWest 92*
**Shideler,** Mary M. 1917- *WrDr 92*
**Shideler,** Robert Weaver 1913- *AmMWSc 92*
**Shiderly,** Phyllis J 1925- *WhoAmP 91*
**Shiefman,** Vicky *DrAPF 91*
**Shieh,** Ching-Chyuan 1950- *AmMWSc 92*
**Shieh,** Francis 1926- *WhoFI 92*
**Shieh,** John Shunen 1946- *AmMWSc 92*
**Shieh,** John Ting-chung 1935- *WhoFI 92*
**Shieh,** Kenneth Kuang-Zen 1936- *AmMWSc 92*
**Shieh,** Leang-San 1934- *AmMWSc 92*
**Shieh,** Paulinus Shee-Shan 1931- *AmMWSc 92*
**Shieh,** Yuch-Ning 1940- *AmMWSc 92, WhoMW 92*
**Shiekman,** Laurence Zeid 1947- *WhoAmL 92*
**Shiel,** M P 1865-1947 *ScFEYrs, TwCSFW 91*
**Shield,** Leslie 1916- *Who 92*
**Shield,** Richard Thorpe 1929- *AmMWSc 92*
**Shieldhouse,** Richard Gerber 1953- *WhoFI 92*
**Shields,** Allen Lowell 1927- *AmMWSc 92*
**Shields,** Brooke 1965- *ConTFT 9, IntMPA 92*
**Shields,** Brooke Christa Camille 1965- *WhoEnt 92*
**Shields,** Bruce Maclean 1922- *AmMWSc 92*
**Shields,** Carol Ann 1935- *IntAu&W 91*
**Shields,** Charles Douglas 1955- *WhoMW 92*
**Shields,** Charles W 1959- *WhoAmP 91*
**Shields,** Charles Woodruff 1825-1904 *BiInAmS*
**Shields,** Clarence L., Jr. 1940- *WhoBlA 92*
**Shields,** Craig M. 1941- *WhoAmL 92*
**Shields,** David *DrAPF 91*
**Shields,** David Lyle Light 1950- *WhoRel 92*
**Shields,** Dennis 1947- *TwCPaSc*
**Shields,** Dennis 1948- *AmMWSc 92*
**Shields,** Elizabeth Lois 1928- *Who 92*
**Shields,** Esther L. M. *WhoBlA 92*
**Shields,** Fletcher Douglas 1926- *AmMWSc 92*
**Shields,** Frank Cox 1944- *WhoFI 92*
**Shields,** George Seamon 1925- *AmMWSc 92*
**Shields,** George Terkel 1928- *WhoAmL 92*
**Shields,** Gerald Francis 1943- *AmMWSc 92*
**Shields,** Howard William 1931- *AmMWSc 92*
**Shields,** James Edwin 1934- *AmMWSc 92*
**Shields,** Jimmie Lee 1934- *AmMWSc 92*
**Shields,** Joan Esther 1934- *AmMWSc 92*
**Shields,** John Allen, Jr. 1946- *WhoMW 92*
**Shields,** John Sinclair 1903- *Who 92*
**Shields,** John William, Jr. 1937- *WhoMW 92*
**Shields,** Jordan David 1956- *WhoFI 92*
**Shields,** Karen Bethea 1949- *WhoBlA 92*
**Shields,** Karen Galloway 1949- *WhoBlA 92*
**Shields,** Landrum Eugene 1927- *WhoBlA 92*
**Shields,** Leslie Stuart 1919- *Who 92*
**Shields,** Lora Maneum 1912- *AmMWSc 92*
**Shields,** Lora Mangum 1912- *WhoWest 92*
**Shields,** Loran Donald 1936- *AmMWSc 92*
**Shields,** Lynnette Adell 1965- *WhoMW 92*
**Shields,** Margaret Kerslake 1941- *IntWW 91*
**Shields,** Michael *Who 92*
**Shields,** Michael Joseph 1938- *IntAu&W 91*
**Shields,** Mildred Jean 1935- *WhoAmP 91*
**Shields,** Neil 1919- *Who 92*
**Shields,** Patrick Thomas, Jr. 1935- *WhoMW 92*
**Shields,** Paul Calvin 1933- *AmMWSc 92*
**Shields,** Perry 1925- *WhoAmL 92*
**Shields,** Richard Lee 1955- *WhoRel 92*
**Shields,** Robert 1930- *IntWW 91, Who 92*
**Shields,** Robert B. d1991 *NewYTBS 91*
**Shields,** Robert Francis 1923- *WhoFI 92, WhoMW 92*
**Shields,** Robert James 1934- *AmMWSc 92*
**Shields,** Robert Lloyd, III 1945- *WhoAmL 92*
**Shields,** Robert Michael 1943- *Who 92*
**Shields,** Robert Pierce 1932- *AmMWSc 92*
**Shields,** Roger L. 1943- *WhoEnt 92*
**Shields,** Ronald Frederick d1991 *Who 92N*
**Shields,** Steven Owen 1952- *WhoEnt 92, WhoMW 92*
**Shields,** Stuart *Who 92*
**Shields,** Tamara West-O'Kelley 1948- *WhoFI 92*
**Shields,** Terrell Michael 1954- *WhoRel 92*
**Shields,** Thomas Todhunter, Jr. 1873-1955 *RelLAm 91*
**Shields,** Thomas William 1922- *AmMWSc 92, WhoMW 92*
**Shields,** Varee, Jr. 1935- *WhoBlA 92*
**Shields,** Vincent O. 1924- *WhoBlA 92*
**Shields,** Walter W. 1935- *WhoWest 92*
**Shields,** William A. 1946- *IntMPA 92*
**Shields,** William A., III 1948- *WhoEnt 92*
**Shields,** William Maurice 1937- *WhoFI 92, WhoWest 92*
**Shields,** William Michael 1958- *WhoFI 92*
**Shiell,** James Wyllie 1912- *Who 92*
**Shiely,** John Stephen 1952- *WhoAmL 92*
**Shier,** Daniel Edward 1939- *WhoWest 92*
**Shier,** Douglas Robert 1946- *AmMWSc 92*
**Shier,** Shelley M. 1957- *WhoEnt 92*
**Shier,** Wayne Thomas 1943- *AmMWSc 92*
**Shierlaw,** Norman Craig 1921- *Who 92*
**Shiers,** Frank Abram 1920- *WhoAmL 92*
**Shiff,** Alan Howard William 1934- *WhoAmL 92*
**Shiff,** Richard 1942- *IntMPA 92*
**Shiff,** Richard Alan 1942- *WhoEnt 92*
**Shiffert,** Edith *DrAPF 91*
**Shifflett,** Crandall A. 1938- *ConAu 135*
**Shifflett,** Lynne Carol *WhoBlA 92*
**Shiffman,** Bernard 1942- *AmMWSc 92*
**Shiffman,** Carl Abraham 1930- *AmMWSc 92*
**Shiffman,** Max 1914- *AmMWSc 92*
**Shiffman,** Melvin Arthur 1931- *WhoWest 92*
**Shiffman,** Morris A 1922- *AmMWSc 92*
**Shiffner,** Henry David 1930- *Who 92*
**Shiffrin,** Steven H. 1941- *WhoAmL 92*
**Shiflet,** Thomas Neal 1930- *AmMWSc 92*
**Shiflet,** W Marion 1927- *WhoAmP 91*
**Shiflett,** Betty *DrAPF 91*
**Shiflett,** Lilburn Thomas 1921- *AmMWSc 92*
**Shiflett,** Pendleton M, III 1946- *WhoIns 92*
**Shiflett,** Ray Calvin 1939- *AmMWSc 92*
**Shifrin,** David A. 1953- *WhoAmL 92*
**Shifrin,** Nisson Abramovich 1892-1961 *SovUnBD*
**Shifrin,** Salvatore John 1958- *WhoFI 92*
**Shifrin,** Seymour 1926-1979 *NewAmDM*
**Shigeishi,** Ronald A 1939- *AmMWSc 92*
**Shigezawa,** Ruth *DrAPF 91*
**Shigley,** Joseph E 1909- *AmMWSc 92*
**Shigo,** Alex Lloyd 1930- *AmMWSc 92*
**Shih Chi-Yang** 1935- *IntWW 91*
**Shih,** Arnold Shang-Teh 1943- *AmMWSc 92*
**Shih,** Benedict Chesang 1935- *WhoWest 92*
**Shih,** Chang-Tai 1934- *AmMWSc 92*
**Shih,** Chia Hsin 1941- *WhoMW 92*
**Shih,** Ching-Yuan G 1934- *AmMWSc 92*
**Shih,** Cornelius Chung-Sheng 1931- *AmMWSc 92*
**Shih,** Frederick F 1936- *AmMWSc 92*
**Shih,** Hansen S T 1942- *AmMWSc 92*
**Shih,** Hsiang 1943- *AmMWSc 92*
**Shih,** Hsio Chang 1937- *AmMWSc 92*
**Shih,** James Waikuo 1941- *AmMWSc 92*
**Shih,** Jason Chia-Hsing 1939- *AmMWSc 92*
**Shih,** Jean Chen 1942- *AmMWSc 92*
**Shih,** Kwang Kuo 1932- *AmMWSc 92*
**Shih,** Thomas Y 1939- *AmMWSc 92*
**Shih,** Tsung-Ming Anthony 1944- *AmMWSc 92*
**Shih,** Vivian Ean 1934- *AmMWSc 92*
**Shih,** Wei Jen 1936- *AmMWSc 92*
**Shih Carducci,** Joan Chia-mo 1933- *WhoFI 92*
**Shihab,** Naomi *DrAPF 91*
**Shihabi,** Samir 1925- *IntWW 91*
**Shihata,** Ibrahim F. I. 1937- *IntWW 91*
**Shihata,** Ibrahim Fahmy Ibrahim 1937- *WhoAmL 92*
**Shikanai,** Nobutaka d1990 *IntWW 91N*
**Shikanai,** Nobutaka 1911-1990 *AnObit 1990, FacFETw*
**Shikata,** Masao 1918- *IntMPA 92*
**Shikes,** Ralph Edmund 1912- *WrDr 92*
**Shiki,** Masaoka 1867-1902 *FacFETw*
**Shikin,** Gennadi Serafimovich 1938- *IntWW 91*
**Shikuma,** Eugene Yujin 1948- *WhoWest 92*
**Shilepsky,** Arnold Charles 1944- *AmMWSc 92*
**Shilepsky,** Nancy Sue 1952- *WhoAmL 92*
**Shilffarth,** Richard A. 1931- *WhoFI 92*
**Shilkofski,** Joseph Robert 1951- *WhoFI 92*
**Shillaber,** Benjamin Penhallow 1814-1890 *BenetAL 91*
**Shilladey,** Ann 1933- *WhoMW 92*
**Shillady,** Donald Douglas 1937- *AmMWSc 92*
**Shiller,** Doris Barker 1933- *WhoAmL 92*
**Shiller,** Helen *WhoAmP 91*
**Shillestad,** John G 1934- *WhoIns 92*
**Shillestad,** John Gardner 1934- *WhoFI 92*
**Shilling,** A. Gary 1937- *WhoFI 92*
**Shilling,** Wilbur Leo 1921- *AmMWSc 92*
**Shillingford,** Arden *Who 92*
**Shillingford,** Arden Coleridge 1936- *IntWW 91*
**Shillingford,** John Parsons 1914- *Who 92*
**Shillingford,** Romeo Arden 1936- *Who 92*
**Shillinglaw,** Ann 1959- *WhoMW 92*
**Shillinglaw,** Gordon 1925- *WrDr 92*
**Shillington,** Graham 1911- *Who 92*
**Shillington,** James Keith 1921- *AmMWSc 92*
**Shillito,** Charles Henry 1922- *Who 92*
**Shillito,** Edward Alan d1991 *Who 92N*
**Shillito,** Robert George 1947- *WhoMW 92*
**Shillitoe,** Edward John 1947- *AmMWSc 92*
**Shilman,** Avner 1923- *AmMWSc 92*
**Shiloh,** Ailon 1924- *WrDr 92*
**Shiloh,** Allen 1947- *WhoEnt 92*
**Shilov,** Aleksandr Maksovich 1943- *IntWW 91*
**Shils,** Maurice Edward 1914- *AmMWSc 92*

**Shilstone,** James Maxwell, Jr 1955- *AmMWSc 92*
**Shilstone,** Margaret Cecile 1950- *WhoEnt 92*
**Shilton,** Peter 1949- *IntWW 91*
**Shim,** Andrew Louis 1964- *WhoWest 92*
**Shim,** Benjamin Kin Chong 1929- *AmMWSc 92*
**Shim,** Jung P 1947- *AmMWSc 92*
**Shim,** Mike L. 1956- *WhoWest 92*
**Shim,** Sang Koo 1942- *WhoFI 92, WhoMW 92*
**Shima,** Richard John 1939- *WhoFI 92*
**Shima,** Shigenobu 1907- *IntWW 91*
**Shimabuku,** Norris M. d1991 *NewYTBS 91*
**Shimabukuro,** Elton Ichio 1950- *WhoWest 92*
**Shimabukuro,** Fred Ichiro 1932- *AmMWSc 92*
**Shimabukuro,** Richard Hideo 1933- *AmMWSc 92*
**Shimada,** Katsunori 1922- *AmMWSc 92*
**Shimada,** Masao 1915- *IntWW 91*
**Shimamoto,** Yoshio 1924- *AmMWSc 92*
**Shimamura,** Tetsuo 1934- *AmMWSc 92*
**Shiman,** Ross 1938- *AmMWSc 92*
**Shimanuki,** Hachiro 1934- *AmMWSc 92*
**Shimaoka,** Katsutaro 1931- *AmMWSc 92*
**Shimasaki,** Hitoshi 1923- *IntWW 91*
**Shimazaki Haruki** 1872-1943 *ConAu 134*
**Shimazaki Toson** *ConAu 134*
**Shimazaki Toson** 1872-1943 *FacFETw*
**Shimazu,** Kiyonobu 1946- *WhoFI 92*
**Shimeall,** Warren Glen 1925- *WhoFI 92*
**Shimek,** Dean Troy 1948- *WhoWest 92*
**Shimer,** Daniel Lewis 1944- *WhoFI 92*
**Shimer,** Donald Albert 1929- *WhoWest 92*
**Shimer,** Henry 1828-1895 *BiInAmS*
**Shimizu,** C Susan 1924- *AmMWSc 92*
**Shimizu,** David *WhoAmP 91*
**Shimizu,** Hiroshi 1924- *AmMWSc 92*
**Shimizu,** Keiichi 1936- *WhoFI 92*
**Shimizu,** Nobumichi 1940- *AmMWSc 92*
**Shimizu,** Nobuyoshi 1941- *AmMWSc 92*
**Shimizu,** Norihiko 1940- *WhoFI 92*
**Shimizu,** Taisuke 1936- *WhoFI 92, WhoWest 92*
**Shimizu,** Yuzuru 1935- *AmMWSc 92*
**Shimkin,** Michael Boris 1912- *AmMWSc 92*
**Shimkin,** Philip 1951- *WhoEnt 92*
**Shimm,** Melvin Gerald 1926- *WhoAmL 92*
**Shimm,** Robert A 1926- *AmMWSc 92*
**Shimmin,** C Gary 1945- *WhoIns 92*
**Shimmon,** Joseph Malick 1896- *WhoWest 92*
**Shimoda,** Takeso 1907- *IntWW 91*
**Shimoff,** Ephraim 1913- *WhoRel 92*
**Shimojo,** Shin'ichiro 1920- *IntWW 91*
**Shimonkevitz,** Richard Phillip 1954- *WhoWest 92*
**Shimono,** Sab 1943- *WhoEnt 92*
**Shimony,** Abner 1928- *AmMWSc 92*
**Shimose,** Pedro 1940- *ConSpAP*
**Shimotake,** Hiroshi 1928- *AmMWSc 92*
**Shimotsu,** Gary Rikikazu 1961- *WhoWest 92*
**Shimp,** Neil Frederick 1927- *AmMWSc 92*
**Shimp,** Richard Lee 1942- *WhoFI 92*
**Shimpfky,** Richard L. *WhoWest 92*
**Shimura,** Goro 1930- *AmMWSc 92*
**Shin,** Ernest Eun-Ho 1935- *AmMWSc 92, WhoWest 92*
**Shin,** Hyung Kyu 1933- *AmMWSc 92*
**Shin,** Kilman 1933- *WhoFI 92*
**Shin,** Kju Hi 1929- *AmMWSc 92*
**Shin,** Moon L 1938- *AmMWSc 92*
**Shin,** Myung Soo 1930- *AmMWSc 92*
**Shin,** Seung-il 1938- *AmMWSc 92*
**Shin,** Soo H 1940- *AmMWSc 92*
**Shin,** Suk-han 1930- *AmMWSc 92, WhoWest 92*
**Shin,** Yong Ae Im 1932- *AmMWSc 92*
**Shin,** Yong-Moo 1931- *AmMWSc 92*
**Shinabery,** Max Lawrence 1939- *WhoAmP 91*
**Shinagawa,** Robert Tetsuro 1956- *WhoWest 92*
**Shinagel,** Michael 1934- *IntAu&W 91, WrDr 92*
**Shinbach,** Bruce D. 1939- *IntMPA 92*
**Shinbrot,** Marvin 1928- *AmMWSc 92*
**Shindala,** Adnan 1937- *AmMWSc 92*
**Shinde,** Amrit Rao 1933- *IntWW 91*
**Shinder,** Jason 1955- *ConAu 133*
**Shindler,** Donald Alan 1946- *WhoAmL 92*
**Shindler,** George John 1922- *Who 92*
**Shindler,** Merrill Karsh 1948- *WhoEnt 92*
**Shindler,** Michael Charles 1951- *WhoAmL 92*
**Shindler,** Steven Hunt 1954- *WhoAmL 92*
**Shindo,** Kaneto 1912- *IntDcF 2-2*
**Shine,** Andrew J 1922- *AmMWSc 92*
**Shine,** Annette Dudek 1954- *AmMWSc 92*
**Shine,** Daniel Phillip 1934- *AmMWSc 92*
**Shine,** David Bruce 1938- *WhoAmP 91*
**Shine,** Frances L. 1927- *WrDr 92*
**Shine,** Frances Louise 1927- *IntAu&W 91*
**Shine,** Henry Joseph 1923- *AmMWSc 92*
**Shine,** Hugh Dunham 1952- *WhoAmP 91*
**Shine,** Joel Matthew 1959- *WhoFI 92*
**Shine,** Kenneth I *AmMWSc 92*
**Shine,** M Carl, Jr 1937- *AmMWSc 92*
**Shine,** Robert John 1941- *AmMWSc 92*
**Shine,** Ted 1931- *WhoBlA 92*
**Shine,** Theodis Wesley 1936- *WhoEnt 92*
**Shine,** Timothy D 1939- *AmMWSc 92*
**Shine,** William Morton 1912- *AmMWSc 92*
**Shinefield,** Henry R 1925- *AmMWSc 92*
**Shinefield,** Henry Robert 1925- *IntWW 91*
**Shineman,** Richard Shubert 1924- *AmMWSc 92*
**Shiner,** Edward Arnold 1924- *AmMWSc 92*
**Shiner,** John Edgar 1956- *WhoEnt 92*
**Shiner,** Ralph Biddle, Jr. 1927- *WhoMW 92*
**Shiner,** Vernon Jack, Jr 1925- *AmMWSc 92*
**Shing,** Yuen Wan 1945- *AmMWSc 92*
**Shing,** Yuh-Han 1941- *AmMWSc 92*
**Shingles,** Godfrey Stephen 1939- *Who 92*
**Shingleton,** Hugh Maurice 1931- *AmMWSc 92*
**Shingo,** Shigeo 1900-1990 *FacFETw*
**Shingu,** Yasuo 1926- *IntWW 91*
**Shinkai,** Ichiro 1941- *AmMWSc 92*
**Shinkle,** John Thomas 1946- *WhoAmL 92*
**Shinkle,** Norman Douglas 1950- *WhoAmP 91*
**Shinkman,** Paul G 1936- *AmMWSc 92*
**Shinn,** Arthur Frederick 1945- *WhoMW 92*
**Shinn,** Clinton Wesley 1947- *WhoAmL 92*
**Shinn,** Dennis Burton 1939- *AmMWSc 92*
**Shinn,** Duane K. 1938- *WhoEnt 92, WhoWest 92*
**Shinn,** Everett 1873-1953 *FacFETw*
**Shinn,** Garland Ray 1931- *WhoRel 92*
**Shinn,** Joseph Hancock 1938- *AmMWSc 92*
**Shinn,** Kevin W. 1963- *WhoRel 92*
**Shinn,** Larry Lee 1937- *WhoMW 92*
**Shinn,** Michael Robert 1947- *WhoAmL 92*
**Shinn,** Richard Randolph 1918- *WhoFI 92*
**Shinn,** Robert C, Jr 1937- *WhoAmP 91*
**Shinn,** Roger Lincoln 1917- *WhoRel 92*
**Shinnar,** Reuel 1923- *AmMWSc 92*
**Shinners,** Carl W 1928- *AmMWSc 92*
**Shinners,** Stanley Marvin 1933- *AmMWSc 92*
**Shinnick-Gallagher,** Patricia L 1947- *AmMWSc 92*
**Shinnie,** Peter Lewis 1915- *Who 92*
**Shinoda,** Masahiro 1931- *IntDcF 2-2 [port]*
**Shinohara,** Makoto 1931- *ConCom 92*
**Shinohara,** Makoto 1937- *AmMWSc 92*
**Shinozaki,** Akihiko 1927- *IntWW 91*
**Shinozuka,** Hisashi *AmMWSc 92*
**Shinozuka,** Masanobu 1930- *AmMWSc 92*
**Shinpoch,** A N *WhoAmP 91*
**Shinskey,** Francis Gregway 1931- *AmMWSc 92*
**Shinwell,** Lord 1884-1986 *FacFETw*
**Shiokawa,** Masajuro 1921- *IntWW 91*
**Shiono,** Ryonosuke 1923- *AmMWSc 92*
**Shiota,** Tetsuo 1923- *AmMWSc 92*
**Shioyama,** Tod Kay 1951- *AmMWSc 92*
**Shiozaki,** Jun *IntWW 91*
**Ship,** Irwin I 1932- *AmMWSc 92*
**Shipchandler,** Mohammed Tyebji 1941- *AmMWSc 92*
**Shipe,** Emerson Russell 1947- *AmMWSc 92*
**Shipe,** Jamesetta Denise Holmes 1956- *WhoBlA 92*
**Shipe,** William Franklin 1920- *AmMWSc 92*
**Shipinski,** John 1932- *AmMWSc 92*
**Shipka,** Ronald Bruce 1938- *WhoMW 92*
**Shipko,** Jeffrey Steven 1953- *WhoMW 92*
**Shipkowitz,** Nathan L 1925- *AmMWSc 92*
**Shipler,** David K. 1942- *WrDr 92*
**Shiplett,** June Lund 1930- *ConAu 36NR*
**Shipley,** Andrew Emil 1959- *WhoAmL 92*
**Shipley,** Anthony J. 1939- *WhoBlA 92*
**Shipley,** David Elliott 1950 *WhoAmL 92*
**Shipley,** Edward Nicholas 1934- *AmMWSc 92*
**Shipley,** Eric Pierson 1956- *WhoEnt 92*
**Shipley,** George Graham 1937- *AmMWSc 92*
**Shipley,** Grant Fredrick 1945- *WhoAmL 92*
**Shipley,** Howard Eugene 1944- *WhoRel 92*
**Shipley,** James Parish, Jr 1945- *AmMWSc 92, WhoWest 92*
**Shipley,** L. Parks, Jr. 1931- *WhoFI 92*
**Shipley,** Michael Thomas 1941- *AmMWSc 92*
**Shipley,** Reginald A 1905- *AmMWSc 92*
**Shipley,** Samuel L 1929- *WhoAmP 91*
**Shipley,** Shelia 1952- *WhoEnt 92*
**Shipley,** Thorne 1927- *AmMWSc 92*
**Shipley,** Tony Lee 1946- *WhoMW 92*
**Shipley,** Vivian *DrAPF 91*
**Shipley,** Walter Vincent 1935- *IntWW 91, WhoFI 92*
**Shipman,** C William 1924- *AmMWSc 92*
**Shipman,** Charles, Jr 1934- *AmMWSc 92*
**Shipman,** David 1932- *IntAu&W 91, WrDr 92*
**Shipman,** David Norval 1939- *WhoMW 92*
**Shipman,** Gordon 1901- *WhoAmP 91*
**Shipman,** Harold R 1911- *AmMWSc 92*
**Shipman,** Harry Longfellow 1948- *AmMWSc 92*
**Shipman,** Henry Longfellow 1948- *WrDr 92*
**Shipman,** Jerry 1943- *AmMWSc 92*
**Shipman,** Lester Lynn 1947- *AmMWSc 92*
**Shipman,** Lynn Karen 1950- *WhoAmL 92*
**Shipman,** Nell 1892-1970 *ReelWom*
**Shipman,** Robert Dean 1921- *AmMWSc 92*
**Shipman,** Robert Jack 1933- *WhoIns 92*
**Shipman,** Ross Lovelace 1926- *AmMWSc 92*
**Shipman,** Samuel 1883-1937 *BenetAL 91*
**Shipman,** Warren Ware, III 1930- *WhoAmL 92*
**Shipmon,** Luther June 1932- *WhoBlA 92*
**Shipov,** Dimitri Nikolayevich 1851-1920 *FacFETw*
**Shipp,** Arthur Roscoe 1959- *WhoEnt 92*
**Shipp,** Dan Shackelford 1946- *WhoAmL 92*
**Shipp,** E. R. 1955- *WhoBlA 92*
**Shipp,** George Fitzhugh 1958- *WhoFI 92*
**Shipp,** Glover Harvey 1927- *WhoRel 92*
**Shipp,** Howard J., Jr. 1938- *WhoBlA 92*
**Shipp,** Joseph Calvin 1927- *AmMWSc 92, WhoWest 92*
**Shipp,** Kerry Donald 1963- *WhoRel 92*
**Shipp,** Maurine Sarah 1913- *WhoBlA 92*
**Shipp,** Melvin Douglas 1948- *WhoBlA 92*
**Shipp,** Oliver Elmo 1928- *AmMWSc 92*
**Shipp,** Olivia 1880-1980 *NotBlAW 92*
**Shipp,** Pamela Louise 1947- *WhoBlA 92*
**Shipp,** Raymond Francis 1931- *AmMWSc 92*
**Shipp,** Robert Lewis 1942- *AmMWSc 92*
**Shipp,** William Lee 1938- *WhoRel 92*
**Shipp,** William Stanley 1939- *AmMWSc 92*
**Shippee-Larson,** Barbara Mett 1927- *WhoAmP 91*
**Shipper,** Frank Martin 1945- *WhoWest 92*
**Shipper,** Todd Jeffrey 1946- *WhoWest 92*
**Shippey,** Sandra Lee 1957- *WhoAmL 92, WhoFI 92*
**Shippey,** T. A. 1943- *WrDr 92*
**Shipps,** Jan 1929- *WhoMW 92, WhoRel 92*
**Shippy,** David James 1931- *AmMWSc 92*
**Shippy,** John D. 1944- *WhoBlA 92*
**Shiprack,** Robert R 1950- *WhoAmP 91*
**Shipsey,** Edward Joseph 1938- *AmMWSc 92*
**Shira,** Bruce Douglas 1956- *WhoRel 92*
**Shirai,** Scott 1942- *WhoEnt 92, WhoWest 92*
**Shiraishi,** Takashi 1921- *IntWW 91*
**Shiraishy,** Yuko 1956- *TwCPaSc*
**Shiraki,** Keizo *AmMWSc 92*
**Shiral,** Scott 1942- *WhoWest 92*
**Shirane,** Gen 1924- *AmMWSc 92*
**Shiras,** Wilmar H 1908-1990 *TwCSFW 91*
**Shiratori,** Rei 1937- *ConAu 133*
**Shirayanagi,** Peter Seiichi 1928- *IntWW 91, WhoRel 92*
**Shirazi,** Mostafa Ayat 1932- *AmMWSc 92*
**Shircliff,** James Vanderburgh 1938- *WhoFI 92*
**Shire,** David 1937- *IntMPA 92*
**Shire,** David Lee 1937- *WhoEnt 92*
**Shire,** Donald Thomas 1930- *WhoFI 92*
**Shire,** Harold Raymond 1910- *WhoAmL 92, WhoWest 92*
**Shire,** Talia 1946- *IntMPA 92*
**Shire,** Talia Rose 1946- *WhoEnt 92*
**Shirek,** John Richard 1926- *WhoFI 92*
**Shireman,** Joan Foster 1933- *WhoWest 92*
**Shireman,** Joseph Alan 1961- *WhoAmP 91*
**Shireman,** Rachel Baker 1940- *AmMWSc 92*
**Shiren,** Norman S 1925- *AmMWSc 92*
**Shirendev,** Badzaryn 1912- *IntWW 91*
**Shirer,** Donald Leroy 1931- *AmMWSc 92*
**Shirer,** Hampton Whiting 1924- *AmMWSc 92*
**Shirer,** Martha Quisenberry 1915- *WhoMW 92*
**Shirer,** William 1904- *BenetAL 91*
**Shirer,** William L 1904- *FacFETw, IntAu&W 91, WrDr 92*
**Shirer,** William Lawrence 1904- *IntWW 91, Who 92*
**Shires,** George Thomas 1925- *AmMWSc 92*
**Shires,** Henry M. 1913-1980 *ConAu 134*
**Shires,** Thomas Kay 1935- *AmMWSc 92*
**Shirey,** Mark Steven 1955- *WhoFI 92*
**Shiriaev,** Alexander S. 1951- *WhoFI 92*
**Shiriashi,** Kazuko 1931- *IntWW 91*
**Shirilau,** Jeffery Micheal 1953- *WhoFI 92*
**Shirilau,** Mark Steven 1955- *WhoFI 92*
**Shirinsky,** Sergey Petrovich 1903-1974 *SovUnBD*
**Shirk,** Adam Hull *ScFEYrs*
**Shirk,** Amy Emiko 1946- *AmMWSc 92*
**Shirk,** B Thomas 1941- *AmMWSc 92*
**Shirk,** David W. 1955- *WhoRel 92, WhoWest 92*
**Shirk,** James Siler 1940- *AmMWSc 92*
**Shirk,** John Curtis 1932- *WhoRel 92*
**Shirk,** Paul David 1948- *AmMWSc 92*
**Shirk,** Richard Jay 1930- *AmMWSc 92*
**Shirkey,** Albert P. 1904-1990 *ConAu 133*
**Shirkey,** Harry Cameron 1916- *AmMWSc 92*
**Shirkey,** William Dan 1951- *WhoFI 92*
**Shirkov,** Dmitriy Vasilevich 1928- *IntWW 91*
**Shirley** *Who 92*
**Shirley,** Aaron 1933- *AmMWSc 92*
**Shirley,** Albert *WhoAmP 91*
**Shirley,** Barbara Anne 1936- *AmMWSc 92*
**Shirley,** Calvin Hylton 1921- *WhoBlA 92*
**Shirley,** David A 1942- *WhoAmP 91*
**Shirley,** David Allen 1918- *AmMWSc 92*
**Shirley,** David Andrew 1926- *Who 92*
**Shirley,** David Arthur 1934- *AmMWSc 92, WhoWest 92*
**Shirley,** Edward Lee 1953- *WhoRel 92*
**Shirley,** Edwin Samuel, Jr. 1922- *WhoBlA 92*
**Shirley,** Frances Ann 1931- *WrDr 92*
**Shirley,** Frank Connard 1933- *AmMWSc 92*
**Shirley,** George 1934- *IntWW 91, NewAmDM*
**Shirley,** George Irving 1934- *WhoEnt 92*
**Shirley,** Herschel Vincent, Jr 1923- *AmMWSc 92*
**Shirley,** J. L., Sr. 1878- *WhoBlA 92*
**Shirley,** James 1596?-1666? *RfGEnL 91*
**Shirley,** James R 1951- *WhoAmP 91*
**Shirley,** Jasper Clyde 1913- *WhoAmP 91*
**Shirley,** John 1953- *IntAu&W 91, TwCSFW 91, WrDr 92*
**Shirley,** John Jeffery 1955- *WhoWest 92*
**Shirley,** John William 1931- *WhoAmP 91*
**Shirley,** Judith Ellen 1942- *WhoRel 92*
**Shirley,** Landona Hortense 1928- *WhoAmP 91*
**Shirley,** Michael James 1941- *WhoWest 92*
**Shirley,** Philip Hammond 1912- *Who 92*
**Shirley,** Ray Louis 1912- *AmMWSc 92*
**Shirley,** Robert Bryce 1951- *WhoFI 92, WhoWest 92*
**Shirley,** Robert Louis 1933- *AmMWSc 92*
**Shirley,** Stephanie *Who 92*
**Shirley,** Thomas Clifton 1947- *AmMWSc 92*
**Shirley,** Vera Stephanie 1933- *Who 92*
**Shirley,** Virginia Lee 1936- *WhoFI 92*
**Shirley,** William 1694-1771 *BenetAL 91*
**Shirley-Quirk,** John 1931- *IntWW 91, NewAmDM*
**Shirley-Quirk,** John Stanton 1931- *Who 92*
**Shirn,** George Aaron 1921- *AmMWSc 92*
**Shirotani,** Yu Yuu 1940- *WhoWest 92*
**Shirras,** Edward Scott 1937- *Who 92*
**Shirreffs,** Gordon D 1914- *TwCWW 91*
**Shirreffs,** Gordon Donald 1914- *IntAu&W 91, WrDr 92*
**Shirtcliff,** John Delzell 1948- *WhoWest 92*
**Shirts,** Randall Brent 1950- *AmMWSc 92*
**Shiryaev,** Aleksandr Viktorovich 1867-1941 *SovUnBD*
**Shiryon,** Kinneret Levine 1955- *WhoRel 92*
**Shishido,** Calvin M. 1933- *WhoWest 92*
**Shishido,** Fumitake 1960- *WhoWest 92*
**Shishido,** Miles Motoyuki 1921- *WhoRel 92*
**Shisler,** Alice Hafling 1923- *WhoEnt 92*
**Shitikov,** Aleksey Pavlovich 1912- *IntWW 91*
**Shito,** Mitsuo 1930- *WhoAmP 91*
**Shitov,** Aleksandr Ivanovich 1925- *IntWW 91*
**Shiu,** Robert P C *AmMWSc 92*
**Shiue,** Chyng-Yann 1941- *AmMWSc 92*
**Shiue,** Joseph P. 1942- *WhoWest 92*
**Shivabalayogi Maharaj,** Shri 1935- *RelLAm 91*
**Shivanandan,** Kandiah 1929- *AmMWSc 92*
**Shivas,** Mark *IntMPA 92*
**Shivas,** Mark 1938- *Who 92*
**Shive,** Donald Wayne 1942- *AmMWSc 92*
**Shive,** John Benjamine, Jr 1945- *AmMWSc 92*
**Shive,** Peter Northrop 1941- *AmMWSc 92*
**Shive,** Richard Byron 1933- *WhoFI 92*
**Shive,** Robert Allen, Jr 1942- *AmMWSc 92*
**Shive,** William *AmMWSc 92*
**Shively,** Carl E 1936- *AmMWSc 92*
**Shively,** Charles Dean 1944- *AmMWSc 92*

**Shively**, Daniel Jerome 1924- *WhoMW 92*
**Shively**, Frank Thomas 1934- *AmMWSc 92*
**Shively**, Jack Jay 1932- *WhoMW 92*
**Shively**, James Nelson 1925- *AmMWSc 92*
**Shively**, Jessup MacLean 1935- *AmMWSc 92*
**Shively**, John Adrian 1922- *AmMWSc 92*
**Shively**, John Ernest 1946- *AmMWSc 92*
**Shively**, John Terry 1943- *WhoWest 92*
**Shively**, Ralph Leland 1921- *AmMWSc 92*
**Shively**, William Phillips 1942- *WhoMW 92*
**Shiver**, John W 1957- *AmMWSc 92*
**Shiver**, Jube, Jr. 1953- *WhoBlA 92*
**Shiverdecker**, Franklin James 1932- *WhoMW 92*
**Shiverick**, Kathleen Thomas 1943- *AmMWSc 92*
**Shivers**, Charles Alex 1932- *AmMWSc 92*
**Shivers**, Edward Thomas 1939- *WhoFI 92*
**Shivers**, Gary Melville 1945- *WhoEnt 92, WhoFI 92*
**Shivers**, Jane 1943- *WhoFI 92*
**Shivers**, Jay 1930- *IntAu&W 91*
**Shivers**, Jay Sanford 1930- *WrDr 92*
**Shivers**, John D, Jr 1951- *WhoAmP 91*
**Shivers**, Peter Derrick 1964- *WhoEnt 92*
**Shivers**, Richard Ray 1940- *AmMWSc 92*
**Shivers**, S. Michael 1935- *WhoBlA 92*
**Shives**, Ronald Dean 1934- *WhoFI 92, WhoIns 92*
**Shivokevich**, Heather Renee 1960- *WhoEnt 92*
**Shizgal**, Harry M 1938- *AmMWSc 92*
**Shizuka**, Gozen *EncAmaz 91*
**Shkabardnya**, Mikhail Sergeyevich 1930- *IntWW 91*
**Shkadov**, Ivan Nikolaevich 1913- *IntWW 91*
**Shkapskaya**, Mariya Mikhaylovna 1891-1952 *SovUnBD*
**Shkarofsky**, Issie Peter 1931- *AmMWSc 92*
**Shkiryatov**, Matvey Fedorovich 1883-1954 *SovUnBD*
**Shklar**, Gerald 1924- *AmMWSc 92*
**Shklar**, Michael Charles 1960- *WhoAmL 92*
**Shklov**, Nathan 1918- *AmMWSc 92*
**Shklovsky**, Iosif Samuilovich 1916-1985 *FacFETw*
**Shklovsky**, Viktor Borisovich 1893-1984 *SovUnBD*
**Shkolnikov**, Moisey B *AmMWSc 92*
**Shkurat**, Stepan Iosifovich 1886-1973 *SovUnBD*
**Shkurkin**, Ekaterina Vladimirovna 1955- *WhoWest 92*
**Shkurti**, William John 1946- *WhoMW 92*
**Shlafer**, Marshal *AmMWSc 92*
**Shlanta**, Alexis 1937- *AmMWSc 92*
**Shlaudeman**, Harry Walter 1926- *IntWW 91, WhoAmP 91*
**Shleien**, Bernard 1934- *AmMWSc 92*
**Shlevin**, Harold H 1949- *AmMWSc 92*
**Shlikhter**, Aleksandr Grigorovich 1868-1940 *SovUnBD*
**Shlonsky**, Abraham 1900-1973 *FacFETw*
**Shloss**, Stephen R. 1947- *WhoFI 92*
**Shlyapina**, Galina Arkadyevna 1951- *IntWW 91*
**Shlyapnikov**, Aleksandr Gavrilovich 1884-1943 *SovUnBD*
**Shlyapnikov**, German Evlampevich 1929- *IntWW 91*
**Shmaefsky**, Brian Robert 1956- *AmMWSc 92*
**Shmal'gauzen**, Ivan Ivanovich 1884-1963 *SovUnBD*
**Shmarinov**, Dementiy Alekseevich 1907- *SovUnBD*
**Shmelev**, Nikolai 1936- *IntWW 91*
**Shmelev**, Nikolay Petrovich 1936- *SovUnBD*
**Shmerling**, James Edward 1954- *WhoMW 92*
**Shmidt**, Otto Yul'evich 1891-1956 *SovUnBD*
**Shmoys**, Jerry 1923- *AmMWSc 92*
**Shmukler**, Stanford 1930- *WhoAmL 92*
**Shneidman**, Edwin S. 1918- *ConAu 36NR*
**Shneidman**, J. Lee 1929- *WrDr 92*
**Shneour**, Elie Alexis 1925- *AmMWSc 92, WrDr 92*
**Shnider**, Bruce I 1920- *AmMWSc 92*
**Shnider**, Bruce Jay 1950- *WhoAmL 92*
**Shnider**, Ruth Wolkow 1915- *AmMWSc 92*
**Shnider**, Sol M 1929- *AmMWSc 92*
**Shnitka**, Theodor Khyam 1927- *AmMWSc 92*
**Shoaf**, Charles Jefferson 1930- *AmMWSc 92*
**Shoaf**, John Lester 1950- *WhoAmP 91*
**Shoaf**, Mary La Salle 1932- *AmMWSc 92*
**Shoaff**, Thomas Mitchell 1941- *WhoMW 92*
**Shoafstall**, Earl Fred 1936- *WhoMW 92*
**Shobe**, L Raymon 1913- *AmMWSc 92*
**Shober**, Robert Anthony 1948- *AmMWSc 92*
**Shobert**, Donald Lynn 1952- *WhoRel 92*
**Shobert**, Erle Irwin, II 1913- *AmMWSc 92*
**Shoch**, David Eugene 1918- *AmMWSc 92*
**Shoch**, John F *AmMWSc 92*
**Shochet**, Melvyn Jay 1944- *AmMWSc 92, WhoMW 92*
**Shock**, Clinton C 1944- *AmMWSc 92*
**Shock**, D'Arcy Adriance 1911- *AmMWSc 92*
**Shock**, Frank 1954- *WhoRel 92*
**Shock**, James Eugene 1942- *WhoRel 92*
**Shock**, Julian *ConAu 34NR*
**Shock**, Maurice 1926- *IntWW 91, Who 92*
**Shock**, Nathan Wetherill 1906- *AmMWSc 92*
**Shock**, Robert Charles 1940- *AmMWSc 92*
**Shockey**, Donald Albert 1941- *AmMWSc 92*
**Shockey**, Thomas Edward 1926- *WhoFI 92*
**Shockey**, William Lee 1953- *AmMWSc 92*
**Shockley**, Alice Ann 1910- *WhoAmP 91*
**Shockley**, Alonzo Hilton, Jr. 1920- *WhoBlA 92*
**Shockley**, Ann Allen *DrAPF 91*
**Shockley**, Ann Allen 1927- *WhoBlA 92, WrDr 92*
**Shockley**, Dolores Cooper 1930- *AmMWSc 92*
**Shockley**, Elizabeth Virginia 1947- *WhoWest 92*
**Shockley**, Gilbert R 1919- *AmMWSc 92*
**Shockley**, Grant S. 1919- *WhoBlA 92*
**Shockley**, J B 1929- *WhoAmP 91*
**Shockley**, James Edgar 1931- *AmMWSc 92*
**Shockley**, Myrtle 1926- *WhoAmP 91*
**Shockley**, Thomas D, Jr 1923- *AmMWSc 92*
**Shockley**, Thomas E 1929- *AmMWSc 92*
**Shockley**, Thomas Edward 1929- *WhoBlA 92*
**Shockley**, W G 1914- *AmMWSc 92*
**Shockley**, William 1910- *AmMWSc 92*
**Shockley**, William Bradford 1910-1989 *FacFETw, WhoNob 90*
**Shockman**, Gerald David 1925- *AmMWSc 92*
**Shockman**, Kelly *WhoAmP 91*
**Shockney**, Thomas Dean 1934- *WhoMW 92*
**Shoctor**, Joseph Harvey 1922- *WhoWest 92*
**Shodell**, Michael J 1941- *AmMWSc 92*
**Shoe**, Stephen Charles 1935- *WhoWest 92*
**Shoebotham**, Jonathan Burton 1954- *WhoAmL 92*
**Shoemaker**, Bill *NewYTBS 91 [port]*
**Shoemaker**, Bob C, Jr 1927- *WhoAmP 91*
**Shoemaker**, Cameron David James 1940- *WhoWest 92*
**Shoemaker**, Carlyle Edward 1923- *AmMWSc 92*
**Shoemaker**, Christine Annette 1944- *AmMWSc 92*
**Shoemaker**, Clara Brink 1921- *AmMWSc 92*
**Shoemaker**, Dale *AmMWSc 92*
**Shoemaker**, David Powell 1920- *AmMWSc 92*
**Shoemaker**, Dean Alan 1966- *WhoMW 92*
**Shoemaker**, Edward Milton 1929- *AmMWSc 92*
**Shoemaker**, Eleanor Boggs 1935- *WhoEnt 92, WhoFI 92*
**Shoemaker**, Eugene Merle 1928- *AmMWSc 92, IntWW 91*
**Shoemaker**, Faith Elaine 1952- *WhoAmL 92*
**Shoemaker**, Frank Crawford 1922- *AmMWSc 92*
**Shoemaker**, Gradus Lawrence 1921- *AmMWSc 92*
**Shoemaker**, Hal Alan 1950- *WhoFI 92*
**Shoemaker**, Harold Lloyd 1923- *WhoWest 92*
**Shoemaker**, Jeff 1955- *WhoAmP 91*
**Shoemaker**, Joanie 1950- *WhoEnt 92, WhoWest 92*
**Shoemaker**, John Daniel, Jr 1939- *AmMWSc 92*
**Shoemaker**, Lloyd R. 1921- *ConAu 133*
**Shoemaker**, Lynn *DrAPF 91*
**Shoemaker**, Melvin Hugh 1940- *WhoRel 92*
**Shoemaker**, Michael C 1945- *WhoAmP 91*
**Shoemaker**, Patricia Nuss 1960- *WhoRel 92*
**Shoemaker**, Paul Beck 1941- *AmMWSc 92*
**Shoemaker**, Paul Frederick 1957- *WhoMW 92*
**Shoemaker**, Peter 1920- *WhoWest 92*
**Shoemaker**, Richard A 1951- *WhoAmP 91*
**Shoemaker**, Richard Lee 1944- *AmMWSc 92*
**Shoemaker**, Richard Leonard 1931- *AmMWSc 92*
**Shoemaker**, Richard Nelson 1921- *AmMWSc 92*
**Shoemaker**, Richard W 1918- *AmMWSc 92*
**Shoemaker**, Robert Alan 1928- *AmMWSc 92*
**Shoemaker**, Robert Comly, Jr. 1932- *WhoWest 92*
**Shoemaker**, Robert Harold 1921- *AmMWSc 92*
**Shoemaker**, Robert Shern 1953- *WhoMW 92*
**Shoemaker**, Roy H 1923- *AmMWSc 92*
**Shoemaker**, Roy Thomas 1923- *WhoFI 92*
**Shoemaker**, Samuel Moor, Jr. 1893-1963 *RelLAm 91*
**Shoemaker**, Scott David 1958- *WhoWest 92*
**Shoemaker**, Selma Sealey 1923- *WhoAmP 91*
**Shoemaker**, Vaughan Hurst 1938- *AmMWSc 92*
**Shoemaker**, Vaughn d1991 *NewYTBS 91*
**Shoemaker**, Veronica Sapp 1929- *WhoBlA 92*
**Shoemaker**, William C 1923- *AmMWSc 92*
**Shoemaker**, William Edward 1945- *WhoFI 92*
**Shoemaker**, Willie 1931- *FacFETw, IntWW 91*
**Shoeman**, Don Walter 1941- *AmMWSc 92*
**Shoemate**, C. Richard 1939- *IntWW 91*
**Shoemate**, Charles Richard 1939- *WhoFI 92*
**Shoen**, Edward Joseph *WhoWest 92*
**Shoenberg**, David 1911- *IntWW 91, Who 92*
**Shoenberger**, Allen Edward 1944- *WhoAmL 92*
**Shoener**, Arthur Lee 1946- *WhoFI 92*
**Shoenfelt**, Catherine Ruth 1954- *WhoFI 92*
**Shoenfelt**, Oscar Leroy, III 1954- *WhoAmL 92*
**Shoenfield**, Joseph Robert 1927- *AmMWSc 92*
**Shoesmith**, Kathleen A 1938- *IntAu&W 91, WrDr 92*
**Shoesmith**, Thomas P 1922- *WhoAmP 91*
**Shoffner**, Clarence L. 1921- *WhoBlA 92*
**Shoffner**, James Priest 1928- *AmMWSc 92, WhoBlA 92*
**Shoffner**, Robert Nurman 1916- *AmMWSc 92*
**Shofner**, Jim 1935- *WhoMW 92*
**Shoger**, Ross L 1930- *AmMWSc 92*
**Shoghi Effendi Rabboni** 1897-1957 *RelLAm 91*
**Shogo**, Watanabe 1915- *IntWW 91*
**Shogren**, Merle Dennis 1926- *AmMWSc 92*
**Shoham**, Menachem 1944- *WhoMW 92*
**Shohet**, Albert Jacob 1938- *WhoFI 92*
**Shohet**, Juda Leon 1937- *AmMWSc 92*
**Shokeir**, Mohamed Hassan Kamel 1938- *AmMWSc 92, WhoWest 92*
**Sholander**, Marlow 1915- *AmMWSc 92*
**Sholander**, Marlow Canon 1915- *WhoMW 92*
**Sholdt**, Lester Lance 1938- *AmMWSc 92*
**Sholes**, David 1943- *WhoAmP 91*
**Sholes**, Ronald W 1939- *WhoIns 92*
**Sholes**, Ronald William 1939- *WhoFI 92, WhoMW 92*
**Sholevar**, Bahman *DrAPF 91*
**Sholl**, Anna McClure *ScFEYrs*
**Sholl**, Betsy *DrAPF 91*
**Sholl**, Howard Alfred 1938- *AmMWSc 92*
**Sholl**, Reginald 1902- *Who 92*
**Sholl**, Robert Knowlton 1954- *WhoAmL 92*
**Shollenberger**, Franklin Leroy 1925- *WhoAmP 91*
**Sholokhov**, Mikhail Aleksandrovich 1905-1984 *SovUnBD*
**Sholokhov**, Mikhail Alexandrovich 1905-1984 *FacFETw*
**Sholokov**, Mikhail Aleksandrovich 1905-1984 *WhoNob 90*
**Sholtis**, Joseph Arnold, Jr. 1948- *WhoWest 92*
**Sholts**, Thomas Earl 1932- *WhoAmL 92*
**Sholty**, David Martin 1959- *WhoEnt 92*
**Sholtz**, Jerrold 1943- *WhoFI 92*
**Shomaker**, John Wayne 1942- *AmMWSc 92*
**Shomay**, David 1924- *AmMWSc 92*
**Shombert**, Donald James 1928- *AmMWSc 92*
**Shome**, Pradipta Lal 1945- *WhoWest 92*
**Shomer**, Enid *DrAPF 91*
**Shomer**, Robert Baker 1943- *WhoWest 92*
**Shon**, Frederick John 1926- *AmMWSc 92*
**Shon**, James T 1947- *WhoAmP 91*
**Shone**, John Terence 1935- *Who 92*
**Shone**, Patric *ConAu 36NR*
**Shone**, Robert L 1937- *AmMWSc 92*
**Shone**, Robert Minshull 1906- *IntWW 91, Who 92*
**Shone**, Robert Tilden 1928- *AmMWSc 92*
**Shone**, Ronald 1946- *WrDr 92*
**Shonebarger**, F J 1924- *AmMWSc 92*
**Shoner**, Patricia Ann 1946- *WhoRel 92*
**Shonfeld**, Edwin Marshall 1936- *WhoWest 92*
**Shonick**, William 1919- *AmMWSc 92*
**Shoning**, Don 1915- *WhoAmP 91*
**Shonk**, Albert Davenport, Jr. 1932- *WhoFI 92, WhoWest 92*
**Shonk**, Carl Ellsworth 1922- *AmMWSc 92*
**Shonkwiler**, Richard Wayne, II 1953- *WhoRel 92*
**Shonkwiler**, Ronald Wesley 1942- *AmMWSc 92*
**Shonle**, John Irwin 1933- *AmMWSc 92*
**Shono**, Senkichi 1913- *IntWW 91*
**Shons**, Alan R *AmMWSc 92*
**Shontz**, Charles Jack 1926- *AmMWSc 92*
**Shontz**, Franklin C. 1926- *WrDr 92*
**Shontz**, John Paul 1940- *AmMWSc 92*
**Shontz**, Nancy Nickerson 1942- *AmMWSc 92*
**Shoob**, Marvin H. 1923- *WhoAmL 92*
**Shook**, Ann Jones 1925- *WhoAmL 92*
**Shook**, Brenda Lee 1952- *AmMWSc 92*
**Shook**, Clifton Arnold 1934- *AmMWSc 92*
**Shook**, Dale Alford, Jr. 1945- *WhoRel 92*
**Shook**, George Brezger 1945- *WhoMW 92*
**Shook**, James Creighton 1931- *WhoMW 92*
**Shook**, Leslie *WhoEnt 92*
**Shook**, Mark Roger 1954- *WhoWest 92*
**Shook**, Patricia Louise 1919- *WhoBlA 92*
**Shook**, Thomas Eugene 1928- *AmMWSc 92*
**Shook**, William Beattie 1928- *AmMWSc 92*
**Shook**, Winthrop Curtis 1926- *WhoAmP 91*
**Shoolery**, James Nelson 1925- *AmMWSc 92*
**Shoolman**, Henry Morton 1941- *WhoFI 92*
**Shooman**, Martin L 1934- *AmMWSc 92*
**Shoop**, C Robert 1935- *AmMWSc 92*
**Shoop**, David Miller 1946- *WhoEnt 92*
**Shoop**, Glenn Powell 1920- *WhoFI 92*
**Shoop**, Robert Hale, Jr. 1938- *WhoAmL 92*
**Shoop**, Robert Leigh 1954- *WhoAmL 92*
**Shoosmith**, John Norman 1934- *AmMWSc 92*
**Shooster**, Frank Mallory 1954- *WhoAmL 92*
**Shoot**, Kent Douglas 1960- *WhoFI 92*
**Shoot**, Vladislav 1941- *ConCom 92*
**Shooter**, Christine Gay 1964- *WhoMW 92*
**Shooter**, Eric Manvers 1924- *AmMWSc 92, Who 92*
**Shooter**, Jack Allen 1940- *AmMWSc 92*
**Shooter**, Reginald Arthur 1916- *Who 92*
**Shope**, John Francis 1959- *WhoFI 92*
**Shope**, Richard Edwin, Jr 1926- *AmMWSc 92*
**Shope**, Robert Ellis 1929- *AmMWSc 92*
**Shopnick**, Rinah Ilene 1960- *WhoMW 92*
**Shopp**, George Milton, Jr 1955- *AmMWSc 92, WhoWest 92*
**Shoppee**, Charles William 1904- *IntWW 91, Who 92*
**Shopshire**, James Maynard 1942- *WhoBlA 92*
**Shopsis**, Charles S *AmMWSc 92*
**Shoquist**, Mary Lucille 1932- *WhoAmP 91*
**Shor**, Aaron Louis 1924- *AmMWSc 92*
**Shor**, Arthur Joseph 1923- *AmMWSc 92*
**Shor**, George G, Jr 1923- *AmMWSc 92*
**Shor**, Steven Michael 1944- *AmMWSc 92*
**Shorb**, Alan McKean 1938- *AmMWSc 92*
**Shore**, Bruce Walter 1935- *AmMWSc 92*
**Shore**, Caron Dean 1949- *WhoMW 92*
**Shore**, Clare 1954- *WhoEnt 92*
**Shore**, David Teignmouth 1928- *Who 92*
**Shore**, Dinah *LesBEnT 92*
**Shore**, Dinah 1917- *IntMPA 92, NewAmDM*
**Shore**, Dinah 1921- *WhoEnt 92*
**Shore**, Elizabeth Catherine 1927- *Who 92*
**Shore**, Eugene L 1936- *WhoAmP 91*
**Shore**, Ferdinand John 1919- *AmMWSc 92*
**Shore**, Fred L 1942- *AmMWSc 92*
**Shore**, Gordon Charles *AmMWSc 92*
**Shore**, Harvey Harris 1940- *WhoFI 92*
**Shore**, Herbert 1924- *WhoEnt 92*
**Shore**, Herbert Barry 1939- *AmMWSc 92*
**Shore**, Howard *IntMPA 92*
**Shore**, Howard Leslie 1946- *WhoEnt 92*
**Shore**, Jack 1922- *Who 92*
**Shore**, James H 1940- *AmMWSc 92*
**Shore**, Jane *DrAPF 91*
**Shore**, John Edward 1946- *AmMWSc 92*
**Shore**, Joseph D 1934- *AmMWSc 92*
**Shore**, Laura Jan *DrAPF 91*
**Shore**, Laurence Stuart 1944- *AmMWSc 92*

**Shore**, Lawrence Arthur 1928- WhoFI 92, WhoIns 92
**Shore**, Miles Frederick 1929- AmMWSc 92
**Shore**, Moris Lawrence 1927- AmMWSc 92
**Shore**, Nomie Abraham 1923- AmMWSc 92
**Shore**, Norman WrDr 92
**Shore**, Peter 1924- IntWW 91, Who 92
**Shore**, Richard 1932- WhoEnt 92
**Shore**, Richard A 1946- AmMWSc 92
**Shore**, Richard Allan 1956- WhoAmL 92
**Shore**, Roy E 1940- AmMWSc 92
**Shore**, Samuel 1924- WhoAmL 92
**Shore**, Samuel David 1937- AmMWSc 92
**Shore**, Samuel Franklin 1935- WhoAmP 91
**Shore**, Sheldon Gerald 1930- AmMWSc 92
**Shore**, Steven Neil 1953- AmMWSc 92
**Shore**, Virgie Guinn 1928- AmMWSc 92
**Shorer**, Philip 1951- AmMWSc 92
**Shores**, Allen Gray 1943- WhoAmP 91
**Shores**, David Arthur 1941- AmMWSc 92
**Shores**, David Lewis 1945- WhoFI 92
**Shores**, Henry Clay 1930- WhoAmP 91
**Shores**, Janie Ledlow 1932- WhoAmL 92, WhoAmP 91
**Shores**, Robert Scott 1959- WhoFI 92
**Shores**, Stephen Dale 1954- WhoRel 92
**Shores**, Thomas Stephen 1942- AmMWSc 92
**Shorett**, Alice Judy 1944- WhoWest 92
**Shorey**, Gregory Day, Jr 1924- WhoAmP 91
**Shorey-Kutschke**, Rose-Ann AmMWSc 92
**Shorin**, Aleksandr Fedorovich 1890-1941 SovUnBD
**Shorney**, George Herbert 1931- WhoEnt 92, WhoFI 92, WhoRel 92
**Shorney**, John Leith 1961- WhoEnt 92
**Shorr**, Alan Lee 1953- WhoFI 92
**Shorr**, Bernard 1928- AmMWSc 92
**Shorris**, Earl 1936- ConAu 34NR
**Shorrock**, John Michael 1943- Who 92
**Short** Who 92
**Short**, Barbara Ann 1940- WhoRel 92
**Short**, Bernard David 1935- Who 92
**Short**, Bobby 1924- WhoBlA 92
**Short**, Brian Patrick 1950- WhoAmL 92, WhoFI 92
**Short**, Byron Elliott 1901- AmMWSc 92
**Short**, C. Brant 1955- WhoWest 92
**Short**, Carroll Dale DrAPF 91
**Short**, Charles Robert 1938- AmMWSc 92
**Short**, Charles Wilkins 1794-1863 BiInAmS
**Short**, Clare 1946- Who 92
**Short**, David Bruce 1953- WhoWest 92
**Short**, David LeRoy 1955- WhoRel 92
**Short**, David Somerset 1918- Who 92
**Short**, De Ronda Miniard 1943- WhoAmP 91
**Short**, Dean Chilton, II 1948- WhoAmL 92
**Short**, Donald James 1942- WhoFI 92
**Short**, Donald Ray, Jr 1944- AmMWSc 92
**Short**, Edward Watson IntWW 91
**Short**, Everett C, Jr 1931- AmMWSc 92
**Short**, Frank DrAPF 91
**Short**, Frank 1857-1945 TwCPaSc
**Short**, Franklin Willard 1928- AmMWSc 92
**Short**, Hedley Vicars Roycraft 1914- Who 92, WhoRel 92
**Short**, Henry Laughton 1934- AmMWSc 92
**Short**, James Edward 1914- WhoBlA 92
**Short**, James Harold 1928- AmMWSc 92
**Short**, James N 1922- AmMWSc 92
**Short**, John 1896- Who 92
**Short**, John Albert 1936- AmMWSc 92
**Short**, John Lawson 1946- AmMWSc 92
**Short**, John Richard 1944- WhoRel 92
**Short**, Kenneth Herbert 1927- Who 92
**Short**, Kenneth L. 1943- WhoBlA 92
**Short**, Kenneth Lowell, Jr. 1956- WhoFI 92
**Short**, Lester Le Roy 1933- AmMWSc 92
**Short**, Luke 1908-1975 BenetAL 91, TwCWW 91
**Short**, Mark, Jr. 1929- WhoRel 92
**Short**, Martin 1950- IntMPA 92
**Short**, Martin 1951- WhoEnt 92
**Short**, Mary Christine 1947- WhoWest 92
**Short**, Mary Elizabeth Haile 1938- WhoAmP 91
**Short**, Michael 1937- SmATA 65
**Short**, Michael Arthur 1930- AmMWSc 92
**Short**, Nicholas Martin 1927- AmMWSc 92
**Short**, Noel 1916- Who 92
**Short**, Paul Edgar, Jr 1947- WhoAmP 91
**Short**, Peter 1945- Who 92
**Short**, Philip 1945- IntAu&W 91, WrDr 92
**Short**, Phillip Dean 1945- WhoFI 92
**Short**, Ray Everett 1919- WhoRel 92
**Short**, Raymond W 1934- WhoAmP 91
**Short**, Renee Who 92
**Short**, Richard James 1931- WhoAmP 91
**Short**, Robert Allen 1927- AmMWSc 92
**Short**, Robert Brown 1920- AmMWSc 92
**Short**, Robert Cecil 1946- WhoAmP 91
**Short**, Robert Henry 1924- WhoFI 92
**Short**, Robert Stuart 1938- WrDr 92
**Short**, Robert Waltrip 1924- WhoEnt 92
**Short**, Robert Yates 1950- WhoEnt 92
**Short**, Roger, Jr. ConAu 134
**Short**, Roger Valentine 1930- IntWW 91, Who 92
**Short**, Rolland William Phillip 1922- AmMWSc 92
**Short**, Ruth Elizabeth 1908- WhoAmP 91
**Short**, Sarah Harvey 1924- AmMWSc 92
**Short**, Seldon 1933- WhoEnt 92
**Short**, Sidney Howe 1858-1902 BiInAmS
**Short**, Skip 1951- WhoAmL 92
**Short**, Ted WhoBlA 92
**Short**, Ted H 1942- AmMWSc 92
**Short**, Vicky Salena 1952- WhoEnt 92
**Short**, W Leigh 1935- AmMWSc 92
**Short**, W Marcus 1930- WhoAmP 91
**Short**, Wallace W 1930- AmMWSc 92
**Short**, Wallace Walter 1930- WhoWest 92
**Short**, William Arthur 1925- AmMWSc 92
**Short**, William Harrison 1868-1935 AmPeW
**Short**, William J. WhoRel 92
**Short**, William Richard 1952- WhoFI 92
**Shortal**, Helen Mary 1961- WhoEnt 92
**Shortbull**, Thomas H 1946- WhoAmP 91
**Shortell**, Stephen M 1944- AmMWSc 92
**Shorten**, Harry d1991 NewYTBS 91
**Shorten**, Martyn Robert 1955- WhoWest 92
**Shorter**, Daniel Albert 1927- AmMWSc 92
**Shorter**, Edward 1941- WrDr 92
**Shorter**, Kenneth Livingston 1915- WhoBlA 92
**Shorter**, Roy Gerrard 1925- AmMWSc 92, WhoMW 92
**Shorter**, Wayne 1933- IntWW 91, NewAmDM, WhoEnt 92
**Shorter**, William Howard, Jr. 1959- WhoFI 92
**Shortes**, Melvin A WhoAmP 91
**Shortess**, David Keen 1930- AmMWSc 92
**Shorthouse**, Joseph Henry 1834-1903 RfGEnL 91
**Shortis**, Colin Terry 1934- Who 92
**Shortle**, Walter Charles 1945- AmMWSc 92
**Shortliffe**, Edward Hance 1947- AmMWSc 92, WhoWest 92
**Shortridge**, James Robert 1944- WhoMW 92
**Shortridge**, Robert Glenn, Jr 1945- AmMWSc 92
**Shortridge**, Robert William 1918- AmMWSc 92
**Shortridge**, Sherie Suzanne Bell 1956- WhoAmL 92
**Shortt**, James Chadwick, Jr. 1938- WhoMW 92
**Shorty**, Vernon James 1943- WhoBlA 92
**Shortz**, Richard Alan 1945- WhoAmL 92, WhoFI 92
**Shoshani**, Jeheskel Hezy 1943- WhoMW 92
**Shoss**, Cynthia Renee 1950- WhoAmL 92, WhoFI 92
**Shostak**, Stanley 1938- AmMWSc 92
**Shostakovich**, Dmitri 1906-1975 NewAmDM
**Shostakovich**, Dmitri Dmitrievich 1906-1975 FacFETw [port]
**Shostakovich**, Dmitriy Dmitrievich 1906-1975 SovUnBD
**Shostakovich**, Maksim Dmitrievich 1938- SovUnBD
**Shostakovich**, Maksim Dmitriyevich 1938- IntWW 91
**Shostakovich**, Maxim 1938- NewAmDM
**Shotland**, Edwin 1908- AmMWSc 92
**Shotland**, Lawrence Martin 1947- WhoFI 92
**Shott**, Gerald Lee 1934- WhoFI 92
**Shott**, John Cary 1924- WhoAmP 91
**Shott**, Leonard D 1934- AmMWSc 92
**Shottafer**, James Edward 1930- AmMWSc 92
**Shotter**, Edward Frank 1933- Who 92
**Shotton**, Edward 1910- Who 92
**Shotton**, Frederick William d1990 IntWW 91N
**Shotton**, Keith Crawford 1943- Who 92
**Shotts**, Adolph Calveran 1925- AmMWSc 92
**Shotts**, Emmett Booker, Jr 1931- AmMWSc 92
**Shotwell**, Ada Christena 1940- WhoBlA 92
**Shotwell**, Bob Edd 1932- WhoRel 92
**Shotwell**, Charles Bland 1955- WhoAmL 92
**Shotwell**, James Thomson 1874-1965 AmPeW
**Shotwell**, John Ralph 1926- WhoMW 92, WhoRel 92
**Shotwell**, Odette Louise 1922- AmMWSc 92
**Shotwell**, Thomas Knight 1934- AmMWSc 92
**Shotwell**, Willis Allen 1920- WhoRel 92
**Shotzberger**, Gregory Steven 1948- AmMWSc 92
**Shoub**, Earle Phelps 1915- AmMWSc 92, WhoFI 92
**Shoubridge**, Eric Alan 1951- AmMWSc 92
**Shough**, Herbert Richard 1942- AmMWSc 92
**Shoukas**, Artin Andrew AmMWSc 92
**Shoukry**, Mohammed Anwar 1905- IntWW 91
**Shoulders**, Ramon Henkiz 1924- WhoBlA 92
**Shoulders**, Raymond H. 1924- WhoMW 92
**Shoulson**, Bruce Dove 1940- WhoAmL 92
**Shoulta**, William Edward 1953- WhoRel 92
**Shoults**, Harold WhoMW 92
**Shoultz**, Donald L 1936- WhoAmP 91
**Shoultz**, Rudolph Samuel 1918- WhoBlA 92
**Shouman**, A R 1929- AmMWSc 92
**Shoup**, Alona Jean 1963- WhoMW 92
**Shoup**, Carl Sumner 1902- WhoFI 92
**Shoup**, Charles Samuel, Jr 1935- AmMWSc 92, WhoMW 92
**Shoup**, James Raymond 1932- WhoFI 92
**Shoup**, Jane Rearick 1941- AmMWSc 92
**Shoup**, Paul Connelly 1938- WhoFI 92
**Shoup**, Robert D 1933- AmMWSc 92
**Shoup**, Terry Emerson 1944- AmMWSc 92, WhoWest 92
**Shouse**, Allen Lee 1947- WhoRel 92
**Shouse**, Kenneth L. 1934- WhoRel 92
**Shoval**, Zalman 1930- NewYTBS 91 [port]
**Shove**, Gene C 1927- AmMWSc 92
**Shovelton**, David Scott 1925- Who 92
**Shovelton**, Patrick 1919- Who 92
**Shover**, Michael Phillip 1957- WhoMW 92
**Shovlin**, Francis Edward 1929- AmMWSc 92
**Show**, Ivan Tristan 1943- AmMWSc 92
**Show**, Mark Alan 1967- WhoEnt 92
**Showalter**, Dennis Edwin 1942- WhoWest 92
**Showalter**, Donald Lee 1943- AmMWSc 92
**Showalter**, Douglas Keith 1948- WhoRel 92
**Showalter**, Elaine 1941- WrDr 92
**Showalter**, Howard Daniel Hollis 1948- AmMWSc 92
**Showalter**, Joanne Marie 1935- WhoAmP 91
**Showalter**, Judy Marie 1944- WhoRel 92
**Showalter**, Kenneth 1949- AmMWSc 92
**Showalter**, Max 1917- IntMPA 92
**Showalter**, Robert Kenneth 1916- AmMWSc 92
**Showell**, Hazel Jarmon 1945- WhoBlA 92
**Showell**, John Sheldon 1925- AmMWSc 92
**Showell**, Milton W. 1936- WhoBlA 92
**Shower**, Robert Wesley 1937- WhoFI 92
**Showers**, Harold Robert, Jr. 1955- WhoRel 92
**Showers**, John R 1952- WhoAmP 91
**Showers**, Mary Jane C 1920- AmMWSc 92
**Showers**, Ralph M 1918- AmMWSc 92
**Showers**, William Broze, Jr 1931- AmMWSc 92
**Showkeir**, James David 1952- WhoMW 92
**Shown**, Suzan DrAPF 91
**Shows**, Thomas Byron 1938- AmMWSc 92
**Shozda**, Raymond John 1931- AmMWSc 92
**Shpeen**, Scott Louis 1957- WhoRel 92
**Shpet**, Gustav Gustavovich 1879-1937 SovUnBD
**Shpinel'**, Iosif Aronovich 1892-1980 SovUnBD
**Shrader**, Carl Michael 1928- WhoFI 92
**Shrader**, John Stanley 1922- AmMWSc 92
**Shrader**, Kenneth Ray 1920- AmMWSc 92
**Shrader**, Marianne Louise 1944- WhoMW 92
**Shrader**, Stephen DrAPF 91
**Shrader**, William D 1912- AmMWSc 92
**Shrader**, William Whitney 1930- AmMWSc 92
**Shrady**, George Frederick 1837-1907 BiInAmS
**Shrager**, Peter George 1941- AmMWSc 92
**Shrago**, Earl 1928- AmMWSc 92
**Shrake**, Andrew 1941- AmMWSc 92
**Shrake**, Edwin 1931- TwCWW 91, WrDr 92
**Shramek**, Dennis DrAPF 91
**Shrand**, David 1913- WrDr 92
**Shrapnel**, Norman 1912- IntAu&W 91, Who 92, WrDr 92
**Shrauner**, Barbara Abraham 1934- AmMWSc 92
**Shrauner**, James Ely 1933- AmMWSc 92
**Shrawder**, Elsie June 1938- AmMWSc 92
**Shrayer-Petrov**, David 1936- WhoEnt 92
**Shreeve**, David Herbert 1934- Who 92
**Shreeve**, Jean'ne Marie 1933- AmMWSc 92
**Shreeve**, Walton Wallace 1921- AmMWSc 92
**Shreffler**, Donald Cecil 1933- AmMWSc 92
**Shreffler**, Jack Henry 1944- AmMWSc 92
**Shreibman**, Henry M. 1952- WhoRel 92
**Shrem**, Charles Joseph 1930- WhoFI 92
**Shremshock**, Gerald Stephen 1944- WhoMW 92
**Shrensel**, J 1922- AmMWSc 92
**Shrestha**, Marich Man Singh 1942- IntWW 91
**Shreve**, David Carr 1942- AmMWSc 92
**Shreve**, Gene Russell 1943- WhoAmL 92, WhoMW 92
**Shreve**, George Wilcox 1913- AmMWSc 92
**Shreve**, Judith Hull 1930- WhoAmP 91
**Shreve**, Leslie Carolyn 1945- WhoEnt 92
**Shreve**, Loy William 1926- AmMWSc 92
**Shreve**, Peg 1927- WhoAmP 91
**Shreve**, Ronald Lee 1930- AmMWSc 92
**Shreve**, Susan R. 1939- WrDr 92
**Shreve**, Susan Richards DrAPF 91
**Shreve**, Susan Richards 1939- IntWW 91
**Shreve**, Theodore Norris 1919- WhoFI 92, WhoWest 92
**Shrewsbury**, Bishop of 1919- Who 92
**Shrewsbury**, Bishop Suffragan of 1927- Who 92
**Shrewsbury**, James Francis 1955- WhoAmP 91
**Shrewsbury**, Lisa Gail 1959- WhoAmL 92
**Shrewsbury And Waterford**, Earl of 1952- Who 92
**Shrider**, Ed 1952- WhoEnt 92
**Shrier**, Adam Louis 1938- AmMWSc 92, WhoFI 92
**Shrier**, Stefan 1942- AmMWSc 92
**Shrieves**, George Matthews 1935- WhoFI 92
**Shrift**, Alex 1923- AmMWSc 92
**Shrigley**, Robert Leroy 1929- AmMWSc 92
**Shrimali**, Kalu Lal 1909- IntWW 91
**Shrime**, George P 1940- AmMWSc 92
**Shrimplin**, John Steven 1934- Who 92
**Shrimpton**, Douglas Malcolm 1935- AmMWSc 92
**Shrimsley**, Bernard 1931- IntAu&W 91, Who 92, WrDr 92
**Shriner**, David Sylva 1945- AmMWSc 92
**Shriner**, Herb d1970 LesBEnT 92
**Shriner**, John Franklin, Jr 1957- AmMWSc 92
**Shriner**, Ralph Lloyd 1899- AmMWSc 92
**Shriner**, Thomas L., Jr. 1947- WhoAmL 92
**Shrinsky**, Jason Lee 1937- WhoAmL 92, WhoEnt 92
**Shrivastava**, Chinmaya Anand 1951- WhoWest 92
**Shrivastava**, Paul 1951- ConAu 133
**Shrivastava**, Prakash Narayan 1940- AmMWSc 92
**Shriver**, Bruce Douglas 1940- AmMWSc 92
**Shriver**, David A 1942- AmMWSc 92
**Shriver**, Donald Woods, Jr. 1927- WhoRel 92
**Shriver**, Duward F 1934- AmMWSc 92
**Shriver**, Harry Roland 1932- WhoEnt 92
**Shriver**, Jack WhoAmP 91
**Shriver**, John William 1949- AmMWSc 92
**Shriver**, Joyce Elizabeth 1937- AmMWSc 92
**Shriver**, Lionel 1957- ConAu 134
**Shriver**, M Kathleen AmMWSc 92
**Shriver**, Maria LesBEnT 92 [port]
**Shriver**, Maria 1955- CurBio 91 [port]
**Shriver**, Maria Owings 1955- WhoEnt 92
**Shriver**, Mary J WhoAmP 91
**Shriver**, Peggy Ann Leu 1931- WhoRel 92
**Shriver**, Phillip Raymond 1922 WhoMW 92
**Shriver**, Rick Craig 1954- WhoEnt 92
**Shriver**, Robert Sargent, Jr 1915- WhoAmP 91
**Shriver**, Rosalia 1927-1987 ConAu 135
**Shriver**, Sargent 1915- FacFETw, Who 92
**Shriver**, Sargent, Jr. 1915- IntWW 91
**Shroat**, Jerry T 1941- WhoIns 92
**Shrock**, Alice Almond 1946- WhoMW 92
**Shrock**, Michael E. 1956- WhoRel 92
**Shrock**, Robert Rakes 1904- AmMWSc 92
**Shrode**, Robert Ray 1919- AmMWSc 92
**Shroder**, John Ford, Jr 1939- AmMWSc 92, WhoMW 92
**Shroff**, Arvin Pranlal 1933- AmMWSc 92
**Shroff**, Firoz Sardar 1950- WhoFI 92
**Shroff**, Ramesh N 1937- AmMWSc 92
**Shrontz**, Frank Anderson 1931- IntWW 91, WhoFI 92, WhoWest 92
**Shrontz**, John William 1916- AmMWSc 92

**Shropshire,** Anne 1954- *WhoFI 92*
**Shropshire,** Arthur C. 1909- *WhoBlA 92*
**Shropshire,** Claudius Napoleon, Jr. 1925-1990 *WhoBlA 92N*
**Shropshire,** Donald Gray 1927- *WhoFI 92, WhoWest 92*
**Shropshire,** Harry W. 1934- *WhoBlA 92*
**Shropshire,** Helen Mae 1909- *WhoWest 92*
**Shropshire,** John Sherwin 1938- *WhoBlA 92*
**Shropshire,** Thomas B. 1925- *WhoBlA 92*
**Shropshire,** Walter, Jr 1932- *AmMWSc 92*
**Shrout,** David Irvin 1952- *WhoRel 92*
**Shrout,** Larry Wayne 1953- *WhoRel 92*
**Shroyer,** Thomas Jerome 1952- *WhoAmL 92*
**Shrubsole,** Alison Cheveley 1925- *Who 92*
**Shrum,** Christine Ruth King 1949- *IntAu&W 91*
**Shrum,** David Leon 1952- *WhoMW 92*
**Shrum,** James David 1956- *WhoAmP 91*
**Shrum,** John W 1925- *AmMWSc 92*
**Shrumm,** Donald Arthur 1959- *WhoRel 92*
**Shryock,** A Jerry 1930- *AmMWSc 92*
**Shryock,** Benjamin Charles 1962- *WhoWest 92*
**Shryock,** Carl Michael 1952- *WhoRel 92*
**Shryock,** Gerald Duane 1933- *AmMWSc 92*
**Shtasel,** Laurence Scott 1956- *WhoAmL 92*
**Shtemenko,** Sergey Matveevich 1907-1976 *SovUnBD*
**Shterenberg,** David Petrovich 1881-1948 *SovUnBD*
**Shterev,** Kiril 1918- *Who 92*
**Shtofman,** Norman Maurice 1928- *WhoAmP 91*
**Shtokolov,** Boris 1930- *IntWW 91*
**Shtraukh,** Maksim Maksimovich 1900-1974 *SovUnBD*
**Shtrikman,** Shmuel 1930- *AmMWSc 92*
**Shtromas,** Aleksandras 1931- *WhoMW 92*
**Shtull,** Jacob 1925- *WhoRel 92*
**Shu Tong** 1906- *IntWW 91*
**Shu,** Florence P. 1947- *WhoFI 92*
**Shu,** Frank H 1943- *AmMWSc 92*
**Shu,** Larry Steven 1936- *AmMWSc 92*
**Shub,** Esfir' Il'inichna 1894-1959 *SovUnBD*
**Shub,** Esther 1894-1959 *IntDcF 2-2, ReelWom*
**Shub,** Michael I 1943- *AmMWSc 92*
**Shube,** Eugene E 1927- *AmMWSc 92*
**Shubeck,** Paul Peter 1926- *AmMWSc 92*
**Shubert,** Bruno Otto 1934- *AmMWSc 92*
**Shubert,** L Elliot 1943- *AmMWSc 92*
**Shubik,** Philippe 1921- *AmMWSc 92*
**Shubin,** Seymour *WrDr 92*
**Shubin,** Seymour 1921- *IntAu&W 91*
**Shubin,** Tatiana 1950- *WhoWest 92*
**Shubkin,** Ronald Lee 1940- *AmMWSc 92*
**Shucard,** Alan *DrAPF 91*
**Shuchat,** Alan Howard 1942- *AmMWSc 92*
**Shuck,** Dee Ross 1941- *WhoMW 92*
**Shuck,** Frank O 1936- *AmMWSc 92*
**Shuck,** John Winfield 1940- *AmMWSc 92*
**Shuck,** Lowell Zane 1936- *AmMWSc 92*
**Shuck,** Robert Fletcher, III 1937- *WhoFI 92*
**Shuck,** Terry Alfred 1934- *WhoFI 92*
**Shuckburgh,** Charles Arthur Evelyn 1909- *Who 92*
**Shuckburgh,** Evelyn *Who 92*
**Shuckburgh,** Evelyn 1909- *IntWW 91*
**Shuckburgh,** Rupert 1949- *Who 92*
**Shuckford,** Samuel 1694?-1754 *BlkwCEP*
**Shuckra,** Christopher C. 1966- *WhoFI 92*
**Shudde,** Rex Hawkins 1929- *AmMWSc 92*
**Shue,** Elisabeth 1963- *IntMPA 92*
**Shue,** Robert Sidney 1943- *AmMWSc 92*
**Shuee,** Charles Edward 1916- *WhoAmP 91*
**Shuel,** David Alan 1961- *WhoWest 92*
**Shuey,** Carolyn Ann 1943- *WhoAmL 92*
**Shuey,** Merlin Arthur 1936- *AmMWSc 92*
**Shuey,** R L 1920- *AmMWSc 92*
**Shuey,** Robert Alton 1911- *WhoFI 92*
**Shuey,** William Carpenter 1924- *AmMWSc 92*
**Shuff,** Herbert R 1919- *WhoIns 92*
**Shuffer,** George Macon, Jr. 1923- *WhoBlA 92*
**Shuffield,** Lynna Kay 1957- *WhoAmP 91*
**Shuffman,** David Kenneth 1947- *WhoAmL 92*
**Shuffrey,** Ralph Frederick Dendy 1925- *Who 92*
**Shuford,** Bill, Jr. 1950- *WhoAmL 92*
**Shuford,** C Robert 1945- *WhoAmP 91*
**Shuford,** Humphrey Lewis 1945- *WhoBlA 92*
**Shuford,** Jerry 1936- *WhoAmL 92*
**Shuford,** Richard Joseph 1944- *AmMWSc 92*
**Shufro,** Salwyn 1905- *WhoFI 92*
**Shugarman,** Peter Melvin 1927- *AmMWSc 92*
**Shugars,** Dale L *WhoAmP 91*
**Shugars,** Jonas P 1934- *AmMWSc 92*
**Shugart,** Alan F. 1930- *WhoWest 92*
**Shugart,** Cecil G 1930- *AmMWSc 92*
**Shugart,** Herman Henry, Jr 1944- *AmMWSc 92*
**Shugart,** Howard Alan 1931- *AmMWSc 92*
**Shugart,** Lee Raleigh 1931- *AmMWSc 92*
**Shughart,** Donald Louis 1926- *WhoAmL 92*
**Shugoll,** Gene *WhoFI 92*
**Shugrue,** J. Edward 1950- *WhoEnt 92*
**Shugrue,** Jim *DrAPF 91*
**Shugrue,** Martin Roger, Jr. 1940- *WhoFI 92*
**Shugrue,** Michael Francis 1934- *WrDr 92*
**Shukairy,** Ahmed 1907-1980 *FacFETw*
**Shukat,** Scott 1937- *WhoEnt 92*
**Shukhaev,** Vasiliy Ivanovich 1887-1973 *SovUnBD*
**Shukhmin,** Petr Mitrofanovich 1894-1955 *SovUnBD*
**Shukla,** Atul J 1957- *AmMWSc 92*
**Shukla,** Kamal Kant 1942- *AmMWSc 92*
**Shukla,** Pradip Kantilal 1956- *WhoWest 92*
**Shukla,** Ravi Kumar 1959- *WhoFI 92*
**Shukla,** Shivendra Dutt 1951- *AmMWSc 92*
**Shukla,** Vidya Charan 1929- *IntWW 91*
**Shukman,** Harold 1931- *IntAu&W 91, WrDr 92*
**Shukry,** Ibrahim 1916- *IntWW 91*
**Shukshin,** V. *ConAu 135*
**Shukshin,** V.M. *ConAu 135*
**Shukshin,** Vasiliy Makarovich 1929-1974 *SovUnBD*
**Shukshin,** Vasily 1929-1974 *ConAu 135*
**Shula,** Don 1930- *News 92-2 [port]*
**Shulaw,** Richard Allen 1934- *WhoAmL 92*
**Shuldiner,** Paul W 1930- *AmMWSc 92*
**Shulenburger,** David Edwin 1945- *WhoFI 92, WhoMW 92*
**Shuler,** Charles F 1953- *AmMWSc 92*
**Shuler,** Craig Edward 1938- *AmMWSc 92*
**Shuler,** Kurt Egon 1922- *AmMWSc 92*
**Shuler,** Michael Louis 1947- *AmMWSc 92*
**Shuler,** Patrick James 1948- *AmMWSc 92*
**Shuler,** Robert Lee 1926- *AmMWSc 92*
**Shuler,** Robert Pierce 1880-1965 *RelLAm 91*
**Shuler,** Sally Ann Smith 1934- *WhoMW 92*
**Shuler-Donner,** Lauren *IntMPA 92*
**Shulkin,** Jerome 1929- *WhoAmL 92*
**Shull,** Charles Morell, Jr 1922- *AmMWSc 92*
**Shull,** Clifford Glenwood 1915- *AmMWSc 92*
**Shull,** Don Louis 1935- *AmMWSc 92*
**Shull,** Douglas K 1943- *WhoAmP 91*
**Shull,** Franklin Buckley 1918- *AmMWSc 92, WhoMW 92*
**Shull,** Harrison 1923- *AmMWSc 92, IntWW 91*
**Shull,** James Jay 1929- *AmMWSc 92*
**Shull,** Merlin Grosh 1927- *WhoRel 92*
**Shull,** Peter Otto, Jr 1954- *AmMWSc 92*
**Shull,** Richard B. 1929- *IntMPA 92*
**Shull,** Richard Bruce 1929- *WhoEnt 92*
**Shull,** Willard Charles, III 1940- *WhoFI 92*
**Shullenberger,** Bonnie Lowry Alexander 1948- *WhoRel 92*
**Shulls,** Wells Alexander 1916- *AmMWSc 92*
**Shulman,** Albert Maimon 1902- *WhoRel 92*
**Shulman,** Alix Kates *DrAPF 91*
**Shulman,** Alvin David 1930- *WhoAmL 92*
**Shulman,** Carl 1917- *AmMWSc 92*
**Shulman,** Daniel Rees 1944- *WhoAmL 92*
**Shulman,** David-Dima 1958- *AmMWSc 92*
**Shulman,** David George 1943- *WhoFI 92*
**Shulman,** Donald Carl 1949- *WhoEnt 92*
**Shulman,** Drusilla Norman *Who 92*
**Shulman,** Fay Grissom Stanley 1925?-1990 *ConAu 133*
**Shulman,** George 1914- *AmMWSc 92*
**Shulman,** Harold 1925- *AmMWSc 92*
**Shulman,** Herbert Byron 1947- *AmMWSc 92*
**Shulman,** Herman L 1922- *AmMWSc 92*
**Shulman,** Ira Andrew 1949- *AmMWSc 92*
**Shulman,** Irving 1913- *WrDr 92*
**Shulman,** Jones A 1936- *AmMWSc 92*
**Shulman,** Lawrence Edward 1919- *AmMWSc 92, IntWW 91*
**Shulman,** Marshall D. 1916- *WrDr 92*
**Shulman,** Martin 1945- *WhoAmL 92*
**Shulman,** Max *DrAPF 91*
**Shulman,** Milton *Who 92*
**Shulman,** Milton 1913- *WrDr 92*
**Shulman,** Morton 1933- *AmMWSc 92*
**Shulman,** N Raphael 1925- *AmMWSc 92*
**Shulman,** Nisson Elchanan 1931- *WhoRel 92*
**Shulman,** Robert Gerson 1924- *AmMWSc 92, IntWW 91*
**Shulman,** Robert Jay 1950- *AmMWSc 92*
**Shulman,** Seth David 1943- *AmMWSc 92*
**Shulman,** Sidney 1923- *AmMWSc 92*
**Shulman,** Sol 1929- *AmMWSc 92*
**Shulman,** Sondra *DrAPF 91*
**Shulman,** Stanford Taylor 1942- *AmMWSc 92*
**Shulman,** Stephen Neal 1933- *WhoAmL 92*
**Shulman,** Warren Scott 1942- *WhoAmL 92*
**Shulman,** Yechiel 1930- *AmMWSc 92*
**Shulmister,** M. Ross 1940- *WhoAmL 92*
**Shult,** Ernest E 1933- *AmMWSc 92*
**Shulte,** Albert Philip 1934- *WhoMW 92*
**Shulte,** Francis *WhoRel 92*
**Shulte,** Joann Cheryl 1936- *WhoRel 92*
**Shultis,** J Kenneth 1941- *AmMWSc 92*
**Shults,** Garry Lynn 1949- *WhoEnt 92*
**Shults,** Robert Lee 1936- *WhoFI 92*
**Shults,** Wilbur Dotry, II 1929- *AmMWSc 92*
**Shultz,** Al *DrAPF 91*
**Shultz,** Allan R 1926- *AmMWSc 92*
**Shultz,** Charles E. *WhoWest 92*
**Shultz,** Charles H 1936- *AmMWSc 92*
**Shultz,** Clifford Glen 1924- *AmMWSc 92*
**Shultz,** Dan McLloyd 1938- *WhoEnt 92*
**Shultz,** Dana Howard 1949- *WhoAmL 92*
**Shultz,** Emmet Lavel 1934- *WhoFI 92, WhoWest 92*
**Shultz,** Fred Townsend 1923- *AmMWSc 92, WhoWest 92*
**Shultz,** Gary Lee 1954- *WhoMW 92*
**Shultz,** George P. 1920- *WrDr 92*
**Shultz,** George Pratt 1920- *AmPolLe [port], IntWW 91, Who 92, WhoAmP 91, WhoFI 92, WhoWest 92*
**Shultz,** John David 1939- *WhoAmL 92, WhoFI 92*
**Shultz,** John Franklin 1951- *WhoAmL 92*
**Shultz,** Joseph Randolph 1927- *WhoMW 92, WhoRel 92*
**Shultz,** Kenneth Scott 1962- *WhoWest 92*
**Shultz,** Leila McReynolds 1946- *AmMWSc 92*
**Shultz,** Leonard Donald 1945- *AmMWSc 92*
**Shultz,** Linda Joyce 1931- *WhoMW 92*
**Shultz,** Retha Mills 1914- *WhoMW 92, WhoRel 92*
**Shultz,** Richard 1942- *WhoAmP 91*
**Shultz,** Sherrie Lee 1961- *WhoEnt 92*
**Shultz,** Silas Harold 1938- *WhoAmL 92*
**Shultz,** Terry D 1947- *AmMWSc 92*
**Shultz,** Walter 1931- *AmMWSc 92*
**Shulze,** Frederick Bennett 1935- *WhoMW 92*
**Shum,** Annie Waiching *AmMWSc 92*
**Shum,** Archie Chue 1942- *AmMWSc 92*
**Shumacker,** Harris B, Jr 1908- *AmMWSc 92*
**Shumake,** Glynn *WhoAmP 91*
**Shumake,** Hildred W *WhoAmP 91*
**Shumake,** James Martin *WhoMW 92*
**Shumaker,** Anne Williamson 1944- *WhoAmP 91*
**Shumaker,** Edward Earl, III 1948- *WhoAmL 92*
**Shumaker,** Gregory Alexander 1958- *WhoMW 92*
**Shumaker,** Harold Dennis 1946- *WhoAmL 92*
**Shumaker,** John Benjamin, Jr 1926- *AmMWSc 92*
**Shumaker,** John J 1929- *WhoAmP 91*
**Shumaker,** Peggy *DrAPF 91*
**Shumaker,** Peter Elliott 1953- *WhoMW 92*
**Shumaker,** Robert C 1931- *AmMWSc 92*
**Shumaker,** Robert Harper 1933- *WhoMW 92*
**Shumaker,** Wayne 1910- *WrDr 92*
**Shuman,** Bertram Marvin 1931- *AmMWSc 92*
**Shuman,** Charles Ross 1918- *AmMWSc 92*
**Shuman,** Charles Wilson 1935- *WhoAmP 91*
**Shuman,** Howard E 1924- *WhoAmP 91*
**Shuman,** Irving Michael 1932- *WhoEnt 92*
**Shuman,** Jerome 1937- *WhoBlA 92*
**Shuman,** Larry Myers 1944- *AmMWSc 92*
**Shuman,** Mark S 1936- *AmMWSc 92*
**Shuman,** Melvin Richard 1954- *WhoAmL 92*
**Shuman,** Mort d1991 *NewYTBS 91*
**Shuman,** Samuel I. 1925- *WrDr 92*
**Shuman,** Stanley S. 1935- *WhoFI 92*
**Shuman,** Thomas Alan 1946- *WhoWest 92*
**Shuman,** Willard Edward 1943- *WhoIns 92*
**Shumard,** Benjamin Franklin 1820-1869 *BiInAmS*
**Shumard-Sauer,** Christine Marie 1961- *WhoMW 92*
**Shumate,** Charles Albert 1904- *WhoWest 92*
**Shumate,** Glen 1958- *WhoBlA 92*
**Shumate,** Kenneth McClellan 1936- *AmMWSc 92*
**Shumate,** Paul William, Jr 1941- *AmMWSc 92*
**Shumate,** Rosemarie 1948- *WhoEnt 92*
**Shumate,** Sidney Ellis 1952- *WhoEnt 92*
**Shumate,** Starling Everett, II 1947- *AmMWSc 92*
**Shumlin,** Peter E 1956- *WhoAmP 91*
**Shumrick,** Donald A 1925- *AmMWSc 92*
**Shumsky,** Jack 1932- *WhoEnt 92*
**Shumsky,** Oscar 1917- *NewAmDM*
**Shumsky,** Zena *WrDr 92*
**Shumway,** Bettie Sue 1924- *WhoAmP 91*
**Shumway,** Clare Nelson 1925- *AmMWSc 92*
**Shumway,** Forrest Nelson 1927- *IntWW 91*
**Shumway,** Jim *WhoAmP 91*
**Shumway,** Lewis Kay 1934- *AmMWSc 92*
**Shumway,** Mary *DrAPF 91*
**Shumway,** Norman D 1934- *WhoAmP 91, WhoWest 92*
**Shumway,** Norman Edward 1923- *IntWW 91, WhoWest 92*
**Shumway,** Richard Phil 1921- *AmMWSc 92*
**Shumway,** Sandra Elisabeth 1952- *AmMWSc 92*
**Shumyatsky,** Boris Zakharovich 1886-1938 *SovUnBD*
**Shung,** K Kirk 1945- *AmMWSc 92*
**Shunn,** Maxine Faye 1917- *WhoAmP 91*
**Shupack,** Paul Martin 1940- *WhoAmL 92*
**Shupe,** Dean Stanley 1937- *AmMWSc 92*
**Shupe,** Donald Vane 1933- *WhoWest 92*
**Shupe,** James LeGrande 1918- *AmMWSc 92*
**Shupe,** John W 1924- *AmMWSc 92*
**Shupe,** Robert Eugene 1934- *AmMWSc 92*
**Shupnik,** Fred Joseph 1916- *WhoAmP 91*
**Shur,** Barry David 1950- *AmMWSc 92*
**Shur,** Michael 1942- *AmMWSc 92*
**Shur,** Walter 1929- *WhoFI 92, WhoIns 92*
**Shura,** Mary Francis *ConAu 133, SmATA 65*
**Shurbet,** Deskin Hunt, Jr 1925- *AmMWSc 92*
**Shurden,** Frank 1940- *WhoAmP 91*
**Shure,** Donald Joseph 1939- *AmMWSc 92*
**Shure,** Fred C 1934- *AmMWSc 92*
**Shure,** Kalman 1925- *AmMWSc 92*
**Shure,** Leonard 1910- *NewAmDM*
**Shurick,** Edward Palmes 1912- *WhoEnt 92*
**Shurin,** Aaron *DrAPF 91*
**Shurin,** Aaron Ben-Zion 1914- *WhoRel 92*
**Shurman,** Laurence Paul Lyons 1930- *Who 92*
**Shurman,** Louis Wayne 1939- *WhoMW 92*
**Shurman,** Michael Mendelsohn 1921- *AmMWSc 92*
**Shurn,** Peter Joseph, III 1946- *WhoAmL 92*
**Shurpin,** Sol 1914- *IntMPA 92*
**Shurtleff,** Bertrand L 1895- *ScFEYrs*
**Shurtleff,** David B 1930- *AmMWSc 92*
**Shurtleff,** Leonard Grant 1940- *WhoAmP 91*
**Shurtleff,** Malcolm C, Jr 1922- *AmMWSc 92*
**Shurts,** Richard Layne 1940- *WhoMW 92*
**Shurvell,** Herbert Francis 1934- *AmMWSc 92*
**Shushan,** Morris 1907- *AmMWSc 92*
**Shushan,** Sam 1922- *AmMWSc 92*
**Shuskus,** Alexander J 1929- *AmMWSc 92*
**Shusman,** T 1920- *AmMWSc 92*
**Shussett,** Steven Harold 1963- *WhoRel 92*
**Shusted,** Thomas J 1926- *WhoAmP 91*
**Shuster,** Bud 1932- *WhoAmP 91*
**Shuster,** Carl Nathaniel, Jr 1919- *AmMWSc 92*
**Shuster,** Charles W *AmMWSc 92*
**Shuster,** E. G. 1932- *AlmAP 92 [port]*
**Shuster,** Jacob 1927- *WhoAmL 92*
**Shuster,** John A. 1939- *WhoFI 92*
**Shuster,** Joseph 1937- *AmMWSc 92*
**Shuster,** Kenneth Ashton 1946- *AmMWSc 92*
**Shuster,** Louis 1929- *AmMWSc 92*
**Shuster,** Marguerite 1947- *WhoRel 92*
**Shuster,** Mark Jon 1957- *WhoEnt 92*
**Shuster,** Robert C 1932- *AmMWSc 92*
**Shusterman,** Nathan 1927- *WhoFI 92*
**Shusterman,** Neal 1962- *ConAu 133*
**Shustitzky,** John Wilson 1951- *WhoMW 92*
**Shute,** Charles Cameron Donald 1917- *Who 92*
**Shute,** David 1931- *WhoAmL 92, WhoFI 92*
**Shute,** Henry Augustus 1856-1943 *BenetAL 91*
**Shute,** John Lawson 1901- *Who 92*
**Shute,** Nevil 1899-1960 *TwCSFW 91*
**Shuter,** Adrienne Joan 1937- *WhoMW 92*
**Shuter,** Eli Ronald 1935- *AmMWSc 92*
**Shuter,** William Leslie Hazlewood 1936- *AmMWSc 92*
**Shutes,** Robert Steven 1949- *WhoRel 92*

**Shutler**, Kenneth Eugene 1938- *WhoWest 92*
**Shutler**, Rex 1933- *Who 92*
**Shutrump**, Mary Jill 1964- *WhoMW 92*
**Shutske**, Gregory Michael *AmMWSc 92*
**Shutt**, Bob 1951- *WhoAmP 91*
**Shutt**, Buffy *IntMPA 92*
**Shutters**, Daniel Moyer 1942- *WhoRel 92*
**Shuttle**, Penelope 1947- *ConPo 91, Who 92, WrDr 92*
**Shuttle**, Penelope Diane 1947- *IntAu&W 91*
**Shuttlesworth**, Fred L. 1922- *WhoBlA 92*
**Shuttleworth**, Baron 1948- *Who 92*
**Shuttleworth**, Natalie Ownbey 1945- *WhoWest 92*
**Shuttleworth**, Paul *DrAPF 91*
**Shutze**, John V 1924- *AmMWSc 92*
**Shuval**, Hillel Isaiah 1926- *AmMWSc 92*
**Shvarts**, Yevgeny L'vovich 1896-1958 *SovUnBD*
**Shvartz**, Esar 1935- *AmMWSc 92*
**Shvernik**, Nikolay Mikhaylovich 1888-1970 *SovUnBD*
**Shvyrkov**, Vladislav V. 1931- *WhoWest 92*
**Shwartz**, Susan 1949- *TwCSFW 91*
**Shwarzstein**, Meyer 1956- *WhoWest 92*
**Shwe**, Hla 1934- *AmMWSc 92*
**Shwide**, Herman 1925- *WhoIns 92*
**Shyamsunder**, Erramilli 1957- *AmMWSc 92*
**Shybut**, George Theodore *WhoMW 92*
**Shykind**, David *AmMWSc 92*
**Shykind**, Edwin B 1931- *AmMWSc 92*
**Shymkus**, James Lowery 1939- *WhoFI 92*
**Shyne**, J C 1925- *AmMWSc 92*
**Shypulefski**, John 1942- *WhoRel 92*
**Shysh**, Alec 1936- *AmMWSc 92*
**Si Siman**, E.E., Jr. 1921- *WhoEnt 92*
**Siad Barre**, Mohamed 1921- *IntWW 91*
**Siadat**, Mohammad Vali 1945- *WhoMW 92*
**Siaguru**, Anthony 1946- *IntWW 91*
**Siakotos**, Aristotle N 1928- *AmMWSc 92*
**Sialom**, Sedat Sami 1940- *WhoFI 92*
**Siano**, Donald Bruce 1942- *AmMWSc 92*
**Siano**, Jerry J. *WhoFI 92*
**Siantz**, Mary Lou deLeon 1947- *WhoHisp 92*
**Siapno**, William David 1926- *AmMWSc 92*
**Siart**, William Eric Baxter 1946- *WhoWest 92*
**Sias**, Fred R, Jr 1931- *AmMWSc 92*
**Sias**, Frederick Ralph 1905- *AmMWSc 92*
**Sias**, John B. *LesBEnT 92 [port]*
**Sias**, John B. 1927- *WhoEnt 92, WhoFI 92*
**Sias**, Richard James 1942- *WhoEnt 92*
**Sias**, Solomon 1829- *BiInAmS*
**Siatkowski**, Ronald E 1950- *AmMWSc 92*
**Siatu'u**, Fiaaoga P *WhoAmP 91*
**Siatu'u**, Peseta Fiaaoga 1934- *WhoAmP 91*
**Siau**, John Finn 1921- *AmMWSc 92*
**Sibal**, Louis Richard 1927- *AmMWSc 92*
**Sibarium**, Michael Leonard 1959- *WhoAmL 92*
**Sibbach**, William Robert 1927- *AmMWSc 92*
**Sibbald**, Ian Ramsay 1931- *AmMWSc 92*
**Sibbald**, John Ristow 1936- *WhoFI 92*
**Sibbald**, Peter Frank Aubrey 1928- *Who 92*
**Sibbald**, William John 1946- *AmMWSc 92*
**Sibbio**, Michael Gregory 1955- *WhoEnt 92, WhoWest 92*
**Sibelius**, Jean 1865-1957 *FacFETw [port], NewAmDM*
**Sibener**, Steven Jay 1954- *AmMWSc 92*
**Siberry**, Jane 1950?- *ConMus 6 [port]*
**Siberry**, John William Morgan 1913- *Who 92*
**Siberry**, William Richard 1950- *Who 92*
**Sibert**, Elbert Ernest 1941- *AmMWSc 92*
**Sibert**, John Rickard 1940- *AmMWSc 92*
**Sibila**, Kenneth Francis 1911- *AmMWSc 92*
**Sibilia**, John Philip 1933- *AmMWSc 92*
**Sibiski**, Kendel Lee 1961- *WhoAmL 92*
**Sibley**, Antoinette 1939- *IntWW 91, Who 92*
**Sibley**, Carol Hopkins 1943- *AmMWSc 92*
**Sibley**, Charles Gald 1917- *AmMWSc 92*
**Sibley**, David McAdams 1947- *WhoAmP 91*
**Sibley**, Dawn Bunnell 1939- *WhoFI 92*
**Sibley**, Duncan Fawcett 1946- *AmMWSc 92*
**Sibley**, Ellen C. 1918- *WhoBlA 92*
**Sibley**, Gordon Wright 1938- *WhoRel 92*
**Sibley**, James Malcolm 1919- *WhoAmL 92*
**Sibley**, Joyce Gregory 1934- *WhoRel 92*
**Sibley**, Lucy Roy 1934- *AmMWSc 92*
**Sibley**, Mulford Quickert 1912-1989 *AmPeW*
**Sibley**, Quintus Whitaker 1956- *WhoAmL 92*
**Sibley**, William Arthur 1932- *AmMWSc 92*
**Sibley**, William Austin 1925- *AmMWSc 92*
**Sibley**, Willis Elbridge 1930- *WhoMW 92*
**Sibolski**, John Alfred, Jr. 1946- *WhoFI 92*
**Sibomana**, Adrien *IntWW 91*
**Siboo**, Russell 1930- *AmMWSc 92*
**Sibrel**, Bart Winfield 1964- *WhoEnt 92*
**Sibul**, Leon Henry 1932- *AmMWSc 92*
**Sibulkin**, Merwin 1926- *AmMWSc 92*
**Sibuya**, Yasutaka 1930- *AmMWSc 92*
**Sica**, Alan Meyer 1949- *WhoMW 92*
**Sica**, John 1962- *WhoAmL 92*
**Sica**, Louis 1935- *AmMWSc 92*
**Sicard**, Guillermo Rafael 1937- *WhoMW 92*
**Sicard**, Maurice-Ivan 1910- *BiDExR*
**Sicard**, Raymond Edward 1948- *AmMWSc 92*
**Sicat**, Gerardo P. 1935- *IntWW 91*
**Siccama**, Thomas G 1936- *AmMWSc 92*
**Sich**, Jeffrey John 1954- *AmMWSc 92*
**Sich**, Rupert 1908- *Who 92*
**Sichel**, Enid Keil 1946- *AmMWSc 92*
**Sichel**, John Martin 1943- *AmMWSc 92*
**Sichel**, Martin 1928- *AmMWSc 92, WhoMW 92*
**Sichel**, Werner 1934- *WhoFI 92, WhoMW 92, WrDr 92*
**Sichelgaita** *EncAmaz 91*
**Sicherman**, Carol 1937- *ConAu 135*
**Sicherman**, Marvin Allen 1934- *WhoAmL 92, WhoMW 92*
**Sicherman**, Michael Robert 1950- *WhoMW 92*
**Sichler**, Jiri Jan 1941- *AmMWSc 92*
**Sichol**, Marcia W. 1940- *ConAu 135*
**Sicilian**, James Michael 1947- *AmMWSc 92*
**Sicilian**, Joseph Michael 1948- *WhoFI 92*
**Siciliano**, Edward Ronald 1948- *AmMWSc 92*
**Siciliano**, Enzo 1934- *IntWW 91*
**Siciliano**, Jean Marie 1954- *WhoMW 92*
**Siciliano**, Joseph Anthony 1959- *WhoAmL 92*
**Siciliano**, Michael J 1937- *AmMWSc 92*
**Siciliano**, Rocco C 1922- *WhoAmP 91*
**Siciliano**, Rocco Carmine 1922- *WhoFI 92*
**Sicilio**, Fred 1920- *AmMWSc 92*
**Sick**, Gary Gordon 1935- *WhoFI 92*
**Sick**, Lowell Victor 1944- *AmMWSc 92*
**Sick**, Thomas J *AmMWSc 92*
**Sick**, William Norman, Jr. 1935- *WhoFI 92*
**Sicka**, Richard Walter 1938- *AmMWSc 92*
**Sickafus**, Edward N 1931- *AmMWSc 92*
**Sickel**, George William 1926- *WhoMW 92*
**Sickel**, Joan Sottilare 1941- *WhoWest 92*
**Sickels**, Quentin Brian 1953- *WhoEnt 92*
**Sickert**, Bernard 1863?-1932 *TwCPaSc*
**Sickert**, Walter Richard 1860-1942 *ThHEIm, TwCPaSc*
**Sickinger**, Kenneth T. 1943- *WhoEnt 92*
**Sickinghe**, Feyo Onno Joost 1926- *IntWW 91*
**Sickler**, Jennifer Susan 1961- *WhoAmL 92*
**Sickles**, Carlton R 1921- *WhoAmP 91*
**Sickles**, William Paul 1961- *WhoMW 92*
**Sicko-Goad**, Linda May 1948- *AmMWSc 92*
**Sicoli**, Dan *DrAPF 91*
**Siconolfi**, Michael Thomas 1942- *WhoEnt 92*
**Sicotte**, Raymond L 1939- *AmMWSc 92*
**Sicotte**, Yvon 1930- *AmMWSc 92*
**Sicular**, George M 1921- *AmMWSc 92*
**Sida**, Derek William 1926- *AmMWSc 92*
**Sidamon-Eristoff**, Constantine 1930- *WhoAmL 92*
**Sidaris**, Andrew W. *LesBEnT 92*
**Sidaris**, Andy 1932- *IntMPA 92*
**Sidbury**, Harold David 1940- *WhoBlA 92*
**Sidbury**, James Buren, Jr 1922- *AmMWSc 92*
**Siddall**, Ernest 1919- *AmMWSc 92*
**Siddall**, Norman 1918- *IntWW 91, Who 92*
**Siddall**, Thomas Henry, III 1922- *AmMWSc 92*
**Siddeley** *Who 92*
**Siddeley**, Randle *Who 92*
**Siddell**, Derreck 1942- *AmMWSc 92*
**Sidder**, Gary Brian 1954- *AmMWSc 92*
**Siddhi Savetsila** 1919- *IntWW 91*
**Siddiky**, B. A. 1915- *IntWW 91*
**Siddiqee**, Muhammad Waheeduddin 1931- *AmMWSc 92*
**Siddiqi**, M. Raziuddin 1908- *IntWW 91*
**Siddiqi**, Obaid 1932- *Who 92*
**Siddique**, Irtaza H 1929- *AmMWSc 92*
**Siddiqui**, Abdul Mannan 1935- *IntWW 91*
**Siddiqui**, Aslam Rasheed 1946- *AmMWSc 92*
**Siddiqui**, Habib 1953- *AmMWSc 92*
**Siddiqui**, Iqbal Rafat 1931- *AmMWSc 92*
**Siddiqui**, M A Q 1937- *AmMWSc 92*
**Siddiqui**, Mohammed Moinuddin 1928- *AmMWSc 92*
**Siddiqui**, Salimuzzaman 1897- *Who 92*
**Siddiqui**, Waheed Hasan 1939- *AmMWSc 92*
**Siddiqui**, Wasim A 1934- *AmMWSc 92*
**Siddon**, Thomas Edward 1941- *IntWW 91*
**Siddons**, Anne Rivers 1928- *IntAu&W 91*
**Siddons**, Arthur Harold Makins 1911- *Who 92*
**Siddons**, James DeWitt 1948- *WhoEnt 92*
**Siddons**, Sarah 1755-1831 *BlkwCEP*
**Siddoway**, Thane R 1953- *WhoAmP 91*
**Sidebottom**, Edward John 1918- *Who 92*
**Sidebottom**, Irvin Eldred 1924- *WhoRel 92*
**Sidebottom**, Omar M 1919- *AmMWSc 92*
**Sidel**, Ruth *WrDr 92*
**Sidel**, Victor William 1931- *AmMWSc 92*
**Sidell**, Bruce David 1948- *AmMWSc 92*
**Sidell**, Frederick R 1934- *AmMWSc 92*
**Sidell**, Ron Daniel 1941- *Who 92*
**Siden**, Edward Joel 1947- *AmMWSc 92*
**Sidenbladh**, Goran 1912- *IntWW 91*
**Sider**, E. Morris 1928- *WhoRel 92*
**Sider**, Harvey Ray 1930- *WhoRel 92*
**Sider**, Ronald Ray 1933- *WhoEnt 92*
**Sideropoulos**, Aris S 1937- *AmMWSc 92*
**Sides**, Charles 1949- *WhoAmP 91*
**Sides**, Gary Donald 1947- *AmMWSc 92*
**Sides**, Jack Davis, Jr. 1939- *WhoAmL 92*
**Sides**, James Ralph 1936- *WhoFI 92*
**Sides**, Julian Earl, Jr 1925- *WhoAmP 91*
**Sides**, Paul Joseph 1951- *AmMWSc 92*
**Sides**, Susan Hatley 1943- *WhoRel 92*
**Sides**, Terry Alan 1960- *WhoAmL 92*
**Sidey**, Ernest 1913- *Who 92*
**Sidey**, John MacNaughton d1990 *Who 92N*
**Sidey**, Thomas Kay Stuart 1908- *Who 92*
**Sidgwick and Jackson Limited** *DcLB 112*
**Sidhu**, Bhag Singh 1929- *AmMWSc 92*
**Sidhu**, Deepinder Pal 1944- *AmMWSc 92*
**Sidhu**, Gurbachan Singh 1920- *IntWW 91*
**Sidhu**, Gurmel Singh 1940- *AmMWSc 92*
**Sidhu**, Gurmel Singh 1943- *WhoWest 92*
**Sidhu**, Nancy Dayton 1941- *WhoFI 92*
**Sidhu**, Victor S. 1938- *WhoFI 92, WhoWest 92*
**Sidi**, Henri 1919- *AmMWSc 92*
**Sidi**, Jacques Albert 1928- *WhoAmP 91*
**Sidi Baba**, Dey Ould 1921- *IntWW 91*
**Sidie**, James Michael 1941- *AmMWSc 92*
**Sidikman**, Paul Henry 1945- *WhoFI 92*
**Sidjakov**, Nicolas 1924- *WhoEnt 92*
**Sidki**, Aziz 1920- *IntWW 91*
**Sidky**, Younan Abdel Malik 1928- *AmMWSc 92*
**Sidle**, Roy Carl 1948- *AmMWSc 92*
**Sidler**, Jack D 1939- *AmMWSc 92*
**Sidlin**, Murray 1940- *NewAmDM*
**Sidlin**, Murry 1940- *IntWW 91*
**Sidman**, Richard Leon 1928- *AmMWSc 92*
**Sidman**, Robert John 1943- *WhoAmL 92*
**Sidmouth**, Viscount 1914- *Who 92*
**Sidney** *Who 92*
**Sidney**, Edward William 1784-1851 *ScFEYrs*
**Sidney**, George 1916- *IntMPA 92, WhoEnt 92*
**Sidney**, Joan Seliger *DrAPF 91*
**Sidney**, Larry Eugene 1952- *WhoMW 92*
**Sidney**, Neilma 1922- *WrDr 92*
**Sidney**, Philip 1554-1586 *CnDBLB 1 [port], RfGEnL 91*
**Sidney**, Stuart Jay 1941- *AmMWSc 92*
**Sidney**, Sylvia 1910- *ConTFT 9, IntMPA 92, WhoEnt 92*
**Sidney**, William Wright 1929- *WhoFI 92, WhoWest 92*
**Sidon**, Weslea *DrAPF 91*
**Sidonius Apollinaris** 430?-487? *EncEarC*
**Sidor**, Karol 1901-1953 *BiDExR*
**Sidorak**, Stephen James, Jr. 1949- *WhoRel 92*
**Sidorov**, Veniamin Aleksandrovich 1930- *IntWW 91*
**Sidorov**, Vladimir Vasilevich 1924- *IntWW 91*
**Sidorowicz**, Wladyslaw 1945- *IntWW 91*
**Sidos**, Pierre Lucien Jerome 1927- *BiDExR*
**Sidote**, Sam 1921- *WhoEnt 92*
**Sidoti**, Daniel Robert 1921- *AmMWSc 92*
**Sidoti**, Raymond Benjamin 1929- *WhoEnt 92*
**Sidran**, Miriam 1920- *AmMWSc 92*
**Sidransky**, Herschel 1925- *AmMWSc 92*
**Sidransky**, Ruth 1929- *ConAu 135*
**Sidwell**, Gregory Allen 1960- *WhoMW 92*
**Sidwell**, Martindale 1916- *Who 92*
**Sidwell**, Robert William 1937- *AmMWSc 92*
**Sidwell**, Scott Edward 1950- *WhoAmP 91*
**Sie**, Banja T. *Who 92*
**Sie**, Charles H 1934- *AmMWSc 92*
**Sie**, Edward Hsien Choh 1925- *AmMWSc 92*
**Sie**, John *LesBEnT 92*
**Siebein**, Gary Walter 1951- *AmMWSc 92*
**Siebel**, John Ewald 1845-1919 *BiInAmS*
**Siebel**, Julia *DrAPF 91*
**Siebel**, M P L 1924- *AmMWSc 92*
**Siebel**, Richard Allan 1939- *WhoAmP 91*
**Siebeling**, Ronald Jon 1937- *AmMWSc 92*
**Siebels-Kilnes**, Jane Marie 1960- *WhoFI 92*
**Sieben**, Harry A, Jr 1943- *WhoAmP 91*
**Sieben**, Todd 1945- *WhoAmP 91*
**Siebenaler**, Agnes Gertrude 1922- *WhoRel 92*
**Siebeneck**, Ronald Paul 1950- *WhoMW 92*
**Siebenmorgen**, Paul 1920- *WhoRel 92*
**Siebens**, Arthur Alexandre 1921- *AmMWSc 92*
**Siebentritt**, Carl R, Jr 1922- *AmMWSc 92*
**Sieber**, Fritz 1946- *AmMWSc 92, WhoMW 92*
**Sieber**, James Leo 1936- *AmMWSc 92*
**Sieber**, Joan E. 1937- *ConAu 35NR*
**Sieber-Fabro**, Susan M 1942- *AmMWSc 92*
**Sieberg**, Jacob *DcAmImH*
**Siebert**, Alan Roger 1930- *AmMWSc 92*
**Siebert**, Calvin D. 1934- *WhoMW 92*
**Siebert**, Donald Robert 1946- *AmMWSc 92*
**Siebert**, Eleanor Dantzler 1941- *AmMWSc 92*
**Siebert**, Jerome Bernard 1938- *AmMWSc 92*
**Siebert**, John 1940- *AmMWSc 92*
**Siebert**, Karl Joseph 1945- *AmMWSc 92*
**Siebert**, Lynn Laitman 1946- *WhoEnt 92*
**Siebert**, Manfred Fritz Eduard Walter 1925- *IntWW 91*
**Siebert**, Stephanie Ray 1949- *WhoWest 92*
**Siebert**, W M 1925- *AmMWSc 92*
**Siebert Held**, Bruno *IntWW 91*
**Sieberts**, Jan Kristian 1942- *WhoWest 92*
**Siebes**, Maria 1958- *AmMWSc 92*
**Siebman**, Clyde Moody 1958- *WhoAmL 92*
**Siebrand**, Willem 1932- *AmMWSc 92*
**Siebrasse**, Richard W. 1926- *WhoFI 92*
**Siebring**, Barteld Richard 1924- *AmMWSc 92*
**Sieburg**, Friedrich 1893-1964 *EncTR 91*
**Sieburth**, John McNeill 1927- *AmMWSc 92*
**Sieck**, Greg R. 1956- *WhoWest 92*
**Sieck**, Harold F 1916- *WhoAmP 91*
**Sieckhaus**, John Francis 1939- *AmMWSc 92*
**Sieckmann**, Donna G 1946- *AmMWSc 92*
**Sieckmann**, Everett Frederick 1928- *AmMWSc 92*
**Siedel**, George John, III 1945- *WhoAmL 92*
**Siederer**, Martin Andrew 1955- *WhoEnt 92*
**Siedle**, Allen R *AmMWSc 92*
**Siedlecki**, Nancy Therese 1954- *WhoAmL 92*
**Siedlecki**, Peter *DrAPF 91*
**Siedler**, Arthur James 1927- *AmMWSc 92*
**Siedlinski**, John E. 1953- *WhoMW 92*
**Siedow**, James N 1947- *AmMWSc 92*
**Siedschlag**, Karl Glenn, Jr 1920- *AmMWSc 92*
**Siedzikowski**, Henry Francis 1953- *WhoAmL 92*
**Siefein**, William Naguib 1939- *IntWW 91*
**Siefert**, David Michael 1951- *WhoMW 92*
**Siefert**, Diane Lynn 1948- *WhoFI 92*
**Siefert**, Richard Carl 1946- *WhoAmL 92*
**Siefert**, Thomas Paul 1950- *WhoRel 92*
**Siefert-Kazanjian**, Donna *WhoFI 92*
**Sieff** *Who 92*
**Sieff**, David Daniel 1939- *Who 92*
**Sieff**, Jeanloup 1933- *IntWW 91*
**Sieff**, John Philip 1928- *WhoFI 92*
**Sieff Of Brimpton**, Baron 1913- *IntWW 91, Who 92*
**Siefferman**, Floyd Earl, Jr. 1932- *WhoAmL 92, WhoMW 92*
**Siefken**, Hugh Edward 1940- *AmMWSc 92*
**Siefken**, John Henry 1939- *WhoRel 92*
**Siefken**, Mark William 1939- *AmMWSc 92*
**Siefker**, Gregory William 1945- *WhoEnt 92*
**Siefker**, Joseph Roy 1933- *AmMWSc 92, WhoMW 92*
**Siefkes**, Philip Dean 1959- *WhoRel 92*
**Siefkin**, Randy Richardson 1942- *WhoAmP 91*
**Siefkin**, William Charles 1946- *WhoFI 92*
**Sieg**, Albert Louis 1930- *AmMWSc 92*
**Sieg**, Daniel Richard 1963- *WhoFI 92*
**Siegal**, Bernard 1924- *AmMWSc 92*
**Siegal**, Burton L 1931- *AmMWSc 92*
**Siegal**, Frederick Paul 1939- *AmMWSc 92*
**Siegal**, Gene Philip 1948- *AmMWSc 92*
**Siegal**, Jeffrey Marc 1960- *WhoFI 92*
**Siegal**, Joel Davis 1937- *WhoAmL 92*
**Siegal**, Marvyn Emanuel 1930- *WhoFI 92*
**Siegan**, Bernard Herbert 1924- *WhoAmL 92*
**Siegart**, William Raymond 1931- *AmMWSc 92*

**Signac**, Paul 1863-1935 *ThHEIm*
**Signell**, Peter Stuart 1928- *AmMWSc 92*
**Signer**, Ethan Royal 1937- *AmMWSc 92*
**Signer**, William A 1949- *WhoAmP 91*
**Signor**, Philip White 1950- *WhoWest 92*
**Signor**, Randy Michael *DrAPF 91*
**Signore**, Robert Joseph 1960- *WhoMW 92*
**Signorelli**, Ernest Leonard 1929- *WhoAmL 92*
**Signorelli**, Michael 1906- *WhoEnt 92*
**Signorelli**, Philip Joseph, III 1941- *WhoWest 92*
**Signoret**, Simone 1921-1985 *ConAu 135, FacFETw [port]*
**Signoriello**, Vincent James 1954- *WhoFI 92*
**Signorile**, Claudio 1937- *IntWW 91*
**Signorile**, Vincent Anthony 1959- *WhoAmL 92*
**Signorino**, Charles A. 1932- *WhoFI 92*
**Signorino**, Charles Anthony 1932- *AmMWSc 92*
**Signorovitch**, Dennis James 1945- *WhoFI 92*
**Sigogne**, Philippe 1943- *IntWW 91*
**Sigourney**, Lydia Howard Huntley 1791-1865 *AmPeW, BenetAL 91*
**Sigrist**, Helmut 1919- *IntWW 91*
**Siguenza**, Herbert 1959- *WhoHisp 92*
**Siguenza**, Peter C *WhoAmP 91*
**Siguenza y Gongora**, Carlos de 1645-1700 *HisDSpE*
**Siguion-Reyna**, Leonardo 1921- *WhoFI 92*
**Siguler**, George William 1947- *WhoFI 92*
**Sigur**, Wanda Anne Alexander 1958- *WhoBlA 92*
**Sigurana**, Catherine *EncAmaz 91*
**Sigurbjornsson**, Einar 1944- *WhoRel 92*
**Sigurdardottir**, Johanna 1942- *IntWW 91*
**Sigurdsen**, Gertrud 1923- *IntWW 91*
**Sigurdson**, Edwin D. 1942- *WhoFI 92*
**Sigurdson**, Jon Frederick Page 1933- *WhoWest 92*
**Sigurdson**, Larry LeRoy 1950- *WhoWest 92*
**Sigurdsson**, Haraldur 1939- *AmMWSc 92*
**Sigurdsson**, Jon 1934- *IntWW 91*
**Sigurdsson**, Jon 1941- *IntWW 91*
**Sigurdsson**, Niels P. 1926- *IntWW 91, Who 92*
**Sigurdsson**, Thordur Baldur 1929- *WhoFI 92*
**Sigworth**, George Fredrick 1956- *WhoAmP 91*
**Sigworth**, Oliver F. 1921- *WrDr 92*
**Sih**, Andrew 1954- *AmMWSc 92*
**Sih**, Charles John *AmMWSc 92*
**Sihag**, Ram K 1950- *AmMWSc 92*
**Sihanouk**, Norodom *IntWW 91*
**Sihanouk**, Norodom 1922- *FacFETw [port]*
**Sihler**, William Wooding 1937- *WhoFI 92*
**Siig**, Arvi 1938- *IntWW 91*
**Siilasvuo**, Ensio 1922- *IntWW 91*
**Siimes**, Jouko 1960- *WhoFI 92*
**Siino**, Lawrence J. 1963- *WhoRel 92*
**Siirala**, Aarne Johannes 1919- *WrDr 92*
**Siirola**, Jeffrey John 1945- *AmMWSc 92*
**Siiteri**, Pentti Kasper 1926- *AmMWSc 92*
**Sij**, John William 1943- *AmMWSc 92*
**Sijpesteijn**, Pieter Johannes 1934- *IntWW 91*
**Sijthoff**, Hendrik Albert Henri 1915- *IntWW 91*
**Sik**, Ota 1919- *IntWW 91*
**Sikand**, Rajinder S *AmMWSc 92*
**Sikarskie**, David L 1937- *AmMWSc 92*
**Sikdar**, Dhirendra N 1930- *AmMWSc 92*
**Sikder**, Santosh K 1949- *AmMWSc 92*
**Sikes**, Alfred C. *LesBEnT 92 [port], WhoAmP 91*
**Sikes**, Alfred C. 1939- *WhoEnt 92, WhoFI 92*
**Sikes**, Cynthia Lee 1954- *WhoEnt 92*
**Sikes**, James Klingman 1924- *AmMWSc 92*
**Sikes**, Melvin Patterson 1917- *WhoBlA 92*
**Sikes**, Shirley *DrAPF 91*
**Sikina**, Thomas 1950- *AmMWSc 92*
**Sikivou**, Semesa Koroikilai 1917- *IntWW 91*
**Sikkema**, Ken *WhoAmP 91*
**Sikkema**, Randal Charles 1960- *WhoRel 92*
**Sikking**, James B. 1934- *IntMPA 92*
**Siklar**, Osman 1929- *IntWW 91*
**Siklosi**, Michael Peter 1948- *AmMWSc 92*
**Siklossy**, Laurent *AmMWSc 92*
**Sikora**, Eugene Stanley 1924- *WhoFI 92*
**Sikora**, Jerome Paul 1947- *AmMWSc 92*
**Sikora**, Joseph Anthony 1953- *WhoFI 92*
**Sikora**, Karol 1948- *Who 92*
**Sikora**, Suzanne Marie 1952- *WhoMW 92*
**Sikorovsky**, Eugene Frank 1927- *WhoAmL 92, WhoFI 92*
**Sikorska**, Hanna 1950- *AmMWSc 92*
**Sikorska**, Marianna 1944- *AmMWSc 92*
**Sikorski**, Gerry 1948- *AlmAP 92 [port], WhoAmP 91, WhoMW 92*
**Sikorski**, James Alan 1948- *AmMWSc 92, WhoMW 92*
**Sikorski**, Wladyslaw 1881-1943 *EncTR 91 [port], FacFETw*
**Sikorsky**, Igor 1889-1972 *DcTwDes [port]*
**Sikorsky**, Igor Ivanovich 1889-1972 *FacFETw*
**Sikoryak**, Kim Eugene 1949- *WhoWest 92*
**Sikov**, Melvin Richard 1928- *AmMWSc 92*
**Sikri**, Atam P 1939- *AmMWSc 92*
**Sikri**, Sarv Mittra 1908- *Who 92*
**Sikula**, Vincent 1936- *IntAu&W 91*
**Sila-On**, Amaret 1933- *IntWW 91*
**Silacci**, Helen Bernadette 1943- *WhoWest 92*
**Silagi**, Selma 1916- *AmMWSc 92*
**Silander**, John August, Jr 1945- *AmMWSc 92*
**Silang**, Diego *HisDSpE*
**Silas**, His Excellency Metropolitan 1919- *WhoRel 92*
**Silas**, Cecil Jesse 1932- *IntWW 91, WhoFI 92*
**Silas**, Dolores Irene *WhoBlA 92*
**Silas**, Jacqueline Ann 1959- *WhoBlA 92*
**Silas**, Paul Theron 1943- *WhoBlA 92*
**Silas**, Richard A 1938- *WhoIns 92*
**Silayev**, Ivan Stepanovich 1930- *IntWW 91*
**Silbajoris**, Frank Rimvydas 1926- *WhoMW 92*
**Silbar**, Richard R 1937- *AmMWSc 92*
**Silbart**, Lawrence K 1958- *AmMWSc 92*
**Silbaugh**, Preston Norwood 1918- *WhoAmL 92, WhoWest 92*
**Silbaugh**, Rudy Lamont 1930- *WhoAmP 91*
**Silbaugh**, Steven A 1949- *AmMWSc 92*
**Silber**, Diana 1936- *ConAu 134*
**Silber**, Frederic Samuel 1952- *WhoEnt 92*
**Silber**, Herbert Bruce 1941- *AmMWSc 92*
**Silber**, Joan *DrAPF 91*
**Silber**, Joan Karen 1945- *IntAu&W 91*
**Silber**, John 1926- *WrDr 92*
**Silber**, John Robert 1926- *IntWW 91*
**Silber**, Norman Isaac 1951- *WhoAmL 92*
**Silber**, Norman Jules 1945- *WhoAmL 92*
**Silber**, Robert 1931- *AmMWSc 92*
**Silber**, Robert 1937- *AmMWSc 92*
**Silber**, Ronald 1946- *WhoAmL 92*
**Silber**, Sherman J. 1941- *WrDr 92*
**Silber**, Stephen Robert 1944- *Who 92*
**Silber**, William L. 1942- *WhoFI 92, WrDr 92*
**Silberberg**, Donald H 1934- *AmMWSc 92*
**Silberberg**, I Harold 1926- *AmMWSc 92*
**Silberberg**, Mary Bickley 1956- *WhoIns 92*
**Silberberg**, Michael Cousins 1940- *WhoAmL 92*
**Silberberg**, Rein 1932- *AmMWSc 92*
**Silberberg**, Ruth 1906- *AmMWSc 92*
**Silberfeld**, Michel 1946- *AmMWSc 92*
**Silberg**, Richard *DrAPF 91*
**Silberg**, Stanley Louis 1927- *AmMWSc 92*
**Silbergeld**, Arthur F. 1942- *WhoAmL 92, WhoWest 92*
**Silbergeld**, Ellen K 1945- *AmMWSc 92*
**Silbergeld**, Mae Driscoll 1923- *AmMWSc 92*
**Silbergeld**, Sam 1918- *AmMWSc 92*
**Silberger**, Allan Joseph 1933- *AmMWSc 92*
**Silberger**, Donald Morison 1930- *AmMWSc 92*
**Silbergleid**, Michael Ian 1964- *WhoEnt 92*
**Silbergleit**, Allen 1928- *AmMWSc 92*
**Silberglitt**, Richard Stephen 1942- *AmMWSc 92*
**Silberhorn**, Gene Michael 1938- *AmMWSc 92*
**Silberling**, Norman John 1928- *AmMWSc 92*
**Silberman**, Arlene *ConAu 133*
**Silberman**, Cary J. 1958- *WhoEnt 92*
**Silberman**, Charles Eliot 1925- *WrDr 92*
**Silberman**, Curt C. 1908- *WhoAmL 92*
**Silberman**, Edward 1914- *AmMWSc 92*
**Silberman**, Enrique 1921- *AmMWSc 92*
**Silberman**, Gregory Alan 1953- *WhoEnt 92*
**Silberman**, H. Lee 1919- *WhoFI 92*
**Silberman**, Irwin Alan 1932- *WhoWest 92*
**Silberman**, James H. 1927- *ConAu 133*
**Silberman**, James Henry 1927- *IntAu&W 91*
**Silberman**, Jeffery Martin 1952- *WhoRel 92*
**Silberman**, Laurence Hirsch 1935- *IntWW 91, WhoAmL 92, WhoAmP 91*
**Silberman**, Lou Hackett 1914- *WhoRel 92*
**Silberman**, Miles Louis 1940- *AmMWSc 92*
**Silberman**, Richard Theodore 1929- *WhoAmP 91*
**Silberman**, Robert G 1939- *AmMWSc 92*
**Silberman**, Ronald 1932- *AmMWSc 92*
**Silberman**, Rosalie Gaull 1937- *WhoAmP 91*
**Silbermann**, Gottfried 1683-1753 *NewAmDM*
**Silbernagel**, Bernard George 1940- *AmMWSc 92*
**Silbernagel**, Matt Joseph 1933- *AmMWSc 92*
**Silberschatz**, Abraham 1947- *AmMWSc 92*
**Silberstein**, Edward B 1936- *AmMWSc 92*
**Silberstein**, Edward Bernard 1936- *WhoMW 92*
**Silberstein**, N. Ronald 1927- *WhoAmL 92, WhoFI 92*
**Silberstein**, Otmar Otto 1921- *AmMWSc 92*
**Silberston**, Aubrey 1922- *IntWW 91, Who 92*
**Silbert**, Amy Foxman 1953- *WhoWest 92*
**Silbert**, David Frederick *AmMWSc 92*
**Silbert**, Irene Selma 1952- *WhoEnt 92*
**Silbert**, Jeremiah Eli *AmMWSc 92*
**Silbert**, Layle *DrAPF 91*
**Silbert**, Leonard Stanton 1920- *AmMWSc 92*
**Silbert**, Stephen D. 1942- *IntMPA 92*
**Silbey**, Joel H 1933- *IntAu&W 91*
**Silbey**, Paul Magic 1938- *WhoEnt 92*
**Silbey**, Robert James 1940- *AmMWSc 92*
**Silcott**, Marvin Leo 1928- *WhoFI 92*
**Silcott**, William L. 1899- *WhoBlA 92*
**Silcox**, Gordon Bruce 1938- *WhoFI 92*
**Silcox**, John 1935- *AmMWSc 92*
**Silcox**, William Henry 1922- *AmMWSc 92*
**Silen**, William 1927- *AmMWSc 92*
**Siler**, Brenda Claire 1953- *WhoBlA 92*
**Siler**, Charles Lewis 1929- *WhoAmP 91*
**Siler**, Eugene Edward, Jr. 1936- *WhoAmL 92*
**Siler**, Freddie Bush 1956- *WhoBlA 92*
**Siler**, Joyce B. 1945- *WhoBlA 92*
**Siler**, Lari Field *DrAPF 91*
**Siler**, Timothy Alan 1951- *WhoAmL 92*
**Siler**, William MacDowell 1920- *AmMWSc 92*
**Siler-Khodr**, Theresa M 1947- *AmMWSc 92*
**Siles Zuazo**, Hernan 1914- *IntWW 91*
**Silesky**, Barry *DrAPF 91*
**Silesky**, Barry 1949- *ConAu 135*
**Silets**, Harvey Marvin 1931- *WhoAmL 92, WhoMW 92*
**Siletti**, Mario d1991 *NewYTBS 91*
**Sileven**, Everett Glen 1939- *WhoRel 92*
**Silevich**, Michael B 1942- *AmMWSc 92*
**Silevitch**, Michael B *AmMWSc 92*
**Silfen**, Lauren B. 1960- *WhoFI 92*
**Silfen**, Martin Elliott 1935- *WhoEnt 92*
**Silfin**, Ira E. 1964- *WhoAmL 92*
**Silflow**, Carolyn Dorothy 1950- *AmMWSc 92*
**Silfvast**, William Thomas 1937- *AmMWSc 92*
**Silhacek**, Donald Le Roy 1937- *AmMWSc 92*
**Silhan**, Paul Henry 1949- *WhoAmL 92*
**Silhavy**, Thomas J 1948- *AmMWSc 92*
**Silja**, Anja 1940- *IntWW 91*
**Siljak**, Dragoslav 1933- *AmMWSc 92*
**Silk**, Alvin John 1935- *WhoFI 92*
**Silk**, David *Who 92*
**Silk**, Dennis 1928- *WrDr 92*
**Silk**, Dennis Raoul Whitehall 1931- *Who 92*
**Silk**, Eleana S. 1951- *WhoRel 92*
**Silk**, Frederick Charles Ziervogel 1934- *WhoFI 92*
**Silk**, Gerald 1947- *ConAu 133*
**Silk**, John Kevin 1938- *AmMWSc 92*
**Silk**, Joseph 1942- *WrDr 92*
**Silk**, Joseph Ivor 1942- *AmMWSc 92*
**Silk**, Leonard 1918- *IntAu&W 91*
**Silk**, Leonard S. 1918- *WrDr 92*
**Silk**, Margaret Wendy Kuhn 1946- *AmMWSc 92*
**Silk**, Marshall Bruce 1955- *WhoWest 92*
**Silk**, Robert David 1936- *Who 92*
**Silk**, Robert K. *Who 92*
**Silke**, William James 1929- *Who 92*
**Silkenat**, James Robert 1947- *WhoAmL 92*
**Silkett**, Robert Tillson 1929- *WhoFI 92*
**Silkin**, Baron *Who 92*
**Silkin**, Lord 1918-1988 *FacFETw*
**Silkin**, Arthur 1916- *Who 92*
**Silkin**, John 1923-1987 *FacFETw*
**Silkin**, Jon 1930- *ConPo 91, IntAu&W 91, IntWW 91, Who 92, WrDr 92*
**Silko**, Leslie 1948- *WrDr 92*
**Silko**, Leslie Marmon *DrAPF 91*
**Silko**, Leslie Marmon 1948- *BenetAL 91, ConNov 91, ConPo 91, TwCWW 91*
**Silkwood**, Karen 1946-1974 *FacFETw*
**Sill**, Alice H *ScFEYrs*
**Sill**, Arthur DeWitt 1921- *AmMWSc 92*
**Sill**, Claude Woodrow 1918- *AmMWSc 92*
**Sill**, Edward Rowland 1841-1887 *BenetAL 91*
**Sill**, Gerald de Schrenck 1917- *WhoFI 92*
**Sill**, Larry R 1937- *AmMWSc 92*
**Sill**, William Lyman, III 1959- *WhoMW 92*
**Sill**, William Robert 1937- *AmMWSc 92*
**Silla**, Harry 1929- *AmMWSc 92*
**Sillah**, Marion Rogers 1945- *WhoBlA 92*
**Sillanpaa**, Frans Eemil 1888-1964 *WhoNob 90*
**Sillanpaa**, Frans Emil 1888-1967 *FacFETw*
**Sillard**, Yves 1936- *IntWW 91*
**Sillari**, Enn-Arno Augustovich 1944- *IntWW 91, SovUnBD*
**Sillars**, James 1937- *Who 92*
**Sillars**, Margo *Who 92*
**Sillars**, Rodger James 1946- *WhoMW 92*
**Sillas**, Herman *WhoHisp 92*
**Sillcocks**, Henry Jackson 1907- *WhoAmL 92*
**Silleck**, Clarence Frederick 1909- *AmMWSc 92*
**Siller**, Stephen I. 1949- *WhoAmL 92, WhoFI 92*
**Sillerman**, Robert F. X. 1948- *WhoFI 92*
**Sillers**, Douglas Hugh 1915- *WhoAmP 91*
**Sillery**, William Moore 1941- *Who 92*
**Sillik**, Dale Alvin 1950- *WhoRel 92*
**Silliker**, John Harold 1922- *AmMWSc 92*
**Silliman**, Benjamin 1779-1864 *BenetAL 91*
**Silliman**, Benjamin, Jr 1816-1885 *BiInAmS*
**Silliman**, Benjamin, Sr 1779-1864 *BiInAmS*
**Silliman**, Benjamin Douglas 1805-1901 *BiInAmS*
**Silliman**, Howard Jeffrey 1944- *WhoRel 92*
**Silliman**, John Emory 1953- *WhoEnt 92*
**Silliman**, Justus Mitchell 1842-1896 *BiInAmS*
**Silliman**, Ralph Parks 1913- *AmMWSc 92*
**Silliman**, Ron *DrAPF 91*
**Silliman**, Ron 1946- *ConPo 91, WrDr 92*
**Sillings**, William H. 1953- *WhoRel 92*
**Silliphant**, Stirling *LesBEnT 92*
**Silliphant**, Stirling 1918- *IntMPA 92*
**Silliphant**, Stirling Dale 1918- *WhoEnt 92*
**Sillitoe**, Alan 1928- *CnDBLB 8 [port], ConNov 91, ConPo 91, FacFETw, IntAu&W 91, IntWW 91, RfGEnL 91, Who 92, WrDr 92*
**Sillitoe**, Leslie Richard 1915- *Who 92*
**Sillman**, Emmanuel I 1915- *AmMWSc 92*
**Sillman**, Herbert Phillip 1927- *WhoFI 92*
**Silloway**, Benton, Jr. 1941- *WhoFI 92*
**Sills**, Beverly 1929- *FacFETw, IntWW 91, NewAmDM, Who 92, WhoEnt 92*
**Sills**, Brian George 1960- *WhoMW 92*
**Sills**, David George 1938- *WhoWest 92*
**Sills**, Gregory D. 1950- *WhoBlA 92*
**Sills**, James H, Jr *WhoAmP 91*
**Sills**, Marvin G. 1949- *WhoBlA 92*
**Sills**, Matthew A 1955- *AmMWSc 92*
**Sills**, Paul 1927- *WhoEnt 92*
**Sills**, Thomas Albert 1914- *WhoBlA 92*
**Sills**, William Henry, III 1936- *WhoFI 92, WhoMW 92*
**Sills-Docherty**, Jonathon John 1941- *IntAu&W 91*
**Silly**, E. S. *SmATA 65*
**Silman**, Roberta *DrAPF 91*
**Silman**, Roberta 1934- *IntAu&W 91, WrDr 92*
**Silon**, Theodore Clifford 1961- *WhoEnt 92*
**Silone**, Ignazio 1900-1978 *ConAu 34NR, FacFETw, LiExTwC*
**Silsbee**, Henry Briggs 1923- *AmMWSc 92*
**Silsbee**, Robert Herman 1929- *AmMWSc 92*
**Silsoe**, Baron 1930- *Who 92*
**Siltanen**, John Carl 1913- *WhoFI 92*
**Silungwe**, Annel Musenga 1936- *IntWW 91*
**Silva**, Aida L. 1963- *WhoHisp 92*
**Silva**, Albert M. 1959- *WhoFI 92*
**Silva**, Alejandro *WhoHisp 92*
**Silva**, Alvaro 1949- *WhoHisp 92*
**Silva**, Antonio Vidal 1951- *WhoHisp 92*
**Silva**, Armand Joseph 1931- *AmMWSc 92*
**Silva**, Arthur P. 1950- *WhoBlA 92*
**Silva**, Aurelia Davila de 1946- *WhoHisp 92*
**Silva**, Beverly *DrAPF 91*
**Silva**, Cesar E. 1955- *WhoHisp 92*
**Silva**, Daniel P *WhoAmP 91, WhoHisp 92*
**Silva**, David 1944- *WhoHisp 92*
**Silva**, David B. 1939- *WhoHisp 92*
**Silva**, Don 1936- *WhoHisp 92*
**Silva**, Donald George 1936- *WhoAmP 91*
**Silva**, Edward John 1944- *WhoHisp 92*
**Silva**, Eugene Joseph 1942- *WhoAmL 92*
**Silva**, Felipe 1919- *WhoHisp 92*
**Silva**, Felipe Rafael, Jr. 1949- *WhoHisp 92*
**Silva**, Flavio J. 1946- *WhoHisp 92*
**Silva**, Francisco 1942- *WhoHisp 92*
**Silva**, Gaston 1953- *WhoHisp 92*
**Silva**, Henriquez Raul 1907- *WhoRel 92*
**Silva**, Henry 1928- *IntMPA 92, WhoHisp 92*
**Silva**, Henry Andrew 1924- *WhoBlA 92*

**Silva,** James Anthony 1930- *AmMWSc 92*
**Silva,** Joan *DrAPF 91*
**Silva,** Jose 1914- *WhoHisp 92*
**Silva,** Jose A., Jr. *WhoHisp 92*
**Silva,** Jose A., Sr. *WhoHisp 92*
**Silva,** Jose Asuncion 1865-1896 *BenetAL 91*
**Silva,** Joseph *TwCSFW 91*
**Silva,** Juan L. 1957- *WhoHisp 92*
**Silva,** Kittim 1950- *WhoRel 92*
**Silva,** Leonel B. 1940- *WhoHisp 92*
**Silva,** Mary Delores 1932- *WhoRel 92*
**Silva,** Moises 1945- *WhoHisp 92*
**Silva,** Omega C. Logan 1936- *WhoBlA 92*
**Silva,** Omega Logan 1936- *AmMWSc 92*
**Silva,** Patricio 1939- *AmMWSc 92*
**Silva,** Paul Claude 1922- *AmMWSc 92*
**Silva,** Pedro 1943- *WhoHisp 92*
**Silva,** Ricardo 1931- *AmMWSc 92*
**Silva,** Richard Robert 1922- *WhoAmP 91*
**Silva,** Ro 1959- *WhoWest 92*
**Silva,** Robert Joseph 1927- *AmMWSc 92*
**Silva,** Robert Owen 1935- *WhoWest 92*
**Silva,** Robert Russell 1928- *WhoHisp 92*
**Silva,** Rolando A 1945- *WhoAmP 91, WhoHisp 92*
**Silva,** Ruth Caridad 1920- *WhoHisp 92*
**Silva,** Ubirajara Da Costa E. 1921- *WhoFI 92*
**Silva,** Victor Daniel 1955- *WhoHisp 92*
**Silva-Ayala,** Jose Enrique 1946- *WhoHisp 92*
**Silva-Concha,** Mario 1924- *IntWW 91*
**Silva-Corvalan,** Carmen 1941- *WhoHisp 92*
**Silva Fuentes,** Ramon 1933- *WhoHisp 92*
**Silva Henriquez,** Raul 1907- *IntWW 91*
**Silva Herzog,** Jesus *IntWW 91*
**Silva-Hutner,** Margarita 1915- *AmMWSc 92*
**Silva-Netto,** Benoni Reyes 1944- *WhoRel 92*
**Silva Ortiz,** Walter Ivan 1956- *WhoHisp 92*
**Silva-Ruiz,** Pedro F. 1943- *WhoHisp 92*
**Silvati,** John Donald 1937- *WhoFI 92*
**Silveira,** Augustine, Jr 1934- *AmMWSc 92*
**Silveira,** Milton Anthony 1929- *AmMWSc 92*
**Silver,** Abba Hillel 1893-1963 *RelLAm 91*
**Silver,** Adele Zeidman 1932- *WhoMW 92*
**Silver,** Alain Joel 1947- *WhoEnt 92*
**Silver,** Alain Irving 1949- *WhoAmL 92*
**Silver,** Alan Richard 1952- *WhoAmP 91*
**Silver,** Alene Freudenheim 1916- *AmMWSc 92*
**Silver,** Andrew James 1956- *WhoFI 92*
**Silver,** Arnold Herbert 1931- *AmMWSc 92*
**Silver,** B Jean 1926- *WhoAmP 91*
**Silver,** Barnard Stewart 1933- *AmMWSc 92, WhoFI 92, WhoWest 92*
**Silver,** Barry Morris 1956- *WhoAmL 92*
**Silver,** Bella Wolfson 1937- *WhoMW 92*
**Silver,** Bert 1931- *WhoAmP 91*
**Silver,** Carol Ruth 1938- *WhoAmL 92*
**Silver,** Christopher *DrAPF 91*
**Silver,** Clinton Vita 1929- *Who 92*
**Silver,** Daniel Ben 1941- *WhoAmL 92*
**Silver,** David Martin 1941- *AmMWSc 92*
**Silver,** David Mitchell 1960- *WhoRel 92*
**Silver,** Donald 1929- *AmMWSc 92, WhoMW 92*
**Silver,** Edward A 1948- *AmMWSc 92*
**Silver,** Edward Allan 1937- *AmMWSc 92*
**Silver,** Eli Alfred 1942- *AmMWSc 92*
**Silver,** Eliezer 1882-1968 *RelLAm 91*
**Silver,** Eric 1935- *WrDr 92*
**Silver,** Eric Aaron 1942- *WhoRel 92*
**Silver,** Ernest Gerard 1929- *AmMWSc 92*
**Silver,** Ethel Marie 1926- *WhoAmP 91*
**Silver,** Francis 1916- *AmMWSc 92*
**Silver,** Franelle Lynne 1952- *WhoEnt 92*
**Silver,** Frank Morris 1943- *AmMWSc 92*
**Silver,** Gary Lee 1936- *AmMWSc 92*
**Silver,** George 1918- *WhoFI 92, WhoMW 92*
**Silver,** George Albert 1913- *AmMWSc 92*
**Silver,** Harold 1928- *WrDr 92*
**Silver,** Henry K 1918- *AmMWSc 92*
**Silver,** Herbert Graham 1938- *AmMWSc 92*
**Silver,** Horace 1928- *NewAmDM*
**Silver,** Horace Ward Martin Tavares 1928- *WhoBlA 92*
**Silver,** Howard *DrAPF 91*
**Silver,** Howard 1925- *WhoAmL 92*
**Silver,** Howard Findlay 1930- *AmMWSc 92*
**Silver,** Howard I 1939- *AmMWSc 92*
**Silver,** Hulbert Keyes Belford 1941- *AmMWSc 92*
**Silver,** Ian Adair 1927- *Who 92*
**Silver,** Idora 1948- *WhoWest 92*
**Silver,** Jack *AmMWSc 92*
**Silver,** James Allen 1933- *WhoWest 92*
**Silver,** Jane Hastings 1938- *WhoAmL 92*
**Silver,** Joan Micklin *ReelWom*
**Silver,** Joan Micklin 1935- *IntDcF 2-2 [port], IntMPA 92, IntWW 91, WhoEnt 92*
**Silver,** Joel *IntMPA 92*
**Silver,** Joel 1939- *ConTFT 9*
**Silver,** Jonathan Edward 1949- *WhoFI 92, WhoWest 92*
**Silver,** Joseph Howard, Sr. 1953- *WhoBlA 92*
**Silver,** Lani Judith 1948- *WhoWest 92*
**Silver,** Lawrence 1921- *AmMWSc 92*
**Silver,** Lawrence Alan 1943- *WhoFI 92*
**Silver,** Lee Merrill 1952- *AmMWSc 92*
**Silver,** Leon J. 1918- *IntMPA 92*
**Silver,** Leon Theodore 1925- *AmMWSc 92*
**Silver,** Lynn Alison 1959- *WhoWest 92*
**Silver,** Malcolm David 1933- *AmMWSc 92*
**Silver,** Marc 1951- *WhoRel 92*
**Silver,** Marc Laurence 1953- *WhoFI 92*
**Silver,** Marc Stamm 1934- *AmMWSc 92*
**Silver,** Marisa 1960- *IntMPA 92*
**Silver,** Marshall Lawrence 1942- *AmMWSc 92*
**Silver,** Martin 1941- *WhoAmL 92*
**Silver,** Marvin 1924- *AmMWSc 92*
**Silver,** Mary Wilcox 1941- *AmMWSc 92*
**Silver,** Melvin Joel 1920- *AmMWSc 92*
**Silver,** Meyer 1926- *AmMWSc 92*
**Silver,** Michael Joel 1955- *WhoAmL 92*
**Silver,** Milton *IntMPA 92*
**Silver,** Nicholas *TwCWW 91*
**Silver,** Nina *DrAPF 91*
**Silver,** Paul Allen 1950- *WhoAmL 92*
**Silver,** Paul J 1951- *AmMWSc 92*
**Silver,** Paul Matthew 1951- *WhoAmL 92*
**Silver,** Paul Robert 1931- *WhoFI 92*
**Silver,** Perrys Samuel 1946- *WhoAmL 92*
**Silver,** Peter Hele S. *Who 92*
**Silver,** Raphael D. 1930- *IntMPA 92*
**Silver,** Richard *IntAu&W 91X, WrDr 92*
**Silver,** Richard N 1945- *AmMWSc 92*
**Silver,** Richard Tobias 1929- *AmMWSc 92*
**Silver,** Robert 1921- *AmMWSc 92*
**Silver,** Robert Simpson 1913- *IntWW 91, Who 92*
**Silver,** Roger Allen 1945- *WhoAmL 92*
**Silver,** Ron 1946- *IntMPA 92, WhoEnt 92*
**Silver,** Ronald A 1943- *WhoAmP 91*
**Silver,** Ruth M. *DrAPF 91*
**Silver,** Samuel Manuel 1912- *WhoRel 92*
**Silver,** Scott Roger 1953- *WhoWest 92*
**Silver,** Sheldon 1944- *WhoAmP 91*
**Silver,** Simon David 1936- *AmMWSc 92*
**Silver,** Stanley Marvin 1920- *WhoFI 92*
**Silver,** Steve 1944- *WhoEnt 92*
**Silver,** Steven Harris 1941- *WhoMW 92*
**Silver,** Steven William 1951- *WhoAmL 92*
**Silver,** Susan Lee 1952- *WhoEnt 92*
**Silver,** Sylvia 1942- *AmMWSc 92*
**Silver,** Warren Seymour 1924- *AmMWSc 92*
**Silvera,** Isaac F 1937- *AmMWSc 92*
**Silverbach,** Alan M. *LesBEnT 92*
**Silverberg,** Herbert Myron 1939- *WhoAmL 92*
**Silverberg,** Mark Victor 1957- *WhoAmL 92*
**Silverberg,** Robert 1935- *BenetAL 91, ConAu 36NR, IntAu&W 91, TwCSFW 91, WhoWest 92, WrDr 92*
**Silverberg,** Stanley J. 1940- *WhoAmL 92*
**Silverberg,** Steven George 1938- *AmMWSc 92*
**Silverberg,** Steven Mark 1947- *WhoAmL 92*
**Silverberg,** Stuart Owen 1931- *WhoWest 92*
**Silverborg,** Savel Benhard 1913- *AmMWSc 92*
**Silverfine,** Jeremy I. 1957- *WhoAmL 92*
**Silverglat,** Alan Gregory 1946- *WhoFI 92*
**Silverleaf,** Alexander 1920- *Who 92*
**Silverlock,** Anne *WrDr 92*
**Silverman,** Alan H. 1954- *WhoAmL 92, WhoEnt 92*
**Silverman,** Albert 1919- *AmMWSc 92*
**Silverman,** Albert A. 1908- *WhoAmL 92, WhoFI 92, WhoMW 92*
**Silverman,** Albert Jack 1925- *AmMWSc 92*
**Silverman,** Ann Judith 1946- *AmMWSc 92*
**Silverman,** Arnold Barry 1937- *WhoAmL 92, WhoFI 92*
**Silverman,** Arthur Charles 1938- *WhoAmL 92*
**Silverman,** Benjamin David 1931- *AmMWSc 92*
**Silverman,** Bernard 1922- *AmMWSc 92*
**Silverman,** Charlotte 1913- *AmMWSc 92*
**Silverman,** David Charles 1947- *WhoMW 92*
**Silverman,** David J 1943- *AmMWSc 92*
**Silverman,** David Norman 1942- *AmMWSc 92*
**Silverman,** Dennis Joseph 1941- *AmMWSc 92*
**Silverman,** Edward 1917- *AmMWSc 92*
**Silverman,** Ellen 1942- *WhoMW 92*
**Silverman,** Ellen-Marie 1942- *AmMWSc 92*
**Silverman,** Eric F. 1954- *WhoFI 92*
**Silverman,** Faye-Ellen 1947- *WhoEnt 92*
**Silverman,** Franklin Harold 1933- *AmMWSc 92*
**Silverman,** Fred *LesBEnT 92*
**Silverman,** Fred 1937- *IntMPA 92, IntWW 91, WhoEnt 92*
**Silverman,** Gary Mark 1961- *WhoFI 92*
**Silverman,** Gary Wayne 1939- *WhoMW 92*
**Silverman,** George Alan 1946- *WhoEnt 92*
**Silverman,** Gerald 1925- *AmMWSc 92*
**Silverman,** Gerry 1938- *ConAu 133*
**Silverman,** Gordon 1934- *AmMWSc 92*
**Silverman,** Harold 1950- *AmMWSc 92*
**Silverman,** Harold I 1928- *AmMWSc 92*
**Silverman,** Herbert Philip 1924- *AmMWSc 92*
**Silverman,** Herschel *DrAPF 91*
**Silverman,** Hillel E. 1924- *WhoRel 92*
**Silverman,** Hirsch Lazaar *IntAu&W 91*
**Silverman,** Howard 1936- *TwCPaSc*
**Silverman,** Hugh Richard 1940- *Who 92*
**Silverman,** Ira 1945-1991 *NewYTBS 91*
**Silverman,** Ira Norton 1935- *WhoEnt 92*
**Silverman,** Jacob 1923- *AmMWSc 92*
**Silverman,** Jeffrey Alan *AmMWSc 92*
**Silverman,** Jerald 1942- *AmMWSc 92*
**Silverman,** Jerome 1936- *WhoWest 92*
**Silverman,** Jerry 1931- *WrDr 92*
**Silverman,** Jim 1950- *IntMPA 92*
**Silverman,** Joel 1952- *WhoEnt 92*
**Silverman,** Joseph 1922- *AmMWSc 92*
**Silverman,** Joseph Elias 1931- *WhoAmL 92*
**Silverman,** Judith Louise 1947- *WhoMW 92*
**Silverman,** Julius 1905- *Who 92*
**Silverman,** Kenneth 1936- *DcLB 111 [port]*
**Silverman,** Lee C. 1962- *WhoAmL 92*
**Silverman,** Leonard *AmMWSc 92*
**Silverman,** Martin Isaac 1927- *WhoRel 92*
**Silverman,** Mary Delson *WhoEnt 92*
**Silverman,** Maxine *DrAPF 91*
**Silverman,** Melvin 1940- *AmMWSc 92*
**Silverman,** Meyer David 1915- *AmMWSc 92*
**Silverman,** Michael Robert 1943- *AmMWSc 92*
**Silverman,** Michael William 1957- *WhoMW 92*
**Silverman,** Morris 1926- *AmMWSc 92*
**Silverman,** Morris Bernard 1924- *AmMWSc 92*
**Silverman,** Myron Simeon 1915- *AmMWSc 92*
**Silverman,** Norman A 1946- *AmMWSc 92*
**Silverman,** Paul Hyman 1924- *AmMWSc 92*
**Silverman,** Philip Michael 1942- *AmMWSc 92*
**Silverman,** Richard 1925- *WhoFI 92*
**Silverman,** Richard Bruce 1946- *AmMWSc 92*
**Silverman,** Richard Lee 1945- *WhoWest 92*
**Silverman,** Robert 1928- *AmMWSc 92, WhoMW 92*
**Silverman,** Robert 1938- *WhoEnt 92*
**Silverman,** Robert 1945- *WhoFI 92*
**Silverman,** Robert Alan 1947- *WhoAmL 92*
**Silverman,** Robert Eliot 1950- *AmMWSc 92*
**Silverman,** Robert Hugh 1948- *AmMWSc 92*
**Silverman,** Robert Joseph 1925- *WhoEnt 92*
**Silverman,** Robert Joseph 1942- *WhoAmL 92*
**Silverman,** Robert Malcolm Reuven 1947- *WhoRel 92*
**Silverman,** Ron 1933- *IntMPA 92*
**Silverman,** Ronald I. 1939- *WhoAmL 92, WhoWest 92*
**Silverman,** Sam M 1925- *AmMWSc 92*
**Silverman,** Sherri *DrAPF 91*
**Silverman,** Sol Richard 1911- *AmMWSc 92*
**Silverman,** Sol Robert 1918- *AmMWSc 92*
**Silverman,** Stanley J. 1938- *NewAmDM*
**Silverman,** Stanley Wayne 1947- *WhoFI 92*
**Silverman,** Stephen M. 1951- *ConAu 135*
**Silverman,** Steven 1957- *WhoAmL 92*
**Silverman,** Syd 1932- *IntMPA 92*
**Silverman,** William Bernard 1932- *AmMWSc 92*
**Silverman,** Zita 1949- *WhoIns 92*
**Silvern,** Leonard C. 1919- *WrDr 92*
**Silvern,** Leonard Charles 1919- *AmMWSc 92, WhoWest 92*
**Silvernail,** Roy Marck 1956- *WhoEnt 92*
**Silvernail,** Walter Lawrence 1921- *AmMWSc 92, WhoMW 92*
**Silvers,** J P 1920- *AmMWSc 92*
**Silvers,** Phil d1985 *LesBEnT 92*
**Silvers,** Phil 1912-1985 *FacFETw*
**Silvers,** Willys Kent 1929- *AmMWSc 92*
**Silversmith,** Ernest Frank 1930- *AmMWSc 92*
**Silverstein,** Abe 1908- *AmMWSc 92*
**Silverstein,** Alexander 1900- *AmMWSc 92*
**Silverstein,** Alvin 1933- *ChlLR 25 [port]*
**Silverstein,** Arthur M 1928- *AmMWSc 92*
**Silverstein,** Barry David 1948- *WhoFI 92*
**Silverstein,** Calvin C 1929- *AmMWSc 92*
**Silverstein,** David 1955- *WhoRel 92, WhoWest 92*
**Silverstein,** Edward Allen 1930- *AmMWSc 92*
**Silverstein,** Elliot 1927- *IntMPA 92*
**Silverstein,** Elliot Morton 1928- *AmMWSc 92*
**Silverstein,** Emanuel 1930- *AmMWSc 92*
**Silverstein,** Herbert 1935- *AmMWSc 92*
**Silverstein,** Herma 1945- *IntAu&W 91*
**Silverstein,** Jack 1915- *WhoAmP 91*
**Silverstein,** Joseph 1932- *NewAmDM*
**Silverstein,** Joseph Harry 1932- *WhoWest 92*
**Silverstein,** Martin Elliot 1922- *AmMWSc 92, WhoWest 92*
**Silverstein,** Martin L 1939- *AmMWSc 92*
**Silverstein,** Maurice 1912- *IntMPA 92*
**Silverstein,** Michael 1954- *WhoFI 92, WhoMW 92*
**Silverstein,** Morton *LesBEnT 92*
**Silverstein,** Richard *WhoWest 92*
**Silverstein,** Richard 1939- *AmMWSc 92*
**Silverstein,** Robert Milton 1916- *AmMWSc 92*
**Silverstein,** Samuel Charles 1937- *AmMWSc 92*
**Silverstein,** Saul Jay 1946- *AmMWSc 92*
**Silverstein,** Shel 1932- *IntAu&W 91, WrDr 92*
**Silverstein,** Theodore 1904- *WrDr 92*
**Silverstein,** Virginia B 1937- *ChlLR 25 [port]*
**Silverstone,** Harris Julian 1939- *AmMWSc 92*
**Silvert,** William Lawrence 1937- *AmMWSc 92*
**Silverthorn,** Dee Unglaub 1948- *AmMWSc 92*
**Silverthorn,** Gloria Jean 1951- *WhoEnt 92, WhoWest 92*
**Silverton,** James Vincent 1934- *AmMWSc 92*
**Silverton,** Mike *DrAPF 91*
**Silvertooth-Stewart,** John 1952- *WhoAmP 91*
**Silvertrust,** Raymond Harvey Rawlins 1946- *WhoMW 92*
**Silverwood,** Harry Edward, Jr. 1934- *WhoAmL 92*
**Silverwood,** Jane *WrDr 92*
**Silverwood-Cope,** Maclachlan Alan Carl 1915- *Who 92*
**Silvester,** Frank *IntAu&W 91X, TwCWW 91*
**Silvester,** Frederick John 1933- *Who 92*
**Silvester,** John Andrew 1950- *AmMWSc 92, WhoWest 92*
**Silvester,** P.P. 1935- *ConAu 135*
**Silvester,** Peter 1934- *ConAu 133*
**Silvester,** Peter Peet 1935- *AmMWSc 92*
**Silveston,** Peter Lewis 1931- *AmMWSc 92*
**Silvestre,** Armand 1837-1901 *ThHEIm*
**Silvestre,** Theophile 1823-1876 *ThHEIm*
**Silvestri,** Anthony John 1936- *AmMWSc 92*
**Silvestri,** George J, Jr 1927- *AmMWSc 92*
**Silvestri,** Michael Joseph 1958- *WhoFI 92*
**Silvestrini,** Achille 1923- *IntWW 91, WhoRel 92*
**Silvestris,** Elaine Joy 1943- *WhoFI 92*
**Silvestro,** Brian Thomas 1949- *WhoAmL 92*
**Silvette,** Herbert 1907- *AmMWSc 92*
**Silvey,** Daniel Joseph 1956- *WhoFI 92*
**Silvey,** Edward 1937- *WhoBlA 92*
**Silvey,** Gregory Gordon 1960- *WhoAmL 92*
**Silvey,** J K Gwynn 1907- *AmMWSc 92*
**Silvey,** Len 1943- *WhoWest 92*
**Silvia,** Charles E *WhoAmP 91*
**Silvia,** John Edwin 1948- *WhoFI 92*
**Silvidi,** Anthony Alfred 1920- *AmMWSc 92*
**Silvious,** Stephen Calvin 1953- *WhoEnt 92*
**Silvis,** Donn Eugene 1942- *WhoWest 92*
**Silvis,** Randall *DrAPF 91*
**Silvius,** Douglas Dean 1962- *WhoAmL 92*
**Silvius,** John Edward 1947- *AmMWSc 92*
**Silzars,** Aris 1940- *AmMWSc 92*
**Silzer,** Scot A. 1952- *WhoAmL 92*
**Sim,** Finlay Bruce 1954- *WhoFI 92*
**Sim,** Georges *ConAu 35NR*
**Sim,** John Kim-Chye 1957- *WhoRel 92*
**Sim,** John Mackay 1917- *Who 92*
**Sim,** Katharine Phyllis 1913- *WrDr 92*
**Sima,** Edward Donald 1929- *WhoFI 92*

**Sima**, Horia 1906- *BiDExR, EncTR 91 [port]*
**Simaan**, Marwan 1946- *AmMWSc 92*
**Simai**, Mihaly 1930- *IntWW 91*
**Simak**, Clifford D. 1904- *BenetAL 91, IntAu&W 91*
**Simak**, Clifford D 1904-1988 *ConAu 35NR, TwCSFW 91*
**Siman**, Jaime Ernesto 1954- *WhoWest 92*
**Siman**, Scott Foster 1954- *WhoEnt 92*
**Simanek**, Eugen 1933- *AmMWSc 92*
**Simanski**, John Francis, Jr. 1951- *WhoAmL 92*
**Simantel**, Gerald M 1934- *AmMWSc 92*
**Simapichaicheth**, Pratak 1941- *WhoFI 92*
**Simard**, Albert Joseph 1942- *AmMWSc 92*
**Simard**, Gerald Lionel 1912- *AmMWSc 92*
**Simard**, Rene 1935- *AmMWSc 92*
**Simard**, Ronald E 1939- *AmMWSc 92*
**Simard**, Therese Gabrielle 1928- *AmMWSc 92*
**Simas**, Joseph Hamilton 1958- *IntAu&W 91*
**Simatupang**, Tahi Bonar 1920- *IntWW 91*
**Simatupang**, Tahi Bonar 1920-1990 *DcEcMov*
**Simba**, Iddi 1935- *IntWW 91*
**Simbanaiye**, Artemon 1935- *IntWW 91*
**Simberloff**, Daniel S 1942- *AmMWSc 92*
**Simbomana**, Adrien *IntWW 91*
**Simburg**, Earl Joseph 1915- *WhoWest 92*
**Simchowitz**, Louis *AmMWSc 92*
**Simckes**, Lazare Seymore *DrAPF 91*
**Simco**, Bill Al 1938- *AmMWSc 92*
**Simcock**, Jack 1929- *TwCPaSc*
**Simcox**, Edwin Jesse 1945- *WhoAmP 91*
**Simcox**, Jeffrey Horace 1948- *WhoAmL 92*
**Simcox**, Jesse Willard 1915- *WhoAmP 91*
**Simcox**, Richard Alfred 1915- *Who 92*
**Sime**, David Gilbert 1948- *AmMWSc 92*
**Sime**, Mary 1911- *WrDr 92*
**Sime**, Rodney J 1931- *AmMWSc 92*
**Sime**, Ruth Lewin 1939- *AmMWSc 92*
**Simenon**, Georges 1903- *IntAu&W 91*
**Simenon**, Georges 1903-1989 *ConAu 35NR, FacFETw, GuFrLit 1*
**Simenstad**, Charles Arthur 1947- *AmMWSc 92*
**Simeon**, Bettie Louise Ross 1948- *WhoEnt 92, WhoWest 92*
**Simeon**, George John 1934- *AmMWSc 92*
**Simeon**, John Edmund Barrington 1911- *Who 92*
**Simeon**, John Power Barrington 1929- *Who 92*
**Simeon Negrin**, Rosa Elena 1943- *IntWW 91*
**Simeone**, Fiorindo Anthony 1908- *AmMWSc 92*
**Simeone**, John Babtista 1919- *AmMWSc 92*
**Simeone**, Reginald Nicola 1927- *Who 92*
**Simeonov**, Konstantin Arsen'evich 1910- *SovUnBD*
**Simeons**, Charles Fitzmaurice Creighton 1921- *Who 92*
**Simeral**, Robert Thomas 1922- *WhoEnt 92*
**Simeral**, William Goodrich 1926- *AmMWSc 92*
**Simerl**, L E 1911- *AmMWSc 92*
**Simerly**, Robert G. 1939- *WhoMW 92*
**Simes**, Stephen Mark 1951- *WhoMW 92*
**Simha**, Bharat Kesher 1934- *Who 92*
**Simha**, Robert 1912- *AmMWSc 92, WhoMW 92*
**Simhai**, Faramarz 1946- *WhoMW 92*
**Simhan**, Raj 1933- *AmMWSc 92*
**Simhauser**, Val C. 1954- *WhoAmL 92*
**Simic**, Charles *DrAPF 91*
**Simic**, Charles 1938- *BenetAL 91, ConLC 68 [port], ConPo 91, IntWW 91, WrDr 92*
**Simic**, Michael G 1932- *AmMWSc 92*
**Simien**, Cynthia Regina 1952- *WhoAmP 91*
**Similon**, Philippe Louis 1953- *AmMWSc 92*
**Simini**, Joseph Peter 1921- *WhoWest 92*
**Siminoff**, Paul 1923- *AmMWSc 92*
**Siminovitch**, Louis 1920- *AmMWSc 92, IntWW 91, Who 92*
**Simion**, Eugen I. 1933- *IntWW 91*
**Simionato**, Giulietta 1910- *NewAmDM*
**Simionato**, Giulietta 1912- *WhoEnt 92*
**Simionescu**, Mircea Horia 1928- *IntAu&W 91*
**Simitis**, Constantine 1936- *IntWW 91*
**Simitses**, George John 1932- *AmMWSc 92*
**Simiu**, Emil 1934- *AmMWSc 92*
**Simkanich**, John Joseph 1941- *WhoAmL 92*
**Simkhovitch**, Mary Kingsbury 1867- *DcAmImH*
**Simkin**, Benjamin 1921- *AmMWSc 92*
**Simkin**, Donald Jules 1925- *AmMWSc 92*
**Simkin**, Morris N. 1941- *WhoAmL 92, WhoFI 92*
**Simkin**, Susan Marguerite 1940- *AmMWSc 92*
**Simkin**, Thomas Edward 1933- *AmMWSc 92*
**Simkin**, William E. 1907- *IntWW 91*
**Simkins**, Charles Abraham 1923- *AmMWSc 92*
**Simkins**, Charles Anthony Goodall 1912- *Who 92*
**Simkins**, George Christopher 1924- *WhoBlA 92*
**Simkins**, Karl LeRoy, Jr 1939- *AmMWSc 92*
**Simkins**, Lawrence David 1933- *WhoMW 92*
**Simkins**, Modjeska 1899- *NotBlAW 92 [port]*
**Simkover**, Harold George 1923- *AmMWSc 92*
**Simkovich**, George 1928- *AmMWSc 92*
**Simler**, Cecil Murl 1915- *WhoMW 92*
**Simler**, George B 1921-1972 *FacFETw*
**Simmang**, C M 1912- *AmMWSc 92*
**Simmel**, Edward Clemens 1932- *AmMWSc 92, WhoWest 92*
**Simmel**, Marianne Lenore *WhoEnt 92*
**Simmelkjaer**, Robert T. *WhoBlA 92*
**Simmer**, Thomas Frank 1951- *WhoMW 92*
**Simmerman**, Jim *DrAPF 91*
**Simmerman**, Jim 1952- *IntAu&W 91*
**Simmie**, James 1941- *WrDr 92*
**Simmon**, Vincent Fowler 1943- *AmMWSc 92, WhoFI 92*
**Simmonds**, Andrew Jeffrey 1943- *WhoWest 92*
**Simmonds**, Donald Lee 1935- *WhoRel 92*
**Simmonds**, James G 1935- *AmMWSc 92*
**Simmonds**, John 1942- *ConAu 135*
**Simmonds**, Kennedy Alphonse 1936- *IntWW 91, Who 92*
**Simmonds**, Kenneth Royston 1927- *Who 92*
**Simmonds**, Kenneth Willison 1912- *Who 92*
**Simmonds**, Posy 1945- *Who 92*
**Simmonds**, Randy James 1951- *WhoRel 92*
**Simmonds**, Richard Carroll 1940- *AmMWSc 92*
**Simmonds**, Richard James 1944- *Who 92*
**Simmonds**, Robert T 1932- *AmMWSc 92*
**Simmonds**, Sidney Herbert 1931- *AmMWSc 92*
**Simmonds**, Sofia 1917- *AmMWSc 92*
**Simmonds**, Stanley 1917- *TwCPaSc*
**Simmonds**, Wilfred John 1918- *IntWW 91*
**Simmonds**, William 1876-1968 *TwCPaSc*
**Simmons**, Adele Smith 1941- *CurBio 91 [port], IntWW 91*
**Simmons**, Alan Gerald 1936- *Who 92*
**Simmons**, Alan J 1924- *AmMWSc 92*
**Simmons**, Albert Bufort, Jr. 1943- *WhoBlA 92*
**Simmons**, Allison Paul 1934- *WhoAmP 91*
**Simmons**, Althea T L 1924-1990 *NotBlAW 92, WhoBlA 92N*
**Simmons**, Annie Marie 1949- *WhoBlA 92*
**Simmons**, Anthony *IntMPA 92*
**Simmons**, Arthur Hugh 1899- *WhoBlA 92*
**Simmons**, Barbara Lett 1927- *WhoAmP 91*
**Simmons**, Belva Tereshia 1927- *WhoBlA 92*
**Simmons**, Beverly Janet 1950- *WhoEnt 92*
**Simmons**, Blake *ConAu 35NR*
**Simmons**, Bonnie Anderson 1943- *WhoMW 92*
**Simmons**, Brad Lee 1960- *WhoFI 92*
**Simmons**, Bradley Williams 1941- *WhoFI 92, WhoWest 92*
**Simmons**, Calvin 1950-1982 *NewAmDM*
**Simmons**, Cecil Lamar 1946- *WhoAmP 91*
**Simmons**, Charles *DrAPF 91*
**Simmons**, Charles Bedford, Jr. 1956- *WhoAmL 92*
**Simmons**, Charles Douglas 1953- *WhoAmL 92*
**Simmons**, Charles Edward 1927- *AmMWSc 92*
**Simmons**, Charles Ferdinand 1910- *AmMWSc 92*
**Simmons**, Charles William 1938- *WhoBlA 92*
**Simmons**, Chester R. *LesBEnT 92*
**Simmons**, Christopher Lanny 1963- *WhoRel 92*
**Simmons**, Clayton Lloyd 1918- *WhoBlA 92*
**Simmons**, Clinton Craig 1947- *WhoFI 92*
**Simmons**, D. R. 1930- *WrDr 92*
**Simmons**, Daniel Harold 1919- *AmMWSc 92*
**Simmons**, Daniel L 1955- *AmMWSc 92*
**Simmons**, Daniel Lee 1946- *WhoAmL 92*
**Simmons**, Daryl Michael 1952- *AmMWSc 92*
**Simmons**, David J 1931- *AmMWSc 92*
**Simmons**, David Norman 1957- *WhoAmL 92*
**Simmons**, David Rae 1940- *AmMWSc 92*
**Simmons**, Deidre Warner 1955- *WhoEnt 92*
**Simmons**, Devane T., Jr. 1956- *WhoRel 92*
**Simmons**, Dick Bedford 1937- *AmMWSc 92*
**Simmons**, Donald Glick 1938- *AmMWSc 92*
**Simmons**, Donald M. 1935- *WhoBlA 92*
**Simmons**, Earl Melvin 1931- *WhoBlA 92*
**Simmons**, Ellamae 1919- *WhoBlA 92*
**Simmons**, Emmett Bryson, III 1953- *WhoBlA 92, WhoEnt 92*
**Simmons**, Emory Guy 1920- *AmMWSc 92*
**Simmons**, Eric 1920- *WhoBlA 92*
**Simmons**, Eric 1930- *Who 92*
**Simmons**, Eric Leslie 1917- *AmMWSc 92*
**Simmons**, Ernest Lee, Jr. 1947- *WhoRel 92*
**Simmons**, Esmeralda 1950- *WhoBlA 92*
**Simmons**, Francis Blair 1930- *AmMWSc 92*
**Simmons**, Gary Adair 1944- *AmMWSc 92*
**Simmons**, Gary Wayne 1939- *AmMWSc 92*
**Simmons**, Gene 1929- *AmMWSc 92*
**Simmons**, Gene 1949- *WhoEnt 92*
**Simmons**, George Allen 1926- *AmMWSc 92*
**Simmons**, George Finlay 1925- *AmMWSc 92*
**Simmons**, George Matthew, Jr 1942- *AmMWSc 92*
**Simmons**, George Michael 1943- *WhoWest 92*
**Simmons**, Geraldine Crossley 1939- *WhoBlA 92*
**Simmons**, Gustavus James 1930- *AmMWSc 92*
**Simmons**, Guy Held, Jr 1936- *AmMWSc 92*
**Simmons**, Guy Lintorn 1925- *Who 92*
**Simmons**, Hardwick 1940- *WhoFI 92*
**Simmons**, Harold C. 1931- *WhoFI 92, WhoWest 92*
**Simmons**, Harold Lee 1947- *WhoBlA 92*
**Simmons**, Harris H. 1954- *WhoFI 92, WhoWest 92*
**Simmons**, Harry Dady, Jr 1938- *AmMWSc 92*
**Simmons**, Herbert *WhoBlA 92*
**Simmons**, Howard Ensign, Jr 1929- *AmMWSc 92, WhoFI 92*
**Simmons**, Howard Koorken 1902- *WhoAmL 92*
**Simmons**, Howard L. 1938- *WhoBlA 92*
**Simmons**, Isaac Tyrone 1946- *WhoBlA 92*
**Simmons**, Jack *WrDr 92*
**Simmons**, Jack 1915- *IntAu&W 91, Who 92*
**Simmons**, James 1933- *ConPo 91, WrDr 92*
**Simmons**, James Boyd 1944- *WhoFI 92*
**Simmons**, James E 1925- *AmMWSc 92*
**Simmons**, James E. 1927- *WhoBlA 92*
**Simmons**, James Edwin 1923- *AmMWSc 92*
**Simmons**, James Michael 1947- *WhoRel 92*
**Simmons**, James Quimby, III 1925- *AmMWSc 92*
**Simmons**, James Richard 1939- *WhoBlA 92*
**Simmons**, James Stewart Alexander 1933- *IntAu&W 91*
**Simmons**, James Wood 1916- *AmMWSc 92*
**Simmons**, Jarette 1927- *WhoAmP 91*
**Simmons**, Jean 1929- *IntMPA 92, IntWW 91, Who 92, WhoEnt 92*
**Simmons**, Jean Elizabeth Margaret 1914- *AmMWSc 92*
**Simmons**, Jerold Lee 1941- *WhoMW 92*
**Simmons**, Jerry Raymond 1944- *WhoMW 92*
**Simmons**, Jesse Doyle 1926- *WhoRel 92*
**Simmons**, Jim 1916- *WhoAmP 91*
**Simmons**, Joe Denton 1938- *AmMWSc 92*
**Simmons**, John Arthur 1932- *AmMWSc 92*
**Simmons**, John Barry Eves 1937- *Who 92*
**Simmons**, John Derek 1931- *WhoFI 92*
**Simmons**, John Edward 1955- *WhoRel 92*
**Simmons**, John Emmett 1936- *WhoBlA 92*
**Simmons**, John Franklin 1945- *WhoEnt 92*
**Simmons**, John Robert 1928- *AmMWSc 92*
**Simmons**, Joseph 1923- *WhoBlA 92*
**Simmons**, Joseph Gottlieb 1955- *WhoAmL 92*
**Simmons**, Joseph Habib 1941- *AmMWSc 92*
**Simmons**, Joseph Jacob, III 1925- *WhoAmL 92, WhoAmP 91, WhoBlA 92, WhoFI 92*
**Simmons**, Joseph Thomas 1936- *WhoFI 92, WhoMW 92*
**Simmons**, Joyce Hobson 1947- *WhoBlA 92*
**Simmons**, Judy 1944- *NotBlAW 92*
**Simmons**, Judy Dothard *DrAPF 91*
**Simmons**, Julius Caesar, Sr. 1925- *WhoBlA 92*
**Simmons**, Kelly J. 1967- *WhoFI 92*
**Simmons**, Kenneth H. 1933- *WhoBlA 92*
**Simmons**, Kenneth N. 1945- *WhoAmL 92*
**Simmons**, Kenneth Rogers 1926- *AmMWSc 92*
**Simmons**, Larry G 1948- *WhoIns 92*
**Simmons**, Leonard 1920- *WhoBlA 92*
**Simmons**, Leonard Micajah, Jr 1937- *AmMWSc 92*
**Simmons**, Lionel J. 1968- *WhoBlA 92*
**Simmons**, Marc 1937- *WrDr 92*
**Simmons**, Mark F. 1959- *WhoFI 92*
**Simmons**, Mark George 1962- *WhoFI 92*
**Simmons**, Marshall Francis 1936- *WhoIns 92*
**Simmons**, Matty *IntMPA 92*
**Simmons**, Maurice Clyde 1957- *WhoBlA 92*
**Simmons**, Michael 1937- *Who 92*
**Simmons**, Michael Eugene 1954- *WhoAmL 92*
**Simmons**, Michael Paul 1953- *WhoMW 92*
**Simmons**, Miriam Quinn 1928- *WhoAmP 91*
**Simmons**, Myron Perry 1941- *WhoFI 92*
**Simmons**, Neville Keith 1938- *IntWW 91*
**Simmons**, Noel Alexander 1947- *WhoWest 92*
**Simmons**, Norman Stanley 1915- *AmMWSc 92*
**Simmons**, Paul A. 1921- *WhoBlA 92*
**Simmons**, Paul Allen 1921- *WhoAmL 92*
**Simmons**, Paul Barrett *WhoAmP 91*
**Simmons**, Paul C 1932- *AmMWSc 92*
**Simmons**, Paul Dewayne 1936- *WhoRel 92*
**Simmons**, Perry, Jr. 1947- *WhoRel 92*
**Simmons**, Peter 1931- *WhoAmL 92*
**Simmons**, Ralph Oliver 1928- *AmMWSc 92*
**Simmons**, Richard D. 1934- *IntWW 91*
**Simmons**, Richard Lawrence 1934- *AmMWSc 92*
**Simmons**, Richard Milton Teagle 1948- *WhoEnt 92*
**Simmons**, Richard Paul 1931- *AmMWSc 92*
**Simmons**, Richard S. d1991 *IntWW 91N*
**Simmons**, Richard Sheridan d1991 *NewYTBS 91 [port]*
**Simmons**, Robert Lewis 1934- *WhoEnt 92*
**Simmons**, Robert Malcolm 1938- *Who 92*
**Simmons**, Robert Michael 1948- *WhoAmL 92*
**Simmons**, Robert S. 1956- *WhoMW 92*
**Simmons**, Robert Wayne 1946- *WhoWest 92*
**Simmons**, Roberta Johnson 1947- *WhoMW 92*
**Simmons**, Roy William 1916- *WhoFI 92, WhoWest 92*
**Simmons**, Russell 1957?- *ConBlB 1, ConMus 7 [port]*
**Simmons**, S. Dallas 1940- *WhoBlA 92*
**Simmons**, Samuel J. 1927- *WhoBlA 92*
**Simmons**, Samuel Lee 1929- *WhoFI 92*
**Simmons**, Sheila Anne 1965- *WhoBlA 92*
**Simmons**, Sherwin Palmer 1931- *WhoAmL 92*
**Simmons**, Shirley Davis 1941- *WhoBlA 92*
**Simmons**, Shirley J. *DrAPF 91*
**Simmons**, Shirley Mae 1931- *WhoAmP 91*
**Simmons**, Stanley Clifford 1927- *Who 92*
**Simmons**, Susan Annette 1947- *WhoFI 92*
**Simmons**, Sylvia J. 1935- *WhoBlA 92*
**Simmons**, Ted Conrad 1916- *WhoWest 92*
**Simmons**, Tedd C. 1956- *WhoRel 92*
**Simmons**, Thelma M. 1942- *WhoBlA 92*
**Simmons**, Thomas Carl 1920- *AmMWSc 92*
**Simmons**, Thomas M. 1932- *WhoBlA 92*
**Simmons**, Victor J. 1945- *WhoFI 92, WhoWest 92*
**Simmons**, W. Louis, Jr. 1952- *WhoEnt 92*
**Simmons**, William Allen 1946- *WhoWest 92*
**Simmons**, William Bruce, Jr 1943- *AmMWSc 92*
**Simmons**, William Frederick 1938- *AmMWSc 92*
**Simmons**, William Howard 1947- *AmMWSc 92, WhoMW 92*
**Simmons**, William J. 1849-1890 *RelLAm 91*
**Simmons**, William Wells 1933- *WhoRel 92*
**Simmons**, Williams A. 1957- *WhoFI 92*
**Simmons**, Willie, Jr. 1939- *WhoBlA 92*
**Simmons**, Woodrow Jennings 1912- *WhoAmP 91*
**Simmons-Edelstein**, Dee 1937- *WhoBlA 92*
**Simmons-Evoy**, Lisa Susanne 1960- *WhoMW 92*
**Simms and M'Intyre** *DcLB 106*
**Simms**, Albert Egerton 1918- *WhoRel 92*
**Simms**, Albert L. 1931- *WhoBlA 92*
**Simms**, Carroll Harris 1924- *WhoBlA 92*
**Simms**, David John 1933- *IntWW 91*
**Simms**, Eric 1921- *WrDr 92*
**Simms**, Ernest S. 1917-1983 *WhoBlA 92N*
**Simms**, Garth *WhoAmP 91*

**Simms**, George Otto 1910- *IntWW 91, Who 92*
**Simms**, Gregory Frame 1928- *WhoBlA 92*
**Simms**, Hilda 1920- *NotBlAW 92*
**Simms**, James Edward 1943- *WhoBlA 92*
**Simms**, Jeffrey 1947- *WhoAmP 91*
**Simms**, John Alvin 1931- *AmMWSc 92*
**Simms**, John Carson 1952- *WhoMW 92*
**Simms**, Laura *DrAPF 91*
**Simms**, Margaret Constance 1946- *WhoBlA 92*
**Simms**, Maria Ester 1938- *WhoWest 92*
**Simms**, Michael *DrAPF 91*
**Simms**, Nathan Frank, Jr 1932- *AmMWSc 92*
**Simms**, Paul C 1932- *AmMWSc 92*
**Simms**, Robert D *WhoAmP 91*
**Simms**, Robert D. 1926- *WhoAmL 92*
**Simms**, Robert H. 1927- *WhoBlA 92*
**Simms**, Stuart Oswald *WhoBlA 92*
**Simms**, W Timothy 1943- *WhoAmP 91*
**Simms**, William E. 1944- *WhoBlA 92*
**Simms**, William Gilmore 1806-1870 *BenetAL 91*
**Simnad**, Massoud T 1920- *AmMWSc 92*
**Simo**, Ana Maria *DrAPF 91*
**Simoes**, Ronald Alan 1949- *WhoFI 92*
**Simojoki**, Lauri Elias 1899-1940 *BiDExR*
**Simon** *Who 92*
**Simon and Garfunkel** *FacFETw, NewAmDM*
**Simon Magus** *EncEarC*
**Simon**, Viscount 1902- *Who 92*
**Simon**, Albert 1924- *AmMWSc 92*
**Simon**, Alexander 1906- *AmMWSc 92*
**Simon**, Alexander Nathan 1951- *WhoAmP 91*
**Simon**, Alfred 1907-1991 *ConAu 134*
**Simon**, Alfred E. d1991 *NewYTBS 91*
**Simon**, Alfred L. 1940- *WhoFI 92*
**Simon**, Allan Lester 1934- *AmMWSc 92*
**Simon**, Andrew L 1930- *AmMWSc 92*
**Simon**, Anthony Olivier 1936- *WhoMW 92*
**Simon**, Armando P. 1914- *WhoHisp 92*
**Simon**, Art 1945- *WhoAmP 91*
**Simon**, Arthur 1930- *WhoRel 92, WrDr 92*
**Simon**, Arthur Bernard 1927- *AmMWSc 92*
**Simon**, Arthur Bernard 1939- *WhoMW 92*
**Simon**, Arthur Robert 1930- *IntAu&W 91*
**Simon**, Barry Martin 1946- *AmMWSc 92*
**Simon**, Barry Philip 1942- *WhoFI 92*
**Simon**, Betty Atkins 1929- *WhoEnt 92*
**Simon**, Bob *LesBEnT 92 [port]*
**Simon**, Brian 1915- *Who 92*
**Simon**, Bruce T 1942- *WhoAmP 91*
**Simon**, Carl Paul 1945- *AmMWSc 92*
**Simon**, Carly 1945- *FacFETw, NewAmDM, WhoEnt 92*
**Simon**, Caroline Klein *WhoAmL 92*
**Simon**, Charles Robert 1947- *WhoMW 92*
**Simon**, Christine Mae 1949- *AmMWSc 92*
**Simon**, Claude 1913- *FacFETw, IntAu&W 91, IntWW 91, Who 92*
**Simon**, Claude 1913-1984 *GuFrLit 1*
**Simon**, Claude Eugene Henri 1913- *WhoNob 90*
**Simon**, David Alec Gwyn 1939- *IntWW 91, Who 92*
**Simon**, David Harold 1930- *WhoWest 92*
**Simon**, David Robert 1934- *WhoAmL 92*
**Simon**, David Zvi 1929- *AmMWSc 92*
**Simon**, Dorothy Martin 1919- *AmMWSc 92*
**Simon**, Edith *TwCPaSc*
**Simon**, Edith 1917- *WrDr 92*
**Simon**, Edward 1927- *AmMWSc 92*
**Simon**, Edward Dave 1927- *WhoFI 92*
**Simon**, Edward Harvey 1934- *AmMWSc 92*
**Simon**, Elaine 1944- *WhoBlA 92*
**Simon**, Ellen McMurtrie 1919- *AmMWSc 92, WhoMW 92*
**Simon**, Eric 1920- *AmMWSc 92*
**Simon**, Eric Jacob 1924- *AmMWSc 92*
**Simon**, Fabrice Jule 1951- *WhoBlA 92*
**Simon**, Francoise Louise 1946- *WhoFI 92*
**Simon**, Frederick Otto 1939- *AmMWSc 92*
**Simon**, Frederick Tyler 1917- *AmMWSc 92*
**Simon**, Gary Albert 1945- *AmMWSc 92*
**Simon**, George 1963- *WhoFI 92*
**Simon**, George Warren 1934- *AmMWSc 92*
**Simon**, Gerald Austin 1927- *WhoFI 92, WhoWest 92*
**Simon**, Geza 1941- *AmMWSc 92*
**Simon**, Gustav 1900-1945 *BiDExR, EncTR 91 [port]*
**Simon**, Harold Barnette 1961- *WhoEnt 92*
**Simon**, Harold J 1928- *AmMWSc 92*
**Simon**, Henry Francis 1944- *WhoMW 92*
**Simon**, Henry John 1939- *AmMWSc 92*
**Simon**, Herbert *WhoMW 92*
**Simon**, Herbert A 1916- *AmMWSc 92, IntWW 91, Who 92, WrDr 92*
**Simon**, Herbert Alexander 1916- *WhoFI 92, WhoNob 90*
**Simon**, Horst D 1953- *AmMWSc 92*
**Simon**, Huey Paul 1923- *WhoAmL 92, WhoFI 92*
**Simon**, Jack Aaron 1919- *AmMWSc 92*
**Simon**, James F. 1938- *WhoAmL 92*
**Simon**, James F. 1939- *ConAu 134*
**Simon**, James Lowell 1944- *WhoAmL 92*
**Simon**, Jane *DrAPF 91*
**Simon**, Jerome Barnet 1939- *AmMWSc 92*
**Simon**, Jewel Woodard 1911- *WhoBlA 92*
**Simon**, Jimmy L 1930- *AmMWSc 92*
**Simon**, John 1873-1954 *EncTR 91*
**Simon**, John 1925- *LiExTwC*
**Simon**, John Allsebrook 1873-1954 *FacFETw*
**Simon**, John Douglas 1957- *AmMWSc 92*
**Simon**, John Ivan 1925- *WhoEnt 92*
**Simon**, John Oliver *DrAPF 91*
**Simon**, John William 1949- *WhoAmL 92, WhoAmP 91*
**Simon**, Jonathan Paul 1967- *WhoFI 92*
**Simon**, Joseph 1918- *AmMWSc 92*
**Simon**, Joseph Donald 1932- *WhoBlA 92*
**Simon**, Joseph Leslie 1937- *AmMWSc 92*
**Simon**, Joseph Matthew 1941- *AmMWSc 92*
**Simon**, Julian L. 1932- *WrDr 92*
**Simon**, Justin Daniel 1947- *WhoAmL 92*
**Simon**, Karen Leslie 1942- *WhoAmP 91*
**Simon**, Karl Gunter 1933- *IntAu&W 91*
**Simon**, Karla Weber 1947- *WhoAmL 92*
**Simon**, Kate 1912-1990 *AnObit 1990*
**Simon**, Kathryn Irene 1953- *WhoFI 92, WhoWest 92*
**Simon**, Keith 1922- *TwCPaSc*
**Simon**, Kenneth Bernard 1953- *WhoBlA 92*
**Simon**, Leah Lynn 1965- *WhoEnt 92*
**Simon**, Lee Will 1940- *AmMWSc 92*
**Simon**, Lewis Bryant 1940- *WhoMW 92*
**Simon**, Lonnie A. 1925- *WhoBlA 92*
**Simon**, Marilyn 1941- *WhoAmL 92*
**Simon**, Mark 1946- *WhoFI 92*
**Simon**, Mark Robert 1941- *AmMWSc 92*
**Simon**, Martha Nichols 1940- *AmMWSc 92*
**Simon**, Marvin Kenneth 1939- *AmMWSc 92*
**Simon**, Maurya *DrAPF 91*
**Simon**, Melvin 1926- *IntMPA 92, WhoMW 92*
**Simon**, Melvin 1937- *AmMWSc 92*
**Simon**, Michael A. 1936- *WrDr 92*
**Simon**, Michael Alexander 1936- *WhoMW 92*
**Simon**, Michael Richard 1943- *AmMWSc 92*
**Simon**, Michael Scott 1954- *WhoAmL 92*
**Simon**, Michal 1940- *AmMWSc 92*
**Simon**, Mordecai 1925- *WhoRel 92*
**Simon**, Myron Sydney 1926- *AmMWSc 92*
**Simon**, Nancy Jane 1939- *AmMWSc 92*
**Simon**, Neil *LesBEnT 92, NewYTBS 91 [port]*
**Simon**, Neil 1927- *BenetAL 91, FacFETw, IntAu&W 91, IntMPA 92, IntWW 91, Who 92, WhoEnt 92, WrDr 92*
**Simon**, Neil A. 1958- *WhoAmL 92*
**Simon**, Norma 1927- *SmATA 68 [port]*
**Simon**, Norman M 1929- *AmMWSc 92*
**Simon**, Norman Robert *AmMWSc 92*
**Simon**, Paul *IntWW 91*
**Simon**, Paul 1928- *AlmAP 92 [port], IntWW 91, WhoAmP 91, WhoMW 92*
**Simon**, Paul 1941- *IntMPA 92, WhoEnt 92*
**Simon**, Paul 1942- *NewAmDM, News 92-2 [port]*
**Simon**, Paul Jerome 1954- *WhoMW 92*
**Simon**, Peregrine Charles Hugo 1950- *Who 92*
**Simon**, Peter M 1950- *WhoAmP 91*
**Simon**, Philipp William 1950- *AmMWSc 92*
**Simon**, Ralph 1906- *WhoRel 92*
**Simon**, Ralph E. 1930- *WhoWest 92*
**Simon**, Ralph Emanuel 1930- *AmMWSc 92*
**Simon**, Renee B 1928- *WhoAmP 91*
**Simon**, Richard 1638-1712 *BlkwCEP*
**Simon**, Richard Alan 1938- *WhoIns 92*
**Simon**, Richard Hege 1911- *WhoAmL 92*
**Simon**, Richard L 1950- *AmMWSc 92*
**Simon**, Richard Macy 1943- *AmMWSc 92*
**Simon**, Rita J. 1931- *WrDr 92*
**Simon**, Rita James 1931- *WhoAmL 92*
**Simon**, Robert *WrDr 92*
**Simon**, Robert Abraham 1918- *WhoAmL 92*
**Simon**, Robert D. 1954- *WhoEnt 92*
**Simon**, Robert David 1945- *AmMWSc 92*
**Simon**, Robert Eli 1952- *WhoEnt 92*
**Simon**, Robert G. 1927- *WhoAmL 92*
**Simon**, Robert H 1920- *AmMWSc 92*
**Simon**, Robert H M 1924- *AmMWSc 92*
**Simon**, Robert Michael 1947- *WhoMW 92*
**Simon**, Robert Michael 1956- *AmMWSc 92*
**Simon**, Robert Scott 1926- *TwCPaSc*
**Simon**, Robert Wayne 1947- *WhoIns 92*
**Simon**, Robet *IntAu&W 91X*
**Simon**, Roger *Who 92*
**Simon**, Roger 1948- *WrDr 92*
**Simon**, Roger Bennett 1940- *WhoFI 92*
**Simon**, Roger Hendricks 1942- *WhoEnt 92*
**Simon**, Roger L. 1943- *WrDr 92*
**Simon**, Ronald I. 1938- *WhoFI 92, WhoWest 92*
**Simon**, Ronn Ward 1963- *WhoAmP 91*
**Simon**, Rosalyn McCord 1946- *WhoBlA 92*
**Simon**, Sanford Ralph 1942- *AmMWSc 92*
**Simon**, Selwyn 1925- *AmMWSc 92, WhoMW 92*
**Simon**, Seymour 1915- *WhoAmL 92, WhoAmP 91, WhoMW 92*
**Simon**, Seymour 1931- *WrDr 92*
**Simon**, Sharlene Michele 1947- *WhoWest 92*
**Simon**, Sheldon Weiss 1937- *IntAu&W 91, WrDr 92*
**Simon**, Shena 1883-1972 *BiDBrF 2*
**Simon**, Sheridan Alan 1947- *AmMWSc 92*
**Simon**, Sidney Arthur 1943- *AmMWSc 92*
**Simon**, Simone 1911- *IntMPA 92*
**Simon**, Stephen G 1942- *WhoAmP 91*
**Simon**, Terrence William 1946- *AmMWSc 92*
**Simon**, Ulrich Ernst 1913- *Who 92*
**Simon**, Walter J. 1941- *WhoBlA 92*
**Simon**, Werner 1914- *IntAu&W 91*
**Simon**, Wilbur 1917- *AmMWSc 92*
**Simon**, William 1844-1916 *BiInAmS*
**Simon**, William 1929- *AmMWSc 92*
**Simon**, William Dien 1954- *WhoAmP 91*
**Simon**, William E 1927- *WhoAmP 91*
**Simon**, William Edward 1927- *IntWW 91, Who 92*
**Simon**, William H. 1947- *WhoAmL 92*
**Simon**, William Leonard 1930- *WhoEnt 92, WhoWest 92*
**Simon Dominguez**, Pedro 1581-1627? *HisDSpE*
**Simon Of Glaisdale**, Baron 1911- *IntWW 91, Who 92*
**Simon of Wythenshawe**, Baron 1913- *Who 92*
**Simon Walhout**, Justine I 1930- *AmMWSc 92*
**Simonaitis**, Romualdas 1934- *AmMWSc 92*
**Simonard**, Andre 1917- *IntWW 91*
**Simonds**, Charles 1945- *WorArt 1980 [port]*
**Simonds**, John Ormsbee 1913- *AmMWSc 92*
**Simonds**, Milford Dale 1944- *WhoRel 92*
**Simonds**, Paul Emery 1932- *WhoWest 92*
**Simonds**, Richard Kimball 1927- *WhoFI 92*
**Simonds**, Stephen Paige 1924- *WhoAmP 91*
**Simonds**, Walter Stearns 1943- *WhoAmL 92*
**Simonds-Gooding**, Anthony James Joseph 1937- *Who 92*
**Simone**, Albert Joseph 1935- *WhoWest 92*
**Simone**, James 1954- *WhoMW 92*
**Simone**, Joseph 1924- *WhoRel 92*
**Simone**, Joseph R. 1949- *WhoAmL 92*
**Simone**, Joseph Vincent 1935- *AmMWSc 92*
**Simone**, Leo Daniel 1935- *AmMWSc 92*
**Simone**, Nina 1933- *IntWW 91, NotBlAW 92*
**Simone**, Nina 1940- *WhoBlA 92*
**Simone**, Peggy 1935- *WhoAmP 91*
**Simone**, Stephen Albert, Jr. 1948- *WhoWest 92*
**Simoneau**, Leopold 1918- *NewAmDM*
**Simoneau**, Wayne Anthony 1935- *WhoAmP 91*
**Simoneaux**, Michel S. 1939- *WhoRel 92*
**Simoneit**, Bernd Rolf Tatsuo 1937- *WhoWest 92*
**Simonelli**, Anthony Peter 1924- *AmMWSc 92*
**Simonelli**, Jerry 1952- *WhoAmP 91*
**Simonelli**, John Justin 1963- *WhoFI 92*
**Simonen**, Thomas Charles 1938- *AmMWSc 92*
**Simonet**, Donald Edward 1946- *AmMWSc 92*
**Simonet**, Henri Francois 1931- *IntWW 91, Who 92*
**Simonet**, Pierre 1934- *Who 92*
**Simonett**, John E *WhoAmP 91*
**Simonett**, John E. 1924- *WhoAmL 92, WhoMW 92*
**Simonetta** *IntWW 91*
**Simoni**, Robert Dario 1939- *AmMWSc 92*
**Simonia**, Nodari 1932- *SovUnBD*
**Simonian**, James Karop 1964- *WhoAmL 92*
**Simonian**, John S *WhoAmP 91*
**Simonian**, Vartkes Hovanes 1911- *AmMWSc 92*
**Simonis**, Adrianus J. 1931- *IntWW 91*
**Simonis**, Adrianus Johannes 1931- *WhoRel 92*
**Simonis**, George Jerome 1946- *AmMWSc 92*
**Simonis**, John Charles 1940- *AmMWSc 92*
**Simonis**, Matthew Jay 1962- *WhoEnt 92*
**Simonnard**, Michel Andre 1933- *WhoFI 92*
**Simonoff**, Robert 1920- *AmMWSc 92*
**Simonov**, Konstantin Mikhailovich 1915-1979 *FacFETw*
**Simonov**, Konstantin Mikhaylovich 1915-1979 *SovUnBD*
**Simonov**, Pavel 1926- *IntWW 91*
**Simonov**, Ruben Nikolaevich 1899-1968 *SovUnBD*
**Simonov**, Yevgeniy Rubenovich 1925- *IntWW 91*
**Simonov**, Yuriy Ivanovich 1941- *IntWW 91*
**Simonpietri**, Arturo A 1917- *WhoIns 92*
**Simons**, Alfred Murray 1927- *Who 92*
**Simons**, Arthur D 1919-1979 *FacFETw*
**Simons**, Barbara Bluestein 1941- *AmMWSc 92, WhoWest 92*
**Simons**, Barbara M. 1929- *WhoAmL 92*
**Simons**, Beverley 1938- *WrDr 92*
**Simons**, Charles Earl, Jr. 1916- *WhoAmL 92*
**Simons**, Daniel J 1940- *AmMWSc 92*
**Simons**, Daryl B 1918- *AmMWSc 92*
**Simons**, Edward Louis 1921- *AmMWSc 92*
**Simons**, Elizabeth Reiman 1929- *AmMWSc 92*
**Simons**, Elwyn LaVerne 1930- *AmMWSc 92, IntWW 91*
**Simons**, Eric Ward 1958- *WhoFI 92*
**Simons**, Frank 1917- *AmMWSc 92*
**Simons**, Gail Derese 1959- *WhoBlA 92*
**Simons**, Gene R 1936- *AmMWSc 92*
**Simons**, Harold Lee 1926- *AmMWSc 92*
**Simons**, Janet Ann 1949- *WhoMW 92*
**Simons**, John Norton 1926- *AmMWSc 92*
**Simons**, John Peter 1945- *AmMWSc 92*
**Simons**, John Philip 1934- *Who 92*
**Simons**, Lawrence Brook 1924- *WhoAmL 92, WhoAmP 91*
**Simons**, Lisa Dale 1960- *WhoEnt 92*
**Simons**, Louise *DrAPF 91*
**Simons**, Lynn Osborn 1934- *WhoAmP 91, WhoWest 92*
**Simons**, Marc V. 1948- *WhoFI 92*
**Simons**, Marlene J 1935- *WhoAmP 91, WhoWest 92*
**Simons**, Marr Dixon 1925- *AmMWSc 92*
**Simons**, Mary Crescenzo *DrAPF 91*
**Simons**, Mary Diane 1944- *WhoEnt 92*
**Simons**, Mayrant, Jr 1936- *AmMWSc 92*
**Simons**, Ray D. 1946- *WhoFI 92*
**Simons**, Renee V. H. 1949- *WhoBlA 92*
**Simons**, Richard D 1927- *WhoAmP 91*
**Simons**, Richard Duncan 1927- *WhoAmL 92*
**Simons**, Robert Philip 1955- *WhoAmL 92*
**Simons**, Robert W 1945- *AmMWSc 92*
**Simons**, Robert Walter 1945- *WhoWest 92*
**Simons**, Roger Alan 1943- *AmMWSc 92*
**Simons**, Roger Mayfield 1926- *AmMWSc 92*
**Simons**, Roy Kenneth 1920- *AmMWSc 92*
**Simons**, Samuel Stoney, Jr 1945- *AmMWSc 92*
**Simons**, Sanford L 1922- *AmMWSc 92*
**Simons**, Stephen 1938- *AmMWSc 92, WhoWest 92*
**Simons**, Thomas W 1938- *WhoAmP 91*
**Simons**, Thomas W., Jr. 1938- *ConAu 134*
**Simons**, William Haddock 1914- *AmMWSc 92*
**Simons**, William Harris 1938- *AmMWSc 92*
**Simonsen**, Bernard Lee 1945- *WhoFI 92*
**Simonsen**, David Raymond 1916- *AmMWSc 92*
**Simonsen**, Donald Howard 1921- *AmMWSc 92*
**Simonsen**, Eric A 1945- *WhoIns 92*
**Simonsen**, Mario Henrique 1935- *IntWW 91*
**Simonsen**, Palle 1933- *IntWW 91*
**Simonsen**, Paul Herbert 1954- *WhoEnt 92*
**Simonsen**, Robert Alan 1956- *WhoMW 92*
**Simonsen**, Stanley Harold 1918- *AmMWSc 92*
**Simonson**, Beryl David 1949- *WhoFI 92*
**Simonson**, Bruce Miller 1950- *WhoMW 92*
**Simonson**, Charles Henry 1940- *WhoRel 92*
**Simonson**, Gerald Herman 1927- *AmMWSc 92*
**Simonson**, Harold P. 1926- *WrDr 92*
**Simonson**, John Alexander 1945- *WhoFI 92*
**Simonson**, John C 1960- *AmMWSc 92*
**Simonson**, Kenneth Wayne, Jr. 1955- *WhoFI 92, WhoWest 92*
**Simonson**, Lee Stuart 1948- *WhoEnt 92*
**Simonson**, Lloyd Grant 1943- *AmMWSc 92*
**Simonson**, Mary Ellen 1949- *WhoAmP 91*

**Simonson,** Michael 1950- *WhoAmL 92, WhoWest 92*
**Simonson,** Miles Kevin 1950- *WhoWest 92*
**Simonson,** Richard D 1950- *WhoAmP 91*
**Simonson,** Solomon S. d1991 *NewYTBS 91*
**Simonson,** Susan Kay 1946- *WhoWest 92*
**Simonsuuri,** Kirsti Katariina 1945- *IntAu&W 91*
**Simonton,** David Paul 1960- *WhoAmL 92*
**Simonton,** Gail Maureen 1951- *WhoAmL 92*
**Simonton,** George Louis 1947- *WhoAmP 91*
**Simonton,** Russ *ScFEYrs*
**Simonyan,** Rayr Rayrovich 1947- *IntWW 91, SovUnBD*
**Simopoulos,** Artemis Panageotis 1933- *AmMWSc 92*
**Simovic,** Laszlo 1957- *WhoMW 92*
**Simovici,** Dan 1943- *AmMWSc 92*
**Simpers,** Mary P 1934- *WhoAmP 91*
**Simpkins,** Cuthbert O. 1925- *WhoBlA 92*
**Simpkins,** J. Edward 1932- *WhoBlA 92*
**Simpkins,** James W 1948- *AmMWSc 92*
**Simpkins,** Kirk Gates 1956- *WhoAmP 91*
**Simpkins,** Marcia Carl 1953- *WhoFI 92*
**Simpkins,** Peter G 1934- *AmMWSc 92*
**Simpkins,** Richard D 1934- *WhoAmP 91*
**Simpkins,** Robert David Thomas 1932- *WhoAmP 91*
**Simpkins,** Victor Alfred 1954- *WhoEnt 92*
**Simpkins,** William Joseph 1934- *WhoBlA 92*
**Simpkinson,** Charles Hoffman 1934- *WhoRel 92*
**Simple,** Peter *IntAu&W 91X, Who 92*
**Simplicio,** Jon 1942- *AmMWSc 92*
**Simplicius** *EncEarC*
**Simplot,** John R. 1909- *WhoWest 92*
**Simpson,** A. W. B. 1931- *WhoAmL 92*
**Simpson,** A. W. Brian 1931- *WrDr 92*
**Simpson,** Alan 1912- *IntWW 91, Who 92*
**Simpson,** Alan 1929- *IntAu&W 91, Who 92*
**Simpson,** Alan 1937- *Who 92*
**Simpson,** Alan K. 1931- *AlmAP 92 [port], WhoAmP 91*
**Simpson,** Alan Kooi 1931- *IntWW 91, WhoWest 92*
**Simpson,** Alfred 1914- *Who 92*
**Simpson,** Alfred Moxon 1910- *Who 92*
**Simpson,** Alfred William Brian 1931- *Who 92*
**Simpson,** Allan Boyd 1948- *WhoFI 92*
**Simpson,** Andrea Lynn 1948- *WhoFI 92, WhoWest 92*
**Simpson,** Anthony Maurice Herbert 1935- *Who 92*
**Simpson,** Antony Michael 1941- *AmMWSc 92*
**Simpson,** Athol John Dundas 1932- *Who 92*
**Simpson,** Audrey 1946- *TwCPaSc*
**Simpson,** Beryl Brintnall 1942- *AmMWSc 92*
**Simpson,** Billy Doyle 1929- *AmMWSc 92*
**Simpson,** Brian *Who 92*
**Simpson,** Brian 1931- *IntWW 91*
**Simpson,** Brian 1953- *Who 92*
**Simpson,** C. Dene 1936- *WhoWest 92*
**Simpson,** Carol Louise 1937- *WhoFI 92*
**Simpson,** Carole 1940- *NotBlAW 92, WhoBlA 92*
**Simpson,** Cary Hatcher 1927- *WhoEnt 92*
**Simpson,** Cathy Ann 1953- *WhoFI 92*
**Simpson,** Charles Baird 1877-1907 *BiInAmS*
**Simpson,** Charles Ednam 1929- *Who 92*
**Simpson,** Charles Edward 1948- *WhoRel 92*
**Simpson,** Charles Floyd 1919- *AmMWSc 92*
**Simpson,** Charles R., III 1945- *WhoAmL 92*
**Simpson,** Charles William 1936- *WhoAmP 91*
**Simpson,** Christopher 1605?-1669 *NewAmDM*
**Simpson,** Corlandt James Woore 1911- *Who 92*
**Simpson,** Craig Evan 1952- *WhoAmL 92*
**Simpson,** Dale R 1930- *AmMWSc 92*
**Simpson,** Daniel H *WhoAmP 91*
**Simpson,** Daniel Reid 1927- *WhoAmL 92, WhoAmP 91*
**Simpson,** David Alexander 1943- *AmMWSc 92*
**Simpson,** David Gordon 1920- *AmMWSc 92*
**Simpson,** David Patten 1930- *AmMWSc 92*
**Simpson,** David Penistan 1917- *IntAu&W 91, WrDr 92*
**Simpson,** David Rae Fisher 1936- *Who 92*
**Simpson,** David Richard Salisbury 1945- *Who 92*
**Simpson,** David Sackville Bruce 1930- *Who 92*
**Simpson,** Dazelle Dean 1924- *WhoBlA 92*
**Simpson,** Deanna Lynn 1956- *WhoRel 92*
**Simpson,** Dennis Arden 1944- *WhoFI 92*
**Simpson,** Dennis Charles 1931- *Who 92*
**Simpson,** Diane Jeannette 1952- *WhoBlA 92*
**Simpson,** Dick 1940- *WrDr 92*
**Simpson,** Dick Weldon 1940- *WhoMW 92*
**Simpson,** Don *WhoEnt 92*
**Simpson,** Don 1945- *IntMPA 92*
**Simpson,** Donnie 1954- *WhoBlA 92*
**Simpson,** Dorothy 1933- *IntAu&W 91, WrDr 92*
**Simpson,** Duncan Andrew 1956- *WhoAmP 91*
**Simpson,** E. Budd 1951- *WhoAmL 92*
**Simpson,** E. P. Y. 1911- *WrDr 92*
**Simpson,** Edward Hugh 1922- *Who 92*
**Simpson,** Edward W, Jr 1916- *WhoAmP 91*
**Simpson,** Esther Eleanor 1919- *Who 92*
**Simpson,** Eugene Sidney 1917- *AmMWSc 92*
**Simpson,** Evan Rutherford *AmMWSc 92*
**Simpson,** Everett Coy 1925- *AmMWSc 92*
**Simpson,** Ffreebairn Liddon 1916- *Who 92*
**Simpson,** Frank 1941- *AmMWSc 92*
**Simpson,** Frank B. 1919- *WhoBlA 92*
**Simpson,** Frankie Joe 1933- *WhoFI 92*
**Simpson,** Frederick James 1922- *AmMWSc 92*
**Simpson,** Garry *IntMPA 92*
**Simpson,** Garry 1914- *WhoEnt 92*
**Simpson,** Gary Martin 1950- *WhoRel 92*
**Simpson,** Gary William 1965- *WhoRel 92*
**Simpson,** Geddes Wilson 1908- *AmMWSc 92*
**Simpson,** George 1942- *Who 92*
**Simpson,** George B d1901 *BiInAmS*
**Simpson,** George Edward 1944- *WhoEnt 92*
**Simpson,** Gordon Russell 1917- *Who 92*
**Simpson,** Grace Willis 1947- *WhoFI 92*
**Simpson,** Gregory Louis 1958- *WhoBlA 92*
**Simpson,** H. Kent 1951- *WhoRel 92*
**Simpson,** Helen *ConAu 134*
**Simpson,** Henry 1853-1921 *TwCPaSc*
**Simpson,** Howard Douglas 1937- *AmMWSc 92*
**Simpson,** Howard Douglas 1959- *WhoEnt 92*
**Simpson,** Howard Edwin 1917- *AmMWSc 92*
**Simpson,** Howard Matthew 1918- *WhoMW 92*
**Simpson,** Ian 1933- *Who 92*
**Simpson,** Ian Alexander 1948- *AmMWSc 92*
**Simpson,** Ian Christopher 1949- *Who 92*
**Simpson,** Jack Benjamin 1937- *WhoFI 92, WhoMW 92*
**Simpson,** Jack Ward 1941- *WhoMW 92*
**Simpson,** Jacqueline 1930- *WrDr 92*
**Simpson,** James 1908- *Who 92*
**Simpson,** James Arlington 1931- *WhoBlA 92*
**Simpson,** James Carroll 1931- *WhoAmP 91*
**Simpson,** James Charles 1930- *WhoAmP 91*
**Simpson,** James Edward 1931- *AmMWSc 92*
**Simpson,** James Henry 1929- *AmMWSc 92*
**Simpson,** James R 1911- *AmMWSc 92*
**Simpson,** James Ray 1945- *WhoFI 92*
**Simpson,** Jerry 1842-1905 *AmPolLe*
**Simpson,** Jim *LesBEnT 92*
**Simpson,** Joanne 1923- *AmMWSc 92*
**Simpson,** John *WhoAmP 91*
**Simpson,** John 1944- *TwCPaSc*
**Simpson,** John Alexander 1916- *AmMWSc 92*
**Simpson,** John Andrew 1953- *Who 92*
**Simpson,** John Arol 1923- *AmMWSc 92*
**Simpson,** John Arthur 1933- *Who 92*
**Simpson,** John Barclay 1947- *AmMWSc 92*
**Simpson,** John Cody Fidler 1944- *IntAu&W 91, Who 92*
**Simpson,** John Ernest 1942- *AmMWSc 92*
**Simpson,** John Ernest Peter 1942- *Who 92*
**Simpson,** John Ferguson 1902- *Who 92*
**Simpson,** John Hamilton 1915- *AmMWSc 92*
**Simpson,** John Liddle 1912- *Who 92*
**Simpson,** John P *WhoAmP 91*
**Simpson,** John W 1914- *AmMWSc 92*
**Simpson,** John Wayne 1935- *AmMWSc 92*
**Simpson,** Johnny 1948- *WhoAmL 92*
**Simpson,** Joyce Michelle 1959- *WhoBlA 92*
**Simpson,** Juanita H. 1925- *WhoBlA 92*
**Simpson,** Keith Taylor 1934- *Who 92*
**Simpson,** Kenneth John 1914- *Who 92*
**Simpson,** Kenneth L 1931- *AmMWSc 92*
**Simpson,** Kenneth W. *DrAPF 91*
**Simpson,** Larry P 1940- *AmMWSc 92*
**Simpson,** Laura Kay 1960- *WhoAmL 92*
**Simpson,** Leland J 1914- *WhoAmP 91*
**Simpson,** Leonard 1932- *AmMWSc 92*
**Simpson,** Leonard Angus 1939- *AmMWSc 92*
**Simpson,** Lewis P. 1916- *WrDr 92*
**Simpson,** Linda Marie 1962- *WhoRel 92*
**Simpson,** Louis *DrAPF 91*
**Simpson,** Louis 1923- *BenetAL 91, ConPo 91, FacFETw, WrDr 92*
**Simpson,** Louis A. 1936- *WhoFI 92*
**Simpson,** Louis Allen 1936- *WhoIns 92*
**Simpson,** Louis Aston Marantz 1923- *IntAu&W 91, IntWW 91*
**Simpson,** Lyle Lee 1937- *WhoAmL 92*
**Simpson,** Malcolm Carter 1929- *Who 92*
**Simpson,** Margaret 1935- *AmMWSc 92*
**Simpson,** Marion Emma 1927- *AmMWSc 92*
**Simpson,** Mark Kelvin 1960- *WhoFI 92*
**Simpson,** Mary Michael 1925- *WhoRel 92*
**Simpson,** Matt 1936- *IntAu&W 91*
**Simpson,** Melvin Vernon 1921- *AmMWSc 92*
**Simpson,** Merton Daniel 1928- *WhoBlA 92*
**Simpson,** Michael 1938- *WhoFI 92*
**Simpson,** Michael 1940- *TwCPaSc*
**Simpson,** Michael Andrew 1944- *WrDr 92*
**Simpson,** Michael Frank 1928- *Who 92*
**Simpson,** Michael Howard 1946- *WhoAmL 92*
**Simpson,** Michael K *WhoAmP 91*
**Simpson,** Michael Wayne 1959- *WhoAmL 92*
**Simpson,** Milton Crawford 1963- *WhoWest 92*
**Simpson,** Mona *DrAPF 91*
**Simpson,** Mona 1957- *ConAu 135, WrDr 92*
**Simpson,** Morag *Who 92*
**Simpson,** Murray 1921- *AmMWSc 92*
**Simpson,** Myrtle Lillias 1931- *WrDr 92*
**Simpson,** N F 1919- *IntAu&W 91, RfGEnL 91, WrDr 92*
**Simpson,** Nancy *DrAPF 91*
**Simpson,** Nancy E 1924- *AmMWSc 92*
**Simpson,** Norman Frederick 1919- *IntWW 91*
**Simpson,** Norvell J. 1931- *WhoBlA 92*
**Simpson,** O. J. *LesBEnT 92 [port]*
**Simpson,** O J 1947- *FacFETw, IntMPA 92, WhoBlA 92*
**Simpson,** Ocleris C 1939- *AmMWSc 92*
**Simpson,** Oliver 1924- *Who 92*
**Simpson,** P Kelley *WhoAmP 91*
**Simpson,** Paul Byron 1914- *WhoFI 92*
**Simpson,** Paula Gail 1938- *WhoFI 92*
**Simpson,** Peter Kooi 1930- *WhoAmP 91, WhoWest 92*
**Simpson,** Peter L. *DrAPF 91*
**Simpson,** Peter Robert 1936- *Who 92*
**Simpson,** R. A. 1929- *ConPo 91, WrDr 92*
**Simpson,** R. Smith 1906- *WrDr 92*
**Simpson,** Ralph Derek 1949- *WhoBlA 92*
**Simpson,** Rennie 1920- *Who 92*
**Simpson,** Richard Alan 1952- *WhoMW 92*
**Simpson,** Richard Allan 1945- *AmMWSc 92*
**Simpson,** Richard John 1953- *WhoWest 92*
**Simpson,** Richard Newton 1951- *WhoWest 92*
**Simpson,** Richard S 1935- *AmMWSc 92*
**Simpson,** Robert 1921- *ConCom 92, WrDr 92*
**Simpson,** Robert 1923- *Who 92*
**Simpson,** Robert Blake *AmMWSc 92*
**Simpson,** Robert Edward, Jr. 1951- *WhoAmL 92*
**Simpson,** Robert Foster 1928- *WhoAmP 91*
**Simpson,** Robert Gene 1925- *AmMWSc 92*
**Simpson,** Robert Glenn 1932- *WhoAmL 92*
**Simpson,** Robert John 1927- *AmMWSc 92*
**Simpson,** Robert L. 1927- *WhoRel 92*
**Simpson,** Robert Leatham 1915- *WhoRel 92*
**Simpson,** Robert Lee 1942- *AmMWSc 92*
**Simpson,** Robert Todd 1938- *AmMWSc 92*
**Simpson,** Robert Watson 1940- *Who 92*
**Simpson,** Robert Wayne 1928- *AmMWSc 92*
**Simpson,** Robert Wilfred Levick 1921- *Who 92*
**Simpson,** Robert Wilfrid Levick 1921- *IntWW 91*
**Simpson,** Robin *Who 92*
**Simpson,** Robin Muschamp Garry 1927- *Who 92*
**Simpson,** Roger Lyndon 1942- *AmMWSc 92*
**Simpson,** Ron West 1940- *WhoEnt 92*
**Simpson,** Ronald Abert 1929- *IntAu&W 91*
**Simpson,** Ruby Laird 1910- *WhoFI 92, WhoWest 92*
**Simpson,** Russell Bruce 1942- *AmMWSc 92*
**Simpson,** Russell Gordon 1927- *WhoAmL 92*
**Simpson,** Ruth 1889-1964 *TwCPaSc*
**Simpson,** S H, Jr 1907- *AmMWSc 92*
**Simpson,** Samuel G. 1931- *WhoBlA 92*
**Simpson,** Sidney Burgess, Jr 1935- *AmMWSc 92*
**Simpson,** Stephen G 1945- *AmMWSc 92*
**Simpson,** Stephen Whittington 1945- *WhoBlA 92*
**Simpson,** Steven Drexell 1953- *WhoAmL 92*
**Simpson,** Stuart Bartley 1960- *WhoEnt 92*
**Simpson,** T B *ScFEYrs*
**Simpson,** Thomas A 1925- *AmMWSc 92*
**Simpson,** Thomas Clyde 1941- *WhoWest 92*
**Simpson,** Tracy L 1937- *AmMWSc 92*
**Simpson,** Valerie *WhoBlA 92*
**Simpson,** Velma Southall 1948- *WhoWest 92*
**Simpson,** Vi 1946- *WhoAmP 91*
**Simpson,** Wallis Warfield *FacFETw*
**Simpson,** Walter 1941- *WhoBlA 92*
**Simpson,** Walter Robert, Jr. 1926- *WhoRel 92*
**Simpson,** Wilburn Dwain 1937- *AmMWSc 92*
**Simpson,** Willa Jean 1943- *WhoBlA 92*
**Simpson,** William 1920- *Who 92*
**Simpson,** William A. 1935- *WhoRel 92*
**Simpson,** William Albert 1934- *AmMWSc 92*
**Simpson,** William Andrew 1946- *WhoWest 92*
**Simpson,** William Arthur 1939- *WhoIns 92, WhoWest 92*
**Simpson,** William Brand 1919- *WhoWest 92*
**Simpson,** William E. 1950- *WhoFI 92*
**Simpson,** William George 1945- *Who 92*
**Simpson,** William H 1938- *WhoIns 92*
**Simpson,** William Henry 1942- *AmMWSc 92*
**Simpson,** William Hood 1888-1980 *FacFETw*
**Simpson,** William Kelly 1855-1914 *BiInAmS*
**Simpson,** William Marshall 1943- *WhoMW 92*
**Simpson,** William Roy 1924- *AmMWSc 92*
**Simpson,** William Stewart 1924- *AmMWSc 92*
**Simpson,** William Tilden 1934- *WhoMW 92*
**Simpson,** William Tracy 1920- *AmMWSc 92*
**Simpson-Herren,** Linda 1927- *AmMWSc 92*
**Simpson-Jones,** Peter Trevor 1914- *Who 92*
**Simpson-Orlebar,** Michael Keith Orlebar 1932- *Who 92*
**Simpson-Watson,** Ora Lee 1943- *WhoBlA 92*
**Simrall,** Harry C F 1912- *AmMWSc 92*
**Simring,** Marvin 1922- *AmMWSc 92*
**Simrock,** Nicolaus 1751-1832 *NewAmDM*
**Sims,** A.K. *TwCWW 91*
**Sims,** Adrienne 1952- *WhoBlA 92*
**Sims,** Andrew Charles Petter 1938- *Who 92*
**Sims,** Asa C, Jr 1919- *AmMWSc 92*
**Sims,** August Charles 1948- *WhoAmL 92*
**Sims,** Barbara M. *WhoBlA 92*
**Sims,** Barbara W 1940- *WhoAmP 91*
**Sims,** Benjamin Turner 1934- *AmMWSc 92*
**Sims,** Bennett Jones 1920- *WhoRel 92*
**Sims,** Bernard John 1915- *IntAu&W 91, WrDr 92*
**Sims,** Bill 1932- *WhoAmP 91*
**Sims,** Billy 1955- *WhoBlA 92*
**Sims,** Calvin Gene 1963- *WhoBlA 92*
**Sims,** Carl W. 1941- *WhoBlA 92*
**Sims,** Carolyn Denise 1960- *WhoAmL 92*
**Sims,** Charles 1873-1928 *TwCPaSc*
**Sims,** Charles, Jr. 1952- *WhoFI 92*
**Sims,** Chester Thomas 1923- *AmMWSc 92*
**Sims,** Constance Arlette 1940- *WhoBlA 92*
**Sims,** David Aaron 1964- *WhoAmL 92*
**Sims,** David Lee 1949- *WhoMW 92*
**Sims,** Dennis C. *WhoEnt 92*
**Sims,** Dorothy Clay 1957- *WhoAmL 92*
**Sims,** Ed 1941- *WhoAmP 91*
**Sims,** Edward Hackney 1944- *WhoBlA 92*
**Sims,** Ernest Theodore, Jr 1932- *AmMWSc 92*
**Sims,** Ethan Allen Hitchcock 1916- *AmMWSc 92*
**Sims,** Eugene Ralph, Jr. 1920- *WhoFI 92*
**Sims,** Ezra 1928- *ConCom 92, NewAmDM, WhoEnt 92*
**Sims,** Frank McNair 1932- *WhoFI 92*
**Sims,** Genevieve Constance 1947- *WhoBlA 92*

**Sims**, Geoffrey Donald 1926- *IntWW 91, Who 92*
**Sims**, George 1923- *WrDr 92*
**Sims**, George Frederick Robert 1923- *IntAu&W 91*
**Sims**, Harold Rudolph 1935- *WhoBlA 92*
**Sims**, James Edward, Jr. 1957- *WhoMW 92*
**Sims**, James Joseph 1937- *AmMWSc 92*
**Sims**, James Marion, Jr. 1957- *WhoWest 92*
**Sims**, James R 1918- *AmMWSc 92*
**Sims**, Jeffrey Lloyd 1958- *WhoFI 92*
**Sims**, Joan 1930- *IntMPA 92*
**Sims**, Joe 1944- *WhoAmL 92*
**Sims**, John *TwCWW 91*
**Sims**, John David 1939- *AmMWSc 92*
**Sims**, John Edward, Jr. 1946- *WhoWest 92*
**Sims**, John Haley 1925-1985 *FacFETw*
**Sims**, John Leonard 1934- *WhoBlA 92*
**Sims**, John Leonidas 1930- *AmMWSc 92*
**Sims**, John LeRoy 1912- *AmMWSc 92*
**Sims**, John Revis 1944- *WhoAmL 92*
**Sims**, John Thomas 1956- *WhoBlA 92*
**Sims**, Johna Lee 1943- *WhoAmP 91*
**Sims**, Joseph Daryl 1959- *WhoRel 92*
**Sims**, Joseph Kirkland 1950- *WhoAmP 91*
**Sims**, Joseph William 1937- *WhoBlA 92*
**Sims**, Laura Mack 1914- *WhoBlA 92*
**Sims**, Leslie Berl 1937- *AmMWSc 92*
**Sims**, Lieutenant A.K. *BenetAL 91*
**Sims**, Lowery Stokes 1949- *WhoBlA 92*
**Sims**, Lydia Theresa 1920- *WhoBlA 92*
**Sims**, Melvin Thomas, Jr 1933- *WhoAmP 91*
**Sims**, Monica Louie *Who 92*
**Sims**, Naomi 1948- *NotBlAW 92*
**Sims**, Naomi R. 1949- *WhoBlA 92*
**Sims**, Patsy 1938- *ConAu 135, WrDr 92*
**Sims**, Paul A. 1922-1988 *WhoBlA 92N*
**Sims**, Paul Kibler 1918- *AmMWSc 92, WhoWest 92*
**Sims**, Pete, Jr. 1924- *WhoBlA 92*
**Sims**, Peter Jay *AmMWSc 92*
**Sims**, Phillip C. 1932-1987 *WhoBlA 92N*
**Sims**, Phillip Leon 1940- *AmMWSc 92*
**Sims**, Randy Rook 1953- *WhoMW 92*
**Sims**, Rex J 1922- *AmMWSc 92*
**Sims**, Ripley Singleton 1907- *WhoBlA 92*
**Sims**, Robert Alan 1936- *AmMWSc 92*
**Sims**, Robert Bell 1934- *WhoAmP 91*
**Sims**, Robert Carl 1936- *WhoWest 92*
**Sims**, Roger Edward 1930- *Who 92*
**Sims**, Ronald 1944- *TwCPaSc*
**Sims**, Ronald Cordell 1948- *WhoBlA 92*
**Sims**, Ronald LaMar 1949- *WhoMW 92*
**Sims**, Ruth Leiserson 1920- *WhoAmP 91*
**Sims**, Samuel John 1934- *AmMWSc 92*
**Sims**, Theophlous Aron, Sr. 1939- *WhoBlA 92*
**Sims**, Victor Dwayne 1959- *WhoMW 92*
**Sims**, William 1922- *WhoBlA 92*
**Sims**, William Dale 1941- *WhoIns 92*
**Sims**, William E. 1921- *WhoBlA 92*
**Sims**, William Josephus 1920- *WhoWest 92*
**Sims**, William Lynn 1924- *AmMWSc 92*
**Sims**, Zoot 1925-1985 *NewAmDM*
**Sims-Davis**, Edith R. 1932- *WhoBlA 92*
**Sims-Roberts**, Priscilla 1957- *WhoBlA 92*
**Sims-Williams**, Nicholas John 1949- *Who 92*
**Simson**, Gary Joseph 1950- *WhoAmL 92*
**Simson**, Jo Anne V 1936- *AmMWSc 92*
**Simson**, Michael Ronald Fraser 1913- *Who 92*
**Simson**, Otto von 1912- *IntWW 91*
**Simton**, Chester 1937- *WhoBlA 92*
**Simunich**, Mary Elizabeth Hedrick *WhoWest 92*
**Sin**, Jaime L. 1928- *IntWW 91*
**Sin**, Jaime Lachica 1928- *WhoRel 92*
**Sin Hyok**, Chong *WhoRel 92*
**Sinacore-Guinn**, David Earl 1952- *WhoAmL 92*
**Sinagege R M**, Utu *WhoAmP 91*
**Sinagra**, Anthony Carl 1940- *WhoAmP 91*
**Sinai**, Allen Leo 1939- *WhoFI 92*
**Sinai**, John Joseph 1930- *AmMWSc 92*
**Sinanoglu**, Oktay 1935- *AmMWSc 92*
**Sinard**, Craig Paul 1951- *WhoEnt 92*
**Sinatra**, Francis Albert 1915- *Who 92*
**Sinatra**, Frank *LesBEnT 92*
**Sinatra**, Frank 1915- *ConTFT 9, FacFETw [port], IntMPA 92, IntWW 91, NewAmDM, RComAH, WhoEnt 92*
**Sinay**, Florence Tsu 1949- *WhoEnt 92*
**Sinay**, Hershel David 1938- *WhoEnt 92*
**Sinbad** *WhoEnt 92*
**Sinbad** 1957?- *ConBlB 1 [port], WhoBlA 92*
**Sinberg**, Ulo Lembit 1931- *WhoEnt 92*
**Sincerbeaux**, Robert Abbott 1913- *WhoAmL 92*
**Sincius**, Joseph Anthony 1926- *AmMWSc 92*
**Sinclair** *Who 92*
**Sinclair**, Lord 1914- *Who 92*
**Sinclair**, Master of 1968- *Who 92*
**Sinclair**, A Richard 1940- *AmMWSc 92*
**Sinclair**, Abiola *DrAPF 91*
**Sinclair**, Alastair James 1935- *AmMWSc 92*
**Sinclair**, Alexander Riddell 1917- *Who 92*
**Sinclair**, Andrew 1935- *ConNov 91, IntMPA 92, WrDr 92*
**Sinclair**, Andrew Annandale 1935- *IntAu&W 91, Who 92*
**Sinclair**, Annette 1916- *AmMWSc 92*
**Sinclair**, Benito A. 1931- *WhoBlA 92*
**Sinclair**, Bennie Lee *DrAPF 91*
**Sinclair**, Bradley Howard 1957- *WhoAmL 92*
**Sinclair**, Brett Jason *AmMWSc 92*
**Sinclair**, Carol Louise 1955- *IntAu&W 91*
**Sinclair**, Charles James Francis 1948- *Who 92*
**Sinclair**, Charles Kent 1938- *AmMWSc 92*
**Sinclair**, Clayton, Jr. 1933- *WhoBlA 92*
**Sinclair**, Clive 1940- *DcTwDes, Who 92*
**Sinclair**, Clive Marles 1940- *IntWW 91*
**Sinclair**, D G 1933- *AmMWSc 92*
**Sinclair**, David Cecil 1915- *Who 92*
**Sinclair**, Douglas C 1938- *AmMWSc 92*
**Sinclair**, Emil 1877-1962 *WhoNob 90*
**Sinclair**, Ernest Keith 1914- *IntWW 91, Who 92*
**Sinclair**, Erroll Norman 1909- *Who 92*
**Sinclair**, Gary Marc 1950- *WhoMW 92*
**Sinclair**, George 1912- *AmMWSc 92*
**Sinclair**, George Brian 1928- *Who 92*
**Sinclair**, George Evelyn 1912- *Who 92*
**Sinclair**, George M 1922- *AmMWSc 92*
**Sinclair**, Glenn Bruce 1946- *AmMWSc 92*
**Sinclair**, Grace *ConAu 35NR*
**Sinclair**, Harold 1907-1966 *BenetAL 91*
**Sinclair**, Henry Beall 1930- *AmMWSc 92*
**Sinclair**, Hugh 1910-1990 *AnObit 1990*
**Sinclair**, Iain 1943- *ConPo 91, WrDr 92*
**Sinclair**, Ian David 1913- *IntWW 91, Who 92*
**Sinclair**, Ian McCahon 1929- *IntWW 91, Who 92*
**Sinclair**, Ian McTaggart 1926- *Who 92*
**Sinclair**, Isabel Lillias *Who 92*
**Sinclair**, Ivan Benjamin 1933- *WhoAmL 92*
**Sinclair**, Ivan Earl 1937- *WhoAmP 91*
**Sinclair**, J Cameron 1918- *AmMWSc 92*
**Sinclair**, J. W. *WhoRel 92*
**Sinclair**, J. Walter 1953- *WhoAmL 92*
**Sinclair**, James *WrDr 92*
**Sinclair**, James 1852?-1915 *BiInAmS*
**Sinclair**, James Brimmer 1947- *WhoEnt 92*
**Sinclair**, James Burton 1927- *AmMWSc 92, WhoMW 92*
**Sinclair**, James Douglas 1945- *AmMWSc 92*
**Sinclair**, John Elbridge 1838-1915 *BiInAmS*
**Sinclair**, John G 1940- *AmMWSc 92*
**Sinclair**, John Henry 1935- *AmMWSc 92*
**Sinclair**, John McHardy 1933- *Who 92*
**Sinclair**, John Richley 1935- *WhoAmP 91*
**Sinclair**, Joseph Samuels 1922- *WhoEnt 92*
**Sinclair**, Judson William 1920- *WhoFI 92*
**Sinclair**, Keith 1922- *Who 92, WrDr 92*
**Sinclair**, Keith Val 1926- *IntWW 91, WrDr 92*
**Sinclair**, Kenneth F 1925- *AmMWSc 92*
**Sinclair**, Kent 1946- *WhoAmL 92*
**Sinclair**, Laurence 1908- *Who 92*
**Sinclair**, Lawrence Albert 1930- *WhoRel 92*
**Sinclair**, Lister 1921- *BenetAL 91*
**Sinclair**, Lonnie Ray 1952- *WhoMW 92*
**Sinclair**, Madge *WhoEnt 92*
**Sinclair**, Madge 1938- *IntMPA 92*
**Sinclair**, Madge 1940- *WhoBlA 92*
**Sinclair**, Margaret Katherine 1941- *WhoEnt 92*
**Sinclair**, Maurice Walter *Who 92*
**Sinclair**, May 1863-1946 *RfGEnL 91*
**Sinclair**, Michael *Who 92*
**Sinclair**, Michael Mackay 1944- *AmMWSc 92*
**Sinclair**, Nicholas Roderick 1936- *AmMWSc 92*
**Sinclair**, Norval A 1935- *AmMWSc 92*
**Sinclair**, Olga 1923- *WrDr 92*
**Sinclair**, Olga Ellen 1923- *IntAu&W 91*
**Sinclair**, Orriette Coiner 1921- *WhoAmP 91*
**Sinclair**, Patrick 1936- *Who 92*
**Sinclair**, Peter C 1929- *AmMWSc 92*
**Sinclair**, Peter Robert 1942- *AmMWSc 92*
**Sinclair**, Peter Ross 1934- *Who 92*
**Sinclair**, Richard Carroll 1948- *WhoAmL 92*
**Sinclair**, Richard Glenn, II 1933- *AmMWSc 92*
**Sinclair**, Robert 1947- *AmMWSc 92*
**Sinclair**, Rolf Malcolm 1929- *AmMWSc 92*
**Sinclair**, Ronald 1931- *AmMWSc 92*
**Sinclair**, Ronald Ormiston 1903- *IntWW 91, Who 92*
**Sinclair**, Sara Voris 1942- *WhoWest 92*
**Sinclair**, Scott B. T. 1953- *WhoWest 92*
**Sinclair**, Sonia 1928- *IntAu&W 91*
**Sinclair**, Thomas Russell 1944- *AmMWSc 92*
**Sinclair**, Upton 1878-1968 *BenetAL 91, DcAmImH, ScFEYrs, TwCSFW 91*
**Sinclair**, Upton Beall 1878-1968 *FacFETw [port]*
**Sinclair**, Warren Keith 1924- *AmMWSc 92*
**Sinclair**, Wayne A 1936- *AmMWSc 92*
**Sinclair**, William Donald *WhoRel 92, WhoWest 92*
**Sinclair**, William Robert 1924- *AmMWSc 92*
**Sinclair De Rochemont**, Hugues Alexandre 1901-1942 *BiDExR*
**Sinclair-Lockhart**, Simon 1941- *Who 92*
**Sinclair of Cleeve**, Baron 1953- *Who 92*
**Sinclair of Freswick**, David Boyd A. *Who 92*
**Sinclair Oyaneder**, Santiago 1927- *IntWW 91*
**Sinclair-Stevenson**, Christopher Terence 1939- *Who 92*
**Sincoff**, Michael Z. 1943- *WhoFI 92*
**Sincoff**, Steven Lawrence 1948- *WhoWest 92*
**Sincovec**, Richard Frank 1942- *AmMWSc 92*
**Sindall**, Adrian John 1937- *Who 92*
**Sindelar**, Jody Louise 1951- *WhoFI 92*
**Sindelar**, Robert D 1952- *AmMWSc 92*
**Sindell**, David Irwin 1912- *WhoAmL 92*
**Sindell**, Marion Harwood 1925- *Who 92*
**Sinden**, Donald 1923- *IntMPA 92*
**Sinden**, Donald Alfred 1923- *IntWW 91, Who 92, WhoEnt 92*
**Sinden**, James Whaples 1902- *AmMWSc 92*
**Sinden**, Jeremy 1950- *ConTFT 9*
**Sinder**, Mike 1946- *WhoAmP 91, WhoHisp 92*
**Sindermann**, Carl James 1922- *AmMWSc 92*
**Sinderoff**, Rita Joyce 1932- *WhoFI 92*
**Sindi**, Kamil 1932- *IntWW 91*
**Sinding**, Christian 1856-1941 *NewAmDM*
**Sindle**, Harvey Bertrand 1930- *WhoAmL 92*
**Sindler**, Bob 1952- *WhoAmP 91*
**Sindler**, Michael H. 1943- *WhoBlA 92*
**Sindos**, Louise King 1930- *WhoBlA 92*
**Sindt**, Carol Anne Wold 1949- *WhoAmP 91*
**Sine**, Amy J. 1962- *WhoAmL 92*
**Sine**, Robert C 1936- *AmMWSc 92*
**Sine**, Wesley Franklin 1936- *WhoWest 92*
**Sinegal**, James D. 1936- *WhoWest 92*
**Sinel**, Norman Mark 1941- *WhoAmL 92*
**Sinensky**, Michael 1945- *AmMWSc 92*
**Sines**, George, Jr 1923- *AmMWSc 92*
**Sines**, Randy Dwain 1948- *WhoWest 92*
**Sines**, Raymond E *WhoAmP 91*
**Sinesio**, Ronald Val 1949- *WhoEnt 92*
**Sinessios** *WhoRel 92*
**Sinex**, Francis Marott 1923- *AmMWSc 92*
**Siney**, John 1831-1880 *DcAmImH*
**Sinfelt**, John Henry 1931- *AmMWSc 92, IntWW 91*
**Sing**, Charles F 1936- *AmMWSc 92*
**Sing**, David Brian 1959- *WhoMW 92*
**Sing**, William Bender 1947- *WhoAmL 92*
**Singal**, Dharam Parkash 1934- *AmMWSc 92*
**Singal**, Pawan Kumar 1946- *AmMWSc 92*
**Singal**, Vijay 1954- *WhoFI 92*
**Singaram**, Bakthan 1950- *AmMWSc 92*
**Singel**, Mark Stephen 1953- *WhoAmP 91*
**Singer**, Adam *WrDr 92*
**Singer**, Alan G 1940- *AmMWSc 92*
**Singer**, Alexander Theodore 1945- *WhoAmP 91*
**Singer**, Alfred 1946- *AmMWSc 92*
**Singer**, Alfred Ernst 1924- *Who 92*
**Singer**, Alma I. 1907- *WhoFI 92*
**Singer**, Arlene 1948- *WhoAmP 91*
**Singer**, Arnold J 1915- *AmMWSc 92*
**Singer**, Arthur Chester 1936- *AmMWSc 92*
**Singer**, Aubrey Edward 1927- *Who 92*
**Singer**, B *AmMWSc 92*
**Singer**, Barney 1961- *WhoAmL 92*
**Singer**, Barry Edward 1945- *WhoEnt 92*
**Singer**, Barry M 1940- *AmMWSc 92*
**Singer**, Benjamin D. 1931- *WrDr 92*
**Singer**, Burton Herbert 1938- *AmMWSc 92*
**Singer**, Carl Norman 1916- *WhoFI 92*
**Singer**, Cecile D *WhoAmP 91*
**Singer**, Charlie 1961- *WhoEnt 92*
**Singer**, Daniel Morris 1930- *WhoFI 92*
**Singer**, David Michael 1957- *WhoEnt 92, WhoFI 92*
**Singer**, Davida *DrAPF 91*
**Singer**, Don B 1934- *AmMWSc 92*
**Singer**, Donald Allen 1943- *AmMWSc 92*
**Singer**, Donald H 1929- *AmMWSc 92*
**Singer**, Donald Henry 1929- *WhoMW 92*
**Singer**, Eugen 1926- *AmMWSc 92*
**Singer**, Frieda *DrAPF 91*
**Singer**, Frieda 1938- *IntAu&W 91*
**Singer**, Gary Ira 1954- *WhoMW 92*
**Singer**, Gary James 1952- *WhoAmL 92*
**Singer**, George 1937- *AmMWSc 92*
**Singer**, George Alan 1948- *WhoEnt 92*
**Singer**, Harold Samuel 1935- *Who 92*
**Singer**, Harry Bruce 1921- *Who 92*
**Singer**, Howard Joseph 1944- *AmMWSc 92*
**Singer**, Ira 1923- *AmMWSc 92*
**Singer**, Ira Michael 1944- *WhoFI 92*
**Singer**, Irwin *AmMWSc 92*
**Singer**, Irwin I 1943- *AmMWSc 92*
**Singer**, Isaac *ConAu 134, SmATA 68*
**Singer**, Isaac B. *DrAPF 91*
**Singer**, Isaac Bashevis d1991 *Who 92N*
**Singer**, Isaac Bashevis 1904- *BenetAL 91, FacFETw, IntAu&W 91, IntWW 91, LiExTwC, WhoNob 90, WrDr 92*
**Singer**, Isaac Bashevis 1904-1991 *ConAu 134, ConLC 69 [port], CurBio 91N, DcLB Y91N [port], NewYTBS 91 [port], News 92-1, SmATA 68*
**Singer**, Isabelle Gibbs 1939- *WhoEnt 92*
**Singer**, Isadore Manual 1924- *AmMWSc 92*
**Singer**, Isadore Manuel 1924- *IntWW 91*
**Singer**, Israel Joshua 1893-1944 *BenetAL 91, LiExTwC*
**Singer**, J. David 1925- *WrDr 92*
**Singer**, Jack W 1942- *AmMWSc 92*
**Singer**, Jan Peter 1944- *Who 92*
**Singer**, Jeanne 1924- *WhoEnt 92*
**Singer**, Jeffrey 1950- *WhoAmL 92*
**Singer**, Jeffrey Alan 1952- *WhoWest 92*
**Singer**, Jerome Ralph 1921- *AmMWSc 92*
**Singer**, John 1947- *WhoAmP 91*
**Singer**, Joshua J 1942- *AmMWSc 92*
**Singer**, Kay Hiemstra *AmMWSc 92*
**Singer**, Kurt Deutsch 1911- *IntAu&W 91*
**Singer**, Lawrence Alan 1936- *AmMWSc 92*
**Singer**, Leon 1918- *AmMWSc 92*
**Singer**, Leonard Sidney 1923- *AmMWSc 92*
**Singer**, Linda Carol 1950- *WhoAmL 92*
**Singer**, Lisa Ilene 1959- *WhoFI 92*
**Singer**, Lori 1962- *IntMPA 92*
**Singer**, Marc *IntMPA 92*
**Singer**, Marcus 1914- *AmMWSc 92*
**Singer**, Marcus George 1926- *WrDr 92*
**Singer**, Marilyn 1948- *SmATA 13AS [port]*
**Singer**, Mark Douglas 1952- *WhoAmL 92*
**Singer**, Maxine 1931- *IntWW 91*
**Singer**, Maxine Frank 1931- *AmMWSc 92*
**Singer**, Merle Elliot 1939- *WhoRel 92*
**Singer**, Michael 1950- *AmMWSc 92*
**Singer**, Michael Gerald 1941- *WhoAmL 92*
**Singer**, Michael Howard 1941- *WhoAmL 92, WhoWest 92*
**Singer**, Miriam 1959- *WhoHisp 92*
**Singer**, Myer Richard 1938- *WhoAmL 92*
**Singer**, Norbert 1931- *Who 92*
**Singer**, Norman Sol 1937- *WhoMW 92*
**Singer**, Oscar 1920- *IntAu&W 91*
**Singer**, Paul A 1949- *AmMWSc 92*
**Singer**, Paul H., Mrs. 1941- *WhoEnt 92*
**Singer**, Paul Meyer 1943- *WhoAmL 92*
**Singer**, Paula Noyes 1944- *WhoAmL 92*
**Singer**, Paulette Miller 1936- *WhoEnt 92*
**Singer**, Peter *Who 92*
**Singer**, Peter 1946- *CurBio 91 [port], WrDr 92*
**Singer**, Peter Albert David 1946- *IntWW 91*
**Singer**, Philip C 1942- *AmMWSc 92*
**Singer**, Ray Eleazer 1916- *WhoEnt 92*
**Singer**, Richard Alan 1945- *AmMWSc 92*
**Singer**, Robert *IntMPA 92*
**Singer**, Robert Mark 1943- *AmMWSc 92*
**Singer**, Robert W 1947- *WhoAmP 91*
**Singer**, Rolf 1906- *AmMWSc 92*
**Singer**, Ronald 1924- *AmMWSc 92*
**Singer**, Rose M. d1991 *NewYTBS 91 [port]*
**Singer**, S Fred 1924- *AmMWSc 92*
**Singer**, S J 1924- *AmMWSc 92*
**Singer**, Samuel 1927- *AmMWSc 92*
**Singer**, Sanford Robert 1930- *WhoFI 92*
**Singer**, Sanford Sandy 1940- *AmMWSc 92*
**Singer**, Sarah *DrAPF 91*
**Singer**, Sarah Beth 1915- *WrDr 92*
**Singer**, Solomon Elias 1919- *AmMWSc 92*
**Singer**, Stanley 1925- *AmMWSc 92*
**Singer**, Stanley Thomas, Jr. 1933- *WhoMW 92*
**Singer**, Stuart H. 1956- *WhoAmL 92*
**Singer**, Susan Rundell 1959- *AmMWSc 92*
**Singer**, Thomas Peter 1920- *AmMWSc 92*
**Singer**, William Merrill 1942- *AmMWSc 92*
**Singer-Delmonico**, Rina Dawn 1956- *WhoWest 92*
**Singewald**, Martin Louis 1909- *AmMWSc 92*

**Singewald**, Quentin Dreyer 1902- *AmMWSc 92*
**Singh**, Ajaib 1935- *AmMWSc 92*
**Singh**, Ajit 1932- *AmMWSc 92*
**Singh**, Amarjit 1924- *AmMWSc 92*
**Singh**, Amreek 1935- *AmMWSc 92*
**Singh**, Amritjit 1945- *WrDr 92*
**Singh**, Arjun 1943- *AmMWSc 92*
**Singh**, Avtar 1947- *WhoWest 92*
**Singh**, Baldev 1931- *WhoAmP 91*
**Singh**, Baldev 1939- *AmMWSc 92*
**Singh**, Balwant 1934- *AmMWSc 92*
**Singh**, Bhagat 1940- *WhoMW 92*
**Singh**, Bhagirath 1946- *AmMWSc 92*
**Singh**, Bharat 1939- *AmMWSc 92*
**Singh**, Bhishma Narain 1933- *IntWW 91*
**Singh**, Bipin 1918- *IntWW 91*
**Singh**, Buta 1934- *IntWW 91*
**Singh**, Chanchal 1934- *AmMWSc 92*
**Singh**, Charan 1916- *RelLAm 91*
**Singh**, Darshan 1921- *ConAu 133, IntAu&W 91*
**Singh**, Darshan 1921-1989 *RelLAm 91*
**Singh**, Daulat 1939- *AmMWSc 92*
**Singh**, Dilbagh 1934- *AmMWSc 92*
**Singh**, Dinesh 1925- *IntWW 91*
**Singh**, Garnish Benedict 1927- *WhoRel 92*
**Singh**, Giani Zail 1916- *IntWW 91, Who 92*
**Singh**, Gopal 1919- *IntWW 91*
**Singh**, Gurcharan 1917- *IntAu&W 91*
**Singh**, Gurdial 1934- *AmMWSc 92*
**Singh**, Gurmukh 1950- *AmMWSc 92*
**Singh**, Hakam 1928- *AmMWSc 92*
**Singh**, Harbans *WhoRel 92*
**Singh**, Harbha Jan 1941- *WhoMW 92*
**Singh**, Harbhajan 1941- *AmMWSc 92*
**Singh**, Harpal P 1941- *AmMWSc 92*
**Singh**, Harwant 1934- *AmMWSc 92*
**Singh**, Inder Jit 1939- *AmMWSc 92*
**Singh**, Inderjit 1943- *AmMWSc 92*
**Singh**, Iqbal 1926- *AmMWSc 92*
**Singh**, Jag Jeet 1926- *AmMWSc 92*
**Singh**, Jagbir 1940- *AmMWSc 92*
**Singh**, Jarnail 1941- *AmMWSc 92*
**Singh**, Jaswant 1937- *AmMWSc 92*
**Singh**, Kanhaya Lal 1944- *AmMWSc 92*
**Singh**, Kanwar N. *Who 92*
**Singh**, Karan 1931- *IntWW 91*
**Singh**, Kewal 1915- *IntWW 91*
**Singh**, Khushwant 1915- *ConNov 91, IntWW 91, RfGEnL 91, Who 92, WrDr 92*
**Singh**, Kirpal 1894-1974 *RelLAm 91*
**Singh**, Laxman 1944- *AmMWSc 92*
**Singh**, Madan Gopal 1946- *AmMWSc 92*
**Singh**, Madho 1936- *AmMWSc 92*
**Singh**, Mahendra Pal 1941- *AmMWSc 92*
**Singh**, Mahendra Pratap 1950- *WhoWest 92*
**Singh**, Malathy 1942- *AmMWSc 92*
**Singh**, Manmohan 1940- *WhoMW 92*
**Singh**, Manohar 1930- *AmMWSc 92*
**Singh**, Mansa C 1928- *AmMWSc 92*
**Singh**, Mota 1930- *Who 92*
**Singh**, Mrityunjay 1957- *AmMWSc 92*
**Singh**, Naresh Pratap 1959- *WhoWest 92*
**Singh**, Param Indar 1946- *AmMWSc 92*
**Singh**, Preetam 1914- *Who 92*
**Singh**, Prithe Paul 1930- *AmMWSc 92*
**Singh**, Prithipal 1939- *AmMWSc 92*
**Singh**, Rabindar Nath 1931- *AmMWSc 92*
**Singh**, Raghbir 1931- *AmMWSc 92*
**Singh**, Raj Kumari 1948- *AmMWSc 92*
**Singh**, Raja Roy 1918- *IntWW 91*
**Singh**, Rajendra 1950- *AmMWSc 92*
**Singh**, Rajendra P. 1934- *WhoBlA 92*
**Singh**, Rajinder 1931- *AmMWSc 92*
**Singh**, Rama Shankar 1938- *AmMWSc 92*
**Singh**, Rama Shankar 1945- *AmMWSc 92*
**Singh**, Raman J 1940- *AmMWSc 92*
**Singh**, Rameshwar 1937- *AmMWSc 92*
**Singh**, Ravi *DrAPF 91*
**Singh**, Ripu Daman *AmMWSc 92*
**Singh**, Roderick Pataudi 1935- *AmMWSc 92*
**Singh**, Rudra Prasad 1940- *AmMWSc 92*
**Singh**, Sankatha Prasad 1937- *AmMWSc 92*
**Singh**, Sant Parkash 1936- *AmMWSc 92*
**Singh**, Sant Thakar 1929- *RelLAm 91*
**Singh**, Sardar Swaran 1907- *IntWW 91, Who 92*
**Singh**, Sawan 1858-1948 *RelLAm 91*
**Singh**, Shiva Pujan 1947- *AmMWSc 92*
**Singh**, Shobha 1928- *AmMWSc 92*
**Singh**, Shyam N 1952- *AmMWSc 92*
**Singh**, Sukhjit 1941- *AmMWSc 92*
**Singh**, Sukhmander *IntWW 91*
**Singh**, Suman Priyadarshi Narain 1941- *AmMWSc 92*
**Singh**, Surendra Pal 1953- *AmMWSc 92*
**Singh**, Surinder Shah 1937- *AmMWSc 92*
**Singh**, Surjit 1931- *AmMWSc 92*
**Singh**, Tara 1921- *WhoWest 92*
**Singh**, Teja 1928- *AmMWSc 92*
**Singh**, Trilochan 1937- *AmMWSc 92*
**Singh**, Vijay P 1946- *AmMWSc 92*
**Singh**, Vijay Pal 1947- *AmMWSc 92*
**Singh**, Vijendra Kumar 1947- *AmMWSc 92, WhoWest 92*
**Singh**, Vishwa Nath 1936- *AmMWSc 92*
**Singh**, Vishwanath Pratap 1931- *IntWW 91, Who 92*
**Singhal**, Avinash Chandra 1941- *AmMWSc 92*
**Singhal**, Radhey Lal 1940- *AmMWSc 92*
**Singhal**, Ram P 1939- *AmMWSc 92*
**Singhal**, Sharwan Kumar 1939- *AmMWSc 92*
**Singham**, Archibald W. d1991 *NewYTBS 91*
**Singhania**, D. C. 1932- *IntWW 91*
**Singhania**, Padampat 1905- *Who 92*
**Singhasaneh**, Suthee 1928- *IntWW 91*
**Singher**, Martial 1904-1990 *NewAmDM*
**Singhvi**, Laxmi Mall 1931- *IntWW 91, Who 92*
**Singhvi**, Sampat Manakchand 1947- *AmMWSc 92*
**Singiser**, Robert Eugene 1930- *AmMWSc 92*
**Single**, Richard Wayne, Sr. 1938- *WhoAmL 92*
**Singlehurst**, Dona Geisenheyner 1928- *WhoWest 92*
**Singler**, Robert Edward 1941- *AmMWSc 92*
**Singletary**, Alvin D. 1942- *WhoAmL 92, WhoFI 92*
**Singletary**, Inez M. *WhoBlA 92*
**Singletary**, John Boon 1928- *AmMWSc 92*
**Singletary**, Lillian Darlington *AmMWSc 92*
**Singletary**, Mike 1958- *WhoBlA 92*
**Singletary**, Patricia Ann 1948- *WhoRel 92*
**Singletary**, Reggie 1964- *WhoBlA 92*
**Singletary**, Robert Lombard 1941- *AmMWSc 92*
**Singletary**, Thomas Alexander 1937- *AmMWSc 92*
**Singletary**, William Hale 1951- *WhoAmP 91*
**Singleterry**, Gary Lee 1948- *WhoFI 92*
**Singleton**, Alan Herbert 1936- *AmMWSc 92*
**Singleton**, Alice Faye *WhoWest 92*
**Singleton**, Alvin 1940- *ConCom 92*
**Singleton**, Barry Neill 1946- *Who 92*
**Singleton**, Benjamin, Sr. 1943- *WhoBlA 92*
**Singleton**, Bert 1928- *AmMWSc 92*
**Singleton**, Chloe Joi 1943- *AmMWSc 92*
**Singleton**, Chris 1967- *WhoBlA 92*
**Singleton**, David Michael 1939- *AmMWSc 92*
**Singleton**, Donald Lee 1944- *AmMWSc 92*
**Singleton**, E. Byron 1909- *WhoFI 92*
**Singleton**, Edgar Bryson 1926- *AmMWSc 92*
**Singleton**, Edward 1921- *Who 92*
**Singleton**, Ernie *WhoBlA 92*
**Singleton**, George Terrell 1927- *AmMWSc 92*
**Singleton**, Gregory Alan 1952- *WhoRel 92*
**Singleton**, Harold Craig 1950- *WhoWest 92*
**Singleton**, Harold Douglas 1908- *WhoBlA 92*
**Singleton**, Harry M 1949- *WhoAmP 91, WhoBlA 92*
**Singleton**, Henry E 1916- *AmMWSc 92*
**Singleton**, Henry Earl 1916- *WhoWest 92*
**Singleton**, Herbert 1947- *WhoBlA 92*
**Singleton**, Isaac, Sr. 1928- *WhoBlA 92*
**Singleton**, Jack Howard 1926- *AmMWSc 92*
**Singleton**, James Benjamin, Jr. 1902- *WhoBlA 92*
**Singleton**, James L 1920- *AmMWSc 92*
**Singleton**, James LeRoy 1944- *WhoBlA 92*
**Singleton**, James M 1933- *WhoAmP 91*
**Singleton**, James Milton 1933- *WhoBlA 92*
**Singleton**, John *NewYTBS 91 [port]*
**Singleton**, John 1968- *ConBlB 2 [port]*
**Singleton**, John Alan 1960- *WhoMW 92*
**Singleton**, John Byrne 1930- *AmMWSc 92*
**Singleton**, John Virgil, Jr. 1918- *WhoAmL 92*
**Singleton**, Kenneth Wayne 1947- *WhoBlA 92*
**Singleton**, Leroy, Sr. 1941- *WhoBlA 92*
**Singleton**, Lisa Michelle 1961- *WhoWest 92*
**Singleton**, Margeaux 1950- *WhoEnt 92*
**Singleton**, Marvin 1939- *WhoAmP 91*
**Singleton**, Mary Clyde 1912- *AmMWSc 92*
**Singleton**, Norman 1913- *Who 92*
**Singleton**, Penny 1908- *IntMPA 92*
**Singleton**, Ralph Stuart 1940- *WhoEnt 92*
**Singleton**, Richard Collom 1928- *AmMWSc 92*
**Singleton**, Rivers, Jr 1939- *AmMWSc 92*
**Singleton**, Robert 1936- *WhoBlA 92*
**Singleton**, Robert Richmond 1913- *AmMWSc 92*
**Singleton**, Roger 1942- *Who 92*
**Singleton**, Tommy Clark 1928- *AmMWSc 92*
**Singleton**, Valerie 1937- *Who 92*
**Singleton**, Vernon LeRoy 1923- *AmMWSc 92*
**Singleton**, W James 1949- *WhoAmP 91*
**Singleton**, Wayne Louis 1944- *AmMWSc 92*
**Singleton**, William Brian 1923- *Who 92*
**Singleton**, William Dean 1951- *IntWW 91, WhoWest 92*
**Singleton**, William Matthew 1924- *WhoBlA 92*
**Singleton**, Woodard L., Jr. 1942- *WhoRel 92*
**Singleton**, Zutty 1898-1975 *NewAmDM*
**Singley**, Elijah 1935- *WhoBlA 92*
**Singley**, John Edward 1924- *AmMWSc 92*
**Singley**, Mark E 1921- *AmMWSc 92*
**Singley**, Yvonne Jean 1947- *WhoBlA 92*
**Singman**, Bruce Howard 1941- *WhoEnt 92, WhoWest 92*
**Singmaster**, Edwin Henry 1911- *WhoAmP 91*
**Singmaster**, Elsie 1879-1958 *BenetAL 91*
**Singmaster-Hernandez**, Karen Amalia 1960- *WhoHisp 92*
**Singpurwalla**, Nozer Drabsha 1939- *AmMWSc 92*
**Singwi**, Kundan Singh 1919- *AmMWSc 92*
**Sinha**, Baron 1920- *Who 92*
**Sinha**, Akhouri Achyutanand 1933- *AmMWSc 92*
**Sinha**, Akhouri Suresh Chandra 1938- *AmMWSc 92*
**Sinha**, Akhuary Krishna 1941- *AmMWSc 92*
**Sinha**, Arabinda Kumar 1933- *AmMWSc 92*
**Sinha**, Asru Kumar 1943- *AmMWSc 92*
**Sinha**, Bidhu Bhushan Prasad *AmMWSc 92*
**Sinha**, Birandra Kumar 1945- *AmMWSc 92*
**Sinha**, Dipen N 1951- *AmMWSc 92*
**Sinha**, Dipendra Kumar 1945- *WhoWest 92*
**Sinha**, Helen Luella 1936- *AmMWSc 92*
**Sinha**, Indranand 1931- *AmMWSc 92*
**Sinha**, Kumares C 1942- *AmMWSc 92*
**Sinha**, Mahendra Kumar 1931- *AmMWSc 92*
**Sinha**, Mihir Kumar *WhoFI 92*
**Sinha**, Naresh Kumar 1927- *AmMWSc 92*
**Sinha**, Navin Kumar 1945- *AmMWSc 92*
**Sinha**, Om Prakash *AmMWSc 92*
**Sinha**, Raj P 1934- *AmMWSc 92*
**Sinha**, Rajiv Krishna 1959- *WhoWest 92*
**Sinha**, Ramesh Chandra 1934- *AmMWSc 92*
**Sinha**, Ranendra Nath 1930- *AmMWSc 92*
**Sinha**, Shome Nath 1952- *AmMWSc 92*
**Sinha**, Snehesh Kumar *AmMWSc 92*
**Sinha**, Sunil K 1939- *AmMWSc 92*
**Sinha**, Vinod T 1941- *AmMWSc 92*
**Sinha**, Yagya Nand 1936- *AmMWSc 92*
**Sinibaldi**, Ralph Michael 1947- *AmMWSc 92*
**Sinicropi**, Michael Wilson 1925- *WhoAmP 91*
**Siniff**, Donald Blair 1935- *AmMWSc 92*
**Sinise**, Gary *ConTFT 9, WhoEnt 92*
**Sinisgalli**, Leonardo 1908-1981 *DcLB 114 [port]*
**Sinishta**, Gjon 1930- *WhoRel 92, WhoWest 92*
**Sink**, David Scott 1950- *AmMWSc 92*
**Sink**, Donald Woodfin 1937- *AmMWSc 92*
**Sink**, Henry Ray 1934- *WhoRel 92*
**Sink**, John Davis 1934- *AmMWSc 92*
**Sink**, John Davis 1949- *WhoWest 92*
**Sink**, Kenneth C, Jr 1937- *AmMWSc 92*
**Sink**, Robert L. 1952- *WhoMW 92*
**Sinkankas**, John 1915- *WrDr 92*
**Sinke**, Carl 1928- *AmMWSc 92*
**Sinker**, Michael Roy 1908- *Who 92*
**Sinkey**, Joseph Francis, Jr. 1944- *WhoFI 92*
**Sinkfield**, Georganna T *WhoAmP 91*
**Sinkfield**, Richard H. 1942- *WhoAmL 92*
**Sinkford**, Jeanne C 1933- *AmMWSc 92*
**Sinkler**, George 1927- *WhoBlA 92*
**Sinkler**, Wharton 1845-1910 *BiInAmS*
**Sinkovics**, Joseph G 1924- *AmMWSc 92*
**Sinks**, John R 1929- *WhoAmP 91*
**Sinks**, Lucius Frederick 1931- *AmMWSc 92*
**Sinkula**, Anthony Arthur 1938- *AmMWSc 92*
**Sinn**, James Micheal 1950- *WhoMW 92*
**Sinn**, Robert Samuel 1930- *WhoFI 92*
**Sinn**, Steven Lawrence 1945- *WhoFI 92*
**Sinnamon**, Hercules Vincent 1899- *Who 92*
**Sinnatt**, Martin Henry 1928- *Who 92*
**Sinnema**, Donald Wilfred 1947- *WhoRel 92*
**Sinnema**, Elizabeth Jane *WhoFI 92*
**Sinner**, Donald H 1937- *AmMWSc 92*
**Sinner**, George A. 1928- *AlmAP 92 [port], WhoAmP 91*
**Sinner**, George Albert 1928- *IntWW 91, WhoMW 92*
**Sinnett**, Carl E 1922- *AmMWSc 92*
**Sinnett**, William McNair 1951- *WhoFI 92*
**Sinnette**, Calvin Herman 1924- *WhoBlA 92*
**Sinnette**, Elinor DesVerney 1925- *WhoBlA 92*
**Sinnhuber**, Russell Otto 1917- *AmMWSc 92*
**Sinni**, Frank Alexander 1948- *WhoFI 92*
**Sinninger**, Dwight Virgil 1901- *WhoFI 92*
**Sinnis**, James Constantine 1935- *AmMWSc 92*
**Sinnott**, Anneliese 1937- *WhoRel 92*
**Sinnott**, Barbara J 1933- *WhoAmP 91*
**Sinnott**, Ernest d1989 *Who 92N*
**Sinnott**, George 1932- *AmMWSc 92*
**Sinnott**, John Patrick 1931- *WhoAmL 92*
**Sinnott**, Joseph John, III 1954- *WhoRel 92*
**Sinnott**, Kevin 1947- *TwCPaSc*
**Sinnott**, M J 1916- *AmMWSc 92*
**Sinnott**, Richard James 1926- *WhoEnt 92*
**Sinopoli**, Giuseppe 1946- *CurBio 91 [port], IntWW 91, NewAmDM*
**Sinor**, Denis 1916- *WhoMW 92, WrDr 92*
**Sinor**, Howard Earl, Jr. 1949- *WhoAmL 92*
**Sinor**, Lyle Tolbot 1957- *AmMWSc 92*
**Sinoto**, Yosihiko Hiko 1924- *WhoWest 92*
**Sinotte**, Louis Paul 1927- *AmMWSc 92*
**Sinou**, Kira 1923- *IntAu&W 91*
**Sinowatz**, Fred 1929- *IntWW 91*
**Sinsheimer**, Joseph Eugene 1922- *AmMWSc 92*
**Sinsheimer**, Robert Louis 1920- *AmMWSc 92, IntWW 91*
**Sinsheimer**, Warren Jack 1927- *WhoFI 92*
**Sinskey**, Anthony J 1940- *AmMWSc 92*
**Sinski**, James Thomas 1927- *AmMWSc 92*
**Sinstead**, Ronel Edmund 1930- *WhoRel 92*
**Sint**, Marjanne 1949- *IntWW 91*
**Sintetos**, Christopher Peter 1954- *WhoFI 92*
**Sinton**, John Maynard 1946- *AmMWSc 92*
**Sinton**, Steven Williams *AmMWSc 92*
**Sinton**, William Merz 1925- *AmMWSc 92, WhoWest 92*
**Sinyavskaya**, Tamara Ilyinichna 1943- *IntWW 91*
**Sinyavsky**, Andrei 1925- *FacFETw*
**Sinyavsky**, Andrei Donatovich 1925- *LiExTwC*
**Sinyavsky**, Andrey Donatovich 1925- *IntWW 91, SovUnBD*
**Siodmak**, Curt *WhoEnt 92*
**Siodmak**, Curt 1902- *IntMPA 92*
**Siodmak**, Curt 1902-1988 *TwCSFW 91*
**Siodmak**, Kurt 1902- *ScFEYrs*
**Siodmak**, Robert 1900-1973 *IntDcF 2-2 [port]*
**Sion**, Edward Michael 1946- *AmMWSc 92*
**Sion**, Maurice 1928- *AmMWSc 92*
**Sionil Jose**, F. 1924- *ConNov 91*
**Siopes**, Thomas David 1939- *AmMWSc 92*
**Sioui**, Richard Henry 1937- *AmMWSc 92*
**Sioukas**, Jack 1936- *WhoWest 92*
**Siouxa**, Susan Gwendolyn Patel *IntAu&W 91*
**Sipe**, David Michael 1959- *AmMWSc 92*
**Sipe**, Harry Craig 1917- *AmMWSc 92*
**Sipe**, Herbert James, Jr 1940- *AmMWSc 92*
**Sipe**, Jerry Eugene 1942- *AmMWSc 92*
**Sipe**, Roger Wayne 1950- *WhoMW 92*
**Sipek**, Meridith Paul 1946- *WhoWest 92*
**Siperstein**, Marvin David 1925- *AmMWSc 92*
**Sipes**, Bill 1946- *WhoAmP 91*
**Sipes**, Donald 1928- *IntMPA 92*
**Sipes**, Ivan Glenn 1942- *AmMWSc 92, WhoWest 92*
**Sipes**, Theodore Lee 1944- *WhoMW 92*
**Sipes**, Timothy Lane 1951- *WhoRel 92*
**Sipes**, William Donal, Jr. 1958- *WhoRel 92*
**Sipfle**, David Arthur 1932- *WhoMW 92*
**Sipher**, Allen James 1927- *WhoAmP 91*
**Sipherd**, Ray 1935- *WhoEnt 92*
**Siphron**, Joseph Rider 1933- *WhoAmL 92*
**Sipila**, Helvi Linnea 1915- *IntWW 91*
**Sipkoski**, Michael George 1957- *WhoMW 92*
**Sipos**, Chiquita Agnes 1939- *WhoWest 92*
**Sipos**, Frank 1926- *AmMWSc 92*
**Sipos**, Ronald Albert 1957- *WhoAmL 92*
**Sipos**, Tibor 1935- *AmMWSc 92*
**Siposs**, George G 1931- *AmMWSc 92*
**Sippel**, Eric Martin 1961- *WhoFI 92*
**Sippel**, Heinz 1922- *IntWW 91*
**Sippel**, Richard Leo 1938- *WhoAmL 92*
**Sippel**, Theodore Otto 1927- *AmMWSc 92*
**Sippel**, William Leroy 1948- *WhoAmL 92*
**Sipple**, James Francis 1924- *WhoMW 92*
**Sippy**, David Dean 1953- *WhoMW 92*
**Sipress**, Jack M 1935- *AmMWSc 92*

**Sipress**, Morton 1938- WhoAmP 91, WhoMW 92
**Sipson**, Roger Fredrick 1940- AmMWSc 92
**Siquig**, Richard Anthony 1942- AmMWSc 92
**Siracusa**, John 1929- WhoAmP 91
**Siradze**, Viktoria Moiseyevna 1929- IntWW 91
**Siraganian**, Reuben Paul 1940- AmMWSc 92
**Sirat**, Rene-Samuel 1930- IntWW 91, WhoRel 92
**Sirbasku**, David Andrew 1941- AmMWSc 92
**Sirc**, Ljubo 1920- WrDr 92
**Sircar**, Anil Kumer 1928- AmMWSc 92
**Sircar**, Ila 1938- AmMWSc 92
**Sircar**, Jagadish Chandra 1935- AmMWSc 92
**Sircus**, Jan Martin 1949- WhoEnt 92
**Siregar**, Melanchton 1913- IntWW 91
**Sirek**, Anna 1921- AmMWSc 92
**Sirek**, Otakar Victor 1921- AmMWSc 92
**Siren**, Heikki 1918- IntWW 91
**Siren**, Katri Anna-Maija Helena 1920- IntWW 91
**Siri**, Jean Brandenburg 1920- WhoWest 92
**Sirianni**, Carmel A 1922- WhoAmP 91
**Sirianni**, Joyce E 1942- AmMWSc 92
**Sirica**, Alphonse Eugene 1944- AmMWSc 92
**Sirica**, John J 1904- FacFETw
**Sirica**, John Joseph 1904- IntWW 91
**Siricius** EncEarC
**Sirignano**, William Alfonso 1938- AmMWSc 92
**Siringo**, Charles A. 1855-1928 BenetAL 91
**Sirisamphan**, Thienchai 1924- IntWW 91
**Sirius** IntAu&W 91X
**Sirius**, Eye Ehm 1951- WhoEnt 92
**Sirius**, Jean DrAPF 91
**Siriwardane**, Upali 1950- AmMWSc 92
**Sirk**, Artur 1900-1937 BiDExR
**Sirk**, Douglas 1900-1987 FacFETw, IntDcF 2-2 [port]
**Sirken**, Monroe Gilbert 1921- AmMWSc 92
**Sirkin**, Alan N 1944- AmMWSc 92
**Sirkin**, Joel H. 1946- WhoAmL 92
**Sirkin**, Leslie A 1933- AmMWSc 92
**Sirkis**, Jon 1958- WhoEnt 92
**Sirlin**, Alberto 1930- AmMWSc 92
**Sirlin**, Julio Leo 1926- AmMWSc 92
**Sirlin**, Philip Jack 1953- WhoFI 92
**Sirmans**, Meredith Franklin 1939- WhoBlA 92
**Sirocky**, Gerard Joseph 1944- WhoWest 92
**Sirof**, Harriet DrAPF 91
**Sirof**, Harriet Toby 1930- IntAu&W 91
**Sirohi**, Rajpal Singh 1943- AmMWSc 92
**Sirois**, David Leon 1933- AmMWSc 92
**Sirois**, Paul Kermit 1956- WhoFI 92
**Sirois**, Pierre 1945- AmMWSc 92
**Sirota**, Fredric James 1945- WhoAmL 92
**Sirota**, Jonas H 1916- AmMWSc 92
**Sirotkin**, Phillip Leonard 1923- WhoWest 92
**Sirotko**, Theodore Francis 1936- WhoRel 92
**Sirotnak**, Francis Michael 1929- AmMWSc 92
**Sirott**, Bob 1949- WhoEnt 92
**Sirovich**, Lawrence 1933- AmMWSc 92
**Sirow**, Richard Lawrence 1950- WhoFI 92
**Sirowitz**, Hal DrAPF 91
**Sirridge**, Marjorie Spurrier 1921- AmMWSc 92
**Sirs**, William 1920- Who 92
**Siry**, Joseph William 1920- AmMWSc 92
**Sis**, Peter 1949- SmATA 67 [port]
**Sis**, Raymond Francis 1931- AmMWSc 92
**Sisak**, James Robert 1949- WhoMW 92
**Sisakyan**, Norayr Martirosovich 1907-1966 SovUnBD
**Sisam**, David Michael 1961- WhoWest 92
**Sisco**, Joseph John 1919- IntWW 91
**Siscoe**, George L 1937- AmMWSc 92
**Siscovick**, David Stuart 1951- AmMWSc 92
**Sisel**, Eric Desbiens 1932- WhoRel 92
**Sisemore**, Claudia 1937- WhoEnt 92, WhoWest 92
**Sisenwine**, Samuel Fred 1940- AmMWSc 92
**Sisisky**, Norman 1927- AlmAP 92 [port], WhoAmP 91
**Sisitsky**, Alan David 1942- WhoAmP 91
**Sisk**, Albert Fletcher, Jr. 1928- WhoFI 92
**Sisk**, Dudley Byrd 1938- AmMWSc 92
**Sisk**, Mark Sean 1942- WhoMW 92, WhoRel 92
**Sisk**, Philip Laurence 1914- WhoAmL 92
**Sisk**, Robert Atwood 1954- WhoMW 92
**Sisk**, Wm. Mark 1960- WhoFI 92
**Siska**, Peter Emil 1943- AmMWSc 92
**Siska**, Richard Stanly 1948- WhoMW 92
**Siske**, Roger Charles 1944- WhoAmL 92, WhoFI 92
**Siskel & Ebert** LesBEnT 92 [port]
**Siskel**, Gene 1946- WhoEnt 92, WhoMW 92
**Sisken**, Jesse Ernest 1930- AmMWSc 92
**Siskin**, Milton 1921- AmMWSc 92
**Siskind**, Aaron 1903-1991 NewYTBS 91 [port]
**Siskind**, Donald Henry 1937- WhoAmL 92
**Siskind**, Gregory William 1934- AmMWSc 92
**Siskind**, Lawrence Jay 1952- WhoWest 92
**Sislen**, David Benjamin 1966- WhoEnt 92
**Sisler**, Charles Carleton 1922- AmMWSc 92
**Sisler**, Edward C 1930- AmMWSc 92
**Sisler**, George C 1923- AmMWSc 92
**Sisler**, Harry Hall 1917- AmMWSc 92, IntAu&W 91, WrDr 92
**Sisler**, Hugh Delane 1922- AmMWSc 92
**Sisler**, Paul Brink 1959- WhoEnt 92
**Sisley**, Alfred 1839-1899 ThHEIm
**Sismondi**, Jean-Charles-Leonard S. de 1773-1842 BlkwCEP
**Sisneros**, Joe M. 1935- WhoHisp 92
**Sisneros**, Jose WhoHisp 92
**Sisneros**, Michael John 1949- WhoHisp 92
**Sisneros**, Raymond A. 1958- WhoHisp 92
**Sisney**, Ricardo 1939- WhoBlA 92
**Sisodia**, Chaturbhuj Singh 1934- AmMWSc 92
**Sison**, Maria Rosario 1957- WhoMW 92
**Sissel**, George Allen 1936- WhoAmL 92
**Sisselman**, David I. 1955- WhoAmL 92
**Sissenwine**, Michael P 1947- AmMWSc 92
**Sissle**, Noble 1889-1975 NewAmDM
**Sissom**, Leighton E 1934- AmMWSc 92
**Sissom**, Stanley Lewis 1932- AmMWSc 92
**Sisson**, Albert E. 1940- WhoMW 92
**Sisson**, C. H. 1914- ConPo 91, FacFETw, WrDr 92
**Sisson**, Charles Hubert 1914- IntAu&W 91, IntWW 91, Who 92
**Sisson**, Donald Victor 1934- AmMWSc 92
**Sisson**, Donna Gayle 1962- WhoRel 92
**Sisson**, Everett Arnold 1920- WhoFI 92
**Sisson**, George Allen 1920- AmMWSc 92
**Sisson**, George Maynard 1922- AmMWSc 92
**Sisson**, H. Michael 1921- WhoEnt 92
**Sisson**, Harriet E 1916- AmMWSc 92
**Sisson**, Jerry Allan 1956- WhoAmL 92
**Sisson**, John Ross 1926- WhoWest 92
**Sisson**, Jonathan DrAPF 91
**Sisson**, Joseph A 1930- AmMWSc 92
**Sisson**, Ray L 1934- AmMWSc 92
**Sisson**, Rosemary Anne 1923- IntAu&W 91, Who 92, WrDr 92
**Sisson**, Roy 1914- Who 92
**Sisson**, Steven Louis 1949- WhoRel 92
**Sisson**, Thomas Randolph Clinton 1920- AmMWSc 92
**Sisson**, Virginia Evans 1927- WhoAmP 91
**Sissons**, John Gerald Patrick 1945- Who 92
**Sissons**, Peter George 1942- Who 92
**Sissons**, Thomas Michael 1934- Who 92
**Sistek**, Vladimir 1931- AmMWSc 92
**Sister Mary Jeremy** ConAu 135
**Sisterson**, Janet M 1940- AmMWSc 92
**Sisti**, Anthony Joseph 1928- AmMWSc 92
**Sisto**, Fernando 1924- AmMWSc 92
**Sistrom**, William R 1927- AmMWSc 92
**Sistrunk**, Oscar, Jr. 1930- WhoBlA 92
**Sistrunk**, William Allen 1919- AmMWSc 92
**Sisulu**, Nontsikelelo Albertina 1919- IntWW 91
**Sisulu**, Walter Max Ulyate 1912- IntWW 91
**Sit**, Eugene C. 1938- WhoMW 92
**Sit**, Hong Chan 1921- WhoRel 92
**Sit**, William Yu 1944- AmMWSc 92
**Sita**, Michael John 1953- WhoMW 92
**Sitar**, Daniel Samuel 1944- AmMWSc 92
**Sitaraman**, Yegnaseshan 1936- AmMWSc 92
**Sitarz**, Anneliese Lotte 1928- AmMWSc 92
**Sites**, Donald Wayne 1958- WhoFI 92
**Sites**, Jack W., Jr. 1951- WhoWest 92
**Sites**, Jack Walter, Jr 1951- AmMWSc 92
**Sites**, James Philip 1948- WhoAmL 92
**Sites**, James Russell 1943- AmMWSc 92
**Sithole**, Ndabaningi 1920- IntWW 91
**Sitka**, Charles Howard 1952- WhoFI 92
**Sitko**, Jeanne Anne 1948- WhoWest 92
**Sitkovetsky**, Dmitry 1954- IntWW 91
**Sitkovsky**, Michail V 1947- AmMWSc 92
**Sitney**, Lawrence Raymond 1923- AmMWSc 92
**Sitnikov**, Vasiliy Ivanovich 1927- IntWW 91
**Sitomer**, Sheila Marie 1951- WhoEnt 92
**Sitrick**, James Baker 1935- WhoAmL 92
**Sitrick**, Michael Steven 1947- WhoFI 92
**Sitrick**, Ronald M. 1956- WhoAmL 92
**Sitrin**, Michael David 1948- AmMWSc 92
**Sitrin**, Robert David 1945- AmMWSc 92
**Sitruk**, Jo 1944- IntWW 91
**Sitruk**, Joseph 1944- WhoRel 92
**Sittason**, Charles Rex 1944- WhoFI 92
**Sittel**, Chester Nachand 1941- AmMWSc 92
**Sittel**, Karl 1916- AmMWSc 92
**Sittenfeld**, Paul George 1947- WhoMW 92
**Sittenfield**, Marcus 1919- AmMWSc 92
**Sitter**, Troy Gordon 1929- WhoMW 92
**Sitter**, William Hall 1939- WhoFI 92
**Sitterle**, Harold 1910- DcTwDes
**Sitterle**, Trudi 1920?- DcTwDes
**Sitterly**, Charlotte 1898-1990 AnObit 1990
**Sitterly**, Charlotte Moore 1898- AmMWSc 92
**Sitterly**, Connie Sue 1953- WhoFI 92
**Sittig**, C Dale 1940- WhoAmP 91
**Sittig**, Dean Forrest 1961- AmMWSc 92
**Sitting Bull** 1831?-1890 BenetAL 91, RelLAm 91
**Sitting Bull** 1834?-1890 RComAH
**Sittler**, Edward Charles, Jr 1947- AmMWSc 92
**Sitton**, Carl Vernon 1928- WhoEnt 92
**Sitton**, Claude Shem 1937- WhoAmP 91
**Sitton**, Frances 1925- WhoEnt 92
**Sitton**, Maryiann WhoRel 92
**Sitty**, Janet L 1942- WhoAmP 91
**Situ Huimin** d1989 IntWW 91N
**Sitwell**, Edith 1887-1964 CnDBLB 7 [port], ConAu 35NR, ConLC 67 [port], FacFETw, PoeCrit 3 [port], RfGEnL 91
**Sitwell**, Francis Gerard 1906- Who 92
**Sitwell**, Osbert 1892-1969 FacFETw, RfGEnL 91
**Sitwell**, Pauline IntAu&W 91
**Sitwell**, Peter Sacheverell W. Who 92
**Sitwell**, Reresby 1927- Who 92
**Sitwell**, Sacheverell 1897- IntAu&W 91
**Sitwell**, Sacheverell 1897-1988 FacFETw, RfGEnL 91
**Sitwells**, The FacFETw
**Sitz**, Thomas O 1944- AmMWSc 92
**Siu**, Chi-Hung 1947- AmMWSc 92
**Siu**, David Patrick 1957- WhoRel 92
**Siu**, Gerald AmMWSc 92
**Siu**, Tsunpui Oswald 1945- AmMWSc 92
**Siu**, Yum-Tong 1943- AmMWSc 92
**Siuru**, William D, Jr 1938- AmMWSc 92
**Siuta**, Gerald Joseph 1947- AmMWSc 92
**Sivack**, Denis DrAPF 91
**Sivadas**, Iraja 1950- WhoWest 92
**Sivadon**, Paul Daniel 1907- IntWW 91
**Sivak**, Andrew 1931- AmMWSc 92
**Sivak**, Jacob Gershon 1944- AmMWSc 92
**Sivak**, Michael 1949- WhoMW 92
**Sivan**, Amiram 1938- IntWW 91
**Sivananda Saraswati**, Swami 1887-1963 RelLAm 91
**Sivasithamparam**, Murgugesu 1923- IntWW 91
**Sivasubramanian**, Pakkirisamy 1939- AmMWSc 92
**Sivazlian**, Boghos D 1936- AmMWSc 92
**Sivco**, Deborah L 1957- AmMWSc 92
**Sive**, Rebecca Anne 1950- WhoMW 92
**Sivec**, Carl Richard 1935- WhoFI 92
**Siverd**, Bonnie Marie 1949- WhoMW 92
**Siverd**, Robert Joseph 1948- WhoAmL 92
**Sivers**, Dennis Wayne 1944- AmMWSc 92
**Siverson**, Randolph Martin 1940- WhoWest 92
**Siverson**, Susan Jo 1960- WhoWest 92
**Sivewright**, Robert Charles Townsend 1923- Who 92
**Sivgin**, Halil 1950- IntWW 91
**Sivie**, John Charles 1945- WhoFI 92, WhoWest 92
**Sivier**, Kenneth R 1928- AmMWSc 92
**Sivin**, Nathan 1931- WhoRel 92
**Sivinski**, Jacek Stefan 1926- AmMWSc 92
**Sivinski**, James Anthony 1938- WhoFI 92
**Sivinski**, John A 1938- AmMWSc 92
**Sivjee**, Gulamabas Gulamhusen 1938- AmMWSc 92
**Sivley**, Paul Allen 1958- WhoAmP 91
**Sivright**, John Avery 1929- WhoFI 92
**Siwe**, Thomas Valentine 1935- WhoEnt 92
**Siwek**, Carol A WhoAmP 91
**Siwicki**, Florian 1925- IntWW 91
**Six**, Les FacFETw, NewAmDM
**Six**, Bradley Bertram 1940- WhoEnt 92
**Six**, Erich Walther 1926- AmMWSc 92
**Six**, Fred N. 1929- WhoAmL 92, WhoMW 92
**Six**, Frederick N WhoAmP 91
**Six**, Howard R 1942- AmMWSc 92
**Six**, Norman Frank, Jr 1935- AmMWSc 92
**Sixto**, Ramiro Ares 1935- WhoFI 92
**Sixtus I** EncEarC
**Sixtus II** EncEarC
**Sixtus III** EncEarC
**Siyad Barre**, Muhammad IntWW 91
**Siyan**, Karanjit Singh 1954- WhoWest 92
**Size**, Dennis Michael 1954- WhoEnt 92
**Size**, William Bachtrup 1943- AmMWSc 92
**Sizemore**, Barbara 1927- NotBlAW 92
**Sizemore**, Barbara A. 1927- WhoBlA 92
**Sizemore**, Christine Wick 1945- ConAu 134
**Sizemore**, Douglas Reece 1947- AmMWSc 92
**Sizemore**, Frank J, III WhoAmP 91
**Sizemore**, Herman Mason, Jr. 1941- WhoWest 92
**Sizemore**, James Middleton, Jr 1942- WhoAmP 91
**Sizemore**, Robert Carlen 1951- AmMWSc 92
**Sizemore**, Ronald Kelly 1947- AmMWSc 92
**Sizenko**, Yevgeny Ivanovich 1931- IntWW 91
**Sizer**, Irwin Whiting 1910- AmMWSc 92
**Sizer**, John 1938- IntAu&W 91, Who 92, WrDr 92
**Sizer**, Michael Gene 1953- WhoAmP 91
**Sizer**, Theodore Ryland 1932- WrDr 92
**Sizer**, Walter Scott 1947- AmMWSc 92, WhoMW 92
**Sizova**, Alla Ivanovna 1939- IntWW 91, SovUnBD
**Sjaastad**, Anders Christian 1942- IntWW 91
**Sjadzali**, Munawir 1924- IntWW 91
**Sjoberg**, Alf 1903-1980 IntDcF 2-2 [port]
**Sjoberg**, Donald WhoRel 92
**Sjoberg**, Sigurd A AmMWSc 92
**Sjoblad**, Roy David 1947- AmMWSc 92
**Sjodin**, Raymond Andrew 1927- AmMWSc 92
**Sjoerdsma**, Albert 1924- AmMWSc 92
**Sjogren**, Clifford Frank, Jr. 1928- WhoWest 92
**Sjogren**, Donald Ernest 1932- WhoMW 92
**Sjogren**, Jon Arne 1951- AmMWSc 92
**Sjogren**, Robert Erik 1931- AmMWSc 92
**Sjogren**, Robert W, Jr 1945- AmMWSc 92
**Sjolander**, Gary Walfred 1942- WhoWest 92
**Sjolander**, John Rogers 1924- AmMWSc 92
**Sjolund**, Richard David 1939- AmMWSc 92
**Sjostrand**, Fritiof S 1912- AmMWSc 92
**Sjostrom**, Rex William 1930- WhoWest 92
**Sjostrom**, Victor 1879-1960 IntDcF 2-2 [port]
**Sjostrom**, William Benno 1956- WhoMW 92
**Sjulin**, R Paul 1939- WhoAmP 91
**Ska**, Jean Louis 1946- WhoRel 92
**Skadden**, Nancy Lee Mackey 1939- WhoAmP 91
**Skadeland**, Dean Ray 1957- WhoMW 92
**Skadron**, George 1936- AmMWSc 92
**Skadron**, Peter 1934- AmMWSc 92
**Skaff**, Michael Samuel 1936- AmMWSc 92
**Skagerberg**, Donna Clare 1928- WhoAmP 91
**Skaggs**, Bill 1942- WhoAmP 91
**Skaggs**, David E. 1943- AlmAP 92 [port], WhoWest 92
**Skaggs**, David Evans 1943- WhoAmP 91
**Skaggs**, Fred Randall 1933- WhoRel 92
**Skaggs**, Hazel Ghazarian 1924- WhoEnt 92
**Skaggs**, Kathy Cheryl 1956- WhoAmL 92
**Skaggs**, L. Sam 1922- WhoFI 92, WhoWest 92
**Skaggs**, Lester S 1911- AmMWSc 92
**Skaggs**, Neil Thomas 1953- WhoFI 92
**Skaggs**, Raymond Leo 1933- WhoAmP 91
**Skaggs**, Richard Wayne 1942- AmMWSc 92
**Skaggs**, Ricky WhoEnt 92
**Skaggs**, Ricky 1954- NewAmDM
**Skaggs**, Robert L 1932- AmMWSc 92
**Skaggs**, Samuel Robert 1936- AmMWSc 92, WhoWest 92
**Skaggs**, Sanford Merle 1939- WhoAmL 92
**Skaggs**, Warren Leslie 1921- WhoEnt 92
**Skaggs**, Wayne Gerard 1929- WhoFI 92
**Skak-Nielsen**, Niels Verner 1922- IntWW 91
**Skakun**, Mark John, III 1950- WhoAmL 92
**Skala**, Gary Dennis 1946- WhoMW 92
**Skala**, Ivan 1922- IntAu&W 91, IntWW 91
**Skala**, James Herbert 1929- AmMWSc 92
**Skala**, Josef Petr 1941- AmMWSc 92
**Skalagard**, Hans Martin 1924- WhoWest 92
**Skalak**, Richard 1923- AmMWSc 92
**Skaldaspillir**, Sigfriour IntAu&W 91X, WrDr 92
**Skalka**, Anna Marie 1938- AmMWSc 92
**Skalko**, Richard G 1936- AmMWSc 92
**Skalkottas**, Nikos 1904-1949 NewAmDM
**Skall**, Gregg P. 1944- WhoAmL 92, WhoEnt 92

**Skalnik,** J G 1923- *AmMWSc 92*
**Skalny,** Jan Peter 1935- *AmMWSc 92*
**Skalski,** Stanislaus 1934- *AmMWSc 92*
**Skalweit,** Stephan 1914- *IntWW 91*
**Skamene,** Emil 1941- *AmMWSc 92*
**Skan,** Peter Henry O. *Who 92*
**Skancke,** Nancy Jean 1950- *WhoAmL 92*
**Skancke,** Ragnar Sigvald 1890-1948 *BiDExR*
**Skandalakis,** John Elias 1920- *AmMWSc 92*
**Skanland,** Hermod 1925- *IntWW 91*
**Skanse,** John Edward 1950- *WhoRel 92*
**Skaperdas,** George T 1914- *AmMWSc 92*
**Skar,** Brian T *WhoAmP 91*
**Skarda,** R Vencil, Jr 1940- *AmMWSc 92*
**Skarda,** Richard Joseph 1952- *WhoWest 92*
**Skardon,** William James 1904-1987 *FacFETw*
**Skarlos,** Leonidas 1941- *AmMWSc 92*
**Skarmeta,** Antonio 1940- *LiExTwC*
**Skarpetowski,** Carol 1958- *WhoAmL 92*
**Skarsaune,** Sandra Kaye 1943- *AmMWSc 92*
**Skarsgard,** Harvey Milton 1929- *AmMWSc 92*
**Skarsgard,** J. Stellan 1951- *IntWW 91*
**Skarsgard,** Lloyd Donald 1933- *AmMWSc 92*
**Skarstedt,** Mark T 1943- *AmMWSc 92*
**Skarsten,** Malvin Olai 1892- *WrDr 92*
**Skarulis,** John Anthony 1917- *AmMWSc 92*
**Skase,** Christopher *LesBEnT 92*
**Skase,** Christopher 1946- *IntMPA 92*
**Skates,** Ronald Louis 1941- *WhoFI 92*
**Skatrud,** Thomas Joseph 1953- *AmMWSc 92*
**Skatzes,** Dawerance Horace 1914- *WhoMW 92*
**Skau,** Kenneth Anthony 1947- *AmMWSc 92*
**Skau,** Michael *DrAPF 91*
**Skau,** Michael W. 1944- *WhoMW 92*
**Skauen,** Donald M 1916- *AmMWSc 92*
**Skauge,** Arne 1948- *IntWW 91*
**Skavaril,** Russell Vincent 1936- *AmMWSc 92*
**Skavdahl,** R E 1934- *AmMWSc 92*
**Skavenski,** Alexander Anthony 1943- *AmMWSc 92*
**Skean,** James Dan 1932- *AmMWSc 92*
**Skeans,** Carolou 1932- *WhoMW 92*
**Skeaping,** John 1901-1980 *TwCPaSc*
**Skeat,** Theodore Cressy 1907- *IntWW 91, Who 92*
**Skeates,** Basil George 1929- *Who 92*
**Skeath,** J Edward 1936- *AmMWSc 92*
**Skeel,** Peter Brooks 1954- *WhoAmL 92*
**Skeel,** Robert David 1947- *AmMWSc 92*
**Skeeles,** John Kirkpatrick 1945- *AmMWSc 92*
**Skeels,** Jack William 1929- *WhoFI 92, WhoMW 92*
**Skeen,** Anita *DrAPF 91*
**Skeen,** Cliff *WhoAmP 91*
**Skeen,** James Norman 1942- *AmMWSc 92*
**Skeen,** Joe 1927- *AlmAP 92 [port]*
**Skeen,** Joseph Richard 1927- *WhoAmP 91, WhoWest 92*
**Skeen,** Leslie Carlisle 1942- *AmMWSc 92*
**Skeene,** Linell De-Silva 1938- *WhoBlA 92*
**Skees,** Hugh Benedict 1927- *AmMWSc 92*
**Skeet,** Muriel Harvey 1926- *Who 92*
**Skeet,** Trevor 1918- *Who 92*
**Skeete,** F. Herbert 1930- *WhoRel 92*
**Skeeter,** Sharyn Jeanne *DrAPF 91*
**Skeever,** Jim *BenetAL 91*
**Skeffington** *Who 92*
**Skeffington and Son** *DcLB 106*
**Skeffington and Southwell** *DcLB 106*
**Skeffington,** John M, Jr 1938- *WhoAmP 91*
**Skeffington,** William *DcLB 106*
**Skeffington-Lodge,** Thomas Cecil 1905- *Who 92*
**Skeggs,** Clifford 1931- *Who 92*
**Skeggs,** Douglas 1952- *IntAu&W 91*
**Skeggs,** Leonard Tucker, Jr 1918- *AmMWSc 92, IntWW 91*
**Skehan,** James William 1923- *AmMWSc 92*
**Skehel,** John James 1941- *Who 92*
**Skeist,** Irving 1915- *AmMWSc 92*
**Skelcey,** James Stanley 1933- *AmMWSc 92*
**Skell,** Philip S 1918- *AmMWSc 92*
**Skelley,** Dean Sutherland 1938- *AmMWSc 92*
**Skelley,** George Calvin, Jr 1937- *AmMWSc 92*
**Skelley,** Jack *DrAPF 91*
**Skelley,** Stephen Vincent 1944- *WhoEnt 92*
**Skellings,** Edmund *DrAPF 91*
**Skelly,** David W 1938- *AmMWSc 92*
**Skelly,** Jerome Philip, Sr 1932- *AmMWSc 92*
**Skelly,** Jim 1933- *WhoAmP 91*
**Skelly,** Joseph Gordon 1935- *WhoAmL 92*
**Skelly,** Michael Francis 1950- *AmMWSc 92*
**Skelly,** Norman Edward 1928- *AmMWSc 92*
**Skelly,** Richard Francis 1937- *WhoFI 92*
**Skelly,** Richard Jon 1962- *WhoEnt 92*
**Skelly,** Thomas Francis 1934- *WhoFI 92*
**Skelmersdale,** Baron 1945- *Who 92*
**Skelos,** Dean G 1948- *WhoAmP 91*
**Skelton,** Bobby Joe 1935- *AmMWSc 92*
**Skelton,** Byron George 1905- *WhoAmL 92, WhoAmP 91*
**Skelton,** Don Richard 1931- *WhoIns 92*
**Skelton,** Earl Franklin 1940- *AmMWSc 92*
**Skelton,** Geoffrey 1916- *WrDr 92*
**Skelton,** Geoffrey David 1916- *IntAu&W 91*
**Skelton,** George Albert 1963- *WhoWest 92*
**Skelton,** Howard Clifton 1932- *WhoFI 92*
**Skelton,** Hugh Bolding 1929- *WhoRel 92*
**Skelton,** Ike 1931- *AlmAP 92 [port]*
**Skelton,** Ike N, Jr 1931- *WhoAmP 91*
**Skelton,** Isaac Newton, IV 1931- *WhoMW 92*
**Skelton,** James Maurice 1939- *WhoIns 92*
**Skelton,** John 1460?-1529 *RfGEnL 91*
**Skelton,** John 1923- *TwCPaSc*
**Skelton,** John Stephen 1954- *WhoWest 92*
**Skelton,** Kenneth John Fraser 1918- *Who 92*
**Skelton,** Marilyn Mae 1936- *AmMWSc 92*
**Skelton,** Mark Albert 1957- *WhoAmL 92*
**Skelton,** Monty Wayne 1941- *WhoIns 92*
**Skelton,** Pam 1949- *TwCPaSc*
**Skelton,** Peter 1901- *Who 92*
**Skelton,** Peter 1929- *IntAu&W 91, WrDr 92*
**Skelton,** Red *LesBEnT 92*
**Skelton,** Red 1913- *IntMPA 92, WhoEnt 92*
**Skelton,** Robert Eugene 1938- *AmMWSc 92*
**Skelton,** Robert William 1929- *Who 92*
**Skelton,** Robin *DrAPF 91*
**Skelton,** Robin 1925- *ConPo 91, IntAu&W 91, Who 92, WrDr 92*
**Skelton,** Steven B. 1949- *WhoAmL 92*
**Skelton,** Thomas Eugene 1930- *AmMWSc 92*
**Skelton,** Thomas Reginald, Jr. 1927- *WhoEnt 92*
**Skema,** Antanas 1911-1961 *LiExTwC*
**Skemp,** Joseph Bright 1910- *IntAu&W 91, Who 92, WrDr 92*
**Skemp,** Richard Rowland 1919- *WrDr 92*
**Skemp,** Terence Rowland Frazer 1915- *Who 92*
**Skempton,** Alec Westley 1914- *IntWW 91, Who 92*
**Skempton,** Howard 1947- *ConCom 92*
**Skender,** LaVerne Janet 1935- *WhoMW 92*
**Skene,** Anthony *IntAu&W 91*
**Skene,** Jeremy Francis 1949- *WhoFI 92*
**Skene,** Laurence Farthing 1911- *WhoWest 92*
**Skerman,** Ronald Sidney 1914- *Who 92*
**Skerrett,** Philip Vincent 1923- *WhoBlA 92*
**Skerritt,** Tom 1933- *IntMPA 92*
**Skerry,** Philip John 1944- *WhoMW 92*
**Sketchley,** Arthur 1817-1882 *ScFEYrs*
**Skewes,** Richard S 1935- *WhoIns 92*
**Skewes-Cox,** Bennet 1918- *WhoWest 92*
**Skewis,** Iain 1936- *Who 92*
**Skewis,** John David 1932- *AmMWSc 92*
**Ski,** Paul Alexander 1947- *WhoEnt 92*
**Skialf** *EncAmaz 91*
**Skibbe,** Eugene Moritz 1930- *WhoMW 92, WhoRel 92*
**Skibinsky,** Morris 1925- *AmMWSc 92*
**Skibniewska,** Halina 1921- *IntWW 91*
**Skibniewski,** Miroslaw Jan 1957- *AmMWSc 92*
**Skibski,** John Leon 1964- *WhoFI 92*
**Skiddell,** Elliot Lewis 1951- *WhoRel 92*
**Skidelsky** *Who 92*
**Skidelsky,** Baron 1939- *Who 92*
**Skidelsky,** Barry David 1951- *WhoAmL 92*
**Skidgel,** Randal Allen 1952- *WhoMW 92*
**Skidmore,** Owings & Merrill *DcTwDes*
**Skidmore,** Donald Earl, Jr. 1944- *WhoFI 92, WhoWest 92*
**Skidmore,** Duane R 1927- *AmMWSc 92*
**Skidmore,** Edward Lyman 1933- *AmMWSc 92*
**Skidmore,** Eric Arthur 1952- *WhoWest 92*
**Skidmore,** Francis Joseph, Jr. 1943- *WhoFI 92*
**Skidmore,** Louis 1897-1962 *DcTwDes*
**Skidmore,** Max J. 1933- *WrDr 92*
**Skidmore,** Paul Harold 1918- *WhoMW 92*
**Skidmore,** Rex O 1947- *WhoIns 92*
**Skidmore,** Wesley Dean 1931- *AmMWSc 92*
**Skieller,** Christian 1948- *WhoWest 92*
**Skiff,** David Michael 1957- *WhoRel 92*
**Skiff,** Frederick Norman 1957- *AmMWSc 92*
**Skiff,** Peter Duane 1938- *AmMWSc 92*
**Skigen,** Dennis 1946- *WhoWest 92*
**Skigen,** Patricia Sue 1942- *WhoAmL 92*
**Skilbeck,** Diana Margaret 1942- *Who 92*
**Skilbeck,** Malcolm 1932- *IntWW 91, Who 92*
**Skiles,** Don *DrAPF 91*
**Skiles,** James J 1928- *AmMWSc 92*
**Skillet Lickers** *NewAmDM*
**Skillin,** Therese Jeno 1956- *WhoWest 92*
**Skilling,** Darroll Dean 1931- *AmMWSc 92*
**Skilling,** David van Diest 1933- *WhoFI 92*
**Skilling,** Hugh 1905- *AmMWSc 92*
**Skilling,** John Bower 1921- *AmMWSc 92*
**Skilling,** Raymond I 1939- *WhoIns 92*
**Skilling,** Raymond Inwood 1939- *WhoAmL 92, WhoFI 92, WhoMW 92*
**Skilling,** Thomas Ethelbert, III 1952- *WhoEnt 92*
**Skillings,** R.D. *DrAPF 91*
**Skillington,** William Patrick Denny 1913- *Who 92*
**Skillken,** Ralph A., Jr. 1941- *WhoAmL 92*
**Skillman,** Becky Sue 1950- *WhoAmP 91*
**Skillman,** Henry Howson 1926- *WhoAmL 92*
**Skillman,** Michael John 1963- *WhoWest 92*
**Skillman,** Richard McKay 1955- *WhoEnt 92*
**Skillman,** Robert Allen 1941- *AmMWSc 92*
**Skillman,** Thomas G 1925- *AmMWSc 92*
**Skillman,** William A 1928- *AmMWSc 92*
**Skillrud,** Harold Clayton 1928- *WhoRel 92*
**Skilton,** Charles Sanford 1868-1941 *NewAmDM*
**Skilton,** John S. 1944- *WhoAmL 92*
**Skingsley,** Anthony 1933- *Who 92*
**Skinner,** Aaron Nichols 1845-1918 *BiInAmS*
**Skinner,** Ainslie *WrDr 92*
**Skinner,** Andrew Forrester 1902- *Who 92*
**Skinner,** Angus M. C. 1950- *Who 92*
**Skinner,** Anita Marier 1933- *WhoEnt 92*
**Skinner,** B. F. 1904-1990 *AnObit 1990, BenetAL 91, FacFETw [port], News 91*
**Skinner,** B. Franklin 1931- *WhoFI 92*
**Skinner,** Brian John 1928- *AmMWSc 92*
**Skinner,** Burrhus Frederic d1990 *IntWW 91N*
**Skinner,** Byron R. *WhoBlA 92*
**Skinner,** Calvin L, Jr 1942- *WhoAmP 91*
**Skinner,** Charles Gordon 1923- *AmMWSc 92*
**Skinner,** Charles Scofield 1940- *WhoMW 92*
**Skinner,** Clementine Anna 1916- *WhoBlA 92*
**Skinner,** Constance Lindsay 1879-1939 *BenetAL 91*
**Skinner,** Cornelia Otis 1901-1979 *BenetAL 91*
**Skinner,** Dale Dean 1931- *AmMWSc 92*
**Skinner,** David Bernt 1935- *AmMWSc 92*
**Skinner,** David Olen 1949- *WhoEnt 92*
**Skinner,** Dennis Edward 1932- *Who 92*
**Skinner,** Dorothy M 1930- *AmMWSc 92*
**Skinner,** Edwin 1940- *BlkOlyM*
**Skinner,** Elihu Barnes 1938- *WhoWest 92*
**Skinner,** Elliott P. 1924- *WhoBlA 92*
**Skinner,** Ernest E. 1943- *WhoEnt 92*
**Skinner,** Eugene W. 1935- *WhoBlA 92*
**Skinner,** Ewart C. 1949- *WhoBlA 92*
**Skinner,** G M 1909- *AmMWSc 92*
**Skinner,** George Douglas 1918- *WhoEnt 92*
**Skinner,** George T 1923- *AmMWSc 92*
**Skinner,** Georja Ann 1952- *WhoWest 92*
**Skinner,** Gordon Bannatyne 1926- *AmMWSc 92*
**Skinner,** H Catherine W 1931- *AmMWSc 92*
**Skinner,** Hubert Clayton 1929- *AmMWSc 92*
**Skinner,** Jacque Lewis 1941- *WhoAmP 91*
**Skinner,** James Ernest 1940- *AmMWSc 92*
**Skinner,** James John 1923- *IntWW 91, Who 92*
**Skinner,** James Lauriston 1953- *AmMWSc 92*
**Skinner,** James Stanford 1936- *AmMWSc 92*
**Skinner,** James Wilbert 1933- *WhoAmP 91*
**Skinner,** Jeffrey 1949- *IntAu&W 91*
**Skinner,** John 1953- *TwCPaSc*
**Skinner,** John Vernon 1938- *WhoFI 92*
**Skinner,** Joseph John 1842-1919 *BiInAmS*
**Skinner,** Joseph L 1931- *AmMWSc 92*
**Skinner,** Joyce Eva 1920- *Who 92*
**Skinner,** Karma Dianne 1962- *WhoMW 92*
**Skinner,** Keith *Who 92*
**Skinner,** Knute *DrAPF 91*
**Skinner,** Knute 1929- *ConPo 91, WrDr 92*
**Skinner,** Leary George 1941- *WhoAmP 91*
**Skinner,** Lindsay A 1938- *AmMWSc 92*
**Skinner,** Loren Courtland, II 1940- *AmMWSc 92*
**Skinner,** Margaret Sheppard 1938- *AmMWSc 92*
**Skinner,** Martyn 1906- *Who 92, WrDr 92*
**Skinner,** Mary Just 1946- *WhoAmP 91*
**Skinner,** Maurice Edward, IV 1962- *WhoFI 92*
**Skinner,** Michael 1953- *ConAu 134*
**Skinner,** Michael Timothy 1931- *Who 92*
**Skinner,** Michael William 1941- *WhoAmP 91*
**Skinner,** Mike 1924- *TwCWW 91*
**Skinner,** Morris Fredrick 1906- *AmMWSc 92*
**Skinner,** Nancy Jo 1956- *WhoWest 92*
**Skinner,** Newman Sheldon, Jr 1934- *AmMWSc 92*
**Skinner,** Otis 1858-1942 *BenetAL 91*
**Skinner,** Patricia Morag 1932- *WhoAmP 91*
**Skinner,** Peter Graeme 1944- *WhoAmL 92*
**Skinner,** Quentin 1940- *WrDr 92*
**Skinner,** Quentin Robert Duthie 1940- *IntWW 91, Who 92*
**Skinner,** Ray 1927- *AmMWSc 92*
**Skinner,** Richard Emery 1934- *AmMWSc 92*
**Skinner,** Robert Dowell 1942- *AmMWSc 92*
**Skinner,** Robert Eugene 1948- *WhoRel 92*
**Skinner,** Robert L 1930- *AmMWSc 92*
**Skinner,** Robert L., Jr. 1941- *WhoBlA 92*
**Skinner,** Russell Everett 1929- *WhoAmP 91*
**Skinner,** Samuel Knox 1938- *NewYTBS 91 [port], WhoAmP 91, WhoFI 92*
**Skinner,** Thomas 1909- *Who 92*
**Skinner,** Thomas Dale 1954- *WhoRel 92*
**Skinner,** Thomas Keith 1927- *Who 92*
**Skinner,** Thomas Monier 1913- *Who 92*
**Skinner,** Timothy Alan 1946- *WhoMW 92*
**Skinner,** Todd Warren 1959- *WhoFI 92*
**Skinner,** Tom 1942- *RelLAm 91*
**Skinner,** Ubaldo V. 1951- *WhoWest 92*
**Skinner,** Walter Jay 1927- *WhoAmL 92*
**Skinner,** Walter Swart 1921- *AmMWSc 92*
**Skinner,** Wilfred Aubrey, Jr 1923- *AmMWSc 92*
**Skinner,** William French Cochran, Jr. 1943- *WhoAmL 92*
**Skinner,** William Polk 1951- *WhoAmL 92*
**Skinner,** William Robert 1930- *AmMWSc 92*
**Skinner,** Willis Dean 1932- *WhoMW 92*
**Skinnider,** Leo F 1929- *AmMWSc 92*
**Skiold,** Birgit 1923-1982 *TwCPaSc*
**Skipp,** Betty Ann 1928- *AmMWSc 92*
**Skipp,** Victor 1925- *WrDr 92*
**Skipper,** David John 1931- *Who 92*
**Skipper,** Floyd E 1925- *WhoIns 92*
**Skipper,** James Marrin, Jr 1952- *WhoAmP 91*
**Skipper,** Nathan Richard, Jr. 1934- *WhoAmL 92*
**Skipski,** Vlaidimir P 1913- *AmMWSc 92*
**Skipwith,** Patrick Alexander d'E 1938- *Who 92*
**Skirball,** Henry Franc 1929- *WhoRel 92*
**Skirball,** William N. *IntMPA 92*
**Skirnick,** Robert Andrew 1938- *WhoAmL 92, WhoFI 92*
**Skirvin,** Robert Michael 1947- *AmMWSc 92*
**Skirvin,** William David 1952- *WhoWest 92*
**Skitt,** Baden Henry 1941- *Who 92*
**Skjaerstad,** Ragnar 1944- *WhoFI 92*
**Skjegstad,** Kenneth 1931- *AmMWSc 92*
**Skjerven,** W C *WhoAmP 91*
**Skjervold,** Geraldine Reid 1944- *WhoMW 92*
**Skjold,** Arthur Christopher 1943- *AmMWSc 92*
**Skjonsby,** Harold Samuel 1937- *AmMWSc 92*
**Skladal,** Elizabeth Lee 1937- *WhoWest 92*
**Skladany,** Linda Arey 1944- *WhoAmL 92*
**Sklansky,** J 1928- *AmMWSc 92*
**Sklansky,** Jack 1928- *WhoWest 92*
**Sklar,** Alexander 1915- *WhoFI 92*
**Sklar,** Bradley Jerome 1961- *WhoAmL 92*
**Sklar,** George *DrAPF 91*
**Sklar,** George 1908- *BenetAL 91*
**Sklar,** Holly Lyn 1955- *AmPeW*
**Sklar,** Jerald Harris 1937- *WhoAmL 92*
**Sklar,** Kathryn Kish 1939- *WrDr 92*
**Sklar,** Larry A *AmMWSc 92*
**Sklar,** Morty *DrAPF 91*
**Sklar,** Pamela *WhoEnt 92*
**Sklar,** Richard J. 1929- *WhoEnt 92*
**Sklar,** Robert 1936- *WrDr 92*
**Sklar,** Robert Anthony 1936- *WhoEnt 92*
**Sklar,** Stanley 1937- *AmMWSc 92*
**Sklare,** Marshall 1921- *WrDr 92*

**Sklarek,** Norma Merrick 1928- *NotBlAW 92, WhoBlA 92*
**Sklarew,** Deborah S 1950- *AmMWSc 92*
**Sklarew,** Myra *DrAPF 91*
**Sklarew,** Robert J 1941- *AmMWSc 92*
**Sklba,** Richard J. 1935- *WhoRel 92*
**Sklenar,** Herbert Anthony 1931- *WhoFI 92*
**Sklenar,** John Mark 1952- *WhoFI 92*
**Sklerov,** Gloria Jean *WhoEnt 92*
**Sklivas,** Steven Demetrios 1960- *WhoFI 92*
**Sklodowska,** Maria 1867-1934 *WhoNob 90*
**Skloot,** Floyd *DrAPF 91*
**Sklovsky,** Robert Joel 1952- *WhoWest 92*
**Sklute,** Adam *WhoEnt 92*
**Sklyarov,** Yuri Aleksandrovich 1925- *IntWW 91*
**Skobe,** Ziedomis 1941- *AmMWSc 92*
**Skoblykova,** Lidiya Pavlovna 1939- *SovUnBD*
**Skochdopole,** Richard E 1927- *AmMWSc 92*
**Skoe,** Raymond Clifford 1923- *WhoMW 92*
**Skoff,** Melissa 1950- *WhoEnt 92*
**Skofronick,** James Gust 1931- *AmMWSc 92*
**Skog,** Laurence Edgar 1943- *AmMWSc 92*
**Skogen,** Haven Sherman 1927- *AmMWSc 92, WhoWest 92*
**Skogerboe,** Gaylord Vincent 1935- *AmMWSc 92*
**Skogerboe,** Rodney K 1931- *AmMWSc 92*
**Skogerson,** Lawrence Eugene 1942- *AmMWSc 92*
**Skogley,** Conrad Richard 1924- *AmMWSc 92*
**Skogley,** Earl O 1933- *AmMWSc 92*
**Skoglund,** Elizabeth 1937- *ConAu 34NR*
**Skoglund,** James G *WhoAmP 91*
**Skoglund,** John E. 1912- *WrDr 92*
**Skoglund,** Wesley John 1945- *WhoAmP 91*
**Skoglund,** Winthrop Charles 1916- *AmMWSc 92*
**Skogsberg,** Duncan Eric 1949- *WhoMW 92*
**Skok,** John 1909- *AmMWSc 92*
**Skok,** Paul Joseph 1947- *WhoAmL 92*
**Skok,** Richard Arnold 1928- *AmMWSc 92*
**Skola,** Arthur Henry 1953- *WhoAmL 92*
**Skold,** Laurence Nelson 1917- *AmMWSc 92*
**Skolimowski,** Jerzy 1938- *IntDcF 2-2 [port], IntMPA 92, IntWW 91*
**Skoller,** Stephen Hinshaw 1958- *WhoAmL 92*
**Skolmen,** Roger Godfrey 1929- *AmMWSc 92*
**Skolnick,** Herbert 1919- *AmMWSc 92*
**Skolnick,** Jeffrey 1953- *AmMWSc 92*
**Skolnick,** Jerome H. 1931- *WhoAmL 92*
**Skolnick,** Malcolm Harris 1935- *AmMWSc 92*
**Skolnick,** Mark Henry 1946- *AmMWSc 92*
**Skolnick,** Phil 1947- *AmMWSc 92*
**Skolnick,** S. Harold 1915- *WhoAmL 92*
**Skolnik,** Barnet David 1941- *WhoAmL 92*
**Skolnik,** David Erwin 1949- *WhoMW 92*
**Skolnik,** Herman 1914- *AmMWSc 92*
**Skolnik,** Merrill I 1927- *AmMWSc 92*
**Skolnik,** Richard S 1945- *WhoIns 92*
**Skolnikoff,** Eugene B 1928- *AmMWSc 92, WrDr 92*
**Skoloff,** Gary Neil 1933- *WhoAmL 92*
**Skolovsky,** Zadel *WhoEnt 92*
**Skolrood,** Robert Kenneth 1928- *WhoAmL 92*
**Skolsky,** Elizabeth Ellen 1943- *WhoMW 92*
**Skomal,** Edward N 1926- *AmMWSc 92*
**Skomski,** Charles 1927- *WhoAmL 92*
**Skone James,** Edmund Purcell 1927- *Who 92*
**Skoner,** Peter Raymond 1957- *AmMWSc 92*
**Skoog,** Douglas Arvid 1918- *AmMWSc 92*
**Skoog,** Folke 1908- *AmMWSc 92, IntWW 91*
**Skoog,** Gary R. 1946- *WhoFI 92*
**Skoog,** Ivan Hooglund 1928- *AmMWSc 92*
**Skoog,** William Arthur 1925- *AmMWSc 92, WhoWest 92*
**Skoor,** John Brian 1939- *WhoWest 92*
**Skop,** Richard Allen 1943- *AmMWSc 92*
**Skopik,** Steven D 1940- *AmMWSc 92*
**Skopil,** Otto Richard, Jr. 1919- *WhoAmL 92*
**Skopitz,** Laurence Martin 1948- *WhoRel 92*
**Skopp,** Joseph Michael 1949- *AmMWSc 92*
**Skora,** Susan Sundman 1947- *WhoAmL 92, WhoFI 92, WhoMW 92*
**Skorcz,** Joseph Anthony 1936- *AmMWSc 92*
**Skorinko,** George 1930- *AmMWSc 92*
**Skorka-Navai,** Aniko 1948- *WhoEnt 92*
**Skornia,** Harry Jay 1910- *WrDr 92*
**Skoropad,** William Peter 1918- *AmMWSc 92*
**Skorus-Neely,** Janina Marie 1961- *WhoMW 92*
**Skoryna,** Stanley C 1920- *AmMWSc 92*
**Skorzeny,** Otto 1908-1975 *BiDExR, EncTR 91 [port]*
**Skosey,** John Lyle 1936- *AmMWSc 92, WhoMW 92*
**Skotak,** Robert F. *WhoEnt 92*
**Skotheim,** Robert Allen 1933- *WhoWest 92*
**Skotnicki,** Jerauld S 1951- *AmMWSc 92*
**Skou,** Jens Christian 1918- *IntWW 91*
**Skouen,** Synne 1950- *ConCom 92*
**Skoug,** David L 1937- *AmMWSc 92*
**Skougstad,** Marvin Wilmer 1918- *AmMWSc 92*
**Skoula Periferaki,** Marlena *IntAu&W 91*
**Skoularikis,** Ioannis P. 1929- *IntWW 91*
**Skoultchi,** Arthur 1940- *AmMWSc 92*
**Skoultchi,** Martin Milton 1933- *AmMWSc 92*
**Skouras,** Thanos 1943- *IntWW 91*
**Skousen,** Ervin M 1915- *WhoAmP 91*
**Skoutakis,** Vasilios A 1943- *AmMWSc 92*
**Skov,** Charles E 1933- *AmMWSc 92*
**Skov,** Leif 1946- *WhoEnt 92*
**Skov,** Niels A 1919- *AmMWSc 92*
**Skove,** Malcolm John 1931- *AmMWSc 92*
**Skovlin,** Jon Matthew 1930- *AmMWSc 92*
**Skovron,** David Alan 1939- *WhoFI 92*
**Skovronek,** Herbert Samuel 1936- *AmMWSc 92*
**Skow,** Bob 1952- *WhoAmP 91*
**Skow,** Loren Curtis 1946- *AmMWSc 92*
**Skowronski,** Eugene Anthony 1944- *WhoAmP 91*
**Skowronski,** Fred Stanley 1918- *WhoMW 92*
**Skowronski,** George Victor 1928- *WhoMW 92*
**Skowronski,** John Joseph 1955- *WhoMW 92*
**Skowronski,** Paul Alexander 1947- *WhoEnt 92*
**Skowronski,** Raymund Paul 1948- *AmMWSc 92*
**Skowronski,** Timothy George Nicholas 1965- *WhoMW 92*
**Skowronski,** Vincent Paul 1944- *WhoEnt 92, WhoMW 92*
**Skoyles,** John *DrAPF 91*
**Skrabek,** Emanuel Andrew 1934- *AmMWSc 92*
**Skrable,** Kenneth William 1935- *AmMWSc 92*
**Skramstad,** Harold Kenneth 1908- *AmMWSc 92*
**Skramstad,** Harold Kenneth 1941- *WhoMW 92*
**Skratek,** Sylvia P *WhoAmP 91*
**Skratek,** Sylvia Paulette 1950- *WhoWest 92*
**Skratz,** G.P. *DrAPF 91*
**Skrdla,** Willis Howard 1920- *AmMWSc 92*
**Skrebneski,** Victor 1929- *WhoMW 92*
**Skrepek,** Roman 1931- *WhoEnt 92*
**Skrinar,** Gary Stephen 1942- *AmMWSc 92*
**Skrinde,** Rolf T 1928- *AmMWSc 92*
**Skrinsky,** Aleksandr Nikolayevich 1936- *IntWW 91*
**Skrivan,** J F 1931- *AmMWSc 92*
**Skroch,** Walter Arthur 1937- *AmMWSc 92*
**Skromme,** Lawrence H 1913- *AmMWSc 92*
**Skrowaczewski,** Stanislaw 1923- *IntWW 91, NewAmDM, WhoEnt 92*
**Skryabin** *NewAmDM*
**Skrypa,** Michael John 1927- *AmMWSc 92*
**Skrypnyk,** Mstyslav Stepan 1898- *WhoRel 92*
**Skrzynecki,** Peter 1945- *ConPo 91, WrDr 92*
**Skrzypek,** Josef *AmMWSc 92*
**Skubatz,** Hanna 1951- *WhoWest 92*
**Skubic,** Patrick Louis 1947- *AmMWSc 92*
**Skubiszewski,** Krzysztof 1926- *IntWW 91*
**Skucas,** Jovitas 1936- *AmMWSc 92*
**Skud,** Bernard Einar 1927- *AmMWSc 92*
**Skudrzyk,** Frank J 1943- *AmMWSc 92*
**Skujins,** John Janis 1926- *AmMWSc 92*
**Skulan,** Thomas William 1932- *AmMWSc 92*
**Skulason,** Olafur *WhoRel 92*
**Skulina,** Thomas Raymond 1933- *WhoAmL 92, WhoFI 92, WhoMW 92*
**Skulme,** Dzhemma Ottovna 1925- *SovUnBD*
**Skulmis,** Vilis Hugo 1953- *WhoFI 92*
**Skultety,** Francis Miles 1922- *AmMWSc 92*
**Skumanich,** Andrew P 1929- *AmMWSc 92*
**Skumatz,** Lisa Anne 1954- *WhoFI 92*
**Skup,** Daniel 1951- *AmMWSc 92*
**Skupsky,** Donald S. 1948- *WrDr 92*
**Skurdahl,** Dale Maynard 1927- *WhoFI 92*
**Skurdal,** Arlie James 1946- *WhoFI 92*
**Skurkis,** Barry A. 1951- *WhoMW 92*
**Skurla,** Laurus 1928- *WhoRel 92*
**Skurnick,** David 1942- *WhoIns 92*
**Skuta,** Gregory Louis 1956- *WhoMW 92*
**Skutch,** Alexander F. 1904- *WrDr 92*
**Skutches,** Charles L 1941- *AmMWSc 92*
**Skutnik,** Bolesh 1941- *WhoRel 92*
**Skutnik,** Bolesh Joseph 1941- *AmMWSc 92*
**Skutsch,** Otto d1990 *Who 92N*
**Skutt,** Richard Michael 1947- *WhoAmL 92, WhoMW 92*
**Skutt,** Thomas J 1930- *WhoIns 92*
**Skutt,** Thomas James 1930- *WhoFI 92, WhoMW 92*
**Skutt,** V J *WhoIns 92*
**Skvorecky,** Josef 1924- *ConAu 34NR, ConLC 69 [port], FacFETw, IntWW 91, LiExTwC, WrDr 92*
**Skwaryk,** Robert Francis 1948- *WhoAmL 92*
**Skwire,** David 1936- *WhoMW 92*
**Skwor,** Edward Paul 1955- *WhoMW 92*
**Sky,** Kathleen *ConAu 133*
**Sky,** Kathleen 1943- *TwCSFW 91, WrDr 92*
**Sky-Peck,** Howard H 1923- *AmMWSc 92*
**Skydsgaard,** Kristen Ejner 1902- *DcEcMov*
**Skye,** Ione 1971- *ConTFT 9, IntMPA 92*
**Skye,** Maggie *ConAu 34NR*
**Skye,** William Charles 1954- *WhoAmL 92*
**Skylstad,** William S. 1934- *WhoRel 92, WhoWest 92*
**Skynner,** Robin 1922- *Who 92*
**Skypek,** Dora Helen 1915- *AmMWSc 92*
**Skyrme,** Thomas 1913- *Who 92*
**Slaats,** Gary William 1945- *WhoMW 92*
**Slaatte,** Howard Alexander 1919- *WhoRel 92*
**Slabaugh,** Darrell Eugene 1943- *WhoMW 92*
**Slabbert,** F. Van Zyl 1940- *ConAu 133*
**Slabbert,** Frederik van Zyl 1940- *IntWW 91, Who 92*
**Slabe,** James F. 1940- *WhoFI 92*
**Slabo,** Alexander 1941- *WhoWest 92*
**Slabosz,** Lawrence Joseph 1960- *WhoFI 92*
**Slabotsky,** Scott Merrill 1953- *WhoFI 92*
**Slaby,** Frank 1936- *WhoFI 92, WhoMW 92*
**Slaby,** Frank J *AmMWSc 92*
**Slaby,** Harold Theodore 1920- *AmMWSc 92, WhoMW 92*
**Slabyj,** Bohdan M 1931- *AmMWSc 92*
**Slachta,** Gregory Andrew 1946- *WhoFI 92*
**Slack,** Charles Roger 1937- *Who 92*
**Slack,** David B 1798-1871 *BiInAmS*
**Slack,** Derald Allen 1924- *AmMWSc 92*
**Slack,** Donald Carl 1942- *WhoWest 92*
**Slack,** Edwin Brian 1923- *WrDr 92*
**Slack,** Geoffrey Layton d1991 *Who 92N*
**Slack,** George Granville 1906- *Who 92*
**Slack,** George Henry 1926- *WhoIns 92*
**Slack,** Glen Alfred 1928- *AmMWSc 92*
**Slack,** Jerald David 1936- *WhoMW 92*
**Slack,** Jim L. 1958- *WhoRel 92*
**Slack,** Jim Marshall 1931- *AmMWSc 92*
**Slack,** John Hamilton 1834-1874 *BiInAmS*
**Slack,** John Kenneth Edward 1930- *Who 92*
**Slack,** John Louis 1938- *WhoFI 92*
**Slack,** John Madison 1914- *AmMWSc 92*
**Slack,** Karen Kershner 1951- *WhoFI 92*
**Slack,** Keith Vollmer 1924- *AmMWSc 92*
**Slack,** Lewis 1924- *AmMWSc 92*
**Slack,** Lyle Howard 1937- *AmMWSc 92*
**Slack,** Nancy G 1930- *AmMWSc 92*
**Slack,** Nelson Hosking 1935- *AmMWSc 92*
**Slack,** Paul Alexander 1943- *Who 92*
**Slack,** Robert A 1934- *WhoAmP 91*
**Slack,** Steven Allen 1947- *AmMWSc 92*
**Slack,** Timothy Willatt 1928- *Who 92*
**Slack,** Warner Vincent 1933- *AmMWSc 92*
**Slack,** William 1925- *Who 92*
**Slade,** Adrian Carnegie 1936- *Who 92*
**Slade,** Arthur Laird 1937- *AmMWSc 92*
**Slade,** Benjamin Julian Alfred 1946- *Who 92*
**Slade,** Bernard *LesBEnT 92*
**Slade,** Bernard 1930- *IntAu&W 91, WhoEnt 92, WrDr 92*
**Slade,** Bernard Newton 1923- *AmMWSc 92*
**Slade,** Brian John 1931- *Who 92*
**Slade,** Christopher John 1927- *IntWW 91, Who 92*
**Slade,** Daniel Denison 1823-1896 *BiInAmS*
**Slade,** Edward Colin 1935- *AmMWSc 92, WhoFI 92*
**Slade,** George Kemble, Jr. 1949- *WhoAmL 92*
**Slade,** H Clyde 1918- *AmMWSc 92*
**Slade,** Joel S 1947- *AmMWSc 92*
**Slade,** John F, III 1943- *WhoAmP 91*
**Slade,** Julian Penkivil 1930- *Who 92*
**Slade,** Larry Malcom 1936- *AmMWSc 92*
**Slade,** Leslie William 1915- *Who 92*
**Slade,** Martin Alphonse, III *AmMWSc 92*
**Slade,** Norman Andrew 1943- *AmMWSc 92*
**Slade,** Patrick Buxton M. *Who 92*
**Slade,** Paul Graham 1941- *AmMWSc 92*
**Slade,** Peter 1912- *IntAu&W 91, WrDr 92*
**Slade,** Philip Earl, Jr 1929- *AmMWSc 92*
**Slade,** Phoebe J. 1935- *WhoBlA 92*
**Slade,** Roy 1933- *WhoMW 92*
**Slade,** Sandra Lynn 1946- *WhoWest 92*
**Slade,** Thomas Bog, III 1931- *WhoAmL 92*
**Slade,** Walter R., Jr. 1918- *WhoBlA 92*
**Sladek,** Celia Davis 1944- *AmMWSc 92*
**Sladek,** John 1937- *TwCSFW 91, WrDr 92*
**Sladek,** John Richard, Jr 1943- *AmMWSc 92*
**Sladek,** Milan 1938- *WhoEnt 92*
**Sladek,** Norman Elmer 1939- *AmMWSc 92*
**Sladek,** Ronald John 1926- *AmMWSc 92*
**Sladen,** Bernard Jacob 1952- *WhoMW 92*
**Sladen,** Teresa 1939- *Who 92*
**Sladich,** Harry Hamill 1938- *WhoWest 92*
**Sladkevicius,** Vincentas 1920- *IntWW 91, WhoRel 92*
**Sladkus,** Harvey Ira 1929- *WhoAmL 92*
**Sladon,** Stephanie Jacoba 1954- *WhoEnt 92*
**Sladowsky,** Yitzchak Alfred 1932- *WhoRel 92*
**Slaga,** Thomas Joseph 1941- *AmMWSc 92*
**Slage,** John Kendall 1959- *WhoMW 92*
**Slagel,** Brian Nelson 1961- *WhoEnt 92*
**Slagel,** Donald E 1930- *AmMWSc 92*
**Slagel,** Robert Clayton 1937- *AmMWSc 92*
**Slager,** Ursula Traugott 1925- *AmMWSc 92*
**Slagg,** Norman 1931- *AmMWSc 92*
**Slagg,** Stanley Dunbar 1931- *WhoAmL 92*
**Slaggie,** Thomas Joseph *WhoAmP 91*
**Slagle,** Gene 1914- *WhoMW 92*
**Slagle,** James R 1934- *AmMWSc 92*
**Slagle,** James Robert 1934- *WhoMW 92*
**Slagle,** Robert Cleveland, III 1935- *WhoAmP 91*
**Slagle,** Wayne Grey 1934- *AmMWSc 92*
**Slakey,** Linda Louise 1939- *AmMWSc 92*
**Slakis,** Albert G 1929- *WhoIns 92*
**Slakoff,** Mort *LesBEnT 92*
**Slama,** Francis J 1939- *AmMWSc 92*
**Slama,** James Albert 1960- *WhoFI 92*
**Slamecka,** Vladimir 1928- *AmMWSc 92*
**Slampyak,** Stephen Michael 1961- *WhoFI 92*
**Slampyak,** Theodore John 1965- *WhoEnt 92*
**Slane,** Viscount 1975- *Who 92*
**Slaney,** Geoffrey 1922- *IntWW 91, Who 92*
**Slanina,** Mary Ann 1961- *WhoMW 92*
**Slansky,** Cyril M 1913- *AmMWSc 92*
**Slansky,** Richard Cyril 1940- *AmMWSc 92*
**Slaoui,** Driss 1926- *IntWW 91*
**Slap,** Charles S. 1933- *WhoRel 92*
**Slapar,** Frank Milton 1929- *WhoMW 92*
**Slapikoff,** Saul Abraham 1931- *AmMWSc 92*
**Slappey,** Mary McGowan *DrAPF 91*
**Slash,** Joseph A. 1943- *WhoBlA 92*
**Slatcher,** William A 1926- *WhoAmP 91*
**Slatcher,** William Kenneth 1926- *Who 92*
**Slate,** C. Philip 1935- *WhoRel 92*
**Slate,** Floyd Owen 1920- *AmMWSc 92*
**Slaten,** Warren Colbert 1935- *WhoEnt 92*
**Slater,** Benjamin Richard, III 1950- *WhoAmL 92*
**Slater,** Bill *Who 92*
**Slater,** C Stewart 1957- *AmMWSc 92*
**Slater,** Carl David 1933- *AmMWSc 92*
**Slater,** Christian 1969- *ConTFT 9, IntMPA 92*
**Slater,** Christopher Peter 1934- *WhoRel 92*
**Slater,** Clifford David 1933- *WhoWest 92*
**Slater,** Dan 1949- *WhoEnt 92, WhoWest 92*
**Slater,** Daphne 1928- *IntMPA 92*
**Slater,** David Homfray 1940- *Who 92*
**Slater,** David Matthew 1961- *WhoAmL 92*
**Slater,** Don Austin 1938- *WhoWest 92*
**Slater,** Donald Carlin 1945- *AmMWSc 92*
**Slater,** Doris Ernestine Wilke *WhoFI 92*
**Slater,** Douglas Bryant 1963- *WhoEnt 92*
**Slater,** Duncan 1934- *Who 92*
**Slater,** Edward Charles 1917- *IntWW 91, Who 92*
**Slater,** Eleanor F *WhoAmP 91*
**Slater,** Eve Elizabeth 1945- *AmMWSc 92*
**Slater,** Gary 1947- *WorArt 1980 [port]*
**Slater,** George P 1932- *AmMWSc 92*
**Slater,** George Richard 1924- *WhoFI 92*
**Slater,** Gordon Charles Henry 1903- *Who 92*

**Slater,** Gordon James Augustus 1922- *IntWW 91, Who 92*
**Slater,** Grant Gay 1918- *AmMWSc 92, WhoWest 92*
**Slater,** Helen 1963- *IntMPA 92*
**Slater,** Helen Mae 1925- *WhoWest 92*
**Slater,** Helene Ford Southern *WhoBlA 92*
**Slater,** Ian 1941- *ConAu 34NR*
**Slater,** Jackie Ray 1954- *WhoBlA 92*
**Slater,** James Alexander 1920- *AmMWSc 92*
**Slater,** James Derrick 1929- *IntWW 91, Who 92*
**Slater,** James Louis 1944- *AmMWSc 92*
**Slater,** James Munro 1929- *AmMWSc 92*
**Slater,** Jill Sherry 1943- *WhoAmL 92*
**Slater,** John Christopher Nash 1946- *Who 92*
**Slater,** John Cunningham Kirkwood 1938- *Who 92*
**Slater,** John Fell 1924- *Who 92*
**Slater,** Joseph Elliott 1922- *IntWW 91*
**Slater,** Karen Reynders 1952- *WhoMW 92*
**Slater,** Kay Ross 1942- *WhoWest 92*
**Slater,** Keith 1935- *AmMWSc 92*
**Slater,** Kenneth Frederick 1925- *Who 92*
**Slater,** Kent 1945- *WhoAmP 91*
**Slater,** Leonard 1908- *Who 92*
**Slater,** Leonard 1920- *WhoWest 92*
**Slater,** Manning 1917- *WhoEnt 92*
**Slater,** Marilee Hebert 1949- *WhoEnt 92*
**Slater,** Mark Harold 1954- *WhoEnt 92*
**Slater,** Mary Jo 1946- *WhoEnt 92*
**Slater,** Michael R 1940- *WhoIns 92*
**Slater,** Oliver Eugene 1906- *WhoRel 92*
**Slater,** Peter James Bramwell 1942- *Who 92*
**Slater,** Peter John 1946- *AmMWSc 92*
**Slater,** Philip Nicholas 1932- *AmMWSc 92*
**Slater,** Phyllis Hill 1945- *WhoBlA 92*
**Slater,** Richard Craig 1946- *AmMWSc 92*
**Slater,** Richard Mercer Keene 1915- *Who 92*
**Slater,** Rodney E. 1955- *WhoBlA 92*
**Slater,** Ron *WhoAmP 91*
**Slater,** Samuel 1768-1835 *BiInAmS*
**Slater,** Schuyler G 1923- *AmMWSc 92*
**Slater,** Scott Edward 1954- *WhoFI 92*
**Slater,** Scott Steven 1958- *WhoAmL 92*
**Slater,** Terry d1991 *NewYTBS 91*
**Slater,** Thomas Bowie 1952- *WhoRel 92*
**Slater,** William Adcock 1933- *WhoMW 92*
**Slater,** William Bell 1925- *Who 92*
**Slater,** William E 1931- *AmMWSc 92*
**Slater,** William John 1927- *Who 92*
**Slater,** William Thomas 1942- *WhoMW 92*
**Slater-Foley,** Margaret Mary 1962- *WhoEnt 92*
**Slates,** Harry Lovell 1923- *AmMWSc 92*
**Slatkin,** Daniel Nathan 1934- *AmMWSc 92*
**Slatkin,** Leonard 1944- *IntWW 91, NewAmDM*
**Slatkin,** Leonard Edward 1944- *WhoEnt 92, WhoMW 92*
**Slatkin,** Marcia *DrAPF 91*
**Slatkin,** Montgomery 1945- *AmMWSc 92*
**Slatkin,** Murray 1905- *WhoFI 92*
**Slatky,** Larry Ira 1950- *WhoFI 92*
**Slatoff,** Walter J. 1922-1991 *ConAu 133*
**Slaton,** Alice Misrahi 1944- *WhoWest 92*
**Slaton,** Gwendolyn C. 1945- *WhoBlA 92*
**Slaton,** Jack H 1925- *AmMWSc 92*
**Slaton,** Lewis Roger 1922- *WhoAmL 92*
**Slaton,** Steven Charles 1953- *WhoEnt 92*
**Slatopolsky,** Eduardo 1934- *AmMWSc 92*
**Slatta,** Richard W. 1947- *ConAu 133*
**Slattery,** Charles Wilbur 1937- *AmMWSc 92*
**Slattery,** David Antony Douglas 1930- *Who 92*
**Slattery,** Eugene William *WhoIns 92*
**Slattery,** James Arthur 1942- *WhoFI 92*
**Slattery,** James Charles 1948- *WhoAmP 91, WhoMW 92*
**Slattery,** James Joseph 1922- *WhoEnt 92*
**Slattery,** James P *WhoIns 92*
**Slattery,** Jim 1948- *AlmAP 92 [port]*
**Slattery,** John C 1932- *AmMWSc 92*
**Slattery,** Louis R 1908- *AmMWSc 92*
**Slattery,** Margaret P. *WhoRel 92*
**Slattery,** Marty 1938- *ConAu 134*
**Slattery,** Matthew 1902-1990 *AnObit 1990*
**Slattery,** Michael Kevin 1953- *WhoAmL 92*
**Slattery,** Paul Francis 1940- *AmMWSc 92*
**Slattery,** Thomas Edward 1940- *WhoAmP 91*
**Slattery,** William Henry 1943- *WhoAmL 92*
**Slatton,** James Hoyt 1933- *WhoRel 92*
**Slatton,** John Louis 1923- *WhoEnt 92*
**Slatton,** Paul Sanders 1937- *WhoRel 92*
**Slatyer,** Ralph Owen 1929- *IntWW 91, Who 92*
**Slatzer,** Robert 1927- *IntAu&W 91, WrDr 92*
**Slatzer,** Robert Franklin 1927- *IntMPA 92*
**Slaughter,** Anson *TwCWW 91*
**Slaughter,** Audrey Cecelia 1930- *Who 92*
**Slaughter,** Carole D. 1945- *WhoBlA 92*
**Slaughter,** Carolyn 1946- *ConNov 91, WrDr 92*
**Slaughter,** Carolyn 1947- *IntAu&W 91*
**Slaughter,** Charles D 1936- *AmMWSc 92*
**Slaughter,** Charles Wesley 1941- *AmMWSc 92, WhoWest 92*
**Slaughter,** D. French, Jr. 1925- *AlmAP 92 [port], WhoAmP 91*
**Slaughter,** Eugene Edward 1909- *WrDr 92*
**Slaughter,** Frank G. 1908- *BenetAL 91, WrDr 92*
**Slaughter,** Frank Gill 1908- *IntAu&W 91, Who 92*
**Slaughter,** Frank Gill, Jr 1940- *AmMWSc 92*
**Slaughter,** Fred Leon 1942- *WhoBlA 92*
**Slaughter,** Gerald M 1928- *AmMWSc 92*
**Slaughter,** Giles David 1937- *Who 92*
**Slaughter,** James Bruce 1960- *WhoAmL 92*
**Slaughter,** James C. 1927- *WhoFI 92*
**Slaughter,** James Luther, III 1944- *WhoEnt 92, WhoMW 92*
**Slaughter,** Jim *TwCWW 91*
**Slaughter,** John Brooks 1934- *AmMWSc 92, WhoBlA 92, WhoWest 92*
**Slaughter,** John Etta 1929- *WhoBlA 92*
**Slaughter,** John Sim 1943- *AmMWSc 92*
**Slaughter,** Louise M. 1929- *AlmAP 92 [port]*
**Slaughter,** Louise McIntosh 1929- *WhoAmP 91*
**Slaughter,** Lynnard J 1938- *AmMWSc 92*
**Slaughter,** Marshall Glenn 1940- *WhoAmL 92*
**Slaughter,** Maynard 1934- *AmMWSc 92*
**Slaughter,** Milton Dean 1944- *AmMWSc 92*
**Slaughter,** Peter 1928- *WhoBlA 92*
**Slaughter,** Richard Lee 1952- *WhoMW 92*
**Slaughter,** Robert L 1933- *WhoAmP 91*
**Slaughter,** Robert L 1950- *WhoAmP 91*
**Slaughter,** Sharon Louise 1950- *WhoWest 92*
**Slaughter,** Susan Lee Brundige 1947- *WhoEnt 92*
**Slaughter,** Vernon L. *WhoBlA 92*
**Slaughter,** Vernon Leroy 1950- *WhoWest 92*
**Slaughter,** Webster M. 1964- *WhoBlA 92*
**Slaughter,** William M *WhoAmP 91*
**Slaughter Andrew,** Anne 1955- *WhoAmL 92*
**Slaughter-Defoe,** Diana T. 1941- *WhoBlA 92*
**Slaunwhite,** Wilson Roy, Jr 1919- *AmMWSc 92*
**Slauson,** John Gordon 1940- *WhoAmL 92*
**Slautterback,** David Buell 1926- *AmMWSc 92*
**Slaven,** Robert Walter 1948- *AmMWSc 92*
**Slavich,** Denis Michael 1940- *WhoFI 92*
**Slavicky,** Klement 1910- *ConCom 92*
**Slavik,** Donald Harlan 1956- *WhoAmL 92*
**Slavik,** Milan 1930- *AmMWSc 92, WhoMW 92*
**Slavik,** Nelson Sigman 1948- *AmMWSc 92*
**Slavin,** Alexandra Nadal 1943- *WhoEnt 92*
**Slavin,** Bernard Geoffrey 1936- *AmMWSc 92*
**Slavin,** George 1916- *IntMPA 92*
**Slavin,** Joanne Louise 1952- *AmMWSc 92, WhoMW 92*
**Slavin,** John Jeremiah 1921- *WhoMW 92*
**Slavin,** Joseph 1924- *WhoAmL 92*
**Slavin,** Joseph Thomas 1958- *WhoFI 92*
**Slavin,** Kenneth Dwan 1937- *WhoMW 92*
**Slavin,** Ovid 1921- *AmMWSc 92*
**Slavin,** Raymond Granam 1930- *AmMWSc 92*
**Slavitt,** David 1935- *ConPo 91, IntAu&W 91, WrDr 92*
**Slavitt,** David R. *DrAPF 91*
**Slavitt,** David Rytman 1935- *IntWW 91*
**Slavitt,** Evan Meyer 1957- *WhoAmL 92*
**Slavkin,** Harold Charles 1938- *AmMWSc 92*
**Slavov,** Atanas Vasilev 1925?- *LiExTwC*
**Slavutin,** Lee Jacob 1951- *WhoFI 92*
**Slavutych,** Yar 1918- *WrDr 92*
**Slawiak,** Sheila Iaquinto 1956- *WhoFI 92*
**Slawsky,** Zaka I 1910- *AmMWSc 92*
**Slawson,** Peter 1939- *AmMWSc 92*
**Slay,** Francis P 1927- *WhoAmP 91*
**Slayden,** Suzanne Weems 1948- *AmMWSc 92*
**Slaymaker,** Frank Harris 1914- *AmMWSc 92*
**Slaymaker,** Gene Arthur 1928- *WhoEnt 92*
**Slaymaker,** Herbert Olav 1939- *AmMWSc 92*
**Slayman,** Carolyn Walch 1937- *AmMWSc 92*
**Slayman,** Clifford L 1936- *AmMWSc 92*
**Slayton,** Donald 1924- *FacFETw*
**Slayton,** Frank Marshall 1932- *WhoAmP 91*
**Slayton,** Joel Charles 1948- *WhoRel 92*
**Slayton,** John Howard 1955- *WhoAmL 92, WhoFI 92*
**Slayton,** Richard Courtney 1937- *WhoFI 92*
**Sleasman,** William Jacob 1927- *WhoRel 92*
**Sleator,** William 1945- *SmATA 68 [port], WrDr 92*
**Sleator,** William Warner, Jr 1917- *AmMWSc 92*
**Slechta,** Robert Frank 1928- *AmMWSc 92*
**Sledd,** William T 1935- *AmMWSc 92*
**Sledge,** Darcy MacKinnon 1958- *WhoFI 92*
**Sledge,** Eugene Bondurant 1923- *AmMWSc 92*
**Sledge,** Larry Dale 1936- *WhoRel 92*
**Sledge,** Larry Gene 1952- *WhoEnt 92*
**Sledge,** P Nevin 1921- *WhoAmP 91*
**Sledge,** Reginald Leon 1954- *WhoFI 92*
**Sledge,** Richard Kitson 1930- *Who 92*
**Sledge,** Terry Lynn 1951- *WhoRel 92*
**Slee,** Frederick Watford 1937- *AmMWSc 92*
**Slee,** Richard *ScFEYrs*
**Slee,** Richard & Pratt, Cornelia Atwood *ScFEYrs*
**Sleem,** Hatem Ameen 1956- *WhoMW 92*
**Sleeman,** Colin *Who 92*
**Sleeman,** Keith 1922- *TwCPaSc*
**Sleeman,** Richard Alexander 1926- *AmMWSc 92*
**Sleeman,** Thomas Barrett 1932- *WhoFI 92, WhoWest 92*
**Sleep,** Norman H 1945- *AmMWSc 92*
**Sleep,** Wayne 1948- *IntWW 91, Who 92*
**Sleeper,** David Allanbrook 1922- *AmMWSc 92*
**Sleeper,** Elbert Launee 1927- *AmMWSc 92*
**Sleeper,** James A. 1947- *ConAu 133*
**Sleeper,** Jim *ConAu 133*
**Sleet,** Moneta J., Jr. 1926- *WhoBlA 92*
**Sleeter,** Thomas David 1952- *AmMWSc 92*
**Sleeth,** Bailey 1900- *AmMWSc 92*
**Sleeth,** David Thompson 1957- *WhoAmL 92*
**Sleeth,** Rhule Bailey 1929- *AmMWSc 92*
**Sleezer,** Paul David 1936- *AmMWSc 92*
**Slegman,** Betty Harvey 1922- *WhoMW 92*
**Sleicher,** Charles A 1924- *AmMWSc 92*
**Sleight,** Arthur William 1939- *AmMWSc 92, WhoWest 92*
**Sleight,** Peter 1929- *Who 92*
**Sleight,** Richard 1946- *Who 92*
**Sleight,** Stuart Duane 1927- *AmMWSc 92*
**Sleight,** Thomas Perry 1943- *AmMWSc 92*
**Slein,** Milton Wilbur 1919- *AmMWSc 92*
**Sleisenger,** Marvin Herbert 1924- *AmMWSc 92*
**Slemmons,** David Burton 1922- *AmMWSc 92*
**Slemmons,** Robert Sheldon 1922- *WhoFI 92, WhoMW 92*
**Slemon,** Charles Roy 1904- *Who 92*
**Slemon,** Gordon R 1924- *AmMWSc 92*
**Slemon,** Gordon Richard 1924- *WrDr 92*
**Slenker,** Norman Frederick 1929- *WhoAmL 92*
**Slensker,** Glenn Alan 1950- *WhoFI 92*
**Slentz,** Daniel Eugene 1963- *WhoEnt 92*
**Slepecky,** Ralph Andrew 1924- *AmMWSc 92*
**Sleper,** David Allen 1945- *AmMWSc 92*
**Slepetys,** Richard Algimantas 1928- *AmMWSc 92*
**Slepian,** David 1923- *AmMWSc 92*
**Slepian,** Jacob Zeiger 1938- *WhoEnt 92*
**Slepian,** Paul 1923- *AmMWSc 92*
**Slepoy,** Ephraim P. 1958- *WhoRel 92*
**Sleppin,** Stuart Arthur 1955- *WhoEnt 92*
**Slesar,** Henry *DrAPF 91*
**Slesar,** Henry 1927- *IntAu&W 91, WrDr 92*
**Slesiensky,** Deloris *DrAPF 91*
**Slesinger,** Reuben Emanuel 1916- *WhoFI 92*
**Slesinger,** Tess 1900-1945 *BenetAL 91*
**Slesinger,** Warren *DrAPF 91*
**Slesinger,** Warren 1933- *WrDr 92*
**Slesnick,** Irwin Leonard 1926- *AmMWSc 92*
**Slesnick,** William Ellis 1925- *AmMWSc 92*
**Slessor,** Keith Norman 1938- *AmMWSc 92*
**Slessor,** Kenneth 1901-1971 *RfGEnL 91*
**Slettebak,** Arne 1925- *AmMWSc 92*
**Slevin,** Brian Francis Patrick 1926- *Who 92*
**Slevin,** Joseph Raymond 1918- *WhoFI 92*
**Slevin,** Margarita H. 1953- *WhoWest 92*
**Slevin,** Patrick Joseph 1951- *WhoFI 92*
**Slezak,** Erika Alma 1946- *WhoEnt 92*
**Slezak,** Frank Bier 1928- *AmMWSc 92*
**Slezak,** Jane Ann *AmMWSc 92*
**Slezak,** Jerzy 1939- *IntWW 91*
**Slezak,** Leo 1873-1946 *NewAmDM*
**Slezko,** Pyotr Yakovlevich 1931- *IntWW 91*
**Slice,** Paul Owens 1932- *WhoRel 92*
**Slichter,** Charles Pence 1924- *AmMWSc 92, IntWW 91*
**Slichter,** William Pence 1922- *AmMWSc 92*
**Slick,** Gary L. 1941- *WhoMW 92*
**Slick,** Grace Wing 1939- *WhoEnt 92*
**Slick,** Jewel Cherie 1934- *WhoMW 92*
**Slick,** Sam *BenetAL 91*
**Slicker,** Frederick Kent 1943- *WhoAmL 92*
**Slide,** Anthony 1944- *WrDr 92*
**Slide,** Anthony Clifford 1944- *IntAu&W 91*
**Slidell,** John 1793-1871 *AmPolLe*
**Slider,** Daniel M. 1958- *WhoEnt 92*
**Slider,** H C 1924- *AmMWSc 92*
**Slie,** Samuel N. *WhoRel 92*
**Slie,** Samuel N. 1925- *WhoBlA 92*
**Sliemers,** Francis Anthony, Jr 1929- *AmMWSc 92*
**Sliepcevich,** Cedomir M 1920- *AmMWSc 92*
**Slife,** Charles W 1949- *AmMWSc 92*
**Slife,** Fred Warren 1923- *AmMWSc 92*
**Slife,** Harry *WhoAmP 91*
**Slifka,** Robert S 1941- *WhoIns 92*
**Slifkin,** Lawrence 1925- *AmMWSc 92*
**Slifkin,** Malcolm 1933- *AmMWSc 92*
**Sligar,** Stephen Gary 1948- *AmMWSc 92*
**Sliger,** Bernard Francis 1924- *IntWW 91*
**Sliger,** Wilburn Andrew 1940- *AmMWSc 92*
**Sligo,** Marquess of 1908- *Who 92*
**Sliker,** Alan 1927- *AmMWSc 92*
**Sliker,** Todd Richard 1936- *AmMWSc 92, WhoWest 92*
**Slikker,** William, Jr *AmMWSc 92*
**Slilaty,** Steve N 1952- *AmMWSc 92*
**Slim** *Who 92*
**Slim,** Viscount 1927- *Who 92*
**Slim,** Taieb 1919- *IntWW 91*
**Slim,** William Joseph 1891-1970 *FacFETw*
**Slimko,** Stella Ann 1939- *WhoFI 92*
**Slimmings,** William Kenneth MacLeod 1912- *Who 92*
**Slinde,** Elizabeth M *WhoAmP 91*
**Sliney,** B W *ScFEYrs*
**Sliney,** David H 1941- *AmMWSc 92*
**Sliney,** James Gilmore, Jr. 1940- *WhoWest 92*
**Slinger,** Brigetta *WhoRel 92*
**Slinger,** Grant 1952- *WhoMW 92*
**Slinger,** Penelope 1947- *TwCPaSc*
**Slinger,** William 1917- *Who 92*
**Slingerland,** Mark Vernon 1864-1909 *BiInAmS*
**Slingerland,** Rudy Lynn 1947- *AmMWSc 92*
**Slingluff,** Charles Haines, Jr. 1929- *WhoFI 92*
**Slinkard,** Alfred Eugene 1931- *AmMWSc 92*
**Slinkard,** Phillip Matthew 1956- *WhoAmL 92*
**Slinkard,** William Earl 1943- *AmMWSc 92*
**Slipman,** Ronald 1939- *WhoFI 92*
**Slipman,** Sue 1949- *Who 92*
**Slipuas,** Jonas *DcAmImH*
**Slipy,** Iosyf 1892-1984 *SovUnBD*
**Slisz,** Jozef 1934- *IntWW 91*
**Sliteris,** E. Joanne 1942- *WhoAmL 92*
**Sliva,** Philip Oscar 1938- *AmMWSc 92*
**Slive,** Seymour 1920- *Who 92, WrDr 92*
**Slivinsky,** Charles R 1941- *AmMWSc 92*
**Slivinsky,** Sandra Harriet *AmMWSc 92*
**Slivka,** Michael Andrew 1955- *WhoAmL 92*
**Slivka,** William John 1947- *WhoFI 92*
**Sliwinski,** Robert Leo 1935- *WhoMW 92*
**Slizeski,** Marilyn Lenore 1953- *WhoWest 92*
**Sloan,** Alan David 1945- *AmMWSc 92*
**Sloan,** Alfred Pritchard, Jr 1875-1966 *FacFETw*
**Sloan,** Andrew 1931- *Who 92*
**Sloan,** Benjamin *DrAPF 91*
**Sloan,** Bob 1940- *TwCPaSc*
**Sloan,** David E. 1923- *WhoBlA 92*
**Sloan,** David W 1937- *WhoAmP 91*
**Sloan,** David Walter 1937- *WhoEnt 92*
**Sloan,** Denise Elizabeth 1950- *WhoEnt 92*
**Sloan,** Donald Leroy, Jr 1944- *AmMWSc 92*
**Sloan,** Donnie Robert, Jr. 1946- *WhoAmL 92*
**Sloan,** Earle Dendy, Jr. 1944- *WhoWest 92*
**Sloan,** Edith Barksdale 1940- *NotBlAW 92, WhoBlA 92*
**Sloan,** Edna Mae 1946- *WhoWest 92*
**Sloan,** Ellis 1958- *WhoFI 92*
**Sloan,** Frank A 1942- *AmMWSc 92*

**Sloan**, Frank Blaine 1920- WhoAmL 92
**Sloan**, Frank Keenan 1921- WhoAmP 91
**Sloan**, Gerald Eugene 1942- WhoWest 92
**Sloan**, Gilbert Jacob 1928- AmMWSc 92
**Sloan**, Harold Paul 1881-1961 RelLAm 91
**Sloan**, Herbert 1914- AmMWSc 92
**Sloan**, James Lloyd 1934- WhoRel 92
**Sloan**, James Park DrAPF 91
**Sloan**, James Park 1916- WhoAmP 91
**Sloan**, Jerry Lee 1936- WhoMW 92
**Sloan**, John 1871-1951 FacFETw
**Sloan**, John R. IntMPA 92
**Sloan**, Johnny Wade 1949- WhoMW 92, WhoRel 92
**Sloan**, Joyce WhoEnt 92
**Sloan**, Judy Beckner 1945- WhoAmL 92
**Sloan**, Lane Everett 1947- WhoFI 92
**Sloan**, Lanny Gene 1945- WhoWest 92
**Sloan**, Maceo Archibald 1913- WhoBlA 92
**Sloan**, Maceo Kennedy 1949- WhoAmL 92, WhoBlA 92, WhoFI 92
**Sloan**, Martin Frank 1934- AmMWSc 92
**Sloan**, Michael 1946- WhoEnt 92
**Sloan**, Michael Dana 1960- WhoWest 92
**Sloan**, Michael Eugene 1943- WhoWest 92
**Sloan**, Norman Alexander 1914- Who 92
**Sloan**, Norman F 1934- AmMWSc 92
**Sloan**, Norman Grady 1937- AmMWSc 92
**Sloan**, Ralph Wayne 1959- WhoAmL 92
**Sloan**, Robert Bryan 1949- WhoRel 92
**Sloan**, Robert Dye 1918- AmMWSc 92
**Sloan**, Robert Evan 1929- AmMWSc 92
**Sloan**, Robert W 1924- AmMWSc 92
**Sloan**, Sheldon Harold 1935- WhoAmP 91
**Sloan**, Sonia Schorr 1928- WhoAmP 91
**Sloan**, Stephen 1951- WhoAmP 91
**Sloan**, Thomas Edwin 1937- WhoMW 92
**Sloan**, Victor 1945- TwCPaSc
**Sloan**, William Cooper 1927- AmMWSc 92
**Sloane**, Ann Brownell 1938- WhoFI 92
**Sloane**, Bernard A. 1921- WhoFI 92
**Sloane**, Beverly LeBov 1936- WhoWest 92
**Sloane**, Christine Scheid 1945- AmMWSc 92
**Sloane**, Hans 1660-1753 BlkwCEP
**Sloane**, Harvey I 1936- WhoAmP 91
**Sloane**, Howard J 1931- AmMWSc 92
**Sloane**, Nathan Howard 1917- AmMWSc 92
**Sloane**, Neil James Alexander 1939- AmMWSc 92
**Sloane**, Owen Jay WhoEnt 92
**Sloane**, Peter J. 1942- WrDr 92
**Sloane**, Peter James 1942- Who 92
**Sloane**, Robert Bruce 1923- AmMWSc 92
**Sloane**, Robert Malcolm 1933- WhoWest 92
**Sloane**, Thompson Milton 1945- AmMWSc 92
**Sloane**, William M 1906-1974 TwCSFW 91
**Sloane**, William Martin 1951- WhoAmP 91
**Sloat**, Barbara Furin 1942- AmMWSc 92
**Sloat**, Charles Allen 1898- AmMWSc 92
**Slobig**, Robert J. 1957- WhoAmL 92
**Slobin**, Dan Isaac 1939- WhoWest 92
**Slobin**, Lawrence I 1938- AmMWSc 92
**Sloboda**, Adolph Edward 1928- AmMWSc 92
**Sloboda**, Roger D 1948- AmMWSc 92
**Slobodchikoff**, Constantine Nicholas 1944- AmMWSc 92
**Slobodkin**, Lawrence Basil 1928- AmMWSc 92
**Slobodkin**, Louis 1903-1975 BenetAL 91
**Slobodkina**, Esphyr 1908- WrDr 92
**Slobodrian**, Rodolfo Jose 1930- AmMWSc 92
**Slochower**, Harry d1991 NewYTBS 91
**Slochower**, Harry 1900-1991 ConAu 134
**Slocombe**, Douglas 1913- IntMPA 92
**Slocombe**, Joseph Owen Douglas 1931- AmMWSc 92
**Slocombe**, Robert Jackson 1917- AmMWSc 92
**Slocombe**, Walter Becker 1941- WhoAmL 92
**Slocum**, Charles Bruce 1958- WhoEnt 92, WhoRel 92
**Slocum**, Donald Hillman 1930- WhoFI 92
**Slocum**, Donald Warren AmMWSc 92
**Slocum**, Harry Kim 1947- AmMWSc 92
**Slocum**, John 1841-1897 RelLAm 91
**Slocum**, Joshua 1844-1909? BenetAL 91
**Slocum**, Milton Jonathan 1905- IntAu&W 91
**Slocum**, Richard William 1934- AmMWSc 92
**Slocum**, Robert Earle 1938- AmMWSc 92
**Slocum**, Robert Richard 1931- AmMWSc 92
**Slocum**, Rosemarie R. 1948- WhoMW 92
**Slocum**, Shaun Michael 1951- WhoAmL 92
**Slocum**, Stephen E., Jr. WhoRel 92
**Slocum**, William Bennett 1936- WhoEnt 92
**Slodki**, Morey Eli 1928- AmMWSc 92
**Slodowski**, Thomas R 1926- AmMWSc 92
**Sloe**, John Edward 1953- WhoMW 92
**Sloger**, Charles 1938- AmMWSc 92
**Sloggett**, Bruce Scott 1951- WhoWest 92
**Sloggett**, Jolyon Edward 1933- Who 92
**Sloggy**, John Edward 1952- WhoFI 92
**Sloluck**, J. Milton BenetAL 91
**Sloma**, Leonard Vincent 1920- AmMWSc 92
**Sloman**, Albert 1921- Who 92
**Sloman**, Albert Edward 1921- IntWW 91, WrDr 92
**Sloman**, Anne 1944- IntAu&W 91
**Sloman**, Barbara 1925- Who 92
**Sloman**, Joel DrAPF 91
**Sloman**, Marvin Sherk 1925- WhoAmL 92
**Sloman**, Peter 1919- Who 92
**Slomanson**, William Reed 1945- WhoAmL 92, WhoWest 92
**Slomiak**, Mitchel Jay 1959- WhoFI 92
**Slomiany**, Amalia AmMWSc 92
**Slomkowski**, Cynthia Sue Olson 1953- WhoWest 92
**Slomovits**, Laszlo 1949- WhoEnt 92
**Slomovitz-Glaser**, Penny Sandra 1964- WhoAmL 92
**Slomp**, George 1922- AmMWSc 92
**Slonczewski**, Joan 1956- TwCSFW 91
**Slonczewski**, Joan Lyn 1956- AmMWSc 92
**Slonczewski**, John Casimir 1929- AmMWSc 92
**Slone**, R. Wayne WhoFI 92, WhoMW 92
**Slonecker**, Charles Edward 1938- AmMWSc 92
**Slonim**, Arnold Robert 1926- AmMWSc 92, WhoMW 92
**Slonim**, Jacob 1945- AmMWSc 92
**Slonim**, Mark 1894-1976 LiExTwC
**Slonim**, Reuben 1914- WrDr 92
**Slonimski**, Piotr 1922- IntWW 91
**Slonimsky**, Nicolas 1894- CurBio 91 [port], IntWW 91, WhoEnt 92
**Slonimsky**, Sergey Mikhailovich 1932- IntWW 91
**Slonimsky**, Sergey Mikhaylovich 1932- SovUnBD
**Slonimsky**, Yuriy Iosifovich 1902-1978 SovUnBD
**Slook**, George Francis 1946- WhoFI 92
**Sloop**, Charles Henry AmMWSc 92
**Sloop**, Gregory Todd 1962- WhoRel 92
**Sloope**, Billy Warren 1924- AmMWSc 92
**Slopek**, Stefan 1914- IntWW 91
**Slosberg**, Mike 1934- WrDr 92
**Sloser**, Michael Edward 1941- WhoEnt 92
**Sloss** Who 92
**Sloss**, James M 1931- AmMWSc 92
**Sloss**, Minerva A. 1921- WhoBlA 92
**Sloss**, Peter William 1942- AmMWSc 92
**Slosser**, Jeffrey Eric 1943- AmMWSc 92
**Slosson**, James E 1923- AmMWSc 92
**Slosson**, James Edward 1923- WhoWest 92
**Slot**, Peter Maurice Joseph 1932- Who 92
**Slota**, Peter John, Jr 1924- AmMWSc 92
**Slota**, Richard DrAPF 91
**Slote**, A. R. 1935- IntMPA 92
**Slote**, Alfred WrDr 92
**Slote**, Lawrence 1924- AmMWSc 92
**Slotkin**, Jacquelyn Hersh 1942- WhoAmL 92
**Slotkin**, Theodore Alan 1947- AmMWSc 92
**Slotnick**, Daniel Leonid 1931- AmMWSc 92
**Slotnick**, Herbert 1928- AmMWSc 92
**Slotnick**, Vicki S. 1963- WhoEnt 92
**Slotnick**, Victor Bernard 1931- AmMWSc 92
**Slotsky**, Myron Norton 1935- AmMWSc 92
**Slotta**, Larry Stewart 1934- AmMWSc 92
**Slotter**, Richard Arden 1932- AmMWSc 92
**Slotterbeck-Baker**, Oberta Ann 1936- AmMWSc 92
**Slouber**, James Kirk 1952- WhoWest 92
**Slough**, John Edward 1942- WhoAmL 92
**Slough**, Kenneth D., Jr. WhoRel 92
**Slovacek**, Bob Leo 1948- WhoFI 92
**Slovacek**, Rudolf Edward 1948- AmMWSc 92
**Slovenko**, Ralph 1927- IntAu&W 91, WhoAmL 92, WhoMW 92, WrDr 92
**Slover**, Archy F. 1920- WhoWest 92
**Slover**, Philip Ray 1947- WhoMW 92
**Sloves**, Marvin 1933- IntWW 91, WhoFI 92
**Slovik**, Eddie 1921-1945 FacFETw
**Slovikowski**, Gerald Jude 1949- WhoFI 92
**Slovin**, Susan Faith 1953- AmMWSc 92
**Sloviter**, Dolores K WhoAmP 91
**Sloviter**, Dolores Korman 1932- WhoAmL 92
**Sloviter**, Henry Allan 1914- AmMWSc 92
**Sloviter**, Robert Seth 1950- AmMWSc 92
**Slovo**, Joe 1926- IntWW 91
**Slowe**, Lucy Diggs 1885-1937 NotBlAW 92
**Slowen**, Warren Thomas 1943- WhoAmL 92
**Slowey**, Jack William 1932- AmMWSc 92
**Slowik**, Edward Casimir 1938- WhoFI 92
**Slowik**, John Henry 1945- AmMWSc 92
**Slowikowski**, Mary Kay 1940- WhoFI 92
**Slowinski**, Emil J, Jr 1922- AmMWSc 92
**Sloyan**, Gerard Stephen 1919- WhoRel 92
**Sloyan**, Mary Stephanie 1918- AmMWSc 92
**Sloyer**, Clifford W, Jr 1934- AmMWSc 92
**Sloyer**, Gary Stephen 1960- WhoEnt 92
**Sluberski**, Thomas Richard 1939- WhoRel 92
**Sluder**, Earl Ray 1930- AmMWSc 92
**Sluder**, Greenfield AmMWSc 92
**Sluiter**, Jack 1945- WhoAmP 91
**Slusarchyk**, William Allen 1940- AmMWSc 92
**Slusarczuk**, George Marcelius Jaremias 1932- AmMWSc 92
**Slusarek**, Lidia AmMWSc 92
**Slusher**, Michael Dennis 1949- WhoEnt 92
**Slusher**, Richart Elliott 1938- AmMWSc 92
**Slusky**, Joseph 1942- WhoWest 92
**Slusky**, Susan E G 1949- AmMWSc 92
**Sluss**, Robert Reginald 1928- AmMWSc 92
**Sluss**, Stephen Craig 1959- WhoAmP 91
**Slusser**, Eugene Alvin 1922- WhoFI 92
**Slusser**, Lester Robert 1921- WhoRel 92
**Slusser**, M L 1919- AmMWSc 92
**Slusser**, Robert Wyman 1938- WhoFI 92, WhoWest 92
**Slutsky**, Arthur 1948- AmMWSc 92
**Slutsky**, Boris Abramovich 1919-1986 SovUnBD
**Slutsky**, Herbert L 1925- AmMWSc 92
**Slutsky**, Leon Judah 1932- AmMWSc 92
**Slutsky**, Leonard Alan 1945- WhoFI 92
**Slutz**, Anthony Lee 1942- WhoRel 92
**Slutz**, Jerome Lee 1927- WhoMW 92
**Slutz**, Ralph Jeffery 1917- AmMWSc 92
**Slutzky**, Elliot Howard WhoWest 92
**Slutzky**, Gale David 1952- AmMWSc 92, WhoMW 92
**Slutzky**, Richard Owen 1956- WhoRel 92
**Sluyter**, David John 1943- WhoMW 92
**Sluyter**, Scott Burritt 1963- WhoFI 92
**Sly and the Family Stone** NewAmDM
**Sly Stone** 1944- NewAmDM
**Sly**, Peter G 1939- AmMWSc 92
**Sly**, Richard Allen 1935- WhoAmL 92
**Sly**, Ridge Michael 1933- AmMWSc 92
**Sly**, William Glenn 1922- AmMWSc 92
**Sly**, William S 1932- AmMWSc 92
**Slye**, John Marshall 1923- AmMWSc 92
**Slyh**, John A 1913- AmMWSc 92
**Slyh**, Raymond Edward 1965- WhoMW 92
**Slyk**, Marek 1953- IntAu&W 91
**Slynn**, Gordon 1930- IntWW 91, Who 92
**Slysh**, Roman Stephan 1926- AmMWSc 92
**Slyter**, Arthur Lowell 1941- AmMWSc 92
**Slyter**, Leonard L 1933- AmMWSc 92
**Slyunkov**, Nikolay Nikitovich 1929- IntWW 91, SovUnBD
**Slywka**, Gerald William Alexander 1939- AmMWSc 92
**Smaga**, Janice 1948- WhoFI 92
**Smagorinsky**, Joseph 1924- AmMWSc 92
**Smail**, James Richard 1934- AmMWSc 92
**Smailes**, George Mason 1916- Who 92
**Smale**, Fred ScFEYrs
**Smale**, John Arthur 1895- Who 92
**Smale**, John G. 1927- IntWW 91
**Smale**, John Gray 1927- WhoFI 92
**Smale**, Stephen 1930- AmMWSc 92, IntWW 91
**Smalheiser**, Harvey 1942- WhoFI 92
**Smalkin**, Frederic N. WhoAmL 92
**Small**, Albert Harrison 1925- WhoFI 92
**Small**, Arnold McCollum 1929- WhoMW 92
**Small**, Arnold McCollum, Jr 1929- AmMWSc 92
**Small**, Arthur A., Jr. 1933- WhoAmL 92, WhoAmP 91, WhoMW 92
**Small**, Austin J d1929 ScFEYrs
**Small**, Ben Francis, III 1947- WhoAmL 92
**Small**, Bertrice 1937- WrDr 92
**Small**, Britton Britt Robert 1947- WhoEnt 92
**Small**, Bruce W. 1950- WhoMW 92
**Small**, Charles John 1919- IntWW 91, Who 92
**Small**, David DrAPF 91
**Small**, David Michael 1958- WhoMW 92
**Small**, David Purvis 1930- Who 92
**Small**, Donald Bridgham 1935- AmMWSc 92
**Small**, Emilie Rose 1946- WhoEnt 92
**Small**, Ernest IntAu&W 91X, WrDr 92
**Small**, Ernest 1940- AmMWSc 92
**Small**, Erwin 1924- AmMWSc 92, WhoMW 92
**Small**, Eugene Beach 1931- AmMWSc 92
**Small**, Gary D 1937- AmMWSc 92
**Small**, Hamish 1929- AmMWSc 92, WhoMW 92
**Small**, Henry Gilbert 1941- AmMWSc 92
**Small**, Isadore, III 1944- WhoBlA 92
**Small**, Israel G. 1941- WhoBlA 92
**Small**, Iver Francis 1923- AmMWSc 92
**Small**, James Graydon 1945- AmMWSc 92
**Small**, Janice Mason 1953- WhoMW 92
**Small**, Jeffrey 1941- WhoAmL 92
**Small**, Jerome Kuhn, Jr. 1947- WhoMW 92
**Small**, John Who 92
**Small**, John Rankin 1933- Who 92
**Small**, Jonathan Andrew 1942- WhoAmL 92
**Small**, Jonathan Andrew 1959- WhoAmL 92
**Small**, Joseph Dunnell 1941- WhoRel 92
**Small**, Joyce G 1931- AmMWSc 92
**Small**, Karna WhoAmP 91
**Small**, Keith Rudolph 1954- WhoAmL 92
**Small**, Kenneth Alan 1945- WhoFI 92
**Small**, Kenneth Lester 1957- WhoBlA 92, WhoHisp 92
**Small**, Kimberley Ann 1950- WhoRel 92
**Small**, Lance W 1941- AmMWSc 92
**Small**, LaVerne Doreyn 1916- AmMWSc 92
**Small**, Lawrence Farnsworth 1925- WhoWest 92
**Small**, Lawrence Francis 1950- WhoWest 92
**Small**, Lawrence Frederick 1934- AmMWSc 92
**Small**, Lawrence Malcolm 1941- WhoBlA 92
**Small**, Lily B. 1934- WhoBlA 92
**Small**, Mark James 1950- WhoFI 92
**Small**, Marshall Lee 1927- WhoAmL 92
**Small**, Mary Eleanor 1954- WhoAmP 91
**Small**, Millie 1924- WhoAmP 91
**Small**, Neal WhoAmP 91
**Small**, Neal 1937- DcTwDes
**Small**, Oscar James, Sr 1931- WhoAmP 91
**Small**, Parker Adams, Jr 1932- AmMWSc 92
**Small**, Pearlie Grace H 1942- WhoAmP 91
**Small**, Ramsay George 1930- Who 92
**Small**, Rebecca Elaine 1946- WhoFI 92
**Small**, Richard Donald 1929- WhoFI 92, WhoMW 92
**Small**, Richard F. 1936- WhoWest 92
**Small**, Robert James 1938- AmMWSc 92
**Small**, Robert Leonard 1905- Who 92
**Small**, S Mouchly 1913- AmMWSc 92
**Small**, Stanley Joseph 1946- WhoBlA 92
**Small**, Sydney L. 1941- WhoBlA 92
**Small**, Timothy Michael 1940- AmMWSc 92
**Small**, William 1734-1775 BiInAmS
**Small**, William 1940- WhoBlA 92
**Small**, William Andrew 1914- AmMWSc 92
**Small**, William J. LesBEnT 92
**Small**, William Jack 1926- IntWW 91
**Smallbone**, Graham 1934- Who 92
**Smallens**, Alexander 1889-1972 NewAmDM
**Smalley**, Alfred Evans 1928- AmMWSc 92
**Smalley**, Arnold Winfred 1933- AmMWSc 92
**Smalley**, Denis 1946- ConCom 92
**Smalley**, Eugene Byron 1926- AmMWSc 92, WhoMW 92
**Smalley**, George W. 1833-1916 BenetAL 91
**Smalley**, Glendon William 1928- AmMWSc 92
**Smalley**, Harry Edwin 1924- AmMWSc 92
**Smalley**, I M 1904- WhoAmP 91
**Smalley**, Jack Peter 1927- WhoEnt 92
**Smalley**, K Maxine 1920- WhoAmP 91
**Smalley**, Katherine N 1935- AmMWSc 92
**Smalley**, Larry L 1937- AmMWSc 92
**Smalley**, LeRoy Dale 1952- WhoRel 92
**Smalley**, Paul 1935- WhoAmP 91, WhoBlA 92
**Smalley**, Ralph Ray 1919- AmMWSc 92
**Smalley**, Richard Errett 1943- AmMWSc 92
**Smalley**, Robert Gordon 1921- AmMWSc 92
**Smalley**, Robert M 1925- WhoAmP 91
**Smalley**, Robin Allinson 1956- WhoEnt 92
**Smalley**, Roger 1943- NewAmDM
**Smalley**, Stephen Mark 1953- WhoRel 92
**Smalley**, Stephen S. 1931- WrDr 92
**Smalley**, Stephen Stewart 1931- IntAu&W 91, Who 92
**Smalley**, Webster Leroy C. 1921- WhoEnt 92
**Smalley**, William Edward 1940- WhoMW 92, WhoRel 92
**Smalley**, William Henry 1943- WhoAmP 91
**Smalley**, William Richard 1928- WhoRel 92

**Smallfield,** Edward *DrAPF 91*
**Smallman,** Barry Granger 1924- *IntWW 91, Who 92*
**Smallman,** Raymond Edward 1929- *IntWW 91, Who 92*
**Smallpeice,** Basil 1906- *IntWW 91, Who 92*
**Smalls,** Charley Mae 1943- *WhoBlA 92*
**Smalls,** Charlie E. 1943-1987 *WhoBlA 92N*
**Smalls,** Dorothy M. 1920- *WhoBlA 92*
**Smalls,** Jacquelyn Elaine 1946- *WhoBlA 92*
**Smalls,** Marcella E. 1946- *WhoBlA 92*
**Smalls,** O'Neal 1941- *WhoBlA 92*
**Smallwood,** Anne Hunter 1922- *Who 92*
**Smallwood,** Charles, Jr 1920- *AmMWSc 92*
**Smallwood,** Denis 1918- *Who 92*
**Smallwood,** Edward Louis 1950- *WhoRel 92*
**Smallwood,** Glenn Walter, Jr. 1956- *WhoFI 92, WhoMW 92*
**Smallwood,** James Edgar 1945- *AmMWSc 92*
**Smallwood,** John Frank Monton 1926- *Who 92*
**Smallwood,** Joseph R. 1900-1991 *NewYTBS 91*
**Smallwood,** Osborn Tucker 1911- *WhoBlA 92*
**Smallwood,** Richard Dale 1935- *AmMWSc 92*
**Smallwood,** Robert H. M. 1947- *WhoFI 92*
**Smalter,** Donald Joseph 1926- *WhoFI 92*
**Smaltz,** Jacob Jay 1917- *AmMWSc 92*
**Smarandache,** Florentin 1954- *AmMWSc 92, WhoWest 92*
**Smardon,** Richard Clay 1948- *AmMWSc 92*
**Smardzewski,** Richard Roman 1942- *AmMWSc 92*
**Smario,** Tom *DrAPF 91*
**Smarr,** Larry Lee 1948- *AmMWSc 92, WhoMW 92*
**Smart,** Alastair 1922- *WrDr 92*
**Smart,** Alexander Basil Peter 1932- *IntWW 91, Who 92*
**Smart,** Andrew 1924- *Who 92*
**Smart,** Anthony 1949- *TwCPaSc*
**Smart,** Arthur David Gerald 1925- *Who 92*
**Smart,** Bruce Edmund 1945- *AmMWSc 92*
**Smart,** Christopher 1722-1771 *BlkwCEP, DcLB 109 [port], RfGEnL 91*
**Smart,** Claude Harlan, Jr. 1927- *WhoAmL 92*
**Smart,** Edward Bernard, Jr. 1949- *WhoBlA 92*
**Smart,** Edwin *Who 92*
**Smart,** Elizabeth 1914- *BenetAL 91*
**Smart,** Elnora Sue 1953- *WhoMW 92*
**Smart,** G N Russell 1921- *AmMWSc 92*
**Smart,** George 1913- *Who 92*
**Smart,** Gerald *Who 92*
**Smart,** Grover Cleveland, Jr 1929- *AmMWSc 92*
**Smart,** Irene Balogh 1921- *WhoAmP 91*
**Smart,** J. J. C. 1920- *ConAu 36NR*
**Smart,** Jack *Who 92*
**Smart,** Jack 1920- *Who 92*
**Smart,** James Blair 1936- *AmMWSc 92*
**Smart,** James Samuel 1919- *AmMWSc 92*
**Smart,** Jean 1951?- *ConTFT 9*
**Smart,** Jerry Don 1935- *WhoMW 92*
**Smart,** Jesse Ray 1939- *WhoAmP 91*
**Smart,** John Jamieson Carswell 1920- *IntWW 91, WrDr 92*
**Smart,** John Roderick 1934- *AmMWSc 92*
**Smart,** Joseph Edward 1937- *WhoMW 92*
**Smart,** Lewis Isaac 1936- *AmMWSc 92*
**Smart,** Louis Edwin 1923- *IntWW 91, Who 92*
**Smart,** Ninian *Who 92*
**Smart,** Ninian 1927- *IntWW 91, WhoRel 92, WrDr 92*
**Smart,** Peter *Who 92*
**Smart,** R. Borlase 1881-1947 *TwCPaSc*
**Smart,** Raymond Jack 1917- *Who 92*
**Smart,** Reginald Piers Alexander de B. *Who 92*
**Smart,** Roderick Ninian 1927- *Who 92*
**Smart,** Stephen Bruce, Jr. 1923- *IntWW 91*
**Smart,** Trey 1956- *WhoRel 92*
**Smart,** Wesley Mitchell 1938- *AmMWSc 92*
**Smart,** William Donald 1927- *AmMWSc 92*
**Smart,** William Norman H. *Who 92*
**Smart Sanchez,** Barbara Ann 1948- *WhoHisp 92*
**Smartt,** John Madison 1919- *WhoAmL 92*
**Smat,** Robert Joseph 1938- *AmMWSc 92*
**Smathers,** Garrett Arthur 1926- *AmMWSc 92*
**Smathers,** George Armistead 1913- *WhoAmP 91*
**Smathers,** James Burton 1935- *AmMWSc 92, WhoWest 92*
**Smatresk,** Neal Joseph 1951- *AmMWSc 92*
**Smatt,** Eddie George 1951- *WhoRel 92*
**Smay,** David Paul, III 1940- *WhoFI 92, WhoWest 92*
**Smay,** Terry A 1935- *AmMWSc 92*
**Smayda,** Theodore John 1931- *AmMWSc 92*
**Smayling,** Lyda Mozella 1923- *WhoMW 92*
**Smeach,** Stephen Charles 1945- *AmMWSc 92*
**Smead,** Burton Armstrong, Jr. 1913- *WhoAmL 92*
**Smeal,** Eleanor *WhoAmP 91*
**Smeal,** Paul Lester 1932- *AmMWSc 92*
**Smeall,** James Leathley 1907- *Who 92*
**Smeaton,** Melvin Douglas 1949- *WhoFI 92*
**Smeaton,** Oliphant 1856-1914 *ScFEYrs*
**Smeby,** Robert Rudolph 1926- *AmMWSc 92, WhoMW 92*
**Smeck,** Neil Edward 1941- *AmMWSc 92*
**Smedberg,** Barry *WhoRel 92*
**Smedes,** Harry Wynn 1926- *AmMWSc 92*
**Smedes,** Lewis B. 1921- *ConAu 36NR*
**Smedfjeld,** John B 1935- *AmMWSc 92*
**Smedley,** Agnes 1892-1950 *TwCWW 91*
**Smedley,** Brian 1934- *Who 92*
**Smedley,** Geoffrey 1927- *IntWW 91*
**Smedley,** George *Who 92*
**Smedley,** Harold 1920- *IntWW 91, Who 92*
**Smedley,** John C. *DrAPF 91*
**Smedley,** Philip Marsden *ConAu 135*
**Smedley,** Robert William 1927- *WhoAmP 91*
**Smedley,** Roscoe Relph George 1919- *Who 92*
**Smedley,** Stanley M 1939- *WhoAmP 91*
**Smedley,** Susan M. *Who 92*
**Smedley,** William Michael 1916- *AmMWSc 92*
**Smeds,** Dave 1955- *IntAu&W 91*
**Smeds,** Edward William 1936- *WhoFI 92*
**Smedskjaer,** Lars Christian 1944- *AmMWSc 92*
**Smedt,** Aemilius Josephus de 1909- *IntWW 91*
**Smee,** Clive Harrod 1942- *Who 92*
**Smee,** John Charles O. *Who 92*
**Smeed,** Frances *IntAu&W 91X*
**Smeeton,** Donald Dean 1946- *WhoRel 92*
**Smeeton,** Richard Michael 1912- *Who 92*
**Smeets,** Maurice, Jr. 1955- *WhoMW 92*
**Smegal,** Thomas Frank, Jr. 1935- *WhoAmL 92*
**Smeins,** Fred E 1941- *AmMWSc 92*
**Smelcer,** Wilma Jean 1949- *WhoFI 92*
**Smelick,** Robert Malcolm 1942- *WhoFI 92, WhoWest 92*
**Smellie,** Jim 1955- *ConAu 133*
**Smellie,** Robert Henderson, Jr 1920- *AmMWSc 92*
**Smellie,** William 1740-1795 *BlkwCEP*
**Smelser,** Charles Harold 1920- *WhoAmP 91*
**Smelser,** John Mark 1948- *WhoMW 92, WhoRel 92*
**Smelser,** Marshall 1912-1978 *ConAu 135*
**Smelser,** Neil Joseph 1930- *WrDr 92*
**Smeltz,** Judith Anne 1942- *WhoRel 92*
**Smeltzer,** Dale Gardner 1920- *AmMWSc 92*
**Smeltzer,** Mary Susan 1941- *WhoEnt 92*
**Smeltzer,** Phyllis *WhoRel 92*
**Smeltzer,** Richard Homer 1940- *AmMWSc 92*
**Smeltzer,** Robert Beryl 1941- *WhoRel 92*
**Smeltzer,** Walter William 1924- *AmMWSc 92*
**Smelyakov,** Yaroslav Vasil'evich 1913-1972 *SovUnBD*
**Smend,** Rudolf 1932- *WhoRel 92*
**Smerage,** Glen H 1937- *AmMWSc 92*
**Smercina,** Charles Joseph 1932- *WhoMW 92*
**Smerdon,** Ernest Thomas 1930- *AmMWSc 92, WhoWest 92*
**Smerdon,** Michael John *AmMWSc 92*
**Smeriglio,** Alfred John 1937- *AmMWSc 92*
**Smerk,** George M. 1933- *WrDr 92*
**Smernoff,** Richard Louis 1941- *WhoFI 92*
**Smet,** Pierre-Jean de 1801-1873 *BenetAL 91*
**Smetana,** Ales 1931- *AmMWSc 92*
**Smetana,** Bedrich 1824-1884 *NewAmDM*
**Smetana,** Frederick Otto 1928- *AmMWSc 92*
**Smetana,** Joseph C 1937- *WhoIns 92*
**Smetanka,** Joseph Walter 1960- *WhoFI 92*
**Smetham,** Andrew James 1937- *Who 92*
**Smethie,** William Massie, Jr 1945- *AmMWSc 92*
**Smethills,** Harold Reginald 1948- *WhoFI 92*
**Smethurst,** Edward William, Jr. 1930- *WhoFI 92*
**Smethurst,** John Michael 1934- *Who 92*
**Smethurst,** Mae J. 1935- *ConAu 133*
**Smethurst,** Richard Good 1941- *Who 92*
**Smets,** Georges Joseph G. R. d1991 *IntWW 91N*
**Smette,** Beth B 1928- *WhoAmP 91*
**Smettem,** Colin William 1916- *Who 92*
**Smetzer,** Michael *DrAPF 91*
**Smeyak,** Gerald Paul 1940- *WhoEnt 92*
**Smeykal,** Patricia Anne 1962- *WhoAmL 92*
**Smialek,** Robert Louis 1948- *WhoIns 92*
**Smibert,** Robert Merrall, II 1930- *AmMWSc 92*
**Smick,** Elmer Bernard 1921- *WhoRel 92*
**Smid,** Johannes 1931- *AmMWSc 92*
**Smid,** Robert John *AmMWSc 92*
**Smidovich,** Sof'ya Nikolaevna 1872-1934 *SovUnBD*
**Smidt,** Fred August, Jr 1932- *AmMWSc 92*
**Smietanka,** John Allen 1941- *WhoAmL 92*
**Smieton,** Mary Guillan 1902- *Who 92*
**Smight,** Jack 1926- *IntMPA 92*
**Smijth-Windham,** William Russell 1907- *Who 92*
**Smika,** Darryl Eugene 1933- *AmMWSc 92*
**Smile,** R Elton *ScFEYrs*
**Smilen,** Lowell I 1931- *AmMWSc 92*
**Smiles,** Kenneth Albert 1944- *AmMWSc 92*
**Smiles,** Leon 1917- *WhoAmP 91*
**Smiles,** Ronald 1933- *WhoFI 92*
**Smiles,** Terri-Lynne Baird 1961- *WhoAmL 92*
**Smiley,** Albert Keith 1910- *WhoRel 92*
**Smiley,** David Bruce 1942- *WhoFI 92, WhoMW 92*
**Smiley,** Emmett L. 1922- *WhoBlA 92*
**Smiley,** Guy Ian 1938- *WhoAmL 92*
**Smiley,** Harry M 1933- *AmMWSc 92*
**Smiley,** Howard Dwight 1877- *ScFEYrs*
**Smiley,** Hugh Houston d1990 *Who 92N*
**Smiley,** James Donald 1930- *AmMWSc 92*
**Smiley,** James Richard 1951- *AmMWSc 92*
**Smiley,** James Walker, Sr. 1928- *WhoBlA 92*
**Smiley,** James Watson 1940- *AmMWSc 92*
**Smiley,** Jane 1949- *WrDr 92*
**Smiley,** John 1934- *Who 92*
**Smiley,** Jones Hazelwood 1933- *AmMWSc 92*
**Smiley,** Joseph Elbert, Jr. 1922- *WhoFI 92*
**Smiley,** Marilynn Jean 1932- *WhoEnt 92*
**Smiley,** Pril 1943- *WhoEnt 92*
**Smiley,** Richard Wayne 1943- *AmMWSc 92, WhoWest 92*
**Smiley,** Robert Arthur 1925- *AmMWSc 92*
**Smiley,** Robert William 1919- *WhoFI 92, WhoWest 92*
**Smiley,** Robert William, Jr. 1943- *WhoFI 92*
**Smiley,** Ronald Michael 1949- *WhoEnt 92*
**Smiley,** Terah Leroy 1914- *AmMWSc 92*
**Smiley,** Teresa Marlene 1951- *WhoHisp 92*
**Smiley,** Timothy John 1930- *Who 92*
**Smiley,** Vern Newton 1930- *AmMWSc 92*
**Smiley,** Virginia Louise 1950- *WhoEnt 92*
**Smiley,** William L. 1912- *WhoBlA 92*
**Smiley-Robertson,** Carolyn 1954- *WhoBlA 92*
**Smilie,** James William, Jr. 1962- *WhoEnt 92*
**Smilkstein,** Laura Lee 1959- *WhoEnt 92*
**Smillie,** Douglas James 1956- *WhoAmL 92*
**Smillie,** Lawrence Bruce 1928- *AmMWSc 92*
**Smillie,** Thomson John 1942- *WhoEnt 92*
**Smillie,** William John Jones 1940- *Who 92*
**Smilowitz,** Bernard *AmMWSc 92*
**Smilowitz,** Henry Martin 1946- *AmMWSc 92*
**Smilowitz,** Zane 1933- *AmMWSc 92*
**Smirk,** Horace d1991 *Who 92N*
**Smirl,** Jody Guthrie 1935- *WhoAmP 91*
**Smirni,** Allan Desmond 1939- *WhoBlA 92*
**Smirnoff,** Joel *WhoEnt 92*
**Smirnoff,** Steve Ross 1939- *WhoWest 92*
**Smirnoff,** Yakov 1951- *WhoEnt 92*
**Smirnov,** Dmitri 1948- *ConCom 92*
**Smirnov,** Georgiy Lukich 1922- *IntWW 91, SovUnBD*
**Smirnov,** Igor Pavlovich 1941- *IntWW 91*
**Smirnov,** Ivan Nikitich 1881-1936 *SovUnBD*
**Smirnov,** Leonid Vasiliyevich 1916- *IntWW 91*
**Smirnov,** Nikolay Ivanovich 1917- *IntWW 91*
**Smirnov,** Viktor Ilyich 1929- *IntWW 91*
**Smirnov,** Vilyam Viktorovich 1941- *IntWW 91, SovUnBD*
**Smirnov,** Vitaliy Stepanovich 1930- *IntWW 91*
**Smirnov,** Vladimir Nikolaevich 1937- *IntWW 91*
**Smirnovsky,** Mikhail Nikolaevich 1921- *Who 92*
**Smirnovsky,** Mikhail Nikolayevich 1921- *IntWW 91*
**Smirnow,** Diane Elaine 1947- *WhoEnt 92*
**Smirnow,** Zoya *EncAmaz 91*
**Smisko,** Richard G. 1936- *WhoRel 92*
**Smisson,** David Clayton 1933- *WhoWest 92*
**Smit,** Christian Jacobus Bester 1927- *AmMWSc 92*
**Smit,** David Ernst 1942- *AmMWSc 92*
**Smit,** Hendrik Hanekom 1925- *IntWW 91*
**Smit,** Jan 1921- *AmMWSc 92*
**Smit,** Kenneth Dale 1960- *WhoMW 92*
**Smit,** Leo 1921- *NewAmDM*
**Smit,** Michael Jay 1955- *WhoFI 92*
**Smit-Kroes,** Neelie 1941- *IntWW 91*
**Smith** *Who 92*
**Smith and Dale** *FacFETw*
**Smith,** Baron 1914- *Who 92*
**Smith,** A C H 1935- *IntAu&W 91*
**Smith,** A Dale 1958- *WhoAmP 91*
**Smith,** A.J.M. 1902-1980 *RfGEnL 91*
**Smith,** A Ledyard, Jr 1932- *WhoAmP 91*
**Smith,** A Lee 1924- *AmMWSc 92*
**Smith,** A. Lockwood *IntWW 91*
**Smith,** A M O 1911- *AmMWSc 92*
**Smith,** A. Maceo 1903-1977 *WhoBlA 92N*
**Smith,** A Mason *AmMWSc 92*
**Smith,** A N 1921- *AmMWSc 92*
**Smith,** A. Wade 1950- *WhoBlA 92*
**Smith,** A. Z. 1938- *WhoBlA 92*
**Smith,** Aaron 1930- *AmMWSc 92*
**Smith,** Abram Alexander 1847-1915 *BiInAmS*
**Smith,** Ada 1894-1984 *NotBlAW 92*
**Smith,** Ada L 1945- *WhoAmP 91*
**Smith,** Adam *RfGEnL 91, WhoAmP 91*
**Smith,** Adam 1723-1790 *BlkwCEP, BlkwEAR*
**Smith,** Adrian *WhoRel 92*
**Smith,** Adrienne Jean 1934- *WhoMW 92*
**Smith,** Adrienne Robinson 1969- *WhoEnt 92*
**Smith,** Al Fredrick 1964- *WhoBlA 92*
**Smith,** Alan 1917- *Who 92*
**Smith,** Alan 1930- *Who 92*
**Smith,** Alan B 1924- *AmMWSc 92*
**Smith,** Alan Bradford 1932- *AmMWSc 92*
**Smith,** Alan Bronson, III 1944- *WhoAmL 92*
**Smith,** Alan Bronson, Jr. 1917- *WhoMW 92*
**Smith,** Alan Christopher 1936- *Who 92*
**Smith,** Alan Frederick 1944- *Who 92*
**Smith,** Alan Guy E. *Who 92*
**Smith,** Alan Jay 1949- *AmMWSc 92, WhoWest 92*
**Smith,** Alan Jerrard 1929- *AmMWSc 92*
**Smith,** Alan Lyle 1941- *AmMWSc 92*
**Smith,** Alan Oliver 1929- *Who 92*
**Smith,** Alan Paul 1945- *AmMWSc 92*
**Smith,** Alan Reid 1943- *AmMWSc 92*
**Smith,** Alastair Macleod M. *Who 92*
**Smith,** Albert A, Jr 1935- *AmMWSc 92*
**Smith,** Albert Carl 1934- *AmMWSc 92*
**Smith,** Albert Charles 1906- *AmMWSc 92, IntWW 91*
**Smith,** Albert Cromwell, Jr. 1925- *WhoFI 92, WhoWest 92*
**Smith,** Albert E. 1932- *WhoBlA 92*
**Smith,** Albert Ernest 1927- *AmMWSc 92*
**Smith,** Albert Ernest, Jr 1938- *AmMWSc 92*
**Smith,** Albert F 1913- *WhoAmP 91*
**Smith,** Albert Goodin 1924- *AmMWSc 92*
**Smith,** Albert J 1914- *WhoAmP 91*
**Smith,** Albert Lee 1924- *WhoMW 92*
**Smith,** Albert Matthews 1927- *AmMWSc 92*
**Smith,** Alden Ernest 1923- *AmMWSc 92*
**Smith,** Aldo Ralston, Jr. 1947- *WhoFI 92*
**Smith,** Alex *Who 92*
**Smith,** Alexander 1943- *Who 92*
**Smith,** Alexander, Jr 1944- *WhoIns 92*
**Smith,** Alexander Crampton 1917- *Who 92*
**Smith,** Alexander Forbes, III 1929- *WhoFI 92*
**Smith,** Alexander Goudy 1919- *AmMWSc 92*
**Smith,** Alexander Mair 1922- *Who 92*
**Smith,** Alexis 1921- *IntMPA 92*
**Smith,** Alfred E. 1873-1944 *BenetAL 91, FacFETw [port]*
**Smith,** Alfred Emanuel 1873-1944 *AmPolLe [port]*
**Smith,** Alfred G 1921- *IntAu&W 91, WrDr 92*
**Smith,** Alfred J., Jr. 1948- *WhoBlA 92*
**Smith,** Alfreda Alice 1928- *WhoAmP 91*
**Smith,** Alice *WhoBlA 92*
**Smith,** Alice Lorraine *AmMWSc 92*
**Smith,** Alistair *Who 92*
**Smith,** Allan Edward 1937- *AmMWSc 92*
**Smith,** Allan Laslett 1938- *AmMWSc 92*
**Smith,** Allen Anderson *AmMWSc 92*
**Smith,** Allen Harold 1925- *WhoAmL 92, WhoFI 92*
**Smith,** Allen Joseph, Sr. 1936- *WhoBlA 92*
**Smith,** Allen Lewis 1936- *WhoAmL 92*
**Smith,** Allen P d1898 *BiInAmS*
**Smith,** Allie Maitland 1934- *AmMWSc 92*

**Smith,** Allison London 1942- *WhoMW 92*
**Smith,** Alonzo Nelson 1940- *WhoBlA 92*
**Smith,** Alphonso Lehman 1937- *WhoBlA 92*
**Smith,** Alson Howard, Jr 1928- *WhoAmP 91*
**Smith,** Alton Hutchison 1930- *AmMWSc 92*
**Smith,** Alvin 1933- *WhoBlA 92*
**Smith,** Alvin Curtis 1938- *WhoAmP 91*
**Smith,** Alvin Winfred 1933- *AmMWSc 92*
**Smith,** Alwyn *Who 92*
**Smith,** Amanda *WhoEnt 92*
**Smith,** Amanda 1837-1915 *RelLAm 91*
**Smith,** Amanda Berry 1837-1915 *NotBlAW 92 [port]*
**Smith,** Amber Lee 1949- *WhoAmL 92*
**Smith,** Amelia Lillian 1924- *AmMWSc 92*
**Smith,** Anderson Dodd 1944- *AmMWSc 92*
**Smith,** Andreas W. *Who 92*
**Smith,** Andrew Alfred, Jr. 1947- *WhoFI 92*
**Smith,** Andrew Charles 1947- *Who 92*
**Smith,** Andrew David 1951- *Who 92*
**Smith,** Andrew George 1918- *AmMWSc 92*
**Smith,** Andrew Heermance 1837-1910 *BiInAmS*
**Smith,** Andrew Leonard 1949- *WhoWest 92*
**Smith,** Andrew Porter 1955- *WhoFI 92*
**Smith,** Andrew Thomas 1946- *AmMWSc 92*
**Smith,** Andrew Vaughn 1924- *WhoFI 92, WhoWest 92*
**Smith,** Andrew W. 1941- *WhoBlA 92*
**Smith,** Angie Frank 1889-1962 *RelLAm 91*
**Smith,** Ann 1946- *AmMWSc 92*
**Smith,** Ann Catherine 1947- *WhoMW 92*
**Smith,** Ann Elizabeth 1939- *WhoBlA 92*
**Smith,** Ann Hamill 1929- *WhoRel 92*
**Smith,** Anna Deavere 1950- *ConAu 133*
**Smith,** Anna DuVal 1944- *WhoFI 92*
**Smith,** Anson B 1911- *WhoIns 92*
**Smith,** Anthony 1926- *WrDr 92*
**Smith,** Anthony 1967- *WhoBlA 92*
**Smith,** Anthony Arthur D. *Who 92*
**Smith,** Anthony David 1938- *IntWW 91, Who 92*
**Smith,** Anthony Edward 1961- *WhoBlA 92*
**Smith,** Anthony Felstead 1936- *IntWW 91*
**Smith,** Anthony James 1918- *AmMWSc 92*
**Smith,** Anthony John Francis 1926- *Who 92*
**Smith,** Anthony Michael Percival 1924- *Who 92*
**Smith,** Anthony Patrick 1939- *Who 92*
**Smith,** Anthony Thomas 1935- *Who 92*
**Smith,** Anthony Wayne *WhoAmL 92*
**Smith,** Anthony Younger 1955- *WhoWest 92*
**Smith,** April Elaine 1963- *WhoAmL 92*
**Smith,** Archibald William 1930- *AmMWSc 92*
**Smith,** Arden Jess 1934- *WhoAmP 91*
**Smith,** Arlo Irving 1911- *AmMWSc 92*
**Smith,** Arnold Cantwell 1915- *IntWW 91, Who 92*
**Smith,** Arnold Terence 1922- *Who 92*
**Smith,** Arthur *DrAPF 91*
**Smith,** Arthur 1898-1971 *NewAmDM*
**Smith,** Arthur 1921- *NewAmDM, WhoEnt 92*
**Smith,** Arthur Beverly, Jr. 1944- *WhoAmL 92, WhoMW 92*
**Smith,** Arthur Clarke 1929- *AmMWSc 92*
**Smith,** Arthur Cyril 1909- *Who 92*
**Smith,** Arthur D. *WhoBlA 92*
**Smith,** Arthur D. 1913- *WhoBlA 92*
**Smith,** Arthur E. 1926- *WhoMW 92*
**Smith,** Arthur George 1868-1916 *BiInAmS*
**Smith,** Arthur Gerald 1929- *AmMWSc 92*
**Smith,** Arthur Hamilton 1916- *AmMWSc 92*
**Smith,** Arthur James Mitchall 1902-1980 *BenetAL 91*
**Smith,** Arthur John Stewart 1938- *AmMWSc 92*
**Smith,** Arthur Kittredge, Jr. 1937- *WhoWest 92*
**Smith,** Arthur L. *WrDr 92*
**Smith,** Arthur L., Jr. 1927- *WrDr 92*
**Smith,** Arthur L., Jr. 1942- *WhoBlA 92*
**Smith,** Arthur Lee 1941- *WhoAmL 92*
**Smith,** Arthur R 1931- *AmMWSc 92*
**Smith,** Arthur Reginald 1871-1934 *TwCPaSc*
**Smith,** Arthur Roy 1953- *WhoMW 92*
**Smith,** Arthur W 1922- *WhoAmP 91*
**Smith,** Ashby Gordon, Jr. 1932- *WhoBlA 92*
**Smith,** Aston Carpenter 1957- *WhoRel 92*
**Smith,** Aubrey Carl, Jr. 1942- *WhoBlA 92*
**Smith,** Audrey S. 1940- *WhoBlA 92*
**Smith,** Augustine 1956- *WhoMW 92*
**Smith,** Augustus William 1802-1866 *BiInAmS*
**Smith,** B D, Jr 1925- *AmMWSc 92*
**Smith,** B P *WhoAmP 91*
**Smith,** Badley F 1931- *IntAu&W 91*
**Smith,** Bailey Eugene 1939- *WhoRel 92*
**Smith,** Baker Armstrong 1947- *WhoAmP 91*
**Smith,** Barbara *DrAPF 91*
**Smith,** Barbara 1946- *WhoBlA 92*
**Smith,** Barbara Ann 1941- *WhoRel 92*
**Smith,** Barbara Barnard 1920- *WhoEnt 92*
**Smith,** Barbara D 1943- *AmMWSc 92*
**Smith,** Barbara Herrnstein 1932- *WrDr 92*
**Smith,** Barbara J. 1948- *WhoWest 92*
**Smith,** Barbara Jean 1948- *WhoMW 92*
**Smith,** Barbara Leavell *DrAPF 91*
**Smith,** Bardwell Leith 1925- *WhoRel 92*
**Smith,** Barney Oveyette, Jr. 1952- *WhoAmL 92*
**Smith,** Barry Edward 1939- *Who 92*
**Smith,** Barry H 1949- *WhoIns 92*
**Smith,** Barry Keith 1960- *WhoRel 92*
**Smith,** Barton D 1947- *WhoIns 92*
**Smith,** Basil Gerald P. *Who 92*
**Smith,** Basil Gerrard 1911- *Who 92*
**Smith,** Ben 1967- *WhoBlA 92*
**Smith,** Benjamin A., II d1991 *NewYTBS 91*
**Smith,** Benjamin Eric 1915- *WhoFI 92*
**Smith,** Benjamin Franklin *WhoBlA 92*
**Smith,** Benjamin Williams 1918- *AmMWSc 92*
**Smith,** Bennett W., Sr. 1933- *WhoBlA 92*
**Smith,** Bennett Walker 1933- *WhoRel 92*
**Smith,** Benny Richard 1940- *WhoFI 92*
**Smith,** Berl Ammons 1960- *WhoAmL 92*
**Smith,** Bernald Stephen 1926- *WhoFI 92*
**Smith,** Bernard 1916- *WrDr 92*
**Smith,** Bernard 1927- *AmMWSc 92*
**Smith,** Bernard Chester 1924- *WhoAmP 91*
**Smith,** Bernard Joseph 1900- *WhoFI 92, WhoWest 92*
**Smith,** Bernard Joseph Connolly 1930- *WhoWest 92*
**Smith,** Bernard William 1916- *IntAu&W 91, IntWW 91*
**Smith,** Bernice Lewis *WhoBlA 92*
**Smith,** Bert Kruger 1915- *WrDr 92*
**Smith,** Bertram Bryan, Jr 1942- *AmMWSc 92*
**Smith,** Bessie 1894-1937 *NewAmDM, NotBlAW 92 [port]*
**Smith,** Bessie 1898-1937 *FacFETw [port], HanAmWH*
**Smith,** Beth Michele 1955- *WhoAmP 91*
**Smith,** Bettie M. 1914- *WhoBlA 92*
**Smith,** Betty 1904-1972 *BenetAL 91*
**Smith,** Betty Anne 1934- *WhoMW 92*
**Smith,** Betty Denny 1932- *WhoWest 92*
**Smith,** Betty F 1930- *AmMWSc 92*
**Smith,** Betty Walker 1918- *WhoAmP 91*
**Smith,** Beverley *Who 92*
**Smith,** Beverly Evans 1948- *WhoBlA 92*
**Smith,** Bill Gordon 1938- *WhoAmP 91*
**Smith,** Bill James 1932- *WhoAmP 91*
**Smith,** Bill Ross 1941- *AmMWSc 92*
**Smith,** Billy Kenneth 1928- *WhoRel 92*
**Smith,** Billy Ray 1944- *WhoAmP 91*
**Smith,** Bob 1941- *AlmAP 92 [port]*
**Smith,** Bob L 1926- *AmMWSc 92*
**Smith,** Bobby Antonia 1949- *WhoBlA 92*
**Smith,** Bobby Eugene 1947- *WhoAmP 91*
**Smith,** Bobby Ray 1953- *WhoRel 92*
**Smith,** Bodrell Joer'dan 1931- *WhoFI 92*
**Smith,** Bonnie Beatrice 1948- *WhoMW 92*
**Smith,** Brad Keller 1955- *AmMWSc 92*
**Smith,** Bradford Adelbert 1931- *AmMWSc 92*
**Smith,** Bradley Edgerton 1933- *AmMWSc 92*
**Smith,** Bradley F. 1931- *WrDr 92*
**Smith,** Bradley Joel 1959- *WhoRel 92*
**Smith,** Bradley Richard 1956- *AmMWSc 92*
**Smith,** Brenda Hensley 1946- *WhoAmP 91*
**Smith,** Brent Phillip 1953- *WhoAmP 91*
**Smith,** Brian *Who 92*
**Smith,** Brian 1935- *IntWW 91, Who 92*
**Smith,** Brian 1938- *WrDr 92*
**Smith,** Brian 1947- *Who 92*
**Smith,** Brian Arthur 1943- *Who 92*
**Smith,** Brian David 1953- *WhoAmL 92*
**Smith,** Brian John 1933- *Who 92*
**Smith,** Brian M. 1955- *WhoMW 92*
**Smith,** Brian Percival 1919- *Who 92*
**Smith,** Brian Richard 1952- *AmMWSc 92*
**Smith,** Brian Richard 1955- *WhoAmL 92*
**Smith,** Brian Stanley 1932- *Who 92*
**Smith,** Brian Thomas 1942- *AmMWSc 92*
**Smith,** Brian W. *Who 92*
**Smith,** Brian William 1938- *Who 92*
**Smith,** Brian William 1947- *WhoAmL 92*
**Smith,** Bridget Janeen 1960- *WhoAmP 91*
**Smith,** Brooke Ellen 1956- *WhoAmL 92*
**Smith,** Bruce Barton 1941- *AmMWSc 92*
**Smith,** Bruce Bernard 1963- *WhoBlA 92*
**Smith,** Bruce Douglas 1950- *WhoMW 92*
**Smith,** Bruce H 1919- *AmMWSc 92*
**Smith,** Bruce I 1934- *WhoAmP 91*
**Smith,** Bruce James 1937- *WhoFI 92*
**Smith,** Bruce Leonard 1946- *WhoFI 92*
**Smith,** Bruce Nephi 1934- *AmMWSc 92, WhoWest 92*
**Smith,** Bruce Warren 1952- *WhoWest 92*
**Smith,** Bruce William 1932- *WhoMW 92*
**Smith,** Bryan *IntAu&W 91X*
**Smith,** Bryan Crossley 1925- *Who 92*
**Smith,** Bryce Everton 1930- *AmMWSc 92*
**Smith,** Bubba 1947- *WhoBlA 92*
**Smith,** Buffalo Bob *LesBEnT 92*
**Smith,** Buford Don 1925- *AmMWSc 92*
**Smith,** Burton Jordan 1941- *AmMWSc 92*
**Smith,** Byron Colman 1924- *AmMWSc 92*
**Smith,** Byron Owen 1916- *WhoAmL 92*
**Smith,** C. Busby *WrDr 92*
**Smith,** C. R. 1899-1990 *AnObit 1990*
**Smith,** C. U. M. 1930- *WrDr 92*
**Smith,** C.W. *DrAPF 91*
**Smith,** C William 1926- *AmMWSc 92*
**Smith,** Caesar *WrDr 92*
**Smith,** Calvert H. *WhoBlA 92*
**Smith,** Calvin 1961- *BlkOlyM*
**Smith,** Calvin Albert 1935- *AmMWSc 92*
**Smith,** Calvin George 1951- *WhoFI 92*
**Smith,** Calvin Miles 1924- *WhoBlA 92*
**Smith,** Cameron Mitchell 1935- *ConAu 133*
**Smith,** Campbell 1906- *Who 92*
**Smith,** Capers F, Jr 1945- *WhoIns 92*
**Smith,** Capers Franklin, Jr. 1945- *WhoFI 92*
**Smith,** Carey Daniel 1932- *AmMWSc 92*
**Smith,** Carl B *WhoAmP 91*
**Smith,** Carl Clinton 1914- *AmMWSc 92*
**Smith,** Carl Edwin 1906- *WhoMW 92*
**Smith,** Carl Hofland 1942- *AmMWSc 92*
**Smith,** Carl Hugh 1934- *AmMWSc 92*
**Smith,** Carl Stanley, III 1961- *WhoFI 92*
**Smith,** Carl W 1924- *WhoAmP 91*
**Smith,** Carl Walter 1937- *AmMWSc 92*
**Smith,** Carl Walter, Jr 1927- *AmMWSc 92*
**Smith,** Carl William 1931- *WhoBlA 92*
**Smith,** Carlton Ray 1960- *WhoFI 92*
**Smith,** Carlyle 1939- *WhoAmP 91*
**Smith,** Carlyle Shreeve 1915- *WhoMW 92*
**Smith,** Carol Barlow 1945- *WhoBlA 92*
**Smith,** Carol J. 1923- *WhoBlA 92*
**Smith,** Carol Lee 1938- *WhoFI 92*
**Smith,** Carol Lou Stubbs 1944- *WhoRel 92*
**Smith,** Carol Sturm *DrAPF 91*
**Smith,** Carole 1944- *WhoWest 92*
**Smith,** Carolyn Jean *AmMWSc 92*
**Smith,** Carolyn Lee 1942- *WhoBlA 92*
**Smith,** Carolyn Williams 1937- *WhoAmP 91*
**Smith,** Carroll B 1936- *WhoIns 92*
**Smith,** Carroll N 1909- *AmMWSc 92*
**Smith,** Carroll Ward 1927- *AmMWSc 92*
**Smith,** Carson Eugene 1943- *WhoBlA 92*
**Smith,** Carter Blakemore 1937- *WhoEnt 92, WhoWest 92*
**Smith,** Cassandra Lynn 1947- *AmMWSc 92, WhoWest 92*
**Smith,** Catharine Mary S. *Who 92*
**Smith,** Catherine Agnes 1914- *AmMWSc 92*
**Smith,** Catherine Parsons 1933- *WhoWest 92*
**Smith,** Cecil Randolph, Jr 1924- *AmMWSc 92, WhoWest 92*
**Smith,** Cedric Martin 1927- *AmMWSc 92*
**Smith,** Chard Powers 1894-1977 *BenetAL 91*
**Smith,** Charles *TwCWW 91*
**Smith,** Charles 1914- *WhoBlA 92*
**Smith,** Charles 1930- *Who 92*
**Smith,** Charles Allen 1944- *AmMWSc 92*
**Smith,** Charles Aloysius 1939- *AmMWSc 92*
**Smith,** Charles Anthony 1939- *WhoWest 92*
**Smith,** Charles B. *Who 92*
**Smith,** Charles Bruce 1936- *AmMWSc 92*
**Smith,** Charles C., Jr. 1948- *WhoFI 92*
**Smith,** Charles Carroll, Jr 1944- *WhoAmP 91*
**Smith,** Charles D 1965- *BlkOlyM*
**Smith,** Charles Daniel, Jr. 1965- *WhoBlA 92*
**Smith,** Charles E 1917- *AmMWSc 92*
**Smith,** Charles E, IV 1967- *BlkOlyM*
**Smith,** Charles Edison *WhoBlA 92*
**Smith,** Charles Edward 1934- *AmMWSc 92*
**Smith,** Charles Edward, Jr 1927- *AmMWSc 92*
**Smith,** Charles Edward Gordon d1991 *Who 92N*
**Smith,** Charles Edward Gordon 1924- *IntWW 91*
**Smith,** Charles Eugene 1948- *WhoAmP 91*
**Smith,** Charles Eugene 1950- *AmMWSc 92*
**Smith,** Charles F., Jr. 1933- *WhoBlA 92*
**Smith,** Charles Francis 1936- *WhoWest 92*
**Smith,** Charles Francis, Jr 1936- *AmMWSc 92*
**Smith,** Charles G 1927- *AmMWSc 92*
**Smith,** Charles Gerard 1960- *WhoAmL 92*
**Smith,** Charles Glenn 1950- *WhoEnt 92*
**Smith,** Charles H. 1826-1903 *BenetAL 91*
**Smith,** Charles Haddon 1926- *AmMWSc 92*
**Smith,** Charles Hayden 1933- *WhoFI 92*
**Smith,** Charles Hooper 1917- *AmMWSc 92*
**Smith,** Charles Irvel 1923- *AmMWSc 92*
**Smith,** Charles Isaac 1931- *AmMWSc 92*
**Smith,** Charles James 1925- *AmMWSc 92*
**Smith,** Charles James, III 1926- *WhoBlA 92*
**Smith,** Charles Joe, Sr. 1951- *WhoEnt 92*
**Smith,** Charles Lavester, Jr 1954- *WhoAmP 91*
**Smith,** Charles Lea 1918- *AmMWSc 92*
**Smith,** Charles Lebanon 1938- *WhoBlA 92*
**Smith,** Charles Lee 1887-1964 *RelLAm 91*
**Smith,** Charles Leon 1953- *WhoBlA 92*
**Smith,** Charles Lewis 1920- *WhoWest 92*
**Smith,** Charles Madison 1948- *WhoFI 92*
**Smith,** Charles Martin 1953- *IntMPA 92*
**Smith,** Charles O 1920- *AmMWSc 92*
**Smith,** Charles Philip 1926- *WhoAmP 91*
**Smith,** Charles Plympton, IV 1954- *WhoAmP 91*
**Smith,** Charles R 1928- *WhoAmP 91*
**Smith,** Charles R 1936- *AmMWSc 92*
**Smith,** Charles Ray 1933- *AmMWSc 92*
**Smith,** Charles Richard 1932- *WhoWest 92*
**Smith,** Charles Roger 1941- *WhoWest 92*
**Smith,** Charles Russell 1925- *Who 92*
**Smith,** Charles S 1950- *WhoAmP 91*
**Smith,** Charles Scott 1960- *WhoMW 92*
**Smith,** Charles Stuart d1991 *Who 92N*
**Smith,** Charles Sydney, Jr 1916- *AmMWSc 92*
**Smith,** Charles U. *WhoBlA 92*
**Smith,** Charles Ullman 1923- *WhoAmP 91*
**Smith,** Charles Vinton 1932- *WhoWest 92*
**Smith,** Charles Watson 1932- *WhoAmP 91*
**Smith,** Charles Welstead 1927- *AmMWSc 92*
**Smith,** Charles William, Jr 1940- *AmMWSc 92*
**Smith,** Charles Winfred, Jr. 1946- *WhoAmL 92*
**Smith,** Charles Z. 1927- *WhoAmL 92, WhoAmP 91, WhoWest 92*
**Smith,** Charlie *DrAPF 91*
**Smith,** Charlie Calvin 1943- *WhoBlA 92*
**Smith,** Charline Galloway 1925- *AmMWSc 92*
**Smith,** Charlotte 1749-1806 *BlkwCEP, DcLB 109 [port], RfGEnL 91*
**Smith,** Charlotte Damron 1919- *AmMWSc 92*
**Smith,** Charlotte Therese Wertz 1959- *WhoAmL 92*
**Smith,** Cheryl Lynn 1943- *WhoMW 92*
**Smith,** Chester 1930- *WhoEnt 92, WhoFI 92, WhoWest 92*
**Smith,** Chester Allen, Jr. 1932- *WhoRel 92*
**Smith,** Chester B. 1954- *WhoBlA 92*
**Smith,** Chester Horace 1919- *WhoAmP 91*
**Smith,** Chester Junior 1942- *WhoRel 92*
**Smith,** Chester Martin, Jr 1935- *AmMWSc 92*
**Smith,** Christian Reverdy 1948- *WhoWest 92*
**Smith,** Christie Lisa 1954- *WhoEnt 92*
**Smith,** Christina Mayem 1962- *WhoWest 92*
**Smith,** Christine H *AmMWSc 92*
**Smith,** Christopher Carlisle 1938- *AmMWSc 92*
**Smith,** Christopher Colin 1927- *Who 92*
**Smith,** Christopher Duncan 1950- *WhoWest 92*
**Smith,** Christopher H. 1953- *AlmAP 92 [port]*
**Smith,** Christopher Henry 1953- *NewYTBS 91, WhoAmP 91*
**Smith,** Christopher Hughes 1929- *Who 92*
**Smith,** Christopher Lee 1970- *WhoMW 92, WhoRel 92*
**Smith,** Christopher Robert 1951- *Who 92*
**Smith,** Christopher Sydney Winwood 1906- *Who 92*
**Smith,** Chuck E. 1950- *WhoWest 92*
**Smith,** Cladys 1908-1991 *NewYTBS 91*
**Smith,** Claibourne Davis 1938- *AmMWSc 92*
**Smith,** Claire 1949- *TwCPaSc*
**Smith,** Claire Leroy 1923- *AmMWSc 92*
**Smith,** Clara 1894-1935 *NotBlAW 92*
**Smith,** Clara May Freeman 1912- *IntAu&W 91*
**Smith,** Clarence Lavett 1927- *AmMWSc 92*
**Smith,** Clarence LeRoy 1941- *WhoFI 92*
**Smith,** Clarence O. 1933- *WhoBlA 92*
**Smith,** Clark Ashton 1893-1961 *ScFEYrs, TwCSFW 91*
**Smith,** Claude C. *Who 92*
**Smith,** Clay Taylor 1917- *AmMWSc 92, WhoWest 92*
**Smith,** Clayton Albert, Jr 1934- *AmMWSc 92*

**Smith**, Clayton Gordon 1955- *WhoFI 92*
**Smith**, Cleveland Emanuel 1924- *WhoBlA 92*
**Smith**, Clifford Bertram Bruce H. *Who 92*
**Smith**, Clifford James 1938- *AmMWSc 92, WhoMW 92*
**Smith**, Clifford Thorpe 1924- *WrDr 92*
**Smith**, Clifford V., Jr. 1931- *WhoBlA 92*
**Smith**, Clifford Weldon, Jr. 1946- *WhoFI 92*
**Smith**, Clinton DeWitt 1854-1916 *BiInAmS*
**Smith**, Cloyd Virgil, Jr 1936- *AmMWSc 92*
**Smith**, Clyde B 1926- *WhoAmP 91*
**Smith**, Clyde Curry 1929- *WhoMW 92, WhoRel 92*
**Smith**, Clyde F 1913- *AmMWSc 92*
**Smith**, Clyde Konrad 1925- *AmMWSc 92*
**Smith**, Clyde R. 1933- *WhoMW 92*
**Smith**, Colin *Who 92*
**Smith**, Colin 1941- *Who 92*
**Smith**, Colin 1953- *TwCPaSc*
**Smith**, Colin McPherson 1927- *AmMWSc 92*
**Smith**, Colin Milner 1936- *Who 92*
**Smith**, Colin Roderick *Who 92*
**Smith**, Colin S. *Who 92*
**Smith**, Colleen Mary 1943- *AmMWSc 92*
**Smith**, Conrad P. 1932- *WhoBlA 92*
**Smith**, Constance Meta 1949- *AmMWSc 92*
**Smith**, Cordwainer 1913-1966 *TwCSFW 91*
**Smith**, Cornelia Marschall 1895- *AmMWSc 92*
**Smith**, Courtney Charles 1947- *WhoIns 92*
**Smith**, Covey Leroy 1942- *WhoIns 92*
**Smith**, Craig Bennett 1943- *WhoAmL 92*
**Smith**, Craig C. 1944- *WhoWest 92*
**Smith**, Craig La Salle 1943- *AmMWSc 92*
**Smith**, Craig Malcolm 1952- *WhoMW 92*
**Smith**, Craig Richey 1925- *WhoMW 92*
**Smith**, Curtis 1932- *WhoAmP 91*
**Smith**, Curtis Alan 1948- *AmMWSc 92*
**Smith**, Curtis Alfonso, Jr. 1934- *WhoMW 92*
**Smith**, Curtis Griffin 1923- *AmMWSc 92*
**Smith**, Curtis P 1916- *WhoAmP 91*
**Smith**, Curtis Page 1938- *AmMWSc 92*
**Smith**, Curtis R 1936- *AmMWSc 92*
**Smith**, Curtis William 1918- *AmMWSc 92*
**Smith**, Cyril 1928- *Who 92*
**Smith**, Cyril Beverley 1921- *AmMWSc 92*
**Smith**, Cyril Robert 1907- *Who 92*
**Smith**, Cyril Stanley 1903- *AmMWSc 92, IntWW 91*
**Smith**, Cyril Stanley 1925- *Who 92*
**Smith**, Cyrus Rowlett 1899-1990 *FacFETw*
**Smith**, DaCosta, Jr. 1917- *WhoAmL 92*
**Smith**, Dale 1915- *AmMWSc 92*
**Smith**, Dale 1937- *WhoAmP 91*
**Smith**, Dale Metz 1928- *AmMWSc 92*
**Smith**, Dallas Glen, Jr 1940- *AmMWSc 92*
**Smith**, Dalton 1947- *WhoAmP 91*
**Smith**, Dan *Who 92*
**Smith**, Dana Kruse 1957- *WhoWest 92*
**Smith**, Dane F, Jr 1940- *WhoAmP 91*
**Smith**, Daniel Albin 1956- *WhoRel 92*
**Smith**, Daniel B 1792-1883 *BiInAmS*
**Smith**, Daniel H., Jr. 1933- *WhoBlA 92*
**Smith**, Daniel Harold 1933- *WhoRel 92*
**Smith**, Daniel James 1944- *AmMWSc 92*
**Smith**, Daniel John 1946- *AmMWSc 92*
**Smith**, Daniel Larsen 1929- *WhoMW 92*
**Smith**, Daniel Montague 1932- *AmMWSc 92*
**Smith**, Daniel Patrick 1920- *WhoWest 92*
**Smith**, Daniel R. 1934- *WhoFI 92, WhoMW 92*
**Smith**, Danny Lee 1953- *WhoRel 92*
**Smith**, Darrell Wayne 1937- *AmMWSc 92*
**Smith**, Darryl Lyle 1946- *AmMWSc 92*
**Smith**, Darwin Eatna 1926- *IntWW 91, WhoAmL 92, WhoFI 92*
**Smith**, Darwin Waldron 1931- *AmMWSc 92*
**Smith**, Daryl Kent 1942- *WhoFI 92*
**Smith**, Dave *DrAPF 91*
**Smith**, Dave 1942- *BenetAL 91, ConPo 91, WrDr 92*
**Smith**, David *Who 92*
**Smith**, David 1927- *Who 92*
**Smith**, David 1935- *Who 92*
**Smith**, David 1939- *AmMWSc 92*
**Smith**, David Alexander 1938- *AmMWSc 92*
**Smith**, David Allen 1933- *AmMWSc 92*
**Smith**, David Allen 1943- *WhoWest 92*
**Smith**, David Arthur 1938- *Who 92*
**Smith**, David Arthur George 1934- *Who 92*
**Smith**, David Asher 1946- *WhoWest 92*
**Smith**, David B. 1932- *DcTwDes*
**Smith**, David Beach 1911- *AmMWSc 92*
**Smith**, David Brookman 1951- *WhoAmL 92*
**Smith**, David Bruce 1948- *WhoAmP 91*
**Smith**, David Buchanan 1936- *Who 92*
**Smith**, David Burnell 1941- *WhoAmL 92*
**Smith**, David Burrard 1916- *AmMWSc 92*
**Smith**, David C. *Who 92*
**Smith**, David Cecil 1930- *IntWW 91, Who 92*
**Smith**, David Clayton 1929- *WhoAmP 91*
**Smith**, David Clement, IV 1951- *AmMWSc 92*
**Smith**, David Collville 1922- *IntWW 91*
**Smith**, David Douglas 1959- *WhoAmL 92*
**Smith**, David Douglas R. *Who 92*
**Smith**, David Dury H. *Who 92*
**Smith**, David E. 1939- *WrDr 92*
**Smith**, David Edmund 1934- *AmMWSc 92*
**Smith**, David Edward 1939- *WhoFI 92*
**Smith**, David Elvin 1939- *WhoWest 92*
**Smith**, David English 1920- *AmMWSc 92*
**Smith**, David Eugene 1941- *WhoFI 92*
**Smith**, David Fletcher 1946- *AmMWSc 92*
**Smith**, David Grahame G. *Who 92*
**Smith**, David H. *Who 92*
**Smith**, David Harrison, Jr 1926- *AmMWSc 92*
**Smith**, David Harry Watrous 1938- *WhoEnt 92*
**Smith**, David Henry 1954- *Who 92*
**Smith**, David Hibbard 1941- *AmMWSc 92, WhoMW 92*
**Smith**, David Huggans 1954- *WhoMW 92*
**Smith**, David Huston 1937- *AmMWSc 92*
**Smith**, David I 1954- *AmMWSc 92*
**Smith**, David Iser 1933- *Who 92*
**Smith**, David James *Who 92*
**Smith**, David John 1948- *AmMWSc 92*
**Smith**, David John Leslie 1938- *Who 92*
**Smith**, David Joseph 1943- *AmMWSc 92*
**Smith**, David Lee 1944- *AmMWSc 92*
**Smith**, David Lee 1961- *WhoMW 92*
**Smith**, David M. 1959- *WhoEnt 92*
**Smith**, David MacIntyre Bell Armour 1923- *Who 92*
**Smith**, David Marshall 1936- *WrDr 92*
**Smith**, David Marshall 1943- *AmMWSc 92*
**Smith**, David Martyn 1921- *AmMWSc 92*
**Smith**, David Michael 1944- *WhoFI 92*
**Smith**, David Michael 1949- *WhoFI 92*
**Smith**, David Philip 1935- *AmMWSc 92*
**Smith**, David R 1936- *AmMWSc 92*
**Smith**, David R. 1940- *IntMPA 92*
**Smith**, David R. 1946- *WhoBlA 92*
**Smith**, David Reeder 1938- *AmMWSc 92*
**Smith**, David Rollin 1940- *WhoWest 92*
**Smith**, David Rollins 1937- *AmMWSc 92*
**Smith**, David Royce 1939- *WhoRel 92*
**Smith**, David S 1921- *AmMWSc 92*
**Smith**, David Spencer 1934- *AmMWSc 92*
**Smith**, David Thomas 1944- *WhoWest 92*
**Smith**, David Varley 1943- *AmMWSc 92*
**Smith**, David Waldo Edward 1934- *AmMWSc 92*
**Smith**, David Warren 1939- *AmMWSc 92*
**Smith**, David Wayne 1963- *WhoRel 92*
**Smith**, David Webster 1938- *WhoAmP 91*
**Smith**, David William 1933- *AmMWSc 92*
**Smith**, David William 1938- *AmMWSc 92*
**Smith**, David William 1948- *AmMWSc 92*
**Smith**, David Young 1943- *AmMWSc 92*
**Smith**, Dawn C. F. 1960- *WhoBlA 92*
**Smith**, Dean Francis 1942- *AmMWSc 92*
**Smith**, Dean Gordon 1959- *WhoMW 92*
**Smith**, Dean Harley 1922- *AmMWSc 92*
**Smith**, Dean Orren 1944- *AmMWSc 92*
**Smith**, Dean Wesley 1950- *IntAu&W 91*
**Smith**, Deane Kingsley, Jr 1930- *AmMWSc 92*
**Smith**, Deborah Lynn 1951- *WhoEnt 92*
**Smith**, Deborah P. 1951- *WhoBlA 92*
**Smith**, Deborah Ruth 1961- *WhoAmL 92*
**Smith**, Debra Lynn 1956- *WhoEnt 92*
**Smith**, DeHaven L. 1928- *WhoBlA 92*
**Smith**, DeLancey Allan 1916- *WhoMW 92*
**Smith**, DeLancey Allan, Jr. 1947- *WhoEnt 92*
**Smith**, Delia *IntAu&W 91, Who 92, WrDr 92*
**Smith**, Delmont K 1927- *AmMWSc 92*
**Smith**, Delos V., Jr. 1906- *WhoEnt 92, WhoMW 92*
**Smith**, Denis M. *Who 92*
**Smith**, Denise Louise 1957- *WhoAmP 91*
**Smith**, Denise Myrtle 1955- *AmMWSc 92*
**Smith**, Dennis *DrAPF 91*
**Smith**, Dennis 1959- *WhoBlA 92*
**Smith**, Dennis Clifford 1928- *AmMWSc 92*
**Smith**, Dennis Dustin 1949- *WhoAmL 92*
**Smith**, Dennis Edwin 1944- *WhoRel 92*
**Smith**, Dennis Eugene 1949- *AmMWSc 92*
**Smith**, Dennis Jack 1955- *WhoRel 92*
**Smith**, Dennis LeBron 1962- *WhoRel 92*
**Smith**, Dennis Matthew 1952- *AmMWSc 92*
**Smith**, Dennis Rae 1961- *WhoBlA 92*
**Smith**, Dennis W 1942- *WhoAmP 91*
**Smith**, Dennis Wayne 1964- *WhoEnt 92*
**Smith**, Dennison A 1943- *AmMWSc 92*
**Smith**, Denny 1938- *WhoAmP 91*
**Smith**, Derek B. *Who 92*
**Smith**, Derek Cyril 1927- *Who 92*
**Smith**, Derek Edward H. *Who 92*
**Smith**, Derek Ervin 1961- *WhoBlA 92*
**Smith**, Derek Frank 1929- *Who 92*
**Smith**, Derek Geoffrey 1931- *WhoEnt 92*
**Smith**, Derek V *WhoIns 92*
**Smith**, Desmond *Who 92*
**Smith**, Desmond Milton 1937- *WhoRel 92*
**Smith**, Detta Renee 1959- *WhoEnt 92*
**Smith**, Deuel Coily, Jr. 1943- *WhoRel 92*
**Smith**, Dewey Wayne 1953- *WhoRel 92*
**Smith**, Diana Lynn Briant 1945- *WhoMW 92*
**Smith**, Diane Elizabeth 1937- *AmMWSc 92*
**Smith**, Diane Karen 1954- *WhoAmL 92*
**Smith**, Dinitia *DrAPF 91*
**Smith**, Doc *TwCSFW 91*
**Smith**, Dodie *ConAu 133, SmATA 65*
**Smith**, Dodie d1990 *IntWW 91N, Who 92N*
**Smith**, Dodie 1896- *IntAu&W 91*
**Smith**, Dodie 1896-1990 *AnObit 1990*
**Smith**, Dolores J. 1936- *WhoBlA 92*
**Smith**, Dolores Maxine Plunk 1926- *WhoEnt 92, WhoMW 92*
**Smith**, Don C *WhoAmP 91*
**Smith**, Don Wiley 1936- *AmMWSc 92*
**Smith**, Donald Alan 1930- *AmMWSc 92*
**Smith**, Donald Archie 1934- *WhoRel 92*
**Smith**, Donald Arnold 1931- *WhoAmP 91*
**Smith**, Donald Arthur 1926- *AmMWSc 92*
**Smith**, Donald Arthur 1935- *WhoMW 92*
**Smith**, Donald Charles 1910- *Who 92*
**Smith**, Donald E. 1930- *WhoWest 92*
**Smith**, Donald Eugene 1934- *AmMWSc 92*
**Smith**, Donald Eugene 1944- *AmMWSc 92*
**Smith**, Donald Eugene 1953- *WhoMW 92*
**Smith**, Donald Evans 1915- *WhoWest 92*
**Smith**, Donald Foss 1913- *AmMWSc 92*
**Smith**, Donald Frederick 1949- *AmMWSc 92*
**Smith**, Donald Gene 1941- *WhoFI 92*
**Smith**, Donald Hugh 1932- *WhoBlA 92*
**Smith**, Donald John 1926- *Who 92*
**Smith**, Donald Joseph 1947- *WhoMW 92*
**Smith**, Donald Kaye 1932- *WhoAmL 92, WhoIns 92*
**Smith**, Donald Kendall 1929- *WhoWest 92*
**Smith**, Donald L 1924- *WhoAmP 91*
**Smith**, Donald Larned 1940- *AmMWSc 92*
**Smith**, Donald Lee 1958- *WhoFI 92*
**Smith**, Donald M. 1931- *WhoBlA 92*
**Smith**, Donald MacKeen 1923- *Who 92*
**Smith**, Donald MacLean 1930- *WhoEnt 92*
**Smith**, Donald Norbert 1931- *WhoFI 92*
**Smith**, Donald Ray 1934- *WhoFI 92*
**Smith**, Donald Ray 1939- *AmMWSc 92*
**Smith**, Donald Reed 1936- *AmMWSc 92*
**Smith**, Donald Richard 1932- *WhoWest 92*
**Smith**, Donald Ross 1940- *AmMWSc 92*
**Smith**, Donald Roy 1926- *WhoMW 92*
**Smith**, Donald Stanley 1926- *AmMWSc 92*
**Smith**, Donald Terry, Jr. 1955- *WhoMW 92*
**Smith**, Donald W. d1991 *NewYTBS 91*
**Smith**, Donald W 1923- *AmMWSc 92*
**Smith**, Donald Ward 1926- *AmMWSc 92*
**Smith**, Donn Leroy 1915- *AmMWSc 92*
**Smith**, Donna *WhoAmP 91*
**Smith**, Donna 1954- *WhoWest 92*
**Smith**, Donna Hacker 1954- *WhoRel 92*
**Smith**, Donna Lee 1941- *WhoAmP 91*
**Smith**, Donnie Louise 1952- *WhoWest 92*
**Smith**, Dorian Glen Whitney 1934- *AmMWSc 92*
**Smith**, Doris Buchanan 1934- *WrDr 92*
**Smith**, Doris Helen 1930- *WhoRel 92*
**Smith**, Dorothy E. 1926- *WomSoc*
**Smith**, Dorothy Gladys 1896-1990 *ConAu 133, SmATA 65*
**Smith**, Dorothy Gordon 1918- *AmMWSc 92*
**Smith**, Dorothy J. 1948- *WhoBlA 92*
**Smith**, Dorothy Louise White 1939- *WhoBlA 92*
**Smith**, Dorothy O. 1943- *WhoBlA 92*
**Smith**, Dorsett David 1937- *WhoWest 92*
**Smith**, Douglas *Who 92*
**Smith**, Douglas 1940- *AmMWSc 92*
**Smith**, Douglas Alan 1959- *AmMWSc 92*
**Smith**, Douglas Boucher 1932- *Who 92*
**Smith**, Douglas Calvin 1949- *AmMWSc 92*
**Smith**, Douglas D *AmMWSc 92*
**Smith**, Douglas Dee 1954- *WhoAmL 92*
**Smith**, Douglas LaRue 1917- *WhoFI 92*
**Smith**, Douglas Lee 1930- *AmMWSc 92*
**Smith**, Douglas Lee 1937- *AmMWSc 92*
**Smith**, Douglas Lee 1943- *AmMWSc 92*
**Smith**, Douglas Leslie B. *Who 92*
**Smith**, Douglas M. 1942- *WhoBlA 92*
**Smith**, Douglas Myles 1946- *WhoAmP 91*
**Smith**, Douglas Roane 1930- *AmMWSc 92*
**Smith**, Douglas Stewart 1924- *AmMWSc 92*
**Smith**, Douglas Warren 1954- *WhoEnt 92*
**Smith**, Douglas Wemp 1938- *AmMWSc 92*
**Smith**, Drew *Who 92*
**Smith**, Duane A 1937- *WhoAmP 91*
**Smith**, Duane Allan 1937- *WhoWest 92, WrDr 92*
**Smith**, Duane Robert 1953- *WhoRel 92*
**Smith**, Dudley 1926- *IntAu&W 91, Who 92, WrDr 92*
**Smith**, Dudley-Brian 1954- *WhoEnt 92*
**Smith**, Dudley Renwick 1937- *WhoIns 92*
**Smith**, Dudley Templeton 1940- *AmMWSc 92*
**Smith**, Dudley Winn, Mrs. 1905- *WhoEnt 92*
**Smith**, Dugal N. *Who 92*
**Smith**, Duncan McLaurin, Jr. 1926- *WhoAmL 92*
**Smith**, Durward A 1947- *AmMWSc 92*
**Smith**, Dwight Glenn 1943- *AmMWSc 92*
**Smith**, Dwight L. 1918- *WrDr 92*
**Smith**, Dwight Leon 1946- *WhoFI 92*
**Smith**, Dwight Morrell 1931- *AmMWSc 92*
**Smith**, Dwight Raymond 1921- *AmMWSc 92*
**Smith**, E 1897- *AmMWSc 92*
**Smith**, E Ashley 1946- *WhoAmP 91*
**Smith**, E. Berry 1926- *WhoEnt 92, WhoMW 92*
**Smith**, E. Brian 1933- *IntWW 91*
**Smith**, E E 1890-1965 *TwCSFW 91*
**Smith**, E. Kendrick 1956- *WhoAmL 92*
**Smith**, Earl Bradford 1953- *WhoBlA 92*
**Smith**, Earl Cooper 1906- *WhoMW 92*
**Smith**, Earl E.T. 1903-1991 *NewYTBS 91*
**Smith**, Earl W 1940- *AmMWSc 92*
**Smith**, Ed 1937- *WhoWest 92*
**Smith**, Ed 1962- *WhoEnt 92*
**Smith**, Ed H 1945- *WhoAmP 91*
**Smith**, Eddie Carol 1937- *AmMWSc 92*
**Smith**, Eddie D. 1920- *WhoBlA 92*
**Smith**, Eddie D., Sr. 1946- *WhoBlA 92*
**Smith**, Eddie Glenn, Jr. 1926- *WhoBlA 92*
**Smith**, Edgar Clarence, Jr 1926- *AmMWSc 92*
**Smith**, Edgar Dumont 1918- *AmMWSc 92*
**Smith**, Edgar E. 1934- *WhoBlA 92*
**Smith**, Edgar Eugene 1934- *AmMWSc 92*
**Smith**, Edgar Fitzhugh 1919- *AmMWSc 92*
**Smith**, Edgar Wright, Jr. 1939- *WhoRel 92*
**Smith**, Edith B. *WhoEnt 92*
**Smith**, Edith B. 1952- *WhoBlA 92*
**Smith**, Edith Lucile 1913- *AmMWSc 92*
**Smith**, Edward 1934- *AmMWSc 92*
**Smith**, Edward Alistair 1939- *Who 92*
**Smith**, Edward Baker 1955- *WhoMW 92*
**Smith**, Edward Bruce 1920- *WhoAmP 91*
**Smith**, Edward Charles 1949- *WhoBlA 92*
**Smith**, Edward Darrell 1778-1819 *BiInAmS*
**Smith**, Edward F 1950- *WhoAmP 91*
**Smith**, Edward Holman 1915- *AmMWSc 92*
**Smith**, Edward J 1920- *AmMWSc 92*
**Smith**, Edward John 1927- *AmMWSc 92*
**Smith**, Edward Joseph 1927- *WhoAmP 91*
**Smith**, Edward Lee 1932- *AmMWSc 92*
**Smith**, Edward Lewis, Jr 1937- *WhoAmP 91*
**Smith**, Edward M 1925- *AmMWSc 92*
**Smith**, Edward Nathaniel, Jr. 1955- *WhoBlA 92*
**Smith**, Edward O'dell 1929- *WhoRel 92*
**Smith**, Edward Paul, Jr. 1939- *WhoFI 92*
**Smith**, Edward Robert 1952- *WhoAmL 92*
**Smith**, Edward Russell 1944- *AmMWSc 92*
**Smith**, Edward S 1924- *AmMWSc 92*
**Smith**, Edward Samuel 1919- *WhoAmL 92*
**Smith**, Edwin 1851-1912 *BiInAmS*
**Smith**, Edwin Ball 1937- *WhoMW 92, WhoRel 92*
**Smith**, Edwin Burnell 1936- *AmMWSc 92*
**Smith**, Edwin Dudley 1936- *WhoAmL 92*
**Smith**, Edwin Eric 1946- *WhoAmL 92*
**Smith**, Edwin Lamar, Jr 1936- *AmMWSc 92*
**Smith**, Edwin Lee 1907- *AmMWSc 92*
**Smith**, Edwin Mark 1927- *AmMWSc 92*
**Smith**, Edwin Milton 1950- *WhoWest 92*
**Smith**, Edwin Steeves 1938- *WhoAmP 91*
**Smith**, Eileen Patricia 1941- *AmMWSc 92*
**Smith**, Eileen S. *Who 92*
**Smith**, Elaine Campbell *DrAPF 91*
**Smith**, Elaine Marie 1947- *WhoBlA 92*
**Smith**, Elbert George 1913- *AmMWSc 92*
**Smith**, Eldon Raymond 1939- *AmMWSc 92*
**Smith**, Eldred Gee 1907- *WhoRel 92*
**Smith**, Eleanor Jane 1933- *WhoBlA 92*
**Smith**, Eleanor Ruth 1932- *WhoFI 92*
**Smith**, Elihu Hubbard 1771-1798 *BenetAL 91*
**Smith**, Elijah 1939- *WhoBlA 92*
**Smith**, Elinor Bellingham 1906-1988 *TwCPaSc*
**Smith**, Eliot Randall 1950- *WhoMW 92*
**Smith**, Elizabeth A. T. 1958- *ConAu 133*
**Smith**, Elizabeth Adams 1944- *WhoEnt 92*
**Smith**, Elizabeth Ann 1948- *WhoAmL 92*

**Smith,** Elizabeth Knapp 1917- *AmMWSc 92*
**Smith,** Elizabeth Marie 1965- *WhoMW 92*
**Smith,** Elizabeth Martinez 1943- *WhoHisp 92*
**Smith,** Elizabeth Melva 1943- *AmMWSc 92*
**Smith,** Elizabeth Oakes 1806-1893 *BenetAL 91*
**Smith,** Elizabeth Patience 1949- *WhoFI 92*
**Smith,** Elizabeth Straubel 1934- *WhoAmP 91*
**Smith,** Ella 1933- *WrDr 92*
**Smith,** Ellison DuRant 1864-1944 *FacFETw*
**Smith,** Elmer G., Jr. 1957- *WhoBlA 92*
**Smith,** Elmer Robert 1923- *AmMWSc 92*
**Smith,** Elouise Beard 1920- *WhoFI 92*
**Smith,** Elsdon Coles 1903- *WhoAmL 92, WrDr 92*
**Smith,** Elsie Mae 1927- *WhoBlA 92*
**Smith,** Elske van Panhuys 1929- *AmMWSc 92*
**Smith,** Elton Edward 1915- *WrDr 92*
**Smith,** Elvie Lawrence 1926- *WhoFI 92*
**Smith,** Emil L 1911- *AmMWSc 92, IntWW 91*
**Smith,** Emil Richard 1931- *AmMWSc 92*
**Smith,** Emma 1923- *ConNov 91, IntAu&W 91, Who 92, WrDr 92*
**Smith,** Emma Breedlove 1931- *AmMWSc 92*
**Smith,** Emmitt J., III 1969- *WhoBlA 92*
**Smith,** Emmitt Mozart 1905- *WhoBlA 92*
**Smith,** Ephraim Philip 1942- *WhoFI 92*
**Smith,** Eric Brian 1933- *Who 92*
**Smith,** Eric Howard 1943- *AmMWSc 92*
**Smith,** Eric John R. *Who 92*
**Smith,** Eric Morgan 1953- *AmMWSc 92*
**Smith,** Eric Norman 1922- *Who 92*
**Smith,** Eric Parkman 1910- *WhoFI 92*
**Smith,** Eric Trent 1959- *WhoEnt 92*
**Smith,** Eric W. 1952- *WhoAmL 92*
**Smith,** Erla Ring 1938- *AmMWSc 92*
**Smith,** Erminnie Adele Platt 1836-1886 *BiInAmS*
**Smith,** Ernest Alwyn 1925- *Who 92*
**Smith,** Ernest Howard 1931- *WhoBlA 92*
**Smith,** Ernest Ketcham 1922- *AmMWSc 92, WhoWest 92*
**Smith,** Ernest Lee, Jr 1934- *AmMWSc 92*
**Smith,** Ernest Lester 1904- *Who 92*
**Smith,** Estella W. *WhoBlA 92*
**Smith,** Estus 1930- *WhoBlA 92*
**Smith,** Euclid O'Neal 1947- *AmMWSc 92*
**Smith,** Eugene 1860-1912 *BiInAmS*
**Smith,** Eugene 1929- *WhoBlA 92*
**Smith,** Eugene 1938- *WhoBlA 92*
**Smith,** Eugene Alfred 1864-1914 *BiInAmS*
**Smith,** Eugene DuBois 1955- *WhoBlA 92*
**Smith,** Eugene Herbert 1927- *WhoWest 92*
**Smith,** Eugene I 1944- *AmMWSc 92*
**Smith,** Eugene Joseph 1929- *AmMWSc 92*
**Smith,** Evangeline Chrisman Davey 1911- *WhoMW 92*
**Smith,** Evelyn E 1937- *TwCSFW 91*
**Smith,** Everett d1991 *NewYTBS 91*
**Smith,** Everett Gregor 1939- *WhoWest 92*
**Smith,** Ewart *Who 92*
**Smith,** Ewart Brian 1938- *WhoWest 92*
**Smith,** F Dow 1921- *AmMWSc 92*
**Smith,** F Harrell 1918- *AmMWSc 92*
**Smith,** F. Hopkinson 1838-1915 *BenetAL 91*
**Smith,** F M *WhoAmP 91*
**Smith,** Felix Teisseire 1920- *AmMWSc 92*
**Smith,** Fenwick *WhoEnt 92*
**Smith,** Fern M. 1933- *WhoAmL 92, WhoWest 92*
**Smith,** Fernando Leon Jorge 1954- *WhoHisp 92*
**Smith,** Florence Margaret 1902-1971 *ConAu 35NR*
**Smith,** Floyd Leslie 1931- *WhoFI 92*
**Smith,** Floyd W 1920- *AmMWSc 92*
**Smith,** Ford *TwCWW 91*
**Smith,** Frances C. *WhoBlA 92*
**Smith,** Frances Harter Roberts 1945- *WhoAmL 92*
**Smith,** Francis Barrymore 1932- *IntWW 91*
**Smith,** Francis Brian W. *Who 92*
**Smith,** Francis Graham 1923- *IntWW 91, Who 92*
**Smith,** Francis J. *DrAPF 91*
**Smith,** Francis Marion 1923- *AmMWSc 92*
**Smith,** Francis Taylor 1933- *Who 92*
**Smith,** Francis White 1931- *AmMWSc 92*
**Smith,** Francis Xavier 1945- *AmMWSc 92*
**Smith,** Frank 1910- *WhoBlA 92*
**Smith,** Frank, Jr *WhoAmP 91*
**Smith,** Frank A 1937- *AmMWSc 92*
**Smith,** Frank Ackroyd 1919- *AmMWSc 92*
**Smith,** Frank David 1950- *WhoRel 92*
**Smith,** Frank E 1936- *AmMWSc 92*
**Smith,** Frank Earl 1931- *WhoFI 92, WhoMW 92*
**Smith,** Frank Ewart 1897- *Who 92*
**Smith,** Frank F., Jr. 1942- *WhoAmL 92*
**Smith,** Frank Houston 1903- *AmMWSc 92*
**Smith,** Frank Junius 1937- *WhoBlA 92*
**Smith,** Frank Roylance 1932- *AmMWSc 92*
**Smith,** Frank Thomas 1948- *IntWW 91, Who 92*
**Smith,** Frank W 1919- *AmMWSc 92*
**Smith,** Frank William G. *Who 92*
**Smith,** Frank Winfred 1909- *WhoRel 92*
**Smith,** Frank Winston, Jr. 1933- *WhoAmL 92*
**Smith,** Franklin L. 1943- *WhoBlA 92*
**Smith,** Fraser Drew 1950- *Who 92*
**Smith,** Fred Dempsey, Jr. 1947- *WhoAmL 92*
**Smith,** Fred George, Jr 1928- *AmMWSc 92*
**Smith,** Fred R, Jr 1940- *AmMWSc 92*
**Smith,** Freddie Alphonso 1924- *WhoBlA 92*
**Smith,** Frederic Newcomb 1925- *WhoAmP 91*
**Smith,** Frederick Adair, Jr 1921- *AmMWSc 92*
**Smith,** Frederick Albert 1911- *AmMWSc 92*
**Smith,** Frederick D. 1917- *WhoBlA 92*
**Smith,** Frederick E 1922- *IntAu&W 91, WrDr 92*
**Smith,** Frederick Edward 1920- *AmMWSc 92*
**Smith,** Frederick Ellis 1928- *WhoBlA 92*
**Smith,** Frederick F., III 1947- *WhoFI 92*
**Smith,** Frederick George 1917- *AmMWSc 92*
**Smith,** Frederick George Walton 1909- *AmMWSc 92*
**Smith,** Frederick Gladstone 1924- *IntWW 91*
**Smith,** Frederick Madison 1874-1946 *RelLAm 91*
**Smith,** Frederick Orville, II 1934- *WhoAmP 91*
**Smith,** Frederick Paul 1951- *AmMWSc 92*
**Smith,** Frederick T 1920- *AmMWSc 92*
**Smith,** Frederick Viggers 1912- *Who 92*
**Smith,** Frederick W 1917- *AmMWSc 92*
**Smith,** Frederick Wallace 1944- *WhoFI 92*
**Smith,** Frederick William 1942- *AmMWSc 92*
**Smith,** Frederick Williams 1922- *AmMWSc 92*
**Smith,** Frederick Willis 1938- *AmMWSc 92*
**Smith,** Fredrick E. 1935- *WhoBlA 92*
**Smith,** Freeman Holmes, III 1943- *WhoAmP 91*
**Smith,** G. Kent 1957- *WhoRel 92*
**Smith,** G V 1916- *AmMWSc 92*
**Smith,** Gail Preston 1915- *AmMWSc 92*
**Smith,** Gale Eugene 1933- *AmMWSc 92*
**Smith,** Galen Eugene *WhoMW 92, WhoRel 92*
**Smith,** Gardner Watkins 1931- *AmMWSc 92*
**Smith,** Garland M., Jr. 1935- *WhoBlA 92*
**Smith,** Garmond Stanley 1932- *AmMWSc 92*
**Smith,** Garret 1876?-1954 *ScFEYrs*
**Smith,** Garry Austin 1940- *AmMWSc 92*
**Smith,** Gary Chester 1938- *AmMWSc 92*
**Smith,** Gary Eugene 1932- *AmMWSc 92*
**Smith,** Gary Joseph *AmMWSc 92*
**Smith,** Gary Keith 1952- *AmMWSc 92*
**Smith,** Gary Lee 1936- *WhoMW 92*
**Smith,** Gary Lee 1947- *AmMWSc 92*
**Smith,** Gary Lee 1961- *WhoAmL 92*
**Smith,** Gary Leroy 1935- *AmMWSc 92*
**Smith,** Gary Richard 1948- *AmMWSc 92*
**Smith,** Gary Richard 1952- *WhoWest 92*
**Smith,** Gary Scott 1950- *WhoRel 92*
**Smith,** Gary Soren 1938- *WhoEnt 92*
**Smith,** Gary W 1947- *WhoIns 92*
**Smith,** Gary W. 1954- *WhoRel 92*
**Smith,** Gaston 1927- *AmMWSc 92*
**Smith,** Gene E 1936- *AmMWSc 92*
**Smith,** Genevieve Grant 1922- *WhoWest 92*
**Smith,** Geoffrey Adams 1947- *WhoFI 92*
**Smith,** Geoffrey J. *Who 92*
**Smith,** Geoffrey M. *Who 92*
**Smith,** Geoffrey W 1939- *AmMWSc 92*
**Smith,** George 1914- *Who 92*
**Smith,** George 1919- *Who 92*
**Smith,** George Albert 1870-1951 *RelLAm 91*
**Smith,** George B *ScFEYrs*
**Smith,** George Bundy 1937- *WhoBlA 92*
**Smith,** George Byron 1933- *AmMWSc 92*
**Smith,** George C 1926- *AmMWSc 92*
**Smith,** George C 1935- *AmMWSc 92*
**Smith,** George Cruice 1945- *WhoAmL 92*
**Smith,** George Curtis 1935- *WhoAmL 92, WhoMW 92*
**Smith,** George David 1941- *AmMWSc 92*
**Smith,** George Elwood 1930- *AmMWSc 92*
**Smith,** George Foster 1922- *AmMWSc 92*
**Smith,** George Graham 1957- *WhoFI 92*
**Smith,** George Grainger 1892-1961 *TwCPaSc*
**Smith,** George H 1922- *IntAu&W 91, TwCSFW 91, WrDr 92*
**Smith,** George Irving 1927- *AmMWSc 92, WhoWest 92*
**Smith,** George Ivan 1915- *IntWW 91*
**Smith,** George Larry 1951- *WhoWest 92*
**Smith,** George Leonard, Jr 1935- *AmMWSc 92, WhoMW 92*
**Smith,** George Neil 1936- *Who 92*
**Smith,** George O 1911- *TwCSFW 91*
**Smith,** George P *WhoAmP 91*
**Smith,** George Pedro 1923- *AmMWSc 92*
**Smith,** George S. 1940- *WhoBlA 92*
**Smith,** George S., Jr. 1948- *WhoEnt 92, WhoFI 92*
**Smith,** George T 1916- *WhoAmP 91*
**Smith,** George Thomas 1931- *AmMWSc 92*
**Smith,** George Thornewell 1916- *WhoAmL 92*
**Smith,** George V. 1926- *WhoBlA 92*
**Smith,** George V R 1937- *WhoIns 92*
**Smith,** George Van Riper 1937- *WhoWest 92*
**Smith,** George Walker 1929- *WhoBlA 92*
**Smith,** George Wolfram 1932- *AmMWSc 92, WhoMW 92*
**Smith,** George Wynn, Jr. 1934- *WhoAmL 92*
**Smith,** Georgia Floyd 1949- *WhoWest 92*
**Smith,** Gerald A 1936- *AmMWSc 92*
**Smith,** Gerald Duane 1942- *AmMWSc 92*
**Smith,** Gerald Floyd 1942- *AmMWSc 92*
**Smith,** Gerald Francis 1928- *AmMWSc 92*
**Smith,** Gerald Kendall 1936- *WhoFI 92*
**Smith,** Gerald L. K. 1898-1976 *FacFETw*
**Smith,** Gerald Lyman Kenneth 1898-1976 *BiDExR, RelLAm 91*
**Smith,** Gerald Lynn 1934- *AmMWSc 92*
**Smith,** Gerald M 1920- *AmMWSc 92*
**Smith,** Gerald R 1928- *WhoAmP 91*
**Smith,** Gerald Ralph 1944- *AmMWSc 92*
**Smith,** Gerald Ray 1935- *AmMWSc 92*
**Smith,** Gerald Ray 1952- *AmMWSc 92*
**Smith,** Gerald Stanton 1938- *Who 92*
**Smith,** Gerald Wavern 1929- *AmMWSc 92*
**Smith,** Gerald Wayne 1950- *WhoBlA 92*
**Smith,** Geraldine T. 1918- *WhoBlA 92*
**Smith,** Gerard Coad 1914- *IntWW 91, WhoAmP 91*
**Smith,** Gerard Peter 1935- *AmMWSc 92*
**Smith,** Gerard Thomas C. *Who 92*
**Smith,** Gerard Vinton 1931- *AmMWSc 92*
**Smith,** Gerrit 1797-1874 *AmPeW*
**Smith,** Gerrit Joseph 1938- *AmMWSc 92*
**Smith,** Gibson Locke, Jr. 1940- *WhoAmL 92*
**Smith,** Gilbert *Who 92*
**Smith,** Gilbert Edwin 1922- *AmMWSc 92*
**Smith,** Gilbert Howlett 1938- *AmMWSc 92*
**Smith,** Ginger Elaine 1957- *WhoRel 92*
**Smith,** Gipsy 1860-1947 *RelLAm 91*
**Smith,** Glee Sidney, Jr. 1921- *WhoAmL 92*
**Smith,** Glen D 1937- *WhoIns 92*
**Smith,** Glenn Edward 1923- *AmMWSc 92*
**Smith,** Glenn R. 1945- *WhoBlA 92*
**Smith,** Glenn S 1952- *AmMWSc 92*
**Smith,** Glenn Sanborn 1907- *AmMWSc 92*
**Smith,** Gloria Ann 1943- *WhoMW 92*
**Smith,** Gloria R. 1934- *WhoBlA 92*
**Smith,** Godfrey 1926- *Who 92*
**Smith,** Goff 1916- *WhoFI 92*
**Smith,** Gordon Allen 1933- *WhoBlA 92*
**Smith,** Gordon C. 1929- *WhoWest 92*
**Smith,** Gordon Drummond 1946- *WhoFI 92*
**Smith,** Gordon E. *Who 92*
**Smith,** Gordon Edward C. *Who 92*
**Smith,** Gordon Eugene 1953- *WhoWest 92*
**Smith,** Gordon Henry 1951- *WhoAmP 91*
**Smith,** Gordon Luther 1958- *WhoFI 92*
**Smith,** Gordon Meade 1930- *AmMWSc 92*
**Smith,** Gordon Russell 1933- *WhoMW 92*
**Smith,** Gordon Scott 1941- *IntWW 91*
**Smith,** Gordon Stuart 1928- *WhoWest 92*
**Smith,** Gracie Bernon 1932- *WhoFI 92, WhoMW 92*
**Smith,** Graham Gable 1914- *WhoMW 92*
**Smith,** Graham Monro 1947- *AmMWSc 92*
**Smith,** Grahame J C 1942- *AmMWSc 92*
**Smith,** Grant Gill 1921- *AmMWSc 92*
**Smith,** Grant Warren, II 1941- *AmMWSc 92, WhoFI 92*
**Smith,** Granville L. *WhoBlA 92*
**Smith,** Granville N. 1927- *WhoBlA 92*
**Smith,** Greg E. 1963- *WhoHisp 92*
**Smith,** Greg M. 1953- *WhoMW 92*
**Smith,** Gregg 1931- *NewAmDM*
**Smith,** Gregory *WhoEnt 92*
**Smith,** Gregory 1946- *WhoAmP 91*
**Smith,** Gregory Allen 1952- *WhoBlA 92*
**Smith,** Gregory Blake 1951- *IntAu&W 91, WrDr 92*
**Smith,** Gregory Butler 1946- *WhoAmL 92*
**Smith,** Gregory James 1955- *WhoAmL 92*
**Smith,** Gregory K. 1949- *WhoRel 92*
**Smith,** Gregory K 1951- *WhoAmP 91*
**Smith,** Gregory Loucks 1936- *WhoMW 92*
**Smith,** Gregory Michael 1941- *WhoRel 92*
**Smith,** Gregory Robert 1954- *WhoAmL 92*
**Smith,** Gregory Stanley 1964- *WhoRel 92*
**Smith,** Gregory Wayne 1962- *WhoFI 92*
**Smith,** Grover Cleveland 1923- *WrDr 92*
**Smith,** Guy Charles 1962- *WhoAmL 92*
**Smith,** Guy Lincoln, IV 1949- *WhoBlA 92, WhoFI 92*
**Smith,** Gwen Evans 1953- *WhoAmP 91*
**Smith,** Gwendolyn G. 1945- *WhoBlA 92*
**Smith,** Gwynne P 1924- *WhoAmP 91*
**Smith,** H. Allen 1907-1976 *BenetAL 91*
**Smith,** H. Vance 1942- *WhoAmL 92*
**Smith,** H Vernon, Jr *AmMWSc 92*
**Smith,** H Zack, Jr 1924- *WhoAmP 91*
**Smith,** Hadley J 1918- *AmMWSc 92*
**Smith,** Hal Leslie 1947- *AmMWSc 92*
**Smith,** Hale 1925- *NewAmDM, WhoBlA 92*
**Smith,** Hamilton Allen 1923- *WhoWest 92*
**Smith,** Hamilton Lanphere 1818-1903 *BiInAmS*
**Smith,** Hamilton O. 1931- *IntWW 91*
**Smith,** Hamilton Othanel 1931- *AmMWSc 92, Who 92, WhoNob 90*
**Smith,** Hannah Whitall 1832-1911 *RelLAm 91*
**Smith,** Harding Eugene 1947- *AmMWSc 92*
**Smith,** Harlan Eugene 1920- *AmMWSc 92*
**Smith,** Harlan J. d1991 *NewYTBS 91*
**Smith,** Harlan J 1924- *AmMWSc 92*
**Smith,** Harlan Millard 1921- *AmMWSc 92*
**Smith,** Harmon Lee, Jr. 1930- *WhoRel 92*
**Smith,** Harold Byron, Jr 1933- *WhoAmP 91, WhoFI 92*
**Smith,** Harold Carter 1920- *AmMWSc 92*
**Smith,** Harold Charles 1934- *WhoFI 92*
**Smith,** Harold Glenn 1927- *AmMWSc 92*
**Smith,** Harold Hill 1910- *AmMWSc 92*
**Smith,** Harold Linwood 1927- *AmMWSc 92*
**Smith,** Harold Philip 1915- *WhoRel 92*
**Smith,** Harold Victor, Jr. 1943- *WhoRel 92*
**Smith,** Harold W 1923- *AmMWSc 92*
**Smith,** Harold William 1928- *AmMWSc 92*
**Smith,** Harry *DrAPF 91, LesBEnT 92*
**Smith,** Harry 1921- *Who 92*
**Smith,** Harry Andrew 1933- *AmMWSc 92*
**Smith,** Harry B. 1860-1936 *BenetAL 91*
**Smith,** Harry Buchanan, Jr. 1924- *WhoMW 92*
**Smith,** Harry C. *DrAPF 91*
**Smith,** Harry Francis 1941- *AmMWSc 92*
**Smith,** Harry John 1927- *AmMWSc 92*
**Smith,** Harry Logan, Jr 1930- *AmMWSc 92*
**Smith,** Harry Mendell, Jr. 1943- *WhoWest 92*
**Smith,** Harvey *IntWW 91, Who 92*
**Smith,** Harvey Alvin 1932- *AmMWSc 92*
**Smith,** Hastings Alexander, Jr 1943- *AmMWSc 92*
**Smith,** Haywood Clark, Jr 1945- *AmMWSc 92*
**Smith,** Hedrick 1933- *CurBio 91 [port], WrDr 92*
**Smith,** Hedworth Cunningham 1912- *Who 92*
**Smith,** Helen Sylvester 1942- *Who 92*
**Smith,** Helene Sheila 1941- *AmMWSc 92*
**Smith,** Heman Bernard 1929- *WhoBlA 92*
**Smith,** Henry d1991 *NewYTBS 91*
**Smith,** Henry Charles, III 1931- *WhoEnt 92, WhoMW 92*
**Smith,** Henry Clay 1945- *WhoEnt 92*
**Smith,** Henry I *AmMWSc 92*
**Smith,** Henry Nash 1906-1986 *BenetAL 91*
**Smith,** Henry P, III 1911- *WhoAmP 91*
**Smith,** Henry R., Jr. 1917- *WhoBlA 92*
**Smith,** Henry Sidney 1928- *IntWW 91, Who 92*
**Smith,** Henry Thomas 1937- *WhoBlA 92*
**Smith,** Herald Leonydus 1909- *WhoBlA 92*
**Smith,** Herbert Huntington 1851-1919 *BiInAmS*
**Smith,** Herbert L 1929- *AmMWSc 92*
**Smith,** Herbert Lavon 1935- *WhoMW 92*
**Smith,** Herbert Roger 1936- *WhoMW 92*
**Smith,** Herman Brunell, Jr. 1927- *WhoBlA 92*
**Smith,** Herman Talliferrio 1915- *WhoBlA 92*
**Smith,** Herschel Bret 1959- *WhoRel 92*
**Smith,** Hilary Cranwell Bowen 1937- *WhoFI 92*
**Smith,** Hobart Muir 1912- *AmMWSc 92, WrDr 92*
**Smith,** Holland McTyeire 1882-1967 *FacFETw*
**Smith,** Homer Alvin, Jr 1932- *AmMWSc 92*
**Smith,** Horace Carroll 1922- *WhoAmP 91*
**Smith,** Horace Earl, II 1949- *WhoRel 92*

**Smith,** Horace Vernon, Jr 1942- *AmMWSc 92*
**Smith,** Horton 1925- *WhoAmL 92*
**Smith,** Howard 1919- *Who 92*
**Smith,** Howard C. *WhoBlA 92*
**Smith,** Howard Duane 1941- *AmMWSc 92*
**Smith,** Howard E 1925- *AmMWSc 92*
**Smith,** Howard E., Jr. 1927- *WrDr 92*
**Smith,** Howard Edwin 1923- *AmMWSc 92*
**Smith,** Howard Everett, Jr 1927- *IntAu&W 91*
**Smith,** Howard Frank Trayton 1919- *IntWW 91*
**Smith,** Howard Jay 1950- *WhoEnt 92*
**Smith,** Howard John Treweek 1937- *AmMWSc 92*
**Smith,** Howard K. *LesBEnT 92*
**Smith,** Howard K 1914- *IntMPA 92*
**Smith,** Howard Leroy 1924- *AmMWSc 92*
**Smith,** Howard Ross 1917- *WrDr 92*
**Smith,** Howard Russell 1914- *WhoWest 92*
**Smith,** Howard Thompson 1937- *WhoFI 92*
**Smith,** Howard Wesley 1929- *AmMWSc 92*
**Smith,** Howlett P. 1933- *WhoBlA 92*
**Smith,** Huey 1934- *NewAmDM*
**Smith,** Hugh Lansden 1940- *WhoRel 92*
**Smith,** Hugo Dunlap 1923- *AmMWSc 92*
**Smith,** Hulett Carlson 1918- *WhoAmP 91*
**Smith,** Huston 1919- *WhoRel 92*
**Smith,** Hy 1934- *IntMPA 92*
**Smith,** Hyrum Wayne 1943- *WhoWest 92*
**Smith,** Iain Crichton 1928- *ConNov 91, ConPo 91, IntAu&W 91, WrDr 92*
**Smith,** Iain-Mor L. *Who 92*
**Smith,** Ian 1919- *FacFETw [port]*
**Smith,** Ian Cormack Palmer 1939- *AmMWSc 92*
**Smith,** Ian Douglas 1919- *IntWW 91, Who 92*
**Smith,** Ian Maclean 1922- *AmMWSc 92*
**Smith,** Ian McKenzie 1935- *TwCPaSc*
**Smith,** Idalia Luna 1956- *WhoHisp 92*
**Smith,** Ieuan Trevor 1933- *AmMWSc 92*
**Smith,** Irene M 1910- *WhoAmP 91*
**Smith,** Irene Patricia *WhoAmP 91*
**Smith,** Irv 1929- *WhoAmP 91*
**Smith,** Irvin Aloysious, III 1939- *WhoFI 92*
**Smith,** Isaac Dixon 1932- *WhoBlA 92*
**Smith,** Isaac Litton *AmMWSc 92*
**Smith,** Isabel Francis 1935- *WhoFI 92*
**Smith,** Isabelle R. 1924- *WhoBlA 92*
**Smith,** Israel Alexander 1876-1958 *RelLAm 91*
**Smith,** Issar 1933- *AmMWSc 92*
**Smith,** Ivor Otterbein 1907- *Who 92*
**Smith,** Ivor Ramsay 1929- *Who 92*
**Smith,** Ivy 1945- *TwCPaSc*
**Smith,** J. Alfred, Sr. 1931- *WhoBlA 92*
**Smith,** J. C. 1930- *WhoBlA 92*
**Smith,** J C 1933- *AmMWSc 92*
**Smith,** J. Clay, Jr. 1942- *WhoBlA 92*
**Smith,** J Dungan 1939- *AmMWSc 92*
**Smith,** J Gregory, Mrs. 1818-1905 *ScFEYrs*
**Smith,** J. Harry 1922- *WhoBlA 92*
**Smith,** J Richard 1924- *AmMWSc 92*
**Smith,** J Roland 1933- *WhoAmP 91*
**Smith,** J. T. 1955- *WhoBlA 92*
**Smith,** J. Timothy 1955- *WhoAmL 92*
**Smith,** Jabbo 1908- *NewAmDM*
**Smith,** Jack 1927- *AmMWSc 92*
**Smith,** Jack 1928- *IntWW 91, TwCPaSc, Who 92*
**Smith,** Jack C. 1945- *WhoFI 92*
**Smith,** Jack Carlton 1913- *AmMWSc 92*
**Smith,** Jack D *WhoAmP 91*
**Smith,** Jack Edward 1929- *WhoWest 92*
**Smith,** Jack Howard 1921- *AmMWSc 92*
**Smith,** Jack John Carter 1943- *WhoWest 92*
**Smith,** Jack Lee 1948- *WhoFI 92*
**Smith,** Jack Louis 1934- *AmMWSc 92*
**Smith,** Jack Phalen 1953- *WhoMW 92*
**Smith,** Jack R 1935- *AmMWSc 92*
**Smith,** Jack Stanley 1916- *Who 92*
**Smith,** Jacklyn J 1934- *WhoAmP 91*
**Smith,** Jackson Bruce 1938- *AmMWSc 92*
**Smith,** Jaclyn 1947- *IntMPA 92, WhoEnt 92*
**Smith,** Jacqueline 1933- *IntMPA 92*
**Smith,** James 1737?-1814? *BenetAL 91*
**Smith,** James 1740-1812 *BiInAmS*
**Smith,** James, Jr. 1932- *WhoBlA 92*
**Smith,** James A. 1927- *WhoBlA 92*
**Smith,** James A. 1930- *WhoAmL 92*
**Smith,** James Aikman 1914- *Who 92*
**Smith,** James Alan 1942- *AmMWSc 92*
**Smith,** James Albert 1942- *WhoAmL 92*
**Smith,** James Alexander 1926- *WhoWest 92*
**Smith,** James Alfred 1913- *Who 92*
**Smith,** James Allbee 1937- *AmMWSc 92*
**Smith,** James Allen 1959- *WhoAmL 92*
**Smith,** James Almer, III 1950- *WhoBlA 92*
**Smith,** James Almer, Jr. 1923- *WhoBlA 92*
**Smith,** James Andrew Buchan 1906- *Who 92*
**Smith,** James Archibald Bruce 1929- *Who 92*
**Smith,** James Arthur 1955- *WhoAmL 92*
**Smith,** James B, Jr 1948- *WhoIns 92*
**Smith,** James Bonner 1950- *WhoAmL 92*
**Smith,** James C 1937- *WhoIns 92*
**Smith,** James C 1940- *WhoAmP 91*
**Smith,** James Cadzow 1927- *Who 92*
**Smith,** James Cecil 1934- *AmMWSc 92*
**Smith,** James Clarence, Jr 1939- *AmMWSc 92*
**Smith,** James Copeland 1945- *WhoFI 92*
**Smith,** James David 1930- *WhoBlA 92*
**Smith,** James David Blackhall 1940- *AmMWSc 92*
**Smith,** James Dean 1955- *WhoWest 92*
**Smith,** James Derrill 1952- *WhoRel 92*
**Smith,** James Desmond 1911- *Who 92*
**Smith,** James Donaldson 1922- *AmMWSc 92*
**Smith,** James Douglas 1927- *AmMWSc 92*
**Smith,** James Doyle 1921- *AmMWSc 92*
**Smith,** James Dwight 1956- *WhoAmL 92*
**Smith,** James E 1929- *WhoIns 92*
**Smith,** James Earl 1949- *AmMWSc 92*
**Smith,** James Edward 1935- *AmMWSc 92*
**Smith,** James Edward 1946- *WhoAmP 91*
**Smith,** James Edward, Jr 1941- *AmMWSc 92*
**Smith,** James Eldon 1928- *AmMWSc 92*
**Smith,** James Eric d1990 *IntWW 91N*
**Smith,** James Everett 1927- *WhoRel 92*
**Smith,** James F 1930- *AmMWSc 92*
**Smith,** James Finley 1938- *WhoFI 92*
**Smith,** James Francis 1936- *WhoFI 92*
**Smith,** James Frederick 1944- *WhoFI 92*
**Smith,** James G d1900 *BiInAmS*
**Smith,** James G 1930- *AmMWSc 92*
**Smith,** James G. 1937- *WhoRel 92*
**Smith,** James Graham 1928- *AmMWSc 92*
**Smith,** James H 1934- *AmMWSc 92*
**Smith,** James H, Jr 1909-1982 *FacFETw*
**Smith,** James Hamilton 1931- *IntWW 91*
**Smith,** James Hammond 1925- *AmMWSc 92*
**Smith,** James Hart 1942- *AmMWSc 92*
**Smith,** James Herbert 1947- *IntWW 91*
**Smith,** James Howard 1947- *WhoFI 92*
**Smith,** James Ian 1924- *Who 92*
**Smith,** James John 1914- *AmMWSc 92*
**Smith,** James Joseph 1940- *WhoMW 92*
**Smith,** James Kirk 1950- *WhoFI 92*
**Smith,** James L 1929- *AmMWSc 92*
**Smith,** James L. 1936- *WrDr 92*
**Smith,** James Lawrence 1943- *AmMWSc 92, WhoWest 92*
**Smith,** James Lawrence, III 1960- *WhoFI 92*
**Smith,** James Lee 1928- *AmMWSc 92*
**Smith,** James Lee 1935- *AmMWSc 92*
**Smith,** James Lee 1937- *AmMWSc 92*
**Smith,** James Lee 1940- *WhoRel 92*
**Smith,** James Lewis 1949- *AmMWSc 92*
**Smith,** James Lynn 1940- *AmMWSc 92*
**Smith,** James Michael 1954- *WhoAmL 92*
**Smith,** James Odell 1953- *WhoBlA 92*
**Smith,** James Oscar 1928- *WhoBlA 92*
**Smith,** James P 1950- *WhoAmP 91*
**Smith,** James Payne, Jr 1941- *AmMWSc 92*
**Smith,** James Peyton 1956- *WhoAmL 92*
**Smith,** James R 1941- *AmMWSc 92*
**Smith,** James Randolph 1948- *WhoEnt 92*
**Smith,** James Reaves 1942- *AmMWSc 92*
**Smith,** James Richard 1947- *WhoEnt 92*
**Smith,** James Robert 1945- *WhoEnt 92*
**Smith,** James Ronald 1952- *WhoRel 92*
**Smith,** James Ross 1943- *AmMWSc 92*
**Smith,** James Russell 1931- *WhoBlA 92*
**Smith,** James S 1917- *AmMWSc 92*
**Smith,** James Scott 1955- *WhoAmP 91*
**Smith,** James Stanley 1939- *AmMWSc 92*
**Smith,** James Thomas 1939- *AmMWSc 92, WhoWest 92*
**Smith,** James W 1931- *AmMWSc 92*
**Smith,** James W. 1944- *WhoWest 92*
**Smith,** James Warren 1934- *AmMWSc 92, WhoMW 92*
**Smith,** James Willie, Jr 1944- *AmMWSc 92*
**Smith,** James Winfred 1943- *AmMWSc 92*
**Smith,** Jan D 1939- *AmMWSc 92*
**Smith,** Jan G 1938- *AmMWSc 92*
**Smith,** Jane Schneberger 1928- *WhoMW 92*
**Smith,** Janet A. *Who 92*
**Smith,** Janet Hilary 1940- *Who 92*
**Smith,** Janice Evon 1952- *WhoBlA 92*
**Smith,** Janice Lynne 1952- *WhoMW 92*
**Smith,** Jared *DrAPF 91*
**Smith,** Jay Hamilton 1927- *AmMWSc 92*
**Smith,** Jay Lawrence 1954- *WhoFI 92*
**Smith,** Jay William 1951- *WhoFI 92*
**Smith,** Jean *WhoWest 92*
**Smith,** Jean Blair 1942- *AmMWSc 92*
**Smith,** Jean E 1932- *AmMWSc 92*
**Smith,** Jean Edward 1932- *WrDr 92*
**Smith,** Jean M. 1943- *WhoBlA 92*
**Smith,** Jean McAnulty 1943- *WhoMW 92*
**Smith,** Jedediah Strong 1798-1831 *BenetAL 91*
**Smith,** Jeff 1939- *CurBio 91 [port], News 91 [port], WrDr 92*
**Smith,** Jefferson Verne, III 1948- *WhoAmP 91*
**Smith,** Jefferson Verne, Jr 1925- *WhoAmP 91*
**Smith,** Jeffery Richard 1956- *WhoEnt 92*
**Smith,** Jeffrey Bordeaux 1926- *WhoAmL 92*
**Smith,** Jeffrey Drew 1922- *AmMWSc 92*
**Smith,** Jeffrey E. 1956- *WhoMW 92*
**Smith,** Jeffrey Hartman 1944- *WhoAmL 92*
**Smith,** Jeffrey Howard 1956- *WhoMW 92*
**Smith,** Jeffrey Lewis 1956- *WhoMW 92*
**Smith,** Jeffrey Michael 1947- *WhoAmL 92*
**Smith,** Jeffrey R. 1947- *WhoAmL 92*
**Smith,** Jeffrey Robert 1961- *WhoMW 92*
**Smith,** Jeffrey Wahlstrom 1958- *WhoFI 92*
**Smith,** Jeffry Alan 1943- *WhoWest 92*
**Smith,** Jenkyn Beverley 1931- *Who 92*
**Smith,** Jennifer C. 1952- *WhoBlA 92*
**Smith,** Jeraldine Williams 1946- *WhoBlA 92*
**Smith,** Jeremy Fox Eric 1928- *Who 92*
**Smith,** Jeremy James Russell 1947- *Who 92*
**Smith,** Jerome Allan 1940- *AmMWSc 92*
**Smith,** Jerome H 1936- *AmMWSc 92*
**Smith,** Jerome Paul 1946- *AmMWSc 92*
**Smith,** Jerry Edwin 1946- *WhoAmL 92, WhoAmP 91*
**Smith,** Jerry Eugene 1947- *WhoRel 92*
**Smith,** Jerry Howard 1944- *AmMWSc 92*
**Smith,** Jerry Joseph 1939- *AmMWSc 92*
**Smith,** Jerry L 1943- *WhoAmP 91*
**Smith,** Jerry Morgan 1934- *AmMWSc 92*
**Smith,** Jerry Neil 1935- *WhoEnt 92*
**Smith,** Jerry Warren 1942- *AmMWSc 92*
**Smith,** Jesse Graham, Jr 1928- *AmMWSc 92*
**Smith,** Jesse Owens 1942- *WhoBlA 92*
**Smith,** Jessie *ConAu 134, SmATA 67*
**Smith,** Jessie Carney *WhoBlA 92*
**Smith,** Jessie Mae 1937- *WhoAmP 91*
**Smith,** Jimmy 1925- *NewAmDM*
**Smith,** Joan 1938- *IntAu&W 91, WrDr 92*
**Smith,** Joan Hunter 1951- *WhoEnt 92*
**Smith,** Joann H 1934- *WhoAmP 91*
**Smith,** Joanne Hamlin 1954- *WhoBlA 92, WhoWest 92*
**Smith,** Joanne Kaye 1954- *WhoAmP 91*
**Smith,** Job Lewis 1827-1897 *BiInAmS*
**Smith,** Jock *Who 92*
**Smith,** Jock Michael 1948- *WhoBlA 92*
**Smith,** Joe 1884-1981 *FacFETw*
**Smith,** Joe Elliott 1938- *WhoBlA 92*
**Smith,** Joe K 1930- *AmMWSc 92*
**Smith,** Joe Lee 1936- *WhoBlA 92*
**Smith,** Joe M 1916- *AmMWSc 92*
**Smith,** Joe Nelson, Jr 1932- *AmMWSc 92*
**Smith,** Joel Franklin 1932- *WhoMW 92*
**Smith,** John 1580-1631 *BenetAL 91, RComAH*
**Smith,** John 1913- *Who 92*
**Smith,** John 1924- *ConPo 91, IntAu&W 91, WrDr 92*
**Smith,** John 1938- *AmMWSc 92, IntWW 91, Who 92*
**Smith,** John A. 1943- *WhoFI 92*
**Smith,** John Alfred 1938- *Who 92*
**Smith,** John Arthur 1937- *WhoBlA 92*
**Smith,** John Arthur 1941- *WhoAmP 91*
**Smith,** John Bernhard 1858-1912 *BiInAmS*
**Smith,** John Bryan 1942- *AmMWSc 92*
**Smith,** John Charles 1850- *BiInAmS*
**Smith,** John Charles 1942- *WhoAmL 92*
**Smith,** John Clay, Jr. 1942- *WhoAmL 92*
**Smith,** John Cole 1935- *AmMWSc 92*
**Smith,** John Cyril 1922- *Who 92*
**Smith,** John Derek 1924- *IntWW 91, Who 92*
**Smith,** John Drake, Jr. 1950- *WhoAmL 92*
**Smith,** John Edgar 1939- *AmMWSc 92*
**Smith,** John Edward 1924- *Who 92*
**Smith,** John Edward D. *Who 92*
**Smith,** John Edward L. *Who 92*
**Smith,** John Elvans 1929- *AmMWSc 92*
**Smith,** John F 1923- *AmMWSc 92*
**Smith,** John Francis, Jr. 1938- *IntWW 91, WhoFI 92*
**Smith,** John Frederick 1934- *Who 92*
**Smith,** John Gelston 1923- *WhoAmL 92*
**Smith,** John H 1923- *WhoAmP 91*
**Smith,** John Henry 1904- *AmMWSc 92*
**Smith,** John Henry 1937- *AmMWSc 92*
**Smith,** John Herbert 1918- *IntWW 91, Who 92*
**Smith,** John Hilary 1928- *Who 92*
**Smith,** John Holmes 1857-1919 *BiInAmS*
**Smith,** John Howard 1937- *AmMWSc 92*
**Smith,** John Kenneth N. *Who 92*
**Smith,** John Kerwin 1926- *WhoAmL 92*
**Smith,** John Lawrence 1818-1883 *BiInAmS*
**Smith,** John Lee, Jr. 1920- *WhoRel 92*
**Smith,** John Leslie, Jr 1924- *AmMWSc 92*
**Smith,** John Lindsay Eric 1923- *Who 92*
**Smith,** John M. *Who 92*
**Smith,** John M 1922- *AmMWSc 92*
**Smith,** John M. 1935- *WhoRel 92*
**Smith,** John Melvin 1937- *AmMWSc 92*
**Smith,** John Mitchell Melvin 1930- *Who 92*
**Smith,** John P. *Who 92*
**Smith,** John Paul 1948- *WhoAmP 91*
**Smith,** John Paul, Jr. 1949- *WhoMW 92*
**Smith,** John R 1941- *WhoAmP 91*
**Smith,** John Raye 1941- *WhoBlA 92*
**Smith,** John Robert 1940- *AmMWSc 92*
**Smith,** John Robert 1948- *AmMWSc 92*
**Smith,** John Roger B. *Who 92*
**Smith,** John Sam 1947- *WhoMW 92*
**Smith,** John Stafford 1750-1836 *NewAmDM*
**Smith,** John Thomas 1919- *WhoBlA 92*
**Smith,** John Thurmond 1925- *AmMWSc 92*
**Smith,** John W 1943- *AmMWSc 92*
**Smith,** John Wallace 1931- *WhoMW 92*
**Smith,** John William Hugh 1937- *WhoMW 92*
**Smith,** John William Patrick 1951- *Who 92*
**Smith,** John Wilson 1920- *Who 92*
**Smith,** John Wolfgang 1930- *AmMWSc 92*
**Smith,** Johnnie M. 1934- *WhoBlA 92*
**Smith,** Johnston *BenetAL 91*
**Smith,** Jonathan A. *Who 92*
**Smith,** Jonathan C. 1946- *WhoMW 92*
**Smith,** Jonathan Jeremy Berkeley 1940- *AmMWSc 92*
**Smith,** Jonathan Simon Christopher R. *Who 92*
**Smith,** Jordan *DrAPF 91*
**Smith,** Joscelyn E. 1918- *WhoBlA 92*
**Smith,** Josef Riley 1926- *AmMWSc 92*
**Smith,** Joseph 1805-1844 *BenetAL 91, RComAH*
**Smith,** Joseph, III 1832-1914 *RelLAm 91*
**Smith,** Joseph Benjamin 1928- *WhoEnt 92*
**Smith,** Joseph Collins 1928- *AmMWSc 92*
**Smith,** Joseph Donald 1943- *AmMWSc 92*
**Smith,** Joseph Edward 1925- *WhoBlA 92*
**Smith,** Joseph Edward 1938- *WhoBlA 92*
**Smith,** Joseph Emmitt 1938- *AmMWSc 92*
**Smith,** Joseph F *WhoAmP 91*
**Smith,** Joseph F. 1945- *WhoBlA 92*
**Smith,** Joseph Fielding, Jr. 1876-1972 *RelLAm 91*
**Smith,** Joseph Fielding, Sr. 1838-1918 *RelLAm 91*
**Smith,** Joseph H, Jr 1925- *AmMWSc 92*
**Smith,** Joseph Harold 1914- *AmMWSc 92*
**Smith,** Joseph James 1921- *AmMWSc 92*
**Smith,** Joseph Jay 1915- *AmMWSc 92*
**Smith,** Joseph LeConte, Jr 1929- *AmMWSc 92*
**Smith,** Joseph Lee 1929- *WhoMW 92*
**Smith,** Joseph P. *IntMPA 92*
**Smith,** Joseph Patrick 1951- *AmMWSc 92*
**Smith,** Joseph Phelan *WhoEnt 92*
**Smith,** Joseph Victor 1928- *AmMWSc 92, Who 92*
**Smith,** Joseph William Grenville 1930- *Who 92*
**Smith,** Josephine Reist 1929- *AmMWSc 92*
**Smith,** Joshua Isaac 1941- *WhoBlA 92*
**Smith,** Joshua L. 1934- *WhoBlA 92*
**Smith,** Juanita Jane 1923- *WhoBlA 92*
**Smith,** Juanita Smith 1927- *WhoBlA 92*
**Smith,** Judith Moore 1948- *WhoBlA 92*
**Smith,** Judith Terry 1940- *AmMWSc 92*
**Smith,** Judson Lord 1917- *WhoFI 92*
**Smith,** Judy Seriale 1953- *WhoAmP 91, WhoBlA 92*
**Smith,** Jules Louis 1947- *WhoAmL 92*
**Smith,** Julia Frances 1911-1989 *NewAmDM*
**Smith,** Julian Cleveland 1919- *AmMWSc 92*
**Smith,** Julie *IntAu&W 91*
**Smith,** Julie 1944- *WrDr 92*
**Smith,** Julie Leonard 1938- *WhoAmP 91*
**Smith,** Julious Perry, Jr. 1943- *WhoAmL 92*
**Smith,** Justin Wilson 1934- *WhoRel 92*
**Smith,** K. Clay 1937- *WhoFI 92*
**Smith,** Karen Ann 1958- *AmMWSc 92*
**Smith,** Karen Lynette 1962- *WhoBlA 92*
**Smith,** Karen Lynn 1944- *WhoEnt 92*
**Smith,** Karl Joseph 1943- *WhoWest 92*
**Smith,** Kate d1986 *LesBEnT 92*
**Smith,** Kate 1909-1986 *FacFETw*
**Smith,** Kathleen 1922- *AmMWSc 92*
**Smith,** Kathleen J. 1929- *WrDr 92*
**Smith,** Kathleen Susan 1950- *WhoAmL 92*
**Smith,** Kathy Ann 1944- *WhoAmP 91*
**Smith,** Kathy Ann 1951- *WhoEnt 92*
**Smith,** Kathy Jane 1952- *WhoRel 92*
**Smith,** Katrina Lynn 1958- *WhoWest 92*

**Smith**, Katrina Marita 1958- *WhoBlA 92*
**Smith**, Kay Nolte 1932- *IntAu&W 91, WrDr 92*
**Smith**, Keir 1950- *TwCPaSc*
**Smith**, Keith Davis 1930- *AmMWSc 92*
**Smith**, Keith Dryden, Jr. 1951- *WhoBlA 92*
**Smith**, Keith Fitzgerald 1964- *WhoWest 92*
**Smith**, Keith James 1937- *AmMWSc 92*
**Smith**, Keith Larue 1917- *WhoWest 92*
**Smith**, Keith Paul 1939- *WhoFI 92*
**Smith**, Kelley R 1946- *WhoAmP 91*
**Smith**, Kelly L 1951- *AmMWSc 92*
**Smith**, Kelvin Wayne 1962- *WhoRel 92*
**Smith**, Ken *DrAPF 91*
**Smith**, Ken 1938- *ConPo 91, IntAu&W 91, WrDr 92*
**Smith**, Kendall A 1942- *AmMWSc 92*
**Smith**, Kendall O 1928- *AmMWSc 92*
**Smith**, Kendric Charles 1926- *AmMWSc 92*
**Smith**, Kennan Taylor 1926- *AmMWSc 92*
**Smith**, Kenneth A 1936- *AmMWSc 92*
**Smith**, Kenneth Arnink 1947- *WhoRel 92*
**Smith**, Kenneth Avery 1941- *WhoWest 92*
**Smith**, Kenneth Bryant 1931- *WhoBlA 92, WhoRel 92*
**Smith**, Kenneth Carless 1932- *AmMWSc 92*
**Smith**, Kenneth Charles, Sr 1932- *WhoAmP 91*
**Smith**, Kenneth D, Jr 1956- *WhoAmP 91*
**Smith**, Kenneth Darin 1966- *WhoMW 92*
**Smith**, Kenneth Edward 1943- *AmMWSc 92*
**Smith**, Kenneth Edward 1949- *WhoRel 92*
**Smith**, Kenneth Edwin 1939- *WhoFI 92*
**Smith**, Kenneth George 1920- *Who 92*
**Smith**, Kenneth Graeme Stewart 1918- *Who 92*
**Smith**, Kenneth James 1948- *WhoWest 92*
**Smith**, Kenneth Judson, Jr 1930- *AmMWSc 92*
**Smith**, Kenneth L *WhoAmP 91*
**Smith**, Kenneth Larry 1941- *AmMWSc 92*
**Smith**, Kenneth Leon 1947- *WhoFI 92*
**Smith**, Kenneth Leroy 1931- *AmMWSc 92*
**Smith**, Kenneth McGregor 1923- *AmMWSc 92*
**Smith**, Kenneth Morris 1949- *WhoWest 92*
**Smith**, Kenneth R 1947- *WhoAmP 91*
**Smith**, Kenneth Rupert, Jr 1932- *AmMWSc 92*
**Smith**, Kenneth Thomas 1949- *AmMWSc 92*
**Smith**, Kent Ernest 1939- *WhoMW 92*
**Smith**, Kent Farrell 1935- *AmMWSc 92*
**Smith**, Kenyon Ray 1963- *WhoRel 92*
**Smith**, Kermit A 1928- *WhoAmP 91*
**Smith**, Kerry Clark 1935- *WhoAmL 92*
**Smith**, Kevin Alan 1954- *WhoWest 92*
**Smith**, Kevin Charles 1957- *WhoMW 92*
**Smith**, Kevin Harvey 1948- *WhoEnt 92*
**Smith**, Kevin L. *WhoBlA 92*
**Smith**, Kevin Leyon 1956- *WhoRel 92*
**Smith**, Kevin Malcolm 1942- *AmMWSc 92*
**Smith**, Kevin Neil 1964- *WhoRel 92*
**Smith**, Kimberly Gray 1948- *AmMWSc 92*
**Smith**, Kingsley Ward 1946- *Who 92*
**Smith**, Kirby Campbell 1940- *AmMWSc 92*
**Smith**, Kristine Jensen 1949- *WhoMW 92*
**Smith**, Kurtwood 1942- *IntMPA 92*
**Smith**, Kurtwood Larson 1943- *WhoEnt 92*
**Smith**, L Dennis *AmMWSc 92*
**Smith**, L Eugene 1921- *WhoAmP 91*
**Smith**, L H, Jr 1928- *AmMWSc 92*
**Smith**, L Neil *IntAu&W 91, WrDr 92*
**Smith**, Laadan Hart 1921- *WhoRel 92*
**Smith**, Lacey Baldwin 1922- *IntAu&W 91, WrDr 92*
**Smith**, Lafayette Kenneth 1947- *WhoBlA 92*
**Smith**, Lamar S. 1947- *AlmAP 92 [port]*
**Smith**, Lamar Seeligson 1947- *WhoAmP 91*
**Smith**, Lance 1950- *TwCPaSc*
**Smith**, Langdon G, Jr 1953- *WhoAmP 91*
**Smith**, Lani Kamiki 1934- *WhoEnt 92*
**Smith**, Larry *DrAPF 91*
**Smith**, Larry 1942- *AmMWSc 92*
**Smith**, Larry 1944- *AmMWSc 92*
**Smith**, Larry Dean 1939- *AmMWSc 92*
**Smith**, Larry Don 1947- *WhoRel 92*
**Smith**, Larry E *WhoAmP 91*
**Smith**, Larry Earl 1949- *WhoRel 92*
**Smith**, Larry Rae 1943- *WhoMW 92*
**Smith**, Larry Steven 1950- *WhoFI 92*
**Smith**, LaSalle, Sr. 1947- *WhoBlA 92*
**Smith**, Laura *Who 92*
**Smith**, Laura Lee Weisbrodt 1903- *AmMWSc 92*
**Smith**, Laura Whitlock 1931- *WhoAmP 91*
**Smith**, Lauren Ashley 1924- *WhoAmL 92, WhoFI 92, WhoMW 92*
**Smith**, Laurence Daniel 1950- *IntAu&W 91*
**Smith**, Laurence Roger 1939- *WhoFI 92*
**Smith**, Laurie 1964- *WhoRel 92*
**Smith**, Lawrence A., Jr. 1936- *WhoAmL 92*
**Smith**, Lawrence Delpre 1905- *Who 92*
**Smith**, Lawrence F 1938- *WhoIns 92*
**Smith**, Lawrence Hartley 1934- *WhoFI 92*
**Smith**, Lawrence Howard 1942- *WhoWest 92*
**Smith**, Lawrence Hubert 1930- *AmMWSc 92*
**Smith**, Lawrence J. *WhoRel 92*
**Smith**, Lawrence J. 1941- *AlmAP 92 [port], WhoAmP 91*
**Smith**, Lawrence John, Jr. 1947- *WhoBlA 92*
**Smith**, Lawrence Joseph *Who 92*
**Smith**, Lawrence Leighton 1936- *NewAmDM, WhoEnt 92*
**Smith**, Lawrence Olford, Jr. 1935- *WhoMW 92*
**Smith**, Lawrence Paul 1945- *WhoAmP 91*
**Smith**, Lawrence R. *DrAPF 91*
**Smith**, Lawrence Rackley 1932- *WhoMW 92*
**Smith**, Lawrence Reed 1964- *WhoFI 92*
**Smith**, Lawrence Roger Hines 1941- *Who 92*
**Smith**, Lawton Harcourt 1924- *AmMWSc 92*
**Smith**, Le Roi Matthew-Pierre, III 1946- *WhoWest 92*
**Smith**, Leah Johnson 1943- *WhoFI 92*
**Smith**, Lee *DrAPF 91*
**Smith**, Lee Arthur 1957- *WhoBlA 92*
**Smith**, Lee L. 1936- *WhoWest 92*
**Smith**, Lee Randall 1952- *WhoAmL 92*
**Smith**, Lehi Tingen 1927- *AmMWSc 92*
**Smith**, Leila Hentzen 1932- *WhoMW 92*
**Smith**, Leland C. 1925- *NewAmDM*
**Smith**, Leland Leroy 1926- *AmMWSc 92*
**Smith**, Leo Anthony 1940- *AmMWSc 92*
**Smith**, Leo Emmet 1927- *WhoAmL 92*
**Smith**, Leo Grant 1940- *WhoBlA 92*
**Smith**, Leon Arthur 1917- *WhoFI 92*
**Smith**, Leonard A *WhoAmP 91*
**Smith**, Leonard Bingley 1915- *WhoEnt 92*
**Smith**, Leonard Charles 1921- *AmMWSc 92*
**Smith**, Leonard Clinton Geoffrey 1944- *WhoIns 92*
**Smith**, Leonard Phillip 1960- *WhoBlA 92*
**Smith**, Leonard Ware 1938- *WhoAmL 92*
**Smith**, Leora Skolkin *DrAPF 91*
**Smith**, LeRoi Matthew-Pierre, III 1946- *WhoBlA 92*
**Smith**, Leroy H, Jr *AmMWSc 92*
**Smith**, LeRoy Spencer 1926- *WhoRel 92*
**Smith**, LeRoy Victor 1933- *WhoBlA 92*
**Smith**, Leslie Charles 1918- *Who 92*
**Smith**, Leslie E 1941- *AmMWSc 92*
**Smith**, Leslie Edward 1919- *IntWW 91*
**Smith**, Leslie Edward George 1919- *Who 92*
**Smith**, Leslie Garrett 1927- *AmMWSc 92*
**Smith**, Leslie Gene 1946- *WhoWest 92*
**Smith**, Leslie Jack 1939- *WhoFI 92*
**Smith**, Lester Martin 1919- *WhoEnt 92*
**Smith**, Leverett Ralph 1949- *AmMWSc 92*
**Smith**, Levering 1910- *AmMWSc 92, WhoWest 92*
**Smith**, Lew *IntAu&W 91X, TwCWW 91*
**Smith**, Lewis Dennis 1938- *AmMWSc 92*
**Smith**, Lewis Oliver, Jr 1922- *AmMWSc 92*
**Smith**, Lewis Spivey 1923- *WhoWest 92*
**Smith**, Lewis Taylor 1925- *AmMWSc 92*
**Smith**, Lewis Wilbert 1937- *AmMWSc 92*
**Smith**, Lila *WhoBlA 92*
**Smith**, Lillian 1897-1966 *BenetAL 91, FacFETw*
**Smith**, Linda *WhoAmP 91*
**Smith**, Linda Joyce 1940- *WhoMW 92*
**Smith**, Linda Kay 1959- *WhoFI 92*
**Smith**, Linda Sue 1946- *WhoMW 92*
**Smith**, Lisa Rexann 1959- *WhoMW 92*
**Smith**, Liz 1925- *ConTFT 9*
**Smith**, Llewellyn 1944- *Who 92*
**Smith**, Lloyd Barnaby 1945- *Who 92*
**Smith**, Lloyd Bruce 1920- *IntWW 91*
**Smith**, Lloyd Hollingworth, Jr 1924- *AmMWSc 92*
**Smith**, Lloyd Muir 1917- *AmMWSc 92*
**Smith**, Lloyd P 1903- *AmMWSc 92*
**Smith**, Logan Pearsall 1865-1946 *BenetAL 91*
**Smith**, Lois Ann 1941- *WhoMW 92*
**Smith**, Lois Arlene *WhoEnt 92*
**Smith**, Lois Eudora 1903- *WhoMW 92*
**Smith**, Lon A 1939- *WhoIns 92*
**Smith**, Lonnie 1955- *WhoBlA 92*
**Smith**, Lonnie Max 1944- *WhoFI 92*
**Smith**, Lora Lee 1953- *WhoRel 92*
**Smith**, Loren Allan 1944- *WhoAmL 92*
**Smith**, Lorraine Catherine 1931- *AmMWSc 92*
**Smith**, Louis 1934- *WhoWest 92*
**Smith**, Louis 1939- *WhoBlA 92*
**Smith**, Louis C 1937- *AmMWSc 92*
**Smith**, Louis Charles 1918- *AmMWSc 92*
**Smith**, Louis De Spain 1910- *AmMWSc 92*
**Smith**, Louis Livingston 1925- *AmMWSc 92*
**Smith**, Louis M, Jr 1937- *WhoIns 92*
**Smith**, Louise Eileen *WhoWest 92*
**Smith**, Lowell *WhoEnt 92*
**Smith**, Lowell R 1933- *AmMWSc 92*
**Smith**, Lowell Scott 1950- *AmMWSc 92*
**Smith**, Lucian Anderson 1910- *AmMWSc 92*
**Smith**, Lucie Wilmot 1861-1888 *NotBlAW 92*
**Smith**, Lucius Skinner, III 1919- *WhoMW 92*
**Smith**, Luther Edward, Jr. 1947- *WhoBlA 92*
**Smith**, Luther Michael 1948- *AmMWSc 92*
**Smith**, Luther W 1932- *AmMWSc 92*
**Smith**, Lyle W 1920- *AmMWSc 92*
**Smith**, Lynn Howard 1936- *WhoMW 92*
**Smith**, Lynn Stanford 1951- *WhoBlA 92*
**Smith**, Lynwood S 1928- *AmMWSc 92*
**Smith**, Lynwood Stephen 1928- *WhoWest 92*
**Smith**, M. Frances 1927- *WhoWest 92*
**Smith**, M Susan 1942- *AmMWSc 92*
**Smith**, Maggie 1934- *FacFETw, IntMPA 92, Who 92, WhoEnt 92*
**Smith**, Maggie Natalie 1934- *IntWW 91*
**Smith**, Malcolm 1919- *AmMWSc 92*
**Smith**, Malcolm Andrew F. *Who 92*
**Smith**, Malcolm Crawford, Jr 1936- *AmMWSc 92*
**Smith**, Malcolm Greville 1941- *WhoWest 92*
**Smith**, Malcolm Sommerville 1933- *WhoEnt 92*
**Smith**, Mamie 1883-1946 *NewAmDM, NotBlAW 92*
**Smith**, Manis James, Jr 1940- *AmMWSc 92*
**Smith**, Marc Taintor 1952- *WhoFI 92*
**Smith**, Marcia Jean 1947- *WhoFI 92*
**Smith**, Marcia Sue 1951- *AmMWSc 92*
**Smith**, Margaret *WhoAmP 91, WhoMW 92*
**Smith**, Margaret Bayard 1778-1844 *BenetAL 91*
**Smith**, Margaret Chase 1897- *IntWW 91, WhoAmP 91*
**Smith**, Margaret Court 1942- *FacFETw*
**Smith**, Margaret Madeline Chase 1897- *AmPolLe*
**Smith**, Margot 1918- *Who 92*
**Smith**, Marian Jose 1915- *AmMWSc 92*
**Smith**, Marianne Freundlich 1922- *AmMWSc 92*
**Smith**, Marie Edmonds 1927- *WhoFI 92*
**Smith**, Marie Evans 1928- *WhoBlA 92*
**Smith**, Marietta Culbreath 1933- *WhoBlA 92*
**Smith**, Marilyn Noeltner 1933- *WhoWest 92*
**Smith**, Marilyn Viola 1934- *WhoRel 92*
**Smith**, Marina Valenzuela 1932- *WhoWest 92*
**Smith**, Marion Bush, Jr 1929- *AmMWSc 92*
**Smith**, Marion Edmonds 1926- *AmMWSc 92*
**Smith**, Marion L. 1901- *WhoBlA 92*
**Smith**, Marion L 1923- *AmMWSc 92*
**Smith**, Marjorie Wiederspan Betzer 1917- *IntAu&W 91*
**Smith**, Mark *DrAPF 91*
**Smith**, Mark 1935- *WrDr 92*
**Smith**, Mark Allington 1948- *WhoRel 92*
**Smith**, Mark Andrew 1947- *AmMWSc 92*
**Smith**, Mark Anthony, III 1947- *WhoAmL 92*
**Smith**, Mark Barnet 1917- *Who 92*
**Smith**, Mark Hudson 1961- *WhoAmL 92*
**Smith**, Mark K 1928- *AmMWSc 92*
**Smith**, Mark Lee 1957- *WhoWest 92*
**Smith**, Mark Leroy 1966- *WhoFI 92*
**Smith**, Mark Richard 1935- *IntAu&W 91*
**Smith**, Mark Roy 1959- *WhoAmL 92*
**Smith**, Mark Stephen *AmMWSc 92*
**Smith**, Mark Townsend 1959- *WhoAmL 92*
**Smith**, Marlyn Stansbury 1942- *WhoBlA 92*
**Smith**, Marshall Savidge 1937- *WhoWest 92*
**Smith**, Martha Kathleen 1944- *AmMWSc 92*
**Smith**, Martin Bristow 1916- *AmMWSc 92*
**Smith**, Martin Cruz 1942- *BenetAL 91, IntAu&W 91, IntWW 91, WrDr 92*
**Smith**, Martin John 1957- *WhoAmP 91*
**Smith**, Martin Travis *WhoAmP 91*
**Smith**, Martyn Thomas 1955- *AmMWSc 92*
**Smith**, Marvin Artell 1936- *AmMWSc 92*
**Smith**, Marvin E *WhoAmP 91*
**Smith**, Marvin LaVerne 1952- *WhoRel 92*
**Smith**, Marvin M. 1952- *WhoAmL 92*
**Smith**, Mary Alice 1941- *WhoEnt 92*
**Smith**, Mary Ann *WhoAmP 91*
**Smith**, Mary Ann Harvey 1940- *AmMWSc 92*
**Smith**, Mary Bunting 1910- *AmMWSc 92*
**Smith**, Mary Carter 1919- *WhoBlA 92*
**Smith**, Mary Levi 1936- *WhoBlA 92*
**Smith**, Mary Louise 1914- *WhoAmP 91*
**Smith**, Mary Louise 1935- *WhoFI 92, WhoMW 92*
**Smith**, Mary Lynn 1965- *WhoWest 92*
**Smith**, Mary Pearl 1937- *WhoWest 92*
**Smith**, Mary Perkins 1949- *WhoFI 92*
**Smith**, Marzell 1936- *WhoBlA 92*
**Smith**, Mason *DrAPF 91*
**Smith**, Matilda H d1910 *BiInAmS*
**Smith**, Matthew 1879-1959 *TwCPaSc*
**Smith**, Matthew J 1941- *WhoAmP 91*
**Smith**, Maura 1926- *WhoRel 92*
**Smith**, Maureen Hamm 1942- *WhoAmL 92*
**Smith**, Maureen McBride 1952- *WhoWest 92*
**Smith**, Maurice 1939- *IntMPA 92*
**Smith**, Maurice George 1915- *Who 92*
**Smith**, Maurice John Vernon 1929- *AmMWSc 92*
**Smith**, Maurice Vernon 1920- *AmMWSc 92*
**Smith**, Max Eugene 1940- *WhoMW 92*
**Smith**, Maxine A *WhoAmP 91*
**Smith**, Maxine Atkins *WhoBlA 92*
**Smith**, Maxine Steward 1921- *WhoAmL 92*
**Smith**, Maynard Dwight 1921- *WhoRel 92*
**Smith**, Maynard E 1916- *AmMWSc 92*
**Smith**, Melancton 1744-1798 *BlkwEAR*
**Smith**, Melissa Ann 1962- *WhoBlA 92*
**Smith**, Melvin *WhoAmP 91*
**Smith**, Melvin 1943- *WhoMW 92*
**Smith**, Melvin I 1924- *AmMWSc 92*
**Smith**, Melvin Kenneth 1952- *Who 92*
**Smith**, Meredith Ford *AmMWSc 92*
**Smith**, Merilyn Roberta 1933- *WhoMW 92*
**Smith**, Michael *IntAu&W 91, Who 92*
**Smith**, Michael 1932- *AmMWSc 92, IntWW 91, Who 92*
**Smith**, Michael 1935- *WrDr 92*
**Smith**, Michael 1942- *WrDr 92*
**Smith**, Michael A 1944- *AmMWSc 92*
**Smith**, Michael Adger 1957- *WhoRel 92*
**Smith**, Michael Alan 1947- *WhoFI 92*
**Smith**, Michael Atwol 1954- *WhoRel 92*
**Smith**, Michael Claude 1949- *AmMWSc 92*
**Smith**, Michael Dennis 1961- *WhoEnt 92*
**Smith**, Michael E. 1935- *WhoAmL 92*
**Smith**, Michael Edward 1956- *WhoAmP 91*
**Smith**, Michael Edward C. *Who 92*
**Smith**, Michael G. 1921- *Who 92*
**Smith**, Michael Gerard A. *Who 92*
**Smith**, Michael Henry 1959- *WhoRel 92*
**Smith**, Michael Howard 1938- *AmMWSc 92*
**Smith**, Michael J 1945-1986 *FacFETw*
**Smith**, Michael James 1945- *AmMWSc 92*
**Smith**, Michael Joseph 1939- *AmMWSc 92*
**Smith**, Michael K. *Who 92*
**Smith**, Michael Kavanagh 1949- *AmMWSc 92*
**Smith**, Michael Lee 1953- *WhoMW 92, WhoRel 92*
**Smith**, Michael Lew *AmMWSc 92*
**Smith**, Michael Lloyd 1955- *WhoAmL 92*
**Smith**, Michael Morgan 1948- *WhoMW 92*
**Smith**, Michael R 1945- *AmMWSc 92*
**Smith**, Michael Robert 1947- *WhoWest 92*
**Smith**, Michael Sidney 1934- *WhoEnt 92*
**Smith**, Michael Steven 1956- *WhoWest 92*
**Smith**, Mildred B. 1935- *WhoBlA 92*
**Smith**, Millard, Jr. 1948- *WhoBlA 92*
**Smith**, Milton Curtis 1937- *WhoAmL 92*
**Smith**, Milton Louis 1939- *AmMWSc 92*
**Smith**, Milton Reynolds 1934- *AmMWSc 92*
**Smith**, Mitchell Cameron 1955- *WhoAmL 92*
**Smith**, Monica LaVonne 1966- *WhoBlA 92*
**Smith**, Mont James, Jr. 1946- *WhoWest 92*
**Smith**, Monte Warren 1953- *WhoFI 92*
**Smith**, Morris Leslie 1933- *WhoBlA 92*
**Smith**, Morris Wade 1938- *AmMWSc 92*
**Smith**, Morton d1991 *NewYTBS 91 [port]*
**Smith**, Morton 1915- *IntAu&W 91, WrDr 92*
**Smith**, Morton 1915-1991 *ConAu 134*
**Smith**, Morton Alan 1931- *WhoAmL 92*
**Smith**, Morton Howison 1923- *WhoRel 92*
**Smith**, Murray Robert 1941- *IntWW 91*
**Smith**, Murray Thomas 1939- *WhoFI 92, WhoMW 92*
**Smith**, Myrl Elden 1938- *WhoRel 92*
**Smith**, N. Clark 1877-1933 *NewAmDM*
**Smith**, N. V. *ConAu 133*

**Smith,** Nancy Hohendorf 1943- *WhoFI 92, WhoMW 92*
**Smith,** Nancy Jo 1955- *WhoWest 92*
**Smith,** Nancy Kay 1944- *WhoEnt 92*
**Smith,** Naomi Ruth 1958- *WhoMW 92*
**Smith,** Nat E 1922- *AmMWSc 92*
**Smith,** Nathan 1762-1829 *BiInAmS*
**Smith,** Nathan Elbert 1936- *AmMWSc 92*
**Smith,** Nathan James 1921- *AmMWSc 92*
**Smith,** Nathan Lewis, III 1943- *AmMWSc 92*
**Smith,** Nathan McKay 1935- *AmMWSc 92, WhoWest 92*
**Smith,** Nathaniel 1929- *WhoBlA 92*
**Smith,** Nathaniel, Jr. *WhoBlA 92*
**Smith,** Neal 1920- *AlmAP 92 [port], WhoAmP 91*
**Smith,** Neal A 1919- *AmMWSc 92*
**Smith,** Neal Edward 1920- *WhoMW 92*
**Smith,** Ned Alan 1928- *WhoMW 92*
**Smith,** Ned Allan 1940- *AmMWSc 92*
**Smith,** Ned Philip 1942- *AmMWSc 92*
**Smith,** Ned R *WhoAmP 91*
**Smith,** Neil *Who 92*
**Smith,** Neil 1939- *ConAu 133*
**Smith,** Neil 1966- *WhoBlA 92*
**Smith,** Neilson Voyne 1939- *Who 92*
**Smith,** Nell W 1929- *WhoAmP 91*
**Smith,** Nellie J. 1932- *WhoBlA 92*
**Smith,** Nels Jensen 1939- *WhoAmP 91*
**Smith,** Nelson S, Jr 1929- *AmMWSc 92*
**Smith,** Neville Vincent 1942- *AmMWSc 92*
**Smith,** Newman Donald 1936- *WhoFI 92*
**Smith,** Nick 1934- *WhoMW 92*
**Smith,** Nick H 1934- *WhoAmP 91*
**Smith,** Nico J. 1929- *IntWW 91*
**Smith,** Nora Archibald 1859?-1934 *BenetAL 91*
**Smith,** Norma Guest 1925- *WhoWest 92*
**Smith,** Norman B 1927- *AmMWSc 92*
**Smith,** Norman Brian 1928- *IntWW 91, Who 92*
**Smith,** Norman Cutler 1915- *AmMWSc 92*
**Smith,** Norman Dwight 1941- *AmMWSc 92*
**Smith,** Norman Edward Mace 1914- *WrDr 92*
**Smith,** Norman Frederick 1920- *WhoAmP 91*
**Smith,** Norman Henry 1925- *IntWW 91*
**Smith,** Norman Jack 1936- *Who 92*
**Smith,** Norman John David 1931- *Who 92*
**Smith,** Norman Obed 1914- *AmMWSc 92*
**Smith,** Norman Raymond 1944- *WhoBlA 92*
**Smith,** Norman Sherrill 1932- *AmMWSc 92*
**Smith,** Norman T. 1935- *WhoAmL 92*
**Smith,** Norman Ty 1932- *AmMWSc 92*
**Smith,** Olin Dail 1931- *AmMWSc 92*
**Smith,** Oliver 1918- *IntWW 91, WhoEnt 92*
**Smith,** Oliver Hugh 1929- *AmMWSc 92*
**Smith,** Omar Ewing, Jr 1931- *AmMWSc 92*
**Smith,** Ora 1900- *AmMWSc 92*
**Smith,** Ora Kingsley 1927- *AmMWSc 92*
**Smith,** Orin Robert 1935- *IntWW 91, WhoFI 92*
**Smith,** Orrin Ernest 1935- *AmMWSc 92*
**Smith,** Orville Auverne 1927- *AmMWSc 92*
**Smith,** Oscar Samuel, Jr. 1929- *WhoBlA 92*
**Smith,** Oswald Garrison 1915- *WhoBlA 92*
**Smith,** Oswald Jeffery 1889-1986 *RelLAm 91*
**Smith,** Otis Benton, Jr. 1939- *WhoBlA 92*
**Smith,** Otis David 1831-1905 *BiInAmS*
**Smith,** Otis Fitzgerald 1964- *WhoBlA 92*
**Smith,** Otis M. 1922- *WhoBlA 92*
**Smith,** Otis Milton 1922- *WhoAmP 91*
**Smith,** Otrie 1936- *WhoBlA 92*
**Smith,** Otto J M 1917- *AmMWSc 92, WhoWest 92*
**Smith,** Owen Chabot 1941- *WhoAmL 92*
**Smith,** Owen Telfair *WhoAmL 92*
**Smith,** Ozzie 1954- *WhoBlA 92, WhoMW 92*
**Smith,** P R *WhoAmP 91*
**Smith,** P Scott 1922- *AmMWSc 92*
**Smith,** Page 1917- *IntAu&W 91, WrDr 92*
**Smith,** Pat Everett 1930- *WhoFI 92*
**Smith,** Patricia *WhoWest 92*
**Smith,** Patricia A. 1950- *WhoAmL 92*
**Smith,** Patricia Ann 1933- *WhoWest 92*
**Smith,** Patricia Ann 1939- *WhoRel 92*
**Smith,** Patricia Anne 1935- *AmMWSc 92*
**Smith,** Patricia Elaine Bostdorff 1949- *WhoMW 92*
**Smith,** Patricia G. 1947- *WhoBlA 92*
**Smith,** Patricia Jacquline 1944- *WhoWest 92*
**Smith,** Patricia Jean 1947- *WhoFI 92*
**Smith,** Patricia Kay 1959- *WhoMW 92*
**Smith,** Patricia Lahr *WhoAmP 91*
**Smith,** Patricia Lee 1946- *AmMWSc 92*
**Smith,** Patrick D. *DrAPF 91*
**Smith,** Patrick Edmund 1937- *WhoEnt 92*
**Smith,** Patrick Stephen 1959- *WhoAmL 92*
**Smith,** Patrick Wells 1953- *WhoWest 92*
**Smith,** Patrick William 1962- *WhoEnt 92*
**Smith,** Patti *DrAPF 91*
**Smith,** Patti 1946- *WhoEnt 92*
**Smith,** Paul 1935- *WhoBlA 92*
**Smith,** Paul Aiken 1934- *AmMWSc 92*
**Smith,** Paul Aikin 1934- *WhoAmP 91, WhoMW 92*
**Smith,** Paul Alexander 1949- *WhoWest 92*
**Smith,** Paul B. 1946- *IntWW 91*
**Smith,** Paul Bernard 1931- *WhoBlA 92*
**Smith,** Paul Clay 1934- *AmMWSc 92*
**Smith,** Paul Daniel 1947- *WhoMW 92*
**Smith,** Paul Dennis 1942- *AmMWSc 92*
**Smith,** Paul E *WhoAmP 91*
**Smith,** Paul E, Jr 1923- *AmMWSc 92*
**Smith,** Paul Edward 1933- *AmMWSc 92*
**Smith,** Paul Edward 1961- *WhoRel 92*
**Smith,** Paul Francis 1927- *AmMWSc 92*
**Smith,** Paul Frederick 1916- *AmMWSc 92*
**Smith,** Paul Gordon 1915- *AmMWSc 92*
**Smith,** Paul Henry 1952- *WhoAmP 91*
**Smith,** Paul Howard 1924- *AmMWSc 92*
**Smith,** Paul John 1943- *AmMWSc 92*
**Smith,** Paul Kent 1935- *AmMWSc 92*
**Smith,** Paul Kevin 1958- *WhoAmL 92*
**Smith,** Paul L 1950- *AmMWSc 92*
**Smith,** Paul Lester 1935- *WhoFI 92*
**Smith,** Paul Letton, Jr 1932- *AmMWSc 92*
**Smith,** Paul M., Jr. 1920- *WhoBlA 92*
**Smith,** Paul Richard 1937- *WhoRel 92*
**Smith,** Paul Russell 1937- *WhoEnt 92*
**Smith,** Paul S 1927- *WhoAmP 91*
**Smith,** Paul Vergon, Jr 1921- *AmMWSc 92*
**Smith,** Paula Beth 1956- *AmMWSc 92*
**Smith,** Paula Suzanne 1950- *WhoWest 92*
**Smith,** Pearlena W. 1916- *WhoBlA 92*
**Smith,** Percival *Who 92*
**Smith,** Percy Leighton 1919- *AmMWSc 92*
**Smith,** Perrin Gary 1912- *AmMWSc 92*
**Smith,** Perry Anderson, III 1934- *WhoBlA 92, WhoRel 92*
**Smith,** Perry Scott 1962- *WhoMW 92*
**Smith,** Peter 1924- *AmMWSc 92*
**Smith,** Peter 1926- *Who 92*
**Smith,** Peter 1945- *WhoAmP 91*
**Smith,** Peter A S 1920- *AmMWSc 92*
**Smith,** Peter Alexander Charles 1920- *Who 92*
**Smith,** Peter Bennett 1934- *WhoFI 92*
**Smith,** Peter Blaise *AmMWSc 92*
**Smith,** Peter Bruce 1944- *Who 92*
**Smith,** Peter Charles Horstead 1940- *IntAu&W 91, WrDr 92*
**Smith,** Peter Clarke 1958- *WhoAmP 91*
**Smith,** Peter Claudius G. *Who 92*
**Smith,** Peter David 1938- *AmMWSc 92*
**Smith,** Peter George 1954- *WhoFI 92*
**Smith,** Peter Graham 1929- *Who 92*
**Smith,** Peter J. *Who 92*
**Smith,** Peter J. 1931- *WrDr 92*
**Smith,** Peter John 1936- *Who 92*
**Smith,** Peter Lloyd 1944- *AmMWSc 92*
**Smith,** Peter Mario 1950- *WhoAmL 92*
**Smith,** Peter Norris 1949- *WhoEnt 92*
**Smith,** Peter Vivian Henworth 1928- *Who 92*
**Smith,** Peter Walker 1923- *WhoFI 92*
**Smith,** Peter William 1936- *WhoMW 92*
**Smith,** Peter William E 1937- *AmMWSc 92*
**Smith,** Peter Wilson 1938- *WhoEnt 92, WhoMW 92*
**Smith,** Philip 1913- *Who 92*
**Smith,** Philip Alan 1938- *WhoRel 92*
**Smith,** Philip Edward 1916- *AmMWSc 92*
**Smith,** Philip G 1946- *WhoAmP 91*
**Smith,** Philip Gene 1928- *WhoBlA 92*
**Smith,** Philip George 1911- *Who 92*
**Smith,** Philip Hardy 1931- *WhoAmP 91*
**Smith,** Philip Jones 1941- *WhoAmL 92*
**Smith,** Philip Lees 1945- *AmMWSc 92*
**Smith,** Philip Meek 1932- *WhoBlA 92*
**Smith,** Philip Wesley 1946- *AmMWSc 92*
**Smith,** Phillip Dale 1952- *WhoWest 92*
**Smith,** Phillip Doyle 1946- *AmMWSc 92*
**Smith,** Phillip Harden 1936- *WhoAmL 92*
**Smith,** Phillip J 1938- *AmMWSc 92, WhoMW 92*
**Smith,** Phillip M. 1937- *WhoBlA 92*
**Smith,** Phyllis Joy 1944- *WhoEnt 92*
**Smith,** Pierce Reiland 1943- *WhoFI 92*
**Smith,** Pierre Frank 1920- *AmMWSc 92*
**Smith,** Pine Top 1904-1929 *NewAmDM*
**Smith,** Preston Gibson 1941- *WhoFI 92*
**Smith,** Priscilla Agnes 1941- *WhoHisp 92*
**Smith,** Quentin P. 1918- *WhoBlA 92*
**Smith,** Quentin Paige, Jr. 1951- *WhoBlA 92*
**Smith,** Quentin T. 1937- *WhoBlA 92*
**Smith,** Quenton Terrill 1929- *AmMWSc 92*
**Smith,** Queon Paul 1935- *WhoRel 92*
**Smith,** R.E. *DrAPF 91*
**Smith,** R Elton *ScFEYrs*
**Smith,** R. Evan 1941- *WhoAmL 92*
**Smith,** R Hal 1917- *WhoAmP 91*
**Smith,** R Jay 1922- *AmMWSc 92*
**Smith,** R L 1924- *AmMWSc 92*
**Smith,** R Lowell 1940- *AmMWSc 92*
**Smith,** R.T. *DrAPF 91*
**Smith,** Rachel Norcom 1925- *WhoBlA 92*
**Smith,** Ralph Bernard 1939- *IntAu&W 91, WrDr 92*
**Smith,** Ralph Carlisle 1910- *AmMWSc 92*
**Smith,** Ralph E 1923- *AmMWSc 92*
**Smith,** Ralph E 1940- *AmMWSc 92*
**Smith,** Ralph E. K. T. *Who 92*
**Smith,** Ralph Earl 1940- *WhoWest 92*
**Smith,** Ralph Edward 1953- *WhoMW 92*
**Smith,** Ralph Emerson 1916- *AmMWSc 92*
**Smith,** Ralph Frederick 1950- *WhoMW 92*
**Smith,** Ralph G 1920- *AmMWSc 92*
**Smith,** Ralph Grafton 1900- *AmMWSc 92*
**Smith,** Ralph Ingram 1916- *AmMWSc 92*
**Smith,** Ralph J 1916- *AmMWSc 92*
**Smith,** Ralph Lee 1927- *WrDr 92*
**Smith,** Ralph Maynard 1904-1964 *TwCPaSc*
**Smith,** Ralph Morgan 1931- *WhoRel 92*
**Smith,** Randal Fane 1961- *WhoRel 92*
**Smith,** Randall 1950- *WhoAmL 92*
**Smith,** Randall Gene 1947- *WhoWest 92*
**Smith,** Randall Morris 1958- *WhoRel 92*
**Smith,** Raoul Normand 1938- *AmMWSc 92*
**Smith,** Raoul P 1935- *WhoAmP 91*
**Smith,** Raphael Ford 1933- *AmMWSc 92*
**Smith,** Ray 1949- *TwCPaSc*
**Smith,** Ray 1962- *WhoRel 92*
**Smith,** Ray Fred 1919- *AmMWSc 92, IntWW 91*
**Smith,** Ray S, Jr *WhoAmP 91*
**Smith,** Ray William 1952- *WhoRel 92*
**Smith,** Raymond Calvin 1934- *AmMWSc 92*
**Smith,** Raymond Edward 1932- *WhoWest 92*
**Smith,** Raymond Everett 1932- *WhoRel 92*
**Smith,** Raymond Gordon *Who 92*
**Smith,** Raymond Horace 1917- *Who 92*
**Smith,** Raymond James 1924- *AmMWSc 92*
**Smith,** Raymond V 1919- *AmMWSc 92*
**Smith,** Raymond Victor 1926- *WhoFI 92, WhoWest 92*
**Smith,** Raymond W. 1937- *WhoFI 92*
**Smith,** Rebecca Anstine 1955- *WhoEnt 92*
**Smith,** Rebecca Beach 1949- *WhoAmL 92*
**Smith,** Red *ConAu 36NR*
**Smith,** Red 1905-1982 *BenetAL 91*
**Smith,** Reed Williams 1949- *WhoEnt 92*
**Smith,** Regan Granville 1938- *WhoMW 92*
**Smith,** Reggie 1945- *WhoBlA 92*
**Smith,** Reginald Brian 1931- *AmMWSc 92*
**Smith,** Reginald D. 1918- *WhoBlA 92*
**Smith,** Reginald J *WhoAmP 91*
**Smith,** Reginald James 1953- *WhoMW 92*
**Smith,** Reginald Verdon *Who 92*
**Smith,** Reid Garfield 1946- *AmMWSc 92*
**Smith,** Reilly Richard 1953- *WhoRel 92*
**Smith,** Reliford Orvin, Jr. 1945- *WhoAmL 92*
**Smith,** Renee Yvonne 1957- *WhoAmL 92*
**Smith,** Reuben R, Jr *WhoAmP 91*
**Smith,** Rex 1957- *WhoAmP 91*
**Smith,** Rex L 1929- *AmMWSc 92*
**Smith,** Rhea Dawn 1951- *WhoMW 92*
**Smith,** Richard *Who 92*
**Smith,** Richard 1931- *IntWW 91*
**Smith,** Richard 1938- *WhoAmP 91*
**Smith,** Richard A 1932- *AmMWSc 92*
**Smith,** Richard Alan 1940- *AmMWSc 92*
**Smith,** Richard Alfred 1932- *WhoBlA 92*
**Smith,** Richard Andrew 1950- *AmMWSc 92*
**Smith,** Richard Avery 1924- *AmMWSc 92*
**Smith,** Richard Barrie 1934- *AmMWSc 92*
**Smith,** Richard Carper 1938- *AmMWSc 92*
**Smith,** Richard Cecil 1940- *AmMWSc 92*
**Smith,** Richard Chandler 1913- *AmMWSc 92*
**Smith,** Richard Clark 1927- *AmMWSc 92*
**Smith,** Richard Cory 1960- *WhoMW 92*
**Smith,** Richard Craig 1949- *WhoFI 92*
**Smith,** Richard D. 1954- *WhoWest 92*
**Smith,** Richard Dale 1949- *AmMWSc 92*
**Smith,** Richard Dean 1922- *AmMWSc 92*
**Smith,** Richard Donald 1928- *WhoIns 92*
**Smith,** Richard Elbridge 1932- *AmMWSc 92*
**Smith,** Richard Emerson 1922- *WhoEnt 92*
**Smith,** Richard Frederick 1929- *AmMWSc 92*
**Smith,** Richard G 1937- *AmMWSc 92*
**Smith,** Richard Graeme 1945- *WhoRel 92*
**Smith,** Richard H. S. *Who 92*
**Smith,** Richard Harding 1950- *AmMWSc 92*
**Smith,** Richard Harrison 1920- *AmMWSc 92*
**Smith,** Richard Harvey 1923- *WhoAmP 91*
**Smith,** Richard Hilbert Edwin, II 1954- *WhoFI 92*
**Smith,** Richard Howard 1927- *WhoFI 92*
**Smith,** Richard James 1947- *AmMWSc 92*
**Smith,** Richard Jay 1948- *AmMWSc 92, WhoMW 92*
**Smith,** Richard John 1934- *Who 92*
**Smith,** Richard Joseph 1942- *WhoWest 92*
**Smith,** Richard Joseph 1950- *WhoFI 92*
**Smith,** Richard Lamar 1952- *WhoRel 92*
**Smith,** Richard Lawrence 1933- *WhoWest 92*
**Smith,** Richard Lawrence 1939- *AmMWSc 92*
**Smith,** Richard Lee 1950- *WhoEnt 92*
**Smith,** Richard Lloyd 1945- *AmMWSc 92*
**Smith,** Richard Lynn 1951- *WhoRel 92*
**Smith,** Richard Maybury H. *Who 92*
**Smith,** Richard Merrill 1942- *AmMWSc 92*
**Smith,** Richard Michael 1946- *Who 92*
**Smith,** Richard Neilson 1918- *AmMWSc 92*
**Smith,** Richard P. *Who 92*
**Smith,** Richard Paul 1943- *AmMWSc 92, WhoWest 92*
**Smith,** Richard Pearson 1926- *AmMWSc 92*
**Smith,** Richard Penn 1799-1854 *BenetAL 91*
**Smith,** Richard R 1936- *AmMWSc 92*
**Smith,** Richard R. V. *Who 92*
**Smith,** Richard Racine 1928- *WhoFI 92*
**Smith,** Richard Robert L. *Who 92*
**Smith,** Richard S, Jr 1930- *AmMWSc 92*
**Smith,** Richard Scott 1939- *AmMWSc 92*
**Smith,** Richard Selby 1914- *Who 92*
**Smith,** Richard Sidney 1933- *AmMWSc 92*
**Smith,** Richard Sydney William 1952- *Who 92*
**Smith,** Richard Thomas 1924- *AmMWSc 92*
**Smith,** Richard Thomas 1925- *AmMWSc 92*
**Smith,** Richard Wendell 1912- *WhoAmL 92*
**Smith,** Richard Yeadon, III 1943- *WhoFI 92*
**Smith,** Richardson Culver 1948- *WhoEnt 92*
**Smith,** Richey 1933- *WhoFI 92, WhoMW 92*
**Smith,** Rick *DrAPF 91*
**Smith,** Rick 1942- *WhoAmP 91*
**Smith,** Rick A. 1948- *WhoMW 92*
**Smith,** Ricky James 1958- *WhoMW 92*
**Smith,** Rita 1932- *LiExTwC*
**Smith,** Robbie 1948- *WhoBlA 92*
**Smith,** Robert 1757-1842 *AmPolLe*
**Smith,** Robert 1921- *AmMWSc 92*
**Smith,** Robert 1937- *WhoBlA 92*
**Smith,** Robert, Jr. 1951- *WhoBlA 92*
**Smith,** Robert Alan 1939- *AmMWSc 92*
**Smith,** Robert Allen 1936- *WhoFI 92*
**Smith,** Robert Baer 1938- *AmMWSc 92*
**Smith,** Robert Bernard, Jr. 1959- *WhoAmL 92*
**Smith,** Robert Blakeman 1949- *WhoAmL 92*
**Smith,** Robert Bruce 1937- *AmMWSc 92*
**Smith,** Robert Burns 1929- *WhoMW 92*
**Smith,** Robert C 1932- *AmMWSc 92*
**Smith,** Robert Carr 1935- *Who 92*
**Smith,** Robert Charles 1947- *WhoBlA 92*
**Smith,** Robert Clinton 1932- *AmMWSc 92*
**Smith,** Robert Clinton 1941- *IntWW 91, WhoAmP 91*
**Smith,** Robert Courtney 1927- *IntWW 91, Who 92*
**Smith,** Robert D. 1932- *WhoBlA 92*
**Smith,** Robert Doyle 1952- *WhoRel 92*
**Smith,** Robert Drake 1944- *WhoFI 92*
**Smith,** Robert E. 1917- *WhoEnt 92*
**Smith,** Robert Earl 1923- *AmMWSc 92*
**Smith,** Robert Earl 1936- *WhoMW 92*
**Smith,** Robert Edward 1929- *AmMWSc 92*
**Smith,** Robert Edward 1943- *WhoBlA 92*
**Smith,** Robert Elijah 1911- *AmMWSc 92*
**Smith,** Robert Ellis 1940- *WhoAmL 92, WhoAmP 91, WrDr 92*
**Smith,** Robert Elmer 1929- *WhoAmP 91*
**Smith,** Robert Elphin 1929- *AmMWSc 92*
**Smith,** Robert Emery 1942- *AmMWSc 92*
**Smith,** Robert Eugene 1931- *WhoRel 92*
**Smith,** Robert Everett 1936- *WhoAmL 92*
**Smith,** Robert Ewing 1934- *AmMWSc 92*
**Smith,** Robert F. 1931- *AlmAP 92 [port]*
**Smith,** Robert Forshay, Jr. 1957- *WhoEnt 92*
**Smith,** Robert Francis 1943- *AmMWSc 92, WhoFI 92*
**Smith,** Robert Frederick 1958- *WhoAmL 92*
**Smith,** Robert Freeman 1930- *WhoMW 92*
**Smith,** Robert Freeman 1931- *WhoAmP 91, WhoWest 92*
**Smith,** Robert G 1947- *WhoAmP 91, WhoFI 92*
**Smith,** Robert H. *WhoBlA 92*

**Smith,** Robert H 1951- *WhoAmP 91*
**Smith,** Robert Hamil 1927- *WhoWest 92*
**Smith,** Robert Harold 1937- *WhoAmL 92*
**Smith,** Robert Harvey 1938- *IntWW 91, Who 92*
**Smith,** Robert Henry Tufrey 1935- *Who 92*
**Smith,** Robert Hill 1958- *Who 92*
**Smith,** Robert Houston 1931- *WhoRel 92*
**Smith,** Robert Howard 1935- *WhoWest 92*
**Smith,** Robert James 1944- *AmMWSc 92*
**Smith,** Robert John 1943- *WhoRel 92*
**Smith,** Robert Johnie 1935- *WhoMW 92*
**Smith,** Robert Johnson 1916- *AmMWSc 92*
**Smith,** Robert Johnson 1920- *WhoBlA 92*
**Smith,** Robert Johnson, II 1960- *WhoRel 92*
**Smith,** Robert Kingston 1924- *AmMWSc 92*
**Smith,** Robert Kirk, Jr. 1952- *WhoFI 92*
**Smith,** Robert L. *DrAPF 91*
**Smith,** Robert L 1941- *AmMWSc 92*
**Smith,** Robert L. T., Sr. 1902- *WhoBlA 92*
**Smith,** Robert Lawrence 1939- *AmMWSc 92*
**Smith,** Robert Lawrence, Sr. 1923- *WhoBlA 92*
**Smith,** Robert Lee 1921- *WhoMW 92*
**Smith,** Robert Lee 1923- *AmMWSc 92*
**Smith,** Robert Lee 1930- *WhoMW 92*
**Smith,** Robert Leland 1920- *AmMWSc 92*
**Smith,** Robert Leo 1925- *AmMWSc 92*
**Smith,** Robert Leonard 1944- *AmMWSc 92*
**Smith,** Robert Lewis 1938- *AmMWSc 92*
**Smith,** Robert Lloyd 1935- *AmMWSc 92*
**Smith,** Robert Lloyd 1941- *AmMWSc 92*
**Smith,** Robert London 1919- *WhoBlA 92*
**Smith,** Robert Lowell 1931- *WhoMW 92*
**Smith,** Robert Mason 1945- *WhoFI 92*
**Smith,** Robert Michael 1940- *WhoWest 92*
**Smith,** Robert Michael 1951- *WhoAmL 92*
**Smith,** Robert Nelson 1920- *WhoAmP 91*
**Smith,** Robert Norton 1930- *WhoEnt 92*
**Smith,** Robert Owens 1937- *AmMWSc 92*
**Smith,** Robert P., Jr. 1923- *WhoBlA 92*
**Smith,** Robert Paul 1942- *AmMWSc 92*
**Smith,** Robert Rex 1933- *WhoAmL 92*
**Smith,** Robert Sefton 1941- *AmMWSc 92*
**Smith,** Robert T., III 1949-1991 *WhoBlA 92N*
**Smith,** Robert Victor 1942- *AmMWSc 92*
**Smith,** Robert W. *WhoBlA 92*
**Smith,** Robert W 1909- *AmMWSc 92*
**Smith,** Robert W. 1952- *WrDr 92*
**Smith,** Robert W., Jr. 1918- *WhoBlA 92*
**Smith,** Robert Weston 1938- *WhoEnt 92*
**Smith,** Robert William 1939- *AmMWSc 92*
**Smith,** Robert William 1943- *AmMWSc 92*
**Smith,** Roberta Hawkins 1945- *AmMWSc 92*
**Smith,** Roberts Angus 1928- *AmMWSc 92*
**Smith,** Robin Jonathan Norman *Who 92*
**Smith,** Roderick MacDowell 1944- *AmMWSc 92*
**Smith,** Rodger Chapman 1915- *AmMWSc 92*
**Smith,** Rodger Hayward *Who 92*
**Smith,** Rodney Martin 1944- *WhoFI 92*
**Smith,** Rodney Russell 1946- *WhoFI 92*
**Smith,** Rodney Wike 1944- *WhoFI 92*
**Smith,** Roger 1932- *IntMPA 92*
**Smith,** Roger A 1932- *WhoAmP 91*
**Smith,** Roger Alan 1947- *AmMWSc 92*
**Smith,** Roger B. 1925- *IntWW 91*
**Smith,** Roger Bonham 1925- *Who 92, WhoFI 92, WhoMW 92*
**Smith,** Roger Bruce 1947- *AmMWSc 92*
**Smith,** Roger Dean 1932- *AmMWSc 92*
**Smith,** Roger Elton 1941- *AmMWSc 92*
**Smith,** Roger Francis Cooper 1940- *AmMWSc 92*
**Smith,** Roger John 1939- *Who 92*
**Smith,** Roger Leroy 1946- *WhoBlA 92*
**Smith,** Roger M 1918- *AmMWSc 92*
**Smith,** Roger Powell 1932- *AmMWSc 92*
**Smith,** Roland 1928- *IntWW 91, Who 92*
**Smith,** Roland Blair, Jr. 1946- *WhoBlA 92*
**Smith,** Roland Hedley 1943- *Who 92*
**Smith,** Rolf C, Jr *AmMWSc 92*
**Smith,** Rolf Colleaux 1940- *WhoFI 92*
**Smith,** Ron *DrAPF 91*
**Smith,** Ron 1915- *Who 92*
**Smith,** Ronald A. D. *Who 92*
**Smith,** Ronald Allen 1954- *WhoMW 92*
**Smith,** Ronald E 1936- *AmMWSc 92*
**Smith,** Ronald Ehlbert 1947- *WhoAmL 92*
**Smith,** Ronald Gene 1944- *AmMWSc 92*
**Smith,** Ronald George 1948- *WhoEnt 92*
**Smith,** Ronald Good 1933- *Who 92*
**Smith,** Ronald L. 1952- *ConAu 36NR*
**Smith,** Ronald Louis 1949- *WhoMW 92*
**Smith,** Ronald Noel 1946- *WhoMW 92*
**Smith,** Ronald Scott 1947- *WhoAmL 92*
**Smith,** Ronald W 1936- *AmMWSc 92*
**Smith,** Ronald Wayne 1944- *WhoWest 92*
**Smith,** Ronnie *WhoAmP 91*
**Smith,** Ronnie Ray 1949- *BlkOlyM*
**Smith,** Rosalie Ann 1950- *WhoMW 92*
**Smith,** Rosamond *WrDr 92*
**Smith,** Rose Marie 1934- *AmMWSc 92*
**Smith,** Rosemary Ann 1932- *Who 92*
**Smith,** Ross Quentin 1959- *WhoWest 92*
**Smith,** Ross W 1927- *AmMWSc 92*
**Smith,** Roulette William 1942- *WhoBlA 92*
**Smith,** Rowland 1938- *WrDr 92*
**Smith,** Roy 1924- *WhoAmP 91*
**Smith,** Roy David A. *Who 92*
**Smith,** Roy E 1926- *AmMWSc 92*
**Smith,** Roy Edgar 1931- *WhoAmP 91*
**Smith,** Roy Jefferson, Jr 1929- *AmMWSc 92*
**Smith,** Roy Martin 1927- *AmMWSc 92*
**Smith,** Roy Philip 1933- *WhoAmL 92*
**Smith,** Royd R 1932- *WhoAmP 91*
**Smith,** Ruben A *WhoAmP 91, WhoHisp 92*
**Smith,** Rufus Albert, Jr 1932- *AmMWSc 92*
**Smith,** Rufus Burnett, Jr. 1943- *WhoBlA 92*
**Smith,** Rufus Herman 1950- *WhoBlA 92*
**Smith,** Rufus Z. d1991 *NewYTBS 91*
**Smith,** Russell Aubrey 1936- *AmMWSc 92*
**Smith,** Russell Bryan 1936- *WhoEnt 92*
**Smith,** Russell D 1950- *AmMWSc 92*
**Smith,** Russell Francis 1944- *WhoFI 92*
**Smith,** Russell Lamar 1959- *AmMWSc 92*
**Smith,** Russell Lynn, Jr. 1919- *WhoWest 92*
**Smith,** Russell Wesley 1947- *WhoFI 92*
**Smith,** Ruth R 1924- *WhoAmP 91*
**Smith,** Sallie P. 1880- *WhoBlA 92*
**Smith,** Sally Ann 1942- *WhoWest 92*
**Smith,** Sam 1922- *WhoBlA 92*
**Smith,** Sam Corry 1922- *AmMWSc 92, WhoWest 92*
**Smith,** Sam J 1922- *WhoAmP 91*
**Smith,** Sammie Lee 1967- *WhoBlA 92*
**Smith,** Samuel 1720-1776 *BenetAL 91*
**Smith,** Samuel 1927- *AmMWSc 92, WhoMW 92*
**Smith,** Samuel Cooper 1934- *AmMWSc 92*
**Smith,** Samuel Doyle 1949- *WhoMW 92*
**Smith,** Samuel Francis *BenetAL 91*
**Smith,** Samuel H 1940- *AmMWSc 92*
**Smith,** Samuel H 1955- *WhoAmP 91*
**Smith,** Samuel Howard 1940- *WhoWest 92*
**Smith,** Samuel Joseph 1939- *AmMWSc 92*
**Smith,** Samuel Stanhope 1750-1819 *BenetAL 91*
**Smith,** Samuel Stuart 1936- *WhoAmL 92*
**Smith,** Sanderson 1832-1915 *BiInAmS*
**Smith,** Sandra Elaine 1964- *WhoEnt 92*
**Smith,** Sandra Kay 1966- *WhoEnt 92*
**Smith,** Sandra Sue *WhoEnt 92*
**Smith,** Sarah Curry 1942- *WhoAmL 92*
**Smith,** Sarah J *WhoAmP 91*
**Smith,** Scott A. 1953- *WhoAmL 92*
**Smith,** Scott Burrows 1955- *WhoFI 92*
**Smith,** Scott Clybourn 1950- *WhoFI 92*
**Smith,** Scott Douglas 1953- *WhoEnt 92*
**Smith,** Scott Edward 1954- *WhoFI 92*
**Smith,** Scott Fenton 1952- *WhoMW 92*
**Smith,** Scott Roy 1959- *WhoEnt 92*
**Smith,** Scott Sherwood 1955- *WhoEnt 92*
**Smith,** Seba 1792-1868 *BenetAL 91*
**Smith,** Selma Moidel 1919- *WhoWest 92*
**Smith,** Selwyn Michael 1942- *AmMWSc 92*
**Smith,** Seymour Howard 1919- *WhoEnt 92*
**Smith,** Shane Dale 1954- *WhoWest 92*
**Smith,** Sharber Wayne 1943- *WhoRel 92*
**Smith,** Shari Lee 1959- *WhoAmL 92*
**Smith,** Sharon 1960- *WhoEnt 92*
**Smith,** Sharon Louise 1945- *AmMWSc 92*
**Smith,** Sharon Patricia 1948- *WhoFI 92*
**Smith,** Sharron Williams 1941- *AmMWSc 92*
**Smith,** Sheila 1933- *WhoEnt 92*
**Smith,** Shelby Dean 1923- *AmMWSc 92*
**Smith,** Sheldon Harold 1948- *WhoAmL 92*
**Smith,** Sheldon LeRoy 1942- *WhoFI 92*
**Smith,** Sheldon Magill 1931- *AmMWSc 92*
**Smith,** Shelley 1912- *WrDr 92*
**Smith,** Shelton Leo 1942- *WhoRel 92*
**Smith,** Sherman 1957- *WhoBlA 92*
**Smith,** Sherman Scott 1946- *WhoFI 92*
**Smith,** Sherry L. 1951- *ConAu 133*
**Smith,** Sherwood Hubbard, Jr. 1934- *WhoFI 92*
**Smith,** Shirley LaVerne 1951- *WhoBlA 92*
**Smith,** Sidney F. R. *LesBEnT 92*
**Smith,** Sidney R, Jr 1935- *AmMWSc 92*
**Smith,** Sidney Ruven 1920- *AmMWSc 92*
**Smith,** Sidney Sharp 1928- *WhoWest 92*
**Smith,** Sidney Taylor 1918- *AmMWSc 92*
**Smith,** Sidney William 1920- *Who 92*
**Smith,** Sol *BenetAL 91*
**Smith,** Spencer B 1927- *AmMWSc 92*
**Smith,** Spencer Thomas 1943- *WhoAmL 92*
**Smith,** Spurgeon Eugene 1925- *AmMWSc 92*
**Smith,** Stacey Lee 1960- *WhoAmL 92*
**Smith,** Stamford Dennis 1939- *AmMWSc 92*
**Smith,** Stan Richard 1941- *WhoMW 92*
**Smith,** Stanford Lee 1935- *AmMWSc 92*
**Smith,** Stanford S 1923- *WhoAmP 91*
**Smith,** Stanford Sidney 1923- *WhoWest 92*
**Smith,** Stanley David 1935- *WhoAmL 92*
**Smith,** Stanley Dean 1951- *WhoWest 92*
**Smith,** Stanley Desmond 1931- *Who 92*
**Smith,** Stanley Frank 1924- *Who 92*
**Smith,** Stanley G. 1940- *WhoBlA 92*
**Smith,** Stanley Galen 1926- *AmMWSc 92*
**Smith,** Stanley Glen 1931- *AmMWSc 92*
**Smith,** Stanley Kent 1945- *WhoFI 92*
**Smith,** Stanton Kinnie, Jr. 1931- *WhoAmL 92, WhoFI 92*
**Smith,** Starita Ann 1949- *WhoBlA 92*
**Smith,** Stephen Alexander 1941- *WhoFI 92*
**Smith,** Stephen Allen 1942- *AmMWSc 92*
**Smith,** Stephen Arnold 1946- *WhoWest 92*
**Smith,** Stephen Charles 1946- *WhoAmP 91*
**Smith,** Stephen Charles 1951- *WhoBlA 92*
**Smith,** Stephen D 1939- *AmMWSc 92*
**Smith,** Stephen D 1948- *AmMWSc 92*
**Smith,** Stephen Eric 1953- *WhoMW 92*
**Smith,** Stephen F 1940- *WhoIns 92*
**Smith,** Stephen F., Jr. 1942- *WhoAmL 92*
**Smith,** Stephen Judson 1924- *AmMWSc 92*
**Smith,** Stephen Kevin 1951- *Who 92*
**Smith,** Stephen Roger 1939- *AmMWSc 92*
**Smith,** Stephen Shelton 1940- *WhoFI 92*
**Smith,** Stephen Sinclair 1947- *WhoFI 92*
**Smith,** Stephen W. 1954- *WhoRel 92*
**Smith,** Steve 1949- *WhoAmP 91*
**Smith,** Steve 1950- *WhoAmP 91*
**Smith,** Steve Austin 1949- *WhoAmP 91*
**Smith,** Steven Albert 1939- *WhoWest 92*
**Smith,** Steven Craig 1957- *WhoAmL 92*
**Smith,** Steven D 1941- *WhoIns 92*
**Smith,** Steven David 1959- *WhoAmL 92*
**Smith,** Steven F *WhoAmP 91*
**Smith,** Steven Frederick 1954- *WhoRel 92*
**Smith,** Steven George 1951- *WhoFI 92*
**Smith,** Steven James 1945- *WhoFI 92, WhoIns 92*
**Smith,** Steven Joel 1940- *AmMWSc 92*
**Smith,** Steven Lee 1952- *WhoAmL 92*
**Smith,** Steven Patrick Decland 1939- *AmMWSc 92*
**Smith,** Steven Phillip *DrAPF 91*
**Smith,** Steven R. 1954- *WhoFI 92*
**Smith,** Steven Ray 1946- *WhoAmL 92, WhoMW 92*
**Smith,** Steven Sidney 1946- *AmMWSc 92, WhoWest 92*
**Smith,** Stevie *ConAu 35NR*
**Smith,** Stevie 1902-1971 *FacFETw, RfGEnL 91*
**Smith,** Stewart Edward 1937- *AmMWSc 92*
**Smith,** Stewart Ranson 1931- *Who 92*
**Smith,** Stewart Russell 1946- *WhoFI 92*
**Smith,** Stewart W 1932- *AmMWSc 92*
**Smith,** Stuart 1940- *AmMWSc 92*
**Smith,** Stuart Brian 1944- *Who 92*
**Smith,** Stuart Craig 1949- *WhoEnt 92*
**Smith,** Stuart D 1941- *AmMWSc 92*
**Smith,** Stuart Robert 1942- *WhoWest 92*
**Smith,** Stuff 1909-1967 *NewAmDM*
**Smith,** Sukie 1964- *WhoEnt 92*
**Smith,** Sunday 1934- *WhoEnt 92*
**Smith,** Sundra Shealey 1948- *WhoBlA 92*
**Smith,** Susan Bitter 1955- *WhoAmP 91, WhoWest 92*
**Smith,** Susan Lee 1953- *WhoFI 92*
**Smith,** Susan May 1942- *AmMWSc 92*
**Smith,** Susan T 1937- *AmMWSc 92*
**Smith,** Sydney 1771-1845 *BenetAL 91, DcLB 107 [port]*
**Smith,** Sydney David 1947- *WhoMW 92*
**Smith,** Sydney Goodsir 1915-1975 *RfGEnL 91*
**Smith,** Sydney Strother, III 1941- *WhoAmL 92, WhoAmP 91*
**Smith,** Sylvester, Jr. 1946- *WhoMW 92*
**Smith,** Symuel Harold 1922- *WhoBlA 92*
**Smith,** T. Arthur 1923- *WhoFI 92*
**Smith,** T Dan 1915- *Who 92*
**Smith,** Tad Randolph 1928- *WhoAmL 92, WhoFI 92*
**Smith,** Teasther West 1941- *WhoBlA 92*
**Smith,** Terence E 1936- *AmMWSc 92*
**Smith,** Terence Fitzgerald 1938- *IntAu&W 91*
**Smith,** Terrance Lewis 1942- *WhoAmL 92*
**Smith,** Terri McFerrin *DrAPF 91*
**Smith,** Terry Douglas 1942- *AmMWSc 92*
**Smith,** Terry Edward 1940- *AmMWSc 92*
**Smith,** Terry G. 1954- *WhoMW 92*
**Smith,** Terry L. 1955- *WhoRel 92*
**Smith,** Terry Lynn 1944- *WhoMW 92*
**Smith,** Terry Mason 1953- *WhoEnt 92*
**Smith,** Terry Ray 1960- *WhoRel 92*
**Smith,** Thelma J. *WhoBlA 92*
**Smith,** Theodate Louise 1859-1914 *BiInAmS*
**Smith,** Theodore Anthony 1934- *WhoFI 92*
**Smith,** Theodore Beaton 1918- *AmMWSc 92*
**Smith,** Theodore Craig 1930- *AmMWSc 92*
**Smith,** Theodore DeWitt 1947- *WhoRel 92*
**Smith,** Theodore G 1934- *AmMWSc 92*
**Smith,** Theodore Isaac Jogues 1945- *AmMWSc 92*
**Smith,** Theresa Marie 1963- *WhoEnt 92*
**Smith,** Thom E. 1936- *WhoEnt 92, WhoFI 92*
**Smith,** Thomas 1956- *WhoRel 92*
**Smith,** Thomas Allen 1931- *WhoWest 92*
**Smith,** Thomas Arthur 1954- *WhoFI 92*
**Smith,** Thomas Benton 1948- *WhoAmP 91*
**Smith,** Thomas Bruce, II 1938- *WhoAmP 91*
**Smith,** Thomas Caldwell 1941- *AmMWSc 92*
**Smith,** Thomas Charles 1925- *AmMWSc 92*
**Smith,** Thomas David 1923- *AmMWSc 92*
**Smith,** Thomas Earle, Jr 1938- *WhoAmP 91*
**Smith,** Thomas Elijah 1933- *AmMWSc 92*
**Smith,** Thomas Gilbert 1937- *Who 92*
**Smith,** Thomas Graves, Jr 1931- *AmMWSc 92*
**Smith,** Thomas Harry Francis 1928- *AmMWSc 92*
**Smith,** Thomas Henry 1947- *AmMWSc 92*
**Smith,** Thomas Jay 1940- *AmMWSc 92*
**Smith,** Thomas Jefferson 1930- *AmMWSc 92*
**Smith,** Thomas Joseph 1938- *WhoFI 92*
**Smith,** Thomas Kent 1939- *WhoMW 92*
**Smith,** Thomas Lauren 1936- *WhoAmP 91*
**Smith,** Thomas Lowell *AmMWSc 92*
**Smith,** Thomas O. 1944- *WhoAmL 92*
**Smith,** Thomas Peters 1776?-1802 *BiInAmS*
**Smith,** Thomas Richard 1955- *WhoMW 92*
**Smith,** Thomas Shore 1924- *WhoAmL 92*
**Smith,** Thomas Stevenson 1921- *AmMWSc 92*
**Smith,** Thomas W 1936- *AmMWSc 92*
**Smith,** Thomas Walter 1955- *WhoFI 92*
**Smith,** Thomas Wesley 1952- *WhoRel 92*
**Smith,** Thomas Whitener 1952- *WhoFI 92*
**Smith,** Thomas Winston 1935- *WhoFI 92, WhoWest 92*
**Smith,** Thomas Woods 1943- *AmMWSc 92*
**Smith,** Thor L. 1920- *WhoWest 92*
**Smith,** Thor Lowe 1920- *AmMWSc 92*
**Smith,** Thorne 1892-1934 *BenetAL 91*
**Smith,** Thorne 1893-1934 *TwCSFW 91*
**Smith,** Tim Denis 1946- *AmMWSc 92*
**Smith,** Timothy Andre 1937- *AmMWSc 92*
**Smith,** Timothy Balderson 1958- *WhoRel 92*
**Smith,** Timothy Charles 1955- *WhoEnt 92*
**Smith,** Timothy D. *Who 92*
**Smith,** Timothy Dean 1952- *WhoRel 92*
**Smith,** Timothy James 1957- *WhoRel 92*
**Smith,** Timothy John 1947- *Who 92*
**Smith,** Timothy Mark 1952- *WhoRel 92*
**Smith,** Timothy Randolph 1945- *WhoRel 92*
**Smith,** Timothy Roland 1958- *WhoFI 92*
**Smith,** Timothy Scott 1962- *WhoRel 92*
**Smith,** Titus K *ScFEYrs*
**Smith,** Titus Keiper 1855- *ScFEYrs*
**Smith,** Todd Iversen 1940- *AmMWSc 92*
**Smith,** Todd P 1959- *WhoAmP 91*
**Smith,** Tom *DrAPF 91*
**Smith,** Tom 1935- *WhoAmP 91*
**Smith,** Tom Eugene 1941- *WhoFI 92*
**Smith,** Tom O 1945- *WhoAmP 91*
**Smith,** Tom O'Dell 1958- *WhoAmP 91*
**Smith,** Tommie 1944- *WhoBlA 92*
**Smith,** Tommie C 1944- *BlkOlyM*
**Smith,** Tommie M. 1919- *WhoBlA 92*
**Smith,** Tommy 1950- *WhoAmP 91*
**Smith,** Tony 1968- *WhoBlA 92*
**Smith,** Tony F. 1943- *WhoMW 92*
**Smith,** Toukie A. *WhoBlA 92*
**Smith,** Townsend Jackson 1910- *AmMWSc 92*
**Smith,** Trevor Arthur 1937- *Who 92*
**Smith,** Tricia 1952- *WhoAmP 91*
**Smith,** Trudy Enzer 1924- *AmMWSc 92*
**Smith,** Uriah 1832-1903 *AmPeW, RelLAm 91*
**Smith,** Van P 1928- *WhoAmP 91*
**Smith,** Vance Carlton, Jr 1952- *WhoAmP 91*
**Smith,** Vangy Edith 1937- *WhoFI 92*
**Smith,** Vann Elliott 1940- *AmMWSc 92*
**Smith,** Vasco A. 1920- *WhoBlA 92*

**Smith,** Vasco Albert, Jr 1920- *WhoAmP 91*
**Smith,** Velma Merriline 1940- *AmMWSc 92*
**Smith,** Venture *DcAmImH*
**Smith,** Vernel Hap 1924- *WhoBlA 92*
**Smith,** Vernon G 1944- *WhoAmP 91, WhoBlA 92*
**Smith,** Vernon Howard 1920- *WhoWest 92*
**Smith,** Vernon Leon 1944- *WhoEnt 92*
**Smith,** Vernon Olivier 1930- *Who 92*
**Smith,** Vicki Lynn 1949- *WhoAmL 92*
**Smith,** Victor 1913- *Who 92*
**Smith,** Victor Earle 1914- *WhoMW 92*
**Smith,** Victor Herbert 1925- *AmMWSc 92*
**Smith,** Victoria Lynn 1959- *AmMWSc 92*
**Smith,** Vin 1944- *WhoWest 92*
**Smith,** Vincent C 1914- *AmMWSc 92*
**Smith,** Vincent D. 1929- *WhoBlA 92*
**Smith,** Vincent Milton 1940- *WhoAmL 92*
**Smith,** Virgie Jackson *WhoMW 92*
**Smith,** Virgil Clark, Jr 1947- *WhoAmP 91, WhoBlA 92*
**Smith,** Virginia 1931- *WhoRel 92*
**Smith,** Virginia Beatrice 1923- *WhoAmL 92*
**Smith,** Virginia Dodd 1911- *WhoAmP 91*
**Smith,** Virginia E. *DrAPF 91*
**Smith,** Virginia M. 1929- *WhoBlA 92*
**Smith,** Vivian 1933- *ConPo 91, WrDr 92*
**Smith,** Vivian Brian 1933- *IntAu&W 91*
**Smith,** Vivianne C 1938- *AmMWSc 92*
**Smith,** W. Alan 1949- *WhoRel 92*
**Smith,** W.H. d1855 *DcLB 106*
**Smith,** W. H. d1891 *DcLB 106 [port]*
**Smith,** W.H., and Son *DcLB 106*
**Smith,** W John 1934- *AmMWSc 92*
**Smith,** W. Lee 1940- *WhoMW 92*
**Smith,** W P 1915- *AmMWSc 92*
**Smith,** Wade *TwCWW 91*
**Smith,** Wade Kilgore 1937- *AmMWSc 92*
**Smith,** Waldo E 1900- *AmMWSc 92*
**Smith,** Waldo Gregorius 1911- *WhoWest 92*
**Smith,** Walker O, Jr 1950- *AmMWSc 92*
**Smith,** Wallace Britton 1941- *AmMWSc 92*
**Smith,** Wallace Bunnell 1929- *RelLAm 91, WhoRel 92*
**Smith,** Wallace Charles 1948- *WhoBlA 92*
**Smith,** Wallace Morgan 1958- *WhoAmL 92*
**Smith,** Wally 1947- *WhoWest 92*
**Smith,** Walter B, Jr 1915- *WhoIns 92*
**Smith,** Walter DeLos 1936- *WhoMW 92*
**Smith,** Walter J. 1921- *WhoWest 92*
**Smith,** Walter Joseph, Jr. 1936- *WhoAmL 92*
**Smith,** Walter L. 1935- *WhoBlA 92*
**Smith,** Walter Laws 1926- *AmMWSc 92*
**Smith,** Walter Lee 1948- *AmMWSc 92*
**Smith,** Walter Purvis 1920- *Who 92*
**Smith,** Walter Richard 1926- *Who 92*
**Smith,** Walter Rogers 1945- *WhoWest 92*
**Smith,** Walter S., Jr. 1940- *WhoAmL 92*
**Smith,** Walter T. 1927- *WhoBlA 92*
**Smith,** Walter Thomas, Jr 1922- *AmMWSc 92*
**Smith,** Walter W. 1905-1982 *ConAu 36NR*
**Smith,** Walter Wellesley *BenetAL 91*
**Smith,** Walter Wellesley 1905-1982 *FacFETw*
**Smith,** Walton Napier 1942- *WhoAmL 92*
**Smith,** Walton Ramsay 1948- *AmMWSc 92*
**Smith,** Wanda Joyce 1945- *WhoWest 92*
**Smith,** Wanda VanHoy 1926- *ConAu 133, SmATA 65 [port]*
**Smith,** Ward 1930- *WhoMW 92*
**Smith,** Waring Grant 1916- *WhoMW 92*
**Smith,** Warren 1949- *WhoBlA 92*
**Smith,** Warren Allen 1921- *WhoEnt 92*
**Smith,** Warren Drew 1942- *AmMWSc 92*
**Smith,** Warren Harvey 1935- *AmMWSc 92*
**Smith,** Warren LaVerne 1924- *AmMWSc 92*
**Smith,** Warren Thomas 1923- *WhoRel 92*
**Smith,** Wayman F., III 1940- *WhoBlA 92*
**Smith,** Wayman Flynn, III 1940- *WhoAmP 91*
**Smith,** Wayne Alan 1962- *WhoAmP 91*
**Smith,** Wayne Arthur 1945- *WhoMW 92*
**Smith,** Wayne Delarmie 1928- *WhoAmP 91*
**Smith,** Wayne Earl 1927- *AmMWSc 92*
**Smith,** Wayne H 1938- *AmMWSc 92*
**Smith,** Wayne Harold 1950- *WhoRel 92*
**Smith,** Wayne Howard 1946- *AmMWSc 92*
**Smith,** Wayne L. *WhoRel 92*
**Smith,** Wayne Lee 1936- *AmMWSc 92*
**Smith,** Wayne Michael 1947- *WhoMW 92*
**Smith,** Wayne Richard 1934- *WhoAmL 92, WhoMW 92*
**Smith,** Wendell Eugene 1950- *WhoRel 92*
**Smith,** Wendell Vandervort 1912- *AmMWSc 92*
**Smith,** Wendy Anne 1954- *AmMWSc 92*
**Smith,** Wendy Hope 1957- *WhoAmL 92*
**Smith,** Wesley R 1928- *AmMWSc 92*
**Smith,** Wesley W. *WhoRel 92*
**Smith,** Wilber G 1935- *WhoAmP 91*
**Smith,** Wilber Gene 1935- *WhoBlA 92*
**Smith,** Wilbur 1933- *WrDr 92*
**Smith,** Wilbur Addison 1933- *IntAu&W 91, IntWW 91, Who 92*
**Smith,** Wilbur Cowan 1914- *WhoAmL 92, WhoMW 92*
**Smith,** Wilbur Moorehead 1894-1976 *RelLAm 91*
**Smith,** Wilbur S 1911- *AmMWSc 92*
**Smith,** Wilburn Jackson, Jr. 1921- *WhoFI 92*
**Smith,** Wilfred Cantwell 1916- *IntWW 91, WhoRel 92, WrDr 92*
**Smith,** Will *ScFEYrs*
**Smith,** Will & Robbins, R J *ScFEYrs*
**Smith,** Willard Grant 1934- *WhoWest 92*
**Smith,** Willard Newell 1926- *AmMWSc 92*
**Smith,** William 1727-1803 *BenetAL 91, BlkwEAR*
**Smith,** William 1728-1793 *BenetAL 91*
**Smith,** William 1728-1795 *BlkwEAR*
**Smith,** William 1932- *IntMPA 92*
**Smith,** William A 1948- *WhoIns 92*
**Smith,** William Adams, Jr 1929- *AmMWSc 92*
**Smith,** William Allen 1940- *AmMWSc 92*
**Smith,** William Allen 1949- *WhoMW 92*
**Smith,** William Ashley 1944- *WhoFI 92*
**Smith,** William Austin N. *Who 92*
**Smith,** William Basil 1936- *WhoMW 92*
**Smith,** William Boyce 1938- *AmMWSc 92*
**Smith,** William Bridges 1944- *AmMWSc 92*
**Smith,** William Burton 1927- *AmMWSc 92*
**Smith,** William Cason, III 1961- *WhoWest 92*
**Smith,** William Clarke 1926- *WhoRel 92*
**Smith,** William Clay 1959- *WhoRel 92*
**Smith,** William Conrad 1937- *AmMWSc 92*
**Smith,** William Edmond 1939- *AmMWSc 92*
**Smith,** William Edward 1938- *AmMWSc 92*
**Smith,** William Forrest 1929- *WhoAmP 91*
**Smith,** William Fortune 1931- *AmMWSc 92*
**Smith,** William Fred 1938- *WhoBlA 92*
**Smith,** William Frederick Bottrill 1903- *Who 92*
**Smith,** William French d1990 *IntWW 91N, Who 92N*
**Smith,** William French 1917-1990 *AnObit 1990, CurBio 91N, FacFETw*
**Smith,** William French 1941- *WhoBlA 92*
**Smith,** William Grady 1937- *AmMWSc 92*
**Smith,** William Grey 1922- *WhoAmP 91*
**Smith,** William H 1929- *AmMWSc 92*
**Smith,** William Hawley 1845-1943 *ScFEYrs*
**Smith,** William Hayden 1940- *AmMWSc 92*
**Smith,** William Holt 1949- *WhoAmL 92*
**Smith,** William Hopkins 1947- *WhoRel 92*
**Smith,** William Howard 1912- *WhoBlA 92*
**Smith,** William Hulse 1939- *AmMWSc 92*
**Smith,** William James 1946- *WhoBlA 92*
**Smith,** William Jay *DrAPF 91*
**Smith,** William Jay 1918- *BenetAL 91, ConPo 91, SmATA 68 [port], WrDr 92*
**Smith,** William Jeffrey 1916- *Who 92*
**Smith,** William K 1920- *AmMWSc 92*
**Smith,** William Kirby 1947- *AmMWSc 92*
**Smith,** William Kirk 1959- *WhoEnt 92*
**Smith,** William Lawrence 1946- *WhoRel 92*
**Smith,** William Lee 1922- *AmMWSc 92*
**Smith,** William Lee 1945- *AmMWSc 92*
**Smith,** William Leslie 1931- *WhoRel 92*
**Smith,** William M., Jr. 1934-1987 *WhoBlA 92N*
**Smith,** William Marion 1932- *WhoAmL 92*
**Smith,** William Mayo 1917- *AmMWSc 92*
**Smith,** William McGregor 1910- *Who 92*
**Smith,** William Milton 1918- *WhoBlA 92, WhoRel 92*
**Smith,** William Novis, Jr 1937- *AmMWSc 92*
**Smith,** William Ogg 1925- *AmMWSc 92*
**Smith,** William Owen 1941- *AmMWSc 92*
**Smith,** William Pernell 1919- *WhoBlA 92*
**Smith,** William R 1828?-1912 *BiInAmS*
**Smith,** William R 1925- *AmMWSc 92*
**Smith,** William Randolph 1928- *WhoAmL 92*
**Smith,** William Randolph 1948- *WhoFI 92*
**Smith,** William Ray 1925- *WhoWest 92*
**Smith,** William Reardon Reardon- 1911- *Who 92*
**Smith,** William Reece, Jr. 1925- *IntWW 91*
**Smith,** William Reginald Verdon *Who 92*
**Smith,** William Richard, III 1946- *WhoFI 92*
**Smith,** William Robert 1916- *WhoFI 92*
**Smith,** William Robert 1935- *AmMWSc 92, WhoRel 92*
**Smith,** William Russell 1917- *AmMWSc 92*
**Smith,** William S 1918- *AmMWSc 92*
**Smith,** William Sidney 1944- *WhoAmL 92*
**Smith,** William Stanley, Jr. 1942- *WhoRel 92*
**Smith,** William T, II 1916- *WhoAmP 91*
**Smith,** William Thayer 1839-1909 *BiInAmS*
**Smith,** William Walker 1940- *AmMWSc 92*
**Smith,** William Wallace 1900- *WhoRel 92*
**Smith,** William Wallace 1900-1989 *RelLAm 91*
**Smith,** William Ward 1914- *AmMWSc 92*
**Smith,** William Xavier 1934- *WhoBlA 92*
**Smith,** Willie 1897-1973 *NewAmDM*
**Smith,** Willie A Wilson 1929- *WhoAmP 91*
**Smith,** Willie Mae Ford 1904- *NotBlAW 92*
**Smith,** Willie Tesreau, Jr. 1920- *WhoAmL 92*
**Smith,** Willis Allen 1919- *WhoFI 92*
**Smith,** Willis Ballard 1931- *WhoFI 92*
**Smith,** Willis Dean 1942- *AmMWSc 92*
**Smith,** Willou Copeland 1939- *WhoAmP 91*
**Smith,** Wilma Janice 1926- *IntAu&W 91*
**Smith,** Winchell 1871-1933 *BenetAL 91*
**Smith,** Winfield Scott 1941- *AmMWSc 92*
**Smith,** Winston Glenn 1920- *WhoAmL 92*
**Smith,** Winthrop Hiram, Jr. 1949- *WhoFI 92*
**Smith,** Winthrop Ware 1936- *AmMWSc 92*
**Smith,** Wirt Wilsey 1920- *AmMWSc 92*
**Smith,** Woodrow Michael 1946- *WhoRel 92*
**Smith,** Wynne 1953- *WhoEnt 92*
**Smith,** Wyre 1939- *WhoBlA 92*
**Smith,** Yolanda Yvette 1957- *WhoRel 92, WhoWest 92*
**Smith,** Young Merritt, Jr. 1944- *WhoFI 92*
**Smith,** Z Z *IntAu&W 91X*
**Smith,** Zachary Alden 1953- *WhoWest 92*
**Smith,** Zdenka Kopal 1943- *WhoWest 92*
**Smith-Alexander,** Melanie Sue 1959- *WhoMW 92*
**Smith Brindle,** Reginald 1917- *IntAu&W 91, NewAmDM*
**Smith-Chall,** Barbara J. 1947- *WhoAmL 92*
**Smith-Davis,** Vanlada 1961- *WhoWest 92*
**Smith-Dodsworth,** John 1935- *Who 92*
**Smith-Epps,** E. Paulette 1947- *WhoBlA 92*
**Smith-Epstein,** Mary Kathleen 1940- *WhoEnt 92*
**Smith-Evernden,** Roberta Katherine *AmMWSc 92*
**Smith Freeman,** Patricia M. 1937- *WhoBlA 92*
**Smith-Gaston,** Linda Ann 1949- *WhoBlA 92*
**Smith-Gill,** Sandra Joyce 1944- *AmMWSc 92*
**Smith-Gordon,** Eldred 1935- *Who 92*
**Smith-Graves,** Sandra Patricia 1947- *WhoMW 92*
**Smith-Gray,** Cassandra Elaine 1947- *WhoBlA 92*
**Smith-Marriott,** Hugh Cavendish 1925- *Who 92*
**Smith McCain,** Dorothy R 1925- *WhoAmP 91*
**Smith-Pierce,** Patricia A. 1939- *WhoMW 92*
**Smith-Sanchez,** Sharon Louise 1949- *WhoAmL 92*
**Smith-Somerville,** Harriett Elizabeth 1944- *AmMWSc 92*
**Smith-Sonneborn,** Joan 1935- *AmMWSc 92*
**Smith-Surles,** Carol Diann 1946- *WhoBlA 92*
**Smith-Thomas,** Barbara 1942- *AmMWSc 92*
**Smith-Whitaker,** Audrey N. 1953- *WhoBlA 92*
**Smithberg,** Morris 1924- *AmMWSc 92*
**Smithburg,** Donald Rowan 1960- *WhoMW 92*
**Smithburg,** William Dean 1938- *WhoFI 92, WhoMW 92*
**Smithee,** John T 1951- *WhoAmP 91*
**Smither,** Elizabeth 1941- *ConPo 91, WrDr 92*
**Smither,** Elizabeth Edwina 1941- *IntAu&W 91*
**Smither,** Gertrude Jackson 1937- *WhoRel 92*
**Smither,** Robert Karl 1929- *AmMWSc 92*
**Smither,** Thomas Dailey, Sr. 1944- *WhoFI 92*
**Smitherman,** Bill *WhoAmP 91*
**Smitherman,** Frank 1913- *Who 92*
**Smitherman,** Geneva *WhoBlA 92*
**Smitherman,** Renford Oneal 1937- *AmMWSc 92*
**Smithers,** David 1908- *Who 92*
**Smithers,** Geoffrey Victor 1909- *Who 92*
**Smithers,** Leonard 1861-1907 *DcLB 112 [port]*
**Smithers,** Oral Lester, Jr. 1940- *WhoBlA 92*
**Smithers,** Peter 1913- *Who 92, WrDr 92*
**Smithers,** Peter Henry Berry Otway 1913- *IntWW 91*
**Smithers,** Priscilla Jane 1942- *WhoBlA 92*
**Smithers,** Reginald 1903- *Who 92*
**Smithey,** Robert Arthur 1925- *WhoBlA 92*
**Smithhisler,** James Edward, II 1954- *WhoMW 92*
**Smithies,** Frederick Albert 1929- *Who 92*
**Smithies,** Kenneth Charles Lester 1927- *Who 92*
**Smithies,** Oliver 1925- *AmMWSc 92*
**Smithing,** Robert Thomas 1956- *WhoWest 92*
**Smithson,** Alan *Who 92*
**Smithson,** Alison 1928- *WrDr 92*
**Smithson,** Alison Margaret 1928- *IntWW 91*
**Smithson,** Charles Wayne 1946- *WhoFI 92*
**Smithson,** George Raymond, Jr 1926- *AmMWSc 92*
**Smithson,** James Louis Macie 1765-1829 *BiInAmS*
**Smithson,** John W 1946- *WhoIns 92*
**Smithson,** Lowell Lee 1930- *WhoAmL 92*
**Smithson,** Peter 1923- *WrDr 92*
**Smithson,** Peter Denham 1923- *IntWW 91, Who 92*
**Smithson,** Richard Joseph 1923- *WhoFI 92*
**Smithson,** Ricky Don 1957- *WhoRel 92*
**Smithson,** Scott Busby 1930- *AmMWSc 92*
**Smithwick,** Elizabeth Mary 1928- *AmMWSc 92*
**Smithyman,** Kendrick 1922- *ConPo 91, IntAu&W 91, WrDr 92*
**Smitka,** John Francis, Jr. 1948- *WhoAmL 92*
**Smitka,** Michael John 1953- *WhoFI 92*
**Smitrovich,** Bill 1947- *IntMPA 92*
**Smits,** Friedolf M 1924- *AmMWSc 92*
**Smits,** Jimmy *WhoEnt 92*
**Smits,** Jimmy 1955- *IntMPA 92, WhoHisp 92*
**Smits,** Pip Nathalie 1964- *WhoEnt 92*
**Smits,** Ronald F. *DrAPF 91*
**Smits,** Talivaldis I 1936- *AmMWSc 92*
**Smitsendonk,** Anton G. O. 1928- *IntWW 91*
**Smitter,** Ronald Warren 1951- *WhoAmL 92*
**Smittle,** Burrell Joe 1934- *AmMWSc 92*
**Smittle,** Doyle Allen 1939- *AmMWSc 92*
**Smittle,** Richard Baird 1943- *AmMWSc 92*
**Smoake,** James Alvin 1942- *AmMWSc 92*
**Smock,** Arthur Reseau, Jr. 1920- *WhoFI 92*
**Smock,** Dale Owen 1915- *AmMWSc 92*
**Smock,** Emerson 1922- *WhoAmP 91*
**Smock,** Frederick *DrAPF 91*
**Smohalla** 1815?-1907 *RelLAm 91*
**Smoke,** Mary E 1931- *AmMWSc 92*
**Smoke,** Richard Edwin 1945- *WhoAmL 92, WhoMW 92*
**Smoke,** William Henry 1928- *AmMWSc 92*
**Smoker,** Richard E *WhoIns 92*
**Smoker,** William Alexander 1915- *AmMWSc 92*
**Smoker,** William Williams 1945- *AmMWSc 92*
**Smoko,** Ronald L *WhoAmP 91*
**Smokovitis,** Athanassios A 1935- *AmMWSc 92*
**Smoktunovsky,** Innokenty Mikhailovich 1925- *IntWW 91*
**Smoktunovsky,** Innokenty Mikhaylovich 1925- *SovUnBD*
**Smol,** John Paul 1955- *AmMWSc 92*
**Smolan,** Richard Scott 1949- *WhoWest 92*
**Smolander,** Martti Juhani 1955- *AmMWSc 92*
**Smolderen,** Luc Hippolyte Marie 1924- *IntWW 91*
**Smoldt,** Robert Keith 1945- *WhoMW 92*
**Smolen,** Donald E. 1923- *IntMPA 92*
**Smolen,** Stephen Adams 1944- *WhoWest 92*
**Smolenski,** Donald John 1955- *WhoMW 92*
**Smolensky,** Eugene 1932- *WhoWest 92*
**Smolensky,** Michael Hale 1942- *AmMWSc 92*
**Smoliar,** Stephen William 1946- *AmMWSc 92*
**Smolich,** Dmitri Nikolaevich 1919- *IntWW 91*
**Smolik,** James Darrell 1942- *AmMWSc 92*
**Smolin,** Lee 1955- *AmMWSc 92*
**Smolinske,** Cora Alice 1919- *WhoAmP 91*

**Smolinski**, Adam Karol 1910- *IntWW 91*
**Smolinski**, Edward Albert 1928- *WhoFI 92, WhoRel 92*
**Smolinski**, Michael Stephen 1957- *WhoEnt 92*
**Smolinsky**, Gerald 1933- *AmMWSc 92*
**Smolinsky**, Sidney Joseph 1932- *WhoAmL 92*
**Smolka**, James William 1950- *WhoWest 92*
**Smolker**, Gary Steven 1945- *WhoAmL 92*
**Smolla**, Rodney Alan 1953- *WhoAmL 92*
**Smollan**, David Leslie 1928- *WhoWest 92*
**Smollar**, Paul Robert 1944- *WhoAmL 92*
**Smollen**, Leonard Elliott 1930- *WhoFI 92*
**Smoller**, Joel A 1939- *AmMWSc 92*
**Smoller**, Sylvia Wassertheil 1932- *AmMWSc 92*
**Smollett**, Tobias 1721-1771 *CnDBLB 2 [port], RfGEnL 91*
**Smollett**, Tobias George 1721?-1771 *BlkwCEP*
**Smollins**, John F, Jr 1940- *WhoAmP 91*
**Smoluchowski**, Roman 1910- *AmMWSc 92*
**Smook**, John T. 1927- *WhoFI 92*
**Smook**, Malcolm Andrew 1924- *AmMWSc 92*
**Smooke**, Mitchell D 1951- *AmMWSc 92*
**Smoose**, Larry Victor 1946- *WhoRel 92*
**Smoot**, Albertha Pearl 1914- *WhoBlA 92*
**Smoot**, Andrew Christopher 1961- *WhoMW 92*
**Smoot**, Carolyn Elizabeth 1945- *WhoBlA 92*
**Smoot**, Charles Richard 1928- *AmMWSc 92*
**Smoot**, David Riley 1954- *WhoEnt 92*
**Smoot**, Edith L 1951- *AmMWSc 92*
**Smoot**, George Fitzgerald 1922- *AmMWSc 92*
**Smoot**, George Fitzgerald, III 1945- *AmMWSc 92*
**Smoot**, Hazel Lampkin 1916- *WhoEnt 92*
**Smoot**, Joseph Grady 1932- *WhoMW 92*
**Smoot**, Leon Douglas 1934- *AmMWSc 92, WhoWest 92*
**Smoot**, Oliver Reed, Jr. 1940- *WhoAmL 92*
**Smoot**, Reed 1862-1941 *RelLAm 91*
**Smoot**, Richard Leonard 1940- *WhoFI 92*
**Smoot**, Wendell McMeans, Jr. 1921- *WhoWest 92*
**Smorol**, Albert Edward, Jr. 1940- *WhoFI 92*
**Smosna**, Richard Allan 1945- *AmMWSc 92*
**Smothers Brothers** *IntMPA 92, LesBEnT 92*
**Smothers**, Dick 1939- *IntMPA 92, WhoEnt 92*
**Smothers**, James Llewellyn 1930- *AmMWSc 92*
**Smothers**, Norman P. *WhoFI 92*
**Smothers**, Ronald *WhoBlA 92*
**Smothers**, Ronald Eric 1946- *WhoBlA 92*
**Smothers**, Tom 1937- *IntMPA 92, WhoEnt 92*
**Smothers**, William Joseph 1919- *AmMWSc 92*
**Smotherson**, Melvin 1936- *WhoBlA 92*
**Smouse**, Hervey Russell *WhoAmL 92*
**Smouse**, Peter Edgar 1942- *AmMWSc 92*
**Smouse**, Thomas Hadley 1936- *AmMWSc 92*
**Smout**, Thomas Christopher 1933- *IntWW 91, Who 92*
**Smoyer**, Claude B 1934- *AmMWSc 92*
**Smrekar**, Karl George, Jr. 1954- *WhoFI 92*
**Smuck**, Harold Vernon 1920- *WhoRel 92*
**Smucker**, Arthur Allan 1923- *AmMWSc 92*
**Smucker**, Barbara Claassen 1915- *WrDr 92*
**Smucker**, Silas Jonathan 1904- *AmMWSc 92*
**Smuckler**, Edward Aaron 1931- *AmMWSc 92*
**Smuckler**, Jack Dennis 1946- *WhoMW 92*
**Smudski**, James W 1925- *AmMWSc 92*
**Smuin**, Michael 1938- *ConTFT 9, WhoEnt 92A*
**Smuk**, John Michael 1932- *AmMWSc 92*
**Smukler**, Linda *DrAPF 91*
**Smukler**, Victor 1931- *WhoAmL 92*
**Smuland**, Philip Lee 1951- *WhoRel 92*
**Smulders**, Anthony Peter 1942- *AmMWSc 92*
**Smullen**, Todd Thomas 1967- *WhoWest 92*
**Smullin**, Donald Evan 1947- *WhoWest 92*
**Smullin**, Louis Dijour 1916- *AmMWSc 92*
**Smulow**, Jerome B 1930- *AmMWSc 92*
**Smulson**, Mark Elliott 1936- *AmMWSc 92*
**Smulyan**, Harold 1929- *AmMWSc 92*
**Smulyan**, Jeffrey *WhoWest 92*
**Smura**, Bronislaw Bernard 1930- *AmMWSc 92*
**Smurfit**, Michael William Joseph *IntWW 91*
**Smurl**, James Frederick 1934- *WhoRel 92*
**Smutny**, Edgar Josef 1928- *AmMWSc 92*
**Smuts**, Jan 1870-1950 *FacFETw*
**Smuts**, Mary Elizabeth 1948- *AmMWSc 92*
**Smutz**, Morton 1918- *AmMWSc 92*
**Smyer**, Myrna Ruth 1946- *WhoEnt 92*
**Smyers**, William Hays 1901- *AmMWSc 92*
**Smykowski**, James George 1934- *WhoAmP 91*
**Smylie**, Douglas Edwin 1925- *AmMWSc 92*
**Smylie**, Michael 1914- *WhoAmP 91*
**Smylie**, Robert Edwin 1929- *AmMWSc 92*
**Smyllie**, J. S. *ConAu 133*
**Smyntek**, John Eugene, Jr. 1950- *WhoEnt 92*
**Smyre**, Calvin *WhoAmP 91, WhoBlA 92*
**Smyrl**, William Hiram 1938- *AmMWSc 92*
**Smyrski**, Lawrence Anthony 1968- *WhoMW 92*
**Smyrski**, Martha Marguerite 1953- *WhoAmL 92*
**Smyser**, Adam Albert 1920- *WhoWest 92*
**Smyser**, C A 1949- *WhoAmP 91*
**Smyser**, Charles Arvil 1949- *WhoWest 92*
**Smyser**, Craig 1951- *WhoAmL 92*
**Smyslov**, Valentin Ivanovich 1928- *IntWW 91*
**Smyslov**, Vasiliy Vasil'evich 1921- *SovUnBD*
**Smyslovsky**, Boris 1897-1988 *FacFETw*
**Smyth**, Bernard Bryan 1843-1913 *BiInAmS*
**Smyth**, Charles Phelps 1895- *AmMWSc 92*
**Smyth**, Clifford 1866-1943 *ScFEYrs*
**Smyth**, Craig Hugh 1915- *IntWW 91*
**Smyth**, David John 1936- *WhoFI 92*
**Smyth**, David Shannon 1943- *WhoWest 92*
**Smyth**, Desmond *Who 92*
**Smyth**, Donald Morgan 1930- *AmMWSc 92*
**Smyth**, Ethel 1858-1944 *NewAmDM*
**Smyth**, Harriet Rucker 1926- *IntAu&W 91, WrDr 92*
**Smyth**, Henry 1898-1986 *FacFETw*
**Smyth**, James Desmond 1917- *WrDr 92*
**Smyth**, James Robert Staples 1926- *Who 92*
**Smyth**, Jay Russell 1939- *AmMWSc 92*
**Smyth**, John Jackson 1941- *Who 92*
**Smyth**, John McDonnell, III 1915- *WhoMW 92*
**Smyth**, Joseph Desmond 1950- *Who 92*
**Smyth**, Joseph Richard 1944- *AmMWSc 92*
**Smyth**, Kelvin Paul 1950- *WhoAmP 91*
**Smyth**, Margaret Jane 1897- *Who 92*
**Smyth**, Martin *Who 92*
**Smyth**, Michael P 1934- *AmMWSc 92*
**Smyth**, Michel 1959- *WhoAmP 91*
**Smyth**, Nicholas Patrick Dillon 1924- *AmMWSc 92*
**Smyth**, Paul *DrAPF 91*
**Smyth**, Reginald 1917- *Who 92, WhoEnt 92*
**Smyth**, Robert Staples *Who 92*
**Smyth**, Theodore Hilton 1915- *WhoWest 92*
**Smyth**, Thomas, Jr 1927- *AmMWSc 92*
**Smyth**, Thomas Weyland Bowyer- 1960- *Who 92*
**Smyth**, Timothy 1953- *Who 92*
**Smyth**, William 1797-1868 *BiInAmS*
**Smyth**, William J. 1949- *ConAu 135*
**Smyth**, William Martin 1931- *Who 92*
**Smythe**, Alfred *ScFEYrs*
**Smythe**, Cheves McCord 1924- *AmMWSc 92*
**Smythe**, Clifford Anthony 1938- *Who 92*
**Smythe**, Patricia Rosemary K. *Who 92*
**Smythe**, Quentin George Murray 1916- *Who 92*
**Smythe**, Reginald *Who 92*
**Smythe**, Richard Vincent 1939- *AmMWSc 92*
**Smythe**, Robert C *AmMWSc 92*
**Smythe**, Tony *Who 92*
**Smythe**, Victor N. *WhoBlA 92*
**Smythe**, William Rodman 1930- *AmMWSc 92*
**Smythe-Haith**, Mabel Murphy 1918- *WhoAmP 91, WhoBlA 92*
**Smythe-Haithe**, Mabel Murphy 1918- *NotBlAW 92*
**Smythies**, John R. 1922- *WrDr 92*
**Snader**, Kenneth Means 1938- *AmMWSc 92*
**Snader**, Robert Miles 1925- *WhoWest 92*
**Snagge**, John Derrick Mordaunt 1904- *Who 92*
**Snagge**, Nancy 1906- *Who 92*
**Snaggs**, Carmen *WhoBlA 92*
**Snaid**, Leon Jeffrey 1946- *WhoAmL 92*
**Snaith**, George Robert 1930- *Who 92*
**Snaith**, J C 1876-1936 *ScFEYrs*
**Snape**, Edwin Allen, III 1931- *WhoEnt 92*
**Snape**, Peter Charles 1942- *Who 92*
**Snape**, Royden Eric 1922- *Who 92*
**Snape**, Thomas Peter 1925- *Who 92*
**Snape**, William J 1912- *AmMWSc 92*
**Snape**, William J, Jr 1943- *AmMWSc 92*
**Snape**, William John, Jr. 1943- *WhoWest 92*
**Snaper**, Alvin Allyn 1927- *AmMWSc 92*
**Snapp**, Thomas Carter, Jr 1938- *AmMWSc 92*
**Snapper**, Ernst 1913- *AmMWSc 92*
**Snapper**, James Robert 1948- *AmMWSc 92*
**Snare**, Carl Lawrence, Jr. 1936- *WhoFI 92, WhoWest 92*
**Snare**, Leroy Earl 1931- *AmMWSc 92*
**Snarr**, Brian B. 1956- *WhoAmL 92*
**Snarr**, John Frederic 1939- *AmMWSc 92*
**Snasdell**, Susan Kathleen 1948- *WhoWest 92*
**Snavely**, Benjamin Breneman 1936- *AmMWSc 92*
**Snavely**, Cynthia Ann 1959- *WhoRel 92*
**Snavely**, Deanne Lynn 1951- *AmMWSc 92*
**Snavely**, Earl Samuel, Jr 1927- *AmMWSc 92*
**Snavely**, Frank Richardson 1920- *WhoRel 92*
**Snavely**, Fred Allen 1919- *AmMWSc 92*
**Snavely**, Parke Detweiler, Jr 1919- *AmMWSc 92*
**Snavely**, William Brant 1951- *WhoMW 92*
**Snavely**, William Pennington 1920- *WhoFI 92*
**Snazelle**, Theodore Edward 1941- *AmMWSc 92*
**Snead**, Clarence Lewis, Jr 1936- *AmMWSc 92*
**Snead**, John D. 1917- *WhoBlA 92*
**Snead**, Kathleen Marie 1948- *WhoAmL 92*
**Snead**, Michael James 1927- *WhoIns 92*
**Snead**, O Carter, III 1943- *AmMWSc 92*
**Snead**, Samuel Jackson 1912- *FacFETw, IntWW 91*
**Sneade**, Barbara Herbert 1947- *AmMWSc 92*
**Sneary**, Max Eugene 1930- *WhoMW 92*
**Snechkus**, Antanas Yuozovich 1903-1974 *SovUnBD*
**Sneck**, Henry James 1926- *AmMWSc 92*
**Sneckenberger**, John Edward 1937- *AmMWSc 92*
**Snedaker**, Samuel Curry 1938- *AmMWSc 92*
**Snedden**, Billy 1926-1987 *FacFETw*
**Snedden**, David King 1933- *Who 92*
**Snedden**, Walter 1936- *AmMWSc 92*
**Sneddon**, Hutchison Burt 1929- *Who 92*
**Sneddon**, Ian Naismith 1919- *IntWW 91, Who 92, WrDr 92*
**Sneddon**, Leigh *AmMWSc 92*
**Sneddon**, Robert 1920- *Who 92*
**Snedecor**, James George 1917- *AmMWSc 92*
**Snedegar**, William H 1926- *AmMWSc 92*
**Snedeker**, James Phyfe 1948- *WhoIns 92*
**Snedeker**, Robert A 1928- *AmMWSc 92*
**Snedeker**, Sedgwick 1909- *WhoFI 92*
**Snee**, Ronald D 1941- *AmMWSc 92*
**Sneed**, Dan Calvin 1944- *WhoRel 92*
**Sneed**, Joseph Tyree, III 1920- *WhoAmL 92*
**Sneed**, Kevin A. 1969- *WhoRel 92*
**Sneed**, Marie Eleanor Wilkey 1915- *WhoMW 92*
**Sneed**, Paula A. 1947- *WhoBlA 92*
**Sneed**, Sherrie Lynn 1954- *WhoRel 92*
**Sneed**, Tommy Lynn 1947- *WhoRel 92*
**Sneen**, Richard Allen 1930- *AmMWSc 92*
**Sneeringer**, Alfred Lauren 1918- *WhoMW 92*
**Sneeringer**, Stephen Geddes 1949- *WhoAmL 92, WhoMW 92*
**Snegirev**, Vladimir Vsevolodovich 1923- *IntWW 91*
**Sneh**, Moshe 1909-1972 *FacFETw*
**Sneider**, Norman Harry 1951- *WhoMW 92*
**Sneider**, Robert Morton 1929- *AmMWSc 92*
**Sneider**, Roberto 1962- *WhoEnt 92*
**Sneider**, Thomas W 1938- *AmMWSc 92*
**Snelgrove**, Donald George *Who 92*
**Snelgrove**, James Lewis 1942- *AmMWSc 92*
**Snelgrove**, Rich *WhoAmP 91*
**Snell**, A W 1924- *AmMWSc 92*
**Snell**, Alden Henry 1953- *WhoRel 92*
**Snell**, Arthur Hawley 1909- *AmMWSc 92*
**Snell**, Bruce M., Jr. 1929- *WhoAmL 92, WhoAmP 91, WhoMW 92*
**Snell**, Charles Murrell 1946- *AmMWSc 92*
**Snell**, Daniel Clair 1947- *WhoRel 92*
**Snell**, Ebenezer Strong 1801-1876 *BiInAmS*
**Snell**, Edmund 1889- *ScFEYrs*
**Snell**, Esmond Emerson 1914- *AmMWSc 92, IntWW 91*
**Snell**, Fred Manget 1921- *AmMWSc 92*
**Snell**, Fred William 1910- *WhoAmP 91*
**Snell**, Frederick Rowlandson d1991 *Who 92N*
**Snell**, George Boyd 1907- *Who 92*
**Snell**, George Davis 1903- *AmMWSc 92, IntWW 91, Who 92, WhoNob 90*
**Snell**, Hannah 1723-1792 *EncAmaz 91*
**Snell**, Hilary Fred 1934- *WhoAmL 92*
**Snell**, James Laurie 1925- *AmMWSc 92*
**Snell**, Jimmy Gregory 1927- *WhoBlA 92*
**Snell**, Joan Yvonne Ervin 1932- *WhoBlA 92*
**Snell**, John B 1936- *AmMWSc 92*
**Snell**, John Nicholas B. *Who 92*
**Snell**, Junius Fielding 1921- *AmMWSc 92*
**Snell**, Kenneth Dwayne 1954- *WhoMW 92*
**Snell**, Luke Murray 1945- *WhoMW 92*
**Snell**, Ned Colwell 1944- *WhoWest 92*
**Snell**, Paul Alan, Sr. 1957- *WhoWest 92*
**Snell**, Peter R.E. 1941- *IntMPA 92*
**Snell**, Philip D. 1915- *Who 92*
**Snell**, Richard 1930- *WhoFI 92, WhoWest 92*
**Snell**, Richard Saxon 1925- *AmMWSc 92*
**Snell**, Robert Isaac 1937- *AmMWSc 92*
**Snell**, Robert L 1925- *AmMWSc 92*
**Snell**, Robert Ross 1932- *AmMWSc 92*
**Snell**, Roger Douglas 1956- *WhoFI 92*
**Snell**, Ronald Lee 1951- *AmMWSc 92*
**Snell**, Thaddeus Stevens, III 1919- *WhoAmL 92*
**Snell**, Verlyn Reid 1934- *WhoRel 92*
**Snell**, William Edward d1990 *Who 92N*
**Snell**, William J 1946- *AmMWSc 92*
**Snellen**, Deborah Sue 1956- *WhoMW 92*
**Sneller**, Phillip Paul 1951- *WhoRel 92*
**Snellgrove**, Anthony *Who 92*
**Snellgrove**, David Llewellyn 1920- *Who 92*
**Snellgrove**, David Llewelyn 1920- *IntWW 91*
**Snellgrove**, John Anthony 1922- *Who 92*
**Snellgrove**, Laurence Ernest 1928- *IntAu&W 91, WrDr 92*
**Snelling**, Arthur 1914- *Who 92*
**Snelling**, Charles Darwin 1931- *WhoAmP 91, WhoFI 92*
**Snelling**, Christopher 1935- *AmMWSc 92*
**Snelling**, George Arthur 1929- *WhoFI 92*
**Snelling**, Lonie Eugene, Jr. 1937- *WhoRel 92*
**Snelling**, Richard A. 1927- *AlmAP 92 [port], IntWW 91*
**Snelling**, Richard A. 1927-1991 *NewYTBS 91 [port]*
**Snelling**, Richard Arkwright 1927- *WhoAmP 91*
**Snelling**, Richard Kelly 1931- *WhoFI 92*
**Snelling**, William Joseph 1804-1848 *BenetAL 91*
**Snelling**, William Lee 1931- *WhoFI 92*
**Snelling**, William Rodman 1931- *WhoFI 92*
**Snellings**, Rolland 1938- *WhoBlA 92*
**Snellings**, William Moran 1947- *AmMWSc 92*
**Snellman**, Leonard W 1920- *AmMWSc 92*
**Snelsire**, Robert W 1933- *AmMWSc 92*
**Snelson**, Alan 1934- *AmMWSc 92*
**Snelson**, Edward Alec Abbott 1904- *Who 92*
**Snelson**, Franklin F, Jr 1943- *AmMWSc 92*
**Snelson**, Sigmund 1932- *AmMWSc 92*
**Snetkov**, Boris Vasilevich 1925- *IntWW 91*
**Snetsinger**, David Clarence 1930- *AmMWSc 92*
**Snetsinger**, Kenneth George 1939- *AmMWSc 92*
**Snetsinger**, Robert J 1928- *AmMWSc 92*
**Snetzer**, Michael Alan 1940- *WhoFI 92*
**Snezhnevsky**, Aleksandr Vladimirovich 1904- *SovUnBD*
**Snider**, Albert Monroe, Jr *AmMWSc 92*
**Snider**, Allen Wesley 1953- *WhoRel 92*
**Snider**, Arthur David 1940- *AmMWSc 92*
**Snider**, Barry B 1950- *AmMWSc 92*
**Snider**, Bill Carl F 1920- *AmMWSc 92*
**Snider**, Clifton *DrAPF 91*
**Snider**, Dale Reynolds 1938- *AmMWSc 92*
**Snider**, Davida Jane 1951- *WhoEnt 92*
**Snider**, Dixie Edward, Jr 1943- *AmMWSc 92*
**Snider**, Donald Edward 1944- *AmMWSc 92*
**Snider**, Dorothy Elizabeth 1923- *WhoRel 92*
**Snider**, Duke 1926- *FacFETw*
**Snider**, Eric Ross 1954- *WhoEnt 92*
**Snider**, George D 1931- *WhoAmP 91*
**Snider**, Gordon Lloyd 1922- *AmMWSc 92*
**Snider**, Howard J 1929- *WhoAmP 91*
**Snider**, James Rhodes 1931- *WhoFI 92*
**Snider**, Jerry Allen 1937- *AmMWSc 92*
**Snider**, John William 1924- *AmMWSc 92, WhoMW 92*
**Snider**, Joseph Lyons 1934- *AmMWSc 92, WhoMW 92*
**Snider**, Karl 1960- *WhoWest 92*
**Snider**, Kenneth C 1946- *WhoAmP 91*
**Snider**, Louis Beckham 1902- *WhoRel 92*

**Snider,** Neil Stanley 1938- *AmMWSc 92*
**Snider,** Patricia Faye 1931- *WhoEnt 92*
**Snider,** Paul Raymond 1952- *WhoEnt 92*
**Snider,** Philip Joel 1952- *WhoRel 92*
**Snider,** Philip Joseph 1929- *AmMWSc 92*
**Snider,** Ray Michael 1948- *AmMWSc 92*
**Snider,** Robert Folinsbee 1931- *AmMWSc 92*
**Snider,** Robert Larry 1932- *WhoFI 92*
**Snider,** Ronald Albert 1931- *WhoRel 92*
**Snider,** Ronald Lynn 1950- *WhoRel 92*
**Snider,** Theodore Eugene 1943- *AmMWSc 92*
**Snider,** William Alan 1967- *WhoEnt 92*
**Snider,** William Don 1941- *WhoMW 92*
**Sniderman,** Howard Irwin 1953- *WhoFI 92*
**Snieckus,** Antanas 1903-1974 *SovUnBD*
**Snieckus,** Victor A 1937- *AmMWSc 92*
**Sniezek,** Patrick William 1964- *WhoWest 92*
**Snihur,** William Joseph, Jr. 1959- *WhoAmL 92*
**Snijders,** Wouter 1928- *IntWW 91*
**Snipes,** Al M 1921- *WhoAmP 91*
**Snipes,** Charles Andrew 1936- *AmMWSc 92*
**Snipes,** David Strange 1928- *AmMWSc 92*
**Snipes,** Juanita Krentzman 1926- *WhoAmP 91*
**Snipes,** Kenneth 1938- *WhoBlA 92*
**Snipes,** Morris Burton 1940- *AmMWSc 92*
**Snipes,** Wallace Clayton 1937- *AmMWSc 92*
**Snipes,** Wesley *WhoBlA 92*
**Snipes,** Wesley 1963- *IntMPA 92*
**Snipp,** Robert Leo 1936- *AmMWSc 92*
**Snipstead,** Richard *WhoRel 92*
**Snite,** Albert John, Jr. 1948- *WhoAmL 92*
**Snitgen,** Donald Albert 1936- *AmMWSc 92*
**Snitzer,** Elias 1925- *AmMWSc 92*
**Snively,** David Allan, Sr. 1940- *WhoMW 92*
**Snively,** Leslie O 1953- *AmMWSc 92*
**Snively,** Stephen Wayne 1949- *WhoAmL 92*
**Snoble,** Joseph Jerry 1931- *AmMWSc 92*
**Snoddon,** Larry E. 1945- *WhoFI 92*
**Snoddy,** Charles Edison, Jr. 1923- *WhoFI 92*
**Snoddy,** Edward L 1933- *AmMWSc 92*
**Snoddy,** Glenn Thomas 1922- *WhoEnt 92*
**Snoderly,** Donald Lynn 1947- *WhoAmP 91*
**Snodgrass,** Anthony McElrea 1934- *IntWW 91, Who 92, WrDr 92*
**Snodgrass,** Herschel Roy 1913- *AmMWSc 92*
**Snodgrass,** Hugh Edwin 1946- *WhoFI 92*
**Snodgrass,** John Michael Owen 1928- *Who 92*
**Snodgrass,** Klyne Ryland 1944- *WhoRel 92*
**Snodgrass,** Michael Jens 1941- *AmMWSc 92*
**Snodgrass,** Quentin Curtius *ConAu 135*
**Snodgrass,** Rex Jackson 1934- *AmMWSc 92*
**Snodgrass,** Robert A. 1957- *WhoFI 92*
**Snodgrass,** Sally E 1936- *WhoAmP 91*
**Snodgrass,** Thomas Jefferson *ConAu 135*
**Snodgrass,** W.D. *DrAPF 91*
**Snodgrass,** W. D. 1926- *BenetAL 91, ConAu 36NR, ConLC 68 [port], ConPo 91, IntAu&W 91, WrDr 92*
**Snodgrass,** William Albert 1933- *WhoIns 92*
**Snodgrass,** William DeWitt 1926- *IntWW 91*
**Snodgress,** Carrie 1945- *IntMPA 92*
**Snoeyenbos,** Glenn Howard 1922- *AmMWSc 92*
**Snoeyink,** Vernon Leroy 1940- *AmMWSc 92*
**Snoke,** Arthur Wilmot 1945- *AmMWSc 92*
**Snoke,** J Arthur 1940- *AmMWSc 92*
**Snoke,** Martin Lee 1914- *WhoMW 92*
**Snoke,** Roy Eugene 1943- *AmMWSc 92*
**Snook,** Billy Jay 1934- *WhoAmP 91*
**Snook,** Harry 1944- *TwCPaSc*
**Snook,** J Carlton 1943- *WhoAmP 91*
**Snook,** James Ronald 1930- *AmMWSc 92*
**Snook,** John Ramsey 1938- *WhoFI 92*
**Snook,** Quinton 1925- *WhoWest 92*
**Snook,** Theodore 1907- *AmMWSc 92*
**Snope,** Andrew John 1939- *AmMWSc 92*
**Snorf,** Lowell Delford, Jr. 1919- *WhoAmL 92, WhoIns 92*
**Snortland,** Howard Jerome 1912- *WhoAmP 91*
**Snover,** James Edward 1920- *AmMWSc 92*
**Snover,** Kurt Albert 1943- *AmMWSc 92*
**Snow,** Adolph Isaac 1921- *AmMWSc 92*
**Snow,** Adrian John 1939- *Who 92*
**Snow,** Alan Albert 1946- *WhoRel 92, WhoWest 92*
**Snow,** Anne E 1943- *AmMWSc 92*
**Snow,** Antony Edmund 1932- *Who 92*
**Snow,** Beatrice Lee 1941- *AmMWSc 92*
**Snow,** Bonnie *DrAPF 91*
**Snow,** C. P. 1905-1980 *CnDBLB 7 [port], FacFETw, RfGEnL 91*
**Snow,** Charles H 1877-1967 *TwCWW 91*
**Snow,** Christopher John 1951- *WhoAmL 92*
**Snow,** Claude Henry, Jr. 1954- *WhoFI 92*
**Snow,** Clyde Collins 1928- *AmMWSc 92*
**Snow,** David Baker 1941- *AmMWSc 92*
**Snow,** Donald L 1917- *AmMWSc 92*
**Snow,** Donald Ray 1931- *AmMWSc 92*
**Snow,** Douglas Oscar 1917- *AmMWSc 92*
**Snow,** Edgar Parks 1905-1972 *BenetAL 91*
**Snow,** Edward Hunter 1936- *AmMWSc 92*
**Snow,** Eleanour Anne 1960- *AmMWSc 92*
**Snow,** Eliza Roxey 1804-1887 *RelLAm 91*
**Snow,** Frances Compton *ConAu 133*
**Snow,** Francis Huntington 1840-1908 *BilnAmS*
**Snow,** George Abraham 1926- *AmMWSc 92*
**Snow,** George Earle 1947- *WhoFI 92*
**Snow,** George Edward 1945- *AmMWSc 92*
**Snow,** Hank 1914- *NewAmDM*
**Snow,** Harold Edwin 1951- *WhoMW 92, WhoRel 92*
**Snow,** Helen Foster 1907- *IntAu&W 91, WrDr 92*
**Snow,** James Byron, Jr 1932- *AmMWSc 92*
**Snow,** Jean Anthony 1932- *AmMWSc 92*
**Snow,** Jeffrey Elliott 1960- *WhoWest 92*
**Snow,** Joel A 1937- *AmMWSc 92*
**Snow,** John Elbridge 1915- *AmMWSc 92*
**Snow,** John J, Jr 1929- *WhoAmP 91*
**Snow,** John Thomas 1943- *AmMWSc 92*
**Snow,** John Thomas 1945- *AmMWSc 92*
**Snow,** John William 1939- *WhoFI 92*
**Snow,** Johnnie Park 1942- *AmMWSc 92*
**Snow,** Jonathan George 1947- *Who 92*
**Snow,** Joseph William 1939- *AmMWSc 92*
**Snow,** Karl Nelson, Jr 1930- *WhoAmP 91*
**Snow,** Keith Ronald 1943- *WrDr 92*
**Snow,** Kenneth Arthur 1934- *Who 92*
**Snow,** Lee Erlin 1924- *WhoWest 92*
**Snow,** Leida *WhoEnt 92*
**Snow,** Lorenzo 1814-1901 *RelLAm 91*
**Snow,** Loudell Fromme 1933- *AmMWSc 92*
**Snow,** Marcellus Scowcroft 1942- *WhoWest 92*
**Snow,** Mark 1946- *IntMPA 92*
**Snow,** Mark Eugene 1955- *WhoMW 92, WhoRel 92*
**Snow,** Michael 1929- *IntDcF 2-2*
**Snow,** Michael Dennis 1942- *AmMWSc 92*
**Snow,** Michael R 1949- *IntAu&W 91*
**Snow,** Mike M *WhoAmP 91*
**Snow,** Mikel Henry 1944- *AmMWSc 92*
**Snow,** Milton Leonard 1930- *AmMWSc 92*
**Snow,** Percy Lee 1967- *WhoBlA 92*
**Snow,** Peter 1927- *TwCPaSc*
**Snow,** Peter John 1938- *Who 92*
**Snow,** Philip 1915- *WrDr 92*
**Snow,** Philip Albert 1915- *Who 92*
**Snow,** Philip Anthony 1951- *AmMWSc 92*
**Snow,** Richard F. 1947- *WrDr 92*
**Snow,** Richard Huntley 1928- *AmMWSc 92*
**Snow,** Richard L 1930- *AmMWSc 92*
**Snow,** Ronald Edward 1933- *Who 92*
**Snow,** Ronald James 1952- *WhoAmL 92*
**Snow,** Sidney Richard 1929- *AmMWSc 92*
**Snow,** Theodore Peck 1947- *AmMWSc 92*
**Snow,** Thomas 1929- *Who 92*
**Snow,** Thomas Gerard 1955- *WhoAmL 92*
**Snow,** Thomas Maitland 1890- *Who 92*
**Snow,** Thomas Righter 1947- *WhoEnt 92*
**Snow,** Thomas Russell 1944- *AmMWSc 92*
**Snow,** Thomas Wayne, Jr 1936- *WhoAmP 91*
**Snow,** Tower Charles, Jr. 1947- *WhoAmL 92*
**Snow,** Valaida 1900?-1956 *NotBlAW 92*
**Snow,** Vanburen Lowry 1950- *WhoAmL 92*
**Snow,** W. Sterling 1947- *WhoWest 92*
**Snow,** Wilbert 1884-1977 *BenetAL 91*
**Snow,** William Appleton 1869-1899 *BilnAmS*
**Snow,** William Richard 1951- *WhoFI 92*
**Snow,** William Rosebrook 1930- *AmMWSc 92*
**Snow,** Wolfe 1938- *AmMWSc 92*
**Snow-Neumann,** Joanne 1947- *WhoAmP 91*
**Snowbarger,** Vincent Keith 1949- *WhoAmL 92, WhoAmP 91*
**Snowberger,** Charlotte Ann 1931- *WhoRel 92*
**Snowden,** Carl O 1953- *WhoAmP 91*
**Snowden,** Diana Emily 1947- *WhoWest 92*
**Snowden,** Donald Philip 1931- *AmMWSc 92*
**Snowden,** Frank Walter 1939- *WhoBlA 92*
**Snowden,** Fredrick 1936- *WhoBlA 92*
**Snowden,** Gail 1945- *WhoBlA 92*
**Snowden,** Gene 1928- *WhoAmP 91*
**Snowden,** Gilda 1954- *WhoBlA 92*
**Snowden,** Guy Bernhard 1945- *WhoFI 92*
**Snowden,** Jesse O 1937- *AmMWSc 92*
**Snowden,** John Samuel Philip *Who 92, WhoRel 92, WhoWest 92*
**Snowden,** Phillip Ray 1951- *WhoBlA 92*
**Snowden,** Raymond C. 1937- *WhoBlA 92*
**Snowdon,** Earl of 1930- *IntWW 91, Who 92*
**Snowdon,** Charles Thomas 1941- *AmMWSc 92, WhoMW 92*
**Snowdowne,** Kenneth William 1947- *AmMWSc 92*
**Snowe,** Olympia J. 1947- *AlmAP 92 [port]*
**Snowe,** Olympia Jean 1947- *WhoAmP 91*
**Snowiss,** Alvin L 1930- *WhoAmP 91*
**Snowling,** Christopher 1934- *Who 92*
**Snowman,** A. Kenneth 1919- *IntWW 91*
**Snowman,** Alfred 1936- *AmMWSc 92*
**Snowman,** Daniel 1938- *IntAu&W 91, WrDr 92*
**Snowman,** Nicholas 1944- *Who 92, WhoEnt 92*
**Snowman,** Nicholas Michael 1944- *IntWW 91*
**Snoy Et d'Oppuers,** Jean-Charles d1991 *Who 92N*
**Snoy Et D'Oppuers,** Jean-Charles 1907- *IntWW 91*
**Snudden,** Birdell Harry 1935- *AmMWSc 92*
**Snustad,** Donald Peter 1940- *AmMWSc 92*
**Snydal,** James M. *DrAPF 91*
**Snydal,** James Matthew 1949- *IntAu&W 91*
**Snyder,** Albert W 1925- *AmMWSc 92*
**Snyder,** Allan Gregory 1954- *WhoWest 92*
**Snyder,** Allan Whitenack 1940- *IntWW 91, Who 92*
**Snyder,** Allegra Fuller 1927- *WhoEnt 92, WhoWest 92*
**Snyder,** Andrew Kagey 1937- *AmMWSc 92*
**Snyder,** Ann C 1951- *AmMWSc 92*
**Snyder,** Ann Knabb 1944- *AmMWSc 92*
**Snyder,** Anne 1922- *WrDr 92*
**Snyder,** Arlen Dean 1933- *WhoEnt 92*
**Snyder,** Arnold Lee, Jr 1937- *AmMWSc 92*
**Snyder,** Arthur Kress 1932- *WhoAmL 92*
**Snyder,** Benjamin Willard 1939- *AmMWSc 92*
**Snyder,** C Robert 1937- *WhoIns 92*
**Snyder,** Carl Edward 1921- *AmMWSc 92*
**Snyder,** Carl Henry 1931- *AmMWSc 92*
**Snyder,** Carol 1946- *WhoAmP 91*
**Snyder,** Carolyn M 1938- *WhoAmP 91*
**Snyder,** Cecil 1927- *WrDr 92*
**Snyder,** Charles Aubrey 1941- *WhoAmL 92*
**Snyder,** Charles Theodore 1912- *AmMWSc 92*
**Snyder,** Charles Thomas 1938- *AmMWSc 92*
**Snyder,** Clair Allison 1921- *WhoFI 92*
**Snyder,** Clarise Elaine 1955- *WhoEnt 92*
**Snyder,** Claude Robert 1937- *WhoFI 92*
**Snyder,** Clifford Charles 1916- *AmMWSc 92*
**Snyder,** Conway Wilson 1918- *AmMWSc 92*
**Snyder,** Cooper 1928- *WhoAmP 91*
**Snyder,** Dana Paul 1922- *AmMWSc 92*
**Snyder,** Daniel Raphael 1940- *AmMWSc 92*
**Snyder,** David Hilton 1938- *AmMWSc 92*
**Snyder,** David John 1955- *WhoRel 92*
**Snyder,** David L. 1944- *WhoEnt 92, WhoWest 92*
**Snyder,** David Scott 1960- *WhoMW 92*
**Snyder,** Dexter Dean 1942- *AmMWSc 92, WhoMW 92*
**Snyder,** Don J 1950- *IntAu&W 91*
**Snyder,** Dona Joy 1932- *WhoMW 92*
**Snyder,** Donald Benjamin 1935- *AmMWSc 92*
**Snyder,** Donald DuWayne 1928- *AmMWSc 92*
**Snyder,** Donald Lee 1943- *AmMWSc 92*
**Snyder,** Donald W 1951- *WhoAmP 91*
**Snyder,** Edd G. 1947- *WhoBlA 92*
**Snyder,** Edward Adams 1953- *WhoFI 92*
**Snyder,** Eugene Harold 1929- *WhoRel 92*
**Snyder,** Evan Samuel 1923- *AmMWSc 92*
**Snyder,** Francis Gregory 1942- *IntAu&W 91, WrDr 92*
**Snyder,** Franklin F 1910- *AmMWSc 92*
**Snyder,** Fred Calvin 1916- *AmMWSc 92*
**Snyder,** Fred Leonard 1931- *AmMWSc 92*
**Snyder,** Freeman Woodrow 1917- *AmMWSc 92*
**Snyder,** Gary *DrAPF 91*
**Snyder,** Gary 1930- *BenetAL 91, ConPo 91, WrDr 92*
**Snyder,** Gary Dean 1947- *AmMWSc 92*
**Snyder,** Gary E. 1947- *WhoAmL 92*
**Snyder,** Gary James 1959- *AmMWSc 92*
**Snyder,** Gary Wayne 1954- *AmMWSc 92*
**Snyder,** George Anna 1934- *WhoAmP 91*
**Snyder,** George Heft 1939- *AmMWSc 92*
**Snyder,** George Leonard 1927- *WhoWest 92*
**Snyder,** George Richard 1929- *AmMWSc 92*
**Snyder,** George Stephen 1949- *WhoWest 92*
**Snyder,** George W. 1944- *WhoBlA 92*
**Snyder,** Glenn J 1923- *AmMWSc 92*
**Snyder,** Graydon 1930- *WrDr 92*
**Snyder,** Gregory Kirk 1939- *AmMWSc 92*
**Snyder,** Gregory Maurice 1953- *WhoAmP 91*
**Snyder,** Harold Lee 1952- *AmMWSc 92*
**Snyder,** Harry E 1930- *AmMWSc 92*
**Snyder,** Harry Raymond, Jr 1924- *AmMWSc 92*
**Snyder,** Hartley Deal 1903- *WhoWest 92*
**Snyder,** Herbert Howard 1927- *AmMWSc 92*
**Snyder,** Howard A 1940- *ConAu 34NR*
**Snyder,** Howard Arthur 1930- *AmMWSc 92, WhoWest 92*
**Snyder,** Hugh Donald 1923- *AmMWSc 92*
**Snyder,** J Edward, Jr 1924- *AmMWSc 92*
**Snyder,** Jack Austin 1927- *AmMWSc 92*
**Snyder,** James Frederick, Jr. 1944- *WhoFI 92*
**Snyder,** James L. 1946- *WhoMW 92*
**Snyder,** James Newton 1923- *AmMWSc 92*
**Snyder,** James Patrick 1964- *WhoEnt 92*
**Snyder,** James William, Jr. 1948- *WhoFI 92, WhoMW 92*
**Snyder,** Janet Ruth 1932- *WhoEnt 92*
**Snyder,** Jeanne Anne 1945- *WhoMW 92*
**Snyder,** Jed Cobb 1955- *WhoFI 92*
**Snyder,** Jedidiah Newell 1944- *WhoRel 92*
**Snyder,** Johanna *WhoEnt 92*
**Snyder,** John Bennett 1929- *WhoFI 92*
**Snyder,** John Crayton 1910- *AmMWSc 92*
**Snyder,** John Joseph 1908- *WhoWest 92*
**Snyder,** John Joseph 1925- *WhoRel 92*
**Snyder,** John L 1930- *AmMWSc 92*
**Snyder,** John William 1940- *AmMWSc 92*
**Snyder,** Joseph John 1946- *WhoFI 92*
**Snyder,** Joseph Quincy 1920- *AmMWSc 92*
**Snyder,** Judith Armstrong 1946- *AmMWSc 92, WhoWest 92*
**Snyder,** Karen Lee 1946- *WhoWest 92*
**Snyder,** Karl Daniel 1926- *WhoEnt 92*
**Snyder,** Laman CG 1945- *WhoWest 92*
**Snyder,** Larry Hayden 1943- *WhoFI 92*
**Snyder,** Laverne 1937- *WhoFI 92*
**Snyder,** Lawrence Clement 1932- *AmMWSc 92*
**Snyder,** Lee *WhoAmP 91*
**Snyder,** Lee Charles 1950- *WhoEnt 92*
**Snyder,** Leon Allen 1920- *AmMWSc 92*
**Snyder,** Lewis Emil 1939- *AmMWSc 92*
**Snyder,** Lloyd Robert 1931- *AmMWSc 92*
**Snyder,** Loren Russell 1941- *AmMWSc 92*
**Snyder,** Louis L 1907- *ConAu 34NR, WrDr 92*
**Snyder,** Louis Leo 1907- *IntAu&W 91*
**Snyder,** Louis Michael 1935- *AmMWSc 92*
**Snyder,** Margaret Judith 1940- *WhoWest 92*
**Snyder,** Marion Gene 1928- *WhoAmP 91*
**Snyder,** Mark 1946- *WhoAmP 91*
**Snyder,** Mark Jeffrey 1947- *WhoFI 92*
**Snyder,** Martin Bradford 1942- *WhoWest 92*
**Snyder,** Mary Cowden 1937- *WhoEnt 92*
**Snyder,** Maryhelen *DrAPF 91*
**Snyder,** Melvin H, Jr 1921- *AmMWSc 92*
**Snyder,** Merrill J 1919- *AmMWSc 92*
**Snyder,** Michael Anthony 1962- *WhoFI 92*
**Snyder,** Mildred Anne 1924- *WhoAmP 91*
**Snyder,** Milton Jack 1921- *AmMWSc 92*
**Snyder,** Mitch 1944-1990 *AnObit 1990, News 91*
**Snyder,** Mitchell 1938- *AmMWSc 92*
**Snyder,** Nathan W 1918- *AmMWSc 92*
**Snyder,** Oliver Page 1927- *WhoFI 92*
**Snyder,** Pamela Jane 1956- *WhoFI 92*
**Snyder,** Patricia Ann 1940- *AmMWSc 92*
**Snyder,** Peter B. 1954- *WhoEnt 92*
**Snyder,** R L 1911- *AmMWSc 92*
**Snyder,** Rachel A. 1953- *WhoMW 92*
**Snyder,** Ralph Sheldon 1922- *WhoAmL 92*
**Snyder,** Randall Louis 1944- *WhoEnt 92*
**Snyder,** Richard A 1910- *WhoAmP 91*
**Snyder,** Richard E. *NewYTBS 91 [port]*
**Snyder,** Richard Elliot 1933- *WhoFI 92*
**Snyder,** Richard Gerald 1928- *AmMWSc 92, WhoWest 92*
**Snyder,** Richard Joseph 1939- *WhoAmL 92, WhoFI 92*
**Snyder,** Richard Lee 1940- *WhoFI 92*
**Snyder,** Robert 1935- *AmMWSc 92*
**Snyder,** Robert Carl 1937- *WhoRel 92*
**Snyder,** Robert Douglas 1934- *AmMWSc 92*
**Snyder,** Robert Gene 1929- *AmMWSc 92*
**Snyder,** Robert James 1936- *WhoRel 92*
**Snyder,** Robert John 1959- *WhoEnt 92*
**Snyder,** Robert L 1934- *AmMWSc 92*
**Snyder,** Robert Lee 1952- *WhoMW 92*

Snyder, Robert Lee, II 1952- *WhoAmL 92*
Snyder, Robert LeRoy 1920- *WhoAmP 91*
Snyder, Robert LeRoy 1926- *AmMWSc 92*
Snyder, Robert Lyman 1941- *AmMWSc 92*
Snyder, Robert Martin 1912- *WhoFI 92*
Snyder, Robert Michael 1954- *WhoWest 92*
Snyder, Robert Raboin 1946- *WhoEnt 92*
Snyder, Rowan 1947- *WhoFI 92*
Snyder, Ruth Evelyn 1911- *AmMWSc 92*
Snyder, Sam A. 1930- *WhoAmL 92*
Snyder, Sid *WhoAmP 91*
Snyder, Solomon H 1938- *AmMWSc 92*
Snyder, Stacey Marie 1964- *WhoFI 92*
Snyder, Stanley Paul 1942- *AmMWSc 92*
Snyder, Stephen Foster 1946- *WhoAmP 91*
Snyder, Stephen Laurie 1942- *AmMWSc 92*
Snyder, Susan Barker 1964- *WhoAmL 92*
Snyder, Thoma Mees 1916- *AmMWSc 92*
Snyder, Thomas Gene 1943- *WhoMW 92*
Snyder, Thomas John 1950- *WhoMW 92*
Snyder, Timothy David 1962- *WhoRel 92*
Snyder, Tom *LesBEnT 92*
Snyder, Tom 1936- *IntMPA 92*
Snyder, Victor F 1947- *WhoAmP 91*
Snyder, Virgil W 1934- *AmMWSc 92*
Snyder, Virginia 1957- *AmMWSc 92*
Snyder, Wadell D. 1929- *WhoBlA 92*
Snyder, Walter Stanley 1949- *AmMWSc 92*
Snyder, Warren Edward 1922- *AmMWSc 92*
Snyder, Wayne William 1928- *WhoMW 92*
Snyder, Wesley Edwin 1946- *AmMWSc 92*
Snyder, Wilbert Frank 1904- *AmMWSc 92*
Snyder, Willard Breidenthal 1940- *WhoAmL 92, WhoFI 92, WhoMW 92*
Snyder, Willard Monroe 1918- *AmMWSc 92*
Snyder, Willetta H 1943- *WhoAmP 91*
Snyder, William Albert 1946- *WhoAmL 92*
Snyder, William Arthur, Jr. 1940- *WhoAmL 92*
Snyder, William Burton 1929- *WhoFI 92, WhoIns 92*
Snyder, William James 1941- *AmMWSc 92*
Snyder, William James 1942- *WhoWest 92*
Snyder, William L. 1920- *IntMPA 92*
Snyder, William Regis, Jr. 1954- *WhoWest 92*
Snyder, William Richard 1929- *WhoRel 92*
Snyder, William Richard 1947- *AmMWSc 92*
Snyder, William Robert 1946- *AmMWSc 92*
Snyder, William Thomas 1931- *AmMWSc 92*
Snyder, Zacharia Xenophon 1850-1915 *BiInAmS*
Snyder, Zilpha Keatley 1927- *IntAu&W 91, WrDr 92*
Snyder Swanson, Carolyn Ann 1951- *WhoWest 92*
Snyderman, Ralph 1940- *AmMWSc 92*
Snyderman, Selma Eleanore 1916- *AmMWSc 92*
Snygg, John Morrow 1937- *AmMWSc 92*
So, Antero Go 1932- *AmMWSc 92*
So, Ronald Ming Cho 1939- *AmMWSc 92*
Soady, William C. 1943- *IntMPA 92*
Soame, Charles Buckworth-Herne- 1932- *Who 92*
Soames, Lady 1922- *Who 92*
Soames, Lord 1920-1987 *FacFETw*
Soames, Nicholas 1948- *Who 92*
Soames, Richard 1936- *IntMPA 92*
Soames, Richard M.F. 1936- *WhoEnt 92*
Soane, Leslie James 1926- *Who 92*
Soards, William L 1942- *WhoAmP 91*
Soare, Robert I 1940- *AmMWSc 92*
Soare, Thomas Fulton 1936- *WhoEnt 92*
Soares, Eugene Robbins 1945- *AmMWSc 92*
Soares, Joseph Henry, Jr 1941- *AmMWSc 92*
Soares, Mario Alberto Nobre Lopes 1924- *IntWW 91, Who 92*
Soares, Wilfred 1929- *WhoAmP 91*
Soares Alves, Francisco Jose 1942- *IntWW 91*
Soares de Mello, Adelino Jose Rodrigues 1931- *WhoFI 92*
Soaries, Raynes L., Jr. 1924- *WhoBlA 92*
Soave, Rosemary 1949- *AmMWSc 92*
Sobchak, Anatoliy Aleksandrovich 1937- *IntWW 91, SovUnBD*
Sobczak, Rosine 1942- *WhoMW 92*
Sobczak, Thomas Victor 1937- *AmMWSc 92*
Sobek, Irvin Gene 1934- *WhoWest 92*
Sobel, Alan 1928- *AmMWSc 92*
Sobel, Edna H 1918- *AmMWSc 92*
Sobel, Erwin 1938- *WhoAmL 92*
Sobel, Henry Wayne *AmMWSc 92*
Sobel, Irwin Philip d1991 *NewYTBS 91*
Sobel, Irwin Philip 1901-1991 *ConAu 134*
Sobel, Jael Sabina 1935- *AmMWSc 92*
Sobel, Kenneth Jay 1960- *WhoAmL 92*
Sobel, Kenneth Mark 1954- *AmMWSc 92*
Sobel, Mark E 1949- *AmMWSc 92*
Sobel, Michael I 1939- *AmMWSc 92*
Sobel, Robert Edward 1941- *AmMWSc 92*
Sobel, Walter Howard 1913- *WhoMW 92*
Sobell, Henry Martinique 1935- *AmMWSc 92*
Sobell, Linda Carter 1948- *AmMWSc 92*
Sobell, Mark Barry 1944- *AmMWSc 92*
Sobell, Michael 1892- *IntWW 91, Who 92*
Soben, Howard David 1942- *WhoFI 92*
Sober, Daniel Isaac 1942- *AmMWSc 92*
Sober, Phillip 1931- *Who 92*
Soberman, Robert K 1930- *AmMWSc 92*
Soberon-Ferrer, Horacio 1954- *WhoFI 92, WhoHisp 92*
Sobers, Austin W. 1914- *WhoBlA 92*
Sobers, Garfield St. Auburn 1936- *IntWW 91*
Sobers, Gary 1936- *FacFETw*
Sobers, Gerfield 1936- *Who 92*
Sobers, Waynett A., Jr. 1937- *WhoBlA 92*
Sobery, Julie Sterner 1953- *WhoFI 92*
Sobey, Arthur Edward, Jr 1924- *AmMWSc 92*
Sobey, David F. 1931- *WhoFI 92*
Sobey, Donald Creighton Rae *WhoFI 92*
Sobhi, Mohamed Ibrahim 1925- *IntWW 91, Who 92*
Sobhuza II 1899-1982 *FacFETw*
Sobie, Merril 1939- *WhoAmL 92*
Sobieski, Carol 1939-1990 *ConTFT 9*
Sobieski, Daniel J. 1948- *WhoMW 92*
Sobieski, James Fulton 1940- *AmMWSc 92*
Sobieszczanski-Sobieski, Jaroslaw 1934- *AmMWSc 92*
Sobin, A.G. *DrAPF 91*
Sobin, Gustaf 1935- *ConPo 91, IntAu&W 91, WrDr 92*
Sobin, Leslie Howard 1934- *AmMWSc 92*
Sobin, Sidney S 1914- *AmMWSc 92*
Sobinov, Leonid Vital'evich 1872-1934 *SovUnBD*
Sobkowicz, Hanna Maria 1931- *AmMWSc 92*
Soble, Mark Richard 1964- *WhoAmL 92*
Soble, Richard Steven 1956- *WhoAmL 92*
Soble, Ron 1932- *IntMPA 92*
Sobocinski, Philip Zygmund 1934- *AmMWSc 92*
Soboczenski, Edward John 1929- *AmMWSc 92*
Sobol, Bruce J 1923- *AmMWSc 92*
Sobol, Donald J 1924- *IntAu&W 91, WrDr 92*
Sobol, Harold 1930- *AmMWSc 92*
Sobol, Ken 1938- *WrDr 92*
Sobol, Lawrence Raymond 1950- *WhoFI 92*
Sobol, Marion Gross 1930- *AmMWSc 92*
Sobol, Stanley Paul 1937- *AmMWSc 92*
Sobolev, Igor 1931- *AmMWSc 92*
Sobolev, Sergey L'vovich 1908- *SovUnBD*
Sobolev, Viktor Viktorovich 1915- *IntWW 91*
Sobolev, Vladimir Mikhailovich 1924- *IntWW 91*
Sobolevsky, Andre Rafail 1958- *WhoAmL 92*
Sobolik, Dennis Merlin 1931- *WhoAmP 91*
Sobon, Paul Morrell 1957- *WhoMW 92*
Sobota, Anthony E 1938- *AmMWSc 92*
Sobota, Walter Louis 1946- *AmMWSc 92, WhoMW 92*
Sobotka, Bette Teresa 1961- *WhoFI 92*
Sobotka, Gabriella Pessl d1991 *NewYTBS 91*
Sobotka, Mark Joseph 1954- *WhoMW 92*
Sobotka, Thomas Joseph 1942- *AmMWSc 92*
Sobottka, Stanley Earl 1930- *AmMWSc 92*
Sobral, Bruno Walther 1958- *WhoWest 92*
Sobrino, Josephine 1915- *ConAu 36NR*
Sobrino, Oswald Paul 1962- *WhoAmL 92*
Sobsey, Mark David 1943- *AmMWSc 92*
Sobukwe, Robert Mangaliso 1924-1978 *FacFETw*
Sobus, Katherine Anthony 1959- *WhoMW 92*
Socci, Anthony Domenic 1948- *WhoMW 92*
Soccio, Judeth Rose 1950- *WhoMW 92*
Socha, Donald Edward 1950- *WhoHisp 92*
Socha, Wladyslaw Wojciech 1926- *AmMWSc 92*
Sochalski, Matthew Michael 1947- *WhoAmP 91*
Socher, Susan Helen 1944- *AmMWSc 92*
Socie, Darrell Frederick 1948- *AmMWSc 92*
Socier, Michael James 1957- *WhoEnt 92*
Sockman, Ralph Washington 1889-1970 *RelLAm 91*
Sockwell, Oliver R., Jr. 1943- *WhoBlA 92*
Socol, Sheldon Eleazer 1936- *WhoFI 92*
Socolar, Sidney Joseph 1924- *AmMWSc 92*
Socolofsky, Homer Edward 1922- *IntAu&W 91, WhoMW 92, WrDr 92*
Socolofsky, Iris Kay 1952- *WhoAmL 92*
Socolofsky, Marion David 1931- *AmMWSc 92*
Socolow, Arthur A 1921- *AmMWSc 92*
Socolow, Elizabeth Anne *DrAPF 91*
Socolow, Robert H 1937- *AmMWSc 92*
Socolow, Sanford *LesBEnT 92*
Socolow, Sanford 1928- *WhoFI 92*
Socrates 469BC-399BC *EncEarC*
Socrates Scholasticus 380?-450 *EncEarC*
Soczka, Kevin Martin 1960- *WhoAmP 91*
Sodal, Ingvar E 1934- *AmMWSc 92*
Sodano, Angelo 1927- *WhoRel 92*
Sodano, Charles Stanley 1939- *AmMWSc 92*
Sodd, Vincent J 1934- *AmMWSc 92*
Sodders, Judith Townsend 1941- *WhoAmP 91*
Sodders, Richard Phillip 1940- *WhoEnt 92*
Soddy, Frederick 1877-1956 *WhoNob 90*
Sodeman, William A 1936- *AmMWSc 92*
Soden, Dennis L. 1953- *WhoWest 92*
Soden, Paul Anthony 1944- *WhoAmL 92*
Soden, Richard Allan 1945- *WhoAmL 92, WhoBlA 92*
Soder, Jon Darwin 1943- *WhoFI 92*
Soder, Karin A. M. 1928- *IntWW 91*
Soderbaum, Kristina 1912- *EncTR 91 [port]*
Soderberg, Erik Axel Olof R:son 1926- *IntWW 91*
Soderberg, Lee Stephen Freeman 1946- *AmMWSc 92*
Soderberg, Roger Hamilton 1936- *AmMWSc 92*
Soderbergh, Steven *IntWW 91, NewYTBS 91 [port]*
Soderbergh, Steven Andrew 1963- *WhoEnt 92*
Soderblom, Laurence Albert 1944- *AmMWSc 92*
Soderblom, Nathan 1866-1931 *DcEcMov [port], FacFETw, WhoNob 90*
Soderling, Thomas Richard 1944- *AmMWSc 92*
Soderlund, David Matthew 1950- *AmMWSc 92*
Soderman, J William 1935- *AmMWSc 92*
Soderquist, David Richard 1936- *AmMWSc 92*
Soderquist, Donald G. 1934- *WhoFI 92*
Soderquist, Larry Dean 1944- *WhoAmL 92*
Soderqvist, Kjell Olof 1938- *WhoEnt 92*
Soderstrom, Edwin Loren 1931- *AmMWSc 92*
Soderstrom, Elisabeth 1927- *NewAmDM*
Soderstrom, Elisabeth Anna 1927- *IntWW 91*
Soderstrom, Hans Tson 1945- *WhoFI 92*
Soderstrom, Kenneth G 1936- *AmMWSc 92*
Soderwall, Arnold Larson 1914- *AmMWSc 92*
Sodetz, James M 1948- *AmMWSc 92*
Sodha, Piyush 1958- *WhoFI 92*
Sodickson, Lester A 1937- *AmMWSc 92*
Sodicoff, Marvin 1937- *AmMWSc 92*
Sodl, Matthew Joseph 1966- *WhoFI 92*
Sodnom, Dumaagiyn 1933- *IntWW 91*
Sodor And Man, Bishop of 1932- *Who 92*
Sodowick, George Yates 1941- *WhoAmL 92*
Sodowsky, Roland 1938- *ConAu 134*
Sodowsky, Roland E. *DrAPF 91*
Soechting, John F 1943- *AmMWSc 92*
Soedarsono, Nani 1928- *IntWW 91*
Soedel, Werner 1936- *AmMWSc 92, WhoMW 92*
Soeder, Robert W 1935- *AmMWSc 92*
Soederstrom, Elisabeth Anna 1927- *WhoEnt 92*
Soedjarwo 1922- *IntWW 91*
Soeharto, General 1921- *Who 92*
Soeiro, Ruy 1932- *AmMWSc 92*
Soekoto, Leo *WhoRel 92*
Soeldner, John Stuart 1932- *AmMWSc 92, WhoWest 92*
Soens, Adolph Lewis, Jr. 1931- *WhoMW 92*
Soens, Lawrence D. 1926- *WhoRel 92*
Soerens, Dave Allen 1952- *AmMWSc 92*
Soerensen, Svend Otto 1916- *SmATA 67 [port]*
Soergel, Konrad H 1929- *AmMWSc 92*
Soet, Henry David 1935- *WhoAmP 91*
Soetebier, Virginia Marie 1930- *WhoAmP 91*
Sofaer, Abraham David 1938- *IntWW 91*
Sofer, Anne Hallowell 1937- *Who 92*
Sofer, Eugene F 1948- *WhoAmP 91*
Sofer, Samir Salim 1945- *AmMWSc 92*
Sofer, William Howard 1941- *AmMWSc 92*
Soffen, Gerald A 1926- *AmMWSc 92*
Soffer, Alfred 1922- *AmMWSc 92*
Soffer, Bernard Harold 1931- *AmMWSc 92*
Soffer, Lowell Charles 1954- *WhoEnt 92*
Soffer, Milton David 1914- *AmMWSc 92*
Soffer, Philip J. 1954- *WhoWest 92*
Soffer, Richard Luber 1932- *AmMWSc 92*
Soffer, Sheldon 1927- *WhoEnt 92*
Soffici, Ardengo 1879-1964 *BiDExR, DcLB 114 [port]*
Sofia, R Duane 1942- *AmMWSc 92*
Sofia, Sabatino 1939- *AmMWSc 92*
Sofia, Zuheir 1944- *WhoFI 92, WhoMW 92*
Sofio, Richard A 1946- *WhoAmP 91*
Sofola, Idowu 1934- *IntWW 91*
Sofos, Stephany Louise 1954- *WhoWest 92*
Sofronitsky, Vladimir Vladimirovich 1901-1961 *SovUnBD*
Sofronski, Bernard *LesBEnT 92*
Softly, Barbara 1924- *WrDr 92*
Softly, Edgar *ConAu 133*
Softly, Edward *ConAu 133*
Soga, Michio Nishi 1956- *WhoFI 92*
Sogaard, Poul 1923- *IntWW 91*
Sogah, Dotsevi Y. 1945- *WhoBlA 92*
Sogah, Dotsevi Yao 1945- *AmMWSc 92*
Sogandares-Bernal, Franklin 1931- *AmMWSc 92*
Sogg, Wilton Sherman 1935- *WhoAmL 92*
Sogin, H H 1920- *AmMWSc 92*
Soglin, Paul R. 1945- *WhoMW 92*
Soglin, Paul Richard 1945- *WhoAmP 91*
Soglo, Nicephore 1934- *IntWW 91*
Soglow, Otto 1900-1975 *BenetAL 91*
Sogn, John Allen 1946- *AmMWSc 92*
Sognefest, Peter William 1941- *AmMWSc 92, WhoFI 92*
Sogo, Power Bunmei 1925- *AmMWSc 92*
Soh, Sung Kuk 1951- *AmMWSc 92*
Sohacki, Leonard Paul 1933- *AmMWSc 92*
Sohahong-Kombet, Jean-Pierre 1935- *IntWW 91*
Sohal, Gurkirpal Singh 1948- *AmMWSc 92*
Sohal, Manohar Singh 1943- *AmMWSc 92*
Sohal, Naresh 1939- *ConCom 92*
Sohal, Parmjit S 1959- *AmMWSc 92*
Sohal, Rajindar Singh 1936- *AmMWSc 92*
Sohappy, David d1991 *NewYTBS 91*
Sohl, Cary Hugh *AmMWSc 92*
Sohl, Gerald A 1913- *IntAu&W 91*
Sohl, Jerry *IntAu&W 91X*
Sohl, Jerry 1913- *TwCSFW 91, WrDr 92*
Sohl, Norman Frederick 1924- *AmMWSc 92*
Sohl, Raymond, Jr. 1949- *WhoEnt 92*
Sohler, Arthur 1927- *AmMWSc 92*
Sohler, Katherine Berridge 1919- *AmMWSc 92*
Sohm, Jim *WhoEnt 92*
Sohmer, Bernard 1929- *AmMWSc 92*
Sohmer, Seymour H 1941- *AmMWSc 92*
Sohmer, Seymour Hans 1941- *WhoWest 92*
Sohmer, Steve *LesBEnT 92, WhoWest 92*
Sohmer, Steve 1942- *IntMPA 92*
Sohmers, Barbara Pearl 1930- *WhoEnt 92*
Sohn, David 1926- *AmMWSc 92*
Sohn, David Youngwhan 1942- *WhoFI 92*
Sohn, Hong Yong 1941- *AmMWSc 92*
Sohn, Howard A 1929- *WhoIns 92*
Sohn, Israel Gregory 1911- *AmMWSc 92*
Sohn, Kenneth S 1933- *AmMWSc 92*
Sohn, Louis B. 1914- *WrDr 92*
Sohn, Stephen 1941- *WhoFI 92*
Sohn, Yung Jai *AmMWSc 92*
Sohnen-Moe, Cherie Marilyn 1956- *WhoWest 92*
Sohnrey, Heinrich 1859-1948 *EncTR 91*
Sohr, Robert Trueman 1937- *AmMWSc 92, WhoMW 92*
Sohy, Gerard Jean 1947- *WhoEnt 92*
Soifer, David 1937- *AmMWSc 92*
Soifer, Herman *AmMWSc 92*
Soifer, Jan 1957- *WhoAmL 92*
Soifertis, Leonid Vladimirovich 1911- *SovUnBD*
Soika, Helmut Emil 1941- *WhoFI 92*
Soike, Kenneth Fieroe 1927- *AmMWSc 92*
Soileau, Curtis Lloyd 1961- *WhoAmL 92, WhoAmP 91*
Soileau, Jerri H 1951- *WhoAmP 91*
Soisson, Jean-Pierre Henri Robert 1934- *IntWW 91*
Soja, Eugene Robert 1930- *WhoAmP 91*
Sojka, Gary Allan 1940- *AmMWSc 92*
Sojka, Robert E 1947- *AmMWSc 92*
Sojka, Stanley Anthony 1946- *AmMWSc 92*
Sojo, Luis 1966- *WhoHisp 92*
Sokal, Michael Mark 1945- *WhoFI 92*
Sokal, Robert Reuven 1926- *AmMWSc 92*

**Sokatch**, John Robert 1928- *AmMWSc 92*
**Soken**, Judith Breen *WhoAmL 92*
**Sokler**, Bruce Douglas 1949- *WhoAmL 92*
**Sokobin**, Alan Mayor 1926- *WhoRel 92*
**Sokol**, David Martin 1942- *WhoMW 92*
**Sokol**, Dennis Allen 1945- *WhoMW 92*
**Sokol**, Frank Carl 1947- *WhoRel 92*
**Sokol**, George 1912- *WhoAmL 92*
**Sokol**, Hilda Weyl 1928- *AmMWSc 92*
**Sokol**, John *DrAPF 91*
**Sokol**, Larry Nides 1946- *WhoAmL 92*
**Sokol**, Robert James 1941- *AmMWSc 92, WhoMW 92*
**Sokol**, Ronald Jay 1950- *AmMWSc 92*
**Sokol**, Sherry Lynn 1960- *WhoMW 92*
**Sokola**, David P *WhoAmP 91*
**Sokol'nikov**, Grigoriy Yakovlevich 1888-1939 *SovUnBD*
**Sokolnikov**, Gregory Yakovlevich 1888-1939 *FacFETw*
**Sokoloff**, Alexander 1920- *AmMWSc 92*
**Sokoloff**, Alexander Dimitrovitch 1920- *WhoWest 92*
**Sokoloff**, Jack 1922- *AmMWSc 92*
**Sokoloff**, Jeffrey Bruce 1941- *AmMWSc 92*
**Sokoloff**, Leon 1919- *AmMWSc 92*
**Sokoloff**, Louis 1921- *AmMWSc 92, IntWW 91*
**Sokoloff**, Vladimir P 1904- *AmMWSc 92*
**Sokoloski**, Adam Anthony 1938- *WhoFI 92*
**Sokoloski**, Martin Michael 1937- *AmMWSc 92*
**Sokoloski**, Theodore Daniel 1933- *AmMWSc 92*
**Sokolov**, Aleksandr Vsevolodovich 1943- *IntWW 91, SovUnBD*
**Sokolov**, Boris Matveevich 1889-1930 *SovUnBD*
**Sokolov**, Boris Sergeyevich 1914- *IntWW 91*
**Sokolov**, Jacque Jenning 1954- *WhoWest 92*
**Sokolov**, Raymond *DrAPF 91*
**Sokolov**, Sacha 1950- *LiExTwC*
**Sokolov**, Sergey Leonidovich 1911- *IntWW 91, SovUnBD*
**Sokolov**, Yefrem Yevseevich 1926- *IntWW 91, SovUnBD*
**Sokolov**, Yuriy Matveevich 1889-1941 *SovUnBD*
**Sokolove**, Phillip Gary 1942- *AmMWSc 92*
**Sokolovsky**, Vasiliy Danilovich 1897-1968 *SovUnBD*
**Sokolow**, Asa D. 1919- *WhoAmL 92*
**Sokolow**, David Simon 1949- *WhoAmL 92*
**Sokolow**, Diane *IntMPA 92*
**Sokolow**, Howard Michael 1951- *WhoAmL 92*
**Sokolow**, Lloyd Bruce 1949- *WhoAmL 92*
**Sokolow**, Maurice 1911- *AmMWSc 92*
**Sokolow**, Moshe 1947- *WhoRel 92*
**Sokolowski**, Chesterlyn 1923- *WhoAmP 91*
**Sokolowski**, Danny Hale 1938- *AmMWSc 92*
**Sokolowski**, Henry Alfred 1923- *AmMWSc 92*
**Sokolski**, Henry David 1951- *WhoFI 92*
**Sokolski**, Walter Thomas 1916- *AmMWSc 92, WhoMW 92*
**Sokolsky**, Helen Leslie *DrAPF 91*
**Sokomanu**, George *IntWW 91*
**Sokorski**, Wlodzimierz 1908- *IntWW 91*
**Sola**, Michael E., Jr. 1953- *WhoHisp 92*
**Solaita**, Milovale *WhoAmP 91*
**Solan**, Miriam *DrAPF 91*
**Solana**, Jose L. 1928- *WhoHisp 92*
**Solana Madariaga**, Javier 1942- *IntWW 91*
**Solana Madariaga**, Luis 1935- *IntWW 91*
**Solana Morales**, Fernando *IntWW 91*
**Solanas**, Fernando E. 1936- *IntDcF 2-2*
**Solanas**, Fernando E., and Octavia Getino *IntDcF 2-2*
**Soland**, Randall Joseph 1953- *WhoMW 92*
**Soland**, Richard Martin 1940- *AmMWSc 92*
**Solandt**, Omond McKillop 1909- *AmMWSc 92, IntWW 91*
**Solanki**, Ramniklal Chhaganlal 1931- *Who 92*
**Solanky**, Hemant 1955- *WhoMW 92*
**Solano**, Faustina Venecia 1962- *WhoHisp 92*
**Solano**, Henry L. 1950- *WhoHisp 92*
**Solano**, Hernando M. 1939- *WhoHisp 92*
**Solano**, Juan A. 1950- *WhoHisp 92*
**Solano**, Nancy Vogt 1958- *WhoMW 92*
**Solano**, Romeo Israel 1957- *WhoMW 92*
**Solar**, Samuel Louis 1919- *AmMWSc 92*
**Solarana**, Philip *WhoHisp 92*
**Solares**, Alberto E. 1922- *WhoHisp 92*
**Solares**, Maria 1842-1923 *RelLAm 91*
**Solari**, Fred John 1951- *WhoEnt 92*
**Solari**, Mario Jose Adolfo 1948- *AmMWSc 92*
**Solaro**, R John *AmMWSc 92*
**Solarz**, Richard William 1947- *AmMWSc 92*
**Solarz**, Stephen J. 1940- *AlmAP 92 [port], WhoAmP 91*
**Solarz**, Stephen Joshua 1940- *NewYTBS 91 [port]*
**Solas**, Humberto 1942- *IntDcF 2-2 [port]*
**Solbach**, John Martin, III 1947- *WhoAmP 91*
**Solberg**, Ingvald 1904- *WhoAmP 91*
**Solberg**, James J 1942- *AmMWSc 92*
**Solberg**, Ken 1940- *WhoAmP 91*
**Solberg**, Loren Albin 1941- *WhoAmP 91*
**Solberg**, Myron 1931- *AmMWSc 92*
**Solberg**, Oscar 1911- *WhoAmP 91*
**Solberg**, Richard Allen 1932- *AmMWSc 92*
**Solberg**, Richard L *WhoAmP 91*
**Solberg**, Richard William 1917- *IntAu&W 91, WrDr 92*
**Solberg**, Ruell Floyd, Jr 1939- *AmMWSc 92*
**Solbrig**, Ingeborg Hildegard 1923- *WhoMW 92*
**Solbrig**, Otto Thomas 1930- *AmMWSc 92, WrDr 92*
**Solc**, Josef 1943- *WhoRel 92*
**Solc**, Karel 1933- *AmMWSc 92*
**Solchaga Catalan**, Carlos 1944- *IntWW 91*
**Solda**, Paul Joseph 1963- *WhoAmL 92*
**Soldano**, Benny A 1921- *AmMWSc 92*
**Soldat**, Joseph Kenneth 1926- *AmMWSc 92*
**Soldati**, Francisco d1991 *NewYTBS 91*
**Soldati**, Gianluigi 1937- *AmMWSc 92*
**Soldati**, Jennifer G 1947- *WhoAmP 91*
**Soldati**, Mario 1906- *LiExTwC*
**Soldatov**, Aleksandr Alekseyevich 1915- *Who 92*
**Soldevila**, Jaime 1944- *WhoAmP 91*
**Soldevilla**, Fernando Gonzalo 1944- *WhoMW 92*
**Soldini**, John Louis 1935- *WhoAmP 91*
**Soldner**, Paul Edmund *WhoWest 92*
**Soldo**, Anthony Thomas 1927- *AmMWSc 92*
**Soldo**, Beth Jean 1948- *AmMWSc 92*
**Soldo**, John J. *DrAPF 91*
**Soldwedel**, K. J. 1947- *WhoFI 92*
**Sole**, Carlos A. 1938- *WhoHisp 92*
**Sole**, Michael Joseph 1940- *AmMWSc 92*
**Sole-Romeo**, Luis Alberto 1934- *Who 92*
**Solecki**, Roman 1925- *AmMWSc 92*
**Soled**, Stuart 1948- *AmMWSc 92*
**Soledad** *DrAPF 91*
**Solem**, G Alan 1931- *AmMWSc 92*
**Solem**, Johndale Christian 1941- *AmMWSc 92*
**Solenberger**, John Carl 1941- *AmMWSc 92*
**Solender**, Sanford 1914- *WhoRel 92*
**Solender**, Stephen David 1938- *WhoRel 92*
**Solensten**, John M *DrAPF 91*
**Soler**, Alan I 1936- *AmMWSc 92*
**Soler**, Ana Picaza 1948- *WhoHisp 92*
**Soler**, Antonio 1729-1783 *NewAmDM*
**Soler**, Antonio R. *Who 92*
**Soler**, E. Ivan 1924- *WhoHisp 92*
**Soler**, Ernesto Miguel 1962- *WhoFI 92*
**Soler**, Frank *WhoHisp 92*
**Soler**, Gladys Pumariega 1930- *WhoHisp 92*
**Soler**, Jaime 1949- *WhoHisp 92*
**Soler**, Rita *WhoHisp 92*
**Soler**, Terrell Diane *WhoEnt 92*
**Soler-Favale**, Santiago C. 1937- *WhoHisp 92*
**Soler-Martinez**, Mercedes C. 1963- *WhoHisp 92*
**Soler-Zapata**, Jose E *WhoAmP 91*
**Soleri**, Paolo 1919- *IntWW 91, WhoWest 92, WrDr 92*
**Solero**, Frank J. 1939- *WhoHisp 92*
**Soles**, Ada Leigh 1937- *WhoAmP 91*
**Soles**, G. Edward 1939- *WhoEnt 92*
**Soles**, James Ralph 1935- *WhoAmP 91*
**Soles**, Robert Charles, Jr 1934- *WhoAmP 91*
**Soles**, W Roger 1920- *WhoIns 92*
**Soles**, William Roger 1920- *WhoFI 92*
**Solesbury**, William Booth 1940- *Who 92*
**Solesby**, Tessa Audrey Hilda 1932- *IntWW 91, Who 92*
**Solet**, Maxwell David 1948- *WhoAmL 92*
**Soley**, Clive Stafford 1939- *Who 92*
**Solez**, Kim 1946- *AmMWSc 92*
**Solf**, Johanna 1887-1954 *EncTR 91 [port]*
**Solf**, W.H. 1862-1936 *EncTR 91*
**Solfisburg**, Roy John, III 1943- *WhoMW 92*
**Solganik**, Marvin 1930- *WhoFI 92*
**Solh**, Rashid 1926- *IntWW 91*
**Solheim**, James *DrAPF 91*
**Solheim**, James Edward 1939- *WhoRel 92*
**Soli**, Giorgio 1920- *AmMWSc 92*
**Solidum**, James 1925- *WhoFI 92*
**Solie**, Leland Peter 1941- *AmMWSc 92*
**Solie**, Thomas Norman 1931- *AmMWSc 92*
**Soliman**, Afifi Hassan 1931- *AmMWSc 92*
**Soliman**, Karam Farag Attia 1944- *AmMWSc 92*
**Soliman**, Magdi R I 1942- *AmMWSc 92*
**Soliman**, Mohammed Sidky 1919- *IntWW 91*
**Soliman**, Mostafa Amin *WhoFI 92*
**Soliman**, Soliman Metwally 1927- *IntWW 91*
**Solimando**, Dominic Anthony, Jr. 1950- *WhoWest 92*
**Solin**, John Jacob 1947- *WhoFI 92*
**Solin**, Stuart Allan 1942- *AmMWSc 92*
**Solinger**, Alan M 1948- *AmMWSc 92*
**Solis**, Alfonso 1948- *WhoHisp 92*
**Solis**, Arturo, Sr. 1931- *WhoHisp 92*
**Solis**, Carlos 1961- *WhoHisp 92*
**Solis**, Dan *WhoHisp 92*
**Solis**, Daniel Gomez 1956- *WhoRel 92*
**Solis**, Ernest V. *WhoHisp 92*
**Solis**, Gary *WhoHisp 92*
**Solis**, Hilda L. 1957- *WhoHisp 92*
**Solis**, Joel 1954- *WhoEnt 92, WhoHisp 92*
**Solis**, Jorge A. *WhoHisp 92*
**Solis**, Joseph A. *WhoHisp 92*
**Solis**, Juan Diaz de 1470-1516 *HisDSpE*
**Solis**, Juan F., III *WhoHisp 92*
**Solis**, Librado L. 1923- *WhoHisp 92*
**Solis**, Octavio 1958- *WhoHisp 92*
**Solis**, Rafael 1967- *WhoHisp 92*
**Solis**, Richard M. 1947- *WhoEnt 92*
**Solis Folch de Cardona**, Jose 1713-1770 *HisDSpE*
**Solis-Gaffar**, Maria Corazon 1939- *AmMWSc 92*
**Solis Palma**, Manuel *IntWW 91*
**Solis Ruiz**, Jose 1913- *IntWW 91*
**Solish**, George Irving 1920- *AmMWSc 92*
**Solish**, Jonathan Craig 1949- *WhoAmL 92*
**Solito**, Peter S. *WhoHisp 92*
**Soliunas**, Francine Stewart 1948- *WhoBlA 92*
**Soliz**, Joseph Guy 1954- *WhoAmL 92, WhoHisp 92*
**Soliz**, Juan 1949- *WhoHisp 92*
**Soliz**, Juan M 1950- *WhoAmP 91*
**Soliz**, Olga *WhoHisp 92*
**Soliz**, Olga Yvonne 1936- *WhoAmP 91*
**Soliz**, Oscar 1934- *WhoHisp 92*
**Soliz**, Salvador G. 1932- *WhoHisp 92*
**Solkalski**, Annie *EncAmaz 91*
**Solkoff**, Jerome Ira 1939- *WhoAmL 92*
**Solkoff**, Joel 1947- *ConAu 133*
**Soll**, Andrew H 1945- *AmMWSc 92*
**Soll**, David Richard 1942- *AmMWSc 92*
**Soll**, Dieter Gerhard 1935- *AmMWSc 92*
**Soll**, William Michael 1953- *WhoRel 92*
**Solla**, Sara A 1950- *AmMWSc 92*
**Sollazo**, Jerry Jon 1953- *WhoIns 92*
**Sollberger**, Arne Rudolph 1924- *AmMWSc 92*
**Sollberger**, Dwight Ellsworth 1908- *AmMWSc 92*
**Sollberger**, Harvey 1938- *NewAmDM*
**Soller**, Arthur 1936- *AmMWSc 92*
**Soller**, Roger William 1946- *AmMWSc 92*
**Sollero**, Lauro 1916- *IntWW 91*
**Sollers-Riedel**, Helen 1911- *AmMWSc 92*
**Solley**, Stephen Malcolm 1946- *Who 92*
**Sollfrey**, Stacey *DrAPF 91*
**Sollfrey**, William 1925- *AmMWSc 92*
**Sollid**, Jon Erik 1939- *AmMWSc 92*
**Sollie**, Solveig 1939- *IntWW 91*
**Sollin**, Ingmar Adolph 1918- *WhoMW 92*
**Sollitt**, Charles Kevin 1943- *AmMWSc 92*
**Sollman**, Paul Benjamin 1920- *AmMWSc 92*
**Sollner-Webb**, Barbara Thea 1948- *AmMWSc 92*
**Sollo**, Wallace R. 1907- *WhoAmL 92*
**Sollott**, Gilbert Paul 1927- *AmMWSc 92*
**Sollov**, Jacques *DrAPF 91*
**Sollov**, Jacques 1935- *IntAu&W 91*
**Solman**, Victor Edward Frick 1916- *AmMWSc 92*
**Solmi**, Sergio 1899-1981 *DcLB 114 [port]*
**Solmitz**, Fritz 1893-1933 *EncTR 91*
**Solmon**, Donald Clyde 1945- *AmMWSc 92*
**Solms**, Kenny Alan 1942- *WhoEnt 92*
**Soln**, Josip Zvonimir 1934- *AmMWSc 92*
**Solnica**, Hershel 1938- *WhoRel 92*
**Solnit**, Albert J 1919- *AmMWSc 92*
**Solntseva**, Yul'ya Ippolitovna 1901- *SovUnBD*
**Solo**, Alan Jere 1933- *AmMWSc 92*
**Solo**, Robert H. 1932- *IntMPA 92*
**Solochek**, Harold 1934- *WhoIns 92*
**Solodar**, Arthur John 1940- *AmMWSc 92*
**Solodar**, Warren E 1925- *AmMWSc 92*
**Soloff**, Bernard Leroy 1931- *AmMWSc 92*
**Soloff**, Louis Alexander 1904- *AmMWSc 92*
**Soloff**, Melvyn Stanley 1938- *AmMWSc 92*
**Soloff**, Mordecai Isaac 1901- *WhoRel 92*
**Soloff**, Rav Asher 1927- *WhoRel 92*
**Sologub**, Fedor Kuz'mich 1863-1927 *SovUnBD*
**Sologuren**, Javier 1921- *ConSpAP*
**Solomenko**, Nikolai Stepanovich 1923- *IntWW 91*
**Solomentsev**, Mikhail Sergeevich 1913- *SovUnBD*
**Solomon** *EncEarC*
**Solomon** 1902-1988 *FacFETw, NewAmDM*
**Solomon**, A Malama 1951- *WhoAmP 91*
**Solomon**, Alan 1933- *AmMWSc 92*
**Solomon**, Alan Lester 1951- *WhoMW 92*
**Solomon**, Alan Peter 1923- *Who 92*
**Solomon**, Allen M 1943- *AmMWSc 92*
**Solomon**, Alvin Arnold 1937- *AmMWSc 92*
**Solomon**, Andrew Alan 1951- *WhoAmL 92*
**Solomon**, Andrew Martin 1961- *WhoAmL 92*
**Solomon**, Anthony Joseph 1932- *WhoAmP 91*
**Solomon**, Anthony Morton 1919- *IntWW 91*
**Solomon**, Arthur Charles 1947- *WhoFI 92*
**Solomon**, Arthur Kaskel 1912- *AmMWSc 92, IntWW 91*
**Solomon**, Barbara J. 1934- *WhoBlA 92*
**Solomon**, Barbara Probst *DrAPF 91*
**Solomon**, Carol Ann 1953- *WhoMW 92*
**Solomon**, Dan Eugene 1936- *WhoRel 92*
**Solomon**, David 1907- *Who 92*
**Solomon**, David 1944- *WhoBlA 92*
**Solomon**, David Eugene 1931- *AmMWSc 92*
**Solomon**, David H. 1923- *IntWW 91*
**Solomon**, David Harris 1923- *AmMWSc 92*
**Solomon**, David Henry 1929- *IntWW 91*
**Solomon**, Denzil Kenneth 1952- *WhoBlA 92*
**Solomon**, Donald L. 1932- *WhoBlA 92*
**Solomon**, Donald W 1941- *AmMWSc 92*
**Solomon**, Donald William 1944- *WhoMW 92*
**Solomon**, Eddie, Jr. 1951-1986 *WhoBlA 92N*
**Solomon**, Edward I 1946- *AmMWSc 92*
**Solomon**, Elinor Harris 1923- *WhoFI 92*
**Solomon**, Emmett Webster 1936- *WhoRel 92*
**Solomon**, Esther Riva 1921-1969 *ConAu 135*
**Solomon**, Ezra 1920- *IntWW 91, WhoFI 92, WrDr 92*
**Solomon**, Frank I 1924- *AmMWSc 92*
**Solomon**, Frank S. *WhoRel 92*
**Solomon**, George E 1925- *AmMWSc 92*
**Solomon**, George Freeman 1931- *AmMWSc 92, WhoWest 92*
**Solomon**, Gerald B 1930- *WhoAmP 91*
**Solomon**, Gerald B. H. 1930- *AlmAP 92 [port]*
**Solomon**, Gilbert Stanley 1936- *WhoAmL 92*
**Solomon**, Glen David 1955- *WhoMW 92*
**Solomon**, Goody L 1929- *IntAu&W 91*
**Solomon**, Gordon Charles 1924- *AmMWSc 92*
**Solomon**, Hannah Greenebaum 1858-1942 *HanAmWH*
**Solomon**, Harry 1937- *Who 92*
**Solomon**, Harvey Donald 1941- *AmMWSc 92*
**Solomon**, Herbert 1919- *AmMWSc 92*
**Solomon**, Hollis *IntWW 91*
**Solomon**, Ionel 1929- *IntWW 91*
**Solomon**, Jack 1941- *AmMWSc 92*
**Solomon**, James Daniel 1913- *WhoBlA 92*
**Solomon**, James Doyle 1934- *AmMWSc 92*
**Solomon**, Jay 1960- *ConAu 135*
**Solomon**, Jay Murrie 1936- *AmMWSc 92*
**Solomon**, Jerome Jay 1945- *AmMWSc 92*
**Solomon**, Jerrold 1946- *WhoAmL 92*
**Solomon**, Jimmy Lloyd 1941- *AmMWSc 92*
**Solomon**, Joel Martin 1932- *AmMWSc 92*
**Solomon**, Jolane Baumgarten 1927- *AmMWSc 92*
**Solomon**, Jonathan Hilali Moise 1939- *Who 92*
**Solomon**, Joseph Alvin 1925- *AmMWSc 92*
**Solomon**, Judith Anne 1943- *WhoEnt 92*
**Solomon**, Julius 1936- *AmMWSc 92*
**Solomon**, Julius Oscar Lee 1917- *WhoWest 92*
**Solomon**, Kenneth 1947- *AmMWSc 92*
**Solomon**, Lawrence Marvin 1931- *AmMWSc 92*
**Solomon**, Lee A *WhoAmP 91*
**Solomon**, Lewis David 1941- *WhoAmL 92*
**Solomon**, Lon Neal 1948- *WhoRel 92*
**Solomon**, Louis 1931- *AmMWSc 92*
**Solomon**, M Michael 1924- *AmMWSc 92*
**Solomon**, Malcolm David 1942- *AmMWSc 92*
**Solomon**, Mark Raymond 1945- *WhoAmL 92*
**Solomon**, Martin M 1950- *WhoAmP 91*
**Solomon**, Marvin H 1949- *AmMWSc 92*

**Solomon,** Max Marshall 1920- *WhoAmP 91*
**Solomon,** Maximilian 1946- *WhoFI 92*
**Solomon,** Maynard Elliott 1930- *WhoEnt 92*
**Solomon,** Michael Jay *LesBEnT 92*
**Solomon,** Michael Jay 1938- *IntMPA 92*
**Solomon,** Michelle Faye 1961- *WhoEnt 92*
**Solomon,** Morris J. 1919- *WhoFI 92*
**Solomon,** Neil 1932- *AmMWSc 92*
**Solomon,** Norman King 1944- *WhoAmP 91*
**Solomon,** Patrick Vincent Joseph 1910- *Who 92*
**Solomon,** Peter *Who 92*
**Solomon,** Peter R 1939- *AmMWSc 92*
**Solomon,** Philip M 1939- *AmMWSc 92*
**Solomon,** Richard H 1937- *WhoAmP 91, WrDr 92*
**Solomon,** Richard L. 1918- *IntWW 91*
**Solomon,** Robert 1921- *IntWW 91*
**Solomon,** Robert C. 1942- *WrDr 92*
**Solomon,** Robert Douglas 1917- *AmMWSc 92*
**Solomon,** Robert Elliott 1947- *WhoRel 92*
**Solomon,** Robert H. 1958- *WhoAmL 92*
**Solomon,** Rodney Jeff 1949- *WhoAmL 92*
**Solomon,** Ron *WhoRel 92*
**Solomon,** Ruth *WhoAmP 91*
**Solomon,** Samuel 1925- *AmMWSc 92*
**Solomon,** Sean Carl 1945- *AmMWSc 92*
**Solomon,** Seymour 1924- *AmMWSc 92*
**Solomon,** Sidney 1923- *AmMWSc 92, WhoWest 92*
**Solomon,** Solomon Sidney 1936- *AmMWSc 92*
**Solomon,** Steven Benjamin *WhoAmL 92*
**Solomon,** Susan 1956- *AmMWSc 92*
**Solomon,** T.G. 1920- *IntMPA 92*
**Solomon,** Terri Marcia 1955- *WhoAmL 92*
**Solomon,** Thomas Allan 1941- *AmMWSc 92*
**Solomon,** Vasanth Balan 1935- *AmMWSc 92*
**Solomon,** Wilbert F. 1942- *WhoBlA 92*
**Solomon,** Yonty 1938- *IntWW 91*
**Solomonides,** Valerie Ann *Who 92*
**Solomonow,** Moshe 1944- *AmMWSc 92*
**Solomons,** Adrian *Who 92*
**Solomons,** Anthony Nathan 1930- *Who 92*
**Solomons,** Clive 1931- *AmMWSc 92*
**Solomons,** David 1912- *IntAu&W 91, Who 92, WrDr 92*
**Solomons,** Gerald 1921- *AmMWSc 92*
**Solomons,** Gus Martinez, Jr. *WhoEnt 92*
**Solomons,** Louis Adrian 1922- *Who 92*
**Solomons,** Noel Willis 1944- *AmMWSc 92*
**Solomons,** Thomas William Graham 1934- *AmMWSc 92*
**Solomons,** William Ebenezer 1943- *AmMWSc 92*
**Solomonson,** Charles D. *WhoMW 92*
**Solomonson,** Larry Paul 1941- *AmMWSc 92*
**Solon,** Leonard Raymond 1925- *AmMWSc 92*
**Solon,** Sam George 1931- *WhoAmP 91*
**Solon,** Thomas Peter 1941- *WhoMW 92*
**Solon,** Thomas Robert 1966- *WhoMW 92*
**Solonche,** David Joshua 1945- *AmMWSc 92*
**Solonche,** J.R. *DrAPF 91*
**Solone,** Raymond Joseph 1960- *WhoWest 92*
**Solonitz,** Ralph 1947- *WhoEnt 92*
**Solorio,** Christina Lynn 1963- *WhoWest 92*
**Solorio,** Nancy Acosta 1958- *WhoHisp 92*
**Solorio,** Robert Stephen 1957- *WhoMW 92*
**Solorza,** Carlos Victor 1937- *WhoHisp 92*
**Solorzano,** Robert Francis 1929- *AmMWSc 92*
**Solorzano Pereira,** Juan de 1575-1655 *HisDSpE*
**Solotaroff,** Robert David 1937- *WhoMW 92*
**Solotaroff,** Theodore *DrAPF 91*
**Solotorovsky,** Morris 1913- *AmMWSc 92*
**Soloukhin,** Vladimir Alekseevich 1924- *SovUnBD*
**Soloukhin,** Vladimir Alekseyevich 1924- *IntWW 91*
**Solov,** Zachary 1923- *WhoEnt 92*
**Solovay,** Robert M *AmMWSc 92*
**Solov'ev,** Yuriy Filippovich 1925- *SovUnBD*
**Solov'ev-Sedoy,** Vasiliy Pavlovich 1907-1979 *SovUnBD*
**Solovey,** Yelena Yakovlevna 1947- *IntWW 91*
**Solovic,** Jan 1934- *IntWW 91*
**Soloviev,** Vladimir 1853-1900 *DcEcMov*
**Solovy,** Jonathan Stuart 1959- *WhoAmL 92*
**Solovyev,** Nikolay Nikolayevich 1931- *IntWW 91*
**Solovyov,** Gleb Mikhailovich 1928- *IntWW 91*
**Solovyov,** Yuri Filippovich 1925- *IntWW 91*
**Solow,** Daniel 1949- *AmMWSc 92*
**Solow,** Herbert Franklin 1930- *WhoEnt 92, WhoWest 92*
**Solow,** John Lewis 1954- *WhoMW 92*
**Solow,** Lee Howard 1953- *WhoWest 92*
**Solow,** Martin 1920-1991 *ConAu 135*
**Solow,** Martin X. d1991 *NewYTBS 91*
**Solow,** Max 1916- *AmMWSc 92*
**Solow,** Robert 1924- *WrDr 92*
**Solow,** Robert A. 1925- *WhoWest 92*
**Solow,** Robert Merton 1924- *IntWW 91, Who 92, WhoFI 92, WhoNob 90*
**Soloway,** Albert Herman 1925- *AmMWSc 92, WhoMW 92*
**Soloway,** Daniel Mark 1959- *WhoAmL 92*
**Soloway,** Harold 1917- *AmMWSc 92*
**Soloway,** S Barney 1915- *AmMWSc 92*
**Soloway,** Saul 1916- *AmMWSc 92*
**Soloway,** Scott Michael 1961- *WhoAmL 92*
**Solowsky,** Jay Howard 1951- *WhoAmL 92*
**Soloyanis,** Susan Constance 1952- *AmMWSc 92*
**Solsberry,** R. Frazier 1948- *WhoAmL 92*
**Solsky,** Joseph Fay 1949- *AmMWSc 92*
**Solt,** Andrew W. 1947- *IntMPA 92*
**Solt,** Dennis Byron *AmMWSc 92*
**Solt,** Mary Ellen *DrAPF 91*
**Solt,** Mary Ellen 1920- *WrDr 92*
**Solt,** Paul E 1929- *AmMWSc 92*
**Soltan,** Hubert Constantine 1932- *AmMWSc 92*
**Soltan,** Jerzy 1913- *IntWW 91*
**Soltanpour,** Parviz Neil 1937- *AmMWSc 92*
**Solter,** Davor 1941- *AmMWSc 92*
**Soltero,** Raymond Arthur 1943- *AmMWSc 92*
**Soltero,** Victor *WhoHisp 92*
**Soltes,** Edward John 1941- *AmMWSc 92*
**Solti,** Georg 1912- *IntWW 91, NewAmDM, Who 92, WhoEnt 92, WhoMW 92*
**Solti,** George 1912- *FacFETw*
**Soltis,** Jonas F. 1931- *WrDr 92*
**Soltis,** Robert Alan 1955- *WhoAmL 92*
**Soltisiak,** Christina Ann 1945- *WhoWest 92*
**Soltykiewicz,** Dariusz Joseph 1961- *WhoMW 92*
**Soltys,** John Joseph, Jr. 1942- *WhoAmL 92*
**Soltys,** Ted John, Sr. 1929- *WhoMW 92*
**Soltysik,** Edward A 1929- *AmMWSc 92*
**Soltysik,** Szczesny Stefan 1929- *AmMWSc 92*
**Soltysinski,** Stanislaw J. 1939- *WhoAmL 92*
**Soltz,** Charlene E *IntMPA 92*
**Soltz,** David Lee 1946- *AmMWSc 92*
**Soltzberg,** Leonard Jay 1944- *AmMWSc 92*
**Solum,** Burdette C *WhoAmP 91*
**Solum,** James Maurice 1951- *WhoMW 92*
**Solum,** John Henry 1935- *WhoEnt 92*
**Solum,** Lawrence Byard 1954- *WhoWest 92*
**Solum,** Stephen Edward 1948- *WhoEnt 92*
**Solursh,** Michael 1942- *AmMWSc 92*
**Solvay,** Jacques Ernest 1920- *IntWW 91*
**Solvik,** R S 1924- *AmMWSc 92*
**Solway,** Richard Joel 1960- *WhoFI 92*
**Solway,** Susan 1952- *WhoMW 92*
**Solwitz,** Sharon *DrAPF 91*
**Solymar,** Laszlo 1930- *Who 92*
**Solyn,** Paul B. *DrAPF 91*
**Solzhenitsyn,** Aleksandr Isaevich 1918- *LiExTwC, SovUnBD*
**Solzhenitsyn,** Aleksandr Isayevich 1918- *IntAu&W 91, IntWW 91*
**Solzhenitsyn,** Alexander 1918- *BenetAL 91, WhoNob 90*
**Solzhenitsyn,** Alexander Isayevich 1918- *FacFETw [port]*
**Solzhenitsyn,** Alexander Isayevitch 1918- *Who 92*
**Som,** Mihir Kumar 1943- *WhoFI 92*
**Som,** Prantika 1942- *AmMWSc 92*
**Soma,** Lawrence R 1933- *AmMWSc 92*
**Somach,** S. Dennis 1952- *WhoEnt 92*
**Somach,** Stuart Leslie 1948- *WhoAmL 92*
**Somah,** Harrison 1950- *WhoRel 92*
**Soman,** Alfred 1934- *ConAu 36NR*
**Somani,** Arun Kumar 1951- *AmMWSc 92, WhoWest 92*
**Somani,** Pitambar 1937- *AmMWSc 92*
**Somani,** Satu M 1937- *AmMWSc 92*
**Somare,** Michael Thomas 1936- *IntWW 91, Who 92*
**Somary,** Johannes Felix 1935- *WhoEnt 92*
**Somasundaran,** P 1939- *AmMWSc 92*
**Sombart,** Paul C 1920- *WhoAmP 91*
**Somberg,** John Charin 1948- *WhoMW 92*
**Somcynsky,** Jean-Francois 1943- *IntAu&W 91*
**Some,** Steven Edward 1955- *WhoAmP 91*
**Somekh,** George S 1935- *AmMWSc 92*
**Somelofske,** Robert Joseph 1947- *WhoIns 92*
**Somer,** Stanley Jerome 1943- *WhoAmL 92*
**Somerfield,** Neil 1953- *WhoEnt 92*
**Somerfield,** Stafford William 1911- *Who 92*
**Somerleyton,** Baron 1928- *Who 92*
**Somero,** George Nicholls 1940- *AmMWSc 92*
**Somers,** Baron 1907- *Who 92*
**Somers,** Anne R 1913- *AmMWSc 92*
**Somers,** Armonia 1920- *SpAmWW*
**Somers,** Clifford Louis 1940- *WhoAmL 92*
**Somers,** Deborah Joan 1954- *WhoAmL 92*
**Somers,** Edward 1928- *Who 92*
**Somers,** Emmanuel 1927- *AmMWSc 92*
**Somers,** Fred Leonard, Jr. 1936- *WhoAmL 92*
**Somers,** George Fredrick, Jr 1914- *AmMWSc 92*
**Somers,** George Warren 1947- *WhoAmL 92*
**Somers,** Harry 1925- *NewAmDM*
**Somers,** Herman Miles 1911-1991 *ConAu 134, NewYTBS 91 [port]*
**Somers,** James Lavaughn 1944- *WhoFI 92*
**Somers,** Jane *IntAu&W 91X, WrDr 92*
**Somers,** John A 1944- *WhoIns 92*
**Somers,** John Arthur 1944- *WhoFI 92*
**Somers,** Karl Brent 1948- *WhoFI 92*
**Somers,** Kenneth Donald 1938- *AmMWSc 92*
**Somers,** Michael Eugene 1929- *AmMWSc 92*
**Somers,** Nicholas Emmanuel 1962- *WhoFI 92*
**Somers,** Paul *WrDr 92*
**Somers,** Paul Preston, Jr. 1942- *WhoMW 92*
**Somers,** Perrie Daniel 1918- *AmMWSc 92*
**Somers,** Rebecca Michelle 1953- *WhoWest 92*
**Somers,** Robert Vance 1937- *WhoAmP 91*
**Somers,** Ronald Eugene 1951- *WhoRel 92*
**Somers,** Suzanne *IntAu&W 91X, WrDr 92*
**Somers,** Suzanne 1946- *IntMPA 92, WhoEnt 92*
**Somers Cocks,** Anna Gwenllian 1950- *Who 92*
**Somersalo,** Arne Sakari 1891-1941 *BiDExR*
**Somerscales,** Euan Francis Cuthbert 1931- *AmMWSc 92*
**Somerscales,** Thomas Lawrence 1913- *Who 92*
**Somerset** *Who 92*
**Somerset,** Duke of 1952- *Who 92*
**Somerset,** David Henry Fitzroy 1930- *Who 92*
**Somerset,** Harold Richard 1935- *WhoFI 92, WhoWest 92*
**Somerset,** Henry Beaufort 1906- *Who 92*
**Somerset,** James H 1938- *AmMWSc 92*
**Somerset,** Leo L., Jr. 1945- *WhoBlA 92*
**Somerset Fry,** Peter George Robin P 1931- *IntAu&W 91, Who 92*
**Somerset Fry,** Plantagenet 1931- *WrDr 92*
**Somerset Jones,** Eric 1925- *Who 92*
**Somerson,** Norman L 1928- *AmMWSc 92*
**Somerton,** Viscount 1982- *Who 92*
**Somervill,** Cynthia Belle 1959- *WhoAmL 92*
**Somerville and Ross** *FacFETw, RfGEnL 91*
**Somerville,** Addison Wimbs 1927- *WhoBlA 92*
**Somerville,** Christopher Roland 1947- *AmMWSc 92, Who 92*
**Somerville,** David 1917- *Who 92*
**Somerville,** Dora B. 1920- *WhoBlA 92*
**Somerville,** Edith 1858-1949 *RfGEnL 91*
**Somerville,** Edith Onone 1858-1949 *FacFETw*
**Somerville,** George R *AmMWSc 92*
**Somerville,** James Hugh Miller 1922- *WrDr 92*
**Somerville,** Jane *DrAPF 91*
**Somerville,** Jane 1933- *Who 92*
**Somerville,** John Arthur Fownes 1917- *Who 92*
**Somerville,** John Nicholas 1924- *Who 92*
**Somerville,** John Spenser 1910- *Who 92*
**Somerville,** Mary Temple 1952- *WhoAmP 91*
**Somerville,** Nicholas *Who 92*
**Somerville,** Paul Noble 1925- *AmMWSc 92*
**Somerville,** Peggy 1918-1975 *TwCPaSc*
**Somerville,** Quentin Charles Somerville A *Who 92*
**Somerville,** Richard Chapin James 1941- *AmMWSc 92*
**Somerville,** Robert 1906- *Who 92*
**Somerville,** Robert Alston 1920- *WhoBlA 92*
**Somerville,** Robert Eugene *WhoRel 92*
**Somerville,** Robert Stanley 1938- *WhoRel 92*
**Somerville,** Robin Bruce 1942- *WhoMW 92*
**Somerville,** Ronald Lamont 1935- *AmMWSc 92*
**Somerville,** Ronald Macaulay d1991 *Who 92N*
**Somerville,** Stuart Scott 1908- *TwCPaSc*
**Somerville,** Thomas David 1915- *Who 92*
**Somerville,** Walter 1913- *Who 92*
**Somerville,** William 1675-1742 *RfGEnL 91*
**Somerville,** William Glassell, Jr. 1933- *WhoAmL 92*
**Somerville-Large,** Peter 1928- *WrDr 92*
**Somes,** Grant William 1947- *AmMWSc 92*
**Somes,** Michael 1917- *Who 92*
**Somes,** Ralph Gilmore, Jr 1929- *AmMWSc 92*
**Somjen,** George G 1929- *AmMWSc 92*
**Somkaite,** Rozalija 1925- *AmMWSc 92*
**Somkuti,** George A 1936- *AmMWSc 92*
**Somlyo,** Andrew Paul 1930- *AmMWSc 92*
**Somlyo,** Avril Virginia 1939- *AmMWSc 92*
**Somlyo,** Gyorgy 1920- *IntAu&W 91, IntWW 91*
**Somma,** Robert 1944- *WhoAmL 92*
**Somma,** Stephen R 1961- *WhoAmP 91*
**Sommaruga,** Cornelio 1932- *IntWW 91, Who 92*
**Sommer,** Alfred 1942- *AmMWSc 92*
**Sommer,** Alfred Hermann 1909- *AmMWSc 92*
**Sommer,** Alphonse Adam, Jr. 1924- *WhoAmL 92, WhoFI 92*
**Sommer,** Armin Brewster, Jr. 1952- *WhoRel 92*
**Sommer,** Charles John 1951- *AmMWSc 92*
**Sommer,** Elke 1940- *IntMPA 92, IntWW 91*
**Sommer,** Elke 1941- *WhoEnt 92*
**Sommer,** Harry Edward 1941- *AmMWSc 92*
**Sommer,** Helmut 1922- *AmMWSc 92*
**Sommer,** Holger Thomas 1950- *AmMWSc 92*
**Sommer,** Joachim Rainer 1924- *AmMWSc 92*
**Sommer,** John G 1926- *AmMWSc 92*
**Sommer,** Josef 1934- *IntMPA 92*
**Sommer,** Kathleen Ruth 1947- *AmMWSc 92*
**Sommer,** Leo Harry 1917- *AmMWSc 92*
**Sommer,** Leonard Samuel 1924- *AmMWSc 92*
**Sommer,** Noel Frederick 1920- *AmMWSc 92*
**Sommer,** Richard Samuel 1941- *WhoFI 92*
**Sommer,** Sheldon E 1937- *AmMWSc 92*
**Sommer,** Theo 1930- *IntWW 91*
**Sommer,** Tiane Lynda 1955- *WhoAmL 92*
**Sommer Smith,** Sally K 1953- *AmMWSc 92*
**Sommerfeld,** David William 1942- *WhoAmL 92*
**Sommerfeld,** Jude T 1936- *AmMWSc 92*
**Sommerfeld,** Milton R 1940- *AmMWSc 92*
**Sommerfeld,** Richard Arthur 1933- *AmMWSc 92*
**Sommerfeldt,** Theron G 1923- *AmMWSc 92*
**Sommerfelt,** Soren Christian 1916- *IntWW 91*
**Sommerfield,** Charles Michael 1933- *AmMWSc 92*
**Sommerhalder,** John Edward 1934- *WhoWest 92*
**Sommerkamp,** Theo Enoch 1929- *WhoRel 92*
**Sommerlatte,** Karl Ewald 1922- *WhoFI 92*
**Sommerman,** George 1909- *AmMWSc 92*
**Sommerman,** Kathryn Martha 1915- *AmMWSc 92*
**Sommers,** Armiger Henry 1920- *AmMWSc 92*
**Sommers,** Dana Eugene 1953- *WhoMW 92*
**Sommers,** David Lynn 1949- *WhoMW 92*
**Sommers,** Duane C 1932- *WhoAmP 91*
**Sommers,** Ella Blanche 1908- *AmMWSc 92*
**Sommers,** Gordon L. *WhoRel 92*
**Sommers,** Helen Elizabeth 1932- *WhoAmP 91*
**Sommers,** Henry Stern, Jr 1914- *AmMWSc 92*
**Sommers,** Herbert M 1925- *AmMWSc 92*
**Sommers,** Jay Richard 1939- *AmMWSc 92*
**Sommers,** Lawrence M *AmMWSc 92*
**Sommers,** Lee Edwin 1944- *AmMWSc 92*
**Sommers,** Mark Richard 1945- *WhoMW 92*
**Sommers,** Paul Edward 1949- *WhoFI 92*
**Sommers,** Raymond A 1931- *AmMWSc 92*
**Sommers,** Robert Thomas 1926- *IntAu&W 91*
**Sommers,** Sheldon Charles 1916- *AmMWSc 92*
**Sommers,** Steven M. 1951- *WhoAmL 92*
**Sommers,** William P 1933- *AmMWSc 92*
**Sommerville,** Joseph C. 1926- *WhoBlA 92*

**Sommese**, Andrew John 1948- AmMWSc 92
**Sommier**, Francois-Clement 1844-1907 ThHEIm
**Somoano**, Robert Bonner 1940- AmMWSc 92
**Somoff**, Ralff John 1952- WhoEnt 92
**Somogi**, Judith 1937-1988 NewAmDM
**Somogyi**, Jozsef 1916- IntWW 91
**Somogyi**, Laszlo 1932- IntWW 91
**Somogyi**, Laszlo P 1931- AmMWSc 92
**Somogyi**, Laszlo Peter 1931- WhoFI 92, WhoWest 92
**Somorjai**, Gabor Arpad 1935- AmMWSc 92, IntWW 91, WhoWest 92
**Somorjai**, Rajmund Lewis 1937- AmMWSc 92
**Somoza**, Joe WhoHisp 92
**Somoza**, Joseph DrAPF 91
**Somoza Debayle**, Anastasio 1925-1980 FacFETw
**Somsen**, Roger Alan 1931- AmMWSc 92
**Somsky**, David Paul 1946- WhoAmP 91
**Somtow**, S P TwCSFW 91, WrDr 92
**Son Sann** 1911- IntWW 91
**Son Sen** 1930?- IntWW 91
**Son**, Chung Hyun 1917- AmMWSc 92
**Sonawane**, Babasaheb R 1940- AmMWSc 92
**Sondak**, Arthur 1929- WhoFI 92
**Sondak**, Bradley Wayne 1962- WhoWest 92
**Sondak**, Norman Edward 1931- AmMWSc 92
**Sondall**, Steven Marion 1949- WhoMW 92
**Sonde**, Susan DrAPF 91
**Sondel**, Paul Mark 1950- AmMWSc 92
**Sonder**, Edward 1928- AmMWSc 92
**Sonderby**, Susan Pierson 1947- WhoAmP 91
**Sonderegger**, Emil 1898-1934 BiDExR
**Sonderegger**, Theo Brown 1925- AmMWSc 92, WhoMW 92
**Sondergaard**, Neal Albert 1949- AmMWSc 92
**Sondergeld**, Carl Henderson 1947- AmMWSc 92
**Sondericker**, Jerome 1859-1904 BiInAmS
**Sonderman**, Wilma 1927- WhoAmP 91
**Sonders**, Scott Alexander DrAPF 91
**Sondes**, Earl 1940- Who 92
**Sondhaus**, Charles Anderson 1924- AmMWSc 92
**Sondheim**, Alan DrAPF 91
**Sondheim**, Stephen 1930- BenetAL 91, ConCom 92, FacFETw, IntMPA 92, NewAmDM, WrDr 92
**Sondheim**, Stephen Joshua 1930- IntWW 91, Who 92, WhoEnt 92
**Sondheimer**, Ernst Helmut 1923- Who 92
**Sondhi**, Ranjit 1950- Who 92
**Sondock**, Ruby Kless 1926- WhoAmL 92
**Sondreal**, Kory Ryn 1961- WhoMW 92
**Sone**, Monica 1919- BenetAL 91
**Sone**, Philip Geary 1949- WhoWest 92
**Sonenberg**, Martin 1920- AmMWSc 92
**Sonenberg**, Maya DrAPF 91
**Sonenshein**, Abraham Lincoln 1944- AmMWSc 92
**Sonenshine**, Daniel E 1933- AmMWSc 92
**Sonenshine**, H. Marshall 1960- WhoAmL 92
**Sonett**, Charles Philip 1924- AmMWSc 92, WhoWest 92
**Song Chengzhi** IntWW 91
**Song Hanliang** 1934- IntWW 91
**Song Hong-Zhao** 1915- IntWW 91
**Song Jian** 1931- IntWW 91
**Song Jiwen** 1920- IntWW 91
**Song Ping** 1917- IntWW 91
**Song Renqiong** 1903- IntWW 91
**Song Zhenming** d1990 IntWW 91N
**Song Zhiguang** 1916- IntWW 91
**Song**, Ben Chunho 1937- WhoRel 92
**Song**, Byoung-Joon 1950- AmMWSc 92
**Song**, Cathy 1955- BenetAL 91
**Song**, Chang Won 1932- AmMWSc 92
**Song**, Charles Chieh-Shyang 1931- AmMWSc 92
**Song**, Douglas 1967- WhoFI 92
**Song**, Jiakun 1944- AmMWSc 92
**Song**, John Doo 1935- WhoWest 92
**Song**, Joseph 1927- AmMWSc 92
**Song**, Kong-Sop Augustin 1934- AmMWSc 92
**Song**, Moon K 1931- AmMWSc 92
**Song**, Moon Ki 1931- WhoWest 92
**Song**, Pill-Soon 1936- AmMWSc 92
**Song**, Seh-Hoon 1936- AmMWSc 92
**Song**, Sun Kyu 1927- AmMWSc 92
**Song**, Tae-Sung 1941- WhoWest 92
**Song**, Won-Ryul AmMWSc 92
**Song**, Yo Taik 1932- AmMWSc 92
**Song Davenport**, Cathy DrAPF 91
**Song Ong**, Roxanne Kay 1953- WhoAmL 92
**Songaila**, Ringaudas-Bronislovas Ignovich 1929- IntWW 91
**Songer**, H S 1940- WhoIns 92
**Songer**, Hugo Charles 1931- WhoAmL 92
**Songer**, Joseph Richard 1926- AmMWSc 92
**Songstad**, Sheldon R WhoAmP 91
**Songster**, Gerard F 1927- AmMWSc 92
**Songster**, John Hugh 1934- WhoFI 92
**Soni**, Atmaram Harilal 1935- AmMWSc 92
**Soni**, Kusum 1930- AmMWSc 92
**Soni**, Prem Sarita 1948- AmMWSc 92
**Soni**, Surjit Paul 1954- WhoAmL 92
**Soniat**, Katherine DrAPF 91
**Sonin**, Ain A 1937- AmMWSc 92
**Sonis**, Meyer 1919- AmMWSc 92
**Sonis**, Stephen Thomas 1945- AmMWSc 92
**Sonju**, Scott Dennis 1954- WhoAmL 92
**Sonka**, Steven T. 1948- WhoMW 92
**Sonkowsky**, Robert Paul 1931- WhoMW 92
**Sonleitner**, Frank Joseph 1932- AmMWSc 92
**Sonmor**, Marilyn Idelle 1933- WhoWest 92
**Sonn**, George Frank 1936- AmMWSc 92
**Sonn**, William Jacob 1948- WhoWest 92
**Sonnabend**, Yolanda 1935- TwCPaSc
**Sonneborn**, Daniel Atesh 1949- WhoEnt 92
**Sonneborn**, David R 1936- AmMWSc 92
**Sonneborn**, Lee Meyers 1931- AmMWSc 92
**Sonneborn**, Rudolf Goldschmid 1898-1986 FacFETw
**Sonnemaker**, Randall Kent 1958- WhoFI 92
**Sonnemann**, George 1926- AmMWSc 92
**Sonnenberg**, Ben 1936- WhoEnt 92
**Sonnenberg**, Hardy 1939- AmMWSc 92
**Sonnenblick**, Edmund H 1932- AmMWSc 92
**Sonnenfeld**, Albert 1934- WhoWest 92
**Sonnenfeld**, Gerald 1949- AmMWSc 92
**Sonnenfeld**, Marc Jay 1946- WhoAmL 92
**Sonnenfeld**, Peter 1922- AmMWSc 92
**Sonnenfeld**, Richard John 1919- AmMWSc 92
**Sonnenfeldt**, Helmut 1926- IntWW 91, WhoAmP 91
**Sonnenfels**, Josef von 1733-1817 BlkwCEP
**Sonnenschein**, Allan 1941- ConAu 133
**Sonnenschein**, Carlos AmMWSc 92
**Sonnenschein**, Hugo Freund 1940- WhoFI 92
**Sonnenschein**, Ralph Robert 1923- AmMWSc 92
**Sonnenwirth**, Alexander Coleman 1923- AmMWSc 92
**Sonner**, Johann 1924- AmMWSc 92
**Sonnerup**, Bengt Ulf osten 1931- AmMWSc 92
**Sonnet**, Philip E 1935- AmMWSc 92
**Sonnichsen**, C. L. 1901- WrDr 92
**Sonnichsen**, George Carl 1941- AmMWSc 92
**Sonnichsen**, Harold Marvin 1912- AmMWSc 92
**Sonnino**, Carlo Benvenuto 1904- AmMWSc 92
**Sonnleitner**, Thomas Gerald 1940- WhoMW 92
**Sonntag**, Bernard H 1940- AmMWSc 92
**Sonntag**, Douglas F 1926- WhoAmP 91
**Sonntag**, Linda Denise 1952- WhoWest 92
**Sonntag**, Norman Oscar Victor 1919- AmMWSc 92
**Sonntag**, Richard E 1933- AmMWSc 92
**Sonntag**, Roy Windham 1929- AmMWSc 92
**Sonntag**, William Edmund 1950- AmMWSc 92
**Sonny & Cher** LesBEnT 92
**Sono**, Ayako ConAu 133
**Sono-jo and Kiku-jo** EncAmaz 91
**Sonoda**, Kiyomitsu 1929- IntWW 91
**Sonoda**, Ronald Masahiro 1939- AmMWSc 92
**Sonora**, Myrna 1959- WhoHisp 92
**Sons of the Pioneers** NewAmDM
**Sons**, Linda Ruth 1939- AmMWSc 92, WhoMW 92
**Sons**, Michael Edward 1947- WhoMW 92
**Sonsino**, Rifat 1938- WhoRel 92
**Sonstegaard**, Miles Harry 1924- WhoFI 92
**Sonstelie**, Richard Robert 1945- WhoFI 92, WhoWest 92
**Sontag**, David Burt 1934- WhoEnt 92
**Sontag**, Eduardo Daniel 1951- AmMWSc 92
**Sontag**, Frederick Earl 1924- WhoWest 92
**Sontag**, Frederick H 1924- WhoAmP 91
**Sontag**, Glennon Christy 1949- WhoFI 92
**Sontag**, Harvey 1943- WhoFI 92
**Sontag**, Henriette 1806-1854 NewAmDM
**Sontag**, Susan DrAPF 91
**Sontag**, Susan 1933- BenetAL 91, ConNov 91, FacFETw, HanAmWH, IntWW 91, LiExTwC, ModAWWr, Who 92, WrDr 92
**Sontgerath**, Mary WhoRel 92
**Sontheimer**, Richard Dennis 1945- AmMWSc 92
**Sonti**, Babu Venkatesh 1956- WhoMW 92
**Sonza**, Eustaquia de EncAmaz 91
**Sonzogno**, Edoardo 1836-1920 NewAmDM
**Sonzski**, William DrAPF 91
**Soo**, Shao-Lee 1922- AmMWSc 92
**Soocher**, Stan 1951- WhoEnt 92
**Sood**, Arvind K. 1958- WhoFI 92
**Sood**, Manmohan K 1941- AmMWSc 92
**Sood**, Satya P 1923- AmMWSc 92
**Sood**, Vijay Kumar 1951- AmMWSc 92
**Soodsma**, James Franklin 1938- AmMWSc 92
**Soohoo**, Ronald Franklin 1928- AmMWSc 92
**Sookne**, Arnold Maurice 1915- AmMWSc 92
**Sooky**, Attila A 1932- AmMWSc 92
**Soong Chang-Chih** 1916- IntWW 91
**Soong Ching-ling** 1892-1981 FacFETw
**Soong Mei-ling** 1897- FacFETw
**Soong**, James Chu-yul 1942- IntWW 91
**Soong**, Tsu-Teh 1934- AmMWSc 92
**Soong**, Yin Shang 1947- AmMWSc 92
**Soonpaa**, Henn H 1930- AmMWSc 92
**Soora**, Siva Shunmugam 1957- AmMWSc 92
**Soorholtz**, John E 1930- WhoAmP 91
**Soos**, R., Jr. DrAPF 91
**Soos**, Zoltan Geza 1941- AmMWSc 92
**Soost**, Robert Kenneth 1920- AmMWSc 92
**Soothill**, Keith 1941- WrDr 92
**Sooy**, Brian Gordon 1961- WhoMW 92
**Sooy**, Francis Adrian 1915- AmMWSc 92
**Sooy**, Walter Richard 1932- AmMWSc 92
**Sooysmith**, Charles 1856-1916 BiInAmS
**Sopanen**, Jeri Rainer 1929- WhoEnt 92
**Soper** Who 92
**Soper**, Baron 1903- IntWW 91, Who 92
**Soper**, Lord 1903- WrDr 92
**Soper**, Davison Eugene 1943- AmMWSc 92
**Soper**, Gordon Knowles 1938- AmMWSc 92
**Soper**, James C 1907- WhoAmP 91
**Soper**, James Herbert 1916- AmMWSc 92
**Soper**, Jon Allen 1936- AmMWSc 92
**Soper**, Laurence 1943- Who 92
**Soper**, Marsha Ann Paulson 1954- WhoMW 92
**Soper**, Mary Ellen 1934- WhoWest 92
**Soper**, Quentin Francis 1919- AmMWSc 92
**Soper**, Richard Graves 1950- AmMWSc 92
**Soper**, Robert Joseph 1927- AmMWSc 92
**Soper**, Robert Tunnicliff 1925- AmMWSc 92
**Soper**, Tony WrDr 92
**Sopher**, Roger Louis 1936- AmMWSc 92
**Sophianopoulos**, Alkis John 1925- AmMWSc 92
**Sophie Elisabeth** 1613-1676 NewAmDM
**Sophocles** 496?BC-406?BC DramC 1 [port]
**Sophronius** EncEarC
**Sophusson**, Fridrik 1943- IntWW 91
**Sopkin**, George 1914- WhoEnt 92
**Sopko**, P. Jeffrey 1962- WhoFI 92
**Sopori**, Mohan L 1942- AmMWSc 92
**Sopp**, Samuel William 1934- AmMWSc 92
**Sopper**, Dale W 1941- WhoAmP 91
**Sopper**, William Edward 1928- AmMWSc 92
**Sopr**, Alois 1913- IntWW 91
**Soprani**, Luciano 1946- IntWW 91
**Sopwith**, Charles 1905- Who 92
**Sopwith**, Thomas Octave Murdoch 1888-1989 FacFETw
**Sor**, Fernando 1780-1839 NewAmDM
**Sorabji**, Richard Rustom Kharsedji 1934- Who 92
**Soraci**, Paul Michael 1955- WhoFI 92
**Sorak**, Nancy Beckett 1942- WhoAmL 92
**Sorato**, Bruno 1922- IntWW 91
**Sorauf**, James E 1931- AmMWSc 92
**Sorbello**, Richard Salvatore 1942- AmMWSc 92
**Sorber**, Charles Arthur 1939- AmMWSc 92
**Sorbo**, Allen Jon 1953- WhoMW 92
**Sorbo**, Josephine Cusato 1921- WhoRel 92
**Sorby**, Donald Lloyd 1933- AmMWSc 92, WhoWest 92
**Sorce**, Christopher Neal 1952- WhoFI 92
**Sorce**, Gregory Joseph 1955- WhoFI 92
**Sorcsek**, Jerome Paul 1949- WhoWest 92
**Sordahl**, Louis A 1936- AmMWSc 92
**Sordello**, Frank John 1937- WhoWest 92
**Sordi**, Alberto 1919- IntMPA 92
**Soref**, Dror 1950- WhoEnt 92
**Soref**, Harold Benjamin 1916- Who 92
**Soref**, Richard Allan 1936- AmMWSc 92
**Soreide**, David Christien 1945- AmMWSc 92
**Sorel**, Claudette Marguerite WhoEnt 92
**Sorel**, Edward 1929- SmATA 65 [port]
**Sorel**, Elizabeth d1991 NewYTBS 91
**Sorel**, Georges 1847-1922 BiDExR
**Sorel**, Julia IntAu&W 91X, WrDr 92
**Sorel**, Nancy Caldwell 1934- IntAu&W 91, WrDr 92
**Sorell**, Henry P 1923- AmMWSc 92
**Sorell**, Michael 1947- WhoFI 92
**Sorem**, Michael Scott 1945- AmMWSc 92
**Sorem**, Ronald Keith 1924- AmMWSc 92, WhoWest 92
**Soren**, Arnold 1910- AmMWSc 92
**Soren**, David 1946- WhoWest 92
**Sorens**, William Bryan 1955- WhoRel 92
**Sorensen**, Andrew Aaron 1938- AmMWSc 92
**Sorensen**, Bengt Algot 1927- IntWW 91
**Sorensen**, Bent 1958- ConCom 92
**Sorensen**, Bill H WhoAmP 91
**Sorensen**, Carl David 1958- WhoWest 92
**Sorensen**, Charles W. WhoMW 92
**Sorensen**, Christina Marie 1968- WhoRel 92
**Sorensen**, Christopher Michael 1947- AmMWSc 92, WhoMW 92
**Sorensen**, Craig Burg 1946- WhoAmP 91
**Sorensen**, Craig Michael 1954- AmMWSc 92
**Sorensen**, Dale Kenwood 1924- AmMWSc 92
**Sorensen**, Daniel Duane 1964- WhoMW 92
**Sorensen**, David Perry 1930- AmMWSc 92
**Sorensen**, David T 1927- AmMWSc 92
**Sorensen**, Dean E WhoAmP 91
**Sorensen**, Debra Lynnette 1954- WhoWest 92
**Sorensen**, Donald Edwin 1948- WhoFI 92
**Sorensen**, Edgar Lavell 1918- AmMWSc 92
**Sorensen**, Eric 1942- Who 92
**Sorensen**, Frederick Allen 1926- AmMWSc 92
**Sorensen**, Gil 1935- WhoEnt 92
**Sorensen**, Harold C 1934- AmMWSc 92
**Sorensen**, Harvey R. 1947- WhoAmL 92
**Sorensen**, Jacki Faye 1942- WhoEnt 92
**Sorensen**, Jane Forester 1942- WhoFI 92
**Sorensen**, Jimmy Louis 1927- WhoMW 92
**Sorensen**, John Frederick 1923- WhoRel 92
**Sorensen**, John Kousgard 1925- IntWW 91
**Sorensen**, Kenneth Alan 1944- AmMWSc 92
**Sorensen**, Knud 1928- IntWW 91
**Sorensen**, Lauralee Huffman 1935- WhoWest 92
**Sorensen**, Lazern Otto 1927- AmMWSc 92
**Sorensen**, Leif Boge 1928- AmMWSc 92
**Sorensen**, Mark N 1948- WhoAmP 91
**Sorensen**, Paul Davidsen 1934- AmMWSc 92
**Sorensen**, Ralph Albrecht 1945- AmMWSc 92
**Sorensen**, Raymond Andrew 1931- AmMWSc 92
**Sorensen**, Ricardo U 1939- AmMWSc 92
**Sorensen**, Robert Carl 1933- AmMWSc 92
**Sorensen**, Robert Carmine 1952- WhoAmP 91
**Sorensen**, Robert Samuel 1955- WhoMW 92
**Sorensen**, Roberta Ann 1954- WhoAmP 91
**Sorensen**, Sally Jo DrAPF 91
**Sorensen**, Sheila Anne 1947- WhoAmP 91
**Sorensen**, Steven Leonard 1949- WhoRel 92
**Sorensen**, Steven Michael 1953- WhoWest 92
**Sorensen**, Svend Otto SmATA 67 [port]
**Sorensen**, Theodore 1928- WrDr 92
**Sorensen**, Theodore Chaikin 1928- IntWW 91, WhoAmL 92, WhoAmP 91
**Sorensen**, Theodore Strang 1934- AmMWSc 92
**Sorensen**, Thomas Chaikin 1926- IntAu&W 91, WrDr 92
**Sorensen**, Virginia 1912- BenetAL 91, TwCWW 91, WrDr 92
**Sorensen**, William Walter 1948- WhoMW 92
**Sorenson**, C. Peter 1951- WhoAmL 92
**Sorenson**, Carol Johnson 1953- WhoRel 92
**Sorenson**, Craig Allen 1954- WhoWest 92
**Sorenson**, Dean Philip 1939- WhoAmP 91, WhoEnt 92
**Sorenson**, Fred M 1927- AmMWSc 92
**Sorenson**, Harold Wayne 1936- AmMWSc 92
**Sorenson**, James Alfred 1938- AmMWSc 92
**Sorenson**, John R J 1934- AmMWSc 92
**Sorenson**, Marion W 1926- AmMWSc 92
**Sorenson**, Patrick Roy 1966- WhoEnt 92
**Sorenson**, Robert Lowell 1940- AmMWSc 92
**Sorenson**, Russell Allen 1926- WhoAmL 92

**Sorenson,** Shelli Austen 1954- *WhoWest 92*
**Sorenson,** Wayne Richard 1926- *AmMWSc 92*
**Sorenson,** William George 1935- *AmMWSc 92*
**Sorescu,** Marin 1936- *IntWW 91*
**Sorett,** Stephen Michael 1949- *WhoAmL 92*
**Sorge,** Richard 1895-1944 *EncTR 91 [port]*
**Sorge,** Robert Harold 1958- *WhoAmL 92*
**Sorgen,** Michael Steven 1942- *WhoAmL 92*
**Sorgen,** Richard Jesse 1945- *WhoMW 92*
**Sorgenfrei,** Robert Kern 1946- *WhoFI 92*
**Sorgenti,** Harold Andrew 1934- *WhoFI 92*
**Sorger,** George Joseph 1937- *AmMWSc 92*
**Soria,** Rodolfo M 1917- *AmMWSc 92*
**Soria,** Sharon Smith-Fliesher 1960- *WhoEnt 92*
**Soria,** Sixto *BlkOlyM*
**Soriano,** Dale *IntMPA 92*
**Soriano,** David S 1953- *AmMWSc 92*
**Soriano,** Enrique Carlos 1922- *WhoHisp 92*
**Soriano,** Hugo R. 1936- *WhoHisp 92*
**Soriano,** Marcel 1942- *WhoHisp 92*
**Soriano,** Osvaldo 1943- *LiExTwC*
**Soriero,** Alice Ann 1947- *AmMWSc 92*
**Sorinj,** L. T. *Who 92*
**Sorkin,** Alan Lowell 1941- *WhoFI 92*
**Sorkin,** Barry Gerald 1941- *WhoFI 92*
**Sorkin,** Charles K. 1907- *WhoFI 92*
**Sorkin,** Dan 1927- *WhoWest 92*
**Sorkin,** Ellis Robert 1955- *WhoEnt 92*
**Sorkin,** Howard 1933- *AmMWSc 92*
**Sorkin,** Marshall 1928- *AmMWSc 92*
**Sorko-Ram,** Ari 1941- *WhoRel 92*
**Sorko-Ram,** Shira 1940- *WhoRel 92*
**Sorley,** Charles Hamilton 1895-1915 *RfGEnL 91*
**Sorley Walker,** Kathrine *WrDr 92*
**Sorlie,** Oscar James, Jr. 1939- *WhoAmL 92*
**Sormani,** Charles Robert 1938- *WhoIns 92*
**Sorof,** Sam 1922- *AmMWSc 92*
**Soroff,** Harry S 1926- *AmMWSc 92*
**Sorokas,** Eileen Marie 1947- *WhoAmP 91*
**Sorokin,** Aleksey Ivanovich 1922- *IntWW 91*
**Sorokin,** Mikhail Ivanovich 1922- *SovUnBD*
**Sorokin,** Peter 1931- *AmMWSc 92*
**Sorokin,** Sergei Pitirimovitch 1933- *AmMWSc 92*
**Sorokin,** Stephan S. *WhoRel 92*
**Sorokos,** John A. 1917- *Who 92*
**Sorom,** Terry Allen 1940- *WhoWest 92*
**Sorooshian,** Soroosh 1948- *AmMWSc 92*
**Soros,** George 1930- *WhoFI 92*
**Sorrell,** Alan 1904-1974 *TwCPaSc*
**Sorrell,** Alec Albert 1925- *Who 92*
**Sorrell,** Esther Hartigan *WhoAmP 91*
**Sorrell,** Furman Y, Jr 1938- *AmMWSc 92*
**Sorrell,** Gary Lee 1943- *AmMWSc 92*
**Sorrell,** Martin Stuart 1945- *IntWW 91, Who 92, WhoFI 92*
**Sorrell,** Michael Floyd 1935- *AmMWSc 92*
**Sorrells,** Frank Douglas 1931- *AmMWSc 92*
**Sorrells,** Gordon Guthrey 1934- *AmMWSc 92*
**Sorrells,** Helen *DrAPF 91*
**Sorrells,** Mark Earl 1950- *AmMWSc 92*
**Sorrells,** Robert T. *DrAPF 91*
**Sorrels,** John David 1927- *AmMWSc 92*
**Sorrenson,** Maurice Peter Keith 1932- *WrDr 92*
**Sorrenti,** J.J., II 1966- *WhoFI 92*
**Sorrentino,** Gilbert *DrAPF 91*
**Sorrentino,** Gilbert 1929- *BenetAL 91, ConNov 91, ConPo 91, IntAu&W 91, WhoWest 92, WrDr 92*
**Sorrentino,** Peter Augustine 1959- *WhoFI 92*
**Sorrentino,** Sandy, Jr 1943- *AmMWSc 92*
**Sorrie,** George Strath 1933- *Who 92*
**Sorrows,** Howard Earle 1918- *AmMWSc 92*
**Sorsa,** Kalevi 1930- *IntWW 91*
**Sorscher,** Alan J 1934- *AmMWSc 92*
**Sorstokke,** Susan Eileen 1955- *WhoFI 92, WhoWest 92*
**Sorteberg,** Kenneth Warren 1945- *WhoMW 92*
**Sorter,** George Hans 1927- *WhoAmL 92*
**Sorter,** Peter F 1933- *AmMWSc 92*
**Sortland,** Paul Allan 1953- *WhoAmL 92, WhoMW 92*
**Sorvino,** Paul *WhoEnt 92*
**Sorvino,** Paul 1939- *IntMPA 92*
**Sorvoja,** Markku 1955- *WhoWest 92*
**Sosa,** America 1938- *WhoHisp 92*
**Sosa,** Aristides A. 1936- *WhoHisp 92*
**Sosa,** Arnie 1949- *WhoHisp 92*
**Sosa,** Blanca 1954- *WhoHisp 92*
**Sosa,** Dan, Jr *WhoAmP 91*
**Sosa,** Dan, Jr. 1923- *WhoAmL 92, WhoHisp 92, WhoWest 92*
**Sosa,** Enrique J. *WhoHisp 92*
**Sosa,** Esteban *WhoHisp 92*
**Sosa,** Hector V. *WhoHisp 92*
**Sosa,** Juan B. 1941- *WhoHisp 92*
**Sosa,** Juan Jorge 1947- *WhoHisp 92*
**Sosa,** Lionel 1939- *WhoHisp 92*
**Sosa,** Manuel A. 1947- *WhoHisp 92*
**Sosa,** Omelio, Jr 1939- *AmMWSc 92*
**Sosa,** Pura O. 1942- *WhoHisp 92*
**Sosa,** Rebecca 1955- *WhoHisp 92*
**Sosa,** Roberto 1930- *ConSpAP*
**Sosa,** Sammy 1968- *WhoHisp 92*
**Sosa,** Samuel 1968- *WhoBlA 92*
**Sosa,** Teri 1946- *WhoHisp 92*
**Sosa-Riddell,** Adaljiza 1937- *WhoHisp 92*
**Sosa Salinas,** Alicia 1947- *WhoHisp 92*
**Sosebee,** Ronald Eugene 1942- *AmMWSc 92*
**Sosenko,** Roma Myroslawa 1960- *WhoEnt 92*
**Sosin,** Judith Leightman 1943- *WhoRel 92*
**Sosinsky,** Barrie Alan 1952- *AmMWSc 92*
**Soska,** Geary Victor 1948- *AmMWSc 92, WhoMW 92*
**Soskin,** Mark David 1947- *WhoFI 92*
**Soskin,** V H *IntAu&W 91X, WrDr 92*
**Soslau,** Gerald 1944- *AmMWSc 92*
**Sosna,** Robert William 1941- *WhoIns 92*
**Sosnik,** Harry 1906- *WhoEnt 92*
**Sosnovsky,** George 1920- *AmMWSc 92*
**Sosnowski,** Thomas Patrick 1936- *AmMWSc 92*
**Sosrodarsono,** Suyono 1926- *IntWW 91*
**Soss,** Alexander Lester 1938- *WhoWest 92*
**Soss,** Neal Martin 1949- *WhoFI 92*
**Sossaman,** Carolyn Sue 1933- *WhoAmP 91*
**Sossaman,** James J 1932- *WhoAmP 91, WhoWest 92*
**Sossaman,** Stephen *DrAPF 91*
**Sossaman,** William Lynwood 1947- *WhoAmL 92*
**Sossong,** Norman D 1939- *AmMWSc 92*
**Sostar,** Victor John 1955- *WhoFI 92*
**Sostarich,** John Mark 1956- *WhoRel 92*
**Sostarich,** Mark Edward 1953- *WhoAmP 91*
**Sostek,** Edward Leon 1926- *WhoEnt 92*
**Sosulski,** Frank Walter 1929- *AmMWSc 92*
**Sotelo,** Andrew 1951- *WhoHisp 92*
**Sotelo,** Antonio Andres, Jr. 1932- *WhoHisp 92*
**Sotelo,** Sabino 1959- *WhoHisp 92*
**Soter** *EncEarC*
**Soter,** Nicholas Gregory 1947- *WhoWest 92*
**Soteriades,** Michael C 1923- *AmMWSc 92*
**Sotero,** Raymond Augustine 1953- *WhoHisp 92*
**Soth,** Lauren 1934- *WhoMW 92*
**Sothern,** Ann 1909- *IntMPA 92*
**Sothern,** Robert B. 1946- *WhoMW 92*
**Sotin,** Hans 1939- *IntWW 91*
**Sotirchos,** Stratis V 1956- *AmMWSc 92*
**Sotirhos,** Michael 1928- *IntWW 91, WhoAmP 91, WhoHisp 92*
**Sotirios of Toronto,** Bishop 1936- *WhoRel 92*
**Soto,** Aida R 1931- *AmMWSc 92, WhoHisp 92*
**Soto,** Antonio Juan *WhoHisp 92*
**Soto,** Benjamin *WhoAmP 91*
**Soto,** Carlos *WhoHisp 92*
**Soto,** Debra Jean 1958- *WhoWest 92*
**Soto,** Domingo de 1495-1560 *HisDSpE*
**Soto,** Frederick E., Jr. 1954- *WhoHisp 92*
**Soto,** Gary *DrAPF 91*
**Soto,** Gary 1952- *ConPo 91, WhoHisp 92, WrDr 92*
**Soto,** Gerardo H 1922- *AmMWSc 92*
**Soto,** Heli Rafael 1964- *WhoEnt 92*
**Soto,** Hernando de 1500?-1542 *HisDSpE*
**Soto,** Jesus-Rafael 1923- *IntWW 91, WorArt 1980*
**Soto,** Jock *WhoHisp 92*
**Soto,** John 1932- *WhoHisp 92*
**Soto,** John Anthony, Sr. 1945- *WhoHisp 92*
**Soto,** Karen I. 1952- *WhoHisp 92*
**Soto,** Leandro P. *WhoHisp 92*
**Soto,** Louis Humberto 1912- *WhoHisp 92*
**Soto,** Lourdes Diaz *WhoHisp 92*
**Soto,** Maria Enid 1957- *WhoHisp 92*
**Soto,** Nell G. *WhoHisp 92*
**Soto,** Osvaldo *WhoHisp 92*
**Soto,** Pedro Juan 1928- *WhoHisp 92*
**Soto,** Philip L. 1959- *WhoHisp 92*
**Soto,** Radames Jose 1959- *WhoHisp 92*
**Soto,** Ramona 1963- *WhoMW 92*
**Soto,** Richard Gil *WhoHisp 92*
**Soto,** Robert Louis 1949- *WhoHisp 92*
**Soto,** Roberto Fernando Eduardo 1950- *WhoHisp 92*
**Soto,** Roberto Manuel 1950- *WhoHisp 92*
**Soto,** Ronald Steven 1948- *WhoHisp 92*
**Soto,** Rose Marie *WhoHisp 92*
**Soto,** Shirlene Ann 1950- *WhoHisp 92*
**Soto,** Victor *WhoHisp 92*
**Soto Mendez,** Benjamin *WhoHisp 92*
**Soto-Tamames,** Eduardo 1943- *WhoHisp 92*
**Soto Velez,** Clemente 1905- *WhoHisp 92*
**Sotolongo,** Alfredo *WhoHisp 92*
**Sotolongo,** Raul O. *WhoHisp 92*
**Sotomayer,** Javier *NewYTBS 91 [port]*
**Sotomayor,** Antonio 1904- *IntWW 91*
**Sotomayor,** Ernie *WhoHisp 92*
**Sotomayor,** Frank O. 1943- *WhoHisp 92*
**Sotomayor,** Javier *NewYTBS 91 [port]*
**Sotomayor,** John A. 1928- *WhoHisp 92*
**Sotomayor,** Lilian Judith 1956- *WhoHisp 92*
**Sotomayor,** Manuel F. 1953- *WhoFI 92*
**Sotomayor,** Marta 1939- *WhoHisp 92*
**Sotomayor,** Rene Eduardo 1937- *AmMWSc 92*
**Sotomayor,** Sonia 1954- *WhoAmL 92*
**Sotos,** Hercules Peter 1933- *WhoFI 92*
**Sotos,** Juan Fernandez 1927- *AmMWSc 92*
**Sottery,** Theodore Walter 1927- *AmMWSc 92*
**Sottile,** Benjamin 1937- *WhoMW 92*
**Sottsass,** Ettore, Jr. 1917- *DcTwDes*
**Sou-Hwan,** Stephen *WhoRel 92*
**Soublette,** Carlos 1789-1870 *HisDSpE*
**Souby,** Armand Max 1917- *AmMWSc 92*
**Soucek,** Raymond F. 1945- *WhoRel 92*
**Soucie,** William George 1942- *AmMWSc 92*
**Soucy,** Donna M 1967- *WhoAmP 91*
**Soucy,** Frederick F *WhoAmP 91*
**Soucy,** Lillian E 1935- *WhoAmP 91*
**Soucy,** Thomas Edward 1945- *WhoMW 92*
**Soudack,** Avrum Chaim 1934- *AmMWSc 92*
**Soudek,** Dushan Edward 1920- *AmMWSc 92*
**Souder,** Paul A 1944- *AmMWSc 92*
**Souder,** Wallace William 1937- *AmMWSc 92*
**Souers,** William Sidney 1892-1973 *FacFETw*
**Souerwine,** Andrew Harry 1924- *WhoFI 92*
**Soufflot,** Jacques Germain 1713?-1780 *BlkwCEP*
**Souhami,** Mark 1935- *Who 92*
**Souhami,** Robert Leon 1938- *Who 92*
**Souhrada,** Frank 1937- *AmMWSc 92*
**Souki,** Joseph M 1932- *WhoAmP 91*
**Soukop,** Wilhelm Josef 1907- *Who 92*
**Soukoup,** Willi 1907- *TwCPaSc*
**Soukup,** Al *WhoAmP 91*
**Soukup,** Erwin Myron 1921- *WhoRel 92*
**Soukup,** Jane Klinkner 1958- *WhoMW 92*
**Soukup,** Rodney Joseph 1939- *AmMWSc 92, WhoMW 92*
**Soul,** David 1943- *IntMPA 92*
**Soul,** David R. *WhoEnt 92*
**Soulages,** Pierre 1919- *IntWW 91*
**Soulas,** Robert Neff 1921- *WhoAmP 91*
**Soulbury,** Viscount 1915- *Who 92*
**Soule,** Caroline Gray 1855-1920 *BiInAmS*
**Soule,** David Elliot 1925- *AmMWSc 92*
**Soule,** Dorothy 1923- *AmMWSc 92*
**Soule,** Gardner 1913- *IntAu&W 91*
**Soule,** George Alan 1930- *WhoMW 92*
**Soule,** James 1920- *AmMWSc 92*
**Soule,** John Dutcher 1920- *AmMWSc 92*
**Soule,** Maris Anne 1939- *IntAu&W 91*
**Soule,** Olan 1909- *ConTFT 9*
**Soule,** Oscar Hommel 1940- *AmMWSc 92*
**Soule,** Phillip E 1950- *WhoIns 92*
**Soule,** Richard Herman 1849-1908 *BiInAmS*
**Soule,** Roger Gilbert 1935- *AmMWSc 92*
**Soule,** Samuel David 1904- *AmMWSc 92*
**Soule,** William 1834-1914 *BiInAmS*
**Soulen,** John Richard 1927- *AmMWSc 92*
**Soulen,** Renate Leroi 1933- *AmMWSc 92*
**Soulen,** Robert J, Jr 1940- *AmMWSc 92*
**Soulen,** Robert Lewis 1932- *AmMWSc 92*
**Soulen,** Thomas Kay 1935- *AmMWSc 92*
**Soules,** Georges Raymond 1907- *BiDExR*
**Soules,** Jack Arbuthnott 1928- *AmMWSc 92*
**Soules,** Terrill Shepard *DrAPF 91*
**Soules,** William Anderson *WhoMW 92*
**Soulet,** Sal 1952- *WhoHisp 92*
**Soulioti,** Stella 1920- *IntWW 91*
**Soulsby** *Who 92*
**Soulsby,** E. J. L. 1926- *WrDr 92*
**Soulsby,** Michael Edward 1941- *AmMWSc 92*
**Soulsby of Swaffham Prior,** Baron 1926- *Who 92*
**Soultz,** Jerry Lee 1949- *WhoMW 92*
**Soundgarden** *ConMus 6 [port]*
**Soung,** Wen Y 1945- *AmMWSc 92*
**Soung-Soo,** Simon Kim *WhoRel 92*
**Soupault,** Philippe 1897- *IntAu&W 91*
**Soupault,** Philippe 1897-1990 *AnObit 1990, ConLC 68 [port], FacFETw, GuFrLit 1*
**Souper,** Patrick C. 1928- *WrDr 92*
**Souphanouvong** 1902- *IntWW 91*
**Souphanouvong** 1909- *FacFETw*
**Sour,** Arthur W, Jr 1924- *WhoAmP 91*
**Sourapas,** Steve James 1935- *WhoWest 92*
**Sourbrine,** Richard Don, II 1965- *WhoMW 92*
**Soureli-Grigoriadou,** Galatia 1930- *IntAu&W 91*
**Soures,** John Michael 1943- *AmMWSc 92*
**Sourian,** Peter *DrAPF 91*
**Souritz,** Elizabeth 1923- *ConAu 135*
**Sourkes,** Theodore Lionel 1919- *AmMWSc 92*
**Sourozh,** Metropolitan of *Who 92*
**Sourrouille,** Juan Vital 1940- *IntWW 91*
**Sours,** Richard Eugene 1941- *AmMWSc 92*
**Sourwine,** Julien Gillen 1939- *WhoAmL 92*
**Sousa,** John Philip 1854-1932 *BenetAL 91, NewAmDM*
**Sousa,** Lynn Robert 1943- *AmMWSc 92*
**Sousa,** Ronald Wayne 1943- *WhoMW 92*
**Soustelle,** Jacques d1990 *IntWW 91N*
**Soustelle,** Jacques 1912-1990 *AnObit 1990*
**Soustelle,** Jacques Emile 1912-1990 *FacFETw*
**Souster,** Raymond 1921- *BenetAL 91, ConAu 14AS [port], ConPo 91, IntAu&W 91, RfGEnL 91, WrDr 92*
**Soutar,** Charles 1920- *Who 92*
**Soutas-Little,** Robert William 1933- *AmMWSc 92, WhoMW 92*
**Soutendijk,** Dirk Rutger 1938- *WhoAmL 92*
**Souter** *Who 92*
**Souter,** Camille 1929- *TwCPaSc*
**Souter,** David 1939- *FacFETw, News 91 [port], -91-3 [port]*
**Souter,** David H. 1939- *CurBio 91 [port], WhoAmP 91*
**Souter,** David Hackett 1939- *IntWW 91, WhoAmL 92*
**Souter,** John Bulloch 1890-1972 *TwCPaSc*
**Souter,** Sydney Scull 1931- *WhoAmL 92*
**South,** Amaryllis Jean 1937- *WhoMW 92*
**South,** Arthur 1914- *Who 92*
**South,** Cris *DrAPF 91*
**South,** Frank E 1924- *AmMWSc 92*
**South,** Graham Robin 1940- *AmMWSc 92*
**South,** Hugh Miles 1947- *AmMWSc 92*
**South,** James Dwight 1957- *WhoEnt 92*
**South,** Karen *DrAPF 91*
**South,** Leonard *WhoEnt 92*
**South,** Mary Ann 1933- *AmMWSc 92*
**South,** Pamela Dawn 1948- *WhoEnt 92*
**South,** Wesley W. 1914- *WhoBlA 92*
**Southack,** Cyprian 1662-1745 *BiInAmS*
**Southall,** Charles 1937- *WhoBlA 92*
**Southall,** Geneva H. 1925- *WhoBlA 92*
**Southall,** Herbert Howardton, Sr. 1907- *WhoBlA 92*
**Southall,** Ivan 1921- *SmATA 68 [port], WrDr 92*
**Southall,** Ivan Francis 1921- *IntAu&W 91, IntWW 91*
**Southall,** Joseph Edward 1861-1944 *TwCPaSc*
**Southall,** Kenneth Charles 1922- *Who 92*
**Southall,** Spalding 1912- *WhoIns 92*
**Southall,** Walter Delbert 1926- *WhoAmP 91*
**Southam,** B C 1931- *IntAu&W 91, WrDr 92*
**Southam,** Chester Milton 1919- *AmMWSc 92*
**Southam,** Donald Lee 1929- *AmMWSc 92*
**Southam,** Frederick William 1924- *AmMWSc 92*
**Southam,** Gordon Hamilton 1916- *IntWW 91*
**Southam,** Gordon Ronald 1918- *Who 92*
**Southam,** John Ralph 1942- *AmMWSc 92*
**Southampton,** Baron 1928- *Who 92*
**Southampton,** Bishop Suffragan of 1935- *Who 92*
**Southan,** Robert Joseph 1928- *Who 92*
**Southard,** Alvin Reid 1926- *AmMWSc 92*
**Southard,** Elmer Ernest 1876-1920 *BiInAmS*
**Southard,** John Brelsford 1938- *AmMWSc 92*
**Southard,** Samuel 1925- *WhoRel 92, WhoWest 92*
**Southard,** Wendell Homer 1927- *AmMWSc 92*
**Southards,** Carroll J 1932- *AmMWSc 92*
**Southards,** William Thomas 1952- *WhoMW 92*
**Southborough,** Baron 1922- *Who 92*
**Southby,** John 1948- *Who 92*
**Southend,** Archdeacon of *Who 92*
**Souther,** Jean Lorraine *WhoFI 92*
**Southerington,** Theresa Koogler 1950- *WhoEnt 92*
**Southerland,** Ellease *DrAPF 91*
**Southerland,** Ellease 1943- *WhoBlA 92*
**Southerland,** William M *AmMWSc 92*
**Southern,** Byron Wayne 1946- *AmMWSc 92*
**Southern,** Charles O. 1920- *WhoBlA 92*
**Southern,** Duane 1948- *WhoAmP 91*

**Southern,** Eileen 1920- *NotBlAW 92*
**Southern,** Eileen Jackson 1920- *WhoBlA 92*
**Southern,** Herbert B. 1926- *WhoBlA 92*
**Southern,** Jeri d1991 *NewYTBS 91*
**Southern,** John Stephen 1953- *WhoEnt 92*
**Southern,** Joseph 1919- *WhoBlA 92*
**Southern,** Lonnie Steven 1947- *WhoMW 92, WhoRel 92*
**Southern,** Michael William 1918- *Who 92*
**Southern,** Richard 1912- *IntWW 91, Who 92*
**Southern,** Robert 1907- *Who 92*
**Southern,** Robert Allen 1930- *WhoAmL 92*
**Southern,** Ronald Donald 1930- *WhoWest 92*
**Southern,** Terry *DrAPF 91*
**Southern,** Terry 1924- *ConNov 91, IntAu&W 91, WrDr 92*
**Southern,** Thomas Martin 1942- *AmMWSc 92*
**Southern,** William Edward 1933- *AmMWSc 92*
**Southerne,** Thomas 1660-1746 *RfGEnL 91*
**Southerton,** Thomas Henry 1917- *Who 92*
**Southesk,** Earl of 1893- *Who 92*
**Southey,** Robert 1774-1843 *DcLB 107 [port], RfGEnL 91*
**Southey,** Robert 1922- *Who 92*
**Southgate,** Colin Grieve 1938- *Who 92*
**Southgate,** Frank 1872-1916 *TwCPaSc*
**Southgate,** Harry Charles 1921- *Who 92*
**Southgate,** John Eliot 1926- *Who 92*
**Southgate,** Malcolm John 1933- *Who 92*
**Southgate,** Peter David 1928- *AmMWSc 92*
**Southin,** John L 1939- *AmMWSc 92*
**Southren,** A Louis 1926- *AmMWSc 92*
**Southward,** Glen Morris 1927- *AmMWSc 92*
**Southward,** Harold Dean 1930- *AmMWSc 92*
**Southward,** Leonard 1905- *Who 92*
**Southward,** Nigel Ralph 1941- *Who 92*
**Southward,** Ralph 1908- *Who 92*
**Southward,** Walter William 1936- *WhoWest 92*
**Southwark,** Archbishop & Metropolitan of 1930- *Who 92*
**Southwark,** Archdeacon of *Who 92*
**Southwark,** Auxiliary Bishops in *Who 92*
**Southwark,** Bishop of 1932- *Who 92*
**Southwark,** Provost of *Who 92*
**Southwell** *Who 92*
**Southwell,** Bishop of 1934- *Who 92*
**Southwell,** Provost of *Who 92*
**Southwell,** Viscount 1930- *Who 92*
**Southwell,** P H 1924- *AmMWSc 92*
**Southwell,** Richard Charles *Who 92*
**Southwell,** Robert 1561-1595 *RfGEnL 91*
**Southwell,** Roy 1914- *Who 92*
**Southwell,** Samuel B. *DrAPF 91*
**Southwell-Keely,** Terry 1908-1985 *FacFETw*
**Southwick,** Charles Henry 1928- *AmMWSc 92, WhoWest 92*
**Southwick,** Christopher Lyn 1956- *WhoMW 92*
**Southwick,** David Leroy 1936- *AmMWSc 92*
**Southwick,** Edward Earle *AmMWSc 92*
**Southwick,** Everett West 1941- *AmMWSc 92*
**Southwick,** Franklin Wallburg 1917- *AmMWSc 92*
**Southwick,** Harry W 1918- *AmMWSc 92*
**Southwick,** Lawrence 1912- *AmMWSc 92*
**Southwick,** Marcia *DrAPF 91*
**Southwick,** Philip Lee 1916- *AmMWSc 92*
**Southwick,** Richard Arthur 1924- *AmMWSc 92*
**Southwick,** Russell Duty 1931- *AmMWSc 92*
**Southwick,** Solomon 1773-1839 *BenetAL 91*
**Southwick,** Stephen Mark 1956- *WhoWest 92*
**Southwick,** Wayne Orin 1923- *AmMWSc 92*
**Southwood,** Horace Gerald 1912- *Who 92*
**Southwood,** Richard 1931- *Who 92, WrDr 92*
**Southwood,** Richard Edmund 1931- *IntWW 91*
**Southwood,** William Frederick Walter 1925- *Who 92*
**Southworth,** Bruce Alan 1951- *WhoRel 92*
**Southworth,** E.D.E.N. 1819-1899 *BenetAL 91*
**Southworth,** Frederick 1910- *Who 92*
**Southworth,** Hamilton 1907- *AmMWSc 92*
**Southworth,** Jean May 1926- *Who 92*
**Southworth,** Jim O 1929- *WhoAmP 91*
**Southworth,** Raymond W 1920- *AmMWSc 92*
**Southworth,** Richard Paul 1944- *WhoMW 92*
**Southworth,** Warren H. 1912- *WrDr 92*
**Southworth,** Warren Hilbourne 1912- *AmMWSc 92*
**Souto,** Javier 1939- *WhoAmP 91*
**Souto,** Javier D. 1939- *WhoHisp 92*
**Souto,** Jose A. *WhoHisp 92*
**Souto Bachiller,** Fernando Alberto 1951- *AmMWSc 92*
**Soutou,** Jean-Marie Leon 1912- *IntWW 91*
**Souttar,** Margaret 1914- *TwCPaSc*
**Soutter,** Thomas D. 1934- *WhoAmL 92, WhoFI 92*
**Souvanna Phouma,** Prince 1901-1984 *FacFETw*
**Souveroff,** Vernon William, Jr. 1934- *WhoFI 92*
**Souyave,** Georges 1926- *Who 92*
**Souza,** Blase Camacho 1918- *WhoWest 92*
**Souza,** Everett J 1945- *WhoIns 92*
**Souza,** F.N. 1924- *TwCPaSc*
**Souza,** Francis Newton 1924- *IntWW 91*
**Souza,** Wade Anthony 1958- *WhoWest 92*
**Souza e Silva,** Celso de 1924- *Who 92*
**Souzay,** Gerard 1918- *NewAmDM*
**Souzay,** Gerard 1920- *IntWW 91*
**Souzay,** Gerard 1921- *Who 92*
**Soven,** Paul 1939- *AmMWSc 92*
**Sovern,** Michael Ira 1931- *IntWW 91, WhoAmL 92*
**Soverow,** Kathy Sylvester 1953- *WhoWest 92*
**Sovers,** Ojars Juris 1937- *AmMWSc 92*
**Sovetky,** Jack 1930- *WhoWest 92*
**Sovey,** William Pierre 1933- *WhoFI 92, WhoMW 92*
**Sovie,** Margaret D *AmMWSc 92*
**Sovish,** Richard Charles 1925- *AmMWSc 92, WhoWest 92*
**Sovocool,** G Wayne 1942- *AmMWSc 92*
**Sowa,** Frank Joseph 1914- *WhoRel 92*
**Sowa,** Frank Xavier 1957- *WhoFI 92*
**Sowa,** John Robert 1934- *AmMWSc 92*
**Sowa,** Larry 1938- *WhoAmP 91*
**Sowa,** Walter 1933- *AmMWSc 92*
**Sowada,** Alphonse Augustus 1933- *WhoRel 92*
**Soward,** Andrew Michael 1943- *Who 92*
**Sowards,** Paul Michael 1967- *WhoAmP 91*
**Sowden,** John Percival 1917- *Who 92*
**Sowden,** Terence Cubitt 1929- *Who 92*
**Sowden,** William Carl 1951- *WhoWest 92*
**Sowder,** Fred Allen 1940- *WhoMW 92*
**Sowder,** Larry K 1938- *AmMWSc 92*
**Sowell,** Ernest Eugene 1950- *WhoAmL 92*
**Sowell,** Jack Robson 1932- *WhoAmL 92*
**Sowell,** Jerry Felix, Jr. 1958- *WhoFI 92*
**Sowell,** John Basil 1958- *AmMWSc 92*
**Sowell,** John Gregory 1941- *AmMWSc 92*
**Sowell,** Katye Marie Oliver 1934- *AmMWSc 92*
**Sowell,** Madison Upshaw 1952- *WhoWest 92*
**Sowell,** Myzell 1924- *WhoBlA 92*
**Sowell,** Polly Rollins *WhoAmP 91*
**Sowell,** Thomas 1930- *ConBlB 2 [port], WhoBlA 92, WrDr 92*
**Sowell,** W. R. 1920- *WhoFI 92*
**Sowell,** William Hilton 1956- *WhoWest 92*
**Sowell,** William Raymond 1928- *WhoWest 92*
**Sower,** Stacia Ann 1950- *AmMWSc 92*
**Sowerbutts,** Bill 1911-1990 *AnObit 1990*
**Sowerby,** Leo 1895-1968 *NewAmDM*
**Sowers,** Arthur Edward 1943- *AmMWSc 92*
**Sowers,** David Eric 1946- *WhoAmL 92*
**Sowers,** Edward Eugene 1942- *AmMWSc 92*
**Sowers,** George F 1921- *AmMWSc 92*
**Sowers,** Jerry Allen 1950- *WhoRel 92*
**Sowers,** Miriam Ruth 1922- *WhoWest 92*
**Sowers,** Richard Louis 1954- *WhoEnt 92*
**Sowers,** Sidney Gerald 1935- *WhoRel 92*
**Sowers,** Wesley H 1905- *WhoAmP 91*
**Sowerwine,** Elbert Orla, Jr. 1915- *WhoFI 92, WhoWest 92*
**Sowinski,** Joseph Matthew 1960- *WhoEnt 92*
**Sowinski,** Mieczyslaw 1930- *IntWW 91*
**Sowinski,** Raymond 1924- *AmMWSc 92*
**Sowinski,** Stanislaus Joseph 1927- *WhoWest 92*
**Sowle,** John Steven 1944- *WhoWest 92*
**Sowles,** Marcia Kay 1950- *WhoAmL 92*
**Sowls,** Lyle Kenneth 1916- *AmMWSc 92*
**Sowman,** Harold G 1923- *AmMWSc 92*
**Sowrey,** Frederick 1922- *Who 92*
**Sowry,** Clive 1917- *Who 92*
**Soyer,** David 1923- *WhoEnt 92*
**Soyinka,** Wole 1934- *BlkLC [port], ConPo 91, DramC 2 [port], FacFETw [port], IntWW 91, LiExTwC, RfGEnL 91, Who 92, WhoNob 90, WrDr 92*
**Soyinkya,** Akinwande Oluiwole 1934- *LiExTwC*
**Soyka,** Lester F 1931- *AmMWSc 92*
**Soysa,** Warusahennedige Abraham Bastian *Who 92*
**Soyster,** Margaret Blair 1951- *WhoAmL 92*
**Soza,** William 1936- *WhoHisp 92*
**Sozansky,** Michael William, Jr. 1949- *WhoAmL 92*
**Sozen,** M A 1930- *AmMWSc 92*
**Sozomen** *EncEarC*
**Spaak,** Paul-Henri 1899-1972 *FacFETw*
**Spaatz,** Carl 1891-1974 *FacFETw*
**Space,** Ace *DrAPF 91*
**Space,** Theodore Maxwell 1938- *WhoAmL 92, WhoFI 92*
**Spacek,** Mary Elizabeth 1949- *IntWW 91*
**Spacek,** Sissy 1949- *IntMPA 92*
**Spacey,** Kevin 1959- *ConTFT 9, IntMPA 92, WhoEnt 92*
**Spach,** James DeHart 1954- *WhoEnt 92*
**Spach,** John Thom *DrAPF 91*
**Spach,** Jule Christian 1923- *WhoRel 92*
**Spach,** Madison Stockton 1926- *AmMWSc 92*
**Spache,** George D. 1909- *WrDr 92*
**Spache,** George Daniel 1909- *IntAu&W 91*
**Spacie,** Anne 1945- *AmMWSc 92*
**Spacie,** Keith 1935- *Who 92*
**Spackman,** Darrel H 1924- *AmMWSc 92*
**Spackman,** John William Charles 1932- *Who 92*
**Spackman,** Michael John 1936- *Who 92*
**Spackman,** Sarah 1958- *TwCPaSc*
**Spackman,** William, Jr 1919- *AmMWSc 92*
**Spacks,** Barry *DrAPF 91*
**Spacks,** Barry 1931- *ConPo 91, WrDr 92*
**Spacks,** Patricia Meyer 1929- *IntAu&W 91, WrDr 92*
**Spada,** Lawrence John 1951- *WhoAmL 92*
**Spadafino,** Leonard Peter 1931- *AmMWSc 92*
**Spadaro,** Charlotte *WhoAmP 91*
**Spadaro,** William Thomas 1967- *WhoEnt 92*
**Spade,** George Lawrence 1945- *WhoWest 92*
**Spade,** Phyllis Dixee 1925- *WhoMW 92*
**Spade,** Rupert *WrDr 92*
**Spader,** Dann Laverne 1951- *WhoRel 92*
**Spader,** James 1960- *IntMPA 92, News 91 [port], WhoEnt 92*
**Spader,** James 1961- *ConTFT 9*
**Spadolini,** Giovanni 1925- *IntWW 91*
**Spadoni,** Leon R 1930- *AmMWSc 92*
**Spadoro,** George A 1948- *WhoAmP 91*
**Spaeder,** Carl Edward, Jr 1935- *AmMWSc 92*
**Spaeder,** Roger Campbell 1943- *WhoAmL 92*
**Spaeh,** Winfried Heinrich 1930- *WhoFI 92*
**Spaepen,** Frans 1948- *AmMWSc 92*
**Spaet,** Theodore H 1920- *AmMWSc 92*
**Spaeth,** Anthony 1955- *ConAu 133*
**Spaeth,** Gary Lewis 1945- *WhoAmP 91*
**Spaeth,** George L 1932- *AmMWSc 92*
**Spaeth,** Joseph Louis 1940- *WhoWest 92*
**Spaeth,** Karl Henry 1929- *WhoAmL 92, WhoFI 92*
**Spaeth,** Nicholas 1950- *WhoAmP 91*
**Spaeth,** Nicholas John 1950- *WhoAmL 92, WhoMW 92*
**Spaeth,** Ralph 1905- *AmMWSc 92*
**Spaeth,** Terry L. 1954- *WhoMW 92*
**Spafford,** Christopher Garnett Howsin 1924- *Who 92*
**Spafford,** George Christopher Howsin 1921- *Who 92*
**Spafford,** Michael Charles 1935- *WhoWest 92*
**Spafford,** Roswell *DrAPF 91*
**Spaggiari,** Albert d1989 *FacFETw*
**Spaght,** Monroe E. 1909- *Who 92*
**Spaght,** Monroe Edward 1909- *AmMWSc 92, IntWW 91*
**Spahle,** Michael Thomas 1952- *WhoWest 92*
**Spahn,** Gerard Joseph 1938- *AmMWSc 92, WhoWest 92*
**Spahn,** John Nick 1928- *WhoAmP 91*
**Spahn,** Kathy Martha 1954- *WhoEnt 92*
**Spahn,** Robert Joseph 1936- *AmMWSc 92*
**Spahn,** Warren 1921- *FacFETw*
**Spahr,** Charles Eugene 1913- *IntWW 91*
**Spahr,** Jean Marie 1943- *WhoMW 92*
**Spahr,** Sidney Louis 1935- *AmMWSc 92*
**Spaht,** Carlos G, II 1942- *AmMWSc 92*
**Spaid,** Frank William 1938- *AmMWSc 92*
**Spaights,** Ernest 1935- *WhoBlA 92*
**Spain,** Hiram, Jr. 1936- *WhoBlA 92*
**Spain,** Ian L 1940- *AmMWSc 92*
**Spain,** Jack Holland, Jr. 1939- *WhoAmL 92*
**Spain,** James Dorris, Jr 1929- *AmMWSc 92*
**Spain,** James Earl 1934- *WhoAmP 91*
**Spain,** James S. 1939- *WhoBlA 92*
**Spain,** James W. 1926- *IntWW 91, WhoAmP 91*
**Spain,** John David 1948- *WhoRel 92*
**Spain,** Richard Kenneth 1952- *WhoRel 92*
**Spain,** Ricky 1949- *WhoRel 92*
**Spain,** Robert Hitchcock 1925- *WhoRel 92*
**Spain,** Thomas *WhoAmP 91*
**Spainhour,** John Edward 1951- *WhoAmL 92*
**Spainhour,** Kyle 1960- *WhoMW 92*
**Spainhower,** James Ivan 1928- *WhoRel 92*
**Spal,** Edward Scott 1953- *WhoMW 92*
**Spalatin,** Ivo Joseph 1946- *WhoAmP 91*
**Spalatin,** Josip 1913- *AmMWSc 92*
**Spalding,** Albert 1888-1953 *NewAmDM*
**Spalding,** Almut Marianne 1957- *WhoRel 92*
**Spalding,** Anne 1911- *TwCPaSc*
**Spalding,** Brian 1923- *Who 92*
**Spalding,** D. Brian 1923- *IntWW 91*
**Spalding,** Daniel Charles 1952- *WhoEnt 92*
**Spalding,** Edward Wyman 1918- *WhoWest 92*
**Spalding,** Eliza Hart 1807-1851 *HanAmWH*
**Spalding,** Frances 1950- *WrDr 92*
**Spalding,** Frederick James 1938- *WhoFI 92*
**Spalding,** George Robert 1927- *AmMWSc 92*
**Spalding,** Henry Cannon, Jr. 1938- *WhoFI 92*
**Spalding,** Ian Jaffery L. *Who 92*
**Spalding,** James Colwell 1921- *WhoRel 92*
**Spalding,** James Hilary, Jr. 1947- *WhoWest 92*
**Spalding,** James Stuart 1934- *WhoFI 92*
**Spalding,** John Oliver 1924- *Who 92*
**Spalding,** Julian 1947- *Who 92*
**Spalding,** Keith 1913- *WrDr 92*
**Spalding,** Lyman 1775-1821 *BiInAmS*
**Spalding,** Martha Knecht 1953- *WhoFI 92*
**Spalding,** Richard Daniel 1948- *WhoFI 92*
**Spalding,** Ruth *WrDr 92*
**Spalding,** Steven Lynn 1960- *WhoAmL 92*
**Spalding,** Thomas James 1948- *WhoFI 92*
**Spalding,** Thomas William 1945- *WhoWest 92*
**Spalding,** Volney Morgan 1849-1918 *BiInAmS*
**Spall,** Henry Roger 1938- *AmMWSc 92*
**Spall,** Walter Dale 1943- *AmMWSc 92*
**Spallholz,** Julian Ernest 1943- *AmMWSc 92*
**Spallone,** Henry J *WhoAmP 91*
**Spalt,** Stella Mickey 1943- *WhoMW 92*
**Spalten,** Rona *DrAPF 91*
**Spalvins,** Janis Gunars 1936- *IntWW 91, Who 92*
**Spamford,** Bryant 1946- *AmMWSc 92*
**Span,** Robert Steven 1947- *WhoAmL 92*
**Spanbauer,** Tom *DrAPF 91*
**Spanberger,** Kathryn Maryanne 1956- *WhoEnt 92*
**Spanbock,** Maurice Samuel 1924- *WhoAmL 92*
**Spandau,** James Irving 1929- *WhoAmL 92*
**Spande,** Thomas Frederick 1937- *AmMWSc 92*
**Spandorfer,** Lester M 1925- *AmMWSc 92*
**Spanel,** Abram Nathaniel 1901-1985 *FacFETw*
**Spanel,** Harriet *WhoAmP 91*
**Spanel,** Leslie Edward 1937- *AmMWSc 92*
**Spanfelner,** Robert Bruce 1939- *WhoIns 92*
**Spang,** Arthur William 1917- *AmMWSc 92*
**Spang,** H Austin, III 1934- *AmMWSc 92*
**Spang,** James Thomas, Jr 1957- *WhoAmP 91*
**Spang,** Sara Crosby 1947- *WhoWest 92*
**Spang-Hanssen,** Ebbe 1928- *IntWW 91*
**Spangenberg,** Carol Anne 1941- *WhoRel 92*
**Spangenberg,** Christa 1928- *IntWW 91*
**Spangenberg,** Dorothy Breslin 1931- *AmMWSc 92*
**Spangler,** Charles William 1938- *AmMWSc 92*
**Spangler,** Daniel Patrick 1934- *AmMWSc 92*
**Spangler,** David 1945- *RelLAm 91*
**Spangler,** David Benjamin 1950- *WhoAmL 92*
**Spangler,** David Sheridan 1948- *WhoEnt 92*
**Spangler,** Fred Walter 1918- *AmMWSc 92*
**Spangler,** George Russell 1942- *AmMWSc 92*
**Spangler,** Glenn Edward 1942- *AmMWSc 92*
**Spangler,** Grant Edward 1926- *AmMWSc 92*
**Spangler,** Hayward Gosse 1938- *AmMWSc 92*
**Spangler,** Henry Wilson 1858-1912 *BiInAmS*
**Spangler,** Jerry L 1952- *WhoAmP 91*
**Spangler,** John Allen 1918- *AmMWSc 92*
**Spangler,** John David 1936- *AmMWSc 92*
**Spangler,** Kenneth Lee 1940- *WhoAmL 92*

**Spangler**, Martin Ord Lee 1928- *AmMWSc 92*
**Spangler**, Paul Junior 1924- *AmMWSc 92*
**Spangler**, Robert Alan 1933- *AmMWSc 92*
**Spangler**, Ronald Leroy 1937- *WhoFI 92*
**Spangler**, Steven Randall 1950- *AmMWSc 92*
**Spaniardi**, Richard J 1936- *WhoIns 92*
**Spanier**, Arthur M 1948- *AmMWSc 92*
**Spanier**, Edward J 1937- *AmMWSc 92*
**Spanier**, Edward Jacob 1937- *WhoFI 92*
**Spanier**, Edwin Henry 1921- *AmMWSc 92*
**Spanier**, Graham Basil 1948- *WhoWest 92*
**Spanier**, Jerome 1930- *AmMWSc 92, WhoWest 92*
**Spanier**, Muggsy 1906-1967 *NewAmDM*
**Spanier**, Muriel *DrAPF 91*
**Spanier**, Nancy Louise 1942- *WhoEnt 92*
**Spanier**, Suzy Peta *Who 92*
**Spaniol**, Craig 1944- *AmMWSc 92*
**Spaniol**, Dennis J *WhoAmP 91*
**Spaniola**, Francis Richard 1935- *WhoAmP 91*
**Spanis**, Curt William 1932- *AmMWSc 92*
**Spankie**, Hugh Oliver 1936- *Who 92*
**Spann**, Ann Olive 1917- *WhoAmP 91*
**Spann**, Bettye Jean Patterson 1930- *WhoMW 92*
**Spann**, Charles Henry 1939- *AmMWSc 92*
**Spann**, David *WhoRel 92*
**Spann**, George William 1946- *WhoFI 92*
**Spann**, Hyman Dale, Jr. 1935- *WhoMW 92*
**Spann**, James Fletcher 1935- *AmMWSc 92*
**Spann**, Katharine Doyle *WhoWest 92*
**Spann**, Keith 1922- *Who 92*
**Spann**, Noah Atterson, Jr. 1938- *WhoBlA 92*
**Spann**, Othmar 1878-1950 *BiDExR, EncTR 91*
**Spann**, Ronald Thomas 1949- *WhoAmL 92*
**Spann**, Stephen Allison 1941- *WhoWest 92*
**Spann**, Theresa Tieuel 1918- *WhoBlA 92*
**Spann**, Weldon Oma 1924- *WrDr 92*
**Spannaus**, Warren Richard 1930- *WhoAmP 91*
**Spanner**, E F 1888- *ScFEYrs*
**Spanninger**, Philip Andrew 1943- *AmMWSc 92*
**Spano**, August John 1921- *WhoAmP 91*
**Spano**, Francis A 1931- *AmMWSc 92*
**Spano**, Frank Joseph 1958- *WhoFI 92*
**Spano**, Joseph 1946- *WhoEnt 92*
**Spano**, Nicholas A 1953- *WhoAmP 91*
**Spano**, Vincent 1962- *IntMPA 92*
**Spanogle**, John Andrew 1934- *WhoAmL 92*
**Spanos**, Alexander Gus 1923- *WhoWest 92*
**Spanos**, Evanthia 1957- *WhoAmL 92*
**Spanos**, Harry V 1926- *WhoAmP 91*
**Spanos**, Marcos 1932- *IntWW 91*
**Spanos**, Peter Robert 1948- *WhoAmL 92*
**Spanos**, Priscilla Hastings 1928- *WhoAmP 91*
**Spanswick**, Roger Morgan 1939- *AmMWSc 92*
**Spanton**, Merrik 1924- *Who 92*
**Spanutius**, Frederick William 1868?-1915 *BiInAmS*
**Spar**, Irving Leo 1926- *AmMWSc 92*
**Spar**, Jerome 1918- *AmMWSc 92*
**Spar**, Michael Roy 1956- *WhoAmL 92*
**Spar**, Robert Alan 1963- *WhoAmL 92*
**Spar**, Warren Hal 1950- *WhoFI 92*
**Sparacino**, Charles Morgan 1941- *AmMWSc 92*
**Sparacino**, Robert R 1927- *AmMWSc 92*
**Sparano**, Benjamin Michael 1928- *AmMWSc 92*
**Sparapany**, John Joseph 1928- *AmMWSc 92*
**Sparber**, Byron Lee 1932- *WhoAmL 92*
**Sparber**, Dale Paul 1948- *WhoMW 92*
**Sparber**, Sheldon B 1938- *AmMWSc 92*
**Sparberg**, Esther Braun 1922- *AmMWSc 92*
**Sparby**, Wallace A *WhoAmP 91*
**Spare**, Austin Osman 1888-1956 *TwCPaSc*
**Sparer**, Malcolm Martin *WhoRel 92*
**Sparey**, John Raymond 1924- *Who 92*
**Sparey**, John William 1927- *WhoEnt 92*
**Sparger**, Rex *LesBEnT 92*
**Spargo**, Benjamin H 1919- *AmMWSc 92*
**Spargo**, John 1876-1966 *DcAmImH*
**Spargo**, Peter Ernest 1937- *IntWW 91*
**Spargur**, Arlie Yon 1956- *WhoRel 92*
**Spark**, Muriel *WrDr 92*
**Spark**, Muriel 1918- *CnDBLB 7 [port], ConAu 36NR, ConNov 91, ConPo 91, FacFETw, LiExTwC, RfGEnL 91*
**Spark**, Muriel Sarah *IntAu&W 91, IntWW 91, Who 92*
**Sparkes**, Robert Lyndley 1929- *Who 92*
**Sparkes**, Robert Stanley 1930- *AmMWSc 92*
**Sparkman**, Dennis Raymond 1954- *AmMWSc 92*
**Sparkman**, Donal Ross 1907- *AmMWSc 92*
**Sparkman**, John J 1899-1985 *FacFETw*
**Sparkman**, Marjorie Frances 1923- *AmMWSc 92*
**Sparkman**, Robert Satterfield 1912- *AmMWSc 92*
**Sparks**, Albert Kirk 1923- *AmMWSc 92*
**Sparks**, Alton Neal 1932- *AmMWSc 92*
**Sparks**, Archie Gilchrist, III 1944- *WhoAmL 92*
**Sparks**, Arthur Charles 1914- *Who 92*
**Sparks**, Arthur Godwin 1938- *AmMWSc 92*
**Sparks**, Billy Schley 1923- *WhoAmL 92, WhoFI 92, WhoMW 92*
**Sparks**, Bobby Lee 1946- *WhoRel 92*
**Sparks**, Cecil Ray 1930- *AmMWSc 92*
**Sparks**, Charles Edward 1940- *AmMWSc 92*
**Sparks**, Cullie J, Jr 1929- *AmMWSc 92*
**Sparks**, Darrell 1938- *AmMWSc 92*
**Sparks**, David Glen 1948- *WhoIns 92*
**Sparks**, David Lee 1937- *AmMWSc 92*
**Sparks**, Edward Franklin 1937- *WhoBlA 92*
**Sparks**, Ella Warden 1912- *WhoAmP 91*
**Sparks**, Gary Dean 1959- *WhoAmP 91*
**Sparks**, Gordon 1935- *WhoAmP 91*
**Sparks**, Harvey Vise 1938- *AmMWSc 92*
**Sparks**, Harvey Vise, Jr. 1938- *WhoMW 92*
**Sparks**, Hedley Frederick Davis 1908- *Who 92*
**Sparks**, Ian Leslie 1943- *Who 92*
**Sparks**, Irving Alan 1933- *WhoRel 92, WhoWest 92*
**Sparks**, Jack Norman 1928- *WhoWest 92*
**Sparks**, James A. 1933- *WhoRel 92*
**Sparks**, Jared 1789-1866 *BenetAL 91*
**Sparks**, John Edward 1930- *WhoAmL 92*
**Sparks**, Larry Wade 1953- *WhoEnt 92*
**Sparks**, Loice Greer 1925- *WhoRel 92*
**Sparks**, Melvin 1921- *WhoMW 92*
**Sparks**, Merrill 1922- *WhoEnt 92, WhoMW 92*
**Sparks**, Morgan 1916- *AmMWSc 92*
**Sparks**, Peter Robert 1947- *AmMWSc 92*
**Sparks**, Richard Edward 1942- *AmMWSc 92*
**Sparks**, Richard Harry 1935- *WhoWest 92*
**Sparks**, Ricky Lynn 1954- *WhoRel 92*
**Sparks**, Robert Andrew 1937- *WhoFI 92*
**Sparks**, Robert D 1932- *AmMWSc 92*
**Sparks**, Robert Dean 1932- *WhoMW 92*
**Sparks**, Robert Edward 1930- *AmMWSc 92*
**Sparks**, Robert Stephen John 1949- *IntWW 91, Who 92*
**Sparks**, Thomas E., Jr. 1942- *WhoAmL 92*
**Sparks**, Walter Chappel 1918- *AmMWSc 92, WhoWest 92*
**Sparks**, William Sheral 1924- *WhoRel 92*
**Sparlin**, Don Merle 1937- *AmMWSc 92*
**Sparling**, Arthur Bambridge 1930- *AmMWSc 92*
**Sparling**, Dale R 1929- *AmMWSc 92*
**Sparling**, Dale Richard 1929- *WhoMW 92*
**Sparling**, Donald Wesley, Jr 1949- *AmMWSc 92*
**Sparling**, James Milton, Jr 1928- *WhoAmP 91*
**Sparling**, Mary Lee 1934- *AmMWSc 92*
**Sparling**, Philip Frederick 1936- *AmMWSc 92*
**Sparling**, Rebecca Hall 1910- *AmMWSc 92*
**Sparling**, Shirley 1929- *AmMWSc 92*
**Sparnins**, Velta L 1928- *AmMWSc 92*
**Sparrazza**, Lucille Angela 1954- *WhoFI 92*
**Sparrevohn**, Frederic Reidtz 1943- *WhoWest 92*
**Sparrgrove**, Dewain A 1941- *WhoIns 92*
**Sparrow**, Albert Charles 1925- *Who 92*
**Sparrow**, Bryan 1933- *Who 92*
**Sparrow**, Charles *Who 92*
**Sparrow**, D A 1947- *AmMWSc 92*
**Sparrow**, E M 1928- *AmMWSc 92*
**Sparrow**, Elena Bautista *AmMWSc 92*
**Sparrow**, Ephraim Maurice 1928- *WhoMW 92*
**Sparrow**, Fox *DrAPF 91*
**Sparrow**, Gregory Brennan 1951- *WhoAmP 91*
**Sparrow**, John 1933- *Who 92*
**Sparrow**, John Hanbury Angus 1906- *Who 92*
**Sparrow**, Rory Darnell 1958- *WhoBlA 92*
**Sparrow**, Victor Howard, III 1945- *WhoBlA 92*
**Sparrow**, William Holliday 1943- *WhoFI 92*
**Sparrowk**, Cora Catherine 1917- *WhoRel 92*
**Sparshott**, Francis 1926- *ConAu 15AS [port], ConPo 91, WrDr 92*
**Sparshott**, Francis Edward 1926- *IntAu&W 91*
**Sparso**, Henning Hempel 1929- *WhoFI 92*
**Sparta**, Nicholas Joseph 1951- *WhoFI 92*
**Sparti**, Cheryl Diane 1930- *WhoWest 92*
**Spassky**, Boris 1937- *FacFETw*
**Spassky**, Boris Vasil'evich 1937- *SovUnBD*
**Spassky**, Boris Vasiliyevich 1937- *IntWW 91*
**Spataro**, Lucian Peter 1957- *WhoWest 92*
**Spater**, Thomas C 1937- *WhoAmP 91*
**Spates**, Frank Harris *WhoAmP 91*
**Spath**, Gregg Anthony 1952- *WhoAmL 92*
**Spath**, Lothar 1937- *IntWW 91*
**Spatny**, Mark Scott 1965- *WhoEnt 92*
**Spatola**, Arno F 1944- *AmMWSc 92*
**Spatt**, Arthur D. 1925- *WhoAmL 92*
**Spatt**, Robert Edward 1956- *WhoAmL 92*
**Spatz**, David Mark 1946- *AmMWSc 92*
**Spatz**, Kenneth Christopher, Jr 1940- *IntAu&W 91, WrDr 92*
**Spatz**, Maria *AmMWSc 92*
**Spatz**, Ronald *DrAPF 91*
**Spatz**, Sidney S 1924- *AmMWSc 92*
**Spatz**, Sydney Martin 1912- *AmMWSc 92*
**Spaulding**, Aaron Lowery 1943- *WhoBlA 92*
**Spaulding**, Asa T. 1902-1990 *WhoBlA 92N*
**Spaulding**, Dale Lloyd 1949- *WhoWest 92*
**Spaulding**, Daniel Alexander 1963- *WhoMW 92*
**Spaulding**, Daniel W. 1909- *WhoBlA 92*
**Spaulding**, Ernest Neil 1946- *WhoMW 92*
**Spaulding**, Harry Samuel, Jr 1930- *AmMWSc 92*
**Spaulding**, Harvey Daniel 1945- *WhoMW 92*
**Spaulding**, Jeb 1952- *WhoAmP 91*
**Spaulding**, John *DrAPF 91*
**Spaulding**, John Pierson 1917- *WhoWest 92*
**Spaulding**, Josiah A 1923- *WhoAmP 91*
**Spaulding**, Keith Bruden 1951- *WhoMW 92*
**Spaulding**, Kenneth Bridgeforth 1944- *WhoBlA 92*
**Spaulding**, Larry R. 1949- *WhoMW 92*
**Spaulding**, Len Davis 1942- *AmMWSc 92*
**Spaulding**, Leonard *IntAu&W 91X*
**Spaulding**, Lynette Victoria 1954- *WhoBlA 92*
**Spaulding**, Malcolm Lindhurst 1947- *AmMWSc 92*
**Spaulding**, Peter J 1944- *WhoAmP 91*
**Spaulding**, Richard W 1949- *WhoIns 92*
**Spaulding**, Robert Alan 1948- *WhoFI 92*
**Spaulding**, Roma Alma 1914- *WhoAmP 91*
**Spaulding**, Romeo Orlando 1940- *WhoBlA 92*
**Spaulding**, Stephen Waasa 1940- *AmMWSc 92*
**Spaulding**, Theodore Charles *AmMWSc 92*
**Spaulding**, William *WhoAmP 91*
**Spaulding**, William Ridley *WhoBlA 92*
**Spaulding**, William Rowe 1915- *WhoFI 92*
**Spaulding**, Winston *IntWW 91*
**Spaunhorst**, Bradley Vincent 1954- *WhoAmL 92*
**Spauschus**, Hans O 1923- *AmMWSc 92*
**Spaventa**, Luigi 1934- *IntWW 91*
**Spawforth**, David Meredith 1938- *Who 92*
**Spayd**, Richard W 1932- *AmMWSc 92*
**Spaziani**, Eugene 1930- *AmMWSc 92, WhoMW 92*
**Spaziani**, Maria Luisa 1924- *IntAu&W 91*
**Speace**, David Dudley 1948- *WhoEnt 92*
**Speaight**, George 1914- *WrDr 92*
**Speake**, Theresa Alvillar 1940- *WhoHisp 92*
**Speaker**, Fred 1930- *WhoAmL 92*
**Speaker**, Susan Jane 1946- *WhoAmL 92*
**Speaker**, Tris 1888-1958 *FacFETw*
**Speakes**, Larry 1939- *WhoAmP 91*
**Speakes**, Larry Melvin 1939- *IntWW 91, WhoFI 92*
**Speakman-Pitt**, William 1927- *Who 92*
**Speaks**, Jerry Mark 1956- *WhoFI 92, WhoMW 92*
**Speaks**, Oley 1874-1948 *NewAmDM*
**Speaks**, Ruben Lee 1920- *WhoRel 92*
**Spear**, Allan Henry 1937- *WhoAmP 91, WhoMW 92, WrDr 92*
**Spear**, Amy M 1962- *WhoAmP 91*
**Spear**, Brian Blackburn 1947- *AmMWSc 92*
**Spear**, Carl D 1927- *AmMWSc 92*
**Spear**, Clay 1916- *WhoAmP 91*
**Spear**, E. Eugene 1938- *WhoBlA 92*
**Spear**, Gerald Sanford 1928- *AmMWSc 92*
**Spear**, Harold Cumming 1909- *Who 92*
**Spear**, Harry Bingham, III 1942- *WhoRel 92*
**Spear**, Hilda D. 1926- *WrDr 92*
**Spear**, Irwin 1924- *AmMWSc 92*
**Spear**, Jean *DrAPF 91*
**Spear**, Jo-Walter 1942- *AmMWSc 92*
**Spear**, Joseph Francis 1943- *AmMWSc 92*
**Spear**, Larry Ross 1941- *WhoRel 92*
**Spear**, Mitchell Lee 1958- *WhoEnt 92*
**Spear**, Patricia Gail 1942- *AmMWSc 92*
**Spear**, Paul Wilburn 1926- *WhoRel 92*
**Spear**, Paul William 1908- *AmMWSc 92*
**Spear**, Robert Clinton 1939- *AmMWSc 92*
**Spear**, Robert W 1943- *WhoAmP 91*
**Spear**, Roberta L. *DrAPF 91*
**Spear**, Ruskin 1911-1990 *AnObit 1990, TwCPaSc*
**Spear**, S. Patricia 1947- *WhoAmL 92*
**Spear**, Sherilynn Ferrario 1944- *WhoMW 92*
**Spear**, Susan *WhoAmP 91*
**Spear**, Timothy George 1962- *WhoRel 92*
**Spear**, Walter Eric 1921- *IntWW 91, Who 92*
**Spear**, Wayne, Jr 1952- *WhoAmP 91*
**Speare**, Daniel Bernard 1929- *WhoEnt 92, WhoWest 92*
**Speare**, Edward Phelps 1921- *AmMWSc 92*
**Speare**, Elizabeth George 1908- *WrDr 92*
**Speare**, Patricia Follett 1923- *WhoEnt 92*
**Spearing**, Ann Marie 1947- *AmMWSc 92*
**Spearing**, Anthony Colin 1936- *Who 92*
**Spearing**, Cecilia W 1927- *AmMWSc 92*
**Spearing**, George David 1927- *Who 92*
**Spearing**, Nigel John 1930- *Who 92*
**Spearly**, James Luther 1950- *WhoWest 92*
**Spearman**, Alexander Young Richard M 1969- *Who 92*
**Spearman**, Clement 1919- *Who 92*
**Spearman**, Frank H 1859-1937 *TwCWW 91*
**Spearman**, Larna Kaye 1945- *WhoBlA 92*
**Spearman**, Leonard H O, Sr 1929- *WhoAmP 91*
**Spearman**, Leonard Hall O'Connell, Sr. 1929- *WhoBlA 92*
**Spearman**, Lionel 1964- *WhoFI 92*
**Spearman**, Maxie Ann 1942- *WhoFI 92*
**Spearman**, Patsy Cordle 1934- *WhoFI 92*
**Spearman**, Robert Worthington 1943- *WhoAmP 91*
**Spearman**, Thomas David 1937- *IntWW 91*
**Spearman**, William Glenn 1927- *WhoRel 92*
**Spears**, Alexander White, III 1932- *AmMWSc 92, WhoFI 92*
**Spears**, Brian Merle 1950- *AmMWSc 92*
**Spears**, Carleton Blaise 1958- *WhoAmL 92*
**Spears**, Carolyn Lee 1944- *WhoWest 92*
**Spears**, Carolyn Sue 1941- *WhoEnt 92*
**Spears**, Charles *WhoBlA 92*
**Spears**, Daniel B. 1959- *WhoEnt 92*
**Spears**, David Lewis 1940- *AmMWSc 92*
**Spears**, Frank 1906- *TwCPaSc*
**Spears**, Franklin Scott 1931- *WhoAmP 91*
**Spears**, George Newton 1916- *WhoMW 92*
**Spears**, Harold T., Jr. 1929- *IntMPA 92*
**Spears**, Heather 1934- *WrDr 92*
**Spears**, Henry Albert, Sr. 1928- *WhoBlA 92*
**Spears**, Jack 1919- *WhoEnt 92*
**Spears**, Jae *WhoAmP 91*
**Spears**, Jo Ann Smith 1936- *WhoAmP 91*
**Spears**, Joseph Faulconer 1915- *AmMWSc 92*
**Spears**, Kenneth George 1943- *AmMWSc 92, WhoMW 92*
**Spears**, Larry Jonell 1953- *WhoAmL 92*
**Spears**, Mack J. 1912-1988 *WhoBlA 92N*
**Spears**, Melvin Stanley 1927- *WhoAmL 92*
**Spears**, Monroe K. 1916- *WrDr 92*
**Spears**, Pamela 1955- *WhoWest 92*
**Spears**, Richard Kent 1937- *AmMWSc 92*
**Spears**, Robert Fields 1943- *WhoAmL 92*
**Spears**, Robert Lee 1932- *WhoWest 92*
**Spears**, Robert Rae 1918- *WhoRel 92*
**Spears**, Sally 1938- *WhoAmL 92*
**Spears**, Sandra Calvette 1964- *WhoBlA 92*
**Spears**, Sholto Marion 1900- *AmMWSc 92*
**Spears**, Terrence Michael 1957- *WhoAmL 92*
**Spears**, Warren 1954- *WhoEnt 92*
**Spears-Jones**, Patricia Kay 1951- *WhoBlA 92*
**Speas**, Charles Stuart 1944- *WhoMW 92*
**Speca**, Bruce Robert 1956- *WhoFI 92*
**Specht**, Donald Francis 1933- *AmMWSc 92*
**Specht**, Edward John 1915- *AmMWSc 92*
**Specht**, Harold Balfour 1927- *AmMWSc 92*
**Specht**, Heinz *AmMWSc 92*
**Specht**, James Eugene 1945- *AmMWSc 92*
**Specht**, Lawrence W 1928- *AmMWSc 92*
**Specht**, Robert Dickerson 1913- *AmMWSc 92*
**Specia**, John J., Jr. *WhoHisp 92*
**Speciale**, Paul Alessandro 1964- *WhoWest 92*
**Speciale**, Richard 1945- *WhoFI 92*
**Specian**, Robert David 1950- *AmMWSc 92*
**Speck**, David George 1945- *WhoAmP 91*

**Speck,** David Ralph 1927- *AmMWSc 92*
**Speck,** Frank G. 1881-1950 *BenetAL 91*
**Speck,** Gregory Otis 1951- *WhoMW 92, WhoRel 92*
**Speck,** Hilda 1916- *WhoMW 92*
**Speck,** John Clarence, Jr 1917- *AmMWSc 92*
**Speck,** John Edward 1925- *AmMWSc 92*
**Speck,** Marvin Luther 1913- *AmMWSc 92*
**Speck,** Reinhard Staniford 1922- *AmMWSc 92*
**Speck,** Rhoads McClellan 1920- *AmMWSc 92*
**Speck,** Richard 1941-1991 *NewYTBS 91 [port]*
**Speck,** Robert Charles 1944- *WhoWest 92*
**Speck,** Samuel W, Jr 1937- *WhoAmP 91*
**Speckman,** John Thomas 1945- *WhoIns 92*
**Speckmann,** Elwood W 1936- *AmMWSc 92*
**Speckmann,** Elwood William 1936- *WhoMW 92*
**Speckmann,** Gunter Wilhelm-Otto 1934- *AmMWSc 92*
**Specktor,** Frederick 1933- *IntMPA 92*
**Specktor,** Peggy G 1940- *WhoAmP 91*
**Specter,** Arlen 1930- *AlmAP 92 [port], IntWW 91, WhoAmP 91*
**Specter,** Howard Alan 1939- *WhoAmL 92*
**Specter,** Melvin Harold 1903- *WhoAmL 92, WhoMW 92*
**Specter,** Richard Bruce 1952- *WhoAmL 92*
**Specter,** Steven Carl 1947- *AmMWSc 92*
**Spector,** Abraham 1926- *AmMWSc 92*
**Spector,** Albert *DrAPF 91*
**Spector,** Arthur Abraham 1936- *AmMWSc 92*
**Spector,** Bertram 1921- *AmMWSc 92*
**Spector,** Brian Fred 1952- *WhoAmL 92*
**Spector,** Carlos *WhoHisp 92*
**Spector,** Clarence J 1927- *AmMWSc 92*
**Spector,** David M. 1946- *WhoAmL 92*
**Spector,** Donna *DrAPF 91*
**Spector,** Harold 1921- *WhoFI 92, WhoWest 92*
**Spector,** Harold Norman 1935- *AmMWSc 92*
**Spector,** Jack Jerome 1925- *WrDr 92*
**Spector,** Jean 1937- *WhoMW 92*
**Spector,** Joel George 1945- *WhoEnt 92*
**Spector,** Leo Francis 1923- *AmMWSc 92*
**Spector,** Leonard B 1918- *AmMWSc 92*
**Spector,** Leonard S. 1945- *WrDr 92*
**Spector,** Martin Wolf 1938- *WhoAmL 92*
**Spector,** Novera Herbert 1919- *AmMWSc 92*
**Spector,** Phil 1940- *WhoEnt 92, WhoWest 92*
**Spector,** Phillip Louis 1950- *WhoAmL 92*
**Spector,** Reynold 1940- *AmMWSc 92*
**Spector,** Richard M 1938- *AmMWSc 92*
**Spector,** Robert D. 1922- *WrDr 92*
**Spector,** Ronnie 1943- *WhoEnt 92*
**Spector,** Roy Geoffrey 1931- *Who 92*
**Spector,** Samuel 1914- *AmMWSc 92*
**Spector,** Sheldon Laurence 1939- *AmMWSc 92*
**Spector,** Sherman David 1927- *WrDr 92*
**Spector,** Sydney 1923- *AmMWSc 92*
**Spector,** Thomas 1944- *AmMWSc 92*
**Spedale,** Vincent John 1929- *WhoMW 92*
**Spedden,** H Rush 1916- *AmMWSc 92*
**Spedding,** Colin Raymond William 1925- *Who 92*
**Spedding,** David Rolland 1943- *Who 92*
**Spedding,** Robert H 1931- *AmMWSc 92*
**Spede,** Lucie Rosa Judith 1936- *IntAu&W 91*
**Speden,** Ian Gordon 1932- *IntWW 91*
**Speece,** Herbert E 1914- *AmMWSc 92*
**Speece,** Susan Phillips 1945- *AmMWSc 92*
**Speed,** Carol *DrAPF 91*
**Speed,** Edwin Maurice 1918- *AmMWSc 92*
**Speed,** F. Maurice 1912- *WrDr 92*
**Speed,** Frank Warren 1911- *WrDr 92*
**Speed,** Harold 1872-1957 *TwCPaSc*
**Speed,** James D *WhoAmP 91*
**Speed,** James Thomas 1939- *WhoAmP 91*
**Speed,** John William 1935- *WhoWest 92*
**Speed,** Keith 1934- *Who 92*
**Speed,** Martha Ray Matthews 1927- *WhoAmP 91*
**Speed,** Nell *ConAu 135*
**Speed,** Nell 1878-1913 *ConAu 135, SmATA 68*
**Speed,** Raymond A 1922- *AmMWSc 92*
**Speed,** Robert 1905- *Who 92*
**Speed,** Robert Clarke 1933- *AmMWSc 92*
**Speede-Franklin,** Wanda A. 1956- *WhoBlA 92*
**Speedie,** Marilyn Kay 1947- *AmMWSc 92*
**Speelman,** Cornelis Jacob 1917- *Who 92*
**Speen,** Gerald Bruce 1930- *AmMWSc 92*
**Speer,** Albert 1905-1981 *BiDExR, EncTR 91 [port], FacFETw*
**Speer,** Cindy Kay 1958- *WhoEnt 92*
**Speer,** Clarence Arvon 1945- *AmMWSc 92*
**Speer,** David Blakeney 1951- *WhoMW 92*
**Speer,** David James 1927- *WhoMW 92*
**Speer,** Fridtjof Alfred 1923- *AmMWSc 92*
**Speer,** Janet Barton 1947- *WhoEnt 92*
**Speer,** Kathleen A 1942- *WhoAmP 91*
**Speer,** Laurel *DrAPF 91*
**Speer,** Lena Ruth *WhoAmP 91*
**Speer,** Margaret Marion 1918- *WhoAmP 91*
**Speer,** Michael Lee 1934- *WhoFI 92*
**Speer,** Paul Alan 1952- *WhoEnt 92*
**Speer,** Richard Norwood, Jr. 1948- *WhoFI 92*
**Speer,** Robert Elliott 1867-1947 *RelLAm 91*
**Speer,** Vaughn C 1924- *AmMWSc 92*
**Speers,** George M 1940- *AmMWSc 92*
**Speers,** J. Alvin 1930- *WhoWest 92*
**Speers,** Louise 1919- *AmMWSc 92*
**Speers,** Misako Terui 1962- *WhoFI 92*
**Speers,** Wendell Carl *AmMWSc 92*
**Speert,** Arnold 1945- *AmMWSc 92*
**Spees,** Steven Tremble, Jr 1933- *AmMWSc 92*
**Speese,** James Stanley 1911- *WhoRel 92*
**Speet,** Kirtland Paul, II 1963- *WhoEnt 92*
**Speheger,** Stevan Walter 1944- *WhoRel 92*
**Spehrley,** Charles W, Jr 1944- *AmMWSc 92*
**Speich,** G R 1928- *AmMWSc 92*
**Speicher,** Benjamin Robert 1909- *AmMWSc 92*
**Speicher,** Carl Eugene 1933- *AmMWSc 92*
**Speicher,** Gary Dean 1947- *WhoMW 92*
**Speicher,** Robert S 1928- *WhoAmP 91*
**Speidel,** David H 1938- *AmMWSc 92*
**Speidel,** Edna W 1908- *AmMWSc 92*
**Speidel,** Hans 1897-1984 *ConAu 133, EncTR 91 [port]*
**Speidel,** John Joseph 1937- *AmMWSc 92*
**Speidel,** Richard Eli 1933- *WhoAmL 92*
**Speidel,** T Michael 1936- *AmMWSc 92*
**Speier,** John Leo, Jr 1918- *AmMWSc 92*
**Speier,** K Jacqueline 1951- *WhoAmP 91*
**Speight,** Ceole 1928- *WhoAmP 91*
**Speight,** Eva B. 1930- *WhoBlA 92*
**Speight,** Graham 1921- *Who 92*
**Speight,** James G 1940- *AmMWSc 92*
**Speight,** John Blain 1940- *WhoWest 92*
**Speight,** Johnny 1920- *IntAu&W 91, Who 92*
**Speight,** Johnny 1921- *WrDr 92*
**Speight,** Robert 1947- *TwCPaSc*
**Speight,** Velma R. 1932- *WhoBlA 92*
**Speights,** James Byron, II 1952- *WhoAmP 91*
**Speights,** John D. 1926- *WhoBlA 92*
**Speights,** Nathaniel H. 1949- *WhoAmL 92, WhoBlA 92*
**Speiginer,** Gertha 1917- *WhoBlA 92*
**Speil,** Sidney 1917- *AmMWSc 92*
**Speir,** Betty Smith 1928- *WhoAmP 91*
**Speir,** Rupert 1910- *Who 92*
**Speirs,** Graham Hamilton 1927- *Who 92*
**Speirs,** William James McLaren 1924- *Who 92*
**Speiser,** James Warren 1949- *WhoMW 92*
**Speiser,** Lawrence d1991 *NewYTBS 91 [port]*
**Speiser,** Robert David 1943- *AmMWSc 92*
**Speiser,** Theodore Wesley 1934- *AmMWSc 92, WhoWest 92*
**Speisman,** Gerald 1930- *AmMWSc 92*
**Speizer,** Frank Erwin 1935- *AmMWSc 92*
**Speizer,** Mark Adler 1943- *WhoIns 92*
**Spejewski,** Eugene Henry 1938- *AmMWSc 92*
**Spekreijse,** Henk *IntWW 91*
**Spelfogel,** Scott David 1960- *WhoAmL 92*
**Speliotis,** Dennis Elias 1933- *AmMWSc 92*
**Speliotis,** Theodore C 1953- *WhoAmP 91*
**Spelke,** Elizabeth Shilin 1949- *AmMWSc 92*
**Spell,** Aldenlee 1920- *AmMWSc 92*
**Spell,** Eldred 1953- *WhoEnt 92*
**Spellacy,** Leo Michael 1934- *WhoAmL 92*
**Spellacy,** William Nelson 1934- *AmMWSc 92*
**Spellenberg,** Richard 1940- *AmMWSc 92*
**Speller,** Antony 1929- *Who 92*
**Speller,** Charles K. 1933- *WhoBlA 92*
**Speller,** Eugene Thurley 1928- *WhoBlA 92*
**Speller,** J. Finton 1909- *WhoBlA 92*
**Speller,** Norman Henry 1921- *Who 92*
**Speller,** Robert and Speller, Jane *ScFEYrs*
**Speller,** Stanley Wayne 1942- *AmMWSc 92*
**Spelling,** Aaron *LesBEnT 92 [port], NewYTBS 91 [port]*
**Spelling,** Aaron 1923- *WhoEnt 92*
**Spelling,** Aaron 1928- *IntMPA 92, IntWW 91*
**Spellissey,** Gary Joseph 1950- *WhoEnt 92*
**Spellman,** Alfred B. 1935- *WhoBlA 92*
**Spellman,** Cathy Cash *WrDr 92*
**Spellman,** Craig William 1946- *AmMWSc 92*
**Spellman,** Douglas Toby 1942- *WhoFI 92, WhoWest 92*
**Spellman,** Eugene P. d1991 *NewYTBS 91*
**Spellman,** Francis Edward 1889-1967 *RelLAm 91*
**Spellman,** Francis J 1889-1967 *FacFETw*
**Spellman,** John D. 1926- *IntWW 91, WhoAmP 91*
**Spellman,** John David 1935- *WhoWest 92*
**Spellman,** John W 1941- *AmMWSc 92*
**Spellman,** Mitchell Wright 1919- *AmMWSc 92*
**Spellman,** Oliver B., Jr. 1953- *WhoBlA 92*
**Spellman,** Robert Edward 1925- *WhoAmP 91*
**Spellman,** Roger G *IntAu&W 91X, TwCWW 91*
**Spellman,** Steven *WhoAmP 91*
**Spellmire,** Sandra Marie 1950- *WhoMW 92*
**Spelman,** Michael John 1939- *AmMWSc 92*
**Spelman,** Philip Ohel 1923- *WhoMW 92*
**Spelsberg,** Thomas Coonan 1940- *AmMWSc 92*
**Spelts,** Richard John 1939- *WhoAmL 92, WhoWest 92*
**Speltz,** George Henry 1912- *WhoRel 92*
**Speltz,** Paul William 1947- *WhoFI 92*
**Spemann,** Hans 1869-1941 *WhoNob 90*
**Spenadel,** Lawrence 1932- *AmMWSc 92*
**Spence** 1932- *TwCPaSc*
**Spence,** A. Michael 1943- *WhoFI 92, WhoWest 92*
**Spence,** Alan 1947- *ConNov 91*
**Spence,** Alastair Andrew 1936- *Who 92*
**Spence,** Alexander Perkins 1929- *AmMWSc 92*
**Spence,** Basil 1907-1976 *FacFETw*
**Spence,** Bill *WrDr 92*
**Spence,** Carole Jane 1949- *WhoWest 92*
**Spence,** Clark Christian 1923- *WhoMW 92*
**Spence,** Dale William 1934- *AmMWSc 92*
**Spence,** David 1941- *AmMWSc 92*
**Spence,** David Wendell d1917 *BiInAmS*
**Spence,** Donald Dale 1926- *WhoBlA 92*
**Spence,** Douglas Morcom 1928- *WhoRel 92*
**Spence,** Duncan *WrDr 92*
**Spence,** Eleanor 1928- *ChlLR 26 [port], WrDr 92*
**Spence,** Eulalie 1894-1981 *NotBlAW 92*
**Spence,** Fay Frances 1962- *WhoAmL 92*
**Spence,** Floyd D. 1928- *AlmAP 92 [port]*
**Spence,** Floyd Davidson 1928- *WhoAmP 91*
**Spence,** Francis John *Who 92*
**Spence,** Francis John 1926- *WhoRel 92*
**Spence,** Frederick Michael T. *Who 92*
**Spence,** Gabriel John 1924- *Who 92*
**Spence,** Gavin Gary 1942- *AmMWSc 92*
**Spence,** Gerald Leonard 1929- *WhoAmL 92, WhoWest 92*
**Spence,** Glen Oscar 1927- *WhoRel 92*
**Spence,** Harlan Ernest 1961- *AmMWSc 92*
**Spence,** Hilda Adele 1929- *AmMWSc 92*
**Spence,** Howard Tee Devon 1949- *WhoMW 92*
**Spence,** Hubert Talmadge, II 1948- *WhoRel 92*
**Spence,** Jack Taylor 1929- *AmMWSc 92*
**Spence,** James Robert, Jr. 1936- *WhoEnt 92*
**Spence,** Janet Taylor 1923- *WomPsyc*
**Spence,** John 1918- *TwCPaSc*
**Spence,** John Edwin 1934- *AmMWSc 92*
**Spence,** Jonathan D. 1936- *WrDr 92*
**Spence,** Joseph Samuel, Sr. 1950- *WhoBlA 92*
**Spence,** Joseph Stephen 1949- *WhoRel 92*
**Spence,** Kemet Dean 1937- *AmMWSc 92*
**Spence,** Kenneth Frederick 1943- *WhoRel 92*
**Spence,** Leslie Percival 1922- *AmMWSc 92*
**Spence,** Malcolm 1936- *BlkOlyM*
**Spence,** Malcolm Hugh 1934- *Who 92*
**Spence,** Mary Anne 1944- *AmMWSc 92*
**Spence,** Michael *DrAPF 91*
**Spence,** Robert 1933- *Who 92*
**Spence,** Robert Dean 1917- *AmMWSc 92*
**Spence,** Russell Morgan 1937- *WhoAmL 92*
**Spence,** Sharon Lloyd 1953- *WhoEnt 92*
**Spence,** Stanley Brian 1937- *Who 92*
**Spence,** Sydney P 1921- *AmMWSc 92*
**Spence,** Terry R 1941- *WhoAmP 91*
**Spence,** Thomas Wayne 1938- *AmMWSc 92*
**Spence,** Willard Lewis 1935- *AmMWSc 92*
**Spence,** William J 1937- *AmMWSc 92*
**Spence,** William John Duncan 1923- *IntAu&W 91, WrDr 92*
**Spence-Allen,** Pamela Jean 1948- *WhoFI 92*
**Spencer** *Who 92*
**Spencer,** Countess 1929- *Who 92*
**Spencer,** Earl 1924- *Who 92*
**Spencer,** Alan Douglas 1920- *Who 92*
**Spencer,** Alan Gerald 1941- *WhoEnt 92*
**Spencer,** Alan H 1937- *WhoIns 92*
**Spencer,** Alan Lee 1960- *WhoRel 92*
**Spencer,** Albert William 1929- *AmMWSc 92*
**Spencer,** Alexander Burke 1932- *AmMWSc 92*
**Spencer,** Alvie Glenn, Jr 1933- *WhoAmP 91*
**Spencer,** Andrew Nigel 1945- *AmMWSc 92*
**Spencer,** Andrew R *AmMWSc 92*
**Spencer,** Anna Carpenter Garlin 1851-1931 *AmPeW*
**Spencer,** Anna Garlin 1851-1932 *WomSoc*
**Spencer,** Anne 1882-1975 *NotBlAW 92 [port]*
**Spencer,** Anne Christine 1938- *Who 92*
**Spencer,** Anthony James Merrill 1929- *IntWW 91, Who 92*
**Spencer,** Anthony Lawrence 1946- *WhoBlA 92*
**Spencer,** Armond E 1933- *AmMWSc 92*
**Spencer,** Arthur Coe, II 1939- *AmMWSc 92*
**Spencer,** Arthur Milton, Jr 1920- *AmMWSc 92*
**Spencer,** Bernard 1909-1963 *RfGEnL 91*
**Spencer,** Billie Jane 1949- *WhoFI 92*
**Spencer,** Brenda L. 1951- *WhoBlA 92*
**Spencer,** Brock 1939- *AmMWSc 92*
**Spencer,** Carol Brown 1936- *WhoWest 92*
**Spencer,** Charles 1920- *WrDr 92*
**Spencer,** Charles A 1813-1881 *BiInAmS*
**Spencer,** Charles Keith 1935- *WhoFI 92*
**Spencer,** Charles Winthrop 1930- *AmMWSc 92*
**Spencer,** Cherrill Melanie 1948- *AmMWSc 92*
**Spencer,** Chester W 1924- *AmMWSc 92*
**Spencer,** Christopher 1930- *WrDr 92*
**Spencer,** Claude Franklin 1919- *AmMWSc 92*
**Spencer,** Colin 1933- *ConNov 91, IntAu&W 91, WrDr 92*
**Spencer,** Cornelia Phillips 1825-1908 *BenetAL 91*
**Spencer,** Cyril 1924- *Who 92*
**Spencer,** Cyril Charles 1912- *Who 92*
**Spencer,** Daniel P 1948- *WhoIns 92*
**Spencer,** David James 1943- *WhoAmL 92*
**Spencer,** David R 1942- *AmMWSc 92*
**Spencer,** Dennis Norman 1953- *WhoEnt 92*
**Spencer,** Derek Harold 1936- *Who 92*
**Spencer,** Derek W 1934- *AmMWSc 92*
**Spencer,** Domina Eberle 1920- *AmMWSc 92*
**Spencer,** Donald Andrew 1915- *WhoBlA 92*
**Spencer,** Donald Clayton 1912- *AmMWSc 92, IntWW 91*
**Spencer,** Donald Jay 1928- *AmMWSc 92*
**Spencer,** Donald L. 1937- *WhoMW 92*
**Spencer,** Donald Lee 1920- *AmMWSc 92*
**Spencer,** Dora 1916- *WrDr 92*
**Spencer,** Doris *TwCPaSc*
**Spencer,** Douglas Charles 1959- *WhoFI 92*
**Spencer,** Douglas Lloyd 1952- *WhoWest 92*
**Spencer,** Dwight Louis 1924- *AmMWSc 92*
**Spencer,** E Martin 1929- *AmMWSc 92*
**Spencer,** Edgar Winston 1931- *AmMWSc 92*
**Spencer,** Edward *ScFEYrs*
**Spencer,** Edward G 1920- *AmMWSc 92*
**Spencer,** Elaine 1919- *AmMWSc 92*
**Spencer,** Elden A 1929- *WhoAmP 91*
**Spencer,** Elizabeth *DrAPF 91, IntAu&W 91, IntWW 91*
**Spencer,** Elizabeth 1921- *BenetAL 91, ConNov 91, WrDr 92*
**Spencer,** Elvins Yuill 1914- *AmMWSc 92*
**Spencer,** Faith M. 1937- *WhoMW 92, WhoRel 92*
**Spencer,** Felton LaFrance 1968- *WhoBlA 92*
**Spencer,** Frances Heaton 1927- *WhoMW 92*
**Spencer,** Frank 1941- *AmMWSc 92*
**Spencer,** Frank Cole 1925- *AmMWSc 92*
**Spencer,** Frederick J 1923- *AmMWSc 92*
**Spencer,** Gilbert 1892-1979 *TwCPaSc*
**Spencer,** Gordon Reed 1925- *AmMWSc 92*
**Spencer,** Guilford Lawson, II 1923- *AmMWSc 92*
**Spencer,** Harold Garth 1930- *AmMWSc 92*
**Spencer,** Harry Chadwick 1905- *WhoRel 92*
**Spencer,** Harry Edwin 1927- *AmMWSc 92*
**Spencer,** Herbert 1915- *Who 92*
**Spencer,** Herbert 1924- *Who 92*
**Spencer,** Herbert W, III 1945- *AmMWSc 92*
**Spencer,** Herbert Ward, III 1945- *WhoWest 92*
**Spencer,** Herta *AmMWSc 92*
**Spencer,** Hubert J. 1901-1964 *RelLAm 91*
**Spencer,** Hugh Miller 1897- *AmMWSc 92*

**Spencer,** Ian James 1916- *Who 92*
**Spencer,** Isobel *Who 92*
**Spencer,** Jack T 1912- *AmMWSc 92*
**Spencer,** James 1947- *Who 92*
**Spencer,** James Alphus 1930- *AmMWSc 92*
**Spencer,** James Brookes 1926- *AmMWSc 92*
**Spencer,** James Eugene 1938- *AmMWSc 92*
**Spencer,** James Nelson 1941- *AmMWSc 92*
**Spencer,** James R. *WhoAmL 92*
**Spencer,** James W 1927- *AmMWSc 92*
**Spencer,** Jean 1942- *TwCPaSc*
**Spencer,** Jeremy Lawrence 1958- *WhoRel 92*
**Spencer,** Jesse G 1935- *AmMWSc 92*
**Spencer,** Joan Moore 1932- *WhoBlA 92*
**Spencer,** Joanna Miriam 1910- *Who 92*
**Spencer,** John *TwCPaSc*
**Spencer,** John 1922- *WrDr 92*
**Spencer,** John 1925- *TwCPaSc*
**Spencer,** John Brockett 1939- *WhoMW 92*
**Spencer,** John Edward 1949- *AmMWSc 92*
**Spencer,** John Francis Theodore 1922- *AmMWSc 92*
**Spencer,** John Hedley 1933- *AmMWSc 92*
**Spencer,** John-K Joseph 1938- *WhoFI 92*
**Spencer,** John Lawrence 1932- *AmMWSc 92*
**Spencer,** John Loraine 1923- *Who 92*
**Spencer,** John Merrill 1919- *WhoAmP 91*
**Spencer,** John Randall, Jr. 1953- *WhoMW 92*
**Spencer,** Joseph Edward 1945- *WhoMW 92*
**Spencer,** Joseph Walter 1921- *AmMWSc 92*
**Spencer,** Kelvin 1898- *Who 92*
**Spencer,** Kenneth Mason 1945- *WhoMW 92*
**Spencer,** Larry T 1941- *AmMWSc 92*
**Spencer,** Laura-Ann 1966- *WhoHisp 92*
**Spencer,** LaVyrle *WrDr 92*
**Spencer,** LaVyrle 1943- *ConAu 34NR, IntAu&W 91*
**Spencer,** Leo 1941- *WhoAmP 91*
**Spencer,** Leonard G. *ConAu 36NR*
**Spencer,** Lewis Grant, III 1952- *WhoRel 92*
**Spencer,** Lilly Martin 1822-1902 *HanAmWH*
**Spencer,** Lorraine Barney 1924- *AmMWSc 92*
**Spencer,** Margaret Beale 1944- *WhoBlA 92*
**Spencer,** Marian A. 1920- *WhoBlA 92*
**Spencer,** Marian Alexander 1920- *WhoAmP 91*
**Spencer,** Marion Wood 1916- *WhoAmP 91*
**Spencer,** Mark Edward 1954- *WhoFI 92, WhoMW 92*
**Spencer,** Mark William 1955- *WhoRel 92*
**Spencer,** Mary Stapleton 1923- *AmMWSc 92*
**Spencer,** Max M 1935- *AmMWSc 92*
**Spencer,** Merrill Parker 1922- *AmMWSc 92*
**Spencer,** Michael Clifford 1936- *IntWW 91*
**Spencer,** Michael Gerald 1947- *Who 92*
**Spencer,** Michael Gregg 1952- *WhoBlA 92*
**Spencer,** Neal Raymond 1936- *WhoWest 92*
**Spencer,** Oscar Alan 1913- *Who 92*
**Spencer,** Paul 1932- *WrDr 92*
**Spencer,** Paul Roger 1941- *AmMWSc 92, WhoWest 92*
**Spencer,** Peter LeValley 1938- *WhoRel 92*
**Spencer,** Peter Simner 1946- *AmMWSc 92*
**Spencer,** Ralph Donald 1920- *AmMWSc 92*
**Spencer,** Randall Scott 1937- *AmMWSc 92*
**Spencer,** Ray Carlos 1957- *WhoAmP 91, WhoFI 92*
**Spencer,** Richard A. 1944- *WhoAmL 92*
**Spencer,** Richard L 1934- *AmMWSc 92*
**Spencer,** Richard Paul 1929- *AmMWSc 92*
**Spencer,** Robert Henry 1950- *WhoFI 92*
**Spencer,** Robert Scott 1956- *WhoEnt 92*
**Spencer,** Robert Wilford 1938- *WhoWest 92*
**Spencer,** Rosemary Jane 1941- *Who 92*
**Spencer,** Ross H 1921- *IntAu&W 91, WrDr 92*
**Spencer,** Roy 1918- *TwCPaSc*
**Spencer,** Samuel Burchard 1942- *WhoAmP 91, WhoFI 92*
**Spencer,** Sarah Ann 1952- *Who 92*
**Spencer,** Scott *DrAPF 91, IntAu&W 91, WrDr 92*
**Spencer,** Scott W. 1956- *WhoAmL 92*
**Spencer,** Selden J 1923- *AmMWSc 92*
**Spencer,** Shanita Rene 1960- *WhoBlA 92*
**Spencer,** Sharon *DrAPF 91*
**Spencer,** Sharon 1947- *WhoAmP 91*
**Spencer,** Sharon A. *WhoBlA 92*
**Spencer,** Shaun Michael 1944- *Who 92*
**Spencer,** Stanley 1891-1959 *FacFETw, TwCPaSc*
**Spencer,** Stuart Krieg 1927- *WhoWest 92*
**Spencer,** Terry Warren 1930- *AmMWSc 92*
**Spencer,** Theodore 1902-1949 *BenetAL 91*
**Spencer,** Thomas 1946- *AmMWSc 92*
**Spencer,** Thomas A 1934- *AmMWSc 92*
**Spencer,** Thomas H *AmMWSc 92*
**Spencer,** Thomas Lee, Jr. 1943- *WhoMW 92*
**Spencer,** Thomas Melvin, III 1949- *WhoFI 92*
**Spencer,** Thomas Newnham Bayley 1948- *Who 92*
**Spencer,** Tim 1960- *WhoBlA 92*
**Spencer,** Vera *TwCPaSc*
**Spencer,** Walter Thomas 1928- *WhoAmL 92*
**Spencer,** Walter William 1933- *AmMWSc 92*
**Spencer,** William 1922- *IntAu&W 91, WrDr 92*
**Spencer,** William Albert 1922- *AmMWSc 92*
**Spencer,** William Arthur 1921- *WhoMW 92*
**Spencer,** William Browning 1946- *ConAu 133*
**Spencer,** William Edwin 1926- *WhoFI 92, WhoMW 92*
**Spencer,** William F 1923- *AmMWSc 92*
**Spencer,** William I. 1917- *IntWW 91*
**Spencer,** William I 1932- *WhoAmP 91*
**Spencer,** William J 1930- *AmMWSc 92*
**Spencer-Churchill** *Who 92*
**Spencer Churchill,** John George *Who 92*
**Spencer-Nairn,** Robert 1933- *Who 92*
**Spencer-Olind,** Rebecca 1953- *WhoHisp 92*
**Spencer Paterson,** Arthur *Who 92*
**Spencer-Silver,** Peter Hele 1922- *Who 92*
**Spencer Smith,** David 1934- *Who 92*
**Spencer-Smith,** John Hamilton- 1947- *Who 92*
**Spencer Wills** *Who 92*
**Spencley,** Joseph Thomas, Jr. 1955- *WhoMW 92*
**Spender,** Humphrey 1910- *TwCPaSc*
**Spender,** Matthew 1945- *TwCPaSc*
**Spender,** Robert Don 1945- *WhoRel 92*
**Spender,** Stephen 1909- *CnDBLB 7 [port], ConPo 91, FacFETw, IntAu&W 91, IntWW 91, RfGEnL 91, Who 92, WrDr 92*
**Spendlove,** John Clifton 1925- *AmMWSc 92*
**Spendlove,** Peter Roy 1925- *Who 92*
**Spendlove,** Rex S 1926- *AmMWSc 92*
**Spendyarov,** Aleksandr Afanas'evich 1871-1928 *SovUnBD*
**Spendyaryan,** Aleksandr Afanas'evich 1871-1928 *SovUnBD*
**Spenger,** Robert E 1924- *AmMWSc 92*
**Spengler,** Christine Jean 1949- *WhoMW 92*
**Spengler,** Joseph J. d1991 *NewYTBS 91*
**Spengler,** Karen Ann 1952- *WhoFI 92*
**Spengler,** Kenneth C *AmMWSc 92*
**Spengler,** Oswald 1880-1936 *BiDExR, EncTR 91 [port], FacFETw*
**Spengler,** Pierre 1947- *IntMPA 92*
**Spenner,** Frank J 1901- *AmMWSc 92*
**Spenner,** Gregory Alan 1964- *WhoAmP 91*
**Spenny,** David Lorin 1943- *AmMWSc 92*
**Spens** *Who 92*
**Spens,** Baron 1942- *Who 92*
**Spens,** Colin Hope 1906- *Who 92*
**Spens,** John Alexander 1933- *Who 92*
**Spenser,** Edmund 1552?-1599 *CnDBLB 1 [port], RfGEnL 91*
**Spenser,** Ian Daniel 1924- *AmMWSc 92*
**Spenser,** Jeremy 1937- *IntMPA 92*
**Spensko,** Salvacion Vargas 1953- *WhoWest 92*
**Spensley,** Philip Calvert 1920- *Who 92*
**Sper,** Sheldon *WhoRel 92*
**Spera,** Frank John 1950- *AmMWSc 92*
**Spera,** Joseph Anthony 1947- *WhoMW 92*
**Sperandio,** Glen Joseph 1918- *AmMWSc 92*
**Speranza,** George Phillip 1924- *AmMWSc 92*
**Speranza,** Gino Charles 1872-1927 *DcAmImH*
**Sperati,** Carleton Angelo 1918- *AmMWSc 92*
**Sperber,** A M *IntAu&W 91*
**Sperber,** Daniel 1930- *AmMWSc 92*
**Sperber,** David Sol 1939- *WhoAmL 92*
**Sperber,** Geoffrey Hilliard 1933- *AmMWSc 92*
**Sperber,** Manes 1905-1984 *LiExTwC*
**Sperber,** Murray Arnold 1940- *WhoMW 92*
**Sperber,** Steven Irwin 1945- *AmMWSc 92*
**Sperber,** William H 1941- *AmMWSc 92*
**Sperelakis,** Nicholas 1930- *WhoMW 92*
**Sperelakis,** Nick 1930- *AmMWSc 92*
**Sperelakis,** Steve Andrew 1965- *WhoMW 92*
**Spergel,** David Nathaniel 1961- *AmMWSc 92*
**Spergel,** Martin Samuel 1937- *AmMWSc 92*
**Spergel,** Philip 1926- *AmMWSc 92*
**Sperley,** Richard Jon 1939- *AmMWSc 92*
**Sperlich,** Harold K. 1929- *IntWW 91*
**Sperlich,** Peter W. 1934- *WrDr 92*
**Sperlich,** Peter Werner 1934- *IntWW 91*
**Sperling,** Allan George 1942- *WhoAmL 92*
**Sperling,** Dan 1949- *SmATA 65*
**Sperling,** David H. 1951- *WhoEnt 92*
**Sperling,** Frederick 1913- *AmMWSc 92*
**Sperling,** George *AmMWSc 92*
**Sperling,** Harry George 1924- *AmMWSc 92*
**Sperling,** Jacob L 1949- *AmMWSc 92*
**Sperling,** John Glen 1921- *WhoFI 92, WhoWest 92*
**Sperling,** Leslie Howard 1932- *AmMWSc 92*
**Sperling,** Mark Alexander 1938- *AmMWSc 92*
**Spero,** Brian J *WhoAmP 91*
**Spero,** Caesar A, Jr 1921- *AmMWSc 92*
**Spero,** Joan Edelman 1944- *WhoFI 92*
**Spero,** Karen Weaver 1943- *WhoFI 92*
**Spero,** Keith Erwin 1933- *WhoAmL 92, WhoMW 92*
**Spero,** Leonard 1921- *AmMWSc 92*
**Spero,** Morton Bertram 1920- *WhoAmL 92*
**Spero,** Shubert 1923- *WhoRel 92*
**Spero,** Stanley Leonard 1919- *WhoEnt 92*
**Speronello,** Barry Keven 1950- *AmMWSc 92*
**Sperr,** Franz 1878-1945 *EncTR 91*
**Sperrle,** Hugo 1885-1953 *EncTR 91 [port]*
**Sperry,** Burt Weldon 1916- *WhoAmP 91*
**Sperry,** Claude J, Jr 1925- *AmMWSc 92*
**Sperry,** Floyd Benjamin 1905- *WhoAmL 92*
**Sperry,** Francis Louis d1906 *BiInAmS*
**Sperry,** John Reginald 1924- *Who 92, WhoRel 92*
**Sperry,** Kip 1940- *WhoWest 92*
**Sperry,** Paul *WhoEnt 92*
**Sperry,** Philip Roger 1920- *AmMWSc 92*
**Sperry,** Roger Wolcott 1913- *AmMWSc 92, IntWW 91, Who 92, WhoNob 90, WhoWest 92*
**Sperry,** Theodore Melrose 1907- *AmMWSc 92, WhoMW 92*
**Sperry,** Victoria B. 1943- *WhoWest 92*
**Sperry,** Willard Charles 1931- *AmMWSc 92*
**Sperryn,** Simon George 1946- *Who 92*
**Sperti,** George Speri d1991 *NewYTBS 91*
**Sperti,** George Speri 1900- *IntWW 91*
**Sperti,** George Speri 1900-1991 *CurBio 91N*
**Spesert,** Douglas William 1951- *WhoEnt 92*
**Spessard,** Dwight Rinehart 1919- *AmMWSc 92*
**Spessard,** Gary Oliver 1944- *AmMWSc 92, WhoMW 92*
**Spessivtzeva,** Olga d1991 *NewYTBS 91 [port]*
**Speth,** Gerald Lennus 1934- *WhoMW 92*
**Spethmann,** Dorothy Marie 1935- *WhoMW 92*
**Spethmann,** Robert Edwin 1931- *WhoMW 92*
**Spetnagel,** Theodore John 1948- *AmMWSc 92*
**Spetrino,** Russell John 1926- *WhoFI 92*
**Spetter,** Ruth Marguerite 1950- *WhoAmL 92*
**Spevacek,** JoAnn M 1935- *WhoAmP 91*
**Spewack,** Bella 1899-1990 *AnObit 1990, BenetAL 91*
**Spewack,** Samuel 1899-1971 *BenetAL 91*
**Speyer,** Debra Gail 1959- *WhoAmL 92*
**Speyer,** Jason L 1938- *AmMWSc 92*
**Speyer,** Leonora 1872-1955 *BenetAL 91*
**Speyers,** Clarence Livingston 1863-1912 *BiInAmS*
**Speyrer,** Jude 1929- *WhoRel 92*
**Spheeris,** Penelope 1945- *IntMPA 92, WhoEnt 92*
**Sphire,** Raymond Daniel 1927- *WhoMW 92*
**Sphon,** James Ambrose 1939- *AmMWSc 92*
**Spialek,** Hans 1894-1983 *NewAmDM*
**Spialter,** Leonard 1923- *AmMWSc 92*
**Spicak,** Doris Elizabeth 1943- *WhoFI 92*
**Spice,** James Alan 1946- *WhoMW 92*
**Spicer,** Carmelita 1946- *WhoBlA 92*
**Spicer,** Charles Walling, Jr. 1930- *WhoRel 92*
**Spicer,** Chester William, Jr. 1946- *WhoMW 92*
**Spicer,** Clifford W 1919- *AmMWSc 92*
**Spicer,** Clive Colquhoun 1917- *Who 92*
**Spicer,** David *DrAPF 91*
**Spicer,** Donald Z 1937- *AmMWSc 92*
**Spicer,** Eldon M *WhoAmP 91*
**Spicer,** Holt Vandercook 1928- *WhoEnt 92*
**Spicer,** Jack 1925-1965 *BenetAL 91*
**Spicer,** James 1925- *Who 92*
**Spicer,** Janeth Lee 1936- *WhoWest 92*
**Spicer,** John Austin 1930- *WhoFI 92*
**Spicer,** Kenneth, Sr. 1949- *WhoBlA 92*
**Spicer,** Leonard Dale 1942- *AmMWSc 92*
**Spicer,** Michael *Who 92*
**Spicer,** Michael 1943- *ConAu 135*
**Spicer,** Osker, Jr. 1949- *WhoBlA 92*
**Spicer,** Peter James 1921- *Who 92*
**Spicer,** Robert J 1936- *WhoIns 92*
**Spicer,** Samuel Gary 1942- *WhoEnt 92*
**Spicer,** Samuel Sherman, Jr 1914- *AmMWSc 92*
**Spicer,** Warwick Charles Richard 1929- *IntWW 91*
**Spicer,** William Ambrose 1865-1952 *RelLAm 91*
**Spicer,** William Edward 1929- *AmMWSc 92*
**Spicer,** William Michael 1943- *Who 92*
**Spicer-Brooks,** Marianna Chase 1951- *WhoEnt 92*
**Spicher,** John L 1935- *AmMWSc 92*
**Spicher,** Lawrence Franklin 1949- *WhoFI 92*
**Spicher,** Robert G 1935- *AmMWSc 92*
**Spicka,** George Francis 1947- *WhoEnt 92*
**Spickerman,** William Reed 1925- *AmMWSc 92*
**Spickernell,** Derek Garland 1921- *Who 92*
**Spicola,** Guy William 1938- *WhoAmP 91*
**Spidle,** Craig Alan 1954- *WhoMW 92*
**Spieckerman,** Leland William 1959- *WhoEnt 92*
**Spiegel,** Albert A 1916- *WhoAmP 91*
**Spiegel,** Allen David 1927- *AmMWSc 92*
**Spiegel,** Allen J 1932- *AmMWSc 92*
**Spiegel,** Allen M *AmMWSc 92*
**Spiegel,** Anita Andersson 1943- *WhoEnt 92*
**Spiegel,** Barry J *WhoIns 92*
**Spiegel,** Edward A 1931- *AmMWSc 92*
**Spiegel,** Eugene 1941- *AmMWSc 92*
**Spiegel,** Evelyn Sclufer 1924- *AmMWSc 92*
**Spiegel,** Francis Herman, Jr. 1935- *WhoFI 92*
**Spiegel,** George 1924- *WhoFI 92*
**Spiegel,** H. Jay 1952- *WhoAmL 92*
**Spiegel,** Hart Hunter 1918- *WhoAmL 92*
**Spiegel,** Henry William 1911- *IntWW 91, WrDr 92*
**Spiegel,** Herbert Eli 1933- *AmMWSc 92*
**Spiegel,** Jayson Leslie 1959- *WhoAmL 92*
**Spiegel,** Jerrold Bruce 1949- *WhoAmL 92*
**Spiegel,** John P. d1991 *NewYTBS 91*
**Spiegel,** John P. 1911-1991 *ConAu 135*
**Spiegel,** John William 1941- *WhoFI 92*
**Spiegel,** Larry *IntMPA 92*
**Spiegel,** Larry J. *WhoEnt 92*
**Spiegel,** Laurie 1945- *NewAmDM, WhoEnt 92*
**Spiegel,** Leonard Emile 1924- *AmMWSc 92*
**Spiegel,** Linda F. 1953- *WhoAmL 92*
**Spiegel,** Marc Jeffrey 1959- *WhoFI 92*
**Spiegel,** Melvin 1925- *AmMWSc 92*
**Spiegel,** Robert 1928- *AmMWSc 92*
**Spiegel,** Robert Moore 1950- *WhoWest 92*
**Spiegel,** Ronald Stuart 1942- *WhoWest 92*
**Spiegel,** S. Arthur 1920- *WhoAmL 92, WhoMW 92*
**Spiegel,** Siegmund 1919- *WhoFI 92*
**Spiegel,** Stanley Lawrence 1935- *AmMWSc 92*
**Spiegel,** Ted *IntMPA 92*
**Spiegel,** Zane 1926- *AmMWSc 92*
**Spiegelberg,** Hans L 1933- *AmMWSc 92*
**Spiegelberg,** Harry Lester 1936- *AmMWSc 92*
**Spiegelhalter,** Roland Robert 1923- *AmMWSc 92*
**Spiegelman,** Bruce M 1952- *AmMWSc 92*
**Spiegelman,** Gerald Henry 1938- *AmMWSc 92*
**Spiegelman,** Martha 1936- *AmMWSc 92*
**Spiegelman,** Rande Lester 1956- *WhoRel 92*
**Spiegelman,** Robert Gerald 1928- *WhoMW 92*
**Spiegl,** Fritz 1926- *Who 92*
**Spiegl,** Steven Howard 1949- *WhoEnt 92*
**Spiegler,** Kurt Samuel 1920- *AmMWSc 92*
**Spiek,** John Robert, Jr. 1947- *WhoWest 92*
**Spieker,** Andrew Maute 1932- *AmMWSc 92*
**Spiel,** Hilde 1911- *IntAu&W 91*
**Spiel,** Hilde 1911-1990 *ConAu 133*
**Spielberg,** David 1939- *WhoEnt 92*
**Spielberg,** Edith D. *DrAPF 91*
**Spielberg,** Nathan 1926- *AmMWSc 92, WhoMW 92*
**Spielberg,** Peter *DrAPF 91*
**Spielberg,** Peter 1929- *WrDr 92*

**Spielberg,** Stephen E 1934- *AmMWSc 92*
**Spielberg,** Stephen Esrael 1934- *WhoMW 92*
**Spielberg,** Steven *LesBEnT 92*
**Spielberg,** Steven 1947- *Au&Arts 8 [port], BenetAL 91, FacFETw [port], IntDcF 2-2 [port], IntMPA 92, IntWW 91, Who 92, WhoEnt 92*
**Spielberger,** Charles Donald 1927- *AmMWSc 92*
**Spieler,** Cliff 1930- *WhoFI 92*
**Spieler,** Helmuth 1945- *AmMWSc 92*
**Spieler,** Richard Arno 1932- *AmMWSc 92*
**Spieler,** Richard Earl 1942- *AmMWSc 92*
**Spielholtz,** Gerald I 1937- *AmMWSc 92*
**Spielman,** Andrew 1930- *AmMWSc 92*
**Spielman,** Barry 1942- *AmMWSc 92*
**Spielman,** David Vernon 1929- *WhoFI 92*
**Spielman,** Harold S 1914- *AmMWSc 92*
**Spielman,** Kim Morgan 1953- *WhoAmL 92, WhoMW 92*
**Spielman,** Richard Saul 1946- *AmMWSc 92*
**Spielman,** William Sloan 1947- *AmMWSc 92*
**Spielvogel,** Bernard Franklin 1937- *AmMWSc 92*
**Spielvogel,** Carl 1928- *IntWW 91, WhoFI 92*
**Spielvogel,** Lawrence George 1938- *AmMWSc 92, WhoFI 92*
**Spielvogel,** Lester Q 1937- *AmMWSc 92*
**Spier,** Edward Ellis 1921- *AmMWSc 92*
**Spier,** Jerome Bertram 1928- *WhoMW 92*
**Spier,** Luise Emma 1928- *WhoWest 92*
**Spierdijk,** Renee 1957- *TwCPaSc*
**Spierer,** Pierre 1948- *AmMWSc 92*
**Spierman,** Michael 1943- *WhoEnt 92*
**Spiers,** Donald Ellis 1948- *AmMWSc 92*
**Spiers,** Donald Maurice 1934- *Who 92*
**Spiers,** Edward M. 1947- *WrDr 92*
**Spiers,** Finn Robert Camillo 1931- *WhoMW 92*
**Spiers,** Frederick William 1907- *Who 92*
**Spiers,** Graeme Hendry Gordon 1925- *Who 92*
**Spiers,** James Monroe 1940- *AmMWSc 92*
**Spiers,** Reginald James 1928- *Who 92*
**Spiers,** Ronald Ian 1925- *IntWW 91, Who 92, WhoAmP 91*
**Spies,** Claudio 1925- *NewAmDM*
**Spies,** Frank Stadler 1939- *WhoAmL 92*
**Spies,** Gary Jacob 1955- *WhoMW 92*
**Spies,** Greg Thomas 1958- *WhoAmL 92*
**Spies,** Harold Glen 1934- *AmMWSc 92, WhoWest 92*
**Spies,** Joseph Reuben *AmMWSc 92*
**Spies,** Karen Bornemann 1949- *WhoWest 92*
**Spies,** Leon Fred 1950- *WhoAmL 92*
**Spies,** Robert Bernard 1943- *AmMWSc 92*
**Spies,** Ronald Herbert 1946- *WhoMW 92*
**Spies,** William Lyle 1961- *WhoEnt 92*
**Spies von Bullesheim,** Adolf Wilhelm 1929- *IntWW 91*
**Spiess,** Eliot Bruce 1921- *AmMWSc 92*
**Spiess,** Fred Noel 1919- *AmMWSc 92*
**Spiess,** Joachim 1940- *AmMWSc 92*
**Spiess,** Kevin John 1946- *WhoMW 92*
**Spieth,** Donald Edward 1941- *WhoEnt 92*
**Spieth,** Herman Theodore 1905- *AmMWSc 92*
**Spieth,** John *AmMWSc 92*
**Spieth,** Philip Theodore 1941- *AmMWSc 92*
**Spiezio,** James Mark 1948- *WhoFI 92*
**Spiezio,** Judith 1949- *WhoMW 92*
**Spigarelli,** Steven Alan 1942- *AmMWSc 92*
**Spight,** Benita Lynn 1963- *WhoBlA 92*
**Spigner,** Archie 1928- *WhoAmP 91*
**Spigner,** Clarence 1946- *WhoBlA 92*
**Spigner,** Donald Wayne 1940- *WhoBlA 92*
**Spike,** Clark Ghael 1921- *AmMWSc 92, WhoMW 92*
**Spike,** Paul *DrAPF 91*
**Spike,** Peter William 1941- *WhoMW 92*
**Spiker,** Steven L 1941- *AmMWSc 92*
**Spikerman,** Richard C. 1940- *WhoFI 92*
**Spikes,** Dolores R. *WhoBlA 92*
**Spikes,** John Daniel 1918- *AmMWSc 92*
**Spikes,** Paul Wenton 1931- *AmMWSc 92*
**Spikes,** W. Franklin 1949- *WhoMW 92*
**Spikings,** Barry 1939- *IntMPA 92*
**Spikings,** Barry Peter 1939- *Who 92, WhoEnt 92*
**Spilatro,** Douglas Allen 1957- *WhoEnt 92*
**Spilburg,** Curtis Allen 1945- *AmMWSc 92*
**Spilhaus,** Athelstan 1911- *WrDr 92*
**Spilhaus,** Athelstan Frederick 1911- *AmMWSc 92, IntWW 91*
**Spilhaus,** Athelstan Frederick, Jr 1938- *AmMWSc 92*
**Spilka,** Louis R. 1942- *WhoMW 92*
**Spilker,** Barbara Jo 1938- *WhoAmP 91*
**Spilker,** Bert 1941- *AmMWSc 92*
**Spilker,** Clarence William 1922- *AmMWSc 92*
**Spillane,** Frank Morrison 1918- *IntAu&W 91, SmATA 66*
**Spillane,** John Michael 1956- *WhoAmL 92*
**Spillane,** Mary Catherine 1956- *WhoEnt 92*
**Spillane,** Mickey *SmATA 66*
**Spillane,** Mickey 1918- *BenetAL 91, FacFETw, WrDr 92*
**Spillemaeckers,** Werner Lodewijk 1936- *IntAu&W 91*
**Spiller,** Eberhard Adolf 1933- *AmMWSc 92*
**Spiller,** Gene A. 1927- *ConAu 133*
**Spiller,** Gene Alan 1927- *AmMWSc 92, WhoWest 92*
**Spiller,** Isabele Taliaferro 1888-1974 *NotBlAW 92*
**Spiller,** John Anthony Walsh 1942- *Who 92*
**Spiller,** Pablo Tomas 1951- *WhoFI 92, WhoMW 92*
**Spiller,** Robert E. 1896-1988 *BenetAL 91*
**Spiller,** Stephen Richard 1944- *WhoAmL 92*
**Spillers,** Hortense 1942- *NotBlAW 92*
**Spillers,** William R 1934- *AmMWSc 92*
**Spillett,** James Juan 1932- *AmMWSc 92*
**Spillman,** Charles Kennard 1934- *AmMWSc 92*
**Spillman,** Eugene Raymond, Jr. 1947- *WhoRel 92*
**Spillman,** George Raymond 1934- *AmMWSc 92*
**Spillman,** Marjorie Rose *WhoEnt 92*
**Spillman,** Richard Jay 1949- *AmMWSc 92*
**Spillman,** William Bert, Jr 1946- *AmMWSc 92*
**Spilman,** Charles Hadley 1942- *AmMWSc 92*
**Spilman,** James Bruce 1947- *WhoWest 92*
**Spilman,** Raymond 1911- *DcTwDes*
**Spilman,** Richard Allen 1947- *WhoFI 92*
**Spilman,** Robert Henkel 1927- *WhoFI 92*
**Spilman,** Timothy Frank 1961- *WhoMW 92*
**Spilsbury,** Edmund Gybbon 1845-1920 *BilnAmS*
**Spina,** Anthony Ferdinand 1937- *WhoAmL 92, WhoMW 92*
**Spina,** Gary Anthony 1958- *WhoWest 92*
**Spina,** Samuel A 1930- *WhoAmP 91*
**Spina,** Vincent *DrAPF 91*
**Spinar,** Leo Harold 1929- *AmMWSc 92*
**Spindel,** Reva Darlene 1960- *WhoWest 92*
**Spindel,** William 1922- *AmMWSc 92*
**Spindler,** George Dearborn 1920- *WrDr 92*
**Spindler,** George S. *WhoAmL 92*
**Spindler,** James Walter 1939- *WhoAmL 92*
**Spindler,** Marc Robert 1930- *WhoRel 92*
**Spindler,** Max 1938- *AmMWSc 92*
**Spindler,** Stephen R. 1943- *WhoWest 92*
**Spindola-Franco,** Hugo 1938- *WhoHisp 92*
**Spindt,** Roderick Sidney 1919- *AmMWSc 92*
**Spinella,** Christopher D. 1960- *WhoWest 92*
**Spinella,** Edward Francis 1952- *WhoAmL 92*
**Spinella,** Joseph Dominic 1934- *WhoRel 92*
**Spinelli,** Eileen *DrAPF 91*
**Spinelli,** Jerry 1941- *ChlLR 26 [port]*
**Spinelli,** John 1925- *AmMWSc 92*
**Spiner,** Brent *ConTFT 9*
**Spinetti,** Victor 1933- *IntMPA 92*
**Spingarn,** Joel *DcAmImH*
**Spingarn,** Joel E. 1875-1939 *BenetAL 91*
**Spingarn,** Lawrence *DrAPF 91*
**Spingarn,** Lawrence 1917- *WrDr 92*
**Spingler,** William A 1941- *WhoAmP 91*
**Spingola,** Frank 1937- *AmMWSc 92*
**Spining,** Arthur Milton, III 1933- *AmMWSc 92*
**Spink,** Charles Harlan 1936- *AmMWSc 92*
**Spink,** D R 1923- *AmMWSc 92*
**Spink,** Gordon Clayton 1935- *AmMWSc 92*
**Spink,** Ian 1932- *WrDr 92*
**Spink,** Reginald 1905- *WrDr 92*
**Spink,** Walter John 1933- *AmMWSc 92*
**Spink,** Wesley William 1904- *AmMWSc 92*
**Spinka,** Harold M 1945- *AmMWSc 92*
**Spinks,** Daniel Owen 1918- *AmMWSc 92*
**Spinks,** John Lee 1924- *AmMWSc 92*
**Spinks,** John William Tranter 1908- *AmMWSc 92*
**Spinks,** Leon 1953- *BlkOlyM*
**Spinks,** Leroy Culver 1941- *WhoRel 92*
**Spinks,** Mary C. 1946- *WhoRel 92*
**Spinks,** Michael 1956- *BlkOlyM, WhoBlA 92*
**Spinner,** Irving Herbert 1922- *AmMWSc 92*
**Spinner,** Lee Louis 1948- *WhoFI 92, WhoMW 92*
**Spinners,** The *NewAmDM*
**Spinnler,** Joseph F 1931- *AmMWSc 92*
**Spino,** Albert Benjamin, Jr. 1927- *WhoWest 92*
**Spinola,** Antonio Sebastiao Ribeiro de 1910- *IntWW 91*
**Spinola,** Joseph Patrick 1958- *WhoAmL 92*
**Spinosa,** Claude 1937- *AmMWSc 92*
**Spinoza,** Baruch 1632-1677 *BlkwCEP*
**Spinrad,** Alan Matthew 1950- *WhoAmL 92*
**Spinrad,** Bernard Israel 1924- *AmMWSc 92*
**Spinrad,** Hyron 1934- *AmMWSc 92*
**Spinrad,** Norman *DrAPF 91*
**Spinrad,** Norman 1940- *IntAu&W 91, TwCSFW 91, WrDr 92*
**Spinrad,** Richard William 1954- *AmMWSc 92*
**Spinrad,** Robert J 1932- *AmMWSc 92*
**Spinweber,** Cheryl Lynn 1950- *WhoWest 92*
**Spiotto,** James Ernest 1946- *WhoAmL 92*
**Spira,** Arthur William 1941- *AmMWSc 92*
**Spira,** Joel Solon 1927- *AmMWSc 92*
**Spira,** Melvin 1925- *AmMWSc 92*
**Spira,** Patricia G. *WhoEnt 92*
**Spira,** Robert Alan 1932- *WhoFI 92*
**Spira,** S. Franklin 1924- *WhoFI 92*
**Spira,** Steven S. 1955- *IntMPA 92*
**Spira-Solomon,** Darlene Joy 1959- *WhoWest 92*
**Spire,** Andre 1868-1966 *GuFrLit 1*
**Spire,** Robert 1925- *WhoAmP 91*
**Spires,** Elizabeth *DrAPF 91*
**Spires,** John B. *IntMPA 92*
**Spires,** Robert Cecil 1936- *WhoMW 92*
**Spirgel,** Gary James 1945- *WhoFI 92*
**Spiridakis,** Tony *WhoEnt 92*
**Spiridonov,** Ivan Vasil'evich 1905- *SovUnBD*
**Spiridonov,** Lev Nikolayevich 1931- *IntWW 91*
**Spirin,** Aleksandr Sergeevich 1931- *SovUnBD*
**Spirin,** Aleksandr Sergeyevich 1931- *IntWW 91*
**Spirito,** Carl Peter 1941- *AmMWSc 92*
**Spirito,** Ugo 1896-1979 *BiDExR*
**Spirkovska,** Lilly 1964- *WhoWest 92*
**Spirn,** Michele Sobel 1943- *WhoFI 92*
**Spirn,** Stuart Douglas 1945- *WhoAmL 92*
**Spiro,** Claudia Alison 1956- *AmMWSc 92*
**Spiro,** Herbert 1924- *WrDr 92*
**Spiro,** Herzl Robert 1935- *AmMWSc 92*
**Spiro,** Howard Marget 1924- *AmMWSc 92*
**Spiro,** Irving J 1913- *AmMWSc 92*
**Spiro,** Julius 1921- *AmMWSc 92*
**Spiro,** Loida Velazquez *WhoHisp 92*
**Spiro,** Mary Jane 1930- *AmMWSc 92*
**Spiro,** Miriam Ellen 1963- *WhoEnt 92*
**Spiro,** Peter *DrAPF 91*
**Spiro,** Richard Glenn 1964- *WhoFI 92*
**Spiro,** Robert Gunter 1929- *AmMWSc 92*
**Spiro,** Sidney 1914- *IntWW 91, Who 92*
**Spiro,** Thomas 1947- *AmMWSc 92*
**Spiro,** Thomas George 1935- *AmMWSc 92*
**Spiroff,** Boris E N 1925- *AmMWSc 92*
**Spirou,** Chris 1942- *WhoAmP 91*
**Spirtos,** Nicholas George 1950- *WhoAmL 92, WhoWest 92*
**Spisak,** Dennis Stephen 1959- *WhoEnt 92*
**Spital,** Hermann Josef Silvester 1925- *IntWW 91*
**Spitaleri,** Vernon Rosario 1922- *WhoWest 92*
**Spitalny,** Frank Jay 1929- *WhoIns 92*
**Spitalny,** George Leonard 1947- *AmMWSc 92*
**Spitalny,** Phil 1890-1970 *NewAmDM*
**Spiteri,** Lino 1938- *IntWW 91*
**Spitler,** Brian Keith 1957- *WhoEnt 92*
**Spitler,** Larry *WhoAmP 91*
**Spitler,** Lynn E 1938- *AmMWSc 92*
**Spitler,** Mark Thomas 1950- *AmMWSc 92*
**Spitler,** Michael Curran 1953- *WhoFI 92*
**Spitler,** Stacey Denise 1963- *WhoEnt 92*
**Spitsbergen,** James Clifford 1926- *AmMWSc 92*
**Spitta,** Heinrich 1902-1972 *EncTR 91*
**Spitteler,** Carl Friedrich Georg 1845-1924 *WhoNob 90*
**Spittell,** John A, Jr 1925- *AmMWSc 92*
**Spitters,** Michael John 1961- *WhoRel 92*
**Spittle,** James Pratt 1952- *WhoEnt 92, WhoMW 92*
**Spittler,** Ernest George 1928- *AmMWSc 92*
**Spittler,** Russell Paul 1931- *WhoRel 92*
**Spittler,** Terry Dale 1943- *AmMWSc 92*
**Spitz,** Arnoldt John 1929- *WhoFI 92*
**Spitz,** Charles Thomas, Jr. 1921- *WhoRel 92*
**Spitz,** Debbie *WhoEnt 92*
**Spitz,** Hugo Max 1927- *WhoAmL 92, WhoFI 92*
**Spitz,** Irving Manfred 1939- *AmMWSc 92*
**Spitz,** James R. 1940- *IntMPA 92*
**Spitz,** James Robert 1940- *WhoEnt 92*
**Spitz,** Kathleen Emily *Who 92*
**Spitz,** Lewis 1939- *Who 92*
**Spitz,** Lewis William 1922- *WhoWest 92, WrDr 92*
**Spitz,** Mark Andrew 1950- *FacFETw [port]*
**Spitz,** Robert John 1947- *WhoRel 92*
**Spitz,** Stephen Lincoln 1947- *WhoAmL 92*
**Spitz,** Werner Uri 1926- *AmMWSc 92*
**Spitzbart,** Abraham 1915- *AmMWSc 92*
**Spitzberg,** Irving Joseph, Jr. 1942- *WhoAmL 92*
**Spitze,** LeRoy Alvin 1917- *AmMWSc 92*
**Spitzer,** Adrian 1927- *AmMWSc 92*
**Spitzer,** Cary Redford 1937- *AmMWSc 92*
**Spitzer,** Frank L 1926- *AmMWSc 92*
**Spitzer,** Hugh Davidson 1949- *WhoAmP 91*
**Spitzer,** Irwin Asher 1922- *AmMWSc 92*
**Spitzer,** Jeffrey Chandler 1940- *AmMWSc 92*
**Spitzer,** John J 1927- *AmMWSc 92*
**Spitzer,** Judy A 1931- *AmMWSc 92*
**Spitzer,** Kenneth Curtis 1947- *WhoEnt 92*
**Spitzer,** Lee Barnett 1957- *WhoRel 92*
**Spitzer,** Lyman 1914- *Who 92, WrDr 92*
**Spitzer,** Lyman, Jr 1914- *AmMWSc 92, IntAu&W 91, IntWW 91*
**Spitzer,** Lynn Christian 1963- *WhoWest 92*
**Spitzer,** Matthew L. 1929- *WhoWest 92*
**Spitzer,** Nicholas Canaday 1942- *AmMWSc 92*
**Spitzer,** Peter George 1956- *WhoFI 92, WhoWest 92*
**Spitzer,** Ralph 1918- *AmMWSc 92*
**Spitzer,** Robert Harry 1929- *AmMWSc 92*
**Spitzer,** Robert Ralph 1922- *WhoMW 92*
**Spitzer,** Roger Earl 1935- *AmMWSc 92*
**Spitzer,** S. Brian 1953- *WhoRel 92*
**Spitzer,** Walter O 1937- *AmMWSc 92*
**Spitzer,** William Carl 1914- *AmMWSc 92*
**Spitzer,** William George 1927- *AmMWSc 92*
**Spitzer-Lehmann,** Roxane 1939- *WhoWest 92*
**Spitzfaden,** Paul Riley 1920- *WhoAmP 91*
**Spitzig,** Norman J., Jr. 1950- *WhoMW 92*
**Spitzig,** William Andrew 1931- *AmMWSc 92*
**Spitzka,** Edward Charles 1852-1914 *BilnAmS*
**Spitzli,** Donald Hawkes, Jr. 1934- *WhoAmL 92*
**Spitznagel,** Edward Lawrence, Jr 1941- *AmMWSc 92*
**Spitznagel,** John A 1941- *AmMWSc 92*
**Spitznagel,** John Keith 1923- *AmMWSc 92*
**Spitznagle,** Larry Allen 1943- *AmMWSc 92*
**Spiva,** Ulysses Van 1931- *WhoBlA 92*
**Spivack,** Charlotte 1926- *IntAu&W 91, WrDr 92*
**Spivack,** Gordon Bernard 1929- *WhoAmL 92*
**Spivack,** Harvey Marvin 1948- *AmMWSc 92*
**Spivack,** Henry Archer 1919- *WhoFI 92*
**Spivack,** Kathleen *DrAPF 91*
**Spivack,** Kathleen 1938- *WrDr 92*
**Spivack,** Susan Fantl *DrAPF 91*
**Spivak,** Jacque R. 1929- *WhoWest 92*
**Spivak,** Jerry Lepow 1938- *AmMWSc 92*
**Spivak,** Lawrence E. 1900- *IntMPA 92*
**Spivak,** Lawrence Edmund 1900- *WhoEnt 92*
**Spivak,** Peter Beeching 1934- *WhoEnt 92*
**Spivak,** Robert Elliot 1936- *WhoFI 92*
**Spivak,** Steven Mark 1942- *AmMWSc 92*
**Spivakovsky,** Tossy 1907- *IntWW 91*
**Spivey,** Broadus Autry 1936- *WhoAmL 92*
**Spivey,** Bruce E. 1934- *WhoWest 92*
**Spivey,** Bruce Eldon 1934- *AmMWSc 92*
**Spivey,** Donald 1948- *WhoBlA 92*
**Spivey,** Ebbie 1938- *WhoAmP 91*
**Spivey,** Ed L. 1933- *WhoRel 92*
**Spivey,** Gary H 1943- *AmMWSc 92*
**Spivey,** Howard Olin 1931- *AmMWSc 92*
**Spivey,** Hubert Michael 1948- *WhoAmP 91*
**Spivey,** Robert Charles 1909- *AmMWSc 92*
**Spivey,** S. Brett 1968- *WhoEnt 92*
**Spivey,** Victoria 1906-1976 *NotBlAW 92*
**Spivey,** Walter Allen 1926- *AmMWSc 92*
**Spivey,** William Lee *WhoRel 92*
**Spivey,** William Michael 1956- *WhoRel 92*
**Spiwak,** Jerome 1933- *WhoFI 92*
**Spizizen,** John 1917- *AmMWSc 92, WhoWest 92*
**Spizizen,** Louise Myers *WhoEnt 92, WhoWest 92*
**Spizziri,** John A 1934- *WhoAmP 91*
**Spizzirri,** Richard Dominic 1933- *WhoAmL 92*
**Spizzo-Serrano,** Christine 1953- *WhoEnt 92*
**Spjeldvik,** Walther Nordmann 1945- *WhoWest 92*

**Spjut,** Harlan Jacobson 1922- *AmMWSc 92*
**Splain,** Francis J, Jr 1955- *WhoIns 92*
**Splaine,** David Arthur 1959- *WhoFI 92*
**Splaine,** James Raymond 1947- *WhoAmP 91*
**Splaine,** John E 1912- *WhoAmP 91*
**Splake,** T. Kilgore *DrAPF 91*
**Splettstoesser,** John Frederick 1933- *AmMWSc 92*
**Splies,** Robert Glenn 1925- *AmMWSc 92*
**Spliethoff,** William Ludwig 1926- *AmMWSc 92*
**Splinter,** William Eldon 1925- *AmMWSc 92*
**Splitt,** David Alan 1945- *WhoAmL 92*
**Splitter,** Earl John 1920- *AmMWSc 92*
**Splitter,** Gary Allen 1945- *AmMWSc 92*
**Splittgerber,** George H 1918- *AmMWSc 92*
**Splittstoesser,** Clara Quinnell 1929- *AmMWSc 92*
**Splittstoesser,** Don Frederick 1927- *AmMWSc 92*
**Splittstoesser,** Walter E 1937- *AmMWSc 92*
**Splittstoesser,** Walter Emil 1937- *WhoMW 92*
**Spock,** Alexander 1929- *AmMWSc 92*
**Spock,** Benjamin 1903- *AmPeW, ConAu 35NR, FacFETw, RComAH, WhoAmP 91, WrDr 92*
**Spock,** Benjamin McLane 1903- *IntWW 91, Who 92*
**Spodek,** Bernard 1931- *WhoMW 92*
**Spodek,** Jules L 1928- *WhoAmP 91*
**Spodick,** David Howard 1927- *AmMWSc 92*
**Spodick,** Robert C. 1919- *IntMPA 92*
**Spoehr,** Albert Frederick 1918- *AmMWSc 92*
**Spoehr,** Alexander 1913- *IntWW 91, WhoWest 92*
**Spoelhof,** Charles Peter 1930- *AmMWSc 92*
**Spoerel,** Wolfgang Eberhart G 1923- *AmMWSc 92*
**Spoerlein,** Marie Teresa 1925- *AmMWSc 92*
**Spoerli,** Heinz 1940- *WhoEnt 92*
**Spofford,** Charles M. 1902-1991 *CurBio 91N, NewYTBS 91 [port]*
**Spofford,** Charles Merville d1991 *Who 92N*
**Spofford,** Harriet Prescott 1835-1921 *BenetAL 91*
**Spofford,** Janice Brogue 1925- *AmMWSc 92*
**Spofford,** Robert Houston 1941- *WhoWest 92*
**Spofford,** Sally Hoyt 1914- *AmMWSc 92*
**Spofford,** Walter O, Jr 1936- *AmMWSc 92*
**Spofford,** Walter Richardson, II 1908- *AmMWSc 92*
**Spofford,** William B. 1921- *WhoRel 92*
**Spofford,** William Knowlton 1944- *WhoMW 92*
**Spohn,** Daniel Jay 1956- *WhoWest 92*
**Spohn,** Herbert Emil 1923- *AmMWSc 92*
**Spohn,** Ralph Joseph *AmMWSc 92*
**Spohn,** William Gideon, Jr 1923- *AmMWSc 92*
**Spohnholz,** Ann *WhoAmP 91*
**Spohr,** Arnold Theodore 1927- *IntWW 91, WhoEnt 92A*
**Spohr,** Daniel Arthur 1927- *AmMWSc 92*
**Spohr,** Louis 1784-1859 *NewAmDM*
**Spokas,** John J 1928- *AmMWSc 92*
**Spokes,** Ann *Who 92*
**Spokes,** Ernest M 1916- *AmMWSc 92*
**Spokes,** G Neil 1935- *AmMWSc 92*
**Spokes,** John Arthur Clayton 1931- *Who 92*
**Spokes Symonds,** Ann 1925- *Who 92*
**Spoljaric,** Nenad 1934- *AmMWSc 92*
**Spolsky,** Christina Maria 1945- *AmMWSc 92*
**Spolter,** Pari Dokht 1930- *WhoWest 92*
**Spolyar,** Louis William 1908- *AmMWSc 92*
**Spomar,** John Peter, Jr. 1945- *WhoRel 92*
**Spomer,** George Guy 1937- *AmMWSc 92*
**Spomer,** Louis Arthur 1940- *AmMWSc 92*
**Spong,** John 1931- *News 91 [port], -91-3 [port]*
**Spong,** John Shelby 1931- *IntWW 91, WhoRel 92*
**Spong,** Mark William 1952- *WhoMW 92*
**Spong,** William B, Jr *WhoAmP 91*
**Spongberg,** Stephen Alan 1942- *AmMWSc 92*
**Sponholz,** Joseph Gerald 1944- *WhoFI 92*
**Sponsel,** William Eric 1955- *WhoMW 92*
**Sponseller,** D L 1931- *AmMWSc 92*
**Sponsler,** George C 1927- *AmMWSc 92*
**Spontini,** Gaspare 1774-1851 *NewAmDM*
**Spontzis,** Steve F. 1945- *WhoWest 92*
**Spoo,** James *WhoAmP 91*
**Spoo,** Randy L 1948- *WhoAmP 91*
**Spoolstra,** Linda Carol 1947- *WhoRel 92*
**Spoon,** Alan Gary 1951- *WhoFI 92*
**Spoon,** Bruce Pebbles 1931- *WhoAmL 92*
**Spoon,** Roy *WhoAmP 91*
**Spoonamore,** Doris Jean 1910- *WhoMW 92*
**Spoonauer,** John W 1948- *WhoIns 92*
**Spooner,** Arthur Elmon 1920- *AmMWSc 92*
**Spooner,** Bernard Myrick 1934- *WhoRel 92*
**Spooner,** Brian Sandford 1937- *AmMWSc 92*
**Spooner,** Charles Edward, Jr 1932- *AmMWSc 92*
**Spooner,** Charles Michael 1950- *WhoAmP 91*
**Spooner,** Ed Thornton Casswell 1950- *AmMWSc 92*
**Spooner,** Edward Tenney Casswell 1904- *Who 92*
**Spooner,** Frank 1937- *WhoAmP 91*
**Spooner,** Frank Clyffurde 1924- *Who 92*
**Spooner,** George Hansford 1927- *AmMWSc 92*
**Spooner,** James 1932- *Who 92*
**Spooner,** James Douglas 1932- *IntWW 91*
**Spooner,** John C. 1950- *WhoBlA 92*
**Spooner,** John D 1935- *AmMWSc 92*
**Spooner,** Linda Greer 1950- *WhoAmL 92*
**Spooner,** M G 1924- *AmMWSc 92*
**Spooner,** Mark Jordan 1945- *WhoAmL 92*
**Spooner,** Peter Michael 1942- *AmMWSc 92*
**Spooner,** Richard C. 1945- *WhoBlA 92*
**Spooner,** Robert Bruce 1920- *AmMWSc 92*
**Spooner,** Stephen 1937- *AmMWSc 92*
**Spoonhour,** James Michael 1946- *WhoAmL 92*
**Spoor,** James Edward 1936- *WhoWest 92*
**Spoor,** Leslee Peyton Sherrill 1958- *WhoAmP 91*
**Spoor,** Ryk Peter 1935- *AmMWSc 92*
**Spoor,** William Arthur 1908- *AmMWSc 92*
**Spoor,** William Howard 1923- *WhoFI 92, WhoMW 92*
**Sporborg,** Christopher Henry 1939- *IntWW 91, Who 92*
**Spore,** Keith Kent 1942- *WhoMW 92*
**Sporek,** Karel Frantisek 1919- *AmMWSc 92*
**Sporer,** Alfred Herbert 1929- *AmMWSc 92*
**Sporkin,** Stanley 1932- *WhoAmL 92*
**Sporn,** Eugene Milton 1925- *AmMWSc 92*
**Sporn,** Michael Benjamin 1933- *AmMWSc 92*
**Spornick,** Lynna 1947- *AmMWSc 92*
**Sporre,** Dennis John 1944- *WhoEnt 92*
**Sporrenberg,** Jacob 1902-1950 *EncTR 91*
**Sposito,** Garrison 1939- *AmMWSc 92, WhoHisp 92*
**Sposito,** Vincent Anthony 1936- *AmMWSc 92*
**Spotnitz,** Henry Michael 1940- *AmMWSc 92*
**Spoto,** Donald 1941- *IntAu&W 91, WhoEnt 92*
**Spotswood,** Alexander 1676-1740 *BenetAL 91*
**Spotswood,** Denis 1916- *IntWW 91, Who 92*
**Spotswood,** Robert Keeling 1952- *WhoAmL 92*
**Spottiswood,** David James 1944- *AmMWSc 92*
**Spottiswood,** James Donald 1934- *Who 92*
**Spottiswoode,** Roger *IntMPA 92*
**Spotts,** Charles Russell 1933- *AmMWSc 92*
**Spotts,** John Hugh 1927- *AmMWSc 92*
**Spotts,** M F 1895- *AmMWSc 92*
**Spotts,** Robert Allen 1945- *AmMWSc 92*
**Spotts,** Roger Hamilton 1928- *WhoEnt 92*
**Spottsville,** Clifford M. 1911- *WhoBlA 92*
**Sprackling,** Ian Oliver John 1936- *Who 92*
**Sprackling,** Michael Thomas 1934- *WrDr 92*
**Spradbery,** Walter 1889-1969 *TwCPaSc*
**Spradley,** Frank Sanford 1946- *WhoBlA 92*
**Spradley,** Hershall Wesley, II 1945- *WhoRel 92*
**Spradley,** Joseph Leonard 1932- *AmMWSc 92, WhoMW 92*
**Spradley,** Mark Merritt *WhoBlA 92*
**Spradlin,** Byron Lee 1949- *WhoRel 92*
**Spradlin,** G.D. *IntMPA 92*
**Spradlin,** Gervase Duan 1920- *WhoWest 92*
**Spradlin,** Harold William 1931- *WhoFI 92*
**Spradlin,** Joseph E 1929- *AmMWSc 92*
**Spradlin,** Karen Sue 1944- *WhoMW 92*
**Spradlin,** Mary Jo 1918- *WhoAmP 91*
**Spradlin,** Roger Lee 1955- *WhoRel 92*
**Spradlin,** Thomas Richard 1937- *WhoAmL 92*
**Spradlin,** Wilford W 1932- *AmMWSc 92*
**Spradling,** Allan C *AmMWSc 92*
**Spradling,** Donald Ray 1943- *WhoRel 92*
**Spradling,** Mark Raymond 1956- *WhoAmL 92*
**Spradling,** Mary Elizabeth Mace *WhoBlA 92*
**Sprafka,** Robert J 1938- *AmMWSc 92*
**Sprafkin,** Samuel Martin 1911- *WhoAmL 92*
**Spragg,** Jocelyn 1940- *AmMWSc 92*
**Spraggins,** Robert Lee 1939- *AmMWSc 92*
**Spraggins,** Stewart 1936- *WhoBlA 92*
**Spraggins,** Thomas Reginald 1930- *WhoAmP 91*
**Spraggs,** Trevor Owen Keith 1926- *Who 92*
**Spragins,** Melchijah 1919- *AmMWSc 92*
**Sprague,** Asa William 1935- *WhoRel 92*
**Sprague,** Basil Sheldon 1920- *AmMWSc 92*
**Sprague,** Carter *TwCSFW 91*
**Sprague,** Charles 1791-1875 *BenetAL 91*
**Sprague,** Charles Cameron 1916- *AmMWSc 92*
**Sprague,** Charles James 1823-1903 *BiInAmS*
**Sprague,** Dale M *WhoAmP 91*
**Sprague,** David Keith 1935- *Who 92*
**Sprague,** Dewey Dean 1954- *WhoWest 92*
**Sprague,** Estel Dean 1944- *AmMWSc 92*
**Sprague,** G Sidney 1918- *AmMWSc 92*
**Sprague,** George Frederick 1902- *AmMWSc 92*
**Sprague,** Gwen Elaine 1951- *WhoMW 92*
**Sprague,** Howard Bennett 1898- *AmMWSc 92*
**Sprague,** Irvine H 1921- *WhoAmP 91*
**Sprague,** Isabelle Baird 1916- *AmMWSc 92*
**Sprague,** James Alan 1943- *AmMWSc 92*
**Sprague,** James Clyde 1928- *AmMWSc 92*
**Sprague,** James Mather 1916- *AmMWSc 92*
**Sprague,** Jane Lucretia Barnes 1943- *WhoAmL 92*
**Sprague,** John Booty 1931- *AmMWSc 92*
**Sprague,** John Reno 1915- *WhoAmL 92*
**Sprague,** John Reno, Jr. 1941- *WhoMW 92*
**Sprague,** Lucian Matthew 1926- *AmMWSc 92*
**Sprague,** Marion Wright 1923- *WhoFI 92*
**Sprague,** Mary L *WhoIns 92*
**Sprague,** Michael James 1940- *WhoAmP 91*
**Sprague,** Milton Alan 1914- *AmMWSc 92*
**Sprague,** Newton G 1914- *AmMWSc 92*
**Sprague,** Peter Julian 1939- *WhoFI 92, WhoWest 92*
**Sprague,** Peter Whitney 1941- *AmMWSc 92*
**Sprague,** Phillip W. 1959- *WhoFI 92*
**Sprague,** R. C. 1900-1991 *CurBio 91N*
**Sprague,** Randall George 1906- *AmMWSc 92*
**Sprague,** Raymond 1947- *WhoEnt 92*
**Sprague,** Richard Howard 1924- *AmMWSc 92*
**Sprague,** Robert Arthur *AmMWSc 92*
**Sprague,** Robert C d1991 *NewYTBS 91*
**Sprague,** Robert C 1900- *AmMWSc 92*
**Sprague,** Robert Elmer 1955- *WhoMW 92*
**Sprague,** Robert Hicks 1914- *AmMWSc 92*
**Sprague,** Robert Joseph 1944- *WhoAmP 91*
**Sprague,** Robert W 1923- *AmMWSc 92*
**Sprague,** Roderick, III 1933- *WhoWest 92*
**Sprague,** Stuart Russell 1947- *WhoRel 92*
**Sprague,** Ted 1939- *WhoEnt 92*
**Sprague,** Vance Glover, Jr 1941- *AmMWSc 92*
**Sprague,** William Douglas 1941- *WhoAmL 92*
**Sprague,** William Leigh 1938- *IntAu&W 91*
**Sprague de Camp,** L. *DrAPF 91*
**Sprain,** Wilbur 1925- *AmMWSc 92*
**Sprainss,** Violet Evelyn 1930- *WhoWest 92*
**Spraker,** Charles Edward 1933- *WhoRel 92*
**Spraker,** Harold Stephen 1929- *AmMWSc 92*
**Sprandel,** Dennis Steuart 1941- *WhoFI 92, WhoMW 92*
**Sprang,** Milton LeRoy 1944- *WhoMW 92*
**Sprangers,** John C. 1956- *WhoAmL 92*
**Spratlen,** Thaddeus H. 1930- *WhoBlA 92*
**Spratley,** Richard Denis 1938- *AmMWSc 92*
**Spratt,** Greville 1927- *Who 92*
**Spratt,** Greville Douglas 1927- *IntWW 91*
**Spratt,** James Leo 1932- *AmMWSc 92, WhoMW 92*
**Spratt,** John M., Jr. 1942- *AlmAP 92 [port], WhoAmP 91*
**Spratt,** John Stricklin 1929- *AmMWSc 92*
**Spratt,** Lewis G *WhoAmP 91, WhoBlA 92*
**Spratto,** George R 1940- *AmMWSc 92*
**Spratto,** John Anthony 1951- *WhoFI 92*
**Spraugh,** W. Herbert 1896- *RelLAm 91*
**Sprauve,** Gilbert A. 1937- *WhoBlA 92*
**Sprawls,** Perry, Jr 1934- *AmMWSc 92*
**Sprawson,** Derek 1955- *TwCPaSc*
**Spray,** Clive Robert 1953- *AmMWSc 92*
**Spray,** David Conover 1946- *AmMWSc 92*
**Spray,** Elwin L 1948- *WhoAmP 91*
**Sprecher,** David A 1930- *AmMWSc 92*
**Sprecher,** Howard W 1936- *AmMWSc 92*
**Sprecher,** William Gunther 1924- *WhoEnt 92*
**Spreckley,** John Nicholas Teague 1934- *IntWW 91*
**Spreckley,** Nicholas 1934- *Who 92*
**Spreiregen,** Paul 1931- *WrDr 92*
**Spreiter,** John R 1921- *AmMWSc 92*
**Spreitzer,** Cynthia Ann 1953- *WhoWest 92*
**Spreitzer,** William Matthew 1929- *AmMWSc 92*
**Spremulli,** Gertrude H 1912- *AmMWSc 92*
**Spremulli,** Linda Lucy 1947- *AmMWSc 92*
**Spreng,** Alfred Carl 1923- *AmMWSc 92*
**Sprenger,** Curtis Donald 1934- *WhoEnt 92*
**Sprenger,** Gordon M. 1937- *WhoMW 92*
**Sprengnether,** Madelon *DrAPF 91*
**Sprenkel,** Richard Keiser 1943- *AmMWSc 92*
**Sprenkle,** Arthur C *WhoAmP 91*
**Sprenkle,** Elaine Elizabeth 1935- *WhoEnt 92*
**Sprent,** John Frederick Adrian 1915- *IntWW 91*
**Spresser,** Diane Mar 1943- *AmMWSc 92*
**Spreull,** James 1908- *Who 92*
**Spriddell,** Peter Henry 1928- *Who 92*
**Sprigge,** Timothy 1932- *WrDr 92*
**Sprigge,** Timothy Lauro Squire 1932- *IntAu&W 91, Who 92*
**Spriggs,** Alfred Samuel 1922- *AmMWSc 92*
**Spriggs,** David William 1949- *WhoMW 92*
**Spriggs,** Edward S. 1934- *WhoBlA 92*
**Spriggs,** Everett Lee 1930- *WhoAmL 92, WhoWest 92*
**Spriggs,** G. Max 1925- *WhoBlA 92*
**Spriggs,** Gaylyn J 1943- *WhoAmP 91*
**Spriggs,** Julia Anne 1951- *WhoMW 92*
**Spriggs,** Leslie 1910- *Who 92*
**Spriggs,** Ray V. 1937- *WhoBlA 92*
**Spriggs,** Richard Moore 1931- *AmMWSc 92*
**Sprik,** Dale Robert 1937- *WhoAmP 91*
**Sprince,** Herbert 1912- *AmMWSc 92*
**Spring,** Arthur Thomas 1935- *WhoFI 92*
**Spring,** Bonnie Joan 1949- *AmMWSc 92*
**Spring,** Dee 1934- *WhoWest 92*
**Spring,** Frank Stuart 1907- *Who 92*
**Spring,** Glenn Ernest 1939- *WhoWest 92*
**Spring,** James C. 1937- *WhoFI 92*
**Spring,** Jeffrey H 1950- *AmMWSc 92*
**Spring,** Linda Kay 1948- *WhoFI 92*
**Spring,** Michael 1941- *IntAu&W 91*
**Spring,** Paull E. *WhoRel 92*
**Spring,** Ray Frederick 1925- *AmMWSc 92*
**Spring,** Richard 1950- *IntWW 91, Who 92*
**Spring,** Stanley Lloyde 1942- *WhoFI 92*
**Spring,** Stephen Royston 1945- *WhoAmL 92*
**Spring,** Susan B 1943- *AmMWSc 92*
**Spring,** Wilbur, Jr 1921- *WhoAmP 91*
**Spring Rice** *Who 92*
**Springberg,** Gerald Harvey 1933- *WhoFI 92*
**Springborn,** Robert Carl 1929- *AmMWSc 92*
**Springer,** Alan David 1948- *AmMWSc 92*
**Springer,** Allan Matthew 1944- *AmMWSc 92*
**Springer,** Ashton, Jr. 1930- *WhoBlA 92, WhoEnt 92*
**Springer,** Axel 1912-1985 *FacFETw*
**Springer,** Bernard G 1935- *AmMWSc 92*
**Springer,** Carol *WhoAmP 91*
**Springer,** Charles Edward 1928- *WhoAmL 92, WhoAmP 91, WhoWest 92*
**Springer,** Charles Eugene 1903- *AmMWSc 92*
**Springer,** Charles Sinclair, Jr 1940- *AmMWSc 92*
**Springer,** David Edward 1953- *WhoAmP 91*
**Springer,** Dick 1948- *WhoAmP 91*
**Springer,** Donald Donner 1938- *WhoFI 92*
**Springer,** Donald Lee 1933- *AmMWSc 92*
**Springer,** Douglas Richard 1945- *WhoMW 92*
**Springer,** Dwight Sylvan 1943- *AmMWSc 92*
**Springer,** Edward L 1931- *AmMWSc 92*
**Springer,** Eric Winston 1929- *WhoBlA 92*
**Springer,** Georg F 1924- *AmMWSc 92*
**Springer,** George 1924- *AmMWSc 92, WhoMW 92*
**Springer,** George C., Jr. 1963- *WhoAmL 92*

**Springer**, George Chelston 1932- WhoBlA 92
**Springer**, George Henry 1918- AmMWSc 92
**Springer**, George S 1933- AmMWSc 92
**Springer**, George Stephen 1933- WhoWest 92
**Springer**, Gerald William 1943- WhoWest 92
**Springer**, Harry Aaron 1937- WhoMW 92
**Springer**, Heinrich WhoAmP 91
**Springer**, Hugh 1913- Who 92
**Springer**, Hugh Worrell 1913- IntWW 91
**Springer**, Jack Mackellar 1930- WhoFI 92
**Springer**, James Berne 1943- WhoMW 92
**Springer**, Jeffrey Alan 1950- WhoAmL 92
**Springer**, John Kenneth 1929- AmMWSc 92
**Springer**, John Mervin 1941- AmMWSc 92
**Springer**, Karl d1991 NewYTBS 91
**Springer**, Karl Goerge 1949- WhoRel 92, WhoWest 92
**Springer**, Karl Joseph 1935- AmMWSc 92
**Springer**, Kenneth N WhoAmP 91
**Springer**, Konrad Ferdinand 1925- IntWW 91
**Springer**, Lorene Hargrove 1927- WhoEnt 92
**Springer**, Martha Edith 1916- AmMWSc 92
**Springer**, Maxwell Elsworth 1913- AmMWSc 92
**Springer**, Melvin Dale 1918- AmMWSc 92
**Springer**, Nancy DrAPF 91
**Springer**, Nancy 1948- IntAu&W 91, SmATA 65, TwCSFW 91
**Springer**, Neil Allen 1938- WhoFI 92
**Springer**, Norman 1887- ScFEYrs
**Springer**, P. Gregory 1949- WhoEnt 92
**Springer**, Paul D. IntMPA 92
**Springer**, Paul David 1942- WhoAmL 92, WhoEnt 92, WhoFI 92, WhoWest 92
**Springer**, Paul Frederick 1922- AmMWSc 92
**Springer**, Robert Harold 1932- AmMWSc 92
**Springer**, Robert Louis 1945- WhoEnt 92
**Springer**, Sally Pearl 1947- WhoWest 92
**Springer**, Timothy Alan AmMWSc 92
**Springer**, Tobias 1907- Who 92
**Springer**, Victor Gruschka 1928- AmMWSc 92
**Springer**, Wayne Gilbert 1951- WhoFI 92
**Springer**, Wayne Richard 1946- AmMWSc 92
**Springer**, William H. 1929- WhoFI 92
**Springer**, William Kenneth 1948- WhoWest 92
**Springett**, Brian E 1936- AmMWSc 92
**Springett**, David Roy 1935- AmMWSc 92
**Springett**, Jack Allan 1916- Who 92
**Springfield**, Harry Wayne 1920- AmMWSc 92
**Springfield**, James Francis 1929- WhoAmL 92
**Springfield**, Rick 1949- IntMPA 92
**Springford**, John Frederick Charles 1919- Who 92
**Springman**, Paul W 1951- WhoIns 92
**Springmeyer**, Don 1954- WhoAmL 92
**Springs**, Lenny F. 1947- WhoBlA 92
**Springs**, Nadia ConAu 135
**Springstead**, Alan Phillip 1933- WhoWest 92
**Springstead**, Paul Steven 1953- WhoMW 92
**Springsted**, Eric Osmon 1951- WhoRel 92
**Springsteen**, Bruce 1949- ConMus 6 [port], FacFETw, IntWW 91, NewAmDM, WhoEnt 92
**Springsteen**, David Folger 1932- WhoFI 92
**Springston**, Benjamin N WhoAmP 91
**Springstubb**, Tricia DrAPF 91
**Sprinkel**, Beryl 1923- WrDr 92
**Sprinkel**, Beryl Wayne 1923- IntWW 91, WhoFI 92
**Sprinkel**, Warren Reed 1922- WhoAmP 91
**Sprinkle**, James 1943- AmMWSc 92
**Sprinkle**, James Kent, Jr 1952- AmMWSc 92
**Sprinkle**, Patricia Houck 1943- ConAu 133
**Sprinkle**, Philip Martin 1926- AmMWSc 92
**Sprinkle**, Robert Shields, III 1935- AmMWSc 92
**Sprinkle**, Stephen Venable 1951- WhoRel 92
**Sprinkle-Hamlin**, Sylvia Yvonne 1945- WhoBlA 92
**Sprinkles**, Catherine Childe WhoAmL 92
**Sprinson**, David Benjamin 1910- AmMWSc 92
**Sprinz**, Helmuth 1911- AmMWSc 92
**Spritz**, Norton 1928- AmMWSc 92
**Spritz**, Richard Andrew 1950- AmMWSc 92
**Spritzer**, Albert A 1927- AmMWSc 92
**Spritzer**, Marlene Alpern 1955- WhoAmL 92
**Spritzer**, Michael Stephen 1939- AmMWSc 92
**Spritzer**, Samuel Lewis 1954- WhoFI 92
**Sprizzo**, John Emilio 1934- WhoAmL 92
**Sproat**, Iain Mac Donald 1938- Who 92
**Sproger**, Charles Edmund 1933- WhoMW 92
**Sprokel**, Gerard J 1921- AmMWSc 92
**Sprot**, Aidan Mark 1919- Who 92
**Sprott**, David Arthur 1930- AmMWSc 92
**Sprott**, Gordon Dennis 1945- AmMWSc 92
**Sprott**, Julien Clinton 1942- AmMWSc 92, WhoMW 92
**Sprott**, Richard Lawrence 1940- AmMWSc 92
**Sprott**, Rodney McDowell 1953- WhoRel 92
**Sproul**, Gordon Duane 1944- AmMWSc 92
**Sproul**, Harvey Leonard 1933- WhoAmL 92, WhoAmP 91
**Sproul**, John Allan 1924- WhoFI 92, WhoWest 92
**Sproul**, Otis J 1930- AmMWSc 92
**Sproul**, William Dallas 1943- AmMWSc 92
**Sproule**, Betty Ann 1948- WhoWest 92
**Sproule**, Brian J 1925- AmMWSc 92
**Sproull**, Robert Fletcher 1947- AmMWSc 92
**Sproull**, Robert Lamb 1918- AmMWSc 92
**Sproull**, Wayne Treber 1906- AmMWSc 92
**Sprouse**, Gene Denson 1941- AmMWSc 92
**Sprouse**, James Edward 1943- WhoAmL 92
**Sprouse**, James M 1923- WhoAmP 91
**Sprouse**, James Marshall 1923- WhoAmL 92
**Sprouse**, John Alwyn 1908- WhoWest 92
**Sprouse**, Robert Allen, II 1935- WhoFI 92, WhoWest 92
**Sprout**, Francis Allen 1940- WhoBlA 92
**Sprowl**, Charles Riggs 1910- WhoAmL 92
**Sprowl**, James Alexander 1941- WhoAmL 92
**Sprowles**, Jolyon Charles 1944- AmMWSc 92
**Sprowls**, Donald O 1919- AmMWSc 92
**Sprowls**, Riley Clay 1921- AmMWSc 92
**Spruance**, Raymond Ames 1886-1969 FacFETw
**Spruance**, Thomas Willing 1947- WhoAmP 91
**Spruce**, George W 1947- WhoAmP 91
**Spruce**, Kenneth L. 1956- WhoBlA 92
**Spruch**, Grace Marmor 1926- AmMWSc 92
**Spruch**, Larry 1923- AmMWSc 92
**Spruell**, Alyce Manley 1958- WhoAmL 92
**Sprugel**, Douglas George 1948- AmMWSc 92
**Sprugel**, George, Jr 1919- AmMWSc 92
**Spruiell**, Joseph E 1935- AmMWSc 92
**Spruill**, Albert Westley 1926- WhoBlA 92
**Spruill**, Howard Vernon 1919- WhoRel 92
**Spruill**, James Arthur 1937- WhoBlA 92
**Spruill**, Nancy Lyon 1949- AmMWSc 92
**Spruill**, Norman Louis 1933- WhoIns 92
**Spruill**, Robert I. 1947- WhoBlA 92
**Spruill**, Steven 1946- TwCSFW 91, WrDr 92
**Sprules**, William Gary 1944- AmMWSc 92
**Sprung**, Donald Whitfield Loyal 1934- AmMWSc 92
**Sprung**, Joseph Asher 1915- AmMWSc 92
**Sprung**, Roger Howard 1930- WhoEnt 92
**Sprunger**, Keith L. 1935- WhoRel 92
**Sprunger**, Meredith Justin 1915- WhoRel 92
**Sprunger**, Virgil Lewis 1921- WhoRel 92
**Sprungl**, Janice Marie 1960- WhoWest 92
**Sprungl**, Katherine Louise 1961- WhoMW 92
**Sprunt**, Eve Silver 1951- AmMWSc 92
**Spry**, Charles Chambers Fowell 1910- Who 92
**Spry**, Christopher John 1946- Who 92
**Spry**, Donald Francis, II 1947- WhoAmL 92
**Spry**, John 1910- Who 92
**Spry**, Robert James 1938- AmMWSc 92
**Spudich**, James Anthony 1942- AmMWSc 92
**Spuehler**, Donald Roy 1934- WhoAmL 92
**Spuhl**, Tola Manzano 1942- WhoAmP 91
**Spuhler**, Willy 1902- IntWW 91
**Spulber**, Daniel Francis 1953- WhoFI 92
**Spulber**, Nicolas 1915- WhoFI 92, WhoMW 92
**Spuler**, Bertold IntWW 91N
**Spuller**, Robert L 1937- AmMWSc 92
**Spungin**, Joel D. 1937- WhoFI 92, WhoMW 92
**Spunt**, Shepard Armin 1931- WhoFI 92
**Spurdle**, John W., Jr. 1937- WhoFI 92
**Spurgeon**, Charles Haddon 1936- WhoMW 92
**Spurgeon**, Edward Dutcher 1939- WhoAmL 92
**Spurgeon**, Karen Elaine 1942- WhoEnt 92
**Spurgeon**, Leeman Clarence 1924- WhoAmP 91
**Spurgeon**, Peter Lester 1927- Who 92
**Spurgeon**, William Marion 1917- AmMWSc 92
**Spurlin**, Harold Morton 1905- AmMWSc 92
**Spurling**, David A. 1953- WhoWest 92
**Spurling**, Hilary 1940- IntAu&W 91, Who 92, WrDr 92
**Spurling**, John 1936- WrDr 92
**Spurling**, John Antony 1936- IntAu&W 91
**Spurling**, Richard G., Jr. 1858-1935 RelLAm 91
**Spurlock**, Benjamin Hill, Jr 1907- AmMWSc 92
**Spurlock**, Carola Henrich 1926- AmMWSc 92
**Spurlock**, Charles T. 1917- WhoBlA 92
**Spurlock**, Delbert L 1941- WhoAmP 91
**Spurlock**, Dorothy A. 1956- WhoBlA 92
**Spurlock**, Jack Marion 1930- AmMWSc 92
**Spurlock**, James B., Jr. 1936- WhoBlA 92
**Spurlock**, Jeanne WhoBlA 92
**Spurlock**, Jeanne 1921- NotBlAW 92
**Spurlock**, Lallah Jean 1924- WhoAmP 91
**Spurlock**, Langley Augustine 1939- AmMWSc 92, WhoBlA 92
**Spurlock**, LaVerne B. 1930- WhoBlA 92
**Spurlock**, Luther T 1945- WhoAmP 91
**Spurlock-Evans**, Karla Jeanne 1949- WhoBlA 92
**Spurr**, Arthur Richard 1915- AmMWSc 92
**Spurr**, Charles Lewis 1913- AmMWSc 92
**Spurr**, Clinton TwCWW 91
**Spurr**, David Tupper 1938- AmMWSc 92
**Spurr**, Gerald Baxter 1928- AmMWSc 92
**Spurr**, Harvey Wesley, Jr 1934- AmMWSc 92
**Spurr**, Margaret Anne 1933- Who 92
**Spurr**, Orson Kirk, Jr 1930- AmMWSc 92
**Spurr**, Stephen Hopkins 1918- AmMWSc 92
**Spurrell**, Francis Arthur 1919- AmMWSc 92
**Spurrier**, Elmer R 1920- AmMWSc 92
**Spurrier**, James Joseph 1946- WhoEnt 92, WhoMW 92
**Spurrier**, Wilma A AmMWSc 92
**Spurzem**, Richard Taliaferro 1960- WhoFI 92
**Spy**, James 1952- Who 92
**Spyber**, John DrAPF 91
**Spyhalski**, Edward James 1925- AmMWSc 92
**Spykman**, Gordon John 1926- WhoRel 92
**Spyropoulos**, Jannis 1912- IntWW 91
**Squair**, George Alexander 1929- Who 92
**Squanto** d1622 BenetAL 91
**Squaw Sachem** EncAmaz 91
**Squazzo**, Mildred Katherine WhoFI 92
**Squeri**, Stephen J. 1954- WhoAmL 92
**Squibb**, Edward Robinson 1819-1900 BiInAmS
**Squibb**, George Drewry 1906- Who 92
**Squibb**, Robert E 1942- AmMWSc 92
**Squibb**, Samuel Dexter 1931- AmMWSc 92
**Squier**, Charles DrAPF 91
**Squier**, Charles LaBarge 1931- WhoWest 92
**Squier**, Donald Platte 1929- AmMWSc 92
**Squier**, E. G. 1821-1888 BenetAL 91
**Squier**, Emma-Lindsay ScFEYrs
**Squier**, Ephraim George 1821-1888 BiInAmS
**Squier**, Robert LesBEnT 92
**Squiers**, Edwin Richard 1948- AmMWSc 92
**Squillace**, Alexander Paul 1945- WhoFI 92
**Squillacote**, Michael Edward 1950- AmMWSc 92
**Squinto**, Stephen P 1956- AmMWSc 92
**Squire**, Alexander 1917- AmMWSc 92
**Squire**, Anne Marguerite 1920- WhoRel 92
**Squire**, Clifford William 1928- IntWW 91, Who 92
**Squire**, Daniel Harris 1954- WhoAmL 92
**Squire**, David R 1935- AmMWSc 92
**Squire**, Larry Ryan 1941- AmMWSc 92
**Squire**, Laurie Rubin 1953- WhoEnt 92
**Squire**, Peter John 1937- Who 92
**Squire**, Raglan 1912- Who 92
**Squire**, Richard Douglas 1940- AmMWSc 92
**Squire**, Robert Alfred 1930- AmMWSc 92
**Squire**, Robin Clifford 1944- Who 92
**Squire**, Rose Elizabeth 1861-1938 BiDBrF 2
**Squire**, Russel Nelson 1908- WhoEnt 92
**Squire**, Walter Charles 1945- WhoAmL 92, WhoEnt 92
**Squire**, Warwick Nevison 1921- Who 92
**Squire**, William Who 92
**Squire**, William 1920- AmMWSc 92
**Squires**, Arthur Morton 1916- AmMWSc 92
**Squires**, Carolyn 1940- WhoAmP 91
**Squires**, Catherine L 1941- AmMWSc 92
**Squires**, Dale Edward 1950- AmMWSc 92, WhoFI 92
**Squires**, Donald Fleming 1927- AmMWSc 92
**Squires**, James Ralph 1940- WhoFI 92
**Squires**, Jay Thomas 1961- WhoAmL 92
**Squires**, John Henry 1946- WhoAmL 92
**Squires**, Lombard AmMWSc 92
**Squires**, Maudest Kelly 1903- WhoBlA 92
**Squires**, Paul Herman 1931- AmMWSc 92
**Squires**, Radcliffe 1917- ConPo 91, WrDr 92
**Squires**, Richard Felt 1933- AmMWSc 92
**Squires**, Robert George 1935- AmMWSc 92
**Squires**, Robert Wright 1921- AmMWSc 92
**Squires**, Ronald M 1951- WhoAmP 91
**Squires**, Scott WhoEnt 92
**Squires**, William Allen 1949- WhoFI 92
**Squirrell**, Leonard 1893-1979 TwCPaSc
**Squyres**, Mary Margaret 1950- WhoAmL 92
**Sramek**, Richard Anthony 1943- AmMWSc 92
**Sraon**, Harbans Singh 1941- WhoRel 92
**Srb**, Adrian Morris 1917- AmMWSc 92, IntWW 91
**Srebnik**, Herbert Harry 1923- AmMWSc 92
**Srebro**, Richard 1936- AmMWSc 92
**Sree Harsha**, Karnamadakala S 1936- AmMWSc 92
**Sreebny**, Leo Morris 1922- AmMWSc 92
**Sreekantan**, Badanaval Venkata 1925- IntWW 91
**Sreenan**, Patrick Hugh 1959- WhoFI 92
**Sreenivasan**, Katepalli Raju 1947- AmMWSc 92
**Sreenivasan**, Sreenivasa Ranga 1933- AmMWSc 92
**Sreevalsan**, Thazepadath 1935- AmMWSc 92
**Srere**, Linda Jean 1955- WhoFI 92
**Srere**, Paul Arnold 1925- AmMWSc 92
**Sreter**, Frank A 1921- AmMWSc 92
**Sribney**, Michael 1927- AmMWSc 92
**Sridaran**, Rajagopala 1950- AmMWSc 92
**Sridhar**, Champa Guha AmMWSc 92
**Sridhar**, Rajagopalan 1941- AmMWSc 92
**Sridhara Maharaja**, Sripad Bhakti Raksaka 1895-1988 RelLAm 91
**Sridhara**, S AmMWSc 92
**Sridharan**, Natesa S 1946- AmMWSc 92
**Srihari**, Sargur N 1950- AmMWSc 92
**Srinath**, Mandyam Dhati 1935- AmMWSc 92
**Srinivas**, Krishna 1913- IntAu&W 91
**Srinivasan**, Asoka 1939- AmMWSc 92
**Srinivasan**, Bhama 1935- AmMWSc 92
**Srinivasan**, G R AmMWSc 92
**Srinivasan**, Makuteswaran 1945- AmMWSc 92
**Srinivasan**, P R 1927- AmMWSc 92
**Srinivasan**, Ramachandra Srini 1939- AmMWSc 92
**Srinivasan**, Rangaswamy 1929- AmMWSc 92
**Srinivasan**, Sathanur Ramachandran 1938- AmMWSc 92
**Srinivasan**, Srini 1940- WhoFI 92
**Srinivasan**, Vadake Ram 1925- AmMWSc 92
**Srinivasan**, Vakula S 1936- AmMWSc 92
**Srinivasan**, Vijay 1954- AmMWSc 92
**Srinivasaraghavan**, Rengachari 1948- AmMWSc 92
**Sripada**, Pavanaram Kameswara 1933- AmMWSc 92
**Sriskandan**, Kanagaretnam 1930- Who 92
**Srithirath**, Soubanh 1936- IntWW 91
**Srivastav**, Ram Prasad 1934- AmMWSc 92
**Srivastava**, Arun 1951- WhoMW 92
**Srivastava**, Ashok Kumar 1951- AmMWSc 92
**Srivastava**, Bejai Inder Sahai 1932- AmMWSc 92
**Srivastava**, Chandrika Prasad 1920- IntWW 91, Who 92
**Srivastava**, Hari Mohan 1940- AmMWSc 92, WhoWest 92
**Srivastava**, Jagdish Narain 1933- AmMWSc 92
**Srivastava**, Krishan 1931- AmMWSc 92
**Srivastava**, Lalit Mohan 1932- AmMWSc 92
**Srivastava**, Laxmi Shanker 1938- AmMWSc 92
**Srivastava**, Muni Shanker 1936- AmMWSc 92
**Srivastava**, Prakash Narain 1929- AmMWSc 92

Srivastava, Rekha 1945- AmMWSc 92
Srivastava, Satish Kumar 1937- AmMWSc 92
Srivastava, Surat Prasad 1937- AmMWSc 92
Srivastava, Suresh Chandra 1939- AmMWSc 92
Srivastava, Trilokv N 1936- AmMWSc 92
Srivastava, Uma Shanker 1934- AmMWSc 92
Srivatsan, Tirumalai Srinivas 1957- AmMWSc 92
Srnka, Leonard James 1946- AmMWSc 92
Sroka, Elliott Frank 1950- WhoEnt 92
Sroka, Rebecca Sue 1952- WhoFI 92
Srolovitz, David Joseph 1957- AmMWSc 92
Sroog, Cyrus Efrem 1922- AmMWSc 92
Sroufe, Clinton Scott 1964- WhoRel 92
Srour, Joseph Ralph 1941- AmMWSc 92
Srp, Karel IntWW 91
Srygley, Fletcher Douglas 1938- AmMWSc 92
Ssemogerere, Paul Kawanga IntWW 91
Staab, Heinz A. 1926- IntWW 91
Staab, Robert R 1938- WhoAmP 91
Staab, Thomas Eugene 1941- WhoFI 92
Staab, Willodine Leah 1927- WhoAmP 91
Staake, Robert Frederick 1951- WhoMW 92
Staal, Gerardus Benardus 1925- AmMWSc 92
Staar, Richard F 1923- IntAu&W 91, WrDr 92
Staas, John William 1942- WhoMW 92
Staat, Robert Henry 1942- AmMWSc 92
Staats, Charles Tolbert, Jr. 1967- WhoWest 92
Staats, Elmer Boyd 1914- IntWW 91, WhoAmP 91
Staats, Florence Joan 1940- WhoBlA 92
Staats, Gustav W 1919- AmMWSc 92
Staats, Norman Lansing 1926- WhoFI 92
Staats, Percy Anderson 1921- AmMWSc 92
Staats, William Austin 1938- WhoMW 92
Staats, William R 1935- AmMWSc 92
Staatz, Mortimer Hay 1918- AmMWSc 92
Staatz, William D AmMWSc 92
Staba, Emil John 1928- AmMWSc 92
Staback, Edward G 1937- WhoAmP 91
Stabb, William 1913- Who 92
Stabe, Donald Wayne 1957- WhoRel 92
Stabej, Rudolph John 1952- WhoMW 92
Stabenfeldt, George H 1930- AmMWSc 92
Stabenow, Deborah Ann 1950- WhoAmP 91
Stabile, Donald Robert 1944- WhoFI 92
Stabile, John P WhoAmP 91
Stable, Owen 1923- Who 92
Stableford, Brian M 1948- TwCSFW 91, WrDr 92
Stableford, Louis Tranter 1914- AmMWSc 92
Stablein, John Joseph, III 1951- WhoFI 92
Stablein, Marilyn DrAPF 91
Stabler, Arthur Fletcher 1919- Who 92
Stabler, Nancy Rae 1946- WhoMW 92
Stabler, Richard H 1820?-1878 BiInAmS
Stabler, Timothy Allen 1940- AmMWSc 92
Stabler, W Laird, Jr 1930- WhoAmP 91
Stables, Gordon 1840-1910 ScFEYrs
Stace-Smith, Richard 1924- AmMWSc 92
Stacey, Carol Ann 1938- WhoIns 92
Stacey, Carol Horning 1934- WhoAmP 91
Stacey, Frank Arthur 1923-1977 ConAu 135
Stacey, Frank Donald 1929- IntWW 91
Stacey, James Allen 1925- WhoAmL 92
Stacey, John Nichol 1920- Who 92
Stacey, John Sydney 1927- AmMWSc 92
Stacey, John William 1949- WhoEnt 92
Stacey, Judith 1943- WrDr 92
Stacey, Lad S 1926- WhoAmP 91
Stacey, Larry Milton 1940- AmMWSc 92
Stacey, Margaret 1922- Who 92, WrDr 92
Stacey, Maurice 1907- IntWW 91, Who 92
Stacey, Michael Lawrence 1924- Who 92
Stacey, Morna Dorothy Who 92
Stacey, Nicholas WrDr 92
Stacey, Nicholas Anthony Howard IntAu&W 91
Stacey, Nicolas David 1927- Who 92
Stacey, Norma Elaine 1925- WhoFI 92
Stacey, Susannah ConAu 133, WrDr 92
Stacey, Tom 1930- IntAu&W 91, WrDr 92
Stacey, Weston Monroe, Jr AmMWSc 92
Stach, David Alan 1953- WhoEnt 92
Stach, Joseph 1938- AmMWSc 92
Stach, Robert William 1945- AmMWSc 92
Stachel, Johanna 1954- AmMWSc 92
Stachel, John Jay 1928- AmMWSc 92
Stachler, Robert G. 1929- WhoAmL 92
Stachowske, Vicki L 1952- WhoAmP 91
Stachowski, William T 1949- WhoAmP 91
Stacia, Kevin Maurice 1958- WhoBlA 92
Stack, Ann Prunella 1914- Who 92
Stack, B R 1924- AmMWSc 92
Stack, Beatriz de Greiff 1939- WhoAmL 92
Stack, Charlie Ray 1929- WhoAmP 91
Stack, Daniel 1928- WhoAmL 92
Stack, Diane Virginia 1958- WhoFI 92
Stack, Edward MacGregor 1919- WrDr 92
Stack, George 1932- WrDr 92
Stack, George 1946- Who 92
Stack, George Joseph 1932- IntAu&W 91
Stack, George Samuel 1961- WhoRel 92
Stack, Gerald Francis 1953- WhoAmL 92
Stack, Jane Marcia 1928- WhoAmL 92
Stack, Joan Murphy 1928- WhoEnt 92
Stack, Joanne Tunney 1952- WhoAmL 92
Stack, John Charles 1962- WhoRel 92
Stack, John D 1938- AmMWSc 92
Stack, Kathleen Griffin WhoFI 92
Stack, Nancy Susan 1943- WhoMW 92
Stack, Neville Who 92
Stack, Neville 1928- Who 92
Stack, Paul Francis 1946- WhoMW 92
Stack, Prunella Who 92
Stack, Raymond John, Jr. 1936- WhoFI 92
Stack, Robert LesBEnT 92
Stack, Robert 1919- IntMPA 92
Stack, Robert Douglas 1956- WhoEnt 92, WhoFI 92
Stack, Robert Langford 1919- WhoEnt 92
Stack, Stephen M 1943- AmMWSc 92
Stack, Stephen S. 1934- WhoFI 92
Stack, Thomas Neville 1919- Who 92
Stackelberg, John Roderick 1935- WhoWest 92
Stackelberg, Olaf Patrick 1932- AmMWSc 92
Stackhouse, David William, Jr. 1926- WhoMW 92
Stackhouse, E. Marilyn 1955- WhoBlA 92
Stackhouse, Jean WhoEnt 92
Stackhouse, Max Lynn 1935- WhoRel 92
Stackhouse, Reginald 1925- WhoRel 92
Stackhouse, Richard Gilbert 1929- WhoFI 92
Stackman, Robert W 1935- AmMWSc 92
Stackman, Robert William 1935- WhoMW 92
Stackpole, John Duke 1935- AmMWSc 92
Stacpoole, John Wentworth 1926- Who 92
Stacpoole, W H 1846- ScFEYrs
Stacy, Carl J 1929- AmMWSc 92
Stacy, David Harry 1949- WhoAmL 92
Stacy, David Lowell 1950- AmMWSc 92
Stacy, Dennis William 1945- WhoFI 92
Stacy, Galen Dwight 1934- WhoWest 92
Stacy, Gardner W 1921- AmMWSc 92
Stacy, Gaylon L 1934- WhoAmP 91
Stacy, Jess 1904- NewAmDM
Stacy, John William 1942- WhoRel 92
Stacy, Orville Briggs 1832?-1912 BiInAmS
Stacy, Pauline French 1915- IntAu&W 91
Stacy, Ralph Winston 1920- AmMWSc 92
Stacy, Richard A. 1942- WhoAmL 92
Stacy, Roy Lee 1950- WhoAmL 92
Stacy, T D 1934- AmMWSc 92
Stacy, T. Don 1934- IntWW 91
Stacy, Theodore 1923- WhoAmP 91
Stacy, Thomas WhoEnt 92
Stacy, Verna Mae 1931- WhoAmP 91
Stadd, Arlene WhoEnt 92
Stade, Frederica von NewAmDM
Stade, George 1933- WrDr 92
Stadelmaier, H H 1922- AmMWSc 92
Stadelman, William Jacob 1917- AmMWSc 92
Stadelmann, Eduard Joseph 1920- AmMWSc 92
Stadelmann, Richard William 1932- WhoRel 92
Stadem, Paul David 1953- WhoMW 92
Staden, Berndt von 1919- IntWW 91
Staden, Johann 1581-1634 NewAmDM
Stadil, Bjorn 1951- WhoFI 92
Stadlen, Nicholas Felix 1950- Who 92
Stadlen, Richard William 1949- WhoEnt 92
Stadler, Anton 1753-1812 NewAmDM
Stadler, David Ross 1925- AmMWSc 92
Stadler, James Robert 1964- WhoAmL 92
Stadler, Joseph F BlkOlyM
Stadler, Louis Benjamin 1926- AmMWSc 92
Stadley, Pat Anna May Gough 1918- WhoWest 92
Stadnicki, Stanley Walter, Jr 1943- AmMWSc 92
Stadnyuk, Ivan Fotievich 1920- IntWW 91
Stadter, James Thomas AmMWSc 92
Stadtherr, Leon 1942- AmMWSc 92
Stadtherr, Mark Allen 1950- AmMWSc 92
Stadtherr, Richard James 1919- AmMWSc 92
Stadtler, Beatrice 1921- IntAu&W 91
Stadtman, Earl R. 1919- IntWW 91
Stadtman, Earl Reece 1919- AmMWSc 92
Stadtman, Theresa Campbell 1920- IntWW 91
Stadtman, Thressa Campbell 1920- AmMWSc 92
Stadtman, Verne August 1926- WrDr 92
Stadtmauer, David 1934- WhoAmL 92
Stadtmueller, Diana Lynne 1946- WhoAmP 91
Stadtmueller, Joseph Peter 1942- WhoAmL 92, WhoMW 92
Stadum, Tony WhoAmP 91
Staebell, Ronald Thomas 1945- WhoMW 92
Staebler, Bruce Gary 1943- WhoWest 92
Staebler, David Lloyd 1940- AmMWSc 92
Staebler, Neil 1905- WhoAmP 91
Staehelin, Lucas Andrew 1939- AmMWSc 92
Staehle, Alan Wallace 1941- WhoWest 92
Staehle, Roger Washburne 1934- AmMWSc 92
Stael, Mme de 1766-1817 BlkwCEP
Stael, Germaine de 1766-1817 GuFrLit 1
Stael, Germaine Necker, Baronne de 1766-1817 FrenWW
Stael-Holstein, Anne-Louise, baronne de 1766-1817 BlkwCEP
Staelin, David Hudson 1938- AmMWSc 92
Staes, Beverly N. WhoBlA 92
Staetz, Charles Alan 1945- AmMWSc 92
Staff Of The Clarion and Others ScFEYrs
Staff, Charles Bancroft, Jr. 1929- WhoEnt 92
Staff, Frank William 1908- WrDr 92
Staff, Karen Leslie 1961- WhoAmL 92
Staffin, Bryan Drayton 1961- WhoMW 92
Stafford, Archdeaconry of Who 92
Stafford, Baron 1954- Who 92
Stafford, Bishop Suffragan of 1943- Who 92
Stafford, Arthur Charles 1947- WhoMW 92
Stafford, Barbara M WhoAmP 91
Stafford, Bernice 1925- WhoRel 92
Stafford, Bruce H 1922- AmMWSc 92
Stafford, Darrel Wayne 1935- AmMWSc 92
Stafford, David Valentine 1930- Who 92
Stafford, Don 1934- WhoBlA 92
Stafford, Earl WhoEnt 92A
Stafford, Edward Peary 1918- ConAu 135
Stafford, Edwin J WhoAmP 91
Stafford, Frank Edmund 1895- Who 92
Stafford, Fred E 1935- AmMWSc 92
Stafford, Gilbert Wayne 1938- WhoRel 92
Stafford, Godfrey Harry 1920- IntWW 91, Who 92
Stafford, Gordon N 1938- WhoAmP 91
Stafford, Harry, Jr 1943- WhoAmP 91
Stafford, Helen Adele 1922- AmMWSc 92
Stafford, J. Francis 1932- WhoRel 92, WhoWest 92
Stafford, Jean 1915-1979 BenetAL 91, ConLC 68 [port], FacFETw, TwCWW 91
Stafford, John 1920- Who 92
Stafford, John Michael 1940- WhoWest 92
Stafford, John R. 1968- WhoWest 92
Stafford, John Rogers 1937- IntWW 91, WhoFI 92
Stafford, John Warner 1932- WhoFI 92
Stafford, John William 1932- AmMWSc 92
Stafford, Kenneth Victor, Sr. 1926- WhoRel 92
Stafford, Kim R. DrAPF 91
Stafford, Leonor Maldonado 1948- WhoHisp 92
Stafford, Magdalen Marrow 1942- AmMWSc 92
Stafford, Mary D 1927- WhoAmP 91
Stafford, Michael Alan 1955- WhoMW 92
Stafford, Moody Frank 1932- WhoAmP 91
Stafford, Preston Clay 1961- WhoEnt 92
Stafford, Richard Wesley, Jr 1952- WhoAmP 91
Stafford, Robert A 1912- WhoAmP 91
Stafford, Robert A. 1953- ConAu 133
Stafford, Robert Oppen 1920- AmMWSc 92
Stafford, Robert T 1913- WhoAmP 91
Stafford, Ronald B 1935- WhoAmP 91
Stafford, Ronald Lee 1938- WhoMW 92
Stafford, Shane Ludwig 1955- WhoAmL 92
Stafford, Thomas 1930- FacFETw
Stafford, Tim ConAu 135
Stafford, Tony Jason 1935- WhoEnt 92
Stafford, Tracy 1948- WhoAmP 91
Stafford, Ulick 1965- WhoMW 92
Stafford, Warren S. 1928- WhoAmL 92
Stafford, William 1914- BenetAL 91, ConPo 91, WrDr 92
Stafford, William 1950- WhoWest 92
Stafford, William Geiger 1959- WhoFI 92
Stafford, William Henry, Jr. 1931- WhoAmL 92
Stafford-Baker, Julius 1904-1988 TwCPaSc
Stafford-Baker, Philip 1908-1955 TwCPaSc
Stafford-Clark, David 1916- Who 92
Stafford-Clark, Max 1941- IntWW 91, Who 92
Stafleu, Frans Antonie 1921- IntWW 91
Stafsudd, Oscar M, Jr 1936- AmMWSc 92
Stagaman, David John 1935- WhoRel 92
Stage, Richard Lee 1936- WhoFI 92, WhoMW 92
Stageman, Paul Jerome 1916- AmMWSc 92
Stager, Carl Vinton 1935- AmMWSc 92
Stager, Donald K. WhoFI 92
Stager, Harold Keith 1921- AmMWSc 92
Stager, Steven Frank 1952- WhoRel 92
Stagg, Amos Alonzo 1862-1965 FacFETw
Stagg, Clyde Lawrence 1935- WhoAmL 92
Stagg, Evelyn W 1916- WhoAmP 91
Stagg, Frank 1911- WrDr 92
Stagg, Geoffrey Leonard 1913- Who 92
Stagg, Ronald M AmMWSc 92
Stagg, Tom 1923- WhoAmL 92
Stagg, William Ray 1937- AmMWSc 92
Staggers, Frank Eugene 1926- WhoBlA 92
Staggers, Harley O. 1907-1991 CurBio 91N
Staggers, Harley O., Jr. 1951- AlmAP 92 [port]
Staggers, Harley O., Sr. d1991 NewYTBS 91 [port]
Staggers, Harley Orrin, Jr 1951- WhoAmP 91
Staggers, Harley Orrin, Sr 1907- WhoAmP 91
Staggs, Frank Maurice, Jr. 1953- WhoAmL 92
Staggs, Ralph E 1922- WhoAmP 91
Stagman, Barry William 1946- WhoMW 92
Stagner, Robert Dean 1950- WhoAmL 92
Stagno, Sergio Bruno 1941- AmMWSc 92
Stahel, Edward P 1934- AmMWSc 92
Stahl, Al IntMPA 92
Stahl, Andrew 1954- TwCPaSc
Stahl, Barbara Jaffe 1930- AmMWSc 92
Stahl, C D 1923- AmMWSc 92
Stahl, Charles Eugene 1944- WhoAmL 92
Stahl, David 1949- WhoEnt 92
Stahl, Ernest Ludwig 1902- Who 92
Stahl, Franklin Phillip, II 1956- WhoRel 92
Stahl, Franklin William 1929- AmMWSc 92
Stahl, Frieda A 1922- AmMWSc 92
Stahl, Georg Ernst 1660-1734 BlkwCEP
Stahl, Glenn Allan 1945- AmMWSc 92
Stahl, Hilda Ann 1938- IntAu&W 91
Stahl, Jack 1934- WhoAmP 91
Stahl, Jack Leland 1934- WhoWest 92
Stahl, Jayne Lyn DrAPF 91
Stahl, Joel S 1918- AmMWSc 92
Stahl, Joel Sol 1918- WhoFI 92
Stahl, John Benton 1930- AmMWSc 92
Stahl, John M. 1886-1950 IntDcF 2-2 [port]
Stahl, John Wendell 1956- AmMWSc 92
Stahl, Keith John 1933- WhoFI 92
Stahl, Laddie L 1921- AmMWSc 92
Stahl, Lesley LesBEnT 92 [port]
Stahl, Madonna 1928- WhoAmL 92
Stahl, Neil 1942- AmMWSc 92
Stahl, Philip Cornelius 1948- WhoAmL 92
Stahl, Philip Damien 1941- AmMWSc 92
Stahl, Ralph Henry 1926- AmMWSc 92
Stahl, Richard G. C. 1934- WhoWest 92
Stahl, Roland Edgar 1925- AmMWSc 92
Stahl, S Sigmund 1925- AmMWSc 92
Stahl, Samuel Morton 1939- WhoRel 92
Stahl, Saul 1942- AmMWSc 92
Stahl, Stephen Lee 1949- WhoEnt 92
Stahl, William J 1939- AmMWSc 92
Stahl, William Louis 1936- AmMWSc 92
Stahle, Anders Oscar Kase 1901- IntWW 91
Stahle, Hans 1923- IntWW 91
Stahler, John Patrick 1957- WhoWest 92
Stahley, William 1928- AmMWSc 92
Stahlgren, Leroy Henry 1924- WhoWest 92
Stahlman, Edward John 1963- WhoWest 92
Stahlman, John Richard 1937- WhoRel 92
Stahlman, Mildred 1922- AmMWSc 92
Stahlman, Phillip Wayne 1948- AmMWSc 92
Stahly, Donald Paul 1937- AmMWSc 92
Stahly, Eldon Everett 1908- AmMWSc 92
Stahmann, Mark Arnold 1914- AmMWSc 92
Stahmer, Harold Martin, Jr. 1929- WhoRel 92
Stahnke, Herbert Ludwig 1902- AmMWSc 92
Stahnke, William E. WhoBlA 92
Stahr, Curtis Brent 1946- WhoMW 92
Stahr, Elvis J., Jr. 1916- IntWW 91
Stahr, Elvis Jacob, Jr. 1916- WhoAmL 92, WhoFI 92
Stahr, Henry Michael 1931- AmMWSc 92
Staiano, Edward F. 1936- WhoMW 92
Staib, Jon Albert 1940- AmMWSc 92

**Staicar**, Thomas Edward 1946- *IntAu&W 91*
**Staiff**, Donald C 1936- *AmMWSc 92*
**Staiger**, Roger Powell 1921- *AmMWSc 92*
**Staikos**, Dimitri Nickolas 1919- *AmMWSc 92*
**Stainback**, Susan Bray 1947- *WhoMW 92*
**Stainbrook**, James Ralph, Jr. 1936- *WhoMW 92*
**Stainer**, Dennis William 1932- *AmMWSc 92*
**Stainer**, John 1840-1901 *NewAmDM*
**Staines**, Michael Laurence 1949- *WhoMW 92*
**Staines**, Trevor *IntAu&W 91X*
**Stainforth**, Charles Herbert 1914- *Who 92*
**Stains**, Howard James 1924- *AmMWSc 92*
**Stainsby**, Wendell Nicholls 1928- *AmMWSc 92*
**Stainton**, Albert *DrAPF 91*
**Stainton**, John Ross 1914- *Who 92*
**Stainton**, Keith 1921- *Who 92*
**Stainton**, Ross *Who 92*
**Stair**, Earl of 1906- *Who 92*
**Stair**, Michael Marvin 1947- *WhoEnt 92*
**Stair**, Peter Curran 1950- *AmMWSc 92*
**Stair**, William K 1920- *AmMWSc 92*
**Stairs**, Gordon *TwCWW 91*
**Stairs**, Gordon R 1932- *AmMWSc 92*
**Stairs**, Jess M 1942- *WhoAmP 91*
**Stairs**, Robert Ardagh 1925- *AmMWSc 92*
**Stake**, Brent Dennis 1950- *WhoRel 92*
**Stake**, Dorothy M 1924- *WhoAmP 91*
**Stake**, Paul Erik 1944- *AmMWSc 92*
**Stake**, Ronald David 1958- *WhoMW 92*
**Stake**, William Floyd 1920- *WhoAmP 91*
**Staker**, Donald David 1926- *AmMWSc 92*
**Staker**, Everon Lee 1944- *WhoAmP 91*
**Staker**, Michael Ray 1947- *AmMWSc 92*
**Staker**, Robert D 1945- *AmMWSc 92*
**Staker**, Robert Jackson 1925- *WhoAmL 92*
**Staker**, William Paul 1919- *AmMWSc 92*
**Stakes**, Debra Sue 1951- *AmMWSc 92*
**Stakgold**, Ivar 1925- *AmMWSc 92*
**Stakis**, Reo 1913- *Who 92*
**Staklis**, Andris A 1939- *AmMWSc 92*
**Staknis**, Victor Richard 1920- *AmMWSc 92*
**Stakutis**, Vincent John 1920- *AmMWSc 92*
**Stalbaum**, Lynn E 1920- *WhoAmP 91*
**Stalcup**, Marvel C 1931- *AmMWSc 92*
**Stalcup**, Robert Edward, Sr 1923- *WhoAmP 91*
**Stalder**, Robert Dean 1955- *WhoWest 92*
**Staler**, William Langdon 1953- *WhoFI 92*
**Staley**, Charles Earl 1927- *WhoFI 92*
**Staley**, Charles Ralls 1938- *WhoAmL 92*
**Staley**, Clinton Andrew 1958- *WhoWest 92*
**Staley**, David H 1930- *AmMWSc 92*
**Staley**, David Horton 1930- *WhoAmP 91*
**Staley**, Dean Oden 1926- *AmMWSc 92*
**Staley**, Delbert C. 1924- *WhoFI 92*
**Staley**, James Randall 1948- *WhoEnt 92*
**Staley**, James T 1934- *AmMWSc 92*
**Staley**, James Trotter 1938- *AmMWSc 92*
**Staley**, Jeffrey Lloyd 1951- *WhoRel 92*
**Staley**, John Charles 1941- *WhoMW 92*
**Staley**, John Fredric 1943- *WhoAmL 92*
**Staley**, John M 1929- *AmMWSc 92*
**Staley**, L M 1926- *AmMWSc 92*
**Staley**, Patrick Aurel 1948- *WhoWest 92*
**Staley**, Ralph Horton 1945- *AmMWSc 92*
**Staley**, Robert Newton 1935- *AmMWSc 92, WhoMW 92*
**Staley**, Robert W. 1935- *WhoFI 92*
**Staley**, Stuart Warner 1938- *AmMWSc 92*
**Staley**, Valeria Howard 1925- *WhoBlA 92*
**Stalford**, Harold Lenn 1942- *AmMWSc 92*
**Stalheim**, Ole H Viking 1917- *AmMWSc 92*
**Stalick**, Wayne Myron 1942- *AmMWSc 92*
**Staliiski**, Aleksandur 1893-1945 *BiDExR*
**Stalin**, Iosif Vissarionovich 1879-1953 *SovUnBD*
**Stalin**, Joseph 1879-1953 *EncTR 91 [port]*
**Stalin**, Joseph Vissarionovich 1879-1953 *FacFETw*
**Stalker**, Archibald MacSween 1924- *AmMWSc 92*
**Stalker**, Harold Thomas 1950- *AmMWSc 92*
**Stalker**, Harrison Dailey 1915- *AmMWSc 92*
**Stalker**, Jacqueline D'Aoust 1933- *WhoMW 92*
**Stalker**, Milliken 1842?-1909 *BiInAmS*
**Stalker**, Robert E 1951- *WhoIns 92*
**Stalker**, Suzy Wooster 1948- *WhoFI 92*
**Stalker**, Timothy Wayne 1950- *WhoAmL 92*
**Stalks**, Larrie W. 1925- *WhoBlA 92*
**Stalkup**, Fred I, Jr 1936- *AmMWSc 92*
**Stall**, Alan David 1951- *WhoFI 92, WhoMW 92*
**Stall**, Robert Eugene 1931- *AmMWSc 92*
**Stall**, William Martin 1944- *AmMWSc 92*
**Stallard** *Who 92*
**Stallard**, Baron 1921- *Who 92*
**Stallard**, George Thomas 1937- *WhoWest 92*
**Stallard**, Michael Lee 1959- *WhoFI 92*
**Stallard**, Peter 1915- *Who 92*
**Stallard**, Richard E 1934- *AmMWSc 92*
**Stallard**, Troy Francis 1944- *WhoFI 92*
**Stallard**, Wayne Minor 1927- *WhoAmL 92, WhoMW 92*
**Stallcup**, Michael R 1947- *AmMWSc 92*
**Stallcup**, Odie Talmadge 1918- *AmMWSc 92*
**Stallcup**, William Blackburn, Jr 1920- *AmMWSc 92*
**Stalley**, Robert Delmer 1924- *AmMWSc 92, WhoWest 92*
**Stalley**, Rodney Edward 1930- *WhoFI 92*
**Stallibrass**, Geoffrey Ward 1911- *Who 92*
**Stalling**, David Laurence 1941- *AmMWSc 92*
**Stalling**, Gustav Heinrich, III 1930- *WhoFI 92*
**Stalling**, Ronald Eugene 1946- *WhoBlA 92*
**Stallings**, Charles Henry 1941- *AmMWSc 92*
**Stallings**, Frank, Jr. 1954- *WhoFI 92*
**Stallings**, Gary Dean 1951- *WhoMW 92*
**Stallings**, George Augustus, Jr. 1948- *RelLAm 91, WhoBlA 92*
**Stallings**, Gregory Ralph 1957- *WhoBlA 92*
**Stallings**, James Cameron 1919- *AmMWSc 92*
**Stallings**, James Raiford 1936- *WhoBlA 92*
**Stallings**, John Robert, Jr 1935- *AmMWSc 92*
**Stallings**, Laurence 1894-1968 *BenetAL 91*
**Stallings**, M. Ronald 1944- *WhoFI 92*
**Stallings**, Margit Sabine Dora 1956- *WhoWest 92*
**Stallings**, Mark Edmond 1956- *WhoRel 92*
**Stallings**, Moody E, Jr 1947- *WhoAmP 91*
**Stallings**, Phillip Kurtis 1957- *WhoAmL 92*
**Stallings**, Raymond Louis 1954- *WhoWest 92*
**Stallings**, Richard H. 1940- *AlmAP 92 [port]*
**Stallings**, Richard Howard 1940- *WhoAmP 91, WhoWest 92*
**Stallings**, Robert S 1927- *WhoAmP 91*
**Stallings**, Ronald Denis 1943- *WhoAmL 92*
**Stallings-Lippert**, Carla Katherine 1958- *WhoEnt 92*
**Stallknecht**, Gilbert Franklin 1935- *AmMWSc 92*
**Stallman**, Robert 1930-1980 *TwCSFW 91*
**Stallmann**, Friedemann Wilhelm 1921- *AmMWSc 92*
**Stallmeyer**, J E 1926- *AmMWSc 92*
**Stallo**, Johann Bernhard 1823-1900 *BiInAmS*
**Stallone**, Sylvester 1946- *IntMPA 92*
**Stallone**, Sylvester Enzio 1946- *IntWW 91, WhoEnt 92*
**Stallone**, Thomas M. 1952- *WhoWest 92*
**Stallones**, Reuel 1923- *IntWW 91*
**Stalls**, Madlyn Alberta 1947- *WhoBlA 92*
**Stallwood**, Burton 1939- *WhoAmP 91*
**Stallwood**, Robert Antony 1925- *AmMWSc 92*
**Stallworth**, Alma G. 1932- *WhoBlA 92*
**Stallworth**, Alma Grace 1932- *WhoAmP 91*
**Stallworth**, Ann P. 1932- *WhoBlA 92*
**Stallworth**, Charles Derothea 1906- *WhoBlA 92*
**Stallworth**, Daisy M. 1939- *WhoWest 92*
**Stallworth**, John Lee 1952- *WhoBlA 92*
**Stallworth**, Johnny Van 1945- *WhoMW 92*
**Stallworth**, Oscar B. 1944- *WhoBlA 92*
**Stallworth**, Thomas Fontaine, III *WhoBlA 92*
**Stallworth**, William Fred 1954- *WhoBlA 92*
**Stallworthy**, John 1906- *Who 92, WrDr 92*
**Stallworthy**, Jon 1935- *ConPo 91, IntAu&W 91, WrDr 92*
**Stallworthy**, Jon Howie 1935- *Who 92*
**Stalnaker**, Clair B 1938- *AmMWSc 92*
**Stalnaker**, John Hulbert 1918- *WhoWest 92*
**Staloch**, James Edward, Jr. 1946- *WhoMW 92*
**Staloff**, Arnold Fred 1944- *WhoFI 92*
**Stalon**, Charles Gary 1929- *WhoAmP 91*
**Stals**, Christian Lodewyk 1935- *IntWW 91*
**Stalter**, Richard 1942- *AmMWSc 92*
**Stalzer**, David *DrAPF 91*
**Stalzer**, Richard Francis 1936- *WhoFI 92*
**Stam**, Jos 1924- *AmMWSc 92*
**Stam**, Mart 1899- *DcTwDes*
**Stam**, Paul B, Jr *WhoAmP 91*
**Stamas**, Stephen 1931- *WhoEnt 92*
**Stamatakis**, Carol Marie 1960- *WhoAmP 91*
**Stamatakos**, Louis Constantine 1925- *WhoMW 92*
**Stamatoyannopoulos**, George 1934- *AmMWSc 92, WhoWest 92*
**Stambaugh**, Curvin Donald 1939- *WhoRel 92*
**Stambaugh**, Edgel Pryce 1922- *AmMWSc 92*
**Stambaugh**, Harriett Wynn McCardell 1922- *WhoWest 92*
**Stambaugh**, John Edgar, Jr 1940- *AmMWSc 92*
**Stambaugh**, Phillip F. 1944- *WhoFI 92*
**Stambaugh**, Richard L 1936- *AmMWSc 92*
**Stambaugh**, William James 1927- *AmMWSc 92*
**Stamberg**, Susan Levitt 1938- *WhoEnt 92*
**Stamberger**, Edwin Henry 1916- *WhoFI 92, WhoMW 92*
**Stamberger**, G. Richard 1947- *WhoFI 92*
**Stambler**, Irwin 1924- *IntAu&W 91, WrDr 92*
**Stambler**, Peter *DrAPF 91*
**Stambolian**, George d1991 *NewYTBS 91*
**Stambolic**, Petar 1912- *IntWW 91*
**Stambolisky**, Alexander 1879-1923 *FacFETw*
**Stamboulidis**, George Alexander 1961- *WhoAmL 92*
**Stambrook**, Peter J 1941- *AmMWSc 92*
**Stamenkovic**, Dragi 1920- *Who 92*
**Stamer**, Anthony 1917- *Who 92*
**Stamer**, John Richard 1925- *AmMWSc 92*
**Stamer**, Peter Eric 1939- *AmMWSc 92*
**Stamers-Smith**, Eileen 1929- *Who 92*
**Stames**, William Alexander 1917- *WhoWest 92*
**Stamey**, Judy Johnson 1942- *WhoRel 92*
**Stamey**, Margaret 1933- *WhoAmP 91*
**Stamey**, Sara 1953- *IntAu&W 91*
**Stamey**, Thomas Alexander 1928- *AmMWSc 92*
**Stamey**, William Lee 1922- *AmMWSc 92*
**Stamitz**, Johann 1717?-1757 *BlkwCEP, NewAmDM*
**Stamler**, Jeremiah 1919- *AmMWSc 92*
**Stamler**, Samuel Aaron 1925- *Who 92*
**Stamm**, Charles H 1938- *WhoIns 92*
**Stamm**, Gerald Lee 1936- *WhoMW 92*
**Stamm**, Richard William 1944- *WhoWest 92*
**Stamm**, Robert Franz 1915- *AmMWSc 92*
**Stamm**, Stanley Jerome 1924- *AmMWSc 92*
**Stamm**, Temple Theodore 1905- *Who 92*
**Stammer**, Charles Hugh 1925- *AmMWSc 92*
**Stammler**, Bradley Wright 1955- *WhoFI 92*
**Stamnes**, Knut Henrik 1943- *WhoWest 92*
**Stamos**, James William 1959- *WhoWest 92*
**Stamos**, John J 1924- *WhoAmP 91*
**Stamos**, John James 1924- *WhoAmL 92, WhoMW 92*
**Stamoulis**, Paul Apostle 1952- *WhoAmL 92*
**Stamp** *Who 92*
**Stamp**, Baron 1935- *Who 92*
**Stamp**, Gavin Mark 1948- *IntWW 91, Who 92*
**Stamp**, Robert Miles 1937- *IntAu&W 91*
**Stamp**, Terence 1938- *IntWW 91, WrDr 92*
**Stamp**, Terence 1939- *IntMPA 92*
**Stamp**, Terence Henry 1938- *Who 92*
**Stamper**, Alex *IntAu&W 91X, WrDr 92*
**Stamper**, Alva Walker 1871-1918 *BiInAmS*
**Stamper**, Eugene 1928- *AmMWSc 92*
**Stamper**, Henry J. *WhoBlA 92*
**Stamper**, Hugh Blair 1943- *AmMWSc 92*
**Stamper**, James Harris 1938- *AmMWSc 92*
**Stamper**, Joe Allen 1914- *WhoAmL 92*
**Stamper**, John Andrew 1930- *AmMWSc 92*
**Stamper**, John Trevor 1926- *Who 92*
**Stamper**, Malcolm T. 1925- *IntWW 91*
**Stamper**, Malcolm Theodore 1925- *WhoFI 92, WhoWest 92*
**Stamper**, Martha C 1925- *AmMWSc 92*
**Stampf**, Edward John, Jr 1949- *AmMWSc 92*
**Stampfer**, Friedrich 1874-1957 *EncTR 91*
**Stampfer**, Joseph Frederick 1930- *AmMWSc 92*
**Stampfl**, Rudolf A 1926- *AmMWSc 92*
**Stampfli**, Joseph 1932- *AmMWSc 92*
**Stampfli**, Peter 1937- *WorArt 1980*
**Stampiglia**, Fausto S. 1935- *WhoRel 92*
**Stampley**, Eugene, Jr. 1963- *WhoBlA 92*
**Stampley**, Gilbert Elvin 1943- *WhoBlA 92*
**Stampp**, Kenneth M 1912- *IntAu&W 91, WrDr 92*
**Stamps**, Delores Bolden 1947- *WhoBlA 92*
**Stamps**, George Moreland 1924- *WhoFI 92*
**Stamps**, Herman Franklin 1924- *WhoBlA 92*
**Stamps**, Joe, Jr. 1939- *WhoBlA 92*
**Stamps**, Judy Ann 1947- *AmMWSc 92*
**Stamps**, Leon Preist 1953- *WhoBlA 92*
**Stamps**, Lynman A., Sr. 1940- *WhoBlA 92*
**Stamps**, Randall H 1959- *WhoAmP 91*
**Stamps**, Ranzie Washington 1908- *WhoFI 92*
**Stamps**, Thomas Paty 1952- *WhoAmL 92, WhoFI 92*
**Stamps**, V. O. 1892-1940 *NewAmDM*
**Stamps**, Virgil Oliver 1892-1940 *RelLAm 91*
**Stana**, Regis Richard 1941- *AmMWSc 92*
**Stanaback**, Robert John 1930- *AmMWSc 92*
**Stanacev**, Nikola Ziva 1928- *AmMWSc 92*
**Stanage**, Thomas Shaun *Who 92*
**Stanage**, Willis Franklin 1921- *WhoMW 92*
**Stanaland**, William Whit, Jr. 1930- *WhoFI 92*
**Stanard**, James Earl 1944- *WhoEnt 92*
**Stanasolovich**, Louis Peter 1957- *WhoFI 92*
**Stanat**, Donald Ford 1937- *AmMWSc 92*
**Stanat**, Ruth Ellen 1947- *WhoFI 92*
**Stanaway**, Anne 1931- *WhoEnt 92*
**Stanback**, Thurman W. 1922- *WhoBlA 92*
**Stanberry**, Lawrence Raymond 1948- *AmMWSc 92*
**Stanbery**, Robert Charles 1947- *WhoMW 92*
**Stanbridge**, Brian 1924- *Who 92*
**Stanbridge**, Eric John 1942- *AmMWSc 92*
**Stanbridge**, Leslie Cyril 1920- *Who 92*
**Stanbridge**, Roger Philip 1941- *WhoFI 92*
**Stanbro**, William David 1946- *AmMWSc 92*
**Stanbrook**, Clive St George Clement 1948- *Who 92*
**Stanbrook**, Ivor Robert 1924- *Who 92*
**Stanbrough**, Jesse Hedrick, Jr 1918- *AmMWSc 92*
**Stanbury**, David McNeil 1952- *AmMWSc 92*
**Stanbury**, John Bruton 1915- *AmMWSc 92*
**Stanbury**, Richard Vivian Macaulay 1916- *Who 92*
**Stanbury**, Robert Douglas George 1929- *IntWW 91*
**Stanbury**, Sydney William 1919- *Who 92*
**Stancampiano**, Charles Vincent 1948- *AmMWSc 92*
**Stancati**, John F 1935- *WhoAmP 91*
**Stancel**, George Michael 1944- *AmMWSc 92*
**Stancell**, Arnold F. 1936- *WhoBlA 92*
**Stancell**, Dolores Wilson Pegram 1936- *WhoBlA 92*
**Stancer**, Harvey C 1926- *AmMWSc 92*
**Stanchfield**, James Ernest 1952- *AmMWSc 92*
**Stanchik**, Dennis John 1954- *WhoAmL 92*
**Stancik**, Violet Joan Gower 1925- *WhoFI 92, WhoMW 92*
**Stancil**, Frank E *WhoAmP 91*
**Stancil**, Steven Lyle 1952- *WhoAmP 91*
**Stancl**, Donald Lee 1940- *AmMWSc 92*
**Stancl**, Mildred Luzader *AmMWSc 92*
**Stancliffe**, David Staffurth 1942- *Who 92*
**Stancliffe**, Martin John 1944- *Who 92*
**Stanculescu**, Victor Atanasie 1928- *IntWW 91*
**Stancyk**, Stephen Edward 1946- *AmMWSc 92*
**Stanczyk**, Frank Zygmunt 1936- *AmMWSc 92*
**Stanczyk**, Martin Henry 1930- *AmMWSc 92*
**Stanczyk**, Matthew John 1961- *WhoAmL 92*
**Standaert**, Frank George 1929- *AmMWSc 92*
**Standaert**, James V 1938- *WhoIns 92*
**Standard**, Franklin 1949- *BlkOlyM*
**Standard**, Kenneth 1920- *Who 92*
**Standard**, Raymond Linwood 1925- *WhoBlA 92*
**Standberry**, Herman Lee 1945- *WhoMW 92*
**Standefer**, Jimmy Clayton 1941- *AmMWSc 92*
**Standen**, John Derek 1937- *WrDr 92*
**Stander**, Jay Randy 1951- *WhoEnt 92*
**Stander**, Joseph W 1928- *AmMWSc 92*
**Stander**, Lionel 1908- *IntMPA 92*
**Stander**, Richard Ramsay, Sr. 1919- *WhoFI 92*
**Stander**, Siegfried 1935- *WrDr 92*
**Standford**, Geoffery Brian 1916- *AmMWSc 92*
**Standifer**, Ben H. 1934- *WhoBlA 92*
**Standifer**, Leonides Calmet, Jr 1925- *AmMWSc 92*
**Standifer**, Lonnie Nathaniel 1926- *AmMWSc 92, WhoBlA 92*

**Standiford**, Les *DrAPF 91*
**Standil**, Sidney 1926- *AmMWSc 92*
**Standing**, Charles Nicholas 1943- *AmMWSc 92*
**Standing**, John *Who 92*
**Standing**, Keith M 1928- *AmMWSc 92*
**Standing**, Kenneth Graham 1925- *AmMWSc 92*
**Standing**, Marshall B *AmMWSc 92*
**Standing**, Sue *DrAPF 91*
**Standing Bear**, Luther 1868-1947? *BenetAL 91*
**Standish**, Buck *TwCWW 91*
**Standish**, Burt L. *BenetAL 91*
**Standish**, Charles Junior 1926- *AmMWSc 92*
**Standish**, Craig Peter 1953- *IntAu&W 91*
**Standish**, E Myles, Jr 1939- *AmMWSc 92*
**Standish**, John Spencer 1925- *WhoFI 92*
**Standish**, Lorraine *DrAPF 91*
**Standish**, Miles 1584?-1656 *BenetAL 91*
**Standish**, Norman Weston 1930- *AmMWSc 92, WhoMW 92*
**Standish**, Samuel Miles 1923- *AmMWSc 92*
**Standish**, William Lloyd 1930- *WhoAmL 92*
**Standlee**, William Jasper 1929- *AmMWSc 92*
**Standley**, Robert Dean 1935- *AmMWSc 92*
**Standley**, Sherrianne Maddox 1945- *WhoMW 92*
**Standring**, James Douglas 1951- *WhoWest 92*
**Stanek**, Alan Edward 1939- *WhoEnt 92, WhoWest 92*
**Stanek**, Eldon Keith 1941- *AmMWSc 92*
**Stanek**, Karen Ann 1950- *AmMWSc 92*
**Stanek**, Peter 1937- *AmMWSc 92*
**Stanesby**, Derek Malcolm 1931- *Who 92*
**Stanevich**, Kenneth William 1958- *WhoMW 92*
**Stanfield**, Andrew William 1927-198-? *BlkOlyM*
**Stanfield**, Anne *IntAu&W 91X, WrDr 92*
**Stanfield**, James Armond 1917- *AmMWSc 92*
**Stanfield**, James Caleb 1923- *WhoAmL 92*
**Stanfield**, Kenneth Charles 1942- *AmMWSc 92*
**Stanfield**, Manie K 1931- *AmMWSc 92*
**Stanfield**, Michael Dean 1943- *WhoWest 92*
**Stanfield**, Robert Lorne 1914- *IntWW 91, Who 92*
**Stanfill**, Dennis C. 1927- *IntMPA 92*
**Stanfill**, Dennis Carothers 1927- *WhoWest 92*
**Stanfill**, Dorothy *DrAPF 91*
**Stanfill**, Jeffery Kenneth 1961- *WhoRel 92*
**Stanford**, Alice Louise 1946- *WhoFI 92*
**Stanford**, Augustus Lamar, Jr 1931- *AmMWSc 92*
**Stanford**, Barbara 1943- *WrDr 92*
**Stanford**, Charles Villiers 1852-1924 *NewAmDM*
**Stanford**, Derek 1918- *WrDr 92*
**Stanford**, Don 1913- *WrDr 92*
**Stanford**, Geoffrey 1916- *AmMWSc 92*
**Stanford**, George Stailing 1928- *AmMWSc 92, WhoMW 92*
**Stanford**, Jack Arthur 1947- *AmMWSc 92, WhoWest 92*
**Stanford**, Jack Wayne 1935- *AmMWSc 92*
**Stanford**, James M. *WhoFI 92, WhoWest 92*
**Stanford**, John Henry 1938- *WhoBlA 92*
**Stanford**, John R. 1916- *WhoRel 92*
**Stanford**, Lynn d1991 *NewYTBS 91*
**Stanford**, Marlene A *AmMWSc 92*
**Stanford**, Melvin Joseph 1932- *WhoMW 92*
**Stanford**, Peter James 1961- *Who 92*
**Stanford**, Peter Maxwell d1991 *Who 92N*
**Stanford**, Robert August 1927- *WhoWest 92*
**Stanford**, Sondra 1942- *WrDr 92*
**Stanford-Tuck**, Robert 1916-1987 *FacFETw*
**Stang**, Arnold 1927- *IntMPA 92*
**Stang**, Arnold 1928- *WhoEnt 92*
**Stang**, Axel 1904-1974 *BiDExR*
**Stang**, Barry 1950- *WhoAmP 91*
**Stang**, Elden James 1940- *AmMWSc 92*
**Stang**, Jeanette Teresa 1928- *WhoRel 92*
**Stang**, Louis George 1919- *AmMWSc 92*
**Stang**, Mary Assunta 1920- *WhoRel 92*
**Stang**, Paul David 1954- *WhoAmL 92*
**Stang**, Peter John 1941- *AmMWSc 92*
**Stang**, Robert George 1938- *AmMWSc 92, WhoWest 92*
**Stanga**, Luzia *EncAmaz 91*
**Stangberg**, Einar V. 1933- *WhoFI 92*
**Stange**, Hugo 1921- *AmMWSc 92*
**Stange**, James Henry 1930- *WhoMW 92*
**Stange**, James R 1945- *WhoAmP 91*
**Stange**, Lionel Alvin 1935- *AmMWSc 92*
**Stangeby**, Peter Christian 1943- *AmMWSc 92*
**Stangeland**, Arlan Inghart 1930- *WhoAmP 91*
**Stangeland**, Ole Ingvaldson 1903- *WhoMW 92*
**Stangeland**, Roger Earl 1929- *WhoWest 92*
**Stanger**, Andrew L 1948- *AmMWSc 92*
**Stanger**, David Harry 1939- *Who 92*
**Stanger**, David N. 1926- *WhoFI 92*
**Stanger**, Philip Charles 1920- *AmMWSc 92*
**Stanger**, Richard Leonard 1935- *WhoRel 92*
**Stanghellini**, Michael Eugene 1940- *AmMWSc 92*
**Stangl**, Franz 1908-1971 *EncTR 91 [port]*
**Stangl**, Jean 1928- *SmATA 67 [port]*
**Stangland**, Eider Clifford 1922- *WhoEnt 92*
**Stangland**, Thomas Carl 1947- *WhoEnt 92*
**Stanhagen**, William Harold 1928- *WhoAmP 91*
**Stanhaus**, James Steven 1945- *WhoAmL 92*
**Stanhope** *Who 92*
**Stanhope**, Andrew 1946- *WhoFI 92*
**Stanhope**, Charles 1753-1816 *BlkwCEP*
**Stanhope**, William Henry 1951- *WhoAmL 92*
**Staniar**, Burton B. *LesBEnT 92 [port]*
**Staniec**, Marjan Peter 1914- *WhoAmL 92*
**Staniecki**, H. Mark 1959- *WhoRel 92*
**Stanier**, Alexander Beville Gibbons 1899- *Who 92*
**Stanier**, Germaine 1920- *IntWW 91*
**Stanier**, John 1925- *Who 92*
**Stanier**, John Wilfred 1925- *IntWW 91*
**Staniforth**, David William 1919- *AmMWSc 92*
**Staniforth**, John Arthur Reginald 1912- *Who 92*
**Staniforth**, Richard John 1946- *AmMWSc 92*
**Staniforth**, Robert Arthur 1917- *AmMWSc 92*
**Stanionis**, Victor Adam 1938- *AmMWSc 92*
**Stanish**, John Richard 1945- *WhoAmP 91*
**Stanislao**, Bettie Chloe Carter 1934- *AmMWSc 92*
**Stanislao**, Joseph 1928- *AmMWSc 92*
**Stanislaus**, Gregory K. 1957- *WhoBlA 92*
**Stanislaus**, Lamuel A. 1921- *IntWW 91*
**Stanislavsky**, Konstantin Sergeevich 1863-1938 *SovUnBD*
**Stanislavsky**, Konstantin Sergeyevich 1865-1938 *FacFETw*
**Stanislaw I** *BlkwCEP*
**Stanislaw II** *BlkwCEP*
**Stanislaw**, Richard John 1939- *WhoMW 92*
**Stanislawski**, Jeanne Florence 1947- *WhoEnt 92*
**Staniswalis**, Chip 1949- *WhoAmP 91*
**Stanisz**, Andrzej Maciej 1961- *AmMWSc 92*
**Staniszewski**, Stefan 1931- *IntWW 91, Who 92*
**Stanitski**, Conrad Leon 1939- *AmMWSc 92, WhoMW 92*
**Staniukynas**, Antanas *DcAmImH*
**Stanius**, Brad G 1946- *WhoAmP 91*
**Stankard**, Francis Xavier 1932- *WhoFI 92*
**Stankavage**, David Edwin 1955- *WhoEnt 92*
**Stankee**, Glen Allen 1953- *WhoAmL 92*
**Stankevich**, Mark Anthony 1953- *WhoEnt 92*
**Stankevich**, Sergey Borisovich 1954- *SovUnBD*
**Stankewicz**, Mary Jane 1944- *WhoMW 92*
**Stankiewicz**, Raymond 1932- *AmMWSc 92*
**Stankiewicz**, William Roy Stanley 1955- *WhoMW 92*
**Stankiewicz**, Witold 1919- *IntWW 91*
**Stankiewicz**, Wladyslaw Jozef 1922- *WrDr 92*
**Stanko**, Joseph Anthony 1941- *AmMWSc 92*
**Stankovich**, Marian Theresa 1947- *AmMWSc 92*
**Stanley** *Who 92*
**Stanley Brothers** *NewAmDM*
**Stanley**, Anthony Dumond 1810-1853 *BiInAmS*
**Stanley**, Arthur Jehu, Jr. 1901- *WhoAmL 92, WhoMW 92*
**Stanley**, Arthur W. *WhoBlA 92*
**Stanley**, Bennett *IntAu&W 91X, WrDr 92*
**Stanley**, Billy Glenn 1953- *WhoWest 92*
**Stanley**, Bruce McLaren 1948- *WhoAmL 92*
**Stanley**, Carol Jones 1947- *WhoBlA 92*
**Stanley**, Carter 1926-1966 *NewAmDM*
**Stanley**, Charles Frazier 1932- *WhoRel 92*
**Stanley**, Charles Malcolm, Jr. 1933- *WhoWest 92*
**Stanley**, Chuck *TwCWW 91*
**Stanley**, Columbus Landon, Sr. 1922- *WhoBlA 92*
**Stanley**, Curtis E. 1917- *WhoBlA 92*
**Stanley**, Daniel Calvin, Jr. 1948- *WhoAmL 92*
**Stanley**, Daniel Jean 1934- *AmMWSc 92*
**Stanley**, Darryl Scott 1966- *WhoRel 92*
**Stanley**, David 1935- *WhoMW 92*
**Stanley**, David G *WhoAmP 91*
**Stanley**, David Warwick 1939- *AmMWSc 92*
**Stanley**, Denise Ramsburg 1954- *WhoAmL 92*
**Stanley**, Diane 1943- *WrDr 92*
**Stanley**, Edward Livingston 1919- *AmMWSc 92*
**Stanley**, Ellis M., Sr. 1951- *WhoBlA 92*
**Stanley**, Eric Gerald 1923- *IntWW 91, Who 92*
**Stanley**, Eugene 1916- *WhoBlA 92*
**Stanley**, Evan Richard 1944- *AmMWSc 92*
**Stanley**, Fay Grissom *ConAu 133*
**Stanley**, Forrest Edwin 1942- *WhoWest 92*
**Stanley**, Fred 1955- *WhoAmP 91*
**Stanley**, George Dabney, Jr. 1948- *WhoWest 92*
**Stanley**, George Geoffrey 1953- *AmMWSc 92*
**Stanley**, George M 1905- *AmMWSc 92*
**Stanley**, Gerald R 1943- *AmMWSc 92*
**Stanley**, Glynne Roy 1954- *WhoAmP 91*
**Stanley**, H Eugene 1941- *AmMWSc 92*
**Stanley**, Harold Russell 1923- *AmMWSc 92*
**Stanley**, Helen Camille *WhoEnt 92*
**Stanley**, Henry M. 1841-1904 *BenetAL 91*
**Stanley**, Henry Sydney Herbert Cloete 1920- *IntWW 91, Who 92*
**Stanley**, Hilbert Dennis 1931- *WhoBlA 92*
**Stanley**, Hugh P 1926- *AmMWSc 92*
**Stanley**, Jack R. 1943- *WhoEnt 92*
**Stanley**, James Richard 1931- *WhoAmL 92*
**Stanley**, Jeanie Ricketts 1946- *WhoAmP 91*
**Stanley**, Jerome Merlin 1941- *WhoMW 92*
**Stanley**, John Langley 1937- *WhoWest 92*
**Stanley**, John Mallalieu 1941- *Who 92*
**Stanley**, John Paul 1942- *Who 92*
**Stanley**, John Pearson 1915- *AmMWSc 92*
**Stanley**, Jon G 1937- *AmMWSc 92*
**Stanley**, Julian C., Jr. 1918- *WrDr 92*
**Stanley**, Julian Cecil, Jr. 1918- *IntWW 91*
**Stanley**, Justin Armstrong 1911- *WhoAmL 92*
**Stanley**, Kathleen Goold 1943- *WhoAmP 91*
**Stanley**, Kenneth Earl 1947- *AmMWSc 92*
**Stanley**, Kerry Jo 1965- *WhoWest 92*
**Stanley**, Kim 1925- *IntMPA 92*
**Stanley**, LaNett Lorraine 1962- *WhoAmP 91*
**Stanley**, Luticious Bryan, Jr *AmMWSc 92*
**Stanley**, Malcolm McClain 1916- *AmMWSc 92*
**Stanley**, Marc Gene 1943- *WhoAmP 91*
**Stanley**, Margaret Dureta Sexton 1931- *WhoMW 92*
**Stanley**, Margaret King 1929- *WhoEnt 92*
**Stanley**, Marjorie Thines 1928- *WhoFI 92*
**Stanley**, Marlyse Reed 1934- *WhoWest 92*
**Stanley**, Melissa Sue Millam 1931- *AmMWSc 92*
**Stanley**, Norman Francis 1916- *AmMWSc 92*
**Stanley**, Oliver 1925- *WrDr 92*
**Stanley**, Oliver Duncan 1925- *Who 92*
**Stanley**, Pamela Margaret d1991 *Who 92N*
**Stanley**, Pamela Mary 1947- *AmMWSc 92*
**Stanley**, Patricia Mary 1948- *AmMWSc 92*
**Stanley**, Paul Loyd 1953- *WhoMW 92*
**Stanley**, Ralph 1927- *NewAmDM, WhoEnt 92*
**Stanley**, Richard Daniel 1960- *WhoFI 92*
**Stanley**, Richard Holt 1932- *WhoMW 92*
**Stanley**, Richard Peter 1944- *AmMWSc 92*
**Stanley**, Richard W 1928- *AmMWSc 92*
**Stanley**, Robert Lauren 1921- *AmMWSc 92*
**Stanley**, Robert Lee, Jr 1940- *AmMWSc 92*
**Stanley**, Robert Weir 1925- *AmMWSc 92*
**Stanley**, Rolfe S 1931- *AmMWSc 92*
**Stanley**, Ronald Alwin 1939- *AmMWSc 92*
**Stanley**, Stephen Charles 1958- *WhoAmL 92*
**Stanley**, Steven Mitchell 1941- *AmMWSc 92*
**Stanley**, Susie Cunningham 1948- *WhoRel 92*
**Stanley**, Theodore H 1940- *AmMWSc 92*
**Stanley**, Thomas 1625?-1678 *RfGEnL 91*
**Stanley**, Vaughan 1950- *WhoRel 92*
**Stanley**, Vincent Cotton 1952- *WhoFI 92*
**Stanley**, Warren S 1948- *WhoIns 92*
**Stanley**, Wendell Meredith 1904-1971 *WhoNob 90*
**Stanley**, Wendell Meredith, Jr 1932- *AmMWSc 92*
**Stanley**, William 1829-1909 *ScFEYrs*
**Stanley**, William 1858-1916 *BiInAmS*
**Stanley**, William, Jr. 1919- *WhoAmL 92*
**Stanley**, William Buteau 1929- *WhoFI 92*
**Stanley**, William Daniel 1937- *AmMWSc 92*
**Stanley**, William Foster 1952- *WhoMW 92*
**Stanley**, William Lyons 1916- *AmMWSc 92*
**Stanley**, Winifred Claire *WhoAmL 92*
**Stanley**, Woodrow 1950- *WhoAmP 91, WhoBlA 92*
**Stanley of Alderley**, Baron 1927- *Who 92*
**Stanley Price**, Peter 1911- *Who 92*
**Stanley-Soulen**, Melanie 1959- *WhoRel 92*
**Stanmore**, Roger Dale 1957- *WhoBlA 92*
**Stann**, John Anthony 1947- *WhoFI 92*
**Stann**, Robert 1938- *WhoIns 92*
**Stannard**, Carl R, Jr 1935- *AmMWSc 92*
**Stannard**, Colin Percy 1924- *Who 92*
**Stannard**, Daphne Evon 1963- *WhoWest 92*
**Stannard**, J Newell 1910- *AmMWSc 92*
**Stannard**, John Anthony 1931- *Who 92*
**Stannard**, Martin 1947- *WrDr 92*
**Stannard**, Robert J 1951- *WhoAmP 91*
**Stannard**, W M *ScFEYrs*
**Stannard**, William A 1931- *AmMWSc 92*
**Stanners**, Clifford Paul 1937- *AmMWSc 92*
**Stannett**, Vivian Thomas 1917- *AmMWSc 92*
**Stanny**, Gary 1953- *WhoMW 92*
**Stano**, Jerome *WhoAmP 91*
**Stano**, Lester Paul 1947- *WhoRel 92*
**Stanojevic**, Caslav V 1928- *AmMWSc 92*
**Stanonis**, David Joseph 1926- *AmMWSc 92*
**Stanonis**, Francis Leo 1931- *AmMWSc 92*
**Stanovnik**, Janez 1922- *IntWW 91*
**Stanovsky**, Joseph Jerry 1928- *AmMWSc 92*
**Stans**, Maurice H 1908- *WhoAmP 91*
**Stans**, Maurice Hubert 1908- *IntWW 91*
**Stansberry**, Domenic *DrAPF 91*
**Stansberry**, Mark A 1956- *WhoAmP 91*
**Stansbery**, David Honor 1926- *AmMWSc 92*
**Stansbrey**, John Joseph 1918- *AmMWSc 92, WhoMW 92*
**Stansbury**, Benjamin H, Jr *WhoAmP 91*
**Stansbury**, Clayton Cresvell 1932- *WhoBlA 92*
**Stansbury**, E E 1918- *AmMWSc 92*
**Stansbury**, Harry Adams, Jr 1917- *AmMWSc 92*
**Stansbury**, Joseph 1742?-1809 *BenetAL 91*
**Stansbury**, Markhum L. 1942- *WhoBlA 92*
**Stansbury**, Philip Roger 1931- *WhoAmL 92*
**Stansbury**, Terence R. 1961- *WhoBlA 92*
**Stansbury**, Vernon Carver, Jr. 1939- *WhoBlA 92*
**Stansby**, John 1930- *Who 92*
**Stansby**, Maurice Earl 1908- *AmMWSc 92*
**Stansel**, John Charles 1935- *AmMWSc 92*
**Stansell**, Leland Edwin, Jr. 1934- *WhoAmL 92*
**Stansell**, Ronald Bruce 1945- *WhoFI 92*
**Stansfield**, Barry Lionel 1942- *AmMWSc 92*
**Stansfield**, George Norman 1926- *IntWW 91, Who 92*
**Stansfield**, James Warden 1906- *Who 92*
**Stansfield**, Mary Jo 1924- *WhoAmP 91*
**Stansfield**, Roger Ellis 1926- *AmMWSc 92, WhoMW 92*
**Stansfield**, William D 1930- *AmMWSc 92*
**Stansfield Smith**, Colin 1932- *Who 92*
**Stansgate**, Viscountcy of *Who 92*
**Stanskas**, Helen Marie 1964- *WhoFI 92*
**Stansky**, Peter 1932- *WrDr 92*
**Stansky**, Peter David Lyman 1932- *IntAu&W 91*
**Stansloski**, Donald Wayne 1939- *AmMWSc 92*
**Stansly**, Philip Gerald *AmMWSc 92*
**Stanton**, Audrey Ann 1922- *WhoAmP 91*
**Stanton**, Benjamin R. 1930- *WhoFI 92*
**Stanton**, Bethelene 1931- *WhoWest 92*
**Stanton**, Beverly A. 1944- *WhoBlA 92*
**Stanton**, Bruce Alan 1952- *AmMWSc 92*
**Stanton**, Charles Madison 1942- *AmMWSc 92*
**Stanton**, David 1942- *Who 92*
**Stanton**, Edwin McMasters 1814-1869 *AmPolLe*
**Stanton**, Elizabeth Cady 1815-1902 *BenetAL 91, HanAmWH, PorAmW [port], RComAH*
**Stanton**, Frank *LesBEnT 92*
**Stanton**, Frank 1908- *IntWW 91*
**Stanton**, Frank 1929- *WhoFI 92*
**Stanton**, Frank L. 1857-1927 *BenetAL 91*
**Stanton**, Garth Michael 1933- *AmMWSc 92*

**Stanton,** George Edwin 1944- *AmMWSc 92*
**Stanton,** George Patrick, Jr. 1933- *WhoAmL 92*
**Stanton,** Gregory Ray 1958- *WhoFI 92*
**Stanton,** Harry Dean 1926- *IntMPA 92, WhoEnt 92*
**Stanton,** Hubert Coleman 1930- *AmMWSc 92*
**Stanton,** James Alexander, IV 1949- *WhoAmL 92*
**Stanton,** James Vincent 1932- *WhoAmP 91*
**Stanton,** Janice D. 1928- *WhoBlA 92*
**Stanton,** Jeanne Frances 1920- *WhoMW 92*
**Stanton,** John Maurice 1918- *Who 92*
**Stanton,** John William 1924- *WhoAmP 91*
**Stanton,** Joseph *DrAPF 91*
**Stanton,** K Neil *AmMWSc 92*
**Stanton,** Kathleen Susanne 1962- *WhoRel 92*
**Stanton,** Lewis Harris 1954- *WhoWest 92*
**Stanton,** Louis Lee 1927- *WhoAmL 92*
**Stanton,** Margaret Elizabeth 1948- *WhoEnt 92*
**Stanton,** Marietta 1948- *ConAu 134*
**Stanton,** Martin Baron 1960- *WhoAmL 92*
**Stanton,** Maura *DrAPF 91*
**Stanton,** Mearl Fredrick 1922- *AmMWSc 92*
**Stanton,** Nancy Kahn 1948- *AmMWSc 92*
**Stanton,** Nancy Lea 1944- *AmMWSc 92*
**Stanton,** Noel Russell 1937- *AmMWSc 92*
**Stanton,** Paul *IntAu&W 91X, WrDr 92*
**Stanton,** Richard Edmund 1931- *AmMWSc 92*
**Stanton,** Robert E 1947- *AmMWSc 92*
**Stanton,** Robert James, Jr 1931- *AmMWSc 92*
**Stanton,** Robert Joseph 1947- *AmMWSc 92*
**Stanton,** Roger D. 1938- *WhoAmL 92, WhoMW 92*
**Stanton,** Sandra Sunquist 1946- *WhoMW 92*
**Stanton,** Thaddeus Brian 1951- *AmMWSc 92*
**Stanton,** Thomas H. *WhoAmL 92*
**Stanton,** Thomas Joyce, Jr. 1928- *WhoFI 92*
**Stanton,** Thomas Mitchell 1922- *WhoAmL 92*
**Stanton,** Tom Arden 1957- *WhoRel 92*
**Stanton,** Toni Lynn 1944- *AmMWSc 92*
**Stanton,** Vance *WrDr 92*
**Stanton,** Will *DrAPF 91*
**Stanton,** William Alexander 1915- *AmMWSc 92*
**Stanton,** William John, Jr. 1919- *WhoWest 92*
**Stanton,** William Taylor 1926- *WhoMW 92*
**Stanton-Hicks,** Michael D'Arcy 1931- *WhoMW 92*
**Stanton-Jones,** Richard d1991 *Who 92N*
**Stanuszek,** Mark Edward 1948- *WhoMW 92*
**Stanwick,** Glenn 1928- *AmMWSc 92*
**Stanwicks,** Thomas Francis 1963- *WhoEnt 92*
**Stanwyck,** Barbara 1907-1990 *AnObit 1990, FacFETw*
**Stanwyck,** Steven Jay 1944- *WhoAmL 92*
**Stanyard,** Hermine P. 1928- *WhoBlA 92*
**Stanyer,** John Turner 1920- *Who 92*
**Stanyer,** Peter 1952- *TwCPaSc*
**Stanzak,** Joseph Stanley 1953- *WhoAmL 92*
**Stanzel,** Franz Karl 1923- *IntWW 91*
**Stapel,** Paul Frederick 1940- *WhoEnt 92*
**Stapelbroek,** Maryn G 1947- *AmMWSc 92*
**Stapella,** Paul Stanley 1959- *WhoMW 92*
**Stapert,** John Charles 1942- *WhoRel 92*
**Staph,** Horace E 1921- *AmMWSc 92*
**Staple,** David 1930- *Who 92*
**Staple,** Peter Hugh 1917- *AmMWSc 92*
**Staple,** Tom Weinberg 1931- *AmMWSc 92*
**Stapledon,** Olaf 1886-1950 *ScFEYrs, TwCSFW 91*
**Staples,** Basil George 1914- *AmMWSc 92*
**Staples,** Danny Lew 1935- *WhoAmP 91*
**Staples,** Edward Eric 1910- *Who 92*
**Staples,** Emily Anne 1929- *WhoAmP 91*
**Staples,** Gary Victor 1940- *WhoAmP 91*
**Staples,** Gracie Bonds 1957- *WhoBlA 92*
**Staples,** Hubert Anthony Justin 1929- *Who 92*
**Staples,** James Alan 1938- *WhoAmP 91*
**Staples,** Jeffery Mark 1961- *WhoFI 92*
**Staples,** Jon T 1938- *AmMWSc 92*
**Staples,** Justin *Who 92*
**Staples,** Lloyd William 1908- *AmMWSc 92*
**Staples,** Lyle Newton 1945- *WhoAmL 92, WhoFI 92*
**Staples,** M. J. *WrDr 92*
**Staples,** Michael 1949- *WhoFI 92*
**Staples,** Reginald 1911- *WrDr 92*
**Staples,** Reginald Thomas 1911- *IntAu&W 91*
**Staples,** Richard Cromwell 1926- *AmMWSc 92*
**Staples,** Robert 1916- *AmMWSc 92*
**Staples,** Robert E. 1942- *WhoBlA 92*
**Staples,** Robert Edward 1931- *AmMWSc 92*
**Staples,** Robert Eugene 1942- *IntAu&W 91, WhoWest 92, WrDr 92*
**Staples,** Thomas 1905- *Who 92*
**Staples,** William Cabell 1922- *WhoAmP 91*
**Stapleton,** Alfred *Who 92*
**Stapleton,** Charles M 1939- *WhoIns 92*
**Stapleton,** Deryck Cameron 1918- *Who 92*
**Stapleton,** Guy 1935- *Who 92*
**Stapleton,** Harvey James 1934- *AmMWSc 92*
**Stapleton,** Henry Alfred 1913- *Who 92*
**Stapleton,** Henry Edward Champneys 1932- *Who 92*
**Stapleton,** Henry F 1930- *WhoAmP 91*
**Stapleton,** James H 1931- *AmMWSc 92*
**Stapleton,** Jean *IntMPA 92, WhoEnt 92*
**Stapleton,** John F 1921- *AmMWSc 92*
**Stapleton,** John Mason 1932- *WhoRel 92*
**Stapleton,** John Owen 1951- *WhoAmL 92*
**Stapleton,** Judy *TwCPaSc*
**Stapleton,** Katharine Hall 1919- *WhoWest 92*
**Stapleton,** Kathleen Louise 1933- *WhoWest 92*
**Stapleton,** Kenneth Ray 1959- *WhoEnt 92*
**Stapleton,** Larrick B. 1936- *WhoAmL 92*
**Stapleton,** Laurence *DrAPF 91*
**Stapleton,** Laurence 1911- *WrDr 92*
**Stapleton,** Marylyn *WhoAmP 91*
**Stapleton,** Marylyn A. 1936- *WhoBlA 92*
**Stapleton,** Maureen 1925- *IntMPA 92, WhoEnt 92*
**Stapleton,** Patrick J *WhoAmP 91*
**Stapleton,** Richard Christopher 1942- *Who 92*
**Stapleton,** Ronald James 1941- *WhoFI 92*
**Stapleton,** Shirley Ann 1936- *WhoWest 92*
**Stapleton,** Thomas Joseph, Jr 1947- *WhoAmP 91*
**Stapleton,** Walter K 1934- *WhoAmP 91*
**Stapleton,** Walter King 1934- *WhoAmL 92*
**Stapleton-Cotton** *Who 92*
**Stapley,** Edward Olley 1927- *AmMWSc 92*
**Staponski,** Earle F 1926- *WhoAmP 91*
**Stapp,** Henry P 1928- *AmMWSc 92*
**Stapp,** John Paul 1910- *AmMWSc 92, IntWW 91*
**Stapp,** William B 1929- *AmMWSc 92*
**Stapp,** William Beebe 1929- *WhoMW 92*
**Stapper,** Charles Henri 1934- *AmMWSc 92*
**Staprans,** Armand 1931- *AmMWSc 92*
**Staprans,** Raimonds 1926- *WhoWest 92*
**Star,** Aura E 1930- *AmMWSc 92*
**Star,** Jeffrey L 1953- *AmMWSc 92*
**Star,** Joseph 1916- *AmMWSc 92*
**Star,** Martin Leon 1928- *AmMWSc 92*
**Star,** Solomon Emanuel 1910- *WhoAmL 92*
**Starace,** Achille 1889-1945 *BiDExR*
**Starace,** Anthony Francis 1945- *AmMWSc 92*
**Staran,** John D. 1957- *WhoAmL 92*
**Staravoytova,** Galina Vasil'evna 1946- *SovUnBD*
**Starbird,** Alfred D 1912- *AmMWSc 92*
**Starbird,** Michael Peter 1948- *AmMWSc 92*
**Starbird,** Robert William 1949- *WhoEnt 92*
**Starbuck,** George *DrAPF 91*
**Starbuck,** George 1931- *ConPo 91, WrDr 92*
**Starcevich,** Bradley Kim 1954- *WhoMW 92*
**Starch,** Daniel 1883-1979 *ConAu 133*
**Starcher,** Barry Chapin 1938- *AmMWSc 92*
**Starcher,** Cody A 1945- *WhoAmP 91*
**Starcher,** Virginia Jolliffe *WhoAmP 91*
**Starchman,** Dale Edward 1941- *AmMWSc 92*
**Starck,** Christian 1937- *IntWW 91*
**Starck,** Philippe 1940- *DcTwDes*
**Starck,** Philippe-Patrick 1949- *IntWW 91*
**Stare,** Fredrick J 1910- *AmMWSc 92*
**Starer,** Robert 1924- *NewAmDM, WhoEnt 92*
**Starewicz,** Artur 1917- *Who 92*
**Starfield,** Barbara 1932- *IntWW 91*
**Starfield,** Barbara Helen 1932- *AmMWSc 92*
**Stargell,** Willie 1940- *FacFETw*
**Stargell,** Willie 1941- *WhoBlA 92*
**Starger,** Martin *LesBEnT 92*
**Starger,** Martin 1932- *IntMPA 92*
**Starhawk** 1951- *RelLAm 91*
**Starhemberg,** Ernst Rudiger 1899-1956 *EncTR 91*
**Starhemberg,** Ernst Rudiger C, Prince of 1899-1956 *BiDExR*
**Starich,** Gale Hanson *AmMWSc 92*
**Staring,** Graydon Shaw 1923- *WhoAmL 92, WhoWest 92*
**Stark,** Andrew 1916- *Who 92*
**Stark,** Andrew Alexander Steel 1916- *IntWW 91*
**Stark,** Antony Albert 1953- *AmMWSc 92*
**Stark,** Barbara Joan 1952- *WhoAmL 92*
**Stark,** Benjamin Chapman 1949- *AmMWSc 92*
**Stark,** Benjamin Louis 1960- *WhoEnt 92*
**Stark,** Charles B. 1947- *WhoAmL 92*
**Stark,** Claude Alan 1935-1980 *ConAu 134*
**Stark,** Cordelia *EncAmaz 91*
**Stark,** Debra Pogrund 1961- *WhoAmL 92*
**Stark,** Dennis Michael 1942- *AmMWSc 92*
**Stark,** Donald Morrison 1945- *WhoEnt 92*
**Stark,** Egon 1920- *AmMWSc 92*
**Stark,** Ethel 1916- *WhoEnt 92*
**Stark,** Forrest Otto 1930- *AmMWSc 92*
**Stark,** Fortney H. 1931- *AlmAP 92 [port], WhoAmP 91*
**Stark,** Fortney Hillman 1931- *WhoWest 92*
**Stark,** Francis C, Jr 1919- *AmMWSc 92*
**Stark,** Freya 1893- *Who 92, WrDr 92*
**Stark,** Freya Madeline 1893- *IntWW 91*
**Stark,** George Robert 1933- *AmMWSc 92, Who 92*
**Stark,** Gregory Francis 1955- *WhoFI 92*
**Stark,** Harold Emil 1920- *AmMWSc 92*
**Stark,** Harold Mead 1939- *AmMWSc 92*
**Stark,** Harold R 1880-1972 *FacFETw*
**Stark,** Harriet *ScFEYrs A*
**Stark,** Henry 1938- *AmMWSc 92*
**Stark,** J P, Jr 1938- *AmMWSc 92*
**Stark,** Jack Everett 1931- *WhoWest 92*
**Stark,** Jack Lee 1934- *WhoWest 92*
**Stark,** James Cornelius 1941- *AmMWSc 92*
**Stark,** Jay Irwin 1944- *WhoFI 92*
**Stark,** Jeremiah Milton 1922- *AmMWSc 92*
**Stark,** Jerry Keith 1952- *WhoRel 92*
**Stark,** Joel 1930- *AmMWSc 92*
**Stark,** Johannes 1874-1957 *EncTR 91 [port], WhoNob 90*
**Stark,** John *WrDr 92*
**Stark,** John, Jr 1921- *AmMWSc 92*
**Stark,** John Howard 1941- *AmMWSc 92*
**Stark,** John Thomas 1955- *WhoAmL 92, WhoFI 92*
**Stark,** Jonathan 1926-1944 *EncTR 91*
**Stark,** Joshua *IntAu&W 91X, TwCWW 91, WrDr 92*
**Stark,** Larry Gene 1938- *AmMWSc 92*
**Stark,** Lawrence 1926- *AmMWSc 92*
**Stark,** Martin J. 1941- *WhoWest 92*
**Stark,** Marvin Michael 1921- *AmMWSc 92*
**Stark,** Maxine Jan 1941- *WhoMW 92*
**Stark,** Milton Dale 1932- *WhoWest 92*
**Stark,** Nathan J. 1920- *IntWW 91*
**Stark,** Nathan Julius 1920- *AmMWSc 92*
**Stark,** Nellie May 1933- *AmMWSc 92*
**Stark,** Otto Gene 1928- *WhoMW 92*
**Stark,** Patricia Ann 1937- *WhoMW 92*
**Stark,** Paul 1929- *AmMWSc 92*
**Stark,** Paul Seidler 1946- *WhoFI 92*
**Stark,** Philip Herald 1936- *AmMWSc 92*
**Stark,** Ray *IntMPA 92, WhoEnt 92, WhoWest 92*
**Stark,** Richard *IntAu&W 91X, WrDr 92*
**Stark,** Richard B 1915- *AmMWSc 92*
**Stark,** Richard Harlan 1916- *AmMWSc 92*
**Stark,** Robert M 1930- *AmMWSc 92*
**Stark,** Ronald William 1922- *AmMWSc 92*
**Stark,** Royal William 1937- *AmMWSc 92*
**Stark,** Ruth E 1950- *AmMWSc 92*
**Stark,** S. Daniel, Jr. 1953- *WhoWest 92*
**Stark,** Sharon Sheehe *DrAPF 91*
**Stark,** Sheldon 1909- *WhoEnt 92*
**Stark,** Shirley J. 1927- *WhoBlA 92*
**Stark,** Stephen *DrAPF 91*
**Stark,** Steven 1943- *WhoFI 92*
**Stark,** Steven Michael 1964- *WhoFI 92*
**Stark,** Temple Cunningham 1946- *WhoIns 92*
**Stark,** Terri Lynne 1961- *WhoFI 92*
**Stark,** Walter Alfred, Jr 1940- *AmMWSc 92*
**Stark,** Werner 1909- *WrDr 92*
**Stark,** Wilbur 1922- *IntMPA 92*
**Stark,** William Polson 1943- *AmMWSc 92*
**Stark,** William Richard 1945- *AmMWSc 92*
**Starke,** Albert Carl, Jr 1916- *AmMWSc 92*
**Starke,** Catherine Juanita 1913- *WhoBlA 92*
**Starke,** Edgar Arlin, Jr 1936- *AmMWSc 92*
**Starke,** H. F. Gerhard 1916- *IntWW 91*
**Starke,** Heinz 1911- *IntWW 91*
**Starke,** John Erskine 1913- *Who 92*
**Starke,** Joseph Gabriel 1911- *WrDr 92*
**Starke,** Roland Adrian Malan *IntAu&W 91*
**Starke,** William H *WhoAmP 91*
**Starker,** Janos 1924- *FacFETw, IntWW 91, NewAmDM, Who 92, WhoEnt 92*
**Starkes,** Dale Joseph 1953- *WhoAmL 92*
**Starkey,** Eugene Edward 1926- *AmMWSc 92*
**Starkey,** Frank David 1944- *AmMWSc 92, WhoBlA 92*
**Starkey,** George 1628-1665 *BiInAmS*
**Starkey,** Harry Charles 1925- *WhoWest 92*
**Starkey,** James G. 1933- *WhoAmL 92*
**Starkey,** James Henry, III 1940- *WhoFI 92*
**Starkey,** John 1936- *AmMWSc 92*
**Starkey,** John 1938- *Who 92*
**Starkey,** Nelson R, Jr 1929- *WhoAmP 91*
**Starkey,** Paul Edward 1920- *AmMWSc 92*
**Starkey,** Robert Eric 1939- *WhoRel 92*
**Starkey,** Russell Bruce, Jr. 1942- *WhoFI 92*
**Starkey,** Walter L 1920- *AmMWSc 92*
**Starkman,** Betty Provizer 1929- *WhoMW 92*
**Starkman,** Elaine *DrAPF 91*
**Starkman,** Stephen Stanley 1957- *WhoEnt 92*
**Starkov,** Vladislav Andreyevich 1940- *IntWW 91*
**Starkovsky,** Nicolas Alexis 1922- *AmMWSc 92*
**Starks,** Aubrie Neal, Jr 1946- *AmMWSc 92*
**Starks,** Charles Wiley 1954- *WhoRel 92*
**Starks,** John *WhoBlA 92*
**Starks,** Kenneth James 1924- *AmMWSc 92*
**Starks,** Norman Lester 1938- *WhoRel 92*
**Starks,** Rick 1948- *WhoBlA 92*
**Starks,** Robert J 1945- *WhoAmP 91*
**Starks,** Robert Terry 1944- *WhoBlA 92*
**Starks,** Thomas Harold 1930- *AmMWSc 92*
**Starks,** Thomas Leroy 1947- *AmMWSc 92*
**Starks,** Tom 1963- *WhoEnt 92, WhoMW 92*
**Starkweather,** Frederick Thomas 1933- *WhoFI 92, WhoWest 92*
**Starkweather,** Gary Keith 1938- *AmMWSc 92*
**Starkweather,** George Pratt 1873-1901 *BiInAmS*
**Starkweather,** Howard Warner, Jr 1926- *AmMWSc 92*
**Starkweather,** Peter Lathrop 1948- *AmMWSc 92*
**Starkweather,** William Henry 1944- *WhoWest 92*
**Starleaf,** Dennis Roy 1938- *WhoFI 92, WhoMW 92*
**Starling,** Albert Gregory 1939- *AmMWSc 92*
**Starling,** Dorothy Mae 1939- *WhoAmP 91*
**Starling,** George Edward 1927- *WhoRel 92*
**Starling,** James Lyne 1930- *AmMWSc 92*
**Starling,** Jane Ann 1946- *AmMWSc 92*
**Starling,** John Crawford 1916- *WhoBlA 92*
**Starling,** Kenneth Earl 1935- *AmMWSc 92*
**Starling,** Thomas *DrAPF 91*
**Starling,** Thomas Madison 1923- *AmMWSc 92*
**Starlinger,** Peter 1931- *IntWW 91*
**Starmer,** C Frank 1941- *AmMWSc 92*
**Starner,** Craig Leslie 1934- *WhoFI 92*
**Starnes,** Edgar Vance 1956- *WhoAmP 91*
**Starnes,** Hal Fletcher, Jr. 1952- *WhoWest 92*
**Starnes,** James Wright 1933- *WhoAmL 92*
**Starnes,** John Kennett 1918- *IntAu&W 91*
**Starnes,** Paul M 1934- *WhoAmP 91*
**Starnes,** Rebecca L 1941- *WhoAmP 91*
**Starnes,** Ruth 1929- *WhoAmP 91*
**Starnes,** Timothy Jackson 1966- *WhoEnt 92*
**Starnes,** William Herbert, Jr 1934- *AmMWSc 92, WhoFI 92*
**Starobin,** Becky 1951- *WhoEnt 92*
**Starobin,** David Simon 1949- *WhoEnt 92*
**Starobinski,** Jean 1920- *IntWW 91*
**Staron,** Debi 1958- *WhoEnt 92*
**Staros,** James Vaughan 1947- *AmMWSc 92*
**Starostyn,** Andrey Petrovich 1906- *SovUnBD*
**Starova,** Vulnet 1934- *IntWW 91*
**Starovoytova,** Galina Vasilevna 1946- *IntWW 91*
**Starr,** Albert 1926- *AmMWSc 92*
**Starr,** Allan H. 1944- *WhoAmL 92*
**Starr,** Arnold 1932- *AmMWSc 92*
**Starr,** Belle 1848-1889 *EncAmaz 91*
**Starr,** Bob Tate 1932- *WhoEnt 92*
**Starr,** C Dean 1921- *AmMWSc 92*
**Starr,** Charles Marion 1925- *WhoRel 92*
**Starr,** Chauncey 1912- *AmMWSc 92*
**Starr,** Chester G. 1914- *ConAu 36NR, WrDr 92*
**Starr,** David 1950- *WhoWest 92*
**Starr,** David Evan 1962- *WhoMW 92*
**Starr,** David Wright 1912- *AmMWSc 92*

**Starr,** Duane Frank 1942- *AmMWSc 92*
**Starr,** E C 1901- *AmMWSc 92*
**Starr,** Eliza Allen 1824-1901 *RelLAm 91*
**Starr,** Ellen Gates 1859-1940 *HanAmWH*
**Starr,** Frederick 1858-1933 *BenetAL 91*
**Starr,** Grier Forsythe 1926- *WhoWest 92*
**Starr,** Henry *IntAu&W 91X, TwCWW 91*
**Starr,** Isidore 1911- *WhoAmL 92*
**Starr,** Ivar Miles 1950- *WhoAmL 92*
**Starr,** James Edward 1944- *WhoWest 92*
**Starr,** James LeRoy 1939- *AmMWSc 92*
**Starr,** James Milton 1961- *WhoRel 92*
**Starr,** Jason Leonard 1928- *AmMWSc 92*
**Starr,** John Carroll, Jr 1940- *WhoAmP 91*
**Starr,** John Edward 1939- *AmMWSc 92*
**Starr,** Kate *WrDr 92*
**Starr,** Kenneth Winston 1946- *WhoAmL 92*
**Starr,** Lori 1954- *WhoWest 92*
**Starr,** Matthew C *AmMWSc 92*
**Starr,** Melvin Lee 1922- *WhoWest 92*
**Starr,** Michael 1948- *WhoAmL 92*
**Starr,** Miriam Carolyn 1951- *WhoFI 92*
**Starr,** Mortimer Paul 1917- *AmMWSc 92*
**Starr,** Norbert T., II 1954- *WhoAmL 92*
**Starr,** Norman 1933- *AmMWSc 92*
**Starr,** Norton 1936- *AmMWSc 92*
**Starr,** Patricia Rae 1935- *AmMWSc 92*
**Starr,** Patrick Joseph 1939- *AmMWSc 92*
**Starr,** Phillip Henry 1920- *AmMWSc 92*
**Starr,** Randy Joe 1951- *WhoRel 92*
**Starr,** Richard Cawthon 1924- *AmMWSc 92*
**Starr,** Rick 1947- *WhoMW 92*
**Starr,** Ringo 1940- *IntMPA 92, IntWW 91, NewAmDM, WhoEnt 92*
**Starr,** Robert A, Jr 1942- *WhoAmP 91*
**Starr,** Robert I 1932- *AmMWSc 92*
**Starr,** Robert Irving 1932- *WhoWest 92*
**Starr,** Ruth Isabel 1963- *WhoAmL 92*
**Starr,** Stephen Frederick 1940- *WhoMW 92*
**Starr,** Susan Colleen Getroh 1959- *WhoAmP 91*
**Starr,** Sydney 1857-1925 *TwCPaSc*
**Starr,** Terrell *WhoAmP 91*
**Starr,** Theodore Jack 1924- *AmMWSc 92*
**Starr,** Thomas Arthur 1960- *WhoMW 92*
**Starr,** Thomas Louis 1949- *AmMWSc 92*
**Starr,** Walter LeRoy 1924- *AmMWSc 92*
**Starr-White,** Debi 1947- *WhoBlA 92*
**Starratt,** Alvin Neil 1936- *AmMWSc 92*
**Starratt,** Patricia Elizabeth 1943- *WhoEnt 92*
**Starrett,** Andrew 1930- *AmMWSc 92*
**Starrett,** Frederick Kent 1947- *WhoAmL 92*
**Starrett,** John David 1952- *WhoWest 92*
**Starrett,** Richmond Mullins 1943- *AmMWSc 92*
**Starrett,** Stanley Young 1936- *WhoMW 92, WhoRel 92*
**Starrett,** Vincent 1886-1974 *BenetAL 91*
**Starrfield,** Sumner Grosby 1940- *AmMWSc 92, WhoWest 92*
**Starrfield,** Susan Lee 1945- *WhoWest 92*
**Starrs,** Elizabeth Anne 1954- *WhoAmL 92*
**Starrs,** James Edward 1930- *WhoAmL 92*
**Starry,** Mary Jane *WhoAmP 91*
**Starszakowna,** Norma 1945- *TwCPaSc*
**Startup,** Peter 1921-1976 *TwCPaSc*
**Startup,** Vivian Margaret 1913- *WhoAmP 91*
**Startz,** Jane Ellen 1947- *WhoEnt 92*
**Startzman,** Gary Robert 1951- *WhoMW 92*
**Staruszkiewicz,** Walter Frank, Jr 1939- *AmMWSc 92*
**Stary,** Frank Edward 1941- *AmMWSc 92*
**Staryk,** Steven S. 1932- *WhoEnt 92*
**Starzak,** Michael Edward 1942- *AmMWSc 92*
**Starzl,** R F 1899-1976 *ScFEYrs*
**Starzl,** Thomas E 1926- *AmMWSc 92*
**Starzyk,** Marvin John 1935- *AmMWSc 92*
**Staser,** Betty Jo 1921- *WhoWest 92*
**Stasheff,** Christopher 1944- *TwCSFW 91, WrDr 92*
**Stasheff,** James Dillon 1936- *AmMWSc 92*
**Stashenkov,** Nikolai Alekseevich 1934- *IntWW 91*
**Stashower,** Arthur L. 1930- *WhoAmL 92*
**Stasi,** Bernard 1930- *IntWW 91*
**Stasiak,** Barbara Castellana 1947- *WhoAmP 91*
**Stasiukevicius,** Kazimieras V. 1964- *WhoAmL 92*
**Stasiw,** Roman Orest 1941- *AmMWSc 92*
**Staskiewicz,** Bernard Alexander 1924- *AmMWSc 92*
**Stasko,** Aivars B 1937- *AmMWSc 92*
**Stasko,** James Leroy 1935- *WhoEnt 92*
**Stasova,** Yelena 1873-1966 *SovUnBD*
**Stassen,** Harold Edward 1907- *FacFETw, Who 92*
**Stassen,** Hendrik Gerard 1935- *IntWW 91*
**Stassen,** John Henry 1943- *WhoAmL 92, WhoMW 92*
**Stassinopoulos,** Arianna 1950- *WrDr 92*
**Stassinopoulos,** Michael 1905- *IntWW 91*
**Stastny,** John Anton 1921- *WhoFI 92*
**Staszak,** David John 1944- *AmMWSc 92*
**Staszak,** Lawrence Robert 1941- *WhoMW 92*
**Staszeky,** Francis M 1918- *AmMWSc 92*
**Staszyc,** Stanislaw Alexander 1956- *WhoAmL 92*
**Statchen,** Robert Theodore 1935- *WhoAmL 92*
**State,** David 1914- *AmMWSc 92*
**State,** Harold M 1910- *AmMWSc 92*
**Staten,** Randolph 1944- *WhoAmP 91*
**Staten,** Raymond Dale 1922- *AmMWSc 92*
**States,** Alan E 1946- *WhoAmP 91*
**States,** Bert Olen 1929- *IntWW 91*
**States,** Jack Sterling 1941- *AmMWSc 92*
**Statescu,** Constantin 1927- *IntWW 91*
**Stathakis,** Jonathan G. 1945- *WhoEnt 92*
**Statham,** Bill R. 1934- *WhoFI 92*
**Statham,** Carl 1950- *WhoBlA 92*
**Statham,** Frances Patton *IntAu&W 91*
**Statham,** Norman 1922- *Who 92*
**Statham,** Stan 1939- *WhoAmP 91*
**Stathatos,** Stephanos 1922- *Who 92*
**Stathis,** Nicholas John 1924- *WhoAmL 92*
**Stathopoulos,** Theodore 1947- *AmMWSc 92*
**Statira** d331BC *EncAmaz 91*
**Statler Brothers** *NewAmDM*
**Statler,** Charles Daniel 1938- *WhoFI 92*
**Statler,** Irving C 1923- *AmMWSc 92*
**Statler,** Oliver 1915- *WrDr 92*
**Statler,** Stuart M 1943- *WhoAmP 91*
**Staton,** Cecil Pope, Jr. 1958- *WhoRel 92*
**Staton,** David Michael 1940- *WhoAmP 91*
**Staton,** John Emmett, Jr. 1954- *WhoEnt 92*
**Staton,** Knofel L. 1934- *ConAu 35NR*
**Staton,** Rick W 1958- *WhoAmP 91*
**Staton,** Rocker Theodore, Jr 1920- *AmMWSc 92*
**Staton,** William W *WhoAmP 91*
**Statt,** Terry G 1953- *AmMWSc 92*
**Statten,** Vargo *TwCSFW 91*
**Statton,** Gary Lewis 1937- *AmMWSc 92*
**Statum,** Hayward S. 1942- *WhoBlA 92*
**Statz,** Hermann 1928- *AmMWSc 92*
**Statz,** Joyce Ann 1947- *AmMWSc 92*
**Staub,** August William 1931- *WhoEnt 92*
**Staub,** E Brian 1927- *WhoIns 92*
**Staub,** Ervin 1938- *ConAu 133*
**Staub,** Fred W 1928- *AmMWSc 92*
**Staub,** Gerald Francis 1935- *WhoMW 92*
**Staub,** Herbert Warren 1927- *AmMWSc 92*
**Staub,** James Richard 1938- *WhoMW 92*
**Staub,** John Thomas 1932- *WhoEnt 92*
**Staub,** Nancy Lohman 1933- *WhoEnt 92*
**Staub,** Norman Croft 1929- *AmMWSc 92*
**Staub,** Peter *DcAmImH*
**Staub,** Rex Bryan 1963- *WhoAmL 92*
**Staub,** Robert J 1922- *AmMWSc 92*
**Stauber,** Marilyn Jean 1938- *WhoMW 92*
**Stauber,** Ronald Joseph 1940- *WhoAmL 92*
**Stauber,** William Taliaferro 1943- *AmMWSc 92*
**Staubitz,** Arthur Frederick 1939- *WhoAmL 92, WhoFI 92*
**Staubitz,** Sheldon Harrison 1940- *WhoMW 92*
**Staubitz,** William Joseph 1915- *AmMWSc 92*
**Staublin,** Judith Ann 1936- *WhoFI 92*
**Staubus,** Alfred Elsworth 1947- *AmMWSc 92*
**Staubus,** John Reginald 1926- *AmMWSc 92*
**Staudenmayer,** Ralph 1942- *AmMWSc 92*
**Staudenmayer,** William J 1936- *AmMWSc 92*
**Stauder,** William 1922- *AmMWSc 92*
**Staudhammer,** John 1932- *AmMWSc 92*
**Staudhammer,** Peter 1934- *AmMWSc 92*
**Staudinger,** Hermann 1881-1965 *WhoNob 90*
**Staudinger,** Ulrich 1935- *IntWW 91*
**Staudt,** Ronald William 1946- *WhoAmL 92*
**Staudte,** Wolfgang 1906-1984 *IntDcF 2-2 [port]*
**Stauffenberg,** Claus Schenk von 1907-1944 *EncTR 91 [port], FacFETw*
**Stauffer,** Alan C 1945- *WhoAmP 91*
**Stauffer,** Allan Daniel 1939- *AmMWSc 92*
**Stauffer,** Bruce W. 1963- *WhoRel 92*
**Stauffer,** Charles Henry 1913- *AmMWSc 92*
**Stauffer,** Clyde E 1935- *AmMWSc 92*
**Stauffer,** Clyde Eugene 1935- *WhoMW 92*
**Stauffer,** Edward Keith 1941- *AmMWSc 92*
**Stauffer,** Gary Dean 1944- *AmMWSc 92*
**Stauffer,** George Franklin 1907- *AmMWSc 92*
**Stauffer,** Helen Winter 1922- *WhoMW 92*
**Stauffer,** Howard Boyer 1941- *AmMWSc 92*
**Stauffer,** Jack B 1928- *AmMWSc 92*
**Stauffer,** Jay Richard, Jr 1951- *AmMWSc 92*
**Stauffer,** John *WhoAmP 91*
**Stauffer,** John Richard 1952- *AmMWSc 92*
**Stauffer,** Mel R 1937- *AmMWSc 92*
**Stauffer,** Richard Blaine 1903- *WhoMW 92*
**Stauffer,** Robert Eliot 1913- *AmMWSc 92*
**Stauffer,** Ronald Eugene 1949- *WhoAmL 92*
**Stauffer,** Sarah Ann 1915- *WhoAmP 91*
**Stauffer,** Suzan Lee 1953- *WhoAmL 92*
**Stauffer,** Thomas Miel 1926- *AmMWSc 92*
**Stauffer,** Truman Parker, Sr 1919- *AmMWSc 92*
**Staugaard,** Burton Christian 1929- *AmMWSc 92*
**Staughton,** Christopher 1933- *Who 92*
**Staum,** Muni M 1921- *AmMWSc 92*
**Staunton,** John Joseph Jameson 1911- *AmMWSc 92*
**Staunton,** Marie 1952- *Who 92*
**Staunton,** Schuyler *ConAu 133*
**Staupers,** Mabel Keaton 1890-1989 *NotBlAW 92 [port], WhoBlA 92N*
**Staur,** Martin John 1933- *WhoFI 92*
**Stauss,** George Henry 1932- *AmMWSc 92*
**Staut,** Ronald 1941- *AmMWSc 92*
**Stauter,** Susan Ellen 1949- *WhoWest 92*
**Stavans,** Ilan 1961- *WhoHisp 92*
**Stavans,** Judyth Gladstein 1955- *WhoEnt 92*
**Stavchansky,** Salomon Ayzenman 1947- *AmMWSc 92*
**Stave,** Bruce M 1937- *IntAu&W 91, WrDr 92*
**Staveley,** John 1914- *Who 92*
**Staveley,** Martin Samuel 1921- *Who 92*
**Staveley,** Robert 1928- *Who 92*
**Staveley,** William 1928- *IntWW 91, Who 92*
**Stavely,** Joseph Rennie 1939- *AmMWSc 92*
**Stavely,** Margaret *DrAPF 91*
**Staver,** Allen Ernest 1923- *AmMWSc 92*
**Stavert,** Alexander Bruce *Who 92*
**Stavetski,** Edward John 1956- *WhoFI 92*
**Stavinoha,** William Bernard 1928- *AmMWSc 92*
**Stavins,** Robert Norman 1948- *WhoFI 92*
**Stavis,** Barrie 1906- *WrDr 92*
**Stavis,** Gus 1921- *AmMWSc 92*
**Stavis,** Roger Lee 1958- *WhoAmL 92*
**Stavisky,** Leonard Price 1925- *WhoAmP 91*
**Stavitsky,** Abram Benjamin 1919- *AmMWSc 92*
**Stavn,** Robert Hans 1940- *AmMWSc 92*
**Stavrianos,** Leften S. 1913- *WrDr 92*
**Stavric,** Bozidar 1926- *AmMWSc 92*
**Stavric,** Stanislava 1933- *AmMWSc 92*
**Stavrolakis,** J A 1921- *AmMWSc 92*
**Stavropoulos,** Dionysos John 1933- *WhoFI 92*
**Stavropoulos,** George 1920-1990 *CurBio 91N*
**Stavros,** Dennis Constantine 1940- *WhoMW 92*
**Stavros,** Mary-Jo 1932- *WhoWest 92*
**Stavroudis,** Orestes Nicholas 1923- *AmMWSc 92*
**Stawicki,** Joseph John, Jr. 1944- *WhoFI 92*
**Stawski,** Henryk Tadeusz 1929- *IntWW 91*
**Stay,** Barbara 1926- *AmMWSc 92*
**Stayer,** Benjamin Clay 1963- *WhoRel 92*
**Stayin,** Randolph John 1942- *WhoAmL 92*
**Stayman,** Samuel M. 1909- *WhoFI 92*
**Staynes,** Jill *ConAu 133*
**Stayton,** Michael Bruce 1946- *WhoMW 92*
**Stayton,** Thomas George 1948- *WhoAmL 92*
**Stea,** David 1936- *WhoWest 92*
**Stead,** C. K. 1932- *ConNov 91, ConPo 91, IntAu&W 91, RfGEnL 91, WrDr 92*
**Stead,** Christina 1902-1983 *RfGEnL 91*
**Stead,** Christina Ellen 1902-1983 *FacFETw*
**Stead,** Christina Ellen 1920-1983 *LiExTwC*
**Stead,** Christopher 1913- *Who 92, WhoRel 92*
**Stead,** Chuck *DrAPF 91*
**Stead,** Eugene A., Jr. 1908- *IntWW 91*
**Stead,** Eugene Anson, Jr 1908- *AmMWSc 92*
**Stead,** Frederick L 1923- *AmMWSc 92*
**Stead,** George Christopher 1913- *IntWW 91*
**Stead,** Ian Mathieson 1936- *Who 92*
**Stead,** James Joseph, Jr. 1930- *WhoFI 92, WhoMW 92*
**Stead,** Jerre L. 1943- *WhoMW 92*
**Stead,** Philip John 1916- *WrDr 92*
**Stead,** Ralph Edmund 1917- *Who 92*
**Stead,** Robert 1909- *Who 92*
**Stead,** Robert Everrett 1933- *WhoAmL 92*
**Stead,** Robert J.C. 1880-1959 *BenetAL 91, TwCWW 91*
**Stead,** William Thomas 1849-1912 *BenetAL 91*
**Stead,** William Wallace 1948- *AmMWSc 92*
**Stead,** William White 1919- *AmMWSc 92*
**Stead Lee,** Polly Jae 1929- *WhoWest 92*
**Steadham,** Charles Victor, Jr. 1944- *WhoEnt 92, WhoFI 92*
**Steadman,** Dale Edward 1946- *WhoEnt 92*
**Steadman,** David Wilton 1936- *WhoMW 92*
**Steadman,** J. P. *WhoRel 92*
**Steadman,** Jack W. 1928- *WhoMW 92*
**Steadman,** James Robert 1942- *AmMWSc 92*
**Steadman,** John Bonneau 1938- *WhoFI 92*
**Steadman,** John Hubert 1938- *Who 92*
**Steadman,** John M *WhoAmP 91*
**Steadman,** John Montague 1930- *WhoAmL 92*
**Steadman,** John William 1943- *AmMWSc 92*
**Steadman,** Mark *DrAPF 91*
**Steadman,** Ralph Idris 1936- *IntWW 91, Who 92*
**Steadman,** Richard Anderson, Jr. 1954- *WhoAmL 92*
**Steadman,** Robert George 1939- *AmMWSc 92*
**Steadman,** Robert Kempton 1943- *WhoWest 92*
**Steadman,** Thomas Ree 1917- *AmMWSc 92*
**Steadman,** Wade Hopkins 1959- *WhoEnt 92*
**Steagald,** Thomas Ray 1955- *WhoRel 92*
**Steagall,** Henry Bascom, II 1922- *WhoAmL 92, WhoAmP 91*
**Steagall,** Jeffrey Wayne 1964- *WhoFI 92*
**Steakley,** Zollie Coffer, Jr 1908- *WhoAmP 91*
**Steane,** J. B. 1928- *WrDr 92*
**Steans,** Edith Elizabeth 1929- *WhoBlA 92*
**Steans,** Phillip Michael 1943- *WhoAmL 92*
**Stear,** David Spring 1925- *WhoAmP 91*
**Stear,** Edwin Byron 1932- *AmMWSc 92*
**Stear,** Michael 1938- *Who 92*
**Stearman,** Roebert L 1923- *AmMWSc 92*
**Stearman,** Ronald Oran 1932- *AmMWSc 92*
**Stearn,** Colin William 1928- *AmMWSc 92*
**Stearn,** Jess *WrDr 92*
**Stearn,** William Thomas 1911- *Who 92, WrDr 92*
**Stearner,** Sigrid Phyllis 1919- *AmMWSc 92*
**Stearney,** Ronald A 1939- *WhoAmP 91*
**Stearns,** Brenton Fisk 1928- *AmMWSc 92*
**Stearns,** Charles Edward 1920- *AmMWSc 92*
**Stearns,** Charles R 1925- *AmMWSc 92*
**Stearns,** Clifford B. 1941- *AlmAP 92 [port]*
**Stearns,** Clifford Bundy 1941- *WhoAmP 91*
**Stearns,** David Winrod 1929- *AmMWSc 92*
**Stearns,** Donald Edison 1948- *AmMWSc 92*
**Stearns,** Edwin Ira 1911- *AmMWSc 92*
**Stearns,** Eugene Marion, Jr 1932- *AmMWSc 92*
**Stearns,** Forest 1918- *AmMWSc 92*
**Stearns,** Frank Warren 1949- *WhoAmL 92*
**Stearns,** H Myrl 1916- *AmMWSc 92*
**Stearns,** Harold 1891-1943 *BenetAL 91*
**Stearns,** Herman DeClercq 1865-1907 *BiInAmS*
**Stearns,** James Gerry 1922- *WhoFI 92*
**Stearns,** John H 1934- *WhoIns 92*
**Stearns,** John Warren 1933- *AmMWSc 92*
**Stearns,** Lillard G. 1941- *WhoBlA 92*
**Stearns,** Lutie Eugenia 1866-1943 *HanAmWH*
**Stearns,** Martin 1916- *AmMWSc 92*
**Stearns,** Mary Beth Gorman *AmMWSc 92*
**Stearns,** Monteagle 1924- *WhoAmP 91*
**Stearns,** Richard Edwin 1936- *AmMWSc 92*
**Stearns,** Richard Gordon 1927- *AmMWSc 92*
**Stearns,** Robert Edwards Carter 1827-1909 *BiInAmS*
**Stearns,** Robert Inman 1932- *AmMWSc 92*
**Stearns,** Robert L 1926- *AmMWSc 92*
**Stearns,** S Russell 1915- *AmMWSc 92*
**Stearns,** Silas 1859-1888 *BiInAmS*
**Stearns,** Stephanie *DrAPF 91*
**Stearns,** Stephen Curtis 1946- *AmMWSc 92*
**Stearns,** Suzanne Anderson 1944- *WhoEnt 92*
**Stearns,** Thomas W 1909- *AmMWSc 92*

**Stearns Miller**, Camille Louise 1956- WhoBlA 92
**Stears**, John Cameron 1928- WhoWest 92
**Stebben**, Gregg 1961- WhoEnt 92
**Stebbing**, Nowell 1941- AmMWSc 92
**Stebbings**, George Donald, Jr. 1945- WhoWest 92
**Stebbings**, James Henry 1937- AmMWSc 92
**Stebbings**, Robert Yeo 1942- WhoAmL 92, WhoFI 92
**Stebbings**, Ronald Frederick 1929- AmMWSc 92
**Stebbings**, William Lee 1945- AmMWSc 92, WhoMW 92
**Stebbins**, Dana Brewington 1946- WhoBlA 92
**Stebbins**, Dean Waldo 1913- AmMWSc 92
**Stebbins**, George Ledyard 1906- AmMWSc 92, IntWW 91
**Stebbins**, Gregory Kellogg 1951- WhoFI 92
**Stebbins**, Henry Blanchard 1951- WhoAmL 92
**Stebbins**, Richard 1945- BlkOlyM
**Stebbins**, Richard Gilbert 1943- AmMWSc 92
**Stebbins**, Richard Henderson 1938- WhoFI 92
**Stebbins**, Robert A. 1938- WrDr 92
**Stebbins**, Robert C. 1915- WrDr 92
**Stebbins**, Robert Cyril 1915- AmMWSc 92, IntAu&W 91
**Stebbins**, Robert H 1924- AmMWSc 92
**Stebbins**, Robin Tucker 1948- AmMWSc 92
**Stebbins**, William Cooper 1929- AmMWSc 92, WhoMW 92
**Stebel**, Sidney Leo 1923- WhoEnt 92
**Stebelsky**, Ihor 1939- AmMWSc 92
**Steben**, John D 1936- AmMWSc 92
**Steber**, A R TwCSFW 91
**Steber**, Eleanor 1914-1990 AnObit 1990, FacFETw
**Steber**, Eleanor 1916-1990 CurBio 91N, NewAmDM
**Steber**, George Rudolph 1938- AmMWSc 92
**Stebinger**, Peter Arnold Robichaud 1954- WhoRel 92
**Steblay**, Craig Douglas 1948- WhoWest 92
**Stec**, John Zygment 1925- WhoMW 92
**Stec**, Robert Gerard 1961- WhoRel 92
**Steccato**, Joseph 1965- WhoFI 92
**Stecher**, Emma Dietz 1905- AmMWSc 92
**Stecher**, Michael 1942- AmMWSc 92
**Stecher**, Theodore P 1930- AmMWSc 92
**Stechman**, John Vance 1934- WhoWest 92
**Stechschulte**, Agnes Louise 1924- AmMWSc 92
**Stechschulte**, Mark Joseph 1953- WhoAmL 92
**Steciuk**, George L 1942- WhoIns 92
**Steck**, Daniel John 1946- AmMWSc 92
**Steck**, Edgar Alfred 1918- AmMWSc 92
**Steck**, Ernest Gustave, III 1952- WhoEnt 92
**Steck**, Theodore Lyle 1939- AmMWSc 92
**Steck**, Warren Franklin 1939- AmMWSc 92
**Steckel**, Richard Hall 1944- WhoMW 92
**Steckel**, Richard J 1936- AmMWSc 92, WhoWest 92
**Steckelberg**, Dob Darryl 1947- WhoMW 92
**Stecker**, Carl S 1916- WhoIns 92
**Stecker**, Floyd William 1942- AmMWSc 92
**Steckl**, Andrew Jules AmMWSc 92
**Steckler**, Arthur 1921-1985 SmATA 65
**Steckler**, Bernard Michael 1932- AmMWSc 92
**Steckler**, David Russell 1956- WhoMW 92
**Steckler**, Phyllis Betty WhoWest 92
**Steckler**, William Elwood 1913- WhoAmL 92, WhoMW 92
**Steckley**, Dennis Allen 1950- WhoMW 92
**Steczo**, Terry Allen 1949- WhoAmP 91
**Stedinger**, Jery Russell 1951- AmMWSc 92
**Stedman** Who 92
**Stedman**, Baroness 1916- Who 92
**Stedman**, Donald Hugh 1943- AmMWSc 92
**Stedman**, Edmund Clarence 1833-1908 BenetAL 91
**Stedman**, James Murphey 1938- AmMWSc 92
**Stedman**, Jane Winifred 1920- WhoMW 92
**Stedman**, Richard Ralph 1936- WhoAmL 92
**Stedman**, Robert John 1929- AmMWSc 92
**Stedronsky**, Frank 1935- WhoEnt 92, WhoFI 92
**Steeb**, Merrill Miller 1924- WhoAmL 92
**Steece**, Bert Maurice 1945- WhoWest 92
**Steed**, Diane Kay 1945- WhoAmP 91
**Steed**, Ernest Horace Joseph 1925- WhoRel 92
**Steed**, Tom Alan 1950- WhoRel 92
**Steed**, Tyrone 1948- WhoBlA 92
**Steedman**, Alasdair 1922- Who 92
**Steedman**, Martha Who 92
**Steedman**, Robert Russell 1929- Who 92
**Steeds**, John Wickham 1940- IntWW 91, Who 92
**Steeg**, Moise S., Jr. 1916- WhoAmL 92
**Steege**, Deborah Anderson 1946- AmMWSc 92
**Steeger**, Henry 1903-1990 ConAu 133
**Steeger**, William Paul 1945- WhoRel 92
**Steegmann**, Albert Theodore, Jr 1936- AmMWSc 92
**Steegmuller**, Francis DrAPF 91
**Steegmuller**, Francis 1906- BenetAL 91, DcLB 111 [port], IntAu&W 91, Who 92, WrDr 92
**Steel**, Anne Heather 1940- Who 92
**Steel**, Byron DrAPF 91, Who 92, WrDr 92
**Steel**, Charles Deane 1901- Who 92
**Steel**, Colin 1933- AmMWSc 92
**Steel**, Colin Geoffrey Hendry 1946- AmMWSc 92
**Steel**, D. R. 1948- WrDr 92
**Steel**, Danielle 1947- ConAu 36NR, SmATA 66 [port], WrDr 92
**Steel**, Danielle 1950- IntWW 91
**Steel**, David 1910- Who 92
**Steel**, David 1916- IntWW 91, Who 92
**Steel**, David 1938- FacFETw, Who 92, WrDr 92
**Steel**, David Martin Scott 1938- IntWW 91
**Steel**, David William 1943- Who 92
**Steel**, Dawn ReelWom
**Steel**, Dawn 1946- IntMPA 92, IntWW 91, WhoEnt 92, WhoWest 92
**Steel**, Donald MacLennan Arklay 1937- Who 92
**Steel**, Fiennes William Strang 1912- Who 92
**Steel**, George Edwin, Jr 1945- WhoAmP 91
**Steel**, Henry 1926- Who 92
**Steel**, Howard Haldeman 1921- AmMWSc 92
**Steel**, James 1909- Who 92
**Steel**, Joan Elizabeth 1953- WhoFI 92, WhoIns 92
**Steel**, John Honeywood 1780-1838 BiInAmS
**Steel**, Patricia Ann 1941- Who 92
**Steel**, R Knight 1939- AmMWSc 92
**Steel**, Robert 1920- Who 92
**Steel**, Robert 1923- AmMWSc 92
**Steel**, Robert George Douglas 1917- AmMWSc 92
**Steel**, Robert Walter 1915- Who 92
**Steel**, Ronald 1931- IntAu&W 91, WrDr 92
**Steel**, Rupert Oliver 1922- Who 92
**Steel**, Stan 1942- WhoEnt 92
**Steel**, Warren G 1920- AmMWSc 92
**Steel**, William Strang Who 92
**Steele**, Alan John 1916- Who 92
**Steele**, Annelle Brenee 1957- WhoMW 92
**Steele**, Arnold Edward 1925- AmMWSc 92
**Steele**, Barbara W 1939- WhoAmP 91
**Steele**, Bernard Robert 1929- Who 92
**Steele**, Byron IntAu&W 91X
**Steele**, Carl Lavern 1934- WhoMW 92
**Steele**, Charles Richard 1933- AmMWSc 92
**Steele**, Claude Mason 1946- WhoBlA 92
**Steele**, Cleophas R., Jr. 1945- WhoBlA 92
**Steele**, Craig William 1954- AmMWSc 92
**Steele**, Danielle IntAu&W 91
**Steele**, David Christopher 1964- WhoBlA 92
**Steele**, David Gentry 1941- AmMWSc 92
**Steele**, David H 1949- WhoAmP 91
**Steele**, Donald Harold 1932- AmMWSc 92
**Steele**, Dorise Weller 1953- WhoEnt 92
**Steele**, Earl L 1923- AmMWSc 92
**Steele**, Ellen Lively 1936- WhoAmP 91, WhoFI 92
**Steele**, Emmett Mitchell WhoEnt 92
**Steele**, Frank Fenwick 1923- Who 92
**Steele**, George Peabody 1924- WhoFI 92
**Steele**, Harold B. 1922- WhoFI 92
**Steele**, Harwood E 1897- TwCWW 91
**Steele**, Ian McKay 1944- AmMWSc 92
**Steele**, Jack 1942- AmMWSc 92
**Steele**, Jack Ellwood 1924- AmMWSc 92
**Steele**, James Harlan 1913- AmMWSc 92
**Steele**, James Isaac, Jr. 1959- WhoRel 92
**Steele**, James Patrick 1919- AmMWSc 92
**Steele**, Jane Riddel 1930- WhoAmP 91
**Steele**, Jeffrey 1931- TwCPaSc
**Steele**, Joel Dorman 1836-1886 BiInAmS
**Steele**, John WhoAmP 91
**Steele**, John D 1923- WhoIns 92
**Steele**, John Earle 1932- AmMWSc 92
**Steele**, John Ernest 1935- Who 92
**Steele**, John H 1926- AmMWSc 92
**Steele**, John Hyslop 1926- IntWW 91, Who 92
**Steele**, John Martin 1938- Who 92
**Steele**, John Patrick Henry 1948- WhoWest 92
**Steele**, John Roderic 1929- IntWW 91, Who 92
**Steele**, John Roy 1945- WhoFI 92
**Steele**, John Wiseman 1934- AmMWSc 92
**Steele**, Joyce Yvonne 1930- WhoBlA 92
**Steele**, Karen Kiarsis 1942- WhoAmP 91
**Steele**, Kathleen F 1960- WhoAmP 91
**Steele**, Kenneth F 1944- AmMWSc 92
**Steele**, Kenneth Walter Lawrence 1914- Who 92
**Steele**, Kurt D. 1945- WhoAmL 92
**Steele**, Lawrence Russell 1935- AmMWSc 92
**Steele**, Lendell Eugene 1928- AmMWSc 92
**Steele**, Leon 1915- AmMWSc 92
**Steele**, Martin Carl 1919- AmMWSc 92
**Steele**, Mary Q 1922- IntAu&W 91, WrDr 92
**Steele**, Max DrAPF 91
**Steele**, Max 1922- WrDr 92
**Steele**, Michael Chandos Merrett 1931- Who 92
**Steele**, Michael Glynn 1955- WhoAmP 91
**Steele**, Michael Leo 1950- WhoRel 92
**Steele**, Michael W. WhoBlA 92
**Steele**, Morris J TwCSFW 91
**Steele**, Myron Thomas 1945- WhoAmP 91
**Steele**, Paul Curry DrAPF 91
**Steele**, Paul Eugene 1933- WhoRel 92
**Steele**, Percy H., Jr. 1920- WhoBlA 92
**Steele**, Peter 1935- WrDr 92
**Steele**, Philip John Rupert 1920- Who 92
**Steele**, R. David 1931- ConAu 135
**Steele**, Railey A 1934- WhoAmP 91
**Steele**, Ralph J WhoAmP 91
**Steele**, Rhea Lynn 1958- WhoMW 92
**Steele**, Richard 1672?-1729 BlkwCEP, CnDBLB 2 [port], LitC 18, RfGEnL 91
**Steele**, Richard 1921- AmMWSc 92
**Steele**, Richard Charles 1928- Who 92
**Steele**, Richard Harold 1919- AmMWSc 92
**Steele**, Richard Kepple 1920- WhoWest 92
**Steele**, Richard W. 1934- ConAu 134
**Steele**, Robert WhoAmP 91
**Steele**, Robert 1929- AmMWSc 92
**Steele**, Robert Charles 1959- WhoWest 92
**Steele**, Robert Darryl 1946- AmMWSc 92
**Steele**, Robert Dennis 1956- WhoEnt 92
**Steele**, Robert Edward 1954- WhoIns 92
**Steele**, Robert Howe 1913- WhoAmP 91
**Steele**, Robert Wilbur 1920- AmMWSc 92
**Steele**, Ronald Edward 1943- AmMWSc 92
**Steele**, Ruby L. WhoBlA 92
**Steele**, Rupert Who 92
**Steele**, Shelby 1946- News 91 [port], WhoBlA 92, WrDr 92
**Steele**, Sidney Russell 1917- AmMWSc 92
**Steele**, Theodore Karl 1922- AmMWSc 92
**Steele**, Thomas Joseph 1933- WhoWest 92
**Steele**, Thomas McKnight 1948- WhoAmL 92
**Steele**, Timothy DrAPF 91
**Steele**, Timothy 1948- ConPo 91, WrDr 92
**Steele**, Timothy Doak 1941- AmMWSc 92
**Steele**, Timothy Reid 1948- IntAu&W 91
**Steele**, Tommy 1936- IntMPA 92, IntWW 91, Who 92
**Steele**, Valerie Fahnestock 1955- WhoEnt 92
**Steele**, Vernon Eugene 1946- AmMWSc 92
**Steele**, Vladislava Julie 1934- AmMWSc 92
**Steele**, Warren Bell 1923- WhoBlA 92
**Steele**, Warren Cavanaugh 1929- AmMWSc 92
**Steele**, Warren Merrill 1874-1910 BiInAmS
**Steele**, Wilbur Daniel 1886-1970 BenetAL 91
**Steele**, William A 1930- AmMWSc 92
**Steele**, William Arthur 1953- WhoWest 92
**Steele**, William F 1920- AmMWSc 92
**Steele**, William Frank 1920- WhoMW 92
**Steele**, William John 1929- AmMWSc 92
**Steele**, William Kenneth 1942- AmMWSc 92
**Steele**, William O 1917-1979 TwCWW 91
**Steele**, William S 1923- BlkOlyM
**Steele-Bodger**, Alasdair 1924- Who 92
**Steele-Bodger**, Michael Roland 1925- Who 92
**Steele-Morgan**, Tony 1931- TwCPaSc
**Steele-Perkins**, Christopher Horace 1947- IntWW 91
**Steele-Perkins**, Derek 1908- Who 92
**Steelink**, Cornelius 1922- AmMWSc 92
**Steelman**, Carrol Dayton 1938- AmMWSc 92
**Steelman**, David Lloyd 1953- WhoAmP 91
**Steelman**, Earlene Mae 1927- WhoAmP 91
**Steelman**, Josie Acosta 1939- WhoHisp 92
**Steelman**, Robert J 1914- TwCWW 91, WrDr 92
**Steelman**, Sanford Lewis 1922- AmMWSc 92
**Steelman**, Sara G 1946- WhoAmP 91
**Steely Dan** NewAmDM
**Steen**, Anthony David 1939- Who 92
**Steen**, Carl Jean, Jr. 1960- WhoMW 92
**Steen**, Don 1949- WhoAmP 91
**Steen**, Donald Mariner 1924- WhoAmP 91
**Steen**, Edwin Benzel 1901- AmMWSc 92
**Steen**, James Southworth 1940- AmMWSc 92
**Steen**, James Wilson 1916- WhoAmP 91
**Steen**, Jerome Bridges 1933- WhoAmL 92
**Steen**, John Gerald 1936- WhoEnt 92
**Steen**, John Thomas, Jr. 1949- WhoFI 92
**Steen**, Lowell Harrison 1923- WhoMW 92
**Steen**, Lynn Arthur 1941- AmMWSc 92
**Steen**, Malcolm Harold 1928-1983 ConAu 135
**Steen**, Mary Beth 1959- WhoWest 92
**Steen**, Michael Bradley 1948- WhoRel 92
**Steen**, Mike ConAu 135
**Steen**, Paul Joseph 1932- WhoEnt 92, WhoWest 92
**Steen**, Reiulf 1933- IntWW 91
**Steen**, Robert Frederick 1942- AmMWSc 92
**Steen**, Ronald Ardis 1954- WhoRel 92
**Steen**, Stephen N 1923- AmMWSc 92
**Steen**, Wesley Wilson 1946- WhoAmL 92
**Steen-McIntyre**, Virginia Carol 1936- AmMWSc 92
**Steenbergen**, James Franklin 1939- AmMWSc 92
**Steenburg**, Richard Wesley 1925- AmMWSc 92
**Steenburgen**, Mary 1953- IntMPA 92, WhoEnt 92
**Steendam**, Jacob 1616?-1672? BenetAL 91
**Steeneck**, Lee R 1948- WhoIns 92
**Steensberg**, Axel 1906- IntWW 91
**Steensen**, Donald H J 1929- AmMWSc 92
**Steensgaard**, Niels Palle 1932- IntWW 91
**Steensma**, Andy 1942- WhoAmP 91
**Steensnaes**, Einar 1942- IntWW 91
**Steenson**, Bernard O 1922- AmMWSc 92
**Steeples**, Donald Wallace 1945- AmMWSc 92
**Steer**, Dulaney Gordon 1956- WhoAmL 92
**Steer**, John Richardson 1928- Who 92
**Steer**, Kenneth Arthur 1913- Who 92
**Steer**, Martin William 1942- AmMWSc 92
**Steer**, Max David 1910- AmMWSc 92
**Steer**, Michael Bernard 1955- AmMWSc 92
**Steer**, Philip Wilson 1860-1942 TwCPaSc
**Steer**, Ronald Paul 1943- AmMWSc 92
**Steer**, Stanley Charles Who 92
**Steer**, Wilfred Reed 1926- Who 92
**Steer**, William Reed Hornby 1899- Who 92
**Steere**, Ernest H. L. Who 92
**Steere**, Peter Kormann 1929- WhoAmL 92
**Steere**, Richard 1643?-1721 BenetAL 91
**Steere**, William Campbell 1907- AmMWSc 92
**Steerman**, James Beach 1936- WhoEnt 92
**Steers**, Edward, Jr 1937- AmMWSc 92
**Steers**, Newton Ivan, Jr 1917- WhoAmP 91
**Steese**, Charles Walter 1963- WhoAmL 92
**Steeves**, Borden Palmer 1913- WhoAmP 91
**Steeves**, Doriene Melendy 1937- WhoAmP 91
**Steeves**, Edna Leake 1909- WhoEnt 92
**Steeves**, Harrison Ross, III 1937- AmMWSc 92
**Steeves**, John Douglas 1952- AmMWSc 92
**Steeves**, Mark Aaron 1958- WhoEnt 92, WhoWest 92
**Steeves**, Richard Allison 1938- AmMWSc 92
**Steeves**, Taylor Armstrong 1926- AmMWSc 92
**Stefan**, Heinz G 1936- AmMWSc 92
**Stefanakos**, Elias Kyriakos 1940- AmMWSc 92
**Stefancin**, Joseph Frank 1957- WhoRel 92
**Stefancsik**, Ernest Anton 1923- AmMWSc 92
**Stefanescu**, Doru Michael 1942- AmMWSc 92
**Stefanescu**, I. Stefan 1929- IntWW 91
**Stefani**, Andrew Peter 1926- AmMWSc 92
**Stefani**, Stefano 1929- AmMWSc 92
**Stefaniak**, Alice Mary 1948- WhoRel 92
**Stefaniak**, Robert C 1935- WhoAmP 91
**Stefanides**, Steven Arthur 1949- WhoAmP 91
**Stefanik**, Janet Ruth 1938- WhoMW 92
**Stefanile**, Felix DrAPF 91
**Stefanile**, James Francis 1950- WhoEnt 92
**Stefanko**, Leona Evans 1945- WhoRel 92
**Stefanko**, Robert Allen 1943- WhoFI 92
**Stefano**, Giuseppe di NewAmDM
**Stefano**, Joseph William 1922- WhoEnt 92
**Stefanon**, Anthony 1949- WhoAmL 92
**Stefanopoulos**, Constantine 1926- IntWW 91

**Stefanou**, Harry 1947- *AmMWSc 92*
**Stefanowicz**, Janusz 1932- *IntWW 91*
**Stefanschi**, Sergiu 1941- *WhoEnt 92*
**Stefanski**, Piotr 1931- *IntWW 91*
**Stefanski**, Raymond Joseph 1941- *AmMWSc 92*
**Stefansson**, Alexander 1922- *IntWW 91*
**Stefansson**, Baldur Rosmund *AmMWSc 92*
**Stefansson**, Vilhjalmur 1879-1962 *BenetAL 91*
**Steff-Langston**, John Antony 1926- *Who 92*
**Steffan**, Wallace Allan 1934- *AmMWSc 92, WhoWest 92*
**Steffani**, Agostino 1654-1728 *NewAmDM*
**Steffanson**, Con *TwCSFW 91, WrDr 92*
**Steffany**, Alo W 1911- *WhoAmP 91*
**Steffany**, Alo William 1911- *WhoWest 92*
**Steffe**, Horst-Otto 1919- *IntWW 91*
**Steffek**, Anthony J 1935- *AmMWSc 92*
**Steffel**, Martin Henry 1938- *WhoAmP 91*
**Steffen**, Alan Leslie 1927- *WhoMW 92*
**Steffen**, Albert Harry 1914- *AmMWSc 92*
**Steffen**, Daniel G 1948- *AmMWSc 92*
**Steffen**, Daniel J. 1962- *WhoMW 92*
**Steffen**, Frederick John 1946- *WhoAmP 91*
**Steffen**, Jerry Adrian 1956- *WhoEnt 92*
**Steffen**, Jonathan 1958- *ConAu 135*
**Steffen**, Joseph J, Jr 1957- *WhoAmP 91*
**Steffen**, Juerg 1942- *AmMWSc 92*
**Steffen**, Lloyd Howard 1951- *WhoRel 92*
**Steffen**, Robert Alan 1960- *WhoMW 92*
**Steffen**, Rolf Marcel 1922- *AmMWSc 92*
**Steffen**, Thomas Lee 1930- *WhoAmL 92, WhoAmP 91, WhoWest 92*
**Steffens**, George Louis 1930- *AmMWSc 92*
**Steffens**, John Howard 1941- *WhoMW 92*
**Steffens**, John Laundon 1941- *WhoFI 92*
**Steffens**, Lincoln *SourALJ*
**Steffens**, Lincoln 1866-1936 *BenetAL 91, FacFETw*
**Steffens**, Lincoln 1886-1936 *DcAmImH*
**Steffens**, Vic Charles 1952- *WhoEnt 92*
**Steffensen**, Dale Marriott 1922- *AmMWSc 92*
**Steffenson**, David Conrad 1937- *WhoRel 92*
**Steffes**, Don C. 1930- *WhoFI 92*
**Steffey**, Eugene P 1942- *AmMWSc 92*
**Steffey**, Eugene Paul 1942- *WhoWest 92*
**Steffey**, Kathryn Elizabeth 1943- *WhoMW 92*
**Steffey**, Lela Gardner 1928- *WhoAmP 91*
**Steffey**, Oran Dean 1921- *AmMWSc 92*
**Steffey**, Richard Dudley 1929- *WhoWest 92*
**Steffey**, Stewart H, Jr *WhoIns 92*
**Steffgen**, Frederick Williams 1926- *AmMWSc 92*
**Steffler**, John Earl 1947- *IntAu&W 91*
**Stefko**, Paul Lowell 1915- *AmMWSc 92*
**Steflik**, Joseph J., Jr. 1946- *WhoAmL 92*
**Steg**, L 1922- *AmMWSc 92*
**Stegall**, Danny James 1955- *WhoMW 92*
**Stegall**, Joel Ringgold 1939- *WhoRel 92*
**Stegall**, Sydney Wallace 1941- *WhoEnt 92*
**Stegelmann**, Erich J 1914- *AmMWSc 92*
**Stegeman**, George I 1942- *AmMWSc 92*
**Stegeman**, Thomas Albert 1948- *WhoAmL 92*
**Stegemeier**, Richard Joseph 1928- *IntWW 91, WhoFI 92, WhoWest 92*
**Stegen**, Gilbert Rolland 1939- *AmMWSc 92*
**Stegenga**, David A. 1946- *WhoWest 92*
**Stegenga**, James A. 1937- *WrDr 92*
**Steger**, C. Donald 1936- *WhoBlA 92*
**Steger**, Herm 1926- *WhoAmP 91*
**Steger**, Joseph A. 1937- *IntWW 91*
**Steger**, Norbert 1944- *IntWW 91*
**Steger**, Richard Warren 1948- *AmMWSc 92*
**Steger**, William Merritt 1920- *WhoAmP 91*
**Stegerwald**, Adam 1874-1945 *EncTR 91*
**Stegge**, Diane Faye 1948- *WhoMW 92*
**Steggle**, Terence Harry 1932- *Who 92*
**Steggles**, Harold *TwCPaSc*
**Steggles**, Walter J. 1902- *TwCPaSc*
**Stegink**, David Wayne 1964- *WhoMW 92*
**Stegink**, Lewis D 1937- *AmMWSc 92*
**Stegmaier**, David 1947- *WhoAmP 91*
**Stegman**, Cathy Anne 1964- *WhoMW 92*
**Stegman**, Charles Alexander 1959- *WhoFI 92*
**Stegman**, Rose Bertha 1946- *WhoRel 92*
**Stegmann**, Johannes Augustus 1926- *IntWW 91*
**Stegmueller**, Wolfgang 1923- *IntWW 91*
**Stegner**, Lynn Nadene 1955- *WhoMW 92*
**Stegner**, Wallace *DrAPF 91*
**Stegner**, Wallace 1909- *BenetAL 91, ConNov 91, IntAu&W 91, TwCWW 91, WrDr 92*
**Steguweit**, Heinz 1897-1964 *EncTR 91*
**Stehbens**, William Ellis 1926- *AmMWSc 92*
**Stehelin**, Dominique Jean Bernard 1943- *IntWW 91*
**Stehle**, Philip McLellan 1919- *AmMWSc 92*
**Stehli**, Francis Greenough 1924- *AmMWSc 92*
**Stehlik**, Loren Joe 1946- *WhoAmP 91*
**Stehlin**, Kenneth Ervan 1949- *WhoMW 92*
**Stehling**, Ferdinand Christian 1930- *AmMWSc 92*
**Stehly**, David Norvin 1933- *AmMWSc 92*
**Stehman**, Betty Kohls 1952- *WhoFI 92*
**Stehman**, John *DrAPF 91*
**Stehney**, Andrew Frank 1920- *AmMWSc 92*
**Stehney**, Ann Kathryn 1946- *AmMWSc 92*
**Stehouwer**, David Mark 1943- *AmMWSc 92*
**Stehr**, Frederick William 1932- *AmMWSc 92*
**Stehr**, Hermann 1864-1940 *EncTR 91 [port]*
**Stehr**, John William 1911- *WhoRel 92*
**Stehsel**, Melvin Louis 1924- *AmMWSc 92*
**Steib**, James T. 1940- *WhoBlA 92*
**Steib**, James Terry *WhoRel 92*
**Steib**, Rene J 1918- *AmMWSc 92*
**Steichen**, Edward 1879-1973 *BenetAL 91, FacFETw [port], RComAH*
**Steichen**, Edward Jean 1879-1973 *DcTwDes*
**Steichen**, James Matthew 1947- *WhoMW 92*
**Steichen**, Richard John 1944- *AmMWSc 92*
**Steicke**, Lance Graham 1933- *WhoRel 92*
**Steidel**, Robert F, Jr 1926- *AmMWSc 92*
**Steidle**, Richard 1881-1940 *BiDExR*
**Steidley**, Jeffrey W. 1953- *WhoAmL 92*
**Steidley**, Juan Dwayne 1959- *WhoAmP 91*
**Steidtmann**, James R 1938- *AmMWSc 92*
**Steier**, M. David 1955- *WhoFI 92*
**Steier**, Rod *DrAPF 91*
**Steier**, William H 1933- *AmMWSc 92*
**Steig**, William 1907- *BenetAL 91, WrDr 92*
**Steigelmann**, William Henry 1935- *AmMWSc 92*
**Steiger**, Dale Arlen 1928- *WhoFI 92*
**Steiger**, Fred Harold 1929- *AmMWSc 92*
**Steiger**, Janet D 1939- *WhoAmP 91*
**Steiger**, Janet Dempsey 1939- *WhoFI 92*
**Steiger**, Rod 1925- *IntMPA 92, IntWW 91, WhoEnt 92*
**Steiger**, Roger Arthur 1939- *AmMWSc 92*
**Steiger**, Sam 1929- *WhoAmP 91*
**Steiger**, Walter Richard 1923- *AmMWSc 92*
**Steiger**, William Lee 1939- *AmMWSc 92*
**Steigers**, Chad Frank 1960- *WhoFI 92*
**Steigerwald**, Louis John, III 1953- *WhoFI 92*
**Steigerwald**, Paul James 1958- *WhoMW 92*
**Steigerwalt**, William J 1939- *WhoIns 92*
**Steighner**, Joseph A 1950- *WhoAmP 91*
**Steigleder**, Karl Zeiner 1958- *WhoMW 92*
**Steiglitz**, Kenneth 1939- *AmMWSc 92*
**Steigman**, Ernest R. 1940- *WhoAmL 92*
**Steigman**, Gary 1941- *AmMWSc 92*
**Steigmann**, Frederick 1905- *AmMWSc 92*
**Steigmann**, Robert James 1944- *WhoMW 92*
**Steigmeier**, Roger *DrAPF 91*
**Steil**, Ludwig 1900-1945 *EncTR 91*
**Steila**, Donald 1939- *AmMWSc 92*
**Steiman**, Henry Robert 1938- *AmMWSc 92*
**Steimberg**, Alicia 1933- *IntAu&W 91*
**Steimle**, Paul R. 1930- *WhoRel 92*
**Steimle**, Timothy C 1951- *AmMWSc 92*
**Steimling**, Frederick Ralph 1961- *WhoRel 92*
**Stein**, Abraham Morton 1923- *AmMWSc 92*
**Stein**, Agnes *DrAPF 91*
**Stein**, Alan H 1947- *AmMWSc 92*
**Stein**, Alan Harvey 1947- *WhoFI 92*
**Stein**, Alice P. *DrAPF 91*
**Stein**, Allan Mark 1951- *WhoAmL 92*
**Stein**, Allan Rudolph 1938- *AmMWSc 92*
**Stein**, Arthur 1918- *AmMWSc 92*
**Stein**, Arthur A 1922- *AmMWSc 92*
**Stein**, Arthur Oscar 1932- *WhoWest 92*
**Stein**, Barry Edward 1944- *AmMWSc 92*
**Stein**, Barry Fred 1937- *AmMWSc 92*
**Stein**, Benjamin 1944- *WrDr 92*
**Stein**, Bennett M 1931- *AmMWSc 92*
**Stein**, Bernard 1913- *WhoFI 92*
**Stein**, Bertha Sperber 1913- *WhoAmP 91*
**Stein**, Beth Ellen 1952- *WhoMW 92*
**Stein**, Beverly *WhoAmP 91*
**Stein**, Bland Allen 1934- *AmMWSc 92*
**Stein**, Bruno 1930- *WrDr 92*
**Stein**, Carey M. 1947- *WhoAmL 92*
**Stein**, Carol B 1937- *AmMWSc 92*
**Stein**, Cassandra Monroe 1944- *WhoAmP 91*
**Stein**, Charles *DrAPF 91*
**Stein**, Charles M *AmMWSc 92*
**Stein**, Charles W C 1914- *AmMWSc 92*
**Stein**, Cheri 1961- *WhoMW 92*
**Stein**, Cheryl Denise 1953- *WhoAmL 92*
**Stein**, Clarence 1883-1975 *DcTwDes*
**Stein**, Cyril *IntWW 91*
**Stein**, Cyril 1928- *Who 92*
**Stein**, Dale Franklin 1935- *AmMWSc 92, WhoMW 92*
**Stein**, Daryl Lee 1949- *AmMWSc 92*
**Stein**, David Morris *AmMWSc 92*
**Stein**, David Timothy 1936- *WhoRel 92*
**Stein**, Dean K. 1955- *WhoEnt 92*
**Stein**, Deborah Lee 1960- *WhoAmL 92*
**Stein**, Diana B 1937- *AmMWSc 92*
**Stein**, Dona *DrAPF 91*
**Stein**, Donald Gerald 1939- *AmMWSc 92*
**Stein**, Edith 1891-1942 *EncTR 91 [port]*
**Stein**, Eleanor Bankoff 1923- *WhoAmL 92, WhoMW 92*
**Stein**, Elias M 1931- *AmMWSc 92, IntWW 91*
**Stein**, Elizabeth Ann 1931- *WhoWest 92*
**Stein**, Eric 1913- *WhoAmL 92*
**Stein**, Ernest D. *WhoAmL 92*
**Stein**, Frank S 1921- *AmMWSc 92*
**Stein**, Fred P 1934- *AmMWSc 92*
**Stein**, Frederick Max 1919- *AmMWSc 92*
**Stein**, Fritz 1897-1961 *EncTR 91 [port]*
**Stein**, Gary Allen 1948- *WhoAmL 92*
**Stein**, Gary S. 1933- *WhoAmL 92, WhoAmP 91*
**Stein**, Gary S 1943- *AmMWSc 92*
**Stein**, George Nathan 1917- *AmMWSc 92*
**Stein**, Gertrude 1874-1946 *BenetAL 91, FacFETw [port], HanAmWH, LiExTwC, ModAWWr, RComAH*
**Stein**, Gertrude Emilie *WhoEnt 92*
**Stein**, Gretchen Herpel 1945- *AmMWSc 92, WhoWest 92*
**Stein**, Hadassah *DrAPF 91*
**Stein**, Hannah *DrAPF 91*
**Stein**, Harvey Philip 1940- *AmMWSc 92*
**Stein**, Herbert 1916- *IntWW 91, WhoFI 92, WrDr 92*
**Stein**, Herbert Joseph 1928- *AmMWSc 92*
**Stein**, Herman David 1917- *WhoMW 92*
**Stein**, Herman H 1930- *AmMWSc 92*
**Stein**, Holly Jayne 1954- *WhoWest 92*
**Stein**, Howard 1952- *WhoFI 92, WhoMW 92*
**Stein**, Howard Jay 1933- *AmMWSc 92*
**Stein**, Irving F, Jr 1918- *AmMWSc 92*
**Stein**, Ivie, Jr 1940- *AmMWSc 92*
**Stein**, Jack J 1938- *AmMWSc 92*
**Stein**, Jacob K. 1931- *WhoAmL 92*
**Stein**, James D, Jr 1941- *AmMWSc 92*
**Stein**, James Ronald 1950- *WhoEnt 92*
**Stein**, Janet Lee Swinehart 1946- *AmMWSc 92*
**Stein**, Jeff D. 1951- *WhoEnt 92*
**Stein**, Jeffrey Howard 1960- *WhoWest 92*
**Stein**, Jeremy Chaim 1960- *WhoFI 92*
**Stein**, Jerome Leon 1928- *WhoFI 92*
**Stein**, Jerry Michael 1952- *AmMWSc 92*
**Stein**, Jerry Sanford 1942- *WhoMW 92*
**Stein**, Joel Kenneth 1961- *WhoMW 92*
**Stein**, John 1944- *WhoFI 92*
**Stein**, John Christopher 1961- *WhoMW 92, WhoRel 92*
**Stein**, John Edward 1965- *WhoMW 92*
**Stein**, John Magrish 1967- *WhoFI 92*
**Stein**, John Michael 1935- *AmMWSc 92*
**Stein**, Joseph *WhoEnt 92*
**Stein**, Julia *DrAPF 91*
**Stein**, Kathryn E *AmMWSc 92*
**Stein**, Kenneth James 1929- *WhoRel 92*
**Stein**, Kenneth Michael 1957- *WhoEnt 92*
**Stein**, Larry 1931- *AmMWSc 92*
**Stein**, Lawrence 1922- *AmMWSc 92*
**Stein**, Leon 1910- *NewAmDM, WhoEnt 92*
**Stein**, Marjorie Leiter *AmMWSc 92*
**Stein**, Mark Avrum 1951- *WhoEnt 92*
**Stein**, Martin Matthew 1946- *WhoFI 92*
**Stein**, Marvin 1923- *AmMWSc 92*
**Stein**, Marvin L 1924- *AmMWSc 92*
**Stein**, Michael B. 1940- *WrDr 92*
**Stein**, Michael Ray 1952- *WhoMW 92*
**Stein**, Michael Roger 1943- *AmMWSc 92*
**Stein**, Milton Michael 1936- *WhoAmL 92*
**Stein**, Myron 1925- *AmMWSc 92*
**Stein**, Otto Ludwig 1925- *AmMWSc 92*
**Stein**, Paul Arthur 1937- *WhoFI 92*
**Stein**, Paul David 1934- *AmMWSc 92, WhoMW 92*
**Stein**, Paul John 1950- *AmMWSc 92*
**Stein**, Paul Lloyd 1943- *WhoMW 92*
**Stein**, Paul S G 1943- *AmMWSc 92*
**Stein**, Paula Barton 1929- *WhoFI 92*
**Stein**, Paula Jean Anne Barton 1929- *WhoMW 92*
**Stein**, Peter 1926- *WrDr 92*
**Stein**, Peter Gonville 1926- *IntAu&W 91, IntWW 91, Who 92*
**Stein**, Philip 1932- *AmMWSc 92*
**Stein**, Ralph Michael 1943- *WhoAmL 92*
**Stein**, Reinhardt P 1935- *AmMWSc 92*
**Stein**, Richard Adolph 1937- *AmMWSc 92*
**Stein**, Richard Allen 1953- *WhoEnt 92, WhoWest 92*
**Stein**, Richard Bernard 1940- *AmMWSc 92*
**Stein**, Richard James 1930- *AmMWSc 92*
**Stein**, Richard Jay 1946- *AmMWSc 92*
**Stein**, Richard L. 1957- *WhoFI 92*
**Stein**, Richard Paul 1925- *WhoFI 92*
**Stein**, Richard Stephen 1925- *AmMWSc 92*
**Stein**, Robert Alfred 1933- *AmMWSc 92*
**Stein**, Robert Allen 1938- *WhoAmL 92*
**Stein**, Robert Foster 1935- *AmMWSc 92, WhoMW 92*
**Stein**, Robert George 1939- *WhoWest 92*
**Stein**, Robert Harry 1935- *WhoRel 92*
**Stein**, Robert Jacob *AmMWSc 92*
**Stein**, Ronald Bley 1935- *WhoWest 92*
**Stein**, Roy Allen 1947- *AmMWSc 92*
**Stein**, Ruth E K 1941- *AmMWSc 92*
**Stein**, Samuel H 1937- *AmMWSc 92*
**Stein**, Samuel Richard 1946- *AmMWSc 92*
**Stein**, Seymour Norman 1913- *AmMWSc 92*
**Stein**, Sherman Kopald 1926- *AmMWSc 92, WhoWest 92*
**Stein**, Sol 1926- *IntAu&W 91, WhoEnt 92, WrDr 92*
**Stein**, Stephen 1943- *WhoWest 92*
**Stein**, Stephen Ellery 1948- *AmMWSc 92*
**Stein**, Stephen Jay 1952- *WhoRel 92*
**Stein**, Stuart Leonard 1946- *WhoAmL 92*
**Stein**, Sylvester *LiExTwC*
**Stein**, T Peter 1941- *AmMWSc 92*
**Stein**, Talbert Sheldon 1941- *AmMWSc 92*
**Stein**, Theodore Anthony 1938- *AmMWSc 92*
**Stein**, Toby *DrAPF 91*
**Stein**, Wayne Alfred 1937- *AmMWSc 92*
**Stein**, William Allan 1956- *WhoWest 92*
**Stein**, William Earl 1924- *AmMWSc 92*
**Stein**, William Edward 1946- *AmMWSc 92*
**Stein**, William Howard 1911-1980 *WhoNob 90*
**Stein**, William Ivo 1922- *AmMWSc 92*
**Stein-Taylor**, Janet Ruth *AmMWSc 92*
**Steinau**, Richard David 1947- *WhoFI 92*
**Steinbach**, Alan Henry 1930- *WhoMW 92, WhoRel 92*
**Steinbach**, Charles Albert 1951- *WhoMW 92*
**Steinbach**, Harold I. 1956- *WhoAmL 92*
**Steinbach**, Leonard 1927- *AmMWSc 92*
**Steinbach**, Lynne Susan 1953- *WhoWest 92*
**Steinbach**, Meredith *DrAPF 91*
**Steinbach**, Meredith Lynn 1949- *IntAu&W 91*
**Steinbacher**, John Adam 1925- *WhoWest 92*
**Steinback**, Thomas R. 1950- *WhoFI 92*
**Steinbeck**, John *SourALJ*
**Steinbeck**, John 1902-1968 *BenetAL 91, ConAu 35NR, FacFETw [port], RComAH, TwCWW 91*
**Steinbeck**, John, IV d1991 *NewYTBS 91*
**Steinbeck**, John Ernst 1902-1968 *WhoNob 90*
**Steinbeck**, John Witherup, II 1931- *WhoWest 92*
**Steinbeck**, Klaus 1937- *AmMWSc 92*
**Steinberg**, Alan L. *DrAPF 91*
**Steinberg**, Alfred David 1940- *AmMWSc 92*
**Steinberg**, Arnold David 1930- *WhoMW 92*
**Steinberg**, Arthur Gerald 1912- *AmMWSc 92*
**Steinberg**, Barry Paul 1941- *WhoAmL 92*
**Steinberg**, Bernard Albert 1924- *AmMWSc 92*
**Steinberg**, Bernhard 1897- *AmMWSc 92*
**Steinberg**, Bettie Murray 1937- *AmMWSc 92*
**Steinberg**, Bradley D. 1933- *WhoAmL 92*
**Steinberg**, Carolyn 1956- *ConCom 92*
**Steinberg**, Cathey Weiss 1942- *WhoAmP 91*
**Steinberg**, Daniel 1922- *AmMWSc 92, WhoWest 92*
**Steinberg**, Daniel J 1935- *AmMWSc 92*
**Steinberg**, David 1942- *IntMPA 92, WhoEnt 92*
**Steinberg**, David H 1929- *AmMWSc 92*
**Steinberg**, David Israel 1942- *AmMWSc 92*
**Steinberg**, David Joseph 1934- *WhoEnt 92*
**Steinberg**, Eliot 1923- *AmMWSc 92*
**Steinberg**, Ellis Philip 1920- *AmMWSc 92*
**Steinberg**, Erwin R. 1920- *WrDr 92*
**Steinberg**, George Milton *AmMWSc 92*
**Steinberg**, Gerald Neil 1945- *Who 92*
**Steinberg**, Gregg Martin 1962- *WhoMW 92*
**Steinberg**, Gunther 1924- *AmMWSc 92*
**Steinberg**, Hannah *Who 92*
**Steinberg**, Harold I 1935- *WhoAmP 91*
**Steinberg**, Herb 1921- *IntMPA 92*

**Steinberg,** Herbert Aaron 1929- *AmMWSc 92*
**Steinberg,** Howard 1926- *AmMWSc 92, WhoWest 92*
**Steinberg,** Howard E. 1944- *WhoAmL 92, WhoFI 92*
**Steinberg,** Irwin Hugh 1921- *WhoEnt 92*
**Steinberg,** Jack d1991 *Who 92N*
**Steinberg,** Jack 1915- *WhoAmL 92, WhoWest 92*
**Steinberg,** Joan Emily 1932- *WhoWest 92*
**Steinberg,** Jonathan 1934- *WrDr 92*
**Steinberg,** Jonathan Robert 1939- *WhoAmL 92, WhoAmP 91*
**Steinberg,** Joseph 1920- *AmMWSc 92*
**Steinberg,** Joseph Lawrence 1928- *WhoAmL 92*
**Steinberg,** Leo 1920- *WrDr 92*
**Steinberg,** Lois Saxelby 1926- *WhoMW 92*
**Steinberg,** M A 1920- *AmMWSc 92*
**Steinberg,** Malcolm Saul 1930- *AmMWSc 92*
**Steinberg,** Marcia Irene 1944- *AmMWSc 92*
**Steinberg,** Mark Robert 1945- *WhoAmL 92*
**Steinberg,** Marshall 1932- *AmMWSc 92*
**Steinberg,** Martin 1920- *AmMWSc 92*
**Steinberg,** Martin H 1936- *AmMWSc 92*
**Steinberg,** Marvin Phillip 1922- *AmMWSc 92*
**Steinberg,** Melvin Allen 1933- *WhoAmP 91*
**Steinberg,** Melvin Sanford 1928- *AmMWSc 92*
**Steinberg,** Meyer 1924- *AmMWSc 92*
**Steinberg,** Michael 1928- *WhoEnt 92*
**Steinberg,** Michael Ward 1952- *WhoAmL 92*
**Steinberg,** Mitchell I 1944- *AmMWSc 92*
**Steinberg,** Paul B 1940- *WhoAmP 91*
**Steinberg,** Philip Arthur 1945- *WhoAmL 92*
**Steinberg,** Phillip Henry 1931- *AmMWSc 92*
**Steinberg,** Richard 1930- *AmMWSc 92*
**Steinberg,** Richard Howard 1936- *WhoAmL 92*
**Steinberg,** Richard Steven 1955- *WhoFI 92*
**Steinberg,** Robert 1922- *AmMWSc 92*
**Steinberg,** Robert Eric 1954- *WhoAmP 91*
**Steinberg,** Robert Lee 1951- *WhoAmL 92*
**Steinberg,** Robert M 1942- *WhoIns 92*
**Steinberg,** Robert M. 1945- *WhoFI 92*
**Steinberg,** Robert Martin 1941- *WhoWest 92*
**Steinberg,** Ronald T 1929- *AmMWSc 92*
**Steinberg,** Roy Bennett 1951- *WhoEnt 92*
**Steinberg,** Roy Herbert 1935- *AmMWSc 92*
**Steinberg,** Saul 1914- *BenetAL 91, IntWW 91, SmATA 67 [port]*
**Steinberg,** Saul Phillip 1939- *Who 92*
**Steinberg,** Scott A. 1957- *WhoAmL 92*
**Steinberg,** Seth Michael 1958- *AmMWSc 92*
**Steinberg,** Stanly 1940- *AmMWSc 92*
**Steinberg,** Stephen Cobbett d1991 *NewYTBS 91*
**Steinberg,** Stuart Alvin 1941- *AmMWSc 92*
**Steinberg,** Thomas Ivan 1924- *WhoWest 92*
**Steinberg,** Warren Linnington 1924- *WhoWest 92*
**Steinberg,** William 1899-1978 *FacFETw, NewAmDM*
**Steinberg-Podgorny,** Judy Ellen *WhoWest 92*
**Steinberger,** Anna 1928- *AmMWSc 92*
**Steinberger,** Jack 1921- *AmMWSc 92, IntWW 91, Who 92, WhoNob 90*
**Steinberger,** Richard Lynn 1939- *WhoAmL 92*
**Steinbergh,** Judith W. *DrAPF 91*
**Steinbock,** John T. 1937- *WhoRel 92*
**Steinborn,** David M 1936- *WhoAmP 91*
**Steinbrecher,** Lester 1927- *AmMWSc 92*
**Steinbrenner,** Arthur H 1917- *AmMWSc 92*
**Steinbrenner,** Eugene Clarence 1921- *AmMWSc 92*
**Steinbrenner,** George *NewYTBS 91 [port]*
**Steinbrenner,** George 1930- *News 91 [port]*
**Steinbrenner,** George Edward 1947- *WhoMW 92*
**Steinbrenner,** Lowell *WhoAmP 91*
**Steinbruck,** John Frederick *WhoRel 92*
**Steinbruegge,** Kenneth Brian 1939- *AmMWSc 92*
**Steinbrugge,** Karl V 1919- *AmMWSc 92*
**Steindl,** Frank George 1935- *WhoFI 92*
**Steindler,** Arthur 1878-1959 *FacFETw*
**Steindler,** Martin Joseph 1928- *AmMWSc 92, WhoMW 92*
**Steindler,** Walter G. 1927- *WhoAmL 92*
**Steineck,** Paul Lewis 1942- *AmMWSc 92*
**Steineger,** Joe *WhoAmP 91*
**Steineger,** John Francis, Jr 1924- *WhoAmP 91*
**Steineger,** Margaret Leisy 1926- *WhoMW 92*
**Steinem,** Gloria 1934- *BenetAL 91, FacFETw, HanAmWH, IntAu&W 91, IntWW 91, RComAH*
**Steinem,** Robert *DrAPF 91*
**Steiner,** Andre Louis 1928- *AmMWSc 92*
**Steiner,** Anne Kercheval 1936- *AmMWSc 92*
**Steiner,** Barbara A. 1934- *SmATA 13AS [port]*
**Steiner,** Bruce 1931- *AmMWSc 92*
**Steiner,** Corky Philip Harry 1943- *WhoFI 92*
**Steiner,** David Randall 1963- *WhoMW 92*
**Steiner,** Diana 1932- *WhoEnt 92*
**Steiner,** Donald Frederick 1930- *AmMWSc 92*
**Steiner,** Edward Earl 1955- *WhoMW 92*
**Steiner,** Erich E 1919- *AmMWSc 92*
**Steiner,** Eugene Francis 1934- *AmMWSc 92*
**Steiner,** Felix 1869-1966 *EncTR 91*
**Steiner,** Frances Josephine 1937- *WhoEnt 92*
**Steiner,** Francis Charles 1925- *WhoMW 92*
**Steiner,** Gary A. d1966 *LesBEnT 92*
**Steiner,** Gene 1948- *WhoEnt 92*
**Steiner,** George 1929- *IntAu&W 91, IntWW 91, Who 92, WrDr 92*
**Steiner,** George 1936- *AmMWSc 92*
**Steiner,** George 1947- *AmMWSc 92*
**Steiner,** George A. *WrDr 92*
**Steiner,** George Albert 1912- *IntAu&W 91*
**Steiner,** George Francis 1929- *LiExTwC*
**Steiner,** Gilbert 1937- *AmMWSc 92*
**Steiner,** Henry Jacob 1930- *WhoAmL 92*
**Steiner,** Henry M 1923- *AmMWSc 92*
**Steiner,** Herbert M 1927- *AmMWSc 92*
**Steiner,** Jack William, Jr. 1950- *WhoAmL 92*
**Steiner,** Jacque 1929- *WhoAmP 91*
**Steiner,** James W 1926- *AmMWSc 92*
**Steiner,** Jan Wilson 1916- *WhoMW 92*
**Steiner,** Jean Louise 1951- *AmMWSc 92*
**Steiner,** Jeffrey Josef 1937- *WhoFI 92*
**Steiner,** John Edward 1917- *AmMWSc 92*
**Steiner,** John F 1908- *AmMWSc 92*
**Steiner,** Julius Michael 1946- *WhoAmL 92*
**Steiner,** Kenneth Donald 1936- *WhoRel 92, WhoWest 92*
**Steiner,** Kim Carlyle 1948- *AmMWSc 92*
**Steiner,** Kurt 1912- *IntAu&W 91, WhoAmL 92, WrDr 92*
**Steiner,** Kurt Edric 1946- *AmMWSc 92*
**Steiner,** Laurie Glandt 1957- *WhoAmL 92*
**Steiner,** Lee Anne S 1935- *WhoAmP 91*
**Steiner,** Lee Nathan 1922- *WhoAmL 92*
**Steiner,** Lewis Henry 1827-1892 *BiInAmS*
**Steiner,** Lisa Amelia 1933- *AmMWSc 92*
**Steiner,** Luke Joseph 1930- *WhoRel 92*
**Steiner,** Manfred *AmMWSc 92*
**Steiner,** Marion Rothberg 1941- *AmMWSc 92*
**Steiner,** Martha Lane 1957- *WhoAmP 91*
**Steiner,** Max 1888-1971 *FacFETw, NewAmDM*
**Steiner,** Michael Patrick 1951- *WhoEnt 92*
**Steiner,** Morris 1904- *AmMWSc 92*
**Steiner,** Ottokar Harold Mojmir St John 1916- *Who 92*
**Steiner,** Paul *WhoEnt 92*
**Steiner,** Paul A 1929- *WhoIns 92*
**Steiner,** Peter Otto 1922- *WhoAmL 92*
**Steiner,** Pinckney Alston, III 1938- *AmMWSc 92*
**Steiner,** Ray Phillip 1941- *AmMWSc 92*
**Steiner,** Richard Russell 1923- *WhoWest 92*
**Steiner,** Robert *DrAPF 91*
**Steiner,** Robert Alan 1947- *AmMWSc 92*
**Steiner,** Robert C 1950- *WhoAmP 91*
**Steiner,** Robert Emil 1918- *Who 92*
**Steiner,** Robert Frank 1926- *AmMWSc 92*
**Steiner,** Roger William 1963- *WhoAmL 92*
**Steiner,** Rudolf 1861-1925 *RelLAm 91*
**Steiner,** Russell Irwin 1927- *AmMWSc 92*
**Steiner,** Sheldon 1940- *AmMWSc 92*
**Steiner,** Werner Douglas 1932- *AmMWSc 92*
**Steinert,** Floyd Henry 1920- *WhoAmP 91*
**Steinert,** Leon Albert 1930- *AmMWSc 92*
**Steinert,** Peter Malcolm *AmMWSc 92*
**Steinert,** Rocky Brent 1951- *WhoMW 92*
**Steinetz,** Bernard George, Jr 1927- *AmMWSc 92*
**Steinfeld,** Alan Geoffrey 1946- *Who 92*
**Steinfeld,** Jeffrey Irwin 1940- *AmMWSc 92*
**Steinfeld,** Jesse Leonard 1927- *AmMWSc 92*
**Steinfeld,** Leonard 1925- *AmMWSc 92*
**Steinfeld,** Reid Layne 1953- *WhoAmL 92*
**Steinfink,** Hugo 1924- *AmMWSc 92*
**Steingass,** David *DrAPF 91*
**Steingesser,** Martin *DrAPF 91*
**Steingiser,** Samuel 1918- *AmMWSc 92*
**Steingold,** Harold 1929- *AmMWSc 92*
**Steingraber,** Frederick George 1938- *WhoFI 92, WhoMW 92*
**Steinhagen,** William Herrick 1948- *AmMWSc 92*
**Steinhardt,** Charles Kendall 1935- *AmMWSc 92*
**Steinhardt,** Emil J 1937- *AmMWSc 92*
**Steinhardt,** Gary C. 1944- *WhoMW 92*
**Steinhardt,** Gary Carl 1944- *AmMWSc 92*
**Steinhardt,** J Michael 1942- *WhoIns 92*
**Steinhardt,** Nancy Shatzman 1954- *ConAu 135*
**Steinhardt,** Paul Joseph 1952- *AmMWSc 92*
**Steinhardt,** Ralph Gustav, III 1954- *WhoAmL 92*
**Steinhardt,** Richard Antony 1939- *AmMWSc 92*
**Steinhart,** Carol Elder 1935- *AmMWSc 92*
**Steinhart,** John Shannon 1929- *AmMWSc 92*
**Steinhart,** William Lee 1942- *AmMWSc 92*
**Steinhauer,** Allen Laurence 1931- *AmMWSc 92*
**Steinhauer,** Gillian 1938- *WhoAmL 92*
**Steinhauer,** John M 1925- *WhoAmP 91*
**Steinhauer,** Kurt Gerard 1949- *WhoIns 92*
**Steinhauer,** Lillian R *IntAu&W 91*
**Steinhauer,** Paul David 1933- *AmMWSc 92*
**Steinhaus,** David Walter 1919- *AmMWSc 92*
**Steinhaus,** John Edward 1917- *AmMWSc 92*
**Steinhaus,** O. Otto 1929- *WhoRel 92*
**Steinhaus,** Ralph K 1939- *AmMWSc 92*
**Steinhauser,** Delores Wingard 1955- *WhoFI 92*
**Steinhauser,** John Jack Stuart 1958- *WhoFI 92*
**Steinhauser,** John William 1924- *WhoFI 92*
**Steinhauser,** Sheldon Eli 1930- *WhoWest 92*
**Steinheimer,** Judy Morales 1941- *WhoHisp 92*
**Steinheimer,** Walter 1955- *WhoFI 92*
**Steinhilber,** August William 1932- *WhoAmL 92*
**Steinhoff,** Donald Dewey 1954- *WhoAmL 92*
**Steinhoff,** Hans 1882-1945 *EncTR 91 [port]*
**Steinhoff,** Monika Anneliese 1941- *WhoWest 92*
**Steinhorn,** Irwin Harry 1940- *WhoAmL 92*
**Steinhouse,** Carl Lewis 1931- *WhoAmL 92*
**Steinhouse,** Edward 1940- *WhoAmL 92*
**Steinig,** Stephen Nelson 1945- *WhoFI 92*
**Steinitz,** Michael Otto 1944- *AmMWSc 92*
**Steinkamp,** James Robert 1954- *WhoMW 92*
**Steinkamp,** Mary Kathleen 1935- *WhoRel 92*
**Steinkamp,** Myrna Pratt 1938- *AmMWSc 92*
**Steinke,** Ann E 1946- *IntAu&W 91*
**Steinke,** Frederich H 1935- *AmMWSc 92*
**Steinke,** Greg A. 1942- *WhoEnt 92*
**Steinke,** Letha May *WhoWest 92*
**Steinke,** Paul Karl Willi 1921- *AmMWSc 92*
**Steinke,** Peter Louis 1938- *WhoRel 92*
**Steinke,** Russell *DrAPF 91*
**Steinker,** Don Cooper 1936- *AmMWSc 92, WhoMW 92*
**Steinkerchner,** Barbara Lynn 1957- *WhoMW 92*
**Steinkraus,** Donald Curtiss 1950- *AmMWSc 92*
**Steinkraus,** Keith Hartley 1918- *AmMWSc 92*
**Steinkuhler,** Franz 1937- *IntWW 91*
**Steinlage,** Paul Nicholas 1941- *WhoIns 92*
**Steinlage,** Ralph Cletus 1940- *AmMWSc 92, WhoMW 92*
**Steinlage,** William Scott 1946- *WhoMW 92*
**Steinlauf,** Marvin Ira 1938- *WhoFI 92*
**Steinle,** Edmund Charles, Jr 1924- *AmMWSc 92*
**Steinman,** Charles Hunter 1958- *WhoMW 92*
**Steinman,** Charles Robert 1938- *AmMWSc 92*
**Steinman,** Clayton Marshall 1950- *WhoWest 92*
**Steinman,** Harry Gordon 1913- *AmMWSc 92*
**Steinman,** Howard Mark 1944- *AmMWSc 92*
**Steinman,** Irvin David 1924- *AmMWSc 92*
**Steinman,** Jerry 1924- *WhoFI 92*
**Steinman,** John Francis 1916- *WhoWest 92*
**Steinman,** Lisa Malinowski *DrAPF 91*
**Steinman,** Lisa Malinowski 1950- *WhoWest 92*
**Steinman,** Martin 1937- *AmMWSc 92*
**Steinman,** Michael 1952- *ConAu 134*
**Steinman,** Monte 1955- *IntMPA 92*
**Steinman,** Peter Edwin 1948- *WhoAmL 92*
**Steinman,** Ralph R 1910- *AmMWSc 92*
**Steinman,** Robert 1918- *AmMWSc 92*
**Steinman,** Scott Brad 1956- *WhoMW 92*
**Steinman,** Shirley P 1938- *WhoIns 92*
**Steinmann,** Andrew Erwin 1954- *WhoRel 92*
**Steinmann,** John Colburn 1941- *WhoWest 92*
**Steinmeier,** Robert C 1943- *AmMWSc 92*
**Steinmetz,** Charles 1865-1923 *FacFETw*
**Steinmetz,** Charles Henry 1929- *AmMWSc 92*
**Steinmetz,** Donald W 1924- *WhoAmP 91*
**Steinmetz,** Donald Walter 1924- *WhoAmL 92, WhoMW 92*
**Steinmetz,** Eulalie *ConAu 134*
**Steinmetz,** John Charles 1947- *WhoWest 92*
**Steinmetz,** Jon David 1940- *WhoMW 92*
**Steinmetz,** Joseph Edward 1955- *WhoMW 92*
**Steinmetz,** Kaye H *WhoAmP 91*
**Steinmetz,** Lawrence L 1938- *IntAu&W 91*
**Steinmetz,** Lawrence Leo 1938- *WrDr 92*
**Steinmetz,** Manning Louis, III 1942- *WhoFI 92*
**Steinmetz,** Michael Anthony 1951- *AmMWSc 92*
**Steinmetz,** Paul B. 1928- *ConAu 135*
**Steinmetz,** Peter Emile 1941- *WhoEnt 92*
**Steinmetz,** Philip R 1927- *AmMWSc 92*
**Steinmetz,** Walter Edmund 1921- *AmMWSc 92*
**Steinmetz,** Wayne Edward 1945- *AmMWSc 92, WhoWest 92*
**Steinmetz,** William John 1939- *AmMWSc 92*
**Steinmetz Cosmic,** Rachel Ela 1956- *WhoEnt 92*
**Steinmuller,** David 1934- *AmMWSc 92*
**Steinnes,** Eiliv 1938- *IntWW 91*
**Steinohrt,** William John 1937- *WhoEnt 92, WhoMW 92*
**Steinrauf,** Larry King 1931- *AmMWSc 92*
**Steinschneider,** Alfred 1929- *AmMWSc 92*
**Steinwachs,** Donald Michael 1946- *AmMWSc 92*
**Steinwurzel,** David Moshe 1934- *WhoRel 92*
**Steiringer,** Luther 1845?-1903 *BiInAmS*
**Steis,** William Burton 1907- *WhoAmP 91*
**Steiss,** Alan Walter 1937- *WhoMW 92*
**Steitz,** Joan Argetsinger 1941- *AmMWSc 92*
**Steitz,** Thomas Arthur 1940- *AmMWSc 92*
**Stejskal,** Edward Otto 1932- *AmMWSc 92*
**Stejskal,** Rudolf 1931- *AmMWSc 92*
**Stekel,** Frank D 1941- *AmMWSc 92*
**Stekiel,** William John 1928- *AmMWSc 92*
**Stekly,** Z J John 1933- *AmMWSc 92*
**Stekoll,** Michael Steven 1947- *AmMWSc 92, WhoWest 92*
**Stelck,** Charles Richard 1917- *AmMWSc 92*
**Stell,** George Roger 1933- *AmMWSc 92*
**Stell,** Joe M *WhoAmP 91*
**Stell,** John Elwin, Jr. 1954- *WhoAmL 92*
**Stell,** Michelle Lucille 1955- *WhoFI 92*
**Stell,** Philip Michael 1934- *Who 92*
**Stell,** Walter Joseph, III 1936- *WhoEnt 92*
**Stell,** William Kenyon 1939- *AmMWSc 92*
**Stella,** Antonio 1868-1927 *DcAmImH*
**Stella,** David M. 1958- *WhoFI 92*
**Stella,** Frank 1936- *FacFETw*
**Stella,** Frank D 1919- *WhoAmP 91*
**Stella,** Frank Dante 1919- *WhoMW 92*
**Stella,** Paul M 1944- *AmMWSc 92*
**Stella,** Valentino John 1946- *AmMWSc 92*
**Stella,** William J 1942- *WhoIns 92*
**Stellar,** Eliot 1919- *AmMWSc 92*
**Stellbrink,** Karl Friedrich 1894-1943 *EncTR 91*
**Steller,** Kenneth Eugene 1941- *AmMWSc 92*
**Stellers,** Thomas Joe 1940- *WhoMW 92*
**Stelling,** James Henry, III 1942- *WhoAmP 91*
**Stelling,** Nancy Joan 1937- *WhoRel 92*
**Stellingwerf,** Robert Francis 1947- *AmMWSc 92*
**Stelljes,** George 1961- *WhoFI 92*
**Stellmacher,** Jon Michael 1956- *WhoMW 92*
**Stellwag,** George William 1921- *WhoIns 92*
**Stellwagen,** Earle C 1933- *AmMWSc 92*
**Stellwagen,** Robert Harwood 1941- *AmMWSc 92, WhoWest 92*
**Stelly,** Matthias 1916- *AmMWSc 92*
**Stelly,** Vic *WhoAmP 91*
**Stelmach,** Marie Anna 1945- *WhoRel 92*
**Stelmachowicz,** Michael Joseph 1927- *WhoRel 92*

**Stelmachowski**, Andrzej 1925- IntWW 91
**Steloff**, Arthur 1925- IntMPA 92
**Stelos**, Peter 1923- AmMWSc 92
**Stelson**, Kim Adair 1952- WhoMW 92
**Stelson**, Paul Hugh 1927- AmMWSc 92
**Stelson**, T E 1928- AmMWSc 92
**Steltenkamp**, Robert John 1936- AmMWSc 92
**Stelting**, Kathleen Marie 1942- AmMWSc 92
**Stelts**, Marion Lee 1940- AmMWSc 92
**Steltzlen**, Janelle Hicks 1937- WhoAmL 92
**Stelzel**, Walter Tell, Jr. 1940- WhoFI 92
**Stelzer**, Kerry Lynn 1959- WhoAmL 92
**Stelzer**, Lorin Roy 1931- AmMWSc 92
**Stelzig**, Eugene L. DrAPF 91
**Stelzner**, Paul Burke 1935- WhoFI 92
**Stem**, Carl Herbert 1935- WhoFI 92
**Stem**, Ronald Leon 1948- WhoMW 92
**Stember**, Charles Herbert 1916-1982 ConAu 135
**Stembler**, John H. 1913- IntMPA 92
**Stembler**, William J. 1946- IntMPA 92
**Stembridge**, David Harry 1932- Who 92
**Stembridge**, Rudy, Jr. 1956- WhoRel 92
**Stembridge**, Vernie A 1924- AmMWSc 92
**Stemer**, Werner Hubert 1955- WhoEnt 92
**Stemke**, Gerald W 1935- AmMWSc 92
**Stemler**, Alan James 1943- AmMWSc 92
**Stemmer**, Edward Alan 1930- AmMWSc 92
**Stemmer**, Jay John 1939- WhoWest 92
**Stemmermann**, Grant N 1918- AmMWSc 92
**Stemmler**, Edward J 1929- AmMWSc 92
**Stemmons**, Robert Earl 1960- WhoAmL 92
**Stemniski**, John Roman 1933- AmMWSc 92
**Stempak**, Jerome G 1931- AmMWSc 92
**Stempel**, Arthur 1917- AmMWSc 92
**Stempel**, Edward 1926- AmMWSc 92
**Stempel**, Ernest Edward 1916- WhoFI 92, WhoIns 92
**Stempel**, Robert 1933- News 91 [port], -91-3 [port]
**Stempel**, Robert C 1933- AmMWSc 92, IntWW 91, WhoFI 92, WhoMW 92
**Stempen**, Henry 1924- AmMWSc 92
**Stemper**, William Herman, Jr. WhoRel 92
**Stempien**, Martin F, Jr 1930- AmMWSc 92
**Stemple**, Donald L 1930- WhoAmP 91
**Stemple**, Joel G 1942- AmMWSc 92
**Stempson**, William H 1948- WhoIns 92
**Stemshorn**, Barry William 1947- AmMWSc 92
**Sten**, Anna 1908- SovUnBD
**Stenack**, Richard John 1945- WhoMW 92
**Stenback**, Par Olav Mikael 1941- IntWW 91
**Stenback**, Wayne Albert 1929- AmMWSc 92
**Stenbaek-Nielsen**, Hans C AmMWSc 92
**Stenberg**, Charles Gustave 1935- AmMWSc 92
**Stenberg**, Donald B. 1948- WhoAmL 92, WhoAmP 91, WhoMW 92
**Stenberg**, Georgiy Avgustovich 1900-1933 SovUnBD
**Stenberg**, Paula E 1953- AmMWSc 92
**Stenberg**, Richard Stephen 1937- WhoRel 92
**Stenberg**, Virgil Irvin 1935- AmMWSc 92
**Stenberg**, Vladimir Avgustovich 1899-1982 SovUnBD
**Stencel**, Carol Frances 1934- WhoMW 92
**Stencel**, Robert Edward 1950- AmMWSc 92
**Stenchever**, Morton Albert 1931- AmMWSc 92
**Stendahl**, Krister 1921- WhoRel 92
**Stendell**, Rey Carl 1941- AmMWSc 92
**Stender**, Charles Frederick 1940- WhoWest 92
**Stendhal** 1783-1842 GuFrLit 1
**Stenehjem**, Allan WhoAmP 91
**Stenehjem**, Wayne 1953- WhoAmP 91
**Stenehjem**, Wayne Kevin 1953- WhoMW 92
**Stenerson**, Georgiann 1934- WhoAmP 91
**Stenesh**, Jochanan 1927- AmMWSc 92
**Stenflo**, Jan Olof 1942- IntWW 91
**Stengel**, Charles Dillon 1889-1975 FacFETw
**Stengel**, Robert Frank 1938- AmMWSc 92
**Stenger**, Frank 1938- AmMWSc 92
**Stenger**, Richard J 1927- AmMWSc 92
**Stenger**, Vernon Arthur 1908- AmMWSc 92
**Stenger**, Victor John 1935- AmMWSc 92
**Stenger**, William 1942- AmMWSc 92
**Stenger**, William J, Sr 1926- AmMWSc 92
**Stengle**, Thomas Richard 1929- AmMWSc 92
**Stengle**, William Bernard 1923- AmMWSc 92
**Stenham**, Anthony William Paul 1932- Who 92
**Stenhammer**, Wilhelm 1871-1927 NewAmDM
**Stenholm**, Charles W. 1938- AlmAP 92 [port], WhoFI 92
**Stenholm**, Charles Walter 1938- WhoAmP 91
**Stenhouse**, David 1932- WrDr 92
**Stenhouse**, Everett Ray 1931- WhoRel 92
**Stenhouse**, John Godwyn 1908- Who 92
**Stenhouse**, Nicol 1911- Who 92
**Stening**, George 1904- Who 92
**Stenkamp**, Ronald Eugene 1948- AmMWSc 92
**Stenlake**, Rodney Lee 1957- WhoAmL 92
**Stenlund**, Bengt Gustav Verner 1939- IntWW 91
**Stenmark**, Ingemar 1956- FacFETw
**Stenn**, Kurt S 1940- AmMWSc 92
**Stenner**, Charles Edwin 1926- WhoRel 92
**Stennes**, Walter 1895-1973 EncTR 91
**Stennett**, W Clinton 1956- WhoAmP 91
**Stennis**, John Cornelius 1901- IntWW 91, WhoAmP 91
**Stennis**, John Hampton 1935- WhoAmP 91
**Stennis**, Willie James 1923- WhoBlA 92
**Stensaas**, Larry J 1932- AmMWSc 92
**Stensaas**, Sharon Gail 1948- WhoWest 92
**Stensaas**, Suzanne Sperling 1939- AmMWSc 92
**Stenseth**, Raymond Eugene 1931- AmMWSc 92
**Stensether**, John Eldon 1944- WhoRel 92
**Stensland**, Linda L WhoAmP 91
**Stenson**, William F 1945- AmMWSc 92
**Stensrud**, Howard Lewis 1936- AmMWSc 92
**Stenstrom**, Michael Knudson 1948- AmMWSc 92, WhoWest 92
**Stenstrom**, Richard Charles 1936- AmMWSc 92
**Stensvaag**, Saul George 1950- WhoRel 92
**Stensvad**, Allan Maurice 1934- WhoRel 92
**Stent**, Gunther S. 1924- WrDr 92
**Stent**, Gunther Siegmund 1924- AmMWSc 92, IntWW 91
**Stent**, Madelon Delany 1933- WhoBlA 92
**Stent**, Michelle Dorene 1955- WhoBlA 92
**Stent**, Nicole M. 1960- WhoBlA 92
**Stent**, Theodore R. 1924- WhoBlA 92
**Stentz**, Steven Thomas 1951- WhoWest 92
**Stenuf**, Theodore Joseph 1924- AmMWSc 92
**Stenulson**, Sonya Helen WhoMW 92
**Stenz**, Donald John 1937- WhoEnt 92
**Stenzel**, Kurt Hodgson 1932- AmMWSc 92
**Stenzel**, Reiner Ludwig 1940- AmMWSc 92
**Stenzel**, Wolfram G 1919- AmMWSc 92
**Step**, Eugene Lee 1929- WhoFI 92, WhoMW 92
**Stepakov**, Vladimir Il'ich 1912-1987 SovUnBD
**Stepan**, Alfred Henry 1920- AmMWSc 92
**Stepanchev**, Stephen DrAPF 91
**Stepanchev**, Stephen 1915- ConPo 91, WrDr 92
**Stepanek**, Joseph Edward 1917- WhoWest 92
**Stepanian**, Ira 1936- WhoFI 92
**Stepanian**, Steven Arvid, II 1935- WhoAmL 92
**Stepanishen**, Peter Richard 1942- AmMWSc 92
**Stepanov**, Vladimir Sevastyanovich 1927- IntWW 91
**Stepanova**, Varvar Fedorovna 1894-1958 SovUnBD
**Stepanovicius**, Julijonas 1911- IntWW 91
**Stepanski**, Anthony Francis, Jr. 1941- WhoFI 92
**Stepenuck**, Stephen Joseph, Jr 1937- AmMWSc 92
**Stephan**, Ann WhoAmP 91
**Stephan**, Bodo 1939- WhoFI 92
**Stephan**, Charles Michael 1949- WhoAmL 92
**Stephan**, Daniel Leroy 1947- WhoAmP 91
**Stephan**, David George 1930- AmMWSc 92
**Stephan**, Edmund Anton 1911- WhoAmL 92
**Stephan**, Egon, Sr. 1933- WhoEnt 92
**Stephan**, George Peter 1933- WhoAmL 92
**Stephan**, John Jason 1941- IntAu&W 91
**Stephan**, Richard Albert 1929- WhoEnt 92
**Stephan**, Robert Conrad 1952- WhoFI 92
**Stephan**, Robert T 1933- WhoAmP 91
**Stephan**, Robert Taft 1933- WhoAmL 92, WhoMW 92
**Stephanakis**, Stavros John 1940- AmMWSc 92
**Stephanedes**, Yorgos Jordan 1951- AmMWSc 92
**Stephani**, Christakis 1926- IntWW 91
**Stephanopoulos**, Constantine IntWW 91
**Stephanopoulos**, Stephanos 1898- FacFETw
**Stephanou**, Stephen Emmanuel 1919- AmMWSc 92
**Stephans**, Richard A 1935- AmMWSc 92
**Stephans**, William Walter Thomas 1942- WhoFI 92
**Stephansson**, Stephan G. 1853-1927 BenetAL 91
**Stephany**, Edward O 1916- AmMWSc 92
**Stephany**, Judith Buckley 1944- WhoAmP 91
**Stephas**, Paul 1929- AmMWSc 92
**Stephen** EncEarC
**Stephen I** EncEarC
**Stephen**, Bishop 1857-1933 RelLAm 91
**Stephen Gobarus** EncEarC
**Stephen**, Charles Ronald 1916- AmMWSc 92
**Stephen**, David Who 92
**Stephen**, Derek Ronald James 1922- Who 92
**Stephen**, Edison J WhoAmP 91
**Stephen**, Edith 1939- WhoEnt 92
**Stephen**, Frederick Malcolm, Jr 1943- AmMWSc 92
**Stephen**, George Martin 1949- Who 92
**Stephen**, Harbourne Mackay 1916- Who 92
**Stephen**, Henrietta Hamilton 1925- Who 92
**Stephen**, James Barnett 1925- WhoAmP 91
**Stephen**, John David 1942- Who 92
**Stephen**, John Erle 1918- WhoAmL 92, WhoFI 92
**Stephen**, John Low 1912- Who 92
**Stephen**, Keith H 1934- AmMWSc 92
**Stephen**, Lessel Bruce 1920- Who 92
**Stephen**, Martin Who 92
**Stephen**, Martin 1949- ConAu 135
**Stephen**, Michael John 1933- AmMWSc 92
**Stephen**, Ninian 1923- Who 92
**Stephen**, Ninian Martin 1923- IntWW 91
**Stephen**, Norman McIntyre 1931- WhoAmP 91
**Stephen**, Norman Scott 1941- WhoIns 92
**Stephen**, Ralph A 1951- AmMWSc 92
**Stephen**, Richard Joseph 1945- WhoMW 92
**Stephen**, Rita Who 92
**Stephen**, Robert 1939- WhoAmP 91
**Stephen**, Thomas Gregory 1949- WhoMW 92
**Stephen**, William Procuronoff 1927- AmMWSc 92
**Stephens**, Aidan Patrick 1938- WhoMW 92
**Stephens**, Alan 1925- ConPo 91, WrDr 92
**Stephens**, Alan J WhoAmP 91
**Stephens**, Albert Hugh 1937- WhoAmL 92
**Stephens**, Alexander Hamilton 1812-1883 BenetAL 91
**Stephens**, Alice Barber 1858-1932 SmATA 66
**Stephens**, Allen Charles, Jr. 1966- WhoEnt 92
**Stephens**, Ann S. 1813-1886 BenetAL 91
**Stephens**, Anne 1912- Who 92
**Stephens**, Anthony William 1930- Who 92
**Stephens**, Arthur Brooke 1942- AmMWSc 92
**Stephens**, Arthur Veryan 1908- Who 92
**Stephens**, Bill Downey 1951- WhoMW 92
**Stephens**, Blythe WrDr 92
**Stephens**, Booker T 1944- WhoAmP 91, WhoBlA 92
**Stephens**, Brenda Wilson 1952- WhoBlA 92
**Stephens**, C. Michael 1949- WhoFI 92
**Stephens**, Casey WrDr 92
**Stephens**, Cedric John 1921- Who 92
**Stephens**, Charles Arthur Lloyd, Jr 1917- AmMWSc 92
**Stephens**, Charles Richard 1938- WhoBlA 92
**Stephens**, Charles W AmMWSc 92
**Stephens**, Christine Taylor 1951- AmMWSc 92
**Stephens**, Christopher Wilson T. Who 92
**Stephens**, Clarence Francis 1917- AmMWSc 92
**Stephens**, Craig Robert 1954- WhoWest 92
**Stephens**, Cynthia Diane 1951- WhoBlA 92
**Stephens**, Dale Nelson 1941- AmMWSc 92
**Stephens**, David Bisel 1944- WhoWest 92
**Stephens**, Douglas Robert 1935- AmMWSc 92
**Stephens**, Eddie A. 1946- WhoAmL 92
**Stephens**, Edgar Ray 1924- AmMWSc 92
**Stephens**, Elsie Marie 1948- WhoBlA 92
**Stephens**, F. Douglas 1913- WrDr 92
**Stephens**, Floris Elaine 1942- WhoWest 92
**Stephens**, Frances 1926- IntAu&W 91
**Stephens**, Frank Samuel 1931- AmMWSc 92
**Stephens**, Frederick Howard, Jr. 1931- WhoFI 92
**Stephens**, Fredric Milo 1955- WhoWest 92
**Stephens**, G Douglas 1951- WhoAmP 91
**Stephens**, Gay 1951- WhoMW 92
**Stephens**, George Benjamin Davis 1904- WhoBlA 92
**Stephens**, George Edward, Jr. 1936- WhoAmL 92, WhoWest 92
**Stephens**, George Myers 1930- WhoFI 92
**Stephens**, George Robert 1929- AmMWSc 92
**Stephens**, Gerald D 1932- WhoIns 92
**Stephens**, Gregory A 1947- AmMWSc 92
**Stephens**, Grover Cleveland 1925- AmMWSc 92
**Stephens**, Harold 1954- WhoAmL 92
**Stephens**, Harold W 1919- AmMWSc 92
**Stephens**, Heather R 1949- AmMWSc 92
**Stephens**, Herbert Malone 1918- WhoBlA 92
**Stephens**, Herman Alvin 1914- WhoBlA 92
**Stephens**, Howard L 1919- AmMWSc 92
**Stephens**, Jack DrAPF 91
**Stephens**, Jack E 1923- AmMWSc 92
**Stephens**, Jack Edward 1955- ConAu 133
**Stephens**, Jack LeRol 1927- WhoAmP 91
**Stephens**, Jackson Thomas 1923- WhoFI 92
**Stephens**, James 1880?-1950 RfGEnL 91
**Stephens**, James 1882-1950 FacFETw
**Stephens**, James Anthony 1914- WhoBlA 92
**Stephens**, James Briscoe 1936- AmMWSc 92
**Stephens**, James Fred 1932- AmMWSc 92
**Stephens**, James M 1946- WhoAmP 91, WhoFI 92
**Stephens**, James Regis 1925- AmMWSc 92
**Stephens**, Jay B. 1946- WhoAmL 92
**Stephens**, Jeffrey Alan 1958- AmMWSc 92
**Stephens**, Jeffrey Todd 1956- WhoMW 92
**Stephens**, Jerry Caldwell, Jr. 1954- WhoRel 92
**Stephens**, Jesse Jerald 1933- AmMWSc 92
**Stephens**, John C 1910- AmMWSc 92
**Stephens**, John Lloyd 1805-1852 BenetAL 91
**Stephens**, John Stewart, Jr 1932- AmMWSc 92
**Stephens**, Karen Lorene WhoFI 92
**Stephens**, Keith Fielding 1910- Who 92
**Stephens**, Kenneth Gilbert 1931- Who 92
**Stephens**, Kenneth S 1932- AmMWSc 92
**Stephens**, Larry Dean 1937- WhoWest 92
**Stephens**, Lawrence James 1940- AmMWSc 92
**Stephens**, Lawton Evans 1954- WhoAmP 91
**Stephens**, Lee Amiel 1962- WhoWest 92
**Stephens**, Lee B., Jr. 1925- WhoBlA 92
**Stephens**, Lee Bishop, Jr 1925- AmMWSc 92
**Stephens**, Lester John, Jr. 1943- WhoFI 92
**Stephens**, Lowell Gregory 1939- WhoMW 92
**Stephens**, Malcolm George 1937- Who 92
**Stephens**, Marion Lee 1935- WhoMW 92
**Stephens**, Martin Who 92
**Stephens**, Martin R 1954- WhoAmP 91
**Stephens**, Marvin Wayne 1943- AmMWSc 92
**Stephens**, Maynard Moody 1908- AmMWSc 92
**Stephens**, Meic 1938- WrDr 92
**Stephens**, Michael DrAPF 91
**Stephens**, Michael A 1927- AmMWSc 92
**Stephens**, Michael Allen 1962- WhoEnt 92
**Stephens**, Michael Jon 1948- WhoFI 92, WhoMW 92
**Stephens**, N Thomas 1932- AmMWSc 92
**Stephens**, Neal Eric 1954- WhoWest 92
**Stephens**, Newman Lloyd 1926- AmMWSc 92
**Stephens**, Nicholas Andrew 1954- WhoFI 92
**Stephens**, Noel, Jr 1928- AmMWSc 92
**Stephens**, Norman Edmund 1920- WhoAmP 91
**Stephens**, Olin J. 1908- DcTwDes, FacFETw
**Stephens**, Olin James, II 1908- IntWW 91
**Stephens**, Paul A. 1921- WhoBlA 92
**Stephens**, Paul Alfred 1921- WhoMW 92
**Stephens**, Peter Norman Stuart 1927- Who 92
**Stephens**, Peter Wesley 1951- AmMWSc 92
**Stephens**, Philip J 1940- AmMWSc 92
**Stephens**, Phillip 1940- WhoWest 92
**Stephens**, Phygenau 1923- WhoBlA 92
**Stephens**, Ralph Ivan 1934- AmMWSc 92
**Stephens**, Ray Garrett 1943- WhoFI 92
**Stephens**, Raymond Edward 1940- AmMWSc 92
**Stephens**, Raymond Weathers, Jr 1928- AmMWSc 92
**Stephens**, Richard Allen 1956- WhoEnt 92
**Stephens**, Richard Harry 1945- AmMWSc 92
**Stephens**, Robert 1909- Who 92

**Stephens,** Robert 1931- *IntMPA 92, IntWW 91, Who 92*
**Stephens,** Robert F. 1927- *WhoAmL 92, WhoAmP 91*
**Stephens,** Robert James *AmMWSc 92*
**Stephens,** Robert Lawrence 1921- *AmMWSc 92*
**Stephens,** Robert Neilson 1867-1906 *BenetAL 91*
**Stephens,** Robert Oren 1928- *IntAu&W 91, WrDr 92*
**Stephens,** Roderick S., Jr. *DcTwDes*
**Stephens,** Ronald Earl 1948- *WhoAmP 91*
**Stephens,** Ronald L 1933- *WhoAmP 91*
**Stephens,** Ronald Louis 1950- *WhoMW 92*
**Stephens,** Rosemary *DrAPF 91*
**Stephens,** Shand Scott 1949- *WhoAmL 92, WhoWest 92*
**Stephens,** Sheryl Lynne 1949- *WhoMW 92*
**Stephens,** Sidney Dee 1945- *WhoFI 92*
**Stephens,** Stan 1929- *AlmAP 92 [port]*
**Stephens,** Stanley Graham 1929- *WhoAmP 91, WhoWest 92*
**Stephens,** Stanley LaVerne 1943- *AmMWSc 92*
**Stephens,** Stephen Martin 1939- *Who 92*
**Stephens,** Stevi *WhoAmP 91*
**Stephens,** Taylor Lane 1937- *WhoFI 92*
**Stephens,** Thomas M. 1931- *WrDr 92*
**Stephens,** Thomas Maron 1931- *WhoMW 92*
**Stephens,** Timothy Lee 1944- *AmMWSc 92*
**Stephens,** Trent Dee 1948- *AmMWSc 92*
**Stephens,** Vivian 1942- *WhoBlA 92*
**Stephens,** W. R. d1991 *NewYTBS 91 [port]*
**Stephens,** Wallace O'Leary 1942- *WhoBlA 92*
**Stephens,** Walter David 1955- *WhoAmL 92*
**Stephens,** Warren E. 1933- *WhoBlA 92*
**Stephens,** Wayne J. 1949- *WhoWest 92*
**Stephens,** William 1932- *DcTwDes, WhoAmP 91*
**Stephens,** William D 1932- *AmMWSc 92*
**Stephens,** William Haynes 1935- *WhoBlA 92*
**Stephens,** William Henry 1913- *Who 92*
**Stephens,** William Leonard 1929- *AmMWSc 92, WhoWest 92*
**Stephens,** William Mark 1952- *WhoFI 92*
**Stephens,** William Peter 1934- *WrDr 92*
**Stephens,** William Powell 1948- *AmMWSc 92*
**Stephens,** William Richard 1932- *WhoRel 92*
**Stephens,** William Theodore 1922- *WhoAmL 92*
**Stephens,** William Thomas *WhoWest 92*
**Stephens,** Willie Oved 1929- *WhoAmP 91*
**Stephens,** Willis H 1925- *WhoAmP 91*
**Stephens,** Wilson 1912- *Who 92*
**Stephens-Newsham,** Lloyd G 1921- *AmMWSc 92*
**Stephenson,** Alan Clements 1944- *WhoFI 92*
**Stephenson,** Alfred Benjamin 1912- *AmMWSc 92*
**Stephenson,** Allan Anthony 1937- *WhoBlA 92*
**Stephenson,** Andrew George 1950- *AmMWSc 92*
**Stephenson,** Andrew M 1946- *TwCSFW 91, WrDr 92*
**Stephenson,** Ashley *Who 92*
**Stephenson,** Barbera Wertz 1938- *WhoAmL 92, WhoWest 92*
**Stephenson,** Blair Y. 1947- *WhoFI 92*
**Stephenson,** Carolyn L. 1945- *WhoBlA 92*
**Stephenson,** Cecil 1889-1965 *TwCPaSc*
**Stephenson,** Chaim 1926- *TwCPaSc*
**Stephenson,** Charles A. 1922- *WhoEnt 92*
**Stephenson,** Charles Bruce 1929- *AmMWSc 92*
**Stephenson,** Charles E., III *WhoBlA 92*
**Stephenson,** Charles V 1924- *AmMWSc 92*
**Stephenson,** Danny Lon 1937- *AmMWSc 92*
**Stephenson,** David 1944- *WhoAmL 92*
**Stephenson,** David Allen 1942- *AmMWSc 92*
**Stephenson,** David Town 1937- *AmMWSc 92*
**Stephenson,** Devin Garry 1953- *WhoRel 92*
**Stephenson,** Donald 1909- *Who 92*
**Stephenson,** Dorothy Maxine 1925- *WhoMW 92*
**Stephenson,** Dwight Eugene 1957- *WhoBlA 92*
**Stephenson,** Edward James 1947- *AmMWSc 92*
**Stephenson,** Edward Luther 1923- *AmMWSc 92*
**Stephenson,** Edward T 1929- *AmMWSc 92*
**Stephenson,** Elizabeth Weiss 1927- *AmMWSc 92*
**Stephenson,** Francis Creighton 1924- *AmMWSc 92, WhoMW 92*
**Stephenson,** Frederick William 1939- *AmMWSc 92*
**Stephenson,** Gary Van 1958- *WhoWest 92*
**Stephenson,** George V. 1926- *TwCPaSc*
**Stephenson,** Gerard J, Jr 1937- *AmMWSc 92*
**Stephenson,** Gordon 1908- *IntWW 91, Who 92*
**Stephenson,** Harold Patty 1925- *AmMWSc 92*
**Stephenson,** Henry Shepherd 1905- *Who 92*
**Stephenson,** Henry Upton 1926- *Who 92*
**Stephenson,** Herman Howard 1929- *WhoFI 92, WhoWest 92*
**Stephenson,** Hugh 1938- *IntAu&W 91, IntWW 91, Who 92*
**Stephenson,** Hugh Edward, Jr 1922- *AmMWSc 92*
**Stephenson,** Ian 1934- *IntWW 91, TwCPaSc*
**Stephenson,** Irene Hamlen 1923- *WhoFI 92, WhoWest 92*
**Stephenson,** J Gregg 1917- *AmMWSc 92*
**Stephenson,** James Bennett 1916- *WhoAmL 92, WhoAmP 91*
**Stephenson,** James Ian 1934- *Who 92*
**Stephenson,** Jerry L. 1949- *WhoBlA 92*
**Stephenson,** Jill Annette 1961- *WhoMW 92*
**Stephenson,** Jim 1932- *Who 92*
**Stephenson,** John 1939- *AmMWSc 92*
**Stephenson,** John Andrew 1966- *WhoWest 92*
**Stephenson,** John Aubrey 1929- *Who 92*
**Stephenson,** John Carter *AmMWSc 92*
**Stephenson,** John Frederick Eustace 1910- *Who 92*
**Stephenson,** John Leslie 1921- *AmMWSc 92*
**Stephenson,** John Robin 1931- *Who 92*
**Stephenson,** Kenneth Edward 1951- *AmMWSc 92*
**Stephenson,** Lani Sue 1948- *AmMWSc 92*
**Stephenson,** Larry Kirk 1944- *WhoWest 92*
**Stephenson,** Lee Palmer 1923- *AmMWSc 92*
**Stephenson,** Linda Sue 1939- *WhoFI 92*
**Stephenson,** Lou Ann 1954- *AmMWSc 92*
**Stephenson,** Lynne *Who 92*
**Stephenson,** Margaret Maud *Who 92*
**Stephenson,** Mark Curran 1949- *WhoAmL 92*
**Stephenson,** Mary Johnson 1935- *WhoFI 92*
**Stephenson,** Mary Louise 1921- *AmMWSc 92*
**Stephenson,** Michael Murray 1943- *WhoAmL 92*
**Stephenson,** Ned Eldon 1957- *WhoFI 92*
**Stephenson,** Norman Robert 1917- *AmMWSc 92*
**Stephenson,** Patrick Hay 1916- *Who 92*
**Stephenson,** Paul 1937- *Who 92*
**Stephenson,** Paul Andrew 1966- *WhoFI 92*
**Stephenson,** Paul Bernard 1937- *AmMWSc 92*
**Stephenson,** Philip Robert 1914- *Who 92*
**Stephenson,** Richard Allen 1931- *AmMWSc 92*
**Stephenson,** Richard Ismert 1937- *WhoAmL 92*
**Stephenson,** Robert Ashley 1927- *Who 92*
**Stephenson,** Robert Bruce 1946- *AmMWSc 92*
**Stephenson,** Robert Charles 1916- *AmMWSc 92*
**Stephenson,** Robert E 1919- *AmMWSc 92*
**Stephenson,** Robert L 1913- *AmMWSc 92*
**Stephenson,** Robert M. 1948- *WhoAmL 92*
**Stephenson,** Robert Moffatt, Jr 1940- *AmMWSc 92*
**Stephenson,** Robert Storer 1943- *AmMWSc 92*
**Stephenson,** Roscoe Bolar, Jr. 1922- *WhoAmL 92, WhoAmP 91*
**Stephenson,** Rufus Scott 1943- *WhoMW 92*
**Stephenson,** Samuel Edward, Jr 1926- *AmMWSc 92*
**Stephenson,** Shelby *DrAPF 91*
**Stephenson,** Stanley 1926- *Who 92*
**Stephenson,** Stanley E 1926- *AmMWSc 92*
**Stephenson,** Stephen Neil 1933- *AmMWSc 92*
**Stephenson,** Steven Lee 1943- *AmMWSc 92*
**Stephenson,** Thomas E 1922- *AmMWSc 92*
**Stephenson,** Tom 1892-1987 *FacFETw*
**Stephenson,** Tom Birkett 1926- *Who 92*
**Stephenson,** William B 1933- *WhoIns 92*
**Stephenson,** William Boyd, Jr. 1933- *WhoFI 92*
**Stephenson,** William Kay 1927- *AmMWSc 92*
**Stephenson,** William S 1896-1989 *FacFETw*
**Stepinac,** Aloysius 1898-1960 *FacFETw*
**Stepka,** William 1917- *AmMWSc 92*
**Stepkoski,** Robert John 1933- *WhoFI 92*
**Stepleman,** Robert Saul 1942- *AmMWSc 92*
**Steplewski,** Zenon 1929- *AmMWSc 92*
**Stepner,** Daniel *WhoEnt 92*
**Stepney,** Area Bishop of *Who 92*
**Steponavicius,** Julijonas 1911- *SovUnBD*
**Steponkus,** Peter Leo 1941- *AmMWSc 92*
**Steponkus,** William Peter 1935- *WhoAmP 91*
**Stepovich,** Michael Leo 1929- *WhoWest 92*
**Stepp,** George Allan, Jr. 1922- *WhoFI 92, WhoWest 92*
**Stepp,** Marc 1923- *WhoAmP 91, WhoBlA 92*
**Stepp,** William Rigby 1943- *WhoRel 92*
**Stepp Bejarano,** Linda Sue 1950- *WhoHisp 92*
**Steppe,** Cecil H. 1933- *WhoBlA 92*
**Steppenwolf** *NewAmDM*
**Steppler,** Don 1954- *WhoAmP 91*
**Steppling,** Richard Carew 1935- *WhoAmP 91*
**Stepto,** Robert Burns 1945- *WhoBlA 92*
**Stepto,** Robert Charles 1920- *AmMWSc 92, WhoBlA 92*
**Steptoe,** John Lewis 1950-1989 *WhoBlA 92N*
**Steptoe,** Lamont Brown 1949- *WhoBlA 92*
**Steptoe,** Patrick Christopher 1913-1988 *FacFETw*
**Steptoe,** Robert M *WhoAmP 91*
**Steptoe,** Roger 1953- *ConCom 92*
**Steptoe,** Roosevelt 1934- *WhoBlA 92*
**Steptoe,** Sonja 1960- *WhoBlA 92*
**Steptoe,** Thomas Wetherell, Jr 1951- *WhoAmP 91*
**Steranka,** Larry Richard *AmMWSc 92*
**Sterba,** Richard 1898-1989 *FacFETw*
**Sterbakov,** Irwin 1952- *WhoEnt 92*
**Sterbenz,** Francis Joseph 1924- *AmMWSc 92*
**Sterbick,** Peter Lawrence, I 1917- *WhoAmL 92, WhoWest 92*
**Sterchi,** Beat 1949- *ConLC 65 [port]*
**Sterck,** Gregory Leo 1949- *WhoFI 92*
**Stercken,** Hans 1923- *IntWW 91*
**Stere,** Athleen Jacobs 1921- *AmMWSc 92*
**Stergios,** Peter Doe 1942- *WhoAmL 92*
**Stergiou,** E James 1949- *WhoIns 92*
**Stergioulas,** Nikolaos Athanassios 1951- *WhoFI 92*
**Stergis,** Christos George 1919- *AmMWSc 92*
**Steriade,** Mircea 1924- *AmMWSc 92*
**Sterk,** Andrew A 1919- *AmMWSc 92*
**Sterken,** Gordon Jay 1930- *AmMWSc 92*
**Sterky,** Hakan Karl August 1900- *IntWW 91*
**Sterle,** Francine *DrAPF 91*
**Sterling** *Who 92*
**Sterling,** A. Mary Fackler 1955- *WhoFI 92*
**Sterling,** Arthur MacLean 1938- *AmMWSc 92*
**Sterling,** Brett *TwCSFW 91*
**Sterling,** Bruce 1954- *IntAu&W 91, TwCSFW 91, WrDr 92*
**Sterling,** Charles A. 1932- *WhoBlA 92*
**Sterling,** Claire 1919- *WrDr 92*
**Sterling,** Clarence 1919- *AmMWSc 92*
**Sterling,** David Alan 1956- *WhoFI 92*
**Sterling,** Donald T. *WhoWest 92*
**Sterling,** Eric Edward 1949- *WhoAmL 92*
**Sterling,** Erik 1955- *WhoEnt 92*
**Sterling,** Gary C. *DrAPF 91*
**Sterling,** George 1869-1926 *BenetAL 91*
**Sterling,** Graham Lee, III 1929- *WhoAmL 92*
**Sterling,** Harry Michael 1935- *WhoAmL 92*
**Sterling,** Helen *SmATA 65*
**Sterling,** Howard David 1941- *WhoAmL 92*
**Sterling,** James 1701?-1763 *BenetAL 91*
**Sterling,** James A. 1942- *WhoRel 92*
**Sterling,** Jan 1923- *IntMPA 92*
**Sterling,** Jeffrey Emery 1964- *WhoBlA 92*
**Sterling,** Jody *DrAPF 91*
**Sterling,** John Harrison 1950- *WhoFI 92*
**Sterling,** Kevin M. 1954- *WhoAmL 92*
**Sterling,** Leon Samuel 1955- *AmMWSc 92*
**Sterling,** Maria Sandra *IntAu&W 91X, TwCWW 91*
**Sterling,** Michael John Howard 1946- *IntWW 91, Who 92*
**Sterling,** Nicholas J 1934- *AmMWSc 92*
**Sterling,** Peter 1940- *AmMWSc 92*
**Sterling,** Phillip *DrAPF 91*
**Sterling,** Raymond Leslie 1949- *AmMWSc 92*
**Sterling,** Rex Elliott 1924- *AmMWSc 92*
**Sterling,** Robert 1917- *IntMPA 92*
**Sterling,** Robert Fillmore 1919- *AmMWSc 92*
**Sterling,** Robert Lee, Jr. 1933- *WhoFI 92*
**Sterling,** Sandra *TwCWW 91*
**Sterling,** Theodor David 1923- *AmMWSc 92*
**Sterling,** Wallace Stine 1935- *WhoMW 92*
**Sterling,** Warren Martin 1947- *AmMWSc 92*
**Sterling,** William Clinton, Jr. 1934- *WhoAmL 92*
**Sterling,** Winfield Lincoln 1936- *AmMWSc 92*
**Sterling Of Plaistow,** Baron 1934- *IntWW 91, Who 92*
**Sterman,** Melvin David 1930- *AmMWSc 92*
**Sterman,** Samuel 1918- *AmMWSc 92*
**Sterman,** Wesley David 1960- *WhoFI 92*
**Stermer,** Dugald Robert 1936- *WhoWest 92*
**Stermer,** Raymond A 1924- *AmMWSc 92*
**Stermer,** Robert L, Jr 1935- *AmMWSc 92*
**Stermitz,** Frank 1928- *AmMWSc 92*
**Stern,** A C 1909- *AmMWSc 92*
**Stern,** Aaron Milton 1920- *AmMWSc 92*
**Stern,** Albert Victor 1923- *AmMWSc 92*
**Stern,** Alfred E.F. *IntMPA 92*
**Stern,** Allan David Reis 1932- *WhoFI 92*
**Stern,** Allan Martin 1947- *WhoAmL 92*
**Stern,** Andrew Joseph 1960- *WhoAmL 92*
**Stern,** Angela Marie 1960- *WhoFI 92*
**Stern,** Arthur Irving 1930- *AmMWSc 92*
**Stern,** Arthur Paul 1925- *AmMWSc 92, WhoFI 92, WhoWest 92*
**Stern,** Barry H 1946- *WhoAmP 91*
**Stern,** Bernard 1920- *TwCPaSc*
**Stern,** Bruce Elliot 1954- *WhoAmL 92*
**Stern,** Bruce H. 1956- *WhoAmL 92*
**Stern,** Carl *LesBEnT 92*
**Stern,** Carl William, Jr. 1946- *WhoMW 92*
**Stern,** Cassandra Silverstone *WhoEnt 92*
**Stern,** Catharini 1925- *TwCPaSc*
**Stern,** Charles M. 1943- *WhoAmL 92*
**Stern,** Clarence A. 1913- *WrDr 92*
**Stern,** Curt 1902-1981 *FacFETw*
**Stern,** Daniel *DrAPF 91*
**Stern,** Daniel 1928- *WrDr 92*
**Stern,** Daniel 1957- *IntMPA 92*
**Stern,** Daniel Henry 1934- *AmMWSc 92*
**Stern,** Daniel William 1953- *WhoAmL 92*
**Stern,** David 1942- *CurBio 91 [port], News 91 [port]*
**Stern,** David P 1931- *AmMWSc 92*
**Stern,** Deborah 1938- *TwCPaSc*
**Stern,** Deborah 1948- *TwCPaSc*
**Stern,** Douglas Donald 1939- *WhoFI 92*
**Stern,** Eddie 1917- *IntMPA 92*
**Stern,** Edward Abraham 1930- *AmMWSc 92*
**Stern,** Elizabeth Kay 1945- *AmMWSc 92*
**Stern,** Ellen Norman 1927- *IntAu&W 91, WrDr 92*
**Stern,** Eric Wolfgang 1930- *AmMWSc 92*
**Stern,** Ernest 1928- *AmMWSc 92*
**Stern,** Ernest 1933- *IntWW 91*
**Stern,** Ezra E. 1908- *IntMPA 92*
**Stern,** Franc N 1934- *WhoAmP 91*
**Stern,** Frank 1928- *AmMWSc 92*
**Stern,** Frank 1936- *WhoRel 92*
**Stern,** Frank Irvin 1929- *WhoFI 92*
**Stern,** Fritz 1926- *IntWW 91, WrDr 92*
**Stern,** Gene Gennadij 1946- *WhoFI 92*
**Stern,** George Leon 1937- *WhoFI 92, WhoMW 92*
**Stern,** Gerald *DrAPF 91*
**Stern,** Gerald 1925- *ConPo 91, WrDr 92*
**Stern,** Gerald M. 1937- *WhoAmL 92*
**Stern,** Grace Mary 1925- *WhoAmP 91*
**Stern,** Herbert 1918- *AmMWSc 92*
**Stern,** Herbert L 1915- *WhoAmP 91*
**Stern,** Irving B 1920- *AmMWSc 92*
**Stern,** Isaac 1920- *ConMus 7 [port], FacFETw, IntWW 91, NewAmDM, Who 92, WhoEnt 92*
**Stern,** Israel Jerome 1910- *WhoAmL 92*
**Stern,** Ivan J 1930- *AmMWSc 92*
**Stern,** Jack Tuteur, Jr 1942- *AmMWSc 92*
**Stern,** Jacques 1932- *IntWW 91*
**Stern,** James 1904- *WrDr 92*
**Stern,** James Andrew 1904- *IntAu&W 91*
**Stern,** James Andrew 1950- *WhoFI 92*
**Stern,** James Coper 1925- *WhoWest 92*
**Stern,** Jay 1929- *IntAu&W 91*
**Stern,** Jay B. 1929- *WrDr 92*
**Stern,** Jay Benjamin 1929- *WhoRel 92*
**Stern,** Jerome H 1929- *WhoIns 92*
**Stern,** Jill Abeshouse 1953- *WhoAmL 92*
**Stern,** Joanne Barbara 1945- *WhoAmL 92*
**Stern,** John Hanus 1928- *AmMWSc 92*
**Stern,** John Jules 1955- *WhoAmL 92*
**Stern,** John Michael 1949- *WhoMW 92*
**Stern,** Joseph Aaron 1927- *AmMWSc 92*
**Stern,** Joseph Peter Maria 1920- *Who 92*
**Stern,** Judith S 1943- *AmMWSc 92*
**Stern,** Karen M. 1940- *WhoMW 92*
**Stern,** Kenneth Alan 1946- *WhoFI 92*
**Stern,** Kingsley Rowland 1927- *AmMWSc 92*
**Stern,** Klaus 1932- *IntWW 91*
**Stern,** Kurt 1909- *AmMWSc 92*

**Stern,** Kurt Heinz 1926- AmMWSc 92
**Stern,** Larry N 1941- WhoAmP 91
**Stern,** Laurence Michael 1951- WhoAmL 92
**Stern,** Lawrence Irving 1947- WhoAmL 92
**Stern,** Lawrence N. 1942- WhoFI 92
**Stern,** Leo 1931- AmMWSc 92
**Stern,** Leonard 1938- CurBio 91 [port]
**Stern,** Leonard B. LesBEnT 92
**Stern,** Leonard Bernard 1923- WhoEnt 92
**Stern,** Leonard Norman 1938- WhoFI 92
**Stern,** Lewis Arthur 1934- WhoAmL 92
**Stern,** Linda Joy 1941- Who 92
**Stern,** Louis 1945- WhoWest 92
**Stern,** Louis C d1918 BiInAmS
**Stern,** Madeleine B. 1912- DcLB 111 [port], WrDr 92
**Stern,** Madeleine Bettina 1912- IntAu&W 91
**Stern,** Malcolm Henry 1915- WhoRel 92
**Stern,** Marc Irwin 1944- WhoFI 92, WhoWest 92
**Stern,** Marc Steven 1954- WhoAmL 92
**Stern,** Marianne 1950- WhoFI 92
**Stern,** Marshall Dana 1949- AmMWSc 92
**Stern,** Martin 1933- AmMWSc 92
**Stern,** Marvin 1916- AmMWSc 92
**Stern,** Max TwCWW 91
**Stern,** Max Herman 1920- AmMWSc 92
**Stern,** Melvin Ernest 1929- AmMWSc 92
**Stern,** Michael 1910- IntAu&W 91
**Stern,** Michael Charles 1942- Who 92
**Stern,** Michele Suchard 1943- AmMWSc 92
**Stern,** Miklos 1957- AmMWSc 92
**Stern,** Milton 1927- AmMWSc 92
**Stern,** Milton Reid 1918- WhoWest 92
**Stern,** Morris 1930- AmMWSc 92
**Stern,** Neal M 1951- WhoIns 92
**Stern,** Nicholas Herbert 1946- Who 92
**Stern,** Norissa Cynthia 1947- WhoMW 92
**Stern,** Otto 1888-1969 WhoNob 90
**Stern,** Paul Elihu 1957- WhoAmL 92
**Stern,** Paula 1945- WhoAmP 91
**Stern,** Paula Helene 1938- AmMWSc 92
**Stern,** Philip Van Doren 1900-1984 BenetAL 91
**Stern,** Phyllis DrAPF 91
**Stern,** Raul A 1928- AmMWSc 92
**Stern,** Rhoda Helen 1940- WhoFI 92
**Stern,** Richard DrAPF 91
**Stern,** Richard 1929- AmMWSc 92
**Stern,** Richard Benjamin 1929- WhoFI 92
**Stern,** Richard Cecil 1942- AmMWSc 92
**Stern,** Richard David 1936- WhoFI 92
**Stern,** Richard G. 1928- BenetAL 91, ConNov 91, IntAu&W 91, WrDr 92
**Stern,** Richard Martin 1915- IntAu&W 91, WrDr 92
**Stern,** Richard Martin, Jr 1948- AmMWSc 92
**Stern,** Robert 1936- AmMWSc 92
**Stern,** Robert A.M. 1939- DcTwDes, WrDr 92
**Stern,** Robert Louis 1908- WhoAmL 92
**Stern,** Robert Louis 1935- AmMWSc 92
**Stern,** Robert Mason 1944- WhoAmL 92
**Stern,** Ronald John 1947- AmMWSc 92
**Stern,** Ronald William 1957- WhoAmL 92
**Stern,** Roy Dalton 1943- WhoMW 92
**Stern,** Samuel T 1928- AmMWSc 92
**Stern,** Sandor 1936- WhoEnt 92
**Stern,** Seymour Sholom 1920- WhoRel 92
**Stern,** Shira 1956- WhoRel 92
**Stern,** Silviu Alexander 1921- AmMWSc 92
**Stern,** Stanley 1933- WhoWest 92
**Stern,** Steve 1947- IntAu&W 91
**Stern,** Steven Alan 1943- WhoFI 92, WhoWest 92
**Stern,** Steven N. 1958- WhoFI 92
**Stern,** Stewart 1922- IntMPA 92
**Stern,** Stuart IntAu&W 91X, WrDr 92
**Stern,** Sydney Ladensohn 1947- ConAu 134
**Stern,** Theodore 1929- AmMWSc 92, WhoFI 92
**Stern,** Thomas Lee 1920- WhoMW 92
**Stern,** Thomas Whital 1922- AmMWSc 92
**Stern,** Vernon Mark 1923- AmMWSc 92, WhoWest 92
**Stern,** Vivien Helen 1941- Who 92
**Stern,** W Eugene 1920- AmMWSc 92
**Stern,** Warren C 1944- AmMWSc 92
**Stern,** Wayne Brian 1948- WhoFI 92
**Stern,** William 1946- AmMWSc 92
**Stern,** William Louis 1926- AmMWSc 92
**Stern,** William Michael 1941- WhoWest 92
**Stern,** William Samuel 1952- WhoAmL 92
**Stern-Chaves,** Elidieth I. 1960- WhoHisp 92
**Sternbach,** Daniel David 1949- AmMWSc 92
**Sternberg,** Ben Kollock 1947- WhoWest 92
**Sternberg,** Daniel Arie 1913- WhoEnt 92
**Sternberg,** Daniel S. 1954- WhoAmL 92
**Sternberg,** David Edward 1946- WhoMW 92
**Sternberg,** Eli IntWW 91N
**Sternberg,** Eli 1917- AmMWSc 92
**Sternberg,** George Miller 1838-1915 BiInAmS
**Sternberg,** Hilgard O'Reilly 1917- AmMWSc 92
**Sternberg,** John Richard 1920- WhoRel 92
**Sternberg,** Jonathan 1919- WhoEnt 92
**Sternberg,** Josef von 1894-1969 BenetAL 91, FacFETw
**Sternberg,** Joseph 1921- AmMWSc 92
**Sternberg,** Moshe 1929- AmMWSc 92
**Sternberg,** Paul J. 1933- WhoAmL 92
**Sternberg,** Richard Walter 1934- AmMWSc 92
**Sternberg,** Robert J 1949- IntAu&W 91, WrDr 92
**Sternberg,** Robert Jeffrey 1949- AmMWSc 92
**Sternberg,** Robert Langley 1922- AmMWSc 92
**Sternberg,** Rolf Max 1945- WhoAmL 92
**Sternberg,** Seymour 1943- WhoIns 92
**Sternberg,** Sigmund 1921- Who 92
**Sternberg,** Stephen Stanley 1920- AmMWSc 92
**Sternberg,** Vita Shlomo 1936- AmMWSc 92
**Sternberg,** Yaron Moshe 1936- AmMWSc 92
**Sternberger,** Dolf IntWW 91N
**Sternberger,** Dolf 1907- IntAu&W 91
**Sternberger,** Ludwig Amadeus 1921- AmMWSc 92
**Sternburg,** James Gordon 1919- AmMWSc 92
**Sternburg,** Janet DrAPF 91
**Sterne,** Emma Gelders 1894-1971 AmPeW
**Sterne,** Laurence 1713-1768 BlkwCEP, CnDBLB 2 [port], RfGEnL 91
**Sterne,** Laurence Henry Gordon 1916- Who 92
**Sterne,** Richard S. 1921- WrDr 92
**Sterner,** Carl D 1935- AmMWSc 92
**Sterner,** James Hervi 1904- AmMWSc 92
**Sterner,** Jerry Joseph 1938- WhoEnt 92
**Sterner,** Michael James 1939- WhoMW 92
**Sterner,** Robert Warner 1958- AmMWSc 92
**Sternfeld,** Leon 1913- AmMWSc 92
**Sternfeld,** Marvin 1927- AmMWSc 92
**Sternfeld,** Reuben 1924- IntWW 91
**Sternglanz,** Rolf 1939- AmMWSc 92
**Sternglass,** Ernest Joachim 1923- AmMWSc 92
**Sternhagen,** Frances 1930- IntMPA 92, WhoEnt 92
**Sternhagen,** Fred Brian 1954- WhoMW 92
**Sternheim,** Morton Maynard 1933- AmMWSc 92
**Sternheimer,** Rudolph Max 1926- AmMWSc 92
**Sternick,** Edward Selby 1939- AmMWSc 92
**Sternick,** Michael John 1958- WhoAmL 92
**Sternklar,** Avraham Albert 1930- WhoEnt 92
**Sternlicht,** B 1928- AmMWSc 92
**Sternlicht,** Himan 1936- AmMWSc 92
**Sternlicht,** Mark Leo 1929- WhoFI 92
**Sternlicht,** Sanford 1931- IntAu&W 91, WrDr 92
**Sternlieb,** George 1928- WhoFI 92
**Sternlieb,** Irmin 1923- AmMWSc 92
**Sternlight,** Jean Renee 1958- WhoAmL 92
**Sternlight,** Peter Donn 1928- WhoFI 92
**Sternling,** Charles V 1924- AmMWSc 92
**Sternman,** Joel W. 1943- WhoAmL 92
**Sterns,** Jay Barry 1960- WhoMW 92
**Sterns,** Patricia Margaret 1952- WhoAmL 92, WhoWest 92
**Sternstein,** Joseph Philip 1925- WhoRel 92
**Sternstein,** Martin 1945- AmMWSc 92
**Sternstein,** Sanford Samuel 1936- AmMWSc 92
**Sterpetti,** Antonio Vittorio 1956- AmMWSc 92
**Sterquell,** Steve Wright 1953- WhoFI 92
**Sterrett,** A. Wayne 1932- WhoMW 92
**Sterrett,** Andrew 1924- AmMWSc 92
**Sterrett,** Frances Susan 1913- AmMWSc 92
**Sterrett,** John Paul 1924- AmMWSc 92
**Sterrett,** Kay Fife 1931- AmMWSc 92
**Sterrett,** Malcolm McCurdy Burdett 1942- WhoAmP 91
**Sterrett,** Roy Stewart 1903- WhoEnt 92
**Sterzer,** Fred 1929- AmMWSc 92
**Sterzinsky,** Georg Maximilian WhoRel 92
**Stesemann,** Gustav 1878-1929 FacFETw
**Stesky,** Robert Michael 1945- AmMWSc 92
**Stessel,** Harry DrAPF 91
**Stessel,** Larry Robert 1953- WhoEnt 92
**Stessin,** Herbert WhoEnt 92
**Stetefeldt,** Carl August 1838-1896 BiInAmS
**Stetler,** C. Joseph 1917- WhoAmL 92
**Stetler,** Charles Edward 1927- WhoWest 92
**Stetler,** David Albert 1935- AmMWSc 92
**Stetler,** David Samuel 1946- WhoAmP 91
**Stetler,** Dean Allen 1954- AmMWSc 92
**Stetler,** Kirby 1951- WhoMW 92
**Stetler,** Margaret DrAPF 91
**Stetler,** Stephen H 1949- WhoAmP 91
**Stetson,** Alvin Rae 1926- AmMWSc 92
**Stetson,** Ernest Kent 1948- IntAu&W 91
**Stetson,** Eugene William, III 1951- WhoFI 92
**Stetson,** Harold W 1926- AmMWSc 92
**Stetson,** Jeffrey P. 1948- WhoBlA 92
**Stetson,** Karl Andrew 1937- AmMWSc 92
**Stetson,** Kenneth F 1924- AmMWSc 92
**Stetson,** Milton H 1943- AmMWSc 92
**Stetson,** Robert F 1928- AmMWSc 92
**Stetson,** Robert Franklin 1932- AmMWSc 92
**Stetson,** Rufus Edwin, Jr 1922- WhoAmP 91
**Stetten,** DeWitt, Jr. d1990 IntWW 91N
**Stetten,** DeWitt, Jr 1909- AmMWSc 92
**Stettenheim,** Peter 1928- AmMWSc 92
**Stetter,** Ib 1917- IntWW 91
**Stetter,** Joseph Robert 1946- AmMWSc 92, WhoMW 92
**Stettinius,** Edward R 1900-1949 FacFETw
**Stettinius,** Edward Reilly 1900-1949 EncTR 91
**Stettinius,** Edward Riley, Jr. 1900-1949 AmPolLe
**Stettler,** John Dietrich 1934- AmMWSc 92
**Stettler,** Reinhard Friederich 1929- AmMWSc 92
**Stettner,** Irving DrAPF 91
**Stetz,** Sylvia Ann 1941- WhoMW 92
**Stetzner,** Leah Manning 1948- WhoAmL 92
**Steuben,** Friedrich Wilhelm Ludolf G 1730-1794 BlkwEAR
**Steuben,** Fritz EncTR 91
**Steucek,** Guy Linsley 1942- AmMWSc 92
**Steudel,** Harold Jude 1945- AmMWSc 92
**Steuer,** David Sidney 1957- WhoAmL 92
**Steuer,** Malcolm F 1928- AmMWSc 92
**Steuer,** Richard Marc 1948- WhoAmL 92
**Steuer,** Robert B. 1937- IntMPA 92
**Steuerle,** C. Eugene 1946- WhoFI 92
**Steuermann,** Edward 1892-1964 NewAmDM
**Steunenberg,** Robert Keppel 1924- AmMWSc 92, WhoMW 92
**Steuver,** JoDell Kaye 1948- WhoMW 92
**Stevanzboyan,** Steven WhoAmP 91
**Stevas** Who 92
**Steven,** Alasdair C 1947- AmMWSc 92
**Steven,** Andy IntAu&W 91X
**Steven,** Jeffrey Charles 1954- WhoMW 92
**Steven,** Stewart 1938- Who 92
**Steven,** William P. d1991 NewYTBS 91
**Stevens** Who 92
**Stevens,** Abel 1815-1897 BenetAL 91
**Stevens,** Alan Douglas 1926- AmMWSc 92
**Stevens,** Albert G, Jr WhoAmP 91
**Stevens,** Alex DrAPF 91
**Stevens,** Alfred 1823-1906 ThHEIm
**Stevens,** Althea Williams 1931- WhoBlA 92
**Stevens,** Andrew 1955- IntMPA 92, WhoEnt 92
**Stevens,** Ann Rebecca 1939- AmMWSc 92
**Stevens,** Anthony John 1926- Who 92
**Stevens,** Art 1935- WhoFI 92
**Stevens,** Arthur Edwin 1905- Who 92
**Stevens,** Arthur Wilber, Jr. 1921- WhoWest 92
**Stevens,** Audrey L 1932- AmMWSc 92
**Stevens,** Austin WrDr 92
**Stevens,** Ben Dee 1942- WhoAmL 92
**Stevens,** Benjamin Franklin 1833-1902 BenetAL 91
**Stevens,** Brian 1924- AmMWSc 92
**Stevens,** Bruce Russell 1952- AmMWSc 92
**Stevens,** Bryna 1924- SmATA 65 [port]
**Stevens,** C. Glenn 1941- WhoAmL 92
**Stevens,** Calvin H 1934- AmMWSc 92
**Stevens,** Calvin Lee 1923- AmMWSc 92
**Stevens,** Carolyn Kay Schisler 1934- WhoAmP 91
**Stevens,** Carroll Douglas 1949- WhoAmL 92
**Stevens,** Cat 1947- NewAmDM
**Stevens,** Charles Aiken 1953- WhoEnt 92
**Stevens,** Charles David 1912- AmMWSc 92
**Stevens,** Charles Edward 1927- AmMWSc 92
**Stevens,** Charles F 1934- AmMWSc 92
**Stevens,** Charles Le Roy 1931- AmMWSc 92
**Stevens,** Chester Wayne 1925- WhoFI 92, WhoMW 92
**Stevens,** Chris 1956- TwCPaSc
**Stevens,** Christina Lea 1948- WhoEnt 92
**Stevens,** Christopher 1948- WrDr 92
**Stevens,** Christopher 1961- TwCPaSc
**Stevens,** Clark 1921- AmMWSc 92
**Stevens,** Cleveland 1927- WhoBlA 92
**Stevens,** Clifford David 1941- Who 92
**Stevens,** Connie 1938- IntMPA 92, WhoEnt 92
**Stevens,** Correale F 1946- WhoAmP 91
**Stevens,** Craig 1918- IntMPA 92
**Stevens,** Dale John 1936- AmMWSc 92, WhoWest 92
**Stevens,** Dan J TwCWW 91, WrDr 92
**Stevens,** Daniel Louis 1961- WhoRel 92
**Stevens,** David 1926- WhoWest 92
**Stevens,** David Allen 1957- WhoRel 92
**Stevens,** David King 1954- WhoWest 92
**Stevens,** David Robert 1949- AmMWSc 92
**Stevens,** Dean Finley 1923- AmMWSc 92
**Stevens,** Deborah Irene 1959- WhoRel 92
**Stevens,** Denis William 1922- IntWW 91, Who 92, WhoEnt 92
**Stevens,** Dennis Leroy 1941- WhoWest 92
**Stevens,** Dennis Max 1944- WhoFI 92
**Stevens,** Donald Keith 1922- AmMWSc 92
**Stevens,** Donald Meade 1947- AmMWSc 92
**Stevens,** Earl Patrick 1925- WhoRel 92
**Stevens,** Edward 1755?-1834 BiInAmS
**Stevens,** Edward Franklin 1940- WhoRel 92, WhoWest 92
**Stevens,** Edwin Who 92
**Stevens,** Eleanor Sandra 1932- WhoWest 92
**Stevens,** Elisabeth DrAPF 91
**Stevens,** Elliot Leslie 1948- WhoRel 92
**Stevens,** Elsie E. TwCPaSc
**Stevens,** Ernest Donald 1941- AmMWSc 92
**Stevens,** Fisher 1963- IntMPA 92
**Stevens,** Floris Elaine 1942- WhoWest 92
**Stevens,** Forrest Wayne 1928- WhoFI 92
**Stevens,** Francis 1884-1939? TwCSFW 91
**Stevens,** Francis 1884-1940? ScFEYrs
**Stevens,** Frank Joseph 1919- AmMWSc 92
**Stevens,** Frank Leonard d1991 Who 92N
**Stevens,** Fred Jay 1949- AmMWSc 92
**Stevens,** Frederic Allan 1916- WhoAmP 91
**Stevens,** Frits Christiaan 1938- AmMWSc 92
**Stevens,** George 1904-1975 FacFETw, IntDcF 2-2 [port]
**Stevens,** George, Jr. LesBEnT 92
**Stevens,** George, Jr. 1932- IntMPA 92, WhoEnt 92
**Stevens,** George Edward, Jr. 1942- WhoBlA 92
**Stevens,** George L. 1932- WhoBlA 92
**Stevens,** George Richard 1931- AmMWSc 92
**Stevens,** Gerald Fairlie 1938- WhoAmP 91
**Stevens,** Gerald M. WhoAmL 92
**Stevens,** Gladstone Taylor, Jr 1930- AmMWSc 92
**Stevens,** Glenn Douglas 1947- WhoRel 92
**Stevens,** Gloria Jean 1954- WhoHisp 92
**Stevens,** Graeme Roy 1932- IntAu&W 91, IntWW 91
**Stevens,** Halsey 1908- NewAmDM
**Stevens,** Handley Michael Gambrell 1941- Who 92
**Stevens,** Harold 1911- AmMWSc 92
**Stevens,** Harold A. 1907-1990 WhoBlA 92N
**Stevens,** Henry 1819-1886 BenetAL 91
**Stevens,** Henry Conrad 1918- AmMWSc 92
**Stevens,** Herbert Francis 1948- WhoAmL 92
**Stevens,** Herbert H, Jr 1913- AmMWSc 92
**Stevens,** Howard Odell 1940- AmMWSc 92
**Stevens,** Isaac Ingalls 1818-1862 BiInAmS
**Stevens,** J.D. TwCWW 91
**Stevens,** J I 1920- AmMWSc 92
**Stevens,** J. Paul 1942- WhoFI 92, WhoMW 92
**Stevens,** Jack G 1937- WhoAmP 91
**Stevens,** Jack Gerald 1933- AmMWSc 92
**Stevens,** Jadene Felina DrAPF 91
**Stevens,** James 1892-1971 BenetAL 91, TwCWW 91
**Stevens,** James Everell 1950- AmMWSc 92
**Stevens,** James Hervey, Jr. 1944- WhoFI 92
**Stevens,** James Levon 1947- AmMWSc 92
**Stevens,** James R. 1940- WrDr 92
**Stevens,** James T 1946- AmMWSc 92
**Stevens,** Jane Alden 1952- WhoMW 92
**Stevens,** Janice R AmMWSc 92
**Stevens,** Jeannette Eloise 1913- WhoAmP 91
**Stevens,** Jeron Lynn 1942- WhoAmL 92
**Stevens,** Jerry W. 1932- WhoRel 92
**Stevens,** Joan Kelley 1922- WhoAmP 91
**Stevens,** Jocelyn Edward Greville 1932- Who 92
**Stevens,** John IntAu&W 91X, WrDr 92
**Stevens,** John 1749-1838 BiInAmS, BlkwEAR

**Stevens,** John 1921- *WrDr 92*
**Stevens,** John A 1921- *AmMWSc 92*
**Stevens,** John Bagshaw 1941- *AmMWSc 92*
**Stevens,** John Christopher Courtenay 1955- *Who 92*
**Stevens,** John David 1951- *WhoMW 92*
**Stevens,** John Edgar 1921- *IntWW 91, Who 92*
**Stevens,** John Flournoy 1914- *WhoRel 92*
**Stevens,** John Floyd d1918 *BiInAmS*
**Stevens,** John G 1943- *AmMWSc 92*
**Stevens,** John Gehret 1941- *AmMWSc 92*
**Stevens,** John Joseph 1941- *AmMWSc 92*
**Stevens,** John Paul 1920- *IntWW 91, Who 92, WhoAmL 92, WhoAmP 91*
**Stevens,** John Paul, III 1920- *FacFETw*
**Stevens,** John Randell 1957- *WhoAmL 92*
**Stevens,** John Theodore, Sr. 1924- *WhoBlA 92*
**Stevens,** John Williams 1929- *Who 92*
**Stevens,** Jonathan Lee 1948- *WhoMW 92*
**Stevens,** Joseph Alfred 1927- *AmMWSc 92*
**Stevens,** Joseph Charles 1929- *AmMWSc 92*
**Stevens,** Joseph Edward, Jr. 1928- *WhoAmL 92, WhoMW 92*
**Stevens,** K. T. 1919- *IntMPA 92*
**Stevens,** Karl Kent 1939- *AmMWSc 92*
**Stevens,** Kay *WrDr 92*
**Stevens,** Kenneth Henry 1922- *Who 92*
**Stevens,** Kenneth N 1924- *AmMWSc 92*
**Stevens,** Kenneth William Harry 1922- *Who 92*
**Stevens,** Larry Otis 1948- *WhoRel 92*
**Stevens,** Laurence 1920- *Who 92*
**Stevens,** Lee *ConAu 135*
**Stevens,** Leland Robert 1929- *WhoRel 92, WhoWest 92*
**Stevens,** Leonard A. 1920- *SmATA 67*
**Stevens,** Leota Mae 1921- *WhoMW 92*
**Stevens,** Leroy Carlton, Jr 1920- *AmMWSc 92*
**Stevens,** Leslie *LesBEnT 92*
**Stevens,** Leslie 1924- *IntMPA 92*
**Stevens,** Lewis Axtell 1913- *AmMWSc 92*
**Stevens,** Lewis David 1936- *Who 92*
**Stevens,** Lloyd Weakley 1914- *AmMWSc 92*
**Stevens,** Lou *DrAPF 91*
**Stevens,** Lydia Hastings 1918- *WhoAmP 91*
**Stevens,** Malcolm Peter 1934- *AmMWSc 92*
**Stevens,** Marilyn Ruth 1943- *WhoFI 92*
**Stevens,** Marion Bennion *AmMWSc 92*
**Stevens,** Marion Eugene 1926- *WhoRel 92*
**Stevens,** Mark 1922- *IntMPA 92*
**Stevens,** Mark 1951- *WrDr 92*
**Stevens,** Mark Anthony 1960- *WhoFI 92*
**Stevens,** Martin Brian 1957- *WhoFI 92*
**Stevens,** Mary Ann *WhoAmP 91*
**Stevens,** Masters B *ScFEYrs*
**Stevens,** Maxwell McDew 1942- *WhoBlA 92*
**Stevens,** Michael Dale 1958- *WhoRel 92*
**Stevens,** Michael Fred 1941- *AmMWSc 92*
**Stevens,** Milton Lewis, Jr. 1942- *WhoEnt 92*
**Stevens,** Morton d1991 *NewYTBS 91*
**Stevens,** Nancy Williams 1927- *WhoAmP 91*
**Stevens,** Nettie Maria 1861-1912 *BiInAmS*
**Stevens,** Norman 1937- *TwCPaSc*
**Stevens,** Patricia 1942- *WhoAmP 91*
**Stevens,** Patricia Ann 1946- *WhoBlA 92*
**Stevens,** Perry G 1931- *WhoIns 92*
**Stevens,** Peter 1927- *ConPo 91, WrDr 92*
**Stevens,** Peter Francis 1944- *AmMWSc 92*
**Stevens,** Philip 1953- *TwCPaSc*
**Stevens,** Philip Theodore 1906- *Who 92*
**Stevens,** Ray 1939- *ConMus 7 [port]*
**Stevens,** Reatha J. 1931- *WhoBlA 92*
**Stevens,** Richard Edward 1932- *AmMWSc 92*
**Stevens,** Richard F 1902- *AmMWSc 92*
**Stevens,** Richard Francis 1927- *WhoMW 92*
**Stevens,** Richard Joseph 1941- *AmMWSc 92*
**Stevens,** Richard Kingsbury, Jr. 1936- *WhoAmL 92*
**Stevens,** Richard P. 1931- *WrDr 92*
**Stevens,** Richard S 1925- *AmMWSc 92*
**Stevens,** Richard William 1924- *Who 92*
**Stevens,** Rick Daryl 1948- *WhoEnt 92*
**Stevens,** Rise 1913- *FacFETw, NewAmDM*
**Stevens,** Robert Bocking 1933- *WhoWest 92*
**Stevens,** Robert Edward 1924- *AmMWSc 92*
**Stevens,** Robert Edward 1957- *WhoFI 92, WhoMW 92*
**Stevens,** Robert Edwin 1927- *WhoFI 92*
**Stevens,** Robert Livingston 1787-1856 *BiInAmS*
**Stevens,** Robert T 1899-1983 *FacFETw*
**Stevens,** Robert Tindall 1951- *WhoRel 92*
**Stevens,** Robert Tyler *WrDr 92*
**Stevens,** Robert William 1936- *WhoRel 92*
**Stevens,** Roger Dale 1950- *WhoRel 92*
**Stevens,** Roger Lacey 1910- *WhoEnt 92*
**Stevens,** Roger Templeton 1927- *AmMWSc 92*
**Stevens,** Ronald David 1953- *WhoMW 92, WhoRel 92*
**Stevens,** Ronald Henry 1946- *AmMWSc 92*
**Stevens,** Rosemary 1935- *WrDr 92*
**Stevens,** Rosemary Anne 1935- *AmMWSc 92, IntWW 91*
**Stevens,** Rowan, Sterling, Yates, Jr. *ScFEYrs*
**Stevens,** Roy Harris 1948- *AmMWSc 92*
**Stevens,** Roy W. 1924- *WhoFI 92*
**Stevens,** Roy White 1934- *AmMWSc 92*
**Stevens,** Ruth Marie 1933- *WhoAmP 91*
**Stevens,** Sanford S. 1933- *WhoAmL 92*
**Stevens,** Scott *WhoEnt 92*
**Stevens,** Shane *DrAPF 91*
**Stevens,** Shane 1951- *WhoEnt 92*
**Stevens,** Sharon A. 1949- *WhoBlA 92*
**Stevens,** Shirley Sue 1939- *WhoRel 92*
**Stevens,** Siaka 1905-1988 *FacFETw*
**Stevens,** Sinclair McKnight 1927- *IntWW 91*
**Stevens,** Stanley Edward, Jr 1944- *AmMWSc 92*
**Stevens,** Stella 1938- *IntMPA 92*
**Stevens,** Stephen Edward *WhoWest 92*
**Stevens,** Steven B. 1941- *WhoEnt 92*
**Stevens,** Steven B. 1956- *WhoAmL 92*
**Stevens,** Sue Cassell *AmMWSc 92*
**Stevens,** Ted 1923- *AlmAP 92 [port]*
**Stevens,** Thaddeus 1792-1868 *AmPolLe [port], RComAH*
**Stevens,** Theodore Fulton 1923- *IntWW 91, WhoAmP 91, WhoWest 92*
**Stevens,** Thomas L 1930- *WhoIns 92*
**Stevens,** Thomas Lee 1930- *WhoAmL 92*
**Stevens,** Thomas Lorenzo, Jr. 1933- *WhoBlA 92*
**Stevens,** Thomas McConnell 1927- *AmMWSc 92*
**Stevens,** Thomas Stevens 1900- *IntWW 91, Who 92*
**Stevens,** Timothy John 1940- *Who 92*
**Stevens,** Timothy John 1946- *Who 92*
**Stevens,** Timothy S. *WhoBlA 92*
**Stevens,** Travis Edward 1927- *AmMWSc 92*
**Stevens,** Vernon Lewis 1930- *AmMWSc 92*
**Stevens,** Vincent Leroy 1930- *AmMWSc 92*
**Stevens,** Violete L 1942- *AmMWSc 92*
**Stevens,** W Tris *WhoIns 92*
**Stevens,** Wallace 1879-1955 *BenetAL 91, FacFETw, RComAH*
**Stevens,** Walter 1933- *AmMWSc 92*
**Stevens,** Walter Joseph 1944- *AmMWSc 92*
**Stevens,** Warren 1919- *WhoEnt 92*
**Stevens,** Warren Douglas 1944- *AmMWSc 92*
**Stevens,** Warren Sherwood 1941- *WhoBlA 92*
**Stevens,** Wendell Claire 1931- *WhoWest 92*
**Stevens,** Wendy *DrAPF 91*
**Stevens,** Wesley Foster 1932- *WhoRel 92*
**Stevens,** Wilbur Hunt 1918- *WhoWest 92*
**Stevens,** William Christopher *WrDr 92*
**Stevens,** William D *AmMWSc 92*
**Stevens,** William David 1934- *Who 92, WhoFI 92*
**Stevens,** William F 1922- *AmMWSc 92*
**Stevens,** William Frederick, III 1954- *WhoMW 92*
**Stevens,** William George 1938- *AmMWSc 92*
**Stevens,** William Grant 1953- *WhoWest 92*
**Stevens,** William John 1915- *WhoFI 92*
**Stevens,** William Kenneth 1917- *WhoAmL 92*
**Stevens,** William Louis 1932- *WhoRel 92*
**Stevens,** William McGee 1946- *WhoMW 92*
**Stevens,** William Talbert 1952- *WhoFI 92*
**Stevens,** William Y 1931- *AmMWSc 92*
**Stevens,** Wilma 1937- *WhoAmP 91*
**Stevens,** Winifred Kera 1917- *IntAu&W 91*
**Stevens,** Woodie James 1951- *WhoRel 92, WhoWest 92*
**Stevens-Arroyo,** Antonio M. 1941- *WhoHisp 92*
**Stevens Of Ludgate,** Baron 1936- *IntWW 91, Who 92*
**Stevens-Silver,** Emily Fabella 1928- *WhoEnt 92*
**Stevenson,** Adlai E. 1900-1965 *BenetAL 91*
**Stevenson,** Adlai E., III 1930- *IntWW 91*
**Stevenson,** Adlai Ewing 1835-1914 *AmPolLe*
**Stevenson,** Adlai Ewing 1900-1965 *AmPolLe [port]*
**Stevenson,** Adlai Ewing, II 1900-1965 *FacFETw [port]*
**Stevenson,** Adlai Ewing, III 1930- *WhoAmL 92, WhoAmP 91*
**Stevenson,** Alan Carruth 1909- *Who 92*
**Stevenson,** Amanda 1943- *WhoEnt 92*
**Stevenson,** Andrew 1784-1857 *AmPolLe*
**Stevenson,** Anne *DrAPF 91, WrDr 92*
**Stevenson,** Anne 1933- *ConPo 91, WrDr 92*
**Stevenson,** Anne Katharine 1933- *IntAu&W 91*
**Stevenson,** Benjamin Howard 1929- *WhoRel 92*
**Stevenson,** Bruce R 1952- *AmMWSc 92*
**Stevenson,** Bryan Allen 1959- *WhoAmL 92*
**Stevenson,** Burton 1872-1962 *ScFEYrs*
**Stevenson,** Burton E. 1872-1962 *BenetAL 91*
**Stevenson,** Charles Edward 1913- *AmMWSc 92*
**Stevenson,** Christopher Terence S. *Who 92*
**Stevenson,** David *Who 92*
**Stevenson,** David 1942- *IntAu&W 91, WrDr 92*
**Stevenson,** David Austin 1928- *AmMWSc 92*
**Stevenson,** David John 1948- *AmMWSc 92*
**Stevenson,** David Michael 1938- *AmMWSc 92*
**Stevenson,** David P 1914- *AmMWSc 92*
**Stevenson,** David Stuart 1924- *AmMWSc 92*
**Stevenson,** Denise L. 1946- *WhoFI 92*
**Stevenson,** Dennis *Who 92*
**Stevenson,** Dennis A 1944- *AmMWSc 92*
**Stevenson,** Derek Paul 1911- *Who 92*
**Stevenson,** Diane *DrAPF 91*
**Stevenson,** Don R 1944- *AmMWSc 92*
**Stevenson,** Donald Thomas 1923- *AmMWSc 92*
**Stevenson,** Dwight Eshelman 1906- *WrDr 92*
**Stevenson,** Elizabeth 1919- *IntAu&W 91, WrDr 92*
**Stevenson,** Elmer Clark 1915- *AmMWSc 92*
**Stevenson,** Enola L 1939- *AmMWSc 92*
**Stevenson,** Eugene Hamilton 1919- *AmMWSc 92*
**Stevenson,** Everett E 1923- *AmMWSc 92*
**Stevenson,** F Dee 1933- *AmMWSc 92*
**Stevenson,** Florence *IntAu&W 91, WrDr 92*
**Stevenson,** Forrest Frederick 1916- *AmMWSc 92*
**Stevenson,** Frances Grace 1921- *WhoWest 92*
**Stevenson,** Frank Jay 1922- *AmMWSc 92*
**Stevenson,** Frank John 1938- *WhoFI 92*
**Stevenson,** Frank Robert 1931- *AmMWSc 92*
**Stevenson,** G W 1951- *AmMWSc 92*
**Stevenson,** Garfield William 1927- *WhoWest 92*
**Stevenson,** George Franklin 1922- *AmMWSc 92*
**Stevenson,** George Telford 1932- *Who 92*
**Stevenson,** George William 1938- *Who 92*
**Stevenson,** Gerald Lee 1937- *WhoFI 92*
**Stevenson,** Harlan Quinn 1927- *AmMWSc 92*
**Stevenson,** Henry C 1948- *AmMWSc 92*
**Stevenson,** Henry Dennistoun 1945- *Who 92*
**Stevenson,** Henry Miller 1914- *AmMWSc 92*
**Stevenson,** Hugh David 1918- *Who 92*
**Stevenson,** Ian 1918- *AmMWSc 92, WrDr 92*
**Stevenson,** Ian Lawrie 1926- *AmMWSc 92*
**Stevenson,** Irone Edmund, Jr 1930- *AmMWSc 92*
**Stevenson,** J Ross 1931- *AmMWSc 92, WhoMW 92*
**Stevenson,** James 1840-1888 *BiInAmS*
**Stevenson,** James 1929- *WrDr 92*
**Stevenson,** James A. 1938- *WhoFI 92*
**Stevenson,** James Earl 1946-1989 *WhoBlA 92N*
**Stevenson,** James Francis 1943- *AmMWSc 92, WhoMW 92*
**Stevenson,** James Laraway 1938- *WhoMW 92*
**Stevenson,** James Ralph 1949- *WhoWest 92*
**Stevenson,** James Richard 1937- *WhoAmL 92, WhoWest 92*
**Stevenson,** James Rufus 1925- *AmMWSc 92*
**Stevenson,** Jean Moorhead 1904- *AmMWSc 92*
**Stevenson,** Jeffery Scott 1956- *WhoRel 92*
**Stevenson,** Jeffrey Smith 1951- *AmMWSc 92*
**Stevenson,** Jeffrey Taylor 1960- *WhoEnt 92*
**Stevenson,** Jim 1937- *Who 92*
**Stevenson,** John 1926- *IntAu&W 91*
**Stevenson,** John 1927- *Who 92*
**Stevenson,** John Crabtree 1937- *AmMWSc 92*
**Stevenson,** John David 1950- *AmMWSc 92*
**Stevenson,** John Martin 1956- *WhoAmL 92*
**Stevenson,** John P. *WrDr 92*
**Stevenson,** John Ray 1943- *AmMWSc 92, WhoMW 92*
**Stevenson,** John Reese 1921- *WhoAmL 92*
**Stevenson,** Jon Wayne 1946- *WhoRel 92*
**Stevenson,** Joseph Aidan 1931- *Who 92*
**Stevenson,** Joseph Ross 1866-1939 *RelLAm 91*
**Stevenson,** Justin Jason, III 1941- *WhoAmL 92*
**Stevenson,** Kenneth Eugene 1942- *AmMWSc 92*
**Stevenson,** Kenneth James 1941- *AmMWSc 92*
**Stevenson,** Kenneth Lee 1939- *AmMWSc 92*
**Stevenson,** Kenneth Roy 1955- *WhoMW 92*
**Stevenson,** L Harold 1940- *AmMWSc 92*
**Stevenson,** Lillian 1922- *WhoBlA 92*
**Stevenson,** Louise Stevens 1912- *AmMWSc 92*
**Stevenson,** Lynn Shaw 1959- *WhoEnt 92*
**Stevenson,** Madeline D *WhoAmP 91*
**Stevenson,** Mark Joseph Tomlinson 1961- *WhoFI 92*
**Stevenson,** Mary M 1951- *AmMWSc 92*
**Stevenson,** Matilda Coxe Evans 1849-1915 *BiInAmS*
**Stevenson,** Melford 1902-1987 *FacFETw*
**Stevenson,** Merlon Lynn 1923- *AmMWSc 92*
**Stevenson,** Michael Gail 1943- *AmMWSc 92*
**Stevenson,** Michael Ray 1958- *WhoMW 92*
**Stevenson,** Morton Coleman *WhoBlA 92*
**Stevenson,** Nancy Backer 1928- *WhoAmP 91*
**Stevenson,** Nancy Roberta 1938- *AmMWSc 92*
**Stevenson,** Olive 1930- *Who 92*
**Stevenson,** Parker 1953- *IntMPA 92*
**Stevenson,** Paul Michael 1954- *AmMWSc 92*
**Stevenson,** Philip Davis 1936- *WhoAmL 92*
**Stevenson,** R.A.M. 1847-1900 *ThHEIm*
**Stevenson,** Ralph Girard, Jr 1925- *AmMWSc 92*
**Stevenson,** Randall 1953- *IntAu&W 91*
**Stevenson,** Ray 1937- *WhoFI 92*
**Stevenson,** Richard Gray, III 1958- *WhoWest 92*
**Stevenson,** Richard Marshall 1923- *AmMWSc 92*
**Stevenson,** Richard William 1955- *WhoEnt 92*
**Stevenson,** Robert 1905-1986 *IntDcF 2-2 [port]*
**Stevenson,** Robert Barron Kerr 1913- *Who 92*
**Stevenson,** Robert Benjamin, III 1950- *WhoMW 92*
**Stevenson,** Robert Bruce 1951- *WhoAmL 92*
**Stevenson,** Robert Bryce 1926- *Who 92*
**Stevenson,** Robert Edward 1932- *WhoFI 92*
**Stevenson,** Robert Edwin 1926- *AmMWSc 92*
**Stevenson,** Robert Evans 1916- *AmMWSc 92*
**Stevenson,** Robert Everett 1921- *AmMWSc 92*
**Stevenson,** Robert Jan 1952- *AmMWSc 92*
**Stevenson,** Robert Louis 1850-1894 *BenetAL 91, CnDBLB 5 [port], RfGEnL 91*
**Stevenson,** Robert Louis 1854-1894 *ScFEYrs*
**Stevenson,** Robert Louis 1932- *AmMWSc 92*
**Stevenson,** Robert Lovell *AmMWSc 92*
**Stevenson,** Robert Macaulay 1854-1952 *TwCPaSc*
**Stevenson,** Robert Murrell 1916- *WhoEnt 92, WhoWest 92*
**Stevenson,** Robert Thomas 1916- *AmMWSc 92*
**Stevenson,** Robert Wilfrid 1947- *IntWW 91, Who 92*
**Stevenson,** Robert William 1930- *AmMWSc 92*
**Stevenson,** Robin 1923- *AmMWSc 92*
**Stevenson,** Robin 1946- *AmMWSc 92*
**Stevenson,** Ronald James 1951- *WhoFI 92*
**Stevenson,** Russell A. 1923- *WhoBlA 92*

**Stevenson,** Simpson 1921- *Who 92*
**Stevenson,** Stansmore Dean 1866-1944 *TwCPaSc*
**Stevenson,** Stuart Shelton 1914- *AmMWSc 92*
**Stevenson,** Teofilo 1952- *BlkOlyM [port]*
**Stevenson,** Thomas Dickson 1924- *AmMWSc 92*
**Stevenson,** Thomas Herbert 1951- *WhoFI 92, WhoMW 92*
**Stevenson,** Unice Teen 1950- *WhoBlA 92*
**Stevenson,** Walter Roe 1946- *AmMWSc 92*
**Stevenson,** Warren H 1938- *AmMWSc 92*
**Stevenson,** Wilf *Who 92*
**Stevenson,** William 1924- *WrDr 92*
**Stevenson,** William Campbell 1931- *AmMWSc 92*
**Stevenson,** William D, Jr 1912- *AmMWSc 92*
**Stevenson,** William Edwards 1900-1985 *FacFETw*
**Stevenson,** William Trevor 1921- *Who 92*
**Stever,** Donald W., Jr. 1944- *WhoAmL 92*
**Stever,** Edward William *DrAPF 91*
**Stever,** H Guyford 1916- *AmMWSc 92*
**Stever,** Horton Guyford 1916- *IntWW 91, WhoAmP 91*
**Stever,** Margo *DrAPF 91*
**Stevermer,** Emmett J 1932- *AmMWSc 92*
**Steveson,** Boyd Donald 1950- *WhoAmP 91*
**Stevinson,** Harry Thompson 1915- *AmMWSc 92*
**Steward,** Carlos Warren 1950- *WhoEnt 92, WhoFI 92*
**Steward,** Cedric John 1931- *Who 92*
**Steward,** D.E. *DrAPF 91*
**Steward,** Emanuel 1944- *WhoBlA 92*
**Steward,** Frederick Campion 1904- *AmMWSc 92, Who 92*
**Steward,** James Brian 1946- *WhoAmL 92*
**Steward,** John P 1927- *AmMWSc 92*
**Steward,** Julian Haynes 1902-1972 *FacFETw*
**Steward,** Kerry Kalen 1930- *AmMWSc 92*
**Steward,** Loretta 1918- *WhoAmP 91*
**Steward,** Lowell C. 1919- *WhoBlA 92*
**Steward,** Nigel Oliver Willoughby d1991 *Who 92N*
**Steward,** Omar Waddington 1932- *AmMWSc 92*
**Steward,** Patricia Ann Rupert 1945- *WhoFI 92, WhoWest 92*
**Steward,** Robert F 1923- *AmMWSc 92*
**Steward,** Stanley Feargus 1904- *Who 92*
**Steward,** Susan McKinney 1847-1918 *NotBlAW 92 [port]*
**Steward,** W G 1930- *AmMWSc 92*
**Stewart** *Who 92*
**Stewart,** A. C. 1915- *WrDr 92*
**Stewart,** Adelle Wright 1922- *WhoBlA 92*
**Stewart,** Alan 1917- *Who 92*
**Stewart,** Alan 1928- *IntAu&W 91*
**Stewart,** Alan 1932- *Who 92*
**Stewart,** Alastair Lindsay 1938- *Who 92*
**Stewart,** Albert C. *WhoBlA 92*
**Stewart,** Albert Clifton 1919- *AmMWSc 92*
**Stewart,** Albert Elisha 1927- *WhoMW 92*
**Stewart,** Alec Thompson 1925- *AmMWSc 92*
**Stewart,** Alexander Doig 1926- *WhoFI 92, WhoRel 92*
**Stewart,** Alexander Ronald, III 1945- *WhoRel 92*
**Stewart,** Allan *Who 92*
**Stewart,** Allen Warren 1938- *WhoAmL 92*
**Stewart,** Andrew d1990 *Who 92N*
**Stewart,** Andrew 1907- *Who 92*
**Stewart,** Andrew Struthers 1937- *Who 92*
**Stewart,** Angus 1946- *Who 92*
**Stewart,** Ann Harleman *WrDr 92*
**Stewart,** Arlene Jean Golden 1943- *WhoFI 92*
**Stewart,** Arthur Van 1938- *AmMWSc 92*
**Stewart,** B T *ScFEYrs*
**Stewart,** Barbara D 1943- *WhoIns 92*
**Stewart,** Barbara Dean 1941- *WhoEnt 92*
**Stewart,** Barbara Dunbar 1943- *WhoFI 92*
**Stewart,** Barbara Yost 1932- *AmMWSc 92*
**Stewart,** Bennett McVey 1915- *WhoAmP 91*
**Stewart,** Bernard 1950- *WhoBlA 92*
**Stewart,** Bernard Harold Ian 1935- *IntWW 91, Who 92*
**Stewart,** Bert James 1924- *WhoAmP 91*
**Stewart,** Bobby Alton 1932- *AmMWSc 92*
**Stewart,** Bonnie 1947- *WhoAmP 91*
**Stewart,** Bonnie Madison 1914- *AmMWSc 92, WhoMW 92*
**Stewart,** Bradley Clayton 1954- *AmMWSc 92*
**Stewart,** Brent Scott 1954- *AmMWSc 92*
**Stewart,** Brian John 1945- *Who 92*
**Stewart,** Brian Thomas Webster 1922- *Who 92*
**Stewart,** Brice Horace 1911- *WhoAmP 91*
**Stewart,** Bruce C. *WhoRel 92*
**Stewart,** Bruce Robert 1927- *IntAu&W 91*
**Stewart,** Carl L. 1936- *WhoBlA 92*
**Stewart,** Carleton C 1940- *AmMWSc 92*
**Stewart,** Carlyle Veeder, Jr 1927- *WhoAmP 91*
**Stewart,** Cecil R 1937- *AmMWSc 92*
**Stewart,** Charles Andrew, III 1959- *WhoAmL 92*
**Stewart,** Charles Edward, Jr. 1916- *WhoAmL 92*
**Stewart,** Charles Evan 1952- *WhoAmL 92*
**Stewart,** Charles Franklin, Jr. 1942- *WhoRel 92, WhoWest 92*
**Stewart,** Charles J. 1930- *WhoBlA 92*
**Stewart,** Charles Jack 1929- *AmMWSc 92*
**Stewart,** Charles Neil 1945- *AmMWSc 92*
**Stewart,** Charles Newby 1931- *AmMWSc 92*
**Stewart,** Charles Ranous 1940- *AmMWSc 92*
**Stewart,** Charles Robert Crombie *WhoWest 92*
**Stewart,** Charles Thorp 1918- *WhoAmL 92*
**Stewart,** Charles Vuille 1941- *WhoAmL 92*
**Stewart,** Charles Walter 1937- *WhoIns 92*
**Stewart,** Charles Wesley 1930- *WhoRel 92*
**Stewart,** Charles Wesley, Jr 1927- *WhoAmP 91*
**Stewart,** Charles William 1930- *WhoWest 92*
**Stewart,** Charles Winfield, Sr 1940- *AmMWSc 92*
**Stewart,** Chester Bryant 1910- *AmMWSc 92*
**Stewart,** Clarence P 1922- *WhoAmP 91*
**Stewart,** Colin MacDonald 1922- *Who 92*
**Stewart,** Colin Murray d1990 *Who 92N*
**Stewart,** Dan *TwCWW 91*
**Stewart,** Daniel I 1932- *WhoAmP 91*
**Stewart,** Daniel Kenneth 1925- *WrDr 92*
**Stewart,** Daniel Robert 1938- *AmMWSc 92*
**Stewart,** Darneau V. 1928- *WhoBlA 92*
**Stewart,** Daryl Michael 1947- *WhoEnt 92*
**Stewart,** Dave 1957- *News 91 [port]*
**Stewart,** David *WrDr 92*
**Stewart,** David 1813-1899 *BiInAmS*
**Stewart,** David 1913- *Who 92*
**Stewart,** David Benjamin 1928- *AmMWSc 92*
**Stewart,** David Denison 1858-1905 *BiInAmS*
**Stewart,** David James H. *Who 92*
**Stewart,** David K. 1937- *WhoEnt 92*
**Stewart,** David Keith 1957- *WhoBlA 92, WhoWest 92*
**Stewart,** David Pentland 1943- *WhoAmL 92*
**Stewart,** David Perry 1916- *AmMWSc 92*
**Stewart,** David Tabb 1949- *WhoRel 92*
**Stewart,** David Wayne 1951- *WhoFI 92, WhoWest 92*
**Stewart,** Dolores Ann 1947- *WhoAmL 92*
**Stewart,** Don M 1937- *WhoIns 92*
**Stewart,** Donald A 1946- *WhoIns 92*
**Stewart,** Donald Borden 1917- *AmMWSc 92*
**Stewart,** Donald Bruce *WhoEnt 92*
**Stewart,** Donald Charles 1912- *AmMWSc 92*
**Stewart,** Donald Charles 1930- *IntAu&W 91, WrDr 92*
**Stewart,** Donald George 1933- *AmMWSc 92*
**Stewart,** Donald George 1935- *WhoEnt 92*
**Stewart,** Donald H. 1911- *WrDr 92*
**Stewart,** Donald James 1920- *IntWW 91, Who 92*
**Stewart,** Donald Mitchell 1938- *WhoBlA 92*
**Stewart,** Donald Ogden 1894-1980 *BenetAL 91*
**Stewart,** Donald W 1940- *WhoAmP 91*
**Stewart,** Donovan 1903- *WhoAmP 91*
**Stewart,** Dorathy Anne 1937- *AmMWSc 92*
**Stewart,** Doris Mae 1927- *AmMWSc 92*
**Stewart,** Dorothy 1905- *TwCPaSc*
**Stewart,** Dorothy Nell 1949- *WhoBlA 92*
**Stewart,** Douglas 1913-1985 *RfGEnL 91*
**Stewart,** Douglas Day *IntMPA 92*
**Stewart,** Dugald 1753-1828 *BlkwCEP*
**Stewart,** Duncan James 1939- *WhoAmL 92*
**Stewart,** Duncan Montgomery 1930- *Who 92*
**Stewart,** Dwight Calvert 1930- *WhoRel 92*
**Stewart,** Edward 1923- *Who 92*
**Stewart,** Edward Nicholson 1940- *WhoFI 92*
**Stewart,** Edward William 1931- *AmMWSc 92*
**Stewart,** Elaine 1929- *IntMPA 92*
**Stewart,** Elinore Pruitt *TwCWW 91*
**Stewart,** Elinore Rupert 1876-1933 *HanAmWH*
**Stewart,** Elizabeth Pierce 1947- *WhoBlA 92*
**Stewart,** Ella P. 1893-1987 *NotBlAW 92 [port]*
**Stewart,** Elwin Lynn 1940- *AmMWSc 92*
**Stewart,** Emily Jones 1937- *WhoBlA 92*
**Stewart,** Eugene Lawrence 1920- *WhoAmL 92*
**Stewart,** Ewen 1926- *Who 92*
**Stewart,** Frank *DrAPF 91*
**Stewart,** Frank Edwin 1941- *AmMWSc 92*
**Stewart,** Frank Moore 1917- *AmMWSc 92*
**Stewart,** Frank Ruben, Sr. 1949- *WhoMW 92*
**Stewart,** Fred M 1936- *IntAu&W 91, WrDr 92*
**Stewart,** Frederick 1916- *Who 92*
**Stewart,** Frederick Henry 1916- *IntWW 91*
**Stewart,** G Russell, II 1933- *WhoAmP 91*
**Stewart,** Gary Franklin 1935- *AmMWSc 92*
**Stewart,** Geoffrey S. 1951- *WhoAmL 92*
**Stewart,** George E. 1915- *WhoRel 92*
**Stewart,** George Girdwood 1919- *Who 92*
**Stewart,** George Hamill 1925- *AmMWSc 92*
**Stewart,** George Hudson 1925- *AmMWSc 92*
**Stewart,** George Louis 1944- *AmMWSc 92*
**Stewart,** George R. 1895-1980 *BenetAL 91, TwCSFW 91*
**Stewart,** George Robert Gordon 1924- *Who 92*
**Stewart,** George Russell 1944- *Who 92*
**Stewart,** George Taylor 1924- *WhoFI 92, WhoIns 92*
**Stewart,** Gerald Walter 1944- *AmMWSc 92*
**Stewart,** Glen Jay 1949- *WhoRel 92*
**Stewart,** Glenn Alexander 1941- *AmMWSc 92*
**Stewart,** Glenn Raymond 1936- *AmMWSc 92*
**Stewart,** Glenn W 1914- *WhoAmP 91*
**Stewart,** Gordon Arnold 1934- *AmMWSc 92*
**Stewart,** Gordon Ervin 1934- *AmMWSc 92*
**Stewart,** Gordon Thallon 1919- *Who 92*
**Stewart,** Gregory 1958- *WhoBlA 92*
**Stewart,** Gregory Randall 1949- *AmMWSc 92*
**Stewart,** Gwendolyn Jane 1926- *AmMWSc 92*
**Stewart,** H J 1915- *AmMWSc 92*
**Stewart,** Hal Aldridge 1937- *WhoRel 92*
**Stewart,** Hal H. 1942- *WhoMW 92*
**Stewart,** Harold 1916- *WrDr 92*
**Stewart,** Harold Brown 1921- *AmMWSc 92*
**Stewart,** Harold Charles 1906- *Who 92*
**Stewart,** Harold Frederick 1916- *IntAu&W 91*
**Stewart,** Harold L 1899- *AmMWSc 92*
**Stewart,** Harris B, Jr. 1922- *ConAu 35NR*
**Stewart,** Harris Bates, Jr 1922- *AmMWSc 92*
**Stewart,** Helen Ivaska 1954- *WhoFI 92*
**Stewart,** Herbert 1928- *AmMWSc 92*
**Stewart,** Horace W. 1910- *WhoBlA 92*
**Stewart,** Houston Mark S. *Who 92*
**Stewart,** Hugh Angus 1882-1917 *BiInAmS*
**Stewart,** Hugh Charlie Godfray 1897- *Who 92*
**Stewart,** Hugh Parker 1934- *Who 92*
**Stewart,** Ian *Who 92*
**Stewart,** Ian George 1923- *Who 92*
**Stewart,** Imogene Bigham 1942- *WhoBlA 92*
**Stewart,** Inez 1956- *WhoHisp 92*
**Stewart,** Isaac Daniel, Jr. 1932- *WhoAmL 92, WhoWest 92*
**Stewart,** Ivan 1922- *AmMWSc 92*
**Stewart,** J. I. M. 1906- *ConNov 91, WrDr 92*
**Stewart,** J R, Jr 1926- *AmMWSc 92*
**Stewart,** J W 1946- *AmMWSc 92*
**Stewart,** Jack Lauren 1924- *AmMWSc 92*
**Stewart,** Jack M. 1926- *WhoFI 92*
**Stewart,** Jackie *Who 92*
**Stewart,** Jackie 1939- *FacFETw*
**Stewart,** Jacques *WhoRel 92*
**Stewart,** James d1991 *NewYTBS 91*
**Stewart,** James 1908- *FacFETw, IntMPA 92, IntWW 91*
**Stewart,** James 1951- *WhoWest 92*
**Stewart,** James A 1920- *AmMWSc 92*
**Stewart,** James A., III *WhoBlA 92*
**Stewart,** James Allan 1953- *WhoMW 92*
**Stewart,** James Allen 1927- *AmMWSc 92*
**Stewart,** James Anthony 1938- *AmMWSc 92*
**Stewart,** James Benjamin 1947- *WhoBlA 92*
**Stewart,** James Cecil Campbell 1916- *Who 92*
**Stewart,** James Clifton, III 1957- *WhoRel 92*
**Stewart,** James Douglas 1925- *Who 92*
**Stewart,** James Drewry 1941- *AmMWSc 92*
**Stewart,** James Edward 1928- *AmMWSc 92*
**Stewart,** James Gathings 1942- *WhoFI 92*
**Stewart,** James George 1937- *WhoEnt 92*
**Stewart,** James Gill d1991 *Who 92N*
**Stewart,** James H, Jr 1926- *WhoAmP 91*
**Stewart,** James Hamilton, III 1943- *WhoAmL 92*
**Stewart,** James Harvey 1939- *Who 92*
**Stewart,** James Joseph 1944- *WhoRel 92*
**Stewart,** James Joseph Patrick 1946- *AmMWSc 92*
**Stewart,** James Kevin 1942- *WhoAmL 92*
**Stewart,** James L. *IntMPA 92*
**Stewart,** James Lablache *Who 92*
**Stewart,** James Lloyd 1918- *AmMWSc 92*
**Stewart,** James M. 1946- *WhoWest 92*
**Stewart,** James Maitland 1908- *Who 92, WhoEnt 92*
**Stewart,** James McDonald 1941- *AmMWSc 92*
**Stewart,** James Monroe 1946- *AmMWSc 92*
**Stewart,** James Montgomery 1939- *WhoFI 92*
**Stewart,** James Moray 1938- *Who 92*
**Stewart,** James Ray 1937- *AmMWSc 92*
**Stewart,** James Robertson 1917- *Who 92*
**Stewart,** James Simeon Hamilton 1943- *Who 92*
**Stewart,** James T 1938- *AmMWSc 92*
**Stewart,** James Vahl 1947- *WhoWest 92*
**Stewart,** Janell Pinkston 1946- *WhoWest 92*
**Stewart,** Janet Lynn 1940- *WhoWest 92*
**Stewart,** Janice Mae 1951- *WhoAmL 92*
**Stewart,** Janson *WhoAmP 91*
**Stewart,** Jean *IntAu&W 91X*
**Stewart,** Jeffrey Bayrd 1952- *WhoAmL 92*
**Stewart,** Jennifer Keys 1947- *AmMWSc 92*
**Stewart,** Jewel Hope 1948- *WhoBlA 92*
**Stewart,** Joan Godsil *AmMWSc 92*
**Stewart,** Joe William 1928- *WhoAmP 91*
**Stewart,** John *DrAPF 91*
**Stewart,** John 1929- *AmMWSc 92*
**Stewart,** John A., Jr. 1942- *WhoAmL 92*
**Stewart,** John Allan 1924- *AmMWSc 92*
**Stewart,** John Allan 1939- *WhoEnt 92*
**Stewart,** John Allan 1942- *Who 92*
**Stewart,** John Antenen 1920- *WhoMW 92*
**Stewart,** John Anthony Benedict 1927- *IntWW 91, Who 92*
**Stewart,** John B., Jr. 1930- *WhoBlA 92*
**Stewart,** John Conyngham 1930- *AmMWSc 92*
**Stewart,** John Craig 1940- *Who 92*
**Stewart,** John Frith 1937- *WhoAmL 92*
**Stewart,** John Gilman 1935- *WhoAmP 91*
**Stewart,** John Hall 1944- *Who 92*
**Stewart,** John Harger *WhoEnt 92*
**Stewart,** John Harris 1928- *AmMWSc 92*
**Stewart,** John Innes Mackintosh 1906- *Who 92*
**Stewart,** John Joseph 1946- *AmMWSc 92*
**Stewart,** John L 1925- *AmMWSc 92*
**Stewart,** John Mathews 1920- *AmMWSc 92*
**Stewart,** John Michael 1956- *WhoMW 92*
**Stewart,** John Morrow 1924- *AmMWSc 92, WhoWest 92*
**Stewart,** John Norman 1940- *WhoEnt 92*
**Stewart,** John O. 1935- *WhoBlA 92*
**Stewart,** John Othneil 1933- *WhoBlA 92*
**Stewart,** John Simon 1955- *Who 92*
**Stewart,** John Thomas, Jr. 1928- *WhoAmL 92*
**Stewart,** John Westcott 1926- *AmMWSc 92*
**Stewart,** John Woods 1942- *AmMWSc 92*
**Stewart,** John Wray Black 1936- *AmMWSc 92, WhoWest 92*
**Stewart,** John Young 1939- *IntWW 91, Who 92*
**Stewart,** Joseph Grier 1941- *WhoAmL 92*
**Stewart,** Joseph Letie 1927- *AmMWSc 92*
**Stewart,** Joseph M. 1942- *WhoBlA 92*
**Stewart,** Judith *WrDr 92*
**Stewart,** Ken *IntMPA 92*
**Stewart,** Kendall Leuomon 1950- *WhoMW 92*
**Stewart,** Kenneth Albert 1925- *Who 92*
**Stewart,** Kenneth C. 1939- *WhoBlA 92*
**Stewart,** Kenneth Hope 1922- *Who 92*
**Stewart,** Kenneth Wilson 1935- *AmMWSc 92*
**Stewart,** Kent Kallam 1934- *AmMWSc 92*
**Stewart,** Kenton M 1931- *AmMWSc 92*
**Stewart,** Kevin James 1928- *Who 92*
**Stewart,** Kimberly Clarice 1968- *WhoRel 92*
**Stewart,** Larry Alan 1950- *WhoMW 92*
**Stewart,** Larry R. 1948- *WhoWest 92*
**Stewart,** Larry Wayne 1947- *WhoRel 92*
**Stewart,** Lawrence Colm 1955- *AmMWSc 92*
**Stewart,** Lee Anne 1961- *WhoAmL 92*
**Stewart,** Leland Perry 1928- *WhoRel 92, WhoWest 92*

**Stewart**, Leland Taylor 1928- AmMWSc 92
**Stewart**, Leon Holmes 1900-1987 WhoBlA 92N
**Stewart**, Leon Otto 1929- WhoRel 92
**Stewart**, Leslie 1949- IntAu&W 91
**Stewart**, Linda Rae WhoEnt 92
**Stewart**, Lindsay D. WhoAmL 92
**Stewart**, Lyman 1840-1923 RelLAm 91
**Stewart**, Mac A. 1942- WhoBlA 92
**Stewart**, Mae E. 1926- WhoBlA 92
**Stewart**, Malcolm M. 1920- WhoBlA 92
**Stewart**, Margaret McBride 1927- AmMWSc 92
**Stewart**, Maria W. 1803-1879 NotBlAW 92
**Stewart**, Marilyn IntMPA 92
**Stewart**, Mark Armstrong 1929- AmMWSc 92
**Stewart**, Mark Steven 1950- WhoAmL 92
**Stewart**, Mark Thomas 1948- WhoFI 92
**Stewart**, Mark Thurston 1948- AmMWSc 92
**Stewart**, Marlene Metzger 1937- WhoFI 92, WhoWest 92
**Stewart**, Martha 1942?- News 92-1 [port]
**Stewart**, Mary 1916- Who 92, WrDr 92
**Stewart**, Mary E 1939- AmMWSc 92
**Stewart**, Mary Florence Elinor 1916- IntAu&W 91
**Stewart**, Mary Ruth 1929- WhoAmP 91
**Stewart**, Maurice L 1929- WhoIns 92
**Stewart**, Melbourne George 1927- AmMWSc 92
**Stewart**, Melinda Jane 1949- WhoAmL 92
**Stewart**, Melville Yorke 1935- WhoMW 92
**Stewart**, Michael DrAPF 91
**Stewart**, Michael 1933- WrDr 92
**Stewart**, Michael C. 1938- WhoAmL 92
**Stewart**, Michael Eugene 1947- WhoAmP 91
**Stewart**, Michael James 1933- Who 92
**Stewart**, Michael McFadden 1938- WhoFI 92
**Stewart**, Michael Norman Francis 1911- Who 92
**Stewart**, Michael Steven 1956- WhoRel 92
**Stewart**, Moray Who 92
**Stewart**, Muriel 1905- Who 92
**Stewart**, Nancy Potter 1936- WhoAmP 91
**Stewart**, Nicholas John Cameron 1947- Who 92
**Stewart**, Nora Scott 1936- WhoAmP 91
**Stewart**, Norma Lee 1925- WhoWest 92
**Stewart**, Norman MacLeod 1934- Who 92
**Stewart**, Patrice Lafferty 1933- WhoFI 92
**Stewart**, Patricia Carry 1928- WhoFI 92
**Stewart**, Paul Alva 1909- AmMWSc 92
**Stewart**, Paul Anthony, II 1952- WhoWest 92
**Stewart**, Paul Arthur 1955- WhoMW 92
**Stewart**, Paul Kennedy 1930- WhoEnt 92
**Stewart**, Paul Wilbur 1925- WhoBlA 92
**Stewart**, Peggy O'Rourke 1923- WhoEnt 92
**Stewart**, Peter Arthur 1921- AmMWSc 92
**Stewart**, Phyllis A. 1939- WhoMW 92
**Stewart**, Porter DrAPF 91
**Stewart**, Potter 1915-1985 FacFETw
**Stewart**, Rachel Ann 1943- WhoAmP 91
**Stewart**, Raymond 1965- BlkOlyM
**Stewart**, Reginald Bruce 1928- AmMWSc 92
**Stewart**, Richard d1991 Who 92N
**Stewart**, Richard Alfred 1945- WhoWest 92
**Stewart**, Richard Burleson 1940- WhoAmL 92
**Stewart**, Richard Byron 1924- AmMWSc 92
**Stewart**, Richard Donald 1926- AmMWSc 92
**Stewart**, Richard E 1933- WhoIns 92
**Stewart**, Richard Jarrett 1949- WhoWest 92
**Stewart**, Richard John 1942- AmMWSc 92
**Stewart**, Richard William 1946- AmMWSc 92
**Stewart**, Richard Williams 1948- WhoAmL 92
**Stewart**, Richard Willis 1936- AmMWSc 92
**Stewart**, Robert DrAPF 91, TwCPaSc
**Stewart**, Robert 1918- WhoEnt 92
**Stewart**, Robert Archie, II 1942- AmMWSc 92
**Stewart**, Robert Blaylock 1926- AmMWSc 92
**Stewart**, Robert Bruce 1926- AmMWSc 92
**Stewart**, Robert Christie 1926- Who 92
**Stewart**, Robert Clarence 1921- AmMWSc 92
**Stewart**, Robert Clarence, Jr. 1936- WhoRel 92
**Stewart**, Robert Daniel 1923- AmMWSc 92
**Stewart**, Robert Douglas 1949- WhoAmL 92
**Stewart**, Robert Earl 1935- AmMWSc 92
**Stewart**, Robert F 1936- AmMWSc 92
**Stewart**, Robert Francis 1926- AmMWSc 92
**Stewart**, Robert Henry 1941- AmMWSc 92
**Stewart**, Robert Jackson 1958- WhoMW 92
**Stewart**, Robert John 1951- WhoEnt 92
**Stewart**, Robert Murray, Jr 1924- AmMWSc 92
**Stewart**, Robert Ray 1938- WhoRel 92
**Stewart**, Robert W. 1923- IntWW 91
**Stewart**, Robert William 1923- AmMWSc 92, Who 92
**Stewart**, Roberta A 1923- AmMWSc 92
**Stewart**, Robertson 1913- Who 92
**Stewart**, Robin Kenny 1937- AmMWSc 92
**Stewart**, Robin Milton 1938- Who 92
**Stewart**, Rod 1945- IntWW 91, NewAmDM
**Stewart**, Roderick David 1945- WhoEnt 92A
**Stewart**, Rodney Milton 1953- WhoMW 92
**Stewart**, Roger 1920- WhoAmP 91
**Stewart**, Ronald 1903- Who 92
**Stewart**, Ronald Eugene 1937- WhoAmP 91
**Stewart**, Ronald K 1948- WhoAmP 91
**Stewart**, Ronald L. 1936- WhoBlA 92
**Stewart**, Ronald Patrick 1942- WhoBlA 92
**Stewart**, Rosemary WrDr 92
**Stewart**, Ross 1924- AmMWSc 92
**Stewart**, Ruth Ann 1942- WhoBlA 92
**Stewart**, Ruth Carol 1928- AmMWSc 92
**Stewart**, S. Jay 1938- IntWW 91
**Stewart**, Samuel B. 1908- WhoAmL 92
**Stewart**, Sheila Frances 1927- AmMWSc 92
**Stewart**, Shelton E 1934- AmMWSc 92
**Stewart**, Simon Who 92
**Stewart**, Stanley Lukeman 1961- WhoAmL 92
**Stewart**, Stanley Toft 1910- Who 92
**Stewart**, Stephen Malcolm 1914- Who 92
**Stewart**, Sue Stern 1942- WhoAmL 92
**Stewart**, Suzanne Freda Who 92
**Stewart**, T Bonner 1924- AmMWSc 92
**Stewart**, Terence Patrick 1948- WhoAmL 92
**Stewart**, Terry Lynn 1943- WhoFI 92
**Stewart**, Terry Sanford 1951- AmMWSc 92
**Stewart**, Thomas 1928- IntWW 91, NewAmDM
**Stewart**, Thomas 1940- AmMWSc 92
**Stewart**, Thomas Glynn 1949- WhoAmP 91
**Stewart**, Thomas Henry McKenzie 1930- AmMWSc 92
**Stewart**, Thomas James, Jr. 1928- WhoEnt 92
**Stewart**, Thomas Leon 1949- WhoAmL 92
**Stewart**, Thomas Penney 1927- WhoRel 92
**Stewart**, Thomas Simrall 1949- WhoMW 92
**Stewart**, Thomas William Wallace 1924- AmMWSc 92
**Stewart**, Tonea Harris 1947- WhoEnt 92
**Stewart**, Vern Bonham 1888-1918 BiInAmS
**Stewart**, Vernon Edwin 1938- WhoRel 92
**Stewart**, Victor Colvin 1921- Who 92
**Stewart**, Victor F, Jr 1926- WhoAmP 91
**Stewart**, W.A. 1882-1953 TwCPaSc
**Stewart**, W. Douglas 1938- WhoBlA 92
**Stewart**, W E 1924- AmMWSc 92
**Stewart**, Warren Hampton, Sr. 1951- WhoBlA 92, WhoRel 92
**Stewart**, Wellington Buel 1920- AmMWSc 92
**Stewart**, Wesley Holmgreen 1948- WhoAmL 92
**Stewart**, Will IntAu&W 91X, TwCSFW 91
**Stewart**, William WhoRel 92
**Stewart**, William 1921- Who 92
**Stewart**, William A, Jr 1929- WhoAmP 91
**Stewart**, William Alexander Campbell 1915- Who 92, WrDr 92
**Stewart**, William Andrew 1933- AmMWSc 92
**Stewart**, William D. P. 1935- IntWW 91
**Stewart**, William Duncan Paterson 1935- Who 92
**Stewart**, William E 1928- WhoAmP 91
**Stewart**, William E. L. 1917- WhoBlA 92
**Stewart**, William Earl 1946- WhoWest 92
**Stewart**, William H. 1935- WhoBlA 92
**Stewart**, William Henry 1949- AmMWSc 92
**Stewart**, William Hiram 1935- WhoRel 92
**Stewart**, William Hogue, Jr 1936- AmMWSc 92
**Stewart**, William Huffman 1921- AmMWSc 92
**Stewart**, William Ian Who 92
**Stewart**, William J 1950- WhoAmP 91
**Stewart**, William Kaye 1936- WhoMW 92
**Stewart**, William O 1925- WhoAmP 91, WhoBlA 92
**Stewart-Clark**, John 1929- Who 92
**Stewart-Clarke**, John Ernest 1928- WhoFI 92
**Stewart Cox**, Arthur George Ernest 1925- Who 92
**Stewart-Jones**, Richard, Mrs. Who 92
**Stewart-Liberty**, Arthur 1916-1990 AnObit 1990
**Stewart-Moore**, Alexander Wyndham Hume 1915- Who 92
**Stewart of Fulham**, Lord 1906-1990 AnObit 1990
**Stewart-Richardson**, Simon 1947- Who 92
**Stewart-Roberts**, Phyllida Katharine 1933- Who 92
**Stewart-Smith**, Christopher Dudley 1941- Who 92
**Stewart-Smith**, David Cree 1913- Who 92
**Stewart-Smith**, Geoffrey 1933- Who 92
**Stewart-Wilson**, Blair Aubyn 1929- Who 92
**Steyer**, Roy Henry 1918- WhoAmL 92, WhoFI 92
**Steyert**, William Albert 1932- AmMWSc 92
**Steyn**, Carole 1938- TwCPaSc
**Steyn**, Daniel Wynand 1923- IntWW 91
**Steyn**, Johan 1932- Who 92
**Steyn**, Marais 1914- Who 92
**Steyn**, S. J. Marais 1914- IntWW 91
**Steyrer**, Kurt 1920- IntWW 91
**Stezoski**, Lorise Ann 1963- WhoWest 92
**Stibbard**, Peter Jack 1936- Who 92
**Stibbe**, Austin Jule 1930- WhoMW 92
**Stibbe**, Philip Godfrey 1921- Who 92
**Stibbon**, John 1935- Who 92
**Stibbs**, Douglas Walter Noble 1919- Who 92
**Stibbs**, Gerald Denike 1910- AmMWSc 92
**Stiber**, Alex DrAPF 91
**Stiberth**, Amanda Lee 1965- WhoMW 92
**Stibitz**, George Robert 1904- AmMWSc 92
**Stich**, Hans F 1927- AmMWSc 92
**Stich**, Michael NewYTBS 91 [port]
**Stich**, Otto 1927- IntWW 91
**Stich**, Sally Simon 1950- WhoWest 92
**Stich-Randall**, Teresa 1927- NewAmDM
**Sticha**, Ernest August 1911- AmMWSc 92
**Stichel**, H. Mark 1958- WhoAmL 92
**Sticht**, Frank Davis 1919- AmMWSc 92
**Sticht**, J. Paul 1917- IntWW 91
**Stick**, Alyce Cushing 1944- WhoFI 92
**Stick**, Thomas Howard Fitchett 1938- WhoFI 92
**Stickel**, Delford LeFew 1927- AmMWSc 92
**Stickel**, Frederick George, III 1915- WhoAmL 92
**Stickel**, John Wesley 1954- WhoWest 92
**Stickel**, Patrick Francis 1950- WhoWest 92
**Stickells**, Austin T. 1914- WhoAmL 92
**Stickelman-Dillinger**, Lisa Suzanne 1956- WhoEnt 92
**Stickels**, Charles A 1933- AmMWSc 92
**Stickels**, Charles Arthur 1933- WhoMW 92
**Sticker**, Robert Earl 1930- AmMWSc 92
**Stickland**, David Peter 1954- AmMWSc 92
**Stickland**, Eugene Gordon 1956- IntAu&W 91
**Stickle**, Gene P 1929- AmMWSc 92
**Stickle**, Robert E., Jr. 1943- WhoMW 92
**Stickle**, Rodney Duane 1961- WhoFI 92
**Stickler**, Alfons 1910- IntWW 91
**Stickler**, Alfons Maria 1910- WhoRel 92
**Stickler**, Chris Alan 1963- WhoMW 92
**Stickler**, David Bruce 1941- AmMWSc 92
**Stickler**, David Collier 1933- AmMWSc 92
**Stickler**, Fred Charles 1931- AmMWSc 92
**Stickler**, Gunnar B 1925- AmMWSc 92
**Stickler**, Mitchell Gene 1934- AmMWSc 92
**Stickler**, Robert Hill 1950- WhoAmL 92
**Stickler**, William Carl 1918- AmMWSc 92
**Stickley**, C Martin 1933- AmMWSc 92
**Stickley**, Glenn David 1964- WhoEnt 92
**Stickley**, Gustav 1857-1942 DcTwDes, FacFETw
**Stickney**, Alan Craig 1947- AmMWSc 92
**Stickney**, Albert, III 1944- WhoFI 92
**Stickney**, Alden Parkhurst 1922- AmMWSc 92
**Stickney**, Benjamin D. 1940- ConAu 135
**Stickney**, Clifton Howard, Jr 1932- WhoAmP 91
**Stickney**, Dean William 1954- WhoMW 92
**Stickney**, Janice L. 1941- WhoBlA 92
**Stickney**, Janice Lee 1941- AmMWSc 92
**Stickney**, Jessica 1929- WhoAmP 91
**Stickney**, John DrAPF 91
**Stickney**, John Moore 1926- WhoAmL 92
**Stickney**, Palmer Blaine 1915- AmMWSc 92
**Stickney**, Phyllis Yvonne WhoEnt 92
**Stickney**, Robert Roy 1941- WhoWest 92
**Stickney**, Trumbull 1874-1904 BenetAL 91
**Stickney**, William Homer, Jr. 1945- WhoBlA 92
**Sticksel**, Philip Rice 1930- AmMWSc 92, WhoMW 92
**Stidd**, Benton Maurice 1936- AmMWSc 92
**Stidd**, Charles Ketchum 1918- AmMWSc 92
**Stidham**, Chuck Ray 1951- WhoAmL 92
**Stidham**, Howard Donathan 1925- AmMWSc 92
**Stidham**, Shaler, Jr 1941- AmMWSc 92
**Stidworthy**, George H 1924- AmMWSc 92
**Stieber**, Jack 1919- WhoMW 92
**Stieber**, Michael Thomas 1943- AmMWSc 92
**Stief**, Louis J 1933- AmMWSc 92
**Stiefbold**, Marguerite Mary 1948- WhoMW 92
**Stiefel**, D L 1945- WhoAmP 91
**Stiefel**, Edward 1942- AmMWSc 92
**Stiefel**, Robert Carl 1934- AmMWSc 92
**Stiefel**, Sheryl Kay 1958- WhoWest 92
**Stieff**, Hellmuth 1901-1944 EncTR 91 [port]
**Stieffen**, Spiros Wallace 1925- WhoAmP 91
**Stiegel**, Michael Allen 1946- WhoAmL 92, WhoMW 92
**Stiegler**, James O 1934- AmMWSc 92
**Stiegler**, T Donald 1934- AmMWSc 92
**Stieglitz**, Alfred 1864-1946 DcTwDes, FacFETw
**Stieglitz**, Ronald D. 1941- WhoMW 92
**Stieglitz**, Ronald Dennis 1941- AmMWSc 92
**Stiehl**, Richard Borg 1942- AmMWSc 92
**Stiehl**, Roy Thomas, Jr 1928- AmMWSc 92
**Stiehl**, William D. 1925- WhoAmL 92, WhoMW 92
**Stiehm**, E Richard 1933- AmMWSc 92
**Stiel**, Edsel Ford 1933- AmMWSc 92
**Stiel**, Leonard Irwin 1937- AmMWSc 92
**Stieler**, Carol Mae 1946- AmMWSc 92
**Stiemke**, Frederick Adolf 1929- WhoRel 92
**Stien**, Howard M 1926- AmMWSc 92
**Stiening**, Rae Frank 1937- AmMWSc 92
**Stiens**, Donald George, Jr. 1966- WhoMW 92
**Stienstra**, Bradley Richard 1949- WhoRel 92
**Stienstra**, Ward C. 1941- WhoMW 92
**Stienstra**, Ward Curtis 1941- AmMWSc 92
**Stier**, Elizabeth Fleming 1925- AmMWSc 92
**Stier**, Howard Livingston 1910- AmMWSc 92
**Stier**, Michael Frederick 1961- WhoEnt 92
**Stier**, Paul Max 1924- AmMWSc 92
**Stier**, Robert Gordon 1947- WhoRel 92
**Stier**, Theodore James Blanchard 1903- AmMWSc 92
**Stierle**, Edward d1991 NewYTBS 91 [port]
**Stierlin**, Helm 1926- WrDr 92
**Stierman**, Donald John 1947- AmMWSc 92
**Stiers**, David Ogden 1942- IntMPA 92, WhoEnt 92
**Stierwalt**, Donald L 1926- AmMWSc 92
**Stifel**, Fred B 1940- AmMWSc 92
**Stifel**, Frederick Benton 1940- WhoRel 92, WhoWest 92
**Stifel**, Peter Beekman 1936- AmMWSc 92
**Stiff**, Hugh Vernon 1916- Who 92
**Stiff**, P. Enoch 1947- WhoMW 92
**Stiff**, Robert H 1923- AmMWSc 92
**Stiffey**, Arthur V 1918- AmMWSc 92
**Stiffler**, Daniel F 1942- AmMWSc 92
**Stiffler**, Jack Justin 1934- AmMWSc 92
**Stiffman**, Jeffrey Barry 1939- WhoRel 92
**Stifler**, Venetia Chakos 1950- WhoEnt 92
**Stigers**, Harold Gene 1917- WhoRel 92
**Stigler**, David Mack 1943- WhoAmL 92
**Stigler**, George J. 1911- WrDr 92
**Stigler**, George Joseph d1991 NewYTBS 91 [port]
**Stigler**, George Joseph 1911- IntWW 91, Who 92, WhoFI 92, WhoNob 90
**Stigler**, Stephen Mack 1941- AmMWSc 92
**Stiglich**, Jacob John, Jr. 1938- WhoWest 92
**Stiglich**, John Charles 1958- WhoMW 92
**Stiglitz**, Irvin G 1936- AmMWSc 92
**Stiglitz**, Joseph Eugene 1943- Who 92, WhoFI 92, WhoWest 92
**Stiglitz**, Martin F. 1946- WhoEnt 92
**Stignani**, Ebe 1907-1974 CurBio 91N
**Stigwood**, Robert 1934- IntMPA 92
**Stigwood**, Robert Colin 1934- IntWW 91, WhoEnt 92
**Stikla** EncAmaz 91
**Stiles**, A B 1909- AmMWSc 92
**Stiles**, B. J. 1933- WhoRel 92
**Stiles**, Charles Dean 1946- AmMWSc 92

**Stiles,** David A 1938- *AmMWSc 92*
**Stiles,** Donald Alan 1951- *WhoMW 92*
**Stiles,** Ezra 1727-1795 *BenetAL 91, BiInAmS, BlkwCEP, BlkwEAR*
**Stiles,** Gary L 1949- *AmMWSc 92*
**Stiles,** Kendall Wayne 1960- *WhoFI 92*
**Stiles,** Lucille E 1947- *AmMWSc 92*
**Stiles,** Lynn F, Jr 1942- *AmMWSc 92*
**Stiles,** Mark Wayne 1948- *WhoAmP 91*
**Stiles,** Martha Bennett *DrAPF 91*
**Stiles,** Mervin 1917- *WhoRel 92*
**Stiles,** Michael Edgecombe 1934- *AmMWSc 92*
**Stiles,** Philip Glenn 1931- *AmMWSc 92*
**Stiles,** Phillip John 1934- *AmMWSc 92*
**Stiles,** Robert Neal 1933- *AmMWSc 92*
**Stiles,** Thomas Beveridge, II 1940- *WhoFI 92*
**Stiles,** Walter A 1922- *WhoAmP 91*
**Stiles,** Warren Cryder 1933- *AmMWSc 92*
**Stiles,** Wilbur J 1932- *AmMWSc 92*
**Stiles,** William Augustus 1837-1897 *BiInAmS*
**Stiles,** William Cobban 1936- *WhoMW 92*
**Stilgenbauer,** Thomas E. *WhoMW 92*
**Stilgoe,** Richard Henry Simpson 1943- *Who 92*
**Still,** Art Barry 1955- *WhoBlA 92*
**Still,** Charles Henry 1942- *WhoAmL 92*
**Still,** Charles Neal 1929- *AmMWSc 92*
**Still,** Clifford 1904-1980 *FacFETw*
**Still,** Edwin Tanner 1935- *AmMWSc 92*
**Still,** Eugene Updike *AmMWSc 92*
**Still,** Gerald G 1933- *AmMWSc 92*
**Still,** Gloria *DrAPF 91*
**Still,** Harold Henry, Jr. 1925- *WhoFI 92, WhoWest 92*
**Still,** Ian William James 1937- *AmMWSc 92*
**Still,** James *DrAPF 91*
**Still,** James 1906- *BenetAL 91*
**Still,** John C, III 1952- *WhoAmP 91*
**Still,** Judith Anne 1942- *WhoEnt 92*
**Still,** Ray 1920- *IntWW 91, WhoEnt 92*
**Still,** Richard 1921- *WrDr 92*
**Still,** Robert T 1954- *WhoAmP 91*
**Still,** W Clark, Jr 1946- *AmMWSc 92*
**Still,** William Grant 1895-1978 *FacFETw, NewAmDM*
**Still,** William James Sangster 1923- *AmMWSc 92*
**Still,** William N. 1932- *WrDr 92*
**Stille,** Alfred 1813-1900 *BiInAmS*
**Stille,** John Kenneth 1930- *AmMWSc 92*
**Stiller,** Brian Carl 1942- *WhoRel 92*
**Stiller,** Calvin R 1941- *AmMWSc 92*
**Stiller,** David 1931- *AmMWSc 92*
**Stiller,** Jerry *WhoEnt 92*
**Stiller,** Mary Louise 1931- *AmMWSc 92*
**Stiller,** Mauritz 1883-1928 *IntDcF 2-2 [port]*
**Stiller,** Patricia H. 1946- *WhoAmL 92*
**Stiller,** Peter Frederick *AmMWSc 92*
**Stiller,** Richard L 1933- *AmMWSc 92*
**Stillinger,** Frank Henry 1934- *AmMWSc 92*
**Stillinger,** Jack 1931- *IntAu&W 91, WrDr 92*
**Stillings,** Bruce Robert 1937- *AmMWSc 92*
**Stillings,** Dennis Otto 1942- *WhoMW 92*
**Stillings,** Richard Wallace 1928- *WhoAmP 91*
**Stillions,** Merle C 1929- *AmMWSc 92*
**Stillman,** Alfred William, Jr. 1942- *WhoFI 92, WhoWest 92*
**Stillman,** Ann Therese 1960- *WhoAmL 92*
**Stillman,** Anne Walker 1951- *WhoFI 92*
**Stillman,** Damie 1933- *ConAu 36NR*
**Stillman,** Elinor Hadley 1938- *WhoAmL 92*
**Stillman,** Gregory Eugene 1936- *AmMWSc 92*
**Stillman,** John Edgar 1945- *AmMWSc 92*
**Stillman,** John Sterling 1918- *WhoAmP 91*
**Stillman,** Kristin Marie 1952- *WhoMW 92*
**Stillman,** Larry Barr 1941- *WhoFI 92*
**Stillman,** Marc Alan 1963- *WhoMW 92*
**Stillman,** Martin John 1947- *AmMWSc 92*
**Stillman,** Paul O. 1933- *WhoFI 92, WhoIns 92*
**Stillman,** Richard Ernest 1929- *AmMWSc 92*
**Stillman,** Richard J. 1917- *ConAu 34NR, WrDr 92*
**Stillman,** Richard Joseph 1917- *IntAu&W 91*
**Stillman,** Richard Wayne 1959- *WhoMW 92*
**Stillman,** Thomas Bliss 1852-1915 *BiInAmS*
**Stillway,** Lewis William 1939- *AmMWSc 92*
**Stillwell,** Edgar Feldman 1929- *AmMWSc 92*
**Stillwell,** Ephraim Posey, Jr 1934- *AmMWSc 92*
**Stillwell,** George Keith 1918- *AmMWSc 92*
**Stillwell,** Harold Daniel 1931- *AmMWSc 92*
**Stillwell,** Mary Kathryn *DrAPF 91*
**Stillwell,** Richard Newhall 1935- *AmMWSc 92*
**Stillwell,** Tina Chasteen 1950- *WhoMW 92*
**Stillwell,** Walter Brooks, III 1946- *WhoAmL 92*
**Stillwell,** William Harry 1946- *AmMWSc 92*
**Stilson,** Bruce Wainwright 1933- *WhoAmL 92*
**Stilson,** Charles B *ScFEYrs*
**Stilson,** David Charles 1933- *WhoRel 92*
**Stilson,** Walter Leslie 1908- *WhoWest 92*
**Stilwell,** Dean Paxton 1952- *WhoWest 92*
**Stilwell,** Donald Lonson 1918- *AmMWSc 92*
**Stilwell,** Frank Barton, III 1957- *WhoAmL 92*
**Stilwell,** H Samuel 1935- *WhoAmP 91*
**Stilwell,** Hart 1902- *TwCWW 91*
**Stilwell,** Joseph W 1883-1946 *FacFETw*
**Stilwell,** Kenneth James 1934- *AmMWSc 92*
**Stilwell,** Richard 1942- *NewAmDM*
**Stilwell,** Richard Dale 1942- *IntWW 91*
**Stilwell,** Richard G. d1991 *NewYTBS 91 [port]*
**Stilwell,** Richard William 1936- *WhoIns 92*
**Stilwill,** Belle Jean 1955- *WhoWest 92*
**Stimac,** Matthew James 1962- *WhoMW 92*
**Stimac,** Patrick Joseph 1956- *WhoAmL 92*
**Stimatz,** Lawrence G 1919- *WhoAmP 91*
**Stimler,** Suzanne Stokes 1928- *AmMWSc 92*
**Stimley,** Leonard David 1946- *WhoFI 92*
**Stimmel,** Glen Lewis 1949- *AmMWSc 92*
**Stimmel,** John Robert 1946- *WhoRel 92*
**Stimmel,** Todd Richard 1954- *WhoAmL 92*
**Stimmell,** K G *AmMWSc 92*
**Stimpfling,** Jack Herman 1924- *AmMWSc 92*
**Stimpson,** William 1832-1872 *BiInAmS*
**Stimson,** Delton Gerald, Jr. 1949- *WhoRel 92*
**Stimson,** Frederic Jesup 1855-1943 *BenetAL 91*
**Stimson,** Frederick Jesup 1855-1943 *ScFEYrs*
**Stimson,** Henry L 1867-1950 *RComAH*
**Stimson,** Henry Lewis 1867-1950 *AmPolLe, EncTR 91, FacFETw*
**Stimson,** Judith Ann 1957- *WhoMW 92*
**Stimson,** Judith Nemeth 1942- *WhoAmL 92*
**Stimson,** Lewis Atterbury 1844-1917 *BiInAmS*
**Stimson,** Miriam Michael 1913- *AmMWSc 92, WhoMW 92*
**Stimson,** Robert Frederick 1939- *Who 92*
**Stimson,** Terry 1943- *WhoAmP 91*
**Stinaff,** Russell Dalton 1940- *AmMWSc 92*
**Stinchcomb,** Thomas Glenn 1922- *AmMWSc 92, WhoMW 92*
**Stinchcomb,** Wayne Webster 1943- *AmMWSc 92*
**Stinchfield,** Carleton Paul 1928- *AmMWSc 92*
**Stinchfield,** Frank E 1910- *AmMWSc 92*
**Stinchfield,** John Edward 1947- *WhoFI 92*
**Stine,** Charles Maxwell 1925- *AmMWSc 92*
**Stine,** Dennis Neal 1952- *WhoAmP 91*
**Stine,** G Harry 1928- *TwCSFW 91, WrDr 92*
**Stine,** George Harry 1928- *IntAu&W 91, WhoWest 92*
**Stine,** Gerald James 1935- *AmMWSc 92*
**Stine,** Gordan Bernard 1924- *WhoAmP 91*
**Stine,** Hank *ConAu 133*
**Stine,** Hank 1945- *WrDr 92*
**Stine,** Henry Eugene 1945- *ConAu 133*
**Stine,** Philip Andrew 1944- *AmMWSc 92*
**Stine,** Timothy D 1956- *WhoAmP 91*
**Stine,** William H, Jr 1926- *AmMWSc 92*
**Stine,** William R 1938- *AmMWSc 92*
**Stinecipher,** Mary Margaret 1940- *AmMWSc 92*
**Stinehart,** Roger Ray 1945- *WhoAmL 92*
**Stinehart,** William, Jr. 1943- *WhoAmL 92*
**Stinemetz,** Steven Douglas 1957- *WhoAmL 92*
**Stiner,** Frederic Matthew, Jr. 1946- *WhoFI 92*
**Stines,** James William 1934- *WhoRel 92*
**Sting** *IntWW 91*
**Sting** 1951- *IntMPA 92, NewAmDM, News 91 [port], WhoEnt 92*
**Stingelin,** Ronald Werner 1935- *AmMWSc 92*
**Stinger,** Henry J 1920- *AmMWSc 92*
**Stingl,** Georg 1948- *AmMWSc 92*
**Stingl,** Hans Alfred 1927- *AmMWSc 92*
**Stingl,** Josef 1919- *IntWW 91*
**Stingley,** Jeff J 1952- *WhoAmP 91*
**Stini,** William Arthur 1930- *AmMWSc 92, WhoWest 92*
**Stinner,** Ronald Edwin 1943- *AmMWSc 92*
**Stinnett,** Henry Orr *AmMWSc 92*
**Stinnett,** Mary K Scott *WhoAmP 91*
**Stinnett,** Terrance Lloyd 1940- *WhoAmL 92*
**Stinnette,** Timothy Earl 1956- *WhoRel 92*
**Stinski,** Mark Francis 1941- *AmMWSc 92*
**Stinson,** Al Worth 1926- *AmMWSc 92*
**Stinson,** Barry Auvil 1946- *WhoEnt 92*
**Stinson,** Constance Robinson *WhoBlA 92*
**Stinson,** David Donnel 1957- *WhoWest 92*
**Stinson,** David John 1921- *Who 92*
**Stinson,** Deane Brian 1930- *WhoFI 92*
**Stinson,** Donald Cline 1925- *AmMWSc 92*
**Stinson,** Donald Leo 1930- *AmMWSc 92*
**Stinson,** Donald R. 1929- *WhoBlA 92*
**Stinson,** Douglas G 1953- *AmMWSc 92*
**Stinson,** Edgar Erwin 1927- *AmMWSc 92*
**Stinson,** George Arthur 1915- *IntWW 91*
**Stinson,** Glen Monette 1939- *AmMWSc 92*
**Stinson,** Harry Theodore, Jr 1926- *AmMWSc 92*
**Stinson,** James Robert 1921- *AmMWSc 92*
**Stinson,** Jim 1937- *WrDr 92*
**Stinson,** Joseph McLester 1939- *AmMWSc 92, WhoBlA 92*
**Stinson,** Katherine 1891-1977 *HanAmWH*
**Stinson,** Kathy 1952- *IntAu&W 91*
**Stinson,** Linda 1965- *WhoBlA 92*
**Stinson,** Margaret E d1912 *BiInAmS*
**Stinson,** Mary Krystyna *AmMWSc 92*
**Stinson,** Perri June *AmMWSc 92*
**Stinson,** Richard Floyd 1921- *AmMWSc 92*
**Stinson,** Robert Anthony 1941- *AmMWSc 92*
**Stinson,** Robert Charles 1946- *WhoAmL 92*
**Stinson,** Robert Henry 1931- *AmMWSc 92*
**Stinson,** Robert Wayne 1936- *WhoFI 92*
**Stinson,** Stanley Thomas 1961- *WhoFI 92*
**Stinson,** Steven Leonis 1958- *WhoFI 92*
**Stinson,** Susan *DrAPF 91*
**Stinson,** Thomas Franklin 1942- *WhoMW 92*
**Stinson,** William W. 1933- *WhoFI 92*
**Stinziano,** Michael Peter 1944- *WhoAmP 91*
**Stio,** Peter M 1913- *WhoAmP 91*
**Stion,** Rebekah 1943- *IntAu&W 91*
**Stipanovic,** Bozidar J 1933- *AmMWSc 92*
**Stipanovic,** Robert Douglas 1939- *AmMWSc 92*
**Stipanowich,** Joseph Jean 1921- *AmMWSc 92*
**Stipe,** Edwin, III 1931- *WhoFI 92*
**Stipe,** Gene 1926- *WhoAmP 91*
**Stipetich,** James Matthew 1962- *WhoEnt 92*
**Stirdivant,** Michael T. *WhoEnt 92*
**Stires,** Patrick Wayne 1948- *WhoMW 92*
**Stirewalt,** Harvey Lee 1932- *AmMWSc 92*
**Stirewalt,** John Newman 1931- *WhoFI 92*
**Stiritz,** Hans Austin 1963- *WhoEnt 92*
**Stiritz,** William P. 1934- *WhoFI 92, WhoMW 92*
**Stirling,** Alexander 1926- *Who 92*
**Stirling,** Andrew John 1944- *AmMWSc 92*
**Stirling,** Angus Duncan Aeneas 1933- *Who 92*
**Stirling,** Charles E 1933- *AmMWSc 92*
**Stirling,** Charles James Matthew 1930- *IntWW 91, Who 92*
**Stirling,** Dale Alexander 1956- *WhoWest 92*
**Stirling,** David d1990 *Who 92N*
**Stirling,** David 1915-1990 *AnObit 1990, FacFETw*
**Stirling,** Edwin Tillman 1927- *WhoAmL 92*
**Stirling,** Geoffrey William 1925- *WhoEnt 92*
**Stirling,** Ian G 1941- *AmMWSc 92*
**Stirling,** James 1926- *IntWW 91*
**Stirling,** James Frazer 1926- *Who 92*
**Stirling,** Jessica *IntAu&W 91X, WrDr 92*
**Stirling,** Lawrence 1942- *WhoAmP 91*
**Stirling,** Michael Grote 1915- *Who 92*
**Stirling,** S M 1953- *TwCSFW 91*
**Stirling-Hamilton,** Malcolm William Bruce 1979- *Who 92*
**Stirling of Fairburn,** Roderick William K 1932- *Who 92*
**Stirling of Garden,** James 1930- *Who 92*
**Stirm,** Eugene Robert 1945- *WhoEnt 92, WhoWest 92*
**Stirn,** Olivier 1936- *IntWW 91*
**Stirn,** Richard J 1933- *AmMWSc 92*
**Stirnaman,** Paul Herbert, Jr 1944- *WhoAmP 91*
**Stirrat,** Gordon Macmillan 1940- *Who 92*
**Stish,** Thomas B 1950- *WhoAmP 91*
**Stiska,** John C. 1942- *WhoAmL 92*
**Stitch,** Malcolm Lane 1923- *AmMWSc 92*
**Stitch,** Sharon Anne 1947- *WhoWest 92*
**Stiteler,** William Merle, III 1942- *AmMWSc 92*
**Stites,** J T 1928- *WhoAmP 91*
**Stites,** Joseph Gant, Jr 1921- *AmMWSc 92*
**Stites,** Ray Dean 1946- *WhoRel 92*
**Stith,** Antoinette Freeman 1958- *WhoBlA 92*
**Stith,** Bradley James 1952- *AmMWSc 92*
**Stith,** Charles Richard 1949- *WhoBlA 92*
**Stith,** Forrest C. 1934- *WhoRel 92*
**Stith,** Francis Blackwell 1939- *WhoAmL 92*
**Stith,** James Herman 1941- *AmMWSc 92*
**Stith,** Jeffrey Len 1950- *AmMWSc 92*
**Stith,** Joseph 1962- *WhoMW 92*
**Stith,** Lee S 1918- *AmMWSc 92*
**Stith,** Marice Wilbur *WhoEnt 92*
**Stith,** Melvin Thomas 1946- *WhoBlA 92*
**Stith,** Rex David 1942- *AmMWSc 92*
**Stith,** William 1707-1755 *BenetAL 91*
**Stith,** William Joseph 1942- *AmMWSc 92*
**Stitley,** James Walter, Jr. 1944- *WhoFI 92*
**Stitnizky,** John Louis 1939- *WhoWest 92*
**Stitt,** Don 1956- *WhoEnt 92*
**Stitt,** Donald K 1944- *WhoAmP 91*
**Stitt,** E. Don 1942- *WhoBlA 92*
**Stitt,** Guy Ames 1957- *WhoWest 92*
**Stitt,** James Harry 1939- *AmMWSc 92*
**Stitt,** John Thomas 1942- *AmMWSc 92*
**Stitt,** Mari Leipper 1923- *WhoRel 92*
**Stitt,** Milan 1941- *WhoEnt 92*
**Stitt,** Richard P. 1926- *WhoFI 92*
**Stitt,** Robert R. 1941- *WhoWest 92*
**Stitt,** Robert Sharp d1991 *NewYTBS 91*
**Stitt,** Sonny d1982 *FacFETw*
**Stitt,** Sonny 1924-1982 *NewAmDM*
**Stitt,** Thomas Paul, Sr. 1943- *WhoAmL 92*
**Stitt,** Walter Boston, Jr. 1924- *WhoRel 92*
**Stittich,** Eleanor Maryann *WhoWest 92*
**Stitzel,** Robert Eli 1937- *AmMWSc 92*
**Stitzinger,** Ernest Lester 1940- *AmMWSc 92*
**Stitzinger,** James Franklin 1950- *WhoRel 92*
**Stivala,** Salvatore Silvio 1923- *AmMWSc 92*
**Stiven,** Alan Ernest 1935- *AmMWSc 92*
**Stivender,** Donald Lewis 1932- *AmMWSc 92, WhoMW 92*
**Stivens,** Dal 1911- *IntAu&W 91*
**Stiver,** James Frederick 1943- *AmMWSc 92, WhoMW 92*
**Stivers,** Elizabeth Ann 1958- *WhoMW 92*
**Stivers,** Joe Alan 1948- *WhoAmP 91*
**Stivers,** Mary 1927- *WhoAmP 91*
**Stivers,** Russell Kennedy 1917- *AmMWSc 92*
**Stivers,** Thomas Walter 1918- *WhoAmP 91*
**Stivers,** William Charles 1938- *WhoFI 92*
**Stivison,** David Vaughn 1946- *WhoAmL 92*
**Stivison,** Ron 1947- *WhoAmP 91*
**Stivison,** Thomas Homer 1948- *WhoWest 92*
**Stix,** John 1920- *WhoEnt 92*
**Stix,** Thomas Howard 1924- *AmMWSc 92*
**Stjernholm,** Paul David 1959- *WhoRel 92*
**Stjernholm,** Rune Leonard 1924- *AmMWSc 92*
**Stoakes,** Richmond Bruce 1940- *WhoRel 92*
**Stoate,** Isabel Dorothy 1927- *Who 92*
**Stob,** Martin 1926- *AmMWSc 92*
**Stob,** Michael J. 1952- *WhoMW 92*
**Stob,** Michael Jay 1952- *AmMWSc 92*
**Stobart,** Patrick Desmond 1920- *Who 92*
**Stobaugh,** Robert Earl 1927- *AmMWSc 92*
**Stobbe,** Elmer Henry 1936- *AmMWSc 92*
**Stobbe,** Leslie Harold 1930- *WhoRel 92*
**Stober,** Henry Carl 1935- *AmMWSc 92*
**Stober,** Quentin Jerome 1938- *AmMWSc 92*
**Stobo,** John David 1941- *AmMWSc 92*
**Stobo,** Robert 1727-1772? *BenetAL 91*
**Stobo,** Wayne Thomas 1944- *AmMWSc 92*
**Stock,** Anita 1938- *WhoMW 92*
**Stock,** B.E. *DrAPF 91*
**Stock,** Ben 1948- *WhoRel 92*
**Stock,** Catherine 1952- *SmATA 65*
**Stock,** Catherine Julia 1952- *IntAu&W 91*
**Stock,** Charles Chester 1910- *AmMWSc 92*
**Stock,** David 1939- *NewAmDM*
**Stock,** David Allen 1941- *AmMWSc 92*
**Stock,** David Earl 1939- *AmMWSc 92*
**Stock,** David Frederick 1939- *WhoEnt 92*
**Stock,** Elliot d1911 *DcLB 106 [port]*
**Stock,** Francis Edgar 1914- *Who 92*
**Stock,** Frederick 1872-1942 *FacFETw, NewAmDM*
**Stock,** Garfield Raymond 1931- *WhoMW 92*
**Stock,** John Thomas 1911- *AmMWSc 92*
**Stock,** Larry Dean 1946- *WhoMW 92*
**Stock,** Leon M 1930- *AmMWSc 92*
**Stock,** Leroy A, Jr 1942- *WhoIns 92*
**Stock,** Michael Z. 1959- *WhoFI 92*
**Stock,** Molly Wilford 1942- *AmMWSc 92*
**Stock,** Norman *DrAPF 91*

**Stock,** Raymond 1913- *Who 92*
**Stock,** Robert Douglas 1941- *WhoMW 92*
**Stock,** Stuart Chase 1946- *WhoAmL 92*
**Stockage,** Steven Edward 1948- *WhoEnt 92*
**Stockanes,** Anthony E. *DrAPF 91*
**Stockard,** Bruce Anthony 1959- *WhoAmL 92*
**Stockbauer,** Roger Lewis 1944- *AmMWSc 92*
**Stockbridge,** Robert R 1910- *AmMWSc 92*
**Stockburger,** George Joseph 1927- *AmMWSc 92*
**Stockdale,** Arthur Noel 1920- *Who 92*
**Stockdale,** Eric 1929- *Who 92*
**Stockdale,** Frank Edward 1936- *AmMWSc 92*
**Stockdale,** Gayle Sue 1955- *WhoFI 92*
**Stockdale,** George William d1990 *Who 92N*
**Stockdale,** Harold James 1931- *AmMWSc 92*
**Stockdale,** John Alexander Douglas 1936- *AmMWSc 92*
**Stockdale,** Noel *Who 92*
**Stockdale,** Thomas 1940- *Who 92*
**Stockdale,** William K 1928- *AmMWSc 92*
**Stockel,** Ivar H 1927- *AmMWSc 92*
**Stockell-Hartree,** Anne 1926- *AmMWSc 92*
**Stocker,** Adolf 1835-1909 *BiDExR*
**Stocker,** Bruce Arnold Dunbar 1917- *Who 92*
**Stocker,** Donald V 1927- *AmMWSc 92*
**Stocker,** Fred Butler 1931- *AmMWSc 92*
**Stocker,** Harold Le Roy 1929- *WhoFI 92*
**Stocker,** Jack H 1924- *AmMWSc 92*
**Stocker,** Jeffrey David 1954- *WhoEnt 92*
**Stocker,** John 1918- *Who 92*
**Stocker,** Midge 1960- *WhoMW 92*
**Stocker,** Richard Louis 1941- *AmMWSc 92*
**Stockert,** Elisabeth 1930- *AmMWSc 92*
**Stockert,** Thomas Lothe, Jr. 1913- *WhoAmL 92*
**Stockett,** Peter McKenzie 1932- *WhoAmP 91*
**Stockglausner,** William George 1950- *WhoMW 92*
**Stockham,** Alf 1933- *TwCPaSc*
**Stockham,** Nancy Heath 1931- *WhoMW 92*
**Stockham,** Thomas Greenway, Jr 1933- *AmMWSc 92*
**Stockhammer,** Karl Adolf 1926- *AmMWSc 92*
**Stockhausen,** Karlheinz 1928- *ConCom 92, FacFETw, IntWW 91, NewAmDM, Who 92*
**Stocking,** Clifford Ralph 1913- *AmMWSc 92*
**Stocking,** Edward Carl 1962- *WhoMW 92*
**Stocking,** Gordon Gary 1924- *AmMWSc 92*
**Stocking,** Holly 1945- *WhoMW 92*
**Stocking,** Kathleen 1945- *ConAu 135*
**Stocking,** Sherl Dee 1945- *WhoWest 92*
**Stockland,** Alan E. 1938- *WhoWest 92*
**Stockland,** Alan Eugene 1938- *AmMWSc 92*
**Stockland,** Wayne Luvern 1942- *AmMWSc 92*
**Stockley,** Jim *WhoAmP 91*
**Stockli,** Martin P 1949- *AmMWSc 92*
**Stocklin,** Alma Katherine 1926- *WhoFI 92*
**Stockman,** Charles H 1922- *AmMWSc 92*
**Stockman,** Charles Henry 1922- *WhoMW 92*
**Stockman,** David A. 1946- *WrDr 92*
**Stockman,** David Allen *WhoAmP 91*
**Stockman,** David Allen 1946- *IntWW 91, WhoFI 92*
**Stockman,** George C 1943- *AmMWSc 92*
**Stockman,** Gerald R 1935- *WhoAmP 91*
**Stockman,** Harry E 1905- *AmMWSc 92*
**Stockman,** Hervey S, Jr 1946- *AmMWSc 92*
**Stockman,** Ida J. 1942- *WhoBlA 92*
**Stockman,** Robert Harold 1953- *WhoRel 92*
**Stockmar,** J. Brian 1950- *WhoFI 92*
**Stockmayer,** Walter Hugo 1914- *AmMWSc 92*
**Stockmeyer,** Larry Joseph 1948- *AmMWSc 92*
**Stockmeyer,** Norman Otto, Jr. 1938- *WhoMW 92*
**Stockmeyer,** Paul Kelly 1943- *AmMWSc 92*
**Stockmeyer,** Steven F 1941- *WhoAmP 91*
**Stockner,** John G 1940- *AmMWSc 92*
**Stockner,** Robert David 1958- *WhoEnt 92*
**Stockport,** Bishop Suffragan of 1932- *Who 92*
**Stocks,** Chester Lee, Jr. 1928- *WhoWest 92*
**Stocks,** Douglas Roscoe, Jr 1932- *AmMWSc 92*
**Stocks,** Eleanor Louise 1943- *WhoBlA 92*
**Stocks,** George Malcolm 1943- *AmMWSc 92*
**Stocks,** Gerald Richard 1932- *WhoMW 92*
**Stockstill,** Charles Michael 1949- *WhoWest 92*
**Stockstill,** Maria Muterspaugh 1963- *WhoRel 92*
**Stockton,** Earl of 1943- *IntWW 91, Who 92*
**Stockton,** Adrian James 1935-1981 *ConAu 134*
**Stockton,** Annis Boudinot 1736-1801 *BlkwEAR*
**Stockton,** Barbara Marshall 1923- *WhoBlA 92*
**Stockton,** Bayard 1930- *ConAu 134*
**Stockton,** Beverly Ann 1939- *WhoMW 92*
**Stockton,** Carl R. 1935- *WhoMW 92, WhoRel 92*
**Stockton,** Cecil Eugene 1934- *WhoAmP 91*
**Stockton,** Clifford, Sr. 1932- *WhoBlA 92*
**Stockton,** Dick *LesBEnT 92*
**Stockton,** Doris S 1924- *AmMWSc 92*
**Stockton,** Francis R. 1834-1902 *BenetAL 91*
**Stockton,** Frank 1834-1902 *ScFEYrs*
**Stockton,** Frank R 1834-1902 *TwCSFW 91*
**Stockton,** James Evan 1931- *AmMWSc 92*
**Stockton,** John Richard 1917- *AmMWSc 92*
**Stockton,** Richard 1730-1781 *AmPolLe*
**Stockton,** Richard Lee 1949- *WhoAmL 92*
**Stockton,** Roderick Alan 1951- *WhoWest 92*
**Stockton,** Ruth S 1916- *WhoAmP 91*
**Stockton,** Stephen Finch 1947- *WhoFI 92*
**Stockton,** Thomas B. 1930- *WhoRel 92*
**Stockwell,** Charles Warren 1940- *AmMWSc 92*
**Stockwell,** Dean 1935?- *CurBio 91 [port], IntMPA 92*
**Stockwell,** Dean 1936- *WhoEnt 92A*
**Stockwell,** Edmund Arthur 1911- *Who 92*
**Stockwell,** Evangelina Ramirez *WhoHisp 92*
**Stockwell,** Hugh 1903-1986 *FacFETw*
**Stockwell,** John 1961- *IntMPA 92*
**Stockwell,** John Nelson 1832-1920 *BiInAmS*
**Stockwell,** Linwood Burton 1947- *WhoFI 92*
**Stockwell,** Nicholas John 1946- *WhoMW 92*
**Stockwell,** Oliver Perkins 1907- *WhoAmL 92, WhoFI 92*
**Stockwin,** Arthur 1935- *WrDr 92*
**Stockwin,** James Arthur Ainscow 1935- *Who 92*
**Stockwood,** Mervyn 1913- *IntWW 91, Who 92, WrDr 92*
**Stoclet,** Eric Philippe 1953- *WhoFI 92*
**Stocum,** David Leon 1939- *AmMWSc 92*
**Stodart** *Who 92*
**Stodart of Leaston,** Baron 1916- *Who 92*
**Stoddard,** Alan 1915- *IntAu&W 91, WrDr 92*
**Stoddard,** Alexandra Hope 1942- *WhoMW 92*
**Stoddard,** Alonzo Edwin, Jr 1926- *AmMWSc 92*
**Stoddard,** Arthur Grant 1947- *WhoWest 92*
**Stoddard,** Brandon *LesBEnT 92 [port]*
**Stoddard,** Brandon 1937- *IntMPA 92, WhoEnt 92*
**Stoddard,** C Kerby 1907- *AmMWSc 92*
**Stoddard,** Charles Warren 1843-1909 *BenetAL 91, BibAL 8*
**Stoddard,** Donald B 1951- *WhoIns 92*
**Stoddard,** Elizabeth Barstow 1823-1902 *BenetAL 91*
**Stoddard,** Elizabeth Drew Barstow 1823-1902 *BibAL 8*
**Stoddard,** Eugene C 1927- *WhoAmP 91*
**Stoddard,** George Edward 1921- *AmMWSc 92*
**Stoddard,** James H 1930- *AmMWSc 92*
**Stoddard,** James Reed 1959- *WhoWest 92*
**Stoddard,** John Fair 1825-1873 *BiInAmS*
**Stoddard,** John Tappan 1852-1919 *BiInAmS*
**Stoddard,** Leland Douglas 1919- *AmMWSc 92*
**Stoddard,** Nathaniel Clark 1945- *WhoFI 92*
**Stoddard,** Orange Nash 1812-1892 *BiInAmS*
**Stoddard,** Richard Ethridge 1950- *WhoFI 92*
**Stoddard,** Richard Henry 1825-1903 *BenetAL 91, BibAL 8*
**Stoddard,** Robert H. 1928- *ConAu 133*
**Stoddard,** Robert Lee 1918- *WhoAmL 92*
**Stoddard,** Solomon 1643-1729 *BenetAL 91*
**Stoddard,** Stephen D 1925- *AmMWSc 92*
**Stoddard,** Stephen Davidson 1925- *WhoAmP 91, WhoWest 92*
**Stoddard,** Susan 1942- *WhoWest 92*
**Stoddard,** Theodore Lothrop 1883-1950 *DcAmImH*
**Stoddard,** William Bert, Jr. 1926- *WhoFI 92*
**Stoddard,** William Osborn 1835-1925 *BenetAL 91*
**Stoddard,** Willis Joseph 1945- *WhoWest 92*
**Stoddart** *Who 92*
**Stoddart,** Anne Elizabeth 1937- *Who 92*
**Stoddart,** Charles Norman 1948- *Who 92*
**Stoddart,** Douglas W *WhoAmP 91*
**Stoddart,** John Little 1933- *Who 92*
**Stoddart,** John Maurice 1938- *Who 92*
**Stoddart,** Kenneth 1914- *Who 92*
**Stoddart,** Michael Craig 1932- *Who 92*
**Stoddart,** Richard Sylvester, Jr. 1963- *WhoMW 92*
**Stoddart of Swindon,** Baron 1926- *Who 92*
**Stodder,** Charles 1808?-1884 *BiInAmS*
**Stodghill,** Labrenda Garrett 1953- *WhoAmL 92*
**Stodghill,** Ronald 1939- *WhoBlA 92*
**Stodghill,** William 1940- *WhoBlA 92*
**Stodghill,** William Wardell 1927- *WhoIns 92*
**Stodola,** Edwin King *AmMWSc 92*
**Stodola,** Mark Allen 1949- *WhoAmP 91*
**Stodolsky,** Marvin 1939- *AmMWSc 92*
**Stoebe,** Thomas Gaines 1939- *AmMWSc 92, WhoWest 92*
**Stoeber,** Werner 1925- *AmMWSc 92*
**Stoebuck,** William Brees 1929- *WhoAmL 92*
**Stoeckenius,** Walther 1921- *AmMWSc 92*
**Stoecker,** Adolf 1835-1909 *EncTR 91 [port]*
**Stoecker,** Dietrich 1915- *IntWW 91*
**Stoeckert,** George Ian 1948- *WhoFI 92*
**Stoeckle,** John Duane 1922- *AmMWSc 92*
**Stoeckler,** Johanna D *AmMWSc 92*
**Stoeckley,** Thomas Robert 1942- *AmMWSc 92*
**Stoeckly,** Robert E 1938- *AmMWSc 92*
**Stoefen,** Gary E 1939- *WhoIns 92*
**Stoefen,** Gary Edwin 1939- *WhoFI 92*
**Stoehr,** Richard Allen 1932- *WhoRel 92*
**Stoehr,** Robert Allen 1930- *AmMWSc 92*
**Stoen,** J. Thomas 1939- *WhoWest 92*
**Stoenner,** Herbert George 1919- *AmMWSc 92*
**Stoermer,** Eugene F 1934- *AmMWSc 92*
**Stoessel,** Albert 1894-1943 *NewAmDM*
**Stoessinger,** John G. 1927- *WrDr 92*
**Stoesz,** David Paul 1947- *WhoWest 92*
**Stoesz,** James Darrel 1950- *AmMWSc 92*
**Stoesz,** Willis Milton 1930- *WhoMW 92, WhoRel 92*
**Stoetzel,** Manya Brooke 1940- *AmMWSc 92*
**Stoetzer,** Gerald Louis 1914- *WhoAmL 92*
**Stoever,** Edward Carl, Jr 1926- *AmMWSc 92*
**Stoever,** William Alfred 1939- *WhoFI 92*
**Stoewsand,** Gilbert Saari 1932- *AmMWSc 92*
**Stoff,** Thomas Patrick 1949- *WhoAmP 91*
**Stoffa,** Paul L 1948- *AmMWSc 92*
**Stoffel,** Klaus Peter 1957- *WhoAmL 92*
**Stoffella,** Peter Joseph 1954- *AmMWSc 92*
**Stoffer,** Henry J *WhoAmP 91*
**Stoffer,** James Myron, Jr. 1952- *WhoAmL 92*
**Stoffer,** James Osber 1935- *AmMWSc 92*
**Stoffer,** Richard Lawrence 1948- *AmMWSc 92*
**Stoffer,** Robert Llewellyn 1927- *AmMWSc 92*
**Stofferahn,** Kenneth Darrell 1934- *WhoAmP 91*
**Stofferahn,** Scott B 1957- *WhoAmP 91*
**Stofferson,** Terry Lee 1957- *WhoFI 92*
**Stoffolano,** John George, Jr 1939- *AmMWSc 92*
**Stoffregen,** Philip Allen 1951- *WhoAmL 92*
**Stoffregen,** Philip Eugene 1947- *WhoMW 92*
**Stogdill,** Thomas Bryan 1935- *WhoMW 92*
**Stogdon,** Norman Francis 1909- *Who 92*
**Stogner,** Joseph Thomas 1939- *WhoAmP 91*
**Stogsdill,** Daniel Ray 1957- *WhoAmL 92*
**Stohler,** Dona Siebler 1957- *WhoMW 92*
**Stohler,** Michael Joe 1956- *WhoMW 92*
**Stohler,** Rudolf 1901- *AmMWSc 92*
**Stohlgren,** Kurt Arnold 1954- *WhoAmL 92*
**Stohlman,** Stephen Arnold 1946- *AmMWSc 92*
**Stohlman,** Stephen Christian 1942- *WhoRel 92*
**Stohr,** Donald J. 1934- *WhoAmL 92*
**Stohr,** Joachim 1947- *AmMWSc 92*
**Stohrer,** Gerhard 1939- *AmMWSc 92*
**Stohry,** William E. 1943- *WhoFI 92*
**Stoia,** Viorel G. 1924- *WhoFI 92, WhoMW 92*
**Stoiber,** Richard Edwin 1911- *AmMWSc 92*
**Stoica,** Chivu 1908-1975 *FacFETw*
**Stoicheff,** Boris Peter 1924- *AmMWSc 92, IntWW 91, Who 92*
**Stoicheff,** James F 1927- *WhoAmP 91*
**Stoick,** James L *WhoAmP 91*
**Stojak,** Richard Michael 1941- *WhoRel 92*
**Stojanovic,** Borislav Jovan 1919- *AmMWSc 92*
**Stojanovic,** Svetozar 1931- *ConAu 134*
**Stoke,** E. G. 1919- *WrDr 92*
**Stoke,** Jonathan Henry 1958- *WhoWest 92*
**Stoke-Upon-Trent,** Archdeacon of *Who 92*
**Stokely,** Craig Ranford 1945- *WhoFI 92*
**Stokely,** Edith Margaret Dawley 1922- *WhoMW 92*
**Stokely,** Ernest Mitchell 1937- *AmMWSc 92*
**Stoker,** Alan 1930- *IntAu&W 91*
**Stoker,** Betty Anderson 1927- *WhoAmP 91*
**Stoker,** Bram 1847-1912 *CnDBLB 5 [port], RfGEnL 91*
**Stoker,** Christopher Lee 1956- *WhoRel 92*
**Stoker,** Dennis James 1928- *Who 92*
**Stoker,** Howard Stephen 1939- *AmMWSc 92*
**Stoker,** James Johnston 1905- *AmMWSc 92*
**Stoker,** Jeff *WhoAmP 91*
**Stoker,** Michael 1918- *Who 92*
**Stoker,** Michael George Parke 1918- *IntWW 91*
**Stoker,** Richard 1938- *ConCom 92*
**Stoker,** Warren C 1912- *AmMWSc 92*
**Stokes** *Who 92*
**Stokes,** Baron 1914- *IntWW 91, Who 92*
**Stokes,** Adrian 1854-1935 *TwCPaSc*
**Stokes,** Adrian 1902-1972 *TwCPaSc*
**Stokes,** Adrian Victor 1945- *Who 92*
**Stokes,** Alistair Michael 1948- *Who 92*
**Stokes,** Allison 1942- *WhoRel 92*
**Stokes,** Arch Yow 1946- *WhoAmL 92*
**Stokes,** Arnold Paul 1932- *AmMWSc 92*
**Stokes,** Barbara S. *WhoFI 92*
**Stokes,** Barry Owen 1945- *AmMWSc 92*
**Stokes,** Bob *DrAPF 91*
**Stokes,** Bradford Taylor 1944- *AmMWSc 92*
**Stokes,** Bunny, Jr. *WhoBlA 92*
**Stokes,** Carl Burton 1927- *WhoAmP 91, WhoBlA 92*
**Stokes,** Carl Nicholas 1907- *WhoAmL 92*
**Stokes,** Carol Lynn 1962- *WhoBlA 92*
**Stokes,** Carolyn Ashe 1925- *WhoBlA 92*
**Stokes,** Charles Eugene, Jr. 1926- *WhoFI 92*
**Stokes,** Charles Sommers 1929- *AmMWSc 92*
**Stokes,** Daniel M. *DrAPF 91*
**Stokes,** David Kershaw, Jr 1927- *AmMWSc 92*
**Stokes,** David Mayhew Allen 1944- *Who 92*
**Stokes,** David Wesley 1946- *WhoRel 92*
**Stokes,** Deborah Cynthia 1957- *WhoMW 92*
**Stokes,** Donald Eugene 1931- *AmMWSc 92*
**Stokes,** Edmond Harold 1940- *WhoFI 92*
**Stokes,** Francis Joseph, III 1940- *WhoMW 92*
**Stokes,** Geoffrey 1940- *ConAu 36NR*
**Stokes,** Gerald Madison 1947- *AmMWSc 92, WhoWest 92*
**Stokes,** Gerald V 1943- *AmMWSc 92*
**Stokes,** Gerald Virgil 1943- *WhoBlA 92*
**Stokes,** Gordon Arthur 1929- *WhoWest 92*
**Stokes,** Gordon Ellis 1933- *AmMWSc 92*
**Stokes,** Harold T 1947- *AmMWSc 92*
**Stokes,** Harry Michael 1926- *Who 92*
**Stokes,** Jacob Leo 1912- *AmMWSc 92*
**Stokes,** James David 1943- *WhoMW 92*
**Stokes,** James Digby 1914- *WhoWest 92*
**Stokes,** James Harold 1938- *WhoEnt 92*
**Stokes,** James Milton 1938- *WhoAmP 91*
**Stokes,** James Sewell 1944- *WhoAmL 92*
**Stokes,** Jimmy Cleveland 1944- *AmMWSc 92*
**Stokes,** John *DrAPF 91*
**Stokes,** John 1917- *Who 92*
**Stokes,** John Fisher 1912- *Who 92*
**Stokes,** John Lemacks, II 1908- *WhoRel 92*
**Stokes,** Johnnie Mae 1941- *WhoBlA 92*
**Stokes,** Joseph Franklin 1934- *AmMWSc 92*
**Stokes,** Joseph Powell 1946- *WhoMW 92*
**Stokes,** Kenneth Irving 1928- *WhoMW 92, WhoRel 92*
**Stokes,** Lana Hughes 1948- *WhoMW 92*
**Stokes,** Lillian Gatlin 1942- *WhoBlA 92*
**Stokes,** Louis 1925- *AlmAP 92 [port], WhoAmP 91, WhoBlA 92, WhoMW 92*
**Stokes,** Mack Marion Boyd 1911- *WhoRel 92*
**Stokes,** Margaret Smith 1950- *WhoBlA 92*
**Stokes,** Marian 1926- *WhoAmP 91*
**Stokes,** Marianne 1855-1927 *TwCPaSc*
**Stokes,** Michael David 1953- *WhoRel 92*

Stokes, Michael Donald 1960- *WhoAmL 92*
Stokes, Pamela Mary 1935- *AmMWSc 92*
Stokes, Patrick T. 1942- *WhoMW 92*
Stokes, Paul Mason 1946- *WhoAmL 92*
Stokes, Peter E 1926- *AmMWSc 92*
Stokes, Rembert Edwards 1917- *WhoBlA 92*
Stokes, Richard Hivling 1921- *AmMWSc 92*
Stokes, Robert Allan 1942- *AmMWSc 92*
Stokes, Robert Mitchell 1936- *AmMWSc 92*
Stokes, Russell Aubrey 1922- *AmMWSc 92*
Stokes, Ruth S 1942- *WhoAmP 91*
Stokes, Sheila Woods 1949- *WhoBlA 92*
Stokes, Sterling J. *WhoBlA 92*
Stokes, Susan B *WhoAmP 91*
Stokes, Terry *DrAPF 91*
Stokes, Theresa Emma 1943- *WhoFI 92*
Stokes, Thomas F 1948- *WhoIns 92*
Stokes, Thomas S. 1946- *WhoRel 92*
Stokes, William Glenn 1921- *AmMWSc 92*
Stokes, William Lee 1915- *AmMWSc 92, WhoWest 92*
Stokes, William Moore 1921- *AmMWSc 92*
Stokesbury, Leon *DrAPF 91*
Stokey, Angel Jeanne 1946- *WhoEnt 92*
Stokey, W F 1917- *AmMWSc 92*
Stokinger, Herbert Ellsworth 1909- *AmMWSc 92*
Stokley, James 1900- *AmMWSc 92*
Stokoe, E G 1919- *TwCWW 91*
Stokowski, Anne K *WhoAmP 91*
Stokowski, Eugene E 1921- *WhoAmP 91*
Stokowski, Leopold 1882-1977 *FacFETw [port], NewAmDM*
Stokowski, Stanley E 1941- *AmMWSc 92*
Stokstad, Evan Ludvig Robert 1913- *AmMWSc 92*
Stokstad, Robert G 1940- *AmMWSc 92*
Stol, Marten 1940- *IntWW 91*
Stolar, Henry Samuel 1939- *WhoAmL 92*
Stolarik, Eugene 1919- *AmMWSc 92*
Stolarik, Robert J. 1929- *WhoAmL 92*
Stolarsky, Kenneth B 1942- *AmMWSc 92*
Stolbach, Leo Lucien 1933- *AmMWSc 92*
Stolber, Dean 1944- *IntMPA 92*
Stolberg, Christian, Graf von 1748-1821 *BlkwCEP*
Stolberg, Friedrich Leopold, Graf von 1750-1819 *BlkwCEP*
Stolberg, Harold Josef 1940- *AmMWSc 92*
Stolberg, Irving Jules 1936- *WhoAmP 91*
Stolberg, Marvin Arnold 1925- *AmMWSc 92*
Stolc, Viktor 1932- *AmMWSc 92*
Stolder, Steven Edward 1957- *WhoEnt 92*
Stoldt, Robert James 1925- *WhoAmP 91*
Stoldt, Stephen Howard 1938- *AmMWSc 92*
Stolee, Michael Joseph 1930- *WhoMW 92*
Stolen, Joanne Siu 1943- *AmMWSc 92*
Stolen, Rogers Hall 1937- *AmMWSc 92*
Stoler, David 1936- *AmMWSc 92*
Stoler, Paul 1938- *AmMWSc 92*
Stoleru, Lionel 1937- *WhoFI 92*
Stolfi, Robert Louis 1938- *AmMWSc 92*
Stolfo, Salvatore Joseph 1954- *AmMWSc 92*
Stoline, Michael Ross 1940- *AmMWSc 92*
Stolk, Jon Martin 1942- *AmMWSc 92*
Stoll, Forrest Duane 1921- *WhoEnt 92*
Stoll, Hans Reiner 1939- *WhoFI 92*
Stoll, Harry Lloyd 1930- *WhoRel 92*
Stoll, Irma 1929- *ConAu 135*
Stoll, Jeffrey William 1957- *WhoMW 92, WhoRel 92*
Stoll, John Raymond 1951- *WhoFI 92*
Stoll, John Robert 1950- *WhoAmL 92, WhoMW 92*
Stoll, Manfred 1944- *AmMWSc 92*
Stoll, Myron Saunders 1934- *WhoAmL 92*
Stoll, Neal Richard 1948- *WhoAmL 92*
Stoll, Norman Robert 1942- *WhoAmL 92, WhoWest 92*
Stoll, Paul James 1933- *AmMWSc 92*
Stoll, Peter Alan 1948- *WhoWest 92*
Stoll, Randall Jaye 1958- *WhoFI 92*
Stoll, Richard E *AmMWSc 92*
Stoll, Richard Edmund 1927- *WhoFI 92, WhoMW 92*
Stoll, Richard Giles 1946- *WhoAmL 92*
Stoll, Robert D 1931- *AmMWSc 92*
Stoll, Rosanna *WhoHisp 92*
Stoll, Wilhelm 1923- *AmMWSc 92, WhoMW 92*
Stoll, William Francis 1932- *AmMWSc 92*
Stoll, William Russell 1931- *AmMWSc 92*
Stollar, Bernard David 1936- *AmMWSc 92*
Stollar, Victor 1933- *AmMWSc 92*
Stollberg, Robert 1915- *AmMWSc 92*
Stollenwerk, John Joseph 1940- *WhoFI 92*
Stoller, Benjamin Boris 1907- *AmMWSc 92*
Stoller, Edward W 1937- *AmMWSc 92*
Stoller, Melissa Berger 1965- *WhoAmL 92*
Stoller, Michael Alan 1944- *WhoFI 92*
Stoller, Richard Sheldon 1944- *WhoFI 92*
Stoller, Robert J d1991 *NewYTBS 91*
Stoller, Robert J. 1924-1991 *ConAu 135*
Stoller, William Lewis 1934- *WhoMW 92*
Stollerman, Gene Howard 1920- *AmMWSc 92*
Stollery, John Leslie 1930- *Who 92*
Stolley, Paul David 1937- *AmMWSc 92, IntWW 91*
Stolley, Richard Brockway 1928- *WhoFI 92*
Stollmeyer, David Rex 1943- *WhoWest 92*
Stolnitz, Art 1928- *IntMPA 92*
Stolnitz, Arthur H 1928- *WhoEnt 92*
Stoloff, Carolyn *DrAPF 91*
Stoloff, Carolyn 1927- *IntAu&W 91*
Stoloff, Irwin Lester 1927- *AmMWSc 92*
Stoloff, Leonard 1915- *AmMWSc 92*
Stoloff, Norman Stanley 1934- *AmMWSc 92*
Stoloff, Victor 1913- *IntMPA 92, WhoEnt 92*
Stolojan, Theodor *IntWW 91*
Stolov, Harold L 1921- *AmMWSc 92*
Stolovy, Alexander 1926- *AmMWSc 92*
Stolow, Nathan 1928- *AmMWSc 92*
Stolow, Robert David 1932- *AmMWSc 92*
Stolowitz, Micah David 1954- *WhoAmL 92*
Stolpe, Manfred 1936- *IntWW 91*
Stolper, Charles Nichols 1953- *WhoFI 92*
Stolper, Edward Manin 1952- *AmMWSc 92*
Stolper, Pinchas Aryeh 1931- *WhoRel 92*
Stolper, Wolfgang Friedrich 1912- *WhoFI 92, WhoMW 92*
Stolpman, Thomas Gerard 1949- *WhoWest 92*
Stolte, Charles 1933- *AmMWSc 92*
Stolte, Dieter 1934- *IntWW 91*
Stolte, Larry Gene 1945- *WhoMW 92*
Stoltenberg, Carl H 1924- *AmMWSc 92*
Stoltenberg, Carl Henry 1924- *WhoWest 92*
Stoltenberg, Gerhard 1928- *IntWW 91, Who 92*
Stoltenberg, Thorvald 1931- *IntWW 91*
Stoltman, Joseph Paul 1940- *WhoMW 92*
Stoltz, Charles Edward 1936- *WhoMW 92*
Stoltz, Eric *WhoEnt 92*
Stoltz, Eric 1961- *IntMPA 92*
Stoltz, Eric Michael 1960- *WhoFI 92*
Stoltz, Joseph Francis 1943- *WhoFI 92*
Stoltz, Leonard Paul 1927- *AmMWSc 92*
Stoltz, Mary Ann 1937- *WhoRel 92*
Stoltz, Michael Rae 1951- *WhoAmL 92*
Stoltz, Paul Gordon 1960- *WhoWest 92*
Stoltz, Robert Lewis 1945- *AmMWSc 92*
Stoltzfus, Ben *DrAPF 91*
Stoltzfus, Ben Frank 1927- *IntAu&W 91, WhoWest 92, WrDr 92*
Stoltzfus, J Lowell *WhoAmP 91*
Stoltzfus, Milton Leroy 1961- *WhoRel 92*
Stoltzfus, Neal W 1946- *AmMWSc 92*
Stoltzfus, William Bryan 1932- *AmMWSc 92*
Stoltzman, Richard Leslie 1942- *WhoEnt 92*
Stoltzmann, David Eugene 1949- *WhoMW 92*
Stoltzmann, William A 1948- *WhoIns 92*
Stolwijk, Jan Adrianus Jozef 1927- *AmMWSc 92*
Stolypin, Peter Arkadyevich 1862-1911 *FacFETw*
Stolz, Mary 1920- *Au&Arts 8 [port], IntAu&W 91, WrDr 92*
Stolz, Mary Slattery 1920- *BenetAL 91*
Stolz, Preble 1931- *WhoAmL 92*
Stolz, Richard James 1959- *WhoMW 92*
Stolz, Robert 1880-1975 *NewAmDM*
Stolz, Walter S 1938- *AmMWSc 92*
Stolzberg, Maxwell 1942- *WhoAmL 92*
Stolzberg, Richard Jay 1948- *AmMWSc 92*
Stolzenbach, Keith Densmore 1944- *AmMWSc 92*
Stolzenberg, Gary Eric 1939- *AmMWSc 92*
Stolzenberg, Sidney Joseph 1927- *AmMWSc 92*
Stolzy, Lewis Hal 1920- *AmMWSc 92*
Stombaugh, Tom Atkins 1921- *AmMWSc 92*
Stombler, Milton Philip 1939- *AmMWSc 92*
Stomer, Raymond S 1925- *WhoAmP 91*
Stommel, Henry Melson 1920- *AmMWSc 92*
Stompro, Keith Harold 1947- *WhoWest 92*
Stone, Alan 1928- *WhoFI 92*
Stone, Alan A. 1929- *WhoAmL 92, WrDr 92*
Stone, Alan Abraham 1929- *IntAu&W 91*
Stone, Alan Jay 1942- *WhoMW 92*
Stone, Alan John 1940- *WhoFI 92*
Stone, Albert Leo, Jr. 1943- *WhoAmL 92*
Stone, Albert Mordecai 1913- *AmMWSc 92*
Stone, Alexander Glattstein 1916- *AmMWSc 92*
Stone, Alexander James 1923- *WhoIns 92*
Stone, Alexander Paul 1928- *AmMWSc 92, WhoWest 92*
Stone, Alma *DrAPF 91*
Stone, Alton Levon, Jr. 1953- *WhoRel 92*
Stone, Alvin Marion 1919- *WhoRel 92*
Stone, Andrew Grover 1942- *WhoAmL 92*
Stone, Andrew L. 1902- *IntMPA 92*
Stone, Anne Frances 1949- *WhoEnt 92*
Stone, Anthony Charles Peter 1939- *Who 92*
Stone, Arlene *DrAPF 91*
Stone, Arthur Harold 1916- *AmMWSc 92*
Stone, Ben Harry 1935- *WhoAmP 91*
Stone, Benjamin Clemens 1933- *AmMWSc 92*
Stone, Benjamin P 1935- *AmMWSc 92*
Stone, Bernard Leonard 1927- *WhoAmP 91, WhoMW 92*
Stone, Bertram Allen 1915- *WhoAmL 92*
Stone, Bobbie Dean 1927- *AmMWSc 92*
Stone, Bonnie Domrose 1941- *ConAu 133*
Stone, Bradford 1929- *WhoAmL 92*
Stone, Brian 1919- *WrDr 92*
Stone, Brinton Harvey 1907- *WhoWest 92*
Stone, Burton J. 1928- *IntMPA 92*
Stone, Carole *DrAPF 91*
Stone, Charles Dean 1926- *AmMWSc 92*
Stone, Charles Joel 1936- *AmMWSc 92*
Stone, Charles John 1827-1886 *ScFEYrs*
Stone, Charles Porter 1937- *AmMWSc 92*
Stone, Charles Richard 1921- *AmMWSc 92*
Stone, Chester B., Jr. 1935- *WhoFI 92*
Stone, Chuck 1924- *WhoBlA 92*
Stone, Clement A 1923- *AmMWSc 92*
Stone, Connie J 1943- *AmMWSc 92*
Stone, Daniel Boxall 1925- *AmMWSc 92*
Stone, Daniel Joseph 1918- *AmMWSc 92*
Stone, Daniel M. 1942- *WhoBlA 92*
Stone, David B 1933- *AmMWSc 92*
Stone, David Guy 1957- *WhoWest 92*
Stone, David Philip 1944- *WhoAmL 92*
Stone, David Randal 1956- *WhoMW 92*
Stone, David Ross 1942- *AmMWSc 92*
Stone, David Ulric 1927- *WhoWest 92*
Stone, David Warren 1954- *WhoMW 92*
Stone, Deborah Bennett 1938- *AmMWSc 92*
Stone, Dee Wallace 1948- *IntMPA 92*
Stone, Dianne S. 1964- *WhoFI 92*
Stone, Dolores June 1939- *WhoBlA 92*
Stone, Don 1949- *WhoEnt 92*
Stone, Donald Crawford 1903- *IntWW 91*
Stone, Donald D. 1924- *WhoFI 92, WhoWest 92*
Stone, Donald Eugene 1930- *AmMWSc 92*
Stone, Donald Raymond 1938- *WhoAmL 92*
Stone, Dorothy Maharam 1917- *AmMWSc 92*
Stone, Douglas Roy 1948- *AmMWSc 92*
Stone, Dwight Albert 1951- *WhoEnt 92*
Stone, Earl Lewis, Jr 1915- *AmMWSc 92*
Stone, Earl Stanley 1914- *WhoRel 92*
Stone, Earle Joshua *DrAPF 91*
Stone, Edward 1932- *AmMWSc 92*
Stone, Edward 1940- *TwCPaSc*
Stone, Edward Carroll 1936- *WhoWest 92*
Stone, Edward Carroll, Jr 1936- *AmMWSc 92*
Stone, Edward Curry 1917- *AmMWSc 92*
Stone, Edward Durell 1902- *DcTwDes*
Stone, Edward Durell 1902-1978 *FacFETw*
Stone, Edward Herman 1939- *WhoAmL 92*
Stone, Edward John 1930- *AmMWSc 92*
Stone, Elliot Edward 1939- *WhoEnt 92*
Stone, Elmer John 1919- *WhoAmL 92*
Stone, Erika Mares 1938- *AmMWSc 92*
Stone, Evan David Robert 1928- *Who 92*
Stone, Ezra *LesBEnT 92*
Stone, Ezra C. 1917- *IntMPA 92*
Stone, Ezra Chaim 1917- *WhoEnt 92*
Stone, Francis Gordon 1925- *Who 92*
Stone, Francis Gordon Albert 1925- *IntWW 91*
Stone, Frank 1947- *WhoAmP 91*
Stone, Fred Michael 1943- *WhoFI 92*
Stone, Frederick Alistair 1927- *Who 92*
Stone, Garrett Allen 1958- *WhoAmL 92*
Stone, Gayle Hallenbeck 1945- *IntAu&W 91*
Stone, Gene d1991 *NewYTBS 91*
Stone, Geoffrey 1931- *TwCPaSc*
Stone, Geoffrey Richard 1946- *WhoAmL 92*
Stone, George Hapgood 1841-1917 *BiInAmS*
Stone, George L 1934- *WhoIns 92*
Stone, Georgia Gossom 1939- *WhoRel 92*
Stone, Gerald 1932- *WrDr 92*
Stone, Gerald Charles 1932- *IntAu&W 91*
Stone, Gerald Lee 1941- *WhoMW 92*
Stone, Gilbert Seymour 1915- *Who 92*
Stone, Gordon *Who 92*
Stone, Gordon Emory 1933- *AmMWSc 92*
Stone, Grace Zaring d1991 *NewYTBS 91 [port]*
Stone, Grace Zaring 1891-1991 *ConAu 135*
Stone, Grace Zaring 1896- *BenetAL 91*
Stone, H Nathan 1920- *AmMWSc 92*
Stone, Harlan Fiske 1872-1946 *AmPolLe, FacFETw, RComAH*
Stone, Harold 1930- *WhoEnt 92*
Stone, Harold Anthony 1949- *WhoBlA 92*
Stone, Harold S 1938- *AmMWSc 92*
Stone, Harris B 1923- *AmMWSc 92*
Stone, Harry 1926- *WhoWest 92*
Stone, Henry E 1922- *AmMWSc 92*
Stone, Henry Otto, Jr 1936- *AmMWSc 92*
Stone, Herbert 1934- *AmMWSc 92*
Stone, Herbert L 1928- *AmMWSc 92*
Stone, Herbert Lynn 1941- *WhoRel 92*
Stone, Herbert Steven 1953- *WhoFI 92*
Stone, Herman 1924- *AmMWSc 92*
Stone, Herman, Jr. 1919- *WhoBlA 92*
Stone, Howard Anderson 1940- *AmMWSc 92*
Stone, Howard Lawrence 1941- *WhoAmL 92*
Stone, Howard N 1922- *AmMWSc 92*
Stone, Hubert Dean 1924- *WhoFI 92*
Stone, I F 1907-1989 *FacFETw [port]*
Stone, Irene Mildred 1928- *WhoMW 92*
Stone, Irving 1903- *IntAu&W 91*
Stone, Irving 1903-1989 *BenetAL 91, FacFETw*
Stone, Irving Charles, Jr 1930- *AmMWSc 92*
Stone, Irving I. 1909- *WhoMW 92*
Stone, Isidor Feinstein 1907-1989 *AmPeW*
Stone, J L 1941- *AmMWSc 92*
Stone, Jack *WhoRel 92*
Stone, Jack I. 1920- *WhoFI 92*
Stone, Jacqueline *TwCPaSc*
Stone, James Howard 1939- *WhoFI 92, WhoMW 92*
Stone, James Robert 1948- *WhoWest 92*
Stone, Janet Marie 1945- *WhoFI 92*
Stone, Jay Cail 1952- *WhoEnt 92*
Stone, Jay D 1944- *AmMWSc 92*
Stone, Jed 1949- *WhoAmL 92*
Stone, Jennifer *DrAPF 91*
Stone, Jerry Hurd 1926- *WhoRel 92*
Stone, Jesse Nealand, Jr. 1924- *WhoBlA 92*
Stone, Jo Slagle 1925- *WhoFI 92*
Stone, Joan *DrAPF 91*
Stone, Joan Elizabeth 1930- *IntAu&W 91*
Stone, Joe Allan 1948- *WhoAmP 91, WhoFI 92, WhoWest 92*
Stone, Joe Thomas 1941- *AmMWSc 92*
Stone, Joel Richard 1949- *WhoEnt 92*
Stone, John *DrAPF 91*
Stone, John Augustus 1800-1834 *BenetAL 91*
Stone, John Austin 1935- *AmMWSc 92*
Stone, John Bruce 1930- *AmMWSc 92*
Stone, John Elmer 1931- *AmMWSc 92*
Stone, John Floyd 1928- *AmMWSc 92*
Stone, John Grover, II 1933- *AmMWSc 92*
Stone, John Morris 1948- *WhoFI 92*
Stone, John O. 1929- *IntWW 91*
Stone, John Patrick 1939- *AmMWSc 92*
Stone, John Richard 1913- *IntWW 91, Who 92*
Stone, John Richard Nicholas 1913- *WhoNob 90*
Stone, John S. 1930- *WhoBlA 92*
Stone, John Timothy, Jr. 1933- *WhoMW 92*
Stone, Jon 1931- *WhoEnt 92*
Stone, Jon Robert 1959- *WhoRel 92*
Stone, Joseph 1920- *AmMWSc 92, WhoEnt 92*
Stone, Joseph Louis 1918- *AmMWSc 92*
Stone, Judson Irwin 1952- *WhoRel 92*
Stone, Julian 1929- *AmMWSc 92*
Stone, Julie L. *DrAPF 91*
Stone, Kara Lynn 1929- *WhoBlA 92*
Stone, Kathleen Sexton 1947- *AmMWSc 92*
Stone, Ken *DrAPF 91*
Stone, Laird Bruce 1953- *WhoAmL 92*
Stone, Laurie *DrAPF 91*
Stone, Lawrence 1919- *IntWW 91, Who 92, WrDr 92*
Stone, Lawrence David 1942- *AmMWSc 92*
Stone, Lawrence E *WhoAmP 91*
Stone, Lesley *WrDr 92*
Stone, Lewis Bart 1938- *WhoAmL 92*
Stone, Linda 1941- *WhoWest 92*
Stone, Livingston 1835-1912 *BiInAmS*
Stone, Loyd Raymond 1945- *AmMWSc 92, WhoMW 92*
Stone, Lucy 1818-1893 *BenetAL 91, HanAmWH*
Stone, M D 1902- *AmMWSc 92*
Stone, Marcus 1840-1921 *TwCPaSc*
Stone, Marcus 1921- *Who 92*
Stone, Margaret Hodgman 1914- *AmMWSc 92*
Stone, Marianne *IntMPA 92*

**Stone**, Marshall Harvey 1903- AmMWSc 92
**Stone**, Marshall Harvey 1903-1989 FacFETw
**Stone**, Martha Barnes 1952- AmMWSc 92
**Stone**, Martin L 1920- AmMWSc 92
**Stone**, Marvin J 1937- AmMWSc 92
**Stone**, Mary Alice 1940- WhoFI 92
**Stone**, Matthew Peter 1961- WhoAmL 92
**Stone**, Maurine Rainer 1940- WhoFI 92
**Stone**, Max Wendell 1929- AmMWSc 92
**Stone**, Melvin Lewis 1921- WhoEnt 92
**Stone**, Merlin 1948- WrDr 92
**Stone**, Merrill Brent 1951- WhoAmL 92
**Stone**, Michael WhoEnt 92
**Stone**, Michael David 1953- WhoWest 92
**Stone**, Michael Gates 1938- AmMWSc 92
**Stone**, Norman 1941- IntWW 91, Who 92
**Stone**, Norman Michael 1949- WhoWest 92
**Stone**, Norman R, Jr 1935- WhoAmP 91
**Stone**, Oliver 1946- IntDcF 2-2 [port], IntMPA 92, IntWW 91, WhoEnt 92
**Stone**, Orville L 1921- AmMWSc 92
**Stone**, Patrick Philip Dennant 1939- Who 92
**Stone**, Paul Stanley 1951- WhoMW 92
**Stone**, Peter 1930- IntAu&W 91, SmATA 65, WhoEnt 92
**Stone**, Peter George 1937- WhoAmL 92
**Stone**, Peter H. 1930- IntMPA 92
**Stone**, Peter H 1948- AmMWSc 92
**Stone**, Peter Hunter 1937- AmMWSc 92
**Stone**, Philip M 1933- AmMWSc 92
**Stone**, R. Gregg 1952- WhoFI 92
**Stone**, Ralph B. 1943- WhoWest 92
**Stone**, Randolph Noel 1946- WhoAmL 92
**Stone**, Reese J., Jr. 1947- WhoBlA 92
**Stone**, Richard IntWW 91, Who 92
**Stone**, Richard 1913- WrDr 92
**Stone**, Richard B. 1943- WhoAmL 92
**Stone**, Richard Bernard 1928- WhoAmP 91
**Stone**, Richard E 1937- WhoIns 92
**Stone**, Richard Frederick 1928- Who 92
**Stone**, Richard Gilbert 1935- WhoFI 92
**Stone**, Richard James 1945- WhoAmL 92
**Stone**, Richard Lee 1963- WhoMW 92
**Stone**, Richard Lehman 1916- WhoWest 92
**Stone**, Richard Nicholas 1913- WhoFI 92
**Stone**, Richard Spillane 1925- AmMWSc 92
**Stone**, Robert DrAPF 91
**Stone**, Robert 1937- BenetAL 91, ConNov 91, IntAu&W 91, WrDr 92
**Stone**, Robert Edward, Jr 1937- AmMWSc 92
**Stone**, Robert Finley 1962- WhoEnt 92
**Stone**, Robert K 1920- AmMWSc 92
**Stone**, Robert Louis 1921- AmMWSc 92
**Stone**, Robert P 1918- AmMWSc 92
**Stone**, Robert Sidney 1923- AmMWSc 92
**Stone**, Robert Thomas 1946- WhoWest 92
**Stone**, Roger 1935- IntWW 91
**Stone**, Roger Alan 1951- WhoFI 92
**Stone**, Roger Jason, Jr 1952- WhoAmP 91
**Stone**, Roger W 1954- WhoAmP 91
**Stone**, Roger Warren 1935- WhoFI 92, WhoMW 92
**Stone**, Ronald F 1945- WhoIns 92
**Stone**, Ronald M. WhoFI 92
**Stone**, Rosetta ConAu 135, SmATA 67
**Stone**, Royce 1836?-1905 BiInAmS
**Stone**, Ruby R WhoAmP 91
**Stone**, Ruth DrAPF 91
**Stone**, Ruth 1915- ConPo 91, WrDr 92
**Stone**, Samuel 1602-1663 BenetAL 91
**Stone**, Samuel Edwin 1936- WhoRel 92
**Stone**, Sandra WhoEnt 92
**Stone**, Sanford Herbert 1921- AmMWSc 92
**Stone**, Saul 1906- WhoAmL 92
**Stone**, Sheldon Leslie 1946- AmMWSc 92
**Stone**, Sheldon Lloyd 1955- WhoMW 92
**Stone**, Sid LesBEnT 92
**Stone**, Sidney Norman 1922- AmMWSc 92
**Stone**, Sly NewAmDM
**Stone**, Solon Allen 1928- AmMWSc 92
**Stone**, Stanley S 1921- AmMWSc 92
**Stone**, Stanley Warren 1953- WhoRel 92
**Stone**, Stephen Edward 1940- WhoAmL 92
**Stone**, Stephen Paul 1941- WhoMW 92
**Stone**, Steven Jay 1953- WhoMW 92
**Stone**, Susan Berman 1957- WhoRel 92
**Stone**, Tammy Lynn 1958- WhoEnt 92
**Stone**, Teena Marie 1948- WhoWest 92
**Stone**, Terence Frederick 1934- WhoMW 92
**Stone**, Thomas Edward 1952- WhoWest 92
**Stone**, Thomas H. WrDr 92
**Stone**, Victor J. 1921- WhoAmL 92
**Stone**, Vivian Rene 1957- WhoFI 92
**Stone**, W Clement 1902- WhoAmP 91, WhoIns 92
**Stone**, Warren Gerald 1950- WhoRel 92
**Stone**, William, Jr. 1916- WhoWest 92
**Stone**, William E 1940- WhoAmP 91
**Stone**, William Ellis 1911- AmMWSc 92
**Stone**, William Frazier 1944- WhoEnt 92
**Stone**, William Harold 1924- AmMWSc 92
**Stone**, William Jack Hanson 1932- AmMWSc 92
**Stone**, William John AmMWSc 92
**Stone**, William Lawrence 1944- AmMWSc 92
**Stone**, William Leete 1792-1844 BenetAL 91
**Stone**, William Lyndon 1926- WhoMW 92, WhoRel 92
**Stone**, William Philip 1911- WhoAmP 91
**Stone**, William Ross 1947- AmMWSc 92
**Stone**, William S. 1928- WrDr 92
**Stone**, William T. 1931- WhoBlA 92
**Stone**, Zachary WrDr 92
**Stonebarger**, C. William 1926- WhoEnt 92
**Stonebraker**, Peter Michael 1945- AmMWSc 92
**Stonebraker**, Peter William 1942- WhoMW 92
**Stoneburner**, Daniel Lee 1945- AmMWSc 92
**Stonecipher**, David A 1941- WhoIns 92
**Stonecypher**, Roy W 1933- AmMWSc 92
**Stonecypher**, Thomas E 1934- AmMWSc 92
**Stonefield**, Liz Topete 1955- WhoHisp 92
**Stonefrost**, Maurice Frank 1927- Who 92
**Stoneham**, Arthur Marshall 1940- Who 92
**Stoneham**, Horace 1903-1990 AnObit 1990
**Stoneham**, Horace Charles 1904-1990 FacFETw
**Stoneham**, Richard George 1920- AmMWSc 92
**Stonehill**, Brian Allan 1953- WhoWest 92
**Stonehill**, Elliott H 1928- AmMWSc 92
**Stonehill**, Lloyd Herschel 1927- WhoMW 92
**Stonehill**, Robert Berrell 1921- AmMWSc 92
**Stonehouse**, Bernard 1926- WrDr 92
**Stonehouse**, Harold Bertram 1922- AmMWSc 92
**Stonehouse**, James Adam 1937- WhoWest 92
**Stonehouse**, Jeffrey Thomas WhoEnt 92
**Stonehouse**, John 1925-1988 FacFETw
**Stonehouse**, John Thomson 1925- IntAu&W 91
**Stonehouse**, Ruth 1893-1941 ReelWom [port]
**Stoneking**, Jerry Edward 1942- AmMWSc 92
**Stoneman**, David McNeel 1939- AmMWSc 92
**Stoneman**, Douglas Grayson 1931- WhoFI 92
**Stoneman**, Maurice 1922- WhoAmP 91
**Stoneman**, Paul 1947- WrDr 92
**Stoneman**, Richard 1951- WrDr 92
**Stoneman**, Samuel Sidney 1911- WhoEnt 92
**Stoneman**, William, III 1927- AmMWSc 92
**Stoner**, Abigail Coburn 1939- WhoAmP 91
**Stoner**, Adair 1928- AmMWSc 92
**Stoner**, Allan K 1939- AmMWSc 92
**Stoner**, Allan Wilbur 1931- AmMWSc 92
**Stoner**, Clinton Dale 1933- AmMWSc 92
**Stoner**, Edward Norris, II 1947- WhoAmL 92
**Stoner**, Elaine Blatt 1939- WhoMW 92
**Stoner**, Elaine Carol Blatt 1939- AmMWSc 92
**Stoner**, Gary David 1942- AmMWSc 92
**Stoner**, George Green 1912- AmMWSc 92
**Stoner**, Glenn Earl 1940- AmMWSc 92
**Stoner**, Graham Alexander 1929- AmMWSc 92
**Stoner**, James Lloyd 1920- WhoRel 92
**Stoner**, John Clark 1933- AmMWSc 92
**Stoner**, John Oliver, Jr 1936- AmMWSc 92
**Stoner**, Larry Clinton 1943- AmMWSc 92
**Stoner**, Laura Marie 1938- WhoRel 92
**Stoner**, Leonard Dudley 1950- WhoFI 92, WhoMW 92
**Stoner**, Madeleine Ruskin 1937- WhoWest 92
**Stoner**, Marshall Robert 1938- AmMWSc 92, WhoMW 92
**Stoner**, Martin Franklin 1942- AmMWSc 92
**Stoner**, Michael Alan 1944- WhoAmL 92
**Stoner**, Oliver Gerald 1922- IntWW 91
**Stoner**, Philip James 1943- WhoMW 92
**Stoner**, Richard Burkett 1920- WhoAmP 91, WhoFI 92
**Stoner**, Richard Dean 1919- AmMWSc 92
**Stoner**, Ronald Edward 1937- AmMWSc 92
**Stoner**, Sandra Wise 1957- WhoAmL 92
**Stoner**, Sherri Lynn 1959- WhoEnt 92
**Stoner**, Warren Norton 1922- AmMWSc 92
**Stoner**, William Patrick 1947- WhoEnt 92
**Stoner**, William Weber 1944- AmMWSc 92
**Stones**, Alan 1947- TwCPaSc
**Stones**, John Stanley 1957- WhoRel 92
**Stones**, Margaret 1920- Who 92
**Stones**, Robert C 1937- AmMWSc 92
**Stones**, William 1923- Who 92
**Stonesifer**, Robert Bruce 1955- WhoFI 92
**Stoney**, Gordon Adair 1930- WhoWest 92
**Stoney**, Larry D WhoAmP 91
**Stoney**, Ralph Francis Ewart 1903- Who 92
**Stoney**, Samuel David, Jr 1939- AmMWSc 92
**Stong**, Elizabeth Snow 1957- WhoAmL 92
**Stong**, John Elliott 1921- WhoFI 92, WhoWest 92
**Stong**, Phil 1899-1957 BenetAL 91
**Stonhouse**, Philip 1916- Who 92
**Stonich**, Timothy Whitman 1947- WhoFI 92
**Stonier**, Tom Ted 1927- AmMWSc 92
**Stonionis**, Douglas James 1965- WhoMW 92
**Stonis**, Richard DcTwDes
**Stonitch**, William Jon 1951- WhoMW 92
**Stonner**, Richard C 1945- WhoAmP 91
**Stonor** Who 92
**Stonor**, Thomas 1936- Who 92
**Stonum**, Elizabeth Ann 1926- WhoAmP 91
**Stoodley**, Peter Ernest William 1925- Who 92
**Stookey**, George K 1935- AmMWSc 92
**Stookey**, John Hoyt 1930- IntWW 91, WhoFI 92
**Stookey**, Laurence Hull 1937- WhoRel 92
**Stookey**, Noel Paul 1937- WhoEnt 92
**Stookey**, Stanley Donald 1915- AmMWSc 92
**Stoolman**, Herbert Leonard 1917- WhoFI 92
**Stoolman**, Leo 1918- AmMWSc 92
**Stoolmiller**, Allen Charles 1940- AmMWSc 92
**Stoops**, Bradley Neil 1951- WhoFI 92, WhoMW 92
**Stoops**, Charles E, Jr 1914- AmMWSc 92
**Stoops**, Daniel J. 1934- WhoAmL 92
**Stoops**, James King 1937- AmMWSc 92
**Stoops**, R F 1921- AmMWSc 92
**Stopczynski**, Stanley 1934- WhoAmP 91
**Stopford** Who 92
**Stopford**, Viscount 1988- Who 92
**Stopford**, Stephen Robert Anthony 1934- Who 92
**Stopford**, Woodhall 1943- AmMWSc 92
**Stoph**, Willi 1914- IntWW 91
**Stopher**, Edward Harden 1943- WhoAmL 92
**Stopher**, Peter Robert 1943- AmMWSc 92
**Stopkie**, Roger John 1939- AmMWSc 92
**Stoppani**, Andres Oscar Manuel 1915- AmMWSc 92
**Stoppard**, Miriam 1937- IntAu&W 91, Who 92, WrDr 92
**Stoppard**, Tom 1937- CnDBLB 8 [port], FacFETw, IntAu&W 91, IntMPA 92, IntWW 91, RfGEnL 91, Who 92, WhoEnt 92, WrDr 92
**Stops** Who 92
**Stora**, Clementine 1845-1917 ThHEIm
**Storaasli**, John Phillip 1921- AmMWSc 92
**Storace**, Nancy 1765-1817 NewAmDM
**Storace**, Stephen 1762-1796 NewAmDM
**Storar**, John Robert Allan Montague 1925- Who 92
**Storar**, Leonore Elizabeth Therese 1920- Who 92
**Storaro**, Vittorio 1940- IntMPA 92, IntWW 91, WhoEnt 92
**Storb**, Ursula AmMWSc 92
**Storch**, Arthur 1925- WhoEnt 92
**Storch**, Donn Marvin 1950- WhoWest 92
**Storch**, Laurence 1950- WhoAmL 92
**Storch**, Marcus 1942- IntWW 91
**Storch**, Richard Harry 1937- AmMWSc 92
**Storck**, Henri 1907- IntDcF 2-2 [port]
**Stord**, Alberta Herrigel 1929- WhoAmP 91
**Storella**, Robert J, Jr 1956- AmMWSc 92
**Storen**, Thomas, Jr. 1933- WhoEnt 92
**Storer**, David George 1929- Who 92
**Storer**, David Humphreys 1804-1891 BiInAmS
**Storer**, Francis Humphreys 1832-1914 BiInAmS
**Storer**, George B. d1975 LesBEnT 92
**Storer**, James Donald 1928- Who 92, WrDr 92
**Storer**, James E 1927- AmMWSc 92
**Storer**, James Frederick 1960- WhoAmL 92
**Storer**, John B 1923- AmMWSc 92
**Storer**, Robert Winthrop 1914- AmMWSc 92
**Storer**, Roy 1928- Who 92
**Storer**, Thomas AmMWSc 92
**Storette**, Ronald Frank 1943- WhoAmL 92
**Storey**, Anthony 1928- IntAu&W 91, WrDr 92
**Storey**, Arthur Thomas 1929- AmMWSc 92
**Storey**, Arthur William 1945- WhoRel 92
**Storey**, Bayard Thayer 1932- AmMWSc 92
**Storey**, Boyd Kay 1926- WhoAmP 91
**Storey**, Brit Allan 1941- WhoWest 92
**Storey**, Charles F. 1926- WhoBlA 92
**Storey**, Christopher 1908- Who 92
**Storey**, David 1933- ConAu 36NR, ConNov 91, FacFETw, RfGEnL 91, WrDr 92
**Storey**, David Malcolm 1933- IntAu&W 91, IntWW 91, Who 92
**Storey**, Edward 1930- IntAu&W 91, WrDr 92
**Storey**, Francis Harold 1933- WhoWest 92
**Storey**, Frederick 1909- IntMPA 92
**Storey**, Gail Donohue DrAPF 91
**Storey**, Graham 1920- Who 92, WrDr 92
**Storey**, Isabel Nagy 1955- WhoEnt 92
**Storey**, James Benton 1928- AmMWSc 92
**Storey**, James Moorfield 1931- WhoAmL 92
**Storey**, JoAnn 1951- WhoAmL 92
**Storey**, Joseph Dale 1962- WhoFI 92
**Storey**, Kenneth Bruce 1949- AmMWSc 92
**Storey**, Lee Herold 1959- WhoAmL 92
**Storey**, M. Karyl 1945- WhoFI 92
**Storey**, Margaret 1926- WrDr 92
**Storey**, Maude 1930- Who 92
**Storey**, Paul 1957- TwCPaSc
**Storey**, R. L. 1927- WrDr 92
**Storey**, Richard 1937- Who 92
**Storey**, Richard Drake 1944- AmMWSc 92
**Storey**, Robert D. 1936- WhoBlA 92
**Storey**, Robert Samuel 1930- AmMWSc 92
**Storey**, Theodore George 1923- AmMWSc 92
**Storfer**, Stanley J 1930- AmMWSc 92
**Storfjell**, Johan Bjornar 1944- WhoMW 92, WhoRel 92
**Storhoff**, Bruce Norman 1942- AmMWSc 92
**Storie-Pahlitzsch**, Lori DrAPF 91
**Storie-Pugh**, Peter David 1919- Who 92
**Storjohann**, Darlys William 1959- WhoFI 92
**Storjohann**, Kenneth Ray 1945- WhoAmP 91
**Stork**, Charles Wharton 1881- BenetAL 91
**Stork**, Donald Arthur 1939- WhoFI 92, WhoMW 92
**Stork**, Donald Harvey 1926- AmMWSc 92
**Stork**, Francis J 1952- WhoAmP 91
**Stork**, Frank James 1952- WhoAmL 92
**Stork**, Gilbert 1921- AmMWSc 92, IntWW 91
**Storke**, William F. IntMPA 92
**Storke**, William Frederick Joseph 1922- WhoEnt 92
**Storm**, Carlyle Bell 1935- AmMWSc 92
**Storm**, Christopher IntAu&W 91X, WrDr 92
**Storm**, Daniel Ralph 1944- AmMWSc 92
**Storm**, Donald A 1932- WhoAmP 91
**Storm**, Doris 1926- WhoEnt 92
**Storm**, Dorothy WhoAmP 91
**Storm**, Edward Francis 1929- AmMWSc 92
**Storm**, Eric TwCSFW 91
**Storm**, Gale 1922- IntMPA 92
**Storm**, Jonathan Morris WhoEnt 92
**Storm**, Leo Eugene 1928- AmMWSc 92
**Storm**, Nicolaas Gerard 1961- WhoAmL 92
**Storm**, Robert MacLeod 1918- AmMWSc 92
**Storm**, Virginia ConAu 34NR
**Storment**, William Ray 1943- WhoWest 92
**Stormer**, Horst Ludwig 1949- AmMWSc 92
**Stormer**, John Anthony 1928- WhoRel 92
**Stormer**, John Charles, Jr 1941- AmMWSc 92
**Stormes**, John Max 1927- WhoWest 92
**Stormo**, Charles O 1929- WhoAmP 91
**Stormont**, Master of 1988- Who 92
**Stormont**, Viscount 1956- Who 92
**Stormont**, Clyde J 1916- AmMWSc 92
**Stormont**, Clyde Junior 1916- WhoFI 92, WhoWest 92
**Stormonth Darling**, James Carlisle 1918- Who 92
**Stormonth Darling**, Peter 1932- Who 92
**Stormonth-Darling**, Robin Andrew 1926- Who 92
**Storms**, Clifford Beekman 1932- WhoAmL 92, WhoFI 92
**Storms**, Lowell H 1928- AmMWSc 92
**Storms**, Margaret LaRue 1938- WhoRel 92
**Storms**, Stephanie Ann 1950- WhoEnt 92
**Stormshak**, Fredrick 1936- AmMWSc 92
**Storni**, Alfonsina 1892-1938 BenetAL 91, SpAmWW
**Storr**, Anthony 1920- IntAu&W 91, IntWW 91, Who 92, WrDr 92
**Storr**, Catherine 1913- IntAu&W 91, WrDr 92
**Storr**, John Frederick 1915- AmMWSc 92

Storrie, Brian 1946- AmMWSc 92
Storrie, James Brien 1962- WhoRel 92
Storrow, Hugh Alan 1926- AmMWSc 92
Storrow, Margaret Tileston 1954- WhoMW 92
Storrs, Charles Lysander 1925- AmMWSc 92
Storrs, Eleanor Emerett 1926- AmMWSc 92
Storrs, Eleanor Reynolds Ring 1905- WhoAmP 91
Storry, Junis O 1920- AmMWSc 92
Storry, Junis Oliver 1920- WhoMW 92
Storti, Robert V 1944- AmMWSc 92
Storts, Ralph Woodrow 1933- AmMWSc 92
Stortz, Clarence B 1933- AmMWSc 92
Storvick, Clara A 1906- AmMWSc 92
Storvick, David A 1929- AmMWSc 92
Storvick, Truman S 1928- AmMWSc 92
Storwick, Robert Martin 1942- AmMWSc 92
Story, Anne Winthrop AmMWSc 92
Story, Anthony F. d1991 NewYTBS 91
Story, Benjamin Sprague 1924- WhoRel 92
Story, Charles Irvin 1954- WhoBlA 92
Story, Christopher, VI 1925- WhoEnt 92
Story, Cullen Ik 1916- WhoRel 92
Story, Cynthia Stinson 1956- WhoAmP 91
Story, Harold S 1927- AmMWSc 92
Story, Isaac 1774-1803 BenetAL 91
Story, Jack Trevor 1917- IntAu&W 91, WrDr 92
Story, James DrAPF 91
Story, Jim Lewis 1931- AmMWSc 92
Story, Jon Alan 1946- AmMWSc 92
Story, Joseph 1779-1845 AmPolLe, BenetAL 91
Story, Norman L. WhoMW 92
Story, Otis Leon, Sr. 1951- WhoBlA 92
Story, Peter Reinald 1932- WhoAmP 91
Story, Richard Wayne 1953- WhoAmL 92
Story, Sam Ernest, Jr 1955- WhoAmP 91
Story, Thomas Lane 1947- WhoAmL 92
Story, Troy Lee, Jr 1940- AmMWSc 92
Story, W. W. 1934- WhoRel 92
Story, William Wetmore 1819-1895 BenetAL 91, BibAL 8
Storz, Edwin Neil 1949- WhoAmL 92
Storz, Johannes 1931- AmMWSc 92
Stosberg, David Thomas 1946- WhoAmL 92
Stosch, Walter Allen 1936- WhoAmP 91
Stose, Gil 1961- WhoEnt 92
Stosic, Michael Richard 1953- WhoWest 92
Stosick, Arthur James 1914- AmMWSc 92
Stoskopf, Michael Kerry 1950- AmMWSc 92
Stoskopf, N C 1934- AmMWSc 92
Stossel, John 1947- IntMPA 92
Stossel, Thomas Peter 1941- AmMWSc 92
Stotesbury, Sidney Dykes 1936- WhoMW 92
Stothart, Herbert 1885-1949 NewAmDM
Stothers, David Marvyn 1946- WhoMW 92
Stothers, John Bailie 1931- AmMWSc 92
Stotland, Ezra 1924- WrDr 92
Stotler, Alicemarie H. 1942- WhoAmL 92
Stotler, Edith Ann 1946- WhoFI 92
Stotler, Raymond Eugene 1940- AmMWSc 92
Stotler, Raymond T 1916- AmMWSc 92
Stotsbery, Lisa Marie 1960- WhoAmL 92
Stotsky, Bernard A 1926- AmMWSc 92
Stott, Lord 1909- Who 92
Stott, Adrian 1948- Who 92
Stott, Brian 1941- AmMWSc 92, WhoWest 92
Stott, Charlotte Mary 1907- IntAu&W 91, Who 92
Stott, Donald Franklin 1928- AmMWSc 92
Stott, Dorothy 1958- ConAu 134, SmATA 67
Stott, Dot ConAu 134, SmATA 67
Stott, Edward 1859-1918 TwCPaSc
Stott, George Gordon Who 92
Stott, James Charles 1945- WhoWest 92
Stott, John R. W. 1921- WhoRel 92
Stott, John Robert Walmsley 1921- Who 92, WrDr 92
Stott, Kenhelm Welburn, Jr 1920- AmMWSc 92
Stott, Mary Who 92
Stott, Mary 1907- WrDr 92
Stott, Mike 1944- WrDr 92
Stott, Paul Edwin 1948- AmMWSc 92
Stott, Peter Frank 1927- Who 92
Stott, Peter Walter 1944- WhoFI 92, WhoWest 92
Stott, Richard Keith 1943- IntAu&W 91, Who 92
Stott, Roger 1943- Who 92
Stotter, Lawrence Henry 1929- WhoAmL 92
Stotter, Mike 1957- TwCWW 91, WrDr 92
Stottlemyre, Gary Allen 1948- WhoAmP 91
Stottlemyre, James Arthur 1948- AmMWSc 92
Stotts, Jane 1939- AmMWSc 92
Stotts, Valmon D. 1925- WhoBlA 92
Stotz, Robert William 1942- AmMWSc 92
Stotz, Thomas Duane 1955- WhoMW 92
Stotzer, Beatriz Olvera 1950- WhoHisp 92
Stotzky, Guenther 1931- AmMWSc 92
Stoudt, Emily Laws 1943- AmMWSc 92
Stoudt, Howard Webster 1925- AmMWSc 92
Stoudt, Thomas Henry 1922- AmMWSc 92
Stoufer, Robert Carl 1930- AmMWSc 92
Stouffer, Austin Hitchins 1941- WhoRel 92, WhoWest 92
Stouffer, Daniel Henry, Jr. 1937- WhoWest 92
Stouffer, Donald Carl 1938- AmMWSc 92
Stouffer, James L 1935- AmMWSc 92
Stouffer, James Ray 1929- AmMWSc 92
Stouffer, John Emerson 1925- AmMWSc 92
Stouffer, Mark J. 1951- WhoEnt 92
Stouffer, Nancy Kathleen 1951- WhoFI 92
Stouffer, Richard Franklin 1932- AmMWSc 92
Stouffer, Richard Lee 1949- AmMWSc 92
Stouffer, Richard Ray 1923- WhoRel 92
Stouffer, Ronald Jay 1954- AmMWSc 92
Stough, Charles Daniel 1914- WhoAmL 92, WhoMW 92
Stough, Charles Senour 1918- WhoAmP 91
Stough, Furman Charles 1928- WhoRel 92
Stough, Stephen Alan 1950- WhoFI 92
Stough, William Allen 1949- WhoFI 92
Stoughton, Alice Casady 1927- WhoMW 92
Stoughton, Raymond Woodford 1916- AmMWSc 92
Stoughton, Richard Baker 1923- AmMWSc 92
Stoughton, Stephen H 1944- WhoAmP 91
Stoughton, William 1631-1701 BenetAL 91
Stoughton-Harris, Anthony Geoffrey 1932- Who 92
Stoumen, Lou 1916-1991 NewYTBS 91
Stoup, Arthur Harry 1925- WhoMW 92
Stourton Who 92
Stourton, John Joseph 1899- Who 92
Stout, Alan B. 1932- NewAmDM
Stout, Andrew V 1930- WhoAmP 91
Stout, Arthur Paul 1932- WhoRel 92
Stout, Barbara Elizabeth 1962- AmMWSc 92
Stout, Benjamin Boreman 1924- AmMWSc 92
Stout, Bill A 1932- AmMWSc 92
Stout, Charles Allison 1930- AmMWSc 92
Stout, Chris Edward 1959- WhoMW 92
Stout, Christine Elizabeth 1949- WhoMW 92
Stout, Darryl Glen 1944- AmMWSc 92
Stout, David Ker 1932- Who 92
Stout, David Michael 1947- AmMWSc 92
Stout, Dennis Lee 1948- WhoAmP 91
Stout, Donald Everett 1926- WhoFI 92
Stout, Edgar Lee 1938- AmMWSc 92
Stout, Edward Irvin 1939- AmMWSc 92, WhoMW 92
Stout, Ernest Ray 1938- AmMWSc 92
Stout, Glen Alan 1957- WhoFI 92
Stout, Glenn Emanuel 1920- AmMWSc 92
Stout, Glenna Faye 1947- WhoRel 92
Stout, Harry S. WrDr 92
Stout, Isaac Jack 1939- AmMWSc 92
Stout, J Barry 1936- WhoAmP 91
Stout, James Dudley 1947- WhoAmL 92
Stout, John Frederick 1936- AmMWSc 92
Stout, John Willard 1912- AmMWSc 92
Stout, Jon E. WhoRel 92
Stout, Joseph A., Jr. 1939- WrDr 92
Stout, Juanita Kidd WhoAmP 91
Stout, Juanita Kidd 1919- NotBlAW 92, WhoBlA 92
Stout, Kenneth Oliver 1929- WhoAmP 91
Stout, Koehler 1922- AmMWSc 92
Stout, Landon Clarke, Jr 1933- AmMWSc 92
Stout, Leatrice Joy 1924- WhoAmP 91
Stout, Lowell 1928- WhoAmL 92
Stout, Lynn Andrea 1957- WhoAmL 92
Stout, Marguerite Annette 1943- AmMWSc 92
Stout, Martin Lindy 1934- AmMWSc 92
Stout, Maye Alma 1920- WhoMW 92
Stout, Patrick Michael 1951- WhoEnt 92
Stout, Phil WhoAmP 91
Stout, Phillip Ray 1956- WhoRel 92
Stout, Quentin Fielden 1949- AmMWSc 92
Stout, Ray Bernard 1939- AmMWSc 92
Stout, Rex 1886-1975 BenetAL 91, ScFEYrs
Stout, Rex 1896-1975 FacFETw
Stout, Richard A 1927- WhoIns 92
Stout, Robert Daniel 1915- AmMWSc 92
Stout, Robert Daniel 1945- AmMWSc 92
Stout, Samuel Coredon 1913- Who 92
Stout, Shirley Ruth 1926- WhoAmP 91
Stout, Stephanie Lee WhoAmL 92
Stout, Thomas Melville 1925- AmMWSc 92
Stout, Thompson Mylan 1914- AmMWSc 92
Stout, Virgil L 1921- AmMWSc 92
Stout, Virginia Falk 1932- AmMWSc 92
Stout, Wayne Everett 1930- WhoRel 92
Stout, William 1949- IntAu&W 91
Stout, William B. 1880-1956 DcTwDes
Stout, William Bushnell 1880-1956 FacFETw
Stout, William F 1940- AmMWSc 92
Stout, William Ferguson 1907- Who 92
Stoutamire, Donald Wesley 1931- AmMWSc 92
Stoutamire, Warren Petrie 1928- AmMWSc 92
Stoute, Michael Ronald 1945- Who 92
Stoutenburg, Jane Sue Williamson 1949- WhoMW 92
Stouter, Vincent Paul 1924- AmMWSc 92
Stovall, Arthur Jean 1941- WhoMW 92
Stovall, Audrean 1933- WhoBlA 92
Stovall, Dan Harris 1948- WhoFI 92
Stovall, Gerald Thomas 1940- WhoRel 92
Stovall, Jerry C 1936- WhoIns 92
Stovall, Mary Kate 1921- WhoAmP 91, WhoBlA 92
Stovall, Melody S. 1952- WhoBlA 92
Stovall, Richard L. 1944- WhoMW 92
Stovall, Stanley V. 1953- WhoBlA 92
Stovall, Thelma Loyace 1919- WhoAmP 91
Stove, David Charles 1927- IntWW 91
Stover, Courtney E WhoAmP 91
Stover, David Frank 1941- WhoAmL 92
Stover, Dennis Eugene 1944- AmMWSc 92
Stover, Donald Rae 1934- WhoMW 92
Stover, E R 1929- AmMWSc 92
Stover, Enos Loy 1948- AmMWSc 92
Stover, F. Gary, Sr. 1945- WhoFI 92
Stover, Franklin Fredrick 1936- WhoRel 92
Stover, James Anderson, Jr 1937- AmMWSc 92
Stover, James Robert 1927- WhoFI 92, WhoMW 92
Stover, John Ford 1912- WrDr 92
Stover, Kathy A. 1956- WhoAmL 92
Stover, Leon 1929- WrDr 92
Stover, Lewis Eugene 1925- AmMWSc 92
Stover, Mark Edward 1955- WhoFI 92, WhoMW 92
Stover, Merry Beth 1950- WhoMW 92
Stover, Raymond Webster 1938- AmMWSc 92
Stover, Samuel Landis 1930- AmMWSc 92
Stover, Stacey Anne 1962- WhoWest 92
Stover, W. Robert 1921- WhoRel 92
Stover, Wendy IntMPA 92
Stover, William R 1922- WhoIns 92
Stover, William Ruffner 1922- WhoFI 92, WhoMW 92
Stover-McBride, Tama Sue 1957- WhoWest 92
Stow, Archdeacon of Who 92
Stow, Christopher P. Who 92
Stow, Frederick Markley 1954- WhoFI 92
Stow, John 1525-1605 RfGEnL 91
Stow, John Montague 1911- Who 92
Stow, Julian Randolph 1935- Who 92
Stow, Ralph Conyers 1916- Who 92
Stow, Randolph Who 92
Stow, Randolph 1935- ConNov 91, IntAu&W 91, LiExTwC, RfGEnL 91, WrDr 92
Stow, Stephen Harrington 1940- AmMWSc 92
Stow, Timothy Montague Fenwick 1943- Who 92
Stowe, Andrea Marie 1959- WhoFI 92
Stowe, Ann Lynn 1958- WhoEnt 92
Stowe, Bruce Bernot 1927- AmMWSc 92
Stowe, Charles Robinson Beecher 1949- WhoAmL 92
Stowe, Clarence M 1922- AmMWSc 92
Stowe, David F 1945- AmMWSc 92
Stowe, David Henry, Jr. 1936- IntWW 91, WhoFI 92, WhoMW 92
Stowe, David Metz 1919- WhoRel 92, WrDr 92
Stowe, David William 1944- AmMWSc 92
Stowe, Harriet Beecher 1811-1896 BenetAL 91, BibAL 8, HanAmWH, RComAH
Stowe, Howard Denison 1927- AmMWSc 92
Stowe, James L. DrAPF 91
Stowe, Keith S 1943- AmMWSc 92
Stowe, Kenneth 1927- Who 92
Stowe, Leland 1899- IntAu&W 91, IntWW 91
Stowe, Louise Pitts 1932- WhoBlA 92
Stowe, Madeleine IntMPA 92
Stowe, Noel James 1942- WhoWest 92
Stowe, Nonnie 1934- WhoIns 92
Stowe, Robert Allen 1924- AmMWSc 92
Stowe, Robert Lee, III 1954- WhoFI 92
Stowe, Walter Allen 1955- WhoWest 92
Stowe, William Gordon 1925- WhoAmP 91
Stowell, Christopher R. 1966- WhoEnt 92
Stowell, Don A. 1959- WhoRel 92
Stowell, Ewell Addison 1922- AmMWSc 92, WhoMW 92
Stowell, Francis Edward 1948- WhoMW 92
Stowell, Geraldine Case 1942- WhoWest 92
Stowell, James Kent 1936- AmMWSc 92
Stowell, John Charles 1938- AmMWSc 92
Stowell, Joseph, III WhoRel 92
Stowell, Kent 1939- WhoWest 92
Stowell, Kimberly Jean 1960- WhoRel 92
Stowell, Linda Rae 1947- WhoAmP 91
Stowell, Michael James 1935- Who 92
Stowell, Phyllis DrAPF 91
Stowell, Robert Eugene 1914- AmMWSc 92
Stowell, Warren 1941- WhoAmP 91
Stowens, Daniel 1919- AmMWSc 92
Stower, Harvey 1944- WhoAmP 91
Stowers, Harry E, Jr WhoAmP 91
Stowes, Patricia Anne 1948- WhoRel 92
Stoy, Philip Joseph 1906- Who 92
Stoy, Roger William, Jr. 1945- WhoFI 92
Stoy, William S 1925- AmMWSc 92
Stoyanoff, Edward Michael 1939- WhoMW 92
Stoyanov, Milan 1933- WhoWest 92
Stoyle, Roger John B. Who 92
Stozharov, Vladimir Fedorovich 1926-1973 SovUnBD
Stozich, John P 1927- WhoAmP 91
Straach, Mildred Eileen 1928- WhoAmP 91
Straat, Patricia Ann 1936- AmMWSc 92
Straatsma, Bradley Ralph 1927- AmMWSc 92
Straavaldsen, Richard Hans 1932- WhoWest 92
Strabolgi, Baron 1914- Who 92
Stracey, John 1938- Who 92
Strachan, Alan Lockhart Thomson 1946- Who 92
Strachan, Alexander William Bruce 1917- Who 92
Strachan, Benjamin Leckie 1924- Who 92
Strachan, Donald Stewart 1932- AmMWSc 92
Strachan, Douglas Frederick 1933- Who 92
Strachan, Douglas Mark Arthur 1946- Who 92
Strachan, Graham Robert 1931- Who 92
Strachan, J. George 1910- WrDr 92
Strachan, John R. 1916- WhoBlA 92
Strachan, Lloyd Calvin, Jr. 1954- WhoBlA 92
Strachan, Michael Francis 1919- Who 92
Strachan, Richard James 1928- WhoBlA 92
Strachan, Robert Martin Who 92N
Strachan, Valerie Patricia Marie 1940- Who 92
Strachan, Walter 1910- Who 92
Strachan, William Merion 1955- WhoMW 92
Strachan, William Michael John 1937- AmMWSc 92
Stracher, Alfred 1930- AmMWSc 92
Strachey Who 92
Strachey, Alix 1892-1973 ConAu 133
Strachey, Charles 1934- Who 92
Strachey, John 1901-1963 FacFETw
Strachey, Lytton 1880-1932 FacFETw
Strachey, Rosemary TwCPaSc
Strachey, William BenetAL 91
Strack, Otto Dirk Leo 1943- WhoMW 92
Stracke, Win d1991 NewYTBS 91
Straczynski, Joseph Michael 1954- WhoWest 92
Strada, Samuel Joseph 1942- AmMWSc 92
Stradal, Walter John 1927- WhoMW 92
Stradbroke, Earl of 1937- Who 92
Stradella, Alessandro 1644-1682 NewAmDM
Strader, Douglas J. 1957- WhoRel 92
Strader, Gayle Gilbert 1937- WhoMW 92
Strader, John Jacob, IV 1923- WhoEnt 92
Strader, Karl David 1929- WhoRel 92
Strader, Laurie Ann 1968- WhoRel 92
Strader, Timothy Richards 1956- WhoAmL 92
Stradivari, Antonio 1644-1737 NewAmDM
Stradley, James Grant 1932- AmMWSc 92
Stradley, Mark Edward 1959- WhoAmL 92
Stradley, Norman H 1924- AmMWSc 92
Stradley, Richard Lee WhoAmL 92

**Stradley**, William Jackson 1939- *WhoAmL 92*
**Stradley**, William Lamar 1940- *WhoFI 92*
**Stradling**, Donald George 1929- *Who 92*
**Stradling**, Harry, Jr. 1925- *IntMPA 92*
**Stradling**, Leslie Edward 1908- *IntWW 91, Who 92, WrDr 92*
**Stradling**, Lester J, Jr 1916- *AmMWSc 92*
**Stradling**, Samuel Stuart 1937- *AmMWSc 92*
**Stradling Thomas**, John d1991 *Who 92N*
**Straeter**, Jane L. 1919- *WhoMW 92*
**Straf**, Miron L 1943- *AmMWSc 92*
**Straffin**, Philip Douglas, Jr. 1943- *WhoMW 92*
**Straffon**, Ralph Atwood 1928- *AmMWSc 92, WhoMW 92*
**Strafford**, Earl of 1936- *Who 92*
**Strafuss**, Albert Charles 1928- *AmMWSc 92*
**Stragalas**, George, III 1946- *WhoAmP 91*
**Straham**, Clarence Clifford, Jr. 1956- *WhoBlA 92*
**Strahan**, Alexander *DcLB 106 [port]*
**Strahan**, Bradley R. *DrAPF 91*
**Strahan**, Julia Celestine 1938- *WhoWest 92*
**Strahan**, William 1715-1785 *BlkwCEP*
**Strahl**, Erwin Otto 1930- *AmMWSc 92*
**Strahle**, Ronald H 1921- *WhoAmP 91*
**Strahle**, Warren C 1938- *AmMWSc 92*
**Strahler**, Arthur Newell 1918- *WhoWest 92*
**Strahm**, Norman Dale 1940- *AmMWSc 92*
**Strahs**, Gerald 1938- *AmMWSc 92*
**Strahs**, Kenneth Robert *AmMWSc 92*
**Straiges**, Tony *ConTFT 9*
**Straight**, Beatrice 1918- *IntMPA 92*
**Straight**, Beatrice Whitney 1918- *WhoEnt 92*
**Straight**, Cathy A. 1963- *WhoBlA 92*
**Straight**, Clio Edwin d1991 *NewYTBS 91*
**Straight**, Earl Kenneth 1960- *WhoAmL 92*
**Straight**, H Joseph 1951- *AmMWSc 92*
**Straight**, James William 1940- *AmMWSc 92*
**Straight**, Michael 1916- *TwCWW 91, WrDr 92*
**Straight**, Richard Coleman 1937- *AmMWSc 92*
**Straile**, William Edwin 1931- *AmMWSc 92*
**Strain**, Boyd Ray 1935- *AmMWSc 92*
**Strain**, Herbert Arthur, III 1954- *WhoMW 92*
**Strain**, James Alexandria 1944- *WhoAmL 92*
**Strain**, James E 1923- *AmMWSc 92*
**Strain**, John Dennis 1946- *WhoRel 92*
**Strain**, John Henry 1922- *AmMWSc 92*
**Strain**, John Thomas 1939- *WhoWest 92*
**Strain**, Larry Alan 1958- *WhoFI 92*
**Strain**, R H 1941- *WhoAmP 91*
**Strain**, Robert W 1924- *WhoIns 92*
**Strain**, Suzy Barbara *WhoEnt 92*
**Strain**, Wesley Baker 1958- *WhoAmL 92*
**Strait**, Bradley Justus 1932- *AmMWSc 92*
**Strait**, Clifford Neil 1934- *WhoRel 92*
**Strait**, George 1952- *WhoEnt 92*
**Strait**, George A. 1914- *WhoBlA 92*
**Strait**, George Alfred, Jr. 1945- *WhoBlA 92*
**Strait**, John 1915- *AmMWSc 92*
**Strait**, Lindsy Edward 1955- *WhoWest 92*
**Strait**, Peggy 1933- *AmMWSc 92*
**Strait**, Ralph 1936- *WhoEnt 92*
**Straiton**, Archie Waugh 1907- *AmMWSc 92*
**Straka**, George John 1937- *WhoWest 92*
**Straka**, Laszlo Richard 1934- *WhoFI 92*
**Straka**, William Charles 1940- *AmMWSc 92*
**Straka**, William Charles, II 1940- *WhoWest 92*
**Strake**, George W, Jr 1935- *WhoAmP 91*
**Straker**, Bryan John 1929- *Who 92*
**Straker**, Ivan Charles 1928- *Who 92*
**Straker**, J F 1904- *IntAu&W 91, WrDr 92*
**Straker**, Michael 1928- *Who 92*
**Straley**, Joseph Paul 1942- *AmMWSc 92*
**Straley**, Joseph Ward 1914- *AmMWSc 92*
**Straley**, Tina 1943- *AmMWSc 92*
**Straling**, Phillip Francis 1933- *WhoRel 92, WhoWest 92*
**Stralka**, Albert R 1940- *AmMWSc 92*
**Stram**, Karen D 1940- *WhoAmP 91*
**Stranahan**, Robert Paul, Jr. 1929- *WhoFI 92*
**Strand**, Ann S 1929- *WhoAmP 91*
**Strand**, Barbara Joan 1949- *WhoFI 92*
**Strand**, Curt Robert 1920- *WhoFI 92*
**Strand**, David Arthur 1952- *WhoWest 92*
**Strand**, Dean Paul 1963- *WhoEnt 92*
**Strand**, Fleur Lillian 1928- *AmMWSc 92*
**Strand**, Gregory Dwaine 1957- *WhoFI 92*
**Strand**, James Cameron 1943- *AmMWSc 92*
**Strand**, John A, III 1938- *AmMWSc 92*
**Strand**, John Gregory 1951- *WhoAmP 91*
**Strand**, Kaj Aage 1907- *AmMWSc 92*
**Strand**, Kenneth A. 1927- *WrDr 92*
**Strand**, Kenneth Albert 1927- *WhoRel 92*
**Strand**, Kenneth T. 1931- *Who 92*
**Strand**, Leof Thomas 1944- *WhoAmL 92*
**Strand**, Mark *DrAPF 91*
**Strand**, Mark 1934- *BenetAL 91, ConPo 91, WrDr 92*
**Strand**, Paul 1890-1976 *DcTwDes, FacFETw*
**Strand**, Ray Walter 1924- *WhoWest 92*
**Strand**, Richard Alvin 1926- *AmMWSc 92*
**Strand**, Richard Carl 1933- *AmMWSc 92*
**Strand**, Roger Gordon 1934- *WhoAmL 92, WhoWest 92*
**Strand**, Ted Raymond, Jr. 1945- *WhoMW 92*
**Strand**, Thomas *DrAPF 91*
**Strand**, Timothy Carl 1948- *AmMWSc 92*
**Strandberg**, Keith William 1957- *IntAu&W 91*
**Strandberg**, Lee R. 1945- *WhoWest 92*
**Strandberg**, Malcom Woodrow Pershing 1919- *AmMWSc 92*
**Strandberg**, Newton Dwight 1921- *WhoEnt 92*
**Strandberg**, Rebecca Newman 1951- *WhoAmL 92*
**Strandhagen**, Adolf G 1914- *AmMWSc 92*
**Strandhagen**, Adolf Gustav 1914- *WhoMW 92*
**Strandhoy**, Jack W 1944- *AmMWSc 92*
**Strandjord**, Paul Edphil 1931- *AmMWSc 92*
**Strandjord**, Ronald Millard 1932- *WhoFI 92*
**Strandness**, Donald Eugene, Jr 1928- *AmMWSc 92*
**Strang** *Who 92*
**Strang**, Baron 1922- *Who 92*
**Strang**, Charles Daniel 1921- *WhoFI 92, WhoMW 92*
**Strang**, Charles Ward 1932- *WhoWest 92*
**Strang**, Gavin Steel 1943- *Who 92*
**Strang**, Gilbert 1934- *AmMWSc 92*
**Strang**, Ian 1886-1952 *TwCPaSc*
**Strang**, Michael L 1929- *WhoAmP 91*
**Strang**, Robert M 1926- *AmMWSc 92*
**Strang**, Robyn 1927- *WhoAmP 91*
**Strang**, Ruth Hancock 1923- *AmMWSc 92*
**Strang**, Stephen Edward 1951- *WhoRel 92*
**Strang**, W Gilbert 1934- *AmMWSc 92*
**Strang**, William 1859-1921 *TwCPaSc*
**Strang**, William 1893-1978 *FacFETw*
**Strang**, William John 1921- *Who 92*
**Strang Burgess**, Meredith Nancy 1956- *WhoAmP 91*
**Strang Steel**, William *Who 92*
**Strange**, Baroness 1928- *Who 92*
**Strange**, Alonzo, Jr. 1947- *WhoBlA 92*
**Strange**, Curtis *IntWW 91*
**Strange**, Donald Ernest 1944- *WhoFI 92*
**Strange**, Gerald Leon 1931- *WhoBlA 92*
**Strange**, James Francis 1938- *IntAu&W 91, WhoRel 92*
**Strange**, Lloyd K 1922- *AmMWSc 92*
**Strange**, Oliver 1871-1952 *TwCWW 91*
**Strange**, Richard Eugene 1928- *WhoEnt 92, WhoWest 92*
**Strange**, Ronald Stephen 1943- *AmMWSc 92*
**Strange**, Sidney Barth 1943- *WhoAmL 92*
**Strange**, Susan 1923- *Who 92*
**Strange**, William Austin 1922- *WhoAmP 91*
**Strange**, William Bazzle, Jr. 1946- *WhoRel 92*
**Stranger**, Joyce *IntAu&W 91, WrDr 92*
**Stranger**, Peter 1949- *WhoFI 92*
**Stranges**, Anthony Nicholas 1936- *AmMWSc 92*
**Stranges**, Frank Ernest 1927- *WhoRel 92*
**Strangfeld**, Diana Kay 1962- *WhoEnt 92*
**Strangi**, Thomas Carl 1957- *WhoFI 92*
**Strangis**, Gregory Joseph 1951- *WhoEnt 92*
**Strangway**, David W 1934- *AmMWSc 92*
**Strangway**, David William 1934- *IntWW 91, WhoWest 92*
**Strangways** *Who 92*
**Straniere**, Robert A 1941- *WhoAmP 91*
**Strano**, Alfonso J 1927- *AmMWSc 92*
**Strano**, Joseph J 1937- *AmMWSc 92*
**Stranraer-Mull**, Gerald 1942- *Who 92*
**Stransky**, Charles Arthur 1946- *WhoEnt 92*
**Stransky**, John Janos 1923- *AmMWSc 92*
**Stranz**, Benon 1918- *IntWW 91*
**Strappello**, Richard L. 1953- *WhoRel 92*
**Strasberg**, Lee 1901-1982 *FacFETw*
**Strasberg**, Murray 1917- *AmMWSc 92*
**Strasberg**, Susan 1938- *IntMPA 92, WhoEnt 92*
**Strasburger**, Janusz 1925- *IntAu&W 91*
**Strasburger**, John Hunter 1937- *WhoAmL 92*
**Strasburger**, Victor C. 1949- *WhoWest 92*
**Strasfogel**, Ian 1940- *WhoEnt 92*
**Strasfogel**, Ignace 1909- *WhoEnt 92*
**Strasma**, John Drinan 1932- *WhoMW 92*
**Strasmich**, Michael 1954- *WhoEnt 92*
**Strassberg**, Stephen *IntMPA 92*
**Strassburger**, John Harvey 1948- *WhoMW 92*
**Strassburger**, John R. 1942- *WhoMW 92*
**Strassenburg**, Arnold Adolph 1927- *AmMWSc 92*
**Strasser**, Alfred Anthony 1927- *AmMWSc 92*
**Strasser**, Daniel Charles Joachim 1929- *IntWW 91*
**Strasser**, Elvira Rapaport *AmMWSc 92*
**Strasser**, Gregor 1892-1934 *BiDExR, EncTR 91 [port]*
**Strasser**, Hans 1919- *IntWW 91*
**Strasser**, John Albert 1945- *AmMWSc 92*
**Strasser**, Otto 1897-1974 *BiDExR, EncTR 91 [port]*
**Strasser**, Stephan 1905- *ConAu 133*
**Strasser**, Todd *DrAPF 91*
**Strasser**, Todd 1950- *WrDr 92*
**Strasshofer**, Roland Henry, Jr. 1924- *WhoAmL 92*
**Stratas**, Jack George 1942- *WhoRel 92*
**Stratas**, Teresa 1938- *FacFETw, IntWW 91, NewAmDM*
**Stratemeyer**, Edward 1863-1930 *BenetAL 91*
**Stratemeyer**, Edward L. 1862-1930 *SmATA 67 [port]*
**Straten**, Allan Roy 1940- *WhoEnt 92*
**Strater**, Henry 1896-1987 *FacFETw*
**Stratford**, Dale E *WhoAmP 91*
**Stratford**, Eugene Scott 1942- *AmMWSc 92*
**Stratford**, H Philip *TwCSFW 91*
**Stratford**, Joseph 1923- *AmMWSc 92*
**Stratford**, Neil Martin 1938- *Who 92*
**Stratford**, R P 1925- *AmMWSc 92*
**Stratford**, William 1844-1908 *BiInAmS*
**Strathairn**, David *IntMPA 92*
**Strathallan**, Viscount 1935- *Who 92*
**Strathalmond**, Baron 1947- *Who 92*
**Strathcarron**, Baron 1924- *Who 92*
**Strathclyde**, Baron 1960- *Who 92*
**Strathcona And Mount Royal**, Baron 1923- *Who 92*
**Strathdee**, Graeme Gilroy 1942- *AmMWSc 92*
**Stratheden**, Baron 1934- *Who 92*
**Strather**, Vivian Carpenter 1952- *WhoBlA 92*
**Strathern**, Andrew Jamieson 1939- *Who 92*
**Strathern**, Jeffrey Neal 1948- *AmMWSc 92*
**Strathern**, Marilyn 1941- *Who 92*
**Strathmann**, Richard Ray 1941- *AmMWSc 92*
**Strathmore And Kinghorne**, Earl of 1957- *Who 92*
**Strathnaver**, Lord 1947- *Who 92*
**Strathspey**, Baron 1912- *Who 92*
**Stratidakis**, Eileen H. *DrAPF 91*
**Stratman**, Frederick William 1927- *AmMWSc 92*
**Stratmeyer**, Melvin Edward 1942- *AmMWSc 92*
**Straton**, George Douglas 1916- *WhoRel 92*
**Straton**, John Roach 1875-1929 *RelLAm 91*
**Stratonice** *EncAmaz 91*
**Stratt**, Randy Allen 1956- *WhoFI 92*
**Stratt**, Richard Mark 1954- *AmMWSc 92*
**Strattan**, Eric Jesse 1956- *WhoRel 92*
**Strattan**, Robert Dean 1936- *AmMWSc 92*
**Stratton**, Andrew 1918- *Who 92*
**Stratton**, Basil 1906- *Who 92*
**Stratton**, Cedric 1931- *AmMWSc 92*
**Stratton**, Charles Abner 1916- *AmMWSc 92*
**Stratton**, Charles Edward 1941- *WhoAmL 92*
**Stratton**, Charlotte Dianne 1929- *AmMWSc 92*
**Stratton**, Clifford James 1945- *AmMWSc 92*
**Stratton**, David Hodges 1927- *WhoWest 92*
**Stratton**, Donald Brendan 1941- *AmMWSc 92*
**Stratton**, Edith Lou 1930- *WhoAmP 91*
**Stratton**, Frank E 1937- *AmMWSc 92*
**Stratton**, George Frederic 1852- *ScFEYrs*
**Stratton**, Gregory Alexander 1946- *WhoAmP 91*
**Stratton**, Hal 1950- *WhoAmP 91*
**Stratton**, J. M. *WrDr 92*
**Stratton**, James Forrest 1943- *AmMWSc 92, WhoMW 92*
**Stratton**, James Thompson 1830-1903 *BiInAmS*
**Stratton**, Jessie Gray 1947- *WhoAmP 91*
**Stratton**, John 1925- *IntMPA 92*
**Stratton**, John Caryl 1920- *WhoFI 92*
**Stratton**, Julius A. 1901- *IntWW 91*
**Stratton**, Julius Adams 1901- *AmMWSc 92, Who 92*
**Stratton**, Julius Augustus 1924- *WhoMW 92*
**Stratton**, Kenneth Ray 1962- *WhoMW 92*
**Stratton**, Kerry 1952- *WhoEnt 92*
**Stratton**, Lewis Palmer 1937- *AmMWSc 92*
**Stratton**, Lois Jean 1927- *WhoAmP 91*
**Stratton**, Owen Bradley 1963- *WhoFI 92, WhoMW 92*
**Stratton**, Peter Hunt 1948- *WhoMW 92*
**Stratton**, Rebecca *IntAu&W 91*
**Stratton**, Richard LeRoy 1925- *WhoMW 92*
**Stratton**, Robert 1928- *AmMWSc 92*
**Stratton**, Robert Alan 1936- *AmMWSc 92*
**Stratton**, Robert John 1928- *WhoAmP 91*
**Stratton**, Roy Franklin, Jr 1929- *AmMWSc 92*
**Stratton**, Roy Olin, Mrs. *Who 92*
**Stratton**, Samuel S. 1916-1990 *CurBio 91N*
**Stratton**, Thomas *TwCSFW 91, WrDr 92*
**Stratton**, Thomas Fairlamb 1929- *AmMWSc 92*
**Stratton**, Walter Love 1926- *WhoAmL 92*
**Stratton**, Wayne Thomas 1933- *WhoAmL 92*
**Stratton**, William Grant 1914- *WhoAmP 91*
**Stratton**, William Hector 1916- *Who 92*
**Stratton**, William R 1922- *AmMWSc 92*
**Stratton**, Wilmer Joseph 1932- *AmMWSc 92*
**Stratton-Morris**, Madeline Robinson M. 1906- *WhoBlA 92*
**Stratton-Porter**, Gene *BenetAL 91*
**Straty**, Richard Robert 1929- *AmMWSc 92*
**Straub**, Cheryl Ann 1952- *WhoMW 92*
**Straub**, Chester John 1937- *WhoAmL 92*
**Straub**, Conrad P 1916- *AmMWSc 92*
**Straub**, Darel K 1935- *AmMWSc 92*
**Straub**, F. Bruno 1914- *IntWW 91*
**Straub**, Gerard Thomas 1947- *IntAu&W 91*
**Straub**, Jean-Marie 1933- *IntDcF 2-2*
**Straub**, Jean-Marie, and Daniele Huillet *IntDcF 2-2*
**Straub**, Joseph John 1930- *WhoAmP 91*
**Straub**, Larry Gene 1959- *WhoMW 92*
**Straub**, Marianne 1909- *Who 92*
**Straub**, Peter 1943- *WrDr 92*
**Straub**, Peter Francis 1943- *IntAu&W 91, WhoEnt 92*
**Straub**, Peter Thornton 1939- *WhoAmL 92*
**Straub**, Richard Wayne 1940- *AmMWSc 92*
**Straub**, Robert W 1920- *WhoAmP 91*
**Straub**, Steven Otto 1945- *WhoWest 92*
**Straub**, Thomas Stuart 1941- *AmMWSc 92*
**Straub**, William Albert 1931- *AmMWSc 92*
**Straub**, Wolf Deter 1927- *AmMWSc 92*
**Straube**, Robert Leonard 1917- *AmMWSc 92*
**Straubel**, John Frederick 1928- *WhoWest 92*
**Strauber**, Andrew Craig 1952- *WhoEnt 92*
**Straubing**, Harold Elk 1918- *IntAu&W 91*
**Straubinger**, Robert M 1953- *AmMWSc 92*
**Strauch**, Arthur Roger, III *AmMWSc 92*
**Strauch**, Donald William 1926- *WhoAmP 91*
**Strauch**, Eduard 1906-1955 *EncTR 91*
**Strauch**, John L. 1939- *WhoAmL 92*
**Strauch**, Karl 1922- *AmMWSc 92*
**Strauch**, Ralph Eugene 1937- *AmMWSc 92*
**Strauch**, Richard G *AmMWSc 92*
**Straughan**, Gary Marvin 1941- *WhoRel 92*
**Straughan**, Isdale Margaret 1939- *AmMWSc 92*
**Straughn**, Arthur Belknap 1944- *AmMWSc 92*
**Straughn**, James Henry 1877- *RelLAm 91*
**Straughn**, M N d1919 *BiInAmS*
**Straughn**, Robert Oscar, III 1942- *WhoAmL 92, WhoMW 92*
**Straughn**, William Ringgold, Jr 1913 *AmMWSc 92*
**Straughter**, Edgar, Sr. 1929- *WhoBlA 92*
**Straumanis**, John Janis, Jr 1935- *AmMWSc 92*
**Straumann**, Heinrich 1902- *WrDr 92*
**Straumfjord**, Jon Vidalin, Jr 1925- *AmMWSc 92*
**Straus**, Alan Edward 1924- *AmMWSc 92*
**Straus**, Alan Gordon 1952- *WhoAmL 92*
**Straus**, Austin *DrAPF 91*
**Straus**, Daniel Steven 1946- *AmMWSc 92*
**Straus**, David Bradley 1930- *AmMWSc 92*
**Straus**, David Conrad 1947- *AmMWSc 92*
**Straus**, David Edward 1957- *WhoRel 92*
**Straus**, Dennis *DrAPF 91*
**Straus**, Dorothea 1916- *IntAu&W 91, WrDr 92*
**Straus**, Francis Howe 1932- *WhoMW 92*

**Straus**, Francis Howe, II 1932- *AmMWSc 92*
**Straus**, Helen Lorna Puttkammer 1933- *AmMWSc 92*
**Straus**, Jerry Alan 1950- *WhoFI 92*
**Straus**, Joe Melvin 1946- *AmMWSc 92*
**Straus**, Joseph Pennington 1911- *WhoAmL 92*
**Straus**, Jozef 1946- *AmMWSc 92*
**Straus**, Marc J 1943- *AmMWSc 92*
**Straus**, Murray A. 1926- *WrDr 92*
**Straus**, Neil Alexander 1943- *AmMWSc 92*
**Straus**, Oscar 1870-1954 *NewAmDM*
**Straus**, Oscar Solomon 1850-1926 *AmPeW*
**Straus**, Reuben d1991 *NewYTBS 91*
**Straus**, Robert 1923- *AmMWSc 92, IntWW 91*
**Straus**, Roger W., Jr. 1917- *IntWW 91*
**Straus**, Seymour Harold 1939- *WhoFI 92*
**Straus**, Stephen Robert 1947- *WhoFI 92*
**Straus**, Thomas Michael 1931- *AmMWSc 92*
**Straus**, Werner 1911- *AmMWSc 92*
**Strausbauch**, Paul Henry 1941- *AmMWSc 92*
**Strausbaugh**, John *DrAPF 91*
**Strausberg**, Sanford I 1931- *AmMWSc 92*
**Strause**, Sterling Franklin 1931- *AmMWSc 92*
**Strauser**, Charles *WhoRel 92*
**Strauser**, Robert Wayne 1943- *WhoAmL 92*
**Strauser**, Wilbur Alexander 1924- *AmMWSc 92*
**Strauss** *Who 92*
**Strauss**, Baron 1901- *Who 92*
**Strauss**, Alan Jay 1927- *AmMWSc 92*
**Strauss**, Albert James 1910- *WhoFI 92*
**Strauss**, Alvin Manosh 1943- *AmMWSc 92*
**Strauss**, Andrew Alexander 1953- *WhoFI 92*
**Strauss**, Annette *WhoAmP 91*
**Strauss**, Arnold Wilbur 1945- *AmMWSc 92*
**Strauss**, Arthur Joseph Louis 1933- *AmMWSc 92*
**Strauss**, Audrey 1947- *WhoAmL 92*
**Strauss**, Bella S 1920- *AmMWSc 92*
**Strauss**, Bernard 1904- *AmMWSc 92*
**Strauss**, Bernard S 1927- *AmMWSc 92*
**Strauss**, Botho 1944- *IntAu&W 91, IntWW 91*
**Strauss**, Bruce Paul 1942- *AmMWSc 92*
**Strauss**, Carl Richard 1936- *AmMWSc 92*
**Strauss**, Catherine B. 1947- *WhoFI 92*
**Strauss**, Charles A 1935- *WhoIns 92*
**Strauss**, Charles Michael 1938- *AmMWSc 92*
**Strauss**, Claude L. *Who 92*
**Strauss**, David Levi *DrAPF 91*
**Strauss**, Ellen Glowacki 1938- *AmMWSc 92*
**Strauss**, Elliott William 1923- *AmMWSc 92*
**Strauss**, Emil 1866-1960 *EncTR 91 [port]*
**Strauss**, Eric James 1947- *WhoMW 92*
**Strauss**, Eric L 1923- *AmMWSc 92*
**Strauss**, Erich 1911-1981 *ConAu 135*
**Strauss**, Frances Goetzmann 1904-1991 *ConAu 134*
**Strauss**, Franz Josef 1915-1988 *FacFETw*
**Strauss**, Fred 1925- *WhoEnt 92*
**Strauss**, Frederick Bodo 1931- *AmMWSc 92*
**Strauss**, Gary J. 1949- *WhoAmL 92*
**Strauss**, Gary Joseph 1953- *WhoFI 92*
**Strauss**, George 1921- *AmMWSc 92*
**Strauss**, H J 1920- *AmMWSc 92*
**Strauss**, Harlee S 1950- *AmMWSc 92*
**Strauss**, Harold C 1940- *AmMWSc 92*
**Strauss**, Henry L 1927- *WhoAmP 91*
**Strauss**, Herbert A. 1918- *ConAu 133*
**Strauss**, Herbert L 1936- *AmMWSc 92*
**Strauss**, Jacobus Gideon Nel 1900- *Who 92*
**Strauss**, James Henry 1938- *AmMWSc 92*
**Strauss**, James Lester 1944- *WhoMW 92*
**Strauss**, Jay Jerald 1936- *WhoFI 92*
**Strauss**, Jennifer 1933- *ConPo 91, WrDr 92*
**Strauss**, Jerome Frank, III 1947- *AmMWSc 92*
**Strauss**, Johann, Jr. 1825-1899 *NewAmDM*
**Strauss**, Johann, Sr. 1804-1849 *NewAmDM*
**Strauss**, John S 1926- *AmMWSc 92*
**Strauss**, John Steinert 1926- *WhoMW 92*
**Strauss**, Leon Frank 1925- *WhoFI 92*
**Strauss**, Leonard 1927- *AmMWSc 92*
**Strauss**, Lewis Lictenstein 1896-1974 *FacFETw*
**Strauss**, Lotte 1913- *AmMWSc 92*
**Strauss**, Marjorie *DrAPF 91*
**Strauss**, Mary Jo 1927- *AmMWSc 92*
**Strauss**, Michael S 1947- *AmMWSc 92*
**Strauss**, Monty Joseph 1945- *AmMWSc 92*
**Strauss**, Nicholas Albert 1942- *Who 92*
**Strauss**, Olin Bernard 1940- *WhoAmP 91*
**Strauss**, Peter 1947- *IntMPA 92, WhoEnt 92*
**Strauss**, Peter E. 1940- *IntMPA 92*
**Strauss**, Peter J 1942- *WhoAmP 91*
**Strauss**, Peter Lester 1940- *WhoAmL 92*
**Strauss**, Phyllis R 1943- *AmMWSc 92*
**Strauss**, Randy Keith 1954- *WhoMW 92*
**Strauss**, Richard 1864-1949 *EncTR 91 [port], FacFETw [port], NewAmDM*
**Strauss**, Richard Harry *AmMWSc 92*
**Strauss**, Richard L. 1933- *ConAu 36NR*
**Strauss**, Robert 1918- *News 91 [port]*
**Strauss**, Robert David 1951- *WhoAmL 92*
**Strauss**, Robert Lynn 1959- *WhoRel 92*
**Strauss**, Robert Philip *WhoFI 92*
**Strauss**, Robert R 1929- *AmMWSc 92*
**Strauss**, Robert S 1918- *WhoAmP 91*
**Strauss**, Robert Schwarz 1918- *IntWW 91, NewYTBS 91*
**Strauss**, Rodolfo *WhoHisp 92*
**Strauss**, Roger William 1927- *AmMWSc 92*
**Strauss**, Ronald George 1939- *AmMWSc 92*
**Strauss**, Simon Wolf 1920- *AmMWSc 92*
**Strauss**, Stephen Barclay 1943- *WhoAmP 91*
**Strauss**, Steven 1930- *AmMWSc 92*
**Strauss**, Stuart *ScFEYrs*
**Strauss**, Thomas W. 1942- *WhoFI 92*
**Strauss**, Ulrich Paul 1920- *AmMWSc 92*
**Strauss**, Walter 1923- *AmMWSc 92*
**Strauss**, Walter A 1937- *AmMWSc 92*
**Strauss**, William Victor 1942- *WhoAmL 92*
**Strauss und Torney**, Lulu von 1873-1956 *EncTR 91 [port]*
**Strausser**, Helen R 1922- *AmMWSc 92*
**Strausz**, Otto Peter 1924- *AmMWSc 92*
**Strausz-Hupe**, Robert 1903- *IntWW 91, WhoAmP 91*
**Strautz**, Robert Lee 1935- *AmMWSc 92*
**Stravers**, David Eugene 1949- *WhoRel 92*
**Stravinsky**, Igor 1882-1971 *NewAmDM, RComAH*
**Stravinsky**, Igor Fedorovich 1882-1971 *FacFETw [port]*
**Straw**, Alice Elizabeth *Who 92*
**Straw**, Gary Robert 1951- *WhoMW 92*
**Straw**, Gerald Kingsley 1943- *WhoMW 92*
**Straw**, Jack 1946- *Who 92*
**Straw**, James Ashley 1932- *AmMWSc 92*
**Straw**, Lawrence Joseph, Jr. 1945- *WhoAmL 92*
**Straw**, Robert Niccolls 1938- *AmMWSc 92*
**Straw**, Syd *WhoEnt 92*
**Straw**, Thomas Eugene 1936- *AmMWSc 92*
**Straw**, William Thomas 1931- *AmMWSc 92*
**Strawberry**, Darryl 1962- *WhoBlA 92, WhoWest 92*
**Strawbridge**, Jesse Ronald 1950- *WhoMW 92*
**Strawbridge**, Peter S. 1938- *WhoFI 92*
**Strawbridge**, Steven James 1948- *WhoAmL 92*
**Strawderman**, Wayne Alan 1936- *AmMWSc 92*
**Strawhecker**, Kurt James 1954- *WhoMW 92*
**Strawhecker**, Paul Joseph 1947- *WhoMW 92*
**Strawn**, Aimee Williams 1925- *WhoBlA 92*
**Strawn**, David Updegraff 1936- *WhoAmL 92*
**Strawn**, Harry Culp 1918- *WhoAmP 91*
**Strawn**, John 1950- *WhoWest 92*
**Strawn**, Oliver P, Jr 1925- *AmMWSc 92*
**Strawn**, Oliver Perry, Jr 1925- *WhoAmP 91*
**Strawn**, Robert Kirk 1922- *AmMWSc 92*
**Strawn-Hamilton**, Frank 1934- *WhoEnt 92*
**Strawson**, Galen 1952- *ConAu 133*
**Strawson**, Galen J. *WrDr 92*
**Strawson**, John Michael 1921- *Who 92*
**Strawson**, Peter 1919- *Who 92, WrDr 92*
**Strawson**, Peter Frederick 1919- *IntAu&W 91, IntWW 91*
**Stray**, Svenn Thorkild 1922- *IntWW 91*
**Strayer**, David Lowell 1955- *AmMWSc 92*
**Strayer**, E. Ward *SmATA 67*
**Strayer**, Gene Paul 1942- *WhoRel 92*
**Strayer**, Richard Lee 1934- *WhoFI 92*
**Strayhorn**, Billy 1915-1967 *NewAmDM*
**Strayhorn**, Earl Carlton 1948- *WhoBlA 92*
**Strayhorn**, Earl E. 1918- *WhoBlA 92*
**Strayhorn**, Lloyd *WhoBlA 92*
**Strayhorn**, Ralph Nichols, Jr. 1923- *WhoAmL 92*
**Strayhorne**, Pauline 1926- *WhoBlA 92*
**Strazanac**, Joann Marie 1954- *WhoMW 92*
**Strazdins**, Edward 1918- *AmMWSc 92*
**Strazewski**, John William 1951- *WhoMW 92*
**Strazzella**, James Anthony 1939- *WhoAmL 92*
**Stream**, Arnold 1950- *WhoAmL 92*
**Streamer**, Col D *IntAu&W 91X*
**Streams**, Frederick Arthur 1933- *AmMWSc 92*
**Streams**, Peter John 1935- *Who 92*
**Strean**, Richard Lockey 1939- *WhoFI 92*
**Streat**, Van, Sr 1954- *WhoAmP 91*
**Streatfeild**, Timothy Stuart Champion 1926- *Who 92*
**Streatfeild-James**, John Jocelyn 1929- *Who 92*
**Streator**, Edward James 1930- *Who 92*
**Strebe**, David Diedrich 1918- *AmMWSc 92*
**Streby**, John A. 1951- *WhoAmL 92*
**Strecker**, David Eugene 1950- *WhoAmL 92*
**Strecker**, E. Bradley 1957- *WhoMW 92*
**Strecker**, George Edison 1938- *AmMWSc 92, WhoMW 92*
**Strecker**, Harold Arthur 1918- *AmMWSc 92*
**Strecker**, Herman 1836-1901 *BiInAmS*
**Strecker**, Ian 1939- *WhoFI 92*
**Strecker**, Ignatius J. 1917- *WhoRel 92*
**Strecker**, Joseph Lawrence 1932- *AmMWSc 92*
**Strecker**, William D *AmMWSc 92*
**Streckfus**, George Martin 1956- *WhoAmL 92*
**Streckfuss**, Joseph Larry 1931- *AmMWSc 92*
**Streckfuss**, Robert John 1944- *WhoEnt 92*
**Stredder**, James Cecil 1912- *Who 92*
**Streeb**, Gordon 1935- *WhoAmP 91*
**Streebin**, Leale E 1934- *AmMWSc 92*
**Streel**, Lucien Alphonse Joseph 1911-1946 *BiDExR*
**Streelman**, Bryan Peter 1947- *WhoAmL 92*
**Streep**, Meryl *NewYTBS 91 [port]*
**Streep**, Meryl 1949- *IntMPA 92, IntWW 91, Who 92, WhoEnt 92*
**Streep**, Meryl 1951- *FacFETw*
**Streeruwitz**, William H Ritter Von 1833- *BiInAmS*
**Street**, Alfred Billings 1811-1881 *BenetAL 91*
**Street**, Anne A. 1942- *WhoBlA 92*
**Street**, Anthony Austin 1926- *IntWW 91, Who 92*
**Street**, Brian Jeffrey 1955- *ConAu 133*
**Street**, Cyrus H. 1843-1913 *AmPeW*
**Street**, Dana Morris 1910- *AmMWSc 92*
**Street**, David Hargett 1943- *WhoFI 92*
**Street**, David Keith 1962- *WhoEnt 92*
**Street**, David Prince 1945- *WhoAmL 92*
**Street**, Douglas Dean 1935- *WhoFI 92*
**Street**, Erica Catherine 1958- *WhoAmL 92*
**Street**, Evelyn *TwCPaSc*
**Street**, Jabez Curry 1906- *AmMWSc 92*
**Street**, James 1903-1954 *BenetAL 91*
**Street**, James Stewart 1934- *AmMWSc 92*
**Street**, Jimmy Joe 1945- *AmMWSc 92*
**Street**, John Edmund Dudley 1918- *Who 92*
**Street**, John F *WhoAmP 91*
**Street**, John Malcolm 1924- *AmMWSc 92*
**Street**, Julia Montgomery *IntAu&W 91*
**Street**, Julia Montgomery 1898- *WrDr 92*
**Street**, Julian 1879-1947 *BenetAL 91*
**Street**, Laurence 1926- *Who 92*
**Street**, Laurence Whistler 1926- *IntWW 91*
**Street**, Michael James 1959- *WhoMW 92*
**Street**, Pamela 1921- *IntAu&W 91*
**Street**, Peter 1951- *TwCPaSc*
**Street**, Robert 1920- *IntWW 91, Who 92*
**Street**, Robert Elliott 1912- *AmMWSc 92*
**Street**, Robert L 1934- *AmMWSc 92*
**Street**, Robert Lewis 1928- *AmMWSc 92*
**Street**, Robert Lynnwood 1934- *WhoWest 92*
**Street**, Sandra Dierker 1942- *WhoMW 92*
**Street**, Stephan Edward 1960- *WhoRel 92*
**Street**, T. Milton 1941- *WhoBlA 92*
**Street**, Vivian Sue 1954- *WhoBlA 92*
**Street**, Walter Scott, III 1944- *WhoAmL 92*
**Street**, William G 1917- *AmMWSc 92*
**Street**, Woodrow W. 1955- *WhoRel 92*
**Street-Kidd**, Mae *WhoBlA 92*
**Streeten**, David Henry Palmer 1921- *AmMWSc 92*
**Streeten**, Frank *Who 92*
**Streeten**, Paul Patrick 1917- *IntAu&W 91, Who 92, WhoFI 92, WrDr 92*
**Streeten**, Reginald Hawkins 1928- *Who 92*
**Streeter**, Alan 1934- *WhoAmP 91*
**Streeter**, Anne Paul 1926- *WhoAmP 91*
**Streeter**, Bernard A, Jr 1935- *WhoAmP 91*
**Streeter**, Debra Brister 1956- *WhoBlA 92*
**Streeter**, Denise Williams 1962- *WhoBlA 92*
**Streeter**, Ed 1891-1976 *BenetAL 91*
**Streeter**, Elwood James 1930- *WhoBlA 92*
**Streeter**, Jarvis, VII 1949- *WhoRel 92*
**Streeter**, Jean M 1950- *WhoAmP 91*
**Streeter**, John Gemmil 1936- *AmMWSc 92*
**Streeter**, John Stuart 1920- *Who 92*
**Streeter**, John Willis 1947- *WhoMW 92*
**Streeter**, Myron Merle 1926- *WhoFI 92*
**Streeter**, Richard Edward 1934- *WhoAmL 92*
**Streeter**, Richard Gordon 1930- *WhoEnt 92*
**Streeter**, Robert Glen 1941- *AmMWSc 92*
**Streeter**, Ruth Cheney 1895-1990 *CurBio 91N*
**Streeter**, William Wolf 1950- *WhoFI 92, WhoMW 92*
**Streetman**, Ben Garland 1939- *AmMWSc 92*
**Streetman**, John Robert 1930- *AmMWSc 92*
**Streetman**, John William, III 1941- *WhoMW 92*
**Streetman**, Nancy Katherine 1933- *WhoEnt 92*
**Streeto**, Joseph Michael 1942- *WhoMW 92*
**Streeton**, Terence 1930- *Who 92*
**Streeton**, Terence George 1930- *IntWW 91*
**Streets**, David George 1947- *AmMWSc 92*
**Streets**, Rubert Burley, Jr 1929- *AmMWSc 92*
**Streett**, Donald Howard 1934- *WhoFI 92*
**Streett**, Richard Alan 1946- *WhoRel 92*
**Streett**, William Bernard 1932- *AmMWSc 92*
**Streever**, Ralph L 1934- *AmMWSc 92*
**Streff**, Clyde E *WhoAmP 91*
**Streff**, Francine K 1950- *WhoAmP 91*
**Streff**, Rodney Joseph 1947- *WhoAmP 91*
**Streff**, William Albert, Jr. 1949- *WhoAmL 92*
**Strege**, Merle Dennis 1947- *WhoRel 92*
**Stregevsky**, Barry Michael 1955- *WhoMW 92*
**Strehler**, Bernard Louis 1925- *AmMWSc 92*
**Strehler**, Giorgio 1921- *CurBio 91 [port]*
**Strehlow**, Clifford David 1940- *AmMWSc 92*
**Strehlow**, Richard Alan 1927- *AmMWSc 92*
**Strehlow**, Roger Albert 1925- *AmMWSc 92*
**Streib**, John Fredrick 1915- *AmMWSc 92*
**Streib**, W C 1920- *AmMWSc 92*
**Streib**, William E 1931- *AmMWSc 92*
**Streibel**, Bryce 1922- *WhoAmP 91, WhoMW 92*
**Streibich**, Harold Cecil 1928- *WhoAmL 92*
**Streibl**, Max 1932- *IntWW 91*
**Streich**, Eric 1959- *WhoAmL 92*
**Streich**, Frank 1922- *WhoEnt 92*
**Streich**, Rita 1920-1987 *NewAmDM*
**Streicher**, Eugene 1926- *AmMWSc 92*
**Streicher**, James Franklin 1940- *WhoAmL 92*
**Streicher**, Julius 1885-1946 *BiDExR, EncTR 91 [port]*
**Streicher**, Michael A 1921- *AmMWSc 92*
**Streicher**, Michael Alfred 1921- *WhoFI 92*
**Streicker**, James Richard 1944- *WhoAmL 92*
**Streifer**, William 1936- *AmMWSc 92*
**Streiff**, Anton Joseph 1915- *AmMWSc 92*
**Streiff**, Richard Reinhart 1929- *AmMWSc 92*
**Streiff**, Thomas F 1958- *WhoIns 92*
**Streiker**, Lowell Dean 1939- *WhoRel 92*
**Streilein**, Jacob Wayne 1935- *AmMWSc 92*
**Streips**, Uldis Normunds 1942- *AmMWSc 92*
**Streisand**, Barbra *ReelWom*
**Streisand**, Barbra 1942- *FacFETw, IntMPA 92, NewAmDM, News 92-2 [port]*
**Streisand**, Barbra Joan 1942- *IntWW 91, WhoEnt 92*
**Streisel**, Leonard William 1941- *WhoMW 92*
**Streissler**, Erich W. 1933- *IntWW 91*
**Streit**, Clarence Kirshman 1896-1986 *AmPeW*
**Streit**, Gary James 1950- *WhoAmL 92*
**Streit**, Gerald Edward 1948- *AmMWSc 92*
**Streit**, Lawrence Carson, Jr. 1918- *WhoWest 92*
**Streit**, Richard John 1943- *WhoMW 92*
**Streit**, Roy Leon 1947- *AmMWSc 92*
**Streitfeld**, Murray Mark 1922- *AmMWSc 92*
**Streitwieser**, Andrew, Jr 1927- *AmMWSc 92, IntWW 91, WhoWest 92, WrDr 92*
**Streitwieser**, Franz Xaver 1939- *WhoEnt 92*
**Strejan**, Gill Henric 1930- *AmMWSc 92*
**Strek**, John Otto 1961- *WhoFI 92*
**Strekal**, Debra Joan 1952- *WhoMW 92*
**Strekas**, Thomas C 1947- *AmMWSc 92*
**Strelan**, John Gerhard 1936- *WhoRel 92*

Streletzky, Kathryn Diane 1957- WhoFI 92
Streltsova, Tatiana D AmMWSc 92
Strelzer, Martin 1925- WhoRel 92
Strelzoff, Alan G 1937- AmMWSc 92
Strem, Michael Edward 1936- AmMWSc 92
Strembitsky, Michael Alexander 1935- WhoWest 92
Stremler, Ferrel G 1933- AmMWSc 92
Stremming, Dennis Ray 1949- WhoRel 92
Strena, Robert Victor 1929- AmMWSc 92
Streng, Frederick John 1933- WhoRel 92, WrDr 92
Streng, William Harold 1944- AmMWSc 92, WhoMW 92
Streng, William Paul 1937- WhoAmL 92
Strengell, Marianne 1909- DcTwDes
Strenger, Christian H. 1943- WhoFI 92
Strenger, George 1906- WhoWest 92
Strenger, Hermann-Josef 1928- IntWW 91
Strength, Delphin Ralph 1925- AmMWSc 92
Strength, Robert Samuel 1929- WhoFI 92
Strenio, Andrew John, Jr. 1952- WhoFI 92
Strenk, Timothy James 1964- WhoWest 92
Strentz, Herbert J. 1938- WhoMW 92
Strenzwilk, Denis Frank 1940- AmMWSc 92
Strepponi, Giuseppina 1815-1897 NewAmDM
Streseman, Gustav 1878-1929 WhoNob 90
Stresemann, Gustav 1878-1929 EncTR 91 [port]
Stresen-Reuter, Frederick Arthur, II 1942- WhoFI 92
Streshinsky, Shirley 1934- IntAu&W 91
Strete, Craig 1950- TwCSFW 91, WrDr 92
Strete, Jane DrAPF 91
Stretton, Antony Oliver Ward 1936- AmMWSc 92
Stretton, Eric Hugh Alexander 1916- Who 92
Stretton, Hugh 1924- WrDr 92
Stretton, Peter John 1938- Who 92
Stretton, Thomas Richard, Jr. 1942- WhoEnt 92
Stretz, Lawrence Albert 1946- WhoWest 92
Streu, Herbert Thomas 1927- AmMWSc 92
Streuli, Carl Arthur 1922- AmMWSc 92
Strever, Kevin Kirk 1960- WhoAmL 92
Strevey, Guy Donald 1932- WhoMW 92
Strianse, Sabbat J. d1991 NewYTBS 91
Stribley, Rexford Carl 1918- AmMWSc 92
Stribling, Ken 1959- WhoAmP 91
Stribling, T. S. 1881-1965 BenetAL 91, ScFEYrs
Stribrny, Jiri 1880-1955 BiDExR
Strichartz, James Leonard 1951- WhoWest 92
Strichartz, Robert Stephen 1943- AmMWSc 92
Strick, Ellis 1921- AmMWSc 92
Strick, John, Jr WhoAmP 91
Strick, Joseph 1923- WhoEnt 92
Strick, Robert Charles Gordon 1931- Who 92
Strickberger, Monroe Wolf 1925- AmMWSc 92
Stricker, Barry Arthur 1957- WhoRel 92
Stricker, Edward Michael 1941- AmMWSc 92
Stricker, Frank Aloysius 1943- WhoWest 92
Stricker, Irwin Jesse 1932- WhoFI 92
Stricker, Raphael Becher 1950- WhoWest 92
Stricker, Stephev Alexander 1954- AmMWSc 92
Strickert, Frederick M. 1948- WhoRel 92
Strickert, Walter Frederick 1916- WhoRel 92
Strickholm, Alfred 1928- AmMWSc 92
Strickholm, Karen 1958- WhoEnt 92
Strickland, Annie Ruth 1949- WhoRel 92
Strickland, Arvarh E. 1930- WhoBlA 92
Strickland, Benjamin Vincent Michael 1939- Who 92
Strickland, Bonnie Ruth 1936- WomPsyc
Strickland, Brad DrAPF 91
Strickland, Charles D 1928- WhoAmP 91
Strickland, Clinton Vernal, Jr. 1950- WhoBlA 92
Strickland, Daniel John 1959- WhoEnt 92
Strickland, Dorothy S. 1933- WhoBlA 92
Strickland, Erasmus Hardin 1936- AmMWSc 92
Strickland, Frank 1928- Who 92
Strickland, Frederick William, Jr. 1944- WhoBlA 92
Strickland, Gail IntMPA 92
Strickland, George Thomas 1934- AmMWSc 92
Strickland, Gordon Edward, Jr 1929- AmMWSc 92
Strickland, Hugh Alfred 1931- WhoAmL 92
Strickland, James Arthur 1961- AmMWSc 92
Strickland, James Shive 1929- AmMWSc 92
Strickland, Jerald Allen 1949- WhoFI 92
Strickland, John Arthur Van 1952- WhoRel 92
Strickland, John Willis 1925- AmMWSc 92
Strickland, Kathleen 1949- WhoAmL 92
Strickland, Kenneth Percy 1927- AmMWSc 92
Strickland, Larry Dean 1938- AmMWSc 92
Strickland, Lily 1887-1958 NewAmDM
Strickland, Margot Teresa 1937- IntAu&W 91
Strickland, Nancy Arnette Stanley 1949- WhoFI 92
Strickland, R. James 1930- WhoBlA 92
Strickland, Rebecca Jane 1958- WhoEnt 92
Strickland, Robert 1927- WhoFI 92
Strickland, Robert Louis 1931- WhoFI 92
Strickland, Rodney 1966- WhoBlA 92
Strickland, Stephanie DrAPF 91
Strickland, Sylvia Raye 1945- WhoWest 92
Strickland, Ted L 1932- WhoAmP 91
Strickland, Vernon Lee 1962- WhoAmL 92
Strickland, Virginia Ann 1952- WhoAmL 92
Strickland, William Jesse 1942- WhoAmL 92
Strickland, William R. d1991 NewYTBS 91
Strickland-Constable, Robert 1903- Who 92
Strickler, Ivan K. 1921- WhoMW 92
Strickler, Stewart Jeffery 1934- AmMWSc 92
Strickler, Thomas David 1922- AmMWSc 92
Stricklin, Buck 1922- AmMWSc 92
Stricklin, James 1934- WhoBlA 92
Stricklin, Kathrine Komenak 1951- WhoRel 92
Stricklin, Mark L. 1951- WhoEnt 92
Stricklin, Robert DrAPF 91
Stricklin, William Ray 1946- AmMWSc 92
Strickling, Edward 1916- AmMWSc 92
Stricklyn, Ray 1930- IntMPA 92
Strickman, Arthur Edwin 1924- WhoFI 92
Strickmeier, Henry Bernard, Jr 1940- AmMWSc 92
Strickon, Harvey Alan 1947- WhoAmL 92
Stricoff, Eric Harold 1950- WhoEnt 92
Strid, Richard Eric 1952- WhoWest 92
Stride, Jeffrey 1946- TwCPaSc
Stride, Sally TwCPaSc
Strider, David Lewis 1929- AmMWSc 92
Strider, Maurice William 1913- WhoBlA 92
Stridiron, Iver A 1945- WhoAmP 91
Stridsberg, Albert Borden 1929- WhoFI 92
Strieber, Louis Whitley 1945- WhoEnt 92
Strieder, William 1938- AmMWSc 92
Strieder, William Christian 1938- WhoMW 92
Striefel, Sebastian 1941- AmMWSc 92
Striefsy, Linda Ann 1952- WhoAmL 92
Striem, Kaarl Javier 1961- WhoFI 92
Striepling, Mark Thomas 1960- WhoFI 92
Strier, Karen Barbara 1959- AmMWSc 92
Strier, Murray Paul 1923- AmMWSc 92
Strieter, Frederick John 1934- AmMWSc 92
Strife, James Richard 1949- AmMWSc 92
Striffler, David Frank 1922- AmMWSc 92
Striffler, William D 1929- AmMWSc 92
Striggio, Alessandro 1535?-1590? NewAmDM
Striggles, Matthew C 1927- WhoAmP 91
Stright, Paul Leonard 1930- AmMWSc 92
Strijdom, Johannes Gerhardus 1893-1958 FacFETw
Strike, Anthony Young 1955- WhoMW 92
Strike, Donald Peter 1936- AmMWSc 92
Striker, G E 1934- AmMWSc 92
Strikwerda, John Charles 1947- AmMWSc 92
Strimbu, Jerry Lee 1945- WhoMW 92
Strimbu, Victor, Jr. 1932- WhoAmL 92
Strimling, Richard Barry 1938- WhoMW 92
Strimling, Walter Eugene 1926- AmMWSc 92
Strindberg, August 1849-1912 ConAu 135, FacFETw
Strindberg, Madeleine TwCPaSc
Strinden, Earl Stanford 1931- WhoAmP 91
Strinden, Sarah Taylor 1955- AmMWSc 92
Stringall, Robert William 1933- AmMWSc 92
Stringam, Elwood Williams 1917- AmMWSc 92
Stringer, Arthur 1874-1950 BenetAL 91, ScFEYrs
Stringer, Arthur and Holman, Russell ScFEYrs
Stringer, C. Vivian 1948- WhoBlA 92
Stringer, Donald Arthur 1922- Who 92
Stringer, Edward Charles 1935- WhoAmL 92
Stringer, Emerson WhoAmP 91
Stringer, Francis William 1941- WhoEnt 92
Stringer, Gene Arthur 1939- AmMWSc 92
Stringer, Harold 1944- WhoAmP 91
Stringer, Howard LesBEnT 92 [port]
Stringer, Howard 1942- IntMPA 92, WhoEnt 92
Stringer, John 1934- AmMWSc 92
Stringer, Johnny William 1950- WhoAmP 91
Stringer, L. E. Dean 1936- WhoAmL 92
Stringer, L F 1925- AmMWSc 92
Stringer, Melyin, Sr. 1927- WhoBlA 92
Stringer, Nelson Howard, Jr. 1948- WhoBlA 92
Stringer, Pamela Mary 1928- Who 92
Stringer, Simon 1960- TwCPaSc
Stringer, Thomas Edward, Sr. 1944- WhoBlA 92
Stringer, William Clayton 1946- AmMWSc 92
Stringer, William Jeremy 1944- WhoFI 92, WhoWest 92
Stringfellow, Dale Alan 1944- AmMWSc 92
Stringfellow, Eric DeVaughn 1960- WhoBlA 92
Stringfellow, Frank 1940- AmMWSc 92
Stringfellow, Gerald B 1942- AmMWSc 92
Stringfield, Victor Timothy 1902- AmMWSc 92
Stringham, Glen Evan 1929- AmMWSc 92
Stringham, Jack Fred, II 1946- WhoAmL 92
Stringham, Reed Millington, Jr AmMWSc 92
Stringham, Washington Irving 1847-1909 BiInAmS
Strintzis, Michael Gerassimos 1944- AmMWSc 92
Striplin, Harry Lynn 1958- WhoFI 92
Stripling, George Michael 1949- WhoAmL 92
Stripling, Hortense M. 1950- WhoHisp 92
Stripling, Luther 1935- WhoBlA 92
Stritch, Elaine 1925- IntWW 91
Stritch, Elaine 1926- IntMPA 92, WhoEnt 92
Stritch, Samuel Alphonsus 1887-1958 FacFETw, RelLAm 91
Strite, Jacob Jay Miller 1904- WhoRel 92
Strittmater, Richard Carlton 1923- AmMWSc 92
Strittmatter, Cornelius Frederick 1926- AmMWSc 92
Strittmatter, Jere L 1950- WhoAmP 91
Strittmatter, Peter Albert 1939- AmMWSc 92, WhoWest 92
Strittmatter, Philipp 1928- AmMWSc 92
Stritzel, Joseph Andrew 1922- AmMWSc 92
Stritzke, Jimmy Franklin 1937- AmMWSc 92
Striz, Alfred Gerhard 1952- AmMWSc 92
Strizek, Norman Francis 1947- WhoAmL 92
Strizich, William S 1949- WhoAmP 91
Strnad, Leonard James 1941- WhoMW 92
Strnat, Karl J 1929- AmMWSc 92
Strnisa, Fred V 1941- AmMWSc 92
Strniste, Gary F 1944- AmMWSc 92
Strobach, Donald Roy 1933- AmMWSc 92
Strobeck, Charles LeRoy 1928- WhoMW 92
Strobeck, Curtis 1940- AmMWSc 92
Strobel, Darrell Fred 1942- AmMWSc 92
Strobel, Desmond Atis 1963- WhoEnt 92
Strobel, Edward 1947- AmMWSc 92
Strobel, Frederick Richard 1937- WhoMW 92
Strobel, Fredric Andrew 1935- WhoEnt 92
Strobel, Gary A 1938- AmMWSc 92
Strobel, George L 1937- AmMWSc 92
Strobel, Howard Austin 1920- AmMWSc 92
Strobel, James Walter 1933- AmMWSc 92
Strobel, Kate 1907- IntWW 91
Strobel, Martin Jack 1940- WhoAmL 92, WhoFI 92
Strobel, Rudolf G K 1927- AmMWSc 92
Strobel, Rudolf Gottfried Karl 1927- WhoMW 92
Strobel, Shirley Holcomb 1929- WhoRel 92
Strobell, John Dixon, Jr 1917- AmMWSc 92
Strober, Samuel 1940- AmMWSc 92
Strober, Warren 1937- AmMWSc 92
Strobl, Gottlieb Maximilian 1916- IntWW 91
Stroblas, Laurie DrAPF 91
Stroble, Francis Anthony 1930- WhoFI 92
Stroble, Robert Eugene 1940- WhoAmP 91
Strobridge, Richard Craig 1958- WhoWest 92
Strock, Herbert L 1918- IntMPA 92
Strock, Herbert Leonard 1918- WhoEnt 92
Strock, James M 1956- WhoAmP 91
Strode, Joseph Arlin 1946- WhoAmL 92
Strode, Velma McEwen 1919- WhoBlA 92
Strode, William 1601?-1645 RfGEnL 91
Strode, Woody 1914- IntMPA 92
Stroebel, Charles Frederick, III 1936- AmMWSc 92
Stroehlein, Jack Lee 1932- AmMWSc 92
Stroesenreuther, George Dale 1954- WhoMW 92
Stroessner, Alfredo 1912- FacFETw, IntWW 91
Stroev, Yegor Semenovich 1937- SovUnBD
Stroev, Yegor Semyonovich 1937- IntWW 91
Stroeve, Pieter 1945- AmMWSc 92
Stroger, John Herman, Jr. 1929- WhoBlA 92
Strogovich, Mikhail Solomonovich 1894-1984 SovUnBD
Stroh, James E. 1937- WhoMW 92
Stroh, Peter Wetherill 1927- WhoMW 92
Stroh, Raymond Eugene 1942- WhoMW 92
Stroh, Robert Carl 1937- AmMWSc 92
Stroh, William Richard 1923- AmMWSc 92
Strohbehn, John Walter 1936- AmMWSc 92
Strohbehn, Kim 1953- AmMWSc 92
Strohecker, Henry Frederick 1905- AmMWSc 92
Stroheim, Erich von IntDcF 2-2
Stroheim, Erich von 1885-1957 FacFETw
Strohl, George Ralph, Jr 1919- AmMWSc 92
Strohl, James A. 1937- WhoFI 92, WhoIns 92
Strohl, John Henry 1938- AmMWSc 92
Strohl, Joseph Allen 1946- WhoAmP 91
Strohl, Kingman P 1949- AmMWSc 92
Strohl, William Allen 1933- AmMWSc 92
Strohm, Gregor MacDonald 1947- WhoFI 92
Strohm, Jerry Lee 1937- AmMWSc 92
Strohm, Paul F 1935- AmMWSc 92
Strohm, Raymond William 1924- WhoFI 92
Strohm, Warren B 1925- AmMWSc 92
Strohmaier, A J 1915- AmMWSc 92
Strohmaier, Debra Lee 1952- WhoMW 92
Strohmaier, Thomas Edward 1943- WhoMW 92
Strohman, Richard Campbell 1927- AmMWSc 92
Strohman, Rollin Dean 1939- AmMWSc 92
Strohmeier, William Walter 1963- WhoEnt 92
Strohmer, Charles Richard 1949- WhoRel 92
Strojny, Edwin Joseph 1926- AmMWSc 92
Strojny, Mariano 1906- WhoRel 92
Stroke, Edgar Daniel 1958- WhoEnt 92
Stroke, George Wilhelm 1924- WhoFI 92
Stroke, Hinko Henry 1927- AmMWSc 92
Stroker, Nancy Elizabeth 1960- WhoFI 92
Stroker, William Dettwiller 1938- WhoRel 92
Strolin, Maryann 1943- WhoIns 92
Strolle, Jon Martin 1940- WhoWest 92
Stroller, Louis A. 1942- IntMPA 92, WhoEnt 92
Strom, Brian Leslie 1949- AmMWSc 92
Strom, Dennis R 1950- WhoAmP 91
Strom, E Thomas 1936- AmMWSc 92
Strom, Everald Hanson 1921- WhoRel 92
Strom, Gordon H 1914- AmMWSc 92
Strom, Lyle Elmer 1925- WhoAmL 92, WhoMW 92
Strom, Mark Alan 1962- WhoWest 92
Strom, Michael A. 1952- WhoAmL 92
Strom, Milton Gary 1942- WhoAmL 92, WhoFI 92
Strom, Oren Grant 1931- AmMWSc 92
Strom, Richard Nelsen 1942- AmMWSc 92
Strom, Robert 1935- WrDr 92
Strom, Robert Duane 1935- IntAu&W 91
Strom, Robert Gregson 1933- AmMWSc 92
Strom, Robert Michael 1951- AmMWSc 92
Strom, Shirley Longeteig 1931- WhoAmP 91
Strom, Stephen 1942- AmMWSc 92
Strom, Terry Barton 1941- AmMWSc 92
Strom-Olsen, John Olaf AmMWSc 92

**Strom-Paikin,** Joyce Elizabeth 1946- *IntAu&W 91*
**Stroman,** Cheryl Delores 1956- *WhoBlA 92*
**Stroman,** David Womack 1944- *AmMWSc 92*
**Stroman,** Kenneth 1948- *WhoBlA 92*
**Stromatt,** Robert Weldon 1929- *AmMWSc 92*
**Stromberg,** Bert Edwin, Jr 1944- *AmMWSc 92*
**Stromberg,** Karl Robert 1931- *AmMWSc 92*
**Stromberg,** Kurt 1939- *AmMWSc 92*
**Stromberg,** LaWayne Roland 1929- *AmMWSc 92*
**Stromberg,** Melvin Willard 1925- *AmMWSc 92*
**Stromberg,** Monica Nell 1963- *WhoRel 92*
**Stromberg,** Robert Remson 1925- *AmMWSc 92*
**Stromberg,** Ross Ernest 1940- *WhoAmL 92*
**Stromberg,** Thorsten Frederick 1936- *AmMWSc 92*
**Stromborg,** Marilyn Laura 1942- *WhoMW 92*
**Strombotne,** Richard L 1933- *AmMWSc 92*
**Strome,** Forrest C, Jr 1924- *AmMWSc 92*
**Strome,** Stephen 1945- *WhoFI 92, WhoMW 92*
**Stromei,** Frank C. 1940- *WhoFI 92, WhoWest 92*
**Stromer,** Delwyn Dean 1930- *WhoAmP 91*
**Stromer,** Marvin Henry 1936- *AmMWSc 92, WhoMW 92*
**Stromer,** Peter Robert 1929- *WhoWest 92*
**Stromgren,** Bengt 1907-1987 *FacFETw*
**Stromholm,** Stig Fredrik 1931- *IntWW 91*
**Strominger,** Jack L 1925- *AmMWSc 92, IntWW 91*
**Strominger,** Norman Lewis 1934- *AmMWSc 92*
**Stromme,** Floyd J *WhoAmP 91*
**Stromme,** Gary L. 1939- *WhoAmL 92, WhoWest 92*
**Strommen,** Dennis Patrick 1938- *AmMWSc 92*
**Strommen,** Norton Duane 1932- *AmMWSc 92*
**Strommen,** Sherwood Van 1946- *WhoMW 92*
**Stromquist,** Peter Stubbee 1952- *WhoEnt 92*
**Stromsta,** Courtney Paul 1922- *AmMWSc 92*
**Stronach,** Carey E 1940- *AmMWSc 92*
**Stronach,** David Brian 1931- *Who 92*
**Stronach,** Frank *WhoFI 92*
**Stroner,** Frederick Maione 1961- *WhoMW 92*
**Strong,** Alan Earl 1941- *AmMWSc 92*
**Strong,** Amanda L. 1935- *WhoBlA 92*
**Strong,** Arthur Mason 1954- *WhoAmL 92*
**Strong,** Arturo Carrillo 1930- *WhoHisp 92*
**Strong,** Augustus Hopkins 1836-1921 *RelLAm 91*
**Strong,** Austin 1881-1952 *BenetAL 91*
**Strong,** Beatrice Marie 1910- *WhoAmP 91*
**Strong,** Blondell McDonald 1943- *WhoBlA 92*
**Strong,** Bradley Scott 1940- *WhoMW 92*
**Strong,** Cameron Gordon 1934- *AmMWSc 92*
**Strong,** Charles S *TwCWW 91*
**Strong,** Craig Stephen 1947- *WhoBlA 92*
**Strong,** David F 1944- *AmMWSc 92, IntWW 91*
**Strong,** David Malcolm 1913- *Who 92*
**Strong,** Don R 1939- *WhoAmP 91*
**Strong,** Donald Raymond, Jr 1944- *AmMWSc 92*
**Strong,** Donsia 1960- *WhoAmL 92*
**Strong,** Dorothy Swearengen 1934- *WhoMW 92*
**Strong,** Douglas Donald 1938- *WhoBlA 92*
**Strong,** E R 1919- *AmMWSc 92*
**Strong,** Edwin Atson 1834-1920 *BiInAmS*
**Strong,** Eithne 1923- *IntAu&W 91, WrDr 92*
**Strong,** Franklin Wallace, Jr. 1949- *WhoAmL 92*
**Strong,** Frederick Carl, III 1917- *AmMWSc 92*
**Strong,** Gary Eugene 1944- *WhoWest 92*
**Strong,** George Gordon, Jr. 1947- *WhoAmL 92, WhoFI 92*
**Strong,** George Hotham 1926- *WhoFI 92*
**Strong,** George Templeton *BenetAL 91*
**Strong,** George Walter 1937- *WhoFI 92*
**Strong,** Helen Francine 1947- *WhoBlA 92*
**Strong,** Herbert Maxwell 1908- *AmMWSc 92*
**Strong,** Ian B 1930- *AmMWSc 92*
**Strong,** Jack Perry 1928- *AmMWSc 92*
**Strong,** James R 1921- *WhoAmP 91*
**Strong,** James Woodward 1833-1913 *RelLAm 91*
**Strong,** Jane *DrAPF 91*
**Strong,** Jerome Anton 1947- *WhoAmP 91, WhoMW 92*
**Strong,** Jerry Glenn 1941- *AmMWSc 92*
**Strong,** John *IntMPA 92*
**Strong,** John 1905- *AmMWSc 92*
**Strong,** John Anderson 1915- *Who 92*
**Strong,** John Clifford 1922- *Who 92*
**Strong,** John D 1936- *WhoIns 92*
**Strong,** John David 1936- *WhoMW 92*
**Strong,** John Oliver 1930- *WhoWest 92*
**Strong,** John Scott 1956- *WhoFI 92*
**Strong,** John Stiven 1948- *WhoRel 92*
**Strong,** John Van Rensselaer 1912- *WhoAmL 92*
**Strong,** John William 1952- *WhoMW 92*
**Strong,** Jonathan *DrAPF 91*
**Strong,** Josiah 1847-1916 *BenetAL 91, RelLAm 91*
**Strong,** Judith Ann 1941- *AmMWSc 92*
**Strong,** Julia Trevelyan *Who 92*
**Strong,** June 1928- *IntAu&W 91*
**Strong,** L.A.G. 1896-1958 *RfGEnL 91*
**Strong,** Laurence Edward 1914- *AmMWSc 92*
**Strong,** Leslie Thomas, III 1961- *WhoRel 92*
**Strong,** Louise Connally 1944- *AmMWSc 92*
**Strong,** Louise J *ScFEYrs A*
**Strong,** Marilyn Terry 1929- *WhoBlA 92*
**Strong,** Maurice F. 1929- *IntWW 91, Who 92*
**Strong,** Mayda Nel 1942- *WhoWest 92*
**Strong,** Mervyn Stuart 1924- *AmMWSc 92*
**Strong,** Moses d1877 *BiInAmS*
**Strong,** Moses McCure 1810-1894 *BiInAmS*
**Strong,** Otis Reginald, III 1954- *WhoBlA 92*
**Strong,** Pamela Kay 1950- *WhoWest 92*
**Strong,** Pat *IntAu&W 91X, WrDr 92*
**Strong,** Patience 1907-1990 *AnObit 1990*
**Strong,** Pearl *WhoAmP 91*
**Strong,** Peter E. 1930- *WhoBlA 92*
**Strong,** Peter Hansen 1952- *WhoWest 92*
**Strong,** Robert Campbell 1915- *WhoAmP 91*
**Strong,** Robert George 1916- *WhoFI 92, WhoWest 92*
**Strong,** Robert Lyman 1928- *AmMWSc 92*
**Strong,** Robert Michael 1943- *AmMWSc 92*
**Strong,** Robert Stanley 1924- *AmMWSc 92*
**Strong,** Ronald Dean 1936- *AmMWSc 92*
**Strong,** Roy 1935- *IntAu&W 91, Who 92, WrDr 92*
**Strong,** Roy Colin 1935- *IntWW 91*
**Strong,** Rudolph Greer 1924- *AmMWSc 92*
**Strong,** Sidney Dix 1860-1938 *AmPeW*
**Strong,** Susan *WrDr 92*
**Strong,** Theodore 1790-1869 *BiInAmS*
**Strong,** Walter L. *WhoBlA 92*
**Strong,** William J 1934- *AmMWSc 92*
**Strong,** William R 1943- *WhoAmP 91*
**Strong,** William Sutherland 1951- *WhoAmL 92*
**Strong,** Zachary *TwCWW 91*
**Stronge,** Christopher James 1933- *Who 92*
**Stronge,** James Anselan Maxwell 1946- *Who 92*
**Stronge,** James Jonathan 1931- *WhoFI 92, WhoMW 92*
**Strongin,** Lynn *DrAPF 91*
**Strongin,** Myron 1936- *AmMWSc 92*
**Stronstad,** Roger Jonathan 1944- *WhoRel 92*
**Stroock,** Thomas F 1925- *WhoAmP 91*
**Stroock,** Thomas Frank 1925- *WhoWest 92*
**Stroop,** Jurgen 1895-1952 *EncTR 91 [port]*
**Strop,** Hans R 1931- *AmMWSc 92*
**Strope,** Dora Diaz 1943- *WhoHisp 92*
**Strope,** Kevin Lind 1957- *WhoRel 92*
**Stropp,** Robert H., Jr. 1947- *WhoAmL 92*
**Strosberg,** Arthur Martin 1940- *AmMWSc 92*
**Stroschein,** Sharon Marie 1944- *WhoAmP 91*
**Stroscio,** Michael Anthony 1949- *AmMWSc 92*
**Stross,** Fred Helmut 1910- *AmMWSc 92*
**Stross,** Raymond George 1930- *AmMWSc 92*
**Strossen,** Nadine 1950- *NewYTBS 91 [port]*
**Strossmayer,** Josip Juraj *DcAmImH*
**Strote,** Joel Richard 1939- *WhoEnt 92*
**Strother,** Allen 1928- *AmMWSc 92*
**Strother,** Greenville Kash 1920- *AmMWSc 92*
**Strother,** J A 1927- *AmMWSc 92*
**Strother,** James French 1938- *WhoAmL 92*
**Strother,** Patrick Joseph 1953- *WhoFI 92*
**Strothman,** Wendy Jo 1950- *WhoRel 92*
**Strottman,** Daniel 1943- *AmMWSc 92*
**Stroube,** Edward W 1927- *AmMWSc 92*
**Stroube,** William Bryan, Jr 1951- *AmMWSc 92, WhoMW 92*
**Stroube,** William Hugh 1924- *AmMWSc 92*
**Stroud,** Bill Aubrey 1963- *WhoRel 92*
**Stroud,** Carlos Ray 1942- *AmMWSc 92*
**Stroud,** Charles Eric 1924- *Who 92*
**Stroud,** David Allen 1952- *WhoRel 92*
**Stroud,** David Gordon 1943- *AmMWSc 92*
**Stroud,** Derek H. *Who 92*
**Stroud,** Don 1937- *IntMPA 92*
**Stroud,** Dorothy Nancy 1910- *Who 92*
**Stroud,** Drew McCord *DrAPF 91*
**Stroud,** Drew McCord 1944- *IntAu&W 91*
**Stroud,** Eric *Who 92*
**Stroud,** Ernest Charles Frederick 1931- *Who 92*
**Stroud,** Herschel Leon 1930- *WhoMW 92*
**Stroud,** Howard Burnett, Sr. 1939- *WhoBlA 92*
**Stroud,** Jackson Swavely 1931- *AmMWSc 92*
**Stroud,** Joe Hinton 1936- *WhoMW 92*
**Stroud,** John Nathan 1948- *WhoRel 92*
**Stroud,** Junius Brutus 1929- *AmMWSc 92*
**Stroud,** Lawrence Lowell 1935- *WhoBlA 92*
**Stroud,** Louis Winston 1946- *WhoBlA 92*
**Stroud,** Malcolm Herbert 1920- *AmMWSc 92*
**Stroud,** Milton *WhoBlA 92*
**Stroud,** Richard Hamilton 1918- *AmMWSc 92*
**Stroud,** Richard Kim 1943- *AmMWSc 92*
**Stroud,** Robert Church 1918- *AmMWSc 92*
**Stroud,** Robert Edward 1934- *WhoAmL 92*
**Stroud,** Robert Malone 1931- *AmMWSc 92*
**Stroud,** Robert Michael 1942- *AmMWSc 92*
**Stroud,** Robert Wayne 1929- *AmMWSc 92*
**Stroud,** Thomas William Felix 1936- *AmMWSc 92*
**Stroud,** William Joseph 1937- *WhoRel 92*
**Strougal,** Lubomir 1924- *IntWW 91*
**Strough,** Robert I 1920- *AmMWSc 92*
**Strougo,** Robert 1943- *WhoAmL 92*
**Stroup,** Cynthia Roxane 1948- *AmMWSc 92*
**Stroup,** Dorothy *DrAPF 91*
**Stroup,** Elizabeth Faye 1939- *WhoWest 92*
**Stroup,** Herbert *WhoRel 92*
**Stroup,** Herbert 1916- *WrDr 92*
**Stroup,** Jerry Donald 1939- *WhoRel 92*
**Stroup,** Kala Mays *WhoMW 92*
**Stroup,** Robert Lee, III 1961- *WhoAmL 92, WhoEnt 92*
**Stroup,** Stanley Stephenson 1944- *WhoAmL 92*
**Stroup,** Timothy Jules 1953- *WhoMW 92*
**Strous,** Ger J 1944- *AmMWSc 92*
**Strouse,** Charles 1928- *NewAmDM*
**Strouse,** Charles Earl 1944- *AmMWSc 92*
**Strouse,** Harry D., Jr. 1923- *WhoAmL 92*
**Strouse,** Jean 1945- *DcLB 111 [port]*
**Strouse,** Richard B. d1991 *NewYTBS 91*
**Strouse,** Thomas Morton 1945- *WhoRel 92*
**Strout,** Barbara E *WhoAmP 91*
**Strout,** Donald A *WhoAmP 91*
**Strout,** John Robert 1941- *WhoWest 92*
**Strout,** Joseph Milton 1956- *WhoMW 92*
**Strout,** Richard 1898-1990 *AnObit 1990*
**Strout,** Richard Goold 1927- *AmMWSc 92*
**Strovink,** Mark William 1944- *AmMWSc 92*
**Strowger,** Gaston Jack 1916- *Who 92*
**Stroyan,** Ronald Angus Ropner 1924- *Who 92*
**Stroyd,** Arthur Heister 1945- *WhoAmL 92*
**Stroynowski,** Iwona T 1950- *AmMWSc 92*
**Stroz,** Daniel 1943- *LiExTwC*
**Strozier,** James Kinard 1933- *AmMWSc 92*
**Strozier,** John Allen, Jr 1934- *AmMWSc 92*
**Strozier,** Yvonne Iglehart 1938- *WhoBlA 92*
**Strub,** Gerald Robert, Jr. 1957- *WhoFI 92*
**Strub,** Mike Robert 1948- *AmMWSc 92*
**Strubbe,** John Lewis 1921- *WhoMW 92*
**Strubbe,** William Burrows 1952- *WhoAmL 92*
**Strube,** Christine Lynn 1966- *WhoMW 92*
**Struble,** Craig Bruce 1950- *AmMWSc 92*
**Struble,** Dean L 1936- *AmMWSc 92*
**Struble,** George W 1932- *AmMWSc 92*
**Struble,** Gordon Lee 1937- *AmMWSc 92*
**Struble,** Raimond Aldrich 1924- *AmMWSc 92*
**Struchkova,** Raisa Stepanovna 1925- *IntWW 91*
**Struchtemeyer,** Roland August 1918- *AmMWSc 92*
**Struck,** Christopher John 1962- *WhoEnt 92*
**Struck,** John Seward 1952- *WhoFI 92*
**Struck,** Richard Charles 1938- *WhoMW 92*
**Struck,** Robert Frederick 1932- *AmMWSc 92*
**Struck,** Robert T 1921- *AmMWSc 92*
**Struck,** William Anthony 1920- *AmMWSc 92*
**Struck-Marcell,** Curtis John 1954- *AmMWSc 92*
**Struckmeyer,** Alan Dean 1959- *WhoRel 92*
**Struckmeyer,** Fred C, Jr 1912- *WhoAmP 91*
**Strudler,** Robert Jacob 1942- *WhoFI 92*
**Strudwick,** Arthur Sidney Ronald 1921- *Who 92*
**Strudwick,** John Philip 1914- *Who 92*
**Strudwick,** Lindsey H., Sr. 1946- *WhoBlA 92*
**Strudwick,** Lindsey Howard 1946- *WhoWest 92*
**Strudwick,** Warren James 1923- *WhoBlA 92*
**Struebing,** Janis R. 1950- *WhoMW 92*
**Struempler,** Arthur W 1920- *AmMWSc 92*
**Struensee,** Johan Friedrich 1737-1772 *BlkwCEP*
**Strugatskii,** Arkadii 1925-1991 *ConAu 135*
**Strugatsky,** Arkadiy Natanovich 1925- *IntWW 91, SovUnBD*
**Strugatsky,** Arkady 1925- *TwCSFW 91A*
**Strugatsky,** Boris 1933- *TwCSFW 91A*
**Strugatsky,** Boris Natanovich 1933- *IntWW 91, SovUnBD*
**Strugnell,** John 1930- *WhoRel 92*
**Struhl,** Kevin 1952- *AmMWSc 92*
**Struhl,** Stanley Frederick 1939- *WhoWest 92*
**Struif,** L. James 1931- *WhoAmL 92*
**Struik,** Dirk Jan 1894- *AmMWSc 92*
**Struik,** Ruth Rebekka 1928- *AmMWSc 92*
**Strukoff,** Rudolf Stephen 1935- *WhoEnt 92*
**Strul,** Gene M. 1927- *WhoFI 92*
**Strull,** Gene 1929- *AmMWSc 92*
**Strum,** Brian J. 1939- *WhoFI 92*
**Strum,** Jay Gerson 1938- *WhoAmL 92*
**Strum,** Judy May 1938- *AmMWSc 92*
**Strumeyer,** David H 1934- *AmMWSc 92*
**Strumilin,** Stanislav Gustavovich 1877-1974 *SovUnBD*
**Struminsky,** Vladimir Vasiliyevich 1914- *IntWW 91*
**Strumwasser,** Felix 1934- *AmMWSc 92*
**Strunck,** Theodor 1895-1945 *EncTR 91*
**Strunk,** Duane H 1920- *AmMWSc 92*
**Strunk,** Klaus Albert 1930- *IntWW 91*
**Strunk,** Mailand Rainey 1919- *AmMWSc 92*
**Strunk,** Richard John 1941- *AmMWSc 92*
**Strunk,** Robert Charles 1942- *AmMWSc 92*
**Strunsky,** Robert d1991 *NewYTBS 91*
**Strunz,** G M 1938- *AmMWSc 92*
**Strupp,** David John 1938- *WhoAmL 92*
**Strupp,** Hans H 1921- *AmMWSc 92*
**Strussion,** Ronald Alexander 1942- *WhoMW 92*
**Struth,** Sandy *WhoEnt 92*
**Struthers,** Barbara Joan Oft 1940- *AmMWSc 92*
**Struthers,** Ralph Charles 1933- *WhoWest 92*
**Struthers,** Robert Claflin 1928- *AmMWSc 92*
**Struthers,** Sally 1948- *IntMPA 92*
**Strutt** *Who 92*
**Strutt,** John William 1842-1919 *WhoNob 90*
**Strutt,** Nigel 1916- *Who 92*
**Strutt,** Thomas L. 1960- *WhoMW 92*
**Strutton,** Bill 1918- *IntAu&W 91, WrDr 92*
**Strutton,** Robert James 1948- *WhoFI 92*
**Strutzel,** Jod Christopher 1947- *WhoWest 92*
**Struve,** Guy Miller 1943- *WhoAmL 92*
**Struve,** Irene B. 1925- *WhoEnt 92*
**Struve,** Larry D. 1942- *WhoAmL 92*
**Struve,** Peter Bernardovich 1870-1944 *FacFETw*
**Struve,** Walter Scott 1945- *AmMWSc 92*
**Struve,** William George 1938- *AmMWSc 92*
**Struve,** William Scott 1915- *AmMWSc 92*
**Struyk,** Raymond J. 1944- *ConAu 134*
**Struyk,** Raymond Jay 1944- *WhoFI 92*
**Struyk,** Robert John 1932- *WhoAmL 92*
**Struzak,** Ryszard G 1933- *AmMWSc 92*
**Struzek,** Boleslaw 1920- *IntWW 91*
**Struzynski,** Raymond Edward 1937- *AmMWSc 92*
**Strycker,** Stanley Julian 1931- *AmMWSc 92*
**Stryer,** Lubert 1938- *AmMWSc 92*
**Strygler,** Bernardo 1959- *WhoWest 92*
**Stryk,** Lucien *DrAPF 91*
**Stryk,** Lucien 1924- *BenetAL 91, ConPo 91, WrDr 92*
**Stryker,** Daniel *ConAu 133, SmATA 66*
**Stryker,** Dennis James 1958- *WhoAmL 92*

**Stryker**, Hal *TwCSFW 91*
**Stryker**, Lynden Joel 1943- *AmMWSc 92*
**Stryker**, Martin H 1943- *AmMWSc 92*
**Stryker**, Michael Paul 1947- *AmMWSc 92*
**Stryker**, Steven Charles 1944- *WhoAmL 92, WhoFI 92*
**Strynkowski**, John J. *WhoRel 92*
**Strzelchik**, Vladislav Ignatevich 1921- *IntWW 91*
**Strzembosz**, Adam Justyn 1930- *IntWW 91*
**Stuart** *Who 92*
**Stuart**, Viscount 1953- *Who 92*
**Stuart**, Alex R. *WrDr 92*
**Stuart**, Alexander *IntAu&W 91*
**Stuart**, Alexander 1955- *WrDr 92*
**Stuart**, Alexander Friedlander 1955- *WhoAmL 92*
**Stuart**, Alfred Herbert 1913- *AmMWSc 92*
**Stuart**, Alfred Wright 1932- *AmMWSc 92*
**Stuart**, Alice Melissa 1957- *WhoAmL 92, WhoFI 92*
**Stuart**, Allan Reeves 1929- *WhoRel 92*
**Stuart**, Ambrose Pascal Sevilon 1820-1899 *BiInAmS*
**Stuart**, Andrew Christopher 1928- *Who 92*
**Stuart**, Ann Elizabeth 1943- *AmMWSc 92*
**Stuart**, Antony James Cobham E. *Who 92*
**Stuart**, Brian Michael 1961- *WhoWest 92*
**Stuart**, Calvin Thomas 1958- *WhoFI 92*
**Stuart**, Charles 1783-1865 *BenetAL 91*
**Stuart**, Charles Murray 1933- *Who 92*
**Stuart**, Charles Rowell 1928- *Who 92*
**Stuart**, Dabney *DrAPF 91*
**Stuart**, Dabney 1937- *ConPo 91, WrDr 92*
**Stuart**, David Edward 1945- *WhoWest 92*
**Stuart**, David Marshall 1928- *AmMWSc 92*
**Stuart**, David Michael 1952- *WhoRel 92*
**Stuart**, David W 1932- *AmMWSc 92*
**Stuart**, Derald Archie 1925- *AmMWSc 92*
**Stuart**, Don A. *ConAu 34NR*
**Stuart**, Dorothy Mae 1933- *WhoWest 92*
**Stuart**, Douglas Gordon 1931- *AmMWSc 92*
**Stuart**, Duncan 1934- *Who 92*
**Stuart**, Edward Marchand 1943- *WhoFI 92*
**Stuart**, Elsie Sutherland Rast 1931- *WhoAmP 91*
**Stuart**, Eugene Page 1927- *WhoAmP 91*
**Stuart**, Floyd C. *DrAPF 91*
**Stuart**, Francis 1902- *ConNov 91, IntWW 91, Who 92, WrDr 92*
**Stuart**, Gary Lester 1939- *WhoAmL 92, WhoWest 92*
**Stuart**, Gary Miller 1940- *WhoFI 92*
**Stuart**, George, Jr 1946- *WhoAmP 91*
**Stuart**, George Wallace 1924- *AmMWSc 92*
**Stuart**, Gerard William, Jr. 1939- *WhoFI 92, WhoWest 92*
**Stuart**, Glenn Douglas 1932- *WhoEnt 92*
**Stuart**, Gordon Edgar 1951- *WhoMW 92*
**Stuart**, Harold Cutliff 1912- *WhoAmL 92, WhoFI 92*
**Stuart**, Herbert James 1926- *Who 92*
**Stuart**, Ian 1927- *IntAu&W 91, WrDr 92*
**Stuart**, Ivan I. *WhoBlA 92*
**Stuart**, James 1713-1788 *BlkwCEP*
**Stuart**, James Carey 1947- *WhoMW 92*
**Stuart**, James Davies 1941- *AmMWSc 92*
**Stuart**, James Fortier 1928- *WhoEnt 92*
**Stuart**, James Glen 1948- *AmMWSc 92*
**Stuart**, James Keith 1940- *Who 92*
**Stuart**, Jesse 1907- *BenetAL 91*
**Stuart**, Joe Don 1932- *AmMWSc 92*
**Stuart**, John 1718-1779 *BlkwEAR*
**Stuart**, John Bruce 1948- *WhoAmL 92*
**Stuart**, John M. 1927- *WhoAmL 92, WhoFI 92*
**Stuart**, John Trevor 1929- *Who 92*
**Stuart**, John W 1924- *AmMWSc 92*
**Stuart**, Jonathan 1946- *WhoEnt 92*
**Stuart**, Joseph B. *Who 92*
**Stuart**, Keith *Who 92*
**Stuart**, Kenneth 1920- *Who 92*
**Stuart**, Kenneth Daniel 1940- *AmMWSc 92*
**Stuart**, Kenneth Lamonte 1920- *IntWW 91*
**Stuart**, Larry Stephen 1948- *WhoMW 92*
**Stuart**, Lawrence David, Jr. 1944- *WhoAmL 92*
**Stuart**, Logan *TwCWW 91*
**Stuart**, Lyle 1922- *IntWW 91*
**Stuart**, Malcolm Moncrieff d1991 *Who 92N*
**Stuart**, Marian Elizabeth 1944- *Who 92*
**Stuart**, Marjorie Mann 1921- *WhoBlA 92*
**Stuart**, Mary *WhoEnt 92*
**Stuart**, Matt *TwCWW 91*
**Stuart**, Mel *LesBEnT 92*
**Stuart**, Michael Francis Harvey 1926- *Who 92*
**Stuart**, Michael George 1951- *WhoAmL 92*
**Stuart**, Muriel d1991 *NewYTBS 91*
**Stuart**, Murray *Who 92*
**Stuart**, Nicholas Willoughby 1942- *Who 92*
**Stuart**, Phillip 1937- *Who 92*
**Stuart**, Preston Alan 1952- *WhoEnt 92*
**Stuart**, Reginald A. 1948- *WhoBlA 92*
**Stuart**, Richard Thompson 1943- *WhoRel 92*
**Stuart**, Robert 1785-1848 *BenetAL 91*
**Stuart**, Robert 1921- *WhoFI 92*
**Stuart**, Robert D, Jr 1916- *WhoAmP 91*
**Stuart**, Robert Douglas, Jr. 1916- *IntWW 91*
**Stuart**, Robert Franklin 1920- *WhoRel 92*
**Stuart**, Robert Henry 1929- *WhoWest 92*
**Stuart**, Ronald S 1919- *AmMWSc 92*
**Stuart**, Ruth McEnery 1849-1917 *BenetAL 91*
**Stuart**, Sandra Joyce 1950- *WhoFI 92, WhoMW 92*
**Stuart**, Sidney *WrDr 92*
**Stuart**, Simon 1930- *WrDr 92*
**Stuart**, Thomas Andrew 1941- *AmMWSc 92*
**Stuart**, Walter Bynum, IV 1946- *WhoAmL 92*
**Stuart**, William Corwin 1920- *WhoAmL 92, WhoMW 92*
**Stuart**, William Dorsey 1939- *AmMWSc 92*
**Stuart-Alexander**, Desiree Elizabeth 1930- *AmMWSc 92*
**Stuart-Cole**, James 1916- *Who 92*
**Stuart-Forbes**, Charles Edward *Who 92*
**Stuart-Harris**, Charles 1909- *Who 92*
**Stuart-Menteth**, James *Who 92*
**Stuart-Moore**, Michael 1944- *Who 92*
**Stuart of Findhorn**, Viscount 1924- *Who 92*
**Stuart-Paul**, Ronald 1934- *Who 92*
**Stuart-Shaw**, Max 1912- *Who 92*
**Stuart-Smith**, James 1919- *Who 92*
**Stuart-Smith**, Murray 1927- *Who 92*
**Stuart Taylor**, Nicholas 1952- *Who 92*
**Stuart-White**, Christopher Stuart 1933- *Who 92*
**Stub**, Hans Gerhard 1849-1931 *RelLAm 91*
**Stuban**, Michael L 1958- *WhoAmP 91*
**Stuban**, Ted 1928- *WhoAmP 91*
**Stubbe**, John Sunapee 1919- *AmMWSc 92*
**Stubbe**, Ray William 1938- *WhoRel 92*
**Stubbeman**, David *WhoAmP 91*
**Stubbeman**, Robert Frank 1935- *AmMWSc 92*
**Stubberud**, Allen Roger 1934- *AmMWSc 92, WhoWest 92*
**Stubbing**, Tony 1921- *TwCPaSc*
**Stubbins**, James Fiske 1931- *AmMWSc 92*
**Stubbins**, James Frederick 1948- *AmMWSc 92*
**Stubblebine**, Warren 1917- *AmMWSc 92*
**Stubblefield**, Beauregard 1923- *AmMWSc 92*
**Stubblefield**, Charles Bryan 1931- *AmMWSc 92*
**Stubblefield**, Frank Milton 1911- *AmMWSc 92*
**Stubblefield**, James 1901- *Who 92*
**Stubblefield**, James Irvin 1953- *WhoWest 92*
**Stubblefield**, Jennye Washington 1925- *WhoBlA 92*
**Stubblefield**, Jerry Mason 1936- *WhoRel 92*
**Stubblefield**, Raymond M. 1945- *WhoBlA 92*
**Stubblefield**, Robert Douglas 1936- *AmMWSc 92*
**Stubblefield**, Thomas Mason 1922- *WhoWest 92*
**Stubblefield**, Travis Elton 1935- *AmMWSc 92*
**Stubblefield**, William Lynn 1940- *AmMWSc 92*
**Stubbles**, Beverly Ann 1947- *WhoMW 92*
**Stubbs**, Archie Roy 1910- *WhoAmP 91*
**Stubbs**, Daniel, II 1965- *WhoBlA 92*
**Stubbs**, Daniel Gaie 1940- *WhoWest 92*
**Stubbs**, Donald William 1932- *AmMWSc 92*
**Stubbs**, Franklin Lee 1960- *WhoBlA 92*
**Stubbs**, Genevieve Graffeo 1956- *WhoAmL 92*
**Stubbs**, George 1724-1806 *BlkwCEP*
**Stubbs**, George Winston 1942- *WhoBlA 92*
**Stubbs**, Harold K. 1940- *WhoBlA 92*
**Stubbs**, Harry Clement *WrDr 92*
**Stubbs**, Imogen 1961- *IntMPA 92*
**Stubbs**, James 1910- *Who 92*
**Stubbs**, Jan Didra 1937- *WhoFI 92, WhoMW 92*
**Stubbs**, Jean 1926- *IntAu&W 91, WrDr 92*
**Stubbs**, John Dorton 1938- *AmMWSc 92*
**Stubbs**, John F. A. H. *Who 92*
**Stubbs**, Judy Hertz 1946- *WhoAmP 91*
**Stubbs**, Levi *WhoBlA 92*
**Stubbs**, Mark Darwin 1950- *WhoAmP 91, WhoWest 92*
**Stubbs**, Michael Wesley 1947- *Who 92*
**Stubbs**, Morris Frank 1898- *AmMWSc 92*
**Stubbs**, Norris 1948- *AmMWSc 92*
**Stubbs**, Peter Charles 1937- *WrDr 92*
**Stubbs**, Randall Arthur 1952- *WhoWest 92*
**Stubbs**, Robert G 1932- *WhoAmP 91*
**Stubbs**, Robert Sherwood, II 1922- *WhoAmL 92*
**Stubbs**, Robert Sherwood, III 1947- *WhoAmL 92*
**Stubbs**, Thomas 1926- *Who 92*
**Stubbs**, Thomas Hubert 1944- *WhoFI 92*
**Stubbs**, W Terrell *WhoAmP 91*
**Stubbs**, William Frederick 1934- *Who 92*
**Stubbs**, William Hamilton 1937- *Who 92*
**Stubenrauch**, Arnold Valentine 1871-1917 *BiInAmS*
**Stuber**, Charles William 1931- *AmMWSc 92*
**Stuber**, Fred A 1933- *AmMWSc 92*
**Stuber**, William Charles 1951- *WhoEnt 92*
**Stubican**, Vladimir S 1924- *AmMWSc 92*
**Stubley**, Trevor 1932- *TwCPaSc*
**Stuchka**, Petr Ivanovich 1865-1932 *SovUnBD*
**Stuchly**, Maria Anna 1939- *AmMWSc 92*
**Stuchly**, Stanislaw S 1931- *AmMWSc 92*
**Stuck**, Barton W 1946- *AmMWSc 92*
**Stuck**, Hudson 1863-1920 *BenetAL 91, RelLAm 91*
**Stuckart**, Wilhelm 1902-1953 *BiDExR, EncTR 91 [port]*
**Stuckenberg**, John Henry Wilbrandt 1835-1903 *RelLAm 91*
**Stucker**, Darren Michael 1947- *WhoEnt 92*
**Stucker**, Harry T 1925- *AmMWSc 92*
**Stucker**, Joseph Bernard 1914- *AmMWSc 92*
**Stucker**, Richard Ryan 1944- *WhoEnt 92*
**Stucker**, Robert Evan 1936- *AmMWSc 92*
**Stucker**, Robert Jay 1960- *WhoMW 92*
**Stuckey**, A Nelson, Jr 1935- *AmMWSc 92*
**Stuckey**, Ann Monkhouse 1940- *WhoEnt 92*
**Stuckey**, Brent 1953- *WhoAmL 92*
**Stuckey**, Dean Vance 1937- *WhoRel 92*
**Stuckey**, James Edward 1939- *WhoRel 92*
**Stuckey**, John *WhoAmP 91*
**Stuckey**, John Edmund 1929- *AmMWSc 92*
**Stuckey**, Richard Jorian 1943- *WhoMW 92*
**Stuckey**, Ronald Lewis 1938- *AmMWSc 92*
**Stuckey**, Walter Jackson, Jr 1927- *AmMWSc 92*
**Stuckey**, Wayne Keith 1940- *WhoWest 92*
**Stuckey**, Williamson Sylvester, Jr 1935- *WhoAmP 91*
**Stucki**, Eugene B *WhoAmP 91*
**Stucki**, Jacob Calvin 1926- *AmMWSc 92*
**Stucki**, Joseph William 1946- *AmMWSc 92*
**Stucki**, Spencer Eugene 1943- *WhoAmP 91*
**Stucki**, William Paul 1931- *AmMWSc 92*
**Stucklen**, Richard 1916- *IntWW 91, Who 92*
**Stuckwisch**, Clarence George 1916- *AmMWSc 92*
**Stucky**, Galen Dean 1936- *AmMWSc 92*
**Stucky**, Gary Lee 1941- *AmMWSc 92*
**Stucky**, James Bruce 1945- *WhoFI 92*
**Stucky**, Richard K 1949- *AmMWSc 92*
**Stucley**, Hugh 1945- *Who 92*
**Stuczko**, Richard Julian 1929- *WhoRel 92*
**Studd**, Edward 1929- *Who 92*
**Studd**, Peter Malden 1916- *Who 92*
**Studden**, William John 1935- *AmMWSc 92*
**Studds**, Gerry E. 1937- *AlmAP 92 [port]*
**Studds**, Gerry Eastman 1937- *WhoAmP 91*
**Stude**, Michael Edwin 1953- *WhoMW 92*
**Studebaker**, Alden Henry 1957- *WhoRel 92*
**Studebaker**, Gerald A 1932- *AmMWSc 92*
**Studebaker**, Glenn Wayne 1939- *WhoMW 92*
**Studebaker**, Irving Glen 1931- *WhoWest 92*
**Studebaker**, William *DrAPF 91*
**Studemeister**, Paul Alexander 1954- *WhoWest 92*
**Studencki**, Anna Bronislawa 1948- *WhoMW 92*
**Student**, Kurt 1890-1978 *FacFETw*
**Student**, Marjorie Marie 1948- *WhoAmL 92*
**Studer**, Cheryl *NewYTBS 91 [port]*
**Studer**, Cheryl 1957- *WhoEnt 92*
**Studer**, Constance E. *DrAPF 91*
**Studer**, Constance Elaine Browne 1942- *IntAu&W 91*
**Studer**, Gerald Clyde 1927- *WhoRel 92*
**Studer**, Jimmy Joe 1941- *WhoRel 92*
**Studer**, Michael Thomas 1950- *WhoFI 92*
**Studer**, Patricia S. 1942- *WhoMW 92*
**Studer**, Rebecca Kathryn 1943- *AmMWSc 92*
**Studham**, Lynn 1936- *TwCPaSc*
**Studholme**, Henry 1958 *Who 92*
**Studier**, Eugene H 1940- *AmMWSc 92*
**Studier**, Frederick William 1936- *AmMWSc 92*
**Studier**, Martin Herman 1917- *AmMWSc 92*
**Studl**, Peter John 1949- *WhoFI 92*
**Studlar**, Susan Moyle 1944- *AmMWSc 92*
**Studley**, Helen Ormson 1937- *WhoWest 92*
**Studley**, Jamienne Shayne 1951- *WhoAmL 92*
**Studness**, Charles Michael 1935- *WhoFI 92*
**Studt**, William Lyon 1947- *AmMWSc 92*
**Studtmann**, George H 1930- *AmMWSc 92*
**Studtmann**, Robert H. *WhoRel 92*
**Studwell**, William Emmett 1936- *WhoMW 92*
**Studzinski**, George P 1932- *AmMWSc 92*
**Stuebbe**, Robert *WhoRel 92*
**Stueben**, Edmund Bruno 1920- *AmMWSc 92*
**Stueber**, Alan Michael 1937- *AmMWSc 92*
**Stuebing**, Edward Willis 1942- *AmMWSc 92*
**Stuebner**, James Cloyd 1931- *WhoMW 92*
**Stueckemann**, Walter Frederick 1926- *WhoAmP 91*
**Stuedemann**, John Alfred 1942- *AmMWSc 92*
**Stuehr**, John Edward 1935- *AmMWSc 92*
**Stuehrenberg**, Paul Frederick 1947- *WhoRel 92*
**Stueland**, Dean T 1950- *AmMWSc 92*
**Stueland**, Victor 1920- *WhoAmP 91*
**Stuelpnagel**, John Clay 1936- *AmMWSc 92*
**Stuenkel**, Wayne E 1953- *WhoIns 92*
**Stuermer**, Emil Frank 1935- *WhoMW 92*
**Stuesse**, Sherry Lynn 1944- *AmMWSc 92*
**Stuessy**, Clarence Joseph, Jr. 1943- *WhoEnt 92*
**Stuessy**, Tod Falor 1943- *AmMWSc 92, WhoMW 92*
**Stuewer**, Roger Harry 1934- *AmMWSc 92*
**Stuffle**, Roy Eugene 1944- *AmMWSc 92*
**Stufflebeam**, Charles Edward 1933- *AmMWSc 92*
**Stufflebeam**, H Kent 1931- *WhoAmP 91*
**Stufflebeam**, Norma Colleen 1928- *WhoAmP 91*
**Stuhan**, Richard George 1951- *WhoAmL 92*
**Stuhl**, Louis Sheldon 1951- *AmMWSc 92*
**Stuhl**, Oskar Paul 1949- *WhoFI 92*
**Stuhldreher**, Donald J. 1935- *WhoMW 92*
**Stuhlinger**, Ernst 1913- *AmMWSc 92*
**Stuhlman**, Robert August 1939- *AmMWSc 92*
**Stuhlmiller**, Gary Michael *AmMWSc 92*
**Stuhlmiller**, John Christopher 1963- *WhoWest 92*
**Stuhlmueller**, Carroll 1923- *IntAu&W 91, WhoMW 92, WhoRel 92, WrDr 92*
**Stuhlreyer**, Paul Augustus, III 1952- *WhoEnt 92*
**Stuhltrager**, Gary W 1955- *WhoAmP 91*
**Stuhmiller**, James Hamilton 1943- *AmMWSc 92*
**Stuhr**, Walter M. 1932- *WhoRel 92*
**Stuiver**, Minze 1929- *AmMWSc 92, IntWW 91*
**Stuiver**, W 1927- *AmMWSc 92*
**Stukalin**, Boris Ivanovich 1923- *IntWW 91*
**Stukalin**, Viktor Fyodorovich 1927- *IntWW 91*
**Stukel**, James Joseph 1937- *AmMWSc 92*
**Stukeley**, William 1687-1765 *BlkwCEP*
**Stukus**, Philip Eugene 1942- *AmMWSc 92*
**Stula**, Edwin Francis 1924- *AmMWSc 92*
**Stulberg**, Gordon 1922- *IntMPA 92*
**Stulberg**, Melvin Philip 1925- *AmMWSc 92*
**Stulgis**, Frank Edward 1950- *WhoMW 92*
**Stull**, Dean P *AmMWSc 92*
**Stull**, Denver *DrAPF 91*
**Stull**, Donald L. 1937- *WhoBlA 92*
**Stull**, Elisabeth Ann 1943 *AmMWSc 92*
**Stull**, G A 1933- *AmMWSc 92*
**Stull**, James Travis 1944- *AmMWSc 92*
**Stull**, John Leete 1930- *AmMWSc 92*
**Stull**, John Warren 1921- *AmMWSc 92*
**Stull**, Mark Alan 1962- *WhoFI 92*
**Stull**, Mary Beth 1942- *WhoEnt 92*
**Stull**, Richard *DrAPF 91*
**Stull**, Robert J. 1935- *WhoBlA 92*
**Stull**, Steven Dale 1961- *WhoEnt 92*
**Stull**, Virginia Elizabeth 1939- *WhoBlA 92*
**Stulpnagel**, Karl Heinrich von 1886-1944 *EncTR 91 [port]*
**Stulpnagel**, Otto von 1878-1948 *EncTR 91 [port]*
**Stulting**, Robert Doyle, Jr 1948- *AmMWSc 92*
**Stults**, Frederick Howard 1948- *AmMWSc 92*

**Stults**, Marion Berdette 1925- WhoWest 92
**Stults**, Taylor 1936- WhoMW 92
**Stults**, Theodore McConnell, II 1937- WhoMW 92
**Stults**, Vala Jean 1942- AmMWSc 92
**Stultz**, Robert Lee, Jr. 1926- WhoFI 92
**Stultz**, Walter Alva 1904- AmMWSc 92
**Stumacher**, Eric 1946- WhoEnt 92
**Stumbaugh**, Lawrence 1940- WhoAmP 91
**Stumbles**, James Rubidge Washington 1939- WhoWest 92
**Stumbo**, Grady WhoAmP 91
**Stumbo**, Gregory Damron 1951- WhoAmP 91
**Stumm**, Werner 1924- AmMWSc 92
**Stumme**, Wayne Curtis 1929- WhoRel 92
**Stump**, Billy Lee 1930- AmMWSc 92
**Stump**, Bob 1927- AlmAP 92 [port], WhoAmP 91, WhoWest 92
**Stump**, Christopher Keith 1949- WhoAmL 92
**Stump**, D L ScFEYrs
**Stump**, D. Michael 1947- WhoWest 92
**Stump**, David Griffith 1953- WhoEnt 92
**Stump**, Earl Spencer 1943- WhoMW 92
**Stump**, Edmund 1946- AmMWSc 92
**Stump**, Eugene Curtis, Jr 1930- AmMWSc 92
**Stump**, Jackie T 1948- WhoAmP 91
**Stump**, Jane Barr 1936- ConAu 133
**Stump**, John Edward 1934- AmMWSc 92
**Stump**, John M 1938- AmMWSc 92
**Stump**, John William, III 1949- WhoAmL 92
**Stump**, Miriam Ellen 1928- WhoRel 92
**Stump**, Mitchell Lynn 1949- WhoFI 92
**Stump**, Randall Walker 1947- WhoEnt 92
**Stump**, Robert 1921- AmMWSc 92
**Stump**, Terry Lee 1955- WhoEnt 92
**Stump**, Walter Ray 1934- WhoEnt 92
**Stump**, Wayne H 1935- WhoAmP 91
**Stumpe**, Warren Robert 1925- AmMWSc 92
**Stumpers**, Frans Louis H M 1911- AmMWSc 92
**Stumpf**, Bernhard Josef 1948- WhoWest 92
**Stumpf**, David Allen 1945- WhoMW 92
**Stumpf**, Earlwayne Schwarze 1951- WhoEnt 92
**Stumpf**, Folden Burt 1928- AmMWSc 92, WhoMW 92
**Stumpf**, H C 1918- AmMWSc 92
**Stumpf**, LeRoy A 1944- WhoAmP 91
**Stumpf**, Lowell Clinton 1917- WhoMW 92
**Stumpf**, Lynne Carole 1956- WhoFI 92
**Stumpf**, Michael Howard 1952- WhoWest 92
**Stumpf**, Paul Karl 1919- AmMWSc 92, IntWW 91
**Stumpf**, Peter Philip 1948- WhoAmP 91
**Stumpf**, Samuel 1918- WrDr 92
**Stumpf**, Stephen A 1949- ConAu 34NR
**Stumpf**, Walter Erich 1927- AmMWSc 92
**Stumpf**, William 1936- DcTwDes
**Stumpff**, Howard Keith 1930- AmMWSc 92
**Stumpff-Burnett**, Deborah Kay 1958- WhoMW 92
**Stumph**, William Edward 1948- AmMWSc 92
**Stumpo**, Ronald A. 1957- WhoFI 92
**Stumpp**, Loren Vernon 1931- WhoMW 92
**Stumreiter**, John Jeffrery 1945- WhoAmL 92
**Stunkard**, Albert J 1922- AmMWSc 92
**Stunkard**, Jim A 1935- AmMWSc 92
**Stuntebeck**, Clinton A. 1938- WhoAmL 92
**Stuntz**, Calvin Frederick 1918- AmMWSc 92
**Stuntz**, Gordon Frederick 1952- AmMWSc 92
**Stunz**, John Henry, Jr. 1921- WhoMW 92
**Stunz**, Stephen Conrad 1875-1918 BiInAmS
**Stup**, J Anita WhoAmP 91
**Stupack**, Robert Louis 1956- WhoFI 92
**Stupak**, Bart WhoAmP 91
**Stuparich**, John Nicholas 1954- WhoAmL 92
**Stuper**, Andrew John 1950- AmMWSc 92
**Stupian**, Gary Wendell 1939- AmMWSc 92
**Stupin**, Susan Lee 1954- WhoFI 92
**Stupp**, Edward Henry 1932- AmMWSc 92
**Stupples**, Peter 1936- ConAu 133
**Sturbaum**, Barbara Ann 1936- AmMWSc 92
**Sturch**, Conrad Ray 1937- AmMWSc 92
**Sturcken**, Edward Francis 1927- AmMWSc 92
**Sturcken**, Frank 1929- ConAu 135
**Sturdee**, Arthur Rodney Barry 1919- Who 92
**Sturdevant**, Eugene J 1930- AmMWSc 92
**Sturdevant**, James Cosgriff 1947- WhoAmL 92
**Sturdivant**, James M. 1937- WhoAmL 92
**Sturdivant**, John Nathan 1938- WhoBlA 92
**Sturdy**, Henry William 1919- Who 92
**Sture**, Stein 1947- WhoWest 92
**Sturek**, Walter Beynon 1937- AmMWSc 92
**Sturen**, Olle 1919- IntWW 91
**Sturett**, Michael Steven 1950- WhoWest 92
**Sturge**, Harold Francis Ralph 1902- Who 92
**Sturge**, John 1925- Who 92
**Sturge**, Michael Dudley 1931- AmMWSc 92
**Sturgeon**, Al 1956- WhoAmP 91
**Sturgeon**, Charles Edwin 1928- WhoFI 92
**Sturgeon**, David Hamilton 1953- WhoRel 92
**Sturgeon**, Edward Earl 1916- AmMWSc 92
**Sturgeon**, George Dennis 1937- AmMWSc 92
**Sturgeon**, Karla Sue 1961- WhoRel 92
**Sturgeon**, Lang Stocker 1950- WhoEnt 92
**Sturgeon**, Mark B. 1954- WhoFI 92
**Sturgeon**, Myron Thomas 1908- AmMWSc 92
**Sturgeon**, Roy V, Jr 1924- AmMWSc 92
**Sturgeon**, Russ Campbell, Sr. 1952- WhoEnt 92
**Sturgeon**, Theodore 1918-1985 BenetAL 91, TwCSFW 91
**Sturges**, David L 1938- AmMWSc 92
**Sturges**, Jeffery Alan 1946- WhoEnt 92
**Sturges**, John 1911- IntDcF 2-2 [port]
**Sturges**, John Eliot 1910- IntMPA 92, WhoEnt 92
**Sturges**, John Siebrand 1939- WhoFI 92
**Sturges**, Leroy D 1945- AmMWSc 92
**Sturges**, Preston 1898-1959 BenetAL 91, FacFETw, IntDcF 2-2 [port]
**Sturges**, Robert Alfred 1920- WhoMW 92
**Sturges**, Sherry Lynn 1946- WhoEnt 92
**Sturges**, Stuart 1913- AmMWSc 92
**Sturges**, Wilton, III 1935- AmMWSc 92
**Sturgess**, Jennifer Mary 1944- AmMWSc 92
**Sturgess**, Robert Alan 1944- WhoWest 92
**Sturgies**, Calvin Henry, Jr. 1933- WhoBlA 92
**Sturgill**, Benjamin Caleb 1934- AmMWSc 92
**Sturgis**, Bernard Miller 1911- AmMWSc 92
**Sturgis**, Howard Ewing 1936- AmMWSc 92
**Sturgis**, Russell 1836-1909 FacFETw
**Sturgis**, Somers Hayes d1991 NewYTBS 91
**Sturgulewski**, Arliss 1927- WhoWest 92
**Sturgulewski**, Jane Arliss 1927- WhoAmP 91
**Sturhahn**, Lawrence DrAPF 91
**Sturino**, Eugenio 1961- WhoFI 92
**Sturkey**, Douglas 1935- Who 92
**Sturkie**, C Lenoir 1951- WhoAmP 91
**Sturkie**, Paul David 1909- AmMWSc 92
**Sturla**, P Michael 1956- WhoAmP 91
**Sturley**, Eric Avern 1915- AmMWSc 92
**Sturley**, Michael F. 1955- WhoAmL 92
**Sturm**, Blaine Carey 1962- WhoMW 92
**Sturm**, Cheryl Johns 1948- WhoAmL 92
**Sturm**, Douglas Earl 1929- WhoRel 92
**Sturm**, Edith S. 1947- WhoFI 92
**Sturm**, Edward AmMWSc 92
**Sturm**, Ephraim H. 1924- WhoRel 92
**Sturm**, George 1930- WhoEnt 92
**Sturm**, James Edward 1930- AmMWSc 92
**Sturm**, James Marvin Gray 1964- WhoMW 92
**Sturm**, Michel Robert 1947- WhoMW 92
**Sturm**, Terence Laurie 1941- IntAu&W 91
**Sturm**, Thomas Paul 1946- WhoMW 92
**Sturm**, Walter Allan 1930- AmMWSc 92
**Sturm**, Walter Carson 1935- WhoMW 92
**Sturm**, William Charles 1941- WhoAmL 92
**Sturm**, William James 1917- AmMWSc 92
**Sturman**, John Andrew 1941- AmMWSc 92
**Sturman**, John Rollin 1952- IntAu&W 91
**Sturman**, Joseph Howard 1931- WhoAmL 92
**Sturman**, Lawrence Stuart 1938- AmMWSc 92
**Sturman**, Robert Harries 1923- WhoMW 92
**Sturmer**, Boris Vladimirovich 1848-1917 FacFETw
**Sturmer**, David Michael 1940- AmMWSc 92
**Sturr**, James William, Jr. 1946- WhoEnt 92
**Sturr**, Joseph Francis 1933- AmMWSc 92
**Sturridge**, Charles IntWW 91
**Sturrock**, Jeremy WrDr 92
**Sturrock**, Peter Andrew 1924- AmMWSc 92, WhoWest 92
**Sturrock**, Peter Earle 1929- AmMWSc 92
**Sturrock**, Philip James 1947- Who 92
**Stursberg**, Carl W., Jr. d1991 NewYTBS 91 [port]
**Sturtevant**, Bradford 1933- AmMWSc 92
**Sturtevant**, Deborah Sue 1954- WhoMW 92
**Sturtevant**, Edward Lewis 1842-1898 BiInAmS
**Sturtevant**, Frank Milton 1927- AmMWSc 92
**Sturtevant**, Julian Munson 1908- AmMWSc 92, IntWW 91
**Sturtevant**, Roger 1937- WhoEnt 92
**Sturtevant**, Ruthann Patterson 1927- AmMWSc 92
**Sturua**, Robert 1938- IntWW 91
**Sturzenegger**, August 1921- AmMWSc 92
**Stushnoff**, Cecil 1940- AmMWSc 92
**Stusnick**, Eric 1939- AmMWSc 92
**Stuteville**, Donald Lee 1930- AmMWSc 92
**Stuth**, Charles James 1932- AmMWSc 92
**Stuthman**, Deon Dean 1940- AmMWSc 92
**Stutler**, Eddie Lionel 1941- WhoMW 92
**Stutman**, Harris Ronald 1947- WhoWest 92
**Stutman**, Leonard Jay 1928- AmMWSc 92
**Stutman**, Osias 1933- AmMWSc 92
**Stutt**, Charles A 1921- AmMWSc 92
**Stuttaford**, Thomas 1931- Who 92
**Stuttaford**, William Royden 1928- Who 92
**Stutte**, Charles A 1933- AmMWSc 92
**Stutte**, Linda Gail 1946- AmMWSc 92
**Stutts**, David Hugh 1949- WhoRel 92
**Stutz**, Conley I 1932- AmMWSc 92
**Stutz**, Howard Coombs 1918- AmMWSc 92
**Stutz**, I. Harold 1924- WhoFI 92, WhoMW 92
**Stutz**, Kenneth Louis 1947- WhoEnt 92
**Stutz**, Robert L 1931- AmMWSc 92
**Stutzenberger**, Fred John 1940- AmMWSc 92
**Stutzle**, Walther K. A. 1941- IntWW 91
**Stutzman**, Ervin Ray 1953- WhoRel 92
**Stutzman**, L. Lee 1953- WhoRel 92
**Stutzman**, Leroy F 1917- AmMWSc 92
**Stutzman**, Myron David 1941- WhoAmL 92
**Stutzman**, Warren Lee 1941- AmMWSc 92
**Stuve**, Eric Michael 1956- AmMWSc 92
**Stuvinski**, B. C. 1953- WhoEnt 92
**Stuy**, Johan Harrie 1925- AmMWSc 92
**Stuyck**, Guy 1921- IntWW 91
**Stuyt**, L. B. J. 1914- IntWW 91
**Stuyvesant**, Peter 1592-1672 BenetAL 91
**Stuyvesant**, Peter 1610?-1672 RComAH
**Stuyvesant**, Phillip Wayne 1940- WhoMW 92
**Stwalley**, William Calvin 1942- AmMWSc 92, WhoMW 92
**Styan**, J. L. 1923- WrDr 92
**Styblinski**, Maciej A 1942- AmMWSc 92
**Styczinski**, Teddy George 1925- WhoAmP 91
**Styer**, Daniel F 1955- AmMWSc 92
**Styer**, Jane Marie 1957- WhoAmL 92
**Styer**, Wilhelm 1893-1975 FacFETw
**Styffe**, Edwin Howard, Jr. 1937- WhoMW 92
**Style**, Godfrey 1915- Who 92
**Style**, William Frederick 1945- Who 92
**Styles**, Beverly 1923- WhoEnt 92, WhoWest 92
**Styles**, Eric Todd 1963- WhoEnt 92
**Styles**, Ernest Derek 1926- AmMWSc 92
**Styles**, Frank Showell WrDr 92
**Styles**, Frank Showell 1908- Who 92
**Styles**, Freddie L. 1944- WhoBlA 92
**Styles**, Fredrick William 1914- Who 92
**Styles**, George Who 92
**Styles**, Julian English 1924- WhoBlA 92
**Styles**, Kathleen Ann 1949- WhoBlA 92
**Styles**, Margretta 1930- IntWW 91
**Styles**, Margretta M 1930- AmMWSc 92
**Styles**, Mark 1956- WhoAmL 92
**Styles**, Marvalene H. 1937- WhoBlA 92
**Styles**, Richard Geoffrey Pentland 1930- IntWW 91
**Styles**, Richard Wayne 1939- WhoBlA 92
**Styles**, Showell Who 92
**Styles**, Showell 1908- IntAu&W 91
**Styles**, Stephen George 1928- Who 92
**Styles**, Teresa Jo 1950- IntAu&W 91, WhoEnt 92
**Styles**, Twitty Junius 1927- AmMWSc 92
**Stylianou**, Petros Savva 1933- IntWW 91
**Stylos**, William A 1927- AmMWSc 92
**Styne**, Jule 1905- FacFETw, IntMPA 92, IntWW 91, NewAmDM
**Stynes**, Stanley K 1932- AmMWSc 92
**Styring**, Ralph E 1921- AmMWSc 92
**Styris**, David Lee 1932- AmMWSc 92
**Styron**, Charles Woodrow 1913- AmMWSc 92
**Styron**, Clarence Edward, Jr 1941- AmMWSc 92
**Styron**, William DrAPF 91
**Styron**, William 1925- BenetAL 91, ConNov 91, FacFETw, IntWW 91, WrDr 92
**Styron**, William, Jr 1925- IntAu&W 91
**Styrsky**, Dennis Martan 1944- WhoFI 92, WhoMW 92
**Styrt**, Paul Joseph 1958- WhoWest 92
**Su Buqing** 1902- IntWW 91
**Su Gang** 1920- IntWW 91
**Su Shaozhi** 1923- IntWW 91
**Su Wei** 1953- LiExTwC
**Su Xiaokang** LiExTwC
**Su Yiran** IntWW 91
**Su**, Chau-Hsing 1935- AmMWSc 92
**Su**, Cheh-Jen 1934- AmMWSc 92
**Su**, George Chung-Chi 1939- AmMWSc 92
**Su**, Helen Chien-Fan 1922- AmMWSc 92
**Su**, Jin-Chen 1932- AmMWSc 92
**Su**, Judy Ya-Hwa Lin 1938- AmMWSc 92
**Su**, Kendall L 1926- AmMWSc 92
**Su**, Kenneth Shyan-Ell 1941- AmMWSc 92
**Su**, Kwei Lee 1942- AmMWSc 92
**Su**, Lao-Sou 1932- AmMWSc 92
**Su**, Robert Tzyh-Chuan 1945- AmMWSc 92
**Su**, Shin-Yi 1940- AmMWSc 92
**Su**, Stanley Y W 1940- AmMWSc 92
**Su**, Stephen Y H 1938- AmMWSc 92
**Su**, Tah-Mun 1939- AmMWSc 92
**Su**, Yao Sin 1929- AmMWSc 92
**Suarez**, Duke of 1932- IntWW 91
**Suarez**, Adrian 1954- WhoHisp 92
**Suarez**, Carlos Esteban 1953- WhoWest 92
**Suarez**, Celia Cristina 1943- WhoHisp 92
**Suarez**, David Mark 1961- WhoMW 92
**Suarez**, Diego WhoHisp 92
**Suarez**, Diego A. 1928- WhoHisp 92
**Suarez**, Ernest 1958- WhoHisp 92
**Suarez**, Francisco 1548-1617 HisDSpE
**Suarez**, Francisco Herminio 1929- WhoHisp 92
**Suarez**, Hector E. 1949- WhoHisp 92
**Suarez**, Inez EncAmaz 91
**Suarez**, Jerry 1960- WhoEnt 92
**Suarez**, Jesus WhoHisp 92
**Suarez**, Jorge Mario 1932- WhoHisp 92
**Suarez**, Jose Gerardo 1962- WhoWest 92
**Suarez**, Jose Ignacio 1951- WhoHisp 92
**Suarez**, Juan L. Who 92
**Suarez**, Kenneth Alfred 1944- AmMWSc 92, WhoMW 92
**Suarez**, Leo 1957- WhoHisp 92
**Suarez**, Lionel WhoHisp 92
**Suarez**, Luis 1934- WhoHisp 92
**Suarez**, Luis Edgardo 1957- WhoHisp 92
**Suarez**, Manuel, Jr. 1930- WhoHisp 92
**Suarez**, Marcos N. 1949- WhoHisp 92
**Suarez**, Margarita M. W. 1957- WhoHisp 92
**Suarez**, Maria D. 1958- WhoHisp 92
**Suarez**, Mariano Arroyo 1910- WhoHisp 92
**Suarez**, Mario Jesus 1952- WhoAmL 92
**Suarez**, Michael Anthony 1948- WhoFI 92
**Suarez**, Omero 1947- WhoHisp 92
**Suarez**, Paco 1931- WhoEnt 92
**Suarez**, R. A. WhoHisp 92
**Suarez**, Rafael Angel, Jr. 1957- WhoHisp 92, WhoMW 92
**Suarez**, Ray WhoAmP 91
**Suarez**, Regner WhoHisp 92
**Suarez**, Roberto 1928- WhoHisp 92
**Suarez**, Ruben Dario 1925- WhoHisp 92
**Suarez**, Tem WhoHisp 92
**Suarez**, Thomas H 1936- AmMWSc 92
**Suarez**, Victor Omar 1934- WhoHisp 92
**Suarez**, Virgil 1962- WhoHisp 92
**Suarez**, Xavier L. 1949- WhoHisp 92
**Suarez**, Xavier Louis 1949- WhoAmP 91
**Suarez-Barrio**, Antonio Valentin 1933- WhoHisp 92
**Suarez de Peralta**, Juan 153-?-1590? HisDSpE
**Suarez Lynch**, B IntAu&W 91X
**Suarez-Quian**, Carlos Andres 1953- WhoHisp 92
**Suarez Rivera**, Adolfo Antonio 1927- WhoRel 92
**Suarez-Rivero**, Eliana 1940- WhoHisp 92
**Suarez-Rogers**, Barbara Jeanne 1938- WhoWest 92
**Suarez-Villa**, Luis 1947- WhoFI 92, WhoHisp 92
**Suarez y Romero**, Anselmo 1818-1878 HisDSpE
**Suazo**, Robert Carl 1951- WhoMW 92
**Subach**, Daniel James 1947- AmMWSc 92
**Subach**, James Alan 1948- WhoWest 92
**Subak-Sharpe**, John Herbert 1924- Who 92
**Subandrio** 1914- IntWW 91
**Subba Row**, Raman 1932- Who 92
**Subbaiah**, Papasani Venkata 1943- AmMWSc 92
**Subbaswamy**, Kumble R 1951- AmMWSc 92
**Subbotin**, Aleksandr Mikhailovich 1924- IntWW 91
**Subbulakshmi**, Madurai Shanmugavadivu 1916- IntWW 91
**Suben**, Joel Eric 1946- WhoEnt 92

**Suber,** Martin Gay 1937- *WhoAmP 91*
**Suber,** Tommie Lee 1947- *WhoMW 92*
**Suberkropp,** Keller Francis 1943- *AmMWSc 92*
**Subich,** Linda Mezydlo 1956- *WhoMW 92*
**Subin,** Bertram W. d1991 *NewYTBS 91*
**Subin,** Florence 1935- *WhoAmL 92*
**Subjeck,** John Robert *AmMWSc 92*
**Sublett,** Bobby Jones 1931- *AmMWSc 92*
**Sublett,** Charles William, Jr *WhoAmP 91*
**Sublett,** Marvin Thomas 1935- *WhoRel 92*
**Sublett,** Norma Raedean 1925- *WhoAmP 91*
**Sublett,** Robert L 1921- *AmMWSc 92*
**Sublette,** C M 1887-1939 *TwCWW 91*
**Sublette,** Ivan H 1929- *AmMWSc 92*
**Sublette,** James Edward 1928- *AmMWSc 92*
**Sublette,** Walter *DrAPF 91*
**Subotnick,** Morton 1933- *ConCom 92, NewAmDM, WhoEnt 92*
**Subotnick,** Morton Leon 1933- *IntWW 91*
**Subrahmanian,** Kalpakasseri Pattom 1946- *WhoMW 92*
**Subrahmanyam,** D 1948- *AmMWSc 92*
**Subraman,** Belinda *DrAPF 91, IntAu&W 91*
**Subramani,** Suresh 1952- *AmMWSc 92*
**Subramaniam,** Chandra Shekar 1952- *WhoFI 92*
**Subramaniam,** Chidambaram 1910- *IntWW 91, Who 92*
**Subramaniam,** Shivan S 1949- *WhoIns 92*
**Subramanian,** Alap Raman 1935- *AmMWSc 92*
**Subramanian,** Gopal 1937- *AmMWSc 92*
**Subramanian,** K N 1938- *AmMWSc 92*
**Subramanian,** Mani M 1934- *AmMWSc 92*
**Subramanian,** Marappa G 1938- *AmMWSc 92*
**Subramanian,** Pallatheri Manackal 1931- *AmMWSc 92*
**Subramanian,** Pazhayannur Ramanathan 1956- *WhoMW 92*
**Subramanian,** Ram Shankar 1947- *AmMWSc 92*
**Subramanian,** Ravanasamudram V. 1933- *WhoWest 92*
**Subramanian,** Ravanasamudram Venkatachala 1933- *AmMWSc 92*
**Subramanian,** Sesha 1935- *AmMWSc 92*
**Subramanian,** Sethuraman 1940- *AmMWSc 92*
**Subramanian,** Sundaram 1934- *WhoWest 92*
**Subramanya,** Shiva 1933- *AmMWSc 92, WhoWest 92*
**Subramanyam,** Dilip Kumar 1955- *AmMWSc 92*
**Subramanyan,** Kalpathi Ganapathi 1924- *IntWW 91*
**Subramuniyaswami,** Sivaya 1927- *RelLAm 91*
**Subroto** 1928- *IntWW 91*
**Subryan,** Carmen 1944- *WhoBlA 92*
**Subudhi,** Manomohan 1946- *AmMWSc 92*
**Subuh,** Muhammad 1901- *RelLAm 91*
**Sucec,** James 1940- *AmMWSc 92*
**Such,** Frederick Rudolph Charles 1936- *Who 92*
**Such,** Mary Jane 1942- *WhoMW 92*
**Suchannek,** Rudolf Gerhard 1921- *AmMWSc 92*
**Suchard,** Steven Norman 1944- *AmMWSc 92*
**Sucharitkul,** Sompong 1931- *IntWW 91*
**Sucharitkul,** Somtow 1952- *TwCSFW 91, WrDr 92*
**Sucher,** Cynthia Clayton Crumb 1943- *WhoFI 92*
**Sucher,** Dorothy Glassman 1933- *IntAu&W 91*
**Sucher,** Vivian Madeline 1923- *WhoWest 92*
**Sucheston,** Martha Elaine 1939- *AmMWSc 92*
**Suchet,** David 1946- *Who 92*
**Suchil,** Sally 1951- *WhoAmL 92*
**Suchin,** Milton Bernard 1944- *WhoEnt 92*
**Suchlicki,** Jaime 1939- *WhoHisp 92*
**Suchman,** David 1947- *AmMWSc 92*
**Suchodolski,** Bogdan 1903- *IntWW 91*
**Suchoff,** Daniel 1954- *WhoFI 92*
**Suchomel,** Jeffrey Raymond 1956- *WhoMW 92*
**Suchon,** Eugen 1908- *IntWW 91*
**Suchow,** Lawrence 1923- *AmMWSc 92*
**Suchsland,** Otto 1928- *AmMWSc 92*
**Suciu,** George Dan 1934- *AmMWSc 92*
**Suciu,** S N 1921- *AmMWSc 92*
**Sucke,** John Howard, III 1942- *WhoAmL 92, WhoEnt 92*
**Suckewer,** Szymon 1938- *AmMWSc 92*
**Suckiel,** Ellen Kappy 1943- *WhoWest 92*
**Suckley,** George 1830-1869 *BiInAmS*
**Suckley,** Margaret L. d1991 *NewYTBS 91*
**Suckling,** Charles W. 1920- *IntWW 91*
**Suckling,** Charles Walter 1920- *Who 92*
**Suckling,** John 1609?-1641? *RfGEnL 91*
**Suckow,** Robert William 1919- *WhoMW 92*
**Suckow,** Ruth 1892-1960 *BenetAL 91, TwCWW 91*
**Suckow,** Steven Edward 1960- *WhoMW 92*
**Sucksdorff,** Ake, Mrs. *Who 92*
**Sucksdorff,** Arne 1917- *IntDcF 2-2*
**Sucksdorff,** Arne Edvard 1917- *IntWW 91*
**Sucoff,** Edward Ira 1931- *AmMWSc 92*
**Sucov,** E W 1922- *AmMWSc 92*
**Sucre,** Guillermo 1933- *ConSpAP*
**Sucre Alcala,** Antonio Jose de 1795-1830 *HisDSpE*
**Sucre-Figarella,** Jose Francisco 1931- *IntWW 91*
**Sucsy,** Steven McDonald 1952- *WhoAmL 92*
**Suczek,** Christopher A. 1942- *WhoWest 92*
**Suczek,** Christopher Anne 1942- *AmMWSc 92*
**Sud,** Ish 1949- *AmMWSc 92*
**Suda,** Zdenek Ludvik 1920- *WrDr 92*
**Sudak,** Jill Roxanne 1963- *WhoMW 92*
**Sudakov,** Il'ya Yakovlevich 1890-1969 *SovUnBD*
**Sudalnik,** James Edward 1951- *WhoEnt 92*
**Sudan,** Ravindra Nath 1931- *AmMWSc 92*
**Sudarkasa,** Niara 1938- *NotBlAW 92 [port], WhoBlA 92*
**Sudarshan,** Ennackel Chandy George 1931- *AmMWSc 92*
**Sudarshan,** T S 1955- *AmMWSc 92*
**Sudarshan,** Tangali S *AmMWSc 92*
**Sudarsky,** Jerry M. 1918- *WhoFI 92*
**Sudbeck,** Richard James 1957- *WhoWest 92*
**Sudberry,** Johnny Ray 1958- *WhoRel 92*
**Sudbery,** Rodie 1943- *WrDr 92*
**Sudborough,** Ivan Hal 1943- *AmMWSc 92*
**Sudborough,** Lois Engle 1921- *WhoWest 92*
**Sudborough,** Richard Rainer 1953- *WhoEnt 92*
**Sudbury,** Archdeacon of *Who 92*
**Sudbury,** David Marshall 1945- *WhoAmL 92*
**Sudbury,** John Dean 1925- *AmMWSc 92, WhoRel 92*
**Sudbury,** Leslie G. 1939- *WhoBlA 92*
**Suddaby,** Arthur 1919- *Who 92*
**Suddaby,** Rowland 1912-1972 *TwCPaSc*
**Suddards,** Gaunt 1910- *Who 92*
**Suddards,** Roger Whitley 1930- *Who 92*
**Suddarth,** Deborah K. 1951- *WhoRel 92*
**Suddarth,** Roscoe Seldon 1935- *WhoAmP 91*
**Suddarth,** Stanley Kendrick 1921- *AmMWSc 92*
**Suddath,** Fred LeRoy 1942- *AmMWSc 92*
**Sudderth,** William David 1940- *AmMWSc 92, WhoMW 92*
**Sudderth,** William H. 1924- *WhoBlA 92*
**Suddick,** Richard Phillips 1934- *AmMWSc 92*
**Suddock,** Frances Suter Thorson 1914- *WhoWest 92*
**Sudds,** Richard Huyette, Jr 1927- *AmMWSc 92*
**Sudeary,** Abdelmuhsin M. Al- 1936- *IntWW 91*
**Sudekum,** William Anthony, Jr. 1949- *WhoWest 92*
**Sudeley,** Baron 1939- *Who 92*
**Suder,** Robert Braswell 1945- *WhoAmL 92*
**Suderman,** Harold Julius 1921- *AmMWSc 92*
**Suderman,** Linda Mary 1946- *WhoMW 92*
**Sudgrove,** Sidney Henry 1920- *IntAu&W 91*
**Sudharmono** 1927- *IntWW 91*
**Sudia,** Theodore William 1925- *AmMWSc 92*
**Sudia,** William Daniel 1922- *AmMWSc 92*
**Sudijono,** John Leonard 1966- *WhoMW 92*
**Sudik,** James William 1952- *WhoEnt 92*
**Sudman,** Seymour 1928- *WhoMW 92*
**Sudman,** Susan K. 1949- *WhoMW 92*
**Sudmeier,** James Lee 1938- *AmMWSc 92*
**Sudol,** Barbara 1942- *WhoRel 92*
**Sudol,** Rita A. 1949- *WhoHisp 92*
**Sudol,** Walter Edward 1942- *WhoAmL 92*
**Sudolcan,** Catherine Eleaine 1953- *WhoWest 92*
**Sudomo** 1926- *IntWW 91*
**Sudreau,** Pierre Robert 1919- *IntWW 91*
**Suduiko,** Ronald Paul 1949- *WhoAmP 91*
**Sudweeks,** Earl Max 1933- *AmMWSc 92*
**Sudweeks,** Walter Bentley 1940- *AmMWSc 92*
**Sue,** Alan Kwai Keong 1946- *WhoWest 92*
**Sue,** Lawrence Gene 1939- *WhoWest 92*
**Su'e,** Lefao Fuimaono 1930- *WhoAmP 91*
**Sue,** Louis 1875-1968 *DcTwDes, FacFETw*
**Sue,** Marie-Joseph 1804-1857 *GuFrLit 1*
**Suelflow,** August R. 1922- *WrDr 92*
**Suelflow,** August Robert 1922- *WhoMW 92*
**Suell,** Robert May 1917- *WhoAmP 91*
**Sueltenfuss,** Elizabeth Anne 1921- *WhoRel 92*
**Suelter,** Clarence Henry 1928- *AmMWSc 92*
**Suen,** Ching Yee 1942- *AmMWSc 92*
**Suen,** T J 1912- *AmMWSc 92*
**Suenaga,** Masaki 1937- *AmMWSc 92*
**Suenens,** Leo Joseph 1904- *Who 92, WhoRel 92*
**Suenens,** Leo Jozef 1904- *IntWW 91*
**Suenram,** Richard Dee 1945- *AmMWSc 92*
**Suenson-Taylor** *Who 92*
**Sueoka,** Noboru 1929- *AmMWSc 92, WhoWest 92*
**Sueppel,** William *WhoAmP 91*
**Suer,** H S 1926- *AmMWSc 92*
**Suerth,** Margaret Agnes 1932- *WhoMW 92*
**Suess,** Gene Guy 1941- *AmMWSc 92*
**Suess,** Hans Eduard 1909- *AmMWSc 92*
**Suess,** James Francis 1919- *AmMWSc 92*
**Suess,** John Gunther 1929- *WhoMW 92*
**Suess,** Steven Tyler 1942- *AmMWSc 92*
**Suetonius,** Gaius Tranquillus 70?-140? *EncEarC*
**Suff,** David 1955- *TwCPaSc*
**Suffern,** Edward William 1957- *WhoRel 92*
**Suffet,** I H 1939- *AmMWSc 92*
**Suffian,** Mohamed 1917- *Who 92*
**Suffield,** Baron 1922- *Who 92*
**Suffield,** Lester 1911- *Who 92*
**Suffin,** Stephen Chester 1947- *AmMWSc 92*
**Suffolk,** Archdeacon of *Who 92*
**Suffolk And Berkshire,** Earl of 1935- *Who 92*
**Sufit,** Robert Louis 1950- *AmMWSc 92, WhoMW 92*
**Sufrin,** Janice Richman 1941- *AmMWSc 92*
**Sufrin,** Jodi Lee 1955- *WhoRel 92*
**Suga,** Hiroyuki 1941- *AmMWSc 92*
**Suga,** Nobuo 1933- *AmMWSc 92*
**Sugai,** Iwao 1928- *AmMWSc 92*
**Sugai,** Kumi 1919- *IntWW 91*
**Sugala** *EncAmaz 91*
**Sugam,** Richard Jay 1951- *AmMWSc 92*
**Sugano,** Katsuhito 1948- *AmMWSc 92*
**Suganuma,** Eric Kazuto 1958- *WhoWest 92*
**Sugar,** Alan 1944- *WhoMW 92*
**Sugar,** Alan Michael 1947- *IntWW 91, Who 92*
**Sugar,** George R 1925- *AmMWSc 92*
**Sugar,** Jack 1929- *AmMWSc 92*
**Sugar,** Joseph M. 1922- *IntMPA 92*
**Sugar,** Joseph Robert 1928- *WhoEnt 92*
**Sugar,** Larry 1945- *IntMPA 92, WhoEnt 92*
**Sugar,** Oscar 1914- *AmMWSc 92*
**Sugar,** Robert Louis 1938- *AmMWSc 92*
**Sugar,** Samuel John 1958- *WhoAmL 92*
**Sugarbaker,** Evan Roy 1949- *AmMWSc 92*
**Sugarman,** Burt *IntMPA 92*
**Sugarman,** George 1912- *WorArt 1980*
**Sugarman,** Jule Meyer 1927- *WhoAmP 91*
**Sugarman,** Myron George 1942- *WhoAmL 92*
**Sugarman,** Nathan 1917- *AmMWSc 92*
**Sugarman,** Paul Ronald 1931- *WhoAmL 92*
**Sugarman,** Robert Gary 1939- *WhoAmL 92, WhoEnt 92*
**Sugarman,** Ronald Samuel 1941- *WhoAmL 92*
**Sugarman,** Stephen D. 1942- *WhoAmL 92*
**Sugathan,** Kanneth Kochappan 1926- *AmMWSc 92*
**Sugaya,** Hiroshi 1931- *AmMWSc 92*
**Sugden,** Arthur 1918- *Who 92*
**Sugden,** Evan A 1952- *AmMWSc 92*
**Sugden,** Francis George 1938- *Who 92*
**Sugden,** John Goldthorp 1921- *Who 92*
**Sugden,** Richard Lee 1959- *WhoMW 92, WhoRel 92*
**Sugerman,** Abraham Arthur 1929- *AmMWSc 92*
**Sugerman,** David F. 1959- *WhoAmL 92*
**Sugerman,** Leonard Richard 1920- *AmMWSc 92*
**Sugerman,** Lewis Martin 1946- *WhoFI 92*
**Sugerman,** Richard Alan 1944- *WhoWest 92*
**Sugg,** Aldhelm St John 1909- *Who 92*
**Sugg,** Margaret Joyce 1929- *WhoAmP 91*
**Sugg,** William Edward, Jr. 1951- *WhoFI 92*
**Suggitt,** Robert Murray 1925- *AmMWSc 92*
**Suggs,** Charles Wilson 1928- *AmMWSc 92*
**Suggs,** John William 1948- *AmMWSc 92*
**Suggs,** M. Jack 1924- *WrDr 92*
**Suggs,** Marion Jack 1924- *WhoRel 92*
**Suggs,** Morris Talmage, Jr 1927- *AmMWSc 92*
**Suggs,** Robert Chinelo 1943- *WhoBlA 92*
**Suggs,** William Albert 1922- *WhoBlA 92*
**Suggs,** William Terry 1945- *AmMWSc 92*
**Sughrue,** Jack *DrAPF 91*
**Sughrue,** Kathryn Eileen *WhoAmP 91*
**Sugihara,** James Masanobu 1918- *AmMWSc 92*
**Sugihara,** Thomas Tamotsu 1924- *AmMWSc 92*
**Sugiki,** Shigemi 1936- *WhoWest 92*
**Sugimoto,** Yoshio 1939- *WrDr 92*
**Sugioka,** Kenneth 1920- *AmMWSc 92*
**Sugita,** Edwin T 1937- *AmMWSc 92*
**Sugiura,** Binsuke 1911- *IntWW 91*
**Sugiura,** Masahisa 1925- *AmMWSc 92*
**Sugrue,** Dennis Patrick 1949- *WhoMW 92*
**Suh,** Chung-Ha 1932- *AmMWSc 92*
**Suh,** John Taiyoung *AmMWSc 92*
**Suh,** Nam Pyo 1936- *AmMWSc 92*
**Suh,** Paul Mansoo 1939- *WhoRel 92*
**Suh,** Tae-il 1928- *AmMWSc 92*
**Suhadolnik,** Gary C 1950- *WhoAmP 91*
**Suhadolnik,** Robert J 1925- *AmMWSc 92*
**Suharto** 1921- *FacFETw, IntWW 91, NewYTBS 91 [port]*
**Suharto,** Gen. *Who 92*
**Suhartoyo,** S. 1926- *Who 92*
**Suhayda,** Joseph Nicholas 1944- *AmMWSc 92*
**Suhir,** Ephraim 1937- *AmMWSc 92*
**Suhl,** Harry 1922- *AmMWSc 92, IntWW 91*
**Suhling,** June *WhoAmP 91*
**Suhm,** Raymond Walter 1941- *AmMWSc 92*
**Suhor,** Mary Lou 1929- *WhoRel 92*
**Suhoski,** Chester A 1941- *WhoAmP 91*
**Suhosky,** Bob 1928- *IntMPA 92*
**Suhovecky,** Albert J 1926- *AmMWSc 92*
**Suhr,** Moon Ja Minn 1940- *WhoEnt 92*
**Suhr,** Norman Henry 1930- *AmMWSc 92*
**Suhre,** Carol Ann 1958- *WhoAmL 92*
**Suhre,** Walter Anthony, Jr. 1933- *WhoAmL 92, WhoFI 92*
**Suhrheinrich,** Richard *WhoAmP 91*
**Suhrheinrich,** Richard Fred 1936- *WhoAmL 92*
**Suhrland,** Leif George 1919- *AmMWSc 92*
**Suib,** Steven L 1953- *AmMWSc 92*
**Suica,** David Earl 1957- *WhoMW 92*
**Suich,** John Edward 1936- *AmMWSc 92*
**Suich,** Maxwell Victor 1938- *IntWW 91*
**Suich,** Ronald Charles 1940- *AmMWSc 92*
**Suinn,** Richard M 1933- *AmMWSc 92, WrDr 92*
**Suinn,** Richard Michael 1933- *WhoWest 92*
**Suirdale,** Viscount 1952- *Who 92*
**Suiseth,** Riccardus *DcLB 115*
**Suisman,** Edward d1991 *NewYTBS 91*
**Suit,** Herman Day 1929- *AmMWSc 92*
**Suit,** Joan C 1931- *AmMWSc 92*
**Suiter,** Marilyn J *AmMWSc 92*
**Suiter,** Norma Jean 1936- *WhoRel 92*
**Suitner,** Otmar 1922- *IntWW 91*
**Suits,** C. G. 1905-1991 *CurBio 91N*
**Suits,** Chauncey Guy d1991 *NewYTBS 91 [port]*
**Suits,** Chauncey Guy 1905- *AmMWSc 92, IntWW 91*
**Suits,** Christopher Daniel 1959- *WhoFI 92*
**Suits,** James Carr 1932- *AmMWSc 92*
**Sujack,** Edwin Thomas 1927- *WhoAmL 92*
**Sujishi,** Sei 1921- *AmMWSc 92*
**Sujo,** Glenn 1952- *TwCPaSc*
**Suk,** Josef 1874-1935 *NewAmDM*
**Suk,** Josef 1929- *IntWW 91, NewAmDM*
**Suk,** Julie *DrAPF 91*
**Suk,** William Alfred 1945- *AmMWSc 92*
**Sukachev,** Vladimir Nikolaevich 1880-1967 *SovUnBD*
**Sukanek,** Peter Charles 1947- *AmMWSc 92*
**Sukarno** 1901-1970 *FacFETw [port]*
**Sukatschew,** Vladimir Nikolaevich 1880-1967 *SovUnBD*
**Sukava,** Armas John 1917- *AmMWSc 92*
**Sukenick,** Lynn *DrAPF 91*
**Sukenick,** Ronald *DrAPF 91*
**Sukenick,** Ronald 1932- *ConNov 91, IntAu&W 91, WrDr 92*
**Sukenik,** Ronald 1932- *BenetAL 91*
**Suker,** Jacob Robert 1926- *AmMWSc 92*
**Sukharev,** Aleksander Yakovlevich 1923- *SovUnBD*
**Sukharev,** Aleksandr Yakovlevich 1923- *IntWW 91*
**Sukhatme,** Balkrishna Vasudeo 1924- *AmMWSc 92*
**Sukhatme,** Shashikala Balkrishna *AmMWSc 92*
**Sukhatme,** Shashikala Balkrishna 1932- *WhoMW 92*
**Sukhatme,** Uday Pandurang 1945- *AmMWSc 92*

**Sukhia,** Kenneth Wayne 1953- *WhoAmL 92*
**Suki,** Wadi Nagib 1934- *AmMWSc 92*
**Sukiennicka,** Halina 1906- *TwCPaSc*
**Suknaski,** Andrew, Jr. 1942- *ConPo 91, WrDr 92*
**Sukov,** Richard Joel 1944- *WhoWest 92*
**Sukow,** Wayne William 1936- *AmMWSc 92*
**Sukowski,** Ernest John 1932- *AmMWSc 92*
**Sukrija,** Ali 1919- *IntWW 91*
**Sukselainen,** Vieno Johannes 1906- *IntWW 91*
**Sukun,** Ziya 1958- *WhoFI 92*
**Sul-Te-Wan,** Madame 1873-1959 *NotBlAW 92*
**Sulaim,** Suliman Abd al aziz as- 1941- *IntWW 91*
**Sulak,** Lawrence Richard 1944- *AmMWSc 92*
**Sulak,** Timothy Martin 1952- *WhoAmL 92*
**Sulakhe,** Prakash Vinayak 1941- *AmMWSc 92*
**Sulavik,** Stephen B 1930- *AmMWSc 92*
**Sulcer,** Frederick Durham 1932- *WhoFI 92*
**Sulcer,** James R 1928- *WhoIns 92*
**Suleiman,** Michael W 1934- *IntAu&W 91*
**Suleiman,** Michael Wadie 1934- *WrDr 92*
**Suleiman,** Susan Rubin 1939- *WrDr 92*
**Sulentic,** Jack William 1947- *AmMWSc 92*
**Sulerud,** Ralph L 1932- *AmMWSc 92*
**Suleski,** James 1953- *WhoIns 92*
**Sulewski,** Paul Eric 1960- *AmMWSc 92*
**Sulg,** Madis 1943- *WhoMW 92*
**Sulg,** Mary Diane 1946- *WhoEnt 92*
**Sulger,** Francis Xavier 1942- *WhoAmL 92*
**Sulick,** Peter, Jr. 1950- *WhoEnt 92*
**Sulick,** Robert John 1947- *WhoMW 92*
**Sulieman,** Jamil *WhoBlA 92*
**Sulik,** Edwin 1957- *WhoFI 92*
**Sulik,** Kathleen Kay 1948- *AmMWSc 92*
**Sulima-Kamiminski,** Jerzy 1928- *IntAu&W 91*
**Suliman,** Douglas Morton 1955- *WhoFI 92*
**Sulimov,** Daniil Yegorovich 1890-1937 *SovUnBD*
**Sulin,** Victor A *WhoAmP 91*
**Suling,** William John 1940- *AmMWSc 92*
**Suliotis,** Elena 1943- *IntWW 91*
**Sulitzer,** Paul-Loup 1946- *IntAu&W 91*
**Sulkin,** Allan Michael 1954- *WhoFI 92*
**Sulkin,** Howard Allen 1941- *WhoMW 92, WhoRel 92*
**Sulkin,** Sidney *DrAPF 91*
**Sulkowski,** Eugene 1934- *AmMWSc 92*
**Sulkowski,** John Peter 1955- *WhoFI 92*
**Sullender,** Jack F. 1958- *WhoMW 92*
**Sullender,** Richard John 1952- *WhoRel 92*
**Sullenger,** Don Bruce 1929- *AmMWSc 92, WhoMW 92*
**Sullinger,** William Stancil 1954- *WhoRel 92*
**Sullivan,** A. M. 1896-1980 *BenetAL 91*
**Sullivan,** Alan 1868-1947 *ScFEYrs*
**Sullivan,** Alfred A. 1926- *WhoAmL 92*
**Sullivan,** Alfred Dewitt 1942- *AmMWSc 92*
**Sullivan,** Allen R. 1941- *WhoBlA 92*
**Sullivan,** Alvin D 1942- *IntAu&W 91, WrDr 92*
**Sullivan,** Andrew Jackson 1926- *AmMWSc 92*
**Sullivan,** Anna Mannevillette 1913- *AmMWSc 92*
**Sullivan,** Archie E. 1917- *WhoEnt 92*
**Sullivan,** Arthur Forrest 1948- *WhoAmP 91*
**Sullivan,** Arthur Lyon 1940- *AmMWSc 92*
**Sullivan,** Arthur S. 1842-1900 *NewAmDM*
**Sullivan,** Barry 1912- *IntMPA 92*
**Sullivan,** Barry 1949- *WhoAmL 92*
**Sullivan,** Barry F. 1930- *IntWW 91, WhoFI 92, WhoMW 92*
**Sullivan,** Barry Michael 1945- *WhoFI 92*
**Sullivan,** Bernard James 1927- *WhoMW 92*
**Sullivan,** Betty J 1902- *AmMWSc 92*
**Sullivan,** Betty Julia 1902- *WhoMW 92*
**Sullivan,** Bradley Wayne 1956- *WhoAmL 92*
**Sullivan,** Brenda Ann 1955- *WhoBlA 92*
**Sullivan,** Brian Francis 1961- *WhoFI 92*
**Sullivan,** Brian Patrick 1949- *AmMWSc 92*
**Sullivan,** Brian R. 1954- *WhoAmL 92*
**Sullivan,** Bruce M. 1951- *WhoRel 92*
**Sullivan,** Carley Hayden 1927- *WhoAmP 91*
**Sullivan,** Caroline Elizabeth 1925- *WhoMW 92*
**Sullivan,** Charles A. *WhoMW 92*
**Sullivan,** Charles Henry 1952- *AmMWSc 92*
**Sullivan,** Charles Irving 1918- *AmMWSc 92*
**Sullivan,** Charlotte Murdoch 1919- *AmMWSc 92*
**Sullivan,** Chuck *DrAPF 91*
**Sullivan,** Claire Ferguson 1937- *WhoFI 92, WhoWest 92*
**Sullivan,** Clara K 1915- *IntAu&W 91, WrDr 92*
**Sullivan,** Colleen 1950-1991 *ConAu 133*
**Sullivan,** Colleen M. d1991 *NewYTBS 91*
**Sullivan,** Connie Castleberry 1934- *WhoMW 92*
**Sullivan,** Cornelius Francis, Jr. 1960- *WhoFI 92*
**Sullivan,** Cornelius Patrick, Jr 1929- *AmMWSc 92*
**Sullivan,** Cornelius Wayne 1943- *WhoWest 92*
**Sullivan,** Dan 1935- *ConAu 135*
**Sullivan,** Dan 1943- *WhoAmP 91*
**Sullivan,** Daniel J. 1940- *WhoEnt 92, WhoWest 92*
**Sullivan,** Daniel Joseph 1928- *AmMWSc 92*
**Sullivan,** Daniel Joseph 1935- *WhoEnt 92*
**Sullivan,** Daniel Mercer 1940- *WhoEnt 92*
**Sullivan,** Daniel Richard 1951- *WhoAmL 92*
**Sullivan,** David Anthony *AmMWSc 92*
**Sullivan,** David Douglas Hooper 1926- *Who 92*
**Sullivan,** David Edward 1952- *WhoAmP 91*
**Sullivan,** David Ignatius 1951- *WhoIns 92*
**Sullivan,** David Thomas 1940- *AmMWSc 92*
**Sullivan,** Dennis James, Jr. 1932- *WhoFI 92*
**Sullivan,** Dennis John 1940- *WhoWest 92*
**Sullivan,** Dennis Michael 1945- *WhoAmL 92*
**Sullivan,** Dennis P 1941- *AmMWSc 92, IntWW 91*
**Sullivan,** Desmond 1920- *Who 92*
**Sullivan,** Don 1946- *WhoAmP 91*
**Sullivan,** Donald 1930- *WhoRel 92*
**Sullivan,** Donald 1936- *AmMWSc 92*
**Sullivan,** Donald Barrett 1939- *AmMWSc 92*
**Sullivan,** Donald Jerome 1929- *WhoAmL 92*
**Sullivan,** Donita B 1931- *AmMWSc 92*
**Sullivan,** Donovan Michael 1916- *Who 92*
**Sullivan,** Dori Dziedzivia 1963- *WhoWest 92*
**Sullivan,** Ed d1974 *LesBEnT 92*
**Sullivan,** Ed 1902-1974 *FacFETw [port]*
**Sullivan,** Edmund Wendell 1925- *Who 92*
**Sullivan,** Edward Augustine 1929- *AmMWSc 92*
**Sullivan,** Edward Christian 1933- *WhoAmP 91*
**Sullivan,** Edward Francis 1920- *AmMWSc 92*
**Sullivan,** Edward Holden, Jr. 1941- *WhoFI 92*
**Sullivan,** Edward James 1932- *WhoBlA 92*
**Sullivan,** Edward Joseph 1915- *WhoFI 92*
**Sullivan,** Edward T 1920- *AmMWSc 92*
**Sullivan,** Eleanor Regis d1991 *NewYTBS 91*
**Sullivan,** Elizabeth 1961- *WhoFI 92*
**Sullivan,** Elizabeth Gary 1937- *WhoEnt 92*
**Sullivan,** Ernest Lee 1952- *WhoMW 92*
**Sullivan,** Eugene John 1920- *IntWW 91*
**Sullivan,** Eugene John 1946- *WhoAmL 92*
**Sullivan,** F W, III 1923- *AmMWSc 92*
**Sullivan,** Faith 1933- *ConAu 134*
**Sullivan,** Faith H. 1933- *WhoMW 92*
**Sullivan,** Frances 1935- *WhoAmP 91*
**Sullivan,** Francis E 1941- *AmMWSc 92*
**Sullivan,** Francis T *WhoAmP 91*
**Sullivan,** Frank 1892-1976 *BenetAL 91*
**Sullivan,** George Allen 1935- *AmMWSc 92*
**Sullivan,** George Anderson *WhoWest 92*
**Sullivan,** George E. 1927- *WrDr 92*
**Sullivan,** George Murray 1922- *WhoAmP 91*
**Sullivan,** Gerald James 1937- *WhoWest 92*
**Sullivan,** Gregory William 1952- *WhoAmP 91*
**Sullivan,** Harry Morton 1921- *AmMWSc 92*
**Sullivan,** Henry P 1917- *WhoAmP 91*
**Sullivan,** Herbert J 1933- *AmMWSc 92*
**Sullivan,** Herbert Patrick 1932- *WhoRel 92*
**Sullivan,** Hugh D 1939- *AmMWSc 92*
**Sullivan,** Hugh David 1958- *WhoFI 92*
**Sullivan,** Hugh R, Jr 1926- *AmMWSc 92*
**Sullivan,** Hugh Richard, Jr. 1926- *WhoMW 92*
**Sullivan,** J Al 1937- *AmMWSc 92*
**Sullivan,** J. Christopher 1932- *WhoBlA 92*
**Sullivan,** J F 1853-1936 *ScFEYrs*
**Sullivan,** Jack, Jr. 1959- *WhoBlA 92*
**Sullivan,** James *DrAPF 91*
**Sullivan,** James Anderson 1924- *WhoAmL 92*
**Sullivan,** James Ash 1946- *WhoFI 92*
**Sullivan,** James Bolling 1940- *AmMWSc 92*
**Sullivan,** James C 1934- *WhoIns 92*
**Sullivan,** James Douglas 1940- *AmMWSc 92*
**Sullivan,** James E. 1920- *WhoRel 92*
**Sullivan,** James F 1924- *AmMWSc 92*
**Sullivan,** James Haddon, Jr 1937- *AmMWSc 92*
**Sullivan,** James Jerome 1943- *WhoAmL 92, WhoWest 92*
**Sullivan,** James Joseph 1922- *WhoFI 92*
**Sullivan,** James Kirk 1935- *WhoWest 92*
**Sullivan,** James Lenox 1910- *WhoRel 92*
**Sullivan,** James Leo 1925- *WhoFI 92*
**Sullivan,** James Michael 1934- *AmMWSc 92*
**Sullivan,** James Stephen 1929- *WhoRel 92*
**Sullivan,** James Thomas 1939- *WhoFI 92*
**Sullivan,** James Thomas, Jr 1928- *AmMWSc 92*
**Sullivan,** Jay Michael 1936- *AmMWSc 92*
**Sullivan,** Jean 1928- *WhoAmP 91*
**Sullivan,** Jeremy Mirth 1945- *Who 92*
**Sullivan,** Jerry Stephen 1945- *AmMWSc 92, WhoFI 92*
**Sullivan,** John *WhoWest 92*
**Sullivan,** John 1740-1795 *BenetAL 91, BlkwEAR*
**Sullivan,** John 1940- *TwCPaSc*
**Sullivan,** John Brendan 1944- *AmMWSc 92*
**Sullivan,** John Dennis 1928- *AmMWSc 92*
**Sullivan,** John Henry 1919- *AmMWSc 92*
**Sullivan,** John Henry Jack 1935- *WhoFI 92*
**Sullivan,** John James, Jr. 1938- *WhoFI 92*
**Sullivan,** John Joseph 1920- *WhoMW 92, WhoRel 92*
**Sullivan,** John Joseph 1921- *WhoAmL 92*
**Sullivan,** John Joseph 1935- *AmMWSc 92*
**Sullivan,** John Joseph 1960- *WhoAmL 92*
**Sullivan,** John Langdon 1777 1865 *BiInAmS*
**Sullivan,** John Lawrence 1941- *WhoAmP 91*
**Sullivan,** John Lawrence 1943- *AmMWSc 92*
**Sullivan,** John Lawrence, Jr. 1959- *WhoFI 92*
**Sullivan,** John Leslie 1917- *AmMWSc 92*
**Sullivan,** John M 1932- *AmMWSc 92*
**Sullivan,** John Magruder 1959- *WhoFI 92*
**Sullivan,** John Matthew 1963- *WhoMW 92*
**Sullivan,** John Patrick 1930- *WrDr 92*
**Sullivan,** John W 1932- *AmMWSc 92*
**Sullivan,** John William 1939- *AmMWSc 92*
**Sullivan,** Jonathan Dennis 1946- *WhoEnt 92*
**Sullivan,** Joseph Arthur 1923- *AmMWSc 92*
**Sullivan,** Joseph M. 1930- *WhoRel 92*
**Sullivan,** Joseph R. *WhoRel 92*
**Sullivan,** Julia Benitez 1957- *WhoHisp 92*
**Sullivan,** Karen A *AmMWSc 92*
**Sullivan,** Kathleen *WhoRel 92*
**Sullivan,** Kathleen Theresa 1953- *WhoAmP 91*
**Sullivan,** Kathryn Ann 1954- *WhoMW 92*
**Sullivan,** Kevin 1918?-1987 *ConAu 34NR*
**Sullivan,** Kevin B 1949- *WhoAmP 91*
**Sullivan,** Kevin E. 1960- *WhoFI 92*
**Sullivan,** Kevin Patrick 1953- *WhoAmL 92*
**Sullivan,** Laura Patricia 1947- *WhoAmL 92, WhoFI 92*
**Sullivan,** Lawrence A. 1923- *WhoAmL 92*
**Sullivan,** Lawrence Paul 1931- *AmMWSc 92*
**Sullivan,** Leo Eugene 1918- *WhoAmP 91*
**Sullivan,** Leon Howard 1922- *WhoBlA 92, WhoRel 92*
**Sullivan,** Leonard, Jr 1925- *WhoAmP 91*
**Sullivan,** Leonard E 1934- *WhoAmP 91*
**Sullivan,** Lillie d1903 *BiInAmS*
**Sullivan,** Lloyd John 1923- *AmMWSc 92*
**Sullivan,** Louis 1856-1924 *FacFETw*
**Sullivan,** Louis 1951- *ConAu 134*
**Sullivan,** Louis H. 1856-1924 *DcTwDes, RComAH*
**Sullivan,** Louis W 1933- *WhoAmP 91*
**Sullivan,** Louis Wade 1933- *AmMWSc 92, IntWW 91, WhoBlA 92*
**Sullivan,** Marcia Waite 1950- *WhoAmL 92*
**Sullivan,** Margaret P 1922- *AmMWSc 92*
**Sullivan,** Marion Frances 1899- *IntAu&W 91*
**Sullivan,** Mark 1874-1952 *BenetAL 91*
**Sullivan,** Mark Andrew 1959- *WhoAmL 92*
**Sullivan,** Mark Anthony, Jr. 1946- *WhoAmL 92*
**Sullivan,** Mark David 1934- *WhoEnt 92*
**Sullivan,** Mark William 1953- *WhoFI 92*
**Sullivan,** Martha Adams 1952- *WhoBlA 92*
**Sullivan,** Mary E 1932- *WhoAmP 91*
**Sullivan,** Mary J 1919- *WhoAmP 91*
**Sullivan,** Mary Jane Leahy 1939- *WhoMW 92*
**Sullivan,** Mary Louise 1906- *AmMWSc 92*
**Sullivan,** Mary M 1952- *WhoAmP 91*
**Sullivan,** Mary Wilson 1907- *IntAu&W 91*
**Sullivan,** Maureen 1954- *WhoAmL 92*
**Sullivan,** Maurice Francis 1922- *AmMWSc 92*
**Sullivan,** Maxine 1911- *NewAmDM*
**Sullivan,** Michael *Who 92*
**Sullivan,** Michael 1916- *WrDr 92*
**Sullivan,** Michael Cornelius 1948- *WhoAmL 92*
**Sullivan,** Michael D 1938- *WhoAmP 91*
**Sullivan,** Michael David 1938- *WhoAmL 92*
**Sullivan,** Michael Evan 1940- *WhoFI 92, WhoWest 92*
**Sullivan,** Michael Francis 1942- *AmMWSc 92, WhoAmL 92*
**Sullivan,** Michael Frederick 1940- *Who 92*
**Sullivan,** Michael J *WhoAmP 91*
**Sullivan,** Michael J. 1939- *AlmAP 92 [port], IntWW 91, WhoAmP 91*
**Sullivan,** Michael John 1939- *WhoWest 92*
**Sullivan,** Michael Joseph, Jr 1942- *AmMWSc 92*
**Sullivan,** Michael Kennedy 1961- *WhoAmL 92*
**Sullivan,** Michael Patrick 1934- *WhoMW 92*
**Sullivan,** Michelle Cornejo 1958- *WhoAmL 92*
**Sullivan,** Morey B. 1951- *WhoEnt 92*
**Sullivan,** Mortimer Allen, Jr. 1930- *WhoAmL 92*
**Sullivan,** Nancy *DrAPF 91*
**Sullivan,** Nancy Achin *WhoAmP 91*
**Sullivan,** Neil Maxwell 1942- *WhoFI 92*
**Sullivan,** Neil Samuel 1942- *AmMWSc 92*
**Sullivan,** Nicholas P. 1958- *WhoFI 92*
**Sullivan,** P.J. 1940- *TwCPaSc*
**Sullivan,** Pat 1936 *WhoAmP 91*
**Sullivan,** Patricia Ann Nagengast 1939- *AmMWSc 92*
**Sullivan,** Patricia W. 1936- *WhoFI 92, WhoMW 92*
**Sullivan,** Patrick Allen 1932- *WhoWest 92*
**Sullivan,** Patrick J. 1920- *IntMPA 92*
**Sullivan,** Paul 1951- *ConAu 133*
**Sullivan,** Paul A 1934- *WhoIns 92*
**Sullivan,** Paul Aloysius 1934- *WhoFI 92*
**Sullivan,** Paul Jerome 1957- *WhoWest 92*
**Sullivan,** Paul Joseph 1939- *AmMWSc 92*
**Sullivan,** Peter Kevin 1938- *AmMWSc 92*
**Sullivan,** Peter M 1938- *WhoAmP 91*
**Sullivan,** Philip Albert 1937- *AmMWSc 92*
**Sullivan,** Preddis Leroy 1959- *WhoMW 92*
**Sullivan,** Raymond 1934- *AmMWSc 92*
**Sullivan,** Reese *TwCWW 91*
**Sullivan,** Richard Arthur 1931- *Who 92*
**Sullivan,** Richard Frederick 1929- *AmMWSc 92*
**Sullivan,** Richard H. 1941- *WhoBlA 92*
**Sullivan,** Richard John 1949- *WhoFI 92*
**Sullivan,** Richard Joseph 1917- *WhoAmP 91*
**Sullivan,** Richard Michael 1950- *WhoFI 92*
**Sullivan,** Robert Charles 1949- *WhoMW 92*
**Sullivan,** Robert E. 1947- *ConAu 135*
**Sullivan,** Robert Edward 1936- *WhoAmL 92*
**Sullivan,** Robert Emmet, Jr. 1955- *WhoAmL 92*
**Sullivan,** Robert Emmett 1932- *AmMWSc 92*
**Sullivan,** Robert J 1949- *WhoIns 92*
**Sullivan,** Robert Little 1928- *AmMWSc 92*
**Sullivan,** Robert Scott 1955- *WhoWest 92*
**Sullivan,** Roger Charles, Jr. 1946- *WhoFI 92*
**Sullivan,** Roger William 1947- *WhoRel 92*
**Sullivan,** Rosemarie 1921- *WhoEnt 92*
**Sullivan,** Samuel Lane, Jr 1935- *AmMWSc 92*
**Sullivan,** Sean Mei *IntAu&W 91X, WrDr 92*
**Sullivan,** Sean Michael *AmMWSc 92*
**Sullivan,** Sharlene 1966- *WhoEnt 92*
**Sullivan,** Shaun S. 1940- *WhoAmL 92*
**Sullivan,** Steve Dwayne 1963- *WhoRel 92*
**Sullivan,** Stuart F 1928- *AmMWSc 92*
**Sullivan,** Stuart Francis 1928- *WhoWest 92*
**Sullivan,** Susan Jean *AmMWSc 92*
**Sullivan,** Teresa Ann 1949- *WhoAmL 92*
**Sullivan,** Terrance Charles 1950- *WhoAmL 92*
**Sullivan,** Thomas 1941- *WhoAmL 92*
**Sullivan,** Thomas Christopher 1937- *WhoFI 92*
**Sullivan,** Thomas Donald 1912- *AmMWSc 92*
**Sullivan,** Thomas Eugene 1948- *WhoAmL 92*
**Sullivan,** Thomas Hathaway 1941- *WhoMW 92*
**Sullivan,** Thomas J *WhoAmP 91*
**Sullivan,** Thomas J 1926- *WhoAmP 91*
**Sullivan,** Thomas J 1928- *WhoIns 92*

**Sullivan**, Thomas J. 1962- WhoFI 92
**Sullivan**, Thomas Joseph 1947- WhoAmP 91
**Sullivan**, Thomas M. d1991 NewYTBS 91 [port]
**Sullivan**, Thomas Michael 1943- WhoAmL 92, WhoMW 92
**Sullivan**, Thomas Patrick 1956- WhoAmL 92
**Sullivan**, Thomas Quinn 1933- WhoAmP 91
**Sullivan**, Thomas Wesley 1930- AmMWSc 92
**Sullivan**, Thomas William 1940- IntAu&W 91
**Sullivan**, Timothy Gerard 1955- WhoAmP 91
**Sullivan**, Timothy Jackson 1944- WhoAmL 92
**Sullivan**, Timothy Patrick 1942- WhoFI 92
**Sullivan**, Timothy Paul 1945- AmMWSc 92
**Sullivan**, Timothy Xavier 1949- WhoAmL 92
**Sullivan**, Tod 1934- Who 92
**Sullivan**, Tom 1947- WhoEnt 92
**Sullivan**, Victoria DrAPF 91
**Sullivan**, Victoria I 1941- AmMWSc 92
**Sullivan**, W Albert, Jr 1924- AmMWSc 92
**Sullivan**, W James 1925- AmMWSc 92
**Sullivan**, Walter 1918- WrDr 92
**Sullivan**, Walter 1924- WrDr 92
**Sullivan**, Walter Clay 1933- WhoFI 92
**Sullivan**, Walter Francis 1928- WhoRel 92
**Sullivan**, Walter J WhoAmP 91
**Sullivan**, Walter Seager 1918- AmMWSc 92, IntAu&W 91, IntWW 91
**Sullivan**, William Alan 1951- WhoFI 92, WhoMW 92
**Sullivan**, William Beaumont 1945- WhoAmL 92
**Sullivan**, William Courtney 1928- WhoAmL 92
**Sullivan**, William Craig 1956- WhoEnt 92
**Sullivan**, William Daniel 1918- AmMWSc 92
**Sullivan**, William Francis 1941- WhoEnt 92
**Sullivan**, William Francis 1950- WhoAmP 91
**Sullivan**, William Francis 1952- WhoAmL 92
**Sullivan**, William H. 1922- ConAu 133
**Sullivan**, William J 1937- WhoAmP 91
**Sullivan**, William James 1930- WhoRel 92, WhoWest 92
**Sullivan**, William Johnson 1928- WhoAmP 91
**Sullivan**, William Litsey 1921- WhoAmP 91
**Sullivan**, William R 1945- WhoAmP 91
**Sullivan**, Woodruff Turner, III 1944- AmMWSc 92
**Sullivan**, Zola Jiles 1921- WhoBlA 92
**Sullivan-Boyle**, Kathleen Marie 1958- WhoWest 92
**Sullivan-Kessler**, Ann Clare 1943- AmMWSc 92
**Sullivant**, Erin Elizabeth 1969- WhoEnt 92
**Sullivant**, Wayne Arthur 1954- WhoEnt 92
**Sullivant**, William Benton 1940- WhoAmP 91
**Sullivant**, William Starling 1803-1873 BiInAmS
**Sullo**, Fiorentino 1921- IntWW 91
**Sullwold**, Harold H 1916- AmMWSc 92
**Sully**, Frank 1898- TwCPaSc
**Sully**, Ira Bennett 1947- WhoAmL 92, WhoMW 92
**Sully**, Leonard Thomas George 1909- Who 92
**Sully-Prudhomme**, Rene 1839-1907 FacFETw
**Sully Prudhomme**, Rene-Francois-Armand 1839-1907 GuFrLit 1
**Sully Prudhomme**, Rene-Francois-Armend 1839-1907 WhoNob 90
**Sulman Al-Khalifa**, Isa bin IntWW 91
**Sulpicius Severus** 360?-420? EncEarC
**Sulser**, Fridolin 1926- AmMWSc 92
**Sulski**, Leonard C 1936- AmMWSc 92
**Sulsona**, Michael WhoHisp 92
**Sulston**, John Edward 1942- IntWW 91, Who 92
**Sult**, Jeffery Scot 1956- WhoEnt 92
**Sultan Ibn Abdul Aziz**, Prince 1922- IntWW 91
**Sultan**, Donald 1951- WorArt 1980 [port]
**Sultan**, Fouad 1931- IntWW 91
**Sultan**, Hassan Ahmed 1936- AmMWSc 92
**Sultan**, Stanley DrAPF 91
**Sultan**, Stanley 1928- WrDr 92
**Sultan**, Syed Abdus d1991 Who 92N
**Sultan-Galiev**, Mirza Said 1892-1939? SovUnBD
**Sultana**, Donald Edward 1924- WrDr 92
**Sultanof**, Jeffrey Brad 1954- WhoEnt 92
**Sulton**, Jacqueline Rhoda 1957- WhoBlA 92
**Sulton**, John D. 1912- WhoBlA 92
**Sultzer**, Barnet Martin 1929- AmMWSc 92
**Sulya**, Louis Leon 1911- AmMWSc 92
**Sulyk**, Stephen 1924- WhoRel 92
**Sulyok**, Peter Arpad 1955- WhoRel 92
**Sulzberg**, Theodore 1936- AmMWSc 92
**Sulzberger**, Arthur Ochs 1926- IntWW 91, Who 92
**Sulzberger**, Arthur Ochs, Sr. 1926- WhoFI 92
**Sulzberger**, C. L. 1912- WrDr 92
**Sulzberger**, Cyrus Leo 1912- IntWW 91
**Sulzberger**, Eugene William 1926- WhoAmL 92
**Sulzberger**, Iphigene Ochs 1892-1990 AnObit 1990
**Sulzby**, Elizabeth Fay 1942- WhoMW 92
**Sulzer**, Alexander Jackson 1922- AmMWSc 92
**Sulzer**, Johann Georg 1720-1779 BlkwCEP
**Sulzer-Azaroff**, Beth AmMWSc 92
**Sulzman**, Frank Michael 1944- AmMWSc 92
**Sumac**, Yma 1927- NewAmDM
**Suman**, Daniel Oscar 1950- AmMWSc 92
**Sumanth**, David Jonnakoty 1946- WhoFI 92
**Sumarno**, Ishak 1943- WhoFI 92
**Sumarokov**, Aleksandr Petrovich 1717-1777 BlkwCEP
**Sumartojo**, Jojok 1937- AmMWSc 92
**Sumaya**, Ciro Valent 1941- WhoHisp 92
**Sumberg**, David A 1942- AmMWSc 92
**Sumberg**, David Anthony Gerald 1941- Who 92
**Sumerlin**, Neal Gordon 1950- AmMWSc 92
**Sumi**, Barbara Elizabeth 1950- WhoFI 92
**Sumida**, Gerald Aquinas 1944- WhoAmL 92, WhoFI 92, WhoWest 92
**Sumida**, Kevin P.H. 1954- WhoAmL 92
**Sumita**, Satoshi 1916- IntWW 91
**Sumler-Lewis**, Janice L. 1948- WhoBlA 92
**Sumlin**, John Robert 1952- WhoAmP 91
**Sumlin**, Roger Lewis 1942- WhoFI 92
**Sumlin**, William WhoAmP 91
**Summer**, Cree WhoBlA 92
**Summer**, Donna 1948- IntWW 91, WhoEnt 92
**Summer**, Donna Andrea 1948- WhoBlA 92
**Summer**, George Kendrick 1923- AmMWSc 92
**Summerall**, Pat LesBEnT 92 [port]
**Summerfelt**, Robert C 1935- AmMWSc 92
**Summerfield**, Arthur 1923- IntWW 91, Who 92
**Summerfield**, George Clark 1937- AmMWSc 92
**Summerfield**, James Zane 1924- WhoAmP 91
**Summerfield**, John 1920- Who 92
**Summerfield**, Martin 1916- AmMWSc 92
**Summerford**, Sherry R. 1948- WhoFI 92
**Summerforest**, Ivy B IntAu&W 91X
**Summerhayes**, Colin Peter 1942- Who 92
**Summerhayes**, David Michael 1922- Who 92
**Summerhayes**, Gerald Victor 1928- Who 92
**Summerhays**, Jane ConTFT 9
**Summerlin**, Jack Blaine 1957- WhoMW 92
**Summerlin**, Lee R 1934- AmMWSc 92
**Summerlin**, Philip Harbin 1940- WhoRel 92
**Summerlin**, Sam 1928- ConAu 34NR
**Summerlin**, Travis Lamar 1954- WhoRel 92
**Summerlot**, Raymond Darrell 1925- WhoFI 92
**Summerour-Perry**, Lisa 1962- WhoBlA 92
**Summers**, Alfred Lawrence, Jr. 1950- WhoFI 92, WhoMW 92
**Summers**, Anne O 1942- AmMWSc 92
**Summers**, Anthony 1942- IntAu&W 91, WrDr 92
**Summers**, Anthony J. DrAPF 91
**Summers**, Audrey Lorraine 1928- AmMWSc 92
**Summers**, Carter B. 1943- WhoMW 92
**Summers**, Charles E WhoAmP 91
**Summers**, Charles Geddes 1941- AmMWSc 92
**Summers**, Charles Keith 1957- WhoWest 92
**Summers**, Claude M 1903- AmMWSc 92
**Summers**, Clifford L 1915- WhoAmP 91
**Summers**, D.B. TwCWW 91, WrDr 92
**Summers**, David 1941- WrDr 92
**Summers**, David Archibold 1944- AmMWSc 92
**Summers**, David Stewart 1932- WhoBlA 92
**Summers**, Dennis Brian 1943- AmMWSc 92
**Summers**, Diana WrDr 92
**Summers**, Donald Balch 1902- AmMWSc 92
**Summers**, Donald F 1934- AmMWSc 92
**Summers**, Donald Lee 1933- AmMWSc 92
**Summers**, Edna White 1919- WhoBlA 92
**Summers**, Essie 1912- IntAu&W 91, WrDr 92
**Summers**, Felix Roland Brattan Who 92
**Summers**, Frank Leslie WhoMW 92
**Summers**, Gene 1939- WhoEnt 92
**Summers**, Gene F. 1936- WrDr 92
**Summers**, Geoffrey P AmMWSc 92
**Summers**, George Donald 1927- AmMWSc 92
**Summers**, Gerald 1902- DcTwDes
**Summers**, Gregory Lawson 1951- AmMWSc 92
**Summers**, Hal 1911- WrDr 92
**Summers**, Hardy 1933- WhoAmL 92, WhoAmP 91
**Summers**, Henry Forbes 1911- IntAu&W 91, Who 92
**Summers**, Hugh B, Jr 1921- AmMWSc 92
**Summers**, Iris DrAPF 91
**Summers**, James Irvin 1921- WhoFI 92
**Summers**, James Richard 1962- WhoFI 92
**Summers**, James Thomas 1938- AmMWSc 92
**Summers**, James William 1940- AmMWSc 92, WhoMW 92
**Summers**, Janet Margaret Who 92
**Summers**, Jerry Andy 1939- WhoMW 92
**Summers**, Jerry C 1942- AmMWSc 92
**Summers**, John Clifford 1936- AmMWSc 92
**Summers**, John David 1929- AmMWSc 92
**Summers**, Joseph Holmes 1920- WrDr 92
**Summers**, Joseph W 1930- WhoAmP 91, WhoBlA 92
**Summers**, Judith 1953- IntAu&W 91, WrDr 92
**Summers**, Keith John 1957- WhoMW 92
**Summers**, Lawrence IntWW 91
**Summers**, Leslie 1919- TwCPaSc
**Summers**, Luis Henry 1939- AmMWSc 92
**Summers**, Marcia Anne 1955- WhoMW 92
**Summers**, Max Duane 1938- AmMWSc 92
**Summers**, Michael Earl 1954- AmMWSc 92
**Summers**, Nancy Jean 1952- WhoEnt 92
**Summers**, Nicholas 1939- Who 92
**Summers**, Phillip Dale 1943- AmMWSc 92
**Summers**, Raymond AmMWSc 92
**Summers**, Retha 1953- WhoBlA 92
**Summers**, Richard James 1943- AmMWSc 92
**Summers**, Richard Lee 1935- AmMWSc 92
**Summers**, Richard Lyle 1938- WhoMW 92
**Summers**, Robert 1922- WhoFI 92
**Summers**, Robert Gentry, Jr 1943- AmMWSc 92
**Summers**, Robert Samuel 1933- WhoAmL 92
**Summers**, Robert Wendell 1938- AmMWSc 92
**Summers**, Rodger 1945- WhoBlA 92
**Summers**, Rowena WrDr 92
**Summers**, Scott Brooks 1948- WhoFI 92
**Summers**, Terry Allen 1966- WhoWest 92
**Summers**, Thomas Abram 1934- WhoRel 92
**Summers**, Thomas Osmond 1812-1882 RelLAm 91
**Summers**, Thomas Osmond 1852?-1899 BiInAmS
**Summers**, Timothy 1942- WhoBlA 92
**Summers**, William Allen, Jr 1944- AmMWSc 92
**Summers**, William Allen, Sr 1914- AmMWSc 92
**Summers**, William Clarke 1936- AmMWSc 92
**Summers**, William Cofield 1939- AmMWSc 92
**Summers**, William E., III 1918- WhoBlA 92
**Summers**, William E., IV 1943- WhoBlA 92
**Summers**, William Hunley 1936- AmMWSc 92
**Summers**, William M. 1961- WhoEnt 92
**Summers**, Wilma Poos 1937- AmMWSc 92
**Summers-Dossena**, Ann 1931- WhoEnt 92
**Summers-Gill**, Robert George 1929- AmMWSc 92
**Summersby**, Kay 1909-1975 FacFETw
**Summerscale**, David Michael 1937- Who 92
**Summerscale**, Peter Wayne 1935- Who 92
**Summersett**, Kenneth George 1922- WhoMW 92
**Summersgill**, Derek H. 1940- TwCPaSc
**Summerskill**, Edith C 1901-1980 FacFETw
**Summerskill**, Edith Clara 1901-1980 BiDBrF 2
**Summerskill**, Shirley Catherine Wynne 1931- Who 92
**Summerson**, Charles Henry 1914- AmMWSc 92
**Summerson**, Hugo Hawksley Fitzthomas 1950- Who 92
**Summerson**, John 1904- Who 92, WrDr 92
**Summerson**, John Newenham 1904- IntAu&W 91, IntWW 91
**Summerton**, Neil William 1942- Who 92
**Summertree**, Katonah WrDr 92
**Summerville**, James DrAPF 91
**Summerville**, Richard Marion 1938- AmMWSc 92
**Summerville**, Tommie Lewis 1928- WhoBlA 92
**Summey**, James Allen 1955- WhoRel 92
**Summey**, Steven Michael 1946- WhoFI 92
**Summit**, Paul Eliot 1949- WhoAmL 92
**Summitt**, Gazella Ann 1941- WhoBlA 92
**Summitt**, Robert L 1932- AmMWSc 92
**Summitt**, W Robert 1935- AmMWSc 92
**Summy**, Gary Alan 1950- WhoMW 92
**Summy**, Gene Warren, Jr. 1958- WhoFI 92
**Summy-Long**, Joan Yvette AmMWSc 92
**Sumner**, Aurea 1913- WrDr 92
**Sumner**, Barbara Elaine 1942- AmMWSc 92
**Sumner**, Charles 1811-1874 AmPeW, AmPolLe [port], BenetAL 91, RComAH
**Sumner**, Christopher John 1939- Who 92
**Sumner**, Daniel Alan 1950- WhoFI 92
**Sumner**, Darrell Dean 1941- AmMWSc 92
**Sumner**, Donald Ray 1937- AmMWSc 92
**Sumner**, Edward D 1925- AmMWSc 92
**Sumner**, Eric E 1924- AmMWSc 92
**Sumner**, Geoffrey 1908-1989 ConTFT 9
**Sumner**, Gordon, Jr. 1924- WhoWest 92
**Sumner**, Gordon Matthew 1951- IntWW 91
**Sumner**, James Batcheller 1887-1955 WhoNob 90
**Sumner**, John Randolph 1944- AmMWSc 92
**Sumner**, John Stewart 1921- AmMWSc 92
**Sumner**, Mark Reese 1923- WhoEnt 92
**Sumner**, Richard Lawrence 1938- AmMWSc 92
**Sumner**, Robert Leslie 1922- WhoRel 92
**Sumner**, Roger D 1934- AmMWSc 92
**Sumner**, Thomas Hubbard 1807-1851 BiInAmS
**Sumner**, Thomas Robert 1949- WhoBlA 92
**Sumner**, Victor Emmanuel 1929- Who 92
**Sumner**, William Graham 1840-1910 BenetAL 91
**Sumners**, DeWitt L 1941- AmMWSc 92
**Sumners**, William Glenn, Jr. 1928- WhoAmL 92
**Sumney**, Jerry Lee 1955- WhoRel 92
**Sumney**, Larry W 1940- AmMWSc 92
**Sumney**, Roland L 1933- WhoIns 92
**Sump**, Cord H 1914- AmMWSc 92
**Sumption**, Anthony James Chadwick 1919- Who 92
**Sumption**, Jonathan 1948- WrDr 92
**Sumption**, Jonathan Philip Chadwick 1948- Who 92
**Sumrall**, Amber Coverdale DrAPF 91
**Sumrall**, H Glenn 1942- AmMWSc 92
**Sumrall**, Joe E. 1957- WhoWest 92
**Sumrall**, Kathryn Helen 1950- WhoAmL 92
**Sumrall**, Lester Frank 1913- RelLAm 91, WhoEnt 92, WhoMW 92, WhoRel 92
**Sumrall**, Robert Lavern 1942- WhoAmP 91
**Sumray**, Maurice 1920- TwCPaSc
**Sumray**, Monty 1918- Who 92
**Sumrell**, Gene 1919- AmMWSc 92, WhoFI 92
**Sumrow**, Kathie 1947- WhoEnt 92
**Sumsion**, H T 1912- AmMWSc 92
**Sumsion**, Herbert Whitton 1899- Who 92
**Sumsion**, John Walbridge 1928- Who 92
**Sumter**, Thomas 1734-1832 BlkwEAR
**Sun Bear** 1929- RelLAm 91
**Sun Daguang** 1917- IntWW 91
**Sun Guozhi** IntWW 91
**Sun Honglie** 1932- IntWW 91
**Sun Jiabo** 1939- IntWW 91
**Sun Jingwen** 1916- IntWW 91
**Sun Qi** 1930- IntWW 91
**Sun Ra** 1914- FacFETw, NewAmDM
**Sun Ra Le Sony'r Ra** WhoEnt 92
**Sun Weiben** 1928- IntWW 91
**Sun Xiaocun** 1906- IntWW 91
**Sun Yat-sen** 1867-1925 FacFETw
**Sun Yefang** 1907-1983 FacFETw
**Sun Yun-hsuan** 1930- FacFETw
**Sun Yun-Suan** 1913- IntWW 91
**Sun**, Albert Yung-Kwang 1932- AmMWSc 92
**Sun**, Alexander Shihkaung 1939- AmMWSc 92
**Sun**, Anthony Mein-Fang 1935- AmMWSc 92
**Sun**, Arthur Hai-Chau 1942- WhoWest 92
**Sun**, Bernard Ching-Huey 1937- AmMWSc 92
**Sun**, Big Daddy 1952- WhoEnt 92

**Sun**, Chang-Tsan 1928- *AmMWSc 92*
**Sun**, Chao Nien 1914- *AmMWSc 92*
**Sun**, Cheng 1937- *AmMWSc 92*
**Sun**, Chih-Ree 1923- *AmMWSc 92*
**Sun**, Chin-Teh 1939- *AmMWSc 92*
**Sun**, Christopher I-Chum 1953- *WhoWest 92*
**Sun**, Cossette Tsung-hung Wu 1937- *WhoAmL 92*
**Sun**, Deming 1947- *AmMWSc 92*
**Sun**, Fang-Kuo 1946- *AmMWSc 92*
**Sun**, Frank F 1938- *AmMWSc 92*
**Sun**, George Chi 1930- *WhoFI 92*
**Sun**, Hugo Sui-Hwan 1940- *AmMWSc 92, WhoWest 92*
**Sun**, Hun H 1925- *AmMWSc 92*
**Sun**, James Dean 1951- *AmMWSc 92*
**Sun**, James Ming-Shan 1918- *AmMWSc 92*
**Sun**, Joe 1943- *WhoEnt 92*
**Sun**, Li-Teh 1939- *WhoFI 92*
**Sun**, Pu-Ning 1932- *AmMWSc 92*
**Sun**, Raymond C. 1963- *WhoAmL 92*
**Sun**, Robert Zu Jei 1948- *WhoFI 92*
**Sun**, Samuel Sai-Ming 1942- *AmMWSc 92*
**Sun**, Siao Fang 1922- *AmMWSc 92*
**Sun**, Tung-Tien 1947- *AmMWSc 92*
**Sun**, Wen-Yin *AmMWSc 92*
**Sun**, Yan 1956- *AmMWSc 92*
**Sun**, Yun-Chung 1937- *AmMWSc 92*
**Sunada**, Daniel K 1936- *AmMWSc 92*
**Sunada**, Shigetami *IntWW 91*
**Sunahara**, Fred Akira 1924- *AmMWSc 92*
**Sunahara**, Yoshifumi 1927- *AmMWSc 92*
**Sunay**, Cevdet 1899-1982 *FacFETw*
**Sund**, Eldon H 1930- *AmMWSc 92*
**Sund**, Jeffrey O. 1940- *WhoMW 92*
**Sund**, John L *WhoAmP 91*
**Sund**, John Leonard 1949- *WhoWest 92*
**Sund**, Michael Warren 1943- *WhoWest 92*
**Sund**, Paul N 1932- *AmMWSc 92*
**Sund**, Raymond Earl 1932- *AmMWSc 92*
**Sund**, Robert *DrAPF 91*
**Sund**, Robert B. 1926- *ConAu 36NR*
**Sunda**, William George 1945- *AmMWSc 92*
**Sundahl**, Robert Charles, Jr 1936- *AmMWSc 92*
**Sundar**, P 1954- *AmMWSc 92*
**Sundaralingam**, Muttaiya 1931- *AmMWSc 92*
**Sundaram**, Kalyan 1932- *AmMWSc 92*
**Sundaram**, Panchanatham N 1939- *AmMWSc 92*
**Sundaram**, R Meenakshi 1942- *AmMWSc 92*
**Sundaram**, Swaminatha 1924- *AmMWSc 92*
**Sundaran**, Soma Thayyadath 1940- *WhoFI 92*
**Sundararajan**, Pudupadi Ranganathan 1943- *AmMWSc 92*
**Sundaravadivelu**, Neyyadupakkam D 1912- *Who 92*
**Sundaresan**, Mosur Kalyanaraman 1929- *AmMWSc 92*
**Sundaresan**, Peruvemba Ramnathan 1930- *AmMWSc 92*
**Sundaresan**, Sankaran 1955- *AmMWSc 92*
**Sundaresh**, Subramanian 1956- *WhoWest 92*
**Sundarraj**, Nirmala *AmMWSc 92*
**Sunday**, Alexander Alan 1943- *WhoFI 92*
**Sunday**, Billy 1862-1935 *RelLAm 91*
**Sunday**, Billy 1863-1935 *FacFETw*
**Sundberg**, David K *AmMWSc 92*
**Sundberg**, Delbert F *WhoAmP 91*
**Sundberg**, Donald Charles 1942- *AmMWSc 92*
**Sundberg**, Edgar Leonard 1920- *WhoWest 92*
**Sundberg**, Edward August 1947- *WhoFI 92*
**Sundberg**, John Edwin 1947- *AmMWSc 92*
**Sundberg**, Kenneth Randall 1945- *AmMWSc 92*
**Sundberg**, Michael William *AmMWSc 92*
**Sundberg**, Norman Dale 1922- *WhoWest 92*
**Sundberg**, Richard J 1938- *AmMWSc 92*
**Sundberg**, Ruth Dorothy 1915- *AmMWSc 92*
**Sundberg**, Trudy James 1925- *WhoEnt 92*
**Sundberg**, Walter James 1939- *AmMWSc 92*
**Sundby**, Olof 1917- *IntWW 91*
**Sunde**, Dean 1932- *WhoAmP 91*
**Sunde**, Milton Lester 1921- *AmMWSc 92*
**Sunde**, Roger Allan 1950- *AmMWSc 92, WhoMW 92*
**Sundeen**, Daniel Alvin 1937- *AmMWSc 92*
**Sundeen**, Joseph Edward 1943- *AmMWSc 92*
**Sundeen**, Neal Sherman 1942- *WhoAmL 92*
**Sundel**, Harvey H. 1944- *WhoFI 92, WhoWest 92*
**Sundelin**, Kurt Gustav Ragnar 1937- *AmMWSc 92*
**Sundelin**, Ronald M 1939- *AmMWSc 92*
**Sundelius**, Harold Wesley 1930- *AmMWSc 92*
**Sundell**, Hakan W 1936- *AmMWSc 92*
**Sunder**, Sham 1942- *AmMWSc 92*
**Sunder**, Shyam 1944- *WhoFI 92*
**Sunderland**, Arthur John 1932- *Who 92*
**Sunderland**, Eric 1930- *IntAu&W 91, IntWW 91, Who 92, WrDr 92*
**Sunderland**, Godfrey Russell 1936- *Who 92*
**Sunderland**, Jabez Thomas 1842-1936 *RelLAm 91*
**Sunderland**, James Cornelius 1924- *WhoRel 92*
**Sunderland**, James Edward 1932- *AmMWSc 92*
**Sunderland**, John *Who 92*
**Sunderland**, Ronald Harry 1929- *WhoRel 92*
**Sunderland**, Russell *Who 92*
**Sunderland**, Sydney 1910- *IntWW 91, Who 92, WrDr 92*
**Sunderland**, Thomas E. 1907-1991 *CurBio 91N, NewYTBS 91*
**Sunderland**, Thomas Elbert 1907- *IntWW 91*
**Sunderlin**, Charles Eugene 1911- *AmMWSc 92*
**Sunderman**, Duane Neuman 1928- *AmMWSc 92*
**Sunderman**, F William, Jr 1931- *AmMWSc 92*
**Sunderman**, Frederick William 1898- *AmMWSc 92*
**Sunderman**, Herbert D 1937- *AmMWSc 92*
**Sunderman**, William Anthony 1946- *WhoAmL 92*
**Sundermeyer**, Daryl Albert 1947- *WhoEnt 92*
**Sundet**, Edwin Odell Stuart 1929- *WhoWest 92*
**Sundet**, Sherman Archie 1918- *AmMWSc 92*
**Sundfors**, Ronald Kent 1932- *AmMWSc 92*
**Sundgaard**, Arnold Olaf 1909- *WhoEnt 92*
**Sundiata**, Sekou *DrAPF 91*
**Sundiata**, Shaka A. *DrAPF 91*
**Sundick**, Roy 1944- *AmMWSc 92*
**Sundin**, Theodore Alan 1932- *WhoWest 92*
**Sundlun**, Bruce 1920- *AlmAP 92 [port], WhoAmP 91*
**Sundlun**, Bruce George 1920- *IntWW 91*
**Sundquist**, Don 1936- *AlmAP 92 [port]*
**Sundquist**, Donald Kenneth 1936- *WhoAmP 91*
**Sundquist**, James 1915- *WrDr 92*
**Sundqvist**, Ulf Lundvig 1945- *IntWW 91*
**Sundram**, P. Sandy 1957- *WhoMW 92*
**Sundry**, Arthur P. 1928- *WhoMW 92*
**Sundsten**, John Wallin 1933- *AmMWSc 92*
**Sundstrom**, Nancy Marie 1956- *WhoEnt 92*
**Sundstrom**, Richard Carl 1953- *WhoMW 92*
**Sundt**, Harry Wilson 1932- *WhoWest 92*
**Sundt**, Robert Stout 1926- *WhoWest 92*
**Sundy**, George Joseph, Jr. 1936- *WhoMW 92*
**Suneja**, Sudhir Kumar 1954- *WhoBlA 92*
**Sung**, Andrew Hsi-Lin 1953- *AmMWSc 92, WhoWest 92*
**Sung**, C. B. 1925- *WhoFI 92*
**Sung**, Changmo 1955- *AmMWSc 92*
**Sung**, Chen-Yu 1915- *AmMWSc 92*
**Sung**, Cheng-Po 1935- *AmMWSc 92*
**Sung**, Chi Ching 1936- *AmMWSc 92*
**Sung**, Chia-Hsiaing 1939- *AmMWSc 92*
**Sung**, Chin Kyung 1957- *WhoWest 92*
**Sung**, Joo Ho 1927- *AmMWSc 92*
**Sung**, Michael Tse Li 1940- *AmMWSc 92*
**Sung**, Ruwang 1956- *WhoMW 92*
**Sung**, Susan Chu 1947- *WhoWest 92*
**Sung**, Yun-Chen *WhoEnt 92*
**Sung**, Zinmay Renee 1947- *AmMWSc 92*
**Sungenis**, Nancy Louise 1939- *WhoAmP 91*
**Sungurlu**, Mahmut Oltan 1936- *IntWW 91*
**Sunier**, John Henry 1936- *WhoEnt 92*
**Sunier**, Jules Willy 1934- *AmMWSc 92*
**Sunim**, Mu Ryang 1959- *WhoRel 92*
**Sunin**, Samu 1941- *RelLAm 91*
**Sunkara**, Sai Prasad 1948- *AmMWSc 92*
**Sunley**, Judith S 1946- *AmMWSc 92*
**Sunley**, Margaret 1921-1990 *ConAu 134*
**Sunlight**, Ben 1935- *TwCPaSc*
**Sunnquist**, Bryan Reed 1963- *WhoMW 92*
**Sunrise**, Diana 1942- *WhoEnt 92*
**Sunseri**, Ron 1948- *WhoAmP 91*
**Sunshine**, Geoffrey H 1948- *AmMWSc 92*
**Sunshine**, Irving 1916- *AmMWSc 92*
**Sunshine**, Melvin Gilbert 1936- *AmMWSc 92*
**Sunshine**, Robert Howard 1946- *IntMPA 92*
**Sunshine**, Warren Lewis 1947- *AmMWSc 92*
**Suntharalingam**, Nagalingam 1933- *AmMWSc 92*
**Suntrangkoon**, Prachuab 1920- *IntWW 91*
**Sununu**, John H. 1939- *IntWW 91, WhoAmP 91*
**Sununu**, John Henry 1939- *AmMWSc 92*
**Suojanen**, Wayne William 1950- *WhoAmL 92*
**Suomi**, Stephen John 1945- *AmMWSc 92*
**Suomi**, Verner Edward 1915- *AmMWSc 92*
**Suominen**, Ilkka Olavi 1939- *IntWW 91*
**Suomisto**, Laurel Kenner 1954- *WhoWest 92*
**Suonio**, Kaarina Elisabet 1941- *IntWW 91*
**Suozzi**, Joseph John 1926- *AmMWSc 92*
**Suozzo**, Frank Vincent 1928- *WhoIns 92*
**Sup**, Stuart Allen 1943- *WhoEnt 92, WhoFI 92*
**Supancheck**, Norman Anthony 1942- *WhoRel 92*
**Super**, Robert Henry 1914- *IntAu&W 91, WrDr 92*
**Super**, William Alan 1953- *WhoMW 92*
**Supernaw**, William Michael 1938- *WhoEnt 92*
**Supersad**, Jankie Nanan 1929- *AmMWSc 92*
**Supervielle**, Jules 1884-1960 *GuFrLit 1*
**Suphamongkhon**, Konthi 1916- *Who 92*
**Supica**, James William, Jr. 1952- *WhoAmL 92*
**Suplee**, Dennis Raymond 1943- *WhoAmL 92*
**Suplee**, Thomas Raymond 1946- *WhoFI 92*
**Suplinskas**, Raymond Joseph 1939- *AmMWSc 92*
**Suplizio**, Samuel Victor 1932- *WhoWest 92*
**Supowit**, Jeffrey Alan 1955- *WhoAmL 92*
**Suppa**, Ronald Anthony 1948- *WhoEnt 92*
**Suppe**, Francis J. 1940- *WhoIns 92*
**Suppe**, Franz von 1819-1895 *NewAmDM*
**Suppe**, Frederick 1940- *AmMWSc 92*
**Suppe**, John 1942- *AmMWSc 92*
**Supperstone**, Michael Alan 1950- *Who 92*
**Suppes**, Patrick 1922- *AmMWSc 92, IntWW 91*
**Suppiger**, Joseph d1857 *DcAmImH*
**Supple**, Barry E. 1930- *WrDr 92*
**Supple**, Barry Emanuel 1930- *IntWW 91, Who 92*
**Supple**, Diane Marie 1956- *WhoFI 92*
**Supple**, Jerome Henry 1936- *AmMWSc 92*
**Supran**, Michael Kenneth 1939- *AmMWSc 92*
**Supraner**, Robyn *DrAPF 91*
**Supremes**, The *ConMus 6 [port], FacFETw, NewAmDM*
**Suprenant**, Bruce A 1952- *AmMWSc 92*
**Suprunowicz**, Konrad 1919- *AmMWSc 92*
**Suprynowicz**, Vincent A 1923- *AmMWSc 92*
**Suquet**, Jose S. 1956- *WhoHisp 92*
**Suquia Goicoechea**, Angel 1916- *IntWW 91, WhoRel 92*
**Sura**, Phillip George 1956- *WhoWest 92*
**Surace**, Mildred Cooper 1937- *WhoMW 92*
**Surak**, John Godfrey 1948- *AmMWSc 92*
**Surampalli**, Rao Yadagiri 1949- *AmMWSc 92*
**Suran**, Jerome J 1926- *AmMWSc 92*
**Suranyi**, Peter 1935- *AmMWSc 92*
**Surawicz**, Borys 1917- *AmMWSc 92*
**Surbey**, Donald Lee 1940- *AmMWSc 92*
**Surdell**, Steven Martin 1959- *WhoFI 92*
**Surdoval**, Donald James 1932- *WhoFI 92*
**Surdoval**, Lawrence Anthony, Jr. 1930- *WhoFI 92*
**Surdy**, Ted E 1925- *AmMWSc 92*
**Sureau**, Claude 1927- *IntWW 91*
**Suren**, Choynoryn 1932- *IntWW 91*
**Suren**, Hans 1885-1972 *EncTR 91*
**Suresh**, Bangalore Ananthaswami 1951- *WhoMW 92*
**Suresh**, Mavanur Rangarajan 1953- *AmMWSc 92*
**Suresh**, Subra *AmMWSc 92*
**Surface**, Chuck L 1944- *WhoAmP 91*
**Surface**, David *DrAPF 91*
**Surface**, James Louis, Sr. 1941- *WhoFI 92*
**Surface**, Stephen Walter 1943- *WhoWest 92*
**Surgalla**, Michael Joseph 1920- *AmMWSc 92*
**Surgenor**, Douglas MacNevin 1918- *AmMWSc 92*
**Surgi**, Elizabeth Benson 1955- *WhoMW 92*
**Surgi**, Marion Rene 1956- *WhoMW 92*
**Surh**, Michael T. 1934- *WhoFI 92*
**Suri**, Ashok 1943- *AmMWSc 92*
**Suri**, Rajan 1952- *AmMWSc 92*
**Suria**, Amin 1942- *AmMWSc 92*
**Suriano**, F J 1937- *AmMWSc 92*
**Surillo Rodriguez**, Jose A *WhoAmP 91, WhoHisp 92*
**Surina**, John Carroll 1944- *WhoAmP 91*
**Surinach**, Carlos 1915- *ConCom 92, NewAmDM*
**Surinach Carreras**, Ricardo Antonio 1928- *WhoRel 92*
**Surinak**, John Joseph 1945- *WhoFI 92*
**Suris**, Oscar, III 1964- *WhoHisp 92*
**Surits**, Yelizaveta Yakovlevna 1923- *IntWW 91, SovUnBD*
**Surjan**, Laszlo 1941- *IntWW 91*
**Surjaningrat**, Suwardjono 1923- *IntWW 91*
**Surkamp**, Richard Edward, Jr. 1964- *WhoAmL 92*
**Surkan**, Alvin John 1934- *AmMWSc 92*
**Surkin**, Elliot Mark 1942- *WhoFI 92*
**Surko**, Clifford Michael 1941- *AmMWSc 92*
**Surko**, Pamela Toni 1942- *AmMWSc 92*
**Surkov**, Aleksey Aleksandrovich 1899-1983 *SovUnBD*
**Surles**, Richard Hurlbut, Jr. 1943- *WhoAmL 92*
**Surlyk**, Finn C. 1943- *IntWW 91*
**Surma**, Louis John, Jr. 1947- *WhoMW 92*
**Surmacz**, Cynthia Ann 1957- *AmMWSc 92*
**Surnamer**, Shulamith *DrAPF 91*
**Surnock**, Richard William 1932- *WhoEnt 92*
**Suro**, David Guillermo 1961- *WhoHisp 92*
**Surovell**, Hariette *DrAPF 91*
**Surowitz**, Marvin Howard 1941- *WhoMW 92*
**Surprenant**, H George 1939- *WhoIns 92*
**Surr**, Jeremy Bernard 1938- *Who 92*
**Surra**, Dan A 1953- *WhoAmP 91*
**Surrett**, David Cofield 1958- *WhoRel 92*
**Surrey**, Archdeacon of *Who 92*
**Surrey**, Earl of 1517?-1547 *RfGEnL 91*
**Surrey**, Alexander Robert 1914- *AmMWSc 92*
**Surrey**, Kenneth 1922- *AmMWSc 92*
**Surridge**, Rex d1990 *Who 92N*
**Surridge**, Robert Caldwell, III 1951- *WhoFI 92*
**Surrusco**, Mark B. 1950- *WhoFI 92*
**Sursa**, Charles David 1925- *WhoMW 92*
**Surtees**, Bruce *IntMPA 92*
**Surtees**, John 1934- *IntWW 91, Who 92*
**Surtees**, R.S. 1805-1864 *RfGEnL 91*
**Surtees**, Virginia *WrDr 92*
**Surti**, Vasant H 1931- *AmMWSc 92*
**Survant**, Joe *DrAPF 91*
**Survant**, Rebecca Ann 1952- *WhoMW 92*
**Survant**, William G 1907- *AmMWSc 92*
**Surver**, William Merle, Jr 1943- *AmMWSc 92*
**Surwill**, Benedict Joseph, Jr. 1925- *WhoWest 92*
**Surwillo**, Walter Wallace 1926- *AmMWSc 92*
**Surwit**, Richard Samuel 1946- *AmMWSc 92*
**Sury**, Earl Ravon 1937- *WhoFI 92*
**Suryanarayana**, Narasipur Venkataram 1931- *AmMWSc 92*
**Suryanarayanan**, Raj Gopalan 1955- *AmMWSc 92, WhoMW 92*
**Suryaraman**, Maruthuvakudi Gopalasastri 1925- *AmMWSc 92*
**Suryavanshi**, O.P.S. 1961- *WhoFI 92*
**Surz**, Ronald Joseph 1945- *WhoMW 92*
**Surzycki**, Stefan Jan 1936- *AmMWSc 92*
**Susag**, Russell H 1930- *AmMWSc 92*
**Susalla**, Anne A *AmMWSc 92*
**Susano**, Charles Daniel, Jr 1936- *WhoAmP 91*
**Susato**, Tielman 1500?-1564? *NewAmDM*
**Suschitzky**, Peter *IntMPA 92*
**Suschitzky**, Wolfgang 1912- *IntWW 91*
**Susens**, Millicent Milanovich *WhoEnt 92*
**Susi**, Frank Robert 1936- *AmMWSc 92*
**Susi**, Peter Vincent 1928- *AmMWSc 92*
**Susina**, Stanley V 1923- *AmMWSc 92*
**Susino**, Louis 1954- *WhoEnt 92*
**Suski**, Henry M 1918- *AmMWSc 92*
**Suskin**, Amy Lawing 1951- *WhoMW 92*
**Suskind**, Raymond Robert 1913- *AmMWSc 92, WhoMW 92*
**Suskind**, Sigmund Richard 1926- *AmMWSc 92*
**Suslick**, Kenneth Sanders 1952- *AmMWSc 92, WhoMW 92*
**Suslin**, Viktor 1942- *ConCom 92*
**Suslov**, Mikhail Andreevich 1902-1982 *SovUnBD*
**Suslov**, Vladimir Pavlovich 1923- *IntWW 91*
**Suslow**, Valerie Yvonne 1958- *WhoMW 92*
**Susman**, Alan Howard 1945- *WhoAmL 92*
**Susman**, Alan L *WhoAmP 91*
**Susman**, Barbara Ann 1958- *WhoAmL 92*
**Susman**, Frank 1941- *WhoAmL 92*
**Susman**, Karen Lee 1942- *WhoAmL 92*
**Susman**, Leon 1936- *AmMWSc 92*
**Susman**, Louis B 1937- *WhoAmP 91*
**Susman**, Millard 1934- *AmMWSc 92*
**Susman**, Morton Lee 1934- *WhoAmL 92*

**Susman,** Randall Lee 1948- *AmMWSc 92*
**Susman,** Thomas Michael 1943- *WhoAmL 92, WhoAmP 91*
**Susman,** Tom L 1959- *WhoAmP 91*
**Susmano,** Armando 1932- *WhoMW 92*
**Susor,** Dorothy Marie Alma Leffel 1922- *WhoMW 92*
**Sussan,** Sidney Martin 1944- *WhoFI 92*
**Sussdorf,** Dieter Hans 1930- *AmMWSc 92*
**Sussenbach,** Ward Virgil 1944- *WhoRel 92*
**Sussenguth,** Edward H 1932- *AmMWSc 92*
**Sussenguth,** Hans 1913- *IntWW 91*
**Susser,** Mervyn W 1921- *AmMWSc 92*
**Sussex,** Ian Mitchell 1927- *AmMWSc 92*
**Sussex,** James Neil 1917- *AmMWSc 92*
**Susskind,** Alfred K 1923- *AmMWSc 92*
**Susskind,** Charles *AmMWSc 92*
**Susskind,** David d1987 *LesBEnT 92*
**Susskind,** David 1920-1987 *FacFETw*
**Susskind,** Harriet *DrAPF 91*
**Susskind,** Herbert 1929- *AmMWSc 92*
**Susskind,** Walter 1913-1980 *NewAmDM*
**Sussman,** Alexander Ralph 1946- *WhoAmL 92*
**Sussman,** Alfred Sheppard 1919- *AmMWSc 92*
**Sussman,** Barry 1934- *WrDr 92*
**Sussman,** Harold Louis 1955- *WhoWest 92*
**Sussman,** Howard H 1934- *AmMWSc 92*
**Sussman,** Josephine Carr *DrAPF 91*
**Sussman,** Karen Ann 1947- *WhoWest 92*
**Sussman,** Karl Edgar 1929- *AmMWSc 92*
**Sussman,** M V *AmMWSc 92*
**Sussman,** Marc Mitchell 1956- *WhoFI 92*
**Sussman,** Mark Richard 1952- *WhoAmL 92*
**Sussman,** Marvin 1927- *WhoAmL 92*
**Sussman,** Maurice 1922- *AmMWSc 92*
**Sussman,** Michael R 1950- *AmMWSc 92*
**Sussman,** Myron Maurice 1945- *AmMWSc 92*
**Sussman,** Raquel Rotman 1921- *AmMWSc 92*
**Sussman,** Steven David 1946- *WhoFI 92*
**Sussmayr,** Franz Xaver 1766-1803 *NewAmDM*
**Sustar,** Christopher David 1966- *WhoRel 92*
**Suster,** Ronald 1942- *WhoAmP 91*
**Susumu Ishii** d1991 *NewYTBS 91*
**Sutch,** Richard C 1942- *ConAu 34NR*
**Sutcliff,** Rosemary 1920- *IntAu&W 91, Who 92, WrDr 92*
**Sutcliffe,** Allan 1936- *Who 92*
**Sutcliffe,** Anthony 1942- *ConAu 34NR*
**Sutcliffe,** David Miller 1947- *WhoFI 92*
**Sutcliffe,** Edward Davis 1917- *Who 92*
**Sutcliffe,** Eric G 1945- *WhoAmP 91*
**Sutcliffe,** Geoffrey 1929- *TwCPaSc*
**Sutcliffe,** Geoffrey Scott 1912- *Who 92*
**Sutcliffe,** James H. 1956- *WhoMW 92*
**Sutcliffe,** John Harold Vick 1931- *Who 92*
**Sutcliffe,** Kenneth Edward 1911- *Who 92*
**Sutcliffe,** Reginald Cockcroft d1991 *Who 92N*
**Sutcliffe,** Reginald Cockcroft 1904- *IntWW 91, WrDr 92*
**Sutcliffe,** Samuel 1934- *AmMWSc 92*
**Sutcliffe,** Stuart 1940-1962 *TwCPaSc*
**Sutcliffe,** Walter Philip d1990 *Who 92N*
**Sutcliffe,** William George 1937- *AmMWSc 92*
**Sutcliffe,** William Humphrey, Jr 1923- *AmMWSc 92*
**Suter,** Albert Edward 1935- *IntWW 91, WhoFI 92*
**Suter,** Bernard Reynold 1954- *WhoAmL 92*
**Suter,** Bruce H 1921- *WhoIns 92*
**Suter,** Bruce Wilsey 1949- *AmMWSc 92*
**Suter,** Daniel B 1920- *AmMWSc 92*
**Suter,** David Winston 1942- *WhoRel 92*
**Suter,** Douglas James 1962- *WhoAmL 92*
**Suter,** Eugene Wayne 1949- *WhoFI 92*
**Suter,** George August 1934- *WhoFI 92*
**Suter,** Glenn Walter, II 1948- *AmMWSc 92*
**Suter,** Martha Wright 1926- *WhoMW 92*
**Suter,** Michael 1944- *Who 92*
**Suter,** Robert Winford 1941- *AmMWSc 92*
**Suter,** Ronald 1930- *WhoMW 92*
**Suter,** Stuart Ross 1941- *AmMWSc 92*
**Sutera,** Salvatore P 1933- *AmMWSc 92*
**Sutermeister,** Heinrich 1910- *IntWW 91*
**Sutheim,** Peter Ernest 1940- *WhoEnt 92*
**Sutherin,** Daniel Nevin 1954- *WhoMW 92*
**Sutherland** *Who 92*
**Sutherland,** Countess of 1921- *Who 92*
**Sutherland,** Duke of 1915- *Who 92*
**Sutherland,** Lord 1932- *Who 92*
**Sutherland,** Anthony 1916- *Who 92*
**Sutherland,** Barbara L 1954- *WhoIns 92*
**Sutherland,** Betsy Middleton 1943- *AmMWSc 92*
**Sutherland,** Bill 1942- *AmMWSc 92*
**Sutherland,** Bruce *WhoEnt 92, WhoWest 92*
**Sutherland,** Carol Ann 1952- *TwCPaSc*
**Sutherland,** Cathy Ann 1946- *WhoMW 92*
**Sutherland,** Charles 1830?-1895 *BiInAmS*
**Sutherland,** Charles Daniel 1950- *WhoMW 92*
**Sutherland,** Charles F 1921- *AmMWSc 92*
**Sutherland,** Charles William 1941- *AmMWSc 92*
**Sutherland,** Colin John MacLean 1954- *Who 92*
**Sutherland,** David M 1940- *AmMWSc 92*
**Sutherland,** David McBeth 1883-1973 *TwCPaSc*
**Sutherland,** David Russell 1945- *WhoEnt 92*
**Sutherland,** Dean Alan 1954- *WhoAmP 91*
**Sutherland,** Donald 1935- *IntMPA 92, WhoEnt 92*
**Sutherland,** Donald James 1929- *AmMWSc 92*
**Sutherland,** Donald McNichol 1935- *IntWW 91*
**Sutherland,** Doug 1937- *WhoAmP 91*
**Sutherland,** Earl C 1923- *AmMWSc 92*
**Sutherland,** Earl Christian 1923- *WhoWest 92*
**Sutherland,** Earl Wilbur, Jr. 1915-1974 *WhoNob 90*
**Sutherland,** Edwin H. *DcAmImH*
**Sutherland,** Efua 1924- *WrDr 92*
**Sutherland,** Elizabeth *WrDr 92*
**Sutherland,** Francis A 1940- *WhoIns 92*
**Sutherland,** G Russell 1923- *AmMWSc 92*
**Sutherland,** George 1862-1942 *FacFETw*
**Sutherland,** George Leslie 1922- *AmMWSc 92, WhoFI 92*
**Sutherland,** Graham 1903-1980 *FacFETw, TwCPaSc*
**Sutherland,** H. W. 1917-1981 *ConAu 134*
**Sutherland,** Herbert James 1943- *AmMWSc 92*
**Sutherland,** Ian 1926- *Who 92*
**Sutherland,** Ian Boyd 1926- *Who 92*
**Sutherland,** Ian Duncan Whittaker 1933- *WhoAmL 92*
**Sutherland,** Ivan Edward 1938- *AmMWSc 92*
**Sutherland,** James 1900- *IntAu&W 91, WrDr 92*
**Sutherland,** James 1920- *IntWW 91, Who 92*
**Sutherland,** James Henry Richardson 1923- *AmMWSc 92*
**Sutherland,** James McKenzie 1923- *AmMWSc 92*
**Sutherland,** James Robert 1942- *WhoWest 92*
**Sutherland,** James Runcieman 1900- *Who 92*
**Sutherland,** Joan 1926- *FacFETw [port], IntWW 91, NewAmDM, Who 92, WhoEnt 92*
**Sutherland,** Joe Allen 1934- *WhoAmL 92*
**Sutherland,** John 1938- *WrDr 92*
**Sutherland,** John Alexander Muir 1933- *Who 92*
**Sutherland,** John B 1918- *AmMWSc 92*
**Sutherland,** John Brewer 1931- *Who 92*
**Sutherland,** John Bruce, IV 1945- *AmMWSc 92*
**Sutherland,** John Campbell 1921- *WhoWest 92*
**Sutherland,** John Clark 1940- *AmMWSc 92*
**Sutherland,** John Elliott 1915- *WhoEnt 92, WhoWest 92*
**Sutherland,** John Menzies 1928- *Who 92*
**Sutherland,** John Patrick 1942- *AmMWSc 92*
**Sutherland,** Judith Elliott 1924- *AmMWSc 92*
**Sutherland,** Kiefer 1966?- *ConTFT 9, IntMPA 92*
**Sutherland,** Kiefer 1967- *WhoEnt 92*
**Sutherland,** Louis Carr 1926- *AmMWSc 92*
**Sutherland,** Lowell Francis 1939- *WhoAmL 92, WhoWest 92*
**Sutherland,** Malcolm Read, Jr. 1916- *WhoRel 92*
**Sutherland,** Margaret 1897-1984 *NewAmDM*
**Sutherland,** Margaret 1941- *IntAu&W 91, WrDr 92*
**Sutherland,** Maurice 1915- *Who 92*
**Sutherland,** Muir *Who 92*
**Sutherland,** Norman Stuart 1927- *IntWW 91, Who 92, WrDr 92*
**Sutherland,** Patrick Kennedy 1925- *AmMWSc 92*
**Sutherland,** Paul Kirchmaier 1947- *WhoAmL 92*
**Sutherland,** Peter Adams 1933- *WhoAmP 91*
**Sutherland,** Peter D. 1946- *IntWW 91*
**Sutherland,** Peter Denis 1946- *Who 92*
**Sutherland,** Peter Gordon 1946- *AmMWSc 92*
**Sutherland,** Ranald Iain *Who 92*
**Sutherland,** Raymond Carter 1917- *WhoRel 92*
**Sutherland,** Raymond Elwood 1937- *WhoFI 92*
**Sutherland,** Richard Earl 1930- *WhoAmP 91*
**Sutherland,** Robert L 1916- *AmMWSc 92*
**Sutherland,** Robert Melvin 1940- *AmMWSc 92*
**Sutherland,** Ronald Byron 1960- *WhoMW 92*
**Sutherland,** Ronald George 1935- *AmMWSc 92*
**Sutherland,** Stewart Ross 1941- *IntWW 91, Who 92*
**Sutherland,** Stuart *Who 92*
**Sutherland,** Terry Michael 1954- *WhoRel 92*
**Sutherland,** Veronica Evelyn 1939- *Who 92*
**Sutherland,** William 1933- *Who 92*
**Sutherland,** William Neil 1927- *AmMWSc 92*
**Sutherland,** William Robert 1936- *AmMWSc 92*
**Sutherland-Brown,** Atholl 1923- *AmMWSc 92*
**Sutherland Smith,** Beverley Margaret 1935- *IntAu&W 91*
**Sutherlund,** David Arvid 1929- *WhoAmL 92*
**Suthers,** Roderick Atkins 1937- *AmMWSc 92*
**Suthiwart-Narueput,** Owart 1926- *Who 92*
**Sutin,** Jerome 1930- *AmMWSc 92*
**Sutin,** Lawrence 1951- *ConAu 135*
**Sutin,** Michael Gary 1935- *WhoAmL 92*
**Sutin,** Norman 1928- *AmMWSc 92*
**Sutjipto,** Suganto 1946- *WhoWest 92*
**Sutker,** Calvin R 1923- *WhoAmP 91*
**Sutman,** Frank X 1927- *AmMWSc 92*
**Sutnar,** Ladislav 1897-1976 *DcTwDes*
**Sutnick,** Alton Ivan 1928- *AmMWSc 92*
**Suto,** Andras 1927- *IntAu&W 91, IntWW 91*
**Sutorius,** Darryl Jon 1940- *WhoMW 92*
**Sutowski,** Thor Brian 1945- *WhoEnt 92*
**Sutphen,** Robert Ray 1950- *WhoWest 92*
**Sutphen,** Van Tassel 1861-1945 *ScFEYrs*
**Sutresna,** Nana S. 1933- *IntWW 91*
**Sutrisno,** Tri *IntWW 91*
**Sutro,** Alfred 1863-1933 *RfGEnL 91*
**Sutro,** John A., Jr. 1936- *WhoAmL 92*
**Sutro,** John Alfred 1905- *WhoAmL 92*
**Suttell,** Paul Allyn 1949- *WhoAmP 91, WhoFI 92*
**Sutter,** Barton *DrAPF 91*
**Sutter,** Brian *WhoMW 92*
**Sutter,** David Franklin 1935- *AmMWSc 92*
**Sutter,** Diane 1950- *WhoEnt 92*
**Sutter,** Elizabeth Henby 1912- *WhoMW 92*
**Sutter,** Gerald Rodney 1937- *AmMWSc 92*
**Sutter,** Harvey Mack 1906- *WhoWest 92*
**Sutter,** Johann August *DcAmImH*
**Sutter,** John Augustus 1803-1880 *BenetAL 91*
**Sutter,** John F *WhoAmP 91*
**Sutter,** John Frederick 1943- *AmMWSc 92*
**Sutter,** John Herbert 1928- *WhoAmL 92*
**Sutter,** John Richard 1937- *WhoMW 92*
**Sutter,** John Ritter 1930- *AmMWSc 92*
**Sutter,** Joseph F 1921- *AmMWSc 92*
**Sutter,** Larabie *TwCWW 91*
**Sutter,** Morley Carman 1933- *AmMWSc 92*
**Sutter,** Philip Henry 1930- *AmMWSc 92*
**Sutter,** Richard Anthony 1909- *WhoMW 92*
**Sutter,** Richard P 1937- *AmMWSc 92*
**Sutter,** Wayne Elmer 1930- *WhoMW 92*
**Sutterby,** John Lloyd 1936- *AmMWSc 92*
**Sutterby,** Larry Quentin 1950- *WhoWest 92*
**Sutterfield,** James Kirby 1957- *WhoRel 92*
**Sutterfield,** James Ray *WhoAmL 92*
**Sutterlein,** Ludwig 1865-1917 *EncTR 91*
**Suttie,** John Weston 1934- *AmMWSc 92*
**Suttie,** Philip Grant- 1938- *Who 92*
**Suttill,** Margaret Joan *Who 92*
**Suttkus,** Royal Dallas 1920- *AmMWSc 92*
**Suttle,** Andrew Dillard, Jr 1926- *AmMWSc 92*
**Suttle,** Dorwin Wallace 1906- *WhoAmL 92*
**Suttle,** Helen Jayson 1925- *WhoAmP 91*
**Suttle,** Jeffrey Charles 1952- *AmMWSc 92*
**Suttle,** Jimmie Ray 1932- *AmMWSc 92*
**Suttle,** Stephen Hungate 1940- *WhoAmL 92*
**Suttles,** Virginia Grant 1931- *WhoWest 92*
**Suttman,** Lori Anne 1962- *WhoMW 92*
**Suttner,** Lee Joseph 1939- *AmMWSc 92*
**Sutton,** Alan John 1936- *Who 92*
**Sutton,** Andrew *TwCSFW 91*
**Sutton,** Anne C 1921- *WhoAmP 91*
**Sutton,** Barbara Jean 1949- *WhoWest 92*
**Sutton,** Barbara Kathryn Powderly 1940- *WhoWest 92*
**Sutton,** Barry Bridge 1937- *Who 92*
**Sutton,** Blaine Mote 1921- *AmMWSc 92*
**Sutton,** Charles Franklin 1944- *WhoIns 92*
**Sutton,** Charles Samuel 1913- *AmMWSc 92*
**Sutton,** Charyn Diane *WhoBlA 92*
**Sutton,** Claudius Henry 1939- *WhoRel 92*
**Sutton,** Clive *TwCPaSc*
**Sutton,** Clive 1937- *WrDr 92*
**Sutton,** Colin Bertie John 1938- *Who 92*
**Sutton,** Dallas Albert 1911- *AmMWSc 92*
**Sutton,** David 1917- *WrDr 92*
**Sutton,** David Brian 1958- *WhoMW 92*
**Sutton,** David Bruce 1949- *WhoRel 92*
**Sutton,** David C 1933- *AmMWSc 92*
**Sutton,** David George 1944- *AmMWSc 92*
**Sutton,** David John 1944- *WrDr 92*
**Sutton,** Denys 1917-1991 *ConAu 133, NewYTBS 91*
**Sutton,** Denys Miller d1991 *Who 92N*
**Sutton,** Derek 1937- *AmMWSc 92*
**Sutton,** Dianne Floyd 1948- *WhoBlA 92*
**Sutton,** Donald Dunsmore 1927- *AmMWSc 92*
**Sutton,** Dorothy Moseley *DrAPF 91*
**Sutton,** Emmett Albert 1935- *AmMWSc 92*
**Sutton,** Eve 1906- *WrDr 92*
**Sutton,** Frederick 1915- *Who 92*
**Sutton,** Frederick Isler, Jr. 1916- *WhoFI 92*
**Sutton,** George E 1923- *AmMWSc 92*
**Sutton,** George Harry 1927- *AmMWSc 92*
**Sutton,** George W 1927- *AmMWSc 92*
**Sutton,** George Walter 1927- *WhoWest 92*
**Sutton,** Gloria W. 1952- *WhoBlA 92*
**Sutton,** Harry Eldon 1927- *AmMWSc 92*
**Sutton,** Henry *DrAPF 91, WrDr 92*
**Sutton,** Henry V 1932- *WhoAmP 91*
**Sutton,** Horace d1991 *NewYTBS 91*
**Sutton,** Horace 1919-1991 *ConAu 135*
**Sutton,** J L 1931- *AmMWSc 92*
**Sutton,** James Andrew 1934- *WhoFI 92*
**Sutton,** James Carter 1945- *WhoBlA 92*
**Sutton,** James T. *IntMPA 92*
**Sutton,** Jane 1950- *WrDr 92*
**Sutton,** Jean 1916- *TwCSFW 91*
**Sutton,** Jeff 1913-1979 *TwCSFW 91*
**Sutton,** Jesse Noel 1926- *WhoRel 92*
**Sutton,** John 1919- *Who 92*
**Sutton,** John 1932- *Who 92*
**Sutton,** John 1935- *TwCPaSc*
**Sutton,** John Clifford 1941- *AmMWSc 92*
**Sutton,** John Curtis 1942- *AmMWSc 92*
**Sutton,** John Ewing 1950- *WhoAmL 92*
**Sutton,** John F., Jr. 1918- *WhoAmL 92*
**Sutton,** John Martin 1922- *WhoMW 92*
**Sutton,** John Phillip 1960- *WhoFI 92*
**Sutton,** John R. 1962- *WhoFI 92, WhoMW 92*
**Sutton,** John Sydney 1936- *Who 92*
**Sutton,** Joseph Cornelius 1959- *WhoRel 92*
**Sutton,** Julia Sumberg 1928- *WhoEnt 92*
**Sutton,** Keith Norman *Who 92*
**Sutton,** Kelso Furbush 1939- *WhoFI 92*
**Sutton,** Larry Allen 1961- *WhoRel 92*
**Sutton,** Leonard von Bibra 1914- *WhoAmP 91, WhoFI 92*
**Sutton,** Leslie Ernest 1906- *IntWW 91, Who 92*
**Sutton,** Lewis McMechan 1946- *AmMWSc 92*
**Sutton,** Linda 1947- *TwCPaSc*
**Sutton,** Lorraine J. *DrAPF 91*
**Sutton,** Lou Nelle *WhoAmP 91*
**Sutton,** Louise Nixon 1925- *AmMWSc 92*
**Sutton,** Marcella French 1946- *WhoWest 92*
**Sutton,** Mary A. 1945- *WhoBlA 92*
**Sutton,** Matthew Albert 1923- *AmMWSc 92*
**Sutton,** Michael Arnold 1951- *WhoRel 92*
**Sutton,** Michael Scott 1962- *WhoFI 92*
**Sutton,** Moses 1920- *WhoBlA 92*
**Sutton,** Norma J. 1952- *WhoBlA 92*
**Sutton,** Oliver Carter, II 1948- *WhoBlA 92*
**Sutton,** Ozell 1925- *WhoBlA 92*
**Sutton,** Paul 1929- *AmMWSc 92*
**Sutton,** Paul Eugene, II 1943- *WhoAmL 92*
**Sutton,** Paul McCullough 1921- *AmMWSc 92*
**Sutton,** Percy E *WhoAmP 91*
**Sutton,** Percy E. 1920- *WhoBlA 92*
**Sutton,** Peter 1923- *Who 92*
**Sutton,** Peter Alfred 1934- *WhoRel 92*
**Sutton,** Peter Morgan 1932- *Who 92*
**Sutton,** Philip 1928- *TwCPaSc*
**Sutton,** Philip John 1928- *IntWW 91, Who 92*
**Sutton,** Pierre Monte 1947- *WhoBlA 92*
**Sutton,** Ray Frederick 1931- *WhoWest 92*
**Sutton,** Ray Ronny 1950- *WhoRel 92*
**Sutton,** Remar Marion 1941- *IntAu&W 91*
**Sutton,** Richard 1940- *Who 92*
**Sutton,** Richard Lewis 1923- *Who 92*
**Sutton,** Richard Lexington 1937- *Who 92*
**Sutton,** Richard Ruel 1934- *WhoRel 92*
**Sutton,** Robert George 1925- *AmMWSc 92*

**Sutton,** Robert Paul 1951- *WhoMW 92*
**Sutton,** Robert Randolph 1947- *WhoFI 92*
**Sutton,** Robert William 1905- *Who 92*
**Sutton,** Roger Beatty 1916- *AmMWSc 92*
**Sutton,** Russell Paul 1929- *AmMWSc 92*
**Sutton,** S. B. 1940- *WrDr 92*
**Sutton,** S. Robert 1955- *WhoAmL 92*
**Sutton,** Samuel J. 1941- *WhoAmL 92*
**Sutton,** Scott Elder 1952- *IntAu&W 91*
**Sutton,** Sharon Egretta 1941- *WhoBlA 92, WhoMW 92*
**Sutton,** Shaun Alfred Graham 1919- *IntAu&W 91, Who 92*
**Sutton,** Stack 1927- *TwCWW 91, WrDr 92*
**Sutton,** Stafford William Powell F. *Who 92*
**Sutton,** Stanley R. 1949- *WhoRel 92*
**Sutton,** Sterling E. 1928- *WhoBlA 92*
**Sutton,** Susan Lyn 1948- *WhoEnt 92*
**Sutton,** Thomas 1918- *WhoBlA 92*
**Sutton,** Thomas C 1942- *WhoIns 92, WhoWest 92*
**Sutton,** Thomas Francis 1923- *Who 92*
**Sutton,** Timothy Wayne 1960- *WhoWest 92*
**Sutton,** Trevor 1948- *TwCPaSc*
**Sutton,** Turner Bond 1945- *AmMWSc 92*
**Sutton,** W H 1930- *AmMWSc 92*
**Sutton,** Walter C. 1927- *WhoRel 92*
**Sutton,** Walter L. 1917- *WhoBlA 92*
**Sutton,** Walter Stanborough 1877-1916 *BiInAmS*
**Sutton,** Wayne 1922- *WhoAmP 91*
**Sutton,** William Anthony 1951- *WhoMW 92*
**Sutton,** William Blaylock 1942- *WhoRel 92*
**Sutton,** William John 1859-1915 *BiInAmS*
**Sutton,** William Joseph 1945- *WhoFI 92*
**Sutton,** William Wallace 1930- *AmMWSc 92, WhoBlA 92*
**Sutton,** William Wallace 1943- *AmMWSc 92*
**Sutton,** Willie 1901-1980 *FacFETw*
**Sutton,** Wilma Jean 1933- *WhoBlA 92*
**Sutton-Salley,** Virginia B. *WhoFI 92*
**Sutula,** Chester Louis 1933- *AmMWSc 92*
**Suu Kyi,** Aung San 1945?- *News 92-2 [port]*
**Suuberg,** Eric Michael 1951- *AmMWSc 92*
**Suura,** Hiroshi 1925- *AmMWSc 92*
**Suva,** Archbishop of 1933- *Who 92*
**Suviranta,** Antti Johannes 1923- *IntWW 91*
**Suy,** Erik 1933- *IntWW 91*
**Suyama,** Yoshitaka 1931- *AmMWSc 92*
**Suyat,** Stanley Donald 1943- *WhoAmL 92*
**Suydam,** Frederick Henry 1923- *AmMWSc 92*
**Suyematsu,** Toshiro 1918- *WhoAmL 92*
**Suyetsugu,** Grace Tamiko 1957- *WhoWest 92*
**Suyin** *Who 92*
**Suzman,** Helen 1917- *IntWW 91, Who 92*
**Suzman,** Janet 1939- *IntMPA 92, IntWW 91, Who 92, WhoEnt 92*
**Suzue,** Ginzaburo 1932- *AmMWSc 92*
**Suzuki,** Bob H. *WhoWest 92*
**Suzuki,** Daisetz Teitaro 1870-1966 *RelLAm 91*
**Suzuki,** David Takayoshi 1936- *AmMWSc 92*
**Suzuki,** Gengo 1904- *IntWW 91, WhoFI 92*
**Suzuki,** Haruo 1913- *IntWW 91*
**Suzuki,** Hideo 1917- *IntWW 91*
**Suzuki,** Hidetaro 1937- *WhoEnt 92*
**Suzuki,** Howard Kazuro 1927- *AmMWSc 92*
**Suzuki,** Isamu 1930- *AmMWSc 92*
**Suzuki,** Jon Byron 1947- *AmMWSc 92*
**Suzuki,** Kinuko 1933- *AmMWSc 92*
**Suzuki,** Kunihiko 1932- *AmMWSc 92*
**Suzuki,** Mahiko 1938- *AmMWSc 92*
**Suzuki,** Michio 1926- *AmMWSc 92*
**Suzuki,** Michio 1927- *AmMWSc 92*
**Suzuki,** Norihisa 1935- *WhoRel 92*
**Suzuki,** Osamu 1930- *IntWW 91*
**Suzuki,** Seiji 1953- *WhoMW 92*
**Suzuki,** Shigeto 1925- *AmMWSc 92*
**Suzuki,** Shin'ichi 1898- *NewAmDM*
**Suzuki,** Shunichi 1910- *IntWW 91*
**Suzuki,** Shunryu 1904-1971 *RelLAm 91*
**Suzuki,** Tadashi 1939- *IntWW 91*
**Suzuki,** Tsuneo 1931- *AmMWSc 92*
**Suzuki,** Zenko 1911- *IntWW 91*
**Svacha,** Anna Johnson 1928- *AmMWSc 92*
**Svahn,** John A 1943- *WhoAmP 91*
**Svalya,** Phillip Gordon 1943- *WhoAmL 92*
**Svanes,** Torgny *AmMWSc 92*
**Svard,** Trygve N. *WhoMW 92*
**Svartvik,** Jan 1931- *IntWW 91, WrDr 92*
**Svarzman,** Norberto Luis 1937- *WhoHisp 92*
**Svashenko,** Semen Andreevich 1904-1969 *SovUnBD*
**Svatek,** Rebecca Ann 1961- *WhoMW 92*
**Sve,** Charles 1940- *AmMWSc 92*
**Svec,** Harry John 1918- *AmMWSc 92*
**Svec,** Janice Lynn 1948- *WhoFI 92*
**Svec,** Leroy Vernon 1942- *AmMWSc 92, WhoMW 92*
**Svec,** Richard Stanley 1942- *WhoWest 92*
**Sveda,** Michael 1912- *AmMWSc 92*
**Svedberg,** Bjoern 1937- *IntWW 91*
**Svedberg,** Theodor H.E. 1884-1971 *WhoNob 90*
**Svedjan,** Ken *WhoAmP 91*
**Svejda,** Felicitas Julia 1920- *AmMWSc 92*
**Svejgaard,** Arne 1937- *IntWW 91*
**Svendsen,** Gerald Eugene 1940- *AmMWSc 92*
**Svendsen,** Hanne Marie 1933- *ConAu 134*
**Svendsen,** Ib Arne 1937- *AmMWSc 92*
**Svendsen,** Kendall Lorraine 1919- *AmMWSc 92*
**Svendsen,** Linda *DrAPF 91*
**Svengalis,** Kendall Frayne 1947- *WhoAmL 92*
**Svenne,** Juris Peteris 1939- *AmMWSc 92*
**Svenson,** Beryl *Who 92*
**Svenson,** Bo 1941- *IntMPA 92, WhoEnt 92*
**Svensson,** Don Arne 1947- *WhoWest 92*
**Svensson,** Eric Carl 1940- *AmMWSc 92*
**Sventeck,** Dale Richard 1951- *WhoFI 92*
**Sverdlov,** Yakov Mikhailovich 1885-1919 *FacFETw*
**Sverdlov,** Yakov Mikhaylovich 1885-1919 *SovUnBD*
**Sverdlove,** Ronald 1948- *AmMWSc 92*
**Sverdrup,** Edward F 1930- *AmMWSc 92*
**Sverdrup,** Georg 1848-1907 *DcAmImH*
**Sverdrup,** George Michael 1949- *AmMWSc 92*
**Sverdsten,** Terry 1932- *WhoAmP 91*
**Svetanics,** Milton F, Jr 1937- *WhoAmP 91*
**Svetanics,** Neil *WhoMW 92*
**Svetlanov,** Yevgeniy Fedorovich 1928- *SovUnBD*
**Svetlanov,** Yevgeniy Fyodorovich 1928- *IntWW 91, WhoEnt 92*
**Svetlic,** Michael Joseph 1951- *WhoAmP 91*
**Svetlik,** Joseph Frank 1918- *AmMWSc 92*
**Svetlov,** Mikhail Arkad'evich 1903-1964 *SovUnBD*
**Svetlova,** Marina 1922- *WhoEnt 92*
**Svevo,** Italo 1861-1928 *FacFETw*
**Svich,** Caridad 1963- *WhoEnt 92, WhoHisp 92*
**Svien,** Don J 1924- *WhoAmP 91*
**Sviggum,** Steve A 1951- *WhoAmP 91*
**Svihel,** Riley Lenard 1934- *WhoMW 92, WhoRel 92*
**Svikhart,** Edwin Gladdin 1930- *WhoWest 92*
**Svilar,** Daniel Paul 1929- *WhoAmL 92*
**Svilova,** Yelizaveta Ignat'evna 1900-1976 *SovUnBD*
**Svirbely,** Joseph Edward 1947- *WhoMW 92*
**Sviridov,** Georgiy Vasilevich 1915- *IntWW 91, SovUnBD*
**Sviridov,** Georgy 1915- *ConCom 92*
**Svirsky,** Gregory Caesarivich 1921- *LiExTwC*
**Svirsky,** Grigoriy Tsezarevich 1921- *IntWW 91*
**Svoboda,** Elizabeth Jane 1944- *WhoAmP 91*
**Svoboda,** Frederic Joseph 1949- *WhoMW 92*
**Svoboda,** Glenn Richard 1930- *AmMWSc 92*
**Svoboda,** Gordon H 1922- *AmMWSc 92*
**Svoboda,** James Arvid 1934- *AmMWSc 92*
**Svoboda,** Josef 1920- *IntWW 91, Who 92*
**Svoboda,** Josef 1929- *AmMWSc 92*
**Svoboda,** Ludvik 1895-1979 *FacFETw*
**Svoboda,** Rudy George 1941- *AmMWSc 92*
**Svoboda,** Terese *DrAPF 91*
**Svokos,** Steve George 1934- *AmMWSc 92*
**Svrcek,** Paul Rapp 1955- *WhoAmP 91*
**Swab,** Janice Coffey 1941- *AmMWSc 92*
**Swaback,** Raymond Syvert 1954- *WhoMW 92*
**Swabb,** Edward Allen 1947- *WhoMW 92*
**Swabb,** Lawrence E, Jr 1922- *AmMWSc 92*
**Swacha,** Stanley Joseph 1953- *WhoRel 92*
**Swacker,** Frank Warren 1922- *WhoAmL 92*
**Swackhammer,** C E *WhoAmP 91*
**Swadener,** Mark William 1954- *WhoRel 92*
**Swader,** Fred Nicholas 1934- *AmMWSc 92*
**Swadley,** J. Paul 1928- *WhoRel 92*
**Swadley,** William Martin 1956- *WhoEnt 92*
**Swadlow,** Harvey A *AmMWSc 92*
**Swados,** Harvey 1920-1972 *BenetAL 91*
**Swados,** Lincoln J. 1942-1989 *NewYTBS 91 [port]*
**Swaelen,** Frank 1930- *IntWW 91*
**Swaffield,** James 1924- *IntWW 91, Who 92*
**Swaffield,** William Robert 1934- *WhoRel 92*
**Swafford,** Claude Galbreath 1925- *WhoAmP 91*
**Swafford,** Darrel Keith 1936- *WhoMW 92*
**Swafford,** Jan Johnson 1946- *WhoEnt 92*
**Swafford,** Wade K 1917- *WhoAmP 91*
**Swagel,** Dennis Jay 1946- *WhoWest 92*
**Swager,** Norvin Leroy 1931- *WhoAmP 91*
**Swaggart,** Jimmy Lee 1935- *RelLAm 91, WhoRel 92*
**Swaiko,** Joseph *WhoRel 92*
**Swaim,** Alice Mackenzie 1911- *IntAu&W 91, WrDr 92*
**Swaim,** Bob 1943- *IntMPA 92*
**Swaim,** Charles Hall 1939- *WhoAmL 92*
**Swaim,** Jeffrey Lynn 1956- *WhoRel 92*
**Swaim,** John A. 1946- *WhoFI 92*
**Swaim,** John Franklin 1935- *WhoFI 92*
**Swaim,** John Joseph 1949- *WhoAmP 91*
**Swaim,** Joseph Carter, Jr. 1934- *WhoAmL 92*
**Swaim,** Robert Harold 1946- *WhoFI 92*
**Swaim,** Robert Lee 1935- *AmMWSc 92*
**Swaiman,** Kenneth F 1931- *AmMWSc 92*
**Swaiman,** Kenneth Fred 1931- *WhoMW 92*
**Swain,** Alice M. 1924- *WhoBlA 92*
**Swain,** Brian Kenneth 1957- *WhoFI 92*
**Swain,** Charles Gardner 1917- *AmMWSc 92*
**Swain,** Christopher Paul 1961- *WhoAmP 91*
**Swain,** Courtenay C 1945- *WhoAmP 91*
**Swain,** David Wood 1942- *AmMWSc 92*
**Swain,** Elisabeth Ramsay 1917- *AmMWSc 92*
**Swain,** Frederick Morrill, Jr 1916- *AmMWSc 92*
**Swain,** Geoffrey W *AmMWSc 92*
**Swain,** Hamp 1929- *WhoBlA 92*
**Swain,** Henry Huntington 1923 *AmMWSc 92*
**Swain,** Henry Thornhill 1924- *Who 92*
**Swain,** Howard Aldred, Jr 1928- *AmMWSc 92*
**Swain,** Howard Lyle 1946- *WhoWest 92*
**Swain,** James H. 1954- *WhoBlA 92*
**Swain,** Jane Alison 1954- *WhoFI 92*
**Swain,** John D *ScFEYrs*
**Swain,** Nola V. 1942- *WhoWest 92*
**Swain,** Philip C., Jr. 1957- *WhoAmL 92*
**Swain,** Philip Raymond 1929- *WhoFI 92*
**Swain,** Ralph Warner 1944- *AmMWSc 92*
**Swain,** Richard Russell 1939- *AmMWSc 92*
**Swain,** Robert Charles 1958- *WhoAmL 92*
**Swain,** Robert Francis 1942- *WhoMW 92*
**Swain,** Robert J. 1919- *WhoBlA 92*
**Swain,** Robert James 1928- *AmMWSc 92*
**Swain,** Ronald L. 1948- *WhoBlA 92*
**Swainbank,** Louise Robinson 1917- *WhoAmP 91*
**Swaine,** Edward Thomas William 1907- *Who 92*
**Swaine,** Howard Ralph 1928- *WhoFI 92, WhoMW 92*
**Swaine,** Robert Leslie, Jr. 1950- *WhoFI 92*
**Swainson,** Eric 1926- *Who 92*
**Swaisgood,** Harold Everett 1936- *AmMWSc 92*
**Swakon,** Doreen H D 1953- *AmMWSc 92*
**Swale,** Suzan 1946- *TwCPaSc*
**Swalen,** Jerome Douglas 1928- *AmMWSc 92*
**Swales,** William Edward 1925- *IntWW 91, WhoFI 92*
**Swalgen,** Steven John 1960- *WhoFI 92*
**Swalin,** Richard Arthur 1929- *AmMWSc 92*
**Swallow,** Daphne Patricia 1932- *Who 92*
**Swallow,** Earl Connor 1941- *AmMWSc 92*
**Swallow,** George Clinton 1817-1899 *BiInAmS*
**Swallow,** John Crossley 1923- *IntWW 91, Who 92*
**Swallow,** LaLee L. 1952- *WhoHisp 92*
**Swallow,** Mark 1963- *ConAu 134*
**Swallow,** Norman 1921- *IntMPA 92, WrDr 92*
**Swallow,** Patricia *Who 92*
**Swallow,** Richard Louis 1939- *AmMWSc 92*
**Swallow,** Sydney 1919- *Who 92*
**Swallow,** William 1905- *Who 92*
**Swallow,** William Hutchinson 1941- *AmMWSc 92*
**Swalm,** Ralph Oehrle 1915- *AmMWSc 92*
**Swamer,** Frederic Wurl 1918- *AmMWSc 92*
**Swaminathan,** Balasubramanian 1946- *AmMWSc 92*
**Swaminathan,** Jagdish 1928- *IntWW 91*
**Swaminathan,** Lakshmi *EncAmaz 91*
**Swaminathan,** Monkombu Sambasivan 1925- *IntWW 91, Who 92*
**Swaminathan,** Srinivasa 1926- *AmMWSc 92*
**Swamy,** Mayasandra Nanjundiah Srikanta 1935- *AmMWSc 92*
**Swamy,** Padmanabha Narayana 1937- *AmMWSc 92*
**Swamy,** Vijay Chinnaswamy 1938- *AmMWSc 92*
**Swan,** Alfred J. 1890-1970 *NewAmDM*
**Swan,** Algernon Gordon 1923- *AmMWSc 92*
**Swan,** Allan Hollister 1929- *WhoRel 92, WhoWest 92*
**Swan,** Allen George 1946- *WhoAmL 92*
**Swan,** Charles H d1899 *BiInAmS*
**Swan,** Conrad Marshall John Fisher 1924- *Who 92*
**Swan,** D 1920- *AmMWSc 92*
**Swan,** Dean George 1923- *AmMWSc 92*
**Swan,** Dennis Charles Tarrant 1900- *Who 92*
**Swan,** Dermot Joseph 1917- *Who 92*
**Swan,** Douglas 1935- *TwCPaSc*
**Swan,** Frederick Robbins, Jr 1937- *AmMWSc 92*
**Swan,** George Steven 1948- *WhoAmL 92*
**Swan,** Gladys *DrAPF 91*
**Swan,** Gladys 1934- *ConLC 69 [port], IntAu&W 91*
**Swan,** H E *ScFEYrs*
**Swan,** Harold James Charles 1922- *AmMWSc 92*
**Swan,** James Byron 1933- *AmMWSc 92*
**Swan,** John 1935- *Who 92*
**Swan,** John W. 1935- *WhoBlA 92*
**Swan,** John William David 1935- *IntWW 91*
**Swan,** Joseph Bishop, Jr. 1942- *WhoAmL 92*
**Swan,** Joshua Augustus 1823-1871 *BiInAmS*
**Swan,** Karl G 1931- *WhoAmP 91*
**Swan,** Kenneth Carl 1912- *AmMWSc 92, WhoWest 92*
**Swan,** Kenneth G 1934- *AmMWSc 92*
**Swan,** L. Alex 1938- *WhoBlA 92*
**Swan,** Lawrence Wesley 1922- *AmMWSc 92*
**Swan,** Lionel F. 1909- *WhoBlA 92*
**Swan,** Michael 1948- *WhoEnt 92*
**Swan,** Monroe 1937- *WhoAmP 91, WhoBlA 92*
**Swan,** Patricia B 1937- *AmMWSc 92*
**Swan,** Peter 1935- *TwCPaSc*
**Swan,** Peter Nachant 1936- *WhoAmL 92*
**Swan,** Richard Alan 1944- *WhoWest 92*
**Swan,** Richard Gordon 1933- *AmMWSc 92, IntWW 91*
**Swan,** Roy Craig, Jr 1920- *AmMWSc 92*
**Swan,** Shanna Helen 1936- *AmMWSc 92*
**Swan,** Sharon L. 1944- *WhoFI 92*
**Swan,** Sheila Tobie 1953- *WhoAmL 92*
**Swan,** William Bertram d1990 *Who 92N*
**Swan,** William Hall 1932- *WhoEnt 92*
**Swan Sonnenschein and Allen** *DcLB 106*
**Swan Sonnenschein,** Lowrey and Company *DcLB 106*
**Swanay,** Russ 1950- *WhoAmP 91*
**Swanberg,** Chandler A 1942- *AmMWSc 92*
**Swanberg,** Edmund Raymond 1921- *WhoFI 92*
**Swanberg,** Ingrid *DrAPF 91*
**Swanberg,** W. A. 1907- *WrDr 92*
**Swanborg,** Robert Harry 1938- *AmMWSc 92*
**Swandby,** Nancy Nelson 1948- *WhoWest 92*
**Swander,** Mary *DrAPF 91*
**Swaner,** Leland Scowcroft *WhoFI 92*
**Swaner,** Paula Margetts 1927- *WhoWest 92*
**Swaney,** John Brewster 1944- *AmMWSc 92*
**Swaney,** Larry Arlen 1930- *WhoMW 92*
**Swaney,** Lois Mae 1928- *AmMWSc 92*
**Swanger,** David *DrAPF 91*
**Swango,** William Franklin 1942- *WhoMW 92*
**Swanigan,** Jesse Calvin 1933- *WhoBlA 92*
**Swank,** Emory Coblentz 1922- *IntWW 91*
**Swank,** Katherine Elizabeth 1960- *WhoAmL 92*
**Swank,** Richard Tilghman 1942- *AmMWSc 92*
**Swank,** Robert Roy, Jr 1939- *AmMWSc 92*
**Swank,** Rolland Laverne 1942- *AmMWSc 92*
**Swank,** Roy Laver 1909- *AmMWSc 92*
**Swank,** Thomas Francis 1937- *AmMWSc 92*
**Swank,** Wayne T 1936- *AmMWSc 92*
**Swann,** Baron d1990 *IntWW 91N*
**Swann,** Lord 1920-1990 *AnObit 1990*
**Swann,** Anthony Charles Christopher d1991 *Who 92N*
**Swann,** Arthur M *WhoAmP 91*
**Swann,** Benjamin Colin Lewis 1922- *Who 92*
**Swann,** Brian *DrAPF 91*
**Swann,** Charles Paul 1918- *AmMWSc 92*
**Swann,** Dale William 1929- *AmMWSc 92*
**Swann,** David A 1936- *AmMWSc 92*
**Swann,** Donald 1923- *WrDr 92*

**Swann**, Donald Ibrahim 1923- IntWW 91, Who 92
**Swann**, Eugene Merwyn 1934- WhoBlA 92
**Swann**, Frederick Lewis 1931- WhoEnt 92
**Swann**, Frederick Ralph Holland 1904- Who 92
**Swann**, Gordon Alfred 1931- AmMWSc 92
**Swann**, Harold S 1942- WhoIns 92
**Swann**, Howard Story Gray 1936- AmMWSc 92
**Swann**, James Howard 1943- WhoMW 92
**Swann**, Jerre Bailey 1939- WhoAmL 92
**Swann**, Julian Dana Nimmo H. Who 92
**Swann**, Larry D 1952- WhoAmP 91
**Swann**, Lois DrAPF 91
**Swann**, Lynn Curtis 1952- WhoBlA 92
**Swann**, Madeline Bruce 1951- AmMWSc 92
**Swann**, Michael 1941- Who 92
**Swann**, Roberta 1948- WhoEnt 92
**Swann**, Roberta M. DrAPF 91
**Swann**, Samuel Douglas 1963- WhoRel 92
**Swann**, Thomas Burnett 1928-1976 TwCSFW 91
**Swann**, William Shirley 1947- WhoRel 92
**Swansea**, Baron 1925- Who 92
**Swansea**, Charleen Whisnant DrAPF 91
**Swansea And Brecon**, Bishop of 1933- Who 92
**Swanson**, Alan Wayne 1944- AmMWSc 92
**Swanson**, Allan Frederick 1929- WhoMW 92
**Swanson**, Allen John 1934- WhoRel 92
**Swanson**, Anne Barrett 1948- AmMWSc 92
**Swanson**, Arnold Arthur 1923- AmMWSc 92
**Swanson**, Arthur Dean 1934- WhoAmL 92
**Swanson**, August George 1925- IntWW 91
**Swanson**, Barry Grant 1944- AmMWSc 92
**Swanson**, Basil Ian 1944- AmMWSc 92
**Swanson**, Bernet S 1921- AmMWSc 92
**Swanson**, Beverly Jane 1949- WhoMW 92
**Swanson**, Byron Ralph 1930- WhoRel 92
**Swanson**, Carl Gustav, Jr. 1921- WhoMW 92
**Swanson**, Carl Pontius 1911- AmMWSc 92
**Swanson**, Carroll Arthur 1915- AmMWSc 92
**Swanson**, Charles 1949- WhoBlA 92
**Swanson**, Charles Andrew 1929- AmMWSc 92
**Swanson**, Charles Howard 1935- WhoEnt 92
**Swanson**, Charles Richard 1953- WhoFI 92
**Swanson**, Curtis James 1941- AmMWSc 92
**Swanson**, Dale Charles 1927- WhoFI 92
**Swanson**, David Bernard 1935- AmMWSc 92
**Swanson**, David G, Jr 1941- AmMWSc 92
**Swanson**, David Heath 1942- IntWW 91, WhoFI 92, WhoMW 92
**Swanson**, David Henry 1930- AmMWSc 92, WhoFI 92
**Swanson**, David Wendell 1930- AmMWSc 92
**Swanson**, Don R 1924- AmMWSc 92
**Swanson**, Donald Alan 1938- AmMWSc 92, WhoWest 92
**Swanson**, Donald Charles 1926- AmMWSc 92
**Swanson**, Donald F. 1928- WhoMW 92
**Swanson**, Donald Frederick 1927- WhoMW 92
**Swanson**, Donald G 1935- AmMWSc 92
**Swanson**, Donald Leroy 1923- AmMWSc 92
**Swanson**, Donald Roland 1927- WhoMW 92
**Swanson**, Dwain V. 1934- WhoFI 92
**Swanson**, Edith 1934- WhoBlA 92
**Swanson**, Edwin Archie 1908- WhoWest 92
**Swanson**, Eleonora 1916- IntAu&W 91
**Swanson**, Eric Rice 1946- AmMWSc 92
**Swanson**, Eric Richmond 1934- AmMWSc 92
**Swanson**, Ernest Allen, Jr 1936- AmMWSc 92
**Swanson**, Eva Lisa Saarinen 1905-1979 DcTwDes
**Swanson**, George D 1942- AmMWSc 92
**Swanson**, Gertrude Gay WhoAmP 91
**Swanson**, Gladys M 1926- WhoAmP 91
**Swanson**, Gloria 1899-1983 FacFETw
**Swanson**, Gustav Adolph 1910- AmMWSc 92
**Swanson**, H.N. d1991 NewYTBS 91
**Swanson**, Harold Dueker 1930- AmMWSc 92
**Swanson**, Heather 1949- ConAu 135
**Swanson**, Howard 1907-1978 NewAmDM
**Swanson**, J Robert 1939- AmMWSc 92
**Swanson**, Jack Lee 1934- AmMWSc 92
**Swanson**, James A 1935- AmMWSc 92
**Swanson**, James C 1934- WhoAmP 91
**Swanson**, Jay Dixon 1933- WhoAmP 91
**Swanson**, Jennifer Ann 1964- WhoEnt 92
**Swanson**, Joanne Thatcher 1932- WhoAmL 92
**Swanson**, John L 1936- AmMWSc 92
**Swanson**, John William 1917- AmMWSc 92
**Swanson**, Jon Charles 1958- WhoMW 92
**Swanson**, Lawrence Ray 1936- AmMWSc 92
**Swanson**, Lee Richard 1957- WhoWest 92
**Swanson**, Leonard George 1940- AmMWSc 92
**Swanson**, Leslie Martin, Jr. 1940- WhoAmL 92
**Swanson**, Lloyd Vernon 1938- AmMWSc 92
**Swanson**, Lynn Allen 1942- AmMWSc 92, WhoMW 92
**Swanson**, Lynwood Walter 1934- AmMWSc 92
**Swanson**, Marvin F 1935- WhoIns 92
**Swanson**, Mary Helen 1926- WhoAmP 91
**Swanson**, Max Lynn 1931- AmMWSc 92
**Swanson**, Maxine Marie 1927- WhoAmP 91
**Swanson**, Melodie Christine 1957- WhoAmL 92
**Swanson**, Michael David 1958- WhoEnt 92
**Swanson**, Neil H. 1896-1983 BenetAL 91
**Swanson**, O'Neil D. WhoBlA 92
**Swanson**, Paul John, Jr. 1934- WhoFI 92
**Swanson**, Paul N 1936- AmMWSc 92
**Swanson**, Paul Reginald 1928- WhoRel 92
**Swanson**, Peggy Eubanks 1936- WhoFI 92
**Swanson**, Phillip D 1932- AmMWSc 92
**Swanson**, Ralph John 1920- WhoAmL 92
**Swanson**, Reuben Theodore 1922- WhoRel 92
**Swanson**, Richard William 1934- WhoWest 92
**Swanson**, Robert A. DrAPF 91
**Swanson**, Robert Allan 1928- AmMWSc 92
**Swanson**, Robert Boudinot, II 1936- WhoEnt 92
**Swanson**, Robert E 1924- AmMWSc 92
**Swanson**, Robert Harold 1933- AmMWSc 92
**Swanson**, Robert James 1945- AmMWSc 92
**Swanson**, Robert Killen 1932- WhoWest 92
**Swanson**, Robert Lawrence 1938- AmMWSc 92
**Swanson**, Robert Martin 1940- WhoMW 92
**Swanson**, Robert Mclean 1920- WhoMW 92
**Swanson**, Robert Nels 1932- AmMWSc 92
**Swanson**, Ronald WhoRel 92
**Swanson**, Roy Joel 1945- WhoAmL 92
**Swanson**, Samuel Edward 1946- AmMWSc 92
**Swanson**, Sheila Sue 1956- WhoMW 92
**Swanson**, Steve DrAPF 91
**Swanson**, Susan Marie DrAPF 91
**Swanson**, Sydney Alan Vasey 1931- Who 92
**Swanson**, Thomas Joseph 1928- WhoFI 92
**Swanson**, Thomas Richard 1954- WhoMW 92
**Swanson**, Thomas Willard 1943- WhoWest 92
**Swanson**, Vernon E 1922- AmMWSc 92
**Swanson**, Virginia Lee 1922- AmMWSc 92
**Swanson**, Wallace Martin 1941- WhoAmL 92
**Swanson**, Warren Lloyd 1933- WhoAmL 92
**Swanson**, Wayne Harold 1943- WhoAmL 92
**Swanson**, William Paul 1931- AmMWSc 92
**Swanson**, William Russell 1949- WhoMW 92
**Swanston**, Clarence Eugene 1947- WhoBlA 92
**Swanston**, Douglas Neil 1938- AmMWSc 92
**Swanston**, Julie 1962- WhoMW 92
**Swanstrom**, Nord Lee 1949- WhoAmP 91
**Swanton**, Ernest William 1907- IntAu&W 91, Who 92
**Swanton**, H Rae 1918- WhoAmP 91
**Swanwick**, Betty 1915-1989 TwCPaSc
**Swanwick**, Graham Russell 1906- Who 92
**Swanwick**, Joseph Harold 1866-1929 TwCPaSc
**Swanwick**, Michael 1950- TwCSFW 91
**Swanz**, Donald Joseph 1933- WhoAmP 91
**Swanzey**, Robert Joseph 1935- WhoFI 92
**Swar Al-Dahab** IntWW 91
**Swarbrick**, Deanna Marie 1957- WhoEnt 92
**Swarbrick**, James 1934- AmMWSc 92, Who 92
**Sward**, Andrea Jeanne 1951- WhoEnt 92
**Sward**, Edward Lawrence, Jr 1933- AmMWSc 92
**Sward**, Robert DrAPF 91
**Sward**, Robert 1933- ConPo 91
**Sward**, Robert S. 1933- WrDr 92
**Sward**, Robert Stuart 1933- IntAu&W 91, WhoWest 92
**Swardson**, Mary Anne 1928- AmMWSc 92, WhoMW 92
**Swarin**, Stephen John 1945- AmMWSc 92, WhoMW 92
**Swaringen**, Roy Archibald, Jr 1942- AmMWSc 92
**Swarm**, H Myron 1916- AmMWSc 92
**Swarm**, Richard L 1927- AmMWSc 92
**Swarner**, Thomas Herbert 1941- WhoWest 92
**Swarowsky**, Hans 1899-1975 NewAmDM
**Swart**, Charles 1893-1982 FacFETw
**Swart**, Janice Lynn 1964- WhoMW 92
**Swart**, Karel 1921- IntWW 91
**Swart**, Vernon David, Jr. 1955- WhoFI 92, WhoWest 92
**Swart**, William Lee 1930- AmMWSc 92
**Swart**, William W 1944- AmMWSc 92
**Swarthout**, Barbara Ann 1947- WhoMW 92
**Swarthout**, Barbara Elaine 1930- WhoMW 92
**Swarthout**, Gladys 1900-1969 NewAmDM
**Swarthout**, Glendon DrAPF 91
**Swarthout**, Glendon 1918- BenetAL 91, ConNov 91, IntAu&W 91, TwCWW 91, WrDr 92
**Swartley**, Willard Myers 1936- WhoRel 92
**Swartout**, Glen Martin 1956- WhoWest 92
**Swartout**, Robert Ray, Jr. 1946- WhoWest 92
**Swarts**, Elwyn Lowell 1929- AmMWSc 92
**Swarts**, Joseph Andrew 1917- WhoAmP 91
**Swarts**, William DrAPF 91
**Swartwood**, Bernard Craig 1955- WhoWest 92
**Swartwood**, Charles Brown 1915- WhoAmL 92
**Swartz**, Barbara Ellen 1945- WhoAmL 92
**Swartz**, Benjamin Kinsell, Jr. 1931- WhoMW 92
**Swartz**, Beth Ames 1936- WorArt 1980 [port]
**Swartz**, Blair Kinch 1932- AmMWSc 92
**Swartz**, Bruce Elliott 1948- WhoWest 92
**Swartz**, Carolyn Elizabeth 1936- WhoMW 92
**Swartz**, Charles Dana 1915- AmMWSc 92
**Swartz**, Charles S. 1939- WhoEnt 92
**Swartz**, Charles W 1938- AmMWSc 92
**Swartz**, Charles Wayne 1938- WhoWest 92
**Swartz**, Christopher John 1951- WhoEnt 92
**Swartz**, Clifford Edward 1925- AmMWSc 92
**Swartz**, Donald Everett 1916- WhoEnt 92
**Swartz**, Donald Howard 1931- WhoWest 92
**Swartz**, Donald Percy 1921- AmMWSc 92
**Swartz**, Edward M. 1934- WhoAmL 92
**Swartz**, Elizabeth Anne 1943- WhoRel 92
**Swartz**, Frank Joseph 1927- AmMWSc 92
**Swartz**, George Alfred 1928- Who 92
**Swartz**, George Allan 1930- AmMWSc 92
**Swartz**, Gordon Elmer 1917- AmMWSc 92
**Swartz**, Grace Lynn 1943- AmMWSc 92
**Swartz**, Harold M 1935- AmMWSc 92
**Swartz**, Harry 1911- AmMWSc 92
**Swartz**, Harry Sip 1925- AmMWSc 92
**Swartz**, Jack 1932- WhoMW 92
**Swartz**, James E 1951- AmMWSc 92
**Swartz**, James Franklin, Jr. 1930- WhoFI 92
**Swartz**, James Lawrence 1939- AmMWSc 92
**Swartz**, James Richard 1942- WhoFI 92
**Swartz**, John Croucher 1924- AmMWSc 92
**Swartz**, Jon David 1934- IntAu&W 91, WrDr 92
**Swartz**, Leslie Gerard 1930- AmMWSc 92
**Swartz**, Malcolm Gilbert 1931- WhoFI 92
**Swartz**, Marjorie Louise 1924- AmMWSc 92
**Swartz**, Melvin Jay 1930- WhoAmL 92
**Swartz**, Morton N 1923- AmMWSc 92
**Swartz**, Paul Frederick 1943- WhoMW 92, WhoRel 92
**Swartz**, Ray 1952- WhoWest 92
**Swartz**, Reginald 1911- Who 92
**Swartz**, Reginald William Colin 1911- IntWW 91
**Swartz**, Robert David 1937- WhoMW 92
**Swartz**, Russell Bruce 1915- WhoFI 92
**Swartz**, Stephen Arthur 1941- WhoFI 92
**Swartz**, Stuart Endsley 1938- AmMWSc 92
**Swartz**, Teresa Anne 1953- WhoWest 92
**Swartz**, Thomas 1946- WhoAmP 91
**Swartz**, Tim Ray 1958- WhoEnt 92
**Swartz**, William Edward, Jr 1944- AmMWSc 92
**Swartz**, William John 1920- AmMWSc 92
**Swartz**, William John 1934- IntWW 91, WhoFI 92, WhoMW 92
**Swartzbaugh**, John Stuart 1953- WhoAmP 91
**Swartzbaugh**, Marc L. 1937- WhoAmL 92
**Swartzendruber**, Dale 1925- AmMWSc 92, WhoMW 92
**Swartzendruber**, Donald Clair 1930- AmMWSc 92
**Swartzendruber**, Douglas Edward 1946- AmMWSc 92
**Swartzendruber**, Lydon James 1933- AmMWSc 92
**Swartzentruber**, Keith Eldon 1956- WhoMW 92
**Swartzentruber**, Paul Edwin 1931- AmMWSc 92
**Swartzlander**, Earl Eugene, Jr 1945- AmMWSc 92
**Swartzman**, Gordon Leni 1943- AmMWSc 92
**Swartzwelder**, John Clyde 1911- AmMWSc 92
**Swartzwelder**, John Joseph 1949- WhoEnt 92, WhoWest 92
**Swarup**, Govind 1929- Who 92
**Swarz**, Jeffrey Robert 1949- WhoFI 92
**Swash**, Stanley Victor 1896- Who 92
**Swatek**, Frank Edward 1929- AmMWSc 92
**Swathirajan**, S 1952- AmMWSc 92
**Swatos**, William Henry, Jr. 1946- WhoRel 92
**Swatridge**, Charles d1964 ConAu 34NR
**Swatridge**, Irene Maude ConAu 34NR
**Swauger**, Paul Landis, Sr. 1930- WhoRel 92
**Swaybill**, Roger E. d1991 NewYTBS 91
**Swaybill**, Roger E. 1943-1991 ConAu 133
**Swayne**, Giles 1946- ConCom 92
**Swayne**, Martin 1884-1953 ScFEYrs
**Swayne**, Ronald 1918- Who 92
**Swayne**, Steven Robert 1957- WhoBlA 92
**Swaythling**, Baron 1928- IntWW 91, Who 92
**Swaythling**, Jean Marcia 1908- Who 92
**Swayze**, John Cameron LesBEnT 92 [port]
**Swayze**, John Cameron 1906- IntMPA 92
**Swayze**, John Cameron, Sr. 1906- WhoEnt 92
**Swayze**, Pat ConTFT 9
**Swayze**, Patrick 1952- CurBio 91 [port]
**Swayze**, Patrick 1954?- ConTFT 9, IntMPA 92, IntWW 91, WhoEnt 92
**Swazey**, E Michael WhoAmP 91
**Swazey**, Judith P 1939- AmMWSc 92
**Swe**, U Ba 1915- IntWW 91
**Sweadner**, Kathleen Joan 1949- AmMWSc 92
**Sweaney**, William Douglas 1912- Who 92
**Swearengen**, Jack Clayton 1940- AmMWSc 92
**Swearengen**, Jack Clayton, II 1940- WhoWest 92
**Swearengin**, Gary Lee 1957- WhoMW 92, WhoRel 92
**Swearer**, Donald K. 1934- WrDr 92
**Swearer**, Donald Keeney 1934- IntAu&W 91, WhoRel 92
**Swearer**, Howard R. d1991 NewYTBS 91 [port]
**Swearingen**, Bert Charles 1936- WhoRel 92
**Swearingen**, Edward Hicks 1948- WhoAmP 91
**Swearingen**, George Robert 1923- WhoAmP 91
**Swearingen**, Jeffrey Anthan 1964- WhoMW 92
**Swearingen**, Jeffrey Rea 1964- WhoRel 92
**Swearingen**, John Eldred 1918- AmMWSc 92, IntWW 91, WhoMW 92
**Swearingen**, Judson Sterling 1907- AmMWSc 92, WhoFI 92
**Swearingen**, Lawson L, Jr 1944- WhoAmP 91
**Swearingen**, Mary Addie 1906- WhoWest 92
**Swearingin**, Marvin Laverne 1931- AmMWSc 92
**Sweat**, Bruce Pierre 1950- WhoWest 92
**Sweat**, Floyd Walter 1941- AmMWSc 92
**Sweat**, Robert Lee 1931- AmMWSc 92
**Sweat**, Sheila Diane 1961- WhoBlA 92
**Sweat**, Vincent Eugene 1941- AmMWSc 92
**Sweatman**, Arthur 1834-1909 RelLAm 91
**Sweatman**, Phillip Jay 1955- WhoFI 92, WhoMW 92
**Sweatt**, Heman 1913-1982 FacFETw
**Sweda**, Edward Leon, Jr. 1955- WhoAmL 92
**Sweda**, Gerald James 1942- WhoFI 92, WhoMW 92
**Swedback**, James M. 1935- WhoFI 92
**Swedberg**, Gertrude Laliah 1933- WhoWest 92
**Swedberg**, Kenneth C 1930- AmMWSc 92

**Swede**, George 1940- *IntAu&W 91, SmATA 67 [port]*
**Swedeen**, Hollie Joel 1927- *WhoMW 92*
**Sweden**, King of *IntWW 91*
**Swedenborg**, Emanuel 1688-1772 *BenetAL 91*
**Swedien**, Bruce Frederik 1934- *WhoEnt 92*
**Swedlow**, Jerold Lindsay 1935- *AmMWSc 92*
**Swedlund**, Alan Charles 1943- *AmMWSc 92*
**Sweebe**, Richard Dale 1951- *WhoAmL 92*
**Sweed**, Norman Harris 1943- *AmMWSc 92*
**Sweedler**, Alan R 1942- *AmMWSc 92*
**Sweeley**, Charles Crawford 1930- *AmMWSc 92*
**Sweelinck**, Jan Pieterszoon 1562-1621 *NewAmDM*
**Sweem**, Billy Don 1942- *WhoRel 92*
**Sweeney**, Asher William 1920- *WhoAmL 92, WhoAmP 91, WhoMW 92*
**Sweeney**, Beatrice Marcy 1914- *AmMWSc 92*
**Sweeney**, Bob *LesBEnT 92*
**Sweeney**, Bruce L 1932- *WhoAmP 91*
**Sweeney**, Christopher Lee 1959- *WhoWest 92*
**Sweeney**, Claudine 1965- *WhoEnt 92*
**Sweeney**, Clayton Anthony 1931- *WhoAmL 92*
**Sweeney**, D.B. 1961- *IntMPA 92*
**Sweeney**, Daniel Bryan, Jr. 1946- *WhoFI 92, WhoWest 92*
**Sweeney**, Daniel Robert 1948- *WhoAmL 92*
**Sweeney**, Daniel Thomas 1929- *WhoEnt 92*
**Sweeney**, Daryl Charles 1936- *AmMWSc 92*
**Sweeney**, David McCann 1955- *WhoAmP 91*
**Sweeney**, Deborah Leah 1945- *WhoFI 92*
**Sweeney**, Deidre Ann 1953- *WhoAmL 92*
**Sweeney**, Dennis Joseph 1941- *WhoMW 92*
**Sweeney**, Donald Lee 1932- *WhoWest 92*
**Sweeney**, Donald Wesley 1946- *AmMWSc 92*
**Sweeney**, Dorothy Love 1922- *WhoRel 92*
**Sweeney**, Edward 1947- *WhoAmP 91*
**Sweeney**, Edward Arthur 1931- *AmMWSc 92*
**Sweeney**, Elizabeth Ann 1946- *WhoFI 92*
**Sweeney**, George Bernard, Jr. 1933- *WhoEnt 92, WhoFI 92*
**Sweeney**, George Douglas 1934- *AmMWSc 92*
**Sweeney**, Gerald H 1928- *WhoAmP 91*
**Sweeney**, Harry David 1944- *WhoFI 92*
**Sweeney**, James Aloysius, Jr 1934- *WhoAmP 91*
**Sweeney**, James Augustus 1912- *WhoWest 92*
**Sweeney**, James Lawrence 1951- *WhoIns 92*
**Sweeney**, James Lee 1930- *WhoFI 92, WhoMW 92*
**Sweeney**, James Lee 1944- *AmMWSc 92, WhoFI 92*
**Sweeney**, James Michael 1945- *AmMWSc 92*
**Sweeney**, James Patrick 1952- *WhoFI 92*
**Sweeney**, James Raymond 1928- *WhoAmL 92*
**Sweeney**, John Albert 1925- *WhoBlA 92*
**Sweeney**, John Robert 1945- *AmMWSc 92*
**Sweeney**, Joyce 1955- *ConAu 35NR, SmATA 65, -68 [port]*
**Sweeney**, Lawrence Earl, Jr 1942- *AmMWSc 92*
**Sweeney**, Leo 1918- *ConAu 34NR, WrDr 92*
**Sweeney**, Mark Owen 1942- *WhoRel 92*
**Sweeney**, Marvin A. 1953- *WhoRel 92*
**Sweeney**, Mary Ann 1945- *AmMWSc 92*
**Sweeney**, Mary Carolyn *WhoFI 92*
**Sweeney**, Mary Devota 1921- *WhoRel 92*
**Sweeney**, Mary Margaret 1957- *WhoEnt 92*
**Sweeney**, Matthew 1952- *ConPo 91, WrDr 92*
**Sweeney**, Michael *WhoAmP 91*
**Sweeney**, Michael 1950- *WhoWest 92*
**Sweeney**, Michael Anthony 1931- *AmMWSc 92*
**Sweeney**, Michael Joseph 1939- *AmMWSc 92*
**Sweeney**, Neal James 1957- *WhoAmL 92*
**Sweeney**, Patrick A 1941- *WhoAmP 91*
**Sweeney**, Patrick Dennis 1954- *WhoEnt 92*
**Sweeney**, Patrick Shepard 1966- *WhoEnt 92*
**Sweeney**, Paula Fisette 1957- *WhoAmL 92*
**Sweeney**, Phillip P. *DrAPF 91*
**Sweeney**, Robert 1949- *WhoAmP 91*
**Sweeney**, Robert Anderson 1940- *AmMWSc 92*
**Sweeney**, Robert Emmet 1931- *WhoAmP 91*
**Sweeney**, Robert Lucien 1895- *WhoBlA 92*
**Sweeney**, Roger Lee 1936- *WhoWest 92*
**Sweeney**, Stephen Joseph 1928- *WhoFI 92*
**Sweeney**, Terrance Allen 1945- *WhoEnt 92*
**Sweeney**, Thomas Francis 1933- *WhoAmP 91*
**Sweeney**, Thomas Frederick 1943- *WhoAmL 92*
**Sweeney**, Thomas Kevin 1923- *Who 92*
**Sweeney**, Thomas L 1936- *AmMWSc 92*
**Sweeney**, Thomas Patrick 1929- *AmMWSc 92*
**Sweeney**, Thomas Richard 1914- *AmMWSc 92*
**Sweeney**, Thomas William 1947- *WhoMW 92*
**Sweeney**, Vonny Hilton 1947- *WhoEnt 92*
**Sweeney**, William 1950- *ConCom 92*
**Sweeney**, William Alan 1926- *AmMWSc 92, WhoWest 92*
**Sweeney**, William Edward 1933- *WhoIns 92*
**Sweeney**, William John 1940- *AmMWSc 92*
**Sweeney**, William Mortimer 1923- *AmMWSc 92*
**Sweeney**, William R, Jr *WhoAmP 91*
**Sweeney**, William Victor 1947- *AmMWSc 92*
**Sweeny**, A. Neil 1951- *WhoFI 92*
**Sweeny**, Charlie 1957- *WhoFI 92*
**Sweeny**, Daniel Michael 1930- *AmMWSc 92*
**Sweeny**, Hale Caterson 1925- *AmMWSc 92*
**Sweeny**, James Gilbert 1944- *AmMWSc 92*
**Sweeny**, Kenneth S. 1948- *WhoEnt 92*
**Sweeny**, Lauren J *AmMWSc 92*
**Sweeny**, Mary K 1923- *IntAu&W 91*
**Sweeny**, Robert F 1931- *AmMWSc 92*
**Sweet Singer of Michigan**, The *BenetAL 91*
**Sweet**, Andrew Arnold 1956- *WhoWest 92*
**Sweet**, Ann Kielty 1935- *WhoAmP 91*
**Sweet**, Arnold Lawrence 1935- *AmMWSc 92, WhoMW 92*
**Sweet**, Arthur 1920- *WhoMW 92*
**Sweet**, Arthur Thomas, Jr 1920- *AmMWSc 92*
**Sweet**, Benjamin Hersh 1924- *AmMWSc 92*
**Sweet**, Bruce *DrAPF 91*
**Sweet**, Charles Edward 1933- *AmMWSc 92*
**Sweet**, Charles Samuel 1942- *AmMWSc 92*
**Sweet**, Charles Wheeler 1943- *WhoFI 92*
**Sweet**, Christopher William 1963- *WhoFI 92*
**Sweet**, Clifford C. 1936- *WhoBlA 92*
**Sweet**, Cody *WhoEnt 92*
**Sweet**, David 1945- *TwCPaSc*
**Sweet**, David Allen 1950- *WhoFI 92*
**Sweet**, David Paul 1948- *AmMWSc 92*
**Sweet**, David W. 1948- *WhoAmL 92, WhoAmP 91*
**Sweet**, Elnathan 1837-1903 *BiInAmS*
**Sweet**, Frederick 1938- *AmMWSc 92*
**Sweet**, George Elliott 1904- *IntAu&W 91*
**Sweet**, George H 1934- *AmMWSc 92*
**Sweet**, Gertrude Evans 1906- *AmMWSc 92*
**Sweet**, Gregory Allen 1956- *WhoMW 92*
**Sweet**, Harvey 1943- *WhoEnt 92*
**Sweet**, Haven C 1942- *AmMWSc 92*
**Sweet**, Herman Royden 1909- *AmMWSc 92*
**Sweet**, James Dale 1952- *WhoAmL 92*
**Sweet**, Jeffrey Warren 1950- *WhoEnt 92*
**Sweet**, Jerry James 1951- *WhoMW 92*
**Sweet**, John Edson 1832-1916 *BiInAmS*
**Sweet**, John W 1910- *AmMWSc 92*
**Sweet**, Joseph John 1914- *WhoAmP 91*
**Sweet**, Justin 1929- *WhoAmL 92*
**Sweet**, Larry Ross 1940- *AmMWSc 92*
**Sweet**, Leonard 1925- *AmMWSc 92*
**Sweet**, Lewis Taber, Jr. 1932- *WhoAmL 92*
**Sweet**, Lowell Elwin 1931- *WhoAmL 92, WhoAmP 91, WhoFI 92*
**Sweet**, Malcolm Stuart 1905- *WhoRel 92*
**Sweet**, Marc Steven 1945- *WhoFI 92*
**Sweet**, Melvin Millard *AmMWSc 92*
**Sweet**, Merrill Henry, II 1935- *AmMWSc 92*
**Sweet**, Peter Alan 1921- *Who 92*
**Sweet**, Philip W. K., Jr. 1927- *WhoMW 92*
**Sweet**, Richard Clark 1921- *AmMWSc 92*
**Sweet**, Robert Burdette *DrAPF 91*
**Sweet**, Robert Dean 1915- *AmMWSc 92*
**Sweet**, Robert Mahlon 1943- *AmMWSc 92*
**Sweet**, Robert W., Jr. 1937- *WhoAmL 92*
**Sweet**, Robert Workman 1922- *WhoAmL 92*
**Sweet**, Ronald Lancelot 1923- *AmMWSc 92*
**Sweet**, Stuart J 1953- *WhoAmP 91*
**Sweet**, Terrecia W. 1955- *WhoBlA 92*
**Sweet**, Terry Thomas 1951- *WhoFI 92*
**Sweet**, Thomas Richard 1921- *AmMWSc 92*
**Sweet**, William Herbert 1910- *AmMWSc 92*
**Sweeten**, Gary Ray 1938- *WhoRel 92*
**Sweeting**, George 1924- *WhoRel 92, WrDr 92*
**Sweeting**, Linda Marie 1941- *AmMWSc 92*
**Sweeting**, William Hart 1909- *Who 92*
**Sweetland**, Arthur E d1903 *BiInAmS*
**Sweetland**, Monroe Mark 1910- *WhoAmP 91*
**Sweetland**, Nancy Rose 1934- *WrDr 92*
**Sweetman**, Brian Jack 1936- *AmMWSc 92*
**Sweetman**, David 1943- *WrDr 92*
**Sweetman**, Doris Dwan 1918- *WhoAmP 91*
**Sweetman**, Jennifer Joan *Who 92*
**Sweetman**, John Francis 1930- *Who 92*
**Sweetman**, Joseph David, Jr. 1948- *WhoWest 92*
**Sweetman**, Lawrence 1942- *AmMWSc 92*
**Sweetman**, Loretta Vinette 1941- *WhoWest 92*
**Sweetnam**, Rodney 1927- *Who 92*
**Sweetow**, Elizabeth Swoope 1947- *WhoFI 92, WhoWest 92*
**Sweetow**, Susan Lee 1937- *WhoWest 92*
**Sweets**, Ellen Adrienne 1941- *WhoBlA 92*
**Sweets**, Henry Hayes, III 1949- *WhoMW 92*
**Sweetser**, Arthur 1888-1968 *AmPeW*
**Sweetser**, Gene 1948- *WhoAmP 91*
**Sweetser**, Ruth Emilie Ziemann 1945- *WhoMW 92*
**Sweetser**, Susan W. 1958- *WhoAmL 92*
**Sweetser**, Wesley 1919- *WrDr 92*
**Sweetser**, Wesley Duaine 1919- *IntAu&W 91*
**Sweett**, Cyril 1903- *Who 92*
**Sweezey**, Charles Otis 1947- *WhoEnt 92, WhoMW 92*
**Sweezy**, John W 1932- *WhoAmP 91*
**Sweezy**, John William 1932- *WhoMW 92*
**Swegal**, Franz B. 1944- *WhoEnt 92*
**Sweigart**, John Andrew 1954- *WhoRel 92*
**Sweitzer**, David Eugene 1962- *WhoAmL 92*
**Sweitzer**, Harry Averil 1943- *WhoAmL 92*
**Sweitzer**, Harry Phillips 1916- *WhoRel 92*
**Sweitzer**, James Adair 1928- *WhoFI 92*
**Sweitzer**, James M 1947- *WhoIns 92*
**Sweitzer**, James Stuart 1951- *AmMWSc 92*
**Swell**, Leon 1927- *AmMWSc 92*
**Swenberg**, Charles Edward 1940- *AmMWSc 92*
**Swenberg**, James Arthur 1942- *AmMWSc 92*
**Swendseid**, Marian Edna 1918- *AmMWSc 92*
**Swendsen**, Robert Haakon 1943- *AmMWSc 92*
**Swenerton**, Helene 1925- *AmMWSc 92*
**Sweney**, William Homer 1948- *WhoEnt 92*
**Swenka**, Arthur John 1937- *WhoWest 92*
**Swensen**, Clifford Henrik, Jr. 1926- *WhoMW 92*
**Swensen**, Mary Jean Hamilton 1910- *WhoWest 92*
**Swensen**, Oscar Warren 1931- *WhoRel 92*
**Swensen**, Philip Romney 1943- *WhoWest 92*
**Swensen**, Ruth *DrAPF 91*
**Swenski**, Mark Charles 1951- *WhoMW 92*
**Swenson**, Betty 1933- *WhoAmP 91*
**Swenson**, Betty Howliston 1923- *WhoEnt 92*
**Swenson**, Bruce Henry 1932- *WhoRel 92*
**Swenson**, Charles Allyn 1933- *AmMWSc 92*
**Swenson**, Charles William 1947- *WhoFI 92*
**Swenson**, Clayton Albert 1923- *AmMWSc 92*
**Swenson**, Courtland Sevander 1936- *WhoEnt 92*
**Swenson**, Daniel Lee 1928- *WhoRel 92*
**Swenson**, David Harold 1948- *AmMWSc 92*
**Swenson**, Donald Adolph 1932- *AmMWSc 92*
**Swenson**, Donald Otis 1937- *AmMWSc 92*
**Swenson**, Douglas 1945- *WhoAmP 91*
**Swenson**, Frank Albert 1912- *AmMWSc 92*
**Swenson**, G W, Jr 1922- *AmMWSc 92*
**Swenson**, Gary Lee 1937- *WhoFI 92*
**Swenson**, Gary Russell 1941- *AmMWSc 92*
**Swenson**, Harold A 1927- *WhoAmP 91*
**Swenson**, Henry Maurice 1916- *AmMWSc 92*
**Swenson**, Hugo Nathanael 1904- *AmMWSc 92*
**Swenson**, Joy A 1921- *WhoAmP 91*
**Swenson**, Karen *DrAPF 91*
**Swenson**, Kathleen Susan 1938- *WhoEnt 92, WhoWest 92*
**Swenson**, Leonard Wayne 1931- *AmMWSc 92*
**Swenson**, Mark Gregory 1949- *WhoMW 92*
**Swenson**, May 1913- *HanAmWH*
**Swenson**, May 1919-1989 *BenetAL 91, ConAu 36NR*
**Swenson**, Melvin John 1917- *AmMWSc 92*
**Swenson**, Orvar 1909- *AmMWSc 92*
**Swenson**, Paul Arthur 1920- *AmMWSc 92*
**Swenson**, Raymond Takashi 1949- *WhoFI 92, WhoWest 92*
**Swenson**, Richard Paul 1949- *AmMWSc 92*
**Swenson**, Richard Waltner 1923- *AmMWSc 92*
**Swenson**, Robert J 1934- *AmMWSc 92*
**Swenson**, Ruth Ann *WhoEnt 92*
**Swenson**, Severt, Jr 1940- *WhoAmP 91*
**Swenson**, Stephen Douglas 1949- *WhoRel 92*
**Swenson**, Theresa Lynn 1957- *AmMWSc 92*
**Swensson**, Elsie Louise 1922- *WhoAmP 91*
**Swensson**, Evelyn Dickenson 1928- *WhoEnt 92*
**Swenton**, John Stephen 1940- *AmMWSc 92*
**Swerbilow**, Howard Marc 1949- *WhoAmL 92*
**Swerczek**, Thomas Walter 1939- *AmMWSc 92*
**Swerda**, Patricia Fine 1916- *WhoWest 92*
**Swerdloff**, Ileen Pollock 1945- *WhoAmL 92*
**Swerdloff**, Ronald S 1938- *AmMWSc 92*
**Swerdlove**, Dorothy Louise 1928- *WhoEnt 92*
**Swerdlow**, Jeffrey Morris 1940- *WhoEnt 92*
**Swerdlow**, Martin A 1923- *AmMWSc 92*
**Swerdlow**, Max 1915- *AmMWSc 92*
**Swerdlow**, Stanley d1991 *NewYTBS 91*
**Swerlick**, Isadore 1921- *AmMWSc 92*
**Swerling**, Jack Bruce 1946- *WhoAmL 92*
**Swerling**, Jo 1897- *IntMPA 92*
**Swerling**, Jo, Jr. 1931- *IntMPA 92*
**Swerling**, Peter 1929- *AmMWSc 92*
**Swet**, Peter 1942- *WhoEnt 92*
**Swetenham**, Violet Hilda 1911- *IntAu&W 91*
**Swetharanyam**, Lalitha *AmMWSc 92*
**Swetits**, John Joseph 1942- *AmMWSc 92*
**Swetland**, David Wightman 1916- *WhoMW 92*
**Swetlik**, William Philip 1950- *WhoMW 92*
**Swetman**, Glenn R. 1936- *WrDr 92*
**Swetman**, Glenn Robert *DrAPF 91*
**Swetmon**, Billy Robert 1943- *WhoRel 92*
**Swetnam**, Daniel Richard 1957- *WhoAmL 92*
**Swetnam**, James Hubbard 1928- *WhoRel 92*
**Swetnick**, Robert N. 1949- *WhoAmL 92*
**Swets**, Don Eugene 1930- *AmMWSc 92*
**Swett**, Chester Parker 1939- *AmMWSc 92*
**Swett**, Dale Everett 1937- *WhoWest 92*
**Swett**, Dana Malcolm 1925- *WhoAmP 91*
**Swett**, Dick *WhoAmP 91*
**Swett**, Dick 1957- *AlmAP 92 [port]*
**Swett**, John Eben 1929- *WhoAmL 92*
**Swett**, John Emery 1932- *AmMWSc 92*
**Swett**, Keene 1932- *AmMWSc 92*
**Swett**, Robert E 1928- *WhoIns 92*
**Swetz**, Frank J. 1937- *ConAu 135*
**Sweven**, Godfrey 1846-1935 *ScFEYrs*
**Swez**, John Adam 1941- *AmMWSc 92*
**Swezey**, Charles Mason 1935- *WhoRel 92*
**Swezey**, Robert Leonard 1925- *AmMWSc 92*
**Swezey**, William Albert, II 1969- *WhoEnt 92*
**Swhier**, Claudia Versfelt 1950- *WhoAmL 92*
**Swiatek**, Kenneth Robert 1935- *AmMWSc 92*
**Swibel**, Steven Warren 1946- *WhoAmL 92*
**Swicegood**, Steven Lloyd 1965- *WhoEnt 92*
**Swichar**, Edward Irving 1940- *WhoAmL 92*
**Swichkow**, Louis Judah 1912- *WhoRel 92*
**Swick**, Kenneth Eugene 1936- *AmMWSc 92*
**Swick**, Larry Marvin 1932- *WhoMW 92*
**Swick**, Marly 1949- *ConAu 135*
**Swick**, Robert Winfield 1925- *AmMWSc 92*
**Swickard**, David *DrAPF 91*
**Swicklik**, Leonard Joseph 1928- *AmMWSc 92*
**Swid**, Stephen Claar 1940- *WhoEnt 92*
**Swiden**, LaDell Ray 1938- *AmMWSc 92, WhoFI 92, WhoMW 92*
**Swider**, Christopher 1950- *WhoEnt 92*
**Swider**, Joseph Charles 1908- *WhoAmP 91*
**Swider**, William, Jr 1934- *AmMWSc 92*
**Swidler**, Ronald 1929- *AmMWSc 92*
**Swiecicki**, Marcin 1947- *IntWW 91*
**Swierenga**, Robert P. 1935- *WrDr 92*

**Swierkiewicz**, Akos 1946- WhoIns 92
**Swierstra**, Ernest Emke 1930- AmMWSc 92
**Swieszkowski**, Dominick WhoAmP 91
**Swieten**, Gerhard van 1700-1772 BlkwCEP
**Swieten**, Gottfried, Freiherr van 1733-1803 BlkwCEP
**Swift**, Al 1935- AlmAP 92 [port], WhoAmP 91, WhoWest 92
**Swift**, Arthur Reynders 1938- AmMWSc 92
**Swift**, Augustus ConAu 133
**Swift**, Bernie 1922- WhoAmP 91
**Swift**, Brinton L 1926- AmMWSc 92
**Swift**, Bryan WrDr 92
**Swift**, Calvin Thomas 1937- AmMWSc 92
**Swift**, Camm Churchill 1940- AmMWSc 92
**Swift**, Charles Moore, Jr 1940- AmMWSc 92
**Swift**, Daniel W 1935- AmMWSc 92
**Swift**, David 1919- IntMPA 92
**Swift**, David Leslie 1935- AmMWSc 92
**Swift**, Dolores Monica Marcinkevich 1936- WhoMW 92
**Swift**, Donald J P 1935- AmMWSc 92
**Swift**, Dorothy Garrison 1939- AmMWSc 92
**Swift**, E. Clinton 1945- WhoFI 92
**Swift**, Edward John, Jr. 1954- WhoMW 92
**Swift**, Elijah, V 1938- AmMWSc 92
**Swift**, Fred Calvin 1926- AmMWSc 92
**Swift**, George W 1930- AmMWSc 92
**Swift**, Glenn W 1932- AmMWSc 92
**Swift**, Graham 1939- AmMWSc 92
**Swift**, Graham 1949- ConNov 91, WrDr 92
**Swift**, Graham Colin 1949- IntAu&W 91, IntWW 91
**Swift**, Harold Eugene 1936- AmMWSc 92
**Swift**, Hewson Hoyt 1920- AmMWSc 92, IntWW 91
**Swift**, Howard R 1920- AmMWSc 92
**Swift**, Ivan 1927- WhoAmP 91
**Swift**, J. J. 1954- WhoMW 92
**Swift**, Jack Bernard 1942- AmMWSc 92
**Swift**, Jane Maria 1965- WhoAmP 91
**Swift**, Jay James 1926- WhoBlA 92
**Swift**, Joan DrAPF 91
**Swift**, John Anthony 1940- Who 92
**Swift**, John Goulding 1955- WhoAmL 92
**Swift**, Jonathan 1667-1745 BlkwCEP, CnDBLB 2 [port], RfGEnL 91, ScFEYrs
**Swift**, Lela IntMPA 92
**Swift**, Leroy V. 1936- WhoBlA 92
**Swift**, Lewis 1820-1913 BiInAmS
**Swift**, Linda Denise 1965- WhoBlA 92
**Swift**, Lionel 1931- Who 92
**Swift**, Lloyd Harrison 1920- AmMWSc 92
**Swift**, Lloyd Wesley, Jr 1932- AmMWSc 92
**Swift**, Malcolm Robin 1948- Who 92
**Swift**, Mary Grace 1927- WrDr 92
**Swift**, Michael 1935- AmMWSc 92
**Swift**, Michael Charles 1921- Who 92
**Swift**, Michael Crane 1944- AmMWSc 92
**Swift**, Pattie Pratt 1959- WhoAmL 92
**Swift**, Reginald Stanley 1914- Who 92
**Swift**, Richard 1927- ConCom 92
**Swift**, Richard E, Jr 1951- WhoAmP 91
**Swift**, Richard Gene 1927- WhoEnt 92
**Swift**, Richard N 1924- ConAu 34NR
**Swift**, Richard Newton 1924- IntAu&W 91, WrDr 92
**Swift**, Robert 1799-1872 BiInAmS
**Swift**, Robert Walter 1956- WhoFI 92
**Swift**, Robinson Marden 1918- AmMWSc 92
**Swift**, Stephen Jensen 1943- WhoAmL 92
**Swift**, Terrence James 1937- AmMWSc 92
**Swift**, Tom 1944- WhoAmP 91
**Swift**, W. Porter 1914- WrDr 92
**Swift**, William Charles 1931- WhoIns 92
**Swift**, William Clement 1928- AmMWSc 92
**Swig**, Richard Lewis, Jr. 1951- WhoEnt 92
**Swigar**, Mary Eva 1940- AmMWSc 92
**Swigart**, James A. 1942- WhoWest 92
**Swigart**, Richard Hanawalt 1925- AmMWSc 92
**Swigart**, Rob DrAPF 91
**Swiger**, Elizabeth Davis 1926- AmMWSc 92
**Swiger**, Louis Andre 1932- AmMWSc 92
**Swiger**, William F 1916- AmMWSc 92
**Swiggett**, Ernest L. WhoBlA 92
**Swihart**, Fred Jacob 1919- WhoAmL 92, WhoFI 92, WhoMW 92
**Swihart**, G R 1920- AmMWSc 92
**Swihart**, H. Gregg 1938- WhoWest 92
**Swihart**, James Calvin 1927- AmMWSc 92
**Swihart**, John Marion 1923- WhoWest 92
**Swihart**, Thomas L. 1929- WrDr 92
**Swihart**, Thomas Lee 1929- AmMWSc 92, IntAu&W 91
**Swilky**, Jody DrAPF 91
**Swille**, Philip Wesley 1937- WhoWest 92
**Swilley**, Barbara Joyce 1950- WhoRel 92
**Swillinger**, Daniel James 1942- WhoAmP 91
**Swim**, Helen Wilson 1928- WhoWest 92
**Swim**, William B 1931- AmMWSc 92
**Swimmer**, Tom 1932- TwCPaSc
**Swinburn**, Richard 1937- Who 92
**Swinburne**, Algernon Charles 1837-1909 CnDBLB 4 [port], RfGEnL 91
**Swinburne**, Ivan Archie 1908- Who 92
**Swinburne**, John 1939- TwCPaSc
**Swinburne**, Nora 1902- Who 92
**Swinburne**, Ralph 1805?-1895 BiInAmS
**Swinburne**, Richard 1934- WrDr 92
**Swinburne**, Richard Granville 1934- IntAu&W 91, Who 92
**Swinburne**, Terence Reginald 1936- Who 92
**Swindale**, Leslie D 1928- AmMWSc 92
**Swindall**, Marshall Guy 1951- WhoRel 92
**Swindell**, Albin B 1945- WhoAmP 91
**Swindell**, John Thomas 1944- WhoFI 92
**Swindell**, Robert Thomas 1938- AmMWSc 92
**Swindell**, Warren C. 1934- WhoBlA 92
**Swindells**, Madge WrDr 92
**Swindells**, Michael 1930- Who 92
**Swindells**, Philip Roy 1945- IntAu&W 91
**Swindells**, Robert 1939- SmATA 14AS [port], WrDr 92
**Swindells**, William, Jr. 1930- WhoWest 92
**Swindeman**, Robert W 1933- AmMWSc 92
**Swinden**, Alan 1915- Who 92
**Swindle**, Albert Brintwood, Jr. 1949- WhoMW 92
**Swindle**, Stephen Daniel 1940- WhoAmL 92
**Swindle**, Timothy Dale 1955- AmMWSc 92
**Swindlehurst**, Owen Francis 1928- Who 92
**Swindler**, Daris Ray 1925- WhoWest 92
**Swindon**, Archdeacon of Who 92
**Swinebroad**, Jeff 1926- AmMWSc 92
**Swinehart**, Bruce Arden 1929- AmMWSc 92
**Swinehart**, Carl Francis 1907- AmMWSc 92
**Swinehart**, James Herbert 1936- AmMWSc 92
**Swinehart**, James Stephen 1929- AmMWSc 92
**Swinehart**, Leonard Robert WhoAmP 91
**Swinehart**, Philip Ross 1945- AmMWSc 92
**Swinehart**, Robert Dane 1937- WhoFI 92
**Swiner**, Connie, III 1959- WhoBlA 92, WhoMW 92
**Swinerton**, William Arthur 1917- WhoFI 92
**Swineshead**, Richard DcLB 115
**Swiney**, Willie Lee 1948- WhoRel 92
**Swinfen**, Baron 1938- Who 92
**Swinford**, David 1941- WhoAmP 91
**Swinford**, Jerry Wayne 1952- WhoMW 92
**Swinford**, Kenneth Roberts 1916- AmMWSc 92
**Swinford**, Maurice Lysle 1928- WhoRel 92
**Swing**, David 1830-1894 RelLAm 91
**Swing**, Peter Gram 1922- WhoEnt 92
**Swing**, Raymond Edwards 1887-1968 AmPeW
**Swing**, William Edwin 1936- WhoRel 92, WhoWest 92
**Swing**, William Lacy 1934- IntWW 91, WhoAmP 91
**Swinger**, Hershel Kendell 1939- WhoBlA 92
**Swingland**, Owen Merlin Webb 1919- Who 92
**Swingle Singers** NewAmDM
**Swingle**, Donald Morgan 1922- AmMWSc 92, WhoWest 92
**Swingle**, Homer Dale 1916- AmMWSc 92
**Swingle**, Karl F 1935- AmMWSc 92
**Swingle**, Karl Frederick 1915- AmMWSc 92
**Swingle**, Roy Spencer 1944- AmMWSc 92, WhoWest 92
**Swingle**, Ward 1927- NewAmDM
**Swingler**, Bryan Edwin 1924- Who 92
**Swingler**, Raymond John Peter 1933- Who 92
**Swingley**, Charles Stephen 1943- AmMWSc 92
**Swink**, David Wesley 1948- WhoRel 92
**Swink**, Laurence N 1934- AmMWSc 92
**Swink**, Mark Edgar WhoFI 92
**Swink**, Robert E. 1918- IntMPA 92
**Swinley**, Margaret Albinia Joanna 1935- Who 92
**Swinnerton-Dyer**, Peter 1927- Who 92
**Swinnerton-Dyer**, Peter Francis 1927- IntWW 91
**Swinney**, Chauncey Melvin 1918- AmMWSc 92
**Swinney**, Donald Henry 1919- WhoEnt 92
**Swinney**, Harry Leonard 1939- AmMWSc 92
**Swinney**, T. Lewis 1946- WhoBlA 92
**Swinson**, Christopher 1948- Who 92
**Swinson**, Derek Bertram 1938- AmMWSc 92, WhoWest 92
**Swinson**, John 1922- Who 92
**Swinton**, Countess of Who 92
**Swinton**, Earl of 1937- Who 92
**Swinton**, David Charles 1943- AmMWSc 92
**Swinton**, John 1830-1901 DcAmImH
**Swinton**, John 1925- Who 92
**Swinton**, Lee Vertis 1922- WhoBlA 92
**Swinton**, Patricia Ann 1954- WhoBlA 92
**Swinton**, Richard Bruce 1950- WhoWest 92
**Swinton**, Sylvia P. 1909- WhoBlA 92
**Swinton**, William 1833-1892 BenetAL 91
**Swinyard**, Ewart Ainslie 1909- AmMWSc 92
**Swiontek**, Steven J 1954- WhoAmP 91
**Swire**, Adrian 1932- Who 92
**Swire**, Edith Wypler 1943- WhoEnt 92
**Swire**, John 1927- Who 92
**Swire**, Lawrence Jay 1939- WhoAmL 92
**Swire**, Willard 1910-1991 NewYTBS 91
**Swirnoff**, Michael A. 1936- WhoAmL 92
**Swirsky**, Benjamin WhoFI 92
**Swischuk**, Leonard Edward 1937- AmMWSc 92
**Swisher**, Donald Everett 1921- WhoFI 92
**Swisher**, Ely Martin 1915- AmMWSc 92
**Swisher**, George Monroe 1943- AmMWSc 92
**Swisher**, Horton Edward 1909- AmMWSc 92
**Swisher**, Joseph Vincent 1932- AmMWSc 92
**Swisher**, Robert Donald 1910- AmMWSc 92
**Swisher**, Ronald Dale 1936- WhoFI 92
**Swisher**, Scott Neil 1918- AmMWSc 92
**Swislocki**, Norbert Ira 1936- AmMWSc 92
**Swiss**, Fern IntMPA 92
**Swiss**, Rodney 1904- Who 92
**Swiss**, Thomas DrAPF 91
**Swissler**, Thomas James 1941- AmMWSc 92
**Swist**, Wally DrAPF 91
**Swiszcz**, Paul Gerard 1958- WhoWest 92
**Swit**, Loretta 1937- IntMPA 92, WhoEnt 92
**Swit**, Michael Adlai 1956- WhoAmL 92
**Switala**, Edward Daniel 1947- WhoMW 92
**Switendick**, Alfred Carl 1931- AmMWSc 92
**Switkes**, Eugene 1943- AmMWSc 92
**Switzer**, Barbara 1940- Who 92
**Switzer**, Boyd Ray 1943- AmMWSc 92
**Switzer**, Clarence Barton, Sr 1936- WhoAmP 91
**Switzer**, Clayton Macfie 1929- AmMWSc 92
**Switzer**, George Lester 1924- AmMWSc 92
**Switzer**, Jay Alan 1950- AmMWSc 92
**Switzer**, Jon Rex 1937- WhoFI 92, WhoMW 92
**Switzer**, L Dean 1918- WhoAmP 91
**Switzer**, Laura Mae 1941- AmMWSc 92
**Switzer**, Lou 1948- WhoBlA 92
**Switzer**, Mary Ellen Phelan 1945- AmMWSc 92
**Switzer**, Mary Kay WhoEnt 92
**Switzer**, Paul 1939- AmMWSc 92
**Switzer**, Robert Earl 1929- WhoAmL 92
**Switzer**, Robert L 1918- AmMWSc 92
**Switzer**, Robert Lee 1940- AmMWSc 92, WhoMW 92
**Switzer**, Veryl A. 1932- WhoBlA 92
**Switzer**, William Paul 1927- AmMWSc 92
**Switzky**, Harvey Newton 1942- WhoMW 92
**Swizer**, John Warren 1945- WhoWest 92
**Swoap**, David Bruce 1937- WhoAmP 91
**Swobe**, Caryn Coe 1960- WhoWest 92
**Swoboda**, James John 1948- WhoMW 92
**Swoboda**, Larry Joseph 1939- WhoAmP 91
**Swoboda**, Peter 1937- IntWW 91
**Swofford**, Harold S, Jr 1936- AmMWSc 92
**Swofford**, Robert Lewis 1948- AmMWSc 92
**Swoger**, James Wesley 1918- WhoEnt 92
**Swogger**, Kurt William 1950- WhoFI 92, WhoMW 92
**Swol**, Stanley Mathew 1950- WhoEnt 92
**Swomley**, John Montgomery, Jr. 1915- AmPeW
**Swonigan**, Howard Ferdinand 1925- WhoMW 92
**Swoope**, Charles C 1934- AmMWSc 92
**Swope**, Fred C 1935- AmMWSc 92
**Swope**, George Wendell 1916- WhoRel 92
**Swope**, Herbert Bayard, Jr. IntMPA 92
**Swope**, John Franklin 1938- WhoFI 92, WhoIns 92
**Swope**, Mary DrAPF 91
**Swope**, Richard Dale 1938- AmMWSc 92
**Swope**, Richard McAllister 1940- WhoAmL 92
**Swope**, Steven Edward 1957- WhoMW 92, WhoRel 92
**Swope**, Warren L 1921- WhoAmP 91
**Sword**, Carl Harry 1947- WhoAmL 92
**Sword**, Christopher Patrick 1928- AmMWSc 92
**Sword**, James Howard 1924- AmMWSc 92
**Sword**, John Howe 1915- Who 92
**Sword**, Robert Randolph 1954- WhoWest 92
**Sword**, Wiley 1937- WrDr 92
**Sworder**, David D 1937- AmMWSc 92
**Swords**, Gary A 1947- WhoIns 92
**Swords**, Henry Logan, II 1948- WhoFI 92
**Swords**, Michael Dennis 1940- WhoMW 92
**Sworski**, Thomas John 1920- AmMWSc 92
**Swortzell**, Lowell Stanley 1930- WhoEnt 92
**Swovick**, Melvin Joseph 1926- AmMWSc 92, WhoMW 92
**Swoyer**, Ann Myrtle 1922- WhoEnt 92
**Swoyer**, Vincent Harry 1932- AmMWSc 92
**Swyer**, Gerald Isaac Macdonald 1917- Who 92
**Swyer**, Paul Robert 1921- AmMWSc 92
**Swygert**, Haywood Patrick 1943- WhoBlA 92
**Swynnerton**, Annie 1844-1933 TwCPaSc
**Swynnerton**, Roger 1911- Who 92
**Swysgood**, Charles 1939- WhoAmP 91
**Sy**, Jose 1944- AmMWSc 92, WhoWest 92
**Sy**, Man-Sun AmMWSc 92
**Syage**, Jack A 1954- AmMWSc 92
**Syal**, Jang B. 1948- WhoFI 92
**Syberberg**, Hans-Jurgen 1935- IntDcF 2-2, IntWW 91
**Sybers**, Harley D 1933- AmMWSc 92
**Sybert**, James Ray 1934- AmMWSc 92
**Sybert**, Paul Dean 1954- AmMWSc 92
**Sybert**, Richard P. 1952- WhoAmL 92
**Sybesma**, Kenneth L. 1961- WhoRel 92
**Syddall**, Joseph 1864-1942 TwCPaSc
**Sydeman**, William 1928- NewAmDM
**Sydenham**, Michael John 1923- WrDr 92
**Sydiskis**, Robert Joseph 1936- AmMWSc 92
**Sydney**, Archbishop of 1922- Who 92
**Sydney**, Archbishop of 1923- Who 92
**Sydney**, Assistant Bishops of Who 92
**Sydney**, Dean of Who 92
**Sydney**, Berenice 1944-1983 TwCPaSc
**Sydney North**, Bishop of Who 92
**Sydney South**, Bishop of Who 92
**Sydnor**, Douglas Bryan 1952- WhoFI 92
**Sydnor**, Robert Hadley 1947- WhoWest 92
**Sydnor**, Thomas Davis 1940- AmMWSc 92
**Sydor**, Michael 1936- AmMWSc 92
**Sydoriak**, Stephen George 1918- AmMWSc 92
**Sydow**, Erik von 1912- IntWW 91
**Sydow**, John Philip 1944- WhoMW 92
**Sydow**, Max von 1929- IntWW 91
**Sydow**, Michael David 1950- WhoAmL 92
**Sydow**, Ronald Larry 1944- WhoEnt 92
**Syed Putra Bin Syed Hassan Jamalullail** IntWW 91
**Syed**, Ashfaquzzaman 1952- AmMWSc 92
**Syed**, Ibrahim Bijli 1939- AmMWSc 92
**Syeduzzaman**, M. 1934- IntWW 91
**Syeklocha**, Delfa 1933- AmMWSc 92
**Syers**, William Edward 1926- WhoWest 92
**Syfert**, Samuel Ray 1928- WhoMW 92
**Sygitowicz**, Leo S. 1911- WhoWest 92
**Sygusch**, Jurgen 1945- AmMWSc 92
**Syke**, Cameron John 1957- WhoWest 92
**Sykee**, Gloria DrAPF 91
**Sykes**, Abel B., Jr. 1934- WhoBlA 92
**Sykes**, Alan Larry 1952- WhoAmP 91
**Sykes**, Alan O'Neil 1925- AmMWSc 92
**Sykes**, Arthur Patrick 1906- Who 92
**Sykes**, Bonar Hugh Charles 1922- Who 92
**Sykes**, Brian Douglas 1943- AmMWSc 92
**Sykes**, Caroline TwCPaSc
**Sykes**, Donald Armstrong 1930- Who 92
**Sykes**, Donald Joseph 1936- AmMWSc 92
**Sykes**, Donald Kunkel, Jr. 1956- WhoMW 92
**Sykes**, Edward 1935- WhoMW 92
**Sykes**, Edwin Leonard 1914- Who 92
**Sykes**, Eric 1923- IntMPA 92
**Sykes**, Francis John 1942- Who 92
**Sykes**, Gerald 1903-1984 ConAu 134
**Sykes**, James Aubrey, Jr 1941- AmMWSc 92
**Sykes**, James Enoch 1923- AmMWSc 92
**Sykes**, James Richard 1934- Who 92
**Sykes**, James Thurman 1935- WhoAmP 91
**Sykes**, John Who 92
**Sykes**, John Bradbury 1929- Who 92
**Sykes**, John Charles Anthony le Gallais 1928- Who 92
**Sykes**, John Gutteridge 1866-1941 TwCPaSc
**Sykes**, Joseph Walter 1915- Who 92
**Sykes**, Keble Watson 1921- Who 92
**Sykes**, Keith Who 92
**Sykes**, L Bonsall 1920- WhoAmP 91

**Sykes**, Lynn R. 1937- *IntWW 91*
**Sykes**, Lynn Ray 1937- *AmMWSc 92*
**Sykes**, Malcolm Keith 1925- *Who 92*
**Sykes**, Michael *DrAPF 91*
**Sykes**, Paul Jay, Jr 1918- *AmMWSc 92*
**Sykes**, Paul John 1957- *WhoMW 92*
**Sykes**, Peter 1923- *IntWW 91*
**Sykes**, Ray *WhoBlA 92*
**Sykes**, Richard *Who 92*
**Sykes**, Richard Brook 1942- *AmMWSc 92*
**Sykes**, Richard Eddy 1932- *WhoMW 92*
**Sykes**, Richard Macrae 1940- *WhoFI 92*
**Sykes**, Robert A. 1947- *WhoBlA 92*
**Sykes**, Robert Bruce 1948- *WhoAmP 91*
**Sykes**, Robert Martin 1943- *AmMWSc 92*
**Sykes**, Sandy 1944- *TwCPaSc*
**Sykes**, Stephen Whitefield *Who 92*
**Sykes**, Tatton 1943- *Who 92*
**Sykes**, Vernon L 1951- *WhoAmP 91*
**Sykes**, Vernon Lee 1951- *WhoBlA 92*
**Sykes**, Weathers Y. 1927-1990 *WhoBlA 92N*
**Sykes**, William d1991 *Who 92N*
**Sykes**, William Richard, Jr. 1948- *WhoBlA 92*
**Sykes**, William Roland 1948- *WhoFI 92*
**Sykora**, Barbara Zwach 1941- *WhoAmP 91*
**Sykora**, Harold James 1939- *WhoMW 92*
**Sykora**, Oskar P 1929- *AmMWSc 92*
**Sylak**, Charles John, Jr. 1950- *WhoFI 92*
**Sylbert**, Anthea 1939- *ConTFT 9, IntMPA 92*
**Sylbert**, Dick *ConTFT 9*
**Sylbert**, Paul 1928- *ConTFT 9*
**Sylbert**, Richard 1928- *ConTFT 9*
**Syler**, M. Rene 1963- *WhoBlA 92*
**Sylk**, Leonard Allen 1941- *WhoFI 92*
**Sylla**, Maodo *WhoRel 92*
**Sylla**, Richard Eugene 1940- *WhoFI 92*
**Sylte**, Judith Ann Osterberg 1943- *WhoWest 92*
**Sylvas**, Lionel B. 1940- *WhoBlA 92*
**Sylvern**, Glenn Leslie 1957- *WhoWest 92*
**Sylvester I** *EncEarC*
**Sylvester**, Arthur Gibbs 1938- *AmMWSc 92*
**Sylvester**, Barbara Thornton 1929- *WhoAmP 91*
**Sylvester**, Bill *DrAPF 91*
**Sylvester**, Christopher Urdahl 1929- *WhoAmP 91*
**Sylvester**, David 1924- *Who 92*
**Sylvester**, Donna 1945- *WhoEnt 92*
**Sylvester**, Edward Sanford 1920- *AmMWSc 92*
**Sylvester**, George Harold 1907- *Who 92*
**Sylvester**, Geraldine F 1931- *WhoAmP 91*
**Sylvester**, James Edward 1947- *AmMWSc 92*
**Sylvester**, James Joseph 1814-1897 *BilnAmS*
**Sylvester**, Janet *DrAPF 91*
**Sylvester**, Johnny 1915-1990 *AnObit 1990*
**Sylvester**, Joseph Robert 1942- *AmMWSc 92*
**Sylvester**, Joshua 1563-1618 *RfGEnL 91*
**Sylvester**, Lynette Marie 1946- *WhoAmP 91*
**Sylvester**, Melvin R. 1939- *WhoBlA 92*
**Sylvester**, Nicholas Dominic 1942- *AmMWSc 92*
**Sylvester**, Odell Howard, Jr. 1924- *WhoBlA 92*
**Sylvester**, Patrick Joseph *WhoBlA 92*
**Sylvester**, Philip *IntAu&W 91X, WrDr 92*
**Sylvester**, Richard Russell 1938- *WhoFI 92*
**Sylvester**, Robert O 1914- *AmMWSc 92*
**Sylvester**, Tangela Ann 1958- *WhoMW 92*
**Sylvester**, Terry Lee 1949- *WhoFI 92, WhoMW 92*
**Sylvester**, Torrey Aiden 1936- *WhoAmL 92*
**Sylvester**, William 1918- *ConAu 34NR*
**Sylvester-Evans**, Alun 1918- *Who 92*
**Sylvestre**, Guy 1918- *IntWW 91*
**Sylvia**, Avis Latham 1938- *AmMWSc 92*
**Sylvia**, Frank J 1928- *WhoAmP 91*
**Sylvia**, James *DrAPF 91*
**Sylvin**, Francis *WrDr 92*
**Symbas**, Panagiotis N 1925- *AmMWSc 92*
**Symchowicz**, Samson 1923- *AmMWSc 92*
**Symcox**, Geoffrey Walter 1938- *WhoWest 92*
**Syme**, Daniel Bailey 1946- *WhoRel 92*
**Syme**, James 1930- *Who 92*
**Syme**, Ronald 1910- *WrDr 92*
**Syme**, S Leonard 1932- *AmMWSc 92*
**Symens**, Paul N *WhoAmP 91*
**Symens**, Ronald Edwin 1951- *WhoMW 92*
**Symeon Stylites** 390?-459 *EncEarC*
**Symes**, Lawrence Richard 1942- *AmMWSc 92*
**Symes**, Mary 1912- *Who 92*
**Symington**, Fife *WhoAmP 91*
**Symington**, Fife 1945- *WhoWest 92*
**Symington**, Fife, III 1945- *AlmAP 92 [port]*
**Symington**, James W 1927- *WhoAmP 91*
**Symington**, Janey 1928- *AmMWSc 92*
**Symington**, Stuart 1901-1988 *FacFETw*
**Symington**, Thomas 1915- *Who 92*
**Symko**, Orest George 1939- *AmMWSc 92*
**Symmachus** *EncEarC*
**Symmachus**, Quintus Aurelius 340?-402? *EncEarC*
**Symmers**, William St Clair 1917- *Who 92*
**Symmes**, Americus *ScFEYrs B*
**Symmes**, Daniel Leslie 1949- *WhoEnt 92, WhoWest 92*
**Symmes**, David 1929- *AmMWSc 92*
**Symmes**, William Daniel 1938- *WhoAmL 92*
**Symmonds**, Algernon Washington 1926- *Who 92*
**Symmons-Symonolewicz**, Konstantin 1909- *WrDr 92*
**Symms**, Steve D. 1938- *WhoWest 92*
**Symms**, Steven D. 1938- *AlmAP 92 [port], WhoAmP 91*
**Symms**, Steven Douglas 1938- *IntWW 91*
**Symon**, Keith Randolph 1920- *AmMWSc 92*
**Symon**, Lindsay 1929- *Who 92*
**Symonds**, Ann Hazel S. *Who 92*
**Symonds**, Elsa Ornelas 1939- *WhoAmL 92*
**Symonds**, Genevieve Ellen 1931- *WhoAmP 91*
**Symonds**, Jane Ursula *Who 92*
**Symonds**, John *WrDr 92*
**Symonds**, John Addington 1840-1893 *NinCLC 34 [port]*
**Symonds**, John Richard 1918- *Who 92*
**Symonds**, Matthew John 1953- *Who 92*
**Symonds**, Pamela 1916- *WrDr 92*
**Symonds**, Paul S 1916- *AmMWSc 92*
**Symonds**, Richard *Who 92*
**Symonds**, Richard 1918- *WrDr 92*
**Symonds**, Robert B 1959- *AmMWSc 92*
**Symonds**, Ronald Charters 1916- *Who 92*
**Symonette**, Jerome Alphonza 1961- *WhoRel 92*
**Symons**, A P *WhoIns 92*
**Symons**, Arthur 1865-1945 *RfGEnL 91*
**Symons**, Christopher John Maurice 1949- *Who 92*
**Symons**, David Thorburn Arthur 1937- *AmMWSc 92*
**Symons**, Edward Allan 1943- *AmMWSc 92*
**Symons**, Edward Leonard, Jr. 1941- *WhoAmL 92*
**Symons**, Elizabeth Conway 1951- *Who 92*
**Symons**, Ernest Vize d1990 *Who 92N*
**Symons**, George E 1903- *AmMWSc 92*
**Symons**, Geraldine 1909- *WrDr 92*
**Symons**, Hugh William 1927- *AmMWSc 92*
**Symons**, J. Keith 1932- *WhoRel 92*
**Symons**, James M 1931- *AmMWSc 92*
**Symons**, Joyce 1927- *WhoAmP 91*
**Symons**, Julian 1912- *ConNov 91, ConPo 91, WrDr 92*
**Symons**, Julian Gustave 1912- *IntAu&W 91, IntWW 91, Who 92*
**Symons**, Leslie John 1926- *WrDr 92*
**Symons**, Mark 1886-1935 *TwCPaSc*
**Symons**, Martyn Christian Raymond 1925- *Who 92*
**Symons**, Patrick 1925- *TwCPaSc*
**Symons**, Patrick 1933- *Who 92*
**Symons**, Patrick Stewart 1925- *IntWW 91, Who 92*
**Symons**, Philip Charles 1939- *AmMWSc 92*
**Symons**, Robert Henry 1934- *Who 92*
**Symons**, Robert Spencer 1925- *WhoWest 92*
**Symons**, Scott 1933- *WrDr 92*
**Symons**, Timothy J 1951- *AmMWSc 92*
**Sympson**, Robert F 1927- *AmMWSc 92*
**Syms**, John Grenville St George 1913- *Who 92*
**Syms**, Sylvia 1934- *IntMPA 92*
**Symuleski**, Richard Aloysius 1947- *WhoMW 92*
**Synan**, Edward A 1918- *IntAu&W 91, WrDr 92*
**Synan**, Edward Aloysius, Jr. 1918- *WhoRel 92*
**Synan**, Harold Vinson 1934- *RelLAm 91, WhoRel 92*
**Synan**, Joseph Alexander 1905-1984 *RelLAm 91*
**Synan**, Vinson 1934- *WrDr 92*
**Synar**, Alan Edmond 1955- *WhoAmL 92*
**Synar**, Michael L. 1950- *AlmAP 92 [port], WhoAmP 91*
**Synder**, Margaret Judith 1940- *WhoWest 92*
**Synek**, Miroslav 1930- *AmMWSc 92*
**Synesius of Cyrene** 370?-414? *EncEarC*
**Synge**, Henry Millington 1921- *IntWW 91, Who 92*
**Synge**, J.M. 1871-1909 *RfGEnL 91*
**Synge**, John Lighton 1897- *IntWW 91, Who 92*
**Synge**, John Millington 1871-1909 *CnDBLB 5 [port], DramC 2 [port], FacFETw*
**Synge**, Richard Laurence Millington 1914- *IntWW 91, Who 92, WhoNob 90*
**Synge**, Robert Carson 1922- *Who 92*
**Synge**, Ursula 1930- *WrDr 92*
**Synnett**, Robert John 1958- *WhoFI 92*
**Synnot**, Anthony 1922- *Who 92*
**Synnott**, Hilary Nicholas Hugh 1945- *Who 92*
**Synnott**, Linda Kay 1949- *WhoAmL 92*
**Synnott**, Paul A, Jr 1939- *WhoIns 92*
**Synnott**, William Raymond 1929- *WhoFI 92*
**Synodi**, Helen Constance 1933- *WhoFI 92*
**Synolakis**, Costas Emmanuel 1956- *AmMWSc 92*
**Synoppe** *EncAmaz 91*
**Synovitz**, Robert J 1931- *AmMWSc 92*
**Synowiec**, John A 1937- *AmMWSc 92*
**Synsteby**, Aaron Oliver 1943- *WhoMW 92*
**Sypert**, George Walter 1941- *AmMWSc 92*
**Syphax**, Burke 1910- *WhoBlA 92*
**Syphax**, Margarite R. 1923- *WhoBlA 92*
**Syphax**, William Thomas 1920- *WhoBlA 92*
**Sypherd**, Paul Starr 1936- *AmMWSc 92*
**Syquia**, Enrique 1930- *IntWW 91*
**Syquia**, Luis Salvador *DrAPF 91*
**Syracusa**, Anthony 1933- *WhoAmP 91*
**Syrcle**, Reginald Nelson 1942- *WhoMW 92*
**Syrek**, Daniel Bruce 1925- *WhoWest 92*
**Syrett**, Barry 1934- *WhoWest 92*
**Syrett**, Barry Christopher 1943- *AmMWSc 92*
**Syrimis**, George 1921- *IntWW 91*
**Syring**, James John 1942- *WhoWest 92*
**Syrop**, Konrad 1914- *WrDr 92*
**Syrtsov**, Sergey Ivanovich 1893-1937 *SovUnBD*
**Syryjczyk**, Tadeusz 1948- *IntWW 91*
**Sysak**, Ronald Francis 1938- *WhoAmL 92*
**Syse**, Glenna Marie Lowes *WhoEnt 92*
**Syse**, Jan P. 1930- *IntWW 91*
**Syski**, Ryszard 1924- *AmMWSc 92*
**Sysonby**, Baron 1945- *Who 92*
**Sysoyev**, Vyacheslav Vyacheslavovich 1937- *IntWW 91*
**Systsov**, Apollon Sergeyevich 1929- *IntWW 91*
**Sytek**, Donna Page 1944- *WhoAmP 91*
**Sytek**, John J *WhoAmP 91*
**Sytenko**, Mikhail Dmitrievich 1918- *IntWW 91*
**Sythes**, Percy Arthur 1915- *Who 92*
**Sytsma**, Kenneth Jay 1954- *AmMWSc 92*
**Sytsma**, Louis Frederick 1946- *AmMWSc 92, WhoMW 92*
**Syty**, Augusta *AmMWSc 92*
**Syverson**, Aldrich 1914- *AmMWSc 92*
**Syvertsen**, Edwin Thor, Jr. 1923- *WhoMW 92*
**Syvertson**, Clarence A 1926- *AmMWSc 92*
**Syvertson**, Clarence Alfred 1926- *WhoWest 92*
**Syz**, Hans d1991 *NewYTBS 91*
**Szabad**, Gyorgy 1924- *IntWW 91*
**Szablya**, Helen Mary 1934- *IntAu&W 91, WhoWest 92*
**Szablya**, John F 1924- *AmMWSc 92*
**Szabo**, A J 1921- *AmMWSc 92*
**Szabo**, Alexander 1931- *AmMWSc 92*
**Szabo**, Arlene Slogoff 1945- *AmMWSc 92*
**Szabo**, Attila 1947- *AmMWSc 92*
**Szabo**, Barna Aladar 1935- *AmMWSc 92*
**Szabo**, Barney Julius 1929- *AmMWSc 92*
**Szabo**, Daniel 1933- *WhoAmP 91*
**Szabo**, Denis 1929- *IntWW 91*
**Szabo**, Emery D 1933- *AmMWSc 92*
**Szabo**, Gabor 1941- *AmMWSc 92*
**Szabo**, Gabor 1941-1982 *FacFETw*
**Szabo**, Istvan 1938- *IntAu&W 91, IntDcF 2-2 [port], IntMPA 92, IntWW 91*
**Szabo**, Kalman Tibor 1921- *AmMWSc 92*
**Szabo**, Lynn Christine 1951- *WhoEnt 92*
**Szabo**, Magda 1917- *IntAu&W 91, IntWW 91*
**Szabo**, Miklos Tamas 1937- *AmMWSc 92*
**Szabo**, Nicholas 1930- *WhoWest 92*
**Szabo**, Piroska Ludwig 1940- *AmMWSc 92*
**Szabo**, Richard Wayne 1956- *WhoEnt 92*
**Szabo**, Robert Joseph 1962- *WhoWest 92*
**Szabo**, Sandor 1944- *AmMWSc 92*
**Szabo**, Steve Stanley 1927- *AmMWSc 92*
**Szabo**, Tibor Imre 1934- *AmMWSc 92*
**Szabo**, Zoltan 1914- *IntWW 91*
**Szabo**, Zoltan 1943- *WhoWest 92*
**Szabolcsi**, Miklos 1921- *IntWW 91*
**Szabuniewicz**, Michael 1909- *AmMWSc 92*
**Szafranski**, Joseph Paul 1944- *WhoMW 92*
**Szajna**, Jozef 1922- *IntWW 91*
**Szakal**, Andras Kalman 1936- *AmMWSc 92*
**Szalacsi**, Joseph Salvatore 1946- *WhoEnt 92*
**Szalai**, Beatrice Benner 1942- *WhoFI 92*
**Szalajda**, Zbigniew 1934- *IntWW 91*
**Szalasi**, Ferenc 1897-1946 *BiDExR, EncTR 91*
**Szalay**, Jeanne 1938- *AmMWSc 92*
**Szalda**, David Joseph 1950- *AmMWSc 92*
**Szalecki**, Wojciech Josef 1935- *AmMWSc 92*
**Szalewicz**, Krzysztof 1950- *AmMWSc 92*
**Szalkowski**, Charles Conrad 1948- *WhoAmL 92*
**Szaller**, James Francis 1945- *WhoAmL 92*
**Szambelan**, Lawrence John 1938- *WhoFI 92*
**Szamosi**, Geza 1922- *AmMWSc 92*
**Szamosi**, Janos 1955- *AmMWSc 92*
**Szaniszlo**, Paul Joseph 1939- *AmMWSc 92*
**Szanto**, Joseph 1931- *AmMWSc 92*
**Szap**, Peter Charles 1929- *AmMWSc 92*
**Szapocznik**, Jose 1947- *WhoHisp 92*
**Szara**, Romuald Joseph 1925- *WhoMW 92*
**Szara**, Stephen Istvan 1923- *AmMWSc 92*
**Szarek**, Stanley Richard 1947- *AmMWSc 92*
**Szarek**, Walter Anthony 1938- *AmMWSc 92*
**Szarka**, Laszlo Joseph 1935- *AmMWSc 92*
**Szarwark**, Ernest John 1951- *WhoAmL 92*
**Szary**, Richard M. *WhoMW 92*
**Szasz**, Bela 1910- *LiExTwC*
**Szasz**, Thomas Stephen 1920- *AmMWSc 92, IntAu&W 91, IntWW 91, WrDr 92*
**Szaszy**, Miraka Petricevich 1921- *Who 92*
**Szczarba**, Robert Henry 1932- *AmMWSc 92*
**Szczech**, George Marion *AmMWSc 92*
**Szczepaniak**, Krystyna 1934- *AmMWSc 92*
**Szczepanski**, David Joel 1949- *WhoMW 92*
**Szczepanski**, Jan 1913- *IntWW 91*
**Szczepanski**, Marek Michal 1941- *AmMWSc 92*
**Szczepek**, John S 1942- *WhoIns 92*
**Szczerbicki**, Edward 1952- *WhoMW 92*
**Szczesniak**, Alina Surmacka 1925- *AmMWSc 92*
**Szczesniak**, Edward Joseph 1943- *WhoAmP 91*
**Szczesniak**, Raymond Albin 1940- *AmMWSc 92*
**Szczesny**, Ronald William 1940- *WhoAmL 92*
**Szczurek**, Thomas Eugene 1957- *WhoMW 92*
**Szczypiorski**, Andrzej 1924- *ConAu 133*
**Sze**, Andrew Wei Tseng 1926- *WhoFI 92*
**Sze**, Arthur *DrAPF 91*
**Sze**, Heven 1947- *AmMWSc 92*
**Sze**, Morgan Chuan-Yuan 1917- *AmMWSc 92*
**Sze**, Paul Yi Ling *AmMWSc 92*
**Sze**, Philip 1945- *AmMWSc 92*
**Sze**, Robert Chia-Ting 1941- *AmMWSc 92*
**Sze**, Tsung Wei 1922- *AmMWSc 92*
**Sze**, Yu-Keung 1944- *AmMWSc 92*
**Szebehely**, Victor 1921- *AmMWSc 92*
**Szebenyi**, Doletha M E 1947- *AmMWSc 92*
**Szebenyi**, Emil 1920- *AmMWSc 92*
**Szedon**, John R 1937- *AmMWSc 92*
**Szego**, Clara Marian 1916- *AmMWSc 92, WhoWest 92*
**Szego**, George C 1919- *AmMWSc 92*
**Szego**, Peter A 1925- *AmMWSc 92*
**Szekely**, Andrew Geza 1925- *AmMWSc 92*
**Szekely**, Gabor 1944- *IntWW 91*
**Szekely**, Ivan J 1919- *AmMWSc 92*
**Szekely**, Joseph George 1940- *AmMWSc 92*
**Szekely**, Julian 1934- *AmMWSc 92*
**Szekeres**, Cyndy 1933- *SmATA 13AS [port]*
**Szekeres**, Szabolcs 1942- *WhoFI 92*
**Szeless**, Adorjan Gyula 1927- *AmMWSc 92*
**Szell**, George 1897-1970 *FacFETw, NewAmDM*
**Szeman**, Sherri *DrAPF 91*
**Szemerenyi**, Oswald John Louis 1913- *Who 92*
**Szenes**, Hanna 1921-1944 *EncTR 91*
**Szent-Gyorgyi**, Albert 1893-1986 *FacFETw*
**Szent-Gyorgyi**, Albert von Nagyrapolt 1893-1986 *WhoNob 90*
**Szent-Gyorgyi**, Andrew Gabriel 1924- *AmMWSc 92*
**Szentagothai**, Janos 1912- *IntWW 91*
**Szentirmai**, George 1928- *AmMWSc 92*
**Szentivanyi**, Andor 1926- *AmMWSc 92*
**Szentkuthy**, Miklos 1908- *IntAu&W 91*
**Szentmihalyi Szabo**, Peter 1945- *IntAu&W 91*
**Szepe**, Stephen 1932- *AmMWSc 92*
**Szepesi**, Bela 1938- *AmMWSc 92*
**Szepesi**, Zoltan Paul John 1912- *AmMWSc 92*

# T

**T**, Mr. 1952- *WhoBlA 92*
**T**, Mr. 1953- *IntMPA 92*
**Ta Van Tai** 1938- *ConAu 133*
**Ta**, Tai Van 1938- *WhoAmL 92*
**Taaffe**, Claire Louise 1925- *WhoWest 92*
**Taaffe**, Edward James 1921- *WhoMW 92*
**Taaffe**, Philip 1955- *WorArt 1980 [port]*
**Taaffe**, Robert Griffin 1951- *WhoFI 92*
**Taagepera**, Mare 1938- *AmMWSc 92*
**Taam**, Brenda Joy 1965- *WhoWest 92*
**Taam**, Ronald Everett 1948- *AmMWSc 92, WhoMW 92*
**Taata** 1888-1964 *WhoNob 90*
**Tabachnick**, Irving I A 1924- *AmMWSc 92*
**Tabachnick**, Joseph 1919- *AmMWSc 92*
**Tabachnick**, Milton 1922- *AmMWSc 92*
**Tabachnick**, Walter J 1947- *AmMWSc 92*
**Tabachnick**, Walter Jay 1947- *WhoWest 92*
**Tabachnik**, Eldred 1943- *Who 92*
**Taback**, Gary A. 1937- *WhoAmL 92*
**Tabai**, Ieremia T. 1950- *IntWW 91*
**Tabak**, Daniel 1934- *AmMWSc 92*
**Tabak**, Israel d1991 *NewYTBS 91*
**Tabak**, Mark David 1937- *AmMWSc 92*
**Tabak**, Ronald Jerome 1949- *WhoAmL 92*
**Tabakin**, Burton Samuel 1921- *AmMWSc 92*
**Tabakin**, Frank 1935- *AmMWSc 92*
**Tabakoff**, Boris 1942- *AmMWSc 92*
**Tabakoff**, Widen 1919- *AmMWSc 92*
**Tabakov**, Emil 1947- *WhoEnt 92*
**Tabakov**, Oleg Pavlovich 1935- *IntWW 91*
**Tabard**, Peter *IntAu&W 91X*
**Tabarly**, Eric Marcel Guy 1931- *IntWW 91*
**Tabarrok**, B 1938- *AmMWSc 92*
**Tabata**, Susumu 1925- *AmMWSc 92*
**Tabata**, Yukio 1948- *WhoFI 92*
**Tabatabai**, Louisa Braal 1939- *AmMWSc 92*
**Tabatabai**, M Ali 1934- *AmMWSc 92*
**Tabatoni**, Pierre 1923- *IntWW 91*
**Tabb**, Charles Jordan 1955- *WhoMW 92*
**Tabb**, David Leo 1946- *AmMWSc 92*
**Tabb**, John Banister 1845-1909 *BenetAL 91, BibAL 8*
**Tabb**, William Howard 1951- *WhoWest 92*
**Tabb**, William Murray 1952- *WhoAmL 92*
**Tabbara**, Hani Bahjat 1939- *Who 92*
**Tabbert**, Robert L 1928- *AmMWSc 92*
**Tabbutt**, Frederick Dean 1931- *AmMWSc 92*
**Taben**, Stanley 1932- *WhoIns 92*
**Taber**, Charles Alec 1937- *AmMWSc 92*
**Taber**, Charles Russell 1928- *WhoRel 92*
**Taber**, David 1922- *AmMWSc 92*
**Taber**, Douglass Fleming 1948- *AmMWSc 92*
**Taber**, Elsie 1915- *AmMWSc 92*
**Taber**, Harry Warren 1935- *AmMWSc 92*
**Taber**, Joseph John 1920- *AmMWSc 92*
**Taber**, Richard Douglas 1920- *AmMWSc 92*
**Taber**, Richard Lawrence 1935- *AmMWSc 92*
**Taber**, Robert Irving 1936- *AmMWSc 92*
**Taber**, Stephen, III 1924- *AmMWSc 92*
**Taber**, Willard Allen 1925- *AmMWSc 92*
**Tabers**, Katherine Elizabeth 1950- *WhoMW 92*
**Tabesh**, Hamid *WhoFI 92*
**Tabet**, Jean-Claude Marie 1955- *WhoMW 92*
**Tabeyev**, Fikhryat Akhmedzhanovich 1928- *IntWW 91*
**Tabi**, Rifat 1938- *AmMWSc 92*
**Tabib-Azar**, Massood 1958- *WhoMW 92*
**Tabibian**, Richard 1929- *AmMWSc 92*
**Tabio**, Eduardo Luis 1959- *WhoHisp 92*
**Tabisz**, George Conrad 1939- *AmMWSc 92*
**Tabiszewski**, Edward Kazimierz 1927- *WhoFI 92*
**Tabita**, F Robert 1943- *AmMWSc 92*
**Tabler**, Bryan G. 1943- *WhoAmL 92*
**Tabler**, Norman Gardner, Jr. 1944- *WhoAmL 92*
**Tabler**, Ronald Dwight 1937- *AmMWSc 92, WhoWest 92*
**Tabner**, Len 1946- *TwCPaSc*
**Taboada**, John 1943- *AmMWSc 92*
**Tabone**, Anton 1937- *IntWW 91*
**Tabone**, Vincent 1913- *IntWW 91, Who 92*
**Tabor**, Celia White 1918- *AmMWSc 92*
**Tabor**, Christopher Alan 1937- *AmMWSc 92*
**Tabor**, David 1913- *IntWW 91, Who 92*
**Tabor**, David John St Maur 1922- *Who 92*
**Tabor**, Edward 1947- *AmMWSc 92*
**Tabor**, Hans 1922- *IntWW 91*
**Tabor**, Herbert 1918- *AmMWSc 92*
**Tabor**, James Daniel 1946- *WhoRel 92*
**Tabor**, John Kaye 1921- *WhoAmP 91*
**Tabor**, John Malcolm 1952- *AmMWSc 92*
**Tabor**, Lillie Montague 1933- *WhoBlA 92*
**Tabor**, Marvin Wilson 1944- *AmMWSc 92*
**Tabor**, Nancy Spindler 1958- *WhoAmL 92*
**Tabor**, Randall Arden 1956- *WhoMW 92*
**Tabor**, Rowland Whitney 1932- *AmMWSc 92*
**Tabor**, Samuel Lynn 1945- *AmMWSc 92*
**Tabor**, Sandra Eileen 1954- *WhoMW 92*
**Tabor**, Theodore Emmett 1940- *AmMWSc 92*
**Tabori**, George 1914- *WrDr 92*
**Tabori**, Paul 1908-1974 *LiExTwC*
**Taborn**, David 1947- *TwCPaSc*
**Taborn**, John Marvin 1935- *WhoBlA 92*
**Taborsak**, Lynn H 1943- *WhoAmP 91*
**Taborski**, Boleslaw 1927- *IntAu&W 91*
**Taborsky**, Edward J. 1910- *WrDr 92*
**Taborsky**, George 1928- *AmMWSc 92*
**Taborsky**, Gerald J, Jr 1948- *AmMWSc 92*
**Tabrisky**, Joseph 1931- *WhoWest 92*
**Taburimai**, Koae 1936- *WhoRel 92*
**Tabuteau**, Marcel 1887-1966 *NewAmDM*
**Taccarino**, John Robert 1941- *WhoMW 92*
**Tacchino**, Gabriel 1934- *WhoEnt 92*
**Tacha**, Athena 1936- *WhoMW 92*
**Tacha**, Deanell Reece *WhoAmP 91*
**Tacha**, Deanell Reece 1946- *WhoAmL 92, WhoMW 92, WhoWest 92*
**Tache**, Alexandre 1926- *WhoRel 92*
**Tache**, Alexandre Antonin 1823-1894 *RelLAm 91*
**Tacheny**, John Charles 1948- *WhoFI 92*
**Tacher**, Robert Frederick 1951- *WhoAmL 92*
**Tachi**, Ryuichiro 1921- *IntWW 91*
**Tachibana Hime** *EncAmaz 91*
**Tachibana**, Dora K 1934- *AmMWSc 92*
**Tachibana**, Hideo 1925- *AmMWSc 92*
**Tachibana**, Takehiko 1928- *AmMWSc 92*
**Tachmindji**, Alexander John 1928- *AmMWSc 92*
**Tachoir**, Jerry Robert 1955- *WhoEnt 92*
**Tachouet**, John James 1943- *WhoWest 92*
**Tachovsky**, Thomas Gregory 1947- *AmMWSc 92*
**Tacitus**, Cornelius 56?-113? *EncEarC*
**Tack**, Peter Isaac 1911- *AmMWSc 92*
**Tackaberry**, John Antony 1939- *Who 92*
**Tacker**, Martha McClelland 1943- *AmMWSc 92*
**Tacker**, Willis Arnold, Jr 1942- *AmMWSc 92*
**Tackett**, James Edwin, Jr 1937- *AmMWSc 92*
**Tackett**, Jesse Lee 1935- *AmMWSc 92*
**Tackett**, Stanford L 1930- *AmMWSc 92*
**Tackling**, Ellen 1946- *WhoFI 92*
**Tackman**, Arthur Lester 1916- *WhoWest 92*
**Tacon**, Ernest William 1917- *Who 92*
**Tacon**, Miguel 1775-1855 *HisDSpE*
**Taddei**, Giuseppe *WhoEnt 92*
**Taddei**, Giuseppe 1916- *NewAmDM*
**Taddei**, Mirian H. 1930- *WhoWest 92*
**Taddeo**, Angelo A 1927- *WhoIns 92*
**Taddesse**, Samuel 1944- *WhoFI 92*
**Taddie**, Daniel Lawrence 1949- *WhoEnt 92*
**Taddonio**, Lee C *WhoAmP 91*
**Tade**, William Howard 1923- *AmMWSc 92*
**Tadepalli**, Anjaneyulu S *AmMWSc 92*
**Tadesse**, Tesfaye 1943- *IntWW 91*
**Tadeusz**, Rozewicz 1921- *IntAu&W 91*
**Tadie**, Jean-Yves 1936- *Who 92*
**Tadjeran**, Hamid 1952- *AmMWSc 92*
**Taege**, Judith Diane 1943- *WhoWest 92*
**Taegtmeyer**, Heinrich 1941- *AmMWSc 92*
**Taeuber**, Irene B. 1906-1974 *WomSoc*
**Taeusch**, H William *AmMWSc 92*
**Tafel**, Edgar 1912- *WrDr 92*
**Tafel**, Richard H. *WhoRel 92*
**Tafelski**, Michael Dennis 1949- *WhoMW 92*
**Taff**, Clyde L. 1924- *WhoFI 92*
**Taff**, Warren Russell 1947- *WhoWest 92*
**Taffanel**, Paul 1844-1908 *NewAmDM*
**Taffany**, David James 1957- *WhoAmL 92*
**Taffe**, Betty Jo 1942- *WhoAmP 91*
**Taffe**, William John 1943- *AmMWSc 92*
**Taffer**, Jack J 1937- *WhoAmP 91*
**Taffner**, Donald L *IntMPA 92, LesBEnT 92*
**Taflove**, Allen 1949- *AmMWSc 92*
**Tafolla**, Carmen *DrAPF 91*
**Tafolla**, Carmen 1951- *WhoHisp 92*
**Tafoya**, Arthur N. 1933- *WhoRel 92*
**Tafoya**, Charles P. *WhoHisp 92*
**Tafoya**, Marcelo H. 1939- *WhoHisp 92*
**Tafoya**, Renee Claire 1954- *WhoEnt 92*
**Taft**, Adon Calvin 1925- *WhoRel 92*
**Taft**, Bruce A 1930- *AmMWSc 92*
**Taft**, Charles John 1938- *WhoRel 92*
**Taft**, Charles Kirkland 1928- *AmMWSc 92*
**Taft**, Chester M *WhoAmP 91*
**Taft**, David Dakin 1938- *AmMWSc 92*
**Taft**, Earl J 1931- *AmMWSc 92*
**Taft**, Edgar Breck 1916- *AmMWSc 92*
**Taft**, Henry Waters, II d1991 *NewYTBS 91*
**Taft**, Jay Leslie 1944- *AmMWSc 92*
**Taft**, Jessie 1882-1961 *WomSoc*
**Taft**, John 1950- *ConAu 133*
**Taft**, John Ailes, Jr. 1927- *WhoFI 92, WhoMW 92*
**Taft**, John Thomas 1950- *WhoEnt 92*
**Taft**, Kathie 1945- *WhoMW 92*
**Taft**, Kingsley Arter, Jr 1930- *AmMWSc 92*
**Taft**, Martin C 1942- *WhoIns 92*
**Taft**, Nathaniel Belmont 1919- *WhoAmL 92*
**Taft**, Peter R. 1936- *WhoWest 92*
**Taft**, Robert 1917- *WhoAmP 91*
**Taft**, Robert, Jr. 1917- *IntWW 91, WhoMW 92*
**Taft**, Robert A. 1889-1953 *BenetAL 91*
**Taft**, Robert A, II 1942- *WhoAmP 91*
**Taft**, Robert Alphonso 1889-1953 *AmPolLe, FacFETw*
**Taft**, Robert Wheaton, Jr 1922- *AmMWSc 92*
**Taft**, Seth Chase 1922- *WhoAmL 92, WhoAmP 91, WhoMW 92*
**Taft**, Sheldon Ashley 1937- *WhoAmL 92*
**Taft**, Thomas F *WhoAmP 91*
**Taft**, William Howard 1857-1930 *AmPeW, AmPolLe [port], BenetAL 91, FacFETw [port], RComAH*
**Taft**, William Howard 1945- *Who 92*
**Taft**, William Howard, III d1991 *NewYTBS 91*
**Taft**, William Howard, IV 1945- *IntWW 91, WhoAmP 91*
**Tafti**, Hassan Barnaba D. *Who 92*
**Tafuri**, John Francis 1924- *AmMWSc 92*
**Tafuri**, Nancy 1946- *SmATA 14AS [port]*
**Tafuri**, Spencer Andrew 1952- *WhoFI 92*
**Tag**, Paul Mark 1945- *AmMWSc 92*
**Tagala**, Isabel Martinez 1930- *WhoFI 92*
**Tagaloa**, Reupena S T *WhoAmP 91*
**Tagawa**, Seiichi 1919- *IntWW 91*
**Tager**, Ira Bruce *AmMWSc 92*
**Tager**, Marcia *DrAPF 91*
**Tager**, Pavel Grigor'evich 1903- *SovUnBD*
**Tagett**, Richard *DrAPF 91*
**Tagg**, Alan 1928- *Who 92*
**Tagg**, Robert 1942- *TwCPaSc*
**Taggard**, Genevieve 1894-1948 *BenetAL 91*
**Taggart**, Cal S 1924- *WhoAmP 91*
**Taggart**, David 1937- *TwCPaSc*
**Taggart**, Dennis DeVere 1938- *WhoWest 92*
**Taggart**, Elizabeth Ottley 1939- *WhoWest 92*
**Taggart**, G Bruce 1942- *AmMWSc 92*
**Taggart**, John *DrAPF 91*
**Taggart**, John Victor 1916- *AmMWSc 92*
**Taggart**, John Y., Mrs. 1932- *WhoAmL 92*
**Taggart**, John Yeatman 1932- *WhoAmL 92*
**Taggart**, Keith Anthony 1944- *AmMWSc 92*
**Taggart**, R Thomas 1951- *AmMWSc 92*
**Taggart**, Raymond 1922- *AmMWSc 92*
**Taggart**, Robert Alexander, Jr. 1946- *WhoFI 92*
**Taggart**, Robert Raymond, Jr. 1948- *WhoFI 92*
**Taggart**, Sondra 1934- *WhoFI 92, WhoWest 92*
**Taggart**, Thomas Michael 1937- *WhoAmL 92*

**Taggart,** Timothy Alan 1955- *WhoMW 92*
**Tagle,** Hilda Gloria 1946- *WhoAmL 92, WhoHisp 92*
**Tagliabue,** Carlo 1898-1978 *NewAmDM*
**Tagliabue,** Giuseppe 1812-1878 *BiInAmS*
**Tagliabue,** John *DrAPF 91*
**Tagliabue,** John 1923- *IntAu&W 91, WrDr 92*
**Tagliabue,** Paul John 1940- *WhoAmL 92*
**Tagliacozzo,** Rhoda S. *DrAPF 91*
**Tagliaferri,** Lee Gene 1931- *WhoFI 92*
**Tagliaferro,** John Anthony 1944- *WhoEnt 92, WhoFI 92*
**Tagliarino,** Scott Alan 1953- *WhoFI 92*
**Tagliavini,** Ferruccio 1913- *NewAmDM*
**Tago,** Ativalu A, Jr *WhoAmP 91*
**Tagore,** Rabindranath 1861-1941 *FacFETw, RfGEnL 91, WhoNob 90*
**Tague,** Barry Elwert 1938- *WhoFI 92*
**Taha,** Hamdy Abdelaziz 1937- *AmMWSc 92*
**Taha,** Mohammed Fathi 1914- *IntWW 91*
**Tahan,** Theodore Wahba 1936- *AmMWSc 92*
**Taher,** Abdul Hadi 1930- *IntWW 91*
**Tahiliani,** Vasu H 1942- *AmMWSc 92*
**Tahir,** Achmad 1924- *IntWW 91*
**Tahir,** Mary Elizabeth 1933- *WhoFI 92*
**Tahir-Kheli,** Raza Ali 1936- *AmMWSc 92*
**Tahkamaa,** Taisto Toivo Johannes 1924- *IntWW 91*
**Tahl,** Mikhail Nekhem'evich 1936- *SovUnBD*
**Tahourdin,** John Gabriel 1913- *Who 92*
**Tahy,** Michael John 1933- *WhoMW 92*
**Tai,** Chen-To 1915- *AmMWSc 92*
**Tai,** Douglas L 1940- *AmMWSc 92*
**Tai,** Gleni *WhoEnt 92*
**Tai,** Han 1924- *AmMWSc 92*
**Tai,** Julia Chow 1935- *AmMWSc 92*
**Tai,** Peter Yao-Po 1937- *AmMWSc 92*
**Tai,** Tsze Cheng 1933- *AmMWSc 92*
**Tai,** William 1934- *AmMWSc 92, WhoMW 92*
**Taibbi,** Robert *WhoEnt 92*
**Taibleson,** Mitchell H 1929- *AmMWSc 92*
**Taibleson,** Mitchell Herbert 1929- *WhoMW 92*
**Taibo,** Paco Ignacio 1949- *IntAu&W 91*
**Taichman,** Norton Stanley 1936- *AmMWSc 92*
**Taiganides,** E Paul 1934- *AmMWSc 92, WhoMW 92*
**Taigen,** Theodore Lee 1952- *AmMWSc 92*
**Tailfer,** Patrick *BenetAL 91*
**Taillard,** Willy Francis 1924- *IntWW 91*
**Tailleferre,** Germaine 1892-1983 *NewAmDM*
**Taillibert,** Roger Rene 1926- *IntWW 91*
**Taillon,** James Howard 1946- *WhoMW 92*
**Taillon,** Roger de Boucherville 1946- *WhoFI 92*
**Taimuty,** Samuel Isaac 1917- *AmMWSc 92, WhoWest 92*
**Tain,** Michael 1927- *TwCPaSc*
**Taine,** Hippolyte 1828-1893 *GuFrLit 1*
**Taine,** John 1883-1960 *ScFEYrs, TwCSFW 91*
**Tainer,** Evelina Margherita 1958- *WhoFI 92, WhoMW 92*
**Tainter,** James Patrick 1961- *WhoMW 92*
**Taipale,** Vappu Tuulikki 1940- *IntWW 91*
**Taira,** Frances Snow 1935- *WhoMW 92*
**Taira,** Masa Morioka 1923- *WhoWest 92*
**Tairov,** Aleksandr Yakovlevich 1885-1950 *SovUnBD*
**Tairov,** Alexander Yakovlevich 1885-1950 *FacFETw*
**Taishoff,** Sol J. d1982 *LesBEnT 92*
**Tait,** Alan Anderson 1934- *Who 92*
**Tait,** Alice Ann 1948- *WhoMW 92*
**Tait,** Allan Gordon 1921- *Who 92*
**Tait,** Andrew Wilson 1922- *Who 92*
**Tait,** Eric 1945- *Who 92*
**Tait,** George Edward 1910- *WrDr 92*
**Tait,** James 1912- *Who 92*
**Tait,** James Francis 1925- *IntWW 91, Who 92*
**Tait,** James Simpson 1930- *AmMWSc 92*
**Tait,** John Charles 1945- *AmMWSc 92*
**Tait,** John Reid 1946- *WhoAmL 92, WhoAmP 91*
**Tait,** Joseph Edward 1957- *WhoWest 92*
**Tait,** Kevin S 1933- *AmMWSc 92*
**Tait,** Michael Logan 1936- *Who 92*
**Tait,** Peter 1915- *Who 92*
**Tait,** Robert James 1937- *AmMWSc 92*
**Tait,** Sylvia Agnes Sophia *Who 92*
**Tait,** William Charles 1932- *AmMWSc 92*
**Taitt,** Branford Mayhew 1938- *IntWW 91*
**Taittinger,** Jean 1923- *IntWW 91*
**Taittinger,** Pierre Charles 1887-1965 *BiDExR*
**Taiz,** Lincoln 1942- *AmMWSc 92*
**Taj Mahal** 1942- *ConMus 6 [port]*
**Tajima,** Toshiki 1948- *AmMWSc 92*
**Tajiri,** Harvey S 1944- *WhoAmP 91*
**Tajo,** Italo 1915- *NewAmDM, WhoEnt 92*
**Tajon,** Encarnacion Fontecha 1920- *WhoWest 92*
**TAK** *Who 92*
**Takacs,** Dalma Sarolta 1933- *WhoEnt 92*
**Takacs,** Gerald Alan 1943- *AmMWSc 92*
**Takacs,** James Eric 1935- *WhoWest 92*
**Takacs-Nagy,** Gabor 1956- *IntWW 91*
**Takada,** Naofumi 1956- *WhoFI 92*
**Takagaki,** Tasuku 1928- *IntWW 91*
**Takagi,** Shozo 1943- *AmMWSc 92*
**Takahama,** Kazuhide 1930- *DcTwDes*
**Takahara,** Sumiko *IntWW 91*
**Takahashi** 1924- *IntWW 91*
**Takahashi,** Akio 1932- *AmMWSc 92*
**Takahashi,** Brian Toshio 1954- *WhoWest 92*
**Takahashi,** Ellen Shizuko *AmMWSc 92*
**Takahashi,** Hironori 1942- *AmMWSc 92*
**Takahashi,** Joseph S 1951- *AmMWSc 92*
**Takahashi,** Kozo 1948- *AmMWSc 92*
**Takahashi,** Lorey K 1953- *AmMWSc 92*
**Takahashi,** Mark T 1936- *AmMWSc 92*
**Takahashi,** Patrick Kenji 1940- *AmMWSc 92*
**Takahashi,** Taro 1930- *AmMWSc 92*
**Takahashi,** Wataru 1925- *WhoWest 92*
**Takahashi,** Yasundo 1912- *AmMWSc 92*
**Takahashi,** Yasushi 1924- *AmMWSc 92*
**Takai,** Ronald T. 1939- *WrDr 92*
**Takai,** Yasuyuki 1951- *AmMWSc 92*
**Takaki,** Melvin Hiroyuki *WhoAmP 91*
**Takamine,** Dwight Y 1953- *WhoAmP 91*
**Takano,** Akiyoshi *WhoWest 92*
**Takano,** Masaharu 1935- *AmMWSc 92*
**Takaro,** Timothy 1920- *AmMWSc 92*
**Takashima,** Hideo 1919- *WhoAmL 92*
**Takashima,** Shiro 1923- *AmMWSc 92*
**Takasugi,** Mitsuo 1928- *AmMWSc 92*
**Takasugi,** Nao *WhoAmP 91*
**Takasugi,** Nao 1922- *WhoWest 92*
**Takasugi,** Robert Mitsuhiro 1930- *WhoAmL 92, WhoWest 92*
**Takata,** Nobu 1938- *WhoWest 92*
**Takata,** Roy Ryoichi 1929- *WhoFI 92*
**Takata,** Sayoko 1937- *WhoWest 92*
**Takatori,** Osamu 1929- *IntWW 91*
**Takats,** Stephen Tibor 1930- *AmMWSc 92*
**Takayama,** Akira *WhoFI 92, WhoMW 92*
**Takayama,** Kuni 1932- *AmMWSc 92*
**Take 6** *ConMus 6 [port]*
**Takebayashi,** Yasuo 1947- *WhoFI 92*
**Takeda,** Timothy Scott 1956- *WhoWest 92*
**Takeda,** Yasuhiko 1927- *AmMWSc 92*
**Takeda,** Yutaka 1914- *IntWW 91*
**Takefuji,** Yoshiyasu 1955- *WhoMW 92*
**Takei,** George 1937- *IntMPA 92*
**Takei,** George Hosato 1937- *WhoEnt 92*
**Takei,** Kei *WhoEnt 92*
**Takei,** Toshihisa 1931- *WhoWest 92*
**Takeiri,** Yoshikatsu 1926- *IntWW 91*
**Takemi,** Taro 1904- *IntWW 91*
**Takemitsu,** Toru 1920- *ConMus 6*
**Takemitsu,** Toru 1930- *ConCom 92, NewAmDM*
**Takemori,** Akira Eddie 1929- *AmMWSc 92*
**Takemoto,** Dolores Jean 1949- *AmMWSc 92*
**Takemoto,** Jon Yutaka 1944- *AmMWSc 92*
**Takemura,** Kaz H 1921- *AmMWSc 92*
**Takemura,** Michael Francis 1961- *WhoMW 92*
**Takenaka,** Masao 1925- *DcEcMov*
**Takesaki,** Masamichi 1933- *AmMWSc 92*
**Takeshita,** Noboru 1924- *FacFETw, IntWW 91*
**Takeshita,** Tsuneichi 1926- *AmMWSc 92*
**Taketa,** Fumito 1926- *AmMWSc 92*
**Taketomo,** Yasuhiko *AmMWSc 92*
**Takeuchi,** Esther Sans 1953- *AmMWSc 92*
**Takeuchi,** Kenji 1934- *AmMWSc 92*
**Takeuchi,** Kiyoshi Hiro 1948- *AmMWSc 92*
**Takeuchi,** Shokoh Akira 1920- *WhoRel 92*
**Takeuchi,** Sylvia Fujie 1939- *WhoWest 92*
**Takeuchi,** Timothy Stephen 1963- *WhoWest 92*
**Takeuti,** Gaisi 1926- *AmMWSc 92*
**Takeyama,** Eiichi 1935- *WhoFI 92*
**Takeyama,** Roy Yoshi 1928- *WhoAmL 92*
**Taki** 1937- *IntAu&W 91*
**Takiff,** Jonathan Henry B. 1946- *WhoEnt 92*
**Takitani,** Henry T 1924- *WhoAmP 91*
**Takiyasha Hime** *EncAmaz 91*
**Takla,** Philippe 1915- *IntWW 91*
**Takle,** Roberta Piper 1940- *WhoAmP 91*
**Takman,** Bertil Herbert 1921- *AmMWSc 92*
**Takriti,** Saddam Hussein *IntWW 91*
**Taksa,** Patti Sullivan 1950- *WhoAmL 92*
**Taktakishvili,** Otar Vasil'evich 1924- *SovUnBD*
**Takvorian,** Kenneth Bedrose 1943- *AmMWSc 92*
**Tal,** Josef 1910- *NewAmDM*
**Tal,** Mikhail Nakhemyevich 1936- *FacFETw*
**Talaat,** Ahmed Samih 1920- *IntWW 91*
**Talaat,** Mehmed 1874-1921 *FacFETw*
**Talaat,** Mostafa E 1924- *AmMWSc 92*
**Talaber,** David Joseph 1951- *WhoWest 92*
**Talafous,** Joseph John 1929- *WhoAmL 92*
**Talal Ibn Abdul Aziz,** Prince 1934- *IntWW 91*
**Talal,** Marilynn *DrAPF 91*
**Talalay,** Paul 1923- *AmMWSc 92*
**Talamantes,** Florence 1931- *WhoHisp 92*
**Talamantes,** Florence Williams 1931- *IntAu&W 91*
**Talamantes,** Frank 1943- *AmMWSc 92, WhoHisp 92*
**Talamantez,** Connie Juarez 1947- *WhoHisp 92*
**Talamo,** Barbara Lisann 1939- *AmMWSc 92*
**Talan,** David B 1948- *WhoAmP 91*
**Talapatra,** Dipak Chandra 1942- *AmMWSc 92*
**Talarico,** Maria Theresa 1960- *WhoMW 92*
**Talarico,** Ross *DrAPF 91*
**Talarzyk,** W. Wayne 1940- *WrDr 92*
**Talaski,** Paul 1953- *WhoEnt 92*
**Talaty,** Erach R *AmMWSc 92*
**Talavera,** Sandra 1956- *WhoHisp 92*
**Talbert,** Charles H. 1934- *WhoRel 92*
**Talbert,** George Brayton 1921- *AmMWSc 92*
**Talbert,** Hamilton Bowen, Jr 1929- *WhoAmP 91*
**Talbert,** Hugh Mathis 1937- *WhoAmL 92*
**Talbert,** James Lewis 1931- *AmMWSc 92*
**Talbert,** Keith Edward 1961- *WhoMW 92*
**Talbert,** Luther M 1926- *AmMWSc 92*
**Talbert,** Marc 1953- *SmATA 68*
**Talbert,** Mary Burnett 1866-1923 *HanAmWH*
**Talbert,** Mary Morris 1866-1923 *NotBlAW 92 [port]*
**Talbert,** Melvin George 1934- *WhoBlA 92, WhoRel 92, WhoWest 92*
**Talbert,** Norwood K 1921- *AmMWSc 92*
**Talbert,** Preston Tidball 1925- *AmMWSc 92*
**Talbert,** Ronald Edward 1936- *AmMWSc 92*
**Talbert,** Willard Lindley, Jr 1932- *AmMWSc 92*
**Talbot,** Alfred Kenneth, Jr. 1916- *WhoBlA 92*
**Talbot,** Arthur Allison FitzRoy 1909- *Who 92*
**Talbot,** Bernard 1937- *AmMWSc 92*
**Talbot,** David Arlington Roberts, Sr. 1916- *WhoBlA 92*
**Talbot,** Dennis Edmund Blaquiere 1908- *Who 92*
**Talbot,** Donald R 1931- *AmMWSc 92*
**Talbot,** Ethelbert 1848-1928 *RelLAm 91*
**Talbot,** Eugene L 1921- *AmMWSc 92*
**Talbot,** FitzRoy *Who 92*
**Talbot,** Frank Hamilton 1930- *IntWW 91*
**Talbot,** Frederick Hilborn 1927- *WhoRel 92*
**Talbot,** Gerald E 1931- *WhoAmP 91*
**Talbot,** Gerald Edgerton 1931- *WhoBlA 92*
**Talbot,** Godfrey Walker 1908- *IntAu&W 91, IntWW 91, Who 92, WrDr 92*
**Talbot,** Hilary Gwynne 1912- *Who 92*
**Talbot,** Howard 1865-1928 *NewAmDM*
**Talbot,** James Lawrence 1932- *AmMWSc 92*
**Talbot,** James Patterson, Sr. 1950- *WhoBlA 92*
**Talbot,** John Mayo 1913- *AmMWSc 92*
**Talbot,** John Michael 1954- *ConMus 6 [port]*
**Talbot,** Lawrence 1925- *AmMWSc 92, WhoWest 92*
**Talbot,** Lee Merriam 1930- *AmMWSc 92*
**Talbot,** Louis Thompson 1889-1976 *RelLAm 91*
**Talbot,** Lyle 1904- *IntMPA 92*
**Talbot,** Marion 1858-1947 *WomSoc*
**Talbot,** Marion 1858-1948 *HanAmWH*
**Talbot,** Mary *TwCPaSc*
**Talbot,** Mary 1922- *Who 92*
**Talbot,** Mary Anne *EncAmaz 91*
**Talbot,** Mary Lee 1953- *WhoRel 92*
**Talbot,** Maurice John 1912- *Who 92*
**Talbot,** Michael 1953- *WrDr 92*
**Talbot,** Michael Owen 1943- *Who 92*
**Talbot,** Nathan Bill 1909- *AmMWSc 92*
**Talbot,** Norman Clare 1936- *IntAu&W 91, WrDr 92*
**Talbot,** Pamela 1946- *WhoFI 92*
**Talbot,** Patrick James 1948- *WhoWest 92*
**Talbot,** Patrick John 1946- *Who 92*
**Talbot,** Paul *LesBEnT 92*
**Talbot,** Peter Henry 1948- *WhoEnt 92*
**Talbot,** Pierre J 1956- *AmMWSc 92*
**Talbot,** Prudence 1944- *AmMWSc 92*
**Talbot,** Raymond James, Jr 1941- *AmMWSc 92*
**Talbot,** Richard 1956- *TwCPaSc*
**Talbot,** Richard Burritt 1933- *AmMWSc 92*
**Talbot,** Richard Michael Arthur Chetwynd 1911- *Who 92*
**Talbot,** T F 1930- *AmMWSc 92*
**Talbot,** Theodore A. 1923- *WhoBlA 92*
**Talbot,** Thomas George 1904- *Who 92*
**Talbot,** Timothy Ralph, Jr 1916- *AmMWSc 92*
**Talbot,** Winthrop d1937 *DcAmImH*
**Talbot-Koehl,** Linda Ann 1956- *WhoEnt 92*
**Talbot of Malahide,** Baron 1931- *Who 92*
**Talbott,** Ben Johnson, Jr. 1940- *WhoAmL 92*
**Talbott,** Edwin M 1923- *AmMWSc 92*
**Talbott,** Everett Guy 1883-1945 *AmPeW*
**Talbott,** George Robert 1925- *WhoWest 92*
**Talbott,** Richard David 1930- *WhoWest 92*
**Talbott,** Richard Lloyd 1935- *AmMWSc 92*
**Talbott,** Robert Dean 1928- *WhoMW 92*
**Talbott,** Strobe 1946- *WrDr 92*
**Talbott,** Ted Delwyn 1929- *AmMWSc 92*
**Talbott,** William B 1949- *WhoAmP 91*
**Talboys,** Brian Edward 1921- *IntWW 91, Who 92*
**Talburt,** Medford Lane 1939- *WhoMW 92*
**Talcott,** John Curtis 1954- *WhoWest 92*
**Talcott,** Patricia Lou 1961- *WhoAmL 92*
**Talcott,** William *DrAPF 91*
**Taleb,** Yusef Sabri Abu 1929- *IntWW 91*
**Talent,** David Leroy 1952- *AmMWSc 92*
**Talent,** James M 1956- *WhoAmP 91*
**Talent,** Larry Gene 1946- *AmMWSc 92*
**Talese,** Gay *SourALJ*
**Talese,** Gay 1932- *WrDr 92*
**Talesnick,** Alan Lee 1945- *WhoAmL 92*
**Talesnick,** Stanley 1927- *WhoAmL 92*
**Talesnik,** Jaime 1916- *AmMWSc 92*
**Taleyarkhan,** Homi J. H. 1917- *IntWW 91*
**Talham,** Robert J 1929- *AmMWSc 92*
**Talhelm,** Daniel Roderick 1941- *WhoFI 92*
**Talhouk,** Rabih Shakib 1959- *AmMWSc 92*
**Talhouni,** Bahjat 1913- *IntWW 91*
**Taliaferro,** Addison 1936- *WhoBlA 92*
**Taliaferro,** Cecil R. 1942- *WhoBlA 92*
**Taliaferro,** Charles M 1940- *AmMWSc 92*
**Taliaferro,** Gary Day 1940- *WhoRel 92*
**Taliaferro,** George 1927- *WhoBlA 92*
**Taliaferro,** Harden E. 1818-1875 *BenetAL 91*
**Taliaferro,** Henry Beauford, Jr. 1932- *WhoAmL 92*
**Taliaferro,** Nettie Howard 1944- *WhoBlA 92*
**Taliaferro,** Paul Anthony 1934- *WhoAmP 91*
**Taliaferro,** Steven Douglas 1949- *AmMWSc 92*
**Talib,** Naji 1917- *IntWW 91*
**Talich,** Vaclav 1883-1961 *NewAmDM*
**Talintyre,** Douglas George 1932- *Who 92*
**Talisman,** Mark Elliott 1941- *WhoAmP 91*
**Talking Heads** *NewAmDM*
**Talkington,** Robert Van 1929- *WhoAmL 92, WhoAmP 91*
**Talks,** John Poole 1954- *WhoMW 92*
**Tall Brothers** *EncEarC*
**Tall,** Booker T. 1928- *WhoBlA 92*
**Tall,** Deborah *DrAPF 91*
**Tall,** Franklin David 1944- *AmMWSc 92*
**Tall,** Stephen 1908-1981 *TwCSFW 91*
**Tallackson,** Harvey D. 1925- *WhoMW 92*
**Tallackson,** Harvey Dean 1925- *WhoAmP 91*
**Tallaksen,** Turner E. 1928- *WhoRel 92*
**Tallal,** Paula 1947- *AmMWSc 92*
**Tallan,** Harris H 1924- *AmMWSc 92*
**Tallan,** Irwin 1927- *AmMWSc 92*
**Tallan,** Norman M 1932- *AmMWSc 92*
**Tallant,** David, Jr. 1931- *WhoAmL 92*
**Tallant,** Robert 1909-1957 *BenetAL 91*
**Tallarida,** Ronald Joseph 1937- *AmMWSc 92*
**Tallas,** Jim 1937- *WhoAmP 91*
**Tallawy,** Mervat 1937- *IntWW 91*
**Tallboys,** Richard Gilbert 1931- *IntWW 91, Who 92*
**Tallchief,** Maria 1925- *FacFETw, HanAmWH, WhoEnt 92, WhoMW 92*
**Tallchief,** Marjorie 1927- *IntWW 91*
**Talleda,** Miguel L. 1919- *WhoHisp 92*
**Talledo,** Oscar Eduardo 1929- *AmMWSc 92*
**Tallent,** Elizabeth *DrAPF 91*
**Tallent,** Elizabeth 1954- *BenetAL 91*
**Tallent,** Norman 1921- *IntAu&W 91, WrDr 92*
**Tallent,** Stephen Edison 1937- *WhoAmL 92*
**Tallent,** Timothy N *WhoAmP 91*
**Tallent,** William Hugh 1928- *AmMWSc 92*
**Taller,** Joe Anthony 1933- *WhoAmP 91*
**Tallerico,** Paul Joseph 1938- *AmMWSc 92*
**Talley,** Charles Peter 1941- *AmMWSc 92*

**Talley**, Clarence, Sr. 1951- *WhoBlA 92*
**Talley**, Clarence Hollis 1945- *WhoRel 92*
**Talley**, Curtiss J. 1939- *WhoBlA 92*
**Talley**, Darryl Victor 1960- *WhoBlA 92*
**Talley**, David Lee 1961- *WhoMW 92*
**Talley**, Denver 1938- *WhoAmP 91*
**Talley**, Eugene Alton 1911- *AmMWSc 92*
**Talley**, James Edward 1940- *WhoBlA 92*
**Talley**, Jim Allen 1942- *WhoRel 92*
**Talley**, John D. *WhoRel 92*
**Talley**, John Herbert 1944- *AmMWSc 92*
**Talley**, John Stephen 1930- *WhoBlA 92*
**Talley**, Kevin David 1951- *WhoAmP 91*
**Talley**, Lee Robert 1956- *WhoEnt 92*
**Talley**, Paul 1949- *WhoRel 92*
**Talley**, Richard Bates 1947- *WhoAmL 92*
**Talley**, Robert Boyd 1931- *AmMWSc 92*
**Talley**, Robert Laverne 1959- *WhoRel 92*
**Talley**, Robert Morrell 1924- *AmMWSc 92*
**Talley**, Ronnie Dale 1961- *WhoAmL 92*
**Talley**, Spurgeon Morris 1918- *AmMWSc 92*
**Talley**, Thurman Lamar 1937- *AmMWSc 92*
**Talley**, William Francis, III 1958- *WhoFI 92*
**Talley**, William Giles, Jr. 1939- *WhoFI 92*
**Talley**, William LeRoy 1935- *WhoWest 92*
**Talley**, Wilson K 1935- *AmMWSc 92*
**Talley-Starks**, Monica Dianne 1958- *WhoMW 92*
**Talleyrand**, Charles-Maurice de 1754-1838 *BlkwCEP*
**Talleyrand-Perigord**, Charles-Maurice de 1754-1838 *BlkwCEP*
**Tallgren**, Leif Johan Gustav 1928- *WhoFI 92*
**Tallian**, Tibor E 1920- *AmMWSc 92*
**Tallichet**, Jan Bowen 1936- *WhoFI 92*
**Tallichet Wyler**, Margaret d1991 *NewYTBS 91*
**Talling**, John Francis 1929- *IntWW 91, Who 92*
**Tallis**, Cedric d1991 *NewYTBS 91*
**Tallis**, Thomas 1505?-1585 *NewAmDM*
**Tallitsch**, Robert Boyde 1950- *AmMWSc 92*
**Tallmadge**, Diane Joyce 1934- *WhoWest 92*
**Tallmadge**, Guy Kasten 1932- *WhoWest 92*
**Tallmadge**, J A, Jr 1928- *AmMWSc 92*
**Tallmadge**, James 1778-1853 *AmPolLe*
**Tallman**, Charles Darren 1960- *WhoAmL 92*
**Tallman**, Dennis Earl 1942- *AmMWSc 92*
**Tallman**, J C 1918- *AmMWSc 92*
**Tallman**, John Francis 1947- *AmMWSc 92*
**Tallman**, John Gary 1950- *AmMWSc 92*
**Tallman**, Lori A. 1964- *WhoAmL 92*
**Tallman**, Richard Dale *AmMWSc 92*
**Tallman**, Richard Louis 1931- *AmMWSc 92*
**Tallman**, Samuel V. 1947- *WhoFI 92*
**TallMountain**, Mary *DrAPF 91*
**Tallon**, James R, Jr 1941- *WhoAmP 91*
**Tallon**, Robert M, Jr 1946- *WhoAmP 91*
**Tallon**, Robin M. 1946- *AlmAP 92 [port]*
**Tallon**, Roger 1929- *DcTwDes*
**Tally**, Lura Self 1921- *WhoAmP 91*
**Tally**, Ted 1952- *WrDr 92*
**Talma**, Louise 1906- *NewAmDM*
**Talmadge**, Mary Christine 1940- *WhoWest 92*
**Talmadge**, Philip A 1952- *WhoAmP 91*
**Talmadge**, Philip Albert 1952- *WhoWest 92*
**Talmadge**, Wooddall Wells 1958- *WhoWest 92*
**Talmage**, Algernon 1871-1939 *TwCPaSc*
**Talmage**, Anne *WrDr 92*
**Talmage**, David Wilson 1919- *AmMWSc 92*
**Talmage**, James Edward 1862-1933 *RelLAm 91*
**Talmage**, Kenneth Kellogg 1946- *WhoWest 92*
**Talmage**, Lance Allen 1938- *WhoMW 92*
**Talmage**, Roy Van Neste 1917- *AmMWSc 92*
**Talmage**, T. De Witt 1832-1902 *BenetAL 91*
**Talmage**, Thomas DeWitt 1832-1902 *RelLAm 91*
**Talman**, James Davis 1931- *AmMWSc 92*
**Talman**, Richard Michael 1934- *AmMWSc 92*
**Talmers**, William Nichols 1919- *WhoFI 92*
**Talmi**, Igal 1925- *IntWW 91*
**Talmi**, Yoav 1943- *WhoEnt 92, WhoWest 92*
**Talner**, Norman Stanley 1925- *AmMWSc 92*
**Talomie**, Frank G, Sr 1921- *WhoAmP 91*
**Talton**, Chester Lovelle 1941- *WhoRel 92, WhoWest 92*
**Talu**, Naim 1919- *IntWW 91*
**Talvacchio**, John 1955- *AmMWSc 92*
**Talve**, Susan Andrea 1952- *WhoRel 92*
**Talvela**, Martti 1935-1989 *FacFETw, NewAmDM*
**Talvi**, Ilkka Ilari 1948- *WhoEnt 92*
**Talwani**, Manik 1933- *AmMWSc 92*
**Talyzin**, Nikolai V. d1991 *NewYTBS 91 [port]*
**Talyzin**, Nikolai Vladimirovich d1991 *IntWW 91N*
**Talyzin**, Nikolay Vladimirovich 1929- *SovUnBD*
**Tam**, Andrew Ching 1944- *AmMWSc 92*
**Tam**, Chick F 1946- *AmMWSc 92*
**Tam**, Christopher K W *AmMWSc 92*
**Tam**, James Pingkwan 1947- *AmMWSc 92*
**Tam**, Kwok Kuen 1938- *AmMWSc 92*
**Tam**, Kwok-Wai 1938- *AmMWSc 92*
**Tam**, Patrick Yui-Chiu 1948- *AmMWSc 92*
**Tam**, Rod 1953- *WhoAmP 91*
**Tam**, Roland Fook Seng 1946- *WhoWest 92*
**Tam**, Sang William *AmMWSc 92*
**Tam**, Tommy Tit-Kwan 1951- *WhoFI 92*
**Tam**, Wing-Gay *AmMWSc 92*
**Tam**, Wing Yim 1953- *AmMWSc 92*
**Tamagnini**, Giulio 1921- *IntWW 91*
**Tamagno**, Francesco 1850-1905 *NewAmDM*
**Tamames Gomez**, Ramon 1933- *IntWW 91*
**Tamano**, Teruo 1937- *AmMWSc 92*
**Tamanoi**, Fuyuhiko 1948- *WhoMW 92*
**Tamaoki**, Taiki 1928- *AmMWSc 92*
**Tamaori Hime** *EncAmaz 91*
**Tamar**, Henry 1929- *AmMWSc 92*
**Tamara**, Queen of Georgia 1160-1212 *EncAmaz 91*
**Tamarelli**, Alan Wayne 1941- *AmMWSc 92*
**Tamari**, Dov 1911- *AmMWSc 92*
**Tamari**, Moshe 1910- *IntAu&W 91*
**Tamarin**, Arnold 1923- *AmMWSc 92*
**Tamarin**, Robert Harvey 1942- *AmMWSc 92*
**Tamarkin**, Jeffrey Mitchell 1952- *IntAu&W 91, WhoEnt 92*
**Tamashiro**, Minoru 1924- *AmMWSc 92*
**Tamayo**, Carlos T. *WhoHisp 92*
**Tamayo**, Charles, Jr. 1951- *WhoHisp 92*
**Tamayo**, Fernando M. 1942- *WhoHisp 92*
**Tamayo**, James Anthony 1949- *WhoHisp 92*
**Tamayo**, Jose, Jr. 1936- *WhoMW 92*
**Tamayo**, Mario Alejandro *WhoHisp 92*
**Tamayo**, Rufino 1899-1991 *NewYTBS 91 [port], News 92-1*
**Tamayo**, Rufino 1900-1991 *CurBio 91N*
**Tamayo-Mendez**, Arnaldo 1942- *FacFETw*
**Tambasco**, Anthony Joseph 1939- *WhoRel 92*
**Tambasco**, Daniel Joseph 1936- *AmMWSc 92*
**Tamberlik**, Enrico 1820-1889 *NewAmDM*
**Tamberrino**, Frank Michael 1955- *WhoFI 92*
**Tamblin**, Pamela Joy 1926- *Who 92*
**Tambling**, Jeremy Charles Richard 1948- *IntAu&W 91*
**Tamblyn**, Russ 1935- *ConTFT 9, IntMPA 92*
**Tambo**, Oliver 1917- *FacFETw, IntWW 91, News 91 [port], -91-3 [port]*
**Tambor**, Jeffrey *IntMPA 92*
**Tamborlane**, William Valentine 1946- *AmMWSc 92*
**Tamborski**, Christ 1926- *AmMWSc 92*
**Tambs**, Lewis Arthur 1927- *WhoAmP 91*
**Tamburin**, Henry John 1944- *AmMWSc 92*
**Tamburini**, Antonio 1800-1876 *NewAmDM*
**Tamburini**, Tullio 1892- *BiDExR*
**Tamburino**, Louis A 1936- *AmMWSc 92*
**Tamburri**, Anthony Julian 1949- *WhoMW 92*
**Tamburro**, Carlo Horace 1936- *AmMWSc 92*
**Tamburro**, Kathleen O'Connell 1942- *AmMWSc 92*
**Tamburro**, Wendell Biddle 1916- *WhoAmP 91*
**Tambuzi**, Jitu *DrAPF 91*
**Tamby**, Marie Cassese 1925- *WhoAmP 91*
**Tambyraja**, Samuel Muthuveloe 1942- *WhoMW 92*
**Tame**, William Charles 1909- *Who 92*
**Tamerius**, John 1945- *AmMWSc 92*
**Tames**, Richard 1946- *SmATA 67*
**Tames**, Richard Lawrence 1946- *IntAu&W 91, WrDr 92*
**Tamez**, Eloisa G. 1935- *WhoHisp 92*
**Tamez**, George N. *WhoHisp 92*
**Tamez**, Gilberto A. 1951- *WhoHisp 92*
**Tamez**, Israel 1946- *WhoHisp 92*
**Tamez**, Jesse 1957- *WhoHisp 92*
**Tamhane**, Ajit Chintaman 1946- *AmMWSc 92*
**Tamimi**, Sargon Frederick 1944- *WhoEnt 92*
**Tamimi**, Yusuf Nimr 1931- *AmMWSc 92*
**Tamiolakis**, Emmanuel 1957- *WhoFI 92*
**Tamir**, Hadassah 1930- *AmMWSc 92*
**Tamir**, Theodor 1927- *AmMWSc 92*
**Tamkevicius**, Sigitas 1938- *SovUnBD*
**Tamkin**, Curtis Sloane 1936- *WhoFI 92, WhoWest 92*
**Tamm**, Ditlev 1946- *IntWW 91*
**Tamm**, Igor 1922- *AmMWSc 92, IntWW 91*
**Tamm**, Igor Evgenevich 1895-1971 *WhoNob 90*
**Tamm**, James Eugene 1960- *WhoAmL 92*
**Tamm**, Peter 1928- *IntWW 91*
**Tamm**, Rudra 1946- *WhoAmL 92*
**Tammadge**, Alan Richard 1921- *Who 92*
**Tammany**, Albert Squire, III 1946- *WhoWest 92*
**Tammaro**, Antonio J *WhoAmP 91*
**Tammelleo**, A. David 1935- *WhoAmL 92*
**Tammeus**, William D 1945- *IntAu&W 91*
**Tammeus**, William David 1945- *WhoMW 92*
**Tammi**, Bruce Allan 1950- *WhoAmL 92*
**Tamminen**, Kalevi Reino 1928- *WhoRel 92*
**Tamminga**, Carol Ann 1946- *AmMWSc 92*
**Tamminga**, Frederick W. 1934- *ConAu 135*
**Tamminga**, Frederick William 1934- *SmATA 66 [port]*
**Tammuz**, Benjamin 1919-1989 *ConAu 36NR*
**Tamor**, Stephen 1925- *AmMWSc 92*
**Tamorria**, Christopher Richard 1932- *AmMWSc 92*
**Tampas**, John Peter 1929- *AmMWSc 92*
**Tampico**, Joseph 1916- *AmMWSc 92*
**Tampkins**, Erma 1938- *WhoRel 92*
**Tamplin**, Mark Lewis 1955- *AmMWSc 92*
**Tamposi**, Betty 1955- *WhoAmP 91*
**Tamposi**, Elizabeth Marian 1955- *WhoAmP 91*
**Tamres**, Milton 1922- *AmMWSc 92, WhoMW 92*
**Tamsitt**, James Ray 1928- *AmMWSc 92*
**Tamsky**, Morgan Jerome 1942- *AmMWSc 92*
**Tamulonis**, Frank Louis, Jr. 1946- *WhoAmL 92*
**Tamuno**, Tekena Nitonye 1932- *Who 92*
**Tamura**, Hajime 1924- *IntWW 91*
**Tamura**, Neal Noboru 1953- *WhoWest 92*
**Tamura**, Tsuneo 1925- *AmMWSc 92*
**Tamworth**, Viscount 1952- *Who 92*
**Tan Dun** 1957- *IntWW 91*
**Tan Jiazhen** 1910- *IntWW 91*
**Tan Qilong** 1912- *IntWW 91*
**Tan Youlin** 1916- *IntWW 91*
**Tan**, Ah-Ti Chu 1935- *AmMWSc 92*
**Tan**, Amy *DrAPF 91*
**Tan**, Amy 1952- *IntAu&W 91*
**Tan**, Arjun 1943- *AmMWSc 92*
**Tan**, Barrie 1953- *AmMWSc 92*
**Tan**, Boen Hie 1926- *AmMWSc 92*
**Tan**, Charlotte 1923- *AmMWSc 92*
**Tan**, Chin Sheng 1947- *AmMWSc 92*
**Tan**, Chor-Weng 1936- *AmMWSc 92*
**Tan**, Diane May Lew 1951- *WhoAmL 92*
**Tan**, Eng M 1926- *AmMWSc 92*
**Tan**, Francis C 1939- *AmMWSc 92*
**Tan**, Henry Harry 1924- *AmMWSc 92*
**Tan**, Henry S I 1932- *AmMWSc 92, WhoMW 92*
**Tan**, James Chien-Hua 1935- *AmMWSc 92*
**Tan**, John K. 1934- *WhoFI 92*
**Tan**, Julia S *AmMWSc 92*
**Tan**, Kim H 1926- *AmMWSc 92*
**Tan**, Kok-Keong 1943- *AmMWSc 92*
**Tan**, Liat 1929- *AmMWSc 92*
**Tan**, Meng Hee 1942- *AmMWSc 92*
**Tan**, Owen T 1931- *AmMWSc 92*
**Tan**, Victor 1944- *AmMWSc 92*
**Tan**, Wai-Yuan 1934- *AmMWSc 92*
**Tan**, William Lew 1949- *WhoWest 92*
**Tan**, Y H 1941- *AmMWSc 92*
**Tan**, Yen T 1940- *AmMWSc 92*
**Tan Keng Yam**, Tony 1940- *IntWW 91*
**Tan-Wilson**, Anna L 1946- *AmMWSc 92*
**Tan-Wong**, Lily 1947- *WhoWest 92*
**Tana**, Patti *DrAPF 91*
**Tanabe**, Masato 1925- *AmMWSc 92*
**Tanabe**, Michael John 1947- *AmMWSc 92*
**Tanada**, Takuma 1919- *AmMWSc 92*
**Tanada**, Yoshinori 1917- *AmMWSc 92*
**Tanahira**, Takeshi 1937- *WhoFI 92*
**Tanaka**, Dave Hiro 1963- *WhoEnt 92*
**Tanaka**, Eiji 1955- *WhoFI 92*
**Tanaka**, Floyd Hideo 1924- *WhoFI 92*
**Tanaka**, Fred Shigeru 1937- *AmMWSc 92, WhoMW 92*
**Tanaka**, Janice Diane 1955- *WhoEnt 92*
**Tanaka**, Jeannie E. 1942- *WhoAmL 92, WhoWest 92*
**Tanaka**, John 1924- *AmMWSc 92*
**Tanaka**, John Augustus 1955- *WhoWest 92*
**Tanaka**, Kakuei 1918- *FacFETw, IntWW 91*
**Tanaka**, Karen 1961- *ConCom 92*
**Tanaka**, Katsumi 1925- *AmMWSc 92*
**Tanaka**, Kay 1929- *AmMWSc 92*
**Tanaka**, Kouichi Robert 1926- *AmMWSc 92*
**Tanaka**, Leila Chiyako 1954- *WhoAmL 92*
**Tanaka**, Naoko *WhoEnt 92*
**Tanaka**, Nobuyuki 1937- *AmMWSc 92*
**Tanaka**, Stanley Katsuki 1932- *WhoWest 92*
**Tanaka**, Tatsuo 1910- *IntWW 91*
**Tanaka**, Thomas Victor Camacho 1940- *WhoAmP 91*
**Tanaka**, Tod Zenho 1957- *WhoAmL 92*
**Tanaka**, Togo William 1916- *WhoFI 92, WhoWest 92*
**Tanaka**, Toyoichi 1946- *AmMWSc 92*
**Tanaka**, Yasuomi 1939- *AmMWSc 92*
**Tananbaum**, Harvey Dale 1942- *AmMWSc 92*
**Tanarro**, Fernando Manuel 1933- *WhoFI 92*
**Tanase**, Barbara Colby 1955- *WhoAmL 92*
**Tanasie**, Petre 1927- *IntWW 91*
**Tanburn**, Jennifer Jephcott 1929- *Who 92*
**Tancock**, John 1942- *WrDr 92*
**Tancred**, H. L. *Who 92*
**Tancrell**, Roger Henry 1935- *AmMWSc 92*
**Tanczos**, Frank I 1921- *AmMWSc 92*
**Tandberg-Hanssen**, Einar Andreas 1921- *AmMWSc 92*
**Tandler**, Bernard 1933- *AmMWSc 92*
**Tandy**, Charles C *WhoAmP 91*
**Tandy**, Jessica 1909- *FacFETw, IntMPA 92, IntWW 91, Who 92, WhoEnt 92*
**Tandy**, John 1905-1982 *TwCPaSc*
**Tandy**, Mary B. *WhoBlA 92*
**Taneja**, Vidya Sagar 1931- *AmMWSc 92*
**Tanella**, Dean Garrett 1960- *WhoFI 92*
**Tanen**, Ned 1931- *IntMPA 92*
**Tanenbaum**, Allan Jay 1946- *WhoAmL 92*
**Tanenbaum**, Basil Samuel 1934- *AmMWSc 92, WhoWest 92*
**Tanenbaum**, David Frederick 1956- *WhoEnt 92*
**Tanenbaum**, Elias 1924- *WhoEnt 92*
**Tanenbaum**, Gerald Stephen 1945- *WhoFI 92*
**Tanenbaum**, Jay Harvey 1933- *WhoAmL 92*
**Tanenbaum**, Jill Nancy 1954- *WhoEnt 92*
**Tanenbaum**, Marc Herman 1925- *WhoRel 92*
**Tanenbaum**, Morris 1928- *AmMWSc 92, WhoFI 92*
**Tanenbaum**, Robert Earl 1936- *WhoWest 92*
**Tanenbaum**, Stuart William 1924- *AmMWSc 92*
**Tanenbaum**, William Alan 1954- *WhoAmL 92*
**Taney**, Roger B 1777-1864 *RComAH*
**Taney**, Roger Brooke 1777-1864 *AmPolLe [port]*
**Taneyev**, Sergey 1856-1915 *NewAmDM*
**Tanford**, Charles 1921- *AmMWSc 92, IntWW 91*
**Tanford**, James Alexander 1950- *WhoAmL 92*
**Tang Aoqing** 1915- *IntWW 91*
**Tang Ke** *IntWW 91*
**Tang Mingzhao** 1910- *IntWW 91*
**Tang Peisung** 1903- *IntWW 91*
**Tang Yijie** 1927- *IntWW 91*
**Tang Zhongwen** 1930- *IntWW 91*
**Tang**, Alfred Sho-Yu 1934- *AmMWSc 92*
**Tang**, Andrew H 1936- *AmMWSc 92*
**Tang**, Chung Liang 1934- *AmMWSc 92*
**Tang**, Chung-Muh 1936- *AmMWSc 92*
**Tang**, Chung-Shih 1938- *AmMWSc 92*
**Tang**, Cynthia Jean 1951- *WhoMW 92*
**Tang**, Deborah Canada 1947- *WhoBlA 92*
**Tang**, Denny Duan-Lee *AmMWSc 92*
**Tang**, Dominic 1908- *IntWW 91*
**Tang**, Donald T 1932- *AmMWSc 92*
**Tang**, Homer H 1934- *AmMWSc 92*
**Tang**, Hwa-Tsang 1937- *AmMWSc 92*
**Tang**, Ignatius Ning-Bang 1933- *AmMWSc 92*
**Tang**, James Juh-Ling 1937- *AmMWSc 92*
**Tang**, Jordan Cho-Tung 1948- *WhoEnt 92*
**Tang**, Jordan J N 1931- *AmMWSc 92*
**Tang**, Kunikyo 1966- *WhoWest 92*
**Tang**, Kwong-Tin 1936- *AmMWSc 92*
**Tang**, Pei Chin 1914- *AmMWSc 92*
**Tang**, Roger Yin Wu 1947- *WhoFI 92, WhoMW 92*
**Tang**, Ruen Chiu 1934- *AmMWSc 92*
**Tang**, Samuel 1961- *WhoWest 92*
**Tang**, Stephen Shien-Pu 1935- *AmMWSc 92*
**Tang**, Stephen Shun-Chien 1960- *WhoFI 92*
**Tang**, Thomas *WhoAmP 91*

**Tang,** Thomas 1922- *WhoAmL 92, WhoWest 92*
**Tang,** Ting-Wei 1934- *AmMWSc 92*
**Tang,** Tom 1946- *WhoWest 92*
**Tang,** Victor Kuang-Tao 1929- *AmMWSc 92*
**Tang,** Walter Kwei-Yuan 1929- *AmMWSc 92*
**Tang,** Wilson H 1943- *AmMWSc 92*
**Tang,** Wilson Hon-chung 1943- *WhoMW 92*
**Tang,** Wing Tsang 1958- *WhoWest 92*
**Tang,** Y S 1922- *AmMWSc 92*
**Tang,** Yau-Chien 1928- *AmMWSc 92*
**Tang,** Yi-Noo 1938- *AmMWSc 92*
**Tangaroa,** Tangaroa 1921- *IntWW 91, Who 92*
**Tange,** Arthur 1914- *Who 92*
**Tange,** Arthur Harold 1914- *IntWW 91*
**Tange,** Kenzo 1913- *IntWW 91*
**Tangel,** O F 1910- *AmMWSc 92*
**Tangen,** Einar 1960- *WhoAmL 92*
**Tangherlini,** Frank R 1924- *AmMWSc 92*
**Tangney,** John Francis 1949- *AmMWSc 92*
**Tangonan,** Gregory Ligot 1947- *AmMWSc 92*
**Tangora,** Martin Charles 1936- *AmMWSc 92*
**Tangprasertchai,** Peter Seri 1946- *WhoMW 92*
**Tangretti,** Thomas A 1946- *WhoAmP 91*
**Tanguay,** A R 1924- *AmMWSc 92*
**Tanguay,** Anita Walburga 1936- *WhoFI 92*
**Tanguay,** Eva 1878-1947 *NewAmDM*
**Tanguay,** Robert M 1944- *AmMWSc 92*
**Tanguma,** Baldemar *WhoHisp 92*
**Tanguy,** Julien 1825-1894 *ThHEIm [port]*
**Tanguy,** Nicole Renee 1950- *WhoAmL 92*
**Tanguy,** Yves 1900-1955 *FacFETw*
**Tangye,** Derek *IntAu&W 91*
**Tanham,** George Kilpatrick 1922- *WrDr 92*
**Tani,** Smio 1925- *AmMWSc 92*
**Tani,** Tetsuo 1941- *WhoFI 92*
**Tania** *EncAmaz 91*
**Tanick,** Marshall Howard 1947- *WhoAmL 92*
**Tanigaki,** Nobuyuki 1929- *AmMWSc 92*
**Taniguchi,** Brian T 1951- *WhoAmP 91*
**Taniguchi,** Izumi 1926- *WhoWest 92*
**Taniguchi,** Makoto 1930- *IntWW 91*
**Taniguchi,** Masaharu 1893-1985 *RelLAm 91*
**Taniguchi,** Raymond Masayuki 1934- *WhoWest 92*
**Taniguchi,** Richard Ryuzo 1913- *WhoFI 92, WhoWest 92*
**Taniguchi,** Tokuso 1915- *WhoWest 92*
**Tanikawa,** Kazuo 1930- *IntWW 91*
**Tanikella,** Murty Sundara Sitarama 1938- *AmMWSc 92*
**Tanimoto,** George 1926- *WhoWest 92*
**Tanimoto,** Steven Larry 1949- *WhoWest 92*
**Tanimoto,** Taffee Tadashi 1917- *AmMWSc 92*
**Tanimura,** Hiroshi 1916- *IntWW 91*
**Tanin,** Gary Steven 1952- *WhoEnt 92*
**Tanino,** Karen Kikumi 1958- *AmMWSc 92*
**Tanis,** David Owen 1940- *WhoMW 92*
**Tanis,** Elliot Alan 1934- *AmMWSc 92, WhoMW 92*
**Tanis,** James Iran 1934- *AmMWSc 92*
**Tanis,** James Robert 1928- *WhoRel 92*
**Tanis,** Richard Conrad 1948- *WhoMW 92*
**Tanis,** Steven Paul 1952- *AmMWSc 92*
**Taniuchi,** Hiroshi 1930- *AmMWSc 92*
**Taniyama,** Tadayoshi 1947- *AmMWSc 92*
**Tanji,** Lydia Hanako 1952- *WhoEnt 92*
**Tank,** Patrick Wayne 1950- *AmMWSc 92*
**Tank,** Rajesh Shivlal 1968- *WhoMW 92*
**Tankard,** Anthony James 1942- *AmMWSc 92*
**Tanke,** Thomas John 1944- *WhoWest 92*
**Tankelevich,** Roman Lvovich 1941- *WhoWest 92*
**Tankersley,** Dan *WhoAmP 91*
**Tankersley,** Donald 1939- *AmMWSc 92*
**Tankersley,** Michael Edward 1960- *WhoAmL 92*
**Tankersley,** Robert K. 1927- *IntMPA 92*
**Tankersley,** Robert Walker, Jr 1927- *AmMWSc 92*
**Tankerson,** Richard E. 1940- *WhoBlA 92*
**Tankerville,** Earl of 1956- *Who 92*
**Tankin,** Richard S 1924- *AmMWSc 92*
**Tankins,** Edwin S 1927- *AmMWSc 92*
**Tanlaw,** Baron 1934- *Who 92*
**Tann,** Jennifer 1939- *WrDr 92*
**Tannahill,** Mary Margaret 1944- *AmMWSc 92*
**Tannahill,** Reay 1929- *WrDr 92*
**Tannebaum,** Samuel Hugo 1933- *WhoFI 92*
**Tannehill,** John C. 1943- *WhoMW 92*
**Tannehill,** John Charles 1943- *AmMWSc 92*
**Tannehill,** Wilkins 1787-1858 *BenetAL 91*
**Tannen,** Jack d1991 *NewYTBS 91*
**Tannen,** Leonard Phillip 1937- *WhoFI 92*
**Tannen,** Paul 1937- *WhoEnt 92*
**Tannen,** Richard L 1937- *AmMWSc 92*
**Tannenbaum,** Arthur 1931- *WhoRel 92*
**Tannenbaum,** Bernice Salpeter *WhoRel 92*
**Tannenbaum,** Carl Martin 1940- *AmMWSc 92*
**Tannenbaum,** Doris M 1935- *WhoAmP 91*
**Tannenbaum,** Gloria Shaffer 1938- *AmMWSc 92*
**Tannenbaum,** Harold E 1914- *AmMWSc 92*
**Tannenbaum,** Harvey 1923- *AmMWSc 92*
**Tannenbaum,** Irving Robert 1926- *AmMWSc 92*
**Tannenbaum,** Janet *AmMWSc 92*
**Tannenbaum,** Judith *DrAPF 91*
**Tannenbaum,** Michael Glen 1953- *AmMWSc 92*
**Tannenbaum,** Michael J 1939- *AmMWSc 92*
**Tannenbaum,** Peter 1946- *WhoWest 92*
**Tannenbaum,** Sally 1952- *WhoMW 92*
**Tannenbaum,** Stanley 1925- *AmMWSc 92*
**Tannenbaum,** Steven Robert 1937- *AmMWSc 92*
**Tannenberg,** Dieter E. A. 1932- *WhoFI 92, WhoMW 92*
**Tannenwald,** Peter 1943- *WhoAmL 92*
**Tannenwald,** Peter Ernest 1926- *AmMWSc 92*
**Tannenwald,** Theodore, Jr. 1916- *WhoAmL 92*
**Tanner,** Alain 1929- *IntDcF 2-2 [port]*
**Tanner,** Alain 1933- *IntWW 91*
**Tanner,** Alan Roger 1941- *AmMWSc 92*
**Tanner,** Allan Bain 1930- *AmMWSc 92*
**Tanner,** Anne *TwCPaSc*
**Tanner,** Arthur *TwCPaSc*
**Tanner,** Bernice Alture 1917- *Who 92*
**Tanner,** Brian Michael 1941- *Who 92*
**Tanner,** Champ Bean d1990 *IntWW 91N*
**Tanner,** Champ Bean 1920- *AmMWSc 92*
**Tanner,** Charles E 1932- *AmMWSc 92*
**Tanner,** Daniel 1926- *AmMWSc 92*
**Tanner,** David 1928- *AmMWSc 92*
**Tanner,** David Earl 1948- *WhoWest 92*
**Tanner,** David Williamson 1930- *Who 92*
**Tanner,** Dee Boshard 1913- *WhoAmL 92*
**Tanner,** Denis Alan 1961- *WhoRel 92*
**Tanner,** Dennis David 1930- *AmMWSc 92*
**Tanner,** Douglas Howard 1935- *WhoAmP 91*
**Tanner,** George Albert 1938- *AmMWSc 92, WhoMW 92*
**Tanner,** Gerry Edward 1948- *WhoFI 92*
**Tanner,** Gloria Geraldine 1935- *WhoAmP 91*
**Tanner,** Gloria Travis 1935- *WhoBlA 92*
**Tanner,** Harry Max 1926- *WhoFI 92*
**Tanner,** Henry Ossawa 1859-1937 *ConBlB 1 [port]*
**Tanner,** Henry Schenck 1786-1858 *BiInAmS*
**Tanner,** Jack E. 1919- *WhoBlA 92*
**Tanner,** Jack Edward 1919- *WhoAmL 92*
**Tanner,** Jacqui Dian 1946- *WhoFI 92*
**Tanner,** James Clark, Jr. 1960- *WhoRel 92*
**Tanner,** James Mervil 1934- *AmMWSc 92*
**Tanner,** James Michael 1960- *WhoFI 92*
**Tanner,** James Taylor 1914- *AmMWSc 92*
**Tanner,** James Thomas 1939- *AmMWSc 92*
**Tanner,** James W., Jr. 1936- *WhoBlA 92*
**Tanner,** Joe *WhoAmP 91*
**Tanner,** John *DrAPF 91*
**Tanner,** John 1780?-1847 *BenetAL 91*
**Tanner,** John 1927- *WrDr 92*
**Tanner,** John 1944- *AlmAP 92 [port]*
**Tanner,** John Douglas, Jr. 1943- *WhoWest 92*
**Tanner,** John Eyer, Jr 1930- *AmMWSc 92*
**Tanner,** John Ian 1927- *IntAu&W 91, Who 92*
**Tanner,** John S 1944- *WhoAmP 91, WhoFI 92*
**Tanner,** John W. 1923- *Who 92*
**Tanner,** Jordan 1931- *WhoAmP 91*
**Tanner,** Lee Elliot 1931- *AmMWSc 92*
**Tanner,** Lloyd George 1918- *AmMWSc 92*
**Tanner,** Lynn 1953- *WhoWest 92*
**Tanner,** Martin Abba 1957- *AmMWSc 92*
**Tanner,** Meg *Who 92*
**Tanner,** Noall Stevan 1934- *AmMWSc 92*
**Tanner,** Noel 1941- *TwCPaSc*
**Tanner,** Paul Antony 1935- *Who 92*
**Tanner,** Paul O. W. 1917- *WhoEnt 92*
**Tanner,** Raymond Lewis 1931- *AmMWSc 92*
**Tanner,** Rebecca J. 1949- *WhoRel 92*
**Tanner,** Richard Dean 1952- *WhoWest 92*
**Tanner,** Richard Thomas 1940- *WhoFI 92*
**Tanner,** Robert Dennis 1939- *AmMWSc 92*
**Tanner,** Robert H 1915- *AmMWSc 92*
**Tanner,** Robert Michael 1946- *AmMWSc 92*
**Tanner,** Robin 1904-1988 *TwCPaSc*
**Tanner,** Roger Ian 1933- *AmMWSc 92, IntWW 91*
**Tanner,** Roger Lee 1943- *AmMWSc 92*
**Tanner,** Ron *DrAPF 91*
**Tanner,** Rosamond Fairchild 1906- *WhoEnt 92*
**Tanner,** Sally *WhoAmP 91*
**Tanner,** Stephen L. 1938- *WrDr 92*
**Tanner,** Terence A. 1948- *ConAu 135*
**Tanner,** Terence Arthur 1948- *WhoMW 92*
**Tanner,** Thomas William 1952- *WhoWest 92*
**Tanner,** Tony 1935- *IntAu&W 91, WrDr 92*
**Tanner,** Walter Rhett 1938- *WhoAmL 92*
**Tanner,** Ward Dean, Jr 1918- *AmMWSc 92*
**Tanner,** William B., Jr. 1944- *WhoEnt 92*
**Tanner,** William Coats, Jr. 1920- *WhoWest 92*
**Tanner,** William Dale 1943- *WhoEnt 92*
**Tanner,** William Francis, Jr 1917- *AmMWSc 92*
**Tanner,** Zera Luther 1835-1906 *BiInAmS*
**Tannery,** Jean-Paul 1911- *IntWW 91*
**Tanneyhill,** Ann 1906- *NotBlAW 92*
**Tannhauser** 1205?-1270? *NewAmDM*
**Tanno,** Ronald Louis 1937- *WhoWest 92*
**Tannock,** Ian Frederick 1943- *AmMWSc 92*
**Tannous,** Afif I. 1905- *IntWW 91*
**Tannura,** Nicholas Donald 1960- *WhoFI 92*
**Tanny,** Gerald Brian 1945- *AmMWSc 92*
**Tanous,** Michael Allan 1939- *WhoWest 92*
**Tanous,** Peter Joseph 1938- *WhoFI 92*
**Tanphaichitr,** Vichai 1940- *AmMWSc 92*
**Tanquary,** Albert Charles 1929- *AmMWSc 92*
**Tanquary,** Janice Rae 1946- *WhoWest 92*
**Tanquary,** Oliver Leo 1918- *WhoRel 92*
**Tanselle,** G. Thomas 1934- *WrDr 92*
**Tansey,** Francis 1959- *TwCPaSc*
**Tansey,** Iva Lee Marie 1930- *WhoAmP 91*
**Tansey,** Michael Richard 1943- *AmMWSc 92*
**Tansey,** Nancy Anne 1962- *WhoFI 92*
**Tansey,** Robert Paul, Sr 1914- *AmMWSc 92*
**Tanski,** Adam 1946- *IntWW 91*
**Tansley,** Eric 1901- *Who 92*
**Tansman,** Alexandre 1897-1986 *NewAmDM*
**Tansy,** Martin F 1937- *AmMWSc 92*
**Tant,** Jefferson Davis 1861-1941 *RelLAm 91*
**Tantawi,** Muhammad Sayed Attiyah *WhoRel 92*
**Tanter,** Raymond 1938- *WhoBlA 92*
**Tantillo,** Charles Robert 1936- *WhoMW 92*
**Tantimedh,** Adisakdi 1967- *IntAu&W 91*
**Tantraporn,** Wirojana 1931- *AmMWSc 92*
**Tanttila,** Walter H 1922- *AmMWSc 92*
**Tanuma,** Toshiyuki Mel 1953- *WhoWest 92*
**Tanz,** Ralph 1925- *AmMWSc 92*
**Tanzania,** Archbishop of 1932- *Who 92*
**Tanzer,** Charles 1912- *AmMWSc 92*
**Tanzer,** Jacob 1935- *WhoAmL 92*
**Tanzer,** Jed Samuel 1947- *WhoFI 92*
**Tanzer,** Jennifer Elizabeth 1966- *WhoEnt 92*
**Tanzer,** Marvin Lawrence 1935- *AmMWSc 92*
**Tanzer,** Matthew Owen 1960- *WhoAmL 92*
**Tanzi,** Diane *DrAPF 91*
**Tanzmann,** Virginia Ward 1945- *WhoWest 92*
**Tao Dayong** 1918- *IntWW 91*
**Tao Siju** 1935- *IntWW 91*
**Tao,** Frank F *AmMWSc 92*
**Tao,** L C 1922- *AmMWSc 92*
**Tao,** Liang Neng 1927- *AmMWSc 92*
**Tao,** Mariano 1938- *AmMWSc 92*
**Tao,** Rongjia 1947- *AmMWSc 92*
**Tao,** Shu-Jen 1928- *AmMWSc 92*
**Tao,** Young 1940- *WhoRel 92*
**Taofinu'u,** Pio 1923- *IntWW 91, WhoRel 92*
**Taoka,** George Takashi 1935- *AmMWSc 92*
**Tapanes,** Ernesto Luis, Jr. 1959- *WhoHisp 92*
**Tapang,** Carlos Cortes 1953- *WhoWest 92*
**Taparowsky,** Elizabeth Jane 1954- *AmMWSc 92*
**Tape,** Gerald Frederick 1915- *AmMWSc 92, IntWW 91*
**Taper** *IntAu&W 91X*
**Taper,** Lillian Janette *AmMWSc 92*
**Tapia,** Daniel 1933- *WhoHisp 92*
**Tapia,** Don *WhoHisp 92*
**Tapia,** Fernando 1922- *AmMWSc 92*
**Tapia,** John Reyna 1922- *WhoWest 92*
**Tapia,** Lorenzo E. 1931- *WhoHisp 92*
**Tapia,** Louis Florencio 1945- *WhoHisp 92*
**Tapia,** M A 1935- *AmMWSc 92*
**Tapia,** Mario E. 1947- *WhoHisp 92*
**Tapia,** Richard 1939- *AmMWSc 92*
**Tapia,** Richard Alfred 1939- *WhoHisp 92*
**Tapia,** Santiago 1939- *AmMWSc 92*
**Tapia,** Steven Paul 1955- *WhoAmL 92*
**Tapia-Videla,** Jorge *WhoHisp 92*
**Tapie,** Bernard Roger 1943- *IntWW 91*
**Tapies Puig,** Antoni 1923- *IntWW 91*
**Tapiovaara,** Ilmari 1914- *DcTwDes*
**Tapking,** Douglas Allen 1949- *WhoWest 92*
**Taplett,** Lloyd Melvin 1924- *WhoMW 92*
**Tapley,** Byron D 1933- *AmMWSc 92*
**Tapley,** Donald Fraser 1927- *AmMWSc 92*
**Tapley,** James Leroy 1923- *WhoAmL 92*
**Taplin,** David Michael Robert 1939- *AmMWSc 92*
**Taplin,** Jonathan 1947- *IntMPA 92*
**Taplin,** Lael Brent 1927- *AmMWSc 92*
**Taplin,** Oliver 1943- *WrDr 92*
**Tapp,** Charles Millard 1936- *AmMWSc 92*
**Tapp,** Jesse Washington, Jr. 1930- *WhoWest 92*
**Tapp,** Lawrence G. 1937- *WhoFI 92*
**Tapp,** Nigel Prior Hanson d1991 *Who 92N*
**Tapp,** Ronald Gene 1941- *WhoFI 92, WhoWest 92*
**Tapp,** William Jouette 1918- *AmMWSc 92*
**Tappan,** Cindy Beard 1930- *WhoRel 92*
**Tappan,** David S., Jr. 1922- *WhoWest 92*
**Tappan,** Donald Vester 1925- *AmMWSc 92*
**Tappan,** Janice Ruth Vogel 1948- *WhoWest 92*
**Tappan,** Major William 1924- *WhoBlA 92*
**Tappe,** Mary Lou 1935- *WhoAmP 91*
**Tappeiner,** John Cummings, II 1934- *AmMWSc 92*
**Tappel,** Aloys Louis 1926- *AmMWSc 92*
**Tappen,** Neil Campbell 1920- *AmMWSc 92*
**Tapper,** Colin Frederick Herbert 1934- *Who 92*
**Tapper,** Daniel Naphtali 1929- *AmMWSc 92*
**Tapper,** David Alfred 1928- *WhoEnt 92*
**Tapper,** Joan Judith 1947- *WhoWest 92*
**Tapper-Jones,** Sydney d1991 *Who 92N*
**Tappert,** Frederick Drach 1940- *AmMWSc 92*
**Tappes,** Shelton 1911-1991 *WhoBlA 92N*
**Tapphorn,** Ralph M 1944- *AmMWSc 92*
**Tappin,** Anthony Gerald 1925- *WhoFI 92*
**Tappin,** Suzanne 1959- *WhoFI 92*
**Tapply,** William G *IntAu&W 91*
**Tapply,** William G. 1940- *WrDr 92*
**Tappmeyer,** Wilbur Paul 1922- *AmMWSc 92*
**Tapps Gervis Meyrick** *Who 92*
**Taps,** Jonie *IntMPA 92*
**Tapscott,** Robert Edwin 1938- *AmMWSc 92*
**Tapscott,** Stephen J. *DrAPF 91*
**Tapsell,** Peter 1930- *IntWW 91, Who 92*
**Tara** 1921- *WhoWest 92*
**Tarabai of Rajasthan** *EncAmaz 91*
**Tarachow,** Michael *DrAPF 91*
**Tarack,** Gerald 1929- *NewAmDM*
**Taradash,** Daniel 1913- *IntMPA 92*
**Taradash,** Daniel Irwin 1913- *WhoEnt 92*
**Taragano,** Howard Jay 1957- *WhoMW 92*
**Taragin,** Morton Frank 1944- *AmMWSc 92*
**Tarallo,** Angelo Nicholas 1940- *WhoFI 92*
**Tarallo,** Barry Joseph *WhoEnt 92*
**Taraman,** Khalil Showky 1939- *AmMWSc 92*
**Taran,** Carole *WhoEnt 92*
**Tarango,** Anthony 1937- *WhoHisp 92*
**Tarango,** Yolanda 1948- *WhoHisp 92*
**Taranik,** James Vladimir 1940- *AmMWSc 92, WhoWest 92*
**Tarantine,** Frank J 1935- *AmMWSc 92*
**Tarantino,** Laura M 1947- *AmMWSc 92*
**Tarantino,** Louis Gerald 1934- *WhoFI 92*
**Tarantino,** Thomas Edward 1954- *WhoAmL 92*
**Taranto,** Joseph Victor 1949- *WhoIns 92*
**Taranto,** Judith E. 1952- *WhoHisp 92*
**Taranu,** Cornel 1934- *IntWW 91*
**Tarapchak,** Stephen J 1942- *AmMWSc 92*
**Taras,** John 1919- *WhoEnt 92*
**Taras,** Michael Andrew 1921- *AmMWSc 92*
**Taras,** Paul 1941- *AmMWSc 92*
**Tarascio,** Vincent Joseph 1930- *WhoFI 92*
**Tarasevich,** Lev Aleksandrovich 1868-1927 *SovUnBD*
**Tarasov-Rodionov,** Aleksandr Ignat'evich 1885-1938 *SovUnBD*
**Tarasova,** Alla Konstantinovna 1898-1973 *SovUnBD*
**Tarasovic,** Marcia M. *DrAPF 91*
**Tarassov,** Nikolai Konstantinovich 1923- *IntWW 91*
**Tarasuk,** John David 1936- *AmMWSc 92*
**Taraszewski,** William John 1956- *WhoMW 92*

**Taraszka,** Anthony John 1935- *AmMWSc 92*
**Taraszkiewicz,** Waldemar 1936- *WhoMW 92*
**Taratuta,** Vasily Nikolaevich 1930- *IntWW 91*
**Taravella,** Christopher Anthony 1951- *WhoAmL 92*
**Tarazevich,** Georgiy Stanislavovich 1937- *IntWW 91, SovUnBD*
**Tarazi,** Paul Nadim 1943- *WhoRel 92*
**Tarbat,** Viscount 1987- *Who 92*
**Tarbell,** Dean Stanley 1913- *AmMWSc 92, IntWW 91*
**Tarbell,** Ida 1857-1944 *FacFETw, HanAmWH*
**Tarbell,** Ida M. 1857-1944 *BenetAL 91*
**Tarbell,** Theodore Dean 1950- *AmMWSc 92*
**Tarbox,** Loretta Jeanne 1926- *WhoAmP 91*
**Tarbutton,** Roger Lynn 1951- *WhoAmL 92*
**Tarby,** Stephen Kenneth 1934- *AmMWSc 92*
**Tarby,** Theodore John 1941- *AmMWSc 92*
**Tarcher,** Jeremy Phillip 1932- *IntWW 91*
**Tarde,** Gabriel De 1843-1904 *ScFEYrs*
**Tardieu,** Jean 1903- *FacFETw, GuFrLit 1, IntWW 91*
**Tardif,** Gilman Normand 1947- *WhoWest 92*
**Tardif,** Henri Pierre *AmMWSc 92*
**Tardiff,** Robert G 1942- *AmMWSc 92*
**Tardiff,** Susan Alice 1952- *WhoAmP 91*
**Tardivo,** Giuseppe 1948- *WhoFI 92*
**Tardos,** Marton 1928- *IntWW 91*
**Tardy,** Robert J *WhoAmP 91*
**Tardy,** Walter J., Jr. 1941- *WhoBlA 92*
**Taren,** James A 1924- *AmMWSc 92*
**Tareski,** Val Gerard 1941- *AmMWSc 92*
**Targ,** Russell 1934- *AmMWSc 92*
**Targan,** Barry *DrAPF 91*
**Target,** George William 1924- *WrDr 92*
**Targett,** Geoffrey Arthur Trevor 1935- *Who 92*
**Targett,** Nancy McKeever 1950- *AmMWSc 92*
**Targett,** Timothy Erwin 1950- *AmMWSc 92*
**Targoff,** Michael Bart 1944- *WhoFI 92*
**Targowski,** Andrew Stanislaw 1937- *WhoFI 92*
**Targowski,** Stanislaw P 1940- *AmMWSc 92*
**Taricco,** Todd Lawrence 1957- *WhoWest 92*
**Tarich,** Yuriy Viktorovich 1885-1967 *SovUnBD*
**Tariche,** Roberto 1948- *WhoHisp 92*
**Tariki,** Abdallah 1919- *IntWW 91*
**Tarin,** Sam U. 1935- *WhoHisp 92*
**Tarin,** William Michael 1942- *WhoWest 92*
**Tario,** Terry Charles 1950- *WhoEnt 92, WhoWest 92*
**Tarjan,** Armen Charles 1920- *AmMWSc 92*
**Tarjan,** George 1912- *AmMWSc 92*
**Tarjan,** Imre 1912- *IntWW 91*
**Tarjan,** Robert Endre 1948- *AmMWSc 92*
**Tarjanne,** Pekka 1937- *Who 92*
**Tarkenton,** Fran 1940- *FacFETw*
**Tarkington,** Booth 1869-1946 *BenetAL 91, FacFETw*
**Tarkka,** Asko 1929- *IntWW 91*
**Tarkoff,** Michael Harris 1946- *WhoAmL 92*
**Tarkovsky,** Andrei 1932-1986 *IntDcF 2-2 [port]*
**Tarkovsky,** Andrey Arsen'evich 1932-1986 *SovUnBD*
**Tarkoy,** Peter J 1941- *AmMWSc 92*
**Tarle,** Gregory 1951- *AmMWSc 92*
**Tarlen,** Carol *DrAPF 91*
**Tarleton,** Banastre 1754-1833 *BlkwEAR*
**Tarleton,** Bennett 1943- *WhoEnt 92*
**Tarleton,** Gadson Jack, Jr 1920- *AmMWSc 92*
**Tarleton,** Kevin Walter 1953- *WhoEnt 92*
**Tarling,** Nicholas 1931 *WrDr 92*
**Tarlock,** Anthony Dan 1940- *WhoAmL 92*
**Tarloff,** Erik Sheppard 1948- *WhoEnt 92*
**Tarlov,** Alvin Richard 1929- *AmMWSc 92, WhoWest 92*
**Tarlow,** Peter Everett 1946- *WhoRel 92*
**Tarlson,** Nick Glenn 1955- *WhoFI 92*
**Tarlton,** Jimmie 1892-1979 *NewAmDM*
**Tarn,** Adam 1902-1975 *LiExTwC*
**Tarn,** John Nelson 1934- *Who 92*
**Tarn,** Nathaniel *DrAPF 91*
**Tarn,** Nathaniel 1928- *ConPo 91, WrDr 92*
**Tarn,** Tzyh-Jong 1937- *AmMWSc 92*
**Tarnacki,** Stanley Peter 1954- *WhoEnt 92*
**Tarnavs'kyj,** Ostap 1917- *LiExTwC*
**Tarnawski,** Feliks 1939- *WhoEnt 92*
**Tarnawsky,** Marta 1930- *WhoAmL 92*
**Tarnawsky,** Yuriy *DrAPF 91*
**Tarnay,** Dennis B. 1952- *WhoFI 92*
**Tarney,** Robert Edward 1931- *AmMWSc 92*
**Tarnoff,** Jerome 1931- *WhoAmP 91*
**Tarnoff,** John B. 1952- *IntMPA 92*
**Tarnoff,** John Brooks 1952- *WhoEnt 92*
**Tarnoky,** Andras Laszlo 1920- *WrDr 92*
**Tarnopol,** Michael L. 1936- *WhoFI 92*
**Tarnopolsky,** Vladimir 1955- *ConCom 92*
**Tarnopolsky,** Walter Surma 1932- *IntWW 91*
**Tarone,** Robert Ernest 1946- *AmMWSc 92*
**Tarpey,** Thomas Anthony 1911- *WhoFI 92*
**Tarpley,** Anderson Ray, Jr 1944- *AmMWSc 92*
**Tarpley,** Jerald Dan 1942- *AmMWSc 92*
**Tarpley,** Margaret Johnson 1944- *WhoRel 92*
**Tarpley,** Nancy Lane 1946- *WhoAmP 91*
**Tarpley,** Roy James, Jr. 1964- *WhoBlA 92*
**Tarpley,** Wallace Armell 1934- *AmMWSc 92*
**Tarpy,** Thomas Michael 1945- *WhoAmL 92*
**Tarquin,** Anthony Joseph 1941- *AmMWSc 92*
**Tarr,** Bruce E *WhoAmP 91*
**Tarr,** Charles Edwin 1940- *AmMWSc 92*
**Tarr,** Curtis William 1924- *WhoAmP 91*
**Tarr,** David Eugene 1932- *WhoWest 92*
**Tarr,** Donald Arthur 1932- *AmMWSc 92*
**Tarr,** Edward H. 1936- *NewAmDM*
**Tarr,** Herbert *DrAPF 91*
**Tarr,** James 1905- *TwCPaSc*
**Tarr,** James Lee 1931- *WhoEnt 92*
**Tarr,** Joel Arthur 1934- *AmMWSc 92, WrDr 92*
**Tarr,** Judith 1955- *TwCSFW 91*
**Tarr,** Melinda Jean 1948- *AmMWSc 92*
**Tarr,** Paul C, III 1933- *WhoIns 92*
**Tarr,** Ralph Stockman 1864-1912 *BiInAmS*
**Tarr,** Raymond Frederick 1932- *WhoWest 92*
**Tarr,** Robert James 1944- *Who 92*
**Tarr,** Robert Joseph, Jr. 1943- *WhoFI 92*
**Tarr-Whelan,** Linda Jane 1940- *WhoFI 92*
**Tarrant,** John *IntAu&W 91X, WrDr 92*
**Tarrant,** John Rex 1941- *WrDr 92*
**Tarrant,** Margaret 1888-1959 *TwCPaSc*
**Tarrant,** Paul 1914- *AmMWSc 92*
**Tarrant,** Peter 1943- *TwCPaSc*
**Tarrants,** William Eugene 1927- *AmMWSc 92*
**Tarry,** Ellen 1906- *ChILR 26 [port], NotBlAW 92, WhoBlA 92*
**Tarses,** Jay *LesBEnT 92*
**Tarses,** Jay 1939- *IntMPA 92, WhoEnt 92*
**Tarshis,** Irvin Barry 1914- *AmMWSc 92*
**Tarsis,** Valery 1906- *LiExTwC*
**Tarson,** Herbert Harvey 1910- *WhoWest 92*
**Tart,** Charles T. 1937- *WrDr 92*
**Tart,** Indrek 1946- *IntAu&W 91*
**Tart,** John *WhoAmP 91*
**Tartabull,** Danny 1962- *WhoBlA 92, WhoHisp 92*
**Tartaglia,** Paul Edward 1944- *AmMWSc 92*
**Tartar,** Vance 1911- *AmMWSc 92*
**Tarter,** Blodwen 1954- *WhoWest 92*
**Tarter,** Curtis Bruce 1939- *AmMWSc 92*
**Tarter,** Donald Cain 1936- *AmMWSc 92*
**Tarter,** Fred Barry 1943- *WhoEnt 92*
**Tarter,** James H., III 1927- *WhoBlA 92*
**Tarter,** James H., Sr. 1904- *WhoBlA 92*
**Tarter,** Michael E 1938- *AmMWSc 92*
**Tarter,** Robert R., Jr. 1948- *WhoBlA 92*
**Tartikoff,** Brandon *LesBEnT 92 [port]*
**Tartikoff,** Brandon 1949- *IntMPA 92, WhoEnt 92, WhoWest 92*
**Tartikoff,** Peter Allen 1941- *WhoFI 92*
**Tartini,** Giuseppe 1692-1770 *NewAmDM*
**Tartof,** David 1945- *AmMWSc 92*
**Tartof,** Kenneth D 1941- *AmMWSc 92*
**Tartt,** Thomas Edward 1940- *AmMWSc 92*
**Tarua,** Ilinome Frank 1941- *Who 92*
**Tarui,** Yasuo 1929- *AmMWSc 92*
**Tarun,** Robert Walter 1949- *WhoAmL 92*
**Tarver,** Charles Melvin 1945- *WhoFI 92*
**Tarver,** Elking, Jr. 1953- *WhoBlA 92*
**Tarver,** Fred Russell, Jr 1925- *AmMWSc 92*
**Tarver,** Gregory W. 1946- *WhoBlA 92*
**Tarver,** Gregory Williams, Sr 1946- *WhoAmP 91*
**Tarver,** Harold 1908- *AmMWSc 92*
**Tarver,** Mae-Goodwin 1916- *AmMWSc 92*
**Tarver,** Margaret Leggett 1942- *WhoAmL 92*
**Tarver,** Marie Nero 1925- *WhoBlA 92*
**Tarvid,** Kevin G 1954- *WhoAmP 91*
**Tarvid,** Mitchell Joseph 1958- *WhoFI 92*
**Tarvin,** Robert Floyd 1942- *AmMWSc 92*
**Tarwater,** Dwight Edward 1955- *WhoAmL 92*
**Tarwater,** Jan Dalton 1937- *AmMWSc 92*
**Tarwater,** Oliver Reed 1944- *AmMWSc 92*
**Tarzwell,** Clarence Matthew 1907- *AmMWSc 92*
**Tasaka,** Masaichi 1925- *WhoWest 92*
**Tasaki,** Ichiji 1910- *AmMWSc 92*
**Tasca,** Catherine 1941- *IntWW 91*
**Tasca,** Jules Edward 1938- *WhoEnt 92*
**Tasch,** Al Felix, Jr 1941- *AmMWSc 92*
**Tasch,** Paul 1910- *AmMWSc 92*
**Taschek,** Richard Ferdinand 1915- *AmMWSc 92*
**Taschereau,** Elzear Alexandre 1820-1898 *RelLAm 91*
**Taschereau,** Pierre 1920- *IntWW 91*
**Taschner,** Michael J 1953- *AmMWSc 92*
**Tascioglu,** Mukerrem 1926- *IntWW 91*
**Tasco,** Frank J 1927- *WhoIns 92*
**Tasco,** Marian 1937- *WhoAmP 91*
**Tasco,** Marian B. *WhoBlA 92*
**Tasco,** Rai 1917- *IntMPA 92*
**Tashi** *NewAmDM*
**Tashian,** Richard Earl 1922- *AmMWSc 92*
**Tashima,** Atsushi Wallace 1934- *WhoAmL 92*
**Tashiro,** Haruo 1917- *AmMWSc 92*
**Tashiro,** Kikuo 1917- *IntWW 91*
**Tashjian,** Armen H, Jr 1932- *AmMWSc 92*
**Tashjian,** Joy Marie 1958- *WhoEnt 92*
**Tashjian,** Julia Harriet 1938- *WhoAmP 91*
**Tashjian,** Robert John 1930- *AmMWSc 92*
**Tashlin,** Frank 1913-1972 *IntDcF 2-2 [port]*
**Tasi,** James 1933- *AmMWSc 92*
**Tasiemski,** Victor Mariano 1961- *WhoWest 92*
**Tasker,** Clinton Waldorf 1918- *AmMWSc 92*
**Tasker,** John B 1933- *AmMWSc 92*
**Tasker,** Ronald Reginald 1927- *AmMWSc 92*
**Taslitz,** Norman 1929- *AmMWSc 92*
**Tasman,** William S *AmMWSc 92*
**Tasmania,** Bishop of 1930- *Who 92*
**Tassani,** Sally Marie 1948- *WhoMW 92*
**Tassava,** Roy A 1937- *AmMWSc 92*
**Tassie,** Robert V. *WhoBlA 92*
**Tassin,** Leslie Paul, Sr 1946- *WhoAmP 91*
**Tassin,** Wirt de Vivier 1868-1915 *BiInAmS*
**Tassinari,** Silvio John 1922- *AmMWSc 92*
**Tassone,** Bruce Anthony 1960- *WhoFI 92*
**Tassone,** Gelsomina 1944- *WhoFI 92*
**Tassoul,** Jean-Louis 1938- *AmMWSc 92*
**Tassoul,** Monique 1942- *AmMWSc 92*
**Taswell,** Harold Langmead Taylor 1910- *IntWW 91*
**Taswell,** Howard Filmore 1928- *AmMWSc 92*
**Tat,** Vincent T. 1955- *WhoWest 92*
**Tata,** Giovanni 1954- *WhoWest 92*
**Tata,** Jamshed Rustom 1930- *IntWW 91, Who 92*
**Tata,** Jehangir Ratanji Dadabhoy 1904- *IntWW 91*
**Tata,** Robert 1930- *WhoAmP 91*
**Tata,** Vijay Srinivas 1954- *WhoAmL 92*
**Tata,** Xerxes Ramyar 1954- *AmMWSc 92*
**Tatangelo,** Aldo 1913- *WhoAmP 91, WhoHisp 92*
**Tatar,** Jerome Arthur 1949- *WhoMW 92*
**Tatarczuk,** Joseph Richard 1936- *AmMWSc 92*
**Tatarinov,** Leonid Petrovich 1926- *IntWW 91*
**Tatarintsev,** Vladimir Mikhailovich 1941- *IntWW 91*
**Tatarowicz,** Philip Mario 1954- *WhoAmL 92*
**Tatay,** Sandor 1910- *IntWW 91*
**Tate,** Adolphus, Jr. 1942- *WhoBlA 92*
**Tate,** Albert, Jr 1920- *WhoAmP 91*
**Tate,** Allen 1899-1979 *BenetAL 91, FacFETw*
**Tate,** Benjamin Franklin 1953- *WhoMW 92*
**Tate,** Bryce Eugene 1920- *AmMWSc 92*
**Tate,** Buddy 1913- *NewAmDM*
**Tate,** Charles Edwin 1961- *WhoAmL 92*
**Tate,** Charlotte Anne 1944- *AmMWSc 92*
**Tate,** Dane Arlon 1965- *WhoEnt 92*
**Tate,** Darryl Allen 1961- *WhoRel 92*
**Tate,** David Kirk 1939- *WhoBlA 92*
**Tate,** David Orey 1935- *WhoAmP 91*
**Tate,** David Paul 1931- *AmMWSc 92*
**Tate,** Deborah M. 1955- *WhoAmL 92*
**Tate,** Dennis Armfield 1931- *WhoWest 92*
**Tate,** Dennis Ray 1943- *WhoRel 92*
**Tate,** Eleanora E. *DrAPF 91*
**Tate,** Eleanora Elaine 1948- *WhoBlA 92*
**Tate,** Elizabeth 1948- *TwCPaSc*
**Tate,** Ellalice *IntAu&W 91X, Who 92, WrDr 92*
**Tate,** Eula Booker 1948- *WhoBlA 92*
**Tate,** Fran M. 1929- *WhoFI 92*
**Tate,** Francis Herbert 1913- *Who 92*
**Tate,** Frank 1964- *BlkOlyM*
**Tate,** Frederick George 1925- *WhoAmL 92*
**Tate,** George Lawrence 1948- *WhoRel 92*
**Tate,** Grady B. 1932- *WhoBlA 92*
**Tate,** Hardy Hagen *WhoAmP 91*
**Tate,** Harold Simmons, Jr. 1930- *WhoAmL 92*
**Tate,** Henry 1902- *Who 92*
**Tate,** Henry Saxon 1931- *Who 92*
**Tate,** Herbert Holmes, Jr. 1953- *WhoBlA 92*
**Tate,** Horace Edward 1922- *WhoAmP 91, WhoBlA 92*
**Tate,** James *DrAPF 91*
**Tate,** James 1943- *BenetAL 91, ConPo 91, WrDr 92*
**Tate,** James A. 1927- *WhoBlA 92*
**Tate,** Jeffrey Philip 1943- *IntWW 91, Who 92*
**Tate,** Jeffrey S 1957- *WhoIns 92*
**Tate,** Jerry Allen 1956- *WhoWest 92*
**Tate,** Jerry Wayne *WhoEnt 92*
**Tate,** Joan 1922- *IntAu&W 91, WrDr 92*
**Tate,** Joan C 1946- *WhoAmP 91*
**Tate,** John 1955- *BlkOlyM*
**Tate,** John T 1925- *AmMWSc 92*
**Tate,** Kathryn Willcox 1939- *WhoAmL 92*
**Tate,** Lars Jamel 1966- *WhoBlA 92*
**Tate,** Laurence Gray 1945- *AmMWSc 92*
**Tate,** Leonard E. 1943- *WhoBlA 92*
**Tate,** Loretta Hitchings 1936- *WhoAmP 91*
**Tate,** Mable Leigh 1947- *WhoAmP 91*
**Tate,** Margaret Townsend 1934- *WhoAmP 91*
**Tate,** Mary Magdalena Lewis 1871-1930 *RelLAm 91*
**Tate,** Matthew 1940- *WhoBlA 92*
**Tate,** Maybird Constance 1893-1947 *BiDBrF 2*
**Tate,** Merze 1905- *WhoBlA 92*
**Tate,** Michael Emil 1950- *WhoMW 92*
**Tate,** Michael J 1954- *WhoAmP 91*
**Tate,** Nahum 1652?-1715 *RfGEnL 91*
**Tate,** Nairne *TwCPaSc*
**Tate,** Peter *TwCSFW 91, WrDr 92*
**Tate,** Phil *WhoAmP 91*
**Tate,** Phil 1946- *WhoAmP 91*
**Tate,** R W 1925- *AmMWSc 92*
**Tate,** Ralph Richards, Jr 1941- *WhoAmP 91*
**Tate,** Randy *WhoAmP 91*
**Tate,** Robert Brian 1921- *IntWW 91, Who 92*
**Tate,** Robert Flemming 1921- *AmMWSc 92*
**Tate,** Robert Lee, III 1944- *AmMWSc 92*
**Tate,** Saxon *Who 92*
**Tate,** Sherman E. 1945- *WhoBlA 92*
**Tate,** Stonewall Shepherd 1917- *WhoAmL 92*
**Tate,** Suresh S 1936- *AmMWSc 92*
**Tate,** Tommy Harrison 1955- *WhoEnt 92*
**Tate,** Walter Erton 1959- *WhoAmL 92*
**Tatebe,** Hiroko 1950- *WhoFI 92*
**Tatelman,** Maurice 1917- *AmMWSc 92*
**Tatelman,** Milton Joseph 1943- *WhoEnt 92*
**Tatem,** Moira 1928- *ConAu 133*
**Tatem,** Patricia Ann 1946- *WhoBlA 92*
**Tateoka,** Reid 1954- *WhoAmL 92*
**Tatge,** Douglas A. 1948- *WhoMW 92*
**Tathagatananda,** Swami *WhoRel 92*
**Tatham,** David Everard 1939- *Who 92*
**Tatham,** Francis Hugh Currer 1916- *Who 92*
**Tatham,** Gregory Arthur 1953- *WhoWest 92*
**Tatham,** John 1610?- *RfGEnL 91*
**Tatham,** William 1752-1819 *BiInAmS*
**Tati,** Jacques 1908-1982 *FacFETw, IntDcF 2-2*
**Tatian** *EncEarC*
**Tatibouet,** Jane B *WhoAmP 91*
**Tatina,** Robert Edward 1942- *AmMWSc 92*
**Tatina,** Scott Alfred 1956- *WhoEnt 92*
**Tatini,** Sita Ramayya 1935- *AmMWSc 92*
**Tatishchev,** Vasily Nikitich 1686-1750 *BlkwCEP*
**Tatishvili,** Tsisana Bezhanovna 1939- *IntWW 91*
**Tatliev,** Suleyman Bayram ogly 1925- *IntWW 91*
**Tatlin,** Vladimir 1885-1953 *DcTwDes, FacFETw*
**Tatlin,** Vladimir Yevgrafovich 1885-1953 *SovUnBD*
**Tatlock,** Anne M. 1939- *WhoFI 92*
**Tatlow,** John Colin 1923- *Who 92*
**Tatlow,** Richard H, III 1906- *AmMWSc 92*
**Tatman,** Edward J. 1949- *WhoMW 92*
**Tatman,** Robin Reich 1959- *WhoWest 92*
**Tatmon,** Eugene 1941- *WhoBlA 92*
**Tatnall,** Thomas Scott 1959- *WhoWest 92*
**Tatom,** John Anthony 1945- *WhoFI 92, WhoMW 92*
**Tatomer,** Harry Nicholas 1913- *AmMWSc 92*
**Tatomer,** William John 1938- *WhoWest 92*
**Taton,** Rene 1915- *IntWW 91*
**Tator,** Charles Haskell 1936- *AmMWSc 92*
**Tatrai,** Vilmos 1912- *IntWW 91*
**Tatro,** Clement A 1924- *AmMWSc 92*

**Tatro**, Peter Richard 1936- *AmMWSc 92*
**Tatsumi**, Sotoo 1923- *IntWW 91*
**Tatsumoto**, Mitsunobu 1923- *AmMWSc 92*
**Tatta**, John Louis 1920- *WhoEnt 92*
**Tattar**, Terry Alan 1943- *AmMWSc 92*
**Tatter**, Dorothy 1922- *AmMWSc 92*
**Tattersall**, Fred T. 1948- *WhoFI 92*
**Tattersall**, Ian Michael 1945- *AmMWSc 92*
**Tattersall**, Jill 1931- *WrDr 92*
**Tattersall**, Laura Catherine Mary 1922- *IntAu&W 91*
**Tattersall**, William James 1932- *WhoAmL 92, WhoFI 92*
**Tattoli**, Oronzo Larry 1961- *WhoEnt 92*
**Tatton Brown**, William Eden 1910- *Who 92*
**Tatum**, Art 1909-1956 *FacFETw*
**Tatum**, Art 1910-1956 *NewAmDM*
**Tatum**, Beatrice Elizabeth 1954- *WhoWest 92*
**Tatum**, Brooking Parsons 1908- *WhoWest 92*
**Tatum**, Carol Evora 1943- *WhoBlA 92*
**Tatum**, Charles Maris 1947- *AmMWSc 92*
**Tatum**, Colin Curtiss 1935- *WhoRel 92*
**Tatum**, Donn B. 1913- *IntMPA 92*
**Tatum**, Donn Benjamin 1913- *WhoEnt 92*
**Tatum**, Edward Lawrie 1909-1975 *WhoNob 90*
**Tatum**, Ezra Carl, Jr 1926- *WhoAmP 91*
**Tatum**, Fred Menefee, Jr. 1927- *WhoAmL 92*
**Tatum**, Gordon, Jr. 1940- *WhoEnt 92*
**Tatum**, Grace Martinez 1960- *WhoHisp 92*
**Tatum**, James Bernard 1925- *WhoAmP 91*
**Tatum**, James Patrick 1938- *AmMWSc 92*
**Tatum**, Jerry *WhoBlA 92*
**Tatum**, John Benjamin 1968- *WhoWest 92*
**Tatum**, Linda Gail 1943- *WhoWest 92*
**Tatum**, Lynn Wayne 1954- *WhoRel 92*
**Tatum**, Mildred Carthan 1940- *WhoBlA 92*
**Tatum**, Omar Lee 1926- *WhoFI 92*
**Tatum**, Sledge d1916 *BiInAmS*
**Tatum**, Thomas Deskins 1946- *WhoEnt 92, WhoWest 92*
**Tatum**, Wilbert A. 1933- *WhoBlA 92*
**Tatum**, William Earl 1933- *AmMWSc 92*
**Tatyrek**, Alfred Frank 1930- *AmMWSc 92*
**Taub**, Aaron M 1935- *AmMWSc 92*
**Taub**, Abraham 1901- *AmMWSc 92*
**Taub**, Abraham Haskel 1911- *AmMWSc 92, WhoWest 92*
**Taub**, Arthur 1932- *AmMWSc 92*
**Taub**, David 1919- *AmMWSc 92*
**Taub**, Edward 1931- *AmMWSc 92*
**Taub**, Eli Irwin 1938- *WhoAmL 92*
**Taub**, Frieda B 1934- *AmMWSc 92*
**Taub**, Haskell Joseph 1945- *AmMWSc 92*
**Taub**, Henry 1927- *WhoFI 92*
**Taub**, Herbert 1918- *AmMWSc 92*
**Taub**, Irwin A 1934- *AmMWSc 92*
**Taub**, James M 1918- *AmMWSc 92*
**Taub**, Jesse 1923- *WhoFI 92*
**Taub**, Jesse J 1927- *AmMWSc 92*
**Taub**, John Marcus 1947- *AmMWSc 92*
**Taub**, Mary L 1948- *AmMWSc 92*
**Taub**, Robert Norman 1936- *AmMWSc 92*
**Taub**, Stephan Robert 1933- *AmMWSc 92*
**Taube**, Henry 1915- *AmMWSc 92, IntWW 91, Who 92, WhoNob 90, WhoWest 92*
**Taube**, Myron *DrAPF 91*
**Taube**, Nicholas 1944- *WhoIns 92*
**Taube**, Robert Roy 1936- *WhoMW 92*
**Taube**, Sheila Efron 1941- *AmMWSc 92*
**Taubeneck**, William Harris 1923- *AmMWSc 92*
**Taubenfeld**, Harry Samuel 1929- *WhoAmL 92, WhoRel 92*
**Taubenfeld**, Marc Whitman 1962- *WhoEnt 92*
**Taubenheim**, Toby Charles 1952- *WhoMW 92*
**Tauber**, Alfred Imre 1947- *AmMWSc 92*
**Tauber**, Arthur 1928- *AmMWSc 92*
**Tauber**, Catherine A *AmMWSc 92*
**Tauber**, Gerald Erich 1922- *AmMWSc 92*
**Tauber**, Maurice Jesse 1937- *AmMWSc 92*
**Tauber**, Richard 1891-1948 *NewAmDM*
**Tauber**, Richard 1892-1948 *FacFETw*
**Tauber**, Richard Norman 1940- *AmMWSc 92*
**Tauber**, Selmo 1920- *AmMWSc 92*
**Tauber**, William Charles 1945- *WhoEnt 92*
**Taubert**, Kathryn Anne 1945- *AmMWSc 92*
**Taubert**, Lyall Warren 1920- *WhoAmP 91*
**Taubitz**, Fredricka 1944- *WhoFI 92*
**Taubler**, James H 1935- *AmMWSc 92*
**Taubman**, A. Alfred 1925- *IntWW 91, WhoFI 92, WhoMW 92*
**Taubman**, Howard 1907- *IntWW 91*
**Taubman**, Martin Arnold 1940- *AmMWSc 92*
**Taubman**, Robert Edward 1921- *AmMWSc 92*
**Taubman**, Robert S. 1953- *WhoFI 92*
**Taubman**, Sheldon Bailey 1936- *AmMWSc 92*
**Tauc**, Jan 1922- *AmMWSc 92*
**Taucher**, Fred Horace 1933- *WhoWest 92*
**Tauchert**, Theodore R 1935- *AmMWSc 92*
**Tauer**, Kenneth J 1923- *AmMWSc 92*
**Tauer**, Paul E *WhoAmP 91*
**Tauer**, Paul E. 1941- *WhoWest 92*
**Taufa'ahau TupouIV** 1918- *IntWW 91*
**Taufer**, Jiri d1986 *IntWW 91N*
**Taukalo**, Dawea 1920- *Who 92*
**Tauke**, Steven Donald 1955- *WhoMW 92*
**Tauke**, Thomas J 1950- *WhoAmP 91*
**Taulbee**, Carl D 1928- *AmMWSc 92*
**Taulbee**, Dale B 1936- *AmMWSc 92*
**Taulbee**, Frances Laverne 1937- *WhoAmP 91*
**Taulbert**, Clifton LeMoure 1945- *WhoBlA 92*
**Tauns**, Linard 1922-1968 *LiExTwC*
**Taunt**, Robert B. 1950- *WhoMW 92*
**Taunton**, Archdeacon of *Who 92*
**Taunton**, Bishop Suffragan of 1942- *Who 92*
**Taunton**, Doidge Estcourt 1902- *Who 92*
**Taunton-Rigby**, Alison 1944- *AmMWSc 92*
**Taura**, Yoshinori *WhoWest 92*
**Taurel**, Sidney Afriat 1949- *WhoMW 92*
**Taurman**, John David 1946- *WhoAmL 92*
**Tauro**, Joseph Louis 1931- *WhoAmL 92*
**Taurog**, Alvin 1915- *AmMWSc 92*
**Taus**, Josef 1933- *IntWW 91*
**Taus**, Roger *DrAPF 91*
**Tauschek**, Terrence Alan 1948- *WhoWest 92*
**Tauscher**, William Young 1950- *WhoWest 92*
**Tausig**, Carl 1841-1871 *NewAmDM*
**Tausig**, Michael Robert 1948- *WhoWest 92*
**Tausky**, Vilem 1910- *Who 92*
**Taussig**, Andrew 1929- *AmMWSc 92*
**Taussig**, Andrew Richard 1951- *WhoFI 92*
**Taussig**, Frederick 1913- *WhoMW 92*
**Taussig**, Helen Brooke 1899-1986 *FacFETw*
**Taussig**, Robert Trimble 1938- *WhoWest 92*
**Taussig**, Steven J 1914- *AmMWSc 92*
**Taussky**, Olga 1906- *AmMWSc 92*
**Tautolo**, Agaoleatu Charlie *WhoAmP 91*
**Tautvydas**, Kestutis Jonas 1940- *AmMWSc 92*
**Tauxe**, Welby Newlon 1924- *AmMWSc 92*
**Tauzin**, W.J. 1943- *AlmAP 92 [port], WhoAmP 91*
**Tavaiqia**, Josaia 1930- *Who 92*
**Tavano**, Donald C 1936- *AmMWSc 92*
**Tavard**, Georges Henri 1922- *IntWW 91*
**Tavare**, Andrew Kenneth 1918- *Who 92*
**Tavare**, John 1920- *Who 92*
**Tavares**, Dennis Joseph 1951- *WhoWest 92*
**Tavares**, Donald Francis 1931- *AmMWSc 92*
**Tavares**, Hannibal Manuel 1919- *WhoAmP 91*
**Tavares**, Isabelle Irene 1921- *AmMWSc 92*
**Tavares**, John Manuel 1954- *WhoFI 92, WhoMW 92*
**Tavares**, Joseph 1945- *WhoFI 92*
**Tavares**, Stafford Emanuel 1940- *AmMWSc 92*
**Tavarez**, Jose Luis 1968- *WhoHisp 92*
**Tavassoli**, Mehdi 1933- *AmMWSc 92*
**Tave**, Douglas 1949- *AmMWSc 92*
**Tave**, Stuart Malcolm 1923- *WhoMW 92*
**Taveggia**, Thomas Charles 1943- *WhoWest 92*
**Tavel**, Andrew Gary 1956- *WhoEnt 92*
**Tavel**, James Wilson 1945- *WhoAmL 92*
**Tavel**, Morton 1939- *AmMWSc 92*
**Tavel**, Ronald *DrAPF 91*
**Tavel**, Ronald 1941- *WhoEnt 92, WrDr 92*
**Tavener**, John 1944- *ConCom 92, IntWW 91, Who 92*
**Tavenner**, Herbert Gale 1928- *WhoRel 92*
**Tavenner**, Patricia May *WhoWest 92*
**Taveras**, Juan M 1919- *AmMWSc 92*
**Taverna**, Darice Marie 1951- *WhoFI 92*
**Taverna**, Rodney Elward 1947- *WhoWest 92*
**Tavernas-Guzman**, Juan Aristides 1936- *IntWW 91*
**Taverne**, Dick 1928- *Who 92, WrDr 92*
**Taverner**, John 1490?-1545 *NewAmDM*
**Taverner**, Sonia 1936- *IntWW 91*
**Taverney**, Thomas D. 1946- *WhoWest 92*
**Tavernier**, Bertrand 1941- *IntDcF 2-2 [port], IntMPA 92*
**Tavernier**, Bertrand Rene Maurice 1941- *IntWW 91, WhoEnt 92*
**Taves**, Milton Arthur 1925- *AmMWSc 92*
**Taviani**, Paolo 1931- *IntDcF 2-2, IntMPA 92, IntWW 91*
**Taviani**, Paolo Emilio 1912- *IntWW 91*
**Taviani**, Vittorio 1929- *IntDcF 2-2, IntWW 91*
**Taviano**, Vittorio 1929- *IntMPA 92*
**Tavill**, Anthony Sydney 1936- *AmMWSc 92*
**Tavistock**, Marquess of 1940- *Who 92*
**Tavlarides**, Lawrence Lasky 1942- *AmMWSc 92*
**Tavoularis**, Stavros 1950- *AmMWSc 92*
**Tavrow**, Richard Lawrence 1935- *WhoAmL 92, WhoFI 92*
**Tawarangkoon**, Wuttipan Noi 1959- *WhoFI 92*
**Tawil**, Joseph E. 1913- *WhoRel 92*
**Tax**, Anne 1944- *AmMWSc 92*
**Tax**, Meredith *DrAPF 91*
**Tax**, Sol 1907- *IntWW 91*
**Taxell**, Christoffer 1948- *IntWW 91*
**Tay**, Michael Kie-seng 1935- *WhoMW 92*
**Tay**, Moses Leng Kong *WhoRel 92*
**Taya**, Maawiya Ould Sid'Ahmed 1943- *IntWW 91*
**Taya**, Minoru 1944- *AmMWSc 92*
**Tayama**, Harry K 1935- *AmMWSc 92*
**Tayari**, Kabili 1950- *WhoBlA 92*
**Tayback**, Matthew 1919- *AmMWSc 92*
**Tayback**, Vic 1930?-1990 *ConTFT 9*
**Tayer**, Donald S. 1932- *WhoEnt 92*
**Tayler**, Albert Chevallier 1862-1925 *TwCPaSc*
**Tayler**, Harold Clive 1932- *Who 92*
**Tayler**, John Lionel 1874-1930 *ScFEYrs*
**Tayloe**, Marjorie Ellen Zaerr *WhoEnt 92*
**Taylor** *Who 92*
**Taylor**, Lady 1914- *Who 92*
**Taylor**, A 1911- *AmMWSc 92*
**Taylor**, A. J. P. 1906-1990 *AnObit 1990, FacFETw*
**Taylor**, Adam David 1917- *WhoFI 92*
**Taylor**, Alan *Who 92*
**Taylor**, Alan Broughton 1939- *Who 92*
**Taylor**, Alan D 1947- *AmMWSc 92*
**Taylor**, Alan John Percivale d1990 *IntWW 91N*
**Taylor**, Alan John Percivale 1906- *IntAu&W 91*
**Taylor**, Alan Neil 1934- *AmMWSc 92*
**Taylor**, Albert, Jr. 1957- *WhoBlA 92*
**Taylor**, Albert Cecil 1905- *AmMWSc 92*
**Taylor**, Albert Spencer 1917- *WhoRel 92*
**Taylor**, Alex *NewAmDM*
**Taylor**, Alexander *DrAPF 91*
**Taylor**, Allan 1919- *Who 92*
**Taylor**, Allan Richard 1932- *IntWW 91, WhoFI 92*
**Taylor**, Allen 1946- *AmMWSc 92*
**Taylor**, Alphonse 1937- *WhoAmP 91*
**Taylor**, Anderson *WhoBlA 92*
**Taylor**, Andre Jerome 1946- *WhoBlA 92*
**Taylor**, Andrew 1940- *ConPo 91, WrDr 92*
**Taylor**, Andrew 1951- *WrDr 92*
**Taylor**, Andrew James 1902- *Who 92*
**Taylor**, Andrew John Robert 1951- *IntAu&W 91*
**Taylor**, Andrew McDonald 1940- *IntAu&W 91*
**Taylor**, Andrew Ronald Argo 1921- *AmMWSc 92*
**Taylor**, Angus Ellis 1911- *AmMWSc 92*
**Taylor**, Ann *Who 92*
**Taylor**, Ann R. *DrAPF 91*
**Taylor**, Anna Bernice 1919- *WhoAmP 91*
**Taylor**, Anna Diggs 1932- *NotBlAW 92, WhoAmL 92, WhoBlA 92, WhoMW 92*
**Taylor**, Anna Newman 1933- *AmMWSc 92*
**Taylor**, Anthony Louis 1958- *WhoMW 92*
**Taylor**, Archer S 1916- *AmMWSc 92*
**Taylor**, Ardell Nichols 1917- *AmMWSc 92*
**Taylor**, Arlene M. J. 1955- *WhoBlA 92*
**Taylor**, Arnold H. 1929- *WhoBlA 92*
**Taylor**, Arnold Joseph 1911- *IntWW 91, Who 92*
**Taylor**, Arthur Duane 1920- *WhoBlA 92*
**Taylor**, Arthur Godfrey 1925- *Who 92*
**Taylor**, Arthur John 1919- *Who 92*
**Taylor**, Arthur R. *LesBEnT 92*
**Taylor**, Arthur Robert 1935- *IntWW 91, Who 92*
**Taylor**, Arthur Ronald 1921- *Who 92*
**Taylor**, Arthur William Charles 1913- *Who 92*
**Taylor**, Aubrey Elmo 1933- *AmMWSc 92*
**Taylor**, Austin Laurence 1932- *AmMWSc 92*
**Taylor**, Austin Starke, Jr 1922- *WhoAmP 91*
**Taylor**, B Gray 1924- *AmMWSc 92*
**Taylor**, Barney Edsel 1951- *AmMWSc 92*
**Taylor**, Barrie Frederick 1939- *AmMWSc 92*
**Taylor**, Barry Edward 1947- *AmMWSc 92*
**Taylor**, Barry L 1937- *AmMWSc 92*
**Taylor**, Barry Michael 1958- *WhoAmL 92*
**Taylor**, Barry Norman 1936- *AmMWSc 92*
**Taylor**, Bayard 1825-1878 *BenetAL 91, BibAL 8*
**Taylor**, Benjamin Joseph 1942- *AmMWSc 92*
**Taylor**, Bernard David 1935- *IntWW 91, Who 92*
**Taylor**, Bernard Franklin 1930- *AmMWSc 92*
**Taylor**, Bert Leston 1866-1921 *BenetAL 91*
**Taylor**, Bert Leston, and Ward, Edward *ScFEYrs*
**Taylor**, Betty Jo 1933- *WhoEnt 92*
**Taylor**, Beverley Ann Price 1951- *AmMWSc 92*
**Taylor**, Billy 1921- *FacFETw, NewAmDM*
**Taylor**, Bobby Joe 1943- *WhoAmP 91*
**Taylor**, Brenda Elizabeth 1955- *WhoWest 92*
**Taylor**, Brenda L. 1949- *WhoBlA 92*
**Taylor**, Brian *DrAPF 91*
**Taylor**, Brian David 1954- *WhoWest 92*
**Taylor**, Brian Hyde 1931- *Who 92*
**Taylor**, Brian William 1933- *Who 92*
**Taylor**, Bruce *DrAPF 91*
**Taylor**, Bruce 1921- *TwCPaSc*
**Taylor**, Bruce Cahill 1942- *AmMWSc 92*
**Taylor**, Burton d1991 *NewYTBS 91*
**Taylor**, Byron Keith 1955- *WhoMW 92*
**Taylor**, C E 1924- *AmMWSc 92*
**Taylor**, C P S 1930- *AmMWSc 92*
**Taylor**, Camille Kay 1948- *WhoEnt 92*
**Taylor**, Carl Ernest 1916- *AmMWSc 92, IntWW 91*
**Taylor**, Carl Larsen 1937- *WhoAmL 92*
**Taylor**, Carole Lillian *WhoBlA 92*
**Taylor**, Carolyn *WhoAmP 91*
**Taylor**, Carroll Stribling 1944- *WhoAmL 92*
**Taylor**, Carson William 1942- *AmMWSc 92*
**Taylor**, Casper R, Jr 1934- *WhoAmP 91*
**Taylor**, Cassandra W. 1951- *WhoBlA 92*
**Taylor**, Cavan 1935- *Who 92*
**Taylor**, Cecil 1933- *NewAmDM*
**Taylor**, Cecil P 1929-1981 *FacFETw*
**Taylor**, Celianna I. *WhoMW 92*
**Taylor**, Charity *Who 92*
**Taylor**, Charles 1922- *WrDr 92*
**Taylor**, Charles 1931- *IntWW 91*
**Taylor**, Charles 1941- *WhoAmP 91*
**Taylor**, Charles, Jr 1929- *WhoAmP 91*
**Taylor**, Charles Avon *WhoBlA 92*
**Taylor**, Charles Avon 1951- *WhoMW 92*
**Taylor**, Charles Bruce 1915- *AmMWSc 92*
**Taylor**, Charles E. 1944- *WhoBlA 92*
**Taylor**, Charles Edward 1931- *WhoAmL 92, WhoBlA 92*
**Taylor**, Charles Ellett 1945- *AmMWSc 92*
**Taylor**, Charles Emery 1940- *AmMWSc 92*
**Taylor**, Charles H. 1941- *AlmAP 92 [port]*
**Taylor**, Charles Joel 1919- *AmMWSc 92*
**Taylor**, Charles Margrave 1931- *Who 92*
**Taylor**, Charles Owen 1949- *WhoAmL 92*
**Taylor**, Charles Richard 1939- *AmMWSc 92*
**Taylor**, Charles Wade 1956- *WhoWest 92*
**Taylor**, Charles William 1878-1960 *TwCPaSc*
**Taylor**, Charles William 1930- *AmMWSc 92*
**Taylor**, Charley R. 1942- *WhoBlA 92*
**Taylor**, Charlotte DeBernier Scarbrough 1806-1861 *BiInAmS*
**Taylor**, Chris 1948- *WhoEnt 92*
**Taylor**, Christine *TwCPaSc*
**Taylor**, Christopher E *AmMWSc 92*
**Taylor**, Christopher Lenard 1923- *WhoBlA 92*
**Taylor**, Claire McKechnie 1927- *WhoEnt 92*
**Taylor**, Clarence B. 1937- *WhoBlA 92*
**Taylor**, Claude I. 1925- *WhoFI 92*
**Taylor**, Clayborne D 1938- *AmMWSc 92*
**Taylor**, Cledie Collins 1926- *WhoBlA 92*
**Taylor**, Clifford 1941- *Who 92*
**Taylor**, Clive Roy 1944- *AmMWSc 92*
**Taylor**, Clyde D 1937- *WhoAmP 91*
**Taylor**, Comer L., Jr. 1949- *WhoBlA 92*
**Taylor**, Conciere *DrAPF 91*
**Taylor**, Constance Elaine Southern 1937- *AmMWSc 92*
**Taylor**, Constance Lindsay *WrDr 92*
**Taylor**, Cordy 1925- *WhoAmP 91*
**Taylor**, Craig P 1957- *WhoAmP 91*
**Taylor**, Cyril 1935- *Who 92*
**Taylor**, D Dax 1937- *AmMWSc 92*
**Taylor**, D Jane *AmMWSc 92*
**Taylor**, D Lansing 1946- *AmMWSc 92*
**Taylor**, Daisy Curry 1948- *WhoBlA 92*
**Taylor**, Dale B. 1939- *WhoBlA 92*
**Taylor**, Dale Frederick 1944- *AmMWSc 92*
**Taylor**, Dallas Jeffrey 1944- *WhoFI 92*
**Taylor**, Dalmas A. 1933- *WhoBlA 92*
**Taylor**, Daniel Brumhall Cochrane 1921- *Who 92*
**Taylor**, David 1928- *WhoFI 92*
**Taylor**, David 1934- *WrDr 92*
**Taylor**, David Brooke 1942- *WhoAmL 92*
**Taylor**, David Byron 1953- *WhoMW 92*
**Taylor**, David Cobb 1939- *AmMWSc 92*
**Taylor**, David G. 1966- *WhoEnt 92*

**Taylor,** David George Pendleton 1933- Who 92
**Taylor,** David James 1951- AmMWSc 92
**Taylor,** David John 1947- Who 92
**Taylor,** David Lee 1944- WhoMW 92
**Taylor,** David Neely 1948- AmMWSc 92
**Taylor,** David Neil 1954- WhoRel 92
**Taylor,** David Vassar 1945- WhoBlA 92
**Taylor,** David Ward 1938- AmMWSc 92
**Taylor,** David Wyatt Aiken 1925- WhoRel 92
**Taylor,** Dawn TwCPaSc
**Taylor,** Deems 1885-1966 NewAmDM
**Taylor,** DeForrest Walker 1933- WhoBlA 92
**Taylor,** Delbert Harry, Jr. 1934- WhoRel 92
**Taylor,** Delores 1939- IntMPA 92
**Taylor,** Dennis Del 1943- WhoMW 92
**Taylor,** Dennis Howard 1944- WhoFI 92
**Taylor,** Derek 1930- Who 92
**Taylor,** Dermot Brownrigg 1915- AmMWSc 92
**Taylor,** Desmond S. Who 92
**Taylor,** Diane Wallace AmMWSc 92
**Taylor,** Domini WrDr 92
**Taylor,** Don 1920- IntMPA 92
**Taylor,** Don Lee 1932- WhoAmP 91
**Taylor,** Donald 1945- TwCPaSc
**Taylor,** Donald Curtis 1939- AmMWSc 92
**Taylor,** Donald Eldridge, III 1953- WhoMW 92
**Taylor,** Donald Fulton, Sr. 1932- WhoBlA 92
**Taylor,** Donald James 1933- AmMWSc 92
**Taylor,** Donald Leon 1938- WhoRel 92
**Taylor,** Doris Denice 1955- WhoMW 92
**Taylor,** Dorothy Francine 1907- WhoAmP 91
**Taylor,** Dorothy Harris 1931- WhoFI 92
**Taylor,** Douglas Hiram 1939- AmMWSc 92
**Taylor,** Douglas Hugh Charles 1938- Who 92
**Taylor,** Duane Francis 1925- AmMWSc 92
**Taylor,** Duncan Paul 1949- AmMWSc 92
**Taylor,** Dwight Willard 1932- AmMWSc 92
**Taylor,** E. Douglas 1941- WhoFI 92, WhoWest 92
**Taylor,** Earl Chip 1950- WhoEnt 92
**Taylor,** Eddie Milton 1945- WhoWest 92
**Taylor,** Edna Jane 1934- WhoWest 92
**Taylor,** Edward 1642?-1729 BenetAL 91
**Taylor,** Edward Curtis 1923- AmMWSc 92
**Taylor,** Edward Donald 1940- AmMWSc 92
**Taylor,** Edward Macmillan 1937- Who 92
**Taylor,** Edward McKinley, Jr. 1928- WhoAmL 92
**Taylor,** Edward Morgan 1933- AmMWSc 92
**Taylor,** Edward Randolph 1844-1917 BiInAmS
**Taylor,** Edward S. d1991 NewYTBS 91
**Taylor,** Edward S 1903- AmMWSc 92
**Taylor,** Edward Stewart 1911- AmMWSc 92
**Taylor,** Edward Thompson 1793-1871 BenetAL 91
**Taylor,** Edward Walter 1926- WhoBlA 92
**Taylor,** Edward William 1953- WhoFI 92
**Taylor,** Edwin Floriman 1931- AmMWSc 92
**Taylor,** Edwin William 1929- AmMWSc 92, Who 92
**Taylor,** Eleanor Ross DrAPF 91
**Taylor,** Elenor Rita 1959- WhoAmL 92
**Taylor,** Elinor Z 1921- WhoAmP 91
**Taylor,** Elisabeth 1931- ConAu 135
**Taylor,** Elizabeth 1912-1975 FacFETw, RfGEnL 91
**Taylor,** Elizabeth 1932- FacFETw, IntMPA 92, IntWW 91, Who 92, WhoEnt 92
**Taylor,** Elizabeth Ann 1952- WhoFI 92
**Taylor,** Elizabeth Beaman Hesch 1921- AmMWSc 92
**Taylor,** Elizabeth Jane 1941- WhoFI 92
**Taylor,** Ellis Clarence, Sr. 1931- WhoBlA 92
**Taylor,** Ellison Hall 1913- AmMWSc 92
**Taylor,** Eric 1909- TwCPaSc
**Taylor,** Eric 1931- Who 92
**Taylor,** Eric Alan 1924- TwCPaSc
**Taylor,** Eric Robert 1947- AmMWSc 92
**Taylor,** Eric Scollick 1918- Who 92
**Taylor,** Eric W. 1909- Who 92
**Taylor,** Ernest Norman, Jr. 1953- WhoBlA 92
**Taylor,** Ernest Richard 1910- Who 92
**Taylor,** Estelle Wormley 1924- WhoBlA 92
**Taylor,** Eugene Donaldson 1922- WhoBlA 92
**Taylor,** Eugene M 1932- AmMWSc 92
**Taylor,** Eva 1895-1977 NotBlAW 92 [port]
**Taylor,** Eva Marietta WhoMW 92
**Taylor,** Felicia Michelle 1960- WhoBlA 92
**Taylor,** Fletcher Brandon, Jr 1929- AmMWSc 92
**Taylor,** Florietta Mae 1931- WhoAmP 91
**Taylor,** Floyd Heckman 1926- AmMWSc 92
**Taylor,** Francine Marie Conat 1937- WhoEnt 92
**Taylor,** Francis B 1925- AmMWSc 92
**Taylor,** Frank Who 92, WrDr 92
**Taylor,** Frank 1915- Who 92
**Taylor,** Frank Edward 1957- WhoEnt 92
**Taylor,** Frank Eugene 1942- AmMWSc 92
**Taylor,** Frank Henry 1907- Who 92
**Taylor,** Frank Henry 1932- Who 92
**Taylor,** Frank John Rupert 1939- AmMWSc 92
**Taylor,** Fraser 1960- TwCPaSc
**Taylor,** Fred WhoAmP 91
**Taylor,** Fred J. 1919- WrDr 92
**Taylor,** Fred M 1919- AmMWSc 92
**Taylor,** Fred William 1932- AmMWSc 92
**Taylor,** Frederick Clayton 1954- WhoWest 92
**Taylor,** Frederick William, Jr. 1933- WhoAmL 92
**Taylor,** Frederick Winslow 1856-1915 BiInAmS
**Taylor,** Fredric William 1944- AmMWSc 92, Who 92
**Taylor,** Fredrick James 1940- AmMWSc 92
**Taylor,** G Jeffrey 1944- AmMWSc 92
**Taylor,** Gary 1952- AmMWSc 92
**Taylor,** Gary Allen 1961- WhoAmL 92
**Taylor,** Gary Eugene 1953- WhoAmP 91
**Taylor,** Gary N 1942- AmMWSc 92
**Taylor,** Gary S 1943- WhoAmP 91
**Taylor,** Gayland Wayne 1958- WhoBlA 92
**Taylor,** Gene 1928- WhoAmP 91
**Taylor,** Gene 1953- AlmAP 92 [port]
**Taylor,** Gene Warren 1936- AmMWSc 92
**Taylor,** Geoff W AmMWSc 92
**Taylor,** Geoffrey H. Who 92
**Taylor,** Geoffrey William 1927- Who 92
**Taylor,** George 1904- IntWW 91, Who 92
**Taylor,** George Blaney, III 1946- WhoRel 92
**Taylor,** George Evans, Jr 1949- AmMWSc 92
**Taylor,** George N., Jr. 1945- WhoBlA 92
**Taylor,** George Stanley 1920- AmMWSc 92
**Taylor,** George Thomas 1935- AmMWSc 92
**Taylor,** George William 1934- AmMWSc 92
**Taylor,** Gerald C 1919- AmMWSc 92
**Taylor,** Gerald Reed, Jr 1937- AmMWSc 92
**Taylor,** Gerard William 1920- Who 92
**Taylor,** Gilbert Leon 1937- WhoBlA 92
**Taylor,** Gladys Gillman 1926- AmMWSc 92
**Taylor,** Glen H 1904-1984 FacFETw
**Taylor,** Gloria Jean WhoBlA 92
**Taylor,** Godfrey Who 92
**Taylor,** Gordon DrAPF 91
**Taylor,** Gordon 1944- Who 92
**Taylor,** Gordon Stevens 1921- AmMWSc 92
**Taylor,** Gordon William 1928- Who 92
**Taylor,** Graham 1857-1938 DcAmImH
**Taylor,** Graham 1944- Who 92
**Taylor,** Gregory WhoEnt 92
**Taylor,** Gregory Blackwell 1930- WhoRel 92
**Taylor,** Gregory Scott 1960- WhoFI 92
**Taylor,** Greville Laughton 1902- Who 92
**Taylor,** Guy Watson 1919- WhoEnt 92
**Taylor,** H Baldwin IntAu&W 91X, WrDr 92
**Taylor,** Harlin R 1948- WhoAmP 91
**Taylor,** Harold Allison, Jr 1942- AmMWSc 92
**Taylor,** Harold Evans 1939- AmMWSc 92
**Taylor,** Harold Joseph 1904- Who 92
**Taylor,** Harold Leland 1920- AmMWSc 92
**Taylor,** Harold Leon 1946- WhoBlA 92
**Taylor,** Harold McCarter 1907- IntWW 91, Who 92
**Taylor,** Harold Mellon 1929- AmMWSc 92
**Taylor,** Harold Nathaniel 1921- AmMWSc 92
**Taylor,** Harry Danner 1944- WhoFI 92
**Taylor,** Harry Elmer 1931- AmMWSc 92
**Taylor,** Harry Grant 1908- WhoAmP 91
**Taylor,** Harry William 1925- AmMWSc 92
**Taylor,** Helen 1947- ConAu 133
**Taylor,** Henry DrAPF 91
**Taylor,** Henry 1942- IntAu&W 91, WrDr 92
**Taylor,** Henry George 1904- Who 92
**Taylor,** Henry Louis, Jr. 1943- WhoBlA 92
**Taylor,** Henry Marshall 1932- WhoBlA 92
**Taylor,** Henry Milton 1903- IntWW 91, Who 92
**Taylor,** Herbert Charles 1948- WhoBlA 92
**Taylor,** Herbert Douglas 1888?-1918 BiInAmS
**Taylor,** Herbert Lyndon 1931- AmMWSc 92
**Taylor,** Herman Daniel 1937- WhoBlA 92
**Taylor,** Hermon 1905- Who 92
**Taylor,** Howard Edward 1922- AmMWSc 92
**Taylor,** Howard F. 1939- WhoBlA 92
**Taylor,** Howard Lawrence 1938- AmMWSc 92
**Taylor,** Howard Melvin 1924- AmMWSc 92
**Taylor,** Howard Milton, III 1937- AmMWSc 92
**Taylor,** Howard S 1935- AmMWSc 92
**Taylor,** Hubert Lee 1943- WhoAmP 91
**Taylor,** Hugh P, Jr 1932- AmMWSc 92
**Taylor,** Humphrey Vincent Who 92
**Taylor,** Hycel B. 1936- WhoBlA 92
**Taylor,** Iain Edgar Park 1938- AmMWSc 92
**Taylor,** Ian Colin 1945- Who 92
**Taylor,** Ian Galbraith 1924- Who 92
**Taylor,** Iris WhoBlA 92
**Taylor,** Irving 1912- WhoFI 92, WhoWest 92
**Taylor,** Isaac Montrose 1921- AmMWSc 92
**Taylor,** Ivor Ralph 1927- Who 92
**Taylor,** J Herbert 1916- AmMWSc 92
**Taylor,** J Paul WhoAmP 91, WhoHisp 92
**Taylor,** J.R. 1950- WhoMW 92
**Taylor,** Jack 1930- TwCPaSc
**Taylor,** Jack Alvin, Jr. 1949- WhoBlA 92
**Taylor,** Jack Arthur 1935- WhoEnt 92
**Taylor,** Jack Eldon 1926- AmMWSc 92
**Taylor,** Jack Howard 1922- AmMWSc 92
**Taylor,** Jack J WhoAmP 91
**Taylor,** Jackie 1935- WhoAmP 91
**Taylor,** Jackson Johnson 1918- AmMWSc 92
**Taylor,** James DrAPF 91
**Taylor,** James 1902- IntWW 91, Who 92
**Taylor,** James 1922- WhoBlA 92
**Taylor,** James 1948- NewAmDM
**Taylor,** James A 1939- AmMWSc 92
**Taylor,** James Bennett 1943- WhoFI 92
**Taylor,** James Boyd 1919- WhoFI 92
**Taylor,** James C. 1930- WhoBlA 92
**Taylor,** James Coleridge 1922- WhoBlA 92
**Taylor,** James E. WhoAmL 92
**Taylor,** James Earl 1916- AmMWSc 92
**Taylor,** James Ellsworth 1953- WhoWest 92
**Taylor,** James Elton 1947- WhoBlA 92
**Taylor,** James Francis 1951- WhoFI 92
**Taylor,** James Gavin 1932- WhoWest 92
**Taylor,** James H 1929- AmMWSc 92
**Taylor,** James Harry, II 1951- WhoMW 92
**Taylor,** James Herbert 1916- IntWW 91
**Taylor,** James Hugh 1940- AmMWSc 92
**Taylor,** James I WhoIns 92
**Taylor,** James Kenneth 1929- AmMWSc 92
**Taylor,** James Lee 1931- AmMWSc 92
**Taylor,** James Marion, II 1926- WhoFI 92
**Taylor,** James Spratt 1928- WhoAmL 92
**Taylor,** James Vandigriff 1931- AmMWSc 92
**Taylor,** James Vernon 1948- WhoEnt 92
**Taylor,** James Walter 1933- WhoFI 92, WhoWest 92
**Taylor,** James Welch 1935- AmMWSc 92
**Taylor,** Janelle 1944- WrDr 92
**Taylor,** Janice A. 1954- WhoBlA 92
**Taylor,** Javin Morse 1936- AmMWSc 92
**Taylor,** Jay Eugene 1918- AmMWSc 92
**Taylor,** Jayne WrDr 92
**Taylor,** Jean 1916- Who 92
**Taylor,** Jean Ellen 1944- AmMWSc 92
**Taylor,** Jean Marie 1932- AmMWSc 92
**Taylor,** Jeanette Eileen 1960- WhoAmL 92
**Taylor,** Jeff 1960- WhoBlA 92
**Taylor,** Jennifer 1935- WrDr 92
**Taylor,** Jennifer Narog 1957- WhoAmL 92
**Taylor,** Jerome 1940- WhoBlA 92
**Taylor,** Jerry Duncan 1938- AmMWSc 92
**Taylor,** Jerry Lynn 1947- AmMWSc 92
**Taylor,** Jesse Elliott, Jr. WhoBlA 92
**Taylor,** Jessie Who 92
**Taylor,** Jill WhoEnt 92
**Taylor,** Jim 1937- TwCPaSc
**Taylor,** Jim Daniel 1954- WhoRel 92
**Taylor,** Job, III 1942- WhoAmL 92
**Taylor,** Jocelyn Mary 1931- AmMWSc 92, WhoMW 92
**Taylor,** Joe DrAPF 91
**Taylor,** Joe Clinton 1942- WhoAmL 92
**Taylor,** John 1703-1772 BlkwCEP
**Taylor,** John 1753-1824 BenetAL 91
**Taylor,** John 1808-1887 RelLAm 91
**Taylor,** John 1931- WrDr 92
**Taylor,** John 1936- TwCPaSc
**Taylor,** John 1937- WrDr 92
**Taylor,** John 1952- TwCPaSc
**Taylor,** John 1955- WhoAmP 91
**Taylor,** John Alfred DrAPF 91
**Taylor,** John Barrington 1914- Who 92
**Taylor,** John Baxter, Jr 1882-1908 BlkOlyM [port]
**Taylor,** John Bernard Who 92
**Taylor,** John Brian 1946- WhoFI 92
**Taylor,** John Bryan 1928- IntWW 91, Who 92
**Taylor,** John C 1925- WhoAmP 91
**Taylor,** John Charles 1931- Who 92
**Taylor,** John Chestnut, III 1928- WhoAmL 92
**Taylor,** John Christopher 1936- AmMWSc 92
**Taylor,** John Clayton 1930- IntWW 91, Who 92
**Taylor,** John Comer 1953- WhoEnt 92
**Taylor,** John Curtis 1951- WhoEnt 92
**Taylor,** John D. Who 92
**Taylor,** John David 1937- Who 92
**Taylor,** John Dirk 1939- AmMWSc 92
**Taylor,** John Earl 1935- WhoRel 92
**Taylor,** John Edgar 1931- AmMWSc 92
**Taylor,** John Felton, II 1925- WhoWest 92
**Taylor,** John Frederick 1944- WhoWest 92
**Taylor,** John Fuller 1912- AmMWSc 92
**Taylor,** John Gardiner Veitch 1926- AmMWSc 92
**Taylor,** John Gerald 1931- IntAu&W 91, Who 92
**Taylor,** John H. Who 92
**Taylor,** John Hall 1922- AmMWSc 92
**Taylor,** John Jacob 1928- AmMWSc 92
**Taylor,** John Joseph 1922- AmMWSc 92
**Taylor,** John Joseph 1925- AmMWSc 92
**Taylor,** John Keenan 1912- AmMWSc 92
**Taylor,** John L. 1947- WhoBlA 92
**Taylor,** John Lang 1924- Who 92
**Taylor,** John Langdon, Jr 1928- AmMWSc 92
**Taylor,** John Laverack 1937- IntAu&W 91
**Taylor,** John Lee 1933- WhoRel 92
**Taylor,** John Lockhart 1927- WhoWest 92
**Taylor,** John Mark 1941- Who 92
**Taylor,** John Marston 1941- AmMWSc 92
**Taylor,** John Mitchell Who 92
**Taylor,** John Nunlist 1905- WhoFI 92
**Taylor,** John R 1946- WhoAmP 91
**Taylor,** John Ralph Carlisle d1991 Who 92N
**Taylor,** John Read, Jr. 1943- WhoFI 92
**Taylor,** John Richard 1945- WhoFI 92
**Taylor,** John Robert WrDr 92
**Taylor,** John Robert 1939- AmMWSc 92
**Taylor,** John Russell 1935- IntAu&W 91, IntMPA 92, IntWW 91, Who 92, WrDr 92
**Taylor,** John Scott 1955- WhoFI 92
**Taylor,** John Sherrod 1947- WhoAmL 92
**Taylor,** John Vernon 1914- DcEcMov, IntAu&W 91, Who 92, WrDr 92
**Taylor,** John W. 1753-1824 AmPolLe
**Taylor,** John Wilkinson 1906- WhoMW 92
**Taylor,** John William 1946- AmMWSc 92
**Taylor,** John William Ransom 1922- IntAu&W 91, Who 92, WrDr 92
**Taylor,** Jonathan Francis 1935- Who 92
**Taylor,** Jonathan Wardwell 1944- WhoFI 92
**Taylor,** Joseph Christopher 1959- WhoEnt 92
**Taylor,** Joseph Hooton, Jr 1941- AmMWSc 92
**Taylor,** Joseph Lawrence 1941- AmMWSc 92
**Taylor,** Joseph T. 1913- WhoBlA 92
**Taylor,** Judy 1932- IntAu&W 91, Who 92
**Taylor,** Julane Hart 1953- WhoRel 92
**Taylor,** Julia W. WhoFI 92
**Taylor,** Julia W. 1936- WhoBlA 92
**Taylor,** Julius David 1913- AmMWSc 92
**Taylor,** Julius H. 1914- WhoBlA 92
**Taylor,** June Laffoon 1921- WhoAmP 91
**Taylor,** June Ruth 1932- WhoRel 92
**Taylor,** Kate NewAmDM
**Taylor,** Kathleen C 1942- AmMWSc 92
**Taylor,** Keith Breden 1924- Who 92
**Taylor,** Keith Edward 1946- AmMWSc 92
**Taylor,** Keith Henry 1938- Who 92
**Taylor,** Ken 1922- IntWW 91
**Taylor,** Kendrick Jay 1914- WhoWest 92
**Taylor,** Kenneth 1921- Who 92
**Taylor,** Kenneth Boivin 1935- AmMWSc 92
**Taylor,** Kenneth D. 1934- IntWW 91
**Taylor,** Kenneth Doyle 1949- AmMWSc 92, WhoBlA 92
**Taylor,** Kenneth Grant 1936- AmMWSc 92
**Taylor,** Kenneth J W 1939- AmMWSc 92
**Taylor,** Kenneth John 1929- Who 92
**Taylor,** Kenneth Lapham 1941- AmMWSc 92
**Taylor,** Kenneth MacDonald 1947- Who 92
**Taylor,** Kenneth Matthew WhoBlA 92
**Taylor,** Kenneth William 1953- WhoFI 92, WhoMW 92
**Taylor,** Kent DrAPF 91
**Taylor,** Kim Who 92
**Taylor,** Kimberly Hayes 1962- WhoBlA 92

Taylor, Kirman 1920- AmMWSc 92
Taylor, Koko WhoEnt 92, WhoMW 92
Taylor, Larry Lee 1949- WhoRel 92
Taylor, Larry Thomas 1939- AmMWSc 92
Taylor, Laura Anne 1958- WhoAmL 92
Taylor, Laurie DrAPF 91, Who 92
Taylor, Lauriston Sale 1902- AmMWSc 92
Taylor, Lawrence August 1938- AmMWSc 92
Taylor, Lawrence Dow 1932- AmMWSc 92
Taylor, Lawrence Jay 1946- WhoEnt 92
Taylor, Lawrence Julius 1959- WhoBlA 92
Taylor, Leigh Herbert 1941- WhoAmL 92
Taylor, Leighton Robert, Jr 1940- AmMWSc 92, WhoWest 92
Taylor, Len Clive 1922- Who 92
Taylor, Leon Eric Manners 1917- Who 92
Taylor, Leonard Campbell 1874-1969 TwCPaSc
Taylor, Leonard S 1928- AmMWSc 92
Taylor, Leonard Wayne 1946- WhoBlA 92
Taylor, Leslie George 1922- WhoWest 92
Taylor, Lester D 1938- IntAu&W 91, WrDr 92
Taylor, Lester Dean 1938- WhoFI 92
Taylor, Levola WhoAmP 91
Taylor, Lewis Arthur, III 1947- WhoFI 92
Taylor, Lincoln Homer 1920- AmMWSc 92
Taylor, Linda 1959- TwCPaSc
Taylor, Linda Suzanna 1947- WhoBlA 92
Taylor, Lindajean Thorton 1942- WhoWest 92
Taylor, Lisa 1933-1991 ConAu 134, NewYTBS 91 [port]
Taylor, Lisa 1963- WhoEnt 92
Taylor, Lisa Monet 1961- WhoRel 92
Taylor, Livingston NewAmDM
Taylor, Liz McNeill ConAu 135
Taylor, Lloyd David 1933- AmMWSc 92
Taylor, Louis Henry 1944- WhoWest 92
Taylor, Lulu TwCPaSc
Taylor, Luther L, Jr 1949- WhoAmP 91
Taylor, Lyle Herman 1936- AmMWSc 92
Taylor, Lynn Boggess 1945- WhoMW 92
Taylor, Lynn Franklin 1945- WhoAmL 92
Taylor, Lynn Johnston 1936- AmMWSc 92
Taylor, Lynnette Dobbins WhoBlA 92
Taylor, Malcolm Who 92
Taylor, Malcolm 1960- WhoBlA 92
Taylor, Malcolm Herbert 1942- AmMWSc 92
Taylor, Marcella B. DrAPF 91
Taylor, Maretta M 1935- WhoAmP 91
Taylor, Margaret 1917- WhoBlA 92
Taylor, Margaret Condon DrAPF 91
Taylor, Margaret Jessie 1924- Who 92
Taylor, Margaret Turner 1944- WhoFI 92
Taylor, Marie de Porres 1947- WhoBlA 92, WhoRel 92
Taylor, Marigold 1922- TwCPaSc
Taylor, Mark 1954- WhoFI 92
Taylor, Mark Alan 1955- WhoMW 92
Taylor, Mark Alan 1959- WhoWest 92
Taylor, Mark Christopher 1958- Who 92
Taylor, Mark Cooper 1945- WhoRel 92
Taylor, Mark Edward 1953- WhoAmP 91
Taylor, Mark Fletcher 1957- WhoAmP 91
Taylor, Mark Lloyd 1953- WhoRel 92
Taylor, Mark William 1952- WhoEnt 92
Taylor, Marlene Ann Zarecki 1954- WhoEnt 92
Taylor, Martha 1941- WhoBlA 92
Taylor, Martha Loeb 1949- AmMWSc 92
Taylor, Mary Cutis Smith 1937- WhoEnt 92
Taylor, Mary D. 1936- WhoWest 92
Taylor, Mary Elizabeth 1933- WhoWest 92
Taylor, Mary Lowell Branson 1932- AmMWSc 92
Taylor, Matthew Owen John 1963- Who 92
Taylor, Maurice Who 92
Taylor, Maurice Clifton 1950- WhoBlA 92
Taylor, Maxwell Davenport 1901-1987 FacFETw
Taylor, Meldrick 1966- BlkOlyM
Taylor, Merlin Gene 1936- AmMWSc 92
Taylor, Mertz Anderson, Jr 1927- WhoAmP 91
Taylor, Meshach IntMPA 92, WhoBlA 92, WhoEnt 92
Taylor, Michael IntMPA 92
Taylor, Michael 1958- WhoBlA 92
Taylor, Michael Alan 1940- AmMWSc 92
Taylor, Michael Dee 1940- AmMWSc 92
Taylor, Michael E 1939- AmMWSc 92
Taylor, Michael Earl 1952- WhoAmP 91
Taylor, Michael Goodiff d1991 Who 92N
Taylor, Michael Hugh 1936- IntWW 91, Who 92
Taylor, Michael J. 1924- WrDr 92
Taylor, Michael J H 1949- ConAu 34NR
Taylor, Michael James 1941- WhoWest 92
Taylor, Michael Lee 1941- AmMWSc 92
Taylor, Michael Loeb 1947- WhoBlA 92
Taylor, Mildred D IntAu&W 91, WrDr 92
Taylor, Mildred D. 1943- WhoBlA 92
Taylor, Mildred E. Crosby 1919- WhoBlA 92
Taylor, Miles Edward 1964- WhoBlA 92
Taylor, Millard Benjamin 1913- WhoEnt 92
Taylor, Milton William 1931- AmMWSc 92
Taylor, Minna 1947- WhoAmL 92, WhoEnt 92
Taylor, Morris Chapman 1939- AmMWSc 92
Taylor, Morris D 1934- AmMWSc 92
Taylor, Murray East 1915- AmMWSc 92
Taylor, Natch 1948- WhoEnt 92
Taylor, Nathalee Britton 1941- WhoFI 92
Taylor, Neil G. 1950- WhoAmL 92
Taylor, Neville 1930- Who 92
Taylor, Nicholas George Frederick 1917- Who 92
Taylor, Nicholas Richard S. Who 92
Taylor, Nick Ray 1956- WhoAmL 92
Taylor, Noel C 1924- WhoAmP 91, WhoBlA 92
Taylor, Norman Eugene 1948- WhoBlA 92
Taylor, Norman Fletcher 1928- AmMWSc 92
Taylor, Norman Linn 1926- AmMWSc 92
Taylor, Octavia G. 1925- WhoBlA 92
Taylor, Oliver Clifton 1918- AmMWSc 92
Taylor, Orlando L. 1936- WhoBlA 92
Taylor, Palmer William 1938- AmMWSc 92
Taylor, Patricia E. 1942- WhoBlA 92
Taylor, Patricia Tate 1954- WhoBlA 92
Taylor, Patrick Timothy 1938- AmMWSc 92
Taylor, Paul 1930- FacFETw
Taylor, Paul B. 1930- IntWW 91
Taylor, Paul D 1939- WhoAmP 91
Taylor, Paul David 1937- WhoBlA 92
Taylor, Paul Duane 1940- AmMWSc 92
Taylor, Paul John 1939- AmMWSc 92
Taylor, Paul M 1927- AmMWSc 92
Taylor, Paul Peak 1921- AmMWSc 92
Taylor, Pauline J. 1911- WhoBlA 92
Taylor, Perry Lee, Jr. 1948- WhoAmL 92
Taylor, Peter DrAPF 91
Taylor, Peter 1917- BenetAL 91, ConNov 91
Taylor, Peter 1919- WrDr 92
Taylor, Peter 1924- Who 92
Taylor, Peter 1930- Who 92
Taylor, Peter 1949- AmMWSc 92
Taylor, Peter Anthony 1932- AmMWSc 92
Taylor, Peter Berkley 1933- AmMWSc 92
Taylor, Peter D 1942- AmMWSc 92
Taylor, Peter van Voorhees 1934- WhoWest 92
Taylor, Peter William Edward 1917- Who 92
Taylor, Philip Craig 1942- AmMWSc 92
Taylor, Philip Liddon 1937- AmMWSc 92
Taylor, Philippe Arthur 1937- Who 92
Taylor, Phillip R 1948- AmMWSc 92
Taylor, Phyllis Johnstone 1933- WhoRel 92
Taylor, Phyllis Mary Constance 1926- Who 92
Taylor, Prince Albert, Jr. 1907- WhoBlA 92
Taylor, Priscilla G 1931- WhoAmP 91
Taylor, Quintard, Jr. 1948- WhoBlA 92
Taylor, R John 1930- AmMWSc 92
Taylor, Ralph Dale 1945- AmMWSc 92
Taylor, Ralph Orien, Jr. 1919- WhoMW 92
Taylor, Ralph Wilson 1937- AmMWSc 92
Taylor, Randall William 1948- WhoMW 92
Taylor, Randy Steven 1951- WhoWest 92
Taylor, Ray Allen 1923- WhoAmP 91
Taylor, Ray Counsel 1926- WhoAmP 91
Taylor, Raymond Dean 1928- AmMWSc 92
Taylor, Raymond Ellory 1929- AmMWSc 92
Taylor, Raymond L 1930- AmMWSc 92
Taylor, Raynor 1745-1825 NewAmDM
Taylor, Raynor Dunham 1908- WhoRel 92
Taylor, Rebecca HanAmWH
Taylor, Reese Hale, Jr 1928- WhoAmP 91
Taylor, Reginald Redall, Jr. 1939- WhoBlA 92
Taylor, Ren WhoAmP 91
Taylor, Renee 1945- IntMPA 92
Taylor, Richard DrAPF 91
Taylor, Richard Andrew 1944- WhoRel 92
Taylor, Richard Charles 1942- WhoAmL 92
Taylor, Richard Cowling 1789-1851 BiInAmS
Taylor, Richard E. 1929- WhoNob 90
Taylor, Richard Edward 1929- AmMWSc 92, IntWW 91, Who 92, WhoWest 92
Taylor, Richard Fred, Jr. 1933- WhoAmL 92
Taylor, Richard G 1952- AmMWSc 92
Taylor, Richard Henry 1943- WhoRel 92
Taylor, Richard Keith 1949- WhoWest 92
Taylor, Richard L 1939- AmMWSc 92
Taylor, Richard L. 1944- WhoBlA 92
Taylor, Richard Lee 1954- WhoAmL 92
Taylor, Richard Melvin 1929- AmMWSc 92
Taylor, Richard N 1952- AmMWSc 92
Taylor, Richard Powell 1928- WhoAmL 92
Taylor, Richard Randall 1959- WhoEnt 92
Taylor, Richard Timothy 1950- AmMWSc 92
Taylor, Richard William 1926- WhoFI 92
Taylor, Robert 1911-1969 FacFETw
Taylor, Robert 1948- BlkOlyM
Taylor, Robert, III 1946- WhoBlA 92
Taylor, Robert Alan 1944- Who 92
Taylor, Robert Brown 1936- WhoWest 92
Taylor, Robert Burns, Jr 1920- AmMWSc 92
Taylor, Robert Carruthers 1939- Who 92
Taylor, Robert Clement 1935- AmMWSc 92
Taylor, Robert Cooper 1917- AmMWSc 92
Taylor, Robert Craig 1939- AmMWSc 92
Taylor, Robert Dalton 1950- AmMWSc 92
Taylor, Robert E 1920- AmMWSc 92
Taylor, Robert Earlington, Jr. 1937- WhoBlA 92
Taylor, Robert Edward 1931- WhoRel 92
Taylor, Robert Emerald, Jr 1930- AmMWSc 92
Taylor, Robert Frank 1930- WhoAmL 92
Taylor, Robert Gay 1940- AmMWSc 92
Taylor, Robert Gordon, II 1944- WhoAmL 92
Taylor, Robert H. 1951- WhoWest 92
Taylor, Robert Harmon 1922- WhoIns 92
Taylor, Robert Jack 1943- WhoEnt 92
Taylor, Robert James 1943- WhoFI 92, WhoMW 92
Taylor, Robert Joe 1945- AmMWSc 92
Taylor, Robert Joseph 1941- AmMWSc 92
Taylor, Robert Lee 1925- AmMWSc 92
Taylor, Robert Lee 1943- AmMWSc 92
Taylor, Robert Lee 1947- WhoAmL 92
Taylor, Robert Leroy 1934- AmMWSc 92
Taylor, Robert Lewis 1912- BenetAL 91, TwCWW 91, WrDr 92
Taylor, Robert Love 1914- WhoAmL 92
Taylor, Robert Love, Jr. DrAPF 91
Taylor, Robert M 1932- WhoRel 92
Taylor, Robert Martin 1914- Who 92
Taylor, Robert Morgan 1941- AmMWSc 92
Taylor, Robert Richardson 1919- Who 92
Taylor, Robert Ronald 1916- Who 92
Taylor, Robert Selby 1909- IntWW 91, Who 92
Taylor, Robert Thomas 1933- Who 92
Taylor, Robert Thomas 1936- AmMWSc 92
Taylor, Robert Tieche 1932- AmMWSc 92
Taylor, Robert William 1932- AmMWSc 92
Taylor, Robin L WhoAmP 91
Taylor, Rockie 1945- WhoBlA 92
Taylor, Rod 1930- IntMPA 92, WhoEnt 92A
Taylor, Roderick 1937- TwCPaSc
Taylor, Roger Lee 1941- WhoAmL 92
Taylor, Roger Miles Whitworth 1944- Who 92
Taylor, Ronald Who 92
Taylor, Ronald 1932- AmMWSc 92
Taylor, Ronald A. 1948- WhoBlA 92
Taylor, Ronald D 1950- AmMWSc 92
Taylor, Ronald Eric 1950- WhoRel 92
Taylor, Ronald George 1935- Who 92
Taylor, Ronald Lewis 1938- WhoFI 92
Taylor, Ronald Lewis 1942- WhoBlA 92
Taylor, Ronald Oliver 1931- Who 92
Taylor, Ronald Paul 1945- AmMWSc 92
Taylor, Ronald Wentworth 1932- Who 92
Taylor, Ronnie 1924- IntMPA 92
Taylor, Roscoe L 1923- AmMWSc 92
Taylor, Rose M d1918 BiInAmS
Taylor, Rosemary 1899- BenetAL 91
Taylor, Roslyn Donny 1941- WhoWest 92
Taylor, Ross 1954- AmMWSc 92
Taylor, Roy J 1913- WhoAmP 91
Taylor, Roy Jasper 1918- AmMWSc 92
Taylor, Roy Lewis 1932- AmMWSc 92, WhoMW 92
Taylor, Roy Marcellus 1925- WhoBlA 92
Taylor, Rush W, Jr 1934- WhoAmP 91
Taylor, Russell Benton 1925- WhoMW 92
Taylor, Russell James, Jr 1935- AmMWSc 92
Taylor, Ruth Anne 1961- WhoAmL 92
Taylor, Ruth Sloan 1918- WhoBlA 92
Taylor, S. Martin WhoBlA 92
Taylor, Samuel 1912- WrDr 92
Taylor, Samuel Albert 1912- WhoEnt 92
Taylor, Samuel Coleridge NewAmDM
Taylor, Samuel Edwin 1941- AmMWSc 92
Taylor, Samuel G, III 1904- AmMWSc 92
Taylor, Samuel Miles 1929- WhoRel 92
Taylor, Samuel S WhoAmP 91
Taylor, Sandra Elaine 1946- WhoBlA 92, WhoEnt 92
Taylor, Sarah EncAmaz 91
Taylor, Sarah McFerrin 1957- WhoRel 92
Taylor, Scott Douglas 1954- WhoWest 92
Taylor, Scott Henry 1960- WhoRel 92
Taylor, Scott Maxfield 1953- WhoFI 92
Taylor, Scott Morris 1957- WhoBlA 92
Taylor, Seldon Duane 1915- WhoAmP 91
Taylor, Selwyn Francis 1913- Who 92
Taylor, Sharon L. 1945- WhoMW 92
Taylor, Sherril Wightman 1924- WhoEnt 92
Taylor, Sinthy E. 1947- WhoBlA 92
Taylor, Snowden 1924- AmMWSc 92
Taylor, Stanley Thomas 1923- WhoEnt 92
Taylor, Stephen 1948- ConAu 133, IntAu&W 91
Taylor, Stephen Dewitt 1945- WhoFI 92
Taylor, Stephen Keith 1944- AmMWSc 92
Taylor, Stephen Lee 1947- WhoAmL 92, WhoAmP 91
Taylor, Stephen Lloyd 1946- WhoMW 92
Taylor, Sterling R. 1942- WhoBlA 92
Taylor, Steve Henry 1947- WhoMW 92
Taylor, Steve L 1946- AmMWSc 92
Taylor, Steven C 1956- WhoAmP 91
Taylor, Steven James Michael 1956- WhoAmL 92
Taylor, Steven Lloyd 1948- WhoBlA 92
Taylor, Steven Millen 1941- WhoMW 92
Taylor, Stratton 1956- WhoAmL 92, WhoAmP 91
Taylor, Stuart A. 1936- WhoBlA 92
Taylor, Stuart Robert 1937- AmMWSc 92
Taylor, Stuart Ross 1925- IntWW 91
Taylor, Susan L. 1946- NotBlAW 92
Taylor, Susan Merril 1947- WhoEnt 92
Taylor, Susan Serota 1942- AmMWSc 92
Taylor, Susie King 1848-1912 NotBlAW 92 [port]
Taylor, T. Raber 1910- WhoWest 92
Taylor, Teddy Who 92
Taylor, Telford 1908- FacFETw, WrDr 92
Taylor, Terrence Derek 1951- WhoMW 92
Taylor, Thad, Jr. 1937- WhoBlA 92
Taylor, Theadoll Peace 1938- WhoMW 92
Taylor, Theodore DrAPF 91
Taylor, Theodore 1921- WrDr 92
Taylor, Theodore Brewster 1925- AmMWSc 92
Taylor, Theodore D. 1930- WhoBlA 92
Taylor, Theodore Langhans 1921- IntAu&W 91
Taylor, Theodore Roosevelt WhoBlA 92
Taylor, Thomas 1820-1910 BiInAmS
Taylor, Thomas Alfred 1942- WhoIns 92
Taylor, Thomas Bernard 1947- WhoAmL 92
Taylor, Thomas C. 1926- WhoBlA 92
Taylor, Thomas Calvin 1956- WhoAmL 92
Taylor, Thomas Franklin 1951- WhoFI 92
Taylor, Thomas Fuller 1937- WhoRel 92
Taylor, Thomas Hudson, Jr. 1920- WhoFI 92
Taylor, Thomas Maynard 1874-1907 BiInAmS
Taylor, Thomas Newton 1944- AmMWSc 92
Taylor, Thomas Norwood 1937- AmMWSc 92
Taylor, Thomas Roger 1945- WhoMW 92
Taylor, Thomas Tallott, Sr 1921- AmMWSc 92
Taylor, Thomas W. 1944- WhoAmL 92
Taylor, Timothy Davies 1945- WhoWest 92
Taylor, Timothy H 1918- AmMWSc 92
Taylor, Timothy Henry 1918- WhoAmP 91
Taylor, Timothy Merritt 1931- WhoBlA 92
Taylor, Timothy Paul 1962- WhoRel 92
Taylor, Tom 1817-1880 RfGEnL 91
Taylor, Tommie W. 1929- WhoBlA 92
Taylor, Tony 1935- WhoHisp 92
Taylor, Vaughan Edward 1947- WhoAmL 92
Taylor, Vaughn Kemp 1931- WhoMW 92
Taylor, Vernon Frank, III 1947- WhoWest 92
Taylor, Veronica C. 1941- WhoBlA 92
Taylor, Victoria Currie 1949- WhoFI 92
Taylor, Vincent Lopez 1930- WhoRel 92
Taylor, Vivian A. 1924- WhoBlA 92
Taylor, Vivian Lorraine 1948- WhoBlA 92
Taylor, W O 1932- WhoAmP 91
Taylor, W.S. 1920- TwCPaSc
Taylor, Walter 1860-1943 TwCPaSc
Taylor, Walter Frederick, Jr. 1946- WhoRel 92
Taylor, Walter Fuller 1940- AmMWSc 92
Taylor, Walter Harold 1905- WrDr 92
Taylor, Walter Herman, Jr 1931- AmMWSc 92
Taylor, Walter Kingsley 1939- AmMWSc 92

**Taylor**, Walter Reynell 1928- Who 92
**Taylor**, Walter Rowland 1918- AmMWSc 92
**Taylor**, Walter Scott 1916- WhoBlA 92
**Taylor**, Walter Wallace 1925- WhoWest 92
**Taylor**, Walton Perry, III 1936- WhoAmP 91
**Taylor**, Warren Egbert 1920- AmMWSc 92
**Taylor**, Watson Robbins, Jr. 1956- WhoFI 92
**Taylor**, Wayne Michael 1945- WhoWest 92
**Taylor**, Welford Dunaway 1938- WrDr 92
**Taylor**, Welton Ivan 1919- AmMWSc 92, WhoBlA 92
**Taylor**, Wendy 1945- TwCPaSc
**Taylor**, Wendy Ann 1945- IntWW 91, Who 92
**Taylor**, Wesley Alan 1958- WhoFI 92
**Taylor**, Wesley Gordon 1947- AmMWSc 92
**Taylor**, Wilford, Jr. 1950- WhoBlA 92
**Taylor**, William 1821-1902 BenetAL 91
**Taylor**, William 1930- IntWW 91, Who 92
**Taylor**, William 1938- WrDr 92
**Taylor**, William 1947- Who 92
**Taylor**, William Al 1938- WhoRel 92
**Taylor**, William Alexander 1837-1912 ScFEYrs
**Taylor**, William Bernard 1930- Who 92
**Taylor**, William Blake 1948- WhoEnt 92
**Taylor**, William Bower 1821-1895 BiInAmS
**Taylor**, William Clyne 1924- AmMWSc 92
**Taylor**, William Daniel 1934- AmMWSc 92
**Taylor**, William E. DrAPF 91
**Taylor**, William Edward 1921- WhoBlA 92
**Taylor**, William Edward Michael 1944- Who 92
**Taylor**, William Ewart, Jr 1927- IntAu&W 91
**Taylor**, William F 1921- AmMWSc 92
**Taylor**, William Francis 1931- AmMWSc 92
**Taylor**, William George AmMWSc 92
**Taylor**, William Glenn 1942- WhoBlA 92
**Taylor**, William H, II 1938- AmMWSc 92
**Taylor**, William Henderson 1945- WhoWest 92
**Taylor**, William Henry 1835-1917 BiInAmS
**Taylor**, William Henry, Sr. 1931- WhoBlA 92
**Taylor**, William Horace 1908- Who 92
**Taylor**, William Irving 1923- AmMWSc 92
**Taylor**, William James 1944- Who 92
**Taylor**, William James 1948- WhoAmL 92
**Taylor**, William Jape 1924- AmMWSc 92
**Taylor**, William Johnson 1833?-1864 BiInAmS
**Taylor**, William Johnson 1916- AmMWSc 92
**Taylor**, William L 1926- AmMWSc 92
**Taylor**, William L. 1931- WhoBlA 92
**Taylor**, William Leonard d1991 Who 92N
**Taylor**, William M 1923- WhoAmP 91
**Taylor**, William Malcolm 1933- WhoWest 92
**Taylor**, William McCaughey 1926- Who 92
**Taylor**, William Michael 1944- WhoIns 92
**Taylor**, William Randolph 1895- AmMWSc 92
**Taylor**, William Robert 1939- AmMWSc 92
**Taylor**, William Robert 1954- WhoFI 92
**Taylor**, William Rodney E. Who 92
**Taylor**, William Romayne 1926- WhoAmP 91
**Taylor**, William Stuart 1927- WhoAmL 92
**Taylor**, William Waller 1950- AmMWSc 92
**Taylor**, William West 1923- AmMWSc 92
**Taylor**, Willie Marvin 1955- WhoBlA 92
**Taylor**, Wilson H. WhoFI 92
**Taylor**, Winifred Ann 1947- Who 92
**Taylor**, Zachary 1784-1850 AmPolLe [port], BenetAL 91, RComAH
**Taylor-Archer**, Mordean 1947- WhoBlA 92
**Taylor-Cade**, Ruth Ann 1937- AmMWSc 92
**Taylor-Greenfield**, Elizabeth 1809-1876 NewAmDM
**Taylor-Hunt**, Mary Bernis Buchanan 1904- WhoWest 92
**Taylor-Little**, Carol 1941- WhoAmP 91
**Taylor-Mayer**, Rhoda E 1936- AmMWSc 92
**Taylor of Blackburn**, Baron 1929- Who 92
**Taylor of Gryfe**, Baron 1912- Who 92
**Taylor of Hadfield**, Baron 1905- Who 92
**Taylor of Mansfield**, Baron d1991 Who 92N
**Taylor-Pitts**, Twila Paulette 1956- WhoFI 92
**Taylor-Smith**, Ralph Emeric Kasope 1924- Who 92
**Taylor Thompson**, John Derek 1927- Who 92
**Taylor-Young**, Leigh 1945- IntMPA 92
**Taylorson**, John Brown 1931- Who 92
**Taylour** Who 92
**Taymor**, Betty 1921- WhoAmP 91
**Tayon**, Deborah Kay 1956- WhoAmL 92
**Tayoun**, James J 1930- WhoAmP 91
**Taysom**, Elvin David 1917- AmMWSc 92
**Tazawa**, Kichiro 1918- IntWW 91
**Tazieff**, Haroun 1914- IntWW 91
**Tazuma**, James Junkichi 1924- AmMWSc 92
**Tchaikovsky** SovUnBD
**Tchaikovsky**, Boris 1925- ConCom 92
**Tchaikovsky**, Piotr Ilyich 1840-1893 NewAmDM
**Tchao**, Ruy AmMWSc 92
**Tchassov**, Stanislav 1963- WhoEnt 92
**Tchen**, Tche Tsing 1924- AmMWSc 92
**Tcherepnin**, Alexander 1899-1977 NewAmDM
**Tcherepnin**, Ivan 1943- NewAmDM
**Tcherepnin**, Nikolay 1873-1945 NewAmDM
**Tcherepnin**, Serge 1941- NewAmDM
**Tcherepnine**, Jessica 1938- TwCPaSc
**Tcherina**, Ludmila 1924- IntWW 91
**Tchertkoff**, Victor 1919- AmMWSc 92
**Tcheurekdjian**, Noubar 1937- AmMWSc 92
**Tchicaya U Tam'si** 1931-1988 LiExTwC
**Tchilingirian**, Hratch 1962- WhoRel 92
**Tchobanoglous**, George 1935- AmMWSc 92
**Tcholakian**, Robert Kevork 1938- AmMWSc 92
**Tchoryk**, Robert Charles 1956- WhoFI 92
**Tchoungi**, Simon Pierre 1916- IntWW 91
**Tea**, Charles Lewis, Jr 1934- WhoIns 92
**Teabeaut**, James Robert, II 1924- AmMWSc 92
**Teach**, Edward BenetAL 91
**Teach**, Eugene Gordon 1926- AmMWSc 92
**Teachout**, Terry 1956- ConAu 133
**Teaf**, Christopher Morris 1953- AmMWSc 92
**Teaff**, Rodger Lynn 1963- WhoRel 92
**Teaford**, Hamilton Joel 1940- WhoMW 92
**Teaford**, Jane 1935- WhoAmP 91
**Teaford**, Margaret Elaine 1928- AmMWSc 92
**Teagarden**, George 1943- WhoAmP 91
**Teagarden**, Jack 1905-1964 FacFETw, NewAmDM
**Teager**, Herbert Martin 1930- AmMWSc 92
**Teagle**, Terry Michael 1960- WhoBlA 92
**Teague**, Abner F 1919- AmMWSc 92
**Teague**, Barry Douglas 1955- WhoRel 92
**Teague**, Benjamin Claton 1952- WhoRel 92
**Teague**, Bernice Rita 1957- WhoFI 92
**Teague**, Bert F 1917- WhoAmP 91
**Teague**, Bob 1946- WhoAmP 91
**Teague**, Catherine Lynne 1951- WhoWest 92
**Teague**, Charles Steven 1950- WhoRel 92
**Teague**, Claude Edward, Jr 1924- AmMWSc 92
**Teague**, David Boyce 1937- AmMWSc 92
**Teague**, Edward, III WhoAmP 91
**Teague**, Gladys Peters 1921- WhoBlA 92
**Teague**, Harold Don 1942- WhoAmL 92
**Teague**, Harold Junior 1941- AmMWSc 92
**Teague**, Howard Stanley 1922- AmMWSc 92
**Teague**, Jane Lorene 1918- WhoRel 92
**Teague**, Joel R 1939- WhoIns 92
**Teague**, Kefton Harding 1920- AmMWSc 92
**Teague**, Lavette Cox, Jr. 1934- WhoWest 92
**Teague**, Lewis 1941- IntMPA 92
**Teague**, Margaret Ann 1956- WhoAmL 92
**Teague**, Marion Warfield 1941- AmMWSc 92
**Teague**, Mark 1963- SmATA 68 [port]
**Teague**, Perry Owen 1936- AmMWSc 92
**Teague**, Peter Wesley 1952- WhoRel 92
**Teague**, Peyton Clark 1915- AmMWSc 92
**Teague**, Randal Cornell, Sr 1944- WhoAmP 91
**Teague**, Robert 1929- WhoBlA 92
**Teague**, Thomas Morse 1924- WhoAmP 91
**Teague**, Thomas Will 1953- WhoRel 92
**Teague**, Tommy Kay 1943- AmMWSc 92
**Teague**, Walter Dorwin, Jr. 1910- DcTwDes
**Teague**, Walter Dorwin, Sr. 1883-1960 DcTwDes, FacFETw
**Teague**, William J. 1927- WhoRel 92
**Teal**, Ella S. 1947- WhoBlA 92
**Teal**, G. Donn 1932- WrDr 92
**Teal**, Gordon Kidd 1907- AmMWSc 92
**Teal**, John Moline 1929- AmMWSc 92
**Teale**, Alan A 1931- WhoIns 92
**Teale**, Edwin Way 1899-1980 BenetAL 91
**Teale**, Kevin Jerome 1957- WhoMW 92
**Teaman**, Richard Alan 1960- WhoWest 92
**Teamer**, Charles C. 1933- WhoBlA 92
**Teaney**, Dale T 1933- AmMWSc 92
**Teaney**, Robert J. 1915- WhoMW 92
**Tear**, Robert 1939- IntWW 91, NewAmDM, Who 92
**Teare**, Andrew Hubert 1942- Who 92
**Teare**, Douglas d1991 Who 92N
**Teare**, Frederick Wilson 1925- AmMWSc 92
**Teare**, Iwan Dale 1931- AmMWSc 92
**Teare**, John James 1924- WhoBlA 92
**Teare**, Nigel John Martin 1952- Who 92
**Tearle**, Michael Victor 1937- WhoEnt 92
**Tearney**, Russell James 1938- AmMWSc 92, WhoBlA 92
**Tears for Fears** ConMus 6 [port]
**Teas**, Howard Jones 1920- AmMWSc 92
**Teaschner**, Patricia Ann 1943- WhoFI 92
**Teasdale**, Anna TwCPaSc
**Teasdale**, John G 1913- AmMWSc 92
**Teasdale**, Joseph Patrick 1936- WhoAmP 91
**Teasdale**, Kenneth Fulbright 1934- WhoMW 92
**Teasdale**, Paul James 1935- WhoRel 92
**Teasdale**, Sara 1884-1933 BenetAL 91, FacFETw
**Teasdale**, William Brooks 1939- AmMWSc 92
**Teasdall**, Robert Douglas 1920- AmMWSc 92
**Teasley**, Larkin 1936- WhoBlA 92, WhoIns 92
**Teasley**, Marie R. WhoBlA 92
**Teat**, Franklin Alvin, Jr. 1956- WhoRel 92
**Te Atairangikaahu**, Arikinui 1931- Who 92
**Teate**, James Lamar 1932- AmMWSc 92
**Teater**, Dorothy Seath 1931- WhoAmP 91
**Teater**, Robert Woodson 1927- AmMWSc 92
**Teats**, Mark Bates 1945- WhoRel 92
**Tebaldi**, Renata 1922- FacFETw, IntWW 91, NewAmDM, Who 92
**Tebbe**, Dennis Lee 1942- AmMWSc 92
**Tebbel**, John 1912- IntAu&W 91
**Tebbit**, Donald 1920- Who 92
**Tebbit**, Donald Claude 1920- IntWW 91
**Tebbit**, Norman 1931- IntAu&W 91, Who 92
**Tebbit**, Norman Beresford 1931- IntWW 91
**Tebble**, Norman 1924- Who 92
**Tebby**, Susan 1944- TwCPaSc
**Tebeau**, Thomas Gerard 1959- WhoFI 92
**Tebedo**, MaryAnne 1936- WhoAmP 91
**Te Beest**, David Orien 1946- AmMWSc 92
**Tebelius**, Mark Alan 1953- WhoAmL 92
**Tebet**, David W. LesBEnT 92
**Tebet**, David William 1920- WhoEnt 92
**Tebo**, Heyl Gremmer 1916- AmMWSc 92
**Tebo**, Stephen Dwane 1944- WhoWest 92
**Teboul**, Albert 1936- WhoFI 92
**Tecayehuatzin**, Victor Saucedo 1937- WhoHisp 92
**Tecco**, Romuald Gilbert Louis Joseph 1941- WhoEnt 92
**Techo**, Robert 1931- AmMWSc 92
**Teck**, Katherine 1939- WhoEnt 92
**Tecklenburg**, Harry 1927- AmMWSc 92
**Teclaff**, Ludwik Andrzej 1918- WhoAmL 92
**Tecle**, Aregai 1948- WhoWest 92
**Tecotzky**, Melvin 1924- AmMWSc 92
**Tecson**, Joseph A 1928- WhoAmP 91
**Tecum Uman** d1524 HisDSpE
**Tecumseh** 1768?-1813 BenetAL 91, RComAH
**Tedder** Who 92
**Tedder**, Baron 1926- IntWW 91, Who 92
**Tedder**, Arthur William 1890-1967 FacFETw
**Tedder**, David Hampton 1946- WhoAmL 92
**Tedeschi**, David Henry 1930- AmMWSc 92
**Tedeschi**, Henry 1930- AmMWSc 92
**Tedeschi**, Ralph Earl 1927- AmMWSc 92
**Tedeschi**, Robert James 1921- AmMWSc 92
**Tedesco**, Francis J 1944- AmMWSc 92
**Tedesco**, Francis Joseph 1944- WhoFI 92
**Tedesco**, Frank 1936- WhoAmP 91
**Tedesco**, Lou LesBEnT 92
**Tedesco**, Richard Albert 1942- WhoRel 92
**Tedesco**, Samuel Paul 1954- WhoEnt 92
**Tedesco**, Thomas Albert 1935- AmMWSc 92
**Tedesko**, Anton 1903- AmMWSc 92
**Tedford**, Charles Franklin 1928- WhoWest 92
**Tedford**, Jack Nowlan, III 1943- WhoAmP 91, WhoFI 92, WhoWest 92
**Tedford**, John Roy, Jr 1936- WhoAmP 91
**Tedford**, Richard Hall 1929- AmMWSc 92
**Tediashvili**, Levan Kitoevich 1948- SovUnBD
**Tedisco**, James Nicholas 1950- WhoAmP 91
**Tedlock**, Sandra Lynn 1954- WhoAmL 92
**Tedrick**, Marjorie Goodale 1952- WhoAmL 92
**Tedrow**, Harry S ScFEYrs
**Tedrow**, John Charles Fremont 1917- AmMWSc 92
**Tee**, Richard 1943- WhoEnt 92
**Teebor**, George William 1935- AmMWSc 92
**Teed**, Shirley 1933- TwCPaSc
**Teegarden**, Arlo Francis 1941- WhoMW 92
**Teegarden**, Bonnard John 1940- AmMWSc 92
**Teegarden**, David Morrison 1941- AmMWSc 92
**Teegarden**, Kenneth James 1928- AmMWSc 92
**Teegarden**, Kenneth Leroy 1921- WhoRel 92
**Teegen**, Evelyn I 1931- WhoAmP 91
**Teeguarden**, Dennis Earl 1931- AmMWSc 92
**Teekah**, George Anthony 1948- WhoBlA 92
**Teekell**, Roger Alton 1930- AmMWSc 92
**Teel**, Lauren Ruth 1956- WhoFI 92
**Teel**, Robert Lee 1925- WhoMW 92
**Teel**, Ward 1924- WhoAmP 91
**Teele**, Arthur E, Jr 1946- WhoAmP 91
**Teele**, Arthur Earle, Jr. 1946- WhoBlA 92
**Teeley**, Peter Barry 1940- WhoAmP 91
**Teelock**, Boodhun 1922- Who 92
**Teem**, Paul Lloyd, Jr. 1948- WhoFI 92
**Teeple**, Richard Duane 1942- WhoAmL 92
**Teer**, Barbara Ann 1937- WhoBlA 92
**Teer**, Kees 1925- IntWW 91
**Teeri**, Arthur Eino 1916- AmMWSc 92
**Teeri**, James Arthur 1944- AmMWSc 92
**Teerlink**, Joseph Leland 1935- WhoWest 92
**Teesdale**, Edmund Brinsley 1915- Who 92
**Teeter**, James Wallis 1937- AmMWSc 92
**Teeter**, Martha Mary 1944- AmMWSc 92
**Teeter**, Merle Lynn 1965- WhoEnt 92
**Teeter**, Richard Malcolm 1926- AmMWSc 92
**Teeter**, Robert M. 1939- NewYTBS 91 [port]
**Teeters**, Clarence 1933- WhoWest 92
**Teeters**, Dennis Monroe 1951- WhoRel 92
**Teeters**, Donald WhoEnt 92
**Teeters**, Nancy Hays 1930- WhoAmP 91, WhoFI 92
**Teets**, Charles Edward 1947- WhoFI 92
**Teets**, John William 1933- IntWW 91, WhoWest 92
**Teevans**, James William 1963- WhoAmL 92
**Tefft**, Melvin 1932- AmMWSc 92
**Tegeler**, Dorothy 1950- WhoWest 92
**Tegenfeldt**, David 1955- WhoWest 92
**Tegenkamp**, Gary Elton 1946- WhoAmL 92
**Tegetmeier**, Dennis 1895-1987 TwCPaSc
**Tegge**, B R 1917- AmMWSc 92
**Tegge**, Frank Allen 1942- WhoMW 92
**Teggins**, John E 1937- AmMWSc 92
**Tegmeyer**, John H 1821?-1901 BiInAmS
**Tegner**, Ian Nicol 1933- Who 92
**Tegner**, Mia Jean 1947- AmMWSc 92
**Tegtmeier**, Ronald Eugene 1943- WhoWest 92
**Tegtmeyer**, Charles John 1939- AmMWSc 92
**Teh**, Hock-Aun 1950- TwCPaSc
**Teh**, Hung-Sia 1945- AmMWSc 92
**Tehan**, Robert Emmet, Jr. 1931- WhoAmL 92
**Te Heuheu**, Hepi 1919- Who 92
**Tehon**, Stephen Whittier 1920- AmMWSc 92
**Tei**, Takuri 1924- WhoMW 92
**Tei Abal**, Sir 1932- Who 92
**Teibel**, Irv 1938 WhoEnt 92
**Teich**, Albert, Jr 1929- WhoAmP 91
**Teich**, Malvin Carl 1939- AmMWSc 92
**Teicher**, Arthur Mace 1946- WhoFI 92
**Teicher**, Harry 1927- AmMWSc 92
**Teicher**, Henry 1922- AmMWSc 92
**Teicher**, Joseph D 1917- AmMWSc 92
**Teicher**, Lawrence Franklin WhoFI 92
**Teichert**, Curt 1905- AmMWSc 92
**Teichler**, Stephen Lin 1952- WhoAmL 92
**Teichler-Zallen**, Doris 1941- AmMWSc 92
**Teichmann**, Theodor 1923- AmMWSc 92
**Teichroew**, Daniel 1925- AmMWSc 92
**Teig**, Marlowe Gilman 1938- WhoFI 92
**Teigen**, James Arthur 1946- WhoMW 92
**Teiger**, Martin 1936- AmMWSc 92
**Teilhard de Chardin**, Pierre 1881-1955 FacFETw, GuFrLit 1
**Teilhet**, Raoul Edward 1933- WhoAmP 91

**Teillier,** Jorge 1935- *ConSpAP*
**Teipel,** John William 1943- *AmMWSc 92*
**Teirstein,** Alice 1929- *WhoEnt 92*
**Teis,** Robert William, Jr. 1944- *WhoRel 92*
**Teish,** Luisah *RelLAm 91*
**Teissier,** Henri 1929- *WhoRel 92*
**Teitel,** Jeffrey Hale 1943- *WhoAmL 92*
**Teitel,** Robert J 1922- *AmMWSc 92*
**Teitelbaum,** Charles Leonard 1925- *AmMWSc 92*
**Teitelbaum,** Gene W. 1935- *WhoAmL 92*
**Teitelbaum,** Ginnette Cay 1962- *WhoEnt 92*
**Teitelbaum,** Irving 1939- *WhoFI 92*
**Teitelbaum,** Leonard 1931- *WhoAmP 91*
**Teitelbaum,** Pedro 1922- *IntMPA 92*
**Teitelbaum,** Philip 1928- *AmMWSc 92, IntWW 91*
**Teitelbaum,** Rhonda Gale 1955- *WhoAmL 92*
**Teitelbaum,** Richard 1939- *NewAmDM*
**Teitelbaum,** Steven Alan 1956- *WhoAmL 92*
**Teitelbaum,** Steven Usher 1945- *WhoAmL 92*
**Teitelbaum,** William Allen 1950- *WhoFI 92*
**Teitell,** Conrad Laurence 1932- *WhoAmL 92*
**Teitell,** Michael Alan 1959- *WhoWest 92*
**Teitelman,** Jill *DrAPF 91*
**Teitelman,** Richard Bertram 1947- *WhoAmL 92*
**Teitelman,** Robert 1954- *ConAu 135*
**Teitelman,** Robert Baruch 1959- *WhoAmL 92*
**Teitler,** Harold Herman 1936- *WhoAmL 92*
**Teitler,** Sidney 1930- *AmMWSc 92*
**Teitz,** Jeffrey Jonathan 1953- *WhoAmP 91*
**Teixeira,** Arthur Alves 1944- *AmMWSc 92*
**Teja,** Amyn Sadruddin 1946- *AmMWSc 92*
**Tejada,** Marquis de *IntWW 91*
**Tejada,** Celia 1958- *WhoHisp 92*
**Tejada,** Hernando 1956- *WhoEnt 92*
**Tejan-Sie,** Banja 1917- *Who 92*
**Tejeda,** Frank M 1945- *WhoAmP 91, WhoHisp 92*
**Tejeda,** Rennie *WhoHisp 92*
**Tejeda,** Robert *WhoHisp 92*
**Teji,** Darshan Singh 1925- *WhoWest 92*
**Tejidor,** Roberto A. 1942- *WhoHisp 92*
**Tejwani,** Gopi Assudomal 1946- *AmMWSc 92*
**te Kaat,** Erich Heinz 1937- *IntWW 91*
**Te Kanawa,** Kiri 1944- *IntWW 91, NewAmDM, Who 92*
**Tekel,** Ralph 1920- *AmMWSc 92*
**Tekeli,** Sait 1932- *AmMWSc 92*
**Tekeyan,** Vahan 1878-1945 *LiExTwC*
**Teklits,** Joseph Anthony 1952- *WhoAmL 92*
**Tekoah,** Yosef d1991 *IntWW 91N*
**Tekoah,** Yosef 1925-1991 *NewYTBS 91*
**Telang,** Vasant G 1935- *AmMWSc 92*
**Teleb,** Zakaria Ahmed 1949- *AmMWSc 92*
**Telegdi,** Valentine L. 1922- *IntWW 91*
**Telegdi,** Valentine Louis 1922- *AmMWSc 92*
**Telek,** Leona G Lee 1931- *WhoAmP 91*
**Telemann,** Georg Philipp 1681-1767 *NewAmDM*
**Telemaque,** Eleanor Wong *DrAPF 91*
**Telep,** Quentin Lee 1953- *WhoFI 92*
**Telepas,** George Peter 1935- *WhoAmL 92*
**Telepneff,** Andrew 1927- *TwCPaSc*
**Telesca,** Michael Anthony 1929- *WhoAmL 92*
**Telesilla** *EncAmaz 91*
**Telesmanik,** Judith J. 1949- *WhoRel 92*
**Televantos,** John Yiannakis 1952- *WhoFI 92*
**Telfair,** Raymond Clark, II 1941- *AmMWSc 92*
**Telfair,** William Boys 1947- *AmMWSc 92*
**Telfeian,** Henry Frederic 1951- *WhoAmL 92*
**Telfer,** Carlyle Hart 1952- *WhoMW 92*
**Telfer,** Nancy 1930- *AmMWSc 92*
**Telfer,** Robert Gilmour Jamieson 1928- *Who 92*
**Telfer,** William Harrison 1924- *AmMWSc 92*
**Telford,** Barry B 1936- *WhoAmP 91*
**Telford,** Ira Rockwood 1907- *AmMWSc 92*
**Telford,** James Wardrop 1927- *AmMWSc 92*
**Telford,** Robert 1915- *Who 92*
**Telford,** Sam Rountree, III 1961- *AmMWSc 92*
**Telford,** Sam Rountree, Jr 1932- *AmMWSc 92*
**Telford Beasley,** John 1929- *Who 92*
**Telgarsky,** Rastislav Jozef 1943- *WhoWest 92*
**Telge,** Donald Ellis 1933- *WhoMW 92*
**Telingater,** Solomon Benediktovich 1903-1969 *SovUnBD*
**Telionis,** Demetri Pyrros 1941- *AmMWSc 92*
**Telischak,** Dennis Joseph 1946- *WhoFI 92*
**Telkes,** Maria 1900- *AmMWSc 92*
**Tell,** A. Charles 1937- *WhoAmL 92*
**Tell,** Benjamin 1936- *AmMWSc 92*
**Tell,** M. David 1936- *WhoAmL 92*
**Tell,** William Kirn, Jr. 1934- *WhoFI 92*
**Tella,** Guido Jose Mario di 1931- *IntWW 91*
**Tella,** Luigi 1939- *WhoFI 92*
**Telle,** Jack Martin 1962- *WhoAmP 91*
**Telle,** John Martin 1947- *AmMWSc 92*
**Telleen,** Steven Louis 1947- *WhoWest 92*
**Tellem,** Susan Mary 1945- *WhoFI 92, WhoWest 92*
**Tellenbach,** Gerd 1903- *IntWW 91*
**Tellep,** Daniel M 1931- *AmMWSc 92*
**Tellep,** Daniel Michael 1931- *WhoFI 92, WhoWest 92*
**Teller,** Aaron Joseph 1921- *AmMWSc 92*
**Teller,** Alvin Norman 1944- *WhoEnt 92*
**Teller,** Cecil Martin, II 1939- *AmMWSc 92*
**Teller,** Daniel Myron 1930- *AmMWSc 92*
**Teller,** David Chambers 1938- *AmMWSc 92*
**Teller,** David Norton 1936- *AmMWSc 92*
**Teller,** Davida Young 1938- *AmMWSc 92, WhoWest 92*
**Teller,** Edward 1908- *AmMWSc 92, FacFETw, IntWW 91, Who 92*
**Teller,** Gayl *DrAPF 91*
**Teller,** Ira 1940- *IntMPA 92*
**Teller,** James Tobias 1940- *AmMWSc 92*
**Teller,** John Roger 1932- *AmMWSc 92*
**Teller,** Michael Elliot 1936- *WhoMW 92*
**Teller,** Neville 1931- *WrDr 92*
**Teller,** Walter Magnes 1910- *WrDr 92*
**Telles,** Lygia Fagundes 1924- *DcLB 113 [port]*
**Telles,** Rick David 1962- *WhoHisp 92*
**Tellez,** Gorki C. *WhoHisp 92*
**Tellez,** Isabelle Ogaz 1924- *WhoHisp 92*
**Tellez,** Laura E. 1955- *WhoHisp 92*
**Tellez,** Louis *WhoHisp 92*
**Tellinghuisen,** Joel Barton 1943- *AmMWSc 92*
**Tellinghuisen,** Roger *WhoAmP 91*
**Tellini,** Emilio Eugenio 1947- *WhoMW 92*
**Tello,** Donna 1955- *WhoWest 92*
**Tello,** Manuel 1935- *Who 92*
**Tello,** Oldemar 1959- *WhoHisp 92*
**Telloni,** John Louis 1950- *WhoRel 92*
**Telmer,** Frederick H. *WhoFI 92*
**Telmer,** Frederick Harold 1937- *IntWW 91*
**Telnack,** John J. 1937- *DcTwDes, WhoMW 92*
**Telow,** John 1914- *WhoAmP 91*
**Telpaz,** Gideon *DrAPF 91*
**Telpner,** Joel Stephan 1956- *WhoAmL 92*
**Telschow,** Kenneth Louis 1947- *AmMWSc 92*
**Telser,** Alvin Gilbert 1939- *AmMWSc 92*
**Telser,** Lester G. 1931- *WrDr 92*
**Teltschik,** Horst 1940- *IntWW 91*
**Tem,** Steve Rasnic *DrAPF 91*
**Tembandumba** *EncAmaz 91*
**Tembo,** John Zenas Ungapake 1932- *IntWW 91*
**Temerlin,** Leiner 1928- *IntWW 91*
**Temerlin,** Liener 1928- *WhoFI 92*
**Temes,** Clifford Lawrence 1930- *AmMWSc 92*
**Temes,** Gabor Charles 1929- *AmMWSc 92*
**Temeyer,** Kevin Bruce 1951- *AmMWSc 92*
**Temianka,** Henri 1906- *NewAmDM, WhoEnt 92, WhoWest 92*
**Temidis,** George Gabriel 1961- *WhoFI 92*
**Temin,** Howard M. 1934- *IntWW 91, Who 92*
**Temin,** Howard Martin 1934- *AmMWSc 92, FacFETw, WhoMW 92, WhoNob 90*
**Temin,** Peter 1937- *WrDr 92*
**Temin,** Rayla Greenberg 1936- *AmMWSc 92*
**Temin,** Samuel Cantor 1919- *AmMWSc 92*
**Temirkanov,** Yuri Khatuevich 1938- *WhoEnt 92*
**Temirkanov,** Yuriy Khatuyevich 1938- *IntWW 91*
**Temkin,** Aaron 1929- *AmMWSc 92*
**Temkin,** Bruce David 1960- *WhoFI 92*
**Temkin,** Owsei 1902- *AmMWSc 92*
**Temkin,** Richard Joel 1945- *AmMWSc 92*
**Temkin,** Robert Harvey 1943- *WhoFI 92*
**Temkin,** Samuel 1936- *AmMWSc 92*
**Temko,** Allan Bernard 1924- *WhoWest 92*
**Temko,** Edward James 1952- *Who 92*
**Temko,** Stanley Leonard 1920- *WhoAmL 92*
**Temme,** Donald H 1928- *AmMWSc 92*
**Temme,** Jon Mark 1954- *WhoRel 92*
**Temmer,** Georges Maxime 1922- *AmMWSc 92*
**Temmer,** Stephen Francis 1928- *WhoEnt 92*
**Tempany,** Myles McDermott 1924- *Who 92*
**Tempchin,** Jack 1947- *WhoEnt 92*
**Tempel,** George Edward 1944- *AmMWSc 92*
**Tempelis,** Constantine H 1927- *AmMWSc 92*
**Tempelman,** Jerry Henry 1962- *WhoFI 92*
**Tempelman,** Steven Carlos 1967- *WhoWest 92*
**Temperley,** Judith Kantack 1936- *AmMWSc 92*
**Temperley,** Neville 1915- *WrDr 92*
**Temperley,** Nicholas 1932- *WrDr 92*
**Temperly,** Thomas Drew 1948- *WhoMW 92*
**Tempero,** Kenneth Floyd 1939- *WhoMW 92*
**Tempero,** Preston Eugene 1952- *WhoMW 92*
**Tempest,** Bruce Dean 1935- *AmMWSc 92*
**Tempest,** Jan *ConAu 34NR*
**Tempest,** Richard B 1935- *WhoAmP 91*
**Tempest,** Rick 1950- *WhoAmP 91*
**Tempest,** Sara *WrDr 92*
**Tempest,** Victor *WrDr 92*
**Temple,** Ann, Ms *IntAu&W 91X*
**Temple,** Anthony Dominic Afamado 1945- *Who 92*
**Temple,** Austin Limiel 1940- *AmMWSc 92*
**Temple,** Carroll Glenn 1932- *AmMWSc 92*
**Temple,** Dan *IntAu&W 91X, TwCWW 91, WrDr 92*
**Temple,** Davis Littleton, Jr 1943- *AmMWSc 92*
**Temple,** Donald 1933- *WhoMW 92*
**Temple,** Donald Melvin 1953- *WhoBlA 92*
**Temple,** Ernest Sanderson 1921- *Who 92*
**Temple,** Frederick Stephen 1916- *Who 92*
**Temple,** George 1901- *IntWW 91, Who 92*
**Temple,** George Frederick 1933- *Who 92*
**Temple,** Herbert 1919- *WhoBlA 92*
**Temple,** James Clarence 1882-1916 *BiInAmS*
**Temple,** John 1910- *Who 92*
**Temple,** John Wesley 1963- *WhoEnt 92*
**Temple,** Joseph George, Jr. 1929- *IntWW 91, WhoFI 92, WhoMW 92*
**Temple,** Kenneth Loren 1918- *AmMWSc 92*
**Temple,** Kristen Marie 1964- *WhoMW 92*
**Temple,** Lee Brett 1956- *WhoFI 92*
**Temple,** Matthew David 1964- *WhoMW 92*
**Temple,** Nicholas Lawrence 1946- *WhoRel 92*
**Temple,** Nigel 1926- *WrDr 92*
**Temple,** Nigel Hal Longdale 1926- *IntAu&W 91*
**Temple,** Oney D. *WhoBlA 92*
**Temple,** Paul *IntAu&W 91X*
**Temple,** Paul David 1953- *WhoEnt 92*
**Temple,** Peter Lawrence 1946- *AmMWSc 92*
**Temple,** Philip 1939- *IntAu&W 91, WrDr 92*
**Temple,** Rawden 1908- *Who 92*
**Temple,** Reginald Robert 1922- *Who 92*
**Temple,** Richard Anthony Purbeck 1913- *Who 92*
**Temple,** Robert 1831?-1901 *BiInAmS*
**Temple,** Robert 1945- *WrDr 92*
**Temple,** Robert Dwight 1941- *AmMWSc 92*
**Temple,** Robert Winfield 1934- *WhoFI 92*
**Temple,** Ronald J. 1940- *WhoBlA 92*
**Temple,** Sanderson *Who 92*
**Temple,** Shirley *IntWW 91*
**Temple,** Shirley 1928- *FacFETw [port]*
**Temple,** Shirley Jane 1928- *IntMPA 92*
**Temple,** Stanley 1930- *AmMWSc 92*
**Temple,** Stanley A 1946- *AmMWSc 92*
**Temple,** Tyler Logan 1956- *WhoMW 92*
**Temple,** Victor Albert Keith 1944- *AmMWSc 92*
**Temple,** Victor Bevis Afoumado 1941- *Who 92*
**Temple,** Wayne C. 1924- *WrDr 92*
**Temple,** William 1881-1941 *FacFETw*
**Temple,** William 1881-1944 *DcEcMov [port]*
**Temple,** William Benton 1913- *WhoAmP 91*
**Temple,** William F 1914-1989 *TwCSFW 91*
**Temple,** William Harvey Ernest 1931- *WhoAmP 91*
**Temple,** William Nicholas 1940- *WhoEnt 92*
**Temple-Gore-Langton** *Who 92*
**Temple-Morris,** Peter 1938- *Who 92*
**Temple of Stowe,** Earl 1924- *Who 92*
**Temple-Troya,** Jose Carlos 1947- *WhoHisp 92*
**Templeman** *Who 92*
**Templeman,** Baron 1920- *IntWW 91, Who 92*
**Templeman,** Gareth J 1937- *AmMWSc 92*
**Templeman,** Wilfred 1908- *AmMWSc 92*
**Templer,** David Allen 1942- *AmMWSc 92*
**Templer,** James Robert 1936- *Who 92*
**Temples,** Dent Larkin, Jr. 1946- *WhoFI 92*
**Templeton,** Alec 1909-1963 *NewAmDM*
**Templeton,** Allan 1946- *Who 92*
**Templeton,** Arch W 1932- *AmMWSc 92*
**Templeton,** Barbara Ann 1954- *WhoMW 92*
**Templeton,** Bruce Allan 1953- *WhoAmL 92*
**Templeton,** Charles Clark 1921- *AmMWSc 92*
**Templeton,** Darwin Herbert 1922- *Who 92*
**Templeton,** David Henry 1920- *AmMWSc 92*
**Templeton,** David Joseph 1960- *WhoEnt 92*
**Templeton,** Edith 1916- *IntAu&W 91, Who 92, WrDr 92*
**Templeton,** Elizabeth Lindsay 1948- *WhoRel 92*
**Templeton,** Fiona *DrAPF 91*
**Templeton,** Fiona 1951- *IntAu&W 91*
**Templeton,** Frederic Eastland 1905- *AmMWSc 92*
**Templeton,** Garry Lewis 1956- *WhoBlA 92*
**Templeton,** George Earl 1931- *AmMWSc 92*
**Templeton,** Gordon Huffine 1940- *AmMWSc 92*
**Templeton,** Hugh Campbell 1929- *IntWW 91*
**Templeton,** Ian M 1929- *AmMWSc 92*
**Templeton,** Joe Wayne 1941- *AmMWSc 92*
**Templeton,** John 1912- *Who 92*
**Templeton,** John Charles 1943- *AmMWSc 92*
**Templeton,** John M. 1912- *IntWW 91*
**Templeton,** John Y, III 1917- *AmMWSc 92*
**Templeton,** Joseph Leslie 1948- *AmMWSc 92*
**Templeton,** McCormick 1923- *AmMWSc 92*
**Templeton,** Robert Clark d1991 *NewYTBS 91*
**Templeton,** Roy Bennett 1967- *WhoEnt 92*
**Templeton,** William Lees 1926- *AmMWSc 92*
**Templeton,** William Milton 1951- *WhoRel 92*
**Templeton-Cotill,** John Atrill 1920- *Who 92*
**Templin,** Kathleen Ann 1947- *WhoWest 92*
**Temptations,** The *NewAmDM*
**Tems,** Robin Douglas 1952- *AmMWSc 92*
**Temte,** Mark Clifford 1947- *WhoMW 92*
**Temu,** Naftali 1945- *BlkOlyM*
**Tena,** Patricia Beatrice 1963- *WhoHisp 92*
**Tenaglia,** John Franc 1935- *WhoEnt 92*
**Tenaglio,** Francis Xavier 1949- *WhoAmP 91*
**Tenayuca,** Emma 1917- *HanAmWH*
**Tenaza,** Richard Reuben 1939- *AmMWSc 92*
**Ten-Barge,** Anthony Joseph 1950- *WhoFI 92*
**Ten Boom,** Corrie 1892-1983 *FacFETw, RelLAm 91*
**Ten Brink,** Norman Wayne 1943- *AmMWSc 92*
**TenBrink,** Terry Dean 1936- *WhoMW 92*
**Tenbroek,** Bernard John 1924- *AmMWSc 92*
**Tenby,** Viscount 1927- *Who 92*
**Tenca,** Joseph Ignatius 1929- *AmMWSc 92*
**Ten Cate,** Arnold Richard 1933- *AmMWSc 92*
**Tench,** David Edward 1929- *Who 92*
**Tench,** William Henry 1921- *Who 92*
**Tencin,** Claudine-Alexandrine Guerin de 1681-1749 *BlkwCEP*
**Tencin,** Claudine-Alexandrine Guerin de 1682-1749 *FrenWW*
**Tencza,** Thomas Michael 1932- *AmMWSc 92*
**Tenczar,** Alan J. 1956- *WhoMW 92*
**Tendam,** Donald Jan 1916- *AmMWSc 92*
**Tendler,** Moses David 1926- *AmMWSc 92*
**Tendryakov,** Vladimir Fedorovich 1923-1984 *SovUnBD*
**Tene,** Benjamin 1914- *IntAu&W 91*
**Tenebaum,** Terry Kaye 1950- *WhoAmL 92*
**Ten Eick,** Robert Edwin 1937- *AmMWSc 92*
**Tenenbaum,** Bernard Hirsh 1954- *WhoFI 92*
**Tenenbaum,** Henry Lawrence 1946- *WhoEnt 92*
**Tenenbaum,** Irving 1908- *WhoAmL 92*
**Tenenbaum,** Joel 1940- *AmMWSc 92*
**Tenenbaum,** Michael 1913- *AmMWSc 92*
**Tenenbaum,** Samuel Jay 1943- *WhoAmP 91*

**Tenenbaum,** Saul 1917- *AmMWSc 92*
**Tenenhouse,** Alan M 1935- *AmMWSc 92*
**Tenenhouse,** Harriet Susie 1940- *AmMWSc 92*
**Tener,** Gordon Malcolm 1927- *AmMWSc 92*
**Tener,** Robert L. *DrAPF 91*
**Tener,** William Terrence 1941- *WhoWest 92*
**Tenes,** Diana Rodriguez 1957- *WhoHisp 92*
**Ten Eyck,** Edward H, Jr 1923- *AmMWSc 92*
**Tenforde,** Thomas Sebastian 1940- *AmMWSc 92*
**Teng Ying-ch'ao** *EncAmaz 91*
**Teng,** Ching Sung 1937- *AmMWSc 92*
**Teng,** Chojan 1947- *AmMWSc 92*
**Teng,** Christina Wei-Tien Tu 1942- *AmMWSc 92*
**Teng,** Evelyn Lee 1938- *AmMWSc 92*
**Teng,** James 1929- *AmMWSc 92*
**Teng,** Jon Ie 1930- *AmMWSc 92*
**Teng,** Lee Chang-Li 1926- *AmMWSc 92*
**Teng,** Lina Chen 1939- *AmMWSc 92*
**Teng,** Philip Chin Huei 1922- *WhoRel 92*
**Teng,** Ta-Liang 1937- *AmMWSc 92*
**Tengbom,** Anders 1911- *IntWW 91*
**Tengbom,** Luverne Charles 1919- *WhoRel 92*
**Tengerdy,** Robert Paul 1930- *AmMWSc 92*
**Tengi,** Frank R. 1920- *WhoAmL 92*
**Tengroth,** Mirra *WhoEnt 92*
**Ten Haken,** Richard Ervin 1934- *WhoFI 92*
**Ten Holt,** Friso 1921- *IntWW 91*
**Tenhouse,** Art *WhoAmP 91*
**Tenhover,** Michael Alan 1953- *AmMWSc 92*
**Tenhula,** John 1951- *ConAu 135*
**Teniente,** Richard *WhoHisp 92*
**Teninga,** Walter Henry 1928- *WhoFI 92, WhoMW 92*
**Teninty,** Billy L. 1946- *WhoRel 92*
**Tenison** *Who 92*
**Tenji-no-tsubone** *EncAmaz 91*
**Tenn,** Joseph S 1940- *AmMWSc 92*
**Tenn,** William 1919- *TwCSFW 91, WrDr 92*
**Tennankore,** Kannan Nagarajan 1946- *AmMWSc 92*
**Tennant** *Who 92*
**Tennant,** Anthony John 1930- *IntWW 91, Who 92*
**Tennant,** Bernard 1930- *Who 92*
**Tennant,** Bud C 1933- *AmMWSc 92*
**Tennant,** Donald L 1927- *AmMWSc 92*
**Tennant,** Dorothy 1855-1926 *TwCPaSc*
**Tennant,** Emma 1937- *ConNov 91, IntAu&W 91, TwCSFW 91, WrDr 92*
**Tennant,** Emma Christina 1937- *IntWW 91, Who 92*
**Tennant,** George Bill 1948- *WhoAmP 91*
**Tennant,** Harry 1917- *Who 92*
**Tennant,** Howard Edward 1941- *WhoWest 92*
**Tennant,** Iain 1919- *Who 92*
**Tennant,** Kylie 1912- *IntAu&W 91*
**Tennant,** Kylie 1912-1988 *RfGEnL 91*
**Tennant,** Margery Mary Edith 1869-1946 *BiDBrF 2*
**Tennant,** Mary Kent-Miller 1905- *WhoEnt 92*
**Tennant,** Melvin, II 1959- *WhoBlA 92*
**Tennant,** Michael Trenchard 1941- *Who 92*
**Tennant,** Peter 1910- *Who 92, WrDr 92*
**Tennant,** Peter Frank Dalrymple 1910- *IntWW 91*
**Tennant,** Raymond Wallace 1937- *AmMWSc 92*
**Tennant,** Stephen 1906-1986 *TwCPaSc*
**Tennant,** Trevor 1906- *TwCPaSc*
**Tennant,** Veronica 1947- *WhoEnt 92*
**Tennant,** Victoria 1953- *IntMPA 92*
**Tennant,** William *IntMPA 92*
**Tennant,** William Emerson 1945- *AmMWSc 92*
**Tennant of Balfluig,** Mark Iain 1932- *Who 92*
**Tennebaum,** James I 1932- *AmMWSc 92*
**Tennefos,** Jens 1930- *WhoAmP 91*
**Tennekes,** Hendrik 1936- *IntWW 91*
**Tennekoon,** Victor 1914- *Who 92*
**Tennen,** Ken 1949- *WhoWest 92*
**Tennenbaum,** Lloyd 1925- *WhoRel 92*
**Tennenbaum,** Michael Ernest 1935- *WhoFI 92*
**Tennenbaum,** Silvia *DrAPF 91*
**Tennent,** David Maddux 1914- *AmMWSc 92*
**Tennent,** Howard Gordon 1916- *AmMWSc 92*
**Tennent,** John 1926- *TwCPaSc*
**Tennent,** Valentine Leslie 1919- *WhoFI 92*
**Tenner,** Erin K. 1959- *WhoAmL 92*
**Tenner,** Melitta Johanna 1933- *WhoRel 92*
**Tenner,** Thomas Edward, Jr 1949- *AmMWSc 92*
**Tenneshaw,** S. M. *ConAu 36NR, TwCSFW 91*
**Tennessen,** Kenneth Joseph 1946- *AmMWSc 92*
**Tennessen,** Robert J 1939- *WhoAmP 91*
**Tenney,** Agnes *AmMWSc 92*
**Tenney,** Albert Seward, III 1943- *AmMWSc 92*
**Tenney,** Boyd 1915- *WhoAmP 91*
**Tenney,** Charles Henry 1911- *WhoAmL 92*
**Tenney,** Edward Jewett, II 1924- *WhoAmL 92*
**Tenney,** Gerold H 1909- *AmMWSc 92*
**Tenney,** Irene 1941- *WhoHisp 92*
**Tenney,** James 1934- *NewAmDM*
**Tenney,** Mark W 1936- *AmMWSc 92*
**Tenney,** Richard Craig 1926- *WhoWest 92*
**Tenney,** Samuel 1748-1816 *BiInAmS*
**Tenney,** Sanborn 1827-1877 *BiInAmS*
**Tenney,** Stephen Marsh 1922- *AmMWSc 92*
**Tenney,** Tabitha 1762-1837 *BenetAL 91*
**Tenney,** Tom Fred 1933- *WhoRel 92*
**Tenney,** William Frank 1946- *WhoWest 92*
**Tenney,** Wilton R 1928- *AmMWSc 92*
**Tennies,** Arthur Cornelius 1931- *WhoRel 92*
**Tennille,** Aubrey W 1929- *AmMWSc 92*
**Tennille,** Margaret 1917- *WhoAmP 91*
**Tennille,** Newton Bridgewater 1908- *AmMWSc 92*
**Tennis,** Calvin Cabell *WhoRel 92*
**Tennison,** Don 1950- *WhoEnt 92, WhoWest 92*
**Tennison,** Robert L 1933- *AmMWSc 92*
**Tennison,** William Ray, Jr. 1941- *WhoFI 92*
**Tennstedt,** Klaus 1926- *IntWW 91, NewAmDM, Who 92, WhoEnt 92*
**Tennyson** *Who 92*
**Tennyson,** Baron 1919- *Who 92*
**Tennyson,** Alfred 1809-1892 *RfGEnL 91*
**Tennyson,** Alfred, Lord 1809-1892 *CnDBLB 4 [port]*
**Tennyson,** G. B. 1930- *WrDr 92*
**Tennyson,** Georg Bernhard 1930- *WhoWest 92*
**Tennyson,** Joseph Alan 1958- *WhoMW 92*
**Tennyson,** Richard Harvey 1921- *AmMWSc 92*
**Tennyson-d'Eyncourt,** Mark 1967- *Who 92*
**Tenofsky-Ealy,** Deanna V. 1956- *WhoAmL 92, WhoMW 92*
**Tenopir,** Lawrence 1950- *WhoAmP 91*
**Tenopir,** Lawrence Lee 1950- *WhoAmL 92*
**Tenore,** Kenneth Robert 1943- *AmMWSc 92*
**Tenorio,** Froilan C *WhoAmP 91*
**Tenorio,** Juan Iguel *WhoAmP 91*
**Tenorio,** Pedro 1934- *WhoAmP 91*
**Tenorio,** Pedro A *WhoAmP 91*
**Tenorio,** Victor 1937- *WhoWest 92*
**Tenoso,** Harold John *AmMWSc 92*
**Tenove,** M. Glen 1955- *WhoWest 92*
**Tenpas,** Kathleen M. *DrAPF 91*
**Tensas,** Madison, M.D. 1825-1850 *BenetAL 91*
**Tenser,** Arthur Stanley 1929- *WhoAmL 92*
**Tensmeyer,** Lowell George 1928- *AmMWSc 92*
**Tenth Muse,** The *BenetAL 91*
**Tentoni,** Stuart Charles 1949- *WhoMW 92*
**Tenuta,** James Caesar *WhoEnt 92*
**Tenuta,** Luigia 1954- *WhoAmL 92*
**Tenzer,** Frederick Dean 1950- *WhoMW 92*
**Tenzer,** Rudolf Kurt 1920- *AmMWSc 92*
**Tenzin Gyatso** 1935- *Who 92, WhoRel 92*
**Teo,** Kim-See 1948- *WhoFI 92*
**Teo,** Penitala 1911- *Who 92*
**Teodosio,** Alexander Ernest 1924- *WhoAmP 91*
**Teotia,** Arvind Pal Singh 1945- *WhoMW 92*
**Tepaleatero** *DrAPF 91*
**Tepas,** Donald Irving 1933- *AmMWSc 92*
**Te Paske,** Everett Russell 1930- *AmMWSc 92*
**Tepedino,** Francis Joseph 1937- *WhoWest 92*
**Teper,** Douglas Clark 1958- *WhoAmP 91*
**Tepfer,** Sanford Samuel 1918- *AmMWSc 92*
**Tephly,** Thomas R 1936- *AmMWSc 92*
**Tepley,** Norman 1935- *AmMWSc 92*
**Teplick,** Joseph George 1911- *AmMWSc 92*
**Teplitz,** Jerry V. 1947- *WhoFI 92*
**Teplitz,** Vigdor Louis 1937- *AmMWSc 92*
**Teply,** Lester Joseph 1920- *AmMWSc 92*
**Teply,** Mark Lawrence 1942- *AmMWSc 92*
**Tepper,** Albert 1921- *WhoEnt 92*
**Tepper,** Allan 1947- *WhoFI 92*
**Tepper,** Arthur Lewis 1935- *WhoAmL 92*
**Tepper,** Byron Seymour 1930- *AmMWSc 92*
**Tepper,** Frederick 1934- *AmMWSc 92, WhoFI 92*
**Tepper,** Herbert Bernard 1931- *AmMWSc 92*
**Tepper,** Jan David 1950- *WhoWest 92*
**Tepper,** Lloyd Barton 1931- *AmMWSc 92*
**Tepper,** Morris 1916- *AmMWSc 92*
**Tepper,** Robert Bruce, Jr. 1949- *WhoAmL 92, WhoWest 92*
**Tepperman,** Barry Lorne 1947- *AmMWSc 92*
**Tepperman,** Helen Murphy 1917- *AmMWSc 92*
**Tepperman,** Jay 1914- *AmMWSc 92*
**Tepperman,** Katherine Gail 1947- *AmMWSc 92*
**Teppert,** William Allan, Sr 1915- *AmMWSc 92*
**Tepping,** Benjamin Joseph 1913- *AmMWSc 92*
**Terada,** Kazuji 1927- *AmMWSc 92*
**Terada,** Suzanne T. 1954- *WhoAmL 92*
**Terahata,** Jun *IntAu&W 91X*
**Teramond,** Guy De 1869-1957 *ScFEYrs*
**Teramura,** Alan Hiroshi 1948- *AmMWSc 92*
**Teran,** Heriberto *DrAPF 91*
**Teran,** Mary Inez 1924- *WhoRel 92*
**Teran,** Miguel A., Sr. 1941- *WhoHisp 92*
**Terando,** Judy Rae 1943- *WhoRel 92*
**Terango,** Larry 1925- *AmMWSc 92*
**Teranishi,** Roy 1922- *AmMWSc 92*
**Terasaki,** Paul Ichiro 1929- *AmMWSc 92*
**Terasawa,** Ei 1938- *AmMWSc 92*
**Teraskiewicz,** Edward Arnold 1946- *WhoFI 92*
**Terasmae,** Jaan 1926- *AmMWSc 92*
**Ter Beek,** Relus 1944- *IntWW 91*
**Terbell,** Thomas Green, Jr. 1938- *WhoWest 92*
**Terborg-Penn,** Rosalyn M. 1941- *WhoBlA 92*
**Terborgh,** Bert 1945- *WhoEnt 92*
**Terborgh,** Eliot Foster 1942- *WhoWest 92*
**Terborgh,** John J 1936- *AmMWSc 92*
**Terboven,** Josef 1898-1945 *EncTR 91 [port]*
**Terboven,** Josef Antonius Heinrich 1898-1945 *BiDExR*
**Terbush,** Jay Murray, IV 1952- *WhoRel 92*
**Terc,** Alexander *WhoHisp 92*
**Terc,** Miguel Angel, Jr. 1968- *WhoHisp 92*
**Terc,** Sigrid Roslyn 1962- *WhoHisp 92*
**Terdiman,** Joseph Franklin 1940- *AmMWSc 92*
**Terebilov,** Vladimir Ivanovich 1916- *IntWW 91*
**Terekh,** Konrat Zigmundovich 1935- *IntWW 91*
**Terekhova,** Margarita Borisovna 1942- *IntWW 91*
**Terenius,** Lars Yngve 1940- *IntWW 91*
**Terenzi,** Joseph F 1932- *AmMWSc 92*
**Terenzio,** Joseph V 1918- *AmMWSc 92*
**Terenzio,** Pio-Carlo 1921- *IntWW 91*
**Teresa de Jesus,** St. 1515-1582 *LitC 18*
**Teresa,** Mother 1910- *FacFETw [port], IntWW 91, Who 92, WhoNob 90, WhoRel 92*
**Teresa,** George Washington 1923- *AmMWSc 92*
**Tereshkova,** Valentina 1937- *FacFETw [port]*
**Tereshkova,** Valentina N. *Who 92*
**Tereshkova,** Valentina V. Nikolayeva- 1937- *IntWW 91*
**Tereshkova,** Valentina Vladimirovna 1937- *SovUnBD*
**Tereshkovich,** George 1930- *AmMWSc 92*
**Teresi,** Joseph 1941- *WhoEnt 92*
**Teresi,** Joseph Dominic 1915- *AmMWSc 92*
**Teret,** Stephen Paul 1945- *WhoAmL 92*
**Terfera,** Raymond Anthony 1929- *WhoAmL 92*
**Terhaar,** Clarence James 1926- *AmMWSc 92*
**Ter Haar,** Gary L 1936- *AmMWSc 92*
**Terhaar,** Luke Henry 1960- *WhoAmL 92*
**Terhar,** Michael John 1953- *WhoAmL 92*
**Terhark,** Scott Alfred 1946- *WhoEnt 92*
**Terhes,** Joyce Lyons 1940- *WhoAmP 91*
**Terho,** Matti Ilmari 1944- *WhoRel 92*
**Terhune,** Albert Payson 1872-1942 *BenetAL 91*
**Terhune,** Mary Virginia 1830-1922 *BenetAL 91*
**Terhune,** Robert William 1926- *AmMWSc 92*
**Terkel,** Studs *IntAu&W 91, WrDr 92*
**Terkel,** Studs 1912- *BenetAL 91, FacFETw, WhoMW 92*
**Terkel,** Studs Louis 1912- *IntWW 91*
**Terker Perelman,** Jane 1952- *WhoFI 92*
**Terl,** Allan Howard 1946- *WhoAmL 92*
**Terlaje,** David Salas 1937- *WhoAmP 91*
**Terlecki,** Wladyslaw Lech 1933- *IntAu&W 91*
**Terlezki,** Stefan 1927- *Who 92*
**Terlouw,** Jan-Cornelis 1931- *IntWW 91*
**Terman,** Charles Richard 1929- *AmMWSc 92*
**Terman,** Lewis M 1877-1956 *DcAmImH*
**Terman,** Lewis Madison 1935- *AmMWSc 92*
**Terman,** Max R 1945- *AmMWSc 92*
**Termine,** John David 1938- *AmMWSc 92*
**Termini,** Roseann Bridget 1953- *WhoAmL 92*
**Ternay,** Andrew Louis, Jr 1939- *AmMWSc 92*
**Ternberg,** Jessie L 1924- *AmMWSc 92*
**Terner,** Charles 1916- *AmMWSc 92*
**Terner,** James 1951- *AmMWSc 92*
**Ternes,** Donavon Peter 1959- *WhoWest 92*
**Terneuzen,** Roger Michael 1946- *WhoWest 92*
**Terninko,** Margaret B 1936- *WhoAmP 91*
**Ternus,** Jean Ann 1944- *WhoMW 92*
**Tero,** Lawrence 1952- *WhoBlA 92*
**Terp,** Dana George 1953- *WhoMW 92*
**Terp,** Thomas Thomsen 1947- *WhoAmL 92*
**Terpening,** Virginia Ann 1917- *WhoMW 92*
**Terpin,** Michael James 1957- *WhoWest 92*
**Ter-Pogossian,** Michel Mathew 1925- *AmMWSc 92*
**Terpstra,** Vern 1927- *IntAu&W 91, WhoMW 92, WrDr 92*
**Terputac,** Thomas James 1927- *WhoAmL 92*
**Terr,** Jim 1948- *WhoEnt 92*
**Terr,** Lenore 1936- *ConAu 134*
**Terr,** Leonard Brian 1946- *WhoAmL 92*
**Terra,** Dale Edward 1948- *WhoWest 92*
**Terra,** Daniel James 1911- *WhoAmP 91*
**Terra,** Jean M 1931- *WhoAmP 91*
**Terracciano,** Anthony Patrick 1938- *WhoFI 92*
**Terrace,** Herbert S. 1936- *WrDr 92*
**Terraglio,** Frank Peter 1928- *AmMWSc 92*
**Terragno,** Paul James 1938- *WhoFI 92*
**Terragno,** Rodolfo H. 1945- *IntWW 91*
**Terraine,** John Alfred 1921- *IntAu&W 91, IntWW 91, Who 92, WrDr 92*
**Terranova,** Andrew Charles 1935- *AmMWSc 92*
**Terranova,** Elaine *DrAPF 91*
**Terranova,** Hobby Delane 1946- *WhoFI 92*
**Terranova,** Patricia Helen 1952- *WhoWest 92*
**Terras,** Audrey Anne 1942- *AmMWSc 92*
**Terrazas,** Francisco de 1525?-1607? *HisDSpE*
**Terrazas,** Jack C. 1932- *WhoHisp 92*
**Terrazas,** Johnnie Almaguer 1947- *WhoHisp 92*
**Terreault,** Bernard J E J 1940- *AmMWSc 92*
**Terre'blanche,** Eugene Ney 1941- *BiDExR*
**Terrel,** Ronald Lee 1936- *AmMWSc 92*
**Terrell,** A. John 1927- *WhoWest 92*
**Terrell,** C W 1927- *AmMWSc 92*
**Terrell,** Catherine M. 1944- *WhoBlA 92*
**Terrell,** Charles R *AmMWSc 92*
**Terrell,** Dale Paul 1940- *WhoWest 92*
**Terrell,** Dorothy 1945- *WhoBlA 92*
**Terrell,** Edward Everett 1923- *AmMWSc 92*
**Terrell,** Ethel 1926- *WhoAmP 91, WhoBlA 92*
**Terrell,** Francis 1944- *WhoBlA 92*
**Terrell,** Francis D'Arcy 1940- *WhoBlA 92*
**Terrell,** G. Irvin 1946- *WhoAmL 92*
**Terrell,** Gail E. 1943- *WhoMW 92, WhoRel 92*
**Terrell,** Glen Edward 1939- *AmMWSc 92*
**Terrell,** Henry Matthew 1940- *WhoBlA 92*
**Terrell,** Howard Bruce 1952- *WhoWest 92*
**Terrell,** J. Anthony 1943- *WhoAmL 92*
**Terrell,** James Edward 1948- *WhoAmP 91*
**Terrell,** Jerry D. 1944- *WhoRel 92*
**Terrell,** John L. 1930- *WhoBlA 92*
**Terrell,** Joseph William 1946- *WhoRel 92*
**Terrell,** Lawrence P. 1948- *WhoAmL 92, WhoWest 92*
**Terrell,** Mable Jean 1936- *WhoBlA 92*
**Terrell,** Marvin Palmer 1934- *AmMWSc 92*
**Terrell,** Mary Ann 1944- *WhoBlA 92*
**Terrell,** Mary Church 1863-1954 *HanAmWH, NotBlAW 92 [port]*
**Terrell,** Mary Eliza Church 1863-1954 *AmPeW*
**Terrell,** Melvin C. 1949- *WhoBlA 92*
**Terrell,** N James, Jr 1923- *AmMWSc 92*
**Terrell,** Pat 1968- *WhoBlA 92*
**Terrell,** Richard Warren 1946- *WhoBlA 92*
**Terrell,** Robert E. 1943- *WhoBlA 92*
**Terrell,** Robert L. 1943- *WhoBlA 92*
**Terrell,** Stanley E. 1949- *WhoBlA 92*
**Terrell,** Stephen *Who 92*
**Terrell,** Terry Lee Tickhill 1949- *AmMWSc 92*
**Terrell,** Timothy Prater 1949- *WhoAmL 92*
**Terrell,** W. Glenn 1920- *WhoWest 92*
**Terrenoire,** Louis 1908- *IntWW 91*
**Terreri,** Frank John 1922- *WhoWest 92*
**Terreros,** Guillermo 1922- *WhoHisp 92*
**Terres,** Geronimo 1925- *AmMWSc 92*

**Terri**, Marie Ursula 1943- *WhoWest 92*
**Terrick**, Richard James 1936- *WhoAmP 91*
**Terrien**, Lawrence B. *WhoRel 92*
**Terriere**, Robert T 1926- *AmMWSc 92*
**Terrile**, Richard John 1951- *AmMWSc 92*
**Terrill**, Albert Lee 1937- *WhoAmP 91*
**Terrill**, Clair Elman 1910- *AmMWSc 92*
**Terrill**, Kathryn *DrAPF 91*
**Terrill**, Richard C. *DrAPF 91*
**Terrill**, Ross 1938- *ConAu 35NR*
**Terrill**, W.H. Tyrone, Jr. 1954- *WhoBlA 92*
**Terrington**, Baron 1915- *Who 92*
**Terrinoni**, David Michael 1957- *WhoRel 92*
**Terris**, James Murray 1941- *AmMWSc 92*
**Terris**, Milton 1915- *AmMWSc 92*
**Terris**, Susan *DrAPF 91*
**Terris**, Susan 1937- *IntAu&W 91, WrDr 92*
**Terris**, Virginia R. *DrAPF 91*
**Terris**, William 1937- *WhoMW 92*
**Terry**, Adeline Helen 1931- *WhoBlA 92*
**Terry**, Angela Owen 1941- *WhoBlA 92*
**Terry**, Bob 1936- *WhoBlA 92*
**Terry**, C V *IntAu&W 91X, WrDr 92*
**Terry**, Carol Dee 1955- *WhoWest 92*
**Terry**, Carolyn Mary 1940- *IntAu&W 91*
**Terry**, Charles C. 1934- *WhoBlA 92*
**Terry**, Charles Robert 1933- *WhoAmL 92*
**Terry**, Clark 1920- *NewAmDM, WhoBlA 92*
**Terry**, Clifford Lewis 1937- *WhoMW 92*
**Terry**, Conrad Martin 1947- *WhoFI 92*
**Terry**, Cori 1952- *WhoEnt 92*
**Terry**, Dale Randolph 1947- *WhoWest 92*
**Terry**, Darrell Merle 1933- *WhoWest 92*
**Terry**, David Lee 1936- *AmMWSc 92*
**Terry**, Dennis Edward 1957- *WhoRel 92*
**Terry**, Frank W. 1919- *WhoBlA 92*
**Terry**, Fred Herbert 1940- *AmMWSc 92*
**Terry**, Frederick Arthur, Jr. 1932- *WhoAmL 92*
**Terry**, Garland Benjamin 1927- *WhoBlA 92*
**Terry**, George 1921- *Who 92*
**Terry**, Harriet Eleanor 1912- *WhoAmP 91*
**Terry**, Herbert 1922- *AmMWSc 92, WhoFI 92*
**Terry**, Hilda 1914- *WhoEnt 92*
**Terry**, James Joseph, Jr. 1952- *WhoAmL 92*
**Terry**, James Layton 1951- *AmMWSc 92*
**Terry**, Jill L. 1958- *WhoAmL 92*
**Terry**, John 1913- *IntMPA 92*
**Terry**, John A 1933- *WhoAmP 91*
**Terry**, John Alfred 1933- *WhoAmL 92*
**Terry**, John Elliott 1913- *Who 92*
**Terry**, John Hart 1924- *WhoAmL 92, WhoAmP 91*
**Terry**, John Quinlan 1937- *IntWW 91, Who 92*
**Terry**, John William 1925- *WhoBlA 92*
**Terry**, Joseph Ray, Jr. 1938- *WhoAmL 92*
**Terry**, Keith Dwayne 1962- *WhoFI 92*
**Terry**, Leon Cass 1940- *AmMWSc 92*
**Terry**, Lucy Irene 1950- *AmMWSc 92*
**Terry**, Luther Leonidas 1911-1985 *FacFETw*
**Terry**, Mary Sue 1947- *WhoAmL 92, WhoAmP 91*
**Terry**, Megan *DrAPF 91*
**Terry**, Megan 1932- *BenetAL 91, IntAu&W 91, WhoEnt 92, WrDr 92*
**Terry**, Michael Edward Stanley I. *Who 92*
**Terry**, Michael Patrick 1940- *WhoIns 92*
**Terry**, Milton Spencer 1840-1914 *RelLAm 91*
**Terry**, Miriam Janice 1956- *WhoRel 92*
**Terry**, Norman 1939- *AmMWSc 92*
**Terry**, Paul H 1928- *AmMWSc 92*
**Terry**, Peter 1926- *Who 92*
**Terry**, Peyton Huber 1923- *WhoAmP 91*
**Terry**, Preston H, III 1958- *WhoAmP 91*
**Terry**, Quinlan *Who 92*
**Terry**, Randall *News 91 [port]*
**Terry**, Raymond Douglas 1945- *AmMWSc 92*
**Terry**, Richard D 1924- *AmMWSc 92*
**Terry**, Richard Edward 1937- *WhoFI 92, WhoMW 92*
**Terry**, Richard Ellis 1949- *AmMWSc 92*
**Terry**, Richard Frank 1949- *WhoWest 92*
**Terry**, Robert Cushing, Jr. 1932- *WhoFI 92*
**Terry**, Robert Davis 1924- *AmMWSc 92, WhoWest 92*
**Terry**, Robert J. 1943- *WhoHisp 92*
**Terry**, Robert James 1922- *AmMWSc 92*
**Terry**, Robert Lee 1918- *AmMWSc 92*
**Terry**, Roger 1917- *AmMWSc 92*
**Terry**, Roger Harold 1925- *WhoRel 92*
**Terry**, Roger Lyon 1940- *WhoMW 92*
**Terry**, Ronald Anderson 1930- *WhoFI 92*
**Terry**, Roy D. 1944- *WhoBlA 92*
**Terry**, Samuel Matthew 1915- *AmMWSc 92*
**Terry**, Saunders 1911- *WhoBlA 92*
**Terry**, Shirley Reeves 1938- *WhoAmP 91*
**Terry**, Sonny 1911-1986 *NewAmDM*
**Terry**, Steven Spencer 1942- *WhoWest 92*
**Terry**, Stuart Lee 1942- *AmMWSc 92*
**Terry**, Thomas Milton 1939- *AmMWSc 92*
**Terry**, Thomas Randall 1954- *WhoEnt 92*
**Terry**, Wallace Houston, II 1938- *WhoBlA 92*
**Terry**, Walter d1991 *Who 92N*
**Terry**, Walter 1913-1982 *FacFETw*
**Terry**, Walter 1924- *IntAu&W 91*
**Terry**, William *TwCWW 91, WrDr 92*
**Terry**, William David 1933- *AmMWSc 92*
**Terry-Thomas** 1911-1990 *AnObit 1990, FacFETw*
**Terschan**, Frank Robert 1949- *WhoAmL 92, WhoMW 92*
**Tershakovec**, George Andrew 1914- *AmMWSc 92*
**Tersoff**, Jerry David 1955- *AmMWSc 92*
**Tersol**, Teresa Anne 1951- *WhoAmP 91*
**Terson**, Peter 1932- *IntAu&W 91, WrDr 92*
**Terss**, Robert H 1925- *AmMWSc 92*
**Tertocha**, Jean-Paul Richard 1955- *WhoEnt 92*
**Tertullian** *EncEarC*
**Tertz**, Abram *FacFETw*
**Teruel**, Javier G. *WhoHisp 92*
**Terveen**, John Victor 1914- *WhoAmP 91*
**Terveer**, Nancy Marie *WhoFI 92*
**Terwagne**, Anne Joseph *EncAmaz 91*
**Terwedow**, Henry Albert, Jr 1946- *AmMWSc 92*
**Terwiel**, Maria 1910-1943 *EncTR 91*
**Terwilliger**, Cynthia Lou 1955- *WhoWest 92*
**Terwilliger**, Don William 1942- *AmMWSc 92*
**Terwilliger**, George James, III 1950- *WhoAmL 92*
**Terwilliger**, James Paul 1943- *AmMWSc 92*
**Terwilliger**, Kent Melville 1924- *AmMWSc 92*
**Terwilliger**, Nora Barclay 1941- *AmMWSc 92*
**Terwilliger**, Paul M 1955- *AmMWSc 92*
**Terwilliger**, Robert E. 1917-1991 *ConAu 134*
**Terwilliger**, Robert Elwin d1991 *NewYTBS 91*
**Terwilliger**, W. Thomas 1945- *WhoAmL 92*
**Terwische**, David Kenneth 1943- *WhoEnt 92*
**Terzaghi**, Margaret 1941- *AmMWSc 92*
**Terzaghi**, Ruth Doggett 1903- *AmMWSc 92*
**Terzakis**, John A 1935- *AmMWSc 92*
**Terzian**, Harry 1927- *WhoAmL 92*
**Terzian**, James Richard 1961- *WhoWest 92*
**Terzian**, Karnig Yervant 1928- *WhoFI 92*
**Terzian**, Yervant 1939- *AmMWSc 92*
**Terzic**, Branko Dusan 1947- *WhoAmP 91*
**Terzich**, Robert M, Sr 1935- *WhoAmP 91*
**Terzuoli**, Andrew Joseph 1914- *AmMWSc 92*
**Terzuolo**, Carlo A 1925- *AmMWSc 92*
**Tesar**, Delbert 1935- *AmMWSc 92*
**Tesar**, Milo B 1920- *AmMWSc 92*
**Tesarek**, Dennis George 1935- *WhoFI 92*
**Tesauro**, Giuseppe 1942- *IntWW 91*
**Tesch**, Emmanuel Camille Georges Victor 1920- *IntWW 91*
**Teschan**, Paul E 1923- *AmMWSc 92*
**Teschemacher**, Frank 1906-1932 *NewAmDM*
**Teschemacher**, James Englebert 1790-1853 *BiInAmS*
**Teschner**, Anne Farrar 1956- *WhoEnt 92*
**Teschner**, Douglass Paul 1949- *WhoAmP 91*
**Tescon**, Trinidad *EncAmaz 91*
**Teselle**, Eugene 1931- *WrDr 92*
**TeSelle**, Eugene Arthur, Jr. 1931- *WhoRel 92*
**Tesh**, Robert Bradfield 1936- *AmMWSc 92*
**Tesh**, Robert Mathieson 1922- *Who 92*
**Teshighara**, Hiroshi 1927- *IntWW 91*
**Tesich**, Nadja *DrAPF 91*
**Tesich**, Steve 1942- *CurBio 91 [port], IntMPA 92, WhoEnt 92, WrDr 92*
**Tesich**, Steve 1943?- *ConLC 69 [port]*
**Tesk**, John A 1934- *AmMWSc 92*
**Teska**, William Reinhold 1950- *AmMWSc 92*
**Teske**, Richard Glenn 1930- *AmMWSc 92*
**Teske**, Richard H 1939- *AmMWSc 92*
**Teskey**, Herbert Joseph 1928- *AmMWSc 92*
**Tesla**, Nikola *DcAmImH*
**Tesler**, Brian 1929- *IntMPA 92, Who 92*
**Tesler**, Lawrence Gordon 1945- *WhoFI 92, WhoWest 92*
**Tesler**, Marc Stanley 1945- *WhoFI 92*
**Tesmer**, Irving Howard 1926- *AmMWSc 92*
**Tesmer**, Joseph Ransdell 1939- *AmMWSc 92*
**Tesmer**, Louise Marie 1942- *WhoAmP 91*
**Tesoriero**, John Vincent 1941- *AmMWSc 92*
**Tesoro**, Giuliana C 1921- *AmMWSc 92*
**Tess**, Roy William Henry 1915- *AmMWSc 92*
**Tessa**, Delio 1886-1939 *DcLB 114 [port]*
**Tessa**, Marian Lorraine 1950- *WhoEnt 92*
**Tessel**, Richard Earl 1944- *AmMWSc 92*
**Tessema**, Tesfaye 1951- *WhoBlA 92*
**Tessendorf**, Hugh Sheril 1948- *WhoMW 92*
**Tesser**, Herbert 1939- *AmMWSc 92*
**Tesser**, Steven Barry 1955- *WhoMW 92*
**Tessier**, Claire Adrienne 1953- *AmMWSc 92*
**Tessler**, Frank Andrew 1954- *WhoAmL 92*
**Tessieri**, John Edward 1920- *AmMWSc 92*
**Tessler**, Arthur Ned 1927- *AmMWSc 92*
**Tessler**, George 1936- *AmMWSc 92*
**Tessler**, Julia Ann 1959- *WhoMW 92*
**Tessler**, Martin Melvyn 1937- *AmMWSc 92*
**Tessler**, Robert Louis 1938- *WhoAmL 92*
**Tessman**, Alan Orin 1930- *WhoWest 92*
**Tessman**, Irwin 1929- *AmMWSc 92*
**Tessmer**, Carl Frederick 1912- *AmMWSc 92*
**Tessmer**, Charles W. 1920- *WhoAmL 92*
**Tesson**, Philippe 1928- *IntWW 91*
**Test**, Charles Edward 1916- *AmMWSc 92*
**Test**, Frederick L 1925- *AmMWSc 92*
**Testa**, Angelo 1921- *DcTwDes*
**Testa**, Anthony Carmine 1933- *AmMWSc 92*
**Testa**, Douglas 1944- *WhoFI 92*
**Testa**, Gary Joseph 1953- *WhoFI 92*
**Testa**, Michael Harold 1939- *WhoAmL 92*
**Testa**, Michael Terry 1961- *WhoEnt 92*
**Testa**, Raymond Thomas 1937- *AmMWSc 92*
**Testa**, Rene B 1937- *AmMWSc 92*
**Testa**, Richard Joseph 1939- *WhoAmL 92*
**Testa**, Santiago Daniel 1954- *WhoHisp 92*
**Testa**, Stephen M 1951- *AmMWSc 92*
**Testa**, Stephen Michael 1951- *WhoFI 92, WhoWest 92*
**Testaferrata**, Marquis *Who 92*
**Testardi**, Louis Richard 1930- *AmMWSc 92*
**Tester**, Bruce Alan 1941- *WhoAmL 92*
**Tester**, Cecil Fred 1938- *AmMWSc 92*
**Tester**, Jefferson William 1945- *AmMWSc 92*
**Tester**, John Robert 1929- *AmMWSc 92*
**Testerman**, Jack Duane 1933- *AmMWSc 92*
**Testerman**, Michael Ray 1956- *WhoAmL 92*
**Testerman**, Philip *WhoAmP 91*
**Testut**, Charles 1818?-1892 *BenetAL 91*
**Testwuide**, Thomas Reiss 1945- *WhoFI 92*
**Teta**, Rosemarie Frances Stacey 1955- *WhoFI 92*
**Tetelman**, Alice 1941- *WhoAmP 91*
**Tetenbaum**, Marvin 1921- *AmMWSc 92*
**Teter**, Robert Dean 1946- *WhoWest 92*
**Teteris**, Nicholas John 1929- *AmMWSc 92*
**Teterycz**, Barbara Ann 1952- *WhoMW 92*
**Tether**, Anthony John 1941- *WhoWest 92*
**Tether**, Ivan Joseph 1949- *WhoAmL 92*
**Tetirick**, Daniel Hartman 1951- *WhoMW 92*
**Tetka** *EncAmaz 91*
**Tetler**, George William, III 1952- *WhoAmL 92*
**Tetley**, Glen 1926- *FacFETw, IntWW 91, Who 92, WhoEnt 92*
**Tetley**, Herbert 1908- *Who 92*
**Tetley**, John Francis Humphrey 1932- *Who 92*
**Tetley**, Kenneth James 1921- *Who 92*
**Tetlie**, Harold 1926- *WhoRel 92*
**Tetlow**, Elisabeth Meier 1942- *WhoRel 92*
**Tetlow**, L.D. *TwCWW 91*
**Tetlow**, Norman Jay 1934- *AmMWSc 92*
**Tetlow**, William Lloyd 1938- *WhoWest 92*
**Tetrault**, Charles Daniel 1950- *WhoAmL 92*
**Tetrault**, Robert Close 1933- *AmMWSc 92*
**Tetrazzini**, Luisa 1871-1940 *NewAmDM*
**Tetro**, Frank Luverne, Jr. 1919- *WhoRel 92*
**Tett**, Hugh 1906- *Who 92*
**Tett**, Hugh Charles 1906- *IntWW 91*
**Tettenhorst**, Rodney Tampa 1934- *AmMWSc 92*
**Tettlebaum**, Harvey M. *WhoAmL 92*
**Tettlebaum**, Harvey Mandell 1941- *WhoAmP 91*
**Tetu**, Michael A 1955- *WhoAmP 91*
**Tetu**, Randeane *DrAPF 91*
**Tetzlaff**, Ted 1903- *IntMPA 92*
**Tetzner**, Lisa 1894-1963 *EncTR 91 [port]*
**Teubal**, Savina J. 1926- *WhoRel 92*
**Teuber**, Larry Ross 1951- *AmMWSc 92*
**Teukolsky**, Saul Arno 1947- *AmMWSc 92*
**Teuscher**, David Mark 1960- *WhoMW 92*
**Teuscher**, George William 1908- *AmMWSc 92*
**Teusner**, Berthold Herbert 1907- *Who 92*
**Teuta** *EncAmaz 91*
**Teutsch**, Champion Kurt 1921- *WhoWest 92*
**Teutsch**, David Alan 1950- *WhoRel 92*
**Teutsch**, Walter 1909- *WhoEnt 92*
**Tevault**, David Earl 1948- *AmMWSc 92*
**Tevebaugh**, Arthur David 1917- *AmMWSc 92*
**Teverbaugh**, Kerry Dean 1954- *WhoEnt 92*
**Tevethia**, Mary Judith 1939- *AmMWSc 92*
**Tevethia**, Satvir S 1936- *AmMWSc 92*
**Teviot**, Baron 1934- *Who 92*
**Teviotdale**, Beth Luise 1940- *AmMWSc 92*
**Tevis**, Walter 1928-1984 *TwCSFW 91*
**Tevoedjre**, Albert 1929- *IntWW 91*
**Tevosyan**, Ivan Fedorovich 1902-1958 *SovUnBD*
**Tevrizian**, Dickran M., Jr. 1940- *WhoAmL 92, WhoWest 92*
**Tew**, E. James, Jr. 1933- *WhoFI 92*
**Tew**, John Garn 1940- *AmMWSc 92*
**Tew**, John Hedley Brian 1917- *Who 92*
**Tew**, Kenneth David 1952- *AmMWSc 92*
**Tewari**, Sujata 1938- *AmMWSc 92*
**Tewarson**, Reginald P 1930- *AmMWSc 92*
**Tewell**, Joseph Robert 1934- *AmMWSc 92*
**Tewes**, Howard Allan 1924- *AmMWSc 92*
**Tewes**, Mark S. 1957- *WhoRel 92*
**Tewhey**, John David 1943- *AmMWSc 92*
**Tewinkel**, G Carper 1909- *AmMWSc 92*
**Te Winkle**, William Peter 1954- *WhoAmP 91*
**Tewkesbury**, Bishop Suffragan of 1929- *Who 92*
**Tewkesbury**, Joan *ReelWom*
**Tewkesbury**, Joan 1936- *IntMPA 92*
**Tewkesbury**, Joan F. 1936- *WhoEnt 92*
**Tewksbury**, Charles Isaac 1925- *AmMWSc 92*
**Tewksbury**, Duane Allan 1936- *AmMWSc 92*
**Tewksbury**, Jorge Samuel 1949- *WhoHisp 92*
**Tewksbury**, L Blaine 1917- *AmMWSc 92*
**Tewksbury**, Stuart K 1942- *AmMWSc 92*
**Tews**, Jean Kring 1928- *AmMWSc 92*
**Tews**, Leonard L 1934- *AmMWSc 92*
**Texier**, Catherine *DrAPF 91*
**Texon**, Meyer 1909- *AmMWSc 92*
**Texter**, E Clinton, Jr 1923- *AmMWSc 92*
**Texter**, John 1949- *AmMWSc 92*
**Textor**, Robin Edward 1943- *AmMWSc 92*
**Textoris**, Daniel Andrew 1936- *AmMWSc 92*
**Tey**, Josephine 1896-1952 *FacFETw*
**Teyler**, Timothy James 1942- *AmMWSc 92*
**Teynham**, Baron 1928- *Who 92*
**Teyssier**, Edward Matthew 1954- *WhoWest 92*
**Teyte**, Maggie 1888-1976 *FacFETw, NewAmDM*
**Tezduyar**, Hasan Tahsin 1945- *WhoMW 92*
**Thabit**, Abdilkhalik Mutalij 1950- *WhoEnt 92*
**Thach**, Robert Edwards 1939- *AmMWSc 92*
**Thach**, William Thomas 1937- *AmMWSc 92*
**Thachenkary**, Cherian Sebastian 1949- *WhoFI 92*
**Thacher**, Carter P. 1926- *WhoWest 92*
**Thacher**, Henry Clarke, Jr 1918- *AmMWSc 92*
**Thacher**, James 1754-1844 *BenetAL 91*
**Thacher**, Jonathan C. 1947- *WhoAmL 92*
**Thacher**, Philip Duryea 1937- *AmMWSc 92*
**Thacik**, Anne Smith 1918- *WhoAmP 91*
**Thacker**, Acel Kent 1949- *WhoWest 92*
**Thacker**, Daniel Dean 1955- *WhoWest 92*
**Thacker**, Harry B 1947- *AmMWSc 92*
**Thacker**, Herbert Dickey 1929- *WhoFI 92*
**Thacker**, John Charles 1943- *AmMWSc 92*
**Thacker**, Raymond 1932- *AmMWSc 92*
**Thacker**, Russell Isaac 1951- *WhoFI 92*
**Thacker**, Sandra J. d1989 *WhoBlA 92N*
**Thacker**, Stephen Brady 1947- *AmMWSc 92*
**Thacker**, Tom G., II 1962- *WhoAmL 92*
**Thackeray**, Jonathan E. 1936- *WhoAmL 92*
**Thackeray**, Milton Howard 1944- *WhoFI 92*
**Thackeray**, William Makepeace 1811-1863 *CnDBLB 4 [port], RfGEnL 91*
**Thackery**, Joseph *DrAPF 91*
**Thackray**, Arnold 1939- *AmMWSc 92*
**Thackston**, Edward Lee 1937- *AmMWSc 92*

**Thackston**, Robert Edwin 1962- WhoAmL 92
**Thacore**, Harshad Rai 1939- AmMWSc 92
**Thadden**, Adolf von 1921- BiDExR
**Thadden**, Elisabeth von 1890-1944 EncTR 91 [port]
**Thaddeus**, Janice DrAPF 91
**Thaddeus**, Patrick 1932- AmMWSc 92
**Thaden**, Edward Carl 1922- WhoMW 92, WrDr 92
**Thaden**, Steven Arthur 1957- WhoRel 92
**Thaeler**, Charles Schropp, Jr 1932- AmMWSc 92
**Thagard**, Shirley Stafford 1940- WhoWest 92
**Thaggard**, Robert Marshall 1955- WhoFI 92
**Thahane**, Timothy Thahane 1940- IntWW 91
**Thai**, John Dinh-Xuan 1956- WhoEnt 92
**Thailand**, King of IntWW 91
**Thain**, Carl Ernest 1918- WhoAmP 91
**Thain**, Eric Malcolm 1925- Who 92
**Thain**, Gerald J. 1935- WhoAmL 92
**Thajeb**, Sjarif 1920- IntWW 91
**Thakar**, Jay H 1940- AmMWSc 92
**Thaker**, Upendra Natverlal 1960- WhoWest 92
**Thakkar**, Ajit Jamnadas 1950- AmMWSc 92
**Thakkar**, Arvind Lavji 1939- AmMWSc 92
**Thakker**, Dhiren R 1949- AmMWSc 92
**Thakor**, Nitish Vyomesh 1952- AmMWSc 92
**Thakura**, Ravindranatha 1861-1941 WhoNob 90
**Thal**, Michael Lewis 1949- WhoWest 92
**Thalacker**, Arbie Robert 1935- WhoAmL 92
**Thalacker**, Victor Paul 1941- AmMWSc 92
**Thalberg**, Irving G 1899-1936 FacFETw
**Thalberg**, Sigismond 1812-1871 NewAmDM
**Thalden**, Barry R. 1942- WhoMW 92
**Thale**, Thomas Richard 1915- AmMWSc 92
**Thale**, William Joseph 1959- WhoWest 92
**Thalen**, Ingela 1943- IntWW 91
**Thaler**, Alvin Isaac 1938- AmMWSc 92
**Thaler**, Barry Jay 1950- AmMWSc 92
**Thaler**, Eric Ronald 1960- AmMWSc 92
**Thaler**, G J 1918- AmMWSc 92
**Thaler**, Jon Jacob 1947- AmMWSc 92
**Thaler**, M Michael 1934- AmMWSc 92
**Thaler**, M. N. WrDr 92
**Thaler**, Manning Michael 1934- WhoWest 92
**Thaler**, Martin S. 1932- WhoAmL 92
**Thaler**, Otto Felix 1923- AmMWSc 92
**Thaler**, Raphael Morton 1925- AmMWSc 92
**Thaler**, Richard H. 1945- WhoFI 92
**Thaler**, Richard Winston, Jr. 1951- WhoFI 92
**Thaler**, Warren Alan 1934- AmMWSc 92
**Thaler**, William John 1925- AmMWSc 92
**Thalestris** EncAmaz 91
**Thalheim**, Jay Richard 1922- WhoFI 92
**Thalhimer**, Morton G., Jr. 1924- IntMPA 92
**Thalhofer**, Paul Terrance 1954- WhoAmL 92
**Thalia** EncAmaz 91
**Thall**, Peter Francis 1949- AmMWSc 92
**Thall**, Peter Morgan 1942- WhoEnt 92
**Thall**, Richard Vincent 1940- WhoWest 92
**Thallner**, Karl Anton, Jr. 1958- WhoAmL 92
**Thalman**, Mark DrAPF 91
**Thalmann**, Ernesto 1914- Who 92
**Thalmann**, Ernesto A. 1914- IntWW 91
**Thalmann**, Ernst 1886-1944 EncTR 91 [port]
**Thalmann**, Robert H 1939- AmMWSc 92
**Tham**, Hilary DrAPF 91
**Tham**, Min Kwan 1939- AmMWSc 92
**Tham**, Robert Quin-Yew 1952- WhoMW 92
**Thamer**, B J 1921- AmMWSc 92
**Thames**, Billy Howard 1944- WhoAmP 91
**Thames**, C H IntAu&W 91X, WrDr 92
**Thames**, Carroll Thomas 1938- WhoWest 92
**Thames**, Howard Davis, Jr 1941- AmMWSc 92
**Thames**, John Long 1924- AmMWSc 92
**Thames**, Marc 1944- AmMWSc 92
**Thames**, Mark Randall 1961- WhoRel 92
**Thames**, Shelby Freland 1936- AmMWSc 92
**Thames**, Uvena Woodruff 1944- WhoBlA 92
**Thames**, Walter Hendrix, Jr 1918- AmMWSc 92
**Thames**, William Gordon, Jr. 1960- WhoAmL 92
**Thamiris** EncAmaz 91
**Thampi**, Mohan Varghese 1960- WhoFI 92
**Thanassi**, John Walter 1937- AmMWSc 92
**Thanawala**, Kishor Premvadan 1936- WhoWest 92
**Thandeka** 1946- WhoBlA 92
**Thane**, Elswyth 1900- BenetAL 91
**Thane**, Russell T 1926- WhoAmP 91
**Thanedar**, Shri 1955- WhoMW 92
**Thanet**, Neil TwCSFW 91, WrDr 92
**Thanet**, Octave BenetAL 91
**Thangaraj**, Sandy 1934- AmMWSc 92
**Thani**, Abdul Aziz ibn Khalifa al- 1948- IntWW 91
**Thani**, Khalifa bin Hamad al- 1932- IntWW 91
**Thanin Kraivichien** IntWW 91
**Thapa**, Ganesh Bahadur 1936- IntWW 91
**Thapa**, Surya Bahadur 1928- IntWW 91
**Thapar**, Mangat Rai 1939- AmMWSc 92
**Thapar**, Nirwan T 1938- AmMWSc 92
**Thapar**, Romesh 1922- ConAu 133
**Tharalson**, D. N. 1943- WhoEnt 92
**Tharin**, James Cotter 1931- AmMWSc 92
**Tharoor**, Shashi 1956- IntAu&W 91
**Tharp**, A G 1927- AmMWSc 92
**Tharp**, Carleen Sue 1950- WhoMW 92
**Tharp**, Charles Christopher 1950- WhoFI 92
**Tharp**, Donald Andrew 1958- WhoRel 92
**Tharp**, Donald M. 1930- WhoRel 92
**Tharp**, Gerald D 1932- AmMWSc 92
**Tharp**, Gregg Alan 1957- WhoMW 92
**Tharp**, James C. WhoEnt 92
**Tharp**, James Wilson 1942- WhoAmL 92
**Tharp**, Roland DrAPF 91
**Tharp**, Twyla 1941- FacFETw, IntWW 91, WhoEnt 92
**Tharp**, Vernon Lance 1917- AmMWSc 92
**Tharp**, Winston Collins, Jr. 1943- WhoEnt 92
**Tharpe**, Rosetta 1915-1973 NotBlAW 92
**Tharpe**, Sister Rosetta 1915-1973 NewAmDM
**Thatcher**, Anthony Neville 1939- Who 92
**Thatcher**, Arthur ScFEYrs
**Thatcher**, Arthur Roger 1926- Who 92
**Thatcher**, Barbara Trainer 1932- WhoFI 92
**Thatcher**, Benjamin Bussey 1809-1840 BenetAL 91
**Thatcher**, Bruce Donald 1937- WhoMW 92
**Thatcher**, C M 1922- AmMWSc 92
**Thatcher**, David Allan 1945- WhoRel 92
**Thatcher**, Denis 1915- Who 92
**Thatcher**, Everett Whiting 1904- AmMWSc 92
**Thatcher**, Ginger Lynn WhoEnt 92
**Thatcher**, Harold W. 1908- WhoBlA 92
**Thatcher**, Janet Solverson 1946- WhoFI 92
**Thatcher**, Kristine Marie 1950- WhoEnt 92
**Thatcher**, Lori Anne 1964- WhoAmL 92
**Thatcher**, Margaret 1925- Who 92
**Thatcher**, Margaret Hilda 1925- FacFETw [port], IntWW 91
**Thatcher**, Mary Jo 1951- WhoEnt 92
**Thatcher**, Reginald 1927- WhoWest 92
**Thatcher**, Robert Clifford 1929- AmMWSc 92
**Thatcher**, Stephen Richard 1945- WhoWest 92
**Thatcher**, Walter Eugene 1927- AmMWSc 92
**Thatcher**, Wayne Raymond 1942- AmMWSc 92
**Thatcher**, William Watters 1942- AmMWSc 92
**Thau**, Frederick E 1938- AmMWSc 92
**Thau**, Rosemarie B Zischka 1936- AmMWSc 92
**Thauer**, Edwin William, Jr. 1953- WhoMW 92
**Thaw**, Bruce R. 1953- WhoAmL 92
**Thaw**, Clifton Baily Beach, III 1962- WhoAmL 92
**Thaw**, Harry K. d1947 FacFETw
**Thaw**, John 1942- ConTFT 9, Who 92
**Thaw**, Mort WhoEnt 92
**Thaw**, Richard Franklin 1920- AmMWSc 92
**Thaw**, Sheila Who 92
**Thawka**, Mao d1991 NewYTBS 91
**Thawley**, David Gorden 1946- AmMWSc 92
**Thaxter**, Celia 1835-1894 BenetAL 91
**Thaxter**, Celia Laighton 1835-1894 BibAL 8
**Thaxter**, Phyllis 1921- IntMPA 92
**Thaxter**, Phyllis St. Felix 1919- WhoEnt 92
**Thaxton**, Everette Frederick 1938- WhoAmL 92, WhoFI 92
**Thaxton**, George Donald 1931- AmMWSc 92
**Thaxton**, James Paul 1941- AmMWSc 92
**Thaxton**, Judy Evette 1961- WhoBlA 92
**Thayer**, Arthur Ralph 1925- WhoAmP 91
**Thayer**, Charles Paine 1843-1910 BiInAmS
**Thayer**, Charles Walter 1944- AmMWSc 92
**Thayer**, Chester Arthur 1948- AmMWSc 92
**Thayer**, Donald Wayne 1937- AmMWSc 92
**Thayer**, Donald Wayne 1948- WhoWest 92
**Thayer**, Duane M 1934- AmMWSc 92
**Thayer**, Edna Louise 1936- WhoFI 92, WhoMW 92
**Thayer**, Edwin Cabot 1935- WhoEnt 92
**Thayer**, Ernest Lawrence BenetAL 91
**Thayer**, Fred James 1929- WhoMW 92
**Thayer**, Gene 1932- WhoAmP 91
**Thayer**, Gerald Campbell 1943- WhoFI 92
**Thayer**, Geraldine IntAu&W 91X, WrDr 92
**Thayer**, Gordon Wallace 1940- AmMWSc 92
**Thayer**, Hanford 1909- WhoWest 92
**Thayer**, Harold Eugene 1912- WhoMW 92
**Thayer**, Harry E T 1927- WhoAmP 91
**Thayer**, James M. 1941- WhoRel 92
**Thayer**, James Norris 1926- WhoWest 92
**Thayer**, John 1949- WhoEnt 92
**Thayer**, John Stearns 1938- AmMWSc 92, WhoMW 92
**Thayer**, Keith Evans 1928- AmMWSc 92
**Thayer**, LeRoy C 1932- WhoAmP 91
**Thayer**, Marcia Lynn 1948- WhoRel 92
**Thayer**, Martha Ann 1936- WhoWest 92
**Thayer**, Paul Arthur 1940- AmMWSc 92
**Thayer**, Paul Loyd 1928- AmMWSc 92
**Thayer**, Philip Standish 1923- AmMWSc 92
**Thayer**, Robert Wilcox 1927- WhoEnt 92, WhoMW 92
**Thayer**, Roger Edward 1934- WhoAmL 92
**Thayer**, Rollin Harold 1916- AmMWSc 92
**Thayer**, Susan Elizabeth 1954- WhoWest 92
**Thayer**, W Stephen WhoAmP 91
**Thayer**, Walter Raymond, Jr 1929- AmMWSc 92
**Thayer**, Walter Stephen, III 1946- WhoAmL 92
**Thayer**, Webster DcAmImH
**Thayer**, William 1948- AmMWSc 92
**Thayer**, William Wentworth 1926- WhoWest 92
**Thayler**, Carl DrAPF 91
**Thayne**, Emma Lou W. DrAPF 91
**Thayne**, William V 1941- AmMWSc 92
**The Black Phoenix** 1946- WhoEnt 92
**The**, Guy Blaudin de IntWW 91
**The**, Victor 1942- WhoFI 92
**Thebault**, Eugene d1942 ScFEYrs
**Thebeau**, Robert Stephen 1939- WhoMW 92
**Theberge**, James Daniel 1930- IntWW 91, WhoAmP 91
**Thebom**, Blanche 1918- NewAmDM
**Thecla** EncEarC
**Thedford**, Roosevelt 1937- AmMWSc 92
**Thee**, Francis Charles Rudolph 1936- WhoRel 92
**Theeuwes**, Felix 1937- AmMWSc 92
**Theil**, Elizabeth 1936- AmMWSc 92
**Theil**, Henri 1924- WrDr 92
**Theil**, Michael Herbert 1933- AmMWSc 92
**Theilen**, Ernest Otto 1923- AmMWSc 92
**Theilen**, Gordon H 1928- AmMWSc 92
**Theiler**, Max 1899-1972 WhoNob 90
**Theilheimer**, Feodor 1909- AmMWSc 92
**Theilheimer**, William 1914- AmMWSc 92
**Theimer**, Axel Knut 1946- WhoMW 92, WhoRel 92
**Theimer**, Edgar E 1915- AmMWSc 92
**Theimer**, Otto 1918- AmMWSc 92
**Theine**, Alice 1938- AmMWSc 92
**Theiner**, Georg 1927-1985 FacFETw
**Theiner**, George Fredric 1927- IntAu&W 91
**Theiner**, Micha 1936- AmMWSc 92
**Theis**, Adolf 1933- IntWW 91
**Theis**, Frank Gordon 1911- WhoAmL 92, WhoMW 92
**Theis**, Henry Ericsson 1933- WhoFI 92
**Theis**, James Edward 1963- WhoWest 92
**Theis**, James F 1924- WhoIns 92
**Theis**, Jerold Howard 1938- AmMWSc 92
**Theis**, Joan C. 1948- WhoWest 92
**Theis**, Paul Anthony 1923- WhoAmP 91
**Theis**, Richard James 1937- AmMWSc 92
**Theis**, William Harold 1945- WhoAmL 92
**Theisen**, Cynthia Theres AmMWSc 92
**Theisen**, Edwin Mathew 1930- WhoMW 92
**Theisen**, George I. 1926- WhoFI 92
**Theisen**, Michael Jourdan 1961- WhoRel 92
**Theisen**, Sylvester Peter 1924- WhoMW 92
**Theisen**, Wilfred Robert 1929- AmMWSc 92, WhoMW 92
**Theiss**, Bill ConTFT 9
**Theiss**, Jeffrey Charles 1946- AmMWSc 92
**Theiss**, William ConTFT 9
**Theiss**, William Ware ConTFT 9
**Thekdi**, Arvind C 1941- AmMWSc 92
**Thel**, Steve Scott 1954- WhoAmL 92
**Thelen**, Charles John 1921- AmMWSc 92
**Thelen**, David P. 1939- ConAu 134
**Thelen**, John F 1949- WhoIns 92
**Thelen**, Theodore David 1947- WhoAmL 92
**Thelen**, Thomas Harvey 1941- AmMWSc 92
**Thelen**, Trisha Ann 1960- WhoAmP 91
**Thelin**, Jack Horstmann 1912- AmMWSc 92
**Thelin**, Lowell Charles 1946- AmMWSc 92
**Thellmann**, Edward L AmMWSc 92
**Thellusson** Who 92
**Thelman**, John Patrick 1942- AmMWSc 92
**Thelwell**, Norman 1923- IntAu&W 91, TwCPaSc, Who 92
**Themba**, Can 1924-1968 LiExTwC
**Themelis**, John C. 1947- WhoAmL 92
**Themelis**, Nickolas John 1933- AmMWSc 92
**Themerson**, Franciszka 1907-1988 TwCPaSc
**Themerson**, Stefan 1910-1988 SmATA 65
**Themistius** EncEarC
**Themistius** 317?-388 EncEarC
**Themstrup**, Bendt WhoIns 92
**Thenen**, Shirley Warnock AmMWSc 92
**Theno**, Daniel O'Connell 1947- WhoAmP 91
**Theobald**, Charles Edwin, Jr 1927- AmMWSc 92
**Theobald**, Edward Robert 1947- WhoAmL 92, WhoFI 92, WhoMW 92
**Theobald**, Frederick Thompson 1949- WhoAmL 92
**Theobald**, George Peter 1931- Who 92
**Theobald**, J Karl 1921- AmMWSc 92
**Theobald**, John J 1904- AmMWSc 92
**Theobald**, Lewis, Jr. ConAu 133
**Theobald**, Michael Paul 1949- WhoWest 92
**Theobald**, Robert 1929- IntAu&W 91, WrDr 92
**Theobald**, Thomas C. 1937- IntWW 91
**Theobald**, Thomas Charles 1937- WhoFI 92, WhoMW 92
**Theobald**, William L 1936- AmMWSc 92
**Theobald**, William Louis 1936- WhoWest 92
**Theocharis**, Reghinos D. 1929- IntWW 91
**Theocharus**, Gregory 1929- Who 92
**Theodora** 500?-548 EncEarC
**Theodorakis**, Mikis 1925- IntMPA 92, IntWW 91
**Theodore of Mopsuestia** 350?-428 EncEarC
**Theodore**, Ares Nicholas 1933- WhoMW 92
**Theodore**, Carla DrAPF 91
**Theodore**, Joseph M, Jr 1931- AmMWSc 92
**Theodore**, Keith Felix 1948- WhoBlA 92
**Theodore**, Nick Andrew 1928- WhoAmP 91
**Theodore**, Samuel Serban 1952- WhoFI 92
**Theodore**, Ted George 1937- AmMWSc 92
**Theodore**, Terry 1936- WhoEnt 92
**Theodore**, Theodore Spiros 1933- AmMWSc 92
**Theodore**, Yvonne M. 1939- WhoBlA 92
**Theodoret of Cyrus** 393-460? EncEarC
**Theodoric** 455?-526 EncEarC
**Theodorides**, Vassilios John 1931- AmMWSc 92
**Theodoridis**, George Constantin 1935- AmMWSc 92
**Theodorou**, Doros Nicolas 1957- AmMWSc 92
**Theodorou**, Jerry 1959- WhoFI 92
**Theodosius I** 346?-395 EncEarC
**Theodosius II** 401-450 EncEarC
**Theodosius**, His Beatitude Metropolitan 1933- WhoRel 92
**Theodosius**, Metropolitan 1933- RelLAm 91
**Theodotion** EncEarC
**Theodotus** EncEarC
**Theodotus The Banker** EncEarC
**Theodotus The Leatherworker** EncEarC
**Theofanous**, Theofanis George 1942- AmMWSc 92
**Theofilopoulos**, Argyrios N AmMWSc 92
**Theognostus** d282 EncEarC
**Theoharis**, Lakis Efstathios 1952- WhoFI 92
**Theokritoff**, George 1924- AmMWSc 92
**Theologides**, Athanasios 1931- AmMWSc 92
**Theologitis**, John Michael 1956- WhoFI 92
**Theon**, John Speridon 1934- AmMWSc 92
**Theophanides**, Theophile 1932- AmMWSc 92

**Theophilus**, Metropolitan 1874-1950 *RelLAm 91*
**Theophilus of Alexandria** d412 *EncEarC*
**Theophilus of Antioch** *EncEarC*
**Theophilus**, Martin 1946- *WhoEnt 92*
**Theopold**, Klaus Hulmut 1954- *AmMWSc 92*
**Theorell**, Axel Hugo Teodor 1903-1982 *WhoNob 90*
**Theos**, Jerry Nicholas 1957- *WhoAmL 92*
**Theos**, Nick *WhoAmP 91*
**Theresa Figueur of Lyon** *EncAmaz 91*
**Theriault**, Gilles P *AmMWSc 92*
**Theriault**, Lucien J. 1926- *WhoMW 92*
**Theriault**, Raynold 1936- *WhoAmP 91*
**Theriault**, Romeo J 1923- *WhoAmP 91*
**Theriault**, Yves 1915-1983 *BenetAL 91*
**Theriot**, Edward Dennis, Jr 1938- *AmMWSc 92*
**Theriot**, Kevin Jude 1958- *AmMWSc 92*
**Theriot**, Leo Jude 1956- *WhoRel 92*
**Theriot**, Leroy James 1935- *AmMWSc 92*
**Theriot**, Sam, Sr 1914- *WhoAmP 91*
**Theriot**, Sam H, Jr 1954- *WhoAmP 91*
**Theriot**, Steve Joseph 1946- *WhoAmP 91*
**Thern**, Royal Edward 1942- *AmMWSc 92*
**Theroigne de Mericourt** 1762-1817 *BlkwCEP*
**Theroux**, Alexander 1939- *BenetAL 91, ConNov 91, WrDr 92*
**Theroux**, Alexander Louis *DrAPF 91*
**Theroux**, Eugene 1938- *WhoAmL 92*
**Theroux**, Gary Michael 1951- *WhoEnt 92*
**Theroux**, Joseph 1953- *ConAu 133*
**Theroux**, Paul *DrAPF 91, LiExTwC*
**Theroux**, Paul 1941- *BenetAL 91, ConNov 91, IntAu&W 91, WrDr 92*
**Theroux**, Paul Edward 1941- *IntWW 91, Who 92*
**Therriault**, Daniel 1953- *IntAu&W 91*
**Therrien**, Chester Dale 1936- *AmMWSc 92*
**Therrien**, Eileen Marie 1956- *WhoRel 92*
**Therrien**, Francois Xavier, Jr. 1928- *WhoFI 92*
**Therrien**, Valerie Monica 1951- *WhoAmP 91*
**Thesen**, Hjalmar Peter 1925- *WrDr 92*
**Thesen**, Sharon 1946- *ConPo 91, WrDr 92*
**Thesiger** *Who 92*
**Thesiger**, Ernest 1879-1961 *TwCPaSc*
**Thesiger**, Roderic Miles Doughty 1915- *Who 92*
**Thesiger**, Wilfred 1910- *IntWW 91, WrDr 92*
**Thesiger**, Wilfred Patrick 1910- *Who 92*
**Thesing**, James J. 1941- *WhoEnt 92*
**Thesing**, Kenneth Francis 1942- *WhoRel 92*
**Thet**, Lyn Aung *AmMWSc 92*
**Thetford**, Bishop Suffragan of *Who 92*
**Thetford**, Violet Lieu 1949- *WhoFI 92*
**Theuer**, Paul John 1936- *AmMWSc 92, WhoFI 92*
**Theuer**, Richard C 1939- *AmMWSc 92*
**Theuer**, William John 1935- *AmMWSc 92*
**Theuner**, Douglas Edwin 1938- *WhoRel 92*
**Theurer**, Byron W. 1939- *WhoWest 92*
**Theurer**, Clark Brent 1934- *AmMWSc 92*
**Theurer**, Hans D., Jr. 1935- *WhoWest 92*
**Theurer**, Jessop Clair 1928- *AmMWSc 92*
**Theus**, BJ 1947- *WhoEnt 92*
**Theus**, Jeremiah *DcAmImH*
**Theus**, Lucius 1922- *WhoBlA 92*
**Theus**, Reggie 1957- *WhoBlA 92*
**Theusch**, Colleen Joan 1932- *AmMWSc 92*
**Theut**, Clarence Peter 1938- *WhoAmL 92*
**Thevenin**, Denis *ConAu 35NR*
**Thewalt**, F. William 1935- *WhoMW 92*
**Thewes**, Mark Allan 1954- *WhoRel 92*
**Thews**, Daniel Paul 1963- *WhoRel 92*
**Thews**, Gerhard 1926- *IntWW 91*
**Thews**, Robert L 1939- *AmMWSc 92*
**Thews**, Verl Jasper 1923- *WhoAmP 91*
**They Might Be Giants** *ConMus 7 [port]*
**Thiagarajan**, Perumal 1951- *WhoWest 92*
**Thiam**, Habib 1933- *IntWW 91*
**Thian**, Robert Peter 1943- *Who 92*
**Thiandoum**, Hyacinthe 1921- *IntWW 91, WhoRel 92*
**Thibau**, Jacques Henri 1928- *IntWW 91*
**Thibaud**, Jacques 1880-1953 *FacFETw, NewAmDM*
**Thibault**, Jacques Anatole-Francois 1844-1924 *WhoNob 90*
**Thibault**, James Alfred 1966- *WhoFI 92*
**Thibault**, Roger Edward 1947- *AmMWSc 92*
**Thibault**, Thomas Delor 1942- *AmMWSc 92*
**Thibeau**, Jack *DrAPF 91*
**Thibeault**, George Walter 1941- *WhoAmL 92*
**Thibeault**, Jack Claude 1946- *AmMWSc 92*
**Thibeault**, Robert Allen 1948- *WhoAmP 91*
**Thibert**, Roger Joseph 1929- *AmMWSc 92*
**Thibodeau**, Gary A 1938- *AmMWSc 92, WhoMW 92*
**Thibodeau**, Joseph Maurice 1929- *WhoEnt 92*
**Thibodeau**, Phillip Eldridge 1945- *WhoWest 92*
**Thibodeau**, Thomas Raymond 1942- *WhoAmL 92*
**Thibodeaux**, Donald 1937- *WhoAmP 91*
**Thibodeaux**, James Marvin 1930- *WhoAmP 91*
**Thibodeaux**, Joe N. 1953- *WhoFI 92*
**Thibodeaux**, Louis J 1939- *AmMWSc 92*
**Thibodeaux**, Sylvia Marie 1937- *WhoBlA 92*
**Thich**, John Adong 1948- *AmMWSc 92*
**Thicke**, Alan *LesBEnT 92, WhoEnt 92*
**Thickstcn**, Edward F 1947- *WhoAmP 91*
**Thickstun**, William Russell, Jr 1922- *AmMWSc 92*
**Thiebaud**, Wayne 1920- *IntWW 91, News 91*
**Thiebaut**, William, Jr 1947- *WhoAmP 91*
**Thiebauth**, Bruce Edward 1947- *WhoFI 92, WhoMW 92*
**Thiebaux**, Helen Jean 1935- *AmMWSc 92*
**Thieberger**, Peter 1935- *AmMWSc 92*
**Thiede**, Barbara Josephine 1949- *WhoMW 92*
**Thiede**, Edwin C. 1937- *WhoMW 92*
**Thiede**, Edwin Carl 1937- *AmMWSc 92*
**Thiede**, Henry A 1926- *AmMWSc 92*
**Thiede**, Michael Ernest 1947- *WhoRel 92*
**Thiede**, Paul Martin 1947- *WhoAmP 91*
**Thiede**, Richard Wesley 1936- *WhoMW 92*
**Thiel**, Frank Anthony 1928- *WhoIns 92*
**Thiel**, Frank L 1942- *AmMWSc 92*
**Thiel**, John E. 1951- *WhoRel 92*
**Thiel**, Patricia Ann 1953- *AmMWSc 92*
**Thiel**, Philip 1920- *WhoEnt 92*
**Thiel**, Ruth Eleanor 1930- *WhoMW 92*
**Thiel**, Thomas J 1928- *AmMWSc 92*
**Thiel**, Thomas Joseph 1928- *WhoFI 92*
**Thiel**, William Bernard 1927- *WhoMW 92*
**Thiel**, Winfried Werner 1940- *WhoRel 92*
**Thiele**, Colin 1920- *WrDr 92*
**Thiele**, Elizabeth Henriette 1920- *AmMWSc 92*
**Thiele**, Ernest 1895- *AmMWSc 92*
**Thiele**, Gary Allen 1938- *AmMWSc 92*
**Thiele**, Herbert William Albert 1953- *WhoAmL 92*
**Thiele**, Howard Nellis, Jr. 1930- *WhoAmL 92*
**Thiele**, Jonathan Karl 1956- *WhoAmL 92*
**Thiele**, Leslie Kathleen 1952- *WhoAmL 92*
**Thiele**, Margaret 1901- *IntAu&W 91*
**Thiele**, Ron *WhoEnt 92*
**Thiele**, William E 1942- *WhoIns 92*
**Thiele**, William Edward 1942- *WhoFI 92*
**Thielemans**, Toots 1922- *NewAmDM*
**Thielen**, Cynthia *WhoAmP 91*
**Thielen**, Lawrence Eugene 1921- *AmMWSc 92*
**Thielen**, Thoralf Theodore 1921- *WhoRel 92*
**Thielges**, Bart A 1938- *AmMWSc 92*
**Thielmann**, Vernon James 1937- *AmMWSc 92*
**Thiels**, Elizabeth Louise 1944- *WhoEnt 92*
**Thielsch**, Helmut 1922- *AmMWSc 92*
**Thiem**, E. George 1897-1987 *ConAu 134*
**Thiem**, George *ConAu 134*
**Thieman**, Theodore Eugene 1930- *WhoRel 92*
**Thiemann**, Bernd 1943- *IntWW 91*
**Thiemann**, Charles Lee 1937- *WhoFI 92, WhoMW 92*
**Thiemann**, Elke Lucia 1942- *WhoWest 92*
**Thiemann**, Ronald Frank 1946- *WhoRel 92*
**Thieme**, Allan Roy 1937- *WhoMW 92*
**Thieme**, Cornelis Leo Hans 1948- *AmMWSc 92*
**Thieme**, Melvin T 1925- *AmMWSc 92*
**Thieme**, Robert Bunger, Jr. 1918- *RelLAm 91*
**Thiemele**, Amoakon-Edjampan 1941- *IntWW 91*
**Thien**, Leonard B 1938- *AmMWSc 92*
**Thien**, Stephen John 1944- *AmMWSc 92*
**Thiene**, Paul G 1919- *AmMWSc 92*
**Thier**, Samuel Osiah 1937- *AmMWSc 92, IntWW 91*
**Thierack**, Otto 1889-1946 *EncTR 91 [port]*
**Thierack**, Otto Georg 1889-1946 *BiDExR*
**Thierauf**, Robert James 1933- *WrDr 92*
**Thierbach**, Marlene Allen 1951- *WhoAmL 92*
**Thieret**, John William 1926- *AmMWSc 92*
**Thieret**, Mark Lynn 1962- *WhoRel 92*
**Thierfelder**, Paul Edward 1956- *WhoRel 92*
**Thiermann**, Alejandro Bories 1947- *AmMWSc 92*
**Thiernau**, Albert Richard 1927- *WhoMW 92*
**Thierolf**, Richard Burton, Jr. 1948- *WhoAmL 92*
**Thierrin**, Gabriel 1921- *AmMWSc 92*
**Thiers**, Eugene Andres 1941- *AmMWSc 92, WhoHisp 92*
**Thiers**, Harry Delbert 1919- *AmMWSc 92*
**Thierstein**, Gerald E 1931- *AmMWSc 92*
**Thierstein**, Hans Rudolf 1944- *AmMWSc 92*
**Thiery**, Jean Paul 1947- *AmMWSc 92*
**Thies**, Clifford Francis 1952- *WhoFI 92*
**Thies**, Richard Leon 1931- *WhoAmL 92*
**Thies**, Richard William 1941- *AmMWSc 92*
**Thies**, Roger E 1933- *AmMWSc 92*
**Thiesen**, Gregory Alan 1958- *WhoWest 92*
**Thiesfeld**, Virgil Arthur 1937- *AmMWSc 92*
**Thiess**, Frank 1890-1977 *EncTR 91 [port]*
**Thiess**, Leslie Charles 1909- *Who 92*
**Thiessen**, Brian David *WhoAmL 92*
**Thiessen**, Cornie R 1910- *WhoAmP 91*
**Thiessen**, Dan *WhoAmP 91*
**Thiessen**, Donald Barry 1959- *WhoEnt 92*
**Thiessen**, Henry Archer 1940- *AmMWSc 92*
**Thiessen**, Jack 1931- *ConAu 34NR*
**Thiessen**, Jacob Willem 1928- *AmMWSc 92*
**Thiessen**, John *ConAu 34NR*
**Thiessen**, Reinhardt, Jr 1913- *AmMWSc 92*
**Thiessen**, William Ernest 1934- *AmMWSc 92*
**Thieu**, Nguyen Van *IntWW 91*
**Thieu**, Nguyen Van 1923- *FacFETw [port]*
**Thigpen**, Calvin Herritage 1924- *WhoBlA 92*
**Thigpen**, Charles Allen 1926- *WhoRel 92*
**Thigpen**, Edmund Leonard 1930- *WhoBlA 92*
**Thigpen**, J J 1917- *AmMWSc 92*
**Thigpen**, Joe Dennard 1942- *WhoWest 92*
**Thigpen**, Neal Dorsey 1939- *WhoAmP 91*
**Thigpen**, Richard Elton, Jr. 1930- *WhoAmL 92*
**Thilenius**, Otto G 1929- *AmMWSc 92*
**Thill**, Donald Cecil 1950- *AmMWSc 92*
**Thill**, Ronald E 1944- *AmMWSc 92*
**Thilmony**, Magdalena Marie 1932- *WhoMW 92*
**Thimann**, Kenneth Vivian 1904- *AmMWSc 92, IntWW 91, Who 92, WrDr 92*
**Thimmesh**, Hilary Donald 1928- *WhoMW 92*
**Thimon**, Jacques Bernard 1942- *WhoFI 92*
**Thimont**, Bernard Maurice 1920- *Who 92*
**Thimotheose**, Kadakampallil George 1938- *WhoMW 92*
**Thin**, U. Tun *IntWW 91*
**Thind**, Gurdarshan S 1940- *AmMWSc 92*
**Thinnes**, Jeffrey Alan 1956- *WhoFI 92*
**Thinnes**, Roy *WhoEnt 92*
**Thinnes**, Roy 1938- *IntMPA 92*
**Thio**, Alan Poo-An 1931- *AmMWSc 92*
**Third**, Richard Henry McPhail *Who 92*
**Thirgood**, Jack Vincent 1924- *AmMWSc 92*
**Thiriart**, Jean Francois 1922- *BiDExR*
**Thirion**, Jean Paul Joseph 1939- *AmMWSc 92*
**Thirkell**, Angela 1890-1961 *RfGEnL 91*
**Thirkettle**, Ellis 1904- *Who 92*
**Thirkill**, John D 1929- *AmMWSc 92*
**Thirlwall**, George Edwin 1924- *Who 92*
**Thiroux**, Jacques Paul 1928- *WhoWest 92*
**Thirring**, Walter E. 1927- *IntWW 91*
**Thirsk**, Joan 1922- *IntWW 91, Who 92, WrDr 92*
**Thirumalai**, Devarajan 1956- *AmMWSc 92*
**Thiruvathukal**, John Varkey 1939- *AmMWSc 92*
**Thiruvathukal**, Kris V 1925- *AmMWSc 92*
**Thiruvengadam**, Alagu Pillai 1935- *AmMWSc 92*
**Thiry**, Marcel 1897- *IntAu&W 91*
**Thiselton**, Anthony Charles 1937- *Who 92*
**Thissell**, Charles William 1931- *WhoWest 92*
**Thissell**, James Dennis 1935- *WhoWest 92*
**Thissen**, Francine 1933- *WhoEnt 92*
**Thissen**, Wil A *AmMWSc 92*
**Thisted**, Ronald Aaron 1951- *AmMWSc 92*
**Thistel**, Cynthia Grelle 1955- *WhoWest 92*
**Thistle**, Dale *WhoAmP 91*
**Thistlethwaite**, Frank 1915- *IntAu&W 91, Who 92*
**Thistlethwaite**, Morvenna *TwCPaSc*
**Thistlethwaite**, Paul Calvin 1945- *WhoMW 92*
**Thistlewood**, Thomas 1721-1786 *BenetAL 91*
**Thiusen**, Ismar 1836-1909 *ScFEYrs*
**Tho**, Le Duc *IntWW 91*
**Thoburn**, Wilbur Wilson d1899 *BiInAmS*
**Thoday**, John Marion 1916- *Who 92*
**Thode**, E F 1921- *AmMWSc 92*
**Thode**, Henry George 1910- *IntWW 91, Who 92*
**Thode**, Lester Elster 1943- *AmMWSc 92*
**Thodos**, George 1915- *AmMWSc 92*
**Thody**, Philip 1928- *WrDr 92*
**Thody**, Philip Malcolm Waller 1928- *Who 92*
**Thoe**, Robert Steven 1945- *AmMWSc 92*
**Thoele**, Perry Ervin 1943- *WhoEnt 92*
**Thoelen**, Frank Thomas 1948- *WhoFI 92*
**Thoen**, Doris Rae 1925- *WhoAmP 91*
**Thoen**, Roberta 1944- *WhoRel 92*
**Thoene**, Jess Gilbert 1942- *AmMWSc 92*
**Thoene**, Peter *ConAu 34NR*
**Thoft**, Bob 1929- *WhoAmP 91*
**Thogmorton**, James Pleasant 1921- *WhoMW 92*
**Tholborn**, Brett Lewis 1957- *WhoWest 92*
**Tholen**, Albert David 1927- *AmMWSc 92*
**Tholen**, Lawrence Arthur 1938- *WhoFI 92*
**Tholfsen**, Trygve R. 1924- *ConAu 134*
**Thom**, Alexander 1894-1985 *ConAu 133*
**Thom**, Drummond Robert 1936- *WhoRel 92*
**Thom**, James Alexander *DrAPF 91*
**Thom**, James Alexander 1933- *IntAu&W 91, TwCWW 91, WrDr 92*
**Thom**, Kenneth Cadwallader 1922- *Who 92*
**Thom**, Michael Andrew 1953- *WhoMW 92*
**Thom**, Randy 1951- *WhoEnt 92*
**Thom**, Ronald Mark 1948- *AmMWSc 92*
**Thoma**, George Edward 1922- *AmMWSc 92*
**Thoma**, George Ranjan 1944- *AmMWSc 92*
**Thoma**, John Anthony 1932- *AmMWSc 92*
**Thoma**, Klaus Dieter 1945- *WhoAmL 92*
**Thoma**, Kurt Michael 1946- *WhoFI 92, WhoRel 92*
**Thoma**, Richard William 1921- *AmMWSc 92*
**Thoma**, Roy E 1922- *AmMWSc 92*
**Thomae**, Betty Jane Kennedy 1920- *IntAu&W 91*
**Thomae**, Betty Kennedy 1920- *WrDr 92*
**Thoman**, Charles James 1928- *AmMWSc 92*
**Thoman**, Marilyn Louise *AmMWSc 92*
**Thoman**, Mark Edward 1936- *WhoMW 92*
**Thomann**, Gary C 1942- *AmMWSc 92*
**Thomann**, Robert V 1934- *AmMWSc 92*
**Thomas** *EncEarC, Who 92*
**Thomas**, A. E. 1872-1947 *BenetAL 91*
**Thomas**, Adrian Tregerthen 1947- *Who 92*
**Thomas**, Adrian Wesley 1939- *AmMWSc 92*
**Thomas**, Alan *Who 92*
**Thomas**, Alan 1923- *WhoFI 92, WhoMW 92*
**Thomas**, Alan Gradon 1911- *WrDr 92*
**Thomas**, Alan Richard 1942- *WhoFI 92*
**Thomas**, Albert Lee, Jr 1923- *AmMWSc 92*
**Thomas**, Alexander 1914- *AmMWSc 92*
**Thomas**, Alexander Edward, III 1930- *AmMWSc 92*
**Thomas**, Alford Mitchell 1942- *AmMWSc 92*
**Thomas**, Alfred Robert 1927- *WhoAmP 91*
**Thomas**, Alfred Strickland 1900- *IntAu&W 91*
**Thomas**, Alfred Victor 1929- *WhoAmP 91*
**Thomas**, Alice Martin 1963- *WhoAmL 92*
**Thomas**, Alice Waters 1912- *WhoBlA 92*
**Thomas**, Allen Lloyd 1939- *WhoAmL 92*
**Thomas**, Alma 1891-1978 *HanAmWH, NotBlAW 92 [port]*
**Thomas**, Alston Havard Rees 1925- *Who 92*
**Thomas**, Alvin 1951- *WhoBlA 92*
**Thomas**, Alvin David, Jr 1928- *AmMWSc 92*
**Thomas**, Ambler Reginald 1913- *Who 92*
**Thomas**, Ambroise 1811-1896 *NewAmDM*
**Thomas**, Andre Jean 1905- *IntWW 91*
**Thomas**, Andrew Lynn 1963- *WhoRel 92*
**Thomas**, Aneurin Morgan 1921- *Who 92*
**Thomas**, Ann Freda 1951- *WhoAmL 92*
**Thomas**, Ann Victoria 1943- *WhoAmL 92*
**Thomas**, Anthony 1931- *AmMWSc 92*
**Thomas**, Antony Charles 1928- *Who 92*
**Thomas**, Archibald Johns, III 1952- *WhoAmL 92*
**Thomas**, Arthur E. *WhoBlA 92*
**Thomas**, Arthur L 1928- *AmMWSc 92*
**Thomas**, Arthur Norman 1931- *AmMWSc 92*
**Thomas**, Aubrey Damon 1931- *WhoRel 92*
**Thomas**, Aubrey Stephen, Jr 1933- *AmMWSc 92*
**Thomas**, Audrey 1935- *BenetAL 91, ConAu 36NR, ConNov 91, WrDr 92*
**Thomas**, Audrey Grace 1935- *IntAu&W 91*
**Thomas**, Audria Acty 1954- *WhoBlA 92*
**Thomas**, Augustus 1857-1934 *BenetAL 91*
**Thomas**, Barbara Ann 1948- *WhoEnt 92*

Thomas, Barry 1941- *AmMWSc 92*
Thomas, Barry D. 1963- *WhoAmL 92*
Thomas, Barry Dickens 1962- *WhoEnt 92*
Thomas, Barry Holland 1939- *AmMWSc 92*
Thomas, Barry Wyeth 1933- *WhoFI 92*
Thomas, Benita Yvette 1966- *WhoWest 92*
Thomas, Benjamin 1910- *WhoBlA 92*
Thomas, Benjamin, Jr. 1961- *WhoBlA 92*
Thomas, Benjamin Franklin 1850-1911 *BiInAmS*
Thomas, Bert O 1926- *AmMWSc 92*
Thomas, Bertha Sophia 1959- *WhoMW 92*
Thomas, Bertram David 1903- *WhoWest 92*
Thomas, Berwyn Brainerd 1919- *AmMWSc 92*
Thomas, Betty 1948- *IntMPA 92*
Thomas, Bide Lakin 1935- *WhoFI 92, WhoMW 92*
Thomas, Bill Harrold 1950- *WhoEnt 92*
Thomas, Billy 1920- *WhoEnt 92*
Thomas, Billy Joe 1942- *WhoEnt 92*
Thomas, Billy Seay 1926- *AmMWSc 92*
Thomas, Blair *WhoBlA 92*
Thomas, Blythe J 1933- *WhoAmP 91*
Thomas, Booker T. 1936- *WhoBlA 92*
Thomas, Bradford Albert 1953- *WhoAmL 92*
Thomas, Brenda 1950- *TwCPaSc*
Thomas, Brian Gordon 1957- *WhoMW 92*
Thomas, Brinley *Who 92*
Thomas, Broderick 1967- *WhoBlA 92*
Thomas, Bruce *ConAu 134, TwCWW 91*
Thomas, Bruce Lorrey 1930- *WhoMW 92*
Thomas, Bruce Robert 1938- *AmMWSc 92*
Thomas, Byron Henry 1897- *AmMWSc 92*
Thomas, C. Edward 1935- *WhoBlA 92*
Thomas, Caldwell 1932- *WhoRel 92*
Thomas, Calvin Lewis 1960- *WhoBlA 92*
Thomas, Calvin Merrill, II 1936- *WhoEnt 92*
Thomas, Carey 1857-1935 *BenetAL 91*
Thomas, Carl Alan 1924- *WhoBlA 92*
Thomas, Carl D. 1950- *WhoBlA 92*
Thomas, Carl H 1925- *AmMWSc 92*
Thomas, Carol M. 1930- *WhoBlA 92*
Thomas, Carolyn Eyster 1928- *AmMWSc 92*
Thomas, Cecil Owen, Jr 1942- *AmMWSc 92*
Thomas, Cecil Wayne 1941- *AmMWSc 92*
Thomas, Cedric Marshall 1930- *Who 92*
Thomas, Charles *Who 92*
Thomas, Charles 1928- *WrDr 92*
Thomas, Charles, Jr 1948- *WhoAmP 91*
Thomas, Charles Allen 1900-1982 *FacFETw*
Thomas, Charles Allen, Jr 1927- *AmMWSc 92*
Thomas, Charles Carlisle, Jr 1925- *AmMWSc 92, WhoWest 92*
Thomas, Charles Carroll 1930- *WhoFI 92*
Thomas, Charles Columbus *DrAPF 91*
Thomas, Charles Columbus 1940- *WhoBlA 92*
Thomas, Charles Edward 1927- *Who 92*
Thomas, Charles H 1934- *WhoAmP 91*
Thomas, Charles Hill 1922- *AmMWSc 92*
Thomas, Charles L 1905- *AmMWSc 92*
Thomas, Charles Richard 1933- *WhoBlA 92*
Thomas, Charles S. 1945- *WhoWest 92*
Thomas, Charles W. 1940- *WhoBlA 92*
Thomas, Charles William, II 1926- *WhoBlA 92*
Thomas, Chauncey 1822-1898 *ScFEYrs*
Thomas, Chauncey 1872-1941 *ScFEYrs*
Thomas, Chris 1957- *TwCPaSc*
Thomas, Christa Louise 1957- *WhoFI 92*
Thomas, Christian 1655-1728 *BlkwCEP*
Thomas, Christopher David 1960- *WhoAmL 92*
Thomas, Christopher Frederick 1946- *WhoMW 92*
Thomas, Christopher Pearce 1945- *WhoWest 92*
Thomas, Christopher Sydney 1950- *Who 92*
Thomas, Christopher Yancey, III 1923- *WhoMW 92*
Thomas, Cindy L. 1955- *WhoFI 92*
Thomas, Clara McCandless 1919- *WrDr 92*
Thomas, Clarence 1948- *ConBlB 2 [port], NewYTBS 91 [port], News 92-2 [port], WhoAmL 92, WhoAmP 91, WhoBlA 92, WhoFI 92*
Thomas, Claude Earle 1940- *AmMWSc 92*
Thomas, Claude Roderick 1943- *WhoBlA 92*
Thomas, Claudewell Sidney 1932- *AmMWSc 92, WhoWest 92*
Thomas, Clayton Lay 1921- *AmMWSc 92*
Thomas, Clyde Pickney, Jr. 1953- *WhoRel 92*
Thomas, Cogswell *TwCSFW 91*
Thomas, Colin 1912- *TwCPaSc*
Thomas, Colin Agnew 1921- *Who 92*
Thomas, Colin Gordon, Jr 1918- *AmMWSc 92*
Thomas, Craig 1933- *AlmAP 92 [port], WhoAmP 91, WhoWest 92*
Thomas, Craig 1942- *IntAu&W 91, WrDr 92*
Thomas, Craig Eugene 1958- *AmMWSc 92*
Thomas, Cynthia Gail 1956- *WhoMW 92*
Thomas, Cyrus 1825-1910 *BiInAmS*
Thomas, D Kelly, Jr 1952- *WhoAmP 91*
Thomas, D.M. 1935- *CnDBLB 8 [port], ConNov 91, ConPo 91, FacFETw, TwCSFW 91, WrDr 92*
Thomas, Dafydd Elis 1946- *Who 92*
Thomas, Dale 1944- *WhoWest 92*
Thomas, Dale 1951- *WhoEnt 92*
Thomas, Dalie Thaxton 1947- *WhoMW 92*
Thomas, Dan Anderson 1922- *AmMWSc 92*
Thomas, Daniel B. *DrAPF 91*
Thomas, Daniel Foley 1950- *WhoFI 92*
Thomas, Daniel Holcombe 1906- *WhoAmL 92*
Thomas, Danny d1991 *LesBEnT 92*
Thomas, Danny 1912-1991 *NewYTBS 91 [port]*
Thomas, Danny 1914?-1991 *CurBio 91N, News 91, -91-3*
Thomas, Danny Ray 1949- *WhoAmP 91*
Thomas, Darrell Denman 1931- *WhoWest 92*
Thomas, David 1776-1859 *BiInAmS*
Thomas, David 1931- *Who 92, WrDr 92*
Thomas, David 1942- *Who 92*
Thomas, David 1943- *IntWW 91*
Thomas, David 1945- *WhoAmP 91*
Thomas, David 1949- *WhoAmP 91*
Thomas, David Albert 1944- *WhoAmL 92*
Thomas, David Alden 1930- *AmMWSc 92*
Thomas, David Ansell 1917- *WhoFI 92*
Thomas, David Arthur 1925- *IntAu&W 91, WrDr 92*
Thomas, David Bartlett 1937- *AmMWSc 92*
Thomas, David Bowen 1931- *Who 92*
Thomas, David Churchill 1933- *Who 92*
Thomas, David Dale 1949- *AmMWSc 92*
Thomas, David Emrys 1935- *Who 92*
Thomas, David Gilbert 1928- *AmMWSc 92*
Thomas, David Glen 1926- *AmMWSc 92*
Thomas, David H. 1945- *WrDr 92*
Thomas, David Hamilton Pryce 1922- *Who 92*
Thomas, David Henry 1934- *WhoMW 92*
Thomas, David Hurst 1945- *IntAu&W 91*
Thomas, David John 1924- *WhoAmL 92*
Thomas, David Lee 1949- *AmMWSc 92, WhoEnt 92*
Thomas, David Lloyd 1942- *WhoFI 92*
Thomas, David Malcom 1953- *WhoRel 92*
Thomas, David Monro 1915- *Who 92*
Thomas, David Owen 1926- *Who 92*
Thomas, David Robert 1954- *WhoAmL 92, WhoFI 92*
Thomas, David St. John 1929- *WrDr 92*
Thomas, David Stanley 1946- *WhoWest 92*
Thomas, David Tipton 1937- *AmMWSc 92*
Thomas, David Warren *AmMWSc 92*
Thomas, David William 1948- *WhoEnt 92*
Thomas, David William Penrose 1959- *Who 92*
Thomas, Debi 1967- *BlkOlyM [port], WhoBlA 92*
Thomas, Deborah Ann 1953- *WhoEnt 92*
Thomas, Delbert Dale 1930- *WhoWest 92*
Thomas, Denis 1922- *ConAu 34NR, IntAu&W 91, WrDr 92*
Thomas, Denise *DrAPF 91*
Thomas, Dennis R *WhoIns 92*
Thomas, Derek John 1934- *Who 92*
Thomas, Derek Morison David 1929- *IntWW 91, Who 92*
Thomas, Derek Wilfrid 1952- *WhoFI 92*
Thomas, Derrick Vincent 1967- *WhoBlA 92*
Thomas, Dewayne 1954- *WhoAmP 91*
Thomas, Dewi Alun 1917- *Who 92*
Thomas, Dominic *WhoRel 92*
Thomas, Don Wylie 1923- *AmMWSc 92*
Thomas, Donald Charles 1935- *AmMWSc 92*
Thomas, Donald E 1918- *AmMWSc 92*
Thomas, Donald H 1933- *AmMWSc 92*
Thomas, Donald Martin *Who 92*
Thomas, Donald Michael 1935- *IntAu&W 91, IntWW 91, Who 92*
Thomas, Donna Stanley 1928- *WhoRel 92*
Thomas, Donnall *Who 92*
Thomas, Dorothy Lois 1927- *WhoAmP 91*
Thomas, Dorothy Swaine 1899-1977 *WomSoc*
Thomas, Douglas L. 1945- *WhoBlA 92*
Thomas, Dudley Lloyd 1946- *Who 92*
Thomas, Dudley Watson 1920- *AmMWSc 92*
Thomas, Dwaine 1959- *WhoEnt 92*
Thomas, Dylan 1914-1953 *CnDBLB 7 [port], FacFETw [port], RfGEnL 91*
Thomas, E J 1951- *WhoAmP 91*
Thomas, Earle Frederick 1925- *WhoBlA 92*
Thomas, Eberle 1935- *WhoEnt 92*
Thomas, Edgar Albert 1940- *WhoFI 92*
Thomas, Edith Matilda 1854-1925 *BenetAL 91*
Thomas, Edmund Barrington 1929- *WrDr 92*
Thomas, Edna 1886-1974 *NotBlAW 92*
Thomas, Edward d1832 *BiInAmS*
Thomas, Edward 1878-1917 *FacFETw, RfGEnL 91*
Thomas, Edward Donnall 1920- *AmMWSc 92, Who 92, WhoNob 90, WhoWest 92*
Thomas, Edward Francis, Jr. 1937- *WhoFI 92, WhoWest 92*
Thomas, Edward P. 1920- *WhoBlA 92*
Thomas, Edward Sandusky, Jr 1938- *AmMWSc 92*
Thomas, Edward Wilfrid 1940- *AmMWSc 92*
Thomas, Edwin John 1927- *WhoMW 92*
Thomas, Edwin Lee 1943- *AmMWSc 92*
Thomas, Edwin Lorimer 1947- *AmMWSc 92*
Thomas, Elizabeth *Who 92*
Thomas, Elizabeth 1677-1731 *BlkwCEP*
Thomas, Elizabeth Allison 1956- *WhoWest 92*
Thomas, Elizabeth Gray 1924- *WhoAmP 91*
Thomas, Elizabeth Marjorie 1919- *Who 92*
Thomas, Elizabeth Marshall *DrAPF 91*
Thomas, Elizabeth Wadsworth 1944- *AmMWSc 92*
Thomas, Ellidee Dotson 1926- *AmMWSc 92*
Thomas, Elmer Lawrence 1916- *AmMWSc 92*
Thomas, Elvin Elbert 1944- *AmMWSc 92*
Thomas, Emily Ann 1952- *WhoMW 92*
Thomas, Emyr 1920- *Who 92*
Thomas, Eric Jason 1964- *WhoBlA 92*
Thomas, Erma Lee 1928- *WhoBlA 92*
Thomas, Ernest 1938- *WhoRel 92*
Thomas, Eryl Stephen 1910- *Who 92*
Thomas, Estes Centennial, III 1940- *AmMWSc 92*
Thomas, Esther Merlene 1945- *WhoWest 92*
Thomas, Ethel Colvin Nichols 1913- *WhoWest 92*
Thomas, Eugene 1933- *WhoMW 92*
Thomas, Eugene C. 1931- *WhoAmL 92*
Thomas, Eugene Gerard 1947- *WhoEnt 92*
Thomas, Eula Wiley 1948- *WhoBlA 92*
Thomas, Eunice S. *WhoBlA 92*
Thomas, Evan Welling 1890-1974 *AmPeW*
Thomas, Everett Dake 1943- *AmMWSc 92*
Thomas, Everette Earl 1935- *WhoAmL 92*
Thomas, F. Richard *DrAPF 91*
Thomas, Faye Evelyn J. 1933- *WhoMW 92*
Thomas, Floyd W, Jr 1938- *AmMWSc 92*
Thomas, Forrest Dean, II 1930- *AmMWSc 92*
Thomas, Francena B. 1936- *WhoBlA 92*
Thomas, Francis Darrell 1928- *WhoFI 92, WhoMW 92*
Thomas, Francis T 1939- *AmMWSc 92*
Thomas, Frank *Who 92*
Thomas, Frank Bancroft 1922- *AmMWSc 92*
Thomas, Frank Harry 1932- *AmMWSc 92*
Thomas, Frank J 1930- *AmMWSc 92*
Thomas, Frank Joseph 1930- *WhoWest 92*
Thomas, Frankie Taylor 1922- *WhoBlA 92*
Thomas, Franklin 1934- *IntWW 91*
Thomas, Franklin A. 1934- *WhoBlA 92*
Thomas, Franklin Augustine 1934- *Who 92*
Thomas, Franklin Richard 1940- *IntAu&W 91, WhoMW 92*
Thomas, Franklin Whitaker 1925- *WhoBlA 92*
Thomas, Fred 1958- *WhoAmP 91*
Thomas, Frederick Bradley 1949- *WhoAmL 92*
Thomas, Frederick William 1806-1866 *BenetAL 91, BibAL 8*
Thomas, Frederick William 1906- *Who 92*
Thomas, Gail B 1944- *AmMWSc 92*
Thomas, Gareth 1932- *AmMWSc 92, IntWW 91*
Thomas, Gareth 1955- *TwCPaSc*
Thomas, Garland Leon 1920- *AmMWSc 92*
Thomas, Garnett Jett 1920- *WhoFI 92*
Thomas, Garth Johnson 1916- *AmMWSc 92*
Thomas, Gary E 1934- *AmMWSc 92*
Thomas, Gary Lee 1937- *AmMWSc 92*
Thomas, Gary Lee 1947- *AmMWSc 92*
Thomas, Gary Lee 1951- *WhoEnt 92*
Thomas, Gary Lynn 1942- *WhoFI 92*
Thomas, Gary Marshall 1943- *WhoFI 92, WhoMW 92*
Thomas, Gary Wayne 1953- *WhoEnt 92*
Thomas, Geoffrey C. *WhoMW 92*
Thomas, Geoffrey Percy Sansom 1915- *Who 92*
Thomas, George *IntWW 91*
Thomas, George 1909- *IntAu&W 91*
Thomas, George 1941- *WhoRel 92*
Thomas, George Allen, Jr. 1956- *WhoEnt 92*
Thomas, George Arthur 1906- *Who 92*
Thomas, George B 1941- *AmMWSc 92*
Thomas, George Brinton, Jr 1914- *AmMWSc 92*
Thomas, George Havard 1893-1933 *TwCPaSc*
Thomas, George Howard 1936- *AmMWSc 92*
Thomas, George Joseph, Jr 1941- *AmMWSc 92*
Thomas, George Richard 1920- *AmMWSc 92*
Thomas, George Scott 1954- *WhoWest 92*
Thomas, Georgie A 1943- *WhoAmP 91*
Thomas, Gerald 1920- *IntMPA 92*
Thomas, Gerald Andrew 1911- *AmMWSc 92*
Thomas, Gerald Eustis 1929- *WhoBlA 92*
Thomas, Gerald H 1942- *AmMWSc 92*
Thomas, Gloria V. *WhoBlA 92*
Thomas, Godfrey Michael 1925- *Who 92*
Thomas, Gordon 1933- *IntAu&W 91, WrDr 92*
Thomas, Gordon Albert 1943- *AmMWSc 92*
Thomas, Graham Havens 1951- *AmMWSc 92*
Thomas, Graham Stuart 1909- *Who 92, WrDr 92*
Thomas, Grant Worthington 1931- *AmMWSc 92*
Thomas, Gregory Forrest 1949- *WhoWest 92*
Thomas, Gwyn 1936- *IntAu&W 91*
Thomas, Gwyn Edward Ward *Who 92*
Thomas, H Ronald 1942- *AmMWSc 92*
Thomas, Hardy LeRoy Maddox 1939- *WhoAmL 92*
Thomas, Harold A, Jr 1913- *AmMWSc 92*
Thomas, Harold Edward 1954- *WhoEnt 92*
Thomas, Harold Lee 1934- *AmMWSc 92*
Thomas, Harold Todd 1942- *AmMWSc 92*
Thomas, Harrison William 1932- *WhoEnt 92*
Thomas, Harry E 1920- *IntMPA 92*
Thomas, Harry L *WhoAmP 91*
Thomas, Harry Lee 1919- *WhoBlA 92*
Thomas, Harvey *Who 92*
Thomas, Harvey Noake 1939- *IntWW 91*
Thomas, Hayward 1921- *WhoWest 92*
Thomas, Hazel Jeanette 1932- *AmMWSc 92*
Thomas, Helen 1920- *WhoAmP 91*
Thomas, Henri 1912- *IntAu&W 91, IntWW 91*
Thomas, Henry 1971- *IntMPA 92*
Thomas, Henry Coffman 1918- *AmMWSc 92*
Thomas, Henry Evans, IV 1937- *WhoAmP 91*
Thomas, Henry H. 1946- *WhoBlA 92*
Thomas, Henry Lee 1948- *WhoMW 92*
Thomas, Herbert Talmadge 1939- *WhoRel 92*
Thomas, Heriberto Victor 1917- *AmMWSc 92*
Thomas, Herman Edward 1941- *WhoBlA 92*
Thomas, Herman Everett, Jr. 1957- *WhoFI 92*
Thomas, Herman Hoit 1931- *AmMWSc 92*
Thomas, Howard 1909-1986 *FacFETw*
Thomas, Howard Christopher 1945- *Who 92*
Thomas, Howard Johnston 1926- *WhoAmP 91*
Thomas, Howard Major 1918- *AmMWSc 92*
Thomas, Howard Paul 1942- *WhoWest 92*
Thomas, Howe Octavius, Jr. 1950- *WhoRel 92*
Thomas, Howell Moore 1906- *WhoAmP 91*
Thomas, Hubert Jon 1940- *AmMWSc 92*
Thomas, Hugh *Who 92*
Thomas, Hugh 1931- *IntAu&W 91, WrDr 92*
Thomas, Irving *WhoBlA 92*
Thomas, Isaac Daniel, Jr. 1939- *WhoBlA 92*
Thomas, Isaiah 1749-1831 *BenetAL 91, NewAmDM*
Thomas, Isiah Lord 1961- *WhoMW 92*
Thomas, Isiah Lord, III 1961- *WhoBlA 92*
Thomas, Ivor *WrDr 92*
Thomas, Ivor 1928-1980 *TwCPaSc*
Thomas, Ivor B. *Who 92*

Thomas, Ivor Bulmer- 1905- IntWW 91
Thomas, J. Mark 1947- WhoRel 92
Thomas, Jack H. 1941- WhoFI 92
Thomas, Jack Sydney 1926- WhoRel 92
Thomas, Jack Ward 1934- AmMWSc 92, WhoWest 92
Thomas, Jacqueline Marie 1952- WhoBlA 92
Thomas, Jacquelyn Small 1938- WhoBlA 92
Thomas, James DrAPF 91
Thomas, James 1946- AmMWSc 92
Thomas, James Arthur 1938- AmMWSc 92
Thomas, James Brown 1922- WhoIns 92
Thomas, James Dalton 1943- WhoAmL 92
Thomas, James E 1926- AmMWSc 92
Thomas, James Edward, Jr. 1950- WhoFI 92
Thomas, James Egbert 1921- WhoEnt 92
Thomas, James H 1936- AmMWSc 92
Thomas, James H 1955- AmMWSc 92
Thomas, James Havard 1854-1921 TwCPaSc
Thomas, James Henry, III 1960- WhoWest 92
Thomas, James L. 1946- WhoBlA 92
Thomas, James Louis WhoAmP 91
Thomas, James Lyle 1946- WhoAmP 91
Thomas, James O., Jr. 1930- WhoBlA 92
Thomas, James Raymond 1947- WhoFI 92
Thomas, James Samuel 1919- WhoBlA 92, WhoRel 92
Thomas, James Ward AmMWSc 92
Thomas, James William 1941- AmMWSc 92
Thomas, James William 1949- WhoAmL 92, WhoMW 92
Thomas, Janet Marie WhoFI 92
Thomas, Janice Morrell 1946- WhoBlA 92
Thomas, Janis P. 1954- WhoBlA 92
Thomas, Jean Olwen 1942- IntWW 91, Who 92
Thomas, Jeanette Mae 1946- WhoWest 92
Thomas, Jeffery Michael 1955- WhoFI 92
Thomas, Jenkin 1938- Who 92
Thomas, Jeremy IntWW 91
Thomas, Jeremy 1931- IntWW 91, Who 92
Thomas, Jeremy 1949- IntMPA 92
Thomas, Jerome Francis 1922- AmMWSc 92
Thomas, Jerry Aroe WhoAmP 91
Thomas, Jerry Francis 1931- WhoEnt 92
Thomas, Jess 1927- WhoEnt 92
Thomas, Jewel M. WhoBlA 92
Thomas, Jim WhoBlA 92
Thomas, Jimmy Lynn 1941- WhoFI 92
Thomas, Jo WhoHisp 92
Thomas, Joab Langston 1933- AmMWSc 92
Thomas, Joan McHenry Bates 1928- WhoBlA 92
Thomas, Joe Ed 1937- AmMWSc 92
Thomas, John 1805-1871 AmPeW
Thomas, John 1922- WhoBlA 92
Thomas, John 1941- WhoBlA 92
Thomas, John 1946- WhoMW 92
Thomas, John A 1933- AmMWSc 92
Thomas, John Alan 1943- Who 92
Thomas, John Alva 1940- AmMWSc 92
Thomas, John B 1925- AmMWSc 92
Thomas, John Charles 1950- WhoAmP 91, WhoEnt 92
Thomas, John Curtis 1941- BlkOlyM
Thomas, John Darrel 1956- WhoEnt 92
Thomas, John David 1931- Who 92
Thomas, John David 1951- WhoEnt 92, WhoWest 92
Thomas, John David 1953- WhoFI 92
Thomas, John David 1963- WhoFI 92
Thomas, John Frank 1920- Who 92
Thomas, John Franklin 1944- WhoFI 92
Thomas, John Gilbert 1948- WhoEnt 92
Thomas, John Harvey 1939- Who 92
Thomas, John Henderson, III 1950- WhoBlA 92
Thomas, John Hollie 1922- WhoAmP 91
Thomas, John Howard 1941- AmMWSc 92
Thomas, John Hunter 1928- AmMWSc 92
Thomas, John J 1923- WhoAmP 91
Thomas, John James Absalom 1908- Who 92
Thomas, John Jenks 1936- AmMWSc 92
Thomas, John Kerry 1934- AmMWSc 92
Thomas, John L. d1991 NewYTBS 91
Thomas, John Lawrence 1910-1991 ConAu 134
Thomas, John M 1936- AmMWSc 92
Thomas, John Maldwyn 1918- Who 92
Thomas, John Martin 1910- AmMWSc 92, WhoMW 92
Thomas, John Meurig 1932- IntWW 91, Who 92
Thomas, John Michael Robert 1958- WhoFI 92
Thomas, John Owen 1946- AmMWSc 92
Thomas, John Paul 1933- AmMWSc 92
Thomas, John Pelham 1922- AmMWSc 92
Thomas, John Phillip 1965- WhoMW 92
Thomas, John Richard 1921- AmMWSc 92
Thomas, John Russell 1955- WhoRel 92
Thomas, John Thieme 1935- WhoMW 92
Thomas, John Wesley 1932- WhoBlA 92
Thomas, John William 1918- AmMWSc 92, WhoMW 92
Thomas, John Xenia, Jr 1950- AmMWSc 92
Thomas, Johnny B. 1953- WhoBlA 92
Thomas, Jonathan Griffen, Jr. 1928- WhoRel 92
Thomas, Jorge A. 1946- WhoHisp 92
Thomas, Joseph A 1929- WhoIns 92
Thomas, Joseph Allan 1929- WhoAmL 92
Thomas, Joseph Calvin 1933- AmMWSc 92
Thomas, Joseph Charles 1945- AmMWSc 92
Thomas, Joseph Edward 1955- WhoAmL 92
Thomas, Joseph Erumappettical 1937- AmMWSc 92
Thomas, Joseph Francis, Jr 1940- AmMWSc 92
Thomas, Joseph H. 1933- WhoBlA 92
Thomas, Joseph H. 1934- WhoFI 92
Thomas, Joseph H 1940- WhoAmP 91
Thomas, Joseph James 1909- AmMWSc 92
Thomas, Joseph W. 1940- WhoBlA 92
Thomas, Joseph Winand 1940- WhoAmL 92
Thomas, Joyce Carol DrAPF 91
Thomas, Joyce Carol 1938- WhoBlA 92
Thomas, Juanita Ware 1923- WhoBlA 92
Thomas, Judith M 1944- AmMWSc 92
Thomas, Julian Edward, Sr 1937- AmMWSc 92
Thomas, K TwCSFW 91
Thomas, K. John 1947- WhoEnt 92
Thomas, Kalin Normoet 1961- WhoBlA 92
Thomas, Karen P. 1957- WhoEnt 92
Thomas, Kate 1950- WhoEnt 92
Thomas, Keith 1933- ConAu 34NR, WrDr 92
Thomas, Keith Henry Westcott 1923- Who 92
Thomas, Keith Vern 1946- WhoWest 92
Thomas, Keith Vivian 1933- IntWW 91, Who 92
Thomas, Kendall 1957- WhoBlA 92
Thomas, Kenneth Alfred, Jr 1946- AmMWSc 92
Thomas, Kenneth Eugene, III 1954- AmMWSc 92
Thomas, Kenneth Rowland 1927- Who 92
Thomas, Kent Swenson 1955- WhoWest 92
Thomas, Kimberly W 1952- AmMWSc 92
Thomas, L E 1925- WhoAmP 91
Thomas, Larry D. DrAPF 91
Thomas, Larry Emerson 1943- AmMWSc 92
Thomas, Larry James 1948- WhoMW 92
Thomas, Latta R., Sr. 1927- WhoBlA 92
Thomas, Laura Marlene 1936- WhoWest 92
Thomas, Lawrence E 1942- AmMWSc 92
Thomas, Lawrence Eugene 1931- WhoWest 92
Thomas, Lazarus Daniel 1925- AmMWSc 92
Thomas, Lee IntAu&W 91X, TwCWW 91
Thomas, Lee Daniel 1951- WhoAmL 92
Thomas, Lee W 1926- AmMWSc 92
Thomas, Leo 1947- WhoFI 92, WhoWest 92
Thomas, Leo Alvon 1922- AmMWSc 92
Thomas, Leo J. 1936- WhoFI 92
Thomas, Leo John 1936- AmMWSc 92
Thomas, Leona Marlene 1933- WhoMW 92
Thomas, Leonard William, Sr 1909- AmMWSc 92
Thomas, Leroy, Sr. 1923- WhoBlA 92
Thomas, Leslie 1931- WrDr 92
Thomas, Leslie John 1931- IntAu&W 91, Who 92
Thomas, Lewis 1913- AmMWSc 92, IntWW 91, WrDr 92
Thomas, Lewis Edward 1913- AmMWSc 92, WhoMW 92
Thomas, Lewis Jones, Jr 1930- AmMWSc 92
Thomas, Lillian Parker 1857- NotBlAW 92
Thomas, Lillie 1950- WhoBlA 92
Thomas, Linda Craig 1944- WhoAmP 91
Thomas, Lindsay 1943- AlmAP 92 [port], WhoAmP 91
Thomas, Liz A. 1946- WhoBlA 92
Thomas, Llewellyn Hilleth 1903- AmMWSc 92, IntWW 91
Thomas, Lloyd A. 1922- WhoBlA 92
Thomas, Lloyd Brewster 1941- WhoMW 92
Thomas, Llywellyn Murray 1922- AmMWSc 92
Thomas, Lorenzo DrAPF 91
Thomas, Louis Barton 1919- AmMWSc 92
Thomas, Louphenia WhoAmP 91
Thomas, Louphenia 1918- WhoBlA 92
Thomas, Lowell d1981 LesBEnT 92
Thomas, Lowell 1892-1981 BenetAL 91, FacFETw
Thomas, Lowell, Jr 1923- WhoAmP 91
Thomas, Lowell George 1936- WhoMW 92
Thomas, Lowell Shumway, Jr. 1931- WhoAmL 92
Thomas, Lucia Theodosia 1917- WhoBlA 92
Thomas, Lucille Cole 1921- WhoBlA 92
Thomas, Lucille Pauline 1935- WhoAmP 91
Thomas, Lucius Ponder 1925- AmMWSc 92
Thomas, Lydia Waters 1944- WhoBlA 92
Thomas, Lyell Jay, Jr 1925- AmMWSc 92
Thomas, M.M. 1916- DcEcMov
Thomas, Mable WhoAmP 91
Thomas, Mable 1957- WhoBlA 92
Thomas, Mack ConAu 133
Thomas, Malayilmelathethil 1932- WhoRel 92
Thomas, Maldwyn Who 92
Thomas, Margaret 1916- TwCPaSc, Who 92
Thomas, Margaret Jean 1943- WhoRel 92
Thomas, Marilyn Taft 1943- WhoEnt 92
Thomas, Mark Ellis 1955- IntAu&W 91
Thomas, Mark Howard 1955- WhoAmL 92
Thomas, Mark Stanton 1931- WhoEnt 92
Thomas, Mark Stanton 1952- WhoAmL 92
Thomas, Marlin S 1933- WhoAmP 91
Thomas, Marlo LesBEnT 92 [port]
Thomas, Marlo 1938- IntMPA 92
Thomas, Marlo 1943- WhoEnt 92
Thomas, Marsha Dvon 1952- WhoFI 92
Thomas, Martha Jane Bergin 1926- AmMWSc 92
Thomas, Martin 1937- Who 92
Thomas, Martin Lewis Hall 1935- AmMWSc 92
Thomas, Marvette Jeraldine 1953- WhoBlA 92
Thomas, Mary A. 1933- WhoBlA 92
Thomas, Mary Beth 1941- AmMWSc 92
Thomas, Mary Elizabeth 1935- Who 92
Thomas, Mary Francisca 1919- WhoRel 92
Thomas, Mason Blanchard 1866-1912 BiInAmS
Thomas, Maurice McKenzie 1943- WhoBlA 92
Thomas, Maurice William, Jr. 1946- WhoEnt 92
Thomas, Maxine F. 1947- WhoBlA 92
Thomas, Maxine Freddie WhoAmL 92
Thomas, Maxine Freddie 1947- WhoAmP 91
Thomas, Maxine Suzanne 1948- WhoBlA 92
Thomas, Maxwell McNee 1926- Who 92
Thomas, McCalip Joseph 1914- AmMWSc 92, WhoMW 92
Thomas, Mel Allen 1955- WhoMW 92
Thomas, Melbourne d1989 Who 92N
Thomas, Merritt L 1926- WhoAmP 91
Thomas, Michael Who 92
Thomas, Michael Allen 1947- WhoFI 92
Thomas, Michael D. 1958- WhoAmL 92
Thomas, Michael David 1933- Who 92
Thomas, Michael David 1942- AmMWSc 92
Thomas, Michael E 1937- AmMWSc 92
Thomas, Michael Earl 1953- WhoWest 92
Thomas, Michael John Glyn 1938- Who 92
Thomas, Michael Paul 1956- WhoAmL 92
Thomas, Michael Stuart 1944- Who 92
Thomas, Michael T. Who 92
Thomas, Michael Tilson 1944- IntWW 91, NewAmDM, WhoEnt 92
Thomas, Miriam Mason Higgins 1920- AmMWSc 92
Thomas, Mitchell 1936- AmMWSc 92
Thomas, Mitchell, Jr. 1952- WhoBlA 92
Thomas, Monica Maria Primus 1954- WhoBlA 92
Thomas, Montcalm Tom 1936- AmMWSc 92
Thomas, Morley Keith 1918- AmMWSc 92
Thomas, N. Charles 1929- WhoBlA 92
Thomas, Nadine WhoAmP 91
Thomas, Nancy Grayce WhoMW 92
Thomas, Nathaniel 1936- WhoBlA 92
Thomas, Nathaniel 1957- WhoBlA 92
Thomas, Nathaniel Charles 1929- WhoRel 92
Thomas, Ned Albert 1943- WhoMW 92
Thomas, Neville Who 92
Thomas, Nicholas 1960- ConAu 135
Thomas, Nick 1943- WhoEnt 92
Thomas, Nida E. 1914- WhoBlA 92
Thomas, Nina M. 1957- WhoBlA 92
Thomas, Noreen Carol 1935- WhoAmP 91
Thomas, Norman 1884-1968 BenetAL 91, FacFETw
Thomas, Norman 1921- Who 92
Thomas, Norman Ernest 1932- WhoRel 92
Thomas, Norman Mattoon 1884-1968 AmPeW, AmPolLe, DcAmImH
Thomas, Norman Randall 1932- AmMWSc 92
Thomas, Norvin Eugene 1945- WhoMW 92
Thomas, Oliver 1919- TwCPaSc
Thomas, Olivia Smith 1956- WhoBlA 92
Thomas, Oommen Kulangaramadhom 1940- WhoRel 92
Thomas, Ora P. 1935- WhoBlA 92
Thomas, Oscar Otto 1919- AmMWSc 92
Thomas, Owen Clark 1922- WhoRel 92
Thomas, Owen Pestell 1933- AmMWSc 92
Thomas, P D 1905- AmMWSc 92
Thomas, Page Allison 1936- WhoRel 92
Thomas, Pat Franklin 1933- WhoAmP 91
Thomas, Patricia Anne 1940- Who 92
Thomas, Patricia Grafton 1921- WhoMW 92
Thomas, Patricia O'Flynn 1940- WhoBlA 92
Thomas, Paul 1908- IntAu&W 91, WrDr 92
Thomas, Paul A V 1925- AmMWSc 92
Thomas, Paul Clarence 1928- AmMWSc 92
Thomas, Paul David 1926- AmMWSc 92
Thomas, Paul Emery 1927- AmMWSc 92
Thomas, Paul Massenna, Jr. 1935- WhoWest 92
Thomas, Paul Milton 1929- AmMWSc 92
Thomas, Paula Susan 1952- WhoMW 92
Thomas, Peter DrAPF 91
Thomas, Peter 1946- AmMWSc 92
Thomas, Peter W. 1929- WhoAmL 92
Thomas, Philip Michael 1949- IntMPA 92, WhoBlA 92
Thomas, Philip S. 1946- WhoBlA 92
Thomas, Philip Stanley 1928- WhoFI 92, WhoMW 92
Thomas, Phillip Charles 1942- Who 92
Thomas, Piri 1928- WhoHisp 92
Thomas, Priscilla D. 1934- WhoBlA 92
Thomas, Quentin Jeremy 1944- Who 92
Thomas, Quentin Vivian 1949- AmMWSc 92
Thomas, R. David 1932- WhoMW 92
Thomas, R E 1930- AmMWSc 92
Thomas, R. Lar 1958- WhoAmL 92
Thomas, R Noel 1936- AmMWSc 92
Thomas, R P 1932- WhoAmP 91
Thomas, R.S. 1913- CnDBLB 8 [port], ConPo 91, FacFETw, RfGEnL 91, WrDr 92
Thomas, Ralph 1915- IntMPA 92
Thomas, Ralph Albert 1954- WhoBlA 92
Thomas, Ralph Charles, III 1949- WhoBlA 92
Thomas, Ralph Harold 1932- AmMWSc 92
Thomas, Ralph Henry, Sr 1931- AmMWSc 92
Thomas, Ralph Philip Who 92
Thomas, Rance 1932- WhoMW 92
Thomas, Randall Craig 1956- WhoRel 92
Thomas, Randall Stuart 1955- WhoAmL 92
Thomas, Raye Edward 1938- AmMWSc 92
Thomas, Raymond WhoRel 92
Thomas, Raymond Vincent 1963- WhoMW 92
Thomas, Reginald 1928- Who 92
Thomas, Reginald Harry 1954- WhoRel 92
Thomas, Reginald Maurice 1964- WhoBlA 92
Thomas, Reginald Pete 1962- WhoMW 92
Thomas, Rene Francois 1929- IntWW 91
Thomas, Reno Henry 1922- WhoAmP 91
Thomas, Ricardo D'Wayne 1966- WhoFI 92
Thomas, Richard Who 92
Thomas, Richard 1938- AmMWSc 92, Who 92
Thomas, Richard 1951- IntMPA 92, WhoEnt 92
Thomas, Richard Alan 1948- AmMWSc 92
Thomas, Richard Charles 1949- AmMWSc 92
Thomas, Richard Clark d1991 NewYTBS 91
Thomas, Richard Dean 1947- AmMWSc 92
Thomas, Richard Eugene 1925- AmMWSc 92
Thomas, Richard Garland 1923- AmMWSc 92
Thomas, Richard Glyndwr, Jr 1932- WhoAmP 91
Thomas, Richard Herbert 1925- WhoEnt 92
Thomas, Richard James 1949- Who 92

**Thomas**, Richard Joseph 1928- *AmMWSc 92*
**Thomas**, Richard Kenneth 1953- *WhoEnt 92*
**Thomas**, Richard Lee 1931- *IntWW 91, WhoFI 92*
**Thomas**, Richard Nelson 1921- *AmMWSc 92*
**Thomas**, Richard Sanborn 1927- *AmMWSc 92*
**Thomas**, Richard Stephen 1949- *WhoFI 92, WhoMW 92*
**Thomas**, Richard Sylvester 1953- *WhoRel 92*
**Thomas**, Richard V 1932- *WhoAmP 91*
**Thomas**, Richard Van 1932- *WhoWest 92*
**Thomas**, Richards Christopher 1942- *WhoFI 92*
**Thomas**, Ritchie Tucker 1936- *WhoAmL 92*
**Thomas**, Robert 1901- *Who 92*
**Thomas**, Robert 1934- *AmMWSc 92*
**Thomas**, Robert Arnold 1927- *WhoWest 92*
**Thomas**, Robert Bailey *BenetAL 91*
**Thomas**, Robert C. 1922-1981 *WhoBlA 92N*
**Thomas**, Robert Charles 1932- *WhoBlA 92*
**Thomas**, Robert E 1936- *AmMWSc 92*
**Thomas**, Robert Eugene 1919- *AmMWSc 92*
**Thomas**, Robert Eugene 1941- *WhoMW 92*
**Thomas**, Robert G. 1943- *IntMPA 92*
**Thomas**, Robert Gerald 1943- *WhoEnt 92*
**Thomas**, Robert Glenn 1926- *AmMWSc 92*
**Thomas**, Robert J. 1922- *IntMPA 92*
**Thomas**, Robert J 1950- *WhoAmP 91*
**Thomas**, Robert James 1949- *AmMWSc 92*
**Thomas**, Robert Jay 1930- *AmMWSc 92*
**Thomas**, Robert Joseph 1912- *AmMWSc 92*
**Thomas**, Robert Knoll 1933- *WhoFI 92*
**Thomas**, Robert L 1938- *AmMWSc 92*
**Thomas**, Robert Lancefield 1909- *WhoWest 92*
**Thomas**, Robert Lee 1938- *WhoFI 92*
**Thomas**, Robert Lewis 1944- *WhoBlA 92*
**Thomas**, Robert Lloyd 1941- *WhoFI 92*
**Thomas**, Robert Neville 1936- *Who 92*
**Thomas**, Robert P 1821-1864 *BiInAmS*
**Thomas**, Robert Ray 1926- *WhoFI 92*
**Thomas**, Robert Spencer David 1941- *AmMWSc 92*
**Thomas**, Robert Wallace 1954- *WhoEnt 92*
**Thomas**, Robert Wilburn 1937- *WhoEnt 92*
**Thomas**, Robert William 1957- *WhoFI 92*
**Thomas**, Rodney Lamar 1965- *WhoBlA 92*
**Thomas**, Roger Christopher 1939- *Who 92*
**Thomas**, Roger David Keen 1942- *AmMWSc 92*
**Thomas**, Roger Gareth 1925- *Who 92*
**Thomas**, Roger Jerry 1942- *AmMWSc 92*
**Thomas**, Roger John Laugharne 1947- *Who 92*
**Thomas**, Roger Lloyd 1919- *Who 92*
**Thomas**, Roger Parry 1951- *WhoWest 92*
**Thomas**, Roger R. *Who 92*
**Thomas**, Roger Warren 1937- *WhoAmL 92*
**Thomas**, Ronald Blaine 1934- *WhoWest 92*
**Thomas**, Ronald Emerson 1930- *AmMWSc 92*
**Thomas**, Ronald F. 1944- *WhoBlA 92*
**Thomas**, Ronald Leslie 1935- *AmMWSc 92*
**Thomas**, Ronald Richard 1929- *Who 92*
**Thomas**, Ronald Stuart 1913- *IntAu&W 91, IntWW 91, Who 92*
**Thomas**, Rosanne Daryl *DrAPF 91*
**Thomas**, Rosie *IntAu&W 91, WrDr 92*
**Thomas**, Rosie 1947- *ConAu 133*
**Thomas**, Ross 1926- *WrDr 92*
**Thomas**, Roy *TwCPaSc*
**Thomas**, Roy Dale 1936- *AmMWSc 92*
**Thomas**, Roy I 1938- *WhoBlA 92*
**Thomas**, Roy Orlando 1921- *AmMWSc 92*
**Thomas**, Roydon Urquhart 1936- *Who 92*
**Thomas**, Russ d1991 *NewYTBS 91*
**Thomas**, Ruth Beatrice *AmMWSc 92*
**Thomas**, Sally *WhoEnt 92*
**Thomas**, Sam B *WhoAmP 91*
**Thomas**, Samuel 1943- *WhoBlA 92*
**Thomas**, Samuel 1945- *WhoAmP 91*
**Thomas**, Samuel, Jr. 1957- *WhoMW 92, WhoRel 92*
**Thomas**, Samuel Gabriel 1946- *AmMWSc 92*
**Thomas**, Sandra Ann *WhoEnt 92*
**Thomas**, Sandria Howard 1969- *WhoEnt 92*
**Thomas**, Sarah Harding 1954- *WhoAmL 92*
**Thomas**, Sarah Nell *AmMWSc 92*
**Thomas**, Scott E 1953- *WhoAmP 91*
**Thomas**, Scott Junior 1934- *WhoWest 92*
**Thomas**, Sebastian Kuzhiamplavil 1949- *WhoWest 92*
**Thomas**, Seth Richard 1941- *AmMWSc 92*
**Thomas**, Sherri Booker *WhoBlA 92*
**Thomas**, Simon 1960- *TwCPaSc*
**Thomas**, Sirr Daniel 1933- *WhoBlA 92*
**Thomas**, Spencer *WhoBlA 92*
**Thomas**, Stanislaus S 1919- *AmMWSc 92*
**Thomas**, Stanley B., Jr. 1942- *WhoBlA 92*
**Thomas**, Stephen Clair 1952- *WhoMW 92*
**Thomas**, Stephen Paul 1938- *WhoAmL 92*
**Thomas**, Steve D. 1951- *WhoWest 92*
**Thomas**, Steven Lee 1966- *WhoWest 92*
**Thomas**, Steven P 1943- *AmMWSc 92*
**Thomas**, Stuart Denis 1938- *WhoFI 92*
**Thomas**, Stuart James 1944- *WhoMW 92*
**Thomas**, Swinton 1931- *Who 92*
**Thomas**, Sylvia Ann 1947- *WhoWest 92*
**Thomas**, T. Varughese 1948- *WhoRel 92*
**Thomas**, Ted 1920- *TwCSFW 91, WrDr 92*
**Thomas**, Ted, Sr. 1935- *WhoRel 92*
**Thomas**, Telfer Lawson 1932- *AmMWSc 92*
**Thomas**, Terence Michael 1952- *AmMWSc 92, WhoMW 92*
**Thomas**, Teresa Ann 1939- *WhoWest 92*
**Thomas**, Terra Leatherberry 1947- *WhoBlA 92*
**Thomas**, Terry Clifford 1942- *WhoRel 92*
**Thomas**, Theodore 1835-1905 *NewAmDM*
**Thomas**, Thom *WhoEnt 92*
**Thomas**, Thomas Darrah 1932- *AmMWSc 92*
**Thomas**, Thurman L. 1966- *WhoBlA 92*
**Thomas**, Timothy Farragut 1938- *AmMWSc 92*
**Thomas**, Tommy 1949- *WhoAmP 91*
**Thomas**, Tony 1954- *WhoRel 92*
**Thomas**, Trevor 1907- *IntAu&W 91, Who 92*
**Thomas**, Trevor 1959- *WhoWest 92*
**Thomas**, Tudor Lloyd 1921- *AmMWSc 92*
**Thomas**, Vaughan 1934- *WrDr 92*
**Thomas**, Vera 1928- *AmMWSc 92*
**Thomas**, Verneda Estella 1936- *WhoWest 92*
**Thomas**, Victoria *WrDr 92*
**Thomas**, Vincent Robert 1963- *WhoFI 92*
**Thomas**, Violeta de los Angeles 1949- *WhoWest 92*
**Thomas**, Virginia Lynn 1943- *AmMWSc 92*
**Thomas**, Virginia M *WhoAmP 91*
**Thomas**, Vonnie *DrAPF 91*
**Thomas**, W Curtis 1948- *WhoAmP 91, WhoBlA 92*
**Thomas**, W Dennis 1943- *WhoAmP 91*
**Thomas**, Waddell Robert 1909- *WhoBlA 92*
**Thomas**, Wade Hamilton, Sr. 1922- *WhoBlA 92*
**Thomas**, Walter Babington 1919- *Who 92*
**Thomas**, Walter Dill, Jr 1918- *AmMWSc 92*
**Thomas**, Walter E 1922- *AmMWSc 92*
**Thomas**, Walter Ivan 1919- *AmMWSc 92*
**Thomas**, Warren H 1933- *AmMWSc 92*
**Thomas**, Wilbon 1921- *WhoBlA 92*
**Thomas**, Wilbur Addison 1922- *AmMWSc 92*
**Thomas**, Wilbur C. 1916- *WhoBlA 92*
**Thomas**, William 1863-1947 *FacFETw*
**Thomas**, William 1935- *WhoBlA 92*
**Thomas**, William Albert 1950- *AmMWSc 92*
**Thomas**, William Andrew 1936- *AmMWSc 92*
**Thomas**, William Arthur 1952- *WhoMW 92*
**Thomas**, William Bruce 1926- *WhoFI 92*
**Thomas**, William Christopher 1939- *WhoBlA 92*
**Thomas**, William Clark, Jr 1919- *AmMWSc 92*
**Thomas**, William D d1901 *BiInAmS*
**Thomas**, William David 1941- *Who 92*
**Thomas**, William Elwood 1932- *WhoWest 92*
**Thomas**, William Eric 1951- *AmMWSc 92*
**Thomas**, William Esmant, Jr. 1958- *WhoWest 92*
**Thomas**, William Fremlyn Cotter 1935- *Who 92*
**Thomas**, William Grady 1934- *AmMWSc 92*
**Thomas**, William Griffin, Jr. 1935- *WhoFI 92*
**Thomas**, William Henry, III 1949- *WhoAmL 92*
**Thomas**, William Hewitt 1926- *AmMWSc 92*
**Thomas**, William I 1863-1947 *DcAmImH*
**Thomas**, William J 1924- *AmMWSc 92*
**Thomas**, William James Cooper 1919- *Who 92*
**Thomas**, William Jordison 1927- *Who 92*
**Thomas**, William Karl 1933- *WhoEnt 92*
**Thomas**, William Kernahan 1911- *WhoMW 92*
**Thomas**, William L. 1938- *WhoBlA 92*
**Thomas**, William M. 1941- *AlmAP 92 [port], WhoAmP 91*
**Thomas**, William Marshall 1941- *WhoWest 92*
**Thomas**, William Michael 1930- *Who 92*
**Thomas**, William N 1927- *WhoAmP 91*
**Thomas**, William Richard 1932- *Who 92*
**Thomas**, William Robb 1926- *AmMWSc 92*
**Thomas**, William Scott 1949- *WhoAmL 92*
**Thomas**, Winfred 1920- *AmMWSc 92*
**Thomas**, Wyndham 1924- *Who 92*
**Thomas**, Yvette Elizabeth 1957- *WhoAmL 92*
**Thomas-Bowlding**, Harold Clifton 1941- *WhoBlA 92*
**Thomas-Carter**, Jean Cooper 1924- *WhoBlA 92*
**Thomas Jirauch**, Mary 1928- *WhoRel 92*
**Thomas of Gwydir**, Baron 1920- *Who 92*
**Thomas Of Swynnerton**, Baron 1931- *IntWW 91, Who 92*
**Thomas-Richards**, Jose Rodolfo 1944- *WhoBlA 92*
**Thomas-Richardson**, Valerie Jean 1947- *WhoBlA 92*
**Thomas-Williams**, Gloria M. 1938- *WhoBlA 92*
**Thomasch**, Roger Paul 1942- *WhoAmL 92*
**Thomasen**, Ole 1934- *IntWW 91*
**Thomasian**, Aram John 1924- *AmMWSc 92*
**Thomasius**, Christian 1655-1728 *BlkwCEP*
**Thomasma**, David Charles 1939- *WhoRel 92*
**Thomason**, Berenice Miller 1924- *AmMWSc 92*
**Thomason**, Burke Curtis 1943- *WhoWest 92*
**Thomason**, Byron 1941- *WhoAmP 91*
**Thomason**, C. Jo 1937- *WhoWest 92*
**Thomason**, Dana Andrew 1954- *WhoRel 92*
**Thomason**, David Morton 1947- *AmMWSc 92*
**Thomason**, Dawn Melodie 1961- *WhoEnt 92*
**Thomason**, Don Albert 1958- *WhoRel 92*
**Thomason**, Donald Brent 1957- *AmMWSc 92*
**Thomason**, Douglas Naaman 1949- *WhoWest 92*
**Thomason**, George Frederick 1927- *Who 92*
**Thomason**, Hugh *ScFEYrs*
**Thomason**, Ivan J 1925- *AmMWSc 92*
**Thomason**, John W., Jr. 1893-1944 *BenetAL 91, TwCWW 91*
**Thomason**, Larry 1948- *WhoAmP 91*
**Thomason**, Phillip Brian 1949- *WhoWest 92*
**Thomason**, Robert Allen, III 1947- *WhoAmP 91*
**Thomason**, Robert Wayne 1952- *AmMWSc 92*
**Thomason**, Ronald Glenn 1945- *WhoAmL 92*
**Thomason**, Ronny Dale 1950- *WhoRel 92*
**Thomason**, Roy 1944- *Who 92*
**Thomason**, Steven Karl 1940- *AmMWSc 92*
**Thomason**, Terry Dean 1964- *WhoMW 92*
**Thomason**, William Edison, III 1965- *WhoFI 92*
**Thomason**, William Hugh 1945- *AmMWSc 92*
**Thomassen**, David George 1952- *AmMWSc 92*
**Thomassen**, Keith I 1936- *AmMWSc 92*
**Thomassen**, Petter 1941- *IntWW 91*
**Thomasson**, Claude Larry 1932- *AmMWSc 92*
**Thomasson**, George Orin 1937- *WhoWest 92*
**Thomasson**, Joseph R 1946- *AmMWSc 92*
**Thomasson**, Maurice Ray 1930- *AmMWSc 92*
**Thomaz**, Americo 1894-1987 *FacFETw*
**Thomborson**, Clark D 1954- *AmMWSc 92*
**Thome**, Dennis Wesley 1939- *WhoAmL 92*
**Thome**, Diane 1942- *WhoEnt 92*
**Thome**, John Macon 1843-1908 *BiInAmS*
**Thomeier**, Siegfried 1937- *AmMWSc 92*
**Thomerson**, Jamie E 1935- *AmMWSc 92*
**Thomes**, William Henry 1824-1895 *BenetAL 91*
**Thomey**, Tedd 1920- *IntAu&W 91, WrDr 92*
**Thomford**, William Emil 1927- *WhoWest 92*
**Thomforde**, C J 1917- *AmMWSc 92*
**Thomforde**, Christopher Meredith 1947- *WhoRel 92*
**Thomi**, Lois Joy 1927- *WhoMW 92*
**Thomlison**, Ray J. 1943- *WhoWest 92*
**Thommes**, Robert Charles 1928- *AmMWSc 92*
**Thomopoulos**, Anthony D. *LesBEnT 92*
**Thomopoulos**, Anthony D. 1938- *IntMPA 92*
**Thomopoulos**, Nick Ted 1930- *AmMWSc 92*
**Thomopulos**, Gregs G. 1942- *WhoMW 92*
**Thompas**, George Henry, Jr. 1941- *WhoBlA 92*
**Thompkins**, Leon 1936- *AmMWSc 92*
**Thompsen**, Joyce Ann 1946- *WhoMW 92*
**Thompson**, A Ralph 1914- *AmMWSc 92*
**Thompson**, Aaron A. 1930- *WhoBlA 92*
**Thompson**, Adell, Jr. 1932- *WhoBlA 92*
**Thompson**, Alan 1920- *Who 92*
**Thompson**, Alan 1927- *WhoAmP 91*
**Thompson**, Alan Eric 1924- *IntWW 91, Who 92*
**Thompson**, Alan Morley 1925- *AmMWSc 92*
**Thompson**, Albert N. *WhoBlA 92*
**Thompson**, Albert W., Sr. 1922- *WhoBlA 92*
**Thompson**, Alfred, Jr. 1949- *WhoEnt 92*
**Thompson**, Alice Abbott 1933- *WhoWest 92*
**Thompson**, Allan Lloyd 1920- *AmMWSc 92*
**Thompson**, Allan M 1940- *AmMWSc 92*
**Thompson**, Almon Harris 1839-1906 *BiInAmS*
**Thompson**, Almose Alphonse 1942- *WhoFI 92*
**Thompson**, Almose Alphonse, II 1942- *WhoBlA 92*
**Thompson**, Alonzo Crawford 1928- *AmMWSc 92*
**Thompson**, Alton Howard 1849-1914 *BiInAmS*
**Thompson**, Alvin 1939- *WhoAmP 91*
**Thompson**, Alvin J. 1924- *WhoBlA 92*
**Thompson**, Alvin Jerome 1924- *AmMWSc 92*
**Thompson**, Anna Blanche 1914- *WhoWest 92*
**Thompson**, Anne Elise 1934- *WhoAmL 92, WhoBlA 92*
**Thompson**, Anne Kathleen 1954- *WhoEnt 92*
**Thompson**, Anne Marie 1920- *WhoWest 92*
**Thompson**, Annie Figueroa 1941- *WhoHisp 92*
**Thompson**, Ansel Frederick, Jr 1941- *AmMWSc 92, WhoFI 92*
**Thompson**, Anson Ellis 1924- *AmMWSc 92*
**Thompson**, Anthony 1967- *WhoBlA 92*
**Thompson**, Anthony Arthur Richard 1932- *Who 92*
**Thompson**, Anthony Richard 1931- *AmMWSc 92*
**Thompson**, Anthony W 1940- *AmMWSc 92*
**Thompson**, Arlene Rita 1933- *WhoWest 92*
**Thompson**, Arnold R 1935- *WhoAmP 91*
**Thompson**, Arnold Wilbur 1926- *WhoFI 92*
**Thompson**, Art, III 1955- *WhoBlA 92*
**Thompson**, Arthur Howard 1942- *AmMWSc 92*
**Thompson**, Arthur R. 1941- *WhoEnt 92*
**Thompson**, Arthur Robert 1959- *AmMWSc 92*
**Thompson**, Aubrey Gordon D. *Who 92*
**Thompson**, Aylmer Henry 1922- *AmMWSc 92*
**Thompson**, Barbara *DrAPF 91*
**Thompson**, Basil F. 1937- *WhoEnt 92*
**Thompson**, Beatrice *WhoAmP 91*
**Thompson**, Beatrice R. 1934- *WhoBlA 92*
**Thompson**, Benjamin 1753-1814 *BenetAL 91, BiInAmS*
**Thompson**, Benjamin 1918- *DcTwDes*
**Thompson**, Benjamin Franklin 1947- *WhoBlA 92*
**Thompson**, Benjamin Scott 1964- *WhoFI 92*
**Thompson**, Bennie G. 1948- *WhoBlA 92*
**Thompson**, Bert Martin 1928- *WhoIns 92*
**Thompson**, Bette Mae 1939- *WhoBlA 92*
**Thompson**, Betty Anne 1926- *WhoRel 92*
**Thompson**, Betty E. Taylor 1943- *WhoBlA 92*
**Thompson**, Betty Jane 1923- *WhoWest 92*
**Thompson**, Betty Lou 1939- *WhoBlA 92*
**Thompson**, Bill Lawrence 1950- *WhoAmL 92*
**Thompson**, Bobby Blackburn 1933- *AmMWSc 92*
**Thompson**, Bobby E 1937- *WhoAmP 91, WhoBlA 92*
**Thompson**, Bonnie Cecil 1935- *AmMWSc 92*
**Thompson**, Boyd 1921- *WhoWest 92*
**Thompson**, Bradbury 1911- *DcTwDes, WhoEnt 92*

Thompson, Bradley Merrill 1961- *WhoAmL 92, WhoMW 92*
Thompson, Brenda Smith 1948- *WhoBlA 92*
Thompson, Brian 1950- *TwCPaSc*
Thompson, Brian J 1932- *AmMWSc 92*
Thompson, Bruce 1949- *WhoAmP 91*
Thompson, Bruce Edward, Jr. 1949- *WhoFI 92*
Thompson, Bruce Rutherford 1911- *WhoAmL 92, WhoWest 92*
Thompson, Bruce Wayne 1948- *WhoWest 92*
Thompson, Bryan David 1956- *WhoEnt 92*
Thompson, Buck *TwCWW 91*
Thompson, Buford Dale 1922- *AmMWSc 92*
Thompson, Byrd Thomas, Jr 1924- *AmMWSc 92*
Thompson, C. Hall *TwCWW 91*
Thompson, C W Sydnor 1924- *WhoAmP 91*
Thompson, Carey Jerome 1951- *WhoAmL 92*
Thompson, Carl Eugene 1941- *AmMWSc 92*
Thompson, Carl Eugene 1953- *WhoBlA 92*
Thompson, Carl William 1914- *WhoAmP 91*
Thompson, Carol Belita 1951- *WhoBlA 92*
Thompson, Carolyn A 1957- *WhoAmP 91*
Thompson, Carolyn Stallings 1949- *WhoAmL 92*
Thompson, Charlcie White 1932- *WhoAmP 91*
Thompson, Charles d1991 *Who 92N*
Thompson, Charles 1930- *IntWW 91*
Thompson, Charles 1954- *AmMWSc 92*
Thompson, Charles Alfred 1957- *WhoRel 92*
Thompson, Charles Allister 1922- *Who 92*
Thompson, Charles Amos 1945- *WhoAmL 92*
Thompson, Charles Calvin 1935- *AmMWSc 92*
Thompson, Charles Denison 1940- *AmMWSc 92*
Thompson, Charles Frederick 1943- *AmMWSc 92*
Thompson, Charles H. 1945- *WhoBlA 92*
Thompson, Charles Lemuel 1839-1924 *RelLAm 91*
Thompson, Charles Norman 1922- *Who 92*
Thompson, Charles William 1939- *WhoMW 92*
Thompson, Charles William Nelson *AmMWSc 92*
Thompson, Cheryl Lynn 1957- *WhoMW 92*
Thompson, Chester Ray 1915- *AmMWSc 92*
Thompson, Christopher Noel 1932- *Who 92*
Thompson, Christopher Peile 1944- *Who 92*
Thompson, Christopher Ronald 1927- *Who 92*
Thompson, Clarence Henry, Jr 1918- *AmMWSc 92*
Thompson, Clarissa J. 1930- *WhoBlA 92*
Thompson, Claud Charles 1930- *WhoMW 92*
Thompson, Clayton Howard 1939- *WhoWest 92*
Thompson, Cleon Franklyn, Jr. 1931- *WhoBlA 92*
Thompson, Cliff F. 1934- *WhoAmL 92*
Thompson, Clifton C 1939- *AmMWSc 92*
Thompson, Clyde Douglas 1947- *WhoEnt 92*
Thompson, Colin Edward 1919- *Who 92*
Thompson, Consuelo Connie *WhoAmP 91*
Thompson, Craig Snover 1932- *WhoWest 92*
Thompson, Crayton Beville 1920- *AmMWSc 92*
Thompson, Cynthia L. 1943- *WhoRel 92*
Thompson, D W 1933- *AmMWSc 92*
Thompson, Dale E *WhoAmP 91*
Thompson, Daley 1958- *FacFETw, IntWW 91*
Thompson, Daniel Emerson 1947- *WhoFI 92*
Thompson, Daniel James 1942- *AmMWSc 92*
Thompson, Daniel Joseph *WhoBlA 92*
Thompson, Daniel Joseph 1953- *WhoEnt 92*
Thompson, Daniel Pierce 1795-1868 *BenetAL 91, BibAL 8*
Thompson, Daniel Quale 1918- *AmMWSc 92*
Thompson, Danny L 1951- *WhoAmP 91*
Thompson, D'Arcy Wentworth 1860-1948 *DcTwDes*
Thompson, Darrell 1967- *WhoBlA 92*
Thompson, Darrell Robert 1937- *AmMWSc 92*
Thompson, David 1770-1857 *BenetAL 91*
Thompson, David A 1929- *AmMWSc 92*
Thompson, David A 1940- *AmMWSc 92*
Thompson, David Allan 1942- *AmMWSc 92*
Thompson, David Allen 1950- *AmMWSc 92*
Thompson, David Brian 1936- *Who 92*
Thompson, David Charles, Sr. 1942- *WhoWest 92*
Thompson, David Duane 1956- *WhoEnt 92*
Thompson, David Duvall 1922- *AmMWSc 92*
Thompson, David Fred 1941- *AmMWSc 92*
Thompson, David J 1934- *AmMWSc 92*
Thompson, David Jerome 1937- *AmMWSc 92*
Thompson, David John 1945- *AmMWSc 92*
Thompson, David Joseph 1952- *WhoMW 92*
Thompson, David Lester 1955- *WhoMW 92*
Thompson, David M. 1946- *WhoHisp 92*
Thompson, David N 1950- *WhoIns 92*
Thompson, David O. 1954- *WhoBlA 92*
Thompson, David Paige 1943- *WhoAmP 91*
Thompson, David Pollock 1920- *WhoRel 92*
Thompson, David R *WhoAmP 91*
Thompson, David Ralph 1959- *WhoWest 92*
Thompson, David Renwick *WhoAmL 92*
Thompson, David Richard 1916- *Who 92*
Thompson, David Robin Bibby 1946- *Who 92*
Thompson, David Russell 1944- *AmMWSc 92*
Thompson, David Scott 1959- *WhoEnt 92*
Thompson, David Walker 1954- *AmMWSc 92*
Thompson, David Wallace 1942- *AmMWSc 92*
Thompson, Deborah Kaye 1965- *WhoRel 92*
Thompson, Deborah Maria 1958- *WhoBlA 92*
Thompson, Debra Jean 1954- *WhoAmL 92*
Thompson, DeHaven Leslie 1939- *WhoBlA 92*
Thompson, Denman 1833-1911 *BenetAL 91*
Thompson, Dennis Cameron 1914- *Who 92*
Thompson, Dennis Peters 1937- *WhoWest 92*
Thompson, Dennis Roy 1939- *WhoWest 92*
Thompson, Dewey McDonald 1961- *WhoEnt 92*
Thompson, Don Gregory 1953- *WhoWest 92*
Thompson, Donald 1931- *Who 92*
Thompson, Donald B 1948- *AmMWSc 92*
Thompson, Donald E. 1930- *WhoFI 92*
Thompson, Donald Henry 1911- *Who 92*
Thompson, Donald Leo 1943- *AmMWSc 92*
Thompson, Donald Leroy 1932- *AmMWSc 92*
Thompson, Donald Loraine 1921- *AmMWSc 92*
Thompson, Donald Oscar 1927- *AmMWSc 92*
Thompson, Donna Kay *WhoAmP 91*
Thompson, Donnell 1958- *WhoBlA 92*
Thompson, Donnis Hazel 1933- *WhoBlA 92*
Thompson, Donovan Jerome 1919- *AmMWSc 92*
Thompson, Doris Leone Ardolf 1958- *WhoEnt 92*
Thompson, Dorothy 1893-1961 *HanAmWH*
Thompson, Dorothy 1894-1961 *BenetAL 91, FacFETw*
Thompson, Dorothy Brown 1896- *WhoMW 92*
Thompson, Douglas Evan 1947- *WhoWest 92*
Thompson, Douglas Stuart 1939- *AmMWSc 92*
Thompson, Dudley 1913- *AmMWSc 92*
Thompson, Dwight Alan 1955- *WhoWest 92*
Thompson, E. P. 1924- *WrDr 92*
Thompson, E. V. 1931- *WrDr 92*
Thompson, Earl Ryan 1939- *AmMWSc 92*
Thompson, Edgar J. *WhoEnt 92, WhoWest 92*
Thompson, Edward Arthur 1914- *Who 92*
Thompson, Edward Arthur 1947- *WhoRel 92*
Thompson, Edward Cornelious 1958- *WhoEnt 92*
Thompson, Edward Hugh Dudley 1907- *IntWW 91, Who 92*
Thompson, Edward Ivins Bradbridge 1933- *AmMWSc 92*
Thompson, Edward K. 1907- *IntWW 91*
Thompson, Edward K, III 1958- *WhoAmP 91*
Thompson, Edward Valentine 1935- *AmMWSc 92*
Thompson, Edward William 1951- *AmMWSc 92*
Thompson, Edwin A. *WhoBlA 92*
Thompson, Elbert Orson 1910- *WhoWest 92*
Thompson, Eldon Dale 1934- *WhoFI 92*
Thompson, Elizabeth 1962- *WhoRel 92*
Thompson, Eloise Bibb 1878-1928 *NotBlAW 92*
Thompson, Emerson McLean, Jr. 1931- *WhoRel 92*
Thompson, Emma 1959- *IntMPA 92, IntWW 91*
Thompson, Emma M. 1920- *WhoBlA 92*
Thompson, Emmanuel Bandele 1928- *AmMWSc 92*
Thompson, Emmett Frank 1936- *AmMWSc 92*
Thompson, Era Bell d1986 *WhoBlA 92N*
Thompson, Era Bell 1906-1986 *NotBlAW 92*
Thompson, Eric Douglas 1934- *AmMWSc 92*
Thompson, Eric John 1934- *Who 92*
Thompson, Eric R. 1941- *WhoBlA 92*
Thompson, Erik G 1934- *AmMWSc 92*
Thompson, Ernest 1949- *WhoEnt 92*
Thompson, Ernest Aubrey, Jr 1945- *AmMWSc 92*
Thompson, Ernest Heber 1891-1971 *TwCPaSc*
Thompson, Ernest Seton *BenetAL 91*
Thompson, Ernest Victor 1931- *IntAu&W 91*
Thompson, Eugene Edward 1938- *WhoBlA 92*
Thompson, Eugene George 1948- *WhoIns 92*
Thompson, Evan M 1933- *AmMWSc 92*
Thompson, Fay Morgen 1935- *AmMWSc 92*
Thompson, Floyd 1914- *WhoBlA 92*
Thompson, Frances E. 1896- *WhoBlA 92*
Thompson, Francesca 1932- *WhoBlA 92*
Thompson, Francis 1859-1907 *CnDBLB 5 [port], RfGEnL 91*
Thompson, Francis 1958- *BlkOlyM [port]*
Thompson, Francis C 1941- *WhoAmP 91*
Thompson, Francis George 1931- *WrDr 92*
Thompson, Francis Michael Longstreth 1925- *IntWW 91, Who 92*
Thompson, Francis Tracy 1930- *AmMWSc 92*
Thompson, Francis W. B. *WhoRel 92*
Thompson, Frank 1927- *WhoBlA 92*
Thompson, Frank Derek 1939- *Who 92*
Thompson, Frank L. 1903- *WhoBlA 92*
Thompson, Frank V 1874- *DcAmImH*
Thompson, Frank William 1928- *WhoBlA 92*
Thompson, Fred C 1928- *AmMWSc 92*
Thompson, Fred Gilbert 1934- *AmMWSc 92*
Thompson, Fred Priestly, Jr. 1917- *WhoRel 92*
Thompson, Fred Weldon 1932- *WhoRel 92*
Thompson, Frederick Nimrod, Jr 1939- *AmMWSc 92*
Thompson, Frederick William 1914- *Who 92*
Thompson, French F., Jr. 1953- *WhoBlA 92*
Thompson, G Robert 1924- *WhoAmP 91*
Thompson, Gail Kinsey 1944- *WhoMW 92*
Thompson, Gail Nanette 1955- *WhoAmL 92*
Thompson, Garfield W 1916- *WhoAmP 91*
Thompson, Garland Lee 1943- *WhoBlA 92*
Thompson, Gary *DrAPF 91*
Thompson, Gary Dewayne 1948- *WhoRel 92*
Thompson, Gary Gene 1940- *AmMWSc 92*
Thompson, Gary Haughton 1935- *AmMWSc 92*
Thompson, Gayle R 1938- *WhoIns 92*
Thompson, Gene *TwCWW 91*
Thompson, Geneva Florence 1915- *WhoMW 92*
Thompson, Geoffrey 1935- *AmMWSc 92*
Thompson, Geoffrey Acheson 1940- *WhoFI 92*
Thompson, Geoffrey Hewlett *Who 92*
Thompson, George Albert 1919- *AmMWSc 92, WhoWest 92*
Thompson, George Ellsworth 1945- *WhoMW 92*
Thompson, George H. 1928- *Who 92*
Thompson, George Lee 1933- *WhoFI 92*
Thompson, George Ralph 1929- *WhoRel 92*
Thompson, George Rex 1943- *AmMWSc 92*
Thompson, George Richard 1930- *AmMWSc 92*
Thompson, George Walter Murry, Jr. 1931- *WhoRel 92*
Thompson, Gerald Everett 1924- *WhoFI 92, WhoMW 92*
Thompson, Gerald Francis Michael P 1910- *Who 92*
Thompson, Gerald Lee 1945- *AmMWSc 92*
Thompson, Gerald Luther 1923- *AmMWSc 92*
Thompson, Gerald Raymond 1939- *WhoAmP 91*
Thompson, Geraldine *WhoBlA 92*
Thompson, Glenn Judean 1936- *WhoMW 92*
Thompson, Glenn Michael 1946- *WhoWest 92*
Thompson, Gloria Crawford 1942- *WhoBlA 92*
Thompson, Godfrey *Who 92*
Thompson, Godfrey James M. *Who 92*
Thompson, Gordon, Jr. 1929- *WhoAmL 92, WhoWest 92*
Thompson, Gordon William *AmMWSc 92*
Thompson, Grant 1927- *AmMWSc 92*
Thompson, Granville Berry 1929- *AmMWSc 92*
Thompson, Greg Alan 1955- *WhoWest 92*
Thompson, Gregory Lee 1946- *WhoFI 92*
Thompson, Gus Howard 1956- *WhoRel 92*
Thompson, Guy A, Jr 1931- *AmMWSc 92*
Thompson, H. B., Jr. *WhoRel 92*
Thompson, Hank 1925 *NewAmDM*
Thompson, Hannis Woodson, Jr 1928- *AmMWSc 92*
Thompson, Harold Fong 1943- *WhoBlA 92*
Thompson, Harold J. *WhoMW 92*
Thompson, Harold Lee 1945- *WhoAmL 92, WhoMW 92*
Thompson, Harold Lindsay 1929- *IntWW 91*
Thompson, Harold W. 1891-1964 *BenetAL 91*
Thompson, Hartwell Greene, Jr 1924- *AmMWSc 92*
Thompson, Harvey E 1920- *AmMWSc 92*
Thompson, Hazen Spencer 1928- *AmMWSc 92*
Thompson, Henry Joseph 1921- *AmMWSc 92*
Thompson, Henry Orrin *WhoRel 92*
Thompson, Herbert, Jr. *WhoMW 92, WhoRel 92*
Thompson, Herbert Bradford 1927- *AmMWSc 92*
Thompson, Herbert Ernest 1923- *WhoWest 92*
Thompson, Herbert Stanley 1932- *AmMWSc 92*
Thompson, Herman G. *WhoBlA 92*
Thompson, Hewlett *Who 92*
Thompson, Hilton Lond 1927- *WhoBlA 92*
Thompson, Hobson, Jr. 1931- *WhoBlA 92*
Thompson, Holly Ann *AmMWSc 92*
Thompson, Homer Armstrong 1906- *IntWW 91*
Thompson, Howard *Who 92*
Thompson, Howard Doyle 1934- *AmMWSc 92*
Thompson, Howard Elliott 1934- *WhoMW 92*
Thompson, Howard K, Jr 1928- *AmMWSc 92*
Thompson, Hugh 1931- *Who 92*
Thompson, Hugh Allison 1935- *AmMWSc 92*
Thompson, Hugh Ansley 1936- *AmMWSc 92*
Thompson, Hugh Erwin 1917- *AmMWSc 92*
Thompson, Hugh Lee 1934- *WhoMW 92*
Thompson, Hugh Patrick 1935- *Who 92*
Thompson, Hugh Walter 1936- *AmMWSc 92*
Thompson, Humphrey Simon M. *Who 92*
Thompson, Hunter 1939- *FacFETw*
Thompson, Hunter S *SourALJ*
Thompson, Hunter S 1939- *IntAu&W 91, News 92-1 [port], WrDr 92*
Thompson, Ian Bently 1936- *WrDr 92*
Thompson, Ian McKim 1938- *Who 92*
Thompson, Ike 1915- *WhoAmP 91*
Thompson, Imogene A. 1927- *WhoBlA 92*
Thompson, Isaiah 1915- *WhoBlA 92*
Thompson, J G *AmMWSc 92*
Thompson, J. Lee 1914- *IntMPA 92*
Thompson, Jack 1940- *IntMPA 92*
Thompson, Jack Coats 1909- *WhoWest 92*
Thompson, Jacqueline Anne 1948- *WhoFI 92*
Thompson, Jacqueline Kay 1950- *WhoAmP 91*

**Thompson**, Jacqueline Kay 1954- *WhoEnt 92*
**Thompson**, James 1932- *WrDr 92*
**Thompson**, James 1942- *WhoMW 92*
**Thompson**, James Arthur 1931- *AmMWSc 92*
**Thompson**, James B. 1929- *WhoRel 92*
**Thompson**, James Burleigh, Jr 1921- *AmMWSc 92, IntWW 91*
**Thompson**, James Charles 1928- *AmMWSc 92*
**Thompson**, James Charlton 1941- *AmMWSc 92*
**Thompson**, James Chilton 1930- *AmMWSc 92*
**Thompson**, James Clark 1939- *WhoFI 92*
**Thompson**, James Craig 1933- *Who 92*
**Thompson**, James David 1945- *WhoAmL 92, WhoFI 92, WhoIns 92*
**Thompson**, James Edwin 1936- *AmMWSc 92*
**Thompson**, James Eugene 1944- *WhoEnt 92*
**Thompson**, James Henry 1928- *WhoEnt 92*
**Thompson**, James Howard 1942- *Who 92*
**Thompson**, James Jarrard *AmMWSc 92*
**Thompson**, James Joseph 1940- *AmMWSc 92*
**Thompson**, James Kent 1951- *WhoMW 92*
**Thompson**, James Lawton *Who 92*
**Thompson**, James Lowry 1940- *AmMWSc 92*
**Thompson**, James Marion 1926- *AmMWSc 92*
**Thompson**, James Martin 1943- *WhoRel 92*
**Thompson**, James Maurice 1844-1901 *BibAL 8*
**Thompson**, James Neal, Jr 1946- *AmMWSc 92*
**Thompson**, James P. 1948- *WhoEnt 92*
**Thompson**, James R. 1936- *IntWW 91*
**Thompson**, James R 1942- *AmMWSc 92*
**Thompson**, James R, Jr 1936- *WhoAmP 91*
**Thompson**, James Richard 1933- *WhoFI 92*
**Thompson**, James Robert 1936- *WhoMW 92*
**Thompson**, James Robert 1938- *AmMWSc 92*
**Thompson**, James W. 1943- *WhoBlA 92*
**Thompson**, James W., Jr. 1948- *WhoMW 92*
**Thompson**, James Walker, III 1952- *WhoRel 92*
**Thompson**, James William 1936- *WhoWest 92*
**Thompson**, James William 1939- *WhoFI 92*
**Thompson**, Jamie 1962- *WhoEnt 92*
**Thompson**, Jane Ann 1955- *WhoAmL 92*
**Thompson**, Jane Johnson 1951- *WhoFI 92*
**Thompson**, Jay Lee 1914- *IntWW 91*
**Thompson**, Jean *DrAPF 91*
**Thompson**, Jeanie *DrAPF 91*
**Thompson**, Jeffery Elders 1951- *WhoRel 92*
**Thompson**, Jeffery Scott 1952- *AmMWSc 92*
**Thompson**, Jeffrey Earl 1955- *WhoBlA 92*
**Thompson**, Jeffrey Michael 1950- *AmMWSc 92*
**Thompson**, Jere William 1932- *WhoFI 92*
**Thompson**, Jerry Nelson 1939- *AmMWSc 92*
**Thompson**, Jesse *WhoBlA 92*
**Thompson**, Jesse Burl 1953- *WhoWest 92*
**Thompson**, Jesse Clay, Jr 1926- *AmMWSc 92*
**Thompson**, Jesse Eldon 1919- *AmMWSc 92*
**Thompson**, Jesse Jackson 1919- *WhoWest 92*
**Thompson**, Jesse M. 1946- *WhoBlA 92*
**Thompson**, Jill Charlotte 1954- *AmMWSc 92*
**Thompson**, Jim 1906-1976 *ConLC 69 [port]*
**Thompson**, Joan Kathryn 1956- *WhoMW 92*
**Thompson**, Joanna *DrAPF 91*
**Thompson**, Joe 1887-1980 *FacFETw*
**Thompson**, Joe David 1947- *AmMWSc 92*
**Thompson**, Joe Floyd 1939- *AmMWSc 92*
**Thompson**, Joe L 1938- *WhoAmP 91*
**Thompson**, John 1907- *Who 92*
**Thompson**, John 1922- *IntWW 91*
**Thompson**, John 1928- *Who 92*
**Thompson**, John 1945- *Who 92*
**Thompson**, John, Jr 1927- *WhoAmP 91*
**Thompson**, John A. *DrAPF 91*
**Thompson**, John Alan 1926- *Who 92*
**Thompson**, John Alec 1942- *AmMWSc 92*
**Thompson**, John Andrew 1907- *WhoBlA 92*
**Thompson**, John Brian 1928- *Who 92*
**Thompson**, John C, Jr 1930- *AmMWSc 92*
**Thompson**, John Carl 1941- *AmMWSc 92*
**Thompson**, John Clayton 1941- *WhoFI 92*
**Thompson**, John Darrell 1933- *AmMWSc 92*
**Thompson**, John Derek T. *Who 92*
**Thompson**, John Eveleigh 1941- *AmMWSc 92*
**Thompson**, John Fanning 1919- *AmMWSc 92*
**Thompson**, John Frederick 1947- *AmMWSc 92*
**Thompson**, John Griggs 1932- *Who 92*
**Thompson**, John Handby 1929- *Who 92*
**Thompson**, John Harold, Jr 1921- *AmMWSc 92*
**Thompson**, John Henry, III 1938- *WhoFI 92*
**Thompson**, John Jeffrey 1938- *Who 92*
**Thompson**, John Keith Lumley 1923- *Who 92*
**Thompson**, John Lee 1940- *WhoAmP 91*
**Thompson**, John Leonard C. *Who 92*
**Thompson**, John Leslie 1917- *AmMWSc 92*
**Thompson**, John Lester 1926- *WhoRel 92, WhoWest 92*
**Thompson**, John Marlow 1914- *Who 92*
**Thompson**, John Michael *AmMWSc 92*
**Thompson**, John Michael Anthony 1941- *Who 92*
**Thompson**, John Michael Tutill 1937- *Who 92*
**Thompson**, John N 1951- *AmMWSc 92*
**Thompson**, John Peter 1925- *Who 92*
**Thompson**, John R. 1823-1873 *BenetAL 91*
**Thompson**, John R 1918- *AmMWSc 92*
**Thompson**, John Robert 1951- *AmMWSc 92*
**Thompson**, John Robert, Jr. 1941- *WhoBlA 92*
**Thompson**, John Ross 1943- *WhoRel 92*
**Thompson**, John S 1928- *AmMWSc 92*
**Thompson**, John Stewart 1940- *AmMWSc 92*
**Thompson**, John Timothy 1952- *WhoFI 92*
**Thompson**, John W *WhoAmP 91*
**Thompson**, John Wesley 1939- *WhoBlA 92*
**Thompson**, John William McWean 1920- *IntAu&W 91, Who 92*
**Thompson**, John Yelverton 1909- *Who 92*
**Thompson**, Johnnie 1930- *WhoBlA 92*
**Thompson**, Jon H 1942- *AmMWSc 92*
**Thompson**, Joseph Allan 1906- *WhoBlA 92*
**Thompson**, Joseph Earl, Sr. *WhoBlA 92*
**Thompson**, Joseph Edward 1960- *WhoEnt 92*
**Thompson**, Joseph Garth 1935- *AmMWSc 92*
**Thompson**, Joseph Isaac 1922- *WhoBlA 92*
**Thompson**, Joseph Kyle 1920- *AmMWSc 92*
**Thompson**, Joseph Lippard 1932- *AmMWSc 92*
**Thompson**, Joseph P. 1937- *WhoFI 92*
**Thompson**, Joseph Warren 1950- *WhoMW 92*
**Thompson**, Joyce *DrAPF 91*
**Thompson**, Judith Kastrup 1933- *WhoWest 92*
**Thompson**, Julia Ann 1943- *AmMWSc 92*
**Thompson**, Julian *Who 92*
**Thompson**, Julian F 1927- *ChILR 24 [port], SmATA 13AS [port]*
**Thompson**, Julian Howard Atherden 1934- *Who 92*
**Thompson**, Julian O. *Who 92*
**Thompson**, Julius Eric *DrAPF 91*
**Thompson**, Juul Harold 1945- *WhoFI 92*
**Thompson**, Karen Ann 1955- *WhoBlA 92*
**Thompson**, Katherine Genevieve 1945- *WhoAmL 92*
**Thompson**, Kathy Helen 1947- *WhoWest 92*
**Thompson**, Keith Bruce 1932- *Who 92*
**Thompson**, Kenneth David 1940- *AmMWSc 92*
**Thompson**, Kenneth Lane 1943- *AmMWSc 92*
**Thompson**, Kenneth N 1937- *WhoAmP 91*
**Thompson**, Kenneth O 1917- *AmMWSc 92*
**Thompson**, Kenneth Pope 1956- *WhoRel 92*
**Thompson**, Kenneth W 1921- *IntAu&W 91, WrDr 92*
**Thompson**, Kevin Mark 1956- *WhoMW 92*
**Thompson**, Kim 1956- *WhoBlA 92*
**Thompson**, Kristofer Philip 1962- *WhoEnt 92*
**Thompson**, La Salle 1961- *WhoBlA 92*
**Thompson**, Lancelot C. A. 1925- *WhoBlA 92*
**Thompson**, Lancelot Churchill Adalbert 1925- *AmMWSc 92*
**Thompson**, Larry Angelo 1944- *WhoEnt 92*
**Thompson**, Larry Bruce 1954- *WhoRel 92*
**Thompson**, Larry Clark 1935- *AmMWSc 92*
**Thompson**, Larry D. 1945- *WhoBlA 92*
**Thompson**, Larry Dean 1945- *WhoAmL 92*
**Thompson**, Larry Dean 1951- *AmMWSc 92*
**Thompson**, Larry E. *DrAPF 91*
**Thompson**, Larry Flack 1944- *AmMWSc 92*
**Thompson**, Larry Richard 1947- *WhoAmL 92*
**Thompson**, Laurence Graham 1920- *WrDr 92*
**Thompson**, Lauretta Peterson *WhoBlA 92*
**Thompson**, LaVerne Elizabeth Thomas 1945- *WhoMW 92*
**Thompson**, Lawrence Hadley 1941- *AmMWSc 92*
**Thompson**, Lea 1961- *ConTFT 9, IntMPA 92*
**Thompson**, Lee Bennett 1902- *WhoAmL 92, WhoFI 92*
**Thompson**, Lee P 1913- *AmMWSc 92*
**Thompson**, Leif Harry 1943- *AmMWSc 92*
**Thompson**, Leith Stanley 1934- *AmMWSc 92*
**Thompson**, Leonard LeRoy 1934- *WhoRel 92*
**Thompson**, Leonard Monteath 1916- *WrDr 92*
**Thompson**, LeRoy, Jr. 1913- *WhoFI 92*
**Thompson**, Leroy B. 1921- *WhoBlA 92*
**Thompson**, Lewis Chisholm 1926- *AmMWSc 92*
**Thompson**, Lilian Umale *AmMWSc 92*
**Thompson**, Lillian Hurlburt 1947- *WhoFI 92*
**Thompson**, Linda Jo 1953- *WhoBlA 92, WhoFI 92*
**Thompson**, Lindsay Hamilton Simpson 1923- *Who 92*
**Thompson**, Lindsay Taylor 1955- *WhoWest 92*
**Thompson**, Lionel *Who 92*
**Thompson**, Litchfield O'Brien 1937- *WhoBlA 92*
**Thompson**, Lloyd Earl 1934- *WhoBlA 92*
**Thompson**, Lloyd H. *Who 92*
**Thompson**, Lohren Matthew 1926- *WhoWest 92*
**Thompson**, Lola May 1931- *WhoEnt 92*
**Thompson**, Loran Tyson 1947- *WhoAmL 92*
**Thompson**, Loren P *WhoAmP 91*
**Thompson**, Louis Jean 1925- *AmMWSc 92*
**Thompson**, Louise 1901- *NotBlAW 92*
**Thompson**, Lowell Dennis 1947- *WhoBlA 92*
**Thompson**, Lucky 1924- *NewAmDM*
**Thompson**, Lyell 1924- *AmMWSc 92*
**Thompson**, Lyle Eugene 1956- *WhoWest 92*
**Thompson**, Lynne Charles 1944- *AmMWSc 92*
**Thompson**, M. T., Jr. 1951- *WhoBlA 92*
**Thompson**, Mack A 1922- *WhoAmP 91*
**Thompson**, Major Curt 1937- *AmMWSc 92*
**Thompson**, Malcolm Caldwell 1919- *WhoRel 92*
**Thompson**, Malcolm Francis 1921- *WhoWest 92*
**Thompson**, Malcolm J 1927- *AmMWSc 92*
**Thompson**, Marcus *WhoEnt 92*
**Thompson**, Marcus Aurelius 1946- *WhoBlA 92*
**Thompson**, Margaret A Wilson 1920- *AmMWSc 92*
**Thompson**, Margaret Douglas 1947- *AmMWSc 92*
**Thompson**, Marjorie Ellis 1957- *Who 92*
**Thompson**, Mark Duaine 1956- *WhoWest 92*
**Thompson**, Mark Randolph 1955- *WhoBlA 92*
**Thompson**, Marshall 1926- *IntMPA 92*
**Thompson**, Marshall Ray 1938- *AmMWSc 92*
**Thompson**, Martin Flanagan 1951- *WhoAmL 92*
**Thompson**, Martin Leroy 1935- *AmMWSc 92*
**Thompson**, Marttie L. 1930- *WhoBlA 92*
**Thompson**, Marttie Louis 1930- *WhoAmL 92*
**Thompson**, Marvin P 1933- *AmMWSc 92*
**Thompson**, Marvin Pete 1941- *AmMWSc 92*
**Thompson**, Mary E 1928- *AmMWSc 92*
**Thompson**, Mary Eileen 1928- *WhoMW 92*
**Thompson**, Mary Eleanor 1926- *AmMWSc 92*
**Thompson**, Mary Elinore 1944- *AmMWSc 92*
**Thompson**, Mary Jean 1935- *WhoWest 92*
**Thompson**, Mary L 1938- *WhoAmP 91*
**Thompson**, Mary Staples 1955- *WhoMW 92*
**Thompson**, Maurice 1844-1901 *BenetAL 91*
**Thompson**, Maurie 1844-1901 *BiInAmS*
**Thompson**, Mavis Sarah 1927- *WhoBlA 92*
**Thompson**, Max Clyde 1936- *AmMWSc 92*
**Thompson**, Maxine Ethel 1951- *WhoWest 92*
**Thompson**, Maxine Marie 1926- *AmMWSc 92*
**Thompson**, Maynard 1936- *AmMWSc 92, WhoMW 92*
**Thompson**, McKim *Who 92*
**Thompson**, Melissa Ann 1950- *WhoFI 92*
**Thompson**, Mervyn 1936- *WrDr 92*
**Thompson**, Michael 1931- *Who 92*
**Thompson**, Michael Bernard 1951- *WhoMW 92*
**Thompson**, Michael Bruce 1939- *AmMWSc 92*
**Thompson**, Michael Don 1950- *WhoRel 92, WhoWest 92*
**Thompson**, Michael Harry Rex 1931- *Who 92*
**Thompson**, Michael Jacques 1936- *Who 92*
**Thompson**, Michael Neal 1963- *WhoRel 92*
**Thompson**, Michael Warwick 1931- *IntWW 91*
**Thompson**, Michael Welman 1928- *IntAu&W 91*
**Thompson**, Mickey 1928-1988 *FacFETw*
**Thompson**, Mike *WhoAmP 91*
**Thompson**, Mike 1942- *WhoAmP 91*
**Thompson**, Milo, Jr. *WhoRel 92*
**Thompson**, Milton 1926- *FacFETw*
**Thompson**, Milton Avery 1929- *AmMWSc 92*
**Thompson**, Milton Earl 1931- *WhoWest 92*
**Thompson**, Minnie Elisabeth 1910- *WhoEnt 92*
**Thompson**, Morris Lee 1946- *WhoAmL 92*
**Thompson**, Mortimer Neal *BenetAL 91*
**Thompson**, Mychal 1955- *WhoBlA 92*
**Thompson**, Myron H. *WhoAmL 92*
**Thompson**, N David 1934- *WhoIns 92*
**Thompson**, Nancy Lynn 1956- *AmMWSc 92*
**Thompson**, Neal Philip 1936- *AmMWSc 92*
**Thompson**, Neil 1929- *WrDr 92*
**Thompson**, Neil Bruce 1941- *WhoWest 92*
**Thompson**, Nicolas de la Mare 1928- *Who 92*
**Thompson**, Noel Brentnall Watson 1932- *Who 92*
**Thompson**, Noel Page 1929- *AmMWSc 92*
**Thompson**, Norman Sinclair 1920- *Who 92*
**Thompson**, Norman Storm 1923- *AmMWSc 92, WhoMW 92*
**Thompson**, Oliver Frederic 1905- *Who 92*
**Thompson**, Oswald 1926- *WhoBlA 92*
**Thompson**, Owen Edward 1939- *AmMWSc 92*
**Thompson**, Pamela Ann 1960- *WhoMW 92*
**Thompson**, Patricia 1942- *WhoRel 92*
**Thompson**, Patricia Moultrie 1942-1989 *WhoBlA 92N*
**Thompson**, Patrick *Who 92*
**Thompson**, Paul 1939- *Who 92*
**Thompson**, Paul DeVries 1939- *AmMWSc 92*
**Thompson**, Paul O 1921- *AmMWSc 92*
**Thompson**, Paul Richard 1935- *Who 92*
**Thompson**, Paul Vernon 1954- *WhoFI 92*
**Thompson**, Paul Woodard 1909- *AmMWSc 92*
**Thompson**, Peter *Who 92*
**Thompson**, Peter 1928- *Who 92*
**Thompson**, Peter Boyd 1955- *WhoRel 92*
**Thompson**, Peter Ervin 1931- *AmMWSc 92*
**Thompson**, Peter John 1937- *Who 92*
**Thompson**, Peter Kenneth James 1937- *Who 92*
**Thompson**, Peter Nicholas 1946- *WhoAmL 92*
**Thompson**, Peter Russell 1921- *WhoFI 92*
**Thompson**, Peter Trueman 1929- *AmMWSc 92*
**Thompson**, Phebe Kirsten 1897- *AmMWSc 92, WhoMW 92*
**Thompson**, Philip A 1928- *AmMWSc 92*
**Thompson**, Phillip Eugene 1946- *AmMWSc 92*
**Thompson**, Phillip Gerhard 1930- *AmMWSc 92*
**Thompson**, Phillip M. 1959- *WhoAmL 92*
**Thompson**, Phyllis Hoge *DrAPF 91*
**Thompson**, Phyllis Hoge 1926- *ConAu 36NR*
**Thompson**, Portia Wilson 1944- *WhoBlA 92*
**Thompson**, Pratt *Who 92*

**Thompson,** Prince Eustace Shokehu *WhoRel 92*
**Thompson,** Priscilla Angelena 1951- *WhoBlA 92*
**Thompson,** R M *WhoAmP 91*
**Thompson,** Ralph 1916- *Who 92*
**Thompson,** Ralph Gordon 1934- *WhoAmL 92*
**Thompson,** Ralph J 1930- *AmMWSc 92*
**Thompson,** Ralph J, Jr 1928- *AmMWSc 92*
**Thompson,** Ralph Luther 1943- *AmMWSc 92*
**Thompson,** Ralph Newell 1918- *AmMWSc 92*
**Thompson,** Ramie Herbert 1933- *AmMWSc 92*
**Thompson,** Randall 1899-1984 *NewAmDM*
**Thompson,** Ray A. 1953- *WhoHisp 92*
**Thompson,** Raymond 1925- *Who 92*
**Thompson,** Raymond Edward 1936- *WhoAmL 92*
**Thompson,** Raymond G 1952- *AmMWSc 92*
**Thompson,** Rebecca *DrAPF 91*
**Thompson,** Rebecca Sue 1944- *WhoMW 92*
**Thompson,** Regina *WhoBlA 92*
**Thompson,** Reginald Aubrey 1905- *Who 92*
**Thompson,** Reginald Harry 1925- *Who 92*
**Thompson,** Reginald Stanley 1899- *Who 92*
**Thompson,** Richard 1912- *Who 92*
**Thompson,** Richard 1949- *ConMus 7 [port]*
**Thompson,** Richard 1952- *WhoAmL 92*
**Thompson,** Richard A 1934- *WhoAmP 91*
**Thompson,** Richard Baxter 1926- *AmMWSc 92*
**Thompson,** Richard Bruce 1939- *AmMWSc 92*
**Thompson,** Richard Claude 1939- *AmMWSc 92*
**Thompson,** Richard David 1936- *WhoMW 92*
**Thompson,** Richard Deane 1933- *WhoEnt 92*
**Thompson,** Richard Dickson 1955- *WhoAmL 92*
**Thompson,** Richard E 1929- *AmMWSc 92*
**Thompson,** Richard Edward 1946- *AmMWSc 92*
**Thompson,** Richard Ellis 1935- *WhoBlA 92, WhoMW 92*
**Thompson,** Richard Eugene 1951- *WhoMW 92*
**Thompson,** Richard Frederick 1930- *AmMWSc 92*
**Thompson,** Richard Henry 1931- *WhoMW 92*
**Thompson,** Richard John 1927- *AmMWSc 92*
**Thompson,** Richard Leon 1944- *WhoAmL 92*
**Thompson,** Richard Michael 1945- *AmMWSc 92*
**Thompson,** Richard Nelson Christoph 1938- *WhoEnt 92*
**Thompson,** Richard Paul Hepworth 1940- *Who 92*
**Thompson,** Richard Perry 1951- *WhoMW 92*
**Thompson,** Richard Richardo 1955- *WhoRel 92*
**Thompson,** Richard Scott 1939- *AmMWSc 92*
**Thompson,** Richard T. 1948- *WhoFI 92*
**Thompson,** Richard Treadwell 1944- *WhoFI 92*
**Thompson,** Richard Victor, Jr. 1951- *WhoFI 92*
**Thompson,** Rita Marie 1930- *WhoWest 92*
**Thompson,** Robert 1916- *WrDr 92*
**Thompson,** Robert Alan 1937- *AmMWSc 92*
**Thompson,** Robert Bruce 1920- *WrDr 92*
**Thompson,** Robert Bruce 1941- *AmMWSc 92*
**Thompson,** Robert Bruce 1959- *WhoFI 92*
**Thompson,** Robert Charles 1931- *AmMWSc 92*
**Thompson,** Robert Charles 1942- *WhoAmL 92*
**Thompson,** Robert Dewey 1936- *WhoBlA 92*
**Thompson,** Robert Douglas 1944- *WhoMW 92*
**Thompson,** Robert Farris 1932- *WhoBlA 92, WrDr 92*
**Thompson,** Robert Gary 1938- *AmMWSc 92*
**Thompson,** Robert Gene 1931- *AmMWSc 92*
**Thompson,** Robert Grainger Ker 1916- *IntAu&W 91, Who 92*
**Thompson,** Robert H 1929- *WhoIns 92*
**Thompson,** Robert H 1946- *WhoAmP 91*
**Thompson,** Robert Harry 1924- *AmMWSc 92*
**Thompson,** Robert Henry Stewart 1912- *IntWW 91, Who 92*
**Thompson,** Robert James 1930- *AmMWSc 92*
**Thompson,** Robert James 1953- *WhoFI 92*
**Thompson,** Robert Jaye 1951- *WhoRel 92*
**Thompson,** Robert John, Jr 1917- *AmMWSc 92*
**Thompson,** Robert King 1948- *WhoFI 92*
**Thompson,** Robert Kruger 1922- *AmMWSc 92*
**Thompson,** Robert L., Jr. 1944- *WhoAmL 92*
**Thompson,** Robert Lee 1945- *AmMWSc 92, WhoFI 92*
**Thompson,** Robert Lloyd H. *Who 92*
**Thompson,** Robert Loran 1958- *WhoEnt 92*
**Thompson,** Robert M 1927- *WhoAmP 91*
**Thompson,** Robert M 1932- *WhoIns 92*
**Thompson,** Robert Norman 1914- *IntAu&W 91, IntWW 91, WrDr 92*
**Thompson,** Robert Poole 1923- *AmMWSc 92*
**Thompson,** Robert Quinton 1955- *AmMWSc 92*
**Thompson,** Robert Richard 1931- *AmMWSc 92*
**Thompson,** Robert S. *DrAPF 91*
**Thompson,** Robert S 1940- *WhoAmP 91*
**Thompson,** Robert Thomas 1930- *WhoAmL 92*
**Thompson,** Robert Walter 1951- *WhoFI 92*
**Thompson,** Robin Lee 1957- *WhoAmL 92*
**Thompson,** Rodger Irwin 1944- *AmMWSc 92*
**Thompson,** Roger Craig 1941- *WhoWest 92*
**Thompson,** Roger Francis 1933- *WrDr 92*
**Thompson,** Roger Kevin Russell 1945- *AmMWSc 92*
**Thompson,** Roland 1950- *WhoMW 92*
**Thompson,** Ron Everett 1935- *WhoRel 92*
**Thompson,** Ronald Charles 1932- *WhoRel 92*
**Thompson,** Ronald Earl 1931- *WhoMW 92*
**Thompson,** Ronald Edward 1931- *WhoAmL 92, WhoWest 92*
**Thompson,** Ronald G 1960- *AmMWSc 92*
**Thompson,** Ronald Halsey 1926- *AmMWSc 92*
**Thompson,** Ronald Hobart 1935- *AmMWSc 92*
**Thompson,** Ronald M 1951- *WhoAmP 91*
**Thompson,** Rosemary Ann 1945- *AmMWSc 92*
**Thompson,** Rosie L. 1950- *WhoBlA 92*
**Thompson,** Roy Charles, Jr 1920- *AmMWSc 92*
**Thompson,** Roy Lloyd 1927- *AmMWSc 92*
**Thompson,** Roy S, Jr 1917- *WhoIns 92*
**Thompson,** Rupert Julian 1941- *IntWW 91, Who 92*
**Thompson,** Russ *TwCWW 91*
**Thompson,** Russell Douglas 1937- *WhoAmL 92*
**Thompson,** Ruth Plumly 1891-1976 *ConAu 134, SmATA 66*
**Thompson,** Sada 1929- *IntMPA 92*
**Thompson,** Sada Carolyn 1929- *WhoEnt 92*
**Thompson,** Sally Engstrom 1940- *WhoAmP 91, WhoMW 92*
**Thompson,** Sally Gail 1938- *WhoMW 92*
**Thompson,** Samuel, III 1932- *AmMWSc 92*
**Thompson,** Samuel Lee 1941- *AmMWSc 92*
**Thompson,** Samuel Rankin 1833-1896 *BiInAmS*
**Thompson,** Sandra *DrAPF 91*
**Thompson,** Sandra Ann *WhoBlA 92*
**Thompson,** Sandra Jean 1958- *WhoWest 92*
**Thompson,** Sandra S. *DrAPF 91*
**Thompson,** Sandy W. 1955- *WhoFI 92*
**Thompson,** Sarah Sue 1948- *WhoBlA 92*
**Thompson,** Scott Gallatin 1944- *WhoIns 92*
**Thompson,** Scott Stanley 1957- *WhoWest 92*
**Thompson,** Senfronia *WhoAmP 91*
**Thompson,** Seth Charles 1927- *WhoMW 92*
**Thompson,** Sharon *DrAPF 91, WhoAmP 91*
**Thompson,** Sheilah *WhoRel 92*
**Thompson,** Sheldon Lee 1938- *AmMWSc 92*
**Thompson,** Sherman Lee 1934- *WhoWest 92*
**Thompson,** Sherwood 1928- *WhoBlA 92*
**Thompson,** Shirley Jean 1937- *AmMWSc 92*
**Thompson,** Shirley Williams 1941- *AmMWSc 92*
**Thompson,** Stanley *Who 92*
**Thompson,** Starley Lee 1954- *AmMWSc 92*
**Thompson,** Stephen *WhoBlA 92*
**Thompson,** Stephen Lynn 1953- *WhoAmL 92*
**Thompson,** Steve 1950- *WhoAmP 91*
**Thompson,** Steve Delwyn 1935- *WhoAmP 91*
**Thompson,** Steven Risley 1938- *AmMWSc 92*
**Thompson,** Sue Ann 1938- *AmMWSc 92*
**Thompson,** Susan Lynne 1950- *WhoRel 92*
**Thompson,** Sylvia A Davis *WhoAmP 91*
**Thompson,** Sylvia Moore 1937- *WhoBlA 92*
**Thompson,** Sylvia Taylor 1946- *WhoWest 92*
**Thompson,** Tawana Sadiela 1957- *WhoBlA 92*
**Thompson,** Taylor 1919- *WhoBlA 92*
**Thompson,** Tazewell Alfred 1954- *WhoEnt 92*
**Thompson,** Terence William 1952- *WhoAmL 92, WhoFI 92, WhoWest 92*
**Thompson,** Teri Elizabeth 1950- *WhoWest 92*
**Thompson,** Theodis 1944- *WhoBlA 92*
**Thompson,** Theodore Warren, Sr. 1923- *WhoRel 92*
**Thompson,** Thomas 1913- *TwCWW 91, WhoEnt 92, WrDr 92*
**Thompson,** Thomas Adrian 1944- *WhoMW 92*
**Thompson,** Thomas Eaton 1938- *AmMWSc 92*
**Thompson,** Thomas Edward 1926- *AmMWSc 92*
**Thompson,** Thomas Henry 1924- *WhoRel 92*
**Thompson,** Thomas Keith 1938- *WhoAmP 91*
**Thompson,** Thomas Leigh 1941- *AmMWSc 92*
**Thompson,** Thomas Leo 1922- *AmMWSc 92*
**Thompson,** Thomas Lionel 1921- *Who 92*
**Thompson,** Thomas Luman 1927- *AmMWSc 92*
**Thompson,** Thomas Luther 1938- *AmMWSc 92*
**Thompson,** Thomas Milroy 1954- *WhoMW 92*
**Thompson,** Thomas Nolan 1949- *WhoAmP 91*
**Thompson,** Thomas Ronald 1927- *WhoFI 92*
**Thompson,** Thomas William 1936- *AmMWSc 92*
**Thompson,** Timothy J 1949- *AmMWSc 92*
**Thompson,** Tina Lewis Chryar 1929- *WhoWest 92*
**Thompson,** Todd Stephen 1948- *WhoWest 92*
**Thompson,** Tommy Burt 1938- *AmMWSc 92*
**Thompson,** Tommy Earl 1944- *AmMWSc 92*
**Thompson,** Tommy G. 1941- *AlmAP 92 [port]*
**Thompson,** Tommy George 1941- *IntWW 91, WhoAmP 91, WhoMW 92*
**Thompson,** Treva Levi 1951- *WhoFI 92*
**Thompson,** Truet B 1917- *AmMWSc 92*
**Thompson,** Tyler 1915- *WhoRel 92*
**Thompson,** Vance 1863-1925 *BenetAL 91, ScFEYrs*
**Thompson,** Verdine Mae 1941- *WhoFI 92*
**Thompson,** Verla Darlene 1932- *WhoAmP 91*
**Thompson,** Vern *WhoAmP 91*
**Thompson,** Vernon 1943- *WhoAmP 91*
**Thompson,** Vernon Cecil 1905- *Who 92*
**Thompson,** Vinton Newbold 1947- *AmMWSc 92*
**Thompson,** Virginia Lou 1928- *WhoWest 92*
**Thompson,** Vivian L 1911- *IntAu&W 91, WrDr 92*
**Thompson,** W P 1934- *AmMWSc 92*
**Thompson,** Walter 1946- *WhoAmP 91*
**Thompson,** Warren Charles 1922- *AmMWSc 92*
**Thompson,** Warren Elwin 1930- *AmMWSc 92*
**Thompson,** Warren Slater 1929- *AmMWSc 92*
**Thompson,** Wayne Julius 1952- *AmMWSc 92*
**Thompson,** Wendy Jill 1961- *WhoAmL 92*
**Thompson,** Wesley Jay 1947- *AmMWSc 92*
**Thompson,** Wiley Ernest 1941- *AmMWSc 92*
**Thompson,** Will Henry 1848-1918 *BenetAL 91*
**Thompson,** Willard Lee, Jr *WhoAmP 91*
**Thompson,** Willard Scott 1942- *WhoAmP 91*
**Thompson,** William, Jr 1936- *AmMWSc 92*
**Thompson,** William A 1936- *AmMWSc 92*
**Thompson,** William A., III 1954- *WhoAmL 92*
**Thompson,** William Abdiel 1762-1847 *BiInAmS*
**Thompson,** William B. 1914- *WrDr 92*
**Thompson,** William B. D. *WhoBlA 92*
**Thompson,** William Baldwin 1935- *AmMWSc 92*
**Thompson,** William Bell 1922- *AmMWSc 92, Who 92*
**Thompson,** William Benbow, Jr 1923- *AmMWSc 92, WhoWest 92*
**Thompson,** William Cannon, Jr. 1938- *WhoFI 92*
**Thompson,** William Charles 1954- *WhoWest 92*
**Thompson,** William Coleridge 1924- *WhoBlA 92*
**Thompson,** William David 1921- *WhoFI 92*
**Thompson,** William David 1929- *WhoRel 92, WrDr 92*
**Thompson,** William Dean 1950- *WhoAmP 91*
**Thompson,** William Dennison, Jr. 1920- *WhoWest 92*
**Thompson,** William Edward 1948- *WhoAmP 91*
**Thompson,** William Francis, III 1945- *AmMWSc 92*
**Thompson,** William Gilbert 1945- *WhoRel 92*
**Thompson,** William Godfrey 1921- *Who 92*
**Thompson,** William Henry 1933- *WhoBlA 92*
**Thompson,** William Horn 1937- *AmMWSc 92*
**Thompson,** William Irwin 1938- *WrDr 92*
**Thompson,** William L. 1951- *WhoBlA 92*
**Thompson,** William Lay 1930- *AmMWSc 92*
**Thompson,** William Mort d1898 *ScFEYrs*
**Thompson,** William N. 1940- *ConAu 135*
**Thompson,** William Oxley, II 1941- *AmMWSc 92*
**Thompson,** William Paul, Jr. 1934- *WhoWest 92*
**Thompson,** William Pratt 1933- *Who 92*
**Thompson,** William Randall 1946- *WhoWest 92*
**Thompson,** William S. 1914- *WhoBlA 92*
**Thompson,** William Stansbury 1963- *WhoBlA 92*
**Thompson,** William Tappan 1812-1882 *BenetAL 91, BibAL 8*
**Thompson,** Willie Edward 1940- *WhoBlA 92*
**Thompson,** Willie Edward 1947- *WhoBlA 92*
**Thompson,** Willoughby Harry 1919- *Who 92*
**Thompson,** Wilmer Leigh 1938- *AmMWSc 92, WhoMW 92*
**Thompson,** Winston 1940- *IntWW 91*
**Thompson,** Winston Edna 1933- *WhoBlA 92*
**Thompson,** Woodrow Thomas, Jr. 1939- *WhoEnt 92*
**Thompson,** Wynelle Doggett 1914- *AmMWSc 92*
**Thompson,** Yaakov 1954- *WhoRel 92*
**Thompson,** Zadock 1796-1856 *BenetAL 91, BiInAmS*
**Thompson-Clemmons,** Olga Unita 1928- *WhoBlA 92*
**Thompson-Cope,** Nancy L 1948- *WhoAmP 91*
**Thompson Hancock,** P. E. *Who 92*
**Thompson-McCausland,** Benedict Maurice P 1938- *Who 92*
**Thompson-Moore,** Ann 1949- *WhoBlA 92*
**Thoms,** Adah 1870?-1943 *NotBlAW 92*
**Thoms,** Colin 1912- *TwCPaSc*
**Thoms,** David Moore 1948- *WhoMW 92*
**Thoms,** Donald H. 1948- *WhoBlA 92*
**Thoms,** Paul Edward 1936- *WhoEnt 92*
**Thoms,** Richard Edwin 1935- *AmMWSc 92*
**Thomsen,** Darrell Everett, Jr. 1958- *WhoRel 92*
**Thomsen,** Halvard Jessen 1917- *WhoRel 92*
**Thomsen,** Harry Ludwig 1911- *AmMWSc 92*
**Thomsen,** Ib 1925- *IntWW 91*
**Thomsen,** John Stearns 1921- *AmMWSc 92, WhoAmP 91*
**Thomsen,** Leon 1942- *AmMWSc 92*
**Thomsen,** Marjorie *TwCPaSc*
**Thomsen,** Michelle Fluckey 1950- *AmMWSc 92*
**Thomsen,** Niels Jorgen 1930- *IntWW 91*
**Thomsen,** Paula Joan 1961- *WhoWest 92*
**Thomsen,** Steuart Hill 1954- *WhoAmL 92*

**Thomsen,** Thomas Richard 1935- *WhoFI 92*
**Thomsen,** Warren Jessen 1922- *AmMWSc 92*
**Thomson** *Who 92*
**Thomson,** Adam 1926- *IntWW 91, Who 92*
**Thomson,** Alan 1928- *AmMWSc 92*
**Thomson,** Alan B R 1943- *AmMWSc 92*
**Thomson,** Alan John 1946- *AmMWSc 92*
**Thomson,** Alfred R. 1894- *TwCPaSc*
**Thomson,** Andrew Francis 1946- *WhoEnt 92*
**Thomson,** Ashley Edwin 1921- *AmMWSc 92*
**Thomson,** Barbara Jeanne 1929- *WhoFI 92, WhoWest 92*
**Thomson,** Basil Henry, Jr. 1945- *WhoAmL 92*
**Thomson,** Brian 1946- *IntWW 91*
**Thomson,** Brian Harold 1918- *Who 92*
**Thomson,** Bruce Randolph, Jr. 1958- *WhoMW 92*
**Thomson,** Bryden *IntWW 91, Who 92*
**Thomson,** Bryden d1991 *NewYTBS 91*
**Thomson,** Charles 1729-1824 *BlkwEAR, DcAmImH*
**Thomson,** Charles John 1941- *Who 92*
**Thomson,** Charles LeRoy 1924- *WhoWest 92*
**Thomson,** Christine Campbell 1897-1985 *ScFEYrs*
**Thomson,** D. H. 1918- *WrDr 92*
**Thomson,** Dale S 1934- *AmMWSc 92*
**Thomson,** David *Who 92, WhoRel 92*
**Thomson,** David 1914- *IntAu&W 91*
**Thomson,** David Anthony 1952- *WhoAmL 92*
**Thomson,** David James 1944- *AmMWSc 92*
**Thomson,** David Kinnear 1910- *Who 92*
**Thomson,** David M P 1939- *AmMWSc 92*
**Thomson,** David Paget 1931- *Who 92*
**Thomson,** David Spence 1915- *IntWW 91, Who 92*
**Thomson,** Dennis Walter 1941- *AmMWSc 92*
**Thomson,** Derick S. 1921- *WrDr 92*
**Thomson,** Donald A 1932- *AmMWSc 92*
**Thomson,** Dorothy Lampen 1904- *WhoFI 92*
**Thomson,** Duncan 1934- *Who 92*
**Thomson,** E. W. 1849-1924 *BenetAL 91*
**Thomson,** Edward *IntAu&W 91X, TwCSFW 91, WrDr 92*
**Thomson,** Elizabeth 1957- *IntAu&W 91*
**Thomson,** Evan 1919- *Who 92*
**Thomson,** Francis Paul 1914- *Who 92, WrDr 92*
**Thomson,** Frederick Douglas David 1940- *Who 92*
**Thomson,** Garry 1925- *Who 92*
**Thomson,** George 1860-1939 *TwCPaSc*
**Thomson,** George Henry 1924- *WrDr 92*
**Thomson,** George Malcolm 1899- *IntAu&W 91, Who 92, WrDr 92*
**Thomson,** George Paget 1892-1975 *WhoNob 90*
**Thomson,** George Ronald 1959- *WhoAmL 92, WhoMW 92*
**Thomson,** George Willis 1921- *AmMWSc 92*
**Thomson,** Gerald Edmund 1932- *AmMWSc 92, WhoBlA 92*
**Thomson,** Gordon Merle 1941- *AmMWSc 92*
**Thomson,** Grace Marie 1932- *WhoWest 92*
**Thomson,** Harry J, Jr 1928- *WhoAmP 91*
**Thomson,** Heather Anne 1940- *WhoEnt 92*
**Thomson,** Ian *Who 92*
**Thomson,** Ian Mackenzie 1926- *Who 92*
**Thomson,** Ivo Wilfrid Home d1991 *Who 92N*
**Thomson,** James 1700-1748 *BlkwCEP, LitC 16 [port], RfGEnL 91*
**Thomson,** James 1834-1882 *RfGEnL 91*
**Thomson,** James Adolph 1924- *WhoMW 92*
**Thomson,** James Alan 1945- *WhoWest 92*
**Thomson,** James Alex L 1928- *AmMWSc 92*
**Thomson,** James Claude, Jr 1931- *WhoAmP 91*
**Thomson,** James Leonard 1905- *Who 92*
**Thomson,** James McIlhany 1924- *WhoAmP 91*
**Thomson,** James Miln 1921- *WrDr 92*
**Thomson,** Jean Basehore 1947- *WhoMW 92*
**Thomson,** Jeffrey Richard 1942- *WhoEnt 92*
**Thomson,** Joanne 1953- *WhoRel 92*
**Thomson,** John *Who 92*
**Thomson,** John 1908- *IntWW 91, Who 92*
**Thomson,** John 1927- *Who 92*
**Thomson,** John Adam 1927- *IntWW 91*
**Thomson,** John Ansel Armstrong 1911- *AmMWSc 92*
**Thomson,** John C *WhoIns 92*
**Thomson,** John Ferguson 1920- *AmMWSc 92*
**Thomson,** John Oliver 1930- *AmMWSc 92*
**Thomson,** John Rankin 1935- *WhoWest 92*
**Thomson,** John Sutherland 1920- *Who 92*
**Thomson,** John Wanamaker 1928- *WhoFI 92*
**Thomson,** Jonathan H. *WrDr 92*
**Thomson,** Joseph John 1856-1940 *FacFETw, WhoNob 90*
**Thomson,** Joseph McGeachy 1948- *Who 92*
**Thomson,** June 1930- *WrDr 92*
**Thomson,** June Valerie 1930- *IntAu&W 91*
**Thomson,** Keith Stewart 1938- *AmMWSc 92*
**Thomson,** Kenneth Clair 1940- *AmMWSc 92*
**Thomson,** Kenneth James 1936- *WhoFI 92*
**Thomson,** Kenneth R. 1923- *WhoFI 92*
**Thomson,** Kerr Clive 1928- *AmMWSc 92*
**Thomson,** Leonard S 1911- *WhoAmP 91*
**Thomson,** Malcolm George 1950- *Who 92*
**Thomson,** Marjorie Morgan 1954- *WhoAmL 92*
**Thomson,** Mark 1939- *Who 92*
**Thomson,** Matthew Thomas 1962- *WhoMW 92*
**Thomson,** Mortimer Neal 1831-1875 *BenetAL 91, BibAL 8*
**Thomson,** Nigel Ernest Drummond 1926- *Who 92*
**Thomson,** Parvin Darabi 1941- *WhoWest 92*
**Thomson,** Patricia Ayame *WhoEnt 92*
**Thomson,** Paul C 1955- *WhoIns 92*
**Thomson,** Peter d1991 *Who 92N*
**Thomson,** Peter 1938- *WrDr 92*
**Thomson,** Peter Alexander Bremner 1938- *IntWW 91, Who 92*
**Thomson,** Peter William 1929- *IntWW 91*
**Thomson,** Quentin Robert 1918- *AmMWSc 92*
**Thomson,** Richard Edward 1944- *AmMWSc 92*
**Thomson,** Richard Harvey 1959- *WhoFI 92*
**Thomson,** Richard Murray 1933- *IntWW 91, WhoFI 92*
**Thomson,** Richard N 1924- *AmMWSc 92*
**Thomson,** Robb M 1925- *AmMWSc 92*
**Thomson,** Robert 1921- *WrDr 92*
**Thomson,** Robert Francis 1914- *AmMWSc 92*
**Thomson,** Robert Howard Garry *Who 92*
**Thomson,** Robert James 1927- *WhoFI 92*
**Thomson,** Robert John Stewart 1922- *Who 92*
**Thomson,** Robert Norman 1935- *Who 92*
**Thomson,** Robert William 1934- *Who 92*
**Thomson,** Roy Herbert 1894-1978 *FacFETw*
**Thomson,** Ryan J. 1949- *WhoEnt 92*
**Thomson,** Sharon *DrAPF 91*
**Thomson,** Shirley Lavinia 1930- *WhoMW 92*
**Thomson,** Stanley 1923- *AmMWSc 92*
**Thomson,** Thomas Alfred 1954- *WhoMW 92*
**Thomson,** Thomas Harold 1935- *IntWW 91, WhoFI 92*
**Thomson,** Thomas James 1923- *IntWW 91, Who 92*
**Thomson,** Thyra Godfrey 1916- *WhoWest 92*
**Thomson,** Tom Radford 1918- *AmMWSc 92*
**Thomson,** Virgil 1896-1989 *ConCom 92, NewAmDM, RComAH*
**Thomson,** Virgil Garnett 1896-1989 *FacFETw*
**Thomson,** William 1833-1907 *BiInAmS*
**Thomson,** William Cran 1926- *IntWW 91*
**Thomson,** William E, Jr *WhoAmP 91*
**Thomson,** William Edward, Jr. *WhoWest 92*
**Thomson,** William Hanna 1833-1918 *BiInAmS*
**Thomson,** William Joseph 1939- *AmMWSc 92*
**Thomson,** William Oliver 1925- *Who 92*
**Thomson,** William R. *IntWW 91*
**Thomson,** William Tyrrell 1909- *AmMWSc 92*
**Thomson,** William Walter 1930- *AmMWSc 92*
**Thomson Of Fleet,** Baron 1923- *IntWW 91, Who 92*
**Thomson Of Monifieth,** Baron 1921- *IntWW 91, Who 92*
**Thomure,** Anne Elizabeth 1958- *WhoMW 92*
**Thon,** J George 1908- *AmMWSc 92*
**Thon,** Melanie Rae 1957- *ConAu 134*
**Thon,** Richard McMichael 1955- *WhoFI 92*
**Thonar,** Eugene Jean-Marie 1945- *AmMWSc 92*
**Thondavadi,** Nandu N. 1954- *WhoFI 92*
**Thone,** Charles *WhoAmP 91*
**Thone,** Charles 1924- *IntWW 91*
**Thonemann,** Peter Clive 1917- *IntWW 91, Who 92*
**Thonet,** Michael 1796-1871 *DcTwDes*
**Thong,** Tran 1951- *WhoWest 92*
**Thonnard,** Norbert 1943- *AmMWSc 92*
**Thor,** Eyvind 1928- *AmMWSc 92*
**Thor,** Karl Bruce 1954- *AmMWSc 92*
**Thor,** Linda M. 1950- *WhoWest 92*
**Thor,** Richard Marquette 1931- *WhoWest 92*
**Thorak,** Josef 1889-1952 *EncTR 91 [port]*
**Thorbeck,** John Shepard 1952- *WhoFI 92*
**Thorbeck,** Thomas George 1945- *WhoAmL 92*
**Thorbecke,** Geertruida Jeanette 1929- *AmMWSc 92*
**Thorbjornsen,** Arthur Robert 1936- *AmMWSc 92*
**Thorburn,** Andrew 1934- *Who 92*
**Thorburn,** Carolyn Coles 1941- *WhoBlA 92*
**Thorburn,** James Alexander 1923- *IntAu&W 91*
**Thorburn,** Wayne J 1944- *WhoAmP 91*
**Thordarson,** William 1929- *WhoWest 92*
**Thore,** Theophile *ThHEIm*
**Thoreau,** Henry David 1817-1862 *BenetAL 91, BibAL 8, RComAH*
**Thorelli,** Hans B 1921- *IntAu&W 91, WrDr 92*
**Thorelli,** Hans Birger *WhoFI 92*
**Thorelli,** Irene Margareta 1950- *WhoMW 92*
**Thoren-Peden,** Deborah Suzanne 1958- *WhoAmL 92, WhoWest 92*
**Thorens,** Justin Pierre 1931- *IntWW 91*
**Thoresen,** Asa Clifford 1930- *AmMWSc 92*
**Thoreson,** Richard M 1935- *WhoIns 92*
**Thorgeirsson,** Snorri S 1941- *AmMWSc 92*
**Thorgrimson,** Neal James 1960- *WhoEnt 92*
**Thorhaug,** Anitra L 1940- *AmMWSc 92*
**Thorington,** Richard Wainwright, Jr 1937- *AmMWSc 92*
**Thorland,** Rodney Harold 1941- *AmMWSc 92*
**Thorley,** Charles Graham 1914- *Who 92*
**Thorley,** Simon Joe 1950- *Who 92*
**Thorman,** Charles Hadley 1936- *AmMWSc 92*
**Thorman,** Richard *DrAPF 91*
**Thormar,** Halldor 1929- *AmMWSc 92*
**Thorn,** Andrea Papp 1960- *WhoAmL 92*
**Thorn,** Brian Earl 1955- *WhoFI 92*
**Thorn,** Charles Behan, III 1946- *AmMWSc 92*
**Thorn,** Donald Childress 1929- *AmMWSc 92*
**Thorn,** Douglas Robert 1961- *WhoAmL 92*
**Thorn,** E. Gaston 1928- *Who 92*
**Thorn,** Fred Earl 1937- *WhoRel 92*
**Thorn,** Garvin Beaty 1956- *WhoAmP 91*
**Thorn,** Gaston 1928- *IntWW 91*
**Thorn,** George W 1906- *AmMWSc 92*
**Thorn,** George Widmer 1906- *IntWW 91*
**Thorn,** John Leonard 1925- *Who 92*
**Thorn,** John Samuel 1911- *Who 92*
**Thorn,** Michael 1956- *RelLAm 91*
**Thorn,** Niels Anker 1924- *IntWW 91*
**Thorn,** Richard Mark 1947- *AmMWSc 92*
**Thorn,** Robert Nicol 1924- *AmMWSc 92*
**Thorn,** Roger Eric 1948- *Who 92*
**Thorn,** William John 1943- *WhoMW 92*
**Thornber,** James Philip 1934- *AmMWSc 92*
**Thornberry,** Betty Jane 1946- *WhoAmP 91*
**Thornberry,** Halbert Houston 1902- *AmMWSc 92*
**Thornberry,** William Homer 1909- *WhoAmP 91*
**Thornborough,** John Randle 1939- *AmMWSc 92*
**Thornburg,** Donald Richard 1933- *AmMWSc 92*
**Thornburg,** John Elmer 1942- *AmMWSc 92*
**Thornburg,** Lacy H 1929- *WhoAmP 91*
**Thornburg,** Lacy Herman 1929- *WhoAmL 92*
**Thornburg,** Newton *DrAPF 91*
**Thornburgh,** Dale A 1931- *AmMWSc 92*
**Thornburgh,** Daniel Eston 1930- *WhoMW 92*
**Thornburgh,** Dick 1932- *IntWW 91, WhoAmL 92*
**Thornburgh,** Elaine Margaret 1952- *WhoEnt 92*
**Thornburgh,** George E 1923- *AmMWSc 92*
**Thornburgh,** Richard Edward 1952- *WhoFI 92*
**Thornburgh,** Richard L 1932- *WhoAmP 91*
**Thornburgh,** Richard Lewis 1932- *Who 92*
**Thornburgh,** Robert Phillip 1949- *WhoMW 92*
**Thornburn,** Thomas H 1916- *AmMWSc 92*
**Thornbury,** Charlotte R 1920- *WhoAmP 91*
**Thornbury,** John R 1929- *AmMWSc 92*
**Thornbury,** William Mitchell 1944- *WhoAmL 92, WhoWest 92*
**Thorndike,** Alan Moulton 1918- *AmMWSc 92*
**Thorndike,** Edward Harmon 1934- *AmMWSc 92*
**Thorndike,** Edward L 1874-1949 *DcAmImH*
**Thorndike,** Edward Moulton 1905- *AmMWSc 92*
**Thorndike,** John *DrAPF 91*
**Thorndike,** John 1942- *WrDr 92*
**Thorndike,** Joseph J. 1913- *WrDr 92*
**Thorndike,** Nicholas Sturgis 1962- *WhoRel 92*
**Thorndike,** William Downie, Jr. 1953- *WhoFI 92*
**Thorndyke,** Helen Louise *ConAu 134, SmATA 65, -67*
**Thorne,** Anthony *ScFEYrs*
**Thorne,** Benjamin 1922- *Who 92*
**Thorne,** Billy Joe 1937- *AmMWSc 92*
**Thorne,** Cecil Michael 1929- *WhoBlA 92*
**Thorne,** Charles Joseph 1915- *AmMWSc 92*
**Thorne,** Charles M 1921- *AmMWSc 92*
**Thorne,** Christopher 1934- *WrDr 92*
**Thorne,** Christopher Guy 1934- *Who 92*
**Thorne,** Curtis Blaine 1921- *AmMWSc 92*
**Thorne,** David 1933- *Who 92*
**Thorne,** Edward Courtney 1923- *Who 92*
**Thorne,** Edward David 1926- *WhoFI 92*
**Thorne,** Francis 1922- *NewAmDM*
**Thorne,** James Meyers 1937- *AmMWSc 92*
**Thorne,** Jerrold Lewis 1929- *WhoAmP 91*
**Thorne,** John Carl 1943- *AmMWSc 92*
**Thorne,** John Richard 1939- *WhoAmP 91*
**Thorne,** Joseph P. 1926- *WhoAmL 92*
**Thorne,** Kip Stephen 1940- *AmMWSc 92, IntWW 91, WhoWest 92*
**Thorne,** Marlowe Driggs 1918- *AmMWSc 92*
**Thorne,** Melvyn Charles 1932- *AmMWSc 92*
**Thorne,** Mike 1940- *WhoAmP 91*
**Thorne,** Neil Gordon 1932- *Who 92*
**Thorne,** Nicola *IntAu&W 91X, WrDr 92*
**Thorne,** Oakleigh Blakeman 1932- *WhoFI 92*
**Thorne,** Peter 1914- *Who 92*
**Thorne,** Richard Charles 1925- *WhoMW 92*
**Thorne,** Richard Eugene 1943- *AmMWSc 92*
**Thorne,** Richard Mansergh 1942- *AmMWSc 92*
**Thorne,** Robert Folger 1920- *AmMWSc 92*
**Thorne,** Robin Horton John 1917- *Who 92*
**Thorne,** Sabina *DrAPF 91*
**Thorne,** Stanley George 1918- *Who 92*
**Thorne,** Susan Jean 1951- *WhoAmP 91*
**Thorne,** Vail Tucker 1958- *WhoAmL 92*
**Thornell,** Richard Paul 1936- *WhoBlA 92*
**Thornely,** Gervase Michael Cobham 1918- *Who 92*
**Thorner,** David Albert 1948- *WhoAmL 92*
**Thorner,** Jeremy William 1946- *AmMWSc 92*
**Thorner,** Michael Oliver 1945- *AmMWSc 92*
**Thorner,** Reta M. 1924- *WhoEnt 92*
**Thorneycroft** *Who 92*
**Thorneycroft,** Baron 1909- *IntWW 91, Who 92*
**Thorneycroft,** William Hamo 1850-1925 *TwCPaSc*
**Thorngate,** John Hill 1935- *AmMWSc 92, WhoWest 92*
**Thornhill,** Adrine Virginia 1945- *WhoBlA 92*
**Thornhill,** Andrew Robert 1943- *Who 92*
**Thornhill,** Arthur Horace, Jr. 1924- *IntWW 91*
**Thornhill,** Claude 1909-1965 *NewAmDM*
**Thornhill,** Edmund Basil 1898- *Who 92*
**Thornhill,** Georgia L. 1925- *WhoBlA 92*
**Thornhill,** Herbert Louis *WhoBlA 92*
**Thornhill,** James Arthur 1951- *AmMWSc 92*
**Thornhill,** Philip G 1918- *AmMWSc 92*
**Thornhill,** Robert Gordon, Jr. 1948- *WhoAmL 92*
**Thornhill,** Todd M. 1961- *WhoAmL 92*
**Thornhill,** William Gregory, Sr. 1946- *WhoRel 92*
**Thorning-Petersen,** Rudolph 1927- *Who 92*
**Thorning-Petersen,** Rudolph Anton 1927- *IntWW 91*
**Thornley,** Jeffrey Mark 1955- *WhoRel 92*
**Thornlow,** Carolyn 1954- *WhoAmL 92*
**Thorns,** Odail, Jr. 1943- *WhoBlA 92*
**Thornsjo,** Douglas Fredric 1927- *WhoWest 92*

**Thornthwaite,** Jerry T 1948- *AmMWSc 92*
**Thornton,** Alfred 1863-1939 *TwCPaSc*
**Thornton,** Allan Charles 1949- *Who 92*
**Thornton,** Andre 1949- *WhoBlA 92*
**Thornton,** Anthony Christopher Lawrence 1947- *Who 92*
**Thornton,** Arnold William 1943- *AmMWSc 92*
**Thornton,** Arvie Gordon 1928- *WhoRel 92*
**Thornton,** Barry Stanley 1956- *WhoRel 92*
**Thornton,** Big Mama 1926-1984 *NewAmDM*
**Thornton,** Bruce H 1936- *WhoIns 92*
**Thornton,** C G 1925- *AmMWSc 92*
**Thornton,** Charles B 1913-1981 *FacFETw*
**Thornton,** Charles Perkins 1927- *AmMWSc 92*
**Thornton,** Charles V. 1942- *WhoAmL 92*
**Thornton,** Clifford E. 1936- *WhoBlA 92*
**Thornton,** Clinton L. 1907- *WhoBlA 92*
**Thornton,** Clive Edward Ian 1929- *IntWW 91, Who 92*
**Thornton,** Daniel Lee 1944- *WhoFI 92*
**Thornton,** Dean Dickson 1929- *WhoFI 92, WhoWest 92*
**Thornton,** Don Ray *DrAPF 91*
**Thornton,** Donald Carlton 1947- *AmMWSc 92*
**Thornton,** Donald Eugene 1933- *WhoEnt 92*
**Thornton,** Dozier W. 1928- *WhoBlA 92*
**Thornton,** Edmund Braxton 1930- *WhoAmP 91*
**Thornton,** Edward E 1925- *IntAu&W 91*
**Thornton,** Edward Ralph 1935- *AmMWSc 92*
**Thornton,** Elizabeth K 1940- *AmMWSc 92*
**Thornton,** Ernest 1905- *Who 92*
**Thornton,** George Daniel 1910- *AmMWSc 92*
**Thornton,** George Fred 1933- *AmMWSc 92*
**Thornton,** George Malcolm 1939- *Who 92*
**Thornton,** Hall *ConAu 36NR*
**Thornton,** Helen Ann Elizabeth *Who 92*
**Thornton,** Hubert Richard 1932- *AmMWSc 92*
**Thornton,** Ivan Tyrone 1961- *WhoBlA 92*
**Thornton,** J. Duke 1944- *WhoAmL 92*
**Thornton,** Jack Edward Clive 1915- *Who 92*
**Thornton,** Jackie C. 1960- *WhoBlA 92*
**Thornton,** James Scott 1941- *WhoWest 92*
**Thornton,** James William, III 1937- *WhoRel 92*
**Thornton,** Janice Elaine 1952- *AmMWSc 92*
**Thornton,** John C. 1940- *WhoBlA 92*
**Thornton,** John Henry 1930- *Who 92*
**Thornton,** John Irvin 1941- *AmMWSc 92, WhoWest 92*
**Thornton,** John Leonard 1913- *WrDr 92*
**Thornton,** John T. 1937- *WhoFI 92*
**Thornton,** John W., Sr. 1928- *WhoAmL 92, WhoFI 92*
**Thornton,** John William 1936- *AmMWSc 92*
**Thornton,** Joseph Scott 1936- *AmMWSc 92, WhoFI 92*
**Thornton,** Kent W 1944- *AmMWSc 92*
**Thornton,** Lawrence 1937- *WrDr 92*
**Thornton,** Leonard 1916- *Who 92*
**Thornton,** Linda Wierman 1942- *AmMWSc 92, WhoMW 92*
**Thornton,** M. Paul 1952- *WhoFI 92*
**Thornton,** Malcolm *Who 92*
**Thornton,** Mark Andrew 1968- *WhoEnt 92*
**Thornton,** Mark Christopher 1960- *WhoFI 92*
**Thornton,** Maurice 1930- *WhoBlA 92*
**Thornton,** Melvin Chandler 1935- *AmMWSc 92*
**Thornton,** Melvin LeRoy 1928- *AmMWSc 92*
**Thornton,** Michael 1941- *IntAu&W 91, WrDr 92*
**Thornton,** Neil Ross 1950- *Who 92*
**Thornton,** Osie M. 1939- *WhoBlA 92*
**Thornton,** Paul A 1925- *AmMWSc 92*
**Thornton,** Pearl B. 1932- *WhoBlA 92*
**Thornton,** Peter 1917- *Who 92*
**Thornton,** Peter Kai 1925- *Who 92*
**Thornton,** Ray 1928- *AlmAP 92 [port], WhoAmP 91*
**Thornton,** Richard D 1929- *AmMWSc 92*
**Thornton,** Richard Eustace 1922- *Who 92*
**Thornton,** Richard Samuel 1934- *WhoEnt 92*
**Thornton,** Robert A, Jr *WhoAmP 91*
**Thornton,** Robert James, Sr. 1943- *WhoFI 92*
**Thornton,** Robert John 1919- *Who 92*
**Thornton,** Robert Lee 1917- *WhoFI 92*
**Thornton,** Robert Melvin 1937- *AmMWSc 92*
**Thornton,** Robert Ribblesdale 1913- *Who 92*
**Thornton,** Robert Richard 1926- *WhoAmL 92*
**Thornton,** Roger Lea 1935- *AmMWSc 92*
**Thornton,** Roy Fred 1941- *AmMWSc 92*
**Thornton,** Sally *Who 92*
**Thornton,** Stafford E 1934- *AmMWSc 92*
**Thornton,** Stephen Thomas 1941- *AmMWSc 92*
**Thornton,** Sybil Anne 1950- *WhoRel 92*
**Thornton,** Theodore Kean 1949- *WhoFI 92*
**Thornton,** Thomas Jay 1951- *WhoRel 92*
**Thornton,** Valerie 1931- *TwCPaSc*
**Thornton,** Valerie Genestra Marion 1931- *IntWW 91*
**Thornton,** Wayne Hollis, Jr. 1925- *WhoWest 92*
**Thornton,** Wayne T. 1958- *WhoBlA 92*
**Thornton,** William Aloysius 1938- *AmMWSc 92*
**Thornton,** William Andrus, Jr 1923- *AmMWSc 92*
**Thornton,** William Dickson 1930- *Who 92*
**Thornton,** William Edgar 1929- *AmMWSc 92*
**Thornton,** William James, Jr. 1919- *WhoEnt 92*
**Thornton,** William Joseph 1930- *WhoAmP 91*
**Thornton,** Willie Mae 1926- *HanAmWH*
**Thorogood,** Alfreda 1942- *Who 92*
**Thorogood,** Bernard George 1927- *IntWW 91, Who 92*
**Thorogood,** Kenneth Alfred Charles 1924- *IntWW 91, Who 92*
**Thorold,** Anthony 1903- *Who 92*
**Thoroughgood,** Carolyn A 1943- *AmMWSc 92*
**Thorp,** Benjamin A 1938- *AmMWSc 92*
**Thorp,** Charles Philip 1949- *WhoRel 92, WhoWest 92*
**Thorp,** David Oliver 1932- *WhoAmP 91*
**Thorp,** Edward O 1932- *AmMWSc 92*
**Thorp,** Edward Oakley 1932- *WhoWest 92*
**Thorp,** Frank Kedzie 1936- *AmMWSc 92*
**Thorp,** Glen Alan 1944- *WhoRel 92*
**Thorp,** James Harrison, III 1948- *AmMWSc 92*
**Thorp,** James Shelby 1937- *AmMWSc 92*
**Thorp,** James Wilson 1942- *AmMWSc 92*
**Thorp,** Jeremy Walter 1941- *Who 92*
**Thorp,** John 1947- *ConAu 133*
**Thorp,** John Stanislaus, Jr. 1925- *WhoAmL 92*
**Thorp,** Mitchell Leon 1910- *WhoAmP 91*
**Thorp,** Robbin Walker 1933- *AmMWSc 92*
**Thorp,** Roderick 1936- *IntAu&W 91, WrDr 92*
**Thorp,** Willard Long 1899- *IntWW 91*
**Thorpe,** Adrian Charles 1942- *Who 92*
**Thorpe,** Alma Lane Kirkland 1941- *WhoEnt 92*
**Thorpe,** Anthony Geoffrey Younghusband 1941- *Who 92*
**Thorpe,** Bert Duane 1929- *AmMWSc 92*
**Thorpe,** Brian Russell 1929- *Who 92*
**Thorpe,** Colin 1947- *AmMWSc 92*
**Thorpe,** Elwood *WhoAmP 91*
**Thorpe,** Fred *ScFEYrs*
**Thorpe,** Gail Ann 1958- *WhoAmL 92*
**Thorpe,** Gary Stephen 1951- *WhoWest 92*
**Thorpe,** Herbert Clifton 1923- *WhoBlA 92*
**Thorpe,** Howard A 1914- *AmMWSc 92*
**Thorpe,** James 1915- *IntWW 91, WhoWest 92, WrDr 92*
**Thorpe,** James F 1926- *AmMWSc 92*
**Thorpe,** James Francis 1888-1953 *FacFETw [port]*
**Thorpe,** James Stewart 1959- *WhoEnt 92*
**Thorpe,** Jeremy 1929- *FacFETw, IntWW 91, Who 92*
**Thorpe,** Jerry *LesBEnT 92*
**Thorpe,** Jim 1888-1953 *RComAH*
**Thorpe,** John Alden 1936- *AmMWSc 92*
**Thorpe,** Josephine Horsley 1943- *WhoBlA 92*
**Thorpe,** Judith Kathleen 1951- *WhoWest 92*
**Thorpe,** Kay *WrDr 92*
**Thorpe,** Marjorie 1941- *IntWW 91*
**Thorpe,** Martha Campbell 1922- *AmMWSc 92*
**Thorpe,** Mathew Alexander 1938- *Who 92*
**Thorpe,** Michael Fielding 1944- *AmMWSc 92*
**Thorpe,** Neal Owen 1938- *AmMWSc 92*
**Thorpe,** Nigel James 1945- *Who 92*
**Thorpe,** Otis 1962- *WhoBlA 92*
**Thorpe,** Otis L. 1953- *WhoBlA 92*
**Thorpe,** Ralph Irving 1936- *AmMWSc 92*
**Thorpe,** Robert Samuel 1949- *WhoWest 92*
**Thorpe,** Rodney Warren 1935- *AmMWSc 92*
**Thorpe,** Ronald Laurence G. *Who 92*
**Thorpe,** Rose Hartwick 1850-1939 *BenetAL 91*
**Thorpe,** Stephen J. *DrAPF 91*
**Thorpe,** Sylvia 1926- *WrDr 92*
**Thorpe,** Thomas B. 1815-1878 *BenetAL 91*
**Thorpe,** Thomas Bangs 1815-1878 *BibAL 8*
**Thorpe,** Trebor *IntAu&W 91X, TwCSFW 91, WrDr 92*
**Thorpe,** Trevor Alleyne 1936- *AmMWSc 92*
**Thorpe,** Wesley Lee 1926- *WhoBlA 92*
**Thorpe-Bates,** Peggy 1914-1989 *ConTFT 9*
**Thorpe-Tracey,** Stephen Frederick 1929- *Who 92*
**Thorsell,** David Linden 1942- *AmMWSc 92*
**Thorsen,** Arthur C 1934- *AmMWSc 92*
**Thorsen,** Donald Arthur 1955- *WhoRel 92*
**Thorsen,** James Hugh 1943- *WhoWest 92*
**Thorsen,** Nancy Dain 1944- *WhoFI 92*
**Thorsen,** Richard Darrell 1928- *WhoFI 92*
**Thorsen,** Richard Stanley 1940- *AmMWSc 92*
**Thorsen,** Thomas O 1931- *WhoIns 92*
**Thorsen,** Thomas Oliver 1931- *WhoFI 92*
**Thorsett,** Eugene Deloy 1948- *AmMWSc 92*
**Thorsett,** Grant Orel 1940- *AmMWSc 92*
**Thorsness,** Leo K 1932- *WhoAmP 91*
**Thorson,** Alan Glen 1952- *WhoMW 92*
**Thorson,** Douglas Young 1933- *WhoMW 92*
**Thorson,** James A 1946- *AmMWSc 92*
**Thorson,** James Donald 1933- *WhoAmP 91*
**Thorson,** James Llewellyn 1934- *WhoWest 92*
**Thorson,** John Wells 1933- *AmMWSc 92*
**Thorson,** Linda 1947- *ConTFT 9*
**Thorson,** Ralph Edward 1923- *AmMWSc 92*
**Thorson,** Steven Greg 1948- *WhoAmL 92*
**Thorson,** Thomas Bertel 1917- *AmMWSc 92*
**Thorson,** Walter Rollier 1932- *AmMWSc 92*
**Thorsrud,** Solveig Ann 1962- *WhoWest 92*
**Thorsteinsson,** Petur 1917- *IntWW 91*
**Thorstenberg,** Laurence 1925- *WhoEnt 92*
**Thorstensen,** Thomas Clayton 1919- *AmMWSc 92*
**Thorstenson,** Verne E *WhoAmP 91*
**Thorup,** Alvin Robert 1952- *WhoAmL 92*
**Thorup,** James Tat 1930- *AmMWSc 92*
**Thorup,** Oscar Andreas, Jr 1922- *AmMWSc 92*
**Thorup,** Richard M 1930- *AmMWSc 92*
**Thorward,** Richard Frank 1950- *WhoEnt 92*
**Thottumkal,** Thomas Joseph 1934- *WhoRel 92*
**Thouless,** David James 1934- *AmMWSc 92, IntWW 91, Who 92*
**Thouret,** Wolfgang E 1914- *AmMWSc 92*
**Thouron,** John 1908- *Who 92*
**Thoyts,** Robert Francis Newman d1991 *Who 92N*
**Thrailkill,** Daniel B. 1957- *WhoAmL 92*
**Thrailkill,** Francis Marie 1937- *WhoRel 92*
**Thrailkill,** John 1930- *AmMWSc 92*
**Thrale,** Hester Lynch 1741-1821 *BlkwCEP*
**Thrall,** Grant Ian 1947- *WhoFI 92*
**Thrall,** Richard C., Jr. 1929- *WhoEnt 92*
**Thrall,** Robert McDowell 1914- *AmMWSc 92*
**Thrane,** Hans Erik 1918- *IntWW 91*
**Thrane,** Loanne R 1933- *WhoAmP 91*
**Thrane,** Peter Harold 1959- *WhoMW 92*
**Thrash,** Bill 1939- *WhoEnt 92*
**Thrasher,** George W 1931- *AmMWSc 92*
**Thrasher,** L W 1922- *AmMWSc 92*
**Thrasher,** Peter Adam 1923- *WrDr 92*
**Thrasher,** Terry Nicholas *AmMWSc 92*
**Thrasher,** William Edward 1950- *WhoBlA 92*
**Thrasher,** William Lee 1953- *WhoEnt 92*
**Thrasher,** William M d1900 *BiInAmS*
**Threadcraft,** Hal Law, III 1952- *WhoRel 92*
**Threadgill,** Cecil Raymond 1925- *WhoRel 92*
**Threadgill,** Ernest Dale 1942- *AmMWSc 92*
**Threadgill,** W D 1922- *AmMWSc 92*
**Threadgill,** Walter Leonard 1945- *WhoBlA 92*
**Threadgold,** Michael Andrew 1950- *WhoFI 92*
**Threatt,** Robert 1928- *WhoBlA 92*
**Threatt,** Sedale Eugene 1961- *WhoBlA 92*
**Three Dog Night** *NewAmDM*
**Three Stooges,** The *FacFETw*
**Three T's** *NewAmDM*
**Threefoot,** Sam Abraham 1921- *AmMWSc 92*
**Threet,** Richard Lowell 1924- *AmMWSc 92*
**Threlfall,** David 1953- *ConTFT 9, Who 92*
**Threlfall,** John Brooks 1920- *WhoAmP 91*
**Threlfall,** Richard Ian 1920- *Who 92*
**Threlfall,** Robert Gorden 1952- *WhoFI 92, WhoMW 92*
**Threlfall,** William 1939- *AmMWSc 92*
**Threlkeld,** Richard *LesBEnT 92*
**Threlkeld,** Richard D 1937- *WhoAmP 91*
**Threlkeld,** Stephen Francis H 1924- *AmMWSc 92*
**Threlkeld,** Steven Wayne 1956- *WhoFI 92, WhoWest 92*
**Threlkeld-Wesaw,** Sallie Easley 1934- *WhoWest 92*
**Thribb,** E. J. *WrDr 92*
**Thridandam,** Sreenivasan 1933- *WhoWest 92*
**Thrift,** Frederick Aaron 1940- *AmMWSc 92*
**Thring,** George Arthur 1903- *Who 92*
**Thring,** Meredith Wooldridge 1915- *Who 92*
**Thro,** Mary Patricia 1938- *AmMWSc 92*
**Throckmorton,** Anthony 1916- *Who 92*
**Throckmorton,** Clare McLaren *Who 92*
**Throckmorton,** Gaylord Scott 1946- *AmMWSc 92*
**Throckmorton,** Hamilton Coe 1955- *WhoRel 92*
**Throckmorton,** James Rodney 1936- *AmMWSc 92*
**Throckmorton,** John L 1913-1986 *FacFETw*
**Throckmorton,** Lynn Hiram 1927- *AmMWSc 92*
**Throckmorton,** Morford C 1919- *AmMWSc 92*
**Throckmorton,** Peter 1928-1990 *AnObit 1990*
**Throckmorton,** Peter E 1927- *AmMWSc 92*
**Throckmorton,** Peter Eugene 1927- *WhoMW 92*
**Throckmorton,** Rex Denton 1941- *WhoWest 92*
**Throckmorton,** Sonny 1940- *NewAmDM*
**Throdahl,** Monte C 1919- *AmMWSc 92*
**Throener,** Mary Ella 1949- *WhoRel 92*
**Thron,** Jonathan Louis 1954- *AmMWSc 92*
**Thron,** Wolfgang Joseph 1918- *AmMWSc 92*
**Thrond,** Dale Homer 1942- *WhoAmP 91*
**Throne,** James Edward 1954- *AmMWSc 92*
**Throne,** James Louis 1937- *AmMWSc 92*
**Throneberry,** Glyn Ogle 1927- *AmMWSc 92*
**Throner,** Guy Charles 1919- *AmMWSc 92*
**Thronson,** Harley Andrew, Jr 1948- *AmMWSc 92*
**Throop,** John Robert 1956- *WhoRel 92*
**Throop,** Lewis John 1929- *AmMWSc 92*
**Throop,** Tom H 1947- *WhoAmP 91*
**Thropay,** John Paul 1949- *WhoWest 92*
**Throw,** Francis Edward 1912- *AmMWSc 92*
**Thrower,** Charles S. 1920- *WhoBlA 92*
**Thrower,** Ellen E 1947- *WhoIns 92*
**Thrower,** Gregory Michael 1950- *WhoRel 92*
**Thrower,** Julius A. 1917- *WhoBlA 92*
**Thrower,** Julius B. 1938- *WhoBlA 92*
**Thrower,** Peter Albert 1938- *AmMWSc 92*
**Thrun,** Richard William 1941- *WhoMW 92*
**Thrupp,** Lauri David 1930- *AmMWSc 92*
**Thrush,** Brian Arthur 1928- *IntWW 91, Who 92*
**Thrussell,** Paul 1969- *WhoEnt 92*
**Thruston,** Alfred Dorrah, Jr 1934- *AmMWSc 92*
**Thuan,** Trinh Xuan 1948- *AmMWSc 92*
**Thubrikar,** Mano J 1947- *AmMWSc 92*
**Thubron,** Colin 1939- *ConNov 91*
**Thubron,** Colin Gerald Dryden 1939- *IntAu&W 91, IntWW 91, Who 92, WrDr 92*
**Thubron,** Harry 1915-1985 *TwCPaSc*
**Thueme,** William Harold 1945- *WhoMW 92*
**Thuente,** David Joseph 1945- *AmMWSc 92*
**Thuering,** George Lewis 1919- *AmMWSc 92*
**Thuesen,** Barbara Wilcox 1932- *WhoEnt 92*
**Thuesen,** Gerald Jorgen 1938- *AmMWSc 92*
**Thueson,** David Orel 1947- *AmMWSc 92, WhoWest 92*
**Thuille,** Ludwig 1861-1907 *NewAmDM*
**Thuillez,** Dale Marcel 1948- *WhoAmL 92*
**Thuillier,** Leslie de Malapert 1905- *Who 92*
**Thulin,** Adelaide Ann 1925- *WhoMW 92*
**Thulin,** Ingrid 1929- *ConTFT 9, IntMPA 92, IntWW 91, WhoEnt 92*
**Thulin,** Lars Uno 1939- *WhoFI 92*
**Thullbery,** Marion Francis 1954- *WhoRel 92*
**Thullen,** Manfred 1938- *WhoHisp 92*
**Thum,** Alan Bradley 1943- *AmMWSc 92*
**Thum,** Marcella *IntAu&W 91, WrDr 92*
**Thumann,** Albert 1942- *AmMWSc 92*

**Thumm**, Byron Ashley 1923- *AmMWSc 92*
**Thumma**, Samuel Anderson 1962- *WhoFI 92*
**Thums**, Charles William 1945- *WhoFI 92, WhoWest 92*
**Thun**, Rudolf Eduard 1921- *AmMWSc 92*
**Thuna**, Leonora 1929- *IntMPA 92*
**Thunborg**, Anders 1934- *IntWW 91*
**Thunder**, Spencer K 1939- *WhoWest 92*
**Thunder**, Suzanne Jeannette 1958- *WhoRel 92*
**Thunders**, Johnny d1991 *NewYTBS 91*
**Thunholm**, Lars-Erik 1914- *IntWW 91*
**Thuning-Roberson**, Claire Ann 1945- *AmMWSc 92*
**Thurau**, Klaus Walther Christian 1928- *IntWW 91*
**Thurber**, Cleveland, Jr. 1925- *WhoAmL 92, WhoFI 92*
**Thurber**, Clifford Hawes 1954- *AmMWSc 92*
**Thurber**, David Lawrence 1934- *AmMWSc 92*
**Thurber**, Eugene Carleton 1865?-1896 *BiInAmS*
**Thurber**, George 1821-1890 *BiInAmS*
**Thurber**, James 1894-1961 *BenetAL 91, FacFETw [port]*
**Thurber**, James Kent 1933- *AmMWSc 92*
**Thurber**, Robert Eugene 1932- *AmMWSc 92*
**Thurber**, Walter Arthur 1908- *AmMWSc 92*
**Thurber**, William Samuels 1922- *AmMWSc 92*
**Thurber**, Willis Robert 1938- *AmMWSc 92*
**Thurberg**, Frederick Peter 1942- *AmMWSc 92*
**Thurburn**, Gwynneth Loveday 1899- *Who 92*
**Thurburn**, Roy Gilbert d1990 *Who 92N*
**Thureson-Klein**, Asa Kristina 1934- *AmMWSc 92*
**Thurian**, Max 1921- *DcEcMov*
**Thurlbeck**, Kenneth Leigh 1947- *WhoEnt 92*
**Thurlbeck**, William Michael 1929- *AmMWSc 92*
**Thurley**, Allyn Robert 1948- *WhoEnt 92*
**Thurlimann**, Bruno 1923- *AmMWSc 92*
**Thurlow**, Baron 1912- *IntWW 91, Who 92*
**Thurlow**, Alfred Gilbert Goddard d1991 *Who 92N*
**Thurlow**, David 1932- *ConAu 134*
**Thurm**, Joel *WhoEnt 92*
**Thurm**, William Henry 1906- *WhoAmP 91*
**Thurmaier**, Mary Jean 1931- *WhoAmP 91*
**Thurmaier**, Roland Joseph 1928- *AmMWSc 92*
**Thurman**, Alfonzo 1946- *WhoBlA 92*
**Thurman**, Andrew Edward 1954- *WhoAmL 92*
**Thurman**, Frances Ashton 1919- *WhoBlA 92*
**Thurman**, Gary Boyd 1941- *AmMWSc 92*
**Thurman**, Henry L, Jr 1927- *AmMWSc 92*
**Thurman**, Howard 1900-1981 *RelLAm 91*
**Thurman**, Judith *DrAPF 91*
**Thurman**, Karen 1951- *WhoAmP 91*
**Thurman**, Lloy Duane 1933- *AmMWSc 92*
**Thurman**, Lori Denise 1957- *WhoMW 92*
**Thurman**, Lucinda 1849-1918 *NotBlAW 92*
**Thurman**, Marjorie Ellen *WhoBlA 92*
**Thurman**, Ralph Holloway 1949- *WhoFI 92*
**Thurman**, Randy 1954- *WhoAmP 91*
**Thurman**, Richard Gary 1940- *AmMWSc 92*
**Thurman**, Robert Ellis, II 1939- *AmMWSc 92*
**Thurman**, Ronald Glenn 1941- *AmMWSc 92*
**Thurman**, Sue 1903- *NotBlAW 92*
**Thurman**, Theodora 1932- *WhoEnt 92*
**Thurman**, Uma 1970- *IntMPA 92*
**Thurman**, Wallace 1902-1934 *BenetAL 91, BlkLC*
**Thurman**, Wayne Laverne 1923- *AmMWSc 92*
**Thurman**, William Gentry 1928- *AmMWSc 92*
**Thurman**, William Lee 1928- *WhoWest 92*
**Thurman-Swartzwelder**, Ernestine H 1920- *AmMWSc 92*
**Thurmon**, Jack Jewel 1944- *WhoFI 92*
**Thurmon**, John C 1930- *AmMWSc 92*
**Thurmon**, Theodore Francis 1937- *AmMWSc 92*
**Thurmond**, George Robert 1939- *WhoEnt 92*
**Thurmond**, James Strom 1902- *AmPolLe*
**Thurmond**, John Tydings 1941- *AmMWSc 92*
**Thurmond**, Michael L *WhoAmP 91*
**Thurmond**, Nate 1941- *WhoBlA 92*
**Thurmond**, Strom 1902- *AlmAP 92 [port], IntWW 91, WhoAmP 91*
**Thurmond**, William 1926- *AmMWSc 92*
**Thurn und Taxis**, Johannes, Prince von d1990 *IntWW 91N*
**Thurnauer**, Hans 1908- *AmMWSc 92*
**Thurnauer**, Marion Charlotte *AmMWSc 92*
**Thurner**, Joseph John 1920- *AmMWSc 92*
**Thurnham**, Peter Giles 1938- *Who 92*
**Thurow**, Gordon Ray 1929- *AmMWSc 92*
**Thurow**, Lester 1938- *WrDr 92*
**Thurow**, Raymond Carl 1920- *WhoMW 92*
**Thursby**, Gene Robert 1939- *WhoRel 92*
**Thursby**, Marie Currie 1947- *WhoFI 92, WhoMW 92*
**Thursby**, Mary Taylor 1911- *WhoAmP 91*
**Thurso**, Viscount 1922- *Who 92*
**Thurston**, A Donald 1925- *WhoAmP 91*
**Thurston**, Bill 1930- *WhoAmP 91*
**Thurston**, Bonnie Bowman 1952- *WhoRel 92*
**Thurston**, Carol M *IntAu&W 91*
**Thurston**, Charles Sparks 1934- *WhoBlA 92*
**Thurston**, David E. 1957- *WhoAmL 92*
**Thurston**, Earle Laurence 1943- *AmMWSc 92*
**Thurston**, Elwyn Odell 1922- *WhoRel 92*
**Thurston**, Fred Stone 1931- *WhoFI 92*
**Thurston**, Gaylen Aubrey 1929- *AmMWSc 92*
**Thurston**, George Butte 1924- *AmMWSc 92*
**Thurston**, Helen 1916- *ReelWom*
**Thurston**, Herbert David 1927- *AmMWSc 92*
**Thurston**, James N 1915- *AmMWSc 92*
**Thurston**, John Robert 1926- *AmMWSc 92*
**Thurston**, M O 1918- *AmMWSc 92*
**Thurston**, Marlin Oakes 1918- *WhoMW 92*
**Thurston**, Morris Ashcroft 1943- *WhoAmL 92*
**Thurston**, Paul E. 1938- *WhoBlA 92*
**Thurston**, Ralph Lloyd 1952- *WhoWest 92*
**Thurston**, Richard Elliott 1933- *WhoEnt 92*
**Thurston**, Rob Jenkins 1957- *WhoFI 92*
**Thurston**, Robert 1936- *TwCSFW 91, WrDr 92*
**Thurston**, Robert Henry 1839-1903 *BiInAmS*
**Thurston**, Robert Norton 1924- *AmMWSc 92*
**Thurston**, Robert Smith 1954- *WhoAmL 92*
**Thurston**, Rodney Sundbye 1933- *AmMWSc 92*
**Thurston**, Roger Grave 1912-1990 *WhoBlA 92N*
**Thurston**, Ross David, Sr. 1931- *WhoFI 92*
**Thurston**, Stephen John 1952- *WhoRel 92*
**Thurston**, Ted, Mrs. 1921- *WhoEnt 92*
**Thurston**, Thea *Who 92*
**Thurston**, Thomas Michael 1951- *WhoRel 92*
**Thurston**, William A. 1944- *WhoBlA 92*
**Thurston**, William P 1946- *AmMWSc 92*
**Thurston**, William R 1915- *AmMWSc 92*
**Thurston**, William Richardson 1920- *WhoWest 92*
**Thurstone**, Robert Leon 1927- *AmMWSc 92*
**Thurstone**, Thelma Gwinn 1897- *WomPsyc*
**Thurswell**, Gerald Elliott 1944- *WhoAmL 92, WhoMW 92*
**Thurtle**, Dorothy 1890?- *BiDBrF 2*
**Thusnelda** *EncAmaz 91*
**Thut**, Paul Douglas 1943- *AmMWSc 92*
**Thwaite**, Ann 1932- *WrDr 92*
**Thwaite**, Ann Barbara 1932- *Who 92*
**Thwaite**, Anthony 1930- *ConPo 91, WrDr 92*
**Thwaite**, Anthony Simon 1930- *IntAu&W 91, Who 92*
**Thwaites**, Bryan 1923- *Who 92*
**Thwaites**, Jacqueline Ann 1931- *Who 92*
**Thwaites**, Peter Trevenen d1991 *Who 92N*
**Thwaites**, Reuben Gold 1853-1913 *BenetAL 91*
**Thwaites**, Ronald 1946- *Who 92*
**Thwaites**, Roy 1931- *Who 92*
**Thwaites**, Thomas Turville 1931- *AmMWSc 92*
**Thwaites**, William Mueller 1933- *AmMWSc 92*
**Thweatt**, John G 1932- *AmMWSc 92*
**Thyagarajan**, B S 1929- *AmMWSc 92*
**Thyateira & Great Britain**, Archbishop of *Who 92*
**Thye**, Forrest Wallace *AmMWSc 92*
**Thyer**, Norman Harold 1929- *AmMWSc 92*
**Thygesen**, Jacob Christoffer 1901- *IntWW 91*
**Thygesen**, Kenneth Helmer 1937- *AmMWSc 92*
**Thygeson**, John R, Jr 1924- *AmMWSc 92*
**Thymele** *EncAmaz 91*
**Thyne**, Malcolm Tod 1942- *Who 92*
**Thynn**, Alexander *Who 92*
**Thynne** *Who 92*
**Thynne**, John Corelli James 1931- *Who 92*
**Thyr**, Billy Dale 1932- *AmMWSc 92*
**Thyra**, Queen of Denmark *EncAmaz 91*
**Thysen**, Benjamin 1932- *AmMWSc 92*
**Thyssen**, Fritz 1873-1951 *EncTR 91 [port]*
**Thyssen-Bornemisza De Kaszon**, Hans H. 1921- *IntWW 91, Who 92*
**Tiab**, Djebbar 1950- *AmMWSc 92*
**Tiacoh**, Gabriel 1963- *BlkOlyM*
**Tian Jiyun** 1929- *IntWW 91*
**Tian Zhaowu** 1927- *IntWW 91*
**Tiano**, J. Richard 1944- *WhoAmL 92*
**Tiao**, George Ching-Hwuan 1933- *AmMWSc 92*
**Tiarks**, Henry Frederic 1900- *Who 92*
**Tibbals**, Harry Fred, III 1943- *AmMWSc 92*
**Tibber**, Anthony Harris 1926- *Who 92*
**Tibber**, Robert *WrDr 92*
**Tibber**, Rosemary *WrDr 92*
**Tibbets**, Robin Frank 1924- *WhoWest 92*
**Tibbett**, Lawrence 1896-1960 *FacFETw, NewAmDM*
**Tibbetts**, Clark 1947- *AmMWSc 92*
**Tibbetts**, Dennis Oliver 1941- *WhoWest 92*
**Tibbetts**, Gary George 1939- *AmMWSc 92*
**Tibbetts**, Merrick Sawyer 1925- *AmMWSc 92*
**Tibbetts**, Orlando L. 1919- *WrDr 92*
**Tibbits**, David 1911- *Who 92*
**Tibbits**, Donald Fay 1943- *AmMWSc 92*
**Tibbitts**, Forrest Donald 1929- *AmMWSc 92*
**Tibbitts**, Pat A. 1933- *WhoFI 92*
**Tibbitts**, Samuel John 1924- *WhoFI 92*
**Tibbitts**, Theodore William 1929- *AmMWSc 92*
**Tibbitts**, Wesley Steven 1962- *WhoWest 92*
**Tibble**, Douglas Clair 1952- *WhoAmL 92*
**Tibble**, Geoffrey 1909-1952 *TwCPaSc*
**Tibbles**, John James 1924- *AmMWSc 92*
**Tibbs**, Ben *DrAPF 91*
**Tibbs**, Craigie John 1935- *Who 92*
**Tibbs**, Don Vaughn 1924- *WhoAmL 92*
**Tibbs**, Edward A. 1940- *WhoBlA 92*
**Tibbs**, John Francisco 1938- *AmMWSc 92*
**Tibbs**, Michael 1921- *Who 92*
**Tibbs**, Nicholas H 1945- *AmMWSc 92*
**Tibbs**, William M 1949- *WhoAmP 91*
**Tiberii**, Anthony James 1940- *WhoFI 92*
**Tiberius** 42BC-37AD *EncEarC*
**Tibesar**, Leo Joseph, Jr 1942- *WhoAmP 91*
**Tibo**, Gilles 1951- *SmATA 67 [port]*
**Tiburzi**, Bonnie 1948- *SmATA 65*
**Tice**, Clifford R 1927- *WhoAmP 91*
**Tice**, David Anthony 1929- *AmMWSc 92*
**Tice**, Laurie Dietrich 1959- *WhoAmL 92*
**Tice**, Linwood Franklin 1909- *AmMWSc 92*
**Tice**, Raymond Richard 1947- *AmMWSc 92*
**Tice**, Robert Galen 1956- *WhoWest 92*
**Tice**, Russell L 1932- *AmMWSc 92*
**Tice**, Terrence Nelson 1931- *WhoRel 92*
**Tice**, Thomas E 1924- *AmMWSc 92*
**Tice**, Thomas Robert *AmMWSc 92*
**Tice**, William Fleet, Jr. 1942- *WhoRel 92*
**Ticehurst**, Arthur Christopher 1933- *Who 92*
**Tichatschek**, Joseph Alois 1807-1886 *NewAmDM*
**Tichauer**, Erwin Rudolph 1918- *AmMWSc 92*
**Tichenor**, Isaac Taylor 1825-1902 *RelLAm 91*
**Tichenor**, Robert Lauren 1918- *AmMWSc 92*
**Tichik**, Evelyn Kay 1942- *WhoMW 92*
**Tichler**, Rosemarie 1939- *WhoEnt 92*
**Tichman**, Nadya Erica 1958- *WhoEnt 92*
**Ticho**, Harold Klein 1921- *AmMWSc 92*
**Tichy**, Robert J 1951- *AmMWSc 92*
**Tichy**, Susan *DrAPF 91*
**Tick**, Ed *DrAPF 91*
**Tick**, Michael Stanley 1955- *WhoEnt 92*
**Tickell**, Crispin 1930- *IntWW 91, Who 92*
**Tickell**, Marston Eustace 1923- *Who 92*
**Tickell**, Renee Oriana Haynes *ConAu 34NR*
**Tickell**, Thomas 1686-1740 *RfGEnL 91*
**Tickle**, Brian Percival 1921- *Who 92*
**Tickle**, Gerard William 1909- *Who 92*
**Tickle**, Phyllis A 1934- *IntAu&W 91*
**Tickle**, Phyllis Alexander *DrAPF 91*
**Tickle**, Robert Simpson 1930- *AmMWSc 92*
**Tickner**, Kenneth Philip 1949- *WhoAmL 92*
**Ticknor**, Francis Orray 1822-1874 *BenetAL 91*
**Ticknor**, George 1791-1871 *BenetAL 91*
**Ticknor**, Leland Bruce 1922- *AmMWSc 92*
**Ticknor**, Robert Lewis 1926- *AmMWSc 92*
**Ticknor**, William Davis 1810-1864 *BenetAL 91*
**Ticknor-Edwardes**, E *ScFEYrs*
**Ticktin**, Richard Mayer 1928- *WhoAmL 92, WhoEnt 92*
**Ticku**, Maharaj K 1948- *AmMWSc 92*
**Ticotin**, Rachel 1958- *IntMPA 92, WhoHisp 92*
**Tidball**, Charles Stanley 1928- *AmMWSc 92*
**Tidball**, M Elizabeth Peters 1929- *AmMWSc 92*
**Tidbury**, Charles 1926- *Who 92*
**Tidbury**, Charles Henderson 1926- *IntWW 91*
**Tidd**, Bill Warren 1947- *WhoMW 92*
**Tidd**, Marshall M 1827-1895 *BiInAmS*
**Tideman**, David R. 1958- *WhoAmL 92*
**Tidiane Traore**, Ahmed *WhoRel 92*
**Tidman**, Derek Albert 1930- *AmMWSc 92*
**Tidmore**, Eugene F 1940- *AmMWSc 92*
**Tidmore**, Max Tabb 1958- *WhoFI 92*
**Tidwell**, Billy Joe 1942- *WhoBlA 92*
**Tidwell**, Eugene Delbert 1926- *AmMWSc 92*
**Tidwell**, George Ernest 1931- *WhoAmL 92*
**Tidwell**, Harold Rodney 1957- *WhoRel 92*
**Tidwell**, Isaiah 1945- *WhoBlA 92*
**Tidwell**, John Edgar 1945- *WhoBlA 92*
**Tidwell**, Joseph Paul, Jr. 1943- *WhoWest 92*
**Tidwell**, Lloyd David 1939- *WhoRel 92*
**Tidwell**, Moody R. 1939- *WhoAmL 92*
**Tidwell**, Thomas Tinsley 1939- *AmMWSc 92*
**Tidwell**, William C., III 1946- *WhoAmL 92*
**Tidwell**, William Lee 1926- *AmMWSc 92*
**Tidy**, Morley David 1933- *Who 92*
**Tidy**, William Edward 1933- *Who 92*
**Tie Ning** 1957- *IntWW 91*
**Tie Ying** 1916- *IntWW 91*
**Tieckelmann**, Howard 1916- *AmMWSc 92*
**Tiedcke**, Carl Heinrich Wilhelm 1903- *AmMWSc 92*
**Tiede**, David L. 1940- *WhoRel 92*
**Tiede**, Roy John 1933- *WhoMW 92*
**Tiede**, Tom 1937- *IntAu&W 91*
**Tiedeman**, John Denby 1937- *WhoWest 92*
**Tiedemann**, Albert William, Jr 1924- *AmMWSc 92*
**Tiedemann**, Dale Merrit 1944- *WhoWest 92*
**Tiedemann**, Herman Henry 1917- *AmMWSc 92*
**Tiedemann**, William Harold 1943- *AmMWSc 92, WhoMW 92*
**Tieden**, Dale L 1922- *WhoAmP 91*
**Tiederman**, William Gregg, Jr 1938- *AmMWSc 92*
**Tiedje**, J Thomas 1951- *AmMWSc 92*
**Tiedje**, James Michael 1942- *AmMWSc 92*
**Tiedtke**, John Meyer 1907- *WhoEnt 92*
**Tiefel**, Ralph Maurice 1928- *AmMWSc 92*
**Tiefel**, William Reginald 1934- *WhoFI 92*
**Tiefenthal**, Harlan E 1922- *AmMWSc 92, WhoMW 92*
**Tiefenthal**, Marguerite Aurand 1919- *WhoMW 92*
**Tiegs**, Cheryl *WhoEnt 92*
**Tieh**, Thomas Ta-Pin 1934- *AmMWSc 92*
**Tiekotter**, Kenneth Louis 1955- *WhoWest 92*
**Tielebein**, John Theodore 1927- *WhoMW 92*
**Tieleman**, Henry William 1933- *AmMWSc 92*
**Tieman**, Michael LaVerne 1950- *WhoWest 92*
**Tieman**, Suzannah Bliss 1943- *AmMWSc 92*
**Tiemann**, Jerome J 1932- *AmMWSc 92*
**Tiemann**, Norbert Theodore 1924- *IntWW 91*
**Tiemeyer**, Christian *WhoMW 92*
**Tiemeyer**, Hope Elizabeth Johnson 1908- *WhoMW 92*
**Tiemstra**, John Peter 1950- *WhoFI 92, WhoMW 92, WhoRel 92*
**Tiemstra**, Peter J 1923- *AmMWSc 92*
**Tien**, Albert Futsu 1947- *WhoFI 92*
**Tien**, C L 1935- *AmMWSc 92*
**Tien**, Chang-Lin *NewYTBS 91 [port]*
**Tien**, Chang Lin 1935- *WhoWest 92*
**Tien**, Chi 1930- *AmMWSc 92*
**Tien**, H Ti 1928- *AmMWSc 92*
**T'ien**, James Shaw-Tzuu 1942- *AmMWSc 92*
**Tien**, John Kai 1940- *AmMWSc 92*
**Tien**, P K 1919- *AmMWSc 92*
**Tien**, Ping-King 1919- *IntWW 91*
**Tien**, Rex Yuan 1935- *AmMWSc 92*
**Tien**, Tseng-Ying 1924- *AmMWSc 92*
**Tienda**, Marta 1950- *WhoHisp 92*
**Tienken**, Arthur T 1922- *WhoAmP 91*
**Tiepolo**, Giovanni Battista 1692-1769 *BlkwCEP*
**Tier**, Charles 1947- *AmMWSc 92*
**Tierce**, John Forrest 1942- *AmMWSc 92*

**Tierman,** Louis C 1922- *WhoAmP 91*
**Tiernan,** Linda Kay 1947- *WhoRel 92*
**Tiernan,** Mary Spear 1836-1891 *BenetAL 91*
**Tiernan,** Natalie Foote 1932- *WhoMW 92*
**Tiernan,** Robert Joseph 1935- *AmMWSc 92*
**Tiernan,** Robert Owens *WhoAmP 91*
**Tiernan,** S. Gregory 1936- *WhoWest 92*
**Tiernan,** Thomas Orville 1936- *AmMWSc 92*
**Tierney,** Catherine Marie 1947- *WhoMW 92*
**Tierney,** Donald Frank 1931- *AmMWSc 92*
**Tierney,** Francis Alphonsus 1910- *Who 92*
**Tierney,** Gene 1920- *IntMPA 92*
**Tierney,** Gene 1920-1991 *NewYTBS 91 [port]*
**Tierney,** Gordon Paul 1922- *WhoMW 92*
**Tierney,** James E 1947- *WhoAmP 91*
**Tierney,** James Edward 1947- *WhoAmL 92*
**Tierney,** John Patrick 1931- *WhoFI 92*
**Tierney,** John W 1923- *AmMWSc 92*
**Tierney,** Kevin 1942- *WrDr 92*
**Tierney,** Kevin Joseph 1951- *WhoAmL 92*
**Tierney,** Lawrence 1919- *IntMPA 92*
**Tierney,** Margaret Marie 1938- *WhoAmP 91*
**Tierney,** Patricia A. *WhoRel 92*
**Tierney,** Paul E., Jr. 1943- *IntWW 91*
**Tierney,** Sydney 1923- *Who 92*
**Tierney,** Theodore James 1940- *WhoAmL 92*
**Tierney,** Thomas J. 1954- *WhoWest 92*
**Tierney,** Thomas John 1942- *WhoEnt 92*
**Tierney,** William John 1944- *AmMWSc 92*
**Tierno,** Edward Gregory 1948- *WhoMW 92*
**Tierno,** Philip M, Jr 1943- *AmMWSc 92*
**Tierno,** Robert Francis 1949- *WhoMW 92*
**Tiers,** George Van Dyke 1927- *AmMWSc 92*
**Tiersten,** Harry Frank 1930- *AmMWSc 92*
**Tiersten,** Irene *DrAPF 91*
**Tiersten,** Martin Stuart 1931- *AmMWSc 92*
**Tiessen,** John Gerard 1956- *WhoMW 92*
**Tieszen,** Larry L 1940- *AmMWSc 92*
**Tiethof,** Jack Alan 1943- *AmMWSc 92*
**Tietjen,** James Joseph 1933- *AmMWSc 92*
**Tietjen,** John H 1940- *AmMWSc 92*
**Tietjen,** William Leighton 1937- *AmMWSc 92*
**Tietjens,** Eunice 1884-1944 *BenetAL 91*
**Tietmeyer,** Hans 1931- *IntWW 91*
**Tietz,** Christopher Martin 1952- *WhoAmL 92*
**Tietz,** Norbert W 1926- *AmMWSc 92*
**Tietz,** Thomas E 1920- *AmMWSc 92*
**Tietz,** William John, Jr 1927- *AmMWSc 92, WhoWest 92*
**Tietze,** Frank 1924- *AmMWSc 92*
**Tieuel,** Robert C. D. 1914- *WhoBlA 92*
**Tiffany,** Charles F 1929- *AmMWSc 92*
**Tiffany,** Charles Louis 1812-1902 *DcTwDes*
**Tiffany,** John Jewett, II 1932- *WhoAmP 91*
**Tiffany,** Joseph Raymond, II 1949- *WhoAmL 92*
**Tiffany,** Lois Hattery 1924- *AmMWSc 92*
**Tiffany,** Louis Comfort 1848-1933 *DcTwDes*
**Tiffany,** Louis McLane 1844-1916 *BiInAmS*
**Tiffany,** Marian Catherine 1919- *WhoWest 92*
**Tiffany,** Otho Lyle 1919- *AmMWSc 92*
**Tiffany,** William James, III 1944- *AmMWSc 92*
**Tiffen,** Norman Herbert 1930- *WhoMW 92*
**Tiffin,** Pamela 1942- *IntMPA 92*
**Tiffney,** Bruce Haynes 1949- *AmMWSc 92*
**Tifft,** Ellen *DrAPF 91*
**Tifft,** Susan E. 1951- *ConAu 135*
**Tifft,** William Grant 1932- *AmMWSc 92*
**Tigani,** Bruce William 1956- *WhoAmL 92*
**Tigar,** Chad *IntAu&W 91X*
**Tigar,** Michael Edward 1941- *WhoAmL 92*
**Tigay,** Alan Merrill 1947- *WhoRel 92*
**Tigchelaar,** Edward Clarence 1939- *AmMWSc 92*
**Tigchelaar,** Peter Vernon 1941- *AmMWSc 92*
**Tiger,** Donald Henry 1959- *WhoFI 92*
**Tiger,** Lionel 1937- *AmMWSc 92, WrDr 92*
**Tiger,** Madeline J. *DrAPF 91*
**Tigerman,** Stanley 1930- *ConAu 36NR, IntWW 91, WhoMW 92, WrDr 92*
**Tigertt,** William David 1915- *AmMWSc 92*
**Tigges,** James Gene 1962- *WhoWest 92*
**Tigges,** Johannes 1931- *AmMWSc 92*
**Tigges,** John Thomas 1932- *WhoMW 92*
**Tighe,** Barbara Jeanne 1961- *WhoFI 92*
**Tighe Moore,** Barbara Jeanne 1961- *WhoMW 92*
**Tight,** William George 1865-1910 *BiInAmS*
**Tignanelli,** A Andrew 1925- *WhoIns 92*
**Tigner,** James Robert 1936- *AmMWSc 92*
**Tigner,** Maury 1937- *AmMWSc 92*
**Tignor,** Beatrice P *WhoAmP 91*
**Tignor,** Robert L. 1933- *ConAu 134*
**Tigue,** Randall Davis Bryant 1948- *WhoMW 92*
**Tigue,** Thomas M 1945- *WhoAmP 91*
**Tigyi,** Jozsef 1926- *IntWW 91*
**Tihansky,** Diane Rice 1948- *AmMWSc 92*
**Tihen,** Joseph Anton 1918- *AmMWSc 92*
**Tihon,** Claude 1944- *AmMWSc 92*
**Tijdeman,** Robert 1943- *IntWW 91*
**Tijerina,** Amador Guerra 1949- *WhoHisp 92*
**Tijerina,** Antonio A., Jr. 1950- *WhoHisp 92*
**Tijerina,** Kathryn Harris 1950- *WhoFI 92*
**Tijerina,** Pete *WhoHisp 92*
**Tijerina,** Rosaura Palacios 1957- *WhoHisp 92*
**Tikaram,** Moti 1925- *Who 92*
**Tikhomirov,** N. I. 1860-1930 *FacFETw*
**Tikhomirov,** Vasiliy Dmitrievich 1876-1956 *SovUnBD*
**Tikhomirov,** Vasily 1876-1956 *FacFETw*
**Tikhon,** Archbishop 1865-1925 *RelLAm 91*
**Tikhon,** Patriarch 1865-1925 *SovUnBD*
**Tikhonov,** Andrey Nikolayevich 1906- *IntWW 91*
**Tikhonov,** Nicholas Semyonovich 1896-1979 *FacFETw*
**Tikhonov,** Nikolay Aleksandrovich 1905- *SovUnBD*
**Tikhonov,** Nikolay Semenovich 1896-1979 *SovUnBD*
**Tikhonov,** Vladimir Aleksandrovich 1927- *IntWW 91*
**Tikhonravov,** Mikhail K 1900-1974 *FacFETw*
**Tikhvinsky,** Sergej Leonidovich 1918- *IntWW 91*
**Tikoo,** Mohan L 1943- *AmMWSc 92*
**Tikoo,** Mohan Lal 1943- *WhoMW 92*
**Tikson,** Michael 1924- *AmMWSc 92*
**Tiktin,** Carl *DrAPF 91*
**Tiku,** Moti *AmMWSc 92*
**Tilberis,** Elizabeth Jane 1947- *Who 92*
**Tilbury,** Roy Sidney 1932- *AmMWSc 92*
**Tilden,** Bill 1893-1953 *FacFETw, RComAH*
**Tilden,** James Clark 1955- *WhoAmL 92*
**Tilden,** James Martin 1950- *WhoFI 92*
**Tilden,** Samuel J. 1814-1886 *BenetAL 91*
**Tilden,** Samuel Jones 1814-1886 *AmPolLe*
**Tildon,** Charles G., Jr. 1926- *WhoBlA 92*
**Tildon,** J Tyson 1931- *AmMWSc 92*
**Tilenius,** Eric W. 1968- *WhoWest 92*
**Tilewick,** Robert 1956- *WhoAmL 92*
**Tiley,** Arthur 1910- *Who 92*
**Tiley,** John 1941- *Who 92*
**Tilford,** Joseph P. 1949- *WhoEnt 92*
**Tilford,** Shelby G 1937- *AmMWSc 92*
**Tilghman,** Alma G 1923- *WhoAmP 91*
**Tilghman,** Benjamin R. 1927- *ConAu 134*
**Tilghman,** Christopher 1948?- *ConLC 65 [port]*
**Tilghman,** Cyprian O. 1913- *WhoBlA 92*
**Tilghman,** Richard A 1920- *WhoAmP 91*
**Tilghman,** Richard Albert 1824-1899 *BiInAmS*
**Tilghman,** Richard Granville 1940- *WhoFI 92*
**Tilghman,** Shirley Marie *AmMWSc 92*
**Tilis,** Jerome S. *WhoMW 92*
**Tilkin,** Peter Michael 1947- *WhoAmL 92*
**Till,** Barry Dorn 1923- *Who 92, WrDr 92*
**Till,** Beatriz Maria 1952- *WhoHisp 92*
**Till,** Charles Edgar 1934- *AmMWSc 92*
**Till,** James Edgar 1931- *AmMWSc 92*
**Till,** Michael John 1934- *AmMWSc 92*
**Till,** Michael Stanley 1935- *Who 92*
**Tillard,** Jean Marie Roger 1927- *WhoRel 92*
**Tillard,** Philip Blencowe 1923- *Who 92*
**Tillay,** Eldrid Wayne 1925- *AmMWSc 92*
**Tillemont,** Louis Sebastien Le Nain De 1637-1698 *EncEarC*
**Tiller,** Calvin Omah 1925- *AmMWSc 92*
**Tiller,** Carl W. d1991 *NewYTBS 91*
**Tiller,** Carl William 1915- *WhoRel 92*
**Tiller,** F M 1917- *AmMWSc 92*
**Tiller,** John 1938- *Who 92*
**Tiller,** Ralph Earl 1925- *AmMWSc 92*
**Tiller,** Robert Wells 1941- *WhoRel 92*
**Tiller,** William Arthur 1929- *AmMWSc 92*
**Tillery,** Bill W 1938- *AmMWSc 92, WhoWest 92*
**Tillery,** Dwight 1948- *WhoMW 92*
**Tillery,** Marvin Ishmael 1936- *AmMWSc 92*
**Tillery,** R. David 1957- *WhoEnt 92*
**Tilles,** Abe 1907- *AmMWSc 92*
**Tilles,** Alan Steven 1957- *WhoAmL 92, WhoEnt 92*
**Tilles,** Gerald Emerson 1942- *WhoBlA 92*
**Tilles,** Harry 1923- *AmMWSc 92*
**Tillett,** George Edward 1923- *WhoBlA 92*
**Tillett,** Kenneth Erroll 1940- *IntWW 91*
**Tilley,** Barbara Claire 1942- *AmMWSc 92*
**Tilley,** Brian Ahern 1947- *WhoFI 92*
**Tilley,** Brian John 1936- *AmMWSc 92*
**Tilley,** David Ronald 1930- *AmMWSc 92*
**Tilley,** Donald E 1925- *AmMWSc 92*
**Tilley,** Doris Ruth Belk 1924- *WhoRel 92*
**Tilley,** Frank N. 1933- *WhoBlA 92*
**Tilley,** James Michael 1945- *WhoMW 92*
**Tilley,** Jefferson Wright 1946- *AmMWSc 92*
**Tilley,** John Leonard 1928- *AmMWSc 92*
**Tilley,** John Vincent 1941- *Who 92*
**Tilley,** Marcus Randall 1960- *WhoRel 92*
**Tilley,** Norwood Carlton, Jr. *WhoAmL 92*
**Tilley,** Patrick 1928- *TwCSFW 91, WrDr 92*
**Tilley,** Rice Matthews, Jr. 1936- *WhoAmL 92*
**Tilley,** Shermaine Ann 1952- *AmMWSc 92*
**Tilley,** Stanley David 1952- *WhoAmL 92*
**Tilley,** Stephen George 1943- *AmMWSc 92*
**Tilley,** T Don 1954- *AmMWSc 92*
**Tilley,** Terrence William 1947- *WhoRel 92*
**Tillich,** Paul 1886-1965 *BenetAL 91, FacFETw*
**Tillich,** Paul Johannes Oskar 1886-1965 *RelLAm 91*
**Tilling,** George Henry Garfield 1924- *Who 92*
**Tilling,** Robert Ingersoll 1935- *AmMWSc 92*
**Tillinghast,** Charles C., Jr. 1911- *IntWW 91*
**Tillinghast,** Charles Carpenter, Jr. 1911- *Who 92*
**Tillinghast,** David *DrAPF 91*
**Tillinghast,** John Avery 1927- *AmMWSc 92*
**Tillinghast,** Richard *DrAPF 91*
**Tillinghast,** Richard 1940- *ConPo 91, WrDr 92*
**Tillinghast,** Richard Williford 1940- *WhoMW 92*
**Tillion,** Clem Vincent 1925- *WhoAmP 91*
**Tillis,** Frederick C. 1930- *WhoBlA 92*
**Tillis,** Mel 1932- *ConMus 7 [port]*
**Tillis,** Melvin 1932- *WhoEnt 92*
**Tillitson,** Edward Walter 1903- *AmMWSc 92*
**Tillman,** Allen Douglas 1916- *AmMWSc 92*
**Tillman,** Benjamin Ryan 1847-1918 *AmPolLe*
**Tillman,** Caroline Elizabeth 1927- *WhoMW 92*
**Tillman,** Christine L. 1952- *WhoBlA 92*
**Tillman,** Dorothy 1948- *WhoAmP 91*
**Tillman,** Floyd 1914- *NewAmDM*
**Tillman,** Frank A 1937- *AmMWSc 92*
**Tillman,** Gerald Joseph 1948- *WhoMW 92*
**Tillman,** Henry Barrett 1948- *WhoWest 92*
**Tillman,** Henry Duran 1960- *BlkOlyM*
**Tillman,** J D, Jr 1921- *AmMWSc 92*
**Tillman,** Jacqueline 1944- *WhoHisp 92*
**Tillman,** Joseph Nathaniel 1926- *WhoBlA 92*
**Tillman,** June Torrison 1917- *WhoEnt 92*
**Tillman,** Larry Jaubert 1948- *AmMWSc 92*
**Tillman,** Lauralee A 1951- *WhoIns 92*
**Tillman,** Lauralee Agnes 1951- *WhoFI 92*
**Tillman,** Lawyer James, Jr. 1966- *WhoBlA 92*
**Tillman,** Lillian G. 1934- *WhoBlA 92*
**Tillman,** Mary A. T. 1935- *WhoBlA 92*
**Tillman,** Massie Monroe 1937- *WhoAmL 92*
**Tillman,** Mayre Lutha 1928- *WhoAmP 91*
**Tillman,** Michael Francis 1943- *AmMWSc 92*
**Tillman,** Myron Edgar 1932- *WhoAmP 91*
**Tillman,** Paula Sellars 1949- *WhoBlA 92*
**Tillman,** Richard Milton 1928- *AmMWSc 92*
**Tillman,** Robert Erwin 1937- *AmMWSc 92*
**Tillman,** Roderick W 1934- *AmMWSc 92*
**Tillman,** Samuel Dyer 1815-1875 *BiInAmS*
**Tillman,** Stephen Joel 1943- *AmMWSc 92*
**Tillman,** Talmadge Calvin 1925- *WhoFI 92*
**Tillman,** Talmadge Calvin, Jr. 1925- *WhoBlA 92*
**Tillman,** Wheeler Mellette 1941- *WhoAmP 91*
**Tillot,** Charles 1825- *ThHEIm*
**Tillotson,** Henry Michael 1928- *Who 92*
**Tillotson,** James E 1929- *AmMWSc 92*
**Tillotson,** James Glen 1923- *AmMWSc 92*
**Tillotson,** James Richard 1933- *AmMWSc 92*
**Tillotson,** Kathleen Mary 1906- *Who 92*
**Tillotson,** Laura Virginia *WhoEnt 92*
**Tillson,** Henry Charles 1923- *AmMWSc 92*
**Tillstrom,** Burr 1917-1985 *FacFETw*
**Tilly,** Anne Petersen 1915- *WhoAmP 91*
**Tilly,** Earl F 1934- *WhoAmP 91*
**Tilly,** Lois Amelia *WhoRel 92*
**Tilly,** Meg 1960- *IntMPA 92*
**Tilly,** Nancy McFadden *DrAPF 91*
**Tillyard,** Aelfrida 1883- *ScFEYrs*
**Tillyer,** William 1938- *TwCPaSc*
**Tilman,** David Frank 1944- *WhoRel 92*
**Tilman,** Ellen Rosenberg 1949- *WhoRel 92*
**Tilman,** Fred *WhoAmP 91*
**Tilman,** G David 1949- *AmMWSc 92*
**Tilmon,** James A. 1934- *WhoBlA 92*
**Tilmouth,** Sheila 1949- *TwCPaSc*
**Tilney,** Charles Edward 1909- *Who 92*
**Tilney,** Guinevere 1916- *Who 92*
**Tilney,** John 1907- *Who 92*
**Tilney,** Lewis Gawtry *AmMWSc 92*
**Tilney,** Nicholas Lechmere *AmMWSc 92*
**Tilney,** William *WhoAmP 91*
**Tilson,** Bret Ransom 1937- *AmMWSc 92*
**Tilson,** Hugh Arval 1946- *AmMWSc 92*
**Tilson,** Joe 1928- *TwCPaSc*
**Tilson,** Joseph 1928- *IntWW 91*
**Tilson,** Joseph Charles 1928- *Who 92*
**Tilson,** Kyle Gene 1931- *WhoMW 92*
**Tilson,** Philip Alan 1930- *WhoFI 92*
**Tilson,** Robert Ray 1932- *WhoFI 92*
**Tilson Thomas,** Michael 1944- *IntWW 91, Who 92*
**Tilston,** Frederick Albert 1906- *Who 92*
**Tilsworth,** Timothy 1939- *AmMWSc 92, WhoWest 92*
**Tilt and Bogue** *DcLB 106*
**Tilt,** Charles d1861 *DcLB 106*
**Tilton,** David Lloyd 1926- *WhoFI 92*
**Tilton,** Elmira F 1950- *WhoAmP 91*
**Tilton,** George Robert 1923- *AmMWSc 92*
**Tilton,** James Floyd 1937- *WhoEnt 92*
**Tilton,** John Elvin 1939- *WhoFI 92*
**Tilton,** Madonna Elaine 1929- *ConAu 36NR*
**Tilton,** Pamela Anne 1964- *WhoMW 92*
**Tilton,** Rafael *ConAu 36NR*
**Tilton,** Robert Eugene 1930- *WhoAmP 91*
**Tilton,** Roger 1924- *WhoEnt 92*
**Tilton,** Ronald William 1944- *WhoWest 92*
**Tilton,** Theodore 1835-1907 *BenetAL 91*
**Tilton,** Varien Russell 1943- *AmMWSc 92*
**Tilton,** Webster, Jr. 1922- *WhoFI 92*
**Tilus,** Kenneth Wayne 1957- *WhoMW 92*
**Timakata,** Fred 1936- *IntWW 91*
**Timasheff,** Serge Nicholas 1926- *AmMWSc 92*
**Timberg,** Sigmund 1911- *WhoAmL 92*
**Timberlake,** Charles E. *WhoBlA 92*
**Timberlake,** Constance Hector *WhoBlA 92*
**Timberlake,** Herman Leslie Patterson 1914- *Who 92*
**Timberlake,** Jack W 1940- *AmMWSc 92*
**Timberlake,** John Paul 1950- *WhoBlA 92*
**Timberlake,** Joseph William 1940- *AmMWSc 92*
**Timberlake,** Richard Henry, Jr. 1922- *WrDr 92*
**Timberlake,** William Edward 1948- *AmMWSc 92*
**Timbers,** Gordon Ernest 1940- *AmMWSc 92*
**Timbers,** Stephen Bryan 1944- *WhoFI 92*
**Timbers,** William Homer 1915- *WhoAmL 92*
**Timbie,** Peter T 1957- *AmMWSc 92*
**Timblin,** Lloyd O, Jr 1927- *AmMWSc 92, WhoWest 92*
**Timbrell,** Charles 1942- *WhoEnt 92*
**Timbury,** Morag Crichton 1930- *Who 92*
**Timell,** Tore Erik 1921- *AmMWSc 92*
**Timerding,** Eric Francis 1960- *WhoRel 92*
**Times,** Betty J. 1939- *WhoBlA 92*
**Times,** Betty Jean 1939- *WhoAmP 91*
**Times,** Misbrew Louise 1950- *WhoAmP 91*
**Timian,** Roland Gustav 1920- *AmMWSc 92*
**Timiras,** Paola Silvestri 1923- *AmMWSc 92*
**Timko,** John Patrick 1963- *WhoEnt 92*
**Timko,** Joseph Michael 1949- *AmMWSc 92*
**Timkovich,** Russell *AmMWSc 92*
**Timlen,** Thomas M. d1991 *NewYTBS 91*
**Timlin,** James Clifford 1927- *WhoRel 92*
**Timlin,** Robert Christopher, Sr. 1963- *WhoRel 92*
**Timm,** Albert Leonard 1929- *WhoFI 92*
**Timm,** Delmar C 1940- *AmMWSc 92*
**Timm,** Gerald Wayne 1940- *AmMWSc 92*
**Timm,** Jeanne Anderson 1918- *WhoEnt 92*
**Timm,** Jeffrey Thomas 1949- *WhoRel 92*
**Timm,** Jerry Roger 1942- *WhoWest 92*
**Timm,** Kenneth Nickerson 1934- *WhoEnt 92*
**Timm,** Kent Edward 1958- *WhoMW 92*
**Timm,** Mike *WhoAmP 91*
**Timm,** Raymond Stanley 1918- *AmMWSc 92*

**Timm**, Robert Dale 1921- WhoAmP 91
**Timm**, Robert Merle 1949- WhoWest 92
**Timm**, Roger Edwin 1945- WhoRel 92
**Timm**, Terry L 1948- WhoIns 92
**Timma**, Donald Lee 1922- AmMWSc 92
**Timme**, Robert William 1940- AmMWSc 92
**Timmer**, Barbara 1946- WhoAmL 92, WhoFI 92
**Timmer**, David Ernest 1951- WhoMW 92, WhoRel 92
**Timmer**, J. D. 1933- IntWW 91
**Timmer**, John 1931- WhoMW 92
**Timmer**, John L WhoAmP 91
**Timmer**, Kathleen Mae 1942- AmMWSc 92
**Timmerhaus**, K D 1924- AmMWSc 92
**Timmerhaus**, Klaus Dieter 1924- WhoWest 92
**Timmerman**, Joan Hyacinth 1938- WhoRel 92
**Timmerman**, Leon Bernard 1924- WhoFI 92
**Timmerman**, William B. 1946- WhoFI 92
**Timmermann**, Barbara Nawalany 1947- AmMWSc 92
**Timmermann**, Dan, Jr 1933- AmMWSc 92
**Timmers**, Michael George 1957- WhoAmL 92
**Timmins**, Edward Patrick 1955- WhoAmL 92
**Timmins**, James Donald 1955- WhoWest 92
**Timmins**, John Bradford 1932- Who 92
**Timmins**, Michael John 1959- WhoFI 92
**Timmins**, Richard Haseltine 1924- WhoMW 92
**Timmins**, Robert Stone 1933- AmMWSc 92
**Timmins**, William Joseph, Jr 1917- WhoAmP 91
**Timmis**, Gerald C 1930- AmMWSc 92
**Timmis**, Robert 1886-1960 TwCPaSc
**Timmons**, Bonita Terry 1963- WhoBlA 92
**Timmons**, Charles McDonald 1926- WhoIns 92
**Timmons**, Darrol Holt 1940- AmMWSc 92
**Timmons**, Emily Irene WhoEnt 92
**Timmons**, Jay Warner 1962- WhoAmP 91
**Timmons**, Jimmy Hodge WhoAmP 91
**Timmons**, Richard B 1938- AmMWSc 92
**Timmons**, Robert G. 1938- WhoWest 92
**Timmons**, Thomas Joseph AmMWSc 92
**Timmons**, Wiliam R, Jr 1924- WhoIns 92
**Timmons**, William Edward 1924- WhoAmL 92
**Timmons**, William Evan 1930- WhoAmP 91
**Timmons**, William Milton 1933- WhoEnt 92, WhoWest 92
**Timmons**, William Richardson, III 1951- WhoIns 92
**Timmreck**, Joe Edward 1950- WhoWest 92
**Timmreck**, Thomas C. 1946- WhoWest 92
**Timms**, A. Jackson 1938- WhoAmL 92
**Timms**, Cecil 1911- Who 92
**Timms**, Eugene Dale 1932- WhoAmP 91
**Timms**, George Boorne 1910- Who 92
**Timms**, Kathleen 1943- WrDr 92
**Timms**, Leonard Joseph, Jr. 1936- WhoFI 92
**Timms**, Noel Walter 1927- Who 92
**Timms**, Robert J 1923- AmMWSc 92
**Timms**, Vera Kate 1944- Who 92
**Timnick**, Andrew 1918- AmMWSc 92
**Timoclea** EncAmaz 91
**Timofeeff-Ressovsky**, Nikolay V. 1900-1981 SovUnBD
**Timofeev-Resovsky**, Nikolay Vladimirovich 1900-1981 SovUnBD
**Timofeyeva**, Nina Vladimirovna 1935- IntWW 91
**Timon**, William Edward, Jr 1924- AmMWSc 92
**Timoni**, Stephen Anthony 1954- WhoAmL 92
**Timony**, Peter Edward 1943- AmMWSc 92
**Timoshenko**, Gregory Stephen 1904- AmMWSc 92
**Timoshenko**, Semen Konstantinovich 1895-1970 SovUnBD
**Timoshenko**, Semyon Konstantinovich 1895-1970 FacFETw
**Timothy** EncEarC
**Timothy Aelurus** d477 EncEarC
**Timothy**, Bishop 1928- WhoMW 92, WhoRel 92
**Timothy of Jerusalem** EncEarC
**Timothy**, David Harry 1928- AmMWSc 92
**Timothy**, John Gethyn 1942- AmMWSc 92
**Timourian**, Hector 1933- AmMWSc 92
**Timourian**, James Gregory 1941- AmMWSc 92
**Timp**, Laura Anne 1962- WhoMW 92
**Timpanelli**, Gioia DrAPF 91
**Timpany Five** NewAmDM
**Timpe**, Michael Wayne 1951- WhoMW 92
**Timperlake**, Edward Thomas 1946- WhoAmP 91
**Timperley**, Rosemary Kenyon 1920- IntAu&W 91, WrDr 92
**Timpson**, Clarence B. 1933- WhoBlA 92
**Timpson**, John Harry Robert 1928- Who 92
**Timrod**, Henry 1828-1867 BenetAL 91, BibAL 8
**Tims**, Demetra 1935- WhoWest 92
**Tims**, Eugene F 1921- AmMWSc 92
**Tims**, George B, Jr 1918- AmMWSc 92
**Timson**, Keith Stephen 1945- IntAu&W 91
**Timson**, Penelope Anne Constance Who 92
**Timusk**, John 1935- AmMWSc 92
**Timusk**, Thomas 1933- AmMWSc 92
**Tin-Wa**, Maung 1940- AmMWSc 92
**Tinaglia**, Michael Anthony 1962- WhoWest 92
**Tinajero**, Josefina Villamil 1949- WhoHisp 92
**Tinanoff**, Norman 1945- AmMWSc 92
**Tinaztepe**, Cihan 1949- WhoWest 92
**Tinbergen**, Jan 1903- IntWW 91, Who 92, WhoFI 92, WhoNob 90
**Tinbergen**, Nikolaas 1907- AmMWSc 92
**Tinbergen**, Nikolaas 1907-1988 FacFETw, WhoNob 90
**Tincher**, Wayne Coleman 1935- AmMWSc 92
**Tincher**, Wendell Laverne 1936- WhoAmP 91
**Tinctoris**, Johannes 1435?-1511? NewAmDM
**Tindal**, D Leslie 1928- WhoAmP 91
**Tindal**, Matthew 1657?-1733 BlkwCEP
**Tindal-Carill-Worsley**, Geoffrey Nicolas 1908- Who 92
**Tindale**, Gordon Anthony 1938- Who 92
**Tindale**, Lawrence Victor Dolman 1921- IntWW 91, Who 92
**Tindale**, Patricia Randall 1926- Who 92
**Tindall**, Blair Alston Mercer 1960- WhoEnt 92
**Tindall**, Charles Gordon, Jr 1942- AmMWSc 92
**Tindall**, Donald J 1944- AmMWSc 92
**Tindall**, Donald R 1937- AmMWSc 92
**Tindall**, Frederick Cryer 1900- Who 92
**Tindall**, George Taylor 1928- AmMWSc 92
**Tindall**, Gillian 1938- ConNov 91, WrDr 92
**Tindall**, Gillian Elizabeth 1938- IntAu&W 91, Who 92
**Tindall**, James WhoAmP 91
**Tindall**, James Robert 1945- WhoMW 92
**Tindall**, Jill Denise 1958- WhoEnt 92
**Tindall**, Lawrence Bennett 1951- WhoMW 92
**Tindall**, Richard Allen 1934- WhoAmL 92
**Tindall**, Robert James 1948- WhoWest 92
**Tindall**, Sandy Ellen 1956- WhoFI 92, WhoWest 92
**Tindall**, Theron Wayne 1962- WhoRel 92
**Tindall**, Victor Ronald 1928- Who 92
**Tindell**, Harry J WhoAmP 91
**Tindell**, Ralph S 1942- AmMWSc 92
**Tindell**, Richard Wayne 1952- WhoRel 92
**Tindemans**, Leo 1922- IntWW 91, Who 92
**Tinder**, Donald George 1938- WhoRel 92
**Tinder**, John Daniel 1950- WhoMW 92
**Tinder**, Richard F 1930- AmMWSc 92
**Tindle**, David 1932- IntWW 91, TwCPaSc, Who 92
**Tindle**, Ray Stanley 1926- Who 92
**Tindley**, Charles Albert 1851-1933 RelLAm 91
**Tine**, Jacques Wilfrid Jean Francis 1914- IntWW 91
**Tine**, Michael P. 1945- WhoFI 92
**Tiner**, Richard Harold 1951- WhoEnt 92
**Ting Mao** 1913- IntWW 91
**Ting**, Chih-Yuan Charles 1947- AmMWSc 92
**Ting**, Chou-Chik 1939- AmMWSc 92
**Ting**, Francis Ta-Chuan 1934- AmMWSc 92
**Ting**, Irwin Peter 1934- AmMWSc 92
**Ting**, K.H. 1915- DcEcMov
**Ting**, Lu 1925- AmMWSc 92
**Ting**, Ming Tsung 1938- WhoWest 92
**Ting**, Robert Yen-Ying 1942- AmMWSc 92
**Ting**, Samuel C C 1936- AmMWSc 92
**Ting**, Samuel Chao Chung 1936- IntWW 91, Who 92, WhoNob 90
**Ting**, Shih-Fan 1917- AmMWSc 92
**Ting**, Sik Vung 1918- AmMWSc 92
**Ting**, Thomas C T 1933- AmMWSc 92
**Ting**, Tsuan Wu 1922- AmMWSc 92
**Ting**, William Bang-yu 1948- WhoFI 92
**Ting**, Yu-Chen 1920- AmMWSc 92
**Ting-Beall**, Hie Ping 1940- AmMWSc 92
**Tinga**, Jacob Hinnes 1920- AmMWSc 92
**Tingelhoff**, Martin Denny 1954- WhoRel 92
**Tingelstad**, Jon Bunde 1935- AmMWSc 92
**Tingey**, David Thomas 1941- AmMWSc 92
**Tingey**, Garth Leroy 1932- AmMWSc 92
**Tingey**, Ward M 1944- AmMWSc 92
**Tingle**, Frederic Carley 1940- AmMWSc 92
**Tingle**, James O'Malley 1928- WhoAmL 92
**Tingle**, John Bishop 1866-1918 BiInAmS
**Tingle**, Lawrence May 1947- WhoBlA 92
**Tingle**, Marjorie Anne 1938- AmMWSc 92
**Tingle**, William Herbert 1917- AmMWSc 92
**Tingleff**, Thomas Alan 1946- WhoFI 92
**Tingley**, Arnold Jackson 1920- AmMWSc 92
**Tingley**, Katherine Augusta Westcott 1847-1929 AmPeW
**Tinguely**, Jean 1925-1991 CurBio 91N, NewYTBS 91
**Tinianow**, Jerome Curtis 1955- WhoAmL 92
**Tinitali**, Soa P WhoAmP 91
**Tinjum**, Larry Ervin 1947- WhoAmP 91
**Tinker**, Arthur James 1942- WhoMW 92
**Tinker**, Carol Wicks 1920- WhoAmP 91
**Tinker**, David Owen 1940- AmMWSc 92
**Tinker**, Edward Brian 1932- WhoWest 92
**Tinker**, Edward Larocque 1881-1968 BenetAL 91
**Tinker**, Gerald 1951- BlkOlyM
**Tinker**, Grant LesBEnT 92 [port]
**Tinker**, Grant A. 1926- IntMPA 92, WhoEnt 92
**Tinker**, Hugh 1921- WrDr 92
**Tinker**, Hugh Russell 1921- Who 92
**Tinker**, Jack 1936- Who 92
**Tinker**, John Frank 1922- AmMWSc 92
**Tinker**, Philip Bernard Hague 1930- Who 92
**Tinker**, Spencer Wilkie 1909- AmMWSc 92
**Tinkham**, James Jeffrey 1961- WhoAmL 92
**Tinkham**, Michael 1928- AmMWSc 92, IntWW 91
**Tinkham**, Thomas W. 1944- WhoAmL 92
**Tinkle**, F. Lorain 1913- WhoAmL 92
**Tinklepaugh**, J R 1920- AmMWSc 92
**Tinkler**, Jack D 1936- AmMWSc 92
**Tinline**, Robert Davies 1925- AmMWSc 92
**Tinling**, Ted 1910-1990 AnObit 1990
**Tinn**, James 1922- Who 92
**Tinner**, Franziska Paula 1944- WhoMW 92
**Tinnerello**, Mike 1944- WhoAmP 91
**Tinney**, Dee Melvin 1940- WhoFI 92
**Tinney**, Francis John 1938- AmMWSc 92
**Tinney**, William Frank 1921- AmMWSc 92
**Tinnin**, Albert Bradley 1956- WhoRel 92
**Tinnin**, Robert Owen 1943- AmMWSc 92
**Tinnin**, Thomas Peck 1948- WhoWest 92
**Tinniswood**, Maurice Owen 1919- Who 92
**Tinniswood**, Peter 1936- ConNov 91, IntAu&W 91, WrDr 92
**Tinoco**, Ignacio, Jr 1930- AmMWSc 92
**Tinoco**, Joan W H 1932- AmMWSc 92
**Tinoko**, Jose Maria Baluis 1936- WhoRel 92
**Tinsley Brothers** DcLB 106
**Tinsley**, Brian Alfred 1937- AmMWSc 92
**Tinsley**, Charles Henry 1914- Who 92
**Tinsley**, Eleanor 1926- WhoAmP 91
**Tinsley**, Ernest John 1919- IntWW 91, Who 92, WrDr 92
**Tinsley**, Fred Leland, Jr. 1944- WhoAmL 92, WhoAmP 91, WhoBlA 92
**Tinsley**, Ian James 1929- AmMWSc 92
**Tinsley**, Lyn D WhoAmP 91
**Tinsley**, Mary WhoAmP 91
**Tinsley**, Randolph James 1960- WhoAmL 92
**Tinsley**, Richard Sterling 1931- AmMWSc 92
**Tinsley**, Samuel Weaver 1923- AmMWSc 92
**Tinsley**, Thomas Vincent, Jr. 1940- WhoFI 92
**Tinsley-Williams**, Alberta 1954- WhoBlA 92
**Tinsman**, James Herbert, Jr 1930- AmMWSc 92
**Tinsman**, Maggie 1936- WhoAmP 91
**Tinsman**, Margaret Neir 1936- WhoMW 92
**Tinson**, Susan 1943- Who 92
**Tinstman**, Marc Richard 1951- WhoRel 92
**Tint**, Howard 1917- AmMWSc 92
**Tintarev**, Kyril 1956- WhoWest 92
**Tintari**, Martin George 1948- WhoMW 92
**Tinti**, Dino S 1941- AmMWSc 92
**Tintweiss**, Steven Ira 1946- WhoEnt 92
**Tinucci**, Raymond Peter 1927- WhoFI 92
**Tinus**, Richard Willard 1936- AmMWSc 92
**Tio**, Adrian Ricardo 1951- WhoHisp 92
**Tio**, Cesario O 1932- AmMWSc 92
**Tiomkin**, Dimitri 1894-1979 NewAmDM
**Tiomkin**, Dimitri 1899-1979 FacFETw
**Tipei**, Nicolae 1913- AmMWSc 92
**Tipei**, Sever 1943- WhoEnt 92, WhoMW 92
**Tiphaigne De La Roche**, Charles Francois 1729-1774 ScFEYrs
**Tipler**, Frank Jennings, III 1947- AmMWSc 92
**Tipler**, Paul A 1933- AmMWSc 92
**Tippens**, Dorr E F 1923- AmMWSc 92
**Tipper**, Donald John 1935- AmMWSc 92
**Tipper**, Harry, III 1949- WhoFI 92
**Tipper**, Ronald Charles 1942- AmMWSc 92
**Tippet**, Anthony 1928- Who 92
**Tippet**, Michael K. 1905- FacFETw
**Tippets**, Dennis W 1938- WhoAmP 91
**Tippets**, John H 1952- WhoAmP 91
**Tippett**, Andre Bernard 1959- WhoBlA 92
**Tippett**, James S. 1885-1958 ConAu 135, SmATA 66
**Tippett**, James T 1931- AmMWSc 92
**Tippett**, Michael 1905- ConCom 92, NewAmDM, Who 92
**Tippett**, Michael Kemp 1905- IntWW 91
**Tippett**, Willis Paul, Jr. 1932- IntWW 91, WhoFI 92
**Tippette**, Giles 1934- TwCWW 91
**Tippette**, Giles 1936- WrDr 92
**Tippetts**, Rutherford Berriman 1913- Who 92
**Tipping**, Harry A. 1944- WhoAmL 92
**Tipping**, Richard H 1939- AmMWSc 92
**Tipping**, William Malcolm 1931- WhoFI 92
**Tippins**, Timothy Michael 1949- WhoAmL 92
**Tippit**, Jean Deann 1963- WhoRel 92
**Tippler**, John 1929- Who 92
**Tipples**, Keith H 1936- AmMWSc 92
**Tippman**, Pamela Candiece 1950- WhoWest 92
**Tipps**, Paul 1936- WhoAmP 91
**Tippy**, Alan Clay 1953- WhoWest 92
**Tippy**, Worth Marion 1866-1961 RelLAm 91
**Tipsword**, Ray Fenton 1931- AmMWSc 92
**Tipsword**, Rolland Fortner 1925- WhoAmP 91
**Tipton**, C R, Jr 1921- AmMWSc 92
**Tipton**, Carl Lee 1931- AmMWSc 92
**Tipton**, Charles M 1927- AmMWSc 92
**Tipton**, Dale Leo 1930- WhoBlA 92
**Tipton**, Darrell Lee 1948- WhoAmP 91
**Tipton**, David 1934- WrDr 92
**Tipton**, David John 1934- IntAu&W 91
**Tipton**, Elden C 1918- WhoAmP 91
**Tipton**, Elizabeth Howse 1925- WhoBlA 92
**Tipton**, Gary Lee 1941- WhoFI 92, WhoWest 92
**Tipton**, Harry B 1927- WhoAmP 91
**Tipton**, Ian Charles 1937- WrDr 92
**Tipton**, James Ceamon 1938- WhoWest 92
**Tipton**, Jennifer 1937- ConTFT 9, WhoEnt 92
**Tipton**, Jon Paul 1934- WhoMW 92
**Tipton**, Kenneth Warren 1932- AmMWSc 92
**Tipton**, Merlin J 1930- AmMWSc 92
**Tipton**, Thomas H. 1933- WhoBlA 92
**Tipton**, Toni Hamilton 1959- WhoBlA 92
**Tipton**, Vernon John 1920- AmMWSc 92
**Tiptree**, James, Jr. ConAu 34NR
**Tiptree**, James, Jr 1916-1987 TwCSFW 91
**Tipu**, Ioan IntWW 91
**Tirado**, Daniel Ramon 1949- WhoHisp 92
**Tirado**, Isabel A. 1947- WhoHisp 92
**Tirado**, Olga Luz 1960- WhoHisp 92
**Tirado Delgado**, Cirilo 1938- WhoHisp 92
**Tirana**, Bardyl Rifat 1937- WhoAmP 91
**Tirgato of Ixomatae** EncAmaz 91
**Tirikatene-Sullivan**, Tini Whetu Marama 1932- IntWW 91
**Tirimo**, Martino 1942- IntWW 91
**Tirino**, Philip Joseph 1940- WhoFI 92
**Tirkkonen**, Tuomo Johannes 1940- WhoEnt 92
**Tirman**, Alvin 1931- AmMWSc 92
**Tirozzi**, Rocco Joseph 1958- WhoAmL 92
**Tirpak**, Joseph Edward 1937- WhoMW 92
**Tirpak**, Stephen Michael 1946- WhoFI 92
**Tirpitz**, Alfred von 1849-1930 FacFETw
**Tirr**, Willy 1915- TwCPaSc
**Tirrell**, Elvin Drew 1931- WhoAmP 91
**Tirrell**, Matthew Vincent 1950- AmMWSc 92
**Tirres**, Richard Raymond 1950- WhoHisp 92
**Tirro**, Frank Pascale 1935- WhoEnt 92
**Tirumalai**, Srivatsan Srinivas 1957- WhoMW 92
**Tirvengadum**, Harry 1933- Who 92
**Tiryakian**, Edward Ashod 1929- WhoRel 92
**Tisch**, Andrew Herbert 1949- WhoFI 92
**Tisch**, Laurence A. LesBEnT 92 [port]
**Tisch**, Laurence A. 1923- IntMPA 92

**Tisch,** Laurence Alan 1923- *IntWW 91, WhoEnt 92, WhoFI 92*
**Tisch,** Preston Robert 1926- *IntMPA 92, WhoFI 92*
**Tisch,** Steve 1949- *IntMPA 92*
**Tischendorf,** John Allen 1929- *AmMWSc 92*
**Tischer,** Frederick Joseph 1913- *AmMWSc 92*
**Tischer,** Gerald E. 1949- *WhoMW 92*
**Tischer,** Ragnar P 1922- *AmMWSc 92*
**Tischer,** Thomas Norman 1934- *AmMWSc 92*
**Tischfield,** Jay Arnold 1946- *AmMWSc 92*
**Tischio,** John Patrick 1942- *AmMWSc 92*
**Tischler,** David William 1935- *WhoWest 92*
**Tischler,** Hans 1915- *WhoEnt 92, WrDr 92*
**Tischler,** Herbert 1924- *AmMWSc 92*
**Tischler,** Judith Blanche 1933- *WhoEnt 92*
**Tischler,** Lewis Paul 1947- *WhoFI 92*
**Tischler,** Marc Eliot 1949- *AmMWSc 92*
**Tischler,** Oscar 1923- *AmMWSc 92*
**Tisdale,** Celes 1941- *WhoBlA 92*
**Tisdale,** Douglas Michael 1949- *WhoAmL 92, WhoWest 92*
**Tisdale,** Glenn E 1924- *AmMWSc 92*
**Tisdale,** Henry Nehemiah 1944- *WhoBlA 92*
**Tisdale,** Herbert Clifford 1928- *WhoBlA 92*
**Tisdale,** Jeffrey Alan 1949- *WhoFI 92*
**Tisdale,** Stuart Williams 1928- *WhoFI 92, WhoMW 92*
**Tisdale,** Thomas Sumter, Jr. 1939- *WhoAmL 92*
**Tisdale,** Wayman 1964- *BlkOlyM*
**Tisdale,** Wayman Lawrence 1964- *WhoBlA 92*
**Tisdall,** Hans 1910- *TwCPaSc*
**Tisdell,** Clement Allan 1939- *WrDr 92*
**Tise,** Allan Brandon 1955- *WhoAmL 92*
**Tise,** Frank P 1951- *AmMWSc 92*
**Tise,** George Francis, II 1937- *WhoWest 92*
**Tisei,** Richard R *WhoAmP 91*
**Tiselius,** Arne Wilhelm Kaurin 1902-1971 *WhoNob 90*
**Tishby,** Naftali Z 1952- *AmMWSc 92*
**Tishchenko,** Boris 1939- *ConCom 92*
**Tishchenko,** Boris Ivanovich 1939- *IntWW 91*
**Tishk,** Alan Jay 1949- *WhoMW 92*
**Tishko,** Steven Michael 1952- *WhoMW 92*
**Tishkoff,** Garson Harold 1923- *AmMWSc 92*
**Tishler,** Max 1906- *AmMWSc 92*
**Tishler,** Peter Verveer 1937- *AmMWSc 92*
**Tishler,** William Henry 1936- *WhoMW 92*
**Tiso,** Josef 1887-1947 *FacFETw*
**Tiso,** Jozef 1887-1947 *EncTR 91 [port]*
**Tiso,** Jozef Gaspar 1887-1947 *BiDExR*
**Tison,** Ben 1930- *WhoAmP 91*
**Tison,** Richard Perry 1944- *AmMWSc 92*
**Tisone,** Gary C 1937- *AmMWSc 92*
**Tiss,** George John 1925- *WhoWest 92*
**Tisse,** Eduard Kazimirovich 1897-1961 *SovUnBD*
**Tisser,** Doron Moshe 1955- *WhoAmL 92, WhoWest 92*
**Tisserat,** Brent Howard 1951- *AmMWSc 92*
**Tissot,** Jacques Joseph 1836-1902 *ThHEIm [port]*
**Tissot,** Simon-Andre 1728-1797 *BlkwCEP*
**Tissue,** Eric Bruce 1955- *AmMWSc 92*
**Tisue,** George Thomas 1940- *AmMWSc 92*
**Tisza,** Laszlo 1907- *AmMWSc 92*
**Tiszenkel,** Paul Morris 1952- *WhoFI 92*
**Titarenko,** Mikhail Leonidovich *IntWW 91*
**Titchell,** John 1926- *Who 92*
**Titchener,** Alan Ronald 1934- *Who 92*
**Titchener,** Edward Bradford 1927- *AmMWSc 92*
**Titchener,** James Lampton 1922- *AmMWSc 92*
**Titchener,** Lanham 1912- *Who 92*
**Titchener,** Louise 1941- *WrDr 92*
**Titchener-Barrett,** Dennis *Who 92*
**Titcomb,** Bonnie L *WhoAmP 91*
**Titcomb,** Caldwell 1926- *WhoEnt 92*
**Titcomb,** Timothy *BenetAL 91*
**Tite,** Michael Stanley 1938- *Who 92*
**Titelbaum,** Sydney 1913- *AmMWSc 92*
**Titeler,** Milt 1949- *AmMWSc 92*
**Titelman,** Russ 1944- *WhoEnt 92*
**Titford,** Donald George 1925- *Who 92*
**Titheridge,** John Edward 1932- *IntWW 91*
**Titheridge,** Roger Noel 1928- *Who 92*
**Titherington,** Mary 1927- *WhoAmP 91*
**Titialii,** Jacinta Eleina 1955- *WhoAmL 92*
**Titkemeyer,** Charles William 1919- *AmMWSc 92*
**Title,** Peter Stephen 1950- *WhoAmL 92*
**Titlebaum,** Edward Lawrence 1937- *AmMWSc 92*
**Titley,** Gary 1950- *Who 92*
**Titley,** Jane 1940- *Who 92*
**Titley,** Larry J. 1943- *WhoAmL 92*
**Titley,** Spencer Rowe 1928- *AmMWSc 92*
**Titlow,** Frank Graham 1943- *WhoFI 92*
**Titman,** John 1926- *Who 92*
**Titman,** Paul Wilson 1920- *AmMWSc 92*
**Titman,** Rodger Donaldson 1943- *AmMWSc 92*
**Tito,** Josip 1892-1980 *EncTR 91 [port]*
**Tito,** Josip Broz 1892-1980 *FacFETw [port]*
**Tito,** Richard Joseph 1947- *WhoFI 92*
**Titone,** Luke Victor 1911- *AmMWSc 92*
**Titone,** Vito J *WhoAmP 91*
**Titone,** Vito Joseph 1929- *WhoAmL 92*
**Titov,** Gherman 1935- *FacFETw*
**Titov,** Herman Stepanovich 1935- *IntWW 91*
**Titov,** Vitaliy Nikolaevich 1907-1980 *SovUnBD*
**Titov,** Yuriy Evlampevich 1935- *IntWW 91*
**Titov,** Yuriy Yevlamp'evich 1935- *SovUnBD*
**Tits,** Jacques Leon 1930- *IntWW 91*
**Tittel,** Frank K 1933- *AmMWSc 92*
**Titterton,** Ernest 1916-1990 *AnObit 1990*
**Titterton,** Ernest William 1916-1990 *FacFETw*
**Titterton,** Paul James 1940- *AmMWSc 92*
**Tittle,** Charles William 1917- *AmMWSc 92*
**Tittle,** Douglas Lee 1954- *WhoMW 92*
**Tittman,** Jay 1922- *AmMWSc 92*
**Tittmann,** Bernhard R 1935- *AmMWSc 92*
**Tittsworth,** Clayton Magness 1920- *WhoAmL 92*
**Tituba** 1648?-1692 *HanAmWH*
**Titunik,** Irwin Robert 1929- *IntAu&W 91*
**Titus** *EncEarC*
**Titus** 39?-81 *EncEarC*
**Titus of Bostra** d371 *EncEarC*
**Titus,** Alan 1945- *NewAmDM*
**Titus,** Alan Witkowski 1945- *WhoEnt 92*
**Titus,** Alice Cestandina 1950- *WhoAmP 91*
**Titus,** Charles Joseph 1923- *AmMWSc 92*
**Titus,** Charles O 1927- *AmMWSc 92*
**Titus,** Donald Dean 1944- *AmMWSc 92*
**Titus,** Dudley Seymour 1929- *AmMWSc 92*
**Titus,** Elwood Owen 1919- *AmMWSc 92*
**Titus,** Eve 1922- *WrDr 92*
**Titus,** Harold 1930- *AmMWSc 92*
**Titus,** Jack L 1926- *AmMWSc 92*
**Titus,** John Elliott 1949- *AmMWSc 92*
**Titus,** John S 1923- *AmMWSc 92*
**Titus,** Jon Alan 1955- *WhoAmL 92, WhoWest 92*
**Titus,** LeRoy Robert 1938- *WhoBlA 92*
**Titus,** Lewis Robert 1942- *WhoWest 92*
**Titus,** Lonnie Ellis 1950- *WhoRel 92*
**Titus,** Myer L. *WhoBlA 92*
**Titus,** Richard Lee 1934- *AmMWSc 92*
**Titus,** Robert Charles 1946- *AmMWSc 92*
**Titus,** Robert Farren, Jr. 1956- *WhoWest 92*
**Titus,** Robin Brian 1954- *WhoEnt 92*
**Titus,** Theo, III *WhoAmP 91*
**Titus,** William James 1941- *AmMWSc 92*
**Titus,** William Ray 1950- *WhoRel 92*
**Titus-Dillon,** Pauline Y. 1938- *WhoBlA 92*
**Titze,** Ingo Roland 1941- *AmMWSc 92*
**Titzer,** Robert Frederick 1933- *WhoMW 92*
**Tius,** Marcus Antonius 1953- *AmMWSc 92*
**Tivers,** Leslie Hanover 1946- *WhoEnt 92*
**Tiverton,** Viscount *Who 92*
**Tiwari,** Narayan Datt 1925- *IntWW 91, Who 92*
**Tiwari,** Surendra Nath 1938- *AmMWSc 92*
**Tixier,** Claude 1913- *IntWW 91*
**Tixier,** Maurice Pierre 1913- *AmMWSc 92*
**Tixier-Vignancour,** Jean Louis Gilbert 1907- *BiDExR*
**Tizard,** Barbara 1926- *Who 92*
**Tizard,** Catherine 1931- *IntWW 91, Who 92*
**Tizard,** Ian Rodney 1942- *AmMWSc 92*
**Tizard,** Peter 1916- *Who 92*
**Tizard,** Robert James 1924- *IntWW 91, Who 92*
**Tizzio,** Thomas R 1938- *WhoIns 92*
**Tizzio,** Thomas Ralph 1938- *WhoFI 92*
**Tjader,** Cal 1925-1982 *FacFETw, NewAmDM*
**Tjeknavorian,** Loris-Zare 1937- *IntWW 91*
**Tjepkema,** John Dirk 1943- *AmMWSc 92*
**Tjepkes,** Michael *DrAPF 91*
**Tjia,** Rick Gavin 1966- *WhoEnt 92*
**Tjian,** Robert Tse Nan 1949- *AmMWSc 92*
**Tjio,** Joe Hin 1919- *AmMWSc 92*
**Tjioe,** Djoe Tjhoo 1937- *AmMWSc 92*
**Tjioe,** Sarah Archambault 1944- *AmMWSc 92*
**Tjoflat,** Gerald Bard 1929- *WhoAmL 92, WhoAmP 91*
**Tjornhom,** Chris M 1959- *WhoAmP 91*
**Tjostem,** John Leander 1935- *AmMWSc 92*
**Tkach,** Joseph William 1927- *RelLAm 91*
**Tkacheff,** Joseph, Jr 1926- *AmMWSc 92*
**Tkachev,** Aleksey Petrovich 1925- *SovUnBD*
**Tkachev,** Sergey Petrovich 1922- *IntWW 91, SovUnBD*
**Tkachuk,** Russell 1930- *AmMWSc 92*
**Tkacz,** Jan S 1944- *AmMWSc 92*
**Tlali,** Miriam *ConNov 91*
**Tlass,** Mustapha el- 1932- *IntWW 91*
**Tlou,** Thomas 1932- *IntWW 91*
**Tlusty,** Jay Richard 1955- *WhoAmP 91*
**To Huu** 1920- *IntWW 91*
**Toadvine,** JoAnne Elizabeth 1933- *WhoWest 92*
**Toaff,** Elio *WhoRel 92*
**Toal,** Jean Hoefer 1943- *WhoAmL 92, WhoAmP 91*
**Toale,** Thomas Edward 1953- *WhoRel 92*
**To'atolu,** Nua *WhoAmP 91*
**Toba,** H Harold 1932- *AmMWSc 92*
**Tobach,** Ethel 1921- *AmMWSc 92*
**Toback,** F Gary 1941- *AmMWSc 92*
**Toback,** James 1944- *IntMPA 92*
**Tobar,** Lea Martinez 1942- *WhoHisp 92*
**Tobar Zaldumbide,** Carlos 1912- *IntWW 91*
**Tobback,** Louis 1938- *IntWW 91*
**Tobe,** Christopher Bayless 1962- *WhoFI 92*
**Tobe,** Roslyn Thea 1959- *WhoAmL 92*
**Tobe,** Stephen Solomon 1944- *AmMWSc 92*
**Tobe,** Susan Bring 1949- *WhoAmL 92*
**Tober,** Stephen Lloyd 1949- *WhoAmL 92*
**Toberman,** Ralph Owen 1923- *AmMWSc 92*
**Tobes,** Michael Charles 1948- *AmMWSc 92*
**Tobet,** William Clinton, III 1933- *WhoRel 92*
**Tobey,** Arthur Robert 1920- *AmMWSc 92*
**Tobey,** Edward Nelson 1871-1915 *BiInAmS*
**Tobey,** Frank Lindley, Jr 1923- *AmMWSc 92*
**Tobey,** Joel N *WhoIns 92*
**Tobey,** Robert Allen 1937- *AmMWSc 92*
**Tobey,** Stephen Winter 1936- *AmMWSc 92*
**Tobia,** Alfonso Joseph 1942- *AmMWSc 92*
**Tobia,** Ronald Lawrence 1944- *WhoAmL 92*
**Tobia,** Sergio B 1939- *WhoIns 92*
**Tobian,** John 1944- *WhoMW 92, WhoRel 92*
**Tobian,** Louis 1920- *AmMWSc 92*
**Tobias,** Andrew P. 1947- *WrDr 92*
**Tobias,** Arthur *DrAPF 91*
**Tobias,** Benjamin Alan 1951- *WhoFI 92*
**Tobias,** Charles Edward 1957- *WhoRel 92*
**Tobias,** Charles W 1920- *AmMWSc 92*
**Tobias,** Christopher Ord 1962- *WhoWest 92*
**Tobias,** Cornelius Anthony 1918- *AmMWSc 92*
**Tobias,** Cynthia Lee 1945- *WhoWest 92*
**Tobias,** George S 1916- *AmMWSc 92*
**Tobias,** Jay Henry 1960- *WhoEnt 92*
**Tobias,** Jerry Vernon 1929- *AmMWSc 92*
**Tobias,** John Jacob 1925- *WrDr 92*
**Tobias,** Paul Raymond 1953- *WhoEnt 92*
**Tobias,** Philip E 1919- *AmMWSc 92*
**Tobias,** Phillip Vallentine 1925- *IntWW 91*
**Tobias,** Randolf A. 1940- *WhoBlA 92*
**Tobias,** Richard C. 1925- *WrDr 92*
**Tobias,** Robert M., Jr. 1954- *WhoHisp 92*
**Tobias,** Russell Lawrence 1948- *AmMWSc 92*
**Tobias-Turner,** Bessye 1917- *IntAu&W 91*
**Tobiasen,** Joyce Marie 1940- *WhoMW 92*
**Tobiason,** Frederick Lee 1936- *AmMWSc 92*
**Tobiassen,** Thomas Johan 1931- *WhoAmP 91*
**Tobiasz,** Robert Brian 1945- *WhoFI 92*
**Tobiessen,** Peter Laws 1940- *AmMWSc 92*
**Tobin,** A Stephen *WhoAmP 91*
**Tobin,** Albert George 1938- *AmMWSc 92*
**Tobin,** Allan Joshua 1942- *AmMWSc 92*
**Tobin,** Arthur H 1930- *WhoAmP 91*
**Tobin,** Bruce Howard 1955- *WhoAmL 92*
**Tobin,** Calvin Jay 1927- *WhoMW 92*
**Tobin,** Cindee A. 1965- *WhoMW 92*
**Tobin,** Craig Daniel 1954- *WhoAmL 92, WhoMW 92*
**Tobin,** David Elliot 1954- *WhoWest 92*
**Tobin,** David L. 1928- *WhoAmL 92*
**Tobin,** Dennis Michael 1948- *WhoAmL 92*
**Tobin,** Elaine Munsey 1944- *AmMWSc 92*
**Tobin,** Gordon Ross 1943- *AmMWSc 92*
**Tobin,** Harold William 1922- *WhoAmL 92*
**Tobin,** Ilona Lines 1943- *WhoMW 92*
**Tobin,** Jack Norman 1941- *WhoAmP 91*
**Tobin,** James 1918- *IntWW 91, Who 92, WhoFI 92, WhoNob 90, WrDr 92*
**Tobin,** James Michael 1948- *WhoAmL 92*
**Tobin,** James Robert 1944- *WhoFI 92*
**Tobin,** John Everard 1923- *WhoAmL 92*
**Tobin,** John Joseph 1934- *WhoFI 92*
**Tobin,** John Robert, Jr 1916- *AmMWSc 92*
**Tobin,** Karen Thompson 1951- *WhoAmL 92*
**Tobin,** Katherine Colleen 1950- *WhoWest 92*
**Tobin,** Kiefer A. 1937- *WhoWest 92*
**Tobin,** Louise 1918- *WhoEnt 92*
**Tobin,** Martin John 1951- *AmMWSc 92*
**Tobin,** Marvin Charles 1923- *AmMWSc 92*
**Tobin,** Mary Ann *WhoAmP 91*
**Tobin,** Mary Virginia 1946- *WhoMW 92*
**Tobin,** Michael 1913- *AmMWSc 92*
**Tobin,** Michael Alan 1952- *WhoMW 92*
**Tobin,** Michael M. 1931- *WhoAmL 92*
**Tobin,** Patricia L. 1943- *WhoBlA 92*
**Tobin,** Paul Xavier 1956- *WhoAmL 92*
**Tobin,** Richard Bruce 1925- *AmMWSc 92*
**Tobin,** Robert Manford, Jr. 1958- *WhoWest 92*
**Tobin,** Roger Lee 1940- *AmMWSc 92*
**Tobin,** Sara L 1946- *AmMWSc 92*
**Tobin,** Saul 1928- *WhoWest 92*
**Tobin,** Sheldon S. 1931- *ConAu 134*
**Tobin,** Sidney Morris 1923- *AmMWSc 92*
**Tobin,** Stanley Elliot 1930- *WhoAmL 92*
**Tobin,** Steven Michael 1940- *WhoFI 92*
**Tobin,** Thomas 1941- *AmMWSc 92*
**Tobin,** Thomas Herbert 1945- *WhoRel 92*
**Tobin,** Thomas M 1943- *WhoIns 92*
**Tobin,** Thomas Vincent 1926- *AmMWSc 92*
**Tobin,** Timothy Bruce 1956- *WhoWest 92*
**Tobin,** Timothy Patrick 1955- *WhoAmL 92*
**Tobin,** William Joseph 1927- *WhoWest 92*
**Tobin,** William Thomas 1931- *WhoFI 92*
**Tobis,** Jerome Sanford 1915- *AmMWSc 92*
**Tobisch,** Othmar Tardin 1932- *AmMWSc 92*
**Tobkes,** Martin 1928- *AmMWSc 92*
**Tobkes,** Nancy J 1958- *AmMWSc 92*
**Tobkin,** Vincent Henry 1951- *WhoFI 92, WhoWest 92*
**Tobler,** D. Lee 1933- *WhoFI 92*
**Tobler,** Robert 1901-1962 *BiDExR*
**Tobler,** Waldo Rudolph 1930- *WhoWest 92*
**Tobocman,** Marilyn 1934- *WhoAmL 92*
**Tobocman,** William 1926- *AmMWSc 92*
**Tobolowsky,** Stephen *IntMPA 92*
**Tobon,** Hector 1934- *WhoHisp 92*
**Toburen,** Larry Howard 1940- *AmMWSc 92, WhoWest 92*
**Toby,** Dennis Michael *WhoRel 92*
**Toby,** Jerry 1963- *WhoAmP 91*
**Toby,** Sidney 1930- *AmMWSc 92*
**Toby,** William, Jr. 1934- *WhoBlA 92*
**Toca,** Jesse 1958- *WhoHisp 92*
**Tocci,** Dominick P. 1934- *WhoAmL 92*
**Tocci,** Paul M 1933- *AmMWSc 92*
**Tocci,** Ronald C 1941- *WhoAmP 91*
**Tocco,** Dominick Joseph 1930- *AmMWSc 92*
**Tocco,** James 1943- *WhoEnt 92*
**Toch,** Ernst 1887-1964 *NewAmDM*
**Toch,** Henry *WrDr 92*
**Toch,** Henry 1923- *IntAu&W 91*
**Tocher,** Richard Dana 1935- *AmMWSc 92*
**Tock,** Joseph 1954- *WhoAmL 92*
**Tock,** Richard William 1940- *AmMWSc 92*
**Tocklin,** Adrian Martha 1951- *WhoFI 92, WhoIns 92*
**Tocqueville,** Alexis 1805-1859 *GuFrLit 1*
**Tocqueville,** Alexis De *RComAH*
**Tocqueville,** Alexis de 1805-1859 *BenetAL 91, DcAmImH*
**Tocus,** Edward C 1925- *AmMWSc 92*
**Toczek,** Donald Richard 1938- *AmMWSc 92*
**Toczek,** Nick 1950- *WrDr 92*
**Tod,** Edward James 1938- *WhoMW 92*
**Tod,** John Hunter H. *Who 92*
**Tod,** Jonathan James Richard 1939- *Who 92*
**Tod,** Murray 1909-1974 *TwCPaSc*
**Todaro,** Frank Edward 1957- *WhoAmL 92*
**Todaro,** George Joseph 1937- *AmMWSc 92*
**Todaro,** Michael P 1942- *AmMWSc 92*
**Todd** *Who 92*
**Todd,** Baron 1907- *IntWW 91, Who 92*
**Todd,** A.R. Middleton 1891-1966 *TwCPaSc*
**Todd,** A W *WhoAmP 91*
**Todd,** Aaron Rodwell 1942- *AmMWSc 92*
**Todd,** Alastair 1920- *Who 92*
**Todd,** Alexander Robertus 1907- *WhoNob 90*
**Todd,** Ann *Who 92*
**Todd,** Ann 1909- *IntMPA 92*
**Todd,** Arthur Ruric, III 1942- *WhoAmP 91*
**Todd,** Ben 1944- *WhoAmL 92*
**Todd,** Beverly *WhoEnt 92*
**Todd,** Beverly 1946- *IntMPA 92*
**Todd,** Beverly 1955- *WhoBlA 92*

**Todd**, Bosworth Moss, Jr. 1930- *WhoFI 92*
**Todd**, Cathy Diane 1952- *WhoMW 92*
**Todd**, Charles O. 1915- *WhoBlA 92*
**Todd**, Cynthia Jean 1951- *WhoBlA 92*
**Todd**, Daphne 1947- *TwCPaSc*
**Todd**, David Burton 1925- *AmMWSc 92*
**Todd**, David Keith 1923- *AmMWSc 92*
**Todd**, Deborah J. 1951- *WhoWest 92*
**Todd**, Donald d1988 *WhoBlA 92N*
**Todd**, Doug 1929- *WhoAmP 91*
**Todd**, Edward Payson 1920- *AmMWSc 92*
**Todd**, Eric E 1906- *AmMWSc 92*
**Todd**, Ewen Cameron David 1939- *AmMWSc 92*
**Todd**, Flake 1917- *WhoAmP 91*
**Todd**, Frank Arnold 1911- *AmMWSc 92*
**Todd**, Garfield *Who 92*
**Todd**, Glen Cory 1931- *AmMWSc 92*
**Todd**, Glenn William 1927- *AmMWSc 92*
**Todd**, Gordon Livingston 1944- *AmMWSc 92*
**Todd**, Gregory Alan 1955- *WhoMW 92*
**Todd**, H E 1908- *IntAu&W 91*
**Todd**, Harold David 1944- *AmMWSc 92*
**Todd**, Harry Flynn, Jr 1941- *AmMWSc 92*
**Todd**, Harry Frank 1958- *WhoAmL 92*
**Todd**, Harry Williams 1922- *WhoFI 92, WhoWest 92*
**Todd**, Henry Davis 1838-1907 *BiInAmS*
**Todd**, Hollis N 1914- *AmMWSc 92*
**Todd**, Ian 1921- *Who 92*
**Todd**, J R, Jr 1943- *WhoAmP 91*
**Todd**, James Averill, Jr. 1928- *WhoFI 92*
**Todd**, James Dale 1943- *WhoAmL 92*
**Todd**, James Gilbert 1937- *WhoWest 92*
**Todd**, James Wyatt 1942- *AmMWSc 92*
**Todd**, Jerry William 1930- *AmMWSc 92*
**Todd**, Jo Ann 1928- *WhoMW 92*
**Todd**, JoAnn Byrne *DrAPF 91*
**Todd**, Joe Thomas 1940- *WhoAmP 91*
**Todd**, John 1911- *AmMWSc 92*
**Todd**, John Arthur 1908- *Who 92*
**Todd**, John Francis James 1937- *Who 92*
**Todd**, John M. 1918- *WrDr 92*
**Todd**, John Odell 1902- *WhoMW 92*
**Todd**, John Rawling 1929- *Who 92*
**Todd**, John Thomas, III 1943- *WhoEnt 92*
**Todd**, Judith 1936- *WhoWest 92*
**Todd**, Kenneth S, Jr 1936- *AmMWSc 92*
**Todd**, Lee John 1936- *AmMWSc 92*
**Todd**, Leonard 1940- *AmMWSc 92*
**Todd**, Lisa Anderson 1942- *WhoAmL 92*
**Todd**, Lois Jane 1944- *WhoMW 92*
**Todd**, Mabel Loomis 1856-1932 *BenetAL 91*
**Todd**, Malcolm 1939- *Who 92*
**Todd**, Margaret Blake 1962- *WhoAmL 92*
**Todd**, Margaret Edna 1924- *AmMWSc 92*
**Todd**, Marion Marsh 1841- *HanAmWH*
**Todd**, Mary Elizabeth *AmMWSc 92*
**Todd**, Mary Williamson Spottiswoode 1909- *Who 92*
**Todd**, Melvin R. 1933- *WhoBlA 92*
**Todd**, Michael Jeremy 1947- *AmMWSc 92*
**Todd**, Mike 1947- *WhoAmP 91*
**Todd**, Mike 1953- *WhoAmP 91*
**Todd**, Neil Bowman 1936- *AmMWSc 92*
**Todd**, Norman d1990 *Who 92N*
**Todd**, Olivier 1929- *IntWW 91*
**Todd**, Orlando 1958- *WhoBlA 92*
**Todd**, Paul *IntAu&W 91X, WrDr 92*
**Todd**, Paul Harold, Jr 1921- *WhoAmP 91*
**Todd**, Paul Wilson 1936- *AmMWSc 92, WhoWest 92*
**Todd**, Peter Justin 1949- *AmMWSc 92*
**Todd**, Philip Hamish 1956- *AmMWSc 92*
**Todd**, Reginald Stephen Garfield 1908- *IntWW 91, Who 92*
**Todd**, Richard 1919- *IntMPA 92, Who 92*
**Todd**, Richard Andrew Palethorpe 1919- *IntWW 91*
**Todd**, Robin Grenville 1948- *AmMWSc 92*
**Todd**, Ron *WhoAmP 91, WhoIns 92*
**Todd**, Ronald 1927- *IntWW 91, Who 92*
**Todd**, Stephan K. 1945- *WhoAmL 92*
**Todd**, Stephen Max 1941- *WhoAmL 92*
**Todd**, Ted Ralph 1939- *WhoAmL 92*
**Todd**, Terry Ray 1947- *AmMWSc 92*
**Todd**, Theodora *DrAPF 91*
**Todd**, Thomas Edward 1953- *WhoAmL 92*
**Todd**, Thomas N. 1938- *WhoBlA 92*
**Todd**, Thomas W 1927- *WhoAmP 91*
**Todd**, Virgil Holcomb 1921- *WhoRel 92*
**Todd**, Wilbert R *AmMWSc 92*
**Todd**, William Armstrong, Jr. 1949- *WhoMW 92*
**Todd**, William Judson 1928- *WhoAmP 91*
**Todd**, William McClintock 1925- *AmMWSc 92*
**Todd**, William S. 1940- *WhoBlA 92*
**Todd**, Zane Grey 1924- *WhoMW 92*
**Todd Copley**, Judith Ann 1950- *WhoMW 92*
**Todea**, Alexandru 1912- *WhoRel 92*
**Todeschi**, Joseph L. 1935- *WhoWest 92*
**Todhunter**, Elizabeth Neige 1901- *AmMWSc 92*
**Todhunter**, John Anthony 1949- *AmMWSc 92, WhoAmP 91*
**Todman**, Howard 1920- *IntMPA 92*
**Todman**, Jureen Francis 1935- *WhoBlA 92*
**Todman**, Terence A 1926- *WhoAmP 91, WhoBlA 92*
**Todorov**, Stanko 1920- *IntWW 91*
**Todrank**, Robert Lee 1950- *WhoEnt 92*
**Todreas**, Neil Emmanuel 1935- *AmMWSc 92*
**Todsen**, Thomas Kamp 1918- *AmMWSc 92, WhoWest 92*
**Todt**, Fritz 1891-1942 *BiDExR, EncTR 91 [port]*
**Todt**, William Lynn 1954- *AmMWSc 92*
**Toedman**, Gordon Reed, Jr. 1961- *WhoFI 92*
**Toegemann**, Alfred C *WhoIns 92*
**Toelle**, Richard Alan 1949- *WhoWest 92*
**Toenges**, Rolland Carlyle 1934- *WhoMW 92*
**Toeniskoetter**, Richard Henry 1931- *AmMWSc 92*
**Toennies**, Jan Peter 1930- *AmMWSc 92, IntWW 91*
**Toenniessen**, Gary Herbert 1944- *AmMWSc 92*
**Toensing**, C H 1915- *AmMWSc 92*
**Toepfer**, Alan James 1941- *AmMWSc 92*
**Toepfer**, Richard E, Jr 1934- *AmMWSc 92*
**Toepke**, Utz Peter 1940- *WhoAmL 92*
**Toeplitz**, Gideon 1944- *WhoEnt 92*
**Toeplitz**, Jerzy 1909- *IntWW 91*
**Toeppe**, William Joseph, Jr 1931- *WhoWest 92*
**Toerner**, David Paul 1963- *WhoMW 92*
**Toetz**, Dale W 1937- *AmMWSc 92*
**Toews**, Arrel Dwayne 1948- *AmMWSc 92*
**Toews**, Cornelius J 1937- *AmMWSc 92*
**Toews**, Daniel Peter 1941- *AmMWSc 92*
**Tofaute**, George Burton 1938- *WhoMW 92*
**Tofe**, Andrew John 1940- *AmMWSc 92*
**Tofel**, Richard Jeffrey 1957- *WhoAmL 92*
**Toffel**, George Mathias 1911- *AmMWSc 92*
**Toffler**, Alvin 1928- *IntAu&W 91, WrDr 92*
**Tofias**, Allan 1930- *WhoFI 92*
**Toft**, Albert 1862-1949 *TwCPaSc*
**Toft**, Anthony Douglas 1944- *Who 92*
**Toft**, John 1933- *IntAu&W 91, WrDr 92*
**Tofteland**, Curt L. 1952- *WhoEnt 92*
**Toftner**, Richard Orville 1935- *WhoFI 92, WhoMW 92*
**Toftness**, Cecil Gillman 1920- *WhoAmL 92, WhoFI 92, WhoWest 92*
**Toftoy**, Holger N 1902-1967 *FacFETw*
**Togafa**, Malaetasi *WhoAmL 92*
**Togafau**, Malaetasi *WhoAmP 91*
**Togafau**, Malaetasi Mauga 1946- *WhoAmL 92*
**Toganivalu**, Josua Brown 1930- *Who 92*
**Togasaki**, Robert K 1932- *AmMWSc 92*
**Togerson**, John Dennis 1939- *WhoWest 92*
**Toggweiler**, John William 1957- *WhoFI 92*
**Toglia**, Joseph U 1927- *AmMWSc 92*
**Togliatti**, Palmiro 1893?-1964 *ConAu 133*
**Tognacci**, Eugene 1929- *WhoEnt 92*
**Tognacci**, Gene, Jr. 1954- *WhoEnt 92*
**Tognarelli**, Richard Lee 1949- *WhoMW 92*
**Tognetti**, Janet 1957- *WhoFI 92*
**Tognoli**, Carlo 1938- *IntWW 91*
**Tognozzi**, Olando 1927- *WhoEnt 92*
**Togo**, Yukiyasu 1924- *WhoWest 92*
**Toguri**, James M 1930- *AmMWSc 92*
**Toh Chin Chye** 1921- *IntWW 91, Who 92*
**Toh**, Joseph Chin Soo 1938- *WhoRel 92*
**Tohill**, Jim Barnette 1947- *WhoAmL 92*
**Tohline**, Joel Edward 1953- *AmMWSc 92*
**Toht**, David Warren 1949- *WhoRel 92*
**Tohver**, Hanno Tiit 1935- *AmMWSc 92*
**Toida**, Saburo *IntWW 91*
**Toida**, Shunichi 1937- *AmMWSc 92*
**Toirac**, Margarita *WhoHisp 92*
**Toirac**, Seth Thomas 1951- *WhoMW 92*
**Toivo**, Andimba Toivo ja 1924- *IntWW 91*
**Toivola**, Pertti Toivo Kalevi 1946- *AmMWSc 92*
**Tojo**, Hideki 1884-1948 *FacFETw [port]*
**Tojo**, Kakuji *AmMWSc 92*
**Tokach**, Richard M *WhoAmP 91*
**Tokar**, Bette Lewis 1935- *WhoFI 92*
**Tokar**, Daniel 1937- *WhoWest 92*
**Tokar**, Edward 1923- *WhoMW 92*
**Tokar**, Edward Thomas, Jr. 1947- *WhoFI 92*
**Tokar**, Gloria Joyce 1941- *WhoAmP 91*
**Tokar**, Michael 1937- *AmMWSc 92*
**Tokarczyk**, Michelle M. *DrAPF 91*
**Tokarev**, Aleksandr Maksimovich 1921- *IntWW 91*
**Tokasz**, Paul 1946- *WhoAmP 91*
**Tokaty**, Grigori Alexandrovich *Who 92*
**Tokay**, Elbert 1916- *AmMWSc 92*
**Tokay**, F Harry 1936- *AmMWSc 92*
**Tokayer**, Marvin 1936- *WhoRel 92*
**Tokei**, Ferenc 1930- *IntWW 91*
**Tokes**, Laszlo 1952- *IntWW 91*
**Tokes**, Laszlo Gyula 1937- *AmMWSc 92*
**Tokes**, Zoltan Andras 1940- *AmMWSc 92*
**Tokioka**, Franklin M 1936- *WhoIns 92*
**Tokioka**, Franklin Makoto 1936- *WhoFI 92*
**Tokita**, Noboru 1923- *AmMWSc 92*
**Toklas**, Alice B. 1877-1967 *BenetAL 91, HanAmWH*
**Tokle**, Robert John 1957- *WhoFI 92*
**Tokley**, Joanna Nutter *WhoBlA 92*
**Tokmakoff**, George 1928- *WhoWest 92*
**Tokody**, Ilona *IntWW 91*
**Tokofsky**, Jerry H. 1936- *IntMPA 92*
**Tokofsky**, Jerry Herbert 1936- *WhoWest 92*
**Tokoli**, Emery G 1923- *AmMWSc 92*
**Tokombayeva**, Aysylu Asanbekovna 1947- *IntWW 91*
**Toksoz**, Mehmet Nafi 1934- *AmMWSc 92*
**Tokuda**, Sei 1930- *AmMWSc 92*
**Tokuhata**, George K 1924- *AmMWSc 92*
**Tokunaga**, Alan Takashi 1949- *AmMWSc 92*
**Tokunaga**, Emiko 1939- *WhoEnt 92*
**Tokuyasu**, Kiyoteru 1925- *AmMWSc 92*
**Tokyo Rose** 1916- *FacFETw*
**Tol Saut** *IntWW 91*
**Tol**, Peter J 1935- *WhoIns 92*
**Tolan**, David J. 1927- *WhoAmL 92, WhoFI 92*
**Tolan**, Stephanie S. *DrAPF 91*
**Tolan**, Stephanie S. 1942- *ConAu 34NR*
**Tolan**, Thomas Edward 1908-1967 *BlkOlyM [port]*
**Toland**, Frederick Morgan 1939- *WhoWest 92*
**Toland**, John 1670-1722 *BlkwCEP*
**Toland**, John 1912- *WrDr 92*
**Toland**, John Robert 1944- *WhoAmL 92*
**Toland**, John Willard 1912- *WhoEnt 92*
**Tolansky**, Ottilie 1912-1977 *TwCPaSc*
**Tolar**, Billy Joe 1948- *WhoEnt 92*
**Tolba**, Mostafa Kamal 1922- *IntWW 91*
**Tolbert**, Amy Sue Schroeder 1964- *WhoMW 92*
**Tolbert**, Bert Mills 1921- *AmMWSc 92*
**Tolbert**, Bruce Edward 1948- *WhoBlA 92*
**Tolbert**, Charles Ray 1936- *AmMWSc 92*
**Tolbert**, Daniel Lee 1946- *AmMWSc 92*
**Tolbert**, Edward T. 1929- *WhoBlA 92*
**Tolbert**, Frank X. 1912-1984 *TwCWW 91*
**Tolbert**, Gene Edward 1925- *AmMWSc 92*
**Tolbert**, Herman Andre 1948- *WhoBlA 92*
**Tolbert**, Jacquelyn C. 1947- *WhoBlA 92*
**Tolbert**, John W., Jr. 1905- *WhoBlA 92*
**Tolbert**, Laren Malcolm 1949- *AmMWSc 92*
**Tolbert**, Lawrence J. 1914- *WhoBlA 92*
**Tolbert**, Margaret Ellen Mayo 1943- *AmMWSc 92*
**Tolbert**, Nathan Edward 1919- *AmMWSc 92*
**Tolbert**, Odie Henderson, Jr. 1939- *WhoBlA 92*
**Tolbert**, Robert John 1928- *AmMWSc 92*
**Tolbert**, Sharon Renee 1945- *WhoBlA 92*
**Tolbert**, Thomas Warren 1945- *AmMWSc 92*
**Tolbert**, Tommy *WhoAmP 91*
**Tolbert**, Tony Lewis 1967- *WhoBlA 92*
**Tolbert**, Virginia Rose 1948- *AmMWSc 92*
**Tolden**, Verna L 1935- *WhoAmP 91*
**Tolderlund**, Douglas Stanley 1939- *AmMWSc 92*
**Tole**, John Roy 1945- *AmMWSc 92*
**Toledano**, Joseph C. 1934- *WhoRel 92*
**Toledano**, Ralph de 1916- *WrDr 92*
**Toledo**, Angel D. *WhoHisp 92*
**Toledo**, Christopher L. 1960- *WhoHisp 92*
**Toledo**, Domingo 1945- *AmMWSc 92*
**Toledo**, Elizabeth Anne 1962- *WhoHisp 92*
**Toledo**, Jesefino Chino 1959- *WhoEnt 92*
**Toledo**, Lawrence Ralph 1941- *WhoHisp 92*
**Toledo**, Nelida Rivera 1960- *WhoMW 92*
**Toledo**, Robert Anthony 1942- *WhoHisp 92*
**Toledo**, Romeo Trance 1941- *AmMWSc 92*
**Toledo-Feria**, Freya M. 1960- *WhoHisp 92*
**Toledo-Pereyra**, Luis Horacio 1943- *AmMWSc 92*
**Toledo y Figueroa**, Francisco Alvarez de 1515?-1582 *HisDSpE*
**Tolentino**, Casimiro Urbano 1949- *WhoWest 92*
**Tolentino**, Shirley A. 1943- *WhoBlA 92*
**Toler** *Who 92*
**Toler**, Burl Abron 1928- *WhoBlA 92*
**Toler**, David Arthur Hodges 1920- *Who 92*
**Toler**, Desmond Burton 1941- *WhoRel 92*
**Toler**, J C 1936- *AmMWSc 92*
**Toler**, Robert William 1928- *AmMWSc 92*
**Tolerico**, Michael Anthony 1952- *WhoEnt 92*
**Toles**, Alvin 1963- *WhoBlA 92*
**Toles**, Edward Bernard 1909- *WhoAmL 92, WhoBlA 92*
**Toles**, Elwin Bonds 1916- *WhoAmP 91*
**Toles**, James LaFayette, Jr. 1933- *WhoBlA 92*
**Toles**, Mason Jeremy 1942- *WhoAmL 92*
**Toles**, Thomas G 1951- *IntAu&W 91*
**Tolgyesi**, Eva *AmMWSc 92*
**Tolin**, Sue Ann 1938- *AmMWSc 92*
**Toline**, Francis Raymond 1918- *AmMWSc 92*
**Tolisano**, Vincent Paul 1960- *WhoAmL 92*
**Toliver**, Adolphus P 1931- *AmMWSc 92*
**Toliver**, Harold E 1932- *ConAu 34NR*
**Toliver**, Harold Eugene, Jr. 1944- *WhoBlA 92*
**Toliver**, Lee 1921- *WhoWest 92*
**Toliver**, Michael Edward 1949- *AmMWSc 92*
**Toliver**, Raymond F. 1914- *ConAu 35NR*
**Toliver**, Raymond Frederick 1914- *WrDr 92*
**Toliver**, Richard T 1930- *WhoAmP 91*
**Toliver**, Virginia F. 1948- *WhoBlA 92*
**Toliver**, William Henry, Sr. 1925- *WhoBlA 92*
**Tolk**, Norman Henry 1938- *AmMWSc 92*
**Tolkachev**, Vitaly Antonovich 1934- *IntWW 91*
**Tolkan**, James 1931- *IntMPA 92*
**Tolkien**, J. R. R. 1892-1973 *CnDBLB 6 [port], ConAu 36NR, RfGEnL 91, TwCSFW 91*
**Tolkien**, John R R 1892-1973 *FacFETw*
**Tolkowsky**, Marcel d1991 *NewYTBS 91*
**Toll**, Charles Hulbert 1931- *WhoWest 92*
**Toll**, Daniel Roger 1927- *WhoFI 92*
**Toll**, John Sampson 1923- *AmMWSc 92*
**Toll**, Maynard Joy, Jr. 1942- *WhoFI 92*
**Toll**, Perry Mark 1945- *WhoAmL 92*
**Toll**, Robert Charles 1938- *WrDr 92*
**Toll**, Seymour I. 1925- *WhoAmL 92*
**Tolle**, Jon Wright 1939- *AmMWSc 92*
**Tollefsen**, John Jacob 1950- *WhoAmL 92*
**Tollefson**, Ben 1927- *WhoAmP 91*
**Tollefson**, Charles Ivar 1918- *AmMWSc 92*
**Tollefson**, Eric Lars 1921- *AmMWSc 92*
**Tollefson**, Jeffrey L 1942- *AmMWSc 92*
**Tollefson**, John Oliver 1937- *WhoFI 92*
**Tollefson**, Robert John 1927- *WhoRel 92*
**Tollefsrud-Anderson**, Linda Adele 1954- *WhoMW 92*
**Tollemache** *Who 92*
**Tollemache**, Baron 1939- *Who 92*
**Tollemache**, Cedric Reginald 1944- *WhoFI 92*
**Tollemache**, Lyonel 1931- *Who 92*
**Tollenaere**, Lawrence Robert 1922- *WhoFI 92*
**Tollenaere**, Reimond 1909-1942 *BiDExR*
**Toller**, Ernst 1893-1939 *EncTR 91 [port], FacFETw, LiExTwC*
**Toller**, Gary Neil 1950- *AmMWSc 92*
**Toller**, William Robert 1930- *WhoFI 92*
**Tollerud**, Jim *DrAPF 91*
**Tollerud**, Toni Rae 1946- *WhoMW 92*
**Tolles**, Robert Bruce 1825?-1883 *BiInAmS*
**Tolles**, Walter Edwin 1916- *AmMWSc 92*
**Tolles**, William Marshall 1937- *AmMWSc 92*
**Tolleson**, Frederic Leroy 1932- *WhoFI 92*
**Tolleson**, James E *WhoAmP 91*
**Tollestrup**, Alvin V 1924- *AmMWSc 92*
**Tollett**, Charles Albert *WhoBlA 92*
**Tollett**, Glenna Belle 1913- *WhoFI 92*
**Tolley**, Edward Donald 1950- *WhoAmL 92*
**Tolley**, George 1925- *Who 92*
**Tolley**, John Stewart 1953- *WhoWest 92*
**Tolley**, Leslie John 1913- *Who 92*
**Tollin**, Gordon 1930- *AmMWSc 92*
**Tollison**, Grady Franklin, Jr 1937- *WhoAmP 91*
**Tollison**, Robert Lee 1959- *WhoRel 92*
**Tolliver**, James David, Jr. 1938- *WhoWest 92*
**Tolliver**, Joel 1946- *WhoBlA 92*
**Tolliver**, Kevin Paul 1951- *WhoMW 92*
**Tolliver**, Lennie-Marie P. 1928- *WhoBlA 92*
**Tolliver**, Ned, Jr. 1943- *WhoBlA 92*
**Tolliver**, Nila Mozingo 1928- *WhoRel 92*
**Tolliver**, Richard Lamar 1945- *WhoBlA 92*
**Tolliver**, Ruby C. *DrAPF 91*
**Tolliver**, Stanley Eugene, Sr. 1925- *WhoBlA 92*
**Tolliver**, Thomas C., Jr. 1950- *WhoBlA 92*
**Tolliver-Oddo**, Debra H. 1960- *WhoFI 92*
**Tollman**, James Perry 1904- *AmMWSc 92*
**Tolmach**, Jane Louise 1921- *WhoAmP 91*
**Tolmach**, L J 1923- *AmMWSc 92*
**Tolman**, Chadwick Alma 1938- *AmMWSc 92*
**Tolman**, Edward Laurie 1942- *AmMWSc 92*
**Tolman**, Gareth W 1938- *WhoIns 92*
**Tolman**, Richard Lee 1941- *AmMWSc 92*
**Tolman**, Robert Alexander 1924- *AmMWSc 92*
**Tolman**, Suzanne Nelson 1931- *WhoMW 92*

**Tolman,** Warren E *WhoAmP 91*
**Tolman,** William H 1861-1932 *DcAmImH*
**Tolnai,** Susan 1928- *AmMWSc 92*
**Tolo,** Paul Gudvin 1925- *WhoRel 92*
**Toloa,** Letuli 1930- *WhoAmP 91*
**Tololo,** Alkan *Who 92*
**Tolpin,** Richard William 1943- *WhoAmP 91*
**Tolpo,** Carolyn Lee Mary 1940- *WhoWest 92*
**Tolpo,** Vincent Carl 1950- *WhoWest 92*
**Tolsa,** Manuel 1757-1815 *HisDSpE*
**Tolsma,** Jacob 1923- *AmMWSc 92*
**Tolson,** John J., III d1991 *NewYTBS 91 [port]*
**Tolson,** Jon Hart 1939- *WhoWest 92*
**Tolson,** Melvin 1898-1966 *AfrAmW*
**Tolson,** Melvin B. 1898?-1966 *BenetAL 91, BlkLC [port]*
**Tolson,** Robert Heath 1935- *AmMWSc 92*
**Tolstaya,** Tatyana 1951- *IntAu&W 91*
**Tolstead,** William Lawrence 1909- *AmMWSc 92*
**Tolsted,** Elmer Beaumont 1920- *AmMWSc 92*
**Tolstoi,** Alexei Nikolaievich 1882-1945 *ScFEYrs*
**Tolstoy,** Aleksey Nikolaevich 1883-1945 *SovUnBD*
**Tolstoy,** Aleksey Nikolayevich 1883-1945 *FacFETw [port]*
**Tolstoy,** Alexey 1882-1945 *TwCSFW 91A*
**Tolstoy,** Dimitry 1912- *Who 92*
**Tolstoy,** Ivan 1923- *AmMWSc 92*
**Tolstoy,** Leo 1828-1910 *ShSCr 9 [port], TwCLC 44 [port]*
**Tolstykh,** Boris Leont'evich 1936- *SovUnBD*
**Tolstykh,** Boris Leontyevich 1935- *IntWW 91*
**Tolton,** Augustine 1854-1897 *RelLAm 91*
**Tolubko,** Vladimir Fedorovich 1914- *SovUnBD*
**Tolzmann,** Arlyn L. 1943- *WhoRel 92*
**Tolzmann,** Don Heinrich 1945- *WhoMW 92*
**Tom,** Allen Webster Wah-Hon 1952- *WhoAmL 92*
**Tom,** Baldwin Heng 1940- *AmMWSc 92*
**Tom,** C.Y. 1907- *IntMPA 92*
**Tom,** Clarence Yung Chen 1927- *WhoWest 92*
**Tom,** Creighton Harvey 1944- *WhoWest 92*
**Tom,** Glenn McPherson 1949- *AmMWSc 92*
**Tom,** Jack Mung 1950- *WhoEnt 92*
**Tom,** James Leroy 1945- *WhoRel 92*
**Tom,** James Robert 1939- *WhoFI 92*
**Tom,** Lawrence 1950- *WhoWest 92*
**Tom,** Terrance W H 1948- *WhoAmP 91*
**Toma,** David Anthony 1949- *WhoEnt 92*
**Toma,** Maiava Iulai 1940- *IntWW 91*
**Toma,** Ramses Barsoum 1938- *AmMWSc 92*
**Tomac,** Steven W 1953- *WhoAmP 91*
**Tomaino,** Joseph Carmine 1948- *WhoMW 92*
**Tomaja,** David Louis 1946- *AmMWSc 92*
**Tomalia,** Donald Andrew 1938- *AmMWSc 92*
**Tomalin,** Claire 1933- *Who 92, WrDr 92*
**Tomalin,** Ruth *IntAu&W 91, WrDr 92*
**Toman,** Frank R 1939- *AmMWSc 92*
**Toman,** Henry Edward 1944- *WhoAmP 91*
**Toman,** Karel 1924- *AmMWSc 92*
**Toman,** Kurt 1921- *AmMWSc 92*
**Toman,** Michael Allen 1954- *WhoFI 92*
**Toman,** Michael J *WhoIns 92*
**Toman,** William Joseph 1956- *WhoAmL 92*
**Toman-Cubbage,** Cheryl Ann 1956- *WhoAmL 92*
**Tomana,** Milan 1932- *AmMWSc 92*
**Tomanek,** Gerald Wayne 1921- *AmMWSc 92*
**Tomany,** Mark Allen 1955- *WhoMW 92*
**Tomar,** Richard Thomas 1945- *WhoAmL 92*
**Tomar,** Russell H 1937- *AmMWSc 92*
**Tomarchio,** Jack Thomas 1955- *WhoAmL 92*
**Tomarelli,** Rudolph Michael 1917- *AmMWSc 92*
**Tomas,** Francisco 1930- *AmMWSc 92*
**Tomas,** Harry A. 1945- *WhoHisp 92*
**Tomasch,** Walter J 1930- *AmMWSc 92*
**Tomaschke,** Harry E 1929- *AmMWSc 92*
**Tomaschke,** John Edward 1949- *WhoWest 92*
**Tomasek,** Frantisek 1899- *IntWW 91, WhoRel 92*
**Tomasek,** Vaclav Jan Krtitel 1774-1850 *NewAmDM*
**Tomaselli,** Vincent Paul 1941- *AmMWSc 92*
**Tomasetta,** Louis Ralph 1948- *AmMWSc 92*
**Tomashefski,** Joseph Francis 1922- *AmMWSc 92*
**Tomashefsky,** Philip 1924- *AmMWSc 92*
**Tomashevich,** George Vid 1927- *ConAu 133*
**Tomashevsky,** Boris Viktorovich 1890-1957 *SovUnBD*
**Tomasi,** Gordon Ernest 1930- *AmMWSc 92*
**Tomasi,** Henri 1901-1971 *NewAmDM*
**Tomasi,** Thomas B, Jr 1927- *AmMWSc 92*
**Tomasi,** Thomas Edward 1955- *AmMWSc 92*
**Tomasini,** Luigi 1741-1808 *NewAmDM*
**Tomasini,** Roberto Jorge 1929- *IntWW 91*
**Tomasovic,** Stephen Peter 1947- *AmMWSc 92*
**Tomass,** Mark Kharpoutly 1961- *WhoFI 92*
**Tomassini,** Lawrence Anthony 1945- *WhoFI 92*
**Tomasson,** Helgi 1942- *WhoEnt 92, WhoWest 92*
**Tomasson,** Tomas Armann 1929- *IntWW 91*
**Tomasson,** Verna Safran *DrAPF 91*
**Tomasz,** Alexander 1930- *AmMWSc 92*
**Tomasz,** Maria 1932- *AmMWSc 92*
**Tomaszewska,** Marta 1933- *IntAu&W 91*
**Tomaszewski,** Henryk 1919- *IntWW 91*
**Tomaszewski,** Marian Edna 1935- *WhoAmP 91*
**Tomback,** Diana Francine 1949- *AmMWSc 92*
**Tombalakian,** Artin S 1929- *AmMWSc 92*
**Tombaugh,** Clyde W 1906- *AmMWSc 92*
**Tombaugh,** Clyde William 1906- *FacFETw, IntWW 91*
**Tombaugh,** Larry William 1939- *AmMWSc 92*
**Tombaugh,** Richard Franklin 1932- *WhoRel 92*
**Tombaugh,** Wayne H 1910- *WhoAmP 91*
**Tombazian,** Charles Michael 1951- *WhoFI 92*
**Tomber,** Marvin L 1925- *AmMWSc 92*
**Tomberlin,** Charles E. 1966- *WhoRel 92*
**Tombes,** Averett S 1932- *AmMWSc 92*
**Tombes,** Averett Snead 1932- *WhoWest 92*
**Tombesi,** Terry Allen 1947- *WhoEnt 92*
**Tomblin,** Earl Ray 1952- *WhoAmP 91*
**Tomboulian,** Paul 1934- *AmMWSc 92*
**Tombrello,** Thomas Anthony, Jr 1936- *AmMWSc 92*
**Tombs** *Who 92*
**Tombs,** Baron 1924- *IntWW 91, Who 92*
**Tombs,** Leroy Cleveland 1921- *WhoBlA 92*
**Tombs,** Sarah 1961- *TwCPaSc*
**Tomcheff,** Erin Jean 1932- *WhoEnt 92*
**Tomcisin,** Theresa Ann 1960- *WhoMW 92*
**Tomcufcik,** Andrew Stephen 1921- *AmMWSc 92*
**Tomei,** L David 1945- *AmMWSc 92*
**Tomeny,** Lynne Johnson 1945- *WhoAmL 92*
**Tomeo,** Thomas P 1911- *WhoAmP 91*
**Tomer,** Kenneth Beamer 1944- *AmMWSc 92*
**Tomes,** Dwight Travis 1946- *AmMWSc 92*
**Tomes,** Henry, Jr. 1932- *WhoBlA 92*
**Tomes,** Margot d1991 *NewYTBS 91*
**Tomes,** Mark Louis 1917- *AmMWSc 92*
**Tometsko,** Andrew M 1938- *AmMWSc 92*
**Tomeu,** Enrique J. *WhoHisp 92*
**Tomezsko,** Edward Stephen John 1935- *AmMWSc 92*
**Tomfohrde,** Heinn F., III *WhoFI 92*
**Tomhon,** Peter Martin 1963- *WhoMW 92*
**Tomic,** Ernst Alois 1926- *AmMWSc 92*
**Tomich,** Charles Edward 1937- *AmMWSc 92, WhoMW 92*
**Tomich,** John Matthew 1952- *AmMWSc 92*
**Tomich,** Lillian 1935- *WhoAmL 92, WhoFI 92*
**Tomich,** Prosper Quentin 1920- *AmMWSc 92*
**Tomich,** Walter Joseph 1959- *WhoFI 92*
**Tomicich,** Helen Espinoza 1944- *WhoHisp 92*
**Tomick,** David P. 1952- *WhoEnt 92, WhoFI 92*
**Tomikel,** John 1928- *AmMWSc 92*
**Tominaga,** Lynn S *WhoAmP 91*
**Tominomori,** Eiji 1928- *IntWW 91*
**Tomita,** Joseph Tsuneki 1938- *AmMWSc 92*
**Tomita,** Tadanori 1945- *WhoMW 92*
**Tomita,** Tatsuo 1939- *AmMWSc 92*
**Tomiyasu,** Kiyo 1919- *AmMWSc 92*
**Tomizuka,** Carl Tatsuo 1923- *AmMWSc 92*
**Tomkiel,** Judith Irene 1949- *IntAu&W 91, WhoFI 92*
**Tomkies,** Douglas Simpson 1928- *WhoIns 92*
**Tomkiewicz,** Micha 1939- *AmMWSc 92*
**Tomkins,** Ann Marie 1962- *WhoAmL 92*
**Tomkins,** Calvin 1925- *WrDr 92*
**Tomkins,** Edward Emile 1915- *Who 92*
**Tomkins,** Frank Sargent 1915- *AmMWSc 92*
**Tomkins,** Jasper 1946- *WrDr 92*
**Tomkins,** Marion Louise 1926- *AmMWSc 92*
**Tomkins,** Oliver S. 1908- *DcEcMov*
**Tomkins,** Oliver Stratford 1908- *IntWW 91, Who 92, WrDr 92*
**Tomkins,** Ridnan 1941- *TwCPaSc*
**Tomkins,** Robert James 1945- *AmMWSc 92*
**Tomkins,** Silvan Samuel d1991 *NewYTBS 91*
**Tomkins,** Thomas 1572-1656 *NewAmDM*
**Tomkinson,** John Stanley 1916- *IntWW 91, Who 92*
**Tomkiw,** Lydia *DrAPF 91*
**Tomko,** Jozef 1924- *IntWW 91, WhoRel 92*
**Tomkowit,** Thaddeus W 1918- *AmMWSc 92*
**Tomkys,** Roger 1937- *Who 92*
**Tomkys,** W. Roger 1937- *IntWW 91*
**Tomlin,** Alan David 1944- *AmMWSc 92*
**Tomlin,** Don C 1932- *AmMWSc 92*
**Tomlin,** Donald Reid 1933- *WhoFI 92*
**Tomlin,** Josephine D. 1952- *WhoBlA 92*
**Tomlin,** Lily 1939- *IntMPA 92, WhoEnt 92*
**Tomlin,** Stephen 1901-1937 *TwCPaSc*
**Tomlinson,** Alan 1944- *WhoWest 92*
**Tomlinson,** Alfred Charles 1927- *Who 92*
**Tomlinson,** Ambrose Jessup 1865-1943 *RelLAm 91*
**Tomlinson,** Arthur *NewAmDM*
**Tomlinson,** Bernard 1920- *Who 92*
**Tomlinson,** Bill *WhoAmP 91*
**Tomlinson,** Charles *Who 92*
**Tomlinson,** Charles 1927- *ConPo 91, IntAu&W 91, WrDr 92*
**Tomlinson,** David 1917- *Who 92, WhoEnt 92*
**Tomlinson,** David L 1929- *WhoAmP 91*
**Tomlinson,** E. T. 1859-1931 *BenetAL 91*
**Tomlinson,** Everett Parsons 1914- *AmMWSc 92*
**Tomlinson,** Frank Stanley 1912- *Who 92*
**Tomlinson,** George Herbert 1912- *AmMWSc 92*
**Tomlinson,** Gerald 1933- *IntAu&W 91*
**Tomlinson,** Geraldine Ann 1931- *AmMWSc 92*
**Tomlinson,** Harley 1932- *AmMWSc 92*
**Tomlinson,** Harry 1943- *ConAu 135*
**Tomlinson,** Herbert Weston 1930- *WhoAmL 92*
**Tomlinson,** Homer Aubrey 1893-1968 *RelLAm 91*
**Tomlinson,** Jack Trish 1929- *AmMWSc 92*
**Tomlinson,** James Everett 1942- *AmMWSc 92*
**Tomlinson,** John 1946- *IntWW 91, Who 92*
**Tomlinson,** John D 1929- *WhoAmP 91*
**Tomlinson,** John Edward 1939- *Who 92*
**Tomlinson,** John Lashier 1935- *AmMWSc 92*
**Tomlinson,** John Michael 1949- *WhoFI 92*
**Tomlinson,** John Race Godfrey 1932- *Who 92*
**Tomlinson,** Joseph Bradley 1944- *WhoFI 92*
**Tomlinson,** Margaret Lynch 1929- *WhoAmL 92*
**Tomlinson,** Mary Teresa 1935- *IntAu&W 91*
**Tomlinson,** Mel Alexander 1954- *IntWW 91, WhoBlA 92*
**Tomlinson,** Michael 1929- *AmMWSc 92*
**Tomlinson,** Michael James 1958- *WhoFI 92, WhoMW 92*
**Tomlinson,** Michael John 1929- *Who 92*
**Tomlinson,** Michael John 1942- *Who 92*
**Tomlinson,** Milton Ambrose 1906- *WhoRel 92*
**Tomlinson,** Percy Charwood, Jr. 1962- *WhoFI 92*
**Tomlinson,** Philip Barry 1932- *AmMWSc 92*
**Tomlinson,** Randolph R. 1920- *WhoBlA 92*
**Tomlinson,** Rawdon *DrAPF 91*
**Tomlinson,** Raymond Valentine 1927- *AmMWSc 92*
**Tomlinson,** Richard Allan 1932- *Who 92*
**Tomlinson,** Richard Howden 1923- *AmMWSc 92*
**Tomlinson,** Robert 1938- *WhoBlA 92*
**Tomlinson,** Robert Eugene 1931- *WhoWest 92*
**Tomlinson,** Robert M 1945- *WhoAmP 91*
**Tomlinson,** Stanley *Who 92*
**Tomlinson,** Stephen Miles 1952- *Who 92*
**Tomlinson,** Walter John, III 1938- *AmMWSc 92*
**Tomlinson,** William Holmes 1922- *WhoFI 92*
**Tomlinson,** William Lee 1939- *WhoRel 92*
**Tomlinson-Keasey,** Carol Ann 1942- *WhoWest 92*
**Tomljanovich,** Esther *WhoAmP 91*
**Tomljanovich,** Nicholas Matthew 1939- *AmMWSc 92*
**Tomlonson,** John Dean 1929- *WhoRel 92*
**Tomlonson,** Mark Eugene 1954- *WhoEnt 92*
**Tommasini,** Vincenzo 1878-1950 *NewAmDM*
**Tommasone,** Dennis William 1943- *WhoMW 92*
**Tommerdahl,** James B 1926- *AmMWSc 92*
**Tomoe,** Gozen *EncAmaz 91*
**Tomomatsu,** Hideo 1929- *AmMWSc 92, WhoMW 92*
**Tomonaga,** Shinichiro 1906-1979 *WhoNob 90*
**Tomonto,** James R 1932- *AmMWSc 92*
**Tomos** 1932- *IntWW 91*
**Tomov,** George Ivan 1933- *WhoEnt 92*
**Tomowa-Sintow,** Anna 1941- *WhoEnt 92*
**Tomowa-Sintow,** Anna 1943- *IntWW 91*
**Tomozawa,** Yukio 1929- *AmMWSc 92*
**Tompa,** Albert S 1931- *AmMWSc 92*
**Tompa,** Frank William 1948- *AmMWSc 92*
**Tompert,** James Emil 1954- *WhoAmL 92*
**Tompkin,** Gervaise William 1924- *AmMWSc 92*
**Tompkin,** Robert Bruce 1937- *AmMWSc 92*
**Tompkins,** Curtis Johnston 1942- *AmMWSc 92*
**Tompkins,** Daniel D. 1774-1825 *AmPolLe*
**Tompkins,** Daniel Reuben 1931- *AmMWSc 92*
**Tompkins,** David Eugene 1956- *WhoFI 92*
**Tompkins,** Donald Robert 1941- *WhoFI 92*
**Tompkins,** Donald Roy, Jr 1932- *AmMWSc 92*
**Tompkins,** Eileen J 1933- *WhoAmP 91*
**Tompkins,** Frederick Clifford 1910- *IntWW 91, Who 92*
**Tompkins,** George Jonathan 1944- *AmMWSc 92*
**Tompkins,** George Nelson, Jr. 1931- *WhoAmL 92*
**Tompkins,** Howard E 1922- *AmMWSc 92*
**Tompkins,** Joseph Buford, Jr. 1950- *WhoAmL 92*
**Tompkins,** Ralph Joel 1919- *IntAu&W 91*
**Tompkins,** Raymond Edgar 1934- *WhoAmL 92*
**Tompkins,** Richard 1918- *Who 92*
**Tompkins,** Robert Charles 1924- *AmMWSc 92*
**Tompkins,** Ronald K 1934- *AmMWSc 92*
**Tompkins,** Stephen Stern 1938- *AmMWSc 92*
**Tompkins,** Susie *WhoWest 92*
**Tompkins,** Victor Norman 1913- *AmMWSc 92*
**Tompkins,** Walker A 1909-1990? *TwCWW 91*
**Tompkins,** Willis Judson 1941- *AmMWSc 92*
**Tompsett,** Michael F 1939- *AmMWSc 92*
**Tompsett,** Ralph Raymond 1913- *AmMWSc 92*
**Tompson,** Benjamin 1642-1714 *BenetAL 91*
**Tompson,** Clifford Ware 1929- *AmMWSc 92*
**Tompson,** Robert Norman 1920- *AmMWSc 92*
**Toms,** Carl 1927- *Who 92*
**Toms,** Edward Ernest 1920- *Who 92*
**Toms-Robinson,** Dolores C. 1926- *WhoBlA 92*
**Tomsett,** Alan Jeffrey 1922- *Who 92*
**Tomsky,** Judy 1959- *WhoWest 92*
**Tomsky,** Mikhail Pavlovich 1880-1937 *SovUnBD*
**Tomsky,** Nikolay Vasil'evich 1900-1984 *SovUnBD*
**Tomson,** Mason Butler 1946- *AmMWSc 92*
**Tomur Dawamat** 1927- *IntWW 91*
**Tomusiak,** Edward Lawrence 1938- *AmMWSc 92*
**Tomyris** *EncAmaz 91*
**Ton,** Bui An 1937- *AmMWSc 92*
**Ton,** Josef 1934- *WhoRel 92*
**Ton-That Tiet** 1933- *ConCom 92*
**Ton-That,** Tuong 1943- *AmMWSc 92*
**Tonascia,** James A 1944- *AmMWSc 92*
**Tonbridge,** Archdeacon of *Who 92*
**Tonbridge,** Bishop Suffragan of 1929- *Who 92*
**Toncic-Sorinj,** Lujo 1915- *IntWW 91, Who 92*
**Tonda,** Richard Dale 1952- *WhoMW 92*
**Tondeur,** Philippe 1932- *AmMWSc 92*
**Tondeur,** Philippe Maurice 1932- *WhoMW 92*
**Tondra,** Richard John 1943- *AmMWSc 92*
**Tone,** James N 1933- *AmMWSc 92*

**Tone**, L. Gene 1934- *WhoRel 92*
**Tone**, Philip Willis 1923- *WhoAmL 92*
**Tone**, Yasunao *DrAPF 91*
**Tonegawa**, Susumu 1939- *AmMWSc 92, IntWW 91, Who 92, WhoNob 90*
**Tonelli**, Alan Edward 1942- *AmMWSc 92*
**Tonelli**, Edith Ann 1949- *WhoWest 92*
**Tonelli**, George 1921- *AmMWSc 92*
**Tonelli**, John P, Jr 1946- *AmMWSc 92*
**Tonello-Stuart**, Enrica Maria 1926- *WhoWest 92*
**Toner**, John Joseph 1915- *WhoAmL 92*
**Toner**, John Joseph 1955- *AmMWSc 92*
**Toner**, Richard K 1913- *AmMWSc 92*
**Toney**, Adam 1938- *WhoAmP 91*
**Toney**, Andrew 1957- *WhoBlA 92*
**Toney**, Anthony 1962- *WhoBlA 92*
**Toney**, Creola Sarah 1920- *WhoMW 92, WhoRel 92*
**Toney**, Edna 1914- *WhoEnt 92*
**Toney**, Glendall Ralph 1951- *WhoRel 92*
**Toney**, Joe David 1942- *AmMWSc 92*
**Toney**, Kelly Lynne Smith 1959- *WhoEnt 92*
**Toney**, Marcellus E, Jr 1920- *AmMWSc 92*
**Toney**, Mark Anthony 1959- *WhoRel 92*
**Toney**, Thomas Clifford 1958- *WhoRel 92*
**Tong**, Alex W 1952- *AmMWSc 92*
**Tong**, Bok Yin 1934- *AmMWSc 92*
**Tong**, Dalton Arlington 1950- *WhoBlA 92*
**Tong**, Far-Dung 1946- *WhoRel 92*
**Tong**, Gary S. 1942- *ConAu 135, SmATA 66*
**Tong**, James Ying-Peh 1926- *AmMWSc 92*
**Tong**, Long Sun 1915- *AmMWSc 92*
**Tong**, Mary Powderly 1924- *AmMWSc 92*
**Tong**, Pin 1937- *AmMWSc 92*
**Tong**, Raymond 1922- *WrDr 92*
**Tong**, Richard Dare 1930- *WhoWest 92*
**Tong**, Siu Wing 1950- *WhoWest 92*
**Tong**, Stephen S C 1936- *AmMWSc 92*
**Tong**, Theodore G 1942- *AmMWSc 92*
**Tong**, Winton 1927- *AmMWSc 92*
**Tong**, Yulan Chang 1935- *AmMWSc 92*
**Tong**, Yung Liang 1935- *AmMWSc 92*
**Tonga**, H M the King of 1918- *Who 92*
**Tonga**, King of *IntWW 91*
**Tongdonmuan**, Arun 1938- *WhoRel 92*
**Tonge**, Brian Lawrence 1933- *Who 92*
**Tonge**, Cecil Howard 1915- *Who 92*
**Tonge**, David Theophilus 1930- *Who 92*
**Tongue**, Carole 1955- *Who 92*
**Tongue**, James Melvin 1946- *WhoRel 92*
**Tongue**, Paul Graham 1932- *WhoFI 92*
**Tonick**, Illene 1951- *WhoWest 92*
**Tonidandel**, Ron 1933- *WhoAmL 92*
**Tonik**, Ellis J 1921- *AmMWSc 92*
**Tonini**, Leon Richard 1931- *WhoWest 92*
**Tonino**, Robert Henry 1944- *WhoFI 92*
**Tonjes**, Marian Jeannette Benton 1929- *WhoWest 92*
**Tonkens**, Solvin William 1919- *WhoMW 92*
**Tonkin**, David Oliver 1929- *IntWW 91, Who 92*
**Tonkin**, Derek 1929- *Who 92*
**Tonkin**, Peter Francis 1950- *WrDr 92*
**Tonking**, William Harry 1927- *AmMWSc 92*
**Tonko**, Paul 1949- *WhoAmP 91*
**Tonkovich**, Dan Richard 1946- *WhoAmP 91*
**Tonks**, David Bayard 1919- *AmMWSc 92*
**Tonks**, Davis Loel 1947- *AmMWSc 92*
**Tonks**, Henry 1862-1937 *TwCPaSc*
**Tonks**, Robert Stanley *AmMWSc 92*
**Tonkyn**, Richard George 1927- *AmMWSc 92*
**Tonn**, Martin Helmuth 1921- *WhoMW 92*
**Tonn**, Robert James 1927- *AmMWSc 92, WhoMW 92*
**Tonna**, Edgar Anthony 1928- *AmMWSc 92*
**Tonndorf**, Juergen 1914- *AmMWSc 92*
**Tonne**, Philip Charles 1938- *AmMWSc 92*
**Tonner**, Brian P 1953- *AmMWSc 92*
**Tonney**, Frederick Rodger 1926- *WhoFI 92*
**Tonnis**, John A 1939- *AmMWSc 92*
**Tonnos**, Anthony 1935- *WhoRel 92*
**Tonos Florenzan**, Fernando 1956- *WhoAmP 91*
**Tonry**, John Landis *AmMWSc 92*
**Tonsing**, Cecilia Ann Degnan 1943- *WhoRel 92*
**Tonti**, Henry 1650?-1704 *BenetAL 91*
**Tonty**, Henry 1650?-1704 *BenetAL 91*
**Tontz**, Jay Logan 1938- *WhoFI 92, WhoWest 92*
**Tonucci**, Vincent J *WhoAmP 91*
**Tonypandy**, Viscount 1909- *IntWW 91, Who 92*
**Tonzetich**, John 1941- *AmMWSc 92*
**Toobin**, Jerome d1984 *LesBEnT 92*
**Tooher**, Meave Marie 1959- *WhoAmL 92*
**Toohey**, Brian Frederick 1944- *WhoAmL 92, WhoMW 92*
**Toohey**, Edward Joseph 1930- *WhoFI 92*
**Toohey**, Jerome Vincent 1914- *WhoRel 92*
**Toohey**, Joyce 1917- *Who 92*
**Toohey**, Richard Edward 1945- *AmMWSc 92*
**Toohig**, Michael Francis 1924- *WhoFI 92*
**Toohig**, Timothy E 1928- *AmMWSc 92*
**Took**, John Michael Exton 1926- *Who 92*
**Tooke**, William Raymond, Jr 1925- *AmMWSc 92*
**Tooker**, Dick Presley *ScFEYrs*
**Tooker**, Edwin Wilson 1923- *AmMWSc 92*
**Tooker**, Ellis Donald 1915- *WhoMW 92*
**Tooker**, Gary Lamarr 1939- *WhoFI 92, WhoMW 92*
**Tooker**, George 1920- *FacFETw*
**Tooker**, H. C. W. *Who 92*
**Tooker**, Richard 1902- *ScFEYrs*
**Tooker**, William Wallace 1848-1917 *BiInAmS*
**Tookey**, Harvey Llewellyn 1922- *AmMWSc 92*
**Tookey**, Marcia Hickman 1932- *WhoAmP 91*
**Tookey**, Richard William 1934- *Who 92*
**Tookey**, Robert C 1925- *WhoIns 92*
**Tookey**, Robert Clarence 1925- *WhoWest 92*
**Toolan**, David Stuart 1935- *WhoRel 92*
**Toolan**, Helene Wallace *AmMWSc 92*
**Toole**, Bryan Patrick 1940- *AmMWSc 92*
**Toole**, Charles Julian, IV 1956- *WhoRel 92*
**Toole**, Clyde Rowland, Jr. 1933- *WhoWest 92*
**Toole**, Floyd Edward 1938- *AmMWSc 92*
**Toole**, Howard 1949- *WhoAmP 91*
**Toole**, James Francis 1925- *AmMWSc 92*
**Toole**, Joan Trimble 1923- *WhoWest 92*
**Toole**, John Kennedy 1937-1969 *BenetAL 91*
**Toole**, Judith H. 1942- *WhoAmL 92*
**Toole**, Lee K. 1936- *WhoWest 92*
**Tooles**, Calvin W 1921- *AmMWSc 92*
**Tooley**, Charles Frederick 1947- *WhoAmP 91*
**Tooley**, F V 1908- *AmMWSc 92*
**Tooley**, John 1924- *IntWW 91, Who 92*
**Tooley**, R. Eric 1962- *WhoRel 92*
**Tooley**, Richard Douglas 1932- *AmMWSc 92*
**Tooley**, William Henry 1925- *AmMWSc 92*
**Tooley**, William Lander 1934- *WhoFI 92, WhoWest 92*
**Tooliatos**, Nickolas Paul, II 1957- *WhoAmL 92*
**Toolson**, Andy *WhoBlA 92*
**Toom**, Paul Marvin 1942- *AmMWSc 92*
**Toomajian**, William Martin 1943- *WhoAmL 92*
**Toombs**, Charles Phillip 1952- *WhoBlA 92*
**Toombs**, Jane Ellen 1926- *IntAu&W 91*
**Toombs**, Robert T *ScFEYrs*
**Toome**, Voldemar 1924- *AmMWSc 92*
**Toomer**, Clarence 1952- *WhoBlA 92*
**Toomer**, Jean *BenetAL 91*
**Toomer**, Jean 1894-1967 *AfrAmW, BlkLC [port]*
**Toomer**, Kenneth 1943- *WhoBlA 92*
**Toomer**, Nathan Eugene 1894-1967 *BenetAL 91*
**Toomer**, Vann Alma Rosalee *WhoBlA 92*
**Toomey**, Brian Chester 1947- *WhoFI 92*
**Toomey**, Daniel 1938- *WhoAmP 91*
**Toomey**, Daniel Francis 1944- *WhoAmL 92*
**Toomey**, James Michael 1930- *AmMWSc 92*
**Toomey**, Joseph Edward 1943- *AmMWSc 92*
**Toomey**, Joseph Edward, Jr. 1943- *WhoMW 92*
**Toomey**, Kent Edward 1935- *WhoFI 92*
**Toomey**, Ralph 1918- *Who 92*
**Toomey**, Regis 1898- *IntMPA 92*
**Toomey**, Regis 1898-1991 *NewYTBS 91*
**Toomey**, Steven Louis 1964- *WhoMW 92*
**Toomey**, Thomas Murray 1923- *WhoAmL 92*
**Toomey**, William Shenberger 1935- *WhoMW 92*
**Toomre**, Alar 1937- *AmMWSc 92*
**Toomsen**, Duane Arthur 1934- *WhoMW 92*
**Toomy**, Joseph F 1948- *WhoAmP 91*
**Toon**, Al Lee, Jr. 1963- *WhoBlA 92*
**Toon**, Cathy Jean 1957- *WhoRel 92*
**Toon**, Leonard Eugene 1932- *WhoWest 92*
**Toon**, Malcolm 1916- *IntWW 91, WhoAmP 91*
**Toon**, Owen Brian 1947- *AmMWSc 92*
**Toon**, Ronald Lynn 1962- *WhoRel 92*
**Toona Gottschalk**, Elin-Kai 1937- *IntAu&W 91*
**Tooney**, Nancy Marion 1939- *AmMWSc 92*
**Toong**, Tau-Yi 1918- *AmMWSc 92*
**Toop**, Edgar Wesley 1932- *AmMWSc 92*
**Toor**, Arthur 1938- *AmMWSc 92*
**Toor**, H L 1927- *AmMWSc 92*
**Toor**, Harold O. d1991 *NewYTBS 91*
**Toor**, Jon 1960- *WhoWest 92*
**Toot**, Joseph F., Jr. 1935- *WhoFI 92, WhoMW 92*
**Toote**, Gloria E. A. 1931- *WhoBlA 92*
**Tootell**, Thomas Edward 1948- *WhoWest 92*
**Tooth**, Douglas *Who 92N*
**Tooth**, Geoffrey Cuthbert 1908- *Who 92*
**Tooth**, John L. *Who 92*
**Toothill**, Richard B 1936- *AmMWSc 92*
**Toothman**, John William 1954- *WhoAmL 92*
**Toothman**, Tamara Anne 1962- *WhoRel 92*
**Tootikian**, Karoun 1918- *WhoEnt 92*
**Tootikian**, Vahan H. 1935- *WhoRel 92*
**Top**, Don *WhoAmP 91*
**Top**, Franklin Henry, Jr 1936- *AmMWSc 92*
**Topaz**, Muriel *WhoEnt 92*
**Topazian**, Richard G 1930- *AmMWSc 92*
**Topcheyev**, Yuriy Ivanovich 1920- *IntWW 91*
**Topchiev**, Aleksandr Vasil'evich 1907-1962 *SovUnBD*
**Topcik**, Barry 1924- *AmMWSc 92*
**Tope**, Dwight Harold 1918- *WhoFI 92*
**Tope**, Graham Norman 1943- *Who 92*
**Tope**, Trimbak Krishna 1914- *IntWW 91*
**Topel**, David Glen 1937- *AmMWSc 92*
**Topel**, Louis John 1934- *WhoRel 92*
**Topete Stonefield**, Liz 1955- *WhoHisp 92*
**Topfer**, Klaus 1938- *IntWW 91*
**Topfer**, Morton Louis 1936- *WhoFI 92*
**Topham**, Douglas William *WhoWest 92*
**Topham**, Lawrence Garth 1914- *Who 92*
**Topham**, Richard Walton 1943- *AmMWSc 92*
**Topham**, Sally Jane 1933- *WhoEnt 92*
**Topham**, Verl Reed 1934- *WhoWest 92*
**Topich**, Joseph 1948- *AmMWSc 92*
**Topilow**, Carl S. 1947- *WhoEnt 92, WhoWest 92*
**Topinka**, Judy Baar 1944- *WhoAmP 91, WhoMW 92*
**Topjon**, Ann Johnson 1940- *WhoWest 92*
**Topkis**, Jay 1924- *WhoAmL 92*
**Topley**, Keith *Who 92*
**Topley**, Kenneth Wallis Joseph 1922- *Who 92*
**Topley**, William Keith 1936- *Who 92*
**Topliss**, John G 1930- *AmMWSc 92*
**Toplitz**, George Nathan 1936- *WhoAmL 92*
**Toplyn**, Joseph Edward 1953- *WhoEnt 92*
**Topoff**, Howard Ronald 1941- *AmMWSc 92*
**Topol** 1935- *ConTFT 9, IntMPA 92*
**Topol**, Chaim 1935- *IntWW 91*
**Topol**, Leo Eli 1926- *AmMWSc 92*
**Topoleski**, Leonard Daniel 1935- *AmMWSc 92*
**Topolski**, Feliks 1907-1989 *TwCPaSc*
**Topolski**, Jerzy 1928- *IntWW 91*
**Topor**, Carol Marie Vlack 1952- *WhoAmL 92*
**Toporek**, Milton 1920- *AmMWSc 92*
**Topornin**, Boris Nikolaevich 1929- *SovUnBD*
**Toporov**, Vladimir Nikolayevich 1928- *IntWW 91*
**Topp**, Alphonso Axel, Jr. 1920- *WhoWest 92*
**Topp**, G Clarke 1937- *AmMWSc 92*
**Topp**, Roger Leslie 1923- *Who 92*
**Topp**, Stephen V 1937- *AmMWSc 92*
**Topp**, William Carl 1948- *AmMWSc 92*
**Topp**, William Robert 1939- *AmMWSc 92*
**Toppel**, Alan Herman 1933- *WhoFI 92, WhoWest 92*
**Toppel**, Bert Jack 1926- *AmMWSc 92*
**Topper**, Leonard 1929- *AmMWSc 92*
**Topper**, Paul Quinn 1925- *WhoEnt 92*
**Topper**, T H 1936- *AmMWSc 92*
**Topper**, Yale Jerome 1916- *AmMWSc 92*
**Toppeto**, Alphonse A 1925- *AmMWSc 92*
**Toppin**, Clare Thomas 1937- *WhoAmL 92*
**Toppin**, David Paul 1947- *WhoMW 92*
**Toppin**, Edgar Allan 1928- *WhoBlA 92*
**Topping**, Eva Catafygiotu 1920- *WhoRel 92*
**Topping**, Frank 1937- *IntAu&W 91, Who 92*
**Topping**, James 1904- *Who 92*
**Topping**, Joseph John 1942- *AmMWSc 92*
**Topping**, Norman Hawkins 1908- *AmMWSc 92*
**Topping**, Richard Francis 1949- *AmMWSc 92*
**Topping**, Robert Joe 1936- *WhoAmP 91*
**Topuz**, Ertugrul S 1935- *AmMWSc 92*
**Topuzes**, Thomas 1947- *WhoHisp 92*
**Torack**, Richard M 1927- *AmMWSc 92*
**Toradze**, Alexander 1952- *WhoEnt 92*
**Torain**, Tony William 1954- *WhoBlA 92*
**Toralballa**, Gloria C 1915- *AmMWSc 92*
**Toraldo Di Francia**, Giuliano 1916- *IntWW 91*
**Toran**, Anthony 1939- *WhoBlA 92*
**Toran**, Kay Dean 1943- *WhoBlA 92*
**Torano**, Francisco Jose 1944- *WhoHisp 92*
**Torano-Pantin**, Maria Elena 1938- *WhoHisp 92*
**Toraya**, Margarita F. 1940- *WhoHisp 92*
**Torbeck**, Victor Henry 1941- *WhoMW 92*
**Torberg**, Friedrich *ConAu 133*
**Torberg**, Friedrich 1908-1979 *LiExTwC*
**Torbert**, Clement Clay, Jr 1929- *WhoAmP 91*
**Torbert**, William C 1935- *WhoAmP 91*
**Torbet**, John Randolph 1943- *WhoAmL 92*
**Torbet**, Walter 1933- *WhoWest 92*
**Torbett**, Emerson Arlin 1939- *AmMWSc 92*
**Torbett**, Jeanne Aloma 1952- *WhoRel 92*
**Torbett**, Philip David 1954- *WhoEnt 92*
**Torbit**, Charles Allen, Jr 1924- *AmMWSc 92*
**Torborg** *EncAmaz 91*
**Torborg**, Kevin Henry 1963- *WhoMW 92*
**Torch**, Reuben 1926- *AmMWSc 92*
**Torchia**, Dennis Anthony 1939- *AmMWSc 92*
**Torchiana**, Mary Louise 1929- *AmMWSc 92*
**Torchinsky**, Abe 1920- *WhoEnt 92*
**Torchinsky**, Alberto 1944- *AmMWSc 92, WhoHisp 92*
**Torda**, Clara 1910- *AmMWSc 92*
**Torday**, Ursula *WrDr 92*
**Tordoff** *Who 92*
**Tordoff**, Baron 1928- *Who 92*
**Tordoff**, Harrison Bruce 1923- *AmMWSc 92*
**Tordoff**, Walter, III 1943- *AmMWSc 92*
**Torell**, Donald Theodore 1926- *AmMWSc 92*
**Torell**, John R., III 1939- *WhoFI 92*
**Torelli**, Giuseppe 1658-1709 *NewAmDM*
**Toren**, Amikam 1945- *TwCPaSc*
**Toren**, Brian Keith 1935- *WhoMW 92*
**Toren**, Eric Clifford, Jr 1933- *AmMWSc 92*
**Toren**, George Anthony 1924- *AmMWSc 92*
**Toren**, Mark 1950- *WhoFI 92*
**Toren**, Paul Edward 1923- *AmMWSc 92*
**Toren**, Robert 1915- *WhoWest 92*
**Toreson**, Wilfred Earl 1916- *AmMWSc 92*
**Torgersen**, Eric *DrAPF 91*
**Torgersen**, Paul E 1931- *AmMWSc 92*
**Torgersen**, Sue 1944- *WhoRel 92*
**Torgerson**, David Franklyn 1942- *AmMWSc 92*
**Torgerson**, John W 1950- *WhoAmP 91*
**Torgerson**, Larry Keith 1935- *WhoAmL 92, WhoFI 92, WhoMW 92*
**Torgerson**, Les 1946- *WhoAmL 92*
**Torgerson**, Ronald Thomas 1936- *AmMWSc 92*
**Torgeson**, Dewayne Clinton 1925- *AmMWSc 92*
**Torgow**, Eugene N 1925- *AmMWSc 92, WhoFI 92*
**Torian**, Edward Torrence 1933- *WhoBlA 92*
**Torian**, Roberta Griffin 1950- *WhoAmL 92*
**Toribara**, Taft Yutaka 1917- *AmMWSc 92*
**Toridis**, Theodore George 1932- *AmMWSc 92*
**Torigian**, Puzant Crossley 1922- *WhoFI 92*
**Torino**, Christopher Joseph 1961- *WhoEnt 92*
**Torio**, Joyce Clarke 1934- *AmMWSc 92*
**Toriz Cobian**, Alfonso 1913- *WhoRel 92*
**Torjesen**, Karen Jo 1945- *WhoRel 92*
**Torkanowsky**, Werner 1926- *NewAmDM, WhoEnt 92*
**Torkelson**, Anthony Rayburn 1936- *WhoMW 92*
**Torkelson**, Arnold 1922- *AmMWSc 92*
**Torkildsen**, Peter Gerard 1958- *WhoAmP 91*
**Torkildson**, Raymond Maynard 1917- *WhoAmL 92, WhoAmP 91*
**Torklep**, Lynlee 1942- *WhoWest 92*
**Torlesse**, Arthur David 1902- *Who 92*
**Torley**, Luke *SmATA 66*
**Torley**, Robert Edward 1918- *AmMWSc 92*
**Tormala**, Pertti 1945- *IntWW 91*
**Tormanen**, Calvin Douglas 1946- *AmMWSc 92*
**Torme**, Mel 1925- *IntMPA 92, NewAmDM*
**Torme**, Melvin 1925- *WhoEnt 92*
**Tormey**, Douglass Cole 1938- *AmMWSc 92*
**Tormey**, John McDivit 1934- *AmMWSc 92*
**Tormey**, Richard 1959- *TwCPaSc*
**Torn**, Rip 1931- *IntMPA 92, WhoEnt 92*
**Tornabene**, Thomas Guy 1937- *AmMWSc 92*
**Tornaes**, Laurits 1936- *IntWW 91*
**Tornaritis**, Criton George 1902- *Who 92*
**Tornatore**, Giuseppe 1956- *WhoEnt 92*
**Torneden**, Roger Lee 1944- *WhoFI 92*

**Torney**, Thomas William 1915- *Who 92*
**Tornfelt**, John Vincent 1952- *WhoRel 92*
**Torng**, Hwa-Chung 1932- *AmMWSc 92*
**Tornheim**, Patricia Anne 1939- *AmMWSc 92*
**Tornimparte**, Alessandra *ConAu 135*
**Torno**, Michele Elaine 1959- *WhoEnt 92*
**Tornqvist**, Erik Gustav Markus 1924- *AmMWSc 92*
**Tornstrom**, Robert Ernest 1946- *WhoAmL 92*
**Tornudd**, Klaus 1931- *IntWW 91*
**Toro**, Amalia Maria 1920- *WhoAmL 92*
**Toro**, Carlos Hans 1943- *WhoHisp 92*
**Toro**, Eusebio *WhoHisp 92*
**Toro**, Joe *WhoHisp 92*
**Toro**, Manuel A. 1937- *WhoHisp 92*
**Toro**, Richard Frank 1939- *AmMWSc 92*
**Toro-Garland**, Fernando de 1925- *IntAu&W 91*
**ToRobert**, Henry Thomas 1942- *IntWW 91, Who 92*
**Torok**, Andrew, Jr 1925- *AmMWSc 92*
**Torok**, John Anthony, III 1952- *WhoMW 92*
**Torok**, Karl 1950- *TwCPaSc*
**Torok**, Margaret Louise 1922- *WhoFI 92*
**Torok**, Nicholas 1909- *AmMWSc 92*
**Torok**, Raymond Patrick 1946- *WhoMW 92*
**Torok**, Theodore Elwyn 1931- *AmMWSc 92*
**Torokvei**, Peter John 1951- *WhoEnt 92*
**Toron**, Caryl R. 1958- *WhoHisp 92*
**Toronto**, Bishop of 1937- *Who 92*
**Toronto**, Bishops Suffragan of *Who 92*
**Torop**, William 1938- *AmMWSc 92*
**Torosian**, George 1936- *AmMWSc 92*
**Torp**, Bruce Alan 1937- *AmMWSc 92*
**Torpey**, Richard *WhoAmP 91*
**Torpey**, Richard Thomas 1954- *WhoEnt 92*
**Torpey**, Scott Raymond 1955- *WhoAmL 92*
**Torphichen**, Lord 1946- *Who 92*
**Torquato**, Salvatore 1954- *AmMWSc 92*
**Torquemada**, Juan de 1563?-1624 *HisDSpE*
**Torr**, Ann M 1935- *WhoAmP 91*
**Torr**, Franklin 1930- *WhoAmP 91*
**Torr**, Ralph 1931- *WhoAmP 91*
**Torrado**, Alberto M. *WhoHisp 92*
**Torrance**, Daniel J 1921- *AmMWSc 92*
**Torrance**, James Bruce 1923- *Who 92*
**Torrance**, Jerry Badgley, Jr 1941- *AmMWSc 92*
**Torrance**, Kenneth E 1940- *AmMWSc 92*
**Torrance**, Lee 1920- *WrDr 92*
**Torrance**, Thomas Forsyth 1913- *IntAu&W 91, IntWW 91, Who 92, WrDr 92*
**Torrando**, Francisco *WhoHisp 92*
**Torras**, Mary R 1927- *WhoAmP 91*
**Torre**, Carlos 1951- *WhoHisp 92*
**Torre**, Carlos de la 1858-1930 *HisDSpE*
**Torre**, Douglas Paul 1919- *AmMWSc 92*
**Torre**, Elias R. 1932- *WhoHisp 92*
**Torre**, Frank John 1944- *AmMWSc 92*
**Torre**, Joseph Paul 1940- *WhoMW 92*
**Torre-Bueno**, Jose Rollin 1948- *AmMWSc 92*
**Torre Nilsson**, Leopoldo 1924-1978 *IntDcF 2-2*
**Torre Tagle y Portocarrero**, Jose B de 1779-1841 *HisDSpE*
**Torreano**, Alan 1946- *WhoEnt 92*
**Torreano**, Michael J. 1948- *WhoFI 92*
**Torreblanca Reyes**, Magin 1929- *WhoRel 92*
**Torregian**, Sotere *DrAPF 91*
**Torregrossa**, Joseph Anthony 1944- *WhoAmL 92*
**Torregrossa**, Robert Emile 1951- *AmMWSc 92*
**Torrejon y Velasco**, Tomas de 1644-1728 *HisDSpE*
**Torrelio Villa**, Celso 1933- *IntWW 91*
**Torrella**, Carlos Rudolph 1943- *WhoFI 92*
**Torrence**, Billy Hubert 1949- *WhoRel 92*
**Torrence**, Jackie 1944- *NotBlAW 92 [port]*
**Torrence**, Jacquelyn Seals 1944- *WhoBlA 92*
**Torrence**, Margaret Ann 1946- *WhoWest 92*
**Torrence**, Paul Frederick 1943- *AmMWSc 92*
**Torrence**, Ridgely 1875-1950 *BenetAL 91*
**Torrence**, Robert James 1937- *AmMWSc 92*
**Torrens-Spence**, Michael 1914- *Who 92*
**Torrent**, Karen E. 1959- *WhoAmL 92*
**Torres**, Adeline *WhoHisp 92*
**Torres**, Andres A. 1943- *WhoHisp 92*
**Torres**, Andrew M 1931- *AmMWSc 92*
**Torres**, Angel *IntWW 91*
**Torres**, Anthony Ignatius 1929- *WhoMW 92*
**Torres**, Anthony R 1943- *AmMWSc 92*
**Torres**, Antonio 1957- *WhoHisp 92*
**Torres**, Art 1946- *WhoAmP 91, WhoHisp 92*
**Torres**, Arturo D. *WhoHisp 92*
**Torres**, Arturo G. *WhoHisp 92*
**Torres**, Arturo Lopez 1948- *WhoHisp 92*
**Torres**, Baldomero Chapa 1935- *WhoHisp 92*
**Torres**, Camilo 1766-1816 *HisDSpE*
**Torres**, Carlos Alberto 1950- *WhoWest 92*
**Torres**, Celia Margaret 1936- *WhoHisp 92*
**Torres**, Cynthia Ann 1958- *WhoFI 92*
**Torres**, David 1934- *WhoHisp 92*
**Torres**, David P., Jr. *WhoHisp 92*
**Torres**, Diana Cristina 1956- *WhoHisp 92*
**Torres**, Durbal, Jr. 1944- *WhoHisp 92*
**Torres**, Edmundo S., Jr. 1938- *WhoHisp 92*
**Torres**, Eduardo Jose 1961- *WhoHisp 92*
**Torres**, Edwin *WhoHisp 92*
**Torres**, Edwin 1947- *WhoHisp 92*
**Torres**, Eliseo S. 1945- *WhoHisp 92*
**Torres**, Elizabeth 1947- *WhoHisp 92*
**Torres**, Ernest C. 1941- *WhoAmL 92, WhoHisp 92*
**Torres**, Estanislao Tudela *WhoAmP 91*
**Torres**, Esteban E. 1930- *AlmAP 92 [port]*
**Torres**, Esteban Edward 1930- *WhoAmP 91, WhoHisp 92, WhoWest 92*
**Torres**, Esther A. 1949- *WhoHisp 92*
**Torres**, Fernando 1924- *AmMWSc 92*
**Torres**, Frank 1928- *WhoHisp 92*
**Torres**, Frank 1953- *WhoAmL 92*
**Torres**, Frederico M. *WhoHisp 92*
**Torres**, Gerald 1952- *WhoAmL 92, WhoHisp 92*
**Torres**, Gladys 1938- *WhoHisp 92*
**Torres**, Gloria Ann 1957- *WhoHisp 92*
**Torres**, Guillermo M. *WhoHisp 92*
**Torres**, Isidore D. 1947- *WhoHisp 92*
**Torres**, Ivan Lincoln 1948- *WhoHisp 92*
**Torres**, J. Antonio 1949- *WhoHisp 92*
**Torres**, Jake *WhoHisp 92*
**Torres**, Jess G. *WhoHisp 92*
**Torres**, Jesus *WhoHisp 92*
**Torres**, Jesus U 1927- *WhoAmP 91*
**Torres**, Joe H. *WhoHisp 92*
**Torres**, John R. 1959- *WhoHisp 92*
**Torres**, Jose Antonio 1952- *WhoHisp 92*
**Torres**, Jose B. 1946- *WhoHisp 92*
**Torres**, Jose E. 1939- *WhoHisp 92*
**Torres**, Jose Luis 1936- *BlkOlyM, WhoHisp 92*
**Torres**, Jose Manuel 1935- *WhoHisp 92*
**Torres**, Joseph Charles *AmMWSc 92*
**Torres**, Joseph James 1950- *WhoHisp 92*
**Torres**, Joseph L. 1927- *WhoHisp 92*
**Torres**, Juan Carlos 1948- *WhoHisp 92*
**Torres**, Juan S *WhoAmP 91*
**Torres**, Julio *WhoHisp 92*
**Torres**, Lady A. 1948- *WhoHisp 92*
**Torres**, Lawrence E. 1927- *WhoHisp 92*
**Torres**, Lawrence J. 1946- *WhoHisp 92*
**Torres**, Leida I. 1949- *WhoHisp 92*
**Torres**, Leonard 1926- *WhoHisp 92*
**Torres**, Leyda Luz 1955- *WhoHisp 92*
**Torres**, Linda Marie *WhoHisp 92*
**Torres**, Lou C. 1950- *WhoHisp 92*
**Torres**, Lourdes Maria 1957- *AmMWSc 92*
**Torres**, Lucille *WhoHisp 92*
**Torres**, Luis 1943- *WhoHisp 92*
**Torres**, Luis A. 1922- *WhoHisp 92*
**Torres**, Luis A., Jr. *WhoHisp 92*
**Torres**, Luis Ruben 1950- *WhoHisp 92*
**Torres**, Magdalena 1930- *WhoHisp 92*
**Torres**, Magdalena 1944- *WhoHisp 92*
**Torres**, Marta Carmen 1954- *WhoHisp 92*
**Torres**, Martin R. 1943- *WhoHisp 92*
**Torres**, Maximino deJesus 1932- *WhoHisp 92*
**Torres**, Maye 1960- *WhoHisp 92*
**Torres**, Milton J. 1931- *WhoHisp 92*
**Torres**, Myrna A. 1941- *WhoHisp 92*
**Torres**, Noe 1956- *WhoRel 92*
**Torres**, Noe Acosta 1956- *WhoHisp 92*
**Torres**, Omar 1945- *WhoHisp 92*
**Torres**, Oscar *WhoHisp 92*
**Torres**, Oscar L., Sr. *WhoHisp 92*
**Torres**, Oscar Modesto, Jr. 1945- *WhoHisp 92*
**Torres**, Ovidio L. 1962- *WhoHisp 92*
**Torres**, Paul 1952- *WhoHisp 92*
**Torres**, Penny *RelLAm 91*
**Torres**, Rafael *WhoHisp 92*
**Torres**, Rafael Angel 1963- *WhoEnt 92*
**Torres**, Ralph Chon 1948- *WhoRel 92*
**Torres**, Ramon Hernan, Jr. 1953- *WhoHisp 92*
**Torres**, Raymond 1957- *WhoHisp 92*
**Torres**, Raymond Nicholas, Jr. 1962- *WhoAmL 92*
**Torres**, Refugio R. 1925- *WhoHisp 92*
**Torres**, Reinaldo E. 1935- *WhoHisp 92*
**Torres**, Ricardo, Jr. *WhoHisp 92*
**Torres**, Ricardo A. *WhoHisp 92*
**Torres**, Richard Roy 1961- *WhoHisp 92*
**Torres**, Rita A. 1951- *WhoHisp 92*
**Torres**, Robert Alvin 1960- *WhoEnt 92*
**Torres**, Robert Anthony 1948- *WhoHisp 92*
**Torres**, Robert John 1963- *WhoHisp 92*
**Torres**, Rodolfo 1925- *WhoHisp 92*
**Torres**, Rosario *WhoHisp 92*
**Torres**, Roy Arthur 1961- *WhoAmL 92*
**Torres**, Sally *WhoHisp 92*
**Torres**, Salvio 1932- *WhoHisp 92*
**Torres**, Sara 1942- *WhoHisp 92*
**Torres**, Sixto E. 1944- *WhoHisp 92*
**Torres**, Tereska *DrAPF 91*
**Torres**, Veronica Imelda 1965- *WhoHisp 92*
**Torres**, Xiomara *WhoHisp 92*
**Torres-Anjel**, Manuel Jose 1942- *AmMWSc 92*
**Torres-Aybar**, Francisco G. 1934- *WhoHisp 92*
**Torres-Bauza**, Luis Jose 1951- *WhoHisp 92*
**Torres Bernardez**, Santiago 1929- *IntWW 91*
**Torres-Blasini**, Gladys *AmMWSc 92*
**Torres Bollo**, Diego de 1551-1638 *HisDSpE*
**Torres-Comas**, Hortensia M. 1949- *WhoHisp 92*
**Torres De Tolosa**, Alvaro 1946- *IntAu&W 91*
**Torres-Figueroa**, Saul 1948- *WhoHisp 92*
**Torres-Geary**, Miriam Beatriz 1956- *WhoHisp 92*
**Torres-Gil**, Fernando 1948- *WhoHisp 92*
**Torres-Guzman**, Maria E. 1951- *WhoHisp 92*
**Torres-Horwitt**, C. Aida *WhoHisp 92*
**Torres-James**, Alicia 1943- *WhoAmP 91*
**Torres Jurado**, Antonio de 1817-1892 *NewAmDM*
**Torres-Labawld**, Jose D. 1932 *WhoHisp 92*
**Torres-Labawld**, Jose Dimas 1932- *WhoFI 92*
**Torres-Medina**, Alfonso 1945- *AmMWSc 92*
**Torres-Melendez**, Elaine 1957- *WhoHisp 92*
**Torres Moore**, Dominga *WhoHisp 92*
**Torres Oliver**, Juan Fremiot 1925- *WhoRel 92*
**Torres-Ordonez**, Carlos Enrique 1942- *WhoEnt 92*
**Torres-Pinedo**, Ramon 1929- *AmMWSc 92*
**Torres Pohl**, Elizabeth *WhoHisp 92*
**Torres Quiles**, Herbert 1930- *WhoAmP 91, WhoHisp 92*
**Torres-Reaves**, Carmen Nellie 1954- *WhoRel 92*
**Torres Reyes**, Emilio 1935- *WhoHisp 92*
**Torres Rivera**, Lina M. 1953- *WhoHisp 92*
**Torres-Rivera**, Rebeca 1931- *WhoHisp 92*
**Torres Romero**, Alfredo 1922- *WhoRel 92*
**Torres-Santiago**, Jose Manuel 1940- *WhoHisp 92*
**Torres-Santos**, Raymond 1958- *WhoHisp 92*
**Torres-Trujillo**, Maye Carmela 1960- *WhoHisp 92*
**Torres-Velez**, Felix L. 1939- *WhoHisp 92*
**Torres Yribar**, Wilfredo 1933- *IntWW 91*
**Torrescano**, Adolfo Jimenez 1937- *WhoWest 92*
**Torrey**, Bradford 1843-1912 *BenetAL 91, BiInAmS*
**Torrey**, Henry Augustus 1871-1910 *BiInAmS*
**Torrey**, Henry Cutler 1911- *AmMWSc 92*
**Torrey**, John 1796-1873 *BiInAmS*
**Torrey**, John Gordon 1921- *AmMWSc 92*
**Torrey**, Reuben Archer 1865-1928 *RelLAm 91*
**Torrey**, Rubye Prigmore 1926- *AmMWSc 92, WhoBlA 92*
**Torrez**, Ervin E. 1935- *WhoHisp 92*
**Torrez**, Fernando M. 1944- *WhoHisp 92*
**Torrez**, Jerry A. 1943- *WhoHisp 92*
**Torrez**, Mariano A 1939- *WhoAmP 91, WhoHisp 92*
**Torrez**, Robert J. 1949- *WhoHisp 92*
**Torriani Gorini**, Annamaria 1918- *AmMWSc 92*
**Torricelli**, Robert G. 1951- *AlmAP 92 [port], WhoAmP 91*
**Torrijos**, Omar 1929-1981 *FacFETw*
**Torrington**, Viscount 1943- *Who 92*
**Torrison**, William Rahr 1945- *WhoMW 92*
**Torro**, Pel *IntAu&W 91X, TwCSFW 91, WrDr 92*
**Torroja Menendez**, Jose Maria 1916- *IntWW 91*
**Torru**, Katharine Lucas 1964- *WhoWest 92*
**Torruella**, Juan R *WhoAmP 91*
**Torruella**, Juan R. 1933- *WhoAmL 92*
**Torruella**, Radames A. 1940- *WhoHisp 92*
**Tors**, Ivan d1983 *LesBEnT 92*
**Torshen**, Jerome Harold 1929- *WhoAmL 92, WhoMW 92*
**Torsney**, Cheryl B. 1955- *ConAu 135*
**Torson**, Terry Tyrone 1962- *WhoEnt 92*
**Torstendahl**, Rolf 1936- *IntWW 91*
**Torsvan**, Berick Traven *BenetAL 91*
**Tortarolo**, Joann Mary 1948- *WhoAmP 91*
**Tortelier**, Paul d1990 *IntWW 91N, Who 92N*
**Tortelier**, Paul 1914- *NewAmDM*
**Tortelier**, Paul 1914-1990 *AnObit 1990*
**Tortelier**, Yan Pascal 1947- *IntWW 91*
**Tortella-Nossokoff**, Gioia Helen 1959- *WhoEnt 92*
**Tortolero**, Carlos *WhoHisp 92*
**Tortonese**, Marco 1962- *AmMWSc 92*
**Tortorelli**, Kevin Michael 1947- *WhoRel 92*
**Tortorello**, Anthony Joseph 1945- *AmMWSc 92, WhoMW 92*
**Tortorici**, Peter *LesBEnT 92*
**Tortorici**, Peter Frank 1949- *WhoEnt 92*
**Tortoriello**, Robert Laurence 1950- *WhoAmL 92*
**Torumtay**, Necip 1926- *IntWW 91*
**Torun**, Benjamin 1939- *AmMWSc 92*
**Torvik**, Peter J 1938- *AmMWSc 92*
**Torvik**, Peter John 1938- *WhoMW 92*
**Torvill and Dean** *FacFETw*
**Torvill**, Jayne 1957- *FacFETw*
**Tory**, Elmer Melvin 1928- *AmMWSc 92*
**Tory**, Geofroy 1912- *Who 92*
**Torz**, Richard J. 1956- *WhoFI 92*
**Tosar**, Hector A. 1923- *IntWW 91*
**Tosato**, Angelo 1938- *WhoRel 92*
**Tosato**, Giovanna *AmMWSc 92*
**Toscan**, Richard Eric 1941- *WhoWest 92*
**Toscan du Plantier**, Daniel 1941- *IntWW 91*
**Toscanini**, Arturo 1867-1957 *FacFETw [port], NewAmDM*
**Toscano**, Maria Guadalupe 1965- *WhoHisp 92*
**Toscano**, Oscar Ernesto 1951- *WhoAmL 92*
**Toscano**, Patrick Peter, Jr. 1960- *WhoAmL 92*
**Toscano**, Sebastian J. 1955- *WhoHisp 92*
**Toscano**, Vincent N. 1940- *WhoFI 92*
**Toscano**, William Agostino, Jr 1945- *AmMWSc 92*
**Toscano**, William Michael 1945- *AmMWSc 92, WhoFI 92*
**Tosch**, Gilbert B 1939- *WhoIns 92*
**Tosch**, William Conrad 1934- *AmMWSc 92*
**Toseland**, Ronald James 1933- *Who 92*
**Toser**, David *WhoEnt 92*
**Tosh**, Fred Eugene 1930- *AmMWSc 92*
**Tosh**, Robert Lowell 1944- *WhoAmP 91*
**Toshio**, Makimoto 1916- *AmMWSc 92*
**Tosi**, Joseph Andrew, Jr 1921- *AmMWSc 92*
**Tosi**, Oscar I 1929- *AmMWSc 92, WhoMW 92*
**Tosi**, Pier Francesco 1653?-1732 *NewAmDM*
**Tosi**, Umberto Renzo 1937- *WhoWest 92*
**Toskey**, Burnett Roland 1929- *AmMWSc 92*
**Tosney**, Kathryn W 1946- *AmMWSc 92*
**Toson** *ConAu 134*
**Tosovsky**, Josef 1950- *IntWW 91*
**Tostado**, Maria Elena 1940- *WhoHisp 92*
**Toste**, Julie Lynda 1964- *WhoWest 92*
**Tosteson**, Daniel Charles 1925- *AmMWSc 92*
**Tosteson**, Heather *DrAPF 91*
**Tosteson**, Heather 1950- *IntAu&W 91*
**Tostevin**, James Earle 1938- *AmMWSc 92*
**Tosti**, Paolo 1846-1916 *NewAmDM*
**Tosunlar**, Akif Zafer 1950- *WhoFI 92*
**Totaro**, Rosemarie 1933- *WhoAmP 91*
**Totenberg**, Nina 1944- *News 92-2 [port]*
**Totenberg**, Roman 1911- *NewAmDM, WhoEnt 92*
**Toth**, Bela 1931- *AmMWSc 92*
**Toth**, Bruce A. 1953- *WhoAmL 92*
**Toth**, D. Richard 1946- *WhoAmL 92*
**Toth**, Elizabeth Levay *WhoWest 92*
**Toth**, Eugene J 1932- *AmMWSc 92*
**Toth**, Joseph Michael, Jr. 1935- *WhoWest 92*
**Toth**, Jozsef 1933- *AmMWSc 92*
**Toth**, Judith Coggeshall 1937- *WhoAmP 91*
**Toth**, Kenneth Stephen 1934- *AmMWSc 92*
**Toth**, Louis McKenna 1941- *AmMWSc 92*
**Toth**, Paul Eugene 1920- *AmMWSc 92*
**Toth**, Robert Allen 1939- *AmMWSc 92*
**Toth**, Robert S 1931- *AmMWSc 92*
**Toth**, Stephen John 1912- *AmMWSc 92*
**Toth**, Stephen Michael 1946- *WhoFI 92*
**Toth**, Susan Allen *DrAPF 91*
**Toth**, William James 1936- *AmMWSc 92*
**Totnes**, Archdeacon of *Who 92*
**Toto**, Michael Anthony 1958- *WhoAmL 92*
**Toto**, Patrick D 1921- *AmMWSc 92*

**Toton,** Edward Thomas 1942- *AmMWSc 92*
**Tott,** Konrad 1936- *IntWW 91*
**Totta,** Paul Anthony 1930- *AmMWSc 92*
**Totten,** Alfred Edward 1938- *WhoWest 92*
**Totten,** Bernice E. 1921- *WhoBlA 92*
**Totten,** Caroline *DrAPF 91*
**Totten,** Donald Lee 1933- *WhoAmP 91*
**Totten,** George Oakley, III 1922- *WhoWest 92*
**Totten,** Herman Lavon 1938- *WhoBlA 92*
**Totten,** James Edward 1947- *AmMWSc 92*
**Totten,** Joseph Gilbert 1788-1864 *BiInAmS*
**Totten,** Stanley Martin 1936- *AmMWSc 92*
**Tottenham** *Who 92*
**Totter,** Audrey 1923- *IntMPA 92*
**Totter,** John Randolph 1914- *AmMWSc 92*
**Totterdale,** Robert Lewis 1953- *WhoFI 92*
**Totterman,** Richard Evert Bjornson 1926- *IntWW 91, Who 92*
**Tottie,** Thomas 1930- *IntWW 91*
**Tottle,** Charles Ronald 1920- *Who 92, WrDr 92*
**Tottress,** Richard Edward 1917- *WhoBlA 92*
**Totty-Kublawi,** Mary Kay 1963- *WhoRel 92*
**Totusek,** Robert 1926- *AmMWSc 92*
**Tou,** James Chieh 1936- *AmMWSc 92*
**Tou,** Jen-sie Hsu 1936- *AmMWSc 92*
**Tou,** Julius T L 1926- *AmMWSc 92*
**Touba,** Ali R 1925- *AmMWSc 92*
**Toubassi,** Elias Hanna 1943- *AmMWSc 92*
**Toubert,** Pierre Marcel Paul 1932- *IntWW 91*
**Toubes,** Norbert *WhoHisp 92*
**Toubon,** Jacques 1941- *IntWW 91*
**Touby,** Kathleen Anita 1943- *WhoAmL 92*
**Touby,** Michael Brian 1966- *WhoFI 92*
**Touch,** Arthur Gerald 1911- *Who 92*
**Touchberry,** Robert Walton 1921- *AmMWSc 92*
**Touche,** Anthony 1927- *Who 92*
**Touche,** Rodney 1928- *Who 92*
**Touchet,** Donovan Bernard 1949- *WhoFI 92*
**Touchstone,** John E. 1939- *WhoBlA 92*
**Touchstone,** Joseph Cary 1921- *AmMWSc 92*
**Touchton,** Bobby Jay 1962- *WhoRel 92*
**Touchton,** James Wesley 1952- *WhoRel 92*
**Touchy,** Deborah K. P. 1957- *WhoAmL 92*
**Toufexis,** Nicolas Constantin 1957- *WhoFI 92*
**Tougas,** Gerard Raymond 1921- *IntWW 91*
**Tougas,** Roger L *WhoAmP 91*
**Touger,** Jerold Steven 1945- *AmMWSc 92*
**Tough,** Dave 1908-1948 *NewAmDM*
**Tough,** James Thomas 1938- *AmMWSc 92*
**Touhey,** Glenda Jean 1945- *WhoEnt 92*
**Touhill,** Charles Joseph 1938- *AmMWSc 92*
**Touhy,** John P 1919- *WhoAmP 91*
**Toulemon,** Robert 1927- *IntWW 91*
**Toulmin,** John Kelvin 1941- *Who 92*
**Toulmin,** Priestley 1930- *AmMWSc 92*
**Toulmin,** Stephen E. 1922- *WrDr 92*
**Toulmin,** Stephen Edelston 1922- *Who 92*
**Toulouse,** James Raymond 1919- *WhoWest 92*
**Toulouse,** Jean 1948- *AmMWSc 92*
**Toulouse,** Mark G. 1952- *WhoRel 92*
**Toulouse,** Paul Michael 1949- *WhoAmL 92*
**Toulson,** Roger Grenfell 1946- *Who 92*
**Toulson,** Shirley 1924- *WrDr 92*
**Toumpas,** John N. 1901- *IntWW 91*
**Toung,** Brian Roy 1958- *WhoAmL 92*
**Toupin,** Richard A 1926- *AmMWSc 92*
**Tour,** James Mitchell 1959- *AmMWSc 92*
**Tour,** Robert Louis 1918- *WhoWest 92*
**Touraine,** Alain Louis Jules Francois 1925- *IntWW 91*
**Toure,** Amadou Toumani *IntWW 91*
**Toure,** Ismael 1925- *IntWW 91*
**Toure,** Kwame 1941- *WhoBlA 92*
**Toure,** Mamoudou 1928- *IntWW 91*
**Toure,** Mohamed Ali 1949- *WhoFI 92*
**Tourel,** Jennie 1900?-1973 *NewAmDM*
**Touret,** Jacques Leon Robert 1936- *IntWW 91*
**Tourgee,** Albion W. 1838-1905 *BenetAL 91*
**Tourgee,** Albion Winegar 1838-1905 *BibAL 8*
**Tourgee,** Ronald Alan 1938- *AmMWSc 92*
**Tourgeman,** Eli A. 1945- *WhoHisp 92*
**Tourian,** Ara Yervant 1933- *AmMWSc 92*
**Tourin,** Richard Harold 1922- *AmMWSc 92*
**Tourjee,** Eben 1834-1891 *NewAmDM*
**Tourlentes,** Thomas Theodore 1922- *AmMWSc 92*
**Tournas,** Methodios 1946- *WhoRel 92*
**Tournemine,** Rene-Joseph 1661-1739 *BlkwCEP*
**Tournemire,** Charles 1870-1939 *NewAmDM*
**Tourneur,** Cyril 1575?-1626 *RfGEnL 91*
**Tourneur,** Jacques 1904-1977 *IntDcF 2-2 [port]*
**Tourneur,** Maurice 1876-1961 *IntDcF 2-2 [port]*
**Tourney,** Garfield 1927- *AmMWSc 92*
**Tournier,** Michel 1924- *ConAu 36NR, GuFrLit 1, IntWW 91*
**Tournier,** Michel Edouard 1924- *IntAu&W 91*
**Tours,** Hugh Berthold 1910- *IntAu&W 91, WrDr 92*
**Tourte,** Francois 1747-1835 *NewAmDM*
**Tourtellotte,** Charles Dee 1931- *AmMWSc 92*
**Tourtellotte,** James Roll 1935- *WhoAmL 92*
**Tourtellotte,** Mark Eton 1928- *AmMWSc 92*
**Tourtellotte,** Wallace William 1924- *AmMWSc 92*
**Tourtelot,** Harry Allison 1918- *AmMWSc 92*
**Tourtillott,** Eleanor Alice 1909- *WhoMW 92*
**Touryan,** Kenell James 1936- *AmMWSc 92*
**Tousey,** Richard 1908- *AmMWSc 92, IntWW 91*
**Tousignant,** Claude 1932- *IntWW 91*
**Tousignant,** Michel 1945- *AmMWSc 92*
**Tousignaut,** Dwight R 1933- *AmMWSc 92*
**Tousley,** Russell Frederick 1938- *WhoAmL 92*
**Tousley,** Steven Francis 1957- *WhoMW 92*
**Toussaint,** Allen Richard 1938- *WhoEnt 92*
**Toussaint,** Cheryl 1952- *BlkOlyM*
**Toussaint,** Donald Raymond 1952- *WhoFI 92*
**Toussaint,** Francois-Vincent 1715-1772 *BlkwCEP*
**Toussaint,** Rose-Marie 1956- *WhoBlA 92*
**Toussaint L'Ouverture,** Pierre Francois D 1743-1803 *BenetAL 91*
**Toussieng,** Povl Winning 1918- *AmMWSc 92*
**Touster,** Oscar 1921- *AmMWSc 92*
**Tout,** Herbert 1904- *Who 92*
**Toutant,** Jean-Pierre 1944- *AmMWSc 92*
**Toutant,** William Joseph 1946- *WhoMW 92*
**Toutloff,** Betty Jane 1940- *WhoMW 92*
**Touval,** Saadia E. 1932- *ConAu 35NR*
**Tov,** Emanuel 1941- *WhoRel 92*
**Tovar,** Dave R. 1967- *WhoHisp 92*
**Tovar,** Humberto Toby 1911- *WhoHisp 92*
**Tovar,** Irene F 1938- *WhoAmP 91*
**Tovar,** Lorenzo 1942- *WhoHisp 92*
**Tovar,** Nicholas Mario 1960- *WhoWest 92*
**Tove,** Samuel B 1921- *AmMWSc 92*
**Tove,** Shirley Ruth 1925- *AmMWSc 92*
**Tovell,** Laurence 1919- *Who 92*
**Tovell,** Walter Massey 1916- *AmMWSc 92*
**Toverud,** Svein Utheim 1929- *AmMWSc 92*
**Tovey,** Brian 1926- *Who 92*
**Tovey,** Donald 1875-1940 *NewAmDM*
**Tovey,** Joseph 1938- *WhoFI 92*
**Tovey,** Weldon Reynolds 1938- *WhoWest 92*
**Tovstonogov,** Georgiy Aleksandrovich 1915- *SovUnBD*
**Tovstukha,** Ivan Pavlovich 1889-1935 *SovUnBD*
**Tovue,** Ronald 1933- *Who 92*
**Tow,** James 1936- *AmMWSc 92*
**Towarnicki,** Robert Joseph 1951- *WhoWest 92*
**Towarnicky,** Joseph Michael 1950- *WhoMW 92*
**Towbin,** Abraham Robert 1935- *WhoFI 92*
**Towbin,** Eugene Jonas 1918- *AmMWSc 92*
**Towe,** A Darden 1935- *WhoAmP 91*
**Towe,** Arnold Lester 1927- *AmMWSc 92*
**Towe,** George Coffin 1921- *AmMWSc 92*
**Towe,** Harry Lancaster d1991 *NewYTBS 91*
**Towe,** Kenneth McCarn 1935- *AmMWSc 92*
**Towe,** Lee Alan 1957- *WhoFI 92*
**Towe,** Peter Milburn 1922- *IntWW 91*
**Towe,** Thomas Edward 1937- *WhoAmP 91, WhoWest 92*
**Toweett,** Taaitta 1925- *IntWW 91*
**Towell,** David Garrett 1937- *AmMWSc 92*
**Towell,** Sydney Gilmer 1928- *WhoAmL 92*
**Towell,** Timothy L 1934- *WhoAmP 91*
**Towell,** William Earnest 1916- *AmMWSc 92*
**Tower,** Donald Bayley 1919- *AmMWSc 92*
**Tower,** Edward 1943- *WhoFI 92*
**Tower,** Horace Linwood, III 1932- *WhoFI 92*
**Tower,** Ibrook 1948- *WhoEnt 92*
**Tower,** Joan 1938- *ConCom 92, NewAmDM*
**Tower,** Joan Peabody 1938- *WhoEnt 92*
**Tower,** John 1926-1991 *News 91*
**Tower,** John G. 1925-1991 *CurBio 91N, NewYTBS 91*
**Tower,** John Goodwin d1991 *IntWW 91N*
**Tower,** Philip Thomas 1917- *Who 92*
**Tower,** Philip William 1943- *WhoMW 92*
**Tower,** Raymond Camille 1925- *WhoFI 92*
**Towers,** Barry 1938- *AmMWSc 92*
**Towers,** Bernard 1922- *AmMWSc 92*
**Towers,** Constance 1934- *IntMPA 92*
**Towers,** Edward William 1947- *WhoMW 92*
**Towers,** George Hugh Neil 1923- *AmMWSc 92*
**Towers,** Harry Alan 1920- *IntMPA 92*
**Towers,** Lawrence Alan 1952- *WhoAmL 92*
**Towers,** Regina *WrDr 92*
**Towers,** Robert *DrAPF 91*
**Towers,** Robert 1947- *WhoFI 92*
**Towers,** T. Gordon 1919- *WhoWest 92*
**Towery,** Curtis Kent 1954- *WhoAmL 92*
**Towey,** Richard Edward 1928- *WhoWest 92*
**Towill,** Leslie Ruth 1944- *AmMWSc 92*
**Towle,** Albert 1925- *AmMWSc 92*
**Towle,** David Walter 1941- *AmMWSc 92, WhoMW 92*
**Towle,** Doris Reiner 1933- *WhoAmP 91*
**Towle,** Howard Colgate 1947- *AmMWSc 92*
**Towle,** Katherine A 1898-1986 *FacFETw*
**Towle,** Louis Wallace 1908- *AmMWSc 92*
**Towle,** Patrick Michael 1941- *WhoMW 92*
**Towle,** Tony *DrAPF 91*
**Towle,** Tony 1939- *WrDr 92*
**Towler,** Joel Curtis 1938- *WhoRel 92*
**Towler,** Martin Lee 1910- *AmMWSc 92*
**Towles,** Stokley Porter 1935- *WhoFI 92*
**Town,** Donald 1927- *WhoIns 92*
**Town,** Harold Barling d1990 *IntWW 91N*
**Towndrow,** Frank Noel 1911- *Who 92*
**Towne,** Carroll E 1926- *WhoAmP 91*
**Towne,** Charles Hanson 1877-1949 *BenetAL 91*
**Towne,** David John 1947- *WhoMW 92*
**Towne,** Dorothea Alice 1910- *WhoWest 92*
**Towne,** Dudley Herbert 1924- *AmMWSc 92*
**Towne,** Edgar Arthur 1928- *WhoRel 92*
**Towne,** Elizabeth Lois Jones 1865-1961 *RelLAm 91*
**Towne,** Jack C 1927- *AmMWSc 92*
**Towne,** Peter *WrDr 92*
**Towne,** Robert *IntWW 91, WhoEnt 92*
**Towne,** Robert 1936- *IntMPA 92*
**Towne,** Ruth H 1928- *WhoAmP 91*
**Towneley,** Simon Peter Edmund Cosmo W 1921- *Who 92*
**Townend,** James Barrie Stanley 1938- *Who 92*
**Townend,** John Ernest 1934- *Who 92*
**Townend,** John Philip 1935- *Who 92*
**Towner,** Daniel *DrAPF 91*
**Towner,** Donald 1903-1985 *TwCPaSc*
**Towner,** George Rutherford 1933- *WhoWest 92*
**Towner,** Harry H 1949- *AmMWSc 92*
**Towner,** Howard Frost 1943- *AmMWSc 92*
**Towner,** Ian Stuart 1940- *AmMWSc 92*
**Towner,** Larry Edwin 1937- *WhoWest 92*
**Towner,** O W 1903- *AmMWSc 92*
**Towner,** Philip Haines 1953- *WhoRel 92*
**Towner,** R J 1925- *AmMWSc 92*
**Towner,** Richard Henry 1948- *AmMWSc 92*
**Townes,** Alexander Sloan 1929- *AmMWSc 92*
**Townes,** Bobby Joe 1932- *WhoFI 92*
**Townes,** Charles H. 1915- *WrDr 92*
**Townes,** Charles Hard 1915- *AmMWSc 92, FacFETw, IntWW 91, Who 92, WhoNob 90, WhoWest 92*
**Townes,** Clarence L., Sr. 1902- *WhoBlA 92*
**Townes,** Clarence Lee, Jr. 1928- *WhoBlA 92*
**Townes,** Edgar Eggleston, Jr. 1906- *WhoAmL 92*
**Townes,** George Anderson 1943- *AmMWSc 92*
**Townes,** Harry W 1937- *AmMWSc 92*
**Townes,** Henry Keith, Jr 1913- *AmMWSc 92*
**Townes,** Mary McLean 1928- *AmMWSc 92*
**Townes,** Philip Leonard 1927- *AmMWSc 92*
**Townes,** Sandra *WhoBlA 92*
**Townley,** Charles William 1934- *AmMWSc 92*
**Townley,** John Mark 1932- *WhoWest 92*
**Townley,** Jon *WhoEnt 92*
**Townley,** Judy Ann 1946- *AmMWSc 92*
**Townley,** Merrill M 1934- *WhoAmP 91*
**Townley,** Preston 1939- *WhoFI 92*
**Townley,** Ralph 1923- *WrDr 92*
**Townley,** Robert William 1907- *AmMWSc 92*
**Townley-Smith,** Thomas Frederick 1942- *AmMWSc 92*
**Towns,** Clarence, Jr 1916- *AmMWSc 92*
**Towns,** Donald Lionel 1935- *AmMWSc 92*
**Towns,** Edolphus 1934- *AlmAP 92 [port], WhoAmP 91, WhoBlA 92*
**Towns,** Elmer Leon 1932- *WhoRel 92*
**Towns,** Eva Rose 1927- *WhoBlA 92*
**Towns,** Forrest G. d1991 *NewYTBS 91*
**Towns,** Maxine Yvonne 1941- *WhoBlA 92*
**Towns,** Myron B., Jr. 1943- *WhoBlA 92*
**Towns,** Robert Lee Roy 1940- *AmMWSc 92*
**Towns,** Rose Mary 1934- *WhoBlA 92*
**Towns,** Sanna Nimtz 1943- *WhoBlA 92*
**Townsel,** Ronald 1934- *WhoBlA 92*
**Townsell,** Jackie Mae 1936- *WhoBlA 92*
**Townsend,** Albert Alan 1917- *Who 92*
**Townsend,** Alden Miller 1942- *AmMWSc 92*
**Townsend,** Alison *DrAPF 91*
**Townsend,** Andre 1962- *WhoBlA 92*
**Townsend,** Anna Stofflet 1899- *WhoWest 92*
**Townsend,** Arthur P. 1921- *WhoBlA 92*
**Townsend,** Barbara *WhoEnt 92*
**Townsend,** Bruce Walter 1953- *WhoRel 92*
**Townsend,** Bryan Sydney 1930- *Who 92*
**Townsend,** C L, Jr 1942- *WhoAmP 91*
**Townsend,** Charles Austin, II 1945- *WhoEnt 92*
**Townsend,** Charley E 1929- *AmMWSc 92*
**Townsend,** Cheryl Lynn 1951- *WhoWest 92*
**Townsend,** Claire 1952- *IntMPA 92*
**Townsend,** Clayton 1961- *WhoEnt 92*
**Townsend,** Craig Arthur 1947- *AmMWSc 92*
**Townsend,** Cynthia V. 1959- *WhoMW 92*
**Townsend,** Cyril David 1937- *Who 92*
**Townsend,** David H *WhoAmP 91*
**Townsend,** David R, Jr *WhoAmP 91*
**Townsend,** David Warren 1952- *AmMWSc 92*
**Townsend,** Douglas 1921- *WhoEnt 92*
**Townsend,** Douglas Wayne 1948- *AmMWSc 92*
**Townsend,** Earl Cunningham, Jr. 1914- *WhoAmL 92, WhoFI 92, WhoMW 92*
**Townsend,** Edward Waterman 1855-1942 *BenetAL 91*
**Townsend,** Edwin C 1936- *AmMWSc 92*
**Townsend,** Fitzhugh 1872?-1906 *BiInAmS*
**Townsend,** Floyd Darnell 1959- *WhoFI 92*
**Townsend,** Francis Everett 1867-1960 *FacFETw*
**Townsend,** Frank Marion 1914- *AmMWSc 92*
**Townsend,** George A 1950- *WhoAmP 91*
**Townsend,** George Alfred 1841-1914 *BenetAL 91*
**Townsend,** Gordon Frederick *AmMWSc 92*
**Townsend,** Greg 1961- *WhoBlA 92*
**Townsend,** Gus 1932- *WhoAmP 91*
**Townsend,** Harold Guyon, Jr. 1924- *WhoFI 92, WhoMW 92*
**Townsend,** Herbert Earl, Jr 1938- *AmMWSc 92*
**Townsend,** Howard C 1917- *WhoAmP 91*
**Townsend,** Howard Garfield, Jr 1938- *AmMWSc 92*
**Townsend,** Irene Fogleman 1932- *WhoFI 92*
**Townsend,** J Ives 1920- *AmMWSc 92*
**Townsend,** James Baker 1927- *WhoAmP 91*
**Townsend,** James Brierton, Jr. 1923- *WhoMW 92*
**Townsend,** James Douglas 1959- *WhoFI 92, WhoMW 92*
**Townsend,** James H. 1921- *WhoWest 92*
**Townsend,** James Skeoch 1934- *AmMWSc 92*
**Townsend,** James Willis 1936- *AmMWSc 92*
**Townsend,** Jane Kaltenbach 1922- *AmMWSc 92*
**Townsend,** Jeffrey Fred 1953- *WhoWest 92*
**Townsend,** Jim A. 1943- *WhoRel 92*
**Townsend,** Joan 1913- *IntAu&W 91*
**Townsend,** Joan 1936- *Who 92*
**Townsend,** John Ford 1936- *AmMWSc 92*
**Townsend,** John Kirk 1809-1851 *BiInAmS*
**Townsend,** John Marshall 1941- *AmMWSc 92*
**Townsend,** John Robert 1925- *AmMWSc 92*
**Townsend,** John Rowe 1922- *IntAu&W 91, SmATA 68 [port], WrDr 92*
**Townsend,** John Tolson 1927- *WhoRel 92*
**Townsend,** John William, Jr 1924- *AmMWSc 92*
**Townsend,** Jonathan 1922- *AmMWSc 92*
**Townsend,** Kenneth Ross 1927- *WhoRel 92*
**Townsend,** Kiliaen Van Rensselaer 1918- *WhoAmP 91*

**Townsend,** Larry Darwyn 1959- *WhoWest 92*
**Townsend,** Lawrence Willard 1947- *AmMWSc 92*
**Townsend,** Lena Moncrieff 1911- *Who 92*
**Townsend,** Leroy B 1933- *AmMWSc 92*
**Townsend,** Leslie 1924- *Who 92*
**Townsend,** Lloyd Everette, Jr. 1954- *WhoEnt 92*
**Townsend,** Mamie Lee Harrington 1920- *WhoBlA 92*
**Townsend,** Marjorie Rhodes 1930- *AmMWSc 92*
**Townsend,** Mark *ConAu 35NR*
**Townsend,** Mary Ashley 1836-1901 *BenetAL 91*
**Townsend,** Miles Averill 1935- *AmMWSc 92*
**Townsend,** Murray Luke, Jr. 1919- *WhoBlA 92*
**Townsend,** P. A. 1914- *WhoBlA 92*
**Townsend,** Palmer W 1926- *AmMWSc 92*
**Townsend,** Patricia 1926- *TwCPaSc*
**Townsend,** Patricia Ann 1933- *WhoMW 92*
**Townsend,** Paul Brorstrom 1919- *WhoFI 92*
**Townsend,** Paul W. 1961- *WhoEnt 92*
**Townsend,** Peter Brereton 1914- *WrDr 92*
**Townsend,** Peter Brereton 1928- *Who 92*
**Townsend,** Peter Wooldridge 1914- *IntAu&W 91, Who 92, WrDr 92*
**Townsend,** R Reid 1951- *AmMWSc 92*
**Townsend,** Ralph N 1931- *AmMWSc 92*
**Townsend,** Randolph J 1947- *WhoAmP 91*
**Townsend,** Richard K 1939- *WhoIns 92*
**Townsend,** Richard Taylor 1940- *WhoAmP 91*
**Townsend,** Robert *WhoEnt 92*
**Townsend,** Robert 1957- *IntMPA 92, WhoBlA 92*
**Townsend,** Roger Dale 1954- *WhoAmL 92*
**Townsend,** Ron 1941- *WhoBlA 92*
**Townsend,** Ronald *LesBEnT 92*
**Townsend,** Ronald P 1948- *WhoAmP 91*
**Townsend,** Russell Henry 1949- *WhoWest 92*
**Townsend,** Samuel Franklin 1935- *AmMWSc 92*
**Townsend,** Sara M 1919- *WhoAmP 91*
**Townsend,** Sue 1946- *IntAu&W 91, IntWW 91, WrDr 92*
**Townsend,** Susan 1946- *Who 92*
**Townsend,** Tammy M D 1939- *WhoAmP 91*
**Townsend,** Theodore Peter 1937- *WhoFI 92*
**Townsend,** Tom David 1952- *WhoFI 92*
**Townsend,** Vickie McCollum 1948- *WhoMW 92*
**Townsend,** W Wayne *WhoAmP 91*
**Townsend,** William *WhoHisp 92*
**Townsend,** William 1909-1973 *TwCPaSc*
**Townsend,** William H 1914- *WhoAmP 91*
**Townsend,** William Henry 1914- *WhoBlA 92*
**Townsend,** William Howard 1929- *WhoAmL 92*
**Townsend,** William Jackson 1932- *WhoAmL 92*
**Townshend** *Who 92*
**Townshend,** Marquess 1916- *Who 92*
**Townshend,** Aurelian 1583?-1651? *RfGEnL 91*
**Townshend,** Charles 1725-1767 *BlkwEAR*
**Townshend,** Graeme Scott 1965- *WhoBlA 92*
**Townshend,** John Linden 1926- *AmMWSc 92*
**Townshend,** Pete 1945- *NewAmDM*
**Townshend,** Peter 1945- *WhoEnt 92*
**Townshend,** Peter Dennis Blandford 1945- *IntWW 91*
**Townshend,** Samuel Arthur 1950- *WhoMW 92*
**Townsing,** Kenneth 1914- *Who 92*
**Townsley,** Clarence Page, III 1924- *WhoFI 92, WhoMW 92*
**Townsley,** John D 1933- *AmMWSc 92*
**Townsley,** Marshall Wayne 1954- *WhoRel 92*
**Townsley,** Philip McNair 1925- *AmMWSc 92*
**Townsley,** Sidney Joseph 1924- *AmMWSc 92*
**Townzen,** Jack Edward, Jr. 1954- *WhoEnt 92*
**Towry,** Peter *Who 92*
**Towse,** Daniel Charles 1924- *WhoAmP 91*
**Towse,** Donald Frederick 1924- *AmMWSc 92*
**Towsen,** John *WhoEnt 92*
**Toy,** Arthur Dock Fon 1915- *AmMWSc 92*
**Toy,** Arthur John, Jr *AmMWSc 92*
**Toy,** Charles David 1955- *WhoAmL 92*
**Toy,** Crawford Howell 1836-1919 *RelLAm 91*
**Toy,** John 1930- *Who 92*
**Toy,** Madeline Shen 1928- *AmMWSc 92*
**Toy,** Peter Francis 1949- *WhoIns 92*
**Toy,** Sam 1923- *IntWW 91, Who 92*
**Toy,** Terrence J 1946- *AmMWSc 92*
**Toy,** William W 1950- *AmMWSc 92*
**Toy,** Wing N 1926- *AmMWSc 92*
**Toyama,** Jean Yamasaki *DrAPF 91*
**Toye,** George Henry 1922- *WhoAmL 92*
**Toye,** John Francis Joseph 1942- *Who 92*
**Toye,** Wendy 1917- *IntWW 91, Who 92*
**Toyer,** Richard Henry 1944- *WhoWest 92*
**Toyn,** Richard John 1927- *Who 92*
**Toynbee,** Arnold J. 1889-1975 *ConAu 36NR, FacFETw*
**Toynbee,** Lawrence 1922- *TwCPaSc*
**Toynbee,** Polly 1946- *IntAu&W 91, Who 92, WrDr 92*
**Toyne,** Peter 1939- *Who 92*
**Toyne Sewell,** Timothy Patrick 1941- *Who 92*
**Toyomura,** Dennis Takeshi 1926- *WhoFI 92, WhoWest 92*
**Tozer,** Aiden Wilson 1897-1963 *RelLAm 91*
**Tozer,** Basil 1872-1949 *ScFEYrs*
**Tozer,** E T 1924- *AmMWSc 92*
**Tozer,** Theodore William 1957- *WhoMW 92*
**Tozer,** Thomas Nelson 1936- *AmMWSc 92*
**Tozer,** W. James, Jr. 1941- *WhoFI 92*
**Tozer,** William T 1934- *WhoIns 92*
**Tozier,** John E 1942- *AmMWSc 92*
**Tozzer,** Charles Phillip 1953- *WhoWest 92*
**Tozzer,** Jack Carl 1922- *WhoMW 92*
**Tozzi,** Giorgio 1923- *NewAmDM*
**Tozzi,** Salvatore *AmMWSc 92*
**Traat,** Mats 1936- *IntAu&W 91*
**Traba,** Marta 1930-1983 *SpAmWW*
**Trabandt,** Charles Anthony 1941- *WhoAmP 91*
**Trabant,** Dennis Carlyle 1943- *WhoWest 92*
**Trabant,** Edward Arthur 1920- *AmMWSc 92*
**Trabb,** Janet Lyn 1942- *WhoFI 92*
**Traber,** Daniel Lee 1938- *AmMWSc 92*
**Traber,** Maret G 1950- *AmMWSc 92*
**Trabucchi,** Alberto 1907- *IntWW 91*
**Trabue,** Charles Clay 1910- *WhoAmL 92*
**Trabulsi,** Richard Joseph, Jr 1945- *WhoAmP 91*
**Trace,** Robert Denny 1917- *AmMWSc 92*
**Tracey,** Daniel Edward 1947- *AmMWSc 92*
**Tracey,** Joshua Irving, Jr 1915- *AmMWSc 92*
**Tracey,** Martin Louis, Jr 1943- *AmMWSc 92*
**Tracey,** Richard Patrick 1943- *Who 92*
**Tracey,** Russell Lee 1932- *WhoFI 92*
**Tracey,** Stanley William 1926- *Who 92*
**Tracey,** Stephen Frederick T. *Who 92*
**Tracey,** Terence John 1952- *WhoMW 92*
**Tracey,** William Raymond 1922- *WhoFI 92*
**Trachewsky,** Daniel 1940- *AmMWSc 92*
**Trachman,** Edward G 1946- *AmMWSc 92*
**Trachsel,** William Henry 1943- *WhoAmL 92*
**Trachtenberg,** Alan *WrDr 92*
**Trachtenberg,** Alan Israel 1956- *WhoWest 92*
**Trachtenberg,** David 1925- *WhoAmL 92*
**Trachtenberg,** Edward Norman 1927- *AmMWSc 92*
**Trachtenberg,** Inge *DrAPF 91*
**Trachtenberg,** Isaac 1929- *AmMWSc 92*
**Trachtenberg,** Matthew J. 1953- *WhoFI 92*
**Trachtenberg,** Paul *DrAPF 91*
**Trachtenberg,** Peter *DrAPF 91*
**Trachtenberg,** Robert Jay 1961- *WhoAmL 92*
**Trachtman,** Mendel 1929- *AmMWSc 92*
**Trachy,** Stuart David 1954- *WhoAmP 91*
**Traci,** Donald Philip 1927- *WhoAmL 92*
**Traci,** Philip 1934-1984 *ConAu 133*
**Track,** Gerhard 1934- *WhoEnt 92*
**Tract,** Harold M. 1926- *WhoAmL 92, WhoIns 92*
**Tract,** Marc Mitchell 1959- *WhoFI 92*
**Tractenberg,** Craig R. 1956- *WhoAmL 92*
**Tractenberg,** Paul L. 1938- *WhoAmL 92*
**Tracton,** Martin Steven 1945- *AmMWSc 92*
**Tracy** *Who 92*
**Tracy,** Abba Arthur 1899- *WhoEnt 92*
**Tracy,** Alan Thomas 1947- *WhoAmP 91*
**Tracy,** Barbara Marie 1945- *WhoAmL 92, WhoFI 92*
**Tracy,** C Richard 1943- *AmMWSc 92*
**Tracy,** Clarence 1908- *WrDr 92*
**Tracy,** Clarissa Tucker 1818-1905 *BiInAmS*
**Tracy,** Craig Arnold 1945- *AmMWSc 92*
**Tracy,** Daniel LeRoy 1946- *WhoRel 92*
**Tracy,** David 1939- *WhoRel 92*
**Tracy,** David J 1937- *AmMWSc 92*
**Tracy,** David M. 1924- *WhoFI 92*
**Tracy,** Denise Diane 1950- *WhoRel 92*
**Tracy,** Derrick Shannon 1933- *AmMWSc 92*
**Tracy,** Dick O. 1962- *WhoEnt 92*
**Tracy,** Emily Anne Miller 1947- *WhoWest 92*
**Tracy,** Eugene Arthur 1927- *WhoFI 92, WhoMW 92*
**Tracy,** Gregory Lynn 1957- *WhoMW 92*
**Tracy,** Hugh Gordon Henry 1912- *Who 92*
**Tracy,** J. David 1946- *WhoAmL 92*
**Tracy,** James Donald 1938- *WhoMW 92*
**Tracy,** James Frueh 1916- *AmMWSc 92*
**Tracy,** James Wayne 1945- *WhoRel 92*
**Tracy,** Joel Dean 1961- *WhoMW 92*
**Tracy,** Joseph Charles 1943- *AmMWSc 92*
**Tracy,** Joseph Walter 1924- *AmMWSc 92*
**Tracy,** Louis 1863-1928 *ScFEYrs*
**Tracy,** Marie Pintavalle 1936- *WhoEnt 92*
**Tracy,** Mark Luther 1943- *WhoRel 92*
**Tracy,** Michael Alec 1932- *WrDr 92*
**Tracy,** Michael Cameron 1952- *WhoEnt 92*
**Tracy,** Richard E 1934- *AmMWSc 92*
**Tracy,** Richard H C *WhoAmP 91*
**Tracy,** Roger Wahlquist 1938- *WhoAmP 91*
**Tracy,** Samuel Mills 1847-1920 *BiInAmS*
**Tracy,** Spencer 1900-1967 *FacFETw [port]*
**Tracy,** Steven McCrary 1949- *WhoMW 92*
**Tracy,** Susan *WhoAmP 91*
**Tracy,** Walter Valentine 1914- *Who 92*
**Tracy,** William Allan 1940- *WhoAmP 91*
**Tracy,** William B 1943- *WhoIns 92*
**Tracy,** William E 1934- *AmMWSc 92*
**Tracy,** William Francis 1954- *AmMWSc 92*
**Tracz,** Will 1950- *AmMWSc 92*
**Trad,** Phillip G. *WhoAmL 92*
**Trader,** Harriet Peat 1922- *WhoBlA 92*
**Trader,** Joseph Edgar 1946- *WhoMW 92*
**Traeger,** John Andrew 1921- *WhoAmP 91*
**Traeger,** Richard K. 1932- *WhoWest 92*
**Traer,** Robert A. 1943- *WhoRel 92*
**Traetta,** Tommaso 1727-1779 *BlkwCEP, NewAmDM*
**Traexler,** John F 1930- *AmMWSc 92*
**Trafeli,** Robert Mario 1958- *WhoMW 92*
**Trafford** *Who 92*
**Trafford,** Edmund 1948- *WhoEnt 92*
**Trafford,** Ian Colton 1928- *IntAu&W 91, Who 92*
**Traficant,** James A., Jr. 1941- *AlmAP 92 [port], WhoAmP 91, WhoMW 92*
**Traficante,** Michael Anthony 1939- *WhoAmP 91*
**Trafis,** Gerald Anthony 1950- *WhoFI 92*
**Trafton,** Barbara M 1949- *WhoAmP 91*
**Trafton,** Laurence Munro 1938- *AmMWSc 92*
**Trafton,** Richard L *WhoAmP 91*
**Trafton-Dyer,** Nancy Jo 1960- *WhoMW 92*
**Tragarz,** Nancy Dowsett 1943- *WhoMW 92*
**Trager,** David G. 1937- *WhoAmL 92*
**Trager,** James 1925- *ConAu 34NR*
**Trager,** Russell Harlan 1945- *WhoWest 92*
**Trager,** William 1910- *AmMWSc 92, IntWW 91*
**Trager,** William Frank 1937- *AmMWSc 92*
**Trahair,** John Rosewarne 1921- *Who 92*
**Trahan,** Barry G 1954- *WhoAmP 91*
**Trahan,** David Paul 1950- *WhoFI 92*
**Trahan,** Donald Herbert 1930- *AmMWSc 92*
**Trahan,** Margaret Fritchey 1934- *WhoFI 92*
**Trahan,** Russell Edward, Jr 1949- *AmMWSc 92*
**Trahanovsky,** Walter Samuel 1938- *AmMWSc 92*
**Trahern,** George Eugene 1936- *WhoAmP 91, WhoWest 92*
**Traherne,** Cennydd 1910- *Who 92*
**Traherne,** Margaret *TwCPaSc*
**Traherne,** Michael *SmATA 66*
**Traherne,** Thomas 1637-1674 *RfGEnL 91*
**Traicoff,** Ellen Braden *WhoMW 92*
**Trail,** Carroll C 1927- *AmMWSc 92*
**Trail,** George Arthur, III 1936- *WhoAmP 91*
**Traill,** Alan 1935- *IntWW 91*
**Traill,** Alan Towers 1935- *Who 92*
**Traill,** Catharine Parr 1802-1899 *NinCLC 31 [port]*
**Traill,** Catherine Parr 1802-1899 *BenetAL 91*
**Traill,** David Angus 1942- *WhoWest 92*
**Traill,** H D 1842-1900 *ScFEYrs*
**Train,** Arthur 1875-1945 *BenetAL 91, ScFEYrs*
**Train,** Arthur and Wood, Robert Williams *ScFEYrs*
**Train,** Carl T 1939- *AmMWSc 92*
**Train,** Christopher John 1932- *Who 92*
**Train,** David 1919- *Who 92*
**Train,** John 1928- *WhoFI 92*
**Train,** Russell Errol 1920- *IntWW 91*
**Traina,** Paul J 1934- *AmMWSc 92*
**Traina,** Vincent Michael 1943- *AmMWSc 92*
**Trainer,** Daniel Olney 1926- *AmMWSc 92*
**Trainer,** David Gibson 1945- *AmMWSc 92*
**Trainer,** Frank W 1921- *AmMWSc 92*
**Trainer,** John Ezra, Jr 1943- *AmMWSc 92*
**Trainer,** John Ezra, Sr 1914- *AmMWSc 92*
**Trainer,** Michael Norman 1952- *AmMWSc 92*
**Trainer,** Richard Daniel Chieffeau 1944- *WhoFI 92*
**Trainin,** Aron Naumovich 1883-1957 *SovUnBD*
**Trainor,** Carol Ann 1964- *WhoAmL 92*
**Trainor,** Charles Warren 1945- *WhoAmL 92*
**Trainor,** David Bruce 1942- *WhoFI 92*
**Trainor,** Francis Rice 1929- *AmMWSc 92*
**Trainor,** George L 1952- *AmMWSc 92*
**Trainor,** James H 1935- *AmMWSc 92*
**Trainor,** John Felix 1921- *WhoMW 92*
**Trainor,** Joseph James 1961- *WhoFI 92*
**Trainor,** Joseph Sidney 1919- *WhoAmP 91*
**Trainor,** Lynne E H 1921- *AmMWSc 92*
**Trainor,** Robert James 1944- *AmMWSc 92*
**Traintime,** Jeff 1948- *WhoEnt 92*
**Traisman,** Howard Sevin 1923- *AmMWSc 92*
**Traisman,** Kenneth Neil 1958- *WhoAmL 92*
**Traitor,** Charles Eugene 1934- *AmMWSc 92*
**Trajan** 53-117 *EncEarC*
**Trajmar,** Sandor 1931- *AmMWSc 92*
**Trakas,** Deno *DrAPF 91*
**Trakl,** Georg 1887-1914 *FacFETw*
**Tralins,** S Robert 1926- *IntAu&W 91*
**Trama,** Francesco Biagio 1927- *AmMWSc 92*
**Trambarulo,** Ralph 1925- *AmMWSc 92*
**Trambley,** Estela Portillo 1936- *WhoHisp 92*
**Trambukis,** William J. 1926- *IntMPA 92*
**Tramell,** Paul Richard 1943- *AmMWSc 92*
**Tramer,** Bennett Perry 1947- *WhoEnt 92*
**Tramiel,** Jack 1928- *WhoWest 92*
**Tramiel,** Kenneth Ray, Sr. 1946- *WhoBlA 92*
**Tramiel,** Sam 1950- *WhoWest 92*
**Trammel,** Clinton Ellis 1940- *WhoFI 92*
**Trammel,** Kenneth 1937- *AmMWSc 92*
**Trammel,** Niles d1973 *LesBEnT 92*
**Trammell,** George Thomas 1923- *AmMWSc 92*
**Trammell,** Grover J, Jr 1919- *AmMWSc 92*
**Trammell,** Larry Michael 1953- *WhoWest 92*
**Trammell,** Rex Costo 1938- *AmMWSc 92*
**Trammell,** Robert DeWitt 1945- *WhoAmP 91*
**Trammell,** Wilbur *WhoBlA 92*
**Trammell,** William Rivers 1926- *WhoBlA 92*
**Trammer,** Monte Irvin 1951- *WhoBlA 92, WhoFI 92*
**Tramondozzi,** John Edmund 1942- *AmMWSc 92*
**Tramontano,** John Patrick, Jr. 1941- *WhoFI 92*
**Tramonte,** James Albert 1951- *WhoAmL 92*
**Tramontine,** John Orlando 1932- *WhoAmL 92*
**Trampler,** Walter *WhoEnt 92*
**Trampler,** Walter 1915- *NewAmDM*
**Tramposh,** Anne Katherine 1954- *WhoMW 92*
**Trampus,** Anthony 1927- *AmMWSc 92*
**Tran Nam Trung** *IntWW 91*
**Tran Tam Tinh** 1929- *IntWW 91*
**Tran thi Nga** 1927- *LiExTwC*
**Tran Thien Khiem** 1925- *IntWW 91*
**Tran Van Huong** 1903- *IntWW 91*
**Tran Van Tra** 1918- *IntWW 91*
**Tran,** Anthony Doan 1950- *WhoRel 92*
**Tran,** Hung The 1956- *WhoWest 92*
**Tran,** Hung Thien 1953- *WhoMW 92*
**Tran,** Long Trieu 1956- *AmMWSc 92, WhoFI 92*
**Tran,** Nang Tri 1948- *AmMWSc 92*
**Tran,** Nghia T. 1963- *WhoWest 92*
**Tran,** Tan Cao 1939- *WhoMW 92*
**Tranel,** Daniel T 1957- *AmMWSc 92*
**Tranel,** James Michael 1951- *WhoRel 92*
**Tranetzki,** Michael George 1946- *WhoMW 92*
**Trangenstein,** Kathy Ann 1952- *WhoMW 92*
**Traniello,** James Francis Anthony 1952- *AmMWSc 92*
**Trank,** John W 1928- *AmMWSc 92*
**Tranmire,** Baron 1903- *Who 92*
**Tranner,** Frank 1922- *AmMWSc 92*
**Tranquada,** Robert Ernest 1930- *AmMWSc 92, WhoWest 92*

**Transtromer,** Tomas 1931- *ConLC 65 [port]*
**Transue,** Laurence Frederick 1914- *AmMWSc 92*
**Transue,** Pamela Jean 1950- *WhoWest 92*
**Transue,** William Reagle 1914- *AmMWSc 92*
**Trant,** Douglas Allen 1951- *WhoAmL 92*
**Trant,** Richard 1928- *Who 92*
**Tranter,** Clement John 1909- *Who 92, WrDr 92*
**Tranter,** John 1943- *ConPo 91, WrDr 92*
**Tranter,** John E 1943- *IntAu&W 91*
**Tranter,** Nigel 1909- *WrDr 92*
**Tranter,** Nigel Godwin 1909- *IntAu&W 91, Who 92*
**Tranter,** Patrick Edward 1957- *WhoEnt 92*
**Tranter,** Terence Michael 1944- *WhoAmP 91*
**Trantham,** Roy Munsten *WhoAmP 91*
**Trantino,** Joseph Peter 1924- *WhoAmP 91*
**Trantino,** Tommy *DrAPF 91*
**Tranum,** Jean Lorraine 1935- *WhoEnt 92*
**Traore,** Diara *IntWW 91*
**Traore,** Mohamed 1940- *IntWW 91*
**Traore,** Moussa 1936- *IntWW 91*
**Trapani,** Ignatius Louis 1925- *AmMWSc 92*
**Trapani,** Ralph James 1952- *WhoWest 92*
**Trapani,** Robert Don 1939- *WhoRel 92*
**Trapeznikov,** Sergey Pavlovich 1912-1984 *SovUnBD*
**Trapeznikov,** Vadim Aleksandrovich 1905- *IntWW 91*
**Trapido,** Barbara 1941- *WrDr 92*
**Trapido,** Harold d1991 *NewYTBS 91*
**Trapido,** Harold 1916- *AmMWSc 92*
**Trapnell,** Barry Maurice Waller 1924- *Who 92*
**Trapnell,** John Arthur 1913- *Who 92*
**Trapolin,** Frank Winter 1913- *WhoFI 92*
**Trapp Family Singers** *NewAmDM*
**Trapp,** Allan Laverne 1932- *AmMWSc 92, WhoMW 92*
**Trapp,** Charles Anthony 1936- *AmMWSc 92*
**Trapp,** Donald W. 1946- *WhoBlA 92*
**Trapp,** Ellen Simpson 1920- *WhoBlA 92*
**Trapp,** Eric Joseph 1910- *Who 92*
**Trapp,** Gene Robert 1938- *AmMWSc 92*
**Trapp,** George 1948- *TwCPaSc*
**Trapp,** George E, Jr 1944- *AmMWSc 92*
**Trapp,** Howard 1934- *WhoAmP 91*
**Trapp,** Joseph Burney 1925- *IntWW 91, Who 92*
**Trapp,** Robert F 1932- *AmMWSc 92*
**Trapp,** Thomas Harvey 1946- *WhoRel 92*
**Trapp,** Wendell H. 1949- *WhoAmL 92*
**Trapp-Dukes,** Rosa Lee 1942- *WhoBlA 92*
**Trappe,** James Martin 1931- *AmMWSc 92*
**Trappier,** Arthur Shives 1937- *WhoBlA 92*
**Traprock,** Walter E. *BenetAL 91*
**Traquair,** James Alvin 1947- *AmMWSc 92*
**Trasenster,** Michael Augustus Tulk 1923- *Who 92*
**Trasher,** Donald Watson 1937- *AmMWSc 92*
**Trask,** Charles Brian 1944- *AmMWSc 92*
**Trask,** James L 1932- *WhoIns 92*
**Trask,** John Boardman 1824-1879 *BiInAmS*
**Trask,** Laurence Marion 1935- *WhoMW 92*
**Trask,** Linda Ann 1956- *WhoWest 92*
**Trask,** Robert Chauncey Riley 1939- *WhoWest 92*
**Traskos,** Richard Thomas 1940- *AmMWSc 92*
**Trasler,** Daphne Gay 1926- *AmMWSc 92*
**Trasler,** Gordon Blair 1929- *Who 92, WrDr 92*
**Trass,** O 1931- *AmMWSc 92*
**Trasvina,** John D. 1958- *WhoHisp 92*
**Tratner,** Alan Arthur 1947- *WhoFI 92, WhoWest 92*
**Tratt,** David Michael 1955- *WhoWest 92*
**Trattler,** Larry 1947- *WhoAmL 92*
**Trattler,** Ross Alan 1950- *WhoWest 92*
**Trattner,** Walter I. 1936- *WrDr 92*
**Traub,** Alan Cutler 1923- *AmMWSc 92*
**Traub,** David Coleman 1957- *WhoWest 92*
**Traub,** George James 1942- *WhoAmP 91*
**Traub,** George Michael 1958- *WhoRel 92*
**Traub,** Joseph Frederick 1932- *AmMWSc 92*
**Traub,** Judy 1940- *WhoAmP 91*
**Traub,** Marvin Stuart 1925- *WhoFI 92*
**Traub,** Paul 1952- *WhoAmL 92*
**Traub,** Richard Kenneth 1950- *WhoAmL 92*
**Traub,** Richard Kimberley 1934- *AmMWSc 92*
**Traub,** Robert 1916- *AmMWSc 92*
**Traub,** Wesley Arthur 1940- *AmMWSc 92*
**Traube,** Victoria G. 1946- *WhoEnt 92*
**Traubel,** Helen 1899-1972 *NewAmDM*
**Traubel,** Helen 1903-1972 *FacFETw*
**Traubel,** Horace 1858-1919 *BenetAL 91*
**Trauberg,** Il'ya Zakharovich 1905-1948 *SovUnBD*
**Trauberg,** Leonid Zakharovich 1902- *SovUnBD*
**Traubert,** Michael 1957- *WhoAmP 91*
**Trauger,** David Lee 1942- *AmMWSc 92*
**Trauger,** Donald Byron 1920- *AmMWSc 92*
**Trauger,** Frederick Dale 1916- *AmMWSc 92*
**Traugh,** Jolinda Ann *AmMWSc 92*
**Traughber,** Charles M. 1943- *WhoBlA 92*
**Traugott,** Stephen C 1927- *AmMWSc 92*
**Traumann,** Klaus Friedrich 1924- *AmMWSc 92*
**Traurig,** Harold H 1936- *AmMWSc 92*
**Trauring,** Mitchell 1922- *AmMWSc 92*
**Trause,** Paul Karl 1948- *WhoAmP 91*
**Traut,** Donald L, Sr 1932- *WhoIns 92*
**Traut,** Robert Rush 1934- *AmMWSc 92*
**Traut,** Thomas Wolfgang 1943- *AmMWSc 92*
**Traut,** William Raymond 1929- *WhoEnt 92*
**Trautenberg,** David Herbert 1958- *WhoWest 92*
**Trauth,** Joseph Louis, Jr. 1945- *WhoAmL 92*
**Trautlein,** Donald Henry 1926- *IntWW 91*
**Trautman,** Andrzej 1933- *IntWW 91*
**Trautman,** Dale Charles 1941- *WhoRel 92*
**Trautman,** Donald Theodore 1924- *WhoAmL 92*
**Trautman,** Donald W. 1936- *WhoRel 92*
**Trautman,** Harold N *WhoAmP 91*
**Trautman,** Jack Carl 1929- *AmMWSc 92*
**Trautman,** Leo C., Jr. 1954- *WhoWest 92*
**Trautman,** Milton Bernhard 1899- *AmMWSc 92*
**Trautman,** Rodes 1923- *AmMWSc 92*
**Trautman,** Tucker Karl 1947- *WhoAmL 92*
**Trautman,** William Ellsworth 1940- *WhoAmL 92*
**Trautmann,** Conrad Henry, III 1963- *WhoEnt 92*
**Trautschold,** John Ray 1952- *WhoEnt 92*
**Trautvetter,** William Edward 1947- *WhoEnt 92*
**Trautwein,** Betty Baldwin 1947- *WhoFI 92*
**Trautwein,** George William 1927- *WhoEnt 92*
**Trautwine,** John Cresson 1810-1883 *BiInAmS*
**Travancore,** Rajpramukh of d1991 *Who 92N*
**Travanti,** Daniel J. 1940- *IntMPA 92*
**Travanti,** Daniel John *WhoEnt 92*
**Travell,** Janet G. 1901- *IntWW 91*
**Travell,** John Charles 1930- *WhoRel 92*
**Travelli,** Armando 1934- *AmMWSc 92*
**Traven,** B *FacFETw*
**Traven,** B. d1969 *BenetAL 91*
**Traven,** Bruno 1882-1969 *LiExTwC*
**Traver,** Alfred Ellis 1939- *AmMWSc 92*
**Traver,** Janet Hope 1926- *AmMWSc 92*
**Traver,** Nancy Schapanski 1953- *WhoMW 92*
**Traver,** Noel Allen 1959- *WhoMW 92*
**Traver,** Peggy Cox 1935- *WhoAmP 91*
**Traver,** Robert *ConAu 134*
**Traver,** Robert 1903- *WrDr 92*
**Travers,** Basil Holmes 1919- *Who 92, WrDr 92*
**Travers,** Ben 1886-1980 *ConAu 133, RfGEnL 91*
**Travers,** Bill 1922- *IntMPA 92*
**Travers,** Brendan 1931- *Who 92*
**Travers,** David Owens 1934- *WhoRel 92*
**Travers,** J.M. *TwCWW 91*
**Travers,** Judith Lynnette 1950- *WhoFI 92, WhoWest 92*
**Travers,** Kenneth *WrDr 92*
**Travers,** Margaret Strauss 1944- *WhoAmL 92*
**Travers,** P. L. 1906- *WrDr 92*
**Travers,** Thomas 1902- *Who 92*
**Travers,** Will *TwCWW 91*
**Travers,** William Brailsford 1934- *AmMWSc 92*
**Traverse,** Alfred 1925- *AmMWSc 92*
**Traverse-Healy,** Thomas Hector 1923- *Who 92*
**Traverse-Healy,** Tim 1923- *IntWW 91*
**Traversi,** Derek A. 1912- *WrDr 92*
**Traverso,** Peggy Bosworth 1938- *WhoWest 92*
**Travinski,** Marilyn Louise 1947- *WhoAmP 91*
**Travis,** Adrian Paul 1931- *WhoRel 92, WhoWest 92*
**Travis,** Alexander B. 1930- *WhoBlA 92*
**Travis,** Alice 1943- *WhoAmP 91*
**Travis,** Benjamin *WhoBlA 92*
**Travis,** Carole Joan 1942- *WhoMW 92*
**Travis,** David M 1926- *AmMWSc 92*
**Travis,** David M 1948- *WhoAmP 91*
**Travis,** Dempsey J. 1920- *WhoBlA 92, WrDr 92*
**Travis,** Donald K. 1928- *WhoAmL 92*
**Travis,** Elizabeth 1920- *ConAu 134*
**Travis,** Ernest Hampton 1927- *WhoEnt 92*
**Travis,** Frederick F. 1942- *ConAu 135*
**Travis,** Geraldine 1931- *WhoBlA 92*
**Travis,** Geraldine Washington 1931- *WhoAmP 91*
**Travis,** Irven 1904- *AmMWSc 92*
**Travis,** Isaac N d1897 *BiInAmS*
**Travis,** J C 1927- *AmMWSc 92*
**Travis,** J. Mark 1953- *IntMPA 92*
**Travis,** James 1935- *AmMWSc 92*
**Travis,** James Leslie 1923- *WhoRel 92*
**Travis,** James Roland 1925- *AmMWSc 92*
**Travis,** Jill Helene 1948- *WhoFI 92*
**Travis,** Joan Faye Schiller 1939- *WhoAmL 92*
**Travis,** Joe Lane 1931- *WhoAmP 91*
**Travis,** John D 1940- *WhoAmP 91*
**Travis,** John Richard 1942- *AmMWSc 92, WhoWest 92*
**Travis,** Joseph 1953- *AmMWSc 92*
**Travis,** Larry Dean 1943- *AmMWSc 92*
**Travis,** Lawrence Allan 1942- *WhoFI 92, WhoMW 92*
**Travis,** Luther Brisendine 1931- *AmMWSc 92*
**Travis,** Marlene O. *WhoFI 92, WhoMW 92*
**Travis,** Merle 1917-1983 *NewAmDM*
**Travis,** Murray William 1931- *WhoRel 92*
**Travis,** Myron 1963- *WhoBlA 92*
**Travis,** Nancy *IntMPA 92*
**Travis,** Paul Nicholas 1949- *WhoWest 92*
**Travis,** Philip 1940- *WhoAmP 91*
**Travis,** Randall Howard 1924- *AmMWSc 92*
**Travis,** Richard Edward 1933- *WhoMW 92*
**Travis,** Robert LeRoy 1940- *AmMWSc 92*
**Travis,** Robert Victor 1933- *AmMWSc 92*
**Travis,** Roy 1922- *NewAmDM, WhoWest 92*
**Travis,** Russell Burton 1918- *AmMWSc 92*
**Travis,** Susan Kathryn 1940- *WhoFI 92*
**Travis,** T. Richard 1957- *WhoAmL 92*
**Travis,** Will *TwCWW 91*
**Travis Copess,** Joyce Marie 1947- *WhoMW 92*
**Travnicek,** Edward Adolph 1936- *AmMWSc 92*
**Travolta,** John 1954- *IntMPA 92, IntWW 91, WhoEnt 92*
**Traw,** Steven Paul 1947- *WhoRel 92*
**Trawick,** Buckner Beasley 1914- *WrDr 92*
**Trawick,** Leonard *DrAPF 91*
**Trawick,** Louise LaVergne 1917- *WhoBlA 92*
**Trawick,** William George 1924- *AmMWSc 92*
**Trawinski,** Benon John 1924- *AmMWSc 92*
**Trawinski,** Edward John 1948- *WhoAmL 92*
**Trawinski,** Irene Patricia Monahan 1929- *AmMWSc 92*
**Traxler,** Bob 1931- *AlmAP 92 [port], WhoAmP 91, WhoMW 92*
**Traxler,** James Theodore 1929- *AmMWSc 92, WhoMW 92*
**Traxler,** Patricia *DrAPF 91*
**Traxler,** Richard Warwick 1928- *AmMWSc 92*
**Traxler,** William Byrd 1912- *WhoAmL 92*
**Traylor,** Charles Harold 1955- *WhoRel 92*
**Traylor,** Claire 1931- *WhoAmP 91*
**Traylor,** Horace Jerome 1931- *WhoBlA 92*
**Traylor,** Jack R, Sr 1922- *WhoAmP 91*
**Traylor,** John Hardie 1928- *WhoRel 92*
**Traylor,** Lee Clyde 1932- *WhoAmP 91*
**Traylor,** Melvin Alvah, Jr 1915- *AmMWSc 92*
**Traylor,** Orba Forest 1910- *WhoFI 92*
**Traylor,** Patricia Shizuko 1930- *AmMWSc 92*
**Traylor,** Rudolph A. 1918- *WhoBlA 92*
**Traylor,** Teddy G 1925- *AmMWSc 92*
**Traylor,** William Robert 1921- *WhoWest 92*
**Traynham,** James Gibson 1925- *AmMWSc 92*
**Traynor,** Harold Joseph 1899-1972 *FacFETw*
**Traynor,** J. Michael 1934- *WhoAmL 92*
**Traynor,** John T *WhoAmP 91*
**Traynor,** Lee 1938- *AmMWSc 92*
**Traystman,** Richard J 1942- *AmMWSc 92*
**Traywick,** Flo Crisman Neher 1924- *WhoAmP 91*
**Trbovich,** Robert Jeffrey 1943- *WhoFI 92*
**Treacher,** John 1924- *Who 92*
**Treacy,** Colman Maurice 1949- *Who 92*
**Treacy,** David Matthew 1953- *WhoFI 92*
**Treacy,** Edward Thomas 1941- *WhoAmP 91*
**Treacy,** Gerald Bernard 1951- *WhoAmL 92*
**Treacy,** Joan 1944- *WhoRel 92*
**Treacy,** Vincent Edward 1942- *WhoAmL 92*
**Treadgold,** Donald Warren 1922- *WhoRel 92, WrDr 92*
**Treadgold,** Hazel Rhona 1936- *Who 92*
**Treadgold,** John David 1931- *Who 92*
**Treadgold,** Mary 1910- *IntAu&W 91, WrDr 92*
**Treadgold,** Sydney William 1933- *Who 92*
**Treado,** Paul A 1936- *AmMWSc 92*
**Treadway,** James Curran 1943- *WhoAmL 92, WhoFI 92*
**Treadway,** Joseph L 1947- *WhoAmP 91*
**Treadway,** Richard Fowle 1913- *WhoAmP 91*
**Treadway,** William Jack, Jr 1949- *AmMWSc 92*
**Treadwell,** Carleton Raymond 1911- *AmMWSc 92*
**Treadwell,** Charles James 1920- *Who 92*
**Treadwell,** Daniel 1791-1872 *BiInAmS*
**Treadwell,** David Merrill 1940- *WhoBlA 92*
**Treadwell,** Elliott Allen 1947- *AmMWSc 92*
**Treadwell,** Fay Rene Lavern 1935- *WhoBlA 92*
**Treadwell,** Frederick Pearson 1857-1918 *BiInAmS*
**Treadwell,** Fredrick Carlton 1956- *WhoRel 92*
**Treadwell,** George Edward, Jr 1941- *AmMWSc 92*
**Treadwell,** Kenneth Myron 1923- *AmMWSc 92*
**Treadwell,** Robert D, Sr 1933- *WhoAmP 91*
**Treagan,** Lucy 1924- *AmMWSc 92*
**Treanor,** Charles Edward 1924- *AmMWSc 92*
**Treanor,** Patricia L 1942- *WhoAmP 91*
**Treanor,** Walter John 1922- *WhoWest 92*
**Treas,** Jack Hanson 1929- *WhoFI 92*
**Trease,** Geoffrey *Who 92*
**Trease,** Geoffrey 1909- *IntAu&W 91, WrDr 92*
**Trease,** Robert Geoffrey 1909- *Who 92*
**Treasure,** Anne Jordan 1961- *WhoAmL 92*
**Treasure,** John Albert Penberthy 1924- *Who 92*
**Treat,** Charles Herbert 1931- *AmMWSc 92*
**Treat,** Donald Fackler 1925- *AmMWSc 92*
**Treat,** Jay Emery, Jr 1920- *AmMWSc 92*
**Treat,** Jessica *DrAPF 91*
**Treat,** John Elting 1946- *WhoWest 92*
**Treat,** Lawrence 1903- *IntAu&W 91, WrDr 92*
**Treat,** Sharon Anglin *WhoAmP 91*
**Treat-Clemons,** Lynda George 1946- *AmMWSc 92*
**Trebek,** Alex 1940- *WhoEnt 92*
**Trebing,** David Martin 1961- *WhoFI 92*
**Treble,** Donald Harold 1934- *AmMWSc 92*
**Treby,** Ivor C *IntAu&W 91*
**Trechsel,** Stefan 1937- *IntWW 91*
**Trede,** Michael 1928- *IntWW 91*
**Tredgold,** Nye *IntAu&W 91X, WrDr 92*
**Tredicce,** Jorge Raul 1953- *AmMWSc 92*
**Tredinnick,** David Arthur Stephen 1950- *Who 92*
**Tredway,** John Thomas 1935- *WhoMW 92*
**Tredwell,** Jay Maynard 1959- *WhoFI 92*
**Tree,** David L. *WhoFI 92*
**Tree,** David R 1936- *AmMWSc 92*
**Tree,** Marietta d1991 *NewYTBS 91 [port]*
**Tree,** Marietta 1917-1991 *CurBio 91N*
**Tree,** Michael 1934- *WhoEnt 92*
**Treece,** Jack Milan 1932- *AmMWSc 92*
**Treece,** Kenneth James 1961- *WhoAmL 92*
**Treece,** Robert Eugene 1927- *AmMWSc 92*
**Treen,** David C 1928- *WhoAmP 91*
**Treen,** David Conner 1928- *IntWW 91*
**Trees,** Candice D. 1953- *WhoBlA 92*
**Trees,** John Simmons 1932- *WhoFI 92*
**Treese,** Christopher Jennings 1956- *WhoWest 92*
**Treese,** Donald Howard 1930- *WhoRel 92*
**Trefethen,** Florence *DrAPF 91*
**Trefethen,** Joseph Muzzy 1906- *AmMWSc 92*
**Trefethen,** Lloyd MacGregor 1919- *AmMWSc 92*
**Trefethen,** Lloyd Nicholas 1955- *AmMWSc 92*
**Treffer,** Kevin Duane 1961- *WhoMW 92*
**Treffers,** Henry Peter 1912- *AmMWSc 92*
**Treffers,** Richard Rowe 1947- *AmMWSc 92*
**Treffert,** Darold Allen 1933- *AmMWSc 92*
**Trefgarne** *Who 92*
**Trefgarne,** Baron 1941- *Who 92*
**Trefil,** James 1938- *WrDr 92*
**Trefil,** James S 1938- *AmMWSc 92*
**Trefny,** John Ulric 1942- *AmMWSc 92, WhoWest 92*
**Trefonas,** Louis Marco 1931- *AmMWSc 92*

**Trefousse**, Hans Louis 1921- *WrDr 92*
**Trefry**, Richard Greenleaf 1924- *WhoAmP 91*
**Trefsgar**, Theodore Webster, Jr. 1961- *WhoRel 92*
**Trefts**, Albert S. 1929- *WhoMW 92*
**Trefts**, Joan Landenberger 1930- *WhoMW 92*
**Trefusis** *Who 92*
**Trefz**, James Robert 1954- *WhoWest 92*
**Trefzger**, John Dennis 1923- *WhoRel 92*
**Tregarthen**, Timothy Doran 1945- *WhoFI 92*
**Tregarthen Jenkin**, Ian Evers *Who 92*
**Tregear**, Mary 1924- *Who 92*
**Tregellas**, Patricia 1936- *WhoEnt 92*
**Tregenza**, Norman Hughson 1937- *WhoFI 92*
**Treger**, Mark Alan 1938- *WhoWest 92*
**Tregian**, Francis 1574-1619 *NewAmDM*
**Tregidgo**, Philip Sillince 1926- *WrDr 92*
**Tregillus**, Leonard Warren 1921- *AmMWSc 92*
**Tregle**, Linda Marie 1947- *WhoEnt 92*
**Treglia**, Thomas A 1924- *AmMWSc 92*
**Treglio**, James Ronald 1946- *WhoWest 92*
**Treglown**, Jeremy Dickinson 1946- *IntAu&W 91, IntWW 91, Who 92*
**Tregoning**, Joseph E 1941- *WhoAmP 91*
**Tregre**, Louis Severin d1991 *NewYTBS 91*
**Trehan**, Rajender *AmMWSc 92*
**Trehane**, Richard 1913- *Who 92*
**Treharne**, John Edward 1939- *WhoWest 92*
**Trehearne**, Elizabeth *IntAu&W 91X, WrDr 92*
**Trehot**, Lise 1848-1924 *ThHEIm [port]*
**Trehu**, Anne Martine 1955- *AmMWSc 92*
**Trehub**, Arnold 1923- *AmMWSc 92*
**Trei**, John Earl 1939- *AmMWSc 92*
**Treibitz**, C. Howard 1950- *WhoFI 92*
**Treichel**, Paul Morgan, Jr 1936- *AmMWSc 92*
**Treichel**, Robin Stong 1950- *AmMWSc 92, WhoMW 92*
**Treichl**, Heinrich 1913- *IntWW 91*
**Treichler**, Ray 1907- *AmMWSc 92*
**Treick**, Ronald Walter 1934- *AmMWSc 92*
**Treiger**, Irwin Louis 1934- *WhoWest 92*
**Treigle**, Norman 1927-1975 *NewAmDM*
**Treiki**, Ali A. 1938- *IntWW 91*
**Treiman**, Sam Bard 1925- *AmMWSc 92, IntWW 91*
**Treinavicz**, Kathryn Mary 1957- *WhoFI 92, WhoMW 92*
**Treinen**, Sylvester William 1917- *WhoRel 92*
**Treiser**, Richard M. 1953- *WhoAmL 92*
**Treistman**, Steven Neal 1945- *AmMWSc 92*
**Treit**, Elroy Malcolm 1933- *WhoRel 92*
**Treitel**, G. H. 1928- *WrDr 92*
**Treitel**, Guenter Heinz 1928- *IntWW 91, Who 92*
**Treitel**, Margot *DrAPF 91*
**Treitel**, Sven 1929- *AmMWSc 92*
**Treiterer**, Joseph 1918- *AmMWSc 92*
**Trejo**, Arnulfo Duenes 1922- *WhoHisp 92*
**Trejo**, Constantino *WhoHisp 92*
**Trejo**, Ernesto *DrAPF 91*
**Trejo**, Jose Diaz 1948- *WhoMW 92*
**Trejo**, Jose Humberto 1942- *WhoHisp 92*
**Trejo**, Maggie *WhoHisp 92*
**Trejo-Meehan**, Tamiye M. *WhoHisp 92*
**Trejos Fernandez**, Jose Joaquin 1916- *IntWW 91*
**Trela**, Constantine L., Jr. 1955- *WhoAmL 92*
**Trela**, Edward 1912- *AmMWSc 92*
**Trela**, John Michael 1942- *AmMWSc 92*
**Trela**, Walter Joseph 1936- *AmMWSc 92*
**Trelawny**, Edward John 1792-1881 *DcLB 110 [port]*
**Trelawny**, Gilbert Sterling 1929- *AmMWSc 92*
**Trelawny**, John Barry Salusbury- 1934- *Who 92*
**Trelease**, Donald Scott 1950- *WhoMW 92*
**Trelease**, Richard Davis 1917- *AmMWSc 92*
**Trelease**, Richard Mitchell, Jr. 1921- *WhoRel 92*
**Trelease**, Richard Norman 1941- *AmMWSc 92*
**Trelease**, Stephen Waldo 1934- *WhoFI 92*
**Treleven**, Mark Daniel 1954- *WhoMW 92*
**Trelfa**, Richard T 1918- *WhoAmP 91*
**Trelford**, Donald Gilchrist 1937- *IntAu&W 91, IntWW 91, Who 92*
**Trelford**, John D 1931- *AmMWSc 92*
**Trelka**, Dennis George 1940- *AmMWSc 92*
**Trelka**, Janice Margaret Nace 1944- *WhoMW 92*
**Trelles Montes**, Oscar 1904- *IntWW 91*
**Trello**, Fred A 1929- *WhoAmP 91*
**Treloar**, Alan Edward 1902- *AmMWSc 92*
**Trelstad**, Robert Laurence 1940- *AmMWSc 92*
**Trelz**, Eric Martin 1958- *WhoAmL 92*
**Tremain**, James Edward 1947- *WhoMW 92*
**Tremain**, Rose 1943- *ConNov 91, IntAu&W 91, IntWW 91, Who 92, WrDr 92*
**Tremaine**, Burton G. d1991 *NewYTBS 91*
**Tremaine**, Jack H 1928- *AmMWSc 92*
**Tremaine**, Peter Richard 1947- *AmMWSc 92*
**Tremaine**, Scott Duncan 1950- *AmMWSc 92*
**Tremayne**, Les 1913- *IntMPA 92*
**Tremayne**, William Howard 1935- *WhoFI 92*
**Tremblay**, Abraham 1710-1784 *BlkwCEP*
**Tremblay**, Andre-Marie 1953- *AmMWSc 92*
**Tremblay**, Bill *DrAPF 91*
**Tremblay**, Gail *DrAPF 91*
**Tremblay**, Gail Elizabeth 1945- *IntAu&W 91*
**Tremblay**, George Charles 1938- *AmMWSc 92*
**Tremblay**, Gerard 1918- *WhoRel 92*
**Tremblay**, Gilles 1928- *AmMWSc 92*
**Tremblay**, Gilles 1932- *NewAmDM*
**Tremblay**, Marc-Adelard 1922- *IntWW 91, Who 92*
**Tremblay**, Michel 1942- *IntWW 91*
**Tremblay**, Paul Lucien 1949- *WhoEnt 92*
**Trembley**, David Alan 1942- *WhoRel 92*
**Trembley**, Paul Gerard 1953- *WhoEnt 92*
**Trembly**, Dennis Michael 1947- *WhoEnt 92, WhoWest 92*
**Tremelling**, Michael, Jr 1945- *AmMWSc 92*
**Tremens**, Del *ConAu 135*
**Tremier**, Wilbert M 1911- *WhoIns 92*
**Treml**, Vladimir Guy 1929- *WhoFI 92*
**Tremlett**, Anthony Frank 1937- *Who 92*
**Tremlett**, Anthony Paul 1914- *Who 92*
**Tremlett**, David 1945- *TwCPaSc*
**Tremlett**, David Rex 1945- *IntWW 91*
**Tremlett**, George William 1939- *IntAu&W 91, Who 92*
**Tremmel**, Carl George 1933- *AmMWSc 92*
**Tremmel**, William Calloley 1918- *WhoRel 92*
**Tremols**, Guillermo Antonio 1937- *WhoHisp 92*
**Tremor**, John W 1932- *AmMWSc 92*
**Trenaman**, Nancy Kathleen 1919- *Who 92*
**Trenary**, Jill *NewYTBS 91 [port]*
**Trenberth**, Kevin Edward 1944- *AmMWSc 92*
**Trench** *Who 92*
**Trench**, John 1920- *WrDr 92*
**Trench**, John 1932- *Who 92*
**Trench**, Peter 1918- *Who 92*
**Trench**, Richard 1949- *ConAu 133*
**Trench**, Robert Kent 1940- *AmMWSc 92*
**Trench**, William Frederick 1931- *AmMWSc 92*
**Trenchard** *Who 92*
**Trenchard**, Viscount 1951- *Who 92*
**Trenchard**, John 1662-1723 *BlkwCEP*
**Trenchard**, Warren Charles 1944- *WhoRel 92, WhoWest 92*
**Trend**, Lord 1914-1987 *FacFETw*
**Trendall**, Arthur Dale 1909- *Who 92, WrDr 92*
**Treneer**, Paula Christina 1949- *WhoFI 92*
**Treneff**, Craig Paul 1952- *WhoMW 92*
**Trenerry**, Walter N. 1917- *ConAu 135*
**Trenev**, Konstantin Andreevich 1876-1945 *SovUnBD*
**Trengganu**, The Sultan of 1930- *IntWW 91*
**Trengove**, Alan Thomas 1929- *WrDr 92*
**Trenhaile**, John Stevens 1949- *IntAu&W 91, WrDr 92*
**Trenholm**, Andrew Rutledge 1942- *AmMWSc 92*
**Trenholm**, Harold Locksley 1941- *AmMWSc 92*
**Trenholme**, John Burgess 1939- *AmMWSc 92*
**Trenker**, Luis 1892-1990 *EncTR 91 [port]*
**Trenkle**, Allen H 1934- *AmMWSc 92*
**Trennel**, Lawrence William 1955- *WhoMW 92*
**Trennepohl**, Gary Lee 1946- *WhoFI 92*
**Trennert**, Robert Anthony, Jr. 1937- *WhoWest 92*
**Trent**, Bertram J 1918- *WhoAmP 91*
**Trent**, Charles H *WhoAmP 91*
**Trent**, Darrell M 1938- *WhoAmP 91*
**Trent**, Debra Renee 1954- *WhoAmP 91*
**Trent**, Dennis W 1935- *AmMWSc 92*
**Trent**, Donald Stephen 1935- *AmMWSc 92*
**Trent**, Edmund Kiernan 1913- *WhoAmL 92*
**Trent**, George Curtis 1958- *WhoRel 92*
**Trent**, James E. 1936- *WhoBlA 92, WhoMW 92*
**Trent**, Jay Lester 1940- *WhoBlA 92*
**Trent**, John Ellsworth 1942- *AmMWSc 92*
**Trent**, John Jason *ScFEYrs*
**Trent**, John Spencer 1950- *WhoBlA 92*
**Trent**, Judith M 1939- *WhoAmP 91*
**Trent**, Marcia M. 1948- *WhoBlA 92*
**Trent**, Olaf *TwCSFW 91, WrDr 92*
**Trent**, Richard Darrell 1925- *WhoBlA 92*
**Trent**, Richard O 1920- *WhoIns 92*
**Trent**, Richard Owen 1920- *WhoFI 92*
**Trent**, Robert Stephen 1958- *WhoFI 92*
**Trent**, Rose Marie 1943- *WhoFI 92*
**Trent**, William Bret, Jr 1947- *WhoAmP 91*
**Trent**, William Johnson, Jr. 1910- *WhoBlA 92*
**Trentelman**, George Frederick 1944- *AmMWSc 92*
**Trentham**, David R 1938- *AmMWSc 92, IntWW 91*
**Trentham**, David Rostron 1938- *Who 92*
**Trentham**, Jimmy N 1936- *AmMWSc 92*
**Trentin**, John Joseph 1918- *AmMWSc 92*
**Trento**, Alfredo 1950- *AmMWSc 92*
**Trenton**, Gail *WrDr 92*
**Trepanier**, Pierre 1953- *AmMWSc 92*
**Trepel**, Anthony Jerome 1932- *WhoAmL 92, WhoWest 92*
**Trepka**, Robert Dale 1938- *AmMWSc 92*
**Trepka**, William James 1933- *AmMWSc 92*
**Trepov**, Dmitry Fedorovich 1855-1906 *FacFETw*
**Trepp**, Leo 1913- *WhoRel 92, WrDr 92*
**Trepper**, Leopold 1904-1982 *FacFETw*
**Trepper**, Leopold 1904-1983 *EncTR 91*
**Trepper**, Terry Steven 1952- *WhoMW 92*
**Treppler**, Irene E 1926- *WhoAmP 91*
**Treppler**, Irene Esther 1926- *WhoMW 92*
**Trepte**, Paul 1954- *Who 92*
**Treptow**, Richard S 1941- *AmMWSc 92*
**Tres**, Paul Andrew 1951- *WhoMW 92*
**Tresca**, Carlo 1879-1943 *DcAmImH*
**Tresca**, Paul Joseph 1945- *WhoFI 92*
**Trescher**, Robert L. 1912- *WhoAmL 92*
**Trescher**, Susan 1928- *WhoWest 92*
**Tresckow**, Henning von 1901-1944 *EncTR 91 [port]*
**Trescott**, Harold Charles 1938- *WhoIns 92*
**Trescott**, Jacqueline Elaine 1947- *WhoBlA 92*
**Trescott**, Paul Barton 1925- *WhoFI 92*
**Trescott**, Robert Lyman 1945- *WhoAmL 92*
**Trescowthick**, Donald 1930- *Who 92*
**Treseder**, Terry Walton 1956- *SmATA 68*
**Treser**, Gerhard 1929- *AmMWSc 92*
**Treshow**, Michael 1926- *AmMWSc 92*
**Tresidder**, Argus John 1907- *WrDr 92*
**Tresidder**, Gerald Charles 1912- *Who 92*
**Tresnowski**, Bernard Richard 1932- *WhoFI 92*
**Tress**, Ronald Charles 1915- *Who 92*
**Tressell**, Robert 1870?-1911 *RfGEnL 91*
**Tresselt**, Alvin 1916- *IntAu&W 91, WrDr 92*
**Tresser**, Thomas Stewart 1952- *WhoEnt 92, WhoMW 92*
**Tressidy**, Jim *IntAu&W 91X, TwCWW 91*
**Tressillian**, Richard *WrDr 92*
**Tressler**, Charles Thomas 1943- *WhoRel 92*
**Tressler**, Jay Howard 1942- *WhoAmL 92*
**Tressler**, Richard Ernest 1942- *AmMWSc 92*
**Trestrail**, John Harris, III 1944- *WhoMW 92*
**Tresvant**, John Bernard 1938- *WhoBlA 92*
**Tretbar**, Harold Carl 1931- *WhoWest 92*
**Tretheway**, Barton Glenn 1945- *WhoMW 92*
**Tretheway**, J. A. *WhoFI 92*
**Tretheway**, Robert Parker, II 1948- *WhoWest 92*
**Trethon**, Ferenc 1923- *IntWW 91*
**Trethowan**, Ian d1990 *IntWW 91N, Who 92N*
**Trethowan**, Ian 1922-1990 *AnObit 1990*
**Trethowan**, William 1907- *WrDr 92*
**Trethowan**, William 1917- *Who 92*
**Tretiak**, Oleh John 1939- *AmMWSc 92*
**Tretler**, Donald C 1936- *WhoIns 92*
**Tretschok**, Dale Deege 1941- *WhoAmL 92*
**Tretter**, James Ray 1933- *WhoFI 92*
**Tretter**, Steven Alan 1940- *AmMWSc 92*
**Trettin**, Rosemary Elizabeth *WhoMW 92*
**Tret'yak**, Ivan Moiseevich 1923- *SovUnBD*
**Tretyak**, Ivan Moiseyevich 1923- *IntWW 91*
**Tret'yak**, Vladislav Aleksandrovich 1952- *SovUnBD*
**Tretyakov**, Sergei Mikhailovich 1892-1939 *FacFETw*
**Tret'yakov**, Sergey Mikhaylovich 1892-1939 *SovUnBD*
**Tret'yakov**, Viktor Viktorovich 1946- *SovUnBD*
**Treu**, Jesse Isaiah 1947- *AmMWSc 92*
**Treu**, Siegfried 1940- *AmMWSc 92*
**Treuherz**, Julian Benjamin 1947- *Who 92*
**Treumann**, William Borgen 1916- *AmMWSc 92*
**Treurnicht**, Andries 1921- *News 92-2 [port]*
**Treurnicht**, Andries Petrus 1921- *IntWW 91*
**Treusch**, Paul Ellsworth *WhoAmL 92*
**Treutel**, Edward F. *WhoEnt 92*
**Trevanian** *IntAu&W 91X*
**Trevanian** 1925- *WrDr 92*
**Trevathan**, Larry Eugene 1947- *AmMWSc 92*
**Trevathan**, Robert E 1925- *TwCWW 91, WrDr 92*
**Trevelyan**, Benjamin John 1922- *AmMWSc 92*
**Trevelyan**, Dennis John 1929- *Who 92*
**Trevelyan**, George 1906- *Who 92*
**Trevelyan**, George M 1876-1962 *FacFETw*
**Trevelyan**, John 1904-1986 *FacFETw*
**Trevelyan**, Julian 1910-1988 *TwCPaSc*
**Trevelyan**, Norman Irving 1915- *Who 92*
**Trevelyan**, Percy *WrDr 92*
**Trevelyan**, Raleigh 1923- *IntAu&W 91, WrDr 92*
**Trevelyan Oman**, Julia *Who 92*
**Trever**, John Cecil 1915- *WhoRel 92, WrDr 92*
**Treves**, David 1930- *AmMWSc 92*
**Treves**, Jean Francois 1930- *AmMWSc 92*
**Treves**, Ralph 1906- *WrDr 92*
**Treves**, S T 1940- *AmMWSc 92*
**Treves**, Samuel Blain 1925- *AmMWSc 92*
**Treves**, Vanni Emanuele 1940- *Who 92*
**Trevethin**, Baron *Who 92*
**Trevett**, Kenneth Parkhurst 1947- *WhoAmL 92*
**Trevett**, Thomas Neil 1942- *WhoAmL 92*
**Trevillyan**, Alvin Earl 1936- *AmMWSc 92*
**Trevino**, A. L. *WhoHisp 92*
**Trevino**, Alex 1957- *WhoHisp 92*
**Trevino**, Anthony 1950- *WhoHisp 92*
**Trevino**, Carlos 1944- *WhoHisp 92*
**Trevino**, Carlos R. 1938- *WhoHisp 92*
**Trevino**, Daniel Louis 1943- *AmMWSc 92, WhoHisp 92*
**Trevino**, Elizabeth de 1904- *IntAu&W 91*
**Trevino**, Fernando Manuel 1949- *WhoHisp 92*
**Trevino**, Genie 1954- *WhoHisp 92*
**Trevino**, Gilbert Timothy 1944- *WhoHisp 92*
**Trevino**, Jesse *WhoHisp 92*
**Trevino**, Jesse 1947- *WhoHisp 92*
**Trevino**, Jesus Salvador 1946- *WhoEnt 92, WhoHisp 92*
**Trevino**, Jose Adan 1932- *WhoHisp 92*
**Trevino**, Julian G. 1947- *WhoHisp 92*
**Trevino**, Laramie M. 1953- *WhoHisp 92*
**Trevino**, Lee 1939- *WhoHisp 92*
**Trevino**, Lee 1945- *WhoIns 92*
**Trevino**, Lee Buck 1939- *FacFETw, IntWW 91*
**Trevino**, Maria del Carmel 1951- *WhoHisp 92*
**Trevino**, Mario 1952- *WhoHisp 92*
**Trevino**, Miguel Angel 1958- *WhoHisp 92*
**Trevino**, Rafael Maria, Sr. 1932- *WhoHisp 92*
**Trevino**, Richard, Jr. 1957- *WhoHisp 92*
**Trevino**, Rosa Ena 1939- *WhoHisp 92*
**Trevino**, Samuel Francisco 1936- *AmMWSc 92, WhoHisp 92*
**Trevino**, Teresa Roque 1960- *WhoHisp 92*
**Treviranus**, Gottfried 1891-1971 *EncTR 91*
**Treviranus**, Gottfried Reinhold 1776-1837 *BlkwCEP*
**Trevithick**, John Richard 1938- *AmMWSc 92*
**Trevithick**, Ronald James 1944- *WhoFI 92, WhoWest 92*
**Trevor**, Baron 1928- *Who 92*
**Trevor**, Anthony John 1934- *AmMWSc 92*
**Trevor**, Bronson 1910- *WhoFI 92*
**Trevor**, Claire 1909- *ConTFT 9*
**Trevor**, Claire 1910- *IntMPA 92*
**Trevor**, Elleston *Who 92, WrDr 92*
**Trevor**, Kenneth Rowland Swetenham 1914- *Who 92*
**Trevor**, Kirk David Niell 1952- *WhoEnt 92*
**Trevor**, Leigh Barry 1934- *WhoAmL 92*
**Trevor**, Meriol 1919- *IntAu&W 91, Who 92, WrDr 92*
**Trevor**, William 1928- *ConNov 91, FacFETw, IntAu&W 91, IntWW 91, RfGEnL 91, Who 92, WrDr 92*
**Trevor Cox**, Horace Brimson *Who 92*
**Trevor-Roper** *Who 92*
**Trevor-Roper**, Hugh 1914- *FacFETw, WrDr 92*
**Trevor-Roper**, Hugh Redwald *IntWW 91*
**Trevor-Roper**, Patrick 1916- *WrDr 92*
**Trevor-Roper**, Patrick Dacre 1916- *Who 92*
**Trevorrow**, Laverne Everett 1928- *AmMWSc 92*
**Trevors**, Jack Thomas 1953- *AmMWSc 92*
**Trevoy**, Donald James 1922- *AmMWSc 92*
**Trew**, Antony 1906- *WrDr 92*

**Trew**, Francis Sidney Edward 1931- *IntWW 91, Who 92*
**Trew**, Peter John Edward 1932- *Who 92*
**Trewby**, Allan 1917- *Who 92*
**Trewella**, Jeffrey Charles *AmMWSc 92*
**Trewiler**, Carl Edward 1934- *AmMWSc 92*
**Trewin**, John Courtenay 1908- *IntAu&W 91*
**Trewyn**, Ronald William 1943- *AmMWSc 92*
**Trexler**, Charles B. 1916- *IntMPA 92*
**Trexler**, Dennis Thomas 1940- *AmMWSc 92*
**Trexler**, Edgar Ray 1937- *WhoRel 92*
**Trexler**, Frederick David 1942- *AmMWSc 92*
**Trexler**, John Peter 1926- *AmMWSc 92*
**Trexler**, Michael Eric 1967- *WhoRel 92*
**Trexler**, Wynn Ridenhour 1941- *WhoAmL 92*
**Treybig**, James G. 1940- *WhoWest 92*
**Treybig**, Leon Bruce 1931- *AmMWSc 92*
**Treyz**, Oliver E. *LesBEnT 92*
**Treyz**, Russell 1940- *WhoEnt 92*
**Trezek**, George J 1937- *AmMWSc 92*
**Trezevant**, John Gray d1991 *NewYTBS 91*
**Tria**, John Joseph, Jr 1946- *AmMWSc 92*
**Triaca**, Alberto Jorge 1941- *IntWW 91*
**Triana**, Estrella *WhoHisp 92*
**Triandafilidis**, George Emmanuel 1922- *AmMWSc 92*
**Triandis**, Harry Charalambos 1926- *WhoMW 92*
**Triano**, John Joseph 1949- *AmMWSc 92*
**Triantafyllides**, Michalakis Antoniou 1927- *IntWW 91*
**Triantaphyllopoulos**, Demetrios 1920- *AmMWSc 92*
**Triantaphyllopoulos**, Eugenie 1921- *AmMWSc 92*
**Triantaphyllou**, Anastasios Christos 1926- *AmMWSc 92*
**Triantaphyllou**, Hedwig Hirschmann 1927- *AmMWSc 92*
**Triaria**, Empress *EncAmaz 91*
**Trias**, Jose Enrique 1944- *WhoAmL 92*
**Tribbey**, Bert Allen 1938- *AmMWSc 92*
**Tribbitt**, Sherman W *WhoAmP 91*
**Tribble**, B. Jodie 1932- *WhoEnt 92*
**Tribble**, Huerta Cassius 1939- *WhoBlA 92*
**Tribble**, Israel, Jr. 1940- *WhoBlA 92*
**Tribble**, Leland Floyd 1923- *AmMWSc 92*
**Tribble**, Richard Walter 1948- *WhoFI 92, WhoWest 92*
**Tribble**, Robert Edmond 1947- *AmMWSc 92*
**Tribble**, William Roy 1911- *WhoAmL 92*
**Tribe**, Geoffrey Reuben 1924- *Who 92*
**Tribe**, Laurence H. 1941- *ConAu 133, WrDr 92*
**Tribe**, Laurence Henry 1941- *IntWW 91, WhoAmL 92*
**Tribe**, Raymond Haydn 1908- *Who 92*
**Tribett**, A E Gene 1928- *WhoAmP 91*
**Tribken**, Craig L *WhoAmP 91*
**Tribken**, Craig Lewis 1953- *WhoWest 92*
**Trible**, Paul Seward, Jr. 1946- *IntWW 91, WhoAmP 91*
**Tribler**, Willis R 1934- *WhoIns 92*
**Tribone**, Thomas Anthony 1952- *WhoFI 92*
**Triboulet**, Raymond 1906- *IntWW 91*
**Tribus**, Myron 1921- *AmMWSc 92, WrDr 92*
**Tricart**, Jean Leon Francois 1920- *IntWW 91*
**Trice**, Jessie Collins 1929- *WhoBlA 92*
**Trice**, Juniper Yates 1921- *WhoBlA 92*
**Trice**, Luther William 1910- *WhoBlA 92*
**Trice**, Virgil Garnett, Jr 1926- *AmMWSc 92*
**Trice**, William B. 1924- *WhoBlA 92*
**Trice**, William Henry 1933- *AmMWSc 92, WhoFI 92*
**Trich**, Leo J, Jr 1951- *WhoAmP 91*
**Triche**, Arthur, Jr. 1961- *WhoBlA 92*
**Triche**, Timothy J 1944- *AmMWSc 92*
**Triche**, Warren J, Jr 1949- *WhoAmP 91*
**Trichter**, Joseph Gary 1951- *WhoAmL 92*
**Trick**, Charles Gordon 1954- *AmMWSc 92*
**Trick**, Gordon Staples 1927- *AmMWSc 92*
**Trick**, Roger Lee 1950- *WhoWest 92*
**Trick**, Timothy Noel 1939- *AmMWSc 92*
**Trickel**, Neal Edward 1954- *WhoMW 92*
**Trickel**, William, Jr. 1937- *WhoFI 92*
**Tricker**, Robert Ian 1933- *Who 92*
**Trickett**, David George 1949- *WhoRel 92*
**Trickett**, Jon Hedley 1950- *Who 92*
**Trickett**, Joyce 1915- *ConAu 34NR, WrDr 92*
**Trickett**, Rachel 1923- *ConNov 91, Who 92, WrDr 92*
**Trickey**, Edward Lorden 1920- *Who 92*
**Trickey**, Samuel Baldwin 1940- *AmMWSc 92*
**Trickler**, Sally Jo 1948- *WhoMW 92*
**Tricoles**, Gus P 1931- *AmMWSc 92*
**Tricoles**, Gus Peter 1931- *WhoWest 92*
**Tricomi**, Vincent 1921- *AmMWSc 92*
**Triebwasser**, John 1936- *AmMWSc 92*
**Triebwasser**, John Henry 1936- *WhoMW 92*
**Triebwasser**, Sol 1921- *AmMWSc 92*
**Trieff**, Norman Martin 1929- *AmMWSc 92*
**Triem**, Eve *DrAPF 91*
**Triemer**, Richard Ernest *AmMWSc 92*
**Trien**, Jay William 1940- *WhoFI 92*
**Trienens**, Howard Joseph 1923- *WhoAmL 92*
**Trier**, Jerry Steven 1933- *AmMWSc 92*
**Trier**, Peter Eugene 1919- *IntWW 91, Who 92*
**Trier**, William Cronin 1922- *WhoWest 92*
**Trieu Thi Trinh** *EncAmaz 91*
**Trieweile**, Terry 1948- *WhoAmP 91*
**Trieweiler**, Terry Nicholas 1948- *WhoWest 92*
**Trifa**, Valerian 1914-1987 *RelLAm 91*
**Trifan**, Daniel Siegfried 1918- *AmMWSc 92*
**Trifan**, Deonisie 1915- *AmMWSc 92*
**Trifaro**, Jose Maria 1936- *AmMWSc 92*
**Triffet**, Terry 1922- *AmMWSc 92*
**Triffin**, Nicholas 1942- *WhoAmL 92*
**Triffin**, Robert 1911- *IntAu&W 91, IntWW 91, WrDr 92*
**Trifonidis**, Beverly Ann 1947- *WhoEnt 92, WhoWest 92*
**Trifonov**, Yuri Valentinovich 1925-1981 *FacFETw*
**Trifonov**, Yuriy Valentinovich 1925-1981 *SovUnBD*
**Trifunac**, Alexander Dimitrije 1944- *AmMWSc 92*
**Trifunac**, Natalia Pisker 1942- *AmMWSc 92*
**Trigano**, Gilbert 1920- *IntWW 91*
**Trigari**, Giancarlo 1945- *WhoFI 92*
**Trigg**, George Lockwood 1925- *AmMWSc 92*
**Trigg**, William Walker 1931- *AmMWSc 92*
**Trigger**, Bruce Graham 1937- *IntAu&W 91, WrDr 92*
**Trigger**, Kenneth James 1910- *AmMWSc 92*
**Trigger**, Kenneth Roy 1924- *AmMWSc 92*
**Triggiani**, Leonard Vincent 1930- *WhoMW 92*
**Triggiani**, Roberto 1942- *AmMWSc 92*
**Triggle**, David J 1935- *AmMWSc 92*
**Triggs**, Michael Lynn 1953- *WhoAmP 91*
**Triggs**, Vincent L 1948- *WhoAmP 91*
**Triggs**, William Michael 1937- *WhoWest 92*
**Trigiano**, Lucien Lewis 1926- *WhoWest 92*
**Trigiano**, Robert Nicholas 1953- *AmMWSc 92*
**Trigilio**, John Patricio 1962- *WhoRel 92*
**Triglia**, Emil J 1921- *AmMWSc 92*
**Trigoboff**, Joseph *DrAPF 91*
**Trigona**, Alex Sceberras 1950- *IntWW 91*
**Trigueros**, Raul C. 1944- *WhoHisp 92*
**Trikaminas**, Peter A 1943- *WhoIns 92*
**Trikonis**, Gus *IntMPA 92*
**Trillin**, Calvin *DrAPF 91*
**Trillin**, Calvin 1935- *BenetAL 91, WrDr 92*
**Trillin**, Calvin Marshall 1935- *WhoEnt 92A*
**Trilling**, Charles A 1923- *AmMWSc 92*
**Trilling**, Diana 1905- *WrDr 92*
**Trilling**, Diana Rubin 1905- *BenetAL 91*
**Trilling**, George Henry 1930- *AmMWSc 92*
**Trilling**, Leon 1924- *AmMWSc 92*
**Trilling**, Lionel 1905-1975 *BenetAL 91, FacFETw*
**Trillo**, Albert John 1915- *Who 92*
**Trillo**, Manny 1950- *WhoHisp 92*
**Trilussa** 1871-1950 *DcLB 114 [port]*
**Trim**, Claude Albert 1935- *WhoAmP 91*
**Trim**, Cynthia Mary 1947- *AmMWSc 92*
**Trim**, John H. 1931- *WhoBlA 92*
**Trimberger**, George William 1909- *AmMWSc 92*
**Trimble**, Allen C 1948- *WhoAmL 92*
**Trimble**, Barbara Margaret 1921- *IntAu&W 91, WrDr 92*
**Trimble**, Cesar *WhoHisp 92*
**Trimble**, David *Who 92*
**Trimble**, Donald E 1916- *AmMWSc 92*
**Trimble**, Henry 1853-1898 *BiInAmS*
**Trimble**, Jenifer *Who 92*
**Trimble**, John Leonard 1944- *AmMWSc 92*
**Trimble**, Lester 1923-1986 *NewAmDM*
**Trimble**, Louis 1917- *TwCWW 91*
**Trimble**, Louis 1917-1988 *TwCSFW 91*
**Trimble**, Mary Ellen 1936- *AmMWSc 92*
**Trimble**, Paul Joseph 1930- *WhoAmL 92, WhoFI 92*
**Trimble**, Phillip R 1937- *WhoAmP 91*
**Trimble**, Phillip Richard 1937- *WhoAmL 92*
**Trimble**, Robert Bogue 1943- *AmMWSc 92*
**Trimble**, Roy Harvey 1955- *WhoAmP 91*
**Trimble**, Russell Fay 1927- *AmMWSc 92, WhoMW 92*
**Trimble**, Stanley Wayne 1940- *WhoWest 92*
**Trimble**, Stephen Asbury 1933- *WhoAmL 92*
**Trimble**, Steve 1942- *WhoAmP 91*
**Trimble**, Thomas James 1931- *WhoAmL 92, WhoFI 92, WhoWest 92*
**Trimble**, Tony Lynn 1951- *WhoMW 92*
**Trimble**, Tony P *WhoAmP 91*
**Trimble**, Virginia Louise 1943- *AmMWSc 92*
**Trimble**, William David 1944- *Who 92*
**Trimboli**, Steven Richard 1918- *WhoAmP 91*
**Trimiar**, J. Sinclair 1933- *WhoBlA 92*
**Trimitsis**, George B 1939- *AmMWSc 92*
**Trimlestown**, Baron d1990 *Who 92N*
**Trimlestown**, Baron 1928- *Who 92*
**Trimmer**, Dale Irving 1949- *WhoEnt 92*
**Trimmer**, Ellen McKay 1915- *IntAu&W 91*
**Trimmer**, Eric 1923- *IntAu&W 91*
**Trimmer**, Eric J. 1923- *WrDr 92*
**Trimmer**, Robert Whitfield 1937- *AmMWSc 92*
**Trimmer**, William S 1943- *AmMWSc 92*
**Trimmier**, Charles Stephen, Jr. 1943- *WhoAmL 92*
**Trimpl**, Robert Louis 1938- *WhoMW 92*
**Trinchero**, Agnes Theresa *WhoWest 92*
**Trinder**, Frank Noel d1991 *Who 92N*
**Trinder**, Frederick William 1930- *Who 92*
**Trinder**, Rachel Bandele 1955- *WhoAmL 92*
**Trindle**, Carl Otis 1941- *AmMWSc 92*
**Trindle**, Susan 1952- *WhoFI 92*
**Trine**, Ralph Waldo 1866-1958 *RelLAm 91*
**Tringale**, Anthony Rosario 1942- *WhoFI 92*
**Tringides**, Michael Christou 1954- *WhoMW 92*
**Trinh**, Duke 1963- *WhoWest 92*
**Trinh**, Xuan Lang 1927- *IntWW 91*
**Trinh Van-Can**, Joseph-Marie d1990 *IntWW 91N*
**Trinidad**, David *DrAPF 91*
**Trinidad**, Ruben *WhoHisp 92*
**Trinius**, Johann Anton 1722-1784 *BlkwCEP*
**Trinkaus**, Charles 1911- *WrDr 92*
**Trinkaus**, John Philip 1918- *AmMWSc 92*
**Trinkaus-Randall**, Vickery E 1953- *AmMWSc 92*
**Trinklein**, David Herbert 1947- *AmMWSc 92*
**Trinklein**, Michael Charles 1930- *WhoRel 92*
**Trinko**, Joseph Richard, Jr 1939- *AmMWSc 92*
**Trinler**, William A 1929- *AmMWSc 92*
**Trintignant**, Jean-Louis 1930- *ConTFT 9, IntMPA 92, IntWW 91*
**Trinz**, Jeffrey Alan 1953- *WhoAmL 92*
**Trio**, Edward Alan 1952- *WhoAmL 92*
**Triolo**, Anthony J 1932- *AmMWSc 92*
**Trione**, Edward John 1926- *AmMWSc 92*
**Tripard**, Gerald Edward 1940- *AmMWSc 92*
**Tripathi**, Brenda Jennifer 1946- *AmMWSc 92*
**Tripathi**, Gorakh Nath Ram 1944- *WhoMW 92*
**Tripathi**, Govakh Nath Ram 1944- *AmMWSc 92*
**Tripathi**, Kamalapati d1990 *IntWW 91N*
**Tripathi**, Ramesh Chandra 1936- *AmMWSc 92, WhoMW 92*
**Tripathi**, Satish Chandra 1956- *AmMWSc 92*
**Tripathi**, Satish K 1951- *AmMWSc 92*
**Tripathi**, Uma Prasad 1945- *AmMWSc 92*
**Tripathi**, Vijai Kumar 1942- *AmMWSc 92*
**Tripathy**, Deoki Nandan 1933- *AmMWSc 92*
**Tripathy**, Sukant K 1952- *AmMWSc 92*
**Tripician**, Joe Anthony 1953- *WhoEnt 92*
**Triplehorn**, Charles A 1927- *AmMWSc 92*
**Triplehorn**, Don Murray 1934- *AmMWSc 92, WhoWest 92*
**Tripler**, Charles Eastman 1849-1906 *BiInAmS*
**Triplett**, Arlene 1942- *WhoAmP 91*
**Triplett**, Edward Lee 1930- *AmMWSc 92*
**Triplett**, Glover Brown, Jr 1930- *AmMWSc 92*
**Triplett**, Henry Hall, Jr. 1946- *WhoWest 92*
**Triplett**, Kelly B *AmMWSc 92*
**Triplett**, Rosalynd D. 1960- *WhoBlA 92*
**Triplett**, Tom *WhoAmP 91*
**Tripodi**, Daniel 1939- *AmMWSc 92*
**Tripodi**, Tony 1932- *WrDr 92*
**Tripole**, Martin Ralph 1935- *WhoRel 92*
**Tripoli**, Joseph Anthony, Jr 1961- *WhoEnt 92*
**Tripp**, George W *ScFEYrs*
**Tripp**, Harry Ernest 1961- *WhoMW 92*
**Tripp**, Howard George 1927- *Who 92*
**Tripp**, John Rathbone 1939- *AmMWSc 92*
**Tripp**, John Stephen 1938- *AmMWSc 92*
**Tripp**, Karen *IntAu&W 91X*
**Tripp**, Kevin Francis 1942- *WhoRel 92*
**Tripp**, Leonard L 1941- *AmMWSc 92*
**Tripp**, Lucius Charles 1942- *WhoBlA 92*
**Tripp**, Luke Samuel 1941- *WhoBlA 92*
**Tripp**, Marenes Robert 1931- *AmMWSc 92*
**Tripp**, Marian Barlow Loofe *WhoMW 92*
**Tripp**, Miles 1923- *WrDr 92*
**Tripp**, Miles Barton 1923- *IntAu&W 91*
**Tripp**, Minot Weld, Jr 1939- *WhoAmP 91*
**Tripp**, Norman Densmore 1938- *WhoAmL 92*
**Tripp**, Paul 1916- *WhoEnt 92*
**Tripp**, Peter 1921- *IntWW 91, Who 92*
**Tripp**, R Maurice 1916- *AmMWSc 92*
**Tripp**, Randy Lee 1956- *WhoMW 92*
**Tripp**, Raymond Plummer, Jr. 1932- *WhoWest 92*
**Tripp**, Robert D 1927- *AmMWSc 92*
**Tripp**, Ruth Enders 1920- *WhoEnt 92*
**Tripp**, Theodore Lawton, Jr. 1948- *WhoAmL 92*
**Tripp**, Thomas Neal 1942- *WhoAmL 92, WhoFI 92, WhoMW 92*
**Tripp**, Thomas William 1960- *WhoFI 92*
**Tripp**, William Karl 1948- *WhoFI 92*
**Trippe**, Anthony Philip 1943- *AmMWSc 92*
**Trippe**, Charles White 1935- *WhoFI 92*
**Trippe**, Juan Terry 1899-1981 *FacFETw*
**Trippe**, Thomas Gordon 1939- *AmMWSc 92*
**Trippier**, David Austin 1946- *Who 92*
**Trippodo**, Nick Charles 1945- *AmMWSc 92*
**Triqueneaux**, Laurent E. 1962- *WhoEnt 92*
**Triscari**, Joseph 1945- *AmMWSc 92*
**Triscari**, Sebastian B. 1962- *WhoFI 92*
**Trischan**, Glenn M *AmMWSc 92*
**Trischka**, John Wilson 1916- *AmMWSc 92*
**Trischler**, Floyd D 1929- *AmMWSc 92*
**Trisco**, Robert Frederick 1929- *WhoRel 92*
**Triska**, Bradley Frank 1950- *WhoWest 92*
**Triska**, Jan Francis 1922- *WhoWest 92*
**Trisko**, Robert Charles 1947- *WhoEnt 92*
**Trisler**, John Charles 1933- *AmMWSc 92*
**Tristan**, Andrew R. 1936- *WhoHisp 92*
**Tristan**, Dorothy *WhoEnt 92*
**Tristan**, Flora 1803-1844 *FrenWW*
**Tristan**, Theodore A 1924- *AmMWSc 92*
**Tristano**, Lennie 1919-1978 *NewAmDM*
**Tristine**, Martin Patrick 1944- *WhoFI 92*
**Tristram**, Uvedale Francis Barrington 1915- *IntAu&W 91*
**Tristram**, William John 1896- *Who 92*
**Tristram-Nagle**, Stephanie Ann 1948- *AmMWSc 92*
**Tritchler**, David Lynn 1944- *AmMWSc 92*
**Tritel**, Barbara *ConAu 133*
**Trites**, Ronald Wilmot 1929- *AmMWSc 92*
**Tritschler**, Louis George 1927- *AmMWSc 92*
**Tritschler**, Richard Dana 1958- *WhoAmL 92*
**Tritsis**, Antonis 1937- *IntWW 91*
**Tritt**, Travis 1964?- *ConMus 7 [port]*
**Tritter**, Daniel F. 1934- *WhoEnt 92*
**Trittinger**, John George 1945- *WhoEnt 92*
**Tritton**, Alan George 1931- *Who 92*
**Tritton**, Anthony 1927- *Who 92*
**Tritton**, Clare 1935- *Who 92*
**Tritton**, Thomas Richard 1947- *AmMWSc 92*
**Tritz**, Gerald Joseph 1937- *AmMWSc 92*
**Trivedi**, Bharat Kalidas 1951- *WhoMW 92*
**Trivedi**, Kishor Shridharbhai 1946- *AmMWSc 92*
**Trivedi**, Mohan Manubhai 1953- *AmMWSc 92*
**Trivedi**, Nayan B 1947- *AmMWSc 92*
**Trivedi**, Ram Krishna 1921- *IntWW 91*
**Trivedi**, Rohit K 1939- *AmMWSc 92*
**Trivelpiece**, Alvin William 1931- *AmMWSc 92, WhoAmP 91*
**Trivelpiece**, Laurel *DrAPF 91*
**Trivelpiece**, Laurel 1926- *WrDr 92*
**Trives**, Nathaniel 1934- *WhoBlA 92*
**Trivett**, Terrence Lynn 1940- *AmMWSc 92*
**Trivick**, Henry Houghton *TwCPaSc*
**Trivisonno**, Charles F 1924- *AmMWSc 92*
**Trivisonno**, Joseph, Jr 1933- *AmMWSc 92*
**Triviz**, Rita Marilyn 1947- *WhoAmP 91*
**Trivulzio**, Cristina Belgiojoso 1808-1871 *EncAmaz 91*
**Trizna**, Dennis Benedict 1941- *AmMWSc 92*
**Trkula**, David 1927- *AmMWSc 92*
**Troan**, Gordon Trygve 1960- *WhoFI 92, WhoWest 92*
**Troan**, John Trygve 1932- *WhoWest 92*
**Trobairitz**, The *FrenWW*

**Trobaugh,** Frank Edwin, Jr 1920- *AmMWSc 92*
**Troberman,** Richard Jonathan 1946- *WhoAmL 92*
**Troccoli,** Antonio Americo 1925- *IntWW 91*
**Troche,** Pedro Juan, Jr. 1963- *WhoHisp 92*
**Troeger,** Thomas H 1945- *ConAu 34NR*
**Troeger,** Thomas Henry 1945- *WhoRel 92*
**Troeh,** Frederick Roy 1930- *AmMWSc 92, WhoMW 92*
**Troell,** Jan 1931- *IntMPA 92*
**Troelstra,** Arne 1935- *AmMWSc 92*
**Troen,** Philip 1925- *AmMWSc 92*
**Troesch,** Beat Andreas 1920- *AmMWSc 92*
**Trofimenko,** Genrikh Aleksandrovich *IntWW 91*
**Trofimenkoff,** Frederick N 1934- *AmMWSc 92*
**Trofimov,** Boris Alexandrovich 1938- *AmMWSc 92*
**Trofimuk,** Andrey Alekseyevich 1911- *IntWW 91*
**Trogan,** Nicholas Richard, III 1943- *WhoAmL 92*
**Trogdon,** Dewey Leonard, Jr. 1932- *WhoFI 92*
**Trogdon,** William Oren 1920- *AmMWSc 92*
**Trogler,** William C *AmMWSc 92*
**Troglin,** Earl Thomas 1936- *WhoRel 92*
**Troia,** Robert Paul 1943- *WhoRel 92*
**Troiani,** Douglas M *WhoAmP 91*
**Troiani,** Maryann Victoria 1958- *WhoMW 92*
**Troiano,** A R 1908- *AmMWSc 92*
**Troisgros,** Pierre Emile Rene 1928- *IntWW 91*
**Troitsky,** Michael S 1917- *AmMWSc 92*
**Trojan,** Paul K 1931- *AmMWSc 92*
**Trolbridge,** Bretton Edward 1959- *WhoWest 92*
**Trolinger,** James Davis 1940- *AmMWSc 92, WhoWest 92*
**Trolio,** William Michael 1947- *WhoFI 92*
**Troll,** Christian Michael 1954- *WhoFI 92*
**Troll,** Joseph 1920- *AmMWSc 92*
**Troll,** Ralph 1932- *AmMWSc 92*
**Troll,** Walter 1922- *AmMWSc 92*
**Troller,** Fred 1930- *WhoEnt 92*
**Troller,** John Arthur 1933- *AmMWSc 92*
**Trolliet,** Philippe Charles 1940- *WhoEnt 92*
**Trollope,** Andrew David Hedderwick 1948- *Who 92*
**Trollope,** Anthony 1815-1882 *BenetAL 91, CnDBLB 4 [port], NinCLC 33 [port], RfGEnL 91, ScFEYrs*
**Trollope,** Anthony 1945- *Who 92*
**Trollope,** Frances 1780-1863 *BenetAL 91, DcAmImH*
**Trollope,** Joanna 1943- *IntAu&W 91, WrDr 92*
**Tromans,** D 1938- *AmMWSc 92*
**Tromba,** Anthony Joseph 1943- *AmMWSc 92*
**Trombetta,** Carmen Victor 1953- *WhoEnt 92*
**Trombetta,** James Thomas 1946- *WhoEnt 92*
**Trombetta,** Louis David 1946- *AmMWSc 92*
**Trombino,** Roger A. 1939- *WhoFI 92*
**Trombka,** Jacob Israel 1930- *AmMWSc 92*
**Tromble,** John M 1932- *AmMWSc 92*
**Trombley,** Charles C. 1928- *WhoRel 92*
**Trombley,** Fitterer *WhoRel 92*
**Trombley,** Joseph Edward 1935- *WhoFI 92*
**Trombley,** Michael Jerome 1933- *WhoAmL 92*
**Trombley,** Peter G 1948- *WhoAmP 91*
**Trombly,** Preston 1945- *NewAmDM*
**Trombly,** Rick A 1957- *WhoAmP 91*
**Trombold,** Walter Stevenson 1910- *WhoMW 92*
**Tromboncino,** Bartolomeo 1470?-1535? *NewAmDM*
**Trombulak,** Stephen Christopher *AmMWSc 92*
**Troncelliti,** Manrico Alfred, Jr. 1954- *WhoAmL 92*
**Tronchin,** Francois 1704-1798 *BlkwCEP*
**Tronchin,** Theodore 1709-1781 *BlkwCEP*
**Troncoso,** Jaime Jesus 1956- *WhoWest 92*
**Trone,** Donald Burnell 1954- *WhoFI 92*
**Trone,** Donald LeRoy 1937- *WhoWest 92*
**Trone,** James Norcross, Jr. 1958- *WhoEnt 92*
**Tronski,** Bronislaw 1921- *IntAu&W 91*
**Trooboff,** Peter Dennis 1942- *WhoAmL 92*
**Troop,** Andrew Mark 1960- *WhoAmL 92*
**Troop,** H. Grant 1951- *WhoRel 92*
**Troost,** Gerard 1776-1850 *BiInAmS*
**Troost,** Paul Ludwig 1878-1934 *EncTR 91 [port]*
**Troostwyk,** David 1929- *TwCPaSc*
**Tropf,** Cheryl Griffiths 1946- *AmMWSc 92, WhoFI 92*
**Tropf,** William Jacob 1947- *AmMWSc 92*
**Tropp,** Burton E 1940- *AmMWSc 92*
**Tropp,** Henry S 1927- *AmMWSc 92*
**Tropp,** Richard A. 1948- *WhoFI 92*
**Tropper,** Joshua 1955- *WhoWest 92*
**Trorey,** A W 1926- *AmMWSc 92*
**Troscinski,** Edwin S 1928- *AmMWSc 92*
**Trosclair,** Carlton James 1939- *WhoAmL 92*
**Trosclair,** Susan Jeanne 1945- *WhoEnt 92*
**Troske,** L A 1931- *WhoIns 92*
**Trosko,** James Edward 1938- *AmMWSc 92*
**Trosman,** Harry 1924- *AmMWSc 92*
**Trosper,** Guy *IntMPA 92*
**Trosper,** James Hamilton 1944- *AmMWSc 92*
**Tross,** Ralph G 1923- *AmMWSc 92*
**Trost,** Barry M 1941- *AmMWSc 92*
**Trost,** Barry Martin 1941- *IntWW 91, WhoWest 92*
**Trost,** Charles Henry 1934- *AmMWSc 92*
**Trost,** Eileen Bannon 1951- *WhoAmL 92*
**Trost,** Henry Biggs 1920- *AmMWSc 92*
**Trost,** J. Ronald 1932- *WhoAmL 92*
**Trost,** Martha Ann 1951- *WhoWest 92*
**Trost,** Phoebe Scherr 1921- *WhoAmP 91*
**Trostel,** Louis J, Jr 1927- *AmMWSc 92*
**Trotha,** Adolf von 1868-1940 *EncTR 91*
**Trotman,** Jack *IntAu&W 91, WrDr 92*
**Trotman,** Richard Edward 1942- *WhoBlA 92*
**Trotman-Dickenson,** Aubrey 1926- *Who 92*
**Trotman-Dickenson,** Aubrey Fiennes 1926- *WrDr 92*
**Trotsky,** Lev Davidovich 1879-1940 *FacFETw [port], SovUnBD*
**Trott,** Dennis Charles 1946- *WhoAmL 92*
**Trott,** Gene F 1929- *AmMWSc 92*
**Trott,** John Francis Henry 1938- *WhoFI 92*
**Trott,** Rosemary Lavonne Clifford 1914- *IntAu&W 91*
**Trott,** Stephen S 1939- *WhoAmP 91*
**Trott,** Stephen Spangler 1939- *WhoAmL 92*
**Trott,** William Macnider 1946- *WhoAmL 92*
**Trott,** Winfield James 1915- *AmMWSc 92*
**Trott zu Solz,** Adam von 1909-1944 *EncTR 91 [port]*
**Trotta,** Frank P 1955- *WhoAmP 91*
**Trotta,** Frank Paul, Jr. 1955- *WhoAmL 92*
**Trotta,** George Benedict 1930- *WhoIns 92*
**Trotta,** Margarethe von *IntDcF 2-2, ReelWom*
**Trotta,** Paul P 1942- *AmMWSc 92*
**Trotter,** Andrew Leon 1949- *WhoBlA 92*
**Trotter,** Catharine *BlkwCEP*
**Trotter,** Decatur W 1932- *WhoAmP 91*
**Trotter,** Decatur Wayne 1932- *WhoBlA 92*
**Trotter,** Donne E 1950- *WhoAmP 91*
**Trotter,** Frederick Thomas 1926- *WhoRel 92, WhoWest 92*
**Trotter,** Geraldine Pindell 1872-1918 *NotBlAW 92 [port]*
**Trotter,** Gordon Trumbull 1934- *AmMWSc 92*
**Trotter,** Hale Freeman 1931- *AmMWSc 92*
**Trotter,** James 1933- *AmMWSc 92*
**Trotter,** James Michael 1958- *WhoRel 92*
**Trotter,** John Allen 1945- *AmMWSc 92*
**Trotter,** John Wayne 1948- *AmMWSc 92*
**Trotter,** Johnny Ray 1950- *WhoMW 92*
**Trotter,** Josephine 1940- *TwCPaSc*
**Trotter,** Nancy Louisa 1934- *AmMWSc 92*
**Trotter,** Neville Guthrie 1932- *Who 92*
**Trotter,** Patrick Casey 1935- *AmMWSc 92*
**Trotter,** Philip James 1941- *AmMWSc 92*
**Trotter,** Richard Donald 1932- *WhoRel 92*
**Trotter,** Robert Russell 1915- *AmMWSc 92*
**Trotter,** Ronald 1927- *Who 92*
**Trotter,** Ronald Ramsay 1927- *IntWW 91*
**Trotter,** Ruth M 1920- *WhoAmP 91*
**Trotter,** Thomas Andrew 1957- *Who 92*
**Trotter,** William Perry 1919- *WhoAmP 91*
**Trotti,** John Boone 1935- *WhoRel 92*
**Trottman,** Alphonso 1936- *WhoBlA 92*
**Trottman,** Charles Henry 1934- *WhoBlA 92*
**Trottmann,** Stuart Robert, III 1949- *WhoMW 92*
**Trotwood,** John *IntAu&W 91X*
**Trotz,** Samuel Isaac 1927- *AmMWSc 92*
**Trotzky,** Howard M 1940- *WhoAmP 91*
**Troubetzkoy,** Amelie Rives, Princess 1863-1945 *BenetAL 91*
**Troubetzkoy,** Dorothy Livingston Ulrich *IntAu&W 91*
**Troubetzkoy,** Eugene Serge 1931- *AmMWSc 92*
**Troubridge,** Thomas 1955- *Who 92*
**Troughton,** Charles Hugh Willis d1991 *Who 92N*
**Troughton,** Charles Hugh Willis 1916- *IntWW 91*
**Troughton,** Henry Lionel 1914- *Who 92*
**Troughton,** Peter 1943- *Who 92*
**Trounson,** Ronald Charles 1926- *Who 92*
**Troup,** Alistair Mewburn 1927- *Who 92*
**Troup,** Anthony *Who 92*
**Troup,** Bobby 1918- *WhoEnt 92*
**Troup,** Elliott Vanbrugh 1938- *WhoBlA 92*
**Troup,** John Anthony 1921- *Who 92*
**Troup,** Malcolm Graham 1918- *WhoWest 92*
**Troup,** Paul VanCleve 1941- *WhoFI 92*
**Troup,** Ronald Eugene 1952- *WhoRel 92*
**Troup,** Stanley Burton 1925- *AmMWSc 92*
**Troupe,** Charles Quincy 1936- *WhoAmP 91, WhoBlA 92*
**Troupe,** Marilyn Kay 1945- *WhoBlA 92*
**Troupe,** Quincy *DrAPF 91*
**Troupe,** Quincy Thomas, Jr. 1943- *WhoBlA 92*
**Troupe,** Terry Lee 1947- *WhoFI 92*
**Troupe-Frye,** Betty Jean 1935- *WhoBlA 92*
**Trousdale,** William Latimer 1928- *AmMWSc 92*
**Trouse,** Albert Charles 1921- *AmMWSc 92*
**Trout,** Barbara Ann 1927- *WhoAmP 91*
**Trout,** David Linn 1927- *AmMWSc 92*
**Trout,** Dennis Alan 1947- *AmMWSc 92*
**Trout,** Gary Lee 1947- *WhoMW 92*
**Trout,** Jerome Joseph *AmMWSc 92*
**Trout,** Kilgore *ConAu 35NR, DrAPF 91, TwCSFW 91, WrDr 92*
**Trout,** Nelson W. 1920- *WhoBlA 92*
**Trout,** Robert *LesBEnT 92*
**Trout,** Roscoe Marshall, Jr. 1944- *WhoWest 92*
**Trout,** Thomas James 1949- *AmMWSc 92*
**Trout,** William Edgar, III 1937- *AmMWSc 92*
**Troutman,** Andrew Craig 1960- *WhoAmL 92*
**Troutman,** Charles H, III 1944- *WhoAmP 91*
**Troutman,** Conaught M 1955- *WhoIns 92*
**Troutman,** E. Mac 1915- *WhoAmL 92*
**Troutman,** Gerald Stevenson 1933- *WhoRel 92*
**Troutman,** James Scott 1930- *AmMWSc 92*
**Troutman,** John G. 1941- *WhoMW 92*
**Troutman,** Porter Lee, Jr. 1943- *WhoBlA 92*
**Troutman,** Richard Charles 1922- *AmMWSc 92*
**Troutman,** Robert Battey, Jr. d1991 *NewYTBS 91*
**Troutman,** Ronald R *AmMWSc 92*
**Troutner,** David Elliott 1929- *AmMWSc 92*
**Troutt,** Don Ray 1948- *WhoEnt 92, WhoMW 92*
**Troutt,** Louise Leotta 1958- *AmMWSc 92*
**Troutt,** Marvin Dean 1944- *WhoMW 92*
**Trouvelot,** Etienne Leopold 1827-1895 *BiInAmS*
**Trovall,** Carl Curtis 1961- *WhoRel 92*
**Trovato,** James David, Jr. 1955- *WhoWest 92*
**Trover,** Ellen Lloyd 1947- *WhoAmL 92, WhoWest 92*
**Trovoada,** Miguel Anjos da Cunha Lisboa *IntWW 91*
**Trow,** Clifford Wayne 1929- *WhoAmP 91*
**Trow,** George W S 1943- *IntAu&W 91*
**Trow,** James 1922- *AmMWSc 92*
**Trowbridge,** Alexander B., Jr. 1929- *IntWW 91*
**Trowbridge,** Alexander Buel, Jr. 1929- *WhoFI 92*
**Trowbridge,** Amelia Ann 1945- *WhoFI 92*
**Trowbridge,** C Robertson 1932- *WhoAmP 91*
**Trowbridge,** Charles Christopher 1870-1918 *BiInAmS*
**Trowbridge,** Dale Brian 1940- *AmMWSc 92*
**Trowbridge,** Edward K 1928- *WhoIns 92*
**Trowbridge,** Elisabeth Ward 1906- *WhoWest 92*
**Trowbridge,** Frederick Lindsley 1942- *AmMWSc 92*
**Trowbridge,** George Cecil 1938- *AmMWSc 92*
**Trowbridge,** George William Job 1911- *Who 92*
**Trowbridge,** Ian Stuart 1947- *AmMWSc 92*
**Trowbridge,** Jeffery David 1956- *WhoAmL 92*
**Trowbridge,** John F 1924- *WhoAmP 91*
**Trowbridge,** John Townsend 1827-1916 *BenetAL 91, BibAL 8*
**Trowbridge,** Lee Douglas 1949- *AmMWSc 92*
**Trowbridge,** Leslie Walter 1920- *AmMWSc 92*
**Trowbridge,** Martin Edward O'Keeffe 1925- *Who 92*
**Trowbridge,** Richard 1920- *IntWW 91, Who 92*
**Trowbridge,** Richard James 1930- *WhoWest 92*
**Trowbridge,** Richard Stuart 1942- *AmMWSc 92*
**Trowbridge,** Ronald Lee 1937- *WhoMW 92*
**Trowbridge,** Thomas, Jr. 1938- *WhoFI 92, WhoWest 92*
**Trowbridge,** William *DrAPF 91*
**Trowbridge,** William Carroll 1904- *WhoAmP 91*
**Trowbridge,** William Petit 1828-1892 *BiInAmS*
**Trowell,** Brian Lewis 1931- *Who 92*
**Trower,** W Peter 1935- *AmMWSc 92*
**Troxel,** Bennie Wyatt 1920- *AmMWSc 92*
**Troxel,** David Lee 1957- *WhoEnt 92*
**Troxel,** Donald Eugene 1934- *AmMWSc 92*
**Troxel,** John Milton 1960- *WhoWest 92*
**Troxel,** Kent M. 1958- *WhoMW 92*
**Troxel,** Oliver Leonard, Jr 1919- *WhoAmP 91*
**Troxell,** Harry Emerson, Jr 1921- *AmMWSc 92*
**Troxell,** Terry Charles 1944- *AmMWSc 92*
**Troxell,** Wade Oakes 1956- *AmMWSc 92*
**Troxler,** David W 1952- *WhoAmP 91*
**Troxler,** Raymond George 1939- *AmMWSc 92*
**Troxler,** Robert Fulton 1938- *AmMWSc 92*
**Troy,** Anthony Francis 1941- *WhoAmL 92*
**Troy,** Daniel Joseph 1932- *AmMWSc 92, WhoMW 92*
**Troy,** Daniel Patrick 1948- *WhoAmP 91*
**Troy,** Frederic Arthur 1937- *AmMWSc 92*
**Troy,** J. Edward 1931- *WhoRel 92*
**Troy,** James Michael 1955- *WhoFI 92*
**Troy,** Joan Brooks 1938- *WhoFI 92*
**Troy,** Katherine *WrDr 92*
**Troy,** Keith Alan 1953- *WhoRel 92*
**Troy,** Matthew William 1951- *WhoAmP 91*
**Troy,** Richard Hershey 1937- *WhoAmL 92*
**Troy,** Robert Sweeney, Sr. 1949- *WhoAmL 92*
**Troy,** Thomas Charles 1930- *WhoAmL 92*
**Troy,** Una *WrDr 92*
**Troy,** William Christopher 1947- *AmMWSc 92*
**Troya,** Ilion 1947- *WhoHisp 92*
**Troyanos,** Tatiana 1938- *NewAmDM*
**Troyanovich,** Steve *DrAPF 91*
**Troyanovsky,** Oleg Aleksandrovich 1919- *IntWW 91*
**Troyat,** Henri 1911- *GuFrLit 1, IntWW 91, Who 92*
**Troyer,** Alvah Forrest 1929- *AmMWSc 92, WhoFI 92*
**Troyer,** David Allen 1934- *WhoMW 92*
**Troyer,** James Richard 1929- *AmMWSc 92*
**Troyer,** John Robert 1928- *AmMWSc 92*
**Troyer,** Robert James 1928- *AmMWSc 92*
**Troyer,** Stephanie Fantl 1944- *AmMWSc 92*
**Trozzolo,** Anthony Marion 1930- *AmMWSc 92, WhoMW 92*
**Trpis,** Milan 1930- *AmMWSc 92*
**Truan,** Carlos F. 1935- *WhoHisp 92*
**Truan,** Carlos Flores 1935- *WhoAmP 91*
**Truax,** Donald R 1927- *AmMWSc 92*
**Truax,** Donald Robert 1927- *WhoWest 92*
**Truax,** George Lawrence 1954- *WhoMW 92*
**Truax,** Robert Lloyd 1928- *AmMWSc 92*
**Truban,** William A 1924- *WhoAmP 91*
**Trubatch,** Janett 1945- *AmMWSc 92*
**Trubatch,** Sheldon L 1942- *AmMWSc 92*
**Trubek,** Josephine Susan 1942- *WhoAmL 92*
**Trubek,** Max 1898- *AmMWSc 92*
**Trubert,** Marc 1927- *AmMWSc 92*
**Trubey,** David Keith 1928- *AmMWSc 92*
**Trubilin,** Nikolay Timofeyevich 1929- *IntWW 91*
**Trubner,** Henry 1920- *WhoWest 92*
**Trubshaw,** Brian 1924- *Who 92*
**Truby,** William F. 1949- *WhoRel 92*
**Truce,** William Everett 1917- *AmMWSc 92*
**Truchard,** James Joseph 1943- *AmMWSc 92*
**Truck,** Debrah Ann 1957- *WhoMW 92*
**Truck,** Fred *DrAPF 91*
**Truck,** Robert-Paul 1917- *IntAu&W 91*
**Truckenbrod,** John Carl *WhoEnt 92*
**Truckenbrod,** Phillip 1941- *WhoEnt 92*
**Trucker,** Donald Edward 1926- *AmMWSc 92*
**Trucksis,** Theresa A. 1924- *WhoMW 92*
**Trudeau,** Arthur G. 1902-1991 *CurBio 91N*
**Trudeau,** Arthur Gilbert 1902-1991 *NewYTBS 91 [port]*
**Trudeau,** Donald Benjamin 1922- *WhoWest 92*
**Trudeau,** Edward Livingston 1848-1915 *BiInAmS*

**Trudeau,** Garry 1948- *FacFETw, News 91 [port], WrDr 92*
**Trudeau,** Garry B. 1948- *IntWW 91*
**Trudeau,** Patricia Margaret 1931- *WhoWest 92*
**Trudeau,** Pierre Elliott 1919- *FacFETw [port], IntWW 91, Who 92*
**Trudeau,** Roger Jerome 1956- *WhoAmL 92*
**Trudeau,** Terry Murray 1934- *WhoAmP 91*
**Trudel,** John Davis 1942- *WhoWest 92*
**Trudel,** Mary Renee *WhoFI 92*
**Trudel,** Michel D 1944- *AmMWSc 92*
**Trudell,** Dennis *DrAPF 91*
**Truden,** Judith Lucille 1931- *AmMWSc 92*
**Trudgill,** Peter John 1943- *Who 92*
**True,** Diemer D. 1946- *WhoWest 92*
**True,** Diemer Durland 1946- *WhoAmP 91*
**True,** Fred Lewis, Jr. 1923- *WhoAmL 92, WhoAmP 91*
**True,** Frederick William 1858-1914 *BiInAmS*
**True,** Harry Staton 1937- *WhoMW 92*
**True,** Henry Alfonso, Jr. 1915- *WhoWest 92*
**True,** Nancy S 1951- *AmMWSc 92*
**True,** Raymond Stephen 1934- *WhoMW 92*
**True,** Roy Joe 1938- *WhoAmL 92*
**True,** S M, Jr *WhoIns 92*
**True,** Virgil 1925- *WhoWest 92*
**True,** Wendell Cleon 1934- *WhoFI 92, WhoMW 92*
**True,** William Wadsworth 1925- *AmMWSc 92*
**Trueblood,** Benjamin Franklin 1847-1916 *AmPeW*
**Trueblood,** Harry Albert, Jr. 1925- *WhoFI 92, WhoWest 92*
**Trueblood,** Jo Ann Rita 1934- *WhoAmP 91*
**Trueblood,** Kenneth Nyitray 1920- *AmMWSc 92*
**Trueblood,** Paul G. 1905- *WrDr 92*
**Trueblood,** Paul Graham 1905- *IntAu&W 91*
**Trueblood,** Vera J. 1962- *WhoBlA 92*
**Trueheart,** Charles 1951- *IntAu&W 91*
**Trueheart,** William E. 1942- *WhoBlA 92*
**Truehill,** Marshall, Jr. 1948- *WhoRel 92*
**Truell,** James H 1947- *WhoAmP 91*
**Truelove,** Bryan *AmMWSc 92*
**Truelove,** C. Keith 1949- *WhoMW 92*
**Trueman,** Edwin Royden 1922- *Who 92*
**Trueman,** Frederick Sewards 1931- *Who 92*
**Trueman,** Thomas Laurence 1935- *AmMWSc 92*
**Truemper,** David George 1939- *WhoMW 92, WhoRel 92*
**Truer,** Jerome Wesley 1952- *WhoMW 92*
**Truesdale,** C.W. *DrAPF 91*
**Truesdale,** John Cushman 1921- *WhoAmP 91*
**Truesdale,** Larry Kenneth 1947- *AmMWSc 92*
**Truesdell,** Alfred Hemingway 1933- *AmMWSc 92*
**Truesdell,** Carolyn Gilmour 1939- *WhoAmL 92*
**Truesdell,** Clifford Ambrose, III 1919- *AmMWSc 92*
**Truesdell,** Karl, Jr 1882-1955 *FacFETw*
**Truesdell,** Susan Jane 1945- *AmMWSc 92*
**Truesdell,** Walter George 1919- *WhoRel 92*
**Truett,** George Washington 1867-1944 *RelLAm 91*
**Truett,** Harold Joseph, III 1946- *WhoAmL 92, WhoWest 92*
**Truett,** Lila Flory 1947- *WhoFI 92*
**Truex,** Earle Melvin 1937- *WhoRel 92*
**Truex,** Max d1991 *NewYTBS 91*
**Truex,** Raymond Carl 1911- *AmMWSc 92*
**Truex,** Timothy Jay 1945- *AmMWSc 92*
**Trufant,** Samuel Adams 1919- *AmMWSc 92*
**Truffaut,** Francois 1932-1984 *ConAu 34NR, FacFETw, IntDcF 2-2 [port]*
**Truffaut,** Michelle 1942- *WhoEnt 92, WhoWest 92*
**Truglia,** Christel *WhoAmP 91*
**Truhaut,** Rene Charles 1909- *IntWW 91*
**Truhlar,** Donald Gene 1944- *AmMWSc 92*
**Truhlar,** Doris Broaddus 1946- *WhoAmL 92*
**Truho,** Gail L. 1944- *WhoMW 92*
**Truitt,** Anne 1921- *WrDr 92*
**Truitt,** Edward Byrd, Jr 1922- *AmMWSc 92*
**Truitt,** Kenneth Ray 1945- *WhoFI 92*
**Truitt,** Lisa Marie 1962- *WhoEnt 92*
**Truitt,** Marcus M 1921- *AmMWSc 92*
**Truitt,** Mary M. *DrAPF 91*
**Truitt,** Robert Lindell 1946- *AmMWSc 92*
**Truitt,** Robert Ralph, Jr. 1948- *WhoAmL 92*
**Truitt,** Wesley Byron 1939- *WhoWest 92*
**Truitte,** James F. *WhoBlA 92*
**Trujillo,** Anna Marie 1945- *WhoAmP 91*
**Trujillo,** Anthony J. 1933- *WhoHisp 92*
**Trujillo,** Armida Manuela 1937- *WhoHisp 92*
**Trujillo,** Arnold Paul 1951- *WhoHisp 92*
**Trujillo,** Augustine 1940- *WhoHisp 92*
**Trujillo,** C B 1932- *WhoAmP 91*
**Trujillo,** Camilla 1956- *WhoHisp 92*
**Trujillo,** Candelario, Jr. 1932- *WhoHisp 92*
**Trujillo,** Carlos Alberto 1957- *WhoHisp 92*
**Trujillo,** Eddie A. *WhoHisp 92*
**Trujillo,** Eduardo E 1930- *AmMWSc 92*
**Trujillo,** Edward M. 1947- *WhoHisp 92*
**Trujillo,** Edward Michael 1947- *AmMWSc 92*
**Trujillo,** Ingrid 1955- *WhoHisp 92*
**Trujillo,** J. B. *WhoHisp 92*
**Trujillo,** J Frank 1907- *WhoAmP 91*
**Trujillo,** Jacobo Eduardo 1940- *WhoHisp 92*
**Trujillo,** Jake Antonio 1944- *WhoHisp 92*
**Trujillo,** Jimmy E. 1948- *WhoHisp 92*
**Trujillo,** Joe Anthony 1937- *WhoHisp 92*
**Trujillo,** Joe D. 1940- *WhoHisp 92*
**Trujillo,** John J. *WhoHisp 92*
**Trujillo,** John Russell 1950- *WhoWest 92*
**Trujillo,** Joseph Ben 1947- *WhoWest 92*
**Trujillo,** Juan 1940- *WhoAmP 91*
**Trujillo,** Julian 1956- *WhoHisp 92*
**Trujillo,** Larry E. *WhoHisp 92*
**Trujillo,** Larry E, Sr 1940- *WhoAmP 91*
**Trujillo,** Laurence Michael 1955- *WhoHisp 92*
**Trujillo,** Linda K *DrAPF 91*
**Trujillo,** Lionel Gil *WhoHisp 92*
**Trujillo,** Lorenzo A. 1951- *WhoWest 92*
**Trujillo,** Lori Sue 1958- *WhoWest 92*
**Trujillo,** Luis *WhoHisp 92*
**Trujillo,** Marc Allen *WhoHisp 92*
**Trujillo,** Marisela Carrasco 1947- *WhoHisp 92*
**Trujillo,** Michael Joseph 1939- *WhoHisp 92*
**Trujillo,** Mike A. *WhoHisp 92*
**Trujillo,** Patricio Eduardo 1937- *AmMWSc 92*
**Trujillo,** Paul Edward *DrAPF 91*
**Trujillo,** Phillip M., Sr. 1921- *WhoHisp 92*
**Trujillo,** Rafael 1891-1961 *FacFETw*
**Trujillo,** Ralph Eusebio 1940- *AmMWSc 92*
**Trujillo,** Roberto Gabriel 1951- *WhoHisp 92*
**Trujillo,** Rudolpho Andres 1939- *WhoHisp 92*
**Trujillo,** Solomon D. 1951- *WhoHisp 92*
**Trujillo,** Stephen Michael 1932- *AmMWSc 92, WhoWest 92*
**Trujillo,** Virginia Marie 1948- *WhoHisp 92*
**Trujillo,** William Andrew 1946- *WhoHisp 92*
**Trujillo Maestas,** Abby 1949- *WhoHisp 92*
**Trujillo Molina,** Hector Bienvenido 1908- *IntWW 91*
**Trull,** Steven Gregory 1952- *WhoMW 92*
**Trulock,** Paul H *WhoAmP 91*
**Trulove,** Harry David 1927- *WhoRel 92*
**Trulson,** Michael E *AmMWSc 92*
**Truly,** Richard 1937- *FacFETw*
**Truly,** Richard H. 1937- *IntWW 91*
**Truman,** Bennett S 1962- *WhoAmP 91*
**Truman,** Harry S. 1884-1972 *AmPolLe [port], BenetAL 91, EncTR 91, FacFETw [port], RComAH*
**Truman,** James 1826-1914 *BiInAmS*
**Truman,** James William 1945- *AmMWSc 92*
**Truman,** Margaret 1924- *WrDr 92*
**Truman,** Peter D 1935- *WhoAmP 91*
**Truman,** Ruth 1931- *WrDr 92*
**Truman,** Ruth Dixon 1931- *IntAu&W 91*
**Trumbauer,** Frankie 1901-1956 *NewAmDM*
**Trumble,** David Frederick 1948- *WhoMW 92*
**Trumbo,** Bruce Edward 1937- *AmMWSc 92*
**Trumbo,** Dalton 1905-1976 *BenetAL 91, LiExTwC*
**Trumbo,** George William 1926- *WhoBlA 92*
**Trumbo,** Malfourd W 1954- *WhoAmP 91*
**Trumbore,** Conrad Noble 1931- *AmMWSc 92*
**Trumbore,** Forrest Allen 1927- *AmMWSc 92*
**Trumbull,** Benjamin 1735-1820 *BenetAL 91*
**Trumbull,** Douglas 1942- *IntMPA 92*
**Trumbull,** Elmer Roy, Jr 1924- *AmMWSc 92*
**Trumbull,** Gurdon 1841-1903 *BiInAmS*
**Trumbull,** Henry Clay 1830-1903 *RelLAm 91*
**Trumbull,** James Hammond 1821-1897 *BiInAmS*
**Trumbull,** John 1750-1831 *BenetAL 91, BibAL 8*
**Trumbull,** Jonathan 1740-1809 *AmPolLe*
**Trumbull,** Lyman 1813-1896 *AmPolLe*
**Trumbull,** Roy Howard 1939- *WhoEnt 92*
**Trumbull,** Stephen Michael 1954- *WhoEnt 92, WhoFI 92*
**Trumka,** Richard Louis 1949- *IntWW 91, WhoFI 92*
**Trummel,** J Merle 1916- *AmMWSc 92*
**Trummer,** Max Joseph 1924- *AmMWSc 92*
**Trump,** Benjamin Franklin 1932- *AmMWSc 92*
**Trump,** Donald 1946- *FacFETw, WrDr 92*
**Trump,** Donald John 1946- *IntWW 91, WhoFI 92*
**Trumpington,** Baroness *Who 92*
**Trumpler,** Paul R 1914- *AmMWSc 92*
**Trumpower,** Bernard Lee 1943- *AmMWSc 92*
**Trumpy,** D Rudolf 1921- *AmMWSc 92, IntWW 91*
**Trung Nhi** *EncAmaz 91*
**Trung Trac** *EncAmaz 91*
**Trungpa Rinpoche,** Chogyam 1939-1987 *RelLAm 91*
**Truninger,** Lauren L 1918- *WhoAmP 91*
**Trunk,** Gerard Vernon 1942- *AmMWSc 92*
**Trunzo,** Caesar 1926- *WhoAmP 91*
**Trunzo,** Floyd F 1917- *AmMWSc 92*
**Truong Nhu Tang** 1923- *IntWW 91*
**Truong,** Hoa Phu 1953- *WhoWest 92*
**Truong,** Mac 1944- *WhoAmL 92*
**Truong,** Thoi Van 1952- *WhoFI 92*
**Truong,** Xuan Thoai 1930- *AmMWSc 92*
**Trupin,** Joel Sunrise 1934- *AmMWSc 92*
**Trupp,** Robin Jean 1953- *WhoMW 92*
**Truran,** James Wellington, Jr 1940- *AmMWSc 92, WhoMW 92*
**Truran,** William R. 1951- *WhoFI 92*
**Truro,** Bishop of 1932- *Who 92*
**Truro,** Dean of *Who 92*
**Trus,** Benes L 1946- *AmMWSc 92*
**Trusal,** Lynn R 1945- *AmMWSc 92*
**Truscott,** Frederick Herbert 1926- *AmMWSc 92*
**Truscott,** George 1929- *Who 92*
**Truscott,** Harold 1914- *ConCom 92*
**Truscott,** Judith Farren 1939- *WhoRel 92*
**Truscott,** Robert Blake *DrAPF 91*
**Truscott,** Robert Bruce 1928- *AmMWSc 92*
**Truskowski,** John Budd 1945- *WhoAmL 92, WhoMW 92*
**Truskowski,** Suzanne Renee 1962- *WhoMW 92*
**Truslow,** Godfrey Grosvenor 1934- *WhoFI 92*
**Trussel,** Harold Junior 1936- *WhoWest 92*
**Trussell,** Donna *DrAPF 91*
**Trussell,** Grayson Lee 1941- *WhoWest 92*
**Trussell,** Henry Joel 1945- *AmMWSc 92*
**Trussell,** Millard Marvin 1920- *WhoFI 92*
**Trussell,** Paul Chandos 1916- *AmMWSc 92*
**Trussell,** Robert Rhodes *WhoWest 92*
**Trust,** Ronald I 1947- *AmMWSc 92*
**Trust,** Trevor John 1942- *AmMWSc 92*
**Trustram Eve** *Who 92*
**Trusty,** Richard Vincent, Jr. 1955- *WhoMW 92*
**Trusty,** Thomas F 1931- *WhoIns 92*
**Truswell,** Stewart 1928- *Who 92*
**Truszkowska,** Krystyna *AmMWSc 92*
**Truta,** Marianne Patricia 1951- *WhoWest 92*
**Truth,** Sojourner 1795-1883 *HanAmWH*
**Truth,** Sojourner 1797?-1883 *BenetAL 91, NotBlAW 92 [port], RComAH*
**Truthan,** Charles Edwin 1955- *WhoMW 92*
**Trutt,** William J 1937- *WhoIns 92*
**Trutter,** John Thomas 1920- *WhoFI 92, WhoMW 92*
**Trutza,** Pauline 1932- *WhoMW 92*
**Truxal,** Fred Stone 1922- *AmMWSc 92*
**Truxal,** John G 1924- *AmMWSc 92*
**Truxillo,** Stanton George 1941- *AmMWSc 92*
**Tryban,** Esther Elizabeth 1958- *WhoAmL 92*
**Tryber,** Thomas Anthony, Jr. 1943- *WhoFI 92, WhoMW 92*
**Trybus,** Raymond J. 1944- *WhoWest 92*
**Tryfiates,** George P 1935- *AmMWSc 92*
**Tryman,** Mfanya Donald 1948- *WhoBlA 92*
**Trynchy,** Peter 1931- *WhoWest 92*
**Tryon** *Who 92*
**Tryon,** Baron 1940- *Who 92*
**Tryon,** Edward Polk 1940- *AmMWSc 92*
**Tryon,** George Washington 1838-1888 *BiInAmS*
**Tryon,** John G 1920- *AmMWSc 92*
**Tryon,** Rolla Milton, Jr 1916- *AmMWSc 92*
**Tryon,** Thomas 1926- *IntAu&W 91*
**Tryon,** Thomas 1926-1991 *ConAu 135, CurBio 91N, NewYTBS 91 [port]*
**Tryon,** Tom *ConAu 135*
**Tryon,** Warren W 1944- *AmMWSc 92*
**Tryon,** Wyndham 1883-1942 *TwCPaSc*
**Tryon-Wilson,** Charles Edward 1909- *Who 92*
**Tryoshnikov,** Aleksey Fedorovich 1914- *IntWW 91*
**Trypanis,** Constantine Athanasius 1909- *IntWW 91, Who 92*
**Tryphaena** *EncAmaz 91*
**Tryphonas,** Helen 1939- *AmMWSc 92*
**Tryphosa** *EncAmaz 91*
**Trythall,** Anthony John 1927- *Who 92*
**Trythall,** Harry Gilbert 1930- *WhoEnt 92*
**Trythall,** John Douglas d1991 *Who 92N*
**Trytten,** George Norman 1928- *AmMWSc 92*
**Trytten,** Roland Aaker 1913- *AmMWSc 92*
**Trytten,** Steven Earl 1952- *WhoWest 92*
**Trzaskoma,** Patricia Povilitis 1940- *AmMWSc 92*
**Trzcienski,** Walter Edward, Jr 1942- *AmMWSc 92*
**Trzcinka,** Charles Anthony 1951- *WhoFI 92*
**Trzeciak,** Leonard Peter 1945- *WhoMW 92*
**Trzeciakowski,** Witold Mieczyslaw 1926- *IntWW 91*
**Trznadel,** Frank Dwight, Jr. 1942- *WhoFI 92*
**Tsagaris,** Theofilos John 1929- *AmMWSc 92*
**Tsai,** Alan Chung-Hong 1943- *AmMWSc 92*
**Tsai,** Bilin Paula 1949- *AmMWSc 92*
**Tsai,** Boh Chang 1944- *AmMWSc 92*
**Tsai,** Chester E 1935- *AmMWSc 92*
**Tsai,** Chia-Yin 1937- *AmMWSc 92*
**Tsai,** Ching-Long 1945- *AmMWSc 92*
**Tsai,** Chishiun S 1933- *AmMWSc 92*
**Tsai,** Chuang Chuang *AmMWSc 92*
**Tsai,** Chun-Che 1937- *AmMWSc 92*
**Tsai,** Chung-Chieh 1948- *AmMWSc 92*
**Tsai,** Frank Y *AmMWSc 92*
**Tsai,** Gerald 1928- *IntWW 91*
**Tsai,** James Hsi-Cho 1934- *AmMWSc 92*
**Tsai,** Jir Shiong *AmMWSc 92*
**Tsai,** Kuei-Wu 1941- *AmMWSc 92*
**Tsai,** Lin 1922- *AmMWSc 92*
**Tsai,** Lung-Wen 1945- *AmMWSc 92*
**Tsai,** Ming-Daw 1950- *AmMWSc 92, WhoMW 92*
**Tsai,** Ming-Jer 1943- *AmMWSc 92*
**Tsai,** Ming-Jong 1950- *AmMWSc 92*
**Tsai,** Peter Ying-Shih 1923- *WhoRel 92*
**Tsai,** Stephen W 1929- *AmMWSc 92*
**Tsai,** Theodore Fang 1948- *WhoWest 92*
**Tsai,** Tsui Hsien 1935- *AmMWSc 92*
**Tsai,** Wilman 1960- *WhoWest 92*
**Tsai,** Y-M 1937- *AmMWSc 92*
**Tsai,** Young Tong 1952- *WhoWest 92*
**Tsai,** Yung Su 1930- *AmMWSc 92*
**Tsakiridis,** Chris Lazarus 1941- *WhoMW 92*
**Tsakonas,** Stavros 1920- *AmMWSc 92*
**Tsaliovich,** Anatoly 1936- *AmMWSc 92*
**Tsaloumas,** Dimitris 1921- *ConPo 91, WrDr 92*
**Tsaloumas,** Dimitris 1930?- *LiExTwC*
**Tsamis,** Donna Robin 1957- *WhoAmL 92*
**Tsan,** Min-Fu 1942- *AmMWSc 92*
**Tsander,** Fridrikh 1887-1933 *FacFETw*
**Tsandoulas,** Gerasimos Nicholas 1939- *AmMWSc 92*
**Tsang,** Charles Pak Wai *AmMWSc 92*
**Tsang,** Chit-Sang 1952- *WhoWest 92*
**Tsang,** Dean Zensh 1952- *AmMWSc 92*
**Tsang,** Gee 1938- *AmMWSc 92*
**Tsang,** James Chen-Hsiang 1946- *AmMWSc 92*
**Tsang,** Joseph Chiao-Liang 1936- *AmMWSc 92*
**Tsang,** Kang Too *AmMWSc 92*
**Tsang,** Leung 1950- *AmMWSc 92*
**Tsang,** Mun Chiu 1955- *WhoMW 92*
**Tsang,** Reginald C 1940- *AmMWSc 92*
**Tsang,** Sai Ki *WhoWest 92*
**Tsang,** Sien Moo 1912- *AmMWSc 92*
**Tsang,** Tung 1932- *AmMWSc 92*
**Tsang,** Victor Chiu Wana 1947- *AmMWSc 92*
**Tsang,** Wai Lin 1951- *AmMWSc 92*
**T'Sani,** Nolan 1948- *WhoEnt 92*
**Tsankov,** Aleksandur 1897-1959 *BiDExR*
**Ts'ao K'un** 1862-1938 *FacFETw*
**Tsao,** Chen-Hsiang 1929- *AmMWSc 92*
**Tsao,** Chia Kuei 1922- *AmMWSc 92*
**Tsao,** Chich-Hsing Alex 1953- *WhoWest 92*
**Tsao,** Ching H 1920- *AmMWSc 92*
**Ts'ao,** Chung-Hsin 1933- *AmMWSc 92*
**Tsao,** Constance S 1934- *AmMWSc 92*
**Tsao,** Francis Hsiang-Chian 1936- *AmMWSc 92*
**Tsao,** George T 1931- *AmMWSc 92*
**Tsao,** Jeffrey Yeenien 1955- *AmMWSc 92*

**Tsao**, Keh Cheng 1923- *AmMWSc 92*
**Tsao**, Makepeace Uho 1918- *AmMWSc 92*
**Tsao**, Nai-Kuan 1939- *AmMWSc 92*
**Tsao**, Peter Hsing-tsuen 1929- *AmMWSc 92*
**Tsao**, Sai Hoi 1936- *AmMWSc 92*
**Tsao**, Utah 1913- *AmMWSc 92*
**Tsao-Wu**, Nelson Tsin 1934- *AmMWSc 92*
**Tsaros**, C L 1921- *AmMWSc 92*
**Tsaroukis** 1910- *IntWW 91*
**Tsatsos**, Constantine 1899-1987 *FacFETw*
**Tsaur**, Bor-Yeu 1955- *AmMWSc 92*
**Tsay**, Hwai-Min 1955- *WhoWest 92*
**Tschacher**, Darell Ray 1945- *WhoWest 92*
**Tschaeche**, Alden N. 1929- *WhoWest 92*
**Tschammer und Osten**, Hans von 1887-1943 *EncTR 91 [port]*
**Tschang**, Pin-Seng 1934- *AmMWSc 92*
**Tschannen-Moran**, Robert Keith 1954- *WhoRel 92*
**Tschantz**, Bruce A 1938- *AmMWSc 92*
**Tschanz**, Charles McFarland 1926- *AmMWSc 92*
**Tschappat**, Douglas Wilson 1927- *WhoFI 92*
**Tscherny**, George 1924- *DcTwDes, WhoEnt 92*
**Tschetter**, Paul 1905- *WhoAmP 91*
**Tschichold**, Jan 1902-1974 *DcTwDes*
**Tschinkel**, Sheila Lerner 1940- *WhoFI 92*
**Tschinkel**, Walter Rheinhardt 1940- *AmMWSc 92*
**Tschirgi**, Robert Donald 1924- *AmMWSc 92*
**Tschirhart**, John Thomas 1946- *WhoWest 92*
**Tschirley**, Fred Harold 1925- *AmMWSc 92*
**Tschirnhaus**, Ehrenfried Walther 1651-1708 *BlkwCEP*
**Tschoegl**, Nicholas William 1918- *AmMWSc 92*
**Tschoepe**, Thomas 1915- *WhoRel 92*
**Tschohl**, John Steven 1947- *WhoMW 92*
**Tschudi**, Hans-Peter 1913- *IntWW 91*
**Tschudi-Madsen**, Stephan 1923- *IntWW 91*
**Tschudy**, Donald P 1926- *AmMWSc 92*
**Tschuikow-Roux**, Eugene 1936- *AmMWSc 92*
**Tschunko**, Hubert F A 1912- *AmMWSc 92*
**Tse**, Bernard Kapang 1948- *WhoWest 92*
**Tse**, Charles Ka-Sung *WhoMW 92*
**Tse**, Francis Lai-Sing 1952- *AmMWSc 92*
**Tse**, Francis S 1919- *AmMWSc 92*
**Tse**, Harley Y 1947- *AmMWSc 92*
**Tse**, John C. M. *WhoRel 92*
**Tse**, Rose 1927- *AmMWSc 92*
**Tse**, Stephen Yung Nien 1931- *WhoFI 92*
**Tse**, Warren W 1939- *AmMWSc 92*
**Tsedenbal**, Yumjaagiyn 1916-1991 *IntWW 91, -91N*
**Tsedenbal**, Yumzhagiin d1991 *NewYTBS 91 [port]*
**Tselkov**, Oleg 1934- *IntWW 91*
**Tsen**, Cho Ching 1922- *AmMWSc 92*
**Tseng Kwang-Shun** 1924- *IntWW 91*
**Tseng Wen-Shing** 1935- *ConAu 35NR*
**Tseng**, Charles C 1932- *AmMWSc 92*
**Tseng**, Chien Kuei 1934- *AmMWSc 92*
**Tseng**, Chipei P. 1920- *WhoMW 92*
**Tseng**, Fung-I 1936- *AmMWSc 92*
**Tseng**, Howard Shih Chang 1935- *WhoFI 92*
**Tseng**, Hsiang Len 1913- *AmMWSc 92*
**Tseng**, Leon L F 1937- *AmMWSc 92*
**Tseng**, Linda 1936- *AmMWSc 92*
**Tseng**, Michael Tsung 1944- *AmMWSc 92*
**Tseng**, Samuel Chin-Chong 1933- *AmMWSc 92*
**Tseng**, Shin-Shyong 1938- *AmMWSc 92*
**Tsering**, Dago 1941- *IntWW 91*
**Tsering**, Tensin 1935- *WhoNob 90*
**Tsernoglou**, Demetrius 1935- *AmMWSc 92*
**Tseu**, Fred K. 1923- *WhoFI 92, WhoWest 92*
**Tseu**, Joseph Kum Kwong 1935- *WhoWest 92*
**Tshabalala**, Headman d1991 *NewYTBS 91*
**Tshering**, Ugyen 1954- *IntWW 91*
**Tshombe**, Moise 1919-1969 *FacFETw*
**Tsiatis**, Anastasios A 1948- *AmMWSc 92*
**Tsibris**, John-Constantine Michael 1936- *AmMWSc 92*
**Tsien**, Hsienchyang 1939- *AmMWSc 92*
**Tsien**, Richard Winyu 1945- *AmMWSc 92*
**Tsigdinos**, George Andrew 1929- *AmMWSc 92*
**Tsin**, Andrew Tsang Cheung 1950- *AmMWSc 92*
**Tsintsadze**, Sulkhan Fedorovich 1925- *SovUnBD*
**Tsintsadze**, Sulkhan Fyodorovich 1925- *IntWW 91*
**Tsiolkovsky**, Konstantin 1857-1935 *FacFETw, TwCSFW 91A*
**Tsiolkovsky**, Konstantin Eduardovich 1857-1935 *ScFEYrs*
**Tsiongas**, K Nicholas 1952- *WhoAmP 91*
**Tsipis**, Kosta M 1934- *AmMWSc 92*
**Tsipko**, Aleksandr Sergeevich 1941- *SovUnBD*
**Tsiranana**, Philibert 1910-1978 *FacFETw*
**Tsiros**, William 1944- *WhoAmP 91*
**Tsividis**, Yannis P 1946- *AmMWSc 92*
**Tso**, Joseph 1924- *WhoAmL 92*
**Tso**, Mark On-Man 1936- *AmMWSc 92*
**Ts'o**, Paul On Pong 1929- *AmMWSc 92*
**Tso**, Tien Chioh 1917- *AmMWSc 92*
**Ts'o**, Timothy On-To 1934- *AmMWSc 92*
**Tsohantaridis**, Timotheos 1954- *WhoRel 92*
**Tsohatzopoulos**, Apostolos Athanasios 1939- *IntWW 91*
**Tsokos**, Chris Peter 1937- *AmMWSc 92*
**Tsolas**, Orestes 1933- *AmMWSc 92*
**Tsolov**, Tano 1918- *IntWW 91*
**Ts'ong**, Fou *Who 92*
**Tsong**, Ignatius Siu Tung 1943- *AmMWSc 92*
**Tsong**, Tian Yow 1934- *AmMWSc 92*
**Tsong**, Tien Tzou 1934- *AmMWSc 92*
**Tsong**, Yun Yen 1937- *AmMWSc 92*
**Tsongas**, Paul E. 1941- *IntWW 91, WhoAmP 91*
**Tsonopoulos**, Constantine 1941- *AmMWSc 92*
**Tsoris**, Stephen A. 1957- *WhoAmL 92*
**Tsotetsi**, Michael Nkhahle 1938- *IntWW 91*
**Tsou**, Chen-Lu 1923- *AmMWSc 92*
**Tsou**, F K 1922- *AmMWSc 92*
**Tsou**, Tang 1918- *WhoMW 92*
**Tsoucalas**, Nicholas 1926- *WhoAmL 92*
**Tsoulfanidis**, Nicholas 1938- *AmMWSc 92*
**Tsovolas**, Dimitris 1942- *IntWW 91*
**Tsu**, T C 1915- *AmMWSc 92*
**Tsuang**, Ming Tso 1931- *AmMWSc 92*
**Tsubaki**, Andrew Takahisa 1931- *WhoEnt 92*
**Tsuboi**, Kenneth Kaz 1922- *AmMWSc 92*
**Tsuchiya**, Masahiro 1948- *WhoWest 92*
**Tsuchiya**, Mizuki 1929- *AmMWSc 92*
**Tsuchiya**, Takumi 1923- *AmMWSc 92, WhoWest 92*
**Tsuchiya**, Yoshihiko 1926- *IntWW 91*
**Tsuda**, Roy Toshio 1939- *AmMWSc 92*
**Tsuei**, Yeong Ging 1932- *AmMWSc 92*
**Tsuetaki**, Tracy Ken 1960- *WhoMW 92*
**Tsugawa**, Glenn H. 1955- *WhoWest 92*
**Tsui**, Benjamin Ming Wah 1948- *AmMWSc 92*
**Tsui**, Daniel Chee 1939- *AmMWSc 92*
**Tsui**, James Bao-Yen *AmMWSc 92*
**Tsui**, Kitty *DrAPF 91*
**Tsui**, Lap-Chee 1950- *Who 92*
**Tsui**, Sze-Kai Jack 1945- *WhoMW 92*
**Tsuji**, Frederick Ichiro 1923- *AmMWSc 92*
**Tsuji**, Gordon Yukio 1942- *AmMWSc 92*
**Tsuji**, Kiyoshi 1931- *AmMWSc 92, WhoMW 92*
**Tsujimura**, R. Brian 1950- *WhoAmL 92, WhoFI 92*
**Tsuk**, Andrew George 1932- *AmMWSc 92*
**Tsukada**, Matsuo 1930- *AmMWSc 92*
**Tsukada**, Osamu 1929- *WhoRel 92*
**Tsukahara**, Shumpei *IntWW 91*
**Tsukasa**, Kimura 1935- *WhoWest 92*
**Tsukasa**, Yoko 1934- *IntMPA 92*
**Tsukerman**, Vladislav 1939- *WhoEnt 92*
**Tsukiji**, Richard Isao 1946- *WhoWest 92*
**Tsukioka**, Mitsuko 1940- *WhoFI 92*
**Tsukui**, Nobuko 1938- *ConAu 133*
**Tsukuno**, Steven S. 1945- *WhoFI 92, WhoWest 92*
**Tsung**, Yean-Kai 1943- *AmMWSc 92*
**Tsur**, Yaacov 1906- *IntWW 91*
**Tsuruta**, Kuniaki 1936- *WhoFI 92*
**Tsurutani**, Bruce Tadashi 1941- *AmMWSc 92*
**Tsushima**, Yuji *IntWW 91*
**Tsutakawa**, Edward Masao 1921- *WhoWest 92*
**Tsutakawa**, Robert K 1930- *AmMWSc 92*
**Tsutakos**, Panayotis 1920- *IntAu&W 91*
**Tsutani**, Motohiro 1935- *WhoFI 92*
**Tsutras**, Frank Gus 1929- *WhoAmP 91*
**Tsutsui**, Ethel Ashworth 1927- *AmMWSc 92*
**Tsutsumi**, Yoshiaki *IntWW 91*
**Tsuyuki**, Shigeru *IntAu&W 91X*
**Tsvetaeva**, Marina 1892-1941 *FacFETw, LiExTwC*
**Tsvetaeva**, Marina Ivanovna 1892-1941 *SovUnBD*
**Tsvetkov**, Aleksey 1947- *IntWW 91*
**Tsvigun**, Semon Kuz'mich 1917-1982 *SovUnBD*
**Tsybin**, Vladimir Dmitrievich 1932- *SovUnBD*
**Tterlikkis**, Lambros 1934- *AmMWSc 92*
**Tu Guangzhi** 1920- *IntWW 91*
**Tu**, Anthony T 1930- *AmMWSc 92*
**Tu**, Charles Wuching 1951- *AmMWSc 92*
**Tu**, Chen Chuan 1918- *AmMWSc 92*
**Tu**, Chen-Pei David 1948- *AmMWSc 92*
**Tu**, Chin Ming 1932- *AmMWSc 92*
**Tu**, Jui-Chang 1936- *AmMWSc 92*
**Tu**, King-Ning 1937- *AmMWSc 92*
**Tu**, Shiao-chun 1943- *AmMWSc 92*
**Tu**, Shu-i 1943- *AmMWSc 92*
**Tu**, Yih-O 1920- *AmMWSc 92*
**Tuam**, Archbishop of 1933- *Who 92*
**Tuam Killala And Achonry**, Bishop of 1945- *Who 92*
**Tuan**, Debbie Fu-Tai 1930- *AmMWSc 92, WhoMW 92*
**Tuan**, Hang-Sheng 1935- *AmMWSc 92*
**Tuan**, Pham 1947- *FacFETw*
**Tuan**, Rocky Sung-Chi 1951- *AmMWSc 92*
**Tuan**, San Fu 1932- *AmMWSc 92*
**Tuan**, Tai-Fu 1929- *AmMWSc 92*
**Tuazon**, Jesus Ocampo 1940- *WhoWest 92*
**Tuba**, I Stephen 1932- *AmMWSc 92*
**Tubb**, Barry 1963 *IntMPA 92*
**Tubb**, E C 1919- *IntAu&W 91, TwCSFW 91, TwCWW 91, WrDr 92*
**Tubb**, Ernest 1914-1984 *NewAmDM*
**Tubb**, Richard Arnold 1931- *AmMWSc 92*
**Tubbs**, Edward Lane 1920- *WhoFI 92*
**Tubbs**, Eldred Frank 1924- *AmMWSc 92*
**Tubbs**, John Townsend 1918- *WhoFI 92*
**Tubbs**, Kristi Jean 1963- *WhoWest 92*
**Tubbs**, Oswald Sydney 1908- *Who 92*
**Tubbs**, Ralph 1912- *Who 92*
**Tubbs**, Raymond R 1946- *AmMWSc 92*
**Tubbs**, Robert Kenneth 1936- *AmMWSc 92*
**Tubbs**, Vincent Trenton 1915-1989 *WhoBlA 92N*
**Tubbs**, W A *WhoAmP 91*
**Tubbs**, William Reid, Jr. 1950- *WhoWest 92*
**Tubby**, I. M. *SmATA 65*
**Tubby**, Roger W. d1991 *NewYTBS 91 [port]*
**Tubiolo**, Richard Stephen 1956- *WhoAmL 92*
**Tubis**, Arnold 1932- *AmMWSc 92, WhoMW 92*
**Tubis**, Manuel 1909- *AmMWSc 92*
**Tubis**, Seymour 1919- *WhoWest 92*
**Tubman**, Harriet 1815?-1913 *EncAmaz 91, RComAH*
**Tubman**, Harriet 1820?-1913 *NotBlAW 92 [port]*
**Tubman**, Harriet 1821?-1913 *BenetAL 91, HanAmWH*
**Tubman**, Robert Colden 1939- *IntWW 91*
**Tubman**, William Charles 1932- *WhoAmL 92, WhoFI 92, WhoWest 92*
**Tubman**, William Willis, Jr 1947- *WhoAmP 91*
**Tubman**, Winston A. 1941- *IntWW 91*
**Tuccelli**, Cheri Frances 1960- *WhoWest 92*
**Tucceri**, Vincent Anthony 1953- *WhoAmL 92*
**Tucci**, Daniel Patrick 1943- *WhoFI 92*
**Tucci**, Edmond Raymond 1933- *AmMWSc 92*
**Tucci**, Gabriella 1929- *NewAmDM*
**Tucci**, James Vincent 1939- *AmMWSc 92*
**Tucci**, Niccolo *DrAPF 91*
**Tucci**, Niccolo 1908- *ConNov 91, WrDr 92*
**Tucci**, Robert, II 1954- *WhoFI 92*
**Tucciarone**, John Peter 1940- *AmMWSc 92*
**Tuccille**, Jerome 1937- *WrDr 92*
**Tuccio**, Sam Anthony 1939- *WhoFI 92, WhoWest 92*
**Tucevich**, Michael D. *WhoWest 92*
**Tuchfarber**, Charles Orrin 1946- *WhoMW 92*
**Tuchi**, Ben Joseph 1936- *WhoFI 92*
**Tuchinsky**, Philip Martin 1945- *AmMWSc 92*
**Tuchman**, Avraham 1935- *AmMWSc 92*
**Tuchman**, Barbara 1912- *IntAu&W 91*
**Tuchman**, Barbara 1912-1989 *FacFETw*
**Tuchman**, Barbara W. 1912-1989 *BenetAL 91*
**Tuchman**, Gaye 1943- *WrDr 92*
**Tuchman**, Kenneth I. 1950- *WhoFI 92*
**Tuchman**, Louis M. 1924- *WhoRel 92*
**Tuchman**, Maurice Simon 1936- *WhoRel 92*
**Tuchman**, Robert Lloyd 1943- *WhoAmL 92*
**Tuchman**, Steven Leslie 1946- *WhoAmL 92, WhoMW 92*
**Tuchmann**, Robert 1946- *WhoAmL 92*
**Tucholke**, Brian Edward 1946- *AmMWSc 92*
**Tucholsky**, Kurt 1890-1935 *EncTR 91 [port], LiExTwC*
**Tuck**, Anthony *Who 92*
**Tuck**, Bruce 1926- *Who 92*
**Tuck**, Clarence Edward Henry 1925- *Who 92*
**Tuck**, Denise Deringer 1943- *WhoAmP 91*
**Tuck**, Dennis George 1929- *AmMWSc 92*
**Tuck**, Donald Richard 1935- *WhoRel 92*
**Tuck**, George Edward 1942- *WhoMW 92*
**Tuck**, John Anthony 1940- *Who 92*
**Tuck**, John Philip 1911- *Who 92*
**Tuck**, Leo Dallas 1916- *AmMWSc 92*
**Tuck**, Lon 1938?-1987 *ConAu 133*
**Tuck**, Michael Ray 1941- *WhoWest 92*
**Tuck**, Murray 1920- *WhoFI 92*
**Tuck**, Ronald Humphrey 1921- *Who 92*
**Tuck**, Russell R., Jr. 1934- *WhoWest 92*
**Tuck**, William Powell 1934- *WhoRel 92*
**Tucker**, Alan 1947- *AmMWSc 92*
**Tucker**, Alan Curtiss 1943- *AmMWSc 92*
**Tucker**, Albert William 1905- *AmMWSc 92*
**Tucker**, Allen B 1942- *AmMWSc 92*
**Tucker**, Allen Brink 1936- *AmMWSc 92*
**Tucker**, Alvin Leroy 1938- *WhoFI 92*
**Tucker**, Anne Nichols 1942- *AmMWSc 92*
**Tucker**, Anne W. 1945- *WrDr 92*
**Tucker**, Anthony 1924- *WrDr 92*
**Tucker**, Anthony 1957- *WhoBlA 92*
**Tucker**, Arthur Vaughn, Jr. 1949- *WhoMW 92*
**Tucker**, Benjamin Ricketson 1854-1939 *AmPeW*
**Tucker**, Berry Kenneth 1946- *WhoMW 92*
**Tucker**, Beverly Sowers 1936- *WhoMW 92*
**Tucker**, Billy Bob 1928- *AmMWSc 92*
**Tucker**, Billy J. 1934- *WhoBlA 92*
**Tucker**, Bob 1941- *WhoEnt 92*
**Tucker**, Bobby Glenn 1954- *WhoRel 92*
**Tucker**, Bowen Hayward 1938- *WhoAmL 92, WhoMW 92*
**Tucker**, Brian George 1922- *Who 92*
**Tucker**, C. DeLores 1927- *NotBlAW 92, WhoBlA 92*
**Tucker**, Carll 1951- *ConAu 133*
**Tucker**, Carolyn Sue 1939- *WhoAmP 91*
**Tucker**, Carroll M 1927- *WhoIns 92*
**Tucker**, Charles Cyril 1942 *WhoWest 92*
**Tucker**, Charles Eugene 1933- *AmMWSc 92*
**Tucker**, Charles L 1953- *AmMWSc 92*
**Tucker**, Charles Leroy, Jr 1921- *AmMWSc 92*
**Tucker**, Charles Thomas 1936- *AmMWSc 92*
**Tucker**, Christopher John 1961- *WhoMW 92*
**Tucker**, Clarence T. 1940- *WhoBlA 92*
**Tucker**, Clive Fenemore 1944- *Who 92*
**Tucker**, Curtis R, Jr 1954- *WhoAmP 91*
**Tucker**, Cynthia Delores 1927- *WhoAmP 91*
**Tucker**, Cynthia Grant 1941- *ConAu 135*
**Tucker**, Cyril James 1911- *Who 92*
**Tucker**, Darryl Courtney 1960- *WhoMW 92*
**Tucker**, David Allan 1935- *WhoWest 92*
**Tucker**, David Patrick Hislop 1934- *AmMWSc 92*
**Tucker**, Dennis Carl 1945- *WhoMW 92*
**Tucker**, Don Harrell 1930- *AmMWSc 92*
**Tucker**, Donald 1938- *WhoAmP 91, WhoBlA 92*
**Tucker**, Donald Frederick 1946- *WhoAmP 91*
**Tucker**, Dorothy M. 1942- *WhoBlA 92*
**Tucker**, Edmond Glenn 1943- *WhoAmL 92*
**Tucker**, Edmund Belford 1922- *AmMWSc 92*
**Tucker**, Edward William 1908- *Who 92*
**Tucker**, Elizabeth Mary 1936- *Who 92*
**Tucker**, Eric M. 1950- *WhoBlA 92*
**Tucker**, Eric Merle 1954- *WhoFI 92*
**Tucker**, Frank Allan, Jr. 1947- *WhoMW 92*
**Tucker**, Gary Edward 1941- *AmMWSc 92*
**Tucker**, Gary Jay 1934- *AmMWSc 92*
**Tucker**, Gene Milton 1935- *WhoRel 92*
**Tucker**, George 1775-1861 *BenetAL 91, ScFEYrs*
**Tucker**, Geraldine Coleman 1952- *WhoBlA 92*
**Tucker**, Geraldine Jenkins 1948- *WhoBlA 92*
**Tucker**, Hal Beall 1928- *WhoFI 92*
**Tucker**, Harvey Michael 1938- *AmMWSc 92*
**Tucker**, Helen 1926- *IntAu&W 91, WrDr 92*
**Tucker**, Henry John Martin 1930- *Who 92*
**Tucker**, Henry St. George 1874-1959 *RelLAm 91*
**Tucker**, Herbert Allen 1936- *AmMWSc 92*
**Tucker**, Herbert E., Jr. 1915- *WhoBlA 92*
**Tucker**, Herbert Harold 1925- *Who 92*
**Tucker**, Howard Gregory 1922- *AmMWSc 92*
**Tucker**, Irwin William 1914- *AmMWSc 92*
**Tucker**, Jack William Andrew 1944- *WhoEnt 92*
**Tucker**, James 1929- *WrDr 92*
**Tucker**, James Elliott 1914- *WhoAmL 92*
**Tucker**, James F. 1924- *WhoBlA 92*
**Tucker**, James Howard 1950- *WhoFI 92*
**Tucker**, Janet Pike 1944- *WhoWest 92*
**Tucker**, Jim Guy, Jr 1943- *WhoAmP 91*

**Tucker**, JoAnne Klineman 1943- *WhoEnt 92*
**Tucker**, Joe Waverlia, Jr. 1942- *WhoWest 92*
**Tucker**, Joel Lawrence 1932- *WhoWest 92*
**Tucker**, John B 1937- *WhoAmP 91*
**Tucker**, John Edward 1955- *WhoFI 92*
**Tucker**, John Maurice 1916- *AmMWSc 92*
**Tucker**, John Richard 1948- *AmMWSc 92*
**Tucker**, John W, Jr 1950- *WhoAmP 91*
**Tucker**, Karen 1952- *WhoBlA 92*
**Tucker**, Kenneth Wilburn 1924- *AmMWSc 92*
**Tucker**, Lael *ConTFT 9*
**Tucker**, Lemuel d1991 *NewYTBS 91*
**Tucker**, Lemuel 1938-1991 *WhoBlA 92N*
**Tucker**, Leota Marie 1944- *WhoBlA 92*
**Tucker**, Linda Wise 1955- *WhoWest 92*
**Tucker**, Link *IntAu&W 91X, TwCWW 91*
**Tucker**, Lynn Richard 1962- *WhoMW 92*
**Tucker**, M. Belinda 1949- *WhoBlA 92*
**Tucker**, Marcus O., Jr. 1934- *WhoBlA 92*
**Tucker**, Marcus Othello 1934- *WhoAmL 92, WhoWest 92*
**Tucker**, Mark David 1960- *WhoAmL 92*
**Tucker**, Martin *DrAPF 91, Who 92*
**Tucker**, Martin 1928- *IntAu&W 91, WrDr 92*
**Tucker**, Mary 1936- *WhoAmP 91*
**Tucker**, Melville 1916- *IntMPA 92, WhoEnt 92, WhoWest 92*
**Tucker**, Memye Curtis *DrAPF 91*
**Tucker**, Michael *WhoEnt 92*
**Tucker**, Michael 1944- *IntMPA 92*
**Tucker**, Michael Kevin 1957- *WhoBlA 92*
**Tucker**, Michael Thomas 1946- *WhoFI 92*
**Tucker**, Nathaniel Beverley 1784-1851 *BenetAL 91, BibAL 8*
**Tucker**, Norma Jean 1932- *WhoBlA 92*
**Tucker**, O. Ruth *WhoBlA 92*
**Tucker**, Pamela Allyson 1960- *WhoFI 92*
**Tucker**, Paul, Jr. 1943- *WhoBlA 92*
**Tucker**, Paul Arthur 1941- *AmMWSc 92*
**Tucker**, Paul Thomas 1948- *WhoMW 92*
**Tucker**, Peter Louis 1927- *Who 92*
**Tucker**, Preston Thomas 1903-1956 *FacFETw*
**Tucker**, Ray Edwin 1929- *AmMWSc 92*
**Tucker**, Richard 1913-1975 *FacFETw, NewAmDM*
**Tucker**, Richard 1930- *Who 92*
**Tucker**, Richard Frank 1926- *AmMWSc 92, WhoFI 92*
**Tucker**, Richard Howard 1960- *WhoMW 92*
**Tucker**, Richard Lee 1935- *AmMWSc 92*
**Tucker**, Richard Lee 1940- *WhoFI 92*
**Tucker**, Robert B *WhoAmP 91*
**Tucker**, Robert C. 1918- *WrDr 92*
**Tucker**, Robert C, Jr *AmMWSc 92*
**Tucker**, Robert Gene 1918- *AmMWSc 92*
**Tucker**, Robert H., Jr. 1941- *WhoBlA 92*
**Tucker**, Robert Jay 1950- *WhoMW 92*
**Tucker**, Robert L. 1929- *WhoBlA 92*
**Tucker**, Robert S 1921- *WhoAmP 91*
**Tucker**, Robert St John P. *Who 92*
**Tucker**, Robert W. 1924- *ConAu 134*
**Tucker**, Robert Wilson *AmMWSc 92*
**Tucker**, Roy Wilbur 1927- *AmMWSc 92*
**Tucker**, Ruth Emma 1901- *AmMWSc 92*
**Tucker**, Samuel Joseph 1930- *WhoBlA 92*
**Tucker**, Samuel Wilbert 1913-1990 *WhoBlA 92N*
**Tucker**, Sheilah L. Wheeler 1951- *WhoBlA 92*
**Tucker**, Sheridan Gregory 1950- *WhoMW 92*
**Tucker**, Shirleen 1941- *WhoAmP 91*
**Tucker**, Shirley Cotter 1927- *AmMWSc 92*
**Tucker**, St. George 1752-1827 *BenetAL 91*
**Tucker**, Stefan Franklin 1938- *WhoAmL 92*
**Tucker**, Steven Barry 1946- *WhoWest 92*
**Tucker**, Susan C *WhoAmP 91*
**Tucker**, Tanya Denise 1958- *WhoEnt 92*
**Tucker**, Thomas Alan 1948- *WhoMW 92*
**Tucker**, Thomas Curtis 1926- *AmMWSc 92*
**Tucker**, Thomas Randall 1931- *WhoFI 92, WhoMW 92*
**Tucker**, Thomas William 1945- *AmMWSc 92*
**Tucker**, Tim 1944- *WhoAmP 91*
**Tucker**, Tracy L. 1959- *WhoRel 92*
**Tucker**, Trent 1959- *WhoBlA 92*
**Tucker**, Tui St. George 1924- *NewAmDM*
**Tucker**, Vance Alan 1936- *AmMWSc 92*
**Tucker**, W Henry 1920- *AmMWSc 92*
**Tucker**, Wallace Hampton 1939- *AmMWSc 92*
**Tucker**, Wally Sydney 1941- *WhoEnt 92*
**Tucker**, Walter Eugene, Jr 1931- *AmMWSc 92*
**Tucker**, Walter Rayford 1924- *WhoAmP 91*
**Tucker**, Watson Billopp 1940- *WhoAmL 92*
**Tucker**, Wilbur Carey 1943- *WhoBlA 92*
**Tucker**, William 1935- *TwCPaSc*
**Tucker**, William E. 1937- *WhoFI 92*
**Tucker**, William Edward 1932- *WrDr 92*
**Tucker**, William Edward 1935- *WhoAmP 91*
**Tucker**, William Eldon d1991 *Who 92N*
**Tucker**, William Philip 1932- *WhoAmL 92*
**Tucker**, William Preston 1932- *AmMWSc 92*
**Tucker**, Willie George 1934- *AmMWSc 92*
**Tucker**, Wilson 1914- *TwCSFW 91, WrDr 92*
**Tucker**, Woodson Coleman, Jr 1908- *AmMWSc 92*
**Tucker-Allen**, Sallie 1936- *WhoBlA 92, WhoMW 92*
**Tuckerman**, Arthur *ScFEYrs*
**Tuckerman**, David R. 1946- *IntMPA 92*
**Tuckerman**, Edward 1817-1886 *BiInAmS*
**Tuckerman**, Frederick Goddard 1821-1873 *BenetAL 91*
**Tuckerman**, Henry Theodore 1813-1871 *BenetAL 91, BibAL 8*
**Tuckerman**, Joseph 1778-1840 *DcAmImH*
**Tuckerman**, Murray Moses 1928- *AmMWSc 92*
**Tuckett**, LeRoy E. 1932- *WhoBlA 92*
**Tuckett**, Robert P 1943- *AmMWSc 92*
**Tuckey**, Andrew Marmaduke Lane 1943- *Who 92*
**Tuckey**, Simon Lane 1941- *Who 92*
**Tuckey**, Stewart Lawrence 1905- *AmMWSc 92*
**Tuckman**, Bruce W 1938- *IntAu&W 91*
**Tuckman**, Bruce Wayne 1938- *WrDr 92*
**Tuckman**, David Joshua 1939- *WhoWest 92*
**Tuckman**, Frederick Augustus 1922- *Who 92*
**Tuckman**, Howard Paul 1941- *WhoFI 92*
**Tuckwell**, Barry 1931- *NewAmDM*
**Tuckwell**, Barry Emmanuel 1931- *IntWW 91, Who 92*
**Tuculescu**, Constantin 1947- *WhoWest 92*
**Tudbury**, Chester A 1913- *AmMWSc 92*
**Tuddenham**, W Marvin 1924- *AmMWSc 92*
**Tudela**, Juan B *WhoAmP 91*
**Tudesco**, James Patrick 1946- *WhoRel 92*
**Tudhope**, David Hamilton 1921- *Who 92*
**Tudhope**, James Mackenzie 1927- *Who 92*
**Tudman**, Cathi Graves 1953- *WhoWest 92*
**Tudor**, Andrew Frank 1942- *IntAu&W 91, WrDr 92*
**Tudor**, Antony 1909-1987 *FacFETw*
**Tudor**, Constantin Dino 1939- *WhoWest 92*
**Tudor**, David 1926- *NewAmDM*
**Tudor**, David Cyrus 1918- *AmMWSc 92*
**Tudor**, James Cameron 1919- *IntWW 91, Who 92*
**Tudor**, James R 1922- *AmMWSc 92*
**Tudor**, John 1930- *Who 92*
**Tudor**, Mary Louise Drummond 1937- *WhoWest 92*
**Tudor**, Stephen H. *DrAPF 91*
**Tudor**, Tasha 1915- *WrDr 92*
**Tudor**, William 1779-1830 *BenetAL 91*
**Tudor Evans**, Haydn 1920- *Who 92*
**Tudoran**, Dorin 1945- *LiExTwC*
**Tudway Quilter**, David C. *Who 92*
**Tuel**, William Gole, Jr 1941- *AmMWSc 92*
**Tuell**, David R., Jr. 1936- *WhoAmL 92*
**Tuell**, Jack Marvin 1923- *WhoRel 92, WhoWest 92*
**Tueller**, Alden B. 1939- *WhoWest 92*
**Tueller**, Paul T 1934- *AmMWSc 92*
**Tuemmler**, William Bruce 1927- *AmMWSc 92*
**Tueni**, Ghassan 1926- *IntWW 91*
**Tuerff**, James Rodrick 1941- *WhoFI 92, WhoIns 92*
**Tuerk**, Fred James 1922- *WhoAmP 91*
**Tuerpe**, Dieter Rolf 1940- *AmMWSc 92*
**Tuesday**, Charles Sheffield 1927- *AmMWSc 92, WhoMW 92*
**Tufarelli**, Nicola 1923- *IntWW 91*
**Tufariello**, Joseph James 1935- *AmMWSc 92*
**Tufaro**, Richard Chase 1944- *WhoAmL 92*
**Tuff**, Donald Wray 1935- *AmMWSc 92*
**Tuffey**, Thomas J *AmMWSc 92*
**Tuffin**, Alan David 1933- *Who 92*
**Tuffin**, Paul Jonathan 1927- *WhoBlA 92*
**Tuffly**, Bartholomew Louis 1928- *AmMWSc 92*
**Tuffy**, John Charles 1938- *WhoWest 92*
**Tufon**, Chris 1959- *WhoBlA 92*
**Tufte**, Marilyn Jean 1939- *AmMWSc 92*
**Tufte**, Obert Norman 1932- *AmMWSc 92*
**Tufte**, Virginia James *IntAu&W 91*
**Tufton** *Who 92*
**Tufts**, Donald Winston 1933- *AmMWSc 92*
**Tufts**, Frank Leo 1871-1909 *BiInAmS*
**Tufts**, J Arthur 1921- *WhoAmP 91*
**Tufts**, Robert B. 1940- *WhoWest 92*
**Tufty**, Barbara 1923- *WrDr 92*
**Tufty**, Barbara Jean 1923- *IntAu&W 91*
**Tufty**, Christopher Guilford 1952- *WhoEnt 92*
**Tugcu**, Nejat 1945- *WhoFI 92*
**Tugendhat**, Christopher 1937- *Who 92, WrDr 92*
**Tugendhat**, Christopher Samuel 1937- *IntWW 91*
**Tugendhat**, Julia 1941- *IntAu&W 91, WrDr 92*
**Tugendhat**, Michael George 1944- *Who 92*
**Tuggle**, Clyde Cebron 1962- *WhoFI 92*
**Tuggle**, Dorothy V. 1935- *WhoBlA 92*
**Tuggle**, Francis Douglas 1943- *WhoFI 92*
**Tuggle**, Jessie Lloyd 1965- *WhoBlA 92*
**Tuggle**, Mike *DrAPF 91*
**Tuggle**, Reginald 1947- *WhoBlA 92*
**Tuggle**, Richard 1948- *IntMPA 92*
**Tuggle**, Richard Allan 1948- *WhoEnt 92*
**Tuggy**, Arthur Leonard 1929- *WhoRel 92*
**Tugman**, Pat 1941- *WhoAmP 91*
**Tugwell**, Maurice A. J. 1925- *WrDr 92*
**Tugwell**, Peter 1944- *AmMWSc 92*
**Tugwell**, Rexford Guy 1891-1979 *AmPolLe [port]*
**Tugwell**, Rexford Guy 1895-1979 *FacFETw*
**Tuholski**, Elizabeth Murray 1956- *WhoWest 92*
**Tuia**, Tuana'itau F *WhoAmP 91*
**Tuika**, Tuika *WhoAmP 91*
**Tuiolosega**, Tagaloa M 1921- *WhoAmP 91*
**Tu'ipelahake**, Fatafehi 1922- *IntWW 91*
**Tu'ipelehake**, Fatafehi 1922- *Who 92*
**Tuipine**, Soliai F 1938- *WhoAmP 91*
**Tuita**, Siosaia Aleamotu'a Laufilitonga 1920- *IntWW 91*
**Tuite**, Christopher 1949- *Who 92*
**Tuite**, John F 1927- *AmMWSc 92*
**Tuite**, Joseph Patrick 1914- *WhoRel 92*
**Tuite**, Patrick Alan 1937- *WhoAmL 92, WhoMW 92*
**Tuite**, Robert Joseph 1934- *AmMWSc 92*
**Tuites**, Donald Edgar 1925- *AmMWSc 92*
**Tuites**, Richard Clarence 1933- *AmMWSc 92*
**Tuitt**, Jane Eliza 1908- *WhoBlA 92*
**Tuivaga**, Timoci 1931- *IntWW 91, Who 92*
**Tuka**, Vojtech 1880-1946 *BiDExR*
**Tuke**, Anthony 1920- *Who 92*
**Tuke**, Anthony Favill 1920- *IntWW 91*
**Tuke**, Henry Scott 1858-1929 *TwCPaSc*
**Tuke**, Seymour Charles 1903- *Who 92*
**Tukeman**, H *ScFEYrs*
**Tukey**, Harold Bradford, Jr 1934- *AmMWSc 92, WhoWest 92*
**Tukey**, John W. 1915- *IntWW 91*
**Tukey**, John Wilder 1915- *AmMWSc 92*
**Tukey**, Loren Davenport 1921- *AmMWSc 92*
**Tukhachevsky**, Michael Nikolayevich 1893-1937 *FacFETw*
**Tukhachevsky**, Mikhail Nikolaevich 1893-1937 *SovUnBD*
**Tulafono**, Togiola T *WhoAmP 91*
**Tulagin**, Vsevolod 1914- *AmMWSc 92*
**Tulchin**, David Bruce 1947- *WhoAmL 92*
**Tulchin**, Joseph S. 1939- *WrDr 92*
**Tulean**, Ingrid *ConTFT 9*
**Tulecke**, Walt 1924- *AmMWSc 92*
**Tuleen**, David L 1936- *AmMWSc 92*
**Tulenko**, James Stanley 1936- *AmMWSc 92*
**Tulenko**, Thomas Norman 1942- *AmMWSc 92*
**Tuler**, Floyd Robert 1939- *AmMWSc 92*
**Tuley**, Thomas Wayne 1940- *WhoMW 92*
**Tuleya**, Robert E 1947- *AmMWSc 92*
**Tuli**, Jagdish Kumar 1941- *AmMWSc 92*
**Tulin**, Leonard George 1920- *AmMWSc 92*
**Tulin**, Marshall P 1926- *AmMWSc 92*
**Tulinsky**, Alexander 1928- *AmMWSc 92*
**Tulip**, Thomas Hunt 1952- *AmMWSc 92*
**Tulisano**, Richard D 1939- *WhoAmP 91*
**Tulk**, Alexander Stuart 1918- *AmMWSc 92*
**Tulkoff**, Myer Simon 1927- *WhoAmL 92*
**Tull**, C. Thomas 1946- *WhoFI 92*
**Tull**, Jack Phillip 1930- *AmMWSc 92*
**Tull**, James Franklin 1947- *AmMWSc 92*
**Tull**, Jethro 1674-1741 *BlkwCEP*
**Tull**, John Hugh, Jr. 1949- *WhoAmL 92*
**Tull**, Louis Randall 1938- *IntWW 91*
**Tull**, Robert Gordon 1929- *AmMWSc 92*
**Tull**, Theresa Ann 1936- *WhoAmP 91*
**Tull**, William J *AmMWSc 92*
**Tullen**, Colton Skipp 1940- *WhoEnt 92*
**Tuller**, Annita 1910- *AmMWSc 92*
**Tuller**, Coburn Munro 1947- *WhoEnt 92*
**Tuller**, Edwin Hurlbut, Jr. 1942- *WhoMW 92*
**Tuller**, Harry Louis 1945- *AmMWSc 92*
**Tuller**, John 1961- *WhoBlA 92*
**Tullett**, James Stuart 1912- *WrDr 92*
**Tulley**, John 1639?-1701 *BenetAL 91*
**Tulli**, Frank, Jr 1944- *WhoAmP 91*
**Tullia** *EncAmaz 91*
**Tullio**, Victor 1927- *AmMWSc 92*
**Tullis**, Chaille Handy 1913- *WhoMW 92*
**Tullis**, Darlene Carroll 1966- *WhoMW 92*
**Tullis**, Edward Lewis 1917- *WhoRel 92*
**Tullis**, Gene Edward 1950- *WhoWest 92*
**Tullis**, J Paul 1938- *AmMWSc 92*
**Tullis**, James Earl *AmMWSc 92*
**Tullis**, James Lyman 1914- *AmMWSc 92*
**Tullis**, Julia Ann 1943- *AmMWSc 92*
**Tullis**, Ramsey 1916- *Who 92*
**Tullis**, Richard Barclay 1913- *WhoFI 92*
**Tullis**, Richard Eugene 1936- *AmMWSc 92*
**Tullis**, Robert 1951- *WhoAmP 91*
**Tullis**, Terry Edson 1942- *AmMWSc 92*
**Tulloch**, Alexander Patrick 1927- *AmMWSc 92*
**Tulloch**, Edwin Fred 1937- *WhoRel 92*
**Tulloch**, George Sherlock 1906- *AmMWSc 92*
**Tullock**, Gordon 1922- *WhoWest 92*
**Tullock**, Robert Johns 1940- *AmMWSc 92*
**Tullos**, Edna H *WhoAmP 91*
**Tullos**, Kathryn Jane 1959- *WhoAmL 92*
**Tulloss**, Rod *DrAPF 91*
**Tully**, Alice 1902- *NewAmDM*
**Tully**, Daniel Patrick 1932- *WhoFI 92*
**Tully**, Edward Joseph, Jr 1930- *AmMWSc 92*
**Tully**, Frank Paul 1946- *AmMWSc 92*
**Tully**, Jim 1891-1947 *BenetAL 91*
**Tully**, John Charles 1942- *AmMWSc 92*
**Tully**, Jon Robert Calahan 1947- *WhoWest 92*
**Tully**, Joseph George 1925- *AmMWSc 92*
**Tully**, Mark 1935- *Who 92*
**Tully**, Michael J, Jr 1933- *WhoAmP 91*
**Tully**, Michael James 1961- *WhoEnt 92*
**Tully**, Neal Coleman 1948- *WhoAmL 92*
**Tully**, Paul *TwCWW 91, WrDr 92*
**Tully**, Philip C 1923- *AmMWSc 92*
**Tully**, Richard Brent 1943- *AmMWSc 92*
**Tully**, Richard Walton 1877-1945 *BenetAL 91*
**Tully**, Robert Gerard 1955- *WhoAmL 92*
**Tully**, Robert T 1933- *WhoAmP 91*
**Tully**, Stephen James 1956- *WhoAmL 92*
**Tully**, Thomas Alois 1940- *WhoMW 92*
**Tully**, Walton Jeanes 1931- *WhoRel 92*
**Tully**, William 1785-1859 *BiInAmS*
**Tulowitzky**, Max William 1935- *WhoRel 92*
**Tulsky**, Emanuel Goodel 1923- *AmMWSc 92*
**Tulunay-Keesey**, Ulker 1932- *AmMWSc 92*
**Tuma**, Dean J 1941- *AmMWSc 92*
**Tuma**, Gerald 1914- *AmMWSc 92*
**Tuma**, Jan J 1919- *AmMWSc 92*
**Tuma**, Samir Jeffrey 1962- *WhoAmL 92*
**Tuman**, Vladimir Shlimon 1923- *AmMWSc 92*
**Tumanishvili**, Mikhail Ivanovich 1921- *IntWW 91*
**Tumas**, Marc Lionel 1943- *WhoFI 92*
**Tumbleson**, M E 1937- *AmMWSc 92*
**Tumblin**, Randall S. 1957- *WhoRel 92*
**Tumblin**, Thomas Frederick 1958- *WhoRel 92*
**Tumeh**, Amer Mohammad 1962- *WhoWest 92*
**Tumelson**, Ronald Adrian 1939- *WhoWest 92*
**Tumelty**, Paul Francis 1941- *AmMWSc 92*
**Tumen**, Henry Joseph 1902- *AmMWSc 92*
**Tumi**, Christian Wiyghan 1930- *IntWW 91, WhoRel 92*
**Tumielewicz**, Anthony 1914- *WhoAmP 91*
**Tumim**, Stephen 1930- *Who 92*
**Tumin**, Melvin M. 1919- *WrDr 92*
**Tuminello**, William Joseph 1920- *WhoEnt 92*
**Tummala**, Rao Ramamohana 1942- *AmMWSc 92*
**Tummett**, David John 1957- *WhoMW 92*
**Tumminello**, Stephen Charles 1936- *WhoFI 92*
**Tumola**, Thomas Joseph 1941- *WhoAmL 92*
**Tumosa**, Nina Jean 1951- *AmMWSc 92*
**Tumperi**, John Robert 1930- *WhoFI 92*
**Tumpson**, Joan Berna *WhoAmL 92*
**Tumulty**, Gary Allen 1941- *WhoAmP 91*
**Tumulty**, Philip A 1912- *AmMWSc 92*
**Tuna**, Naip 1921- *AmMWSc 92*
**Tunberg**, Karl 1909- *IntMPA 92*
**Tunberg**, Karl Alexander 1960- *WhoWest 92*
**Tunby**, Rolph 1933- *WhoAmP 91*
**Tunc**, Andre Robert 1917- *Who 92*
**Tunc**, Deger Cetin 1936- *AmMWSc 92*
**Tuncap**, Priscilla T 1935- *WhoAmP 91*
**Tuncer**, Cengiz 1942- *IntWW 91*
**Tune**, Bruce Malcolm 1939- *AmMWSc 92*
**Tune**, Michael Thomas 1953- *WhoRel 92*
**Tune**, Tommy 1939- *IntMPA 92, IntWW 91, WhoEnt 92*
**Tunell**, Richard Gavin 1956- *WhoEnt 92*
**Tung Shu-Fang** 1932- *IntWW 91*
**Tung**, C Y 1911-1982 *FacFETw*
**Tung**, Che-Se 1948- *AmMWSc 92*

**Tung**, Chi Chao 1932- *AmMWSc 92*
**Tung**, David Christopher 1961- *WhoWest 92*
**Tung**, Fred Fu 1934- *AmMWSc 92*
**Tung**, John Shih-Hsiung 1928- *AmMWSc 92*
**Tung**, Ka-Kit 1948- *AmMWSc 92*
**Tung**, Ko-Yung 1947- *WhoAmL 92*
**Tung**, Leslie Thomas 1951- *WhoMW 92*
**Tung**, Lu Ho 1923- *AmMWSc 92*
**Tung**, Marvin Arthur 1937- *AmMWSc 92*
**Tung**, Ming Sung 1942- *AmMWSc 92*
**Tung**, Rosalie Lam 1948- *WhoFI 92*
**Tung**, Samuel Shui-Liang 1946- *WhoFI 92*
**Tung**, Simon Chin-Yu 1951- *WhoMW 92*
**Tung**, Theodore Hschum 1934- *WhoFI 92*
**Tung**, Wu-Ki 1939- *AmMWSc 92*
**Tung**, Yeou-Koung 1954- *AmMWSc 92*
**Tungate**, James Lester 1947- *WhoAmL 92*
**Tungpalan**, Eloise Yamashita 1945- *WhoAmP 91*
**Tunheim**, James Ronald 1941- *WhoAmP 91*
**Tunheim**, Jerald Arden 1940- *AmMWSc 92*
**Tunick**, Bonnie Ilyse 1959- *WhoAmL 92*
**Tunick**, Budd Lewis 1949- *WhoEnt 92*
**Tunicka**, Maria Irmina 1936- *WhoEnt 92*
**Tunik**, Bernard D 1921- *AmMWSc 92*
**Tunis**, C J 1932- *AmMWSc 92*
**Tunis**, John R. 1889-1975 *BenetAL 91*
**Tunis**, Marvin 1925- *AmMWSc 92*
**Tunison**, Elizabeth Lamb 1922- *WhoWest 92*
**Tunkel**, Steven Joseph 1929- *AmMWSc 92*
**Tunkin**, Grigoriy Ivanovich 1906- *SovUnBD*
**Tunley**, David Evatt 1930- *IntWW 91*
**Tunley**, Naomi Louise 1936- *WhoBlA 92*
**Tunnard**, John 1900-1971 *TwCPaSc*
**Tunnecliffe**, Daniel Lee 1953- *WhoMW 92*
**Tunnell**, Carolyn Joyce 1947- *WhoRel 92*
**Tunnell**, Hugh James Oliver Redvers 1935- *Who 92*
**Tunnell**, Mark LaMonte 1950- *WhoAmL 92*
**Tunnell**, William C 1915- *AmMWSc 92*
**Tunner**, William H 1906-1983 *FacFETw*
**Tunney**, Gene 1898-1978 *FacFETw*
**Tunney**, John V. 1934- *IntWW 91*
**Tunney**, John Varick 1934- *WhoAmP 91*
**Tunney**, Michael Martin 1948- *WhoWest 92*
**Tunnicliff**, David George 1931- *AmMWSc 92*
**Tunnicliff**, Godfrey 1941- *AmMWSc 92*
**Tunnicliffe**, Denis 1943- *Who 92*
**Tunnicliffe**, Philip Robert 1922- *AmMWSc 92*
**Tunnicliffe**, Verena Julia 1953- *AmMWSc 92*
**Tunon**, Ivan A. 1946- *WhoHisp 92*
**Tunstall**, C. Jeremy 1934- *WrDr 92*
**Tunstall**, Charles Arthur 1912- *WhoBlA 92*
**Tunstall**, Franklin George 1943- *WhoRel 92*
**Tunstall**, Garnett Taylor, Jr. 1950- *WhoAmL 92*
**Tunstall**, June Rebecca 1947- *WhoBlA 92*
**Tunstall**, Lucille Hawkins *WhoBlA 92*
**Tunstall**, Lucille Hawkins 1922- *AmMWSc 92*
**Tunstall-Grant**, Ruth Neal 1945- *WhoBlA 92*
**Tunturi**, Archie Robert 1917- *AmMWSc 92*
**Tuohey**, Mark Henry, III 1946- *WhoAmL 92*
**Tuohy**, Frank 1925- *ConNov 91, WrDr 92*
**Tuohy**, John Francis 1925- *IntAu&W 91, Who 92*
**Tuohy**, Thomas 1917- *Who 92*
**Tuomey**, Michael 1805-1857 *BiInAmS*
**Tuomi**, Donald 1920- *AmMWSc 92*
**Tuominen**, Francis William 1943- *AmMWSc 92*
**Tuomy**, Justin M 1914- *AmMWSc 92*
**Tuovinen**, Olli Heikki 1944- *AmMWSc 92, WhoMW 92*
**Tupac Amaru** 1545-1574 *HisDSpE*
**Tupac Amaru II** 1742-1781 *HisDSpE*
**Tupin**, Joe Paul 1934- *AmMWSc 92, WhoWest 92*
**Tupler**, Harriet 1935- *WhoEnt 92*
**Tupman**, William Ivan 1921- *Who 92*
**Tupolev**, Aleksey Andreyevich 1925- *IntWW 91*
**Tupolev**, Andrei Nikolayevich 1888-1972 *FacFETw*
**Tupolev**, Andrey Nikolaevich 1888-1972 *SovUnBD*
**Tuppan**, Glenda Rana *WhoAmP 91*
**Tupper**, Charles Hibbert 1930- *Who 92*
**Tupper**, Charles John 1920- *AmMWSc 92*
**Tupper**, Earl 1908- *DcTwDes*
**Tupper**, Earl S 1907-1983 *FacFETw*
**Tupper**, Helen M *WhoAmP 91*
**Tupper**, Jean Lorraine *DrAPF 91*
**Tupper**, Martin 1810-1889 *RfGEnL 91*
**Tupper**, Meredith Jane 1964- *WhoEnt 92*
**Tupper**, Rick 1958- *WhoEnt 92*
**Tupper**, Steve R 1944- *WhoAmP 91*
**Tupper**, W R Carl 1915- *AmMWSc 92*
**Tupua**, Le'iato *WhoAmP 91*
**Tura**, David Duncan 1945- *WhoFI 92*
**Tura**, Eshetu 1950- *BlkOlyM*
**Turanski**, Anita Marlene 1951- *WhoWest 92*
**Turati**, Augusto 1888-1955 *BiDExR*
**Turay**, Abdul Rahman 1938- *IntWW 91*
**Turba**, Wilfrid Joseph 1928- *WhoAmP 91*
**Turbak**, Albin Frank 1929- *AmMWSc 92*
**Turbay Ayala**, Julio Cesar 1916- *IntWW 91*
**Turberg**, Phillip Albert 1928- *WhoFI 92*
**Turbervile**, George 1543?-1597? *RfGEnL 91*
**Turberville**, Geoffrey 1899- *Who 92*
**Turbeville**, Caroll Dale 1957- *WhoRel 92*
**Turbeville**, Daniel Eugene, III 1945- *WhoWest 92*
**Turbott**, Ian 1922- *Who 92*
**Turbyfill**, Charles Lewis 1933- *AmMWSc 92*
**Turcan**, Henry Watson 1941- *Who 92*
**Turchan**, Otto Charles 1925- *AmMWSc 92, WhoWest 92*
**Turchaninova**, Yevdokiya Dmitrievna 1870-1963 *SovUnBD*
**Turchen**, Lesta Van Der Wert 1944- *WhoMW 92*
**Turchetta**, Linda Marlene 1950- *WhoEnt 92*
**Turchi**, Joseph J 1933- *AmMWSc 92*
**Turchi**, Patrice Ernest Antoine 1952- *WhoWest 92*
**Turchi**, Peter John 1946- *AmMWSc 92, WhoMW 92*
**Turchin**, Robert Louis 1922- *WhoFI 92*
**Turchinetz**, William Ernest 1928- *AmMWSc 92*
**Turchuk**, Julia Grace 1945- *WhoEnt 92*
**Turchyn**, William, Jr. 1945- *WhoFI 92*
**Turck**, Marvin 1934- *AmMWSc 92*
**Turco**, Charles Paul 1934- *AmMWSc 92*
**Turco**, Jenifer 1950- *AmMWSc 92*
**Turco**, Lewis *DrAPF 91*
**Turco**, Lewis 1934- *ConPo 91, WrDr 92*
**Turco**, Richard 1943- *ConAu 135*
**Turco**, Richard Peter 1943- *AmMWSc 92*
**Turco**, Salvatore J 1932- *AmMWSc 92*
**Turcot**, Marguerite Hogan 1934- *WhoFI 92*
**Turcotte**, Donald Lawson 1932- *AmMWSc 92*
**Turcotte**, Edgar Lewis 1929- *AmMWSc 92*
**Turcotte**, Jean-Claude 1936- *WhoRel 92*
**Turcotte**, Jeremiah G 1933- *AmMWSc 92*
**Turcotte**, Joseph George 1936- *AmMWSc 92*
**Turcotte**, William Arthur 1945- *AmMWSc 92*
**Turczyn-Toles**, Doreen Marie 1958- *WhoMW 92*
**Tureck**, Rosalyn 1914- *IntWW 91, NewAmDM, Who 92, WhoEnt 92, WrDr 92*
**Turek**, Andrew 1935- *AmMWSc 92*
**Turek**, Frank 1914- *WhoAmP 91*
**Turek**, Fred William 1947- *AmMWSc 92*
**Turek**, Ian Francis *TwCSFW 91*
**Turek**, Ione Frances *TwCSFW 91*
**Turek**, William Norbert 1931- *AmMWSc 92*
**Turekian**, Karl Karekin 1927- *AmMWSc 92*
**Turel**, Franziska Lili Margarete 1924- *AmMWSc 92*
**Turel**, Sudi Nese 1929- *IntWW 91*
**Turer**, Jack 1912- *AmMWSc 92*
**Turesky**, Samuel Saul 1916- *AmMWSc 92*
**Turetsky**, Aaron 1951- *WhoAmL 92*
**Turetzky**, Bertram 1933- *NewAmDM*
**Turgeon**, Gregoire *DrAPF 91*
**Turgeon**, Jean 1936- *AmMWSc 92*
**Turgeon**, Judith Lee 1942- *AmMWSc 92*
**Turgeon**, Roger David 1954- *WhoAmL 92*
**Turgeon**, Roland M 1915- *WhoAmP 91*
**Turgot**, Anne-Robert-Jacques 1727-1781 *BlkwCEP*
**Turi**, Michael David 1949- *WhoMW 92*
**Turi**, Paul George 1917- *AmMWSc 92*
**Turi**, Raymond A 1957- *AmMWSc 92*
**Turillo**, Michael Joseph, Jr. 1947- *WhoFI 92*
**Turin**, George L 1930- *AmMWSc 92*
**Turin**, Viktor Aleksandrovich 1895-1945 *SovUnBD*
**Turina**, Joaquin 1882-1949 *NewAmDM*
**Turing**, Alan 1912-1954 *FacFETw*
**Turing**, John Dermot 1961- *Who 92*
**Turino**, Gerard Michael 1924- *AmMWSc 92*
**Turinsky**, Jiri 1935- *AmMWSc 92*
**Turinsky**, Paul Josef 1944- *AmMWSc 92*
**Turishcheva**, Lyudmila Ivanovna 1952- *SovUnBD*
**Turitto**, Vincent Thomas 1944- *AmMWSc 92*
**Turk**, Alfred J., II 1930- *WhoBlA 92*
**Turk**, Amos 1918- *AmMWSc 92*
**Turk**, Dale Warren 1953- *WhoEnt 92*
**Turk**, Daniel Gottlob 1756-1813 *NewAmDM*
**Turk**, Dennis Charles 1946- *AmMWSc 92*
**Turk**, Donald Earle 1931- *AmMWSc 92*
**Turk**, Edmund John 1925- *WhoAmP 91*
**Turk**, Fateh M 1924- *AmMWSc 92*
**Turk**, Frances 1915- *WrDr 92*
**Turk**, Frances Mary 1915- *IntAu&W 91*
**Turk**, Gregory Chester 1951- *AmMWSc 92*
**Turk**, James Clinton 1923- *WhoAmL 92*
**Turk**, James Clinton, Jr. 1956- *WhoAmL 92*
**Turk**, Kenneth Leroy 1908- *AmMWSc 92*
**Turk**, Leland Jan 1938- *AmMWSc 92*
**Turk**, Martin Erwin 1945- *WhoFI 92*
**Turk**, Penelope Bryant 1941- *WhoWest 92*
**Turk**, Randall James 1950- *WhoAmL 92*
**Turk**, Rudy Henry 1927- *WhoWest 92*
**Turkan Kahtun** *EncAmaz 91*
**Turkanis**, Stuart Allen 1936- *AmMWSc 92*
**Turkdogan**, Ethem Tugrul 1923- *AmMWSc 92*
**Turkel**, Miriam Wilen 1950- *WhoFI 92*
**Turkel**, Rickey M 1943- *AmMWSc 92*
**Turkeltaub**, Paul Charles 1944- *AmMWSc 92*
**Turkevich**, Anthony 1916- *AmMWSc 92*
**Turkevich**, Anthony Leonid 1916- *IntWW 91*
**Turkevich**, John 1907- *AmMWSc 92*
**Turkevich**, Leonid Anthony 1950- *WhoMW 92*
**Turkia**, Kalevi Matti 1941- *WhoFI 92*
**Turkiewicz**, Witold Wladyslaw 1930- *WhoEnt 92*
**Turkin**, Marshall William 1926- *WhoEnt 92, WhoWest 92*
**Turkin**, Valentin Konstantinovich 1887-1958 *SovUnBD*
**Turkington**, Eric *WhoAmP 91*
**Turkington**, Robert Albert 1951- *AmMWSc 92*
**Turkington**, Roger W 1936- *AmMWSc 92*
**Turkki**, Pirkko Reetta 1934- *AmMWSc 92*
**Turkle**, Brinton 1915- *WrDr 92*
**Turkmen**, Ilter 1927- *IntWW 91*
**Turkot**, Frank 1929- *AmMWSc 92*
**Turkson**, Albertine Bowie *WhoBlA 92*
**Turkstra**, Carl J 1936- *AmMWSc 92*
**Turlapaty**, Prasad 1942- *AmMWSc 92*
**Turlej**, Zbigniew Stanislaw 1954- *WhoWest 92*
**Turley**, Anne 1953- *WhoEnt 92*
**Turley**, J. Wayne 1951- *WhoAmL 92*
**Turley**, Jonathan Robert 1961- *WhoAmL 92*
**Turley**, June Williams 1929- *AmMWSc 92*
**Turley**, Kevin 1946- *AmMWSc 92*
**Turley**, Marion E. 1938- *WhoRel 92*
**Turley**, Mark Christopher 1949- *WhoEnt 92, WhoWest 92*
**Turley**, Richard Eyring 1930- *AmMWSc 92*
**Turley**, Robert Joe 1926- *WhoAmL 92*
**Turley**, Sheldon Gamage 1922- *AmMWSc 92*
**Turley**, Stanley F 1921- *WhoAmP 91*
**Turley**, Stewart 1934- *WhoFI 92*
**Turley**, Windle 1939- *WhoAmL 92*
**Turlington**, John Edwin 1957- *WhoAmP 91*
**Turman**, Elbert Jerome 1924- *AmMWSc 92*
**Turman**, George 1928- *WhoWest 92*
**Turman**, George F 1928- *WhoAmP 91*
**Turman**, Glynn *WhoBlA 92, WhoEnt 92*
**Turman**, Lawrence 1926- *IntMPA 92*
**Turman**, Robert L. 1926- *WhoBlA 92*
**Turman**, Robert Lloyd 1956- *WhoAmL 92*
**Turmeau**, William Arthur 1929- *Who 92*
**Turnage**, C Gaylon 1935- *WhoAmP 91*
**Turnage**, Jean A. 1926- *WhoAmL 92, WhoAmP 91, WhoWest 92*
**Turnage**, Mark-Anthony 1960- *ConCom 92*
**Turnage**, Thomas K 1923- *WhoAmP 91*
**Turnbaugh**, Hank *WhoAmP 91*
**Turnbaugh**, Ronald Neal 1935- *WhoRel 92*
**Turnbeaugh**, Terry Dean 1954- *WhoRel 92*
**Turnblom**, Ernest Wayne 1946- *AmMWSc 92*
**Turnbole**, Kathleen McCombe 1951- *WhoRel 92*
**Turnbull**, Agnes Sligh 1888-1982 *BenetAL 91*
**Turnbull**, Alexander 1925-1990 *AnObit 1990*
**Turnbull**, Alexander Cuthbert 1925-1990 *IntWW 91, -91N*
**Turnbull**, Alison 1956- *TwCPaSc*
**Turnbull**, Andrew 1945- *Who 92*
**Turnbull**, Anthony Michael *Who 92*
**Turnbull**, Anthony Robert 1944- *WhoWest 92*
**Turnbull**, Bruce Felton 1928- *AmMWSc 92*
**Turnbull**, Bruce William 1946- *AmMWSc 92*
**Turnbull**, Charles Wesley 1935- *WhoBlA 92*
**Turnbull**, Colin M. 1924- *WrDr 92*
**Turnbull**, Craig David 1940- *AmMWSc 92*
**Turnbull**, David 1915- *AmMWSc 92*
**Turnbull**, G Keith 1935- *AmMWSc 92*
**Turnbull**, Gael 1928- *ConAu 14AS [port], ConPo 91, WrDr 92*
**Turnbull**, Gael Lundin 1928- *IntAu&W 91*
**Turnbull**, George 1926- *Who 92*
**Turnbull**, George Henry 1926- *IntWW 91*
**Turnbull**, Horace Hollins 1949- *WhoBlA 92*
**Turnbull**, Jeffrey Alan 1934- *Who 92*
**Turnbull**, Kenneth 1951- *AmMWSc 92*
**Turnbull**, Lyle E. J. L. 1928- *IntWW 91*
**Turnbull**, Malcolm Bligh 1954- *IntWW 91, Who 92*
**Turnbull**, Michael *Who 92*
**Turnbull**, Michael 1950- *TwCPaSc*
**Turnbull**, Michael Gary 1949- *WhoMW 92*
**Turnbull**, Miles Watson 1929- *WhoWest 92*
**Turnbull**, Reginald March 1907- *Who 92*
**Turnbull**, Renaldo Antonio 1963- *WhoBlA 92*
**Turnbull**, Richard 1909- *Who 92*
**Turnbull**, Robert James 1941- *AmMWSc 92*
**Turnbull**, Stephen 1948- *WrDr 92*
**Turnbull**, Thomas Kent 1934- *WhoRel 92*
**Turnbull**, William 1922- *IntWW 91, TwCPaSc*
**Turnbull**, William, Jr. 1935- *IntWW 91*
**Turnbull**, William D. d1991 *NewYTBS 91 [port]*
**Turneaure**, John Paul 1939- *AmMWSc 92*
**Turnell**, Kenneth 1948- *TwCPaSc*
**Turner** *Who 92*
**Turner**, Alan B. *Who 92*
**Turner**, Albert Joseph, Jr 1938- *AmMWSc 92*
**Turner**, Alberta T. *DrAPF 91*
**Turner**, Alberta Tucker 1919- *IntAu&W 91*
**Turner**, Alexander 1901- *Who 92, WrDr 92*
**Turner**, Alfred 1874-1940 *TwCPaSc*
**Turner**, Allen H. 1923- *WhoBlA 92*
**Turner**, Almon George, Jr 1932- *AmMWSc 92*
**Turner**, Alvis Greely 1929- *AmMWSc 92*
**Turner**, Amedee 1929- *WrDr 92*
**Turner**, Amedee Edward 1929- *Who 92*
**Turner**, Andrew 1922- *AmMWSc 92, WhoMW 92*
**Turner**, Andrew B 1940- *AmMWSc 92*
**Turner**, Anne Halligan 1941- *AmMWSc 92*
**Turner**, Annie Uribe 1958- *WhoHisp 92*
**Turner**, Antony Hubert Michael 1930- *Who 92*
**Turner**, Arthur Edward 1931- *WhoFI 92*
**Turner**, Arthur Francis 1906- *AmMWSc 92*
**Turner**, Arthur Francis 1912- *Who 92*
**Turner**, Arthur L 1950- *WhoAmP 91*
**Turner**, Bailey W. 1932- *WhoBlA 92*
**Turner**, Barbara Bush *AmMWSc 92*
**Turner**, Barbara Holman 1926- *AmMWSc 92*
**Turner**, Barry Earl 1936- *AmMWSc 92*
**Turner**, Bernice Hilburn 1937- *WhoEnt 92*
**Turner**, Betty *WhoAmP 91*
**Turner**, Big Joe 1911-1985 *NewAmDM*
**Turner**, Bill *WhoBlA 92*
**Turner**, Billie B. 1930- *WhoMW 92*
**Turner**, Billie Lee 1925- *AmMWSc 92*
**Turner**, Bonese Collins *WhoWest 92*
**Turner**, Bradwell 1907-1990 *AnObit 1990*
**Turner**, Brenda Kaye 1948- *WhoAmP 91*
**Turner**, Brian 1944- *ConPo 91, WrDr 92*
**Turner**, Bruce Jay 1945- *AmMWSc 92*
**Turner**, Bryan S. 1945- *WrDr 92*
**Turner**, Cameron Archer 1915- *Who 92*
**Turner**, Carl Jeane 1933- *WhoFI 92*
**Turner**, Carlton Edgar 1940- *AmMWSc 92*
**Turner**, Carmen Elizabeth *WhoBlA 92*
**Turner**, Castellano Blanchet 1938- *WhoBlA 92*
**Turner**, Cedric Edward 1926- *Who 92*
**Turner**, Charles Carre 1944- *WhoAmL 92*
**Turner**, Charles Hamilton 1936- *WhoAmL 92*
**Turner**, Charles Joseph 1926- *WhoMW 92*
**Turner**, Charles Robert 1910- *WhoBlA 92*
**Turner**, Charles Wayland 1916- *WhoAmP 91*
**Turner**, Charlie Daniel, Jr 1946- *AmMWSc 92*
**Turner**, Charlie Guilford 1944- *WhoFI 92*
**Turner**, Christopher Gilbert 1929- *Who 92*
**Turner**, Christopher John 1933- *Who 92*
**Turner**, Christy Gentry, II 1933- *AmMWSc 92*

**Turner**, Claire Denise Yarbrough 1956- *WhoAmL 92*
**Turner**, Clay *TwCWW 91*
**Turner**, Clifford 1913- *IntMPA 92*
**Turner**, Clifford John 1918- *Who 92*
**Turner**, Clifton B. 1924-1988 *WhoBlA 92N*
**Turner**, Colin Francis 1930- *Who 92*
**Turner**, Colin William 1933- *Who 92*
**Turner**, Colin William Carstairs 1922- *Who 92*
**Turner**, Dain Cameron 1970- *WhoBlA 92*
**Turner**, Dale Bradley 1954- *WhoMW 92*
**Turner**, Daniel Charles 1950- *WhoAmL 92*
**Turner**, Daniel Shelton 1945- *AmMWSc 92*
**Turner**, Daniel Stoughton 1917- *AmMWSc 92, WhoWest 92*
**Turner**, Danny William 1947- *AmMWSc 92*
**Turner**, Darwin T. 1931- *WrDr 92*
**Turner**, Darwin T. 1931-1991 *ConAu 133, WhoBlA 92N*
**Turner**, David Andrew 1947- *Who 92*
**Turner**, David Eldridge 1947- *WhoAmL 92*
**Turner**, David Gerald 1945- *AmMWSc 92*
**Turner**, David L 1949- *AmMWSc 92*
**Turner**, David Scott 1952- *WhoWest 92*
**Turner**, David Warren 1927- *Who 92*
**Turner**, Dean Edson 1927- *WhoWest 92*
**Turner**, Dennis 1942- *Who 92*
**Turner**, Dennis Edward 1960- *WhoRel 92*
**Turner**, Derek T 1926- *AmMWSc 92*
**Turner**, Diane Krupnak 1954- *WhoWest 92*
**Turner**, Diane Young 1950- *WhoBlA 92*
**Turner**, Donald Chisholm 1903-1985 *TwCPaSc*
**Turner**, Donald Frank 1921- *WhoAmL 92*
**Turner**, Donald Lloyd 1937- *AmMWSc 92*
**Turner**, Donald W 1932- *AmMWSc 92*
**Turner**, Donald William 1925- *Who 92*
**Turner**, Doris 1930- *WhoBlA 92*
**Turner**, Doris J. *WhoBlA 92*
**Turner**, Douglas Hugh 1946- *AmMWSc 92*
**Turner**, Dudley Russell Flower 1916- *Who 92*
**Turner**, Dwight Luther 1944- *WhoMW 92*
**Turner**, E. Deane 1928- *WhoAmL 92*
**Turner**, E.P., Mrs. 1856-1938 *HanAmWH*
**Turner**, E. S. 1909- *WrDr 92*
**Turner**, Ed *LesBEnT 92*
**Turner**, Ed Sims 1935- *WhoEnt 92*
**Turner**, Eddie William 1931- *WhoBlA 92*
**Turner**, Edgar *ScFEYrs*
**Turner**, Edgar and Hodder, Raymond *ScFEYrs*
**Turner**, Edna *WhoBlA 92*
**Turner**, Edward C 1943- *AmMWSc 92*
**Turner**, Edward Felix, Jr 1920- *AmMWSc 92*
**Turner**, Edward Harrison 1920- *AmMWSc 92*
**Turner**, Edward L. *WhoBlA 92*
**Turner**, Edward M. 1925- *WhoAmL 92*
**Turner**, Edward V 1913- *AmMWSc 92*
**Turner**, Edwin Lewis 1949- *AmMWSc 92*
**Turner**, Ella Victoria 1946- *AmMWSc 92*
**Turner**, Elmyra G. 1928- *WhoBlA 92*
**Turner**, Ermelinda Miguelita 1932- *WhoWest 92*
**Turner**, Ernest Craig, Jr 1927- *AmMWSc 92*
**Turner**, Ernest John Donaldson 1914- *Who 92*
**Turner**, Ervin 1948- *WhoBlA 92*
**Turner**, Eugene 1934- *WhoBlA 92*
**Turner**, Eugene Bonner 1922- *AmMWSc 92*
**Turner**, Eva 1892-1990 *AnObit 1990, FacFETw*
**Turner**, Evan Hopkins 1927- *WhoMW 92*
**Turner**, Evelyn Evon 1954- *WhoBlA 92*
**Turner**, Evelyn Marguerite *Who 92*
**Turner**, Floyd, Jr. 1966- *WhoBlA 92*
**Turner**, Floyd Ray 1951- *WhoRel 92*
**Turner**, Frances Bernadette 1903- *WhoRel 92*
**Turner**, Francis *Who 92*
**Turner**, Francis A. 1896-1991 *NewYTBS 91 [port]*
**Turner**, Franklin Delton 1933- *WhoRel 92*
**Turner**, Franklin James 1960- *WhoBlA 92*
**Turner**, Fred Allen 1933- *AmMWSc 92, WhoMW 92*
**Turner**, Fred L. 1933- *WhoMW 92*
**Turner**, Fred Lamar 1949- *WhoFI 92*
**Turner**, Frederick *DrAPF 91, IntMPA 92*
**Turner**, Frederick 1937- *ConAu 34NR*
**Turner**, Frederick 1943- *IntAu&W 91*
**Turner**, Frederick Brown 1927- *AmMWSc 92*
**Turner**, Frederick C. 1938- *WrDr 92*
**Turner**, Frederick Jackson 1861-1932 *BenetAL 91, FacFETw, RComAH*
**Turner**, G W 1923- *WhoAmP 91*
**Turner**, Geoffrey Whitney 1948- *WhoWest 92*
**Turner**, George 1916- *ConNov 91, IntAu&W 91, TwCSFW 91, WrDr 92*
**Turner**, George 1935- *IntWW 91*
**Turner**, George Allen 1908- *WhoRel 92*
**Turner**, George Cleveland 1925- *AmMWSc 92*
**Turner**, George E. 1945- *WhoEnt 92*
**Turner**, George Kibbe *DcAmImH*
**Turner**, George R. 1944- *WhoBlA 92*
**Turner**, George Timothy *WhoBlA 92*
**Turner**, George William 1921- *IntAu&W 91, IntWW 91, WrDr 92*
**Turner**, Gerald Henry 1942- *WhoAmP 91*
**Turner**, Glennette Tilley 1933- *ConAu 133*
**Turner**, Grenville 1936- *IntWW 91, Who 92*
**Turner**, Hal Wesley 1932- *WhoWest 92*
**Turner**, Harold Walter 1911- *WrDr 92*
**Turner**, Harry 1942- *WhoEnt 92*
**Turner**, Harry Edward 1927- *WhoAmP 91*
**Turner**, Harry Edward 1935- *Who 92*
**Turner**, Harry Woodruff 1939- *WhoAmL 92*
**Turner**, Henry A. 1919- *WrDr 92*
**Turner**, Henry Brown 1936- *WhoFI 92*
**Turner**, Henry Ernest William 1907- *Who 92*
**Turner**, Henry McNeal 1834-1915 *RelLAm 91*
**Turner**, Herbert Arthur 1919- *Who 92, WrDr 92*
**Turner**, Herbert Branch 1926- *WhoWest 92*
**Turner**, Howard S 1911- *AmMWSc 92*
**Turner**, Hugh Joseph, Jr. 1945- *WhoAmL 92*
**Turner**, Hugh Michael 1942- *AmMWSc 92*
**Turner**, Hugh Wason 1923- *Who 92*
**Turner**, Ike 1933- *NewAmDM*
**Turner**, Isiah 1945- *WhoBlA 92*
**Turner**, J E *WhoAmP 91*
**Turner**, J Howard 1927- *AmMWSc 92*
**Turner**, Jack Allen 1942- *AmMWSc 92*
**Turner**, Jacqueline Paula 1964- *WhoRel 92*
**Turner**, Jacquie 1959- *TwCPaSc*
**Turner**, James A 1948- *AmMWSc 92*
**Turner**, James Benion, Jr. 1949- *WhoRel 92*
**Turner**, James David 1952- *AmMWSc 92*
**Turner**, James Edward 1930- *AmMWSc 92*
**Turner**, James Eldridge 1942- *AmMWSc 92*
**Turner**, James Henry 1922- *AmMWSc 92*
**Turner**, James Howard 1912- *AmMWSc 92*
**Turner**, James Johnson 1935- *Who 92*
**Turner**, James Marshall 1944- *AmMWSc 92*
**Turner**, James N. 1956- *WhoEnt 92*
**Turner**, James P *WhoAmP 91*
**Turner**, James P. 1930- *WhoAmL 92*
**Turner**, James Reginald 1934- *WhoAmP 91*
**Turner**, James S. 1940- *WhoAmL 92*
**Turner**, James Thomas 1938- *WhoAmL 92*
**Turner**, James Thomas 1944- *WhoMW 92*
**Turner**, Jan Ross 1937- *AmMWSc 92*
**Turner**, Janice Butler 1936- *AmMWSc 92*
**Turner**, Jerome 1942- *WhoAmL 92*
**Turner**, Jerry *WhoEnt 92, WhoWest 92*
**Turner**, Jesse Grant 1912- *WhoEnt 92*
**Turner**, Jim 1946- *WhoAmP 91*
**Turner**, Joanna Elizabeth 1923- *Who 92*
**Turner**, Joe 1907- *NewAmDM*
**Turner**, Joe 1907-1990 *AnObit 1990*
**Turner**, John 1946- *Who 92*
**Turner**, John A., Jr. 1948- *WhoBlA 92*
**Turner**, John Andrew 1949- *WhoFI 92*
**Turner**, John B. 1922- *WhoBlA 92*
**Turner**, John Barrimore 1942- *WhoBlA 92*
**Turner**, John Charles 1949- *AmMWSc 92*
**Turner**, John Christopher 1928- *WrDr 92*
**Turner**, John Dean 1930- *AmMWSc 92*
**Turner**, John Derfel 1928- *Who 92*
**Turner**, John Frayn 1923- *WrDr 92*
**Turner**, John Freeland 1942- *WhoAmP 91, WhoWest 92*
**Turner**, John G 1939- *WhoIns 92*
**Turner**, John K 1923- *AmMWSc 92*
**Turner**, John Lindsey 1946- *AmMWSc 92*
**Turner**, John M. 1948- *WhoBlA 92*
**Turner**, John Napier 1929- *FacFETw, IntWW 91, Who 92*
**Turner**, John Stewart 1930- *Who 92*
**Turner**, John Turnage 1929- *Who 92*
**Turner**, Johnnie Rodgers 1940- *WhoBlA 92*
**Turner**, Joseph Addison 1826-1868 *BenetAL 91*
**Turner**, Joseph Ellis 1939- *WhoBlA 92*
**Turner**, Joseph Vernon 1911-1985 *FacFETw*
**Turner**, Judith Ann 1952- *AmMWSc 92*
**Turner**, Judy 1936- *WrDr 92*
**Turner**, Karen M. 1954- *WhoEnt 92*
**Turner**, Katharine Charlotte 1910- *WrDr 92*
**Turner**, Kathleen 1954- *IntMPA 92, IntWW 91, WhoEnt 92*
**Turner**, Keena 1958- *WhoBlA 92*
**Turner**, Keith 1943- *WhoBlA 92*
**Turner**, Kendall Allen 1962- *WhoRel 92*
**Turner**, Kenneth Clyde 1934- *AmMWSc 92*
**Turner**, Kenneth L, Sr 1934- *WhoAmP 91*
**Turner**, Kermit *DrAPF 91*
**Turner**, Kim 1961- *BlkOlyM*
**Turner**, Kim Smith 1959- *WhoBlA 92*
**Turner**, La Ferria Maria 1962- *WhoFI 92*
**Turner**, Lana 1920- *WhoEnt 92*
**Turner**, Lana 1921- *IntMPA 92*
**Turner**, Lana 1950- *WhoBlA 92*
**Turner**, Lanny Meredith 1944- *WhoMW 92*
**Turner**, Larry 1939- *WhoAmP 91*
**Turner**, Leaf 1943- *AmMWSc 92*
**Turner**, Lee Howard 1950- *WhoFI 92*
**Turner**, Leland Smith, Jr. 1936- *WhoEnt 92, WhoRel 92*
**Turner**, Len *IntAu&W 91X, TwCWW 91*
**Turner**, Lester Nathan 1933- *WhoAmL 92*
**Turner**, Lillian Erna 1918- *WhoWest 92*
**Turner**, Lincoln Hulley 1928- *AmMWSc 92*
**Turner**, Linda Darnell 1947- *WhoBlA 92*
**Turner**, Lisa Phillips 1951- *WhoFI 92*
**Turner**, Lloyd Charles 1938- *IntAu&W 91, Who 92*
**Turner**, Lloyd Gardener 1924- *WhoEnt 92*
**Turner**, Louis 1942- *ConAu 34NR*
**Turner**, Louis Edouard 1939- *WhoBlA 92*
**Turner**, Louis Mark 1942- *WrDr 92*
**Turner**, Loyce Warren 1927- *WhoAmP 91*
**Turner**, Lucille Ellen 1956- *WhoAmL 92*
**Turner**, Lynne Alison 1941- *WhoEnt 92*
**Turner**, M. Annette 1953- *WhoBlA 92*
**Turner**, Malcolm Elijah, Jr 1929- *AmMWSc 92*
**Turner**, Manson Don 1928- *AmMWSc 92*
**Turner**, Marcellus 1963- *WhoBlA 92*
**Turner**, Marcus Jared 1966- *WhoBlA 92*
**Turner**, Margot 1910- *Who 92*
**Turner**, Marguerite Rose 1920- *WhoAmP 91*
**Turner**, Mark Anthony 1951- *WhoBlA 92*
**Turner**, Mark Courtney, Sr. 1951- *WhoMW 92*
**Turner**, Marshall Chittenden, Jr. 1941- *WhoFI 92, WhoWest 92*
**Turner**, Marta Dawn 1954- *WhoRel 92*
**Turner**, Martha Anne 1904-1985 *ConAu 134*
**Turner**, Marvin Wentz 1959- *WhoBlA 92*
**Turner**, Mary *IntAu&W 91X*
**Turner**, Mary Louise 1954- *WhoFI 92*
**Turner**, Matthew X 1928- *AmMWSc 92*
**Turner**, Maureen Barbara 1936- *WhoWest 92*
**Turner**, Meir 1948- *WhoRel 92*
**Turner**, Melvin Duval 1949- *WhoBlA 92*
**Turner**, Merfyn 1915- *WrDr 92*
**Turner**, Merfyn 1915-1991 *ConAu 135*
**Turner**, Merfyn Lloyd 1915- *IntAu&W 91*
**Turner**, Michael 1931- *Who 92*
**Turner**, Michael D 1927- *AmMWSc 92*
**Turner**, Michael Griswold 1925- *WhoFI 92*
**Turner**, Michael Ralph 1929- *Who 92*
**Turner**, Michael Seth 1948- *WhoEnt 92, WhoWest 92*
**Turner**, Michael Stanley 1949- *AmMWSc 92*
**Turner**, Michael Wallace 1960- *WhoAmL 92*
**Turner**, Mikoel 1950- *WhoBlA 92*
**Turner**, Mortimer Darling 1920- *AmMWSc 92, WhoWest 92*
**Turner**, Moses 1938- *WhoBlA 92*
**Turner**, Nancy Kay 1947- *WhoWest 92*
**Turner**, Nat 1800-1831 *BenetAL 91*
**Turner**, Natalie Elizabeth 1971- *WhoWest 92*
**Turner**, Noel Hinton 1940- *AmMWSc 92*
**Turner**, Norman Henry 1916- *Who 92*
**Turner**, Otis *WhoAmP 91*
**Turner**, P Eric *WhoAmP 91*
**Turner**, Patricia 1927- *Who 92*
**Turner**, Paul 1917- *WrDr 92*
**Turner**, Paul Jesse 1948- *WhoWest 92*
**Turner**, Peter *Who 92*
**Turner**, Peter 1924- *Who 92*
**Turner**, Peter 1948- *WhoBlA 92*
**Turner**, Peter Helmer 1934- *WhoWest 92*
**Turner**, Peter William *Who 92*
**Turner**, Phil 1939- *Who 92*
**Turner**, Philip 1913- *Who 92*
**Turner**, Philip 1925- *WrDr 92*
**Turner**, Philip Stanley 1905- *Who 92*
**Turner**, Philip William 1925- *IntAu&W 91*
**Turner**, R James 1945- *AmMWSc 92*
**Turner**, Ralph 1919- *WrDr 92*
**Turner**, Ralph 1936- *WrDr 92*
**Turner**, Ralph B 1931- *AmMWSc 92*
**Turner**, Ralph Herbert 1919- *WhoWest 92*
**Turner**, Ralph James 1935- *WhoWest 92*
**Turner**, Ralph Waldo 1938- *AmMWSc 92*
**Turner**, Ralph Wilson, Jr. 1948- *WhoEnt 92, WhoFI 92*
**Turner**, Randall Lee 1961- *WhoMW 92*
**Turner**, Raymond C. *Who 92*
**Turner**, Raymond Marriner 1927- *AmMWSc 92*
**Turner**, Revis Eugene 1947- *WhoRel 92*
**Turner**, Rex A., Jr. *WhoRel 92*
**Turner**, Rex Howell *AmMWSc 92*
**Turner**, Ricardo Cornelius, Sr. 1947- *WhoBlA 92*
**Turner**, Richard 1909- *Who 92*
**Turner**, Richard Allen 1935- *WhoAmP 91*
**Turner**, Richard Arlen 1934- *WhoFI 92*
**Turner**, Richard Lee 1929- *WhoWest 92*
**Turner**, Richard Wainwright Duke 1909- *Who 92*
**Turner**, Robert *WhoAmP 91*
**Turner**, Robert 1925- *AmMWSc 92*
**Turner**, Robert, Jr. 1949- *WhoBlA 92*
**Turner**, Robert Alexander 1937- *AmMWSc 92*
**Turner**, Robert Atwood *AmMWSc 92*
**Turner**, Robert Comrie 1920- *WhoEnt 92*
**Turner**, Robert Davison 1929- *AmMWSc 92*
**Turner**, Robert E L 1936- *AmMWSc 92*
**Turner**, Robert Edward 1938- *IntMPA 92, WhoEnt 92*
**Turner**, Robert Elwood 1937- *WhoMW 92*
**Turner**, Robert Foster 1944- *WhoAmL 92*
**Turner**, Robert H 1923- *WhoAmP 91*
**Turner**, Robert Harold 1941- *AmMWSc 92*
**Turner**, Robert James 1921- *AmMWSc 92*
**Turner**, Robert L 1947- *WhoAmP 91*
**Turner**, Robert Lawrence 1945- *AmMWSc 92*
**Turner**, Robert Lloyd 1947- *WhoBlA 92*
**Turner**, Robert Lockley 1935- *Who 92*
**Turner**, Robert Russell 1950- *WhoEnt 92*
**Turner**, Robert Stuart 1912- *AmMWSc 92*
**Turner**, Roderick L. 1931- *WhoFI 92*
**Turner**, Ronald Lee 1947- *WhoWest 92*
**Turner**, Ross James 1930- *WhoFI 92, WhoWest 92*
**Turner**, Ruth Dixon 1914- *AmMWSc 92*
**Turner**, S Richard 1942- *AmMWSc 92*
**Turner**, Samuel A. 1926- *WhoBlA 92*
**Turner**, Scott Wayne 1962- *WhoMW 92*
**Turner**, Sharon V. 1945- *WhoBlA 92*
**Turner**, Sherrod E 1939- *WhoIns 92*
**Turner**, Shirley 1936- *WhoBlA 92*
**Turner**, Shirley K. 1941- *WhoBlA 92*
**Turner**, Stansfield 1923- *IntWW 91, WhoAmP 91*
**Turner**, Stephen Gordon 1935- *Who 92*
**Turner**, Stephen Miller 1939- *WhoAmL 92, WhoFI 92*
**Turner**, Steven Cornell 1953- *WhoFI 92*
**Turner**, Suzanne A 1952- *WhoIns 92*
**Turner**, Sylvester 1954- *WhoAmP 91*
**Turner**, Ted *LesBEnT 92 [port]*
**Turner**, Ted 1938- *FacFETw, IntWW 91, WhoEnt 92*
**Turner**, Terry Tomo 1945- *AmMWSc 92*
**Turner**, Theodora 1907- *Who 92*
**Turner**, Thomas Bourne 1902- *AmMWSc 92*
**Turner**, Thomas Coke 1930- *WhoFI 92*
**Turner**, Thomas Coleman 1927- *IntAu&W 91, WrDr 92*
**Turner**, Thomas Jenkins 1926- *AmMWSc 92*
**Turner**, Thomas Newell, Jr 1938- *WhoAmP 91*
**Turner**, Thomas Peter 1928- *Who 92*
**Turner**, Thomas Wayne 1949- *WhoRel 92*
**Turner**, Thomas Wyatt 1877-1978 *FacFETw*
**Turner**, Tina 1938- *NewAmDM*
**Turner**, Tina 1939- *IntMPA 92, NotBlAW 92, WhoEnt 92*
**Turner**, Tina 1940- *IntWW 91*
**Turner**, Tina 1941- *WhoBlA 92*
**Turner**, Vivian Love 1947- *WhoBlA 92*
**Turner**, Vivian Vanessa 1955- *WhoBlA 92*
**Turner**, W. Burghardt 1915- *WhoBlA 92*
**Turner**, Wallace E. 1923- *WhoBlA 92*
**Turner**, Walter W 1922- *AmMWSc 92*
**Turner**, Warren Austin 1926- *WhoWest 92*
**Turner**, Warren R. 1963- *WhoFI 92*
**Turner**, Wayne Connelly 1942- *AmMWSc 92*
**Turner**, Wilfred 1921- *IntWW 91, Who 92*
**Turner**, William 1927- *Who 92*
**Turner**, William Christopher 1946- *WhoAmP 91*
**Turner**, William Cochrane 1929- *IntWW 91, WhoFI 92, WhoWest 92*
**Turner**, William Danny 1939- *AmMWSc 92*
**Turner**, William H. 1931- *WhoBlA 92*
**Turner**, William Hobertt 1946- *WhoBlA 92*
**Turner**, William Joseph 1927- *AmMWSc 92*
**Turner**, William Joseph 1955- *WhoAmL 92*
**Turner**, William Junior 1940- *AmMWSc 92*
**Turner**, William L. 1939- *WhoAmL 92*

**Turner,** William O 1914-1980 *TwCWW 91*
**Turner,** William Price 1927- *IntAu&W 91*
**Turner,** William Richard 1936- *AmMWSc 92*
**Turner,** William Rogers 1936- *WhoAmL 92*
**Turner,** William Weyand 1927- *WhoWest 92, WrDr 92*
**Turner,** William Wilberforce *BenetAL 91*
**Turner,** Willie 1935- *AmMWSc 92, WhoBlA 92*
**Turner,** Winifred 1903-1983 *TwCPaSc*
**Turner,** Winston E. 1921- *WhoBlA 92*
**Turner,** Yvonne Williams 1927- *WhoBlA 92*
**Turner Cain,** George Robert 1912- *Who 92*
**Turner-Givens,** Ella Mae 1927- *WhoBlA 92*
**Turner of Camden,** Baroness 1927- *Who 92*
**Turner-Samuels,** David Jessel 1918- *Who 92*
**Turner-Samuels,** Norma Florence *Who 92*
**Turner Ward,** Douglas 1930- *IntAu&W 91*
**Turner-Warwick,** Margaret 1924- *Who 92*
**Turner-Warwick,** Richard Trevor 1925- *Who 92*
**Turney,** Alan Harry 1932- *Who 92*
**Turney,** Howard Ray 1931- *WhoFI 92*
**Turney,** James Bruce 1951- *WhoAmP 91*
**Turney,** James Edward, II 1933- *WhoFI 92*
**Turney,** Kenneth Wayne 1952- *WhoFI 92*
**Turney,** Peter Benjamin Bolton 1946- *WhoFI 92*
**Turney,** Thomas William 1947- *WhoFI 92*
**Turney,** Tully Hubert 1936- *AmMWSc 92*
**Turnham,** Pete Benton *WhoAmP 91*
**Turnheim,** Joy Karen 1965- *WhoAmL 92*
**Turnheim,** Palmer 1921- *WhoFI 92*
**Turnill,** Reginald 1915- *IntAu&W 91, WrDr 92*
**Turnipseed,** Carl Wendell 1947- *WhoBlA 92*
**Turnipseed,** David E 1945- *WhoAmP 91*
**Turnipseed,** Glyn D 1942- *AmMWSc 92*
**Turnipseed,** Marvin Roy 1934- *AmMWSc 92*
**Turnipseed,** Tom 1936- *WhoAmP 91*
**Turnley,** David Carl 1955- *WhoMW 92*
**Turnley,** Richard Dick 1933- *WhoAmP 91*
**Turnley,** Richard Dick, Jr. 1933- *WhoBlA 92*
**Turnlund,** Judith Rae 1936- *AmMWSc 92, WhoWest 92*
**Turnock,** A C 1930- *AmMWSc 92*
**Turnock,** David 1938- *WrDr 92*
**Turnock,** William James 1929- *AmMWSc 92*
**Turnour** *Who 92*
**Turnquest,** Henrietta E *WhoAmP 91*
**Turnquest,** Sandra Close 1954- *WhoBlA 92*
**Turnquist,** Carl Richard 1944- *AmMWSc 92*
**Turnquist,** Larry F 1952- *WhoAmP 91*
**Turnquist,** Mark Alan 1949- *AmMWSc 92*
**Turnquist,** Paul Kenneth 1935- *AmMWSc 92*
**Turnquist,** Ralph Otto 1928- *AmMWSc 92*
**Turnquist,** Richard Lee 1944- *AmMWSc 92*
**Turnquist,** Truman Dale 1940- *AmMWSc 92*
**Turnrose,** Barry Edmund 1947- *AmMWSc 92*
**Turo,** Ron 1955- *WhoAmL 92*
**Turo,** Thomas Christopher 1954- *WhoFI 92*
**Turoczi,** Lester J 1942- *AmMWSc 92*
**Turoff,** Carole Ruth 1937- *WhoAmL 92*
**Turoff,** Marshall Arnold 1927- *WhoWest 92*
**Turoff,** Murray 1936- *AmMWSc 92*
**Turok,** Paul Harris 1929- *WhoEnt 92*
**Turow,** L. Scott 1949- *IntWW 91*
**Turow,** Scott 1949- *CurBio 91 [port], WrDr 92*
**Turow,** Scott F. 1949- *WhoMW 92*
**Turowicz,** Jerzy 1912- *IntWW 91*
**Turpen,** James Baxter 1945- *AmMWSc 92*
**Turpen,** Michael Craig *WhoAmP 91*
**Turpin,** Frank Thomas 1943- *AmMWSc 92*
**Turpin,** James Alexander 1917- *Who 92*
**Turpin,** Joseph Marcel 1887-1943 *RelLAm 91*
**Turpin,** Kenneth Charlton 1915- *Who 92*
**Turpin,** Mel Harrison 1960- *WhoBlA 92*
**Turpin,** Patrick George 1911- *Who 92*
**Turpin,** Richard Harold 1939- *WhoWest 92*
**Turpin,** Robin Sue 1957- *WhoMW 92*
**Turpin,** Samuel R *WhoAmP 91*
**Turpin,** Tom 1873-1922 *NewAmDM*
**Turrell,** Brian George 1938- *AmMWSc 92*
**Turrell,** Eugene Snow 1919- *AmMWSc 92, WhoWest 92*
**Turrell,** George Charles 1931- *AmMWSc 92*
**Turrentine,** Howard Boyd 1914- *WhoWest 92*
**Turrentine,** Lynda Gayle 1941- *WhoWest 92*
**Turrentine,** Rogers 1939- *WhoEnt 92*
**Turret,** Ira A. 1950- *WhoAmL 92*
**Turretini,** Jean Alphonse 1671-1737 *BlkwCEP*
**Turriff,** David Earl 1947- *WhoMW 92*
**Turriff,** Thomas J. 1946- *WhoFI 92*
**Turrin,** Joseph Egidio 1947- *WhoEnt 92*
**Turro,** Nicholas John 1938- *AmMWSc 92, IntWW 91*
**Turrone,** Richard Charles 1936- *WhoAmL 92*
**Turse,** Richard S 1935- *AmMWSc 92*
**Tursky,** Anne Barbara 1960- *WhoRel 92*
**Tursso,** Dennis Joseph 1939- *WhoFI 92, WhoMW 92*
**Turteltaub-Orenstein** *LesBEnT 92*
**Turtle,** Jon 1949- *WhoEnt 92*
**Turtledove,** Harry *TwCSFW 91*
**Turton** *Who 92*
**Turton,** Eugenie Christine 1946- *Who 92*
**Turton,** Victor Ernest 1924- *Who 92*
**Turton-Hart,** Francis 1908- *Who 92*
**Turturro,** John 1957- *ConTFT 9, IntMPA 92, WhoEnt 92*
**Turtz,** Robert Elias 1941- *WhoAmL 92*
**Turunku,** Bakwa *EncAmaz 91*
**Turvey,** Garry 1934- *Who 92*
**Turvey,** Ralph 1927- *Who 92, WrDr 92*
**Tusa,** John 1936- *IntWW 91, Who 92*
**Tuschman,** James Marshall 1941- *WhoFI 92, WhoMW 92*
**Tuseo,** Norbert Joseph John 1950- *WhoFI 92*
**Tusher,** Thomas William 1941- *WhoWest 92*
**Tushingham,** A Douglas 1914- *IntAu&W 91, WrDr 92*
**Tushingham,** Rita 1942- *IntMPA 92, Who 92*
**Tusiani,** Joseph 1924- *IntAu&W 91*
**Tusing,** Thomas William 1920- *AmMWSc 92*
**Tuska,** Agnes 1960- *WhoMW 92*
**Tuso,** Joseph Frederick 1933- *WhoWest 92*
**Tusser,** Thomas 1524?-1580 *RfGEnL 91*
**Tussing,** Aubrey Dale 1935- *WrDr 92*
**Tustanoff,** Eugene Reno 1929- *AmMWSc 92*
**Tustin,** Arnold 1899- *Who 92*
**Tustin,** David *Who 92*
**Tusting,** Robert Frederick 1933- *AmMWSc 92*
**Tustison,** Randal Wayne 1947- *AmMWSc 92*
**Tusty,** James Robert 1949- *WhoEnt 92*
**Tuszynski,** Alfons Alfred 1921- *AmMWSc 92*
**Tuszynski,** Daniel J., Jr. 1947- *WhoFI 92*
**Tuszynski,** George P *AmMWSc 92*
**Tuszynski,** Jack A 1956- *AmMWSc 92*
**Tute,** Sophie 1960- *TwCPaSc*
**Tute,** Warren Stanley 1914- *IntAu&W 91*
**Tutein,** John F 1958- *WhoAmP 91*
**Tutelman,** Jacki Deena 1954- *WhoFI 92*
**Tuten,** Frederic *DrAPF 91*
**Tuteur,** Franz Benjamin 1923- *AmMWSc 92*
**Tuthill,** Arthur F 1916- *AmMWSc 92*
**Tuthill,** Harlan Lloyd 1917- *AmMWSc 92*
**Tuthill,** Samuel James 1925- *AmMWSc 92*
**Tuthill,** Samuel Miller 1919- *AmMWSc 92*
**Tuthill,** Stacy *DrAPF 91*
**Tuti,** Dudley 1919- *Who 92*
**Tutihasi,** Simpei 1922- *AmMWSc 92*
**Tutin,** Barry Michael 1951- *WhoFI 92, WhoMW 92*
**Tutin,** Dorothy 1930- *IntMPA 92, IntWW 91*
**Tutin,** Dorothy 1931- *Who 92*
**Tutin,** Winifred Anne 1915- *Who 92*
**Tutman,** William L. 1931- *WhoBlA 92*
**Tutri,** Juan 1950- *WhoEnt 92*
**Tutt,** Billy Dean 1937- *WhoAmP 91*
**Tutt,** Fred David 1946- *WhoFI 92*
**Tutt,** Lia S. 1960- *WhoBlA 92*
**Tutt,** Louise Thompson 1937- *WhoAmL 92*
**Tutt,** Norman Sydney 1944- *Who 92*
**Tutt,** Walter Cornelius 1918- *WhoBlA 92*
**Tutt,** William Bullard 1941- *WhoWest 92*
**Tutte,** William Thomas 1917- *AmMWSc 92, Who 92*
**Tuttle,** Annie R. 1956- *WhoMW 92*
**Tuttle,** Catherine Vaughn 1957- *WhoEnt 92*
**Tuttle,** Charles Wesley 1829-1881 *BiInAmS*
**Tuttle,** Christine Moe 1949- *WhoWest 92*
**Tuttle,** Daniel Howard 1946- *WhoAmP 91*
**Tuttle,** Daniel Sylvester 1837-1923 *RelLAm 91*
**Tuttle,** David F 1914- *AmMWSc 92*
**Tuttle,** David Kitchell 1835-1915 *BiInAmS*
**Tuttle,** David Terrence 1937- *WhoWest 92*
**Tuttle,** Donald Latham 1934- *WhoFI 92*
**Tuttle,** Donald Monroe 1917- *AmMWSc 92*
**Tuttle,** Donna Claire 1947- *WhoAmP 91*
**Tuttle,** Edwin Ellsworth 1927- *WhoFI 92*
**Tuttle,** Elbert P, Jr 1921- *AmMWSc 92*
**Tuttle,** Elizabeth R 1938- *AmMWSc 92*
**Tuttle,** Elsie Eleanor 1927- *WhoRel 92*
**Tuttle,** Florence Guertin 1869-1951 *AmPeW*
**Tuttle,** Frances Lynch 1947- *WhoMW 92*
**Tuttle,** George B *ScFEYrs*
**Tuttle,** Horace Parnell 1839-1893 *BiInAmS*
**Tuttle,** James Percival 1857-1913 *BiInAmS*
**Tuttle,** John L, Jr *WhoAmP 91*
**Tuttle,** Jon d1991 *NewYTBS 91*
**Tuttle,** Kenneth Lewis 1944- *AmMWSc 92*
**Tuttle,** Leon E. 1934- *WhoWest 92*
**Tuttle,** Lisa 1952- *IntAu&W 91, TwCSFW 91, WrDr 92*
**Tuttle,** Lynda Lee 1947- *WhoFI 92*
**Tuttle,** Merlin Devere 1941- *AmMWSc 92*
**Tuttle,** Richard J *WhoAmP 91*
**Tuttle,** Richard Suneson 1930- *AmMWSc 92*
**Tuttle,** Rick 1940- *WhoWest 92*
**Tuttle,** Robert Allan, Jr. 1946- *WhoWest 92*
**Tuttle,** Robert D. 1925- *WhoFI 92, WhoMW 92*
**Tuttle,** Robert Lewis 1922- *AmMWSc 92*
**Tuttle,** Ronald Ralph 1936- *AmMWSc 92*
**Tuttle,** Russell Howard 1939- *AmMWSc 92, WhoMW 92*
**Tuttle,** Sherwood Dodge 1918- *AmMWSc 92*
**Tuttle,** Thomas R, Jr 1928- *AmMWSc 92*
**Tuttle,** W C 1883- *TwCWW 91*
**Tuttle,** Warren Wilson 1930- *AmMWSc 92*
**Tuttle,** William Julian 1912- *WhoEnt 92*
**Tuttle,** William McCullough 1937- *IntAu&W 91*
**Tuttle,** William McCullough, Jr. 1937- *WrDr 92*
**Tuttle,** William Roger 1939- *WhoAmP 91*
**Tutu,** Desmond 1931- *BlkLC [port], FacFETw [port]*
**Tutu,** Desmond Mpilo *Who 92*
**Tutu,** Desmond Mpilo 1931- *DcEcMov, IntWW 91, WhoNob 90, WhoRel 92*
**Tutuola,** Amos 1920- *BlkLC [port], ConNov 91, IntWW 91, RfGEnL 91, WrDr 92*
**Tutupalli,** Lohit Venkateswara 1945- *AmMWSc 92*
**Tutwiler,** Gene Floyd 1945- *AmMWSc 92*
**Tutwiler,** Margaret DeBardeleben 1950- *WhoAmP 91*
**Tuul,** Johannes 1922- *AmMWSc 92, WhoWest 92*
**Tuve,** Merle A 1901-1982 *FacFETw*
**Tuve,** Richard Larsen 1912- *AmMWSc 92*
**Tuverson,** James Dockray, III 1964- *WhoEnt 92*
**Tuveson,** Robert Williams 1931- *AmMWSc 92*
**Tuvim,** Yuri 1930- *WhoEnt 92*
**Tuwhare,** Hone 1922- *ConPo 91, WrDr 92*
**Tuwin,** Julian 1894-1953 *LiExTwC*
**Tuxworth,** Ian Lindsay 1942- *IntWW 91*
**Tuyn,** William Robert 1937- *WhoRel 92*
**Tuzar,** Jaroslav 1915- *AmMWSc 92*
**Tuzo,** Harry 1917- *Who 92*
**Tuzo,** Harry Craufurd 1917- *IntWW 91*
**Tuzson,** John J 1929- *AmMWSc 92*
**Tuzzolino,** Anthony J 1931- *AmMWSc 92*
**Tuzzolino,** Gina Doreen 1958- *WhoWest 92*
**Tvardovsky,** Aleksander Trifonovich 1910-1971 *SovUnBD*
**Tvardovsky,** Alexander Trifonovich 1910-1971 *FacFETw*
**Tvedt,** John 1938- *IntWW 91*
**Tvedt,** Joseph Arnold, Jr. 1944- *WhoWest 92*
**Tveit,** Larry J 1935- *WhoAmP 91*
**Tveit,** Steven Wayne 1956- *WhoEnt 92*
**Twaddell,** William H 1941- *WhoAmP 91*
**Twain,** Mark *ConAu 135, SourALJ*
**Twain,** Mark 1835-1910 *BenetAL 91, RComAH, ScFEYrs, TwCSFW 91*
**Twaine,** Michael 1939- *IntMPA 92*
**Twait,** Larry Gene 1945- *WhoAmP 91*
**Twanmoh,** Valerie Hurley 1957- *WhoAmL 92*
**Twardock,** Arthur Robert 1931- *AmMWSc 92*
**Twardowski,** Zbylut Jozef 1934- *AmMWSc 92, WhoMW 92*
**Twardy,** Stanley Albert, Jr. 1951- *WhoAmL 92*
**Twarog,** Betty Mack 1927- *AmMWSc 92*
**Twarog,** Bruce Anthony 1952- *AmMWSc 92*
**Twarog,** Robert 1935- *AmMWSc 92*
**Tway,** Patricia C 1945- *AmMWSc 92*
**Twede,** Diana 1954- *WhoMW 92*
**Twedt,** Robert Madsen 1924- *AmMWSc 92*
**Tweed,** Andre R. 1914- *WhoBlA 92*
**Tweed,** David George *AmMWSc 92*
**Tweed,** John 1869-1933 *TwCPaSc*
**Tweed,** John 1942- *AmMWSc 92*
**Tweed,** John Louis 1947- *WhoFI 92*
**Tweed,** Stephen C. 1949- *ConAu 133*
**Tweed,** William Marcy 1823-1878 *AmPolLe*
**Tweeddale,** Marquis of 1947- *Who 92*
**Tweeddale,** Martin George 1940- *AmMWSc 92*
**Tweedell,** Kenyon Stanley 1924- *AmMWSc 92, WhoMW 92*
**Tweedell,** Lynne 1939- *WhoAmP 91*
**Tweedie,** Adelbert Thomas 1931- *AmMWSc 92*
**Tweedie,** Carol E. 1942- *WhoMW 92*
**Tweedie,** Jill Sheila 1936- *IntAu&W 91, Who 92*
**Tweedie,** John William d1991 *Who 92N*
**Tweedie,** Virgil Lee 1918- *AmMWSc 92*
**Tweedle,** Charles David 1944- *AmMWSc 92*
**Tweedsmuir,** Baron 1911- *Who 92*
**Tweedy,** Billy Gene 1934- *AmMWSc 92*
**Tweedy,** Colin David 1953- *Who 92*
**Tweedy,** James Arthur 1939- *AmMWSc 92*
**Tweel,** Nicholas J. 1916- *WhoFI 92*
**Tweet,** Arthur Glenn 1927- *AmMWSc 92*
**Tweito,** Eleanor Marie 1909- *WhoMW 92*
**Twells,** John Lawrence 1934- *WhoMW 92*
**Twelves,** Robert Ralph 1927- *AmMWSc 92*
**Twelvetree,** Eric Alan 1928- *Who 92*
**Twenhofel,** William Stephens 1918- *AmMWSc 92*
**Twente,** John W 1926- *AmMWSc 92*
**Twentyman,** Esther Forbes 1924- *WhoAmP 91*
**Twersky,** Victor 1923- *AmMWSc 92*
**Twesme,** Albert Laverne 1914- *WhoAmL 92*
**Tweten,** Malcolm Stuart 1925- *WhoAmP 91*
**Tweto,** Ogden 1912- *AmMWSc 92*
**Twichell,** Chase *DrAPF 91*
**Twichell,** Joseph 1838-1918 *BenetAL 91*
**Twiddy,** Frances Elizabeth 1947- *WhoFI 92*
**Twidwell,** Carl, Jr 1927- *WhoAmP 91*
**Twidwell,** Larry G 1939- *AmMWSc 92*
**Twieg,** Donald Baker 1944- *AmMWSc 92*
**Twiest,** Gilbert Lee 1937- *AmMWSc 92*
**Twietmeyer,** Don Henry 1954- *WhoAmL 92*
**Twiford,** James 1942- *WhoAmP 91*
**Twigg,** Bernard Alvin 1928- *AmMWSc 92*
**Twigg,** Homer Lee 1926- *AmMWSc 92*
**Twigg,** Lewis Harold 1937- *WhoBlA 92*
**Twigg,** Patrick Alan 1943- *Who 92*
**Twigg-Smith,** Thurston 1921- *WhoWest 92*
**Twiggs,** Jerry T 1933- *WhoAmP 91*
**Twiggs,** Leo Franklin 1934- *WhoBlA 92*
**Twiggs,** Ralph *WhoAmP 91*
**Twiggy** *IntWW 91*
**Twiggy** 1949- *IntMPA 92, Who 92, WhoEnt 92*
**Twilegar,** Ron Jess 1943- *WhoAmP 91*
**Twilley,** Ian Charles 1927- *AmMWSc 92*
**Twilley,** Joshua Marion 1928- *WhoAmP 91*
**Twine,** Edgar Hugh 1935- *WhoBlA 92*
**Twining,** Alexander Catlin 1801-1884 *BiInAmS*
**Twining,** Linda Carol 1952- *AmMWSc 92*
**Twining,** Nathan F 1897-1982 *FacFETw*
**Twining,** Sally Shinew 1947- *AmMWSc 92*
**Twining,** William Lawrence 1934- *Who 92*
**Twinn,** Ian David 1950- *Who 92*
**Twinn,** John Ernest 1921- *Who 92*
**Twiselton,** Steven Glen 1944- *WhoMW 92*
**Twisk,** Russell Godfrey 1941- *IntAu&W 91, Who 92*
**Twisleton-Wykeham-Fiennes** *Who 92*
**Twisleton-Wykeham-Fiennes,** John 1911- *Who 92*
**Twisleton-Wykeham-Fiennes,** Maurice A. 1907- *IntWW 91*
**Twisleton-Wykeham-Fiennes,** Ranulph 1944- *IntAu&W 91*
**Twiss,** Dorothy *DrAPF 91*
**Twiss,** Frank 1910- *Who 92*
**Twiss,** Page Charles 1929- *AmMWSc 92, WhoMW 92*
**Twiss,** Peter 1921- *Who 92*
**Twiss,** Robert John 1942- *AmMWSc 92*
**Twist,** Ananias *IntAu&W 91X, WrDr 92*
**Twist,** Henry Aloysius 1914- *Who 92*
**Twist,** Robert Lanphier 1926- *WhoWest 92*
**Twitchell,** John Paul 1908?-1971 *RelLAm 91*
**Twitchell,** Kent 1942- *WhoWest 92*
**Twitchell,** Paul F 1932- *AmMWSc 92*
**Twitchell,** R Donald *WhoAmP 91*

**Twitchell,** Thomas Evans 1923- *AmMWSc 92*
**Twitchett,** Denis Crispin 1925- *IntWW 91, Who 92*
**Twite,** Robin 1932- *Who 92*
**Twitty,** Conway *WhoEnt 92*
**Twitty,** Conway 1933- *ConMus 6 [port], NewAmDM*
**Two Women of The West** *ScFEYrs*
**Twogood,** Richard Edward 1951- *WhoWest 92*
**Twohy,** Donald Wilfred 1924- *AmMWSc 92*
**Twombly,** Cy 1929- *IntWW 91, WorArt 1980*
**Twombly,** Gerard 1948- *WhoAmP 91*
**Twombly,** John C 1921- *AmMWSc 92*
**Twomey,** Burt Christian 1958- *WhoRel 92*
**Twomey,** Jeremiah John 1934- *AmMWSc 92*
**Twomey,** John J 1934- *WhoIns 92*
**Twomey,** Joseph Gerald 1926- *WhoAmL 92*
**Twomey,** Seamus 1919-1989 *FacFETw*
**Twomey,** Sean Andrew *AmMWSc 92*
**Twomey,** Thomas Aloysius, Jr. 1945- *WhoAmL 92*
**Twomley,** Bruce Clarke 1945- *WhoWest 92*
**Tworek,** Michael Lynn 1948- *WhoWest 92*
**Tworek,** Richard Kenneth 1943- *WhoMW 92*
**Tworuschka,** Udo 1949- *WhoRel 92*
**Twum,** Michael Kyei 1954- *IntAu&W 91*
**Twyford,** Donald Henry 1931- *Who 92*
**Twyman,** Alan P. 1934- *IntMPA 92*
**Twyman,** Luska J. 1914- *WhoBlA 92*
**Twyman,** Paul Hadleigh 1943- *Who 92*
**Ty-Casper,** Linda 1931- *IntAu&W 91, WrDr 92*
**Tyack,** Jim *DrAPF 91*
**Tyack,** Thomas Michael 1940- *WhoAmL 92*
**Tyacke,** David Noel Hugh 1915- *Who 92*
**Tyacke,** Sarah Jacqueline 1945- *Who 92*
**Tyagi,** Suresh C 1955- *AmMWSc 92*
**Tyan,** Marvin L 1926- *AmMWSc 92*
**Tyazhel'nikov,** Yevgeniy Mikhaylovich 1928- *SovUnBD*
**Tyberg,** John Victor 1938- *AmMWSc 92*
**Tybor,** Philip Thomas 1948- *AmMWSc 92*
**Tybout,** Richard Alton 1920- *WhoFI 92, WhoMW 92*
**Tybulewicz,** Albin 1929- *Who 92*
**Tyce,** Francis Anthony 1917- *AmMWSc 92*
**Tyce,** Gertrude Mary 1927- *AmMWSc 92*
**Tyce,** Robert Charles 1947- *AmMWSc 92*
**Tychmini,** Natalie *EncAmaz 91*
**Tychowski,** Christopher Roman 1937- *WhoWest 92*
**Tychsen,** Paul C 1916- *AmMWSc 92*
**Tycko,** Daniel H 1927- *AmMWSc 92*
**Tyconius** *EncEarC*
**Tyczka,** Mieczyslaw 1925- *IntWW 91*
**Tyczkowski,** Edward Albert 1924- *AmMWSc 92*
**Tydeman,** Frank William Edward 1901- *Who 92*
**Tydeman,** John Peter 1936- *Who 92*
**Tydeman,** William 1935- *WrDr 92*
**Tydings,** Joseph D 1928- *WhoAmP 91*
**Tye,** Alan Peter 1933- *Who 92*
**Tye,** Arthur 1909- *AmMWSc 92*
**Tye,** Bik-Kwoon 1947- *AmMWSc 92*
**Tye,** Christopher 1505?-1572? *NewAmDM*
**Tye,** George W 1946- *WhoIns 92*
**Tye,** James 1921- *Who 92*
**Tye,** Roderick 1958- *TwCPaSc*
**Tye,** Sze-Hoi Henry 1947- *AmMWSc 92*
**Tye,** Walter 1912- *Who 92*
**Tyeryar,** Franklin Joseph 1935- *AmMWSc 92*
**Tyhach,** Richard Joseph 1949- *AmMWSc 92, WhoMW 92*
**Tykeson,** Donald Erwin 1927- *WhoWest 92*
**Tykocinski,** Mark L 1952- *AmMWSc 92*
**Tykodi,** Ralph John 1925- *AmMWSc 92*
**Tyl,** Noel Jan 1936- *WhoEnt 92*
**Tyler,** Albert Vincent 1938- *AmMWSc 92*
**Tyler,** Anne *DrAPF 91*
**Tyler,** Anne 1941- *BenetAL 91, ConNov 91, IntAu&W 91, IntWW 91, ModAWWr, WrDr 92*
**Tyler,** Arthur Catchmay 1913- *Who 92*
**Tyler,** Audrey Elayne Quick 1944- *WhoBlA 92*
**Tyler,** Austin Lamont 1936- *AmMWSc 92*
**Tyler,** Bonnie Moreland 1941- *AmMWSc 92*
**Tyler,** Calvin Genota 1942- *WhoMW 92*
**Tyler,** Carol Ann 1951- *WhoWest 92*
**Tyler,** Christopher 1934- *Who 92*
**Tyler,** Christopher William 1943- *AmMWSc 92*
**Tyler,** Cyril 1911- *Who 92, WrDr 92*
**Tyler,** Daniel James 1953- *WhoRel 92*
**Tyler,** Darlene Jasmer 1939- *WhoWest 92*
**Tyler,** David E 1928- *AmMWSc 92*
**Tyler,** David Ralph 1953- *AmMWSc 92*
**Tyler,** Ellis *TwCWW 91*
**Tyler,** Frank Hill 1916- *AmMWSc 92*
**Tyler,** Gail Madeleine 1953- *WhoWest 92*
**Tyler,** George Leonard 1940- *AmMWSc 92*
**Tyler,** Gerald DeForest 1946- *WhoBlA 92*
**Tyler,** H Richard 1927- *AmMWSc 92*
**Tyler,** Hubert 1934- *WhoBlA 92*
**Tyler,** Jack D 1940- *AmMWSc 92*
**Tyler,** James Chase 1935- *AmMWSc 92*
**Tyler,** Jean Mary 1928- *AmMWSc 92*
**Tyler,** John 1790-1862 *AmPolLe [port], BenetAL 91, RComAH*
**Tyler,** John Howard 1935- *AmMWSc 92*
**Tyler,** John Lewis 1914- *WhoBlA 92*
**Tyler,** Kenneth Laurence 1953- *AmMWSc 92*
**Tyler,** Lee Malcolm 1917- *WhoBlA 92*
**Tyler,** Leona E 1906- *WomPsyc*
**Tyler,** Leonard George 1920- *Who 92*
**Tyler,** Leslie 1904- *Who 92*
**Tyler,** Leslie J 1919- *AmMWSc 92*
**Tyler,** Linda *SmATA 65 [port]*
**Tyler,** Linda W 1952- *SmATA 65 [port]*
**Tyler,** Mary Stott 1949- *AmMWSc 92*
**Tyler,** Michael Aaron 1961- *WhoFI 92*
**Tyler,** Mike 1944- *WhoAmP 91*
**Tyler,** Moses Coit 1835-1900 *BenetAL 91*
**Tyler,** Parker 1907-1974 *BenetAL 91*
**Tyler,** Paul Archer 1941- *Who 92*
**Tyler,** Paul Robert, Jr. 1955- *WhoEnt 92*
**Tyler,** R A 1920- *AmMWSc 92*
**Tyler,** Rhonda Sue 1965- *WhoWest 92*
**Tyler,** Richard Sidney 1951- *WhoEnt 92*
**Tyler,** Robert 1965- *WhoBlA 92*
**Tyler,** Robert James, Sr. 1935- *WhoBlA 92*
**Tyler,** Robert Joseph 1948- *WhoFI 92*
**Tyler,** Royall 1757-1826 *BenetAL 91, BibAL 8*
**Tyler,** Seth 1949- *AmMWSc 92*
**Tyler,** Shirley Neizer *WhoBlA 92*
**Tyler,** Stephanie S *WhoAmP 91*
**Tyler,** Stephen Albert 1932- *WrDr 92*
**Tyler,** Stephen Hunter 1959- *WhoAmL 92*
**Tyler,** Steve 1962- *WhoEnt 92*
**Tyler,** Steven Anthony 1964- *WhoWest 92*
**Tyler,** Theresa Campbell 1935- *WhoMW 92*
**Tyler,** Thomas Lee 1933- *WhoMW 92*
**Tyler,** Tim 1946- *WhoWest 92*
**Tyler,** Tipton Ransom 1941- *AmMWSc 92*
**Tyler,** Tom R. 1950- *ConAu 135*
**Tyler,** Tuck *WhoMW 92*
**Tyler,** Varro Eugene 1926- *AmMWSc 92*
**Tyler,** Waldo H. *WhoBlA 92*
**Tyler,** Walter Steele 1925- *AmMWSc 92*
**Tyler,** Wayne B 1939- *WhoIns 92*
**Tyler,** Willard Philip 1909- *AmMWSc 92*
**Tyler,** William Gurdon, III 1939- *WhoFI 92*
**Tyler,** William Royall 1910- *WhoAmP 91*
**Tyler,** Wink 1941- *WhoEnt 92*
**Tyler Browne,** Mary Ann 1939- *WhoWest 92*
**Tyler-Slaughter,** Cecil Lord 1958- *WhoBlA 92*
**Tyler-Whittle,** Michael 1927- *IntAu&W 91, WrDr 92*
**Tylutki,** Beatrice Stella 1936- *WhoAmL 92*
**Tylutki,** Edmund Eugene 1926- *AmMWSc 92*
**Tym,** Ronald D. 1954- *WhoAmL 92*
**Tymchatyn,** Edward Dmytro 1942- *AmMWSc 92*
**Tyminski,** Stanislaw 1948- *IntWW 91*
**Tymoczko,** Walter Michael 1950- *WhoFI 92*
**Tymon,** Marylyn A 1936- *WhoIns 92*
**Tynan,** Kenneth 1920-1980 *FacFETw*
**Tynan,** Michael John 1934- *Who 92*
**Tyndale-Biscoe,** Alec Julian 1906- *Who 92*
**Tyndale-Biscoe,** Cecil Hugh 1929- *IntWW 91*
**Tyndall,** J Paul *WhoAmP 91*
**Tyndall,** Jesse Parker 1925- *AmMWSc 92*
**Tyndall,** John Raymond 1942- *AmMWSc 92*
**Tyndall,** Marshall Clay, Jr. 1943- *WhoFI 92*
**Tyndall,** Nicholas John 1928- *Who 92*
**Tyndall,** Timothy 1925- *Who 92*
**Tyner,** Charles R. 1950- *WhoBlA 92*
**Tyner,** David Anson 1922- *AmMWSc 92*
**Tyner,** Earl Lankford 1918- *WhoAmL 92*
**Tyner,** George S 1916- *AmMWSc 92*
**Tyner,** John C. 1947- *WhoRel 92*
**Tyner,** Mack 1916- *AmMWSc 92*
**Tyner,** Max Raymond 1925- *WhoRel 92*
**Tyner,** McCoy 1938- *ConMus 7 [port], NewAmDM, WhoBlA 92*
**Tyner,** Mitchell Harry 1963- *WhoAmL 92*
**Tyner,** Neal Edward 1930- *WhoFI 92, WhoIns 92, WhoMW 92*
**Tyner,** Regina Lisa 1945- *WhoBlA 92*
**Tyner,** Rob d1991 *NewYTBS 91*
**Tyner,** Rob 1945?-1991 *News 92-2*
**Tynes,** Arthur Richard 1926- *AmMWSc 92*
**Tynes,** Joele Ann 1966- *WhoWest 92*
**Tynes,** Richard H. 1942- *WhoBlA 92*
**Tynyanov,** Yuriy Nikolaevich 1894-1943 *SovUnBD*
**Tyor,** Malcolm Paul 1923- *AmMWSc 92*
**Tyorinoja,** Reijo Juhani 1948- *WhoRel 92*
**Typermass,** Arthur G. 1937- *WhoFI 92*
**Typhoid Mary** 1868-1938 *FacFETw*
**Tyran,** Garry K. 1953- *WhoFI 92*
**Tyree,** Alan Dean 1929- *WhoMW 92, WhoRel 92*
**Tyree,** Bernadette *AmMWSc 92*
**Tyree,** Lewis, Jr. 1922- *WhoFI 92*
**Tyree,** Margaret Elizabeth 1951- *WhoRel 92*
**Tyree,** Melvin Thomas 1946- *AmMWSc 92*
**Tyree,** Patricia Grey 1942- *WhoBlA 92*
**Tyree,** Paul M 1942- *WhoAmP 91*
**Tyree,** Randell Lewis 1940- *WhoAmP 91*
**Tyree,** Sheppard Young, Jr 1920- *AmMWSc 92*
**Tyree,** William 1921- *Who 92*
**Tyrell-Kenyon** *Who 92*
**Tyrer,** Christopher John Meese 1944- *Who 92*
**Tyrer,** Harry Wakeley 1942- *AmMWSc 92*
**Tyrey,** Lee 1937- *AmMWSc 92*
**Tyrie,** Peter Robert 1946- *Who 92*
**Tyrl,** Ronald Jay 1943- *AmMWSc 92*
**Tyroler,** Herman A 1924- *AmMWSc 92*
**Tyrone,** Earl of 1958- *Who 92*
**Tyrone,** Jimmy Walter 1947- *WhoAmP 91*
**Tyror,** John George 1930- *Who 92*
**Tyrrell,** Alan Rupert 1933- *Who 92*
**Tyrrell,** David Arthur John 1925- *IntWW 91, Who 92, WrDr 92*
**Tyrrell,** Eleanore Day 1938- *WhoWest 92*
**Tyrrell,** Elizabeth Ann 1931- *AmMWSc 92*
**Tyrrell,** Elizabeth Dalton 1959- *WhoAmL 92*
**Tyrrell,** Gerald Fraser 1907- *Who 92*
**Tyrrell,** Henry Flansburg 1937- *AmMWSc 92*
**Tyrrell,** Henry John Valentine 1920- *Who 92*
**Tyrrell,** James 1938- *AmMWSc 92*
**Tyrrell,** James A. 1931- *WhoBlA 92*
**Tyrrell,** Karine 1940- *WhoMW 92*
**Tyrrell,** Michael Anthony 1946- *WhoAmL 92*
**Tyrrell,** Murray 1913- *Who 92*
**Tyrrell,** Phillip E 1932- *WhoAmP 91*
**Tyrrell,** Susan 1946- *IntMPA 92*
**Tyrrell,** Thomas Lyal 1935- *WhoMW 92*
**Tyrrell,** Valentine *Who 92*
**Tyrrell,** William Warren 1949- *WhoMW 92*
**Tyrrell,** Willis W, Jr 1930- *AmMWSc 92*
**Tyrsa,** Nikolay Andreevich 1887-1942 *SovUnBD*
**Tyrus,** Judy Elizabeth 1960- *WhoEnt 92*
**Tyrwhitt,** Mary 1903- *Who 92*
**Tyrwhitt,** Reginald 1947- *Who 92*
**Tyrwhitt,** Ursula 1878-1966 *TwCPaSc*
**Tysdahl,** Bjorn Johan 1933- *WrDr 92*
**Tysdal,** Lauris Lloyd 1949- *WhoAmP 91*
**Tyshler,** Aleksandr Grigor'evich 1898-1980 *SovUnBD*
**Tysiac,** Lawrence Leon 1953- *WhoFI 92*
**Tysinger,** James W *WhoAmP 91*
**Tyson,** Alan Walker 1926- *IntWW 91, Who 92*
**Tyson,** Albert Dillard, Jr. 1927- *WhoRel 92*
**Tyson,** Bertrand Oliver 1931- *WhoBlA 92*
**Tyson,** Cicely *WhoEnt 92*
**Tyson,** Cicely 1933- *IntMPA 92, WhoBlA 92*
**Tyson,** Cicely 1942- *NotBlAW 92 [port]*
**Tyson,** Cleveland Allen 1946- *WhoBlA 92*
**Tyson,** Donald John 1930- *WhoFI 92*
**Tyson,** Greta E 1933- *AmMWSc 92*
**Tyson,** H. Michael 1938- *WhoFI 92*
**Tyson,** Harvey Wood 1928- *IntWW 91*
**Tyson,** Henry M *WhoAmP 91*
**Tyson,** Ian 1933- *TwCPaSc*
**Tyson,** J Anthony 1940- *AmMWSc 92*
**Tyson,** J Aubrey 1870-1930 *ScFEYrs*
**Tyson,** James 1841-1919 *BiInAmS*
**Tyson,** James Edward 1959- *WhoWest 92*
**Tyson,** John *WhoEnt 92*
**Tyson,** John C. 1951- *WhoBlA 92*
**Tyson,** John David, Jr. 1937- *WhoFI 92*
**Tyson,** John Edward Alfred 1935- *AmMWSc 92*
**Tyson,** John Jeanes 1947- *AmMWSc 92*
**Tyson,** John Marsh 1953- *WhoFI 92*
**Tyson,** John Rodger 1952- *WhoRel 92*
**Tyson,** Joseph B. 1928- *WrDr 92*
**Tyson,** Joseph Blake 1928- *WhoRel 92*
**Tyson,** Lorena E. 1933- *WhoBlA 92*
**Tyson,** Michael Gerard 1966- *FacFETw*
**Tyson,** Mike *NewYTBS 91 [port]*
**Tyson,** Mike 1966- *WhoBlA 92*
**Tyson,** Mike G. 1966- *IntWW 91*
**Tyson,** Monica Elizabeth 1927- *Who 92*
**Tyson,** Patti Birge *WhoAmL 92, WhoFI 92*
**Tyson,** Patti Birge 1939- *WhoAmP 91*
**Tyson,** Philip Thomas 1799-1877 *BiInAmS*
**Tyson,** Ralph Robert 1920- *AmMWSc 92*
**Tyson,** William Russell 1939- *AmMWSc 92*
**Tysseland,** Terry Lawrence 1941- *WhoWest 92*
**Tysver,** Joseph Bryce 1918- *AmMWSc 92*
**Tyszkiewicz,** Robert Edward 1948- *WhoWest 92*
**Tytanic,** Christopher Alan 1961- *WhoAmL 92*
**Tytler,** Christian Helen F. *Who 92*
**Tytler,** Donald Alexander *Who 92*
**Tytler,** Linda Jean 1947- *WhoAmP 91, WhoWest 92*
**Tyukalov,** Yuriy Antonovich 1930- *SovUnBD*
**Tyus,** E Leroy 1916- *WhoAmP 91*
**Tyus,** Wyomia 1945- *BlkOlyM [port], WhoBlA 92*
**Tyutchev,** Fyodor 1803-1873 *NinCLC 34 [port]*
**Tyzack,** Margaret Maud 1931- *Who 92*
**Tyzack,** Michael 1933- *TwCPaSc*
**Tyzbir,** Robert S *AmMWSc 92*
**Tyznik,** William John 1927- *AmMWSc 92*
**Tzadua,** Paulos 1921- *WhoRel 92*
**Tzafestas,** Spyros G 1939- *AmMWSc 92*
**Tzagournis,** Manuel 1934- *AmMWSc 92*
**Tzall,** Wayne Allen 1946- *WhoFI 92*
**Tzanakou,** M Evangelia *AmMWSc 92*
**Tzangas,** George John 1930- *WhoAmL 92*
**Tzara,** Tristan 1896-1953 *FacFETw*
**Tzara,** Tristan 1896-1963 *LiExTwC*
**Tzavella,** Moscho *EncAmaz 91*
**Tzavella-Evjen,** Hara 1936- *WhoWest 92*
**Tzeng,** Chu 1940- *AmMWSc 92*
**Tzeng,** Chun-Hung 1944- *WhoMW 92*
**Tzeng,** Kenneth Kai-Ming 1937- *AmMWSc 92*
**Tzeng,** Wen-Shian Vincent 1943- *AmMWSc 92*
**Tzianabos,** Theodore 1933- *AmMWSc 92*
**Tzighan,** Margarita Alleman 1949- *WhoEnt 92*
**Tzodikov,** Nathan Robert 1952- *AmMWSc 92*
**Tzoganakis,** Costas 1960- *AmMWSc 92*
**Tzomes,** Chancellor Alfonso 1944- *WhoBlA 92*
**Tzou,** Tsi-Zong 1961- *WhoMW 92*

# U

**U Thant** 1909-1974 *FacFETw*
**U Than Aung,** Alphonse *WhoRel 92*
**U2** *NewAmDM*
**Uathach** *EncAmaz 91*
**Uatioa,** Mere 1924- *Who 92*
**Ubaldini,** Cia degli *EncAmaz 91*
**Uban,** Stephen A 1950- *AmMWSc 92*
**Ubarry,** Grizel 1953- *WhoHisp 92*
**Ubbelohde,** Robert Allen 1942- *WhoMW 92*
**Ubben,** Donald Thomas 1946- *WhoAmL 92*
**Ubee,** Sydney Richard 1903- *Who 92*
**Ubelaker,** Douglas Henry 1946- *AmMWSc 92*
**Ubelaker,** John E 1940- *AmMWSc 92*
**Uber,** David Albert 1921- *WhoEnt 92*
**Uberall,** Herbert Michael 1931- *AmMWSc 92*
**Uberoi,** M S 1924- *AmMWSc 92*
**Ubleis,** Heinrich 1933- *IntWW 91*
**Ubukata,** Taiji 1916- *IntWW 91*
**Ucci,** Pompelio Angelo 1922- *AmMWSc 92*
**Uchida,** Irene Ayako 1917- *AmMWSc 92*
**Uchida,** Mitsuko 1948- *CurBio 91 [port], IntWW 91*
**Uchida,** Richard Noboru 1929- *AmMWSc 92*
**Uchida,** Yoshiko *DrAPF 91*
**Uchida,** Yoshiko 1921- *WrDr 92*
**Uchimura,** Glenn G. 1952- *WhoFI 92*
**Uchimura,** Susan Wiersma 1961- *WhoEnt 92*
**Uchitelle,** Louis 1932- *WhoFI 92*
**Uchupi,** Elazar 1928- *AmMWSc 92*
**Ucko,** David A 1948- *AmMWSc 92*
**Ucko,** David Alan 1948- *WhoFI 92, WhoMW 92*
**ud-Din,** Khair- 1921- *Who 92*
**Udall,** Jan Beaney 1938- *ConAu 35NR*
**Udall,** John Alfred 1929- *AmMWSc 92*
**Udall,** John Nicholas, Jr 1940- *AmMWSc 92*
**Udall,** Morris 1922- *IntWW 91*
**Udall,** Morris K. 1922- *AlmAP 92 [port]*
**Udall,** Morris King 1922- *WhoAmP 91, WhoWest 92*
**Udall,** Nicholas 1504-1556? *RfGEnL 91*
**Udall,** Stewart Lee 1920- *IntWW 91*
**Udall,** Tom 1948- *WhoAmL 92, WhoAmP 91, WhoWest 92*
**Udaltsova,** Nadezhda 1886-1961 *FacFETw*
**Udal'tsova,** Nadezhda Andreevna 1886-1961 *SovUnBD*
**Udani,** Kanakkumar Harilal 1936- *AmMWSc 92*
**Udani,** Lalit Kumar Harilal 1927- *AmMWSc 92*
**Udavchak,** Raymond M 1933- *WhoIns 92*
**Udd,** John Eaman 1937- *AmMWSc 92*
**Uddin,** Shafique 1962- *TwCPaSc*
**Ude,** Wayne *DrAPF 91*
**Ude,** Wayne 1946- *TwCWW 91, WrDr 92*
**Udell,** Charles 1949- *WhoFI 92, WhoMW 92*
**Udell,** Gerald Gail 1936- *WhoMW 92*
**Udell,** Jon Gerald 1935- *WhoFI 92, WhoMW 92*
**Udell,** Richard 1932- *WhoAmL 92, WhoFI 92*
**Udelson,** Daniel G 1929- *AmMWSc 92*
**Udem,** Stephen Alexander 1944- *AmMWSc 92*
**Uden,** Cynthia Kay 1952- *WhoMW 92*
**Uden,** James Edward 1937- *WhoMW 92*
**Uden,** Peter Christopher 1939- *AmMWSc 92*
**Udenfriend,** Sidney 1918- *AmMWSc 92, IntWW 91*
**Udet,** Ernst 1896-1941 *EncTR 91 [port]*
**Udin,** Susan Boymel 1947- *AmMWSc 92*
**Udipi,** Kishore 1940- *AmMWSc 92*
**Udland,** Melvin Orlo 1946- *WhoMW 92*
**Udler,** Dmitry 1954- *AmMWSc 92*
**Udo,** Reuben Kenrick 1935- *ConAu 35NR*
**Udo,** Tatsuo 1925- *AmMWSc 92*
**Udod,** Hryhory 1925- *WhoRel 92*
**Udolf,** Roy 1926- *AmMWSc 92*
**Udoma,** Udo 1917- *IntWW 91, Who 92*
**Udovic,** Daniel 1947- *AmMWSc 92*
**Udry,** J. Richard 1928- *WrDr 92*
**Udry,** Janice 1928- *WrDr 92*
**Udry,** Joe Richard 1928- *AmMWSc 92*
**Udvardy,** Miklos Dezso Ferenc 1919- *AmMWSc 92*
**Udvarhelyi,** George Bela 1920- *AmMWSc 92*
**Udvary,** Alex Thomas 1947- *WhoEnt 92*
**Udwadia,** Firdaus Erach 1947- *WhoFI 92, WhoWest 92*
**Udy,** Lex Lynn 1933- *WhoFI 92*
**Uebbing,** John Julian 1937- *AmMWSc 92*
**Uebel,** Jacob John 1937- *AmMWSc 92*
**Uebele,** Curtis Eugene 1935- *AmMWSc 92*
**Ueberroth,** Peter 1937- *IntWW 91*
**Uebersax,** Mark Alan 1948- *AmMWSc 92*
**Uecker,** Bob 1935- *WhoEnt 92*
**Uecker,** Francis August 1930- *AmMWSc 92*
**Ueckert,** Charlotte 1944- *IntAu&W 91*
**Ueda,** Clarence Tad 1942- *AmMWSc 92*
**Ueda,** Issaku 1924- *WhoWest 92*
**Ueda,** Makoto 1931- *ConAu 34NR, WrDr 92*
**Ueda,** Takeshi 1941- *WhoFI 92*
**Uehara,** Hiroshi 1923- *AmMWSc 92*
**Uehara,** Osamu 1960- *WhoEnt 92*
**Uehlein,** Edward Carl, Jr. 1941- *WhoAmL 92*
**Uehling,** Barbara S. 1932- *IntWW 91*
**Uehling,** Barbara Staner 1932- *WhoWest 92*
**Uehling,** Gordon Alexander, Jr. 1939- *WhoFI 92*
**Uehling,** Leha Karlyn 1963- *WhoMW 92*
**Uehling,** Rick 1953- *WhoAmP 91*
**Ueki,** Shigeaki 1935- *IntWW 91*
**Ueland,** Arnulf, Jr 1920- *WhoAmP 91*
**Ueland,** Kent 1931- *AmMWSc 92*
**Uematsu,** Kunihiko 1931- *IntWW 91*
**Uematsu,** Yoshiaki 1957- *WhoFI 92*
**Uemura,** Joseph Norio 1926- *WhoMW 92, WhoRel 92*
**Uemura,** Yasutomo J 1953- *AmMWSc 92*
**Ueng,** Charles E S 1930- *AmMWSc 92*
**Ueno,** Hiroshi 1950- *AmMWSc 92*
**Ueno,** Taichi 1924- *IntWW 91*
**Uetz,** George William 1946- *AmMWSc 92, WhoMW 92*
**Ufberg,** Murray 1943- *WhoAmL 92*
**Ufema,** John William 1946- *WhoFI 92*
**Uff,** John Francis 1942- *Who 92*
**Uffen,** Kenneth James 1925- *IntWW 91, Who 92*
**Uffen,** Robert James 1923- *AmMWSc 92, IntWW 91*
**Uffen,** Robert L 1937- *AmMWSc 92*
**Uffner,** Beth Marilyn 1942- *WhoEnt 92*
**Uffner,** Michael S. 1945- *WhoFI 92*
**Ufford,** Charles Wilbur, Jr. 1931- *WhoAmL 92*
**Ufholz,** Philip John 1947- *WhoAmP 91*
**Ugai,** Susan Marie 1956- *WhoAmL 92*
**Uganda,** Archbishop of 1927- *Who 92*
**Ugarov,** Boris Sergeevich 1922- *IntWW 91*
**Ugarte,** Eduardo 1935- *AmMWSc 92*
**Ugarte,** Jose M. 1941- *WhoHisp 92*
**Ugaste,** Daniel John 1963- *WhoAmL 92*
**Ugbisien,** Moses 1964- *BlkOlyM*
**Ugent,** Alvin Ronald 1929- *WhoAmL 92*
**Ugent,** Donald 1933- *AmMWSc 92*
**Ugent,** Geoffrey Raymond 1956- *WhoRel 92*
**Ugent,** Warren David 1946- *WhoMW 92*
**Uggams,** Leslie 1943- *IntMPA 92, NewAmDM, WhoBlA 92, WhoEnt 92*
**Uggerud,** Ward Lee 1949- *WhoMW 92*
**Ughetta,** William C. 1954- *WhoAmL 92*
**Ughetti,** Dana Marie 1961- *WhoEnt 92*
**Ughi,** Uto 1944- *IntWW 91*
**Ugincius,** Peter 1936- *AmMWSc 92*
**Uglanov,** Nikolay Aleksandrovich 1886-1940 *SovUnBD*
**Uglem,** Gary Lee 1941- *AmMWSc 92*
**Uglow,** Euan 1932- *IntWW 91, TwCPaSc*
**Uglow,** William Gary 1947- *WhoFI 92*
**Uglum,** John Richard 1909- *WhoAmP 91*
**Ugolini,** Fiorenzo Cesare 1929- *AmMWSc 92*
**Ugolyn,** Victor 1947- *WhoFI 92*
**Ugron,** Duane Lee 1966- *WhoMW 92*
**Ugueto,** Luis 1936- *IntWW 91*
**Ugurbil,** Kamil 1949- *AmMWSc 92*
**Ugwu,** David Egbo 1950- *WhoMW 92*
**Ugwu,** Gabriel Nebechi 1951- *WhoEnt 92, WhoMW 92*
**Uhart,** Michael Scott 1948- *AmMWSc 92*
**Uhde,** Larry Jackson 1939- *WhoWest 92*
**Uhde,** Thomas Whitley *AmMWSc 92*
**Uher,** D R 1937- *WhoAmP 91*
**Uher,** Lorna *WrDr 92*
**Uher,** Richard Anthony 1939- *AmMWSc 92*
**Uherka,** David Jerome 1938- *AmMWSc 92*
**Uherka,** Kenneth L. 1937- *WhoMW 92*
**Uherka,** Kenneth Leroy 1937- *AmMWSc 92*
**Uhl,** Arthur E 1929- *AmMWSc 92*
**Uhl,** Charles Harrison 1918- *AmMWSc 92*
**Uhl,** John Jerry, Jr 1940- *AmMWSc 92, WhoMW 92*
**Uhl,** Melvin John 1915- *ConAu 34NR*
**Uhl,** Petr 1941- *IntWW 91*
**Uhl,** Philip Edward 1949- *WhoWest 92*
**Uhl,** Thomas Edward 1961- *WhoFI 92*
**Uhl,** V W 1917- *AmMWSc 92*
**Uhlaner,** Julius Earl 1917- *WhoWest 92*
**Uhlein,** Gabriele 1952- *WhoRel 92*
**Uhlenbeck,** George Eugene 1900- *AmMWSc 92*
**Uhlenbeck,** Karen K 1942- *AmMWSc 92*
**Uhlenbeck,** Olke Cornelis 1942- *AmMWSc 92*
**Uhlenbrock,** Dietrich A 1937- *AmMWSc 92*
**Uhlenhake,** Helen Idell 1922- *WhoAmP 91*
**Uhlenhop,** Paul Buscher 1936- *WhoMW 92*
**Uhlenhopp,** Elliott Lee 1942- *AmMWSc 92*
**Uhlenhuth,** Eberhard Henry 1927- *AmMWSc 92*
**Uhler,** Michael David 1956- *AmMWSc 92*
**Uhler,** Philip Reese 1835-1913 *BiInAmS*
**Uhlhorn,** Kenneth W 1933- *AmMWSc 92*
**Uhlig,** Herbert H 1907- *AmMWSc 92*
**Uhlig,** John Walter 1952- *WhoWest 92*
**Uhlinger,** Susan J. 1942-1980 *ConAu 34NR*
**Uhlir,** Arthur, Jr 1926- *AmMWSc 92*
**Uhlir,** Golby Cleigh 1932- *WhoAmL 92*
**Uhlman,** Fred 1901- *TwCPaSc*
**Uhlman,** Fred 1901-1985? *ConAu 34NR*
**Uhlman,** Thomas Michael 1947- *WhoWest 92*
**Uhlman,** Wesley Carl 1935- *WhoAmP 91*
**Uhlmann,** Donald Robert 1936- *AmMWSc 92, WhoWest 92*
**Uhnak,** Dorothy 1933- *IntAu&W 91, WrDr 92*
**Uhr,** Jonathan William 1927- *AmMWSc 92*
**Uhr,** Leonard Merrick 1927- *AmMWSc 92*
**Uhran,** John Joseph, Jr *AmMWSc 92*
**Uhran,** John Joseph, Jr. 1935- *WhoMW 92*
**Uhrey,** Robert Lee 1926- *WhoWest 92*
**Uhrich,** David Lee 1939- *AmMWSc 92*
**Uhrich,** Richard Beckley 1932- *WhoWest 92*
**Uhrig,** Jerome Lee *AmMWSc 92*
**Uhrig,** Robert Eugene 1928- *AmMWSc 92*
**Uhrman,** Celia 1927- *IntAu&W 91*
**Uhry,** Alfred 1936- *ConAu 133, WrDr 92*
**Uhry,** Alfred Fox 1936- *WhoEnt 92*
**Uhse,** Bodo 1904-1963 *LiExTwC*
**Uht,** Augustus Kinzel 1955- *WhoWest 92*
**Uicker,** John Joseph, Jr 1938- *AmMWSc 92*
**Uihlein,** Justin Phillip 1949- *WhoMW 92*
**Uipi,** Phil H 1949- *WhoAmP 91*
**Uitti,** Roger William 1934- *WhoRel 92*
**Uitto,** Jouni Jorma 1943- *AmMWSc 92*
**Ujfalussy,** Jozsef 1920- *IntWW 91*
**Ukeles,** Ravenna 1929- *AmMWSc 92*
**Ukena,** Paul d1991 *NewYTBS 91*
**Ukleja,** Paul Leonard Matthew 1946- *AmMWSc 92*
**Ukpong,** Justin Sampson 1940- *WhoRel 92*
**Ukrainetz,** Paul Ruvim 1935- *AmMWSc 92*
**Ukropina,** James Robert 1937- *WhoFI 92, WhoWest 92*
**Uku,** Eustace Oris, Sr. 1947- *WhoBlA 92*
**Ulabarro,** Jose Antonio, Jr. 1933- *WhoHisp 92*
**Ulaby,** Fawwaz Tayssir 1943- *AmMWSc 92*
**Ulagaraj,** Munivandy Seydunganallur 1944- *AmMWSc 92*
**Ulakovich,** Ronald Stephen 1942- *WhoFI 92, WhoMW 92*
**Ulam,** Adam Bruno 1922- *IntAu&W 91, WrDr 92*
**Ulam,** S M 1909-1984 *ConAu 34NR*
**Ulam,** Stanislaw Marcin 1909-1984 *FacFETw*

**Ulano**, Solomon Paul 1920- *WhoEnt 92*
**Ulanova**, Galina Sergeevna 1910- *SovUnBD*
**Ulanova**, Galina Sergeyevna 1910- *FacFETw, IntWW 91, Who 92*
**Ulanowicz**, Robert Edward 1943- *AmMWSc 92*
**Ulanowsky**, Paul 1908-1968 *NewAmDM*
**Ulberg**, Lester Curtiss 1917- *AmMWSc 92*
**Ulbrecht**, Jaromir Josef 1928- *AmMWSc 92*
**Ulbrich**, Carlton Wilbur 1932- *AmMWSc 92*
**Ulbricht**, Walter 1893-1973 *EncTR 91 [port], FacFETw*
**Ulch**, Bryan Dee 1948- *WhoWest 92*
**Ulderich**, Thomas Earl 1955- *WhoRel 92*
**Uldrick**, John Paul 1929- *AmMWSc 92*
**Ulene**, Arthur Lawrence 1936- *WhoEnt 92*
**Ulery**, Dana Lynn 1938- *AmMWSc 92*
**Ulevitch**, Richard Joel 1944- *AmMWSc 92*
**Ulewicz**, Laura Louise *DrAPF 91*
**Ulf**, Franklin Edgar 1931- *WhoFI 92*
**Ulf**, Haerved *ConAu 135*
**Ulf**, Harved *ConAu 135*
**Ulfelder**, Howard 1911- *AmMWSc 92*
**Ulfilas** 311?-383? *EncEarC*
**Ulfung**, Ragnar Sigurd 1927- *WhoEnt 92*
**Uliana**, Joseph M 1965- *WhoAmP 91*
**Ulibarri**, John E. 1939- *WhoHisp 92*
**Ulibarri**, John Elias 1939- *WhoAmP 91*
**Ulibarri**, Sabine R. 1919- *WhoHisp 92*
**Ulibarri**, Yvonne 1956- *WhoHisp 92*
**Ulich**, Bobby Lee 1947- *AmMWSc 92*
**Ulich**, Willie Lee 1920- *AmMWSc 92*
**Ulichny**, Barbara Lynn 1947- *WhoAmP 91*
**Ulin**, Robert Mark 1961- *WhoEnt 92*
**Ulinski**, Philip Steven 1943- *AmMWSc 92*
**Ulisse**, Peter J. *DrAPF 91*
**Ulissey**, Catherine *WhoEnt 92*
**Ulke**, Henry 1821-1910 *BiInAmS*
**Ullal**, Marcia Ann 1955- *WhoWest 92*
**Ullendorff**, Edward 1920- *IntWW 91, Who 92, WrDr 92*
**Ulliman**, Joseph James 1935- *AmMWSc 92, WhoWest 92*
**Ullman**, Arthur William James 1936- *AmMWSc 92*
**Ullman**, Edwin Fisher 1930- *AmMWSc 92*
**Ullman**, Frank Gordon 1926- *AmMWSc 92*
**Ullman**, Jack Donald 1929- *AmMWSc 92*
**Ullman**, James Ramsey 1907-1971 *BenetAL 91*
**Ullman**, Jeffrey D 1942- *AmMWSc 92*
**Ullman**, Jeffrey David 1942- *WhoWest 92*
**Ullman**, Joseph Leonard 1923- *AmMWSc 92*
**Ullman**, Leo Solomon 1939- *WhoAmL 92*
**Ullman**, Leslie *DrAPF 91*
**Ullman**, Marie 1914- *WhoFI 92*
**Ullman**, Myron Edward, III 1946- *WhoFI 92*
**Ullman**, Nelly Szabo 1925- *AmMWSc 92*
**Ullman**, Robert 1920- *AmMWSc 92*
**Ullman**, Tracey 1959?- *ConTFT 9, IntMPA 92, WhoEnt 92*
**Ullmann**, John E 1923- *AmMWSc 92, ConAu 34NR, WrDr 92*
**Ullmann**, Liv 1938- *Who 92, WhoEnt 92*
**Ullmann**, Liv 1939- *IntMPA 92*
**Ullmann**, Liv Johanne 1938- *IntWW 91*
**Ullo**, J Chris 1928- *WhoAmP 91*
**Ulloa**, Antonio de 1716-1795 *BenetAL 91, HisDSpE*
**Ulloa**, Eunice *WhoHisp 92*
**Ulloa**, Sergio E. 1955- *WhoHisp 92*
**Ulloa**, Sergio Eduarod 1955- *WhoMW 92*
**Ulloa Elias**, Manuel 1922- *IntWW 91*
**Ullom**, Marc Fredric 1947- *WhoAmL 92*
**Ullom**, Stephen Virgil 1938- *AmMWSc 92*
**Ulloth**, Dana Royal 1941- *WhoEnt 92*
**Ullrey**, Duane Earl 1928- *AmMWSc 92*
**Ullrich**, David Frederick 1937- *AmMWSc 92*
**Ullrich**, Donald William, Jr. 1952- *WhoAmL 92*
**Ullrich**, Felix Thomas 1939- *AmMWSc 92*
**Ullrich**, John Frederick 1940- *WhoMW 92*
**Ullrich**, Robert Albert 1939- *WhoFI 92*
**Ullrich**, Robert Carl 1940- *AmMWSc 92*
**Ullrich**, Robert Leo 1947- *AmMWSc 92*
**Ullrick**, William Charles 1924- *AmMWSc 92*
**Ullsten**, Ola 1931- *IntWW 91*
**Ullswater**, Viscount 1942- *Who 92*
**Ullyot**, Glenn Edgar 1910- *AmMWSc 92*
**Ulm**, Edgar H 1942- *AmMWSc 92*
**Ulm**, Lester, Jr 1922- *AmMWSc 92*
**Ulman**, Karyn Melanie 1954- *WhoEnt 92*
**Ulman**, Roman Witold 1942- *WhoAmP 91*
**Ulmer**, Daniel P 1950- *WhoAmP 91*
**Ulmer**, Edgar 1904-1972 *IntDcF 2-2 [port]*
**Ulmer**, Eldon Robert 1918- *WhoAmP 91*
**Ulmer**, Frances Ann *WhoAmP 91*
**Ulmer**, Gene Carleton 1937- *AmMWSc 92*
**Ulmer**, James 1942- *NewAmDM*
**Ulmer**, Melville Jack 1911- *WhoFI 92*
**Ulmer**, Melville Paul 1943- *AmMWSc 92*
**Ulmer**, Millard B 1946- *AmMWSc 92*
**Ulmer**, Raymond Arthur 1923- *AmMWSc 92, WhoAmL 92*
**Ulmer**, Richard Clyde 1909- *AmMWSc 92*
**Ulmer**, Ronald Joseph 1929- *WhoRel 92*
**Ulness**, Jeffrey Mark 1960- *WhoAmL 92*
**Ulosevich**, Steven Nils 1947- *WhoWest 92*
**Uloth**, Robert Henry 1927- *AmMWSc 92*
**Ulph**, Owen 1914- *ConAu 133*
**Ulpian**, Carla 1947- *AmMWSc 92*
**Ulrey**, Stephen Scott 1946- *AmMWSc 92*
**Ulrich**, Aaron Jack 1921- *AmMWSc 92*
**Ulrich**, Arthur Raymond, Jr. 1946- *WhoRel 92*
**Ulrich**, Benjamin H, Jr 1922- *AmMWSc 92*
**Ulrich**, Betty Garton 1919- *IntAu&W 91*
**Ulrich**, Celeste 1924- *WhoWest 92*
**Ulrich**, Christian Roy 1953- *WhoMW 92, WhoRel 92*
**Ulrich**, Dale V 1932- *AmMWSc 92*
**Ulrich**, Dave 1953- *WhoMW 92*
**Ulrich**, Delmont Marion 1919- *WhoWest 92*
**Ulrich**, Dennis Nicholas 1949- *WhoMW 92*
**Ulrich**, Diane Lynne 1950- *WhoAmP 91*
**Ulrich**, Frank 1926- *AmMWSc 92*
**Ulrich**, Gael Dennis 1935- *AmMWSc 92*
**Ulrich**, Gerhard Alfred 1957- *WhoMW 92*
**Ulrich**, Gertrude Willems 1927- *WhoAmP 91*
**Ulrich**, Gregory Glenn 1960- *WhoEnt 92*
**Ulrich**, Henri 1925- *AmMWSc 92*
**Ulrich**, Homer 1906-1987 *ConAu 36NR*
**Ulrich**, Jeannette *WhoHisp 92*
**Ulrich**, John August 1915- *AmMWSc 92*
**Ulrich**, Joyce Louise 1956- *WhoFI 92*
**Ulrich**, Martin Dale 1952- *WhoFI 92*
**Ulrich**, Max Marsh 1925- *WhoFI 92*
**Ulrich**, Merwyn Gene 1936- *AmMWSc 92*
**Ulrich**, Paul Graham 1938- *WhoAmL 92, WhoFI 92, WhoWest 92*
**Ulrich**, Reinhard 1929- *WhoRel 92*
**Ulrich**, Richard William 1950- *WhoFI 92*
**Ulrich**, Robert 1933- *WhoAmP 91*
**Ulrich**, Robert Gardner 1935- *WhoAmL 92, WhoFI 92*
**Ulrich**, Roger Steffen 1946- *AmMWSc 92*
**Ulrich**, Shirley Irene 1926- *WhoAmP 91*
**Ulrich**, Theodore Albert 1943- *WhoAmL 92*
**Ulrich**, Valentin 1926- *AmMWSc 92*
**Ulrich**, Walter Otto 1927- *Who 92*
**Ulrich**, Werner 1931- *AmMWSc 92*
**Ulrich**, William Frederick 1926- *AmMWSc 92*
**Ulrichsen**, Wilhelm 1924- *IntWW 91*
**Ulrichson**, Dean LeRoy 1937- *AmMWSc 92*
**Ulrych**, Tadeusz Jan 1935- *AmMWSc 92*
**Ulsamer**, Andrew George, Jr 1941- *AmMWSc 92*
**Ulsenheimer**, Dean 1941- *WhoMW 92*
**Ulseth**, George Walter 1918- *WhoIns 92*
**Ulseth**, Harold Allyn 1928- *WhoRel 92*
**Ulsoy**, Ali Galip 1950- *WhoMW 92*
**Ulster**, Earl of 1974- *Who 92*
**Ulstrom**, Robert 1923- *AmMWSc 92*
**Ulstrup**, Leif Christian 1963- *WhoFI 92*
**Ultan**, Lloyd 1929- *WhoEnt 92*
**Ultee**, Casper Jan 1928- *AmMWSc 92*
**Ultman**, James Stuart 1943- *AmMWSc 92*
**Ultmann**, John Ernest 1925- *AmMWSc 92, WhoMW 92*
**Ulug**, Esin M *AmMWSc 92*
**Ulum**, Jennifer Lynn 1957- *WhoWest 92*
**Ulusu**, Bulent 1923- *IntWW 91*
**Ulvang**, John 1929- *WhoAmP 91*
**Ulvedal**, Frode 1932- *AmMWSc 92*
**Ulveling**, Roger Alan 1943- *WhoWest 92*
**Ulvila**, Jacob Walter 1950- *WhoFI 92*
**Ulyanov**, Mikhail Aleksandrovich 1927- *IntWW 91, SovUnBD*
**Ul'yanov**, Nikolay Pavlovich 1875-1949 *SovUnBD*
**Ul'yanova**, Mariya Ilichna 1878-1937 *SovUnBD*
**Uman**, Martin A 1936- *AmMWSc 92*
**Uman**, Myron F 1939- *AmMWSc 92*
**Umans**, Robert Scott 1941- *AmMWSc 92*
**Umansky**, Raphael Douglas 1950- *WhoAmL 92*
**Umanzio**, Carl Beeman 1907- *AmMWSc 92*
**Umba Di Lutete** 1939- *IntWW 91*
**Umba Kyamitala** 1937- *IntWW 91*
**Umbach**, Eberle *DrAPF 91*
**Umbach**, Lawrence Cutler 1932- *WhoFI 92*
**Umbarger**, H Edwin 1921- *AmMWSc 92*
**UmBayemake Joachim**, Linda 1953- *WhoBlA 92*
**Umbdenstock**, Ronald 1950- *WhoEnt 92*
**Umbeck**, John Robert 1945- *WhoMW 92*
**Umbehagen**, Mark Dean 1960- *WhoRel 92*
**Umbehocker**, Kenneth Sheldon 1934- *WhoRel 92*
**Umberg**, Tom 1955- *WhoAmP 91*
**Umberger**, Debbie Ann Ziegler 1968- *WhoEnt 92*
**Umberger**, Ernest Joy 1909- *AmMWSc 92*
**Umberger**, Wallace Randolph, Jr. 1942- *WhoEnt 92*
**Umbreit**, Gerald Ross 1930- *AmMWSc 92*
**Umbreit**, LeBertha 1952- *WhoBlA 92*
**Umbreit**, Wayne William 1913- *AmMWSc 92*
**Umeda**, Patrick Kaichi *AmMWSc 92*
**Umeda**, Zenji 1913- *IntWW 91*
**Umemoto**, Don George 1945- *WhoWest 92*
**Umen**, Michael Jay 1948- *AmMWSc 92*
**Umetsu**, Dale T. 1951- *WhoWest 92*
**Umezawa**, Hiroomi 1924- *AmMWSc 92, WhoWest 92*
**Umholtz**, Clyde Allan 1947- *AmMWSc 92, WhoFI 92*
**Uminowicz**, William Chester 1944- *WhoMW 92*
**Umland**, Pauline Sawyer 1903- *WhoWest 92*
**Ummel**, J. Wesley 1942- *WhoMW 92, WhoRel 92*
**Ummel**, Stephen 1941- *WhoMW 92*
**Ummer**, James Walter 1945- *WhoAmL 92*
**Umminger**, Bruce Lynn 1941- *AmMWSc 92*
**Umolu**, Mary Harden 1927- *WhoBlA 92*
**Umphlett**, Wiley Lee 1931- *ConAu 34NR*
**Umphres**, Jerry Darmond 1931- *WhoWest 92*
**Umpierre**, Gustavo 1931- *WhoHisp 92*
**Umpierre**, Luz Maria 1947- *WhoHisp 92*
**Umpierre-Herrera**, Luzma 1947- *WhoHisp 92*
**Umpierre-Suarez**, Enrique 1941- *WhoHisp 92*
**Umrath**, Oskar 1913-1943 *EncTR 91*
**Umri**, Hassan *IntWW 91*
**Umscheid**, Christina-Ma *DrAPF 91*
**Umstattd**, Elizabeth Coles 1933- *WhoAmP 91*
**Un**, Chong Kwan 1940- *AmMWSc 92*
**Un**, Howard Ho-Wei 1938- *AmMWSc 92*
**Unada** *WrDr 92*
**Unaeze**, Felix Eme 1952- *WhoBlA 92*
**Unakar**, Nalin J 1935- *AmMWSc 92*
**Unakar**, Nalin Jayantilal 1935- *WhoMW 92*
**Unal**, Aynur 1946- *AmMWSc 92*
**Unamuno**, Miguel de 1864-1936 *DcLB 108 [port], LiExTwC*
**Unangst**, Paul Charles 1944- *AmMWSc 92*
**Unanue**, Emil R 1934- *AmMWSc 92*
**Unanue**, Frank *WhoHisp 92*
**Unanue**, Joseph A. 1926- *WhoHisp 92*
**Unanue**, Joseph F. 1957- *WhoHisp 92*
**Unanue**, Mary Ann 1959- *WhoHisp 92*
**Unbehaun**, Laraine Marie 1940- *AmMWSc 92*
**Uncapher**, Chester Laird 1943- *WhoMW 92*
**Uncas** 1588?-1682? *RComAH*
**Underberg**, Mark Alan 1955- *WhoAmL 92*
**Undercliffe**, Errol *IntAu&W 91X*
**Underdahl**, Norman Russell 1918- *AmMWSc 92*
**Underdown**, Brian James 1941- *AmMWSc 92*
**Underheim**, Gregg 1950- *WhoAmP 91*
**Underhill** *Who 92*
**Underhill**, Baron 1914- *Who 92*
**Underhill**, Anne Barbara 1920- *AmMWSc 92*
**Underhill**, Charles *WrDr 92*
**Underhill**, Christopher Sands 1934- *WhoAmL 92*
**Underhill**, David Stuart 1960- *WhoAmL 92*
**Underhill**, Edward Wesley 1931- *AmMWSc 92*
**Underhill**, Glenn 1925- *AmMWSc 92*
**Underhill**, Herbert Stuart 1914- *Who 92*
**Underhill**, James Campbell 1923- *AmMWSc 92*
**Underhill**, John 1597?-1672 *BenetAL 91*
**Underhill**, Liz 1948- *TwCPaSc*
**Underkofler**, William Leland 1936- *AmMWSc 92*
**Underweiser**, Irwin Philip 1929- *WhoFI 92*
**Underwood**, Arthur Louis, Jr 1924- *AmMWSc 92*
**Underwood**, Barbara Ann 1934- *AmMWSc 92*
**Underwood**, Benjamin Franklin 1839-1914 *RelLAm 91*
**Underwood**, Benton J. 1915- *ConAu 34NR*
**Underwood**, Bernard Edward 1925- *WhoRel 92*
**Underwood**, Blair *ConTFT 9, WhoEnt 92*
**Underwood**, Blair 1964- *WhoBlA 92*
**Underwood**, Cecil H. 1922- *IntWW 91*
**Underwood**, Cecil Harland 1922- *WhoAmP 91*
**Underwood**, Charles David 1957- *WhoRel 92*
**Underwood**, Charles Dunning, Jr. 1946- *WhoAmL 92*
**Underwood**, Cynthia Marie 1962- *WhoMW 92*
**Underwood**, Dennis B *WhoAmP 91*
**Underwood**, Donald Lee 1928- *AmMWSc 92*
**Underwood**, Douglas Haines 1934- *AmMWSc 92*
**Underwood**, Earl Frederick, Jr. 1943- *WhoRel 92*
**Underwood**, Edwin Hill 1920- *WhoAmL 92*
**Underwood**, Ervin E 1918- *AmMWSc 92*
**Underwood**, Frankye Harper 1953- *WhoBlA 92*
**Underwood**, Frederick 1923- *WhoRel 92*
**Underwood**, Glenn 1917- *WhoAmP 91*
**Underwood**, H John 1947- *WhoAmP 91*
**Underwood**, Harry Burnham, II 1943- *WhoFI 92*
**Underwood**, Herbert Arthur, Jr 1945- *AmMWSc 92*
**Underwood**, Herbert G. 1929- *WhoAmL 92*
**Underwood**, James H 1946- *WhoAmP 91*
**Underwood**, James Henry 1938- *AmMWSc 92*
**Underwood**, James Ross, Jr 1927- *AmMWSc 92*
**Underwood**, Jeffrey William 1963- *WhoMW 92*
**Underwood**, John Morris *Who 92*
**Underwood**, John Weeden 1932- *ConAu 35NR*
**Underwood**, Lawrence Statton 1936- *AmMWSc 92*
**Underwood**, Leon 1890-1975 *TwCPaSc*
**Underwood**, Leonard I *WhoAmP 91*
**Underwood**, Lloyd B 1919- *AmMWSc 92*
**Underwood**, Louis Edwin 1937- *AmMWSc 92*
**Underwood**, Lucien Marcus 1853-1907 *BiInAmS*
**Underwood**, Maude Esther 1930- *WhoBlA 92*
**Underwood**, Michael *Who 92*
**Underwood**, Michael 1916- *IntAu&W 91, WrDr 92*
**Underwood**, Oscar Wilder 1862-1929 *AmPolLe, FacFETw*
**Underwood**, Peter 1923- *IntAu&W 91, WrDr 92*
**Underwood**, Ralph Edward 1947- *WhoWest 92*
**Underwood**, Ralph T *WhoAmP 91*
**Underwood**, Rex J 1926- *AmMWSc 92*
**Underwood**, Richard Harvey 1948- *WhoAmL 92*
**Underwood**, Robert Donovan 1956- *WhoAmP 91*
**Underwood**, Robert Gordon 1945- *AmMWSc 92*
**Underwood**, Robert Leigh 1944- *WhoFI 92, WhoMW 92*
**Underwood**, Ron 1953- *IntMPA 92*
**Underwood**, Ronald Brian 1953- *WhoEnt 92*
**Underwood**, Sharry Marie Traver 1922- *WhoEnt 92*
**Underwood**, Thomas Woodbrook 1930- *WhoWest 92*
**Underwood**, Troy Jervis 1932- *WhoMW 92*
**Underwood**, Vernon O., Jr. 1940- *WhoWest 92*
**Underwood**, William Booker, III 1957- *WhoAmL 92*
**Undeutsch**, William Charles 1925- *AmMWSc 92*
**Undlin**, Charles Thomas 1928- *WhoMW 92*
**Undset**, Sigrid 1882-1949 *FacFETw, LiExTwC, WhoNob 90*
**Unekis**, Joseph Keith 1940- *WhoMW 92*
**Unfried**, Dona Lee 1928- *WhoRel 92*
**Unfried**, Stephen Mitchell 1943- *WhoFI 92*
**Ung**, Chinary 1942- *ConCom 92*
**Ung**, Man T 1938- *AmMWSc 92*
**Ungar**, Abraham Albert 1940- *WhoMW 92*
**Ungar**, Edward William 1936- *AmMWSc 92*
**Ungar**, Eric E 1926- *AmMWSc 92*
**Ungar**, Frank 1922- *AmMWSc 92*
**Ungar**, Frederick 1898-1988 *FacFETw*
**Ungar**, Gerald S 1941- *AmMWSc 92*
**Ungar**, Irwin A 1934- *AmMWSc 92*
**Ungar**, Keith Stephan 1959- *WhoMW 92*
**Ungar**, Lawrence Beryl 1930- *WhoAmL 92*
**Ungar**, Robert Arthur 1955- *WhoAmL 92*
**Ungar**, Sanford J. 1945- *WrDr 92*
**Ungaretti**, Giuseppe 1888-1970 *DcLB 114 [port], FacFETw*
**Ungaretti**, Richard Anthony 1942- *WhoAmL 92*
**Ungaro**, Emanuel 1933- *DcTwDes*
**Ungaro**, Emanuel Matteotti 1933- *IntWW 91*
**Ungaro**, Joan 1951- *WhoEnt 92, WhoFI 92*
**Ungaro**, Patrick J 1941- *WhoAmP 91*
**Unger**, Alan Mark 1954- *WhoAmL 92*

**Unger**, Alvin E. d1975 *LesBEnT 92*
**Unger**, Anthony B. 1940- *IntMPA 92*
**Unger**, Arlene Klein 1952- *WhoWest 92*
**Unger**, Barbara *DrAPF 91*
**Unger**, Dan Phillip 1928- *WhoAmL 92, WhoMW 92*
**Unger**, David *DrAPF 91*
**Unger**, David 1950- *WhoHisp 92*
**Unger**, David James 1952- *WhoMW 92*
**Unger**, Douglas 1952- *WrDr 92*
**Unger**, Douglas Arthur 1952- *IntAu&W 91*
**Unger**, Elizabeth Betty 1936- *WhoRel 92*
**Unger**, George D. 1924- *WhoBlA 92*
**Unger**, Gerald 1942- *WhoMW 92*
**Unger**, Hans-Georg 1926- *AmMWSc 92*
**Unger**, Heinz 1895-1965 *NewAmDM*
**Unger**, Israel 1938- *AmMWSc 92*
**Unger**, J. Marshall 1947- *WhoWest 92*
**Unger**, James William 1921- *AmMWSc 92*
**Unger**, Jim 1937- *SmATA 67 [port]*
**Unger**, John Duey 1943- *AmMWSc 92*
**Unger**, John Thomas 1951- *WhoAmL 92*
**Unger**, Kurt 1922- *IntMPA 92*
**Unger**, Leonard 1916- *ConAu 34NR*
**Unger**, Leonard 1917- *WhoAmP 91*
**Unger**, Les 1943- *WhoWest 92*
**Unger**, Lloyd George 1918- *AmMWSc 92*
**Unger**, Marianne Louise 1957- *WhoEnt 92*
**Unger**, Martin Paul 1939- *WhoAmL 92*
**Unger**, Michael Ronald 1943- *IntAu&W 91, IntWW 91, Who 92*
**Unger**, Michael William 1955- *WhoAmL 92*
**Unger**, Paul A. 1914- *WhoMW 92*
**Unger**, Paul Temple 1942- *WhoFI 92*
**Unger**, Paul Vincent 1956- *WhoMW 92*
**Unger**, Paul Walter 1931- *AmMWSc 92*
**Unger**, Peter Van Buren 1957- *WhoAmL 92*
**Unger**, Raymond Frank 1945- *WhoFI 92*
**Unger**, Richard Mahlon 1945- *WhoAmL 92*
**Unger**, Roger Harold 1924- *AmMWSc 92*
**Unger**, S H 1931- *AmMWSc 92*
**Unger**, Sonja Franz 1921- *WhoFI 92*
**Unger**, Stephen A. 1946- *IntMPA 92*
**Unger**, Vernon Edwin, Jr 1935- *AmMWSc 92*
**Unger**, Vincent Tauno 1948- *WhoMW 92*
**Ungerer**, Miriam 1929- *WrDr 92*
**Ungerer**, Tomi 1931- *Who 92*
**Ungerer**, Werner 1927- *IntWW 91*
**Ungerman**, Kimball Reid 1957- *WhoFI 92, WhoWest 92*
**Ungerman**, Roseanna Weeks 1960- *WhoEnt 92*
**Ungers**, Oswald Mathias 1926- *IntWW 91*
**Unglaube**, James M 1942- *AmMWSc 92*
**Ungo**, Guillermo d1991 *NewYTBS 91 [port]*
**Ungvichian**, Vichate 1949- *AmMWSc 92*
**Unhjem**, Michael B 1953- *WhoAmP 91*
**Unhjem**, Michael Bruce 1953- *WhoAmL 92*
**Unice**, Thomas Robert, Jr. 1957- *WhoAmL 92*
**Unik**, John Peter 1934- *AmMWSc 92*
**Unis**, Richard L *WhoAmP 91*
**Unis**, Richard L. 1928- *WhoAmL 92, WhoWest 92*
**Unitas**, John Constantine 1933- *FacFETw*
**Unkefer**, Barbara Morgan Baxter 1939- *WhoMW 92*
**Unklesbay**, Athel Glyde 1914- *AmMWSc 92*
**Unklesbay**, Nan F 1944- *AmMWSc 92*
**Unkovic**, John Clark 1943- *WhoAmL 92*
**Unland**, Mark Leroy 1940- *AmMWSc 92*
**Unlu**, M Selim 1964- *AmMWSc 92*
**Unnam**, Jalaiah 1947- *AmMWSc 92*
**Unnewehr**, Lewis Emory 1925- *WhoMW 92*
**Uno**, Hideo 1929- *AmMWSc 92*
**Uno**, Osamu 1917- *IntWW 91*
**Uno**, Sosuke 1922- *IntWW 91*
**Unowsky**, Joel 1938- *AmMWSc 92*
**Unpingco**, Antonio Reyes 1942- *WhoAmP 91*
**Unrath**, Claude Richard 1941- *AmMWSc 92*
**Unrau**, Abraham Martin 1926- *AmMWSc 92*
**Unrau**, David George 1938- *AmMWSc 92*
**Unrug**, Raphael *AmMWSc 92*
**Unruh**, Dan A. 1930- *WhoWest 92*
**Unruh**, Henry, Jr 1926- *AmMWSc 92*
**Unruh**, James Arlen 1941- *WhoFI 92, WhoMW 92*
**Unruh**, Jerry Dean 1944- *AmMWSc 92*
**Unruh**, JoAnna M 1931- *WhoAmP 91*
**Unruh**, Paula 1929- *WhoAmP 91*
**Unruh**, Philip W. 1950- *WhoAmL 92, WhoAmP 91*
**Unruh**, William George 1945- *AmMWSc 92*
**Unseld**, Siegfried 1924- *IntWW 91*
**Unseld**, Wes 1946- *WhoBlA 92*
**Unsoeld**, Jolene 1931- *AlmAP 92 [port], WhoAmP 91, WhoWest 92*
**Unsold**, Albrecht Otto Johannes 1905- *IntWW 91*
**Unstead**, Robert John 1915- *IntAu&W 91*
**Unsworth**, Barrie John 1934- *IntWW 91*
**Unsworth**, Barry 1930- *WrDr 92*
**Unsworth**, Barry Forster 1930- *IntAu&W 91*
**Unsworth**, Brian Russell 1937- *AmMWSc 92*
**Unsworth**, Edgar 1906- *Who 92*
**Unsworth**, Jim 1958- *TwCPaSc*
**Unsworth**, Peter 1937- *TwCPaSc*
**Unsworth**, Richard Preston 1927- *WhoRel 92*
**Unt**, Hillar 1935- *AmMWSc 92*
**Untch**, Karl George 1931- *AmMWSc 92*
**Untener**, Kenneth E. 1937- *WhoRel 92*
**Unterberger**, Betty Miller *WrDr 92*
**Unterberger**, Robert Mark 1961- *WhoAmL 92*
**Unterberger**, Robert Ruppe 1921- *AmMWSc 92*
**Unterborn**, Lee Robert 1951- *WhoAmL 92*
**Unterecker**, John 1922-1989 *ConAu 34NR*
**Unterharnscheidt**, Friedrich J 1926- *AmMWSc 92*
**Unterkoefler**, Ernest L. 1917- *WhoRel 92*
**Unterman**, Eugene Rex 1953- *WhoMW 92*
**Unterman**, Ira Nathan 1964- *WhoWest 92*
**Unterman**, Thomas Edward 1944- *WhoAmL 92, WhoWest 92*
**Untermann**, Jurgen 1928- *IntWW 91*
**Untermeyer**, Charles Graves 1946- *WhoAmP 91*
**Untermeyer**, Jean Starr 1886-1970 *BenetAL 91*
**Untermeyer**, Louis 1885-1977 *BenetAL 91, FacFETw*
**Unterreiner**, C. Martin 1940- *WhoFI 92*
**Untersteiner**, Norbert 1926- *AmMWSc 92*
**Unthank**, G. Wix 1923- *WhoAmL 92*
**Unthank**, Thomas Roth 1960- *WhoWest 92*
**Unti**, Theodore Wayne Joseph 1931- *AmMWSc 92*
**Unton**, Theodore Francis 1944- *WhoFI 92, WhoMW 92*
**Untrauer**, Raymond E 1926- *AmMWSc 92*
**Unwin**, Brian *Who 92*
**Unwin**, Christopher Philip 1917- *Who 92*
**Unwin**, David 1918- *WrDr 92*
**Unwin**, David Storr 1918- *Who 92*
**Unwin**, Eric Geoffrey 1942- *Who 92*
**Unwin**, Francis 1885-1925 *TwCPaSc*
**Unwin**, James Brian 1935- *Who 92*
**Unwin**, Kenneth 1926- *Who 92*
**Unwin**, Nigel 1942- *Who 92*
**Unwin**, Peter William 1932- *IntWW 91, Who 92*
**Unwin**, Rayner 1925- *WrDr 92*
**Unwin**, Rayner Stephens 1925- *Who 92*
**Unwin**, Stephen Charles 1953- *AmMWSc 92*
**Unwin**, Stephen Forman 1927- *WhoWest 92*
**Unwin**, T. Fisher 1848-1935 *DcLB 106 [port]*
**Unz**, Hillel 1929- *AmMWSc 92*
**Unz**, Richard F 1935- *AmMWSc 92*
**Unzaga De Le Vega**, Oscar 1916-1959 *BiDExR*
**Unzicker**, John Duane 1938- *AmMWSc 92*
**Unzueta**, Manuel 1949- *WhoHisp 92*
**Uoka**, Satele M *WhoAmP 91*
**Uotila**, Urho A 1923- *AmMWSc 92*
**Up De Graff**, Thad. Stevens 1839-1885 *BiInAmS*
**Upadhyay**, Jagdish M 1931- *AmMWSc 92*
**Upadhyay**, Shailendra Kumar 1929- *IntWW 91*
**Upadhyaya**, Belle Raghavendra *AmMWSc 92*
**Upadhyaya**, Shrinivasa Kumbhashi 1950- *WhoWest 92*
**Upadrashta**, Kameswara Rao *WhoFI 92*
**Upatnieks**, Juris 1936- *AmMWSc 92, WhoMW 92*
**Upbin**, Shari *WhoEnt 92*
**Upchurch**, Avery C *WhoAmP 91*
**Upchurch**, Garland Rudolph, Jr. 1952- *WhoWest 92*
**Upchurch**, Hamilton D 1925- *WhoAmP 91*
**Upchurch**, Jonathan Everett 1951- *AmMWSc 92*
**Upchurch**, Leanne Nichols 1960- *WhoEnt 92*
**Upchurch**, Michael *DrAPF 91*
**Upchurch**, Robert Phillip 1928- *AmMWSc 92*
**Upchurch**, Sam Bayliss 1941- *AmMWSc 92*
**Upchurch**, Samuel E., Jr. 1952- *WhoAmL 92*
**Updegraff**, Allan *ScFEYrs*
**Updegraff**, David Maule 1917- *AmMWSc 92*
**Updegrove**, Louis B 1928- *AmMWSc 92*
**Updike**, Charles Bruce 1939- *WhoAmL 92*
**Updike**, Daniel Berkeley 1860-1941 *BenetAL 91*
**Updike**, John *DrAPF 91*
**Updike**, John 1932- *BenetAL 91, ConNov 91, ConPo 91, FacFETw [port], WrDr 92*
**Updike**, John Hoyer 1932- *IntAu&W 91, IntWW 91, Who 92*
**Updike**, Margaret Rachel 1947- *WhoAmP 91*
**Updike**, Michael Lee 1943- *WhoAmL 92*
**Updike**, Otis L, Jr 1920- *AmMWSc 92*
**Upeslacis**, Janis 1946- *AmMWSc 92*
**Upgren**, Arthur Reinhold, Jr 1933- *AmMWSc 92*
**Upham**, Charles Hazlitt 1908- *Who 92*
**Upham**, Charles Wentworth 1802-1875 *BenetAL 91*
**Upham**, Chester R, Jr 1925- *WhoAmP 91*
**Upham**, Edwin Porter 1845-1918 *BiInAmS*
**Upham**, Roy Herbert 1920- *AmMWSc 92*
**Upham**, Roy Walter 1920- *AmMWSc 92*
**Upham**, Steadman 1949- *WhoWest 92*
**Upham**, Thomas C. 1799-1872 *AmPeW*
**Uphoff**, Delta Emma 1922- *AmMWSc 92*
**Uphoff**, Evelyn M 1918- *WhoAmP 91*
**Uphoff**, Joseph 1955- *WhoWest 92*
**Uphoff**, Joseph Anthony 1950- *IntAu&W 91*
**Uphoff**, Louise Joan 1947- *WhoAmP 91*
**Upholt**, William Boyce 1943- *AmMWSc 92*
**Uphus**, Sylvester Bernard 1927- *WhoAmP 91*
**Upjohn**, Gordon Farleigh 1912- *Who 92*
**Upledger**, Michael Cave 1963- *WhoEnt 92*
**Upmeier**, Harald 1950- *AmMWSc 92*
**Uppman**, Theodor 1920- *WhoEnt 92*
**Uppman**, Theodore 1920- *NewAmDM*
**Upponi**, Ashwin Dattatraya 1961- *WhoFI 92*
**Uppuluri**, V R Rao 1931- *AmMWSc 92*
**U'Prichard**, David C 1948- *AmMWSc 92*
**Upright**, J. W. 1937- *WhoMW 92*
**Upshall**, Helen Ruby 1926- *IntAu&W 91*
**Upshaw**, Dawn 1960- *News 91 [port]*
**Upshaw**, Gene 1945- *WhoBlA 92*
**Upshaw**, Lisa Gaye 1959- *WhoFI 92*
**Upshaw**, Sam, Jr. 1964- *WhoBlA 92*
**Upshaw**, Willie Clay 1957- *WhoBlA 92*
**Upshur**, Abel Parker 1791-1844 *AmPolLe*
**Upson**, Dan W 1929- *AmMWSc 92*
**Upson**, Jeannine Martin 1942- *WhoAmP 91*
**Upson**, Roger Ballard 1938- *WhoFI 92*
**Upson**, Stuart Barnard 1925- *WhoFI 92*
**Upson**, Thomas F 1941- *WhoAmP 91*
**Upson**, William Hazlett 1891-1975 *BenetAL 91*
**Upston**, John Edwin 1935- *WhoAmP 91*
**Uptegraff**, Robert Alton, Jr. 1965- *WhoFI 92*
**Upthegrove**, Franklin John 1921- *WhoRel 92*
**Upthegrove**, W R 1928- *AmMWSc 92*
**Uptigrove**, Kenneth R. 1943- *WhoMW 92*
**Upton**, Arthur Canfield 1923- *AmMWSc 92, IntWW 91*
**Upton**, Barbara A 1921- *WhoAmP 91*
**Upton**, Charles *DrAPF 91*
**Upton**, Charles W. 1943- *WhoMW 92*
**Upton**, E. H. 1924- *WhoBlA 92*
**Upton**, Fred 1953- *AlmAP 92 [port]*
**Upton**, Fred Stephen 1953- *WhoAmP 91*
**Upton**, Frederick Stephen 1953- *WhoMW 92*
**Upton**, G Virginia 1929- *AmMWSc 92*
**Upton**, Harriet Taylor 1854-1945 *HanAmWH*
**Upton**, Lee *DrAPF 91*
**Upton**, Mark N. 1951- *WhoWest 92*
**Upton**, Martin 1933- *WrDr 92*
**Upton**, Michael 1938- *TwCPaSc*
**Upton**, Robert *DrAPF 91*
**Upton**, Ronald P 1941- *AmMWSc 92*
**Upton**, Steve Jay 1953- *WhoMW 92*
**Upton**, Thomas Hallworth 1952- *AmMWSc 92*
**Upton**, Thomas Lee 1944- *WhoMW 92*
**Upton**, William Lloyd 1956- *WhoMW 92*
**Upton**, Winslow 1853-1914 *BiInAmS*
**Upward**, Edward 1903- *ConNov 91, RfGEnL 91, WrDr 92*
**Upward**, Janet *Who 92*
**Upward**, Peter 1932- *TwCPaSc*
**Urabe**, Shizutaro 1909- *IntWW 91*
**Uralil**, Francis Stephen 1950- *AmMWSc 92*
**Uram**, Gerald Robert 1941- *WhoAmL 92*
**Uranga**, Jose N. 1946- *WhoHisp 92*
**Uranga McKane**, Steven 1952- *WhoHisp 92*
**Urano**, Muneyasu 1936- *AmMWSc 92*
**Uranov**, Gennadi Vasilevich 1934- *IntWW 91*
**Urbach**, Ephraim Elimelech 1912- *IntWW 91*
**Urbach**, Frederick 1922- *AmMWSc 92*
**Urbach**, Frederick Lewis 1938- *AmMWSc 92*
**Urbach**, Herman B 1923- *AmMWSc 92*
**Urbach**, John C 1934- *AmMWSc 92*
**Urbach**, Karl Frederic 1917- *AmMWSc 92*
**Urbain**, Robert 1930- *IntWW 91*
**Urbain**, Walter Mathias 1910- *AmMWSc 92*
**Urbaitel**, Leon 1945- *WhoFI 92*
**Urban**, Barbara Jean 1960- *WhoEnt 92*
**Urban**, Bohumil 1934- *IntWW 91*
**Urban**, Carl Anthony 1939- *WhoRel 92*
**Urban**, Edmund Gerard, III 1957- *WhoAmL 92*
**Urban**, Emil Karl 1934- *AmMWSc 92*
**Urban**, Eugene Willard 1935- *AmMWSc 92*
**Urban**, Frank Henry 1930- *WhoAmP 91*
**Urban**, Frank M. 1953- *WhoHisp 92*
**Urban**, Guy *WhoEnt 92*
**Urban**, Horst W. 1936- *IntWW 91*
**Urban**, James Arthur 1927- *WhoAmL 92*
**Urban**, James Edward 1942- *AmMWSc 92*
**Urban**, Jerome A 1914-1991 *NewYTBS 91*
**Urban**, Jerzy 1933- *IntWW 91*
**Urban**, Joseph 1872-1933 *DcTwDes*
**Urban**, Joseph 1921- *AmMWSc 92*
**Urban**, Lajos 1934- *IntWW 91*
**Urban**, Lee Donald 1946- *WhoAmL 92*
**Urban**, Michael John, Jr 1951- *WhoAmP 91*
**Urban**, Richard William 1945- *AmMWSc 92*
**Urban**, Ronald James 1947- *WhoMW 92*
**Urban**, Sharon Kay *WhoMW 92*
**Urban**, Theodore Joseph 1926- *AmMWSc 92*
**Urban**, Thomas Charles 1944- *AmMWSc 92, WhoWest 92*
**Urban**, Willard Edward, Jr 1936- *AmMWSc 92*
**Urbanek**, Adam 1928- *IntWW 91*
**Urbanek**, Agnes Clotilda 1909- *WhoEnt 92*
**Urbanek**, Karel 1941- *IntWW 91*
**Urbanek**, Vincent Edward 1927- *AmMWSc 92*
**Urbani**, Anthony, II 1953- *WhoAmL 92*
**Urbaniak**, Stephen Michael 1959- *WhoEnt 92*
**Urbanik**, Arthur Ronald 1939- *AmMWSc 92*
**Urbanik**, Kazimierz 1930- *IntWW 91*
**Urbano**, Anthony Ralph 1935- *WhoEnt 92*
**Urbanowicz**, E. Peter 1963- *WhoAmL 92*
**Urbanowski**, John Richard 1947- *WhoFI 92*
**Urbanski**, Douglas James 1957- *WhoEnt 92, WhoWest 92*
**Urbansky**, Yevgeniy Yakovlevich 1932-1965 *SovUnBD*
**Urbas**, Branko 1929- *AmMWSc 92*
**Urbatsch**, Lowell Edward 1942- *AmMWSc 92*
**Urbigkit**, Walter C., Jr. 1927- *WhoAmL 92, WhoAmP 91, WhoWest 92*
**Urbik**, Jerome Anthony 1929- *WhoFI 92*
**Urbina**, Eduardo 1948- *WhoHisp 92*
**Urbina**, Jeffrey Alan 1955- *WhoHisp 92*
**Urbina**, Manuel, II 1939- *WhoHisp 92*
**Urbina**, Nicasio 1958- *WhoHisp 92*
**Urbina**, Ricardo Manuel 1946- *WhoHisp 92*
**Urbina**, Susana P. 1946- *WhoHisp 92*
**Urbina de Breen**, Marlene Victoria 1958- *WhoHisp 92*
**Urbom**, Warren Keith 1925- *WhoAmL 92, WhoMW 92*
**Urbrock**, William Joseph 1938- *WhoRel 92*
**Urbscheit**, Nancy Lee 1946- *AmMWSc 92*
**Urbsys**, Juozas d1991 *NewYTBS 91*
**Urch**, Elizabeth 1921- *WrDr 92*
**Urch**, George T 1959- *WhoAmP 91*
**Urch**, Umbert Anthony 1946- *AmMWSc 92*
**Urcia**, Ingeborg 1934- *WhoWest 92*
**Urciolo**, John Raphael, II 1947- *WhoFI 92*
**Urdal**, David L *AmMWSc 92*
**Urdan**, James Alan 1931- *WhoAmL 92*
**Urdaneta**, Andres de 1508-1568 *HisDSpE*
**Urdaneta**, Luis Fernando 1936 *WhoHisp 92*
**Urdaneta**, Maria-Luisa 1931- *WhoHisp 92*
**Urdaneta**, Rafael 1789-1845 *HisDSpE*
**Urdang**, Arnold 1928- *AmMWSc 92*
**Urdang**, Constance *DrAPF 91*
**Urdang**, Constance 1922- *ConPo 91, WrDr 92*
**Urdang**, Ivy Paige 1953- *WhoAmL 92*
**Urdiales**, Richard, Sr. 1946- *WhoHisp 92*
**Urdy**, Charles E. 1933- *WhoBlA 92*
**Urdy**, Charles Eugene 1933- *AmMWSc 92, WhoAmP 91*
**Ure**, James Mathie 1925- *Who 92*
**Ure**, Jean 1943- *SmATA 14AS [port], WrDr 92*
**Ure**, Jean Ann 1943- *IntAu&W 91*
**Ure**, John 1931- *Who 92, WrDr 92*

**Ure**, John Burns 1931- *IntWW 91*
**Ureles**, Alvin L 1921- *AmMWSc 92*
**Urello**, Donald Richard 1934- *WhoMW 92*
**Uremovic**, Joseph Anthony 1947- *WhoAmL 92*
**Uren**, Thomas 1921- *IntWW 91*
**Urena**, Luis Francisco 1948- *WhoHisp 92*
**Urena-Alexiades**, Jose Luis 1949- *WhoWest 92*
**Urena de Henriquez**, Salome 1850-1897 *SpAmWW*
**Urenovitch**, Joseph Victor 1937- *AmMWSc 92*
**Uresk**, Daniel William 1943- *AmMWSc 92*
**Uresti**, Gilberto *WhoHisp 92*
**Uretsky**, Jack Leon 1924- *AmMWSc 92*
**Uretsky**, Myron 1940- *AmMWSc 92*
**Uretz**, Robert Benjamin 1924- *AmMWSc 92*
**Urey**, Harold C 1893-1981 *FacFETw*
**Urey**, Harold Clayton 1893-1981 *WhoNob 90*
**Urgelles**, Alejandro *BlkOlyM*
**Urhausen**, James Nicholas 1943- *WhoMW 92*
**Uri**, George Wolfsohn 1920- *WhoWest 92*
**Uri**, Pierre Emmanuel 1911- *IntWW 91*
**Uria**, Alvin Patrick 1952- *WhoHisp 92*
**Uria**, Miguel 1937- *WhoHisp 92*
**Uriarte-Otheguy**, Francisco Javier 1968- *WhoHisp 92*
**Urias**, Carmen Carrasco 1966- *WhoHisp 92*
**Urias**, Rodolfo 1957- *WhoHisp 92*
**Urias-Islas**, Martha Alicia 1960- *WhoHisp 92*
**Uribe**, Alberto Ramiro 1957- *WhoHisp 92*
**Uribe**, Charles 1937- *WhoHisp 92, WhoWest 92*
**Uribe**, Ernest G. 1935- *WhoHisp 92*
**Uribe**, Ernest Gilbert 1935- *AmMWSc 92*
**Uribe**, Ernesto 1937- *WhoHisp 92*
**Uribe**, Hector 1946- *WhoAmP 91*
**Uribe**, Hector R. 1946- *WhoHisp 92*
**Uribe**, Javier Miguel 1941- *WhoFI 92*
**Uribe**, Javier R. *WhoHisp 92*
**Uribe**, John 1937- *WhoHisp 92*
**Uribe**, Jose Alta 1959- *WhoHisp 92*
**Uricchio**, Michael Anthony 1953- *WhoAmL 92*
**Uricchio**, William Andrew 1924- *AmMWSc 92*
**Urice**, John Kraus 1946- *WhoMW 92*
**Urich**, Robert *LesBEnT 92, WhoEnt 92*
**Urich**, Robert 1947- *IntMPA 92*
**Urick**, Kevin *DrAPF 91*
**Urick**, Robert Joseph 1915- *AmMWSc 92*
**Urie**, John Dunlop 1915- *Who 92*
**Urie**, Joseph 1947- *TwCPaSc*
**Urinza**, Ana Lezama de *EncAmaz 91*
**Uris**, Leon 1924- *ConNov 91, WhoRel 92, WrDr 92*
**Uris**, Leon M. 1924- *BenetAL 91*
**Uris**, Leon Marcus 1924- *IntAu&W 91, IntWW 91*
**Urisko**, Richard Francis Xavier 1957- *WhoAmL 92*
**Urista-Heredia**, Alberto 1947- *WhoHisp 92*
**Uritam**, Rein Aarne 1939- *AmMWSc 92*
**Uriu**, Kiyoto 1917- *AmMWSc 92*
**Urkowitz**, Harry 1921- *AmMWSc 92*
**Urkowitz**, Michael 1943- *WhoFI 92*
**Urlacher**, Herbert *WhoAmP 91*
**Urman**, Mark 1952- *IntMPA 92*
**Urmson**, James Opie 1915- *Who 92*
**Urmuz** *ConAu 34NR*
**Urness**, David Edgar 1935- *WhoEnt 92*
**Urness**, Kent D 1948- *WhoIns 92*
**Urness**, Philip Joel 1936- *AmMWSc 92*
**Urone**, Paul 1915- *AmMWSc 92*
**Urone**, Paul Peter 1944- *AmMWSc 92*
**Urowsky**, Richard J. 1946- *WhoAmL 92*
**Urquhart**, Andrew Willard 1939- *AmMWSc 92*
**Urquhart**, Brian 1919- *IntWW 91, Who 92*
**Urquhart**, Brian Edward 1919- *WrDr 92*
**Urquhart**, Donald John 1909- *Who 92*
**Urquhart**, Fred 1912- *ConNov 91, IntAu&W 91, WrDr 92*
**Urquhart**, James Graham 1925- *Who 92*
**Urquhart**, James McCartha 1953- *WhoBlA 92*
**Urquhart**, John 1934- *WhoWest 92*
**Urquhart**, John, III 1934- *AmMWSc 92*
**Urquhart**, Lawrence McAllister 1935- *IntWW 91, Who 92*
**Urquhart**, N Scott 1940- *AmMWSc 92*
**Urquhart**, Robert 1922- *ConTFT 9, IntMPA 92*
**Urquhart**, Stephen E. 1949- *WhoAmL 92*
**Urquidi-MacDonald**, Mirna 1946- *AmMWSc 92*
**Urquilla**, Pedro Ramon 1939- *AmMWSc 92*
**Urrabazo**, Rosendo 1952- *WhoHisp 92*
**Urraca**, Queen of Aragon 1081-1126 *EncAmaz 91*
**Urrechaga**, Jose L. *WhoHisp 92*
**Urrutia**, Esther E. 1956- *WhoHisp 92*
**Urrutia**, Frank 1929- *WhoHisp 92*
**Urrutia**, Jorge Luis 1948- *WhoHisp 92*
**Urrutia**, Lupe G. 1943- *WhoHisp 92*
**Urrutia**, Manuel Lleo 1901-1981 *FacFETw*
**Urry**, Dan Wesley 1935- *AmMWSc 92*
**Urry**, Grant Wayne 1926- *AmMWSc 92*
**Urry**, Lisa Andrea 1953- *AmMWSc 92*
**Urry**, Ronald Lee 1945- *AmMWSc 92*
**Urry**, Wilbert Herbert 1914- *AmMWSc 92*
**Ursache**, Victorin 1912- *WhoRel 92*
**Ursano**, Carol Monda 1962- *WhoEnt 92*
**Ursell**, Fritz Joseph 1923- *Who 92*
**Ursell**, John Henry 1938- *AmMWSc 92*
**Ursell**, Philip Elliott 1942- *Who 92*
**Ursenbach**, Wayne Octave 1923- *AmMWSc 92*
**Urshan**, Nathaniel A. 1920- *WhoRel 92*
**Ursi**, Corrado 1908- *IntWW 91, WhoRel 92*
**Ursic**, Stanley John 1924- *AmMWSc 92*
**Ursich**, Donald Weaver 1939- *WhoRel 92*
**Ursillo**, Richard Carmen 1926- *AmMWSc 92*
**Ursin**, Bjarne Elling 1930- *WhoFI 92, WhoWest 92*
**Ursino**, Donald Joseph 1935- *AmMWSc 92*
**Ursino**, Joseph Anthony 1939- *AmMWSc 92*
**Urso**, Paul 1925- *AmMWSc 92*
**Urstadt**, Charles Deane 1959- *WhoFI 92*
**Urstadt**, Charles Jordan 1928- *WhoFI 92*
**Ursu**, Doru Viorel *IntWW 91*
**Ursu**, Ioan 1928- *IntWW 91*
**Ursua**, Pedro de 1510?-1550 *HisDSpE*
**Ursula**, Saint *EncAmaz 91*
**Urtasun**, Raul C *AmMWSc 92*
**Urtecho**, Elizabeth 1951- *WhoHisp 92*
**Urtiew**, Paul Andrew 1931- *AmMWSc 92*
**Uruguay**, Bishop of 1948- *Who 92*
**Urwick**, Alan 1930- *Who 92*
**Urwick**, Alan Bedford 1930- *IntWW 91*
**Urwiller**, Daniel Gordon 1949- *WhoAmP 91*
**Urwin**, Gregory J. W. 1955- *ConAu 36NR*
**Urwin**, Harry 1915- *Who 92*
**Urwin**, Peter 1948- *Who 92*
**Ury**, Hans Konrad 1924- *AmMWSc 92*
**Ury**, Perry S. 1925- *WhoEnt 92*
**Usabel**, Gaizka Salvador 1933- *WhoHisp 92*
**Usalis**, George Jerome 1948- *WhoMW 92*
**Usami**, Tadanobu 1925- *IntWW 91*
**Usatch**, Sonia *DrAPF 91*
**Usategui**, Ramon 1925- *WhoHisp 92*
**Usborne**, Henry Charles 1909- *Who 92*
**Usborne**, Richard A. 1910- *WrDr 92*
**Usborne**, Richard Alexander 1910- *Who 92*
**Usborne**, William Ronald 1937- *AmMWSc 92*
**Uschold**, Richard L 1928- *AmMWSc 92*
**Uschuk**, Pamela *DrAPF 91*
**Uschuk**, Pamela Marie 1948- *IntAu&W 91*
**Usdane**, Robert B *WhoAmP 91*
**Usdin**, Vera Rudin 1925- *AmMWSc 92*
**Uselton**, James Clayton 1939- *WhoFI 92*
**Usenik**, Edward A 1927- *AmMWSc 92*
**Usera**, John Joseph 1941- *WhoMW 92*
**Usera**, Joseph Andrew 1949- *WhoAmL 92*
**Usey**, Robert Wayne 1940- *WhoAmP 91*
**Ushakov**, Nikolay Aleksandrovich 1918- *IntWW 91*
**Ushenko**, Audrey Andreyevna 1945- *WhoMW 92*
**Usher**, David Anthony 1936- *AmMWSc 92*
**Usher**, Frederick Barrie 1942- *WhoFI 92*
**Usher**, George 1930- *IntAu&W 91, WrDr 92*
**Usher**, Harry Lester 1939- *WhoWest 92*
**Usher**, Juan Oscar 1928- *WhoRel 92*
**Usher**, Leonard 1907- *Who 92*
**Usher**, Peter Denis 1935- *AmMWSc 92*
**Usher**, Robert 1934- *Who 92*
**Usher**, Ronald E *WhoAmP 91*
**Usher**, Ronald Lee 1935- *WhoWest 92*
**Usher**, Wm Mack 1927- *AmMWSc 92*
**Usher Arsene**, Assouan 1930- *IntWW 91*
**Usher-Kerr**, Marva Dianne 1955- *WhoRel 92*
**Usherwood**, Noble Ransom 1938- *AmMWSc 92*
**Usherwood**, Stephen 1907- *WrDr 92*
**Ushijima**, Arthur Akira 1948- *WhoMW 92*
**Ushijima**, Jean M. 1933- *WhoWest 92*
**Ushioda**, Masuko *WhoEnt 92*
**Ushioda**, Sukekatsu 1941- *AmMWSc 92*
**Ushkow**, Charmaine Marie 1955- *WhoEnt 92*
**Ushman**, Neal Leslie 1951- *WhoWest 92*
**Usigli**, Rodolfo 1905- *BenetAL 91*
**Usinger**, Martha Putnam 1912- *WhoWest 92*
**Usinger**, Richard Putnam 1947- *WhoWest 92*
**Usinger**, William R 1951- *AmMWSc 92*
**Usiskin**, Zalman P 1943- *AmMWSc 92*
**Usiskin**, Zalman Philip 1943- *WhoMW 92*
**Usitalo**, Irene Joann 1921- *WhoWest 92*
**Uslan**, Michael E. 1951- *IntMPA 92*
**Uslan**, Michael Elliot 1951- *WhoEnt 92*
**Uslar Pietri**, Arturo 1906- *BenetAL 91, DcLB 113 [port], IntWW 91*
**Uslenghi**, Piergiorgio L 1937- *AmMWSc 92*
**Usmani**, Arthur Mohammad 1940- *WhoMW 92*
**Usmani**, Ishrat Husain 1917- *IntWW 91*
**Usmani**, Riaz Ahmad 1934- *AmMWSc 92*
**Usmankhodzhaev**, Inamzhon Buzrukovich 1930- *SovUnBD*
**Usmanov**, Gumer Ismagilovich 1932- *IntWW 91, SovUnBD*
**Usmiller**, Richard Raymond 1957- *WhoEnt 92*
**Uspensky**, Boris Aleksandrovich 1927- *SovUnBD*
**Uspensky**, Boris Andreevich 1937- *SovUnBD*
**Uspensky**, Boris Andreyevich 1937- *IntWW 91*
**Uspensky**, Nikolay Nikolayevich 1938- *IntWW 91*
**Usrey**, Linda Darlene 1947- *WhoMW 92*
**Usry**, Dona White 1933- *WhoAmP 91*
**Usry**, James L 1922- *WhoAmP 91*
**Usry**, James LeRoy 1922- *WhoBlA 92*
**Ussachevsky**, Vladimir 1911-1990 *NewAmDM*
**Usselman**, Melvyn Charles 1946- *AmMWSc 92*
**Usselman**, Thomas Michael 1947- *AmMWSc 92*
**Ussery**, Albert Travis 1928- *WhoAmL 92*
**Ussery**, Calvin Clifford 1920- *WhoRel 92*
**Ussery**, Dan Kenneth 1948- *WhoRel 92*
**Ussery**, David 1937- *WhoAmP 91*
**Ussery**, E Michael *WhoAmP 91*
**Ussery**, Harry MacRae 1920- *WhoAmL 92*
**Ussery**, Terdema Lamar, II 1958- *WhoBlA 92*
**Ustinov**, D. F. 1908-1984 *ConAu 133*
**Ustinov**, Dimitri Fedorovich 1908-1984 *FacFETw*
**Ustinov**, Dmitriy Fedorovich 1908-1984 *SovUnBD*
**Ustinov**, Peter 1921- *FacFETw, IntAu&W 91, IntMPA 92, Who 92, WrDr 92*
**Ustinov**, Peter Alexander 1921- *IntWW 91, WhoEnt 92*
**Ustinov**, Vyacheslav Aleksandrovich 1925- *IntWW 91*
**Uston**, Ken 1935-1987 *SmATA 65*
**Ustvolskaya**, Galina 1919- *ConCom 92*
**Ustvol'skaya**, Galina Ivanovna 1919- *SovUnBD*
**Usui**, Leslie Raymond 1946- *WhoFI 92, WhoWest 92*
**Utagikar**, Ajit Purushottam 1967- *AmMWSc 92*
**Utchanah**, Mahyendrah *IntWW 91*
**Utech**, Frederick Herbert 1943- *AmMWSc 92*
**Utermohlen**, Virginia 1943- *AmMWSc 92*
**Utesov**, Leonid Osipovich 1895-1982 *SovUnBD*
**Utgaard**, John Edward 1936- *AmMWSc 92*
**Utgard**, Russell Oliver 1933- *AmMWSc 92*
**Utgoff**, Vadym V 1917- *AmMWSc 92*
**Uthe**, John Frederick 1938- *AmMWSc 92*
**Uthe**, P M, Jr 1930- *AmMWSc 92*
**Uthlaut**, Ralph, Jr 1933- *WhoAmP 91*
**Uthoff**, Michael 1943- *WhoEnt 92*
**Uthurusamy**, Keshav *WhoMW 92*
**Uti**, Sunday 1962- *BlkOlyM*
**Utiger**, Ronald Ernest 1926- *IntWW 91, Who 92*
**Utke**, Allen R 1936- *AmMWSc 92*
**Utke**, Robert Ahrens 1933- *WhoRel 92*
**Utkhede**, Rajeshwar Shamrao 1939- *AmMWSc 92*
**Utkin**, Iosif Pavlovich 1903-1944 *SovUnBD*
**Utkin**, Vladimir Fedorovich 1923- *IntWW 91*
**Utku**, Bisulay Bereket 1940- *AmMWSc 92*
**Utku**, Senol 1931- *AmMWSc 92*
**Utlaut**, William Frederick 1922- *AmMWSc 92*
**Utley**, Freda 1898-1978 *FacFETw*
**Utley**, Garrick *LesBEnT 92*
**Utley**, Garrick 1939- *Who 92*
**Utley**, James Henry Paul 1936- *Who 92*
**Utley**, John Eddy 1941- *WhoFI 92*
**Utley**, John Foster, III 1944- *AmMWSc 92*
**Utley**, Jon Basil 1934- *WhoFI 92*
**Utley**, Philip Ray 1941- *AmMWSc 92*
**Utley**, Richard Henry 1949- *WhoBlA 92*
**Utley**, Robert M. 1929- *WrDr 92*
**Utley**, Robert Marshall 1929- *IntAu&W 91*
**Utley**, Steven 1948- *TwCSFW 91*
**Utman**, Cragg Brien 1952- *WhoWest 92*
**Utracki**, Lechoslaw Adam 1931- *AmMWSc 92*
**Utrecht**, Paul F. 1960- *WhoAmL 92*
**Utroska**, Donald Ray 1938- *WhoFI 92*
**Utsick**, Jack Paul 1942- *WhoEnt 92*
**Utsumi**, Hideo 1922- *IntWW 91*
**Utt**, Robert Edward 1948- *WhoEnt 92*
**Uttal-Schlichtman**, Susan E. 1954- *WhoAmL 92*
**Uttamchandanisundri Assandas**, S 1924- *IntAu&W 91*
**Utter**, Annette 1961- *WhoWest 92*
**Utter**, Charles Davey 1941- *WhoEnt 92*
**Utter**, Fred Madison 1931- *AmMWSc 92*
**Utter**, Marilee Ann 1949- *WhoWest 92*
**Utter**, Robert F 1930- *WhoAmP 91*
**Utter**, Robert French 1930- *WhoAmL 92, WhoWest 92*
**Utterback**, Donald D 1904- *AmMWSc 92*
**Utterback**, Everett Emory 1906- *WhoBlA 92*
**Utterback**, Mary W 1917- *WhoAmP 91*
**Utterback**, Nyle Gene 1931- *AmMWSc 92*
**Utterback**, Will Hay, Jr. 1947- *WhoFI 92*
**Utting**, William 1931- *Who 92*
**Uttley**, John William, III 1955- *WhoMW 92*
**Utz**, Carolyn Glover 1913- *WhoEnt 92*
**Utz**, Eugene Joseph 1923- *WhoAmL 92*
**Utz**, John Philip 1922- *AmMWSc 92*
**Utz**, Stephen Gerard 1947- *WhoAmL 92*
**Utz**, Winfield Roy, Jr 1919- *AmMWSc 92, WhoMW 92*
**Utzerath**, Hansjorg 1926- *IntWW 91*
**Utzon**, Jorn 1918- *DcTwDes, IntWW 91*
**Uvarov**, Olga *Who 92*
**Uvena**, Frank John 1934- *WhoFI 92*
**Uviller**, H. Richard 1929- *WhoAmL 92*
**Uwaydah**, Ibrahim Musa 1943- *AmMWSc 92*
**Uxbridge**, Earl of 1950- *Who 92*
**Uxkull-Gyllenband**, Nikolaus, Count von 1877-1944 *EncTR 91*
**Uy**, William Cheng 1940- *AmMWSc 92*
**Uyeda**, Carl Kaoru 1922- *AmMWSc 92*
**Uyeda**, Charles Tsuneo 1929- *AmMWSc 92*
**Uyeda**, Kosaku 1932- *AmMWSc 92*
**Uyeda**, Lance Den 1943- *WhoWest 92*
**Uyeda**, Seiya 1929- *IntWW 91*
**Uyehara**, Otto A 1916- *AmMWSc 92*
**Uyehara**, Otto Arthur 1916- *WhoWest 92*
**Uyeki**, Edwin M 1928- *AmMWSc 92*
**Uyemoto**, Jerry Kazumitsu 1939- *AmMWSc 92*
**Uyeno**, Edward Teiso 1921- *AmMWSc 92*
**Uys**, Jacobus Johannes 1921- *IntWW 91*
**Uys**, Johannes Marthinus 1925- *AmMWSc 92*
**Uys**, Pieter-Dirk 1945- *IntWW 91*
**Uyterhoeven**, Hugo Emil Robert 1931- *WhoFI 92*
**Uyttenbroeck**, Frans 1921- *IntWW 91*
**Uzawa**, Hirofumi 1928- *IntWW 91*
**Uzer**, Ahmet Turgay 1952- *AmMWSc 92*
**Uzes**, Charles Alphonse 1939- *AmMWSc 92*
**Uzgiris**, Egidijus E 1941- *AmMWSc 92*
**Uzieblo**, Jerzy Zygmunt 1942- *IntWW 91*
**Uziel**, Mayo 1930- *AmMWSc 92*
**Uziell-Hamilton**, Adrianne Pauline 1932- *Who 92*
**Uzilevsky**, Marcus 1937- *WhoWest 92*
**Uzodinma**, John E 1929- *AmMWSc 92*
**Uzoigwe**, Godfrey N. 1938- *WhoBlA 92*
**Uzoigwe**, Joshua 1946- *ConCom 92*
**Uztariz**, Jeronimo de 1670-1732 *BlkwCEP*
**Uzzell**, Albert Werner 1931- *WhoEnt 92*
**Uzzell**, Thomas 1932- *AmMWSc 92*

# V

Va, Moananu 1937- *WhoAmP 91*
Vaagenes, Morris George Cornell 1929- *WhoRel 92*
Vaal, Joseph John, Jr. 1947- *WhoMW 92*
Vaaler, Jeffrey David 1948- *AmMWSc 92*
Vaara, Cathie Lynne 1955- *WhoMW 92*
Vaca, Santiago Mauricio 1960- *WhoHisp 92*
Vacca, Anthony Andrew 1940- *WhoMW 92*
Vacca, John Joseph, Jr. 1922- *WhoEnt 92*
Vacca, Linda Lee 1947- *AmMWSc 92*
Vaccai, Nicola 1790-1848 *NewAmDM*
Vaccarezza, Peter E. 1937- *WhoMW 92*
Vaccaro, Brenda 1939- *IntMPA 92, WhoEnt 92*
Vaccaro, Christopher Mark 1959- *WhoAmL 92*
Vaccaro, Richard Francis 1949- *WhoFI 92*
Vacchiano, William 1912- *WhoEnt 92*
Vacco, Dennis C. 1952- *WhoAmL 92*
Vachani, Mohan 1942- *WhoFI 92*
Vache, Claude Charles 1926- *WhoRel 92*
Vache, Warren 1914- *IntAu&W 91*
Vacher De Lapouge, Georges 1854-1936 *BiDExR*
Vacher-Morris, Elizabeth Michele 1963- *WhoRel 92*
Vachher, Prehlad Singh 1933- *WhoMW 92*
Vachnadze, Nato 1904-1953 *SovUnBD*
Vachon, Dennis Paul 1954- *WhoAmL 92*
Vachon, Louis-Albert *Who 92*
Vachon, Louis-Albert 1912- *IntWW 91, RelLAm 91, WhoRel 92*
Vachon, Raymond Normand 1940- *AmMWSc 92*
Vachon, Reginald Irenee 1937- *AmMWSc 92, WhoFI 92*
Vachon, Rogatien Rosaire 1945- *WhoWest 92*
Vachss, Andrew H. 1942- *WrDr 92*
Vachss, Andrew Henry 1942- *IntAu&W 91, WhoAmL 92*
Vacik, James P 1931- *AmMWSc 92*
Vacirca, Salvatore John 1922- *AmMWSc 92*
Vacquier, Victor 1907- *AmMWSc 92*
Vacquier, Victor Dimitri 1940- *AmMWSc 92*
Vactor, Alma Kane 1925- *WhoWest 92*
Vadakin, James C. 1924-1981 *ConAu 134*
Vadalabene, Sam Martin 1914- *WhoAmP 91*
Vadas, Peter 1953- *AmMWSc 92*
Vadas, Robert Louis 1936- *AmMWSc 92*
Vader, Randy W. 1950- *WhoMW 92*
Vadhwa, Om Parkash 1941- *AmMWSc 92*
Vadim, Roger 1928- *IntDcF 2-2 [port], IntMPA 92, IntWW 91*
Vadim, Roger Plemiannikov 1928- *WhoEnt 92*
Vadlamudi, Krishna 1927- *AmMWSc 92*
Vadodaria, Bhupatbhai 1929- *IntAu&W 91*
Vaduva, Leontina 1962- *IntWW 91*
Vaea 1921- *Who 92*
Vaes, Robert 1919- *IntWW 91, Who 92*
Vafai, Kambiz 1953- *WhoMW 92*
Vafakos, William P 1927- *AmMWSc 92*
Vafopoulo, Xanthe 1949- *AmMWSc 92*
Vaganova, Agrippina 1879-1951 *FacFETw*
Vaganova, Agrippina Yakovlevna 1879-1951 *SovUnBD*
Vagelatos, Nicholas 1945- *AmMWSc 92*
Vagelos, P Roy 1929- *AmMWSc 92*
Vagelos, Pindaros Roy 1929- *IntWW 91, WhoFI 92*
Vaggione, Richard Paul 1945- *WhoRel 92*
Vagingeim, Konstantin Konstantinovich 1899-1934 *SovUnBD*
Vaginov, Konstantin Konstantinovich 1899-1934 *SovUnBD*
Vagneur, Kathryn Otto 1946- *WhoFI 92, WhoWest 92*
Vagnieres, Robert Charles, Jr. 1954- *WhoMW 92*
Vagnini, Livio L 1917- *AmMWSc 92*
Vagnozzi, Aldo 1925- *WhoAmP 91*
Vagnucci, Anthony Hillary 1928- *AmMWSc 92*
Vago, Constant 1921- *IntWW 91*
Vago, Pierre 1910- *IntWW 91*
Vagramian-Nishanian, Violet *WhoEnt 92*
Vagris, Jan Janovich 1930- *IntWW 91*
Vagris, Yan Yanovich 1930- *SovUnBD*
Vagts, Detlev Frederick 1929- *WhoAmL 92*
Vahala, George Martin 1946- *AmMWSc 92*
Vahanian, Gabriel 1927- *IntAu&W 91, WrDr 92*
Vahaviolos, Sotirios J 1946- *AmMWSc 92*
Vahey, David William 1944- *AmMWSc 92*
Vahey, Maryanne T *AmMWSc 92*
Vahila, James George 1941- *WhoFI 92*
Vahila, Michael Jerome 1954- *WhoEnt 92, WhoMW 92*
Vahldiek, Fred W 1933- *AmMWSc 92*
Vahouny, George V 1932- *AmMWSc 92*
Vahsholtz, Robert John 1935- *WhoFI 92*
Vaicaitis, Rimas 1941- *AmMWSc 92*
Vaidhyanathan, V S 1933- *AmMWSc 92*
Vaidya, Akhil Babubhai 1947- *AmMWSc 92*
Vail, Charles Brooks 1923- *AmMWSc 92*
Vail, Charles R 1915- *AmMWSc 92*
Vail, Desire *DrAPF 91*
Vail, Edwin George 1921- *AmMWSc 92*
Vail, Frederick Scott 1944- *WhoEnt 92*
Vail, Iris Jennings 1928- *WhoMW 92*
Vail, Joane Rand 1928- *WhoAmP 91*
Vail, Joe Franklin 1928- *WhoFI 92, WhoMW 92*
Vail, John Moncrieff 1931- *AmMWSc 92*
Vail, Larry Dean 1956- *WhoMW 92*
Vail, Luki Styskal 1937- *WhoWest 92*
Vail, Patricia 1941- *WhoAmL 92*
Vail, Patrick Virgil 1937- *AmMWSc 92*
Vail, Peter R 1930- *AmMWSc 92*
Vail, Sidney Lee 1928- *AmMWSc 92*
Vail, Thomas Van Husen 1926- *WhoMW 92*
Vaillancourt, Remi Etienne 1934- *AmMWSc 92*
Vaillant, George Eman 1934- *AmMWSc 92*
Vaillant, Henry Winchester 1936- *AmMWSc 92*
Vaillaud, Michel L. 1931- *IntWW 91*
Vaillaud, Pierre 1935- *IntWW 91*
Vails, Nelson 1960- *BlkOlyM*
Vainisi, Jerome Robert 1941- *WhoMW 92*
Vainshtein, Boris Konstantinovich 1921- *IntWW 91*
Vainshtok, Vladimir Petrovich 1908-1978 *SovUnBD*
Vaira, Peter Francis 1937- *WhoAmL 92*
Vairasse, Denis 1637?-1683? *ScFEYrs*
Vairavan, Kasivisvanathan 1939- *AmMWSc 92*
Vairo, Robert J 1930- *WhoIns 92*
Vaisey, David George 1935- *IntWW 91, Who 92*
Vaisey-Genser, Florence Marion 1929- *AmMWSc 92*
Vaishnav, Ramesh 1934- *AmMWSc 92*
Vaishnava, Prem P 1942- *AmMWSc 92*
Vaisnys, Juozas Rimvydas 1937- *AmMWSc 92*
Vaitkevicius, Vainutis K 1927- *AmMWSc 92*
Vaitl, William Ludwig 1934- *WhoMW 92*
Vaitukaitis, Judith L 1940- *AmMWSc 92*
Vaivads, Sandra N. 1959- *WhoFI 92*
Vaivods, Julijans d1990 *IntWW 91N*
Vaivods, Julijans 1895- *WhoRel 92*
Vaizey, Lady 1938- *Who 92*
Vaizey, Alandra Marina 1938- *IntAu&W 91*
Vaizey, Marina 1938- *WrDr 92*
Vajda, Gyorgy 1927- *IntWW 91*
Vajda, Vladimir 1948- *WhoEnt 92*
Vajeeprasee Thongsak, Thomas 1935- *WhoFI 92*
Vajk, J Peter 1942- *AmMWSc 92*
Vajna, Andrew 1944- *IntMPA 92*
Vajnar, Vratislav 1930- *IntWW 91*
Vajpayee, Atal Bihari 1926- *IntWW 91, Who 92*
Vajra, Lake Rain 1969- *WhoEnt 92*
Vakalo, Emmanuel-George 1946- *WhoMW 92*
Vakhromeyev, Kyril Varfolomeyevich *IntWW 91*
Vakhtangov, Yevgeniy Bagrationovich 1883-1922 *SovUnBD*
Vakhtangov, Yevgeny Bagrationovich 1833-1927 *FacFETw*
Vakil, Jayshree 1957- *WhoWest 92*
Vakil, Nader *WhoMW 92*
Vakili, Nader Gholi 1927- *AmMWSc 92*
Vakilzadeh, Javad 1927- *AmMWSc 92*
Vakula, Alex Benjamin 1961- *WhoAmL 92*
Vala, Martin Thorvald, Jr 1938- *AmMWSc 92*
Vala, Robert 1930- *WhoWest 92*
Valabregue, Antonin 1845-1900 *ThHEIm*
Valach, Miroslav 1926- *AmMWSc 92*
Valachi, Joseph M 1903-1971 *FacFETw*
Valades, Diego 1533-1579 *HisDSpE*
Valadez, Bernadette Dolores 1963- *WhoHisp 92*
Valadez, Gustavo 1952- *WhoHisp 92*
Valadez, John Robert 1944- *WhoHisp 92*
Valadez, Lando X *WhoAmP 91*
Valadez, Mark Alan 1960- *WhoRel 92*
Valadez, Ray Michael 1947- *WhoHisp 92*
Valadez, Stanley David 1924- *WhoHisp 92*
Valadon, Marie Clementine 1867-1938 *ThHEIm [port]*
Valan, Merlyn O 1926- *WhoAmP 91*
Valance, Edward Hatch 1930- *WhoAmL 92*
Valance, Marsha Jeanne 1946- *WhoMW 92*
Valandra, Paul *WhoAmP 91*
Valanis, Barbara Mayleas 1942- *AmMWSc 92*
Valante, Harrison 1936- *WhoEnt 92*
Valasca *EncAmaz 91*
Valasek, Joseph 1897- *AmMWSc 92, WhoMW 92*
Valaskovic, David William 1961- *WhoMW 92*
Valassi, Kyriake V 1917- *AmMWSc 92*
Valberg, Leslie S 1930- *AmMWSc 92*
Valbrun, Marjorie 1963- *WhoBlA 92*
Valcourt, Bernard 1952- *IntWW 91*
Valdar, Colin Gordon 1918- *IntAu&W 91, Who 92*
Valderrabano, Enriquez de 1500?-1560? *NewAmDM*
Valderrama, David M 1933- *WhoAmP 91*
Valdes, Albert Charles 1907- *WhoHisp 92*
Valdes, Alberto 1946- *WhoHisp 92*
Valdes, Berardo A. 1943- *WhoHisp 92*
Valdes, Carlos L 1951- *WhoAmP 91*
Valdes, Carlos Leonardo 1951- *WhoHisp 92*
Valdes, Carmen 1954- *BlkOlyM*
Valdes, Dario 1938- *WhoHisp 92*
Valdes, David Churchill 1950- *WhoEnt 92*
Valdes, Gilberto *WhoHisp 92*
Valdes, Hector Jose, Sr. 1930- *WhoHisp 92*
Valdes, James John 1951- *AmMWSc 92, WhoHisp 92*
Valdes, Jorge E. 1940- *WhoHisp 92*
Valdes, Jorge Nelson 1942- *WhoHisp 92*
Valdes, Juan Jose 1953- *WhoHisp 92*
Valdes, Laura 1919- *WhoBlA 92*
Valdes, Mario J. 1934- *WrDr 92*
Valdes, Maximiano *WhoEnt 92, WhoHisp 92*
Valdes, Othoniel Aurelio 1956- *WhoRel 92*
Valdes, Pedro H. 1945- *WhoBlA 92*
Valdes, Pedro Hilario, Jr. 1945- *WhoHisp 92*
Valdes, Petra G. *WhoHisp 92*
Valdes, Teresa A. 1938- *WhoHisp 92*
Valdes, Victor A., Sr. 1936- *WhoHisp 92*
Valdes-Dapena, Marie A 1921- *AmMWSc 92*
Valdes-Fauli, Gonzalo Francisco 1946- *WhoFI 92*
Valdes-Fauli, Jose *WhoHisp 92*
Valdes-Fauli, Raul Jacinto 1943- *WhoHisp 92*
Valdes Lopez, Lourdes Maria 1959- *WhoAmL 92*
Valdez, Abelardo *WhoHisp 92*
Valdez, Abelardo L. 1942- *WhoHisp 92*
Valdez, Abelardo Lopez 1942- *WhoAmP 91*
Valdez, Albert *WhoHisp 92*
Valdez, Albert R 1948- *WhoAmP 91*
Valdez, Arnold 1954- *WhoWest 92*
Valdez, Bernard R. 1931- *WhoHisp 92*
Valdez, Bert *WhoHisp 92*
Valdez, Betty Jean 1956- *WhoHisp 92*
Valdez, Carlos 1952- *WhoHisp 92*
Valdez, David 1949- *WhoHisp 92*
Valdez, Elizabeth O. de 1945- *WhoHisp 92*
Valdez, Ernest E. 1938- *WhoHisp 92*
Valdez, Frances Juanita 1955- *WhoHisp 92*
Valdez, Frank M. 1927- *WhoHisp 92*
Valdez, Jake Reginaldo 1936- *WhoHisp 92*
Valdez, Joe R. 1947- *WhoHisp 92*
Valdez, Joel D. 1934- *WhoHisp 92*

**Valdez,** Jose A. *WhoHisp 92*
**Valdez,** Joseph Thomas 1950- *WhoHisp 92*
**Valdez,** Joseph Vincent, II 1955- *WhoHisp 92*
**Valdez,** Joyce Ruby 1928- *WhoAmP 91*
**Valdez,** Juan Andres 1950- *WhoAmP 91*
**Valdez,** Jude 1944- *WhoHisp 92*
**Valdez,** Luis 1940- *BenetAL 91, WrDr 92*
**Valdez,** Luis M. 1940- *WhoHisp 92*
**Valdez,** Mary Alejandra 1950- *WhoHisp 92*
**Valdez,** Oscar Jesus 1960- *WhoHisp 92*
**Valdez,** Pedro Patricio 1946- *WhoHisp 92*
**Valdez,** Pete, Jr. 1945- *WhoHisp 92*
**Valdez,** Rebecca Katharine 1954- *WhoHisp 92*
**Valdez,** Robert D. 1956- *WhoFI 92, WhoHisp 92*
**Valdez,** Robert Otto *WhoHisp 92*
**Valdez,** Robert Otto Burciaga 1956- *WhoWest 92*
**Valdez,** Rogelio *WhoHisp 92*
**Valdez,** Sergio 1965- *WhoHisp 92*
**Valdez,** Tereso, Sr. 1928- *WhoHisp 92*
**Valdez,** Troy Harold 1938- *WhoHisp 92*
**Valdez,** Valdamar Eluid 1929- *WhoHisp 92*
**Valdez,** Vicky *WhoHisp 92*
**Valdez,** Victor A. 1949- *WhoHisp 92*
**Valdez,** Victor Raul 1962- *WhoHisp 92*
**Valdez,** Vincent Emilio 1940- *WhoWest 92*
**Valdez-Cantu,** Linda L. 1952- *WhoHisp 92*
**Valdivia,** Enrique *AmMWSc 92*
**Valdivia,** Luis de 1561-1642 *HisDSpE*
**Valdivia,** Pedro de 1502?-1553 *HisDSpE*
**Valdivielso,** Jose Martinez 1934- *WhoHisp 92*
**Valdivieso,** Dario 1936- *AmMWSc 92*
**Valdivieso,** Pedro M. 1932- *WhoHisp 92*
**Valdivieso,** Rafael 1942- *WhoHisp 92*
**Valdivieso-Belaunde,** Felipe 1928- *Who 92*
**Valdman,** Albert 1931- *WhoMW 92*
**Valdovinos,** J. Lauro 1938- *WhoHisp 92*
**Valdsaar,** Herbert 1925- *AmMWSc 92*
**Vale,** Brian 1938- *Who 92*
**Vale,** Eugene *WhoEnt 92*
**Vale,** Eugene 1916- *IntMPA 92*
**Vale,** Malcolm Graham Allan 1942- *WrDr 92*
**Valeani,** Bernard Marie 1945- *WhoFI 92*
**Valega,** Thomas Michael 1937- *AmMWSc 92*
**Valek,** Miroslav 1927- *IntAu&W 91*
**Valencak,** Hannelore 1929- *IntAu&W 91*
**Valencia,** Amalia 1943- *WhoHisp 92*
**Valencia,** Carmen 1962- *WhoHisp 92*
**Valencia,** Cesar 1918- *WhoHisp 92*
**Valencia,** Henry 1942- *WhoHisp 92*
**Valencia,** Henry R. 1924- *WhoHisp 92*
**Valencia,** Lydia J. 1942- *WhoHisp 92*
**Valencia,** Martin de 1473-1534 *HisDSpE*
**Valencia,** Mauro Eduardo 1949- *AmMWSc 92*
**Valencia,** Nestor Alvaro 1934- *WhoHisp 92*
**Valencia,** Richard 1952- *WhoHisp 92*
**Valencia,** Rogelio Pasco 1939- *WhoFI 92, WhoMW 92*
**Valencia,** Shelby Sue 1962- *WhoWest 92*
**Valencia,** Simon Rodolfo 1938- *WhoHisp 92*
**Valencia,** Valerie J. 1951- *WhoHisp 92*
**Valencia-Bogert,** Elizabeth C. 1963- *WhoHisp 92*
**Valencia-Ibanez,** Edmundo 1925- *IntWW 91*
**Valencia-Rodriguez,** Luis 1926- *IntWW 91*
**Valenciano,** Randal Grant Bolosan 1958- *WhoAmL 92*
**Valencich,** Trina J 1943- *AmMWSc 92*
**Valenciennes,** Pierre-Henri de 1750-1819 *BlkwCEP*
**Valency,** Maurice 1903- *IntAu&W 91, WrDr 92*
**Valens** *EncEarC*
**Valens** 328?-378 *EncEarC*
**Valenstein,** Elliot Spiro 1923- *AmMWSc 92*
**Valenta,** Zdenek 1927- *AmMWSc 92*
**Valentas,** Kenneth John 1938- *WhoMW 92*
**Valente,** Benita 1939- *NewAmDM*
**Valente,** Jose Angel 1929- *DcLB 108 [port]*
**Valente,** Michael F. 1937- *WhoWest 92*
**Valente,** Peter Charles 1940- *WhoAmL 92*
**Valentekovich,** Marija Nikoletic 1932- *AmMWSc 92*
**Valenti,** Fernando 1926- *NewAmDM*
**Valenti,** Frederick Alan 1967- *WhoEnt 92*
**Valenti,** Jack *LesBEnT 92*
**Valenti,** Jack 1921- *IntMPA 92, IntWW 91*
**Valenti,** Jack Joseph 1921- *NewYTBS 91 [port], WhoEnt 92*
**Valenti,** Rita *WhoAmP 91*
**Valenti,** Thomas Paul 1952- *WhoMW 92*
**Valentia,** Viscount 1929- *Who 92*
**Valentich,** John David *AmMWSc 92*
**Valentin,** Angel Luis 1955- *WhoHisp 92*
**Valentin,** Jose Rafael 1953- *WhoWest 92*
**Valentin,** Nilda 1950- *WhoHisp 92*
**Valentine,** Alan Darrell 1958- *WhoEnt 92*
**Valentine,** Alex *IntAu&W 91X*
**Valentine,** Amy Young 1916- *WhoAmP 91*
**Valentine,** Barry 1927- *Who 92*
**Valentine,** Barry Dean 1924- *AmMWSc 92*
**Valentine,** Carol Ann 1942- *WhoWest 92*
**Valentine,** Christine Spicer Jones 1942- *WhoWest 92*
**Valentine,** Darnell 1959- *WhoBlA 92*
**Valentine,** David Thomas 1801-1869 *BenetAL 91*
**Valentine,** De Wain 1936- *WhoWest 92*
**Valentine,** Deborah Marie 1951- *WhoBlA 92*
**Valentine,** Donald H, Jr 1940- *AmMWSc 92*
**Valentine,** Doris Mae *WhoEnt 92*
**Valentine,** E S *ScFEYrs*
**Valentine,** Foy Dan 1923- *WhoRel 92*
**Valentine,** Frank Michael 1951- *WhoRel 92*
**Valentine,** Fred Townsend 1934- *AmMWSc 92*
**Valentine,** Fredrick Arthur 1926- *AmMWSc 92*
**Valentine,** Gene C. 1950- *WhoWest 92*
**Valentine,** Harry McWalter, III 1951- *WhoEnt 92*
**Valentine,** Herman E. 1937- *WhoBlA 92*
**Valentine,** Herman Edward 1937- *WhoFI 92*
**Valentine,** I Tim, Jr 1926- *WhoAmP 91*
**Valentine,** J. T. 1918- *WhoBlA 92*
**Valentine,** James K 1942- *AmMWSc 92*
**Valentine,** James William 1926- *AmMWSc 92, WhoWest 92*
**Valentine,** Jean *DrAPF 91*
**Valentine,** Jean 1934- *BenetAL 91, ConAu 34NR, ConPo 91, WrDr 92*
**Valentine,** Jeffrey 1945- *WhoAmL 92*
**Valentine,** Jimmie Lloyd 1940- *AmMWSc 92*
**Valentine,** Joan Selverstone 1945- *AmMWSc 92*
**Valentine,** John L 1949- *WhoAmP 91*
**Valentine,** Joseph Earl 1933- *AmMWSc 92*
**Valentine,** Karen 1947- *IntMPA 92*
**Valentine,** Kid Thomas 1896-1987 *FacFETw*
**Valentine,** Martin Douglas 1935- *AmMWSc 92*
**Valentine,** Milton 1825-1906 *RelLAm 91*
**Valentine,** Raymond Carlyle 1936- *AmMWSc 92*
**Valentine,** Robert Jerome 1943- *WhoRel 92*
**Valentine,** Tim 1926- *AlmAP 92 [port]*
**Valentine,** Tony 1939- *TwCPaSc*
**Valentine,** William Newton 1917- *AmMWSc 92, IntWW 91*
**Valentine,** William R 1944- *WhoAmP 91*
**Valentini,** James Joseph 1950- *AmMWSc 92*
**Valentini Terrani,** Lucia 1946- *IntWW 91*
**Valentinian I** 321-375 *EncEarC*
**Valentinian II** 371-392 *EncEarC*
**Valentinian III** 419-455 *EncEarC*
**Valentino** 1932- *IntWW 91*
**Valentino,** Frank d1991 *NewYTBS 91*
**Valentino,** Mario *DcTwDes*
**Valentino,** Mario d1991 *NewYTBS 91*
**Valentino,** Rene X. 1961- *WhoEnt 92*
**Valentino,** Rudolph 1895-1926 *FacFETw [port]*
**Valentino,** Stephen Eric 1954- *WhoWest 92*
**Valentinus** *EncEarC*
**Valento,** Donald John 1933- *WhoAmP 91*
**Valenty,** Steven Jeffrey 1944- *AmMWSc 92*
**Valenty,** Vivian Briones 1944- *AmMWSc 92*
**Valenzeno,** Dennis Paul 1949- *AmMWSc 92*
**Valenzuela,** Claudio, Jr. 1957- *WhoHisp 92*
**Valenzuela,** Debra Guadalupe 1957- *WhoFI 92*
**Valenzuela,** Edward 1934- *WhoHisp 92*
**Valenzuela,** Edward 1935- *WhoHisp 92*
**Valenzuela,** Fernando 1960- *WhoHisp 92*
**Valenzuela,** Gaspar Rodolfo 1933- *AmMWSc 92*
**Valenzuela,** Henry Emilio 1960- *WhoAmL 92*
**Valenzuela,** Jose Luis 1951- *WhoEnt 92*
**Valenzuela,** Luisa 1938- *BenetAL 91, DcLB 113 [port], IntWW 91, LiExTwC, SpAmWW*
**Valenzuela,** Manuel Anthony, Jr. 1955- *WhoAmL 92, WhoHisp 92*
**Valenzuela,** Patrick 1962- *WhoHisp 92*
**Valenzuela,** Paul Acosta, Jr. 1947- *WhoHisp 92*
**Valenzuela,** Rafael L. *WhoHisp 92*
**Valenzuela,** Reinaldo A 1952- *AmMWSc 92*
**Valenzuela,** Victor 1944- *WhoHisp 92*
**Valenzuela,** William G. *WhoHisp 92*
**Valeo,** Ernest John 1945- *AmMWSc 92*
**Valera,** Julio 1968- *WhoHisp 92*
**Valerian** 200?-260? *EncEarC*
**Valeriano,** Napoleon D 1917-1975 *FacFETw*
**Valerio,** Anthony *DrAPF 91*
**Valerio,** Mark Luke 1954- *WhoFI 92*
**Valeriote,** Frederick Augustus 1941- *AmMWSc 92*
**Valernes,** Evariste de Bernardi de 1816-1896 *ThHEIm*
**Valero,** Rene Arnold 1930- *WhoHisp 92, WhoRel 92*
**Valero,** Roberto 1955- *WhoHisp 92*
**Valery,** Paul 1871-1945 *FacFETw, GuFrLit 1*
**Vales,** Carolyn Jean 1954- *WhoEnt 92*
**Valesco,** Frances Kay 1941- *WhoWest 92*
**Valesh,** Eva McDonald 1866-1956 *HanAmWH*
**Valeta,** Peter James 1953- *WhoAmL 92*
**Valette,** Adolphe 1876-1942 *TwCPaSc*
**Valfer,** Ernst Siegmar 1925- *WhoWest 92*
**Valgardson,** W.D. *DrAPF 91*
**Valgardson,** William Dempsey 1939- *IntAu&W 91*
**Vali,** Gabor 1936- *AmMWSc 92*
**Vali,** Katrin 1956- *IntAu&W 91*
**Valia,** Kirti Himatlal 1950- *WhoMW 92*
**Valiant,** Leslie Gabriel 1949- *Who 92*
**Valianti,** Daniel James 1965- *WhoAmP 91*
**Valiaveedan,** George Devasia 1932- *AmMWSc 92*
**Valicek,** Michael David 1954- *WhoAmL 92*
**Valien,** Preston 1914- *WhoBlA 92*
**Valier,** Max 1895-1930 *ScFEYrs*
**Valiguira,** Keith 1957- *WhoAmP 91*
**Valimahomed,** Salim Akbarali 1948- *WhoFI 92*
**Valimont,** Robert W 1922- *WhoAmP 91*
**Valin,** Jonathan 1947- *IntAu&W 91, WrDr 92*
**Valin,** Reginald Pierre 1938- *Who 92*
**Valine,** Delmar Edmond, Sr. 1919- *WhoMW 92*
**Valine,** Frederick Christ, Jr. 1944- *WhoWest 92*
**Valins,** Fred Franklin 1946- *WhoMW 92*
**Valinsky,** Jay E *AmMWSc 92*
**Valinsky,** Jay Lawrence 1954- *WhoAmL 92*
**Valinsky,** Mark Steven 1951- *WhoMW 92*
**Valios,** Nicholas Paul 1943- *Who 92*
**Valis,** Wayne Harold 1944- *WhoAmP 91*
**Valk,** Henry Snowden 1929- *AmMWSc 92*
**Valk,** William Lowell 1909- *AmMWSc 92*
**Valko,** Terrence Arthur 1960- *WhoAmL 92*
**Valla,** Kristin Hille 1944- *IntWW 91*
**Vallabhan,** C V Girija 1935- *AmMWSc 92*
**Valladares Perez,** Armando F. 1937- *LiExTwC*
**Vallance,** B *ScFEYrs*
**Vallance,** Iain David Thomas 1943- *IntWW 91, Who 92*
**Vallance,** May Louise 1901- *WhoAmP 91*
**Vallance,** Michael Wilson 1933- *Who 92*
**Vallance,** Philip Ian Fergus 1943- *Who 92*
**Vallance-Owen,** John 1920- *IntWW 91, Who 92*
**Vallance White,** James Ashton 1938- *Who 92*
**Vallandigham,** Clement Laird 1820-1871 *AmPolLe*
**Vallano,** Richard David 1931- *WhoIns 92*
**Vallante,** Michael Anthony 1955- *WhoAmP 91*
**Vallarino,** Eduardo 1938- *IntWW 91*
**Vallario,** Joseph Frederick, Jr 1937- *WhoAmP 91*
**Vallat,** Francis Aime 1912- *Who 92*
**Vallat,** Xavier 1891-1972 *BiDExR*
**Vallbona,** Carlos 1927- *AmMWSc 92*
**Vallbona,** R. Nuri 1957- *WhoHisp 92*
**Vallbona,** Rima Gretel Rothe 1931- *WhoHisp 92*
**Vallbona de Rima,** Gretchen 1931- *IntAu&W 91*
**Valle,** Carmen *DrAPF 91*
**Valle,** Dave 1960- *WhoHisp 92*
**Valle,** Dino 1940- *WhoEnt 92*
**Valle,** Georgette *WhoAmP 91*
**Valle,** Isis *WhoHisp 92*
**Valle,** J. Esteban 1942- *WhoHisp 92*
**Valle,** Jose A. 1943- *WhoHisp 92*
**Valle,** Jose B., Jr. 1947- *WhoHisp 92*
**Valle,** Jose Cecilio del 1770-1834 *HisDSpE*
**Valle,** Laurence Francis 1943- *WhoAmL 92*
**Valle,** Mark A. *WhoHisp 92*
**Valle-Riestra,** J Frank 1924- *AmMWSc 92*
**Valle y Caviedes,** Juan *HisDSpE*
**Valleau,** John Philip 1932- *AmMWSc 92*
**Vallee,** Bert L 1919- *AmMWSc 92*
**Vallee,** Bert Lester 1919- *IntWW 91*
**Vallee,** Jacques Fabrice 1939- *WhoFI 92*
**Vallee,** Jacques P 1945- *AmMWSc 92*
**Vallee,** Lillian 1949- *ConAu 135*
**Vallee,** Oliver Robert 1963- *WhoWest 92*
**Vallee,** Richard Bert *AmMWSc 92*
**Vallee,** Richard Earl 1928- *AmMWSc 92*
**Vallee,** Rudy 1901-1986 *FacFETw, NewAmDM*
**Vallejo,** Cesar 1892-1938 *BenetAL 91, FacFETw*
**Vallejo,** Cesar Abraham 1892-1938 *LiExTwC*
**Vallejo,** Eduardo 1942- *WhoHisp 92*
**Vallejo,** Lisa Elena 1965- *WhoHisp 92*
**Vallejos,** Ramon Jose 1953- *WhoHisp 92*
**Vallejos,** Ricardo Paul 1959- *WhoHisp 92*
**Vallejos,** William Arthur 1958- *WhoHisp 92*
**Vallely,** Gwen Meltzer 1943- *WhoFI 92*
**Vallely,** Thomas J *WhoAmP 91*
**Vallen,** Jerome Jay 1928- *WhoWest 92*
**Vallentine,** Benjamin Bennaton 1843-1926 *BenetAL 91*
**Vallentine,** John Franklin 1931- *AmMWSc 92*
**Vallera,** Daniel A 1951- *AmMWSc 92*
**Vallerand,** Philippe Georges 1954- *WhoWest 92*
**Vallerga,** Bernard A *AmMWSc 92*
**Valles,** Evelyn 1953- *WhoHisp 92*
**Valles,** Judith 1933- *WhoHisp 92*
**Valles,** Jules 1832-1885 *GuFrLit 1*
**Vallese,** Frank M 1950- *AmMWSc 92*
**Vallese,** Lucio M 1915- *AmMWSc 92*
**Valleskey,** Carole Anne 1955- *WhoEnt 92*
**Valletta,** Robert M 1931- *AmMWSc 92*
**Valley,** John 1941- *TwCPaSc*
**Valley,** Leonard Maurice 1933- *AmMWSc 92*
**Valley,** Sharon Louise 1941- *AmMWSc 92*
**Valley,** Thomas James 1945- *WhoBlA 92*
**Valli,** Alida 1921- *IntMPA 92*
**Valli,** Frankie 1937- *NewAmDM, WhoEnt 92*
**Valli,** June 1933- *WhoEnt 92*
**Valliant,** John Peden 1947- *WhoAmP 91*
**Vallier,** Tracy L 1936- *AmMWSc 92*
**Valliere,** Roland Edward 1954- *WhoEnt 92*
**Vallin,** Eugene 1856-1922 *DcTwDes*
**Vallings,** George 1932- *Who 92*
**Vallis,** Michael Anthony 1929- *Who 92*
**Vallis,** Val 1916- *WrDr 92*
**Vallis,** Vince 1940- *WhoEnt 92*
**Vallone,** Peter F. *WhoHisp 92*
**Vallone,** Peter F 1934- *WhoAmP 91*
**Vallone,** Raf 1916- *IntMPA 92*
**Vallone,** Ralph, Jr. 1947- *WhoAmL 92*
**Vallotton,** William Wise 1927- *AmMWSc 92*
**Vallowe,** Henry Howard 1924- *AmMWSc 92*
**Valls,** Nicolas J. 1964- *WhoHisp 92*
**Valls,** Oriol Tomas 1947- *AmMWSc 92*
**Valls Arango,** Jorge 1933- *LiExTwC*
**Valner,** Rudy 1960- *WhoAmL 92, WhoWest 92*
**Valocchi,** Albert Joseph 1953- *AmMWSc 92*
**Valoff,** Jo Lynn 1957- *WhoWest 92*
**Valois,** Charles 1924- *WhoRel 92*
**Valois,** Fern L. J. 1946- *WhoEnt 92*
**Valois,** Georges 1878-1945 *BiDExR*
**Valois,** Ninette de *Who 92*
**Valois,** Ninette de 1898- *FacFETw*
**Valois,** Roger 1928- *WhoAmP 91*
**Valone,** Keith Emerson 1953- *WhoWest 92*
**Valor,** Joaquin, Jr. 1944- *WhoHisp 92*
**Valov,** Yuriy Nikolayevich 1934- *IntWW 91*
**Valpey,** Richard Sanborn, III 1956- *WhoMW 92*
**Valsamakis,** Emmanuel 1933- *AmMWSc 92*
**Valsangiacomo,** Oreste Victor, Sr 1919- *WhoAmP 91*
**Valticos,** Nicholas 1918- *IntWW 91*
**Valtin,** Heinz 1926- *AmMWSc 92*
**Valtin,** Jan 1905-1951 *LiExTwC*
**Valvani,** Shri Chand 1940- *AmMWSc 92*
**Valvassori,** Galdino E 1926- *AmMWSc 92*
**Valverde,** Eradio, Jr. 1952- *WhoRel 92*
**Valverde,** Joe A. 1935- *WhoHisp 92*
**Valverde,** Jose Maria 1926- *DcLB 108 [port]*
**Valverde,** Leonard A. 1943- *WhoHisp 92*
**Valverde,** Nelson Alberto 1954- *WhoFI 92*
**Valverde,** Rodrigo Alberto 1952- *WhoHisp 92*
**Valverde,** Sylvia Ann 1956- *WhoHisp 92*
**Valverde,** Vicente de d1541 *HisDSpE*
**Valyi,** Emery I 1911- *AmMWSc 92*
**Vammen,** James Oliver 1932- *WhoMW 92*
**Vamos,** Tibor 1926- *AmMWSc 92, IntWW 91*
**Vamplew,** Wray 1943- *IntAu&W 91, WrDr 92*
**Vampola,** Alfred Ludvik 1934- *AmMWSc 92*
**Van,** Peter 1936- *WhoAmL 92, WhoFI 92*
**Van,** Vester L., Jr. 1941- *WhoBlA 92*

**Van**, Vester Lee 1941- *WhoAmL 92*

**Van Aardenne**, Gijs M. C. 1930- *IntWW 91*

**Vanable**, Joseph William, Jr 1936- *AmMWSc 92*

**Van Ackeren**, Maurice Edward 1911- *WhoMW 92*

**Van Agt**, Andries A. M. *IntWW 91*

**Van Aken**, William Russell 1912- *WhoAmP 91*

**Van Alen**, James d1991 *NewYTBS 91 [port]*

**Van Alfen**, Neal K 1943- *AmMWSc 92*

**Van Allan**, Richard 1935- *IntWW 91, Who 92*

**Van Allburg**, Chris 1949- *WrDr 92*

**Van Allen**, George Howard 1946- *WhoMW 92*

**Van Allen**, James Alfred 1914- *AmMWSc 92, FacFETw, IntWW 91, Who 92*

**Van Allen**, Maurice Wright 1918- *AmMWSc 92*

**VanAllen**, Morton Curtis 1950- *WhoBlA 92*

**Van Allen**, Rodger 1938- *WhoRel 92*

**Van Aller**, Robert Thomas 1933- *AmMWSc 92*

**Van Allman**, Don Thomas 1932- *WhoMW 92*

**Van Alstine**, James Bruce 1949- *AmMWSc 92*

**Van Alstyne**, John Pruyn 1921- *AmMWSc 92*

**Van Alstyne**, Vance Brownell 1924- *WhoFI 92*

**Van Alstyne**, W. Scott, Jr. 1922- *WhoAmL 92*

**Van Alstyne**, William Warner 1934- *WhoAmL 92*

**Van Alten**, Lloyd 1924- *AmMWSc 92*

**Van Alten**, Pierson Jay 1928- *AmMWSc 92*

**Van Altena**, William F 1939- *AmMWSc 92*

**Vanaman**, David Clyde 1954- *WhoFI 92*

**Vanaman**, Sherman Benton 1928- *AmMWSc 92*

**Vanaman**, Thomas Clark 1941- *AmMWSc 92*

**VanAmburg**, Gerald Leroy 1941- *AmMWSc 92*

**VanAmburg**, Lisa Smith 1948- *WhoAmL 92*

**Vanamee**, Parker 1919- *AmMWSc 92*

**Vanamo**, Jorma Jaakko 1913- *IntWW 91*

**Van Amringe**, John Howard 1835-1915 *BiInAmS*

**Van Amson**, George Louis 1952- *WhoBlA 92*

**Van Andel**, Betty Jean 1921- *WhoFI 92, WhoMW 92*

**Van Andel**, Jay 1924- *WhoFI 92, WhoMW 92*

**van Andel**, Katharine Bridget *Who 92*

**Van Andel**, Nan 1953- *WhoFI 92*

**Van Andel**, Tjeerd Hendrik 1923- *AmMWSc 92*

**VanAntwerp**, Craig Lewis 1950- *AmMWSc 92*

**Van Antwerp**, Daniel Janse 1935- *WhoAmL 92*

**Van Antwerp**, James C, Jr 1923- *WhoAmP 91*

**Van Antwerp**, Rosemary Dirkie 1946- *WhoFI 92*

**Van Antwerp**, Walter Robert 1925- *AmMWSc 92*

**Van Antwerpen**, Franklin Stuart 1941- *WhoAmL 92*

**van Appledorn**, Elizabeth Ruth 1918- *WhoRel 92*

**van Appledorn**, Mary Jeanne 1927- *WhoEnt 92*

**Van Ark**, Joan *WhoEnt 92*

**Van Ark**, Joan 1943- *IntMPA 92*

**Van Arman**, Clarence Gordon 1917- *AmMWSc 92*

**Van Arsdale**, Catherine Eva 1917- *WhoAmP 91*

**Van Arsdale**, Curtis Ray 1947- *WhoMW 92*

**Van Arsdale**, Dick 1943- *WhoWest 92*

**Van Arsdale**, Herman Wesley 1925- *WhoRel 92*

**Van Arsdale**, James *WhoWest 92*

**Van Arsdale**, James W 1926- *WhoAmP 91*

**Van Arsdel**, John Hedde 1921- *AmMWSc 92*

**Van Arsdel**, Paul Parr, Jr 1926- *AmMWSc 92, WhoWest 92*

**Van Arsdel**, William Campbell, III 1920- *AmMWSc 92*

**Van Arsdell**, Madelene 1918- *WhoAmP 91*

**Van Arsdol**, Maurice Donald, Jr. 1928- *WhoWest 92*

**Van Artsdalen**, Donald West 1919- *WhoAmL 92*

**Van Artsdalen**, Ervin Robert 1913- *AmMWSc 92*

**Van As**, Tamara Lin 1968- *WhoEnt 92*

**Van Asdall**, Willard 1934- *AmMWSc 92*

**Vanasek**, James George 1944- *WhoFI 92, WhoWest 92*

**Vanasek**, Robert Edward 1949- *WhoAmP 91, WhoMW 92*

**Van Asperen**, Morris Earl 1943- *WhoFI 92, WhoWest 92*

**Vanasse**, Albert J 1918- *WhoAmP 91*

**Vanasse**, Charles Andrew 1959- *WhoMW 92*

**Vanasse**, George Alfred 1924- *AmMWSc 92*

**Van Assendelft**, Onno Willem 1932- *AmMWSc 92*

**Van Atta**, Charles W 1934- *AmMWSc 92*

**Vanatta**, John Crothers, III 1919- *AmMWSc 92*

**Van Atta**, John Reynolds 1939- *WhoMW 92*

**Van Atta**, Lester Clare 1905- *AmMWSc 92*

**Van Auken**, Oscar William 1939- *AmMWSc 92*

**Van Auken**, Richard Anthony 1934- *WhoMW 92*

**Vanauken**, Sheldon 1914- *ConAu 35NR*

**Van Auken-Haight**, Carol Ann 1940- *WhoAmL 92*

**Van Ausdal**, Ray Garrison 1943- *AmMWSc 92*

**Vanaver**, Livia Rebecca Drapkin 1951- *WhoEnt 92*

**Van Baak**, Anthony Edward 1949- *WhoFI 92*

**Van Baak**, David Alan 1952- *AmMWSc 92*

**Van Balen**, Gary Lee 1954- *WhoFI 92*

**Van Beaumont**, Karel William 1930- *AmMWSc 92*

**Van Bebber**, George Thomas 1931- *WhoAmL 92, WhoMW 92*

**van Beeck**, Frans Jozef 1930- *WhoRel 92*

**Van Beinum**, Eduard 1901-1959 *NewAmDM*

**Van Beke**, Charles William 1940- *WhoAmL 92*

**Van Belle**, Gerald 1936- *AmMWSc 92*

**Van Bellinghen**, Jean-Paul 1925- *IntWW 91, Who 92*

**Van Benschoten**, David Bruce 1950- *WhoAmL 92*

**Van Benthuysen**, Gretchen Crosby 1953- *WhoEnt 92*

**Van Bergen**, Frederick Hall 1914- *AmMWSc 92*

**van Bergen**, Johannes Frans A. 1942- *WhoFI 92*

**Van Bibber**, Karl Albert 1950- *AmMWSc 92*

**Van Binh**, Paul Nguyen *WhoRel 92*

**VanBlaricom**, Glenn R 1949- *AmMWSc 92*

**Vanblarigan**, Peter 1952- *AmMWSc 92*

**van Boer**, Bertil Herman 1924- *WhoEnt 92*

**Van Bokkelen**, William Requa 1946- *WhoMW 92*

**Van Booven**, Judy Lee 1952- *WhoMW 92*

**Van Borssum**, John Bernard 1947- *WhoWest 92*

**Van Boven**, D Lauris 1919- *WhoAmP 91*

**Van Breeman**, Cornelis 1936- *AmMWSc 92*

**Van-Breemen**, Bertram 1919- *WhoMW 92*

**VanBremen**, Lee 1938- *WhoMW 92*

**Van Broekhoven**, Harold 1913- *WhoRel 92*

**Van Broekhoven**, Rollin Adrian 1940- *WhoAmL 92*

**VanBruggen**, Ariena H C 1949- *AmMWSc 92*

**Van Bruggen**, John Timothy 1913- *AmMWSc 92*

**Van Bruggen**, Theodore 1926- *AmMWSc 92*

**Vanbrugh**, John 1664?-1726 *BlkwCEP, RfGEnL 91*

**Van Brunt**, Cornelius 1827?-1903 *BiInAmS*

**Van Brunt**, Edmund Ewing 1926- *WhoWest 92*

**Van Brunt**, H. L. *ConAu 35NR*

**Van Brunt**, Lloyd *DrAPF 91*

**Van Brunt**, Lloyd 1936- *ConAu 35NR, ConAu 15AS [port]*

**Van Brunt**, Marcia Adele 1937- *WhoMW 92*

**Van Brunt**, Richard Joseph 1939- *AmMWSc 92*

**Van Bruwaene**, Raymond T. 1938- *WhoFI 92*

**Van Buhler**, Robert Allan 1944- *WhoEnt 92, WhoWest 92*

**Van Buijtenen**, Johannes Petrus 1928- *AmMWSc 92*

**Van Bulck**, Hendrikus Eugenius 1950- *WhoFI 92*

**Van Buren**, Arnie Lee 1939- *AmMWSc 92*

**Van Buren**, David S. *DrAPF 91*

**Van Buren**, James Clifford 1935- *WhoEnt 92*

**Van Buren**, Jerome Paul 1926- *AmMWSc 92*

**Van Buren**, Martin 1782-1862 *AmPolLe [port], BenetAL 91, RComAH*

**Van Buren**, Paul Matthews 1924- *WhoRel 92*

**Van Buren**, Phyllis Eileen 1947- *WhoMW 92*

**Van Buren**, William Ralph, III 1956- *WhoAmL 92*

**Van Burkalow**, Anastasia 1911- *AmMWSc 92*

**Van Caenegem**, Raoul Charles Joseph 1927- *Who 92*

**Van Calsteren**, Marie-Rose 1958- *AmMWSc 92*

**Van Camp**, Ann Jane 1931- *WhoMW 92*

**Van Camp**, Brian Ralph 1940- *WhoAmL 92*

**Van Camp**, Bruce Alan 1958- *WhoMW 92*

**Van Camp**, Mike 1941- *WhoAmP 91*

**VanCamp**, Paul Louis 1954- *WhoEnt 92*

**Van Camp**, W M 1921- *AmMWSc 92*

**Van Campen**, Darrell R 1935- *AmMWSc 92*

**Van Campen**, Karl *ConAu 34NR*

**Van Cantfort**, Dale Edward 1952- *WhoEnt 92*

**Vancas**, Mark Francis 1947- *WhoWest 92*

**Vance**, Benjamin Dwain 1932- *AmMWSc 92*

**Vance**, Bridgid Rowan 1952- *WhoAmP 91*

**Vance**, Buzz Dwane 1954- *WhoRel 92*

**Vance**, Carrie Temple 1944- *WhoWest 92*

**Vance**, Catherine Ann 1953- *WhoMW 92*

**Vance**, Charles Fogle, Jr. 1924- *WhoAmL 92*

**Vance**, Charles Ivan 1929- *Who 92*

**Vance**, Charles Randall 1953- *WhoRel 92*

**Vance**, Christopher M *WhoAmP 91*

**Vance**, Cyrus Roberts 1917- *AmPolLe, IntWW 91, Who 92, WhoAmL 92, WhoAmP 91*

**Vance**, David Alvin 1948- *WhoFI 92*

**Vance**, David Zue 1955- *WhoAmL 92*

**Vance**, Dennis E 1942- *AmMWSc 92*

**Vance**, Dennis William 1938- *AmMWSc 92*

**Vance**, Donald Richard 1957- *WhoRel 92*

**Vance**, Edward F 1929- *AmMWSc 92*

**Vance**, Elbridge Putnam 1915- *AmMWSc 92*

**Vance**, Estil A 1938- *WhoAmP 91*

**Vance**, Ethel *ConAu 135*

**Vance**, Eugene 1934- *IntAu&W 91*

**Vance**, George 1936- *WhoAmP 91*

**Vance**, Gerald *ConAu 36NR, TwCSFW 91*

**Vance**, Howard Grant 1915- *WhoAmP 91*

**Vance**, Hugh Gordon 1924- *AmMWSc 92*

**Vance**, Irvin E. 1928- *WhoBlA 92*

**Vance**, Irvin Elmer 1928- *AmMWSc 92*

**Vance**, Jack 1916- *IntAu&W 91, TwCSFW 91, WrDr 92*

**Vance**, James 1930- *WhoAmL 92, WhoFI 92*

**Vance**, James Richard 1957- *WhoAmL 92*

**Vance**, Jeffrey Michael 1965- *WhoEnt 92*

**Vance**, Joan Emily Jackson 1925- *WhoMW 92*

**Vance**, John Holbrook *WrDr 92*

**Vance**, John Milton 1937- *AmMWSc 92*

**Vance**, Joseph Alan 1930- *AmMWSc 92*

**Vance**, Joseph Francis 1937- *AmMWSc 92*

**Vance**, Kevin Brett 1953- *WhoMW 92*

**Vance**, Kevin Mark 1966- *WhoRel 92*

**Vance**, Lawrence N. 1949- *WhoBlA 92*

**Vance**, Leigh 1922- *IntMPA 92*

**Vance**, Michael C 1951- *WhoAmP 91*

**Vance**, Michael Charles 1951- *WhoAmL 92, WhoMW 92*

**Vance**, Miles Elliott 1932- *AmMWSc 92*

**Vance**, Morag L *WhoAmP 91*

**Vance**, Ollie Lawrence 1937- *AmMWSc 92*

**Vance**, Patricia Eisler 1956- *WhoEnt 92*

**Vance**, Patricia H 1936- *WhoAmP 91*

**Vance**, Paul A, Jr 1930- *AmMWSc 92*

**Vance**, Ray Thomas 1929- *WhoMW 92*

**Vance**, Robert Floyd 1926- *AmMWSc 92*

**Vance**, Robert Mercer 1916- *WhoFI 92*

**Vance**, Robert Smith 1931- *WhoAmP 91*

**Vance**, Ronald *DrAPF 91*

**Vance**, Roy Carroll *WhoAmP 91*

**Vance**, Roy N 1921- *WhoAmP 91*

**Vance**, Sheldon Baird 1917- *WhoAmP 91*

**Vance**, Stephen James 1947- *WhoAmP 91*

**Vance**, Sylvia Phillips 1925- *WhoMW 92*

**Vance**, Thomas Jackson 1955- *WhoMW 92*

**Vance**, Tommie Rowan 1929- *WhoBlA 92*

**Vance**, Velma Joyce 1929- *AmMWSc 92*

**Vance**, Vera R. 1908- *WhoBlA 92*

**Vance**, William E d1986 *TwCWW 91*

**Vance**, William Harrison 1934- *AmMWSc 92*

**Vance**, William J., Sr. 1923- *WhoBlA 92*

**Vance**, William L. 1934- *WrDr 92*

**Vance-Welsh**, Mary Catherine 1957- *WhoRel 92*

**Vancini**, Larry Primo 1956- *WhoEnt 92*

**Van Citters**, Robert L 1926- *AmMWSc 92, IntWW 91*

**Van Citters**, Robert Lee 1926- *WhoWest 92*

**Vancko**, Robert Michael 1942- *AmMWSc 92*

**VanCleave**, Allan Bishop 1910- *AmMWSc 92*

**Van Cleave**, Horace William 1931- *AmMWSc 92*

**Van Cleave**, Peter 1927- *WhoMW 92*

**Van Cleef**, Edward Anson 1944- *WhoEnt 92*

**Van Cleve**, Charles Warren *WhoAmL 92*

**Van Cleve**, John Woodbridge 1914- *AmMWSc 92*

**Van Cleve**, Ruth Gill 1925- *WhoAmP 91*

**Van Cott**, Harold Porter 1925- *AmMWSc 92*

**Van Cott**, Jeffrey Mark 1945- *WhoWest 92*

**Van Cott**, Margaret Newton 1830-1914 *RelLAm 91*

**Vancouver**, Archbishop of d1990 *Who 92N*

**Vancouver**, George 1757-1798 *BenetAL 91*

**Vancrum**, Robert J *WhoAmP 91*

**Van-Culin**, Samuel 1930- *IntWW 91, Who 92, WhoRel 92*

**Vancura**, Barbara Jean *WhoMW 92*

**Van Cura**, Joyce Bennett 1944- *WhoMW 92*

**Vandal**, Steven Offerdal 1948- *WhoWest 92*

**VanDale**, Robert LeRoy 1935- *WhoRel 92*

**Van Dam**, Jose 1940- *IntWW 91, NewAmDM*

**Vandam**, Leroy David 1914- *AmMWSc 92*

**Van Dam**, R. Paul *WhoAmL 92, WhoAmP 91, WhoWest 92*

**Vandame**, Charles *WhoRel 92*

**Van Damm**, Sheila 1922-1987 *FacFETw*

**Van Damme**, Jean-Claude 1961- *IntMPA 92*

**van de Beek**, Abraham 1946- *WhoRel 92*

**Vande Berg**, James L. 1939- *WhoRel 92*

**Vande Berg**, Jerry Stanley 1940- *AmMWSc 92*

**VandeBerg**, John Lee 1947- *AmMWSc 92*

**Vandeberg**, John Thomas 1939- *AmMWSc 92*

**Vande Berg**, Warren James 1943- *AmMWSc 92*

**Van de Bogart**, David Fawdrey 1956- *WhoMW 92*

**Vandebosch**, Jacques 1941- *IntWW 91*

**van de Bunt**, Dirk Wouter 1957- *WhoEnt 92*

**Van Deburg**, William Lloyd 1948- *WhoMW 92*

**Van de Castle**, John F 1933- *AmMWSc 92*

**Van Deerlin**, Lionel *LesBEnT 92*

**Van Deerlin**, Lionel 1914- *WhoAmP 91*

**Vandegaer**, Jan Edmond 1927- *AmMWSc 92*

**Van De Graaf**, Jacobus J 1938- *WhoIns 92*

**Van de Graaf**, Johannes J *WhoAmP 91*

**Van De Graaff**, Kent Marshall 1942- *AmMWSc 92*

**Vandegriff**, Thomas Herman 1949- *WhoMW 92*

**Vandegrift**, Alfred Eugene 1937- *AmMWSc 92, WhoMW 92*

**Vandegrift**, Donald P 1960- *WhoIns 92*

**Vandegrift**, Joseph Thomas 1943- *WhoFI 92*

**Vandegrift**, Vaughn 1946- *AmMWSc 92*

**Vandehey**, Robert C 1924- *AmMWSc 92*

**Vande Hoef**, Richard 1925- *WhoAmP 91*

**Van De Kaa**, Dirk Jan 1933- *IntWW 91*

**Van de Kamp**, John 1936- *WhoAmP 91*

**Van de Kamp**, John Kalar 1936- *WhoAmL 92, WhoWest 92*

**Vande Kamp**, Norman Eugene 1939- *WhoMW 92*

**van de Kamp**, Peter Cornelis 1940- *AmMWSc 92*

**Van de Kar**, Louis David 1947- *AmMWSc 92*

**Vande Kemp**, Hendrika 1948- *WhoRel 92*

**Vande Kieft**, Laurence John 1932- *AmMWSc 92*

**Van Dellen**, Chester, Jr. 1949- *WhoMW 92*

**Vandeman**, George Allen 1940- *WhoAmL 92*

**Van Demark**, Duane R 1936- *AmMWSc 92*

**Vandemark**, Noland Leroy 1919- *AmMWSc 92*

**Van Demark**, Richard Edward 1955- *WhoAmL 92, WhoMW 92*

**Van Demark**, Robert Eugene 1913- *WhoMW 92*

**Van Demark**, Ruth Elaine 1944- *WhoAmL 92, WhoMW 92*

**Van den Akker**, Johannes Archibald 1904- *AmMWSc 92*

**Van Den Avyle**, James Albert 1946- *AmMWSc 92*
**Vanden-Bempde-Johnstone** *Who 92*
**Vandenberg**, Arthur Hendrick 1884-1951 *AmPeW, AmPolLe, FacFETw*
**Vandenberg**, Joanna Maria 1938- *AmMWSc 92*
**Van Den Berg**, L 1929- *AmMWSc 92*
**Vandenberg**, Marvin G 1926- *WhoAmP 91*
**Vanden Berg**, Michael Stewart 1954- *WhoRel 92*
**Vandenberg**, Patricia Clasina 1948- *WhoMW 92*
**Vandenberg**, Peter Ray 1939- *WhoWest 92*
**Vandenberg**, Robert Lee 1951- *WhoWest 92*
**Vandenberg**, Steven Gerritjan 1915- *AmMWSc 92*
**Vandenbergh**, David John 1959- *AmMWSc 92*
**Vandenbergh**, John Garry 1935- *AmMWSc 92*
**Van den Bergh**, Sidney 1929- *AmMWSc 92, IntWW 91, Who 92*
**Vandenberghe**, Ronald Gustave 1937- *WhoFI 92, WhoWest 92*
**Van Den Bogaerde**, Derek Niven 1921- *Who 92*
**Van Den Bold**, Willem Aaldert 1921- *AmMWSc 92*
**Van Den Boom**, Esperanza 1953- *WhoMW 92*
**Van Den Boom**, Wayne Jerome 1953- *WhoMW 92*
**Vanden Born**, William Henry 1932- *AmMWSc 92*
**Vanden Bosch**, James L. 1946- *WhoEnt 92*
**Vandenbosch**, Robert 1932- *AmMWSc 92*
**Vanden Bout**, Paul Adrian 1939- *AmMWSc 92*
**Van Den Broek**, Hans 1936- *IntWW 91*
**Vandenbroucke**, Russell James 1948- *WhoEnt 92, WhoMW 92*
**Vandenburgh**, John Derek 1964- *WhoAmL 92*
**Van Den Essen**, Louis 1939- *WhoHisp 92*
**Vanden Eynden**, Charles Lawrence 1936- *AmMWSc 92, WhoMW 92*
**Van Den Haag**, Ernest 1914- *IntWW 91, WhoAmL 92*
**VandenHazel**, Bessel J 1927- *AmMWSc 92*
**vanden Heuvel**, Katrina 1959- *ConAu 133*
**Vanden Heuvel**, William John Adrian, III 1935- *AmMWSc 92*
**van den Houten**, W.F. 1943- *WhoAmL 92*
**Van Den Hoven**, Helmert Frans *Who 92*
**Van Den Hoven**, Helmert Frans 1923- *IntWW 91*
**Van Den Noort**, Stanley 1930- *AmMWSc 92*
**Vande Noord**, Edwin Lee 1938- *AmMWSc 92*
**Van Den Sype**, Jaak Stefaan 1935- *AmMWSc 92*
**Van De Poel**, Jeffrey Paul 1957- *WhoWest 92*
**Van Depoele**, Charles Joseph 1846-1892 *BiInAmS*
**Vandepopuliere**, Joseph Marcel 1929- *AmMWSc 92*
**Van de Putte**, Leticia 1954- *WhoAmP 91, WhoHisp 92*
**Vandeputte**, Robert M. A. C. 1908- *IntWW 91*
**Vander**, Arthur J 1933- *AmMWSc 92*
**Vander Aarde**, Robert Leon 1936- *WhoRel 92*
**Vander Aarde**, Stanley Bernard 1931- *WhoMW 92*
**Van Der Avoird**, Ad 1943- *IntWW 91*
**VanDerbeck**, James Scott 1953- *WhoAmL 92*
**Vanderbeck**, Ronald Lee 1955- *WhoMW 92*
**Vanderbeek**, Duane Lloyd 1942- *WhoMW 92*
**Vander Beek**, Leo Cornelis 1918- *AmMWSc 92*
**Vanderbeek**, Stan 1927-1984 *IntDcF 2-2*
**VanDerBeets**, Richard 1932- *ConAu 35NR*
**Vanderberg**, Jerome Philip 1935- *AmMWSc 92*
**Van Der Beugel**, Ernst H. *IntWW 91*
**Van Der Biest**, Alain 1943- *IntWW 91*
**Van der Bijl**, William 1920- *AmMWSc 92*
**Vanderbilt**, Arthur T, II 1950- *IntAu&W 91, WhoAmL 92*
**Vanderbilt**, Cornelius 1794-1877 *RComAH*
**Vanderbilt**, David Hamilton 1954- *AmMWSc 92*
**Vanderbilt**, Dean *WhoAmP 91*
**Vanderbilt**, George Washington 1862-1914 *BiInAmS*
**VanderBilt**, Herb Jay 1946- *WhoMW 92*
**Vanderbilt**, Jeffrey James 1951- *AmMWSc 92*
**Vanderbilt**, Kermit 1925- *WhoWest 92*
**Vanderbilt**, Vern C, Jr 1920- *AmMWSc 92*
**Vanderbilt**, Vern Corwin, Jr. 1920- *WhoMW 92*
**Vanderborgh**, Nicholas Ernest 1938- *AmMWSc 92*
**Van Der Bosch**, Susan Hartnett 1935- *WhoMW 92*
**Vanderburg**, Charles R 1956- *AmMWSc 92*
**Vanderburg**, Craig Terrence 1954- *WhoBlA 92*
**Vanderburg**, Paul Stacey 1941- *WhoFI 92*
**Van der Burg**, Sjirk 1926- *AmMWSc 92*
**Vanderburg**, Vance Dilks 1937- *AmMWSc 92, WhoMW 92*
**Van Der Byl**, Pieter K. Fleming-Voltelyn 1923- *IntWW 91*
**Vander Clute**, Norman Roland 1932- *WhoAmL 92*
**Vandercook**, John W. 1902-1963 *BenetAL 91*
**Vander Does**, Michael David 1951- *WhoEnt 92*
**Van der Donck**, Adriaen 1620-1655? *BenetAL 91*
**Van Der Eb**, Alex Jan 1936- *IntWW 91*
**Vander Esch**, Lawrence Merle 1947- *WhoAmP 91*
**Vander Espt**, Georges J. H. 1931- *IntWW 91*
**Vanderet**, Robert Charles 1947- *WhoAmL 92*
**Vanderfelt**, Robin 1921- *Who 92*
**Vanderford**, Thomas Neil, Jr. 1960- *WhoAmL 92*
**Vandergraaf**, Tjalle T 1936- *AmMWSc 92*
**Vandergraff**, Donna Jean 1956- *WhoMW 92*
**Vandergraft**, James Saul 1937- *AmMWSc 92*
**Vandergriff**, Jerry Dodson 1943- *WhoFI 92, WhoWest 92*
**Vandergriff**, Kenneth Lynn 1954- *WhoRel 92*
**Vandergriff**, William P *WhoAmP 91*
**Vandergrift**, Mary 1901-1991 *NewYTBS 91*
**Vandergrit**, Alexander Archer 1887-1973 *FacFETw*
**Vanderhaar**, Gerard Anthony 1931- *WhoRel 92*
**Vanderhaeghe**, Guy Clarence 1951- *IntAu&W 91*
**Vander Hart**, David Lloyd 1941- *AmMWSc 92*
**Van Der Heide**, Be 1933- *TwCPaSc*
**Vander Heide**, G. Peter 1947- *WhoFI 92*
**Vanderheiden**, Gregg 1949- *AmMWSc 92*
**Vanderheiden**, Richard Thomas 1947- *WhoWest 92*
**Van der Heijde**, Paul Karel Maria 1947- *AmMWSc 92*
**Van der Helm**, Dick 1933- *AmMWSc 92*
**van der Hiel**, Rudolph John 1940- *WhoAmL 92*
**Vanderhoef**, Larry Neil 1941- *AmMWSc 92*
**Vander Hoek**, Gerald Wayne 1955- *WhoRel 92*
**Vanderhoek**, Jack Yehudi 1941- *AmMWSc 92*
**Van der Hoeven**, Theo A 1933- *AmMWSc 92*
**Vanderhoff**, James H. 1950- *WhoFI 92*
**Vanderhoff**, John W 1925- *AmMWSc 92*
**Vanderholm**, Dale Henry 1940- *AmMWSc 92*
**Vander Houwen**, Boyd A. 1946- *WhoWest 92*
**Van der Hulst**, Jan Mathijs 1948- *AmMWSc 92*
**Van De Rijn**, Ivo 1946- *AmMWSc 92*
**Van Deripe**, Donald R 1934- *AmMWSc 92*
**Vander Jagt**, David Lee 1942- *AmMWSc 92*
**VanderJagt**, Donald W 1938- *AmMWSc 92*
**Vander Jagt**, Guy 1931- *AlmAP 92 [port], WhoAmP 91, WhoMW 92*
**Vanderkam**, James Clair 1946- *WhoRel 92*
**Van Der Kemp**, Gerald 1912- *IntWW 91*
**Van Der Kiste**, Robert Edgar Guy 1912- *Who 92*
**Van Der Klaauw**, Christoph Albert 1924- *IntWW 91*
**Vander Kloet**, Sam Peter 1942- *AmMWSc 92*
**Van der Kloot**, Albert Peter 1921- *AmMWSc 92*
**Van der Kloot**, William George 1927- *AmMWSc 92*
**Vanderkooi**, Jane M 1944- *AmMWSc 92*
**Vander Kooi**, Kathryn Cornelia 1921- *WhoAmP 91*
**Vander Kooi**, Lambert Ray 1935- *AmMWSc 92*
**Vanderkooi**, William Nicholas 1929- *AmMWSc 92*
**Vanderkooy**, John 1941- *AmMWSc 92*
**Vander Laan**, Mark Alan 1948- *WhoAmL 92*
**Vanderlaan**, Martin 1948- *AmMWSc 92*
**Vanderlaan**, Richard B. 1931- *WhoFI 92, WhoMW 92*
**Vanderlaan**, Robert 1930- *WhoAmP 91*
**VanderLaan**, Robert D. 1952- *WhoAmL 92*
**Vanderlaan**, Willard Parker 1917- *AmMWSc 92*
**VanDerlaske**, Dennis P 1948- *AmMWSc 92*
**Van Der Lijde**, Arnold *BlkOlyM*
**Vanderlind**, Merwyn Ray *AmMWSc 92*
**Vanderlinde**, Mary 1929- *WhoAmP 91*
**Vanderlinde**, Raymond E 1924- *AmMWSc 92*
**Van Der Linde**, Reinhoud H 1929- *AmMWSc 92*
**VanderLinden**, Camilla Denice Dunn 1950- *WhoFI 92, WhoWest 92*
**VanderLinden**, Carl R 1923- *AmMWSc 92*
**VanderLinden**, Carl Rene 1923- *WhoWest 92*
**Van der Linden**, John Edward 1917- *WhoAmP 91*
**Vanderlip**, Narcissa Cox 1880-1966 *HanAmWH*
**Vanderlip**, Richard L 1938- *AmMWSc 92*
**van der Loon**, Piet 1920- *Who 92*
**Vanderloop**, William N *WhoAmP 91*
**Vanderlosk**, Stanley R 1918- *WhoAmP 91*
**Vander Lugt**, Anthony 1937- *AmMWSc 92*
**Vander Lugt**, Karel L 1940- *AmMWSc 92*
**Van Der Maaten**, Martin Junior 1932 *AmMWSc 92*
**VanderMarck**, William Henry 1929- *WhoRel 92*
**VanderMeer**, Canute 1930- *AmMWSc 92*
**Van Der Meer**, Jan 1935- *IntWW 91*
**VanderMeer**, John David 1944- *WhoMW 92*
**Vandermeer**, John H 1940- *AmMWSc 92*
**Van der Meer**, John Peter 1943- *AmMWSc 92*
**Vander Meer**, Johnny 1914- *FacFETw*
**Van Dermeer**, Marc 1953- *WhoEnt 92*
**Vandermeer**, R A 1934- *AmMWSc 92*
**Vander Meer**, Robert Kenneth 1942- *AmMWSc 92*
**Vandermeer**, Roy 1931- *Who 92*
**Van Der Meer**, Simon 1925- *AmMWSc 92, IntWW 91, Who 92, WhoNob 90*
**Van der Merwe**, Barbara Rondelli 1939- *WhoMW 92*
**van der Merwe**, Nikolaas J 1940- *ConAu 35NR*
**Van Der Merwe**, Stoffel 1934- *IntWW 91*
**Vandermeulen**, David John 1959- *WhoAmL 92*
**Vandermeulen**, John Henri 1933- *AmMWSc 92*
**Van Der Meulen**, Joseph Pierre 1929- *AmMWSc 92, WhoWest 92*
**Vandermey**, Herman Ronald 1952- *WhoRel 92*
**Van Der Meyden**, Diederick O. 1960- *WhoWest 92*
**Vander Molen**, Jack Jacobus 1916- *WhoFI 92*
**Vander Molen**, Richard Allen 1948- *WhoAmP 91*
**Vandermolen**, Robert *DrAPF 91*
**VanderMolen**, Robert 1947- *ConAu 36NR*
**Vander Molen**, Thomas Dale 1950- *WhoAmL 92*
**Vander Muelen**, Conrad 1925- *WhoIns 92*
**Vander Myde**, Paul A 1937- *WhoAmP 91*
**Vander Myde**, Philip Louis 1931- *WhoFI 92*
**Vanderperren**, Cletus J 1912- *WhoAmP 91*
**Vanderplaats**, Garret Niel 1944- *AmMWSc 92*
**Vanderploeg**, Henry Alfred 1944- *AmMWSc 92*
**Vanderpoel**, Sally Rouse 1921- *WhoAmP 91*
**Vanderpool**, Crawford Daniel 1944- *WhoRel 92*
**Vanderpool**, Eustace Arthur 1934- *WhoBlA 92*
**Vanderpool**, Ward Melvin 1917- *WhoFI 92, WhoMW 92*
**Vanderpoorten**, Herman 1922- *IntWW 91*
**van der Post**, Laurens 1906- *ConAu 35NR, ConNov 91, LiExTwC, RfGEnL 91, Who 92, WrDr 92*
**Van Der Post**, Laurens Jan 1906- *IntAu&W 91, IntWW 91*
**Vanderryn**, Jack 1930- *AmMWSc 92*
**Vandersall**, John Henry 1928- *AmMWSc 92*
**Vander Sande**, John Bruce 1944- *AmMWSc 92*
**Vandersee**, Charles *DrAPF 91*
**Vanderslice**, Douglas Mark 1961- *WhoFI 92*
**Vanderslice**, Joseph Thomas 1927- *AmMWSc 92*
**Vanderslice**, Thomas Aquinas 1932- *AmMWSc 92, WhoFI 92*
**Vander Sluis**, Kenneth Leroy 1925- *AmMWSc 92*
**Vanderspek**, Peter George 1925- *WhoWest 92*
**Van Der Spiegel**, Jan 1951- *AmMWSc 92*
**Vanderspurt**, Thomas Henry 1946- *AmMWSc 92*
**Van Der Spuy**, Una 1912- *WrDr 92*
**Vanderstar**, John 1933- *WhoAmL 92*
**Van Der Stee**, Alphons Petrus Johannes M. 1928- *IntWW 91*
**Vander Stelt**, Nathan John 1963- *WhoRel 92*
**Van Der Stoel**, Max 1924- *IntWW 91*
**Vander Stoep**, J 1957- *WhoAmP 91*
**Van der Stucken**, Frank 1858-1929 *NewAmDM*
**Van Der Vaart**, Hubertus Robert 1922- *AmMWSc 92*
**Vandervalk**, Charlotte *WhoAmP 91*
**Van Der Vat**, Dan 1939- *IntAu&W 91*
**Van Der Veen**, James Morris 1931- *AmMWSc 92*
**Vanderveen**, John Edward 1934- *AmMWSc 92*
**Vanderveen**, John Warren 1933- *AmMWSc 92*
**Van der Veen**, Steven Roger 1947- *WhoFI 92*
**Vanderveken**, John 1930- *IntWW 91*
**Vander Velde**, George 1943- *AmMWSc 92, WhoMW 92*
**Vander Velde**, John Christian 1930- *AmMWSc 92*
**Vander Velde**, W E 1929- *AmMWSc 92*
**VanderVen**, Ned Stuart 1932- *AmMWSc 92*
**Van der Voo**, Rob 1940- *AmMWSc 92*
**Van Der Voorn**, Peter C 1940- *AmMWSc 92*
**Vander Voort**, Dale Gilbert 1924- *WhoFI 92*
**Vandervoort**, Peter Oliver 1935- *AmMWSc 92*
**Vander Vorst**, Andre 1935- *AmMWSc 92*
**Vander Vorst**, Darlene M. 1937- *WhoRel 92*
**Vander Vorst**, Wilbur *WhoAmP 91*
**Vandervort**, Darrell Lynn 1956- *WhoRel 92*
**Van Der Waals**, J. Henri 1920- *IntWW 91*
**Van der Waals**, Johannes Diderik 1837-1923 *WhoNob 90*
**Vander Wall**, Eugene 1931- *AmMWSc 92*
**Vanderwall**, Mary Elizabeth 1952- *WhoAmP 91*
**Van Der Wall**, Robert J. 1941- *WhoAmL 92*
**van der Wateren**, Jan Floris 1940- *Who 92*
**Van der Wee**, Herman 1928- *ConAu 133*
**Van Der Wee**, Herman Frans Anna 1928- *IntWW 91*
**Vander Weele**, Donald Joseph 1944- *WhoFI 92*
**Vander Wende**, Christina 1930- *AmMWSc 92*
**Van Der Wende**, Kenneth 1955- *WhoMW 92*
**van der Werff**, Jonathan Ervine 1935- *Who 92*
**VanderWerff**, Lyle Lloyd 1934- *WhoMW 92, WhoRel 92*
**Van Der Werff**, Terry J. 1944- *IntWW 91*
**Van der Werff**, Terry Jay 1944- *AmMWSc 92*
**Vanderwerff**, William D 1929- *AmMWSc 92*
**VanderWiel**, Carole Jean 1950- *AmMWSc 92*
**Vander Wiel**, Kenneth Carlton 1933- *WhoFI 92*
**Vander Wiele**, Dean Kenneth 1958- *WhoRel 92*
**Vanderwiele**, James Milton 1958- *AmMWSc 92*
**Vanderwielen**, Adrianus Johannes 1944- *AmMWSc 92*
**Vanderwill**, William Leo 1954- *WhoMW 92*
**Vanderwolf**, Cornelius Hendrik 1935- *AmMWSc 92*
**Van Der Woude**, Adam Simon 1927- *IntWW 91*
**Vanderwoude**, J. Stephen 1944- *WhoMW 92*
**Vanderwyden**, P. William, III 1947- *WhoMW 92, WhoRel 92*
**Vander Zalm**, William N. 1934- *IntWW 91, Who 92*
**Vander Zalm**, William Nick 1934- *WhoWest 92*

**Vanderzanden,** Edwinna Creswick 1946- *WhoAmL 92*
**Vanderzant,** Carl 1925- *AmMWSc 92*
**Vanderzant,** Erma Schumacher 1920- *AmMWSc 92*
**Vanderzee,** Cecil Edward 1912- *AmMWSc 92*
**van der Zee,** Karen 1947- *WrDr 92*
**Van Der Ziel,** Aldert 1910- *AmMWSc 92*
**Van Der Ziel,** Jan Peter 1937- *AmMWSc 92*
**Vander Zwaag,** Roger 1938- *AmMWSc 92*
**Van Der Zwet,** Tom 1932- *AmMWSc 92*
**Van De Sande,** Johan Hubert 1941- *AmMWSc 92*
**Van de Sande,** Theodorus Amandus Maria 1947- *WhoEnt 92*
**Van De Steeg,** Garet Edward 1940- *AmMWSc 92*
**Van De Steene,** Donald Joseph 1949- *WhoFI 92*
**Van Deursen,** Arie Theodorus 1931- *IntWW 91*
**Van Deusen,** Richard L 1926- *AmMWSc 92*
**Van De Vaart,** Herman 1934- *AmMWSc 92*
**van de Vall,** Mark 1923- *WrDr 92*
**Van De Van,** Theodorus Gertrudus Maria 1946- *AmMWSc 92*
**Van de Vate,** Nancy 1930- *ConCom 92*
**Van de Vate,** Nancy Hayes 1930- *NewAmDM*
**Vandeveer,** Michael D 1941- *WhoAmP 91*
**Van De Veere,** Kathleen Dailey 1935- *WhoWest 92*
**Van De Velde,** Henri 1863-1957 *DcTwDes*
**Vandevelde,** Kenneth Joseph 1953- *WhoAmL 92*
**Van De Ven,** Johannes Adrianus 1930- *IntWW 91*
**VanDevender,** John Pace 1947- *AmMWSc 92*
**Vandevender,** Robert Lee, II 1958- *WhoFI 92*
**Vandeventer,** Janice Leigh 1944- *WhoWest 92*
**Van Deventer,** Mills 1862-1942 *FacFETw*
**Van Deventer,** Pieter Gabriel 1945- *WhoRel 92*
**Van Deventer,** William Carlstead 1908- *AmMWSc 92*
**Vandever,** William Dirk 1949- *WhoAmL 92*
**Van Devere,** Trish 1945- *IntMPA 92*
**Van de Vyver,** Mary Francilene 1941- *WhoRel 92*
**Van De Wal,** Ineke 1954- *TwCPaSc*
**VandeWalle,** Don Micheal 1955- *WhoMW 92*
**VandeWalle,** Gerald Wayne 1933- *WhoAmL 92, WhoAmP 91, WhoMW 92*
**Van de Water,** Frederic F. 1890-1968 *BenetAL 91*
**Van De Water,** Joseph M 1934- *AmMWSc 92*
**Van de Water,** Margaret Smith 1919- *WhoAmP 91*
**Van De Weghe,** Raymond Francis 1934- *WhoFI 92*
**Van de Wetering,** Jan Charles 1941- *WhoFI 92*
**Van De Wetering,** Janwillem 1931- *WrDr 92*
**Van de Wetering,** Richard Lee 1928- *AmMWSc 92*
**Van de Workeen,** M. C. 1927- *WhoRel 92*
**Van de Workeen,** Priscilla Townsend 1946- *WhoFI 92*
**Vande Woude,** George 1935- *AmMWSc 92*
**Vandiford,** Douglas Aaron 1947- *WhoAmP 91*
**Van Dijk,** Christiaan Pieter 1915- *AmMWSc 92*
**Van Dijk,** Cornelis Pieter 1931- *IntWW 91*
**Van Dijk,** Petrus 1943- *IntWW 91*
**Van Dilla,** Marvin Albert 1919- *AmMWSc 92*
**Van Dine,** Alan Charles 1933- *IntAu&W 91*
**Van Dine,** Howard Arthur, Jr. 1921- *WhoRel 92*
**Van Dine,** Paul Edwin 1939- *WhoRel 92*
**Van Dine,** S.S. *BenetAL 91*
**Van Dine,** Vance 1925- *WhoFI 92*
**Vandiver,** Bradford B 1927- *AmMWSc 92*
**Vandiver,** Frank Everson 1925- *IntAu&W 91, WrDr 92*
**Vandiver,** Robert Sanford 1937- *WhoWest 92*
**Vandivier,** Blair Robert 1955- *WhoAmL 92*
**Vandiviere,** H Mac 1921- *AmMWSc 92*
**Vandivort,** William Clayton 1947- *WhoAmL 92*
**Vandlen,** Richard Lee 1947- *AmMWSc 92*
**Vando,** Gloria *DrAPF 91*
**Van Doeren,** Richard Edgerly 1937- *AmMWSc 92*
**Van Dolah,** Robert Frederick 1949- *AmMWSc 92*
**Van Dolah,** Robert Wayne 1919- *AmMWSc 92*
**Van Domelen,** Bruce Harold 1933- *AmMWSc 92*
**Van Dommelen,** David B. 1929- *ConAu 35NR*
**Van Dongen,** Cornelis Godefridus 1934- *AmMWSc 92*
**Van Doorne,** William 1937- *AmMWSc 92*
**Vandore,** Peter Kerr 1943- *Who 92*
**Van Doren,** Carl 1885-1950 *BenetAL 91*
**Van Doren,** Carl Clinton 1885-1950 *AmPeW*
**Van Doren,** Donald Huizinga 1942- *WhoFI 92*
**Van Doren,** Emerson Barclay 1940- *WhoAmL 92*
**Van Doren,** Glenn Henry 1927- *WhoFI 92*
**Van Doren,** Harold 1895-1957 *DcTwDes*
**Van Doren,** Mamie 1933- *IntMPA 92*
**Van Doren,** Mark 1894-1972 *BenetAL 91*
**VanDoren,** Vance Jay 1959- *WhoMW 92*
**Van Dorn,** Edward Michael, Jr. 1947- *WhoAmL 92*
**Van Dorn,** Peter Douglas 1941- *WhoFI 92, WhoWest 92*
**Van Dorne,** R. *ConAu 35NR*
**Van Dover,** Donald 1932- *WhoMW 92*
**Van Dreal,** George 1931- *WhoWest 92*
**Van Dreal,** Paul Arthur 1932- *AmMWSc 92*
**Van Dreel,** Mary Lou E 1935- *WhoAmP 91*
**Van Dreser,** Merton Lawrence 1929- *AmMWSc 92*
**Van Driel,** Henry Martin 1946- *AmMWSc 92*
**Van Driessche,** Willy 1940- *AmMWSc 92*
**Vandross,** Luther *IntWW 91, NewYTBS 91 [port], WhoEnt 92*
**Vandross,** Luther 1951- *CurBio 91 [port]*
**Vandross,** Luther R. 1951- *WhoBlA 92*
**VanDruff,** Larry Wayne 1942- *AmMWSc 92*
**Van Druten,** John 1901-1957 *BenetAL 91, FacFETw*
**Van Dusen,** Albert 1916- *WrDr 92*
**Van Dusen,** Ann Brenton 1919- *WhoWest 92*
**Van Dusen,** Eric Lauren 1946- *WhoRel 92*
**Van Dusen,** Francis Lund 1912- *WhoAmL 92*
**Van Dusen,** George Merrill 1936- *WhoMW 92*
**Van Dusen,** Gerald Charles 1946- *WhoMW 92*
**Van Dusen,** Granville Roy 1944- *WhoEnt 92*
**Van Dusen,** Henry Pitney 1897-1975 *RelLAm 91*
**Van Dusen,** Richard William 1945- *WhoAmL 92*
**van Duuren,** Benjamin Louis 1927- *AmMWSc 92*
**Van Duyn,** Mona *DrAPF 91*
**Van Duyn,** Mona 1921- *BenetAL 91, ConPo 91, WrDr 92*
**Van Duyne,** LeRoy 1923- *WhoAmP 91*
**Van Duyne,** Richard Palmer 1945- *AmMWSc 92*
**Van Duzer,** Albert Wiencke 1917- *WhoRel 92*
**Van Dyck,** Wendy *WhoEnt 92*
**van Dyk,** A. S. *WhoRel 92*
**Van Dyk,** John William 1928- *AmMWSc 92*
**Vandyk,** Neville David 1923- *Who 92*
**Van Dyk,** Robert 1953- *WhoFI 92*
**Van Dyke,** Cecil Gerald 1941- *AmMWSc 92*
**Van Dyke,** Charles H 1937- *AmMWSc 92*
**Van Dyke,** Craig 1941- *AmMWSc 92*
**Van Dyke,** Dan Ross 1950- *WhoAmP 91*
**Van Dyke,** Daniel T. 1946- *WhoFI 92*
**Van Dyke,** David John 1959- *WhoAmL 92*
**Van Dyke,** Dick *LesBEnT 92*
**Van Dyke,** Dick 1925- *IntMPA 92, WhoEnt 92*
**Van Dyke,** Elinor Floyd 1929- *WhoAmP 91*
**Van Dyke,** Henry 1852-1933 *BenetAL 91*
**Van Dyke,** Henry 1921- *AmMWSc 92*
**Van Dyke,** Henry 1928- *WhoBlA 92, WrDr 92*
**Van Dyke,** Jan Ellen 1941- *WhoEnt 92*
**Van Dyke,** Jerry *WhoEnt 92*
**Van Dyke,** John Paul 1950- *WhoMW 92*
**Van Dyke,** John William, Jr 1935- *AmMWSc 92*
**Van Dyke,** Joseph Gary Owen 1939- *WhoFI 92*
**Van Dyke,** Knox 1939- *AmMWSc 92*
**Van Dyke,** Milton D 1922- *AmMWSc 92*
**Van Dyke,** Robert Lowell 1922- *WhoAmP 91*
**Van Dyke,** Russell Austin 1930- *AmMWSc 92*
**Van Dyke,** Sandra 1947- *WhoEnt 92*
**Van Dyke,** Thomas Wesley 1938- *WhoAmL 92*
**Van Dyke,** Vernon 1912- *IntAu&W 91*
**Van Dyke,** Vernon B. 1912- *WrDr 92*
**Van Dyke,** W. S. 1889-1943 *IntDcF 2-2 [port]*
**Van Dyke,** Willard 1906-1986 *IntDcF 2-2*
**Van Dyke-Cooper,** Anny Marion 1928- *WhoFI 92*
**Van Dyken,** Lambertus Peter 1910- *WhoAmP 91*
**Van Dyken,** Roger Lee 1945- *WhoAmP 91*
**Van Dyne,** Edith *ConAu 133, -135, SmATA 68*
**Vane** *Who 92*
**Vane,** Arthur B 1915- *AmMWSc 92*
**Vane,** Bert *WrDr 92*
**Vane,** Edwin T. *LesBEnT 92*
**Vane,** Floie Marie 1937- *AmMWSc 92*
**Vane,** John 1927- *Who 92*
**Vane,** John Robert 1927- *AmMWSc 92, IntWW 91, WhoNob 90*
**Vane,** Sylvia Brakke 1918- *WhoWest 92*
**Vane,** Terence G., Jr. 1942- *WhoFI 92*
**Vane-Tempest-Stewart** *Who 92*
**Van Echo,** Andrew 1918- *AmMWSc 92*
**Van Echo,** David Andrew 1947- *AmMWSc 92*
**Van Eck,** Arthur Orville 1925- *WhoRel 92*
**Van Eck,** Edward Arthur 1916- *AmMWSc 92*
**Van Eck,** Willem Adolph 1928- *AmMWSc 92*
**Van Eeden,** Constance 1927- *AmMWSc 92*
**Van Eekelen,** Willem Frederik 1931- *IntWW 91*
**Van Eenenaam,** Jeffrey Alan 1957- *WhoMW 92*
**Van Eessel,** Charles Leon 1961- *WhoFI 92*
**VanEffen,** Richard Michael 1953- *AmMWSc 92*
**Vanegas,** Guillermo J. *WhoHisp 92*
**Vanegas,** Jorge Alberto 1956- *WhoHisp 92, WhoMW 92*
**Van Egmond,** Max *NewAmDM*
**Van Eikeren,** Paul 1946- *AmMWSc 92*
**Vanek,** Elizabeth-Anne 1951- *WhoMW 92*
**Vanek,** Gary M 1940- *WhoAmP 91*
**Van Ek,** Lynn Carol 1947- *WhoRel 92*
**Van Eldik,** Linda Jo *AmMWSc 92*
**Van Elk,** Ger 1941- *WorArt 1980*
**Vanelli,** Ronald Edward 1919- *AmMWSc 92*
**Van Elswyk,** Marinus, Jr 1929- *AmMWSc 92*
**Van Emden,** Maarten Herman *AmMWSc 92*
**Van Enkevort,** Ronald Lee 1939- *AmMWSc 92*
**Van Ens,** Jack Ronald 1946- *WhoRel 92*
**Van Epps,** Dennis Eugene 1946- *AmMWSc 92*
**Van Epps,** George David 1940- *WhoAmL 92*
**Van Eron,** Kevin J. 1957- *WhoMW 92*
**Van Ert,** Barbara Marie 1943- *WhoFI 92*
**Van Eseltine,** William Parker 1924- *AmMWSc 92*
**Vaness,** Carol 1952- *NewAmDM, WhoEnt 92*
**Van Essen,** David Clinton 1945- *AmMWSc 92*
**Van Essen,** W. 1910- *WrDr 92*
**Van Etten,** Alan 1945- *WhoAmL 92*
**Van Etten,** Hans D 1941- *AmMWSc 92*
**Van Etten,** James L 1938- *AmMWSc 92*
**Van Etten,** James P 1922- *AmMWSc 92*
**Van Etten,** Robert Lee 1937- *AmMWSc 92*
**Van Evera,** Richard K. 1948- *WhoAmL 92*
**van Eyck,** Aldo Ernest 1918- *Who 92*
**Van Eys,** Jan 1929- *AmMWSc 92*
**Van Faasen,** Paul 1934- *AmMWSc 92*
**Van Flandern,** Thomas C 1940- *AmMWSc 92*
**Van Fleet,** George Allan 1953- *WhoAmL 92*
**Vanfleet,** Howard Bay 1931- *AmMWSc 92*
**Van Fleet,** Jo 1919- *IntMPA 92*
**Van Fleet,** Jo 1922- *WhoEnt 92*
**Van Fleet,** William Mabry 1915- *WhoWest 92*
**Van Fossan,** Donald Duane 1929- *AmMWSc 92*
**Van Fossen,** Don B 1942- *AmMWSc 92*
**van Fraassen,** Bas C. 1941- *WrDr 92*
**Van Frank,** Richard Mark 1930- *AmMWSc 92*
**Van Furth,** Ralph 1929- *AmMWSc 92*
**Van Geet,** Anthony Leendert 1929- *AmMWSc 92*
**Van Gelder,** Arthur 1938- *AmMWSc 92*
**Van Gelder,** Nico Michel 1933- *AmMWSc 92*
**Van Gelder,** Richard George 1928- *AmMWSc 92*
**Van Gelder,** Robert 1904-1952 *BenetAL 91*
**Van Gelder,** Rudolph *WhoEnt 92*
**Vangelis** *IntWW 91*
**Vangelis** 1943- *IntMPA 92*
**Vangelisti,** Paul *DrAPF 91*
**Vangellow,** Alex Michael 1948- *WhoEnt 92*
**Van Geluwe,** John David 1916- *AmMWSc 92*
**VanGemeren,** Willem Arie 1943- *WhoRel 92*
**Van Gemert,** Barry 1946- *AmMWSc 92*
**Vanger,** Milton Isadore 1925- *ConAu 34NR*
**Van Gerpen,** Edward *WhoAmP 91*
**Van Gerven,** Walter M. 1935- *IntWW 91*
**Van Gheluwe,** Betty Louise 1953- *WhoWest 92*
**Van Gieson,** Ira Thompson 1866-1913 *BiInAmS*
**Van Gilder,** Derek Robert 1950- *WhoAmL 92, WhoFI 92*
**Van Gilst,** Bass 1911- *WhoAmP 91*
**Van Ginneken,** Andreas J 1935- *AmMWSc 92*
**Van Gorden,** Heron A 1926- *WhoAmP 91*
**Van Gorder,** Jan Reid 1947- *WhoFI 92*
**Van Gorder,** John Frederic 1943- *WhoFI 92*
**Van Gorp,** Gary Wayne 1953- *WhoFI 92, WhoRel 92*
**Van Graafeiland,** Ellsworth Alfred 1915- *WhoAmL 92*
**Van Grack,** Steven 1948- *WhoAmP 91*
**VanGrasstek,** Craig Edwin 1959- *WhoFI 92*
**Van Greenaway,** Peter 1929- *IntAu&W 91*
**Van Grit,** William 1937- *WhoWest 92*
**Van Groenewoud,** Herman 1926- *AmMWSc 92*
**Van Grunsven,** Paul Robert 1961- *WhoAmL 92*
**Van Gulick,** Norman Martin 1926- *AmMWSc 92*
**Van Gundy,** Gregory Frank 1945- *WhoAmL 92*
**Van Gundy,** Seymour Dean 1931- *AmMWSc 92*
**VanGunten,** Edward Albert 1937- *WhoAmL 92*
**Van Hagey,** William 1946- *WhoAmL 92, WhoMW 92*
**Vanhal,** Johann Baptist 1739-1813 *NewAmDM*
**Van Halen,** Eddie 1957- *WhoEnt 92*
**Van Hall,** Clayton Edward 1924- *AmMWSc 92*
**van Hamont,** John Edward 1950- *WhoWest 92*
**Van Handel,** Emile 1918- *AmMWSc 92*
**VanHandel,** Ralph Anthony 1919- *WhoMW 92*
**Van Haren,** W. Michael 1948- *WhoAmL 92*
**Van Harn,** Gordon L 1935- *AmMWSc 92*
**Van Hassel,** Henry John 1933- *AmMWSc 92*
**van Hasselt,** Marc 1924- *Who 92*
**Van Haven,** Frank William 1946- *WhoMW 92*
**Van Haverbeke,** David F 1928- *AmMWSc 92*
**Van Hecke,** Gerald Raymond 1939- *AmMWSc 92*
**Van Hecke,** Jim, Jr 1947- *WhoAmP 91*
**Van Hecke,** Mark August 1959- *WhoMW 92*
**van Heeckeren,** Daniel Wigbold 1936- *WhoMW 92*
**Van Heerden,** Augustus *WhoEnt 92*
**Van Heerden,** Lawrence *WhoRel 92*
**Van Heerden,** Neil Peter 1939- *IntWW 91*
**Van Heerden,** Pieter Jacobus 1915- *AmMWSc 92*
**van Heller,** Marcus *WrDr 92*
**Van Hemert,** Judy 1947- *WhoFI 92*
**van Hengel,** Maarten 1927- *WhoFI 92*
**Van Heusen,** Jimmy 1913-1990 *AnObit 1990, FacFETw, NewAmDM*
**Van Heuvelen,** Alan 1938- *AmMWSc 92*
**Van Heyde,** G. James 1944- *WhoAmL 92*
**Van Heyningen,** Earle Marvin 1921- *AmMWSc 92*
**Van Heyningen,** Roger 1927- *AmMWSc 92*
**Van Hise,** Charles Richard 1857-1918 *BiInAmS*
**Van Hise,** James R 1937- *AmMWSc 92*
**Van Holde,** Kensal Edward 1928- *AmMWSc 92*
**VanHollen,** Christopher, Jr *WhoAmP 91*
**Van Hooff,** Jan A. R. A. M. 1936- *IntWW 91*
**Van Hook,** Andrew 1907- *AmMWSc 92*
**Van Hook,** Donald 1945- *WhoEnt 92*
**Van Hook,** Helen 1961- *WhoEnt 92*
**Van Hook,** James Paul 1931- *AmMWSc 92*
**Van Hook,** Robert Irving, Jr 1942- *AmMWSc 92*

**Van Hook**, Warren Kenneth 1920- *WhoBlA 92*
**Van Hook**, William Alexander 1936- *AmMWSc 92*
**Van Hoomissen**, George Albert 1930- *WhoAmL 92, WhoAmP 91, WhoWest 92*
**Van Hoosier**, Gerald L, Jr 1934- *AmMWSc 92*
**Van Hooven**, Eckart 1925- *IntWW 91*
**Van Horn**, D A 1930- *AmMWSc 92*
**Van Horn**, David Downing 1921- *AmMWSc 92*
**Van Horn**, Diane Lillian 1939- *AmMWSc 92*
**Van Horn**, Donald H 1928- *AmMWSc 92*
**Van Horn**, Gene Stanley 1940- *AmMWSc 92*
**Van Horn**, Harold H, Jr 1937- *AmMWSc 92*
**Van Horn**, Hugh Moody 1938- *AmMWSc 92*
**Van Horn**, Kevin Ray 1960- *WhoAmL 92*
**Van Horn**, Lloyd Dixon 1938- *AmMWSc 92*
**Van Horn**, Richard 1920- *WhoWest 92*
**Van Horn**, Ruth Warner 1918- *AmMWSc 92*
**Van Horn**, Wendell Earl 1929- *AmMWSc 92*
**Van Horne**, Robert Loren 1915- *AmMWSc 92*
**Van Horne**, Terry Eugene 1946- *WhoAmP 91*
**Van Horssen**, Charles Arden 1944- *WhoWest 92*
**Van House**, Mark A. 1961- *WhoRel 92*
**Van House**, Robert Wendell 1932- *WhoRel 92*
**Van Housen**, Muriel Arline 1947- *WhoFI 92*
**Van Houten**, Donald Roger 1936- *WhoWest 92*
**Van Houten**, Franklyn Bosworth 1914- *AmMWSc 92*
**Van Houten**, Gene Steven 1946- *WhoWest 92*
**VanHouten**, Jacob Wesley 1958- *WhoMW 92*
**Van Houten**, Lois *DrAPF 91*
**Van Houten**, Lois 1918- *ConAu 34NR*
**Van Houten**, Lyle Carter 1928- *WhoAmP 91*
**van Houten**, Richard Lee 1946- *WhoRel 92*
**Van Houten**, Robert 1923- *AmMWSc 92*
**van Houten**, Robert Jan 1953- *WhoWest 92*
**Van Houten**, Ronald G 1944- *AmMWSc 92*
**Van Houtte**, Jan A. 1913- *IntWW 91*
**Vanhoutte**, Jean Jacques 1932- *AmMWSc 92*
**Vanhoutte**, Paul Michel *AmMWSc 92*
**Van Houweling**, Cornelius Donald 1918- *AmMWSc 92*
**Van Hoven**, Gerard 1932- *AmMWSc 92*
**Van Hoven**, Jay, Mrs. 1945- *WhoMW 92*
**Van Hoy**, Philip Marshall 1947- *WhoAmP 91*
**van Hudson**, Mark Valentines 1949- *WhoRel 92*
**Van Huystee**, Robert Bernard 1931- *AmMWSc 92*
**Van Hyning**, Howard Martin 1936- *WhoEnt 92*
**Vanicek**, C David 1939- *AmMWSc 92*
**Vanicek**, Petr 1935- *AmMWSc 92*
**Vanier**, Jacques 1934- *AmMWSc 92*
**Vanier**, Peter Eugene 1946- *AmMWSc 92*
**van Iersel**, Bastiaan Martinus 1924- *WhoRel 92*
**Vanik**, Charles A 1913- *WhoAmP 91*
**Vanilla Ice** 1967?- *ConMus 6 [port], News 91 [port], -91-3 [port]*
**Vaniman**, Jean Ann 1960- *WhoFI 92*
**Van Impe**, Jack Leo 1931- *RelLAm 91*
**Van Ingen**, Hubert Anthony 1931- *WhoMW 92*
**Van Ingen**, Jennifer 1942- *TwCPaSc*
**van Innis**, Philippe Xavier 1949- *WhoFI 92*
**Van Inwegen**, Richard Glen 1944- *AmMWSc 92*
**van Itallie**, Jean-Claude 1936- *WhoEnt 92, WrDr 92*
**Van Itallie**, Theodore Bertus 1919- *AmMWSc 92*
**Van Ittersum**, Boudewijn F. 1939- *IntWW 91*
**Vanka**, Maxo *DcAmImH*
**Van Kalker**, Richard A. 1962- *WhoAmL 92*
**van Kammen**, Daniel P. 1943- *WhoFI 92*
**Van Kammen**, Daniel Paul 1943- *AmMWSc 92*
**Van Kampen**, Kent Rigby 1936- *AmMWSc 92*
**Van Kampen**, Paul Lewis 1943- *WhoIns 92*
**Van Karsen**, Charles David 1953- *WhoMW 92*
**Van Kempen**, Ties Harold 1949- *WhoWest 92*
**Van Keppel**, Hendrick 1914- *DcTwDes*
**Van Keppel-Green** *DcTwDes*
**Van Kersen**, Christopher P. 1954- *WhoMW 92*
**Vankin**, George Lawrence 1931- *AmMWSc 92*
**Van Kirk**, James William 1858-1946 *AmPeW*
**Van Kirk**, Thomas Lee *WhoAmL 92*
**Van Kirk**, Walter William 1891-1956 *AmPeW*
**Van Klaveren**, Nico 1934- *AmMWSc 92*
**Van Kleeck**, Letitia Hubka 1940- *WhoMW 92*
**Van Kleeck**, Mary 1883-1972 *WomSoc*
**Van Kleek**, Laurence McKee 1944- *WhoRel 92*
**Van Kleek**, Mary 1883- *DcAmImH*
**Van Kleek**, Peter Eric 1929- *ConAu 35NR*
**Van Kley**, Harold 1932- *AmMWSc 92, WhoMW 92*
**Van Koten**, Leland Stanley 1949- *WhoAmL 92*
**Van Kranendonk**, Jan 1924- *AmMWSc 92*
**Van Krey**, Harry P 1931- *AmMWSc 92*
**Van Kula**, George, III 1963- *WhoWest 92*
**Van Laethem**, Gabriel 1918- *IntWW 91*
**Van Lancker**, Julien L 1924- *AmMWSc 92*
**Van Landingham**, Hugh F 1935- *AmMWSc 92*
**Van Landingham**, Leander Shelton, Jr. 1925- *WhoAmL 92, WhoFI 92*
**Van Landingham**, Marian Amelia 1937- *WhoAmP 91*
**Van Lanen**, Robert Jerome 1943- *AmMWSc 92*
**Van Langen**, Cornelus N. J. 1946- *WhoFI 92*
**VanLangeveld**, David Herbert 1941- *WhoAmP 91*
**VanLaningham**, Todd Alan 1956- *WhoRel 92*
**Van Lawick**, Hugo 1937- *WrDr 92*
**Van Lear**, David Hyde 1940- *AmMWSc 92*
**Van Leer**, John Cloud 1940- *AmMWSc 92*
**Van Leeuwen**, Cornelis 1924- *WhoRel 92*
**Van Leeuwen**, Gerard 1929- *AmMWSc 92*
**VanLeeuwen**, Liz 1925- *WhoAmP 91*
**Van Leeuwen**, Raymond Cornelius 1948- *WhoRel 92*
**van Lennep**, Emile 1915- *Who 92*
**Van Lente**, Kenneth Anthony 1903- *AmMWSc 92*
**Van Leuven**, Robert Joseph 1931- *WhoAmL 92, WhoFI 92, WhoMW 92*
**Van Lew**, James H 1934- *WhoIns 92*
**Van Lhin**, Eric *TwCSFW 91*
**Van Lhin**, Erik *IntAu&W 91X*
**Van Lier**, Jan Antonius 1924- *AmMWSc 92*
**Van Lier**, Johannes Ernestinus 1942- *AmMWSc 92*
**Van Lier**, Norm 1947- *WhoBlA 92*
**Van Liere**, Carma Parkhurst 1918- *WhoRel 92*
**Van Lierop**, Robert F. 1939- *IntWW 91, WhoBlA 92*
**Van Lieshout**, David Lyn 1949- *WhoAmL 92*
**Van Liew**, Donald H. 1929- *WhoBlA 92*
**Van Liew**, Hugh Davenport 1930- *AmMWSc 92*
**Van Liew**, Judith Bradford 1930- *AmMWSc 92*
**Van Ligten**, Raoul Fredrick 1932- *AmMWSc 92*
**Van Linh**, Erik *WrDr 92*
**Van Lint**, Jacobus Hendricus 1932- *IntWW 91*
**Van Lint**, Victor Anton Jacobus 1928- *AmMWSc 92, WhoWest 92*
**Van Loan**, Anna S 1912- *WhoAmP 91*
**Van Loon**, Edward John 1911- *AmMWSc 92*
**Van Loon**, Hendrik Willem 1882-1944 *BenetAL 91*
**van Loon**, Jan Thomas 1945- *WhoAmL 92*
**Van Loon**, Jon Clement 1937- *AmMWSc 92*
**Van Lopik**, Jack Richard 1929- *AmMWSc 92*
**Van Loveren**, Henk 1951- *AmMWSc 92*
**Van Lustbader**, Eric 1946- *WrDr 92*
**Van Luven**, Steve 1947- *WhoAmP 91*
**Van Luven**, William Robert 1931- *WhoMW 92*
**Van Maanen**, Evert Florus 1918- *AmMWSc 92*
**Van Maanen**, Harold 1929- *WhoAmP 91*
**Van Maerssen**, Otto L. 1919- *WhoWest 92*
**Van Manen**, Jan Dirk 1923- *IntWW 91*
**Vanmarcke**, Erik Hector 1941- *AmMWSc 92*
**Van Mark**, Jack 1930- *WhoAmP 91*
**Van Marter**, Ronald Albert 1936- *WhoMW 92*
**van Maurik**, Ernest Henry 1916- *Who 92*
**VanMeer**, Mary Ann 1947- *WhoFI 92*
**Van Mell**, Herman T. 1911- *WhoAmL 92*
**Van Melsen**, Andreas G M 1912- *ConAu 34NR*
**van Merkensteijn**, Eric Cornelis 1946- *WhoFI 92*
**Van Meter**, David 1919- *AmMWSc 92*
**Van Meter**, Donald Eugene 1942- *AmMWSc 92*
**Van Meter**, James Gordon 1944- *WhoRel 92, WhoWest 92*
**Van Meter**, John David 1951- *WhoFI 92*
**Van Meter**, Mary E Wilson 1925- *WhoAmP 91*
**Van Meter**, Ruth Frances 1911- *WhoWest 92*
**Van Meter**, Thomas Adams 1943- *WhoAmP 91*
**Van Meter**, Wayne Paul 1926- *AmMWSc 92*
**Van Metre**, Margaret Cheryl 1938- *WhoEnt 92*
**Van Metre**, Thomas Earle, Jr 1923- *AmMWSc 92*
**van Michaels**, Christopher 1924- *WhoWest 92*
**VanMiddlesworth**, Frank L 1955- *AmMWSc 92*
**Van Middlesworth**, Lester 1919- *AmMWSc 92*
**Van Mierop**, Lodewyk H S 1927- *AmMWSc 92*
**Van Miert**, Karel 1942- *IntWW 91, Who 92*
**Van Mol**, Louis John, Jr. 1943- *WhoFI 92*
**Van Montagu**, Marc Charles Ernest 1933- *IntWW 91*
**Van Munster**, Hans 1925- *IntWW 91*
**Vann**, Albert 1934- *WhoAmP 91, WhoBlA 92*
**Vann**, David J 1928- *WhoAmP 91*
**Vann**, Douglas Carroll 1939- *AmMWSc 92*
**Vann**, Gregory Alvin 1954- *WhoBlA 92*
**Vann**, Joseph M 1937- *AmMWSc 92*
**Vann**, Robert Lewis 1938- *WhoWest 92*
**Vann**, Robin Iris 1952- *WhoEnt 92*
**Vann**, Stanley 1910- *Who 92*
**Vann**, W Pennington 1935- *AmMWSc 92*
**Vann**, William L 1923- *AmMWSc 92*
**Vann-Adibe**, Robbie O. 1961- *WhoFI 92*
**VanNaerssen**, Henri Johan 1943- *WhoFI 92*
**Vannan**, Roland Lester 1927- *WhoIns 92*
**Vanneck** *Who 92*
**Vanneck**, Peter Beckford Rutgers 1922- *IntWW 91, Who 92*
**Vanneman**, Edgar, Jr 1919- *WhoAmP 91*
**Vanner**, John F, Jr 1955- *WhoAmP 91*
**Vanness**, Calvin Hann 1926- *WhoWest 92*
**Van Ness**, Hendrick C 1924- *AmMWSc 92*
**Van Ness**, James E 1926- *AmMWSc 92*
**Van Ness**, John Winslow 1936- *AmMWSc 92*
**Van Ness**, Kenneth E *AmMWSc 92*
**Van Ness**, Patricia Catheline 1951- *WhoEnt 92*
**Van Ness**, Robert Clifford *WhoMW 92*
**Van Ness**, Ross Howard 1932- *WhoMW 92*
**Van Ness**, Stanley C. 1934- *WhoBlA 92*
**Van Neste**, Andre 1938- *AmMWSc 92*
**Vannice**, Merlin Albert 1943- *AmMWSc 92*
**Van Niekerk**, Willem Abraham 1937- *IntWW 91*
**Van Niel**, Cornelius Bernardus 1897-1985 *FacFETw*
**Vannier**, Wilton Emile 1924- *AmMWSc 92*
**Vannikov**, Boris L'vovich 1897-1962 *SovUnBD*
**Vannix**, Cecil Robert 1953- *WhoWest 92*
**Van Noord**, Andrew John 1922- *WhoFI 92*
**Van Nordstrand**, Robert Alexander 1917- *WhoWest 92*
**Van Norman**, Gilden Ramon 1932- *AmMWSc 92*
**Van Norman**, John Donald 1934- *AmMWSc 92*
**Van Nostrand**, Henry D d1896 *BiInAmS*
**Van Nostrand**, Richard K. d1991 *NewYTBS 91*
**Van Nostrand**, Walt *WhoAmP 91*
**Vannote**, Robin L 1934- *AmMWSc 92*
**Van Noy**, Terry W 1947- *WhoIns 92*
**Van Noy**, Terry Willard 1947- *WhoWest 92*
**Vannozzi**, Thomas 1951- *WhoEnt 92*
**van Nuis**, Hermine J. 1941- *WhoMW 92*
**Van Nuys**, Peter 1939- *WhoAmL 92*
**Vanocur**, Marc Louis 1969- *WhoFI 92*
**Vanocur**, Sander *LesBEnT 92*
**Vanocur**, Sander 1928- *IntMPA 92*
**Van Oero**, Willem Theodorus Hendricus 1934- *AmMWSc 92*
**Van Oeveren**, Edward Lanier 1954- *WhoAmL 92*
**Vanoff**, Nick d1991 *LesBEnT 92, NewYTBS 91*
**Vanoni**, Vito A 1904- *AmMWSc 92*
**Van Ooij**, William Johan 1941- *WhoMW 92*
**Van Oostenburg**, Gordon L. 1921- *WhoRel 92*
**Van Oosterhout**, Peter Denne 1932- *WhoFI 92*
**Vanora**, Jerome Patrick 1941- *WhoFI 92*
**Van Orden**, Frank Jeffrey 1947- *WhoFI 92*
**Van Orden**, Frederick Parpart 1921- *WhoFI 92*
**Van Orden**, Harris O 1917- *AmMWSc 92*
**Van Orden**, Harris Olson 1917- *WhoWest 92*
**Van Orden**, James C. 1950- *WhoEnt 92*
**Van Orden**, Lucas Schuyler, III 1928- *AmMWSc 92, WhoWest 92*
**Van Order**, Robert Bruce 1915- *AmMWSc 92*
**Van Orman**, Chandler L. 1941- *WhoAmL 92*
**Van Orman**, Richard A 1936- *ConAu 34NR*
**VanOrsow**, Alice Marie 1931- *WhoRel 92*
**Van Os**, David 1950- *WhoAmL 92*
**Van Oss**, Carel J 1923- *AmMWSc 92*
**Van Oss**, David J. 1946- *WhoAmL 92*
**Van Oss**, Oliver 1909- *Who 92*
**Van Osselaer**, Paul J. 1950- *WhoAmL 92*
**Van Ostenburg**, Donald Ora 1929- *AmMWSc 92*
**Van Over**, Raymond 1934- *IntAu&W 91*
**Van Overbeek**, Johannes 1908- *AmMWSc 92*
**Van Overschelde**, Dennis *WhoAmP 91*
**Van Overstraeten**, Roger Joseph 1937- *AmMWSc 92*
**van Paassen**, Pierre 1895-1968 *BenetAL 91*
**Van Pallandt**, Nina 1932- *IntMPA 92*
**Van Pallandt**, Wilprand 1926- *IntWW 91*
**Van Patten**, Denis J. 1947- *WhoWest 92*
**Van Patten**, Dick 1928- *IntMPA 92*
**Van Patten**, Dick Vincent 1928- *WhoEnt 92*
**Van Patten**, Jonathan Keith 1949- *WhoAmL 92*
**Van Patten**, Joyce 1936- *IntMPA 92*
**Van Patten**, Joyce Benignia *WhoEnt 92*
**Van Patter**, Douglas Macpherson 1923- *AmMWSc 92*
**Van Pay**, Randy John 1949- *WhoRel 92*
**Vanpee**, Marcel 1916- *AmMWSc 92*
**Van Peebles**, Mario *NewYTBS 91, WhoBlA 92*
**Van Peebles**, Mario 1957?- *ConBlB 2 [port], IntMPA 92*
**Van Peebles**, Melvin 1932- *IntMPA 92, WhoBlA 92*
**Van Pelt**, Arnold Francis, Jr 1924- *AmMWSc 92*
**Van Pelt**, David Merrill 1958- *WhoWest 92*
**Van Pelt**, Peter Sylvan 1961- *WhoEnt 92*
**Van Pelt**, Richard H 1922- *AmMWSc 92*
**Van Pelt**, Richard W 1933- *AmMWSc 92*
**Van Pelt**, Robert Irving 1931- *WhoMW 92*
**Van Pelt**, Rollo Winslow, Jr 1929- *AmMWSc 92*
**Van Pelt**, Wesley Austin 1930- *WhoRel 92, WhoWest 92*
**Van Pelt**, Wesley Richard 1943- *AmMWSc 92*
**van Peursen**, Cornelis A. 1920- *WrDr 92*
**Van Pilsum**, John Franklin 1922- *AmMWSc 92*
**Van Poolen**, Lambert John 1939- *AmMWSc 92*
**Van Poznak**, Alan 1927- *AmMWSc 92*
**Van Praag**, Alan 1947- *WhoAmL 92*
**Van praag**, Herman M 1929- *AmMWSc 92*
**van Praag**, Louis 1926- *Who 92*
**Van Praag**, William 1924- *IntMPA 92*
**van Praagh**, Peggy 1910-1990 *AnObit 1990*
**VanPraagh**, Richard 1930- *AmMWSc 92*
**Van Putten**, Donald John 1934- *WhoWest 92*
**Van Putten**, James D, Jr 1934- *AmMWSc 92*
**Van Raalte**, A. C. *DcAmImH*
**Van Raalte**, John A 1938- *AmMWSc 92*
**Van Rafelghem**, Carlos H. J. 1925- *IntWW 91*
**Van Reen**, Robert 1921- *AmMWSc 92, WhoWest 92*
**Van Regenmorter**, William *WhoAmP 91*
**Van Remmen**, Roger 1950- *WhoWest 92*
**Van Rennes**, Jerry Wayne 1941- *WhoWest 92*
**Van Rensburg**, Johannes Frederik Janse 1898-1966 *BiDExR*
**Van Rensburg**, Willem Cornelius Janse 1938- *AmMWSc 92*
**Van Rensselaer**, Jeremiah 1793-1871 *BiInAmS*
**Van Rensselaer**, Stephen 1764-1839 *BiInAmS*
**Van Reuth**, Edward C *AmMWSc 92*

**Van Rheenen**, Verlan H 1939- *AmMWSc 92*
**Van Riel**, Christa 1963- *TwCPaSc*
**van Riemsdijk**, John Theodore 1924- *Who 92*
**Vanriet**, Jan 1948- *IntWW 91*
**Van Rij**, Willem Idaniel 1942- *AmMWSc 92*
**Van Rijn**, Jacob Jacobse 1929- *IntWW 91*
**Van Riper**, Charles, III 1943- *AmMWSc 92*
**Van Riper**, Gordon Everett 1917- *AmMWSc 92*
**Van Riper**, Guernsey, Jr. 1909- *WhoMW 92, WrDr 92*
**Van Riper**, Kenneth Alan 1949- *AmMWSc 92*
**Van Riper**, Thomas Peter 1938- *WhoFI 92*
**van Rjndt**, Philippe 1950- *WrDr 92*
**Van Roggen**, Arend 1928- *AmMWSc 92*
**van Roijen**, Jan Herman d1991 *NewYTBS 91*
**van Rooij**, Vincent A. M. *WhoHisp 92*
**Van Roosbroeck**, Willy Werner 1913- *AmMWSc 92*
**Van Roosen**, Donald Collett 1923- *WhoFI 92*
**Van Rossum**, George Donald Victor 1931- *AmMWSc 92*
**Van Royen**, Olivier Henri Aurel 1930- *IntWW 91*
**Van Ryzin**, Martina 1923- *AmMWSc 92*
**Vansa**, Sofie *EncAmaz 91*
**Van Sambeek**, Jerome William 1947- *AmMWSc 92*
**Vansandt**, Van Henry 1961- *WhoRel 92*
**Van Sant**, David Eugene 1950- *WhoWest 92*
**Van Sant**, George Montgomery 1927- *WhoAmP 91*
**Van Sant**, Gus 1952- *NewYTBS 91 [port], News 92-2 [port]*
**Van Sant**, James Hurley, Jr 1933- *AmMWSc 92*
**Van Sant**, John F 1930- *WhoAmP 91*
**Van Sant**, Robert William 1938- *WhoFI 92*
**van Santen**, John Henry, III 1953- *WhoFI 92*
**Van Saun**, William Arthur 1946- *AmMWSc 92*
**Van Schaik**, Peter Hendrik 1927- *AmMWSc 92*
**Van Schalk**, Robert 1927- *IntWW 91*
**Van Schilfgaarde**, Jan 1929- *AmMWSc 92*
**Van Schmus**, William Randall 1938- *AmMWSc 92*
**Van Schoiack**, Dean Allen 1958- *WhoMW 92*
**Van Sciver**, Steven W 1948- *AmMWSc 92*
**Van Scott**, Eugene Joseph 1922- *AmMWSc 92*
**Van Scyoc**, Lee J. 1952- *WhoMW 92*
**Van Scyoc**, Sydney 1939- *WrDr 92*
**Van Scyoc**, Sydney J 1939- *TwCSFW 91*
**Van Scyoc**, Sydney Joyce 1939- *IntAu&W 91*
**Vanselow**, Clarence Hugo 1928- *AmMWSc 92*
**Vanselow**, Duane Robert 1949- *WhoRel 92*
**Vanselow**, Neal A 1932- *AmMWSc 92*
**Vanselow**, Ralf W 1931- *AmMWSc 92*
**Van Seters**, John 1935- *WhoRel 92*
**Van Setter**, George Gerard 1940- *WhoAmL 92*
**van Seventer**, A. 1913- *WhoWest 92*
**Van Severen**, Georges Edmond Edouard 1894-1940 *BiDExR*
**Van Shelton**, Ricky 1952- *WhoEnt 92*
**Vanshenkin**, Konstantin Yakovlevich 1925- *SovUnBD*
**Vansickle**, Barbara Jean 1948- *WhoFI 92, WhoMW 92*
**Van Sickle**, Bruce Marion 1917- *WhoAmL 92, WhoMW 92*
**Van Sickle**, Dale Elbert 1932- *AmMWSc 92*
**Van Sickle**, David C 1934- *AmMWSc 92*
**Van Sickle**, John V 1892- *ConAu 35NR*
**Van Siclen**, DeWitt Clinton 1918- *AmMWSc 92*
**Van Singel**, Donald 1943- *WhoAmP 91*
**Van Sistine**, Jerome 1926- *WhoAmP 91*
**Vansittart**, Peter 1920- *ConNov 91, IntAu&W 91, WrDr 92*
**Vansittart**, Robert Gilbert 1881-1957 *EncTR 91*
**Van Sluyters**, Richard Charles 1945- *AmMWSc 92*
**VanSlyck**, Steven Byron 1956- *WhoMW 92*
**Van Slyke**, Clague Arthur, III 1955- *WhoAmL 92*
**Van Slyke**, J B, Jr 1942- *WhoAmP 91*
**Van Slyke**, James King, II 1957- *WhoAmP 91*
**Van Slyke**, Leonard DuBose, Jr. 1944- *WhoAmL 92*
**Van Slyke**, Paul Christopher 1942- *WhoAmL 92*
**Van Slyke**, Richard M 1937- *AmMWSc 92*
**VanSoest**, Peter John 1929- *AmMWSc 92*
**Van Spanckeren**, Kathryn *DrAPF 91*
**Van Spanckeren**, Kathryn 1945- *IntAu&W 91*
**VanSpeybroeck**, Leon Paul 1935- *AmMWSc 92*
**Van Stee**, Ethard Wendel 1936- *AmMWSc 92*
**Van Steeland**, Ronald Field 1940- *WhoFI 92*
**Van Steenbergen**, Arie 1928- *AmMWSc 92*
**Vansteenberghe**, Alice d1991 *NewYTBS 91*
**Van Stockum**, Hilda 1908- *WrDr 92*
**Vanstone**, J R 1933- *AmMWSc 92*
**Van Stone**, Raymond James 1928- *WhoRel 92*
**Vanstone**, Scott Alexander 1947- *AmMWSc 92*
**Vanstory**, Angela *WhoEnt 92*
**VanStralen**, Eric 1952- *WhoWest 92*
**van Straubenzee**, William 1924- *Who 92*
**Van Strien**, Richard Edward 1920- *AmMWSc 92*
**Van Stryland**, Eric William 1947- *AmMWSc 92*
**Van Swaaij**, Willibrordus Petrus Maria 1942- *IntWW 91*
**Van Swaay**, Maarten 1930- *AmMWSc 92*
**Van Syckle**, William 1942- *WhoIns 92*
**Van't Hof**, Jack 1932- *AmMWSc 92*
**Van't Hof**, William Keith 1930- *WhoAmL 92*
**Van't Hoff**, Jacobus Henricus 1852-1911 *WhoNob 90*
**Vant-Hull**, Lorin Lee 1932- *AmMWSc 92*
**Van't Riet**, Bartholomeus 1922- *AmMWSc 92*
**Van Tamelen**, Eugene Earl 1925- *AmMWSc 92*
**Van Tamelen**, Eugene Earle 1925- *IntWW 91*
**van Tamelen**, Mary Ruth 1930- *WhoWest 92*
**Van Tassel**, David Dirck 1928- *ConAu 35NR*
**Van Tassel**, Dennie L 1939- *ConAu 35NR*
**Van Tassel**, Katrina *DrAPF 91*
**Van Tassel**, Roger A 1936- *AmMWSc 92*
**Van Tassell**, Morgan Howard 1923- *AmMWSc 92*
**Van Thiel**, David H 1941- *AmMWSc 92*
**Van Thiel**, Mathias 1930- *AmMWSc 92*
**Van Thijn**, Eduard 1934- *IntWW 91*
**VantHull**, Lorin L 1932- *AmMWSc 92*
**Van Tiel**, Wouter Jan 1960- *WhoWest 92*
**Van Tienhoven**, Ari 1922- *AmMWSc 92*
**Van Til**, Alyssa Barbara 1936- *WhoRel 92*
**Van Til**, Cornelius 1895- *RelLAm 91*
**Van Til**, William 1911- *WrDr 92*
**Van Tilborg**, Andre Marcel 1953- *AmMWSc 92*
**Van Till**, Howard Jay 1938- *AmMWSc 92*
**Vantine**, Donald Arthur 1919- *WhoRel 92*
**Van Tine**, John William 1946- *WhoRel 92*
**Van Tine**, Kirk Kelso 1948- *WhoAmL 92*
**Vantrease**, Alice Twiggs 1943- *WhoFI 92*
**Vantrease**, Edwin Kyle 1951- *WhoAmL 92*
**Van Trece**, Jackson C. 1928- *WhoBlA 92*
**Van Trump**, James Edmond 1943- *AmMWSc 92*
**Van Tubbergen**, Wayne 1952- *WhoFI 92*
**Van Tuin**, Jon Albert, Jr. 1962- *WhoFI 92*
**Van Tuyl**, Andrew Heuer 1922- *AmMWSc 92*
**Van Tuyl**, Harold Hutchison 1927- *AmMWSc 92*
**Van Tuyle**, Glenn Charles 1943- *AmMWSc 92*
**Van Twiller**, Wouter 1580?-1656? *BenetAL 91*
**Van Tyle**, William Kent 1944- *AmMWSc 92*
**Van Uitert**, LeGrand G 1922- *AmMWSc 92*
**Van Ummersen**, Claire Ann 1935- *AmMWSc 92*
**Van Upp**, Virginia 1902-1970 *ReelWom [port]*
**Vanuxem**, Lardner 1792-1848 *BiInAmS*
**Van Vactor**, David 1906- *NewAmDM*
**Van Valen**, Leigh Maiorana 1935- *AmMWSc 92*
**Van Valer**, Joe Ned 1935- *WhoAmL 92, WhoFI 92, WhoMW 92*
**Van Valin**, Charles Carroll 1929- *AmMWSc 92, WhoWest 92*
**Van Valin**, Clyde Emory 1929- *WhoRel 92*
**Van Valkenburg**, Fred 1948- *WhoAmP 91*
**Van Valkenburg**, Holli Beadell 1950- *WhoWest 92*
**Van Valkenburg**, Jeptha Wade, Jr 1925- *AmMWSc 92*
**Van Valkenburg**, M E 1921- *AmMWSc 92*
**Van Valkenburg**, William Lee 1951- *WhoRel 92*
**Van Vechten**, Carl 1880-1964 *BenetAL 91*
**Van Vechten**, Deborah 1947- *AmMWSc 92*
**Van Vechten**, James Alden 1942- *AmMWSc 92*
**Van Veelen**, Evert 1911- *IntWW 91*
**Van Veen**, Christian *IntWW 91*
**Van Veghten**, Gary Lewis 1936- *WhoEnt 92*
**Van Veldhuizen**, Philip Androcles 1930- *AmMWSc 92*
**Van Velzer**, Verna Jean 1929- *WhoWest 92*
**Van Velzor**, James Daniel 1922- *WhoAmP 91*
**Van Verth**, James Edward 1928- *AmMWSc 92*
**Van Vinkenroye du Waysaeck**, Fedia M. 1932- *WhoFI 92*
**Van Vlack**, Charles W. 1949- *WhoFI 92*
**Van Vlack**, Lawrence H 1920- *AmMWSc 92*
**Van Vlack**, Lawrence Hall 1920- *WhoMW 92*
**Van Vlear**, John Edward 1962- *WhoAmL 92*
**Van Vleck**, Fred Scott 1934- *AmMWSc 92*
**Van Vleck**, James 1930- *WhoFI 92*
**Van Vleck**, John Hasbrouck 1899-1980 *WhoNob 90*
**Van Vleck**, John Monroe 1833-1912 *BiInAmS*
**Van Vleck**, Lloyd Dale 1933- *AmMWSc 92*
**Van Vleet**, John F 1938- *AmMWSc 92*
**Van Vliet**, Antone Cornelis 1930- *AmMWSc 92*
**Van Vliet**, Carolyne Marina 1929- *AmMWSc 92*
**Van Vliet**, David R. 1957- *WhoRel 92*
**Van Vliet**, Tony 1930- *WhoAmP 91*
**Van Vogt**, A. E. 1912- *BenetAL 91, TwCSFW 91, WrDr 92*
**Van Volkenburg**, J.L. d1963 *LesBEnT 92*
**VanVoorhis**, Gail 1946- *WhoEnt 92*
**Van Voris**, Peter 1948- *AmMWSc 92*
**Van Vorous**, Ted 1929- *AmMWSc 92*
**Van Vorst**, Bessie d1927 *DcAmImH*
**Van Vorst**, William D 1919- *AmMWSc 92*
**Van Vranken**, Leah 1953- *WhoEnt 92*
**Van Vunakis**, Helen 1924- *AmMWSc 92*
**van Vuuren**, Nancy 1938- *ConAu 35NR*
**Van Vyven**, Dale Nulsen 1935- *WhoAmP 91*
**van Waardenburg**, Franklin Alphons 1952- *WhoWest 92*
**Van Wachem**, Lodewijk Christiaan 1931- *IntWW 91, Who 92, WhoFI 92*
**Van Wagenen**, Sterling 1947- *WhoEnt 92, WhoWest 92*
**Van Wagner**, Charles Edward 1924- *AmMWSc 92*
**Van Wagner**, Edward M 1924- *AmMWSc 92*
**Van Wagner**, Ellen 1942- *WhoAmL 92*
**Van Wagner**, Nancy Lee 1938- *WhoMW 92*
**Van Wagner**, Richard 1936- *WhoAmP 91*
**Van Wagtendonk**, Jan Willem 1940- *AmMWSc 92*
**Van Wagtendonk**, Willem Johan 1910- *AmMWSc 92*
**Van Walleghen**, Michael Joseph 1938- *WhoMW 92*
**VanWarmer**, Randy 1955- *WhoEnt 92*
**Van Wart**, Harold Edgar 1947- *AmMWSc 92*
**Van Wazer**, John Robert 1918- *AmMWSc 92*
**Van Weert**, Gezinus 1933- *AmMWSc 92*
**Vanwert**, William F. *DrAPF 91*
**Van Wey**, Kim Ellen 1956- *WhoMW 92*
**Van Wie**, Steven Howard 1950- *WhoMW 92*
**Van Wieck**, Nigel 1947- *TwCPaSc*
**van Wieren**, Mona *WrDr 92*
**Van Wijk**, Theodor 1916- *IntWW 91*
**Van Wijngaarden**, Arie 1933- *AmMWSc 92*
**Van Wijngaarden**, Leendert 1932- *IntWW 91*
**Van Winckel**, Nance Lee *DrAPF 91*
**Van Winden**, Jacobus Cornelis Maria 1922- *IntWW 91*
**Van Winkle**, Michael George 1939- *AmMWSc 92*
**Van Winkle**, Quentin 1919- *AmMWSc 92*
**Van Winkle**, Thomas Leo 1922- *AmMWSc 92*
**Van Winkle**, Webster, Jr 1938- *AmMWSc 92*
**Van Winkle**, William 1934- *WhoFI 92*
**Van Winter**, Clasine 1929- *AmMWSc 92*
**Van Witsen**, Leo 1912- *WhoEnt 92*
**Van Witt**, Peggy Salome 1953- *WhoMW 92*
**Van Woert**, Melvin H 1929- *AmMWSc 92*
**Van Wormer**, Kenneth A, Jr 1930- *AmMWSc 92*
**Van Wyck**, George Richard 1928- *WhoIns 92*
**Van Wyk**, Betty Vicha 1939- *WhoMW 92*
**Van Wyk**, Christopher John 1955- *AmMWSc 92*
**Van Wyk**, Judson John 1921- *AmMWSc 92*
**Van Wyk**, Willem 1933- *IntWW 91*
**Van Wylen**, Gordon J 1920- *AmMWSc 92*
**Van Wyngarden**, Sharon Renee 1964- *WhoMW 92*
**Van Yahres**, Mitchell 1926- *WhoAmP 91*
**Vanyo**, James Patrick 1928- *AmMWSc 92, WhoWest 92*
**Vanysek**, Petr 1952- *AmMWSc 92*
**Van Zandt**, J Timothy 1954- *WhoAmP 91*
**Van Zandt**, Lonnie L 1937- *AmMWSc 92*
**Van Zandt**, Paul Doyle 1927- *AmMWSc 92*
**Van Zandt**, Richard Louis 1948- *WhoRel 92*
**Van Zandt**, Roland d1991 *NewYTBS 91*
**Van Zandt**, Roland 1918-1991 *ConAu 134*
**Van Zandt**, Thomas Edward 1929- *AmMWSc 92*
**Van Zant**, Donald Lee 1934- *WhoWest 92*
**Van Zant**, Kent Lee 1947- *AmMWSc 92, WhoWest 92*
**van Zantwijk**, Rudolf 1932- *ConAu 133*
**Van Zee**, Richard Jerry 1947- *AmMWSc 92*
**Vanzi**, Max Bruno 1934- *WhoWest 92*
**Van Zile**, Edward S 1863-1931 *ScFEYrs*
**Van Zile**, Philip Taylor, III 1945- *WhoAmL 92*
**Van Zwalenberg**, George 1930- *AmMWSc 92*
**Van Zwienen**, Ilse Charlotte Koehn 1929-1991 *ConAu 35NR, SmATA 67*
**Van Zwieten**, Matthew Jacobus 1945- *AmMWSc 92*
**Van Zyl Slabbert**, F. *ConAu 133, IntWW 91*
**Van Zytveld**, John Bos 1940- *AmMWSc 92*
**Vaporis**, Michael Nomikos 1954- *WhoAmL 92*
**Vaquer**, Armand Merle 1954- *WhoAmP 91*
**Vara**, Albert C. 1931- *ConAu 35NR*
**Vara**, Madeleine *ConAu 135*
**Vara**, Theresa C. *DrAPF 91*
**Varadan**, Vasundara Venkatraman 1948- *AmMWSc 92*
**Varadan**, Vijay K 1943- *AmMWSc 92*
**Varadarajan**, Kalathoor 1935- *AmMWSc 92*
**Varady**, John Carl 1935- *AmMWSc 92*
**Varah**, Doris Susan 1916- *Who 92*
**Varah**, Edward Chad 1911- *Who 92*
**Varah**, Susan *Who 92*
**Varaiya**, Pravin Pratap 1940- *AmMWSc 92*
**Varan**, Cyrus O 1934- *AmMWSc 92*
**Varanasi**, Prasad 1938- *AmMWSc 92*
**Varanasi**, Suryanarayana Rao 1939- *AmMWSc 92*
**Varanasi**, Usha *AmMWSc 92*
**Varani**, James *AmMWSc 92*
**Varano**, Steven Anthony 1958- *WhoAmL 92*
**Varas**, Manny 1939- *WhoHisp 92*
**Varat**, Jonathan D. 1945- *WhoAmL 92*
**Varat**, Michael Samuel Ring 1966- *WhoWest 92*
**Varberg**, Dale Elthon 1930- *AmMWSc 92*
**Varco-Shea**, Theresa Camille 1959- *AmMWSc 92*
**Varcoe**, Christopher Stephen 1949- *Who 92*
**Varcoe**, Jeremy Richard Lovering G 1937- *Who 92*
**Varcoe**, Stephen *Who 92*
**Varda**, Agnes *ReelWom*
**Varda**, Agnes 1928- *IntDcF 2-2 [port], IntWW 91*
**Vardaman**, James Kimble 1861-1930 *AmPolLe*
**Vardaman**, John Wesley, Jr. 1940- *WhoAmL 92*
**Vardaman**, Patricia Black 1931- *WrDr 92*
**Vardaman**, Robert H, Sr *WhoAmP 91*
**Vardanian**, Yurik 1956- *IntWW 91*
**Vardanis**, Alexander 1933- *AmMWSc 92*
**Vardaris**, Richard Miles 1934- *AmMWSc 92*
**Vardaro**, Anthony Joseph 1954- *WhoAmP 91*
**Vardeman**, Stephen Bruce 1949- *AmMWSc 92*
**Vardi**, Joseph *AmMWSc 92*
**Vardi**, Yehuda *AmMWSc 92*
**Vardiman**, Ronald G 1932- *AmMWSc 92*
**Vardre**, Leslie *TwCSFW 91, WrDr 92*
**Vardy**, Stephen Edward 1963- *WhoEnt 92*
**Vare**, Glenna Collett 1903-1989 *FacFETw*
**Varela**, Anita Jean 1957- *WhoMW 92*
**Varela**, Blanca 1926- *ConSpAP*
**Varela**, Charles Richard 1933- *WhoHisp 92*
**Varela**, Franklyn P. 1949- *WhoHisp 92*

**Varela,** Jesse 1954- *WhoHisp 92*
**Varela,** Julio A. 1959- *WhoHisp 92*
**Varela,** Luciano *WhoAmP 91, WhoHisp 92*
**Varela,** Melvin 1949- *WhoHisp 92*
**Varela,** Raymond M., Jr. 1959- *WhoHisp 92*
**Varela,** Robert 1932- *WhoHisp 92*
**Varela,** William 1950- *WhoEnt 92*
**Varela Fernandez,** Jose A *WhoAmP 91*
**Varela Fernandez,** Jose R. *WhoHisp 92*
**Varela-Ibarra,** Jose L. *DrAPF 91*
**Varela y Morales,** Felix Francisco J M de 1788-1853 *HisDSpE*
**Varellas,** Sandra Motte 1946- *WhoAmL 92*
**Varennikov,** Valentin Ivanovich 1923- *IntWW 91*
**Varese,** Edgar 1883-1965 *FacFETw*
**Varese,** Edgard 1883-1965 *NewAmDM*
**Varese,** William J 1947- *WhoAmP 91*
**Varet,** Michael A. 1942- *WhoFI 92*
**Varey,** John Earl 1922- *IntWW 91, Who 92*
**Varey,** Simon *ConAu 135*
**Vareykis,** Iosif Mikhaylovich 1894-1938 *SovUnBD*
**Varfis,** Grigorios 1927- *IntWW 91*
**Varfis,** Grigoris 1927- *Who 92*
**Varga,** Gabriella Anne 1951- *AmMWSc 92*
**Varga,** Gideon Michael, Jr 1941- *AmMWSc 92*
**Varga,** Ilona 1951- *WhoAmP 91*
**Varga,** Imre 1923- *IntWW 91*
**Varga,** Janos M 1935- *AmMWSc 92*
**Varga,** Louis P 1922- *AmMWSc 92*
**Varga,** Richard S 1928- *AmMWSc 92*
**Varga,** Steven Carl 1952- *WhoWest 92*
**Vargas,** Al Garcia 1943- *WhoFI 92*
**Vargas,** Allen H. 1944- *WhoHisp 92*
**Vargas,** Angel Antonio 1956- *WhoHisp 92*
**Vargas,** Arnulfo *WhoHisp 92*
**Vargas,** Bobbe *WhoAmP 91*
**Vargas,** Carlos 1953- *WhoHisp 92*
**Vargas,** Daniel Gomez 1955- *WhoRel 92*
**Vargas,** David A. 1940- *WhoHisp 92*
**Vargas,** Edward Anthony 1951- *WhoHisp 92*
**Vargas,** Edward Lee 1951- *WhoHisp 92*
**Vargas,** Edwin, Jr. 1949- *WhoHisp 92*
**Vargas,** Fernando Figueroa 1926- *AmMWSc 92*
**Vargas,** Frank, Jr. 1942- *WhoHisp 92*
**Vargas,** George 1939- *WhoHisp 92*
**Vargas,** Gloria M. 1926- *WhoHisp 92*
**Vargas,** Henry Philip 1929- *WhoHisp 92*
**Vargas,** Herminio *DrAPF 91*
**Vargas,** Hernan de Jesus Diaz 1957- *WhoEnt 92*
**Vargas,** J. Hector 1965- *WhoHisp 92*
**Vargas,** Jorge A. 1937- *WhoHisp 92*
**Vargas,** Joseph Martin, Jr 1942- *AmMWSc 92*
**Vargas,** Juan Eduardo 1952- *WhoHisp 92*
**Vargas,** Julie S. 1938- *ConAu 34NR*
**Vargas,** Kathy 1950- *WhoHisp 92*
**Vargas,** Laura Dennison *DrAPF 91*
**Vargas,** Lourdes Hernandez 1963- *WhoHisp 92*
**Vargas,** Manuel John 1919- *WhoMW 92, WhoRel 92*
**Vargas,** Manuel P. 1947- *WhoHisp 92*
**Vargas,** Margarita 1956- *WhoHisp 92*
**Vargas,** Nancy R. 1952- *WhoHisp 92*
**Vargas,** Nyno S. 1938- *WhoHisp 92*
**Vargas,** Quintin, III 1948- *WhoHisp 92*
**Vargas,** Ray M *WhoAmP 91, WhoHisp 92*
**Vargas,** Robert *DrAPF 91*
**Vargas,** Robert J. *WhoHisp 92*
**Vargas,** Roberto H *DrAPF 91*
**Vargas,** Rodolfo, IV 1959- *WhoHisp 92*
**Vargas,** Roger I *AmMWSc 92*
**Vargas,** Sybil Rose Hunt 1912- *WhoAmP 91*
**Vargas,** William 1946- *WhoHisp 92*
**Vargas,** William Jose 1955- *WhoEnt 92*
**Vargas Llosa,** Mario 1936- *BenetAL 91, FacFETw, IntWW 91, LiExTwC*
**Vargas-Vidot,** Jose Antonio 1954- *WhoHisp 92*
**Varghese,** Sankoorikal Lonappan 1943- *AmMWSc 92*
**Vargo,** Edward Paul 1935- *WhoRel 92*
**Vargo,** Steven William 1931- *AmMWSc 92*
**Vargus,** Ione D. 1930- *WhoBlA 92*
**Varian,** Hal Ronald 1947- *WhoFI 92, WhoMW 92*
**Varin,** Robert Andrzej 1946- *AmMWSc 92*
**Varin,** Roger Robert 1925- *AmMWSc 92*
**Varineau,** Verne John 1915- *AmMWSc 92*
**Varkas,** William A *WhoAmP 91*
**Varkey,** Thankamma Eapen 1936- *AmMWSc 92*
**Varki,** Ajit Pothan 1952- *AmMWSc 92*
**Varkonyi,** Peter 1931- *IntWW 91*
**Varlashkin,** Paul 1931- *AmMWSc 92*
**Varley** *Who 92*
**Varley,** Baron 1932- *IntWW 91, Who 92*
**Varley,** Joan 1920- *Who 92*
**Varley,** John 1947- *TwCSFW 91, WrDr 92*
**Varley,** Julia 1871-1952 *BiDBrF 2*
**Varley,** Thomas Arthur 1950- *WhoFI 92*
**Varloot,** Denis 1937- *IntWW 91*
**Varma,** Andre A O 1927- *AmMWSc 92*
**Varma,** Arun Kumar *AmMWSc 92*
**Varma,** Arvind 1947- *AmMWSc 92, WhoMW 92*
**Varma,** Asha 1942- *AmMWSc 92*
**Varma,** Chitra Thirunal Bala Rama d1991 *NewYTBS 91*
**Varma,** Daya Ram *AmMWSc 92*
**Varma,** Man Mohan 1932- *AmMWSc 92*
**Varma,** Matesh Narayan 1943- *AmMWSc 92*
**Varma,** Monika 1916- *WrDr 92*
**Varma,** Rad Srinivasan 1943- *WhoMW 92*
**Varma,** Raj Narayan 1928- *AmMWSc 92*
**Varma,** Rajender S 1951- *AmMWSc 92*
**Varma,** Ranbir 1928- *WhoFI 92*
**Varma,** Ravi Kannadikovilakom 1937- *AmMWSc 92*
**Varma,** Shambhu D *AmMWSc 92*
**Varma,** Surendra K 1939- *AmMWSc 92*
**Varmus,** Harold Eliot 1939- *IntWW 91, Who 92, WhoNob 90, WhoWest 92*
**Varmus,** Harold Elliot 1939- *AmMWSc 92*
**Varn,** Richard J 1958- *WhoAmP 91*
**Varnachev,** Yevgeniy Andreyevich 1932- *IntWW 91*
**Varnado,** Arthur 1932- *WhoBlA 92*
**Varnam,** Ivor 1922- *Who 92*
**Varnava,** Penelope 1961- *WhoMW 92*
**Varnay,** Astrid 1918- *NewAmDM*
**Varnedoe,** Kirk 1946- *CurBio 91 [port]*
**Varnell,** John Dunlap 1941- *WhoAmL 92*
**Varnell,** Thomas Raymond 1931- *AmMWSc 92*
**Varnell,** Van 1967- *WhoWest 92*
**Varner,** Bruce H., Jr. 1946- *WhoWest 92*
**Varner,** Charleen LaVerne McClanahan 1931- *WhoFI 92, WhoMW 92*
**Varner,** David Eugene 1937- *WhoAmL 92*
**Varner,** Henry, Jr 1931- *WhoAmP 91*
**Varner,** Ivory Leon 1948- *WhoRel 92*
**Varner,** James, Sr. 1934- *WhoBlA 92*
**Varner,** Jewell C. 1918- *WhoBlA 92*
**Varner,** John 1906- *WhoAmP 91*
**Varner,** Joseph Elmer 1921- *AmMWSc 92*
**Varner,** Larry Weldon 1944- *AmMWSc 92*
**Varner,** Nellie M. 1935- *WhoBlA 92*
**Varner,** Robert Bernard 1930- *WhoFI 92, WhoMW 92*
**Varner,** Robert Edward 1921- *WhoAmL 92*
**Varner,** Robert Lee 1932- *WhoBlA 92*
**Varner,** Sterling Verl 1919- *WhoFI 92*
**Varnerin,** Lawrence J 1923- *AmMWSc 92*
**Varnes,** David Joseph 1919- *AmMWSc 92, WhoWest 92*
**Varnes,** Marie Elizabeth 1942- *AmMWSc 92*
**Varney,** Charles W, Jr 1912- *WhoIns 92*
**Varney,** Eugene Harvey 1923- *AmMWSc 92*
**Varney,** Jim 1950- *IntMPA 92*
**Varney,** Peter Justin 1942- *WhoWest 92*
**Varney,** Robert Nathan 1910- *AmMWSc 92*
**Varney,** William York 1917- *AmMWSc 92*
**Varnhorn,** Mary Catherine 1914- *AmMWSc 92*
**Varnum,** Charles Henry 1933- *WhoAmP 91*
**Varnum,** Joseph Bradley 1750?-1821 *AmPolLe*
**Varnum,** William Sloan 1941- *AmMWSc 92*
**Varon,** Myron Izak 1930- *AmMWSc 92*
**Varon,** Silvio Salomone 1924- *AmMWSc 92*
**Varona,** Enrique Jose 1849-1933 *HisDSpE*
**Varona,** Oscar *BlkOlyM*
**Varpio,** Veijo Aleksanteri 1928- *WhoEnt 92*
**Varrasso,** Richard Kenneth 1957- *WhoEnt 92*
**Varrelmann,** Robert Gale 1947- *WhoWest 92*
**Varrenti,** Adam, Jr. 1949- *WhoFI 92*
**Varrese,** Francis Raymond *AmMWSc 92*
**Varricchio,** Frederick 1938- *AmMWSc 92*
**Varrone,** John M *WhoAmP 91*
**Varsa,** Edward Charles 1938- *AmMWSc 92*
**Varsamis,** Ioannis 1932- *AmMWSc 92*
**Varsbergs,** Vilis 1929- *WhoRel 92*
**Varsel,** Charles John 1930- *AmMWSc 92*
**Varshavsky,** Ilya 1909- *TwCSFW 91A*
**Varshney,** Pramod Kumar 1952- *AmMWSc 92*
**Varshni,** Yatendra Pal 1932- *AmMWSc 92*
**Varsi,** Diane 1938- *IntMPA 92*
**Vartabedian,** Steven Michael 1950- *WhoAmL 92*
**Vartanian,** Elsie 1930- *WhoAmP 91*
**Vartanian,** Haik 1961- *WhoWest 92*
**Vartanian,** Leo 1933- *AmMWSc 92*
**Vartanian,** Perry H, Jr 1931- *AmMWSc 92*
**Varteressian,** K A 1908- *AmMWSc 92*
**Vartsky,** David 1946- *AmMWSc 92*
**Varty,** Isaac William 1924- *AmMWSc 92*
**Varty,** Keith 1952- *IntWW 91*
**Varvik,** Dagfinn 1924- *IntWW 91*
**Varviso,** Silvio 1924- *NewAmDM*
**Vary,** James Corydon 1939- *AmMWSc 92*
**Vary,** Patricia Susan 1941- *AmMWSc 92*
**Vas,** Istvan 1910- *IntAu&W 91, IntWW 91*
**Vas,** Stephen Istvan 1926- *AmMWSc 92*
**Vas Dias,** Robert 1931- *ConPo 91, IntAu&W 91, WrDr 92*
**Vasallo,** Pedro E. *WhoHisp 92*
**Vasarely,** Victor 1908- *IntWW 91*
**Vasarhelyi,** Desi D 1910- *AmMWSc 92*
**Vasary,** Tamas 1933- *IntWW 91, NewAmDM, Who 92, WhoEnt 92*
**Vasavada,** Kashyap V 1938- *AmMWSc 92*
**Vasavada,** Kashyap Vishnuprasad 1938- *WhoMW 92*
**Vasco,** Donald Wyman 1958- *AmMWSc 92*
**Vasconcellos,** John 1932- *WhoAmP 91, WhoHisp 92*
**Vasconcellos,** Josefina Alys Hermes de *Who 92*
**Vasconcelos,** Aurea C 1935- *AmMWSc 92*
**Vasconcelos,** Wolner V 1937- *AmMWSc 92*
**Vaseen,** V Albert 1917- *AmMWSc 92*
**Vasek,** Frank Charles 1927- *AmMWSc 92*
**Vasel,** Carolynn 1952- *WhoMW 92*
**Vaserstein,** Leonid, IV 1944- *AmMWSc 92*
**Vasey,** Bill 1939- *WhoAmP 91*
**Vasey,** Carey Edward 1927- *AmMWSc 92*
**Vasey,** Edfred H 1933- *AmMWSc 92*
**Vasey,** Frank Barnett 1942- *AmMWSc 92*
**Vasey,** George 1822-1893 *BiInAmS*
**Vasey,** Harvey Elmer 1890-1918 *BiInAmS*
**Vasey,** William Leslie 1943- *WhoRel 92*
**Vashishta,** Priya Darshan 1944- *AmMWSc 92*
**Vasholz,** Lothar A. 1930- *WhoFI 92*
**Vashon,** George 1820-1878 *BenetAL 91*
**Vashon,** Susan Paul 1838-1912 *NotBlAW 92 [port]*
**Vashti** *EncAmaz 91*
**Vasicek,** Daniel J 1942- *AmMWSc 92*
**Vasigh,** Bijan 1950- *WhoFI 92*
**Vasil,** Indra Kumar 1932- *AmMWSc 92*
**Vasil,** Michael Lawrence 1945- *AmMWSc 92*
**Vasil,** Raj Kumar 1931- *WrDr 92*
**Vasil,** Vimla 1932- *AmMWSc 92*
**Vasilakos,** Nicholas Petrou 1954- *AmMWSc 92*
**Vasilas,** Darla Jean 1949- *WhoFI 92*
**Vasilatos-Younken,** Regina 1954- *AmMWSc 92*
**Vasile,** Michael Joseph 1940- *AmMWSc 92*
**Vasil'ev,** Georgiy Nikoaevich 1899-1946 *SovUnBD*
**Vasil'ev,** Pavel Nikolaevich 1910-1937 *SovUnBD*
**Vasil'ev,** Sergey Dmitrievich 1900-1959 *SovUnBD*
**Vasil'ev,** Vladimir Viktorovich 1940- *SovUnBD*
**Vasilevsky,** Aleksandr Mikhaylovich 1895-1977 *SovUnBD*
**Vasiliauskas,** Edmund 1938- *AmMWSc 92*
**Vasiliev and Maximova** *FacFETw*
**Vasiliev,** Anatoli *IntWW 91*
**Vasiliev,** Boris 1924- *IntWW 91*
**Vasiliev,** Georgi 1899-1946 *IntDcF 2-2*
**Vasiliev,** Ivan Afanasivevich 1924- *IntWW 91*
**Vasiliev,** Lev Borisovich 1925- *IntWW 91*
**Vasiliev,** Sergei 1900-1959 *IntDcF 2-2 [port]*
**Vasiliev,** Vladimir Victorovich 1940- *FacFETw*
**Vasiliu,** Emanuel 1929- *IntWW 91*
**Vasiliyev,** German Konstantinovich 1936- *IntWW 91*
**Vasiliyev,** Vladimir Viktorovich 1940- *IntWW 91*
**Vasilos,** Thomas 1929- *AmMWSc 92*
**Vasilyev,** Nikolay Fyodorovich 1916- *IntWW 91*
**Vasington,** Frank D 1928- *AmMWSc 92*
**Vaska,** Lauri 1925- *AmMWSc 92*
**Vasko,** John Stephen 1929- *AmMWSc 92*
**Vasko,** Michael Richard 1948- *AmMWSc 92*
**Vaslef,** Nicholas P. 1930- *WhoEnt 92*
**Vaslett,** Victoria Jean 1955- *WhoEnt 92*
**Vaslow,** Dale Franklin 1945- *AmMWSc 92*
**Vasnetsov,** Yuriy Alekseevich 1900-1973 *SovUnBD*
**Vasofsky,** Richard William 1946- *AmMWSc 92*
**Vasquez,** Alfred 1923- *Who 92*
**Vasquez,** Alphonse Thomas 1938- *AmMWSc 92*
**Vasquez,** Arturo *WhoHisp 92*
**Vasquez,** Cesar Luis 1935- *WhoHisp 92*
**Vasquez,** Edmundo Eusebio 1932- *WhoRel 92*
**Vasquez,** Fernando, Sr. 1955- *WhoHisp 92*
**Vasquez,** Florentino John 1957- *WhoHisp 92*
**Vasquez,** Floyd Estevan, II 1963- *WhoHisp 92*
**Vasquez,** Gabriel Marcus 1960- *WhoHisp 92*
**Vasquez,** Gaddi Holguin 1955- *WhoHisp 92*
**Vasquez,** Gilbert Reynaldo 1939- *WhoHisp 92*
**Vasquez,** Hector Rey 1952- *WhoHisp 92*
**Vasquez,** Irene Sosa 1950- *WhoHisp 92*
**Vasquez,** James Alan 1932- *WhoHisp 92*
**Vasquez,** Jeffery 1956- *WhoHisp 92*
**Vasquez,** Joseph Anthony, Jr. 1950- *WhoHisp 92*
**Vasquez,** Joseph B. *WhoHisp 92*
**Vasquez,** Joseph J. 1927- *WhoHisp 92*
**Vasquez,** Juan *WhoHisp 92*
**Vasquez,** Juanita Sylvia 1919- *WhoHisp 92*
**Vasquez,** Lee 1945- *WhoHisp 92*
**Vasquez,** Lois 1942- *WhoHisp 92*
**Vasquez,** Manuel Daniel 1959- *WhoHisp 92*
**Vasquez,** Nick Antonio 1951- *WhoWest 92*
**Vasquez,** Pablo 1769-1847 *HisDSpE*
**Vasquez,** Paul 1952- *WhoAmP 91, WhoHisp 92*
**Vasquez,** Philip Daniel 1955- *WhoHisp 92*
**Vasquez,** Raul 1954- *WhoHisp 92*
**Vasquez,** Raul Herrera, Jr. 1949- *WhoHisp 92*
**Vasquez,** Richard *DrAPF 91*
**Vasquez,** Richard 1928- *WhoHisp 92*
**Vasquez,** Robert J. 1931- *WhoHisp 92*
**Vasquez-Ajmac,** Luis Alfredo 1961- *WhoHisp 92*
**Vasquez Arce y Ceballos,** Gregorio 1638-1711 *HisDSpE*
**Vasquez de Coronado,** Francisco *HisDSpE*
**Vasquez de Coronado,** Juan *HisDSpE*
**Vasquez de Velasco,** Pedro 1603-1670 *HisDSpE*
**Vasquez Elizalde,** Serafin 1922- *WhoRel 92*
**Vass,** Steven T. 1932- *WhoMW 92*
**Vassa,** Gustavus *BenetAL 91*
**Vassall,** Sidney Austin 1934- *WhoBlA 92*
**Vassalle,** Mario 1928- *AmMWSc 92*
**Vassalli,** Giuliano 1915- *IntWW 91*
**Vassallo,** Donald Arthur 1932- *AmMWSc 92*
**Vassallo,** Efrain David 1928- *WhoHisp 92*
**Vassallo,** Franklin A 1934- *AmMWSc 92*
**Vassallo,** John A. 1937- *WhoAmL 92*
**Vassamillet,** Lawrence Francois 1924- *AmMWSc 92*
**Vassar,** David Anthony 1951- *WhoEnt 92*
**Vassar,** John Dixie, Jr. 1953- *WhoFI 92*
**Vassar,** Milas Robert 1953- *WhoRel 92*
**Vassar-Smith,** Richard Rathborne 1909- *Who 92*
**Vassel,** Bruno 1908- *AmMWSc 92*
**Vassell,** Gregory S 1921- *AmMWSc 92*
**Vassell,** Milton O 1931- *AmMWSc 92*
**Vassil,** Pamela 1943- *WhoEnt 92*
**Vassilaqui,** Alejandro *WhoRel 92*
**Vassilas,** Anastasios Eugene 1949- *WhoFI 92*
**Vassiliades,** Anthony E 1933- *AmMWSc 92*
**Vassiliades-Rokou,** Mapia 1931- *IntAu&W 91*
**Vassilikos,** Vassilis 1934- *LiExTwC*
**Vassiliou,** Andreas H 1936- *AmMWSc 92*
**Vassiliou,** Eustathios 1934- *AmMWSc 92*
**Vassiliou,** George 1931- *Who 92*
**Vassiliou,** George Vassos 1931- *IntWW 91*
**Vassiliou,** Marius Simon 1957- *AmMWSc 92*
**Vassiliou,** Simos G. 1919- *IntWW 91*
**Vassiliyevna,** Larisa 1935- *IntWW 91*
**Vassogne,** Jean Georges 1919- *IntWW 91*
**Vassos,** John 1898-1985 *ScFEYrs*
**Vassos,** Ruth 1896-1965 *ScFEYrs*
**Vasta,** Edward 1928- *WrDr 92*
**Vasta,** Vincent Joseph, Jr. 1944- *WhoAmL 92*
**Vastano,** Andrew Charles 1936- *AmMWSc 92*
**Vastine,** J Robert, Jr 1937- *WhoAmP 91*
**Vastola,** Francis J 1928- *AmMWSc 92*
**Vastola,** Michael J. *WhoFI 92*
**Vasu,** Bangalore Seshachalam *WhoWest 92*
**Vasu,** Bangalore Seshachalam 1929- *AmMWSc 92*
**Vasudeva** *DrAPF 91*
**Vasudeva,** Vishnudayal *WrDr 92*
**Vasyagin,** Semyon Petrovich 1910- *IntWW 91*
**Vatcher,** Cheryl Ann 1961- *WhoMW 92*
**Vatikiotis,** P. J. 1928- *WrDr 92*

**Vatikiotis,** Panayiotis Jerasimos 1928- *IntWW 91*
**Vatistas,** Georgios H 1953- *AmMWSc 92*
**Vatne,** Robert Dahlmeier 1934- *AmMWSc 92*
**Vatolin,** Nikolay Anatolevich 1926- *IntWW 91*
**Vatsis,** Kostas Petros 1945- *AmMWSc 92*
**Vatsures,** Thomas Peter 1958- *WhoAmL 92*
**Vattel,** Emmerich de 1714-1767 *BlkwCEP*
**Vatter,** Harold Goodhue 1910- *WhoFI 92*
**Vaucanson,** Jacques de 1709-1782 *BlkwCEP*
**Vaucher,** Jean G 1942- *AmMWSc 92*
**Vauchez,** Andre Michel 1938- *IntWW 91*
**Vaudo,** Anthony Frank 1946- *AmMWSc 92*
**Vaugeois,** Henri 1864-1916 *BiDExR*
**Vaughan** *Who 92*
**Vaughan,** Viscount 1945- *Who 92*
**Vaughan,** Alden T. 1929- *WrDr 92*
**Vaughan,** Arvin Maynard 1939- *WhoMW 92*
**Vaughan,** Austin Bernard 1927- *WhoRel 92*
**Vaughan,** Benjamin 1751-1835 *BiInAmS*
**Vaughan,** Benjamin Noel Young 1917- *Who 92*
**Vaughan,** Burton Eugene 1926- *AmMWSc 92*
**Vaughan,** Christopher Clayton 1941- *WhoFI 92*
**Vaughan,** Daniel 1818?-1879 *BiInAmS*
**Vaughan,** David Arthur 1923- *AmMWSc 92*
**Vaughan,** David Arthur John 1938- *Who 92*
**Vaughan,** David John 1924- *WhoFI 92, WhoMW 92*
**Vaughan,** David Sherwood 1923- *AmMWSc 92*
**Vaughan,** Deborah Whittaker 1943- *AmMWSc 92*
**Vaughan,** Dennis Ralsten, Jr. 1941- *WhoAmL 92, WhoFI 92*
**Vaughan,** Donald Ray 1952- *WhoAmL 92*
**Vaughan,** Douglas Stanwood 1946- *AmMWSc 92*
**Vaughan,** Edgar *Who 92*
**Vaughan,** Edgar 1907- *IntWW 91*
**Vaughan,** Elizabeth *Who 92*
**Vaughan,** Elizabeth Ardrey 1963- *WhoEnt 92*
**Vaughan,** Elizabeth Crownhart 1929- *WhoWest 92*
**Vaughan,** Eugene H. 1933- *WhoFI 92*
**Vaughan,** George Edgar 1907- *Who 92*
**Vaughan,** Gerald R. 1957- *WhoBlA 92*
**Vaughan,** Gerard 1923- *Who 92*
**Vaughan,** Gregory Neil 1951- *WhoMW 92*
**Vaughan,** H M 1870-1948 *ScFEYrs*
**Vaughan,** Harry H 1893-1981 *FacFETw*
**Vaughan,** Henry 1621-1695 *RfGEnL 91*
**Vaughan,** Henry William Campbell d1991 *Who 92N*
**Vaughan,** Herbert Edward 1911- *AmMWSc 92*
**Vaughan,** Herbert Wiley 1920- *WhoAmL 92, WhoFI 92*
**Vaughan,** J Rodney M 1921- *AmMWSc 92*
**Vaughan,** Jack 1961- *WhoAmP 91*
**Vaughan,** Jack Chapline, Jr. 1943- *WhoAmL 92*
**Vaughan,** James Arthur, Jr. 1914- *WhoWest 92*
**Vaughan,** James Edward 1943- *WhoBlA 92*
**Vaughan,** James Franklin 1937- *WhoFI 92*
**Vaughan,** James Roland 1928- *AmMWSc 92*
**Vaughan,** Janet 1899- *Who 92*
**Vaughan,** Janet Maria 1899- *IntWW 91*
**Vaughan,** Jerald Denny 1947- *WhoMW 92*
**Vaughan,** Jerry Eugene 1939- *AmMWSc 92*
**Vaughan,** John 1756-1841 *BiInAmS*
**Vaughan,** John 1775-1807 *BiInAmS*
**Vaughan,** John Dixon 1925- *AmMWSc 92*
**Vaughan,** John Heath 1921- *AmMWSc 92*
**Vaughan,** John Nolen 1941- *WhoRel 92*
**Vaughan,** John Thomas 1932- *AmMWSc 92*
**Vaughan,** Karen McHugh 1954- *WhoAmL 92*
**Vaughan,** Keith 1912-1976 *TwCPaSc*
**Vaughan,** Larry Clayton 1948- *WhoAmL 92*
**Vaughan,** Larry Dean 1950- *WhoMW 92*
**Vaughan,** Leslie Clifford 1927- *Who 92*
**Vaughan,** Linda Ann 1950- *AmMWSc 92*
**Vaughan,** Loy Ottis, Jr 1945- *AmMWSc 92*
**Vaughan,** Martha 1926- *AmMWSc 92*
**Vaughan,** Mary Kathleen 1943- *AmMWSc 92*
**Vaughan,** Michael 1938- *TwCPaSc*
**Vaughan,** Michael Ray 1944- *AmMWSc 92*
**Vaughan,** Michael Thomas 1940- *AmMWSc 92*
**Vaughan,** Mimi C. R. *WhoHisp 92*
**Vaughan,** Nick Hampton 1923- *AmMWSc 92*
**Vaughan,** Olive Elizabeth 1925- *WhoFI 92*
**Vaughan,** Patrick Joseph 1929- *WhoAmP 91*
**Vaughan,** Paul Irvine 1937- *WhoRel 92*
**Vaughan,** Peter St George *Who 92*
**Vaughan,** Richard Alaric 1965- *WhoWest 92*
**Vaughan,** Richard Allen 1946- *WhoFI 92*
**Vaughan,** Richard Patrick 1919- *WrDr 92*
**Vaughan,** Robert Alan 1953- *WhoAmP 91*
**Vaughan,** Robert Charles 1945- *Who 92*
**Vaughan,** Robert Timothy 1956- *WhoFI 92*
**Vaughan,** Roger 1944- *Who 92*
**Vaughan,** Roger Davison 1923- *Who 92*
**Vaughan,** Sarah 1924-1990 *AnObit 1990, FacFETw, NewAmDM, NotBlAW 92 [port]*
**Vaughan,** Sarah Lois 1924-1990 *WhoBlA 92N*
**Vaughan,** Stevie 1954-1990 *FacFETw*
**Vaughan,** Stevie Ray 1954-1990 *AnObit 1990*
**Vaughan,** Stevie Ray 1956?-1990 *News 91*
**Vaughan,** Terry Alfred 1928- *AmMWSc 92*
**Vaughan,** Theresa Phillips 1941- *AmMWSc 92*
**Vaughan,** Thomas James Gregory 1924- *WhoWest 92*
**Vaughan,** Thomas Marshall 1943- *WhoFI 92*
**Vaughan,** Thomas Martin 1946- *WhoAmL 92*
**Vaughan,** Victor Clarence, III 1919- *AmMWSc 92*
**Vaughan,** Victor Clarence, Jr. 1879-1919 *BiInAmS*
**Vaughan,** Warren Taylor, Jr. 1920- *WhoWest 92*
**Vaughan,** Wayland Edward 1934- *WhoFI 92*
**Vaughan,** William Addison 1935- *WhoAmP 91*
**Vaughan,** William Mace 1942- *AmMWSc 92*
**Vaughan,** William Randal 1912- *Who 92*
**Vaughan,** William Walton 1930- *AmMWSc 92*
**Vaughan,** Worth E 1936- *AmMWSc 92*
**Vaughan,** Wyman Ristine 1916- *AmMWSc 92*
**Vaughan-Jackson,** Oliver James 1907- *Who 92*
**Vaughan-Morgan** *Who 92*
**Vaughan-Thomas,** Wynford 1908- *IntAu&W 91*
**Vaughan-Thomas,** Wynford 1908-1987 *FacFETw*
**Vaughan Williams,** Ralph 1872-1958 *FacFETw [port], NewAmDM*
**Vaughan Williams,** Ursula 1911- *WrDr 92*
**Vaughen,** Victor C A 1933- *AmMWSc 92*
**Vaughn,** Alvin 1939- *WhoBlA 92*
**Vaughn,** Audrey Smith 1958- *WhoBlA 92*
**Vaughn,** Billy d1991 *NewYTBS 91*
**Vaughn,** Charles Arthur 1938- *WhoEnt 92*
**Vaughn,** Charles L 1919- *WhoAmP 91*
**Vaughn,** Charles Melvin 1915- *AmMWSc 92, WhoMW 92*
**Vaughn,** Christopher Clarence 1944- *WhoWest 92*
**Vaughn,** Clarence B. 1928- *WhoBlA 92*
**Vaughn,** Clarence Benjamin 1928- *AmMWSc 92*
**Vaughn,** Clarence Roland, Jr 1921- *WhoAmP 91*
**Vaughn,** Danny Mack 1948- *AmMWSc 92*
**Vaughn,** Donald Charles 1936- *WhoFI 92*
**Vaughn,** Edward 1934- *WhoAmP 91*
**Vaughn,** Elbert Hardy 1946- *WhoFI 92*
**Vaughn,** Eleanor L 1922- *WhoAmP 91*
**Vaughn,** Eugenia Marchelle Washington 1957- *WhoBlA 92*
**Vaughn,** Fred D 1920- *WhoAmP 91*
**Vaughn,** Gordon E. *WhoRel 92*
**Vaughn,** H George, Jr 1939- *WhoAmP 91*
**Vaughn,** Jack C 1937- *AmMWSc 92*
**Vaughn,** Jackie, III *WhoAmP 91*
**Vaughn,** Jackie, III 1939- *WhoBlA 92*
**Vaughn,** Jacqueline Barbara 1935- *WhoBlA 92*
**Vaughn,** James E, Jr 1939- *AmMWSc 92*
**Vaughn,** James Eldon 1925- *WhoEnt 92*
**Vaughn,** James English, Jr. 1939- *WhoWest 92*
**Vaughn,** James L 1934- *AmMWSc 92*
**Vaughn,** James Michael 1939- *WhoMW 92*
**Vaughn,** James T 1925- *WhoAmP 91*
**Vaughn,** Jimmy Fredrick 1965- *WhoRel 92*
**Vaughn,** Joe Warren 1933- *AmMWSc 92*
**Vaughn,** John B 1924- *AmMWSc 92*
**Vaughn,** Karen Iversen 1944- *WhoFI 92*
**Vaughn,** Kirk Andrew 1949- *WhoAmL 92*
**Vaughn,** Leevy Hightower 1928- *WhoMW 92*
**Vaughn,** Lewis R 1934- *WhoAmP 91*
**Vaughn,** Lisa Dawn 1961- *WhoMW 92*
**Vaughn,** Lowry D 1944- *WhoIns 92*
**Vaughn,** Mary Kathryn 1949- *WhoBlA 92*
**Vaughn,** Michael Louis 1948- *WhoAmL 92*
**Vaughn,** Michael Thayer 1936- *AmMWSc 92*
**Vaughn,** Moses William 1913- *AmMWSc 92*
**Vaughn,** Nora Belle 1914- *WhoBlA 92*
**Vaughn,** Percy Joseph, Jr. 1932- *WhoBlA 92*
**Vaughn,** Peter Paul 1928- *AmMWSc 92*
**Vaughn,** Phoebe Juanita Fitzgerald 1939- *IntAu&W 91*
**Vaughn,** Ralph Edwin 1955- *WhoMW 92*
**Vaughn,** Raymond L, Jr 1948- *WhoAmP 91*
**Vaughn,** Reese Haskell 1908- *AmMWSc 92*
**Vaughn,** Richard Clements 1925- *AmMWSc 92*
**Vaughn,** Robert 1932- *IntMPA 92*
**Vaughn,** Stephen Lee 1947- *WhoMW 92*
**Vaughn,** Thomas Hunt 1909- *AmMWSc 92*
**Vaughn,** William James 1834-1912 *BiInAmS*
**Vaughn,** William John 1931- *WhoFI 92*
**Vaughn,** William King 1938- *AmMWSc 92*
**Vaughn,** William Samuel, III 1955- *WhoBlA 92*
**Vaughn,** William Smith 1930- *WhoBlA 92*
**Vaughns,** Fred L. 1923- *WhoBlA 92*
**Vaughns,** John Claude 1914- *WhoBlA 92*
**Vaughns,** Sylvester J., Sr. 1935- *WhoBlA 92*
**Vaught,** David Hall 1947- *WhoFI 92*
**Vaught,** Douglas Stephen 1951- *WhoAmP 91*
**Vaught,** Elmer Richard 1928- *WhoAmP 91*
**Vaught,** Jimmie Barton *AmMWSc 92*
**Vaught,** Loy Stephon 1967- *WhoBlA 92*
**Vaught,** Richard Loren 1933- *WhoMW 92*
**Vaught,** Robert L 1926- *AmMWSc 92*
**Vaun,** William Stratin 1929- *AmMWSc 92*
**Vaupel,** Donald Bruce 1942- *AmMWSc 92*
**Vaupel,** Martin Robert 1928- *AmMWSc 92*
**Vaupen,** Burton 1930- *WhoEnt 92*
**Vause,** Edwin H 1923- *AmMWSc 92*
**Vautin,** William C. 1957- *WhoFI 92*
**Vautrin,** Jean 1933- *IntWW 91*
**Vaux,** Dora Louise 1922- *WhoWest 92*
**Vaux,** Henry James 1912- *AmMWSc 92*
**Vaux,** James Edward, Jr 1932- *AmMWSc 92*
**Vaux,** Marc 1932- *TwCPaSc*
**Vaux,** Nicholas Francis 1936- *Who 92*
**Vaux,** Patrick 1872- *ScFEYrs*
**Vaux,** Thomas 1510-1556 *RfGEnL 91*
**Vaux,** William Sansom 1811-1882 *BiInAmS*
**Vaux of Harrowden,** Baron 1915- *Who 92*
**Vavagiakis,** Efstratios Joeseph 1957- *WhoEnt 92*
**Vavasour,** Geoffrey William 1914- *Who 92*
**Vavich,** Mitchell George 1916- *AmMWSc 92*
**Vavilov,** Nicholas Ivanovich 1887-1943 *FacFETw*
**Vavilov,** Nikolay Ivanovich 1887-1943 *SovUnBD*
**Vavoulis,** George J 1911- *WhoAmP 91*
**Vavra,** James Joseph 1929- *AmMWSc 92*
**Vavra,** Otakar 1911- *IntWW 91*
**Vavrus,** Donald Richard 1958- *WhoEnt 92*
**Vawter,** Alfred Thomas 1943- *AmMWSc 92*
**Vawter,** Donald 1920- *WhoWest 92*
**Vawter,** James Keith 1953- *WhoRel 92*
**Vawter,** Jay 1934- *WhoFI 92*
**Vawter,** Spencer Max 1937- *AmMWSc 92*
**Vayda,** Andrew P. 1931- *WrDr 92*
**Vayda,** Jeffrey George 1953- *WhoRel 92*
**Vayhinger,** John Monroe 1916- *WhoRel 92*
**Vaynonen,** Vasiliy Ivanovich 1901-1964 *SovUnBD*
**Vayo,** Harris Westcott 1935- *AmMWSc 92*
**Vayrynen,** Paavo Matti 1946- *IntWW 91*
**Vaz,** Douglas Crompton 1937- *IntWW 91*
**Vaz,** Keith 1956- *Who 92*
**Vaz,** Maria Joao de Sampaionunes 1952- *WhoMW 92*
**Vaz,** Nuno A 1951- *AmMWSc 92*
**Vaz,** Nuno Artur 1951- *WhoMW 92*
**Vazgen I** 1908- *IntWW 91*
**Vaziri,** Menouchehr 1951- *AmMWSc 92*
**Vazmina,** Shelley Carol Borger 1947- *WhoAmL 92*
**Vazquez,** Albert 1947- *WhoHisp 92*
**Vazquez,** Alfredo Jorge 1937- *AmMWSc 92*
**Vazquez,** Amalia 1956- *WhoHisp 92*
**Vazquez,** Angel Antonio 1949- *WhoHisp 92*
**Vazquez,** Angela M. 1940- *WhoHisp 92*
**Vazquez,** Anna T. 1918- *WhoHisp 92*
**Vazquez,** Arturo, Jr. 1956- *WhoHisp 92*
**Vazquez,** Carlos Alberto 1968- *WhoFI 92*
**Vazquez,** Edna 1952- *WhoHisp 92*
**Vazquez,** Eloy 1935- *WhoHisp 92*
**Vazquez,** Emil C. 1947- *WhoHisp 92*
**Vazquez,** Gilbert Falcon 1952- *WhoAmL 92*
**Vazquez,** J. Michael *WhoHisp 92*
**Vazquez,** John David 1935- *WhoHisp 92*
**Vazquez,** Jorge Alberto 1943- *IntWW 91*
**Vazquez,** Juan M. 1949- *WhoHisp 92*
**Vazquez,** Martha Elisa 1954- *WhoHisp 92*
**Vazquez,** Olga *WhoHisp 92*
**Vazquez,** Raul A. 1939- *WhoHisp 92*
**Vazquez,** Rebecca C. 1957- *WhoHisp 92*
**Vazquez,** Roberto 1923- *WhoHisp 92*
**Vazquez,** Roberto Rodriguez 1923- *WhoMW 92*
**Vazquez Diaz,** Rene 1952- *IntAu&W 91*
**Vazquez-Rana,** Mario 1932- *WhoHisp 92*
**Vazquez Richard,** Juan 1949- *WhoHisp 92*
**Vazsonyi,** Balint 1936- *WhoMW 92*
**Vazzana,** Patricia Anne 1947- *WhoFI 92*
**Vdovin,** Valentin Petrovich 1927- *IntWW 91*
**Veach,** Allen Marshall 1933- *AmMWSc 92*
**Veach,** William David 1959- *WhoWest 92*
**Veal,** Billy Robert 1961- *WhoRel 92*
**Veal,** Boyd William, Jr 1937- *AmMWSc 92*
**Veal,** Donald L 1931- *AmMWSc 92*
**Veal,** Donald Lyle 1931- *WhoWest 92*
**Veal,** Howard Richard 1942- *WhoBlA 92*
**Veal,** John Bartholomew 1909- *Who 92*
**Veal,** Kenneth Wayne 1943- *WhoRel 92*
**Veal,** Rex R. 1956- *WhoAmL 92*
**Veal,** Robert Jeffery 1951- *WhoAmL 92*
**Veal,** Yvonnecris Smith *WhoBlA 92*
**Veale,** Alan 1920- *Who 92*
**Veale,** Alan John Ralph 1920- *IntWW 91*
**Veale,** Alan Keith 1950- *WhoRel 92*
**Veale,** Tinkham, II 1914- *WhoFI 92*
**Veale,** Warren Lorne 1943- *AmMWSc 92*
**Veasel,** Walter 1925- *WhoRel 92*
**Veasey,** Columbus, Jr. 1935- *WhoWest 92*
**Veasey,** Jack *DrAPF 91*
**Veasey,** Josephine 1930- *IntWW 91, Who 92*
**Veatch,** Brian Douglas 1962- *WhoEnt 92*
**Veatch,** John William 1923- *WhoWest 92*
**Veatch,** Marcus Robert 1953- *WhoMW 92*
**Veatch,** Ralph Wilson 1900- *AmMWSc 92*
**Veazey,** Jimmy L. 1960- *WhoRel 92*
**Veazey,** Monty Mobley 1954- *WhoAmP 91*
**Veazey,** Richard Edward 1941- *WhoMW 92*
**Veazey,** Sidney Edwin 1937- *AmMWSc 92*
**Veazey,** Thomas Mabry 1920- *AmMWSc 92*
**Veber,** Daniel Frank 1939- *AmMWSc 92*
**Veber,** Francis 1937- *ConAu 135*
**Veblen,** David Rodli 1947- *AmMWSc 92*
**Veblen,** Thomas Clayton 1929- *WhoFI 92*
**Veblen,** Thorstein 1857-1929 *RComAH*
**Veblen,** Thorstein B. 1857-1929 *BenetAL 91, FacFETw*
**Veblen,** Thorstein Bunde 1857-1929 *AmPeW*
**Veburg,** Ronald Neil 1930- *WhoMW 92*
**Vecchi,** Orazio 1550-1605 *NewAmDM*
**Vecchio,** Raymond 1933- *WhoAmP 91*
**Vecchio,** Robert Peter 1950- *WhoMW 92*
**Vecchione,** Al *LesBEnT 92*
**Vecci,** Raymond Joseph 1943- *WhoFI 92, WhoWest 92*
**Vecellio,** Leo Arthur, Jr. 1946- *WhoFI 92*
**Veciana-Suarez,** Ana 1956- *WhoHisp 92*
**Vedam,** Kuppuswamy 1926- *AmMWSc 92*
**Vedamuthu,** Ebenezer Rajkumar 1932- *AmMWSc 92*
**Vedder,** Elihu 1836-1923 *BenetAL 91*
**Vedder,** Henry Clay 1853-1935 *RelLAm 91*
**Vedder,** James Forrest 1928- *AmMWSc 92*
**Vedder,** Richard Kent 1940- *WhoFI 92*
**Vedejs,** Edwin 1941- *AmMWSc 92*
**Vedel,** Georges 1910- *IntWW 91*
**Vederas,** John Christopher 1947- *AmMWSc 92*
**Vedernikov,** Aleksandr Filippovich 1927- *SovUnBD*
**Vedernikov,** Gennadiy Georgiyevich 1937- *IntWW 91*
**Vedral,** Joyce L 1943- *SmATA 65 [port]*
**Vedros,** Neylan Anthony 1929- *AmMWSc 92*
**Vedvick,** Thomas Scott 1944- *AmMWSc 92*
**Vedvik,** Jerry Donald 1936- *WhoWest 92*
**Vee,** Tommy 1951- *WhoEnt 92, WhoMW 92*
**Veech,** Richard L 1935- *AmMWSc 92*
**Veech,** William Austin 1938- *AmMWSc 92*

**Veeck,** Bill 1914-1986 *FacFETw*
**Veeder,** Major Albert 1848-1915 *BiInAmS*
**Veeder,** Van Vechten 1948- *Who 92*
**Veen-Baigent,** Margaret Joan 1933- *AmMWSc 92*
**Veenema,** Ralph J 1921- *AmMWSc 92*
**Veeneman,** David Cain 1952- *WhoFI 92*
**Veenendaal,** Cornelia *DrAPF 91*
**Veenhuis,** Philip Edward 1935- *WhoMW 92*
**Veening,** Hans 1931- *AmMWSc 92*
**Veenker,** Ronald Allen 1937- *WhoRel 92*
**Veenker,** Russell Ralph 1953- *WhoRel 92*
**Veenstra,** A. Paul 1931- *WhoRel 92*
**Veeravalli,** Madhavan Sevilimedu 1961- *WhoMW 92*
**Veerkamp,** Gregory William 1958- *WhoMW 92*
**Veesart,** Janet Lyle 1961- *WhoWest 92*
**Veesenmayer,** Edmund 1904- *EncTR 91 [port]*
**Veesenmayer,** Edmund 1904-1977 *BiDExR*
**Veeser,** Lynn Raymond 1942- *AmMWSc 92*
**Vega,** Alberto Leon 1947- *WhoHisp 92*
**Vega,** Antony 1919- *WhoHisp 92*
**Vega,** Arturo 1958- *WhoHisp 92*
**Vega,** Aurelio de la 1925- *ConCom 92, NewAmDM*
**Vega,** Benjamin Urbizo 1916- *WhoAmL 92, WhoWest 92*
**Vega,** Beth Susan 1950- *WhoWest 92*
**Vega,** Carlos A. 1953- *WhoHisp 92*
**Vega,** Ed *DrAPF 91*
**Vega,** Ed 1936- *WhoHisp 92*
**Vega,** Flavio 1943- *WhoHisp 92*
**Vega,** Francisco *WhoHisp 92*
**Vega,** Francisco Miguel 1922- *WhoAmP 91*
**Vega,** Frank 1954- *WhoWest 92*
**Vega,** Garcilaso de la *HisDSpE*
**Vega,** Janine Pommy *DrAPF 91*
**Vega,** Jose Guadalupe 1953- *WhoWest 92*
**Vega,** Juan Ramon 1931- *WhoHisp 92*
**Vega,** Lazaro Nava, III 1960- *WhoHisp 92*
**Vega,** Manuel 1929- *WhoHisp 92*
**Vega,** Mariano, Jr. 1949- *WhoHisp 92*
**Vega,** Rafael 1925- *WhoHisp 92*
**Vega,** Rafael Evaristo, Jr. 1934- *WhoHisp 92*
**Vega,** Ralph, Jr. 1953- *WhoHisp 92*
**Vega,** Robeto 1956- *AmMWSc 92*
**Vega,** Rosa Elia 1952- *WhoHisp 92*
**Vega,** Rufino A. *WhoHisp 92*
**Vega,** Valorie *WhoHisp 92*
**Vega,** William M. *WhoHisp 92*
**Vega De Seoane Azpilicueta,** Javier 1947- *IntWW 91*
**Vega-Garcia,** Edna Rosa 1950- *WhoHisp 92*
**Vega Jacome,** Rafael 1944- *WhoHisp 92*
**Vega Trejos,** Guillermo 1927- *Who 92*
**Vega Yunque,** Edgardo 1936- *WhoHisp 92*
**Vegas,** Diana L. 1945- *WhoHisp 92*
**Vegas Latapie,** Eugenio 1907-1985 *BiDExR*
**Vege,** Nageswara Rao 1932- *IntAu&W 91*
**Vegesna,** Vijaya Raju 1949- *WhoWest 92*
**Vegh,** Emanuel 1936- *AmMWSc 92*
**Vegh Villegas,** Alejandro 1928- *IntWW 91*
**Veghte,** Robert Illingworth 1952- *WhoFI 92*
**Vegors,** Stanley H, Jr 1929- *AmMWSc 92*
**Vegotsky,** Allen 1931- *AmMWSc 92*
**Vehar,** August Randall 1950- *WhoAmP 91*
**Vehar,** Gordon Allen 1948- *AmMWSc 92, WhoWest 92*
**Vehrencamp,** Sandra Lee 1948- *AmMWSc 92*
**Vehse,** Robert Chase 1936- *AmMWSc 92*
**Vehse,** William E 1932- *AmMWSc 92*
**Veicsteinas,** Arsenio 1944- *AmMWSc 92*
**Veidis,** Mikelis Valdis 1939- *AmMWSc 92*
**Veigel,** Jon Michael 1938- *AmMWSc 92*
**Veigele,** William John 1925- *AmMWSc 92*
**Veil,** Simone 1927- *IntWW 91*
**Veil,** Simone Annie 1927- *Who 92*
**Veiller,** Bayard 1869-1943 *BenetAL 91*
**Veiller,** Lawrence T d1943 *DcAmImH*
**Veilleux,** Gerard 1942- *WhoFI 92*
**Veilleux,** Marcel Paul 1956- *WhoAmP 91*
**Veillon,** Claude 1940- *AmMWSc 92*
**Veinott,** Arthur Fales, Jr 1934- *AmMWSc 92*
**Veinott,** Cyril G 1905- *AmMWSc 92*
**Veira,** Philip 1921- *Who 92*
**Veirs,** Val Rhodes 1942- *AmMWSc 92*
**Veis,** Arthur 1925- *AmMWSc 92, WhoMW 92*
**Veit,** Bruce Clinton 1942- *AmMWSc 92*
**Veit,** Frederick Charles Otto 1960- *WhoAmL 92, WhoRel 92*
**Veit,** Jiri Joseph 1934- *AmMWSc 92*
**Veit,** Lawrence A. 1938- *WhoFI 92*
**Veit,** William Arthur 1947- *WhoFI 92*
**Veitch,** Boyer Lewis 1930- *WhoFI 92*
**Veitch,** D. Philip 1953- *WhoRel 92*
**Veitch,** Fletcher Pearre, Jr 1908- *AmMWSc 92*
**Veitch,** John 1925- *IntMPA 92*
**Veitch,** Patrick Lee 1944- *WhoEnt 92*
**Veitch,** Tom *DrAPF 91*
**Veitch,** William A 1925- *WhoAmP 91*
**Veith,** Daniel A 1936- *AmMWSc 92*
**Veith,** Frank James 1931- *AmMWSc 92*
**Veizer,** Jan 1941- *AmMWSc 92*
**Veizer,** Keith *DrAPF 91*
**Vejar,** Rudolph Lawrence 1933- *WhoHisp 92*
**Vejnoska,** L. Christopher 1955- *WhoAmL 92*
**Vejvoda,** Edward 1924- *AmMWSc 92*
**Vekert,** Charles Thomas 1948- *WhoAmL 92*
**Vekich,** Max M, Jr 1954- *WhoAmP 91*
**Vela,** Adan Richard 1930- *AmMWSc 92*
**Vela,** Charles Frank 1936- *WhoWest 92*
**Vela,** Emilio Lamar 1939- *WhoHisp 92*
**Vela,** Filemon B. 1935- *WhoAmL 92, WhoHisp 92*
**Vela,** Gerard Roland 1927- *AmMWSc 92, WhoHisp 92*
**Vela,** Librada D. 1953- *WhoHisp 92*
**Vela,** Noelia 1949- *WhoHisp 92*
**Vela,** Ricardo Rene 1956- *WhoHisp 92*
**Vela,** San Juanita Rosario 1947- *WhoHisp 92*
**Vela-Creixell,** Mary I. 1938- *WhoHisp 92*
**Velaer,** Charles Alfred 1932- *WhoMW 92*
**Velarde,** Anita Renee 1966- *WhoHisp 92*
**Velarde,** Carlos E. 1929- *WhoHisp 92*
**Velarde,** Luis Alfonso, Jr. 1936- *WhoHisp 92*
**Velarde,** Randy 1962- *WhoHisp 92*
**Velardo,** Joseph Thomas 1923- *AmMWSc 92, WhoMW 92, WrDr 92*
**Velasco,** Agustin C. *WhoHisp 92*
**Velasco,** Alfredo Frank 1944- *WhoHisp 92*
**Velasco,** Frank E. 1948- *WhoHisp 92*
**Velasco,** Jerry G. *WhoHisp 92*
**Velasco,** Kathy Lynn 1956- *WhoMW 92*
**Velasco,** Luis de 1511-1564 *HisDSpE*
**Velasco,** Ralph E., Jr. 1926- *WhoHisp 92*
**Velasco,** Raymond Lester 1951- *WhoHisp 92*
**Velasco,** Tomas 1962- *WhoHisp 92*
**Velasco Ibarra,** Jose Maria 1893-1979 *FacFETw*
**Velasco y Perez Petroche,** Juan Manuel de 1727-1792 *HisDSpE*
**Velasques,** Daniel Roger 1943- *BlkOlyM*
**Velasquez,** Angelo *WhoHisp 92*
**Velasquez,** Arthur Raymond 1938- *WhoHisp 92*
**Velasquez,** Baldemar 1947- *WhoHisp 92*
**Velasquez,** Benito J. 1956- *WhoHisp 92*
**Velasquez,** Carlos 1948- *WhoHisp 92*
**Velasquez,** Diego 1465-1524 *HisDSpE*
**Velasquez,** Edward Bustos 1946- *WhoHisp 92*
**Velasquez,** Joe 1946- *WhoHisp 92*
**Velasquez,** Jorge H. 1951- *WhoHisp 92*
**Velasquez,** Loreta *EncAmaz 91*
**Velasquez,** Manuel Mel 1952- *WhoHisp 92*
**Velasquez,** Pedro *ScFEYrs*
**Velasquez,** Ruth Lind 1926- *WhoWest 92*
**Velasquez,** Tomasa M. 1938- *WhoHisp 92*
**Velasquez-Gaztelu Ruiz,** Candido 1937- *IntWW 91*
**Velayati,** Ali Akbar 1945- *IntWW 91*
**Velazco y Trianosky,** Gregory 1953- *WhoMW 92*
**Velazquez,** Aramis M. 1956- *WhoHisp 92*
**Velazquez,** Arturo M. 1928- *WhoHisp 92*
**Velazquez,** Cesar 1956- *WhoMW 92*
**Velazquez,** Hector *WhoHisp 92*
**Velazquez,** Irene Jeanne *WhoEnt 92*
**Velazquez de Cancel,** Lourdes 1941- *WhoRel 92*
**Velazquez-Domenech,** Estrella *WhoHisp 92*
**Velde,** James R. 1913- *IntMPA 92*
**Velde,** John Ernest, Jr. 1917- *WhoWest 92*
**Velde,** Thomas James 1957- *WhoWest 92*
**Veldman,** Bruce Richard 1953- *WhoMW 92*
**Veldman,** Donald James 1926- *WhoAmL 92*
**Veleckis,** Ewald 1926- *AmMWSc 92*
**Velella,** Guy J 1944- *WhoAmP 91*
**Velenyi,** Louis Joseph 1934- *AmMWSc 92*
**Veletsos,** A 1927- *AmMWSc 92*
**Velez,** Alejandro *WhoHisp 92*
**Velez,** Anita 1922- *WhoHisp 92*
**Velez,** Carmelo E. *WhoHisp 92*
**Velez,** Isa 1949- *WhoHisp 92*
**Velez,** Ismael A. *WhoHisp 92*
**Velez,** Jose *WhoHisp 92*
**Velez,** Juan 1955- *WhoHisp 92*
**Velez,** Luis 1955- *WhoHisp 92*
**Velez,** Miguel 1949- *WhoAmP 91*
**Velez,** Ralph John 1934- *WhoWest 92*
**Velez,** Randy Anthony 1943- *WhoHisp 92*
**Velez,** Samuel Jose 1945- *AmMWSc 92*
**Velez,** Theresa Lynn 1967- *WhoHisp 92*
**Velez,** Tom *WhoHisp 92*
**Velez,** Tony 1946- *WhoHisp 92*
**Velez,** William 1950- *WhoEnt 92, WhoHisp 92*
**Velez,** William 1951- *WhoHisp 92*
**Velez,** William Yslas 1947- *AmMWSc 92, WhoHisp 92*
**Velez de Acevedo,** Mabel 1944- *WhoAmP 91, WhoHisp 92*
**Velez Hernandez,** Benjamin *WhoAmP 91, WhoHisp 92*
**Velez-Ibanez,** Carlos G. 1936- *WhoHisp 92*
**Velez-Mitchell,** Anita 1922- *WhoHisp 92*
**Velez-Mitchell,** Jane 1955- *WhoHisp 92*
**Velez-Morell,** Jose Antonio 1960- *WhoHisp 92*
**Velichko,** Vladimir Makarovich 1937- *IntWW 91*
**Velick,** Sidney Frederick 1913- *AmMWSc 92*
**Velikhov,** Yevgeniy Pavlovich 1935- *IntWW 91, SovUnBD*
**Velikovsky,** Immanuel 1895-1979 *FacFETw*
**Veliky,** Ivan Alois 1929- *AmMWSc 92*
**Velimirovic,** Milos M. 1922- *WhoEnt 92*
**Veliotes,** Nicholas Alexander 1928- *WhoAmP 91, WhoFI 92*
**Velis,** Peter Arthur 1942- *WhoAmP 91*
**Veliz,** Ana Margarita 1961- *WhoAmL 92*
**Veliz,** Gilbert *WhoHisp 92*
**VelJohnson,** Reggie *ConTFT 9*
**VelJohnson,** Reginald 1952- *ConTFT 9*
**Velk,** Robert James 1938- *WhoWest 92*
**Velkoff,** Henry Rene 1921- *AmMWSc 92*
**Vella,** Carolyn Marie 1948- *WhoFI 92*
**Vella,** Francis 1929- *AmMWSc 92*
**Vella,** Karmenu 1950- *IntWW 91*
**Vella,** Ruth Ann 1942- *WhoFI 92*
**Vella-Coleiro,** George 1941- *AmMWSc 92*
**Vellaccio,** Frank 1948- *AmMWSc 92*
**Vellacott,** Elizabeth 1905- *TwCPaSc*
**Vellekamp,** Gary John 1951- *AmMWSc 92*
**Vellenga,** Kathleen Osborne 1938- *WhoAmP 91*
**Velletri,** Paul A 1950- *AmMWSc 92*
**Velloney,** Richard Andrew 1941- *WhoMW 92*
**Vellturo,** Anthony Francis 1936- *AmMWSc 92*
**Vellucci,** Peter A 1942- *WhoAmP 91*
**Vellutato,** James Lee 1958- *WhoEnt 92*
**Velo,** Luis Fernandez 1950- *WhoWest 92*
**Veloz,** Bradley, Jr. 1948- *WhoHisp 92*
**Veloz,** George A. 1947- *WhoHisp 92*
**Veltri,** Frank 1912- *WhoAmP 91*
**Veltri,** Robert William 1941- *AmMWSc 92*
**Velvet Underground,** The *ConMus 7 [port], NewAmDM*
**Velzy,** Charles O 1930- *AmMWSc 92, WhoFI 92*
**Vemer,** Randall Werth 1953- *WhoEnt 92*
**Vemula,** Subba Rao 1924- *AmMWSc 92*
**Vemuri,** Suryanarayana 1943- *AmMWSc 92*
**Vemuri,** Venkateswararao 1938- *AmMWSc 92*
**Vena,** Joseph Augustus 1931- *AmMWSc 92*
**Venable,** Abraham S. 1930- *WhoBlA 92*
**Venable,** Andrew Alexander, Jr. 1944- *WhoBlA 92*
**Venable,** Charles H 1932- *WhoIns 92*
**Venable,** Charles Scott 1827-1900 *BiInAmS*
**Venable,** Douglas 1920- *AmMWSc 92*
**Venable,** Emerson 1911- *AmMWSc 92*
**Venable,** Howard Phillip 1913- *WhoBlA 92*
**Venable,** Jack Benton 1939- *WhoAmP 91*
**Venable,** John Heinz, Jr 1938- *AmMWSc 92*
**Venable,** Lucy Dent 1926- *WhoEnt 92*
**Venable,** Max 1957- *WhoBlA 92*
**Venable,** Patricia Lengel 1930- *AmMWSc 92*
**Venable,** Richard *WhoAmP 91*
**Venable,** Robert Charles 1950- *WhoBlA 92*
**Venable,** Wallace Starr 1940- *AmMWSc 92*
**Venable,** William Henry 1836-1920 *BenetAL 91*
**Venables,** David 1932- *Who 92*
**Venables,** John Anthony 1936- *AmMWSc 92*
**Venables,** John Duxbury 1927- *AmMWSc 92*
**Venables,** Richard William Ogilvie 1928- *Who 92*
**Venables,** Robert 1947- *Who 92*
**Venables,** Robert L 1933- *WhoAmP 91*
**Venables,** Robert Michael Cochrane 1939- *Who 92*
**Venables,** Terry *WrDr 92*
**Venables-Llewelyn,** John Dillwyn- 1938- *Who 92*
**Venantius Fortunatus** 535?-610? *EncEarC*
**Venard,** Carl Ernest 1909- *AmMWSc 92*
**Vencer,** Agustin Baldonasa, Jr. 1946- *WhoRel 92*
**Vendeland,** Michael C. 1960- *WhoEnt 92*
**Vendelin,** Robin Rae Woods 1951- *WhoRel 92*
**Vendice,** William Vincent 1948- *WhoEnt 92*
**Vendig,** Irving 1902- *WhoEnt 92*
**Venditti,** Clelia Rose *WhoEnt 92*
**Venditti,** John M 1927- *AmMWSc 92*
**Venditto,** James Joseph 1951- *WhoFI 92*
**Vendler,** Helen 1933- *IntAu&W 91, WrDr 92*
**Vendler,** Helen Hennessy 1933- *IntWW 91*
**Vendrell,** John Donald Oromi 1934- *WhoWest 92*
**Venegas,** Arturo, Jr. 1948- *WhoHisp 92*
**Venegas,** Joseph M. 1920- *WhoHisp 92*
**Venegas,** Rafael Adrian 1943- *WhoHisp 92*
**Venegas-Avila,** Haydee E. 1950- *WhoHisp 92*
**Veneklase,** Joseph Earl 1955- *WhoMW 92*
**Venema,** Cornelis Paul 1954- *WhoRel 92*
**Venema,** Gerard Alan 1949- *AmMWSc 92*
**Venema,** Harry J 1922- *AmMWSc 92*
**Venema,** Ronald E. 1937- *WhoMW 92*
**Veneman,** Gerard Earl 1920- *WhoFI 92*
**Veneman,** Peter Lourens Marinus 1947- *AmMWSc 92*
**Vener,** Kirt J 1943- *AmMWSc 92*
**Veneruso,** James John 1951- *WhoAmL 92*
**Venesy,** Bryan Jerome 1963- *WhoAmL 92*
**Venetsanopoulos,** Anastasios Nicolaos 1941- *AmMWSc 92*
**Veney,** Herbert Lee 1953- *WhoBlA 92*
**Venezian,** Giulio 1938- *AmMWSc 92*
**Veneziano,** Philip John 1951- *WhoWest 92*
**Venezky,** David Lester 1924- *AmMWSc 92*
**Venham,** Larry Lee 1941- *AmMWSc 92*
**Venhuizen,** Paul Ralph 1949- *WhoAmP 91*
**Veniamin,** Christodoulos 1922- *IntWW 91*
**Venier,** Clifford George 1939- *AmMWSc 92*
**Veninga,** Karen Ann 1944- *WhoMW 92*
**Venini,** Paolo 1895-1959 *DcTwDes*
**Venit,** Sharyn Diane 1947- *WhoWest 92*
**Venit,** Stewart Mark 1946- *AmMWSc 92*
**Venit,** William Bennett 1931- *WhoFI 92, WhoMW 92*
**Venitis,** Basil 1945- *WhoFI 92*
**Venizelos,** Eleutherios 1864-1936 *FacFETw*
**Venkata,** Subrahmanyam Saraswati 1942- *AmMWSc 92*
**Venkatachalam,** Manjeri A 1940- *AmMWSc 92*
**Venkatachalam,** Taracad Krishnan 1937- *AmMWSc 92*
**Venkataraghavan,** R 1939- *AmMWSc 92*
**Venkataraman,** Krishnamurthy 1925- *IntWW 91*
**Venkataraman,** M 1943- *AmMWSc 92*
**Venkataraman,** Ramaswamy 1910- *IntWW 91, Who 92*
**Venkataramanan,** Raman 1951- *AmMWSc 92*
**Venkatasubbaiah,** Pendekanti 1921- *IntWW 91*
**Venkatesam,** Malabi M 1950- *AmMWSc 92*
**Venkatesan,** Doraswamy *AmMWSc 92*
**Venkatesan,** S *AmMWSc 92*
**Venkatesan,** Thirumalai 1949- *AmMWSc 92*
**Venkatesan,** Vaidyanathan 1944- *WhoWest 92*
**Venkatesh,** Alagiriswami 1946- *WhoWest 92*
**Venkateswaran,** Uma D 1953- *AmMWSc 92*
**Venkatu,** Doulatabad A 1936- *AmMWSc 92*
**Venkayya,** Vipperla 1931- *AmMWSc 92*
**Venketeswaran,** S 1931- *AmMWSc 92*
**Venn,** George *DrAPF 91*
**Vennamo,** Pekka Veikko 1944- *IntWW 91*
**Vennamo,** Veikko Emil Alexsander 1913- *IntWW 91*
**Vennard,** David Leigh 1945- *WhoFI 92*
**Vennart,** George Piercy 1926- *AmMWSc 92*
**Vennen,** Dennis Lee 1944- *WhoWest 92*
**Venner,** Dominique 1935- *BiDExR*
**Vennes,** Jack A 1923- *AmMWSc 92*
**Vennes,** John Wesley 1924- *AmMWSc 92*
**Vennesland,** Birgit 1913- *AmMWSc 92, WhoWest 92*
**Venning,** Philip Duncombe Riley 1947- *Who 92*
**Venning,** Robert Stanley 1943- *WhoAmL 92*
**Venning,** Robert William Dawe 1946- *Who 92*
**Vennos,** Mary Susannah 1931- *AmMWSc 92*
**Veno,** Glen Corey 1951- *WhoMW 92*
**Venora,** Diane 1952- *IntMPA 92*
**Venson,** Clyde R. 1936- *WhoBlA 92*

**Venson,** Jeanine 1962- *WhoBlA 92*
**Venson,** John E. 1922- *WhoBlA 92*
**Vent,** Richard Henry 1941- *WhoFI 92*
**Vent,** Robert Joseph 1940- *AmMWSc 92*
**Venta,** Krishna 1911-1958 *RelLAm 91*
**Venta,** Miguel R. 1956- *WhoHisp 92*
**Venta,** Patrick John 1951- *AmMWSc 92*
**Ventadour,** Fanny *DrAPF 91*
**Venter,** Elizabeth Hendrina 1938- *IntWW 91*
**Venter,** J Craig 1946- *AmMWSc 92*
**Venters,** Carl Vernon, III 1956- *WhoEnt 92*
**Venters,** Michael Dyar *AmMWSc 92*
**Venti,** Steven F. 1953- *WhoFI 92*
**Ventling,** Thomas Lee 1948- *WhoWest 92*
**Vento,** Bruce F. 1940- *AlmAP 92 [port]*
**Vento,** Bruce Frank 1940- *WhoAmP 91, WhoMW 92*
**Vento,** Johann Marie 1965- *WhoRel 92*
**Vento,** M. Therese 1951- *WhoAmL 92*
**Ventola,** Anthony Benito 1964- *WhoEnt 92*
**Venton,** Patrick *TwCPaSc*
**Ventre,** Francis Thomas 1937- *AmMWSc 92*
**Ventres,** Charles Samuel 1942- *AmMWSc 92*
**Ventres,** Judith Martin 1943- *WhoAmL 92, WhoMW 92*
**Ventres,** Romeo John 1924- *WhoFI 92*
**Ventresca,** Carol *AmMWSc 92*
**Ventresca,** Joseph Anthony 1949- *WhoMW 92*
**Ventrice,** Carl Alfred 1930- *AmMWSc 92*
**Ventrice,** Marie Busck 1940- *AmMWSc 92*
**Ventriglia,** Anthony E 1922- *AmMWSc 92*
**Ventry,** Baron 1943- *Who 92*
**Ventry,** Catherine Valerie 1949- *WhoAmL 92, WhoFI 92*
**Ventura,** Alene Stonestreet 1911- *WhoAmP 91*
**Ventura,** Anthony F 1927- *WhoIns 92*
**Ventura,** Brent N. *WhoHisp 92*
**Ventura,** Charlie 1916- *NewAmDM*
**Ventura,** Joaquin Calvo 1929- *AmMWSc 92*
**Ventura,** Jose Antonio 1954- *AmMWSc 92*
**Ventura,** Robin 1967- *WhoHisp 92*
**Ventura,** William Paul 1942- *AmMWSc 92*
**Venturella,** Vincent Steven 1930- *AmMWSc 92*
**Ventures,** The *NewAmDM*
**Venturi,** Franco 1914- *IntWW 91*
**Venturi,** Jack 1950- *WhoAmL 92*
**Venturi,** Lionello 1885-1961 *ThHEIm*
**Venturi,** Rick 1946- *WhoMW 92*
**Venturi,** Robert 1925- *DcTwDes, IntWW 91, Who 92, WrDr 92*
**Venturini,** Donald Joseph 1930- *WhoWest 92*
**Venturo,** Frank Angelo 1940- *WhoAmP 91*
**Venugopal,** Sriramashetty 1933- *Who 92*
**Venugopalan,** Srinivasa I 1944- *AmMWSc 92*
**Venuti,** Joe 1903-1978 *NewAmDM*
**Venuti,** William J 1924- *AmMWSc 92*
**Venuto,** Paul B 1933- *AmMWSc 92*
**Venza,** Jac *LesBEnT 92*
**Venzke,** Walter George 1912- *AmMWSc 92*
**Venzo,** Mario 1900- *IntWW 91*
**Veomett,** George Ector 1944- *AmMWSc 92*
**Veon,** Michael R 1957- *WhoAmP 91*
**Vera,** Harriette Dryden 1909- *AmMWSc 92*
**Vera,** Hernan 1937- *WhoHisp 92*
**Vera,** James Medardo 1949- *WhoHisp 92*
**Vera,** Julio Cesar 1952- *WhoHisp 92*
**Vera,** Marcelo 1957- *WhoHisp 92*
**Vera,** Ndoro Vincent 1933- *WhoBlA 92*
**Vera,** Percy O. 1935- *WhoHisp 92*
**Vera,** Richard 1946- *WhoHisp 92*
**Vera,** Yolanda *WhoHisp 92*
**Vera Cruz,** Alonso de la 1504-1584 *HisDSpE*
**Vera y Pintado,** Bernardo 1780-1827 *HisDSpE*
**Veracini,** Francesco Maria 1690-1768 *NewAmDM*
**Verastegui,** Enrique 1950- *ConSpAP*
**Verba,** Betty Lou 1933- *WhoMW 92*
**Verba,** Sidney 1932- *IntWW 91*
**Verbal,** Claude A. 1942- *WhoBlA 92*
**Verbanac,** Frank 1920- *AmMWSc 92*
**Verbeek,** Earl Raymond 1948- *AmMWSc 92*
**Verbeek,** Paul 1925- *IntWW 91*
**Verbeke,** Judith Ann 1948- *AmMWSc 92*
**Verbelen,** Robert Jan 1911-1990 *NewYTBS 91*
**Verbelun,** Cynthia Fern 1955- *WhoEnt 92*
**Verber,** Carl Michael 1935- *AmMWSc 92*
**Verbic,** Andrew Glen 1962- *WhoMW 92*
**Verbinski,** Victor V 1922- *AmMWSc 92*
**Verbiscar,** Anthony James 1929- *AmMWSc 92*
**Verble,** Patrick Ray 1952- *WhoMW 92*
**Verbrugge,** Calvin James 1937- *AmMWSc 92*
**Verbrugge,** Verlyn David 1942- *WhoRel 92*
**Verburgt,** Paul Adriaan 1935- *IntWW 91*
**Verby,** John E 1923- *AmMWSc 92*
**Verby,** John Edward, Jr. 1923- *WhoMW 92*
**Vercellotti,** John R 1933- *AmMWSc 92*
**Verch,** Richard Lee 1937- *AmMWSc 92*
**Verchenko,** Yuriy N. *SovUnBD*
**Vercheres,** Madeliene de 1678-1766 *EncAmaz 91*
**Verches,** Annabel *WhoHisp 92*
**Verches,** Dan 1956- *WhoHisp 92*
**Verco,** Walter 1907- *Who 92*
**Vercoe,** Barry 1937- *NewAmDM*
**Vercoe,** Elizabeth 1941- *WhoEnt 92*
**Vercoe,** Whakahuihui *Who 92*
**Vercors** *ConAu 134*
**Vercors** d1991 *Who 92N*
**Vercors** 1902- *IntWW 91*
**Vercors** 1902-1991 *TwCSFW 91A*
**Vercors,** J. Bruller *ConAu 134*
**Verdan,** Claude-Edouard 1909- *IntWW 91*
**Verdeal,** Kathey Marie 1949- *AmMWSc 92*
**Verdelot,** Philippe 1475?-1552? *NewAmDM*
**Verderber,** Nadine Lucille 1940- *AmMWSc 92*
**Verderber,** Rudolph Richard, Sr. 1929- *WhoWest 92*
**Verdesi,** Elizabeth Howell 1922- *WhoRel 92*
**Verdet,** Ilie 1925- *IntWW 91*
**Verdeyen,** Joseph T 1932- *AmMWSc 92*
**Verdi,** Barry E. 1937- *WhoHisp 92*
**Verdi,** Giuseppe 1813-1901 *NewAmDM*
**Verdi,** James L 1941- *AmMWSc 92*
**Verdi,** Nejat Hasan 1913- *WhoFI 92*
**Verdi,** Robert William 1946- *WhoMW 92*
**Verdier,** Peter Howard 1931- *AmMWSc 92*
**Verdier,** Quentin Roosevelt 1921- *WhoFI 92, WhoMW 92*
**Verdin,** Clarence 1963- *WhoBlA 92*
**Verdina,** Joseph 1921- *AmMWSc 92*
**Verdon,** Gwen 1925- *IntMPA 92, WhoEnt 92*
**Verdon,** Gwen 1926- *NewAmDM*
**Verdon,** Joseph Michael 1941- *AmMWSc 92*
**Verdon-Smith,** Reginald 1912- *IntWW 91, Who 92*
**Verdone,** Vincent Joseph 1947- *WhoFI 92*
**Verdoorn,** Robert J 1934- *WhoIns 92*
**Verdu,** Sergio 1958- *AmMWSc 92*
**Verdugo,** Fidel 1935- *WhoHisp 92*
**Verduin,** Jacob 1913- *AmMWSc 92*
**Verduin,** John Richard, Jr. 1931- *IntAu&W 91, WrDr 92*
**Verduzco,** J. Jorge *WhoHisp 92*
**Verdy,** Maurice 1933- *AmMWSc 92*
**Vere-Jones,** David 1936- *IntWW 91*
**Verebelyi,** Ernest Raymond 1947- *WhoMW 92*
**Verebey,** Karl G 1938- *AmMWSc 92*
**Verecundus** d552 *EncEarC*
**Vereen,** Ben 1946- *IntMPA 92, WhoEnt 92*
**Vereen,** Ben Augustus 1946- *WhoBlA 92*
**Vereen,** Dixie Diane 1957- *WhoBlA 92*
**Vereen,** Larry Edwin 1940- *AmMWSc 92*
**Vereen,** Michael L. 1965- *WhoBlA 92*
**Vereen,** Nathaniel 1924- *WhoBlA 92*
**Vereen,** Robert Charles 1924- *WhoMW 92*
**Vereen-Gordon,** Mary Alice 1950- *WhoBlA 92*
**Vereker** *Who 92*
**Vereker,** John Michael Medlicott 1944- *Who 92*
**Vereker,** Peter William Medlicott 1939- *Who 92*
**Vereketis,** Constantin Kimon 1908- *WhoFI 92*
**Verell,** Ruth Ann 1935- *AmMWSc 92*
**Verenes,** John Chris 1956- *WhoAmP 91*
**Veresaev** 1867-1945 *SovUnBD*
**Veresayev,** Vikenty Vikentevich 1867-1946 *FacFETw*
**Veress,** Sandor 1907- *NewAmDM*
**Veress,** Sandor A 1927- *AmMWSc 92*
**Verette,** Thomas J. 1940- *WhoMW 92*
**Verey,** David John 1950- *Who 92*
**Verey,** Michael John 1912- *IntWW 91, Who 92*
**Vereysky,** Georgiy Semenich 1886-1962 *SovUnBD*
**Vereysky,** Orest Georgievich 1915- *IntWW 91*
**Vergara,** Alfonso Ignacio 1931- *WhoHisp 92*
**Vergara,** Isabel R. 1951- *WhoHisp 92*
**Vergara,** Lautaro Jorge 1916- *WhoHisp 92*
**Vergara,** Rosalyn Patrice 1952- *WhoAmP 91*
**Vergara,** William Charles 1923- *AmMWSc 92*
**Vergara-Vives,** Alfonso 1931- *WhoHisp 92*
**Verge,** Pierre 1936- *IntWW 91*
**Verge,** Richard John 1957- *WhoFI 92*
**Vergennes** *BlkwEAR*
**Vergenz,** Robert Allan 1956- *AmMWSc 92*
**Vergeront,** Susan B 1945- *WhoAmP 91*
**Verges,** Jacques 1925- *IntWW 91*
**Verghese,** Kuruvilla 1936- *AmMWSc 92*
**Verghese,** Margrith Wehrli 1939- *AmMWSc 92*
**Verghese,** Thadikkal Paul *IntWW 91*
**Vergiels,** John M 1937- *WhoAmP 91, WhoWest 92*
**Vergin,** Timothy Lynn 1962- *WhoFI 92, WhoMW 92*
**Vergon,** Frederick Porter, Jr. 1944- *WhoAmL 92*
**Vergona,** Kathleen Anne Dobrosielski 1948- *AmMWSc 92*
**Verhaeren,** Emile 1855-1916 *GuFrLit 1*
**Verhage,** Harold Glenn 1937- *AmMWSc 92*
**Ver Hagen,** Jan Karol 1937- *WhoFI 92*
**Verhagen,** William Ray 1960- *WhoMW 92*
**Verhalen,** Laval 1941- *AmMWSc 92*
**Verhalen,** Philip A. 1934- *WhoRel 92*
**Verhanovitz,** Richard Frank 1944- *AmMWSc 92*
**Verhey,** Allen Dale 1945- *WhoRel 92*
**Verhey,** Joseph William 1928- *WhoWest 92*
**Verhey,** Roger Frank 1938- *AmMWSc 92*
**Verheyden,** Jack Clyde 1934- *WhoRel 92*
**Verheyden,** Julien P H 1933- *AmMWSc 92*
**Verhoef,** David Donald 1962- *WhoEnt 92*
**Verhoek,** Frank Henry 1909- *AmMWSc 92*
**Verhoek,** Susan Elizabeth *AmMWSc 92*
**Verhoeven,** John Daniel 1934- *AmMWSc 92*
**Verhoeven,** Paul 1938- *IntMPA 92, IntWW 91*
**Verhoogen,** John 1912- *AmMWSc 92, IntWW 91*
**Verich,** Demetrio 1932- *WhoAmP 91*
**Verich,** Michael Gregory 1953- *WhoAmP 91*
**Verigan,** Terrence 1948- *WhoFI 92*
**Verigin,** John J. *WhoRel 92*
**Verink,** Ellis D, Jr 1920- *AmMWSc 92*
**Verissimo,** Erico 1905-1975 *BenetAL 91*
**Verity,** Anthony Courtenay Froude 1939- *Who 92*
**Verity,** Calvin William, Jr. 1917- *IntWW 91*
**Verity,** Charlotte 1954- *TwCPaSc*
**Verity,** Maurice Anthony 1931- *AmMWSc 92*
**Verivakis,** Elevtherios 1935- *IntWW 91*
**Verkade,** John George 1935- *AmMWSc 92*
**Verkade,** Stephen Dunning 1957- *AmMWSc 92*
**Verkamp,** Bernard Joseph 1938- *WhoMW 92*
**Verkauf-Verlon,** Willy Andre 1917- *IntWW 91*
**Verkin,** Boris Yeremievich d1990 *IntWW 91N*
**Verkozen,** Tomas Henry 1946- *WhoWest 92*
**Verkuil,** Paul Robert 1939- *WhoAmL 92*
**Verlag,** Cora *WrDr 92*
**Verlaine,** Paul 1844-1896 *GuFrLit 1*
**Verlangieri,** Anthony Joseph 1945- *AmMWSc 92*
**Ver Lee,** Ronald F. 1948- *WhoRel 92*
**Verleur,** Hans Willem 1932- *AmMWSc 92*
**Verley,** Frank A 1933- *AmMWSc 92*
**Verlinden,** Charles 1907- *IntWW 91*
**Verma,** Ajit K 1944- *AmMWSc 92*
**Verma,** Anil Kumar 1950- *AmMWSc 92*
**Verma,** Deepak Kumar *AmMWSc 92*
**Verma,** Devi C 1946- *AmMWSc 92*
**Verma,** Ghasi Ram 1929- *AmMWSc 92*
**Verma,** Pramode Kumar 1941- *AmMWSc 92*
**Verma,** Ram D 1929- *AmMWSc 92*
**Verma,** Ram S 1946- *AmMWSc 92*
**Verma,** Sadanand 1930- *AmMWSc 92*
**Verma,** Shashi Bhushan 1944- *AmMWSc 92*
**Verma,** Surendra Kumar 1943- *AmMWSc 92*
**Verma,** Surendra P 1941- *AmMWSc 92*
**Vermaas,** Susan Kim 1964- *WhoWest 92*
**Vermaas,** Willem F J 1959- *AmMWSc 92*
**Vermaas,** Willem Frederik Johan 1959- *WhoWest 92*
**Vermeer,** Maureen Dorothy 1945- *WhoFI 92*
**Vermeij,** Geerat Jacobus 1946- *AmMWSc 92*
**Vermes,** Geza 1924- *IntAu&W 91, Who 92, WhoRel 92, WrDr 92*
**Vermeule,** Emily Dickinson Townsend 1928- *Who 92, WrDr 92*
**Vermeulen,** Carl William 1939- *AmMWSc 92*
**Vermeulen,** Theodore 1916- *AmMWSc 92*
**Vermillion,** John F *WhoAmP 91*
**Vermillion,** Lois Jeanne 1945- *WhoAmL 92*
**Vermillion,** Robert Everett 1937- *AmMWSc 92*
**Vermillion,** Tammy Regina 1957- *WhoMW 92*
**Vermilya,** Claire 1919- *IntAu&W 91*
**Vermilya,** Dale Nelson 1959- *WhoFI 92*
**Vermilye,** Peter Hoagland 1920- *WhoFI 92*
**Vermilyea,** Barry Lynn 1941- *AmMWSc 92*
**Vermilyea,** D A 1923- *AmMWSc 92*
**Vermund,** Halvor 1916- *AmMWSc 92*
**Vermund,** Sten Halvor 1954- *AmMWSc 92*
**Vernadakis,** Antonia 1930- *AmMWSc 92*
**Vernadsky,** Vladimir Ivanovich 1863-1945 *FacFETw, SovUnBD*
**Vernarelli,** Michael Joseph 1948- *WhoFI 92*
**Vernazza,** Jorge Enrique 1943- *AmMWSc 92*
**Vernberg,** Frank John 1925- *AmMWSc 92*
**Vernberg,** Winona B 1925- *AmMWSc 92*
**Verne,** Jules 1828-1905 *GuFrLit 1, ScFEYrs, TwCSFW 91A*
**Verne,** Jules, and Grousset, Paschal *ScFEYrs*
**Verne,** Jules, and Michel Verne *ScFEYrs*
**Verne,** Michel 1861- *ScFEYrs*
**Vernejoul,** Robert, Baron De 1890- *IntWW 91*
**Vernekar,** Anandu Devarao 1932- *AmMWSc 92*
**Verner,** James Hamilton 1940- *AmMWSc 92*
**Verner,** Jared 1934- *AmMWSc 92*
**Verner,** MacDonald, Jr. 1928- *WhoMW 92*
**Vernet,** Claude-Joseph 1714-1789 *BlkwCEP*
**Verneuil,** Henri 1920- *IntWW 91*
**Verney** *Who 92*
**Verney,** Douglas 1924- *WrDr 92*
**Verney,** John 1913- *TwCPaSc, Who 92, WrDr 92*
**Verney,** Lawrence John 1924- *Who 92*
**Verney,** Michael Palmer 1923- *WrDr 92*
**Verney,** Peter 1930- *WrDr 92*
**Verney,** Ralph 1915- *Who 92*
**Verney,** Richard Greville 1946- *WhoFI 92*
**Verney,** Stephen Edmund 1919- *IntAu&W 91, Who 92, WrDr 92*
**Verni,** Ralph F 1943- *WhoIns 92*
**Verni,** Ralph Francis 1943- *WhoFI 92*
**Vernick,** Ruth Lina 1934- *WhoFI 92*
**Vernier,** D. Paul, Jr. 1951- *WhoAmL 92*
**Vernier,** Robert L 1924- *AmMWSc 92*
**Vernier,** Vernon George 1924- *AmMWSc 92*
**Vernier-Palliez,** Bernard Maurice A. 1918- *IntWW 91, Who 92*
**Verniero,** Joan Evans 1937- *WhoWest 92*
**Vernikos,** Joan 1934- *AmMWSc 92*
**Vernon** *Who 92*
**Vernon,** Baron 1923- *Who 92*
**Vernon,** Ann S. 1947- *WhoMW 92*
**Vernon,** Anne 1924- *IntMPA 92*
**Vernon,** C Wayne 1939- *AmMWSc 92*
**Vernon,** Christie Dougherty 1929- *WhoAmP 91*
**Vernon,** Darryl Mitchell 1956- *WhoAmL 92*
**Vernon,** David Bowater 1926- *Who 92*
**Vernon,** David Harvey 1925- *WhoAmL 92*
**Vernon,** David Paul 1948- *WhoWest 92*
**Vernon,** Eugene Haworth 1901- *AmMWSc 92*
**Vernon,** Frances 1963-1991 *ConAu 135*
**Vernon,** Francine M. 1939- *WhoBlA 92*
**Vernon,** Frank Lee, Jr 1927- *AmMWSc 92*
**Vernon,** Gregory Allen 1947- *AmMWSc 92*
**Vernon,** James 1910- *IntWW 91, Who 92*
**Vernon,** James William 1915- *Who 92*
**Vernon,** John *DrAPF 91*
**Vernon,** John 1936- *IntMPA 92*
**Vernon,** John Ashbridge 1940- *AmMWSc 92*
**Vernon,** John Leroy, Jr. 1959- *WhoRel 92*
**Vernon,** Kenneth Robert 1923- *Who 92*
**Vernon,** Larry Skip *WhoAmP 91*
**Vernon,** Leo Preston 1925- *AmMWSc 92*
**Vernon,** Lillian *WhoFI 92*
**Vernon,** Lillian Malley 1910- *WhoAmL 92*
**Vernon,** Lonnie William 1922- *AmMWSc 92*
**Vernon,** Mabel 1883-1975 *AmPeW*
**Vernon,** Magdalen Dorothea 1901- *Who 92, WrDr 92*
**Vernon,** Michael *Who 92*
**Vernon,** Michael 1926- *IntWW 91*
**Vernon,** Nigel 1924- *Who 92*
**Vernon,** Philip Ewart 1905-1987 *ConAu 133*
**Vernon,** Ralph Jackson 1920- *AmMWSc 92*
**Vernon,** Raymond 1913- *WhoFI 92, WrDr 92*
**Vernon,** Robert Brian 1954- *WhoWest 92*
**Vernon,** Robert Carey 1923- *AmMWSc 92*
**Vernon,** Robert Gerard 1935- *WhoAmL 92*
**Vernon,** Ronald J 1936- *AmMWSc 92*
**Vernon,** Virginia Lee 1931- *WhoAmP 91*

**Vernon,** Walter Newton, Jr. 1907- *WhoRel 92*
**Vernon,** William Bradford 1951- *WhoAmP 91*
**Vernon,** William Michael 1926- *Who 92*
**Vernon,** William W 1925- *AmMWSc 92*
**Vernon-Chesley,** Michele Joanne 1962- *WhoBlA 92*
**Vernon-Wortzel,** Heidi 1938- *WhoFI 92*
**Vernone,** Michael Jerome 1962- *WhoAmL 92*
**Veron,** J. Michael 1950- *WhoAmL 92*
**Veron de Fortbonnais,** Francois 1722-1800 *BlkwCEP*
**Verona,** David Alan 1954- *WhoAmL 92*
**Verona,** Stephen 1940- *IntMPA 92*
**Verona,** Stephen Frederic 1940- *WhoEnt 92*
**Veronese,** Vittorino d1986 *Who 92N*
**Veronese,** Vittorino 1910- *IntWW 91*
**Veronesi,** Umberto 1925- *WhoFI 92*
**Veronica** *EncEarC*
**Veronica,** Mary 1924-1977 *ConAu 134*
**Veronis,** George 1926- *AmMWSc 92*
**Verosta,** Stephan Eduard 1909- *IntWW 91*
**Verostko,** Roman Joseph 1929- *WhoMW 92*
**Verosub,** Kenneth Lee 1944- *AmMWSc 92, WhoWest 92*
**Verplaetse,** Alfons Remi Emiel 1930- *IntWW 91*
**Verplanck,** G. C. 1786-1870 *BenetAL 91*
**Verpoorte,** Jacob A 1936- *AmMWSc 92*
**Verr,** Harry Coe *ConAu 134, SmATA 67*
**Verral,** Charles Spain 1904-1990 *SmATA 65*
**Verrall,** Ronald Ernest 1937- *AmMWSc 92*
**Verrastro,** Ralph Edward 1933- *WhoEnt 92*
**Verrazano,** Giovanni da 1485?-1528 *BenetAL 91*
**Verrazzano,** Giovanni da 1485?-1528 *BenetAL 91*
**Verren,** Angela 1930- *TwCPaSc*
**Verrett,** Joyce M. 1932- *WhoBlA 92*
**Verrett,** Shirley 1931- *IntWW 91, NewAmDM, WhoEnt 92*
**Verrett,** Shirley 1933- *WhoBlA 92*
**Verri,** Pietro 1728-1797 *BlkwCEP*
**Verrier,** Richard Leonard *AmMWSc 92*
**Verrill,** A. Hyatt 1871-1954 *BenetAL 91, ScFEYrs, TwCSFW 91*
**Verrill,** Charles Owen, Jr. 1937- *WhoAmL 92, WhoFI 92*
**Verrill,** Chester Roland 1912- *WhoAmP 91*
**Verrill,** Clarence Sidney d1918 *BiInAmS*
**Verrillo,** Ronald Thomas 1927- *AmMWSc 92*
**Verrone,** Denise Ann 1963- *WhoEnt 92*
**Verrone,** Patric Miller 1959- *WhoAmL 92, WhoFI 92, WhoWest 92*
**Verrot,** Pascal *WhoEnt 92*
**Versace,** Gianni 1946- *IntWW 91*
**Versaggi,** Joseph Angelo 1961- *WhoFI 92*
**Versaggi,** Matthew Robert 1963- *WhoMW 92*
**Verschingel,** Roger H C 1928- *AmMWSc 92*
**Verschoor,** Curtis Carl 1931- *WhoFI 92*
**Verschoor,** J D 1923- *AmMWSc 92*
**Verschuren,** Jacobus Petrus 1930- *AmMWSc 92*
**Verschuren,** Paul M. *WhoRel 92*
**Verschuur,** Gerrit L 1937- *AmMWSc 92*
**Versen,** Kurt 1901- *DcTwDes*
**Verseput,** Herman Ward 1921- *AmMWSc 92*
**Verser,** Jacqueline Ann 1954- *WhoFI 92*
**Verses,** Christ James 1939- *AmMWSc 92*
**Versey,** Henry Cherry d1990 *Who 92N*
**Versfelt,** Porter LaRoy, III 1957- *WhoEnt 92*
**Vershinin,** Konstantin Andreevich 1900-1973 *SovUnBD*
**Versic,** Ronald James 1942- *AmMWSc 92*
**Ver Steeg,** Donna Lorraine Frank 1929- *WhoWest 92*
**Versteegh,** Larry Robert 1949- *AmMWSc 92*
**Verstraete,** Marc 1925- *IntWW 91*
**Ver Strate,** Gary William 1940- *AmMWSc 92*
**Vertefeuille,** Albert Benoit 1933- *WhoAmP 91*
**Verter,** Herbert Sigmund 1936- *AmMWSc 92*
**Verter,** Joel I 1942- *AmMWSc 92*
**Vertes,** Victor 1927- *AmMWSc 92*
**Vertiz y Salcedo,** Juan Jose de 1719-1799 *HisDSpE*
**Vertlieb,** Stephen Joel 1945- *WhoEnt 92*
**Vertov,** Dziga 1896-1954 *FacFETw, IntDcF 2-2 [port], SovUnBD*
**Vertreace,** Martha M. *DrAPF 91*
**Vertreace,** Walter Charles 1947- *WhoAmL 92, WhoBlA 92*
**Vertrees,** Billy Gene 1949- *WhoWest 92*
**Vertrees,** Robert Layman 1939- *AmMWSc 92*
**Verts,** Lita Jeanne 1935- *WhoWest 92*
**Vertue,** Beryl *LesBEnT 92*
**Verulam,** Earl of 1951- *Who 92*
**Verval,** Alain *IntAu&W 91X, WrDr 92*
**Vervoort,** Gerardus 1933- *AmMWSc 92*
**Ver Vynck-Potter,** Virginia Mary 1940- *WhoMW 92*
**Verwoerd,** Hendrik 1901-1966 *FacFETw*
**Verwoerdt,** Adrian 1927- *AmMWSc 92*
**Verwolf,** William Joseph 1943- *WhoWest 92*
**Very,** Jones 1813-1880 *BenetAL 91, BibAL 8*
**Very,** Lydia Louise Anne 1823-1901 *BenetAL 91*
**Veryan,** Patricia 1923- *WrDr 92*
**Verykios,** Panaghiotis Andrew d1990 *Who 92N*
**Verzone,** Ronald Dickens 1947- *WhoFI 92*
**Vesce,** Joseph C. *WhoWest 92*
**Vescovi,** Selvi 1930- *WhoMW 92*
**Veselits,** Charles Francis 1930- *WhoFI 92*
**Vesell,** Elliot S 1933- *AmMWSc 92*
**Veselsky,** Ernst Eugen 1932- *IntWW 91*
**Vesely,** Alexander 1926- *WhoFI 92*
**Vesely,** Artem 1899-1939 *FacFETw*
**Vesely,** David Lynn 1943- *AmMWSc 92*
**Vesely,** Kenneth Donald 1936- *WhoFI 92*
**Veseth,** Michael 1949- *ConAu 135*
**Vesey** *Who 92*
**Vesey,** Godfrey 1923- *WrDr 92*
**Vesey,** Henry *Who 92*
**Vesey,** Nathaniel Henry 1901- *Who 92*
**Vesey,** Paul 1917- *WrDr 92*
**Vesley,** Donald 1932- *AmMWSc 92*
**Vesnin,** Aleksandr Aleksandrovich 1883-1959 *SovUnBD*
**Vesnin,** Leonid 1880-1933 *SovUnBD*
**Vesnin,** Viktor 1882-1950 *SovUnBD*
**Vespasian** 9-79 *EncEarC*
**Vesper,** Karl H 1932- *IntAu&W 91, WrDr 92*
**Vesper,** Will 1882-1962 *EncTR 91*
**Vespucci,** Amerigo 1451-1512 *HisDSpE*
**Vespucci,** Amerigo 1454-1512 *BenetAL 91*
**Vessel,** Eugene David 1927- *AmMWSc 92*
**Vesselinovitch,** Stan Dushan 1922- *AmMWSc 92*
**Vessey,** Adele Ruth 1947- *AmMWSc 92*
**Vessey,** John W., Jr. 1922- *IntWW 91*
**Vessey,** John William, Jr. 1922- *WhoMW 92*
**Vessey,** Martin Paterson 1936- *Who 92*
**Vessey,** Stephen H 1939- *AmMWSc 92*
**Vessey,** Theodore Alan 1938- *AmMWSc 92*
**Vessot,** Robert F C 1930- *AmMWSc 92*
**Vessup,** Aaron Anthony 1947- *WhoBlA 92*
**Vest,** Ben 1940- *WhoAmP 91*
**Vest,** Charles Marstiller 1941- *AmMWSc 92*
**Vest,** Donald Seymour, Sr. 1930- *WhoBlA 92*
**Vest,** Floyd Russell 1934- *AmMWSc 92*
**Vest,** Frank Harris, Jr. 1936- *WhoRel 92*
**Vest,** Fred G. 1930- *WhoWest 92*
**Vest,** George S *WhoAmP 91*
**Vest,** George S. 1918- *IntWW 91*
**Vest,** Gregory Lee 1963- *WhoMW 92*
**Vest,** Herbie Darwin 1944- *WhoFI 92*
**Vest,** Hilda Freeman 1933- *WhoBlA 92*
**Vest,** Hyrum Grant, Jr 1935- *AmMWSc 92*
**Vest,** Jay Hansford Charles 1951- *WhoRel 92*
**Vest,** Jeffrey Alan 1962- *WhoMW 92*
**Vest,** Robert W 1930- *AmMWSc 92*
**Vestal,** Bedford Mather 1943- *AmMWSc 92*
**Vestal,** Charles Russell 1940- *AmMWSc 92*
**Vestal,** Claude Kendrick 1916- *AmMWSc 92*
**Vestal,** George 1857?-1898 *BiInAmS*
**Vestal,** George Alexander 1927- *WhoFI 92*
**Vestal,** J Robie 1942- *AmMWSc 92*
**Vestal,** Lowell Alan 1934- *WhoAmP 91*
**Vestal,** Robert Elden 1945- *AmMWSc 92*
**Vestal,** Stanley *BenetAL 91*
**Vestal,** Tommy Ray 1939- *WhoAmL 92*
**Vester,** Frederic 1925- *IntAu&W 91*
**Vester,** John William 1924- *AmMWSc 92*
**Vester,** Terry Y. 1955- *WhoBlA 92*
**Vestey** *Who 92*
**Vestey,** Baron 1941- *Who 92*
**Vestey,** Edmund Hoyle 1932- *IntWW 91, Who 92*
**Vestey,** John Derek 1914- *Who 92*
**Vestling,** Carl Swensson 1913- *AmMWSc 92*
**Vestling,** Martha Meredith 1941- *AmMWSc 92*
**Vetelino,** John Frank 1942- *AmMWSc 92*
**Vetemaa,** Enn 1936- *IntAu&W 91*
**Vetere,** Richard *DrAPF 91*
**Vethamany,** Victor Gladstone 1935- *AmMWSc 92*
**Vetlesen,** Vesla 1939- *IntWW 91*
**Veto,** Janine M. *DrAPF 91*
**Vette,** David Edward 1946- *WhoWest 92*
**Vette,** James Ira 1927- *AmMWSc 92*
**Vetter,** Arthur Frederick 1918- *AmMWSc 92*
**Vetter,** Betty M 1924- *AmMWSc 92*
**Vetter,** James Louis 1933- *AmMWSc 92*
**Vetter,** Jan 1934- *WhoAmL 92*
**Vetter,** Mary Margaret 1945- *WhoFI 92*
**Vetter,** Richard 1928- *IntMPA 92*
**Vetter,** Richard J 1943- *AmMWSc 92*
**Vetter,** Richard L 1930- *AmMWSc 92*
**Vetter,** William J *AmMWSc 92*
**Vetterli,** Doris Arlene 1941- *WhoWest 92*
**Vetterling,** John Martin 1934- *AmMWSc 92*
**Vetterling,** William Thomas 1948- *AmMWSc 92*
**Vettori,** Paul Marion 1944- *WhoAmL 92*
**Veum,** Trygve Lauritz 1940- *AmMWSc 92*
**Veverka,** Donald John 1935- *WhoAmL 92*
**Veverka,** Joseph F 1941- *AmMWSc 92*
**VeVerka,** Robert Francis 1946- *WhoMW 92*
**Veyron-Lacroix,** Robert d1991 *NewYTBS 91*
**Veyron-Lacroix,** Robert 1922- *NewAmDM*
**Veysey,** Arthur 1914- *ConAu 133*
**Veytia,** Albert Charles 1958- *WhoHisp 92*
**Veytia,** Edgar Bertolo 1953- *WhoHisp 92*
**Vezelay,** Paule 1892-1984 *TwCPaSc*
**Vezeridis,** Michael Panagiotis 1943- *AmMWSc 92*
**Vezina,** Claude 1926- *AmMWSc 92*
**Vezina,** Monique 1935- *IntWW 91*
**Veziroglu,** T Nejat 1924- *AmMWSc 92*
**Vezirov,** Abdul Rakhman Khalil ogly 1930 *IntWW 91, SovUnBD*
**Via,** Dennis Martin 1952- *WhoIns 92*
**Via,** Francis Anthony *AmMWSc 92*
**Via,** Thomas Henry 1959- *WhoBlA 92*
**Via,** William Fredrick, Jr 1920- *AmMWSc 92*
**Via,** William Randolph 1953- *WhoFI 92*
**Viadana,** Lodovico Grossi da 1560?-1627 *NewAmDM*
**Viagas,** Robert Anthony 1956- *WhoEnt 92*
**Vial,** Armand Richard 1954- *WhoAmL 92*
**Vial,** James Leslie 1924- *AmMWSc 92*
**Vial,** Kenneth Harold 1912- *Who 92*
**Vial,** Lester Joseph, Jr 1944- *AmMWSc 92*
**Vial,** Theodore Merriam 1921- *AmMWSc 92*
**Vialar,** Paul 1898- *IntWW 91*
**Vialis,** Gaston *ConAu 35NR*
**Viall,** Kenneth Warren 1951- *WhoMW 92*
**Vialle,** Karen *WhoAmP 91, WhoWest 92*
**Vialon,** Friedrich Karl 1905- *EncTR 91*
**Viamonte,** Manuel, Jr. 1930- *WhoHisp 92*
**Viamontes,** George Ignacio *AmMWSc 92*
**Vian,** Boris 1920-1959 *GuFrLit 1*
**Viana,** Hector Benjamin 1962- *WhoAmL 92*
**Vianello,** Hugo 1926- *WhoEnt 92*
**Vianna,** Nicholas Joseph 1941- *AmMWSc 92*
**Viano,** David Charles 1946- *AmMWSc 92*
**Vianson,** Paolo Mario 1959- *WhoWest 92*
**Viapree,** Don Irving 1950- *WhoEnt 92*
**Viardot,** Pauline 1821-1910 *NewAmDM*
**Viardot-Garcia,** Pauline 1821-1910 *NewAmDM*
**Viart,** Guy Pascal 1957- *WhoFI 92*
**Viat,** Marijane 1939- *WhoEnt 92*
**Vibe,** Kjeld 1927- *IntWW 91*
**Viberti,** Victor Lawrence 1913- *WhoRel 92*
**Vicari,** Anne Marie 1960- *WhoAmL 92*
**Vicari,** Gary Neal 1953- *WhoEnt 92*
**Vicarion,** Palmiro, Count *IntAu&W 91X*
**Vicars-Harris,** Noel Hedley d1991 *Who 92N*
**Vicary,** Douglas Reginald 1916- *Who 92*
**Viccajee,** Victor Framje 1903- *WhoEnt 92*
**Viccaro,** James Richard 1945- *WhoFI 92*
**Vice,** Charles Loren 1921- *WhoWest 92*
**Vice,** John Leonard 1942- *AmMWSc 92*
**Vice,** LaVonna Lee 1952- *WhoAmL 92*
**Vice,** Lisa *DrAPF 91*
**Vice,** Robert Bruce 1953- *WhoAmL 92*
**Vicens,** Carlos Francisco 1963- *WhoMW 92*
**Vicens,** Enrique 1926- *WhoAmP 91*
**Vicens,** Guillermo Juan 1948- *WhoHisp 92*
**Vicente,** Jose Alberto 1954- *WhoHisp 92*
**Vicente,** Ralph A. 1946- *WhoHisp 92*
**Vicentino,** Nicola 1511-1572 *NewAmDM*
**Viceps-Madore,** Dace I 1947- *AmMWSc 92*
**Vichich,** Thomas E 1917- *AmMWSc 92*
**Vichich,** William Michael 1947- *WhoMW 92*
**Vichit-Vadakan,** Vinyu 1937- *IntWW 91*
**Vicinie,** Albert Frank, III 1959- *WhoMW 92*
**Vicinsky,** Ronald Allan 1952- *WhoWest 92*
**Vick,** Arnold Oughtred Russell 1933- *Who 92*
**Vick,** Arthur 1911- *IntWW 91, Who 92*
**Vick,** Austin Lafayette 1929- *WhoFI 92*
**Vick,** Charles Booker 1932- *AmMWSc 92*
**Vick,** George Beauchamp 1901-1975 *RelLAm 91*
**Vick,** George R 1920- *AmMWSc 92*
**Vick,** Gerald Keith 1930- *AmMWSc 92*
**Vick,** Harvey Oscar, III 1957- *WhoBlA 92*
**Vick,** James 1931- *AmMWSc 92*
**Vick,** James Whitfield 1942- *AmMWSc 92*
**Vick,** Jeffrey Howard 1962- *WhoRel 92*
**Vick,** Kathleen M 1938- *WhoAmP 91*
**Vick,** Marian *WhoBlA 92*
**Vick,** Paul David 1960- *WhoMW 92*
**Vick,** Phillip Layne 1946- *WhoFI 92*
**Vick,** Ralph Lewis 1929- *WhoWest 92*
**Vick,** Richard 1917- *Who 92*
**Vick,** Robert Lore 1929- *AmMWSc 92*
**Vick,** Ronald Greg 1959- *WhoFI 92*
**Vick,** Susan 1945- *WhoEnt 92*
**Vick Roy,** Thomas Rogers 1922- *AmMWSc 92*
**Vickerman,** Jim 1931- *WhoAmP 91*
**Vickerman,** Keith 1933- *Who 92*
**Vickerman,** Sara Elizabeth 1949- *WhoWest 92*
**Vickers** *Who 92*
**Vickers,** Baroness *Who 92*
**Vickers,** Charles Harold 1945- *WhoEnt 92*
**Vickers,** David Hyle 1940- *AmMWSc 92*
**Vickers,** David Leroy 1942- *WhoFI 92*
**Vickers,** Deanna 1940- *WhoAmP 91*
**Vickers,** Dolores Ehlin 1935- *WhoAmP 91*
**Vickers,** Eric 1921- *Who 92*
**Vickers,** Evan James 1954- *WhoWest 92*
**Vickers,** Florence Foster *AmMWSc 92*
**Vickers,** James Hudson 1930- *AmMWSc 92*
**Vickers,** James Oswald Noel 1916- *Who 92*
**Vickers,** John 1916-1976 *ConAu 134*
**Vickers,** John Stuart 1958- *Who 92*
**Vickers,** Jon 1926- *FacFETw, IntWW 91, NewAmDM, Who 92*
**Vickers,** Michael Douglas Allen 1929- *Who 92*
**Vickers,** Michael Edwin *Who 92*
**Vickers,** Milton David 1949- *WhoBlA 92*
**Vickers,** Richard 1928- *Who 92*
**Vickers,** Roger Spencer 1937- *AmMWSc 92*
**Vickers,** Stanley 1939- *AmMWSc 92*
**Vickers,** Thomas Douglas 1916- *Who 92*
**Vickers,** Thomas H. 1949- *WhoEnt 92*
**Vickers,** Thomas J 1939- *AmMWSc 92*
**Vickers,** Tom 1936- *WhoAmP 91*
**Vickers,** Tony 1932- *Who 92*
**Vickers,** William W 1923- *AmMWSc 92*
**Vickers,** Zata Marie 1950- *AmMWSc 92*
**Vickers-Rich,** Patricia 1944- *AmMWSc 92*
**Vickerstaff,** Robert Percy 1935- *WhoIns 92*
**Vickery,** Brian Campbell 1918- *Who 92*
**Vickery,** Byrdean Eyvonne Hughes 1928- *WhoWest 92*
**Vickery,** Glenn Wheeler 1938- *WhoAmL 92*
**Vickery,** James A 1931- *WhoIns 92*
**Vickery,** Larry Edward 1945- *AmMWSc 92*
**Vickery,** Melba 1925- *WhoWest 92*
**Vickery,** Millie Margaret 1920- *WhoMW 92*
**Vickery,** Raymond Ezekiel, Jr 1942- *WhoAmP 91*
**Vickery,** Robert Craig 1958- *WhoFI 92*
**Vickery,** Robert Kingston, Jr 1922- *AmMWSc 92*
**Vickery,** William *WhoMW 92*
**Vickland,** Kathleen Dannehl 1959- *WhoFI 92*
**Vickrey,** C.B., III 1965- *WhoFI 92*
**Vickrey,** Herta Miller *AmMWSc 92*
**Vickroy,** David Gill 1941- *AmMWSc 92*
**Vickroy,** Virgil Vester, Jr 1931- *AmMWSc 92*
**Vico,** Giambattista 1668-1744 *BlkwCEP*
**Vicory,** William Anthony 1958- *AmMWSc 92*
**Vicq d'Azyr,** Felix 1748-1794 *BlkwCEP*
**Victery,** Winona Whitwell 1941- *AmMWSc 92*
**Victor I** *EncEarC*
**Victor Emmanuel III** 1869-1947 *EncTR 91 [port], FacFETw*
**Victor of Vita** *EncEarC*
**Victor,** Andrew C 1934- *AmMWSc 92*
**Victor,** Charlene d1991 *NewYTBS 91*
**Victor,** Charles B. *WrDr 92*
**Victor,** David d1989 *LesBEnT 92*
**Victor,** Ed 1939- *Who 92*
**Victor,** Edward 1914- *WrDr 92*
**Victor,** Frances 1826-1902 *BenetAL 91*
**Victor,** Frances Auretta Fuller 1826-1902 *HanAmWH*
**Victor,** George A 1936- *AmMWSc 92*

**Victor,** James 1939- *IntMPA 92, WhoWest 92*
**Victor,** Joe Mayer 1939- *AmMWSc 92*
**Victor,** Jonathan David 1954- *AmMWSc 92*
**Victor,** Leonard Baker 1934- *AmMWSc 92*
**Victor,** Metta Victoria 1831-1886 *BenetAL 91*
**Victor,** Michael Gary 1945- *WhoAmL 92*
**Victor,** Paul-Emile 1907- *IntWW 91*
**Victor,** Richard Steven 1949- *WhoAmL 92*
**Victor,** Walter K 1922- *AmMWSc 92*
**Victoria,** Edward Jess, Jr 1941- *AmMWSc 92*
**Victoria,** Francisco D. 1955- *WhoHisp 92*
**Victoria,** Guadelupe 1785-1843 *HisDSpE*
**Victoria,** Roger Dale 1959- *WhoRel 92*
**Victoria,** Tomas Luis de 1548-1611 *NewAmDM*
**Victorica,** Benjamin 1936- *AmMWSc 92*
**Victorin,** His Eminence 1912- *WhoRel 92*
**Victorin,** Steven Robert 1961- *WhoFI 92*
**Victorina** d269 *EncAmaz 91*
**Victorinus of Pettau** d304? *EncEarC*
**Victorinus,** Caius Marius d363? *EncEarC*
**Victorius,** Claudius Marius d425? *EncEarC*
**Victorius,** Claus 1923- *AmMWSc 92*
**Victors,** Alexis Peter 1937- *WhoWest 92*
**Victorson,** Michael Bruce 1954- *WhoAmL 92*
**Victory,** Gerard 1921- *ConCom 92*
**Victory,** Joel William 1942- *WhoFI 92*
**Vicuna,** Cecilia 1948- *WhoHisp 92*
**Vicuna,** Francisco O. *Who 92*
**Vicuna,** Patricio Ricardo 1953- *WhoHisp 92*
**Vida,** Julius 1928- *AmMWSc 92*
**Vidal,** Adriana *WhoHisp 92*
**Vidal,** Avis Carlotta 1945- *WhoHisp 92*
**Vidal,** Dagmar Lund 1917- *WhoAmP 91*
**Vidal,** Eduardo R. 1957- *WhoHisp 92*
**Vidal,** Federico S. 1920- *WhoHisp 92*
**Vidal,** Gore *DrAPF 91*
**Vidal,** Gore 1925- *ConNov 91, FacFETw, IntAu&W 91, IntWW 91, LiExTwC, Who 92, WrDr 92*
**Vidal,** Gore 1929- *BenetAL 91*
**Vidal,** Jacques J 1930- *AmMWSc 92*
**Vidal,** James Emeric 1945- *WhoAmP 91*
**Vidal,** Paul 1863-1931 *NewAmDM*
**Vidal,** Ricardo 1931- *IntWW 91, WhoRel 92*
**Vidal,** Ulises *WhoHisp 92*
**Vidale,** Richard F 1936- *AmMWSc 92*
**Vidali,** Gian Franco *AmMWSc 92*
**Vidalon,** Mario Carlos 1946- *WhoMW 92*
**Vidas,** Vincent George 1931- *WhoFI 92*
**Vidaurreta,** Luis E 1920- *AmMWSc 92*
**Vidaurri,** Alfredo Garcia 1930- *WhoHisp 92*
**Vidaurri,** Fernando C, Jr 1939- *AmMWSc 92*
**Vidaver,** Anne Marie Kopecky 1938- *AmMWSc 92*
**Vidaver,** Doris *DrAPF 91*
**Vidaver,** George Alexander 1930- *AmMWSc 92*
**Vidaver,** William Elliott 1921- *AmMWSc 92*
**Videla,** Jorge Rafael 1925- *IntWW 91*
**Videon,** Fred F 1934- *AmMWSc 92*
**Viderman,** Linda Jean 1957- *WhoAmL 92, WhoFI 92*
**Vides,** Alexis *WhoRel 92*
**Vidger,** Leonard Perry 1920- *WrDr 92*
**Vidic,** Dobrivoje 1918- *Who 92*
**Vidisky,** Diana Nita 1944- *WhoWest 92*
**Vidler,** Alec R. *ConAu 135*
**Vidler,** Alexander Roper d1991 *Who 92N*
**Vidler,** Alexander Roper 1899- *WrDr 92*
**Vidler,** Alexander Roper 1899-1991 *ConAu 135*
**Vidmar,** Paul Joseph 1944- *AmMWSc 92*
**Vidmar,** Richard Anthony 1947- *WhoWest 92*
**Vidoli,** Vivian Ann 1941- *AmMWSc 92*
**Vidoloff,** Robert Zaprian Tchomoneff 1915- *WhoEnt 92*
**Vidone,** Romeo Albert 1930- *AmMWSc 92*
**Vidor,** Charles 1900-1959 *IntDcF 2-2 [port]*
**Vidor,** King 1894-1982 *FacFETw, IntDcF 2-2 [port]*
**Vidor,** Miklos Janos 1923- *IntAu&W 91*
**Vidosic,** J P 1909- *AmMWSc 92*
**Vidricksen,** Ben E 1927- *WhoAmP 91*
**Vidricksen,** Ben Eugene 1927- *WhoMW 92*
**Vidrine,** Malcolm Francis 1949- *AmMWSc 92*
**Vidt,** Edward James 1927- *AmMWSc 92*
**Vidueira,** Joe R. 1963- *WhoHisp 92*
**Vidulich,** George A 1931- *AmMWSc 92*
**Vidussoni,** Aldo 1914-1982 *BiDExR*
**Vidyasagar,** Mathukumalli 1947- *AmMWSc 92*
**Vie,** Richard Carl 1937- *WhoFI 92*
**Viebrock,** Frederick William 1935- *AmMWSc 92*
**Viebrock,** Michael Eugene 1949- *WhoEnt 92*
**Viechnicki,** Dennis J 1940- *AmMWSc 92*
**Viegas,** Kenneth Dell 1931- *WhoHisp 92*
**Vieglais,** Nikolajs 1907- *WhoRel 92, WhoWest 92*
**Vieh,** James Edward 1949- *WhoAmL 92*
**Viehe,** Carl Armin 1917- *WhoRel 92*
**Viehe,** Karl William 1943- *WhoAmL 92, WhoFI 92*
**Viehland,** Dennis Warren 1952- *WhoWest 92*
**Viehland,** Larry Alan 1947- *AmMWSc 92*
**Vieillard,** Roger d1989 *IntWW 91N*
**Vieira,** David John 1950- *AmMWSc 92*
**Vieira,** Joao Bernardo 1939- *IntWW 91*
**Vielbig,** Thomas Edward 1964- *WhoMW 92*
**Viele,** Egbert Ludovicus 1863-1937 *BenetAL 91*
**Viele,** George Washington *AmMWSc 92*
**Viele,** Herman K 1856-1908 *ScFEYrs*
**Viele,** Herman Knickerbocker 1856-1908 *BenetAL 91*
**Vieler,** Geoffrey Herbert 1910- *Who 92*
**Vielhauer,** Jeffrey James 1960- *WhoMW 92*
**Vien,** Joseph-Marie 1716-1809 *BlkwCEP*
**Vien,** Steve Hung 1957- *AmMWSc 92*
**Viener,** John D. 1939- *WhoAmL 92, WhoFI 92*
**Vienot,** Marc 1928- *IntWW 91*
**Vier,** Dwayne Trowbridge 1914- *AmMWSc 92*
**Viera,** Antonio Torres 1962- *WhoHisp 92*
**Viera,** John David 1941- *WhoEnt 92*
**Viera,** Meredith *LesBEnT 92*
**Viera,** Pedro *WhoHisp 92*
**Viera,** Rodolfo Elias 1948- *WhoRel 92*
**Viera-Martinez,** Angel 1915- *WhoAmP 91*
**Vierck,** Charles John, Jr 1936- *AmMWSc 92*
**Vierck,** Robert K 1908- *AmMWSc 92*
**Viereck,** George Sylvester 1884-1962 *BenetAL 91*
**Viereck,** Leslie A 1930- *AmMWSc 92*
**Viereck,** Louis 1851-1922 *DcAmImH*
**Viereck,** Peter *DrAPF 91*
**Viereck,** Peter 1916- *BenetAL 91, ConPo 91, IntAu&W 91, IntWW 91, WrDr 92*
**Vieregg,** James Donald 1945- *WhoAmL 92*
**Vierne,** Louis 1870-1937 *NewAmDM*
**Viernstein,** Lawrence J 1919- *AmMWSc 92*
**Vierra,** Brian Coburn 1961- *WhoWest 92*
**Vierros,** Tuure Johannes 1927- *IntAu&W 91*
**Viers,** Jimmy Wayne 1943- *AmMWSc 92*
**Viertel,** Deborah Kerr *Who 92*
**Viertel,** John Richard 1949- *WhoEnt 92*
**Viertel,** Joseph *DrAPF 91*
**Viertel,** Joseph 1915- *IntAu&W 91, WrDr 92*
**Viertl,** John Ruediger Mader 1941- *AmMWSc 92*
**Vieru,** Anatol 1926- *ConCom 92, IntWW 91*
**Vieselmeyer,** Ron R 1941- *WhoAmP 91*
**Viessman,** Warren, Jr 1930- *AmMWSc 92*
**Viest,** Ivan M 1922- *AmMWSc 92*
**Vieth,** G. Duane 1923- *WhoAmL 92*
**Vieth,** Joachim 1925- *AmMWSc 92*
**Vieth,** Wolf R 1934- *AmMWSc 92*
**Vieth von Golssenau,** Arnold *EncTR 91*
**Vietmeyer,** Noel Duncan 1940- *AmMWSc 92*
**Vietor,** Donald Melvin 1945- *AmMWSc 92*
**Vietor,** Harold Duane 1931- *WhoAmL 92, WhoMW 92*
**Viets,** Frank Garfield, Jr 1916- *AmMWSc 92*
**Viets,** Hermann 1943- *AmMWSc 92*
**Viets,** Richard N 1930- *WhoAmP 91*
**Viets,** Robert O. 1943- *WhoFI 92, WhoMW 92*
**Viette,** Michael Anthony 1941- *AmMWSc 92*
**Vietti,** Teresa Jane 1927- *AmMWSc 92*
**Vieux,** Alex Serge 1957- *WhoFI 92*
**Vieuxtemps,** Henry 1820-1881 *NewAmDM*
**Vieweg,** Bruce Wayne 1947- *WhoMW 92*
**Viezer,** Timothy Wayne 1959- *WhoFI 92, WhoMW 92*
**Vig,** Baldev K 1935- *AmMWSc 92*
**Vig,** Baldev Krishan 1935- *WhoWest 92*
**Vig,** Vernon Edward 1937- *WhoAmL 92*
**Vigano,** Vittorio *DcTwDes*
**Vigars,** Della *Who 92*
**Vigars,** Robert Lewis 1923- *Who 92*
**Vigdor,** Steven Elliot 1947- *AmMWSc 92*
**Vigdorova,** Frida Abramovna 1915-1965 *SovUnBD*
**Vigee,** Gerald S 1931- *AmMWSc 92*
**Vigee-Lebrun,** Elisabeth 1755-1842 *BlkwCEP*
**Vigfusson,** Norman V 1930- *AmMWSc 92*
**Viggers,** Peter John 1938- *Who 92*
**Viggers,** Robert F 1923- *AmMWSc 92*
**Viggiano,** Albert 1954- *AmMWSc 92*
**Viggiano,** Paul M 1943- *WhoAmP 91*
**Vigil,** Allan R. 1947- *WhoHisp 92*
**Vigil,** Arthur Margarito 1942- *WhoHisp 92*
**Vigil,** Bernadette 1955- *WhoHisp 92*
**Vigil,** Charles J. 1964- *WhoAmL 92*
**Vigil,** Charles S. 1912- *WhoAmL 92*
**Vigil,** Daniel A. 1947- *WhoHisp 92*
**Vigil,** Daniel Agustin 1947- *WhoAmL 92, WhoWest 92*
**Vigil,** David Anthony 1930- *WhoHisp 92*
**Vigil,** Dolores 1938- *WhoHisp 92*
**Vigil,** Edward Francis 1964- *WhoWest 92*
**Vigil,** Eugene Leon 1941- *AmMWSc 92*
**Vigil,** Evangelina *DrAPF 91*
**Vigil,** James Diego 1938- *WhoHisp 92*
**Vigil,** John Carlos 1939- *AmMWSc 92, WhoHisp 92*
**Vigil,** John Jess 1952- *WhoHisp 92*
**Vigil,** Maurilio Eutimio 1941- *WhoHisp 92, WhoWest 92*
**Vigil,** Michael Edward 1951- *WhoAmL 92*
**Vigil,** Neddy Augustin 1939- *WhoHisp 92*
**Vigil,** Rafael 1951- *WhoEnt 92*
**Vigil,** Ralph H. 1932- *WhoHisp 92*
**Vigil,** Richard Martin, Sr. 1928- *WhoHisp 92*
**Vigil,** Robert 1953- *WhoAmP 91*
**Vigil,** Robert E. 1953- *WhoHisp 92*
**Vigil,** Samuel F *WhoAmP 91*
**Vigil,** Samuel F., Jr. *WhoHisp 92*
**Vigil-Giron,** Rebecca 1954- *WhoAmP 91*
**Vigil-Giron,** Rebecca D. 1954- *WhoHisp 92, WhoWest 92*
**Vigil-Perez,** Angie *WhoHisp 92*
**Vigil-Pinon,** Evangelina *WhoHisp 92*
**Vigilantius** *EncEarC*
**Vigilius** *EncEarC*
**Vigliante,** Mary *DrAPF 91*
**Viglierchio,** David Richard 1925- *AmMWSc 92*
**Viglione,** Eugene Lawrence 1931- *WhoWest 92*
**Viglione,** Sam S 1929- *AmMWSc 92*
**Vigliotti,** Anthony Joseph 1942- *WhoAmP 91*
**Vigliotti,** Louis John 1957- *WhoFI 92*
**Vignal,** Renaud 1943- *IntWW 91*
**Vigneau,** Robert A 1920- *WhoAmP 91*
**Vignelli,** Lella *DcTwDes*
**Vignelli,** Massimo 1931- *DcTwDes*
**Vigneri,** Joseph William 1956- *WhoAmL 92*
**Vignery,** Agnes M C 1949- *AmMWSc 92*
**Vignes,** Louis Joseph 1930- *WhoWest 92*
**Vignola,** Andrew Michael, Sr. 1938- *WhoFI 92*
**Vignoles,** Roger Hutton 1945- *Who 92*
**Vignon,** Victor 1851-1917 *ThHEIm*
**Vignos,** James Henry 1933- *AmMWSc 92*
**Vignos,** Paul Joseph, Jr 1919- *AmMWSc 92*
**Vignovich,** Raymond Lee 1949- *WhoMW 92*
**Vigny,** Alfred de 1797-1863 *GuFrLit 1*
**Vigo,** Benny Richard 1933- *WhoHisp 92*
**Vigo,** Jean 1905-1934 *IntDcF 2-2 [port]*
**Vigo,** Tyrone Lawrence 1939- *AmMWSc 92*
**Vigoda,** Abe 1921- *WhoEnt 92A*
**Vigoda,** David *DrAPF 91*
**Vigolo,** Giorgio 1894-1983 *DcLB 114 [port]*
**Vigran,** Stanley Louis 1926- *WhoFI 92*
**Vigrass,** Laurence William 1929- *AmMWSc 92*
**Vigue,** Henry Joseph, Jr. 1951- *WhoEnt 92*
**Viguerie,** Richard Art 1933- *IntWW 91*
**Vihstadt,** Robert Francis 1941- *WhoWest 92*
**Viirlaid,** Arved 1922- *LiExTwC*
**Vijay,** Hari Mohan *AmMWSc 92*
**Vijay,** Inder Krishan 1940- *AmMWSc 92*
**Vijay,** Mohan Madan 1937- *AmMWSc 92*
**Vijayagopal,** Parakat *AmMWSc 92*
**Vijayan,** Sivaraman 1945- *AmMWSc 92*
**Vijayan,** Vijaya Kumari 1942- *AmMWSc 92*
**Vijayendran,** Bheema R 1941- *AmMWSc 92*
**Vijh,** Ashok Kumar 1938- *AmMWSc 92*
**Vijil,** Alfonso Jose 1956- *WhoHisp 92*
**Vijit,** Supinit *IntWW 91*
**Vijoen,** Gerrit van Niekerk 1926- *IntWW 91*
**Vijoen,** Henri Pieter 1932- *IntWW 91*
**Vijverberg,** Wim Petrus Maria 1955- *WhoFI 92*
**Vik,** Anne 1933- *IntWW 91*
**Vike,** Gregory Jon 1951- *WhoMW 92*
**Viken,** Linda Lea M 1945- *WhoAmP 91*
**Vikis,** Andreas Charalambous 1942- *AmMWSc 92*
**Vikram,** Chandra Shekhar 1950- *AmMWSc 92*
**Vikre,** Peter George 1947- *WhoWest 92*
**Viksne,** Andy 1934- *AmMWSc 92*
**Viksnins,** George Juris 1937- *WhoFI 92*
**Vikstrom,** John Edvin 1931- *IntWW 91*
**Vikstrom,** John Edwin 1931- *WhoRel 92*
**Vikulov,** Sergey Vasil'evich 1922- *SovUnBD*
**Vikulov,** Vladimir Ivanovich 1946- *IntWW 91*
**Vila,** Adis Maria 1953- *WhoAmL 92, WhoHisp 92*
**Vila,** Bob 1946- *WhoHisp 92*
**Vila,** Raul Ivan 1954- *WhoHisp 92*
**Vila,** Robert Joseph 1946- *WhoEnt 92*
**Vila,** Samuel Campderros 1930- *AmMWSc 92*
**Viladecans,** Joan-Pere 1948- *IntWW 91*
**Viladesau,** Richard R., Jr. 1944- *WhoHisp 92*
**Vilaincour,** Leon 1923- *TwCPaSc*
**Vilandre,** Paul Connell 1942- *WhoFI 92*
**Vilaplana,** Jose M. 1927- *WhoHisp 92*
**Vilardell,** Francisco 1926- *IntWW 91*
**Vilardi,** Agnes Francine 1918- *WhoWest 92*
**Vilarino,** Idea 1920- *ConSpAP*
**Vilarino Pintos,** Daria 1928- *IntWW 91*
**Vilas,** Richard W 1918- *WhoIns 92*
**Vilas,** Santiago 1931- *WhoHisp 92*
**Vilato,** Roberto 1952- *WhoHisp 92*
**Vilatte,** Joseph Rene 1854-1929 *RelLAm 91*
**Vilcek,** Jan Tomas 1933- *AmMWSc 92*
**Vilches,** Oscar Edgardo 1936- *AmMWSc 92*
**Vilchez,** Blanca Rosa 1957- *WhoHisp 92*
**Vilcins,** Gunars 1930- *AmMWSc 92*
**Vile,** Maurice John Crawley 1927- *Who 92*
**Vilenkin,** Alexander 1949- *AmMWSc 92*
**Viles,** Timothy Patrick 1958- *WhoWest 92*
**Vilgrain,** Pierre E. 1922- *WhoFI 92*
**Vilhjalmsson,** Thor 1930- *IntWW 91*
**Vilim,** John Robert 1922- *WhoMW 92*
**Viljoen,** Marais 1915- *IntWW 91, Who 92*
**Vilker,** Vincent Lee 1943- *AmMWSc 92*
**Vilker-Kuchment,** Valeria *WhoEnt 92*
**Vilkitis,** James Richard *AmMWSc 92, WhoWest 92*
**Vilkki,** Erkki Uuno 1922- *AmMWSc 92, WhoMW 92*
**Vilks,** Gustavs 1929- *AmMWSc 92*
**Vilks,** Peter 1956- *AmMWSc 92*
**Villa,** Alvaro J. 1940- *WhoHisp 92*
**Villa,** Carlos Cesar 1941- *WhoHisp 92*
**Villa,** Daniel Joseph 1956- *WhoHisp 92*
**Villa,** Dario 1953- *IntAu&W 91*
**Villa,** Edmond Roland, Sr. 1929- *WhoFI 92*
**Villa,** Francisco 1877-1923 *BenetAL 91*
**Villa,** John Joseph 1917- *WhoHisp 92*
**Villa,** John Kazar 1948- *WhoFI 92*
**Villa,** Jose Garcia 1914- *IntWW 91*
**Villa,** Juan Francisco 1941- *AmMWSc 92, WhoHisp 92*
**Villa,** Pancho 1878?-1923 *FacFETw [port]*
**Villa,** Raul Manuel 1940- *WhoHisp 92*
**Villa,** Vicente Domingo 1940- *AmMWSc 92*
**Villa-Gilbert,** Mariana 1937- *WrDr 92*
**Villa-Gilbert,** Mariana Soledad Magdalena 1937- *IntAu&W 91*
**Villa-Komaroff,** Lydia 1947- *AmMWSc 92, WhoHisp 92*
**Villa-Lobos,** Heitor 1887-1959 *FacFETw, NewAmDM*
**Villa-Vicencio,** Charles 1942- *IntWW 91*
**Villablanca,** Jaime Rolando 1929- *AmMWSc 92*
**Villacampa,** Alcides Antonio 1952- *WhoHisp 92*
**Villacorte,** Guillermo Vilar 1933- *AmMWSc 92*
**Villafana,** Allan Francis 1961- *WhoHisp 92*
**Villafana,** Manuel A. 1940- *WhoHisp 92*
**Villafana,** Theodore 1936- *AmMWSc 92, WhoHisp 92*
**Villafane,** Juan, Jr. 1951- *WhoHisp 92*
**Villafane,** Robert 1941- *WhoHisp 92*
**Villafranca,** Joseph John 1944- *AmMWSc 92*
**Villafuerte,** Lisa Marie 1966- *WhoHisp 92*
**Village People,** The *ConMus 7 [port]*
**Villagomez,** Ramon Garrido 1949- *WhoAmL 92*
**Villagomez,** Thomas Pangelinan *WhoAmP 91*
**Villagra,** Gaspar Perez de 1555?-1620? *BenetAL 91*
**Villagran,** Gilbert J. 1948- *WhoHisp 92*
**Villagran De Leon,** Francisco 1954- *IntWW 91*
**Villagran Rodriguez,** Dolores 1954- *WhoHisp 92*
**Villain,** Claude Edouard Louis Etienne 1935- *IntWW 91*
**Villalba,** Jovito 1908- *IntWW 91*
**Villalobos,** Ruben L., Jr. 1946- *WhoHisp 92*
**Villalobos Padilla,** Francisco 1921- *WhoRel 92*

**Villalon,** Dalisay Manuel 1941- WhoMW 92
**Villalon,** Manuel F. 1944- WhoHisp 92
**Villalon,** Pedro Augusto 1925- WhoHisp 92
**Villalpando,** Alberto 1949- WhoHisp 92
**Villalpando,** Catalina Vasquez 1940- WhoHisp 92
**Villalpando,** Jesse M. 1959- WhoHisp 92
**Villalpando,** Jesse Michael 1959- WhoAmP 91
**Villamanan,** Manuel WhoHisp 92
**Villamarin,** Juan A. 1939- WhoHisp 92
**Villamil,** Anne Patricia 1958- WhoFI 92
**Villamil,** Jose Antonio 1946- WhoHisp 92
**Villamil,** Jose de 1788-1866 HisDSpE
**Villamil,** Lydia I. 1951- WhoHisp 92
**Villamor,** Catherine WhoHisp 92
**Villamor,** Enrique 1961- WhoHisp 92
**Villane,** Anthony M, Jr WhoAmP 91
**Villani,** Frank John, Sr 1921- AmMWSc 92
**Villani,** Joseph Trigg 1961- WhoWest 92
**Villani,** Mario A. 1939- WhoHisp 92
**Villanova,** Robert Allan, Sr. 1945- WhoFI 92
**Villanueva,** Alma DrAPF 91
**Villanueva,** Alma Luz 1944- WhoHisp 92
**Villanueva,** Edward Anthony 1946- WhoHisp 92
**Villanueva,** German Baid AmMWSc 92
**Villanueva,** Hector 1964- WhoHisp 92
**Villanueva,** Jose 1937- AmMWSc 92
**Villanueva,** Jose A. WhoHisp 92
**Villanueva,** Jose Antonio WhoHisp 92
**Villanueva,** Miguel Ramon, Sr. 1936- WhoHisp 92
**Villanueva,** Tino DrAPF 91
**Villanueva,** Tino 1941- WhoHisp 92
**Villanueva,** Tomas Ayala 1941- WhoHisp 92
**Villanueva,** Victor, Jr. 1948- WhoHisp 92
**Villanueva,** Vincent C. 1943- WhoHisp 92
**Villapalos-Salas,** Gustavo 1949- IntWW 91
**Villapiano,** John A 1951- WhoAmP 91
**Villar,** Arturo Ignacio 1933- WhoHisp 92
**Villar,** Isabel Elsa 1948- WhoHisp 92
**Villar,** James Walter 1930- AmMWSc 92
**Villar,** Juan C. 1960- WhoHisp 92
**Villar-Palasi,** Carlos 1928- AmMWSc 92
**Villar Y Ortiz De Urdia,** Francisco 1945- IntWW 91
**Villard,** Dimitri Serrano 1943- WhoEnt 92
**Villard,** Helen Frances Garrison 1844-1928 AmPeW
**Villard,** Henry 1835-1900 BenetAL 91
**Villard,** Oswald G, Jr 1916- AmMWSc 92
**Villard,** Oswald Garrison DcAmImH
**Villard,** Oswald Garrison 1872-1949 AmPeW, BenetAL 91
**Villareal,** Dewey R. 1926- WhoAmL 92
**Villareal,** Ramiro 1950- AmMWSc 92
**Villarejo,** Merna 1939- AmMWSc 92
**Villarejos,** Miguel Otto 1943- WhoMW 92
**Villarejos,** Victor Moises 1918- AmMWSc 92
**Villari,** Jack C. 1938- WhoEnt 92
**Villarini,** Pedro WhoHisp 92
**Villaronga,** Raul Gabriel 1938- WhoHisp 92
**Villarreal,** Alfred William 1957- WhoHisp 92
**Villarreal,** David 1958- WhoHisp 92
**Villarreal,** Fernando M. 1956- WhoHisp 92
**Villarreal,** G. Claude 1930- WhoHisp 92
**Villarreal,** Homer Anthony 1952- WhoHisp 92
**Villarreal,** Humberto 1940- WhoHisp 92
**Villarreal,** Jesse James 1913- AmMWSc 92
**Villarreal,** Joaquin WhoHisp 92
**Villarreal,** Jose Antonio 1924- ConAu 133
**Villarreal,** Jose Rolando WhoHisp 92
**Villarreal,** Lorenzo 1951- WhoHisp 92
**Villarreal,** Luis Mario WhoHisp 92
**Villarreal,** Luis Perez 1949- AmMWSc 92
**Villarreal,** Martha Ellen 1942- WhoHisp 92
**Villarreal,** Melecio Mercado, Jr. 1924- WhoHisp 92
**Villarreal,** Mike WhoHisp 92
**Villarreal,** Mike A., Sr. WhoHisp 92
**Villarreal,** Norma 1955- WhoHisp 92
**Villarreal,** Osiel, Jr. 1968- WhoHisp 92
**Villarreal,** Pedro Corona 1964- WhoHisp 92
**Villarreal,** Raul, Sr. WhoHisp 92
**Villarreal,** Rita 1931- WhoHisp 92
**Villarreal,** Robert P. 1951- WhoHisp 92
**Villarreal,** Roberto E. WhoHisp 92
**Villarreal,** Romeo Manuel 1936- WhoHisp 92
**Villarreal,** Rosalva 1957- WhoHisp 92
**Villarroel,** Gaspar de 1587-1665 HisDSpE
**Villarrubia,** Jan DrAPF 91
**Villars,** Felix Marc Hermann 1921- AmMWSc 92
**Villas Boas,** Claudio 1916- IntWW 91
**Villas-Boas,** Jose Manuel P. de 1931- IntWW 91
**Villas Boas,** Orlando 1914- IntWW 91
**Villasenor,** Victor Edmundo DrAPF 91
**Villasenor,** Victor Edmundo 1940- WhoHisp 92
**Villasoto,** Dolores Cruz 1937- WhoAmP 91
**Villasuso,** Raul, Jr. 1965- WhoHisp 92
**Villavaso,** Stephen Donald 1949- WhoAmL 92
**Villaverde,** Cirilo 1812- HisDSpE
**Villaverde,** Roberto 1945- WhoHisp 92
**Villazana-Ruiz,** Maria 1954- WhoEnt 92
**Villechaize,** Herve 1943- IntMPA 92
**Villechaize,** Herve Jean Pierre 1943- WhoEnt 92
**Villedieu,** Marie-Catherine Desjardins de 1640?-1683 FrenWW
**Villee,** Claude Alvin, Jr 1917- AmMWSc 92
**Villee,** Dorothy Balzer 1927- AmMWSc 92
**Villegas,** Carmen Milagros 1954- WhoHisp 92
**Villegas,** Cesareo 1921- AmMWSc 92
**Villegas,** Daniel John 1950- WhoHisp 92
**Villegas,** Emilio 1943- WhoHisp 92
**Villegas,** J. Frank WhoHisp 92
**Villegas,** Joaquin 1946- WhoHisp 92
**Villegas,** Joel 1965- WhoHisp 92
**Villegas,** Kathryn Thompson 1907- WhoAmP 91
**Villegas,** Orlando Luis 1954- WhoMW 92
**Villegas,** Patricia Soule-Perfect de 1922- WhoHisp 92
**Villegas,** Richard Junipero 1938- WhoWest 92
**Villegas,** Rolando Villena WhoRel 92
**Villegas,** Victoria Alano 1960- WhoAmL 92
**Villegas De Clercamp,** Eric Auguste M. de 1924- IntWW 91
**Villella,** Edward 1936- FacFETw, IntWW 91
**Villella,** Edward Joseph 1936- WhoEnt 92
**Villemejane,** Bernard de 1930- IntWW 91
**Villemez,** Clarence Louis, Jr 1938- AmMWSc 92
**Villemure,** M Paul James 1928- AmMWSc 92
**Villeneuve,** A T 1930- AmMWSc 92
**Villeneuve,** Andre 1932- AmMWSc 92
**Villeneuve,** Donald Avila 1930- WhoWest 92
**Villere,** Karen R 1944- AmMWSc 92
**Villers,** John Franklin 1950- WhoMW 92
**Villet,** Ruxton Herrer 1933- AmMWSc 92
**Villeta-Trigo,** Juan Altagracia 1952- WhoFI 92
**Villhard,** Victor Joseph 1957- WhoWest 92
**Villiers** Who 92
**Villiers,** Viscount 1948- Who 92
**Villiers,** Charles 1912- Who 92
**Villiers,** Charles Hyde 1912- IntWW 91
**Villiers,** Charles Nigel 1941- Who 92
**Villiers,** George RfGEnL 91
**Villiers de l'Isle-Adam,** Comte de 1838-1889 GuFrLit 1
**Villiers De L'Isle Adam,** Jean, Comte De 1838-1889 ScFEYrs
**Villiers-Stuart,** Gerald ScFEYrs
**Villines,** Floyd G WhoAmP 91
**Villodas,** Jack WhoHisp 92
**Villwock,** Jeffrey Carlton 1954- WhoFI 92
**Villwock,** Kenneth James 1953- WhoFI 92
**Vilms,** Jaak 1937- AmMWSc 92
**Vilnrotter,** Victor Alpar 1944- WhoWest 92
**Vilter,** Richard William 1911- AmMWSc 92
**Vilutis,** Arv 1944- WhoFI 92
**Vil'yams,** Petr Vladimirovich 1902-1947 SovUnBD
**Vil'yams,** Vasiliy Robertovich 1863-1939 SovUnBD
**Vimeur,** Jean-Baptiste-Donatien de 1725-1807 BlkwEAR
**Vimmerstedt,** John P 1931- AmMWSc 92
**Vimond,** Paul Marcel 1922- IntWW 91
**Vimont,** Jacques Pierre 1911- IntWW 91
**Vimont,** Richard Elgin 1936- WhoAmL 92
**Vina,** Juan R 1956- AmMWSc 92
**Vinal,** Harold 1891-1965 BenetAL 91
**Vinal,** Richard S 1938- AmMWSc 92
**Vinal,** Stuart C 1895?-1918 BiInAmS
**Vinao,** Alejandro 1951- ConCom 92
**Vinar,** Benjamin 1935- WhoAmL 92
**Vinas,** Christopher Andrew 1962- WhoFI 92
**Vinas,** David 1927- IntAu&W 91
**Vinatieri,** James Edward 1947- AmMWSc 92
**Vinay,** Jean-Paul 1910- IntWW 91
**Vince,** Clinton Andrew 1949- WhoAmL 92
**Vince,** George R. 1946- WhoAmL 92
**Vince,** Robert 1940- AmMWSc 92
**Vince,** Robert E 1930- WhoAmP 91
**Vincent of Lerins** d450? EncEarC [port]
**Vincent,** Anthony Lionel 1933- Who 92
**Vincent,** Bennett Frank, Jr. 1930- WhoMW 92
**Vincent,** Biff 1954- WhoEnt 92
**Vincent,** Brian Dale 1956- WhoAmL 92
**Vincent,** Bruce Havird 1947- WhoFI 92
**Vincent,** Charles 1933- WhoBlA 92
**Vincent,** Christopher Thomas 1956- WhoFI 92
**Vincent,** Daniel 1907- IntWW 91
**Vincent,** Daniel Paul 1939- WhoBlA 92
**Vincent,** David Ridgely 1941- WhoWest 92
**Vincent,** Dayton George 1936- AmMWSc 92
**Vincent,** Dietrich H 1925- AmMWSc 92
**Vincent,** Donald Leslie 1921- AmMWSc 92
**Vincent,** Douglas 1916- Who 92
**Vincent,** Dwight Harold 1930- WhoAmP 91
**Vincent,** Edward 1920- WhoEnt 92
**Vincent,** Edward 1934- WhoAmP 91, WhoBlA 92, WhoWest 92
**Vincent,** Ewart Albert 1919- Who 92
**Vincent,** Fay 1938- CurBio 91 [port]
**Vincent,** Francis C 1925- WhoAmP 91
**Vincent,** Francis T 1938- FacFETw
**Vincent,** Francis T., Jr. 1938- IntMPA 92
**Vincent,** Gabrielle IntAu&W 91
**Vincent,** Gene 1935-1971 NewAmDM
**Vincent,** George Paul 1901- AmMWSc 92
**Vincent,** Gerald Glenn 1934- AmMWSc 92
**Vincent,** Harold Arthur 1930- AmMWSc 92
**Vincent,** Irvin James 1932- Who 92
**Vincent,** Irving H. 1934- WhoBlA 92
**Vincent,** Ivor Francis Sutherland 1916- Who 92
**Vincent,** James Louis 1939- WhoFI 92
**Vincent,** James Sidney 1935- AmMWSc 92
**Vincent,** Jan-Michael 1945- IntMPA 92, WhoEnt 92
**Vincent,** Jay Fletcher 1959- WhoBlA 92
**Vincent,** Jean-Pierre 1942- IntWW 91
**Vincent,** Jerry William 1935- AmMWSc 92
**Vincent,** John 1902-1977 NewAmDM
**Vincent,** John 1937- WrDr 92
**Vincent,** John C 1942- WhoAmP 91
**Vincent,** John Heyl 1832-1920 RelLAm 91
**Vincent,** John James 1929- IntAu&W 91, IntWW 91, Who 92, WhoRel 92, WrDr 92
**Vincent,** John Joseph 1907- Who 92
**Vincent,** John Nathaniel, III 1939- WhoEnt 92
**Vincent,** John Russell 1937- Who 92
**Vincent,** Katharine IntMPA 92
**Vincent,** Kent Richard 1950- WhoMW 92
**Vincent,** Larry R 1941- WhoAmP 91
**Vincent,** Leonard Grange 1916- Who 92
**Vincent,** Leonard Stuart 1947- AmMWSc 92
**Vincent,** Lloyd Drexell 1924- AmMWSc 92
**Vincent,** Louis Dale 1932- WhoFI 92
**Vincent,** Marcus Alan 1956- WhoWest 92
**Vincent,** Marjorie Judith 1964- WhoBlA 92
**Vincent,** Marjorie Judith 1965?- ConBlB 2 [port]
**Vincent,** Mark Kent 1959- WhoWest 92
**Vincent,** Mark LaVon 1963- WhoRel 92
**Vincent,** Michael Allen 1961- WhoRel 92
**Vincent,** Monroe Mortimer 1912- AmMWSc 92
**Vincent,** Muriel C 1922- AmMWSc 92
**Vincent,** Norman Fuller 1930- WhoEnt 92
**Vincent,** Norman L. 1933- WhoFI 92
**Vincent,** Olatunde Olabode 1925- IntWW 91
**Vincent,** Oreste 1924- WhoAmL 92
**Vincent,** Phillip Earl 1938- WhoFI 92
**Vincent,** Phillip G 1941- AmMWSc 92
**Vincent,** R. J. 1943-1990 ConAu 133
**Vincent,** Richard 1931- IntWW 91, Who 92
**Vincent,** Richard A. WhoMW 92
**Vincent,** Richard Ainsley 1945- WhoWest 92
**Vincent,** Richard Bernard 1959- WhoFI 92
**Vincent,** Robert Benn 1947- WhoRel 92
**Vincent,** Robert Carr 1930- WhoAmP 91
**Vincent,** Robert David 1942- WhoAmP 91
**Vincent,** Robert Keller 1941- WhoMW 92
**Vincent,** Sam 1963- WhoBlA 92
**Vincent,** Scott Anthony 1957- WhoWest 92
**Vincent,** Stephen DrAPF 91
**Vincent,** Stephen M. 1948- WhoMW 92
**Vincent,** Steven Robert 1954- AmMWSc 92
**Vincent,** Susan Gailey 1957- WhoIns 92
**Vincent,** Thomas Lange 1935- AmMWSc 92
**Vincent,** Timothy Scott 1957- WhoEnt 92
**Vincent,** Val 1948- WhoAmP 91
**Vincent,** Vicki Lynn 1956- WhoMW 92
**Vincent,** Walter Sampson 1921- AmMWSc 92
**Vincent,** William 1945- Who 92
**Vincent,** William Slater 1954- WhoAmL 92
**Vincent Brown,** Kenneth Who 92
**Vincent-Daviss,** Diana 1943- WhoAmL 92
**Vincent-Jones,** Desmond 1912- Who 92
**Vincenti,** Sheldon Arnold 1938- WhoAmL 92, WhoWest 92
**Vincenti,** Walter G 1917- AmMWSc 92
**Vincenz,** Stanislaw Aleksander 1915- AmMWSc 92
**Vincenzi,** Frank Foster 1938- AmMWSc 92
**Vincett,** Paul Stamford 1944- AmMWSc 92
**Vinci,** Leonardo 1690-1730 NewAmDM
**Vinci,** Pietro 1535?-1584 NewAmDM
**Vinciguerra,** Michael Joseph 1945- AmMWSc 92
**Vinciguerra,** Thomas Michael 1953- WhoMW 92
**Vinck,** William Charles 1947- WhoMW 92
**Vincow,** Gershon 1935- AmMWSc 92
**Vincze,** Paul 1907- Who 92
**Vinde,** Pierre L. V. 1931- IntWW 91
**Vindum,** Jorgen Ole 1945- WhoWest 92
**Vine,** Allyn Collins 1914- AmMWSc 92
**Vine,** Barbara WrDr 92
**Vine,** Carl 1954- ConCom 92
**Vine,** Frederick John 1939- Who 92
**Vine,** Gregory S 1955- WhoAmP 91
**Vine,** James David 1921- AmMWSc 92
**Vine,** Janet 1937- IntAu&W 91
**Vine,** Philip Mesban 1919- Who 92
**Vine,** Roland Stephen 1910- Who 92
**Vine,** Roy 1923- Who 92
**Vineberg,** Neil Howard 1953- WhoEnt 92
**Vinella,** Mark Steven 1962- WhoFI 92
**Vinelott,** John 1923- Who 92
**Vinen,** William Frank 1930- Who 92
**Viner,** Michael 1945- IntMPA 92
**Viner,** Monique Sylvaine 1926- Who 92
**Vines,** Benjamin Glenn 1930-1988 WhoBlA 92N
**Vines,** Bill WhoAmP 91
**Vines,** Burl Dewayne 1945- WhoMW 92
**Vines,** Charles Jerry 1937- WhoRel 92
**Vines,** Darrell Lee AmMWSc 92
**Vines,** David Anthony 1949- Who 92
**Vines,** Doyle Ray 1947- WhoWest 92
**Vines,** Eric Victor 1929- Who 92
**Vines,** Henry Ellsworth, III 1950- WhoFI 92
**Vines,** Herbert Max 1918- AmMWSc 92
**Vines,** Leonard Dean 1946- WhoMW 92
**Vines,** Pamela Lynn Dyson 1955- WhoMW 92
**Vines,** William 1916- Who 92
**Vines,** William Joshua 1916- IntWW 91
**Viney,** Anne Margaret 1926- Who 92
**Viney,** Elliott 1913- Who 92
**Vineyard,** Billy Dale 1931- AmMWSc 92
**Vineyard,** Harriett Anderson 1932- WhoRel 92
**Vineyard-Beets,** Peggy Ann 1954- WhoMW 92
**Vinge,** Joan D 1948- IntAu&W 91, TwCSFW 91, WrDr 92
**Vinge,** Vernor 1944- TwCSFW 91, WrDr 92
**Vinge,** Vernor Steffen 1944- IntAu&W 91
**Vingiello,** Frank Anthony 1921- AmMWSc 92
**Vinh,** Nguyen Xuan 1930- AmMWSc 92
**Vinha,** Luiz Augusto Nogueira 1926- WhoFI 92
**Vinhage,** William August 1960- WhoFI 92
**Vinich,** John Paul 1950- WhoAmP 91
**Vinick,** Fredric James 1947- AmMWSc 92
**Vinicombe,** James Morris, Jr. 1922- WhoFI 92
**Vining,** Daniel Rutledge, Jr. 1944- WhoFI 92
**Vining,** Elizabeth Gray 1902- WrDr 92
**Vining,** Joseph 1938- WhoAmL 92
**Vining,** Leo Charles 1925- AmMWSc 92
**Vining,** Linda Louise 1952- WhoAmL 92
**Vining,** Robert Luke, Jr. 1931- WhoAmL 92
**Vining,** Rowena Adelaide 1921- Who 92
**Vinje,** Mary M 1913- AmMWSc 92
**Vinkemulder,** H. Yvonne 1930- WhoAmL 92
**Vinnik,** Anatoliy Yakovlevich 1936- IntWW 91
**Vinograde,** Bernard 1915- AmMWSc 92
**Vinogradoff,** Anna Patricia AmMWSc 92
**Vinogradov,** Oleg Mikhailovich 1937- IntWW 91
**Vinogradov,** Oleg Mikhaylovich 1937- SovUnBD
**Vinogradov,** Serge 1933- AmMWSc 92
**Vinogradov,** Viktor Vladimirovich 1895-1969 SovUnBD
**Vinogradov,** Vladimir Alekseyevich 1921- IntWW 91
**Vinogradov,** Vladimir Mikhailovich 1921- IntWW 91
**Vinokur,** Marcel 1929- AmMWSc 92
**Vinokurov,** Evgeny Mikhailovich 1925- IntWW 91

**Vinokurov,** Yevgeniy Mikhaylovich 1925- *SovUnBD*
**Vinopal,** Timothy John 1959- *WhoWest 92*
**Vinores,** Stanley Anthony 1950- *AmMWSc 92*
**Vinovskis,** Maris Arved 1943- *WhoMW 92*
**Vins,** Georgiy Petrovich 1928- *SovUnBD*
**Vinson** *Who 92*
**Vinson,** Baron 1931- *Who 92*
**Vinson,** Arlone Ann 1920- *WhoAmP 91*
**Vinson,** Bernard L. 1919- *WhoFI 92*
**Vinson,** C. Roger 1940- *WhoAmL 92*
**Vinson,** Carl 1883-1981 *FacFETw*
**Vinson,** Chuck Rallen 1956- *WhoBlA 92*
**Vinson,** David Berwick 1917- *AmMWSc 92*
**Vinson,** Fred M 1890-1953 *FacFETw*
**Vinson,** Frederick Moore 1890-1953 *AmPolLe*
**Vinson,** Gerald D. 1954- *WhoMW 92*
**Vinson,** James A. 1945- *WhoFI 92*
**Vinson,** James S 1941- *AmMWSc 92*
**Vinson,** Joe Allen 1941- *AmMWSc 92*
**Vinson,** John Willis 1960- *WhoAmL 92*
**Vinson,** Julius Ceasar 1926- *WhoBlA 92*
**Vinson,** Kathryn 1911- *WrDr 92*
**Vinson,** Laurence Duncan, Jr. 1947- *WhoAmL 92*
**Vinson,** Leonard J 1915- *AmMWSc 92*
**Vinson,** Richard G 1931- *AmMWSc 92*
**Vinson,** S Bradleigh 1938- *AmMWSc 92*
**Vinson,** William Charles 1949- *WhoRel 92*
**Vinson,** William Ellis 1943- *AmMWSc 92*
**Vinson,** William T. *WhoAmL 92*
**Vinsonhaler,** Charles I 1942- *AmMWSc 92*
**Vint,** Larry Francis 1941- *AmMWSc 92*
**Vint,** Muriel Mosconi *WhoWest 92*
**Vint,** Toomas Endelevich 1944- *SovUnBD*
**Vinter,** Frederick Robert Peter 1914- *Who 92*
**Vinter,** Peter *Who 92*
**Vinters,** Harry Valdis 1950- *AmMWSc 92*
**Vinti,** John Pascal 1907- *AmMWSc 92*
**Vinton,** Alfred Merton 1938- *Who 92*
**Vinton,** Alice Helen 1942- *WhoWest 92*
**Vinton,** Arthur Dudley 1852-1906 *ScFEYrs*
**Vinton,** Bobby *WhoEnt 92*
**Vinton,** John 1937- *WhoEnt 92*
**Vinton,** Lori Jane 1961- *WhoAmL 92*
**Vinton,** Samuel R., Jr. *WhoRel 92*
**Vinton,** Will 1947- *WhoEnt 92*
**Vinyard,** Gary Lee 1949- *AmMWSc 92*
**Vinyard,** George Allen 1949- *WhoAmL 92*
**Vinyard,** Robert Austin 1945- *WhoAmP 91*
**Vinyard,** Roy George, II 1955- *WhoMW 92*
**Vinyard,** William Corwin 1922- *AmMWSc 92*
**Vinz,** Mark *DrAPF 91*
**Vinz,** Mark L. 1942- *WhoMW 92*
**Vinz,** Warren Lang 1932- *WhoRel 92*
**Vinzant,** David Gene 1963- *WhoRel 92*
**Viola,** Alfred 1928- *AmMWSc 92*
**Viola,** John Thomas 1938- *AmMWSc 92*
**Viola,** Lynne 1955- *ConAu 135*
**Viola,** Roberto Eduardo 1924- *IntWW 91*
**Viola,** Ronald Edward 1946- *AmMWSc 92*
**Viola,** Victor E. 1935- *WhoMW 92*
**Viola,** Victor E, Jr 1935- *AmMWSc 92*
**Violante,** Joseph Anthony 1950- *WhoAmL 92*
**Violante,** Michael Robert 1944- *AmMWSc 92*
**Violet,** Arlene 1943- *WhoAmP 91*
**Violet,** Charles Earl 1924- *AmMWSc 92*
**Violet,** John Richard 1946- *WhoFI 92*
**Violet,** Woodrow Wilson, Jr. 1937- *WhoWest 92*
**Violett,** Theodore Dean 1932- *AmMWSc 92*
**Violette,** Betty 1928- *WhoRel 92*
**Violette,** Elmer H 1921- *WhoAmP 91*
**Violette,** Joseph Lawrence Norman 1932- *AmMWSc 92*
**Violette,** Paul Elmer 1955- *WhoAmP 91*
**Violette,** Rodney James 1952- *WhoMW 92*
**Violi,** Paul *DrAPF 91*
**Violis,** G. *ConAu 35NR*
**Viollet,** Paul 1919- *IntWW 91*
**Vionnet,** Madeleine 1876-1975 *DcTwDes*
**Viorst,** Judith *WrDr 92*
**Viorst,** Judith 1931- *BenetAL 91*
**Viorst,** Milton 1930- *BenetAL 91, WrDr 92*
**Viot,** Jacques Edmond 1921- *IntWW 91, Who 92*
**Viot,** Pierre 1925- *IntWW 91*
**Viotti,** Giovanni Battista 1755-1824 *NewAmDM*
**Vipond,** Jonathan, III 1945- *WhoAmL 92*
**Vipont,** Charles *WrDr 92*
**Vique,** Marc J *WhoAmP 91*
**Viramontes,** Julio Cesar *WhoHisp 92*
**Virani,** Nazmudin Gulamhusein 1948- *Who 92*
**Viraraghavan,** Thiruvenkatachari 1934- *AmMWSc 92*
**Virata,** Cesar Enrique 1930- *IntWW 91*
**Virches,** Raul *BlkOlyM*
**Virden,** Mark A. 1950- *WhoMW 92*
**Virdure,** Bernel B. 1923- *WhoBlA 92*
**Virella,** Gabriel T 1943- *AmMWSc 92*
**Virelli,** Louis James, Jr. 1948- *WhoAmL 92*
**Viren,** Lasse 1949- *IntWW 91*
**Virga,** Vincent *DrAPF 91*
**Virgil,** Michael Stephen 1942- *WhoAmL 92*
**Virgil,** Ozzie 1933- *WhoHisp 92*
**Virgil,** Ozzie 1956- *WhoHisp 92*
**Virgili,** Luciano 1948- *AmMWSc 92*
**Virgils,** Katherine 1954- *TwCPaSc*
**Virgin Mary** *EncAmaz 91*
**Virginia Minstrels** *NewAmDM*
**Virgo,** Bruce Barton 1943- *AmMWSc 92*
**Virgo,** John Michael 1943- *WhoFI 92, WhoMW 92*
**Virgo,** Katherine Sue 1959- *WhoMW 92*
**Virgo,** Muriel Agnes 1924- *WhoWest 92*
**Virk,** Kashmir Singh *AmMWSc 92*
**Virkar,** Raghunath Atmaram 1930- *AmMWSc 92*
**Virkhaus,** Taavo 1934- *WhoEnt 92, WhoMW 92*
**Virkki,** Niilo 1924- *AmMWSc 92*
**Virnig,** Michael Joseph 1946- *AmMWSc 92*
**Virnstein,** Robert W 1943- *AmMWSc 92*
**Virolainen,** Johannes 1914- *IntWW 91*
**Virsaladze,** Eliso 1942- *IntWW 91*
**Virsaladze,** Simon Bagratovich 1909- *SovUnBD*
**Virta,** Nikolay Yevgeniyevich 1906- *IntWW 91*
**Virtanen,** Artturi Ilmari 1895-1973 *WhoNob 90*
**Virtue,** Jack Down 1930- *WhoMW 92*
**Virtue,** John 1947- *TwCPaSc*
**Virtue,** Noel 1947- *ConNov 91*
**Virtue,** Robert 1904- *AmMWSc 92*
**Virtue,** Thomas Goodwin 1948- *WhoWest 92*
**Visbal,** Jonathan Ralph 1957- *WhoWest 92*
**Visbord,** Edmund Marks Wolfe 1928- *IntWW 91*
**Viscardi,** Christopher James 1946- *WhoRel 92*
**Viscardi,** Peter G. 1947- *WhoFI 92*
**Visceglia,** Frank D. d1991 *NewYTBS 91*
**Vischer,** Lukas 1926- *DcEcMov*
**Visclosky,** Peter J. 1949- *AlmAP 92 [port], WhoAmP 91*
**Visclosky,** Peter John 1949- *WhoMW 92*
**Visco,** Frank Anthony 1945- *WhoAmP 91*
**Viscomi,** B Vincent 1933- *AmMWSc 92, WhoFI 92*
**Viscomi,** Gregory Phillip 1962- *WhoEnt 92*
**Visconti,** Bianca Maria 1423-1468 *EncAmaz 91*
**Visconti,** James Andrew 1939- *AmMWSc 92*
**Visconti,** Luchino 1906-1976 *FacFETw, IntDcF 2-2 [port]*
**Viscott,** David S 1938- *SmATA 65 [port], WrDr 92*
**Viscuglia,** Lisa Partice 1960- *WhoEnt 92, WhoWest 92*
**Viscusi,** Joe A 1953- *WhoAmP 91*
**Viscusi,** William G. Kip 1949- *WhoFI 92*
**Visek,** Willard James 1922- *AmMWSc 92*
**Viseltear,** Arthur Jack 1938- *AmMWSc 92*
**Visentini,** Bruno 1914- *IntWW 91*
**Vish,** Donald H. 1945- *WhoFI 92*
**Visher,** Emily B. *WhoWest 92*
**Visher,** Frank N 1923- *AmMWSc 92*
**Visher,** Glenn S 1930- *AmMWSc 92*
**Vishnevskaya,** Galina 1926- *FacFETw, NewAmDM, Who 92*
**Vishnevskaya,** Galina Pavlovna 1926- *IntWW 91, SovUnBD*
**Vishnevsky,** Valentina Michailovna *WhoEnt 92*
**Vishnevsky,** Vsevolod 1900-1951 *FacFETw*
**Vishnevsky,** Vsevolod Vital'evich 1900-1951 *SovUnBD*
**Vishniac,** Helen Simpson 1923- *AmMWSc 92*
**Vishniac,** Roman 1897-1990 *AnObit 1990, FacFETw*
**Vishnu Devananda,** Swami 1929- *RelLAm 91*
**Vishnubhotla,** Sarma Raghunadha 1946- *AmMWSc 92*
**Vishny,** Deborah Susan 1955- *WhoAmL 92*
**Visich,** Marian, Jr 1930- *AmMWSc 92*
**Visiedo,** Octavio Jesus 1951- *WhoHisp 92*
**Visintainer,** Carl Louis 1939- *WhoWest 92*
**Viskanta,** Raymond 1931- *AmMWSc 92*
**Visner,** Sidney 1917- *AmMWSc 92*
**Visor,** Julia N. 1949- *WhoBlA 92*
**Visotsky,** Harold M 1924- *AmMWSc 92*
**Visram,** Rozina 1939- *ConAu 133*
**Visscher,** Pieter Bernard 1945- *AmMWSc 92*
**Visscher,** Saralee Neumann 1929- *AmMWSc 92*
**Visscher,** William M 1928- *AmMWSc 92*
**Visser,** John Bancroft 1928- *Who 92*
**Visser,** Richard Edgar 1937- *WhoRel 92*
**Visser 't Hooft,** Willem Adolf 1900-1985 *DcEcMov [port]*
**Visseur,** Pierre 1920- *IntWW 91*
**Visson,** Lynn 1945- *ConAu 134*
**Vistbacka,** Raimo Viljam 1945- *IntWW 91*
**Viste,** Arlen E 1936- *AmMWSc 92*
**Visvanathan,** T R 1922- *AmMWSc 92*
**Viswanadham,** Ramamurthy K 1946- *AmMWSc 92*
**Viswanatha,** Thammaiah 1926- *AmMWSc 92*
**Viswanathan,** C T *AmMWSc 92*
**Viswanathan,** Chand R 1929- *AmMWSc 92*
**Viswanathan,** Kadayam Sankaran 1937- *AmMWSc 92*
**Viswanathan,** R 1938- *AmMWSc 92*
**Viswanathan,** Ramaswami *AmMWSc 92*
**Vita,** Tricia *DrAPF 91*
**Vita-Finzi,** Claudio 1936- *WrDr 92*
**Vita-Finzi,** Penelope 1939- *ConAu 133*
**Vitagliano,** Vincent J 1927- *AmMWSc 92*
**Vital,** David 1927- *WrDr 92*
**Vital,** Tina Jean 1953- *WhoFI 92*
**Vitale,** A. Perry 1940- *WhoRel 92*
**Vitale,** Alberto 1933- *IntWW 91*
**Vitale,** Elena Persis 1949- *WhoEnt 92*
**Vitale,** Gerald Lee 1950- *WhoMW 92*
**Vitale,** Ida 1923- *ConSpAP*
**Vitale,** Joseph A. 1901- *IntMPA 92*
**Vitale,** Joseph John 1924- *AmMWSc 92*
**Vitale,** Philip Albert 1952- *WhoMW 92*
**Vitale,** Richard Albert 1944- *AmMWSc 92*
**Vitale,** Robert L. 1961- *WhoAmL 92*
**Vitale,** Vincent Paul 1947- *WhoWest 92*
**Vitali,** Felice Antonio 1907- *IntWW 91*
**Vitali,** Giovanni Battista 1632-1692 *NewAmDM*
**Vitali,** Julius Michael 1952- *WhoEnt 92*
**Vitaliano,** Charles Joseph 1910- *AmMWSc 92*
**Vitaliano,** Dorothy Brauneck 1916- *AmMWSc 92*
**Vitaliano,** Eric Nicholas 1948- *WhoAmP 91*
**Vitalie,** Carl Lynn 1937- *WhoWest 92*
**Vite,** Frank Anthony 1930- *WhoFI 92, WhoMW 92*
**Vite,** Mark Steven 1956- *WhoMW 92, WhoWest 92*
**Vitek,** Donna *WrDr 92*
**Vitek,** James Allen 1958- *WhoWest 92*
**Vitello,** Peter A 1950- *AmMWSc 92*
**Viterbi,** Andrew J 1935- *AmMWSc 92*
**Viterzovic,** T. *WrDr 92*
**Vitez,** Antoine 1930-1990 *AnObit 1990*
**Vitez,** Laura 1963- *WhoEnt 92*
**Vithavong,** Jean Khamse *WhoRel 92*
**Vitiello,** Mario James 1952- *WhoIns 92*
**Vitier,** Cintio 1921- *ConSpAP*
**Vitkauskas,** Grace *AmMWSc 92*
**Vitkovits,** John A 1921- *AmMWSc 92*
**Vitkowsky,** Vincent Joseph 1955- *WhoAmL 92, WhoFI 92*
**Vitkus-McKinney,** Sally 1944- *WhoAmP 91*
**Vitols,** Visvaldis Alberts 1936- *AmMWSc 92*
**Vitoria,** Francisco de 1480-1560 *HisDSpE*
**Vitosh,** Maurice Lee 1939- *AmMWSc 92*
**Vitosky,** F. Ron 1948- *WhoRel 92*
**Vitousek,** Martin J 1924- *AmMWSc 92*
**Vitousek,** Peter Morrison 1949- *AmMWSc 92*
**Vitovec,** Franz H 1921- *AmMWSc 92*
**Vitria,** Emmanuel 1920-1987 *FacFETw*
**Vitry,** Philippe de 1291-1361 *NewAmDM*
**Vitt,** Dale Hadley 1944- *AmMWSc 92*
**Vitt,** David Aaron 1938- *WhoFI 92*
**Vitt,** Laurie Joseph 1945- *AmMWSc 92*
**Vitt,** Sam B. 1926- *WhoEnt 92, WhoFI 92*
**Vitter,** Jeffrey Scott 1955- *AmMWSc 92*
**Vittetoe,** Marie Clare 1927- *AmMWSc 92*
**Vitti,** Monica 1931- *IntWW 91*
**Vitti,** Monica 1933- *IntMPA 92*
**Vitti,** Trieste Guido 1925- *AmMWSc 92*
**Vittitoe,** Charles Norman 1934- *AmMWSc 92*
**Vittitoe,** Roger Bruce 1953- *WhoFI 92*
**Vittoria** *NewAmDM*
**Vittoria,** Carmine 1941- *AmMWSc 92*
**Vittorini,** Elio 1908-1966 *ConAu 133*
**Vittum,** Morrill Thayer 1919- *AmMWSc 92*
**Vitty,** Roderic Bemis 1933- *WhoFI 92*
**Vitu,** Thomas Leo 1961- *WhoAmL 92*
**Vitulli,** Marie Angela 1949- *WhoWest 92*
**Vitullo,** Anthony Joseph 1948- *WhoFI 92*
**Vitullo,** Victor Patrick 1939- *AmMWSc 92*
**Vitunac,** Eric Alton 1960- *WhoFI 92*
**Vitzthum,** Edward Francis 1936- *WhoMW 92*
**Vivaldi,** Antonio 1678-1741 *NewAmDM*
**Vivanco,** Luis Felipe 1907-1975 *DcLB 108 [port]*
**Vivante,** Arturo *DrAPF 91*
**Vivante,** Arturo 1923- *WrDr 92*
**Vivarelli,** Roberto 1929- *IntWW 91*
**Vivas,** David L. 1967- *WhoRel 92*
**Vivekananda,** Swami 1863-1902 *RelLAm 91*
**Vivenair,** Monsieur *ScFEYrs*
**Vivenot,** Baroness de 1907- *Who 92*
**Viverito,** Margaret E. 1963- *WhoEnt 92*
**Vivian** *Who 92*
**Vivian,** Baron d1991 *Who 92N*
**Vivian,** Baron 1935- *Who 92*
**Vivian,** Cordy Tindell 1924- *WhoBlA 92*
**Vivian,** E Charles 1882-1947 *ScFEYrs*
**Vivian,** J Edward 1913- *AmMWSc 92*
**Vivian,** Linda Bradt 1945- *WhoWest 92*
**Vivian,** Michael Hugh 1919- *Who 92*
**Vivian,** Timothy 1926- *TwCPaSc*
**Vivian,** Virginia M 1923- *AmMWSc 92*
**Vivian,** Weston Edward 1924- *WhoMW 92*
**Viviano,** Charles Anthony 1948- *WhoAmL 92*
**Viviano,** Paul Steven 1953- *WhoWest 92*
**Vivians,** Nathaniel Roosevelt 1937- *WhoBlA 92*
**Viviers,** Jacobus Cornelius 1938- *IntWW 91*
**Vivis,** Geoffrey 1944- *TwCPaSc*
**Vivo,** Paquita *WhoHisp 92*
**Vivo Acrivos,** Juana Luisa Adolfina 1928- *WhoHisp 92*
**Vivona,** Daniel Nicholas 1924- *WhoMW 92*
**Vivona,** Stefano 1919- *AmMWSc 92*
**Vizarrondo-DeSoto,** Maria Elena 1951- *WhoHisp 92*
**Vizcaino,** Henry P. 1918- *WhoFI 92*
**Vizcaino,** Jose Luis Pimental 1968- *WhoHisp 92*
**Vizcarrondo,** Ramon L. 1951- *WhoHisp 92*
**Vize,** Vladimir Yulyevich 1888-1954 *FacFETw*
**Vizenor,** Gerald 1934- *BenetAL 91, TwCWW 91, WrDr 92*
**Vizenor,** Gerald Robert *DrAPF 91*
**Vizenor,** Gerald Robert 1934- *WhoWest 92*
**Vizetelly and Company** *DcLB 106*
**Vizetelly,** Frank 1864-1938 *BenetAL 91*
**Vizinczey,** Stephen 1933- *IntAu&W 91*
**Vizquel,** Omar 1967- *WhoHisp 92*
**Vizthum,** Arthur Warren 1959- *WhoEnt 92*
**Vizueto,** Carmen Carrillo 1960- *WhoHisp 92*
**Vizy,** Kalman Nicholas 1940- *AmMWSc 92*
**Vizzini,** Carlo 1947- *IntWW 91*
**Vlaar,** Nicolaas Jacob 1933- *IntWW 91*
**Vlach,** Jeffrey Allen 1953- *WhoMW 92*
**Vlach,** Jiri 1922- *AmMWSc 92*
**Vlachopoulos,** John A 1942- *AmMWSc 92*
**Vlachos,** Evan Constantine 1935- *WhoWest 92*
**Vlack,** Robert Addison 1927- *WhoAmP 91*
**Vlad,** Alexandru 1950- *IntAu&W 91*
**Vlad,** Roman 1919- *NewAmDM*
**Vladeck,** B Charney 1886-1938 *DcAmImH*
**Vladeck,** Bruce C 1949- *AmMWSc 92*
**Vladeck,** Judith Pomarlen 1923- *WhoAmL 92*
**Vladimir,** Archbishop 1852-1933 *RelLAm 91*
**Vladimir,** Marek 1928- *WhoEnt 92*
**Vladimiroff,** Christine *WhoRel 92*
**Vladimirov,** Igor Petrovich 1919- *IntWW 91*
**Vladimirov,** Vasiliy Sergeyevich 1923- *IntWW 91*
**Vladimirsky,** Mikhail Fedorovich 1874-1951 *SovUnBD*
**Vladimov,** Georgiy Nikolaevich 1931- *SovUnBD*
**Vladimov,** Georgiy Nikolayevich 1931- *IntWW 91*
**Vladutiu,** Adrian O 1940- *AmMWSc 92*
**Vladutiu,** Georgirene Dietrich 1944- *AmMWSc 92*
**Vladutz,** George E 1928- *AmMWSc 92*
**Vladychenko,** Ivan Maximovich 1924- *IntWW 91*
**Vlahakis,** George 1923- *AmMWSc 92*
**Vlahos,** Pete 1930- *WhoAmL 92*
**Vlahoulis,** William John 1959- *WhoMW 92*
**Vlajkovic,** Radovan 1922- *IntWW 91*
**Vlaovic,** Milan Stephen 1936- *AmMWSc 92*
**Vlasak,** Walter Raymond 1938- *WhoWest 92*
**Vlasenko,** Anatoliy Aleksandrovich *IntWW 91*
**Vlases,** George Charpentier 1936- *AmMWSc 92*
**Vlasopolos,** Anca 1948- *WhoMW 92*

**Vlasov**, Aleksandr Vladimirovich 1932- *SovUnBD*
**Vlasov**, Alexander Vladimirovich 1933- *IntWW 91*
**Vlasov**, Andrei 1900-1946 *EncTR 91 [port]*
**Vlasov**, Andrei Andreyevich 1900-1946 *FacFETw*
**Vlasov**, Andrey Andreevich 1900-1946 *SovUnBD*
**Vlasov**, Yuriy Petrovich 1935- *SovUnBD*
**Vlastos**, Carol Jo 1941- *WhoAmP 91*
**Vlastos**, Gregory d1991 *NewYTBS 91*
**Vlastos**, Gregory 1907-1991 *ConAu 135*
**Vlasuk**, George P 1955- *AmMWSc 92*
**Vlatkovic**, Dusan 1938- *IntWW 91*
**Vlattas**, Isidoros 1935- *AmMWSc 92*
**Vlay**, George John 1927- *AmMWSc 92*
**Vlazny**, John George 1937- *WhoMW 92, WhoRel 92*
**Vlcek**, Donald Henry 1918- *AmMWSc 92*
**Vlcek**, Donald Joseph, Jr. 1949- *WhoMW 92*
**Vlcek**, Jan Benes 1943- *WhoAmL 92*
**Vleet Van**, William Benjamin, Jr. 1924- *WhoAmL 92*
**Vleisides**, Gregory William 1950- *WhoAmL 92, WhoMW 92*
**Vliet**, Daniel H 1921- *AmMWSc 92*
**Vliet**, Gary Clark 1933- *AmMWSc 92*
**Vlok**, Adriaan *IntWW 91*
**Vo Chi Cong** 1914- *IntWW 91*
**Vo Nguyen Giap** 1912- *FacFETw [port], IntWW 91*
**Vo Van Kiet** 1922- *IntWW 91*
**Vo**, Huu Dinh 1950- *WhoWest 92*
**Vo-Dinh**, Tuan *AmMWSc 92*
**Vo-Van**, Truong 1948- *AmMWSc 92*
**Voada** *EncAmaz 91*
**Voadicia** *EncAmaz 91*
**Voake**, Richard Charles 1940- *WhoWest 92*
**Vobach**, Arnold R 1932- *AmMWSc 92*
**Vobach**, William H. *WhoMW 92*
**Vobecky**, Josef 1923- *AmMWSc 92*
**Vobejda**, William Frank 1918- *WhoWest 92*
**Voboril**, Lorna Adele 1955- *WhoAmL 92*
**Vocci**, Frank Joseph 1924- *AmMWSc 92*
**Voccola**, Margaret Helen 1928- *WhoAmP 91*
**Vocelle**, Louis Basil, Jr 1956- *WhoAmP 91*
**Vocht**, Michelle Elise 1956- *WhoAmL 92, WhoMW 92*
**Vocke**, Merlyn C 1933- *AmMWSc 92*
**Vockell**, Edward Louis 1945- *WhoMW 92*
**Vockler**, John Charles 1924- *Who 92, WrDr 92*
**Voda**, Isadore Leon 1913- *WhoWest 92*
**Vodenik**, John Russell 1947- *WhoEnt 92*
**Vodenos**, Arna Susan 1959- *WhoEnt 92*
**Voderberg**, Kurt Ernest 1921- *WhoFI 92*
**Vodicnik**, Mary Jo 1951- *AmMWSc 92*
**Vodkin**, Lila Ott 1950- *AmMWSc 92*
**Vodkin**, Linda Maxine 1952- *WhoFI 92*
**Vodkin**, Michael Harold 1942- *AmMWSc 92*
**Vodopyanov**, Mikhail V 1900-1980 *FacFETw*
**Voedisch**, Robert W 1924- *AmMWSc 92*
**Voege**, Jeanne *DrAPF 91*
**Voegtlin**, Rex 1947- *WhoMW 92*
**Voeks**, Robert Allen 1950- *AmMWSc 92*
**Voelcker**, Christopher David 1933- *Who 92*
**Voelcker**, Herbert B 1930- *AmMWSc 92*
**Voelcker**, Hunce *DrAPF 91*
**Voelkel**, Jane Emma 1960- *WhoRel 92*
**Voelker**, Alan Morris 1938- *AmMWSc 92*
**Voelker**, C E 1923- *AmMWSc 92*
**Voelker**, Charles Robert 1944- *WhoRel 92*
**Voelker**, John D. 1903-1991 *ConAu 134, NewYTBS 91*
**Voelker**, Mary I. Van Beck 1944- *WhoMW 92*
**Voelker**, Richard William 1936- *AmMWSc 92*
**Voelker**, Robert Allen 1943- *AmMWSc 92*
**Voelker**, Robert Heth *AmMWSc 92*
**Voelker**, Roy E 1923- *WhoAmP 91*
**Voell**, Richard Allen 1933- *WhoFI 92*
**Voelly**, Richard Walter *AmMWSc 92*
**Voelz**, Frederick 1927- *AmMWSc 92*
**Voelz**, George Leo 1926- *AmMWSc 92*
**Voelz**, Michael H 1956- *AmMWSc 92*
**Voet**, Donald Herman 1938- *AmMWSc 92*
**Voet**, Judith Greenwald 1941- *AmMWSc 92*
**Voet**, Paul C. 1946- *WhoFI 92*
**Vogan**, David A, Jr 1954- *AmMWSc 92*
**Vogan**, Don Kenneth 1928- *WhoAmP 91*
**Vogan**, Eric Lloyd 1924- *AmMWSc 92*
**Vogan**, Sara *DrAPF 91*
**Vogan**, Sara d1991 *NewYTBS 91*
**Vogan**, Sara 1947-1991 *ConAu 134*
**Vogel**, Alfred Morris 1915- *AmMWSc 92*
**Vogel**, Arthur Anton 1924- *WhoMW 92, WhoRel 92*
**Vogel**, Arthur Mark *AmMWSc 92*
**Vogel**, Bernhard 1932- *IntWW 91*
**Vogel**, Carl Edward 1919- *WhoFI 92, WhoMW 92*
**Vogel**, Carl M *WhoAmP 91*
**Vogel**, Carl-Wilhelm E 1951- *AmMWSc 92*
**Vogel**, Cedric Wakelee 1946- *WhoMW 92*
**Vogel**, Charles Stimmel 1932- *WhoAmL 92*
**Vogel**, Daniel James 1960- *WhoFI 92*
**Vogel**, Denis Raymond 1950- *WhoAmL 92*
**Vogel**, Donald Sears *WhoFI 92*
**Vogel**, Eugene L. 1931- *WhoAmL 92*
**Vogel**, Eugenia Jackson 1932- *WhoRel 92*
**Vogel**, Ezra F. 1930- *WrDr 92*
**Vogel**, Francis Stephen 1919- *AmMWSc 92*
**Vogel**, George 1924- *AmMWSc 92*
**Vogel**, Gerald Lee 1943- *AmMWSc 92*
**Vogel**, Glenn Charles 1943- *AmMWSc 92*
**Vogel**, Hans *WrDr 92*
**Vogel**, Hans-Jochen 1926- *IntWW 91, Who 92*
**Vogel**, Henry 1916- *AmMWSc 92*
**Vogel**, Henry Elliott 1925- *AmMWSc 92*
**Vogel**, Howard H, Jr 1914- *AmMWSc 92*
**Vogel**, Howard Stanley 1934- *WhoAmL 92, WhoFI 92*
**Vogel**, James Alan 1935- *AmMWSc 92*
**Vogel**, James John 1935- *AmMWSc 92*
**Vogel**, Joan Elinor 1951- *WhoAmL 92*
**Vogel**, John Arnold 1962- *WhoWest 92*
**Vogel**, John H. 1944- *WhoRel 92*
**Vogel**, John Henry 1944- *WhoFI 92*
**Vogel**, John Walter 1948- *WhoAmL 92*
**Vogel**, Joyce 1957- *WhoMW 92*
**Vogel**, Julius 1835-1899 *ScFEYrs*
**Vogel**, Julius 1924- *WhoIns 92*
**Vogel**, Kathryn Giebler 1942- *AmMWSc 92*
**Vogel**, Linda Jane 1940- *WhoMW 92*
**Vogel**, Malvina Graff 1932- *WhoEnt 92*
**Vogel**, Manfred Henry 1930- *WhoRel 92*
**Vogel**, Martin 1935- *AmMWSc 92*
**Vogel**, Michael F. 1948- *WhoFI 92*
**Vogel**, Nancy *WhoMW 92*
**Vogel**, Norman William 1917- *AmMWSc 92*
**Vogel**, Orville Alvin d1991 *NewYTBS 91*
**Vogel**, Paul William 1919- *AmMWSc 92*
**Vogel**, Paula Anne 1951- *WhoEnt 92*
**Vogel**, Peter 1937- *AmMWSc 92*
**Vogel**, Philip Christian 1941- *AmMWSc 92*
**Vogel**, Ralph A 1923- *AmMWSc 92*
**Vogel**, Richard Clark 1918- *AmMWSc 92*
**Vogel**, Richard E 1930- *AmMWSc 92*
**Vogel**, Robert 1918- *WhoAmL 92*
**Vogel**, Robert 1919- *WhoFI 92*
**Vogel**, Robert Allen 1942- *WhoMW 92*
**Vogel**, Roberta Burrage 1938- *WhoBlA 92*
**Vogel**, Roger Arlen 1955- *WhoWest 92*
**Vogel**, Roger Craig 1947- *WhoEnt 92*
**Vogel**, Roger Frederick 1942- *AmMWSc 92*
**Vogel**, Rudolf 1918- *IntWW 91*
**Vogel**, Sarah *WhoAmP 91*
**Vogel**, Stefanie N *AmMWSc 92*
**Vogel**, Steven 1940- *AmMWSc 92*
**Vogel**, Steven James 1946- *WhoEnt 92*
**Vogel**, Thomas A 1937- *AmMWSc 92*
**Vogel**, Thomas Timothy 1934- *AmMWSc 92, WhoMW 92, WhoRel 92*
**Vogel**, Timothy J. 1958- *WhoMW 92*
**Vogel**, Todd William 1959- *WhoEnt 92*
**Vogel**, Veronica Lee 1943- *AmMWSc 92*
**Vogel**, Werner Paul 1923- *WhoFI 92*
**Vogel**, Willa Hope 1929- *WhoMW 92*
**Vogel**, William Alan 1951- *WhoFI 92*
**Vogel**, Willis Gene 1930- *AmMWSc 92*
**Vogel**, Winston Dan 1943- *WhoEnt 92*
**Vogel**, Wolfgang Hellmut 1930- *AmMWSc 92*
**Vogelberger**, Peter John, Jr 1932- *AmMWSc 92*
**Vogelfanger**, Elliot Aaron 1937- *AmMWSc 92*
**Vogelgesang**, Frederick Lawrence 1920- *WhoEnt 92*
**Vogelgesang**, Laura Jane 1951- *WhoAmL 92*
**Vogelhut**, Paul Otto 1935- *AmMWSc 92*
**Vogeli**, Bruce R 1929- *AmMWSc 92*
**Vogelman**, Joseph H 1920- *AmMWSc 92*
**Vogelman**, Joseph Herbert 1920- *WhoFI 92*
**Vogelman**, Lawrence Allen 1949- *WhoAmL 92*
**Vogelmann**, Hubert Walter 1928- *AmMWSc 92*
**Vogelpoel**, Pauline *Who 92*
**Vogels**, Hanns Arnt 1926- *IntWW 91*
**Vogels**, Walter Alfons 1932- *WhoRel 92*
**Vogelsang**, Arthur *DrAPF 91*
**Vogelsang**, Bernd 1928- *WhoIns 92*
**Vogelsang**, Gunter 1920- *IntWW 91*
**Vogelsang**, Judith Ayers 1945- *WhoEnt 92*
**Vogelzang**, Nicholas John 1949- *WhoMW 92*
**Vogh**, Betty Pohl 1927- *AmMWSc 92*
**Voght**, Geoffrey Michael 1945- *WhoMW 92*
**Vogl**, Otto 1927- *AmMWSc 92*
**Vogl**, Richard J 1932- *AmMWSc 92*
**Vogl**, Thomas Paul 1929- *AmMWSc 92*
**Vogler**, Albert 1877-1945 *EncTR 91 [port]*
**Vogler**, Charles C 1931- *WhoAmP 91*
**Vogler**, Georg Joseph 1749-1814 *NewAmDM*
**Vogler**, Kevin Paul 1957- *WhoWest 92*
**Vogler**, Larry B 1947- *AmMWSc 92*
**Vogler**, Robert E 1928- *WhoAmP 91*
**Vogler**, Roger James 1931- *WhoMW 92*
**Vognild**, Larry L 1932- *WhoAmP 91*
**Vogt**, Albert R 1938- *AmMWSc 92*
**Vogt**, Carl William 1936- *WhoAmL 92*
**Vogt**, Erich Wolfgang 1929- *AmMWSc 92*
**Vogt**, Evon Zartman, III 1946- *WhoWest 92*
**Vogt**, Hermann Josef 1932- *WhoRel 92*
**Vogt**, Hersleb 1912- *IntWW 91*
**Vogt**, Herwart Curt 1929- *AmMWSc 92*
**Vogt**, Hugh Frederick 1916- *WhoRel 92*
**Vogt**, John Henry 1918- *WhoMW 92*
**Vogt**, John W 1936- *WhoAmP 91*
**Vogt**, Kristiina Ann 1949- *AmMWSc 92*
**Vogt**, Linda L. 1949- *WhoMW 92*
**Vogt**, Martha Diane 1952- *WhoAmL 92*
**Vogt**, Marthe Louise 1903- *IntWW 91, Who 92*
**Vogt**, Molly Thomas 1939- *AmMWSc 92*
**Vogt**, Peter K. 1932- *IntWW 91*
**Vogt**, Peter Klaus 1932- *AmMWSc 92*
**Vogt**, Peter Richard 1939- *AmMWSc 92*
**Vogt**, Rochus E 1929- *AmMWSc 92*
**Vogt**, Rochus Eugen 1929- *WhoWest 92*
**Vogt**, Steven Scott 1949- *AmMWSc 92*
**Vogt**, Thomas Clarence, Jr 1932- *AmMWSc 92*
**Vogt**, Thomas R. 1945- *WhoFI 92*
**Vogt**, William G 1931- *AmMWSc 92*
**Vogt Lorentzen**, Fredrik 1946- *IntWW 91*
**Vogue**, Adalbert de 1924- *WhoRel 92*
**Vogue**, Robert *WhoAmP 91*
**Vohr**, John H 1934- *AmMWSc 92*
**Vohra**, Pran Nath 1919- *AmMWSc 92*
**Vohra**, Saroj Kumar 1947- *WhoFI 92*
**Vohs**, Cathy Ann 1957- *WhoAmL 92*
**Vohs**, James A 1928- *AmMWSc 92*
**Vohs**, James Arthur 1928- *IntWW 91*
**Vohs**, Paul Anthony, Jr 1931- *AmMWSc 92*
**Voice**, Jack Wilson, Jr. 1945- *WhoWest 92*
**Voichick**, Michael 1934- *AmMWSc 92*
**Voiculescu**, Dan Dumitru 1946- *WhoFI 92*
**Voige**, William Huntley 1947- *AmMWSc 92*
**Voight**, Barry 1937- *AmMWSc 92*
**Voight**, David K 1941- *WhoAmP 91*
**Voight**, Jerry D. 1937- *WhoAmL 92*
**Voight**, Jon 1938- *IntMPA 92, IntWW 91, WhoEnt 92*
**Voight**, Nancy Lee 1945- *WhoMW 92*
**Voigt**, Adolf F 1914- *AmMWSc 92*
**Voigt**, Charles Frederick 1942- *AmMWSc 92*
**Voigt**, Cynthia 1942- *WrDr 92*
**Voigt**, Donald Bernard 1947- *WhoWest 92*
**Voigt**, Ellen Bryant *DrAPF 91*
**Voigt**, Ellen Bryant 1943- *ConPo 91, IntAu&W 91, WrDr 92*
**Voigt**, Eva-Maria 1928- *AmMWSc 92*
**Voigt**, Friedrich 1882-1945 *EncTR 91*
**Voigt**, Gale E 1936- *WhoAmP 91*
**Voigt**, Garth Kenneth 1923- *AmMWSc 92*
**Voigt**, Gerd-Hannes *AmMWSc 92*
**Voigt**, Hans-Heinrich 1921- *IntWW 91*
**Voigt**, Harry Holmes 1931- *WhoAmL 92*
**Voigt**, Herbert Frederick 1952- *AmMWSc 92*
**Voigt**, John Jacob 1942- *WhoFI 92*
**Voigt**, John Wilbur 1920- *AmMWSc 92*
**Voigt**, Milton 1924- *IntAu&W 91, WhoWest 92, WrDr 92*
**Voigt**, Paul Warren 1940- *AmMWSc 92*
**Voigt**, Richard 1946- *WhoAmL 92*
**Voigt**, Robert Gary 1939- *AmMWSc 92*
**Voigt**, Robert Lee 1924- *AmMWSc 92*
**Voigt**, Scott Kenneth 1964- *WhoWest 92*
**Voigt**, Steven Russell 1952- *WhoAmL 92*
**Voigt**, Valerie 1953- *RelLAm 91*
**Voigt**, Walter 1938- *AmMWSc 92*
**Voigtman**, Edward Walter 1938- *WhoMW 92*
**Voinea**, Radu 1923- *IntWW 91*
**Voinovich**, George V. 1935- *AlmAP 92 [port]*
**Voinovich**, George V 1936- *WhoAmP 91, WhoMW 92*
**Voinovich**, V.N. *SovUnBD*
**Voinovich**, Vladimir 1932- *FacFETw, LiExTwC*
**Voinovich**, Vladimir Nikolayevich 1932- *IntWW 91*
**Voisard**, Walter Bryan 1925- *AmMWSc 92*
**Voisin**, Roger 1918- *NewAmDM*
**Voisinet**, James Raymond 1931- *WhoFI 92*
**Voit**, Eberhard Otto 1953- *AmMWSc 92*
**Voit**, Franz Johann, Jr. 1932- *WhoFI 92*
**Voit**, Todd K. 1961- *WhoFI 92*
**Voitle**, Robert 1919- *WrDr 92*
**Voitle**, Robert Allen 1938- *AmMWSc 92*
**Voitle**, Robert Brown 1919- *IntAu&W 91*
**Vojnovich**, Theodore 1932- *AmMWSc 92*
**Vojta**, Paul Alan 1957- *WhoWest 92*
**Vokac**, Peter Russell 1935- *WhoWest 92*
**Voke**, Richard A *WhoAmP 91*
**Vokes**, Emily Hoskins 1930- *AmMWSc 92*
**Vokes**, Harold Ernest 1908- *AmMWSc 92*
**Vokes**, Howard Dean *WhoEnt 92*
**Voketaitis**, Arnold Mathew 1930- *WhoEnt 92*
**Volans**, Kevin 1949- *ConCom 92*
**Volante**, Ralph Paul 1949- *AmMWSc 92*
**Volante**, Thomas Joseph 1956- *WhoMW 92*
**Volarich**, David Thomas 1951- *WhoMW 92*
**Volavka**, Jan 1934- *AmMWSc 92*
**Volborth**, Alexis 1924- *AmMWSc 92, WhoWest 92*
**Volbrecht**, Richard E., Jr. 1947- *WhoMW 92*
**Volbrecht**, Stanley Gordon 1923- *AmMWSc 92*
**Volcana** *EncAmaz 91*
**Volcani**, Benjamin Elazari 1915- *AmMWSc 92, WhoWest 92*
**Volcker**, Paul A. 1927- *IntWW 91, Who 92, WhoAmP 91, WhoFI 92*
**Volcker**, Paul Adolph 1927- *AmPolLe*
**Volckmann**, Peter Terrel 1941- *WhoWest 92*
**Vold**, Barbara Schneider 1942- *AmMWSc 92*
**Vold**, Carl Leroy 1932- *AmMWSc 92*
**Vold**, Marjorie Jean 1913- *AmMWSc 92*
**Vold**, Regitze Rosenorn 1937- *AmMWSc 92*
**Vold**, Robert Lawrence 1942- *AmMWSc 92*
**Voldemaras**, Augustinas 1883-1942 *BiDExR*
**Voldeng**, Albert Nelson 1938- *AmMWSc 92*
**Voldman**, Steven Howard 1957- *WhoFI 92*
**Volentine**, Kenneth Lee 1941- *WhoAmP 91*
**Volentine**, Richard J., Jr. 1955- *WhoAmL 92*
**Volesky**, Bohumil 1939- *AmMWSc 92*
**Volesky**, Ron James 1954- *WhoAmP 91*
**Volgenau**, Lewis 1940- *AmMWSc 92*
**Volger**, Hendrik Cornelis 1932- *IntWW 91, Who 92*
**Volgy**, Thomas John 1946- *WhoWest 92*
**Volgy**, Tom *WhoAmP 91*
**Volicer**, Ladislav 1935- *AmMWSc 92*
**Volin**, John Joseph 1956- *WhoAmL 92*
**Volin**, Raymond Bradford 1943- *AmMWSc 92*
**Volk**, Bob G 1943- *AmMWSc 92*
**Volk**, Bruno W 1909- *AmMWSc 92*
**Volk**, Claudia Jean 1947- *WhoFI 92*
**Volk**, Craig Francis 1951- *WhoEnt 92*
**Volk**, David Lawrence 1947- *WhoAmP 91*
**Volk**, Deborah Pensack 1959- *WhoAmL 92*
**Volk**, Ernest 1845-1919 *BiInAmS*
**Volk**, Eugene John 1931- *WhoIns 92*
**Volk**, John A 1915- *WhoAmP 91*
**Volk**, Murray Edward 1922- *AmMWSc 92*
**Volk**, Patricia *DrAPF 91*
**Volk**, Richard James 1928- *AmMWSc 92*
**Volk**, Robert Harkins 1932- *WhoWest 92*
**Volk**, Stephen Richard 1936- *WhoAmL 92*
**Volk**, Thomas Lewis 1933- *AmMWSc 92*
**Volk**, Timothy John 1962- *WhoWest 92*
**Volk**, Veril Van 1938- *AmMWSc 92*
**Volk**, Wesley Aaron 1924- *AmMWSc 92*
**Volk**, William David 1956- *WhoWest 92*
**Volkan**, Vamik 1932- *AmMWSc 92*
**Volkening-Quarternik**, Debra Lynn 1962- *WhoEnt 92*
**Volkenstein**, Mikhail Vladimirovich 1912- *IntWW 91*
**Volker**, Dale M 1940- *WhoAmP 91*
**Volker**, Eugene Jeno 1942- *AmMWSc 92*
**Volker**, Joseph Francis 1913- *AmMWSc 92*
**Volkers**, Burton Jay 1957- *WhoMW 92*
**Volkert**, Wynn Arthur 1941- *AmMWSc 92*
**Volkin**, Elliot 1919- *AmMWSc 92*
**Volkman**, Alvin 1926- *AmMWSc 92*
**Volkman**, Douglas Edward 1949- *WhoWest 92*
**Volkmann**, Frances Cooper 1935- *AmMWSc 92*
**Volkmann**, Keith Robert 1942- *AmMWSc 92*
**Volkmann**, M. Fredric 1941- *WhoMW 92*
**Volkmann**, Robert Alfred 1945- *AmMWSc 92*
**Volkmar**, Lloyd Baker 1925- *WhoRel 92*
**Volkmer**, Hans Walter 1953- *WhoMW 92*

**Volkmer**, Harold L. 1931- *AlmAP 92 [port], WhoAmP 91, WhoMW 92*
**Volkoff**, George Michael 1914- *AmMWSc 92*
**Volkonsky**, Andrei 1933- *NewAmDM*
**Volkonsky**, Andrey Mikhaylovich 1933- *SovUnBD*
**Volkov**, Alexander 1885-1942 *IntDcF 2-2*
**Volkov**, Anatole Boris 1924- *AmMWSc 92*
**Volkov**, Vladislav 1935-1971 *FacFETw*
**Volkova**, Bronislava *DrAPF 91*
**Volksen**, Willi 1950- *AmMWSc 92*
**Volkwijn**, Kay-Robert 1938- *WhoRel 92*
**Voll**, Donald Casper 1935- *WhoRel 92*
**Voll**, Mary Jane 1933- *AmMWSc 92*
**Vollack**, Anthony F *WhoAmP 91*
**Vollack**, Anthony F. 1929- *WhoAmL 92, WhoWest 92*
**Volland**, Leonard Allan 1937- *AmMWSc 92*
**Vollard**, Ambroise 1868-1939 *ThHEIm*
**Vollbeer**, Fred H. 1944- *WhoFI 92*
**Volle**, Robert Leon 1930- *AmMWSc 92*
**Vollenweider**, Richard A 1922- *AmMWSc 92*
**Vollero**, Keith Raphael 1956- *WhoFI 92*
**Volley**, Jo 1953- *TwCPaSc*
**Vollhardt**, K Peter C 1946- *AmMWSc 92*
**Vollmann**, Alan Peter 1948- *WhoAmL 92*
**Vollmann**, William T. 1959- *ConAu 134*
**Vollmar**, Arnulf R 1928- *AmMWSc 92*
**Vollmer**, Erwin Paul 1906- *AmMWSc 92*
**Vollmer**, Frederick Wolfer 1956- *AmMWSc 92*
**Vollmer**, Howard Robert 1930- *WhoMW 92*
**Vollmer**, James 1924- *AmMWSc 92*
**Vollmer**, Lulu 18--?-1955 *BenetAL 91*
**Vollmer**, Regis Robert 1946- *AmMWSc 92*
**Vollmer**, Richard Wade 1926- *WhoAmL 92*
**Vollrath**, Lutz Ernst Wolf 1936- *Who 92*
**Vollum**, Robert Boone 1933- *WhoFI 92*
**Volman**, David H 1916- *AmMWSc 92*
**Volmar**, Scott McAllister 1958- *WhoWest 92*
**Volmer**, Everett Anton 1946- *WhoFI 92*
**Volmer**, Nancy Kay 1960- *WhoWest 92*
**Volmer**, Yurii Mikhailovich 1933- *IntWW 91*
**Volney**, Carl Walter 1838- *BiInAmS*
**Volney**, Constantin-Francois, marquis de 1757-1820 *BlkwCEP*
**Volodin**, Boris Mikhailovich 1931- *IntWW 91*
**Volonte**, Gian Maria 1933- *IntMPA 92*
**Volontir**, Mikhail Yermolaevich 1934- *IntWW 91*
**Voloshin**, Arkady S 1946- *AmMWSc 92*
**Voloshin**, Maksimilyan Aleksandrovich 1878-1932 *SovUnBD*
**Voloshin**, Maximilian Alexandrovich 1877-1931 *FacFETw*
**Volp**, Rainer Wilhelm 1931- *WhoRel 92*
**Volp**, Robert Francis 1952- *AmMWSc 92*
**Volpe**, Angelo Anthony 1938- *AmMWSc 92*
**Volpe**, Edmond Loris 1922- *IntAu&W 91*
**Volpe**, Erminio Peter 1927- *AmMWSc 92*
**Volpe**, Gerald T 1935- *AmMWSc 92*
**Volpe**, Joseph J 1938- *AmMWSc 92*
**Volpe**, P J, Jr 1934- *AmMWSc 92*
**Volpe**, Richard Gerard 1950- *WhoWest 92*
**Volpe**, Robert 1926- *AmMWSc 92*
**Volpe**, Rosalind Ann 1954- *AmMWSc 92*
**Volpe**, Vernon L. 1955- *ConAu 135*
**Volpe Landi**, John Baptist, Marquis 1841-1918 *DcAmImH*
**Volpert**, Barry Stuart 1959- *WhoAmL 92*
**Volpert**, Richard Sidney 1935- *WhoAmL 92, WhoWest 92*
**Volpi**, Walter Mark 1946- *WhoAmL 92*
**Volpi di Misurata**, Giuseppe 1887-1947 *BiDExR*
**Volpin**, Aleksandr Sergeyevich 1924- *IntWW 91*
**Volpp**, Gert Paul Justus 1930- *AmMWSc 92*
**Volsky**, Arkadiy Ivanovich 1932- *IntWW 91, SovUnBD*
**Volsky**, Viktor Vatslavovich 1921- *IntWW 91*
**Voltaire** 1694-1778 *BlkwCEP, ScFEYrs*
**Voltz**, Charles Edward 1934- *WhoAmL 92*
**Voltz**, Stephen Mark 1957- *WhoAmL 92*
**Voltz**, Sterling Ernest 1921- *AmMWSc 92*
**Voltzow**, Janice 1958- *AmMWSc 92*
**Voluck**, Allan S. *WhoFI 92*
**Volwiler**, Wade 1917- *AmMWSc 92*
**Volynsky**, Isaak 1949- *WhoWest 92*
**Volz**, Arthur William 1942- *WhoRel 92*
**Volz**, Carl Andrew 1933- *WhoRel 92*
**Volz**, Eugene Richard 1932- *WhoWest 92*
**Volz**, Frederic Ernst 1922- *AmMWSc 92*
**Volz**, John Edward 1940- *AmMWSc 92*
**Volz**, John Phillip 1935- *WhoAmL 92*
**Volz**, Marlin Milton 1917- *WhoAmL 92*
**Volz**, Michael George 1945- *AmMWSc 92*
**Volz**, Paul Albert *WhoMW 92*
**Volz**, Paul Albert 1936- *AmMWSc 92*
**Volz**, Richard A 1937- *AmMWSc 92*
**Volz**, William K 1919- *AmMWSc 92*
**Volzke**, Doris Matilda 1921- *WhoAmP 91*
**vom Baur**, Francis Trowbridge 1908- *WhoAmL 92*
**vom Berg**, Haubold Otto 1952- *WhoFI 92*
**Vomachka**, Archie Joel 1946- *AmMWSc 92*
**Vomhof**, Daniel William 1938- *AmMWSc 92, WhoWest 92*
**Vomocil**, James Arthur 1926- *AmMWSc 92*
**Von**, Isaiah 1918- *AmMWSc 92*
**Vona**, Joseph Albert 1920- *AmMWSc 92*
**Von Almen**, William Frederick I 1928- *AmMWSc 92*
**von Althann**, Natica del Valle 1950- *WhoFI 92*
**Von Arb**, John J. 1952- *WhoWest 92*
**Vonarburg**, Elisabeth 1947- *TwCSFW 91A*
**Von Aulock**, Wilhelm Heinrich 1915- *AmMWSc 92*
**Von Bacho**, Paul Stephan, Jr 1937- *AmMWSc 92*
**Von Baeyer**, Adolf Johann Friedrich W 1835-1917 *WhoNob 90*
**Von Baeyer**, Hans Christian 1938- *AmMWSc 92*
**Von Bargen**, Kenneth Louis 1931- *AmMWSc 92*
**Von Baudissin**, Wolf, Graf 1907- *IntWW 91*
**Von Beckh**, Harald J. 1917- *IntWW 91*
**Von Behren**, Ronald Craig 1946- *WhoRel 92*
**von Behring**, Emil Adolph 1854-1917 *WhoNob 90*
**Von Bekesy**, Georg 1899-1972 *WhoNob 90*
**Von Berg**, Robert L 1918- *AmMWSc 92*
**von Bernuth**, Carl W. *WhoAmL 92*
**von Bittenfeld** *Who 92*
**Von Bodungen**, George Anthony 1940- *AmMWSc 92*
**Von Borstel**, Robert Carsten 1925- *AmMWSc 92*
**von Bressensdorf**, Otto 1927- *WhoFI 92*
**Von Bulow**, Andreas 1937- *IntWW 91*
**von Bulow**, Claus *FacFETw*
**Von Bun**, Friedrich Otto 1925- *AmMWSc 92*
**von Clemm**, Michael 1935- *Who 92*
**von Craigh**, Bertha Theresa 1939- *WhoRel 92*
**von dem Bussche**, Wolf 1934- *WhoWest 92*
**Vondemkamp**, Steven Joseph 1957- *WhoMW 92*
**Von Der Dunk**, Hermann Walther 1928- *IntWW 91*
**von der Esch**, Hans Ulrik 1928- *WhoFI 92*
**Vonderhaar**, Barbara Kay 1943- *AmMWSc 92*
**Vonderhaar**, James Coy 1935- *WhoFI 92*
**Vonder Haar**, Raymond A 1946- *AmMWSc 92*
**Vonderhaar**, Raymond T. 1919- *IntMPA 92*
**Vonder Haar**, Thomas Henry 1942- *AmMWSc 92*
**Vonderheid**, Arda Elizabeth 1925- *WhoWest 92*
**von der Heydt**, James Arnold 1919- *WhoAmL 92, WhoWest 92*
**Von der Porten**, Edward Paul 1933- *WhoWest 92*
**von Destinon**, Mark Alan 1956- *WhoWest 92*
**Von Dohlen**, Tim 1943- *WhoAmP 91*
**Von Dohlen**, William August, II 1954- *WhoRel 92*
**Von Dohnanyi**, Christoph 1929- *IntWW 91, WhoEnt 92, WhoMW 92*
**Von Dohnanyi**, Klaus 1928- *IntWW 91*
**Von Dohrmann**, Jean Ann 1933- *WhoAmP 91*
**Vondra**, Carl Frank 1934- *AmMWSc 92*
**Vondra**, Vladimir 1930- *IntWW 91*
**Vondrak**, Edward Andrew 1938- *AmMWSc 92*
**Vondrak**, Robert Richard 1949- *WhoWest 92*
**Von Dreele**, Robert Bruce 1943- *AmMWSc 92*
**Von Drehle**, Ramon A 1930- *WhoIns 92*
**Vondruska**, Eloise Marie 1950- *WhoMW 92*
**Von Eckardt**, Wolf 1918- *IntAu&W 91*
**Voneida**, Theodore J 1930- *AmMWSc 92, WhoMW 92*
**von Eiff**, Theodore William 1942- *WhoMW 92*
**Von Erffa**, Helmut 1900-1979 *ConAu 133*
**Von Eschen**, Garvin L 1913- *AmMWSc 92*
**Von Essen**, Carl Francois 1926- *AmMWSc 92*
**Von Euler**, Leo Hans 1931- *AmMWSc 92*
**Von Euler**, Ulf Svante *FacFETw*
**von Euler**, Ulf Svante 1905-1983 *WhoNob 90*
**von Ferstel**, Marilou McCarthy 1937- *WhoMW 92*
**von Frisch**, Karl 1886-1982 *WhoNob 90*
**vonFuhrmann**, Eric Loraine 1933- *WhoMW 92*
**von Furstenberg**, Betsy 1931- *WhoEnt 92*
**von Furstenberg**, George Michael 1941- *WhoMW 92*
**Von Gencsy**, Eva 1924- *WhoEnt 92*
**Von Gierke**, Henning Edgar 1917- *AmMWSc 92*
**von Glahn**, Gerhard Ernst 1911- *WrDr 92*
**Von Goeler**, Eberhard 1930- *AmMWSc 92*
**Von Gonten**, Douglas 1934- *AmMWSc 92*
**Von Gonten**, Kevin Paul 1949- *WhoRel 92*
**Von Graffenried**, Christoph *DcAmImH*
**Vongsay**, Kithong 1937- *IntWW 91*
**Von Gutfeld**, Robert J 1934- *AmMWSc 92*
**Von Hagen**, D Stanley 1937- *AmMWSc 92*
**von Harz**, James Lyons 1915- *WhoFI 92*
**von Hase**, Karl-Gunther 1917- *Who 92*
**Von Hassel**, George A 1929- *WhoIns 92*
**von Hassell**, Fey 1918- *ConAu 134*
**Von Heidenstam**, Carl Gustaf Verner 1859-1940 *WhoNob 90*
**von Heimburg**, Roger Lyle 1931- *WhoMW 92*
**Von Herff**, Ferdinand 1820-1912 *DcAmImH*
**vonHernried Ritter vonWasel-Waldingau**, P *WhoEnt 92*
**Von Herzen**, Richard P 1930- *AmMWSc 92*
**Von Heune**, Friedrich 1929- *NewAmDM*
**Von Hippel**, Arthur R 1898- *AmMWSc 92*
**Von Hippel**, Frank 1937- *AmMWSc 92*
**Von Hippel**, Peter Hans 1931- *AmMWSc 92, WhoWest 92*
**Von Hirschberg**, C. F. G. 1926- *IntWW 91*
**Von Hoerner**, Sebastian 1919- *AmMWSc 92*
**von Hoffman**, Nicholas 1929- *ConAu 34NR, WrDr 92*
**von Hoffmann**, William Gerard, III 1956- *WhoAmL 92*
**von Huene**, Roland 1929- *AmMWSc 92*
**Von Hungen**, Kern 1940- *AmMWSc 92*
**von Kalinowski**, Julian Onesime 1916- *WhoAmL 92, WhoFI 92, WhoWest 92*
**Von Klitzing**, Klaus 1943- *AmMWSc 92, IntWW 91, Who 92, WhoNob 90*
**Von Korff**, Richard Walter 1916- *AmMWSc 92*
**von Krenner**, Walther G. 1940- *WhoWest 92*
**von Kunheim**, Eberhard 1928- *Who 92*
**von Lang**, Frederick William 1929- *WhoMW 92*
**Von Laue**, Theodore H. 1916- *WrDr 92*
**Von Leden**, Hans Victor 1918- *AmMWSc 92*
**von Leitis**, Gregorij Hirt 1944- *WhoEnt 92*
**von Leyden**, Wolfgang 1911- *WrDr 92*
**Von Lichtenberg**, Franz 1919- *AmMWSc 92*
**von Linsowe**, Marina Dorothy 1952- *WhoFI 92*
**Von Losberg**, Les *DrAPF 91*
**Von Losch**, Maria Magdalena 1904- *WhoEnt 92*
**von Mallinckrodt**, Georg Wilhelm 1930- *Who 92*
**Von Maltzahn**, Wolf W 1946- *AmMWSc 92*
**Von Manteuffel**, Hasso 1897-1978 *FacFETw*
**Von Meerwall**, Ernst Dieter 1940- *AmMWSc 92*
**Von Mehren**, Arthur Taylor 1922- *IntAu&W 91, WhoAmL 92, WrDr 92*
**von Mehren**, Robert Brandt 1922- *WhoAmL 92*
**Von Minden**, Merle *WhoAmP 91*
**Von Minden**, Milton Charles, Jr. 1936- *WhoWest 92*
**von Molnar**, Anina 1967- *WhoEnt 92*
**Von Molnar**, Stephan 1935- *AmMWSc 92*
**Vonnegut**, Bernard 1914- *AmMWSc 92*
**Vonnegut**, Kurt *DrAPF 91*
**Vonnegut**, Kurt 1922- *BenetAL 91, IntAu&W 91*
**Vonnegut**, Kurt, Jr. 1922- *ConNov 91, CurBio 91 [port], FacFETw, IntWW 91, ShSCr 8 [port], TwCSFW 91, Who 92, WhoEnt 92, WrDr 92*
**Von Neida**, Allyn Robert 1932- *AmMWSc 92*
**Von Neumann**, John 1903-1957 *FacFETw, RComAH*
**Von Noorden**, Gunter Konstantin 1928- *AmMWSc 92*
**Von Ohain**, Hans Joachim 1911- *AmMWSc 92*
**Von Ostwalden**, Peter Weber 1923- *AmMWSc 92*
**Von Otter**, Anne Sofie 1955- *IntWW 91*
**Von Passenheim**, John Burr 1964- *WhoAmL 92*
**Von Raab**, William 1942- *WhoAmP 91*
**Von-Recklinghausen**, Daniel R 1925- *AmMWSc 92*
**Von Reichbauer**, Peter *WhoAmP 91*
**von Reitzenstein**, Hans-Joachim Freiherr *Who 92*
**von Rhein**, John Richard 1945- *WhoEnt 92*
**Von Rheinwald**, Eva 1932- *WhoWest 92*
**von Richthofen**, Hermann 1933- *Who 92*
**Von Riesemann**, Walter Arthur 1930- *AmMWSc 92, WhoWest 92*
**Von Riesen**, Daniel Dean 1943- *AmMWSc 92*
**Von Roenn**, Kelvin Alexander 1949- *WhoMW 92*
**Von Rohr**, Jerry Stanford 1945- *WhoMW 92*
**Von Rosenberg**, Dale Ursini 1928- *AmMWSc 92*
**von Rosenberg**, H E 1926- *AmMWSc 92*
**Von Rosenberg**, Joseph Leslie, Jr 1932- *AmMWSc 92*
**von Rosenvinge**, Tycho Tor 1942- *AmMWSc 92*
**Von Rothkirch**, Edward 1919- *IntMPA 92*
**Von Ruck**, Hurley *ScFEYrs*
**Von Rumker**, Rosmarie 1926- *AmMWSc 92*
**von Sadovszky**, Otto Joseph 1925- *WhoWest 92*
**VonSchimmelmann**, Ronald Harold 1940- *WhoFI 92*
**von Schlabrendorff**, Fabian 1907-1980 *FacFETw*
**Von Schlabrendorff**, Fabian Gotthard H. 1944- *IntWW 91*
**Von Schonfeldt**, Hilmar Armin 1937- *AmMWSc 92*
**von Schramek**, Eric 1921- *Who 92*
**von Schubert**, Andreas 1922- *WhoFI 92*
**Von Schweinitz**, Lewis David *BiInAmS*
**von Seldeneck**, Judith Metcalfe 1940- *WhoFI 92*
**Vonsovskiy**, Sergey Vasiliyevich 1910- *IntWW 91*
**Von Stackelberg**, Peter 1953- *IntAu&W 91*
**Von Stade**, Frederica 1945- *FacFETw, IntWW 91, NewAmDM*
**von Sternberg**, Josef 1894-1969 *IntDcF 2-2 [port]*
**von Sternberg**, Nicholas Josef 1951- *WhoEnt 92*
**von Stietencron**, Heinrich H. 1933- *WhoRel 92*
**Von Strandtmann**, Maximillian 1927- *AmMWSc 92*
**Von Stroh**, Gordon E. 1943- *WhoFI 92*
**von Stroheim**, Erich 1885-1957 *IntDcF 2-2 [port]*
**Von Stryk**, Frederick George 1912- *AmMWSc 92*
**von Studnitz**, Gilbert Alfred 1950- *WhoWest 92*
**vonSuttner**, Bertha Felicie Sophie Kinsky 1843-1914 *WhoNob 90*
**Von Sydow**, Max 1929- *IntMPA 92, WhoEnt 92*
**Von Tersch**, Lawrence W 1923- *AmMWSc 92*
**Von Thaden**, Arthur Gregg 1932- *WhoFI 92*
**Von Tilsit**, Heidemarie 1944- *WhoWest 92*
**Von Tilzer**, Harry 1872-1946 *NewAmDM*
**Von Trapp**, Maria 1905-1987 *FacFETw*
**Von Trotta**, Margarethe 1942- *IntAu&W 91, IntDcF 2-2 [port], IntMPA 92, IntWW 91*
**Von Turkovich**, Branimir F 1924- *AmMWSc 92*
**VonVoigtlander**, Philip Friedrich 1946- *AmMWSc 92*
**von Wahlde**, Urban Camillus 1941- *WhoRel 92*
**von Wechmar**, Rudiger 1923- *Who 92*
**Von Weihe**, Darlene Goltry 1945- *WhoMW 92*
**von Weizsacker**, Carl-Friedrich 1912- *Who 92*
**Von Weizsacker**, Ernst Ulrich 1939- *WhoRel 92*
**von Weizsacker**, Richard 1920- *Who 92*
**Von Wilpert**, Gero 1933- *IntWW 91*
**Von Winbush**, Samuel 1932- *AmMWSc 92*
**Von Winkle**, William A 1928- *AmMWSc 92*
**von Winterfeldt**, Dominik 1937- *Who 92*
**Von Wright**, Victor, Sr. 1953- *WhoWest 92*
**von Wyss**, Marc Robert 1931- *WhoMW 92*
**von Zellen**, Bruce Walfred 1922- *AmMWSc 92*
**Von Zerneck**, Frank 1940- *IntMPA 92*
**von Zerneck**, Frank Ernest 1940- *WhoEnt 92*
**Von Zinzendorf**, Nicholas Louis *DcAmImH*
**von Zweck**, Dina *DrAPF 91*
**Voogt**, James Leonard 1944- *AmMWSc 92*

**Voois,** Judy Ann 1957- *WhoEnt 92*
**Vook,** Frederick Ludwig 1931- *AmMWSc 92*
**Vook,** Richard Werner 1929- *AmMWSc 92*
**Voorhees,** Burton Hamilton 1942- *AmMWSc 92*
**Voorhees,** Donald 1903-1989 *FacFETw*
**Voorhees,** Edward Burnett 1856-1911 *BiInAmS*
**Voorhees,** Frank Ray 1935- *AmMWSc 92*
**Voorhees,** Howard R 1921- *AmMWSc 92*
**Voorhees,** John E 1929- *AmMWSc 92*
**Voorhees,** John Henry 1936- *WhoBlA 92*
**Voorhees,** John James 1938- *AmMWSc 92*
**Voorhees,** Kent Jay 1943- *AmMWSc 92*
**Voorhees,** Larry Donald 1946- *AmMWSc 92*
**Voorhees,** Lorraine Isobel 1947- *WhoWest 92*
**Voorhees,** Mark William 1953- *WhoEnt 92*
**Voorhees,** Peter Willis 1955- *AmMWSc 92*
**Voorhees,** Raymond Carl 1947- *WhoRel 92*
**Voorhees,** Richard A. 1953- *WhoMW 92*
**Voorhees,** Richard Lesley 1941- *WhoAmL 92*
**Voorhees,** Vernon W, II 1942- *WhoIns 92*
**Voorhess,** Mary Louise 1926- *AmMWSc 92*
**Voorhies,** Alexis, Jr 1899- *AmMWSc 92*
**Voorhies,** E. Gregory 1952- *WhoAmL 92*
**Voorhies,** John Davidson 1933- *AmMWSc 92*
**Voorhies,** Michael Reginald 1941- *AmMWSc 92*
**Voorhoeve,** Rudolf Johannes Herman 1938- *AmMWSc 92*
**Voos,** Jane Rhein 1927- *AmMWSc 92*
**Voos,** Kenneth August 1951- *WhoWest 92*
**Voos,** Paula Beth 1949- *WhoFI 92, WhoMW 92*
**Voots,** Richard Joseph 1921- *AmMWSc 92*
**Vopat,** William A 1910- *AmMWSc 92*
**Vora,** Ashok 1947- *WhoFI 92*
**Vora,** Manu Kishandas 1945- *WhoMW 92*
**Vora,** Motilal 1928- *IntWW 91*
**Voran,** Joel Bruce 1952- *WhoAmL 92*
**Vorburger,** Jean-Louis 1958- *WhoFI 92*
**Vorchheimer,** Norman 1935- *AmMWSc 92*
**Vore,** Marvin Esli 1945- *WhoWest 92*
**Vore,** Mary Edith 1947- *AmMWSc 92*
**Voreades,** Demetrios 1942- *AmMWSc 92*
**Vorenberg,** James 1928- *WhoAmL 92*
**Vorenberg,** Stephen Carl 1943- *WhoFI 92*
**Vorhauer,** Delia Villegas 1940- *WhoHisp 92*
**Vorhaus,** James Louis 1950- *AmMWSc 92*
**Vorhaus,** William G., Jr. d1991 *NewYTBS 91*
**Vorhees,** Charles V 1948- *AmMWSc 92*
**Vorherr,** Helmuth Wilhelm 1928- *AmMWSc 92*
**Vorhies,** Carl Brad 1949- *WhoWest 92*
**Vorhies,** Jack McKim 1923- *WhoMW 92*
**Vorhies,** John Rolland 1944- *WhoMW 92*
**Vorhis,** Robert C 1917- *AmMWSc 92*
**Vorholt,** Jeffrey Joseph 1953- *WhoFI 92*
**Vories,** Dennis Lynn 1952- *WhoWest 92*
**Vories,** Eugene Capps 1923- *WhoAmP 91*
**Voris,** David W. 1951- *WhoFI 92*
**Voris,** Harold K 1940- *AmMWSc 92*
**Voris,** William 1924- *WhoFI 92, WhoWest 92*
**Vorisek,** Jan Vaclav 1791-1825 *NewAmDM*
**Vork,** Amy Jean *WhoMW 92*
**Vornberger,** Charles Calvin 1950- *WhoEnt 92*
**VornDick,** William Thomas 1950- *WhoEnt 92*
**Vornle von Haagenfels,** John P. 1958- *WhoFI 92*
**Vorobev,** Arkadiy Nikitich 1924- *SovUnBD*
**Vorobyov,** Ivan Alekseyevich 1921- *IntWW 91*
**Voronaev,** Ivan Yefimovich 1886-1940? *SovUnBD*
**Voronin,** Lev Alekseyevich 1928- *IntWW 91*
**Voronkov,** Mikhail Grigorevich 1921- *IntWW 91*
**Voronov,** Avenir Arkadyevich 1910- *IntWW 91*
**Voronov,** Gennadiy Ivanovich 1910- *SovUnBD*
**Voronsky,** Aleksandr Konstantinovich 1884-1943 *SovUnBD*
**Voronsky,** Alexander Konstantinovich 1884-1935 *FacFETw*
**Vorontsov,** Yuliy Mikhailovich 1929- *IntWW 91*
**Voropayev,** Mikhail Gavrilovich 1919- *IntWW 91*
**Voros,** Gerald John 1930- *WhoFI 92*
**Voroshilov,** Kliment Efremovich 1881-1969 *FacFETw*
**Voroshilov,** Kliment Yefremovich 1881-1969 *SovUnBD*
**Vorosmarti,** James, Jr 1935- *AmMWSc 92*
**Vorotnikov,** Vitaliy Ivanovich 1926- *IntWW 91, SovUnBD*
**Vorpagel,** Wilbur Charles 1926- *WhoWest 92*
**Vorse,** Mary Heaton 1874-1966 *BenetAL 91*
**Vorst,** James J 1942- *AmMWSc 92*
**Vorster,** B J 1915-1983 *FacFETw*
**Vorster,** Gordon 1924- *ConAu 133*
**Vortman,** L J 1920- *AmMWSc 92*
**Vortuba,** Jan 1938- *AmMWSc 92*
**Vorys,** Arthur I 1923- *WhoIns 92*
**Vorys,** Arthur Isaiah 1923- *WhoAmL 92, WhoMW 92*
**Vos,** Bert John *AmMWSc 92*
**Vos,** David Adam 1960- *WhoEnt 92*
**Vos,** Geoffrey Michael 1927- *Who 92*
**Vos,** Hubert Daniel 1933- *WhoFI 92*
**Vos,** Kenneth Dean 1935- *AmMWSc 92*
**Vosburg,** David Lee 1930- *AmMWSc 92*
**Vosburg,** Noble E. 1941- *WhoWest 92*
**Vosburgh,** James 1955- *WhoWest 92*
**Vosburgh,** Kirby Gannett 1944- *AmMWSc 92*
**Vose,** Harry L 1927- *WhoAmP 91*
**Voshall,** Roy Edward 1933- *AmMWSc 92*
**Voska,** Kathryn Caples 1942- *WhoMW 92*
**Voskanyan,** Grant Mushegovich 1924- *IntWW 91*
**Vosko,** Seymour H 1929- *AmMWSc 92*
**Voskuhl,** Sean 1966- *WhoAmP 91*
**Vosler-Hunter,** Richard William 1954- *WhoWest 92*
**Voso,** Deborah Elizabeth 1950- *WhoFI 92*
**Vosper,** F Kent 1921- *WhoAmP 91*
**Voss,** Anne Coble 1946- *AmMWSc 92, WhoMW 92*
**Voss,** August Eduardovich 1916- *IntWW 91*
**Voss,** Avgust Eduardovich 1916- *SovUnBD*
**Voss,** Bernard Jerome 1911- *WhoWest 92*
**Voss,** Carl Hermann 1910- *WhoRel 92*
**Voss,** Charles Henry, Jr 1926- *AmMWSc 92*
**Voss,** Edward Groesbeck 1929- *AmMWSc 92*
**Voss,** Edward William, Jr 1933- *AmMWSc 92*
**Voss,** Gilbert Lincoln 1918- *AmMWSc 92*
**Voss,** Gordon Owen 1938- *WhoAmP 91*
**Voss,** Henry David 1950- *AmMWSc 92*
**Voss,** Jack Donald 1921- *WhoAmL 92, WhoFI 92*
**Voss,** James Leo 1934- *AmMWSc 92*
**Voss,** Johann Heinrich 1751-1826 *BlkwCEP*
**Voss,** Katherine Evelyn 1957- *WhoMW 92*
**Voss,** Kathryn Ann 1933- *WhoRel 92*
**Voss,** Kenneth Edwin 1946- *AmMWSc 92*
**Voss,** Marcus Joseph 1943- *WhoRel 92*
**Voss,** Paul Joseph 1943- *AmMWSc 92*
**Voss,** Regis D 1931- *AmMWSc 92*
**Voss,** Richard Frederick 1948- *AmMWSc 92*
**Voss,** Richard William 1950- *WhoRel 92*
**Voss,** William Charles 1937- *WhoFI 92*
**Vosseler,** Harriet Elaine 1928- *WhoWest 92*
**Vossen,** John Louis 1937- *AmMWSc 92*
**Vostal,** Jaroslav Joseph 1927- *AmMWSc 92*
**Vosti,** Donald Curtis 1927- *AmMWSc 92*
**Votary,** R. E. *WhoRel 92*
**Votava,** Cari Lynn 1957- *WhoAmL 92, WhoFI 92*
**Votava,** Thomas Anthony 1925- *WhoMW 92*
**Votaw,** Carmen Delgado *WhoHisp 92*
**Votaw,** Charles Isac 1933- *AmMWSc 92*
**Votaw,** Dow 1920- *WrDr 92*
**Votaw,** Robert Barnett 1939- *AmMWSc 92*
**Votaw,** Robert Grimm 1938- *AmMWSc 92*
**Voth,** Alden H. 1926- *WhoWest 92*
**Voth,** Andrew C. 1947- *WhoWest 92*
**Voth,** David Richard 1941- *AmMWSc 92*
**Voth,** Harold Moser 1922- *AmMWSc 92*
**Voth,** Richard Theodore 1942- *WhoWest 92*
**Votta,** Ferdinand, Jr 1916- *AmMWSc 92*
**Vouel,** Raymond d1987 *Who 92N*
**Vouel,** Raymond 1923- *IntWW 91*
**Vouga,** Francois 1948- *WhoRel 92*
**Vought,** Eldon Jon 1935- *AmMWSc 92*
**Vought,** John Mark, Jr. 1937- *WhoRel 92*
**Vought,** Robert Howard 1920- *AmMWSc 92*
**Voulgaropoulos,** Emmanuel 1931- *AmMWSc 92*
**Voulkos,** Peter 1924- *WhoWest 92, WorArt 1980*
**Voultsos-Vourtzis,** Pericles Count 1910- *WhoEnt 92*
**Vounas,** Ronald R 1936- *WhoIns 92*
**Vournakis,** John Nicholas 1939- *AmMWSc 92*
**Vouros,** Paul 1938- *AmMWSc 92*
**Vourvopoulos,** George 1936- *AmMWSc 92*
**Voute,** William Joseph 1938- *WhoFI 92*
**Voutsas,** Alexander Matthew 1923- *AmMWSc 92, WhoFI 92*
**Vouyiouklis,** Dorothy *WhoFI 92*
**Vovakis,** Lewis Harry 1934- *WhoAmL 92*
**Vowell,** Jack 1927- *WhoAmP 91*
**Vowell,** Jeff D. 1952- *WhoFI 92*
**Vowell,** Julia Ann 1960- *WhoMW 92*
**Vowell,** Larry Kay 1944- *WhoRel 92*
**Vowles,** Paul Foster 1919- *Who 92*
**Voxman,** Himie 1912- *WhoEnt 92*
**Voxman,** William L 1939- *AmMWSc 92*
**Voyle,** Mary *IntAu&W 91X*
**Voyles,** Mark Clyde 1948- *WhoWest 92*
**Voyles,** Richard Meredith 1962- *WhoWest 92*
**Voyles,** Robb Lawrence 1957- *WhoAmL 92*
**Voynovich,** Vladimir Nikolaevich 1932- *SovUnBD*
**Voysey,** C.F.A. 1857-1941 *DcTwDes*
**Voysey,** Reginald George *Who 92*
**Voytko,** M. Mercedes 1931- *WhoRel 92*
**Voytsik,** Ada Ignat'evna 1905- *SovUnBD*
**Voytuk,** James A 1936- *AmMWSc 92*
**Voyvodic,** Louis 1921- *AmMWSc 92*
**Voznesensky,** Andrei A 1933- *FacFETw*
**Voznesensky,** Andrey Andreevich 1933- *SovUnBD*
**Voznesensky,** Andrey Andreyevich 1933- *IntWW 91*
**Voznesensky,** Nicholas Alekseyevich 1903-1950 *FacFETw*
**Voznesensky,** Nikolay Alekseevich 1903-1950 *SovUnBD*
**Vozoff,** Keeva 1928- *AmMWSc 92*
**Vraalsen,** Tom Eric 1936- *IntWW 91*
**Vracarich,** Carol Ocile 1944- *WhoEnt 92*
**Vradenburg,** Beatrice White 1922- *WhoEnt 92, WhoWest 92*
**Vradenburg,** George, III *WhoAmL 92*
**Vradenburg,** Trish 1946- *WhoEnt 92*
**Vrakas,** Daniel P *WhoAmP 91*
**Vrakatitsis,** Zoe 1919- *WhoAmP 91*
**Vrana,** Norman M 1920- *AmMWSc 92*
**Vranas,** William Paul 1950- *WhoMW 92*
**Vrandecic-Dwyer,** Aurelia Maria 1950- *WhoHisp 92*
**Vranic,** Mladen 1930- *AmMWSc 92*
**Vranicar,** Gregory Leonard 1950- *WhoAmL 92*
**Vranish,** Luise Shelley 1914- *WhoAmP 91*
**Vranitzky,** Franz 1937- *IntWW 91*
**Vratil,** John Logan 1945- *WhoAmL 92*
**Vratsanos,** Spyros M 1920- *AmMWSc 92*
**Vratusa,** Anton 1915- *IntWW 91*
**Vrba,** Frederick John 1949- *AmMWSc 92*
**Vrbanac,** John James 1949- *AmMWSc 92*
**Vrbancic,** John Emerick 1955- *WhoMW 92*
**Vrbovska-Saitta,** Anca *DrAPF 91*
**Vrdolyak,** Edward Robert 1937- *WhoAmP 91*
**Vrdolyak,** Victor 1932- *WhoAmP 91*
**Vrebalovich,** Thomas 1926- *AmMWSc 92*
**Vredeling,** Hendrikus 1924- *Who 92*
**Vredeling,** Henk 1924- *IntWW 91*
**Vredenburgh,** Dorothy McElroy *IntWW 91*
**Vredeveld,** Nicholas Gene 1929- *AmMWSc 92*
**Vredevoe,** Donna Lou 1938- *AmMWSc 92*
**Vredevoe,** Lawrence A 1940- *AmMWSc 92*
**Vree,** Roger Allen 1943- *WhoAmL 92*
**Vreeken,** Johannes 1929- *IntWW 91*
**Vreeland,** Diana Dalziel 1903?-1989 *FacFETw*
**Vreeland,** James P, Jr 1910- *WhoAmP 91*
**Vreeland,** John Allen 1925- *AmMWSc 92*
**Vreeland,** Robert Wilder 1923- *WhoWest 92*
**Vreeland,** Russell Glenn 1960- *WhoFI 92*
**Vreeland,** Ruth Marianne 1935- *WhoAmP 91*
**Vreeland,** Susan *DrAPF 91*
**Vreeland,** Thad, Jr 1924- *AmMWSc 92*
**Vreeland,** Therese Jennings 1959- *WhoEnt 92*
**Vreeland,** Valerie Jane 1943- *AmMWSc 92*
**Vreman,** Hendrik Jan 1939- *AmMWSc 92*
**Vrenios,** Anastasios Nicholas 1940- *WhoEnt 92*
**Vrentas,** Christine Mary 1953- *AmMWSc 92*
**Vrentas,** James Spiro 1936- *AmMWSc 92*
**Vrettakos,** Nikiforos d1991 *NewYTBS 91*
**Vreugdenhil,** Ralph Lyle 1940- *WhoRel 92*
**Vreuls,** Diane *DrAPF 91*
**Vreven,** Alfred 1937- *IntWW 91*
**Vrhovec,** Josip 1926- *IntWW 91*
**Vrieland,** Gail Edwin 1938- *AmMWSc 92*
**Vriens,** Gerard N 1924- *AmMWSc 92*
**Vries,** Egbert de 1901- *IntWW 91*
**Vries,** Klaas de 1944- *ConCom 92*
**Vriesen,** Calvin W 1916- *AmMWSc 92*
**Vriesman,** Todd L. 1956- *WhoAmL 92*
**Vrigny,** Roger 1920- *IntWW 91*
**Vrijenhoek,** Robert Charles 1946- *AmMWSc 92*
**Vroman,** Barbara *DrAPF 91*
**Vroman,** Hugh Egmont 1928- *AmMWSc 92*
**Vroman,** Leo 1915- *AmMWSc 92*
**Vroom,** Alan Heard 1920- *AmMWSc 92*
**Vroom,** David Archie 1941- *AmMWSc 92*
**Vroom,** Victor H. 1932- *WrDr 92*
**Vroon,** Donald Richard 1942- *WhoEnt 92*
**Vroon,** Peter R *WhoAmP 91*
**Vruggink,** Elmer H. 1928- *WhoMW 92*
**Vruggink,** Faith Marlene 1951- *WhoMW 92*
**Vryonis,** Speros, Jr. 1928- *WhoWest 92*
**Vsevolod** *WhoRel 92*
**V'Soske,** Stanislav 1900-1983 *DcTwDes*
**Vu Van Mau** 1914- *IntWW 91*
**Vu,** Hung Viet 1955- *WhoWest 92*
**Vu,** Jean-Pierre 1934- *WhoFI 92*
**Vu,** Truc Quang 1959- *WhoWest 92*
**Vucanovich,** Barbara F. 1921- *AlmAP 92 [port], WhoAmP 91*
**Vucanovich,** Barbara Farrell 1921- *WhoWest 92*
**Vuchetich,** Yevgeniy Viktorovich 1908-1974 *SovUnBD*
**Vuchic,** Vukan R 1935- *AmMWSc 92*
**Vucich,** M G 1926- *AmMWSc 92*
**Vucinich,** Vuk *DcAmImH*
**Vuckovic,** Vladeta 1923- *AmMWSc 92*
**Vuich,** Rose Ann *WhoAmP 91, WhoWest 92*
**Vuillaume,** Jean-Baptiste 1798-1875 *NewAmDM*
**Vuille,** Georges-Alain 1948- *IntMPA 92*
**Vuillemin,** Joseph J 1934- *AmMWSc 92*
**Vuillequez,** Jean J. d1991 *NewYTBS 91 [port]*
**Vuilleumier,** Francois 1938- *AmMWSc 92*
**Vujic,** Jasmina Ljubomir 1953- *WhoMW 92*
**Vukasin,** John Peter, Jr. 1928- *WhoAmL 92, WhoWest 92*
**Vukasovich,** Mark Samuel 1927- *AmMWSc 92*
**Vukov,** Rastko 1942- *AmMWSc 92*
**Vukovic,** Drago Vuko 1934- *WhoFI 92*
**Vukovich,** Fred Matthew 1939- *AmMWSc 92*
**Vukovich,** Joseph John 1945- *WhoAmP 91*
**Vukovich,** Robert Anthony 1943- *AmMWSc 92*
**Vukovich,** Thomas Walter 1952- *WhoMW 92*
**Vuksic,** Nelly 1938- *WhoHisp 92*
**Vuksta,** Michael Joseph 1926- *WhoWest 92*
**Vulgamore,** Melvin L. 1935- *WhoMW 92*
**Vulich,** Joseph Frank, Jr. 1953- *WhoEnt 92*
**Vulk,** Raymond Paul, Sr 1943- *WhoAmP 91*
**Vulliamy,** Edward 1876-1962 *TwCPaSc*
**Vulliamy,** Shirley *Who 92*
**Vulliemoz,** Yvonne *AmMWSc 92*
**Vullo,** William Joseph 1933- *AmMWSc 92*
**Vunderink,** Ralph William 1939- *WhoRel 92*
**Vunibobo,** Berenado 1932- *IntWW 91*
**Vuong Van Bac** 1927- *IntWW 91*
**Vuong,** Lynette Dyer 1938- *IntAu&W 91*
**Vuono,** Carl E. 1934- *IntWW 91*
**Vuorilehto,** Simo 1930- *IntWW 91*
**Vuoristo,** Osmo Jalmari 1929- *IntWW 91*
**Vurek,** Gerald G 1935- *AmMWSc 92*
**Vurek,** Ruth Kathryn 1932- *WhoAmP 91*
**Vurich,** John David 1946- *WhoWest 92*
**Vurobaravu,** Nikenike 1951- *IntWW 91*
**Vuskovic,** Leposava 1941- *AmMWSc 92*
**Vvedensky,** Aleksandr Ivanovich 1904-1941 *SovUnBD*
**Vyalov,** Konstantin Aleksandrovich 1900-1976 *SovUnBD*
**Vyalyas,** Vaino Iosipovich 1931- *IntWW 91*
**Vyalyas,** Vayno Iosipovich 1931- *SovUnBD*
**Vyas,** Brijesh 1948- *AmMWSc 92*
**Vyas,** Girish Narmadashankar 1933- *AmMWSc 92*
**Vyas,** Ravindra Kantilal 1935- *AmMWSc 92*
**Vyas,** Reeta 1953- *AmMWSc 92*
**Vyborny,** Carl Joseph 1950- *AmMWSc 92, WhoMW 92*
**Vydelingum,** Nadarajen Ameerdanaden 1945- *AmMWSc 92*
**Vyden,** John Keith 1933- *WhoWest 92*
**Vye,** John Quentin 1942- *WhoFI 92*
**Vye,** Malcolm Vincent 1936- *AmMWSc 92*
**Vynnychenko,** Volodymyr 1880-1951 *LiExTwC*
**Vyse,** Edward D. H. *Who 92*
**Vyshinsky,** Andrei Yanuaryevich 1883-1954 *FacFETw*
**Vyshinsky,** Andrey Yanuarovich 1883-1955 *SovUnBD*
**Vysotsky,** Vladimir Semenovich 1938-1980 *SovUnBD*
**Vytal,** James Alfred 1936- *WhoFI 92*
**Vyvyan,** John 1916- *Who 92*

# W

**W.** *NewAmDM*
**Waack,** Richard 1931- *AmMWSc 92*
**Waack,** Richard Eugene 1923- *WhoAmP 91*
**Waag,** Charles Joseph 1931- *AmMWSc 92*
**Waag,** Robert Charles 1938- *AmMWSc 92*
**Waage,** Frederick O. *DrAPF 91*
**Waage,** Jonathan King 1944- *AmMWSc 92*
**Waage,** Karl Mensch 1915- *AmMWSc 92*
**Waage,** Mervin Bernard 1944- *WhoAmL 92*
**Waagenaar,** Sam 1908- *IntAu&W 91, WrDr 92*
**Waaland,** Irving T 1927- *AmMWSc 92*
**Waaland,** Joseph Robert 1943- *AmMWSc 92*
**Waaler,** Bjarne Arentz 1925- *IntWW 91*
**Waalkes,** T Phillip 1919- *AmMWSc 92*
**Waanders,** Gerald L. 1944- *WhoWest 92*
**Waara,** Maria Esther 1930- *WhoMW 92*
**Waart,** Edo de 1941- *NewAmDM*
**Waarvik,** Karen Marie 1955- *WhoWest 92*
**Waas,** Julie Rebecca Reby 1961- *WhoAmL 92*
**Waas,** Norman Murray 1961- *WhoAmL 92*
**Wabeck,** Charles J 1938- *AmMWSc 92*
**Waber,** Bernard 1924- *WrDr 92*
**Waber,** James Thomas 1920- *AmMWSc 92*
**Wabler,** Robert Charles, II 1948- *WhoFI 92*
**Wachbrit,** Jill Barrett 1955- *WhoWest 92*
**Wachel,** Martin James, Jr. 1933- *WhoWest 92*
**Wachholz,** Bruce William 1936- *AmMWSc 92*
**Wachman,** Harold Yehuda 1927- *AmMWSc 92*
**Wachman,** Murray 1931- *AmMWSc 92*
**Wachner,** Linda Joy 1946- *WhoFI 92, WhoWest 92*
**Wachowski,** Theodore John 1907- *WhoMW 92*
**Wachs,** Alan Leonard 1959- *AmMWSc 92*
**Wachs,** Gerald N 1937- *AmMWSc 92*
**Wachs,** Kate Mary *WhoMW 92*
**Wachs,** Melvin Walter 1933- *AmMWSc 92*
**Wachs,** Saul Philip 1931- *WhoRel 92*
**Wachsberger,** Clyde Phillip 1945- *WhoEnt 92*
**Wachsberger,** Phyllis Rachelle *AmMWSc 92*
**Wachsman,** Joseph T 1927- *AmMWSc 92*
**Wachsmann,** Konrad 1901-1980 *DcTwDes*
**Wachsmuth,** Charles 1829-1896 *BiInAmS*
**Wachsmuth,** Robert William 1942- *WhoAmL 92*
**Wachspress,** Eugene Leon 1929- *AmMWSc 92*
**Wachtel,** Albert 1939- *WhoEnt 92*
**Wachtel,** Allen W 1925- *AmMWSc 92*
**Wachtel,** Chuck *DrAPF 91*
**Wachtel,** Eleanor 1947- *ConAu 134*
**Wachtel,** Jeffrey Leigh 1953- *WhoEnt 92*
**Wachtel,** Marion Merriman d1991 *NewYTBS 91*
**Wachtel,** Norman Jay 1941- *WhoAmL 92*
**Wachtel,** Paul Spencer 1947- *ConAu 133*
**Wachtel,** Stephen Shoel 1937- *AmMWSc 92*
**Wachtel,** Wendie Lynn 1953- *WhoFI 92*
**Wachtell,** Esther *WhoEnt 92*
**Wachtell,** George Peter 1923- *AmMWSc 92*
**Wachtell,** Marc James 1954- *WhoAmL 92*
**Wachtell,** Richard L 1920- *AmMWSc 92*
**Wachtell,** Thomas 1928- *WhoFI 92, WhoWest 92*
**Wachter,** Eberhard 1929- *IntWW 91*
**Wachter,** Joseph Edward 1933- *WhoMW 92*
**Wachter,** Michael L. 1943- *WhoAmL 92, WhoFI 92*
**Wachter,** Oralee 1935- *WrDr 92*
**Wachter,** Ralph Franklin 1918- *AmMWSc 92*
**Wachter,** Robert Dale 1947- *WhoFI 92*
**Wachtl,** Carl 1906- *AmMWSc 92*
**Wachtler,** Sol *WhoAmP 91*
**Wachtler,** Sol 1930- *WhoAmL 92*
**Wachtman,** John Bryan, Jr 1928- *AmMWSc 92*
**Wachtman,** Lynn R *WhoAmP 91*
**Wachtmeister,** Wilhelm Hans Frederik 1923- *IntWW 91*
**Wack,** Paul Edward 1919- *AmMWSc 92*
**Wackenhut,** George Russell 1919- *WhoFI 92*
**Wackenhut,** Richard Russell 1947- *WhoFI 92*
**Wacker,** Frederick Glade, Jr. 1918- *WhoFI 92*
**Wacker,** George Adolf 1939- *AmMWSc 92*
**Wacker,** John Frederick 1954- *WhoWest 92*
**Wacker,** Margaret Morrissey 1951- *WhoFI 92*
**Wacker,** Waldon Burdette 1923- *AmMWSc 92*
**Wacker,** Warren Ernest Clyde 1924- *AmMWSc 92*
**Wacker,** William Dennis 1941- *AmMWSc 92*
**Wackerbarth,** Estela S. 1944- *WhoAmL 92*
**Wackerle,** Frederick William 1939- *WhoFI 92, WhoMW 92*
**Wackerle,** Jerry Donald 1930- *AmMWSc 92*
**Wackernagel,** Hans Beat 1931- *AmMWSc 92*
**Wackett,** Lawrence Philip 1954- *WhoMW 92*
**Wackman,** Peter Husting 1928- *AmMWSc 92*
**Wada,** George 1927- *AmMWSc 92*
**Wada,** James Yasuo 1934- *AmMWSc 92*
**Wada,** Juhn A 1924- *AmMWSc 92*
**Wada,** Richard Yutaka 1938- *WhoAmL 92*
**Wada,** Walter W 1919- *AmMWSc 92*
**Wadati,** Kiyoo 1902- *IntWW 91*
**Waddell,** Alexander 1913- *Who 92*
**Waddell,** C.G. *TwCPaSc*
**Waddell,** Charles Lindy 1932- *WhoAmP 91*
**Waddell,** Charles M. 1938- *WhoBlA 92*
**Waddell,** Charles Noel 1922- *AmMWSc 92*
**Waddell,** Evelyn Margaret 1918- *IntAu&W 91, WrDr 92*
**Waddell,** Gary Evans 1950- *WhoAmP 91*
**Waddell,** Gordon Herbert 1937- *IntWW 91, Who 92*
**Waddell,** Henry Thomas 1918- *AmMWSc 92*
**Waddell,** Jack 1923- *WhoWest 92*
**Waddell,** James 1914- *Who 92*
**Waddell,** James Madison, Jr 1922- *WhoAmP 91*
**Waddell,** Kidd M 1937- *AmMWSc 92*
**Waddell,** Martin 1941- *ConAu 34NR, IntAu&W 91, WrDr 92*
**Waddell,** Mathis Theron, Jr 1941- *WhoAmP 91*
**Waddell,** Oliver W. 1930- *WhoFI 92, WhoMW 92*
**Waddell,** Phillip Dean 1948- *WhoAmL 92*
**Waddell,** R. Eugene 1932- *WhoRel 92*
**Waddell,** Richard Lord, Jr. 1936- *WhoRel 92*
**Waddell,** Richard W *WhoAmP 91*
**Waddell,** Robert Clinton 1921- *AmMWSc 92, WhoMW 92*
**Waddell,** Robert Gregory 1939- *WhoAmL 92*
**Waddell,** Robert P 1948- *WhoAmP 91*
**Waddell,** Theodore R. 1934- *WhoBlA 92*
**Waddell,** Thomas Groth 1944- *AmMWSc 92*
**Waddell,** Walter Harvey 1947- *AmMWSc 92*
**Waddell,** William Angus 1924- *Who 92*
**Waddell,** William Joseph 1929- *AmMWSc 92*
**Waddell,** William Robert 1940- *WhoAmL 92*
**Waddell-Dill,** Mildred 1939- *WhoMW 92*
**Wadden,** Christopher David 1959- *WhoFI 92*
**Wadden,** Richard Albert *AmMWSc 92*
**Wadden,** Thomas Antony 1952- *AmMWSc 92*
**Waddill,** Van Hulen 1947- *AmMWSc 92*
**Waddilove,** Lewis Edgar 1914- *Who 92*
**Waddington** *Who 92*
**Waddington,** Baron 1929- *IntWW 91, Who 92*
**Waddington,** Bette Hope *WhoEnt 92*
**Waddington,** Cecil Jacob 1929- *AmMWSc 92*
**Waddington,** David James 1932- *Who 92*
**Waddington,** Donald Van Pelt 1931- *AmMWSc 92*
**Waddington,** Gary Lee 1944- *WhoWest 92*
**Waddington,** Gerald Eugene 1909- *Who 92*
**Waddington,** John 1938- *AmMWSc 92*
**Waddington,** John Albert Henry 1910- *Who 92*
**Waddington,** Leslie 1934- *Who 92*
**Waddington,** Miriam 1917- *ConPo 91, IntAu&W 91, WrDr 92*
**Waddington,** Raymond 1962- *AmMWSc 92*
**Waddington,** Raymond B. 1935- *WrDr 92*
**Waddington,** Raymond Bruce 1935- *IntAu&W 91*
**Waddington,** Raymond Bruce, Jr. 1935- *WhoWest 92*
**Waddington,** Robert Murray 1927- *Who 92*
**Waddington-Feather,** John Joseph 1933- *IntAu&W 91, WrDr 92*
**Waddle,** Bradford Avon 1920- *AmMWSc 92*
**Waddle,** David Bourne 1945- *WhoRel 92*
**Waddle,** Ted W 1928- *WhoAmP 91*
**Waddles,** Charleszetta 1912- *NotBlAW 92 [port]*
**Waddles,** Charleszetta Lina 1912- *WhoBlA 92*
**Waddles,** George Wesley, Sr. 1948- *WhoBlA 92*
**Waddoups,** Michael Grant 1948- *WhoAmP 91*
**Wadds,** Jean Casselman 1920- *IntWW 91, Who 92*
**Waddy,** Arthur Robert 1943- *WhoBlA 92*
**Waddy,** Charis 1909- *WrDr 92*
**Waddy,** Lawrence Heber 1914- *IntAu&W 91, Who 92, WhoRel 92, WrDr 92*
**Waddy,** Walter James 1929- *WhoBlA 92*
**Wade** *Who 92*
**Wade,** Achille Melvin 1943- *WhoBlA 92*
**Wade,** Adelbert Elton 1926- *AmMWSc 92*
**Wade,** Adrian Paul 1960- *AmMWSc 92*
**Wade,** Alan *WrDr 92*
**Wade,** Alan Gerard 1946- *WhoEnt 92*
**Wade,** Andrew Thomas 1954- *WhoRel 92*
**Wade,** Ashton 1898- *Who 92*
**Wade,** Benjamin Franklin 1800-1878 *AmPolLe*
**Wade,** Bill *TwCWW 91, WrDr 92*
**Wade,** Brooke Nelson 1953- *WhoFI 92*
**Wade,** Bruce L. 1951- *WhoBlA 92*
**Wade,** Campbell Marion 1930- *AmMWSc 92*
**Wade,** Casey, Jr. 1930- *WhoBlA 92*
**Wade,** Charles *WhoAmP 91*
**Wade,** Charles Gary 1938- *AmMWSc 92*
**Wade,** Charles Gordon 1937- *AmMWSc 92*
**Wade,** Clarence W R 1927- *AmMWSc 92*
**Wade,** Dale A 1928- *AmMWSc 92*
**Wade,** David 1929- *IntAu&W 91*
**Wade,** David 1951- *WhoAmL 92*
**Wade,** David Carlton 1957- *WhoRel 92*
**Wade,** David Robert 1939- *AmMWSc 92*
**Wade,** Donald L 1934- *WhoIns 92*
**Wade,** Dorothy *TwCPaSc*
**Wade,** Earl Kenneth 1914- *AmMWSc 92*
**Wade,** Edwin L 1947- *IntAu&W 91*
**Wade,** Edwin Lee 1932- *WhoAmL 92, WhoMW 92*
**Wade,** Eugene Henry-Peter 1954- *WhoBlA 92*
**Wade,** George Joseph 1938- *WhoAmL 92*
**Wade,** Glen 1921- *AmMWSc 92*
**Wade,** Greta Evona 1897- *WhoAmP 91*
**Wade,** Hardon McDonald, Jr. 1933- *WhoFI 92*
**Wade,** Henry William 1918- *IntWW 91, Who 92*
**Wade,** Jacqueline E. 1940- *WhoBlA 92*
**Wade,** James Alan 1950- *WhoAmL 92*
**Wade,** James B *AmMWSc 92*
**Wade,** James Joseph 1946- *AmMWSc 92*
**Wade,** James Nathaniel 1933- *WhoBlA 92*
**Wade,** James Paul, Jr 1930- *WhoAmP 91*
**Wade,** James Robert *WhoAmL 92*
**Wade,** James Thomas 1954- *WhoWest 92*
**Wade,** Janice Elizabeth 1937- *WhoEnt 92*
**Wade,** Jennifer *WrDr 92*
**Wade,** Jere Dueffort 1935- *WhoEnt 92*
**Wade,** John Stevens *DrAPF 91*
**Wade,** John Webster 1911- *WhoAmL 92*
**Wade,** Joseph Downey 1938- *WhoBlA 92*
**Wade,** Joseph Frederick 1919- *Who 92*
**Wade,** Joyce K. 1949- *WhoBlA 92*
**Wade,** Kenneth 1932- *Who 92*
**Wade,** Kim Mache 1957- *WhoBlA 92*

**Wade,** Larry Edward 1948- *WhoRel 92*
**Wade,** Lawrence S. 1926- *WhoBlA 92*
**Wade,** Leigh d1991 *NewYTBS 91 [port]*
**Wade,** Leroy Grover, Jr 1947- *AmMWSc 92*
**Wade,** Lyndon Anthony 1934- *WhoBlA 92*
**Wade,** Martha Georgie 1939- *WhoWest 92*
**Wade,** Mary Louise Powell 1932- *WhoRel 92*
**Wade,** Mason 1913- *WrDr 92*
**Wade,** Maurice 1917- *TwCPaSc*
**Wade,** Michael George 1941- *AmMWSc 92*
**Wade,** Michael James 1942- *AmMWSc 92*
**Wade,** Michael John 1949- *AmMWSc 92*
**Wade,** Michael Robert Alexander 1945- *WhoFI 92*
**Wade,** Michael Stephen 1948- *WhoWest 92*
**Wade,** Mildred Moncrief 1926- *WhoBlA 92*
**Wade,** Norma Adams 1944- *WhoBlA 92*
**Wade,** Ormand Joseph 1939- *WhoFI 92*
**Wade,** Owen Lyndon 1921- *Who 92*
**Wade,** Patricia Lynne 1950- *WhoWest 92*
**Wade,** Patrick John 1941- *WhoWest 92*
**Wade,** Peter Allen 1946- *AmMWSc 92*
**Wade,** Peter Cawthorn 1944- *AmMWSc 92*
**Wade,** R Hunter 1916- *Who 92*
**Wade,** Rebecca Haygood 1946- *WhoMW 92*
**Wade,** Richard Archer 1930- *AmMWSc 92*
**Wade,** Robert 1920- *WrDr 92*
**Wade,** Robert Glenn 1933- *WhoFI 92*
**Wade,** Robert Harold 1920- *AmMWSc 92*
**Wade,** Robert Hirsch Beard 1916- *WhoAmP 91*
**Wade,** Robert J. 1938- *WhoAmL 92*
**Wade,** Robert Richard 1940- *WhoWest 92*
**Wade,** Robert Simson 1920- *AmMWSc 92*
**Wade,** Rodger Grant 1945- *WhoFI 92, WhoWest 92*
**Wade,** Ronald Eustace 1905- *Who 92*
**Wade,** Rosalind *IntAu&W 91*
**Wade,** Ruthven 1920- *Who 92*
**Wade,** Stephen Eric 1953- *WhoWest 92*
**Wade,** Suzanne 1938- *WhoFI 92*
**Wade,** Thomas Edward 1943- *AmMWSc 92, WhoFI 92*
**Wade,** Virginia 1945- *IntWW 91, Who 92*
**Wade,** William *Who 92*
**Wade,** William 1918- *WrDr 92*
**Wade,** William Allen 1953- *WhoFI 92*
**Wade,** William C., Jr. 1945- *WhoBlA 92*
**Wade,** William Conrad 1943- *WhoWest 92*
**Wade,** William H 1930- *AmMWSc 92*
**Wade,** William Howard 1923- *AmMWSc 92*
**Wade,** William James 1941- *WhoAmL 92*
**Wade,** William Raymond, II 1943- *AmMWSc 92*
**Wade,** Winston Jay 1938- *WhoFI 92, WhoWest 92*
**Wade-Gayles,** Gloria Jean *WhoBlA 92*
**Wade-Gery,** Robert 1929- *IntWW 91, Who 92*
**Wade of Chorlton,** Baron 1932- *Who 92*
**Wadelin,** Coe William 1927- *AmMWSc 92*
**Wadell,** Lyle H 1934- *AmMWSc 92*
**Wadenpfuhl,** Jay *WhoEnt 92*
**Wadewitz,** Nathan Rodolfo 1939- *WhoRel 92*
**Wadey,** Walter Geoffrey 1918- *AmMWSc 92*
**Wadhams,** Peter 1948- *Who 92*
**Wadhams,** Richard Ivory 1955- *WhoAmP 91*
**Wadhams,** Wayne Nathan 1946- *WhoEnt 92*
**Wadia,** Maneck S. 1931- *WrDr 92*
**Wadia,** Maneck Sorabji 1931- *WhoWest 92*
**Wadke,** Deodatt Anant 1938- *AmMWSc 92*
**Wadkins,** Charles L 1929- *AmMWSc 92*
**Wadkins,** Mack Loyd 1937- *WhoAmP 91*
**Wadkins,** Peter Charles, Sr. 1954- *WhoFI 92*
**Wadleigh,** Cecil Herbert 1907- *AmMWSc 92*
**Wadleigh,** Kenneth R 1921- *AmMWSc 92*
**Wadleigh,** Michael 1941- *IntMPA 92*
**Wadler,** Arnold L. 1943- *WhoAmL 92*
**Wadley,** M. Richard 1942- *WhoFI 92, WhoWest 92*
**Wadley,** Margil Warren 1931- *AmMWSc 92*
**Wadlin,** Martha Stedman 1937- *WhoMW 92*
**Wadlinger,** Robert Louis Peter 1932- *AmMWSc 92*
**Wadlington,** Jeff *WhoEnt 92*
**Wadlington,** W. M. 1944- *WhoFI 92, WhoWest 92*
**Wadlington,** Walter James 1931- *WhoAmL 92*
**Wadlow,** David 1950- *AmMWSc 92*
**Wadlow,** Joan Krueger 1932- *WhoWest 92*
**Wadman,** Anne Sijbe 1919- *IntAu&W 91*
**Wadman,** W Hugh 1926- *AmMWSc 92*
**Wadman,** William Wood, III 1936- *WhoFI 92, WhoWest 92*
**Wadsworth,** Charles 1929- *NewAmDM*
**Wadsworth,** Dallas Fremont 1922- *AmMWSc 92*
**Wadsworth,** Dyer Seymour 1936- *WhoAmL 92*
**Wadsworth,** Edward 1889-1949 *TwCPaSc*
**Wadsworth,** Evard William, Jr. 1941- *WhoEnt 92*
**Wadsworth,** Frank H 1915- *AmMWSc 92*
**Wadsworth,** Ginger 1945- *ConAu 134*
**Wadsworth,** Harrison M 1924- *AmMWSc 92*
**Wadsworth,** Herbert Robinson, Jr 1931- *WhoAmP 91*
**Wadsworth,** James Patrick 1940- *Who 92*
**Wadsworth,** James T. *LesBEnT 92*
**Wadsworth,** Jeffrey 1950- *AmMWSc 92*
**Wadsworth,** Karen O 1945- *WhoAmP 91*
**Wadsworth,** Kevin Warren 1948- *WhoWest 92*
**Wadsworth,** Lee Ann 1946- *WhoFI 92*
**Wadsworth,** Lonnie Adren 1946- *WhoRel 92*
**Wadsworth,** Milton E 1922- *AmMWSc 92*
**Wadsworth,** Oliver Fairfield 1838-1911 *BiInAmS*
**Wadsworth,** Robert David 1942- *WhoFI 92*
**Wadsworth,** Vivian Michael 1921- *Who 92*
**Wadsworth,** William Bingham 1934- *AmMWSc 92*
**Wadsworth,** William Steele, Jr 1927- *AmMWSc 92*
**Wadt,** Willard Rogers 1949- *AmMWSc 92*
**Waechter,** Arthur Joseph, Jr. 1913- *WhoAmL 92*
**Waehner,** Kenneth Arthur 1926- *AmMWSc 92*
**Waelbroeck,** Jean Louis 1927- *IntWW 91*
**Waelsch,** Salome G. 1907- *IntWW 91*
**Waelsch,** Salome Gluecksohn 1907- *AmMWSc 92*
**Waelti-Walters,** Jennifer 1942- *WrDr 92*
**Waesche,** R H Woodward 1930- *AmMWSc 92*
**Waetjen,** Herman Charles 1929- *WhoRel 92, WhoWest 92*
**Wafeira** *EncAmaz 91*
**Waffle,** Elizabeth Lenora 1938- *AmMWSc 92*
**Wafford,** Daniel Eugene 1950- *WhoFI 92*
**Wagaman,** Mary Davidson 1943- *WhoAmL 92*
**Wagar,** Joseph Boyanton 1949- *WhoFI 92*
**Wagar,** Willis Franklin 1936- *WhoMW 92*
**Wage,** Michael Lee 1951- *WhoMW 92*
**Wagemaker,** David Isaac 1949- *WhoFI 92, WhoWest 92*
**Wagenaar,** Bernard 1894-1971 *NewAmDM*
**Wagenaar,** Emile B 1923- *AmMWSc 92*
**Wagenaar,** Raphael Omer 1916- *AmMWSc 92, WhoMW 92*
**Wagenbach,** Gary Edward 1940- *AmMWSc 92*
**Wagenecht,** Kraig Alan 1962- *WhoMW 92*
**Wagener,** Donna Lynn 1959- *WhoMW 92*
**Wagener,** Johann Hampton 1941- *WhoWest 92*
**Wagenet,** Robert Jeffrey 1950- *AmMWSc 92*
**Wagenfeld,** Wilhelm 1900- *DcTwDes*
**Wagenhals,** Walter Lincoln 1934- *WhoWest 92*
**Wagenius,** Jean D 1941- *WhoAmP 91*
**Wagenknecht,** Burdette Lewis 1925- *AmMWSc 92*
**Wagenknecht,** Dietmar Manfred 1934- *WhoMW 92*
**Wagenknecht,** Edward 1900- *IntAu&W 91, WrDr 92*
**Wagenknecht,** John Henry 1939- *AmMWSc 92*
**Wagenseil,** Georg Christoph 1715-1777 *NewAmDM*
**Wager,** Bebo 1905-1943 *EncTR 91 [port]*
**Wager,** David Allen 1956- *WhoMW 92*
**Wager,** Jerry William 1937- *WhoWest 92*
**Wager,** John Fisher 1953- *AmMWSc 92*
**Wager,** Walter Herman 1924- *WhoEnt 92*
**Wagers,** Gardner D. 1948- *WhoAmL 92*
**Wagers,** Leonard Gordon 1959- *WhoRel 92*
**Wages,** Bennie G. 1944- *WhoEnt 92*
**Waggaman,** Mackenzie Worthington 1950- *WhoEnt 92*
**Waggener,** Craig Steven 1956- *WhoRel 92*
**Waggener,** Richard *WhoAmP 91*
**Waggener,** Robert Glenn 1932- *AmMWSc 92*
**Waggener,** Ronald E 1926- *AmMWSc 92*
**Waggener,** Susan Lee 1951- *WhoAmL 92*
**Waggener,** Theryn Lee 1941- *WhoWest 92*
**Waggener,** Thomas Barrow 1951- *AmMWSc 92*
**Waggener,** Thomas Runyan 1938- *AmMWSc 92*
**Waggener,** William Cole 1917- *AmMWSc 92*
**Waggle,** Doyle H 1939- *AmMWSc 92*
**Waggoner,** Daniel LeRoy 1934- *WhoMW 92*
**Waggoner,** David Carl 1953- *WhoWest 92*
**Waggoner,** Eugene B *AmMWSc 92*
**Waggoner,** G. Thomas 1953- *WhoRel 92*
**Waggoner,** Geoffrey Howe 1950- *WhoAmL 92*
**Waggoner,** Jack Holmes, Jr 1927- *AmMWSc 92*
**Waggoner,** James Arthur 1931- *AmMWSc 92*
**Waggoner,** James Clyde 1946- *WhoAmL 92, WhoWest 92*
**Waggoner,** James Thomas, Jr 1937- *WhoAmP 91*
**Waggoner,** Jane Byrn 1921- *WhoAmP 91*
**Waggoner,** Laine 1933- *WhoWest 92*
**Waggoner,** Lawrence William 1937- *WhoAmL 92*
**Waggoner,** Leland Tate 1916- *WhoIns 92*
**Waggoner,** Linda Suzette 1947- *WhoWest 92*
**Waggoner,** Lyle 1935- *IntMPA 92*
**Waggoner,** Paul Edward 1923- *AmMWSc 92, IntWW 91*
**Waggoner,** Phillip Ray 1943- *AmMWSc 92*
**Waggoner,** Raymond C 1930- *AmMWSc 92*
**Waggoner,** Raymond Walter 1901- *AmMWSc 92*
**Waggoner,** Richard M. 1948- *WhoMW 92*
**Waggoner,** Samuel Lee 1930- *WhoFI 92*
**Waggoner,** Wilbur J 1924- *AmMWSc 92*
**Waggoner,** William Charles 1936- *AmMWSc 92*
**Waggoner,** William Horace 1924- *AmMWSc 92*
**Wagh,** Meghanad D 1948- *AmMWSc 92*
**Wagh,** Premanand Vinayak 1934- *AmMWSc 92*
**Wagle,** Gilmour Lawrence 1922- *AmMWSc 92*
**Wagle,** Robert Fay 1916- *AmMWSc 92*
**Wagle,** Shreepad R 1931- *AmMWSc 92*
**Wagle,** Susan 1953- *WhoAmP 91*
**Wagley,** Charles d1991 *NewYTBS 91*
**Wagley,** Philip Franklin 1917- *AmMWSc 92*
**Wagman,** David S. 1951- *WhoWest 92*
**Wagman,** Gerald Howard 1926- *AmMWSc 92*
**Wagman,** Robert J 1942- *IntAu&W 91*
**Wagner,** A Keith 1953- *WhoAmP 91*
**Wagner,** Adolf 1890-1944 *BiDExR, EncTR 91 [port]*
**Wagner,** Alan *LesBEnT 92*
**Wagner,** Alan Cyril 1931- *WhoEnt 92*
**Wagner,** Alan R 1923- *AmMWSc 92*
**Wagner,** Albert Fordyce 1945- *AmMWSc 92*
**Wagner,** Alfred Lawrence 1915- *WhoAmP 91*
**Wagner,** Alvin Louis, Jr. 1939- *WhoMW 92*
**Wagner,** Andrew James 1934- *AmMWSc 92, WhoRel 92*
**Wagner,** Anne Marie 1957- *WhoAmL 92*
**Wagner,** Anneliese *DrAPF 91*
**Wagner,** Anthony 1908- *Who 92, WrDr 92*
**Wagner,** Anthony Richard 1908- *IntWW 91*
**Wagner,** Arthur Franklin 1922- *AmMWSc 92*
**Wagner,** Aubrey Joseph 1912- *AmMWSc 92, IntWW 91*
**Wagner,** Barbara F. 1940- *WhoWest 92*
**Wagner,** Bernard Meyer 1928- *AmMWSc 92*
**Wagner,** Betty Valiree 1923- *WhoMW 92*
**Wagner,** Blake Douglas 1931- *WhoRel 92*
**Wagner,** Brian Allen 1958- *WhoMW 92*
**Wagner,** Bruce Stanley 1943- *WhoFI 92*
**Wagner,** C N J 1927- *AmMWSc 92*
**Wagner,** C. Peter 1930- *WhoRel 92, WhoWest 92*
**Wagner,** Carl E 1940- *AmMWSc 92*
**Wagner,** Carl George 1943- *AmMWSc 92*
**Wagner,** Carol Anne 1942- *WhoRel 92*
**Wagner,** Charles Alan 1948- *WhoMW 92*
**Wagner,** Charles Eugene 1923- *AmMWSc 92*
**Wagner,** Charles Kenyon 1943- *AmMWSc 92*
**Wagner,** Charles Roe 1925- *AmMWSc 92*
**Wagner,** Christian Joergen 1960- *WhoWest 92*
**Wagner,** Christina Breuer 1954- *WhoFI 92*
**Wagner,** Clark L. 1932- *WhoAmL 92*
**Wagner,** Clifford Henry *AmMWSc 92*
**Wagner,** Clinton 1837-1914 *BiInAmS*
**Wagner,** Conrad 1929- *AmMWSc 92*
**Wagner,** D. William 1943- *WhoAmL 92*
**Wagner,** Daniel Hobson 1925- *AmMWSc 92*
**Wagner,** David Bruce 1952- *WhoAmP 91*
**Wagner,** David Curran 1959- *WhoFI 92*
**Wagner,** David Darley 1944- *AmMWSc 92*
**Wagner,** David H. 1926- *WhoBlA 92*
**Wagner,** David Henry 1945- *AmMWSc 92*
**Wagner,** David J. 1952- *WhoWest 92*
**Wagner,** David Loren 1942- *AmMWSc 92*
**Wagner,** Diane 1959- *WrDr 92*
**Wagner,** Donald Arthur 1963- *WhoFI 92*
**Wagner,** Donald Edward 1942- *WhoMW 92, WhoRel 92*
**Wagner,** Donald Roger 1926- *WhoFI 92*
**Wagner,** Dorothy Caroline 1917- *WhoRel 92*
**Wagner,** Dorothy Victory *WhoMW 92*
**Wagner,** E. Glenn 1953- *WhoRel 92*
**Wagner,** Edgar Waldemar 1952- *WhoMW 92*
**Wagner,** Edward D 1919- *AmMWSc 92*
**Wagner,** Edward Knapp 1940- *AmMWSc 92*
**Wagner,** Edward Michael 1951- *WhoAmL 92*
**Wagner,** Emilie C 1910- *WhoAmP 91*
**Wagner,** Eric G 1931- *AmMWSc 92*
**Wagner,** Eugene Ross 1937- *AmMWSc 92*
**Wagner,** Eugene Stephen 1934- *AmMWSc 92*
**Wagner,** Falk 1939- *IntWW 91*
**Wagner,** Florence Signaigo 1919- *AmMWSc 92*
**Wagner,** Frank A, Jr 1932- *AmMWSc 92*
**Wagner,** Frank S, Jr 1925- *AmMWSc 92*
**Wagner,** Frederic A 1938- *WhoAmP 91*
**Wagner,** Frederic Hamilton 1926- *AmMWSc 92*
**Wagner,** Frederick William 1940- *AmMWSc 92*
**Wagner,** Friedelind d1991 *NewYTBS 91*
**Wagner,** G. Keith 1929- *WhoFI 92*
**Wagner,** George Hoyt 1914- *AmMWSc 92*
**Wagner,** George Joseph 1943- *AmMWSc 92*
**Wagner,** George O *WhoAmP 91*
**Wagner,** George Richard 1933- *AmMWSc 92*
**Wagner,** Gerald C *AmMWSc 92*
**Wagner,** Gerald Gale 1941- *AmMWSc 92*
**Wagner,** Gerald Roy 1928- *AmMWSc 92*
**Wagner,** Gerhard d1990 *IntWW 91N*
**Wagner,** Gerhard 1888-1939 *EncTR 91 [port]*
**Wagner,** Gerrit Abram 1916- *IntWW 91, Who 92*
**Wagner,** Gilbert Keith 1929- *WhoIns 92*
**Wagner,** Gillian Mary Millicent 1927- *Who 92*
**Wagner,** Glenn Maris 1953- *WhoRel 92*
**Wagner,** Gustav 1911-1980 *EncTR 91*
**Wagner,** Hans 1932- *AmMWSc 92*
**Wagner,** Harold A. 1935- *WhoFI 92*
**Wagner,** Harry Henry 1933- *AmMWSc 92*
**Wagner,** Harry Mahlon 1924- *AmMWSc 92*
**Wagner,** Harvey Arthur 1905- *AmMWSc 92*
**Wagner,** Heinz Georg 1928- *IntWW 91*
**Wagner,** Henry George 1917- *AmMWSc 92*
**Wagner,** Henry N, Jr 1927- *AmMWSc 92*
**Wagner,** Herman Leon 1921- *AmMWSc 92*
**Wagner,** Hunter Owen, Jr 1930- *WhoAmP 91*
**Wagner,** J Robert 1932- *AmMWSc 92*
**Wagner,** Jack Alan 1953- *WhoMW 92*
**Wagner,** James Arthur 1939- *WhoMW 92*
**Wagner,** James Bruce, Jr 1927- *AmMWSc 92*
**Wagner,** James H., Jr. 1951- *WhoEnt 92*
**Wagner,** James Peyton 1939- *WhoAmL 92*
**Wagner,** James Richard 1946- *WhoRel 92*
**Wagner,** Jane 1935- *IntMPA 92*
**Wagner,** Jeames Arthur 1944- *AmMWSc 92*
**Wagner,** Jean 1924- *Who 92*
**Wagner,** Jenny *WrDr 92*
**Wagner,** Joan A 1935- *WhoAmP 91*
**Wagner,** John Alan 1962- *WhoMW 92*
**Wagner,** John Alexander 1935- *AmMWSc 92*
**Wagner,** John Edward 1927- *AmMWSc 92*
**Wagner,** John Edward, II 1966- *WhoRel 92*
**Wagner,** John Garnet 1921- *AmMWSc 92*
**Wagner,** John George 1942- *AmMWSc 92*
**Wagner,** John Julius 1949- *WhoFI 92*
**Wagner,** John Kyle *WhoWest 92*
**Wagner,** John Peter 1874-1955 *FacFETw*
**Wagner,** John Peter 1959- *WhoMW 92*
**Wagner,** John Philip 1940- *AmMWSc 92*
**Wagner,** John Robert 1964- *WhoMW 92*
**Wagner,** John Timothy 1952- *WhoEnt 92*
**Wagner,** John Victor 1947- *WhoIns 92*
**Wagner,** Josef 1899-1945 *BiDExR, EncTR 91 [port]*

**Wagner,** Joseph Crider 1907- *WhoMW 92*
**Wagner,** Joseph Edward 1938- *AmMWSc 92*
**Wagner,** Joseph F. 1900-1974 *NewAmDM*
**Wagner,** Judith Benita 1931- *WhoFI 92*
**Wagner,** Judith Buck 1943- *WhoWest 92*
**Wagner,** K. Peter 1923- *WhoFI 92*
**Wagner,** Karl W. 1925- *WhoMW 92*
**Wagner,** Kaye Marie 1951- *WhoEnt 92*
**Wagner,** Kenneth Lynn 1956- *WhoAmL 92*
**Wagner,** Kit Kern 1947- *AmMWSc 92*
**Wagner,** Lanny Mark 1956- *WhoRel 92*
**Wagner,** Laurence Edward 1949- *WhoFI 92*
**Wagner,** Lavern John 1925- *WhoEnt 92*
**Wagner,** Lawrence Carl 1946- *AmMWSc 92*
**Wagner,** Leslie 1943- *Who 92*
**Wagner,** Lester Thomas 1942- *WhoAmL 92*
**Wagner,** Lilya 1940- *WhoMW 92*
**Wagner,** Linda *DrAPF 91*
**Wagner,** Linda C. 1936- *WrDr 92*
**Wagner,** Lindsay *LesBEnT 92*
**Wagner,** Lindsay 1949- *IntMPA 92*
**Wagner,** Lindsay J. 1949- *WhoEnt 92*
**Wagner,** Lynn Edward 1941- *WhoAmL 92, WhoFI 92*
**Wagner,** Mark Anthony 1958- *WhoEnt 92, WhoMW 92*
**Wagner,** Martin Gerald 1942- *AmMWSc 92*
**Wagner,** Martin James 1931- *AmMWSc 92*
**Wagner,** Mary Ann 1947- *WhoMW 92*
**Wagner,** Mary Anthony 1916- *WhoRel 92*
**Wagner,** Mary Kathryn 1932- *WhoAmP 91, WhoMW 92*
**Wagner,** Maryfrances *DrAPF 91*
**Wagner,** Matthew Jon 1960- *WhoMW 92*
**Wagner,** Melvin Peter 1926- *AmMWSc 92*
**Wagner,** Michael D 1948- *WhoIns 92*
**Wagner,** Michael D 1957- *WhoAmP 91*
**Wagner,** Michael G. 1951- *ConAu 133*
**Wagner,** Michael Grafton 1935- *WhoFI 92*
**Wagner,** Michael J 1941- *WhoAmP 91*
**Wagner,** Milt *WhoBlA 92*
**Wagner,** Morris 1917- *AmMWSc 92*
**Wagner,** Neal Richard 1940- *AmMWSc 92*
**Wagner,** Norman Ernest 1935- *WhoWest 92*
**Wagner,** Norman Keith 1932- *AmMWSc 92*
**Wagner,** Orvin Edson 1930- *AmMWSc 92, WhoWest 92*
**Wagner,** Otto 1841-1918 *DcTwDes*
**Wagner,** Patricia Anthony 1937- *AmMWSc 92*
**Wagner,** Paul Dean 1937- *WhoMW 92*
**Wagner,** Peter Ewing 1929- *AmMWSc 92*
**Wagner,** Peter J 1938- *AmMWSc 92*
**Wagner,** Phil *DrAPF 91*
**Wagner,** Philip Marshall 1904- *IntWW 91*
**Wagner,** Phillip Richard 1962- *WhoEnt 92*
**Wagner,** R Thomas, Jr 1955- *WhoAmP 91*
**Wagner,** Raleigh Ernest 1945- *WhoMW 92*
**Wagner,** Ray David 1924- *WhoWest 92*
**Wagner,** Raymond James 1925- *IntMPA 92*
**Wagner,** Raymond Lee 1946- *AmMWSc 92*
**Wagner,** Raymond Thomas, Jr. 1959- *WhoAmL 92*
**Wagner,** Richard 1813-1883 *EncTR 91 [port], NewAmDM*
**Wagner,** Richard Carl 1941- *AmMWSc 92*
**Wagner,** Richard Charles 1931- *WhoIns 92*
**Wagner,** Richard Elliott 1932- *WhoWest 92*
**Wagner,** Richard Eric 1951- *WhoMW 92*
**Wagner,** Richard John 1932- *AmMWSc 92*
**Wagner,** Richard John 1936- *AmMWSc 92*
**Wagner,** Richard Lloyd 1934- *AmMWSc 92*
**Wagner,** Richard Lorraine, Jr 1936- *AmMWSc 92, WhoAmP 91*
**Wagner,** Richard S 1925- *AmMWSc 92*
**Wagner,** Robert *LesBEnT 92*
**Wagner,** Robert 1895-1945 *EncTR 91 [port]*
**Wagner,** Robert 1895-1946 *BiDExR*
**Wagner,** Robert 1930- *IntMPA 92, IntWW 91, WhoEnt 92*
**Wagner,** Robert Alan 1941- *AmMWSc 92*
**Wagner,** Robert Deuane 1960- *WhoEnt 92*
**Wagner,** Robert E 1920- *AmMWSc 92*
**Wagner,** Robert Edward 1930- *WhoAmL 92*
**Wagner,** Robert Edwin 1920- *AmMWSc 92*
**Wagner,** Robert F., Jr. 1910-1991 *CurBio 91N*
**Wagner,** Robert Ferdinand 1877-1953 *AmPolLe [port]*
**Wagner,** Robert Ferdinand 1910-1991 *NewYTBS 91 [port]*
**Wagner,** Robert G 1934- *AmMWSc 92*
**Wagner,** Robert G 1950- *AmMWSc 92*
**Wagner,** Robert H 1921- *AmMWSc 92*
**Wagner,** Robert Martin 1928- *WhoAmP 91*
**Wagner,** Robert O. 1936- *WhoFI 92*
**Wagner,** Robert Philip 1918- *AmMWSc 92*
**Wagner,** Robert Roderick 1923- *AmMWSc 92*
**Wagner,** Robert Thomas 1923- *AmMWSc 92*
**Wagner,** Robert Todd 1932- *WhoMW 92*
**Wagner,** Robert Walter 1918- *WhoEnt 92*
**Wagner,** Robert Wanner 1913- *AmMWSc 92*
**Wagner,** Robin Samuel Anton 1933- *WhoEnt 92*
**Wagner,** Roger 1914- *NewAmDM*
**Wagner,** Roger Curtis 1943- *AmMWSc 92*
**Wagner,** Roger Frances 1914- *WhoWest 92*
**Wagner,** Ron Jay 1926- *WhoRel 92*
**Wagner,** Ross Irving 1925- *AmMWSc 92*
**Wagner,** Roy Henry, III 1947- *WhoEnt 92*
**Wagner,** Rudolph Fred 1921- *WrDr 92*
**Wagner,** Ruth Joos 1933- *WhoWest 92*
**Wagner,** S. David, Jr. 1942- *WhoMW 92*
**Wagner,** Scott Raymond 1959- *WhoEnt 92*
**Wagner,** Sharon Blythe 1936- *IntAu&W 91, WrDr 92*
**Wagner,** Sheldon Leon 1929- *WhoWest 92*
**Wagner,** Sigurd 1941- *AmMWSc 92*
**Wagner,** Stanley M. 1932- *WhoRel 92*
**Wagner,** Sterling Robacker 1904- *WhoFI 92*
**Wagner,** Steven Marc 1954- *WhoFI 92*
**Wagner,** Sue Ellen 1940- *WhoAmP 91, WhoWest 92*
**Wagner,** Theodore Franklin 1921- *WhoAmP 91*
**Wagner,** Thomas Charles Gordon 1916- *AmMWSc 92*
**Wagner,** Thomas Edward 1937- *WhoMW 92*
**Wagner,** Thomas Edwards 1942- *AmMWSc 92*
**Wagner,** Thomas John 1938- *WhoFI 92*
**Wagner,** Timothy Knight 1939- *AmMWSc 92*
**Wagner,** Vallerie Denise 1959- *WhoBlA 92*
**Wagner,** Vernon E 1926- *WhoAmP 91*
**Wagner,** Vincent, Jr. 1957- *WhoMW 92*
**Wagner,** Vincent Michael 1944- *WhoEnt 92*
**Wagner,** Walter Hermann 1935- *WhoRel 92*
**Wagner,** Warren Herbert, Jr 1920- *AmMWSc 92*
**Wagner,** Wayne 1946- *WhoAmP 91*
**Wagner,** Wenceslas J. 1917- *WrDr 92*
**Wagner,** Wenceslas Joseph 1917- *IntAu&W 91*
**Wagner,** William 1796-1885 *BiInAmS*
**Wagner,** William Bradley 1949- *WhoAmL 92*
**Wagner,** William Charles 1932- *AmMWSc 92*
**Wagner,** William Edward, Jr 1925- *AmMWSc 92*
**Wagner,** William Frederick 1916- *AmMWSc 92*
**Wagner,** William Gerard 1936- *AmMWSc 92, WhoWest 92*
**Wagner,** William John 1938- *AmMWSc 92*
**Wagner,** William Lyle 1936- *WhoRel 92*
**Wagner,** William Robert 1959- *WhoAmL 92*
**Wagner,** William S 1936- *AmMWSc 92*
**Wagner,** William Sherwood 1928- *AmMWSc 92*
**Wagner,** Wiltz Walker, Jr 1939- *AmMWSc 92*
**Wagner,** Winifred 1897-1980 *EncTR 91*
**Wagner,** Wolfgang 1919- *IntWW 91, WhoEnt 92*
**Wagner-Bartak,** Claus Gunter 1937- *AmMWSc 92*
**Wagner-Martin,** Linda C 1936- *IntAu&W 91*
**Wagner Tizon,** Allan 1942- *IntWW 91*
**Wagner von Jaurregg,** Julius 1857-1940 *WhoNob 90*
**Wagnon,** Joan Davis 1940- *WhoAmP 91*
**Wagoner,** Dale E 1936- *AmMWSc 92*
**Wagoner,** Dan 1932- *IntWW 91*
**Wagoner,** David *DrAPF 91*
**Wagoner,** David 1926- *BenetAL 91, ConNov 91, ConPo 91, TwCWW 91, WrDr 92*
**Wagoner,** David Eugene 1949- *AmMWSc 92*
**Wagoner,** David Everett 1928- *WhoAmL 92, WhoWest 92*
**Wagoner,** Dorothy Millie Van Donselaar 1927- *WhoWest 92*
**Wagoner,** Glen 1927- *AmMWSc 92*
**Wagoner,** Harless D. 1918-1973 *ConAu 134*
**Wagoner,** Howard Eugene 1925- *WhoWest 92*
**Wagoner,** Porter 1927- *WhoEnt 92*
**Wagoner,** Porter 1930- *NewAmDM*
**Wagoner,** Ralph Howard 1938- *WhoMW 92*
**Wagoner,** Richard Calvin 1956- *WhoRel 92*
**Wagoner,** Robert H 1952- *AmMWSc 92*
**Wagoner,** Robert Vernon 1938- *AmMWSc 92*
**Wagoner,** Ronald Lewis 1942- *AmMWSc 92*
**Wagoner,** Thomas Frank 1952- *WhoWest 92*
**Wagoner,** Thomas Patrick 1958- *WhoFI 92*
**Wagoner,** Walter Dray, Jr. 1942- *WhoAmL 92*
**Wagoner,** William Douglas 1947- *WhoMW 92*
**Wagram,** Louis-Marie Philippe, Prince de 1883-1917 *ThHElm*
**Wagreich,** Philip Donald 1941- *AmMWSc 92, WhoMW 92*
**Wagschal,** Peter Henry 1944- *WhoWest 92*
**Wagstaff,** Blanche Shoemaker 1888- *BenetAL 91*
**Wagstaff,** Christopher John Harold 1936- *Who 92*
**Wagstaff,** David Jesse 1935- *AmMWSc 92*
**Wagstaff,** David St John Rivers 1930- *Who 92*
**Wagstaff,** Edward Malise Wynter 1930- *Who 92*
**Wagstaff,** Henry Wynter 1890- *Who 92*
**Wagstaff,** Robert Hall 1941- *WhoAmL 92*
**Wagstaff,** Samuel Standfield, Jr 1945- *AmMWSc 92*
**Wah,** Thein 1919- *AmMWSc 92*
**Wahab,** James Hatton 1920- *AmMWSc 92*
**Wahba,** Albert J 1928- *AmMWSc 92*
**Wahba,** Grace *AmMWSc 92, WhoMW 92*
**Wahdan,** Josephine Barrios 1937- *WhoHisp 92*
**Wahi,** Prem Nath 1908- *IntWW 91*
**Wahl,** A J 1920- *AmMWSc 92*
**Wahl,** Arthur Charles 1917- *AmMWSc 92*
**Wahl,** Betsy Hacker 1952- *WhoMW 92*
**Wahl,** Eberhard Wilhelm 1914- *AmMWSc 92*
**Wahl,** Edward Thomas 1957- *WhoAmL 92*
**Wahl,** Floyd Michael 1931- *AmMWSc 92, WhoWest 92*
**Wahl,** George Henry, Jr 1936- *AmMWSc 92*
**Wahl,** Gisela Antje 1946- *WhoWest 92*
**Wahl,** Howard Wayne 1935- *WhoFI 92*
**Wahl,** Jacques Henri 1932- *IntWW 91*
**Wahl,** James Warner 1947- *WhoMW 92*
**Wahl,** Jan 1933- *IntAu&W 91, WrDr 92*
**Wahl,** Jenny Bourne 1957- *WhoMW 92*
**Wahl,** Joan Constance 1921- *WhoWest 92*
**Wahl,** Jonathan Michael 1945- *AmMWSc 92*
**Wahl,** Joseph Anthony 1929- *WhoRel 92*
**Wahl,** Ken 1960- *IntMPA 92*
**Wahl,** Michael James 1952- *WhoEnt 92*
**Wahl,** Patricia Walker 1938- *AmMWSc 92*
**Wahl,** Paul 1922- *WhoFI 92*
**Wahl,** Richard Alan 1952- *WhoWest 92*
**Wahl,** Richard Leo 1952- *WhoMW 92*
**Wahl,** Robert Herman 1920- *WhoAmL 92*
**Wahl,** Rosalie E *WhoAmP 91*
**Wahl,** Rosalie E. 1924- *WhoAmL 92, WhoMW 92*
**Wahl,** Sharon Knudson 1945- *AmMWSc 92*
**Wahl,** Thomas Peter 1931- *WhoRel 92*
**Wahl,** Werner Henry 1930- *AmMWSc 92*
**Wahl,** William G 1930- *AmMWSc 92*
**Wahl,** William Henry 1848-1909 *BiInAmS*
**Wahlbeck,** Phillip Glenn 1933- *AmMWSc 92, WhoMW 92*
**Wahlberg,** Allen Henry 1933- *WhoFI 92*
**Wahlberg,** Philip Lawrence 1924- *WhoRel 92*
**Wahlbrink,** Jeff Curtis 1958- *WhoFI 92*
**Wahle,** F. Keith *DrAPF 91*
**Wahlen,** Bruce Edward 1947- *WhoWest 92*
**Wahlen,** Edwin Alfred 1919- *WhoAmL 92*
**Wahler-Edwards,** David 1951- *WhoEnt 92*
**Wahlers,** Russell Gordon 1948- *WhoMW 92*
**Wahlert,** John Howard 1943- *AmMWSc 92*
**Wahlgren,** Morris A 1929- *AmMWSc 92*
**Wahlgren,** Morris Arnold 1929- *WhoMW 92*
**Wahlgren,** Olof Gustaf Christerson 1927- *IntWW 91*
**Wahlig,** Michael Alexander 1934- *AmMWSc 92*
**Wahlmeier,** James Edward 1954- *WhoMW 92*
**Wahlquist,** Andrew F 1940- *WhoAmP 91*
**Wahlquist,** Jack R 1933- *WhoIns 92*
**Wahlquist,** Jack Rainard 1933- *WhoFI 92*
**Wahls,** Harvey E 1931- *AmMWSc 92*
**Wahls,** Myron H 1931- *WhoAmP 91*
**Wahls,** Myron Hastings 1931- *WhoBlA 92*
**Wahlstrom,** Ernest E 1909- *AmMWSc 92*
**Wahlstrom,** Harold Eugene 1947- *WhoWest 92*
**Wahlstrom,** Jarl Holger 1918- *IntWW 91, Who 92*
**Wahlstrom,** Lawrence F 1915- *AmMWSc 92*
**Wahlstrom,** Linda Nettie 1948- *WhoRel 92*
**Wahlstrom,** Norman O *WhoAmP 91*
**Wahlstrom,** Paul Burr 1947- *WhoEnt 92*
**Wahlstrom,** Richard Carl 1923- *AmMWSc 92*
**Wahnon,** Judith Mascarenhas 1943- *WhoEnt 92*
**Wahnsiedler,** Walter Edward 1947- *AmMWSc 92*
**Wahoske,** Michael James 1953- *WhoAmL 92*
**Wahr,** John Cannon 1926- *AmMWSc 92*
**Wahrhaftig,** Austin Levy 1917- *AmMWSc 92*
**Wahrhaftig,** Clyde 1919- *AmMWSc 92*
**Wai,** Chien Moo 1937- *AmMWSc 92*
**Waiaru,** Amos Stanley *Who 92*
**Waiaru,** Amos Stanley 1944- *WhoRel 92*
**Waibel,** Paul Edward 1927- *AmMWSc 92*
**Waid,** Jim 1942- *WorArt 1980 [port]*
**Waid,** Margaret Cowsar 1941- *AmMWSc 92*
**Waid,** Rex A 1933- *AmMWSc 92*
**Waid,** Ted Henry 1925- *AmMWSc 92*
**Waide,** Bevan 1936- *Who 92*
**Waide,** Jacqueline Ann 1938- *WhoWest 92*
**Waidelich,** Charles J. 1929- *IntWW 91*
**Waidelich,** D L 1915- *AmMWSc 92*
**Waidson,** Herbert Morgan 1916- *WrDr 92*
**Waife,** Sholom Omi 1919- *AmMWSc 92*
**Waigandt,** Alexander 1950- *WhoMW 92*
**Waigel,** Theodor 1939- *IntWW 91, Who 92*
**Waiguchu,** Muruku 1937- *WhoBlA 92*
**Waihee,** John D., III 1946- *AlmAP 92 [port], WhoAmP 91*
**Waihee,** John David, III 1946- *IntWW 91, WhoWest 92*
**Waikato,** Bishop of 1948- *Who 92*
**Wailand,** Adele Rosen 1949- *WhoAmL 92*
**Wailers,** The *FacFETw*
**Wailes,** Benjamin Leonard Covington 1797-1862 *BiInAmS*
**Wailes,** John Leonard 1923- *AmMWSc 92*
**Wailey,** Anthony Paul 1947- *IntAu&W 91*
**Wain,** Christopher Henry, Jr. 1951- *WhoWest 92*
**Wain,** John 1925- *CnDBLB 8 [port], ConNov 91, ConPo 91, WrDr 92*
**Wain,** John Barrington 1925- *IntAu&W 91, IntWW 91, Who 92*
**Wain,** Louis 1860-1939 *TwCPaSc*
**Wain,** Louis 1911- *Who 92*
**Wain,** Margot Crawford 1955- *WhoEnt 92*
**Wain,** Ralph Louis 1911- *IntWW 91*
**Waina,** Richard Baird 1939- *WhoWest 92*
**Wainberg,** Mark Arnold 1945- *AmMWSc 92*
**Waine,** Colin 1936- *Who 92*
**Waine,** John *Who 92*
**Waine,** Martin 1933- *AmMWSc 92*
**Wainer,** Arthur 1938- *AmMWSc 92*
**Wainer,** Cord *IntAu&W 91X*
**Wainer,** Stanley Allen 1926- *WhoWest 92*
**Wainerdi,** Richard E 1931- *AmMWSc 92*
**Wainess,** Marcia Watson 1949- *WhoFI 92, WhoWest 92*
**Wainfan,** Elsie 1926- *AmMWSc 92*
**Wainger,** Stephen *AmMWSc 92*
**Wainio,** Mark Ernest 1953- *WhoFI 92, WhoWest 92*
**Wainio,** Walter W 1914- *AmMWSc 92*
**Wainionpaa,** John William 1946- *WhoWest 92*
**Wainman,** Barbara Walden 1956- *WhoAmP 91*
**Wainright,** Carol *DrAPF 91*
**Wainscott,** James Lawrence 1957- *WhoFI 92*
**Wainscott,** Jeffrey Mize 1946- *WhoAmP 91*
**Waintal,** Fabian W. 1964- *WhoEnt 92*
**Wainwright,** Albert 1898-1943 *TwCPaSc*
**Wainwright,** Arthur William 1925- *WhoRel 92*
**Wainwright,** Carroll Livingston, Jr. 1925- *WhoAmL 92*
**Wainwright,** Charles Anthony 1933- *WhoFI 92*
**Wainwright,** Edwin 1908- *Who 92*
**Wainwright,** Geoffrey 1939- *ConAu 34NR, IntAu&W 91, WrDr 92*
**Wainwright,** Geoffrey John 1937- *Who 92*
**Wainwright,** Gloria Bessie 1950- *WhoBlA 92*
**Wainwright,** Gordon Ray 1937- *WrDr 92*
**Wainwright,** Jeffrey 1944- *ConPo 91, IntAu&W 91, WrDr 92*

**Wainwright**, John 1921- IntAu&W 91, WrDr 92
**Wainwright**, John 1943- AmMWSc 92
**Wainwright**, Jonathan 1883-1953 FacFETw
**Wainwright**, Ken TwCSFW 91
**Wainwright**, Lillian K 1923- AmMWSc 92
**Wainwright**, Oliver O'Connell 1936- WhoBlA 92
**Wainwright**, Ray M 1913- AmMWSc 92
**Wainwright**, Richard Scurrah 1918- Who 92
**Wainwright**, Robert Everard d1990 Who 92N
**Wainwright**, Rupert Charles Purchas d1991 Who 92N
**Wainwright**, Sam 1924- Who 92
**Wainwright**, Stanley D 1927- AmMWSc 92
**Wainwright**, Stephen Andrew 1931- AmMWSc 92
**Wainwright**, Stuyvesant, III 1943- WhoFI 92
**Wainwright**, Thomas Everett 1927- AmMWSc 92
**Wainwright**, William 1947- WhoAmP 91
**Wainwright**, William Lloyd AmMWSc 92
**Waisanen**, Christine M. 1949- WhoAmL 92
**Waisanen**, Melvin Lee 1946- WhoWest 92
**Waisman**, Jerry 1934- AmMWSc 92
**Waisman**, Joseph L 1919- AmMWSc 92
**Waiss**, Anthony C, Jr 1936- AmMWSc 92
**Wait**, Barbara Ellen WhoAmP 91
**Wait**, Charles Valentine 1951- WhoFI 92
**Wait**, David Francis 1933- AmMWSc 92
**Wait**, Frona Eunice 1859- ScFEYrs
**Wait**, James Richard 1924- AmMWSc 92
**Wait**, John V 1932- AmMWSc 92
**Wait**, Lucien Augustus 1846-1913 BiInAmS
**Wait**, Ronald A 1944- WhoAmP 91
**Wait**, Samuel Charles, Jr 1932- AmMWSc 92
**Wait**, Trudy Kay 1960- WhoMW 92
**Waite**, Conrad W 1938- WhoAmP 91
**Waite**, Constance Mason 1952- WhoFI 92
**Waite**, Daniel Elmer 1926- AmMWSc 92
**Waite**, Darvin Danny WhoFI 92, WhoMW 92
**Waite**, David Arthur 1950- WhoMW 92
**Waite**, Gerald Donald 1952- WhoAmL 92, WhoWest 92
**Waite**, John 1932- Who 92
**Waite**, Lawrence Wesley 1951- WhoMW 92
**Waite**, Leonard Charles 1941- AmMWSc 92
**Waite**, Morrison Remick 1816-1888 AmPolLe
**Waite**, Moseley 1936- AmMWSc 92
**Waite**, Norma Lillia 1950- WhoBlA 92
**Waite**, Norman, Jr. 1936- WhoAmL 92
**Waite**, Paul J 1918- AmMWSc 92
**Waite**, Perry D 1943- WhoAmP 91
**Waite**, Peter 1922- WrDr 92
**Waite**, Peter Busby 1922- IntAu&W 91
**Waite**, Ralph 1929- IntMPA 92, WhoEnt 92
**Waite**, Ric IntMPA 92
**Waite**, Ric 1933- WhoEnt 92
**Waite**, Stephen Holden 1936- WhoAmL 92
**Waite**, Terence Hardy 1939- IntWW 91, Who 92
**Waite**, Terry 1940- FacFETw
**Waite**, William McCastline 1939- AmMWSc 92
**Waiter**, Serge-Albert 1930- AmMWSc 92
**Waiters**, Gail Elenoria 1954- WhoBlA 92
**Waiters**, Granville S. 1961- WhoBlA 92
**Waiters**, Lloyd Winferd, Jr. 1948- WhoBlA 92
**Waites**, Candy Y 1943- WhoAmP 91
**Waites**, Robert Ellsworth 1916- AmMWSc 92
**Waites-Howard**, Shirley Jean 1948- WhoBlA 92
**Waith**, Eldridge 1918- WhoBlA 92
**Waithe**, William Irwin 1937- AmMWSc 92
**Waitkins**, George Raymond 1911- AmMWSc 92
**Waiton**, Rudolph O. 1922- WhoWest 92
**Waits**, Bert Kerr 1940- AmMWSc 92
**Waits**, Jim L. WhoRel 92
**Waits**, Thomas Alan 1949- WhoEnt 92
**Waits**, Tom 1949- IntMPA 92
**Waitt**, Don Francis 1956- WhoEnt 92
**Waitz**, Jay Allan 1935- AmMWSc 92
**Waitzman**, Daniel Robert 1943- WhoEnt 92
**Waitzman**, Morton Benjamin 1923- AmMWSc 92
**Waiwood**, Kenneth George 1947- AmMWSc 92
**Waiyaki**, Munyua 1926- IntWW 91
**Wajda**, Andrzej 1926- IntDcF 2-2 [port], IntMPA 92, IntWW 91, Who 92
**Wajda**, Edward John, II 1960- WhoMW 92
**Wajda**, Edward Stanley 1924- AmMWSc 92
**Wajda**, Isabel 1913- AmMWSc 92
**Wajert**, Sean Peter 1960- WhoAmL 92
**Wajnert**, Thomas C. 1943- WhoFI 92
**Wakatsuki**, James H. 1929- WhoAmL 92, WhoWest 92
**Wakatsuki**, James Hiroji 1929- WhoAmP 91
**Wakayama**, Yoshihiro 1945- AmMWSc 92
**Wake**, Charles Staniland 1835-1910 BiInAmS
**Wake**, David Burton 1936- AmMWSc 92, WhoWest 92
**Wake**, Henry Everett 1939- WhoMW 92
**Wake**, Hereward 1916- Who 92
**Wake**, Marvalee H 1939- AmMWSc 92
**Wake**, Marvalee Hendricks 1939- WhoWest 92
**Wake**, Neil Vincent 1948- WhoAmL 92
**Wake**, Robert Alan WhoAmL 92
**Wake**, Thomas Henry 1905- WhoFI 92
**Wakefield**, Bishop of Who 92
**Wakefield Master** RfGEnL 91
**Wakefield**, Provost of Who 92
**Wakefield**, Benton McMillin, Jr. 1920- WhoFI 92
**Wakefield**, Dan DrAPF 91
**Wakefield**, Dan 1932- ConNov 91, WhoEnt 92, WrDr 92
**Wakefield**, David WhoEnt 92
**Wakefield**, Deborah Gay 1952- WhoMW 92
**Wakefield**, Derek John 1922- Who 92
**Wakefield**, Edward Humphry 1936- Who 92
**Wakefield**, Ernest Henry 1915- AmMWSc 92, WhoMW 92
**Wakefield**, Gordon Stevens 1921- Who 92
**Wakefield**, H Russell 1888-1965 ScFEYrs
**Wakefield**, Howard 1936- WhoWest 92
**Wakefield**, Humphry Who 92
**Wakefield**, J. Alvin 1938- WhoBlA 92
**Wakefield**, John Conrad 1947- WhoRel 92
**Wakefield**, Juana Rosella 1955- WhoMW 92
**Wakefield**, Larry 1925- TwCPaSc
**Wakefield**, Lucille Marion 1925- AmMWSc 92
**Wakefield**, Norman 1929- Who 92
**Wakefield**, Peter 1922- Who 92
**Wakefield**, Peter George Arthur 1922- IntWW 91
**Wakefield**, Richard Colin 1947- WhoFI 92
**Wakefield**, Robert Chester 1925- AmMWSc 92
**Wakefield**, Shirley Lorraine 1934- AmMWSc 92
**Wakefield**, Stephen Alan 1940- WhoAmL 92
**Wakefield**, Thomas William 1954- WhoMW 92
**Wakefield**, Wesley Halpenny 1929- WhoRel 92
**Wakefield**, William Barry 1930- Who 92
**Wakeford**, Edward 1914-1973 TwCPaSc
**Wakeford**, Geoffrey Michael Montgomery 1937- Who 92
**Wakeford**, Richard 1922- Who 92
**Wakeham**, Helmut 1916- AmMWSc 92
**Wakeham**, John 1932- IntWW 91, Who 92
**Wakehurst**, Baron 1925- Who 92
**Wakehurst**, Dowager Lady 1899- Who 92
**Wakeland**, Robin Gay 1948- WhoEnt 92
**Wakeland**, William Richard 1921- AmMWSc 92
**Wakeley**, James Stuart 1950- AmMWSc 92
**Wakeley**, John 1926- Who 92
**Wakelin**, David Herbert 1940- AmMWSc 92
**Wakelin**, James Henry, Jr 1911- AmMWSc 92, WhoAmP 91
**Wakeling**, John Denis 1918- Who 92
**Wakely**, Leonard John Dean 1909- Who 92
**Wakelyn**, Phillip Jeffrey 1940- AmMWSc 92
**Wakeman**, Carolyn 1943- IntAu&W 91
**Wakeman**, Charles B 1927- AmMWSc 92
**Wakeman**, David d1991 Who 92N
**Wakeman**, Donald Lee 1929- AmMWSc 92
**Wakeman**, Douglas James 1956- WhoFI 92
**Wakeman**, Edward Offley Bertram 1934- Who 92
**Wakeman**, Evans IntAu&W 91X, WrDr 92
**Wakeman**, Frederic Evans 1937- IntAu&W 91
**Wakeman**, Frederic Evans, Jr. 1937- WrDr 92
**Wakeman**, John 1928- IntAu&W 91
**Wakeman**, John Marshall 1937- AmMWSc 92
**Wakeman**, Mary Lalley 1955- WhoAmL 92
**Wakeman**, Rick WhoEnt 92
**Wakerley**, Richard MacLennon 1942- Who 92
**Wakham**, Bernard Brock 1964- WhoWest 92
**Wakiihuri**, Douglas 1963- BlkOlyM
**Wakil**, Abdul 1945- IntWW 91
**Wakil**, Salih J AmMWSc 92
**Wakim**, Khalil Georges 1907- AmMWSc 92
**Wakim**, Najib G. WhoMW 92
**Wakimoto**, Barbara Toshiko 1954- AmMWSc 92
**Wakley**, Bertram Joseph 1917- Who 92
**Wako**, Gabriel Zubier WhoRel 92
**Wakoski**, Diane DrAPF 91
**Wakoski**, Diane 1937- BenetAL 91, ConPo 91, IntAu&W 91, WrDr 92
**Waks**, Jay Warren 1946- WhoAmL 92
**Waksberg**, Armand L AmMWSc 92
**Waksberg**, Joseph 1915- AmMWSc 92
**Wakschlag**, Milton Samuel 1955- WhoAmL 92
**Waksman**, Byron Halstead 1919- AmMWSc 92
**Waksman**, Selman Abraham 1888-1973 FacFETw, WhoNob 90
**Waksman**, Ted Stewart 1949- WhoAmL 92
**Walakafra-Wills**, Delpaneaux V. 1952- WhoBlA 92
**Walas**, Leonard Anthony 1950- WhoEnt 92
**Walaszek**, Edward Joseph 1927- AmMWSc 92
**Walawender**, Michael John 1939- AmMWSc 92
**Walba**, David Mark 1949- AmMWSc 92, WhoWest 92
**Walba**, Harold 1921- AmMWSc 92
**Walbank**, Frank William 1909- Who 92, WrDr 92
**Walberg**, Clifford Bennett 1915- AmMWSc 92
**Walberg**, Timothy Lee 1951- WhoAmP 91
**Walbey**, Theodosia Emma Draher 1950- WhoBlA 92
**Walborg**, Earl Fredrick, Jr 1935- AmMWSc 92
**Walborn**, Nolan Revere 1944- AmMWSc 92
**Walborsky**, Harry M 1923- AmMWSc 92
**Walbot**, Virginia Elizabeth AmMWSc 92
**Walbrick**, Johnny Mac 1941- AmMWSc 92
**Walbridge**, John Tuthill, Jr 1925- WhoAmP 91
**Walbrook**, Louise WrDr 92
**Walburg**, H E 1932- AmMWSc 92
**Walburg**, Judith Ann 1948- WhoBlA 92
**Walburn**, Frederick J 1951- AmMWSc 92
**Walch**, Henry Andrew, Jr 1922- AmMWSc 92
**Walch**, John MacArthur Dunsmore 1926- WhoAmP 91
**Walch**, W. Stanley 1934- WhoAmL 92
**Walcha**, Helmut 1907- IntWW 91, NewAmDM
**Walcha**, Helmut 1907-1991 NewYTBS 91
**Walcha**, Nancy La Donna 1947- WhoWest 92
**Walcher**, Alan Ernest 1949- WhoAmL 92
**Walchli**, Harold E 1922- AmMWSc 92
**Walck**, Alfred William 1921- WhoRel 92
**Walcoff**, Lawrence 1932- WhoMW 92
**Walcot**, Charles Melton 1816-1868 BenetAL 91
**Walcot**, William 1874-1943 TwCPaSc
**Walcott**, Benjamin 1941- AmMWSc 92
**Walcott**, Charles 1934- AmMWSc 92, WhoFI 92
**Walcott**, Delbert Lee 1930- WhoFI 92
**Walcott**, Derek DrAPF 91, IntWW 91
**Walcott**, Derek 1930- BenetAL 91, BlkLC [port], ConLC 67 [port], ConPo 91, FacFETw, LiExTwC, RfGEnL 91, WrDr 92
**Walcott**, Helena B d1911 BiInAmS
**Walcott**, Jersey Joe 1914- WhoBlA 92
**Walcott**, Michael Lee 1956- WhoAmL 92
**Walcott**, Richard Irving 1933- Who 92
**Walczak**, Hubert R 1934- AmMWSc 92
**Wald**, Alan Maynard 1946- WhoMW 92
**Wald**, Alvin Stanley 1934- AmMWSc 92
**Wald**, Arnold 1942- AmMWSc 92
**Wald**, Bernard Joseph 1932- WhoAmL 92, WhoFI 92
**Wald**, Diane DrAPF 91
**Wald**, Francine Joy Weintraub 1938- AmMWSc 92
**Wald**, Francis John 1935- WhoAmP 91
**Wald**, Fritz Veit 1933- AmMWSc 92
**Wald**, George 1906- AmMWSc 92, IntWW 91, Who 92, WhoNob 90
**Wald**, Jeff Sommers 1944- WhoEnt 92
**Wald**, Lillian 1867-1940 DcAmImH, HanAmWH
**Wald**, Malvin 1917- IntMPA 92
**Wald**, Malvin Daniel 1917- WhoEnt 92
**Wald**, Martin 1934- WhoAmL 92
**Wald**, Michael S. 1941- WhoAmL 92
**Wald**, Milton M 1925- AmMWSc 92
**Wald**, Nicholas John 1944- Who 92
**Wald**, Niel 1925- AmMWSc 92
**Wald**, Patricia M 1928- WhoAmP 91
**Wald**, Patricia McGowan 1928- IntWW 91, WhoAmL 92
**Wald**, Richard C IntAu&W 91, IntWW 91, LesBEnT 92 [port]
**Wald**, Richard C. 1931- IntMPA 92
**Wald**, Robert Gray 1963- WhoWest 92
**Wald**, Robert Lewis 1926- WhoAmL 92
**Wald**, Robert Manuel 1947- AmMWSc 92
**Wald**, Samuel Stanley 1907- AmMWSc 92
**Wald**, Sarah Elizabeth 1953- WhoAmL 92
**Waldauer**, Charles 1935- WhoFI 92
**Waldbauer**, Eugene Charles 1926- AmMWSc 92
**Waldbauer**, Gilbert Peter 1928- AmMWSc 92
**Waldbillig**, Ronald Charles 1943- AmMWSc 92
**Walde**, Ralph Eldon 1943- AmMWSc 92
**Walde**, Thomas 1949- IntWW 91
**Waldeck**, Gary Cranston 1943- WhoWest 92
**Waldeck**, John Walter, Jr. 1949- WhoAmL 92, WhoFI 92, WhoMW 92
**Waldeck-Pyrmont**, J, Hereditary Prince of 1896-1967 EncTR 91
**Waldecker**, Thomas Raymond 1950- WhoMW 92
**Waldegrave** Who 92
**Waldegrave**, Earl 1905- Who 92
**Waldegrave**, William 1946- IntWW 91, Who 92
**Walden**, Alvin Earl 1948- WhoRel 92
**Walden**, Barbara 1936- WhoBlA 92
**Walden**, Brian 1932- IntAu&W 91, IntWW 91, Who 92
**Walden**, C Craig 1921- AmMWSc 92
**Walden**, Carl Eugene 1936- WhoEnt 92
**Walden**, Clyde Harrison 1921- AmMWSc 92
**Walden**, David Burton 1932- AmMWSc 92
**Walden**, Edith M. DrAPF 91
**Walden**, Emerson Coleman 1923- WhoBlA 92
**Walden**, George Gordon Harvey 1939- Who 92
**Walden**, Graham Howard Who 92
**Walden**, Greg 1957- WhoAmP 91
**Walden**, Herbert Richard Charles 1926- Who 92
**Walden**, Jack M 1922- AmMWSc 92
**Walden**, James Lee 1955- WhoWest 92
**Walden**, James William 1936- WhoFI 92, WhoMW 92
**Walden**, John William, Jr. 1941- WhoFI 92
**Walden**, Julia Kay 1960- WhoFI 92
**Walden**, Narada Michael 1952- WhoBlA 92, WhoEnt 92
**Walden**, Robert E., Jr. 1954- WhoEnt 92
**Walden**, Robert Edison 1920- WhoBlA 92
**Walden**, Robert Henry 1939- AmMWSc 92
**Walden**, Robert M., III 1959- WhoFI 92
**Walden**, Stanley Eugene 1932- WhoEnt 92
**Walden**, Thurman L 1926- WhoAmP 91
**Walden**, William DrAPF 91
**Waldenberg**, Adair Louise 1950- WhoFI 92, WhoMW 92
**Waldenfels**, Hans 1931- WhoRel 92
**Waldenstrom**, Erland d1988 IntWW 91N
**Waldenstrom**, Jan Gosta 1906- IntWW 91
**Walder**, Edwin James 1921- Who 92
**Walder**, Justin Perry 1935- WhoAmL 92
**Walder**, Ruth Christabel 1906- Who 92
**Walder**, Steven Richard 1965- WhoFI 92
**Waldera**, Gerald Joseph 1931- WhoAmP 91
**Waldera**, Wayne E. 1933- WhoWest 92
**Waldern**, Donald E 1928- AmMWSc 92
**Waldeyer**, John Thomas, Jr 1948- WhoAmP 91
**Waldhauer**, F D 1927- AmMWSc 92
**Waldhauer**, Fred Donald 1927- WhoWest 92
**Waldhausen**, John Anton 1929- AmMWSc 92
**Waldhauser**, Cathy Howard 1949- WhoIns 92
**Waldheim**, Kurt 1918- FacFETw [port], IntWW 91, Who 92
**Waldholtz**, Joseph P 1963- WhoAmP 91
**Waldichuk**, Michael 1923- AmMWSc 92
**Waldinger**, Ernst 1895-1970 LiExTwC
**Waldinger**, Harlan Albert 1935- WhoAmL 92
**Waldinger**, Hermann V 1923- AmMWSc 92
**Waldinger**, Jesse Seth 1947- WhoAmL 92
**Waldinger**, Richard J 1944- AmMWSc 92

**Waldkoenig,** Gilson Christian 1928- *WhoRel 92*
**Waldman,** Alan S 1959- *AmMWSc 92*
**Waldman,** Anne *DrAPF 91, IntAu&W 91*
**Waldman,** Anne 1945- *ConAu 34NR, ConPo 91, WrDr 92*
**Waldman,** Anne Lesley 1945- *WhoEnt 92*
**Waldman,** Barbara Criscuolo 1956- *AmMWSc 92*
**Waldman,** Barry Jerome 1940- *WhoWest 92*
**Waldman,** Bernard 1913- *AmMWSc 92*
**Waldman,** George D 1932- *AmMWSc 92*
**Waldman,** Jay Carl 1944- *WhoAmL 92*
**Waldman,** Jeffrey 1941- *AmMWSc 92*
**Waldman,** Joseph 1906- *AmMWSc 92*
**Waldman,** Jules Lloyd 1912- *IntAu&W 91*
**Waldman,** L A 1929- *AmMWSc 92*
**Waldman,** Marilyn Robinson 1943- *WhoMW 92*
**Waldman,** Mel *DrAPF 91*
**Waldman,** Michael Lawrence 1960- *WhoAmL 92*
**Waldman,** Milton 1927- *WhoWest 92*
**Waldman,** Robert H 1938- *AmMWSc 92*
**Waldman,** Walter *IntMPA 92*
**Waldman,** Yuval 1946- *WhoEnt 92*
**Waldmann,** Herman 1945- *Who 92*
**Waldmann,** Raymond John 1938- *WhoAmP 91*
**Waldmann,** Thomas A 1930- *AmMWSc 92*
**Waldner,** Michael 1924- *AmMWSc 92*
**Waldo,** Anna Lee 1925- *TwCWW 91, WrDr 92*
**Waldo,** Bradley Wayne 1955- *WhoEnt 92*
**Waldo,** Burton Corlett 1920- *WhoWest 92*
**Waldo,** Carol Dunn *WhoBlA 92*
**Waldo,** Charles N. 1936- *WhoMW 92*
**Waldo,** Dale 1907- *TwCWW 91*
**Waldo,** Frank 1857-1920 *BiInAmS*
**Waldo,** George Van Pelt, Jr 1940- *AmMWSc 92*
**Waldo,** Janet 1930- *ConTFT 9*
**Waldo,** Jeffrey Ralph 1956- *WhoAmL 92*
**Waldo,** Willis Henry 1920- *AmMWSc 92*
**Waldon,** Alton R, Jr 1936- *WhoAmP 91*
**Waldon,** Alton Ronald, Jr. 1936- *WhoBlA 92*
**Waldon,** Dennis C. 1946- *WhoAmL 92*
**Waldon,** Lori Annette 1961- *WhoBlA 92*
**Waldorf,** Eugene 1936- *WhoAmP 91*
**Waldorf,** Geraldine Polack 1942- *WhoAmL 92*
**Waldren,** Charles Allen 1934- *AmMWSc 92*
**Waldrep,** Alfred Carson, Jr 1923- *AmMWSc 92*
**Waldrep,** Kenneth *WhoAmP 91*
**Waldrep,** Thomas William 1934- *AmMWSc 92*
**Waldron,** Acie Chandler 1930- *AmMWSc 92*
**Waldron,** Agnes d1991 *NewYTBS 91*
**Waldron,** Arthur 1948- *ConAu 135*
**Waldron,** Charles A 1922- *AmMWSc 92*
**Waldron,** Donald 1952- *WhoAmL 92*
**Waldron,** Gary L. 1948- *WhoAmL 92*
**Waldron,** Harold Francis 1929- *AmMWSc 92, WhoMW 92*
**Waldron,** Hicks Benjamin 1923- *WhoFI 92*
**Waldron,** Howard Hamilton 1917- *AmMWSc 92*
**Waldron,** Ingrid Lore 1939- *AmMWSc 92*
**Waldron,** Jeremy James 1953- *WhoAmL 92*
**Waldron,** John Graham Claverhouse 1909- *Who 92*
**Waldron,** Kenneth John 1943- *AmMWSc 92*
**Waldron,** Kenneth Lynn 1941- *WhoAmL 92*
**Waldron,** Marcia Mary 1951- *WhoAmL 92*
**Waldron,** Mary Katherine 1954- *WhoMW 92*
**Waldron,** Orval Hubert 1918- *WhoAmP 91*
**Waldron,** Peter 1941- *TwCPaSc*
**Waldron,** Steve 1946- *WhoAmP 91*
**Waldron-Ramsey,** Waldo Emerson 1930- *Who 92*
**Waldrop,** Ann Lyneve 1939- *AmMWSc 92*
**Waldrop,** Dave C, Jr 1943- *WhoAmP 91*
**Waldrop,** Edwin W. 1921- *WhoMW 92*
**Waldrop,** Francis N 1926- *AmMWSc 92*
**Waldrop,** Gerald Wayne 1942- *WhoAmP 91*
**Waldrop,** Gideon William 1919- *WhoEnt 92*
**Waldrop,** Howard 1946- *TwCSFW 91, WrDr 92*
**Waldrop,** Howard Leon 1948- *WhoMW 92*
**Waldrop,** Isaac Merit, Jr 1933- *WhoAmP 91*
**Waldrop,** John Michael 1956- *WhoRel 92*
**Waldrop,** Keith *DrAPF 91*
**Waldrop,** Morgan A 1937- *AmMWSc 92*
**Waldrop,** Rosmarie *DrAPF 91*
**Waldrop,** Rosmarie 1935- *IntAu&W 91*
**Waldroup,** Park William 1937- *AmMWSc 92*
**Waldrup,** Charles E 1925- *WhoAmP 91*
**Waldschmidt,** Paul Edward 1920- *WhoRel 92, WhoWest 92*
**Waldschmidt,** Robert Howard 1951- *WhoAmL 92*
**Waldstein,** Arne *WhoAmP 91*
**Waldstein,** Linda Ruth 1948- *WhoMW 92*
**Waldstein,** Sheldon Saul 1924- *AmMWSc 92*
**Walecka,** Jerrold Alberts 1930- *AmMWSc 92*
**Walecka,** John Dirk 1932- *AmMWSc 92*
**Walek,** Thomas A. 1957- *WhoFI 92*
**Walendowski,** George Jerry 1947- *WhoFI 92*
**Walenga,** Ronald W 1946- *AmMWSc 92*
**Walerian,** Szyszkowski 1945- *AmMWSc 92*
**Wales,** Archbishop of *Who 92*
**Wales,** Prince of 1948 *Who 92R*
**Wales,** The Prince of 1948- *IntWW 91*
**Wales,** The Princess of 1961- *IntWW 91*
**Wales,** Bethany Ellen 1965- *WhoMW 92*
**Wales,** Charles E 1928- *AmMWSc 92*
**Wales,** Daphne Beatrice 1917- *Who 92*
**Wales,** David Bertram 1939- *AmMWSc 92*
**Wales,** Geoffrey 1912-1990 *TwCPaSc*
**Wales,** Ken 1938- *WhoEnt 92*
**Wales,** Nym *IntAu&W 91X, WrDr 92*
**Wales,** Robert 1923- *WrDr 92*
**Wales,** Robert 1933- *IntAu&W 91*
**Wales,** Ross Elliot 1947- *WhoAmL 92*
**Wales,** Stephen Henry, Sr. 1932- *WhoFI 92*
**Wales,** Walter D 1933- *AmMWSc 92*
**Walesa,** Lech 1943- *FacFETw [port], IntWW 91, News 91 [port], Who 92, WhoNob 90*
**Walewski,** Alexandre 1810-1861 *ThHEIm*
**Waley,** Andrew Felix 1926- *Who 92*
**Waley,** Daniel Philip 1921- *Who 92*
**Waley,** Felix *Who 92*
**Waley-Cohen,** Bernard d1991 *NewYTBS 91*
**Waley-Cohen,** Bernard Nathaniel d1991 *Who 92N*
**Waley-Cohen,** Joyce Constance Ina 1920- *Who 92*
**Waley-Cohen,** Stephen 1946- *Who 92*
**Walfish,** Binyamin H. 1925- *WhoRel 92*
**Walford,** A. J. 1906- *WrDr 92*
**Walford,** Christopher Rupert 1935- *Who 92*
**Walford,** Diana Marion 1944- *Who 92*
**Walford,** John Howard 1927- *Who 92*
**Walford,** John Thomas 1933- *Who 92*
**Walford,** Roy Lee, Jr 1924- *AmMWSc 92*
**Walgenbach,** David D 1937- *AmMWSc 92*
**Walgenbach-Telford,** Susan Carol 1952- *AmMWSc 92*
**Walgreen,** Charles Rudolph, III 1935- *WhoFI 92, WhoMW 92*
**Walgren,** Doug 1940- *WhoAmP 91*
**Walgren,** Gordon Lee 1933- *WhoAmP 91*
**Walgren,** Paul Castleton 1922- *WhoAmP 91*
**Walhain,** Michel Octave Marie Louis 1915- *IntWW 91*
**Walhof,** Frederick James 1938- *WhoRel 92*
**Walhout,** Justine Isabel Simon 1930- *AmMWSc 92*
**Wali,** Kameshwar C 1927- *AmMWSc 92*
**Wali,** Mohan Kishen 1937- *AmMWSc 92*
**Walia,** Amrik Singh 1947- *AmMWSc 92*
**Walia,** Jasjit Singh 1934- *AmMWSc 92*
**Waligora,** James 1954- *WhoFI 92*
**Waligorski,** Ewaryst 1937- *IntWW 91*
**Waling,** J L 1916- *AmMWSc 92*
**Walinski,** Nicholas Joseph 1920- *WhoAmL 92, WhoMW 92*
**Walinski,** Richard S. 1943- *WhoAmL 92*
**Waliullah,** Syed 1922-1971 *ConAu 134*
**Walize,** Reuben Thompson, III 1950- *WhoWest 92*
**Walk,** Charles Edmonds *ScFEYrs*
**Walk,** George 1949- *WhoAmP 91*
**Walk,** Leonard 1926- *WhoEnt 92*
**Walke,** Anne 1888?-1965 *TwCPaSc*
**Walke,** Ralph Meade 1944- *WhoAmL 92*
**Walke,** Raymond J 1936- *WhoIns 92*
**Walken,** Christopher 1943- *IntMPA 92, IntWW 91, WhoEnt 92*
**Walkenstein,** Sidney S 1920- *AmMWSc 92*
**Walker,** A Earl 1907- *AmMWSc 92*
**Walker,** A. Harris 1935- *WhoAmL 92*
**Walker,** A Maceo 1909- *WhoIns 92*
**Walker,** A. Maceo, Sr. 1909- *WhoBlA 92*
**Walker,** Ada 1870-1914 *NotBlAW 92 [port]*
**Walker,** Adam 1730?-1821 *BlkwCEP*
**Walker,** Alan 1911- *IntWW 91, Who 92, WhoRel 92, WrDr 92*
**Walker,** Alan 1937- *AmMWSc 92*
**Walker,** Alan Kent 1950- *AmMWSc 92*
**Walker,** Albert L. 1945- *WhoBlA 92*
**Walker,** Albertina 1929- *WhoBlA 92*
**Walker,** Albertina 1930- *NewAmDM*
**Walker,** A'Lelia 1885-1931 *NotBlAW 92 [port]*
**Walker,** Alexander 1930- *IntAu&W 91, Who 92, WrDr 92*
**Walker,** Alfred Cecil 1924- *Who 92*
**Walker,** Alfred L, Jr 1935- *WhoAmP 91*
**Walker,** Alice *DrAPF 91*
**Walker,** Alice 1944- *AfrAmW, BenetAL 91, BlkLC [port], ConBlB 1 [port], ConNov 91, FacFETw, HanAmWH, ModAWWr, NotBlAW 92 [port], WrDr 92*
**Walker,** Alice Davis 1931- *WhoFI 92*
**Walker,** Alice Malsenior 1944- *IntAu&W 91, IntWW 91, WhoBlA 92*
**Walker,** Allan 1907- *Who 92*
**Walker,** Allene Marsha 1953- *WhoBlA 92*
**Walker,** Alma Toevs 1911- *AmMWSc 92*
**Walker,** Alta Sharon 1942- *AmMWSc 92*
**Walker,** Alvin Paul 1958- *WhoAmL 92*
**Walker,** Amasa 1799-1875 *AmPeW*
**Walker,** Ameae M 1951- *AmMWSc 92*
**Walker,** Angus Henry 1935- *Who 92*
**Walker,** Ann B. 1923- *WhoBlA 92*
**Walker,** Annie Mae 1913- *WhoBlA 92*
**Walker,** Antony 1934- *Who 92*
**Walker,** Ardis Manly d1991 *IntWW 91N*
**Walker,** Arthur B. C. 1901- *WhoBlA 92*
**Walker,** Arthur Bertram Cuthbert, Jr 1936- *AmMWSc 92*
**Walker,** Arthur Geoffrey 1909- *Who 92*
**Walker,** Arthur Lonzo 1926- *WhoRel 92*
**Walker,** Augustus Chapman 1923- *AmMWSc 92*
**Walker,** Bailus S *AmMWSc 92*
**Walker,** Baldwin Patrick 1924- *Who 92*
**Walker,** Barth Powell 1914- *WhoAmL 92, WhoFI 92*
**Walker,** Benjamin 1923- *WrDr 92*
**Walker,** Bennie Frank 1937- *AmMWSc 92*
**Walker,** Bernadette Marie 1960- *WhoMW 92*
**Walker,** Betsy Ellen 1953- *WhoFI 92*
**Walker,** Betty Jean *WhoAmP 91*
**Walker,** Betty Stevens 1944- *WhoBlA 92*
**Walker,** Bill *Who 92*
**Walker,** Billy Cummins 1937- *WhoRel 92*
**Walker,** Billy Kenneth 1946- *AmMWSc 92*
**Walker,** Blair Kendall 1962- *WhoFI 92*
**Walker,** Bobby *Who 92*
**Walker,** Bonnie Lee 1939- *WhoEnt 92*
**Walker,** Brent Taylor 1963- *WhoAmP 91*
**Walker,** Brian *DrAPF 91*
**Walker,** Brian Wilson 1930- *Who 92*
**Walker,** Brooks, Jr. 1928- *WhoWest 92*
**Walker,** Bruce David 1952- *AmMWSc 92*
**Walker,** Bruce Edward 1926- *AmMWSc 92*
**Walker,** Bruce Howard 1946- *WhoWest 92*
**Walker,** Bruce J *WhoAmP 91*
**Walker,** Bruce Keppen 1952- *WhoMW 92*
**Walker,** Burton Leith 1927- *WhoWest 92*
**Walker,** C. Edward 1931- *TwCPaSc*
**Walker,** C J 1867-1919 *RComAH*
**Walker,** C.J., Madame 1867-1919 *HanAmWH, NotBlAW 92 [port]*
**Walker,** Carl 1934- *Who 92*
**Walker,** Carl, Jr. 1924- *WhoBlA 92*
**Walker,** Carl Kingsley 1959- *WhoRel 92*
**Walker,** Carol L 1935- *AmMWSc 92*
**Walker,** Carolyn *WhoAmP 91, WhoBlA 92*
**Walker,** Carolyn Louise 1947- *WhoWest 92*
**Walker,** Catherine *IntWW 91*
**Walker,** Catherine 1958- *WhoWest 92*
**Walker,** Cecil *Who 92*
**Walker,** Cedric Frank 1950- *AmMWSc 92*
**Walker,** Charles 1945- *WhoBlA 92*
**Walker,** Charles A. *WhoBlA 92*
**Walker,** Charles A 1914- *AmMWSc 92*
**Walker,** Charles A 1935- *AmMWSc 92*
**Walker,** Charles Douglas 1915- *WhoBlA 92*
**Walker,** Charles E. 1935- *WhoBlA 92*
**Walker,** Charles Edward 1923- *WhoAmP 91*
**Walker,** Charles H. 1951- *WhoBlA 92*
**Walker,** Charles Michael 1916- *Who 92*
**Walker,** Charles R 1928- *AmMWSc 92*
**Walker,** Charles Ray 1927- *WhoAmP 91*
**Walker,** Charles Thomas 1932- *AmMWSc 92*
**Walker,** Charles Urmston 1931- *WhoWest 92*
**Walker,** Charles W 1947- *WhoAmP 91*
**Walker,** Charles Wayne 1947- *AmMWSc 92*
**Walker,** Charlotte Zoe *DrAPF 91*
**Walker,** Charls E. 1923- *Who 92*
**Walker,** Charls Edward 1923- *IntWW 91*
**Walker,** Chauncey Lovelle 1938- *WhoAmL 92*
**Walker,** Cheryl Lyn 1955- *AmMWSc 92*
**Walker,** Chester 1940- *WhoBlA 92*
**Walker,** Christopher Bland 1925- *AmMWSc 92*
**Walker,** Christopher Roy 1934- *Who 92*
**Walker,** Cindy Lee 1952- *WhoBlA 92*
**Walker,** Claud L *WhoAmP 91*
**Walker,** Claude 1934- *WhoBlA 92*
**Walker,** Clint 1927- *IntMPA 92*
**Walker,** Colin 1934- *Who 92*
**Walker,** Constance Mae 1928- *WhoRel 92*
**Walker,** Cora T. 1926- *WhoBlA 92*
**Walker,** Craig J. 1962- *WhoBlA 92*
**Walker,** Craig Michael 1947- *WhoAmL 92*
**Walker,** Cynthia Bush 1956- *WhoBlA 92*
**Walker,** Dale Rush 1943- *WhoFI 92*
**Walker,** Dan B 1945- *AmMWSc 92*
**Walker,** Daniel Alvin 1940- *AmMWSc 92*
**Walker,** Daniel Joshua, Jr. 1915- *WhoAmL 92*
**Walker,** Darrell 1961- *WhoBlA 92*
**Walker,** Darryl 1950- *TwCPaSc*
**Walker,** David 1785-1830 *BenetAL 91, RComAH*
**Walker,** David 1911- *IntAu&W 91, WrDr 92*
**Walker,** David 1920- *WrDr 92*
**Walker,** David 1946- *AmMWSc 92*
**Walker,** David Alan 1928- *IntWW 91, Who 92*
**Walker,** David Alan 1939- *IntWW 91, Who 92*
**Walker,** David Allen 1942- *WhoRel 92*
**Walker,** David Bruce 1934- *IntWW 91, Who 92*
**Walker,** David C. *DrAPF 91*
**Walker,** David Charles 1927- *WhoAmL 92*
**Walker,** David Critchlow 1940- *Who 92*
**Walker,** David Crosby 1934- *AmMWSc 92*
**Walker,** David Dean 1937- *WhoRel 92*
**Walker,** David Elliott 1947- *WhoRel 92*
**Walker,** David Glenn 1927- *WhoMW 92, WhoRel 92*
**Walker,** David H 1925- *WhoAmP 91*
**Walker,** David Harry 1911- *BenetAL 91, Who 92*
**Walker,** David Hughes 1943- *AmMWSc 92*
**Walker,** David Kenneth 1943- *AmMWSc 92*
**Walker,** David Lewis 1950- *WhoMW 92*
**Walker,** David Maxwell 1920- *IntAu&W 91, IntWW 91, Who 92*
**Walker,** David Michael 1951- *WhoFI 92*
**Walker,** David N 1943- *AmMWSc 92*
**Walker,** David Rudger 1929- *AmMWSc 92*
**Walker,** David Todd 1937- *WhoAmL 92*
**Walker,** David Tutherly 1922- *AmMWSc 92*
**Walker,** David Wild 1941- *WhoAmL 92*
**Walker,** Deborah 1950- *WhoFI 92*
**Walker,** Dennis Kendon 1938- *AmMWSc 92*
**Walker,** Dennis William, III 1948- *WhoFI 92*
**Walker,** Derek William Rothwell 1924- *Who 92*
**Walker,** Derrick N. 1967- *WhoBlA 92*
**Walker,** Deward Edgar, Jr. 1935- *WhoWest 92*
**Walker,** Don Wesley 1942- *AmMWSc 92*
**Walker,** Donald 1928- *Who 92*
**Walker,** Donald F 1923- *AmMWSc 92*
**Walker,** Donald I 1922- *AmMWSc 92*
**Walker,** Donald Murray 1938- *WhoRel 92*
**Walker,** Donald Robert, Jr. 1955- *WhoMW 92, WhoRel 92*
**Walker,** Donna Henry 1954- *WhoFI 92*
**Walker,** Donna Lou 1953- *WhoRel 92*
**Walker,** Doreen 1920- *ConAu 135*
**Walker,** Dorothea Bernice 1906- *WhoBlA 92*
**Walker,** Dorothy Keister 1920- *WhoRel 92*
**Walker,** Doug *WhoAmP 91*
**Walker,** Douglas F. 1937- *WhoBlA 92*
**Walker,** Duard Lee 1921- *AmMWSc 92*
**Walker,** Duncan Edward 1942- *WhoWest 92*
**Walker,** E. Cardon 1916- *IntMPA 92*
**Walker,** Edward Bell Mar 1952- *AmMWSc 92*
**Walker,** Edward Bullock, III 1922- *IntWW 91*
**Walker,** Edward John 1927- *AmMWSc 92*
**Walker,** Edward M. 1935- *WhoRel 92*
**Walker,** Edward Robert 1922- *AmMWSc 92*
**Walker,** Edward S, Jr *WhoAmP 91*
**Walker,** Edwin L. 1956- *WhoBlA 92*
**Walker,** Edwin Stuart, III 1928- *WhoRel 92*
**Walker,** Elaine Nogay 1951- *WhoEnt 92*
**Walker,** Elbert Abner 1930- *AmMWSc 92*
**Walker,** Elizabeth Jane 1936- *WhoAmP 91*
**Walker,** Elizabeth Reed 1941- *AmMWSc 92*
**Walker,** Eljana M. du Vall 1924- *WhoWest 92*
**Walker,** Ellen Marcia 1955- *WhoFI 92*
**Walker,** Elva Mae Dawson 1914- *WhoMW 92*
**Walker,** Eric A 1910- *AmMWSc 92*

**Walker,** Eric George 1907-1985 *TwCPaSc*
**Walker,** Ernest L. 1941- *WhoBlA 92*
**Walker,** Ernestein 1926- *WhoBlA 92*
**Walker,** Esme *Who 92*
**Walker,** Esper Lafayette, Jr. 1930- *WhoFI 92*
**Walker,** Ethel 1861-1951 *TwCPaSc*
**Walker,** Ethel Pitts 1943- *WhoBlA 92*
**Walker,** Eugene Henry 1925- *WhoBlA 92*
**Walker,** Eugene P *WhoAmP 91*
**Walker,** Eugene Wilson 1919- *WhoAmP 91*
**Walker,** Evelyn *WhoEnt 92, WhoFI 92*
**Walker,** Frances 1924- *WhoBlA 92*
**Walker,** Frances 1930- *TwCPaSc*
**Walker,** Francis Amasa 1840-1897 *BiInAmS*
**Walker,** Francis Edwin 1931- *AmMWSc 92*
**Walker,** Francis H 1936- *AmMWSc 92*
**Walker,** Francis Joseph 1922- *WhoAmL 92, WhoFI 92, WhoWest 92*
**Walker,** Frank 1934-1985 *WhoBlA 92N*
**Walker,** Frank Banghart 1931- *WhoMW 92*
**Walker,** Frank Stockdale d1989 *Who 92N*
**Walker,** Fred 1910-1982 *FacFETw*
**Walker,** Fred Elmer 1931- *WhoEnt 92*
**Walker,** Fred Leonard 1961- *WhoEnt 92*
**Walker,** Frederick 1934- *Who 92*
**Walker,** Frederick 1954- *AmMWSc 92*
**Walker,** G. Edward 1942- *WhoBlA 92*
**Walker,** Gary S. 1947- *WhoBlA 92*
**Walker,** Gene B 1932- *AmMWSc 92*
**Walker,** George 1908- *DcTwDes*
**Walker,** George 1922- *NewAmDM*
**Walker,** George Alfred 1929- *IntWW 91, Who 92*
**Walker,** George Edward 1940- *AmMWSc 92, WhoBlA 92*
**Walker,** George F. 1947- *WrDr 92*
**Walker,** George Gary 1948- *WhoRel 92*
**Walker,** George Kontz 1938- *WhoAmL 92*
**Walker,** George Moore 1952- *WhoAmL 92*
**Walker,** George P. L. 1926- *IntWW 91*
**Walker,** George Patrick Leonard 1926- *Who 92*
**Walker,** George Raymond 1936- *WhoBlA 92*
**Walker,** George Robert 1915- *WhoIns 92*
**Walker,** George T. 1922- *WhoBlA 92*
**Walker,** George Theophilus, Jr. 1922- *WhoEnt 92*
**Walker,** Gerald *DrAPF 91*
**Walker,** Gerald T 1940- *WhoIns 92*
**Walker,** Gervas 1920- *Who 92*
**Walker,** Glenn Kenneth 1948- *AmMWSc 92*
**Walker,** Gordon Alfred 1924- *WhoRel 92*
**Walker,** Gordon Arthur Hunter 1936- *AmMWSc 92*
**Walker,** Gordon T. 1942- *WhoAmL 92*
**Walker,** Grayson Howard 1938- *AmMWSc 92*
**Walker,** Grayson Watkins 1944- *AmMWSc 92*
**Walker,** Grover Pulliam 1941- *WhoBlA 92*
**Walker,** Gustav Adolphus 1944- *AmMWSc 92*
**Walker,** H. Lawson 1949- *WhoAmL 92*
**Walker,** Hal Wilson 1929- *WhoAmP 91*
**Walker,** Harley Jesse 1921- *AmMWSc 92*
**Walker,** Harold 1927- *Who 92*
**Walker,** Harold 1932- *Who 92*
**Walker,** Harold Blake 1904- *WhoMW 92, WhoRel 92*
**Walker,** Harold Osmonde 1928- *WhoFI 92*
**Walker,** Harold William, Jr. 1946- *WhoAmL 92*
**Walker,** Harrell Lynn 1945- *AmMWSc 92*
**Walker,** Harriette Katherine 1929- *WhoRel 92*
**Walker,** Harry *IntAu&W 91X, Who 92, WrDr 92*
**Walker,** Harry Grey 1924- *WhoAmP 91*
**Walker,** Heather 1959- *TwCPaSc*
**Walker,** Henry Alexander, Jr. 1922- *WhoWest 92*
**Walker,** Henry Lawson, II 1949- *WhoAmP 91*
**Walker,** Herbert John 1919- *IntWW 91*
**Walker,** Herschel 1962- *ConBlB 1 [port], WhoBlA 92*
**Walker,** Hiram H. 1920- *WhoRel 92*
**Walker,** Homer Franklin 1943- *AmMWSc 92, WhoWest 92*
**Walker,** Homer Wayne 1925- *AmMWSc 92, WhoMW 92*
**Walker,** Horace L. 1938- *WhoBlA 92*
**Walker,** Howard David 1925- *AmMWSc 92*
**Walker,** Howard K 1935- *WhoAmP 91*
**Walker,** Howard Kent 1935- *WhoBlA 92*
**Walker,** Howard Lee 1944- *WhoAmL 92*
**Walker,** Howard Painter 1932- *WhoAmL 92*
**Walker,** Hugh 1925- *Who 92*
**Walker,** Hugh S 1935- *AmMWSc 92*
**Walker,** Ian Gardner 1928- *AmMWSc 92*
**Walker,** Ian Munro 1940- *AmMWSc 92*
**Walker,** Irving Edward 1952- *WhoAmL 92*
**Walker,** J. *WrDr 92*
**Walker,** J Bernard 1858- *ScFEYrs*
**Walker,** J Calvin 1935- *AmMWSc 92*
**Walker,** J Knox 1927- *AmMWSc 92*
**Walker,** J. Wilbur 1912- *WhoBlA 92*
**Walker,** Jack D 1922- *WhoAmP 91*
**Walker,** James 1881-1946 *FacFETw*
**Walker,** James 1916- *Who 92*
**Walker,** James 1926- *WhoBlA 92*
**Walker,** James Alvin 1925- *WhoRel 92*
**Walker,** James Benjamin 1922- *AmMWSc 92*
**Walker,** James Bernard 1946- *Who 92*
**Walker,** James Callan Gray 1939- *AmMWSc 92*
**Walker,** James Calvin 1951- *WhoFI 92*
**Walker,** James Elliot Cabot 1926- *AmMWSc 92*
**Walker,** James Faure 1948- *TwCPaSc*
**Walker,** James Findlay 1916- *Who 92*
**Walker,** James Frederick 1904- *AmMWSc 92*
**Walker,** James Frederick, Jr 1937- *AmMWSc 92*
**Walker,** James Glenn 1947- *WhoWest 92*
**Walker,** James Graham 1913- *Who 92*
**Walker,** James Harris 1944- *AmMWSc 92*
**Walker,** James Heron 1914- *Who 92*
**Walker,** James Joseph 1933- *AmMWSc 92*
**Walker,** James King 1935- *AmMWSc 92*
**Walker,** James Lynwood *WhoRel 92, WhoWest 92*
**Walker,** James Martin 1938- *AmMWSc 92*
**Walker,** James Richard 1933- *AmMWSc 92*
**Walker,** James Roderick 1946- *WhoWest 92*
**Walker,** James Ronald 1947- *WhoAmP 91*
**Walker,** James Roy 1937- *AmMWSc 92*
**Walker,** James Silas 1933- *WhoRel 92*
**Walker,** James Willard 1943- *AmMWSc 92*
**Walker,** James William, Jr. 1927- *WhoAmL 92, WhoFI 92*
**Walker,** James Wilson 1922- *AmMWSc 92*
**Walker,** James Zell, II 1932- *WhoBlA 92*
**Walker,** Jana Lynn 1954- *WhoAmL 92*
**Walker,** Jay 1952- *WhoEnt 92*
**Walker,** Jay, III 1947- *WhoAmP 91*
**Walker,** Jay Scott 1955- *WhoFI 92*
**Walker,** Jean Kindy 1933- *WhoAmP 91*
**Walker,** Jean Tweedy 1944- *AmMWSc 92*
**Walker,** Jeanne Murray *DrAPF 91*
**Walker,** Jearl Dalton 1945- *AmMWSc 92*
**Walker,** Jerald Carter 1938- *WhoFI 92*
**Walker,** Jerry Arnold 1948- *AmMWSc 92*
**Walker,** Jerry C 1938- *AmMWSc 92*
**Walker,** Jerry Euclid 1932- *WhoBlA 92*
**Walker,** Jerry Jeff 1942- *WhoEnt 92*
**Walker,** Jerry Quenten 1953- *WhoWest 92*
**Walker,** Jerry Tyler 1930- *AmMWSc 92*
**Walker,** Jesse Marshall 1917- *WhoRel 92*
**Walker,** Jewel Lee 1950- *WhoMW 92*
**Walker,** Jewett Lynius 1930- *WhoRel 92*
**Walker,** Jimmie 1945- *WhoBlA 92*
**Walker,** Jimmy 1947- *WhoBlA 92*
**Walker,** Jimmy Newton 1924- *AmMWSc 92*
**Walker,** Joan Marion 1937- *AmMWSc 92*
**Walker,** Joe 1934- *WhoBlA 92*
**Walker,** John 1732-1807 *BlkwCEP*
**Walker,** John 1906- *IntWW 91, Who 92*
**Walker,** John 1929- *Who 92*
**Walker,** John 1939- *TwCPaSc, WorArt 1980*
**Walker,** John Charles 1893- *IntWW 91*
**Walker,** John David 1924- *Who 92*
**Walker,** John E 1938- *WhoIns 92*
**Walker,** John E. 1948- *WhoRel 92*
**Walker,** John J 1935- *AmMWSc 92*
**Walker,** John Joseph 1950- *WhoIns 92*
**Walker,** John Lawrence, Jr 1931- *AmMWSc 92*
**Walker,** John Leslie 1933- *WhoBlA 92*
**Walker,** John Letham 1946- *WhoAmP 91*
**Walker,** John M, Jr 1940- *WhoAmP 91*
**Walker,** John Malcolm 1930- *Who 92*
**Walker,** John Martin 1935- *AmMWSc 92*
**Walker,** John Mercer, Jr. 1940- *WhoAmL 92*
**Walker,** John Michael 1942- *WhoFI 92*
**Walker,** John Neal 1930- *AmMWSc 92*
**Walker,** John Robert *WhoAmL 92*
**Walker,** John Robert 1931- *AmMWSc 92*
**Walker,** John Scott 1944- *AmMWSc 92*
**Walker,** John Sumpter, Jr. 1921- *WhoAmL 92, WhoWest 92*
**Walker,** John T. 1925-1989 *WhoBlA 92N*
**Walker,** Jonathan Alan 1958- *WhoMW 92*
**Walker,** Jonathan Lee 1948- *WhoAmL 92, WhoMW 92*
**Walker,** Joseph 1892-1985 *FacFETw*
**Walker,** Joseph 1921-1966 *FacFETw*
**Walker,** Joseph 1922- *AmMWSc 92*
**Walker,** Joseph 1935- *BenetAL 91*
**Walker,** Joseph A. 1935- *WhoBlA 92, WrDr 92*
**Walker,** Joseph Allen 1951- *WhoFI 92*
**Walker,** Joseph G *WhoAmP 91*
**Walker,** Joseph Hillary, Jr. 1919- *WhoAmL 92*
**Walker,** Joseph Robert 1942- *WhoWest 92*
**Walker,** Joseph William 1930- *WhoRel 92*
**Walker,** Joseph Wylie 1948- *WhoAmP 91*
**Walker,** Joyce Marie 1948- *WhoWest 92*
**Walker,** Judith 1955- *TwCPaSc*
**Walker,** Julian Fortay 1929- *Who 92*
**Walker,** Julian Guy Hudsmith 1936- *Who 92*
**Walker,** K. Grahame 1937- *WhoFI 92*
**Walker,** Kathryn *IntMPA 92*
**Walker,** Keith Allen 1948- *WhoMW 92*
**Walker,** Keith Gerald 1941- *AmMWSc 92*
**Walker,** Kelsey, Jr 1925- *AmMWSc 92*
**Walker,** Kenneth 1964- *WhoBlA 92*
**Walker,** Kenneth Henry 1940- *WhoFI 92*
**Walker,** Kenneth Merriam 1921- *AmMWSc 92*
**Walker,** Kenneth R. 1930- *WhoBlA 92*
**Walker,** Kenneth R. 1951- *WhoBlA 92*
**Walker,** Kenneth Roland *IntAu&W 91*
**Walker,** Kenneth Roland 1928- *WrDr 92*
**Walker,** Kenneth Russell 1937- *AmMWSc 92*
**Walker,** Kent 1944- *WhoAmL 92*
**Walker,** L. T. *WhoRel 92*
**Walker,** Lannon *WhoAmP 91*
**Walker,** Larry *WhoBlA 92*
**Walker,** Larry C 1942- *WhoAmP 91*
**Walker,** Larry Lee 1948- *WhoRel 92*
**Walker,** Larry M. 1935- *WhoBlA 92*
**Walker,** Larry Vaughn 1939- *WhoBlA 92*
**Walker,** Laurence Colton 1924- *AmMWSc 92*
**Walker,** Lawrence Arthur 1956- *WhoFI 92*
**Walker,** Lawrence Daniel 1928- *WhoAmP 91*
**Walker,** Lee H. 1938- *WhoBlA 92*
**Walker,** Leland J 1923- *AmMWSc 92*
**Walker,** Leland Jasper 1923- *WhoWest 92*
**Walker,** Lelia 1886-1954 *NotBlAW 92*
**Walker,** Leon Bryan, Jr 1925- *AmMWSc 92*
**Walker,** LeRoy Harold 1933- *AmMWSc 92*
**Walker,** Leroy Tashreau 1918- *WhoBlA 92*
**Walker,** Lewis 1936- *WhoBlA 92*
**Walker,** Lisa M 1961- *WhoAmP 91*
**Walker,** Lois S *WhoAmP 91*
**Walker,** Lois V. *DrAPF 91*
**Walker,** Loren Haines 1936- *AmMWSc 92*
**Walker,** Lou Ann 1952- *IntAu&W 91, SmATA 66 [port]*
**Walker,** Lucius *WhoBlA 92*
**Walker,** Lucius, Jr. 1930- *WhoBlA 92*
**Walker,** Lucy 1907- *WrDr 92*
**Walker,** Lula Aquillia 1955- *WhoBlA 92*
**Walker,** Lynn Jones *WhoBlA 92*
**Walker,** M Lucius, Jr 1936- *AmMWSc 92, WhoBlA 92*
**Walker,** Maggie L. 1867-1934 *NotBlAW 92 [port]*
**Walker,** Maggie L. 1918- *WhoBlA 92*
**Walker,** Malcolm Conrad 1946- *Who 92*
**Walker,** Mallory Elton 1935- *WhoEnt 92*
**Walker,** Manuel Lorenzo 1930- *WhoBlA 92*
**Walker,** Margaret *DrAPF 91*
**Walker,** Margaret 1915- *AfrAmW, BlkLC [port], ConNov 91, ConPo 91, NotBlAW 92 [port], WrDr 92*
**Walker,** Margaret Abigail 1915- *BenetAL 91, WhoBlA 92*
**Walker,** Maria Latanya 1957- *WhoBlA 92*
**Walker,** Marie 1934- *WhoWest 92*
**Walker,** Mark A. 1941- *WhoAmL 92*
**Walker,** Mark Lamont 1952- *WhoBlA 92*
**Walker,** Marshall John 1912- *AmMWSc 92*
**Walker,** Martha Jane 1957- *WhoMW 92*
**Walker,** Martha Y 1940- *WhoAmP 91*
**Walker,** Martin D. 1932- *WhoMW 92*
**Walker,** Mary Alexander *DrAPF 91*
**Walker,** Mary Alexander 1927- *IntAu&W 91*
**Walker,** Mary Alice 1941- *WhoBlA 92*
**Walker,** Mary Ann 1953- *WhoAmL 92*
**Walker,** Mary Clare *AmMWSc 92*
**Walker,** Mary Edwards 1832-1919 *HanAmWH*
**Walker,** Mary L 1948- *WhoAmP 91*
**Walker,** Mary L. 1951- *WhoBlA 92*
**Walker,** Maurice Edward 1937- *WhoBlA 92*
**Walker,** Max *WrDr 92*
**Walker,** May 1943- *WhoBlA 92*
**Walker,** Melford Whitfield, Jr. 1958- *WhoBlA 92*
**Walker,** Melvin E., Jr. 1946- *WhoBlA 92*
**Walker,** Merle F 1926- *AmMWSc 92*
**Walker,** Michael *Who 92*
**Walker,** Michael 1931- *Who 92*
**Walker,** Michael Barry *AmMWSc 92*
**Walker,** Michael Charles, Sr. 1940- *WhoFI 92*
**Walker,** Michael Claude 1940- *WhoFI 92, WhoMW 92*
**Walker,** Michael Dirck 1931- *AmMWSc 92*
**Walker,** Michael James 1946- *WhoMW 92*
**Walker,** Michael John 1946- *WhoFI 92*
**Walker,** Michael Leolin F. *Who 92*
**Walker,** Michael Stephen 1939- *AmMWSc 92*
**Walker,** Michael Stephen 1940- *AmMWSc 92*
**Walker,** Mike 1949- *WhoAmP 91*
**Walker,** Mildred 1905- *BenetAL 91*
**Walker,** Miles Rawstron 1940- *IntWW 91, Who 92*
**Walker,** Moira Kaye 1940- *WhoFI 92, WhoWest 92*
**Walker,** Moses Andre 1929- *WhoBlA 92*
**Walker,** Moses L. 1940- *WhoBlA 92*
**Walker,** Nancy *LesBEnT 92*
**Walker,** Nancy 1922- *IntMPA 92, WhoEnt 92*
**Walker,** Nancy Eileen 1951- *WhoFI 92, WhoMW 92*
**Walker,** Nancy Slaughter *EncAmaz 91*
**Walker,** Nathan Belt 1952- *WhoAmP 91*
**Walker,** Nathaniel 1909- *AmMWSc 92*
**Walker,** Neil Allan 1924- *AmMWSc 92*
**Walker,** Nigel 1917- *WrDr 92*
**Walker,** Nigel David 1917- *Who 92*
**Walker,** Noel John 1948- *Who 92*
**Walker,** Olene S 1930- *WhoAmP 91*
**Walker,** Pamela *DrAPF 91*
**Walker,** Patric 1931- *NewYTBS 91 [port]*
**Walker,** Patricia Kathleen Randall *Who 92*
**Walker,** Patrick 1932- *Who 92*
**Walker,** Paul A. d1965 *LesBEnT 92*
**Walker,** Paul Crawford 1940- *Who 92*
**Walker,** Paul Ewing 1943- *WhoEnt 92*
**Walker,** Peggy Ada 1955- *WhoAmL 92*
**Walker,** Peter Edward 1932- *IntWW 91, Who 92*
**Walker,** Peter Knight 1919- *Who 92*
**Walker,** Peter Martin Brabazon 1922- *Who 92*
**Walker,** Peter Roy 1945- *AmMWSc 92*
**Walker,** Philip 1924- *ConAu 133*
**Walker,** Philip Caleb 1911- *AmMWSc 92*
**Walker,** Philip Gordon 1912- *Who 92*
**Walker,** Philip Henry Conyers 1926- *Who 92*
**Walker,** Philip L, Jr 1924- *AmMWSc 92*
**Walker,** Philip Smith 1933- *WhoAmL 92*
**Walker,** Ralph Waldo 1928- *WhoAmL 92*
**Walker,** Randolph Clive 1950- *WhoEnt 92*
**Walker,** Raymond 1945- *TwCPaSc*
**Walker,** Raymond Augustus 1943- *Who 92*
**Walker,** Raymond Francis 1914- *WhoFI 92, WhoWest 92*
**Walker,** Raymond James 1943- *Who 92*
**Walker,** Raymond John 1942- *AmMWSc 92*
**Walker,** Reeve *TwCWW 91*
**Walker,** Richard 1942- *Who 92*
**Walker,** Richard 1954- *TwCPaSc*
**Walker,** Richard 1955- *TwCPaSc*
**Walker,** Richard Allen 1935- *WhoWest 92*
**Walker,** Richard Alwyne F. *Who 92*
**Walker,** Richard Battson 1916- *AmMWSc 92*
**Walker,** Richard Bruce 1948- *WhoAmP 91*
**Walker,** Richard David 1931- *AmMWSc 92*
**Walker,** Richard E 1923- *AmMWSc 92*
**Walker,** Richard Francis 1939- *AmMWSc 92*
**Walker,** Richard Henry 1943- *WhoFI 92*
**Walker,** Richard Ives 1942- *AmMWSc 92*
**Walker,** Richard John Boileau 1916- *Who 92*
**Walker,** Richard L *WhoAmP 91*
**Walker,** Richard Lee 1960- *WhoEnt 92*
**Walker,** Richard V 1918- *AmMWSc 92*
**Walker,** Richard Wayne 1935- *WhoMW 92*
**Walker,** Robert 1924- *Who 92*
**Walker,** Robert 1938- *Who 92*
**Walker,** Robert Arnold 1926- *WhoMW 92*
**Walker,** Robert Bridges 1946- *AmMWSc 92*
**Walker,** Robert D, Jr 1912- *AmMWSc 92*
**Walker,** Robert Eugene 1936- *WhoRel 92*
**Walker,** Robert George 1953- *WhoEnt 92*
**Walker,** Robert Glenn 1929- *WhoRel 92*
**Walker,** Robert Hugh 1935- *AmMWSc 92*
**Walker,** Robert John 1801-1869 *AmPolLe*
**Walker,** Robert Lee 1919- *AmMWSc 92*
**Walker,** Robert Mowbray 1929- *AmMWSc 92, IntWW 91*
**Walker,** Robert Paul 1943- *AmMWSc 92*
**Walker,** Robert S. 1942- *AlmAP 92 [port]*
**Walker,** Robert Scott 1913- *Who 92*
**Walker,** Robert Shackford 1945- *WhoAmL 92*
**Walker,** Robert Smith 1942- *WhoAmP 91*

Walker, Robert W 1933- AmMWSc 92
Walker, Robert W 1948- SmATA 66 [port]
Walker, Robert Wayne 1948- IntAu&W 91
Walker, Robert Winn 1925- AmMWSc 92
Walker, Roger 1942- TwCPaSc
Walker, Roger Antony Martineau- 1940- Who 92
Walker, Roger Geoffrey 1939- AmMWSc 92
Walker, Roland 1907- AmMWSc 92
Walker, Ron E 1947- WhoAmP 91
Walker, Ronald IntWW 91
Walker, Ronald d1988 IntWW 91N
Walker, Ronald F. 1938- WhoFI 92, WhoIns 92, WhoMW 92
Walker, Ronald Jack 1940- Who 92
Walker, Ronald Lee 1934- WhoRel 92
Walker, Ronald Plezz 1953- WhoBlA 92
Walker, Rosalee Taylor 1929- WhoAmP 91
Walker, Roy Who 92
Walker, Russell WhoAmP 91
Walker, Russell Glenn 1931- AmMWSc 92
Walker, Russell Wagner 1924- AmMWSc 92
Walker, Russell Wendell 1955- WhoWest 92
Walker, Ruth Angelina 1920- AmMWSc 92
Walker, Sally Barbara 1921- WhoFI 92
Walker, Sally C. WhoWest 92
Walker, Sally W 1929- WhoAmP 91
Walker, Samuel E. 1942- WrDr 92
Walker, Sandra 1946- WhoEnt 92
Walker, Sandra Venezia 1949- WhoBlA 92
Walker, Sarah Elizabeth Royle IntWW 91, Who 92
Walker, Sears Cook 1805-1853 BiInAmS
Walker, Sebastian d1991 Who 92N
Walker, Sharon Leslie 1958- AmMWSc 92
Walker, Sheila Mosley 1917- Who 92
Walker, Sheila Suzanne 1944- WhoBlA 92
Walker, Sheppard Matthew 1909- AmMWSc 92
Walker, Sherry 1960- WhoAmP 91
Walker, Sidney Harris 1925- WhoBlA 92
Walker, Solomon W., II WhoBlA 92
Walker, Sonia 1937- WhoBlA 92
Walker, Stanley Clay 1923- WhoAmP 91
Walker, Stanley Kenneth 1916- Who 92
Walker, Stanley M. 1942- WhoBlA 92
Walker, Stella Archer WrDr 92
Walker, Sterling Wilson 1912- WhoBlA 92
Walker, Steve Allan 1954- WhoEnt 92
Walker, Steven Dennis 1945- WhoMW 92
Walker, Steven Eugene 1960- WhoRel 92
Walker, Stuart 1888-1941 BenetAL 91
Walker, Stuart Andrew 1963- WhoFI 92
Walker, Sue DrAPF 91
Walker, Susan 1906- Who 92
Walker, Susan 1948- WhoEnt 92
Walker, T-Bone 1910-1975 NewAmDM
Walker, Tanya Rosetta 1953- WhoBlA 92
Walker, Ted DrAPF 91
Walker, Ted 1934- ConPo 91, IntAu&W 91, WrDr 92
Walker, Terence William 1935- Who 92
Walker, Terry M 1938- AmMWSc 92
Walker, Theodore Roscoe 1921- AmMWSc 92
Walker, Theresa Anne 1952- AmMWSc 92
Walker, Thomas Cole 1929- WhoFI 92
Walker, Thomas Eugene 1948- AmMWSc 92
Walker, Thomas F 1916- WhoAmP 91
Walker, Thomas Jefferson 1931- AmMWSc 92
Walker, Thomas L. 1948- WhoBlA 92
Walker, Thomas Overington 1933- Who 92
Walker, Thomas William 1916- Who 92
Walker, Timothy Edward 1946- Who 92
Walker, Timothy Edward Hanson 1945- Who 92
Walker, Valaida Smith 1932 WhoBlA 92
Walker, Vanessa Arlene 1960- WhoMW 92
Walker, Vaughn R. 1944- WhoAmL 92
Walker, Vicki Renee 1959- WhoMW 92, WhoRel 92
Walker, Virgil Wayne 1925- WhoAmP 91
Walker, W H 1827-1895 ScFEYrs
Walker, Waldo Sylvester 1931- AmMWSc 92
Walker, Walter 1912- Who 92
Walker, Walter Basil Scarlett 1915- Who 92
Walker, Walter Lorenzo 1935- WhoBlA 92
Walker, Walter Ray 1958- WhoAmL 92
Walker, Walter W 1924- AmMWSc 92
Walker, Walter Wayne 1938- WhoFI 92
Walker, Walter Willard 1911- WhoMW 92
Walker, Warren Elliott 1942- AmMWSc 92
Walker, Warren Franklin, Jr 1918- AmMWSc 92
Walker, Watson Herchael 1918-1990 WhoBlA 92N
Walker, Wayne 1966- WhoBlA 92
Walker, Wellington Epler 1931- AmMWSc 92
Walker, Wendell P. 1930- WhoBlA 92
Walker, Wendy DrAPF 91
Walker, Wendy Diana Knight 1961- WhoFI 92
Walker, Wendy Lauren 1960- WhoAmP 91
Walker, Wesley Darcel 1955- WhoBlA 92
Walker, Wilbert Lee 1925- IntAu&W 91
Walker, Wilbur Gordon 1926- AmMWSc 92
Walker, Wilbur P. 1936- WhoBlA 92
Walker, William 1809-1875 NewAmDM
Walker, William 1824-1860 BenetAL 91
Walker, William 1931- WhoEnt 92
Walker, William 1960- WhoAmP 91
Walker, William Charles 1928- AmMWSc 92
Walker, William Comstock 1921- AmMWSc 92
Walker, William Connoll 1929- Who 92
Walker, William Delany 1923- AmMWSc 92
Walker, William F 1937- AmMWSc 92
Walker, William G WhoAmP 91
Walker, William George 1928- IntAu&W 91, WrDr 92
Walker, William Hamilton 1934- AmMWSc 92, WhoMW 92
Walker, William Harold 1915- WhoBlA 92
Walker, William Henry 1914-1989 WhoBlA 92N
Walker, William Homer, III 1940- WhoFI 92
Walker, William J, Jr AmMWSc 92
Walker, William Jeffrie 1949- WhoEnt 92
Walker, William Johnson 1790-1865 BiInAmS
Walker, William M 1928- AmMWSc 92
Walker, William MacLelland 1933- Who 92
Walker, William Oliver, Jr. 1930- WhoRel 92
Walker, William Paul, Jr. 1940- WhoBlA 92
Walker, William R 1925- AmMWSc 92
Walker, William Ray 1923- WhoEnt 92
Walker, William Ross 1934- WhoFI 92
Walker, William Sonny 1933- WhoBlA 92
Walker, William Stanley 1940- AmMWSc 92
Walker, William Thomas 1953- WhoEnt 92
Walker, William Waldrum 1933- AmMWSc 92
Walker, William Warner 1958- WhoAmL 92
Walker, Willie F. 1942- WhoBlA 92
Walker, Willie M. 1929- WhoBlA 92
Walker, Willie Mark 1929- WhoMW 92
Walker, Williston 1860-1922 EncEarC
Walker, Woodrow Wilson 1919- WhoAmL 92
Walker, Woodson DuBois 1950- WhoBlA 92
Walker, Wyatt Tee 1929- WhoBlA 92
Walker-Daniels, Kimberly Kayne 1958- WhoFI 92
Walker-Haworth, John Liegh 1944- Who 92
Walker-Johnson, Geneva Marie 1944- WhoBlA 92
Walker-Last, Marie 1917- TwCPaSc
Walker-Okeover, Peter 1947- Who 92
Walker-Shaw, Patricia 1939- WhoBlA 92
Walker-Smith Who 92
Walker-Smith, Angelique Keturah 1958- WhoBlA 92, WhoRel 92
Walker-Smith, John Jonah 1939- Who 92
Walker-Taylor, Yvonne WhoBlA 92
Walker-Thoth, Daphne LaVera 1954- WhoBlA 92
Walker-Williams, Hope Denise 1952- WhoBlA 92
Walkiewicz, Thomas Adam 1939- AmMWSc 92
Walkine, Herbert Cleveland 1929- Who 92
Walking Buffalo 1870-1967 RelLAm 91
Walkington, David L 1930- AmMWSc 92
Walkinshaw, Charles Howard, Jr 1935- AmMWSc 92
Walkling, Robert Adolph 1931- AmMWSc 92
Walkling, Walter Douglas 1939- AmMWSc 92
Walkowiak, Diane Kaye 1958- WhoAmP 91
Walkowiak, Edmund Francis 1935- AmMWSc 92
Walkowicz, Chris 1943- ConAu 135
Walkup, Betsy Skinner 1945- WhoEnt 92
Walkup, Charlotte Lloyd 1910- WhoAmL 92
Walkup, John Frank 1941- AmMWSc 92
Walkup, Mary Roe 1924- WhoAmP 91
Walkwitz, Jon Jeffrey 1949- WhoWest 92
Wall, Aaron 1834-1905 RelLAm 91
Wall, Alfreda Who 92
Wall, Anne 1928- Who 92
Wall, Arthur Edward Patrick 1925- WhoRel 92
Wall, Barron Stephen 1951- WhoIns 92
Wall, Beverly Eyvonne 1955- WhoMW 92
Wall, Brian 1931- IntWW 91, TwCPaSc
Wall, Brian Owen 1933- Who 92
Wall, Brian Raymond 1940- WhoFI 92, WhoWest 92
Wall, Carolyn LesBEnT 92
Wall, Charles Terence Clegg 1936- IntWW 91, Who 92
Wall, Clarence Vinson 1947- WhoAmP 91
Wall, Conrad, III 1939- AmMWSc 92
Wall, David 1946- Who 92
Wall, Donald Arthur 1946- WhoAmL 92
Wall, Donald Dines 1921- AmMWSc 92
Wall, Edward Millard 1929- WhoFI 92
Wall, Edward Thomas 1920- AmMWSc 92
Wall, Eric St Quintin 1915- Who 92
Wall, Erving Henry, Jr 1934- WhoAmP 91
Wall, Francis Joseph 1927- AmMWSc 92
Wall, Frank 1885?-1958 ScFEYrs
Wall, Frank A. 1949- IntWW 91
Wall, Frederick Theodore 1912- AmMWSc 92, IntWW 91
Wall, George 1930-1974 TwCPaSc
Wall, Gerard 1920- Who 92
Wall, Gregory John 1944- AmMWSc 92
Wall, Harold Marvin 1922- WhoWest 92
Wall, James M. 1928- ConAu 134
Wall, James McKendree 1928- WhoAmP 91, WhoRel 92
Wall, Janet G 1949- WhoAmP 91
Wall, Joe Layton 1939- WhoRel 92
Wall, John F 1913- WhoAmP 91
Wall, John Hallett 1924- AmMWSc 92
Wall, John Stephen 1947- Who 92
Wall, John T. 1957- WhoEnt 92
Wall, John William 1942- WhoFI 92
Wall, Joseph Frazier 1920- WrDr 92
Wall, Joseph S 1942- AmMWSc 92
Wall, Joseph Sennen 1923- AmMWSc 92
Wall, Kenneth E., Jr. 1944- WhoAmL 92
Wall, Kevin 1952- WhoEnt 92
Wall, Leonard Wong 1941- AmMWSc 92
Wall, Lloyd L. 1936- WhoWest 92
Wall, Malcolm Jefferson, Jr 1941- AmMWSc 92
Wall, Mark Emanuel 1937- WhoFI 92
Wall, Mary Kate 1912- WhoAmL 92
Wall, Mary Sprague 1916- WhoAmP 91
Wall, Max 1908-1990 AnObit 1990, FacFETw
Wall, Mervyn 1908- IntAu&W 91
Wall, Michael, Mrs. Who 92
Wall, Monroe Eliot 1916- AmMWSc 92
Wall, Nicholas Peter Rathbone 1945- Who 92
Wall, P.Q. Lucius John 1931- WhoWest 92
Wall, Patrick 1916- Who 92, WrDr 92
Wall, Patrick David 1925- IntWW 91, Who 92
Wall, Peter K. 1953- WhoFI 92
Wall, Richard Cook 1944- WhoEnt 92
Wall, Robert 1929- Who 92
Wall, Robert A. 1909- WhoAmL 92
Wall, Robert Ecki 1935- AmMWSc 92
Wall, Robert Gene 1937- AmMWSc 92
Wall, Robert H 1928- WhoIns 92
Wall, Robert Lee, Jr 1936- WhoAmP 91
Wall, Robert Leroy 1921- AmMWSc 92
Wall, Robert Percival Walter 1927- Who 92
Wall, Robert Seth 1958- WhoWest 92
Wall, Ronald Eugene 1936- AmMWSc 92
Wall, Ronald George Robert d1991 Who 92N
Wall, Ronald Lynn 1947- WhoFI 92
Wall, Ronald William 1949- WhoWest 92
Wall, Sonja Eloise 1938- WhoFI 92, WhoWest 92
Wall, Stephen Who 92
Wall, Stephen James 1947- WhoFI 92
Wall, Thomas Edward 1949- WhoAmL 92
Wall, Thomas Randolph 1943- AmMWSc 92
Wall, Thomas Ulrich 1944- WhoWest 92
Wall, William Douglas 1913- Who 92
Wall, William James 1921- AmMWSc 92
Wallace Who 92
Wallace, Aaron 1923- AmMWSc 92
Wallace, Albert Frederick 1921- Who 92
Wallace, Alexander Cameron 1921- AmMWSc 92
Wallace, Alexander Fielding 1918-1991 ConAu 135
Wallace, Alfred Thomas 1935- AmMWSc 92
Wallace, Allen 1953- WhoWest 92
Wallace, Allen F. 1948- WhoAmL 92
Wallace, Alton Smith 1944- AmMWSc 92
Wallace, Amy 1955- WhoWest 92
Wallace, Andrew Grover 1935- AmMWSc 92
Wallace, Andrew Hugh 1926- AmMWSc 92
Wallace, Anne Paterson TwCPaSc
Wallace, Anthony F. C. 1923- IntWW 91
Wallace, Archibald, III 1938- WhoAmL 92
Wallace, Arnold D., Sr. 1932- WhoBlA 92
Wallace, Arnold Delaney, Sr. 1932- WhoEnt 92
Wallace, Arthur 1919- AmMWSc 92
Wallace, Arthur, Jr. 1939- WhoBlA 92, WhoFI 92
Wallace, Atwell Milton 1914- WhoMW 92
Wallace, Barbara Brooks WrDr 92
Wallace, Barry 1953- WhoMW 92
Wallace, Beatrice Leslie 1934- WhoMW 92
Wallace, Betty Frances 1926- IntAu&W 91
Wallace, Betty Jean 1927- WhoRel 92
Wallace, Big-Foot BenetAL 91
Wallace, Bill 1956- WhoAmP 91
Wallace, Brenda Anne 1941- WhoAmP 91
Wallace, Bruce DrAPF 91
Wallace, Bruce 1920- AmMWSc 92, IntWW 91, WrDr 92
Wallace, Bruce Sanford 1958- WhoAmL 92
Wallace, C E 1929- AmMWSc 92
Wallace, C. Everett 1951- WhoBlA 92
Wallace, Carl J 1938- AmMWSc 92
Wallace, Carol Louise 1943- WhoEnt 92
Wallace, Charles A. 1930- WhoEnt 92
Wallace, Charles Isaac, Jr. 1943- WhoRel 92
Wallace, Charles Leslie 1945- WhoBlA 92
Wallace, Charles William 1926- Who 92
Wallace, Chester Alan 1942- AmMWSc 92
Wallace, Chris LesBEnT 92
Wallace, Claudette J. WhoBlA 92
Wallace, Clyde Howard 1924- WhoRel 92
Wallace, Craig Kesting 1928- AmMWSc 92
Wallace, Daniel Baird 1952- WhoRel 92
Wallace, David Foster DrAPF 91
Wallace, David H 1937- AmMWSc 92
Wallace, David James 1945- IntWW 91, Who 92
Wallace, David Lee 1928- AmMWSc 92
Wallace, David Mitchell 1913- Who 92
Wallace, David William 1924- WhoWest 92
Wallace, Derrick D. 1953- WhoBlA 92
Wallace, Dewey D., Jr. 1936- WhoRel 92
Wallace, DeWitt 1889-1981 RComAH
Wallace, Dexter ConAu 133
Wallace, Dillon 1863-1939 BenetAL 91
Wallace, Don, Jr. 1932- WhoAmL 92
Wallace, Donald Ernest 1946- WhoMW 92
Wallace, Donald Howard 1926- AmMWSc 92
Wallace, Donald Macpherson, Jr 1934- AmMWSc 92
Wallace, Dorothy Jacqueline H. Who 92
Wallace, Douglas Cecil 1946- AmMWSc 92
Wallace, Edgar 1875-1932 RfGEnL 91, ScFEYrs, TwCSFW 91
Wallace, Edith Winchell 1935- AmMWSc 92
Wallace, Edwin Garfield 1917- AmMWSc 92
Wallace, Elaine Wendy 1949- WhoAmL 92
Wallace, F L TwCSFW 91, WrDr 92
Wallace, Fleming Who 92
Wallace, Foy Esco, Jr. 1896-1979 RelLAm 91
Wallace, Franklin Gerhard 1909- AmMWSc 92
Wallace, Franklin Sherwood 1927- WhoMW 92
Wallace, Frederic Andrew 1933- AmMWSc 92
Wallace, Gary Dean 1946- AmMWSc 92
Wallace, Gary Oren 1940- AmMWSc 92
Wallace, George DrAPF 91
Wallace, George C 1919- RComAH
Wallace, George C, Jr 1951- WhoAmP 91
Wallace, George Corley 1919- AmPolLe [port], FacFETw [port], IntWW 91, WhoAmP 91
Wallace, George Karren 1958- WhoWest 92
Wallace, George Washington, Jr. 1930- WhoWest 92
Wallace, Gerald Wayne 1933- AmMWSc 92
Wallace, Gordon Dean 1927- AmMWSc 92
Wallace, Gordon Thomas 1942- AmMWSc 92
Wallace, Graham Franklin 1935- AmMWSc 92
Wallace, H. Bruce 1947- WhoWest 92
Wallace, Harden Wilson 1922- WhoBlA 92
Wallace, Harold Dean 1922- AmMWSc 92
Wallace, Harold Gene 1945- WhoBlA 92
Wallace, Harry Leland 1927- WhoAmL 92
Wallace, Helen M 1913- AmMWSc 92

**Wallace**, Helen Margaret 1913- WhoWest 92
**Wallace**, Helen Winfree-Peyton 1927- WhoBlA 92
**Wallace**, Henry A. 1888-1965 BenetAL 91, FacFETw [port]
**Wallace**, Henry Agard 1888-1965 AmPeW, AmPolLe
**Wallace**, Henry Jared, Jr. 1943- WhoAmL 92
**Wallace**, Herbert Norman 1937- WhoAmL 92
**Wallace**, Herbert William 1930- AmMWSc 92
**Wallace**, Homer L. 1941- WhoBlA 92
**Wallace**, Ian 1912- TwCSFW 91, WrDr 92
**Wallace**, Ian 1919- IntWW 91
**Wallace**, Ian 1950- WrDr 92
**Wallace**, Ian Alexander 1917- Who 92
**Wallace**, Ian Bryce 1919- Who 92
**Wallace**, Ian James 1916- Who 92
**Wallace**, Ian Norman Duncan 1922- Who 92
**Wallace**, Ian Robert 1950- IntAu&W 91
**Wallace**, Irving 1916- IntAu&W 91
**Wallace**, Irving 1916-1990 AnObit 1990, FacFETw, News 91
**Wallace**, Ivan Harold Nutt 1935- Who 92
**Wallace**, J. Clifford 1928- WhoAmL 92, WhoAmP 91, WhoWest 92
**Wallace**, Jack E 1934- AmMWSc 92
**Wallace**, James WrDr 92
**Wallace**, James 1932- AmMWSc 92
**Wallace**, James Alfonso 1948- WhoBlA 92
**Wallace**, James Bruce 1939- AmMWSc 92
**Wallace**, James D 1904- AmMWSc 92
**Wallace**, James Fleming 1931- Who 92
**Wallace**, James H, Jr 1942- WhoAmP 91
**Wallace**, James Harold, Jr. 1941- WhoAmL 92
**Wallace**, James John 1946 WhoFI 92
**Wallace**, James M 1939- AmMWSc 92
**Wallace**, James Price 1928- WhoAmP 91
**Wallace**, James Robert 1938- AmMWSc 92
**Wallace**, James Robert 1954- Who 92
**Wallace**, James Wendell 1930- WhoWest 92
**Wallace**, James William, Jr 1940- AmMWSc 92
**Wallace**, Jeannette O 1934- WhoAmP 91
**Wallace**, Jeffrey J. 1946- WhoBlA 92
**Wallace**, Jesse Wyatt 1925- WhoFI 92
**Wallace**, Jessie Irene Turner 1922- WhoEnt 92
**Wallace**, Joan M 1928- AmMWSc 92
**Wallace**, Joan S 1930- WhoAmP 91
**Wallace**, Joan Scott 1930- NotBlAW 92
**Wallace**, Jody Namio 1954- WhoMW 92
**Wallace**, Joel Keith 1933- WhoRel 92, WhoWest 92
**Wallace**, John Andrew 1961- WhoMW 92
**Wallace**, John Craig 1954- WhoAmL 92
**Wallace**, John E., Jr. 1942- WhoBlA 92
**Wallace**, John F 1919- AmMWSc 92
**Wallace**, John Howard 1925- AmMWSc 92, WhoBlA 92
**Wallace**, John Joseph 1947- WhoWest 92
**Wallace**, John M, Jr 1924- AmMWSc 92
**Wallace**, John Malcolm 1928- WrDr 92
**Wallace**, John Malcolm Agnew 1928- Who 92
**Wallace**, John Michael 1940- AmMWSc 92
**Wallace**, John Williamson 1949- Who 92
**Wallace**, Jon Berkley 1939- WhoMW 92
**Wallace**, Jon Marques 1943- AmMWSc 92
**Wallace**, Joseph Fletcher, Jr. 1921- WhoBlA 92
**Wallace**, Karen Smyley 1943- WhoBlA 92
**Wallace**, Keith G. 1926- WhoFI 92
**Wallace**, Keith M. 1956- WhoAmL 92
**Wallace**, Kendall B 1953- AmMWSc 92
**Wallace**, Kenneth Alan 1938- WhoWest 92
**Wallace**, King ScFEYrs
**Wallace**, Kyle David 1943- AmMWSc 92
**Wallace**, Lance Arthur 1938- AmMWSc 92
**Wallace**, Larry J 1937- AmMWSc 92
**Wallace**, Laurence 1952- TwCPaSc
**Wallace**, Lawrence Eugene 1940- WhoRel 92
**Wallace**, Lawrence James 1913- Who 92
**Wallace**, Leigh Allen, Jr. 1927- WhoRel 92
**Wallace**, Lew 1827-1905 BenetAL 91
**Wallace**, Lewis 1827-1905 BibAL 8
**Wallace**, Lou Ella 1936- WhoAmP 91
**Wallace**, Louise Margaret 1942- WhoMW 92
**Wallace**, Mack 1929- WhoAmP 91
**Wallace**, Malcolm Charles Robarts 1947- Who 92
**Wallace**, Marc Charles 1957- WhoWest 92
**Wallace**, Marion Brooks 1917- AmMWSc 92
**Wallace**, Mark Douglas 1949- WhoEnt 92
**Wallace**, Mark Harris 1955- WhoRel 92
**Wallace**, Mark I. 1956- WhoRel 92
**Wallace**, Mary Ann 1939- WhoWest 92
**Wallace**, Matthew Walker 1924- WhoWest 92
**Wallace**, Michael Arthur 1951- WhoMW 92
**Wallace**, Michael Dwight 1947- AmMWSc 92
**Wallace**, Michael Lee 1935- WhoMW 92
**Wallace**, Mike LesBEnT 92 [port]
**Wallace**, Mike 1918- IntMPA 92
**Wallace**, Milton De'Nard 1957- WhoBlA 92
**Wallace**, Minor Gordon, Jr. 1936- WhoFI 92
**Wallace**, Nancy Diane 1958- WhoWest 92
**Wallace**, Paul Francis 1927- AmMWSc 92
**Wallace**, Paul Harvey 1944- WhoAmL 92, WhoWest 92
**Wallace**, Paul Starett, Jr. 1941- WhoBlA 92
**Wallace**, Paul William 1936- AmMWSc 92
**Wallace**, Perry Eugene 1948- WhoBlA 92
**Wallace**, Peter Dart 1943- WhoMW 92
**Wallace**, Peter Rudy 1954- WhoAmP 91
**Wallace**, Philip Russell 1915- AmMWSc 92
**Wallace**, Phyllis A. WhoBlA 92
**Wallace**, Phyllis Ann 192-?- NotBlAW 92
**Wallace**, Ralph Ray, III 1949- WhoAmP 91
**Wallace**, Randall 1954- WhoEnt 92
**Wallace**, Raymond Howard, Jr 1936- AmMWSc 92
**Wallace**, Reginald James 1919- Who 92
**Wallace**, Renee C. WhoBlA 92
**Wallace**, Richard Alexander 1946- Who 92
**Wallace**, Richard Harris, Jr 1944- WhoAmP 91
**Wallace**, Richard Kent 1954- AmMWSc 92
**Wallace**, Richard Warner 1929- WhoBlA 92
**Wallace**, Robert DrAPF 91, WhoMW 92, WrDr 92
**Wallace**, Robert 1697-1771 BlkwCEP
**Wallace**, Robert 1911- Who 92
**Wallace**, Robert Allan 1930- AmMWSc 92
**Wallace**, Robert B. 1935- WhoAmL 92
**Wallace**, Robert B 1937- AmMWSc 92
**Wallace**, Robert Bruce 1933- WhoRel 92
**Wallace**, Robert Bruce 1942- WhoMW 92
**Wallace**, Robert Bruce 1944- WhoAmL 92
**Wallace**, Robert Bruce 1950- AmMWSc 92
**Wallace**, Robert Earl 1916- AmMWSc 92, WhoWest 92
**Wallace**, Robert F. 1965- WhoEnt 92
**Wallace**, Robert Henry AmMWSc 92
**Wallace**, Robert Luther, II 1949- WhoMW 92
**Wallace**, Robert William 1943- AmMWSc 92
**Wallace**, Robin A 1933- AmMWSc 92
**Wallace**, Ronald DrAPF 91
**Wallace**, Ronald Gary 1938- AmMWSc 92
**Wallace**, Ronald Wilfred 1941- WhoBlA 92
**Wallace**, Ronald William 1945- IntAu&W 91, WhoMW 92
**Wallace**, Ronnie Lee 1958- WhoRel 92
**Wallace**, Samuel 1949- WhoBlA 92
**Wallace**, Samuel Taylor 1943- WhoMW 92
**Wallace**, Sharon Ann 1946- WhoWest 92
**Wallace**, Sherwood Lee WhoMW 92
**Wallace**, Sidney 1929- AmMWSc 92
**Wallace**, Sippie 1898-1976 NotBlAW 92
**Wallace**, Sippie 1898-1986 ConBlB 1 [port], ConMus 6 [port]
**Wallace**, Stephen Joseph 1939- AmMWSc 92
**Wallace**, Steven Charles 1953- WhoAmL 92
**Wallace**, Steven Rollinson 1955- WhoMW 92
**Wallace**, Stewart Raynor 1919- AmMWSc 92
**Wallace**, Susan Scholes 1938- AmMWSc 92
**Wallace**, Susan Ulmer 1952- AmMWSc 92
**Wallace**, Sylvia WrDr 92
**Wallace**, Terry Charles 1933- AmMWSc 92
**Wallace**, Terry Charles, Jr 1956- AmMWSc 92
**Wallace**, Terry S. DrAPF 91
**Wallace**, Theodore Calvin 1951- WhoAmP 91
**Wallace**, Theodore Richmond 1949- WhoBlA 92
**Wallace**, Thomas Patrick 1935- AmMWSc 92, WhoMW 92
**Wallace**, Todd 1961- WhoAmL 92
**Wallace**, Tracy I 1924- AmMWSc 92
**Wallace**, Victor Lew 1933- AmMWSc 92
**Wallace**, Vincent 1812-1865 NewAmDM
**Wallace**, Volney 1925- AmMWSc 92
**Wallace**, W Lawrence 1949- WhoAmP 91
**Wallace**, Walter Ian James 1905- Who 92
**Wallace**, Walter Wilkinson 1923- IntWW 91, Who 92
**Wallace**, William 1940- AmMWSc 92, WhoWest 92
**Wallace**, William Alexander Anderson BenetAL 91
**Wallace**, William Arthur, Jr. 1942- WhoWest 92
**Wallace**, William Donald 1933- AmMWSc 92
**Wallace**, William Edward 1917- AmMWSc 92
**Wallace**, William Edward, Jr 1942- AmMWSc 92
**Wallace**, William J 1935- AmMWSc 92
**Wallace**, William James 1935- WhoMW 92
**Wallace**, William James Lord 1908- AmMWSc 92, WhoBlA 92
**Wallace**, William John Lawrence 1941- Who 92
**Wallace**, William Ray 1923- WhoFI 92
**Wallace**, William Ross 1819-1881 BenetAL 91
**Wallace**, William Wales 1959- WhoWest 92
**Wallace-Crabbe**, Chris 1934- ConPo 91
**Wallace-Crabbe**, Christopher 1934- WrDr 92
**Wallace-Crabbe**, Christopher Keith 1934- IntWW 91
**Wallace-Martinez**, Elvia 1948- WhoHisp 92
**Wallace of Campsie**, Baron 1915- Who 92
**Wallace of Coslany**, Baron 1906- Who 92
**Wallace-Padgett**, Debra Kaye 1958- WhoRel 92
**Wallach**, Allan Henry 1927- WhoEnt 92
**Wallach**, Anne Jackson WhoEnt 92
**Wallach**, Benno M. 1923- WhoRel 92
**Wallach**, Edward E 1933- AmMWSc 92
**Wallach**, Eli 1915- IntMPA 92, IntWW 91, WhoEnt 92
**Wallach**, Erica 1922- WrDr 92
**Wallach**, George 1918- IntMPA 92
**Wallach**, Ira 1913- WrDr 92
**Wallach**, Jacques Burton 1926- AmMWSc 92
**Wallach**, Jason Jonathan 1957- WhoFI 92
**Wallach**, Jerome 1938- WhoAmL 92
**Wallach**, Joelle 1952- WhoEnt 92
**Wallach**, Marshall Ben 1940- AmMWSc 92
**Wallach**, Michael Charles 1957- WhoMW 92
**Wallach**, Otto 1847-1931 WhoNob 90
**Wallach**, Paul 1925- WhoWest 92
**Wallach**, Richard Wingard 1927- WhoAmL 92
**Wallach**, Robert P WhoAmP 91
**Wallach**, Stanley 1928- AmMWSc 92
**Wallach**, Sylvan 1914- AmMWSc 92
**Wallack**, Paul Mark 1927- AmMWSc 92
**Wallance**, Don 1909- DcTwDes
**Wallance**, Gregory J. 1948- WhoAmL 92
**Wallander**, Jerome F 1939- AmMWSc 92
**Wallant**, Edward Lewis 1926-1962 BenetAL 91
**Wallbank**, Alfred Mills 1925- AmMWSc 92
**Wallbrunn**, Henry Maurice 1918- AmMWSc 92
**Wallcave**, Lawrence 1926- AmMWSc 92
**Walle**, James Paul 1956- WhoAmL 92, WhoMW 92
**Walleigh**, Robert S 1915- AmMWSc 92
**Wallek**, Lee DrAPF 91
**Wallen**, Clarence Joseph 1916- AmMWSc 92
**Wallen**, Cynthia Anne 1952- AmMWSc 92
**Wallen**, Donald George 1933- AmMWSc 92
**Wallen**, Ella Kathleen 1914- Who 92
**Wallen**, Lowell Lawrence 1921- AmMWSc 92
**Wallen**, Martha Louise 1946- WhoMW 92
**Wallen**, Raeburn Glenn 1931- WhoRel 92
**Wallen**, Richard Lee 1953- WhoMW 92
**Wallen**, Stanley Eugene 1948- AmMWSc 92
**Wallenberg**, Frank A 1936- WhoIns 92
**Wallenberg**, Peter 1926- IntWW 91, Who 92
**Wallenberg**, Raoul 1912-19--? FacFETw
**Wallenberger**, Frederick Theodore 1930- AmMWSc 92
**Wallencheck**, Elizabeth Marie 1956- WhoMW 92
**Wallenda**, Enrico B. 1955- WhoEnt 92
**Wallender**, Michael Todd 1950- WhoAmL 92, WhoFI 92
**Wallender**, Wesley William 1954- AmMWSc 92, WhoWest 92
**Wallenfeldt**, Evert 1904- AmMWSc 92
**Wallenfels**, Miklos 1934- AmMWSc 92
**Wallengren**, Ernest Ferrin 1952- WhoEnt 92
**Wallenhorst**, Timothy James 1954- WhoMW 92
**Wallenius**, Kurt Martti 1893-1984 BiDExR
**Wallenmeyer**, William Anton 1926- AmMWSc 92
**Wallenstein**, Alfred 1898-1983 FacFETw, NewAmDM
**Wallenstein**, Barry DrAPF 91
**Wallenstein**, James Harry 1942- WhoAmL 92
**Wallenstein**, John S. 1950- WhoAmL 92
**Wallenstein**, Martin Cecil AmMWSc 92
**Wallentine**, Max V 1931- AmMWSc 92
**Waller**, Arlou Gill 1922- WhoMW 92
**Waller**, Bradley Allan 1963- WhoWest 92
**Waller**, Bruce Frank 1947- AmMWSc 92, WhoMW 92
**Waller**, Coy Webster 1914- AmMWSc 92
**Waller**, David Percival 1943- AmMWSc 92
**Waller**, Donald Macgregor 1951- AmMWSc 92
**Waller**, Edmund 1606-1687 RfGEnL 91
**Waller**, Elwyn 1846-1919 BiInAmS
**Waller**, Eunice McLean 1921- WhoBlA 92
**Waller**, Fats 1904-1943 ConMus 7 [port], NewAmDM
**Waller**, Francis Joseph 1943- AmMWSc 92
**Waller**, Gary Lee 1950- WhoRel 92
**Waller**, Gary Peter Anthony 1945- Who 92
**Waller**, George Macgregor WrDr 92
**Waller**, George Mark 1940- Who 92
**Waller**, George Rozier, Jr 1927- AmMWSc 92
**Waller**, George Stanley 1911- Who 92
**Waller**, Gordon David 1935- AmMWSc 92
**Waller**, Hardress Jocelyn 1928- AmMWSc 92
**Waller**, Irene Ellen 1928- WrDr 92
**Waller**, J. Garland 1950- WhoEnt 92
**Waller**, J. Michael 1959- WhoAmL 92
**Waller**, James R 1931- AmMWSc 92
**Waller**, John James 1924- WhoWest 92
**Waller**, John Keith 1914- Who 92
**Waller**, John Robert 1946- WhoMW 92
**Waller**, John Stanier 1917- IntAu&W 91, Who 92
**Waller**, John Stevens 1924- Who 92
**Waller**, John Wayne 1937- AmMWSc 92
**Waller**, Jonathan 1956- TwCPaSc
**Waller**, Juanita Ann 1958- WhoBlA 92
**Waller**, Julian Arnold 1932- AmMWSc 92
**Waller**, Keith Who 92
**Waller**, Keith G. 1957- WhoRel 92
**Waller**, Larry 1947- WhoBlA 92
**Waller**, Larry Gene 1948- WhoWest 92
**Waller**, Larry James 1940- WhoMW 92
**Waller**, Leslie 1923- WrDr 92
**Waller**, Louis E. 1928- WhoBlA 92
**Waller**, Mark Who 92
**Waller**, Mary Ella 1855-1938 BenetAL 91
**Waller**, Paul Pressley, Jr. 1924- WhoAmL 92
**Waller**, Peter William 1926- WhoWest 92
**Waller**, Ray Albert 1937- AmMWSc 92
**Waller**, Rhoda DrAPF 91
**Waller**, Richard Conrad 1915- AmMWSc 92
**Waller**, Robert Carl 1931- WhoWest 92
**Waller**, Robert Lee 1924-1990 WhoBlA 92N
**Waller**, Robert Morris 1944- WhoMW 92
**Waller**, Robert Rex 1937- WhoMW 92
**Waller**, Robert William 1934- Who 92
**Waller**, Roger Milton 1926- AmMWSc 92
**Waller**, Samuel Carpenter 1918- WhoAmP 91
**Waller**, Seth 1933- WhoAmL 92, WhoFI 92
**Waller**, Steven Scobee 1947- AmMWSc 92
**Waller**, Thomas 1904-1943 FacFETw [port]
**Waller**, Thomas Richard 1937- AmMWSc 92
**Waller**, William L 1926- WhoAmP 91
**Waller**, William T 1941- AmMWSc 92
**Wallerich**, Peter Kenneth 1931- WhoWest 92
**Wallerstein**, Bruce Lee 1943- WhoWest 92
**Wallerstein**, David Vandermere 1937- AmMWSc 92
**Wallerstein**, Edward Perry 1928- AmMWSc 92
**Wallerstein**, George 1930- AmMWSc 92
**Wallerstein**, Judith S 1921- IntAu&W 91
**Wallerstein**, Ralph O. 1922- IntWW 91
**Wallerstein**, Ralph Oliver 1922- WhoWest 92
**Wallerstein**, Ralph Oliver, Jr 1953- AmMWSc 92
**Wallerstein**, Robert Solomon 1921- AmMWSc 92, WhoWest 92
**Walles**, James Alton 1933- WhoWest 92
**Walles**, Wilhelm Egbert 1925- AmMWSc 92
**Wallestad**, Philip Weston 1922- WhoMW 92

Wallette, Alonzo Vandolph 1940- *WhoBlA 92*
Walley, Francis 1918- *Who 92*
Walley, Joan Lorraine 1949- *Who 92*
Walley, John 1906- *Who 92*
Walley, Keith Henry 1928- *Who 92*
Walley, Page Blakeslee 1957- *WhoAmP 91*
Walley, William W *WhoAmP 91*
Walley, Willis Wayne 1934- *AmMWSc 92*
Wallick, Charles C. 1916- *WhoRel 92*
Wallick, Earl Taylor 1938- *AmMWSc 92*
Wallick, Ernest Herron 1928- *WhoBlA 92*
Wallick, George Castor 1923- *AmMWSc 92*
Wallin, Angie *WhoWest 92*
Wallin, Daniel Guy 1927- *WhoEnt 92*
Wallin, David Ernest 1955- *WhoFI 92*
Wallin, Desna L. 1946- *WhoMW 92*
Wallin, Jack Robb 1915- *AmMWSc 92, WhoMW 92*
Wallin, John David 1937- *AmMWSc 92*
Wallin, Kenneth E 1930- *WhoAmP 91*
Wallin, Norman Elroy 1914- *WhoAmP 91*
Wallin, Richard Franklin 1939- *AmMWSc 92*
Wallin, Winston Roger 1926- *WhoFI 92*
Walling, Albert Clinton, II 1925- *WhoRel 92*
Walling, Cheves 1916- *AmMWSc 92, IntWW 91*
Walling, Cheves T. 1916- *WhoWest 92*
Walling, Derald Dee 1937- *AmMWSc 92*
Walling, Esther Kolb 1940- *WhoAmP 91*
Walling, Henry Francis 1825-1888 *BiInAmS*
Walling, Margaret S 1924- *WhoAmP 91*
Walling, Robert H 1927- *WhoAmP 91*
Walling, Susan Eileen Femrite 1944- *WhoMW 92*
Walling, William English *DcAmImH*
Walling, Willis Ray *WhoAmP 91*
Wallinger, George Arthur 1930- *WhoFI 92*
Wallinger, Mark 1959- *TwCPaSc*
Wallinger, Melvin Bruce 1945- *WhoAmL 92*
Wallingford, Errol E 1928- *AmMWSc 92*
Wallingford, John Stuart 1935- *AmMWSc 92*
Wallington, James R, Jr 1944- *BlkOlyM*
Wallington, Jeremy Francis 1935- *Who 92*
Wallins, Roger Peyton 1941- *WhoWest 92*
Wallis, Alfred 1855-1942 *TwCPaSc*
Wallis, B *ScFEYrs*
Wallis, Barnes Neville 1887-1979 *FacFETw*
Wallis, Ben Alton, Jr. 1936- *WhoAmL 92, WhoFI 92*
Wallis, Clifford Merrill 1904- *AmMWSc 92*
Wallis, Colin 1937- *TwCPaSc*
Wallis, Diana Lynn 1946- *WhoEnt 92*
Wallis, Dick 1931- *WhoAmP 91*
Wallis, Donald Douglas James H 1943- *AmMWSc 92*
Wallis, Donald Wills 1950- *WhoAmL 92*
Wallis, Edmund Arthur 1939- *Who 92*
Wallis, Elizabeth Susan 1953- *WhoMW 92*
Wallis, Frederick Alfred John E. *Who 92*
Wallis, George C *ScFEYrs*
Wallis, George C and Wallis B *ScFEYrs*
Wallis, Graham B 1936- *AmMWSc 92*
Wallis, Hal B 1899-1986 *FacFETw*
Wallis, Hugh Macdonell d1991 *Who 92N*
Wallis, Jeffrey Joseph 1923- *Who 92*
Wallis, Joe D. 1958- *WhoRel 92*
Wallis, Kay F 1944- *WhoAmP 91*
Wallis, Lloyd Randall 1954- *WhoMW 92*
Wallis, Olney Gray 1940- *WhoAmL 92*
Wallis, Peter Gordon 1935- *Who 92*
Wallis, Peter Malcolm 1952- *AmMWSc 92*
Wallis, Peter Ralph 1924- *Who 92*
Wallis, Richard Fisher 1924- *AmMWSc 92*
Wallis, Richard James 1954- *WhoAmL 92*
Wallis, Robert Charles 1921- *AmMWSc 92*
Wallis, Robert L 1934- *AmMWSc 92*
Wallis, Sheran Payne 1944- *WhoMW 92*
Wallis, Thomas Gary 1948- *AmMWSc 92*
Wallis, Victor Harry 1922- *Who 92*
Wallis, W. Allen *LesBEnT 92*
Wallis, W Allen 1912- *AmMWSc 92, WhoAmP 91*
Wallis, Walter Denis 1941- *AmMWSc 92*
Wallis, William *DrAPF 91*
Wallis-Jones, Ewan Perrins 1913- *Who 92*
Wallis-King, Colin Sainthill 1926- *Who 92*
Walliser, Blair A. 1917- *WhoEnt 92, WhoFI 92*
Walliser, Otto Heinrich 1928- *IntWW 91*
Wallison, Frieda K. 1943- *WhoAmL 92*
Wallison, Peter J. 1941- *WhoAmL 92*
Wallman, Charles James 1924- *WhoFI 92, WhoMW 92*
Wallman, Charles Stephen 1953- *WhoFI 92*
Wallman, David Thees 1949- *WhoIns 92*
Wallman, Joshua 1943- *AmMWSc 92*
Wallman, Walter 1932- *IntWW 91*
Wallmann, Jeffrey M 1941- *ConAu 35NR, IntAu&W 91*
Wallmann, Jeffrey Miner 1941- *WhoWest 92*
Wallmark, J Torkel 1919- *AmMWSc 92*
Wallmeyer, Dick *ConAu 133*
Wallmeyer, Richard 1931- *ConAu 133*
Wallnau, Carl Newman 1953- *WhoEnt 92*
Wallner, Jack Devereux 1955- *WhoEnt 92*
Wallner, Mary Jane 1946- *WhoAmP 91*
Wallner, Pete 1949- *WhoIns 92*
Wallner, Stephen John 1945- *AmMWSc 92*
Wallner, William E 1936- *AmMWSc 92*
Walloch, Esther Coto 1938- *WhoHisp 92*
Wallop *Who 92*
Wallop, Douglass *DrAPF 91*
Wallop, Malcolm 1933- *AlmAP 92 [port], IntWW 91, WhoAmP 91, WhoWest 92*
Wallot, Jean-Pierre 1935- *IntWW 91, WhoMW 92*
Wallot, Paul 1841-1912 *EncTR 91*
Wallower, Lucille 1910- *WrDr 92*
Wallraff, Barbara Jean 1953- *WhoFI 92*
Wallraff, Evelyn Bartels 1920- *AmMWSc 92*
Wallrock, John 1922- *Who 92*
Walls, Andrew Finlay 1928- *WhoRel 92*
Walls, Betty Lou 1930- *WhoAmP 91*
Walls, Daniel Frank 1942- *IntWW 91*
Walls, David Robert 1953- *WhoRel 92*
Walls, Doyle Wesley *DrAPF 91*
Walls, Eldred Wright 1912- *Who 92*
Walls, Everson 1959- *WhoBlA 92*
Walls, Forest Wesley 1939- *WhoAmL 92*
Walls, Fredric T. 1935- *WhoBlA 92*
Walls, Geoffrey Nowell 1945- *Who 92*
Walls, George Hilton, Jr. 1942- *WhoBlA 92*
Walls, Glen Alan *WhoMW 92*
Walls, Hugh A 1934- *AmMWSc 92*
Walls, Ian G. 1922- *WrDr 92*
Walls, Ian Gascoigne 1922- *IntAu&W 91*
Walls, James Douglas 1931- *WhoRel 92*
Walls, John William 1927- *WhoMW 92*
Walls, Kenneth W 1928- *AmMWSc 92*
Walls, Margaret Susan 1951- *WhoEnt 92*
Walls, Melvin 1948- *WhoBlA 92*
Walls, Nancy Williams 1930- *AmMWSc 92*
Walls, Patrick Osa 1938- *WhoFI 92*
Walls, Peter 1926- *IntWW 91*
Walls, Robert Blocksom 1905- *WhoAmL 92*
Walls, Robert Clarence 1934- *AmMWSc 92*
Walls, Roland Charles 1917- *Who 92*
Walls, Stephen Roderick 1947- *Who 92*
Walls, William Hamilton 1932- *WhoAmL 92*
Walls, William Jacob 1885-1975 *RelLAm 91*
Wallschlaeger, Michael John 1943- *WhoMW 92*
Wallskog, Joyce Marie 1942- *WhoMW 92*
Wallstrom, Margot 1954- *IntWW 91*
Wallstrom, Wesley Donald 1929- *WhoFI 92, WhoWest 92*
Wallwork, Craig Raymond 1951- *WhoFI 92*
Wallwork, John 1946- *Who 92*
Wallwork, John Sackfield 1918- *Who 92*
Wallworth, Cyril 1916- *Who 92*
Wally, Walter Edward 1929- *WhoFI 92*
Walman, Thomas H 1943- *WhoAmP 91*
Walmer, Edwin Fitch 1930- *WhoAmL 92*
Walmer, James L. 1948- *WhoAmL 92*
Walmsley, Arnold Robert 1912- *Who 92*
Walmsley, Arthur Edward 1928- *WhoRel 92*
Walmsley, Brian 1936- *Who 92*
Walmsley, David George 1938- *IntWW 91*
Walmsley, Francis Joseph 1926- *Who 92*
Walmsley, Frank 1935- *AmMWSc 92*
Walmsley, Ian Alexander 1960- *AmMWSc 92*
Walmsley, Judith Abrams 1936- *AmMWSc 92*
Walmsley, Nigel Norman 1942- *Who 92*
Walmsley, Peter James 1929- *Who 92*
Walmsley, Peter N 1936- *AmMWSc 92*
Walmsley, Robert 1906- *Who 92*
Walmsley, Robert 1941- *Who 92*
Walmsley, Tom 1948- *IntAu&W 91*
Waln, Robert 1794-1825 *BenetAL 91*
Walne, Kathleen 1915- *TwCPaSc*
Walne, Patricia Lee 1932- *AmMWSc 92*
Walner, Robert Joel 1946- *WhoAmL 92, WhoMW 92*
Walnut, Thomas Henry, Jr 1924- *AmMWSc 92*
Waloga, Geraldine 1946- *AmMWSc 92*
Walper, Jack Louis 1916- *AmMWSc 92*
Walpert, George W 1924- *AmMWSc 92*
Walpin, Gerald 1931- *WhoAmL 92*
Walpole *Who 92*
Walpole, Baron 1938- *Who 92*
Walpole, Alton Lewis 1946- *WhoEnt 92*
Walpole, Frederick A 1861-1904 *BiInAmS*
Walpole, Horace 1717-1797 *BlkwCEP, RfGEnL 91*
Walpole, Hugh 1884-1941 *FacFETw, RfGEnL 91*
Walpole, Ronald Edgar 1931- *AmMWSc 92*
Walrad, Charlene Chuck 1946- *WhoWest 92*
Walradt, John Pierce 1942- *AmMWSc 92*
Walrafen, George Edouard 1929- *AmMWSc 92*
Walrath, Harry Rienzi 1926- *WhoRel 92, WhoWest 92*
Walrath, Hugh Earl 1950- *WhoFI 92*
Walrath, Patricia A 1941- *WhoAmP 91*
Walraven, Gary Dennis 1941- *WhoWest 92*
Walraven, Harold Richard 1934- *WhoWest 92*
Walraven, William Frederick 1932- *WhoMW 92*
Walravens, Philip Alfred 1939- *WhoWest 92*
Walrod, David James 1946- *WhoFI 92*
Walrod, Truman S., III 1950- *WhoEnt 92*
Walsberg, Glenn Eric 1949- *AmMWSc 92*
Walser, Armin 1937- *AmMWSc 92*
Walser, David 1923- *Who 92*
Walser, Mackenzie 1924- *AmMWSc 92*
Walser, Martin 1927- *IntAu&W 91, IntWW 91*
Walser, Robert 1878-1956 *FacFETw*
Walser, Ronald Herman 1944- *AmMWSc 92*
Walsh, Alan 1916- *IntWW 91, Who 92*
Walsh, Alan John 1947- *WhoMW 92*
Walsh, Alexander 1947- *TwCPaSc*
Walsh, Andrew Joseph 1930- *WhoFI 92*
Walsh, Ann Briks 1956- *WhoAmL 92*
Walsh, Anthony F. 1942- *WhoAmL 92*
Walsh, Arthur Campbell 1919- *AmMWSc 92*
Walsh, Arthur Stephen 1926- *IntWW 91, Who 92*
Walsh, Barbara Mary 1932- *WhoRel 92*
Walsh, Benjamin Dann 1808-1869 *BiInAmS*
Walsh, Bernard Lawrence, Jr. 1932- *WhoWest 92*
Walsh, Bertram 1938- *AmMWSc 92*
Walsh, Bill d1975 *LesBEnT 92*
Walsh, Bonita A. 1952- *WhoFI 92*
Walsh, Brian *WhoRel 92*
Walsh, Brian 1935- *Who 92*
Walsh, Carolyn Sue 1961- *WhoMW 92*
Walsh, Chad *DrAPF 91*
Walsh, Chad 1914- *ConPo 91, WrDr 92*
Walsh, Chad 1914-1991 *ConAu 133, CurBio 91N, NewYTBS 91*
Walsh, Charles Joseph 1940- *AmMWSc 92*
Walsh, Charles Richard 1939- *WhoFI 92*
Walsh, Christopher Thomas 1944- *AmMWSc 92*
Walsh, Clune Joseph, Jr. 1928- *WhoMW 92*
Walsh, Colin Stephen 1955- *Who 92*
Walsh, Daniel B 1935- *WhoAmP 91*
Walsh, Daniel Francis 1937- *WhoRel 92, WhoWest 92*
Walsh, David 1927- *TwCPaSc*
Walsh, David Allan 1945- *AmMWSc 92*
Walsh, David Ervin 1939- *AmMWSc 92*
Walsh, Delano B. 1945- *WhoBlA 92*
Walsh, Dermot Francis 1901- *Who 92*
Walsh, Diane 1950- *WhoEnt 92*
Walsh, Don 1931- *AmMWSc 92, IntWW 91*
Walsh, Donald James 1949- *WhoMW 92*
Walsh, Donald Peter 1930- *WhoAmL 92*
Walsh, Doris Montague Huntley 1912- *IntAu&W 91*
Walsh, Douglas MacArthur 1942- *WhoMW 92*
Walsh, E. Stephen 1942- *WhoAmL 92*
Walsh, Edmund John 1961- *WhoAmL 92*
Walsh, Edward John 1942- *AmMWSc 92*
Walsh, Edward Joseph 1932- *WhoWest 92*
Walsh, Edward Joseph 1941- *AmMWSc 92*
Walsh, Edward Joseph, Jr 1935- *AmMWSc 92*
Walsh, Edward Kyran 1931- *AmMWSc 92*
Walsh, Edward Nelson 1925- *AmMWSc 92*
Walsh, Ellen Dolores 1953- *WhoFI 92*
Walsh, Everald J. 1938- *WhoBlA 92*
Walsh, Francis Richard 1924- *WhoAmL 92*
Walsh, Frederick Rall, Jr. 1952- *WhoFI 92*
Walsh, Gary Lynn 1940- *AmMWSc 92*
Walsh, Geoffrey 1909- *Who 92*
Walsh, Geoffrey David Jeremy *Who 92*
Walsh, George William 1931- *IntAu&W 91*
Walsh, Gerald Michael 1944- *AmMWSc 92*
Walsh, Gerald Richard 1944- *WhoEnt 92*
Walsh, Gerry 1951- *WhoAmP 91*
Walsh, Goodwin *ScFEYrs*
Walsh, Graham Robert 1939- *Who 92*
Walsh, Henry George 1939- *Who 92*
Walsh, J. T. *ConTFT 9, IntMPA 92*
Walsh, Jack Patrick 1953- *WhoEnt 92*
Walsh, James d1991 *NewYTBS 91*
Walsh, James Aloysius 1933- *AmMWSc 92*
Walsh, James David 1956- *WhoAmL 92*
Walsh, James E. 1960- *WhoFI 92*
Walsh, James Francis 1944- *WhoMW 92*
Walsh, James Hamilton 1947- *WhoAmL 92*
Walsh, James Joseph 1930- *WhoAmL 92*
Walsh, James Lawrence 1962- *WhoEnt 92*
Walsh, James Mark 1909- *Who 92*
Walsh, James Michael 1947- *WhoFI 92*
Walsh, James Patrick, Jr. 1910- *WhoFI 92, WhoMW 92*
Walsh, James Paul 1917- *AmMWSc 92*
Walsh, James T. 1947- *AlmAP 92 [port], WhoAmP 91*
Walsh, Jane Dora West 1952- *WhoRel 92*
Walsh, Janet Claire 1961- *WhoAmL 92*
Walsh, Jason Todd 1963- *WhoFI 92*
Walsh, Jeanne 1924- *WhoEnt 92*
Walsh, Jerome Leo 1932- *WhoAmP 91*
Walsh, Jerome Mikel 1952- *WhoAmP 91*
Walsh, Jill P. *Who 92*
Walsh, John *WrDr 92*
Walsh, John 1937- *Who 92, WhoWest 92*
Walsh, John Breffni 1927- *AmMWSc 92*
Walsh, John Bronson 1927- *WhoAmL 92, WhoFI 92*
Walsh, John Edmond 1939- *AmMWSc 92*
Walsh, John Evangelist 1927- *IntAu&W 91*
Walsh, John G. 1950- *WhoFI 92*
Walsh, John H 1938- *AmMWSc 92*
Walsh, John Heritage 1929- *AmMWSc 92*
Walsh, John James 1917- *Who 92*
Walsh, John Joseph 1924- *AmMWSc 92*
Walsh, John Joseph 1942- *AmMWSc 92*
Walsh, John Joseph 1943- *WhoMW 92*
Walsh, John M 1923- *AmMWSc 92*
Walsh, John P. *Who 92, WhoIns 92*
Walsh, John Patrick 1911- *Who 92*
Walsh, John Paul 1942- *AmMWSc 92*
Walsh, John Richard 1920- *AmMWSc 92*
Walsh, John Robert 1930- *WhoFI 92*
Walsh, John Thomas 1927- *AmMWSc 92*
Walsh, John V 1942- *AmMWSc 92*
Walsh, Joseph B *WhoAmP 91*
Walsh, Joseph Broughton 1930- *AmMWSc 92*
Walsh, Joseph Fidler 1947- *WhoEnt 92A*
Walsh, Joseph T *WhoAmP 91*
Walsh, Joseph Thomas 1930- *WhoAmL 92*
Walsh, Joseph William 1941- *WhoAmP 91*
Walsh, Joy *DrAPF 91*
Walsh, Julia Montgomery 1923- *WhoFI 92*
Walsh, Katherine H *WhoAmP 91*
Walsh, Kenneth Albert 1922- *AmMWSc 92, WhoMW 92*
Walsh, Kenneth Andrew 1931- *AmMWSc 92, WhoWest 92*
Walsh, Lawrence E. 1912- *CurBio 91 [port]*
Walsh, Lawrence Edward 1912- *IntWW 91*
Walsh, Leo M, Jr 1932- *WhoIns 92*
Walsh, Leo Marcellus 1931- *AmMWSc 92*
Walsh, Louis Victor, IV 1962- *WhoFI 92*
Walsh, M. Emmet 1935- *IntMPA 92*
Walsh, Margaret Josephine 1923- *WhoMW 92*
Walsh, Margaret Mary 1920- *WhoAmP 91*
Walsh, Maria Christine 1952- *WhoAmL 92*
Walsh, Marian C *WhoAmP 91*
Walsh, Marie Leclerc 1928- *WhoMW 92*
Walsh, Mary D. Fleming 1913- *WhoWest 92*
Walsh, Mary Noelle 1954- *Who 92*
Walsh, Maurice 1879-1964 *ConAu 133*
Walsh, Maury John 1953- *WhoMW 92*
Walsh, Michael F 1946- *WhoIns 92*
Walsh, Michael Francis 1947- *WhoWest 92*
Walsh, Michael Gregory 1948- *WhoAmL 92*
Walsh, Michael J. 1932- *WhoAmL 92*
Walsh, Michael John Hatley 1927- *Who 92*
Walsh, Michael Patrick 1951- *AmMWSc 92*
Walsh, Michael Patrick 1956- *WhoAmP 91*
Walsh, Michael Thomas 1943- *Who 92*
Walsh, Milton O'Neal 1941- *WhoAmL 92*
Walsh, Noel Perrings 1919- *Who 92*
Walsh, P. G. 1923- *WrDr 92*
Walsh, Patrick Joseph *Who 92*
Walsh, Patrick Noel 1930- *AmMWSc 92*
Walsh, Peter 1929- *AmMWSc 92*
Walsh, Peter Alexander 1935- *IntWW 91*
Walsh, Peter Newton 1935- *AmMWSc 92*

**Walsh**, Ralph Edward 1923- *WhoAmP 91*
**Walsh**, Raoul 1887-1980 *FacFETw, IntDcF 2-2 [port]*
**Walsh**, Raymond Albert 1938- *WhoEnt 92*
**Walsh**, Raymond Robert 1925- *AmMWSc 92*
**Walsh**, Richard A *WhoAmP 91*
**Walsh**, Richard F. 1900- *IntMPA 92*
**Walsh**, Richard Michael 1958- *WhoAmL 92*
**Walsh**, Robert 1784-1859 *BenetAL 91*
**Walsh**, Robert Anthony 1938- *WhoAmL 92, WhoWest 92*
**Walsh**, Robert Francis 1930- *WhoFI 92*
**Walsh**, Robert Gerard 1966- *WhoWest 92*
**Walsh**, Robert Jerome 1929- *AmMWSc 92*
**Walsh**, Robert Lawrence 1933- *WhoAmP 91*
**Walsh**, Robert Michael 1938- *AmMWSc 92*
**Walsh**, Robert R 1927- *AmMWSc 92*
**Walsh**, Robert R 1939- *WhoAmP 91*
**Walsh**, Robin 1940- *Who 92*
**Walsh**, Robin Jo 1956- *WhoWest 92*
**Walsh**, Ruth Elizabeth 1919- *WhoAmP 91*
**Walsh**, Samuel 1951- *TwCPaSc*
**Walsh**, Scott Wesley 1947- *AmMWSc 92*
**Walsh**, Sean Patrick 1950- *WhoAmP 91*
**Walsh**, Sheila 1928- *IntAu&W 91, WrDr 92*
**Walsh**, Stephen 1942- *WrDr 92*
**Walsh**, Stephen G 1947- *AmMWSc 92*
**Walsh**, Teresa Marie 1962- *AmMWSc 92*
**Walsh**, Thelma Louise 1911- *WhoMW 92*
**Walsh**, Thomas Browning 1941- *WhoMW 92*
**Walsh**, Thomas Charles 1940- *WhoAmL 92*
**Walsh**, Thomas David 1936- *AmMWSc 92*
**Walsh**, Thomas G 1942- *WhoIns 92*
**Walsh**, Thomas Gerald 1949- *WhoRel 92*
**Walsh**, Thomas Gerard 1942- *WhoFI 92*
**Walsh**, Thomas James 1859-1933 *AmPeW*
**Walsh**, Thomas John, Sr. 1927- *WhoAmL 92*
**Walsh**, Thomas Joseph 1917- *WhoMW 92*
**Walsh**, Thomas Joseph 1954- *WhoMW 92*
**Walsh**, Thomas Meifeld 1952- *WhoAmL 92, WhoMW 92*
**Walsh**, Thomas P *WhoAmP 91*
**Walsh**, Tom 1937- *WhoAmP 91*
**Walsh**, Tony 1947- *WhoEnt 92*
**Walsh**, Walter J 1929- *WhoIns 92*
**Walsh**, Walter Joseph 1929- *WhoFI 92*
**Walsh**, Walter Michael, Jr 1931- *AmMWSc 92*
**Walsh**, William 1663-1708 *RfGEnL 91*
**Walsh**, William 1916- *Who 92, WrDr 92*
**Walsh**, William Arthur 1954- *AmMWSc 92*
**Walsh**, William Charles 1948- *WhoAmL 92*
**Walsh**, William D 1924- *WhoAmP 91*
**Walsh**, William Desmond 1930- *WhoFI 92*
**Walsh**, William F. 1914- *WhoFI 92*
**Walsh**, William Frank 1947- *WhoWest 92*
**Walsh**, William J. *DrAPF 91*
**Walsh**, William J 1936- *AmMWSc 92*
**Walsh**, William Joseph, Jr 1942- *WhoIns 92*
**Walsh**, William K 1932- *AmMWSc 92*
**Walsh**, William Thomas 1891-1949 *ScFEYrs*
**Walsh-Atkins**, Leonard Brian 1915- *Who 92*
**Walsham**, John Scarlett Warren 1910- *Who 92*
**Walsham**, Margaret Kenyon 1924- *WhoEnt 92*
**Walshe**, R. D. 1923- *WrDr 92*
**Walsingham**, Baron 1925- *Who 92*
**Walske**, Max Carl 1922- *AmMWSc 92*
**Walsmith**, Charles Rodger 1926- *WhoWest 92*
**Walstad**, John Daniel 1944- *AmMWSc 92*
**Walstad**, William Bathurst 1949- *WhoFI 92, WhoMW 92*
**Walstedt**, Russell E 1936- *AmMWSc 92*
**Walston**, Baron d1991 *Who 92N*
**Walston**, Baron 1912- *IntWW 91*
**Walston**, Dale Edouard 1930- *AmMWSc 92*
**Walston**, Lola Inge 1943- *WhoMW 92*
**Walston**, Ray 1918- *IntMPA 92*
**Walston**, Ray 1924- *WhoEnt 92*
**Walston**, Rick Lyle Josh 1954- *WhoWest 92*
**Walston**, Roderick Eugene 1935- *WhoAmL 92*
**Walston**, William H, Jr 1937- *AmMWSc 92*
**Walston**, Woodrow William 1918- *WhoBlA 92*
**Walstrom**, Julie Carter 1956- *WhoAmP 91*
**Walstrom**, Robert John 1922- *AmMWSc 92*
**Walstrom**, Thomas Arvid 1933- *WhoWest 92*
**Walt**, Alexander Jeffrey 1923- *AmMWSc 92, WhoMW 92*
**Walt**, Joseph William 1925- *WhoMW 92*
**Walt**, Martin 1926- *AmMWSc 92*
**Walta**, Raymond J. 1931- *WhoMW 92*
**Waltar**, Alan Edward 1939- *AmMWSc 92*
**Waltcher**, Azelle Brown 1925- *AmMWSc 92*
**Waltcher**, Irving 1917- *AmMWSc 92*
**Waltemeyer**, Robert Victor 1934- *WhoFI 92*
**Waltenbaugh**, Carl 1948- *AmMWSc 92*
**Walter**, Becky Leigh 1964- *WhoMW 92*
**Walter**, Bert Mathew 1915- *WhoWest 92*
**Walter**, Bruce Alexander 1922- *WhoWest 92*
**Walter**, Bruno 1876-1962 *EncTR 91 [port], FacFETw, NewAmDM*
**Walter**, Carl 1905- *AmMWSc 92*
**Walter**, Carlton H 1924- *AmMWSc 92*
**Walter**, Charles Frank 1936- *AmMWSc 92*
**Walter**, Charles Robert, Jr 1922- *AmMWSc 92*
**Walter**, Charlton M 1923- *AmMWSc 92*
**Walter**, Daniel *DrAPF 91*
**Walter**, David 1913- *WhoEnt 92*
**Walter**, David 1949- *WhoFI 92*
**Walter**, David Keith 1944- *WhoAmP 91*
**Walter**, Donald K 1931- *AmMWSc 92*
**Walter**, Douglas Hanson 1941- *WhoAmL 92*
**Walter**, Edward Joseph 1914- *AmMWSc 92*
**Walter**, Elizabeth *WrDr 92*
**Walter**, Eugene 1874-1941 *BenetAL 91*
**Walter**, Eugene LeRoy, Jr 1922- *AmMWSc 92*
**Walter**, Everett L 1929- *AmMWSc 92*
**Walter**, F John 1931- *AmMWSc 92*
**Walter**, Frederick John 1944- *WhoWest 92*
**Walter**, Gary Alan 1948- *WhoMW 92*
**Walter**, Gerry Henry 1947- *WhoRel 92*
**Walter**, Gilbert G 1930- *AmMWSc 92*
**Walter**, Gilbert Gustav 1930- *WhoMW 92*
**Walter**, Glenn Alan 1934- *WhoAmP 91*
**Walter**, Gordon H *AmMWSc 92*
**Walter**, Harold 1920- *Who 92*
**Walter**, Harold Edward 1920- *IntWW 91*
**Walter**, Harry 1930- *AmMWSc 92*
**Walter**, Hartmut 1940- *AmMWSc 92*
**Walter**, Henry Alexander 1912- *AmMWSc 92*
**Walter**, Henry Clement 1919- *AmMWSc 92*
**Walter**, Hollis Clifford, Jr. 1941- *WhoRel 92*
**Walter**, Ingo 1940- *WhoFI 92*
**Walter**, James Andrew 1953- *WhoFI 92*
**Walter**, James W. 1922- *WhoFI 92*
**Walter**, Jessica 1944- *IntMPA 92, WhoEnt 92*
**Walter**, John 1948- *ConAu 134*
**Walter**, John C. 1933- *WhoBlA 92*
**Walter**, John Fitler 1943- *AmMWSc 92*
**Walter**, John Harris 1927- *AmMWSc 92*
**Walter**, John Robert 1947- *WhoFI 92, WhoMW 92*
**Walter**, Joseph David 1939- *AmMWSc 92*
**Walter**, Joseph L 1930- *AmMWSc 92*
**Walter**, Kenneth Burwood 1918- *Who 92*
**Walter**, Louis S 1933- *AmMWSc 92*
**Walter**, Martin Edward 1945- *AmMWSc 92*
**Walter**, Marvin Joseph 1940- *WhoMW 92*
**Walter**, Mary Lou 1939- *WhoAmP 91*
**Walter**, Melinda Kay 1957- *WhoFI 92*
**Walter**, Michael Charles 1956- *WhoWest 92*
**Walter**, Michael David 1960- *WhoBlA 92*
**Walter**, Mildred Pitts *WrDr 92*
**Walter**, Neil Douglas 1942- *Who 92*
**Walter**, Norbert 1944- *IntWW 91*
**Walter**, Paul Hermann Lawrence 1934- *AmMWSc 92*
**Walter**, Paul Ryder 1937- *WhoRel 92*
**Walter**, Paul William *WhoAmL 92*
**Walter**, Priscilla Anne 1943- *WhoAmL 92*
**Walter**, Ralph Collins, III 1946- *WhoMW 92*
**Walter**, Reginald Henry 1933- *AmMWSc 92*
**Walter**, Richard *WhoEnt 92*
**Walter**, Richard D 1921- *AmMWSc 92*
**Walter**, Richard L 1933- *AmMWSc 92*
**Walter**, Richard Webb, Jr 1944- *AmMWSc 92*
**Walter**, Robert Irving 1920- *AmMWSc 92*
**Walter**, Robert John 1950- *AmMWSc 92*
**Walter**, Ronald Anderson 1949- *WhoAmP 91*
**Walter**, Ronald Bruce 1957- *AmMWSc 92*
**Walter**, Sandra K 1942- *WhoAmP 91*
**Walter**, Sheryl Lynn 1956- *WhoAmL 92*
**Walter**, Sibylle Edeltraud 1943- *WhoMW 92*
**Walter**, Thomas 1696-1725 *BenetAL 91*
**Walter**, Thomas 1740?-1789 *BiInAmS*
**Walter**, Thomas James 1939- *AmMWSc 92*
**Walter**, Trevor John 1944- *AmMWSc 92*
**Walter**, Wilbert George 1933- *AmMWSc 92*
**Walter**, William Arnold, Jr 1922- *AmMWSc 92*
**Walter**, William Mood, Jr 1936- *AmMWSc 92*
**Walter**, William Trump 1931- *AmMWSc 92*
**Waltermire**, Donald Eugene, Jr. 1957- *WhoRel 92*
**Walters**, Alan 1926- *Who 92*
**Walters**, Alan Arthur 1926- *IntWW 91, WrDr 92*
**Walters**, Alexander 1858-1917 *RelLAm 91*
**Walters**, Anna Lee *DrAPF 91*
**Walters**, Anna Lee 1946- *WhoWest 92*
**Walters**, Arthur M. 1918- *WhoBlA 92*
**Walters**, Barbara *LesBEnT 92 [port]*
**Walters**, Barbara 1931- *FacFETw, IntMPA 92, IntWW 91, WhoEnt 92*
**Walters**, Bette Jean 1946- *WhoAmL 92*
**Walters**, Betty Jayne 1935- *WhoFI 92*
**Walters**, Bill Peter 1943- *WhoAmP 91*
**Walters**, Bucky d1991 *NewYTBS 91 [port]*
**Walters**, Carl John 1944- *AmMWSc 92*
**Walters**, Carol Price 1941- *AmMWSc 92*
**Walters**, Charles 1911-1982 *IntDcF 2-2 [port]*
**Walters**, Charles Philip 1915- *AmMWSc 92*
**Walters**, Charles Sebastian 1913- *AmMWSc 92*
**Walters**, Christopher Kent 1942- *WhoAmL 92*
**Walters**, Craig Hartley 1955- *WhoWest 92*
**Walters**, Craig Thompson 1940- *AmMWSc 92*
**Walters**, Curla Sybil 1929- *AmMWSc 92, WhoBlA 92*
**Walters**, Daniel Lee 1959- *WhoFI 92*
**Walters**, Daniel Vern 1960- *WhoEnt 92*
**Walters**, David 1951- *AlmAP 92 [port], WhoAmP 91*
**Walters**, Deborah K W 1951- *AmMWSc 92*
**Walters**, Dennis 1928- *Who 92*
**Walters**, Dennis George 1945- *WhoFI 92*
**Walters**, Derrick *Who 92*
**Walters**, Donald 1925- *Who 92*
**Walters**, Donald 1926- *RelLAm 91*
**Walters**, Douglas Bruce 1942- *AmMWSc 92*
**Walters**, Edward Albert 1940- *AmMWSc 92*
**Walters**, Edward Joseph, Jr. 1947- *WhoAmL 92*
**Walters**, Eric 1937- *WhoWest 92*
**Walters**, Fowler McCoy, Jr. 1951- *WhoRel 92*
**Walters**, Fred Henry 1947- *AmMWSc 92*
**Walters**, Geoffrey King 1931- *AmMWSc 92*
**Walters**, George Kauffman 1929- *WhoMW 92*
**Walters**, Geraint Gwynn 1910- *Who 92*
**Walters**, Gomer Winston 1937- *WhoAmL 92*
**Walters**, Helen B. d1987 *ConAu 133*
**Walters**, Hubert Everett 1933- *WhoBlA 92*
**Walters**, Hubert Jack 1915- *AmMWSc 92*
**Walters**, Hugh 1910- *TwCSFW 91, WrDr 92*
**Walters**, J. Donald 1926- *WhoEnt 92*
**Walters**, Jack Edward 1896-1967 *ConAu 134*
**Walters**, Jack Henry 1925- *AmMWSc 92*
**Walters**, James Carter 1948- *AmMWSc 92, WhoMW 92*
**Walters**, James Murray 1959- *WhoEnt 92*
**Walters**, James Vernon 1933- *AmMWSc 92*
**Walters**, James William 1945- *WhoRel 92*
**Walters**, Jeanette West 1953- *WhoRel 92*
**Walters**, Jefferson Brooks 1922- *WhoMW 92*
**Walters**, Jesse Raymond, Jr. 1938- *WhoWest 92*
**Walters**, John Beauchamp 1903- *WrDr 92*
**Walters**, John Philip 1938- *AmMWSc 92*
**Walters**, John Philip 1941- *AmMWSc 92*
**Walters**, John William Townshend 1926- *Who 92*
**Walters**, Joyce Dora *Who 92*
**Walters**, Judith R *AmMWSc 92*
**Walters**, Julie 1950- *IntMPA 92, IntWW 91, Who 92*
**Walters**, Kenn David 1957- *WhoFI 92*
**Walters**, Kenneth 1934- *Who 92*
**Walters**, Lee Rudyard 1928- *AmMWSc 92*
**Walters**, Leon C 1940- *AmMWSc 92*
**Walters**, Lester James, Jr 1940- *AmMWSc 92*
**Walters**, Lowell Eugene 1919- *AmMWSc 92*
**Walters**, Mark David 1959- *AmMWSc 92*
**Walters**, Martha I 1925- *AmMWSc 92*
**Walters**, Mary C 1922- *WhoAmP 91*
**Walters**, Mary Dawson 1923- *WhoBlA 92*
**Walters**, Michael Quentin 1927- *Who 92*
**Walters**, Michael Y. 1943- *WhoMW 92*
**Walters**, Milton James 1942- *WhoFI 92*
**Walters**, Neal Ray 1961- *WhoAmL 92*
**Walters**, Peter Ernest 1913- *Who 92*
**Walters**, Peter Hugh Bennetts Ensor 1912- *Who 92*
**Walters**, Peter Ingram 1931- *IntWW 91, Who 92*
**Walters**, Phyllis Kobel 1939- *WhoAmP 91*
**Walters**, Randall Keith 1943- *AmMWSc 92, WhoMW 92*
**Walters**, Raymond L. 1943- *WhoWest 92*
**Walters**, Rhys Derrick 1932- *Who 92*
**Walters**, Richard Carl 1946- *WhoAmL 92*
**Walters**, Richard Francis 1930- *AmMWSc 92*
**Walters**, Robert F 1914- *AmMWSc 92*
**Walters**, Robert Fred 1914- *WhoMW 92*
**Walters**, Robert Stephen 1941- *WhoFI 92*
**Walters**, Roger 1917- *Who 92*
**Walters**, Roger Talbot 1917- *IntWW 91*
**Walters**, Roland Dick 1920- *AmMWSc 92*
**Walters**, Ronald 1938- *WhoBlA 92*
**Walters**, Ronald Arlen 1940- *AmMWSc 92, WhoWest 92*
**Walters**, Ronald Eugene 1946- *WhoMW 92*
**Walters**, Sarah Jane 1953- *WhoMW 92*
**Walters**, Stanley David 1931- *WhoRel 92*
**Walters**, Stephen Milo 1940- *AmMWSc 92*
**Walters**, Stuart Max 1920- *Who 92*
**Walters**, Sumner J. 1916- *WhoAmL 92*
**Walters**, Sylvia Solochek 1938- *WhoWest 92*
**Walters**, Thomas Lloyd 1937- *WhoWest 92*
**Walters**, Thomas N. *DrAPF 91*
**Walters**, Thomas Richard 1929- *AmMWSc 92*
**Walters**, Timothy Carl 1955- *WhoWest 92*
**Walters**, Tom Frederick 1931- *WhoMW 92*
**Walters**, Tyler *WhoEnt 92*
**Walters**, Vernon A 1917- *WhoAmP 91*
**Walters**, Vernon Anthony 1917- *IntWW 91*
**Walters**, Virginia F 1925- *AmMWSc 92*
**Walters**, Warren W. 1932- *WhoBlA 92*
**Walters**, William A. 1937- *WhoEnt 92*
**Walters**, William Ben 1938- *AmMWSc 92*
**Walters**, William Le Roy 1932- *AmMWSc 92*
**Walters**, William Owen 1952- *WhoAmP 91*
**Walters**, William Peter 1943- *WhoAmL 92*
**Walters**, William Raymond 1934- *WhoRel 92*
**Walterspiel**, Otto Heinrich 1927- *IntWW 91*
**Walthall**, Hugh *DrAPF 91*
**Walthall**, Lee Wade 1953- *WhoEnt 92*
**Waltham**, Tony 1942- *WrDr 92*
**Walther von der Vogelweide** 1170?-1230? *NewAmDM*
**Walther**, Adriaan 1934- *AmMWSc 92*
**Walther**, Alina 1923- *AmMWSc 92*
**Walther**, Carl Ferdinand Wilhelm 1811-1887 *DcAmImH*
**Walther**, Charles Marion, Jr 1935- *WhoAmP 91*
**Walther**, Frank H 1930- *AmMWSc 92*
**Walther**, Fritz R 1921- *AmMWSc 92*
**Walther**, Herbert 1935- *IntWW 91*
**Walther**, James Eugene 1932- *AmMWSc 92*
**Walther**, Johann Gottfried 1684-1748 *NewAmDM*
**Walther-Lee**, Dorianne 1938- *WhoFI 92*
**Walthour**, Bruce Shuey 1949- *WhoRel 92*
**Walthour**, Fred Allen 1943- *WhoRel 92*
**Waltking**, Arthur Ernest 1937- *AmMWSc 92*
**Waltman**, Alfred A *WhoAmP 91*
**Waltman**, Bob 1933- *WhoAmP 91*
**Waltman**, Naomi Brufsky 1963- *WhoAmL 92*
**Waltman**, Paul Elvis 1931- *AmMWSc 92*
**Waltmann**, William Lee 1934- *AmMWSc 92, WhoMW 92*
**Waltner**, Arthur 1914- *AmMWSc 92*
**Waltner**, John Randolph 1938- *WhoMW 92*
**Waltner**, Richard Hege 1931- *WhoWest 92*
**Walton** *Who 92*
**Walton**, Alan George 1936- *AmMWSc 92*
**Walton**, Allan 1892-1948 *TwCPaSc*
**Walton**, Alvin Earl 1964- *WhoBlA 92*
**Walton**, Anthony John 1934- *WhoEnt 92*
**Walton**, Anthony Michael 1925- *Who 92*
**Walton**, Anthony Scott 1965- *WhoBlA 92*
**Walton**, Anthony Warrick 1943- *AmMWSc 92*
**Walton**, Arthur Halsall 1916- *Who 92*
**Walton**, Barbara Ann 1940- *AmMWSc 92*
**Walton**, Booker T., Jr. 1950- *WhoFI 92*

**Walton,** Bryce Calvin 1923- *AmMWSc 92*
**Walton,** Cedar Anthony 1901- *WhoBlA 92*
**Walton,** Charles Anthony 1926- *AmMWSc 92*
**Walton,** Charles D 1948- *WhoAmP 91*
**Walton,** Charles Michael 1941- *AmMWSc 92*
**Walton,** Charles William 1908- *AmMWSc 92*
**Walton,** Clifford Wayne 1954- *WhoMW 92*
**Walton,** Craig 1934- *WhoWest 92*
**Walton,** Daniel C 1934- *AmMWSc 92*
**Walton,** David A. *DrAPF 91*
**Walton,** Deborah Gail 1950- *WhoWest 92*
**Walton,** Derek 1931- *AmMWSc 92*
**Walton,** Derek Nigel 1958- *WhoMW 92*
**Walton,** DeWitt T., Jr. 1937- *WhoBlA 92*
**Walton,** Donald William 1917- *WhoMW 92*
**Walton,** Edmund Lewis, Jr. 1936- *WhoAmL 92, WhoAmP 91*
**Walton,** Edward Arthur 1860-1922 *TwCPaSc*
**Walton,** Elbert Arthur, Jr 1942- *WhoAmP 91, WhoBlA 92*
**Walton,** Ernest Thomas Sinton 1903- *IntWW 91, Who 92, WhoNob 90*
**Walton,** Flavia Batteau 1947- *WhoBlA 92*
**Walton,** Frederick R. *IntMPA 92*
**Walton,** Geoffrey Elmer 1934- *Who 92*
**Walton,** George 1867-1933 *DcTwDes*
**Walton,** George 1914- *AmMWSc 92*
**Walton,** George D 1932- *WhoAmP 91*
**Walton,** Gerald Steven 1935- *AmMWSc 92*
**Walton,** Hanes, Jr. 1942- *WhoBlA 92*
**Walton,** Harold Frederic 1912- *AmMWSc 92*
**Walton,** Harold V 1921- *AmMWSc 92*
**Walton,** Harriet J. 1933- *WhoBlA 92*
**Walton,** Harriett J 1933- *AmMWSc 92*
**Walton,** Harry Vincent 1948- *WhoEnt 92*
**Walton,** Henry J 1924- *ConAu 35NR*
**Walton,** Henry John 1924- *IntWW 91, WrDr 92*
**Walton,** Henry Miller 1912- *AmMWSc 92*
**Walton,** Ian 1943- *TwCPaSc*
**Walton,** Ian 1950- *TwCPaSc*
**Walton,** Izaak 1593?-1683 *CnDBLB 1 [port], RfGEnL 91*
**Walton,** Jack Kemmer, II 1952- *WhoFI 92*
**Walton,** James 1911- *WrDr 92*
**Walton,** James Donald 1952- *WhoBlA 92*
**Walton,** James Edward 1944- *WhoBlA 92*
**Walton,** James Madison 1926- *WhoBlA 92*
**Walton,** James Meade 1947- *WhoWest 92*
**Walton,** Jay R 1946- *AmMWSc 92*
**Walton,** John *TwCPaSc*
**Walton,** John 1922- *WrDr 92*
**Walton,** John Coulter 1946- *WhoEnt 92*
**Walton,** John H 1939- *WhoIns 92*
**Walton,** John Joseph 1934- *AmMWSc 92*
**Walton,** John Robert 1904- *Who 92*
**Walton,** John Wayne 1947- *WhoAmL 92*
**Walton,** John William Scott 1925- *Who 92*
**Walton,** Jon David 1942- *WhoAmL 92*
**Walton,** Jon Maxwell 1947- *WhoRel 92*
**Walton,** Jonathan Taylor 1930- *WhoFI 92, WhoMW 92*
**Walton,** Kenneth Nelson 1935- *AmMWSc 92*
**Walton,** Laurence Roland 1939- *WhoMW 92*
**Walton,** Lludloo Charles 1950- *WhoBlA 92*
**Walton,** Matt Savage 1915- *AmMWSc 92*
**Walton,** Meredith 1936- *WhoRel 92*
**Walton,** Mildred Lee 1926- *WhoBlA 92*
**Walton,** Monty Lewis 1960- *WhoAmL 92*
**Walton,** Ortiz 1933- *WrDr 92*
**Walton,** Ortiz Montaigne *WhoBlA 92*
**Walton,** Peter Dawson 1924- *AmMWSc 92*
**Walton,** Phillip Vernal 1963- *WhoRel 92*
**Walton,** Ray Daniel, Jr 1921- *AmMWSc 92*
**Walton,** Reggie Barnett 1949- *WhoBlA 92*
**Walton,** Richard J. 1928- *WrDr 92*
**Walton,** Richard K 1931- *WhoAmP 91*
**Walton,** Robert Allen 1959- *WhoEnt 92*
**Walton,** Robert Bruce 1915- *AmMWSc 92*
**Walton,** Robert Cutler 1932- *WhoRel 92*
**Walton,** Robert Eugene 1931- *AmMWSc 92*
**Walton,** Robert Prentiss 1938- *WhoAmL 92*
**Walton,** Roddy Burke 1931- *AmMWSc 92*
**Walton,** Rodney Earl 1947- *WhoAmL 92*
**Walton,** Roger Alan 1941- *WhoWest 92*
**Walton,** Roger Michael 1943- *WhoWest 92*
**Walton,** Roland J. *WhoBlA 92*
**Walton,** Ronald C. 1929- *WhoWest 92*
**Walton,** Ronald Linn 1955- *WhoWest 92*
**Walton,** S. Robson 1945- *WhoFI 92*
**Walton,** Sam Moore 1920- *IntWW 91, WhoFI 92*
**Walton,** Sidney F., Jr. 1934- *WhoBlA 92*
**Walton,** Stanley Anthony, III 1939- *WhoAmL 92*
**Walton,** Susan H. 1949- *WhoMW 92*
**Walton,** Theodore Ross 1931- *AmMWSc 92*
**Walton,** Thomas Edward 1940- *AmMWSc 92, WhoWest 92*
**Walton,** Thomas Peyton, III 1922- *AmMWSc 92*
**Walton,** Timothy Paul 1949- *WhoMW 92*
**Walton,** Tony *WhoEnt 92*
**Walton,** Tracy Matthew, Jr. 1930- *WhoBlA 92*
**Walton,** Vincent Michael 1949- *AmMWSc 92*
**Walton,** Warren Lewis 1914- *AmMWSc 92*
**Walton,** Wayne J A, Jr 1941- *AmMWSc 92*
**Walton,** Will Ora, III 1957- *WhoAmL 92*
**Walton,** William 1902-1983 *FacFETw, NewAmDM*
**Walton,** William P. 1935- *WhoMW 92*
**Walton,** William Ralph 1923- *AmMWSc 92*
**Walton,** William Robert 1949- *WhoFI 92*
**Walton,** William Stephen 1933- *Who 92*
**Walton Of Detchant,** Baron 1922- *IntWW 91, Who 92*
**Waltrip,** Mather K. 1960- *WhoWest 92*
**Waltrip,** Robert 1924- *WhoBlA 92*
**Waltrup,** Paul John 1945- *AmMWSc 92*
**Walts,** Lou E 1932- *WhoIns 92*
**Waltz,** Alan Kent 1931- *WhoRel 92*
**Waltz,** Arthur G 1932- *AmMWSc 92*
**Waltz,** Jon Richard 1929- *WhoAmL 92*
**Waltz,** Kenneth N. 1924- *WrDr 92*
**Waltz,** Marcus Ernest 1921- *WhoWest 92*
**Waltz,** Ronald Edward 1943- *AmMWSc 92*
**Waltz,** Thomas William 1940- *WhoFI 92*
**Waltz,** William Lee 1940- *AmMWSc 92*
**Waltzer,** Brenda Weiss 1944- *WhoAmL 92*
**Waltzer,** Wayne C 1948- *AmMWSc 92*
**Walum,** Herbert 1936- *AmMWSc 92*
**Walvekar,** Arun Govind 1942- *AmMWSc 92*
**Walvin,** James 1942- *IntAu&W 91, WrDr 92*
**Walvoord,** Edgar A 1936- *WhoIns 92*
**Walvoord,** John Flipse 1910- *WhoRel 92*
**Walwer,** Frank Kurt 1930- *WhoAmL 92*
**Walwick,** Earle Richard 1929- *AmMWSc 92*
**Walwicz,** Ania 1951- *ConPo 91, WrDr 92*
**Walworth,** Arthur 1903- *WrDr 92*
**Walworth,** Arthur Clarence 1903- *IntAu&W 91*
**Walworth,** Jack 1957- *WhoEnt 92*
**Walwyn,** Fulke Thomas Tyndall d1991 *Who 92N*
**Walwyn,** Peter Tyndall 1933- *Who 92*
**Waly,** Youssef 1930- *IntWW 91*
**Walz,** Alvin Eugene 1919- *AmMWSc 92*
**Walz,** Bruce James 1940- *WhoMW 92*
**Walz,** Daniel Albert 1944- *AmMWSc 92*
**Walz,** Donald Thomas 1924- *AmMWSc 92*
**Walz,** Frederick George 1940- *AmMWSc 92*
**Walz,** Frederick Sutherland 1937- *WhoWest 92*
**Walz,** Jay 1907-1991 *ConAu 135*
**Walz,** Jay Franklin d1991 *NewYTBS 91*
**Walz,** Kenneth Gordon 1942- *WhoEnt 92*
**Walz,** Thomas Anthony 1946- *WhoFI 92*
**Walzer,** James Harvey 1949- *WhoAmL 92*
**Walzer,** Michael 1935- *WrDr 92*
**Walzer,** Norman Charles 1943- *WhoFI 92, WhoMW 92*
**Walzer,** Robert Steven 1932- *WhoAmL 92*
**Walzer,** William Charles 1912- *WhoRel 92*
**Walzog,** Nancy Lee 1963- *WhoEnt 92*
**Wambach,** Peter Cyrano 1916- *WhoAmP 91*
**Wambaugh,** Joseph 1937- *IntAu&W 91, IntWW 91, WrDr 92*
**Wambaugh,** Sarah 1882-1955 *AmPeW*
**Wamble,** Amos Sylvester, Sr. 1916- *WhoBlA 92*
**Wambles,** Lynda England 1937- *WhoMW 92*
**Wambold,** James Charles 1932- *AmMWSc 92*
**Wambold,** Richard Lawrence 1952- *WhoFI 92*
**Wamboldt,** Donald George 1932- *WhoFI 92, WhoIns 92*
**Wambolt,** Thomas Eugene 1938- *WhoFI 92, WhoWest 92*
**Wambsganss,** Jacob Roy 1950- *WhoFI 92, WhoMW 92*
**Wamester,** Blake Hanson 1945- *WhoRel 92*
**Wammer,** Michael Henry 1939- *WhoAmP 91*
**Wampler,** D Eugene 1935- *AmMWSc 92*
**Wampler,** Dee 1940- *WhoAmP 91*
**Wampler,** E Joseph 1933- *AmMWSc 92*
**Wampler,** Fred Benny 1943- *AmMWSc 92*
**Wampler,** Jesse Marion 1936- *AmMWSc 92*
**Wampler,** Joe Forrest 1926- *AmMWSc 92*
**Wampler,** John E *AmMWSc 92*
**Wampler,** Robert Joseph 1936- *WhoAmL 92*
**Wampler,** W. Norman 1907- *WhoWest 92*
**Wampler,** William Creed, Jr 1959- *WhoAmP 91*
**Wamre,** Rick Elliot 1958- *WhoFI 92*
**Wamser,** Carl Christian 1944- *AmMWSc 92, WhoWest 92*
**Wamser,** Christian Albert 1913- *AmMWSc 92*
**Wamsley,** W W 1925- *AmMWSc 92*
**Wamytan,** Rock 1951- *IntWW 91*
**Wan Da** 1918- *IntWW 91*
**Wan Haifeng** *IntWW 91*
**Wan Li** 1916- *IntWW 91*
**Wan Shaofen** 1931- *IntWW 91*
**Wan,** Abraham Tai-Hsin 1928- *AmMWSc 92*
**Wan,** Frederic Yui-Ming 1936- *AmMWSc 92, WhoWest 92*
**Wan,** Jeffrey Kwok-Sing 1934- *AmMWSc 92*
**Wan,** Peter J 1943- *AmMWSc 92*
**Wan,** Shao-Hong 1946- *WhoFI 92*
**Wan,** Yieh-Hei 1947- *AmMWSc 92*
**Wanamaker,** Giles A. 1932- *WhoAmL 92*
**Wanamaker,** John Eric 1961- *WhoMW 92*
**Wanamaker,** Sam 1919- *IntMPA 92, IntWW 91, Who 92, WhoEnt 92*
**Wanat,** Stanley Frank 1939- *AmMWSc 92*
**Wanchow,** Susan Beth 1965- *WhoWest 92*
**Wand,** Mitchell 1948- *AmMWSc 92*
**Wanda of Poland** *EncAmaz 91*
**Wandass,** Joseph Henry 1960- *AmMWSc 92*
**Wander,** Herbert Stanton 1935- *WhoMW 92*
**Wander,** Joseph Day 1941- *AmMWSc 92*
**Wanderer,** Peter John, Jr 1943- *AmMWSc 92*
**Wanderman,** Susan Mae 1947- *WhoAmL 92*
**Wanders,** David Gillet 1955- *WhoFI 92*
**Wandmacher,** Cornelius 1911- *AmMWSc 92*
**Wandor,** Michelene 1940- *WrDr 92*
**Wandor,** Michelene Dinah 1940- *IntAu&W 91*
**Wandrag,** Graham David 1949- *WhoFI 92*
**Wandrei,** Donald 1908-1987 *ScFEYrs*
**Wands,** John Millar 1946- *WhoWest 92*
**Wands,** Ralph Clinton 1919- *AmMWSc 92*
**Wandsworth,** Archdeacon of *Who 92*
**Wane,** Malcolm T 1921- *AmMWSc 92*
**Wanebo,** Harold *AmMWSc 92*
**Wanek,** Jerrold 1958- *WhoAmL 92*
**Wanek,** Ronald Melvin 1938- *WhoMW 92*
**Wang Anyi** 1954- *IntWW 91*
**Wang Bingqian** 1925- *IntWW 91*
**Wang Chang-Ching** 1920- *IntWW 91*
**Wang Chaowen** 1931- *IntWW 91*
**Wang Chengbin** 1928- *IntWW 91*
**Wang Chenghan** *IntWW 91*
**Wang Ching-wei** 1883-1944 *FacFETw*
**Wang Chuanbin** *IntWW 91*
**Wang Congwu** 1905- *IntWW 91*
**Wang Daohan** 1915- *IntWW 91*
**Wang Deyan** 1931- *IntWW 91*
**Wang Dezhao** 1902- *IntWW 91*
**Wang Donghai** 1938- *IntWW 91*
**Wang Dongling** 1945- *IntWW 91*
**Wang Dongxing** 1916- *IntWW 91*
**Wang Enmao** 1912- *IntWW 91*
**Wang Fang** 1920- *IntWW 91*
**Wang Feng** 1907- *IntWW 91*
**Wang Fuzhi** 1923- *IntWW 91*
**Wang Ganchang** 1907- *IntWW 91*
**Wang Guangmei** 1922- *IntWW 91*
**Wang Guangying** 1919- *IntWW 91*
**Wang Guangyu** 1919- *IntWW 91*
**Wang Guangzhong** 1921- *IntWW 91*
**Wang Gungwu** 1930- *IntWW 91, Who 92*
**Wang Hai** 1925- *IntWW 91*
**Wang Hanbin** 1925- *IntWW 91*
**Wang Heshou** 1908- *IntWW 91*
**Wang Hongwen** *FacFETw*
**Wang Hongwen** 1937- *IntWW 91*
**Wang Jida** 1935- *IntWW 91*
**Wang Jun** 1921- *IntWW 91*
**Wang Kefen** 1927- *IntWW 91*
**Wang Kui** 1931- *IntWW 91*
**Wang Lei** 1914- *IntWW 91*
**Wang Lianzheng** 1930- *IntWW 91*
**Wang Lin** *IntWW 91*
**Wang Liusheng** 1912- *IntWW 91*
**Wang Maolin** 1935- *IntWW 91*
**Wang Meng** 1934- *IntWW 91*
**Wang Ping** 1907- *IntWW 91*
**Wang Qun** 1926- *IntWW 91*
**Wang Renzhi** 1933- *IntWW 91*
**Wang Renzhong** 1917- *IntWW 91*
**Wang Senhao** 1932- *IntWW 91*
**Wang Shitai** 1909- *IntWW 91*
**Wang Shouguan** 1923- *IntWW 91*
**Wang Tao** 1931- *IntWW 91*
**Wang Tian-Ren** 1939- *IntWW 91*
**Wang Wenshi** 1921- *IntWW 91*
**Wang Xiaoguang** 1924- *IntWW 91*
**Wang Xuezhen** 1926- *IntWW 91*
**Wang Yinglai** 1907- *IntWW 91*
**Wang You-Tsao** 1925- *IntWW 91*
**Wang Yuan** 1930- *IntWW 91*
**Wang Yuefeng** *IntWW 91*
**Wang Yung-Ching** 1917- *IntWW 91*
**Wang Ze** 1923- *IntWW 91*
**Wang Zengqi** 1920- *IntWW 91*
**Wang Zhaoguo** 1941- *IntWW 91*
**Wang Zhen** 1908- *IntWW 91*
**Wang Zhongfang** 1921- *IntWW 91*
**Wang Zhongshu** 1925- *IntWW 91*
**Wang Zhongyu** 1933- *IntWW 91*
**Wang Zikun** 1929- *IntWW 91*
**Wang,** Albert James 1958- *WhoMW 92*
**Wang,** Albert Show-Dwo 1937- *AmMWSc 92*
**Wang,** An 1920- *AmMWSc 92*
**Wang,** An 1920-1990 *AnObit 1990, FacFETw*
**Wang,** An-Chuan 1936- *AmMWSc 92*
**Wang,** An-Ming 1926- *WhoEnt 92*
**Wang,** Andrew H-J 1945- *AmMWSc 92*
**Wang,** Anyi 1954- *IntAu&W 91*
**Wang,** Arthur Ching-Li 1949- *WhoAmP 91*
**Wang,** Bin *AmMWSc 92*
**Wang,** Bin Ching 1941- *AmMWSc 92*
**Wang,** Bosco Shang 1947- *AmMWSc 92*
**Wang,** C J 1918- *AmMWSc 92*
**Wang,** Carl C T 1935- *AmMWSc 92*
**Wang,** Chang-Yi 1939- *AmMWSc 92*
**Wang,** Chao Chen 1914- *AmMWSc 92*
**Wang,** Chao-Cheng 1938- *AmMWSc 92*
**Wang,** Charles C 1933- *AmMWSc 92*
**Wang,** Charles P 1937- *AmMWSc 92*
**Wang,** Charles T P 1930- *AmMWSc 92*
**Wang,** Chen Chi 1932- *WhoFI 92, WhoWest 92*
**Wang,** Chen-Show *AmMWSc 92*
**Wang,** Chi-Hua 1923- *AmMWSc 92*
**Wang,** Chi-Sun 1942- *AmMWSc 92*
**Wang,** Chia-Lin Jeffrey 1949- *AmMWSc 92*
**Wang,** Chia Ping *AmMWSc 92*
**Wang,** Chien Bang 1941- *AmMWSc 92*
**Wang,** Chien Yi 1942- *AmMWSc 92*
**Wang,** Chih Chun 1932- *AmMWSc 92*
**Wang,** Chih-Chung 1922- *AmMWSc 92*
**Wang,** Chih Hsing 1917- *AmMWSc 92*
**Wang,** Chih-Lueh Albert 1950- *AmMWSc 92*
**Wang,** Chihping 1961- *WhoWest 92*
**Wang,** Chin Hsien 1939- *AmMWSc 92*
**Wang,** Ching Chung 1936- *AmMWSc 92*
**Wang,** Ching-Ping Shih 1947- *AmMWSc 92*
**Wang,** Chiu-Chen 1922- *AmMWSc 92*
**Wang,** Chiu-Sen 1937- *AmMWSc 92*
**Wang,** Christine A 1955- *AmMWSc 92*
**Wang,** Chu Ping 1931- *AmMWSc 92*
**Wang,** Chun-Juan Kao 1928- *AmMWSc 92*
**Wang,** Dalton T *AmMWSc 92*
**Wang,** Daniel I-Chyau 1936- *AmMWSc 92*
**Wang,** David I. J. 1932- *WhoFI 92*
**Wang,** Dazong 1954- *AmMWSc 92*
**Wang,** Edward Yeong 1933- *AmMWSc 92*
**Wang,** Eugenia 1945- *AmMWSc 92*
**Wang,** Francis Wei-Yu 1936- *AmMWSc 92*
**Wang,** Frank Feng Hui 1924- *AmMWSc 92*
**Wang,** Franklin Fu-Yen 1928- *AmMWSc 92*
**Wang,** Frederick E 1932- *AmMWSc 92*
**Wang,** Gary T 1963- *AmMWSc 92*
**Wang,** George Shih Chang 1933- *WhoWest 92*
**Wang,** Guang Tsan 1935- *AmMWSc 92*
**Wang,** Gung H. 1909- *WhoMW 92*
**Wang,** Gwo-Ching 1946- *AmMWSc 92*
**Wang,** H E Frank 1929- *AmMWSc 92*
**Wang,** Hao 1921- *AmMWSc 92*
**Wang,** Henry 1951- *AmMWSc 92*
**Wang,** Herbert Fan 1946- *AmMWSc 92*
**Wang,** Howard Hao 1942- *AmMWSc 92*
**Wang,** Hsiang 1936- *AmMWSc 92*
**Wang,** Hsin-Pang 1946- *AmMWSc 92*
**Wang,** Hsioh-Shan 1928- *AmMWSc 92*
**Wang,** Hsu-Kun 1933- *IntAu&W 91*
**Wang,** Hsueh-Hwa 1923- *AmMWSc 92*
**Wang,** Hui-Ming 1922- *WrDr 92*
**Wang,** Hwa-Chi 1955- *WhoMW 92*
**Wang,** Hwa Lih 1921- *AmMWSc 92*
**Wang,** I-Tung 1933- *WhoWest 92*
**Wang,** James C 1936- *AmMWSc 92*
**Wang,** James Chia-fang 1926- *WhoAmP 91, WhoWest 92*
**Wang,** James Li-Ming 1946- *AmMWSc 92*
**Wang,** James Ting-Shun 1931- *AmMWSc 92*
**Wang,** Janet Colt 1951- *WhoWest 92*
**Wang,** Jaw-Kai 1932- *AmMWSc 92, WhoWest 92*
**Wang,** Jen Yu 1915- *AmMWSc 92*
**Wang,** Jerry Hsueh-Ching 1937- *AmMWSc 92*
**Wang,** Ji Ching 1938- *AmMWSc 92*

Wang, Jia-Chao 1939- *AmMWSc 92*
Wang, Jian 1968- *NewYTBS 91 [port]*
Wang, Jin 1955- *WhoFI 92, WhoMW 92*
Wang, Jin-Liang 1937- *AmMWSc 92, WhoMW 92*
Wang, Jin Tsai 1931- *AmMWSc 92*
Wang, John L 1946- *AmMWSc 92*
Wang, John Ling-Fai 1942- *AmMWSc 92*
Wang, Johnson Jenn-Hwa 1938- *AmMWSc 92*
Wang, Jon Y 1943- *AmMWSc 92*
Wang, Joseph *AmMWSc 92*
Wang, Joseph 1948- *WhoWest 92*
Wang, Joseph Shou-Jen 1933- *WhoRel 92*
Wang, Jui Hsin 1921- *AmMWSc 92*
Wang, Kang-Lung 1941- *AmMWSc 92*
Wang, Karl *DrAPF 91*
Wang, Ke-Chin 1930- *AmMWSc 92*
Wang, Ken Hsi 1934- *AmMWSc 92*
Wang, Kia K 1924- *AmMWSc 92*
Wang, Kuan *AmMWSc 92*
Wang, Kung-Ping 1919- *AmMWSc 92*
Wang, Kuo King 1923- *AmMWSc 92*
Wang, L. Edwin 1919- *WhoRel 92*
Wang, Lawrence Chia-Huang 1940- *AmMWSc 92*
Wang, Lawrence K 1940- *AmMWSc 92*
Wang, Lawrence Kuan-Meen 1939- *WhoFI 92*
Wang, Leon Ru-Liang 1932- *AmMWSc 92*
Wang, Li Chuan *AmMWSc 92*
Wang, Lin 1929- *WhoWest 92*
Wang, Lin-Shu 1938- *AmMWSc 92*
Wang, Lixiao 1955- *WhoMW 92*
Wang, Marian M 1928- *AmMWSc 92*
Wang, Maw Shiu 1925- *AmMWSc 92*
Wang, Muhao S 1942- *AmMWSc 92*
Wang, N. T. *WhoFI 92*
Wang, Nai-San 1936- *AmMWSc 92*
Wang, Nancy Yang 1926- *AmMWSc 92*
Wang, P K C 1934- *AmMWSc 92*
Wang, Pao-Kuan 1949- *AmMWSc 92*
Wang, Paul H. 1954- *WhoRel 92*
Wang, Paul Keng Chieh 1934- *AmMWSc 92, WhoWest 92*
Wang, Paul Shyh-Horng 1944- *AmMWSc 92*
Wang, Paul Weily 1951- *AmMWSc 92*
Wang, Peter Cheng-Chao 1937- *AmMWSc 92*
Wang, Pie-Yi 1940- *AmMWSc 92*
Wang, Ping Chun 1920- *AmMWSc 92*
Wang, Ping-Lieh Thomas 1946- *AmMWSc 92*
Wang, Richard Hsu-Shien 1932- *AmMWSc 92*
Wang, Richard I H 1924- *AmMWSc 92*
Wang, Richard J 1941- *AmMWSc 92, WhoMW 92*
Wang, Richard Ruey-Chyi 1943- *WhoWest 92*
Wang, Robert 1930- *WhoAmL 92*
Wang, Robert T 1941- *AmMWSc 92*
Wang, Ru-Tsang 1928- *AmMWSc 92*
Wang, Sam S Y 1936- *AmMWSc 92*
Wang, San-Pin 1920- *AmMWSc 92*
Wang, Shao-Fu 1922- *AmMWSc 92*
Wang, Shien Tsun 1938- *AmMWSc 92*
Wang, Shih Chun 1910- *AmMWSc 92*
Wang, Shou-Ling 1924- *AmMWSc 92*
Wang, Shu Lung 1925- *AmMWSc 92*
Wang, Shyh 1925- *AmMWSc 92*
Wang, Soo Ray 1940- *AmMWSc 92*
Wang, Stephen 1947- *WhoFI 92*
Wang, Sue Hwa 1948- *WhoFI 92, WhoWest 92*
Wang, Taitzer 1939- *AmMWSc 92*
Wang, Theodore Joseph 1906- *AmMWSc 92*
Wang, Theodore Sheng-Tao 1930- *AmMWSc 92*
Wang, Thomas Nie-Chin 1938- *AmMWSc 92*
Wang, Ting Chung *AmMWSc 92*
Wang, Ting-I 1944- *AmMWSc 92*
Wang, Ting-Tai Helen 1948- *AmMWSc 92*
Wang, Tong-eng 1933- *WhoFI 92*
Wang, Tony Kar-Hung 1952- *WhoWest 92*
Wang, Tsuey Tang 1932- *AmMWSc 92*
Wang, Tung Yue 1921- *AmMWSc 92*
Wang, Tzyy-Cheng 1949- *WhoWest 92*
Wang, Victor Kai-Kuo 1944- *AmMWSc 92*
Wang, Vincent Tsan-Leun 1953- *WhoMW 92*
Wang, Virginia Li 1933- *AmMWSc 92*
Wang, Wayne 1949- *IntMPA 92*
Wang, Wei-Yeh 1944- *AmMWSc 92*
Wang, Wen I 1953- *AmMWSc 92*
Wang, Wun-Cheng W 1936- *AmMWSc 92*
Wang, Xingwu 1953- *AmMWSc 92*
Wang, Ya Ko 1956- *WhoMW 92*
Wang, Ya-Yen Lee 1930- *AmMWSc 92*
Wang, Yang 1923- *AmMWSc 92*
Wang, Yar-Ming 1947- *AmMWSc 92*
Wang, Yen 1928- *AmMWSc 92*
Wang, Yen Chu 1938- *AmMWSc 92*
Wang, Yeu-Ming Alexander 1942- *AmMWSc 92*
Wang, Yi-Ming 1950- *AmMWSc 92*
Wang, Yu-Li *AmMWSc 92*
Wang, Yuan Jian 1929- *IntAu&W 91*
Wang, Yuan R 1934- *AmMWSc 92*
Wang, Yung-Li 1937- *AmMWSc 92*
Wang-Iverson, Patsy 1947- *AmMWSc 92*
Wangaard, Frederick Field 1911- *AmMWSc 92*
Wangaratta, Bishop of 1929- *Who 92*
Wangberg, James Keith 1946- *AmMWSc 92*
Wangberg, Lou M 1941- *WhoAmP 91*
Wangberg, Mark Thomas *DrAPF 91*
Wangchuk, Jigme Singye 1955- *IntWW 91*
Wangemann, Robert Theodore 1933- *AmMWSc 92*
Wangensteen, Ove Douglas 1942- *AmMWSc 92*
Wangensteen, Stephen Lightner 1933- *AmMWSc 92*
Wanger, Oliver Winston 1940- *WhoAmL 92*
Wangerin, Ronald Richard 1931- *WhoMW 92*
Wangerin, Walter J. 1944- *ConAu 34NR*
Wangersky, Peter John 1927- *AmMWSc 92*
Wangila, Robert *BlkOlyM*
Wangler, Mark Adrian 1955- *WhoMW 92*
Wangler, Roger Dean 1950- *AmMWSc 92*
Wangler, Thomas P 1937- *AmMWSc 92*
Wangler, William C 1929- *WhoIns 92*
Wangler, William Clarence 1929- *WhoFI 92*
Wangsness, Paul Jerome 1944- *AmMWSc 92*
Wangsness, Roald Klinkenberg 1922- *AmMWSc 92*
Wanhal, Johann Baptist *NewAmDM*
Wani, Jagannath K 1934- *AmMWSc 92*
Wani, Mansukhlal Chhaganlal 1925- *AmMWSc 92*
Wani, Silvanus 1916- *Who 92*
Waniek, Marilyn Nelson *DrAPF 91*
Waniek, Ralph Walter 1925- *AmMWSc 92*
Wanielista, Martin Paul 1941- *AmMWSc 92*
Wank, Neil N. 1944- *WhoWest 92*
Wank, Roland A. 1898-1970 *DcTwDes*
Wankat, Phillip Charles 1944- *AmMWSc 92, WhoMW 92*
Wanke, Gunther 1939- *WhoRel 92*
Wanke, Ronald Lee 1941- *WhoAmL 92*
Wanke, Sieghard Ernst 1942- *AmMWSc 92*
Wankel, Felix 1902-1988 *DcTwDes, FacFETw*
Wanless, Harold Rogers 1942- *AmMWSc 92*
Wanless, Ronald W. 1946- *WhoEnt 92*
Wann, David L. *DrAPF 91*
Wann, Donald Frederick 1932- *AmMWSc 92*
Wann, Elbert Van 1930- *AmMWSc 92*
Wann, Lois *WhoEnt 92*
Wannamethee, Phan 1924- *Who 92*
Wannebo, Ode 1932- *WhoRel 92*
Wannemacher, Philip 1960- *WhoAmP 91*
Wannemacher, Robert, Jr 1929- *AmMWSc 92*
Wanner, Adam *AmMWSc 92*
Wanner, F Walton 1914- *WhoAmP 91*
Wanner, Irene *DrAPF 91*
Wannier, Peter Gregory 1946- *AmMWSc 92*
Wanniski, Jude 1936- *ConAu 133*
Wanscher, Ole 1903- *DcTwDes*
Wansel, Dexter Gilman 1950- *WhoBlA 92*
Wansink, Brian Charles 1960- *WhoMW 92*
Wanstall, Charles Gray 1912- *Who 92*
Wansten, Daniel Joseph 1959- *WhoRel 92*
Wanta, Theresa Susan 1942- *WhoMW 92*
Wantland, Evelyn Kendrick 1917- *AmMWSc 92*
Wantland, William Charles 1934- *WhoRel 92*
Wanton, Eva C. 1935- *WhoBlA 92*
Wanvig, James Louis 1921- *WhoAmL 92*
Wanzenried, David E 1948- *WhoAmP 91*
Waples, James Touchstone 1935- *WhoMW 92*
Waplington, Paul 1938- *TwCPaSc*
Wapnewski, Peter 1922- *IntWW 91*
Wapnir, Raul A 1930- *AmMWSc 92*
Wapp, James Edward 1955- *WhoMW 92*
Wappner, Rebecca Sue 1944- *AmMWSc 92*
Wapshott, Nicholas 1952- *ConAu 135*
Wapshott, Nicholas Henry 1952- *Who 92*
War Admiral 1934-1959 *FacFETw*
Warach, Bernard 1921- *WhoFI 92*
Warakomski, Alphonse Walter Joseph, Jr. 1943- *WhoMW 92*
Waranch, Seeman *WhoIns 92*
Warapius, Glen Robert 1953- *WhoWest 92*
Waravdekar, Vaman Shivram 1914- *AmMWSc 92*
Warbasse, James Peter 1866-1957 *AmPeW*
Warbasse, Lawrence Hill, III 1955- *WhoMW 92*
Warburg, James Paul 1896-1969 *AmPeW*
Warburg, Otto Heinrich 1883-1970 *WhoNob 90*
Warburton, Alfred Arthur 1913- *Who 92*
Warburton, Anne 1927- *Who 92*
Warburton, Anne Marion 1927- *IntWW 91*
Warburton, Charles E, Jr 1941- *AmMWSc 92*
Warburton, David 1942- *Who 92*
Warburton, David Lewis 1947- *AmMWSc 92*
Warburton, Dorothy 1936- *AmMWSc 92*
Warburton, Ernest Keeling 1928- *AmMWSc 92*
Warburton, Fred *ScFEYrs*
Warburton, Geoffrey Barratt 1924- *Who 92*
Warburton, Ivor William 1946- *Who 92*
Warburton, Jacqueline Williams 1930- *WhoAmP 91*
Warburton, Joan 1920- *TwCPaSc*
Warburton, John Kenneth 1932- *Who 92*
Warburton, Nathaniel Calvin, Jr 1910- *WhoAmP 91*
Warburton, Ralph Joseph 1935- *WhoFI 92*
Warburton, Richard Maurice 1928- *Who 92*
Warburton, Wallace Stanley 1956- *WhoEnt 92*
Warburton, William 1698-1779 *BlkwCEP*
Warburton, William Kurtz 1942- *AmMWSc 92*
Warch, George W 1912- *WhoIns 92*
Warch, Richard 1939- *WhoMW 92*
Ward *Who 92*
Ward and Lock *DcLB 106 [port]*
Ward, Lock, Bowden and Company *DcLB 106*
Ward, Lock and Tyler *DcLB 106*
Ward, Aileen 1919- *DcLB 111 [port]*
Ward, Alan Gordon 1914- *Who 92*
Ward, Alan Hylton 1938- *Who 92*
Ward, Alan J. 1937- *WrDr 92*
Ward, Alan S. 1931- *WhoAmL 92*
Ward, Albert A. 1929- *WhoBlA 92*
Ward, Albert Eugene 1940- *WhoWest 92*
Ward, Albert Joseph Reginald 1927- *Who 92*
Ward, Albert M. 1929- *WhoBlA 92*
Ward, Alford L 1919- *AmMWSc 92*
Ward, Aline Hollopeter 1898- *WhoAmP 91*
Ward, Allen Richard 1959- *WhoRel 92*
Ward, Ann Sarita 1923- *Who 92*
Ward, Anna Elizabeth 1952- *WhoBlA 92*
Ward, Anthony Haines 1949- *WhoRel 92*
Ward, Anthony John 1931- *WhoAmL 92*
Ward, Anthony Thomas 1941- *AmMWSc 92*
Ward, Arnette S. 1937- *WhoBlA 92*
Ward, Artemas 1727-1800 *BlkwEAR*
Ward, Artemus 1834-1867 *BenetAL 91*
Ward, Arthur Allen, Jr 1916- *AmMWSc 92*
Ward, Arthur Frederick 1912- *Who 92*
Ward, Arthur Hugh 1906- *Who 92*
Ward, Barbara 1914-1981 *FacFETw*
Ward, Benjamin 1926- *WhoBlA 92*
Ward, Benjamin F, Jr 1943- *AmMWSc 92*
Ward, Bennie Franklin Leon 1948- *AmMWSc 92*
Ward, Betty Sue 1941- *WhoWest 92*
Ward, Bonnie Jean 1947- *WhoWest 92*
Ward, Brad *TwCWW 91*
Ward, Brad M. 1966- *WhoEnt 92*
Ward, Brendan Noel 1949- *WhoEnt 92*
Ward, Brian Hayden 1948- *WhoWest 92*
Ward, Burke Thomas 1947- *WhoFI 92*
Ward, Burt 1945- *IntMPA 92*
Ward, C. Douglas 1930- *WhoBlA 92*
Ward, Calvin Edouard 1925- *WhoBlA 92*
Ward, Calvin Herbert 1933- *AmMWSc 92*
Ward, Calvin Lucian 1928- *AmMWSc 92*
Ward, Carl Edward 1948- *WhoWest 92*
Ward, Carol Buhner 1947- *WhoMW 92*
Ward, Carole Geneva 1943- *WhoBlA 92*
Ward, Carolyn E. 1945- *WhoMW 92*
Ward, Cecil 1929- *Who 92*
Ward, Charles Albert 1939- *AmMWSc 92*
Ward, Charles Eugene Willoughby 1938- *AmMWSc 92*
Ward, Charles Hamilton 1952- *WhoRel 92*
Ward, Charles Leslie 1916- *Who 92*
Ward, Charles Richard 1940- *AmMWSc 92*
Ward, Charlotte Reed 1929- *AmMWSc 92*
Ward, Christopher *WrDr 92*
Ward, Christopher 1868-1943 *BenetAL 91*
Ward, Christopher John 1942- *Who 92*
Ward, Christopher John Ferguson 1942- *Who 92*
Ward, Clara Mae 1924-1973 *NotBlAW 92 [port]*
Ward, Clarke G. 1930- *WhoBlA 92*
Ward, Coleman Younger 1928- *AmMWSc 92*
Ward, Conley, Jr 1947- *WhoAmP 91*
Ward, Curtis Howard 1927- *AmMWSc 92*
Ward, Cynthia 1944- *TwCPaSc*
Ward, Daniel *WhoRel 92*
Ward, Daniel 1934- *WhoBlA 92*
Ward, Daniel Bertram 1928- *AmMWSc 92*
Ward, Daniel P. 1918- *WhoAmL 92, WhoAmP 91*
Ward, Daniel Patrick 1918- *WhoMW 92*
Ward, Darrell N 1924- *AmMWSc 92*
Ward, David 1937- *Who 92*
Ward, David 1938- *WhoMW 92, WrDr 92*
Ward, David 1940- *AmMWSc 92*
Ward, David 1951- *TwCPaSc*
Ward, David Aloysius 1930- *AmMWSc 92*
Ward, David Christian 1941- *AmMWSc 92*
Ward, David Conisbee 1933- *Who 92*
Ward, David Gene 1949- *AmMWSc 92*
Ward, David L. 1936- *WhoFI 92*
Ward, David S. 1947- *IntMPA 92*
Ward, David Schad 1947- *WhoEnt 92*
Ward, Dean Morris 1925- *WhoMW 92*
Ward, DeeAnn Ellen 1946- *WhoRel 92*
Ward, Diane *DrAPF 91*
Ward, Diane Korosy 1939- *WhoFI 92, WhoWest 92*
Ward, Dick 1937- *TwCPaSc*
Ward, Donald Albert 1920- *Who 92*
Ward, Donald Butler 1919- *WhoRel 92*
Ward, Donald Earl 1946- *WhoMW 92*
Ward, Donald Thomas 1936- *AmMWSc 92*
Ward, Doris Margaret 1932- *WhoBlA 92*
Ward, Douglas Eric 1957- *AmMWSc 92, WhoMW 92*
Ward, Douglas Merrill 1950- *WhoWest 92*
Ward, Douglas Scott 1964- *WhoRel 92*
Ward, Douglas Turner 1930- *WhoBlA 92, WrDr 92*
Ward, Dudley 1905- *Who 92*
Ward, E D 1868-1938 *ScFEYrs*
Ward, Edmund Fisher *Who 92*
Ward, Edmund William Beswick 1930- *AmMWSc 92*
Ward, Edward *Who 92*
Ward, Edward Hilson 1930- *AmMWSc 92*
Ward, Edwin James Greenfield 1919- *Who 92*
Ward, Edwin Jesse 1919- *WhoFI 92*
Ward, Elizabeth Honor 1926- *WrDr 92*
Ward, Elizabeth Stuart Phelps 1844-1911 *BenetAL 91, BibAL 8*
Ward, Ellacott Lyne Stephens 1905- *Who 92*
Ward, Erica Anne 1950- *WhoAmL 92*
Ward, Eugene William 1932- *WhoAmL 92*
Ward, Everett Blair 1958- *WhoAmP 91, WhoBlA 92*
Ward, Felker *WhoBlA 92*
Ward, Floyd Edward, Jr. 1944- *WhoFI 92*
Ward, Frances Ellen 1939- *AmMWSc 92*
Ward, Frances Marie 1964- *WhoBlA 92*
Ward, Francis 1926- *TwCPaSc*
Ward, Frank Alan 1948- *WhoFI 92*
Ward, Frank Dixon *Who 92*
Ward, Frank Kernan 1931- *AmMWSc 92*
Ward, Fraser Prescott 1940- *AmMWSc 92*
Ward, Fred 1943- *ConTFT 9, IntMPA 92*
Ward, Frederick Roger 1940- *AmMWSc 92*
Ward, Fredrick James 1928- *AmMWSc 92*
Ward, Gary Lamell 1953- *WhoBlA 92*
Ward, Gene 1943- *WhoAmP 91*
Ward, Geoffrey C 1940- *IntAu&W 91, WrDr 92*
Ward, George A 1936- *AmMWSc 92*
Ward, George Edward 1941- *WhoAmL 92*
Ward, George Henry 1916- *AmMWSc 92*
Ward, George Truman 1927- *WhoFI 92*
Ward, Gerald Lawrence 1947- *WhoMW 92*
Ward, Gerald Madison 1921- *AmMWSc 92*
Ward, Gerald T 1926- *AmMWSc 92*
Ward, Gertrude Luckhardt 1923- *AmMWSc 92*
Ward, Harold Anson, III 1933- *WhoAmL 92*
Ward, Harold Nathaniel 1936- *AmMWSc 92*
Ward, Harold Richard 1931- *AmMWSc 92*
Ward, Harold Roy 1935- *AmMWSc 92*
Ward, Harry Frederick 1873-1966 *RelLAm 91*
Ward, Harry Lee 1945- *WhoRel 92*
Ward, Harry Merrill 1929- *WrDr 92*
Ward, Haskell G. 1940- *WhoBlA 92*
Ward, Helene Statfeld 1938- *WhoAmP 91*
Ward, Henry Augustus 1834-1906 *BilnAmS*
Ward, Herbert Bailey *AmMWSc 92*
Ward, Herbert D. 1861-1932 *ScFEYrs*
Ward, Hiram Hamilton 1923- *WhoAmL 92*
Ward, Horace T. 1927- *WhoBlA 92*
Ward, Horace Taliaferro 1927- *WhoAmL 92*
Ward, Houston *WhoRel 92*

Ward, Howard 1953- WhoMW 92
Ward, Hubert 1931- Who 92
Ward, Humphry, Mrs. 1851-1920 RfGEnL 91
Ward, Ian Macmillan 1928- IntWW 91, Who 92
Ward, Ingeborg L 1940- AmMWSc 92
Ward, Irene Mary Berwick 1895-1980 BiDBrF 2
Ward, Ivor William 1916- Who 92
Ward, J F 1831?-1902 BiInAmS
Ward, James 1851-1924 TwCPaSc
Ward, James 1964- AmMWSc 92
Ward, James Alto, III 1951- WhoFI 92
Ward, James Andrew 1938- AmMWSc 92
Ward, James Audley 1910- AmMWSc 92
Ward, James B 1931- AmMWSc 92
Ward, James Dale 1959- WhoBlA 92
Ward, James David 1935- WhoAmL 92, WhoWest 92
Ward, James Edward, III 1939- AmMWSc 92
Ward, James Edwin 1933- WhoRel 92
Ward, James Frank 1938- WhoMW 92
Ward, James Gordon 1944- WhoMW 92
Ward, James Hubert 1937- WhoWest 92
Ward, James Vernon 1940- AmMWSc 92
Ward, Jay d1989 LesBEnT 92
Ward, Jeffrey Blair, Sr. 1951- WhoFI 92
Ward, Jerrold Michael 1942- AmMWSc 92
Ward, Jerry W. DrAPF 91
Ward, Jerry Washington, Jr. 1943- WhoBlA 92
Ward, Joe Henry, Jr. 1930- WhoAmL 92
Ward, John Who 92, WhoAmP 91
Ward, John 1571-1638 NewAmDM
Ward, John 1679?-1758 BlkwCEP
Ward, John 1917- TwCPaSc
Ward, John Aloysius Who 92
Ward, John Aloysius 1929- IntWW 91
Ward, John Clive 1924- Who 92
Ward, John Devereux 1925- Who 92
Ward, John Edward 1923- AmMWSc 92
Ward, John Everett, Jr 1941- AmMWSc 92
Ward, John F 1935- AmMWSc 92
Ward, John Frank 1934- AmMWSc 92
Ward, John Guthrie d1991 Who 92N
Ward, John Hamilton 1938- WhoAmL 92
Ward, John Henry 1950- AmMWSc 92
Ward, John Hood 1925- IntAu&W 91
Ward, John J. 1920- WhoRel 92, WhoWest 92
Ward, John K 1927- AmMWSc 92
Ward, John Orson 1942- WhoFI 92
Ward, John Paul 1930- WhoFI 92
Ward, John Powell 1937- IntAu&W 91
Ward, John Robert 1923- AmMWSc 92, WhoWest 92
Ward, John Robert 1929- AmMWSc 92
Ward, John Robert 1941- WhoWest 92
Ward, John Sheridan 1958- WhoAmL 92
Ward, John Stanton 1917- Who 92
Ward, John Stephen Keith 1938- Who 92
Ward, John Wesley 1925- AmMWSc 92
Ward, John William 1929- AmMWSc 92, WhoWest 92
Ward, John William 1937- AmMWSc 92
Ward, John X 1926- WhoAmP 91
Ward, Jonas IntAu&W 91X, TwCWW 91, WrDr 92
Ward, Jonas 1922-1960 TwCWW 91
Ward, Jonathan Bishop, Jr 1943- AmMWSc 92
Ward, Joseph Haggitt 1926- Who 92
Ward, Joseph J 1946- AmMWSc 92
Ward, Joseph James Laffey 1946- Who 92
Ward, Joseph Richard 1942- AmMWSc 92
Ward, Judy Kitchen 1940- WhoFI 92
Ward, Karl Ben 1956- WhoWest 92
Ward, Katheryn Hope 1941- WhoMW 92
Ward, Kathleen W 1928- WhoAmP 91
Ward, Kay K. 1942- WhoRel 92
Ward, Keith Who 92
Ward, Keith 1938- WrDr 92
Ward, Keith Bolen, Jr 1943- AmMWSc 92
Ward, Kenneth 1956- WhoFI 92
Ward, Kevin Joseph 1955- WhoMW 92
Ward, Kevin Michael 1953- WhoAmL 92
Ward, Kyle, Jr 1902- AmMWSc 92
Ward, Laird Gordon Lindsay 1931- AmMWSc 92
Ward, Larry S. 1955- WhoEnt 92
Ward, Lawrence McCue 1944- AmMWSc 92
Ward, Lawrence W 1926- AmMWSc 92
Ward, Lenwood E. WhoBlA 92
Ward, Leo Richard 1951- WhoAmL 92
Ward, Leonard George 1930- AmMWSc 92
Ward, Leslie 1888- TwCPaSc
Ward, Lester F. 1841-1913 BenetAL 91
Ward, Lester Frank 1841-1913 BiInAmS
Ward, Lester Lowe, Jr. 1930- WhoAmL 92, WhoWest 92
Ward, Lew O 1930- WhoAmP 91
Ward, Lewis Edes 1925- WhoWest 92
Ward, Lewis Edes, Jr 1925- AmMWSc 92
Ward, Linda Gayle 1954- WhoAmP 91
Ward, Llewellyn Orcutt, III 1930- WhoFI 92
Ward, Lorene Howelton 1927- WhoBlA 92
Ward, Louis Emmerson 1918- AmMWSc 92
Ward, Lowell Sanford 1949- WhoWest 92
Ward, Lyman Joseph 1941- WhoEnt 92
Ward, Malcolm Beverley 1931- Who 92
Ward, Malcolm Stanley 1951- Who 92
Ward, Marcia 1955- WhoFI 92
Ward, Margaret Motter 1928- WhoEnt 92
Ward, Martin 1944- TwCPaSc
Ward, Martyn Eric 1927- Who 92
Ward, Marvin 1914- WhoAmP 91
Ward, Mary J. 1905- BenetAL 91
Ward, McLain NewYTBS 91
Ward, Melvin A 1940- AmMWSc 92
Ward, Melvin Fitzgerald, Sr. 1918- WhoBlA 92
Ward, Michael D 1951- WhoAmP 91
Ward, Michael George 1951- WhoWest 92
Ward, Michael Jackson 1931- Who 92
Ward, Michael John 1931- Who 92
Ward, Michael Phelps 1925- IntWW 91, Who 92
Ward, Morris J 1924- WhoAmP 91
Ward, Nancy 1738?-1822 EncAmaz 91, PorAmW
Ward, Nathaniel 1578?-1652? BenetAL 91
Ward, Ned d1731 BenetAL 91
Ward, Ned 1667-1731 RfGEnL 91
Ward, Nicholas Donnell 1941- WhoAmL 92, WhoFI 92
Ward, Nolan F. 1945- WhoBlA 92
Ward, Norman 1918- WrDr 92
Ward, Norman McQueen 1918- IntAu&W 91
Ward, Orville Elvin 1926- WhoWest 92
Ward, Oscar Gardien 1932- AmMWSc 92
Ward, Patricia Ann 1940- WhoMW 92
Ward, Patricia Lynn 1966- WhoEnt 92
Ward, Patrick Joseph 1952- WhoAmL 92
Ward, Paul Anthony 1929- WhoAmL 92
Ward, Paul H 1928- AmMWSc 92
Ward, Paul Hutchins 1928- WhoWest 92
Ward, Perry W. WhoBlA 92
Ward, Peter 1943- ConAu 134
Ward, Peter A 1934- AmMWSc 92
Ward, Peter Alexander 1930- Who 92
Ward, Peter Allan 1934- WhoMW 92
Ward, Peter Langdon 1943- AmMWSc 92
Ward, Philip 1924- Who 92
Ward, Philip 1938- IntAu&W 91, WrDr 92
Ward, Phillip Wayne 1935- AmMWSc 92
Ward, R. J. WhoRel 92
Ward, Rachel 1957- IntMPA 92
Ward, Ralph Gerard 1933- WrDr 92
Ward, Ray 1960- TwCPaSc
Ward, Raymond Leland 1932- AmMWSc 92
Ward, Reginald Who 92
Ward, Reginald George 1942- Who 92
Ward, Richard 1937- TwCPaSc
Ward, Richard Compton 1941- WhoMW 92
Ward, Richard Eugene 1931- WhoMW 92
Ward, Richard Floyd 1927- AmMWSc 92
Ward, Richard Gerald 1942- WhoAmL 92
Ward, Richard Halsted 1837-1917 BiInAmS
Ward, Richard Hurley 1939- WhoMW 92
Ward, Richard Jan 1947- WhoAmP 91
Ward, Richard John 1925- AmMWSc 92
Ward, Richard Leo 1942- AmMWSc 92
Ward, Richard S 1920- AmMWSc 92
Ward, Richard S. 1940- WhoFI 92
Ward, Robert 1917- NewAmDM
Ward, Robert Allen, Jr. 1937- WhoFI 92
Ward, Robert C 1932- AmMWSc 92
Ward, Robert Carl 1944- AmMWSc 92
Ward, Robert Cleveland 1944- AmMWSc 92
Ward, Robert D 1940- WhoAmP 91
Ward, Robert De Courcy 1867-1931 DcAmImH
Ward, Robert Edward 1916- WhoWest 92
Ward, Robert Joseph 1926- WhoAmL 92
Ward, Robert L. 1951- WhoFI 92
Ward, Robert M WhoAmP 91
Ward, Robert Paul, III 1951- WhoWest 92
Ward, Robert R. DrAPF 91
Ward, Robert T 1920- AmMWSc 92
Ward, Robert William 1935- Who 92
Ward, Robin William 1931- Who 92
Ward, Rodman, Jr. 1934- WhoAmL 92
Ward, Roger Coursen 1922- WhoAmL 92
Ward, Roger Wilson 1944- AmMWSc 92, WhoWest 92
Ward, Ronald Anthony 1929- AmMWSc 92
Ward, Ronald Wayne 1943- AmMWSc 92
Ward, Ronald Wayne 1944- AmMWSc 92
Ward, Roscoe Fredrick 1930- AmMWSc 92
Ward, Roy Livingstone 1925- Who 92
Ward, Russel 1914- WrDr 92
Ward, Samuel 1814-1884 BenetAL 91
Ward, Samuel 1944- AmMWSc 92
Ward, Samuel Abner 1923- AmMWSc 92
Ward, Samuel Baldwin 1842-1915 BiInAmS
Ward, Samuel Joseph, Jr. 1928- WhoFI 92
Ward, Sarah E. 1920- IntMPA 92
Ward, Sarah Frances 1937- WhoMW 92
Ward, Scott John 1965- WhoWest 92
Ward, Sheila Daneen 1935- WhoMW 92
Ward, Shelby Dean 1938- WhoAmP 91
Ward, Sidney Charles 1929- WhoAmL 92
Ward, Simon 1941- IntMPA 92, IntWW 91
Ward, Simon B. Who 92
Ward, Stephen Michael WhoMW 92
Ward, Stephen Patrick 1959- WhoFI 92, WhoWest 92
Ward, Stephen Rosborough 1948- WhoMW 92
Ward, Susan A 1947- AmMWSc 92
Ward, Tamara Lynn 1961- WhoAmL 92
Ward, Taylor Dudley 1956- WhoAmL 92
Ward, Ted Warren 1930- WhoRel 92
Ward, Terence George 1906- Who 92
Ward, Terry Granville 1941- WhoRel 92
Ward, Theresa 1953- WhoFI 92
Ward, Thomas 1807-1873 BenetAL 91
Ward, Thomas Edmund 1944- AmMWSc 92
Ward, Thomas J 1930- AmMWSc 92
Ward, Thomas Joseph 1950- WhoFI 92
Ward, Thomas Monroe 1952- WhoAmL 92
Ward, Thomas Morgan 1935- WhoAmP 91
Ward, Thomas William 1918- Who 92
Ward, Todd Pope 1938- WhoMW 92
Ward, Truman L 1925- AmMWSc 92
Ward, Vincent 1956- IntWW 91
Ward, W H d1897 BiInAmS
Ward, Wallace Dixon 1924- AmMWSc 92
Ward, Walter 1911- WhoAmP 91
Ward, Walter Frederick 1940- AmMWSc 92
Ward, Walter L, Jr WhoAmP 91
Ward, Walter L., Jr. 1943- WhoBlA 92
Ward, William Alan H. Who 92
Ward, William Alec 1928- Who 92
Ward, William Cruse 1933- AmMWSc 92
Ward, William E WhoAmP 91
Ward, William Edward 1922- WhoMW 92
Ward, William Ernest Frank 1900- Who 92
Ward, William Francis 1928- AmMWSc 92
Ward, William Francis 1951- WhoAmL 92
Ward, William Garrett 1961- WhoEnt 92
Ward, William J, III 1939- AmMWSc 92
Ward, William Joseph 1928- WhoAmL 92
Ward, William Kenneth 1918- Who 92
Ward, William L 1936- WhoIns 92
Ward, William Reed 1918- WhoEnt 92
Ward, Yolanda Jean 1957- WhoMW 92
Ward, Zana Rogers 1915- WhoBlA 92
Ward-Booth, John Antony 1927- Who 92
Ward-Brooks, Joyce Renee 1952- WhoBlA 92
Ward-Jackson, Adrian Alexander d1991 Who 92N
Ward-Jackson, Muriel 1914- Who 92
Ward-Jones, Norman Arthur 1922- Who 92
Ward-McLemore, Ethel 1908- AmMWSc 92
Ward-Shaw, Sheila Theresa 1951- WhoWest 92
Ward-Steinman, David 1936- WhoEnt 92, WhoWest 92
Ward-Thomas, Evelyn Who 92
Ward Thomas, Gwyn Edward 1923- Who 92
Wardale, Geoffrey 1919- Who 92
Warde, Cardinal 1945- AmMWSc 92
Warde, Frederick 1851-1935 BenetAL 91
Warde, John Robins 1920- Who 92
Wardeberg, George E. 1935- IntWW 91
Wardega, Patricia Elaine Hallman 1947- WhoMW 92
Wardell, Charles Willard Bennett, III 1945- WhoFI 92
Wardell, Gareth Lodwig 1944- Who 92
Wardell, J. William 1938- WhoFI 92
Wardell, Jay Howard 1943- WhoFI 92
Wardell, Joe Russell, Jr 1929- AmMWSc 92
Wardell, Phyl 1909- WrDr 92
Wardell, William Michael 1938- AmMWSc 92
Warden, Herbert Edgar 1920- AmMWSc 92
Warden, Ivan Leigh 1943- WhoRel 92
Warden, Jack 1920- IntMPA 92, WhoEnt 92
Warden, John L. 1941- WhoAmL 92
Warden, Joseph Tallman 1946- AmMWSc 92
Warden, Lewis Christopher 1913- WrDr 92
Warden, Margaret Smith 1917- WhoAmP 91
Warder, David Lee 1940- AmMWSc 92
Warder, Frederick L 1912- WhoAmP 91
Warder, John Aston 1812-1883 BiInAmS
Warder, John Morgan 1927- WhoBlA 92
Warder, Richard C, Jr 1936- AmMWSc 92
Warder, Robert Bowne 1848-1905 BiInAmS
Wardeska, Jeffrey Gwynn 1941- AmMWSc 92
Wardhana, Ali 1928- IntWW 91
Wardhaugh, Ronald 1932- WrDr 92
Wardington, Baron 1924- Who 92
Wardlaw, Alvia Jean 1947- WhoBlA 92
Wardlaw, Alvin Holmes 1925- WhoBlA 92
Wardlaw, Henry 1930- Who 92
Wardlaw, Jack 1907- WhoIns 92
Wardlaw, Janet Melville 1924- AmMWSc 92
Wardlaw, McKinley, Jr. 1927- WhoBlA 92
Wardlaw, Norman Claude 1935- AmMWSc 92
Wardlaw, William Patterson 1936- AmMWSc 92
Wardle, Charles Frederick 1939- Who 92
Wardle, Dan TwCWW 91
Wardle, David 1930- WrDr 92
Wardle, Irving 1929- IntAu&W 91, Who 92, WrDr 92
Wardle, John Francis Carleton 1945- AmMWSc 92
Wardle, Thomas 1912- Who 92
Wardlow, Bill 1921- WhoEnt 92
Wardlow, Floyd H, Jr 1921- WhoAmP 91
Wardner, Carl Arthur 1904- AmMWSc 92
Wardner, Rich WhoAmP 91
Wardowski, Wilfred Francis, II 1937- AmMWSc 92
Wardroper, John Edmund 1923- WrDr 92
Wards, George Thexton Who 92
Wardzinski, Georgean 1954- WhoIns 92
Ware, Alan Alfred 1924- AmMWSc 92
Ware, Barbara Ann 1955- WhoBlA 92
Ware, Brendan J 1932- AmMWSc 92
Ware, Carl 1943- WhoBlA 92
Ware, Carl F 1951- AmMWSc 92
Ware, Caroline 1908- DcAmImH
Ware, Carolyn Bogardus 1930- AmMWSc 92
Ware, Charles Harvey, Jr 1927- AmMWSc 92
Ware, Charles Jerome 1948- WhoBlA 92
Ware, Chester Dawson 1920- AmMWSc 92
Ware, Clifton, Jr. 1937- WhoEnt 92
Ware, Cyril George 1922- Who 92
Ware, Donna Marie Eggers 1942- AmMWSc 92
Ware, Dyahanne 1958- WhoBlA 92
Ware, Edwin Oswald, III 1927- WhoAmP 91
Ware, Eliot B 1908- WhoAmP 91
Ware, Eugene Fitch 1841-1911 BenetAL 91
Ware, Frederick 1928- AmMWSc 92
Ware, George Henry 1924- AmMWSc 92, WhoMW 92
Ware, George Whitaker, Jr 1927- AmMWSc 92
Ware, Gilbert 1933- WhoBlA 92
Ware, Glenn Oren 1941- AmMWSc 92
Ware, Henry 1764-1845 BenetAL 91
Ware, Henry, Jr. 1794-1843 BenetAL 91
Ware, Irene Johnson 1935- WhoBlA 92
Ware, J. Lowell 1928- WhoBlA 92
Ware, James Crawford 1915- WhoAmP 91
Ware, James Edman 1937- WhoWest 92
Ware, James Gareth 1929- AmMWSc 92
Ware, James H 1941- AmMWSc 92
Ware, James Howard 1944- WhoWest 92
Ware, Jane 1936- ConAu 133
Ware, Jean 1914- WrDr 92
Ware, John 1795-1864 BenetAL 91
Ware, John H, III 1908- WhoAmP 91
Ware, John Rosswork 1922- WhoEnt 92
Ware, John Thomas, III 1931- WhoAmL 92
Ware, Juanita Glee 1923- WhoBlA 92
Ware, Kallistos 1934- WrDr 92
Ware, Kenneth Dale 1935- AmMWSc 92
Ware, Lanette Raquel 1968- WhoEnt 92
Ware, Lawrence Leslie, Jr 1920- AmMWSc 92
Ware, Martin 1915- Who 92
Ware, Michael John 1932- Who 92
Ware, Omego John Clinton, Jr. 1928- WhoBlA 92
Ware, Patricia J. DrAPF 91
Ware, Robert Alexander, IV 1931- WhoAmL 92
Ware, Roger Perry 1942- AmMWSc 92
Ware, Stewart Alexander 1942- AmMWSc 92
Ware, Susan Davenport 1937- WhoFI 92
Ware, Thomas Edward 1938- WhoIns 92
Ware, Vassie C AmMWSc 92
Ware, W H 1920- AmMWSc 92
Ware, Wallace WrDr 92
Ware, Walter Elisha 1933- AmMWSc 92
Ware, William 1797-1852 BenetAL 91, BibAL 8

**Ware,** William L. 1934- *WhoBlA 92*
**Ware,** William Romaine 1931- *AmMWSc 92*
**Ware,** Willis Howard 1920- *WhoWest 92*
**Warehall,** William Donald 1942- *WhoWest 92*
**Wareham,** Alton L. 1920- *WhoBlA 92*
**Wareham,** Ellsworth Edwin 1914- *AmMWSc 92*
**Wareham,** James L. 1939- *WhoFI 92*
**Wareham,** Levada E 1921- *WhoAmP 91*
**Wareham,** Raymond Noble 1948- *WhoFI 92*
**Wareham,** Ronald James 1944- *WhoFI 92*
**Wareing,** Philip Frank 1914- *Who 92*
**Wareing,** Robert Nelson 1930- *Who 92*
**Waren,** Allan D 1935- *AmMWSc 92*
**Waren,** Allan David 1935- *WhoMW 92*
**Waren,** Florence 1917- *WhoEnt 92*
**Wares,** Bruce Robert 1946- *WhoWest 92*
**Warf,** J H 1904- *WhoAmP 91*
**Warf,** James Curren 1917- *AmMWSc 92*
**Warfel,** David Ross 1942- *AmMWSc 92*
**Warfel,** John Hiatt 1916- *AmMWSc 92*
**Warfield,** Benjamin Breckinridge 1851-1921 *RelLAm 91*
**Warfield,** Carol Larson 1941- *AmMWSc 92*
**Warfield,** Curtis H. 1960- *WhoRel 92*
**Warfield,** Dawn Ellen 1955- *WhoAmL 92*
**Warfield,** George 1919- *AmMWSc 92*
**Warfield,** J N 1925- *AmMWSc 92*
**Warfield,** James Monhollen, Jr. 1918- *WhoRel 92*
**Warfield,** Joseph Alton 1937- *WhoEnt 92*
**Warfield,** Marsha *WhoBlA 92*
**Warfield,** Marsha 1955- *ConBlB 2 [port]*
**Warfield,** Melvin Eugene 1955- *WhoMW 92*
**Warfield,** Paul D. 1942- *WhoBlA 92*
**Warfield,** Peter Foster 1918- *AmMWSc 92*
**Warfield,** Robert Breckinridge, Jr 1940- *AmMWSc 92*
**Warfield,** Robert N. 1948- *WhoBlA 92*
**Warfield,** Robert Welmore 1926- *AmMWSc 92*
**Warfield,** Sandra *WhoEnt 92*
**Warfield,** Sandra 1929- *NewAmDM*
**Warfield,** Virginia McShane 1942- *AmMWSc 92*
**Warfield,** William 1920- *NewAmDM*
**Warfield,** William C. 1920- *WhoBlA 92*
**Warfield,** William Caesar 1920- *WhoEnt 92*
**Warfield-Coppock,** Nsenga Patricia 1949- *WhoBlA 92*
**Warford,** Malcolm Lyle 1942- *WhoRel 92*
**Warford,** William Smith 1921- *WhoRel 92*
**Warg,** Richard Dana 1947- *WhoMW 92*
**Warga,** Jack 1922- *AmMWSc 92*
**Wargel,** Robert Joseph 1940- *AmMWSc 92*
**Wargentin,** Pehr Wilhelm 1717-1783 *BlkwCEP*
**Wargo,** Philip Matthew 1940- *AmMWSc 92*
**Wargo,** Robert Paul 1966- *WhoEnt 92*
**Warhaftig,** Solomon L. 1938- *WhoAmL 92*
**Warham,** John 1919- *WrDr 92*
**Warhol,** Andy 1927-1987 *FacFETw [port]*
**Warhol,** Andy 1928?-1987 *ConAu 34NR, IntDcF 2-2 [port], RComAH*
**Warhol,** Michael J *AmMWSc 92*
**Warhol,** Robyn R. 1955- *ConAu 135*
**Warhurst,** Alan 1927- *Who 92*
**Waring,** Derek Morris Holt 1925- *AmMWSc 92*
**Waring,** Edward Graham, Jr. 1924- *WhoRel 92*
**Waring,** Eloise Botts 1920- *WhoAmP 91*
**Waring,** Fred 1900-1984 *NewAmDM*
**Waring,** Gail L *AmMWSc 92*
**Waring,** George Houstoun, IV 1939- *AmMWSc 92, WhoMW 92*
**Waring,** George O, III 1941- *AmMWSc 92*
**Waring,** Glenn Howell 1948- *WhoFI 92*
**Waring,** Holburt 1933- *Who 92*
**Waring,** Laura Wheeler 1887-1948 *NotBlAW 92 [port]*
**Waring,** Richard *DrAPF 91*
**Waring,** Richard C 1936- *AmMWSc 92*
**Waring,** Richard H 1935- *AmMWSc 92*
**Waring,** Robert Kerr, Jr 1928- *AmMWSc 92*
**Waring,** Virginia 1915- *WhoEnt 92, WhoFI 92*
**Waring,** William Winburn 1923- *AmMWSc 92*
**Waring,** Worden 1915- *AmMWSc 92*
**Warinner,** Douglas Keith 1941- *AmMWSc 92*
**Warioba,** Joseph Sinde 1940- *IntWW 91*
**Waris,** Klaus 1914- *IntWW 91*
**Waris,** Michael, Jr. 1921- *WhoAmL 92*
**Waritz,** Richard David 1954- *WhoEnt 92*
**Waritz,** Richard Stefen 1929- *AmMWSc 92*
**Wark,** John Charles 1959- *WhoWest 92*
**Wark,** Kenneth, Jr 1927- *AmMWSc 92*
**Wark,** Steve *WhoAmP 91*
**Warkany,** Josef 1902- *AmMWSc 92*
**Warke,** Guy Donald 1935- *WhoRel 92*
**Warke,** Robert Alexander *Who 92*
**Warkenthien,** Gene E *WhoAmP 91*
**Warkentin,** Benno Peter 1929- *AmMWSc 92*
**Warkentin,** John 1931- *AmMWSc 92*
**Warkentin,** Larry Ray 1940- *WhoEnt 92*
**Warkomski,** Theodore Robert 1924- *WhoAmP 91*
**Warlich,** Eugene Melvin 1926- *WhoAmL 92*
**Warlick,** Charles Henry 1930- *AmMWSc 92*
**Warlick,** Robert L. 1941- *WhoBlA 92*
**Warlock,** Peter *NewAmDM*
**Warltier,** David Charles 1947- *AmMWSc 92*
**Warlum,** Michael Frank *DrAPF 91*
**Warm,** Joel Seymour 1933- *WhoMW 92*
**Warmack,** Kevin Lavon 1956- *WhoBlA 92, WhoFI 92*
**Warman,** Cy 1855-1914 *BenetAL 91*
**Warman,** Francis Frederic Guy d1991 *Who 92N*
**Warman,** Guy Lee 1929- *WhoAmL 92*
**Warman,** Henry J. 1907-1982 *ConAu 133*
**Warman,** James Clark 1927- *AmMWSc 92*
**Warman,** Linda Sue 1952- *WhoEnt 92*
**Warman,** Oliver Byrne 1932- *Who 92*
**Warman,** Philip Robert 1946- *AmMWSc 92*
**Warman,** Scott L 1949- *WhoIns 92*
**Warmanen,** Richard Duane 1945- *WhoWest 92*
**Warmath,** John T, Jr 1929- *WhoIns 92*
**Warmbrod,** Catharine Phelps 1929- *WhoMW 92*
**Warmbrodt,** Robert Dale 1947- *AmMWSc 92*
**Warme,** Beverly Ring 1941- *WhoFI 92*
**Warme,** John Edward 1937- *AmMWSc 92*
**Warme,** Paul Kenneth 1942- *AmMWSc 92*
**Warmer,** Richard Craig 1936- *WhoAmL 92*
**Warmington,** Marshall George Clitheroe 1910- *Who 92*
**Warmington,** William Allan 1922- *IntAu&W 91, WrDr 92*
**Warmke,** Harry Earl 1907- *AmMWSc 92*
**Warmly,** Leon 1941- *WhoBlA 92*
**Warn,** Emily *DrAPF 91*
**Warnas,** Joseph John 1933- *WhoWest 92*
**Warnath,** Maxine Ammer 1928- *WhoWest 92*
**Warncke,** Edna Wagstaff *WhoMW 92*
**Warne,** Antony M. *Who 92*
**Warne,** Frederick 1825- *DcLB 106 [port]*
**Warne,** John 1926- *Who 92*
**Warne,** Katharine Mulky 1923- *WhoEnt 92*
**Warne,** Ronson Joseph 1932- *AmMWSc 92*
**Warne,** Thomas Martin 1939- *AmMWSc 92*
**Warne,** William Elmo 1905- *WhoWest 92*
**Warner,** Alan 1912- *WrDr 92*
**Warner,** Alden Howard 1937- *AmMWSc 92*
**Warner,** Alex *WhoAmP 91*
**Warner,** Amos Griswold 1861-1900 *DcAmImH*
**Warner,** Ann Marie 1944- *AmMWSc 92*
**Warner,** Anna Bartlett 1824-1915 *BibAL 8*
**Warner,** Anna Bartlett 1827-1915 *BenetAL 91*
**Warner,** Anne Elizabeth 1940- *Who 92*
**Warner,** Barbara Ann 1941- *WhoAmP 91*
**Warner,** Barry Allen 1952- *WhoMW 92*
**Warner,** Bennie D. 1935- *IntWW 91, WhoRel 92*
**Warner,** Bert Joseph 1925- *AmMWSc 92*
**Warner,** Brent A 1953- *AmMWSc 92*
**Warner,** Brian 1939- *IntWW 91*
**Warner,** Bruce Franklyn 1946- *WhoMW 92*
**Warner,** Byron Hilbun, Jr. 1939- *WhoEnt 92*
**Warner,** C. Scott 1966- *WhoEnt 92*
**Warner,** Carol Miller 1946- *AmMWSc 92*
**Warner,** Cecil F 1915- *AmMWSc 92*
**Warner,** Charles Collins 1942- *WhoAmL 92*
**Warner,** Charles D 1945- *AmMWSc 92*
**Warner,** Charles Dudley 1829-1900 *BenetAL 91, BibAL 8*
**Warner,** Charles Robert 1931- *AmMWSc 92*
**Warner,** Charles Y 1934- *AmMWSc 92*
**Warner,** Clarence E 1938- *WhoAmP 91*
**Warner,** Curt 1961- *WhoBlA 92*
**Warner,** Dale J 1929- *WhoAmP 91*
**Warner,** Daniel Douglas 1942- *AmMWSc 92*
**Warner,** David 1941- *IntMPA 92, IntWW 91*
**Warner,** David Charles 1942- *AmMWSc 92*
**Warner,** David Gill 1928- *WhoWest 92*
**Warner,** David Ross, Jr. 1943- *WhoAmL 92*
**Warner,** Deborah 1959- *Who 92*
**Warner,** Denis Ashton 1917- *IntWW 91*
**Warner,** Don Lee 1934- *AmMWSc 92*
**Warner,** Donald R 1918- *AmMWSc 92*
**Warner,** Donald Theodore 1918- *AmMWSc 92*
**Warner,** Dorothy Marie 1922- *WhoAmP 91*
**Warner,** Douglas Alexander, III 1946- *WhoFI 92*
**Warner,** Dwain Willard 1917- *AmMWSc 92*
**Warner,** Edward C. 1948- *WhoMW 92*
**Warner,** Edward Courtenay Henry 1951- *Who 92*
**Warner,** Edward L. 1939- *WhoBlA 92*
**Warner,** Edward Redston 1911- *Who 92*
**Warner,** Edythe Records 1916-1980 *ConAu 134*
**Warner,** Eldon Dezelle 1911- *AmMWSc 92*
**Warner,** Francis 1937- *IntAu&W 91, Who 92, WrDr 92*
**Warner,** Francis James 1897- *AmMWSc 92*
**Warner,** Frank *TwCWW 91*
**Warner,** Frank A. *SmATA 67*
**Warner,** Frank Damian 1952- *WhoEnt 92*
**Warner,** Frank Shrake 1940- *WhoWest 92*
**Warner,** Frank Wilson, III 1938- *AmMWSc 92*
**Warner,** Fred Archibald 1918- *IntWW 91*
**Warner,** Frederic Cooper 1915- *AmMWSc 92*
**Warner,** Frederick 1910- *Who 92*
**Warner,** Frederick Archibald 1918- *Who 92*
**Warner,** Frederick Edward 1910- *IntWW 91*
**Warner,** Garett Robinson 1948- *WhoMW 92*
**Warner,** George Blackburn, Jr 1951- *WhoAmP 91*
**Warner,** George Rayner 1955- *WhoAmL 92*
**Warner,** Gerald Chierici 1931- *Who 92*
**Warner,** Gregory Howard 1941- *WhoAmL 92*
**Warner,** H Jack *AmMWSc 92*
**Warner,** Harlow Lester 1942- *AmMWSc 92*
**Warner,** Harold 1917- *AmMWSc 92*
**Warner,** Harold Walton, Jr. 1929- *WhoRel 92*
**Warner,** Henry *Who 92*
**Warner,** Homer R 1922- *AmMWSc 92*
**Warner,** Horace Everett 1839-1930 *AmPeW*
**Warner,** Howard Wayne 1931- *WhoEnt 92*
**Warner,** Huber Richard 1936- *AmMWSc 92*
**Warner,** Irving *DrAPF 91*
**Warner,** Isaiah H. 1916- *WhoBlA 92*
**Warner,** Isiah Manuel 1946- *AmMWSc 92*
**Warner,** Ivan 1919- *WhoBlA 92*
**Warner,** Jack *IntAu&W 91X*
**Warner,** Jack, Jr. 1916- *IntMPA 92, WhoEnt 92*
**Warner,** Jack L 1892-1978 *FacFETw*
**Warner,** James Bruce 1954- *WhoEnt 92*
**Warner,** James D 1827-1911 *BilnAmS*
**Warner,** James Daniel 1924- *WhoRel 92*
**Warner,** James Howard 1938- *AmMWSc 92*
**Warner,** James LeRoy 1938- *WhoMW 92*
**Warner,** Jean-Pierre Frank Eugene 1924- *Who 92*
**Warner,** Jerome 1927- *WhoAmP 91*
**Warner,** John Charles 1962- *AmMWSc 92*
**Warner,** John Christian 1897- *AmMWSc 92*
**Warner,** John Hilliard, Jr. 1941- *WhoFI 92*
**Warner,** John Scott 1928- *AmMWSc 92*
**Warner,** John W. 1927- *AlmAP 92 [port], IntWW 91*
**Warner,** John William 1927- *WhoAmP 91*
**Warner,** Jonathan Robert 1937- *AmMWSc 92*
**Warner,** Josiah 1798?-1874 *BenetAL 91*
**Warner,** Keith Crandall 1938- *WhoAmP 91*
**Warner,** Kendall 1927- *AmMWSc 92*
**Warner,** Larry 1945- *WhoAmP 91*
**Warner,** Laurance Bliss 1931- *AmMWSc 92*
**Warner,** Lawrence Allen 1914- *AmMWSc 92, WhoWest 92*
**Warner,** Lee Howland 1943- *WhoEnt 92*
**Warner,** Lee Michael 1917- *WhoWest 92*
**Warner,** Malcolm-Jamal *WhoBlA 92*
**Warner,** Malcolm-Jamal 1970- *IntMPA 92, WhoEnt 92*
**Warner,** Marina 1946- *ConNov 91, WrDr 92*
**Warner,** Marina Sarah 1946- *IntAu&W 91, IntWW 91, Who 92*
**Warner,** Mark Clayson 1939- *AmMWSc 92*
**Warner,** Marlene Ryan 1938- *AmMWSc 92*
**Warner,** Marvin 1919- *WhoAmP 91*
**Warner,** Matt *WrDr 92*
**Warner,** Michael D. 1949- *WhoWest 92*
**Warner,** Michael Henry Charles 1927- *Who 92*
**Warner,** Milo Nelson 1949- *WhoMW 92*
**Warner,** Mont Marcellus 1919- *AmMWSc 92*
**Warner,** Nancy Elizabeth 1923- *AmMWSc 92*
**Warner,** Norman Reginald 1940- *Who 92*
**Warner,** Paul Longstreet, Jr 1940- *AmMWSc 92*
**Warner,** Peter 1920- *AmMWSc 92*
**Warner,** Peter Deryk 1938- *WhoWest 92*
**Warner,** Philip 1914- *WrDr 92*
**Warner,** Philip A W 1914- *IntAu&W 91*
**Warner,** Philip Mark 1946- *AmMWSc 92*
**Warner,** Philip T 1931- *WhoAmP 91*
**Warner,** R E 1921- *AmMWSc 92*
**Warner,** Rawleigh, Jr. 1921- *IntWW 91*
**Warner,** Ray Allen 1938- *AmMWSc 92*
**Warner,** Raymond M, Jr 1922- *AmMWSc 92*
**Warner,** Rex 1905-1986 *RfGEnL 91*
**Warner,** Richard Alan 1926- *WhoFI 92*
**Warner,** Richard Alan 1936- *WhoFI 92, WhoWest 92*
**Warner,** Richard Charles 1947- *AmMWSc 92*
**Warner,** Richard Dudley 1944- *AmMWSc 92*
**Warner,** Richard G 1922- *AmMWSc 92*
**Warner,** Robert 1912- *AmMWSc 92*
**Warner,** Robert Collett 1913- *AmMWSc 92*
**Warner,** Robert Edson 1931- *AmMWSc 92*
**Warner,** Robert Edward 1942- *WhoEnt 92*
**Warner,** Robert Lewis 1937- *AmMWSc 92*
**Warner,** Robert Ronald 1946- *AmMWSc 92*
**Warner,** Rollin Miles, Jr. 1930- *WhoFI 92, WhoWest 92*
**Warner,** Seth L 1927- *AmMWSc 92*
**Warner,** Shawn Daniel 1961- *WhoWest 92*
**Warner,** Shirley Ann 1936- *WhoRel 92*
**Warner,** Sidney T 1934- *WhoAmP 91*
**Warner,** Susan 1819-1885 *NinCLC 31 [port]*
**Warner,** Susan Bogert 1819-1885 *BenetAL 91, BibAL 8*
**Warner,** Suzanne Elizabeth *Who 92*
**Warner,** Sylvia Townsend 1893-1978 *RfGEnL 91*
**Warner,** Thomas Clark, Jr 1919- *AmMWSc 92*
**Warner,** Thomas Garrie 1948- *AmMWSc 92*
**Warner,** Thomas R 1935- *WhoAmP 91*
**Warner,** Tracey Jennings 1964- *WhoAmL 92*
**Warner,** Val 1946- *WrDr 92*
**Warner,** Vander, Jr. 1930- *WhoRel 92*
**Warner,** Victor Duane 1943- *AmMWSc 92*
**Warner,** Walter Charles 1920- *AmMWSc 92*
**Warner,** Walter Duke 1952- *WhoWest 92*
**Warner,** Wayne Marshall 1927- *WhoRel 92*
**Warner,** William *AmMWSc 92*
**Warner,** William 1558-1609 *RfGEnL 91*
**Warner,** William Hamer 1929- *AmMWSc 92, WhoMW 92*
**Warner,** William Richard 1836-1901 *BilnAmS*
**Warner,** William W. 1920- *ConAu 134, WrDr 92*
**Warner,** Willis L 1930- *AmMWSc 92*
**Warner,** Wilmot Melville 1933- *WhoBlA 92*
**Warner,** Wilson Keith 1930- *WhoWest 92*
**Warnes,** Carl Edward 1948- *WhoMW 92*
**Warnes,** Dennis Daniel 1933- *AmMWSc 92*
**Warnes,** Richard Harry 1933- *AmMWSc 92*
**Warnhoff,** Edgar William 1929- *AmMWSc 92*
**Warnick,** Alvin Cropper 1920- *AmMWSc 92*
**Warnick,** Boyd L 1930- *WhoAmP 91*
**Warnick,** Charles Terry 1943- *WhoWest 92*
**Warnick,** Joel Stanley 1954- *WhoMW 92*
**Warnick,** Jordan Edward 1942- *AmMWSc 92*
**Warnick,** Kenneth L. 1944- *WhoWest 92*
**Warnick,** Robert Eldredge 1929- *AmMWSc 92*
**Warnick,** Walter Lee 1947- *AmMWSc 92*
**Warnke,** Detlef Andreas 1928- *AmMWSc 92*
**Warnke,** Frank J 1933- *WhoAmP 91*

**Warnke,** Jurgen 1932- *IntWW 91*
**Warnke,** Paul Culliton 1920- *IntWW 91, WhoAmL 92, WhoAmP 91*
**Warnke,** Roger Allen 1945- *WhoWest 92*
**Warnke,** Thomas 1943- *WhoAmL 92, WhoIns 92*
**Warnken,** Byron Leslie 1946- *WhoAmL 92*
**Warnken,** Virginia Muriel Thompson 1927- *WhoWest 92*
**Warnock** *Who 92*
**Warnock,** Baroness 1924- *IntWW 91, Who 92, WrDr 92*
**Warnock,** Bruce Edwin 1936- *WhoMW 92*
**Warnock,** Curtlon Lee 1954- *WhoAmL 92*
**Warnock,** David Gene 1945- *AmMWSc 92*
**Warnock,** Geoffrey 1923- *Who 92, WrDr 92*
**Warnock,** Geoffrey James 1923- *IntWW 91*
**Warnock,** Harold Charles 1912- *WhoWest 92*
**Warnock,** John Alfred 1934- *WhoAmP 91*
**Warnock,** John Edward 1932- *AmMWSc 92*
**Warnock,** Laken Guinn 1928- *AmMWSc 92*
**Warnock,** Martha L 1934- *AmMWSc 92*
**Warnock,** Patric Francis 1951- *WhoWest 92*
**Warnock,** Robert G 1925- *AmMWSc 92*
**Warnock,** Robert Lee 1930- *AmMWSc 92*
**Warnock,** William Reid 1939- *WhoAmL 92*
**Warpehoski,** Martha Anna 1949- *AmMWSc 92*
**Warpula,** Calvin Wayne 1944- *WhoRel 92*
**Warr,** Brian Louis 1946- *WhoAmL 92*
**Warr,** John James 1927- *Who 92*
**Warr,** William Bruce 1933- *AmMWSc 92*
**Warrack,** John 1928- *WrDr 92*
**Warrell,** David Alan 1939- *IntWW 91, Who 92*
**Warrell,** Ernest Herbert 1915- *Who 92*
**Warren,** Alan 1936- *AmMWSc 92*
**Warren,** Alan Christopher 1932- *Who 92*
**Warren,** Alastair Kennedy 1922- *Who 92*
**Warren,** Albert *LesBEnT 92*
**Warren,** Albert 1920- *WhoFI 92*
**Warren,** Alice Josephine *Who 92*
**Warren,** Alvin Clifford, Jr. 1944- *WhoAmL 92*
**Warren,** Andrew *IntAu&W 91X*
**Warren,** Austin 1899-1986 *BenetAL 91*
**Warren,** Bacil Christopher 1948- *WhoWest 92*
**Warren,** Bradley Jay 1962- *WhoFI 92*
**Warren,** Brian *Who 92*
**Warren,** Brian Charles Pennefather 1923- *Who 92*
**Warren,** Bruce Albert 1934- *AmMWSc 92*
**Warren,** Bruce Alfred 1937- *AmMWSc 92*
**Warren,** Bryan C. 1959- *WhoFI 92*
**Warren,** Carol Joan 1940- *WhoWest 92*
**Warren,** Caroline Matilda 1787?-1844 *BenetAL 91*
**Warren,** Cecil Allan 1924- *Who 92*
**Warren,** Charles 1927- *WhoAmP 91*
**Warren,** Charles Earl, Sr. 1939- *WhoWest 92*
**Warren,** Charles Edward 1926- *AmMWSc 92*
**Warren,** Charles Marquis 1912-1990 *AnObit 1990, TwCWW 91*
**Warren,** Charles Reynolds 1913- *AmMWSc 92*
**Warren,** Charles Robert 1956- *WhoMW 92*
**Warren,** Chris William 1963- *WhoEnt 92*
**Warren,** Christopher Charles 1949- *WhoWest 92*
**Warren,** Christopher David 1938- *AmMWSc 92*
**Warren,** Claude Earl 1914- *AmMWSc 92*
**Warren,** Clifford A 1913- *AmMWSc 92*
**Warren,** Craig Bishop 1939- *AmMWSc 92*
**Warren,** Cyrus Moors 1824-1891 *BiInAmS*
**Warren,** Daniel R *WhoAmP 91*
**Warren,** David Henry 1930- *AmMWSc 92*
**Warren,** David S. *DrAPF 91*
**Warren,** Dawn Marie 1962- *WhoMW 92*
**Warren,** Diana Lynn 1946- *WhoMW 92*
**Warren,** Don Cameron 1890- *AmMWSc 92*
**Warren,** Donald W 1935- *AmMWSc 92*
**Warren,** Doug 1935- *ConAu 34NR*
**Warren,** Douglas Edgar 1955- *WhoFI 92*
**Warren,** Douglas Ernest 1918- *Who 92*
**Warren,** Douglas Robson 1916- *AmMWSc 92*
**Warren,** Dwight William, III 1942- *AmMWSc 92, WhoWest 92*
**Warren,** Earl 1891-1974 *AmPolLe [port], FacFETw [port], RComAH*
**Warren,** Earle Ronald 1914- *NewAmDM*
**Warren,** Ed N 1926- *WhoAmP 91*
**Warren,** Eddie Lee 1955- *WhoRel 92*
**Warren,** Eugene Howard, Jr. 1943- *WhoFI 92*
**Warren,** Francis A 1917- *AmMWSc 92*
**Warren,** Francis Shirley 1920- *AmMWSc 92*
**Warren,** Fred Franklin 1922- *WhoBlA 92*
**Warren,** Frederick Lloyd 1911- *Who 92*
**Warren,** Frederick Miles 1929- *IntWW 91, Who 92*
**Warren,** Gene 1916- *IntMPA 92*
**Warren,** George Frederick 1913- *AmMWSc 92, WhoMW 92*
**Warren,** George Harry 1916- *AmMWSc 92*
**Warren,** Gertrude Francois 1929- *WhoBlA 92*
**Warren,** Gina Angelique 1954- *WhoBlA 92*
**Warren,** Glenn E 1943- *WhoAmP 91*
**Warren,** Gouverneur Kemble 1830-1882 *BiInAmS*
**Warren,** Graham Barry 1948- *Who 92*
**Warren,** Gretchen Ward 1945- *WhoEnt 92*
**Warren,** Guylyn Rea 1941- *AmMWSc 92*
**Warren,** H Dale 1932- *AmMWSc 92*
**Warren,** Halleck Burkett, Jr 1922- *AmMWSc 92*
**Warren,** Harold Brian 1914- *Who 92*
**Warren,** Harold Hubbard 1922- *AmMWSc 92*
**Warren,** Harris Gaylord 1906- *WrDr 92*
**Warren,** Harry 1893-1981 *FacFETw, NewAmDM*
**Warren,** Harry Verney 1904- *AmMWSc 92*
**Warren,** Henry L. 1940- *WhoBlA 92*
**Warren,** Herman Lecil 1932- *AmMWSc 92*
**Warren,** Herman Lecil 1933- *WhoBlA 92*
**Warren,** Holland Douglas 1932- *AmMWSc 92*
**Warren,** Ian Scott 1917- *Who 92*
**Warren,** Irene Jacobson 1954- *WhoFI 92*
**Warren,** J E 1926- *AmMWSc 92*
**Warren,** Jack Hamilton 1921- *IntWW 91, Who 92*
**Warren,** James C 1930- *AmMWSc 92*
**Warren,** James Clinton 1929- *WhoAmL 92*
**Warren,** James David, Jr. 1951- *WhoWest 92*
**Warren,** James Donald 1948- *AmMWSc 92*
**Warren,** James E., Jr. *DrAPF 91*
**Warren,** James E, Jr 1908- *IntAu&W 91, WrDr 92*
**Warren,** James Edmond 1934- *WhoAmP 91*
**Warren,** James Kenneth 1947- *WhoBlA 92*
**Warren,** James Vaughn 1915- *AmMWSc 92*
**Warren,** Janet Elaine 1951- *WhoMW 92*
**Warren,** Jeffrey Wayne 1948- *WhoAmL 92*
**Warren,** Jeffry Clary 1949- *WhoWest 92*
**Warren,** Jennifer *WhoEnt 92*
**Warren,** Jennifer 1941- *IntMPA 92*
**Warren,** Joe E 1912- *WhoAmP 91*
**Warren,** Joel 1914- *AmMWSc 92*
**Warren,** John 1753-1815 *BiInAmS*
**Warren,** John Byrne Leicester *RfGEnL 91*
**Warren,** John Collins 1778-1856 *BiInAmS*
**Warren,** John Hertz, III 1946- *WhoAmL 92*
**Warren,** John Lucius 1932- *AmMWSc 92*
**Warren,** John Stanley 1937- *AmMWSc 92*
**Warren,** Johnny Wilmer 1946- *WhoAmL 92*
**Warren,** Jonathan Mason 1811-1867 *BiInAmS*
**Warren,** Joseph 1741-1775 *BlkwEAR*
**Warren,** Joseph David 1938- *WhoAmP 91, WhoBlA 92*
**Warren,** Joseph Lawrence 1952- *WhoAmP 91*
**Warren,** Joseph W. 1949- *WhoBlA 92*
**Warren,** Joseph Weatherhead 1849-1916 *BiInAmS*
**Warren,** Josephine *Who 92*
**Warren,** Josiah 1798-1874 *AmPeW*
**Warren,** Joyce *DrAPF 91*
**Warren,** Joyce Williams 1949- *WhoBlA 92*
**Warren,** Judi Dell 1940- *WhoRel 92*
**Warren,** Kenneth 1931- *WrDr 92*
**Warren,** Kenneth Robin 1926- *Who 92*
**Warren,** Kenneth S 1929- *AmMWSc 92, IntWW 91*
**Warren,** Kenneth Wayne 1940- *AmMWSc 92*
**Warren,** Larkin *DrAPF 91*
**Warren,** Larry Michael 1946- *WhoRel 92, WhoWest 92*
**Warren,** Leben 1836-1905 *BiInAmS*
**Warren,** Lee Alden 1954- *WhoBlA 92*
**Warren,** Leonard 1911-1960 *NewAmDM*
**Warren,** Leonard 1924- *AmMWSc 92*
**Warren,** Lesley Ann 1946- *WhoEnt 92*
**Warren,** Lesley Ann 1947- *IntMPA 92*
**Warren,** Lingan A 1889-1984 *FacFETw*
**Warren,** Lionel Gustave 1926- *AmMWSc 92*
**Warren,** Lloyd Oliver 1915- *AmMWSc 92*
**Warren,** Mark Edward 1938- *WhoBlA 92, WhoEnt 92*
**Warren,** Mark Edward 1951- *WhoAmL 92*
**Warren,** Mary Alice *WhoAmP 91*
**Warren,** Mashuri Laird 1940- *AmMWSc 92*
**Warren,** Maurice Eric 1933- *Who 92*
**Warren,** McWilson 1929- *AmMWSc 92*
**Warren,** Mercy 1728-1814 *HanAmWH*
**Warren,** Mercy Otis 1728-1814 *BenetAL 91, BlkwEAR, PorAmW [port]*
**Warren,** Michael 1946- *WhoBlA 92*
**Warren,** Michael 1950- *TwCPaSc*
**Warren,** Michael Donald 1923- *Who 92*
**Warren,** Mitchum Ellison, Jr 1934- *AmMWSc 92*
**Warren,** Morrison Fulbright 1923- *WhoBlA 92*
**Warren,** Nagueyalti 1947- *WhoBlA 92*
**Warren,** Naomi W 1948- *WhoAmP 91*
**Warren,** Nicholas Walter 1941- *WhoWest 92*
**Warren,** Norman Leonard 1934- *Who 92*
**Warren,** Pamela Christine 1965- *WhoMW 92*
**Warren,** Paul Horton 1953- *AmMWSc 92*
**Warren,** Peter 1938- *AmMWSc 92*
**Warren,** Peter Beach 1922- *WhoFI 92*
**Warren,** Peter Francis 1940- *Who 92*
**Warren,** Peter Grenelle 1952- *WhoAmL 92*
**Warren,** Peter Michael 1938- *Who 92*
**Warren,** Peter Tolman 1937- *Who 92*
**Warren,** Peter Whitson 1941- *WhoWest 92*
**Warren,** Randall Fulton 1949- *WhoRel 92*
**Warren,** Raymond Allan 1957- *WhoAmP 91*
**Warren,** Raymond Henry Charles 1928- *Who 92*
**Warren,** Reed Parley 1942- *AmMWSc 92*
**Warren,** Richard Hawks 1934- *AmMWSc 92*
**Warren,** Richard Joseph 1931- *AmMWSc 92*
**Warren,** Richard Joseph 1933- *AmMWSc 92*
**Warren,** Richard Scott 1942- *AmMWSc 92*
**Warren,** Richard Wayne 1935- *WhoWest 92*
**Warren,** Rick Duane 1954- *WhoRel 92*
**Warren,** Rik *WhoMW 92*
**Warren,** Robert A. 1922- *WhoFI 92*
**Warren,** Robert Clarence, Jr. 1960- *WhoAmL 92*
**Warren,** Robert D 1928- *WhoAmP 91*
**Warren,** Robert Holmes 1941- *AmMWSc 92*
**Warren,** Robert Penn 1905-1989 *BenetAL 91, FacFETw*
**Warren,** Robert Willis 1925- *WhoAmL 92, WhoMW 92*
**Warren,** Ronald 1946- *WhoFI 92*
**Warren,** Ronald Barry 1944- *WhoRel 92*
**Warren,** Rosanna *DrAPF 91*
**Warren,** Rueben Clifton 1945- *WhoBlA 92*
**Warren,** Russell Glen 1942- *WhoMW 92*
**Warren,** Russell James 1938- *WhoFI 92*
**Warren,** S Reid, Jr 1908- *AmMWSc 92*
**Warren,** Samuel Edward 1831-1909 *BiInAmS*
**Warren,** Shirley *DrAPF 91*
**Warren,** Sidney 1916- *WrDr 92*
**Warren,** Stanley 1932- *WhoBlA 92*
**Warren,** Stanley Anthony Treleaven 1925- *Who 92*
**Warren,** Stephen Theodore 1953- *AmMWSc 92*
**Warren,** Steve 1945- *WhoWest 92*
**Warren,** Steven Leon 1960- *WhoEnt 92*
**Warren,** Thomas Bratton 1920- *WhoRel 92*
**Warren,** Thomas Trimble 1942- *WhoFI 92*
**Warren,** Tori Jo 1961- *WhoWest 92*
**Warren,** Virgil 1942- *WhoMW 92, WhoRel 92*
**Warren,** Walter R, Jr 1929- *AmMWSc 92*
**Warren,** Walter Raymond, Jr. 1929- *WhoWest 92*
**Warren,** Wayne Hutchinson, Jr 1940- *AmMWSc 92*
**Warren,** Wilfred Lewis 1929- *IntWW 91, WrDr 92*
**Warren,** Wilfrid d1991 *Who 92N*
**Warren,** William *ScFEYrs*
**Warren,** William A 1936- *AmMWSc 92*
**Warren,** William Bradford 1934- *WhoAmL 92*
**Warren,** William Clements 1909- *WhoAmL 92, WhoFI 92*
**Warren,** William D 1936- *WhoIns 92*
**Warren,** William David 1924- *WhoAmL 92*
**Warren,** William Ernest 1930- *AmMWSc 92*
**Warren,** William Fairfield 1833-1924 *RelLAm 91*
**Warren,** William Frampton, Jr. 1954- *WhoRel 92*
**Warren,** William Gerald 1930- *WhoAmL 92*
**Warren,** William Howard 1951- *WhoMW 92*
**Warren,** William Willard, Jr 1938- *AmMWSc 92*
**Warren Evans,** Roger 1935- *Who 92*
**Warren-Lazenberry,** Lillian Frances 1928- *WhoAmP 91*
**Warrender** *Who 92*
**Warrender,** John Robert 1921- *Who 92*
**Warrender,** Robert Thomas, II 1952- *WhoMW 92*
**Warrender,** Robin Hugh 1927- *Who 92*
**Warrenton,** Lule 1863-1932 *ReelWom [port]*
**Warrick,** Alan Everett 1953- *WhoBlA 92*
**Warrick,** Arthur W 1940- *AmMWSc 92*
**Warrick,** Bryan Anthony 1959- *WhoBlA 92*
**Warrick,** Earl Leathen 1911- *AmMWSc 92*
**Warrick,** Mildred Lorine 1917- *WhoWest 92*
**Warrick,** Percy, Jr 1935- *AmMWSc 92*
**Warrick,** Ruth 1916- *IntMPA 92, WhoEnt 92*
**Warrick,** William W. *WhoFI 92*
**Warrick-Crisman,** Jeri Everett *WhoBlA 92*
**Warriner,** Joseph B 1934- *WhoIns 92*
**Warring,** Charles Bartlett 1825-1907 *BiInAmS*
**Warrington,** Archdeacon of *Who 92*
**Warrington,** Bishop Suffragan of 1928- *Who 92*
**Warrington,** Anthony d1990 *Who 92N*
**Warrington,** Elizabeth Kerr *IntWW 91, Who 92*
**Warrington,** Patrick Douglas 1942- *AmMWSc 92*
**Warrington,** Richard William 1868-1953 *TwCPaSc*
**Warrington,** Terrell L 1940- *AmMWSc 92*
**Warrington,** Thomas John 1951- *WhoEnt 92*
**Warschaw,** Carmen H 1917- *WhoAmP 91*
**Warsh,** Catherine Evelyn 1943- *AmMWSc 92*
**Warsh,** Lewis *DrAPF 91*
**Warsh,** Lewis 1944- *ConPo 91, WrDr 92*
**Warshauer,** Steven Michael 1945- *AmMWSc 92*
**Warshavsky,** Suzanne May 1944- *WhoEnt 92*
**Warshaw,** Douglas Alden 1959- *WhoEnt 92*
**Warshaw,** Israel 1925- *AmMWSc 92*
**Warshaw,** Joseph B *AmMWSc 92*
**Warshaw,** Leon J 1917- *WhoIns 92*
**Warshaw,** Michael Thomas 1950- *WhoAmL 92*
**Warshaw,** Stanley I 1931- *AmMWSc 92*
**Warshaw,** Stephen I 1939- *AmMWSc 92*
**Warshawski,** Morrie *DrAPF 91*
**Warshawsky,** Hershey 1938- *AmMWSc 92*
**Warshawsky,** Jay 1927- *AmMWSc 92*
**Warshawsky,** Laura Beth Margolis 1962- *WhoAmL 92*
**Warshay,** Marvin 1934- *AmMWSc 92*
**Warshel,** Arieh 1940- *AmMWSc 92*
**Warshofsky,** Fred 1931- *WhoEnt 92*
**Warshofsky,** Isaac *ConAu 134, IntAu&W 91X, SmATA 68*
**Warshowsky,** Benjamin 1919- *AmMWSc 92*
**Warsi,** Nazir Ahmed 1939- *AmMWSc 92*
**Warsi,** Zahir U A 1936- *AmMWSc 92*
**Warsinske,** James A., Jr. 1958- *WhoEnt 92*
**Warson,** Toby Gene 1937- *WhoMW 92*
**Warsop,** John Charles 1927- *Who 92*
**Warstler,** Robert Thomas 1942- *WhoMW 92*
**Warta,** Denis Joseph 1927- *WhoMW 92*
**Wartell,** Roger Martin 1945- *AmMWSc 92*
**Warten,** Ralph Martin 1926- *AmMWSc 92*
**Warter,** Janet Kirchner 1933- *AmMWSc 92*
**Warter,** Stuart L 1934- *AmMWSc 92*
**Warters,** Mary 1902- *AmMWSc 92*
**Warters,** Raymond Leon 1945- *AmMWSc 92*
**Warters,** William Dennis 1928- *AmMWSc 92*
**Wartes,** Burleigh d1991 *NewYTBS 91*
**Warth,** Donald Eugene 1932- *WhoRel 92*
**Warthen,** John David, Jr 1939- *AmMWSc 92*
**Warthen,** John Edward 1922- *WhoFI 92*
**Warther,** Richard Owen 1954- *WhoFI 92*
**Wartick,** Ronald D 1942- *WhoIns 92*
**Wartik,** Thomas 1921- *AmMWSc 92*
**Wartiovaara,** Otso Uolevi 1908- *Who 92*
**Wartluft,** David Jonathan 1938- *WhoRel 92*
**Wartnaby,** John 1926- *Who 92*
**Wartner,** Paul Dennis 1939- *WhoAmP 91*
**Wartofsky,** Leonard 1937- *AmMWSc 92*
**Wartofsky,** Victor 1931- *IntAu&W 91, WrDr 92*
**Warton,** Joseph 1722-1800 *DcLB 109 [port], RfGEnL 91*
**Warton,** Thomas 1728-1790 *BlkwCEP, DcLB 109 [port], RfGEnL 91*
**Wartzok,** Douglas 1942- *AmMWSc 92*

Waruinge, Philip 1945- *BlkOlyM*
Warung, Price 1855-1911 *RfGEnL 91*
Warwick *Who 92*
Warwick, Archdeacon of *Who 92*
Warwick, Bishop Suffragan of 1937- *Who 92*
Warwick, Earl of 1934- *Who 92*
Warwick, Alice Elizabeth 1951- *WhoAmL 92*
Warwick, Diana 1945- *Who 92*
Warwick, Dionne 1940- *NotBlAW 92, WhoBlA 92*
Warwick, Dionne 1941- *IntWW 91, NewAmDM, WhoEnt 92*
Warwick, Hannah Cambell Grant *Who 92*
Warwick, James Walter 1924- *AmMWSc 92*
Warwick, Mary Carol 1939- *WhoEnt 92*
Warwick, Robert Franklin 1936- *WhoAmP 91*
Warwick, Roger d1991 *Who 92N*
Warwick, Roger 1912- *WrDr 92*
Warwick, Roger 1912-1991 *ConAu 135*
Warwick, Suzanne Irene 1952- *AmMWSc 92*
Warwick, Thomas J 1932- *WhoAmP 91*
Warwick, Warren J 1928- *AmMWSc 92*
Warwick, William Eldon 1912- *Who 92*
Warzecha, Andrzej 1946- *IntAu&W 91*
Warzel, L A 1925- *AmMWSc 92*
Was (Not Was) *ConMus 6 [port]*
Wasa, Kiyotaka 1937- *AmMWSc 92*
Wasacz, John Peter 1944- *AmMWSc 92*
Wasan, Darsh T 1938- *AmMWSc 92*
Wasan, Madanlal T 1930- *AmMWSc 92*
Wasbauer, Marius Sheridan 1928- *AmMWSc 92*
Wascom, Earl Ray 1930- *AmMWSc 92*
Wascom, Lonnie Louis 1948- *WhoRel 92*
Wascou, Ellen Fern 1950- *WhoEnt 92*
Wasden, Jed W 1919- *WhoAmP 91*
Wasden, Winifred Sawaya 1938- *WhoWest 92*
Wase, Arthur William 1915- *AmMWSc 92*
Waser, Nickolas Merritt 1948- *AmMWSc 92*
Waser, Peter Gaudenz 1918- *IntWW 91*
Waser, Peter Merritt 1945- *AmMWSc 92*
Wasfi, Sadiq Hassan 1937- *AmMWSc 92*
Wash, Glenn Edward 1931- *WhoBlA 92*
Washa, George William 1909- *AmMWSc 92*
Washburn, Abbott M. *LesBEnT 92*
Washburn, Albert Lincoln 1911- *AmMWSc 92*
Washburn, Alphonso Victor, Jr. 1912- *WhoRel 92*
Washburn, Carver L. 1932- *WhoFI 92*
Washburn, David Thacher 1930- *WhoAmL 92*
Washburn, Deric *IntMPA 92*
Washburn, Donald Arthur 1944- *WhoFI 92*
Washburn, Frank Murray 1926- *WhoWest 92*
Washburn, Harold W 1902- *AmMWSc 92*
Washburn, Jack 1921- *AmMWSc 92*
Washburn, James Thomas, II 1958- *WhoRel 92*
Washburn, Jerry Martin 1943- *WhoFI 92, WhoWest 92*
Washburn, John Merrow, Jr. 1927- *WhoFI 92*
Washburn, John Rosser 1943- *WhoFI 92*
Washburn, Kenneth W 1937- *AmMWSc 92*
Washburn, L J 1957- *TwCWW 91, WrDr 92*
Washburn, Lee Cross 1947- *AmMWSc 92*
Washburn, Margaret Floy 1871-1939 *WomPsyc*
Washburn, Monard Kent 1942- *WhoEnt 92*
Washburn, Peter Lloyd 1943- *WhoWest 92*
Washburn, Robert 1928- *NewAmDM*
Washburn, Robert Brooks 1928- *WhoEnt 92*
Washburn, Robert Henry 1936- *AmMWSc 92*
Washburn, Robert Latham 1921- *AmMWSc 92*
Washburn, Sherwood L 1911- *AmMWSc 92*
Washburn, Stewart Alexander 1923- *WhoFI 92*
Washburn, Thomas Dale 1947- *WhoFI 92*
Washburn, William H 1920- *AmMWSc 92*
Washburn-Osborn, Daisy Marie 1925- *WhoRel 92*
Washburne, Elihu Benjamin 1816-1887 *AmPolLe*
Washburne, Stephen Shepard 1942- *AmMWSc 92*
Washburne, Theodore Ludwig 1953- *WhoFI 92*
Washbush, Charles Edward 1929- *WhoFI 92*
Washington, Arna D. 1927- *WhoBlA 92*
Washington, Arnic J. 1934- *WhoBlA 92*
Washington, Arthur, Jr. 1922- *WhoBlA 92*
Washington, Arthur Clover 1939- *AmMWSc 92, WhoBlA 92*
Washington, Ava F. 1949- *WhoBlA 92*
Washington, Bennetta B. 1918- *WhoBlA 92*
Washington, Bennetta Bullock d1991 *NewYTBS 91 [port]*
Washington, Betty Lois 1948- *WhoBlA 92*
Washington, Booker T. *DcAmImH*
Washington, Booker T. 1856-1915 *BenetAL 91, BlkLC [port], FacFETw, RComAH*
Washington, Bushrod 1762-1829 *AmPolLe*
Washington, C. Clifford *WhoBlA 92*
Washington, Carl Douglas 1943- *WhoBlA 92*
Washington, Charles Edward 1933- *WhoWest 92*
Washington, Chester Lloyd 1902-1983 *WhoBlA 92N*
Washington, Claudell 1954- *WhoBlA 92*
Washington, Consuela M. 1948- *WhoBlA 92*
Washington, Craig 1941- *AlmAP 92 [port]*
Washington, Craig A. 1941- *WhoBlA 92*
Washington, Craig Anthony 1941- *WhoAmP 91*
Washington, Darryl McKenzie 1948- *WhoBlA 92*
Washington, David Warren 1949- *WhoBlA 92*
Washington, Denzel *WhoBlA 92, WhoEnt 92*
Washington, Denzel 1954- *ConBlB 1 [port], ConTFT 9, IntMPA 92, IntWW 91*
Washington, Dinah 1924-1963 *NewAmDM, NotBlAW 92*
Washington, Dolores Elizabeth 1936- *WhoWest 92*
Washington, Earl Melvin 1939- *WhoBlA 92*
Washington, Earl S. *WhoBlA 92*
Washington, Earl Stanley 1944- *WhoWest 92*
Washington, Earlene 1951- *WhoBlA 92*
Washington, Edith May Faulkner 1933- *WhoBlA 92*
Washington, Edward 1936- *WhoBlA 92*
Washington, Edward, Jr. 1931- *WhoBlA 92*
Washington, Eli H. 1962- *WhoBlA 92*
Washington, Elmer L 1935- *AmMWSc 92, WhoBlA 92*
Washington, Floyd, Jr. 1943- *WhoBlA 92, WhoFI 92, WhoMW 92*
Washington, Fredi 1903- *NotBlAW 92*
Washington, George 1732-1799 *AmPolLe [port], BenetAL 91, BlkwCEP, BlkwEAR [port], RComAH*
Washington, Gladys J. 1931- *WhoBlA 92*
Washington, Grover, Jr. 1943- *WhoBlA 92, WhoEnt 92*
Washington, Henry L. 1922- *WhoBlA 92*
Washington, Ida Harrison 1924- *ConAu 35NR*
Washington, Isaiah Edward 1908- *WhoBlA 92*
Washington, J. Barry 1947- *WhoBlA 92*
Washington, Jacquelin Edwards 1931- *WhoBlA 92*
Washington, Jacquelyn M. 1965- *WhoBlA 92*
Washington, James A. 1950- *WhoBlA 92*
Washington, James A, Jr 1915- *WhoAmP 91*
Washington, James Edward 1927- *WhoBlA 92*
Washington, James Lee 1948- *WhoBlA 92*
Washington, James M 1938- *AmMWSc 92*
Washington, James Melvin 1948- *WhoBlA 92*
Washington, James W., Jr. *WhoBlA 92*
Washington, Jerome *DrAPF 91*
Washington, Jerry 1940- *WhoAmP 91*
Washington, Joe Dan 1953- *WhoBlA 92*
Washington, John A, II 1936- *AmMWSc 92*
Washington, John Calvin, III 1950- *WhoBlA 92*
Washington, John William 1921- *WhoBlA 92*
Washington, Johnnie M. 1936- *WhoBlA 92*
Washington, Joseph R., Jr. 1930- *WhoBlA 92, WrDr 92*
Washington, Josephine 1861-1949 *NotBlAW 92*
Washington, Josie B. 1943- *WhoBlA 92*
Washington, Judy 1958- *WhoEnt 92*
Washington, Kenneth Dean 1967- *WhoWest 92*
Washington, Kenneth S. 1922- *WhoBlA 92*
Washington, Kermit 1951- *WhoBlA 92*
Washington, Lawrence C 1951- *AmMWSc 92*
Washington, Leroy 1925- *WhoBlA 92*
Washington, Lester Renez 1954- *WhoBlA 92*
Washington, Linda Ann 1949- *WhoRel 92*
Washington, Linda Phaire 1948- *WhoBlA 92*
Washington, Lionel 1960- *WhoBlA 92*
Washington, Luisa 1946- *WhoBlA 92*
Washington, Margaret Murray 1861?-1925 *NotBlAW 92 [port]*
Washington, Margaret Murray 1865-1925 *HanAmWH*
Washington, Mary Helen 1941- *WhoBlA 92*
Washington, Mary Parks *WhoBlA 92*
Washington, McKinley, Jr 1936- *WhoAmP 91*
Washington, Michael Harlan 1950- *WhoBlA 92*
Washington, Nancy Ann 1938- *WhoBlA 92*
Washington, Napoleon, Jr. 1948- *WhoFI 92, WhoWest 92*
Washington, Nat Willis 1914- *WhoAmP 91*
Washington, Olivia Davidson 1854-1889 *NotBlAW 92 [port]*
Washington, Oscar D. 1912- *WhoBlA 92*
Washington, Paul M. 1921- *WhoBlA 92*
Washington, Philemon 1934- *WhoBlA 92*
Washington, Reginald Louis 1949- *WhoWest 92*
Washington, Robert Benjamin, Jr 1942- *WhoAmP 91, WhoBlA 92*
Washington, Robert E *WhoAmP 91*
Washington, Robert E. 1936- *WhoBlA 92*
Washington, Robert Orlanda 1935- *WhoBlA 92*
Washington, Ronald 1952- *WhoBlA 92*
Washington, Roosevelt, Jr. 1932- *WhoBlA 92*
Washington, Ruth 1914-1990 *WhoBlA 92N*
Washington, Ruth V. d1990 *WhoBlA 92N*
Washington, Samuel T. 1901- *WhoBlA 92*
Washington, Sandra Beatrice 1946- *WhoBlA 92*
Washington, Sarah M. 1942- *WhoBlA 92*
Washington, Sarah Spencer 1889- *NotBlAW 92*
Washington, Saundra L. *WhoRel 92*
Washington, Sherry Ann 1956- *WhoBlA 92*
Washington, Thomas 1937- *WhoBlA 92*
Washington, Thomas Kight, Sr. 1937- *WhoBlA 92*
Washington, U. L. 1953- *WhoBlA 92*
Washington, Valdemar Luther 1952- *WhoBlA 92*
Washington, Von Hugo, Sr. 1943- *WhoBlA 92*
Washington, Walter 1923- *WhoBlA 92*
Washington, Walter E. 1915- *IntWW 91, WhoBlA 92*
Washington, Warren Morton 1936- *AmMWSc 92, WhoBlA 92*
Washington, William, III 1959- *WhoMW 92*
Washington, William Montell 1939- *WhoBlA 92*
Washington, Willie James 1942- *AmMWSc 92*
Washington, Wilma J. 1949- *WhoMW 92*
Washington-Walls, Shirley 1962- *WhoBlA 92*
Washino, Robert K 1932- *AmMWSc 92*
Washko, Floyd Victor 1922- *AmMWSc 92*
Washko, Walter William 1920- *AmMWSc 92*
Washow, Paula Burnette 1948- *WhoMW 92*
Washton, Nathan Seymour 1916- *AmMWSc 92*
Wasicsko, Nicolas C 1959- *WhoAmP 91*
Wasielewski, Michael Roman 1949- *AmMWSc 92*
Wasielewski, Paul Francis 1941- *AmMWSc 92*
Wasik, Vincent A. 1944- *WhoFI 92, WhoMW 92*
Wasilewski, Vincent T. *LesBEnT 92*
Wasilik, John H 1925- *AmMWSc 92*
Wasinger, David 1963- *WhoMW 92*
Wasinger, Thomas Michael 1951- *WhoAmP 91*
Wasiolek, Edward 1924- *WrDr 92*
Waska, Ronald Jerome 1942- *WhoAmL 92*
Waskell, Lucy Ann 1942- *WhoWest 92*
Waskom, K. Donavon 1929- *WhoFI 92*
Waskom, Michael Albert 1940- *WhoFI 92*
Waskow, Arthur Ocean 1933- *WhoRel 92*
Wasley, Richard J 1931- *AmMWSc 92*
Waslien, Carol Irene 1940- *AmMWSc 92*
Wasmund, Suzanne 1936- *WhoMW 92*
Wasmus, Robert Theodore 1933- *WhoRel 92*
Wason, Robert Alexander 1874-1955 *ScFEYrs*
Wason, Satish Kumar 1940- *AmMWSc 92*
Wason, Suman 1951- *WhoMW 92*
Wasow, Wolfgang Richard 1909- *AmMWSc 92*
Wass, Carl Gustave 1937- *WhoAmL 92*
Wass, Douglas 1923- *Who 92*
Wass, Douglas William Gretton 1923- *IntWW 91*
Wass, John Alfred 1950- *AmMWSc 92*
Wass, Marvin Leroy 1922- *AmMWSc 92*
Wass, Paul 1925- *WhoAmP 91*
Wass, Wallace M 1929- *AmMWSc 92*
Wass, Wallace Milton 1929- *WhoMW 92*
Wassarman, Paul Michael 1940- *AmMWSc 92*
Wassef, Nabila M 1943- *AmMWSc 92*
Wassell, Loren W. 1948- *WhoMW 92*
Wassenberg, Shirley Mae 1927- *WhoAmP 91*
Wasser, Bonnie Stern 1957- *WhoAmL 92*
Wasser, Clinton Howard 1915- *AmMWSc 92*
Wasser, Joseph 1920- *WhoAmP 91*
Wasser, Richard Barkman 1936- *AmMWSc 92*
Wasserburg, Gerald Joseph 1927- *AmMWSc 92, IntWW 91*
Wasserheit, Judith Nina 1954- *AmMWSc 92*
Wasserlein, John Henry 1941- *WhoFI 92*
Wasserman, Aaron E 1921- *AmMWSc 92*
Wasserman, Aaron Osias 1927- *AmMWSc 92*
Wasserman, Aaron Reuben 1932- *AmMWSc 92*
Wasserman, Al *LesBEnT 92*
Wasserman, Albert J 1928- *AmMWSc 92*
Wasserman, Allen Lowell 1934- *AmMWSc 92*
Wasserman, Arthur Gabriel 1938- *AmMWSc 92*
Wasserman, August von 1866-1925 *FacFETw*
Wasserman, Bert W. *WhoFI 92*
Wasserman, Bruce Arlen 1954- *WhoWest 92*
Wasserman, Bruce P 1953- *AmMWSc 92*
Wasserman, Charles 1929- *WhoFI 92*
Wasserman, Clare 1954- *WhoEnt 92*
Wasserman, Dale *LesBEnT 92*
Wasserman, Dale 1917- *IntMPA 92, WhoEnt 92, WrDr 92*
Wasserman, David 1917- *AmMWSc 92*
Wasserman, Diana 1947- *WhoHisp 92*
Wasserman, Donald Eugene 1939- *AmMWSc 92, WhoMW 92*
Wasserman, Edel 1932- *AmMWSc 92*
Wasserman, Edward 1921- *AmMWSc 92*
Wasserman, Eileen Martin 1945- *WhoMW 92*
Wasserman, Frederick E 1948- *AmMWSc 92*
Wasserman, Gerald Steward 1937- *AmMWSc 92*
Wasserman, Gordon Joshua 1938- *Who 92*
Wasserman, Harry H 1920- *AmMWSc 92*
Wasserman, Jack F 1941- *AmMWSc 92*
Wasserman, Jerry 1931- *AmMWSc 92*
Wasserman, Julia B *WhoAmP 91*
Wasserman, Karlman 1927- *AmMWSc 92*
Wasserman, Lawrence Harvey 1945- *AmMWSc 92*
Wasserman, Lew 1913- *IntMPA 92*
Wasserman, Lew R. 1913- *CurBio 91 [port], IntWW 91, WhoEnt 92, WhoFI 92, WhoWest 92*
Wasserman, Louis Robert 1910- *AmMWSc 92*
Wasserman, Mark Daniel 1964- *WhoWest 92*
Wasserman, Martin Allan 1941- *AmMWSc 92*
Wasserman, Martin S 1938- *AmMWSc 92*
Wasserman, Marvin 1929- *AmMWSc 92*
Wasserman, Morris 1928- *WhoWest 92*
Wasserman, Paul 1924- *WrDr 92*
Wasserman, Richard Leo 1948- *WhoAmL 92*
Wasserman, Robert 1934- *WhoWest 92*
Wasserman, Robert H 1923- *AmMWSc 92*
Wasserman, Robert Harold 1926- *AmMWSc 92, IntWW 91*
Wasserman, Robert Zachary 1947- *WhoWest 92*
Wasserman, Rosanne *DrAPF 91*
Wasserman, Stanley 1951- *AmMWSc 92*
Wasserman, Stephen I *AmMWSc 92*
Wasserman, William Jack 1925- *AmMWSc 92*
Wasserman, William John 1947- *AmMWSc 92*
Wasserman, William Phillip 1945- *WhoAmL 92*
Wasserman, Zelda Rakowitz 1935- *AmMWSc 92*
Wassermann, Felix Emil 1924- *AmMWSc 92*
Wasserstein, Abraham 1921- *Who 92*
Wasserstein, Bruce 1947- *WhoFI 92*

**Wasserstein,** Jeffrey Alan 1958- *WhoFI 92*
**Wasserstein,** Wendy *IntAu&W 91, WrDr 92*
**Wasserstein,** Wendy 1950- *News 91 [port], -91-3 [port], WhoEnt 92*
**Wassersug,** Richard Joel 1946- *AmMWSc 92*
**Wasshausen,** Dieter Carl 1938- *AmMWSc 92*
**Wassink,** Darwin 1934- *WhoFI 92, WhoMW 92*
**Wassmer,** Robert William 1961- *WhoFI 92*
**Wassmundt,** Frederick William 1932- *AmMWSc 92*
**Wassner,** Neil Allen 1941- *WhoFI 92*
**Wassom,** Clyde E 1924- *AmMWSc 92*
**Wasson,** Barbara Hickam 1918- *WhoEnt 92, WhoMW 92*
**Wasson,** Craig 1954- *IntMPA 92*
**Wasson,** Donald DeWitt 1921- *WhoEnt 92*
**Wasson,** Douglas 1927- *WhoRel 92, WhoWest 92*
**Wasson,** James A 1926- *AmMWSc 92*
**Wasson,** James Walter 1951- *AmMWSc 92, WhoWest 92*
**Wasson,** John R 1941- *AmMWSc 92*
**Wasson,** John Taylor 1934- *AmMWSc 92*
**Wasson,** L C 1909- *AmMWSc 92*
**Wasson,** Oren A 1935- *AmMWSc 92*
**Wasson,** Richard Lee 1932- *AmMWSc 92*
**Wasson,** Roy D. 1950- *WhoAmL 92*
**Wasson,** W Dana 1934- *AmMWSc 92*
**Wasswas,** Edgar S. 1939- *WhoBlA 92*
**Wastell,** Cyril Gordon 1916- *Who 92*
**Wasterlain,** Claude Guy 1935- *AmMWSc 92*
**Wasti,** Khizar 1948- *AmMWSc 92*
**Wastie,** Winston Victor 1900- *Who 92*
**Wasylishen,** Roderick Ernest 1944- *AmMWSc 92*
**Wasylkiwskyj,** Wasyl 1935- *AmMWSc 92*
**Wasylyk,** John Stanley 1942- *AmMWSc 92*
**Wasylyk,** Peter N 1957- *WhoAmP 91*
**Wat,** Aleksander 1900-1967 *FacFETw, LiExTwC*
**Wat,** Bo Ying 1925- *AmMWSc 92*
**Wat,** Edward Koon Wah 1940- *AmMWSc 92*
**Wat,** James Kam-Choi 1949- *WhoWest 92*
**Watabe,** Norimitsu 1922- *AmMWSc 92*
**Watada,** Alley E 1930- *AmMWSc 92*
**Watanabe,** Akira 1935- *AmMWSc 92*
**Watanabe,** Bunzo 1907- *IntWW 91*
**Watanabe,** Corinne Kaoru Amemiya 1950- *WhoWest 92*
**Watanabe,** Daniel Seishi 1940- *AmMWSc 92*
**Watanabe,** Eric Katsuji 1951- *WhoWest 92*
**Watanabe,** Gedde *IntMPA 92*
**Watanabe,** Itaru S 1933- *AmMWSc 92*
**Watanabe,** Jeffrey Noboru 1943- *WhoWest 92*
**Watanabe,** Kosei 1957- *WhoAmL 92*
**Watanabe,** Kouichi 1942- *WhoFI 92*
**Watanabe,** Kozo *IntWW 91*
**Watanabe,** Kyoichi A 1935- *AmMWSc 92*
**Watanabe,** Larry Geo 1950- *WhoWest 92*
**Watanabe,** Makoto 1953- *WhoEnt 92*
**Watanabe,** Mamoru 1933- *AmMWSc 92*
**Watanabe,** Michael Jiro 1953- *WhoAmL 92*
**Watanabe,** Michiko 1952- *AmMWSc 92*
**Watanabe,** Michio 1923- *IntWW 91*
**Watanabe,** Philip Glen 1947- *AmMWSc 92*
**Watanabe,** Richard Megumi 1962- *WhoWest 92*
**Watanabe,** Roy Noboru 1947- *WhoAmL 92*
**Watanabe,** Takeji 1913- *IntWW 91*
**Watanabe,** Takeshi 1940- *AmMWSc 92*
**Watanabe,** Tomiya 1927- *AmMWSc 92*
**Watanabe,** Yoshio 1925- *AmMWSc 92*
**Watanabe,** Youji 1923- *IntWW 91*
**Watanen,** John, Jr. 1936- *WhoMW 92*
**Watanuki,** Tamisuke 1927- *IntWW 91*
**Watari,** Sugiichiro 1925- *IntWW 91*
**Watase,** Takanori 1946- *WhoMW 92*
**Watchman,** Leo C *WhoAmP 91*
**Watchorn,** C L F 1945- *WhoIns 92*
**Watchorn,** William Ernest 1943- *WhoFI 92*
**Watelet,** Claude-Henri 1718-1786 *BlkwCEP*
**Watenpaugh,** Keith Donald 1939- *AmMWSc 92*
**Water,** Linda Gail 1946- *WhoMW 92*
**Water-sitting Grizzly** *EncAmaz 91*
**Waterbury,** Jackson DeWitt 1937- *WhoFI 92, WhoMW 92*
**Waterbury,** Lowell David 1942- *AmMWSc 92*
**Waterbury,** Stephen Chauncey 1949- *WhoAmL 92*
**Waterer,** Louis Phillipp 1939- *WhoWest 92*
**Waterfield,** Giles Adrian 1949- *Who 92*
**Waterfield,** Harry Lee, II 1943- *WhoIns 92*
**Waterfield,** John Percival 1921- *Who 92*
**Waterfield,** Michael Derek 1941- *Who 92*
**Waterfield,** Richard A 1939- *WhoAmP 91*
**Waterford,** Marquess of 1933- *Who 92*
**Waterhouse,** Barry D 1949- *AmMWSc 92*
**Waterhouse,** Benjamin 1754-1846 *BiInAmS*
**Waterhouse,** David Martin 1937- *Who 92*
**Waterhouse,** Douglas Frew 1916- *IntWW 91, Who 92*
**Waterhouse,** Frederick Harry 1932- *Who 92*
**Waterhouse,** Howard N 1932- *AmMWSc 92*
**Waterhouse,** John P 1920- *AmMWSc 92*
**Waterhouse,** John William 1849-1917 *TwCPaSc*
**Waterhouse,** Joseph Stallard 1929- *AmMWSc 92*
**Waterhouse,** Keith 1929- *ConNov 91, IntMPA 92, WrDr 92*
**Waterhouse,** Keith R 1929- *AmMWSc 92*
**Waterhouse,** Keith Spencer 1929- *IntAu&W 91, IntWW 91, Who 92*
**Waterhouse,** Olga 1917- *WhoAmP 91*
**Waterhouse,** Rachel 1923- *Who 92*
**Waterhouse,** Richard 1924- *AmMWSc 92*
**Waterhouse,** Ronald 1926- *Who 92*
**Waterhouse,** Stephen Lee 1943- *WhoFI 92*
**Waterhouse,** William Charles 1941- *AmMWSc 92*
**Waterland,** Larry R 1948- *AmMWSc 92*
**Waterloo,** Stanley 1846-1913 *ScFEYrs, TwCSFW 91*
**Waterlow,** Christopher Rupert 1959- *Who 92*
**Waterlow,** Ernest Albert 1850-1919 *TwCPaSc*
**Waterlow,** James Gerard 1939- *Who 92*
**Waterlow,** John Conrad 1916- *IntWW 91, Who 92*
**Waterman,** Alan T, Jr 1918- *AmMWSc 92*
**Waterman,** Andrew 1940- *ConPo 91, WrDr 92*
**Waterman,** Byron Olney 1909- *WhoRel 92*
**Waterman,** Cary *DrAPF 91*
**Waterman,** Charles K. *DrAPF 91*
**Waterman,** Daniel 1927- *AmMWSc 92*
**Waterman,** Fanny 1920- *Who 92*
**Waterman,** Frank Melvin 1938- *AmMWSc 92*
**Waterman,** Homer D. 1915- *WhoBlA 92*
**Waterman,** Lori 1914- *WhoWest 92*
**Waterman,** Merton C *WhoAmP 91*
**Waterman,** Michael Alan 1950- *WhoAmL 92*
**Waterman,** Michael Roberts 1939- *AmMWSc 92*
**Waterman,** Michael S 1942- *AmMWSc 92*
**Waterman,** Mignon Redfield 1944- *WhoAmP 91*
**Waterman,** Peter Lewis 1955- *AmMWSc 92*
**Waterman,** Samuel B. 1907- *WhoAmL 92*
**Waterman,** Talbot H 1914- *AmMWSc 92*
**Waterman,** Thelma M. 1937- *WhoBlA 92*
**Waterman Humber,** Richard 1962- *WhoEnt 92*
**Waterpark,** Baron 1926- *Who 92*
**Waters,** Aaron C. d1991 *NewYTBS 91*
**Waters,** Aaron Clement 1905- *AmMWSc 92, IntWW 91*
**Waters,** Andre 1962- *WhoBlA 92*
**Waters,** Ann Walworth 1957- *WhoAmL 92*
**Waters,** Billie 1896-1979 *TwCPaSc*
**Waters,** Brenda Joyce 1950- *WhoBlA 92*
**Waters,** Brent Philip 1953- *WhoRel 92*
**Waters,** Charles John 1935- *Who 92*
**Waters,** Chocolate *DrAPF 91*
**Waters,** Curtis Jefferson 1929- *WhoRel 92*
**Waters,** David Watkin 1911- *Who 92, WrDr 92*
**Waters,** Dean Allison 1936- *AmMWSc 92*
**Waters,** Donald Henry 1937- *Who 92, WhoFI 92*
**Waters,** Edward Neighbor d1991 *NewYTBS 91*
**Waters,** Edward Sarsfield 1930- *WhoEnt 92*
**Waters,** Elsie 1894-1990 *AnObit 1990*
**Waters,** Enoch P. 1910?-1987 *ConAu 134*
**Waters,** Ethel 1896-1977 *NewAmDM, NotBlAW 92 [port]*
**Waters,** Ethel 1900-1977 *HanAmWH*
**Waters,** Frank *DrAPF 91*
**Waters,** Frank 1902- *TwCWW 91, WrDr 92*
**Waters,** Frank, Mrs. *Who 92*
**Waters,** Garth Rodney 1944- *Who 92*
**Waters,** Greg Henry 1943- *WhoEnt 92*
**Waters,** H. Franklin 1932- *WhoAmL 92*
**Waters,** Harry N 1936- *WhoAmP 91*
**Waters,** Henrietta Davis 1941- *WhoAmL 92*
**Waters,** Henrietta E. 1927- *WhoBlA 92*
**Waters,** Irving Wade 1931- *AmMWSc 92*
**Waters,** J. Kevin 1933- *WhoWest 92*
**Waters,** James Augustus 1931- *AmMWSc 92*
**Waters,** James Frederick 1938- *AmMWSc 92*
**Waters,** James Larry 1953- *WhoAmP 91*
**Waters,** Jennifer Nash 1951- *WhoAmL 92*
**Waters,** Jerry B 1933- *WhoAmP 91*
**Waters,** John *Who 92*
**Waters,** John 1945- *IntDcF 2-2 [port]*
**Waters,** John 1946- *IntMPA 92, WhoEnt 92*
**Waters,** John Albert 1935- *AmMWSc 92*
**Waters,** John F. 1930- *WrDr 92*
**Waters,** John Frederick 1930- *IntAu&W 91*
**Waters,** John M. 1946- *IntAu&W 91*
**Waters,** John W. 1936- *WhoBlA 92, WhoRel 92*
**Waters,** Joseph Hemenway 1930- *AmMWSc 92*
**Waters,** Kenneth Lee 1914- *AmMWSc 92*
**Waters,** King 1950- *WhoAmL 92*
**Waters,** Larry Charles 1939- *AmMWSc 92*
**Waters,** Martin Vincent 1917- *WhoBlA 92*
**Waters,** Maxine *WhoAmP 91, WhoBlA 92*
**Waters,** Maxine 1938- *AlmAP 92 [port], WhoWest 92*
**Waters,** Michael *DrAPF 91*
**Waters,** Michael Dee 1942- *AmMWSc 92*
**Waters,** Montague 1917- *Who 92*
**Waters,** Muddy *NewAmDM*
**Waters,** Neville R., III 1957- *WhoBlA 92*
**Waters,** Norman Dale 1922- *AmMWSc 92*
**Waters,** Norman S 1925- *WhoAmP 91*
**Waters,** Philip Alan 1949- *WhoEnt 92*
**Waters,** Richard C 1950- *AmMWSc 92*
**Waters,** Robert Allen 1955- *WhoAmP 91*
**Waters,** Robert Charles 1930- *AmMWSc 92*
**Waters,** Rodney Lewis 1936- *AmMWSc 92*
**Waters,** Rolland Mayden 1926- *AmMWSc 92*
**Waters,** Rollie Odell 1942- *WhoFI 92*
**Waters,** Stephen Russell 1954- *WhoAmP 91, WhoMW 92*
**Waters,** Sylvia *WhoEnt 92*
**Waters,** Sylvia Ann 1949- *WhoBlA 92*
**Waters,** Theodore *ScFEYrs*
**Waters,** Thomas Alfred 1940- *WhoAmP 91*
**Waters,** Thomas Frank 1926- *AmMWSc 92*
**Waters,** Todd Vern 1947- *WhoMW 92*
**Waters,** Wayne Arthur 1929- *WhoFI 92, WhoMW 92*
**Waters,** William David 1924- *WhoBlA 92*
**Waters,** William E 1922- *AmMWSc 92*
**Waters,** William Ernest 1928- *WhoFI 92*
**Waters,** William F 1943- *AmMWSc 92*
**Waters,** William L. 1941- *WhoBlA 92*
**Waters,** William Roland 1920- *WhoMW 92*
**Waters,** Willie Anthony 1951- *NewAmDM, WhoEnt 92*
**Waters,** Willie Estel 1931- *AmMWSc 92*
**Waters,** Wimbley, Jr. 1943- *WhoBlA 92*
**Waters von Hatten,** Eileen Elizabeth 1959- *WhoMW 92*
**Waterson,** Claire 1947- *WhoFI 92*
**Waterson,** John R 1944- *AmMWSc 92*
**Waterston,** Charles Dewar 1925- *Who 92*
**Waterston,** James Rufus *WhoFI 92*
**Waterston,** Sam 1940- *IntMPA 92*
**Waterston,** Samuel Atkinson 1940- *WhoEnt 92*
**Waterston,** William King 1937- *WhoRel 92*
**Waterstone,** David George Stuart 1935- *Who 92*
**Waterstone,** Timothy John Stuart 1939- *Who 92*
**Waterton,** Betty Marie 1923- *IntAu&W 91*
**Waterton,** William Arthur 1916- *Who 92*
**Waterworth,** Alan William 1931- *Who 92*
**Waterworth,** Edward B *ScFEYrs*
**Waterworth,** Howard E 1936- *AmMWSc 92*
**Wates,** Christopher 1939- *Who 92*
**Wates,** Michael Edward 1935- *Who 92*
**Watford,** Charles Lamar *WhoAmP 91*
**Watford,** Jeanette Patterson 1928- *WhoAmP 91*
**Wathelet,** Melchior 1949- *IntWW 91*
**Wathen,** Daniel E 1939- *WhoAmP 91*
**Wathen,** Daniel Everett 1939- *WhoAmL 92*
**Wathen,** Julian Philip Gerard 1923- *Who 92*
**Wathen,** Richard 1917- *WrDr 92*
**Wathen,** Richard B 1917- *WhoAmP 91*
**Watia,** Tarmo 1938- *WhoWest 92*
**Watiker,** Albert David, Jr. 1938- *WhoBlA 92, WhoMW 92*
**Watkin,** Aelred 1918- *Who 92*
**Watkin,** David 1925- *IntMPA 92, WhoEnt 92*
**Watkin,** David John 1941- *Who 92*
**Watkin,** Donald M *AmMWSc 92*
**Watkin Williams,** Peter 1911- *Who 92*
**Watkins,** Alan 1933- *IntAu&W 91, Who 92, WrDr 92*
**Watkins,** Alan Keith 1938- *IntWW 91, Who 92*
**Watkins,** Allen Harrison 1938- *AmMWSc 92*
**Watkins,** Ann Esther 1949- *WhoWest 92*
**Watkins,** Aretha La Anna 1930- *WhoBlA 92*
**Watkins,** Arthur Goronwy d1990 *Who 92N*
**Watkins,** Benjamin Wilston 1922- *WhoBlA 92*
**Watkins,** Brenton John 1946- *AmMWSc 92*
**Watkins,** Brian 1933- *Who 92*
**Watkins,** Charles B 1942- *AmMWSc 92*
**Watkins,** Charles B., Jr. 1942- *WhoBlA 92*
**Watkins,** Charles Booker 1913- *WhoBlA 92*
**Watkins,** Charles H 1913- *AmMWSc 92*
**Watkins,** Charles Lee 1942- *AmMWSc 92*
**Watkins,** Charles Morgan 1954- *WhoAmL 92, WhoRel 92*
**Watkins,** Charles Reynolds 1951- *WhoWest 92*
**Watkins,** Clyde Andrew 1946- *AmMWSc 92*
**Watkins,** Dane *WhoAmP 91*
**Watkins,** Daniel Joseph 1923- *WhoFI 92*
**Watkins,** Darrell Dwight, Jr 1943- *AmMWSc 92*
**Watkins,** Darton 1928- *TwCPaSc*
**Watkins,** David Hyder 1917- *AmMWSc 92*
**Watkins,** David John 1925- *Who 92*
**Watkins,** Dean Allen 1922- *AmMWSc 92*
**Watkins,** Don Wayne 1940- *AmMWSc 92*
**Watkins,** Dudley T 1938- *AmMWSc 92*
**Watkins,** Elton, Jr 1921- *AmMWSc 92*
**Watkins,** Evan Paul 1946- *WhoWest 92*
**Watkins,** Felix Scott 1946- *WhoFI 92*
**Watkins,** Floyd C 1920- *IntAu&W 91, WrDr 92*
**Watkins,** Frank 1951- *TwCPaSc*
**Watkins,** Frederick D 1915- *WhoIns 92*
**Watkins,** Gary L 1946- *WhoAmP 91*
**Watkins,** George Daniels 1924- *AmMWSc 92*
**Watkins,** Gerrold *WrDr 92*
**Watkins,** Glenn Elson 1927- *WhoEnt 92*
**Watkins,** Gloria Elizabeth 1950- *WhoBlA 92*
**Watkins,** Gordon Derek 1929- *Who 92*
**Watkins,** Gordon R. *DrAPF 91*
**Watkins,** Grath 1922- *IntMPA 92*
**Watkins,** Guy Hansard 1933- *Who 92*
**Watkins,** Hannah Bowman 1924- *WhoBlA 92*
**Watkins,** Harold D., Sr. 1933- *WhoBlA 92*
**Watkins,** Harold R. *WhoRel 92*
**Watkins,** Harold Robert 1928- *WhoRel 92*
**Watkins,** Harold Wade 1946- *WhoWest 92*
**Watkins,** Hays Thomas 1926- *WhoFI 92*
**Watkins,** Herbert Nathaniel 1940- *WhoBlA 92*
**Watkins,** Ivan Warren 1934- *AmMWSc 92*
**Watkins,** Izear Carl 1926- *WhoBlA 92*
**Watkins,** Jackie Lloyd 1932- *AmMWSc 92*
**Watkins,** James D 1927- *WhoAmP 91*
**Watkins,** James Darnell 1949- *WhoBlA 92*
**Watkins,** James David 1927- *IntWW 91, NewYTBS 91 [port], WhoFI 92*
**Watkins,** James Theodore 1957- *WhoAmL 92*
**Watkins,** Jane *DrAPF 91*
**Watkins,** Jay B. 1948- *WhoBlA 92*
**Watkins,** Jeffrey Clifton 1929- *Who 92*
**Watkins,** Jerry D. 1939- *WhoBlA 92*
**Watkins,** Jerry Lynn 1951- *WhoWest 92*
**Watkins,** Jerry West 1931- *WhoFI 92*
**Watkins,** Jesse *TwCPaSc*
**Watkins,** Joel Smith, Jr 1932- *AmMWSc 92*
**Watkins,** John Barr, III 1953- *WhoMW 92*
**Watkins,** John Chewning 1947- *WhoAmP 91*
**Watkins,** John Cumming, Jr. 1935- *WhoAmL 92*
**Watkins,** John Elfreth 1852-1903 *BiInAmS*
**Watkins,** John Goodrich 1913- *WrDr 92*
**Watkins,** John M., Jr. 1942- *WhoBlA 92*
**Watkins,** John W, Jr 1938- *WhoIns 92*
**Watkins,** Jonathan Lee *WhoRel 92*
**Watkins,** Joseph Philip 1953- *WhoBlA 92*
**Watkins,** Juanita *WhoAmP 91*
**Watkins,** Juanita 1939- *WhoBlA 92*
**Watkins,** Judith Ann 1942- *WhoWest 92*
**Watkins,** Julian F, II 1936- *AmMWSc 92*
**Watkins,** Kay Orville 1932- *AmMWSc 92, WhoWest 92*
**Watkins,** Kenneth Walter 1939- *AmMWSc 92*
**Watkins,** Kirk Wheeler 1948- *WhoAmL 92*
**Watkins,** Lenice J. 1933- *WhoBlA 92*
**Watkins,** Levi 1911- *WhoBlA 92*

**Watkins,** Levi, Jr. 1944- *WhoBlA 92*
**Watkins,** Linda Rothblum 1954- *AmMWSc 92*
**Watkins,** Lottie Heywood *WhoAmP 91, WhoBlA 92*
**Watkins,** Lou Rogers 1942- *WhoAmP 91*
**Watkins,** Mark E 1937- *AmMWSc 92*
**Watkins,** Mark Raymond 1958- *WhoMW 92*
**Watkins,** Mary Frances 1925- *WhoBlA 92*
**Watkins,** Maurice 1946- *AmMWSc 92*
**Watkins,** Michael Thomas 1954- *WhoBlA 92*
**Watkins,** Mimi J. 1952- *WhoMW 92*
**Watkins,** Mose 1940- *WhoBlA 92*
**Watkins,** Mozelle Ellis 1924- *WhoBlA 92*
**Watkins,** Nancy Chapman 1939- *AmMWSc 92*
**Watkins,** Oscar S 1883-1919 *BiInAmS*
**Watkins,** Patricia Ellen 1952- *WhoAmL 92*
**Watkins,** Paul Allan 1949- *AmMWSc 92*
**Watkins,** Paul Barnett 1949- *WhoMW 92*
**Watkins,** Paul Donald 1940- *AmMWSc 92*
**Watkins,** Peter 1934- *SmATA 66*
**Watkins,** Peter 1935- *IntDcF 2-2*
**Watkins,** Peter Rodney 1931- *Who 92*
**Watkins,** Price I. 1925- *WhoBlA 92*
**Watkins,** Robert Anthony 1951- *WhoEnt 92*
**Watkins,** Robert Arnold 1926- *AmMWSc 92*
**Watkins,** Robert Charles 1927- *WhoBlA 92*
**Watkins,** Rolanda Rowe 1956- *WhoBlA 92*
**Watkins,** Ronald 1904- *WrDr 92*
**Watkins,** Ronald J. 1945- *ConAu 133*
**Watkins,** Sallie Ann 1922- *AmMWSc 92*
**Watkins,** Sammy Nelson 1935- *WhoWest 92*
**Watkins,** Sara Van Horn 1945- *WhoEnt 92*
**Watkins,** Spencer Hunt 1924- *AmMWSc 92*
**Watkins,** Stanley Read 1929- *AmMWSc 92*
**Watkins,** Steven Douglas 1945- *WhoWest 92*
**Watkins,** Steven F 1940- *AmMWSc 92*
**Watkins,** Susan Gail 1962- *WhoAmL 92*
**Watkins,** Sylvestre C., Sr. 1911- *WhoBlA 92*
**Watkins,** Tasker 1918- *Who 92*
**Watkins,** Ted 1923- *WhoBlA 92*
**Watkins,** Terry Anderson 1938- *AmMWSc 92*
**Watkins,** Thomas Frederick 1914- *Who 92*
**Watkins,** Thomas W 1955- *WhoAmP 91*
**Watkins,** Tobias 1780-1855 *BenetAL 91*
**Watkins,** Tommy, Jr. *WhoBlA 92*
**Watkins,** Vern Richard 1939- *WhoAmP 91*
**Watkins,** Vernon 1906-1967 *RfGEnL 91*
**Watkins,** W David *AmMWSc 92*
**Watkins,** Walter C., Jr. 1946- *WhoBlA 92*
**Watkins,** Warren Hyde 1953- *WhoMW 92*
**Watkins,** Wesley Wade 1938- *WhoAmP 91*
**Watkins,** Wiliam John 1942- *WrDr 92*
**Watkins,** William 1942- *AmMWSc 92*
**Watkins,** William, Jr. 1932- *WhoBlA 92, WhoFI 92*
**Watkins,** William Howard, Jr 1941- *WhoAmP 91*
**Watkins,** William John *DrAPF 91*
**Watkins,** William Jon 1942- *TwCSFW 91*
**Watkins,** William Shepard 1950- *WhoWest 92*
**Watkins,** William T 1921- *WhoAmP 91*
**Watkins,** William Wallace 1939- *WhoRel 92*
**Watkins,** Willie S., III 1941- *WhoBlA 92*
**Watkins,** Winifred May 1924- *IntWW 91, Who 92*
**Watkins,** Wynfred C. 1946- *WhoBlA 92*
**Watkins-Pitchford,** Denys 1905-1990 *AnObit 1990*
**Watkins-Pitchford,** Denys James 1905- *IntAu&W 91*
**Watkins-Pitchford,** Denys James 1905-1990 *SmATA 66*
**Watkins-Pitchford,** John 1912- *Who 92*
**Watkinson** *Who 92*
**Watkinson,** Viscount 1910- *IntWW 91, Who 92*
**Watkinson,** Bob 1914- *TwCPaSc*
**Watkinson,** John Taylor 1941- *Who 92*
**Watkinson,** Patricia Grieve 1946- *WhoWest 92*
**Watkinson,** Thomas G 1931- *WhoAmP 91*
**Watkiss,** David Keith 1924- *WhoAmL 92*
**Watkiss,** Gill 1938- *TwCPaSc*
**Watkiss,** Ronald Frederick d1991 *Who 92N*
**Watley,** Jody 1960- *WhoBlA 92*
**Watley,** Margaret Ann 1925- *WhoBlA 92*
**Watling,** Brian 1935- *Who 92*
**Watling,** James 1933- *SmATA 67 [port]*
**Watling,** Les 1945- *AmMWSc 92*
**Watling,** William J. 1950- *WhoMW 92*
**Watlington,** Arthuro, Jr 1953- *WhoAmP 91*
**Watlington,** Charles Oscar 1932- *AmMWSc 92*
**Watlington,** Janet *WhoAmP 91*
**Watlington,** Janet Berecia 1938- *WhoBlA 92*
**Watlington,** Joseph, Jr. 1924- *WhoFI 92*
**Watlington,** Mario A 1917- *WhoAmP 91, WhoBlA 92*
**Watlington,** Sarah Jane 1938- *WhoMW 92*
**Watman,** Marcia Renee 1958- *WhoMW 92*
**Watmough,** David 1926- *ConNov 91, WrDr 92*
**Watne,** Alvin Lloyd 1927- *AmMWSc 92*
**Watne,** Gene M *WhoAmP 91*
**Watney,** John Basil *IntAu&W 91*
**Watnick,** Arthur Saul 1930- *AmMWSc 92*
**Watrach,** Adolf Michael 1918- *AmMWSc 92*
**Watrel,** Warren George 1935- *AmMWSc 92*
**Watring,** Stephen Alan 1954- *WhoAmL 92*
**Watring,** Watson Glenn 1936- *WhoWest 92*
**Watrous,** James Joseph 1942- *AmMWSc 92*
**Watrous,** Philip Jordan 1933- *WhoFI 92*
**Watrous,** William Theodore 1939- *WhoEnt 92*
**Watschke,** Thomas Lee 1944- *AmMWSc 92*
**Watson** *Who 92*
**Watson,** Adam *Who 92*
**Watson,** Alan *Who 92*
**Watson,** Alan 1933- *WrDr 92*
**Watson,** Alan 1957- *TwCPaSc*
**Watson,** Alan Albert 1929- *Who 92*
**Watson,** Alan Andrew 1938- *Who 92*
**Watson,** Alan Eugene *WhoIns 92*
**Watson,** Alan George *Who 92*
**Watson,** Alan John 1941- *Who 92*
**Watson,** Alan Kemball 1948- *AmMWSc 92*
**Watson,** Alexander F 1939- *WhoAmP 91*
**Watson,** Alexander Fletcher 1939- *IntWW 91*
**Watson,** Alonzo Wallace, Jr. 1922- *WhoAmL 92*
**Watson,** Andrew *Who 92*
**Watson,** Andrew John 1921- *AmMWSc 92*
**Watson,** Andrew Linton 1927- *Who 92*
**Watson,** Andrew Orr 1946- *WhoFI 92*
**Watson,** Andrew Samuel 1920- *AmMWSc 92, WhoAmL 92*
**Watson,** Angus Gavin 1944- *Who 92*
**Watson,** Anita Louise 1953- *WhoRel 92*
**Watson,** Anne 1945- *WhoBlA 92*
**Watson,** Annetta Paule 1948- *AmMWSc 92*
**Watson,** Anthony Gerard 1955- *Who 92*
**Watson,** Anthony Heriot 1912- *Who 92*
**Watson,** Antony Edward Douglas 1945- *Who 92*
**Watson,** Arthur d1991 *LesBEnT 92*
**Watson,** Arthur 1951- *TwCPaSc*
**Watson,** Arthur A. 1930-1991 *NewYTBS 91 [port]*
**Watson,** Arthur Christopher 1927- *IntWW 91, Who 92*
**Watson,** Arthur Dennis 1950- *WhoAmP 91*
**Watson,** Barry 1940- *AmMWSc 92*
**Watson,** Ben 1955- *WhoBlA 92*
**Watson,** Benjamin Marston 1848-1918 *BiInAmS*
**Watson,** Bernard C. 1928- *WhoBlA 92*
**Watson,** Betty Collier 1946- *WhoBlA 92*
**Watson,** Beverly A 1935- *WhoAmP 91*
**Watson,** Bobby 1953- *NewAmDM*
**Watson,** Bruce 1928- *IntWW 91, Who 92*
**Watson,** Carol 1957- *WhoFI 92*
**Watson,** Carol Kay 1949- *WhoAmP 91*
**Watson,** Carole M. 1944- *WhoBlA 92*
**Watson,** Celia *DrAPF 91*
**Watson,** Charles Irwin 1926- *WhoAmP 91*
**Watson,** Charles S 1932- *AmMWSc 92*
**Watson,** Cheryl Ann 1955- *WhoMW 92*
**Watson,** Clarence 1916- *WhoBlA 92*
**Watson,** Clarence Ellis, Jr 1951- *AmMWSc 92*
**Watson,** Clayton Wilbur 1933- *AmMWSc 92*
**Watson,** Cletus Claude 1938- *WhoBlA 92, WhoRel 92*
**Watson,** Clifford D. 1946- *WhoBlA 92*
**Watson,** Clifford Dean, II 1953- *WhoEnt 92*
**Watson,** Clyde 1947- *SmATA 68 [port], WrDr 92*
**Watson,** Clyniece Lois 1948- *WhoBlA 92*
**Watson,** Constance A. 1951- *WhoBlA 92*
**Watson,** Craig *DrAPF 91*
**Watson,** D. Rahim *DrAPF 91*
**Watson,** Dale Alan 1955- *WhoMW 92*
**Watson,** Daniel 1938- *WhoBlA 92*
**Watson,** Daniel Stewart 1911- *Who 92*
**Watson,** David Colquitt 1936- *WhoFI 92, WhoWest 92*
**Watson,** David G. 1948- *WhoEnt 92*
**Watson,** David Goulding 1929- *AmMWSc 92*
**Watson,** David John 1949- *Who 92*
**Watson,** David Livingston 1926- *AmMWSc 92*
**Watson,** David Michael 1956- *WhoEnt 92*
**Watson,** David W. 1963- *WhoAmL 92*
**Watson,** Dennis Rahiim 1953- *WhoBlA 92*
**Watson,** Dennis Ronald 1941- *AmMWSc 92*
**Watson,** Dennis Wallace 1914- *AmMWSc 92*
**Watson,** Derek *TwCPaSc*
**Watson,** Diane Edith 1933- *WhoAmP 91, WhoBlA 92, WhoWest 92*
**Watson,** D'Jaris H. 1928-1989 *WhoBlA 92N*
**Watson,** Doc 1923- *NewAmDM, WhoEnt 92*
**Watson,** Donald Pickett 1912- *AmMWSc 92*
**Watson,** Donald Royce 1930- *WhoMW 92*
**Watson,** Douglas George 1945- *WhoFI 92*
**Watson,** Duane Craig 1930- *AmMWSc 92*
**Watson,** Duncan *Who 92*
**Watson,** Duncan Amos 1926- *Who 92*
**Watson,** Earl Eugene 1939- *AmMWSc 92*
**Watson,** Ed 1943- *WhoAmP 91*
**Watson,** Ed Raymond 1920- *WhoAmP 91*
**Watson,** Edna Sue 1945- *AmMWSc 92*
**Watson,** Elizabeth 1949- *News 91 [port]*
**Watson,** Ernest W. 1884-1969 *ConAu 134*
**Watson,** Eugenia Baskerville 1919- *WhoBlA 92*
**Watson,** Evelyn E 1928- *AmMWSc 92*
**Watson,** Everett Donald 1931- *WhoFI 92, WhoMW 92*
**Watson,** Felicia 1962- *WhoMW 92*
**Watson,** Fletcher Guard 1912- *AmMWSc 92*
**Watson,** Forrest Albert 1951- *WhoAmL 92, WhoFI 92*
**Watson,** Francis 1907- *Who 92*
**Watson,** Francis John Bagott 1907- *IntWW 91*
**Watson,** Frank Charles 1945- *WhoAmP 91*
**Watson,** Frank Yandle 1925- *AmMWSc 92*
**Watson,** Fred 1937- *TwCPaSc*
**Watson,** Fred D. 1919- *WhoBlA 92*
**Watson,** Gary Hunter 1951- *AmMWSc 92*
**Watson,** Gavin *Who 92*
**Watson,** Genevieve 1950- *WhoBlA 92*
**Watson,** Geoffrey Stuart 1921- *AmMWSc 92*
**Watson,** George *LesBEnT 92*
**Watson,** George 1927- *WrDr 92*
**Watson,** George Douglas 1848-1923 *RelLAm 91*
**Watson,** George E, III 1931- *AmMWSc 92*
**Watson,** George Spencer 1869-1934 *TwCPaSc*
**Watson,** George William 1926- *WhoAmL 92*
**Watson,** Georgette 1943- *WhoBlA 92*
**Watson,** Gerald Glenn 1945- *WhoAmL 92*
**Watson,** Gerald Walter 1934- *Who 92*
**Watson,** Geraldine G *WhoAmP 91*
**Watson,** Gladys 1926- *WhoAmP 91*
**Watson,** Glenn Robert 1917- *WhoAmL 92*
**Watson,** Hal, Jr 1939- *AmMWSc 92*
**Watson,** Harold *WhoAmP 91*
**Watson,** Harold George 1931- *WhoWest 92*
**Watson,** Harry 1871-1936 *TwCPaSc*
**Watson,** Hayden D. 1948- *WhoFI 92*
**Watson,** Helen Richter 1926- *WhoWest 92*
**Watson,** Henry 1910- *Who 92*
**Watson,** Henry Brereton Marriott 1863-1921 *ScFEYrs*
**Watson,** Henry Stuart 1922- *Who 92*
**Watson,** Herbert James d1988 *Who 92N*
**Watson,** Herman Doc 1931- *WhoBlA 92*
**Watson,** Hilary 1946- *TwCPaSc*
**Watson,** Hugh Alexander 1926- *AmMWSc 92*
**Watson,** Ian *WhoFI 92*
**Watson,** Ian 1943- *TwCSFW 91, WrDr 92*
**Watson,** Irmatean Yelling 1940- *WhoAmP 91*
**Watson,** J Kenneth 1929- *AmMWSc 92*
**Watson,** J. R. 1934- *WrDr 92*
**Watson,** J. Warren 1923- *WhoBlA 92*
**Watson,** Jack Crozier 1917- *WhoAmP 91*
**Watson,** Jack Crozier 1928- *WhoAmL 92*
**Watson,** Jack Ellsworth 1938- *AmMWSc 92*
**Watson,** Jack Samuel 1935- *AmMWSc 92*
**Watson,** Jack Throck 1939- *AmMWSc 92*
**Watson,** James 1936- *IntAu&W 91, WrDr 92*
**Watson,** James Andrew 1937- *Who 92*
**Watson,** James Craig 1838-1880 *BiInAmS*
**Watson,** James D 1928- *RComAH, WrDr 92*
**Watson,** James Dewey 1928- *AmMWSc 92, FacFETw, IntWW 91, Who 92, WhoNob 90*
**Watson,** James E, Jr 1938- *AmMWSc 92*
**Watson,** James Frederic 1931- *AmMWSc 92*
**Watson,** James Gibson, III 1955- *WhoWest 92*
**Watson,** James Kay Graham 1936- *IntWW 91, Who 92*
**Watson,** James Kenneth 1935- *Who 92*
**Watson,** James L. 1922- *WhoBlA 92*
**Watson,** James Lopez 1922- *WhoAmL 92*
**Watson,** James Patrick 1936- *Who 92*
**Watson,** James Ray, Jr 1935- *AmMWSc 92*
**Watson,** Jeanette Marie 1931- *WhoWest 92*
**Watson,** Jeffrey 1940- *AmMWSc 92*
**Watson,** Jeffrey Lynn 1956- *WhoWest 92*
**Watson,** Jerry Carroll 1943- *WhoFI 92*
**Watson,** Jerry M 1942- *AmMWSc 92*
**Watson,** Jim Albert 1939- *WhoAmL 92*
**Watson,** Joann Nichols 1951- *WhoBlA 92*
**Watson,** John 1914- *Who 92*
**Watson,** John Alfred 1940- *AmMWSc 92*
**Watson,** John Allan 1938- *WhoRel 92*
**Watson,** John Allen 1946- *WhoAmL 92*
**Watson,** John Broadus 1878-1958 *FacFETw*
**Watson,** John C 1932- *WhoIns 92*
**Watson,** John Cecil 1932- *WhoFI 92, WhoMW 92*
**Watson,** John Dargan, Jr. 1954- *WhoAmL 92*
**Watson,** John Dudley 1930- *WhoRel 92*
**Watson,** John Edward 1949- *WhoFI 92*
**Watson,** John Forbes I. *Who 92*
**Watson,** John Garth 1914- *Who 92*
**Watson,** John Grenville Bernard 1943- *Who 92*
**Watson,** John H. *ConAu 35NR*
**Watson,** John H L 1916- *AmMWSc 92*
**Watson,** John Hugh Adam 1914- *Who 92*
**Watson,** John Lawrence, III 1932- *WhoFI 92*
**Watson,** John Michael 1956- *WhoAmL 92, WhoFI 92*
**Watson,** John Richard 1934- *IntAu&W 91*
**Watson,** John S 1924- *WhoAmP 91*
**Watson,** John T. 1904- *Who 92*
**Watson,** John Thomas 1940- *AmMWSc 92*
**Watson,** John Whitaker *BenetAL 91*
**Watson,** Johnny 1935- *WhoBlA 92*
**Watson,** Jolou Trujillo 1963- *WhoHisp 92*
**Watson,** Joseph Alexander 1926- *AmMWSc 92*
**Watson,** Joseph Stanley d1991 *Who 92N*
**Watson,** Joseph W. 1940- *WhoBlA 92*
**Watson,** Juanita 1923- *WhoBlA 92*
**Watson,** Kenneth 1935- *AmMWSc 92*
**Watson,** Kenneth Anthony 1943- *WhoFI 92*
**Watson,** Kenneth De Pencier 1915- *AmMWSc 92*
**Watson,** Kenneth Fredrick 1942- *AmMWSc 92*
**Watson,** Kenneth Marshall 1921- *AmMWSc 92, IntWW 91, WhoWest 92*
**Watson,** Lance Dean 1959- *WhoRel 92*
**Watson,** Lawrence *DrAPF 91*
**Watson,** Leland Hale 1926- *WhoEnt 92*
**Watson,** Leonard Wayne 1923- *WhoBlA 92*
**Watson,** Leonidas 1910- *WhoBlA 92*
**Watson,** Leslie Michael S *Who 92*
**Watson,** Linda Hanson 1941- *WhoAmP 91*
**Watson,** Lyall *TwCPaSc*
**Watson,** Lyall 1939- *IntAu&W 91, IntWW 91, WrDr 92*
**Watson,** Lynn *DrAPF 91*
**Watson,** Madale *WhoAmP 91*
**Watson,** Margaret Elizabeth 1917- *WhoAmP 91*
**Watson,** Margery Jeanette 1943- *WhoRel 92*
**Watson,** Mark Ashley 1960- *WhoEnt 92*
**Watson,** Mark Henry 1938- *WhoAmL 92*
**Watson,** Marshall Tredway 1922- *AmMWSc 92*
**Watson,** Martha F 1935- *AmMWSc 92*
**Watson,** Mary Ann 1944- *WhoWest 92*
**Watson,** Mary Ellen 1931- *WhoFI 92*
**Watson,** Mary Spencer 1913- *TwCPaSc*
**Watson,** Maurice E *AmMWSc 92*
**Watson,** Maxine Amanda 1947- *AmMWSc 92*
**Watson,** Michael d1991 *Who 92N*
**Watson,** Michael Douglas 1936- *AmMWSc 92*
**Watson,** Michael Goodall 1949- *Who 92*
**Watson,** Michael M. *Who 92*
**Watson,** Mildred L. 1923- *WhoBlA 92*
**Watson,** Milton H. 1927- *WhoBlA 92*
**Watson,** Milton Russell 1934- *WhoWest 92*
**Watson,** Nancy Dingman *DrAPF 91*
**Watson,** Nathan Dee 1935- *AmMWSc 92*
**Watson,** Newton Frank 1923- *Who 92*
**Watson,** Noel Duncan 1915- *Who 92*
**Watson,** Norma 1939- *WhoBlA 92*

**Watson,** Odest Jefferson, Sr. 1924- *WhoBlA 92*
**Watson,** Oliver Lee, III 1938- *WhoWest 92*
**Watson,** P Keith 1927- *AmMWSc 92*
**Watson,** Patricia Seets 1930- *IntAu&W 91*
**Watson,** Patrick *LesBEnT 92*
**Watson,** Percy Willis 1951- *WhoAmP 91*
**Watson,** Peter 1944- *Who 92*
**Watson,** Peter Robert 1936- *Who 92*
**Watson,** Phil d1991 *NewYTBS 91 [port]*
**Watson,** Philip 1919- *Who 92*
**Watson,** Philip Donald 1941- *AmMWSc 92*
**Watson,** Philip Richard 1952- *WhoWest 92*
**Watson,** Ralph Phillip 1958- *WhoAmP 91*
**Watson,** Rand Lewis 1940- *AmMWSc 92*
**Watson,** Ray G. 1934- *WhoWest 92*
**Watson,** Raymond Coke, Jr 1926- *AmMWSc 92*
**Watson,** Raymond Leslie 1926- *WhoFI 92*
**Watson,** Reginald Gordon Harry 1928- *Who 92*
**Watson,** Richard *DrAPF 91*
**Watson,** Richard Allan 1931- *AmMWSc 92*
**Watson,** Richard Charles Challinor 1923- *Who 92*
**Watson,** Richard E 1931- *AmMWSc 92*
**Watson,** Richard Eagleson Gordon Burges 1930- *Who 92*
**Watson,** Richard Elvis 1912- *AmMWSc 92*
**Watson,** Richard F. *ConAu 36NR*
**Watson,** Richard Prather 1938- *WhoAmL 92*
**Watson,** Richard White, Jr 1933- *AmMWSc 92*
**Watson,** Robert *DrAPF 91, WhoAmP 91*
**Watson,** Robert 1925- *ConPo 91, WrDr 92*
**Watson,** Robert A *WhoAmP 91*
**Watson,** Robert Barden 1914- *AmMWSc 92*
**Watson,** Robert C. 1947- *WhoBlA 92*
**Watson,** Robert Fletcher 1910- *AmMWSc 92*
**Watson,** Robert Francis 1936- *AmMWSc 92, WhoAmL 92*
**Watson,** Robert James 1954- *WhoAmP 91*
**Watson,** Robert James 1955- *WhoAmL 92*
**Watson,** Robert Jose 1946- *WhoBlA 92*
**Watson,** Robert K 1932- *WhoIns 92*
**Watson,** Robert Lee 1931- *AmMWSc 92*
**Watson,** Robert Lee 1934- *AmMWSc 92*
**Watson,** Robert Lowrie 1946- *AmMWSc 92*
**Watson,** Robert Marion 1914- *WhoAmP 91*
**Watson,** Robert Ogle 1934- *WhoAmP 91*
**Watson,** Roberta C. *WhoBlA 92*
**Watson,** Roberta Casper 1949- *WhoAmL 92*
**Watson,** Roderick 1943- *WrDr 92*
**Watson,** Roderick Anthony 1920- *Who 92*
**Watson,** Ronald Ross 1942- *AmMWSc 92*
**Watson,** Roy H, Jr 1937- *WhoAmP 91*
**Watson,** Roy William 1926- *Who 92*
**Watson,** Sereno 1826-1892 *BiInAmS*
**Watson,** Sharon Gitin 1943- *WhoWest 92*
**Watson,** Sheila 1909- *BenetAL 91*
**Watson,** Solomon B., IV 1944- *WhoBlA 92*
**Watson,** Stanley Arthur 1915- *AmMWSc 92*
**Watson,** Stanley Ellis 1957- *WhoMW 92, WhoRel 92*
**Watson,** Stanley W 1921- *AmMWSc 92*
**Watson,** Stephen E. *WhoMW 92*
**Watson,** Stephen Roger 1943- *Who 92*
**Watson,** Sterling *DrAPF 91*
**Watson,** Steven 1947- *ConAu 135*
**Watson,** Stewart *Who 92*
**Watson,** Stewart Charles 1922- *WhoFI 92*
**Watson,** Stuart *Who 92*
**Watson,** Sue Carter 1933- *WhoAmL 92*
**Watson,** Susan *DrAPF 91*
**Watson,** Susanne Levine 1938- *WhoMW 92*
**Watson,** Sydney d1991 *Who 92N*
**Watson,** Sylvia 1938- *WhoAmP 91*
**Watson,** Terri Lynette 1963- *WhoAmL 92*
**Watson,** Theo Franklin 1931- *AmMWSc 92*
**Watson,** Theresa Grace Lawhorn 1945- *WhoAmL 92*
**Watson,** Theresa Lawhorn 1945- *WhoBlA 92*
**Watson,** Thomas 1557?-1592? *RfGEnL 91*
**Watson,** Thomas Andrew, II 1953- *WhoRel 92*
**Watson,** Thomas Edward 1856-1922 *AmPolLe*
**Watson,** Thomas Frederick 1906- *Who 92*
**Watson,** Thomas J., Jr. 1914- *IntWW 91*
**Watson,** Thomas Philip 1933- *WhoAmP 91*
**Watson,** Thomas S., Jr. *WhoBlA 92*
**Watson,** Thomas Sellers, Jr. *WhoFI 92*
**Watson,** Thomas Sturges 1949- *IntWW 91*
**Watson,** Thomas Wayne 1957- *WhoAmL 92*
**Watson,** Thomas Yirrell 1906- *Who 92*
**Watson,** Tom 1949- *FacFETw*
**Watson,** Vance H 1942- *AmMWSc 92*
**Watson,** Velvin Richard 1932- *AmMWSc 92*
**Watson,** Vernaline 1942- *WhoBlA 92*
**Watson,** Victor Hugo 1928- *Who 92*
**Watson,** W. H. *WhoRel 92*
**Watson,** Wilbur H. 1938- *WhoBlA 92*
**Watson,** Will *IntAu&W 91X, TwCWW 91*
**Watson,** William 1834-1915 *BiInAmS*
**Watson,** William 1858-1935 *RfGEnL 91*
**Watson,** William 1917- *IntWW 91, Who 92*
**Watson,** William 1946- *TwCPaSc*
**Watson,** William Albert 1930- *Who 92*
**Watson,** William Alexander Jardine 1933- *Who 92*
**Watson,** William Alfred, III 1960- *WhoWest 92*
**Watson,** William Crawford 1927- *AmMWSc 92*
**Watson,** William Douglas 1942- *AmMWSc 92*
**Watson,** William Downing, Jr. 1938- *WhoFI 92*
**Watson,** William Edward 1936- *WhoAmP 91*
**Watson,** William Harold, Jr 1931- *AmMWSc 92*
**Watson,** William Martin, Jr 1946- *AmMWSc 92*
**Watson,** William Randy 1950- *WhoWest 92*
**Watson,** Wynnfield Young 1924- *AmMWSc 92*
**Watson-Bell,** Sandra 1955- *WhoBlA 92*
**Watson-Brodnax,** Shirley Jean *WhoWest 92*
**Watt** *Who 92*
**Watt,** Alfred Ian 1934- *Who 92*
**Watt,** Alick Angus 1920- *IntAu&W 91*
**Watt,** Alison 1965- *TwCPaSc*
**Watt,** Andrew 1909- *Who 92*
**Watt,** Bob Everett 1917- *AmMWSc 92*
**Watt,** Charles Vance 1934- *WhoFI 92*
**Watt,** Charlotte Joanne *Who 92*
**Watt,** Daniel Frank 1938- *AmMWSc 92*
**Watt,** David 1932-1987 *ConAu 133*
**Watt,** David Milne, Jr 1942- *AmMWSc 92*
**Watt,** Dean Day 1917- *AmMWSc 92*
**Watt,** Diana Lynn 1956- *WhoWest 92*
**Watt,** Donald Cameron *Who 92, WrDr 92*
**Watt,** Ethel Madsen 1925- *WhoEnt 92*
**Watt,** Garland Wedderick 1932- *WhoBlA 92*
**Watt,** George 1820-1893 *BiInAmS*
**Watt,** Graham Wend 1926- *WhoAmP 91*
**Watt,** Hamish 1925- *Who 92*
**Watt,** Harry 1906-1987 *IntDcF 2-2 [port]*
**Watt,** Ian 1917- *WrDr 92*
**Watt,** James 1736-1819 *BlkwCEP*
**Watt,** James 1914- *Who 92*
**Watt,** James Gaius 1938- *IntWW 91, WhoAmP 91*
**Watt,** James H. *Who 92*
**Watt,** James L 1944- *WhoAmP 91*
**Watt,** James Park 1948- *IntWW 91*
**Watt,** James Peter 1949- *AmMWSc 92*
**Watt,** Jeffrey Xavier 1961- *WhoMW 92*
**Watt,** John 1948- *WhoAmP 91*
**Watt,** John Hayden 1938- *WhoMW 92*
**Watt,** Joseph T, Jr 1933- *AmMWSc 92*
**Watt,** Kenneth Edmund Ferguson 1929- *AmMWSc 92*
**Watt,** Lynn A K 1924- *AmMWSc 92*
**Watt,** Mamadov Hame 1943- *AmMWSc 92*
**Watt,** Melvin L *WhoAmP 91*
**Watt,** Paul Brooks 1946- *WhoRel 92*
**Watt,** Richard Lorimer d1991 *Who 92N*
**Watt,** Robert 1923- *Who 92*
**Watt,** Robert Douglas 1919- *AmMWSc 92*
**Watt,** Robert M 1951- *AmMWSc 92*
**Watt,** Roger 1932- *WhoMW 92*
**Watt,** Stuart George 1934- *WhoFI 92*
**Watt,** W. Montgomery 1909- *WrDr 92*
**Watt,** Ward Belfield 1940- *AmMWSc 92*
**Watt,** William Buell 1919- *WhoFI 92*
**Watt,** William George 1934- *WhoIns 92*
**Watt,** William Joseph 1925- *AmMWSc 92*
**Watt,** William Lee 1959- *WhoAmP 91*
**Watt,** William Montgomery 1909- *Who 92*
**Watt,** William Russell 1920- *AmMWSc 92*
**Watt,** William Smith 1913- *Who 92*
**Watt,** William Stewart 1937- *AmMWSc 92*
**Watt-Evans,** Lawrence 1954- *IntAu&W 91*
**Watt-Morse,** Peter M. 1958- *WhoAmL 92*
**Wattachanackal,** John Thomas 1939- *WhoMW 92*
**Wattel,** Harold Louis 1921- *WhoFI 92*
**Watten,** Barrett *DrAPF 91*
**Wattenberg,** Albert 1917- *AmMWSc 92*
**Wattenberg,** Ben J. 1933- *WrDr 92*
**Wattenberg,** David E 1940- *WhoAmP 91*
**Wattenberg,** Franklin Arvey 1943- *AmMWSc 92*
**Wattenberg,** Lee Wolff 1921- *AmMWSc 92*
**Watterlond,** Wiley Edward 1951- *WhoWest 92*
**Watters,** Belva *WhoAmP 91*
**Watters,** Christopher Deffner 1939- *AmMWSc 92*
**Watters,** David 1947- *WhoMW 92*
**Watters,** David J. 1931- *WhoAmL 92*
**Watters,** Edward C, Jr 1923- *AmMWSc 92*
**Watters,** Edward McLain, III *WhoAmL 92*
**Watters,** Gary Z 1935- *AmMWSc 92*
**Watters,** Gordon Valentine 1928- *AmMWSc 92*
**Watters,** James I 1908- *AmMWSc 92*
**Watters,** Kenneth Lynn 1939- *AmMWSc 92*
**Watters,** Linda A. 1953- *WhoBlA 92*
**Watters,** Mari 1941- *WhoAmP 91*
**Watters,** Richard Campbell 1947- *WhoAmL 92*
**Watters,** Richard Donald 1951- *WhoAmL 92*
**Watters,** Robert James 1946- *AmMWSc 92*
**Watters,** Robert Lisle 1925- *AmMWSc 92*
**Watterson,** Arthur C, Jr 1938- *AmMWSc 92*
**Watterson,** Bill 1958- *ConAu 134, SmATA 66*
**Watterson,** D Martin 1946- *AmMWSc 92*
**Watterson,** Donald Hodges 1929- *WhoRel 92*
**Watterson,** Gene Lee 1929- *WhoRel 92*
**Watterson,** Henry 1840-1921 *BenetAL 91*
**Watterson,** Jon Craig 1944- *AmMWSc 92*
**Watterson,** Kenneth Franklin 1929- *AmMWSc 92*
**Watterson,** Ray Leighton 1915- *AmMWSc 92*
**Watterson,** Richard Harvey 1926- *WhoBlA 92*
**Watterson,** Thomas Batchelor 1938- *WhoMW 92*
**Watterston,** George 1783-1854 *BenetAL 91*
**Watterston,** Kenneth Gordon 1934- *AmMWSc 92*
**Watthey,** Jeffrey William Herbert 1937- *AmMWSc 92*
**Wattles,** Joshua S. *IntMPA 92*
**Wattles,** W D 1860- *ScFEYrs*
**Wattleton,** Alyce Faye 1943- *WhoBlA 92*
**Wattleton,** Faye 1943- *NotBlAW 92, WhoBlA 92*
**Wattleworth,** Roberta Ann 1955- *WhoMW 92*
**Wattley,** Cheryl Brown 1953- *WhoAmL 92*
**Wattley,** Graham Richard 1930- *Who 92*
**Wattley,** Thomas Jefferson 1953- *WhoBlA 92*
**Wattman,** Kenneth E. 1928- *WhoFI 92*
**Wattman,** Malcolm Peter 1941- *WhoAmL 92*
**Watton,** Arthur 1943- *AmMWSc 92*
**Watton,** James Augustus 1915- *Who 92*
**Watts,** Alan 1915-1973 *BenetAL 91*
**Watts,** Alan 1925- *WrDr 92*
**Watts,** Alan Wilson 1915-1973 *RelLAm 91*
**Watts,** Alexander Alfred 1904-1984 *WhoBlA 92N*
**Watts,** Andre 1946- *NewAmDM, WhoBlA 92, WhoEnt 92*
**Watts,** Anthony Brian 1945- *Who 92*
**Watts,** Anthony John 1942- *WrDr 92*
**Watts,** Arthur 1931- *Who 92*
**Watts,** Arthur Desmond 1931- *IntWW 91*
**Watts,** Barry Allen 1943- *WhoWest 92*
**Watts,** Bob 1930- *WhoAmP 91*
**Watts,** Carlton Bedford, Mrs. 1941- *WhoFI 92*
**Watts,** Charles 1953- *TwCPaSc*
**Watts,** Charles D 1917- *AmMWSc 92*
**Watts,** Charles Dewitt 1917- *WhoBlA 92*
**Watts,** Charles Edward 1928- *AmMWSc 92*
**Watts,** Charlie *WhoAmP 91*
**Watts,** Charlie Irving 1943- *WhoEnt 92*
**Watts,** Cynthia Gay 1962- *WhoWest 92*
**Watts,** Daniel Jay 1943- *AmMWSc 92*
**Watts,** Daniel Thomas 1916- *AmMWSc 92*
**Watts,** Dave Henry 1932- *WhoFI 92*
**Watts,** David Eide 1921- *WhoAmL 92*
**Watts,** Dennis Randolph 1943- *AmMWSc 92*
**Watts,** Dey Wadsworth 1923- *WhoAmL 92, WhoMW 92*
**Watts,** Donald George 1933- *AmMWSc 92*
**Watts,** Donald Walter 1934- *IntWW 91, Who 92*
**Watts,** E.B. *TwCPaSc*
**Watts,** Edward 1940- *Who 92*
**Watts,** Edward Quentin 1936- *WhoEnt 92*
**Watts,** Eugene J 1942- *WhoAmP 91*
**Watts,** Exum DeVer 1926- *AmMWSc 92*
**Watts,** Frederick, Jr. 1929- *WhoBlA 92*
**Watts,** Glenn Ellis 1920- *WhoAmP 91*
**Watts,** Guy Leland 1941- *WhoAmP 91*
**Watts,** Harold H. 1906- *WrDr 92*
**Watts,** Harry Emerson 1936- *WhoMW 92*
**Watts,** Helen 1927- *NewAmDM*
**Watts,** Helen Josephine 1927- *IntWW 91, Who 92*
**Watts,** Helen L. Hoke *SmATA 65*
**Watts,** Isaac 1674-1748 *BlkwCEP*
**Watts,** Isaac 1675-1748 *RfGEnL 91*
**Watts,** J C 1957- *WhoAmP 91*
**Watts,** J. C., Jr. 1957- *WhoBlA 92*
**Watts,** James Harrison 1951- *WhoWest 92*
**Watts,** James Lawrence 1949- *WhoFI 92, WhoWest 92*
**Watts,** Jeffrey Alan 1950- *WhoWest 92*
**Watts,** Jeffrey Lynn 1955- *AmMWSc 92*
**Watts,** JoAnn Margaret 1934- *WhoMW 92*
**Watts,** John 1930-1982 *NewAmDM*
**Watts,** John Albert, Jr 1949- *AmMWSc 92*
**Watts,** John Arthur 1947- *Who 92*
**Watts,** John Cadman 1913- *Who 92*
**Watts,** John E. 1896- *WhoBlA 92*
**Watts,** John E. 1936- *WhoBlA 92*
**Watts,** John Francis 1926- *Who 92, WrDr 92*
**Watts,** John Peter Barry Condliffe 1930- *Who 92*
**Watts,** John Ransford 1930- *WhoEnt 92, WhoMW 92*
**Watts,** Ken 1932- *TwCPaSc*
**Watts,** Larry Dean 1955- *WhoFI 92*
**Watts,** Lucile *WhoBlA 92*
**Watts,** Malcolm S M 1915- *AmMWSc 92*
**Watts,** Marvin Lee 1932- *WhoAmP 91, WhoWest 92*
**Watts,** Mary S. 1868-1958 *BenetAL 91*
**Watts,** Michael Dale 1961- *WhoMW 92*
**Watts,** Oliver Edward 1939- *WhoWest 92*
**Watts,** Patsy Jeanne 1943- *WhoWest 92*
**Watts,** Paul Lawrence 1945- *WhoWest 92*
**Watts,** Plato Hilton, Jr 1941- *AmMWSc 92*
**Watts,** Rachel Mary *Who 92*
**Watts,** Richard Eugene 1956- *WhoRel 92*
**Watts,** Richard Gregory 1954- *WhoAmL 92*
**Watts,** Robert B. 1922- *WhoBlA 92*
**Watts,** Roberta Ogletree 1939- *WhoBlA 92*
**Watts,** Ronald George 1914- *Who 92*
**Watts,** Roy 1925- *IntWW 91, Who 92*
**Watts,** Sherrill Glenn 1937- *AmMWSc 92*
**Watts,** Steven Richard 1955- *WhoAmL 92*
**Watts,** Terence Leslie 1935- *AmMWSc 92*
**Watts,** Thomas Rowland 1917- *Who 92*
**Watts,** Victor Brian 1927- *Who 92*
**Watts,** Victor Lewis 1955- *WhoBlA 92*
**Watts,** Vivian E 1940- *WhoAmP 91*
**Watts,** William Arthur 1930- *IntWW 91, Who 92*
**Watts,** William Lord 1850- *BiInAmS*
**Watts,** Wilsonya Richardson *WhoBlA 92*
**Wattson,** Robert K, Jr 1922- *AmMWSc 92*
**Watumull,** Gulab 1924- *WhoWest 92*
**Watwood,** Vernon Bell, Jr 1935- *AmMWSc 92, WhoMW 92*
**Watz,** Martin Charles 1938- *WhoFI 92*
**Watzke,** Robert Coit 1922- *AmMWSc 92*
**Watzman,** Nathan 1926- *AmMWSc 92*
**Wauchope,** Keith Leveret 1941- *WhoAmP 91*
**Wauchope,** Robert Donald 1942- *AmMWSc 92*
**Wauchope,** Roger Don- 1938- *Who 92*
**Waud,** Barbara E 1931- *AmMWSc 92*
**Waud,** Christopher Denis George Pierre 1928- *Who 92*
**Waud,** Douglas Russell 1932- *AmMWSc 92*
**Waud,** Reeve Byron 1963- *WhoFI 92, WhoMW 92*
**Waugh,** Alec 1898-1981 *FacFETw*
**Waugh,** Auberon *FacFETw*
**Waugh,** Auberon 1939- *WrDr 92*
**Waugh,** Auberon Alexander 1939- *IntAu&W 91, IntWW 91, Who 92*
**Waugh,** Daniel Charles 1955- *WhoAmL 92*
**Waugh,** Dorothy *WrDr 92*
**Waugh,** Douglas Oliver William 1918- *AmMWSc 92*
**Waugh,** Eric 1929- *TwCPaSc*
**Waugh,** Eric Alexander 1933- *Who 92*
**Waugh,** Evelyn 1903-1966 *CnDBLB 6 [port], RfGEnL 91*
**Waugh,** Evelyn Arthur St. John 1903-1966 *FacFETw*
**Waugh,** Hillary 1920- *WrDr 92*
**Waugh,** Hillary Baldwin 1920- *IntAu&W 91*
**Waugh,** John David 1932- *AmMWSc 92*
**Waugh,** John Lodovick Thomson 1922- *AmMWSc 92*
**Waugh,** John Stewart 1929- *AmMWSc 92, IntWW 91*
**Waugh,** Judith Ritchie 1939- *WhoBlA 92*
**Waugh,** Margaret H 1923- *AmMWSc 92*
**Waugh,** Richard Roy 1938- *WhoWest 92*
**Waugh,** Richard W 1943- *WhoIns 92*
**Waugh,** Richard William 1943- *WhoFI 92*
**Waugh,** William Howard 1925- *AmMWSc 92*

**Wauhop,** Iles W 1934- *WhoIns 92*
**Wauls,** Inez La Mar 1924- *WhoBlA 92*
**Waun,** George Glen 1927- *WhoRel 92*
**Waun,** William George 1953- *WhoRel 92*
**Wauters,** Duane Francies 1942- *WhoFI 92*
**Wauters,** Shirley Stapleton 1936- *WhoWest 92*
**Wauthier,** Jean-Luc 1950- *IntAu&W 91*
**Wave,** Herbert Edwin 1923- *AmMWSc 92*
**Wavell,** Archibald Percival 1883-1950 *FacFETw*
**Waverley,** Viscount 1949- *Who 92*
**Wavrik,** John J 1941- *AmMWSc 92*
**Wawersik,** Wolfgang R 1936- *AmMWSc 92*
**Wawilow,** Danuta 1942- *IntAu&W 91*
**Wawner,** Franklin Edward, Jr 1933- *AmMWSc 92*
**Wawro,** Walter J., Sr. 1951- *WhoMW 92*
**Wawrzyniak,** Stephen David 1949- *WhoFI 92*
**Wawszkiewicz,** Edward John 1933- *AmMWSc 92*
**Wax,** George Louis 1928- *WhoFI 92*
**Wax,** Harry 1918- *AmMWSc 92*
**Wax,** Joan 1921- *AmMWSc 92*
**Wax,** Mo *IntMPA 92*
**Wax,** Morton Dennis 1932- *IntMPA 92*
**Wax,** Murray L. 1922- *WrDr 92*
**Wax,** Nadine Virginia 1927- *WhoFI 92, WhoMW 92*
**Wax,** Nelson 1917- *AmMWSc 92*
**Wax,** Ray Van 1944- *WhoWest 92*
**Wax,** Robert LeRoy 1938- *AmMWSc 92*
**Wax,** Rosalie 1911- *WomSoc*
**Wax,** Steven T. 1948- *WhoAmL 92*
**Wax,** William Edward 1956- *ConAu 133*
**Waxberg,** Stanley Daum 1911- *WhoAmL 92*
**Waxenberg,** Michael 1954- *WhoAmL 92*
**Waxler,** Glenn Lee 1925- *AmMWSc 92*
**Waxman,** Alan David 1938- *AmMWSc 92*
**Waxman,** Alan N. 1955- *WhoAmL 92*
**Waxman,** Albert Samuel 1935- *WhoEnt 92*
**Waxman,** David 1918- *AmMWSc 92*
**Waxman,** Franz 1906-1967 *NewAmDM*
**Waxman,** Henry A. 1939- *AlmAP 92 [port]*
**Waxman,** Henry Arnold 1939- *WhoAmP 91, WhoWest 92*
**Waxman,** Herbert J. *DrAPF 91*
**Waxman,** Herbert Sumner 1936- *AmMWSc 92*
**Waxman,** Lloyd H *AmMWSc 92*
**Waxman,** Margery Hope 1942- *WhoAmL 92*
**Waxman,** Ronald 1933- *AmMWSc 92*
**Waxman,** Samuel *AmMWSc 92*
**Waxman,** Sheldon Robert 1941- *WhoAmL 92*
**Waxman,** Sidney 1923- *AmMWSc 92*
**Waxman,** Stephen George 1945- *AmMWSc 92*
**Waxse,** David John 1945- *WhoAmL 92*
**Waxter,** Thomas, Jr 1934- *WhoAmP 91*
**Way,** Alva Otis 1929- *IntWW 91*
**Way,** Anthony Gerald 1920- *Who 92*
**Way,** Brenda Bolte 1942- *WhoEnt 92*
**Way,** Carol Jane 1940- *WhoFI 92*
**Way,** Curtis J. 1935- *WhoBlA 92*
**Way,** E Leong 1916- *AmMWSc 92*
**Way,** Edward Leong 1916- *WhoWest 92*
**Way,** Frederick, III 1925- *AmMWSc 92*
**Way,** Gary Darryl 1958- *WhoBlA 92*
**Way,** George H 1930- *AmMWSc 92*
**Way,** Greg 1950- *WhoWest 92*
**Way,** Jacob Edson, III 1947- *WhoWest 92*
**Way,** James Leong 1927- *AmMWSc 92*
**Way,** Jeffry Gardner 1954- *WhoWest 92*
**Way,** Jon Leong 1961- *AmMWSc 92*
**Way,** Katharine 1903- *AmMWSc 92*
**Way,** Kenneth L. 1939- *WhoMW 92*
**Way,** Kermit R 1939- *AmMWSc 92*
**Way,** Lawrence Wellesley 1933- *AmMWSc 92*
**Way,** Margaret *WrDr 92*
**Way,** Paul Edward 1958- *WhoMW 92*
**Way,** Peter 1936- *WrDr 92*
**Way,** Richard 1914- *IntWW 91, Who 92*
**Way,** Scott Alan 1950- *WhoMW 92*
**Way,** Scott Wendell 1960- *WhoRel 92*
**Way,** Walter 1931- *AmMWSc 92*
**Wayans,** Damon 1960- *IntMPA 92*
**Wayans,** Keenen Ivory *WhoBlA 92, WhoEnt 92*
**Wayans,** Keenen Ivory 1958- *IntMPA 92, News 91 [port]*
**Waychunas,** Glenn Alfred 1948- *WhoWest 92*
**Waygood,** Edward Bruce 1945- *AmMWSc 92*
**Waygood,** Ernest Roy 1918- *AmMWSc 92*
**Waylan,** Cecil Jerome 1941- *WhoFI 92*
**Wayland,** Bradford B 1939- *AmMWSc 92*
**Wayland,** Francis 1796-1865 *AmPeW*
**Wayland,** J Harold 1909- *AmMWSc 92*
**Wayland,** James Robert, Jr 1937- *AmMWSc 92*
**Wayland,** L. C. Newton 1909- *WhoWest 92*
**Wayland,** Len *IntMPA 92*
**Wayland,** Newton Hart 1940- *WhoEnt 92*
**Wayland,** Rosser Lee, Jr 1930- *AmMWSc 92*
**Wayland,** Russell Gibson 1913- *AmMWSc 92*
**Wayland-Smith,** Frank 1841-1911 *AmPeW*
**Wayland-Smith,** Robert Dean 1943- *WhoFI 92*
**Wayman,** Alexander Walker 1821-1895 *RelLAm 91*
**Wayman,** Anthony Russell 1929- *WhoEnt 92*
**Wayman,** C Marvin 1930- *AmMWSc 92*
**Wayman,** David Anthony 1950- *WhoMW 92*
**Wayman,** Dennis Lynn 1951- *WhoRel 92*
**Wayman,** Frank Whelon 1946- *WhoMW 92*
**Wayman,** Kathryn 1962- *TwCPaSc*
**Wayman,** Michael Lash 1943- *AmMWSc 92*
**Wayman,** Morris 1915- *AmMWSc 92*
**Wayman,** Oliver 1916- *AmMWSc 92*
**Wayman,** Patrick Arthur 1927- *IntWW 91*
**Wayman,** Tom 1945- *ConPo 91, IntAu&W 91, WrDr 92*
**Wayman,** Vivienne 1926- *WrDr 92*
**Waymer,** David Benjamin, Jr. 1958- *WhoBlA 92*
**Waymer,** Richard Turner 1911- *WhoBlA 92*
**Waymire,** Jack Calvin 1941- *AmMWSc 92*
**Waymon,** Samuel Luther 1944- *WhoEnt 92*
**Waymouth,** Charity 1915- *AmMWSc 92, Who 92, WhoRel 92*
**Waymouth,** John Francis 1926- *AmMWSc 92*
**Wayna Capac** *HisDSpE*
**Waynant,** Ronald William 1940- *AmMWSc 92*
**Wayne,** Anthony 1745-1796 *BlkwEAR*
**Wayne,** Burton Howard 1924- *AmMWSc 92*
**Wayne,** Clarence Eugene 1956- *AmMWSc 92*
**Wayne,** David 1916- *IntMPA 92*
**Wayne,** Donald *WrDr 92*
**Wayne,** Franklin Stanford 1949- *WhoMW 92*
**Wayne,** George Howard, Sr. 1938- *WhoBlA 92*
**Wayne,** George Jerome 1914- *AmMWSc 92*
**Wayne,** Jane O. *DrAPF 91*
**Wayne,** Jim 1948- *WhoAmP 91*
**Wayne,** Joel *IntMPA 92*
**Wayne,** John 1907-1979 *FacFETw, RComAH*
**Wayne,** Johnny 1918-1990 *AnObit 1990*
**Wayne,** Joseph *TwCWW 91, WrDr 92*
**Wayne,** Justine Washington 1945- *WhoBlA 92*
**Wayne,** Kyra Petrovskaya 1918- *WhoWest 92*
**Wayne,** Lawrence Gershon 1926- *AmMWSc 92*
**Wayne,** Lawrence Joseph 1951- *WhoMW 92*
**Wayne,** Lowell Grant 1918- *AmMWSc 92, WhoWest 92*
**Wayne,** Marvin Alan 1943- *WhoWest 92*
**Wayne,** Michael A. 1934- *IntMPA 92*
**Wayne,** Patrick 1939- *IntMPA 92*
**Wayne,** Robert Andrew 1938- *WhoAmL 92*
**Wayne,** Robert Jonathan 1951- *WhoAmL 92*
**Wayne,** Thomas Francis 1954- *WhoFI 92*
**Wayne,** William John 1922- *AmMWSc 92, WhoMW 92*
**Wayner,** Matthew John 1927- *AmMWSc 92*
**Wayner,** Peter C, Jr 1934- *AmMWSc 92*
**Waynes,** Kathleen Yanes 1920- *WhoBlA 92*
**Waynewood,** Freeman Lee 1942- *WhoBlA 92*
**Wayrynen,** Robert Ellis 1924- *AmMWSc 92*
**Wayt,** Gard Russell 1938- *WhoAmP 91*
**Waytula,** Anthony J 1944- *WhoIns 92*
**Waytz,** Ruth 1960- *WhoFI 92*
**Waywell,** Geoffrey Bryan 1944- *Who 92*
**Waz,** Joseph Walter, Jr. 1953- *WhoAmL 92*
**Wazir,** Tadar Jihad 1944- *WhoRel 92*
**Waziri,** Rafiq 1933- *AmMWSc 92*
**Wazzan,** A R Frank 1935- *AmMWSc 92*
**Wazzan,** Chafiq al- 1925- *IntWW 91*
**Wead,** Rodney Sam 1935- *WhoBlA 92*
**Wead,** William Badertscher 1940- *AmMWSc 92*
**Weady,** Louis Stanley Charles-Marie 1940- *WhoAmP 91*
**Weaire,** Denis Lawrence 1942- *IntWW 91*
**Weait,** Christopher Robert 1939- *WhoEnt 92*
**Weakland,** Kevin L. 1963- *IntMPA 92*
**Weakland,** Rembert G. 1927- *WhoMW 92, WhoRel 92*
**Weakley,** Donald Irving, Sr 1936- *WhoAmP 91*
**Weakley,** Martin LeRoy 1925- *AmMWSc 92*
**Weakliem,** Herbert Alfred, Jr 1926- *AmMWSc 92*
**Weaks,** Thomas Elton 1934- *AmMWSc 92*
**Weale,** Anne *WrDr 92*
**Weale,** Gareth Pryce 1963- *AmMWSc 92*
**Weales,** Gerald 1925- *WrDr 92*
**Wean,** Ronald Harry 1953- *WhoRel 92*
**Wear,** James Otto 1937- *AmMWSc 92*
**Wear,** Jean Simmons 1920- *WhoWest 92*
**Wear,** Robert Lee 1924- *AmMWSc 92*
**Wearden,** Stanley 1926- *AmMWSc 92*
**Weare,** Bryan C 1947- *AmMWSc 92*
**Weare,** John H 1940- *AmMWSc 92*
**Weare,** Trevor John 1943- *Who 92*
**Wearly,** William L 1915- *AmMWSc 92*
**Wearly,** William Levi 1915- *WhoWest 92*
**Wearn,** Richard Benjamin 1916- *AmMWSc 92*
**Wearne,** Alan 1948- *ConPo 91, WrDr 92*
**Wearne,** Alan Richard 1948- *IntAu&W 91*
**Wears,** James Russell 1949- *WhoFI 92*
**Weart,** Harry W 1927- *AmMWSc 92*
**Weart,** Richard Claude 1922- *AmMWSc 92*
**Weart,** Spencer R. 1942- *WrDr 92*
**Weart,** Spencer Richard 1942- *AmMWSc 92*
**Weart,** Wendell D 1932- *AmMWSc 92*
**Weary,** Dolphus 1946- *WhoBlA 92*
**Weary,** Dolphus D. 1946- *WhoRel 92*
**Weary,** Lawrence Clifton 1928- *WhoAmP 91*
**Weary,** Marlys E 1939- *AmMWSc 92*
**Weary,** Ogdred *WrDr 92*
**Weary,** Peyton Edwin 1930- *AmMWSc 92*
**Weary,** Thomas Squires 1925- *WhoAmL 92*
**Weast,** Clair Alexander 1913- *AmMWSc 92*
**Weather Report** *FacFETw, NewAmDM*
**Weather,** Leonard, Jr. 1944- *WhoBlA 92*
**Weatherall,** David 1933- *Who 92*
**Weatherall,** David John 1933- *IntWW 91*
**Weatherall,** James 1936- *Who 92*
**Weatherall,** Miles 1920- *Who 92*
**Weatherbee,** Carl 1916- *AmMWSc 92, WhoMW 92*
**Weatherbee,** James A 1943- *AmMWSc 92*
**Weatherby,** Gerald Duncan 1940- *AmMWSc 92*
**Weatherby,** Gregg *DrAPF 91*
**Weatherby,** William John *IntAu&W 91*
**Weatherford,** Thomas Waller, III 1930- *AmMWSc 92*
**Weatherford,** W D, Jr 1923- *AmMWSc 92*
**Weatherhead,** A. Kingsley 1923- *WrDr 92*
**Weatherhead,** Albert John, III 1925- *WhoMW 92*
**Weatherhead,** Alexander Stewart 1931- *Who 92*
**Weatherhead,** Andrea Kathryn 1960- *WhoEnt 92*
**Weatherhead,** Andrew Kingsley 1923- *WhoWest 92*
**Weatherhead,** James Leslie 1931- *IntWW 91, Who 92*
**Weatherhead,** Leslie R. 1956- *WhoAmL 92*
**Weatherhead,** Tim 1964- *TwCPaSc*
**Weatherill,** Bernard 1920- *IntWW 91, Who 92*
**Weatherington,** Randall L. 1949- *WhoEnt 92*
**Weatherley,** Alan Harold 1928- *AmMWSc 92*
**Weatherley,** Paul Egerton 1917- *IntWW 91, Who 92*
**Weatherly,** Georges Lloyd 1942- *AmMWSc 92*
**Weatherly,** John Hugh 1924- *WhoAmP 91*
**Weatherly,** Norman F 1932- *AmMWSc 92*
**Weatherly,** Tom 1942- *WhoBlA 92*
**Weatherred,** Jackie G 1934- *AmMWSc 92*
**Weathers,** Alice Ann 1944- *WhoBlA 92*
**Weathers,** Carl 1947- *WhoBlA 92*
**Weathers,** Carl 1948- *IntMPA 92*
**Weathers,** Clarence 1962- *WhoBlA 92*
**Weathers,** Dwight Ronald 1938- *AmMWSc 92*
**Weathers,** J. Leroy 1936- *WhoBlA 92*
**Weathers,** Lewis Glen 1925- *AmMWSc 92*
**Weathers,** Margaret A. 1922- *WhoBlA 92*
**Weathers,** Milledge Wright 1926- *WhoFI 92, WhoMW 92*
**Weathers,** Philip 1908- *WrDr 92*
**Weathers,** Theodore Michael 1956- *WhoAmL 92*
**Weathers,** W. T. *BenetAL 91*
**Weathers,** Warren Russell 1947- *WhoWest 92*
**Weathers,** Wesley Wayne 1942- *AmMWSc 92*
**Weathersby,** Augustus Burns 1913- *AmMWSc 92*
**Weathersby,** Joseph Brewster 1925- *WhoRel 92*
**Weathersby,** William Cecil 1941- *WhoFI 92*
**Weatherspoon,** Charles Phillip 1942- *AmMWSc 92*
**Weatherspoon,** J. B. 1936- *WhoBlA 92*
**Weatherspoon,** Jimmy Lee 1947- *WhoBlA 92*
**Weatherspoon,** Keith Earl 1949- *WhoBlA 92*
**Weatherspoon,** Teresa 1965- *BlkOlyM*
**Weatherston,** Alastair 1935- *Who 92*
**Weatherstone,** Dennis 1930- *IntWW 91, Who 92, WhoFI 92*
**Weatherstone,** James W 1925- *WhoIns 92*
**Weatherstone,** Robert Bruce 1926- *Who 92*
**Weatherup,** Roy Garfield 1947- *WhoAmL 92*
**Weatherwax,** Michael Dwaine 1945- *WhoFI 92, WhoWest 92*
**Weatherwax,** Thomas K 1942- *WhoAmP 91*
**Weaver,** Albert Bruce 1917- *AmMWSc 92*
**Weaver,** Alfred Charles 1949- *AmMWSc 92*
**Weaver,** Allen Dale 1911- *AmMWSc 92*
**Weaver,** Amanda Louise 1948- *WhoWest 92*
**Weaver,** Amy Myers 1959- *WhoAmL 92*
**Weaver,** Andrew Albert 1926- *AmMWSc 92*
**Weaver,** Arlene Rose 1931- *WhoMW 92*
**Weaver,** Arthur Lawrence 1936- *WhoMW 92*
**Weaver,** Audrey Turner 1913- *WhoBlA 92*
**Weaver,** Carl Harold 1910- *WrDr 92*
**Weaver,** Carolyn Leslie 1952- *WhoFI 92*
**Weaver,** Charles Edward 1925- *AmMWSc 92*
**Weaver,** Charles Hadley 1920- *AmMWSc 92*
**Weaver,** Charles Lyndell, Jr. 1945- *WhoFI 92, WhoMW 92*
**Weaver,** Charles Richard 1928- *WhoWest 92*
**Weaver,** Charlie 1957- *WhoAmP 91*
**Weaver,** Christopher Scot 1951- *AmMWSc 92*
**Weaver,** Clark Everest 1940- *WhoAmL 92*
**Weaver,** Clyde Eugene 1924- *WhoRel 92*
**Weaver,** Connie Marie 1950- *AmMWSc 92, WhoMW 92*
**Weaver,** Cynthia Marie 1948- *WhoAmL 92*
**Weaver,** Dale L 1926- *WhoAmP 91*
**Weaver,** Darrel Allen 1949- *WhoFI 92*
**Weaver,** David Dawson 1939- *AmMWSc 92*
**Weaver,** David Edgar 1952- *WhoMW 92*
**Weaver,** David Hugh 1946- *WhoMW 92*
**Weaver,** David Leo 1937- *AmMWSc 92*
**Weaver,** Delbert Allen 1931- *WhoAmL 92*
**Weaver,** Dennis 1924- *WhoEnt 92*
**Weaver,** Dennis 1925- *IntMPA 92*
**Weaver,** Dennis Alan 1946- *WhoMW 92*
**Weaver,** Donald K, Jr 1924- *AmMWSc 92*
**Weaver,** Donna Rae 1945- *WhoMW 92*
**Weaver,** Earle L. 1960- *WhoFI 92*
**Weaver,** Edwin Snell 1933- *AmMWSc 92*
**Weaver,** Ella Haith d1991 *NewYTBS 91*
**Weaver,** Ellen Cleminshaw 1925- *AmMWSc 92*
**Weaver,** Elvin Paul 1912- *WhoRel 92*
**Weaver,** Ervin Eugene 1923- *AmMWSc 92*
**Weaver,** Frank Cornell 1951- *WhoBlA 92*
**Weaver,** Fritz 1926- *IntMPA 92*
**Weaver,** Fritz William 1926- *WhoEnt 92*
**Weaver,** Gail Norman 1921- *WhoRel 92*
**Weaver,** Garland Rapheal, Jr. 1932- *WhoBlA 92*
**Weaver,** Garrett F. 1948- *WhoBlA 92*
**Weaver,** Gary W. 1952- *WhoBlA 92*
**Weaver,** George Leon Paul 1912- *WhoAmP 91, WhoBlA 92*
**Weaver,** George Thomas 1939- *AmMWSc 92*
**Weaver,** Gordon *DrAPF 91*
**Weaver,** Gordon Allison 1937- *IntAu&W 91*
**Weaver,** Grace Margaret 1909- *WhoRel 92, WhoWest 92*
**Weaver,** Harold Francis 1917- *AmMWSc 92*
**Weaver,** Harriett E. 1908- *SmATA 65 [port]*
**Weaver,** Harry Edward, Jr 1923- *AmMWSc 92*
**Weaver,** Harry Talmadge 1938- *AmMWSc 92*
**Weaver,** Henry D, Jr 1928- *AmMWSc 92*
**Weaver,** Herbert C. *WhoBlA 92*
**Weaver,** Howard Cecil 1950- *WhoWest 92*
**Weaver,** J. Denny 1941- *WhoRel 92*
**Weaver,** James B, Jr 1926- *AmMWSc 92*

**Weaver**, James Baird 1833-1912 *AmPolLe*
**Weaver**, James Cowles 1940- *AmMWSc 92*
**Weaver**, James Howard 1927- *WhoAmP 91*
**Weaver**, James Paul 1933- *WhoRel 92*
**Weaver**, Jane Elizabeth 1937- *WhoMW 92*
**Weaver**, Jeremiah William 1916- *AmMWSc 92*
**Weaver**, Jerry Thomas, Jr. 1948- *WhoWest 92*
**Weaver**, John Arthur 1940- *WhoBlA 92*
**Weaver**, John Borland 1937- *WhoEnt 92*
**Weaver**, John Carrier 1915- *WhoWest 92*
**Weaver**, John Herbert 1946- *AmMWSc 92*
**Weaver**, John L 1928- *WhoAmP 91*
**Weaver**, John Trevor 1932- *AmMWSc 92*
**Weaver**, John V. A. 1893-1938 *BenetAL 91*
**Weaver**, Jon Brendan 1962- *WhoMW 92*
**Weaver**, Joseph D. 1912- *WhoBlA 92*
**Weaver**, Kathie Sue 1951- *WhoMW 92*
**Weaver**, Kenneth Andrew 1951- *WhoMW 92*
**Weaver**, Kenneth Lamar 1950- *WhoRel 92*
**Weaver**, Kenneth Newcomer 1927- *AmMWSc 92*
**Weaver**, L A C 1937- *AmMWSc 92*
**Weaver**, Lawrence Clayton 1924- *AmMWSc 92*
**Weaver**, Lee Jackie 1956- *WhoRel 92*
**Weaver**, Leo James 1924- *AmMWSc 92*
**Weaver**, Leonard John 1936- *Who 92*
**Weaver**, Leslie O 1910- *AmMWSc 92*
**Weaver**, Lloyd Jess 1933- *WhoMW 92*
**Weaver**, Lois Jean 1944- *WhoWest 92*
**Weaver**, Lynn E 1930- *AmMWSc 92*
**Weaver**, Lynne C 1945- *AmMWSc 92*
**Weaver**, Macarthur 1942- *WhoRel 92*
**Weaver**, Marguerite McKinnie 1925- *WhoFI 92*
**Weaver**, Marianne Gruhn 1942- *WhoEnt 92*
**Weaver**, Marvin *DrAPF 91*
**Weaver**, Max Kimball 1941- *WhoWest 92*
**Weaver**, Michael 1952- *IntWW 91*
**Weaver**, Michael D 1961- *IntAu&W 91*
**Weaver**, Michael Glenn 1955- *WhoMW 92*
**Weaver**, Michael James 1946- *WhoAmL 92, WhoWest 92*
**Weaver**, Michael John 1947- *AmMWSc 92*
**Weaver**, Michael L 1947- *WhoAmP 91*
**Weaver**, Michael S. *DrAPF 91*
**Weaver**, Milo Wesley 1913- *AmMWSc 92*
**Weaver**, Morris Eugene 1929- *AmMWSc 92*
**Weaver**, Nevin 1920- *AmMWSc 92*
**Weaver**, Oliver 1942- *Who 92*
**Weaver**, Oliver Laurence 1943- *AmMWSc 92*
**Weaver**, Patricia *WhoAmP 91*
**Weaver**, Paul C. 1937- *WhoAmL 92*
**Weaver**, Paul David 1943- *WhoEnt 92*
**Weaver**, Paul Franklin 1926- *AmMWSc 92*
**Weaver**, R E C 1932- *AmMWSc 92*
**Weaver**, Ralph Sherman 1935- *AmMWSc 92*
**Weaver**, Reginald Lee 1939- *WhoBlA 92*
**Weaver**, Richard *DrAPF 91*
**Weaver**, Richard Donald 1926- *WhoRel 92*
**Weaver**, Richard L., II 1941- *WhoMW 92*
**Weaver**, Richard Wayne 1944- *AmMWSc 92*
**Weaver**, Robert Bradley 1932- *WhoMW 92*
**Weaver**, Robert C. 1907- *IntWW 91, WhoBlA 92*
**Weaver**, Robert Christian, Jr. 1944- *WhoFI 92*
**Weaver**, Robert Clifton 1907- *AmPolLe, FacFETw, WhoAmP 91*
**Weaver**, Robert Edward 1954- *WhoAmP 91*
**Weaver**, Robert F 1942- *AmMWSc 92*
**Weaver**, Robert G. *DrAPF 91*
**Weaver**, Robert Hinchman 1931- *AmMWSc 92*
**Weaver**, Robert Howard 1944- *WhoWest 92*
**Weaver**, Robert John 1917- *AmMWSc 92*
**Weaver**, Robert Michael 1942- *AmMWSc 92*
**Weaver**, Robert Paul 1952- *AmMWSc 92*
**Weaver**, Robin Geoffrey 1948- *WhoAmL 92*
**Weaver**, Roger *DrAPF 91*
**Weaver**, Russell Lee 1952- *WhoAmL 92*
**Weaver**, Scott James 1958- *WhoMW 92*
**Weaver**, Sigourney 1949- *IntMPA 92, IntWW 91, WhoEnt 92*
**Weaver**, Stanley B 1925- *WhoAmP 91*
**Weaver**, Susan Louise 1944- *WhoMW 92*
**Weaver**, Sylvester L., Jr. *LesBEnT 92*
**Weaver**, Sylvester L., Jr. 1908- *IntMPA 92*
**Weaver**, Thomas Arthur 1951-1991 *WhoMW 92*
**Weaver**, Tobias Rushton 1911- *Who 92*
**Weaver**, Velather Val Edwards 1944- *WhoWest 92*
**Weaver**, W Douglas 1945- *AmMWSc 92*
**Weaver**, Warren Eldred 1921- *AmMWSc 92*
**Weaver**, Wayne Willard 1944- *WhoWest 92*
**Weaver**, Wesley James 1944- *WhoRel 92*
**Weaver**, William Bruce 1946- *AmMWSc 92*
**Weaver**, William Cameron 1942- *WhoFI 92*
**Weaver**, William Clair, Jr. 1936- *WhoFI 92, WhoMW 92*
**Weaver**, William Dixon 1857-1919 *BiInAmS*
**Weaver**, William Judson 1936- *AmMWSc 92*
**Weaver**, William Merritt, Jr. 1912- *WhoFI 92*
**Weaver**, William Michael 1931- *AmMWSc 92*
**Weavers**, The *FacFETw, NewAmDM*
**Webb**, Aaron Wayne 1953- *WhoRel 92*
**Webb**, Alan Wendell 1939- *AmMWSc 92*
**Webb**, Alan Whitney 1939- *WhoFI 92*
**Webb**, Albert Dinsmoor 1917- *AmMWSc 92*
**Webb**, Alex Bearce 1942- *WhoFI 92*
**Webb**, Alfreda 1923- *WhoAmP 91*
**Webb**, Alfreda Johnson 1923- *AmMWSc 92*
**Webb**, Allan 1931- *WhoBlA 92*
**Webb**, Allen Nystrom 1921- *AmMWSc 92*
**Webb**, Andrew Clive 1947- *AmMWSc 92*
**Webb**, Andrew Howard 1945- *WhoRel 92*
**Webb**, Anthony 1932- *TwCPaSc*
**Webb**, Anthony Michael Francis 1914- *Who 92*
**Webb**, Arthur Brooke 1918- *Who 92*
**Webb**, Barry 1947- *ConAu 135*
**Webb**, Beatrice 1858-1943 *FacFETw, WomSoc*
**Webb**, Bernice *DrAPF 91, WrDr 92*
**Webb**, Bill D 1928- *AmMWSc 92*
**Webb**, Boyd 1947- *TwCPaSc*
**Webb**, Brainard Troutman, Jr. 1943- *WhoAmL 92*
**Webb**, Brian Lockwood 1949- *WhoAmL 92*
**Webb**, Brian Robert 1942- *WhoFI 92*
**Webb**, Burke Hilliard 1936- *WhoAmP 91*
**Webb**, Burleigh C 1923- *AmMWSc 92*
**Webb**, Byron H 1903- *AmMWSc 92*
**Webb**, Byron Kenneth 1934- *AmMWSc 92*
**Webb**, Charles 1939- *IntAu&W 91, WrDr 92*
**Webb**, Charles Alan 1947- *AmMWSc 92*
**Webb**, Charles H. *DrAPF 91*
**Webb**, Charles Haizlip, Jr. 1933- *WhoEnt 92, WhoMW 92*
**Webb**, Charles Harry 1953- *WhoFI 92*
**Webb**, Charles Henry 1834-1905 *BenetAL 91*
**Webb**, Chick 1909-1939 *FacFETw, NewAmDM*
**Webb**, Chloe *IntMPA 92*
**Webb**, Christopher Robert 1933- *WhoEnt 92*
**Webb**, Clifford 1895-1972 *TwCPaSc*
**Webb**, Clifton 1891-1966 *FacFETw*
**Webb**, Clifton Alan 1950- *WhoBlA 92*
**Webb**, Clyde B *WhoAmP 91*
**Webb**, Colin Edward 1937- *Who 92*
**Webb**, Colin Thomas 1939- *IntAu&W 91, Who 92*
**Webb**, Cynthia Ann Glinert 1947- *AmMWSc 92*
**Webb**, Danny Boy 1947- *WhoAmP 91*
**Webb**, Darrel M *WhoAmP 91*
**Webb**, David Lee 1954- *WhoAmP 91*
**Webb**, David R, Jr 1944- *AmMWSc 92*
**Webb**, David Ritchie 1944- *AmMWSc 92, WhoWest 92*
**Webb**, David Thomas 1945- *AmMWSc 92*
**Webb**, Dean LeRoy 1949- *WhoWest 92*
**Webb**, Denis Conrad 1938- *AmMWSc 92*
**Webb**, Don 1960- *IntAu&W 91*
**Webb**, Donald Wayne 1939- *AmMWSc 92*
**Webb**, Donald Woodford 1939- *WhoAmP 91*
**Webb**, Dorothy Louise 1936- *WhoMW 92*
**Webb**, Dotti M. *WhoEnt 92*
**Webb**, E. N. *WhoRel 92*
**Webb**, Edwin Clifford 1921- *Who 92*
**Webb**, Elizabeth Ann 1947- *WhoWest 92*
**Webb**, Eugene 1938- *WhoRel 92*
**Webb**, Frances *DrAPF 91*
**Webb**, Francis 1925-1973 *RfGEnL 91*
**Webb**, Fred, Jr 1935- *AmMWSc 92*
**Webb**, G. E. C. 1914- *WrDr 92*
**Webb**, George Dayton 1934- *AmMWSc 92*
**Webb**, George Hannam 1929- *Who 92*
**Webb**, George N 1920- *AmMWSc 92*
**Webb**, George Randolph 1938- *AmMWSc 92*
**Webb**, Georgia Houston 1951- *WhoBlA 92*
**Webb**, Glenn Francis 1942- *AmMWSc 92*
**Webb**, Glenn R 1918- *AmMWSc 92*
**Webb**, Gloria O *WhoAmP 91*
**Webb**, Gretchen Marie 1954- *WhoMW 92*
**Webb**, Guy E, Jr 1931- *WhoIns 92*
**Webb**, Guy Edmund, Jr. 1931- *WhoFI 92*
**Webb**, Harold, Sr. 1933- *WhoBlA 92*
**Webb**, Harold Donivan 1909- *AmMWSc 92*
**Webb**, Harold H. 1925- *WhoBlA 92*
**Webb**, Harri 1920- *WrDr 92*
**Webb**, Harvey, Jr. 1929- *WhoBlA 92*
**Webb**, Helen Marguerite 1913- *AmMWSc 92*
**Webb**, Henry Emile 1922- *WhoRel 92*
**Webb**, J Warren 1945- *AmMWSc 92*
**Webb**, Jack d1982 *LesBEnT 92*
**Webb**, James Calvin 1947- *WhoRel 92*
**Webb**, James E 1906- *FacFETw*
**Webb**, James Eugene 1956- *WhoBlA 92*
**Webb**, James H, Jr *WhoAmP 91*
**Webb**, James H., Jr. 1946- *IntWW 91*
**Webb**, James L A 1917- *AmMWSc 92*
**Webb**, James O. 1931- *WhoBlA 92*
**Webb**, James R 1945- *AmMWSc 92*
**Webb**, James Raymond 1954- *AmMWSc 92*
**Webb**, James Robert 1954- *WhoFI 92*
**Webb**, James Robert, III 1943- *WhoFI 92*
**Webb**, Jane 1807-1858 *ScFEYrs*
**Webb**, Jay Michal 1956- *WhoMW 92*
**Webb**, Jean Francis 1910- *WrDr 92*
**Webb**, Jean Francis, IV 1937- *WhoIns 92*
**Webb**, Jeffrey Ray 1960- *WhoMW 92*
**Webb**, Jerry Glen 1938- *AmMWSc 92*
**Webb**, Jimmy 1946- *NewAmDM*
**Webb**, Joe 1935- *WhoBlA 92*
**Webb**, John 1926- *WhoAmL 92, WhoAmP 91*
**Webb**, John Adrian, II 1959- *WhoFI 92*
**Webb**, John Beck 1951- *WhoRel 92*
**Webb**, John Burkitt 1841-1912 *BiInAmS*
**Webb**, John Day 1949- *AmMWSc 92*
**Webb**, John Raymond 1920- *AmMWSc 92*
**Webb**, John Stuart 1920- *Who 92*
**Webb**, John Weber, Jr. 1962- *WhoRel 92*
**Webb**, Joseph 1908-1962 *TwCPaSc*
**Webb**, Joseph Ernest 1915- *Who 92*
**Webb**, Joseph G. 1950- *WhoBlA 92*
**Webb**, Julian 1911- *WhoAmL 92*
**Webb**, Kaye *Who 92*
**Webb**, Kempton Evans 1931- *WrDr 92*
**Webb**, Kenneth 1927- *TwCPaSc*
**Webb**, Kenneth Emerson, Jr 1943- *AmMWSc 92*
**Webb**, Kenneth L 1930- *AmMWSc 92*
**Webb**, Lance 1909- *WhoRel 92*
**Webb**, Leland Frederick 1941- *AmMWSc 92, WhoWest 92*
**Webb**, Leslie Roy 1935- *IntWW 91, Who 92*
**Webb**, Lillian Frier 1926- *WhoRel 92*
**Webb**, Lucious Moses 1928- *WhoBlA 92*
**Webb**, M. Rodney 1944- *WhoRel 92*
**Webb**, Margaret Elizabeth Barbieri *Who 92*
**Webb**, Margaret Taylor 1928- *WhoWest 92*
**Webb**, Margot 1934- *ConAu 134, SmATA 67*
**Webb**, Marianne 1936- *WhoEnt 92*
**Webb**, Martha Jeanne 1947- *WhoEnt 92*
**Webb**, Martin Frank 1947- *WhoMW 92*
**Webb**, Marvin Russell 1918- *WhoMW 92*
**Webb**, Mary 1881-1927 *RfGEnL 91*
**Webb**, Mary 1939- *TwCPaSc*
**Webb**, Mary Alice 1951- *AmMWSc 92*
**Webb**, Maurice Barnett 1926- *AmMWSc 92*
**Webb**, Maysie 1923- *Who 92*
**Webb**, Melvin Richard 1940- *WhoBlA 92*
**Webb**, Michael Dennis Puzey 1937- *WhoWest 92*
**Webb**, Morrison DeSoto 1947- *WhoAmL 92*
**Webb**, Muhammad Alexander Russell 1846-1916 *RelLAm 91*
**Webb**, Muriel S. 1913-1977 *ConAu 134, -36NR*
**Webb**, Neil *TwCWW 91*
**Webb**, Neil Broyles 1930- *AmMWSc 92*
**Webb**, Nina Miller 1953- *WhoFI 92*
**Webb**, Norval Ellsworth, Jr 1927- *AmMWSc 92*
**Webb**, Paul 1923 *AmMWSc 92*
**Webb**, Paul 1945- *AmMWSc 92*
**Webb**, Paul H., Jr. 1955- *WhoEnt 92*
**Webb**, Pauline Mary 1927- *Who 92*
**Webb**, Perry Flynt, Jr. 1925- *WhoRel 92*
**Webb**, Peter Noel 1936- *AmMWSc 92*
**Webb**, Philip 1831-1915 *DcTwDes*
**Webb**, Philip Gilbert 1943- *AmMWSc 92, WhoMW 92*
**Webb**, Phillip Allen 1943- *WhoRel 92*
**Webb**, Phyllis 1927- *BenetAL 91, ConPo 91, WrDr 92*
**Webb**, R Clinton 1948- *AmMWSc 92*
**Webb**, Ralph L 1934- *AmMWSc 92*
**Webb**, Richard 1919- *Who 92*
**Webb**, Richard 1946- *AmMWSc 92*
**Webb**, Richard 1963- *TwCPaSc*
**Webb**, Richard C 1915- *AmMWSc 92*
**Webb**, Richard Gilbert 1932- *WhoFI 92*
**Webb**, Richard Kenton 1959- *TwCPaSc*
**Webb**, Richard Lansing 1923- *AmMWSc 92*
**Webb**, Richard Murton Lumley 1939- *Who 92*
**Webb**, Robert Carroll 1947- *AmMWSc 92*
**Webb**, Robert Donald, Jr. 1943- *WhoMW 92*
**Webb**, Robert Eldridge 1928- *WhoMW 92*
**Webb**, Robert G 1927- *AmMWSc 92*
**Webb**, Robert Howard 1934- *AmMWSc 92*
**Webb**, Robert Lee 1926- *AmMWSc 92*
**Webb**, Robert MacHardy 1915- *AmMWSc 92*
**Webb**, Robert Stopford 1948- *Who 92*
**Webb**, Rodney A 1946- *AmMWSc 92*
**Webb**, Rodney Scott 1935- *WhoAmL 92, WhoMW 92*
**Webb**, Roger P 1936- *AmMWSc 92*
**Webb**, Ron *TwCSFW 91*
**Webb**, Ronald Duane 1949- *WhoMW 92*
**Webb**, Ruth 1942- *WhoWest 92*
**Webb**, Ryland Edwin 1932- *AmMWSc 92*
**Webb**, Samuel Clement 1934- *WhoFI 92*
**Webb**, Sawney David 1936- *AmMWSc 92*
**Webb**, Schuyler Cleveland 1951- *WhoBlA 92*
**Webb**, Sharon *DrAPF 91*
**Webb**, Sharon 1936- *TwCSFW 91, WrDr 92*
**Webb**, Sharon Lynn 1936- *IntAu&W 91*
**Webb**, Sidney 1859-1947 *FacFETw*
**Webb**, Spud 1963- *WhoBlA 92*
**Webb**, Susan Howard 1908- *WhoAmP 91*
**Webb**, Theodore Stratton, Jr 1930- *AmMWSc 92*
**Webb**, Thomas 1908- *Who 92*
**Webb**, Thomas Evan 1932- *AmMWSc 92*
**Webb**, Thomas Harlan 1944- *WhoRel 92*
**Webb**, Thomas Howard 1935- *AmMWSc 92*
**Webb**, Thomas Irwin, Jr. 1948- *WhoAmL 92, WhoFI 92, WhoMW 92*
**Webb**, Thompson, III 1944- *AmMWSc 92*
**Webb**, Timothy 1942- *WrDr 92*
**Webb**, Walter Prescott 1888-1963 *BenetAL 91*
**Webb**, Walter Woodrow 1963- *WhoRel 92*
**Webb**, Watt Wetmore 1927- *AmMWSc 92*
**Webb**, Watts Rankin 1922- *AmMWSc 92*
**Webb**, Wellington E. *WhoWest 92*
**Webb**, Wellington E. 1941- *WhoBlA 92*
**Webb**, Wellington Edward 1941- *WhoAmP 91*
**Webb**, Wilfred D 1921- *WhoAmP 91*
**Webb**, William Albert 1944- *AmMWSc 92*
**Webb**, William Britton 1932- *WhoRel 92*
**Webb**, William Clement 1943- *WhoRel 92*
**Webb**, William Gatewood 1925- *AmMWSc 92*
**Webb**, William Grierson 1947- *Who 92*
**Webb**, William Hess 1905- *WhoAmL 92*
**Webb**, William Logan 1930- *AmMWSc 92*
**Webb**, William Paul 1922- *AmMWSc 92*
**Webb**, William Y. 1935- *WhoEnt 92*
**Webb**, Willis Keith 1928- *AmMWSc 92*
**Webb**, Willis Lee 1923- *AmMWSc 92*
**Webb**, Wilma J 1943- *WhoAmP 91*
**Webb**, Zadie Ozella 1932- *WhoBlA 92*
**Webb Duarte**, Richard Charles 1937- *IntWW 91*
**Webb-Mitchell**, Brett Parker 1955- *WhoRel 92*
**Webbe**, Diana *TwCPaSc*
**Webber** *Who 92*
**Webber**, Alfred Wayne 1947- *WhoMW 92*
**Webber**, Bobby 1937- *WhoAmP 91*
**Webber**, Charles Franklin 1935- *WhoWest 92*
**Webber**, Charles Lewis, Jr 1947- *AmMWSc 92*
**Webber**, Charles Wilkins 1819-1856 *BenetAL 91, BiInAmS*
**Webber**, Donald Salyer 1917- *AmMWSc 92*
**Webber**, E. Ronald 1915- *WrDr 92*
**Webber**, Edgar Ernest 1932- *AmMWSc 92*
**Webber**, Edith Judith 1946- *WhoWest 92*
**Webber**, Edythe Marie 1954- *WhoFI 92, WhoMW 92*
**Webber**, Fernley Douglas d1991 *Who 92N*
**Webber**, Gayle Milton 1931- *AmMWSc 92*
**Webber**, George Roger 1926- *AmMWSc 92*
**Webber**, Herbert H 1941- *AmMWSc 92*
**Webber**, J Alan 1940- *AmMWSc 92*
**Webber**, John Clinton 1943- *AmMWSc 92*
**Webber**, Jon Keith, Jr. 1956- *WhoEnt 92*
**Webber**, Larry Stanford 1945- *AmMWSc 92*
**Webber**, M. L. 1938- *WhoRel 92*
**Webber**, Marion George 1921- *AmMWSc 92*
**Webber**, Milo M 1930- *AmMWSc 92*
**Webber**, Milo Melvin 1930- *WhoWest 92*
**Webber**, Patrick John 1938- *AmMWSc 92*
**Webber**, Patrick Neil 1936- *WhoWest 92*
**Webber**, Paul R., III 1934- *WhoBlA 92*

**Webber,** Paul Rainey, III 1934- *WhoAmL 92*
**Webber,** Peter C 1952- *WhoAmP 91*
**Webber,** Philip Ellsworth 1944- *WhoMW 92*
**Webber,** Richard Harry 1924- *AmMWSc 92*
**Webber,** Richard John 1948- *AmMWSc 92*
**Webber,** Richard Lyle 1935- *AmMWSc 92*
**Webber,** Robert Eugene 1933- *WhoRel 92*
**Webber,** Robert Keller 1948- *WhoAmL 92*
**Webber,** Robert Stanley 1942- *WhoWest 92*
**Webber,** Rolland Lloyd 1932- *WhoAmP 91*
**Webber,** Ronald Keith 1957- *WhoMW 92*
**Webber,** Ross A. 1934- *WrDr 92*
**Webber,** Roy Seymour 1933- *Who 92*
**Webber,** Stanley Eugene 1919- *AmMWSc 92*
**Webber,** Stephen Edward 1940- *AmMWSc 92*
**Webber,** Thomas Charles 1947- *WhoAmP 91*
**Webber,** Thomas Gray 1912- *AmMWSc 92*
**Webber,** William A 1934- *AmMWSc 92*
**Webber,** William Alexander 1934- *WhoWest 92*
**Webber,** William Diderichsen 1930- *WhoRel 92*
**Webber,** William R 1929- *AmMWSc 92*
**Webber,** William Stuart 1942- *WhoBlA 92*
**Webber,** William Wallace, Jr. 1959- *WhoEnt 92*
**Webbink,** Ronald Frederick 1945- *AmMWSc 92*
**Webblow,** Joan Louise 1939- *WhoFI 92*
**Webbon,** Bruce Warren 1945- *AmMWSc 92*
**Webeck,** Alfred Stanley 1913- *WhoMW 92*
**Webel,** James Buell 1923- *WhoMW 92*
**Weber & Fields** *FacFETw*
**Weber,** Alban 1915- *WhoAmL 92*
**Weber,** Albert Vincent 1925- *AmMWSc 92*
**Weber,** Alfons 1927- *AmMWSc 92*
**Weber,** Alfred Herman 1906- *AmMWSc 92*
**Weber,** Allen Howard 1938- *AmMWSc 92*
**Weber,** Allen Thomas 1943- *AmMWSc 92*
**Weber,** Alois Hughes 1910- *WhoWest 92*
**Weber,** Aloysia 1759?-1839 *NewAmDM*
**Weber,** Alvin Francis 1918- *AmMWSc 92*
**Weber,** Annemarie 1923- *AmMWSc 92*
**Weber,** Arnold R. 1929- *WhoMW 92*
**Weber,** Arthur George 1903- *AmMWSc 92*
**Weber,** Arthur L 1943- *AmMWSc 92*
**Weber,** Arthur Phineas 1920- *AmMWSc 92*
**Weber,** Barbara C 1947- *AmMWSc 92*
**Weber,** Barbara M. 1945- *WhoFI 92*
**Weber,** Ben 1916-1979 *NewAmDM*
**Weber,** Brom 1917- *WrDr 92*
**Weber,** Bruce 1946- *IntWW 91*
**Weber,** Bruce Howard 1941- *AmMWSc 92*
**Weber,** Carl Joseph 1954- *AmMWSc 92*
**Weber,** Carl Maria von 1786-1826 *NewAmDM*
**Weber,** Charlene Lydia 1943- *WhoWest 92*
**Weber,** Charles L 1937- *AmMWSc 92*
**Weber,** Charles Walter 1931- *AmMWSc 92*
**Weber,** Charles William 1922- *AmMWSc 92*
**Weber,** Charles William 1946- *WhoAmP 91*
**Weber,** Clifford E 1918- *AmMWSc 92*
**Weber,** Daniel 1942- *WhoBlA 92*
**Weber,** Daniel 1948- *WhoAmL 92*
**Weber,** Darrell J 1933- *AmMWSc 92*
**Weber,** Darrell Jack 1933- *WhoWest 92*
**Weber,** David Alexander 1939- *AmMWSc 92*
**Weber,** David Frederick 1939- *AmMWSc 92*
**Weber,** David Joseph 1940- *WrDr 92*
**Weber,** David Paul 1933- *WhoIns 92*
**Weber,** Deane Fay 1925- *AmMWSc 92*
**Weber,** Delbert Dean 1932- *WhoMW 92*
**Weber,** Dennis Herman 1950- *WhoMW 92*
**Weber,** Dennis Joseph 1934- *AmMWSc 92, WhoMW 92*
**Weber,** Dennis Paul 1952- *WhoAmP 91, WhoWest 92*
**Weber,** Derek 1921- *Who 92*
**Weber,** Donald A. 1953- *WhoRel 92*
**Weber,** Dorothy Jo 1951- *WhoWest 92*
**Weber,** Douglas D. 1954- *WhoRel 92*
**Weber,** Dwight Edward 1951- *WhoFI 92, WhoMW 92*
**Weber,** Edward F 1931- *WhoAmP 91*
**Weber,** Edward Joseph 1948- *AmMWSc 92*
**Weber,** Eicke Richard 1949- *AmMWSc 92*
**Weber,** Elizabeth *DrAPF 91*
**Weber,** Ernst 1901- *AmMWSc 92*
**Weber,** Erwin Wilbur 1931- *AmMWSc 92*
**Weber,** Eugen 1925- *WrDr 92*
**Weber,** Evelyn Joyce 1928- *AmMWSc 92, WhoMW 92*
**Weber,** Faustin N 1911- *AmMWSc 92*
**Weber,** Florence Robinson 1921- *AmMWSc 92*
**Weber,** Frank E 1935- *AmMWSc 92*
**Weber,** Frank Edward 1935- *WhoMW 92*
**Weber,** Frank L 1924- *AmMWSc 92*
**Weber,** Fred J. 1919- *WhoAmL 92, WhoAmP 91, WhoWest 92*
**Weber,** Frederick, Jr 1923- *AmMWSc 92*
**Weber,** Frederick Edwin 1924- *WhoMW 92*
**Weber,** Frederick Henry 1952- *WhoMW 92*
**Weber,** Garry Allen 1936- *WhoAmP 91*
**Weber,** Gary Richard 1950- *WhoRel 92*
**Weber,** George 1922- *AmMWSc 92*
**Weber,** George Richard 1929- *IntAu&W 91, WhoFI 92, WhoWest 92*
**Weber,** George Russell 1911- *AmMWSc 92, WhoMW 92*
**Weber,** Gregorio 1916- *AmMWSc 92*
**Weber,** Hans Josef 1942- *AmMWSc 92*
**Weber,** Hans Jurgen 1939- *AmMWSc 92*
**Weber,** Hans-Ruedi 1923- *DcEcMov*
**Weber,** Harry A 1921- *AmMWSc 92*
**Weber,** Harry P 1931- *AmMWSc 92*
**Weber,** Harvey Allen 1917- *WhoEnt 92*
**Weber,** Heather R Wilson 1943- *AmMWSc 92*
**Weber,** Helene Marie 1824- *EncAmaz 91*
**Weber,** Henry Adam 1845-1912 *BiInAmS*
**Weber,** Herman Jacob 1927- *WhoAmL 92*
**Weber,** Howard W. 1941- *WhoAmL 92*
**Weber,** J K Richard 1957- *AmMWSc 92*
**Weber,** James Alan 1944- *AmMWSc 92*
**Weber,** James Edward 1957- *AmMWSc 92*
**Weber,** James H 1919- *AmMWSc 92*
**Weber,** James Harold 1936- *AmMWSc 92*
**Weber,** James Mitchell 1927- *WhoRel 92*
**Weber,** James R 1945- *AmMWSc 92*
**Weber,** James Robert 1961- *WhoRel 92*
**Weber,** James Stuart 1947- *WhoFI 92, WhoMW 92*
**Weber,** Janet Crosby 1923- *AmMWSc 92*
**Weber,** Janet M. 1958- *WhoWest 92*
**Weber,** Jean Robert 1925- *AmMWSc 92*
**Weber,** Jeffrey Randolph 1952- *WhoEnt 92*
**Weber,** Jerome Bernard 1933- *AmMWSc 92*
**Weber,** Joe 1867-1942 *FacFETw*
**Weber,** John Bertram 1930- *WhoMW 92*
**Weber,** John Donald 1934- *AmMWSc 92*
**Weber,** John R 1924- *AmMWSc 92*
**Weber,** Jon Fredric 1958- *WhoAmL 92*
**Weber,** Joseph 1867-1942 *BenetAL 91*
**Weber,** Joseph 1919- *AmMWSc 92*
**Weber,** Joseph Elliott 1910- *WhoMW 92*
**Weber,** Joseph James 1942- *WhoWest 92*
**Weber,** Joseph M 1939- *AmMWSc 92*
**Weber,** Joseph T 1938- *AmMWSc 92*
**Weber,** Judy Delores 1943- *WhoMW 92*
**Weber,** Julius 1914- *AmMWSc 92*
**Weber,** Karen Jeanne 1960- *WhoRel 92*
**Weber,** Karl T *AmMWSc 92*
**Weber,** Karl William 1953- *WhoFI 92*
**Weber,** Kenneth C 1937- *AmMWSc 92*
**Weber,** Lavern J 1933- *AmMWSc 92*
**Weber,** Lawrence Kirkwood, Jr. 1930- *WhoFI 92*
**Weber,** Leon 1931- *AmMWSc 92*
**Weber,** Lester George 1924- *AmMWSc 92*
**Weber,** Linda Ficklin 1926- *WhoMW 92*
**Weber,** Lois 1882-1939 *HanAmWH, IntDcF 2-2 [port], ReelWom*
**Weber,** Marc *DrAPF 91*
**Weber,** Margaret Laura Jane 1933- *WhoMW 92*
**Weber,** Maria 1919- *IntWW 91*
**Weber,** Mark Charles 1953- *WhoAmL 92*
**Weber,** Marlene Elizabeth 1938- *WhoMW 92*
**Weber,** Marvin John 1932- *AmMWSc 92*
**Weber,** Mary Aquinas 1923- *WhoRel 92*
**Weber,** Marylou Queally 1956- *WhoFI 92*
**Weber,** Max 1864-1920 *FacFETw*
**Weber,** Max O. 1929- *WhoFI 92*
**Weber,** Merrill Evan 1956- *WhoAmL 92*
**Weber,** Michael Joseph 1942- *AmMWSc 92*
**Weber,** Milan George 1908- *WhoMW 92*
**Weber,** Morton M 1922- *AmMWSc 92*
**Weber,** Neal Albert 1908- *AmMWSc 92*
**Weber,** Norman 1934- *AmMWSc 92*
**Weber,** Owen 1946- *WhoEnt 92*
**Weber,** Paul-Egon 1913- *WhoMW 92*
**Weber,** Paul Van Vranken 1921- *AmMWSc 92*
**Weber,** Peter B 1934- *AmMWSc 92*
**Weber,** R.B. *DrAPF 91*
**Weber,** Ralph E. 1926- *WrDr 92*
**Weber,** Richard 1941- *WhoFI 92*
**Weber,** Richard Allen 1949- *WhoMW 92*
**Weber,** Richard Gerald 1939- *AmMWSc 92*
**Weber,** Richard Rand 1938- *AmMWSc 92*
**Weber,** Robert Carl 1950- *WhoAmL 92*
**Weber,** Robert Donald 1935- *WhoRel 92*
**Weber,** Robert Emil 1930- *AmMWSc 92*
**Weber,** Robert Harrison 1919- *AmMWSc 92*
**Weber,** Robert R 1925- *WhoAmP 91*
**Weber,** Ronald J. 1946- *WhoMW 92*
**Weber,** Roy Edwin 1928- *WhoMW 92*
**Weber,** Russell John 1960- *WhoEnt 92*
**Weber,** Sarah Appleton *WrDr 92*
**Weber,** Sharon Ann 1954- *WhoAmL 92*
**Weber,** Shirley Nash 1948- *WhoBlA 92*
**Weber,** Stephen Clark 1954- *WhoRel 92*
**Weber,** Stephen Floyd 1957- *WhoMW 92*
**Weber,** Susan Lee 1951- *WhoEnt 92*
**Weber,** Thomas Alan 1949- *WhoWest 92*
**Weber,** Thomas Byrnes 1925- *AmMWSc 92*
**Weber,** Thomas Scott 1955- *WhoRel 92*
**Weber,** Thomas W 1930- *AmMWSc 92*
**Weber,** Timothy Preston 1947- *WhoRel 92*
**Weber,** Vin 1952- *AlmAP 92 [port], WhoAmP 91, WhoMW 92*
**Weber,** Waldemar Carl 1937- *AmMWSc 92*
**Weber,** Wallace Rudolph 1934- *AmMWSc 92*
**Weber,** Walter J, Jr 1934- *AmMWSc 92*
**Weber,** Wendell W 1925- *AmMWSc 92*
**Weber,** Wilfried T 1936- *AmMWSc 92*
**Weber,** Wilhelm K. 1939- *WhoWest 92*
**Weber,** Willes Henry 1942- *AmMWSc 92, WhoMW 92*
**Weber,** William Alfred 1918- *AmMWSc 92*
**Weber,** William J 1949- *AmMWSc 92*
**Weber,** William Mark 1941- *AmMWSc 92*
**Weber,** William Palmer 1940- *AmMWSc 92, WhoWest 92*
**Weber,** Winnie P *WhoAmP 91*
**Weber-Javers,** Florence Ruth 1953- *WhoWest 92*
**Weberg,** Berton Charles 1930- *AmMWSc 92*
**Weberman,** Ben 1923- *WhoFI 92*
**Weberman,** Phineas 1930- *WhoRel 92*
**Webern,** Anton von 1883-1945 *FacFETw, NewAmDM*
**Webers,** Gerald F 1932- *AmMWSc 92*
**Webers,** Vincent Joseph 1922- *AmMWSc 92*
**Webert,** Henry S 1929- *AmMWSc 92*
**Webiorg** *EncAmaz 91*
**Weblin,** Harold 1930- *Who 92*
**Weborg,** John 1937- *WhoMW 92, WhoRel 92*
**Webre,** Joseph Septime 1961- *WhoEnt 92*
**Webre,** Neil Whitney 1938- *AmMWSc 92*
**Webster,** Aen Walker 1957- *WhoAmP 91*
**Webster,** Alan Brunskill 1918- *Who 92, WrDr 92*
**Webster,** Albert Knickerbocker 1937- *WhoEnt 92*
**Webster,** Alec 1934- *Who 92*
**Webster,** Allen E 1938- *AmMWSc 92*
**Webster,** Allen Eugene 1938- *WhoMW 92*
**Webster,** Barbara Donahue 1929- *AmMWSc 92*
**Webster,** Ben 1909-1973 *NewAmDM*
**Webster,** Bennett Addison 1923- *WhoAmP 91*
**Webster,** Beveridge *WhoEnt 92*
**Webster,** Beveridge 1908- *NewAmDM*
**Webster,** Bruce Ronald 1946- *WhoRel 92*
**Webster,** Bryan Courtney 1931- *Who 92*
**Webster,** Burnice Hoyle 1910- *AmMWSc 92*
**Webster,** Carl M 1956- *WhoIns 92*
**Webster,** Cecil Ray 1954- *WhoBlA 92*
**Webster,** Charles *Who 92*
**Webster,** Charles 1936- *IntWW 91, WhoBlA 92*
**Webster,** Charles M *WhoAmP 91*
**Webster,** Clyde Leroy, Jr 1944- *AmMWSc 92*
**Webster,** Colin Thomas 1937- *WhoMW 92*
**Webster,** Curtis Cleveland 1922- *AmMWSc 92*
**Webster,** Cyril Charles 1909- *Who 92*
**Webster,** D S 1917- *AmMWSc 92*
**Webster,** Dale Arroy 1938- *AmMWSc 92*
**Webster,** Daniel 1782-1852 *AmPolLe [port], BenetAL 91, RComAH*
**Webster,** Daniel 1949- *WhoAmP 91*
**Webster,** David 1931- *Who 92*
**Webster,** David Clark 1927- *WhoFI 92*
**Webster,** David Dyer 1918- *AmMWSc 92*
**Webster,** David Henry 1934- *AmMWSc 92*
**Webster,** David James 1931- *WhoFI 92*
**Webster,** David John 1938- *WhoWest 92*
**Webster,** David MacLaren 1937- *Who 92*
**Webster,** Dennis Burton 1942- *AmMWSc 92*
**Webster,** Derek Adrian 1927- *Who 92*
**Webster,** DeWitt T., Jr. 1932- *WhoBlA 92*
**Webster,** Donald Jordan 1946- *WhoWest 92*
**Webster,** Dorothy Margaret 1920- *WhoWest 92*
**Webster,** Douglas B 1934- *AmMWSc 92*
**Webster,** Edward Mount d1976 *LesBEnT 92*
**Webster,** Edward William 1922- *AmMWSc 92*
**Webster,** Eleanor Rudd 1920- *AmMWSc 92*
**Webster,** Emilia 1950- *AmMWSc 92*
**Webster,** Ferris 1934- *AmMWSc 92*
**Webster,** Francis Marion 1849-1916 *BiInAmS*
**Webster,** Frank V *ScFEYrs, SmATA 67*
**Webster,** Frederic Smith 1849- *BiInAmS*
**Webster,** Frederick A M 1886- *ScFEYrs*
**Webster,** Gary Dean 1934- *AmMWSc 92, WhoWest 92*
**Webster,** George Calvin 1924- *AmMWSc 92*
**Webster,** George Drury 1921- *WhoAmL 92, WhoFI 92*
**Webster,** George V. 1945- *WhoEnt 92*
**Webster,** Gerald Best 1944- *WhoEnt 92*
**Webster,** Gordon Ritchie 1922- *AmMWSc 92*
**Webster,** Gordon Visscher, Jr. 1947- *WhoRel 92*
**Webster,** Grady Linder 1927- *AmMWSc 92*
**Webster,** H. T. 1885-1952 *BenetAL 91*
**Webster,** Harold Frank 1919- *AmMWSc 92*
**Webster,** Harris Duane 1920- *AmMWSc 92*
**Webster,** Harrison Edwin 1841-1906 *BiInAmS*
**Webster,** Harry 1921- *TwCPaSc*
**Webster,** Harry Timothy 1949- *WhoWest 92*
**Webster,** Henry deForest 1927- *AmMWSc 92*
**Webster,** Henry George 1917- *Who 92*
**Webster,** Henry Kitchell 1875-1932 *BenetAL 91, ScFEYrs*
**Webster,** Ian Stevenson 1925- *Who 92*
**Webster,** Isabel Gates 1931- *WhoBlA 92*
**Webster,** Isabella Margaret 1911- *AmMWSc 92*
**Webster,** J Provand *ScFEYrs*
**Webster,** Jackson Dan 1919- *AmMWSc 92*
**Webster,** Jackson Ross 1945- *AmMWSc 92*
**Webster,** James Albert 1928- *AmMWSc 92*
**Webster,** James Allan 1939- *AmMWSc 92*
**Webster,** James Carmody 1938- *WhoAmP 91*
**Webster,** James Douglas 1940- *WhoAmP 91*
**Webster,** James Randolph, Jr 1931- *AmMWSc 92*
**Webster,** Jan 1924- *IntAu&W 91, WrDr 92*
**Webster,** Janice Helen 1944- *Who 92*
**Webster,** Jean 1876-1916 *BenetAL 91*
**Webster,** Jeffrey Leon 1941- *WhoEnt 92, WhoMW 92*
**Webster,** Jerry Lynn 1950- *WhoAmP 91*
**Webster,** Jesse *IntAu&W 91X*
**Webster,** John 1579?-1634? *RfGEnL 91*
**Webster,** John 1580?-1634? *CnDBLB 1, DramC 2*
**Webster,** John Alexander R. *Who 92*
**Webster,** John E, Jr 1938- *WhoAmP 91*
**Webster,** John Goodwin 1932- *AmMWSc 92, WhoMW 92*
**Webster,** John H 1928- *AmMWSc 92*
**Webster,** John Kimball 1934- *WhoFI 92*
**Webster,** John Kingsley Ohl, II 1950- *WhoFI 92*
**Webster,** John Lawrence Harvey 1913- *Who 92*
**Webster,** John M. 1936- *WhoWest 92*
**Webster,** John Morrison 1932- *Who 92*
**Webster,** John Robert 1916- *AmMWSc 92*
**Webster,** John Roger 1926- *Who 92*
**Webster,** John Thomas 1927- *AmMWSc 92*
**Webster,** John W., III 1961- *WhoBlA 92*
**Webster,** John White 1793-1850 *BiInAmS*
**Webster,** Karl Smith 1924- *AmMWSc 92*
**Webster,** Keith Edward 1935- *Who 92*
**Webster,** Larry Dale 1939- *AmMWSc 92*
**Webster,** Lee Alan 1941- *AmMWSc 92*
**Webster,** Lee Sydney 1963- *WhoFI 92*
**Webster,** Lesley Douglass 1949- *WhoBlA 92*
**Webster,** Leslie T, Jr 1926- *AmMWSc 92*
**Webster,** Lois Shand 1929- *WhoFI 92*
**Webster,** Lonnie 1922- *WhoBlA 92*
**Webster,** Marvin Nathaniel 1952- *WhoBlA 92*
**Webster,** Mary Clark 1947- *WhoAmP 91*
**Webster,** Merritt Samuel 1909- *AmMWSc 92*
**Webster,** Michael *Who 92, WhoEnt 92*
**Webster,** Michael George Thomas 1920- *Who 92*
**Webster,** Michael Lee 1949- *WhoRel 92*

**Webster,** Nancy Mulvihill 1953- *WhoWest 92*
**Webster,** Nathan Burnham 1821-1900 *BiInAmS*
**Webster,** Niambi Dyanne *WhoBlA 92*
**Webster,** Nicholas *LesBEnT 92*
**Webster,** Nicholas 1912- *WhoEnt 92*
**Webster,** Noah *IntAu&W 91X, WrDr 92*
**Webster,** Noah 1758-1843 *BenetAL 91, BiInAmS, BlkwCEP, BlkwEAR*
**Webster,** Norman 1924- *TwCPaSc*
**Webster,** Norman William 1920- *IntAu&W 91, WrDr 92*
**Webster,** Orrin John 1913- *AmMWSc 92*
**Webster,** Owen Wright 1929- *AmMWSc 92*
**Webster,** Patrick 1928- *Who 92*
**Webster,** Paul Daniel, III 1930- *AmMWSc 92*
**Webster,** Paul F 1907-1984 *FacFETw*
**Webster,** Pelatiah 1726-1795 *BenetAL 91*
**Webster,** Peletiah 1726-1795 *BlkwEAR*
**Webster,** Peter 1924- *Who 92*
**Webster,** Peter Bridgman 1941- *WhoAmL 92*
**Webster,** Peter David 1949- *WhoAmL 92*
**Webster,** Peter John 1942- *AmMWSc 92*
**Webster,** Philip Jonathan 1939- *WhoEnt 92*
**Webster,** Porter Grigsby 1929- *AmMWSc 92*
**Webster,** R.A. 1933- *IntMPA 92*
**Webster,** Ralph Terrence 1922- *WhoWest 92*
**Webster,** Richard Michael 1942- *Who 92*
**Webster,** Robert Byron 1932- *WhoAmL 92*
**Webster,** Robert Edward 1938- *AmMWSc 92*
**Webster,** Robert G 1932- *AmMWSc 92*
**Webster,** Robert Gordon 1932- *Who 92*
**Webster,** Robert K 1938- *AmMWSc 92*
**Webster,** Robert Loudon 1954- *WhoMW 92*
**Webster,** Robin Welander 1956- *WhoWest 92*
**Webster,** Ronald Arthur 1938- *WhoAmP 91*
**Webster,** Ronald D. 1949- *WhoFI 92*
**Webster,** Roy Edward, II 1933- *WhoRel 92*
**Webster,** Ruth Ann 1949- *WhoAmL 92*
**Webster,** Sharon B. 1937- *WhoFI 92*
**Webster,** Stephen Burtis 1935- *WhoMW 92*
**Webster,** Stephen W 1943- *WhoAmP 91*
**Webster,** Terry R 1938- *AmMWSc 92*
**Webster,** Theodore *WhoBlA 92*
**Webster,** Thomas G 1924- *AmMWSc 92*
**Webster,** Tom *WhoWest 92*
**Webster,** William H 1924- *WhoAmP 91*
**Webster,** William H. 1946- *WhoBlA 92*
**Webster,** William Hedgcock 1924- *IntWW 91*
**Webster,** William John, Jr 1943- *AmMWSc 92*
**Webster,** William L *WhoAmP 91*
**Webster,** William Lawrence 1953- *WhoAmL 92, WhoMW 92*
**Webster,** William Merle 1925- *AmMWSc 92*
**Webster,** William Osceola, Jr. 1955- *WhoRel 92*
**Webster,** William Phillip 1930- *AmMWSc 92*
**Webster,** Winston Roosevelt 1943- *WhoBlA 92*
**Wechmar,** Rudiger, Baron Von 1923- *IntWW 91*
**Wechsberg,** Joseph 1907-1983 *BenetAL 91, ConAu 34NR*
**Wechsler,** Gil 1942- *WhoEnt 92*
**Wechsler,** Jonathan David 1960- *WhoMW 92*
**Wechsler,** Judith Glatzer 1940- *WhoEnt 92*
**Wechsler,** Martin T 1921- *AmMWSc 92*
**Wechsler,** Max 1906- *WhoFI 92*
**Wechsler,** Monroe S 1923- *AmMWSc 92*
**Wechsler,** Sergio 1944- *WhoMW 92*
**Wechsler,** Steven Lewis 1948- *AmMWSc 92*
**Wecht,** Cyril H 1931- *WhoAmP 91*
**Wechter,** Angela Pirolli 1937- *WhoAmP 91*
**Wechter,** Clari Ann 1953- *WhoFI 92, WhoMW 92*
**Wechter,** Margaret Ann 1935- *AmMWSc 92*
**Wechter,** Norman Robert 1926- *WhoMW 92*
**Wechter,** Vivienne Thaul *DrAPF 91*
**Wechter,** William Julius 1932- *AmMWSc 92, WhoWest 92*
**Weck,** Friedrich Josef 1918- *AmMWSc 92*
**Weck,** Kristin Willa 1959- *WhoFI 92, WhoMW 92*
**Wecker,** Lynn 1947- *AmMWSc 92*
**Wecker,** Stanley C 1933- *AmMWSc 92*
**Weckerly,** William Clarence 1937- *WhoRel 92*
**Weckesser,** Elden Christian 1910- *WhoMW 92*
**Weckesser,** Louis Benjamin 1928- *AmMWSc 92*
**Weckler,** Gene Peter 1932- *AmMWSc 92*
**Weckman,** George A. 1939- *WhoRel 92*
**Weckmann,** Matthias 1619?-1674 *NewAmDM*
**Weckmann-Munoz,** Luis 1923- *IntWW 91*
**Weckowicz,** Thaddeus Eugene 1918- *AmMWSc 92*
**Weckstein,** Marvin S. 1929- *WhoMW 92*
**Wecksung,** George William 1931- *AmMWSc 92*
**Weckwerth,** Vernon Ervin 1931- *AmMWSc 92*
**Wecter,** Dixon 1906-1950 *BenetAL 91*
**Wedberg,** Stanley Edward 1913- *AmMWSc 92*
**Wedd,** George Morton 1930- *Who 92*
**Wedde,** Ian 1946- *ConNov 91, ConPo 91, WrDr 92*
**Weddell,** David S 1917- *AmMWSc 92*
**Weddell,** George G 1923- *AmMWSc 92*
**Weddell,** James Blount 1927- *AmMWSc 92*
**Weddell,** Martin *WrDr 92*
**Wedderburn** *Who 92*
**Wedderburn,** Alexander John Maclagan 1942- *WhoRel 92*
**Wedderburn,** Andrew John Alexander O. *Who 92*
**Wedderburn,** Dorothy Enid Cole 1925- *Who 92*
**Wedderburn,** James Edward 1938- *BlkOlyM*
**Wedderburn Of Charlton,** Baron 1927- *IntWW 91, Who 92*
**Wedderspoon,** Alexander Gillan 1931- *Who 92*
**Weddige,** Emil Albert 1907- *WhoMW 92*
**Wedding,** Brent 1936- *AmMWSc 92*
**Wedding,** Randolph Townsend 1921- *AmMWSc 92*
**Wedding,** Scott Dale 1954- *WhoEnt 92*
**Weddington,** Elaine 1964- *WhoBlA 92*
**Weddington,** Elizabeth Gardner 1932- *WhoEnt 92*
**Weddington,** Rachel Thomas 1917- *WhoBlA 92*
**Weddington,** Sarah Ragle 1945- *WhoAmP 91*
**Weddington,** Wayne 1936- *WhoBlA 92*
**Weddington,** Wilburn Harold, Sr. 1924- *WhoBlA 92*
**Weddle,** Judith Ann 1944- *WhoWest 92*
**Weddle,** Michael R 1949- *WhoAmP 91*
**Weddle,** Stephen Shields 1938- *WhoAmL 92, WhoFI 92*
**Weddleton,** Richard Francis 1939- *AmMWSc 92*
**Wedeen,** Richard P 1934- *AmMWSc 92*
**Wedega,** Alice 1905- *Who 92*
**Wedegaertner,** Donald K 1936- *AmMWSc 92*
**Wedekind,** Gilbert Leroy 1933- *AmMWSc 92*
**Wedeking,** Ralph Weinberg 1934- *WhoRel 92*
**Wedel,** Arnold Marion 1928- *AmMWSc 92*
**Wedel,** Cynthia Clark 1908-1986 *DcEcMov, RelLAm 91*
**Wedel,** John Mark 1953- *WhoAmP 91*
**Wedel,** Millie Redmond 1939- *WhoWest 92*
**Wedel,** Victor James 1950- *WhoMW 92*
**Wedell,** Eberhard George 1927- *WrDr 92*
**Wedell,** George 1927- *Who 92*
**Wedell,** Roger William 1948- *WhoRel 92*
**Wedemeier,** Robert Gorham 1942- *WhoWest 92*
**Wedemeyer,** Albert Coady 1897-1989 *FacFETw*
**Wedemeyer,** Gary Alvin 1935- *AmMWSc 92*
**Wedemeyer,** John Mills, Jr. 1945- *WhoWest 92*
**Wedgbury,** David *TwCPaSc*
**Wedge,** Jimmy Joe 1942- *WhoAmP 91*
**Wedge,** Martin *TwCPaSc*
**Wedgeworth,** Ann *WhoEnt 92*
**Wedgeworth,** Ann 1935- *IntMPA 92*
**Wedgeworth,** Robert, Jr. 1937- *WhoBlA 92*
**Wedgle,** Richard Jay 1951- *WhoAmL 92*
**Wedgwood** *Who 92*
**Wedgwood,** Baron 1954- *Who 92*
**Wedgwood,** C V 1910- *IntAu&W 91, WrDr 92*
**Wedgwood,** Cicely Veronica 1910- *Who 92*
**Wedgwood,** Geoffrey Heath 1900- *TwCPaSc*
**Wedgwood,** Hensleigh Cecil d1991 *NewYTBS 91*
**Wedgwood,** Hugo Martin 1933- *Who 92*
**Wedgwood,** John Alleyne 1920- *Who 92*
**Wedgwood,** Ralph Josiah Patrick 1924- *AmMWSc 92*
**Wedgwood,** Ruth *WhoAmL 92*
**Wedgwood,** Veronica *Who 92*
**Wedgwood,** Veronica 1910- *IntWW 91*
**Wedin,** Carolyn E. 1939- *WhoMW 92*
**Wedin,** John Harry, III 1949- *WhoEnt 92*
**Wedin,** Robert John 1953- *WhoMW 92*
**Wedin,** Walter F 1925- *AmMWSc 92*
**Wedl,** Lois Catherine 1931- *WhoMW 92*
**Wedler,** Frederick Charles Oliver, Jr 1941- *AmMWSc 92*
**Wedlick,** Harold Lee 1936- *AmMWSc 92*
**Wedlock,** Bruce D 1934- *AmMWSc 92*
**Wedman,** Elwood Edward 1922- *AmMWSc 92*
**Wedmore,** Frederick 1844-1921 *ThHEIm*
**Wedoff,** Teresa Lynn 1949- *WhoAmP 91*
**Wedum,** John Ahugh 1929- *WhoMW 92*
**Wee Chong Jin** 1917- *IntWW 91, Who 92*
**Wee Kim Wee** 1915- *IntWW 91, Who 92*
**Wee,** William Go 1937- *AmMWSc 92*
**Weech,** Allen Bertell 1922- *WhoWest 92*
**Weed,** Edward Reilly 1940- *WhoFI 92*
**Weed,** Elaine Greening Ames 1932- *AmMWSc 92*
**Weed,** Frederic Augustus 1918- *WhoWest 92*
**Weed,** Gene Leonard 1935- *WhoEnt 92*
**Weed,** Grant B 1935- *AmMWSc 92*
**Weed,** H C 1920- *AmMWSc 92*
**Weed,** Herman Roscoe 1922- *AmMWSc 92, WhoMW 92*
**Weed,** John Conant 1912- *AmMWSc 92*
**Weed,** Lawrence Leonard 1923- *AmMWSc 92*
**Weed,** Lois Cron 1927- *WhoFI 92*
**Weed,** Marlene 1936- *WhoEnt 92*
**Weed,** Mary Theophilos 1928- *WhoMW 92*
**Weed,** Maurice James 1912- *WhoEnt 92*
**Weed,** Ray Arnold 1934- *WhoAmL 92*
**Weed,** Ronald De Vern 1932- *WhoWest 92*
**Weed,** Sterling Barg 1926- *AmMWSc 92*
**Weed,** Thurlow 1797-1882 *BenetAL 91*
**Weeden,** Craig *DrAPF 91*
**Weeden,** Robert Barton 1933- *AmMWSc 92*
**Weeden,** Timothy L 1951- *WhoAmP 91, WhoMW 92*
**Weeding,** Cecil 1934- *WhoAmP 91*
**Weedman,** Daniel Wilson 1942- *AmMWSc 92*
**Weedn,** Trish 1950- *WhoAmP 91*
**Weedn,** Victor Walter 1953- *WhoAmL 92*
**Weedon,** Alan Charles 1951- *AmMWSc 92*
**Weedon,** Basil Charles Leicester 1923- *IntWW 91, Who 92*
**Weedon,** Dudley William 1920- *Who 92*
**Weedon,** Gene Clyde 1936- *AmMWSc 92*
**Weedon,** William Stone 1877-1912 *BiInAmS*
**Weege,** Randall James 1926- *AmMWSc 92*
**Weekes,** Ambrose Walter Marcus 1919- *Who 92*
**Weekes,** Martin Edward 1933- *WhoBlA 92*
**Weekes,** Michael Manning 1938- *WhoRel 92*
**Weekes,** Philip Gordon 1920- *Who 92*
**Weekes,** Trevor Cecil 1940- *AmMWSc 92*
**Weekley,** Augustine Smythe, Jr. 1930- *WhoAmL 92*
**Weekley,** Dewitt Talmage 1911- *WhoRel 92*
**Weekley,** Richard J. *DrAPF 91*
**Weekly,** John William 1931- *WhoFI 92, WhoMW 92*
**Weekman,** Gerald Thomas 1931- *AmMWSc 92*
**Weekman,** Vern W, Jr 1931- *AmMWSc 92*
**Weeks,** Alan Frederick 1923- *Who 92*
**Weeks,** Arthur Andrew 1914- *WhoAmL 92*
**Weeks,** Charles Merritt 1944- *AmMWSc 92*
**Weeks,** Charles Walker 1941- *WhoEnt 92*
**Weeks,** Clifford Myers 1938- *WhoEnt 92*
**Weeks,** David I 1916- *WhoIns 92*
**Weeks,** David Lee 1930- *AmMWSc 92*
**Weeks,** Deborah Redd 1947- *WhoBlA 92*
**Weeks,** Dennis Alan 1943- *AmMWSc 92*
**Weeks,** Donald Paul 1941- *AmMWSc 92*
**Weeks,** Dorothy Walcott 1893- *AmMWSc 92*
**Weeks,** Edward 1898-1989 *ConAu 36NR*
**Weeks,** Edward Olin *ScFEYrs*
**Weeks,** Gary Lynn 1936- *WhoFI 92*
**Weeks,** George Eliot 1939- *AmMWSc 92*
**Weeks,** Gerald 1941- *AmMWSc 92*
**Weeks,** Gregory Paul 1947- *AmMWSc 92*
**Weeks,** Harmon Patrick, Jr 1944- *AmMWSc 92*
**Weeks,** Howard Benjamin 1924- *WhoRel 92*
**Weeks,** Hugh 1904- *Who 92*
**Weeks,** James Page 1946- *WhoMW 92*
**Weeks,** James Robert 1920- *AmMWSc 92*
**Weeks,** James W 1937- *WhoAmP 91*
**Weeks,** Janet H *WhoAmP 91*
**Weeks,** Janet Healy 1932- *WhoAmL 92, WhoWest 92*
**Weeks,** Jeffrey 1945- *WrDr 92*
**Weeks,** John David 1943- *AmMWSc 92*
**Weeks,** John F 1932- *WhoAmP 91*
**Weeks,** John Henry 1938- *Who 92*
**Weeks,** John Leonard 1926- *AmMWSc 92*
**Weeks,** John R, IV 1927- *AmMWSc 92*
**Weeks,** John Stafford 1920- *WhoMW 92, WhoRel 92*
**Weeks,** Joseph Dame 1840-1896 *BiInAmS*
**Weeks,** Joseph Preble 1937- *WhoAmP 91*
**Weeks,** L H 1918- *AmMWSc 92*
**Weeks,** Leo 1925- *AmMWSc 92*
**Weeks,** Leslie Vernon 1918- *AmMWSc 92*
**Weeks,** Lloyd F 1932- *WhoAmP 91*
**Weeks,** M. J. 1942- *WhoFI 92, WhoMW 92*
**Weeks,** Marcia Gail 1938- *WhoAmP 91*
**Weeks,** Maurice Harold 1921- *AmMWSc 92*
**Weeks,** Paul Martin 1932- *AmMWSc 92*
**Weeks,** Ramona Martinez *DrAPF 91*
**Weeks,** Renee Jones 1948- *WhoBlA 92*
**Weeks,** Richard W 1922- *AmMWSc 92*
**Weeks,** Richard William 1942- *AmMWSc 92*
**Weeks,** Robert A 1924- *AmMWSc 92*
**Weeks,** Robert Earl 1925- *WhoMW 92*
**Weeks,** Robert Gray 1936- *WhoFI 92*
**Weeks,** Robert Joe 1929- *AmMWSc 92*
**Weeks,** Robert Lewis *DrAPF 91*
**Weeks,** Robert Walker 1926- *WhoFI 92*
**Weeks,** Stephan John 1950- *AmMWSc 92*
**Weeks,** Stephen P 1949- *AmMWSc 92*
**Weeks,** Thomas F 1935- *AmMWSc 92*
**Weeks,** Thomas Joseph, Jr 1941- *AmMWSc 92*
**Weeks,** Thomas Wesley 1945- *WhoRel 92*
**Weeks,** Wilford Frank 1929- *AmMWSc 92, WhoWest 92*
**Weeks,** William Thomas 1932- *AmMWSc 92*
**Weelkes,** Thomas 1575?-1623 *NewAmDM*
**Weems,** Charles William 1941- *AmMWSc 92*
**Weems,** Howard Vincent, Jr 1922- *AmMWSc 92*
**Weems,** John Edward 1924- *WrDr 92*
**Weems,** Luther B. 1944- *WhoBlA 92*
**Weems,** Malcolm Lee Bruce 1945- *AmMWSc 92*
**Weems,** Marcus Aurelius, III 1954- *WhoEnt 92*
**Weems,** Marion Lee 1948- *WhoRel 92*
**Weems,** Mason Locke 1759-1825 *BenetAL 91*
**Weems,** Rick 1948- *WhoWest 92*
**Weems,** Robert Edwin 1947- *AmMWSc 92*
**Weems,** Rodger Cary 1952- *WhoRel 92*
**Weems,** Vernon Eugene, Jr. 1948- *WhoBlA 92*
**Weems,** William Arthur 1944- *AmMWSc 92*
**Weener,** Jay R. 1927- *WhoRel 92*
**Weenolsen,** Hebe *ConAu 34NR*
**Weeple,** Edward John 1945- *Who 92*
**Weeramantry,** Christopher Gregory 1926- *IntWW 91*
**Weertman,** Johannes 1925- *AmMWSc 92*
**Weertman,** Julia Randall 1926- *AmMWSc 92*
**Weerts,** Hendrik Joseph 1950- *WhoMW 92*
**Weerts,** Richard Kenneth 1928- *WhoEnt 92, WhoMW 92*
**Weese,** Amy Joanne 1968- *WhoRel 92*
**Weese,** Don 1946- *WhoAmP 91*
**Weese,** Harry M. 1915- *IntWW 91*
**Weese,** Richard Henry 1938- *AmMWSc 92*
**Weese,** Samuel H 1935- *WhoIns 92*
**Weesner,** Bertrand Winfred, Sr. 1912- *WhoMW 92*
**Weetall,** Howard H 1936- *AmMWSc 92*
**Weetamoo** *EncAmaz 91*
**Weetch,** Kenneth Thomas 1933- *Who 92*
**Weete,** John Donald 1942- *AmMWSc 92*
**Weetman,** David G 1938- *AmMWSc 92*
**Weetman,** Gordon Frederick 1933- *AmMWSc 92*
**Weevers,** Theodoor 1904- *Who 92*
**Weezorak,** Dennis Robert 1953- *WhoRel 92*
**Wefald,** Jon 1937- *WhoMW 92*
**Wefald,** Robert Ovrom 1942- *WhoAmP 91*
**Wefel,** John Paul 1944- *AmMWSc 92*
**Wefer,** Donald Peters 1933- *WhoAmL 92*
**Wefers,** Karl 1928- *AmMWSc 92*
**Wefler,** Wilson Daniel 1927- *WhoMW 92*
**Weg,** Frank A 1927- *WhoIns 92*
**Weg,** John Gerard 1934- *AmMWSc 92*
**Weg,** Ruth B 1920- *AmMWSc 92*
**Wegbreit,** Ben 1944- *WhoFI 92*
**Wege,** Ann Christene 1956- *AmMWSc 92*
**Wege,** William Richard 1926- *AmMWSc 92*

**Wegelin,** Christof 1911- *WrDr 92*
**Wegeman,** Alvin Paul, Jr. 1964- *WhoWest 92*
**Wegener,** Alfred Lothar 1880-1930 *FacFETw*
**Wegener,** Beverly Joan 1956- *WhoFI 92*
**Wegener,** Paul 1874-1948 *EncTR 91 [port]*
**Wegener,** Peter Paul 1917- *AmMWSc 92*
**Wegener,** Warner Smith 1935- *AmMWSc 92*
**Wegenka,** Lynn Marie 1954- *WhoEnt 92*
**Wegenstein,** Martin Willi 1950- *WhoFI 92*
**Weger,** James Earle 1956- *WhoAmL 92*
**Weger,** Jeffrey Kim 1961- *WhoRel 92*
**Wegermann,** Rodney Edwin 1941- *WhoRel 92*
**Wegge,** David Glen 1948- *WhoMW 92*
**Weggel,** John Richard 1941- *AmMWSc 92*
**Weggel,** Robert John 1943- *AmMWSc 92*
**Weggenman,** James Robert 1949- *WhoWest 92*
**Weghorst,** Brenda Lee 1961- *WhoEnt 92*
**Weglarz,** Joseph 1965- *WhoFI 92*
**Wegman,** David Howe 1940- *AmMWSc 92*
**Wegman,** Edward Joseph 1943- *AmMWSc 92*
**Wegman,** Myron Ezra 1908- *AmMWSc 92*
**Wegman,** Steven M 1953- *AmMWSc 92*
**Wegman,** William 1942?- *News 91 [port], WorArt 1980 [port]*
**Wegmann,** George J 1901- *WhoIns 92*
**Wegmann,** Thomas George 1941- *AmMWSc 92*
**Wegmiller,** Donald Charles 1938- *WhoFI 92*
**Wegner,** Arthur Eduard 1937- *WhoFI 92*
**Wegner,** Carl Fredrick 1964- *WhoRel 92*
**Wegner,** Gene H 1930- *AmMWSc 92*
**Wegner,** Hans 1914- *DcTwDes*
**Wegner,** Harvey E 1925- *AmMWSc 92*
**Wegner,** Karl Heinrich 1930- *AmMWSc 92*
**Wegner,** Marcus Immanuel 1915- *AmMWSc 92*
**Wegner,** Mary Josephine 1934- *WhoMW 92*
**Wegner,** Patrick Andrew 1940- *AmMWSc 92*
**Wegner,** Paul Dean 1956- *WhoRel 92*
**Wegner,** Peter 1932- *AmMWSc 92*
**Wegner,** Robert Carl 1944- *AmMWSc 92*
**Wegner,** Robert E *DrAPF 91*
**Wegner,** Samuel Joseph 1952- *WhoWest 92*
**Wegner,** Thomas Norman 1932- *AmMWSc 92*
**Wegner,** William Edward 1950- *WhoAmL 92*
**Wegrzyn,** Stefan 1925- *IntWW 91*
**Wegs,** Joyce Markert 1942- *WhoMW 92*
**Wegscheid,** Darril 1944- *WhoAmP 91*
**Wegst,** W F 1909- *AmMWSc 92*
**Wegst,** Walter F, Jr 1934- *AmMWSc 92*
**Wegweiser,** Arthur E 1934- *AmMWSc 92*
**Weh,** Allen Edward 1942- *WhoWest 92*
**Wehage,** Rodger John 1949- *WhoAmP 91*
**Wehausen,** John Vrooman 1913- *AmMWSc 92*
**Wehba,** C. Frederick 1947- *WhoWest 92*
**Wehde,** Albert Edward 1935- *WhoAmL 92*
**Wehe,** Robert L 1921- *AmMWSc 92*
**Wehen,** Joy DeWeese 1936- *WrDr 92*
**Wehinger,** Peter Augustus 1938- *AmMWSc 92*
**Wehlau,** Amelia W 1930- *AmMWSc 92*
**Wehlau,** William Henry 1926- *AmMWSc 92*
**Wehle,** Louis Brandeis, Jr 1918- *AmMWSc 92*
**Wehling,** Fred Lowell 1963- *WhoWest 92*
**Wehling,** Robert Louis 1938- *WhoMW 92*
**Wehman,** Adele *WhoEnt 92*
**Wehman,** Anthony Theodore 1942- *AmMWSc 92*
**Wehman,** Guy Thomas 1952- *WhoEnt 92*
**Wehmann,** Alan Ahlers 1940- *AmMWSc 92*
**Wehmeyer,** Josephine Mont 1916- *WhoHisp 92*
**Wehmeyer,** Victor William 1904- *WhoAmP 91*
**Wehmhoefer,** Jerry L. 1945- *WhoMW 92*
**Wehner,** Alfred Peter 1926- *AmMWSc 92*
**Wehner,** Donald C 1929- *AmMWSc 92*
**Wehner,** Gottfried Karl 1910- *AmMWSc 92*
**Wehner,** Herbert 1906-1990 *AnObit 1990*
**Wehner,** Jeanne M *AmMWSc 92*
**Wehner,** Josef Magnus 1891-1973 *EncTR 91 [port]*
**Wehner,** Philip 1917- *AmMWSc 92*
**Wehner,** Stephen Vincent 1954- *WhoAmL 92*
**Wehr,** Allan Gordon 1931- *AmMWSc 92*
**Wehr,** Carl Timothy 1943- *AmMWSc 92*
**Wehr,** Herbert Michael 1943- *AmMWSc 92*
**Wehr,** Polly Jeanne 1962- *WhoRel 92*
**Wehr,** Thomas A 1941- *AmMWSc 92*
**Wehrbein,** Roger 1938- *WhoAmP 91*
**Wehrbein,** William Mead 1948- *AmMWSc 92*
**Wehren,** Rixanne 1947- *WhoEnt 92*
**Wehrenberg,** John P 1927- *AmMWSc 92*
**Wehrheim,** Carol Ann 1940- *WhoRel 92*
**Wehring,** Bernard William 1937- *AmMWSc 92*
**Wehrle,** Martha Gaines 1925- *WhoAmP 91*
**Wehrle,** Paul F 1921- *AmMWSc 92*
**Wehrli,** Eugene S. *WhoRel 92*
**Wehrli,** Jonathan Allen 1962- *WhoFI 92*
**Wehrli,** Peter 1939- *IntAu&W 91*
**Wehrli,** Pius Anton 1933- *AmMWSc 92*
**Wehrly,** Joseph Malachi 1915- *WhoWest 92*
**Wehrly,** Thomas Edward 1947- *AmMWSc 92*
**Wehrman,** Elizabeth Ann 1932- *WhoEnt 92*
**Wehrmann,** Ralph F 1918- *AmMWSc 92*
**Wehrmeister,** Herbert Louis 1920- *AmMWSc 92*
**Wehry,** Earl L, Jr 1941- *AmMWSc 92*
**Wei Chunshu** 1922- *IntWW 91*
**Wei Jianxing** 1931- *IntWW 91*
**Wei Jinshan** 1927- *IntWW 91*
**Wei Mingyi** 1924- *IntWW 91*
**Wei Wei** 1920- *IntWW 91*
**Wei Yung** 1937- *IntWW 91*
**Wei,** Chin Hsuan 1926- *AmMWSc 92*
**Wei,** Ching-Yeu 1948- *AmMWSc 92*
**Wei,** Chung-Chen 1940- *AmMWSc 92*
**Wei,** Diana Yun Dee 1930- *AmMWSc 92*
**Wei,** Edward T 1944- *AmMWSc 92*
**Wei,** Enoch Ping 1942- *AmMWSc 92*
**Wei,** Guang-Jong Jason 1946- *AmMWSc 92*
**Wei,** James 1930- *AmMWSc 92*
**Wei,** L Y 1920- *AmMWSc 92*
**Wei,** Lee-Jen 1948- *AmMWSc 92*
**Wei,** Lester Yeehow 1944- *AmMWSc 92*
**Wei,** Lun-Shin 1929- *AmMWSc 92*
**Wei,** Pax Samuel Pin 1938- *AmMWSc 92*
**Wei,** Peter Hsing-Lien 1922- *AmMWSc 92*
**Wei,** Robert 1939- *AmMWSc 92*
**Wei,** Robert Peh-Ying 1931- *AmMWSc 92*
**Wei,** Stephen Hon Yin 1937- *AmMWSc 92*
**Wei,** Wei-Zen 1951- *AmMWSc 92*
**Wei,** William Wu-Shyong 1940- *AmMWSc 92*
**Wei,** Yen 1957- *AmMWSc 92*
**Wei-Berk,** Caroline 1956- *AmMWSc 92*
**Weibel,** Armella 1920- *AmMWSc 92*
**Weibel,** Bob Wilson 1949- *WhoWest 92*
**Weibel,** Charles Alexander 1950- *AmMWSc 92*
**Weibel,** Dale Eldon 1920- *AmMWSc 92*
**Weibel,** Gladys Helen 1921- *WhoAmP 91*
**Weibell,** Fred John 1927- *AmMWSc 92, WhoWest 92*
**Weiblen,** Paul Willard 1927- *AmMWSc 92*
**Weibrecht,** Walter Eugene 1937- *AmMWSc 92*
**Weibust,** Robert Smith 1942- *AmMWSc 92*
**Weichardt,** Louis Theodor 1894-1985 *BiDExR*
**Weichbrodt,** Thomas Leland 1948- *WhoAmL 92*
**Weichel,** Hugo 1937- *AmMWSc 92*
**Weichenthal,** Burton Arthur 1937- *AmMWSc 92*
**Weichert,** Dieter Horst 1932- *AmMWSc 92*
**Weichlein,** Russell George 1915- *AmMWSc 92*
**Weichman,** Barry Michael *AmMWSc 92*
**Weichman,** Frank Ludwig 1930- *AmMWSc 92*
**Weichman,** Peter Bernard 1959- *AmMWSc 92*
**Weichs,** Maximilian, Baron von 1881-1954 *EncTR 91 [port]*
**Weichsel,** Morton E, Jr 1933- *AmMWSc 92*
**Weichsel,** Paul M 1931- *AmMWSc 92*
**Weick,** Charles Frederick 1931- *AmMWSc 92*
**Weick,** Richard Fred 1934- *AmMWSc 92*
**Weicker,** Jack Edward 1924- *WhoMW 92*
**Weicker,** Lowell *NewYTBS 91 [port]*
**Weicker,** Lowell P., Jr. 1931- *AlmAP 92 [port]*
**Weicker,** Lowell Palmer, Jr. 1931- *IntWW 91, WhoAmP 91*
**Weida,** Bill *ConAu 135*
**Weida,** George Albert F. 1936- *WhoWest 92*
**Weida,** Lewis Dixon 1924- *WhoFI 92*
**Weida,** William J. 1942- *ConAu 135*
**Weidanz,** William P 1935- *AmMWSc 92*
**Weide,** David L 1936- *AmMWSc 92*
**Weide,** William Wolfe 1923- *WhoFI 92, WhoWest 92*
**Weideman,** Virgil Lee 1949- *WhoFI 92*
**Weidemann,** Alfred 1918- *EncTR 91*
**Weidemeyer,** Carleton Lloyd 1933- *WhoAmL 92, WhoEnt 92, WhoFI 92*
**Weiden,** Mathias Herman Joseph 1923- *AmMWSc 92*
**Weidenaar,** Reynold 1945- *NewAmDM*
**Weidenaar,** Reynold Henry 1945- *WhoEnt 92*
**Weidenbaum,** Murray 1927- *WrDr 92*
**Weidenbaum,** Murray Lew 1927- *IntWW 91, Who 92, WhoAmP 91, WhoMW 92*
**Weidenbaum,** Sherman S 1925- *AmMWSc 92*
**Weidenfeld** *Who 92*
**Weidenfeld and Nicolson** *DcLB 112*
**Weidenfeld,** Baron 1919- *IntWW 91, Who 92*
**Weidenfeld,** Edward Lee 1943- *WhoEnt 92*
**Weidenfeld,** Sheila Rabb 1943- *WhoEnt 92*
**Weidenfeld,** Werner 1947- *IntWW 91*
**Weidenhofer,** Neal 1940- *WhoWest 92*
**Weidensaul,** T Craig 1939- *AmMWSc 92*
**Weidenschilling,** Stuart John 1946- *AmMWSc 92*
**Weider,** John Richard 1946- *WhoAmL 92*
**Weidhaas,** Donald E 1928- *AmMWSc 92*
**Weidhaas,** John August, Jr 1925- *AmMWSc 92*
**Weidie,** Alfred Edward 1931- *AmMWSc 92*
**Weidig,** Charles F 1945- *AmMWSc 92*
**Weidinger,** Christine *IntWW 91*
**Weidlein,** James Rea 1949- *WhoWest 92*
**Weidler,** Donald John 1933- *AmMWSc 92*
**Weidler,** Ronald Walter 1950- *WhoRel 92*
**Weidlich,** John Edward, Jr 1919- *AmMWSc 92*
**Weidling,** Frank Carl 1955- *WhoAmL 92*
**Weidlinger,** Paul 1914- *IntWW 91*
**Weidlinger,** Paul 1937- *AmMWSc 92*
**Weidman,** Dick 1940- *WhoAmP 91*
**Weidman,** Harold D 1929- *WhoAmP 91*
**Weidman,** Jerome *DrAPF 91*
**Weidman,** Jerome 1913- *BenetAL 91, ConNov 91, WrDr 92*
**Weidman,** Patrick Dan 1941- *AmMWSc 92*
**Weidman,** Robert McMaster 1923- *AmMWSc 92*
**Weidman,** Robert Stuart 1954- *AmMWSc 92*
**Weidmann,** Silvio 1921- *AmMWSc 92*
**Weidner,** Bruce Van Scoyoc 1908- *AmMWSc 92*
**Weidner,** Earl 1935- *AmMWSc 92*
**Weidner,** Jerry R 1938- *AmMWSc 92*
**Weidner,** Marvin Detweiler 1911- *WhoAmP 91*
**Weidner,** Michael George, Jr 1922- *AmMWSc 92*
**Weidner,** Richard Tilghman 1921- *AmMWSc 92*
**Weidner,** Terry Mohr 1937- *AmMWSc 92*
**Weidner,** Victor Ray 1932- *AmMWSc 92*
**Weidner,** William Jeffrey 1947- *AmMWSc 92*
**Weier,** Gary Wilbert 1943- *WhoRel 92*
**Weier,** Richard Mathias 1940- *AmMWSc 92, WhoMW 92*
**Weiffenbach,** Conrad Venable 1942- *AmMWSc 92*
**Weig,** David William 1943- *WhoFI 92*
**Weigall,** Peter Raymond 1922- *Who 92*
**Weigand,** Heather Lynn 1963- *WhoMW 92*
**Weigand,** Richard G 1938- *WhoAmP 91*
**Weigand,** Richard George 1935- *WhoAmL 92*
**Weigand,** William Adam 1938- *AmMWSc 92*
**Weigand,** William Keith 1937- *WhoRel 92, WhoWest 92*
**Weigel,** Elsie Diven 1948- *WhoFI 92*
**Weigel,** Gustave 1906-1964 *RelLAm 91*
**Weigel,** Hans 1908-1991 *NewYTBS 91*
**Weigel,** Kenneth George 1954- *WhoAmL 92*
**Weigel,** Nancy Kay 1943- *WhoMW 92*
**Weigel,** Ollie J. 1922- *WhoMW 92*
**Weigel,** Paul H 1946- *AmMWSc 92*
**Weigel,** Robert David 1923- *AmMWSc 92*
**Weigel,** Russell C, Jr 1940- *AmMWSc 92*
**Weigel,** Stanley Alexander 1905- *WhoAmL 92*
**Weigel,** Tom *DrAPF 91*
**Weigelt,** Horst Erich 1934- *WhoRel 92*
**Weigelt,** Morris Almor 1934- *WhoRel 92*
**Weigend,** Guido Gustav 1920- *WhoWest 92*
**Weigensberg,** Bernard Irving 1926- *AmMWSc 92*
**Weiger,** Robert W 1927- *AmMWSc 92*
**Weigh,** Brian 1926- *Who 92*
**Weighell,** Sidney 1922- *Who 92*
**Weighill,** Robert Harold George 1920- *Who 92*
**Weight,** Carel 1908- *TwCPaSc*
**Weight,** Carel Victor Morlais 1908- *IntWW 91, Who 92*
**Weight,** Forrest F 1936- *AmMWSc 92*
**Weight,** Frank *TwCSFW 91*
**Weight,** George Dale 1934- *WhoFI 92, WhoWest 92*
**Weight,** Michael Anthony 1940- *WhoAmL 92*
**Weightman,** Donald Sharp 1949- *WhoAmL 92*
**Weightman,** Judy Mae 1941- *WhoAmL 92*
**Weightman,** William 1813-1904 *BiInAmS*
**Weigl,** Bruce *DrAPF 91*
**Weigl,** Etta Ruth *DrAPF 91*
**Weigl,** Joseph 1766-1846 *NewAmDM*
**Weigl,** Karl 1881-1949 *NewAmDM*
**Weigl,** Peter Douglas 1939- *AmMWSc 92*
**Weigle,** Jack LeRoy 1925- *AmMWSc 92*
**Weigle,** Joerg-Peter 1953- *WhoEnt 92*
**Weigle,** Richard S. 1948- *WhoEnt 92*
**Weigle,** Robert Edward 1927- *AmMWSc 92*
**Weigle,** William O 1927- *AmMWSc 92*
**Weigle,** William Oliver 1927- *WhoWest 92*
**Weigman,** Bernard J 1932- *AmMWSc 92*
**Weigner,** Brent James 1949- *WhoWest 92*
**Weigner,** Robert L. 1950- *WhoFI 92*
**Weihaupt,** John George 1930- *AmMWSc 92, WhoWest 92*
**Weihe,** Jeffrey George 1952- *WhoEnt 92*
**Weihe,** Joseph William 1921- *AmMWSc 92*
**Weiher,** James F 1933- *AmMWSc 92*
**Weihing,** John 1921- *WhoAmP 91*
**Weihing,** John Lawson 1921- *AmMWSc 92, WhoMW 92*
**Weihing,** Robert Ralph 1938- *AmMWSc 92*
**Weijer,** Jan 1924- *AmMWSc 92*
**Weik,** David Peter 1947- *WhoEnt 92*
**Weik,** Martin H, Jr 1922- *AmMWSc 92*
**Weikel,** John Henry, Jr 1929- *AmMWSc 92*
**Weikert,** Ralf 1940- *WhoEnt 92*
**Weikert,** Robert Neil 1950- *WhoWest 92*
**Weikl,** Bernd 1942- *IntWW 91*
**Weiksner,** George Bernard, Jr. 1944- *WhoFI 92*
**Weiksner,** Sandra S. 1945- *WhoAmL 92*
**Weikum,** George Arnold 1953- *WhoMW 92*
**Weil,** Andre *AmMWSc 92*
**Weil,** Andrew Thomas 1942- *AmMWSc 92*
**Weil,** Benjamin Henry 1916- *AmMWSc 92*
**Weil,** Carrol S 1917- *AmMWSc 92*
**Weil,** Clifford Edward 1937- *AmMWSc 92*
**Weil,** Constance M. 1959- *WhoMW 92*
**Weil,** Daniel Wilkus 1940- *WhoAmL 92*
**Weil,** David Harris 1953- *WhoWest 92*
**Weil,** Edward David 1928- *AmMWSc 92*
**Weil,** Francis Alphonse 1938- *AmMWSc 92*
**Weil,** Gordon Lee 1937- *WhoAmP 91, WhoFI 92*
**Weil,** Harold G 1942- *WhoAmP 91*
**Weil,** Herschel 1921- *AmMWSc 92*
**Weil,** Jack Baum 1928- *WhoWest 92*
**Weil,** James Beverly 1944- *WhoFI 92*
**Weil,** James L. *DrAPF 91*
**Weil,** James L. 1929- *ConAu 36NR*
**Weil,** Jerry *WhoEnt 92*
**Weil,** Jerry David 1943- *WhoMW 92*
**Weil,** Jesse Leo 1931- *AmMWSc 92*
**Weil,** John A 1929- *AmMWSc 92*
**Weil,** John Victor 1935- *AmMWSc 92*
**Weil,** Jon David 1937- *AmMWSc 92*
**Weil,** Leon Jerome 1927- *WhoAmP 91*
**Weil,** Marvin Lee 1924- *AmMWSc 92*
**Weil,** Max Harry 1927- *AmMWSc 92, WhoMW 92*
**Weil,** Michael Ray 1951- *AmMWSc 92*
**Weil,** Peter Henry 1933- *WhoAmL 92*
**Weil,** Raoul Bloch *AmMWSc 92*
**Weil,** Raymond 1923- *IntWW 91*
**Weil,** Richard 1876-1917 *BiInAmS*
**Weil,** Robert Irving 1922- *WhoAmL 92*
**Weil,** Robert L. 1932- *WhoBIA 92*
**Weil,** Rolf 1926- *AmMWSc 92*
**Weil,** Rolf Alfred 1921- *WhoMW 92*
**Weil,** Roman Lee 1940- *WhoMW 92*
**Weil,** Sidney, Jr 1926- *WhoAmP 91*
**Weil,** Simone 1909-1943 *FacFETw, FrenWW, GuFrLit 1, LiExTwC*
**Weil,** Steven Mark 1949- *WhoWest 92*
**Weil,** Suzanne S. Fern 1933- *WhoWest 92*
**Weil,** Ted Jay 1967- *WhoEnt 92*
**Weil,** Thomas Andre 1944- *AmMWSc 92*
**Weil,** Thomas P 1932- *AmMWSc 92*
**Weil,** William B, Jr 1924- *AmMWSc 92*
**Weiland,** Galen Franklin *WhoAmP 91*
**Weiland,** Stephen Cass 1948- *WhoAmL 92*
**Weiland,** Stephen Robert 1952- *WhoEnt 92*
**Weileder,** Stanley 1933- *WhoIns 92*
**Weiler,** Dorothy Esser 1914- *WhoWest 92*
**Weiler,** Edward John 1949- *AmMWSc 92*
**Weiler,** Ernest Dieter 1939- *AmMWSc 92*
**Weiler,** Gerald E. 1928- *IntMPA 92*

**Weiler**, John Henry, Jr 1925- *AmMWSc 92*
**Weiler**, Joseph Ashby 1946- *WhoMW 92*
**Weiler**, Kurt Walter 1943- *AmMWSc 92*
**Weiler**, Lawrence Stanley 1942- *AmMWSc 92*
**Weiler**, Margaret Horton 1941- *AmMWSc 92*
**Weiler**, Paul Cronin 1939- *WhoAmL 92*
**Weiler**, Richard L 1945- *WhoIns 92*
**Weiler**, Roland R 1936- *AmMWSc 92*
**Weiler**, Scott Michael 1952- *WhoMW 92*
**Weiler**, Terence Gerard 1919- *Who 92*
**Weiler**, Thomas Joseph *WhoMW 92*
**Weiler**, Thomas Joseph 1949- *AmMWSc 92*
**Weiler**, William Alexander 1941- *AmMWSc 92*
**Weilert**, Ronald Lee 1948- *WhoMW 92*
**Weill**, Carol Edwin 1918- *AmMWSc 92*
**Weill**, Claudia *ReelWom*
**Weill**, Claudia 1947- *IntMPA 92*
**Weill**, Daniel Francis 1931- *AmMWSc 92*
**Weill**, Georges Gustave 1926- *AmMWSc 92*
**Weill**, Hans 1933- *AmMWSc 92*
**Weill**, Kurt 1900-1950 *BenetAL 91, EncTR 91 [port], FacFETw, NewAmDM*
**Weill**, Michel Alexandre D. *Who 92*
**Weill**, Patricia Gene 1939- *WhoFI 92*
**Weill**, Richard L. 1943- *WhoAmL 92*
**Weill**, Roger G. d1991 *NewYTBS 91*
**Weill**, Samuel, Jr. 1916- *WhoWest 92*
**Weill**, Sanford I. 1933- *IntWW 91, WhoFI 92*
**Weiller**, David Barry 1957- *WhoWest 92*
**Weiller**, Paul Annik 1933- *WhoFI 92*
**Weiller**, Paul-Louis 1893- *IntWW 91*
**Weiman**, Rita 1889-1954 *BenetAL 91*
**Weimann**, Ludwig Jan 1941- *AmMWSc 92*
**Weimar**, Virginia Lee 1922- *AmMWSc 92*
**Weimberg**, Ralph 1924- *AmMWSc 92*
**Weimer**, Bruce James 1952- *WhoWest 92*
**Weimer**, Constance Lounds 1947- *WhoMW 92*
**Weimer**, David 1919- *AmMWSc 92*
**Weimer**, F Carlin 1917- *AmMWSc 92*
**Weimer**, Ferne Lauraine 1950- *WhoMW 92*
**Weimer**, Franklin E *WhoAmP 91*
**Weimer**, Gary Wilfred 1944- *WhoMW 92*
**Weimer**, Henry Eben 1914- *AmMWSc 92*
**Weimer**, Jean Elaine 1932- *WhoMW 92*
**Weimer**, John Thomas 1930- *AmMWSc 92*
**Weimer**, Maryellen 1947- *ConAu 135*
**Weimer**, Paul Kessler 1914- *AmMWSc 92*
**Weimer**, Peter Dwight 1938- *WhoAmL 92, WhoFI 92*
**Weimer**, Richard Paul 1947- *WhoFI 92*
**Weimer**, Robert Fredrick 1940- *AmMWSc 92*
**Weimer**, Robert J 1926- *AmMWSc 92*
**Weimers**, Eric Harold 1958- *WhoAmL 92*
**Weimers**, Leigh Albert 1935- *WhoWest 92*
**Wein**, Albert W. d1991 *NewYTBS 91*
**Wein**, Bibi *DrAPF 91*
**Wein**, George Theodore 1925- *WhoEnt 92*
**Wein**, Howard J. 1950- *WhoAmL 92*
**Wein**, Ross Wallace 1940- *AmMWSc 92*
**Weinacht**, Richard Jay 1931- *AmMWSc 92*
**Weinbach**, Arthur Frederic 1943- *WhoFI 92*
**Weinbach**, Eugene Clayton 1919- *AmMWSc 92*
**Weinbach**, Lawrence Allen 1940- *WhoFI 92*
**Weinbaum**, Carl Martin 1937- *AmMWSc 92*
**Weinbaum**, George 1932- *AmMWSc 92*
**Weinbaum**, Sheldon 1937- *AmMWSc 92*
**Weinbaum**, Stanley G 1902-1935 *TwCSFW 91*
**Weinbaum**, William 1960- *WhoEnt 92*
**Weinberg**, Allan D. 1959- *WhoAmL 92*
**Weinberg**, Alvin M. 1915 *IntWW 91*
**Weinberg**, Alvin Martin 1915- *AmMWSc 92*
**Weinberg**, Barbara Bickerstaffe 1936- *WhoAmP 91*
**Weinberg**, Barbara Lee Huberman 1934- *AmMWSc 92*
**Weinberg**, Bernd 1940- *AmMWSc 92*
**Weinberg**, Crispin Bernard 1951- *AmMWSc 92*
**Weinberg**, Daniel I 1928- *AmMWSc 92*
**Weinberg**, David Burton 1948- *WhoAmL 92*
**Weinberg**, David Samuel 1938- *AmMWSc 92*
**Weinberg**, Donald Lewis 1931- *AmMWSc 92*
**Weinberg**, Elaine Joseph 1929- *WhoAmP 91*
**Weinberg**, Elbert d1991 *NewYTBS 91*
**Weinberg**, Elliot Carl 1932- *AmMWSc 92*
**Weinberg**, Elliot Hillel 1924- *AmMWSc 92*
**Weinberg**, Eric S 1942- *AmMWSc 92*
**Weinberg**, Erick James 1947- *AmMWSc 92*
**Weinberg**, Eugene David 1922- *AmMWSc 92*
**Weinberg**, Felix Jiri 1928- *IntWW 91, Who 92*
**Weinberg**, Florence M. 1933- *IntAu&W 91, WrDr 92*
**Weinberg**, Fred 1925- *AmMWSc 92*
**Weinberg**, H. Barbara *ConAu 134*
**Weinberg**, I Jack 1935- *AmMWSc 92*
**Weinberg**, Ira Jay 1959- *WhoWest 92*
**Weinberg**, Irving 1918- *AmMWSc 92*
**Weinberg**, Jeffrey J. 1948- *WhoAmL 92*
**Weinberg**, Jerry L 1931- *AmMWSc 92*
**Weinberg**, John Livingston 1925- *WhoFI 92*
**Weinberg**, Jonathan T. 1958- *WhoAmL 92*
**Weinberg**, Kerry *WrDr 92*
**Weinberg**, Louis 1919- *AmMWSc 92*
**Weinberg**, Louise *WhoAmL 92*
**Weinberg**, Marc Steven 1948- *AmMWSc 92*
**Weinberg**, Mark 1931- *Who 92*
**Weinberg**, Martyn S. 1940- *WhoEnt 92*
**Weinberg**, Matthew Basil 1934- *WhoAmL 92*
**Weinberg**, Meyer 1920- *WrDr 92*
**Weinberg**, Michael Allen 1953- *WhoRel 92*
**Weinberg**, Myron Simon 1930- *AmMWSc 92*
**Weinberg**, Norman 1920- *AmMWSc 92*
**Weinberg**, Paul David 1956- *WhoEnt 92*
**Weinberg**, Philip 1925- *AmMWSc 92*
**Weinberg**, Robert A 1942- *AmMWSc 92, IntWW 91*
**Weinberg**, Robert Leonard 1923- *WhoAmL 92*
**Weinberg**, Robert P 1955- *AmMWSc 92*
**Weinberg**, Roger 1931- *AmMWSc 92*
**Weinberg**, Roger David 1954- *WhoEnt 92*
**Weinberg**, Ronald Elliott 1941- *WhoFI 92*
**Weinberg**, Sidney B 1923- *AmMWSc 92*
**Weinberg**, Sidney David 1919- *WhoAmL 92*
**Weinberg**, Steven 1933- *AmMWSc 92, ConAu 36NR, FacFETw, IntWW 91, Who 92, WhoNob 90, WrDr 92*
**Weinberg**, Steven Marc 1952- *WhoAmL 92*
**Weinberg**, Susan C. *DrAPF 91*
**Weinberg**, William Henry 1944- *AmMWSc 92, WhoWest 92*
**Weinberger**, Alan David 1945- *WhoAmL 92, WhoFI 92*
**Weinberger**, Arnold 1924- *AmMWSc 92*
**Weinberger**, Caspar 1917- *AmPolLe*
**Weinberger**, Caspar W. 1917- *ConAu 133*
**Weinberger**, Caspar Willard 1917- *IntWW 91, Who 92, WhoAmP 91, WhoFI 92*
**Weinberger**, Charles Brian 1941- *AmMWSc 92*
**Weinberger**, Daniel R 1947- *AmMWSc 92*
**Weinberger**, Doreen Anne 1954- *AmMWSc 92*
**Weinberger**, Ed *WhoEnt 92*
**Weinberger**, Edward Bertram 1921- *AmMWSc 92*
**Weinberger**, Florence *DrAPF 91*
**Weinberger**, Hans Felix 1928- *AmMWSc 92*
**Weinberger**, Harold 1910- *AmMWSc 92*
**Weinberger**, Harold Paul 1947- *WhoAmL 92*
**Weinberger**, Harry 1924- *TwCPaSc*
**Weinberger**, Leon Joseph 1931- *WhoFI 92, WhoIns 92, WhoMW 92*
**Weinberger**, Leon Judah 1926- *WhoRel 92*
**Weinberger**, Leon Walter 1923- *AmMWSc 92*
**Weinberger**, Lynne Marsha 1955- *WhoWest 92*
**Weinberger**, Marc Robert 1950- *WhoWest 92*
**Weinberger**, Miles 1938- *AmMWSc 92*
**Weinberger**, Miro 1970- *ConAu 135*
**Weinberger**, Myron Hilmar 1937- *AmMWSc 92*
**Weinberger**, Norman Malcolm 1935- *AmMWSc 92*
**Weinberger**, Paul E. 1931-1983? *ConAu 134*
**Weinberger**, Pearl 1926- *AmMWSc 92*
**Weinberger**, Peter Henry 1950- *WhoAmL 92*
**Weinberger**, Peter Jay 1942- *AmMWSc 92*
**Weinberger**, Stanley Robert 1930- *WhoAmL 92*
**Weinberger**, Steven Elliott 1949- *AmMWSc 92*
**Weinberger**, Steven Eric 1960- *WhoAmL 92*
**Weinberger-Daniels** *LesBEnT 92*
**Weinblatt**, Charles Samuel 1952- *WhoMW 92*
**Weinblatt**, Mike 1929- *IntMPA 92*
**Weinblatt**, Stuart Gary 1952- *WhoRel 92*
**Weinbrandt**, Richard M 1944- *AmMWSc 92*
**Weincek**, David Alan 1965- *WhoEnt 92*
**Weindling**, Joachim I 1927- *AmMWSc 92*
**Weindruch**, Linda Sue 1956- *WhoAmL 92*
**Weinel**, William Harvey, III 1954- *WhoEnt 92*
**Weiner**, Alfred 1885-1964 *EncTR 91*
**Weiner**, Andrew 1949- *TwCSFW 91*
**Weiner**, Barry Jay 1948- *WhoFI 92*
**Weiner**, Brian Lewis 1945- *AmMWSc 92*
**Weiner**, Charles 1931- *AmMWSc 92, ConAu 134*
**Weiner**, Claire Zundell 1933- *WhoEnt 92*
**Weiner**, Daniel Lee 1950- *AmMWSc 92*
**Weiner**, Deborah Jane 1951- *WhoRel 92*
**Weiner**, Dora B. 1924- *WhoWest 92*
**Weiner**, Earl David 1939- *WhoAmL 92*
**Weiner**, Edmund Simon Christopher 1950- *Who 92*
**Weiner**, Elliot Alan 1943- *WhoWest 92*
**Weiner**, Eric L. 1954- *WhoMW 92*
**Weiner**, Eugene Robert 1928- *AmMWSc 92*
**Weiner**, Gerald Arne 1941- *WhoMW 92*
**Weiner**, Gerald B. 1944- *WhoEnt 92*
**Weiner**, Gerald T *WhoAmP 91*
**Weiner**, Gerry 1933- *IntWW 91*
**Weiner**, Gershon Ralph 1935- *WhoMW 92*
**Weiner**, Hannah *DrAPF 91*
**Weiner**, Hannah 1928- *IntAu&W 91*
**Weiner**, Harold 1925- *WhoAmP 91*
**Weiner**, Henri *IntAu&W 91X*
**Weiner**, Henry 1937- *AmMWSc 92*
**Weiner**, Herbert 1921- *AmMWSc 92*
**Weiner**, Howard Jacob 1937- *AmMWSc 92*
**Weiner**, Howard L. *DrAPF 91*
**Weiner**, Irwin M 1930- *AmMWSc 92*
**Weiner**, Jacob 1947- *AmMWSc 92*
**Weiner**, Jeffrey David 1956- *WhoMW 92*
**Weiner**, Jeffrey Stuart 1948- *WhoAmL 92*
**Weiner**, Jerome Harris 1923- *AmMWSc 92*
**Weiner**, Joel David 1936- *WhoFI 92*
**Weiner**, Joel Hirsch 1946- *AmMWSc 92*
**Weiner**, John 1943- *AmMWSc 92*
**Weiner**, Lawrence 1942- *WhoAmL 92*
**Weiner**, Lawrence Myron 1923- *AmMWSc 92*
**Weiner**, Lazar 1897-1982 *NewAmDM*
**Weiner**, Leo 1885-1960 *NewAmDM*
**Weiner**, Louis I 1913- *AmMWSc 92*
**Weiner**, Louis Max 1926- *AmMWSc 92*
**Weiner**, Mark Steven 1954- *WhoAmP 91*
**Weiner**, Matei 1933- *AmMWSc 92*
**Weiner**, Mervyn Lester 1922- *IntWW 91*
**Weiner**, Michael A. 1956- *WhoMW 92*
**Weiner**, Michael Joel 1955- *WhoEnt 92*
**Weiner**, Milton Lawrence 1921- *AmMWSc 92*
**Weiner**, Murray 1919- *AmMWSc 92*
**Weiner**, Myron 1943- *AmMWSc 92*
**Weiner**, Norman 1928- *AmMWSc 92, WhoWest 92*
**Weiner**, Patricia Hermann 1941- *WhoEnt 92*
**Weiner**, Paul I. *WhoAmL 92*
**Weiner**, Richard 1936- *AmMWSc 92*
**Weiner**, Richard D 1945- *AmMWSc 92*
**Weiner**, Richard H. 1949- *WhoAmL 92*
**Weiner**, Richard Ira 1940- *AmMWSc 92*
**Weiner**, Robert Allen 1940- *AmMWSc 92*
**Weiner**, Ronald Martin 1942- *AmMWSc 92*
**Weiner**, Sanford Alan 1946- *WhoAmL 92*
**Weiner**, Sharon Rose *WhoWest 92*
**Weiner**, Sigmund Tatar 1942- *WhoAmL 92*
**Weiner**, Stephen Douglas 1941- *AmMWSc 92*
**Weiner**, Steven Allan 1942- *AmMWSc 92*
**Weiner**, Steven R. 1950- *WhoWest 92*
**Weiner**, Stewart George 1945- *WhoWest 92*
**Weiner**, Sydell Sally 1947- *WhoEnt 92*
**Weiner**, Tim 1956- *ConAu 135*
**Weiner**, Walter Herman 1930- *WhoFI 92*
**Weiner**, Zane David 1953- *WhoEnt 92*
**Weinerman**, Chester *DrAPF 91*
**Weinert**, Ann Regan 1933- *WhoAmP 91*
**Weinert**, Hilary Ray 1958- *WhoAmL 92*
**Weinfeld**, Herbert 1921- *AmMWSc 92*
**Weinfeld**, Marsha Kash *DrAPF 91*
**Weinfield**, Henry *DrAPF 91*
**Weinfurter**, Daniel Joseph 1957- *WhoFI 92, WhoMW 92*
**Weinfurter**, John Joseph 1950- *WhoAmP 91*
**Weingarten**, Donald Henry 1945- *AmMWSc 92*
**Weingarten**, Norman C 1947- *AmMWSc 92*
**Weingarten**, Roger *DrAPF 91*
**Weingarten**, Saul Myer 1921- *WhoAmL 92*
**Weingarten**, Victor I 1931- *AmMWSc 92*
**Weingartner**, David Peter 1939- *AmMWSc 92*
**Weingartner**, Felix 1863-1942 *FacFETw, NewAmDM*
**Weingartner**, Hans Martin 1929- *WhoFI 92*
**Weingartner**, Herbert 1935- *AmMWSc 92*
**Weingartner**, Karl Ernst *AmMWSc 92*
**Weinger**, Steven Murray 1954- *WhoAmL 92*
**Weingold**, Allan Byrne 1930- *AmMWSc 92*
**Weingrad**, Stephen Aaron 1939- *WhoAmL 92*
**Weingrod**, Herschel 1947- *IntMPA 92*
**Weinhauer**, Carlin Eugene 1939- *WhoRel 92*
**Weinhauer**, William Gillette 1924- *WhoRel 92*
**Weinheber**, Josef 1892-1945 *EncTR 91 [port]*
**Weinheimer**, Andrew John 1953- *WhoWest 92*
**Weinhoeft**, John Joseph 1952- *WhoMW 92*
**Weinhold**, Albert Raymond 1931- *AmMWSc 92, WhoWest 92*
**Weinhold**, Donald L, Jr 1946- *WhoAmP 91*
**Weinhold**, Paul Allen 1935- *AmMWSc 92*
**Weinholzer**, Bob *WhoAmP 91*
**Weinhouse**, Sidney 1909- *AmMWSc 92*
**Weinig**, Richard Arthur 1940- *WhoAmL 92*
**Weinig**, Sheldon 1928- *AmMWSc 92*
**Weininger**, Stephen Joel 1937- *AmMWSc 92*
**Weinkam**, Lois Anne 1942- *WhoAmP 91*
**Weinkam**, Robert Joseph 1942- *AmMWSc 92*
**Weinkauf**, David Shelley 1940- *WhoEnt 92*
**Weinlander**, Max Martin 1917- *WhoMW 92*
**Weinlein**, Gregg Thomas *DrAPF 91*
**Weinman**, Glenn Alan 1955- *WhoAmL 92*
**Weinman**, Irving 1937- *WrDr 92*
**Weinman**, Paul *DrAPF 91*
**Weinman**, Roberta Sue 1945- *WhoFI 92*
**Weinman**, William Edward 1956- *WhoFI 92*
**Weinmann**, Clarence Jacob 1925- *AmMWSc 92*
**Weinmann**, John Giffen 1928- *WhoAmL 92, WhoAmP 91*
**Weinmann**, Richard Adrian 1917- *WhoAmL 92*
**Weinmann**, Robert Lewis 1935- *WhoWest 92*
**Weinraub**, Alan P 1947- *WhoIns 92*
**Weinraub**, Alan Paul 1947- *WhoFI 92*
**Weinreb**, Alan H. 1958- *WhoAmL 92*
**Weinreb**, Eva Lurie *AmMWSc 92*
**Weinreb**, Ilene Spack 1931- *WhoAmP 91*
**Weinreb**, Lloyd Lobell 1936- *WhoAmL 92*
**Weinreb**, Michael Philip 1939- *AmMWSc 92*
**Weinreb**, Robert Neal 1949- *AmMWSc 92*
**Weinreb**, Sander 1936- *AmMWSc 92*
**Weinreb**, Steven Martin 1941- *AmMWSc 92*
**Weinreich**, Daniel 1942- *AmMWSc 92*
**Weinreich**, Gabriel 1928- *AmMWSc 92*
**Weinrib**, Leonard *LesBEnT 92*
**Weinrich**, A. K. H. 1933- *WrDr 92*
**Weinrich**, Alan Jeffrey 1953- *AmMWSc 92*
**Weinrich**, Carl d1991 *NewYTBS 91*
**Weinrich**, James D 1950- *AmMWSc 92*
**Weinrich**, James Donald 1950- *WhoWest 92*
**Weinrich**, Marcel 1927- *AmMWSc 92*
**Weinroth**, Robert Stuart 1952- *WhoAmL 92*
**Weinryb**, Ira 1940- *AmMWSc 92*
**Weinsberg**, Edgar James 1944- *WhoRel 92*
**Weinschel**, Alan Jay 1946- *WhoAmL 92*
**Weinshank**, Donald Jerome 1937- *AmMWSc 92*
**Weinshenker**, Ned Martin 1942- *AmMWSc 92*
**Weinshienk**, Zita Leeson 1933- *WhoAmL 92, WhoWest 92*
**Weinshilboum**, Richard Merle 1940- *AmMWSc 92*
**Weinsier**, Roland Louis *AmMWSc 92*
**Weinstein**, Abbott Samson 1924- *AmMWSc 92*
**Weinstein**, Adam Cassel 1960- *WhoWest 92*
**Weinstein**, Alan David 1943- *AmMWSc 92*
**Weinstein**, Alan Edward 1945- *WhoAmL 92*
**Weinstein**, Alan Ira 1940- *AmMWSc 92*
**Weinstein**, Alan Jay 1957- *AmMWSc 92*
**Weinstein**, Alexander 1893- *AmMWSc 92*
**Weinstein**, Allan M. 1945- *WhoWest 92*
**Weinstein**, Allen 1937- *WrDr 92*
**Weinstein**, Alvin Elliot 1943- *WhoMW 92*
**Weinstein**, Alvin Seymour 1928- *AmMWSc 92, WhoAmL 92*

**Weinstein**, Arnold 1927- *WrDr 92*
**Weinstein**, Arnold Abraham 1927- *WhoEnt 92*
**Weinstein**, Arthur 1944- *AmMWSc 92*
**Weinstein**, Arthur Howard 1924- *AmMWSc 92*
**Weinstein**, Barry Alan 1943- *WhoMW 92*
**Weinstein**, Bernard Allen 1946- *AmMWSc 92*
**Weinstein**, Berthold Werner 1947- *AmMWSc 92*
**Weinstein**, Constance de Courcy 1924- *AmMWSc 92*
**Weinstein**, Curt David 1951- *AmMWSc 92*
**Weinstein**, David Alan 1951- *AmMWSc 92*
**Weinstein**, Edward Michael 1947- *WhoFI 92*
**Weinstein**, George 1924- *WhoMW 92*
**Weinstein**, George 1928- *WhoAmL 92*
**Weinstein**, Gregory 1864-1931 *DcAmImH*
**Weinstein**, Hannah 1911-1984 *ReelWom*
**Weinstein**, Harel 1945- *AmMWSc 92*
**Weinstein**, Harris *WhoAmL 92*
**Weinstein**, Helene E 1952- *WhoAmP 91*
**Weinstein**, Henry T 1924- *IntMPA 92*
**Weinstein**, Herbert 1933- *AmMWSc 92*
**Weinstein**, Howard *DrAPF 91*
**Weinstein**, Howard 1927- *AmMWSc 92*
**Weinstein**, Hyman Gabriel 1920- *AmMWSc 92*
**Weinstein**, I Bernard 1930- *AmMWSc 92*
**Weinstein**, Ira 1928- *AmMWSc 92*
**Weinstein**, Iram J 1936- *AmMWSc 92*
**Weinstein**, Irwin M 1926- *AmMWSc 92, IntWW 91*
**Weinstein**, Jack B. 1921- *WhoAmL 92*
**Weinstein**, Jeff *DrAPF 91*
**Weinstein**, Jeremy S 1950- *WhoAmP 91*
**Weinstein**, Jeremy Saul 1944- *AmMWSc 92*
**Weinstein**, Jerome William 1942- *WhoFI 92*
**Weinstein**, Joseph 1862?-1917 *BiInAmS*
**Weinstein**, Judith 1927- *WhoWest 92*
**Weinstein**, Leonard Harlan 1926- *AmMWSc 92*
**Weinstein**, Lewis H. 1905- *WhoAmL 92*
**Weinstein**, Louis 1909- *AmMWSc 92*
**Weinstein**, Mark Allen 1937- *WrDr 92*
**Weinstein**, Mark Joel 1945- *AmMWSc 92*
**Weinstein**, Mark Michael 1942- *WhoAmL 92, WhoEnt 92, WhoFI 92*
**Weinstein**, Marvin 1942- *AmMWSc 92*
**Weinstein**, Marvin Stanley 1927- *AmMWSc 92*
**Weinstein**, Merrick Charles 1959- *WhoAmL 92*
**Weinstein**, Norman *DrAPF 91*
**Weinstein**, Norman J 1929- *AmMWSc 92*
**Weinstein**, Paul 1940- *WhoAmL 92*
**Weinstein**, Paul P 1919- *AmMWSc 92*
**Weinstein**, Paul Peter 1919- *WhoMW 92*
**Weinstein**, Paula 1945- *IntMPA 92*
**Weinstein**, Peter M *WhoAmP 91*
**Weinstein**, Robert 1949- *AmMWSc 92*
**Weinstein**, Ronald S 1938- *AmMWSc 92*
**Weinstein**, Roy 1927- *AmMWSc 92*
**Weinstein**, Roy 1943- *WhoFI 92*
**Weinstein**, Sam 1916- *AmMWSc 92*
**Weinstein**, Sharon M. 1944- *WhoMW 92*
**Weinstein**, Stanley 1929- *WhoRel 92*
**Weinstein**, Stanley Edwin 1942- *AmMWSc 92*
**Weinstein**, Stanley Howard 1948- *WhoMW 92*
**Weinstein**, Stephen B 1938- *AmMWSc 92*
**Weinstein**, Stephen Henry 1937- *AmMWSc 92*
**Weinstein**, Stephen Saul 1939- *WhoAmL 92*
**Weinstein**, William Joseph 1917- *WhoAmL 92*
**Weinstine**, Robert R. 1944- *WhoAmL 92*
**Weinstock** *Who 92*
**Weinstock**, Baron 1924- *IntWW 91, Who 92*
**Weinstock**, Alfred 1939- *AmMWSc 92*
**Weinstock**, Barnet Mordecai 1940- *AmMWSc 92*
**Weinstock**, Eleanor 1929- *WhoAmP 91*
**Weinstock**, Frank Joseph 1933- *WhoMW 92*
**Weinstock**, George A. 1937- *WhoWest 92*
**Weinstock**, George David 1937- *WhoFI 92*
**Weinstock**, Gloria 1946- *WhoEnt 92*
**Weinstock**, Grace Evangeline 1904- *WhoMW 92*
**Weinstock**, Harold 1925- *WhoAmL 92*
**Weinstock**, Harold 1934- *AmMWSc 92*
**Weinstock**, Irwin Morton 1925- *AmMWSc 92*
**Weinstock**, Jerome 1933- *AmMWSc 92*
**Weinstock**, Joel Vincent *AmMWSc 92*
**Weinstock**, Joseph 1928- *AmMWSc 92*
**Weinstock**, Leonard M 1927- *AmMWSc 92*
**Weinstock**, Manuel 1927- *AmMWSc 92*
**Weinstock**, Robert 1919- *AmMWSc 92, WhoMW 92*
**Weinstock**, W 1925- *AmMWSc 92*
**Weinswig**, Melvin H 1935- *AmMWSc 92*
**Weintraub**, Arden Loren 1949- *WhoWest 92*
**Weintraub**, Bruce Dale 1940- *AmMWSc 92*
**Weintraub**, Dov 1926- *WrDr 92*
**Weintraub**, Dov 1926-1985 *ConAu 36NR*
**Weintraub**, Fred 1928- *IntMPA 92*
**Weintraub**, Harold M 1945- *AmMWSc 92*
**Weintraub**, Herbert D 1930- *AmMWSc 92*
**Weintraub**, Herschel Jonathan R 1948- *AmMWSc 92*
**Weintraub**, J. *DrAPF 91*
**Weintraub**, Jay Sigmund 1962- *WhoFI 92*
**Weintraub**, Jeff 1949- *WhoAmL 92*
**Weintraub**, Jerry *WhoEnt 92A*
**Weintraub**, Jerry 1937- *IntMPA 92*
**Weintraub**, Joel D 1942- *AmMWSc 92*
**Weintraub**, Karl Joachim 1924- *WhoMW 92*
**Weintraub**, Leonard 1926- *AmMWSc 92*
**Weintraub**, Lester 1924- *AmMWSc 92*
**Weintraub**, Lewis Robert 1934- *AmMWSc 92*
**Weintraub**, Linda 1942- *ConAu 135*
**Weintraub**, Lori 1952- *WhoEnt 92*
**Weintraub**, Marvin 1924- *AmMWSc 92*
**Weintraub**, Philip 1947- *WhoFI 92*
**Weintraub**, Philip Marvin 1939- *AmMWSc 92*
**Weintraub**, Robert Louis 1912- *AmMWSc 92*
**Weintraub**, Samuel Joseph 1917- *WhoAmL 92*
**Weintraub**, Sidney 1922- *WrDr 92*
**Weintraub**, Simkha Yitzkhak 1953- *WhoRel 92*
**Weintraub**, Stanley 1929- *DcLB 111 [port], IntAu&W 91, WhoEnt 92, WrDr 92*
**Weintraub**, Sy 1923- *IntMPA 92*
**Weintz**, Jacob Frederick, Jr. 1926- *WhoFI 92*
**Weinwurm**, George Felix 1935- *WhoFI 92*
**Weiny**, George Azem 1933- *WhoWest 92*
**Weinzaepflen**, Catherine 1946- *IntAu&W 91*
**Weinzetl**, Lawrence Martin 1943- *WhoMW 92*
**Weinzierl**, Thomas Allen 1951- *WhoMW 92*
**Weinzimmer**, Fred 1925- *AmMWSc 92*
**Weinzweig**, Avrum Israel 1926- *AmMWSc 92*
**Weinzweig**, John 1913- *NewAmDM*
**Weipers**, William Lee d1990 *Who 92N*
**Weipert**, Eugene Allen 1931- *AmMWSc 92*
**Weir** *Who 92*
**Weir**, Lord 1931- *Who 92*
**Weir**, Viscount 1933- *Who 92*
**Weir**, Alexander, Jr 1922- *AmMWSc 92, WhoFI 92, WhoWest 92*
**Weir**, Alexander Fortune Rose 1928- *Who 92*
**Weir**, Andrew John 1919- *Who 92*
**Weir**, Bruce Spencer 1943- *AmMWSc 92*
**Weir**, Carol Jean 1929- *WhoMW 92*
**Weir**, Cecil James Mullo 1897- *Who 92*
**Weir**, David Bruce *Who 92*
**Weir**, Dorothy Pauline 1939- *WhoMW 92*
**Weir**, Edward Earl, II 1945- *AmMWSc 92*
**Weir**, Edward Kenneth 1943- *AmMWSc 92*
**Weir**, Gillian Constance 1941- *IntWW 91, Who 92*
**Weir**, Ian Ralph 1956- *IntAu&W 91*
**Weir**, James, Jr 1856-1906 *BiInAmS*
**Weir**, James Henry, III 1932- *AmMWSc 92*
**Weir**, James Robert, Jr 1932- *AmMWSc 92*
**Weir**, Jim Dale 1956- *WhoWest 92*
**Weir**, Joan Sherman 1928- *IntAu&W 91*
**Weir**, John Arnold 1916- *AmMWSc 92*
**Weir**, Judith 1954- *ConCom 92, Who 92*
**Weir**, Julian Paul 1923- *WhoAmP 91*
**Weir**, La Vada *WrDr 92*
**Weir**, Maurice Dean 1939- *WhoWest 92*
**Weir**, Michael 1925- *Who 92*
**Weir**, Michael H 1924- *WhoAmP 91*
**Weir**, Michael Ross 1942- *AmMWSc 92, WhoWest 92*
**Weir**, Molly 1920- *WrDr 92*
**Weir**, Morton Webster 1934- *WhoMW 92*
**Weir**, Peter 1944- *FacFETw, IntDcF 2-2, IntMPA 92*
**Weir**, Peter Frank 1933- *WhoAmL 92*
**Weir**, Peter Lindsay 1944- *IntWW 91, Who 92, WhoEnt 92*
**Weir**, Richard Stanton 1933- *Who 92*
**Weir**, Robert H. 1922- *WhoAmL 92*
**Weir**, Robert James, Jr 1924- *AmMWSc 92*
**Weir**, Roderick 1927- *Who 92*
**Weir**, Ronald Blackwood 1944- *WrDr 92*
**Weir**, Ronald Douglas 1941- *AmMWSc 92*
**Weir**, Rosemary 1905- *WrDr 92*
**Weir**, Sheila A. 1956- *WhoAmL 92*
**Weir**, Stuart Peter 1938- *IntWW 91, Who 92*
**Weir**, Thomas Charles 1933- *WhoFI 92*
**Weir**, Thomas Raymond 1945- *WhoWest 92*
**Weir**, William Carl 1919- *AmMWSc 92*
**Weir**, William David 1941- *AmMWSc 92*
**Weir**, William P. 1940- *WhoAmL 92*
**Weir**, William Thomas 1931- *AmMWSc 92*
**Weires**, Richard William, Jr 1944- *AmMWSc 92*
**Weirich**, Gunter Friedrich 1934- *AmMWSc 92*
**Weirich**, Walter Edward 1938- *AmMWSc 92*
**Weis**, Dale Stern 1924- *AmMWSc 92*
**Weis**, Darlene Marie 1937- *WhoAmP 91*
**Weis**, Don 1922- *IntMPA 92*
**Weis**, Earl August 1923- *WhoRel 92*
**Weis**, Eberhard 1925- *IntWW 91*
**Weis**, Jack 1932- *IntAu&W 91, IntMPA 92*
**Weis**, James R. 1932- *WhoEnt 92*
**Weis**, Jerry Samuel 1935- *AmMWSc 92*
**Weis**, Judith Shulman 1941- *AmMWSc 92*
**Weis**, Konrad Max 1928- *WhoFI 92*
**Weis**, Laura Visser 1961- *WhoAmL 92*
**Weis**, Leonard Walter 1923- *AmMWSc 92*
**Weis**, Margaret 1948- *ConAu 34NR*
**Weis**, Michael Bernell 1961- *WhoFI 92*
**Weis**, Paul Lester 1922- *AmMWSc 92*
**Weis**, Peddrick 1938- *AmMWSc 92*
**Weis**, R. *DrAPF 91*
**Weis**, Robert E 1918- *AmMWSc 92*
**Weisbach**, Jerry Arnold 1933- *AmMWSc 92*
**Weisbard**, Alan J. 1950- *WhoAmL 92*
**Weisbart**, Melvin 1938- *AmMWSc 92*
**Weisbaum**, Earl 1930- *WhoAmL 92*
**Weisbecker**, Henry B 1925- *AmMWSc 92*
**Weisberg**, Arthur 1931- *NewAmDM*
**Weisberg**, David Charles 1938- *WhoAmL 92*
**Weisberg**, Herbert 1931- *AmMWSc 92*
**Weisberg**, Joseph 1937- *WrDr 92*
**Weisberg**, Joseph Simpson 1937- *AmMWSc 92*
**Weisberg**, Leonard R. 1929- *WhoMW 92*
**Weisberg**, Richard Charbourn 1952- *WhoAmL 92*
**Weisberg**, Robert Francis 1950- *WhoFI 92*
**Weisberg**, Robert H 1947- *AmMWSc 92*
**Weisberg**, Ruth Maxine 1956- *WhoEnt 92*
**Weisberg**, Sanford *AmMWSc 92*
**Weisberg**, Seymour William 1910- *WhoMW 92*
**Weisberg**, Stephen Barry 1954- *AmMWSc 92*
**Weisberger**, Barbara 1926- *WhoEnt 92*
**Weisberger**, Joseph R 1920- *WhoAmP 91*
**Weisberger**, Joseph Robert 1920- *WhoAmL 92*
**Weisberger**, William I 1937- *AmMWSc 92*
**Weisblat**, David Irwin 1916- *AmMWSc 92*
**Weisbord**, Norman Edward 1901- *AmMWSc 92*
**Weisbrod**, Burton A. 1931- *IntWW 91*
**Weisbrod**, Ken 1957- *WhoFI 92*
**Weisbrodt**, Norman William 1942- *AmMWSc 92*
**Weisbrot**, David R 1931- *AmMWSc 92*
**Weisbroth**, Steven H 1934- *AmMWSc 92*
**Weisbruch**, Craig Dennis 1949- *WhoFI 92*
**Weisburd**, Steven I. 1949- *WhoAmL 92*
**Weisburger**, Elizabeth Kreiser 1924- *AmMWSc 92*
**Weisburger**, John Hans 1921- *AmMWSc 92*
**Weise**, Charles Martin 1926- *AmMWSc 92*
**Weise**, Jurgen Karl 1937- *AmMWSc 92*
**Weise**, Richard Henry 1935- *WhoAmL 92*
**Weise**, Richard Walter 1944- *WhoEnt 92*
**Weise**, Robert Lewis 1945- *WhoAmP 91*
**Weisel**, George Ferdinand, Jr 1915- *AmMWSc 92*
**Weisenberg**, Harvey 1933- *WhoAmP 91*
**Weisenberg**, Richard Charles 1941- *AmMWSc 92*
**Weisenberger**, Brockton Lamar 1933- *WhoMW 92*
**Weisenberger**, Richard 1938- *WhoAmP 91*
**Weisenborn**, Frank L 1925- *AmMWSc 92*
**Weisenburger**, Theodore M. 1930- *WhoAmL 92, WhoWest 92*
**Weisenburger**, Walter Gerard 1957- *WhoMW 92*
**Weisend**, Martha B 1931- *WhoAmP 91*
**Weisengoff**, Paul Edmund 1932- *WhoAmP 91*
**Weiser**, Alan 1955- *AmMWSc 92*
**Weiser**, Conrad John 1935- *AmMWSc 92*
**Weiser**, Dan 1933- *AmMWSc 92, WhoAmP 91*
**Weiser**, Daniel Jacob 1959- *WhoAmL 92*
**Weiser**, David W 1921- *AmMWSc 92*
**Weiser**, Frank Alan 1953- *WhoAmL 92, WhoWest 92*
**Weiser**, Irving 1947- *WhoFI 92*
**Weiser**, Kurt 1924- *AmMWSc 92*
**Weiser**, Mark David 1952- *WhoWest 92*
**Weiser**, Martin Jay 1943- *WhoAmL 92*
**Weiser**, Norman Sidney 1919- *WhoEnt 92, WhoFI 92*
**Weiser**, Philip Craig 1941- *AmMWSc 92*
**Weiser**, Robert B 1927- *AmMWSc 92*
**Weiser**, Russel Shively 1906- *AmMWSc 92*
**Weiser**, Stanley 1949- *WhoEnt 92*
**Weiser**, Terry Lee 1954- *WhoAmL 92*
**Weiser**, William Elwood 1954- *WhoAmP 91*
**Weisert**, Kent Albert Frederick 1949- *WhoAmL 92, WhoFI 92*
**Weisert**, Lee Nansteel 1949- *WhoEnt 92*
**Weisfeld**, Glenn Ellis 1943- *WhoMW 92*
**Weisfeld**, Lewis Bernard 1929- *AmMWSc 92*
**Weisfeld**, Sheldon 1946- *WhoAmL 92*
**Weisfeld**, Zelma Hope 1931- *WhoEnt 92*
**Weisfeldt**, Myron Lee 1940- *AmMWSc 92*
**Weisgall**, Hugo 1912- *NewAmDM*
**Weisgall**, Jonathan Michael 1949- *WhoAmL 92*
**Weisgard**, Leonard 1916- *BenetAL 91*
**Weisgerber**, David Wendelin 1938- *AmMWSc 92*
**Weisgerber**, George Austin 1918- *AmMWSc 92*
**Weisgerber**, William Denny 1930- *WhoAmP 91*
**Weisgraber**, Karl Heinrich 1941- *AmMWSc 92*
**Weishaus**, Joel *DrAPF 91*
**Weisheit**, Dirk Allen 1958- *WhoWest 92*
**Weisheit**, Jon Carleton 1944- *AmMWSc 92*
**Weisiger**, Joyce Michelle 1950- *WhoEnt 92*
**Weiskel**, Catherine Lacny 1950- *WhoEnt 92*
**Weiskopf**, William Harvard 1938- *WhoFI 92, WhoWest 92*
**Weiskrantz**, Lawrence 1926- *IntWW 91, Who 92*
**Weisleder**, David 1939- *AmMWSc 92*
**Weisler**, Leonard 1912- *AmMWSc 92*
**Weislow**, Owen Stuart 1938- *AmMWSc 92*
**Weisman**, Ann E. *DrAPF 91*
**Weisman**, Ann Elisabeth 1948- *WhoEnt 92*
**Weisman**, Douglas Marc 1956- *WhoEnt 92*
**Weisman**, Gary Raymond 1949- *AmMWSc 92*
**Weisman**, Harold 1928- *AmMWSc 92*
**Weisman**, Harvey 1927- *AmMWSc 92*
**Weisman**, James Lewis 1938- *WhoAmL 92*
**Weisman**, Joel 1928- *AmMWSc 92, WhoMW 92*
**Weisman**, Malcolm *Who 92*
**Weisman**, Marcia Simon d1991 *NewYTBS 91*
**Weisman**, Martin Dwain 1958- *WhoWest 92*
**Weisman**, Martin Jerome 1930- *WhoWest 92*
**Weisman**, Paul Howard 1957- *WhoAmL 92*
**Weisman**, R Bruce 1950- *AmMWSc 92*
**Weisman**, Robert A 1936- *AmMWSc 92*
**Weisman**, Robert Evans 1950- *WhoWest 92*
**Weisman**, Russell 1922- *AmMWSc 92*
**Weisman**, Stewart 1955- *WhoAmL 92*
**Weismann**, Donald L. 1914- *WrDr 92*
**Weismann**, Theodore James 1930- *AmMWSc 92*
**Weismantel**, Gregory Nelson 1940- *WhoFI 92, WhoMW 92*
**Weismantel**, Leo 1888-1962 *EncTR 91 [port]*
**Weismantle**, Peter Anthony 1950- *WhoMW 92*
**Weismehl**, Ronald 1939- *WhoMW 92*
**Weismeyer**, Richard Wayne 1943- *WhoWest 92*
**Weismiller**, David R. 1943- *WhoMW 92*
**Weismiller**, Richard A 1942- *AmMWSc 92*
**Weismuller**, Thomas Paul 1949- *WhoWest 92*
**Weisner**, Joan R 1950- *WhoAmP 91*
**Weisner**, Kenneth *DrAPF 91*
**Weispfenning**, John Thomas 1960- *WhoEnt 92*
**Weiss**, Adolph 1891-1971 *NewAmDM*
**Weiss**, Alan 1955- *AmMWSc 92*
**Weiss**, Alan Michael 1945- *WhoAmL 92*
**Weiss**, Aline Pollitzer d1991 *NewYTBS 91*
**Weiss**, Althea McNish *Who 92*
**Weiss**, Alvin H 1928- *AmMWSc 92*
**Weiss**, Andre 1952- *WhoFI 92*
**Weiss**, Andrew Murray 1947- *WhoFI 92*
**Weiss**, Andrew W 1930- *AmMWSc 92*
**Weiss**, Ann E. 1943- *SmATA 13AS [port]*
**Weiss**, Anthony O. 1928- *WhoMW 92*
**Weiss**, Armand Berl 1931- *WhoFI 92*
**Weiss**, Arnold Hans 1924- *WhoAmL 92*
**Weiss**, Arnold M 1933- *WhoAmP 91*
**Weiss**, Arthur Jacobs 1925- *AmMWSc 92*

**Weiss**, Benjamin 1922- *AmMWSc 92*
**Weiss**, Bernard 1925- *AmMWSc 92*
**Weiss**, Bernard 1936- *AmMWSc 92*
**Weiss**, Bernard 1943- *WhoWest 92*
**Weiss**, Bill 1955- *WhoEnt 92*
**Weiss**, Brett David 1959- *WhoAmL 92*
**Weiss**, Brian 1945- *WhoAmL 92, WhoFI 92*
**Weiss**, C Dennis 1939- *AmMWSc 92*
**Weiss**, Caryl P. 1951- *WhoEnt 92*
**Weiss**, Celia Stinebaugh 1948- *WhoEnt 92*
**Weiss**, Charles, Jr 1937- *AmMWSc 92*
**Weiss**, Charles Frederick 1921- *AmMWSc 92*
**Weiss**, Charles Frederick 1939- *WhoWest 92*
**Weiss**, Charles Karl 1933- *WhoRel 92*
**Weiss**, Charles Manuel 1918- *AmMWSc 92*
**Weiss**, Craig 1956- *WhoWest 92*
**Weiss**, Daniel Leigh 1923- *AmMWSc 92*
**Weiss**, David 1928- *WhoRel 92*
**Weiss**, David Ansel 1922- *WhoFI 92*
**Weiss**, David Edward 1947- *WhoEnt 92*
**Weiss**, David John 1941- *WhoEnt 92*
**Weiss**, David Raymond 1948- *WhoAmL 92*
**Weiss**, David Steven 1944- *AmMWSc 92*
**Weiss**, David Walter 1927- *AmMWSc 92*
**Weiss**, David William 1928- *WhoEnt 92*
**Weiss**, Debra Nancy 1954- *WhoEnt 92*
**Weiss**, Debra S. 1953- *WhoMW 92*
**Weiss**, Denis Anthony 1942- *WhoMW 92*
**Weiss**, Dennis 1940- *AmMWSc 92*
**Weiss**, Donald Herbert 1936- *WhoMW 92*
**Weiss**, Douglas Eugene 1945- *AmMWSc 92*
**Weiss**, Earle Burton 1932- *AmMWSc 92*
**Weiss**, Ed, Jr. *WhoBlA 92*
**Weiss**, Edward Abraham 1931- *WhoAmL 92*
**Weiss**, Edwin 1927- *AmMWSc 92*
**Weiss**, Elaine Carol 1958- *WhoAmL 92*
**Weiss**, Ellen Covner 1947- *WhoAmL 92*
**Weiss**, Elliott B. 1946- *WhoAmL 92*
**Weiss**, Emilio 1918- *AmMWSc 92*
**Weiss**, Eugene 1928- *WhoAmP 91*
**Weiss**, Eva 1919- *WhoAmP 91*
**Weiss**, Fred Geoffrey 1941- *WhoFI 92*
**Weiss**, Fred Toby 1916- *AmMWSc 92*
**Weiss**, Fredric Norman 1949- *WhoEnt 92*
**Weiss**, Gary Bruce 1944- *AmMWSc 92*
**Weiss**, George B 1935- *AmMWSc 92*
**Weiss**, George Herbert 1930- *AmMWSc 92*
**Weiss**, George M 1895-1972 *FacFETw*
**Weiss**, Gerald S 1934- *AmMWSc 92*
**Weiss**, Gerson 1939- *AmMWSc 92*
**Weiss**, Glenn P. 1961- *WhoEnt 92*
**Weiss**, Guido Leopold 1928- *AmMWSc 92, WhoMW 92*
**Weiss**, Harlan Lee 1941- *WhoAmL 92*
**Weiss**, Harold Gilbert 1923- *AmMWSc 92*
**Weiss**, Harold S. 1922- *WhoMW 92*
**Weiss**, Harold Samuel 1922- *AmMWSc 92*
**Weiss**, Harry Joseph 1923- *AmMWSc 92*
**Weiss**, Harvey Jerome 1929- *AmMWSc 92*
**Weiss**, Harvey Richard 1943- *AmMWSc 92*
**Weiss**, Henry Allen 1947- *WhoWest 92*
**Weiss**, Herbert A. 1952- *WhoAmL 92*
**Weiss**, Herbert Klemm 1917- *AmMWSc 92, WhoWest 92*
**Weiss**, Herbert V 1921- *AmMWSc 92*
**Weiss**, Howard A. *WhoEnt 92*
**Weiss**, Ira Paul 1942- *AmMWSc 92*
**Weiss**, Irma Tuck 1913- *AmMWSc 92*
**Weiss**, Irving *DrAPF 91*
**Weiss**, Irving 1919- *AmMWSc 92*
**Weiss**, Irving Norman 1937- *WhoFI 92*
**Weiss**, Jack Meyar 1947- *WhoAmL 92*
**Weiss**, James Allyn 1943- *AmMWSc 92*
**Weiss**, James Michael 1946- *WhoFI 92*
**Weiss**, James Moses Aaron 1921- *AmMWSc 92*
**Weiss**, James Owen 1931- *AmMWSc 92*
**Weiss**, James Robert 1949- *WhoAmL 92*
**Weiss**, Jaqueline Shachter 1926- *SmATA 65 [port]*
**Weiss**, Jason Lee *DrAPF 91*
**Weiss**, Jay M 1941- *AmMWSc 92*
**Weiss**, Jeffrey Martin 1944- *AmMWSc 92*
**Weiss**, Jerald Aubrey 1922- *AmMWSc 92*
**Weiss**, Jerome 1922- *AmMWSc 92*
**Weiss**, Jiri 1913- *IntDcF 2-2 [port]*
**Weiss**, Joel Edwin 1953- *WhoEnt 92*
**Weiss**, John Carroll, III 1948- *WhoFI 92*
**Weiss**, John Jay 1953- *AmMWSc 92*
**Weiss**, Jonas 1934- *AmMWSc 92*
**Weiss**, Jonathan David 1954- *WhoWest 92*
**Weiss**, Joseph Francis 1940- *AmMWSc 92*
**Weiss**, Joseph Henry, Jr 1943- *WhoAmP 91*
**Weiss**, Joseph Jacob 1934- *AmMWSc 92*
**Weiss**, Joseph Samson 1941- *WhoFI 92*
**Weiss**, Joyce Lacey 1941- *WhoBlA 92*
**Weiss**, Karl H 1926- *AmMWSc 92*
**Weiss**, Ken 1948- *WhoEnt 92*
**Weiss**, Kenneth Jay 1941- *WhoRel 92*
**Weiss**, Kenneth Monrad 1941- *AmMWSc 92*
**Weiss**, Klaudiusz Robert 1944- *AmMWSc 92*
**Weiss**, Laurence S 1919- *WhoAmP 91*
**Weiss**, Lawrence H 1938- *AmMWSc 92*
**Weiss**, Lawrence N. 1942- *WhoAmL 92*
**Weiss**, Lawrence Robert 1937- *WhoFI 92, WhoWest 92*
**Weiss**, Leon 1925- *AmMWSc 92*
**Weiss**, Leonard 1928- *AmMWSc 92*
**Weiss**, Leonard 1934- *AmMWSc 92*
**Weiss**, Leonard Winchell 1925- *WhoMW 92*
**Weiss**, Lionel Edward 1927- *AmMWSc 92*
**Weiss**, Lionel Ira 1923- *AmMWSc 92*
**Weiss**, Louis Charles 1925- *AmMWSc 92*
**Weiss**, Malcolm Charles 1956- *WhoAmL 92*
**Weiss**, Malcolm Pickett 1921- *AmMWSc 92*
**Weiss**, Manuel Martin 1952- *WhoAmL 92*
**Weiss**, Mark *DrAPF 91*
**Weiss**, Mark Alan 1953- *WhoEnt 92*
**Weiss**, Mark Anschel 1937- *WhoAmL 92*
**Weiss**, Mark Lawrence 1945- *AmMWSc 92, WhoMW 92*
**Weiss**, Martin 1919- *AmMWSc 92*
**Weiss**, Martin E. 1926- *WhoMW 92*
**Weiss**, Martin George 1911- *AmMWSc 92*
**Weiss**, Martin Harvey 1939- *WhoWest 92*
**Weiss**, Martin Joseph 1923- *AmMWSc 92*
**Weiss**, Marvin 1914- *AmMWSc 92*
**Weiss**, Marvin 1929- *WhoAmL 92*
**Weiss**, Max Leslie 1933- *AmMWSc 92*
**Weiss**, Max Tibor 1922- *AmMWSc 92*
**Weiss**, Michael Allen 1941- *WhoMW 92*
**Weiss**, Michael David 1942- *AmMWSc 92*
**Weiss**, Michael John 1955- *AmMWSc 92*
**Weiss**, Michael Karl 1928- *AmMWSc 92*
**Weiss**, Michael Stephen 1943- *AmMWSc 92*
**Weiss**, Mitchell Joseph 1942- *AmMWSc 92*
**Weiss**, Myron 1939- *WhoEnt 92*
**Weiss**, Nigel Oscar 1936- *Who 92*
**Weiss**, Noel Scott 1943- *AmMWSc 92*
**Weiss**, Norm A. 1935- *WhoWest 92*
**Weiss**, Norman Jay 1942- *AmMWSc 92*
**Weiss**, Paul 1901- *WrDr 92*
**Weiss**, Paul Alfred 1898- *AmMWSc 92*
**Weiss**, Paul Alfred 1898-1989 *FacFETw*
**Weiss**, Paul Storch 1959- *AmMWSc 92*
**Weiss**, Peter 1916-1982 *FacFETw, LiExTwC*
**Weiss**, Peter H. 1956- *WhoWest 92*
**Weiss**, Peter Joseph 1918- *AmMWSc 92*
**Weiss**, Philip 1916- *AmMWSc 92*
**Weiss**, Philip David 1934- *WhoAmL 92*
**Weiss**, Philip Jeffrey 1941- *WhoEnt 92*
**Weiss**, Rainer 1932- *AmMWSc 92*
**Weiss**, Randall Dunn 1946- *WhoFI 92*
**Weiss**, Renee Karol 1923- *IntAu&W 91*
**Weiss**, Rhett Louis 1961- *WhoAmL 92, WhoFI 92*
**Weiss**, Richard Gerald 1942- *AmMWSc 92*
**Weiss**, Richard Jerome 1923- *AmMWSc 92*
**Weiss**, Richard Louis 1944- *AmMWSc 92*
**Weiss**, Richard Raymond 1928- *AmMWSc 92*
**Weiss**, Robert Alan 1950- *AmMWSc 92*
**Weiss**, Robert Anthony 1940- *Who 92*
**Weiss**, Robert Jerome 1917- *AmMWSc 92*
**Weiss**, Robert John 1937- *AmMWSc 92*
**Weiss**, Robert Martin *AmMWSc 92*
**Weiss**, Robert Stephen 1946- *WhoFI 92, WhoWest 92*
**Weiss**, Roger Harvey 1926- *AmMWSc 92*
**Weiss**, Roland George 1949- *AmMWSc 92*
**Weiss**, Ronald 1937- *AmMWSc 92*
**Weiss**, Ronald Phillip 1947- *WhoAmL 92*
**Weiss**, Roy Thomas 1959- *WhoMW 92*
**weiss**, ruth *DrAPF 91*
**Weiss**, S Shirley 1932- *WhoAmP 91*
**Weiss**, Sam 1950- *WhoRel 92*
**Weiss**, Samson Raphael 1910- *WhoRel 92*
**Weiss**, Samuel Abba 1922- *WhoMW 92*
**Weiss**, Samuel Bernard 1926- *AmMWSc 92*
**Weiss**, Sanford *DrAPF 91*
**Weiss**, Sanford Ronald 1931- *WhoWest 92*
**Weiss**, Sara *ScFEYrs*
**Weiss**, Scott S. 1959- *WhoEnt 92*
**Weiss**, Sidney *WhoWest 92*
**Weiss**, Sidney 1920- *AmMWSc 92*
**Weiss**, Sigmund *DrAPF 91*
**Weiss**, Sigmund 1904- *IntAu&W 91*
**Weiss**, Sol 1913- *AmMWSc 92*
**Weiss**, Stanley 1929- *AmMWSc 92*
**Weiss**, Stanley H 1954- *AmMWSc 92*
**Weiss**, Stephen Duffus 1954- *WhoWest 92*
**Weiss**, Stephen Fredrick 1944- *AmMWSc 92*
**Weiss**, Stephen Joel 1938- *WhoAmL 92*
**Weiss**, Steven Alan 1944- *IntMPA 92, WhoEnt 92*
**Weiss**, Steven Joe 1953- *WhoMW 92*
**Weiss**, Stuart Lloyd 1945- *WhoEnt 92*
**Weiss**, Suzanne Terry 1946- *WhoAmL 92*
**Weiss**, Sylvius Leopold 1686-1750 *NewAmDM*
**Weiss**, Ted 1927- *WhoAmP 91*
**Weiss**, Theodore *DrAPF 91*
**Weiss**, Theodore 1916- *BenetAL 91, ConPo 91, WrDr 92*
**Weiss**, Theodore Joel 1919- *AmMWSc 92*
**Weiss**, Theodore S. 1927- *AlmAP 92 [port]*
**Weiss**, Theresa Dominguez 1950- *WhoWest 92*
**Weiss**, Thomas E 1916- *AmMWSc 92*
**Weiss**, Ulrich 1908- *AmMWSc 92*
**Weiss**, Ulrich 1936- *IntWW 91*
**Weiss**, Volker 1930- *AmMWSc 92*
**Weiss**, Walter Stanley 1929- *WhoAmL 92*
**Weiss**, Wilhelm 1892-1950 *EncTR 91 [port]*
**Weiss**, William 1919- *AmMWSc 92*
**Weiss**, William 1923- *AmMWSc 92*
**Weiss**, William Hans 1952- *WhoWest 92*
**Weiss**, William Lee 1929- *WhoFI 92, WhoMW 92*
**Weiss Bizzoco**, Richard Lawrence 1940- *WhoWest 92*
**Weissbach**, Arthur 1927- *AmMWSc 92*
**Weissbach**, Herbert 1932- *AmMWSc 92*
**Weissbard**, David Raymond 1940- *WhoRel 92*
**Weissbard**, Samuel Held 1947- *WhoAmL 92*
**Weissberg**, Alfred 1928- *AmMWSc 92*
**Weissberg**, Robert Murray 1940- *AmMWSc 92*
**Weissberg**, Victor Howard 1927- *WhoRel 92*
**Weissbluth**, Mitchel 1915- *AmMWSc 92*
**Weissbort**, Daniel 1935- *ConPo 91, WrDr 92*
**Weissbrodt**, David Samuel 1944- *WhoAmL 92*
**Weissburg**, Carl Ivan 1930- *WhoAmL 92*
**Weisse**, Allen B 1929- *AmMWSc 92*
**Weisse**, Guenter 1935- *WhoMW 92*
**Weissenberg**, Alexis 1929- *IntWW 91, NewAmDM*
**Weissenberger**, Glen 1946- *WhoAmL 92*
**Weissenberger**, Harry George 1928- *WhoAmL 92*
**Weissenberger**, Stein 1937- *AmMWSc 92*
**Weissenborn**, Sheridan Kendall 1948- *WhoAmL 92*
**Weissenbuehler**, Wayne *WhoRel 92*
**Weissenburger**, Don William 1947- *AmMWSc 92*
**Weissenburger**, Jason T 1932- *AmMWSc 92*
**Weissent**, Alexander Bruce 1950- *WhoMW 92*
**Weisser**, Eugene P 1922- *AmMWSc 92*
**Weisser**, Henry George 1935- *WhoWest 92*
**Weisser**, William James 1948- *WhoRel 92*
**Weissfeld**, Joachim Alexander 1927- *WhoAmL 92*
**Weissgerber**, Rudolph E 1921- *AmMWSc 92*
**Weisshaar**, Milton Leon 1921- *WhoRel 92*
**Weissinger**, Charles Hyde, Jr 1950- *WhoAmP 91*
**Weissinger**, Thomas, Sr. 1951- *WhoBlA 92*
**Weisskopf**, Bernard 1929- *AmMWSc 92*
**Weisskopf**, Martin Charles 1942- *AmMWSc 92*
**Weisskopf**, Victor Frederick 1908- *AmMWSc 92, IntWW 91, Who 92*
**Weissler**, Arnold M 1927- *AmMWSc 92*
**Weissler**, Friedrich 1891-1937 *EncTR 91 [port]*
**Weissler**, Gerhard Ludwig 1918- *AmMWSc 92*
**Weissman**, Albert 1933- *AmMWSc 92*
**Weissman**, Benjamin Aaron 1950- *WhoEnt 92*
**Weissman**, Charles 1951- *AmMWSc 92*
**Weissman**, Charles Barry 1953- *WhoFI 92*
**Weissman**, Dan 1955- *WhoEnt 92*
**Weissman**, David E 1937- *AmMWSc 92*
**Weissman**, Deborah Marlene 1951- *WhoAmL 92*
**Weissman**, Earl Bernard 1942- *AmMWSc 92*
**Weissman**, Eugene Y 1931- *AmMWSc 92*
**Weissman**, Irving L 1939- *AmMWSc 92*
**Weissman**, Michael Benjamin 1949- *AmMWSc 92*
**Weissman**, Michael Herbert 1942- *AmMWSc 92*
**Weissman**, Michael Lewis 1934- *WhoAmL 92*
**Weissman**, Murray *IntMPA 92*
**Weissman**, Myrna Milgram 1935- *AmMWSc 92*
**Weissman**, Norman 1914- *AmMWSc 92*
**Weissman**, Norman 1925- *WhoFI 92*
**Weissman**, Paul Morton 1936- *AmMWSc 92*
**Weissman**, Paul Robert 1947- *AmMWSc 92*
**Weissman**, Robert Allen 1950- *WhoAmL 92*
**Weissman**, Robert Evan 1940- *WhoFI 92*
**Weissman**, Robert Henry 1942- *AmMWSc 92*
**Weissman**, Samuel Isaac 1912- *AmMWSc 92*
**Weissman**, Seymour J 1931- *IntMPA 92*
**Weissman**, Sharon Lee 1955- *WhoEnt 92*
**Weissman**, Sherman Morton 1930- *AmMWSc 92*
**Weissman**, Suzanne Heisler 1949- *AmMWSc 92*
**Weissman**, William 1918- *AmMWSc 92*
**Weissman**, William R. 1940- *WhoAmL 92*
**Weissmann**, Bernard 1917- *AmMWSc 92*
**Weissmann**, David *DrAPF 91*
**Weissmann**, Gerald 1930- *AmMWSc 92*
**Weissmann**, Gerd Friedrich Horst 1923- *AmMWSc 92*
**Weissmann**, N. Charles 1931- *IntWW 91*
**Weissmann**, Robin Lee 1953- *WhoFI 92*
**Weissmann**, Sigmund 1917- *AmMWSc 92*
**Weissmueller**, Charles Donald 1952- *WhoEnt 92*
**Weissmuller**, Alberto Augusto 1927- *Who 92*
**Weissmuller**, Johnny 1904-1984 *FacFETw*
**Weisstein**, Ulrich W. 1925- *WrDr 92*
**Weisstub**, David N. 1944- *WrDr 92*
**Weisstuch**, Donald N. 1935- *WhoFI 92*
**Weist**, Dwight d1991 *NewYTBS 91*
**Weist**, William Bernard 1938- *WhoAmL 92*
**Weist**, William Godfrey, Jr 1931- *AmMWSc 92*
**Weistart**, John C. 1943- *WhoAmL 92*
**Weistrop**, Donna Etta 1944- *AmMWSc 92*
**Weiswasser**, Stephen *LesBEnT 92*
**Weiswasser**, Stephen Anthony 1940- *WhoAmL 92, WhoEnt 92, WhoFI 92*
**Weisz**, George 1951- *WhoAmP 91*
**Weisz**, James Milton 1945- *WhoRel 92*
**Weisz**, Jeffrey Steven 1951- *WhoFI 92*
**Weisz**, Judith 1926- *AmMWSc 92*
**Weisz**, Michael Jay 1957- *WhoAmL 92*
**Weisz**, Paul B 1921- *AmMWSc 92*
**Weisz**, Paul Burg 1919- *AmMWSc 92*
**Weisz**, Peter R. 1953- *WhoAmL 92*
**Weisz**, Rita Lanyce 1951- *WhoMW 92*
**Weisz**, Robert Stephen 1918- *AmMWSc 92*
**Weisz**, Sharon Ann 1950- *WhoEnt 92*
**Weisz**, Steven Gary 1956- *WhoEnt 92*
**Weisz-Carrington**, Paul *AmMWSc 92*
**Weith**, Herbert Lee *AmMWSc 92*
**Weithas**, William Vincent 1929- *WhoFI 92*
**Weithers**, John G. 1933- *WhoFI 92*
**Weithers**, Timothy Martin 1956- *WhoFI 92*
**Weitkamp**, Fredrick John 1927- *WhoWest 92*
**Weitkamp**, John F. 1953- *WhoWest 92*
**Weitkamp**, Lowell R 1936- *AmMWSc 92*
**Weitkamp**, William George 1934- *AmMWSc 92*
**Weitlauf**, Harry 1937- *AmMWSc 92*
**Weitsman**, Allen William 1940- *AmMWSc 92*
**Weitz**, Bernard George Felix 1919- *Who 92*
**Weitz**, Bruce 1943- *WhoEnt 92*
**Weitz**, David L. 1956- *WhoRel 92*
**Weitz**, Eric 1947- *AmMWSc 92*
**Weitz**, John Hills 1916- *AmMWSc 92*
**Weitz**, Joseph Leonard 1922- *AmMWSc 92*
**Weitz**, Martin Mishli 1907- *WhoRel 92*
**Weitz**, Raanan 1913- *IntWW 91*
**Weitz**, Ralph William 1947- *WhoRel 92*
**Weitz**, Ronald George 1954- *WhoAmL 92*
**Weitz**, Sue Dee 1948- *WhoWest 92*
**Weitz**, Theodore Mark 1946- *WhoAmL 92*
**Weitzel**, John Quinn 1928- *WhoRel 92, WhoWest 92*
**Weitzel**, William Conrad, Jr. 1935- *WhoFI 92*
**Weitzenhoffer**, Aaron Max, Jr. 1939- *WhoEnt 92, WhoFI 92*
**Weitzenhoffer**, Frances 1944-1991 *NewYTBS 91*
**Weitzler**, Linda *IntMPA 92*
**Weitzman**, Allan Harvey 1949- *WhoAmL 92*
**Weitzman**, Daniel Michael 1958- *WhoAmL 92, WhoMW 92*
**Weitzman**, Elliot D 1929- *AmMWSc 92*
**Weitzman**, Marc Herschel 1950- *WhoAmL 92*
**Weitzman**, Peter 1926- *Who 92*
**Weitzman**, Sarah Brown *DrAPF 91*
**Weitzman**, Stanley Howard 1927- *AmMWSc 92*
**Weitzmann**, Kurt 1904- *ConAu 35NR*
**Weitzner**, David 1938- *IntMPA 92*
**Weitzner**, David A. 1938- *WhoEnt 92*

**Weitzner,** Harold 1933- *AmMWSc 92*
**Weitzner,** Stanley 1931- *AmMWSc 92*
**Weixlmann,** Joseph Norman, Jr. 1946- *WhoMW 92*
**Weizman,** Ezer 1924- *IntWW 91*
**Weizmann,** Chaim 1874-1952 *EncTR 91 [port], FacFETw*
**Weizsacker,** Carl Friedrich, Freiherr von 1912- *IntWW 91*
**Weizsacker,** Ernst, Baron von 1882-1951 *EncTR 91 [port]*
**Weizsacker,** Richard von 1920- *IntWW 91*
**Wejchert,** Andrzej 1937- *WhoFI 92*
**Wejcman,** Linda *WhoAmP 91*
**Wejksnora,** Peter James 1950- *AmMWSc 92*
**Wekell,** Marleen Marie 1942- *AmMWSc 92*
**Wekezer,** Jerzy Wladyslaw 1946- *WhoWest 92*
**Weksler,** Babette Barbash 1937- *AmMWSc 92*
**Weksler,** Marc Edward 1937- *AmMWSc 92*
**Wekstein,** David Robert 1937- *AmMWSc 92*
**Wekstein,** Morton Nathaniel 1911- *WhoAmL 92*
**Wekwerth,** Manfred 1929- *IntWW 91*
**Welander,** David Charles St Vincent 1925- *Who 92*
**Welbaum,** Jeffrey Mitchell 1952- *WhoAmL 92*
**Welber,** David Alan 1949- *WhoFI 92*
**Welber,** Irwin 1924- *AmMWSc 92*
**Welber,** Nancy Helene 1957- *WhoAmL 92*
**Welborn,** Briney 1948- *WhoAmP 91*
**Welborn,** Jeremy Ray 1970- *WhoRel 92*
**Welborn,** John Alva *WhoAmP 91*
**Welborn,** Marie 1953- *WhoMW 92*
**Welborn,** Reich Lee 1945- *WhoAmL 92*
**Welborn,** W. Wayne 1947- *WhoFI 92*
**Welborn-Weinstock,** Marion Dowling 1961- *WhoAmL 92*
**Welborne,** John Howard 1947- *WhoAmL 92*
**Welbourn,** Richard Burkewood 1919- *Who 92*
**Welburn,** Edward Thomas, Jr. 1950- *WhoBlA 92*
**Welburn,** Ron *DrAPF 91*
**Welburn,** Ronald Garfield 1944- *WhoBlA 92*
**Welburn,** Vivienne C *IntAu&W 91*
**Welby,** Bruno *Who 92*
**Welby,** Charles William 1926- *AmMWSc 92*
**Welby,** Richard Bruno 1928- *Who 92*
**Welby-Everard,** Christopher Earle 1909- *Who 92*
**Welch,** Aaron Waddington 1916- *AmMWSc 92*
**Welch,** Agnes 1924- *WhoAmP 91*
**Welch,** Ann Courtenay 1917- *WrDr 92*
**Welch,** Annemarie S 1937- *AmMWSc 92*
**Welch,** Anthony Edward 1906- *Who 92*
**Welch,** Archie W, Jr 1940- *WhoAmP 91*
**Welch,** Arnold D 1908- *AmMWSc 92*
**Welch,** Ashley James 1933- *AmMWSc 92*
**Welch,** Ashton Everett 1942- *WhoAmP 91*
**Welch,** Barbara Ann 1956- *WhoEnt 92*
**Welch,** Betty Leonora 1961- *WhoFI 92, WhoWest 92*
**Welch,** Bob 1956- *News 91 [port], -91-3 [port]*
**Welch,** Carlos Harlan 1939- *WhoRel 92*
**Welch,** Charles R 1928- *WhoAmP 91*
**Welch,** Charles Smith 1942- *WhoMW 92*
**Welch,** Clark Moore 1925- *AmMWSc 92*
**Welch,** Claude Alton 1921- *AmMWSc 92*
**Welch,** Claude Raymond 1922- *WhoRel 92, WhoWest 92*
**Welch,** Cletus Norman 1937- *AmMWSc 92*
**Welch,** Colin *Who 92*
**Welch,** Colin 1924- *IntAu&W 91*
**Welch,** David A 1940- *WhoAmP 91*
**Welch,** David O 1938- *AmMWSc 92*
**Welch,** David Tyrone 1927- *WhoAmP 91*
**Welch,** David William 1941- *WhoAmL 92, WhoMW 92*
**Welch,** Dean Earl 1937- *AmMWSc 92*
**Welch,** Denton 1915-1948 *RfGEnL 91, TwCPaSc*
**Welch,** Don *DrAPF 91*
**Welch,** Don Meredith 1946- *WhoRel 92*
**Welch,** Edward L. 1928- *WhoBlA 92*
**Welch,** Edward Lawrence C. *Who 92*
**Welch,** Frank Joseph 1929- *AmMWSc 92*
**Welch,** Garth Larry 1937- *AmMWSc 92, WhoWest 92*
**Welch,** Gary Alan 1942- *AmMWSc 92*
**Welch,** Gary William 1943- *AmMWSc 92*
**Welch,** George Burns 1920- *AmMWSc 92*
**Welch,** George Rickey 1947- *AmMWSc 92*
**Welch,** Gordon E 1933- *AmMWSc 92*
**Welch,** Graeme P 1917- *AmMWSc 92*
**Welch,** H William 1920- *AmMWSc 92*
**Welch,** Harry William 1943- *WhoFI 92*
**Welch,** Harvey, Jr. 1932- *WhoBlA 92*
**Welch,** Herbert Alden 1935- *WhoRel 92*
**Welch,** Hugh Gordon 1937- *AmMWSc 92*
**Welch,** J Philip 1933- *AmMWSc 92*
**Welch,** James *DrAPF 91*
**Welch,** James 1940- *BenetAL 91, ConNov 91, ConPo 91, TwCWW 91, WrDr 92*
**Welch,** James Alexander 1924- *AmMWSc 92*
**Welch,** James Colin 1924- *Who 92*
**Welch,** James Edward 1911- *AmMWSc 92*
**Welch,** James Graham 1932- *AmMWSc 92*
**Welch,** James Lee 1946- *AmMWSc 92*
**Welch,** James Milton 1957- *WhoFI 92*
**Welch,** James Scott 1939- *WhoRel 92*
**Welch,** James Stewart 1940- *WhoEnt 92*
**Welch,** James Stirling, Sr. 1929- *WhoAmL 92*
**Welch,** Jane Marie 1950- *AmMWSc 92*
**Welch,** Jasper Arthur, Jr 1931- *AmMWSc 92*
**Welch,** Jennifer *DrAPF 91*
**Welch,** Jerome E 1945- *AmMWSc 92*
**Welch,** Jesse Roy 1949- *WhoBlA 92*
**Welch,** Joan Kathleen 1950- *WhoEnt 92*
**Welch,** John Butler 1940- *WhoEnt 92*
**Welch,** John F, Jr 1935- *AmMWSc 92*
**Welch,** John Francis, Jr. 1935- *IntWW 91, WhoFI 92*
**Welch,** John K. *Who 92*
**Welch,** John L. 1929- *WhoBlA 92*
**Welch,** John Reader 1933- *Who 92*
**Welch,** John Stanley 1920- *WhoAmL 92*
**Welch,** Kevin M. 1956- *WhoFI 92*
**Welch,** Liliane 1937- *IntAu&W 91*
**Welch,** Lin 1927- *AmMWSc 92*
**Welch,** Lloyd Richard 1927- *AmMWSc 92, WhoWest 92*
**Welch,** Louie 1918- *WhoAmP 91*
**Welch,** Louise Banner 1926- *WhoRel 92*
**Welch,** Matt *WhoAmP 91*
**Welch,** Melvin Bruce 1945- *AmMWSc 92*
**Welch,** Michael John 1939- *AmMWSc 92*
**Welch,** Mindy M. 1937- *WhoEnt 92*
**Welch,** Noble 1930- *WhoFI 92*
**Welch,** O. J. 1929- *WhoFI 92*
**Welch,** Odella T. 1934- *WhoBlA 92*
**Welch,** Olga Michele 1948- *WhoBlA 92*
**Welch,** Patricia L 1953- *WhoAmP 91*
**Welch,** Patrick Daniel 1948- *WhoAmP 91, WhoMW 92*
**Welch,** Patrick James 1944- *WhoFI 92*
**Welch,** Patrick Kevin 1951- *WhoWest 92*
**Welch,** Paul Brown, III 1955- *WhoAmL 92*
**Welch,** Peter 1947- *WhoAmP 91*
**Welch,** Peter D 1928- *AmMWSc 92*
**Welch,** Raquel 1940- *IntMPA 92, IntWW 91, WhoEnt 92A, WhoHisp 92*
**Welch,** Raymond Lee 1943- *AmMWSc 92*
**Welch,** Richard Martin 1933- *AmMWSc 92*
**Welch,** Robert 1929- *DcTwDes*
**Welch,** Robert Gibson 1915- *WhoWest 92*
**Welch,** Robert Henry Winborne 1899-1985 *BiDExR*
**Welch,** Robert Morrow, Jr. 1927- *WhoAmL 92*
**Welch,** Robert Radford 1929- *Who 92*
**Welch,** Robert T 1958- *WhoAmP 91*
**Welch,** Robin Ivor 1930- *AmMWSc 92*
**Welch,** Ronald Maurice 1943- *AmMWSc 92*
**Welch,** Ross Maynard 1943- *AmMWSc 92*
**Welch,** Roy Allen 1939- *AmMWSc 92*
**Welch,** Sandra Hopper 1946- *WhoFI 92*
**Welch,** Stephen Melwood 1949- *AmMWSc 92*
**Welch,** Steven Charles 1940- *AmMWSc 92*
**Welch,** Teresa J. *WhoAmL 92*
**Welch,** Thomas Benjamin, III 1956- *WhoMW 92*
**Welch,** Thomas Patrick 1947- *WhoAmP 91*
**Welch,** Timothy LeRoy 1935- *WhoWest 92*
**Welch,** Walter Raynes 1920- *AmMWSc 92*
**Welch,** Wayne Willard 1934- *AmMWSc 92*
**Welch,** Willard McKowan, Jr 1944- *AmMWSc 92*
**Welch,** William Henry, Jr 1940- *AmMWSc 92*
**Welch,** William John 1934- *AmMWSc 92*
**Welch,** William Manual 1951- *WhoWest 92*
**Welch,** William Neville 1906- *Who 92*
**Welch,** Winfred Bruce 1918- *WhoBlA 92*
**Welch,** Winona Hazel 1896- *AmMWSc 92*
**Welch,** Zara D 1915- *AmMWSc 92*
**Welcher,** Jeanne 1922- *ScFEYrs*
**Welcher,** Jeanne & Bush, George E, Jr *ScFEYrs*
**Welcher,** Richard Parke 1919- *AmMWSc 92*
**Welcher,** Rosalind 1922- *WrDr 92*
**Welcome,** John *IntAu&W 91X*
**Welcome,** John 1914- *WrDr 92*
**Welcome,** S Byron *ScFEYrs*
**Welcome,** Verda F. d1990 *WhoBlA 92N*
**Weld,** Charles Beecher 1899- *AmMWSc 92*
**Weld,** Jonathan Minot 1941- *WhoAmL 92*
**Weld,** Joseph William 1909- *Who 92*
**Weld,** Laenas Gifford 1862-1919 *BiInAmS*
**Weld,** Roger Bowen 1953- *WhoRel 92, WhoWest 92*
**Weld,** Theodore Dwight 1803-1895 *BenetAL 91*
**Weld,** Thomas *BenetAL 91*
**Weld,** Tuesday 1943- *IntMPA 92*
**Weld,** Tuesday Ker 1943- *IntWW 91, WhoEnt 92*
**Weld,** William F. *NewYTBS 91 [port], WhoAmP 91*
**Weld,** William F. 1945- *AlmAP 92 [port]*
**Weld,** William Floyd 1945- *IntWW 91, WhoAmL 92*
**Weld Forester** *Who 92*
**Welden,** Arthur Luna 1927- *AmMWSc 92*
**Welden,** Richard W *WhoAmP 91*
**Welden,** Robert Dean 1945- *WhoAmL 92*
**Welder,** Thomas 1940- *WhoRel 92*
**Weldes,** Helmut H 1928- *AmMWSc 92*
**Weldin,** John Clement 1948- *WhoAmL 92*
**Welding,** Minnette Susan 1960- *WhoRel 92*
**Weldon,** Ann 1938- *WhoEnt 92*
**Weldon,** Ann Blain 1911- *WhoRel 92*
**Weldon,** Anthony 1947- *Who 92*
**Weldon,** Barbara Maltby 1931- *WhoWest 92*
**Weldon,** Curt 1947- *AlmAP 92 [port]*
**Weldon,** David Joseph, Jr. 1953- *WhoRel 92*
**Weldon,** David Rollins 1959- *WhoAmL 92*
**Weldon,** Deborah 1951- *WhoBlA 92*
**Weldon,** Doris May 1925- *WhoWest 92*
**Weldon,** Duncan Clark 1941- *Who 92*
**Weldon,** Edward J, Jr 1938- *AmMWSc 92*
**Weldon,** Fay *WrDr 92*
**Weldon,** Fay 1931- *CnDBLB 8 [port], ConNov 91, IntAu&W 91, IntWW 91, RfGEnL 91, Who 92*
**Weldon,** Henry Arthur 1947- *AmMWSc 92*
**Weldon,** Norman Ross 1934- *WhoFI 92*
**Weldon,** Onah Conway 1926- *WhoBlA 92*
**Weldon,** Ramon N. 1932- *WhoBlA 92*
**Weldon,** Robert William 1934- *WhoIns 92*
**Weldon,** Virginia V 1935- *AmMWSc 92, WhoFI 92, WhoMW 92*
**Weldon,** Virginia Verral 1935- *IntWW 91*
**Weldon,** Wayne Curtis 1947- *WhoAmP 91*
**Weldon,** William Forrest 1945- *AmMWSc 92*
**Weldon,** William Kimberly 1921- *WhoAmP 91*
**Weldon-Linne,** C. Michael 1953- *WhoMW 92*
**Weldy,** Norma Jean 1929- *WhoMW 92*
**Welensky,** Roy 1907- *FacFETw, IntWW 91, Who 92*
**Welensky,** Roy 1907-1991 *NewYTBS 91*
**Welfare,** Simon 1946- *ConAu 133*
**Welfeld,** Jack Arnold 1912- *WhoAmL 92*
**Welford,** Norman Traviss 1921- *AmMWSc 92*
**Welford,** Robert Ford, II 1939- *WhoMW 92*
**Welford,** Walter Thompson d1990 *IntWW 91N*
**Welge,** Henry John 1907- *AmMWSc 92*
**Welham,** N. Douglas 1958- *WhoEnt 92*
**Welhan,** John Andrew 1950- *AmMWSc 92*
**Welikson,** Jeffrey Alan 1957- *WhoAmL 92*
**Weliky,** Irving 1924- *AmMWSc 92*
**Weliky,** Norman 1919- *AmMWSc 92*
**Welin,** Karl-Erik 1934- *ConCom 92*
**Welin,** Walter 1908- *WhoFI 92*
**Welinsky,** Howard S 1949- *WhoAmP 91*
**Welinsky,** Howard Steven 1949- *WhoEnt 92*
**Welish,** Marjorie *DrAPF 91*
**Welitsch,** Ljuba 1913- *NewAmDM*
**Weliver,** E. Delmer 1939- *WhoEnt 92*
**Welk,** Lawrence 1903- *ConAu 134, FacFETw, IntMPA 92, NewAmDM*
**Welker,** Edward Philip 1932- *WhoFI 92*
**Welker,** Everett Linus 1911- *AmMWSc 92*
**Welker,** George W 1923- *AmMWSc 92*
**Welker,** J Reed 1936- *AmMWSc 92*
**Welker,** Neil Ernest 1932- *AmMWSc 92*
**Welker,** Ray *WhoAmP 91*
**Welker,** Wallace I 1926- *AmMWSc 92*
**Welker,** William V, Jr 1928- *AmMWSc 92*
**Welkie,** George William 1932- *AmMWSc 92*
**Welkowitz,** Walter 1926- *AmMWSc 92*
**Welks,** David John 1952- *WhoFI 92*
**Well,** Gunther Wilhelm van 1922- *IntWW 91*
**Welland,** Colin 1934- *IntAu&W 91, IntWW 91, Who 92*
**Welland,** Grant Vincent 1940- *AmMWSc 92*
**Welland,** Robert Roy 1933- *AmMWSc 92*
**Wellbeloved,** James 1926- *Who 92*
**Wellborn,** Charles Ivey 1941- *WhoAmL 92*
**Wellborn,** Thomas Michael 1952- *WhoWest 92*
**Wellby,** Roger Stanley 1906- *Who 92*
**Welldon,** Paul Burke 1916- *AmMWSc 92*
**Welle,** Alan W 1945- *WhoAmP 91*
**Welle,** Stephen Leo *AmMWSc 92*
**Wellek,** Rene 1903- *IntWW 91, WrDr 92*
**Wellek,** Rene 1903-1989 *LiExTwC*
**Wellen,** C. W. 1924- *WhoAmL 92*
**Wellen,** Robert Howard 1946- *WhoAmL 92*
**Wellenreiter,** Donald Gene 1949- *WhoMW 92*
**Wellenreiter,** Rodger Henry 1942- *AmMWSc 92*
**Weller,** Albert Hermann 1922- *IntWW 91*
**Weller,** Charles David 1944- *WhoAmL 92*
**Weller,** Charles Stagg, Jr 1940- *AmMWSc 92*
**Weller,** Charles Weston 1948- *WhoMW 92*
**Weller,** David Lloyd 1938- *AmMWSc 92*
**Weller,** Edward Crozier 1946- *WhoWest 92*
**Weller,** Edward F, Jr 1919- *AmMWSc 92*
**Weller,** Frederick Everett 1952- *WhoMW 92*
**Weller,** Gerald C *WhoAmP 91*
**Weller,** Glenn Peter 1943- *AmMWSc 92*
**Weller,** Gunter Ernst 1934- *AmMWSc 92, WhoWest 92*
**Weller,** Harold Leighton 1941- *WhoEnt 92, WhoWest 92*
**Weller,** Henry Richard 1941- *AmMWSc 92*
**Weller,** Janet Louise 1953- *WhoAmL 92*
**Weller,** John Jurgen 1944- *WhoAmL 92*
**Weller,** John Martin 1919- *AmMWSc 92*
**Weller,** Keith Austin 1961- *WhoAmL 92*
**Weller,** Lawrence Allenby 1927- *AmMWSc 92*
**Weller,** Louis Stevan 1949- *WhoWest 92*
**Weller,** Lowell Ernest 1923- *AmMWSc 92, WhoMW 92*
**Weller,** Malcolm Philip Isadore 1935- *IntWW 91*
**Weller,** Mary Louise 1956- *WhoEnt 92*
**Weller,** Michael 1942- *WhoEnt 92, WrDr 92*
**Weller,** Milton Webster 1929- *AmMWSc 92*
**Weller,** Paul Franklin 1935- *AmMWSc 92*
**Weller,** Peter 1947- *IntMPA 92*
**Weller,** Philip Douglas 1948- *WhoAmL 92*
**Weller,** Richard Irwin 1921- *AmMWSc 92*
**Weller,** Robert Andrew 1950- *AmMWSc 92*
**Weller,** Robert G. *WhoHisp 92*
**Weller,** Robert Norman 1939- *WhoFI 92*
**Weller,** S W 1918- *AmMWSc 92*
**Weller,** Sheila *DrAPF 91*
**Weller,** Thomas Huckle 1915- *AmMWSc 92, IntWW 91, Who 92, WhoNob 90*
**Weller,** Walter 1939- *IntWW 91, Who 92*
**Weller,** Wendy Fossgreen 1958- *WhoRel 92*
**Wellershoff,** Dieter 1925- *IntWW 91*
**Wellershoff,** Dieter 1933- *IntWW 91*
**Wellerson,** Ralph, Jr 1924- *AmMWSc 92*
**Welles,** David Wilder 1938- *WhoAmL 92*
**Welles,** Elizabeth *WrDr 92*
**Welles,** George William, III 1940- *WhoEnt 92, WhoMW 92*
**Welles,** Halsted 1906- *WhoEnt 92*
**Welles,** Harry Leslie 1945- *AmMWSc 92*
**Welles,** John Galt 1925- *WhoWest 92*
**Welles,** Melinda Fassett 1943- *WhoWest 92*
**Welles,** Orson 1915-1985 *BenetAL 91, FacFETw [port], RComAH*
**Welles,** Orson 1916-1985 *IntDcF 2-2 [port]*
**Welles,** Samuel P. 1907- *WrDr 92*
**Welles,** Samuel Paul 1907- *AmMWSc 92*
**Welles,** Sumner 1892-1961 *AmPeW, EncTR 91*
**Welles,** Winifred 1893-1939 *BenetAL 91*
**Wellesley** *Who 92*
**Wellesley,** Julian Valerian 1933- *Who 92*
**Wellesley,** Kenneth 1911- *WrDr 92*
**Wellesz,** Egon 1885-1974 *NewAmDM*
**Wellford,** Harry Walker 1924- *WhoAmL 92*
**Wellford,** Priscilla Morris 1944- *WhoFI 92*
**Wellford,** W Harrison 1940- *WhoAmP 91*
**Wellhoefer,** Jon Lewis 1943- *WhoMW 92*
**Welling,** Calvin Don 1951- *WhoFI 92*
**Welling,** Daniel J 1937- *AmMWSc 92*
**Welling,** Eric Clark 1956- *WhoWest 92*
**Welling,** Larry Wayne *AmMWSc 92*
**Welling,** Richard Clayton 1957- *WhoFI 92*
**Wellings,** Jack 1917- *Who 92*
**Wellings,** Victor Gordon 1919- *Who 92*
**Wellington,** Archbishop of 1930- *Who 92*
**Wellington,** Bishop of *Who 92*
**Wellington,** Duke of 1915- *Who 92*
**Wellington,** Arthur Mellen 1847-1895 *BiInAmS*

**Wellington,** Carol Strong 1948- *WhoAmL 92*
**Wellington,** George Harvey 1915- *AmMWSc 92*
**Wellington,** Hubert 1879-1967 *TwCPaSc*
**Wellington,** John Sessions 1921- *AmMWSc 92*
**Wellington,** Monica 1957- *SmATA 67 [port]*
**Wellington,** Peter Scott 1919- *Who 92*
**Wellington,** Ralph Glenn 1946- *WhoAmL 92*
**Wellington,** Robert Hall 1922- *WhoMW 92*
**Wellington,** Robert John 1954- *WhoWest 92*
**Wellington,** William George 1920- *AmMWSc 92*
**Wellington-Tillis,** Joy Anne 1949- *WhoEnt 92*
**Welliver,** Albertus *AmMWSc 92*
**Welliver,** Paul Wesley 1931- *AmMWSc 92*
**Welliver,** Warren Dee 1920- *WhoAmL 92, WhoAmP 91, WhoMW 92*
**Wellman,** Angela Myra 1935- *AmMWSc 92*
**Wellman,** Anthony Donald Emerson 1955- *WhoEnt 92*
**Wellman,** Beth Lucy 1895-1952 *WomPsyc*
**Wellman,** Carl Pierce 1926- *WrDr 92*
**Wellman,** Dennis Lee 1942- *AmMWSc 92*
**Wellman,** Donald *DrAPF 91*
**Wellman,** Harold William 1909- *IntWW 91*
**Wellman,** Henry Nelson 1933- *AmMWSc 92, WhoMW 92*
**Wellman,** Howard 1944- *WhoAmP 91*
**Wellman,** Mac *DrAPF 91*
**Wellman,** Mac 1945- *ConLC 65 [port]*
**Wellman,** Manly Wade 1903- *IntAu&W 91*
**Wellman,** Manly Wade 1903-1986 *ScFEYrs, TwCSFW 91*
**Wellman,** Paul I. 1898-1966 *BenetAL 91, TwCWW 91*
**Wellman,** Richard Kent 1940- *WhoEnt 92*
**Wellman,** Richard Vance 1922- *WhoAmL 92*
**Wellman,** Robin Elizabeth 1945- *WhoWest 92*
**Wellman,** Russel Elmer 1922- *AmMWSc 92*
**Wellman,** Samuel Edison 1951- *WhoEnt 92*
**Wellman,** Samuel Thomas 1847-1919 *BiInAmS*
**Wellman,** Thomas Peter 1932- *WhoAmL 92*
**Wellman,** W. Arvid 1918- *WhoFI 92*
**Wellman,** William 1896-1975 *IntDcF 2-2 [port]*
**Wellman,** William Edward 1932- *AmMWSc 92*
**Wellmann,** Klaus Friedrich 1929- *AmMWSc 92*
**Wellner,** Daniel 1934- *AmMWSc 92*
**Wellner,** Marcel 1930- *AmMWSc 92*
**Wellner,** Vaira Pamiljans 1936- *AmMWSc 92*
**Wellnitz,** Carol Lee 1947- *WhoFI 92*
**Wellnitz,** Craig Otto 1946- *WhoAmL 92*
**Wellon,** Robert G. 1948- *WhoAmL 92*
**Wellons,** Jesse Davis, III 1938- *AmMWSc 92*
**Wells,** Archdeacon of *Who 92*
**Wells,** Dean of *Who 92*
**Wells,** Adoniram Judson 1917- *AmMWSc 92*
**Wells,** Alan Arthur *Who 92*
**Wells,** Angus 1943- *TwCWW 91*
**Wells,** Arthur Stanton 1931- *WhoFI 92*
**Wells,** Aubrey 1954- *WhoRel 92*
**Wells,** Barbara 1960- *WhoRel 92*
**Wells,** Barbara Duryea 1939- *AmMWSc 92*
**Wells,** Barbara Jones 1939- *WhoBlA 92*
**Wells,** Basil E 1912- *IntAu&W 91*
**Wells,** Benjamin B, Jr 1941- *AmMWSc 92*
**Wells,** Betty Ruth 1927- *WhoMW 92*
**Wells,** Billy Gene *WhoBlA 92*
**Wells,** Bobby R 1934- *AmMWSc 92*
**Wells,** Bobby Ray 1956- *WhoBlA 92*
**Wells,** Bowen 1935- *Who 92*
**Wells,** Brian Jeffrey 1960- *WhoRel 92*
**Wells,** Brigid *Who 92*
**Wells,** Bruce Robert 1950- *WhoEnt 92*
**Wells,** Carol Menthe *WhoWest 92*
**Wells,** Carole C 1943- *WhoAmP 91*
**Wells,** Carolyn 1869-1942 *BenetAL 91*
**Wells,** Carveth 1887-1957 *BenetAL 91*
**Wells,** Cecil Harold, Jr. 1927- *WhoWest 92*
**Wells,** Charles Donald 1946- *WhoAmP 91*
**Wells,** Charles Edmon 1929- *AmMWSc 92*
**Wells,** Charles Frederick 1937- *AmMWSc 92*
**Wells,** Charles Henry 1931- *AmMWSc 92*
**Wells,** Charles Maltby 1908- *Who 92*
**Wells,** Charles Marion 1905- *WhoAmL 92*
**Wells,** Charles Van 1937- *AmMWSc 92*
**Wells,** Charles William 1934- *WhoFI 92*
**Wells,** Clayton E 1937- *WhoAmP 91*
**Wells,** Clifford Eugene 1927- *WhoFI 92*
**Wells,** Damon, Jr. 1937- *WhoFI 92*
**Wells,** Daniel R 1921- *AmMWSc 92*
**Wells,** Darrell Gibson 1917- *AmMWSc 92*
**Wells,** Darthon Vernon 1929- *AmMWSc 92*
**Wells,** David *WhoEnt 92*
**Wells,** David Allen 1955- *WhoWest 92*
**Wells,** David Ames 1828-1898 *BiInAmS*
**Wells,** David Arthur 1941- *Who 92*
**Wells,** David Ernest 1939- *AmMWSc 92*
**Wells,** David George 1941- *Who 92*
**Wells,** David John 1949- *WhoFI 92*
**Wells,** Denys 1881-1973 *TwCPaSc*
**Wells,** Dewey Wallace 1929- *WhoAmL 92*
**Wells,** Dickie 1909-1985 *FacFETw*
**Wells,** Dicky 1907-1985 *NewAmDM*
**Wells,** Donald *TwCPaSc*
**Wells,** Donald Austin 1937- *WhoRel 92*
**Wells,** Donna Frances 1948- *WhoFI 92, WhoWest 92*
**Wells,** Doreen Patricia *Who 92*
**Wells,** Dwight Allen 1925- *WhoAmP 91*
**Wells,** Eddie N 1940- *AmMWSc 92*
**Wells,** Edward C 1910-1986 *FacFETw*
**Wells,** Edward Joseph 1936- *AmMWSc 92*
**Wells,** Elaine L *WhoAmP 91*
**Wells,** Eliab Horatio 1836- *BiInAmS*
**Wells,** Elizabeth Fortson 1943- *AmMWSc 92*
**Wells,** Elmer Eugene 1939- *WhoBlA 92*
**Wells,** F J d1904 *BiInAmS*
**Wells,** Fletcher Evan, II 1954- *WhoMW 92*
**Wells,** Frances Jean 1937- *WhoFI 92*
**Wells,** Frank Edward 1925- *AmMWSc 92*
**Wells,** Frank G. 1932- *IntMPA 92, WhoEnt 92, WhoWest 92*
**Wells,** Fred Warren, II 1955- *WhoWest 92*
**Wells,** Frederick Joseph 1944- *AmMWSc 92*
**Wells,** Garland Ray 1936- *AmMWSc 92*
**Wells,** Gary Leroy 1950- *WhoMW 92*
**Wells,** Gary Neil 1941- *AmMWSc 92*
**Wells,** Gary Ray 1938- *WhoFI 92*
**Wells,** George Albert 1926- *Who 92*
**Wells,** George Henry 1940- *WhoRel 92*
**Wells,** George O *ScFEYrs*
**Wells,** Gregory Alan 1951- *WhoMW 92*
**Wells,** Guy Jackson 1930- *WhoAmP 91*
**Wells,** H. G. 1866-1946 *CnDBLB 6 [port], FacFETw [port], RfGEnL 91, ScFEYrs, -A, TwCSFW 91*
**Wells,** Harrington 1952- *AmMWSc 92*
**Wells,** Helena *BenetAL 91*
**Wells,** Henry Bradley *AmMWSc 92*
**Wells,** Henry E 1915- *WhoAmP 91*
**Wells,** Herbert 1930- *AmMWSc 92*
**Wells,** Herbert Arthur 1921- *AmMWSc 92*
**Wells,** Herbert James 1897- *Who 92*
**Wells,** Herman B. 1902- *IntWW 91, WhoMW 92*
**Wells,** Homer Douglas 1923- *AmMWSc 92*
**Wells,** Hondo *TwCWW 91*
**Wells,** Horace 1815-1848 *BiInAmS*
**Wells,** Ibert Clifton 1921- *AmMWSc 92*
**Wells,** Ira J. K., Jr. 1934- *WhoBlA 92*
**Wells,** J. Eugene M. 1925- *WhoMW 92*
**Wells,** J Gordon 1918- *AmMWSc 92*
**Wells,** J Wellington *IntAu&W 91X*
**Wells,** Jack Albert 1951- *WhoEnt 92*
**Wells,** Jack Dennis 1928- *Who 92*
**Wells,** Jack Nulk 1937- *AmMWSc 92*
**Wells,** Jacqueline Gaye 1931- *AmMWSc 92*
**Wells,** James A. 1933- *WhoBlA 92*
**Wells,** James Dale 1928- *WhoAmP 91*
**Wells,** James Howard 1932- *AmMWSc 92*
**Wells,** James Lesesne 1902- *WhoBlA 92*
**Wells,** James Ray 1932- *AmMWSc 92*
**Wells,** James Robert 1940- *AmMWSc 92*
**Wells,** James Wayne 1941- *WhoWest 92*
**Wells,** Jane Frances 1944- *AmMWSc 92*
**Wells,** Jeffrey Frederick 1958- *WhoWest 92*
**Wells,** Jeffrey M 1948- *WhoAmP 91, WhoWest 92*
**Wells,** Jennifer Brigid 1928- *Who 92*
**Wells,** Jere' Leverette 1939- *WhoRel 92*
**Wells,** Jerome Covell 1936- *WhoFI 92*
**Wells,** Joel Freeman 1930- *WrDr 92*
**Wells,** John 1907- *TwCPaSc*
**Wells,** John 1936- *WrDr 92*
**Wells,** John Arthur 1935- *AmMWSc 92*
**Wells,** John Calhoun, Jr 1941- *AmMWSc 92*
**Wells,** John Campbell 1936- *Who 92*
**Wells,** John Christopher 1939- *Who 92*
**Wells,** John J *IntAu&W 91X, TwCSFW 91*
**Wells,** John Julius 1925- *Who 92*
**Wells,** John Marcum 1956- *WhoEnt 92, WhoWest 92*
**Wells,** John Marvin 1918- *WhoAmP 91*
**Wells,** John Morgan, Jr 1940- *AmMWSc 92*
**Wells,** John West 1907- *AmMWSc 92, IntWW 91*
**Wells,** Jon Barrett 1937- *WhoFI 92*
**Wells,** Joseph 1934- *AmMWSc 92*
**Wells,** Joseph S 1930- *AmMWSc 92*
**Wells,** Junior 1934- *NewAmDM*
**Wells,** Kathleen Elizabeth 1961- *WhoFI 92*
**Wells,** Keith Philip 1955- *WhoRel 92*
**Wells,** Kenneth 1927- *AmMWSc 92*
**Wells,** Kenneth Lincoln 1935- *AmMWSc 92*
**Wells,** Kentwood David 1948- *AmMWSc 92*
**Wells,** Kim Bradford 1949- *WhoAmP 91*
**Wells,** Kitty 1919- *ConMus 6 [port], NewAmDM*
**Wells,** L. Rosemary Siplon 1930- *WhoEnt 92*
**Wells,** Larry Gene 1947- *AmMWSc 92*
**Wells,** Lawrence Leon 1933-1983 *WhoBlA 92N*
**Wells,** Linda Ivy 1948- *WhoBlA 92*
**Wells,** Lionelle Dudley 1951- *WhoFI 92*
**Wells,** Lloyd C. A. 1924- *WhoBlA 92*
**Wells,** Lynn Annette 1950- *WhoRel 92*
**Wells,** Malcolm Henry Weston 1927- *Who 92*
**Wells,** Marion Robert 1937- *AmMWSc 92*
**Wells,** Mark *WhoIns 92*
**Wells,** Mark Alan 1960- *WhoWest 92*
**Wells,** Mark Brimhall 1929- *AmMWSc 92*
**Wells,** Martin John 1928- *IntAu&W 91, WrDr 92*
**Wells,** Mary 1943- *NewAmDM*
**Wells,** Max *WhoAmP 91*
**Wells,** Melissa F *WhoAmP 91*
**Wells,** Merle William 1918- *WhoWest 92*
**Wells,** Michael A 1953- *WhoAmP 91*
**Wells,** Michael Arthur 1938- *AmMWSc 92*
**Wells,** Michael Byron 1922- *AmMWSc 92*
**Wells,** Milton Ernest 1932- *AmMWSc 92*
**Wells,** Otho Sylvester 1938- *AmMWSc 92*
**Wells,** Ouida Carolyn 1933- *AmMWSc 92*
**Wells,** Patricia Bennett 1935- *WhoWest 92*
**Wells,** Patrick Harrington 1926- *AmMWSc 92, WhoWest 92*
**Wells,** Patrick Roland 1931- *AmMWSc 92, WhoBlA 92*
**Wells,** Payton R. 1933- *WhoBlA 92*
**Wells,** Peter Boyd, Jr. 1915- *WhoAmL 92*
**Wells,** Peter Frederick 1918- *WrDr 92*
**Wells,** Peter Nathaniel 1938- *WhoAmL 92*
**Wells,** Peter Scoville 1938- *WhoFI 92*
**Wells,** Petrie Bowen *Who 92*
**Wells,** Philip Vincent 1928- *AmMWSc 92*
**Wells,** Phillip Cecil *WhoFI 92*
**Wells,** Phillip Richard 1936- *AmMWSc 92*
**Wells,** Quentin Thomas 1941- *WhoWest 92*
**Wells,** R Michael 1949- *WhoAmP 91*
**Wells,** Ralph Gordon 1915- *AmMWSc 92*
**Wells,** Raymond O'Neil, Jr 1940- *AmMWSc 92*
**Wells,** Richard Burton 1940- *Who 92*
**Wells,** Richard Montraville 1957- *WhoWest 92*
**Wells,** Robert *LesBEnT 92*
**Wells,** Robert 1947- *ConPo 91*
**Wells,** Robert Alfred 1942- *WhoAmL 92*
**Wells,** Robert Benjamin, Jr. 1947- *WhoBlA 92*
**Wells,** Robert Dale 1938- *AmMWSc 92*
**Wells,** Robert Louis 1939- *WhoRel 92*
**Wells,** Robert Michael 1949- *WhoAmL 92*
**Wells,** Robert Steven 1951- *WhoAmL 92*
**Wells,** Roderick John 1936- *Who 92*
**Wells,** Rona Lee 1950- *WhoFI 92*
**Wells,** Ronald Alfred 1920- *Who 92*
**Wells,** Ronald Allen 1942- *AmMWSc 92*
**Wells,** Rosemary 1943- *WrDr 92*
**Wells,** Rufus Michael Grant 1947- *IntWW 91*
**Wells,** Russell Frederick 1937- *AmMWSc 92*
**Wells,** Samuel Alonzo, Jr 1936- *AmMWSc 92*
**Wells,** Samuel Jay 1924- *WhoAmP 91*
**Wells,** Samuel Roberts 1820-1875 *BiInAmS*
**Wells,** Stanley 1930- *WrDr 92*
**Wells,** Stanley, Mrs. *Who 92*
**Wells,** Stanley Dale 1944- *WhoMW 92*
**Wells,** Stanley William 1930- *IntAu&W 91, Who 92*
**Wells,** Stephen Gene 1949- *AmMWSc 92*
**Wells,** Steve C 1944- *WhoAmP 91*
**Wells,** Steve Carroll 1944- *WhoFI 92*
**Wells,** Steven Alan 1955- *WhoMW 92*
**Wells,** Steven Frederick 1948- *WhoWest 92*
**Wells,** Tammara *WhoEnt 92*
**Wells,** Theodora 1926- *ConAu 134*
**Wells,** Theresa Diane 1955- *WhoFI 92*
**Wells,** Thomas B. 1945- *WhoAmL 92*
**Wells,** Thomas Leonard 1930- *Who 92*
**Wells,** Thomas Umfrey 1927- *Who 92*
**Wells,** Tobias *IntAu&W 91X, WrDr 92*
**Wells,** Tomm 1948- *WhoWest 92*
**Wells,** Van L 1941- *WhoIns 92*
**Wells,** Vernon George 1945- *WhoEnt 92*
**Wells,** Walter 1937- *WrDr 92*
**Wells,** Walter Newton 1943- *IntAu&W 91*
**Wells,** Warner Lee, Jr. d1991 *NewYTBS 91*
**Wells,** Warren Brooks 1923- *WhoEnt 92*
**Wells,** Warren F 1926- *AmMWSc 92*
**Wells,** Warren Frey 1926- *WhoMW 92*
**Wells,** Wayne Alton 1946- *WhoAmL 92*
**Wells,** Webster 1851-1916 *BiInAmS*
**Wells,** Willard H 1931- *AmMWSc 92*
**Wells,** William *DrAPF 91*
**Wells,** William Charles 1757-1817 *BiInAmS*
**Wells,** William Henry Weston 1940- *Who 92*
**Wells,** William LeRoy *WhoRel 92*
**Wells,** William Lochridge 1939- *AmMWSc 92*
**Wells,** William Raymond 1936- *AmMWSc 92*
**Wells,** William T 1933- *AmMWSc 92*
**Wells,** William Thomas 1938- *WhoRel 92*
**Wells,** William Vincent 1826-1876 *BenetAL 91*
**Wells,** William Wood 1927- *AmMWSc 92*
**Wells,** William Woodrow, Jr. 1950- *WhoAmL 92*
**Wells-Barnett,** Ida 1862-1931 *PorAmW [port]*
**Wells Barnett,** Ida B. 1862-1930 *NotBlAW 92 [port]*
**Wells-Barnett,** Ida B. 1862-1931 *AmPeW, HanAmWH, RComAH, WomSoc*
**Wells-Davis,** Margie Elaine 1944- *WhoBlA 92*
**Wells-Henderson,** Ronald John 1934- *WhoFI 92*
**Wells-Merrick,** Lorraine Roberta 1938- *WhoBlA 92*
**Wells-Pestell,** Baron d1991 *Who 92N*
**Wells-Schooley,** Jane 1949- *WhoAmP 91*
**Wellsandt,** Vicky Lynn 1962- *WhoMW 92*
**Wellso,** Stanley Gordon 1935- *AmMWSc 92*
**Wellstone,** Paul *NewYTBS 91 [port]*
**Wellstone,** Paul 1944- *WhoAmP 91, WhoMW 92*
**Wellstone,** Paul David 1944- *AlmAP 92 [port]*
**Wellwarth,** George E. 1932- *WrDr 92*
**Welmaker,** Forrest Nolan 1925- *WhoAmL 92*
**Welman,** Douglas Pole 1902- *Who 92*
**Welmers,** Everett Thomas 1912- *AmMWSc 92*
**Welna,** Cecilia *AmMWSc 92*
**Welnetz,** David Charles 1947- *WhoFI 92, WhoMW 92*
**Welninski,** James Jerome 1960- *WhoEnt 92*
**Welply,** Joseph Kevin 1953- *AmMWSc 92*
**Welpott,** Raymond W. d1973 *LesBEnT 92*
**Wels,** Otto 1873-1939 *EncTR 91 [port]*
**Welsby,** John Kay 1938- *Who 92*
**Welsby,** Paul Antony 1920- *Who 92*
**Welsch,** Clifford William, Jr 1935- *AmMWSc 92*
**Welsch,** Federico 1933- *AmMWSc 92*
**Welsch,** Frank 1941- *AmMWSc 92*
**Welsch,** Gerhard Egon 1944- *AmMWSc 92*
**Welsch,** John Armand 1966- *WhoMW 92*
**Welsch,** Joseph P 1928- *WhoAmP 91*
**Welsch,** Roy Elmer 1943- *AmMWSc 92*
**Welser-Most,** Franz 1960- *IntWW 91, WhoEnt 92*
**Welsh,** Alexander 1933- *WrDr 92*
**Welsh,** Alfred John 1947- *WhoAmL 92*
**Welsh,** Andrew Paton 1944- *Who 92*
**Welsh,** Arthur Craig 1947- *WhoEnt 92*
**Welsh,** Barbara Lathrop *AmMWSc 92*
**Welsh,** Charles Victor 1958- *WhoFI 92*
**Welsh,** David Albert 1942- *AmMWSc 92*
**Welsh,** David Edward 1942- *AmMWSc 92, WhoWest 92*
**Welsh,** David Malcolm 1942- *WhoFI 92*
**Welsh,** Frank 1931- *ConAu 135*
**Welsh,** Frank Reeson 1931- *Who 92*
**Welsh,** Gary Morton 1947- *WhoAmL 92*
**Welsh,** George W, III 1920- *AmMWSc 92*
**Welsh,** H. Ronald 1950- *WhoAmL 92*
**Welsh,** James Francis 1930- *AmMWSc 92*
**Welsh,** James Michael 1938- *WhoEnt 92*
**Welsh,** James Neal 1942- *WhoFI 92*
**Welsh,** James P *AmMWSc 92*
**Welsh,** James Ralph 1933- *AmMWSc 92*
**Welsh,** John 1937- *WhoEnt 92*
**Welsh,** John Beresford, Jr. 1940- *WhoAmL 92*
**Welsh,** John Elliott, Sr 1927- *AmMWSc 92*
**Welsh,** Joseph John 1955- *WhoAmP 91*
**Welsh,** Lawrence B 1939- *AmMWSc 92*
**Welsh,** Lawrence H. 1935- *WhoRel 92*
**Welsh,** Mary McAnaw 1920- *WhoWest 92*
**Welsh,** Matthew Empson 1912- *WhoAmP 91*
**Welsh,** Michael Collins 1926- *Who 92*
**Welsh,** Michael James *AmMWSc 92*
**Welsh,** Michael John 1942- *Who 92*
**Welsh,** Moray Meston 1947- *IntWW 91*

**Welsh,** Patrick T 1950- *WhoAmP 91*
**Welsh,** Peter Miles 1930- *Who 92*
**Welsh,** Richard D 1931- *WhoIns 92*
**Welsh,** Richard Stanley 1921- *AmMWSc 92*
**Welsh,** Robert Edward 1932- *AmMWSc 92*
**Welsh,** Ronald 1926- *AmMWSc 92*
**Welsh,** S. Patricia 1956- *IntAu&W 91*
**Welsh,** Stephen George 1948- *WhoFI 92*
**Welsh,** Susan *AmMWSc 92*
**Welsh,** Thomas J. 1921- *WhoRel 92*
**Welsh,** Thomas Laurence 1932- *AmMWSc 92*
**Welsh,** Timothy T. 1934- *WhoFI 92*
**Welsh,** William *DrAPF 91*
**Welsh,** William Brownlee 1924- *WhoAmP 91*
**Welsh,** William Curtis 1952- *WhoRel 92*
**Welsh,** William James 1947- *AmMWSc 92*
**Welsh,** Wilmer Hayden 1932- *WhoEnt 92*
**Welsh-Asante,** Karimau 1949- *WhoEnt 92*
**Welshimer,** Gwen *WhoAmP 91*
**Welshimer,** Herbert Jefferson 1920- *AmMWSc 92*
**Welshons,** William John 1922- *AmMWSc 92*
**Welsing,** Frances Cress 1935- *WhoBlA 92*
**Welstead,** William John, Jr 1935- *AmMWSc 92*
**Welsted,** John Edward 1935- *AmMWSc 92*
**Welt,** Bernard *DrAPF 91*
**Welt,** Isaac Davidson 1922- *AmMWSc 92*
**Welt,** Jan Pieter 1942- *WhoEnt 92*
**Welt,** Martin A 1932- *AmMWSc 92*
**Weltchek,** Robert Jay 1955- *WhoAmL 92*
**Welte** *NewAmDM*
**Welte,** A. Theodore 1944- *WhoFI 92*
**Welter,** Alphonse Nicholas 1925- *AmMWSc 92*
**Welter,** C Joseph 1932- *AmMWSc 92*
**Welter,** Dave Allen 1936- *AmMWSc 92*
**Welter,** Patrick John 1948- *WhoFI 92*
**Welter,** Rush 1923- *WrDr 92*
**Welter,** Rush E 1923- *IntAu&W 91*
**Welters,** Warren William, III 1956- *WhoMW 92*
**Welting,** Ruth Lynn 1948- *IntWW 91*
**Weltman,** Clarence A 1919- *AmMWSc 92*
**Weltman,** Joel Kenneth 1933- *AmMWSc 92*
**Weltman,** Sheldon J. 1936- *WhoRel 92*
**Weltmer,** Sidney A. 1858-1930 *RelLAm 91*
**Weltner,** Charles Longstreet 1927- *WhoAmL 92, WhoAmP 91*
**Weltner,** William, Jr 1922- *AmMWSc 92*
**Welton,** Ann Frances 1947- *AmMWSc 92*
**Welton,** Charles Ephraim 1947- *WhoWest 92*
**Welton,** Evelyn R. 1928- *WhoBlA 92*
**Welton,** James Arthur 1921- *WhoFI 92*
**Welton,** Kathleen Ann 1956- *WhoFI 92*
**Welton,** Michael Peter 1957- *WhoWest 92*
**Welton,** Steven Lee 1954- *WhoFI 92*
**Welton,** Theodore Allen 1918- *AmMWSc 92*
**Welton,** William Arch 1928- *AmMWSc 92*
**Welty,** Eudora *DrAPF 91, Who 92*
**Welty,** Eudora 1909- *BenetAL 91, ConNov 91, FacFETw, IntAu&W 91, IntWW 91, ModAWWr, WrDr 92*
**Welty,** Eudora Alice 1909- *HanAmWH*
**Welty,** Gordon A. 1942- *WhoMW 92*
**Welty,** James Richard 1933- *AmMWSc 92*
**Welty,** John D. 1944- *IntWW 91*
**Welty,** Joseph D 1931- *AmMWSc 92*
**Welty,** Quentin Reed 1925- *WhoEnt 92*
**Welty,** Richard Edward 1942- *WhoAmP 91*
**Welty,** Ronald Earle 1934- *AmMWSc 92*
**Welty,** Willis Edward 1926- *WhoMW 92*
**Welz,** Joey W. 1940- *WhoEnt 92*
**Welz,** Stephen Gary 1950- *WhoAmL 92*
**Welzen,** Lawrence Casimir 1963- *WhoEnt 92*
**Wemcken,** Christoph Michael 1949- *WhoEnt 92*
**Wemmer,** David Earl 1951- *AmMWSc 92*
**Wempe,** Jack 1934- *WhoAmP 91*
**Wempe,** Lawrence Kyran 1941- *AmMWSc 92*
**Wemple,** Clark Cullings 1927- *WhoAmP 91*
**Wemple,** J. Michael 1961- *WhoEnt 92*
**Wemple,** Stuart H 1930- *AmMWSc 92*
**Wempner,** Gerald Arthur 1928- *AmMWSc 92*
**Wemyss,** Earl of 1912- *Who 92*
**Wemyss,** Courtney Titus, Jr 1922- *AmMWSc 92*
**Wemyss,** Francis Courtney 1797-1859 *BenetAL 91*
**Wemyss,** Martin La Touche 1927- *Who 92*
**Wen Jiabao** 1942- *IntWW 91*
**Wen Minsheng** 1910- *IntWW 91*
**Wen,** Chin-Yung 1928- *AmMWSc 92*
**Wen,** Duanzhi 1942- *WhoWest 92*
**Wen,** Eric Hong-Hsu 1947- *WhoFI 92*
**Wen,** Eric Lewis 1953- *Who 92*
**Wen,** Richard Yutze 1930- *AmMWSc 92*
**Wen,** Shih-Liang *AmMWSc 92*
**Wen,** Sung-Feng 1933- *AmMWSc 92*
**Wen,** Wen-Yang 1931- *AmMWSc 92*
**Wenban-Smith,** Nigel *Who 92*
**Wenban-Smith,** William 1908- *Who 92*
**Wenban-Smith,** William Nigel 1936- *Who 92*
**Wenck,** Guy Addison 1943- *WhoRel 92*
**Wenckus,** James R 1941- *WhoIns 92*
**Wenclawiak,** Bernd Wilhelm 1951- *AmMWSc 92*
**Wend,** David Van Vranken 1923- *AmMWSc 92*
**Wende,** Charles David 1941- *AmMWSc 92*
**Wendel,** Carlton Tyrus 1939- *AmMWSc 92*
**Wendel,** Charlotte Selden 1944- *WhoEnt 92*
**Wendel,** Douglas John 1951- *WhoWest 92*
**Wendel,** Elmarie Louise 1935- *WhoEnt 92*
**Wendel,** James G 1922- *AmMWSc 92*
**Wendel,** John Fredric 1936- *WhoAmL 92*
**Wendel,** Otto Theodore, Jr 1948- *AmMWSc 92*
**Wendel,** Samuel Reece 1944- *AmMWSc 92*
**Wendelburg,** Norma Ruth 1918- *WhoEnt 92*
**Wendelken,** Carl Leroy 1925- *WhoEnt 92*
**Wendelken,** John Franklin 1945- *AmMWSc 92*
**Wendelken,** Richard Joseph 1939- *WhoAmL 92*
**Wendell,** Barrett 1855-1921 *BenetAL 91*
**Wendell,** Daniel Wade 1954- *WhoEnt 92*
**Wendell,** Julia *DrAPF 91*
**Wendell,** Leilah *DrAPF 91*
**Wendell,** Oliver Clinton 1845-1912 *BiInAmS*
**Wender,** Irving 1915- *AmMWSc 92*
**Wender,** Paul Anthony *AmMWSc 92*
**Wender,** Paul H 1934- *AmMWSc 92*
**Wender,** Paul Herbert 1934- *WhoWest 92*
**Wender,** Simon Harold 1913- *AmMWSc 92*
**Wenderoth,** Andrea Bull 1961- *WhoAmL 92*
**Wenders,** Wim 1945- *IntDcF 2-2 [port], IntMPA 92, IntWW 91*
**Wendkos,** Paul *LesBEnT 92*
**Wendkos,** Paul 1926- *IntMPA 92*
**Wendland,** Ray Theodore 1911- *AmMWSc 92*
**Wendland,** Wayne Marcel 1934- *AmMWSc 92, WhoMW 92*
**Wendland,** Wolfgang Leopold 1936- *AmMWSc 92*
**Wendlandt,** Wesley W 1927- *AmMWSc 92*
**Wendler,** Gerd Dierk 1939- *AmMWSc 92*
**Wendleton,** Patricia Ann 1942- *WhoAmP 91*
**Wendley,** Richard 1920- *WhoEnt 92*
**Wendoloski,** Anthony Joseph, Jr. 1945- *WhoRel 92*
**Wendorf,** Richard 1948- *ConAu 36NR*
**Wendricks,** Roland N 1930- *AmMWSc 92*
**Wendroff,** Burton 1930- *AmMWSc 92*
**Wendt,** Albert 1939- *ConNov 91, ConPo 91, IntWW 91, WrDr 92*
**Wendt,** Arnold 1922- *AmMWSc 92*
**Wendt,** Charles William 1931- *AmMWSc 92*
**Wendt,** David Allen 1959- *WhoMW 92*
**Wendt,** Edward George, Jr. 1928- *WhoFI 92*
**Wendt,** Elizabeth Warczak 1931- *WhoFI 92, WhoMW 92*
**Wendt,** Frankie 1958- *WhoAmL 92*
**Wendt,** Gary Carl 1942- *WhoFI 92*
**Wendt,** George 1948- *IntMPA 92*
**Wendt,** George Robert *WhoEnt 92*
**Wendt,** George Robert 1923- *WhoMW 92*
**Wendt,** Gregory Allen 1963- *WhoFI 92*
**Wendt,** Henry 1933- *IntWW 91, Who 92*
**Wendt,** Henry, III 1933- *WhoFI 92*
**Wendt,** Ingrid *DrAPF 91*
**Wendt,** Jerry James 1960- *WhoMW 92*
**Wendt,** John Arthur Frederic, Jr. *WhoAmL 92*
**Wendt,** Jost O L 1941- *AmMWSc 92*
**Wendt,** Larry 1946- *NewAmDM*
**Wendt,** Michael James 1948- *WhoWest 92*
**Wendt,** Norman Victor *WhoFI 92*
**Wendt,** Richard K 1932- *WhoIns 92*
**Wendt,** Richard P 1932- *AmMWSc 92*
**Wendt,** Robert Charles 1929- *AmMWSc 92*
**Wendt,** Robert L 1920- *AmMWSc 92*
**Wendt,** Robert Leo *AmMWSc 92*
**Wendt,** Robin Glover 1941- *Who 92*
**Wendt,** Steven William 1948- *WhoWest 92*
**Wendt,** Theodore Mil 1940- *AmMWSc 92*
**Wendt,** Thomas Gene 1951- *WhoFI 92, WhoMW 92*
**Wendte,** Ron 1948- *WhoAmP 91*
**Wendtland,** Anthony Todd 1961- *WhoAmL 92*
**Weneser,** Joseph 1922- *AmMWSc 92*
**Weng,** Lih-Jyh 1937- *AmMWSc 92*
**Weng,** Peter A. 1939- *WhoBlA 92*
**Weng,** Tung Hsiang 1933- *AmMWSc 92*
**Weng,** Tzong-Ruey 1934- *AmMWSc 92*
**Weng,** Wu Tsung 1944- *AmMWSc 92*
**Wengel,** John R. 1966- *WhoRel 92*
**Wenger,** Amos Daniel 1867-1935 *RelLAm 91*
**Wenger,** Antoine 1919- *IntWW 91*
**Wenger,** Byron Sylvester 1919- *AmMWSc 92*
**Wenger,** Christian Bruce 1942- *AmMWSc 92*
**Wenger,** David W. 1954- *WhoAmL 92*
**Wenger,** Derrick Eliot 1961- *WhoFI 92*
**Wenger,** Franz 1925- *AmMWSc 92*
**Wenger,** Galen Rosenberger 1946- *AmMWSc 92*
**Wenger,** J. C. 1910- *WrDr 92*
**Wenger,** James Carl 1958- *WhoRel 92*
**Wenger,** John C 1941- *AmMWSc 92*
**Wenger,** John Earl 1947- *WhoMW 92*
**Wenger,** Larry Bruce 1941- *WhoAmL 92*
**Wenger,** Lowell Edward 1948- *AmMWSc 92*
**Wenger,** Nanette Kass 1930- *AmMWSc 92*
**Wenger,** Noah W 1934- *WhoAmP 91*
**Wenger,** Paul Clement 1932- *WhoMW 92*
**Wenger,** Ronald Harold 1937- *AmMWSc 92*
**Wenger,** Thomas Lee 1945- *AmMWSc 92*
**Wengerd,** Sherman Alexander 1915- *AmMWSc 92*
**Wengertsman,** Carol Ann 1951- *WhoRel 92*
**Wengrow,** Arnold 1944- *WhoEnt 92*
**Wenham,** Brian George 1937- *Who 92*
**Wenig,** Harold G 1924- *AmMWSc 92*
**Wenig,** Harold George 1924- *WhoFI 92*
**Weninger,** Howard L 1904- *WhoAmP 91*
**Weninger,** John Franklin 1939- *WhoMW 92*
**Wenis,** Edward 1919- *AmMWSc 92*
**Wenk,** Charles Herman 1925- *WhoMW 92*
**Wenk,** Edward, Jr 1920- *AmMWSc 92*
**Wenk,** Eugene J 1927- *AmMWSc 92*
**Wenk,** Hans-Rudolf 1941- *AmMWSc 92*
**Wenk,** Martin Lester *AmMWSc 92*
**Wenkam,** Robert George 1920- *WhoEnt 92*
**Wenkert,** Ernest 1925- *AmMWSc 92*
**Wenman,** Thomas Lee 1950- *WhoFI 92*
**Wennberg,** John E 1934- *AmMWSc 92*
**Wenner,** A. Randall 1959- *WhoEnt 92*
**Wenner,** Adrian Manley 1928- *AmMWSc 92*
**Wenner,** Bruce Richard 1938- *AmMWSc 92*
**Wenner,** Charles Earl 1924- *AmMWSc 92*
**Wenner,** David Bruce 1941- *AmMWSc 92*
**Wenner,** Herbert Allan 1912- *AmMWSc 92*
**Wenner,** Jann Simon 1946- *WhoEnt 92*
**Wenner,** Kate *DrAPF 91*
**Wenner,** Michael Alfred 1921- *Who 92*
**Wenner,** Wallis 1919- *WhoEnt 92*
**Wennerberg,** A L 1932- *AmMWSc 92*
**Wennermark,** John David 1940- *WhoAmL 92*
**Wennerstrom,** Arthur J 1935- *AmMWSc 92*
**Wennerstrom,** David E 1945- *AmMWSc 92*
**Wennerstrom,** Mary H. 1939- *ConAu 134*
**Wennes,** Howard E. *WhoRel 92*
**Wenning,** Katherine *WhoEnt 92*
**Wennlund,** Larry 1941- *WhoAmP 91*
**Wenrich,** Karen Jane 1947- *AmMWSc 92, WhoWest 92*
**Wenrich,** Percy 1887-1952 *NewAmDM*
**Wensch,** Glen W 1917- *AmMWSc 92*
**Wenski,** Thomas Gerard 1950- *WhoRel 92*
**Wensley,** Charles Gelen 1949- *AmMWSc 92*
**Wenstrom,** Frank Augustus 1903- *WhoAmP 91*
**Wenstrom,** Gene R 1946- *WhoAmP 91*
**Went,** David 1947- *IntWW 91*
**Went,** Fritz 1903- *AmMWSc 92*
**Went,** Hans Adriaan 1929- *AmMWSc 92*
**Went,** John Stewart 1944- *Who 92*
**Wente,** Henry Christian 1936- *AmMWSc 92*
**Wente,** Patricia Ann *WhoMW 92*
**Wenten,** Robert Peter 1946- *WhoAmL 92*
**Wenthe,** P K 1937- *WhoIns 92*
**Wentink,** Maureen Ann McGuire 1929- *WhoWest 92*
**Wentink,** Tunis, Jr 1920- *AmMWSc 92*
**Wentland,** Mark Philip 1945- *AmMWSc 92*
**Wentland,** Stephen Henry 1940- *AmMWSc 92*
**Wentley,** Richard Taylor 1930- *WhoAmL 92*
**Wentorf,** Robert H, Jr 1926- *AmMWSc 92*
**Wentworth,** Alberta M *WhoAmP 91*
**Wentworth,** Bernard C 1935- *AmMWSc 92*
**Wentworth,** Carl M, Jr 1936- *AmMWSc 92*
**Wentworth,** Carl Merrick 1936- *WhoWest 92*
**Wentworth,** Gary 1939- *AmMWSc 92*
**Wentworth,** George Albert 1835-1906 *BiInAmS*
**Wentworth,** Jack Roberts 1928- *WhoFI 92*
**Wentworth,** Jason David 1966- *WhoAmP 91*
**Wentworth,** Jeff 1940- *WhoAmP 91*
**Wentworth,** John W 1925- *AmMWSc 92*
**Wentworth,** Lydia G. 1858-1947 *AmPeW*
**Wentworth,** Malinda Ann Nachman *WhoFI 92*
**Wentworth,** Maurice Frank Gerard 1908- *Who 92*
**Wentworth,** Richard 1947- *TwCPaSc*
**Wentworth,** Rupert A D 1934- *AmMWSc 92*
**Wentworth,** Stanley Earl 1940- *AmMWSc 92*
**Wentworth,** Stephen 1943- *Who 92*
**Wentworth,** Theodore Sumner 1938- *WhoAmL 92, WhoWest 92*
**Wentworth,** Thomas Ralph 1948- *AmMWSc 92*
**Wentworth,** Wayne 1930- *AmMWSc 92*
**Wentworth,** Winifred Lane 1927- *WhoAmL 92*
**Wentz,** Abdel Ross 1883-1976 *RelLAm 91*
**Wentz,** Charles Alvin, Jr. 1935- *WhoMW 92*
**Wentz,** Howard Beck, Jr. 1930- *WhoFI 92*
**Wentz,** Jack Lawrence 1937- *WhoAmL 92*
**Wentz,** Janet Marie 1937- *WhoAmP 91*
**Wentz,** Wayne Eric 1951- *WhoMW 92*
**Wentz,** Wendell Franklin 1939- *WhoMW 92*
**Wentz,** William Budd 1924- *AmMWSc 92*
**Wentz,** William Henry 1933- *AmMWSc 92*
**Wentzel,** Donat Gotthard 1934- *AmMWSc 92*
**Wentzel,** Herman Karl 1926- *WhoMW 92*
**Wentzel,** Jacob Johannes Greyling 1925- *IntWW 91*
**Wentzel,** Willard LeRoy, Jr. 1955- *WhoAmL 92*
**Wentzien,** Paul Warren 1937- *WhoMW 92*
**Wentzler,** Nancy Anne 1951- *WhoFI 92*
**Wenzel,** Alan Richard 1938- *AmMWSc 92*
**Wenzel,** Alexander B 1936- *AmMWSc 92*
**Wenzel,** Bernice Martha 1921- *AmMWSc 92*
**Wenzel,** Bruce Erickson 1938- *AmMWSc 92*
**Wenzel,** Carol Marion Nagler 1936- *WhoWest 92*
**Wenzel,** David J 1945- *WhoAmP 91*
**Wenzel,** Duane Greve 1920- *AmMWSc 92*
**Wenzel,** Edward Leon 1949- *WhoFI 92*
**Wenzel,** Elizabeth Marie 1954- *WhoWest 92*
**Wenzel,** Frederick J 1930- *AmMWSc 92*
**Wenzel,** Harry G, Jr 1937- *AmMWSc 92*
**Wenzel,** James Gottlieb 1926- *AmMWSc 92*
**Wenzel,** John Albert 1941- *WhoMW 92*
**Wenzel,** John Thompson 1946- *AmMWSc 92*
**Wenzel,** Leonard A 1923- *AmMWSc 92*
**Wenzel,** Richard Louis 1921- *AmMWSc 92*
**Wenzel,** Robert Gale 1932- *AmMWSc 92*
**Wenzel,** Rupert Leon 1915- *AmMWSc 92*
**Wenzel,** Stephen G 1946- *WhoAmP 91*
**Wenzel,** William Alfred 1924- *AmMWSc 92*
**Wenzell,** William Theodore 1829-1913 *BiInAmS*
**Wenzinger,** George Robert 1933- *AmMWSc 92*
**Wenzl,** James E 1935- *AmMWSc 92*
**Wenzler,** Edward William 1954- *WhoMW 92*
**Wenzler,** Paul B. 1947- *WhoFI 92*
**Weores,** Sandor 1913- *IntAu&W 91*
**Wepener,** Willem Jacobus 1927- *IntWW 91*
**Wepfer,** William J 1952- *AmMWSc 92*
**Weppelman,** Roger Michael 1944- *AmMWSc 92*
**Weprin,** Saul 1927- *WhoAmP 91*
**Werb,** Hillel David 1941- *WhoRel 92*
**Werba,** Erik 1918- *NewAmDM*
**Werba,** Gabriel 1930- *WhoFI 92*
**Werbach,** Melvyn Roy 1940- *AmMWSc 92, WhoWest 92*
**Werbalowsky,** Jeffrey Ira 1957- *WhoFI 92*
**Werbel,** Leslie Morton 1931- *AmMWSc 92*
**Werber,** Erna Alture 1909- *AmMWSc 92*
**Werber,** Frank Xavier 1924- *AmMWSc 92*
**Werber,** Stephen Jay 1940- *WhoAmL 92*
**Werbin,** Harold 1922- *AmMWSc 92*
**Werblin,** David A. 1910-1991 *NewYTBS 91 [port]*
**Werblin,** Frank Simon 1937- *AmMWSc 92*
**Werbner,** Eliot *DrAPF 91*

**Werckmeister**, Andreas 1645-1706 *NewAmDM*
**Werdegar**, David 1930- *AmMWSc 92*
**Werdel**, Judith Ann 1937- *AmMWSc 92*
**Werder**, Alvar Arvid 1917- *AmMWSc 92*
**Werderman**, William Robert 1937- *WhoWest 92*
**Werdin**, Andrew Charles 1964- *WhoMW 92*
**Werfel**, David Michael 1947- *WhoAmL 92*
**Werfel**, Franz 1890-1945 *EncTR 91 [port], FacFETw, LiExTwC*
**Wergedal**, Jon E 1936- *AmMWSc 92*
**Werger**, Marinus Johannes Antonius 1944- *IntWW 91*
**Werger**, Paul Myron 1931- *WhoMW 92, WhoRel 92*
**Wergin**, William Peter 1942- *AmMWSc 92*
**Werk**, Allen Arthur 1956- *WhoRel 92*
**Werkema**, George Jan 1936- *AmMWSc 92*
**Werkheiser**, Arthur H, Jr 1935- *AmMWSc 92*
**Werkhoven**, Theunis 1922- *WhoAmP 91*
**Werking**, Robert Junior 1930- *AmMWSc 92*
**Werkman**, Joyce 1940- *AmMWSc 92*
**Werkman**, Sidney Lee 1927- *AmMWSc 92*
**Werkstrom**, Bertil *WhoRel 92*
**Werle**, Charles Robert 1936- *WhoMW 92*
**Werlein**, Ewing, Jr. 1936- *WhoAmL 92*
**Werlin**, Paul Alan 1952- *WhoFI 92*
**Werman**, Robert 1929- *AmMWSc 92*
**Werman**, Thomas Ehrlich 1945- *WhoEnt 92*
**Wermers**, Mary Ann 1946- *WhoWest 92*
**Wermund**, Edmund Gerald, Jr 1926- *AmMWSc 92*
**Wermus**, Gerald R 1938- *AmMWSc 92*
**Wermuth**, Jerome Francis 1936- *AmMWSc 92*
**Wermuth**, Michael Anthony 1946- *WhoAmP 91*
**Wernau**, William Charles 1947- *AmMWSc 92*
**Wernecke**, Heinz 1922- *WhoMW 92*
**Wernecke**, Julia Wagner 1959- *WhoAmL 92*
**Werner**, Abraham Gottlob 1750-1817 *BlkwCEP*
**Werner**, Alfred 1866-1919 *WhoNob 90*
**Werner**, Alfred Emil Anthony 1911- *Who 92*
**Werner**, Arnold 1938- *AmMWSc 92*
**Werner**, Burton Kready 1933- *WhoFI 92, WhoIns 92*
**Werner**, Daniel Paul 1938- *AmMWSc 92*
**Werner**, E. Louis, Jr. *WhoWest 92*
**Werner**, Earl Edward 1944- *AmMWSc 92*
**Werner**, Elmer Louis, Jr 1927- *WhoIns 92*
**Werner**, Ervin Robert, Jr 1932- *AmMWSc 92*
**Werner**, F E 1927- *AmMWSc 92*
**Werner**, Floyd Gerald 1921- *AmMWSc 92*
**Werner**, Frank D 1922- *AmMWSc 92*
**Werner**, Fritz *WhoWest 92*
**Werner**, Gerhard 1921- *AmMWSc 92*
**Werner**, Glenn Allen 1955- *WhoMW 92*
**Werner**, Gloria S. 1940- *WhoWest 92*
**Werner**, Harold Robert 1948- *WhoFI 92*
**Werner**, Harry Emil 1921- *AmMWSc 92*
**Werner**, Helmut 1936- *IntWW 91*
**Werner**, Herma 1926- *ConAu 34NR*
**Werner**, James Edward 1951- *WhoRel 92*
**Werner**, Janet B 1916- *WhoAmP 91*
**Werner**, Jay Steven 1954- *WhoWest 92*
**Werner**, Joan Kathleen 1932- *AmMWSc 92*
**Werner**, Joanne Lucille 1940- *WhoFI 92*
**Werner**, John Ellis 1932- *AmMWSc 92*
**Werner**, John Kirwin 1941- *AmMWSc 92*
**Werner**, Karl Ferdinand 1924- *IntWW 91*
**Werner**, Lincoln Harvey 1918- *AmMWSc 92*
**Werner**, M. R. 1897-1981 *BenetAL 91*
**Werner**, Mario 1931- *AmMWSc 92*
**Werner**, Michael 1912- *TwCPaSc*
**Werner**, Michael Wolock 1942- *AmMWSc 92*
**Werner**, Mort *LesBEnT 92*
**Werner**, Patricia Ann Snyder 1941- *AmMWSc 92*
**Werner**, Peter *IntAu&W 91X*
**Werner**, Peter 1947- *IntMPA 92*
**Werner**, Pierre 1913- *IntWW 91*
**Werner**, Raymond Edmund 1919- *AmMWSc 92*
**Werner**, Richard Allen 1936- *AmMWSc 92, WhoWest 92*
**Werner**, Richard Earle 1918- *WhoFI 92*
**Werner**, Robert Allen 1946- *WhoMW 92*
**Werner**, Robert George 1936- *AmMWSc 92*
**Werner**, Robert John 1951- *WhoMW 92*
**Werner**, Robert L. 1913- *WhoAmL 92*
**Werner**, Roger Harry 1950- *WhoWest 92*
**Werner**, Roger Livingston, Jr. 1950- *WhoEnt 92*
**Werner**, Ronald Louis 1924- *Who 92*
**Werner**, Roy Anthony 1944- *WhoWest 92*
**Werner**, Rudolf 1934- *AmMWSc 92*
**Werner**, Samuel Alfred 1937- *AmMWSc 92*
**Werner**, Sandra Lee 1938- *WhoAmP 91*
**Werner**, Sanford Benson 1939- *AmMWSc 92*
**Werner**, Sidney Charles 1909- *AmMWSc 92*
**Werner**, Stuart Lloyd 1932- *WhoFI 92*
**Werner**, Thomas Clyde 1942- *AmMWSc 92*
**Werner**, Tom *WhoEnt 92*
**Werner**, William Ernest 1930- *WhoMW 92*
**Werner**, William Ernest, Jr 1925- *AmMWSc 92*
**Werner-Robertson**, Gail Marie 1962- *WhoFI 92*
**Wernham**, Richard Bruce 1906- *Who 92*
**Wernheim**, John *TwCSFW 91*
**Wernick**, Jack H 1923- *AmMWSc 92*
**Wernick**, Richard 1934- *ConCom 92, NewAmDM*
**Wernick**, Richard Frank 1934- *WhoEnt 92*
**Wernick**, Robert J 1928- *AmMWSc 92*
**Wernick**, William 1910- *AmMWSc 92*
**Wernimont**, Cheryl Ann 1944- *WhoMW 92*
**Werning**, Waldo John 1921- *WhoRel 92*
**Wernle**, C Henry 1831?-1902 *BiInAmS*
**Wernsman**, Earl Allen 1935- *AmMWSc 92*
**Werntz**, Carl W 1931- *AmMWSc 92*
**Werntz**, Henry Oscar 1930- *AmMWSc 92*
**Werntz**, James Herbert, Jr 1928- *AmMWSc 92*
**Werny**, Frank 1936- *AmMWSc 92*
**Werries**, E. Dean 1929- *WhoFI 92*
**Werry**, Arthur Eugene 1960- *WhoRel 92*
**Wersba**, Barbara 1932- *WrDr 92*
**Wershaw**, Robert Lawrence 1935- *AmMWSc 92*
**Wershba**, Joseph *LesBEnT 92*
**Wershba**, Joseph 1920- *WhoEnt 92*
**Werst**, Kevin Scott 1958- *WhoRel 92*
**Werstiuk**, Nick Henry 1939- *AmMWSc 92*
**Wert**, Charles Allen 1919- *AmMWSc 92*
**Wert**, Frank Shadle 1942- *WhoFI 92*
**Wert**, Giaches de 1535-1596 *NewAmDM*
**Wert**, Harry Emerson 1932- *WhoWest 92*
**Wert**, James J 1933- *AmMWSc 92*
**Wert**, James William 1946- *WhoFI 92*
**Wert**, Jonathan 1939- *WrDr 92*
**Wert**, Jonathan Maxwell, Jr 1939- *AmMWSc 92*
**Wert**, Karl Jerome 1943- *WhoWest 92*
**Wert**, Lawrence Joseph 1956- *WhoMW 92*
**Wert**, Lucille Mathena 1919- *WhoMW 92*
**Wert**, Peter Leigh 1964- *WhoEnt 92*
**Wert**, Robert Clifton 1944- *WhoAmL 92*
**Wertenbaker**, G Peyton 1907- *ScFEYrs*
**Wertenbaker**, L. T. *ConTFT 9*
**Wertenbaker**, Lael *ConTFT 9*
**Wertenbaker**, Lael Tucker *ConTFT 9*
**Wertenbaker**, Lael Tucker 1909- *WrDr 92*
**Wertenbaker**, Timberlake *WrDr 92*
**Wertenbaker**, Timberlake 1909- *ConTFT 9*
**Werth**, Glenn Conrad 1926- *AmMWSc 92*
**Werth**, Jean Marie 1943- *AmMWSc 92*
**Werth**, Richard George 1920- *AmMWSc 92, WhoMW 92*
**Werth**, Robert Joseph 1940- *AmMWSc 92*
**Werthamer**, N Richard 1935- *AmMWSc 92*
**Werthan**, Jeffrey Michael 1954- *WhoAmL 92*
**Wertheim**, Arthur Robert 1915- *AmMWSc 92*
**Wertheim**, Bill *DrAPF 91*
**Wertheim**, Gunther Klaus 1927- *AmMWSc 92*
**Wertheim**, Jay Philip 1952- *WhoAmL 92*
**Wertheim**, Lynda Faye 1949- *WhoFI 92*
**Wertheim**, Mary Ann 1955- *WhoAmL 92*
**Wertheim**, Robert Halley 1922- *AmMWSc 92*
**Wertheim**, Toby 1946- *WhoEnt 92*
**Wertheimer**, Alan Lee 1946- *AmMWSc 92*
**Wertheimer**, Albert I 1942- *AmMWSc 92*
**Wertheimer**, Fred 1939- *WhoAmP 91*
**Wertheimer**, Max 1880-1943 *FacFETw*
**Wertheimer**, Michael Robert 1940- *AmMWSc 92*
**Wertheimer**, Richard Frederick, II 1943- *WhoFI 92*
**Wertheimer**, Richard James 1936- *WhoAmL 92*
**Wertheimer**, Thomas 1938- *IntMPA 92, WhoEnt 92, WhoFI 92*
**Werthen**, Hans Lennart Oscar 1919- *IntWW 91*
**Wertime**, Richard *DrAPF 91*
**Wertman**, Louis 1925- *AmMWSc 92*
**Wertman**, William Thomas 1920- *AmMWSc 92*
**Wertmuller**, Lina 1928- *IntDcF 2-2 [port], IntMPA 92, IntWW 91*
**Wertmuller**, Lina 193-?- *ReelWom [port]*
**Werts**, John Stephen 1945- *WhoAmL 92*
**Werts**, Merrill Harmon 1922- *WhoAmP 91, WhoMW 92*
**Wertz**, Andrew Walter, Sr. 1928- *WhoBlA 92*
**Wertz**, David Lee 1940- *AmMWSc 92*
**Wertz**, Dennis William 1942- *AmMWSc 92*
**Wertz**, Gail T Williams 1943- *AmMWSc 92*
**Wertz**, Glenda M. 1959- *WhoFI 92*
**Wertz**, Harvey J 1936- *AmMWSc 92*
**Wertz**, Harvey Joe 1936- *WhoWest 92*
**Wertz**, Jack Lowell 1931- *WhoAmP 91*
**Wertz**, James Richard 1944- *AmMWSc 92*
**Wertz**, John Edward 1916- *AmMWSc 92*
**Wertz**, Krickett Yarnell 1953- *WhoEnt 92*
**Wertz**, Mark Earl 1957- *WhoAmL 92*
**Wertz**, Philip W. 1949- *WhoMW 92*
**Wertz**, Philip Wesley 1949- *AmMWSc 92*
**Wertz**, Robert Charles 1932- *WhoAmP 91*
**Wertz**, Robert Randy 1947- *WhoAmL 92*
**Wertz**, Ronald Duane 1929- *AmMWSc 92*
**Wertz**, William John 1945- *WhoEnt 92*
**Wesberry**, James Pickett 1906- *WhoRel 92*
**Wesberry**, James Pickett, Jr. 1934- *WhoFI 92*
**Wesbrook**, Frank Fairchild 1868-1918 *BiInAmS*
**Wesbrooks**, Perry 1932- *WhoAmL 92*
**Wesbury**, Stuart Arnold, Jr. 1933- *WhoFI 92, WhoMW 92*
**Wesche**, Percival A 1912- *WhoAmP 91*
**Weschke**, Karl 1925- *TwCPaSc*
**Weschke**, Karl Martin 1925- *IntWW 91*
**Weschler**, Charles John 1948- *AmMWSc 92*
**Weschler**, Lawrence 1952- *ConAu 135*
**Wescoat**, Kyle Burley 1951- *WhoFI 92*
**Wescott**, Don Harlow 1940- *WhoEnt 92*
**Wescott**, Eugene Michael 1932- *AmMWSc 92*
**Wescott**, Glenway 1901-1989 *BenetAL 91*
**Wescott**, Lyle DuMond, Jr 1937- *AmMWSc 92*
**Wescott**, Lynanne Butcher 1951- *WhoAmL 92*
**Wescott**, Richard Breslich 1932- *AmMWSc 92*
**Wescott**, William B 1922- *AmMWSc 92*
**Weseli**, Roger William 1932- *WhoMW 92*
**Weseloh**, Melvin Leslie 1932- *WhoRel 92*
**Weseloh**, Ronald Mack 1944- *AmMWSc 92*
**Wesely**, Don 1954- *WhoAmP 91*
**Wesely**, Donald Raymond 1954- *WhoMW 92*
**Wesely**, Edwin Joseph 1929- *WhoAmL 92, WhoFI 92*
**Wesely**, Marvin Larry 1944- *AmMWSc 92*
**Wesely**, Meridel Ann 1944- *WhoMW 92*
**Wesenberg**, Clarence L 1920- *AmMWSc 92*
**Wesenberg**, Darrell 1939- *AmMWSc 92*
**Weser**, Don Benton 1942- *AmMWSc 92*
**Weser**, Elliot 1932- *AmMWSc 92*
**Wesierska**, George, Mrs. *Who 92*
**Wesil**, Dennis 1915- *Who 92*
**Wesker**, Arnold 1932- *CnDBLB 8 [port], IntAu&W 91, IntWW 91, RfGEnL 91, Who 92, WrDr 92*
**Wesler**, Ken 1964- *WhoEnt 92*
**Wesler**, Oscar 1921- *AmMWSc 92*
**Wesley**, Barbara Ann 1930- *WhoBlA 92*
**Wesley**, Charles 1707-1788 *RfGEnL 91*
**Wesley**, Clarence E. 1940- *WhoBlA 92*
**Wesley**, Clemon Herbert, Jr. 1936- *WhoBlA 92*
**Wesley**, Dean E 1937- *AmMWSc 92*
**Wesley**, Elizabeth *IntAu&W 91X, WrDr 92*
**Wesley**, Gloria Walker 1928- *WhoBlA 92*
**Wesley**, John 1703-1791 *BlkwCEP*
**Wesley**, John Milton *DrAPF 91*
**Wesley**, John Phillip 1950- *WhoRel 92*
**Wesley**, Mary *Who 92*
**Wesley**, Mary 1912- *ConNov 91, IntAu&W 91, SmATA 66 [port], WrDr 92*
**Wesley**, Nathaniel, Jr. 1943- *WhoBlA 92*
**Wesley**, Richard 1945- *WrDr 92*
**Wesley**, Richard C 1949- *WhoAmP 91*
**Wesley**, Richard Errol 1945- *IntAu&W 91, WhoBlA 92*
**Wesley**, Robert Cook 1926- *AmMWSc 92*
**Wesley**, Roy Lewis 1929- *AmMWSc 92*
**Wesley**, Samuel 1766-1837 *NewAmDM*
**Wesley**, Samuel 1810-1876 *NewAmDM*
**Wesley**, Stephen Burton 1949- *WhoFI 92*
**Wesley**, Stephen Harrison 1961- *WhoFI 92*
**Wesley**, Virginia Anne 1951- *WhoWest 92*
**Wesley**, Walter Glen 1938- *AmMWSc 92*
**Wesley**, Yvonne Edith 1936- *WhoRel 92*
**Wesloh**, Ferdinand Joseph 1938- *WhoRel 92*
**Wesner**, James Ermal 1936- *WhoAmL 92*
**Wesner**, John William 1936- *AmMWSc 92*
**Wesnick**, Richard James 1938- *WhoWest 92*
**Wesolowski**, Kurt Scott 1962- *WhoRel 92*
**Wesolowski**, Wayne Edward 1945- *AmMWSc 92*
**Wess**, Glenys *TwCPaSc*
**Wess**, Jim 1933- *TwCPaSc*
**Wess**, Roger George 1940- *WhoMW 92*
**Wesse**, David Joseph 1951- *WhoFI 92, WhoMW 92*
**Wessel**, Carol Sue 1965- *WhoMW 92*
**Wessel**, Colleen Annette 1962- *WhoMW 92*
**Wessel**, Frederick Peter 1941- *WhoEnt 92*
**Wessel**, Gunter Kurt 1920- *AmMWSc 92*
**Wessel**, Hans U 1927- *AmMWSc 92*
**Wessel**, Helen S. 1924- *WrDr 92*
**Wessel**, Horst 1907-1930 *BiDExR, EncTR 91 [port]*
**Wessel**, Jeanette Driver 1942- *WhoAmP 91*
**Wessel**, John Emmit 1942- *AmMWSc 92*
**Wessel**, Jonathan Andrew 1962- *WhoRel 92*
**Wessel**, Milton R. d1991 *NewYTBS 91*
**Wessel**, Nancy Kathryn 1935- *WhoAmP 91*
**Wessel**, Peter 1952- *WhoAmL 92*
**Wessel**, Richard Louis 1931- *WhoMW 92*
**Wessel**, Robert Leslie 1912- *Who 92*
**Wessel**, Roger D. 1957- *WhoRel 92*
**Wessel**, William Roy 1937- *AmMWSc 92, WhoWest 92*
**Wesselink**, David Duwayne 1942- *WhoFI 92*
**Wessells**, Norman Keith 1932- *AmMWSc 92*
**Wesselmann**, Tom 1931- *IntWW 91*
**Wessels**, Bruce Warren 1946- *AmMWSc 92*
**Wessels**, Charles Henry 1940- *WhoAmP 91*
**Wessels**, David Joseph 1945- *WhoRel 92*
**Wessels**, Laura Kay 1965- *WhoRel 92*
**Wessels**, Richard Herbert 1939- *WhoAmL 92*
**Wesselschmidt**, Quentin Frederick 1937- *WhoRel 92*
**Wessely**, Joseph G. 1956- *WhoFI 92*
**Wessely**, Paula 1907- *EncTR 91 [port]*
**Wessenauer**, Gabriel Otto 1906- *AmMWSc 92*
**Wesserling**, Charles Richard 1955- *WhoAmL 92*
**Wessinger**, Noah Frederick 1933- *WhoWest 92*
**Wessinger**, William David 1951- *AmMWSc 92*
**Wessler**, Max Alden 1931- *AmMWSc 92*
**Wessler**, Melvin Dean 1932- *WhoWest 92*
**Wessler**, Ruth Ann Cotter 1938- *WhoMW 92*
**Wessler**, Stanford 1917- *AmMWSc 92*
**Wessling**, Donald Moore 1936- *WhoAmL 92*
**Wessling**, Gregory Jay 1951- *WhoFI 92*
**Wessling**, Mark 1944- *WhoAmL 92*
**Wessling**, Ritchie A 1932- *AmMWSc 92*
**Wessling**, Robert Bruce 1937- *WhoAmL 92*
**Wessman**, Garner Elmer 1920- *AmMWSc 92*
**Wessman**, Henry C 1937- *WhoAmP 91*
**Wessner**, Kenneth Thomas 1922- *WhoFI 92*
**Wesson**, Alphonzo Joshua, III 1960- *WhoEnt 92*
**Wesson**, Chalmers William 1924- *WhoAmP 91*
**Wesson**, Cleo 1924- *WhoBlA 92*
**Wesson**, Edward 1910- *TwCPaSc*
**Wesson**, James Robert 1921- *AmMWSc 92*
**Wesson**, Kenneth Alan 1948- *WhoBlA 92*
**Wesson**, Laurence Goddard, Jr 1917- *AmMWSc 92*
**Wesson**, Paul Stephen 1949- *AmMWSc 92*
**Wesson**, Robert G. 1920- *WrDr 92*
**Wesson**, Robert G. 1920-1991 *ConAu 134*
**Wesson**, Robert Gale d1991 *NewYTBS 91*
**Wesson**, Robert Laughlin 1944- *AmMWSc 92*
**West** *Who 92*
**West**, A Sumner 1922- *AmMWSc 92*
**West**, Adam 1929- *IntMPA 92*
**West**, Anita 1930- *AmMWSc 92*
**West**, Anthony 1914-1987 *BenetAL 91*
**West**, Anthony C. 1910- *ConNov 91, WrDr 92*
**West**, Arthur James, II 1927- *AmMWSc 92*
**West**, Ben, Jr 1941- *WhoAmP 91*
**West**, Benjamin 1730-1813 *BenetAL 91, BiInAmS*
**West**, Billy Gene 1946- *WhoWest 92*
**West**, Bob 1931- *AmMWSc 92*
**West**, Bruce Alan 1948- *WhoWest 92*
**West**, Bruce David 1935- *AmMWSc 92*
**West**, Burl Dwight 1954- *WhoRel 92*
**West**, Byron Kenneth 1933- *WhoMW 92*
**West**, Carol Ann 1938- *WhoRel 92*

West, Carol Catherine 1944- WhoAmL 92
West, Charles Allen 1927- AmMWSc 92
West, Charles David 1937- AmMWSc 92
West, Charles Donald 1920- AmMWSc 92
West, Charles H. 1934- WhoFI 92
West, Charles Hutchison Keesor 1948- AmMWSc 92
West, Charles P 1916- AmMWSc 92
West, Charles P 1921- WhoAmP 91
West, Charles Patrick 1952- AmMWSc 92
West, Charles Ross DrAPF 91
West, Charlotte 1932- WhoMW 92
West, Christopher Drane 1943- AmMWSc 92
West, Christopher John 1936- WhoEnt 92
West, Christopher O. 1915- WhoBlA 92
West, Christopher Robin 1944- Who 92
West, Christopher Wayne 1961- WhoWest 92
West, Claire 1893-1980 ReelWom
West, Clark Darwin 1918- AmMWSc 92
West, Clell Albert 1934- WhoWest 92
West, Colin Douglas 1941- AmMWSc 92
West, Cornel 1953- NewYTBS 91 [port]
West, Dan Carlos 1939- WhoMW 92
West, Daniel 1893-1971 AmPeW
West, Daniel C. 1955- WhoRel 92
West, Danny Lee 1950- WhoMW 92
West, Darby Lindsey 1938- WhoWest 92
West, David 1939- TwCPaSc
West, David Armstrong 1933- AmMWSc 92
West, David Arthur James 1927- Who 92
West, David Eugene 1956- WhoEnt 92
West, David Thomson 1923- Who 92
West, David William 1937- WhoAmP 91
West, Delno Cloyde, Jr. 1936- WhoWest 92
West, Dennis R 1946- AmMWSc 92
West, Donald James 1924- Who 92, WrDr 92
West, Donald K 1929- AmMWSc 92
West, Donald Markham 1925- AmMWSc 92
West, Donald V. 1930- WhoEnt 92
West, Donna L. 1938- WhoWest 92
West, Dorothy ConAu 134, SmATA 65
West, Dorothy 1907- NotBlAW 92 [port], WhoBlA 92
West, Dottie 1932-1991 NewYTBS 91, News 92-2
West, Doug 1967- WhoBlA 92
West, Douglas IntAu&W 91X, TwCSFW 91
West, Douglas Brent 1953- AmMWSc 92
West, Douglas Xavier 1937- AmMWSc 92
West, E P 1820-1892 BiInAmS
West, Earl Irvin 1920- WhoRel 92
West, Earl M. 1912- WhoBlA 92
West, Edward Alan 1928- WhoFI 92, WhoWest 92
West, Edward Mark 1923- IntWW 91, Who 92
West, Edward S. 1957- WhoAmL 92
West, Elmer D. 1907-1991 ConAu 135
West, Elmer Gordon 1914- WhoAmL 92
West, Emery Joseph 1940- WhoFI 92
West, Eric Neil 1941- AmMWSc 92
West, Erick Clay 1962- WhoRel 92
West, Erlene Elaine 1951- WhoWest 92
West, Ernest Patrick, Jr. 1925- WhoFI 92
West, Felicia Emminger 1926- AmMWSc 92
West, Fowler Claude 1940- WhoAmP 91, WhoFI 92
West, Francis 1936- TwCPaSc
West, Francis Horner 1909- Who 92
West, Francis James 1927- IntWW 91, WrDr 92
West, Fred Ralph, Jr 1925- AmMWSc 92
West, Frederic Hadleigh, Jr. 1956- WhoFI 92
West, Gayle Dianne 1944- WhoAmP 91
West, George Arthur Alston-Roberts- 1937- Who 92
West, George Curtiss 1931- AmMWSc 92
West, George Ferdinand, Jr. 1940- WhoBlA 92
West, George M 1923- WhoAmP 91
West, Gerald I. 1937- WhoBlA 92
West, Glenn Edward 1944- WhoFI 92
West, Gordon Fox 1933- AmMWSc 92
West, Harold Dadford 1904- WhoBlA 92
West, Harry Irwin, Jr 1925- AmMWSc 92
West, Henry John 1942- WhoMW 92
West, Henry William 1917- Who 92
West, Herbert Lee, Jr. 1947- WhoBlA 92
West, Herschel J 1937- AmMWSc 92
West, Hugh Sterling 1930- WhoWest 92
West, J Robinson 1946- WhoAmP 91
West, Jack Henry 1934- WhoWest 92
West, Jacqueline Louise WhoEnt 92
West, Jade Christine 1950- WhoAmP 91
West, James A. 1960- WhoAmL 92
West, James C. WhoRel 92
West, James E 1951- WhoAmP 91
West, James Edward 1944- AmMWSc 92
West, James Harold 1926- WhoFI 92
West, James Joe 1936- WhoWest 92
West, James Joseph 1945- WhoAmL 92
West, Jay 1951- WhoAmP 91
West, Jean DrAPF 91
West, Jerome Alan 1938- FacFETw
West, Jerry Alan 1938- WhoWest 92
West, Jerry Lee 1940- AmMWSc 92
West, Jessamyn 1902-1984 BenetAL 91, TwCWW 91
West, Jody Woodward 1957- WhoFI 92
West, John Andrew 1942- WhoBlA 92
West, John Anthony DrAPF 91
West, John B 1925- AmMWSc 92
West, John B 1928- AmMWSc 92
West, John Burnard 1928- WhoWest 92
West, John C. 1922- IntWW 91
West, John Carl 1922- WhoAmP 91
West, John Clifford 1922- Who 92
West, John Foster DrAPF 91
West, John Frederick 1929- WrDr 92
West, John Gregory 1947- WhoAmP 91
West, John Henry, III 1954- WhoRel 92
West, John M 1920- AmMWSc 92
West, John M 1927- AmMWSc 92
West, John Raymond 1931- WhoBlA 92
West, John Wyatt 1923- AmMWSc 92
West, Joseph King 1929- WhoAmL 92, WhoBlA 92
West, Julian ScFEYrs
West, Kathleene DrAPF 91
West, Keith P 1920- AmMWSc 92
West, Kenneth 1930- Who 92
West, Kenneth Calvin 1935- AmMWSc 92
West, Kevin J 1958- AmMWSc 92
West, Kevin James 1958- AmMWSc 92
West, Kingsley TwCWW 91
West, Layton Paul 1950- WhoMW 92
West, Leander 1954- WhoRel 92
West, Lee Roy 1929- WhoAmL 92
West, Louis Jolyon 1924- AmMWSc 92, WhoWest 92
West, M. Holland 1952- WhoAmL 92
West, Mae BenetAL 91
West, Mae 1892-1980 FacFETw
West, Mae 1893-1980 ReelWom [port]
West, Marcella Polite WhoBlA 92
West, Marcellus 1913- WhoBlA 92
West, Mark Andre 1960- WhoBlA 92
West, Martin Litchfield 1937- IntWW 91, Who 92
West, Martin Luther 1936- AmMWSc 92
West, Michael DrAPF 91
West, Michael 1948- WhoMW 92
West, Michael Charles B. Who 92
West, Mike Harold 1948- AmMWSc 92
West, Mitchell 1953- WhoWest 92
West, Morris 1916- ConNov 91, IntAu&W 91, IntWW 91, Who 92, WrDr 92
West, Nathanael 1903-1940 FacFETw, TwCLC 44 [port]
West, Nathanael 1904-1940 BenetAL 91
West, Neil Elliott 1937- AmMWSc 92
West, Nigel Who 92
West, Norman 1935- Who 92
West, Norman Ariel 1928- WhoAmL 92
West, Norman Reed 1943- AmMWSc 92
West, Owen ConAu 36NR, WrDr 92
West, Pamela Marshall 1956- WhoAmL 92
West, Paul DrAPF 91
West, Paul 1930- BenetAL 91, ConNov 91, WrDr 92
West, Peter 1920- Who 92
West, Peter Lawrence 1965- WhoRel 92
West, Pheoris 1950- WhoBlA 92
West, Philip William 1913- AmMWSc 92
West, Pilar Ramirez 1935- WhoHisp 92
West, Prunella Margaret Rumney Who 92
West, Rebecca 1892-1983 BiDBrF 2, FacFETw [port], RfGEnL 91
West, Richard G. 1926- IntWW 91
West, Richard Gilbert 1926- Who 92
West, Richard John 1939- Who 92
West, Richard Lowell 1934- AmMWSc 92
West, Richard Paul 1947- WhoWest 92
West, Richard Rollin 1938- WhoFI 92
West, Richard Vincent 1934- WhoWest 92
West, Robert A 1951- AmMWSc 92
West, Robert Elmer 1938- AmMWSc 92
West, Robert Gerard 1959- WhoEnt 92
West, Robert H. 1938- WhoFI 92, WhoMW 92
West, Robert Lewis 1951- WhoFI 92
West, Robert MacLellan 1942- AmMWSc 92, WhoMW 92
West, Robert Sumner 1935- WhoWest 92
West, Robert V, Jr 1921- WhoAmP 91
West, Roger Seiker, III 1949- WhoFI 92
West, Ronald E 1933- AmMWSc 92
West, Ronald La Vera 1948- WhoMW 92
West, Ronald Robert 1935- AmMWSc 92
West, Rose Gayle 1943- AmMWSc 92
West, Roy 1939- WhoBlA 92
West, Roy A 1930- WhoAmP 91
West, Royce Barry 1952- WhoBlA 92
West, Samuel Edward 1938- WhoFI 92
West, Sarah EncAmaz 91
West, Seymour S 1920- AmMWSc 92
West, Shelby Jay 1938- WhoFI 92, WhoWest 92
West, Sherlie Hill 1927- AmMWSc 92
West, Stephanie Roberta 1937- Who 92
West, Stephen R. 1931- WhoMW 92
West, Stephen Robert 1931- WhoAmP 91
West, Stewart John 1934- IntWW 91
West, Tegan Newton 1959- WhoEnt 92
West, Terence Douglas 1948- WhoFI 92, WhoMW 92
West, Terry Ronald 1936- AmMWSc 92
West, Theodore Clinton 1919- AmMWSc 92
West, Thomas A. DrAPF 91
West, Thomas Dyson 1851-1915 BiInAmS
West, Thomas Edward 1954- WhoEnt 92
West, Thomas Lowell, Jr. 1937- WhoFI 92
West, Thomas Meade 1940- WhoFI 92, WhoMW 92
West, Thomas Moore 1940- WhoWest 92
West, Thomas Patrick 1953- AmMWSc 92
West, Thomas Summers 1927- Who 92
West, Timothy 1934- IntMPA 92, WhoEnt 92
West, Timothy Lancaster 1934- IntWW 91, Who 92
West, Togo Dennis, Jr. 1942- WhoAmL 92, WhoBlA 92
West, Tom 1895-1980? TwCWW 91
West, Tony 1937- WhoAmP 91, WhoWest 92
West, Vikki Lynn 1948- WhoWest 92
West, W. J. 1937- WhoMW 92
West, Wallace 1900- ScFEYrs
West, Walter Scott 1912- AmMWSc 92
West, Ward TwCWW 91
West, Warren John 1943- WhoAmL 92
West, Warwick Reed, Jr 1922- AmMWSc 92
West, Weldon Wallace 1921- WhoWest 92
West, William Dixon 1901- Who 92
West, William Lee 1926- WhoMW 92
West, William Lionel 1923- AmMWSc 92, WhoBlA 92
West, William T 1925- AmMWSc 92
West-Bailey, Stacey Sue 1956- WhoWest 92
West Cumberland, Archdeacon of Who 92
West-Eberhard, Mary J 1941- AmMWSc 92
West Ham, Archdeacon of Who 92
West Indies, Archbishop of 1928- Who 92
West-Russell, David 1921- Who 92
Westall, Frederick Charles 1943- AmMWSc 92
Westall, Robert 1929- WrDr 92
Westall, Robert Atkinson 1929- IntAu&W 91, Who 92
Westall, Rupert Vyvyan Hawksley 1899- Who 92
Westall, William 1834-1903 ScFEYrs
Westaway, Kenneth C 1938- AmMWSc 92
Westbay, Charles Duane 1930- WhoFI 92
Westberg, Helen Groff 1917- WhoAmP 91
Westberg, John Augustin 1931- WhoAmL 92
Westberg, Karl Rogers 1939- AmMWSc 92
Westblade, Donald James 1953- WhoRel 92
Westbo, Leonard Archibald, Jr. 1931- WhoWest 92
Westbrook, April Lynn 1942- WhoAmP 91
Westbrook, Charley Erwin, Jr. 1957- WhoRel 92
Westbrook, David Rex 1937- AmMWSc 92
Westbrook, Don Arlen 1941- WhoRel 92
Westbrook, Edwin Monroe 1948- AmMWSc 92
Westbrook, Elouise WhoBlA 92
Westbrook, Eric Ernest 1915- Who 92
Westbrook, Franklin Solomon 1958- WhoBlA 92
Westbrook, Gilson Howard 1947- WhoBlA 92
Westbrook, J H 1924- AmMWSc 92
Westbrook, Jean Ann 1948- WhoRel 92
Westbrook, Joel Whitsitt, III 1916- WhoAmL 92
Westbrook, Joseph W., III 1919- WhoBlA 92
Westbrook, Karla Renee 1964- WhoWest 92
Westbrook, Kenneth Kirk 1950- WhoWest 92
Westbrook, Michael John David 1936- Who 92
Westbrook, Neil 1917- Who 92
Westbrook, Paul Wayne 1964- WhoRel 92
Westbrook, Perry D. WrDr 92
Westbrook, Peter J 1952- BlkOlyM
Westbrook, Roger 1941- IntWW 91, Who 92
Westbrook, Scott C., III 1939- WhoBlA 92
Westbrook, T. L. WhoRel 92
Westbrook, Walter Winfield 1955- WhoRel 92
Westbrooks, Logan H. 1937- WhoBlA 92
Westbury, Baron 1922- Who 92
Westbury, Gerald 1927- Who 92
Westby, Carl A 1936- AmMWSc 92
Westby, Carl Martin, Jr. 1928- WhoRel 92
Westcott, Brian John 1957- WhoWest 92
Westcott, E. N. 1846-1898 BenetAL 91
Westcott, Edward August, Jr. 1922- WhoRel 92
Westcott, Helen 1929- IntMPA 92
Westcott, Jan 1912- WrDr 92
Westcott, John Hugh 1920- IntWW 91, Who 92
Westcott, John McMahon, Jr. 1944- WhoAmL 92
Westcott, Keith R 1952- AmMWSc 92
Westcott, Peter Walter 1938- AmMWSc 92
Westcott, Robert Frederick 1922- WhoMW 92
Westcott, W F 1949- IntAu&W 91
Westcott, William John 1919- WhoMW 92
Westcott Jones, Kenneth 1921- WrDr 92
Westdal, Paul Harold 1921- AmMWSc 92
Westen, Peter 1943- WhoAmL 92
Westen, Robin 1950- WhoEnt 92
Westenbarger, Don Edward 1928- WhoMW 92
Westenbarger, Gene Arlan 1935- AmMWSc 92
Westenberg, Arthur Ayer 1922- AmMWSc 92
Westenborg, Jack Arthur 1942- WhoWest 92
Westendorf, Wolfhart 1924- IntWW 91
Westenfelder, Christof 1942- AmMWSc 92, WhoWest 92
Westenfelder, Grant Orville 1940- WhoMW 92
Westenra Who 92
Westenskow, Dwayne R 1947- AmMWSc 92
Wester, Derin C 1949- AmMWSc 92
Wester, Donald Gray 1931- WhoRel 92
Wester, Keith Albert 1940- WhoEnt 92, WhoWest 92
Wester, Richard Clark 1945- WhoBlA 92
Wester, Ronald Clarence 1940- AmMWSc 92
Westerbeck, David F 1945- WhoIns 92
Westerberg, Arthur William 1938- AmMWSc 92
Westerberg, Thomas Bates 1930- WhoFI 92
Westerberg, Victor John 1912- WhoAmP 91
Westerdahl, Carolyn Ann Lovejoy 1935- AmMWSc 92
Westerdahl, John Brian 1954- WhoWest 92
Westerdahl, Raymond P 1929- AmMWSc 92
Westerfeld, Wilfred Wiedey 1913- AmMWSc 92
Westerfield, Clifford 1908- AmMWSc 92
Westerfield, H. Bradford 1928- WrDr 92
Westerfield, Hargis DrAPF 91
Westerfield, Louis 1949- WhoBlA 92
Westerfield, Michael Wayne 1952- WhoMW 92
Westerfield, Nancy G. DrAPF 91
Westerfield, Nancy Gillespie 1925- WhoRel 92
Westerfield, Putney 1930- IntWW 91, WhoFI 92
Westergaard, Peter 1931- NewAmDM
Westergaard, Peter Talbot 1931- WhoEnt 92
Westerhaus, Douglas Bernard 1951- WhoAmL 92
Westerhaus, Joseph George, III 1938- WhoMW 92
Westerhof, Nicolaas 1937- AmMWSc 92
Westerholm, Leo Lyder 1922- WhoAmP 91
Westerhout, Gart 1927- AmMWSc 92
Westerlund, Bengt Elis 1921- IntWW 91
Westerlund, Paul Lawrence 1938- WhoRel 92
Westerman, Alan 1913- IntWW 91, Who 92
Westerman, Arthur B 1919- AmMWSc 92
Westerman, David Scott 1946- AmMWSc 92
Westerman, Edwin J 1935- AmMWSc 92
Westerman, Gayl Shaw 1939- WhoAmL 92
Westerman, Howard Robert 1926- AmMWSc 92
Westerman, Ira John 1945- AmMWSc 92
Westerman, Michael Mayer 1948- WhoAmL 92
Westerman, Richard Earl 1935- AmMWSc 92
Westerman, William Joseph, II 1937- AmMWSc 92
Westermann, D T 1941- AmMWSc 92
Westermann, Fred Ernst 1921- AmMWSc 92, WhoMW 92
Westermann, Gerd Ernst Gerold 1927- AmMWSc 92

**Westermann**, H. C. 1922-1981 *WorArt 1980 [port]*
**Westermeier**, John Thomas, Jr. 1941- *WhoAmL 92*
**Westermeyer**, Paul Henry 1940- *WhoRel 92*
**Western**, Arthur Boyd 1944- *AmMWSc 92*
**Western**, Donald Ward 1915- *AmMWSc 92*
**Western**, Mark *WrDr 92*
**Westerterp**, Theodorus Engelbertus 1930- *IntWW 91*
**Westervelt**, Clinton Albert, Jr 1936- *AmMWSc 92*
**Westervelt**, Franklin Herbert 1930- *AmMWSc 92*
**Westervelt**, Frederic Ballard, Jr 1931- *AmMWSc 92*
**Westervelt**, James 1946- *WhoIns 92*
**Westervelt**, James Joseph 1946- *WhoFI 92*
**Westervelt**, Jane McQuaid 1927- *WhoAmP 91*
**Westervelt**, Peter Jocelyn 1919- *AmMWSc 92*
**Westfahl**, Bernard James 1947- *WhoMW 92*
**Westfahl**, Pamela Kay *AmMWSc 92*
**Westfall**, David 1927- *WhoAmL 92*
**Westfall**, David Patrick 1942- *AmMWSc 92, WhoWest 92*
**Westfall**, Dwayne Gene 1938- *AmMWSc 92*
**Westfall**, Helen Naomi 1933- *AmMWSc 92*
**Westfall**, Jane Anne 1928- *AmMWSc 92, WhoMW 92*
**Westfall**, John Edward 1938- *WhoWest 92*
**Westfall**, Lachlan Andrew 1959- *WhoWest 92*
**Westfall**, Michael Merritt 1940- *WhoWest 92*
**Westfall**, Minter Jackson, Jr 1916- *AmMWSc 92*
**Westfall**, Morris Gene 1939- *WhoAmP 91*
**Westfall**, Richard Merrill 1956- *AmMWSc 92, WhoFI 92, WhoWest 92*
**Westfall**, Richard S. 1924- *WrDr 92*
**Westfall**, Thomas Creed 1937- *AmMWSc 92*
**Westfeldt**, Wallace *LesBEnT 92*
**Westfield**, James D 1937- *AmMWSc 92*
**Westgaard**, Thomas Paul 1939- *WhoAmP 91*
**Westgard**, James Blake 1935- *AmMWSc 92*
**Westgate**, John *IntAu&W 91X*
**Westhaus**, Paul Anthony 1938- *AmMWSc 92*
**Westhead**, Edward William, Jr 1930- *AmMWSc 92*
**Westhead**, Paul *WhoWest 92*
**Westheimer**, David *DrAPF 91*
**Westheimer**, David 1917- *IntAu&W 91, WrDr 92*
**Westheimer**, David Kaplan 1917- *WhoEnt 92*
**Westheimer**, Frank Henry 1912- *AmMWSc 92, IntWW 91*
**Westheimer**, Gerald 1924- *AmMWSc 92, Who 92*
**Westheimer**, Ruth 1928- *WrDr 92*
**Westhoff**, Dennis Charles 1942- *AmMWSc 92*
**Westhoff**, Frank Dominic 1933- *WhoRel 92*
**Westin**, Av *LesBEnT 92*
**Westin**, Avram Robert 1929- *WhoEnt 92*
**Westin**, David Lawrence 1952- *WhoAmL 92*
**Westin**, Richard Axel 1945- *WhoAmL 92*
**Westin**, Robert Lee 1932- *WhoWest 92*
**Westine**, Peter Sven 1940- *AmMWSc 92*
**Westing**, Arthur H 1928- *AmMWSc 92*
**Westing**, Harold Jay 1929- *WhoRel 92*
**Westinghouse**, George 1846-1914 *BiInAmS*
**Westkaemper**, John C 1923- *AmMWSc 92*
**Westlake**, Donald E 1933- *IntAu&W 91, WrDr 92*
**Westlake**, Donald Edwin 1933- *WhoEnt 92*
**Westlake**, Donald G 1928- *AmMWSc 92*
**Westlake**, Donald William Speck 1931- *AmMWSc 92*
**Westlake**, Henry Dickinson 1906- *Who 92*
**Westlake**, Peter Alan Grant 1919- *Who 92*
**Westlake**, Robert Elmer, Sr 1918- *AmMWSc 92*
**Westlake**, Vernon L 1921- *WhoAmP 91*
**Westland**, Alan Duane 1929- *AmMWSc 92*
**Westland**, Lynn *TwCWW 91*
**Westland**, Roger D 1928- *AmMWSc 92*
**Westler**, William Milo 1950- *AmMWSc 92*
**Westley**, Ann 1948- *TwCPaSc*
**Westley**, John Leonard 1927- *AmMWSc 92*
**Westley**, John Richard 1939- *WhoFI 92*
**Westley**, John William 1936- *AmMWSc 92*
**Westling**, Carl Edward 1953- *WhoMW 92*
**Westling**, Lester Leon, Jr. 1930- *WhoRel 92*
**Westling**, Louise 1942- *ConAu 133*
**Westling**, Louise Hutchings 1942- *WhoWest 92*
**Westly**, Steven Paul 1956- *WhoAmP 91*
**Westmacott**, Kenneth Harry 1929- *AmMWSc 92*
**Westmacott**, Richard Kelso 1934- *Who 92*
**Westman**, Alida Spaans 1944- *WhoMW 92*
**Westman**, Jack Conrad 1927- *AmMWSc 92*
**Westman**, James *WhoWest 92*
**Westman**, Patricia Ann 1941- *WhoAmP 91*
**Westman**, Richard A 1959- *WhoAmP 91*
**Westman**, Robert Allan 1926- *WhoMW 92*
**Westman**, Steven Ronald 1945- *WhoRel 92*
**Westman**, Walter Emil 1945- *AmMWSc 92*
**Westmann**, Russell A 1936- *AmMWSc 92*
**Westmark**, Paul David 1951- *WhoMW 92*
**Westmark**, Stephen Harold 1949- *WhoMW 92*
**Westmeath**, Earl of 1928- *Who 92*
**Westmeyer**, Paul 1925- *AmMWSc 92*
**Westminster**, Archbishop of 1923- *Who 92*
**Westminster**, Auxiliary Bishops of *Who 92*
**Westminster**, Dean of *Who 92*
**Westminster**, Duke 1951- *IntWW 91*
**Westminster**, Duke of 1951- *Who 92*
**Westminster**, Aynn *ConAu 34NR*
**Westmore**, John Brian 1937- *AmMWSc 92*
**Westmore**, Michael *ConTFT 9*
**Westmore**, Michael G. 1938- *ConTFT 9*
**Westmore**, Michael George 1938- *WhoEnt 92*
**Westmore**, Mike *ConTFT 9*
**Westmoreland**, Barbara Fenn 1940- *AmMWSc 92, WhoMW 92*
**Westmoreland**, David Gray 1946- *AmMWSc 92*
**Westmoreland**, Harry Elmer 1908- *WhoMW 92*
**Westmoreland**, Jim 1937- *WhoAmP 91*
**Westmoreland**, Norma Jane 1936- *WhoAmP 91*
**Westmoreland**, Phillip R 1951- *AmMWSc 92*
**Westmoreland**, Samuel Douglas 1944- *WhoBlA 92*
**Westmoreland**, William C 1914- *FacFETw [port]*
**Westmoreland**, William Childs 1914- *IntWW 91*
**Westmoreland**, Winfred William 1919- *AmMWSc 92*
**Westmorland**, Earl of 1924- *IntWW 91, Who 92*
**Westmorland And Furness**, Archdeacon of *Who 92*
**Westneat**, David French 1929- *AmMWSc 92*
**Westneat**, David French, Jr 1959- *AmMWSc 92*
**Westoff**, Charles F *AmMWSc 92*
**Westoff**, Charles F. 1927- *WrDr 92*
**Westoll**, James 1918- *Who 92*
**Westoll**, Thomas Stanley 1912- *Who 92*
**Weston**, Allen *WrDr 92*
**Weston**, Arthur Walter 1914- *AmMWSc 92*
**Weston**, Bertram John 1907- *Who 92*
**Weston**, Bryan Henry 1930- *Who 92*
**Weston**, Burns H. 1933- *WrDr 92*
**Weston**, Burns Humphrey 1933- *WhoAmL 92, WhoMW 92*
**Weston**, Burton Saul 1952- *WhoAmL 92*
**Weston**, Carol *IntAu&W 91*
**Weston**, Charles Arthur Winfield 1922- *Who 92*
**Weston**, Charles Hartshorne, Jr. 1941- *WhoMW 92*
**Weston**, Charles Richard 1933- *AmMWSc 92*
**Weston**, Christopher John 1937- *Who 92*
**Weston**, Cole *TwCWW 91, WrDr 92*
**Weston**, Corinne Comstock 1919- *WrDr 92*
**Weston**, David Wilfrid Valentine 1937- *Who 92*
**Weston**, Deirdre Denise 1964- *WhoWest 92*
**Weston**, Dennis Paul 1946- *WhoFI 92*
**Weston**, Edmund Brownell 1850-1916 *BiInAmS*
**Weston**, Edward 1886-1958 *DcTwDes, FacFETw*
**Weston**, Edward 1925- *WhoEnt 92, WhoWest 92*
**Weston**, Frances 1954- *WhoAmP 91*
**Weston**, Francine Evans 1946- *WhoEnt 92*
**Weston**, Frank Valentine 1935- *Who 92*
**Weston**, Galen *Who 92*
**Weston**, Garfield Howard 1927- *IntWW 91, Who 92*
**Weston**, Geoffrey Harold 1920- *Who 92*
**Weston**, Helen Gray *IntAu&W 91X, WrDr 92*
**Weston**, Henry Griggs, Jr 1922- *AmMWSc 92*
**Weston**, Jack 1924- *IntMPA 92, WhoEnt 92*
**Weston**, James A 1936- *AmMWSc 92*
**Weston**, Jay 1929- *IntMPA 92*
**Weston**, Jeffrey Allen 1960- *WhoFI 92*
**Weston**, John *Who 92*
**Weston**, John Carruthers *Who 92*
**Weston**, John Colby 1926- *AmMWSc 92*
**Weston**, John Frederick 1916- *WhoFI 92*
**Weston**, John Pix 1920- *Who 92*
**Weston**, John William 1915- *Who 92*
**Weston**, Josh S. 1928- *WhoFI 92*
**Weston**, Kenneth Clayton 1932- *AmMWSc 92*
**Weston**, Kenneth W 1929- *AmMWSc 92*
**Weston**, Larry Carlton 1948- *WhoBlA 92*
**Weston**, M. Moran, II 1910- *WhoBlA 92*
**Weston**, Margaret 1926- *Who 92*
**Weston**, Martin V. 1947- *WhoBlA 92*
**Weston**, Michael Charles Swift 1937- *IntWW 91, Who 92*
**Weston**, Philip John 1938- *Who 92*
**Weston**, Phyllis Jean 1921- *WhoMW 92*
**Weston**, R Timothy 1947- *WhoAmP 91*
**Weston**, Ralph E, Jr 1923- *AmMWSc 92*
**Weston**, Randy 1926- *WhoEnt 92*
**Weston**, Randy 1958- *WhoAmP 91*
**Weston**, Raymond E 1917- *AmMWSc 92*
**Weston**, Raymond Stoner 1941- *WhoEnt 92*
**Weston**, Robert R. *IntMPA 92*
**Weston**, Roger Lance 1943- *WhoFI 92*
**Weston**, Roy Francis 1911- *AmMWSc 92*
**Weston**, Sharon 1956- *WhoBlA 92*
**Weston**, Stephen Burns 1904- *WhoAmL 92*
**Weston**, Susan 1943- *WrDr 92*
**Weston**, Susan B. *DrAPF 91*
**Weston**, Vaughan Hatherley 1931- *AmMWSc 92*
**Weston**, W Galen 1940- *Who 92*
**Weston**, Willard Galen 1940- *WhoFI 92*
**Weston**, William *WrDr 92*
**Weston**, William Kenneth 1904- *Who 92*
**Weston**, William Lee 1938- *AmMWSc 92*
**Weston**, William R 1947- *WhoIns 92*
**Westover**, James Donald 1934- *AmMWSc 92*
**Westover**, Lemoyne Byron 1928- *AmMWSc 92*
**Westover**, Samuel Lee 1955- *WhoWest 92*
**Westover**, Thomas A 1909- *AmMWSc 92*
**Westpfahl**, David John 1953- *AmMWSc 92*
**Westphal**, Arnold Carl 1897- *WhoRel 92*
**Westphal**, Heiner J 1935- *AmMWSc 92*
**Westphal**, Heinz 1924- *IntWW 91*
**Westphal**, James Adolph 1930- *AmMWSc 92*
**Westphal**, Leonard Wyrick 1946- *WhoMW 92*
**Westphal**, Marjorie Lord 1940- *WhoAmL 92*
**Westphal**, Max 1895-1942 *EncTR 91*
**Westphal**, Michael d1991 *NewYTBS 91*
**Westphal**, Milton C, Jr 1926- *AmMWSc 92*
**Westphal**, Warren Henry 1925- *AmMWSc 92*
**Westphalen**, Emilio Adolfo 1911- *ConSpAP*
**Westra**, Mark William 1946- *WhoAmL 92*
**Westra**, Vincent Castelli 1952- *WhoAmL 92*
**Westran**, Roy Alvin 1925- *WhoMW 92*
**Westray**, Kenneth Maurice 1952- *WhoBlA 92*
**Westrick**, Elsie Margaret Beyer 1910- *IntAu&W 91*
**Westrum**, Edgar Francis, Jr 1919- *AmMWSc 92*
**Westrum**, Lesnick Edward 1934- *AmMWSc 92*
**Westwater**, Edgeworth Rupert 1937- *AmMWSc 92*
**Westwater**, J W 1919- *AmMWSc 92*
**Westwell**, Alan Reynolds 1940- *Who 92*
**Westwick**, Roy 1933- *AmMWSc 92*
**Westwood** *Who 92*
**Westwood**, Baron 1907- *Who 92*
**Westwood**, Albert Ronald Clifton 1932- *AmMWSc 92*
**Westwood**, Dennis 1928- *TwCPaSc*
**Westwood**, Gwen 1915- *WrDr 92*
**Westwood**, Jean Miles 1923- *WhoAmP 91*
**Westwood**, John Norton 1931- *WrDr 92*
**Westwood**, Melvin 1923- *AmMWSc 92*
**Westwood**, Perry *TwCWW 91*
**Westwood**, Vivienne *IntWW 91*
**Westwood**, William Dickson 1937- *AmMWSc 92*
**Westwood**, William John *Who 92*
**Weswig**, Paul Henry 1913- *AmMWSc 92*
**Wetegrove**, Robert Lloyd 1948- *AmMWSc 92*
**Wetere**, Koro Tainui 1935- *IntWW 91*
**Wetherald**, Ethelwyn 1857-1940 *BenetAL 91*
**Wetherald**, Margaret Elizabeth 1958- *WhoAmL 92*
**Wetherald**, Richard Tryon 1936- *AmMWSc 92*
**Wetherall**, Theodore Sumner d1990 *Who 92N*
**Wetherbee**, Robert Solon 1959- *WhoMW 92*
**Wetherbee**, Roberta Janis 1948- *WhoEnt 92*
**Wetherby**, Lawrence Winchester 1908- *WhoAmP 91*
**Wethered**, Julian Frank Baldwin 1929- *Who 92*
**Wetherell**, Alan Marmaduke 1932- *Who 92*
**Wetherell**, Claire 1919- *WhoAmP 91*
**Wetherell**, Donald Francis 1927- *AmMWSc 92*
**Wetherell**, Elizabeth *BenetAL 91*
**Wetherell**, Gordon Geoffrey 1948- *Who 92*
**Wetherell**, Herbert Ranson, Jr 1927- *AmMWSc 92*
**Wetherell**, Michael E. 1945- *WhoWest 92*
**Wetherell**, Michael Edward 1945- *WhoAmP 91*
**Wetherell**, Peter Clive 1955- *WhoEnt 92*
**Wetherell**, Thomas Kent 1945- *WhoAmP 91*
**Wetherell**, W.D. *DrAPF 91*
**Wetherhold**, Robert Campbell 1951- *AmMWSc 92*
**Wetherill**, Charles Mayer 1825-1871 *BiInAmS*
**Wetherill**, Eikins 1919- *WhoAmL 92*
**Wetherill**, George West 1925- *AmMWSc 92, IntWW 91*
**Wetherill**, Samuel 1821-1890 *BiInAmS*
**Wetherill**, Tom Oliver 1930- *WhoWest 92*
**Wetherington**, John Mallory 1956- *WhoWest 92*
**Wetherington**, Ronald K 1935- *AmMWSc 92*
**Wetherington**, Tom Lee 1926- *WhoAmP 91*
**Wethern**, James Douglas 1926- *AmMWSc 92*
**Wethers**, Doris L. 1927- *NotBlAW 92*
**Wethington**, John A, Jr 1921- *AmMWSc 92*
**Wethington**, Norbert Anthony 1943- *WhoMW 92, WhoRel 92*
**Wetjen**, Albert Richard 1900-1948 *BenetAL 91*
**Wetlaufer**, Donald Burton 1925- *AmMWSc 92*
**Wetli**, Peggy Marie 1949- *WhoEnt 92, WhoMW 92*
**Wetmore**, Claude H 1862-1944 *ScFEYrs A*
**Wetmore**, Claude H, and Yost, Robert M *ScFEYrs A*
**Wetmore**, Clifford Major 1934- *AmMWSc 92*
**Wetmore**, David Eugene 1935- *AmMWSc 92*
**Wetmore**, Marisa 1944- *WhoMW 92*
**Wetmore**, Ralph Hartley 1892- *AmMWSc 92*
**Wetmore**, Robert D 1930- *WhoAmP 91*
**Wetmore**, Stanley Irwin, Jr 1939- *AmMWSc 92*
**Wetmore**, William *DrAPF 91*
**Wetmur**, James Gerard 1941- *AmMWSc 92*
**Wets**, Roger J B 1937- *AmMWSc 92*
**Wetstein**, Gary M. *WhoFI 92*
**Wetstone**, Howard J 1926- *AmMWSc 92*
**Wetta**, Therese Catherine 1941- *WhoRel 92*
**Wettach**, George Edward 1940- *WhoWest 92*
**Wettach**, Thomas C. 1941- *WhoAmL 92*
**Wettach**, William 1910- *AmMWSc 92*
**Wettack**, F. Sheldon *WhoMW 92*
**Wettack**, F Sheldon 1938- *AmMWSc 92*
**Wettaw**, John 1939- *WhoAmP 91*
**Wette**, Reimut 1927- *AmMWSc 92*
**Wettemann**, Robert Paul 1944- *AmMWSc 92*
**Wettenhall**, Roger 1931- *WrDr 92*
**Wetter**, Edward 1919- *WhoEnt 92*
**Wetter**, Friedrich 1928- *IntWW 91, WhoRel 92*
**Wetter**, Jack 1943- *WhoWest 92*
**Wetter**, Melvin G 1929- *WhoAmP 91*
**Wetterau**, Theodore C. 1927- *WhoFI 92, WhoMW 92*
**Wettergreen**, Richard A 1943- *WhoIns 92*
**Wetterhahn**, Karen E 1948- *AmMWSc 92*
**Wetterschneider**, Larry Kay 1947- *WhoWest 92*
**Wettersten**, Nancy Carla 1954- *WhoAmL 92*

**Wettig**, Patricia *WhoEnt 92*
**Wettig**, Patricia 1951- *ConTFT 9*
**Wetton**, Philip Henry Davan 1937- *Who 92*
**Wettstein**, Diter von 1929- *IntWW 91*
**Wettstein**, Felix O 1932- *AmMWSc 92*
**Wettstein**, Joseph G 1954- *AmMWSc 92*
**Wettstein**, Peter J *AmMWSc 92*
**Wetzel**, Albert John 1917- *AmMWSc 92*
**Wetzel**, Allan Brooke 1933- *AmMWSc 92*
**Wetzel**, Dave 1942- *Who 92*
**Wetzel**, Don 1945- *WhoFI 92*
**Wetzel**, Edward Thomas 1937- *WhoFI 92*
**Wetzel**, Gale Thomas 1937- *WhoRel 92*
**Wetzel**, Gary Erwin 1938- *WhoMW 92*
**Wetzel**, John Edwin 1932- *AmMWSc 92*
**Wetzel**, Karen J. 1953- *WhoMW 92*
**Wetzel**, Karl Joseph 1937- *AmMWSc 92*
**Wetzel**, Lewis *TwCWW 91*
**Wetzel**, Margaret Lou 1922- *WhoAmP 91*
**Wetzel**, Mary Goodwin 1939- *WhoMW 92*
**Wetzel**, Nicholas 1920- *AmMWSc 92*
**Wetzel**, Richard Denney 1937- *WhoMW 92*
**Wetzel**, Robert Ellsworth 1937- *WhoAmL 92*
**Wetzel**, Robert George 1936- *AmMWSc 92*
**Wetzel**, Roland H 1923- *AmMWSc 92*
**Wetzel**, Ronald Burnell 1946- *AmMWSc 92*
**Wetzler**, Monte Edwin 1936- *WhoAmL 92*
**Wetzstein**, H J 1920- *AmMWSc 92*
**Wevill**, David 1935- *ConPo 91*
**Wewer**, William Paul 1947- *WhoAmL 92*
**Wewerka**, Eugene Michael 1938- *AmMWSc 92*
**Wex**, Bernard 1922-1990 *AnObit 1990*
**Wexell**, Dale Richard 1943- *AmMWSc 92*
**Wexler**, Anne 1930- *WhoAmP 91*
**Wexler**, Arthur Samuel 1918- *AmMWSc 92*
**Wexler**, Bernard Carl 1923- *AmMWSc 92*
**Wexler**, Bernard Lester 1945- *AmMWSc 92*
**Wexler**, Dorothy Frankel 1926- *WhoRel 92*
**Wexler**, Evelyn *DrAPF 91*
**Wexler**, Ginia Davis 1923- *WhoEnt 92*
**Wexler**, Haskell 1922- *WhoEnt 92*
**Wexler**, Haskell 1926- *IntMPA 92*
**Wexler**, Howard Adam 1949- *WhoEnt 92*
**Wexler**, Howard B 1951- *WhoIns 92*
**Wexler**, Jonathan David 1937- *AmMWSc 92*
**Wexler**, Judie Gaffin 1945- *WhoWest 92*
**Wexler**, Leonard D. 1924- *WhoAmL 92*
**Wexler**, Marvin 1947- *WhoAmL 92*
**Wexler**, Peter John 1936- *WhoEnt 92*
**Wexler**, Philip *DrAPF 91*
**Wexler**, Richard 1953- *ConAu 135*
**Wexler**, Richard Lewis 1941- *WhoAmL 92*
**Wexler**, Robert 1961- *WhoAmP 91*
**Wexler**, Steven Mark 1955- *WhoRel 92*
**Wexler-Johnson**, Eileen Lugar 1915- *WhoAmP 91*
**Wexley**, John 1907-1985 *BenetAL 91*
**Wexner**, Ira Howard 1929- *WhoAmL 92*
**Wexner**, Leslie Herbert 1937- *WhoFI 92, WhoMW 92*
**Wey**, Albert Chin-Tang 1955- *AmMWSc 92*
**Wey**, Jong-Shinn 1944- *AmMWSc 92*
**Weyand**, Frederick Carlton 1916- *IntWW 91*
**Weyand**, John David 1939- *AmMWSc 92*
**Weybrew**, Joseph Arthur 1915- *AmMWSc 92*
**Weyenberg**, Donald Richard 1930- *AmMWSc 92, WhoFI 92*
**Weyerhaeuser**, George Hunt 1926- *IntWW 91, WhoFI 92, WhoWest 92*
**Weyermann**, Jay Thomas 1945- *WhoWest 92*
**Weyforth Dawson**, Mary Ann 1944- *WhoAmP 91*
**Weygand**, Leroy Charles 1926- *WhoFI 92, WhoWest 92*
**Weygand**, Maxime 1867-1965 *EncTR 91, FacFETw*
**Weygand**, Robert 1948- *WhoAmP 91*
**Weyh**, John Arthur 1942- *AmMWSc 92*
**Weyhenmeyer**, James Alan 1951- *AmMWSc 92*
**Weyhing**, Steven David 1954- *WhoAmL 92*
**Weyhmann**, Walter Victor 1935- *AmMWSc 92*
**Weyl**, Peter K 1924- *AmMWSc 92*
**Weyland**, Gregory Theodore 1952- *WhoWest 92*
**Weyland**, Jack Arnold 1940- *AmMWSc 92*
**Weyland**, Otto P 1902-1979 *FacFETw*
**Weyler**, Kenneth L 1941- *WhoAmP 91*
**Weyler**, Michael E 1940- *AmMWSc 92*
**Weyler**, Valeriano 1838-1930 *HisDSpE*
**Weymann**, Gert 1919- *IntWW 91*
**Weymann**, Ray J 1934- *AmMWSc 92*
**Weymann**, Thomas F. 1950- *WhoAmL 92*
**Weymes**, John Barnard 1927- *Who 92*
**Weymouth**, Viscount 1932- *Who 92*
**Weymouth**, John Walter 1922- *AmMWSc 92*
**Weymouth**, Norman E *WhoAmP 91*
**Weymouth**, Patricia Perkins 1918- *AmMWSc 92*
**Weymouth**, Philip H 1925- *WhoAmP 91*
**Weymouth**, Richard J 1928- *AmMWSc 92*
**Weyna**, Philip Leo 1932- *AmMWSc 92*
**Weynand**, Edmund E 1920- *AmMWSc 92*
**Weynen**, Wolfgang 1913- *IntWW 91*
**Weyrens**, Jerry P 1932- *WhoAmP 91*
**Weyrich**, James Henry 1944- *WhoAmP 91*
**Weyrick**, John Alfred 1948- *WhoEnt 92*
**Weyter**, Frederick William 1934- *AmMWSc 92*
**Wezniak**, Frank J. 1932- *WhoFI 92*
**Whaddon**, Baron 1927- *Who 92*
**Whaite**, Gillian 1934- *TwCPaSc*
**Whale**, James 1889?-1957 *IntDcF 2-2 [port]*
**Whale**, James 1896-1957 *FacFETw*
**Whale**, John 1931- *WrDr 92*
**Whale**, John Hilary 1931- *Who 92*
**Whale**, John Seldon 1896- *Who 92*
**Whalen**, Bernard F., III 1951- *WhoMW 92*
**Whalen**, Brian B. 1939- *WhoMW 92*
**Whalen**, Carol Kupers *AmMWSc 92*
**Whalen**, Geoffrey Henry 1936- *Who 92*
**Whalen**, George Edwin 1919- *WhoAmP 91*
**Whalen**, James F. 1951- *WhoFI 92*
**Whalen**, James Joseph 1935- *AmMWSc 92*
**Whalen**, James William 1923- *AmMWSc 92*
**Whalen**, Joseph R *WhoAmP 91*
**Whalen**, Joseph Wilson 1923- *AmMWSc 92*
**Whalen**, Laurence J. 1941- *WhoAmL 92*
**Whalen**, Lawrence E. *WhoMW 92*
**Whalen**, Margaret Cavanagh 1913- *WhoWest 92*
**Whalen**, Paul Lewellin *WhoAmL 92*
**Whalen**, Philip *DrAPF 91*
**Whalen**, Philip 1923- *BenetAL 91, ConPo 91, WrDr 92*
**Whalen**, Richard James 1935- *WrDr 92*
**Whalen**, Terry Anthony 1944- *IntAu&W 91*
**Whalen**, Thomas 1903-1975 *TwCPaSc*
**Whalen**, Thomas Earl 1938- *WhoWest 92*
**Whalen**, Thomas J 1931- *AmMWSc 92*
**Whalen**, Thomas Michael, III 1934- *WhoAmP 91*
**Whalen**, Timothy J 1956- *WhoAmP 91*
**Whalen**, Tom *DrAPF 91*
**Whalen**, Vermel M *WhoAmP 91*
**Whalen**, William James 1915- *AmMWSc 92*
**Whaley**, Charles Edward 1928- *WhoWest 92*
**Whaley**, Charles Henry, IV 1958- *WhoFI 92*
**Whaley**, Dawn Ellen 1953- *WhoEnt 92*
**Whaley**, Douglas John 1943- *WhoAmL 92*
**Whaley**, Foster 1920- *WhoAmP 91*
**Whaley**, Frank 1963- *IntMPA 92*
**Whaley**, Howard Arnold 1934- *AmMWSc 92*
**Whaley**, Joseph S. 1933- *WhoBlA 92*
**Whaley**, Julian Wendell 1937- *AmMWSc 92*
**Whaley**, Katharine Birgitta 1956- *AmMWSc 92*
**Whaley**, Mary H. *WhoBlA 92*
**Whaley**, Peter Walter 1937- *AmMWSc 92*
**Whaley**, Randall McVay 1915- *AmMWSc 92*
**Whaley**, Ross Samuel 1937- *AmMWSc 92*
**Whaley**, Thomas H. 1949- *WhoEnt 92*
**Whaley**, Thomas Patrick 1923- *AmMWSc 92*
**Whaley**, Thomas Williams 1942- *AmMWSc 92*
**Whaley**, Wayne Edward 1949- *WhoBlA 92*
**Whaley**, Wilson Monroe 1920- *AmMWSc 92*
**Whaley**, Zachary 1932- *WhoRel 92*
**Whalin**, Edwin Ansil, Jr 1924- *AmMWSc 92*
**Whaling**, Frank 1934- *WhoRel 92*
**Whaling**, Ward 1923- *AmMWSc 92*
**Whalley**, Edward 1925- *AmMWSc 92*
**Whalley**, Joanne *ConTFT 9*
**Whalley**, John Mayson 1932- *Who 92*
**Whalley**, Joyce Irene *WrDr 92*
**Whalley**, Judy L. 1950- *WhoAmL 92*
**Whalley**, Peter 1946- *IntAu&W 91, WrDr 92*
**Whalley**, Richard Carlton 1922- *Who 92*
**Whalley**, William Basil 1916- *Who 92*
**Whalley**, William Leonard 1930- *Who 92*
**Whalley-Kilmer**, Joanne 1964- *ConTFT 9, IntMPA 92, IntWW 91*
**Whalley-Tooker**, Hyde Carnock 1900- *Who 92*
**Whallon**, Evan Arthur, Jr. 1923- *WhoEnt 92*
**Whalum**, Kenneth Twigg 1934- *WhoBlA 92*
**Wham**, Dashiel 1959- *WhoWest 92*
**Wham**, David Buffington *DrAPF 91*
**Wham**, David Buffington 1937- *IntAu&W 91*
**Wham**, Dorothy Stonecipher 1925- *WhoAmP 91, WhoWest 92*
**Wham**, Robert S 1926- *WhoAmP 91*
**Whan**, Glenn A 1930- *AmMWSc 92*
**Whan**, Norman Wendell 1943- *WhoRel 92*
**Whan**, Ruth Elaine 1931- *AmMWSc 92*
**Whang**, Robert 1928- *AmMWSc 92*
**Whang**, Sukoo Jack 1934- *AmMWSc 92*
**Whang**, Sung H 1936- *AmMWSc 92*
**Whang**, Un-Young 1954- *WhoMW 92*
**Whang**, Yun Chow 1933- *AmMWSc 92*
**Whangbo**, Myung Hwan 1945- *AmMWSc 92*
**Whanger**, Philip Daniel 1936- *AmMWSc 92*
**Whaples**, Robert MacDonald 1961- *WhoFI 92*
**Wharf**, Brian 1932- *WhoWest 92*
**Wharncliffe**, Earl of 1953- *Who 92*
**Wharram**, Paul F 1954- *WhoIns 92*
**Wharry**, Stephen Mark 1955- *AmMWSc 92*
**Wharton**, Baroness 1934- *Who 92*
**Wharton**, A. C., Jr. 1944- *WhoBlA 92*
**Wharton**, Albert Benjamin 1938- *WhoRel 92*
**Wharton**, Betsy Freeman 1950- *WhoAmP 91*
**Wharton**, Blaze Douglas 1956- *WhoAmP 91*
**Wharton**, Charles, II 1936- *WhoRel 92*
**Wharton**, Charles Benjamin 1926- *AmMWSc 92*
**Wharton**, Charles Ellis 1943- *WhoWest 92*
**Wharton**, Clifton R. 1899-1990 *AnObit 1990*
**Wharton**, Clifton R., Jr. 1926- *IntWW 91, WhoBlA 92, WhoIns 92*
**Wharton**, Clifton Reginald, Jr. 1926- *WhoFI 92*
**Wharton**, Clyde Wilson 1913- *WhoAmP 91*
**Wharton**, David Carrie 1930- *AmMWSc 92*
**Wharton**, David W. 1951- *WhoWest 92*
**Wharton**, Dolores D. 1927- *WhoBlA 92*
**Wharton**, Edith 1862-1937 *BenetAL 91, FacFETw, HanAmWH, ModAWWr, RComAH*
**Wharton**, Ferdinand D., Jr. *WhoBlA 92*
**Wharton**, Gary C. 1940- *WhoMW 92*
**Wharton**, H Whitney 1931- *AmMWSc 92*
**Wharton**, James Henry 1937- *AmMWSc 92*
**Wharton**, Joseph 1826-1909 *BiInAmS*
**Wharton**, Lennard 1933- *AmMWSc 92*
**Wharton**, Marion A 1910- *AmMWSc 92*
**Wharton**, Michael 1933- *TwCPaSc*
**Wharton**, Michael Bernard 1913- *Who 92*
**Wharton**, Milton S. 1946- *WhoBlA 92*
**Wharton**, Peter Stanley 1931- *AmMWSc 92*
**Wharton**, Scott A. 1964- *WhoAmL 92*
**Wharton**, Thomas Heard, Jr. 1930- *WhoAmL 92*
**Wharton**, Thomas William 1943- *WhoWest 92*
**Wharton**, Tom Michael 1950- *WhoWest 92*
**Wharton**, Walter Washington 1926- *AmMWSc 92*
**Wharton**, William 1925- *BenetAL 91, ConNov 91, IntAu&W 91, WrDr 92*
**Wharton**, William Raymond 1943- *AmMWSc 92*
**Wharton-Boyd**, Linda F. 1951- *WhoBlA 92*
**Whatley**, Alfred T 1922- *AmMWSc 92*
**Whatley**, Alfred Thielen 1922- *WhoWest 92*
**Whatley**, Booker Tillman 1915- *AmMWSc 92, WhoBlA 92*
**Whatley**, Ennis 1962- *WhoBlA 92*
**Whatley**, Frederick Robert 1924- *IntWW 91, Who 92*
**Whatley**, Harriette Williford 1918- *WhoAmP 91*
**Whatley**, Jacqueline Beltram 1944- *WhoAmL 92*
**Whatley**, James Arnold 1916- *AmMWSc 92*
**Whatley**, Thomas Alvah 1932- *AmMWSc 92*
**Whatley**, Wallace *DrAPF 91*
**Whatley**, William Henry Potts 1922- *Who 92*
**Whatley**, William Wayne 1958- *WhoAmL 92*
**Whatmore**, George Bernard 1917- *AmMWSc 92*
**Whayne**, Tom French 1905- *AmMWSc 92*
**Wheadon**, A. Wendel 1938- *WhoBlA 92*
**Wheadon**, Richard Anthony 1933- *Who 92*
**Wheadon**, Rosetta Fay 1934-1990 *WhoBlA 92N*
**Whealon**, John Francis d1991 *NewYTBS 91 [port]*
**Whealon**, Robert F 1934- *WhoIns 92*
**Whealton**, John Hobson 1943- *AmMWSc 92*
**Wheare**, Thomas David 1944- *Who 92*
**Wheasler**, Robert 1924- *AmMWSc 92*
**Wheat**, Alan 1951- *AlmAP 92 [port], WhoAmP 91, WhoBlA 92*
**Wheat**, Alan Dupree 1951- *WhoMW 92*
**Wheat**, Charles Donald Edmund 1937- *Who 92*
**Wheat**, James Weldon, Jr. 1948- *WhoBlA 92*
**Wheat**, John David 1921- *AmMWSc 92*
**Wheat**, John Nixon 1952- *WhoAmL 92*
**Wheat**, Joseph Allen 1913- *AmMWSc 92*
**Wheat**, Josiah 1928- *WhoAmL 92*
**Wheat**, Julie Yager 1930- *WhoAmP 91*
**Wheat**, Maxwell Corydon *DrAPF 91*
**Wheat**, Robert Wayne 1926- *AmMWSc 92*
**Wheat**, Zach 1888-1972 *FacFETw*
**Wheatcroft**, Andrew Jonathan Maclean 1944- *IntAu&W 91*
**Wheatcroft**, Geoffrey 1945- *WrDr 92*
**Wheatcroft**, John *DrAPF 91*
**Wheatcroft**, John Stewart 1925- *WrDr 92*
**Wheatcroft**, Stephen Frederick 1921- *Who 92*
**Wheater**, Ashley *WhoEnt 92*
**Wheatland**, David Alan 1940- *AmMWSc 92*
**Wheatley**, Alan Edward 1938- *Who 92*
**Wheatley**, Andrew d1991 *Who 92N*
**Wheatley**, Anthony 1933- *Who 92*
**Wheatley**, Arthur 1931- *Who 92*
**Wheatley**, Charles Moore 1822-1882 *BiInAmS*
**Wheatley**, Curtis Dewayne 1945- *WhoMW 92*
**Wheatley**, Dennis 1897-1977 *TwCSFW 91*
**Wheatley**, Derek Peter Francis 1925- *Who 92*
**Wheatley**, Ford Harry, IV 1953- *WhoWest 92*
**Wheatley**, Grace 1888-1970 *TwCPaSc*
**Wheatley**, Jean George 1936- *WhoWest 92*
**Wheatley**, Jeff R. 1927- *WhoAmL 92, WhoWest 92*
**Wheatley**, John 1892-1955 *TwCPaSc*
**Wheatley**, John Derek 1927- *Who 92*
**Wheatley**, John Francis 1941- *Who 92*
**Wheatley**, Laura Frances *NotBlAW 92*
**Wheatley**, Myron Daniel 1953- *WhoAmL 92*
**Wheatley**, Paul Charles 1938- *Who 92*
**Wheatley**, Phillis 1753-1784 *AfrAmW, BenetAL 91, BlkLC [port], HanAmWH, NotBlAW 92 [port], PoeCrit 3 [port], PorAmW [port]*
**Wheatley**, Phillis 1754-1784 *BlkwEAR [port]*
**Wheatley**, Robert Ray, III 1934- *WhoFI 92*
**Wheatley**, Stanley Harold 1934- *WhoWest 92*
**Wheatley**, Victor Richard 1918- *AmMWSc 92*
**Wheatley**, W A 1923- *AmMWSc 92*
**Wheatley**, William Ogden, Jr. 1944- *WhoEnt 92*
**Wheaton**, Alice Alshuler 1920- *WhoWest 92*
**Wheaton**, Burdette Carl 1938- *AmMWSc 92*
**Wheaton**, David Harry 1930- *Who 92*
**Wheaton**, Elmer Paul 1909- *AmMWSc 92*
**Wheaton**, Gregory Alan 1947- *AmMWSc 92*
**Wheaton**, Harrison H 1884- *DcAmImH*
**Wheaton**, Harry Otis 1923- *WhoAmL 92*
**Wheaton**, Janice C. 1943- *WhoBlA 92*
**Wheaton**, Jonathan Edward 1947- *AmMWSc 92*
**Wheaton**, Robert Miller 1919- *AmMWSc 92*
**Wheaton**, Thelma Kirkpatrick 1907- *WhoBlA 92*
**Wheaton**, Thomas Adair 1936- *AmMWSc 92*
**Wheaton**, Wil 1972- *IntMPA 92*
**Wheatstraw**, Peetie 1902-1941 *NewAmDM*
**Wheby**, Munsey S 1930- *AmMWSc 92*
**Whedon**, John Ogden d1991 *NewYTBS 91*
**Whedon**, Margaret Brunssen *WhoEnt 92*
**Wheeden**, Richard Lee 1940- *AmMWSc 92*
**Wheelan**, Belle Louise 1951- *WhoBlA 92*
**Wheeldon**, John Murray 1929- *IntWW 91*
**Wheeldon**, Philip William 1913- *Who 92*
**Wheeler**, Albert Harold 1915- *AmMWSc 92, WhoBlA 92*
**Wheeler**, Alfred George, Jr 1944- *AmMWSc 92*
**Wheeler**, Alfred Portius 1947- *AmMWSc 92*

**Wheeler**, Allan Gordon 1923- *AmMWSc 92*
**Wheeler**, Amos Dean 1803-1876 *BiInAmS*
**Wheeler**, Anthony *Who 92*
**Wheeler**, Arthur Murray 1928- *WhoMW 92*
**Wheeler**, Arthur Walter 1927- *Who 92*
**Wheeler**, Arthur William Edge 1930- *Who 92*
**Wheeler**, Benita Louise 1939- *WhoWest 92*
**Wheeler**, Bernice Marion 1915- *AmMWSc 92*
**Wheeler**, Beth M *WhoAmP 91*
**Wheeler**, Betty McNeal 1932- *WhoBlA 92*
**Wheeler**, Bonnie G. 1943- *WhoRel 92*
**Wheeler**, Bruce 1948- *WhoHisp 92*
**Wheeler**, Burton Kendall 1882-1975 *AmPolLe*
**Wheeler**, Candice 1827-1923 *DcTwDes*
**Wheeler**, Charles 1892-1974 *TwCPaSc*
**Wheeler**, Charles 1923- *Who 92*
**Wheeler**, Charles B 1926- *WhoAmP 91*
**Wheeler**, Charles Fay 1842-1910 *BiInAmS*
**Wheeler**, Charles Gilbert 1836-1912 *BiInAmS*
**Wheeler**, Charles Lynn 1943- *WhoEnt 92*
**Wheeler**, Claude L d1916 *BiInAmS*
**Wheeler**, Clayton Eugene, Jr 1917- *AmMWSc 92*
**Wheeler**, Darrell Deane 1939- *AmMWSc 92*
**Wheeler**, David John 1927- *Who 92*
**Wheeler**, David K 1959- *WhoAmP 91*
**Wheeler**, David Lee 1946- *WhoRel 92*
**Wheeler**, David Wayne 1952- *WhoFI 92*
**Wheeler**, Desmond Michael Sherlock 1929- *AmMWSc 92*
**Wheeler**, Dolores Verene 1961- *WhoAmL 92*
**Wheeler**, Donald Alsop 1931- *AmMWSc 92*
**Wheeler**, Donald Bingham, Jr 1917- *AmMWSc 92*
**Wheeler**, Donald Keith 1960- *WhoFI 92*
**Wheeler**, Donna Marie 1962- *WhoEnt 92*
**Wheeler**, Douglas Alan 1963- *WhoMW 92*
**Wheeler**, Douglas Hughes *WhoEnt 92*
**Wheeler**, Ebenezer Smith 1839-1913 *BiInAmS*
**Wheeler**, Edd Dudley 1940- *WhoAmL 92*
**Wheeler**, Edward L. *BenetAL 91*
**Wheeler**, Edward Norwood 1927- *AmMWSc 92*
**Wheeler**, Edward Stubbs 1927- *AmMWSc 92*
**Wheeler**, Edwin Yorke 1926- *WhoMW 92*
**Wheeler**, Elton Samuel 1943- *WhoFI 92*
**Wheeler**, Emma B 1916- *WhoAmP 91*
**Wheeler**, Ernest S 1869?-1909 *BiInAmS*
**Wheeler**, Ethel Jenkins 1915- *WhoAmP 91*
**Wheeler**, Frank Basil 1937- *Who 92*
**Wheeler**, Frank Carlisle 1917- *AmMWSc 92*
**Wheeler**, Frank Earl 1952- *WhoRel 92*
**Wheeler**, Frederick 1914- *Who 92*
**Wheeler**, George Carlos 1897- *AmMWSc 92*
**Wheeler**, George Lawrence 1944- *AmMWSc 92*
**Wheeler**, George Montague 1842-1905 *BiInAmS*
**Wheeler**, Gerald William 1943- *WhoRel 92*
**Wheeler**, Gerridee Stenehjem 1927- *WhoAmP 91*
**Wheeler**, Gilbert Vernon 1922- *AmMWSc 92*
**Wheeler**, Glynn Pearce 1919- *AmMWSc 92*
**Wheeler**, Gordon *Who 92*
**Wheeler**, Harold 1943- *WhoBlA 92*
**Wheeler**, Harold A 1903- *AmMWSc 92*
**Wheeler**, Harold H 1929- *WhoAmP 91*
**Wheeler**, Harry Anthony 1919- *Who 92*
**Wheeler**, Harry Ernest 1919- *AmMWSc 92*
**Wheeler**, Helen Rippier *WhoWest 92*
**Wheeler**, Helen Rippier 1926- *WrDr 92*
**Wheeler**, Henry Lord 1867-1914 *BiInAmS*
**Wheeler**, Henry Neil 1917- *Who 92*
**Wheeler**, Henry Orson 1924- *AmMWSc 92*
**Wheeler**, James Donlan 1923- *AmMWSc 92*
**Wheeler**, James English 1938- *AmMWSc 92*
**Wheeler**, James Julian 1921- *WhoAmL 92*
**Wheeler**, James William, Jr 1934- *AmMWSc 92*
**Wheeler**, Jeanette Norris 1918- *AmMWSc 92*
**Wheeler**, Jeffrey Morse 1960- *WhoRel 92*
**Wheeler**, Jerry Barth 1951- *WhoRel 92*
**Wheeler**, Jimmy W. 1948- *WhoMW 92*
**Wheeler**, Joe Darr 1930- *AmMWSc 92*
**Wheeler**, John 1905- *Who 92*
**Wheeler**, John 1940- *Who 92*
**Wheeler**, John Archibald 1911- *AmMWSc 92, IntWW 91, WrDr 92*
**Wheeler**, John C 1941- *AmMWSc 92*
**Wheeler**, John Craig 1943- *AmMWSc 92*
**Wheeler**, John Henry 1959- *WhoRel 92*
**Wheeler**, John Hervey 1908- *WhoBlA 92*
**Wheeler**, John Oliver 1924- *AmMWSc 92*
**Wheeler**, John Watson 1938- *WhoAmL 92*
**Wheeler**, Jos Ridley 1927- *WhoWest 92*
**Wheeler**, Katherine Wells 1940- *WhoAmP 91*
**Wheeler**, Keith Wilson 1918- *AmMWSc 92*
**Wheeler**, Kenneth 1912- *Who 92*
**Wheeler**, Kenneth Theodore, Jr 1940- *AmMWSc 92*
**Wheeler**, Kenneth Theodore, Sr 1911- *WhoAmP 91*
**Wheeler**, Kenny 1930- *NewAmDM*
**Wheeler**, Kimball *WhoEnt 92*
**Wheeler**, Larry Richard 1940- *WhoFI 92, WhoWest 92*
**Wheeler**, Lawrence 1923- *AmMWSc 92*
**Wheeler**, Leslie William Frederick 1930- *Who 92*
**Wheeler**, Lewis Turner 1940- *AmMWSc 92*
**Wheeler**, Lloyd G. 1907- *WhoBlA 92*
**Wheeler**, Malcolm Edward 1944- *WhoAmL 92*
**Wheeler**, Mark Alfred 1961- *WhoRel 92*
**Wheeler**, Marshall Ralph 1917- *AmMWSc 92*
**Wheeler**, Marty L. 1961- *WhoRel 92*
**Wheeler**, Mary Fanett 1938- *AmMWSc 92*
**Wheeler**, Michael Hugh 1940- *AmMWSc 92*
**Wheeler**, Michael Mortimer 1915- *Who 92*
**Wheeler**, Michael R 1952- *WhoAmP 91*
**Wheeler**, Ned Brent 1936- *AmMWSc 92*
**Wheeler**, Neil *Who 92*
**Wheeler**, Nicholas Allan 1933- *AmMWSc 92*
**Wheeler**, Orville Eugene 1932- *AmMWSc 92*
**Wheeler**, Patricia A. 1950- *WhoBlA 92*
**Wheeler**, Paul Leonard 1926- *WhoMW 92*
**Wheeler**, Penny Estes 1943- *WrDr 92*
**Wheeler**, Post 1869-1957 *BenetAL 91*
**Wheeler**, Primus, Jr. 1950- *WhoBlA 92*
**Wheeler**, Ralph John 1929- *AmMWSc 92*
**Wheeler**, Randall David 1945- *WhoEnt 92*
**Wheeler**, Raymond Louis 1945- *WhoAmL 92*
**Wheeler**, Richard d1990 *Who 92N*
**Wheeler**, Richard Henry Littleton 1906- *Who 92*
**Wheeler**, Richard Hunting 1931- *AmMWSc 92*
**Wheeler**, Richard S. 1935- *TwCWW 91, WrDr 92*
**Wheeler**, Robert Francis 1943- *AmMWSc 92*
**Wheeler**, Robert Hobert 1945- *WhoAmL 92*
**Wheeler**, Robert L 1940- *WhoAmP 91*
**Wheeler**, Robert Lee 1944- *AmMWSc 92*
**Wheeler**, Robert LeVan 1936- *WhoMW 92*
**Wheeler**, Robert William 1935- *WhoMW 92*
**Wheeler**, Rod 1944- *WhoEnt 92*
**Wheeler**, Roger Neil 1941- *Who 92*
**Wheeler**, Ronald C. 1957- *WhoBlA 92*
**Wheeler**, Ruric E 1923- *AmMWSc 92*
**Wheeler**, Russell Leonard 1943- *AmMWSc 92*
**Wheeler**, Ruth Etta 1949- *WhoWest 92*
**Wheeler**, Samuel Crane, Jr 1913- *AmMWSc 92*
**Wheeler**, Selwyn Charles *Who 92*
**Wheeler**, Shirley Y. 1935- *WhoBlA 92*
**Wheeler**, Susan *DrAPF 91*
**Wheeler**, Susan Voight 1961- *WhoAmL 92*
**Wheeler**, Susie Weems 1917- *WhoBlA 92*
**Wheeler**, Sylvia *DrAPF 91*
**Wheeler**, Sylvia Griffith 1930- *WhoMW 92*
**Wheeler**, Thaddeus James 1948- *WhoBlA 92*
**Wheeler**, Theodore Stanley 1931- *WhoBlA 92*
**Wheeler**, Thomas Beardsley 1936- *WhoFI 92*
**Wheeler**, Thomas Clay *WhoAmP 91*
**Wheeler**, Thomas Francis 1937- *WhoWest 92*
**Wheeler**, Thomas Neil 1943- *AmMWSc 92*
**Wheeler**, Verl D. 1937- *WhoEnt 92*
**Wheeler**, Walter Hall 1923- *AmMWSc 92*
**Wheeler**, Warren Hervey 1943- *WhoBlA 92*
**Wheeler**, Wayne Cable 1938- *WhoWest 92*
**Wheeler**, William Almon 1819-1887 *AmPolLe*
**Wheeler**, William Bryan, III 1940- *WhoFI 92*
**Wheeler**, William Gordon 1910- *Who 92*
**Wheeler**, William Henry 1907- *Who 92*
**Wheeler**, William Hollis 1946- *AmMWSc 92*
**Wheeler**, William Joe 1940- *AmMWSc 92*
**Wheeler**, William R, Jr 1961- *WhoAmP 91*
**Wheeler**, William Scott 1952- *WhoEnt 92*
**Wheeler**, Willis Boly 1938- *AmMWSc 92*
**Wheeler-Booth**, Michael Addison John 1934- *Who 92*
**Wheeless**, Leon Lum, Jr 1935- *AmMWSc 92*
**Wheeless**, Robert Allen 1932- *WhoIns 92*
**Wheelis**, Mark Lewis 1944- *AmMWSc 92*
**Wheelock**, Earle Frederick 1927- *AmMWSc 92*
**Wheelock**, Eleazar 1711-1779 *BenetAL 91*
**Wheelock**, John Hall 1886-1978 *BenetAL 91*
**Wheelock**, Kenneth Steven 1943- *AmMWSc 92*
**Wheelock**, Martha Ellen 1941- *WhoEnt 92*
**Wheelock**, Robert Dean 1936- *WhoRel 92*
**Wheelock**, Thomas David 1925- *AmMWSc 92*
**Wheelon**, Albert Dewell 1929- *AmMWSc 92, WhoWest 92*
**Wheelwright**, Betty Coon *DrAPF 91*
**Wheelwright**, Earl J 1928- *AmMWSc 92*
**Wheelwright**, Edward Lawrence 1921- *WrDr 92*
**Wheelwright**, John 1592?-1679 *BenetAL 91*
**Wheelwright**, John Brooks 1897-1940 *BenetAL 91*
**Wheelwright**, Rowland 1870-1955 *TwCPaSc*
**Wheetley**, Eugene Lee 1934- *WhoMW 92*
**Wheildon**, W M, Jr 1908- *AmMWSc 92*
**Whelan**, Donald Joseph 1934- *WhoMW 92*
**Whelan**, Elizabeth M 1943- *AmMWSc 92*
**Whelan**, Eugene 1924- *IntWW 91*
**Whelan**, Francis C. 1907- *WhoWest 92*
**Whelan**, Gloria *DrAPF 91*
**Whelan**, James Arthur 1928- *AmMWSc 92*
**Whelan**, Jannice Karen 1952- *WhoAmP 91*
**Whelan**, Jean King 1939- *AmMWSc 92*
**Whelan**, John David 1943- *WhoRel 92*
**Whelan**, John Martin 1944- *WhoFI 92*
**Whelan**, John Michael 1921- *AmMWSc 92*
**Whelan**, Joseph L. 1917- *WhoMW 92*
**Whelan**, Joseph Michael 1954- *WhoFI 92*
**Whelan**, Michael Anthony 1947- *WhoEnt 92*
**Whelan**, Michael John 1931- *IntWW 91, Who 92*
**Whelan**, Noel 1940- *IntWW 91*
**Whelan**, Terence Leonard 1936- *Who 92*
**Whelan**, Thomas, III 1944- *AmMWSc 92*
**Whelan**, William Joseph 1924- *AmMWSc 92*
**Whelan**, William Paul, Jr 1923- *AmMWSc 92*
**Whelchel**, Sandra Jane 1944- *WhoWest 92*
**Wheldon**, Huw d1986 *LesBEnT 92*
**Wheldon**, Huw Prys 1916-1986 *FacFETw*
**Wheldon**, Juliet Louise 1950- *Who 92*
**Whelehan**, David D 1942- *WhoIns 92*
**Wheler**, Edward 1920- *Who 92*
**Whelihan**, Anthony Raymond 1953- *WhoMW 92*
**Whelihan**, James Bruce 1942- *WhoFI 92*
**Whelly**, Sandra Marie 1945- *AmMWSc 92*
**Whelon**, Charles Patrick Clavell 1930- *Who 92*
**Whelpley**, James Davenport 1817-1872 *BiInAmS*
**Whelpley**, Samuel 1766-1817 *AmPeW*
**Whelton**, Andrew 1940- *AmMWSc 92*
**Whelton**, Bartlett David 1941- *AmMWSc 92*
**Whelton**, Clark *DrAPF 91*
**Whent**, Gerald Arthur 1927- *Who 92*
**Whereat**, Arthur Finch 1927- *AmMWSc 92*
**Wherrett**, John Ross *AmMWSc 92*
**Wherry**, Edward John, Jr. 1942- *WhoAmL 92*
**Wherry**, Paul Arthur 1927- *WhoMW 92*
**Whetsel**, Kermit Bazil 1923- *AmMWSc 92*
**Whetstone**, Anthony John 1927- *Who 92*
**Whetstone**, Bernard 1912- *WhoAmL 92*
**Whetstone**, Byron William 1958- *WhoMW 92*
**Whetstone**, George 1544?-1587? *RfGEnL 91*
**Whetstone**, James Dewitt 1935- *WhoRel 92*
**Whetstone**, Keith 1930- *Who 92*
**Whetstone**, Stanley L, Jr 1925- *AmMWSc 92*
**Whetten**, John T 1935- *AmMWSc 92*
**Whetten**, John Theodore 1935- *WhoWest 92*
**Whetten**, Nathan Rey 1928- *AmMWSc 92*
**Whetten**, Robert Lloyd 1959- *AmMWSc 92*
**Wheway**, Albert James 1922- *Who 92*
**Whewell**, Charles Smalley 1912- *Who 92*
**Whichard**, Willis Padgett 1940- *WhoAmL 92, WhoAmP 91*
**Whicher**, Peter George 1929- *Who 92*
**Whicher**, Stephen E. 1915-1961 *DcLB 111 [port]*
**Whicker**, Alan Donald 1925- *IntAu&W 91, IntWW 91, Who 92*
**Whicker**, Donald 1944- *AmMWSc 92*
**Whicker**, Floyd Ward 1937- *AmMWSc 92*
**Whicker**, Lawrence R 1934- *AmMWSc 92*
**Whidby**, Jerry Frank 1943- *AmMWSc 92*
**Whidden**, Patrick Brian 1948- *WhoMW 92*
**Whidden**, Stanley John 1947- *AmMWSc 92*
**Whidden**, Woodrow Wilson, II 1944- *WhoRel 92*
**Whiddon**, Carol Price 1947- *WhoWest 92*
**Whiddon**, Delaine Frasier 1956- *WhoEnt 92*
**Whiddon**, Paul Michael 1952- *WhoRel 92*
**Whiffen**, David Hardy *Who 92*
**Whiffen**, David Hardy 1922- *IntWW 91*
**Whiffen**, James Douglass 1931- *AmMWSc 92*
**Whigan**, Daisy B 1947- *AmMWSc 92*
**Whigham**, David Keith 1938- *AmMWSc 92*
**Whikehart**, David Ralph 1939- *AmMWSc 92*
**Whikehart**, John R 1947- *WhoAmP 91*
**Whilden**, Robert Harral, Jr. 1935- *WhoAmL 92*
**Whilden**, Walter Burleson 1938- *WhoFI 92*
**Whildin**, Eileen Bachman 1955- *WhoAmP 91*
**Whillans**, Ian Morley 1944- *AmMWSc 92*
**Whillock**, David Everett 1952- *WhoEnt 92*
**Whim Wham** *IntAu&W 91X*
**Whinnery**, James Elliott 1946- *AmMWSc 92*
**Whinnery**, John R 1916- *AmMWSc 92*
**Whinnery**, John Roy 1916- *IntWW 91, WhoWest 92*
**Whinney**, Michael Humphrey Dickens 1930- *Who 92*
**Whipkey**, Kenneth Lee 1932- *AmMWSc 92*
**Whipp**, Brian James 1937- *AmMWSc 92*
**Whipp**, Shannon Carl 1931- *AmMWSc 92*
**Whipper**, Ionia Rollin 1872-1953 *NotBlAW 92*
**Whipper**, Lucille Simmons 1928- *WhoAmP 91, WhoBlA 92*
**Whippey**, Patrick William 1940- *AmMWSc 92*
**Whipple**, Amiel Weeks 1816-1863 *BiInAmS*
**Whipple**, Blaine 1930- *WhoAmP 91*
**Whipple**, Bryan Randolph Rogers 1940- *WhoFI 92*
**Whipple**, Charles K. 1808-1900 *AmPeW*
**Whipple**, Charles Lewis d1991 *NewYTBS 91*
**Whipple**, Christopher George 1949- *AmMWSc 92*
**Whipple**, David Pearlman 1951- *WhoWest 92*
**Whipple**, Dean 1938- *WhoAmL 92, WhoMW 92*
**Whipple**, E. P. 1819-1886 *BenetAL 91*
**Whipple**, Earl Bennett 1930- *AmMWSc 92*
**Whipple**, Eleanor Blanche 1916- *WhoRel 92*
**Whipple**, Fred Lawrence 1906- *AmMWSc 92, IntWW 91, Who 92*
**Whipple**, George Hoyt 1878-1976 *WhoNob 90*
**Whipple**, George Stephenson 1950- *WhoWest 92*
**Whipple**, Gerald Howard 1923- *AmMWSc 92*
**Whipple**, Janice U *WhoIns 92*
**Whipple**, Kenneth 1934- *WhoFI 92*
**Whipple**, Royson Newton 1912- *AmMWSc 92*
**Whipple**, Squire 1804-1888 *BiInAmS*
**Whipple**, Thomas Walton 1942- *WhoMW 92*
**Whipple**, V. Thayne, II 1964- *WhoWest 92*
**Whipple**, Walter Leighton 1940- *WhoWest 92*
**Whipple**, William Perry 1913- *WhoMW 92*
**Whippman**, Michael Lewis 1938- *Who 92*
**Whipps**, Edward Franklin 1936- *WhoAmL 92, WhoMW 92*
**Whipps**, Mary N. 1945- *WhoBlA 92*
**Whiren**, Alice Phipps 1941- *WhoMW 92*
**Whirlaway** 1938-1953 *FacFETw*
**Whirlow**, Donald Kent 1938- *AmMWSc 92*
**Whisenand**, James Dudley 1947- *WhoFI 92*
**Whisenhunt**, Donald Wayne 1938- *WhoWest 92*
**Whisenton**, Andre C. 1944- *WhoBlA 92*
**Whisenton**, Joffre T. *WhoBlA 92*
**Whishaw**, Anthony 1930- *IntWW 91, TwCPaSc*

Whishaw, Anthony Popham Law 1930- Who 92
Whishaw, Charles 1909- Who 92
Whisker, James Biser 1939- WhoAmP 91
Whisler, Frank Duane 1934- AmMWSc 92
Whisler, Howard Clinton 1931- AmMWSc 92
Whisler, James Steven 1954- WhoAmL 92, WhoFI 92
Whisler, Kirk 1951- WhoWest 92
Whisler, Walter William 1934- AmMWSc 92
Whisnant, Charleen DrAPF 91
Whisnant, David Marshall 1954- WhoFI 92
Whisnant, Jack Page 1924- AmMWSc 92
Whisnant, Patrick N. 1955- WhoRel 92
Whisnant, Richard B. 1959- WhoAmL 92
Whisonant, Robert Clyde 1941- AmMWSc 92
Whissell-Buechy, Dorothy Y E 1926- AmMWSc 92
Whistler, Alwyne Michael Webster 1909- Who 92
Whistler, David Paul 1940- AmMWSc 92
Whistler, George Washington 1800-1849 BiInAmS
Whistler, James Abbott McNeill 1834-1903 ThHEIm
Whistler, James McNeill 1834-1903 BenetAL 91, RComAH
Whistler, Laurence 1912- ConPo 91, IntWW 91, Who 92, WrDr 92
Whistler, Rex 1905-1944 TwCPaSc
Whistler, Roy Lester 1912- AmMWSc 92
Whiston, Peter Rice 1912- Who 92
Whiston, William 1667-1752 BlkwCEP
Whitacre, Bruce Edward 1956- WhoEnt 92
Whitacre, Caroline C 1949- AmMWSc 92
Whitacre, David Martin 1943- AmMWSc 92
Whitacre, Edward E., Jr. IntWW 91
Whitacre, Edward E., Jr. 1941- WhoFI 92, WhoMW 92
Whitacre, Gale R 1933- AmMWSc 92
Whitacre, Vernon C WhoAmP 91
Whitacre, Wendell Britt 1927- WhoWest 92
Whitaker, Alexander 1585-1617? BenetAL 91
Whitaker, Arthur L. 1921- WhoBlA 92
Whitaker, Audie Dale 1949- WhoMW 92
Whitaker, Ben 1934- WrDr 92
Whitaker, Benjamin Charles George 1934- Who 92
Whitaker, Bruce D. 1948- WhoWest 92
Whitaker, C. Larimore 1943- WhoAmL 92
Whitaker, Clay Westerfield 1924- AmMWSc 92
Whitaker, David 1930-1980 ConAu 134
Whitaker, David Haddon 1931- Who 92
Whitaker, Donald L 1931- WhoAmP 91
Whitaker, Elaine Emanuel 1942- WhoEnt 92
Whitaker, Ellis Hobart 1908- AmMWSc 92
Whitaker, Ewen A 1922- AmMWSc 92
Whitaker, Forest 1961- ConBlB 2 [port], IntMPA 92, WhoBlA 92
Whitaker, George Warren, III 1950- WhoAmL 92
Whitaker, Gilbert R., Jr. 1931- WrDr 92
Whitaker, Gilbert Riley, Jr. 1931- WhoFI 92
Whitaker, Glenn Virgil 1947- WhoAmL 92
Whitaker, Jack LesBEnT 92
Whitaker, James Herbert Ingham 1925- Who 92
Whitaker, John Barclay 1939- WhoAmP 91
Whitaker, John O, Jr 1935- AmMWSc 92
Whitaker, John Robert 1929- AmMWSc 92
Whitaker, John Scott 1948- AmMWSc 92
Whitaker, Louis Rodman 1957- WhoBlA 92
Whitaker, Mack Lee 1931- AmMWSc 92
Whitaker, Mary 1947- WhoWest 92
Whitaker, Meade 1919- WhoAmL 92
Whitaker, Mical Rozier 1941- WhoBlA 92
Whitaker, Morris Duane 1940- WhoWest 92
Whitaker, O'Kelley 1926- WhoRel 92
Whitaker, Pernell 1964- BlkOlyM
Whitaker, Rick D. 1951- WhoRel 92
Whitaker, Robert C 1941- WhoIns 92
Whitaker, Robert Dallas 1933- AmMWSc 92
Whitaker, Robert John 1936- WhoMW 92
Whitaker, Rod WrDr 92
Whitaker, Rodney William 1931- IntAu&W 91
Whitaker, Roger Torr 1951- WhoAmL 92
Whitaker, Ronald Martin 1933- WhoMW 92
Whitaker, Sheila 1936- Who 92
Whitaker, Sidney Hopkins 1940- AmMWSc 92
Whitaker, Thomas Burton 1939- AmMWSc 92
Whitaker, Thomas Kenneth 1916- IntWW 91, Who 92
Whitaker, Thomas Wallace 1905- AmMWSc 92
Whitaker, Tom O'Hara 1953- WhoEnt 92
Whitaker, Wayne Orson 1960- WhoFI 92, WhoWest 92
Whitaker, Willard H. 1912- WhoBlA 92
Whitaker, William Armstrong 1936- AmMWSc 92
Whitaker, William Thomas, Jr. 1944- WhoAmL 92
Whitaker-Azmitia, Patricia Mack 1953- AmMWSc 92
Whitbread, Fatima 1961- IntWW 91
Whitbread, Samuel Charles 1937- IntWW 91, Who 92
Whitbread, Thomas DrAPF 91
Whitbread, William Henry 1900- Who 92
Whitby, Bishop Suffragan of 1934- Who 92
Whitby, Charles Harley 1926- Who 92
Whitby, Joy 1930- IntAu&W 91, Who 92
Whitby, Kenneth T 1925- AmMWSc 92
Whitby, Lionel Gordon 1926- Who 92
Whitby, Owen WhoIns 92
Whitby, Owen 1942- AmMWSc 92
Whitby, Sharon IntAu&W 91X, WrDr 92
Whitby, Von H. 1948- WhoWest 92
Whitcher, Alice DrAPF 91
Whitcher, Frances Miriam 1814-1852 BenetAL 91
Whitchurch, Charles Augustus 1940- WhoWest 92
Whitchurch, Ellwood Falvey 1939- WhoFI 92
Whitcomb, Carl Erwin 1939- AmMWSc 92
Whitcomb, Donald Dooley 1946- WhoRel 92
Whitcomb, Donald Leroy 1925- AmMWSc 92
Whitcomb, Edgar Doud 1917- WhoAmP 91
Whitcomb, Harold Craig 1939- WhoWest 92
Whitcomb, Henry F, Jr 1917- WhoAmP 91
Whitcomb, Ian Timothy 1941- WhoEnt 92
Whitcomb, John C. 1924- WrDr 92
Whitcomb, John Clement, Jr. 1924- WhoRel 92
Whitcomb, Noel 1918- ConAu 134
Whitcomb, Pineapple DrAPF 91
Whitcomb, Ray ScFEYrs
Whitcomb, Richard T 1921- AmMWSc 92
Whitcomb, Stanley Ernest 1951- AmMWSc 92
Whitcomb, Walter E WhoAmP 91
Whitcomb, Walter Henry 1928- AmMWSc 92
Whitcomb, Willard Hall 1915- AmMWSc 92
Whitcomb, William Grandon 1942- WhoAmL 92
Whitcombe, Allan Ronald 1941- IntAu&W 91
Whitcraft, David Main 1962- WhoEnt 92
White Who 92
White, Baroness 1909- IntWW 91, Who 92
White, Addison Hughson 1909- AmMWSc 92
White, Adrian N. S. Who 92
White, Aidan Patrick 1951- IntAu&W 91, Who 92
White, Alan 1930- Who 92
White, Alan George Castle 1916- AmMWSc 92
White, Alan Ray 1941- WhoEnt 92
White, Alan Richard 1922- Who 92, WrDr 92
White, Alan Wayne 1954- AmMWSc 92
White, Alan Whitcomb 1945- AmMWSc 92
White, Albert Cornelius 1927- AmMWSc 92
White, Albert George, Jr 1940- AmMWSc 92
White, Albert M 1926- AmMWSc 92
White, Alberta LaVerne 1913- WhoWest 92
White, Alexander Patrick, Jr. 1932- WhoMW 92
White, Alfred E. WhoRel 92
White, Alfred Kenneth, Jr. 1929- WhoAmL 92
White, Alice Elizabeth 1954- AmMWSc 92
White, Alice June 1905- WhoWest 92
White, Allan WhoAmP 91
White, Alma Birdwell 1862-1946 RelLAm 91
White, Alphonza F. 1935- WhoBlA 92
White, Alvin Murray 1925- AmMWSc 92
White, Andrew 1579-1656 BenetAL 91
White, Andrew D. 1832-1918 BenetAL 91
White, Andrew John, III 1932- WhoRel 92
White, Andrew Michael 1942- AmMWSc 92
White, Andrew Peter 1944- WhoRel 92
White, Andrew Stewart 1941- WhoIns 92
White, Andrew Wilson, Jr 1927- AmMWSc 92
White, Anna 1831-1910 AmPeW, RelLAm 91
White, Anne Terry 1896-1980 ConAu 135
White, Anthony Charles Gunn 1955- WhoBlA 92
White, Arlynn Quinton, Jr 1946- AmMWSc 92
White, Arnold Allen 1923- AmMWSc 92
White, Arthur C 1925- AmMWSc 92
White, Arthur Joe 1933- WhoIns 92
White, Arthur John Stanley d1991 Who 92N
White, Arthur Thomas 1939- WhoMW 92
White, Arthur Thomas, II 1939- AmMWSc 92
White, Arthur W., Jr. 1943- WhoBlA 92
White, Artis Andre 1926- WhoBlA 92
White, Augustus A., III 1936- WhoBlA 92
White, Augustus Aaron, III 1936- AmMWSc 92
White, Barbara Ann 1942- WhoWest 92
White, Barbara Williams 1943- WhoBlA 92
White, Barrington Raymond 1934- Who 92
White, Barry 1944- ConMus 6 [port], WhoBlA 92
White, Beatrice Lockhart 1906- WhoWest 92
White, Benjamin Franklin 1800-1879 NewAmDM
White, Benjamin Steven 1945- AmMWSc 92
White, Bernard Henry 1947- AmMWSc 92
White, Bernard J 1937- AmMWSc 92
White, Bertram Milton 1923- WhoFI 92
White, Betty LesBEnT 92
White, Betty 1922- WhoEnt 92
White, Betty 1924- IntMPA 92
White, Beverly Anita 1960- WhoBlA 92
White, Beverly Jean 1928- WhoAmP 91
White, Bill 1933?- ConBlB 1 [port]
White, Bill 1934- NewYTBS 91 [port], WhoBlA 92
White, Billy Ray 1936- WhoBlA 92
White, Blanche Babette 1905- AmMWSc 92
White, Bonnie Yvonne 1940- WhoWest 92
White, Booker Taliaferro 1907- WhoBlA 92
White, Brenda Black DrAPF 91
White, Brian 1936- AmMWSc 92
White, Brian William 1934- WhoWest 92
White, Brittan Romeo 1936- WhoWest 92
White, Bruce Hilding 1933- WhoMW 92
White, Bruce Langton 1931- AmMWSc 92
White, Bryan Oliver 1929- Who 92
White, Byron R 1917- FacFETw, Who 92, WhoAmL 92, WhoAmP 91
White, C. Dale 1925- WhoRel 92
White, C. Noel 1938- WhoRel 92
White, C. Thomas 1928- WhoAmL 92, WhoAmP 91, WhoMW 92
White, Caroline 1935- WhoAmP 91
White, Caroline 1952- TwCPaSc
White, Carolyn DrAPF 91
White, Carter Hixson 1916- WhoFI 92
White, Catharine Boswell 1958- WhoEnt 92
White, Catherine Kilmurray 1930- WhoAmP 91
White, Cecil Ray 1937- WhoRel 92, WhoWest 92
White, Cecile Holmes 1955- WhoRel 92
White, Cecile Renee Kingsbury 1952- WhoEnt 92
White, Cedric Masey 1898- Who 92
White, Celestino, Sr 1945- WhoAmP 91
White, Chappell 1920- WhoMW 92
White, Charles A. 1829-1892 NewAmDM
White, Charles A, Jr 1922- AmMWSc 92
White, Charles Abiathar 1826-1910 BiInAmS
White, Charles Edward 1920- WhoRel 92
White, Charles Edwin 1952- WhoMW 92
White, Charles F 1913- AmMWSc 92
White, Charles Henry 1943- AmMWSc 92
White, Charles Joyce 1839-1917 BiInAmS
White, Charles R. 1937- WhoBlA 92
White, Charles Raymond 1933- AmMWSc 92
White, Charles Richard 1937- WhoRel 92
White, Charley Monroe 1932- AmMWSc 92
White, Christine Larkin 1946- WhoBlA 92
White, Christopher 1930- WrDr 92
White, Christopher Clarke 1937- AmMWSc 92
White, Christopher John 1930- IntWW 91, Who 92
White, Christopher Minot 1951- WhoFI 92
White, Christopher Robert Meadows 1940- Who 92
White, Christopher Stuart Stuart- Who 92
White, Claire Nicolas DrAPF 91
White, Clara Jo 1927- WhoFI 92
White, Clarence Cameron 1880-1960 NewAmDM
White, Clarence Dean 1946- WhoBlA 92
White, Clark Woody 1940- AmMWSc 92
White, Claude Esley 1949- WhoAmL 92, WhoBlA 92
White, Clayton Cecil 1942- WhoBlA 92
White, Clayton M 1936- AmMWSc 92
White, Clifford Joseph, III 1956- WhoAmL 92
White, Clovis Leland 1953- WhoBlA 92
White, Cohen W. 1887- WhoBlA 92
White, Colin 1913- AmMWSc 92
White, Craig William 1944- WhoIns 92
White, Cynthia Carol 1943- WhoFI 92
White, D. Richard 1947- WhoBlA 92
White, Dale Andrew 1958- IntAu&W 91
White, Damon L. 1934- WhoBlA 92
White, Daniel Eugene 1950- WhoAmL 92
White, Daniel James 1948- WhoMW 92
White, Danny Fernando 1955- WhoWest 92
White, Danny Levius 1956- WhoWest 92
White, Darlene Mary 1945- WhoRel 92
White, Daryl Joseph 1947- WhoFI 92
White, David 1925- AmMWSc 92
White, David 1936- AmMWSc 92
White, David Alan, Jr. 1942- WhoFI 92
White, David Archer 1927- AmMWSc 92
White, David Calvin 1922- AmMWSc 92
White, David Cleaveland 1929- AmMWSc 92
White, David D. 1901- WhoBlA 92
White, David Evans 1932- AmMWSc 92
White, David Gover 1927- AmMWSc 92
White, David Halbert 1945- AmMWSc 92
White, David Harry 1929- Who 92
White, David Hywel 1931- AmMWSc 92
White, David O. 1948- WhoFI 92
White, David Raymond 1940- AmMWSc 92
White, David Sanford 1945- AmMWSc 92
White, David Stuart 1944- WhoFI 92
White, David Thomas 1931- Who 92
White, Dean Kincaid 1944- AmMWSc 92
White, DeAnna H. 1959- WhoWest 92
White, Deidra R. 1958- WhoBlA 92
White, Denis Naldrett 1916- AmMWSc 92
White, Dennis Michael 1946- WhoAmL 92
White, Derek Leslie 1933- Who 92
White, Devon Markes 1962- WhoBlA 92
White, Dewey Anderson, Jr 1923- WhoAmP 91
White, Dezra 1941- WhoBlA 92
White, Diane Edrine 1938- WhoWest 92
White, Dick 1906- Who 92
White, Don Lee WhoBlA 92
White, Don William 1942- WhoFI 92, WhoWest 92
White, Donald Benjamin 1930- AmMWSc 92
White, Donald Edward 1914- AmMWSc 92
White, Donald Edward 1925- WhoBlA 92
White, Donald F. 1908- WhoBlA 92
White, Donald Glenn 1946- AmMWSc 92
White, Donald Harvey 1931- AmMWSc 92, WhoWest 92
White, Donald Henry 1940- AmMWSc 92
White, Donald J 1938- WhoIns 92
White, Donald J. 1956- WhoMW 92
White, Donald L 1949- WhoAmP 91
White, Donald Louis 1934- WhoFI 92
White, Donald Perry 1916- AmMWSc 92
White, Donald R., Jr. 1949- WhoBlA 92
White, Donald Robertson 1924- AmMWSc 92
White, Dorothy Dianne 1940- WhoFI 92
White, Doug WhoAmP 91
White, Dwain Montgomery 1931- AmMWSc 92
White, E. B. 1899-1985 BenetAL 91, FacFETw
White, Earl Craig 1960- WhoRel 92
White, Earl Henry 1959- WhoBlA 92
White, Eartha 1876-1974 NotBlAW 92 [port]
White, Eartha Mary Magdalene 1876-1974 FacFETw
White, Ed Pearson 1911- WhoBlA 92
White, Edmund DrAPF 91
White, Edmund 1940- Au&Arts 7 [port], BenetAL 91, ConAu 36NR, ConNov 91, CurBio 91 [port], IntAu&W 91, WrDr 92
White, Edmund W 1920- AmMWSc 92
White, Edward 1930-1967 FacFETw
White, Edward 1933- AmMWSc 92
White, Edward Alfred 1934- WhoAmL 92
White, Edward Allen 1928- WhoWest 92
White, Edward Austin 1915- AmMWSc 92
White, Edward Clarence, Jr. 1956- WhoBlA 92
White, Edward D 1845-1921 RComAH
White, Edward Douglass 1845-1921 AmPolLe [port], FacFETw
White, Edward George 1923- Who 92

White, Edward Gibson, II 1954- *WhoAmL 92*
White, Edward John 1932- *AmMWSc 92*
White, Edward Lewis 1947- *AmMWSc 92*
White, Edward Lucas 1866-1934 *BenetAL 91, ScFEYrs*
White, Edward M. 1933- *WrDr 92*
White, Edward Martin 1938- *Who 92*
White, Edwin Henry 1937- *AmMWSc 92*
White, Elaine Kontominas 1944- *WhoWest 92*
White, Elizabeth Flad 1954- *WhoWest 92*
White, Elizabeth Lloyd 1916- *AmMWSc 92*
White, Elizabeth Loczi 1936- *AmMWSc 92*
White, Ella Flowers 1941- *WhoBlA 92*
White, Ellen Gould Harmon 1827-1915 *AmPeW, RelLAm 91*
White, Elmer G. 1926-1979 *ConAu 134*
White, Elwyn Brooks 1899-1985 *AmPeW*
White, Emil Henry 1926- *AmMWSc 92*
White, Emily Gruen 1921- *WhoMW 92*
White, Emmons E. 1891-1982 *ConAu 133*
White, Erica d1991 *Who 92N*
White, Ernest G. 1946- *WhoBlA 92*
White, Ernest Howard 1908-1983 *TwCPaSc*
White, Erskine Norman, III 1951- *WhoRel 92*
White, Ethelbert 1891-1972 *TwCPaSc*
White, Eugene 1930- *WhoRel 92*
White, Eugene 1963- *WhoAmP 91*
White, Eugene L 1951- *AmMWSc 92*
White, Eugene M 1937- *WhoAmP 91*
White, Eugene Wilbert 1933- *AmMWSc 92*
White, Floyd H 1932- *WhoIns 92*
White, Frank *LesBEnT 92*
White, Frank 1932- *IntWW 91*
White, Frank, Jr. 1950- *WhoBlA 92*
White, Frank D 1933- *WhoAmP 91*
White, Frank John 1927- *Who 92*
White, Frank N. 1963- *WhoAmL 92*
White, Frank Paul *WhoAmP 91*
White, Frank Richard 1939- *Who 92*
White, Frankie Walton 1945- *WhoBlA 92*
White, Franklin Estabrook 1922- *AmMWSc 92*
White, Franklin Heinritz 1927- *WhoMW 92*
White, Franklin Henry 1919- *AmMWSc 92*
White, Fred D 1918- *AmMWSc 92*
White, Fred G 1928- *AmMWSc 92*
White, Fred M 1859- *ScFEYrs*
White, Fred Newton 1927- *AmMWSc 92*
White, Frederic Paul, Jr. 1948- *WhoBlA 92*
White, Frederick Andrew 1918- *AmMWSc 92*
White, Frederick Howard, Jr 1926- *AmMWSc 92*
White, Frederick William George 1905- *IntWW 91, Who 92*
White, Fredric Paul 1942- *AmMWSc 92*
White, Fredrick John 1952- *WhoMW 92*
White, Gabriel 1902- *TwCPaSc*
White, Gail *DrAPF 91*
White, Garland Anthony 1932- *WhoBlA 92*
White, Garrett Marquet 1953- *WhoRel 92*
White, Gary *WhoAmP 91*
White, Gary Charles 1937- *WhoEnt 92*
White, Gary Leon 1932- *WhoBlA 92*
White, Gayle Clay 1944- *WhoWest 92*
White, George *WhoFI 92*
White, George 1934- *WhoBlA 92*
White, George A 1941- *WhoIns 92*
White, George Alan 1932- *Who 92*
White, George C 1919- *WhoIns 92*
White, George Charles, Jr 1918- *AmMWSc 92*
White, George Cooke 1935- *WhoEnt 92*
White, George Edward 1941- *WhoAmL 92*
White, George Gregory 1953- *WhoBlA 92*
White, George Hal 1946- *WhoRel 92*
White, George Harvey 1939- *WhoWest 92*
White, George Matthews 1941- *AmMWSc 92*
White, George Michael 1939- *AmMWSc 92*
White, George Nichols, Jr 1919- *AmMWSc 92*
White, George Rowland 1929- *AmMWSc 92*
White, George Stanley James 1948- *Who 92*
White, George Timothy 1957- *WhoFI 92*
White, George W. 1931- *WhoAmL 92, WhoBlA 92*
White, George Washington 1918- *WhoMW 92*
White, George Wendell, Jr. 1915- *WhoAmL 92*
White, Gerald M 1929- *AmMWSc 92*
White, Gifford 1912- *AmMWSc 92*
White, Gilbert Anthony 1916- *Who 92*
White, Gilbert F. 1911- *IntWW 91*
White, Gilbert Fowler 1911- *AmMWSc 92*
White, Gillian Mary 1936- *IntAu&W 91, WrDr 92*
White, Glenn E 1957- *AmMWSc 92*
White, Glenn Maxwell 1962- *WhoAmL 92*
White, Gloria Waters 1934- *WhoBlA 92*
White, Gordon Allan 1932- *AmMWSc 92*
White, Gordon E. 1935- *WhoBlA 92*
White, Granville C. 1927- *WhoBlA 92*
White, Gregory 1952- *WhoMW 92*
White, Gregory Durr, Mrs. 1908- *WhoBlA 92*
White, Guy Kendall 1925- *IntWW 91*
White, H. Blair 1927- *WhoAmL 92, WhoMW 92*
White, H. Melton 1924- *WhoBlA 92*
White, Halbert Lynn, Jr. 1950- *WhoFI 92*
White, Harold Bancroft, III 1943- *AmMWSc 92*
White, Harold Birts, Jr 1929- *AmMWSc 92*
White, Harold Clare 1919- *Who 92*
White, Harold Clark Mitchelle 1948- *WhoBlA 92*
White, Harold D 1910- *AmMWSc 92*
White, Harold Edgar 1913- *WhoFI 92, WhoMW 92*
White, Harold J 1920- *AmMWSc 92*
White, Harold Keith 1923- *AmMWSc 92*
White, Harold Leslie 1905- *IntWW 91, Who 92*
White, Harold McCoy 1932- *AmMWSc 92*
White, Harold R. 1936- *WhoFI 92*
White, Harold Rogers 1923- *WhoBlA 92*
White, Harold Tredway, III 1947- *WhoFI 92*
White, Harris Herman 1949- *AmMWSc 92*
White, Harry *TwCWW 91*
White, Harry 1938- *TwCPaSc*
White, Harry Clifford 1930- *WhoRel 92*
White, Harry Edward, Jr. 1939- *WhoAmL 92*
White, Harry Joseph 1931- *AmMWSc 92*
White, Helen Lyng 1930- *AmMWSc 92*
White, Henry 1850-1927 *AmPolLe*
White, Henry Arthur Dalrymple D. *Who 92*
White, Henry W 1941- *AmMWSc 92*
White, Herbert Spencer 1927- *WhoMW 92*
White, Herman Brenner, Jr 1948- *AmMWSc 92*
White, Horace Frederick 1925- *AmMWSc 92*
White, Howard Ashley 1913-1991 *ConAu 133*
White, Howard Dwaine 1946- *AmMWSc 92*
White, Howard Julian, Jr 1920- *AmMWSc 92*
White, Hubert William 1944- *WhoEnt 92, WhoWest 92*
White, Hugh Clayton 1936- *WhoRel 92*
White, Hugh Lawson 1773-1840 *AmPolLe*
White, Hugo Moresby 1939- *Who 92*
White, Ian *Who 92*
White, Ida Margaret 1924- *WhoBlA 92*
White, Irvin Linwood 1932- *AmMWSc 92*
White, J. Arthur 1903-1977 *WhoBlA 92N*
White, J Courtland 1948- *AmMWSc 92*
White, J V 1925- *WhoIns 92*
White, Jack 1935- *WhoAmP 91*
White, Jack Lee 1925- *AmMWSc 92*
White, Jack Raymond 1936- *WhoAmL 92*
White, James *Who 92*
White, James 1821-1881 *RelLAm 91*
White, James 1913- *Who 92*
White, James 1928- *IntAu&W 91, TwCSFW 91, WrDr 92*
White, James 1937- *Who 92*
White, James Allen 1948- *WhoFI 92*
White, James Ashton V. *Who 92*
White, James Boyd 1938- *WhoAmL 92*
White, James Carl 1922- *AmMWSc 92*
White, James Carrick 1916- *AmMWSc 92*
White, James Clarence 1936- *AmMWSc 92*
White, James Clarke 1833-1916 *BiInAmS*
White, James David 1935- *AmMWSc 92*
White, James David 1941- *WhoWest 92*
White, James David 1942- *WhoIns 92*
White, James Edward 1918- *AmMWSc 92, WhoWest 92*
White, James Edwin 1935- *AmMWSc 92*
White, James F. 1932- *WhoRel 92*
White, James Floyd 1932- *WrDr 92*
White, James Frederick, Jr. 1940- *WhoAmL 92*
White, James George 1929- *AmMWSc 92*
White, James Howard 1930- *WhoAmP 91*
White, James J 1929- *WhoAmP 91*
White, James Justesen 1934- *WhoAmL 92*
White, James L 1938- *AmMWSc 92*
White, James Louis, Jr. 1949- *WhoBlA 92*
White, James P. *DrAPF 91*
White, James Patrick 1939- *AmMWSc 92*
White, James Richard 1948- *WhoAmL 92*
White, James Robert 1936- *WhoRel 92*
White, James Rushton 1923- *AmMWSc 92*
White, James Russell 1919- *AmMWSc 92*
White, James S. 1930- *WhoBlA 92*
White, James Springer 1821-1881 *AmPeW*
White, James Ulysses, Jr. 1949- *WhoAmL 92*
White, James Victor 1941- *AmMWSc 92*
White, James William 1850-1916 *BiInAmS*
White, James William 1935- *WhoMW 92*
White, James Wilson 1914- *AmMWSc 92*
White, James Wilson 1926- *WhoAmP 91*
White, Jan Tuttle 1943- *WhoFI 92*
White, Jane Vicknair 1947- *AmMWSc 92*
White, Javier A. 1945- *WhoBlA 92*
White, Jay P. *DrAPF 91*
White, Jean Tillinghast 1934- *WhoAmP 91*
White, Jeffrey Daniel 1960- *WhoEnt 92*
White, Jeffrey Paul 1955- *WhoMW 92*
White, Jere Lee 1954- *WhoAmP 91*
White, Jerry Eugene 1946- *AmMWSc 92*
White, Jesse 1919- *IntMPA 92*
White, Jesse C, Jr 1934- *WhoAmP 91, WhoBlA 92*
White, Jesse Edmund 1927- *AmMWSc 92*
White, Jesse Marc *WhoEnt 92*
White, Jesse Steven 1917- *AmMWSc 92*
White, Jesse Wathen 1955- *WhoFI 92*
White, Jill Carolyn 1934- *WhoAmL 92*
White, Jim 1935- *WhoAmP 91*
White, Jo Jo 1946- *WhoBlA 92*
White, Joan Emily 1946- *WhoWest 92*
White, Job Benton 1931- *WhoRel 92*
White, Joe Lloyd 1921- *AmMWSc 92*
White, Joe Wade 1940- *AmMWSc 92*
White, John *BenetAL 91, BiInAmS, WhoAmP 91*
White, John 1802-1845 *AmPolLe*
White, John 1919- *WrDr 92*
White, John 1936- *ConCom 92*
White, John 1937- *WhoAmP 91*
White, John Aaron, Jr. 1943- *WhoAmL 92*
White, John Abiathar 1948- *WhoWest 92*
White, John Alan 1905- *Who 92*
White, John Anderson 1919- *AmMWSc 92*
White, John Arnold 1933- *AmMWSc 92*
White, John Austin 1942- *Who 92*
White, John Austin, Jr 1939- *AmMWSc 92*
White, John Charles 1911- *Who 92*
White, John Clinton 1942- *WhoBlA 92*
White, John Coyle 1924- *WhoAmP 91*
White, John David 1928- *AmMWSc 92*
White, John David 1931- *WhoEnt 92*
White, John Edward 1924- *WrDr 92*
White, John Edward Clement Twarowski 1924- *Who 92*
White, John F. *LesBEnT 92*
White, John F. 1924- *WhoBlA 92*
White, John F, Jr 1949- *WhoAmP 91*
White, John Francis 1921- *AmMWSc 92*
White, John Francis 1929- *AmMWSc 92*
White, John Francis 1944- *AmMWSc 92*
White, John Francis 1945- *AmMWSc 92*
White, John Glenn, Jr. 1949- *WhoEnt 92*
White, John Greville 1922- *AmMWSc 92*
White, John Joseph 1932- *WhoWest 92*
White, John Joseph, III 1939- *AmMWSc 92*
White, John Joseph, III 1948- *WhoAmL 92*
White, John Kenneth 1952- *WrDr 92*
White, John L 1930- *WhoAmP 91*
White, John Lee 1962- *WhoBlA 92*
White, John Lindsey 1930- *WhoAmL 92*
White, John M 1926- *WhoAmP 91*
White, John Marvin 1937- *AmMWSc 92*
White, John Michael 1938- *AmMWSc 92*
White, John Preston 1945- *WhoMW 92*
White, John Sampson 1916- *Who 92*
White, John Simon 1910- *WhoEnt 92*
White, John Thomas 1931- *AmMWSc 92*
White, John Timothy 1951- *WhoMW 92, WhoRel 92*
White, John W 1933- *AmMWSc 92*
White, John William 1937- *Who 92*
White, John Woolmer 1947- *Who 92*
White, Jon Jay 1955- *WhoMW 92*
White, Jon M *AmMWSc 92*
White, Jon Manchip *DrAPF 91*
White, Jon Manchip 1924- *IntAu&W 91, WrDr 92*
White, Jonathan Bruce 1956- *WhoRel 92*
White, Joseph 1946- *BlkOlyM*
White, Joseph Calvin 1930- *WhoFI 92*
White, Joseph Reeves, Jr. 1930- *WhoAmL 92*
White, Josh 1915-1969 *NewAmDM*
White, Juanita M *WhoAmP 91*
White, Jude Gilliam *WrDr 92*
White, Judith Ann O'Radnik 1943- *WhoMW 92*
White, Julian Eugene, Jr. 1932- *WhoWest 92*
White, Julie Belle 1943- *WhoMW 92*
White, June Broussard 1924- *AmMWSc 92*
White, June Joyce 1949- *WhoBlA 92*
White, Kande 1950- *WhoMW 92*
White, Karin Rose 1959- *WhoAmL 92*
White, Karl Raymond 1950- *WhoWest 92*
White, Katherine Patricia 1948- *WhoAmL 92, WhoFI 92*
White, Kathleen *TwCPaSc*
White, Kathleen Taylor 1949- *WhoEnt 92*
White, Katie Kinnard 1932- *WhoBlA 92*
White, Keith Alan 1958- *WhoFI 92*
White, Kenneth 1936- *ConPo 91, WrDr 92*
White, Kenneth Spencer, Sr. 1939- *WhoAmL 92*
White, Kermit Earle 1917- *WhoBlA 92*
White, Kerr Lachlan 1917- *AmMWSc 92*
White, Kevin Hagan 1929- *WhoAmP 91*
White, Kevin John 1956- *WhoRel 92*
White, Kevin Joseph 1936- *AmMWSc 92*
White, Larry Dale 1940- *AmMWSc 92*
White, Laura Bradstreet d1919 *BiInAmS*
White, Lawrence Gilbert 1963- *WhoAmP 91*
White, Lawrence J. 1943- *WhoFI 92, WrDr 92*
White, Lawrence John 1915- *Who 92*
White, Lawrence Keith 1948- *AmMWSc 92*
White, Lawrence R. *LesBEnT 92*
White, Lawrence R 1926- *IntMPA 92*
White, Lawrence S 1923- *AmMWSc 92*
White, Lee James 1939- *AmMWSc 92*
White, Leland Jennings 1940- *WhoRel 92*
White, Lendell Aaron 1926- *AmMWSc 92*
White, Leonard *IntMPA 92*
White, Leroy Albert 1929- *AmMWSc 92*
White, Lerrill James 1948- *WhoRel 92*
White, Lester *WhoAmP 91*
White, Linda 1964- *WhoMW 92*
White, Linda Diane 1952- *WhoAmL 92*
White, Lionel 1905- *WrDr 92*
White, Lloyd Michael 1949- *WhoRel 92*
White, Lola *DrAPF 91*
White, Lorenzo Maurice 1966- *WhoBlA 92*
White, Lowell Elmond, Jr 1928- *AmMWSc 92*
White, Luther D. 1937- *WhoBlA 92*
White, Luther J. 1936- *WhoBlA 92*
White, Lyle James 1947- *WhoMW 92*
White, Lynn Allen 1950- *WhoRel 92*
White, Lynton 1916- *Who 92*
White, Mabel *WhoBlA 92*
White, Mahlon Thatcher 1936- *WhoWest 92*
White, Major C. 1926- *WhoBlA 92*
White, Malcolm Lunt 1927- *AmMWSc 92*
White, Margareta *LesBEnT 92*
White, Margarette Paulyne Morgan 1934- *WhoBlA 92*
White, Margit Triska 1932- *WhoFI 92*
White, Margita Eklund 1937- *WhoEnt 92*
White, Marilyn Elaine 1944- *BlkOlyM*
White, Marilyn Mildred 1947- *WhoBlA 92*
White, Mark Gilmore 1949- *AmMWSc 92*
White, Mark Thomas 1955- *WhoRel 92*
White, Mark W, Jr *WhoAmP 91*
White, Mark Wells, Jr. 1940- *IntWW 91*
White, Marsha *DrAPF 91*
White, Martin *Who 92*
White, Marvin Hart 1937- *AmMWSc 92*
White, Mary Anne 1953- *AmMWSc 92*
White, Mary Belle 1954- *WhoAmL 92*
White, Mary Jane *DrAPF 91*
White, Mary Louise 1933- *WhoFI 92*
White, Matthew 1941- *WhoWest 92*
White, Matthew Hagy 1956- *WhoEnt 92*
White, Maude Adams 1916- *WhoWest 92*
White, Maurice 1941- *WhoBlA 92*
White, Maurice Leopold 1928- *AmMWSc 92*
White, Max Stewart 1939- *WhoFI 92*
White, Melvyn Lee 1941- *WhoBlA 92*
White, Merit P 1908- *AmMWSc 92*
White, Michael *WhoEnt 92*
White, Michael Dennis 1952- *WhoFI 92*
White, Michael George 1953- *AmMWSc 92*
White, Michael K 1938- *WhoIns 92*
White, Michael Lee 1961- *WhoFI 92*
White, Michael R *WhoAmP 91*
White, Michael Reed 1951- *WhoBlA 92, WhoMW 92*
White, Michael Simon 1936- *IntWW 91, Who 92*
White, Milton *DrAPF 91*
White, Minor 1908-1976 *ModArCr 2 [port]*
White, Moreno J 1948- *AmMWSc 92*
White, Morgan Wilson 1945- *WhoWest 92*
White, Morton 1917- *WrDr 92*
White, Morton Gabriel 1917- *ConAu 35NR*
White, Moses Clarke 1819-1900 *BiInAmS*
White, Myron Edward 1920- *AmMWSc 92*
White, N F 1939- *AmMWSc 92*
White, Nan E. 1931- *WhoBlA 92*
White, Nancy Margaret 1938- *WhoAmP 91*
White, Nathan Emmett, Jr 1941- *WhoAmP 91*
White, Nathaniel B. 1914- *WhoBlA 92*
White, Nathaniel Miller 1941- *AmMWSc 92*

**White,** Nelia Gardner 1894-1957 *BenetAL 91*
**White,** Neville Helme 1931- *Who 92*
**White,** Niles C 1922- *AmMWSc 92*
**White,** Noel 1938- *TwCPaSc*
**White,** Noel David George 1951- *AmMWSc 92*
**White,** Norman A. 1922- *IntWW 91*
**White,** Norman Arthur 1922- *Who 92, WhoFI 92*
**White,** Norman Edward 1917- *AmMWSc 92*
**White,** O. C. 1932- *WhoBlA 92*
**White,** Onna *WhoEnt 92*
**White,** Ora Lee 1945- *WhoMW 92*
**White,** Padraic 1942- *IntWW 91*
**White,** Patricia Denise 1949- *WhoAmL 92, WhoMW 92*
**White,** Patricia Holmes 1948- *WhoAmP 91*
**White,** Patrick d1990 *IntWW 91N*
**White,** Patrick 1912- *IntAu&W 91*
**White,** Patrick 1912-1990 *AnObit 1990, ConLC 65 [port], -69 [port], FacFETw, RfGEnL 91*
**White,** Patrick Victor Martindale d1990 *Who 92N*
**White,** Patrick Victor Martindale 1912- *WhoNob 90*
**White,** Paul *IntMPA 92*
**White,** Paul d1955 *LesBEnT 92*
**White,** Paul A 1915- *AmMWSc 92*
**White,** Paul C 1941- *AmMWSc 92*
**White,** Paul Christopher 1947- *WhoBlA 92*
**White,** Paul Dunbar 1917- *WhoAmL 92, WhoMW 92*
**White,** Paul R 1930- *WhoAmP 91*
**White,** Pearl 1897-1938 *ReelWom [port]*
**White,** Peter 1919- *Who 92*
**White,** Peter 1930- *AmMWSc 92, WhoMW 92*
**White,** Peter Sawyer 1938- *WhoAmP 91*
**White,** Philip Cleaver 1913- *AmMWSc 92*
**White,** Phyllis Margaret *WhoEnt 92*
**White,** Polly Sears 1931- *WhoMW 92, WhoRel 92*
**White,** Preston Charles 1933- *WhoWest 92*
**White,** Quentin Jerome 1952- *WhoRel 92*
**White,** Quenton I. 1960- *WhoAmL 92*
**White,** Quincy 1933- *WhoAmP 91*
**White,** Quitman, Jr. 1945- *WhoBlA 92*
**White,** R. Elton 1942- *WhoFI 92, WhoMW 92*
**White,** R Milford 1932- *AmMWSc 92*
**White,** R. Quincy 1933- *WhoAmL 92, WhoFI 92*
**White,** Ralph E 1942- *AmMWSc 92*
**White,** Ralph L. 1930- *WhoBlA 92*
**White,** Ralph L. 1943- *WhoBlA 92*
**White,** Ralph Lawrence, Jr 1941- *AmMWSc 92*
**White,** Ramy Allison *SmATA 67*
**White,** Randall Allen 1953- *WhoEnt 92*
**White,** Randolph Louis 1897- *WhoBlA 92*
**White,** Randy 1967- *WhoBlA 92*
**White,** Ray Henry 1936- *AmMWSc 92*
**White,** Ray Lewis 1941- *WrDr 92*
**White,** Raymond 1945- *WhoRel 92*
**White,** Raymond Burton 1943- *WhoFI 92*
**White,** Raymond E 1933- *AmMWSc 92*
**White,** Raymond Gene 1930- *AmMWSc 92*
**White,** Raymond P. 1937- *IntWW 91*
**White,** Raymond Petrie, Jr 1937- *AmMWSc 92*
**White,** Raymond Rodney, Sr. 1953- *WhoBlA 92*
**White,** Raymond Walter Ralph 1923- *IntWW 91, Who 92*
**White,** Rebecca 1948- *WhoRel 92*
**White,** Rebecca Anne 1949- *WhoMW 92*
**White,** Reggie 1961- *WhoBlA 92*
**White,** Reginald 1914- *WrDr 92*
**White,** Renee Allyn 1945- *WhoAmL 92*
**White,** Richard 1942- *WhoAmP 91*
**White,** Richard 1949- *WhoAmP 91*
**White,** Richard Alan 1935- *AmMWSc 92*
**White,** Richard Allan 1946- *AmMWSc 92*
**White,** Richard Allen 1936- *WhoMW 92*
**White,** Richard Allen 1948- *WhoRel 92*
**White,** Richard Allen 1957- *WhoEnt 92*
**White,** Richard C. 1941- *WhoBlA 92*
**White,** Richard Clarence 1933- *WhoAmL 92*
**White,** Richard Crawford 1923- *WhoAmP 91*
**White,** Richard David 1953- *WhoFI 92*
**White,** Richard Earl 1933- *AmMWSc 92*
**White,** Richard Edward 1925- *WhoMW 92*
**White,** Richard Edward 1944- *AmMWSc 92*
**White,** Richard Grant 1821-1885 *BenetAL 91*
**White,** Richard H. 1950- *WhoBlA 92*
**White,** Richard Kenneth 1930- *AmMWSc 92*
**White,** Richard Manning 1930- *AmMWSc 92*
**White,** Richard N 1949- *WhoIns 92*
**White,** Richard Norman 1933- *AmMWSc 92*
**White,** Richard Paul 1925- *AmMWSc 92*
**White,** Richard Stanton, Jr. 1934- *WhoFI 92*
**White,** Richard Taylor 1908- *Who 92*
**White,** Robert 1535?-1574 *NewAmDM*
**White,** Robert 1924- *FacFETw*
**White,** Robert Allan 1934- *AmMWSc 92*
**White,** Robert Allen 1944- *AmMWSc 92*
**White,** Robert Andrew 1924- *WhoEnt 92*
**White,** Robert Arnold 1944- *WhoRel 92*
**White,** Robert B 1921- *AmMWSc 92*
**White,** Robert E 1917- *AmMWSc 92*
**White,** Robert Edward 1926- *WhoAmP 91*
**White,** Robert Gordon 1938- *WhoWest 92*
**White,** Robert J 1926- *AmMWSc 92*
**White,** Robert James 1923- *IntWW 91*
**White,** Robert James 1958- *WhoFI 92*
**White,** Robert Joel 1946- *WhoAmL 92, WhoFI 92*
**White,** Robert Keller 1930- *AmMWSc 92*
**White,** Robert L. 1916- *WhoBlA 92*
**White,** Robert L. G., Jr. 1941- *WhoFI 92*
**White,** Robert Lee 1927- *AmMWSc 92, WhoWest 92*
**White,** Robert Lee 1928- *WrDr 92*
**White,** Robert Lester 1953- *AmMWSc 92*
**White,** Robert Louis 1952- *WhoWest 92*
**White,** Robert M 1923- *AmMWSc 92*
**White,** Robert M., II 1915- *IntWW 91*
**White,** Robert Marshall 1938- *AmMWSc 92*
**White,** Robert Mayer 1923- *IntWW 91*
**White,** Robert Michael 1942- *WhoWest 92*
**White,** Robert Miles Ford 1928- *WhoFI 92*
**White,** Robert Milton 1948- *WhoWest 92*
**White,** Robert Mitchell, II 1915- *IntAu&W 91*
**White,** Robert Rankin 1942- *IntAu&W 91, WhoWest 92*
**White,** Robert Stephen 1920- *AmMWSc 92, WhoWest 92*
**White,** Robert Stephen 1952- *Who 92*
**White,** Robert Wellington, Jr 1940- *WhoAmP 91*
**White,** Roberta Jean 1926- *AmMWSc 92*
**White,** Robin *DrAPF 91*
**White,** Robin Bernard G. *Who 92*
**White,** Robin Shepard 1950- *WhoWest 92*
**White,** Roger 1950- *Who 92*
**White,** Roger Lowrey 1928- *Who 92*
**White,** Ronald 1943- *AmMWSc 92*
**White,** Ronald E 1948- *AmMWSc 92*
**White,** Ronald Jerome 1936- *AmMWSc 92*
**White,** Ronald Joseph 1940- *AmMWSc 92*
**White,** Ronald Leon 1930- *WhoFI 92*
**White,** Ronald Lynn 1944- *WhoRel 92*
**White,** Ronald Paul, Sr 1935- *AmMWSc 92*
**White,** Ronnie L *WhoAmP 91*
**White,** Rory Wilbur 1959- *WhoBlA 92*
**White,** Rosanne Teresa 1954- *WhoFI 92*
**White,** Roscoe Beryl 1937- *AmMWSc 92*
**White,** Roseann Spicola 1943- *AmMWSc 92*
**White,** Roy B. 1926- *IntMPA 92*
**White,** Roy Bernard *WhoEnt 92, WhoFI 92*
**White,** Russell Lynn 1950- *WhoWest 92*
**White,** Ruth Bryant 1955- *WhoRel 92*
**White,** Ruth Margaret 1922- *WhoWest 92*
**White,** Ruth S. 1925- *WhoEnt 92*
**White,** Ryan 1971-1990 *FacFETw*
**White,** Samuel Grandford, Jr 1945- *AmMWSc 92*
**White,** Sandra L 1941- *AmMWSc 92*
**White,** Sandra LaVelle 1941- *WhoBlA 92*
**White,** Sandy Bruce 1960- *WhoEnt 92*
**White,** Scott A., Sr. 1909- *WhoBlA 92*
**White,** Sharon Brown 1963- *WhoBlA 92*
**White,** Sidney Edward 1916- *AmMWSc 92*
**White,** Simon David Manton 1951- *AmMWSc 92*
**White,** Stanford 1853-1906 *DcTwDes*
**White,** Stanhope 1913- *IntAu&W 91, WrDr 92*
**White,** Stanley A 1931- *AmMWSc 92*
**White,** Stanley Archibald 1931- *WhoWest 92*
**White,** Stephen 1945- *ConAu 134*
**White,** Stephen Edward 1947- *AmMWSc 92, WhoFI 92*
**White,** Stephen Francis 1949- *WhoAmL 92*
**White,** Stephen Fraser 1922- *Who 92*
**White,** Stephen Halley 1940- *AmMWSc 92*
**White,** Stephen Tracy 1947- *WhoAmP 91*
**White,** Steven D. 1950- *WhoRel 92*
**White,** Steven Douglas 1953- *WhoRel 92*
**White,** Steven F. *DrAPF 91*
**White,** Steven Gregory 1957- *WhoAmL 92*
**White,** Steven James 1951- *WhoFI 92*
**White,** Stewart Edward 1863-1946 *ScFEYrs*
**White,** Stewart Edward 1873-1946 *BenetAL 91, TwCWW 91*
**White,** Stewart Edward & Adams, Samuel H *ScFEYrs*
**White,** Stuart Cossitt 1942- *AmMWSc 92*
**White,** Sylvia Kay 1955- *WhoBlA 92*
**White,** T. H. 1906-1964 *LiExTwC, RfGEnL 91*
**White,** Ted 1938- *TwCSFW 91, WrDr 92*
**White,** Terence D. 1942- *WhoRel 92*
**White,** Terence de Vere 1912- *IntAu&W 91, Who 92, WrDr 92*
**White,** Terence Philip 1932- *Who 92*
**White,** Terrence Harold 1943- *IntWW 91*
**White,** Terry Arthur 1953- *WhoAmL 92*
**White,** Theodore Greely 1872?-1901 *BiInAmS*
**White,** Theodore H. 1915-1986 *BenetAL 91, FacFETw*
**White,** Thomas Anthony B. *Who 92*
**White,** Thomas Astley Woollaston 1904- *Who 92*
**White,** Thomas Dale 1941- *WhoMW 92*
**White,** Thomas Daniel, Jr. 1954- *WhoWest 92*
**White,** Thomas David 1943- *AmMWSc 92*
**White,** Thomas Gailand 1932- *AmMWSc 92*
**White,** Thomas Harrington 1931- *WhoRel 92*
**White,** Thomas James 1945- *AmMWSc 92*
**White,** Thomas Lester 1903- *WhoMW 92*
**White,** Thomas Owen 1940- *WhoAmL 92*
**White,** Thomas P 1950- *WhoAmP 91*
**White,** Thomas Raeburn, III 1938- *WhoAmL 92*
**White,** Thomas S. 1949- *WhoAmL 92*
**White,** Thomas Stuart, Jr. 1943- *WhoFI 92*
**White,** Thomas Taylor 1920- *AmMWSc 92*
**White,** Thomas Vincent 1947- *WhoAmL 92*
**White,** Thomas Wayne 1934- *AmMWSc 92*
**White,** Timothy Lee 1951- *AmMWSc 92*
**White,** Timothy P 1949- *AmMWSc 92*
**White,** Tom *Who 92*
**White,** Tom Martin 1951- *WhoEnt 92*
**White,** Tom Willingham 1943- *WhoFI 92*
**White,** Tommie Lee 1944- *WhoBlA 92*
**White,** Tommy D. 1949- *WhoFI 92*
**White,** Ulysses 1939- *WhoBlA 92*
**White,** Van Freeman 1924- *WhoBlA 92*
**White,** Vanna *LesBEnT 92 [port]*
**White,** Vanna Marie 1957- *WhoHisp 92*
**White,** Vicki Lee 1960- *WhoMW 92*
**White,** Vickie H 1955- *WhoAmP 91*
**White,** Virginia Lou 1932- *WhoAmP 91*
**White,** W Arthur 1916- *AmMWSc 92*
**White,** W. Christopher 1951- *WhoAmL 92*
**White,** W Paul 1945- *WhoAmP 91*
**White,** Walter 1893-1955 *BenetAL 91, BlkLC [port]*
**White,** Walter Francis 1893-1955 *FacFETw*
**White,** Walter Hiawatha, Jr. 1954- *WhoAmL 92, WhoMW 92*
**White,** Walter Preston, Jr. 1923- *WhoAmL 92*
**White,** Warren D 1915- *AmMWSc 92*
**White,** Warren Wurtele 1932- *WhoFI 92*
**White,** Wendell F. 1939- *WhoBlA 92*
**White,** Willard Wentworth 1946- *IntWW 91, Who 92*
**White,** Willard Worster, III 1944- *AmMWSc 92*
**White,** William 1910- *WrDr 92*
**White,** William 1928- *AmMWSc 92*
**White,** William, Jr. 1934- *WrDr 92*
**White,** William Alexander 1906- *AmMWSc 92*
**White,** William Allen 1868-1944 *AmPeW, BenetAL 91*
**White,** William Blaine 1934- *AmMWSc 92*
**White,** William Charles 1922- *AmMWSc 92*
**White,** William E. 1934- *WhoBlA 92*
**White,** William Francis 1957- *WhoAmL 92*
**White,** William H. 1932- *WhoBlA 92*
**White,** William H. 1947- *WhoFI 92*
**White,** William Hale *RfGEnL 91*
**White,** William Hedges 1948- *WhoFI 92*
**White,** William J. 1926- *WhoBlA 92*
**White,** William J. 1935- *WhoBlA 92*
**White,** William J. 1948- *WhoMW 92*
**White,** William James 1938- *IntWW 91, WhoFI 92, WhoMW 92*
**White,** William Joseph 1942- *WhoHisp 92*
**White,** William Kelvin Kennedy 1930- *Who 92*
**White,** William L. 1900-1973 *BenetAL 91*
**White,** William Luther 1931- *WrDr 92*
**White,** William M. *DrAPF 91*
**White,** William Michael 1948- *AmMWSc 92*
**White,** William Nelson 1938- *WhoAmL 92*
**White,** William North 1925- *AmMWSc 92*
**White,** William Smith 1907- *IntWW 91*
**White,** William T., III 1947- *WhoBlA 92*
**White,** William Wallace 1939- *AmMWSc 92*
**White,** William Woods 1957- *WhoAmL 92*
**White,** Willis S, Jr 1926- *AmMWSc 92*
**White,** Willis Sheridan, Jr. 1926- *WhoFI 92, WhoMW 92*
**White,** Willye B 1939- *BlkOlyM*
**White,** Winifred Viaria 1953- *WhoBlA 92*
**White,** Yolanda Simmons 1955- *WhoBlA 92*
**White-Hunt,** Keith 1950- *WhoFI 92, WhoWest 92*
**White-Hurst,** John Marshall 1942- *WhoAmL 92*
**White of Hull,** Baron 1923- *Who 92*
**White-Thomson,** Ian Hugh 1904- *Who 92*
**White-Thomson,** Ian Leonard 1936- *WhoWest 92*
**White-Vondran,** Mary Ellen 1938- *WhoWest 92*
**White-Ware,** Grace E. 1921- *WhoBlA 92*
**Whiteaker,** Linda Joyce 1942- *WhoRel 92*
**Whitebird,** J. *DrAPF 91*
**Whitebrook,** Robert Ballard 1917- *WhoWest 92*
**Whitechurch,** Victor L 1868-1933 *ScFEYrs*
**Whited,** Dean Allen 1940- *AmMWSc 92*
**Whited,** Julie Lynn 1960- *WhoAmL 92*
**Whitefield,** Billie Buntin 1921- *WhoAmP 91*
**Whitefield,** Carolyn Lee 1946- *WhoAmL 92*
**Whitefield,** George 1714-1770 *BenetAL 91*
**Whitefield,** Philip Douglas 1953- *AmMWSc 92*
**Whitefield,** Rodney Joe 1936- *AmMWSc 92*
**Whiteford,** Kate 1952- *TwCPaSc*
**Whiteford,** Micheal Bonneville 1945- *WhoMW 92*
**Whiteford,** Robert Daniel 1922- *AmMWSc 92*
**Whiteford,** Wynne 1915- *TwCSFW 91*
**Whitehair,** Charles Kenneth 1916- *AmMWSc 92*
**Whitehair,** J. Greg 1957- *WhoAmL 92*
**Whitehair,** Leo A 1929- *AmMWSc 92*
**Whitehead,** Alfred 1887-1974 *NewAmDM*
**Whitehead,** Alfred North 1861-1947 *BenetAL 91, FacFETw*
**Whitehead,** Andrew Bruce 1932- *AmMWSc 92*
**Whitehead,** Armand T 1936- *AmMWSc 92*
**Whitehead,** Barbara Elaine 1947- *WhoFI 92*
**Whitehead,** Cabell 1863-1908 *BiInAmS*
**Whitehead,** Carl Francis 1927- *WhoFI 92*
**Whitehead,** Charles A 1935- *WhoAmP 91*
**Whitehead,** Clay T. *LesBEnT 92*
**Whitehead,** Daniel L 1915- *AmMWSc 92*
**Whitehead,** David 1958- *TwCWW 91, WrDr 92*
**Whitehead,** David Barry 1946- *WhoAmL 92, WhoWest 92*
**Whitehead,** David William 1946- *WhoBlA 92*
**Whitehead,** Donald Reed 1932- *AmMWSc 92*
**Whitehead,** Donald Robert 1948- *WhoFI 92*
**Whitehead,** Eddie L. 1944- *WhoBlA 92*
**Whitehead,** Eddie Lee 1944- *WhoEnt 92*
**Whitehead,** Edward Anthony 1933- *IntAu&W 91, Who 92*
**Whitehead,** Eugene Irving 1918- *AmMWSc 92*
**Whitehead,** Floy Eugenia 1913- *AmMWSc 92*
**Whitehead,** Frank 1916- *WrDr 92*
**Whitehead,** Frank Ernest 1930- *Who 92*
**Whitehead,** Fred 1905- *AmMWSc 92*
**Whitehead,** G. Marc 1940- *WhoAmL 92*
**Whitehead,** Geoffrey Michael 1921- *WrDr 92*
**Whitehead,** George 1916- *Who 92*
**Whitehead,** George Sydney 1915- *Who 92*
**Whitehead,** George William 1918- *AmMWSc 92, IntWW 91*
**Whitehead,** Gerald Norman 1947- *WhoWest 92*
**Whitehead,** Gillian 1941- *ConCom 92*
**Whitehead,** Graham Wright *Who 92*
**Whitehead,** Harvey Sterlin, Jr. 1945- *WhoMW 92*
**Whitehead,** Henry S 1882-1932 *ScFEYrs*
**Whitehead,** Howard Allan 1927- *AmMWSc 92*
**Whitehead,** James *DrAPF 91*
**Whitehead,** James 1936- *WrDr 92*
**Whitehead,** James Rennie 1917- *AmMWSc 92*
**Whitehead,** James S. 1948- *WhoAmL 92*
**Whitehead,** James T., Jr. 1934- *WhoBlA 92*
**Whitehead,** Janet *WrDr 92*
**Whitehead,** John 1944- *WhoEnt 92*
**Whitehead,** John Andrews 1941- *AmMWSc 92*
**Whitehead,** John Clark 1934- *WhoWest 92*
**Whitehead,** John Ernest Michael 1920- *IntWW 91, Who 92*

**Whitehead,** John L., Jr. 1924- *WhoBlA 92*
**Whitehead,** John Stainton 1932- *IntWW 91, Who 92*
**Whitehead,** John W. 1946- *WhoAmL 92, WhoFI 92*
**Whitehead,** Kenneth E 1928- *AmMWSc 92*
**Whitehead,** Lloyd Oscar 1939- *WhoAmL 92*
**Whitehead,** Marian Nedra 1922- *AmMWSc 92*
**Whitehead,** Marvin Delbert 1917- *AmMWSc 92*
**Whitehead,** Mary Elizabeth 1922- *WhoAmP 91*
**Whitehead,** Michael Anthony 1935- *AmMWSc 92*
**Whitehead,** Michael Kenneth 1950- *WhoRel 92*
**Whitehead,** Paxton 1937- *WhoEnt 92*
**Whitehead,** Phillip 1937- *IntAu&W 91, Who 92*
**Whitehead,** Reginald Joseph 1945- *WhoEnt 92*
**Whitehead,** Richard Henry 1865-1916 *BiInAmS*
**Whitehead,** Richard Lee 1927- *WhoIns 92*
**Whitehead,** Richard Walter 1937- *WhoFI 92*
**Whitehead,** Robert H 1934- *WhoIns 92*
**Whitehead,** Robert Stewart 1932- *WhoMW 92*
**Whitehead,** Rowland 1930- *Who 92*
**Whitehead,** Samuel Lyman 1937- *WhoAmP 91*
**Whitehead,** Ted *Who 92*
**Whitehead,** Ted 1933- *WrDr 92*
**Whitehead,** Thomas Patterson 1923- *Who 92*
**Whitehead,** Timothy Dwight 1934- *WhoBlA 92*
**Whitehead,** Tom Simmons, Jr. 1928- *WhoEnt 92*
**Whitehead,** Walter Dexter, Jr 1922- *AmMWSc 92*
**Whitehead,** Wayne William, Sr. 1940- *WhoFI 92*
**Whitehead,** Wiley Leon, Jr 1943- *WhoAmP 91*
**Whitehead,** William 1715-1785 *DcLB 109 [port], RfGEnL 91*
**Whitehead,** William C. 1955- *WhoFI 92*
**Whitehead,** William Earl 1945- *AmMWSc 92*
**Whitehead,** William Riddick 1831-1902 *BiInAmS*
**Whitehill,** Angela Elizabeth 1938- *WhoEnt 92*
**Whitehill,** Clifford Lane 1931- *WhoAmL 92, WhoFI 92, WhoHisp 92*
**Whitehill,** Henry W *ScFEYrs*
**Whitehill,** James Arthur 1959- *WhoAmL 92*
**Whitehill,** James Donald 1942- *WhoRel 92*
**Whitehill,** N. James, III 1963- *WhoEnt 92*
**Whitehorn,** John Roland Malcolm 1924- *Who 92*
**Whitehorn,** Katharine *IntAu&W 91, WrDr 92*
**Whitehorn,** Katharine Elizabeth *Who 92*
**Whitehorn,** William Victor 1915- *AmMWSc 92*
**Whitehorne,** Donald 1955- *WhoFI 92*
**Whitehouse,** Anne *DrAPF 91*
**Whitehouse,** Bruce Alan 1939- *AmMWSc 92*
**Whitehouse,** Charles Sheldon 1921- *WhoAmP 91*
**Whitehouse,** David Bryn 1941- *Who 92*
**Whitehouse,** David R 1929- *AmMWSc 92*
**Whitehouse,** David Rae Beckwith 1945- *Who 92*
**Whitehouse,** Frank, Jr 1924- *AmMWSc 92*
**Whitehouse,** Gary E 1938- *AmMWSc 92*
**Whitehouse,** Gerald D 1936- *AmMWSc 92*
**Whitehouse,** Jack Pendleton 1924- *WhoFI 92*
**Whitehouse,** Mary 1910- *Who 92*
**Whitehouse,** Robert Allen 1941- *WhoAmP 91*
**Whitehouse,** Ronald Leslie S 1937- *AmMWSc 92*
**Whitehouse,** Walter Alexander 1915- *Who 92, WrDr 92*
**Whitehouse,** Walter MacIntire, Sr 1916- *AmMWSc 92*
**Whitehurst,** Brooks M 1930- *AmMWSc 92*
**Whitehurst,** Charles A 1929- *AmMWSc 92*
**Whitehurst,** Charles Bernard, Sr. 1938- *WhoBlA 92*
**Whitehurst,** Daniel Keenan 1948- *WhoAmP 91*
**Whitehurst,** Darrell Duayne 1938- *AmMWSc 92*
**Whitehurst,** Eldridge Augustus 1923- *AmMWSc 92*
**Whitehurst,** Garnett Brooks 1952- *AmMWSc 92*
**Whitehurst,** George William 1925- *WhoAmP 91*
**Whitehurst,** Harry Bernard 1922- *AmMWSc 92, WhoWest 92*
**Whitehurst,** Virgil Edwards 1932- *AmMWSc 92*
**Whitehurst,** William Wilfred, Jr. 1937- *WhoFI 92*
**Whiteker,** McElwyn D 1929- *AmMWSc 92*
**Whiteker,** Roy Archie 1927- *AmMWSc 92*
**Whitelaw** *Who 92*
**Whitelaw,** Viscount 1918- *Who 92*
**Whitelaw,** Billie 1932- *IntMPA 92, IntWW 91, Who 92*
**Whitelaw,** James Hunter 1936- *Who 92*
**Whitelaw,** Kenneth David 1947- *WhoAmL 92*
**Whitelaw,** R L 1917- *AmMWSc 92*
**Whitelaw,** Reid Smith 1945- *WhoEnt 92*
**Whitelaw,** William Albert 1941- *AmMWSc 92*
**Whitelaw Of Penrith,** Viscount 1918- *IntWW 91*
**Whiteley** *Who 92*
**Whiteley,** Alfred 1928- *TwCPaSc*
**Whiteley,** Benjamin R 1929- *WhoIns 92*
**Whiteley,** Benjamin Robert 1929- *WhoWest 92*
**Whiteley,** Gerald Abson 1915- *Who 92*
**Whiteley,** Helen Riaboff 1922- *AmMWSc 92*
**Whiteley,** Hugo Baldwin H. *Who 92*
**Whiteley,** Norman Franklin, Jr. 1940- *WhoFI 92*
**Whiteley,** Peter 1920- *Who 92*
**Whiteley,** Phyllis Ellen 1957- *AmMWSc 92*
**Whiteley,** Roger L 1930- *AmMWSc 92*
**Whiteley,** Samuel Lloyd 1913- *Who 92*
**Whiteley,** William Richard, Sr. 1940- *WhoMW 92*
**Whiteley Lucero,** Linda 1951- *WhoWest 92*
**Whitelock,** Richard Lawrence 1930- *WhoAmP 91*
**Whitely,** Donald Harrison 1955- *WhoBlA 92*
**Whitely,** James Lowell 1936- *WhoFI 92*
**Whiteman,** Albert Leon 1915- *AmMWSc 92*
**Whiteman,** Cameron C. 1953- *WhoFI 92*
**Whiteman,** Charles E 1918- *AmMWSc 92*
**Whiteman,** Darrell L. 1947- *WhoRel 92*
**Whiteman,** Donna L 1948- *WhoAmP 91*
**Whiteman,** Eldon Eugene 1913- *AmMWSc 92*
**Whiteman,** Elizabeth Anne Osborn 1918- *Who 92*
**Whiteman,** Harold Bartlett, III 1948- *WhoEnt 92*
**Whiteman,** Herbert Wells, Jr. 1936- *WhoBlA 92*
**Whiteman,** Horace Clifton 1925- *WhoFI 92*
**Whiteman,** Joe V 1919- *AmMWSc 92*
**Whiteman,** John David 1943- *AmMWSc 92*
**Whiteman,** John Robert 1938- *Who 92*
**Whiteman,** Joseph David 1933- *WhoAmL 92*
**Whiteman,** Michael 1906- *WrDr 92*
**Whiteman,** Paul 1890-1967 *NewAmDM*
**Whiteman,** Paul 1891-1967 *FacFETw*
**Whiteman,** Peter George 1942- *Who 92*
**Whiteman,** Richard Frank 1925- *WhoMW 92*
**Whiteman,** Roberta Hill *DrAPF 91*
**Whiteman,** Rodney David Carter 1940- *Who 92*
**Whiteman,** Victor Lee 1939- *WhoMW 92*
**Whitemore,** Hugh 1936- *IntMPA 92, WrDr 92*
**Whitemore,** Hugh John 1936- *IntAu&W 91, Who 92*
**Whiten,** Mark Eldon 1962- *WhoWest 92*
**Whitenberg,** David Calvin 1931- *AmMWSc 92*
**Whiteneck,** John Samuel, Jr. 1905- *WhoRel 92*
**Whitener,** Philip Charles 1920- *WhoWest 92*
**Whitener,** Tommie Wayne 1942- *WhoWest 92*
**Whitener,** William Garnett 1951- *WhoEnt 92*
**Whiteoak,** John Edward Harrison 1947- *Who 92*
**Whitescarver,** Olin Dravo 1936- *WhoWest 92*
**Whitesell,** Jack Wilfred, Jr. 1949- *WhoAmL 92*
**Whitesell,** James Judd 1939- *AmMWSc 92*
**Whitesell,** James Keller 1944- *AmMWSc 92*
**Whitesell,** John Edwin 1938- *WhoEnt 92*
**Whitesell,** Nolan Gary 1953- *WhoFI 92*
**Whitesell,** Theresa Downes 1945- *WhoWest 92*
**Whitesell,** William James 1927- *AmMWSc 92*
**Whiteside,** Alba Lea 1928- *WhoAmL 92*
**Whiteside,** Beverly Lois 1955- *WhoRel 92*
**Whiteside,** Bobby Gene 1940- *AmMWSc 92*
**Whiteside,** Carol Gordon 1942- *WhoAmP 91, WhoWest 92*
**Whiteside,** Charles Hugh 1932- *AmMWSc 92*
**Whiteside,** Dale 1930- *WhoAmP 91*
**Whiteside,** David Powers, Jr. 1950- *WhoAmL 92*
**Whiteside,** Derek Thomas 1932- *Who 92*
**Whiteside,** Ernestyne E. *WhoBlA 92*
**Whiteside,** Eugene Perry 1912- *AmMWSc 92*
**Whiteside,** Jack Oliver 1928- *AmMWSc 92*
**Whiteside,** James Brooks 1942- *AmMWSc 92*
**Whiteside,** Larry W. 1937- *WhoBlA 92*
**Whiteside,** Melbourne C 1937- *AmMWSc 92*
**Whiteside,** Michael Douglas 1946- *WhoFI 92*
**Whiteside,** Theresa L 1939- *AmMWSc 92*
**Whiteside,** Wesley C 1927- *AmMWSc 92*
**Whiteside,** Wesley Cecil 1927- *WhoMW 92*
**Whitesides,** George McClelland 1939- *AmMWSc 92*
**Whitesides,** John Lindsey, Jr 1943- *AmMWSc 92*
**Whitesides,** Lawson Ewing 1910- *WhoMW 92*
**Whitesitt,** John Eldon 1922- *AmMWSc 92*
**Whitesitt,** Linda Marie 1951- *WhoEnt 92*
**Whitest,** Beverly Joyce 1951- *WhoBlA 92*
**Whitestone,** Herbert William 1920- *WhoAmP 91*
**Whiteway,** Stirling Giddings 1927- *AmMWSc 92*
**Whitfield** *Who 92*
**Whitfield,** Adrian 1937- *Who 92*
**Whitfield,** Alan 1939- *Who 92*
**Whitfield,** Carol F 1939- *AmMWSc 92*
**Whitfield,** Carolyn Dickson 1941- *AmMWSc 92*
**Whitfield,** Charles Richard 1927- *Who 92*
**Whitfield,** David Richard 1928- *WhoEnt 92, WhoMW 92*
**Whitfield,** Frances Smith 1946- *WhoAmP 91*
**Whitfield,** George 1909- *WrDr 92*
**Whitfield,** George Buckmaster, Jr 1923- *AmMWSc 92*
**Whitfield,** George Joshua Newbold 1909- *Who 92*
**Whitfield,** Harley A 1930- *WhoIns 92*
**Whitfield,** Harvey James, Jr 1940- *AmMWSc 92*
**Whitfield,** Jack D 1928- *AmMWSc 92*
**Whitfield,** Jack Duane 1928- *WhoFI 92*
**Whitfield,** James F 1931- *AmMWSc 92*
**Whitfield,** James M. 1830-1870 *BenetAL 91*
**Whitfield,** John 1941- *Who 92*
**Whitfield,** John Flett 1922- *Who 92*
**Whitfield,** John H. 1962- *WhoAmL 92*
**Whitfield,** John Howard Mervyn 1939- *AmMWSc 92*
**Whitfield,** John Humphreys 1906- *Who 92, WrDr 92*
**Whitfield,** June Rosemary 1925- *Who 92*
**Whitfield,** Lynn *WhoBlA 92, WhoEnt 92*
**Whitfield,** Malvin Greston 1924- *BlkOlyM*
**Whitfield,** Michael 1940- *Who 92*
**Whitfield,** Richard Allen 1946- *IntMPA 92*
**Whitfield,** Richard George 1951- *AmMWSc 92*
**Whitfield,** Richard Wriston 1942- *WhoWest 92*
**Whitfield,** Robert Edward 1921- *AmMWSc 92*
**Whitfield,** Robert Parr 1828-1910 *BiInAmS*
**Whitfield,** Roderick 1937- *Who 92*
**Whitfield,** Terry Bertland 1953- *WhoBlA 92*
**Whitfield,** Timberly N. 1966- *WhoBlA 92*
**Whitfield,** Vantile E. 1930- *WhoBlA 92*
**Whitfield Lewis,** Herbert John *Who 92*
**Whitfill,** Donald Lee 1939- *AmMWSc 92*
**Whitford,** Albert Edward 1905- *AmMWSc 92*
**Whitford,** Gary M 1937- *AmMWSc 92*
**Whitford,** George V 1914- *WhoIns 92*
**Whitford,** Howard Wayne 1940- *AmMWSc 92*
**Whitford,** John 1913- *Who 92*
**Whitford,** Larry Alston 1902- *AmMWSc 92*
**Whitford,** Philip Burton 1920- *AmMWSc 92*
**Whitford,** Walter George 1936- *AmMWSc 92*
**Whitford-Stark,** James Leslie 1948- *AmMWSc 92*
**Whitham,** Gerald Beresford 1927- *AmMWSc 92, IntWW 91, Who 92*
**Whithorne,** Emerson 1884-1958 *NewAmDM*
**Whiting,** Alan 1946- *Who 92*
**Whiting,** Albert Nathaniel 1917- *WhoBlA 92*
**Whiting,** Allen R *AmMWSc 92*
**Whiting,** Allen Suess 1926- *WhoWest 92*
**Whiting,** Anne Margaret 1941- *AmMWSc 92*
**Whiting,** Arthur Milton 1928- *WhoWest 92*
**Whiting,** Barbara *NewAmDM*
**Whiting,** Barbara E. 1936- *WhoBlA 92*
**Whiting,** Emanuel *WhoBlA 92*
**Whiting,** Frank M 1932- *AmMWSc 92*
**Whiting,** Harold 1855-1895 *BiInAmS*
**Whiting,** Henry H. *WhoAmL 92*
**Whiting,** Henry H 1923- *WhoAmP 91*
**Whiting,** Henry L 1821-1897 *BiInAmS*
**Whiting,** James Vincent 1926- *WhoWest 92*
**Whiting,** John 1917-1963 *RfGEnL 91*
**Whiting,** John Dale, Jr 1947- *AmMWSc 92*
**Whiting,** Leroy 1938- *WhoBlA 92*
**Whiting,** Margaret *NewAmDM*
**Whiting,** Margaret 1924- *FacFETw*
**Whiting,** Maybelle Stevens 1925- *WhoBlA 92*
**Whiting,** Nathan *DrAPF 91*
**Whiting,** Ollie Beth 1953- *WhoBlA 92*
**Whiting,** Peter Graham 1930- *Who 92*
**Whiting,** R L 1918- *AmMWSc 92*
**Whiting,** Richard 1891-1938 *FacFETw*
**Whiting,** Richard A. 1891-1938 *NewAmDM*
**Whiting,** Richard Albert 1922- *WhoAmL 92*
**Whiting,** Robert 1942- *WrDr 92*
**Whiting,** Robert L *WhoAmP 91*
**Whiting,** Stephen Clyde 1952- *WhoAmL 92*
**Whiting,** Steven Jay 1948- *WhoEnt 92*
**Whiting,** Sydney d1875 *ScFEYrs*
**Whiting,** Thomas J. 1923- *WhoBlA 92*
**Whiting,** Van Robert, Jr. 1950- *WhoWest 92*
**Whiting,** Wayne Clark 1926- *WhoMW 92*
**Whiting,** Willie *WhoBlA 92*
**Whitla,** William Alexander 1938- *AmMWSc 92*
**Whitlam,** Gough 1916- *FacFETw, IntWW 91, Who 92, WrDr 92*
**Whitlam,** Michael Richard 1947- *Who 92*
**Whitlam,** Nicholas Richard 1945- *Who 92*
**Whitlatch,** Martha Jane 1956- *WhoMW 92*
**Whitlatch,** Robert Bruce 1948- *AmMWSc 92*
**Whitledge,** William Haynes 1955- *WhoAmL 92*
**Whitley,** Belinda Gail 1961- *WhoWest 92*
**Whitley,** Dan Lee 1940- *WhoAmP 91*
**Whitley,** David Scott 1953- *WhoWest 92*
**Whitley,** Douglas Best 1928- *WhoAmP 91*
**Whitley,** Elizabeth Young 1915- *Who 92*
**Whitley,** Frank James 1894- *WhoBlA 92*
**Whitley,** James Heyward 1926- *AmMWSc 92*
**Whitley,** James R 1921- *AmMWSc 92*
**Whitley,** Joe Daly 1950- *WhoAmL 92*
**Whitley,** John 1905- *Who 92*
**Whitley,** John Reginald 1926- *Who 92*
**Whitley,** Joseph Efird 1931- *AmMWSc 92*
**Whitley,** Juana Lynn 1964- *WhoFI 92*
**Whitley,** Keith 1956?-1989 *ConMus 7 [port]*
**Whitley,** Larry Stephen 1937- *AmMWSc 92*
**Whitley,** Nancy O'Neil 1932- *AmMWSc 92*
**Whitley,** Oliver John 1912- *Who 92*
**Whitley,** R. Joyce 1930- *WhoBlA 92*
**Whitley,** Richard Francis 1954- *WhoEnt 92*
**Whitley,** William N. 1934- *WhoBlA 92*
**Whitley,** William Thurmon 1941- *AmMWSc 92*
**Whitlinger,** Gene P. 1933- *WhoFI 92*
**Whitlock,** Becky Kay Otto 1964- *WhoEnt 92*
**Whitlock,** Billy 1813-1878 *NewAmDM*
**Whitlock,** Brand 1869-1934 *BenetAL 91*
**Whitlock,** Charles Henry 1939- *AmMWSc 92*
**Whitlock,** Charles Wayne 1937- *WhoRel 92*
**Whitlock,** David Graham 1924- *AmMWSc 92*
**Whitlock,** Don E 1929- *WhoAmP 91*
**Whitlock,** Foster Brand d1991 *NewYTBS 91*
**Whitlock,** Francis *ScFEYrs*
**Whitlock,** Fred Henry 1936- *WhoBlA 92*
**Whitlock,** Gaylord Purcell 1917- *AmMWSc 92*

**Whitlock,** George Clinton 1808-1864 *BiInAmS*
**Whitlock,** Irene M 1933- *WhoAmP 91*
**Whitlock,** James C, Jr 1939- *WhoAmP 91*
**Whitlock,** John Hendrick 1913- *AmMWSc 92*
**Whitlock,** John Merrill 1955- *WhoAmL 92*
**Whitlock,** L Ronald 1944- *AmMWSc 92*
**Whitlock,** Lapsley Craig 1942- *AmMWSc 92*
**Whitlock,** Louis M *WhoAmP 91*
**Whitlock,** Luder Gradick, Jr. 1940- *WhoRel 92*
**Whitlock,** Ralph 1914- *WrDr 92*
**Whitlock,** Richard T 1931- *AmMWSc 92*
**Whitlock,** Robert Henry 1941- *AmMWSc 92*
**Whitlock,** William Abel 1929- *WhoAmL 92*
**Whitlock,** William Charles 1918- *Who 92*
**Whitlock,** Willie Walker 1925- *WhoAmL 92, WhoAmP 91*
**Whitlow,** Donald R. 1932- *WhoFI 92*
**Whitlow,** Graham Anthony 1938- *AmMWSc 92*
**Whitlow,** Lon Weidner 1950- *AmMWSc 92*
**Whitlow,** Morton Blanton 1940- *WhoFI 92, WhoMW 92*
**Whitlow,** Tony E 1933- *WhoAmP 91*
**Whitlow,** William Barney, Jr. 1945- *WhoFI 92*
**Whitlow,** William La Fond 1932- *WhoRel 92*
**Whitlow,** Woodrow, Jr. 1952- *WhoBlA 92*
**Whitmal,** Nathaniel 1937- *WhoBlA 92*
**Whitman,** Alan B 1941- *AmMWSc 92*
**Whitman,** Alan M 1937- *AmMWSc 92*
**Whitman,** Albery A. 1851-1901 *BenetAL 91*
**Whitman,** Alden 1913-1990 *DcLB Y91N [port]*
**Whitman,** Andrew Peter 1926- *AmMWSc 92*
**Whitman,** Ann C. d1991 *NewYTBS 91 [port]*
**Whitman,** Barry Tevian 1931- *WhoAmL 92*
**Whitman,** Charles Otis 1842-1910 *BiInAmS*
**Whitman,** Christina Brooks 1947- *WhoAmL 92*
**Whitman,** Constance Smith 1947- *WhoMW 92*
**Whitman,** Donald Ray 1931- *AmMWSc 92*
**Whitman,** Frank Perkins 1853-1919 *BiInAmS*
**Whitman,** Gerald Martin 1941- *AmMWSc 92*
**Whitman,** James Thomas 1940- *WhoWest 92*
**Whitman,** John Emerson 1944- *WhoEnt 92*
**Whitman,** Jules I. 1923- *WhoAmL 92*
**Whitman,** Kenneth Jay 1947- *WhoWest 92*
**Whitman,** Laurie Dee 1959- *WhoEnt 92*
**Whitman,** Leon A. 1936- *WhoEnt 92*
**Whitman,** Manuel S. 1937- *WhoFI 92*
**Whitman,** Mara Arden 1964- *WhoAmL 92*
**Whitman,** Marina von Neumann 1935- *IntWW 91*
**Whitman,** Martin J. 1924- *WhoFI 92*
**Whitman,** Nancy Ellin 1934- *WhoMW 92*
**Whitman,** Philip Martin 1916- *AmMWSc 92*
**Whitman,** Robert V 1928- *AmMWSc 92*
**Whitman,** Rollin Lawrence 1947- *AmMWSc 92*
**Whitman,** Roy Milton 1925- *AmMWSc 92*
**Whitman,** Ruth *DrAPF 91*
**Whitman,** Ruth 1922- *ConPo 91, WrDr 92*
**Whitman,** Sarah Helen 1803-1878 *BenetAL 91*
**Whitman,** Stephen French *ScFEYrs*
**Whitman,** Stuart 1928- *ConTFT 9, IntMPA 92*
**Whitman,** Victor *AmMWSc 92*
**Whitman,** Walt 1819-1892 *BenetAL 91, NinCLC 31 [port], PoeCrit 3 [port], RComAH*
**Whitman,** William *DrAPF 91*
**Whitmarsh,** Clifford John 1946- *AmMWSc 92*
**Whitmer,** Frederick Lee 1947- *WhoAmL 92*
**Whitmer,** Jeffrey Thomas 1948- *AmMWSc 92, WhoMW 92*
**Whitmer,** John Charles 1939- *AmMWSc 92*
**Whitmer,** Kyra Marie Riegle 1940- *WhoMW 92*
**Whitmer,** Robert Morehouse 1908- *AmMWSc 92*
**Whitmer,** Robert V 1923- *WhoAmP 91*
**Whitmire,** Bryant Andrew, Jr. 1946- *WhoAmL 92*
**Whitmire,** Carrie Ella 1926- *AmMWSc 92*
**Whitmire,** John Harris 1949- *WhoAmP 91*
**Whitmire,** Kathryn Jean 1946- *WhoAmP 91*
**Whitmire,** Kenton Herbert 1955- *AmMWSc 92*
**Whitmire,** Melburn G. 1939- *WhoWest 92*
**Whitmore,** Arnold Paul 1940- *WhoBlA 92*
**Whitmore,** Bradley Charles 1953- *AmMWSc 92*
**Whitmore,** Cilla *WrDr 92*
**Whitmore,** Clive 1935- *Who 92*
**Whitmore,** Deborah Harkins 1953- *WhoFI 92*
**Whitmore,** Donald Herbert, Jr 1944- *AmMWSc 92*
**Whitmore,** Edward Hugh 1926- *AmMWSc 92*
**Whitmore,** Frank Clifford, Jr 1915- *AmMWSc 92*
**Whitmore,** Frank William 1932- *AmMWSc 92*
**Whitmore,** George *DrAPF 91*
**Whitmore,** George Merle, Jr. 1928- *WhoFI 92*
**Whitmore,** Gordon Francis 1931- *AmMWSc 92*
**Whitmore,** Howard Lloyd 1935- *AmMWSc 92*
**Whitmore,** James 1921- *IntMPA 92*
**Whitmore,** John 1937- *Who 92*
**Whitmore,** Jon Scott 1945- *WhoEnt 92*
**Whitmore,** Joshua David 1949- *WhoEnt 92*
**Whitmore,** Kay Rex 1932- *IntWW 91, WhoFI 92*
**Whitmore,** Lori K 1958- *WhoAmP 91*
**Whitmore,** Mary Rowe 1936- *AmMWSc 92*
**Whitmore,** Menandra Sabina 1936- *WhoHisp 92*
**Whitmore,** R Peter *WhoAmP 91*
**Whitmore,** Ralph Ervin, Jr. 1932- *WhoWest 92*
**Whitmore,** Ralph M 1917- *AmMWSc 92*
**Whitmore,** Raymond Leslie 1920- *WrDr 92*
**Whitmore,** Robert Vincent 1956- *WhoMW 92*
**Whitmore,** Roy Alvin, Jr 1928- *AmMWSc 92*
**Whitmore,** Roy Walter 1947- *AmMWSc 92*
**Whitmore,** Stephen Carr 1931- *AmMWSc 92*
**Whitmore,** William Francis 1917- *AmMWSc 92, WhoWest 92*
**Whitnah,** Donald Robert 1925- *IntAu&W 91, WrDr 92*
**Whitner,** Donna K. 1951- *WhoBlA 92*
**Whitner,** Jane Marvin 1935- *WhoWest 92*
**Whitney,** A James 1943- *WhoAmP 91*
**Whitney,** Adeline Dutton Train 1824-1906 *HanAmWH*
**Whitney,** Arthur Edwin, Jr 1938- *AmMWSc 92*
**Whitney,** Arthur Sheldon 1933- *AmMWSc 92*
**Whitney,** Barry Lyn 1947- *WhoRel 92*
**Whitney,** Carol Marie 1946- *WhoFI 92*
**Whitney,** Charles Allen 1929- *AmMWSc 92*
**Whitney,** Charles Candee, Jr 1939- *AmMWSc 92*
**Whitney,** Charles Ralph 1943- *WhoWest 92*
**Whitney,** Constance Clein *WhoWest 92*
**Whitney,** Cynthia Kolb 1941- *AmMWSc 92*
**Whitney,** Daniel DeWayne 1937- *WhoWest 92*
**Whitney,** Daniel Eugene 1938- *AmMWSc 92*
**Whitney,** David Clay 1937- *WhoWest 92*
**Whitney,** Donald Ransom 1915- *AmMWSc 92*
**Whitney,** Eli 1765-1825 *BiInAmS, RComAH*
**Whitney,** Ellsworth Dow 1928- *AmMWSc 92*
**Whitney,** Elvin Dale 1928- *AmMWSc 92*
**Whitney,** Enoch Jonathan 1945- *WhoAmL 92*
**Whitney,** Eugene C 1913- *AmMWSc 92*
**Whitney,** George Stephen 1934- *AmMWSc 92*
**Whitney,** George Ward 1924- *WhoAmL 92*
**Whitney,** Gina Marie 1958- *AmMWSc 92*
**Whitney,** Grace Ann 1945- *WhoFI 92*
**Whitney,** Gwin Richard 1932- *WhoMW 92*
**Whitney,** Harvey Stuart 1935- *AmMWSc 92*
**Whitney,** Hassler 1907- *AmMWSc 92*
**Whitney,** J Barry, III 1944- *AmMWSc 92*
**Whitney,** J.D. *DrAPF 91*
**Whitney,** J. Marvin 1948- *WhoRel 92*
**Whitney,** James Arthur 1946- *AmMWSc 92*
**Whitney,** James Martin 1936- *AmMWSc 92*
**Whitney,** Jane 1941- *WhoWest 92*
**Whitney,** Jodie Doyle 1937- *AmMWSc 92*
**Whitney,** Joel Gayton 1937- *AmMWSc 92*
**Whitney,** John Adair 1932- *WhoAmP 91*
**Whitney,** John Barry, Jr 1916- *AmMWSc 92*
**Whitney,** John Clarence 1915- *WhoAmL 92*
**Whitney,** John Freeman, Jr 1944- *WhoAmP 91, WhoMW 92*
**Whitney,** John Glen 1939- *AmMWSc 92*
**Whitney,** John Joseph 1926- *WhoAmL 92*
**Whitney,** John Norton Braithwaite 1930- *IntWW 91, Who 92*
**Whitney,** Josiah Dwight 1819-1896 *BiInAmS*
**Whitney,** Kenneth Dean 1952- *AmMWSc 92*
**Whitney,** Larry Keith 1946- *WhoRel 92*
**Whitney,** Lester F 1928- *AmMWSc 92*
**Whitney,** Malika Lee 1946- *ConAu 133*
**Whitney,** Marion Isabelle 1911- *AmMWSc 92*
**Whitney,** Marylou *NewYTBS 91 [port]*
**Whitney,** Norman John 1925- *AmMWSc 92*
**Whitney,** Philip Roy 1935- *AmMWSc 92*
**Whitney,** Phyllis A 1903- *IntAu&W 91, WrDr 92*
**Whitney,** Raymond William 1930- *Who 92*
**Whitney,** Richard Ralph 1927- *AmMWSc 92*
**Whitney,** Richard Wilbur 1938- *AmMWSc 92*
**Whitney,** Robert 1904-1986 *NewAmDM*
**Whitney,** Robert Arthur, Jr 1935- *AmMWSc 92*
**Whitney,** Robert Byron 1905- *AmMWSc 92*
**Whitney,** Robert C 1919- *AmMWSc 92*
**Whitney,** Robert James 1926- *WhoAmP 91*
**Whitney,** Robert McLaughlin 1911- *AmMWSc 92*
**Whitney,** Ronald Dunn 1954- *WhoFI 92*
**Whitney,** Rosalyn L. 1950- *WhoBlA 92*
**Whitney,** Roy Davidson 1927- *AmMWSc 92*
**Whitney,** Roy P 1913- *AmMWSc 92*
**Whitney,** Ruth Reinke 1928- *ConAu 133*
**Whitney,** Stewart Bowman 1938- *WhoFI 92*
**Whitney,** Thomas Allen 1940- *AmMWSc 92*
**Whitney,** Virginia Koogler 1927- *WhoAmP 91*
**Whitney,** W. Monty 1945- *WhoBlA 92*
**Whitney,** Wendell Keith 1927- *AmMWSc 92*
**Whitney,** William Elliot, Jr. 1933- *WhoFI 92*
**Whitney,** William Gordon 1922- *WhoFI 92*
**Whitney,** William Merrill 1929- *AmMWSc 92*
**Whitney-Welles,** Darla 1949- *WhoAmP 91*
**Whitney-Wise,** Patricia Helen 1953- *WhoRel 92*
**Whiton,** Stephen E 1934- *WhoIns 92*
**Whitsel,** Barry L 1937- *AmMWSc 92*
**Whitsel,** Richard Harry 1931- *WhoWest 92*
**Whitsel,** Robert Malcolm 1929- *WhoIns 92, WhoMW 92*
**Whitsell,** John Crawford, II 1929- *AmMWSc 92*
**Whitsett,** Carolyn F 1945- *AmMWSc 92*
**Whitsett,** Jane Frances 1956- *WhoWest 92*
**Whitsett,** Johnson Mallory, II 1941- *AmMWSc 92*
**Whitsett,** Paul Timothy, Jr. 1943- *WhoEnt 92*
**Whitsett,** Thomas L 1936- *AmMWSc 92*
**Whitsey,** Fred 1919- *Who 92*
**Whitsitt,** Garland B, Jr 1921- *WhoAmP 91*
**Whitsitt,** Michael Eugene 1947- *WhoAmL 92*
**Whitsitt,** Robert James 1956- *WhoWest 92*
**Whitsitt,** William Allen 1943- *WhoRel 92*
**Whitsitt,** William Heth 1841-1911 *RelLAm 91*
**Whitson,** John H 1854-1936 *TwCWW 91*
**Whitson,** John Harvey 1854-1936 *BenetAL 91*
**Whitson,** Lish 1942- *WhoAmL 92*
**Whitson,** Paul David 1940- *AmMWSc 92*
**Whitson,** Robert Edd 1942- *AmMWSc 92, WhoFI 92*
**Whitson,** Thomas Jackson 1930- *Who 92*
**Whitson,** Zane C, Jr 1933- *WhoAmP 91*
**Whitsy,** Charles H., Jr. 1945- *WhoBlA 92*
**Whitt,** Darnell Moses 1913- *AmMWSc 92*
**Whitt,** Dixie Dailey 1939- *AmMWSc 92*
**Whitt,** Dwight Reginald 1949- *WhoBlA 92*
**Whitt,** Gregory Sidney 1938- *AmMWSc 92*
**Whitt,** Laurie Anne *DrAPF 91*
**Whitt,** Mary White 1916- *WhoAmP 91*
**Whitt,** Michael D 1952- *WhoAmP 91*
**Whitt,** Richard Keith 1954- *WhoRel 92*
**Whitt,** Stan Evert 1947- *WhoFI 92*
**Whitt,** Ward 1942- *AmMWSc 92*
**Whittaker,** Alun Howard 1946- *WhoWest 92*
**Whittaker,** Bill Douglas 1943- *WhoRel 92*
**Whittaker,** Carole Ann 1935- *WhoWest 92*
**Whittaker,** Charles E 1901-1973 *FacFETw*
**Whittaker,** Charles Joseph 1938- *WhoFI 92*
**Whittaker,** David 1933- *Who 92*
**Whittaker,** David Jay 1945- *WhoRel 92*
**Whittaker,** Edward 1948- *TwCPaSc*
**Whittaker,** Frederick 1838-1889 *ScFEYrs*
**Whittaker,** Frederick Horace 1928- *AmMWSc 92*
**Whittaker,** Geoffrey Owen 1932- *Who 92*
**Whittaker,** George 1918- *WhoAmP 91*
**Whittaker,** J Richard 1934- *AmMWSc 92*
**Whittaker,** James Victor 1931- *AmMWSc 92*
**Whittaker,** Marion Alma 1947- *WhoAmL 92*
**Whittaker,** Paul 1943- *AmMWSc 92*
**Whittaker,** Robert 1939- *WhoAmP 91*
**Whittaker,** Sheelagh Dillon 1947- *WhoEnt 92, WhoFI 92*
**Whittaker,** Stanley Henry 1935- *Who 92*
**Whittaker,** Terry McKinley 1950- *WhoBlA 92*
**Whittall,** Harold Astley 1925- *Who 92*
**Whittall,** Michael Charlton 1926- *Who 92*
**Whittam,** James Henry 1949- *AmMWSc 92*
**Whittam,** Ronald 1925- *IntWW 91, Who 92*
**Whittam Smith,** Andreas 1937- *IntAu&W 91, IntWW 91, Who 92*
**Whitted,** Andrew Eugene 1924- *WhoBlA 92*
**Whitted,** Earl, Jr. 1931- *WhoBlA 92*
**Whittell,** James Michael Scott 1939- *Who 92*
**Whittembury,** Guillermo 1929- *AmMWSc 92*
**Whittemore,** Alice S 1936- *AmMWSc 92*
**Whittemore,** Anne Marie 1946- *WhoAmL 92*
**Whittemore,** Charles Alan 1935- *AmMWSc 92*
**Whittemore,** Donald Osgood 1944- *AmMWSc 92*
**Whittemore,** Ernest William 1916- *Who 92*
**Whittemore,** Frank N *WhoAmP 91*
**Whittemore,** James A 1914- *WhoAmP 91*
**Whittemore,** Laurence Frederick 1929- *WhoFI 92*
**Whittemore,** O J, Jr 1919- *AmMWSc 92*
**Whittemore,** Reed *DrAPF 91*
**Whittemore,** Reed 1919- *BenetAL 91, ConPo 91, WrDr 92*
**Whittemore,** Ruth 1917- *AmMWSc 92*
**Whittemore,** William Leslie 1924- *AmMWSc 92*
**Whitten,** Barbara L 1946- *AmMWSc 92*
**Whitten,** Benjamin C. 1923- *WhoBlA 92*
**Whitten,** Bertwell Kneeland 1941- *AmMWSc 92*
**Whitten,** Bobby Lee 1930- *WhoAmP 91*
**Whitten,** C. G. 1925- *WhoAmL 92*
**Whitten,** Charles A, Jr 1940- *AmMWSc 92*
**Whitten,** Charles F. 1922- *WhoBlA 92*
**Whitten,** David G 1938- *AmMWSc 92*
**Whitten,** David Owen 1940- *WhoFI 92*
**Whitten,** Elmer Hammond 1927- *AmMWSc 92*
**Whitten,** Eloise Culmer 1929- *WhoBlA 92*
**Whitten,** Eric Harold Timothy 1927- *AmMWSc 92*
**Whitten,** Hubert Fulton, III 1955- *WhoRel 92*
**Whitten,** Jamie L. 1910- *AlmAP 92 [port], WhoBlA 92*
**Whitten,** Jamie Lloyd 1910- *WhoAmP 91*
**Whitten,** Jerry Lynn 1937- *AmMWSc 92*
**Whitten,** Kenneth Wayne 1932- *AmMWSc 92*
**Whitten,** Larry 1938- *WhoAmP 91*
**Whitten,** Leslie H, Jr 1928- *IntAu&W 91*
**Whitten,** Leslie Hunter, Jr. 1928- *WrDr 92*
**Whitten,** Maurice Mason 1923- *AmMWSc 92*
**Whitten,** Norman E, Jr 1937- *IntAu&W 91, WrDr 92*
**Whitten,** Robert Craig, Jr 1926- *AmMWSc 92*
**Whitten,** Stanley Burt 1935- *WhoMW 92*
**Whitten,** Thomas P. 1937- *WhoBlA 92*
**Whittenberg,** Charles 1927-1984 *NewAmDM*
**Whittenberger,** James Laverre 1914- *AmMWSc 92*
**Whittengton,** Robert E *WhoAmP 91*
**Whitteridge,** David 1912- *IntWW 91, Who 92*
**Whitteridge,** Gordon 1908- *Who 92*
**Whitters,** Timothy John 1951- *WhoAmL 92*
**Whittick,** Richard James 1912- *Who 92*

**Whittier,** Angus Charles 1921- *AmMWSc 92*
**Whittier,** Dean Page 1935- *AmMWSc 92*
**Whittier,** Denise 1948- *WhoEnt 92*
**Whittier,** E James 1928- *WhoIns 92*
**Whittier,** Henry O 1937- *AmMWSc 92*
**Whittier,** James S 1935- *AmMWSc 92*
**Whittier,** John Greenleaf 1807-1892 *AmPeW, BenetAL 91*
**Whittier,** John Rensselaer 1919- *AmMWSc 92*
**Whittig,** Lynn D 1922- *AmMWSc 92*
**Whittingdale,** John Flasby Lawrance 1959- *Who 92*
**Whittingham,** Charles Percival 1922- *Who 92, WrDr 92*
**Whittingham,** M Stanley 1941- *AmMWSc 92*
**Whittingham,** Richard 1939- *ConAu 36NR*
**Whittinghill,** Maurice 1909- *AmMWSc 92*
**Whittingslow,** Michaela 1938- *WhoWest 92*
**Whittington,** Aven 1917- *WhoFI 92*
**Whittington,** Bernard W 1920- *AmMWSc 92*
**Whittington,** Charles Richard 1908- *Who 92*
**Whittington,** Geoffrey 1938- *IntAu&W 91, Who 92, WrDr 92*
**Whittington,** Harrison DeWayne 1931- *WhoBlA 92*
**Whittington,** Harry 1915- *IntAu&W 91*
**Whittington,** Harry 1915-1989 *TwCWW 91*
**Whittington,** Harry Blackmore 1916- *Who 92*
**Whittington,** Jeremiah 1946- *WhoWest 92*
**Whittington,** John David 1938- *WhoMW 92*
**Whittington,** Joseph Basil 1921- *Who 92*
**Whittington,** Peter *IntAu&W 91X, WrDr 92*
**Whittington,** Stuart Gordon 1942- *AmMWSc 92*
**Whittington,** Thomas Alan 1916- *Who 92*
**Whittington,** Tony Burnice 1940- *WhoEnt 92*
**Whittington,** Wesley Herbert 1933- *AmMWSc 92*
**Whittington-Smith,** Marianne Christine *Who 92*
**Whittle,** Charles Edward, Jr 1931- *AmMWSc 92*
**Whittle,** Chris *NewYTBS 91*
**Whittle,** Christopher 1947- *CurBio 91 [port]*
**Whittle,** Douglas Alexander 1947- *WhoRel 92*
**Whittle,** Frank 1907- *AmMWSc 92, IntWW 91, Who 92*
**Whittle,** Gail Harding 1920- *WhoAmP 91*
**Whittle,** George Patterson 1925- *AmMWSc 92*
**Whittle,** Jennifer Anne 1961- *WhoWest 92*
**Whittle,** John Antony 1942- *AmMWSc 92*
**Whittle,** John J 1936- *WhoIns 92*
**Whittle,** Kenneth Francis 1922- *Who 92*
**Whittle,** Peter 1927- *IntWW 91, Who 92, WrDr 92*
**Whittle,** Philip Rodger 1943- *AmMWSc 92*
**Whittle,** Stephen Charles 1945- *Who 92*
**Whittle,** Tyler *IntAu&W 91X, WrDr 92*
**Whittle,** William Arthur 1946- *WhoAmP 91*
**Whittlebot,** Hernia *ConAu 35NR*
**Whittlesey,** Charles 1808-1886 *BiInAmS*
**Whittlesey,** Emmet Finlay 1923- *AmMWSc 92*
**Whittlesey,** Eunice Baird *WhoAmP 91*
**Whittlesey,** Faith Ryan 1939- *WhoAmL 92, WhoAmP 91*
**Whittlesey,** John R B 1927- *AmMWSc 92*
**Whittlesey,** John Williams 1917- *WhoAmL 92*
**Whittome,** Alan 1926- *Who 92*
**Whitton,** Cuthbert Henry 1905- *Who 92*
**Whitton,** Leslie 1923- *AmMWSc 92*
**Whitton,** Peter William 1925- *Who 92*
**Whittow,** George Causey 1930- *AmMWSc 92*
**Whittuck,** Gerald Saumarez 1912- *Who 92*
**Whittum,** Norman Rex 1939- *WhoRel 92*
**Whittum-Hudson,** Judith Anne *AmMWSc 92*
**Whitty,** Elmo Benjamin 1937- *AmMWSc 92*
**Whitty,** Jim 1931- *WhoAmP 91*
**Whitty,** John Lawrence 1943- *Who 92*
**Whitty,** Steven C 1956- *WhoIns 92*
**Whitwam,** David Ray 1942- *WhoMW 92*
**Whitwam,** Derek Firth 1932- *Who 92*
**Whitwell,** Stephen John 1920- *Who 92*
**Whitwer,** Glen Sterling, Jr. 1944- *WhoFI 92*
**Whitworth,** Claudia Alexander 1927- *WhoBlA 92*
**Whitworth,** Clyde W 1926- *AmMWSc 92*
**Whitworth,** Douglas Neil 1965- *WhoMW 92*
**Whitworth,** E. Leo, Jr. *WhoBlA 92*
**Whitworth,** Francis John 1925- *Who 92*
**Whitworth,** Frank 1910- *Who 92*
**Whitworth,** Hugh Hope Aston 1914- *Who 92*
**Whitworth,** John McKelvie 1942- *WrDr 92*
**Whitworth,** Reginald Henry 1916- *Who 92*
**Whitworth,** Rex 1916- *WrDr 92*
**Whitworth,** Robert Francis 1961- *WhoRel 92*
**Whitworth,** Walter Richard 1934- *AmMWSc 92*
**Whitworth-Jones,** Anthony 1945- *Who 92, WhoEnt 92*
**Who,** The *FacFETw, NewAmDM*
**Whone,** Herbert 1925- *WrDr 92*
**Whorf,** David Michael 1934- *WhoEnt 92*
**Whorton,** Charles, Jr 1924- *WhoAmP 91*
**Whorton,** Chester D 1903- *AmMWSc 92*
**Whorton,** Elbert Benjamin 1938- *AmMWSc 92*
**Whorton,** M Donald 1943- *AmMWSc 92*
**Whorton,** Rayburn Harlen 1931- *AmMWSc 92*
**Whyatt,** Frances *DrAPF 91*
**Whybrew,** Edward Graham 1938- *Who 92*
**Whybrow,** Peter Charles 1939- *AmMWSc 92*
**Whymper,** Charles 1853-1941 *TwCPaSc*
**Whynott,** Robert Donald 1945- *WhoAmP 91*
**Whyte,** Archie James 1936- *WhoIns 92*
**Whyte,** Bruce Lincoln 1941- *WhoFI 92*
**Whyte,** Donald Edward 1918- *AmMWSc 92*
**Whyte,** Garrett 1915- *WhoBlA 92*
**Whyte,** Hamilton d1990 *IntWW 91N*
**Whyte,** Hartzell J. 1927- *WhoBlA 92*
**Whyte,** Helena Mary 1948- *WhoWest 92*
**Whyte,** James Aitken 1920- *Who 92*
**Whyte,** James McLaurin 1933- *WhoRel 92*
**Whyte,** James Primrose, Jr. 1921- *WhoAmL 92*
**Whyte,** John Stuart 1923- *Who 92*
**Whyte,** John Stuart Scott 1926- *Who 92*
**Whyte,** Michael Peter 1946- *AmMWSc 92*
**Whyte,** Robert *NewAmDM*
**Whyte,** Sibly *ConAu 133*
**Whyte,** Stuart Scott *Who 92*
**Whyte,** Thaddeus E, Jr 1937- *AmMWSc 92*
**Whyte,** William Hollingsworth 1917- *IntWW 91*
**Whythorne,** Thomas 1528-1595 *NewAmDM*
**Whytt,** Robert 1714-1766 *BlkwCEP*
**Wiacek,** Bruce Edward 1943- *WhoAmL 92*
**Wiackley,** Mildred *DrAPF 91*
**Wians,** David Alan 1952- *WhoMW 92*
**Wiant,** Allen John 1924- *WhoAmP 91*
**Wiant,** Harry Vernon, Jr 1932- *AmMWSc 92*
**Wiant,** Keith Alan 1949- *WhoMW 92*
**Wiant,** Sarah Kirsten 1946- *WhoAmL 92*
**Wiard,** Christine Ann 1955- *WhoWest 92*
**Wiard,** Stephen Lee *WhoAmP 91*
**Wiard,** William O. *IntMPA 92*
**Wiatrowski,** Claude Allan 1946- *AmMWSc 92*
**Wiatrowski,** William Joseph 1958- *WhoFI 92*
**Wiatt,** James Anthony 1946- *WhoEnt 92*
**Wiatt,** Sue Boswell 1921- *WhoRel 92*
**Wiazowski,** Konstanty *WhoRel 92*
**Wibaux,** Fernand 1921- *IntWW 91*
**Wibbenmeyer,** Carl Thomas 1959- *WhoAmL 92*
**Wibberley,** Gerald Percy 1915- *Who 92*
**Wiberg,** Donald M 1936- *AmMWSc 92*
**Wiberg,** George Stuart 1920- *AmMWSc 92*
**Wiberg,** John Samuel 1930- *AmMWSc 92*
**Wiberg,** Kenneth Berle 1927- *AmMWSc 92, IntWW 91*
**Wiberg,** V DeMont 1937- *WhoAmP 91*
**Wiberley,** Stephen Edward 1919- *AmMWSc 92*
**Wible,** Charles Stephen 1937- *WhoAmP 91*
**Wible,** Connie *WhoAmP 91*
**Wible,** James Oram 1949- *WhoFI 92, WhoMW 92*
**Wiblin,** Derek John 1933- *Who 92*
**Wiborg,** James Hooker 1924- *WhoWest 92*
**Wicander,** Edwin Reed 1946- *AmMWSc 92*
**Wice,** David Herschel 1908- *WhoRel 92*
**Wich,** Donald Anthony, Jr. 1947- *WhoAmL 92*
**Wicher,** Chris Charles 1956- *WhoRel 92*
**Wicher,** Konrad J 1924- *AmMWSc 92*
**Wicher,** Victoria 1933- *AmMWSc 92*
**Wichern,** Dean William 1942- *AmMWSc 92*
**Wichlenski,** John Joseph 1943- *WhoMW 92*
**Wichman,** Michael Dale 1956- *WhoMW 92*
**Wichman,** William C. d1991 *NewYTBS 91*
**Wichmann,** Eyvind Hugo 1928- *AmMWSc 92*
**Wichmann,** Mary Lynne 1955- *WhoWest 92*
**Wichner,** Robert Paul 1933- *AmMWSc 92*
**Wicholas,** Mark L 1940- *AmMWSc 92*
**Wichterle,** Otto 1913- *IntWW 91*
**Wichterman,** Ralph 1907- *AmMWSc 92*
**Wick,** Albert Marion 1929- *WhoWest 92*
**Wick,** Carter *WrDr 92*
**Wick,** Charles Z. 1917- *IntWW 91*
**Wick,** Daniel Lewis 1944- *WhoWest 92*
**Wick,** David Gunnar 1957- *WhoFI 92*
**Wick,** Donald Gary 1947- *WhoMW 92*
**Wick,** Emily Lippincott 1921- *AmMWSc 92*
**Wick,** Gian Carlo 1909- *AmMWSc 92*
**Wick,** Hal Gerard 1944- *WhoAmP 91*
**Wick,** Hilton 1920- *WhoAmP 91*
**Wick,** James Roy 1912- *AmMWSc 92*
**Wick,** Lawrence Scott 1945- *WhoMW 92*
**Wick,** Margaret 1942- *WhoRel 92*
**Wick,** Michael Kelly 1948- *WhoWest 92*
**Wick,** Norman G. *WhoRel 92*
**Wick,** O J 1914- *AmMWSc 92*
**Wick,** Raymond Victor 1940- *WhoWest 92*
**Wick,** Robert S 1925- *AmMWSc 92*
**Wick,** William Quentin 1927- *AmMWSc 92*
**Wickam,** Gary Lynn 1946- *WhoWest 92*
**Wickard,** Samuel Eugene 1950- *WhoRel 92*
**Wickberg,** Erik E. 1904- *IntWW 91, Who 92*
**Wickbom,** Sten 1931- *IntWW 91*
**Wicke,** Brian Garfield 1944- *AmMWSc 92*
**Wicke,** Howard Henry 1924- *AmMWSc 92*
**Wicke,** John Michael 1945- *WhoFI 92*
**Wickelgren,** Warren Otis 1941- *AmMWSc 92*
**Wickenhauser,** Gerald Martin 1934- *WhoRel 92*
**Wickens,** Alan Herbert 1929- *Who 92*
**Wickens,** Aryness Joy d1991 *NewYTBS 91*
**Wickens,** Aryness Joy 1901-1991 *CurBio 91N*
**Wickens,** Donald Lee 1934- *WhoFI 92*
**Wickens,** Peter Charles 1912- *WrDr 92*
**Wickens,** William George 1905- *WhoAmL 92*
**Wicker,** Allan Wert 1941- *WhoWest 92*
**Wicker,** Brian John 1929- *WrDr 92*
**Wicker,** Dennis A 1952- *WhoAmP 91*
**Wicker,** Elmus Rogers 1926- *WhoFI 92*
**Wicker,** Everett E 1919- *AmMWSc 92*
**Wicker,** Henry Sindos 1928- *WhoBlA 92*
**Wicker,** Isabelle 1944- *WhoBlA 92*
**Wicker,** James Robert 1954- *WhoRel 92*
**Wicker,** Jeremy Charles 1941- *WhoAmL 92*
**Wicker,** Leslie Elizabeth 1966- *WhoWest 92*
**Wicker,** Nina A. *DrAPF 91*
**Wicker,** Ralph David, Jr. 1960- *WhoAmL 92*
**Wicker,** Robert Kirk 1938- *AmMWSc 92*
**Wicker,** Roger Frederick 1951- *WhoAmP 91*
**Wicker,** Terry Craig 1957- *WhoMW 92*
**Wicker,** Thomas Carey, Jr. 1923- *WhoAmL 92*
**Wicker,** Thomas Grey 1926- *IntWW 91*
**Wicker,** Thomas Hamilton, Jr 1923- *AmMWSc 92*
**Wicker,** Tom 1926- *WrDr 92*
**Wicker,** Veronica DiCarlo *WhoAmL 92*
**Wickerhauser,** Milan 1922- *AmMWSc 92*
**Wickersham,** Charles Edward, Jr 1951- *AmMWSc 92*
**Wickersham,** Edward Walker 1932- *AmMWSc 92*
**Wickersham,** George W. *DcAmImH*
**Wickersham,** William *WhoAmP 91*
**Wickersheim,** Bryan Kent 1957- *WhoMW 92*
**Wickersheim,** Kenneth Alan 1928- *AmMWSc 92*
**Wickerson,** John 1937- *Who 92*
**Wickert,** Erwin 1915- *IntWW 91*
**Wickert,** Max A. *DrAPF 91*
**Wickert,** Victor Ray 1956- *WhoRel 92*
**Wickes,** Charles G. *Who 92*
**Wickes,** Frank Bovee 1937- *WhoEnt 92*
**Wickes,** George 1923- *WhoWest 92*
**Wickes,** Harry E 1925- *AmMWSc 92*
**Wickes,** Mary *IntMPA 92, WhoEnt 92, WhoWest 92*
**Wickes,** Richard Paul 1948- *WhoAmL 92*
**Wickes,** Thomas Lee 1947- *WhoRel 92*
**Wickes,** William Castles 1946- *AmMWSc 92, WhoWest 92*
**Wickfield,** Eric Nelson 1953- *WhoFI 92*
**Wickham,** Charles Patrick 1937- *WhoWest 92*
**Wickham,** Daphne Elizabeth 1946- *Who 92*
**Wickham,** DeWayne 1946- *WhoBlA 92*
**Wickham,** Donald G 1922- *AmMWSc 92*
**Wickham,** Edward Ralph 1911- *IntAu&W 91, Who 92, WrDr 92*
**Wickham,** Glynne 1922- *IntAu&W 91, WrDr 92*
**Wickham,** Glynne William Gladstone 1922- *Who 92*
**Wickham,** Harvey 1872-1930 *ScFEYrs A*
**Wickham,** James Edgar, Jr 1933- *AmMWSc 92*
**Wickham,** John Adams, Jr 1928- *WhoAmP 91*
**Wickham,** Leslie Oliver, Jr. 1952- *WhoAmL 92*
**Wickham,** M Gary 1942- *AmMWSc 92*
**Wickham,** Mabel 1901- *TwCPaSc*
**Wickham,** Muriel Jeannette 1957- *WhoBlA 92*
**Wickham,** William Rayley 1926- *Who 92*
**Wickham,** William Terry 1929- *WhoMW 92*
**Wickham,** William Terry, Jr 1929- *AmMWSc 92*
**Wickham-St. Germain,** Margaret Edna 1956- *WhoMW 92*
**Wicki,** Dieter 1931- *WhoFI 92*
**Wicki-Fink,** Agnes 1919- *IntWW 91*
**Wickins,** David Allen 1920- *Who 92*
**Wickizer,** Cindy Louise 1946- *WhoWest 92*
**Wicklein,** John Frederick 1924- *IntAu&W 91*
**Wickler,** Steven John 1952- *AmMWSc 92*
**Wickliff,** Aloysius M., Sr. 1921- *WhoBlA 92*
**Wickliff,** James Leroy 1931- *AmMWSc 92*
**Wickliffe,** Jerry L. 1941- *WhoAmL 92*
**Wickliffe,** Verne Allen 1955- *WhoRel 92*
**Wicklow,** Donald Thomas 1940- *AmMWSc 92*
**Wicklund,** Arthur Barry 1942- *AmMWSc 92*
**Wicklund,** David Wayne 1949- *WhoAmL 92*
**Wicklund,** Millie Mae *DrAPF 91*
**Wicklund,** Peter Vincent 1965- *WhoFI 92*
**Wickman,** Herbert Hollis 1936- *AmMWSc 92*
**Wickman,** John Edward 1929- *WhoMW 92*
**Wickman,** Krister 1924- *IntWW 91*
**Wickman,** Paul Everett 1912- *WhoWest 92*
**Wickmiller,** Margaret Allison 1957- *WhoAmL 92*
**Wickramasinghe,** Nalin Chandra 1939- *IntWW 91, Who 92, WrDr 92*
**Wickre,** Paul Merrill 1936- *WhoEnt 92*
**Wickre,** Terry Michael 1941- *WhoWest 92*
**Wickrema Sinha,** Asoka J 1937- *AmMWSc 92*
**Wickreme,** A. S. K. *Who 92*
**Wickremesinghe,** Walter Gerald 1897- *Who 92*
**Wicks,** Allan 1923- *Who 92*
**Wicks,** Angie Stella 1950- *WhoEnt 92*
**Wicks,** Charles E 1925- *AmMWSc 92*
**Wicks,** Craig Allan 1952- *WhoEnt 92*
**Wicks,** David Vaughan 1918- *Who 92*
**Wicks,** Frederick John 1937- *AmMWSc 92*
**Wicks,** Geoffrey Leonard 1934- *Who 92*
**Wicks,** George Gary 1945- *AmMWSc 92*
**Wicks,** Harry Oliver, III 1931- *WhoFI 92*
**Wicks,** James 1910- *Who 92*
**Wicks,** John Harold 1963- *WhoFI 92*
**Wicks,** John R. 1937- *WhoAmL 92*
**Wicks,** Mark *ScFEYrs*
**Wicks,** Nigel Leonard 1940- *Who 92*
**Wicks,** Ralph Edwin 1921- *Who 92*
**Wicks,** Rita Faye 1961- *WhoMW 92*
**Wicks,** Wesley Doane 1936- *AmMWSc 92*
**Wicks,** Zeno W, Jr 1920- *AmMWSc 92*
**Wickson,** Edward James 1920- *AmMWSc 92*
**Wickstead,** Cyril 1922- *Who 92*
**Wicksten,** Mary Katherine 1948- *AmMWSc 92*
**Wickstrand,** Alan Keith 1953- *WhoWest 92*
**Wickstrom,** Conrad Eugene 1943- *AmMWSc 92*
**Wickstrom,** Eric 1946- *AmMWSc 92*
**Wickstrom,** Jack 1913- *AmMWSc 92*
**Wickstrom,** Lois *DrAPF 91*
**Wickwire,** Emerson MacMillin 1944- *WhoFI 92*
**Wickwire,** James D, Jr *WhoIns 92*
**Wickwire,** Patricia Joanne Nellor *WhoWest 92*
**Widaman,** Gregory Alan 1955- *WhoFI 92, WhoWest 92*
**Widdas,** Wilfred Faraday 1916- *Who 92*
**Widdecombe,** Ann Noreen 1947- *Who 92*
**Widdecombe,** James Murray 1910- *Who 92*
**Widdel,** John Earl, Jr. 1936- *WhoAmL 92*
**Widdemer,** Margaret 1890?-1978 *BenetAL 91*

**Widden,** Paul Rodney 1943- *AmMWSc 92*
**Widder,** Charles Joseph 1941- *WhoIns 92*
**Widder,** James Stone 1935- *AmMWSc 92*
**Widder,** Patricia A. 1953- *WhoWest 92*
**Widdicombe,** David Graham 1924- *Who 92*
**Widdicombe,** Gillian Mary 1943- *IntAu&W 91*
**Widdicombe,** Roland Marc 1950- *WhoWest 92*
**Widdoes,** Lawrence Lewis 1932- *WhoEnt 92*
**Widdows,** Charles *Who 92*
**Widdows,** Roland Hewlett 1921- *Who 92*
**Widdows,** Stanley Charles 1909- *Who 92*
**Widdowson,** Elsie May 1906- *Who 92*
**Widdowson,** Henry George 1935- *Who 92*
**Widdrington,** Peter Nigel Tinling 1930- *IntWW 91, WhoFI 92*
**Widdup,** Malcolm 1920- *Who 92*
**Wideburg,** Norman Earl 1933- *AmMWSc 92*
**Wideman,** Charles James 1936- *AmMWSc 92*
**Wideman,** Cyrilla Helen 1926- *AmMWSc 92*
**Wideman,** John Edgar 1941- *AfrAmW, BenetAL 91, BlkLC [port], ConLC 67 [port], ConNov 91, CurBio 91 [port], IntAu&W 91, WhoBlA 92, WrDr 92*
**Wideman,** Lawson Gibson 1943- *AmMWSc 92*
**Wideman,** Robert Frederick, Jr 1949- *AmMWSc 92*
**Wideman,** Thomas Wayne 1958- *WhoRel 92*
**Widener,** Bill A 1939- *WhoAmP 91*
**Widener,** Bruce E 1948- *WhoAmP 91*
**Widener,** Edward Ladd, Sr 1926- *AmMWSc 92*
**Widener,** H Emory, Jr *WhoAmP 91*
**Widener,** Hiram Emory, Jr. 1923- *WhoAmL 92*
**Widener,** Richard L. 1948- *WhoRel 92*
**Widener,** Warren H 1938- *WhoAmP 91*
**Widener,** Warren Hamilton 1938- *WhoBlA 92*
**Widenor,** William Cramer 1937- *WhoMW 92*
**Widera,** G. E. O. 1938- *WhoMW 92*
**Widera,** Georg Ernst Otto 1938- *AmMWSc 92*
**Widerberg,** Bo 1930- *IntWW 91*
**Widerquist,** V R 1922- *AmMWSc 92*
**Widershien,** Marc *DrAPF 91*
**Widess,** Moses B 1911- *AmMWSc 92*
**Widger,** Rodric Alan 1952- *WhoMW 92*
**Widger,** William Russell *AmMWSc 92*
**Widgery,** Jan *DrAPF 91*
**Widgery,** Jeanne-Anna 1920- *IntAu&W 91*
**Widgoff,** Mildred 1924- *AmMWSc 92*
**Widholm,** Jack Milton 1939- *AmMWSc 92*
**Widin,** Katharine Douglas 1952- *AmMWSc 92*
**Widlar,** Robert J. d1991 *NewYTBS 91*
**Widlus,** Hannah Beverly 1955- *WhoAmL 92*
**Widmaier,** Eric Paul 1957- *AmMWSc 92*
**Widmaier,** Robert George 1948- *AmMWSc 92*
**Widman,** Douglas Jack 1949- *WhoAmL 92*
**Widman,** Joseph James Jake 1952- *WhoWest 92*
**Widman,** Paul Joseph 1936- *WhoAmP 91*
**Widmann,** Frances King 1935- *AmMWSc 92*
**Widmark,** Richard 1914- *IntMPA 92, IntWW 91, WhoEnt 92*
**Widmayer,** Dorothea Jane 1930- *AmMWSc 92*
**Widmer,** Elmer Andreas 1925- *AmMWSc 92, WhoWest 92*
**Widmer,** Frederick William 1915- *WhoRel 92*
**Widmer,** Hans Michael 1933- *WhoFI 92*
**Widmer,** Kemble 1913- *AmMWSc 92*
**Widmer,** Kingsley 1925- *WhoWest 92*
**Widmer,** Richard Ernest 1922- *AmMWSc 92*
**Widmer,** Robert H 1916- *AmMWSc 92*
**Widmer,** Wilbur James 1918- *AmMWSc 92*
**Widmoyer,** Fred Bixler 1920- *AmMWSc 92, WhoAmP 91*
**Widnall,** Sheila Evans 1938- *AmMWSc 92*
**Widnell,** Christopher Courtenay 1940- *AmMWSc 92*
**Widner,** Jimmy Newton 1942- *AmMWSc 92*
**Widner,** William Richard 1920- *AmMWSc 92*
**Widom,** Benjamin 1927- *AmMWSc 92, IntWW 91*
**Widom,** Diane *IntMPA 92*
**Widom,** Harold 1932- *AmMWSc 92*
**Widor,** Charles-Marie 1844-1937 *NewAmDM*
**Widra,** Abe 1924- *AmMWSc 92*
**Widstrom,** Neil Wayne 1933- *AmMWSc 92*
**Wie,** Chu Ryang 1957- *AmMWSc 92*
**Wieand,** Donald Edwin, Jr 1951- *WhoAmP 91*
**Wiebe,** Dallas *DrAPF 91*
**Wiebe,** Donald 1923- *AmMWSc 92*
**Wiebe,** Jacqueline Catherine 1957- *WhoWest 92*
**Wiebe,** John 1926- *AmMWSc 92*
**Wiebe,** John Peter 1938- *AmMWSc 92*
**Wiebe,** Leonard Irving 1941- *AmMWSc 92, WhoWest 92*
**Wiebe,** Michael Eugene 1942- *AmMWSc 92, WhoWest 92*
**Wiebe,** Peter Howard 1940- *AmMWSc 92*
**Wiebe,** Richard Penner 1928- *AmMWSc 92*
**Wiebe,** Robert A 1939- *AmMWSc 92*
**Wiebe,** Rudy 1934- *BenetAL 91, ConNov 91, WrDr 92*
**Wiebe,** Rudy H 1934- *IntAu&W 91*
**Wiebe,** William John *AmMWSc 92*
**Wiebelhaus,** Pamela Sue 1952- *WhoWest 92*
**Wiebenga,** William Martin 1938- *WhoMW 92*
**Wiebold,** William John 1949- *AmMWSc 92*
**Wiebusch,** Charles Fred 1903- *AmMWSc 92*
**Wiebusch,** F B 1923- *AmMWSc 92*
**Wiebusch,** Todd Denton 1962- *WhoFI 92*
**Wiebush,** Joseph Roy 1920- *AmMWSc 92*
**Wiecer,** Stephanie Bernadette 1952- *WhoRel 92*
**Wiech,** Norbert Leonard 1939- *AmMWSc 92*
**Wiechelman,** Karen Janice 1947- *AmMWSc 92*
**Wiechers,** James David 1937- *WhoMW 92*
**Wiechert,** Allen LeRoy 1938- *WhoMW 92*
**Wiechert,** Ernst 1887-1950 *EncTR 91 [port]*
**Wiechmann,** Anke 1951- *WhoAmP 91*
**Wiechmann,** Carol Louise 1959- *WhoMW 92*
**Wiechmann,** Eric Watt 1948- *WhoAmL 92*
**Wiechmann,** Ferdinand Gerhard 1858-1919 *BiInAmS*
**Wiechmann,** Helmut Henry 1909- *WhoRel 92*
**Wieck,** Clara *NewAmDM*
**Wieck,** Hans-Georg 1928- *IntWW 91*
**Wieckowski,** Zdislaw Wladyslaw 1954- *WhoAmL 92*
**Wieczorek,** Dean E *WhoAmP 91*
**Wieczorek,** Gerald Francis 1949- *AmMWSc 92*
**Wieczynski,** Frank Robert 1939- *WhoFI 92*
**Wied,** George Ludwig 1921- *AmMWSc 92, WhoMW 92*
**Wiedebusch,** Larry 1936- *WhoAmP 91*
**Wiedeman,** Paul Edward 1957- *WhoMW 92*
**Wiedeman,** Varley Earl 1933- *AmMWSc 92*
**Wiedemann,** Alfred Max 1931- *AmMWSc 92*
**Wiedemann,** Fritz 1891-1970 *EncTR 91 [port]*
**Wiedemann,** Josef 1910- *IntWW 91*
**Wiedemann,** Joseph R 1928- *WhoIns 92*
**Wiedemann,** Joseph Robert 1928- *WhoFI 92*
**Wiedemeier,** Heribert 1928- *AmMWSc 92*
**Wiedenbeck,** Marcellus Lee 1919- *AmMWSc 92*
**Wiedenheft,** Charles John 1941- *AmMWSc 92*
**Wiedenmann,** Lynn G 1928- *AmMWSc 92*
**Wieder,** Bruce Terrill 1955- *WhoAmL 92*
**Wieder,** Douglas Marx 1952- *WhoFI 92, WhoMW 92*
**Wieder,** Grace Marilyn 1928- *AmMWSc 92*
**Wieder,** Harold 1927- *AmMWSc 92*
**Wieder,** Irwin 1925- *AmMWSc 92*
**Wieder,** Sol 1940- *AmMWSc 92*
**Wiederaenders,** Robert Charles 1922- *WhoRel 92*
**Wiederhold,** Edward W 1921- *AmMWSc 92*
**Wiederhold,** Michael L 1939- *AmMWSc 92*
**Wiederhold,** Pieter Rijk 1928- *AmMWSc 92*
**Wiederholt,** Wigbert C 1931- *AmMWSc 92, WhoWest 92*
**Wiederhorn,** Sheldon M 1933- *AmMWSc 92*
**Wiederick,** Harvey Dale 1937- *AmMWSc 92*
**Wiedersich,** H 1926- *AmMWSc 92*
**Wiederspahn,** Alvin 1949- *WhoAmP 91*
**Wiederspahn,** Alvin Lee 1949- *WhoWest 92*
**Wiedman,** Harold W 1930- *AmMWSc 92*
**Wiedmeier,** Vernon Thomas 1935- *AmMWSc 92*
**Wiedner,** Barbara Anne 1928- *WhoWest 92*
**Wiedow,** Carl Paul 1907- *AmMWSc 92, WhoWest 92*
**Wiegand,** Craig Loren 1933- *AmMWSc 92*
**Wiegand,** Donald Arthur 1927- *AmMWSc 92*
**Wiegand,** Gayl 1939- *AmMWSc 92*
**Wiegand,** George Frederick 1942- *WhoMW 92*
**Wiegand,** Ingrid 1934- *WhoEnt 92*
**Wiegand,** James Albert 1946- *WhoFI 92*
**Wiegand,** James Richard 1928- *WhoMW 92*
**Wiegand,** Oscar Fernando 1921- *AmMWSc 92*
**Wiegand,** Ronald Gay 1929- *AmMWSc 92*
**Wiegand,** Sylvia Margaret 1945- *AmMWSc 92*
**Wiegand,** William *DrAPF 91*
**Wiegand,** William 1928- *WrDr 92*
**Wiegand-Moss,** Richard Clifton 1947- *WhoMW 92*
**Wiegand-Moss,** Richard Clifton, Jr. 1947- *WhoBlA 92*
**Wiegandt,** Herbert F 1917- *AmMWSc 92*
**Wiegel,** Robert L 1922- *AmMWSc 92*
**Wiegers,** Rolland Lee 1930- *WhoIns 92*
**Wiegert,** Philip E 1927- *AmMWSc 92*
**Wiegert,** Raymnond Paul 1935- *WhoWest 92*
**Wiegert,** Raymond Paul 1935- *WhoRel 92*
**Wiegert,** Richard G 1932- *AmMWSc 92*
**Wiegley,** Roger Douglas 1948- *WhoAmL 92*
**Wiegman,** David L *AmMWSc 92*
**Wiegmann,** Roger Henry 1934- *WhoFI 92*
**Wiegner,** Allen W 1947- *AmMWSc 92*
**Wiegner,** Edward A 1939- *WhoIns 92*
**Wiegner,** Edward Alex 1939- *WhoFI 92*
**Wiehahn,** Nicholas E. 1929- *IntWW 91*
**Wiehe,** William Albert 1947- *AmMWSc 92*
**Wiehl,** James George 1954- *WhoAmL 92*
**Wiehl,** Richard Lloyd 1936- *WhoAmL 92*
**Wieland,** Bruce Wendell 1937- *AmMWSc 92*
**Wieland,** Christoph Martin 1733-1813 *BlkwCEP*
**Wieland,** Denton R 1927- *AmMWSc 92*
**Wieland,** Ferdinand 1943- *WhoFI 92*
**Wieland,** Glen David 1957- *WhoAmL 92*
**Wieland,** Heinrich Otto 1877-1957 *WhoNob 90*
**Wieland,** Joyce 1931- *IntDcF 2-2, IntWW 91*
**Wieland,** Sara Jennings 1938- *WhoMW 92*
**Wieland,** Timothy E. 1953- *WhoFI 92*
**Wieland,** William Dean 1948- *WhoFI 92*
**Wiele,** Jef van der 1903-1979 *BiDExR*
**Wielgus,** Charles Joseph 1923- *WhoFI 92*
**Wielkiewicz,** Richard Michael 1949- *WhoMW 92*
**Wielopolski,** Mary Esther 1955- *WhoMW 92*
**Wielowieyski,** Andrzej 1927- *IntWW 91*
**Wieman,** Henry Nelson 1884-1975 *RelLAm 91*
**Wiemann,** John Moritz 1947- *WhoWest 92*
**Wiemann,** Marion Russell, Jr. 1929- *WhoMW 92*
**Wiemer,** David F 1950- *AmMWSc 92*
**Wiemer,** Loyal Hulbert 1914- *WhoRel 92*
**Wiemer,** Robert Ernest 1938- *WhoEnt 92, WhoWest 92*
**Wiemeyer,** Stanley Norton 1940- *AmMWSc 92*
**Wien,** Richard W, Jr 1945- *AmMWSc 92*
**Wien,** Wilhelm Carl Werner Otto Fritz F 1864-1928 *WhoNob 90*
**Wiene,** Robert 1881-1938 *IntDcF 2-2*
**Wiener,** Allen Joel 1943- *IntAu&W 91*
**Wiener,** Daniel Norman 1921- *WhoMW 92*
**Wiener,** David Carl 1947- *WhoFI 92*
**Wiener,** David Stuart 1954- *WhoFI 92*
**Wiener,** Earl Louis 1933- *AmMWSc 92*
**Wiener,** Ed d1991 *NewYTBS 91*
**Wiener,** Frederick Paul 1952- *WhoAmL 92*
**Wiener,** Harry 1924- *WhoFI 92*
**Wiener,** Howard B. 1931- *WhoAmL 92*
**Wiener,** Howard Lawrence 1937- *AmMWSc 92*
**Wiener,** Jack 1926- *IntMPA 92*
**Wiener,** Jacques L, Jr 1934- *WhoAmP 91*
**Wiener,** Jacques Loeb, Jr. 1934- *WhoAmL 92*
**Wiener,** Joel Howard 1937- *IntAu&W 91, WrDr 92*
**Wiener,** Jon 1944- *WhoWest 92*
**Wiener,** Joseph 1828-1904 *BiInAmS*
**Wiener,** Joseph 1927- *AmMWSc 92*
**Wiener,** Joshua M. 1949- *ConAu 133*
**Wiener,** L D 1926- *AmMWSc 92*
**Wiener,** Leo *DrAPF 91*
**Wiener,** Martin *TwCPaSc*
**Wiener,** Marvin S. 1925- *WhoRel 92*
**Wiener,** Michael Charles 1962- *WhoWest 92*
**Wiener,** Morry 1948- *WhoMW 92*
**Wiener,** Norbert 1894-1964 *BenetAL 91, FacFETw*
**Wiener,** Richard Joseph 1945- *WhoAmL 92*
**Wiener,** Richard Neal 1947- *WhoAmP 91*
**Wiener,** Robert Newman 1930- *AmMWSc 92*
**Wiener,** Sidney 1922- *AmMWSc 92*
**Wiener,** Stanley L 1930- *AmMWSc 92*
**Wiener,** Sydney Paul 1918- *WhoWest 92*
**Wiener,** Theodore 1918- *WhoRel 92*
**Wiener,** Thomas Eli 1940- *WhoAmL 92*
**Wiener,** Valerie 1948- *WhoFI 92, WhoWest 92*
**Wieners,** John *DrAPF 91*
**Wieners,** John 1934- *BenetAL 91, ConPo 91, WrDr 92*
**Wieners,** John Joseph 1934- *IntAu&W 91*
**Wienert,** John Geoffrey Wilmann 1951- *WhoAmL 92*
**Wienges,** Malachy George 1940- *WhoEnt 92*
**Wienhorst,** Richard William 1920- *WhoEnt 92*
**Wieniawski,** Henryk 1835-1880 *NewAmDM*
**Wienke,** Bruce Ray 1940- *AmMWSc 92*
**Wienker,** Curtis Wakefield 1945- *AmMWSc 92*
**Wiens,** Delbert 1932- *AmMWSc 92*
**Wiens,** John Anthony 1939- *AmMWSc 92*
**Wier,** Allen *DrAPF 91*
**Wier,** Charles Eugene 1921- *AmMWSc 92*
**Wier,** Dara *DrAPF 91*
**Wier,** David Dewey 1923- *AmMWSc 92*
**Wier,** Ester 1910- *WrDr 92*
**Wier,** Jack Knight 1923- *AmMWSc 92*
**Wier,** Joseph M 1924- *AmMWSc 92*
**Wier,** Karen Elizabeth 1964- *WhoAmL 92*
**Wier,** Patricia Ann 1937- *WhoFI 92, WhoMW 92*
**Wier,** Paul Benjamin 1959- *WhoRel 92*
**Wier,** Richard Jerome 1955- *WhoMW 92*
**Wier,** Withrow Gil 1950- *AmMWSc 92*
**Wierenga,** Peter J 1934- *AmMWSc 92*
**Wierenga,** Wendell 1948- *AmMWSc 92*
**Wierengo,** Cyril John, Jr 1940- *AmMWSc 92*
**Wierman,** John C 1949- *AmMWSc 92*
**Wiersbe,** Warren Wendell 1929- *WhoRel 92*
**Wiersich,** Oswald 1882-1945 *EncTR 91*
**Wiersma,** Daniel 1916- *AmMWSc 92*
**Wiersma,** James H 1940- *AmMWSc 92*
**Wierwille,** Victor Paul 1916-1985 *RelLAm 91*
**Wierwille,** Walter W 1936- *AmMWSc 92*
**Wierzbicki,** Eugeniusz 1909- *IntWW 91*
**Wiesboeck,** Robert A 1930- *AmMWSc 92*
**Wieschenberg,** Klaus 1932- *WhoFI 92*
**Wiese,** Allen F 1925- *AmMWSc 92*
**Wiese,** Alvin Carl 1913- *AmMWSc 92*
**Wiese,** Andrew J *WhoAmP 91*
**Wiese,** Charles Henry, III 1938- *WhoMW 92*
**Wiese,** Clark Mason 1964- *WhoWest 92*
**Wiese,** Daniel Edward 1936- *WhoFI 92*
**Wiese,** Frederick William 1941- *WhoMW 92*
**Wiese,** Helen Jean Coleman 1941- *AmMWSc 92*
**Wiese,** Howard Henry 1943- *WhoMW 92*
**Wiese,** James Douglas *WhoAmL 92*
**Wiese,** James Lorenz 1936- *WhoRel 92*
**Wiese,** John Herbert 1917- *AmMWSc 92*
**Wiese,** John Paul 1934- *WhoAmL 92*
**Wiese,** Kevin Glen 1960- *WhoWest 92*
**Wiese,** Kurt 1887-1974 *BenetAL 91*
**Wiese,** Maurice Victor 1940- *AmMWSc 92*
**Wiese,** Richard Anton 1928- *AmMWSc 92*
**Wiese,** Robert George, Jr 1933- *AmMWSc 92*
**Wiese,** Terry Eugene 1948- *WhoFI 92*
**Wiese,** Warren M 1929- *AmMWSc 92*
**Wiese,** Wolfgang Lothar 1931- *AmMWSc 92*
**Wiesel,** Elie *DrAPF 91*
**Wiesel,** Elie 1928- *Au&Arts 7 [port], BenetAL 91, FacFETw [port], IntAu&W 91, IntWW 91, LiExTwC, Who 92, WhoNob 90, WhoRel 92, WrDr 92*
**Wiesel,** Torsten N. 1924- *WhoNob 90*
**Wiesel,** Torsten Nils 1924- *AmMWSc 92, Who 92*
**Wieseman,** Mary Folliard 1942- *WhoAmL 92*
**Wiesen,** Audray Agnes 1936- *WhoAmP 91*
**Wiesen,** Bernard *IntMPA 92*
**Wiesen,** James D. 1937- *WhoMW 92*
**Wiesenberg,** Jacqueline Leonardi 1928- *WhoFI 92*
**Wiesendanger,** Hans Ulrich David 1928- *AmMWSc 92*
**Wiesenfarth,** Joseph 1933- *WrDr 92*

**Wiesenfarth,** Joseph John 1933- *IntAu&W 91*
**Wiesenfeld,** Jay Martin 1950- *AmMWSc 92*
**Wiesenfeld,** Joel 1918- *AmMWSc 92*
**Wiesenfeld,** John Richard 1944- *AmMWSc 92*
**Wiesenthal,** Andrew Michael 1950- *WhoWest 92*
**Wiesenthal,** Simon 1908- *EncTR 91, FacFETw, IntAu&W 91, IntWW 91*
**Wieser,** Helmut 1935- *AmMWSc 92*
**Wieser,** Jeffrey Noble 1952- *WhoFI 92*
**Wieser,** Joseph Alphonsus 1943- *WhoAmP 91*
**Wieser,** Richard Charles 1952- *WhoEnt 92*
**Wieser,** Siegfried 1933- *WhoWest 92*
**Wiesler,** James Ballard 1927- *WhoFI 92*
**Wiesman,** Melvyn W. 1939- *WhoAmL 92*
**Wiesman,** Ronald 1948- *WhoIns 92*
**Wiesmeyer,** Herbert 1932- *AmMWSc 92*
**Wiesner,** Dallas Charles 1959- *WhoMW 92*
**Wiesner,** Daniel Richard Claude 1947- *WhoEnt 92*
**Wiesner,** Douglas W 1940- *WhoIns 92*
**Wiesner,** J B 1915- *AmMWSc 92*
**Wiesner,** Jerome Bert 1915- *IntWW 91, Who 92*
**Wiesner,** John Joseph 1938- *WhoFI 92*
**Wiesner,** Julie Ann 1961- *WhoEnt 92*
**Wiesner,** Leo 1913- *AmMWSc 92*
**Wiesner,** Loren Elwood 1938- *AmMWSc 92*
**Wiesner,** Michael Ira 1947- *WhoFI 92*
**Wiesner,** Rakoma 1920- *AmMWSc 92*
**Wiesner-Duran,** Eduardo 1934- *IntWW 91*
**Wiesnet,** Andrew John 1954- *WhoEnt 92*
**Wiesnet,** Donald Richard 1927- *AmMWSc 92*
**Wiest,** Claire 1930- *ConAu 34NR*
**Wiest,** Dianne 1948- *IntMPA 92, WhoEnt 92*
**Wiest,** Edward Robert 1954- *WhoAmL 92*
**Wiest,** Grace L. *WrDr 92*
**Wiest,** Joel Rees 1955- *WhoMW 92*
**Wiest,** Nona Harden 1900- *WhoAmP 91*
**Wiest,** Steven Craig 1951- *AmMWSc 92*
**Wiest,** Walter Gibson 1922- *AmMWSc 92*
**Wietecha,** Ronald W 1942- *WhoAmP 91*
**Wiethuchter,** Horst 1928- *IntWW 91*
**Wieting,** Terence James 1935- *AmMWSc 92*
**Wiewel,** Bradford Gerald 1952- *WhoRel 92*
**Wiewiorowski,** Tadeusz Karol 1935- *AmMWSc 92*
**Wiff,** Donald Ray 1936- *AmMWSc 92*
**Witten,** Alfred K. 1896-1968 *TwCPaSc*
**Wigan,** Alan 1913- *Who 92*
**Wigan,** Christopher *IntAu&W 91X, TwCWW 91*
**Wigan,** Gareth 1931- *IntMPA 92*
**Wigdor,** Lucien Simon 1919- *Who 92*
**Wigen,** Philip E 1933- *AmMWSc 92*
**Wiget,** Earl Craig 1950- *WhoMW 92*
**Wigfall,** Robert Paul 1929- *WhoMW 92*
**Wigfall,** Samuel E. 1946- *WhoBlA 92*
**Wigfield,** Donald Compston 1943- *AmMWSc 92*
**Wigg,** Charles Mayes 1889-1969 *TwCPaSc*
**Wigg,** T I G *IntAu&W 91X*
**Wiggans,** Donald Sherman 1925- *AmMWSc 92*
**Wiggans,** Samuel Claude 1922- *AmMWSc 92*
**Wiggenhorn,** Susan Marie 1951- *WhoMW 92*
**Wigger,** G. Eugene 1944- *WhoFI 92*
**Wigger,** H Joachim 1928- *AmMWSc 92*
**Wiggers,** Harold Carl *AmMWSc 92*
**Wiggert,** Barbara Norene 1938- *AmMWSc 92*
**Wiggham,** Barrie 1937- *Who 92*
**Wiggin,** Alfred William 1937- *Who 92*
**Wiggin,** Allen R 1941- *WhoAmP 91*
**Wiggin,** Edwin Albert 1921- *AmMWSc 92*
**Wiggin,** Gordon E 1933- *WhoAmP 91*
**Wiggin,** Jerry *Who 92*
**Wiggin,** John 1921- *Who 92*
**Wiggin,** Kate Douglas 1856-1923 *BenetAL 91*
**Wiggin,** Terry Lynn 1956- *WhoAmP 91*
**Wiggins,** Alan 1958-1991 *WhoBlA 92N*
**Wiggins,** Alvin Dennie 1922- *AmMWSc 92*
**Wiggins,** Anthony John 1938- *Who 92*
**Wiggins,** Carl M 1941- *AmMWSc 92*
**Wiggins,** Charles A. 1943- *WhoBlA 92*
**Wiggins,** Charles E 1942- *WhoAmP 91*
**Wiggins,** Charles Edward 1927- *WhoAmL 92*
**Wiggins,** Clifton Allen, Sr. 1912- *WhoBlA 92*
**Wiggins,** Craig Douglas 1956- *WhoFI 92*
**Wiggins,** Daniel Braxton, Jr. 1952- *WhoRel 92*
**Wiggins,** Daphne Cordelia 1960- *WhoBlA 92*
**Wiggins,** David 1933- *IntWW 91, Who 92, WrDr 92*
**Wiggins,** Dewayne Lee 1949- *WhoFI 92*
**Wiggins,** Earl Lowell 1921- *AmMWSc 92*
**Wiggins,** Edith Mayfield 1942- *WhoBlA 92*
**Wiggins,** Edward A 1933- *WhoAmP 91*
**Wiggins,** Edwin George 1943- *AmMWSc 92*
**Wiggins,** Ernest James 1917- *AmMWSc 92*
**Wiggins,** George I *WhoAmP 91*
**Wiggins,** Glenn Blakely 1927- *AmMWSc 92*
**Wiggins,** Harry *WhoAmP 91*
**Wiggins,** Harry 1934- *WhoMW 92*
**Wiggins,** Ira Loren 1899- *AmMWSc 92*
**Wiggins,** Jack Gillmore, Jr. 1926- *WhoMW 92*
**Wiggins,** James Bryan 1935- *WhoRel 92*
**Wiggins,** James Russell 1903- *ConAu 133, IntWW 91*
**Wiggins,** James Wendell 1942- *AmMWSc 92*
**Wiggins,** James William 1940- *AmMWSc 92*
**Wiggins,** Jay Ross 1947- *AmMWSc 92*
**Wiggins,** John *Who 92*
**Wiggins,** John 1949- *AmMWSc 92*
**Wiggins,** John H, Jr 1931- *AmMWSc 92*
**Wiggins,** John Shearon 1915- *AmMWSc 92*
**Wiggins,** Joseph L. 1944- *WhoBlA 92*
**Wiggins,** Larry Don 1949- *WhoAmP 91*
**Wiggins,** Leslie 1936- *WhoBlA 92*
**Wiggins,** Lillian Cooper 1932- *WhoBlA 92*
**Wiggins,** Marianne 1947- *IntAu&W 91, WrDr 92*
**Wiggins,** Maxwell Lester 1915- *Who 92*
**Wiggins,** Mitchell 1959- *WhoBlA 92*
**Wiggins,** Nancy Bowen 1948- *WhoFI 92*
**Wiggins,** Nina Louise 1961- *WhoMW 92*
**Wiggins,** Norman Adrian 1924- *WhoAmL 92*
**Wiggins,** Peter F 1935- *AmMWSc 92*
**Wiggins,** Ralphe 1940- *AmMWSc 92*
**Wiggins,** Renzo Samuel 1956- *WhoAmL 92*
**Wiggins,** Richard Calvin 1945- *AmMWSc 92*
**Wiggins,** Rosalind Zeldina 1959- *WhoAmL 92*
**Wiggins,** Thomas Arthur 1921- *AmMWSc 92*
**Wiggins,** Thomas Gene 1944- *WhoEnt 92*
**Wiggins,** Todd Keith 1967- *WhoRel 92*
**Wiggins,** Virgil Dale 1931- *AmMWSc 92*
**Wiggins,** Walton Wray 1924- *WhoWest 92*
**Wiggins,** William H., Jr. 1934 *WhoBlA 92*
**Wigglesworth,** David Cunningham 1927- *WhoWest 92*
**Wigglesworth,** Frank 1918- *NewAmDM*
**Wigglesworth,** Frank, Jr. 1918- *WhoEnt 92*
**Wigglesworth,** Gordon Hardy 1920- *Who 92*
**Wigglesworth,** Michael 1631-1705 *BenetAL 91*
**Wigglesworth,** Vincent 1899- *IntWW 91, Who 92*
**Wigglesworth,** William Robert Brian 1937- *Who 92*
**Wiggs,** P. David 1942- *WhoWest 92*
**Wigh,** Russell 1914- *AmMWSc 92*
**Wight,** Darlene 1926- *WhoMW 92*
**Wight,** Doris T. *DrAPF 91*
**Wight,** Dorothea 1944- *TwCPaSc*
**Wight,** Hewitt Glenn 1921- *AmMWSc 92*
**Wight,** James Alfred 1916- *Who 92*
**Wight,** Jerald Ross 1931- *AmMWSc 92*
**Wight,** Joseph Douglas 1930- *WhoWest 92*
**Wight,** Lawrence John *WhoMW 92*
**Wight,** M Arnold, Jr *WhoAmP 91*
**Wight,** Randy Lee 1951- *WhoWest 92*
**Wight,** Robin 1944- *Who 92*
**Wightman,** Ann 1958- *WhoAmL 92*
**Wightman,** Arthur Strong 1922- *AmMWSc 92, IntWW 91*
**Wightman,** Frank 1928- *AmMWSc 92*
**Wightman,** James Pinckney 1935- *AmMWSc 92*
**Wightman,** Robert Harlan 1937- *AmMWSc 92*
**Wightman,** William d1909 *BiInAmS*
**Wightman,** William David 1939- *Who 92*
**Wighton,** John L 1915- *AmMWSc 92*
**Wightwick,** Charles Christopher Brooke 1931- *Who 92*
**Wigington,** Ronald L 1932- *AmMWSc 92*
**Wigington,** Ronald Lee 1932- *WhoMW 92*
**Wiginton,** Dan Allen 1949- *AmMWSc 92*
**Wiginton,** James Bayles 1947- *WhoMW 92*
**Wigle,** Ernest Douglas 1928- *AmMWSc 92*
**Wigler,** Michael H 1947- *AmMWSc 92*
**Wigler,** Paul William 1928- *AmMWSc 92*
**Wigley,** Dafydd 1943- *IntWW 91, Who 92*
**Wigley,** John 1962- *TwCPaSc*
**Wigley,** Neil Marchand 1936- *AmMWSc 92*
**Wigley,** Richard Ellis 1918- *WhoAmP 91*
**Wigley,** Roland L 1923- *AmMWSc 92*
**Wigman,** Mary 1886-1973 *EncTR 91*
**Wigmore,** James Arthur Joseph 1928- *Who 92*
**Wigmore,** John Grant 1928- *WhoAmL 92*
**Wignall,** Frank Stephen 1948- *WhoWest 92*
**Wignall,** George Denis 1941- *AmMWSc 92*
**Wignell,** Edel 1936- *IntAu&W 91*
**Wigner,** Eugene P. 1902- *Who 92*
**Wigner,** Eugene Paul 1902- *AmMWSc 92, FacFETw, IntWW 91, WhoNob 90*
**Wigner,** Larry Raymond 1935- *WhoFI 92*
**Wigoder** *Who 92*
**Wigoder,** Baron 1921- *Who 92*
**Wigodner,** Byron I. 1952- *WhoMW 92*
**Wigodsky,** Herman S 1915- *AmMWSc 92*
**Wigram** *Who 92*
**Wigram,** Baron 1915- *Who 92*
**Wigram,** Clifford Woolmore 1911- *Who 92*
**Wigram,** Derek Roland 1908- *Who 92*
**Wigsten,** Paul Bradley, Jr. 1947- *WhoFI 92*
**Wigton,** Robert Spencer 1911- *AmMWSc 92*
**Wigzell,** Hans 1938- *IntWW 91*
**Wihby,** Linda S 1951- *WhoAmP 91*
**Wihtol,** Arn S. 1944- *IntMPA 92*
**Wiig,** Elisabeth Hemmersam 1935- *AmMWSc 92*
**Wiin-Nielsen,** Aksel Christopher 1924- *Who 92*
**Wiin-Nielsen,** Aksel Christopher 1929- *IntWW 91*
**Wiinblad,** Bjorn 1919- *DcTwDes*
**Wiita,** Paul Joseph 1953- *AmMWSc 92*
**Wiitala,** J. Mark 1961- *WhoWest 92*
**Wiitala,** Stephen Allen 1946- *AmMWSc 92*
**Wiitala,** Stephen John 1942- *WhoAmP 91*
**Wiitanen,** Wayne Alfred 1935- *AmMWSc 92*
**Wijangco,** Antonio Robles 1944- *AmMWSc 92*
**Wijesekera,** Duminda 1957- *WhoMW 92*
**Wijesekera,** Nandadeva 1908- *IntWW 91*
**Wijetunge,** D. B. 1922- *IntWW 91*
**Wijewardane,** Nissanka 1926- *IntWW 91*
**Wijnen,** Joseph M H 1920- *AmMWSc 92*
**Wijsman,** Robert Arthur 1920- *AmMWSc 92*
**Wikarski,** Nancy Susan 1954- *WhoMW 92*
**Wike,** Edward L. 1922- *WrDr 92*
**Wike,** Stephen Michael 1949- *WhoRel 92*
**Wikel,** Stephen Kenneth 1945- *AmMWSc 92*
**Wiker,** Edgar Guy 1932- *WhoRel 92*
**Wikjord,** Alfred George 1943- *AmMWSc 92*
**Wikler,** Yosef 1945- *WhoRel 92*
**Wikman,** Carl Herman 1950- *WhoEnt 92*
**Wikman-Coffelt,** Joan 1929- *AmMWSc 92*
**Wikoff,** Virgil Cornwell 1927- *WhoAmP 91*
**Wiksten,** Barry Frank 1935- *WhoFI 92*
**Wikstrom,** Daryl Lyn 1962- *WhoFI 92*
**Wikstrom,** Jan-Erik 1932- *IntWW 91*
**Wikstrom,** Marilyn 1935- *WhoMW 92*
**Wikstrom,** Per-Olof Helge 1955- *IntAu&W 91*
**Wikswo,** John Peter, Jr 1949- *AmMWSc 92*
**Wiktorowicz,** Andrew Charles 1945- *WhoWest 92*
**Wiktorowicz,** John Edward 1949- *AmMWSc 92*
**Wikum,** Douglas Arnold 1933- *AmMWSc 92*
**Wiland,** Harry Alan 1944- *WhoEnt 92*
**Wilander,** Mats *IntWW 91*
**Wilansky,** Albert 1921- *AmMWSc 92*
**Wilbanks,** John Randall 1938- *AmMWSc 92*
**Wilbanks,** Mark Oliver 1951- *WhoRel 92*
**Wilbarger,** Edward Stanley 1931- *WhoWest 92*
**Wilbarger,** Edward Stanley, Jr 1931- *AmMWSc 92*
**Wilbarger,** John Wesley *BenetAL 91*
**Wilber,** Bernard 1924- *WhoAmP 91*
**Wilber,** Bob 1928- *NewAmDM*
**Wilber,** Charles Grady 1916- *AmMWSc 92*
**Wilber,** Charles K. 1935- *ConAu 134*
**Wilber,** Clare Marie 1928- *WhoWest 92*
**Wilber,** Donald Blaine 1952- *WhoRel 92*
**Wilber,** Donald Newton 1907- *WrDr 92*
**Wilber,** Elinor F *WhoAmP 91*
**Wilber,** Gary 1950- *WhoFI 92*
**Wilber,** Jay Lawrence 1960- *WhoAmL 92*
**Wilber,** Joe Casley, Jr 1929- *AmMWSc 92*
**Wilber,** Kathleen Harriet 1948- *WhoWest 92*
**Wilber,** Laura Ann 1934- *AmMWSc 92*
**Wilber,** Margie Robinson *WhoBlA 92*
**Wilber,** Philip Irving 1927- *WhoFI 92*
**Wilber,** Thomas Craig 1963- *WhoWest 92*
**Wilberforce** *Who 92*
**Wilberforce,** Baron 1907- *IntWW 91, Who 92*
**Wilberforce,** William 1759-1833 *BlkwCEP*
**Wilberforce,** William John Antony 1930- *IntWW 91, Who 92*
**Wilberg,** Richard Willard 1948- *WhoFI 92*
**Wilberger,** James Eldridge 1952- *AmMWSc 92*
**Wilbert,** Brian Kurt 1960- *WhoRel 92*
**Wilbert,** Lawrence J *WhoAmP 91*
**Wilbert,** Martin Inventius 1855-1916 *BiInAmS*
**Wilbon,** Joan Marie 1949- *WhoBlA 92*
**Wilborn,** Letta Grace Smith 1936- *WhoBlA 92*
**Wilborn,** W Stephen 1947- *WhoAmP 91*
**Wilborn,** Walter Harrison 1935- *AmMWSc 92*
**Wilbourn,** Colin 1956- *TwCPaSc*
**Wilbraham** *Who 92*
**Wilbraham,** Antony Charles 1936- *AmMWSc 92*
**Wilbraham,** John Harry George 1944- *IntWW 91*
**Wilbraham,** Richard B. *Who 92*
**Wilbrandt,** Conrad *ScFEYrs*
**Wilbun,** Shepperson A. 1924- *WhoBlA 92*
**Wilbur,** Brayton, Jr. 1935- *WhoWest 92*
**Wilbur,** Daniel Scott 1950- *AmMWSc 92*
**Wilbur,** David Wesley 1937- *AmMWSc 92*
**Wilbur,** Donald Lee 1942- *AmMWSc 92*
**Wilbur,** Dwight Locke 1903- *AmMWSc 92*
**Wilbur,** George Craig 1946- *WhoAmP 91*
**Wilbur,** Henry Miles 1944- *AmMWSc 92*
**Wilbur,** James Myers, Jr 1929- *AmMWSc 92, WhoMW 92*
**Wilbur,** Karl Milton 1912- *AmMWSc 92*
**Wilbur,** Kirby Allen 1953- *WhoAmP 91*
**Wilbur,** L C 1924- *AmMWSc 92*
**Wilbur,** Leslie Eugene 1924- *WhoWest 92*
**Wilbur,** Lyman D 1900- *AmMWSc 92*
**Wilbur,** Marvin Cummings 1914- *WhoRel 92*
**Wilbur,** Paul James 1937- *AmMWSc 92, WhoWest 92*
**Wilbur,** Richard *DrAPF 91*
**Wilbur,** Richard 1921- *BenetAL 91, ConPo 91, IntAu&W 91, IntWW 91, WrDr 92*
**Wilbur,** Richard Purdy 1921- *WhoEnt 92*
**Wilbur,** Richard Sloan 1924- *AmMWSc 92, IntWW 91, WhoMW 92*
**Wilbur,** Robert Daniel 1931- *AmMWSc 92*
**Wilbur,** Robert Lynch 1925- *AmMWSc 92*
**Wilbur,** Sandra Beth 1946- *WhoEnt 92*
**Wilbur,** Sara Elizabeth 1956- *WhoEnt 92*
**Wilbur-Coulter,** Julie Kaye 1960- *WhoWest 92*
**Wilburn,** Howard Lee 1945- *WhoRel 92*
**Wilburn,** Isaac Earphette 1932- *WhoBlA 92*
**Wilburn,** James Richard 1932- *WhoWest 92*
**Wilburn,** Jerry *WhoAmP 91*
**Wilburn,** Kathy 1948- *SmATA 68 [port]*
**Wilburn,** L. Thomas, Jr. 1928- *WhoMW 92*
**Wilburn,** Mary Nelson 1932- *WhoAmL 92*
**Wilburn,** Melissa Lyn 1963- *WhoAmL 92*
**Wilburn,** Norman Patrick 1931- *AmMWSc 92*
**Wilburn,** Raymond Allen 1947- *WhoRel 92*
**Wilburn,** Stephen Sallis 1947- *WhoRel 92*
**Wilburn,** Victor H. 1931- *WhoBlA 92*
**Wilby,** Basil Leslie 1930- *IntAu&W 91, WrDr 92*
**Wilby,** James 1958- *IntMPA 92, IntWW 91*
**Wilbye,** John 1574-1638 *NewAmDM*
**Wilce,** Robert Thayer 1924- *AmMWSc 92*
**Wilcha-Armbruster,** Lynell Felicia 1959- *WhoEnt 92*
**Wilcher,** Denny 1915- *WhoWest 92*
**Wilcher,** Ina Florence 1936- *WhoAmP 91*
**Wilcher,** LaJuana Sue 1954- *WhoAmL 92*
**Wilchinsky,** Zigmond Walter 1915- *AmMWSc 92*
**Wilck,** Carl Thomas 1933- *WhoWest 92*
**Wilckens,** Ulrich 1928- *IntWW 91*
**Wilcock,** Christopher Camplin 1939- *Who 92*
**Wilcock,** Donald F 1913- *AmMWSc 92*
**Wilcock,** William Leslie 1922- *Who 92*
**Wilcott,** Harry W 1936- *WhoIns 92*
**Wilcott,** Harry William 1936- *WhoFI 92*
**Wilcox,** Albert Frederick 1909- *Who 92*
**Wilcox,** Benjamin A 1934- *AmMWSc 92*
**Wilcox,** Benson Reid 1932- *AmMWSc 92*
**Wilcox,** Brian William 1964- *WhoRel 92*
**Wilcox,** Bruce Alexander 1948- *AmMWSc 92*
**Wilcox,** Calvin Hayden 1924- *AmMWSc 92, WhoWest 92*
**Wilcox,** Charles Frederick, Jr 1930- *AmMWSc 92*
**Wilcox,** Charles Hamilton 1929- *AmMWSc 92*
**Wilcox,** Charles John 1946- *WhoAmL 92*
**Wilcox,** Charles Julian 1930- *AmMWSc 92*
**Wilcox,** Christopher Stuart 1942- *AmMWSc 92*

**Wilcox,** Clifford LaVar 1925- *AmMWSc 92*
**Wilcox,** Collin 1924- *IntAu&W 91, WrDr 92*
**Wilcox,** Daniel Edward, III 1946- *WhoWest 92*
**Wilcox,** David Eric 1939- *WhoFI 92*
**Wilcox,** David John Reed 1939- *Who 92*
**Wilcox,** David Peter *Who 92*
**Wilcox,** David Robert 1944- *WhoWest 92*
**Wilcox,** Debra Kay 1955- *WhoAmL 92*
**Wilcox,** Dennis Lee 1941- *WhoWest 92*
**Wilcox,** Desmond John 1931- *Who 92*
**Wilcox,** Donald Alan 1951- *WhoAmL 92, WhoMW 92*
**Wilcox,** Donald Brooks 1911- *AmMWSc 92*
**Wilcox,** Donald J. 1938-1991 *ConAu 134*
**Wilcox,** Earl V *WhoAmP 91, WhoHisp 92*
**Wilcox,** Ella Wheeler 1850-1919 *BenetAL 91, RelLAm 91*
**Wilcox,** Esther Louise *Who 92*
**Wilcox,** Ethelwyn Bernice 1906- *AmMWSc 92*
**Wilcox,** Evlyn *WhoAmP 91, WhoWest 92*
**Wilcox,** Frank H 1927- *AmMWSc 92*
**Wilcox,** Frank Herbert 1927- *WhoMW 92*
**Wilcox,** Gary Lynn 1947- *AmMWSc 92*
**Wilcox,** George Franklin 1937- *WhoMW 92, WhoRel 92*
**Wilcox,** George Latimer *AmMWSc 92*
**Wilcox,** Gerald Eugene 1925- *AmMWSc 92*
**Wilcox,** Harold Edgar 1940- *WhoWest 92*
**Wilcox,** Harold Kendall 1942- *AmMWSc 92*
**Wilcox,** Harry Hammond 1918- *AmMWSc 92*
**Wilcox,** Henry G 1933- *AmMWSc 92*
**Wilcox,** Herbert 1891-1977 *IntDcF 2-2 [port]*
**Wilcox,** Howard Albert 1920- *AmMWSc 92*
**Wilcox,** Howard Joseph 1939- *AmMWSc 92*
**Wilcox,** Hugh Edward 1916- *AmMWSc 92*
**Wilcox,** Jackson Burton 1918- *WhoRel 92*
**Wilcox,** James Raymond 1931- *AmMWSc 92, WhoMW 92*
**Wilcox,** Janice Horde 1940- *WhoBlA 92*
**Wilcox,** Jeffrey Merrill 1963- *WhoMW 92*
**Wilcox,** John Christopher 1951- *WhoEnt 92*
**Wilcox,** Joseph Clifford 1930- *AmMWSc 92*
**Wilcox,** Judith Ann *Who 92*
**Wilcox,** Kent Westbrook 1945- *AmMWSc 92*
**Wilcox,** Laird Maurice 1942- *WhoMW 92*
**Wilcox,** Lee Roy 1912- *AmMWSc 92*
**Wilcox,** Louis Van Inwegen, Jr 1931- *AmMWSc 92*
**Wilcox,** Lyle C 1932- *AmMWSc 92*
**Wilcox,** Lynn E. 1935- *WhoWest 92*
**Wilcox,** Marion Walter 1922- *AmMWSc 92*
**Wilcox,** Mark Dean 1952- *WhoAmL 92*
**Wilcox,** Marsha Ann 1956- *WhoFI 92*
**Wilcox,** Mary Marks 1921- *WhoRel 92*
**Wilcox,** Mary Rose 1949- *WhoAmP 91, WhoHisp 92*
**Wilcox,** Merrill 1929- *AmMWSc 92*
**Wilcox,** Paul Denton 1935- *AmMWSc 92*
**Wilcox,** Paul Horne 1950- *WhoWest 92*
**Wilcox,** Paul Stewart 1948- *WhoAmL 92, WhoAmP 91*
**Wilcox,** Preston 1923- *WhoBlA 92*
**Wilcox,** Ray Everett 1912- *AmMWSc 92*
**Wilcox,** Rhoda Davis 1918- *WhoWest 92*
**Wilcox,** Richard Cecil 1959- *WhoFI 92*
**Wilcox,** Robert Kalleen 1943- *WhoEnt 92*
**Wilcox,** Roberta Arlene 1932- *AmMWSc 92*
**Wilcox,** Roberta Moat 1933- *WhoEnt 92*
**Wilcox,** Ronald Bruce 1934- *AmMWSc 92*
**Wilcox,** Ronald Calvin 1953- *WhoEnt 92*
**Wilcox,** Ronald Erwin 1929- *AmMWSc 92*
**Wilcox,** Ronald Wayne 1941- *WhoRel 92*
**Wilcox,** Roy Carl 1933- *AmMWSc 92*
**Wilcox,** Ted *TwCPaSc*
**Wilcox,** Thomas Jefferson 1942- *AmMWSc 92*
**Wilcox,** W R 1935- *AmMWSc 92*
**Wilcox,** W Wayne 1938- *AmMWSc 92*
**Wilcox,** Walter James, Sr 1949- *WhoAmP 91*
**Wilcox,** Walter Russell, Jr. 1951- *WhoEnt 92*
**Wilcox,** Wesley C 1925- *AmMWSc 92*
**Wilcox,** Wesley Crain 1926- *AmMWSc 92*
**Wilcox,** William Gary 1943- *WhoFI 92*
**Wilcox,** William Harry *WhoAmP 91*
**Wilcox,** William Jenkins, Jr 1923- *AmMWSc 92*
**Wilcox,** Winton Wilfred, Jr. 1945- *WhoWest 92*
**Wilcoxen,** William Merritt 1932- *WhoAmL 92*
**Wilcoxson,** Roy Dell 1926- *AmMWSc 92*
**Wilczek,** Frank Anthony 1951- *AmMWSc 92*
**Wilczek,** Robert Joseph 1944- *WhoAmL 92*
**Wilczynski,** Janusz S *AmMWSc 92*
**Wilczynski,** Walter 1952- *AmMWSc 92*
**Wild,** Bradford Williston 1927- *AmMWSc 92*
**Wild,** Chris 1945- *TwCPaSc*
**Wild,** David 1930- *Who 92*
**Wild,** David Humphrey 1927- *Who 92*
**Wild,** Earl 1915- *IntWW 91, NewAmDM*
**Wild,** Eric d1991 *Who 92N*
**Wild,** Gaynor 1934- *AmMWSc 92*
**Wild,** Gene Muriel 1926- *AmMWSc 92*
**Wild,** Gerald Percy 1908- *Who 92*
**Wild,** Heidi Karin 1948- *WhoFI 92*
**Wild,** James Robert 1945- *AmMWSc 92*
**Wild,** John Frederick 1926- *AmMWSc 92*
**Wild,** John Frederick 1942- *AmMWSc 92*
**Wild,** John Herbert Severn 1904- *Who 92*
**Wild,** John Julian 1914- *AmMWSc 92*
**Wild,** John Paul 1923- *IntWW 91, Who 92*
**Wild,** John Vernon 1915- *Who 92*
**Wild,** Nelson Hopkins 1933- *WhoAmL 92*
**Wild,** Peter *DrAPF 91*
**Wild,** Peter 1940- *ConPo 91, WrDr 92*
**Wild,** Philip 1954- *WhoEnt 92*
**Wild,** Raymond 1940- *Who 92*
**Wild,** Robert 1932- *Who 92*
**Wild,** Robert Anthony 1940- *WhoRel 92*
**Wild,** Robert Lee 1921- *AmMWSc 92*
**Wild,** Stephen Kent 1948- *WhoFI 92*
**Wild,** Steven Daggett 1952- *WhoEnt 92*
**Wild,** Victor Allyn 1946- *WhoAmL 92*
**Wild,** Wayne Grant 1917- *AmMWSc 92*
**Wildasin,** David Earl 1950- *WhoFI 92, WhoMW 92*
**Wildasin,** Harry Lewis 1923- *AmMWSc 92*
**Wildberger,** William Campbell 1914- *AmMWSc 92*
**Wilde,** Alexander G 1948- *WhoIns 92*
**Wilde,** Anthony Flory 1930- *AmMWSc 92*
**Wilde,** Arthur L. *IntMPA 92*
**Wilde,** Bryan Edmund 1934- *AmMWSc 92*
**Wilde,** Carroll Orville 1932- *AmMWSc 92*
**Wilde,** Charles Edward, III 1946- *AmMWSc 92*
**Wilde,** Charles Edward, Jr 1918- *AmMWSc 92*
**Wilde,** D J 1929- *AmMWSc 92*
**Wilde,** David 1931- *TwCPaSc*
**Wilde,** Derek Edward 1912- *Who 92*
**Wilde,** Donald Raymond 1926- *WhoFI 92*
**Wilde,** Fred *TwCPaSc*
**Wilde,** Garner Lee 1926- *AmMWSc 92*
**Wilde,** Gayle Ann 1941- *WhoAmP 91*
**Wilde,** Gerald 1905-1986 *TwCPaSc*
**Wilde,** Gerald Eldon 1939- *AmMWSc 92*
**Wilde,** Helen 1954- *TwCPaSc*
**Wilde,** Kenneth Alfred 1929- *AmMWSc 92*
**Wilde,** Louise *TwCPaSc*
**Wilde,** Neva Maxine 1916- *WhoWest 92*
**Wilde,** Oscar 1854-1900 *CnDBLB 5 [port], RfGEnL 91, TwCLC 41 [port]*
**Wilde,** Pat 1935- *AmMWSc 92*
**Wilde,** Patricia 1928- *WhoEnt 92*
**Wilde,** Paul Cecil 1950- *WhoFI 92*
**Wilde,** Percival 1887-1953 *BenetAL 91*
**Wilde,** Peter Appleton 1925- *Who 92*
**Wilde,** Richard Edward, Jr 1931- *AmMWSc 92*
**Wilde,** Richard Henry 1789-1847 *BenetAL 91*
**Wilde,** Richard Lawrence 1944- *WhoEnt 92*
**Wilde,** Teruko 1945- *WhoWest 92*
**Wilde,** Walter Samuel 1909- *AmMWSc 92*
**Wilde,** William Richard 1953- *WhoAmL 92*
**Wilde,** Wilson 1927- *WhoFI 92, WhoIns 92*
**Wildebush,** Joseph Frederick 1910- *WhoFI 92*
**Wildeman,** Thomas Raymond 1940- *AmMWSc 92*
**Wilden,** Anthony 1935- *WrDr 92*
**Wildenstein,** Daniel Leopold 1917- *IntWW 91, Who 92*
**Wildenthal,** Bryan Hobson 1937- *AmMWSc 92, WhoWest 92*
**Wildenthal,** Kern 1941- *AmMWSc 92*
**Wilder,** Alec 1907-1980 *NewAmDM*
**Wilder,** Billy 1906- *BenetAL 91, FacFETw, IntAu&W 91, IntDcF 2-2 [port], IntMPA 92, IntWW 91, WhoEnt 92*
**Wilder,** Brett Paxton 1939- *WhoFI 92*
**Wilder,** Charles Willoughby 1929- *WhoAmL 92, WhoFI 92*
**Wilder,** Cherry 1930- *IntAu&W 91, TwCSFW 91, WrDr 92*
**Wilder,** Cleo Duke 1925- *AmMWSc 92*
**Wilder,** Cora White 1936- *WhoBlA 92*
**Wilder,** David Randolph 1929- *AmMWSc 92*
**Wilder,** Gene 1935- *IntMPA 92, WhoEnt 92*
**Wilder,** Gene 1950- *WhoRel 92*
**Wilder,** Harry D 1932- *AmMWSc 92*
**Wilder,** James Andrew, Jr 1950- *AmMWSc 92*
**Wilder,** James Curtis 1958- *WhoBlA 92*
**Wilder,** James D. 1935- *WhoWest 92*
**Wilder,** James Sampson, III 1949- *WhoAmL 92*
**Wilder,** John Richard 1955- *IntAu&W 91*
**Wilder,** John S 1921- *WhoAmP 91*
**Wilder,** Joseph Bowers 1923- *WhoAmP 91*
**Wilder,** Joseph R 1920- *AmMWSc 92*
**Wilder,** L. Douglas 1931- *AlmAP 92 [port]*
**Wilder,** Laura Ingalls 1867-1957 *BenetAL 91, TwCWW 91*
**Wilder,** Lawrence Douglas 1931- *IntWW 91, NewYTBS 91 [port], WhoAmP 91, WhoBlA 92*
**Wilder,** Lee Davidson 1951- *WhoFI 92*
**Wilder,** Martin Stuart 1937- *AmMWSc 92*
**Wilder,** Mary A. H. 1924- *WhoBlA 92*
**Wilder,** Michael S 1941- *WhoIns 92*
**Wilder,** Myron F 1934- *WhoIns 92*
**Wilder,** Myron F., Jr. 1934- *WhoFI 92*
**Wilder,** Norma Fredrick R 1924- *WhoAmP 91*
**Wilder,** Pelham, Jr 1920- *AmMWSc 92*
**Wilder,** Roland Percival, Jr. 1940- *WhoAmL 92*
**Wilder,** Ronald Lynn 1947- *AmMWSc 92*
**Wilder,** Thomas, Jr 1946- *WhoAmP 91*
**Wilder,** Thomas Henry 1952- *WhoRel 92*
**Wilder,** Thornton 1897-1975 *BenetAL 91, DramC 1 [port], FacFETw*
**Wilder,** Valerie 1947- *WhoEnt 92*
**Wilder,** Violet Myrtle 1908- *AmMWSc 92*
**Wilder,** William Bruce, Jr. 1957- *WhoRel 92*
**Wilderotter,** James Arthur 1944- *WhoAmL 92*
**Wilderson,** Frank B., Jr. 1931- *WhoBlA 92*
**Wilderson,** Thad 1935- *WhoBlA 92*
**Wildey,** Brian Roger 1941- *WhoWest 92*
**Wildey,** Robert Leroy 1934- *AmMWSc 92, WhoWest 92*
**Wildey,** Sharon Ann 1943- *WhoAmL 92*
**Wildey,** William Edward 1952- *WhoRel 92*
**Wildfeuer,** Marvin Emanuel 1936- *AmMWSc 92*
**Wildi,** Bernard Sylvester 1920- *AmMWSc 92*
**Wildin,** Maurice W 1935- *AmMWSc 92*
**Wilding,** Alison 1948- *TwCPaSc*
**Wilding,** Diane 1942- *WhoFI 92*
**Wilding,** Eric *IntAu&W 91X, TwCSFW 91*
**Wilding,** Griseda *WrDr 92*
**Wilding,** Lawrence Paul 1934- *AmMWSc 92*
**Wilding,** Michael 1942- *ConNov 91, IntAu&W 91, WrDr 92*
**Wilding,** Noel 1903-1966 *TwCPaSc*
**Wilding,** Richard William Longworth 1929- *Who 92*
**Wildish,** Denis Bryan Harvey 1914- *Who 92*
**Wildman,** Eugene *DrAPF 91*
**Wildman,** Gary Cecil 1942- *AmMWSc 92*
**Wildman,** George Thomas 1935- *AmMWSc 92*
**Wildman,** John Hazard *DrAPF 91*
**Wildman,** Peter James Lacey 1936- *AmMWSc 92*
**Wildmann,** Manfred 1930- *AmMWSc 92*
**Wildmon,** Donald *LesBEnT 92*
**Wildnauer,** Richard Harry 1940- *AmMWSc 92, WhoFI 92*
**Wildrick,** Craig Douglas 1951- *WhoWest 92*
**Wildrick,** Kenyon Jones 1933- *WhoRel 92*
**Wilds,** Alfred Lawrence 1915- *AmMWSc 92*
**Wilds,** Constance T. 1941- *WhoBlA 92*
**Wilds,** Jetie Boston, Jr. 1940- *WhoBlA 92*
**Wilds,** Preston Lea 1926- *AmMWSc 92*
**Wilds,** Thomas 1925- *WhoFI 92*
**Wildsmith,** Brian 1930- *ConAu 35NR*
**Wildsmith,** Brian Lawrence 1930- *IntAu&W 91, Who 92*
**Wildt,** David Edwin 1950- *AmMWSc 92*
**Wildung,** Raymond Earl 1941- *AmMWSc 92*
**Wile,** Howard P 1911- *AmMWSc 92*
**Wile,** Joan 1931- *WhoEnt 92*
**Wile,** Kathleen Wrightsman 1963- *WhoMW 92*
**Wileman,** Douglas Brian 1958- *WhoMW 92*
**Wileman,** Margaret Annie 1908- *Who 92*
**Wilemski,** Gerald 1946- *AmMWSc 92*
**Wilen,** Judith Beth 1954- *WhoMW 92*
**Wilen,** Samuel Henry 1931- *AmMWSc 92*
**Wilen,** William Wayne 1943- *WhoMW 92*
**Wilenchik,** Dennis I. 1952- *WhoAmL 92*
**Wilens,** Peter Stephen 1955- *WhoFI 92*
**Wilenski,** Peter Stephen 1939- *IntWW 91*
**Wilenski,** Reginald Howard 1887-1975 *TwCPaSc*
**Wilensky,** Harold L. 1923- *ConAu 34NR, WhoWest 92*
**Wilensky,** Jacob T 1942- *AmMWSc 92*
**Wilensky,** Robert 1951- *AmMWSc 92*
**Wilensky,** Samuel 1937- *AmMWSc 92*
**Wilentz,** Robert N 1927- *WhoAmP 91*
**Wilentz,** Robert Nathan 1927- *WhoAmL 92*
**Wiles,** Andrew John *Who 92*
**Wiles,** Betty Jane 1940- *WhoFI 92*
**Wiles,** David M 1932- *AmMWSc 92*
**Wiles,** Donald 1912- *Who 92*
**Wiles,** Donald Roy 1925- *AmMWSc 92*
**Wiles,** Joseph St. Clair 1914- *WhoBlA 92*
**Wiles,** Leon E. 1947- *WhoBlA 92*
**Wiles,** Mari Elena 1962- *WhoRel 92*
**Wiles,** Maurice Frank 1923- *Who 92, WrDr 92*
**Wiles,** Michael 1940- *AmMWSc 92*
**Wiles,** Peter John de la Fosse 1919- *Who 92*
**Wiles,** Robert Allan 1929- *AmMWSc 92*
**Wiles,** Spencer H. 1944- *WhoBlA 92*
**Wiles,** Viola M 1912- *WhoAmP 91*
**Wilets,** Lawrence 1927- *AmMWSc 92*
**Wiley,** Albert Lee, Jr 1936- *AmMWSc 92*
**Wiley,** Bell *ConAu 134*
**Wiley,** Bill 1928- *WhoEnt 92*
**Wiley,** Bill Beauford 1923- *AmMWSc 92*
**Wiley,** Charles Albert 1925- *WhoEnt 92*
**Wiley,** Don Craig 1944- *AmMWSc 92*
**Wiley,** Donald Paul 1959- *WhoAmL 92*
**Wiley,** Donovon Linn 1938- *WhoWest 92*
**Wiley,** Douglas Walker 1929- *AmMWSc 92*
**Wiley,** E O, III 1944- *AmMWSc 92*
**Wiley,** Edward, III 1959- *WhoBlA 92*
**Wiley,** Edwin Packard 1929- *WhoAmL 92*
**Wiley,** Fletcher Houston 1942- *WhoBlA 92*
**Wiley,** Forrest Parks 1937- *WhoBlA 92*
**Wiley,** Gerald Edward 1948- *WhoBlA 92*
**Wiley,** Herley Wesley 1914- *WhoBlA 92*
**Wiley,** Jack Cleveland 1940- *AmMWSc 92, WhoMW 92*
**Wiley,** James C, Jr 1938- *AmMWSc 92*
**Wiley,** Janet May 1937- *WhoMW 92*
**Wiley,** John *TwCSFW 91*
**Wiley,** John D., Jr. 1938- *WhoBlA 92*
**Wiley,** John Duncan 1942- *AmMWSc 92*
**Wiley,** John Francis, Jr. 1950- *WhoAmL 92*
**Wiley,** John Robert 1946- *AmMWSc 92*
**Wiley,** John W 1949- *AmMWSc 92*
**Wiley,** Junior Lee 1926- *WhoAmP 91*
**Wiley,** Kenneth LeMoyne 1947- *WhoBlA 92*
**Wiley,** Leroy Sherman 1936- *WhoBlA 92*
**Wiley,** Lorraine *AmMWSc 92*
**Wiley,** Lucish D. 1950-1985 *WhoBlA 92N*
**Wiley,** Lynn M 1947- *AmMWSc 92*
**Wiley,** Madeline Dolores 1955- *WhoWest 92*
**Wiley,** Margaret L. *WrDr 92*
**Wiley,** Margaret Z. Richardson 1934- *WhoBlA 92*
**Wiley,** Maria Elena 1947- *WhoWest 92*
**Wiley,** Marilyn E *AmMWSc 92*
**Wiley,** Marshall W 1925- *WhoAmP 91*
**Wiley,** Martin Lee 1935- *AmMWSc 92*
**Wiley,** Maurice 1941- *WhoBlA 92*
**Wiley,** Michael David 1939- *AmMWSc 92, WhoWest 92*
**Wiley,** Morlon David 1966- *WhoBlA 92*
**Wiley,** Paul Fears 1916- *AmMWSc 92*
**Wiley,** Rena Deloris 1953- *WhoBlA 92*
**Wiley,** Richard Arthur 1928- *WhoAmL 92, WhoAmP 91, WhoFI 92*
**Wiley,** Richard E. *LesBEnT 92*
**Wiley,** Richard E 1934- *WhoAmP 91*
**Wiley,** Richard G 1937- *AmMWSc 92*
**Wiley,** Richard Haven 1913- *AmMWSc 92*
**Wiley,** Richard Haven, Jr 1943- *AmMWSc 92*
**Wiley,** Robert A 1934- *AmMWSc 92*
**Wiley,** Robert Craig 1924- *AmMWSc 92*
**Wiley,** Robert Stanley 1942- *WhoAmP 91*
**Wiley,** Ronald Gordon 1947- *AmMWSc 92*
**Wiley,** Ronald Lee 1937- *AmMWSc 92*
**Wiley,** Ronald LeRoy 1936- *WhoMW 92*
**Wiley,** S. Donald 1926- *WhoAmL 92*
**Wiley,** Samuel J 1939- *AmMWSc 92*
**Wiley,** W. Bradford 1910- *IntWW 91*
**Wiley,** William B. 1945- *WhoWest 92*
**Wiley,** William Charles 1924- *AmMWSc 92*
**Wiley,** William R. 1931- *WhoBlA 92*
**Wiley,** William Rodney 1931- *WhoWest 92*
**Wiley,** William Rodney 1932- *AmMWSc 92*
**Wiley-Pickett,** Gloria 1937- *WhoBlA 92*
**Wilfert,** Douglas Edward 1957- *WhoEnt 92*
**Wilfong,** Henry T., Jr. 1933- *WhoBlA 92*
**Wilfong,** John Franklin 1951- *WhoRel 92*
**Wilfong,** John Scott 1950- *WhoFI 92*
**Wilfong,** Robert Edward 1920- *AmMWSc 92*
**Wilford,** Harold C. 1924- *WhoBlA 92*

**Wilford,** John Noble 1933- *IntAu&W 91, WrDr 92*
**Wilford,** Michael 1922- *IntWW 91, Who 92*
**Wilford,** Walton Terry 1937- *WhoFI 92*
**Wilfork,** Andrew Louis 1947- *WhoBlA 92*
**Wilfret,** Gary Joe 1943- *AmMWSc 92*
**Wilgram,** George Friederich 1924- *AmMWSc 92*
**Wilgus,** Donovan Ray 1921- *AmMWSc 92*
**Wilheit,** Thomas Turner 1941- *AmMWSc 92*
**Wilhelm** 1882-1951 *EncTR 91*
**Wilhelm II** 1859-1941 *EncTR 91 [port], FacFETw [port]*
**Wilhelm,** Alan Roy 1936- *AmMWSc 92*
**Wilhelm,** Dale Leroy 1926- *AmMWSc 92*
**Wilhelm,** Eugene J, Jr 1933- *AmMWSc 92*
**Wilhelm,** Harley A 1900- *AmMWSc 92*
**Wilhelm,** James Maurice 1940- *AmMWSc 92*
**Wilhelm,** Jeffry John 1950- *WhoAmP 91*
**Wilhelm,** Jim 1954- *WhoEnt 92*
**Wilhelm,** Joseph Lawrence 1909- *Who 92*
**Wilhelm,** Kate *ConAu 36NR*
**Wilhelm,** Kate 1928- *TwCSFW 91, WrDr 92*
**Wilhelm,** Katie Gertrude 1928- *ConAu 36NR*
**Wilhelm,** Lisa Nizza 1958- *WhoMW 92*
**Wilhelm,** Mary Lou 1937- *WhoWest 92*
**Wilhelm,** Robert Gordon 1944- *WhoMW 92*
**Wilhelm,** Robert Oscar 1918- *WhoAmL 92, WhoWest 92*
**Wilhelm,** Rudolf Ernst 1926- *AmMWSc 92*
**Wilhelm,** Stephen 1919- *AmMWSc 92*
**Wilhelm,** Stephen Paul 1948- *WhoWest 92*
**Wilhelm,** Thomas Allan 1944- *WhoFI 92*
**Wilhelm,** Walter Eugene 1931- *AmMWSc 92*
**Wilhelm,** Wilbert Edward 1942- *AmMWSc 92*
**Wilhelm,** William Jean 1935- *AmMWSc 92, WhoMW 92*
**Wilhelmsson,** Hans K. B. 1929- *IntWW 91*
**Wilhelmy,** Jerry Barnard 1942- *AmMWSc 92*
**Wilhite,** Clayton Edward 1945- *WhoFI 92*
**Wilhite,** Dean Roy 1957- *WhoEnt 92*
**Wilhite,** Douglas Lee 1944- *AmMWSc 92*
**Wilhite,** Elmer Lee 1944- *AmMWSc 92*
**Wilhite,** F. Douglas 1953- *WhoRel 92*
**Wilhite,** Richard English 1924- *WhoAmP 91*
**Wilhite,** Richard James 1938- *WhoWest 92*
**Wilhjelm,** Nils 1936- *IntWW 91*
**Wilhm,** Jerry L 1930- *AmMWSc 92*
**Wilhoft,** Daniel C 1930- *AmMWSc 92*
**Wilhoit,** Carl H. 1935- *WhoBlA 92*
**Wilhoit,** Eugene Dennis 1931- *AmMWSc 92*
**Wilhoit,** Henry Rupert, Jr. 1935- *WhoAmL 92*
**Wilhoit,** James Cammack, Jr 1925- *AmMWSc 92*
**Wilhoit,** Melvin Ross 1948- *WhoRel 92*
**Wilhoit,** Randolph Carroll 1925- *AmMWSc 92*
**Wilhold,** Gilbert A 1934- *AmMWSc 92*
**Wilimovsky,** Norman Joseph 1925- *AmMWSc 92*
**Wilk,** Christopher Henzel 1961- *WhoFI 92*
**Wilk,** David *DrAPF 91*
**Wilk,** David I. 1957- *WhoAmL 92*
**Wilk,** Dennis Keith 1952- *WhoMW 92*
**Wilk,** Leonard Stephen 1927- *AmMWSc 92*
**Wilk,** Max *DrAPF 91*
**Wilk,** Melvin *DrAPF 91*
**Wilk,** Sherwin 1938- *AmMWSc 92*
**Wilk,** Ted 1908- *IntMPA 92*
**Wilk,** Wanda Helen 1921- *WhoEnt 92*
**Wilk,** William David 1942- *AmMWSc 92*
**Wilke,** Beverly Ann 1940- *WhoAmP 91*
**Wilke,** Carl Edward 1920- *WhoMW 92, WhoRel 92*
**Wilke,** Charles R 1917- *AmMWSc 92*
**Wilke,** Frederick Walter 1933- *AmMWSc 92*
**Wilke,** Robert Nielsen 1941- *AmMWSc 92*
**Wilke,** Stephen Kitchens 1955- *WhoMW 92*
**Wilke,** Wayne William 1948- *WhoRel 92*
**Wilken,** David Richard 1934- *AmMWSc 92*
**Wilken,** Dieter H 1944- *AmMWSc 92*
**Wilken,** Donald Rayl 1938- *AmMWSc 92*
**Wilken,** Jimmy Louis 1949- *WhoEnt 92*
**Wilken,** Leon Otto, Jr 1924- *AmMWSc 92*
**Wilken,** Robert Louis 1936- *WhoRel 92*
**Wilkenfeld,** Jason Michael 1939- *AmMWSc 92*
**Wilkening,** Dean Arthur 1950- *AmMWSc 92*
**Wilkening,** George Martin 1923- *AmMWSc 92*
**Wilkening,** Jane Shepard 1943- *WhoWest 92*
**Wilkening,** Laurel Lynn 1944- *AmMWSc 92, WhoWest 92*
**Wilkening,** Marvin C 1920- *AmMWSc 92*
**Wilkening,** Marvin H 1918- *AmMWSc 92*
**Wilkens,** George A 1909- *AmMWSc 92*
**Wilkens,** Jerrel L 1937- *AmMWSc 92*
**Wilkens,** John Albert 1947- *AmMWSc 92*
**Wilkens,** Leonard R. 1937- *WhoBlA 92*
**Wilkens,** Leonard Randolph, Jr. 1937- *WhoMW 92*
**Wilkens,** Lon Allan 1942- *AmMWSc 92*
**Wilkens,** Lucile Shanes 1950- *AmMWSc 92*
**Wilkens,** Robert Allen 1929- *WhoMW 92*
**Wilkens,** Thomas G. 1936- *WhoRel 92*
**Wilkerson,** Charles W 1916- *WhoAmP 91*
**Wilkerson,** Clarence Wendell, Jr 1944- *AmMWSc 92*
**Wilkerson,** Curtis 1926- *WhoAmP 91*
**Wilkerson,** Daniel Jay 1959- *WhoAmL 92*
**Wilkerson,** David Ray 1931- *RelLAm 91*
**Wilkerson,** Dick 1943- *WhoAmP 91*
**Wilkerson,** Henry C. 1922- *WhoBlA 92*
**Wilkerson,** James Edward 1945- *AmMWSc 92*
**Wilkerson,** James Neill 1939- *WhoAmL 92*
**Wilkerson,** Jerry E 1945- *WhoAmP 91*
**Wilkerson,** John Christopher 1926- *AmMWSc 92*
**Wilkerson,** Margaret Buford 1938- *WhoBlA 92*
**Wilkerson,** Marjorie JoAnn Madar 1930- *WhoFI 92*
**Wilkerson,** Mary Piercy 1936- *WhoEnt 92*
**Wilkerson,** Michael *DrAPF 91*
**Wilkerson,** Robert C 1918- *AmMWSc 92*
**Wilkerson,** Robert Douglas 1944- *AmMWSc 92*
**Wilkerson,** Roosevelt, Jr. 1952- *WhoRel 92*
**Wilkerson,** Thomas Delaney 1932- *AmMWSc 92*
**Wilkerson,** Vivian Carol 1939- *WhoEnt 92*
**Wilkerson,** Walter D, Jr 1930- *WhoAmP 91*
**Wilkerson,** William Avery 1938- *WhoAmP 91*
**Wilkerson,** William Holton 1947- *WhoFI 92*
**Wilkes,** Angela Biggs 1952- *WhoMW 92*
**Wilkes,** Charles 1798-1877 *BiInAmS*
**Wilkes,** Charles Eugene 1939- *AmMWSc 92*
**Wilkes,** Charles Fred 1926- *WhoWest 92*
**Wilkes,** Delano Angus 1935- *WhoMW 92*
**Wilkes,** Donald Fancher 1931- *WhoWest 92*
**Wilkes,** Eric 1920- *Who 92*
**Wilkes,** Garth L 1942- *AmMWSc 92*
**Wilkes,** Glenn Richard 1937- *AmMWSc 92*
**Wilkes,** Helen Barbour *WhoAmP 91*
**Wilkes,** Hilbert Garrison, Jr 1937- *AmMWSc 92*
**Wilkes,** Jamaal 1953- *WhoBlA 92*
**Wilkes,** James C 1921- *AmMWSc 92*
**Wilkes,** James Oscroft 1932- *AmMWSc 92*
**Wilkes,** Jennifer Ruth 1960- *WhoWest 92*
**Wilkes,** John 1725-1797 *BlkwEAR*
**Wilkes,** John 1727-1797 *BlkwCEP*
**Wilkes,** John Barker 1916- *AmMWSc 92*
**Wilkes,** John Douglas 1952- *WhoEnt 92*
**Wilkes,** John Joseph 1936- *Who 92*
**Wilkes,** John Stuart 1947- *AmMWSc 92*
**Wilkes,** Joseph Wray 1922- *AmMWSc 92*
**Wilkes,** Lorna M 1943- *WhoAmP 91*
**Wilkes,** Lyall d1991 *Who 92N*
**Wilkes,** Maurice V 1913- *AmMWSc 92*
**Wilkes,** Maurice Vincent 1913- *IntWW 91, Who 92*
**Wilkes,** Michael 1940- *Who 92*
**Wilkes,** Michael Jocelyn James P. *Who 92*
**Wilkes,** Paul 1938- *WhoEnt 92*
**Wilkes,** Penny Ferance 1946- *WhoWest 92*
**Wilkes,** Peter 1937- *WhoRel 92*
**Wilkes,** Reggie Wayman 1956- *WhoBlA 92*
**Wilkes,** Richard Geoffrey 1928- *Who 92*
**Wilkes,** Richard Jeffrey 1945- *AmMWSc 92*
**Wilkes,** Robert Lee 1942- *WhoWest 92*
**Wilkes,** Rodney Adolphus *BlkOlyM*
**Wilkes,** Shelby R. 1950- *WhoBlA 92*
**Wilkes,** Stanley Northrup 1927- *AmMWSc 92*
**Wilkes,** Stella H *AmMWSc 92*
**Wilkes,** Timothy C 1948- *WhoAmP 91*
**Wilkes,** William R. 1902- *WhoBlA 92*
**Wilkes,** William Roy 1939- *AmMWSc 92*
**Wilkey,** Cynthia Denise 1961- *WhoRel 92*
**Wilkie,** Bruce Nicholson 1941- *AmMWSc 92*
**Wilkie,** Charles Arthur 1941- *AmMWSc 92*
**Wilkie,** Donald W 1931- *AmMWSc 92*
**Wilkie,** Donald Walter 1931- *WhoWest 92*
**Wilkie,** Douglas Robert 1922- *IntWW 91, Who 92*
**Wilkie,** Earl A. 1930- *WhoBlA 92*
**Wilkie,** Gerry L *WhoAmP 91*
**Wilkie,** John Frederick 1951- *WhoFI 92*
**Wilkie,** Margery Michelle 1958- *WhoWest 92*
**Wilkin,** Eugene Welch 1923- *WhoEnt 92, WhoWest 92*
**Wilkin,** John 1916- *Who 92*
**Wilkin,** John Martin 1949- *WhoRel 92*
**Wilkin,** Jonathan Keith 1945- *AmMWSc 92*
**Wilkin,** Louis Alden 1939- *AmMWSc 92*
**Wilkin,** Miles Clifford 1948- *WhoEnt 92*
**Wilkin,** Peter J 1943- *AmMWSc 92*
**Wilkin,** Ruth Warren 1918- *WhoAmP 91*
**Wilkins,** Allen Henry 1934- *WhoBlA 92*
**Wilkins,** Arthur Norman 1925- *WhoMW 92*
**Wilkins,** Bert, Jr 1934- *AmMWSc 92*
**Wilkins,** Betty 1922- *WhoBlA 92*
**Wilkins,** Brian John Samuel 1937- *AmMWSc 92*
**Wilkins,** Bruce Tabor 1931- *AmMWSc 92*
**Wilkins,** Bryan James 1961- *WhoRel 92*
**Wilkins,** C Howard, Jr 1938- *WhoAmP 91*
**Wilkins,** Caroline Hanke 1937- *WhoAmP 91, WhoWest 92*
**Wilkins,** Charles H T 1920- *AmMWSc 92*
**Wilkins,** Charles L. 1938- *WhoWest 92*
**Wilkins,** Charles Lee 1938- *AmMWSc 92*
**Wilkins,** Charles O. 1938- *WhoBlA 92*
**Wilkins,** Christopher Putnam 1957- *WhoWest 92*
**Wilkins,** Cletus Walter, Jr 1945- *AmMWSc 92*
**Wilkins,** Curtis C 1935- *AmMWSc 92*
**Wilkins,** David Horton 1946- *WhoAmP 91*
**Wilkins,** David Ray 1940- *WhoEnt 92*
**Wilkins,** Diane Louise 1957- *WhoEnt 92*
**Wilkins,** Dominique 1960- *WhoBlA 92*
**Wilkins,** Ebtisam A M Seoudi 1945- *AmMWSc 92*
**Wilkins,** Eddie Lee 1962- *WhoBlA 92*
**Wilkins,** Ervin W. 1919- *WhoBlA 92*
**Wilkins,** Floyd, Jr. 1925- *WhoAmL 92*
**Wilkins,** Gary Clifton 1963- *WhoBlA 92*
**Wilkins,** Gerald Bernard 1963- *WhoBlA 92*
**Wilkins,** Graham John 1924- *IntWW 91, Who 92*
**Wilkins,** Harold 1933- *AmMWSc 92*
**Wilkins,** Helen Elizabeth 1943- *WhoEnt 92*
**Wilkins,** Henry, III 1930- *WhoAmP 91, WhoBlA 92*
**Wilkins,** Herbert P 1930- *WhoAmP 91*
**Wilkins,** Herbert Priestly 1942- *WhoBlA 92*
**Wilkins,** Herbert Putnam 1930- *WhoAmL 92*
**Wilkins,** Howell Oscar 1922- *WhoRel 92*
**Wilkins,** J Ernest, Jr 1923- *AmMWSc 92*
**Wilkins,** Jerry Lynn 1936- *WhoAmL 92, WhoFI 92*
**Wilkins,** Jesse Theodore 1947- *WhoBlA 92*
**Wilkins,** John Anthony Francis 1936- *Who 92*
**Wilkins,** John Stephen 1945- *WhoEnt 92*
**Wilkins,** John Steven 1952- *WhoFI 92*
**Wilkins,** Judd Rice 1920- *AmMWSc 92*
**Wilkins,** Kay H. 1940- *WhoWest 92*
**Wilkins,** Keith Edward 1952- *WhoRel 92*
**Wilkins,** Kenneth C. 1952- *WhoBlA 92*
**Wilkins,** Leona B. 1922- *WhoBlA 92*
**Wilkins,** Lucy Lee 1934- *WhoAmP 91*
**Wilkins,** Malcolm Barrett 1933- *Who 92*
**Wilkins,** Mark Thomas 1956- *WhoEnt 92*
**Wilkins,** Mary E. *BenetAL 91*
**Wilkins,** Maurice Gray, Jr. 1931- *WhoFI 92*
**Wilkins,** Maurice Hugh Frederick 1916- *IntWW 91, Who 92, WhoNob 90*
**Wilkins,** Merlin James 1928- *WhoRel 92*
**Wilkins,** Michael 1933- *Who 92*
**Wilkins,** Michael James 1949- *WhoRel 92*
**Wilkins,** Mira 1931- *WhoFI 92*
**Wilkins,** Nancy 1932- *Who 92*
**Wilkins,** Ormsby *WhoEnt 92*
**Wilkins,** Ralph G 1927- *AmMWSc 92*
**Wilkins,** Raymond Leslie 1925- *AmMWSc 92*
**Wilkins,** Richard Allan 1938- *WhoEnt 92*
**Wilkins,** Richard Gundersen 1952- *WhoWest 92*
**Wilkins,** Rillastine Roberta 1932- *WhoBlA 92*
**Wilkins,** Robert Pearce, Jr. 1956- *WhoAmL 92*
**Wilkins,** Roger 1932- *ConBlB 2 [port]*
**Wilkins,** Roger C. 1906- *IntWW 91*
**Wilkins,** Roger L. 1928- *WhoBlA 92*
**Wilkins,** Roger Lawrence 1928- *AmMWSc 92*
**Wilkins,** Roger Wood 1932- *WhoBlA 92*
**Wilkins,** Ronald Wayne 1943- *AmMWSc 92*
**Wilkins,** Roy 1901-1981 *FacFETw*
**Wilkins,** S Vance, Jr 1936- *WhoAmP 91*
**Wilkins,** Susan *DrAPF 91*
**Wilkins,** Thomas A. 1930- *WhoBlA 92*
**Wilkins,** Thomas Alphonso 1956- *WhoBlA 92*
**Wilkins,** Thomas Wayne 1958- *WhoRel 92*
**Wilkins,** Tracy Dale 1943- *AmMWSc 92*
**Wilkins,** W. David 1963- *WhoEnt 92*
**Wilkins,** W. Gary 1945- *WhoHisp 92*
**Wilkins,** William S. 1942- *WhoFI 92*
**Wilkins,** William W, Jr *WhoAmP 91*
**Wilkins,** William Walter, Jr. 1942- *WhoAmL 92*
**Wilkins,** Willie T. 1929- *WhoBlA 92*
**Wilkinson,** A Williams 1832-1908 *BiInAmS*
**Wilkinson,** Alan Bassindale 1931- *Who 92*
**Wilkinson,** Alec 1952- *WrDr 92*
**Wilkinson,** Alexander Birrell 1932- *Who 92*
**Wilkinson,** Andrew Wood 1914- *Who 92*
**Wilkinson,** Anne 1910-1961 *BenetAL 91, RfGEnL 91*
**Wilkinson,** Anthony Bawden 1940- *WhoEnt 92*
**Wilkinson,** Brenda 1946- *WhoBlA 92*
**Wilkinson,** Brian James 1946- *AmMWSc 92*
**Wilkinson,** Bruce H 1942- *AmMWSc 92*
**Wilkinson,** Bruce Herbert 1947- *WhoRel 92*
**Wilkinson,** Bruce W 1928- *AmMWSc 92*
**Wilkinson,** Burke 1913- *WrDr 92*
**Wilkinson,** C.E. *DrAPF 91*
**Wilkinson,** Carol Lynn *DrAPF 91*
**Wilkinson,** Cecilia Alta 1949- *WhoWest 92*
**Wilkinson,** Charles Allan 1930- *WhoMW 92*
**Wilkinson,** Charles Brock 1922- *AmMWSc 92, WhoBlA 92*
**Wilkinson,** Charles Francis 1957- *WhoAmL 92*
**Wilkinson,** Christopher Foster 1938- *AmMWSc 92*
**Wilkinson,** Christopher Richard 1941- *Who 92*
**Wilkinson,** Clive Victor 1938- *Who 92*
**Wilkinson,** D. G. B. *Who 92*
**Wilkinson,** Daniel Francis 1940- *WhoFI 92, WhoWest 92*
**Wilkinson,** Daniel R 1938- *AmMWSc 92*
**Wilkinson,** Daniel Ralph 1938- *WhoMW 92*
**Wilkinson,** David Anthony 1947- *Who 92*
**Wilkinson,** David Ian 1932- *AmMWSc 92*
**Wilkinson,** David L 1936- *WhoAmP 91*
**Wilkinson,** David Lawrence 1936- *WhoWest 92*
**Wilkinson,** David Lloyd 1937- *Who 92*
**Wilkinson,** David Lowell 1933- *WhoMW 92*
**Wilkinson,** David Todd 1935- *AmMWSc 92*
**Wilkinson,** Denys 1922- *Who 92, WrDr 92*
**Wilkinson,** Denys Haigh 1922- *IntWW 91*
**Wilkinson,** Donald Charles 1936- *WhoBlA 92*
**Wilkinson,** Donald McLean, Jr. 1938- *WhoFI 92*
**Wilkinson,** Doris Yvonne *WhoBlA 92*
**Wilkinson,** Elizabeth Mary 1909- *Who 92*
**Wilkinson,** Eugene P Dennis 1918- *AmMWSc 92*
**Wilkinson,** Frank Smith, Jr 1939- *WhoIns 92*
**Wilkinson,** Frederick D., Jr. 1921- *WhoBlA 92*
**Wilkinson,** Geoffrey 1921- *AmMWSc 92, IntWW 91, Who 92, WhoNob 90*
**Wilkinson,** Geoffrey Crichton 1926- *Who 92*
**Wilkinson,** Graham 1947- *Who 92*
**Wilkinson,** Grant Robert 1941- *AmMWSc 92*
**Wilkinson,** Harold L 1941- *AmMWSc 92*
**Wilkinson,** Hazel Wiley *AmMWSc 92*
**Wilkinson,** Heather Carol *Who 92*
**Wilkinson,** J Harvie, III *WhoAmP 91*
**Wilkinson,** Jack Dale 1931- *AmMWSc 92*
**Wilkinson,** James 1757-1825 *BenetAL 91*
**Wilkinson,** James Allan 1945- *WhoAmL 92*
**Wilkinson,** James Edward 1948- *WhoFI 92*
**Wilkinson,** James Harvie, III 1944- *WhoAmL 92*
**Wilkinson,** James Wellington 1935- *WhoBlA 92*
**Wilkinson,** Jeffrey Vernon 1930- *Who 92*
**Wilkinson,** John 1929- *WrDr 92*
**Wilkinson,** John Arbuthnot Du Cane 1940- *Who 92*
**Wilkinson,** John Edwin 1942- *AmMWSc 92*
**Wilkinson,** John Francis 1926- *Who 92*
**Wilkinson,** John Frederick 1897- *IntWW 91, Who 92*

**Wilkinson,** John Peter Darrell 1938- *AmMWSc 92*
**Wilkinson,** John Taylor 1955- *WhoWest 92*
**Wilkinson,** John Wesley 1928- *AmMWSc 92*
**Wilkinson,** Kathie Stevens 1952- *WhoRel 92*
**Wilkinson,** Kathleen Diane 1957- *WhoAmL 92*
**Wilkinson,** Keith Howard 1948- *Who 92*
**Wilkinson,** Kenneth Grahame d1990 *IntWW 91N, Who 92N*
**Wilkinson,** Larry Dale 1936- *WhoRel 92*
**Wilkinson,** Lawrence Hamlett 1950- *WhoEnt 92, WhoFI 92*
**Wilkinson,** Leon Guy 1928- *Who 92*
**Wilkinson,** Marguerite 1883-1928 *BenetAL 91*
**Wilkinson,** Marie L. 1910- *WhoBlA 92*
**Wilkinson,** Martin 1911-1990 *AnObit 1990*
**Wilkinson,** Mary Ellen 1947- *WhoWest 92*
**Wilkinson,** Michael Kennerly 1921- *AmMWSc 92*
**Wilkinson,** Nicholas John 1941- *Who 92*
**Wilkinson,** Nicolas Christopher Henry B. *Who 92*
**Wilkinson,** Nigel Vivian Marshall 1949- *Who 92*
**Wilkinson,** Norman 1878-1971 *TwCPaSc*
**Wilkinson,** Paul 1937- *IntWW 91, Who 92, WrDr 92*
**Wilkinson,** Paul Kenneth 1945- *AmMWSc 92*
**Wilkinson,** Paul R 1919- *AmMWSc 92*
**Wilkinson,** Peter 1914- *Who 92*
**Wilkinson,** Philip 1927- *Who 92*
**Wilkinson,** Philip Richard 1961- *WhoAmL 92*
**Wilkinson,** Philip William 1927- *IntWW 91*
**Wilkinson,** Ralph Russell 1930- *AmMWSc 92*
**Wilkinson,** Raymond George 1922- *AmMWSc 92*
**Wilkinson,** Raymond M., Jr. 1943- *WhoBlA 92*
**Wilkinson,** Raymond Stewart 1919- *Who 92*
**Wilkinson,** Richard Denys 1946- *Who 92*
**Wilkinson,** Richard Francis, Jr. 1944- *WhoFI 92*
**Wilkinson,** Richard K. 1957- *WhoAmL 92*
**Wilkinson,** Robert Cleveland, Jr 1923- *AmMWSc 92*
**Wilkinson,** Robert Eugene 1926- *AmMWSc 92*
**Wilkinson,** Robert Haydn 1926- *AmMWSc 92*
**Wilkinson,** Robert Purdy 1933- *Who 92*
**Wilkinson,** Robert Shaw, Jr. 1928- *WhoBlA 92*
**Wilkinson,** Robert Steven 1955- *WhoBlA 92*
**Wilkinson,** Robin Eve 1958- *WhoAmL 92*
**Wilkinson,** Ronald Craig 1943- *AmMWSc 92*
**Wilkinson,** Rose 1940- *WhoEnt 92*
**Wilkinson,** Rosemary C. *DrAPF 91*
**Wilkinson,** Rosemary Regina Challoner 1924- *WhoWest 92*
**Wilkinson,** Sheppard Field *WhoBlA 92*
**Wilkinson,** Stanley R 1931- *AmMWSc 92*
**Wilkinson,** Sylvia *DrAPF 91*
**Wilkinson,** Sylvia J. 1940- *WrDr 92*
**Wilkinson,** Thomas Lloyd, Jr 1939- *AmMWSc 92*
**Wilkinson,** Thomas Lynn 1948- *WhoMW 92*
**Wilkinson,** Thomas Preston 1941- *AmMWSc 92*
**Wilkinson,** Thomas Ross 1937- *AmMWSc 92*
**Wilkinson,** Tim 1912- *WrDr 92*
**Wilkinson,** W C 1914- *AmMWSc 92*
**Wilkinson,** Wallace G. 1941- *AlmAP 92 [port], IntWW 91, WhoAmP 91*
**Wilkinson,** Warren Scripps 1920- *WhoFI 92*
**Wilkinson,** William 1932- *Who 92*
**Wilkinson,** William H 1927- *AmMWSc 92*
**Wilkinson,** William Kenneth 1918- *AmMWSc 92*
**Wilkinson,** William Lionel 1931- *Who 92*
**Wilkinson,** William Lyle 1921- *AmMWSc 92*
**Wilkinson,** Winifred *WrDr 92*
**Wilkinson Herron,** Laura 1957- *WhoWest 92*
**Wilkinson-Latham,** Robert John 1943- *WrDr 92*
**Wilkniss,** Peter Eberhard 1934- *AmMWSc 92*
**Wilkoff,** Lee Joseph 1924- *AmMWSc 92*
**Wilkomirska,** Wanda 1929- *IntWW 91*
**Wilkomirski,** Josef 1926- *WhoEnt 92*
**Wilkov,** Robert Spencer 1943- *AmMWSc 92*
**Wilkow,** Clifton Jack *WhoMW 92*
**Wilkowske,** Howard Hugo 1917- *AmMWSc 92*
**Wilks,** Gertrude 1927- *WhoBlA 92*
**Wilks,** Jean Ruth Fraser 1917- *Who 92*
**Wilks,** Jim *Who 92*
**Wilks,** John William 1944- *AmMWSc 92*
**Wilks,** Larry Dean 1955- *WhoAmL 92*
**Wilks,** Louis Phillip 1913- *AmMWSc 92*
**Wilks,** Stanley David 1920- *Who 92*
**Will,** Clark Bradford 1955- *WhoAmL 92*
**Will,** Clifford Martin 1946- *AmMWSc 92*
**Will,** Edward Edmund 1952- *WhoFI 92*
**Will,** Eric 1959- *WhoAmP 91*
**Will,** Frederic *DrAPF 91*
**Will,** Frit Gustav 1931- *AmMWSc 92*
**Will,** Fritz, III 1926- *AmMWSc 92*
**Will,** George F 1941- *FacFETw, WhoAmP 91, WrDr 92*
**Will,** George Frederick 1941- *IntAu&W 91*
**Will,** Hubert Louis 1914- *WhoAmL 92, WhoMW 92*
**Will,** James Arthur 1930- *AmMWSc 92*
**Will,** James Edward 1928- *WhoRel 92*
**Will,** John Junior 1924- *AmMWSc 92*
**Will,** Paul Arthur 1946- *AmMWSc 92*
**Will,** Peter Milne 1935- *AmMWSc 92, WhoWest 92*
**Will,** Robert John 1963- *WhoAmL 92*
**Will,** Robert Joseph 1957- *WhoFI 92*
**Will,** Ronald Kerr 1918- *Who 92*
**Will,** Theodore A 1937- *AmMWSc 92*
**Will,** Thomas Eric 1949- *WhoMW 92*
**Will,** Timothy Joseph 1960- *WhoWest 92*
**Will,** Trevor Jonathan 1953- *WhoAmL 92*
**Willacy,** Hazel M. 1946- *WhoBlA 92*
**Willacy,** Michael James Ormerod 1933- *Who 92*
**Willaert,** Adrian 1485?-1562 *NewAmDM*
**Willaert,** Andrew Alois, Jr. 1958- *WhoAmL 92*
**Willaman,** Jerry Bruce 1957- *WhoFI 92*
**Willan,** Edward Gervase 1917- *Who 92*
**Willan,** Healey 1880-1968 *NewAmDM*
**Willan,** Thomas Stuart 1910- *Who 92*
**Willans,** Jean Stone 1924- *WhoRel 92*
**Willard,** Barbara 1909- *IntAu&W 91, WrDr 92*
**Willard,** Charles A. d1991 *NewYTBS 91*
**Willard,** Daniel 1926- *AmMWSc 92*
**Willard,** Daniel Edward 1934- *AmMWSc 92*
**Willard,** De Forest 1846-1910 *BiInAmS*
**Willard,** Edward N 1945- *WhoIns 92*
**Willard,** Emma Hart 1787-1870 *BenetAL 91, HanAmWH*
**Willard,** Frances 1839-1898 *RComAH*
**Willard,** Frances E. 1839-1898 *HanAmWH*
**Willard,** Frances Elizabeth 1839-1898 *AmPeW, BenetAL 91, RelLAm 91*
**Willard,** Frederick Harold 1959- *WhoEnt 92*
**Willard,** Gregory Dale 1954- *WhoAmL 92*
**Willard,** Harrison Robert 1933- *WhoFI 92, WhoWest 92*
**Willard,** James Douglas 1945- *WhoWest 92*
**Willard,** James Matthew 1939- *AmMWSc 92*
**Willard,** John Ela 1908- *AmMWSc 92*
**Willard,** John Gerard 1952- *WhoFI 92*
**Willard,** John Martin 1946- *WhoAmL 92*
**Willard,** Joseph 1738-1804 *BiInAmS*
**Willard,** Josiah Flynt 1869-1907 *BenetAL 91*
**Willard,** Mark Alan 1946- *WhoAmL 92*
**Willard,** Mark Benjamin 1943- *AmMWSc 92*
**Willard,** Mildred Wilds 1911-1978 *ConAu 135*
**Willard,** Nancy *DrAPF 91*
**Willard,** Nancy 1936- *ConPo 91*
**Willard,** Nancy Margaret *IntAu&W 91*
**Willard,** Paul Edwin 1919- *AmMWSc 92*
**Willard,** Paul W 1933- *AmMWSc 92*
**Willard,** Robert Edgar 1929- *WhoAmL 92*
**Willard,** Robert Jackson 1929- *AmMWSc 92, WhoMW 92*
**Willard,** Samuel 1640-1707 *BenetAL 91*
**Willard,** Thomas Maxwell 1937- *AmMWSc 92*
**Willard,** Thomas Spaulding 1944- *WhoWest 92*
**Willard,** William Kenneth 1929- *AmMWSc 92*
**Willard-Gallo,** Karen Elizabeth 1953- *AmMWSc 92*
**Willardson,** Lyman S 1927- *AmMWSc 92*
**Willardson,** Robert Kent 1923- *AmMWSc 92*
**Willat,** Boyd I. 1943- *WhoWest 92*
**Willats,** Stephen 1943- *IntWW 91, TwCPaSc*
**Willatt,** Hugh 1909- *IntWW 91, Who 92*
**Willbanks,** Emily West 1930- *AmMWSc 92*
**Willbanks,** Roger Paul 1934- *WhoFI 92, WhoWest 92*
**Willcock,** Kenneth Milner *Who 92*
**Willcock,** Malcolm Maurice 1925- *Who 92*
**Willcocks,** David 1919- *IntWW 91, NewAmDM, Who 92*
**Willcott,** Mark Robert, III 1933- *AmMWSc 92*
**Willcox,** Alfred Burton 1925- *AmMWSc 92*
**Willcox,** Breckinridge Long 1944- *WhoAmL 92*
**Willcox,** James Henry 1923- *Who 92*
**Willcox,** Joseph Karl 1941- *WhoAmL 92*
**Willden,** Charles Ronald 1929- *AmMWSc 92*
**Willden,** Gary Delbert 1946- *WhoWest 92*
**Wille,** Gunnar Edvard 1937- *WhoFI 92*
**Wille,** John Jacob, Jr 1937- *AmMWSc 92*
**Wille,** Lois Jean 1932- *WhoMW 92*
**Wille,** Luc Theo 1956- *AmMWSc 92*
**Willeboordse,** Friso *AmMWSc 92*
**Willebrands,** Johannes Gerardus Maria 1909- *DcEcMov, IntWW 91, Who 92, WhoRel 92*
**Willeford,** Bennett Rufus, Jr 1921- *AmMWSc 92*
**Willeford,** Charles 1919- *IntAu&W 91*
**Willeke,** Gene E. 1934- *WhoMW 92*
**Willeke,** Klaus 1941- *AmMWSc 92*
**Willemot,** Claude 1933- *AmMWSc 92*
**Willems,** Arnold Lee 1942- *WhoWest 92*
**Willems,** Elizabeth Leodena 1937- *WhoRel 92*
**Willems,** Frank J 1919- *WhoAmP 91*
**Willems,** Jan C 1939- *AmMWSc 92*
**Willems,** Nicholas 1924- *AmMWSc 92*
**Willemsen,** Alan Mitchell 1933- *WhoIns 92*
**Willemsen,** Herman William 1945- *AmMWSc 92*
**Willemsen,** Roger Wayne 1944- *AmMWSc 92*
**Willen,** H. Douglas 1959- *WhoAmL 92*
**Willenberg,** Harvey Jack 1945- *AmMWSc 92*
**Willenberger,** Hans 1940- *WhoMW 92*
**Willenbrock,** Frederick Karl 1920- *AmMWSc 92*
**Willens,** Robert 1946- *WhoFI 92*
**Willensky,** Elliot 1933- *IntAu&W 91, WrDr 92*
**Willensky,** Elliot 1933-1990 *AnObit 1990*
**Willenz,** Nicole Valli 1958- *WhoMW 92*
**Willenzik,** David S. 1946- *WhoAmL 92*
**Willer,** Charles Franklin 1954- *WhoEnt 92*
**Willer,** Lynn Michael 1956- *WhoEnt 92*
**Willer,** Rodney Lee 1948- *AmMWSc 92*
**Willermet,** Pierre Andre 1941- *AmMWSc 92*
**Willerson,** James Thornton *AmMWSc 92*
**Willert,** John A 1930- *WhoIns 92*
**Willerton,** Chris *DrAPF 91*
**Willerton,** John Patton, Jr. 1953- *WhoWest 92*
**Willes,** Mark Hinckley 1941- *WhoFI 92*
**Willes,** S Blaine 1934- *WhoAmP 91*
**Willesden,** Area Bishop of *Who 92*
**Willesee,** Donald Robert 1916- *IntWW 91, Who 92*
**Willet,** Gerald L 1934- *WhoAmP 91*
**Willett,** Archibald Anthony 1924- *Who 92*
**Willett,** Colin Sidney 1935- *AmMWSc 92*
**Willett,** Douglas W 1937- *AmMWSc 92*
**Willett,** Edward Farrand, Jr. 1933- *WhoAmL 92*
**Willett,** Frank 1925- *Who 92, WrDr 92*
**Willett,** Frederick John 1922- *Who 92*
**Willett,** Hilda Pope 1923- *AmMWSc 92*
**Willett,** James Delos 1937- *AmMWSc 92*
**Willett,** John 1917- *WrDr 92*
**Willett,** Joseph Erwin 1929- *AmMWSc 92*
**Willett,** Lynn Brunson 1944- *AmMWSc 92*
**Willett,** Norman P 1928- *AmMWSc 92*
**Willett,** Noyes Watters, III 1924- *WhoEnt 92*
**Willett,** Richard Michael 1945- *AmMWSc 92*
**Willett,** Robert Lee 1935- *WhoMW 92*
**Willett,** Roger 1936- *AmMWSc 92*
**Willett,** Roger DuWayne 1936- *WhoWest 92*
**Willett,** Thomas Eugene 1938- *WhoEnt 92*
**Willette,** Gordon Louis 1933- *AmMWSc 92*
**Willette,** Robert Edmond 1933- *AmMWSc 92*
**Willetts,** Bernard Frederick 1927- *IntWW 91, Who 92*
**Willetts,** David Lindsay 1956- *Who 92*
**Willetts,** Jeffory Dean 1959- *WhoRel 92*
**Willetts,** Ronald Frederick 1915- *WrDr 92*
**Willey,** Basil 1897-1978 *ConAu 135*
**Willey,** Charles Wayne 1932- *WhoAmL 92*
**Willey,** Cliff Rufus 1935- *AmMWSc 92*
**Willey,** Craig Leander 1966- *WhoMW 92*
**Willey,** Elizabeth Lou 1952- *WhoAmP 91*
**Willey,** Frank Patrick 1953- *WhoAmL 92*
**Willey,** Gordon Randolph 1913- *IntWW 91*
**Willey,** Henry 1824-1907 *BiInAmS*
**Willey,** James Lee 1953- *WhoMW 92*
**Willey,** Joan DeWitt 1948- *AmMWSc 92*
**Willey,** Lawrence *WhoAmP 91*
**Willey,** Margaret *DrAPF 91*
**Willey,** Mary Louise *DrAPF 91*
**Willey,** N Laurence, Jr 1949- *WhoAmP 91*
**Willey,** Robert Bruce 1930- *AmMWSc 92*
**Willey,** Ruth Lippitt 1928- *AmMWSc 92*
**Willey,** Stephen Douglas 1950- *WhoAmL 92*
**Willford,** Loren 1939- *WhoAmP 91*
**Willham,** Richard Lewis 1932- *AmMWSc 92*
**Willhelm,** Sidney McLarty 1934- *WrDr 92*
**Willhide,** Gary L. 1944- *WhoWest 92*
**Willhite,** Calvin Campbell 1952- *AmMWSc 92*
**Willhite,** Glen Paul 1937- *AmMWSc 92*
**Willhoit,** Donald Gillmor 1934- *AmMWSc 92*
**Willhoit,** Jim 1943- *WhoMW 92, WhoRel 92*
**Willi,** Jim 1948- *WhoEnt 92*
**William of Auvergne** 1190?-1249 *DcLB 115*
**William of Conches** 1090?-1154? *DcLB 115*
**William of Sherwood** 1200?-1266? *DcLB 115*
**William,** David 1926- *IntWW 91*
**William,** James C, Jr *AmMWSc 92*
**William,** Marian *WhoRel 92*
**William,** Thompson E. 1924- *WhoBlA 92*
**Williams** *Who 92*
**Williams,** A Ben, Jr 1919- *WhoIns 92*
**Williams,** A. Cecil 1929- *WhoBlA 92*
**Williams,** A. L. 1917- *WhoRel 92*
**Williams,** Aaron, Jr 1942- *AmMWSc 92*
**Williams,** Ada L. 1933- *WhoBlA 92*
**Williams,** Addie Gatewood 1899- *WhoBlA 92*
**Williams,** Adella J 1918- *WhoAmP 91*
**Williams,** Al 1930- *WhoAmP 91*
**Williams,** Alan 1935- *WrDr 92*
**Williams,** Alan 1952- *WhoRel 92*
**Williams,** Alan Evan 1952- *AmMWSc 92*
**Williams,** Alan Frederick 1945- *Who 92*
**Williams,** Alan Harold 1927- *Who 92*
**Williams,** Alan John 1930- *Who 92*
**Williams,** Alan K 1928- *AmMWSc 92*
**Williams,** Alan Lee 1930- *Who 92, WrDr 92*
**Williams,** Alan Moray 1915- *IntAu&W 91*
**Williams,** Alan Wynne 1945- *Who 92*
**Williams,** Alastair Edgcumbe James D. *Who 92*
**Williams,** Albert 1927- *Who 92*
**Williams,** Albert J, Jr 1903- *AmMWSc 92*
**Williams,** Albert James, III 1940- *AmMWSc 92*
**Williams,** Albert P. *WhoBlA 92*
**Williams,** Albert Paine 1935- *WhoFI 92, WhoWest 92*
**Williams,** Albert Simpson 1924- *AmMWSc 92*
**Williams,** Albert Trevor 1938- *Who 92*
**Williams,** Alexander 1931- *Who 92*
**Williams,** Alexander Stephens, III 1936- *WhoIns 92*
**Williams,** Alfred *ScFEYrs*
**Williams,** Alfred T. 1930- *WhoAmL 92*
**Williams,** Allan Frederick 1956- *WhoMW 92*
**Williams,** Allan Silvio 1925- *WhoAmP 91*
**Williams,** Alma Minton 1937- *WhoBlA 92*
**Williams,** Alphonza 1933- *WhoBlA 92*
**Williams,** Althea Bulls *WhoBlA 92*
**Williams,** Alwyn 1921- *IntWW 91, Who 92*
**Williams,** Andrew 1899- *WhoBlA 92*
**Williams,** Andrew 1946- *WhoAmL 92*
**Williams,** Andrew 1954- *TwCPaSc*
**Williams,** Andrew Mark 1958- *WhoFI 92*
**Williams,** Andy 1930- *WhoEnt 92*
**Williams,** Angie Bass 1939- *WhoBlA 92*
**Williams,** Anita Spencer *WhoBlA 92*
**Williams,** Ann C. 1949- *WhoAmL 92*
**Williams,** Ann Claire 1949- *WhoBlA 92*
**Williams,** Ann E. A. 1946- *WhoBlA 92*
**Williams,** Ann Houston 1943- *AmMWSc 92*
**Williams,** Anna Maria 1927- *AmMWSc 92*
**Williams,** Anna Maureen *Who 92*
**Williams,** Annalisa Stubbs 1956- *WhoBlA 92*
**Williams,** Annette Polly 1937- *WhoAmP 91*
**Williams,** Annie M. 1937- *WhoBlA 92*
**Williams,** Anson 1949- *ConTFT 9*
**Williams,** Anthony 1946- *WhoAmL 92*
**Williams,** Anthony J 1949- *WhoAmP 91*
**Williams,** Archibald 1871-1935 *ScFEYrs*
**Williams,** Archibald Franklin 1915- *BlkOlyM*
**Williams,** Ardis Mae 1919- *AmMWSc 92*
**Williams,** Armstrong 1960- *WhoBlA 92*

**Williams,** Arnette L. *WhoBlA 92*
**Williams,** Arsenia Inez 1957- *WhoAmL 92*
**Williams,** Art S. 1912-1978 *WhoBlA 92N*
**Williams,** Arthur 1928- *Who 92*
**Williams,** Arthur Cozad 1926- *WhoEnt 92*
**Williams,** Arthur Ernest 1955- *WhoEnt 92*
**Williams,** Arthur G., Jr. 1919- *WhoBlA 92*
**Williams,** Arthur K. 1945- *WhoBlA 92*
**Williams,** Arthur Lee 1947- *AmMWSc 92*
**Williams,** Arthur Love 1940- *WhoBlA 92*
**Williams,** Arthur Olney, Jr 1913- *AmMWSc 92*
**Williams,** Arthur Robert 1941- *AmMWSc 92*
**Williams,** Arthur Vivian 1909- *Who 92*
**Williams,** Atanda F. *Who 92*
**Williams,** Ather, Jr. 1943- *WhoBlA 92*
**Williams,** Aubin Bernard 1964- *WhoBlA 92*
**Williams,** Aubrey 1926-1990 *AnObit 1990, TwCPaSc*
**Williams,** Austen *Who 92*
**Williams,** Austin Beatty 1919- *AmMWSc 92*
**Williams,** Avon Nyanza, Jr 1921- *WhoAmP 91, WhoBlA 92*
**Williams,** B. John, Jr. 1949- *WhoAmL 92*
**Williams,** Babette Deanna 1960- *WhoAmL 92*
**Williams,** Barbara *WhoRel 92*
**Williams,** Barbara Ann 1945- *WhoBlA 92*
**Williams,** Barbara Elaine 1952- *WhoEnt 92*
**Williams,** Barbara June 1948- *WhoAmL 92, WhoFI 92*
**Williams,** Barry 1932- *WrDr 92*
**Williams,** Bart 1949- *WhoEnt 92*
**Williams,** Basil Hugh G. *Who 92*
**Williams,** Ben Albert 1946- *WhoWest 92*
**Williams,** Ben Ames 1889-1953 *BenetAL 91*
**Williams,** Benjamin Hayden 1921- *AmMWSc 92*
**Williams,** Benjamin Hayden, Jr. 1921- *WhoMW 92*
**Williams,** Benjamin J. *DrAPF 91*
**Williams,** Benjamin Vernon 1927- *WhoBlA 92*
**Williams,** Bennie B 1922- *AmMWSc 92*
**Williams,** Bernadine 1939- *WhoWest 92*
**Williams,** Bernard 1929- *WrDr 92*
**Williams,** Bernard Arthur Owen 1929- *IntWW 91, Who 92*
**Williams,** Berry *WhoAmP 91*
**Williams,** Bert 1874-1922 *NewAmDM*
**Williams,** Bert 1875-1922 *BenetAL 91*
**Williams,** Bert 1922- *IntMPA 92*
**Williams,** Bert 1930- *WrDr 92*
**Williams,** Bert Nolan 1930- *IntAu&W 91*
**Williams,** Bert R., III 1956- *WhoFI 92*
**Williams,** Bertha Mae 1927- *WhoBlA 92*
**Williams,** Beryl E. W. 1913- *WhoBlA 92*
**Williams,** Betty *Who 92*
**Williams,** Betty 1943- *FacFETw, IntWW 91*
**Williams,** Betty Jo 1928- *WhoAmP 91*
**Williams,** Betty L *AmMWSc 92*
**Williams,** Betty Outhier 1947- *WhoAmL 92*
**Williams,** Betty Smith 1929- *WhoBlA 92*
**Williams,** Beverly Beatrice 1932- *WhoWest 92*
**Williams,** Big Joe 1903-1982 *NewAmDM*
**Williams,** Bill 1916- *IntMPA 92*
**Williams,** Billy Dee 1937- *IntMPA 92, WhoBlA 92, WhoEnt 92*
**Williams,** Billy Leo 1938- *WhoBlA 92*
**Williams,** Billy Myles 1950- *WhoBlA 92*
**Williams,** Bismarck 1928- *WhoBlA 92*
**Williams,** Bob *WhoAmP 91*
**Williams,** Bob 1929- *WhoAmP 91*
**Williams,** Bob 1942- *WhoAmP 91*
**Williams,** Bobby 1936- *WhoEnt 92, WhoMW 92*
**Williams,** Bobby Joe 1930- *AmMWSc 92*
**Williams,** Bonnie Kay 1952- *WhoMW 92*
**Williams,** Booker T. 1920- *WhoBlA 92*
**Williams,** Brenda Paulette 1946-1990 *WhoBlA 92N*
**Williams,** Brian Carroll 1951- *WhoAmP 91*
**Williams,** Bronwyn *WrDr 92*
**Williams,** Brown F 1940- *AmMWSc 92*
**Williams,** Bruce 1919- *IntWW 91, Who 92*
**Williams,** Bruce 1934- *WhoAmP 91*
**Williams,** Bruce E. 1931- *WhoBlA 92*
**Williams,** Bruce Livingston 1945- *WhoFI 92*
**Williams,** Bruce Robin 1949- *WhoMW 92*
**Williams,** Bruce Rodda 1919- *WrDr 92*
**Williams,** Bryan 1925- *AmMWSc 92*
**Williams,** Buck 1960- *WhoBlA 92*
**Williams,** Bunnis Curtis 1939- *WhoAmP 91*
**Williams,** Buster 1942- *WhoBlA 92*
**Williams,** Byron Lee, Jr 1920- *AmMWSc 92*
**Williams,** C. Arthur, Jr. 1924- *WrDr 92*
**Williams,** C. J. F. 1930- *WrDr 92*
**Williams,** C. James, III 1960- *WhoAmL 92*
**Williams,** C.K. *DrAPF 91*
**Williams,** C. K. 1936- *ConPo 91, IntAu&W 91, WrDr 92*
**Williams,** Calvin 1946- *WhoMW 92*
**Williams,** Calvit Herndon, Jr 1936- *AmMWSc 92*
**Williams,** Camilla *WhoBlA 92, WhoEnt 92*
**Williams,** Camilla 1922- *NewAmDM*
**Williams,** Campbell *Who 92*
**Williams,** Cara 1925- *IntMPA 92*
**Williams,** Carl Carnelius, Jr. 1926- *WhoRel 92*
**Williams,** Carl Michael 1928- *WhoAmP 91*
**Williams,** Carl W. 1927- *IntMPA 92*
**Williams,** Carla Renata 1961- *WhoEnt 92*
**Williams,** Carletta Celeste 1956- *WhoBlA 92*
**Williams,** Carlton Ray, Jr. 1957- *WhoBlA 92*
**Williams,** Carol Ann 1940- *AmMWSc 92*
**Williams,** Carole A 1947- *AmMWSc 92*
**Williams,** Carolyn Chandler 1947- *WhoBlA 92*
**Williams,** Carolyn Ruth Armstrong 1944- *WhoBlA 92*
**Williams,** Carrington 1919- *WhoAmP 91*
**Williams,** Carroll Burns, Jr 1929- *AmMWSc 92, WhoBlA 92*
**Williams,** Carroll M. d1991 *NewYTBS 91*
**Williams,** Carroll Milton 1916- *AmMWSc 92, IntWW 91*
**Williams,** Carroll Warner 1931- *WhoEnt 92*
**Williams,** Cassandra Faye 1948- *WhoBlA 92*
**Williams,** Catherine G. 1914- *WhoBlA 92*
**Williams,** Catrin Mary 1922- *Who 92*
**Williams,** Cecil Beaumont 1926- *Who 92*
**Williams,** Charlene J. 1949- *WhoBlA 92*
**Williams,** Charles 1886-1945 *RfGEnL 91*
**Williams,** Charles A. 1942- *WhoBlA 92*
**Williams,** Charles Arthur 1950- *WhoMW 92*
**Williams,** Charles Bernard 1925- *Who 92*
**Williams,** Charles C. 1939- *WhoBlA 92*
**Williams,** Charles D. *WhoRel 92*
**Williams,** Charles Dudley 1933- *WhoFI 92*
**Williams,** Charles E., III 1946- *WhoBlA 92*
**Williams,** Charles Finn, II 1954- *WhoFI 92*
**Williams,** Charles Frederick 1924- *WhoBlA 92*
**Williams,** Charles Haddon, Jr 1932- *AmMWSc 92*
**Williams,** Charles Herbert 1935- *AmMWSc 92*
**Williams,** Charles J., Sr. 1942- *WhoBlA 92*
**Williams,** Charles Judson 1930- *WhoAmL 92*
**Williams,** Charles Lee 1947- *WhoFI 92, WhoWest 92*
**Williams,** Charles Melville 1925- *AmMWSc 92*
**Williams,** Charles Michael *ScFEYrs*
**Williams,** Charles Michael 1955- *WhoAmL 92*
**Williams,** Charles Pickens 1926- *WhoFI 92*
**Williams,** Charles Richard 1948- *WhoBlA 92*
**Williams,** Charles S 1926- *WhoIns 92*
**Williams,** Charles Thomas 1916- *WhoBlA 92*
**Williams,** Charles Thomas 1941- *WhoBlA 92*
**Williams,** Charles Van 1944- *WhoAmP 91*
**Williams,** Charles Wesley 1931- *AmMWSc 92*
**Williams,** Charlie G *WhoAmP 91*
**Williams,** Charlotte Bell 1944- *WhoFI 92*
**Williams,** Charlotte Leola 1928- *WhoBlA 92*
**Williams,** Chester 1921- *TwCPaSc*
**Williams,** Chester Arthur *WhoBlA 92*
**Williams,** Chester Lee 1944- *WhoBlA 92*
**Williams,** Christine 1943- *AmMWSc 92*
**Williams,** Christopher *Who 92*
**Williams,** Christopher 1873-1934 *TwCPaSc*
**Williams,** Christopher Noel 1935- *AmMWSc 92*
**Williams,** Christopher P S 1931- *AmMWSc 92*
**Williams,** Christopher Randolph 1962- *WhoEnt 92*
**Williams,** Cicely Delphine 1893- *Who 92*
**Williams,** Cindy 1947- *IntMPA 92*
**Williams,** Cindy J. 1947- *WhoEnt 92*
**Williams,** Clara Belle 1885- *WhoBlA 92*
**Williams,** Clarence 1898-1965 *NewAmDM*
**Williams,** Clarence 1945- *WhoBlA 92*
**Williams,** Clarence Earl, Jr. 1950- *WhoBlA 92*
**Williams,** Clarence G. 1938- *WhoBlA 92*
**Williams,** Clarice Leona 1936- *WhoBlA 92*
**Williams,** Clark D *WhoAmP 91*
**Williams,** Claudette *WrDr 92*
**Williams,** Clay Rule 1935- *WhoAmL 92, WhoMW 92*
**Williams,** Clayton Drews 1935- *AmMWSc 92*
**Williams,** Clayton Richard 1920- *WhoBlA 92*
**Williams,** Clifford 1926- *Who 92*
**Williams,** Clifford Glyn 1928- *WrDr 92*
**Williams,** Clyde 1939- *WhoBlA 92*
**Williams,** Clyde Michael 1928- *AmMWSc 92*
**Williams,** Coe *TwCWW 91*
**Williams,** Colin *Who 92*
**Williams,** Colin Hartley 1938- *Who 92*
**Williams,** Colin James 1938- *AmMWSc 92*
**Williams,** Conrad Malcolm 1936- *AmMWSc 92*
**Williams,** Cootie 1910-1985 *NewAmDM*
**Williams,** Curtis Alvin, Jr 1927- *AmMWSc 92*
**Williams,** Curtis Chandler, III 1926- *AmMWSc 92*
**Williams,** Cynthia Marie 1954- *WhoBlA 92*
**Williams,** Cyril Robert 1895- *Who 92*
**Williams,** D. Lee 1931- *WhoAmL 92*
**Williams,** Dafydd Wyn J. *Who 92*
**Williams,** Dale Gordon 1929- *AmMWSc 92*
**Williams,** Dan 1947- *WhoAmP 91*
**Williams,** Daniel *DrAPF 91*
**Williams,** Daniel Charles 1935- *IntWW 91*
**Williams,** Daniel Charles 1944- *AmMWSc 92*
**Williams,** Daniel Edwin 1933- *WhoBlA 92*
**Williams,** Daniel Frank 1942- *AmMWSc 92*
**Williams,** Daniel Hale 1856-1931 *ConBlB 2 [port]*
**Williams,** Daniel Louis 1926- *WhoBlA 92*
**Williams,** Daniel Salu 1942- *WhoBlA 92*
**Williams,** Danny 1949- *WhoAmP 91*
**Williams,** Darleen Dorothy 1938- *WhoWest 92*
**Williams,** Darryl Marlowe 1938- *AmMWSc 92*
**Williams,** Dave Harrell 1932- *WhoFI 92*
**Williams,** David 1904- *WhoRel 92*
**Williams,** David 1921- *IntWW 91, Who 92*
**Williams,** David 1926- *IntAu&W 91, WrDr 92*
**Williams,** David 1934- *TwCPaSc*
**Williams,** David 1938- *Who 92*
**Williams,** David 1950- *WhoEnt 92*
**Williams,** David Allan 1949- *WhoMW 92*
**Williams,** David Allen 1938- *AmMWSc 92*
**Williams,** David Apthorp 1911- *Who 92*
**Williams,** David Barry 1931- *Who 92*
**Williams,** David Bernard 1949- *AmMWSc 92*
**Williams,** David Carlton 1912- *Who 92*
**Williams,** David Cary 1935- *AmMWSc 92*
**Williams,** David Claverly 1917- *Who 92*
**Williams,** David Douglas F 1930- *AmMWSc 92*
**Williams,** David Edward 1953- *WhoWest 92*
**Williams,** David Fletcher 1956- *WhoMW 92*
**Williams,** David Francis 1938- *AmMWSc 92*
**Williams,** David G 1935- *AmMWSc 92*
**Williams,** David George 1939- *WhoBlA 92*
**Williams,** David Glyndwr Tudor 1930- *IntWW 91, Who 92*
**Williams,** David Gurth 1930- *WhoFI 92*
**Williams,** David Innes 1919- *Who 92*
**Williams,** David Iorwerth 1913- *Who 92*
**Williams,** David James 1943- *AmMWSc 92*
**Williams,** David James 1947- *AmMWSc 92*
**Williams,** David John 1914- *Who 92*
**Williams,** David John 1937- *AmMWSc 92*
**Williams,** David John 1941- *Who 92*
**Williams,** David John, III 1927- *AmMWSc 92*
**Williams,** David John Delwyn 1938- *Who 92*
**Williams,** David L 1953- *WhoAmP 91*
**Williams,** David Larry 1945- *IntAu&W 91*
**Williams,** David Lee 1939- *AmMWSc 92*
**Williams,** David Lincoln 1937- *Who 92*
**Williams,** David Llewelyn 1937- *AmMWSc 92*
**Williams,** David Lloyd 1935- *AmMWSc 92*
**Williams,** David Michael 1936- *WhoWest 92*
**Williams,** David Newell 1950- *WhoRel 92*
**Williams,** David Noel 1934- *AmMWSc 92*
**Williams,** David Oliver 1926- *Who 92*
**Williams,** David Owen C. *Who 92*
**Williams,** David Perry 1934- *WhoFI 92, WhoMW 92*
**Williams,** David Ralph 1950- *WhoFI 92*
**Williams,** David Raymond 1941- *Who 92*
**Williams,** David Roy 1954- *WhoAmL 92*
**Williams,** David Russell 1932- *WhoEnt 92*
**Williams,** David S., Jr. 1945- *WhoBlA 92*
**Williams,** David Stidum, II 1960- *WhoRel 92*
**Williams,** David Trevor 1940- *AmMWSc 92*
**Williams,** David W. 1910- *WhoBlA 92*
**Williams,** David Wakelin 1913- *Who 92*
**Williams,** David Welford 1910- *WhoAmL 92, WhoWest 92*
**Williams,** Dean E 1924- *AmMWSc 92*
**Williams,** Deborah Ann 1951- *WhoBlA 92*
**Williams,** Deborah Brown 1957- *WhoBlA 92*
**Williams,** Debra Joan 1963- *WhoAmL 92*
**Williams,** Delores J. 1929- *WhoRel 92*
**Williams,** Delwyn *Who 92*
**Williams,** Dena Lorrene Lovett 1953- *WhoWest 92*
**Williams,** Denis John d1990 *Who 92N*
**Williams,** Denise Renee 1958- *WhoBlA 92*
**Williams,** Dennis 1957- *WhoBlA 92*
**Williams,** Dennis B 1943- *WhoIns 92*
**Williams,** Dennis Lee 1958- *WhoRel 92*
**Williams,** Dennis Vaughn 1946- *WhoAmL 92*
**Williams,** Denny 1949- *WhoRel 92*
**Williams,** Denys 1929- *Who 92*
**Williams,** Denys Ambrose 1929- *IntWW 91*
**Williams,** Derek, Jr. 1958- *WhoWest 92*
**Williams,** Derek Alfred H. *Who 92*
**Williams,** Derrick *Who 92*
**Williams,** Desai 1959- *BlkOlyM*
**Williams,** Dewitt 1919- *WhoAmP 91*
**Williams,** Diane Dorothy 1948- *WhoAmP 91*
**Williams,** Diane Wray 1938- *WhoAmP 91*
**Williams,** Dianna Roselle 1961- *WhoAmL 92*
**Williams,** Dillwyn *Who 92*
**Williams,** Doiran George 1926- *Who 92*
**Williams,** Dolores Louise 1937- *WhoFI 92*
**Williams,** Don 1946- *WhoAmP 91*
**Williams,** Donald Allen, Jr. 1955- *WhoEnt 92*
**Williams,** Donald Benjamin 1933- *AmMWSc 92*
**Williams,** Donald C 1939- *WhoAmP 91*
**Williams,** Donald Clinton 1929- *WhoFI 92*
**Williams,** Donald Elmer 1930- *AmMWSc 92*
**Williams,** Donald Eugene 1929- *WhoBlA 92, WhoMW 92, WhoRel 92*
**Williams,** Donald H. 1936- *WhoBlA 92*
**Williams,** Donald Howard 1938- *AmMWSc 92, WhoMW 92*
**Williams,** Donald J 1933- *AmMWSc 92*
**Williams,** Donald Mark 1954- *Who 92*
**Williams,** Donald Robert 1948- *AmMWSc 92*
**Williams,** Donald Spencer 1939- *AmMWSc 92, WhoWest 92*
**Williams,** Donald Victor 1936- *WhoWest 92*
**Williams,** Donnell Sil Dorsey 1960- *WhoRel 92*
**Williams,** Doris Carson 1949- *WhoAmP 91*
**Williams,** Dorothy Daniel 1938- *WhoBlA 92*
**Williams,** Dorothy P. 1938- *WhoBlA 92*
**Williams,** Doug Lee 1955- *WhoBlA 92*
**Williams,** Douglas 1912- *WhoFI 92, WhoWest 92*
**Williams,** Douglas 1917- *Who 92*
**Williams,** Douglas Allan 1938- *WhoWest 92*
**Williams,** Douglas Eric 1949- *WhoAmL 92*
**Williams,** Douglas Francis 1948- *AmMWSc 92*
**Williams,** Douglas L. 1951- *WhoFI 92*
**Williams,** Douglas Lloyd 1957- *WhoFI 92*
**Williams,** Duane Alwin 1935- *AmMWSc 92*
**Williams,** Dudley 1912- *AmMWSc 92*
**Williams,** Dudley Howard 1937- *IntWW 91, Who 92*
**Williams,** E. Faye 1941- *WhoBlA 92*
**Williams,** E P 1918- *AmMWSc 92*
**Williams,** E. Thomas, Jr. 1937- *WhoBlA 92*
**Williams,** Earl 1938- *WhoBlA 92*
**Williams,** Earl, Jr. 1935- *WhoBlA 92*
**Williams,** Earl Duane 1929- *WhoFI 92, WhoWest 92*
**Williams,** Earl West 1928- *WhoBlA 92*
**Williams,** Ebenezer David, Jr 1927- *AmMWSc 92*
**Williams,** Ed E, III 1948- *WhoAmP 91*
**Williams,** Eddie, Sr. *WhoBlA 92*
**Williams,** Eddie Nathan 1932- *WhoBlA 92*
**Williams,** Eddie R 1925- *WhoAmP 91*
**Williams,** Eddie Robert 1945- *AmMWSc 92*
**Williams,** Edgar 1912- *Who 92*
**Williams,** Edgar Purell 1918- *WhoWest 92*
**Williams,** Edith Vernorz 1945- *WhoEnt 92*

**Williams,** Edmond Brady 1943- *AmMWSc 92*
**Williams,** Edna C. 1933- *WhoBlA 92*
**Williams,** Edson Poe 1923- *WhoMW 92*
**Williams,** Edward *WhoRel 92*
**Williams,** Edward Alexander Wilmot 1910- *Who 92*
**Williams,** Edward Aston 1947- *AmMWSc 92*
**Williams,** Edward Bennett 1920-1988 *FacFETw*
**Williams,** Edward David 1932- *WhoFI 92*
**Williams,** Edward Dillwyn 1929- *Who 92*
**Williams,** Edward Earl, Jr. 1945- *WhoFI 92*
**Williams,** Edward Ellis 1938- *WhoBlA 92*
**Williams,** Edward F. *DrAPF 91*
**Williams,** Edward Foster, III 1935- *WhoAmP 91*
**Williams,** Edward G. *DrAPF 91*
**Williams,** Edward James 1926- *AmMWSc 92*
**Williams,** Edward Joseph 1942- *WhoBlA 92*
**Williams,** Edward M. 1933- *WhoBlA 92*
**Williams,** Edward Stanley 1924- *Who 92*
**Williams,** Edward Stratten 1921- *Who 92*
**Williams,** Edward Taylor 1911- *Who 92*
**Williams,** Edward Vinson 1935- *WhoEnt 92*
**Williams,** Edwin Bruce 1918- *AmMWSc 92*
**Williams,** Eleanor Joyce 1936- *WhoMW 92*
**Williams,** Eleanor Ruth 1924- *AmMWSc 92*
**Williams,** Eleazar 1789?-1858 *BenetAL 91*
**Williams,** Eliot Churchill 1913- *AmMWSc 92*
**Williams,** Eliot Penfield 1942- *WhoFI 92*
**Williams,** Elizabeth *IntWW 91*
**Williams,** Elizabeth 1943- *Who 92, WhoNob 90*
**Williams,** Ellen D 1953- *AmMWSc 92*
**Williams,** Ellis 1931- *WhoBlA 92*
**Williams,** Elmer Lee 1929- *AmMWSc 92*
**Williams,** Elmo 1913- *IntMPA 92*
**Williams,** Elmo 1928- *WhoMW 92*
**Williams,** Elynor A. 1946- *WhoBlA 92*
**Williams,** Emlyn 1905-1987 *ConAu 36NR*
**Williams,** Emmett *DrAPF 91*
**Williams,** Emmett 1925- *ConPo 91, WrDr 92*
**Williams,** Emmett Lewis 1933- *AmMWSc 92*
**Williams,** Emrys 1958- *TwCPaSc*
**Williams,** Enoch H 1927- *WhoAmP 91, WhoBlA 92*
**Williams,** Eric 1911-1981 *FacFETw*
**Williams,** Eric Stanton 1958- *WhoFI 92*
**Williams,** Ernest Currant 1944- *WhoWest 92*
**Williams,** Ernest Donald, Jr. 1949- *WhoBlA 92*
**Williams,** Ernest Edward 1914- *AmMWSc 92*
**Williams,** Ernest Going 1915- *WhoFI 92*
**Williams,** Ernest Y. 1900- *WhoBlA 92*
**Williams,** Ervin Eugene 1923- *WhoRel 92*
**Williams,** Esly Bernard, Jr. 1943- *WhoMW 92*
**Williams,** Esther 1923- *IntMPA 92*
**Williams,** Ethel Frances 1928- *WhoRel 92*
**Williams,** Ethel Jean 1922- *WhoBlA 92*
**Williams,** Ethel Langley *WhoBlA 92*
**Williams,** Eugene G 1925- *AmMWSc 92*
**Williams,** Eugene H 1912- *AmMWSc 92*
**Williams,** Euphemia G. 1938- *WhoBlA 92*
**Williams,** Evan Thomas 1936- *AmMWSc 92*
**Williams,** Evelyn 1929- *TwCPaSc*
**Williams,** Evelyn Faithfull M. *Who 92*
**Williams,** Everett Belvin 1932- *WhoBlA 92*
**Williams,** F Campbell 1921- *AmMWSc 92*
**Williams,** Faith *DrAPF 91*
**Williams,** Falba W. 1935- *WhoBlA 92*
**Williams,** Fannie B. 1855-1944 *NotBlAW 92 [port]*
**Williams,** Felton Carl 1946- *WhoBlA 92*
**Williams,** Florence Walters 1926- *WhoAmP 91*
**Williams,** Floyd James 1920- *AmMWSc 92*
**Williams,** Forman A 1934- *AmMWSc 92*
**Williams,** Forrest Wesley 1937- *WhoBlA 92*
**Williams,** Frances *ReelWom*
**Williams,** Francis 1905- *Who 92*
**Williams,** Francis 1927- *AmMWSc 92*
**Williams,** Francis Julian 1927- *Who 92*
**Williams,** Francis Leon 1918- *WhoWest 92*
**Williams,** Frank, Jr. *WhoBlA 92*
**Williams,** Frank Bellows 1942- *WhoWest 92*
**Williams,** Frank Denry Clement 1913- *Who 92*
**Williams,** Frank H *ScFEYrs*
**Williams,** Frank J. 1938- *WhoBlA 92*
**Williams,** Frank J. 1940- *WhoFI 92*
**Williams,** Frank James, Jr. 1938- *WhoAmL 92*
**Williams,** Frank Lynn 1945- *AmMWSc 92*
**Williams,** Frank Purdy 1848- *ScFEYrs*
**Williams,** Frank Vernon, III 1947- *WhoAmL 92*
**Williams,** Franklin H. 1917-1990 *WhoBlA 92N*
**Williams,** Fred 1930-1985 *TwCPaSc*
**Williams,** Fred 1935- *WhoAmP 91*
**Williams,** Fred A 1938- *WhoIns 92*
**Williams,** Fred C. 1922- *WhoBlA 92*
**Williams,** Fred Devoe 1936- *AmMWSc 92*
**Williams,** Fred Eugene 1941- *AmMWSc 92*
**Williams,** Freddye H 1917- *WhoAmP 91*
**Williams,** Freddye Harper 1917- *WhoBlA 92*
**Williams,** Frederick Daniel Crawford 1943- *WhoBlA 92*
**Williams,** Frederick McGee 1934- *AmMWSc 92*
**Williams,** Frederick Wallace 1939- *AmMWSc 92*
**Williams,** Fredric Thomas 1937- *WhoMW 92*
**Williams,** Fredrick David 1937- *AmMWSc 92*
**Williams,** G Brymer 1913- *AmMWSc 92*
**Williams,** Gareth 1937- *AmMWSc 92*
**Williams,** Gareth Howel 1925- *Who 92*
**Williams,** Gareth Lloyd 1935- *Who 92*
**Williams,** Gareth Pierce 1939- *AmMWSc 92*
**Williams,** Gareth R. *Who 92*
**Williams,** Gareth Wyn 1941- *Who 92*
**Williams,** Garry Dean 1937- *WhoWest 92*
**Williams,** Garry Dee 1948- *WhoRel 92*
**Williams,** Garth 1912- *ConAu 134, FacFETw, SmATA 66 [port]*
**Williams,** Garth Montgomery 1912- *BenetAL 91*
**Williams,** Gary *DrAPF 91*
**Williams,** Gary Joseph 1952- *WhoWest 92*
**Williams,** Gary Lynn 1950- *AmMWSc 92*
**Williams,** Gary Murray 1940- *AmMWSc 92*
**Williams,** Gayle Terese 1964- *WhoBlA 92*
**Williams,** Geline Bowman *WhoAmP 91*
**Williams,** Gene R 1932- *AmMWSc 92*
**Williams,** Geoffrey Guy 1930- *Who 92*
**Williams,** George 1919- *WhoAmP 91*
**Williams,** George, Jr 1931- *AmMWSc 92*
**Williams,** George Abiah 1931- *AmMWSc 92*
**Williams,** George Arthur 1918- *AmMWSc 92*
**Williams,** George Arthur 1925- *WhoBlA 92*
**Williams,** George Christopher 1926- *AmMWSc 92*
**Williams,** George Haigh Graeme 1935- *Who 92*
**Williams,** George Harry 1942- *AmMWSc 92*
**Williams,** George Howard 1918- *WhoAmL 92*
**Williams,** George Huntington 1856-1894 *BiInAmS*
**Williams,** George Kenneth 1932- *AmMWSc 92*
**Williams,** George L., Sr. 1929- *WhoBlA 92*
**Williams,** George M. 1930- *RelLAm 91*
**Williams,** George Masayasu 1930- *WhoRel 92*
**Williams,** George Mervyn 1918- *Who 92*
**Williams,** George Nathaniel 1947- *AmMWSc 92*
**Williams,** George Rainey 1926- *AmMWSc 92*
**Williams,** George Ronald 1928- *AmMWSc 92*
**Williams,** George W. *Who 92*
**Williams,** George W 1946- *AmMWSc 92*
**Williams,** George W., III 1946- *WhoBlA 92*
**Williams,** Georgianna M. 1938- *WhoBlA 92*
**Williams,** Gerald 1963- *WhoBlA 92*
**Williams,** Gerald Albert 1921- *AmMWSc 92*
**Williams,** Gerald Arnold 1964- *WhoAmL 92*
**Williams,** Gex 1952- *WhoAmP 91*
**Williams,** Gil *DrAPF 91*
**Williams,** Glanmor 1920- *IntWW 91, Who 92*
**Williams,** Glanville 1911- *WrDr 92*
**Williams,** Glanville Llewelyn 1911- *IntWW 91, Who 92*
**Williams,** Glen Garfield 1923- *Who 92*
**Williams,** Glen Morgan 1920- *WhoAmL 92*
**Williams,** Glen Nordyke 1938- *AmMWSc 92*
**Williams,** Glenn C 1914- *AmMWSc 92*
**Williams,** Glynn 1939- *TwCPaSc*
**Williams,** Gordon 1934- *WrDr 92*
**Williams,** Gordon Bretnell 1929- *WhoFI 92*
**Williams,** Gordon Elam 1948- *WhoFI 92*
**Williams,** Gordon Oliver 1925- *WhoAmP 91*
**Williams,** Grady Carter 1939- *WhoBlA 92*
**Williams,** Graeme *Who 92*
**Williams,** Graham Charles 1937- *Who 92*
**Williams,** Graheme John Bramald 1942- *AmMWSc 92*
**Williams,** Grant B. 1949- *WhoEnt 92*
**Williams,** Gregory Dale 1955- *WhoWest 92*
**Williams,** Gregory Howard 1943- *WhoBlA 92*
**Williams,** Gregory M. *WhoBlA 92*
**Williams,** Gretchen Susan 1945- *WhoEnt 92*
**Williams,** Grier Moffatt 1931- *WhoEnt 92*
**Williams,** Gus 1953- *WhoBlA 92*
**Williams,** Guthrie J. 1914- *WhoBlA 92*
**Williams,** Guy James 1960- *WhoWest 92*
**Williams,** Guy R. 1920- *WrDr 92*
**Williams,** Guy Richard 1920- *IntAu&W 91*
**Williams,** Gwendolyn Ann 1945- *WhoRel 92*
**Williams,** Gwilym Owen d1990 *Who 92N*
**Williams,** Gwyn 1904- *ConPo 91, IntAu&W 91*
**Williams,** Gwynne 1947- *AmMWSc 92*
**Williams,** H. Evan, IV 1950- *WhoAmL 92*
**Williams,** Hal *WhoBlA 92*
**Williams,** Hank 1923-1953 *FacFETw [port], NewAmDM*
**Williams,** Hank, Jr. 1949- *NewAmDM, WhoEnt 92*
**Williams,** Hardy 1931- *WhoAmP 91, WhoBlA 92*
**Williams,** Harold 1934- *AmMWSc 92*
**Williams,** Harold Cleophas 1943- *WhoBlA 92*
**Williams,** Harold Edward 1949- *WhoBlA 92*
**Williams,** Harold Guy L. *Who 92*
**Williams,** Harold Henderson 1907- *AmMWSc 92*
**Williams,** Harold Louis 1924- *WhoBlA 92*
**Williams,** Harri Llwyd H. *Who 92*
**Williams,** Harriette F. 1930- *WhoBlA 92*
**Williams,** Harriette Flowers 1930- *WhoWest 92*
**Williams,** Harrison Arlington, Jr. 1919- *IntWW 91*
**Williams,** Harry Abbott 1919- *Who 92*
**Williams,** Harry Edward 1925- *WhoWest 92*
**Williams,** Harry Edwin 1930- *AmMWSc 92*
**Williams,** Harry George 1925- *WhoRel 92*
**Williams,** Harry Leverne 1916- *AmMWSc 92*
**Williams,** Harry Thomas 1941- *AmMWSc 92*
**Williams,** Harvey *WhoBlA 92*
**Williams,** Harvey Dean 1930- *WhoBlA 92*
**Williams,** Harvey Joseph 1941- *WhoBlA 92*
**Williams,** Hattie Plum 1878-1963 *WomSoc*
**Williams,** Haydon 1942- *TwCPaSc*
**Williams,** Hayward J. 1944- *WhoBlA 92*
**Williams,** Hazel Browne *WhoBlA 92*
**Williams,** Heathcote 1941- *WrDr 92*
**Williams,** Helen B. 1916- *WhoBlA 92*
**Williams,** Helen Cora 1931- *WhoAmP 91*
**Williams,** Helen Elizabeth 1933- *WhoBlA 92*
**Williams,** Helen Elizabeth Webber 1938- *Who 92*
**Williams,** Helen Maria 1762-1827 *BlkwCEP*
**Williams,** Henry *BenetAL 91*
**Williams,** Henry 1923- *WhoBlA 92*
**Williams,** Henry Lawrence 1923- *WhoRel 92*
**Williams,** Henry Leslie 1919- *Who 92*
**Williams,** Henry Livingston 1842- *ScFEYrs*
**Williams,** Henry Newton 1917- *WhoAmL 92*
**Williams,** Henry P. 1941- *WhoBlA 92*
**Williams,** Henry Pogue 1955- *WhoFI 92*
**Williams,** Henry R. 1937- *WhoBlA 92*
**Williams,** Henry Rudolph 1919- *WhoFI 92*
**Williams,** Henry S. 1929- *WhoBlA 92*
**Williams,** Henry Shaler 1847-1918 *BiInAmS*
**Williams,** Henry Stratton 1929- *WhoWest 92*
**Williams,** Henry Sydney 1920- *Who 92*
**Williams,** Henry Ward, Jr. 1930- *WhoAmL 92*
**Williams,** Henry Warrington 1934- *AmMWSc 92*
**Williams,** Henry Willard 1821-1895 *BiInAmS*
**Williams,** Herb E. 1946- *WhoBlA 92*
**Williams,** Herb L. 1958- *WhoBlA 92*
**Williams,** Herbert 1932- *WrDr 92*
**Williams,** Herbert C. 1930- *WhoBlA 92*
**Williams,** Herbert J. *WhoRel 92*
**Williams,** Herbert Lee 1932- *WhoBlA 92*
**Williams,** Herbert Lloyd 1932- *IntAu&W 91*
**Williams,** Herman 1943- *WhoBlA 92*
**Williams,** Herman Michael 1965- *WhoBlA 92*
**Williams,** Hermine Weigel 1933- *WhoEnt 92*
**Williams,** Hibbard E 1932- *AmMWSc 92*
**Williams,** Hilary a'Beckett E. *Who 92*
**Williams,** Hilda Yvonne 1946- *WhoBlA 92*
**Williams,** Homer LaVaughan 1925- *WhoBlA 92*
**Williams,** Hooper Anderson, Jr. 1918- *WhoFI 92*
**Williams,** Hope Denise 1952- *WhoMW 92*
**Williams,** Hosea L. 1926- *WhoBlA 92*
**Williams,** Hosea Lorenzo 1926- *WhoAmP 91*
**Williams,** Hot Rod 1961- *WhoBlA 92*
**Williams,** Howard d1991 *Who 92N*
**Williams,** Howard 1947- *WhoEnt 92*
**Williams,** Howard Copeland 1921- *WhoBlA 92*
**Williams,** Howard Manson 1943- *WhoMW 92*
**Williams,** Howard Russell 1915- *WhoAmL 92, WhoWest 92*
**Williams,** Howard Vernon 1951- *WhoWest 92*
**Williams,** Howard Walter 1937- *WhoWest 92*
**Williams,** Hubert 1939- *WhoBlA 92*
**Williams,** Hubert Glyn 1912- *Who 92*
**Williams,** Hugh Alexander, Jr. 1926- *WhoFI 92, WhoMW 92*
**Williams,** Hugh Cowie 1943- *AmMWSc 92*
**Williams,** Hugh Harrison 1944- *AmMWSc 92*
**Williams,** Hugh Hermes 1945- *WhoBlA 92*
**Williams,** Hugo 1942- *ConPo 91, WrDr 92*
**Williams,** Hugo Mordaunt 1942- *IntAu&W 91, Who 92*
**Williams,** Hulen Brown 1920- *AmMWSc 92*
**Williams,** Huntington, Jr. 1925- *WhoRel 92*
**Williams,** Ian Malcolm Gordon 1914- *Who 92*
**Williams,** Ioan M. 1941- *WrDr 92*
**Williams,** Iola 1936- *WhoBlA 92*
**Williams,** Ira Joseph 1926- *WhoBlA 92*
**Williams,** Ira Lee 1930- *WhoBlA 92*
**Williams,** J. Bedell 1923- *WhoBlA 92*
**Williams,** J. Bryan 1947- *WhoAmL 92*
**Williams,** J. Craig 1957- *WhoAmL 92*
**Williams,** J D 1942- *WhoAmP 91*
**Williams,** J Marshall 1930- *WhoAmP 91*
**Williams,** J. R. *WrDr 92*
**Williams,** Jack A 1926- *AmMWSc 92*
**Williams,** Jack Kenny 1920- *IntWW 91*
**Williams,** Jack L R 1923- *AmMWSc 92*
**Williams,** Jack Marvin 1938- *AmMWSc 92*
**Williams,** Jack Raymond 1923- *WhoMW 92*
**Williams,** Jack Rudolph 1929- *AmMWSc 92*
**Williams,** Jacqueline 1962- *TwCPaSc*
**Williams,** James Arthur 1939- *WhoBlA 92*
**Williams,** James Austin 1956- *WhoFI 92*
**Williams,** James B. 1945- *WhoFI 92*
**Williams,** James B, Jr 1930- *WhoAmP 91*
**Williams,** James Bryan 1933- *WhoFI 92*
**Williams,** James C, III 1928- *AmMWSc 92*
**Williams,** James Carl 1935- *AmMWSc 92*
**Williams,** James Case 1938- *AmMWSc 92*
**Williams,** James Clayton, Jr. 1947- *WhoFI 92*
**Williams,** James D 1932- *AmMWSc 92*
**Williams,** James DeBois 1926- *WhoBlA 92*
**Williams,** James Dennis 1942- *WhoAmL 92*
**Williams,** James E. *WhoWest 92*
**Williams,** James E. 1943- *WhoBlA 92*
**Williams,** James E., Jr. 1936- *WhoBlA 92*
**Williams,** James Earl, Jr 1938- *AmMWSc 92*
**Williams,** James Edward 1955- *WhoBlA 92*
**Williams,** James Francis, Jr. 1938- *WhoRel 92*
**Williams,** James G 1944- *AmMWSc 92*
**Williams,** James Gerard 1941- *AmMWSc 92*
**Williams,** James Gordon 1938- *Who 92*
**Williams,** James H., Jr. 1941- *WhoBlA 92*
**Williams,** James Henry, Jr 1918- *AmMWSc 92*
**Williams,** James Henry, Jr 1941- *AmMWSc 92*
**Williams,** James Hiawatha 1945- *WhoBlA 92*

Williams, James Hutchison 1922- *AmMWSc 92*
Williams, James Kendrick *WhoRel 92*
Williams, James Lovon, Jr 1929- *AmMWSc 92*
Williams, James Marvin 1934- *AmMWSc 92*
Williams, James Melvin 1910- *WhoAmP 91*
Williams, James Melvin 1958- *WhoRel 92*
Williams, James Norman, Jr. 1943- *WhoAmL 92*
Williams, James Oliver 1936- *WhoAmP 91*
Williams, James P., Jr. 1944- *WhoEnt 92*
Williams, James R. 1933- *WhoBlA 92*
Williams, James Richard 1946- *WhoFI 92*
Williams, James Stanley 1934- *AmMWSc 92*
Williams, James Thomas 1933- *AmMWSc 92, WhoBlA 92*
Williams, James Vaughan 1912- *Who 92*
Williams, James Wilbert, Jr. 1953- *WhoEnt 92*
Williams, Jamye Coleman 1918- *WhoBlA 92, WhoRel 92*
Williams, Jane *DrAPF 91*
Williams, Jane A. 1958- *WhoAmL 92*
Williams, Jane E. 1947- *WhoBlA 92*
Williams, Janice Bostic 1934- *WhoAmP 91*
Williams, Janice L. 1938- *WhoBlA 92*
Williams, Jarvis Eric 1965- *WhoBlA 92*
Williams, Jasmin Heidi 1959- *WhoEnt 92*
Williams, Jason Harold 1944- *WhoBlA 92*
Williams, Jay Gomer 1932- *WhoRel 92*
Williams, Jean Carolyn 1956- *WhoBlA 92*
Williams, Jean Paul 1918- *AmMWSc 92*
Williams, Jean Perkins 1951- *WhoBlA 92*
Williams, Jeanette K 1917- *WhoAmP 91*
Williams, Jeanette Marie 1942- *WhoBlA 92*
Williams, Jeanne 1930- *IntAu&W 91, TwCWW 91, WrDr 92*
Williams, Jeffrey C. 1952- *WhoFI 92*
Williams, Jeffrey Clarke 1940- *WhoWest 92*
Williams, Jeffrey F 1942- *AmMWSc 92*
Williams, Jeffrey Keith Benjamin 1957- *WhoFI 92*
Williams, Jeffrey Lee 1958- *WhoFI 92*
Williams, Jeffrey Reed 1948- *WhoFI 92*
Williams, Jeffrey Taylor 1953- *AmMWSc 92*
Williams, Jeffrey Thomas 1952- *WhoWest 92*
Williams, Jeffrey Walter 1951- *AmMWSc 92*
Williams, Jeremiah Galloway 1941- *WhoRel 92*
Williams, Jerome 1926- *AmMWSc 92*
Williams, Jerome D. 1947- *WhoBlA 92*
Williams, Jerome Loren 1949- *WhoEnt 92*
Williams, Jerre Stockton 1916- *WhoAmL 92*
Williams, Jerre Stockton, Jr. 1951- *WhoRel 92*
Williams, Jesse 1922- *WhoBlA 92*
Williams, Jesse Bascom 1917- *AmMWSc 92*
Williams, Jesse J., Jr. 1940- *WhoBlA 92*
Williams, Jesse Lynch 1871-1929 *BenetAL 91*
Williams, Jesse T., Sr. 1940- *WhoBlA 92*
Williams, Jessie Willmon 1907- *WhoRel 92*
Williams, Jester C. 1924- *WhoBlA 92*
Williams, Jewel L. 1937- *WhoBlA 92*
Williams, Jimmy Calvin 1943- *AmMWSc 92*
Williams, Jo Beth 1953- *IntMPA 92*
Williams, Joan *DrAPF 91*
Williams, Joan 1928- *IntAu&W 91*
Williams, Joanne Louise 1949- *WhoBlA 92*
Williams, Joe 1918- *NewAmDM, WhoBlA 92*
Williams, Joe H. 1937- *WhoBlA 92*
Williams, Joe R *WhoAmP 91*
Williams, Joel Jay 1948- *WhoFI 92*
Williams, Joel Lawson 1941- *AmMWSc 92*
Williams, Joel Lee 1957- *WhoAmL 92*
Williams, Joel Mann, Jr 1940- *AmMWSc 92*
Williams, Joel Quitman 1922- *AmMWSc 92*
Williams, John *DrAPF 91*
Williams, John 1664-1729 *BenetAL 91*
Williams, John 1761-1818 *BenetAL 91*
Williams, John 1817-1899 *RelLAm 91*
Williams, John 1922- *ConNov 91, IntAu&W 91, TwCWW 91, WrDr 92*
Williams, John 1932- *FacFETw, IntMPA 92, NewAmDM*
Williams, John 1941- *IntWW 91, Who 92*
Williams, John 1961- *WhoBlA 92*
Williams, John A. *DrAPF 91*
Williams, John A. 1925- *BenetAL 91, BlkLC [port], ConNov 91, IntAu&W 91, TwCSFW 91, WrDr 92*
Williams, John A 1929- *AmMWSc 92*
Williams, John Albert 1937- *AmMWSc 92*
Williams, John Albert 1941- *WhoMW 92*
Williams, John Alden 1928- *WhoRel 92*
Williams, John Alfred 1925- *WhoBlA 92*
Williams, John Andrew 1941- *AmMWSc 92, WhoMW 92*
Williams, John B 1945- *WhoAmP 91*
Williams, John Barry *WrDr 92*
Williams, John Bernard 1949- *WhoMW 92*
Williams, John Brindley 1919- *WhoWest 92*
Williams, John Brinley 1927- *Who 92*
Williams, John Bucknall Kingsley 1927- *Who 92*
Williams, John C 1925- *AmMWSc 92*
Williams, John Charles 1912- *Who 92*
Williams, John Charles 1938- *Who 92*
Williams, John Charles, II 1955- *WhoWest 92*
Williams, John Collins, Jr 1945- *AmMWSc 92*
Williams, John Delane 1938- *AmMWSc 92*
Williams, John E. 1922- *BenetAL 91*
Williams, John Earl 1948- *WhoBlA 92*
Williams, John Eirwyn F. *Who 92*
Williams, John Ellis Caerwyn 1912- *IntWW 91, Who 92*
Williams, John Ernest 1935- *AmMWSc 92*
Williams, John Eryl Hall 1921- *Who 92*
Williams, John F. 1928- *WhoBlA 92*
Williams, John F, Jr 1931- *AmMWSc 92*
Williams, John Francis 1862?-1891 *BiInAmS*
Williams, John Frederick 1923- *AmMWSc 92*
Williams, John Griffith 1944- *Who 92*
Williams, John H. 1934- *WhoBlA 92*
Williams, John Henry 1948- *WhoBlA 92*
Williams, John Herbert 1919- *Who 92*
Williams, John Howard *WhoFI 92*
Williams, John James, Jr. 1949- *WhoFI 92, WhoWest 92*
Williams, John Joseph 1906- *WhoBlA 92*
Williams, John Kyffin 1918- *IntWW 91, Who 92*
Williams, John L. 1937- *WhoBlA 92*
Williams, John L. 1964- *WhoBlA 92*
Williams, John Lee 1942- *WhoAmL 92*
Williams, John Leighton 1941- *Who 92*
Williams, John Leslie 1913- *Who 92*
Williams, John Melville 1931- *Who 92*
Williams, John Meredith 1926- *Who 92*
Williams, John Noctor 1931- *Who 92*
Williams, John Paul 1946- *AmMWSc 92*
Williams, John Pershing 1919- *WhoWest 92*
Williams, John Peter Rhys 1949- *IntWW 91, Who 92*
Williams, John R. 1937- *WhoBlA 92*
Williams, John Richard 1909- *WhoAmP 91*
Williams, John Robert 1922- *IntWW 91, Who 92*
Williams, John Robert 1931- *WhoMW 92*
Williams, John Roderick 1940- *AmMWSc 92*
Williams, John Rodman 1918- *WhoRel 92*
Williams, John Russell 1948- *AmMWSc 92*
Williams, John Sam 1966- *WhoBlA 92*
Williams, John Steven Meurig 1948- *WhoWest 92*
Williams, John Stuart 1920- *WrDr 92*
Williams, John T. 1932- *IntWW 91*
Williams, John Thomas 1931- *WhoAmP 91*
Williams, John Towner 1932- *Who 92, WhoEnt 92*
Williams, John Troy 1924- *WhoMW 92*
Williams, John Tudno 1938- *Who 92*
Williams, John Waldo 1911- *WhoBlA 92*
Williams, John Walter 1953- *WhoAmL 92*
Williams, John Warren 1898- *AmMWSc 92*
Williams, John Watkins, III 1942- *AmMWSc 92*
Williams, John Wesley 1940- *WhoMW 92*
Williams, John Wesley 1944- *AmMWSc 92*
Williams, John Wharton 1945- *AmMWSc 92*
Williams, John Woodbridge 1950- *WhoEnt 92*
Williams, Jonathan *DrAPF 91*
Williams, Jonathan 1750-1815 *BiInAmS*
Williams, Jonathan 1929- *ConPo 91, WrDr 92*
Williams, Joseph Arthur 1958- *WhoWest 92*
Williams, Joseph B. 1921- *WhoBlA 92*
Williams, Joseph Barbour 1945- *WhoBlA 92*
Williams, Joseph Burton 1946- *AmMWSc 92*
Williams, Joseph Dalton 1926- *IntWW 91, WhoFI 92*
Williams, Joseph Francis 1938- *AmMWSc 92*
Williams, Joseph Henry 1931- *WhoBlA 92*
Williams, Joseph Hill 1933- *WhoFI 92*
Williams, Joseph Lee 1936- *AmMWSc 92*
Williams, Joseph Lee 1945- *WhoBlA 92*
Williams, Joseph R. 1918- *WhoBlA 92*
Williams, Joseph Robert 1945- *WhoWest 92*
Williams, Joseph Rulon 1904- *WhoAmP 91*
Williams, Josephine Louise 1926- *AmMWSc 92*
Williams, Josephine P 1921- *WhoAmP 91*
Williams, Joslyn N 1940- *WhoAmP 91*
Williams, Joy *DrAPF 91*
Williams, Joy 1944- *BenetAL 91, WrDr 92*
Williams, Joy Elizabeth P 1929- *AmMWSc 92*
Williams, Juanita Terry *WhoAmP 91*
Williams, Judi *Who 92*
Williams, Julie Belle 1950- *WhoMW 92*
Williams, Julius Penson 1954- *WhoEnt 92*
Williams, Junius W. 1943- *WhoBlA 92*
Williams, Karen Hastie 1944- *WhoBlA 92*
Williams, Karen Lynn 1952- *ConAu 133, SmATA 66*
Williams, Karen R 1950- *WhoAmP 91*
Williams, Karen Renee 1954- *WhoBlA 92*
Williams, Karin Renee 1961- *WhoMW 92*
Williams, Karren Rae 1958- *WhoWest 92*
Williams, Katherine 1941- *WhoBlA 92*
Williams, Kathi *WhoAmP 91*
Williams, Kathleen J. 1945- *WhoWest 92*
Williams, Keith David 1948- *WhoEnt 92*
Williams, Keith David 1956- *WhoBlA 92*
Williams, Keith Wilbur 1928- *WhoRel 92*
Williams, Kenneth Anthony 1961- *WhoAmL 92*
Williams, Kenneth Bock 1930- *AmMWSc 92*
Williams, Kenneth Daniel 1963- *WhoRel 92*
Williams, Kenneth Emerson 1962- *WhoEnt 92*
Williams, Kenneth Eugene 1955- *WhoMW 92*
Williams, Kenneth Herbert 1945- *WhoBlA 92*
Williams, Kenneth James 1924- *WhoWest 92*
Williams, Kenneth L 1934- *AmMWSc 92*
Williams, Kenneth Ogden 1924- *WhoAmP 91*
Williams, Kenneth Raynor 1912-1989 *WhoBlA 92N*
Williams, Kenneth Scott 1955- *WhoEnt 92, WhoFI 92*
Williams, Kenneth Stuart 1940- *AmMWSc 92*
Williams, Kevin A. 1956- *WhoBlA 92*
Williams, Kevin Erroll 1957- *WhoRel 92*
Williams, Kim Eric 1943- *WhoRel 92*
Williams, Kimmika L.H. *DrAPF 91*
Williams, Kimmika L. H. 1959- *WhoBlA 92*
Williams, Kingsley *Who 92*
Williams, Kit 1946- *TwCPaSc*
Williams, Kneely *WhoBlA 92*
Williams, Knox 1928- *WhoWest 92*
Williams, Kyffin *Who 92*
Williams, Kyffin 1918- *TwCPaSc*
Williams, L. Colene 1921- *WhoBlA 92*
Williams, Lacey Kirk 1871-1940 *RelLAm 91*
Williams, Lafayette W. 1937- *WhoBlA 92*
Williams, Lansing Earl 1921- *AmMWSc 92*
Williams, Larry C. 1931- *WhoBlA 92*
Williams, Larry D 1941- *WhoIns 92*
Williams, Larry Emmett 1936- *WhoFI 92*
Williams, Larry G 1935- *AmMWSc 92*
Williams, Larry Gale 1939- *AmMWSc 92*
Williams, Larry McClease *AmMWSc 92*
Williams, Larry McClease 1955- *WhoWest 92*
Williams, Larry Richard 1942- *WhoWest 92*
Williams, Larry Ritchie 1935- *WhoFI 92*
Williams, LaShina Brigette 1957- *WhoBlA 92*
Williams, Lauren S. 1945- *WhoBlA 92*
Williams, Lawrence Ernest 1937- *AmMWSc 92*
Williams, Lawrence Eugene 1949- *WhoEnt 92*
Williams, Lea E. 1947- *WhoBlA 92*
Williams, Leah Ann 1932- *AmMWSc 92*
Williams, Leamon Dale 1935- *AmMWSc 92*
Williams, Lee 1925- *WhoAmP 91*
Williams, Lee Dwain 1950- *WhoAmL 92*
Williams, Lee R. 1936- *WhoBlA 92*
Williams, Leland Hendry 1930- *AmMWSc 92*
Williams, Leon L *WhoAmP 91*
Williams, Leon Lawson 1922- *WhoBlA 92*
Williams, Leona Rae 1928- *WhoWest 92*
Williams, Leonard 1919- *Who 92*
Williams, Leonard, Sr. 1945- *WhoBlA 92*
Williams, Leonard Edmund Henry 1919- *Who 92*
Williams, Leonard Worcester 1875-1912 *BiInAmS*
Williams, Leroy Joseph 1937- *WhoBlA 92*
Williams, Lesley Lattin 1939- *AmMWSc 92*
Williams, Leslie *Who 92*
Williams, Leslie Arthur 1909- *Who 92*
Williams, Leslie Arthur 1945- *WhoEnt 92*
Williams, Leslie Henry d1991 *Who 92N*
Williams, Leslie Henry 1903- *IntWW 91*
Williams, Leslie J. 1947- *WhoBlA 92*
Williams, Letha Dawn 1953- *WhoMW 92*
Williams, Lewis David 1944- *AmMWSc 92*
Williams, Lewis Frederick 1938- *WhoWest 92*
Williams, Lewis Isaac, IV 1949- *WhoWest 92*
Williams, Lewis White 1807?-1876 *BiInAmS*
Williams, Lillian C. 1924- *WhoBlA 92*
Williams, Linda Grant 1950- *WhoAmL 92*
Williams, Linda Jo 1942- *WhoWest 92*
Williams, Linda Turner 1941- *WhoWest 92*
Williams, Lisa Michelle 1966- *WhoEnt 92*
Williams, Lisa Powell 1961- *WhoFI 92*
Williams, Lisl King 1955- *WhoMW 92*
Williams, Lloyd A. *WhoBlA 92*
Williams, Lloyd Edward, Jr. 1934- *WhoAmL 92*
Williams, Lloyd L. 1944- *WhoBlA 92*
Williams, Londell 1939- *WhoBlA 92*
Williams, Lonnie Ray 1954- *WhoBlA 92*
Williams, Lorece P. 1927- *WhoBlA 92*
Williams, Loring Rider 1907- *AmMWSc 92*
Williams, Lorraine A. 1923- *NotBlAW 92*
Williams, Lottie Mae 1931- *WhoBlA 92*
Williams, Louis Allen 1952- *NewYTBS 91 [port]*
Williams, Louis Booth 1916- *WhoFI 92*
Williams, Louis Gressett 1913- *AmMWSc 92*
Williams, Louis James 1944- *WhoAmL 92*
Williams, Louis L 1859- *DcAmImH*
Williams, Louis Nathaniel 1929- *WhoBlA 92*
Williams, Louise Anita 1942- *WhoRel 92*
Williams, Louise Bernice 1937- *WhoBlA 92*
Williams, Lowell Craig 1947- *WhoAmL 92*
Williams, Lowell D. 1931- *WhoRel 92*
Williams, Lu 1947- *WhoBlA 92*
Williams, Lucinda 1937- *BlkOlyM*
Williams, Lucius Lee, Jr. 1927-1990 *WhoBlA 92N*
Williams, Lucretia Murphy 1941- *WhoBlA 92*
Williams, Luther Charles, Jr. *WhoAmL 92*
Williams, Luther Steward 1940- *AmMWSc 92, WhoBlA 92*
Williams, Lyman Neil, Jr. 1936- *WhoAmL 92*
Williams, Lyman O 1934- *AmMWSc 92*
Williams, Lyn *Who 92*
Williams, Lynn Dolores 1944- *AmMWSc 92*
Williams, Lynn Roy 1945- *AmMWSc 92*
Williams, Lynn Russell 1924- *IntWW 91*
Williams, M. Barry 1942- *WhoFI 92*
Williams, M Coburn 1929- *AmMWSc 92*
Williams, Maceo Merton 1939- *WhoBlA 92*
Williams, Mack Geoffrey Denis 1939- *IntWW 91*
Williams, Malcolm David 1939- *IntAu&W 91*
Williams, Malcolm Demosthenes 1909- *WhoBlA 92*
Williams, Malvin A. 1942- *WhoBlA 92*
Williams, Mamie 1872-1951 *NotBlAW 92*
Williams, Mamie Lou 1911- *WhoAmP 91*
Williams, Marcus Doyle 1952- *WhoAmL 92, WhoBlA 92*
Williams, Margaret Frances Howell 1912- *IntAu&W 91*
Williams, Margaret Myrrhene 1962- *WhoEnt 92*
Williams, Margo E. 1947- *WhoBlA 92*
Williams, Marhsall Vance, Jr. 1948- *WhoMW 92*
Williams, Maria Selika 1849?-1937 *NotBlAW 92*
Williams, Marie B 1926- *WhoAmP 91*
Williams, Marion Lester 1933- *WhoWest 92*
Williams, Marion Porter 1946- *AmMWSc 92*
Williams, Mark Alan 1955- *WhoRel 92*
Williams, Mark Allen 1959- *WhoMW 92*

**Williams**, Mark Anthony 1957- *WhoRel 92*
**Williams**, Mark Riley 1952- *WhoEnt 92*
**Williams**, Mark Robert 1950- *WhoEnt 92*
**Williams**, Mark Samuel 1953- *WhoEnt 92*
**Williams**, Marshall Burns 1912- *WhoAmP 91*
**Williams**, Marshall Henry, Jr 1925- *AmMWSc 92*
**Williams**, Marshall MacKenzie 1923- *WhoFI 92, WhoWest 92*
**Williams**, Marshall Vance 1948- *AmMWSc 92*
**Williams**, Martha E *AmMWSc 92*
**Williams**, Martha S. 1921- *WhoBlA 92*
**Williams**, Martin John 1941- *Who 92*
**Williams**, Mary 1943- *WhoIns 92*
**Williams**, Mary Alice *LesBEnT 92*
**Williams**, Mary Ann 1925- *AmMWSc 92*
**Williams**, Mary Ann Sheridan 1945- *WhoBlA 92*
**Williams**, Mary Bearden 1936- *AmMWSc 92*
**Williams**, Mary Beatrice 1938- *WhoAmP 91*
**Williams**, Mary Carol *AmMWSc 92*
**Williams**, Mary Carol 1942- *AmMWSc 92*
**Williams**, Mary Carol 1953- *WhoRel 92*
**Williams**, Mary Carr 1926- *AmMWSc 92*
**Williams**, Mary D. 1922- *WhoBlA 92*
**Williams**, Mary Evelyn Walker 1933- *WhoFI 92*
**Williams**, Mary Haley 1936-1986 *WhoBlA 92N*
**Williams**, Mary Lou 1910-1981 *FacFETw, NotBlAW 92 [port]*
**Williams**, Mary Lou 1914-1981 *NewAmDM*
**Williams**, Maryon Johnston, Jr 1946- *AmMWSc 92*
**Williams**, Matt *LesBEnT 92*
**Williams**, Matthew Albert 1929- *WhoBlA 92*
**Williams**, Maureen R. 1963- *WhoMW 92*
**Williams**, Maurice Jacoutot 1920- *IntWW 91*
**Williams**, Max *Who 92*
**Williams**, Max L, Jr 1922- *AmMWSc 92*
**Williams**, Max W 1930- *AmMWSc 92*
**Williams**, Maxine Eleanor 1940- *WhoMW 92*
**Williams**, McDonald 1917- *WhoBlA 92*
**Williams**, Melba Ruth *WhoAmP 91*
**Williams**, Melva L. 1925- *WhoEnt 92*
**Williams**, Melvin 1944- *WhoBlA 92*
**Williams**, Melvin D. 1933- *WhoBlA 92*
**Williams**, Melvin Donald 1933- *WhoMW 92*
**Williams**, Melvin Pearson 1930- *WhoAmL 92*
**Williams**, Melvin Walker 1939- *WhoBlA 92*
**Williams**, Merlin Charles 1931- *AmMWSc 92*
**Williams**, Michael *ScFEYrs*
**Williams**, Michael 1935- *ConAu 133, Who 92*
**Williams**, Michael 1936- *TwCPaSc*
**Williams**, Michael 1947- *AmMWSc 92*
**Williams**, Michael Alan 1948- *WhoMW 92*
**Williams**, Michael Allen 1946- *WhoRel 92*
**Williams**, Michael Andrew 1946- *WhoEnt 92*
**Williams**, Michael Anthony 1932- *WhoAmL 92*
**Williams**, Michael C 1937- *AmMWSc 92*
**Williams**, Michael Cunningham 1959- *WhoAmL 92*
**Williams**, Michael D 1939- *AmMWSc 92*
**Williams**, Michael D. 1959- *WhoAmL 92*
**Williams**, Michael Dale 1947- *WhoIns 92*
**Williams**, Michael Dean 1955- *WhoFI 92*
**Williams**, Michael Edward 1955- *WhoAmL 92*
**Williams**, Michael Eugene 1940- *AmMWSc 92*
**Williams**, Michael I. 1955- *WhoMW 92*
**Williams**, Michael James 1951- *WhoWest 92*
**Williams**, Michael Joseph 1942- *Who 92*
**Williams**, Michael Ledell 1943- *AmMWSc 92*
**Williams**, Michael Leonard 1935- *Who 92*
**Williams**, Michael Maurice Rudolph 1935- *AmMWSc 92, Who 92*
**Williams**, Michael O. *Who 92*
**Williams**, Michael R 1955- *WhoAmP 91*
**Williams**, Michael S. 1946- *WhoFI 92*
**Williams**, Michael Stewart 1948- *WhoFI 92*
**Williams**, Mikki Terry 1943- *WhoEnt 92*
**Williams**, Miller *DrAPF 91, IntAu&W 91*
**Williams**, Miller 1930- *ConPo 91, WrDr 92*
**Williams**, Milton 1936- *WhoBlA 92*
**Williams**, Milton A. *WhoRel 92*
**Williams**, Milton Lawrence 1932- *WhoBlA 92*
**Williams**, Morris O. *WhoBlA 92*
**Williams**, Moses, Sr. 1932- *WhoBlA 92*
**Williams**, Muriel E. Rasmussen-Kay 1920- *IntAu&W 91*
**Williams**, Myra Nicol 1941- *AmMWSc 92*
**Williams**, Myrna 1929- *WhoAmP 91*
**Williams**, Nancy Dana 1948- *WhoEnt 92*
**Williams**, Nancy Ellen Webb *WhoBlA 92, WhoWest 92*
**Williams**, Naomi 1946- *WhoMW 92*
**Williams**, Naomi B. 1942- *WhoBlA 92*
**Williams**, Naomi Fisher 1913- *WhoBlA 92*
**Williams**, Napoleon 1900- *WhoBlA 92*
**Williams**, Neal Thomas 1921- *AmMWSc 92*
**Williams**, Neil Wynn *ScFEYrs*
**Williams**, Nelson Garrett 1926- *WhoAmL 92*
**Williams**, Nicholas James Donald 1925- *IntWW 91, Who 92*
**Williams**, Nicholas John S. *Who 92*
**Williams**, Nigel 1948- *IntAu&W 91, WrDr 92*
**Williams**, Nigel Christopher Ransome 1937- *IntWW 91, Who 92*
**Williams**, Noel Ignace B. *Who 92*
**Williams**, Noreen 1955- *AmMWSc 92*
**Williams**, Norma Jean 1952- *WhoAmL 92*
**Williams**, Norman *DrAPF 91, Who 92*
**Williams**, Norman 1915- *WhoAmL 92*
**Williams**, Norman Dale 1924- *AmMWSc 92, WhoMW 92*
**Williams**, Norman Eugene 1928- *AmMWSc 92*
**Williams**, Norman Harwood 1928- *WhoWest 92*
**Williams**, Norman S W *AmMWSc 92*
**Williams**, Norris Gerald 1948- *WhoBlA 92*
**Williams**, Norris Hagan 1943- *AmMWSc 92*
**Williams**, Novella Stewart 1927- *WhoAmP 91, WhoBlA 92*
**Williams**, Numan Arthur 1928- *WhoFI 92, WhoIns 92, WhoMW 92*
**Williams**, Oliver F 1939- *ConAu 35NR*
**Williams**, Ora 1926- *WhoBlA 92*
**Williams**, Ora P. 1935- *WhoBlA 92*
**Williams**, Oren Francis 1920- *AmMWSc 92*
**Williams**, Oscar *IntMPA 92*
**Williams**, Oscar 1900-1964 *BenetAL 91*
**Williams**, Osmond 1914- *Who 92*
**Williams**, Otis P. *WhoBlA 92*
**Williams**, Owen Lenn 1914- *Who 92*
**Williams**, Palmer *LesBEnT 92*
**Williams**, Parham Henry, Jr. 1931- *WhoAmL 92*
**Williams**, Pat 1937- *AlmAP 92 [port], WhoAmP 91, WhoWest 92*
**Williams**, Patricia Anne 1943- *WhoBlA 92*
**Williams**, Patricia Bell *AmMWSc 92*
**Williams**, Patricia Hill 1939- *WhoBlA 92*
**Williams**, Patricia R. 1943- *WhoBlA 92*
**Williams**, Patrick Kelly 1943- *AmMWSc 92*
**Williams**, Patrick Moody 1939- *WhoEnt 92*
**Williams**, Patrick Nehemiah 1928- *WhoAmP 91, WhoBlA 92*
**Williams**, Paul *IntMPA 92*
**Williams**, Paul 1929- *WhoBlA 92*
**Williams**, Paul 1940- *IntMPA 92*
**Williams**, Paul Glyn 1922- *Who 92*
**Williams**, Paul H. *Who 92*
**Williams**, Paul Hamilton 1940- *WhoEnt 92*
**Williams**, Paul Hugh 1938- *AmMWSc 92*
**Williams**, Paul L 1953- *WhoAmP 91*
**Williams**, Paul O 1935- *TwCSFW 91, WrDr 92*
**Williams**, Paul Osborne *DrAPF 91*
**Williams**, Paul Randall 1934- *Who 92*
**Williams**, Paul Revere 1895-1980 *FacFETw*
**Williams**, Paul Robert 1937- *WhoMW 92*
**Williams**, Paul Tennyson 1925- *WhoMW 92*
**Williams**, Paul Whitcomb 1903- *WhoAmL 92*
**Williams**, Penny Baldwin 1937- *WhoAmP 91*
**Williams**, Penry Herbert 1925- *Who 92*
**Williams**, Percy Don 1922- *WhoAmL 92*
**Williams**, Peter F. *Who 92*
**Williams**, Peter H. *Who 92*
**Williams**, Peter J 1932- *AmMWSc 92*
**Williams**, Peter James 1956- *WhoFI 92*
**Williams**, Peter Keegan 1938- *Who 92*
**Williams**, Peter Lancelot 1914- *Who 92*
**Williams**, Peter M 1927- *AmMWSc 92*
**Williams**, Peter Michael 1945- *Who 92*
**Williams**, Peter Orchard 1925- *IntWW 91, Who 92*
**Williams**, Peter W. *Who 92*
**Williams**, Peter William 1944- *WhoRel 92*
**Williams**, Peyton, Jr. 1942- *WhoBlA 92*
**Williams**, Philip *Who 92*
**Williams**, Philip B. 1922- *WhoBlA 92*
**Williams**, Philip Carslake 1933- *AmMWSc 92*
**Williams**, Philip Copelain 1917- *WhoMW 92*
**Williams**, Philip F. C. 1956- *WhoWest 92*
**Williams**, Phillip Wayne 1939- *WhoFI 92*
**Williams**, Phletus P 1933- *AmMWSc 92*
**Williams**, Phyllis Cutforth 1917- *WhoWest 92*
**Williams**, Preston N. 1926- *WhoBlA 92*
**Williams**, Quinn Patrick 1949- *WhoAmL 92, WhoWest 92*
**Williams**, Raleigh R. *WhoBlA 92*
**Williams**, Ralph C, Jr 1928- *AmMWSc 92*
**Williams**, Ralph Edward 1943- *AmMWSc 92*
**Williams**, Ralph Edward 1949- *WhoMW 92*
**Williams**, Ralph Vaughan *NewAmDM*
**Williams**, Randolph 1944- *WhoBlA 92*
**Williams**, Randy Luvelle 1953- *BlkOlyM*
**Williams**, Ray Clayton 1944- *AmMWSc 92*
**Williams**, Ray H. 1931-1981 *WhoBlA 92N*
**Williams**, Raymond 1921-1988 *FacFETw, RfGEnL 91*
**Williams**, Raymond, III 1946- *WhoMW 92*
**Williams**, Raymond A 1945- *WhoIns 92*
**Williams**, Raymond Alan 1945- *WhoRel 92*
**Williams**, Raymond Brady 1935- *WhoRel 92*
**Williams**, Raymond Crawford 1924- *AmMWSc 92*
**Williams**, Raymond Lloyd 1927- *Who 92*
**Williams**, Rebecca Lynn 1959- *WhoAmL 92*
**Williams**, Redford Brown, Jr 1940- *AmMWSc 92*
**Williams**, Reed Chester 1941- *AmMWSc 92*
**Williams**, Reggie 1954- *WhoBlA 92*
**Williams**, Reggie 1964- *WhoBlA 92*
**Williams**, Regina E. *DrAPF 91*
**Williams**, Regina Vloyn-Kinchen 1947- *WhoBlA 92*
**Williams**, Reginald Clark 1950- *WhoBlA 92*
**Williams**, Reginald Norman 1917- *Who 92*
**Williams**, Reginald T. 1945- *WhoBlA 92*
**Williams**, Rhys 1929- *WhoRel 92*
**Williams**, Richard 1927- *AmMWSc 92*
**Williams**, Richard 1933- *IntMPA 92*
**Williams**, Richard, Jr. 1933- *WhoBlA 92*
**Williams**, Richard Alvin 1936- *AmMWSc 92*
**Williams**, Richard Anderson 1931- *AmMWSc 92*
**Williams**, Richard Derrick 1926- *Who 92*
**Williams**, Richard Douglas 1947- *WhoWest 92*
**Williams**, Richard Dudley 1946- *WhoWest 92*
**Williams**, Richard E., Jr. 1962- *WhoBlA 92*
**Williams**, Richard Edmund 1933- *IntWW 91*
**Williams**, Richard Edward 1939- *WhoMW 92*
**Williams**, Richard F 1941- *WhoIns 92*
**Williams**, Richard Gail 1934- *WhoAmL 92*
**Williams**, Richard Hall 1926- *Who 92*
**Williams**, Richard Hirschfeld 1929- *WhoWest 92*
**Williams**, Richard James 1942- *WhoFI 92*
**Williams**, Richard James 1951- *WhoWest 92*
**Williams**, Richard John 1944- *AmMWSc 92*
**Williams**, Richard Kelso 1938- *AmMWSc 92*
**Williams**, Richard Laverne 1956- *WhoFI 92, WhoWest 92*
**Williams**, Richard Lee, II 1959- *WhoBlA 92*
**Williams**, Richard Lenwood 1931- *WhoBlA 92*
**Williams**, Richard Leroy 1923- *WhoAmL 92*
**Williams**, Richard Pascal, Jr. 1939- *WhoWest 92*
**Williams**, Richard Stanley 1951- *AmMWSc 92*
**Williams**, Richard Sugden, Jr 1938- *AmMWSc 92*
**Williams**, Richard Taylor 1946- *AmMWSc 92*
**Williams**, Rickey Jay 1942- *AmMWSc 92*
**Williams**, Robert 1916- *Who 92*
**Williams**, Robert Alan, Sr. 1947- *WhoWest 92*
**Williams**, Robert Allen 1945- *AmMWSc 92*
**Williams**, Robert B 1921- *WhoIns 92*
**Williams**, Robert B. 1943- *WhoBlA 92*
**Williams**, Robert Calvin 1944- *AmMWSc 92*
**Williams**, Robert Carl, Sr. 1941- *WhoRel 92*
**Williams**, Robert Cody 1948- *WhoIns 92*
**Williams**, Robert D. 1931- *WhoBlA 92*
**Williams**, Robert D., Sr. 1916- *WhoBlA 92*
**Williams**, Robert Dale, Jr. 1950- *WhoRel 92*
**Williams**, Robert Dana 1939- *WhoAmL 92*
**Williams**, Robert Dee 1932- *AmMWSc 92*
**Williams**, Robert E 1934- *WhoIns 92*
**Williams**, Robert Edward 1933- *WhoEnt 92, WhoMW 92*
**Williams**, Robert Ellis 1930- *AmMWSc 92*
**Williams**, Robert Fones 1928- *AmMWSc 92*
**Williams**, Robert Glenn 1937- *AmMWSc 92*
**Williams**, Robert H. 1938- *WhoBlA 92*
**Williams**, Robert Hackney 1915- *AmMWSc 92*
**Williams**, Robert Haworth 1914- *AmMWSc 92*
**Williams**, Robert Henry 1946- *WhoFI 92*
**Williams**, Robert Hughes 1941- *Who 92*
**Williams**, Robert J 1923- *AmMWSc 92*
**Williams**, Robert Jackson 1928- *WhoMW 92*
**Williams**, Robert Jackson 1931- *AmMWSc 92*
**Williams**, Robert Jene 1931- *WhoAmL 92*
**Williams**, Robert Joseph Paton 1926- *IntWW 91, Who 92*
**Williams**, Robert K *WhoAmP 91*
**Williams**, Robert K 1928- *AmMWSc 92*
**Williams**, Robert L 1922- *AmMWSc 92*
**Williams**, Robert L. 1930- *WhoBlA 92*
**Williams**, Robert Lee 1933- *WhoBlA 92*
**Williams**, Robert Lee 1936- *WhoBlA 92*
**Williams**, Robert Lee, Jr. 1955- *WhoBlA 92*
**Williams**, Robert Leo 1949- *WhoRel 92*
**Williams**, Robert Leroy 1928- *AmMWSc 92*
**Williams**, Robert Lloyd 1933- *AmMWSc 92*
**Williams**, Robert Mann 1940- *WhoFI 92*
**Williams**, Robert Martin 1919- *IntWW 91, Who 92*
**Williams**, Robert Michael 1949- *WhoFI 92*
**Williams**, Robert Moore 1907-1977 *TwCSFW 91*
**Williams**, Robert Neff *WhoEnt 92*
**Williams**, Robert Philip 1950- *Who 92*
**Williams**, Robert Pierce 1920- *AmMWSc 92*
**Williams**, Robert Reynolds 1932- *WhoEnt 92*
**Williams**, Robert Sanders 1948- *AmMWSc 92*
**Williams**, Robert Scott 1955- *WhoMW 92*
**Williams**, Robert Stewart 1944- *WhoEnt 92*
**Williams**, Robert Stone 1952- *WhoWest 92*
**Williams**, Robert W. 1922- *WhoBlA 92*
**Williams**, Robert Walter 1920- *AmMWSc 92*
**Williams**, Robert Wilmot 1943- *WhoWest 92*
**Williams**, Roberta Magdalene 1927- *WhoAmP 91*
**Williams**, Robin *LesBEnT 92, Who 92*
**Williams**, Robin 1941- *AmMWSc 92*
**Williams**, Robin 1951- *WhoEnt 92*
**Williams**, Robin 1952- *IntMPA 92, IntWW 91*
**Williams**, Robin Guy 1930- *Who 92*
**Williams**, Robin L *WhoAmP 91*
**Williams**, Robin Murphy, Jr. 1914- *IntWW 91*
**Williams**, Robin O 1927- *AmMWSc 92*
**Williams**, Robin Philip 1928- *Who 92*
**Williams**, Robley Cook 1908- *AmMWSc 92*
**Williams**, Robley Cook, Jr 1940- *AmMWSc 92*
**Williams**, Rodney Elliott 1928- *WhoBlA 92*
**Williams**, Roger *WhoBlA 92*
**Williams**, Roger 1603-1683 *AmPolLe, BenetAL 91, RComAH*
**Williams**, Roger 1926- *IntMPA 92*
**Williams**, Roger Courtland 1944- *WhoAmL 92*
**Williams**, Roger Harold 1954- *WhoAmL 92, WhoMW 92*
**Williams**, Roger J 1893-1988 *FacFETw*
**Williams**, Roger Kenton 1914-1989 *WhoBlA 92N*
**Williams**, Roger Lea 1941- *AmMWSc 92*
**Williams**, Roger Neal 1935- *AmMWSc 92*
**Williams**, Roger Richard 1944- *AmMWSc 92*
**Williams**, Roger Stanley 1931- *IntWW 91, Who 92*
**Williams**, Roger Stewart 1941- *AmMWSc 92*
**Williams**, Roger Terry 1936- *AmMWSc 92*
**Williams**, Roger Wright 1918- *AmMWSc 92*

**Williams,** Roland 1910- *WrDr 92*
**Williams,** Ron 1945- *WhoIns 92*
**Williams,** Ron Robert 1944- *WhoBlA 92*
**Williams,** Ronald Bethel 1943- *WhoEnt 92*
**Williams,** Ronald Charles 1948- *WhoBlA 92*
**Williams,** Ronald David 1944- *WhoFI 92, WhoWest 92*
**Williams,** Ronald Dean 1940- *WhoRel 92*
**Williams,** Ronald Doherty 1927- *WhoAmL 92*
**Williams,** Ronald Eugene 1942- *WhoRel 92*
**Williams,** Ronald John 1927- *WhoFI 92*
**Williams,** Ronald Lee 1936- *AmMWSc 92, WhoWest 92*
**Williams,** Ronald Lee 1949- *WhoBlA 92*
**Williams,** Ronald Lloyde 1944- *AmMWSc 92*
**Williams,** Ronald Millward 1922- *Who 92*
**Williams,** Ronald Oscar 1940- *WhoFI 92, WhoWest 92*
**Williams,** Ronald Wendell 1939- *AmMWSc 92*
**Williams,** Ronald Wesley 1946- *WhoBlA 92*
**Williams,** Ronald William 1926- *Who 92*
**Williams,** Roosevelt 1944- *WhoBlA 92*
**Williams,** Rosa B. 1933- *WhoBlA 92*
**Williams,** Ross Arnold 1953- *WhoMW 92*
**Williams,** Ross Edward 1922- *AmMWSc 92*
**Williams,** Rowan Douglas 1950- *Who 92*
**Williams,** Roy 1934- *Who 92*
**Williams,** Roy Edward 1938- *AmMWSc 92*
**Williams,** Roy Lee 1937- *AmMWSc 92*
**Williams,** Roy Nolan, Jr 1941- *WhoAmP 91*
**Williams,** Ruby Mai 1904- *WhoBlA 92*
**Williams,** Ruby Ora 1926- *WhoWest 92*
**Williams,** Rudy V. *WhoBlA 92*
**Williams,** Rufus Phillips 1851-1911 *BiInAmS*
**Williams,** Runette Flowers 1945- *WhoBlA 92*
**Williams,** Russ *DrAPF 91*
**Williams,** Russell Raymond 1926- *AmMWSc 92*
**Williams,** Ruth H. 1938- *WhoEnt 92*
**Williams,** Ruth J. *WhoWest 92*
**Williams,** Ruth Lee 1944- *WhoWest 92*
**Williams,** Ruthann Evege 1945- *WhoBlA 92*
**Williams,** Sallie Elizabeth 1937- *WhoAmL 92*
**Williams,** Sam 1934- *WhoAmP 91*
**Williams,** Sam B *AmMWSc 92*
**Williams,** Samm-Art 1946- *WhoBlA 92*
**Williams,** Samuel 1743-1817 *BiInAmS*
**Williams,** Samuel Gardner 1827-1900 *BiInAmS*
**Williams,** Samuel Lewis 1934- *Who 92*
**Williams,** Sandra K. 1954- *WhoBlA 92*
**Williams,** Sandra Roberts 1940- *WhoBlA 92*
**Williams,** Scott *WhoBlA 92*
**Williams,** Scott W. 1943- *WhoBlA 92*
**Williams,** Scott Warner 1943- *AmMWSc 92*
**Williams,** Sean Dick 1956- *WhoMW 92*
**Williams,** Selase 1945- *WhoBlA 92*
**Williams,** Shahron G. 1949- *WhoBlA 92*
**Williams,** Shawnell 1962- *WhoBlA 92*
**Williams,** Sheila Andrea 1966- *WhoBlA 92*
**Williams,** Sherley Anne *DrAPF 91*
**Williams,** Sherley Anne 1944- *BlkLC [port], WhoBlA 92*
**Williams,** Sherman 1961- *WhoBlA 92*
**Williams,** Shirley 1930- *IntWW 91*
**Williams,** Shirley Jean Oostenbroek 1931- *WhoMW 92*
**Williams,** Shirley Stennis *WhoBlA 92*
**Williams,** Shirley Vivien Teresa Brittain 1930- *FacFETw, Who 92*
**Williams,** Shirley Yvonne *WhoBlA 92*
**Williams,** Sidmond Carl 1943- *WhoFI 92*
**Williams,** Sidney Arthur 1933- *AmMWSc 92*
**Williams,** Sidney Austen 1912- *Who 92*
**Williams,** Sidney B., Jr. 1935- *WhoBlA 92*
**Williams,** Simon 1943- *ConAu 133*
**Williams,** Smallwood E. d1991 *NewYTBS 91*
**Williams,** Smallwood Edmond 1907- *WhoAmP 91*
**Williams,** Snowden J. 1959- *WhoBlA 92*
**Williams,** Sonya Denise 1963- *WhoBlA 92*
**Williams,** St Claire Nathaniel 1949- *WhoAmP 91*
**Williams,** Stacy *WhoEnt 92*
**Williams,** Stanley 1925- *WhoEnt 92*
**Williams,** Stanley A 1932- *AmMWSc 92*
**Williams,** Stanley Clark 1939- *AmMWSc 92, WhoWest 92*
**Williams,** Stanley David 1947- *WhoEnt 92*
**Williams,** Stanley King 1948- *WhoBlA 92*
**Williams,** Starks J. 1921- *WhoBlA 92*
**Williams,** Stephen 1926- *IntWW 91*
**Williams,** Stephen Craig 1954- *WhoEnt 92*
**Williams,** Stephen Earl 1948- *AmMWSc 92*
**Williams,** Stephen Edward 1942- *AmMWSc 92*
**Williams,** Stephen F 1936- *WhoAmP 91*
**Williams,** Stephen Fain 1936- *WhoAmL 92*
**Williams,** Stephen Jay 1940- *WhoAmL 92*
**Williams,** Stephen Joseph 1948- *WhoWest 92*
**Williams,** Stephen T 1956- *WhoAmP 91*
**Williams,** Stephen West 1790-1855 *BiInAmS*
**Williams,** Sterling B., Jr. 1941- *WhoBlA 92*
**Williams,** Steve 1952- *WhoIns 92*
**Williams,** Steven Frank 1944- *AmMWSc 92*
**Williams,** Steven Henry 1947- *WhoAmL 92*
**Williams,** Steven Mark 1959- *WhoRel 92*
**Williams,** Steven Mark 1961- *WhoEnt 92*
**Williams,** Steven Orville 1951- *WhoAmP 91*
**Williams,** Sue M. 1942- *WhoFI 92, WhoWest 92*
**Williams,** Susan Eileen 1952- *WhoFI 92*
**Williams,** Susan Elizabeth 1942- *Who 92*
**Williams,** Susan Eva 1915- *Who 92*
**Williams,** Susan Hadley 1956- *WhoAmL 92*
**Williams,** Sydney *Who 92*
**Williams,** Sylvia J. 1939- *WhoBlA 92*
**Williams,** Tad *IntAu&W 91*
**Williams,** Tennessee 1911-1983 *BenetAL 91, FacFETw [port], RComAH*
**Williams,** Terence Heaton 1929- *AmMWSc 92*
**Williams,** Terri Ann 1958- *WhoAmL 92*
**Williams,** Terri L. 1958- *WhoBlA 92*
**Williams,** Terrie Michelle 1954- *WhoBlA 92, WhoEnt 92*
**Williams,** Terry Lee 1950- *WhoAmP 91*
**Williams,** Terry Wayne 1945- *AmMWSc 92*
**Williams,** Theartrice 1934- *WhoBlA 92*
**Williams,** Theodore Burton 1949- *AmMWSc 92*
**Williams,** Theodore E. 1943- *WhoWest 92*
**Williams,** Theodore Earle 1920- *WhoFI 92, WhoWest 92*
**Williams,** Theodore Edward 1943- *WhoBlA 92*
**Williams,** Theodore J 1923- *AmMWSc 92*
**Williams,** Theodore Joseph 1923- *WhoMW 92*
**Williams,** Theodore L 1939- *AmMWSc 92*
**Williams,** Theodore M. 1905-1989 *WhoBlA 92N*
**Williams,** Theodore P 1933- *AmMWSc 92*
**Williams,** Theodore R. 1931- *WhoBlA 92*
**Williams,** Theodore Roosevelt 1930- *AmMWSc 92*
**Williams,** Theodore Samuel 1918- *FacFETw*
**Williams,** Theodore Shields 1911- *AmMWSc 92*
**Williams,** Theopolis Charles 1956- *WhoBlA 92*
**Williams,** Thom Albert 1941- *WhoFI 92, WhoMW 92*
**Williams,** Thomas *DrAPF 91*
**Williams,** Thomas 1926- *IntAu&W 91*
**Williams,** Thomas Alan 1947- *AmMWSc 92*
**Williams,** Thomas Allen 1959- *WhoBlA 92*
**Williams,** Thomas Allison 1936- *WhoAmL 92*
**Williams,** Thomas Arthur 1943- *WhoAmL 92*
**Williams,** Thomas Eifion Hopkins 1923- *Who 92*
**Williams,** Thomas Ffrancon 1928- *AmMWSc 92*
**Williams,** Thomas Franklin 1921- *AmMWSc 92*
**Williams,** Thomas Henry 1934- *AmMWSc 92*
**Williams,** Thomas Henry Lee 1951- *AmMWSc 92*
**Williams,** Thomas Hewett 1936- *WhoMW 92*
**Williams,** Thomas J 1948- *WhoIns 92*
**Williams,** Thomas Pedworth 1910- *WhoBlA 92*
**Williams,** Thomas R 1926- *AmMWSc 92*
**Williams,** Thomas Russell 1928- *WhoFI 92*
**Williams,** Thomas Stafford *Who 92*
**Williams,** Thomas Stafford 1930- *IntWW 91, WhoRel 92*
**Williams,** Thomas T 1925- *WhoAmP 91*
**Williams,** Thornton, Jr. 1942- *WhoRel 92*
**Williams,** Thurmon *WhoMW 92*
**Williams,** Tiffany Johns, Jr. 1929- *WhoMW 92*
**Williams,** Timothy C 1942- *AmMWSc 92*
**Williams,** Todd Robertson 1945- *AmMWSc 92*
**Williams,** Tom 1886-1985 *FacFETw*
**Williams,** Tom Vare 1938- *AmMWSc 92*
**Williams,** Tommye Joyce 1930- *WhoBlA 92*
**Williams,** Tony 1945- *ConMus 6, WhoEnt 92*
**Williams,** Travis d1991 *NewYTBS 91*
**Williams,** Treat 1951- *WhoEnt 92*
**Williams,** Treat 1952- *IntMPA 92*
**Williams,** Trevor *Who 92*
**Williams,** Trevor Illtyd 1921- *Who 92, WrDr 92*
**Williams,** Tuffy 1952- *WhoEnt 92*
**Williams,** Tyrell Clay 1949- *WhoWest 92*
**Williams,** Ulis 1941- *BlkOlyM*
**Williams,** Ulysses Jean 1947- *WhoBlA 92*
**Williams,** Ursula Moray *WrDr 92*
**Williams,** Valena Marie 1948- *WhoWest 92*
**Williams,** Vanessa *WhoBlA 92*
**Williams,** Vaniecia Jenell *WhoEnt 92*
**Williams,** Vaughan *Who 92*
**Williams,** Vera B. 1927- *WrDr 92*
**Williams,** Vernice Louise 1934- *WhoBlA 92*
**Williams,** Vernon 1926- *AmMWSc 92*
**Williams,** Vernon L *WhoAmP 91*
**Williams,** Veronica Ann 1956- *WhoFI 92*
**Williams,** Vesta *WhoBlA 92*
**Williams,** Vick Franklin 1936- *AmMWSc 92*
**Williams,** Virginia Walker *WhoBlA 92*
**Williams,** W. Bill, Jr. 1939- *WhoBlA 92*
**Williams,** W. Clyde *WhoBlA 92*
**Williams,** W. Donald 1936- *WhoBlA 92*
**Williams,** W. Vail 1940- *WhoMW 92*
**Williams,** Wade Allen 1960- *WhoAmP 91*
**Williams,** Walker Richard, Jr. 1928- *WhoBlA 92, WhoMW 92*
**Williams,** Wallace C. *WhoBlA 92*
**Williams,** Wallace Terry 1942- *AmMWSc 92*
**Williams,** Walter 1939- *WhoBlA 92*
**Williams,** Walter Baker 1921- *WhoWest 92*
**Williams,** Walter Bernard 1942- *WhoFI 92*
**Williams,** Walter E. 1936- *WrDr 92*
**Williams,** Walter Ford 1927- *AmMWSc 92*
**Williams,** Walter Fred 1929- *IntWW 91, WhoFI 92*
**Williams,** Walter Gordon Mason 1923- *Who 92*
**Williams,** Walter Harrison 1941- *WhoWest 92*
**Williams,** Walter Jackson, Jr 1925- *AmMWSc 92*
**Williams,** Walter Michael 1943- *AmMWSc 92*
**Williams,** Walter W. *WhoMW 92*
**Williams,** Warren Grey 1962- *WhoFI 92*
**Williams,** Warren Stephen 1943- *WhoMW 92*
**Williams,** Wayne Darnell 1967- *WhoBlA 92*
**Williams,** Wayne Richard 1945- *WhoBlA 92*
**Williams,** Wayne Watson 1922- *AmMWSc 92*
**Williams,** Wells Eldon 1919- *AmMWSc 92*
**Williams,** Wendell P 1950- *WhoAmP 91*
**Williams,** Wendell Sterling 1928- *AmMWSc 92*
**Williams,** Wesley Keith 1953- *WhoRel 92*
**Williams,** Wesley S., Jr. 1942- *WhoBlA 92*
**Williams,** Wesley Samuel, Jr. 1942- *WhoAmL 92*
**Williams,** Wilbert 1924- *WhoBlA 92*
**Williams,** Wilbert Edd 1948- *WhoBlA 92*
**Williams,** Wilbert Lee 1938- *WhoBlA 92*
**Williams,** Wilho Edward 1922- *WhoWest 92*
**Williams,** William, Jr. 1939- *WhoBlA 92*
**Williams,** William Appleman 1921-1990 *AnObit 1990*
**Williams,** William Arnold 1922- *AmMWSc 92, WhoWest 92*
**Williams,** William B 1923-1986 *FacFETw*
**Williams,** William C. *ConAu 34NR*
**Williams,** William Carlos 1883-1963 *BenetAL 91, ConAu 34NR, ConLC 67 [port], FacFETw, RComAH*
**Williams,** William Clark 1941- *WhoWest 92*
**Williams,** William Corey 1937- *WhoRel 92, WhoWest 92*
**Williams,** William David 1917- *Who 92*
**Williams,** William Donald 1928- *AmMWSc 92*
**Williams,** William H. 1936- *ConAu 36NR*
**Williams,** William Henry, II 1931- *WhoFI 92*
**Williams,** William J. 1935- *WhoBlA 92*
**Williams,** William James 1935- *AmMWSc 92*
**Williams,** William John 1928- *IntWW 91, WhoMW 92*
**Williams,** William John, Jr. 1937- *WhoAmL 92*
**Williams,** William Joseph 1915- *WhoIns 92*
**Williams,** William Joseph 1926- *AmMWSc 92*
**Williams,** William Kinsey 1942- *WhoFI 92*
**Williams,** William Lane 1914- *AmMWSc 92*
**Williams,** William Lawrence 1919- *AmMWSc 92*
**Williams,** William Lee 1937- *AmMWSc 92*
**Williams,** William Max 1926- *Who 92*
**Williams,** William Orville 1940- *AmMWSc 92*
**Williams,** William Paul 1948- *WhoAmP 91*
**Williams,** William Stephen 1953- *WhoRel 92*
**Williams,** William Thomas 1913- *Who 92*
**Williams,** William Thomas 1924- *AmMWSc 92*
**Williams,** William Thomas 1942- *WhoBlA 92*
**Williams,** William Trevor 1925- *Who 92*
**Williams,** Willie 1947- *WhoBlA 92*
**Williams,** Willie, Jr. *WhoBlA 92*
**Williams,** Willie, Jr 1947- *AmMWSc 92*
**Williams,** Willie Elbert 1927- *AmMWSc 92, WhoBlA 92*
**Williams,** Willie J. *DrAPF 91*
**Williams,** Willie J. 1949- *WhoBlA 92*
**Williams,** Willie LaVern 1940- *WhoBlA 92*
**Williams,** Willie S. 1932- *WhoBlA 92*
**Williams,** Wilmer Dempsey 1937- *WhoRel 92*
**Williams,** Winston *WhoBlA 92*
**Williams,** Winton Edwin 1935- *WhoAmL 92*
**Williams,** Winton Hugh 1920- *WhoFI 92*
**Williams,** Wirt 1921- *BenetAL 91*
**Williams,** Wyatt Clifford 1921- *WhoBlA 92*
**Williams,** Wynona Bennett 1959- *WhoEnt 92*
**Williams,** Yarborough, Jr. 1950- *WhoBlA 92*
**Williams,** Yarborough Burwell, Jr. 1928- *WhoBlA 92*
**Williams,** Yvonne Carter 1932- *WhoBlA 92*
**Williams,** Yvonne LaVerne 1938- *WhoBlA 92*
**Williams,** Yvonne Lovat 1920- *Who 92*
**Williams-Ashman,** Howard Guy 1925- *AmMWSc 92*
**Williams Boyd,** Sheila Anne 1951- *WhoBlA 92*
**Williams-Bulkeley,** Richard Harry David 1911- *Who 92*
**Williams Davis,** Edith G. 1958- *WhoBlA 92*
**Williams-Dovi,** Joanna 1953- *WhoBlA 92*
**Williams-Ellis,** David 1959- *TwCPaSc*
**Williams-Garner,** Debra 1957- *WhoBlA 92*
**Williams-Green,** Joyce F. 1948- *WhoBlA 92*
**Williams-Harris,** Diane Beatrice 1949- *WhoBlA 92*
**Williams-Jones,** Michael 1947- *IntMPA 92*
**Williams Of Elvel,** Baron 1933- *IntWW 91, Who 92*
**Williams-Thomas,** Reginald Silvers d1990 *Who 92N*
**Williams-Wynn,** Watkin 1940- *Who 92*
**Williams-Wynne,** John Francis 1908- *Who 92*
**Williamson** *Who 92*
**Williamson,** Alan 1944- *WrDr 92*
**Williamson,** Andrew George 1948- *Who 92*
**Williamson,** Arthur Elridge, Jr 1926- *AmMWSc 92*
**Williamson,** Ashley Deas 1947- *AmMWSc 92*
**Williamson,** Barbara Diane 1950- *WhoFI 92, WhoWest 92*
**Williamson,** Bill Logan 1938- *WhoWest 92*
**Williamson,** Brian *Who 92*
**Williamson,** Carl Vance 1955- *WhoBlA 92*
**Williamson,** Carlton 1958- *WhoBlA 92*
**Williamson,** Charles Elvin 1926- *AmMWSc 92*
**Williamson,** Clarence Kelly 1924- *AmMWSc 92*
**Williamson,** Clark Murray 1935- *WhoRel 92*
**Williamson,** Claude F 1933- *AmMWSc 92*
**Williamson,** Coy Colbert, Jr. 1936- *WhoBlA 92*
**Williamson,** Craig *DrAPF 91*
**Williamson,** Craig Edward 1953- *AmMWSc 92*
**Williamson,** David 1927- *ConAu 134*
**Williamson,** David 1942- *WrDr 92*
**Williamson,** David F. 1934- *IntWW 91*
**Williamson,** David Francis 1934- *Who 92*

Williamson, David Gadsby 1941- AmMWSc 92
Williamson, David Geoffrey 1927- IntAu&W 91
Williamson, David Keith 1942- IntAu&W 91, IntWW 91
Williamson, David Lee 1930- AmMWSc 92
Williamson, David Louis 1937- WhoRel 92
Williamson, David Theodore Nelson 1923- IntWW 91, Who 92
Williamson, Denis George 1941- AmMWSc 92
Williamson, Donald Elwin 1913- AmMWSc 92
Williamson, Douglas Harris 1924- AmMWSc 92
Williamson, Douglas Mark 1951- WhoAmL 92
Williamson, Edward Henry 1957- WhoRel 92, WhoWest 92
Williamson, Edward P 1933- AmMWSc 92
Williamson, Elsie Marjorie 1913- Who 92
Williamson, Fletcher Phillips 1923- WhoFI 92
Williamson, Francis Sidney Lanier 1927- AmMWSc 92
Williamson, Frank Edger 1917- Who 92
Williamson, Fred 1937- IntMPA 92
Williamson, George Arthur 1938- WhoAmP 91
Williamson, George Beauchamp 1946- WhoAmP 91
Williamson, George H., Jr. 1929- WhoBlA 92
Williamson, George Malcolm 1939- Who 92
Williamson, Gerald Neal 1932- ConAu 34NR
Williamson, Gilbert P. 1937- IntWW 91
Williamson, Gilbert Pemberton 1937- WhoFI 92, WhoMW 92
Williamson, Gingeree Eletta 1958- WhoAmL 92
Williamson, Gloria Ann 1931- WhoMW 92
Williamson, Handy, Jr 1945- AmMWSc 92, WhoBlA 92
Williamson, Harold 1898-1972 TwCPaSc
Williamson, Harold E 1930- AmMWSc 92
Williamson, Harold Sandys 1892- TwCPaSc
Williamson, Harwood Danford 1932- WhoWest 92
Williamson, Hazel Eleanor 1947- Who 92
Williamson, Henry 1895-1977 ConAu 36NR, RfGEnL 91
Williamson, Henry Gaston, Jr. 1947- WhoFI 92
Williamson, Holly Harvel 1956- WhoAmL 92
Williamson, Hugh 1735-1819 BilnAmS
Williamson, Hugh A 1927- AmMWSc 92
Williamson, Hugh A 1932- AmMWSc 92
Williamson, Hugh Godfrey Maturin 1947- Who 92
Williamson, J David 1933- WhoIns 92
Williamson, J. N. ConAu 34NR, DrAPF 91
Williamson, J N 1932- IntAu&W 91
Williamson, Jack 1908- BenetAL 91, IntAu&W 91, TwCSFW 91, WhoWest 92, WrDr 92
Williamson, Jack DeForrest 1934- WhoWest 92
Williamson, James 1920- Who 92
Williamson, James Allen 1951- WhoAmP 91
Williamson, James Larry 1952- WhoAmP 91
Williamson, James Lawrence 1929- AmMWSc 92
Williamson, Jane 1921- TwCPaSc
Williamson, Jerry Robert 1938- AmMWSc 92
Williamson, Joanne Marcroft 1952- WhoAmL 92
Williamson, Joel 1930- WrDr 92
Williamson, John Arthur 1947- WhoRel 92
Williamson, John Hybert 1938- AmMWSc 92
Williamson, John Maurice 1938- WhoMW 92
Williamson, John Michael 1962- WhoWest 92
Williamson, John Pritchard 1922- WhoWest 92
Williamson, John Richard 1933- AmMWSc 92
Williamson, John S 1958- AmMWSc 92
Williamson, John Thomas 1925- WhoFI 92
Williamson, John W 1933- AmMWSc 92
Williamson, Johnny H 1934- WhoIns 92
Williamson, Karen Elizabeth 1947- WhoBlA 92
Williamson, Keith 1928- IntWW 91, Who 92
Williamson, Kenneth Dale 1920- AmMWSc 92
Williamson, Kenneth Donald, Jr 1935- AmMWSc 92
Williamson, Kenneth Lee 1934- AmMWSc 92
Williamson, Kenneth Paul, Jr. 1942- WhoEnt 92
Williamson, Kenneth Robert 1929- WhoWest 92
Williamson, Laird 1937- WhoEnt 92
Williamson, Lamar, Jr. 1926- WhoRel 92
Williamson, Larry C 1930- WhoAmP 91
Williamson, Linda Jean M 1952- WhoAmP 91
Williamson, Liz WhoEnt 92
Williamson, Lowell James 1923- WhoWest 92
Williamson, Luther Howard 1936- AmMWSc 92
Williamson, Malcolm Who 92
Williamson, Malcolm 1931- ConCom 92, NewAmDM
Williamson, Malcolm Benjamin Graham 1931- IntWW 91
Williamson, Malcolm Benjamin Graham C 1931- Who 92
Williamson, Malcolm Edward 1936- WhoMW 92
Williamson, Marianne 1953?- News 91 [port]
Williamson, Marjorie Who 92
Williamson, Marshall WhoEnt 92
Williamson, Michael Joe 1944- WhoFI 92
Williamson, Neil Robert 1940- WhoWest 92
Williamson, Neil Seymour, III 1935- WhoWest 92
Williamson, Nicholas Frederick Hedworth 1937- Who 92
Williamson, Nicol 1938- IntMPA 92, IntWW 91, Who 92, WhoEnt 92
Williamson, Nigel 1954- Who 92
Williamson, Oliver Eaton 1932- WhoAmL 92, WhoFI 92
Williamson, Patricia Mary 1952- WhoFI 92
Williamson, Patrick 1929- IntMPA 92
Williamson, Patrick Leslie 1948- AmMWSc 92
Williamson, Patrick Michael 1929- WhoEnt 92
Williamson, Paul Alan 1947- WhoMW 92
Williamson, Peter George 1952- AmMWSc 92
Williamson, Peter Roger 1942- Who 92
Williamson, Ralph Edward 1923- AmMWSc 92
Williamson, Raymond Daniel 1938- WhoAmL 92
Williamson, Richard 1935- WrDr 92
Williamson, Richard Arthur 1930- WhoWest 92
Williamson, Richard Arthur 1932- Who 92
Williamson, Richard Cardinal 1939- AmMWSc 92
Williamson, Richard Duane 1948- WhoAmP 91
Williamson, Richard Edmund 1927- AmMWSc 92
Williamson, Richard F 1952- WhoAmP 91
Williamson, Richard Salisbury 1949- WhoAmL 92
Williamson, Robert 1938- Who 92
Williamson, Robert Brady 1933- AmMWSc 92
Williamson, Robert Brian 1945- Who 92
Williamson, Robert C. 1916- WrDr 92
Williamson, Robert Charles 1925- WhoFI 92
Williamson, Robert Elmore 1937- AmMWSc 92
Williamson, Robert Emmett 1937- AmMWSc 92, WhoWest 92
Williamson, Robert Garland 1942- WhoFI 92
Williamson, Robert Kerr Who 92
Williamson, Robert Marshall 1923- AmMWSc 92
Williamson, Robert Samuel 1922- AmMWSc 92
Williamson, Robert Webster 1942- WhoFI 92
Williamson, Robin DrAPF 91
Williamson, Robin 1943- IntAu&W 91, WrDr 92
Williamson, Robin Charles Noel 1942- Who 92
Williamson, Roy 1936-1990 AnObit 1990
Williamson, Samuel Johns 1939- AmMWSc 92
Williamson, Samuel P. 1949- WhoBlA 92
Williamson, Samuel R. 1943- WhoBlA 92
Williamson, Sonny Boy 1897-1965 NewAmDM
Williamson, Sonny Boy 1914?-1948 NewAmDM
Williamson, Stanley Gill 1938- AmMWSc 92
Williamson, Stanley Morris 1936- AmMWSc 92
Williamson, Stephen 1948- Who 92
Williamson, Susan 1936- AmMWSc 92
Williamson, Thomas Daniel 1959- WhoMW 92
Williamson, Thomas Garnett 1934- AmMWSc 92
Williamson, Tony 1932- IntAu&W 91
Williamson, Vikki Lyn 1956- WhoFI 92, WhoMW 92
Williamson, Walter Robert 1921- WhoAmP 91
Williamson, Walton E, Jr 1944- AmMWSc 92
Williamson, William, Jr 1934- AmMWSc 92
Williamson, William Burton 1946- AmMWSc 92
Williamson, William O 1911- AmMWSc 92
Williamson-Ige, Dorothy Kay 1950- WhoBlA 92
Williard, Paul Gregory 1950- AmMWSc 92
Willich, Martin 1945- IntWW 91
Willich, Michael Von 1969- WhoRel 92
Willie, Charles Vert 1927- WhoBlA 92
Willie, Claude Edward, III 1952- WhoRel 92
Willie, Frederick ConAu 133
Willie, John Howard 1943- WhoMW 92
Willie, Louis J. 1923- WhoBlA 92
Williford, Cynthia W. 1917- WhoBlA 92
Williford, Lawrence H WhoIns 92
Williford, Lawrence Harding 1929- WhoFI 92
Williford, Stanley O. 1942- WhoBlA 92
Williford, William Olin 1933- AmMWSc 92
Willig, David S. 1961- WhoAmL 92
Willig, Karl Victor 1944- WhoWest 92
Willig, Leslie August 1926- WhoMW 92
Willig, Michael Robert 1952- AmMWSc 92
Willig, Robert Daniel 1947- WhoAmL 92
Williger, Ervin John 1927- AmMWSc 92
Williges, George Goudie 1924- AmMWSc 92
Williges, Robert Carl 1942- AmMWSc 92
Willihnganz, Paul Waddell 1937- WhoAmL 92, WhoFI 92
Willimon, William Henry 1946- WhoRel 92
Willing, James Richard 1958- WhoWest 92
Willing, Maria Paula Figueiroa Who 92
Willing, Robert Nelson 1934- WhoRel 92
Willing, Victor 1928-1988 TwCPaSc
Willingham, Allan King 1941- AmMWSc 92
Willingham, Ben Hill d1991 NewYTBS 91 [port]
Willingham, Calder DrAPF 91
Willingham, Calder 1922- BenetAL 91, ConNov 91, WrDr 92
Willingham, Clark Suttles 1944- WhoAmL 92
Willingham, Donnie Andrew 1951- WhoFI 92
Willingham, Edward Bacon, Jr. 1934- WhoRel 92
Willingham, Francis Fries, Jr 1942- AmMWSc 92
Willingham, Jeanne Maggart 1923- WhoEnt 92
Willingham, Mark C 1946- AmMWSc 92
Willingham, Thomas W 1945- WhoIns 92
Willingham, Voncile 1935- WhoBlA 92
Willings, David Richard 1932- IntAu&W 91
Willink, Charles 1929- Who 92
Williquette, Gerald F 1940- WhoIns 92
Willis Who 92
Willis, Baron 1918- IntWW 91, Who 92
Willis, Andrew 1938- WhoBlA 92
Willis, Avery Thomas, Jr. 1934- WhoRel 92
Willis, Bradley J. 1952- WhoWest 92
Willis, Bruce 1955- ConTFT 9, IntMPA 92
Willis, Bruce Walter 1955- IntWW 91, WhoEnt 92
Willis, C. Paul 1932- WhoRel 92
Willis, Carl Bertram 1937- AmMWSc 92
Willis, Carl Raeburn, Jr 1939- AmMWSc 92, WhoFI 92
Willis, Cecil B. WhoBlA 92
Willis, Charles Dubois 1925- WhoRel 92
Willis, Charles L. 1926- WhoBlA 92
Willis, Charles Reginald 1906- Who 92
Willis, Charles Richard 1928- AmMWSc 92
Willis, Christopher John 1934- AmMWSc 92
Willis, Clifford Leon 1913- AmMWSc 92, WhoWest 92
Willis, Clive 1939- AmMWSc 92
Willis, Connie 1945- ConAu 35NR, IntAu&W 91, TwCSFW 91, WrDr 92
Willis, D Roger 1933- AmMWSc 92
Willis, Dale Roy 1950- WhoWest 92
Willis, Daryl Brent 1957- WhoRel 92
Willis, David Arthur 1940- WhoFI 92
Willis, David Edwin 1926- AmMWSc 92, WhoWest 92
Willis, David Jackson, Jr. 1956- WhoRel 92
Willis, David Lee 1927- AmMWSc 92
Willis, David Leon 1959- WhoAmL 92
Willis, Dawn Louise 1959- WhoAmL 92
Willis, Doyle 1908- WhoAmP 91
Willis, Edgar E. WrDr 92
Willis, Edward 1918- IntAu&W 91
Willis, Eric 1922- Who 92
Willis, Eric Archibald 1922- IntWW 91
Willis, Everett Irving 1908- WhoAmL 92
Willis, Frances E 1899-1983 FacFETw
Willis, Frank B. 1947- WhoBlA 92
Willis, Frank Marsden 1926- AmMWSc 92
Willis, Frank William 1947- Who 92
Willis, Fred Douglas 1918- WhoBlA 92
Willis, Frederic L. 1937- WhoBlA 92
Willis, Gaspard Who 92
Willis, George Clark 1938- WhoWest 92
Willis, Gerald WhoAmP 91
Willis, Gladys January 1944- WhoBlA 92
Willis, Gordon IntMPA 92, WhoEnt 92
Willis, Grover C, Jr 1921- AmMWSc 92
Willis, Grover Cleveland 1933- WhoAmP 91
Willis, Guido James 1923- Who 92
Willis, Guye Henry 1937- AmMWSc 92
Willis, Harold Lester 1940- AmMWSc 92
Willis, Harold Wendt, Sr. 1927- WhoFI 92, WhoWest 92
Willis, Henry Stokes, Jr. 1947- WhoBlA 92
Willis, Irene DrAPF 91
Willis, Isaac 1940- AmMWSc 92, WhoBlA 92
Willis, Jacalyn Giacalone 1947- AmMWSc 92
Willis, Jack LesBEnT 92
Willis, James Who 92
Willis, James Alfred 1925- IntWW 91
Willis, James Byron 1918- AmMWSc 92
Willis, James Stewart, Jr 1935- AmMWSc 92
Willis, Jeffrey Owen 1948- AmMWSc 92
Willis, Jill Michelle 1952- WhoBlA 92
Willis, Jimmy Roy 1941- WhoWest 92
Willis, John A. 1916- WrDr 92
Willis, John Alvin 1916- WhoEnt 92A
Willis, John Brooke 1906- Who 92
Willis, John Brooker 1926- Who 92
Willis, John Frederick 1937- Who 92
Willis, John Fristoe 1910- WhoEnt 92
Willis, John Patrick 1947- WhoFI 92
Willis, John Steele 1935- AmMWSc 92
Willis, John Trueman 1918- Who 92
Willis, Joseph Robert McKenzie 1909- Who 92
Willis, Judith Horwitz 1935- AmMWSc 92
Willis, Katherine Mary 1916- WhoAmP 91
Willis, Kathi Grant 1959- WhoBlA 92
Willis, Kenneth Henry George Who 92
Willis, Kenneth R 1932- WhoIns 92
Willis, Kevin Andre 1962- WhoBlA 92
Willis, Larryann C 1947- WhoAmP 91
Willis, Lee Lawrence 1944- WhoAmL 92
Willis, Levy WhoRel 92
Willis, Levy E. WhoBlA 92
Willis, Lloyd L, II 1943- AmMWSc 92
Willis, Lucy 1954- TwCPaSc
Willis, Lynn Roger 1942- AmMWSc 92
Willis, Meredith Sue DrAPF 91
Willis, Michael Stephan 1949- WhoEnt 92
Willis, Miechelle Orchid 1954- WhoBlA 92
Willis, Millie WhoMW 92
Willis, Nathaniel Parker 1806-1867 BenetAL 91
Willis, Norma Byers 1931- WhoAmP 91
Willis, Norman David 1933- IntWW 91, Who 92
Willis, Park Weed, III 1925- AmMWSc 92
Willis, Peter Matthew 1967- WhoFI 92
Willis, Phyllida Mave 1918- AmMWSc 92
Willis, Ralph 1938- IntWW 91
Willis, Reginald Erwyn 1934- WhoMW 92
Willis, Richard James 1957- WhoMW 92
Willis, Richard Murat 1929- WhoEnt 92
Willis, Robert D 1948- AmMWSc 92
Willis, Robert Earl 1930- WhoAmL 92
Willis, Robert William Gaspard 1905- Who 92
Willis, Roberta Berk 1951- WhoAmP 91
Willis, Roger Blenkiron 1906- Who 92
Willis, Ronald Porter 1926- AmMWSc 92
Willis, Rose W. 1939- WhoBlA 92
Willis, Sara Payson 1811-1872 BenetAL 91
Willis, Selene Yvette 1958- WhoWest 92

**Willis**, Stephen Michael 1947- *WhoRel 92*
**Willis**, Stephen Murrell 1929- *Who 92*
**Willis**, Sunday 1934- *WhoEnt 92*
**Willis**, Suzanne Eileen 1951- *AmMWSc 92*
**Willis**, Ted *Who 92*
**Willis**, Ted 1918- *IntMPA 92, WrDr 92*
**Willis**, Thomas Newton 1948- *WhoMW 92*
**Willis**, Val 1946- *WrDr 92*
**Willis**, Victor *TwCPaSc*
**Willis**, Wayne O 1928- *AmMWSc 92*
**Willis**, Wesley Robert 1941- *WhoFI 92, WhoRel 92*
**Willis**, William Darrell, Jr 1934- *AmMWSc 92*
**Willis**, William Ervin 1926- *WhoAmL 92*
**Willis**, William Harold, Jr. 1927- *WhoFI 92*
**Willis**, William Hillman 1908- *AmMWSc 92*
**Willis**, William J 1932- *AmMWSc 92*
**Willis**, William Pascal 1910- *WhoAmP 91*
**Willis**, William Russell 1926- *AmMWSc 92*
**Willis**, William Van 1937- *AmMWSc 92*
**Williscroft**, Dagmar Christine 1940- *WhoAmP 91*
**Williscroft**, Robert Grover 1942- *WhoAmP 91*
**Willison**, Bruce Gray 1948- *WhoFI 92, WhoWest 92*
**Willison**, David 1919- *Who 92*
**Willison**, James E 1925- *WhoAmP 91*
**Willison**, John 1914- *Who 92*
**Willison**, Mildred Lucille 1921- *WhoAmP 91*
**Willison**, Sue Kindred 1926- *WhoAmP 91*
**Willistein**, Paul August 1950- *WhoEnt 92*
**Williston**, John Stoddard 1934- *AmMWSc 92*
**Williston**, Samuel Wendell 1851-1918 *BiInAmS*
**Willits**, Bruce Albert 1951- *WhoRel 92*
**Willits**, Charles Haines 1923- *AmMWSc 92*
**Willits**, Lon Kedric 1939- *WhoWest 92*
**Willius**, T. F. *SmATA 66*
**Willke**, John Charles 1925- *WhoRel 92*
**Willke**, Thomas Aloys 1932- *AmMWSc 92*
**Willkie**, Wendell 1892-1944 *FacFETw [port]*
**Willkie**, Wendell L. 1892-1944 *BenetAL 91*
**Willkie**, Wendell Lewis 1882-1944 *AmPeW*
**Willkie**, Wendell Lewis 1892-1944 *AmPolLe [port]*
**Willkie**, Wendell Lewis 1951- *WhoAmP 91*
**Willkie**, Wendell Lewis, II 1951- *WhoAmL 92*
**Willkomm**, Scott Edward 1965- *WhoFI 92*
**Willman**, John 1949- *Who 92*
**Willman**, John Norman 1915- *WhoFI 92*
**Willman**, Joseph F 1931- *AmMWSc 92*
**Willman**, Kenneth William 1954- *WhoMW 92*
**Willman**, Lee A *WhoIns 92*
**Willman**, Vallee L 1925- *AmMWSc 92*
**Willman**, Vincent Marie 1932- *WhoRel 92*
**Willman**, Warren Walton 1943- *AmMWSc 92*
**Willmann**, Robert B 1931- *AmMWSc 92*
**Willmarth**, Mary Sue 1963- *WhoWest 92*
**Willmarth**, William W 1924- *AmMWSc 92*
**Willmer**, Edward Nevill 1902- *Who 92, WrDr 92*
**Willmer**, John Franklin 1930- *Who 92*
**Willmer**, Nevill *Who 92*
**Willmert**, Kenneth Dale 1942- *AmMWSc 92*
**Willmes**, Henry 1939- *AmMWSc 92*
**Willmore**, Larry Neal 1944- *WhoFI 92*
**Willmore**, Peter 1930- *Who 92*
**Willmott**, Cort James 1946- *AmMWSc 92*
**Willmott**, Dennis James 1932- *Who 92*
**Willmott**, Edward George 1936- *Who 92*
**Willmott**, John Charles 1922- *Who 92*
**Willmott**, Nicholas John 1960- *WhoMW 92*
**Willmott**, Peter 1923- *Who 92, WrDr 92*
**Willms**, Charles Ronald 1933- *AmMWSc 92*
**Willms**, Richard Scott 1957- *WhoWest 92*
**Willner**, David 1930- *AmMWSc 92*
**Willner**, Jay R. 1924- *WhoFI 92*
**Willner**, Steven P *AmMWSc 92*
**Willoch**, Kare Isaachsen 1928- *IntWW 91*
**Willochra**, Bishop of 1940- *Who 92*
**Willock**, Colin 1919- *WrDr 92*
**Willock**, David Eldon 1959- *WhoWest 92*
**Willock**, Marcelle Monica 1938- *WhoBlA 92*
**Willott**, Brian *Who 92*
**Willott**, Brian 1940- *IntWW 91*
**Willott**, William Brian 1940- *Who 92*
**Willoughby** *Who 92*
**Willoughby**, Anne D *AmMWSc 92*
**Willoughby**, Cass *IntAu&W 91X, WrDr 92*
**Willoughby**, Christopher R. 1938- *IntWW 91*
**Willoughby**, Christopher Ronald 1938- *WhoFI 92*
**Willoughby**, Clarice E. 1934- *WhoBlA 92*
**Willoughby**, David Albert 1931- *Who 92*
**Willoughby**, David Charles 1940- *WhoMW 92*
**Willoughby**, Ernest Dwight 1932- *WhoMW 92*
**Willoughby**, Gerald *WhoAmP 91*
**Willoughby**, Hugh *WrDr 92*
**Willoughby**, James Russell 1928- *WhoWest 92*
**Willoughby**, Jimmy Ray 1953- *WhoRel 92*
**Willoughby**, John Edward Francis d1991 *Who 92N*
**Willoughby**, Joyce Carol 1939- *WhoAmP 91*
**Willoughby**, Kenneth James 1922- *Who 92*
**Willoughby**, Lee Davis *WrDr 92*
**Willoughby**, Noel Vincent *Who 92*
**Willoughby**, Ralph Arthur 1923- *AmMWSc 92*
**Willoughby**, Richard Rawlings 1947- *WhoWest 92*
**Willoughby**, Robert McEwen 1965- *WhoFI 92*
**Willoughby**, Robin Kay *DrAPF 91*
**Willoughby**, Roger James 1939- *Who 92*
**Willoughby**, Russell A 1933- *AmMWSc 92*
**Willoughby**, Sarah Margaret C 1917- *AmMWSc 92*
**Willoughby**, Stephen Schuyler 1932- *AmMWSc 92*
**Willoughby**, Stuart Carroll 1951- *WhoWest 92*
**Willoughby**, Susan Melita 1925- *WhoBlA 92*
**Willoughby**, Tanyayette Charlaisse 1957- *WhoEnt 92*
**Willoughby**, Trevor 1926- *TwCPaSc*
**Willoughby**, William Franklin 1936- *AmMWSc 92*
**Willoughby**, William George 1917- *WhoRel 92*
**Willoughby**, Winston Churchill 1907- *WhoBlA 92*
**Willoughby De Broke**, Baron 1938- *Who 92*
**Willoughby De Eresby**, Baroness 1934- *Who 92*
**Willour**, David Roger 1939- *WhoFI 92*
**Willows**, Arthur Owen Dennis 1941- *AmMWSc 92*
**Willrich**, Emzy James 1959- *WhoBlA 92*
**Willrich**, Mason 1933- *WrDr 92*
**Wills** *Who 92*
**Wills**, Alfred J. 1927- *WrDr 92*
**Wills**, Alfred John 1927- *IntAu&W 91*
**Wills**, Arthur William 1926- *Who 92*
**Wills**, Audrey Elizabeth 1930- *WhoFI 92*
**Wills**, Bart Francis 1955- *WhoMW 92*
**Wills**, Bob 1905-1975 *ConMus 6 [port], NewAmDM*
**Wills**, Brian Alan 1927- *Who 92*
**Wills**, C J *ScFEYrs*
**Wills**, Chester *TwCWW 91*
**Wills**, Christopher J 1938- *AmMWSc 92*
**Wills**, Colin Spencer 1937- *Who 92*
**Wills**, Cornelia 1953- *WhoBlA 92*
**Wills**, David *Who 92*
**Wills**, David Seton 1939- *Who 92*
**Wills**, David Wood 1942- *WhoRel 92*
**Wills**, Dean Robert 1933- *IntWW 91, Who 92*
**Wills**, Donald L 1924- *AmMWSc 92*
**Wills**, Edward Michael 1958- *WhoEnt 92*
**Wills**, Garry 1934- *FacFETw, WhoMW 92, WhoRel 92, WrDr 92*
**Wills**, Gene David 1934- *AmMWSc 92*
**Wills**, George B 1928- *AmMWSc 92*
**Wills**, Helen *Who 92*
**Wills**, Hugh David 1917- *Who 92*
**Wills**, James E, Jr 1916- *AmMWSc 92*
**Wills**, James Willard 1933- *WhoBlA 92*
**Wills**, Jean 1929- *IntAu&W 91*
**Wills**, John Arthur 1946- *WhoWest 92*
**Wills**, John Clarence 1942- *WhoWest 92*
**Wills**, John G 1931- *AmMWSc 92*
**Wills**, John Spencer 1904- *IntWW 91, Who 92*
**Wills**, John Vernon 1928- *Who 92*
**Wills**, Karen Elizabeth 1956- *WhoMW 92*
**Wills**, Keith Cameron 1917- *WhoRel 92*
**Wills**, Matthew Buckner 1932- *WhoAmL 92*
**Wills**, Nancy Kay 1949- *AmMWSc 92*
**Wills**, Nicholas Kenneth Spencer 1941- *Who 92*
**Wills**, Olan Kennyon 1936- *WhoRel 92*
**Wills**, Peter Gordon Bethune 1931- *Who 92*
**Wills**, Robert Hamilton 1926- *WhoMW 92*
**Wills**, Scott Dean 1964- *WhoMW 92*
**Wills**, Seton *Who 92*
**Wills**, Sylvia Lucy 1964- *WhoEnt 92*
**Wills**, Tom 1937- *WhoAmP 91*
**Wills**, Walter J. 1915- *WrDr 92*
**Wills**, Walter Joe 1915- *WhoFI 92*
**Wills**, Wirt Henry 1924- *AmMWSc 92*
**Willsey**, Lynn W *WhoIns 92*
**Willsher**, Brian 1930- *TwCPaSc*
**Willson**, Alan Neil, Jr 1939- *AmMWSc 92*
**Willson**, Carlton Grant 1939- *AmMWSc 92*
**Willson**, Clyde D 1935- *AmMWSc 92*
**Willson**, Dean David 1945- *WhoFI 92*
**Willson**, Donald Bruce 1941- *AmMWSc 92*
**Willson**, Douglas James 1906- *Who 92*
**Willson**, Francis Michael Glenn 1924- *IntWW 91*
**Willson**, Glenn 1924- *Who 92*
**Willson**, Graeme 1951- *TwCPaSc*
**Willson**, John Ellis 1929- *AmMWSc 92*
**Willson**, John Michael 1931- *Who 92*
**Willson**, John Tucker 1924- *AmMWSc 92*
**Willson**, Laura Faulk 1937- *WhoWest 92*
**Willson**, Lee Anne Mordy 1947- *AmMWSc 92*
**Willson**, Mark Draper 1959- *WhoMW 92*
**Willson**, Mary Frances 1938- *AmMWSc 92*
**Willson**, Meredith 1902-1984 *NewAmDM*
**Willson**, Philip James 1926- *AmMWSc 92*
**Willson**, Prentiss, Jr. 1943- *WhoAmL 92*
**Willson**, Richard Atwood *AmMWSc 92*
**Willson**, Richard Coale, Jr. 1930- *WhoAmL 92*
**Willson**, Robert Newton 1873-1916 *BiInAmS*
**Willson**, Terry 1948- *TwCPaSc*
**Willson**, Thomas Leopold 1860-1915 *BiInAmS*
**Willson**, Warrack Grant 1943- *AmMWSc 92*
**Willstater**, Richard Martin 1872-1942 *WhoNob 90*
**Willwerth**, Lawrence James 1932- *AmMWSc 92*
**Willy**, John G 1942- *WhoAmP 91*
**Willy**, Margaret 1919- *WrDr 92*
**Willy**, Thomas Ralph 1943- *WhoAmL 92*
**Willyoung**, Elmer Grant 1865-1919 *BiInAmS*
**Wilmarth**, Mary Ann 1960- *WhoWest 92*
**Wilmarth**, Richard *DrAPF 91*
**Wilmer**, Clive 1945- *ConPo 91, IntAu&W 91, WrDr 92*
**Wilmer**, Dale *WrDr 92*
**Wilmer**, Harry A 1917- *AmMWSc 92*
**Wilmer**, Michael Emory 1941- *AmMWSc 92*
**Wilmer**, Richard Hooker, Jr. 1918- *WhoRel 92*
**Wilmerding**, John 1938- *WrDr 92*
**Wilmeth**, Don Burton 1939- *WhoEnt 92*
**Wilmington**, Joseph 1932- *Who 92*
**Wilmore**, Gayraud S. 1921- *ConAu 134*
**Wilmore**, Gayraud Stephen 1921- *WhoBlA 92, WhoRel 92*
**Wilmore**, Lillian A. 1943- *WhoAmL 92*
**Wilmot**, David 1814-1868 *AmPolLe*
**Wilmot**, David 1943- *Who 92*
**Wilmot**, David Winston 1944- *WhoBlA 92*
**Wilmot**, George Barwick 1928- *AmMWSc 92*
**Wilmot**, Henry Robert 1967- *Who 92*
**Wilmot**, John *RfGEnL 91*
**Wilmot**, John Assheton E. *Who 92*
**Wilmot**, Robb *Who 92*
**Wilmot**, Robert William 1945- *IntWW 91, Who 92*
**Wilmot-Sitwell**, Peter Sacheverell 1935- *Who 92*
**Wilmoth**, Benton M 1925- *AmMWSc 92*
**Wilmoth**, Wade Franklin 1934- *WhoAmP 91*
**Wilmott**, Peter Graham 1947- *Who 92*
**Wilmotte**, Raymond M 1908- *AmMWSc 92*
**Wilmouth**, Ellen Boyle 1928- *WhoMW 92*
**Wilmouth**, Robert K. 1928- *WhoFI 92, WhoMW 92*
**Wilmowski**, Wendy Ann 1962- *WhoEnt 92*
**Wilms**, Dorothee 1929- *IntWW 91*
**Wilms**, Ernest Victor 1936- *AmMWSc 92*
**Wilms**, Hugo John, Jr 1922- *AmMWSc 92*
**Wilmsen**, Carl William 1934- *AmMWSc 92*
**Wilmshurst**, Jon Barry 1936- *Who 92*
**Wilmshurst**, Michael Joseph 1934- *Who 92*
**Wilner**, Eleanor *DrAPF 91*
**Wilner**, Freeman Marvin 1926- *WhoMW 92*
**Wilner**, George Dubar 1940- *AmMWSc 92*
**Wilner**, Morton Harrison 1908- *WhoAmL 92*
**Wilner**, Thomas Bernard 1944- *WhoAmL 92*
**Wiloch**, Thomas *DrAPF 91*
**Wiloch**, Thomas 1953- *IntAu&W 91*
**Wilsdorf**, Doris Kuhlmann 1922- *AmMWSc 92*
**Wilsdorf**, Heinz G F 1917- *AmMWSc 92*
**Wilsey**, John 1939- *Who 92*
**Wilsey**, Neal David 1937- *AmMWSc 92*
**Wilshire**, David 1943- *Who 92*
**Wilshire**, Howard Gordon 1926- *AmMWSc 92*
**Wilshire**, Robert Vidal 1937- *WhoRel 92*
**Wilska**, Alvar P 1911- *AmMWSc 92*
**Wilsker**, Ira lee 1950- *WhoFI 92*
**Wilsman**, Larry W. d1991 *NewYTBS 91*
**Wilsnack**, Sharon Carlson 1943- *WhoMW 92*
**Wilson** *Who 92*
**Wilson**, Baron 1915- *Who 92*
**Wilson**, A. Jeyaratnam 1928- *WrDr 92*
**Wilson**, A. Kenneth 1949- *WhoRel 92*
**Wilson**, A. N. 1950- *ConNov 91, WrDr 92*
**Wilson**, Abraham 1922- *WhoAmL 92*
**Wilson**, Addison Joe Graves 1947- *WhoAmP 91*
**Wilson**, Alan 1906- *Who 92*
**Wilson**, Alan C 1945- *AmMWSc 92*
**Wilson**, Alan Geoffrey 1939- *IntWW 91, Who 92*
**Wilson**, Alan Herries 1906- *IntWW 91*
**Wilson**, Alan Martin 1940- *Who 92*
**Wilson**, Alan Neal 1940- *WhoMW 92*
**Wilson**, Alastair James Drysdale 1946- *Who 92*
**Wilson**, Albert E 1927- *AmMWSc 92*
**Wilson**, Alexander 1766-1813 *BenetAL 91, BiInAmS*
**Wilson**, Alexander 1921- *IntWW 91, Who 92*
**Wilson**, Alexander D 1945- *AmMWSc 92*
**Wilson**, Alexander Galbraith 1924- *IntAu&W 91, IntWW 91*
**Wilson**, Alexander James 1921- *Who 92*
**Wilson**, Alexander Murray 1922- *WhoFI 92*
**Wilson**, Alexander Wayne 1963- *WhoFI 92*
**Wilson**, Alford M. *WhoRel 92*
**Wilson**, Alicia Santana 1948- *WhoBlA 92*
**Wilson**, Allan Byron 1948- *WhoFI 92*
**Wilson**, Allan C. d1991 *NewYTBS 91 [port]*
**Wilson**, Allan Charles d1991 *Who 92N*
**Wilson**, Allan Charles 1934- *AmMWSc 92*
**Wilson**, Allen Ray 1950- *WhoRel 92*
**Wilson**, Alma *WhoAmP 91*
**Wilson**, Alma D. 1917- *WhoAmL 92*
**Wilson**, Alma McDonald 1929- *AmMWSc 92*
**Wilson**, Alva L. 1922- *WhoBlA 92*
**Wilson**, Andrew *Who 92*
**Wilson**, Andrew 1923- *IntAu&W 91, WrDr 92*
**Wilson**, Andrew James *Who 92*
**Wilson**, Andrew N 1950- *IntAu&W 91, IntWW 91, Who 92*
**Wilson**, Andrew Robert 1941- *AmMWSc 92*
**Wilson**, Andrew Stephen 1947- *AmMWSc 92*
**Wilson**, Andrew Thomas 1926- *Who 92*
**Wilson**, Angus d1991 *NewYTBS 91 [port]*
**Wilson**, Angus 1913- *IntAu&W 91, IntWW 91, RfGEnL 91*
**Wilson**, Angus 1913-1991 *ConAu 134, CurBio 91N*
**Wilson**, Angus 1920- *AmMWSc 92*
**Wilson**, Angus Frank Johnstone d1991 *Who 92N*
**Wilson**, Ann Dustin 1950- *WhoWest 92*
**Wilson**, Annette R. 1956- *WhoAmL 92*
**Wilson**, Anthony 1928- *IntWW 91, Who 92*
**Wilson**, Anthony Joseph 1937- *Who 92*
**Wilson**, Antonia Joy *WhoEnt 92*
**Wilson**, Archie Fredric 1931- *AmMWSc 92*
**Wilson**, Archie Spencer 1921- *AmMWSc 92*
**Wilson**, Armin Guschel 1916- *AmMWSc 92*
**Wilson**, Arnold Jesse 1941- *WhoWest 92*
**Wilson**, Arthur 1929- *TwCPaSc*
**Wilson**, Arthur Gillespie 1900- *Who 92*
**Wilson**, Arthur James Cochran 1914- *IntWW 91, Who 92, WrDr 92*
**Wilson**, August 1945- *BenetAL 91, BlkLC [port], DramC 2 [port], IntAu&W 91, IntWW 91, WhoBlA 92, WhoMW 92, WrDr 92*
**Wilson**, Augusta *BenetAL 91*
**Wilson**, Austin *DrAPF 91*
**Wilson**, Austin George d1987 *Who 92N*
**Wilson**, Austin Peter 1938- *Who 92*
**Wilson**, Avray 1914- *TwCPaSc*
**Wilson**, Barbara *DrAPF 91, WrDr 92*
**Wilson**, Barbara 1950- *TwCWW 91*
**Wilson**, Barbara Ann 1948- *AmMWSc 92*
**Wilson**, Barbara Jean 1940- *WhoBlA 92*
**Wilson**, Barbara Jean 1948- *WhoMW 92*
**Wilson**, Barbara Ker 1929- *WrDr 92*

Wilson, Barbara Louise 1952- WhoWest 92
Wilson, Barron Orlando 1970- WhoRel 92
Wilson, Barry 1936- Who 92
Wilson, Barry William 1931- AmMWSc 92
Wilson, Basil W 1909- AmMWSc 92
Wilson, Benjamin Calvin 1947- WhoMW 92
Wilson, Benjamin F. 1951- WhoAmL 92
Wilson, Benjamin James 1923- AmMWSc 92
Wilson, Betty M 1947- WhoIns 92
Wilson, Betty May 1947- WhoFI 92
Wilson, Bill WhoBlA 92
Wilson, Blair Aubyn S. Who 92
Wilson, Blenda J. 1941- WhoBlA 92
Wilson, Blenda Jacqueline 1941- WhoMW 92
Wilson, Bobby L. 1942- WhoBlA 92
Wilson, Brandon Laine 1953- WhoWest 92
Wilson, Brayton F 1934- AmMWSc 92
Wilson, Brent Lawrence 1952- WhoAmL 92
Wilson, Brian David Henderson 1948- Who 92
Wilson, Brian Douglas 1942- WhoEnt 92
Wilson, Brian G. 1930- IntWW 91
Wilson, Brian Graham 1930- Who 92
Wilson, Brian Harvey 1915- Who 92
Wilson, Brian William John Gregg 1937- Who 92
Wilson, Bruce Allen 1961- WhoAmL 92
Wilson, Bruce Benjamin 1952- WhoEnt 92
Wilson, Bruce Brighton 1936- WhoAmL 92, WhoFI 92
Wilson, Bruce Winston Who 92
Wilson, Bryan R. WrDr 92
Wilson, Bryan Ronald 1926- Who 92
Wilson, Budge 1927- IntAu&W 91
Wilson, Burton David 1932- AmMWSc 92
Wilson, Byron J 1931- AmMWSc 92
Wilson, Calvin T. 1928- WhoBlA 92
Wilson, Carl Arthur 1947- WhoFI 92, WhoWest 92
Wilson, Carl C 1915- AmMWSc 92
Wilson, Carl J., Jr. 1934- WhoAmL 92
Wilson, Carl L. 1921- WhoBlA 92
Wilson, Carl Morris 1947- WhoMW 92
Wilson, Carl Weldon, Jr. 1933- WhoFI 92
Wilson, Carlos Guillermo 1941- WhoHisp 92, WhoWest 92
Wilson, Carol A. 1944- WhoFI 92
Wilson, Carol Maggart 1936- AmMWSc 92
Wilson, Carole ConAu 35NR
Wilson, Carole Winston 1943- WhoAmL 92
Wilson, Carroll Klepper 1917- AmMWSc 92
Wilson, Carroll Lloyd 1937- WhoBlA 92
Wilson, Carter 1941- IntAu&W 91, WrDr 92
Wilson, Cassandra WhoEnt 92
Wilson, Catherine Mary 1945- Who 92
Wilson, Catherine Mary 1957- WhoFI 92
Wilson, Cathryn Prather 1958- WhoAmL 92
Wilson, Charles 1933- AlmAP 92 [port], WhoAmP 91
Wilson, Charles 1935- IntAu&W 91, IntWW 91
Wilson, Charles 1939- ConAu 135
Wilson, Charles B 1929- AmMWSc 92
Wilson, Charles Edward T. Who 92
Wilson, Charles Elmer 1931- AmMWSc 92
Wilson, Charles Erwin 1890-1961 AmPolLe
Wilson, Charles F. 1925- WhoBlA 92
Wilson, Charles Harrison 1941- WhoFI 92
Wilson, Charles Haynes 1909- IntWW 91, Who 92
Wilson, Charles Henry d1991 Who 92N
Wilson, Charles Henry 1916- IntWW 91
Wilson, Charles Julian 1934- WhoAmL 92
Wilson, Charles Martin 1935- Who 92
Wilson, Charles Maye 1916- AmMWSc 92
Wilson, Charles Norman 1947- AmMWSc 92
Wilson, Charles Oren 1926- AmMWSc 92
Wilson, Charles R 1929- AmMWSc 92
Wilson, Charles Stanley, Jr. 1952- WhoBlA 92
Wilson, Charles Thomas 1941- WhoFI 92
Wilson, Charles Thomson Rees 1869-1959 FacFETw, WhoNob 90
Wilson, Charles Woodson, III 1924- AmMWSc 92
Wilson, Charles Z., Jr. 1929- WhoBlA 92
Wilson, Charles Zachary, Jr. 1929- WhoWest 92
Wilson, Christina Mosher 1954- WhoAmP 91
Wilson, Christine IntAu&W 91X, WrDr 92
Wilson, Christine Shearer AmMWSc 92
Wilson, Christopher AmMWSc 92
Wilson, Christopher David 1916- Who 92
Wilson, Christopher Maynard 1928- Who 92
Wilson, Clarence A. 1943- WhoBlA 92
Wilson, Clarence Ivan 1927- WhoFI 92
Wilson, Clarence Northon 1920- WhoBlA 92
Wilson, Clarence S., Jr. WhoBlA 92
Wilson, Clarence Sylvester, Jr. 1945- WhoMW 92
Wilson, Clark Thomas WhoEnt 92
Wilson, Claude Leonard 1905- AmMWSc 92
Wilson, Claude Raymond, Jr. 1933- WhoAmL 92
Wilson, Cleo Francine 1943- WhoBlA 92, WhoEnt 92
Wilson, Clifford 1906- Who 92
Wilson, Clifford Earle 1928- WhoRel 92
Wilson, Clive Hebden 1940- Who 92
Wilson, Clive Howard 1942- WhoEnt 92
Wilson, Clyde Livingston 1922- AmMWSc 92
Wilson, Colin 1931- ConNov 91, FacFETw, WrDr 92
Wilson, Colin Alexander St John 1922- Who 92
Wilson, Colin Henry 1931- IntAu&W 91, IntWW 91, Who 92
Wilson, Collin 1931- TwCSFW 91
Wilson, Colon Hayes, Jr 1932- AmMWSc 92
Wilson, Connie Drake 1953- WhoBlA 92
Wilson, Coyt Taylor 1913- AmMWSc 92
Wilson, Curtis Marshall 1926- AmMWSc 92
Wilson, Cynthia 1926- AmMWSc 92
Wilson, Cyril 1911- TwCPaSc
Wilson, Dale Joseph 1952- WhoEnt 92
Wilson, Dale Owen, Jr. 1955- WhoWest 92
Wilson, Dana E 1937- AmMWSc 92
Wilson, Daniel Crowell 1946- WhoAmL 92
Wilson, Daniel W. 1966- WhoEnt 92
Wilson, Danny Karl 1959- WhoRel 92
Wilson, Danton Thomas 1958- WhoBlA 92
Wilson, Darcy Benoit 1936- AmMWSc 92
Wilson, Dare Who 92
Wilson, Darrell Glenn 1939- WhoMW 92
Wilson, Darryl Benjamin 1957- WhoEnt 92
Wilson, Dave IntAu&W 91X, TwCWW 91
Wilson, David Who 92
Wilson, David 1928- Who 92
Wilson, David 1931- Who 92
Wilson, David 1935- Who 92
Wilson, David 1954- WhoBlA 92
Wilson, David Allen 1926- WhoWest 92
Wilson, David Buckingham 1940- AmMWSc 92
Wilson, David Clive 1935- FacFETw, IntWW 91
Wilson, David E 1929- AmMWSc 92
Wilson, David Eugene 1940- WhoWest 92
Wilson, David F 1938- AmMWSc 92
Wilson, David Forrester 1873-1950 TwCPaSc
Wilson, David Franklin 1941- AmMWSc 92
Wilson, David George 1919- AmMWSc 92
Wilson, David George 1921- AmMWSc 92
Wilson, David Gordon 1928- AmMWSc 92
Wilson, David Henry 1937- WrDr 92
Wilson, David J 1930- AmMWSc 92
Wilson, David Jefferies 1939- WhoRel 92
Wilson, David Louis 1943- AmMWSc 92
Wilson, David M. 1931- WrDr 92
Wilson, David Mackenzie 1931- IntWW 91
Wilson, David Merl 1941- AmMWSc 92
Wilson, David Orin 1937- AmMWSc 92
Wilson, David Palir 1930- WhoRel 92
Wilson, David Ralph 1956- WhoAmL 92
Wilson, David S. 1931- WrDr 92
Wilson, David William 1941- Who 92
Wilson, David William 1958- WhoAmL 92
Wilson, Deborah Gail 1955- WhoFI 92
Wilson, Delano D 1934- AmMWSc 92
Wilson, Delbert Ray 1926- WhoMW 92
Wilson, Demond WhoBlA 92
Wilson, Dempsey MacArthur 1951- WhoMW 92
Wilson, Dennis Edward 1952- WhoEnt 92
Wilson, Des 1941- IntAu&W 91, Who 92, WrDr 92
Wilson, Diane Doerge 1948- WhoFI 92
Wilson, Dierdre Lynn 1945- WhoEnt 92
Wilson, Don 1900-1982 CurBio 91N
Wilson, Don Ellis 1944- AmMWSc 92
Wilson, Don Whitman 1942- WhoAmP 91
Wilson, Donald Who 92
Wilson, Donald Alan 1930- AmMWSc 92
Wilson, Donald Alfred 1941- AmMWSc 92
Wilson, Donald Benjamin 1925- AmMWSc 92
Wilson, Donald Bruce 1933- AmMWSc 92
Wilson, Donald Edward, Jr. 1951- WhoRel 92
Wilson, Donald K, Jr 1935- WhoIns 92
Wilson, Donald Kenneth, Jr. 1954- WhoEnt 92
Wilson, Donald Laurence 1921- AmMWSc 92
Wilson, Donald M. 1925- IntWW 91
Wilson, Donald P. WhoBlA 92
Wilson, Donald Porter 1940- WhoMW 92
Wilson, Donald Richard 1936- AmMWSc 92
Wilson, Donald Wallin 1938- WhoMW 92
Wilson, Donella Joyce 1951- WhoBlA 92
Wilson, Donte 1949- WhoWest 92
Wilson, Doric 1939- WrDr 92
Wilson, Doris Burda 1937- AmMWSc 92
Wilson, Dorothy Clarke 1904- IntAu&W 91, WrDr 92
Wilson, Douglas 1936- TwCPaSc
Wilson, Douglas Downes 1947- WhoAmL 92
Wilson, Douglas Edwin 1917- WhoWest 92
Wilson, Douglas George 1924- Who 92
Wilson, Duane Isaac 1920- WhoMW 92
Wilson, Dwight Elliott, Jr 1932- AmMWSc 92
Wilson, E. Bright 1908- IntWW 91
Wilson, Earl 1907- IntAu&W 91
Wilson, Earl, Jr. 1932- WhoBlA 92
Wilson, Earl Lawrence 1923- WhoBlA 92
Wilson, Earl M 1939- WhoAmP 91
Wilson, Earl Ray 1939- WhoFI 92
Wilson, Ed 1925- WhoBlA 92
Wilson, Edgar Bright 1908- AmMWSc 92
Wilson, Edith 1896-1981 NotBlAW 92
Wilson, Edith Hundley WhoBlA 92
Wilson, Edith N. 1938- WhoBlA 92
Wilson, Edmond Woodrow, Jr 1940- AmMWSc 92
Wilson, Edmund 1895-1972 BenetAL 91, FacFETw
Wilson, Edward Carl 1929- AmMWSc 92
Wilson, Edward Churchill 1940- WhoAmL 92
Wilson, Edward Cox 1938- WhoRel 92
Wilson, Edward Hamilton, Jr 1951- WhoAmP 91
Wilson, Edward John 1946- WhoRel 92
Wilson, Edward L 1931- AmMWSc 92
Wilson, Edward Matthew 1937- AmMWSc 92
Wilson, Edward Nathan 1941- AmMWSc 92
Wilson, Edward O. 1929- WrDr 92
Wilson, Edward Osborne 1929- AmMWSc 92, FacFETw, IntAu&W 91, IntWW 91
Wilson, Edward Raymond 1896-1987 AmPeW
Wilson, Edwina Allison 1961- WhoAmL 92
Wilson, Elaine 1959- TwCPaSc
Wilson, Eldon Ray 1931- WhoRel 92
Wilson, Elizabeth 1925- IntMPA 92
Wilson, Elizabeth 1936- WrDr 92
Wilson, Elizabeth Allen 1950- AmMWSc 92
Wilson, Elizabeth Ann 1941- WhoAmP 91
Wilson, Elizabeth Jane 1948- IntAu&W 91
Wilson, Elizabeth Karsian 1931- WhoAmP 91
Wilson, Elizabeth Mary AmMWSc 92
Wilson, Elwood Justin, Jr 1917- AmMWSc 92
Wilson, Emily Herring DrAPF 91
Wilson, Emily Marie 1951- WhoWest 92
Wilson, Eric DrAPF 91
Wilson, Eric Charles Twelves 1912- Who 92
Wilson, Eric Leroy 1935- AmMWSc 92
Wilson, Eric Paul 1958- WhoFI 92
Wilson, Eric Randall 1964- WhoFI 92, WhoWest 92
Wilson, Ernest 1925- WhoBlA 92
Wilson, Ernest 1936- WhoBlA 92
Wilson, Ernest C. 1896-1982 RelLAm 91
Wilson, Ernest Staton, Jr. 1927- WhoAmL 92
Wilson, Esther Marie 1932- WhoAmP 91
Wilson, Ethel 1888-1980 RfGEnL 91
Wilson, Ethel Davis 1888-1980 BenetAL 91
Wilson, Eugene M 1928- AmMWSc 92
Wilson, Eugene Madison 1943- AmMWSc 92
Wilson, Eugene T 1924- WhoAmP 91
Wilson, Evelyn H 1921- AmMWSc 92
Wilson, Everett D 1928- AmMWSc 92
Wilson, Everett Leroy 1936- WhoRel 92
Wilson, Ezra Herbert 1858-1906 BiInAmS
Wilson, F Douglas 1928- AmMWSc 92
Wilson, F. Leon 1953- WhoBlA 92
Wilson, F Paul 1946- IntAu&W 91, TwCSFW 91, WrDr 92
Wilson, F Wesley, Jr 1939- AmMWSc 92
Wilson, Flip 1933- IntMPA 92, WhoBlA 92, WhoEnt 92
Wilson, Florabelle W. 1927- WhoBlA 92
Wilson, Floyd Edward, Jr. 1935- WhoBlA 92
Wilson, Forest Ray, II 1941- AmMWSc 92
Wilson, Forrest 1883-1942 BenetAL 91
Wilson, Francis 1854-1935 BenetAL 91
Wilson, Frank B 1929- AmMWSc 92
Wilson, Frank Charles 1927- AmMWSc 92
Wilson, Frank Crane 1929- AmMWSc 92
Wilson, Frank Douglas 1928- AmMWSc 92, WhoWest 92
Wilson, Frank Edwin 1928- WhoMW 92
Wilson, Frank Fredrick, III 1936- WhoBlA 92
Wilson, Frank Joseph AmMWSc 92
Wilson, Frank Richard 1920- Who 92
Wilson, Franklyn 1941- TwCPaSc
Wilson, Fred E 1937- AmMWSc 92
Wilson, Fred Lee 1938- AmMWSc 92
Wilson, Frederic Rowland 1947- WhoRel 92
Wilson, Frederick A. 1946- WhoBlA 92
Wilson, Frederick Albert 1928- AmMWSc 92
Wilson, Frederick Allen 1937- AmMWSc 92
Wilson, Frederick Earl 1954- WhoWest 92
Wilson, Frederick Sutphen 1927- AmMWSc 92
Wilson, G Dennis 1946- AmMWSc 92
Wilson, G Howard ScFEYrs
Wilson, Gabriel TwCSFW 91
Wilson, Gary August 1942- AmMWSc 92
Wilson, Gary D. DrAPF 91
Wilson, Gary Dean 1943- WhoAmL 92
Wilson, Gary Ivan 1947- WhoWest 92
Wilson, Gary Lee 1940- WhoFI 92
Wilson, Geoffrey 1920- WrDr 92
Wilson, Geoffrey 1929- Who 92
Wilson, Geoffrey Alan 1934- Who 92
Wilson, Geoffrey Hazlitt 1929- IntWW 91, Who 92
Wilson, Geoffrey Leonard 1924- AmMWSc 92
Wilson, Geoffrey Masterman 1910- Who 92
Wilson, Geoffrey Studholme 1913- Who 92
Wilson, George Who 92
Wilson, George 1942- BlkOlyM
Wilson, George Balch 1927- WhoEnt 92
Wilson, George Donald 1925- AmMWSc 92
Wilson, George G. 1929- WhoBlA 92
Wilson, George Grafton 1863-1951 AmPeW
Wilson, George Harley 1904- WhoRel 92
Wilson, George Hugh 1922- WhoEnt 92
Wilson, George McConnell 1913- WhoMW 92, WhoRel 92
Wilson, George Peter 1939- AmMWSc 92
Wilson, George Porter, III 1927- AmMWSc 92
Wilson, George Pritchard Harvey 1918- Who 92
Wilson, George Rodger 1923- AmMWSc 92
Wilson, George Simpson, III 1932- WhoAmL 92
Wilson, George Spencer 1939- AmMWSc 92
Wilson, George Wilton 1928- WrDr 92
Wilson, Georges 1921- IntWW 91
Wilson, Gerald Alan 1951- WhoWest 92
Wilson, Gerald Gene 1928- AmMWSc 92
Wilson, Gerald Loomis 1939- AmMWSc 92
Wilson, Gerald Robertson 1939- Who 92
Wilson, Gerald Roy 1930- Who 92
Wilson, Gerald Stanley 1918- WhoBlA 92
Wilson, Gilbert 1908- Who 92
Wilson, Gillian Brenda Who 92
Wilson, Gina 1943- IntAu&W 91, WrDr 92
Wilson, Glen Wesley 1930- WhoFI 92
Wilson, Glenn IntAu&W 91
Wilson, Glenn Ashby 1918- WhoAmP 91
Wilson, Golder North 1944- AmMWSc 92
Wilson, Gordon IntWW 91, Who 92
Wilson, Gordon, Jr 1925- AmMWSc 92
Wilson, Gordon Russel 1947- WhoWest 92
Wilson, Gordon Wallace 1926- Who 92
Wilson, Graeme McDonald 1919- Who 92
Wilson, Graham Alastair 1949- WhoFI 92
Wilson, Graham McGregor 1944- WhoFI 92
Wilson, Grant Paul, Jr. 1943- WhoBlA 92
Wilson, Greer Dawson 1943- WhoBlA 92
Wilson, Gregg Steven 1956- WhoMW 92
Wilson, Gregory Bruce 1948- AmMWSc 92
Wilson, Gregory Lee 1954- WhoAmP 91
Wilson, Grosvenor 1866- ScFEYrs
Wilson, Gustavus Edwin 1939- AmMWSc 92
Wilson, Guy Harris, Jr. 1943- WhoRel 92
Wilson, Guy Murray 1950- Who 92
Wilson, H W 1866-1940 ScFEYrs
Wilson, H W & White, Arnold ScFEYrs
Wilson, Harold IntWW 91

**Wilson,** Harold 1916- *FacFETw [port], WrDr 92*
**Wilson,** Harold 1931- *Who 92*
**Wilson,** Harold Albert 1874-1964 *FacFETw*
**Wilson,** Harold Albert 1905- *AmMWSc 92*
**Wilson,** Harold Arthur Cooper B. *Who 92*
**Wilson,** Harold Frederick 1922- *AmMWSc 92*
**Wilson,** Harrell Thomas 1944- *WhoRel 92*
**Wilson,** Harriet 1808-1870? *BenetAL 91*
**Wilson,** Harriet 1827?- *BlkLC*
**Wilson,** Harriet E. Adams 1827?-1870? *NotBlAW 92*
**Wilson,** Harriett C. 1916- *WrDr 92*
**Wilson,** Harrison B. 1928- *WhoBlA 92*
**Wilson,** Harry *Who 92*
**Wilson,** Harry Cochrane 1945- *WhoRel 92*
**Wilson,** Harry David Bruce 1916- *AmMWSc 92*
**Wilson,** Harry Leon 1867-1939 *BenetAL 91, TwCWW 91*
**Wilson,** Harry W. Jr 1924- *AmMWSc 92*
**Wilson,** Hazel Forrow Simmons 1927- *WhoBlA 92*
**Wilson,** Helen 1954- *TwCPaSc*
**Wilson,** Helen Frances 1921- *WhoAmP 91*
**Wilson,** Helen Louise 1921- *WhoAmP 91*
**Wilson,** Helen Marie 1930- *WhoWest 92*
**Wilson,** Helen Tolson *WhoBlA 92*
**Wilson,** Henry 1812-1875 *AmPolLe*
**Wilson,** Henry, Jr. 1938- *WhoBlA 92*
**Wilson,** Henry Arthur, Jr. 1939- *WhoFI 92*
**Wilson,** Henry Braithwaite 1911- *Who 92*
**Wilson,** Henry Dewey 1924- *WhoAmL 92*
**Wilson,** Henry Moir 1910- *Who 92*
**Wilson,** Henry R 1936- *AmMWSc 92*
**Wilson,** Henry Wallace 1923- *Who 92*
**Wilson,** Herbert Alexander, Jr 1914- *AmMWSc 92*
**Wilson,** Herbert Michael 1860-1920 *BiInAmS*
**Wilson,** Herschel Manuel 1930- *WhoWest 92*
**Wilson,** Howard Le Roy 1932- *AmMWSc 92*
**Wilson,** Howell Kenneth 1937- *AmMWSc 92*
**Wilson,** Hugh *LesBEnT 92*
**Wilson,** Hugh 1943- *IntMPA 92*
**Wilson,** Hugh A. 1940- *WhoBlA 92*
**Wilson,** Hugh Daniel 1943- *AmMWSc 92*
**Wilson,** Hugh Mal 1930- *WhoAmP 91*
**Wilson,** Hugh Reid 1943- *AmMWSc 92*
**Wilson,** Hugh Steven 1947- *WhoAmL 92*
**Wilson,** Hughlyne Perkins 1931- *WhoBlA 92*
**Wilson,** Ian *IntAu&W 91*
**Wilson,** Ian D. *Who 92*
**Wilson,** Ian Holroyde 1925- *WhoFI 92*
**Wilson,** Ian Matthew 1926- *Who 92*
**Wilson,** Ira Lee 1927- *WhoWest 92*
**Wilson,** Irene K. *DrAPF 91*
**Wilson,** Irwin B 1921- *AmMWSc 92*
**Wilson,** J.R. 1949- *WhoWest 92*
**Wilson,** J. Ray 1937- *WhoBlA 92*
**Wilson,** J W 1916- *AmMWSc 92*
**Wilson,** Jack 1918-1956 *BlkOlyM*
**Wilson,** Jack 1926- *WhoAmP 91*
**Wilson,** Jack Belmont 1921- *AmMWSc 92*
**Wilson,** Jack Charles 1928- *AmMWSc 92*
**Wilson,** Jack Lowery 1943- *AmMWSc 92*
**Wilson,** Jack Martin 1945- *AmMWSc 92*
**Wilson,** Jackie 1934-1984 *NewAmDM*
**Wilson,** Jacqueline 1945- *IntAu&W 91, WrDr 92*
**Wilson,** Jacqueline Etheridge 1937- *WhoRel 92*
**Wilson,** Jacqueline Prophet 1949- *WhoBlA 92*
**Wilson,** James *Who 92*
**Wilson,** James d1990 *Who 92N*
**Wilson,** James 1742-1798 *BenetAL 91, BlkwCEP, BlkwEAR*
**Wilson,** James 1836-1920 *BiInAmS*
**Wilson,** James 1922- *Who 92*
**Wilson,** James, Jr. 1919- *WhoBlA 92*
**Wilson,** James Albert 1929- *AmMWSc 92*
**Wilson,** James Barker 1926- *WhoAmL 92*
**Wilson,** James Blake 1924- *AmMWSc 92*
**Wilson,** James Caswell, Jr. 1923- *WhoWest 92*
**Wilson,** James Charles, Jr. 1947- *WhoAmL 92*
**Wilson,** James D. 1945- *WhoFI 92*
**Wilson,** James Davis 1937- *WhoBlA 92*
**Wilson,** James Dennis 1940- *AmMWSc 92*
**Wilson,** James Edward, Jr. 1954- *WhoAmL 92*
**Wilson,** James Eldon 1948- *WhoAmL 92*
**Wilson,** James Ernest 1915- *WhoWest 92*
**Wilson,** James Franklin 1920- *AmMWSc 92*
**Wilson,** James Gregory 1950- *WhoAmP 91*
**Wilson,** James Harold 1916- *IntAu&W 91*
**Wilson,** James Howard 1943- *WhoMW 92*
**Wilson,** James Larry 1942- *AmMWSc 92*
**Wilson,** James Lawrence 1936- *WhoFI 92*
**Wilson,** James Lee 1920- *AmMWSc 92*
**Wilson,** James Lester 1925- *AmMWSc 92*
**Wilson,** James M 1950- *AmMWSc 92*
**Wilson,** James Maxwell Glover 1913- *Who 92*
**Wilson,** James Newman 1927- *WhoWest 92*
**Wilson,** James Noel 1919- *Who 92*
**Wilson,** James Paris 1907- *WhoBlA 92*
**Wilson,** James Quinn 1931- *WrDr 92*
**Wilson,** James R 1922- *AmMWSc 92*
**Wilson,** James Ray 1930- *WhoFI 92, WhoMW 92*
**Wilson,** James Reed 1948- *WhoMW 92*
**Wilson,** James Ricker 1922- *WhoRel 92*
**Wilson,** James Robert 1927- *WhoWest 92*
**Wilson,** James Rodney 1937- *WhoMW 92*
**Wilson,** James Ronald 1954- *WhoRel 92*
**Wilson,** James Ross 1939- *WhoEnt 92*
**Wilson,** James Russell 1933- *AmMWSc 92*
**Wilson,** James Stewart 1909- *Who 92*
**Wilson,** James Tylee 1931- *IntWW 91*
**Wilson,** James William 1919- *AmMWSc 92*
**Wilson,** James William 1928- *WhoAmL 92, WhoFI 92*
**Wilson,** James William 1936- *AmMWSc 92*
**Wilson,** James William Alexander 1944- *AmMWSc 92*
**Wilson,** James William Douglas 1960- *Who 92*
**Wilson,** Jane Brownlow 1945- *WhoFI 92*
**Wilson,** Jane Phillipson 1955- *WhoAmL 92*
**Wilson,** Janie Menchaca 1936- *WhoHisp 92*
**Wilson,** Jay D. 1947- *WhoWest 92*
**Wilson,** Jean Donald 1932- *AmMWSc 92, IntWW 91*
**Wilson,** Jean Gaddy 1944- *WhoMW 92*
**Wilson,** Jean L 1928- *WhoAmP 91*
**Wilson,** Jeanette Kurtz 1929- *WhoWest 92*
**Wilson,** Jeffrey A. 1946- *WhoMW 92*
**Wilson,** Jeffrey Alan 1960- *WhoEnt 92*
**Wilson,** Jeffrey R. *WhoBlA 92*
**Wilson,** Jeril B 1938- *WhoAmP 91*
**Wilson,** Jerry D 1937- *AmMWSc 92*
**Wilson,** Jerry Lee 1938- *AmMWSc 92*
**Wilson,** Jill R. 1957- *WhoAmL 92*
**Wilson,** Jimmie L. *WhoBlA 92*
**Wilson,** Jimmie L 1945- *WhoAmP 91*
**Wilson,** Joan Hoff 1937- *ConAu 134*
**Wilson,** Joe *Who 92*
**Wilson,** Joe Bransford 1914- *AmMWSc 92*
**Wilson,** Joe L 1946- *WhoAmP 91*
**Wilson,** Joe Mack 1919- *WhoAmP 91*
**Wilson,** Joe Robert 1923- *AmMWSc 92*
**Wilson,** Joel Montgomery 1964- *WhoFI 92*
**Wilson,** John 1591?-1667 *BenetAL 91*
**Wilson,** John 1595-1674 *NewAmDM*
**Wilson,** John 1626?-1695? *RfGEnL 91*
**Wilson,** John 1785-1854 *DcLB 110 [port]*
**Wilson,** John 1919- *Who 92, WrDr 92*
**Wilson,** John 1922- *WhoBlA 92*
**Wilson,** John 1928- *WrDr 92*
**Wilson,** John A 1943- *WhoAmP 91, WhoBlA 92*
**Wilson,** John Bennett, Jr. 1935- *WhoAmL 92*
**Wilson,** John Burgess *WrDr 92*
**Wilson,** John Cleland 1935- *AmMWSc 92*
**Wilson,** John Coe 1931- *AmMWSc 92*
**Wilson,** John D 1935- *AmMWSc 92*
**Wilson,** John Drennan 1938- *AmMWSc 92*
**Wilson,** John E. 1932- *WhoBlA 92*
**Wilson,** John Edward 1939- *AmMWSc 92*
**Wilson,** John Eric 1919- *AmMWSc 92*
**Wilson,** John F 1922- *AmMWSc 92*
**Wilson,** John Foster 1919- *IntWW 91*
**Wilson,** John Gardiner 1913- *Who 92*
**Wilson,** John Graham 1911- *Who 92*
**Wilson,** John H 1944- *AmMWSc 92*
**Wilson,** John Hewitt 1924- *Who 92*
**Wilson,** John Human 1900- *AmMWSc 92*
**Wilson,** John James 1927- *WhoWest 92*
**Wilson,** John James 1932- *Who 92*
**Wilson,** John Lewis 1943- *WhoWest 92*
**Wilson,** John Louis, Jr. 1899-1989 *WhoBlA 92N*
**Wilson,** John Martindale 1915- *Who 92*
**Wilson,** John Michael 1946- *WhoIns 92*
**Wilson,** John Murray 1926- *Who 92*
**Wilson,** John Neville 1918- *AmMWSc 92*
**Wilson,** John P. 1923- *IntWW 91*
**Wilson,** John Page 1922- *WhoFI 92*
**Wilson,** John Pasley 1933- *WhoAmL 92, WhoWest 92*
**Wilson,** John Philip, Sr. 1922- *WhoMW 92*
**Wilson,** John Phillips 1916- *AmMWSc 92*
**Wilson,** John Randall 1934- *AmMWSc 92*
**Wilson,** John Richard Meredith 1944- *WhoWest 92*
**Wilson,** John Ross, Sr. 1952- *WhoWest 92*
**Wilson,** John Sheridan 1944- *AmMWSc 92*
**Wilson,** John Spark 1922- *Who 92*
**Wilson,** John Steuart 1913- *WhoEnt 92*
**Wilson,** John Stuart Gladstone 1916- *Who 92, WrDr 92*
**Wilson,** John T 1938- *AmMWSc 92*
**Wilson,** John T., Jr. 1924- *WhoBlA 92*
**Wilson,** John Thomas 1944- *AmMWSc 92*
**Wilson,** John Thomas 1947- *AmMWSc 92*
**Wilson,** John Thomas, Jr 1924- *AmMWSc 92*
**Wilson,** John Tuzo 1908- *AmMWSc 92, IntWW 91, Who 92*
**Wilson,** John Veitch D. *Who 92*
**Wilson,** John W. 1928- *WhoBlA 92*
**Wilson,** John Warley 1936- *Who 92*
**Wilson,** John Warwick 1937- *Who 92*
**Wilson,** John Wes 1962- *WhoEnt 92*
**Wilson,** John William 1940- *AmMWSc 92*
**Wilson,** John William, III 1943- *AmMWSc 92*
**Wilson,** Johnny Leaverne 1954- *WhoBlA 92*
**Wilson,** Jon 1955- *WhoBlA 92*
**Wilson,** Jon Louis 1946- *WhoAmL 92*
**Wilson,** Jon Stephen 1935- *WhoWest 92*
**Wilson,** Jonathan Reford 1951- *WhoRel 92*
**Wilson,** Joseph *DrAPF 91*
**Wilson,** Joseph Albert 1922- *Who 92*
**Wilson,** Joseph Edward 1920- *AmMWSc 92*
**Wilson,** Joseph F. 1951- *WhoBlA 92*
**Wilson,** Joseph Lopez 1960- *WhoAmL 92*
**Wilson,** Joseph Miller 1838-1902 *BiInAmS*
**Wilson,** Joseph Morris, III 1945- *WhoAmL 92*
**Wilson,** Joseph Roland 1944- *WhoEnt 92*
**Wilson,** Joseph Trannie 1960- *WhoFI 92*
**Wilson,** Joseph William 1934- *AmMWSc 92*
**Wilson,** Josephine Evadna *WhoAmP 91*
**Wilson,** Josephine Frances 1937- *WhoWest 92*
**Wilson,** Joy Johnson 1954- *WhoBlA 92*
**Wilson,** Joyce Muriel 1921- *IntAu&W 91*
**Wilson,** Joyce Norene 1942- *WhoMW 92*
**Wilson,** Judge Bradley, II 1956- *WhoAmL 92*
**Wilson,** Judy Vantrease 1939- *WhoFI 92*
**Wilson,** Julie 1924?- *ConTFT 9*
**Wilson,** June *WrDr 92*
**Wilson,** Karen Lee 1949- *WhoMW 92*
**Wilson,** Karen LeRohl 1950- *WhoAmL 92*
**Wilson,** Karen M. 1963- *WhoMW 92*
**Wilson,** Karl A 1947- *AmMWSc 92*
**Wilson,** Katherine Muriel 1920- *Who 92*
**Wilson,** Katherine Woods 1923- *AmMWSc 92*
**Wilson,** Kathryn Jay 1948- *AmMWSc 92*
**Wilson,** Kathryn Pippo 1937- *WhoEnt 92*
**Wilson,** Keith *DrAPF 91*
**Wilson,** Keith 1927- *ConPo 91, WrDr 92*
**Wilson,** Keith O 1925- *WhoAmP 91*
**Wilson,** Kenneth Allen 1928- *AmMWSc 92*
**Wilson,** Kenneth Charles 1937- *AmMWSc 92*
**Wilson,** Kenneth Geddes 1936- *AmMWSc 92, Who 92, WhoMW 92, WhoNob 90*
**Wilson,** Kenneth Glade 1940- *AmMWSc 92, WhoMW 92*
**Wilson,** Kenneth Sheridan 1924- *AmMWSc 92*
**Wilson,** Kent Raymond 1937- *AmMWSc 92*
**Wilson,** Kim Alesia 1959- *WhoBlA 92*
**Wilson,** Kirk George 1951- *WhoWest 92*
**Wilson,** L Britt 1960- *AmMWSc 92*
**Wilson,** L Kenneth 1910- *AmMWSc 92*
**Wilson,** L Rule 1909- *Who 92*
**Wilson,** Lance Henry 1948- *WhoAmP 91, WhoBlA 92*
**Wilson,** Lanford 1937- *BenetAL 91, IntAu&W 91, WhoEnt 92, WrDr 92*
**Wilson,** Lanford Eugene 1927- *FacFETw*
**Wilson,** Larry Eugene 1935- *AmMWSc 92*
**Wilson,** Lauren R 1936- *AmMWSc 92*
**Wilson,** Laurence Edward 1930- *AmMWSc 92*
**Wilson,** Laurie Jane Tucker 1952- *WhoWest 92*
**Wilson,** Laval S. 1935- *WhoBlA 92*
**Wilson,** Lawrence Albert, Jr 1925- *AmMWSc 92*
**Wilson,** Lawrence C. 1932- *WhoBlA 92*
**Wilson,** Lawrence E., III 1951- *WhoBlA 92*
**Wilson,** Lawrence Frank 1938- *WhoWest 92*
**Wilson,** Lawrence Graham, III 1944- *WhoFI 92*
**Wilson,** Lee 1942- *AmMWSc 92*
**Wilson,** Leigh Allison *DrAPF 91*
**Wilson,** Lennox Norwood 1932- *AmMWSc 92*
**Wilson,** Leon A. 1930- *WhoBlA 92*
**Wilson,** Leon E., Jr. 1945- *WhoBlA 92*
**Wilson,** Leonard D. 1933- *WhoBlA 92*
**Wilson,** Leonard Gilchrist 1928- *AmMWSc 92*
**Wilson,** Leonard Richard 1906- *AmMWSc 92*
**Wilson,** Leroy, III 1951- *WhoBlA 92*
**Wilson,** Leroy, Jr. 1939- *WhoBlA 92*
**Wilson,** Leslie 1941- *AmMWSc 92*
**Wilson,** Leslie William 1918- *Who 92*
**Wilson,** Lester A, Jr 1917- *AmMWSc 92*
**Wilson,** LeVon Edward 1954- *WhoAmL 92*
**Wilson,** Lewis Lansing 1932- *WhoAmP 91, WhoFI 92*
**Wilson,** Linda S 1936- *AmMWSc 92, IntWW 91*
**Wilson,** Lionel J 1915- *WhoAmP 91, WhoBlA 92*
**Wilson,** Logan 1907-1990 *CurBio 91N*
**Wilson,** Lois 1927- *ConAu 134*
**Wilson,** Lois M. 1927- *WhoRel 92*
**Wilson,** Lois Mayfield 1924- *WhoWest 92*
**Wilson,** Lois Miriam 1927- *DcEcMov, IntWW 91*
**Wilson,** Lon James 1944- *AmMWSc 92*
**Wilson,** Lonnie Alexander 1932- *WhoRel 92*
**Wilson,** Lorenzo George 1938- *AmMWSc 92*
**Wilson,** Lorne Graham 1929- *AmMWSc 92*
**Wilson,** Lorraine Kallinger 1961- *WhoAmL 92*
**Wilson,** Louis Frederick 1932- *AmMWSc 92*
**Wilson,** Louis Hugh 1920- *IntWW 91*
**Wilson,** Lowell D 1933- *AmMWSc 92*
**Wilson,** Lowell L 1936- *AmMWSc 92*
**Wilson,** Lucy R. 1930- *WhoBlA 92*
**Wilson,** Lynn Anthony 1939- *Who 92*
**Wilson,** Lynn Jonathan 1958- *WhoMW 92, WhoRel 92*
**Wilson,** Lynn O 1944- *AmMWSc 92*
**Wilson,** Lynton Ronald 1940- *WhoFI 92*
**Wilson,** Lyons 1892- *TwCPaSc*
**Wilson,** Mabel F 1906- *AmMWSc 92*
**Wilson,** Mannie L. *WhoBlA 92*
**Wilson,** Marc Fraser 1941- *WhoMW 92*
**Wilson,** Marcia Hammerquist 1952- *AmMWSc 92*
**Wilson,** Marcus 1968- *WhoBlA 92*
**Wilson,** Margaret 1882-1973 *BenetAL 91*
**Wilson,** Margaret 1882-1976 *FacFETw*
**Wilson,** Margaret Ann 1957- *WhoMW 92*
**Wilson,** Margaret Bush 1919- *NotBlAW 92, WhoBlA 92*
**Wilson,** Margaret F. 1932- *WhoBlA 92*
**Wilson,** Margaret Sullivan 1924- *WhoAmP 91*
**Wilson,** Margery 1898-1986 *ReelWom*
**Wilson,** Marjorie Price 1924- *AmMWSc 92*
**Wilson,** Mark Allan 1956- *AmMWSc 92, WhoMW 92*
**Wilson,** Mark Curtis 1921- *AmMWSc 92*
**Wilson,** Mark Vincent Hardman 1946- *AmMWSc 92*
**Wilson,** Markly 1947- *WhoBlA 92*
**Wilson,** Marlene Moore 1947- *AmMWSc 92*
**Wilson,** Marshall Ward, Jr. 1948- *WhoFI 92*
**Wilson,** Martha *DrAPF 91*
**Wilson,** Martin d1991 *Who 92N*
**Wilson,** Martin 1913- *AmMWSc 92*
**Wilson,** Marvin Cracraft 1943- *AmMWSc 92*
**Wilson,** Marvin H. 1938- *WhoBlA 92*
**Wilson,** Mary *WrDr 92*
**Wilson,** Mary 1944- *WhoBlA 92*
**Wilson,** Mary Christina 1950- *IntAu&W 91*
**Wilson,** Mason, Jr. 1924- *WhoRel 92*
**Wilson,** Mason P, Jr 1933- *AmMWSc 92*
**Wilson,** Mathew John Anthony 1935- *Who 92*
**Wilson,** Mathew Kent 1920- *AmMWSc 92*
**Wilson,** McClure 1924- *AmMWSc 92*
**Wilson,** Merle R 1932- *AmMWSc 92*
**Wilson,** Michael *WhoBlA 92*
**Wilson,** Michael 1942- *WhoBlA 92*
**Wilson,** Michael 1953- *WhoBlA 92*
**Wilson,** Michael Anthony 1936- *Who 92*
**Wilson,** Michael Bruce 1943- *WhoAmL 92, WhoWest 92*
**Wilson,** Michael Dean 1951- *WhoEnt 92*
**Wilson,** Michael Friend 1927- *AmMWSc 92*
**Wilson,** Michael Holcombe 1937- *IntWW 91*
**Wilson,** Michael John 1942- *AmMWSc 92*
**Wilson,** Michael Joseph 1953- *WhoFI 92*
**Wilson,** Michael K 1944- *WhoAmP 91*
**Wilson,** Michael Moureau 1952- *WhoAmL 92*
**Wilson,** Michael Sumner 1943- *Who 92*
**Wilson,** Miles *DrAPF 91*
**Wilson,** Milton 1915- *WhoBlA 92*
**Wilson,** Minor Keith 1904- *WhoAmL 92*
**Wilson,** Miriam Geisendorfer 1922- *AmMWSc 92*
**Wilson,** Mitchell 1913-1973 *BenetAL 91*

**Wilson,** Monte Dale 1938- *AmMWSc 92*
**Wilson,** Mookie 1956- *WhoBlA 92*
**Wilson,** Muriel *Who 92*
**Wilson,** Myron Robert, Jr. 1932- *WhoWest 92*
**Wilson,** Nan L. 1929- *WhoMW 92*
**Wilson,** Nancy 1937- *NotBlAW 92, WhoBlA 92, WhoEnt 92*
**Wilson,** Nancy Keeler 1937- *AmMWSc 92*
**Wilson,** Natarsha Juliet 1961- *WhoBlA 92*
**Wilson,** Nathaniel J. 1945- *WhoRel 92*
**Wilson,** Neal Clayton 1920- *WhoRel 92*
**Wilson,** Neil 1944- *ConAu 133*
**Wilson,** Newell George 1943- *WhoWest 92*
**Wilson,** Nicholas Allan Roy 1945- *Who 92*
**Wilson,** Nick 1942- *WhoAmP 91*
**Wilson,** Nigel Guy 1935- *IntWW 91, Who 92*
**Wilson,** Nigel Henry Moir 1944- *AmMWSc 92*
**Wilson,** Nixon Albert 1930- *AmMWSc 92*
**Wilson,** Norma F. 1940- *WhoHisp 92*
**Wilson,** Norma June 1940- *WhoBlA 92*
**Wilson,** Norman George 1911- *Who 92*
**Wilson,** Norman Lewis, Jr. 1921- *WhoMW 92*
**Wilson,** Norman Ward 1948- *WhoIns 92*
**Wilson,** Olin C 1909- *AmMWSc 92, IntWW 91*
**Wilson,** Olly 1937- *ConCom 92, NewAmDM*
**Wilson,** Olly W. 1937- *WhoBlA 92*
**Wilson,** Ora Brown 1937- *WhoBlA 92*
**Wilson,** Oscar, Jr. 1935- *WhoAmL 92*
**Wilson,** Oscar Bryan, Jr 1922- *AmMWSc 92*
**Wilson,** Owen Meredith, Jr. 1939- *WhoAmL 92*
**Wilson,** P David 1933- *AmMWSc 92*
**Wilson,** Pamela Jean Compton 1955- *WhoAmL 92*
**Wilson,** Pat 1910- *IntAu&W 91, WrDr 92*
**Wilson,** Patricia A. 1948- *WhoBlA 92*
**Wilson,** Patricia I. 1940- *WhoBlA 92*
**Wilson,** Patricia Jervis 1951- *WhoBlA 92*
**Wilson,** Patrick Elliott 1934- *WhoIns 92*
**Wilson,** Paul Anthony Joseph 1949- *WhoAmL 92*
**Wilson,** Paul Hastings *DrAPF 91*
**Wilson,** Paul Holliday, Jr. 1942- *WhoAmL 92*
**Wilson,** Paul Preston, Jr. 1940- *WhoAmL 92*
**Wilson,** Paul Robert 1939- *AmMWSc 92*
**Wilson,** Paul W., Jr. 1948- *WhoMW 92*
**Wilson,** Paul Wayne 1933- *WhoMW 92*
**Wilson,** Paul Wayne 1958- *WhoFI 92*
**Wilson,** Peggy Ann 1945- *WhoAmP 91*
**Wilson,** Peggy Mayfield Dunlap 1927- *AmMWSc 92, WhoAmP 91*
**Wilson,** Percy Charles 1940- *WhoAmP 91*
**Wilson,** Perry Baker 1927- *AmMWSc 92*
**Wilson,** Pete 1933- *AlmAP 92 [port], CurBio 91 [port], IntWW 91, WhoAmP 91, WhoWest 92*
**Wilson,** Peter Northcote 1928- *Who 92*
**Wilson,** Peter Scott 1955- *WhoAmL 92*
**Wilson,** Peter Sinclair 1958- *WhoAmL 92, WhoFI 92*
**Wilson,** Philip Alexander P. *Who 92*
**Wilson,** Phillip 1922- *WrDr 92*
**Wilson,** Philo Calhoun 1924- *AmMWSc 92*
**Wilson,** Prince E. *WhoBlA 92*
**Wilson,** Quentin Charles 1955- *WhoAmP 91*
**Wilson,** Quintin Campbell 1913- *Who 92*
**Wilson,** Ralph L. 1934- *WhoBlA 92*
**Wilson,** Ramona C. *DrAPF 91*
**Wilson,** Raphael 1925- *AmMWSc 92*
**Wilson,** Ray F. 1926- *WhoBlA 92*
**Wilson,** Ray Floyd 1926- *AmMWSc 92*
**Wilson,** Raymond 1925- *Who 92*
**Wilson,** Raymond Lloyd 1933- *WhoIns 92*
**Wilson,** Reagon Wayne, Jr. 1952- *WhoRel 92*
**Wilson,** Reginald 1905- *Who 92*
**Wilson,** Reginald 1927- *WhoBlA 92*
**Wilson,** Rhys Thaddeus 1955- *WhoAmL 92, WhoFI 92*
**Wilson,** Richard *DrAPF 91*
**Wilson,** Richard d1991 *NewYTBS 91*
**Wilson,** Richard 1714-1782 *BlkwCEP*
**Wilson,** Richard 1920-1987? *TwCSFW 91*
**Wilson,** Richard 1926- *AmMWSc 92*
**Wilson,** Richard Barr 1921- *AmMWSc 92*
**Wilson,** Richard Cushman 1953- *WhoAmP 91*
**Wilson,** Richard Dale 1933- *WhoFI 92*
**Wilson,** Richard Earl 1949- *WhoMW 92*
**Wilson,** Richard Edward 1941- *WhoEnt 92*
**Wilson,** Richard Edward, Jr. 1956- *WhoWest 92*
**Wilson,** Richard Fairfield 1930- *AmMWSc 92*
**Wilson,** Richard Ferrin 1920- *AmMWSc 92*
**Wilson,** Richard Garth 1945- *AmMWSc 92*
**Wilson,** Richard Hansel 1939- *AmMWSc 92*
**Wilson,** Richard Howard 1942- *AmMWSc 92*
**Wilson,** Richard Lee 1939- *AmMWSc 92, WhoMW 92*
**Wilson,** Richard Michael 1945- *AmMWSc 92*
**Wilson,** Richard Middlewood 1908- *Who 92*
**Wilson,** Richard Randolph 1950- *WhoAmL 92, WhoWest 92*
**Wilson,** Richard Thomas James 1942- *Who 92*
**Wilson,** Rita P. 1946- *WhoBlA 92*
**Wilson,** Robert 1543?-1600? *RfGEnL 91*
**Wilson,** Robert 1927- *IntWW 91, Who 92*
**Wilson,** Robert 1931- *DcTwDes*
**Wilson,** Robert, Jr *WhoAmP 91*
**Wilson,** Robert Allen 1936- *WhoRel 92*
**Wilson,** Robert Anton 1932- *IntAu&W 91, TwCSFW 91, WrDr 92*
**Wilson,** Robert Burton 1936- *AmMWSc 92*
**Wilson,** Robert Byron 1936- *WhoMW 92*
**Wilson,** Robert C E *ScFEYrs*
**Wilson,** Robert Charles 1953- *TwCSFW 91*
**Wilson,** Robert Charles, Jr. 1953- *WhoMW 92*
**Wilson,** Robert D 1921- *AmMWSc 92*
**Wilson,** Robert Dale 1952- *WhoAmP 91*
**Wilson,** Robert Donald 1922- *Who 92*
**Wilson,** Robert E 1926- *AmMWSc 92*
**Wilson,** Robert E 1937- *AmMWSc 92*
**Wilson,** Robert Eugene 1932- *AmMWSc 92*
**Wilson,** Robert Foster 1926- *WhoAmL 92, WhoMW 92*
**Wilson,** Robert Francis 1921- *WhoAmP 91*
**Wilson,** Robert Francis 1934- *AmMWSc 92*
**Wilson,** Robert G 1930- *AmMWSc 92*
**Wilson,** Robert Gardner 1948- *WhoAmL 92*
**Wilson,** Robert George, V 1947- *WhoMW 92*
**Wilson,** Robert Gordon 1933- *WhoFI 92*
**Wilson,** Robert Gordon 1938- *IntWW 91, Who 92*
**Wilson,** Robert Gray 1934- *AmMWSc 92*
**Wilson,** Robert H. *WhoBlA 92*
**Wilson,** Robert Hallowell 1924- *AmMWSc 92*
**Wilson,** Robert Henry, Jr. 1965- *WhoFI 92*
**Wilson,** Robert James 1915- *AmMWSc 92*
**Wilson,** Robert Jewell 1943- *WhoAmL 92*
**Wilson,** Robert John 1935- *AmMWSc 92*
**Wilson,** Robert Julian 1933- *Who 92*
**Wilson,** Robert Kinner 1929- *WhoAmP 91*
**Wilson,** Robert L. 1925-1991 *ConAu 134*
**Wilson,** Robert L. 1934- *WhoBlA 92*
**Wilson,** Robert Lake 1924- *AmMWSc 92*
**Wilson,** Robert Lee 1917- *AmMWSc 92*
**Wilson,** Robert Lee 1918- *WhoWest 92*
**Wilson,** Robert Lee 1946- *AmMWSc 92*
**Wilson,** Robert Lee, Jr 1942- *AmMWSc 92*
**Wilson,** Robert Lee Miles 1930- *WhoBlA 92*
**Wilson,** Robert Louis 1939- *WhoMW 92*
**Wilson,** Robert M. 1941- *WhoEnt 92*
**Wilson,** Robert M. 1944- *BenetAL 91*
**Wilson,** Robert M. 1952- *WhoMW 92*
**Wilson,** Robert McLachlan 1916- *IntWW 91, Who 92, WrDr 92*
**Wilson,** Robert Neal 1924- *WrDr 92*
**Wilson,** Robert Norton 1927- *AmMWSc 92*
**Wilson,** Robert Paul 1941- *AmMWSc 92*
**Wilson,** Robert Peter 1943- *Who 92*
**Wilson,** Robert Rathbun 1914- *AmMWSc 92*
**Wilson,** Robert Stanley 1923- *WhoBlA 92*
**Wilson,** Robert Steven 1939- *AmMWSc 92*
**Wilson,** Robert W. 1965- *WhoEnt 92*
**Wilson,** Robert Warren 1909- *AmMWSc 92*
**Wilson,** Robert Woodrow 1936- *AmMWSc 92, IntWW 91, Who 92, WhoNob 90*
**Wilson,** Robin *Who 92*
**Wilson,** Robin Lee 1933- *Who 92*
**Wilson,** Robin Scott 1928- *WhoWest 92*
**Wilson,** Robley *DrAPF 91*
**Wilson,** Robley, Jr. 1930- *WrDr 92*
**Wilson,** Rodney Herbert William 1942- *Who 92*
**Wilson,** Roger B 1948- *WhoAmP 91*
**Wilson,** Roger Cowan d1991 *Who 92N*
**Wilson,** Roger Duane 1938- *WhoWest 92*
**Wilson,** Roger Goodwin 1950- *WhoAmL 92*
**Wilson,** Roger Plumpton 1905- *IntWW 91, Who 92*
**Wilson,** Roland 1904- *IntWW 91, Who 92*
**Wilson,** Ron R 1953- *WhoAmP 91*
**Wilson,** Ronald Amos 1946- *WhoRel 92*
**Wilson,** Ronald Andrew 1941- *Who 92*
**Wilson,** Ronald Dare 1919- *Who 92*
**Wilson,** Ronald Darling 1922- *Who 92*
**Wilson,** Ronald Harvey 1932- *AmMWSc 92*
**Wilson,** Ronald Lee 1967- *WhoRel 92*
**Wilson,** Ronald M. 1949- *WhoBlA 92*
**Wilson,** Ronald Marshall 1923- *Who 92*
**Wilson,** Ronald Ray 1953- *WhoBlA 92*
**Wilson,** Ronald Wayne 1939- *AmMWSc 92*
**Wilson,** Ross 1959- *TwCPaSc*
**Wilson,** Roy *Who 92*
**Wilson,** Roy Edmond 1924- *WhoAmP 91*
**Wilson,** Roy Vernon 1922- *Who 92*
**Wilson,** Ruby Leila 1931- *AmMWSc 92*
**Wilson,** Rudolph George 1935- *WhoBlA 92*
**Wilson,** Sally Angela *Who 92*
**Wilson,** Samuel 1953- *Who 92*
**Wilson,** Samuel H 1939- *AmMWSc 92*
**Wilson,** Sandra 1944- *WrDr 92*
**Wilson,** Sandra E. 1944- *WhoBlA 92*
**Wilson,** Sandra Lee 1957- *WhoFI 92*
**Wilson,** Sandy *Who 92*
**Wilson,** Sandy 1924- *Who 92, WrDr 92*
**Wilson,** Scott 1942- *IntMPA 92*
**Wilson,** Scottie 1889-1972 *TwCPaSc*
**Wilson,** Sherman Arthur 1931- *WhoBlA 92*
**Wilson,** Sid R. 1943- *WhoMW 92*
**Wilson,** Simeon R 1927- *WhoAmP 91*
**Wilson,** Sloan 1920- *BenetAL 91, ConNov 91, WrDr 92*
**Wilson,** Sloan Jacob 1910- *AmMWSc 92*
**Wilson,** Snoo 1948- *IntAu&W 91, Who 92, WrDr 92*
**Wilson,** Sodonia Mae *WhoBlA 92*
**Wilson,** Sonali Bustamante 1958- *WhoBlA 92*
**Wilson,** Sonja Mary 1938- *WhoWest 92*
**Wilson,** Stanley Charles 1947- *WhoBlA 92*
**Wilson,** Stanley John 1921- *IntWW 91, Who 92*
**Wilson,** Stanley Livingstone 1905- *Who 92*
**Wilson,** Stanton Rodger 1923- *WhoRel 92*
**Wilson,** Stephanie Y. 1952- *WhoBlA 92*
**Wilson,** Stephanie Yvette 1952- *WhoFI 92*
**Wilson,** Stephen Harth 1944- *WhoWest 92*
**Wilson,** Stephen Rip 1948- *WhoWest 92*
**Wilson,** Stephen Ross 1946- *AmMWSc 92*
**Wilson,** Stephen Roy 1946- *WhoFI 92*
**Wilson,** Stephen Victor 1941- *WhoAmL 92*
**Wilson,** Stephen W 1952- *AmMWSc 92*
**Wilson,** Stephen White 1943- *WhoAmL 92*
**Wilson,** Steven Paul 1950- *AmMWSc 92*
**Wilson,** Susan Bernadette 1954- *WhoMW 92*
**Wilson,** Sybil *WhoBlA 92*
**Wilson,** Ted *DrAPF 91*
**Wilson,** Teddy 1912-1986 *FacFETw, NewAmDM*
**Wilson,** Terrence Raymond 1943- *WhoFI 92*
**Wilson,** Terry L. 1962- *WhoFI 92*
**Wilson,** Theodore A 1935- *AmMWSc 92*
**Wilson,** Theodore Allen 1940- *WhoMW 92*
**Wilson,** Theodore Henry 1940- *WhoWest 92*
**Wilson,** Thom 1956- *WhoFI 92*
**Wilson,** Thomas 1832-1902 *BiInAmS*
**Wilson,** Thomas 1916- *IntWW 91, Who 92, WrDr 92*
**Wilson,** Thomas 1927- *ConCom 92*
**Wilson,** Thomas Bellerby 1807-1865 *BiInAmS*
**Wilson,** Thomas Bennett, III 1946- *WhoAmL 92*
**Wilson,** Thomas Buck 1939- *WhoAmL 92*
**Wilson,** Thomas Dale 1952- *WhoWest 92*
**Wilson,** Thomas Edward 1918- *WhoEnt 92, WhoWest 92*
**Wilson,** Thomas Edward 1942- *AmMWSc 92*
**Wilson,** Thomas Edward 1954- *WhoEnt 92*
**Wilson,** Thomas G 1926- *AmMWSc 92*
**Wilson,** Thomas H, Capt. *ScFEYrs*
**Wilson,** Thomas Hastings 1925- *AmMWSc 92*
**Wilson,** Thomas Joseph 1957- *WhoFI 92*
**Wilson,** Thomas Kendrick 1931- *AmMWSc 92*
**Wilson,** Thomas Lamont 1914- *AmMWSc 92*
**Wilson,** Thomas Lee 1909- *AmMWSc 92*
**Wilson,** Thomas Leon 1942- *AmMWSc 92*
**Wilson,** Thomas M d1908 *BiInAmS*
**Wilson,** Thomas Marcus 1913- *Who 92*
**Wilson,** Thomas Matthew, III 1936- *WhoAmL 92*
**Wilson,** Thomas Putnam 1918- *AmMWSc 92*
**Wilson,** Thomas R C, II 1935- *WhoAmP 91*
**Wilson,** Thomas Raiford, Jr. 1930- *WhoRel 92*
**Wilson,** Thomas Rayburn, III 1946- *WhoWest 92*
**Wilson,** Thomas Woodrow 1856-1924 *AmPeW, WhoNob 90*
**Wilson,** Thornton Arnold 1921- *AmMWSc 92, IntWW 91*
**Wilson,** Timothy Hugh 1950- *Who 92*
**Wilson,** Timothy M 1938- *AmMWSc 92*
**Wilson,** Timothy Stearns 1957- *WhoFI 92*
**Wilson,** Todd Rodney 1954- *WhoEnt 92*
**Wilson,** Trevor 1968- *WhoBlA 92*
**Wilson,** Trevor Frederick *WrDr 92*
**Wilson,** Trevor Gordon 1928- *IntWW 91, WrDr 92*
**Wilson,** Truman E *WhoAmP 91*
**Wilson,** Valentine L. 1925- *WhoFI 92*
**Wilson,** Valerie *WhoEnt 92*
**Wilson,** Valeta Bene 1942- *WhoEnt 92*
**Wilson,** Victor Joseph 1928- *AmMWSc 92*
**Wilson,** Vincent L 1950- *AmMWSc 92*
**Wilson,** Virgil James, III 1953- *WhoAmL 92*
**Wilson,** Vivian Marie 1955- *WhoMW 92*
**Wilson,** Volney Colvin 1910- *AmMWSc 92*
**Wilson,** Wade 1914- *WhoBlA 92*
**Wilson,** Walter C. 1935- *WhoFI 92*
**Wilson,** Walter Davis 1935- *AmMWSc 92*
**Wilson,** Walter Ervin 1934- *AmMWSc 92*
**Wilson,** Walter James 1966- *WhoBlA 92*
**Wilson,** Walter LeRoy 1918- *AmMWSc 92*
**Wilson,** Walter Leroy 1942- *WhoMW 92*
**Wilson,** Walter Lucien, Jr 1927- *AmMWSc 92*
**Wilson,** Walter R 1919- *AmMWSc 92*
**Wilson,** Wanda Lee 1950- *WhoEnt 92, WhoFI 92, WhoWest 92*
**Wilson,** Warren Bingham 1920- *WhoWest 92*
**Wilson,** Warren Walter, Jr. 1955- *WhoFI 92*
**Wilson,** Warren Witherspoon 1936- *WhoAmL 92*
**Wilson,** Wayne MacArthur 1957- *WhoBlA 92*
**Wilson,** Wesley Campbell 1931- *WhoBlA 92*
**Wilson,** Wesley M. 1927- *WrDr 92*
**Wilson,** Wesley Warren 1958- *WhoFI 92*
**Wilson,** Wilbur William 1948- *AmMWSc 92*
**Wilson,** Wilfred J 1930- *AmMWSc 92*
**Wilson,** Wilfred James 1922- *WhoIns 92*
**Wilson,** William 1905-1972 *TwCPaSc*
**Wilson,** William 1913- *Who 92*
**Wilson,** William 1914- *WhoAmP 91*
**Wilson,** William Adam 1928- *Who 92*
**Wilson,** William Arthur 1931- *WhoMW 92*
**Wilson,** William Arthur 1949- *WhoRel 92*
**Wilson,** William August 1924- *AmMWSc 92*
**Wilson,** William Craig 1951- *WhoFI 92*
**Wilson,** William Curtis 1927- *AmMWSc 92*
**Wilson,** William D 1925- *AmMWSc 92*
**Wilson,** William David 1944- *AmMWSc 92*
**Wilson,** William Dennis 1940- *AmMWSc 92*
**Wilson,** William Desmond 1922- *Who 92*
**Wilson,** William E. 1937- *WhoBlA 92*
**Wilson,** William Edward 1940- *WhoFI 92*
**Wilson,** William Enoch, Jr 1933- *AmMWSc 92*
**Wilson,** William Eugene 1929- *WhoAmP 91*
**Wilson,** William Eugene 1958- *WhoAmL 92*
**Wilson,** William Ewing 1932- *AmMWSc 92*
**Wilson,** William George 1921- *Who 92*
**Wilson,** William Gilbert *Who 92*
**Wilson,** William Huntington 1870- *ScFEYrs*
**Wilson,** William J. *DrAPF 91*
**Wilson,** William James Fitzpatrick 1946- *AmMWSc 92*
**Wilson,** William Jewell 1932- *AmMWSc 92*
**Wilson,** William John 1939- *AmMWSc 92*
**Wilson,** William Julius 1935- *WhoBlA 92, WrDr 92*
**Wilson,** William Lawrence 1912- *Who 92*
**Wilson,** William M 1937- *WhoIns 92*
**Wilson,** William Marion 1958- *WhoRel 92*
**Wilson,** William Mark Dunlop 1949- *AmMWSc 92*
**Wilson,** William Napier M. *Who 92*
**Wilson,** William Preston 1922- *AmMWSc 92*
**Wilson,** William Robert Dunwoody 1941- *AmMWSc 92*
**Wilson,** William S. *DrAPF 91*
**Wilson,** William Thomas 1932- *AmMWSc 92*
**Wilson,** William Thomas 1937- *WhoAmP 91*
**Wilson,** William Warren 1955- *WhoMW 92*
**Wilson,** William Yale 1927- *WhoEnt 92*

**Wilson,** Willie Mae 1942- *WhoBlA 92*
**Wilson,** Wilson W. 1942- *WhoBlA 92*
**Wilson,** Woodrow 1856-1924 *AmPolLe [port], BenetAL 91, FacFETw, RComAH*
**Wilson,** Z. Vance *DrAPF 91*
**Wilson-Barnett,** Jenifer 1944- *Who 92*
**Wilson-Felder,** Cynthia Ann 1951- *WhoBlA 92*
**Wilson-Johnson,** David Robert 1950- *IntWW 91, Who 92*
**Wilson Jones,** Edward 1926- *Who 92*
**Wilson of Langside,** Baron 1916- *Who 92*
**Wilson Of Rievaulx,** Baron 1916- *IntWW 91, Who 92*
**Wilson-Simpson,** Dorothy Andrea 1945- *WhoMW 92*
**Wilson-Smith,** Willie Arrie 1929- *WhoBlA 92*
**Wilson-Spohr,** Melissa Jan 1966- *WhoEnt 92*
**Wilt,** Donald William 1948- *WhoWest 92*
**Wilt,** Fred H 1934- *AmMWSc 92*
**Wilt,** James William 1930- *AmMWSc 92*
**Wilt,** John Charles 1920- *AmMWSc 92*
**Wilt,** Martin Wayne 1962- *WhoMW 92*
**Wilt,** Paxton Marshall 1942- *AmMWSc 92*
**Wilt,** Roy William 1935- *WhoAmP 91*
**Wiltbank,** Joseph Kelley 1950- *WhoAmL 92*
**Wiltbank,** William Joseph 1927- *AmMWSc 92*
**Wiltermood,** Michael Curtis 1958- *WhoWest 92*
**Wiltgen,** Ralph 1921- *WrDr 92*
**Wilton,** Earl of 1921- *Who 92*
**Wilton,** Andrew *Who 92*
**Wilton,** Arthur John 1921- *Who 92*
**Wilton,** Donald Robert 1942- *AmMWSc 92*
**Wilton,** James Andrew 1942- *Who 92*
**Wilton,** John *Who 92*
**Wilton,** Penelope 1946- *ConTFT 9*
**Wilts,** Archdeacon of *Who 92*
**Wilts,** Charles H 1920- *AmMWSc 92*
**Wiltschko,** David Vilander 1949- *AmMWSc 92*
**Wiltse,** Chloryce Jerene 1933- *WhoWest 92*
**Wiltse,** James Burdick 1927- *WhoAmL 92*
**Wiltse,** James Cornelius 1926- *AmMWSc 92*
**Wiltse,** Richard Allan 1951- *WhoMW 92*
**Wiltshire,** Earl of 1969- *Who 92*
**Wiltshire,** Charles Thomas 1941- *AmMWSc 92*
**Wiltshire,** Edward Parr 1910- *Who 92*
**Wiltshire,** Frederick Munro 1911- *Who 92*
**Wiltshire,** Richard Watkins *WhoIns 92*
**Wiltz,** Charles J. 1934- *WhoBlA 92*
**Wiltz,** Philip G., Jr. 1930- *WhoBlA 92*
**Wilunowski,** Al Dominic 1946- *WhoWest 92*
**Wimalasena,** Nanediri 1914- *IntWW 91, Who 92*
**Wiman,** Richard Payne 1950- *WhoRel 92*
**Wimber,** Donald Edward 1930- *AmMWSc 92*
**Wimber,** R Ted 1935- *AmMWSc 92*
**Wimberger,** Kurt Phillip-Peter 1965- *WhoEnt 92*
**Wimberley,** Stanley 1927- *AmMWSc 92*
**Wimberly,** Anne Streaty 1936- *WhoBlA 92*
**Wimberly,** Beadie Reneau 1937- *WhoFI 92*
**Wimberly,** C Ray 1936- *AmMWSc 92*
**Wimberly,** Edward P. 1943- *WhoBlA 92*
**Wimberly,** George E *WhoAmP 91*
**Wimberly,** James Hudson 1935- *WhoBlA 92*
**Wimberly,** John William, Jr. 1947- *WhoRel 92*
**Wimbish,** C Bette *WhoAmP 91*
**Wimbish,** C. Bette 1924- *WhoBlA 92*
**Wimborne,** Viscount 1939- *Who 92*
**Wimbrow,** Peter Ayers, III 1947- *WhoAmL 92*
**Wimbush,** F. Blair 1955- *WhoBlA 92*
**Wimbush,** Gary Lynn 1953- *WhoBlA 92*
**Wimbush,** Mark Howard 1936- *AmMWSc 92*
**Wimbush,** Richard Knyvet 1909- *Who 92*
**Wimenitz,** Francis Nathaniel 1922- *AmMWSc 92*
**Wimer,** Barney Dale 1939- *WhoRel 92*
**Wimer,** Bruce Meade 1922- *AmMWSc 92*
**Wimer,** Cynthia Crosby 1933- *AmMWSc 92*
**Wimer,** David Carlisle 1926- *AmMWSc 92*
**Wimer,** Larry Thomas 1936- *AmMWSc 92*
**Wimer,** Richard E 1932- *AmMWSc 92*
**Wimer,** Sarah Joyce 1951- *WhoEnt 92*
**Wimer,** William John 1934- *WhoFI 92*
**Wimmer,** Dick *DrAPF 91*
**Wimmer,** Donn Braden 1927- *AmMWSc 92*
**Wimmer,** Eckard 1936- *AmMWSc 92*
**Wimmer,** Hans 1907- *IntWW 91*
**Wimmer,** John Charles 1944- *WhoWest 92*
**Wimmer,** John Richard 1956- *WhoRel 92*
**Wimmer,** Joseph E 1934- *WhoAmP 91*
**Wimmer,** Katherine Jones *WhoFI 92*
**Wimmer,** Lance Peter 1944- *WhoFI 92*
**Wimmer,** Maria *IntWW 91*
**Wimmer,** Paul Joseph 1959- *WhoEnt 92*
**Wimmer,** Susanne Mitchell 1946- *WhoAmP 91*
**Wimmer,** William Robert 1950- *WhoMW 92*
**Wimmers,** Steven Harry 1951- *WhoWest 92*
**Wimp,** Edward Lawson 1942- *WhoBlA 92*
**Wimp,** Jet *DrAPF 91*
**Wimpfheimer,** Michael Clark 1944- *WhoAmL 92*
**Wimpfheimer,** Steven 1941- *WhoAmL 92*
**Wimpress,** Gordon Duncan, Jr 1922- *AmMWSc 92*
**Wims,** Andrew Montgomery 1935- *AmMWSc 92*
**Wims,** Mary Ella 1952- *WhoFI 92*
**Winans,** A.D. *DrAPF 91*
**Winans,** Christopher 1950- *ConAu 133*
**Winans,** Edgar Vincent 1930- *WhoWest 92*
**Winans,** Randall Edward 1949- *AmMWSc 92*
**Winans,** William O 1942- *WhoAmP 91*
**Winant,** Ethel *LesBEnT 92*
**Winant,** Fran *DrAPF 91*
**Winant,** William Karl 1953- *WhoWest 92*
**Winard,** Arthur Irving 1916- *WhoAmL 92*
**Winarski,** Daniel James 1948- *WhoWest 92*
**Winarski,** Paul James Felix 1970- *WhoEnt 92*
**Winawer,** Sidney J 1931- *AmMWSc 92*
**Winberg,** Hakan 1931- *IntWW 91*
**Winberg,** Wynn 1957- *WhoEnt 92*
**Winbergh,** Gosta Anders 1948- *WhoEnt 92*
**Winberry,** William Thomas 1949- *WhoEnt 92*
**Winbery,** Carlton Loyd 1937- *WhoRel 92*
**Winborn,** William Burt 1931- *AmMWSc 92*
**Winborne,** George E 1937- *WhoAmP 91*
**Winbow,** Graham Arthur 1943- *AmMWSc 92*
**Winburn,** B. J. 1918- *WhoBlA 92*
**Winburn,** Gene Mack 1937- *WhoAmL 92*
**Winbury,** Martin M 1918- *AmMWSc 92*
**Winbury,** Martin Maurice 1918- *WhoMW 92*
**Winbush,** Clarence, Jr. 1948- *WhoBlA 92*
**Winbush,** LeRoy 1915- *WhoBlA 92*
**Winbush,** Roy L. H. *WhoRel 92*
**Wincenc,** Carol 1949- *WhoEnt 92*
**Wincer,** Simon *ConTFT 9, IntMPA 92*
**Winch,** Donald Norman 1935- *IntWW 91, Who 92*
**Winch,** Fred Everett, Jr 1914- *AmMWSc 92*
**Winch,** Peter 1926- *WrDr 92*
**Winch,** Peter Guy 1926- *IntAu&W 91, IntWW 91*
**Winch,** Terence *DrAPF 91*
**Winchell,** Alexander 1824-1891 *BiInAmS*
**Winchell,** C Paul 1921- *AmMWSc 92*
**Winchell,** Charmaine Louise 1947- *WhoRel 92*
**Winchell,** Harry Saul 1935- *AmMWSc 92*
**Winchell,** Horace 1915- *AmMWSc 92*
**Winchell,** Newton Horace 1839-1914 *BiInAmS*
**Winchell,** Paul 1922- *ConTFT 9, WhoEnt 92*
**Winchell,** Paul 1924- *IntMPA 92*
**Winchell,** Richard Marion 1928- *WhoRel 92*
**Winchell,** Robert Allen 1945- *WhoWest 92*
**Winchell,** Robert E 1931- *AmMWSc 92*
**Winchell,** Walter d1972 *LesBEnT 92*
**Winchell,** Walter 1897-1972 *FacFETw*
**Winchell,** William Olin 1933- *WhoAmL 92, WhoFI 92*
**Winchester,** Archdeacon of *Who 92*
**Winchester,** Bishop of 1926- *Who 92*
**Winchester,** Dean of *Who 92*
**Winchester,** Marquess of 1941- *Who 92*
**Winchester,** Albert McCombs 1908- *AmMWSc 92*
**Winchester,** Ian Sinclair 1931- *Who 92*
**Winchester,** Jack *IntAu&W 91X*
**Winchester,** James Frank 1944- *AmMWSc 92*
**Winchester,** James L. 1961- *WhoFI 92*
**Winchester,** John W 1929- *AmMWSc 92*
**Winchester,** Kennard *WhoBlA 92*
**Winchester,** Lyman Gene 1935- *WhoAmP 91*
**Winchester,** Randall Wayne 1955- *WhoEnt 92*
**Winchester,** Richard Albert *AmMWSc 92*
**Winchester,** Robert C 1945- *WhoAmP 91*
**Winchester,** Robert J 1937- *AmMWSc 92*
**Winchester,** Simon 1944- *WrDr 92*
**Winchevsky,** Morris 1855-1932 *LiExTwC*
**Winchevsky,** Morris 1856-1932 *BenetAL 91*
**Winchilsea,** Countess of 1661-1720 *RfGEnL 91*
**Winchilsea,** Earl of 1936- *Who 92*
**Winchurch,** Richard Albert 1936- *AmMWSc 92*
**Winckelmann,** Johann Joachim 1717-1768 *BlkwCEP*
**Winckler,** John Randolph 1916- *AmMWSc 92*
**Winckler,** Josef 1881-1966 *EncTR 91*
**Winckles,** Kenneth 1918- *Who 92*
**Wincklhofer,** Robert Charles 1926- *AmMWSc 92*
**Winckowski,** Scott Andrew 1964- *WhoAmL 92*
**Wincor,** Michael Z. 1946- *WhoWest 92*
**Wincott,** Jeff Piero *WhoEnt 92*
**Wind,** Herbert Hamilton, Jr 1915- *WhoAmP 91*
**Wind,** James Preslyn 1948- *WhoRel 92*
**Wind,** Willie W. 1913- *WhoEnt 92, WhoMW 92*
**Windaus,** Adolf Otto Reinhold 1876-1959 *WhoNob 90*
**Windecker,** George Henry, Jr. 1949- *WhoFI 92*
**Windeknecht,** Thomas George 1935- *AmMWSc 92*
**Windelen,** Heinrich 1921- *IntWW 91*
**Windeler,** Leon A 1910- *WhoAmP 91*
**Windell,** John Thomas 1930- *AmMWSc 92*
**Windels,** Carol Elizabeth 1948- *AmMWSc 92*
**Windels,** Paul, Jr. 1921- *WhoAmL 92, WhoFI 92*
**Winder,** Alfred M. *WhoBlA 92*
**Winder,** Barbara *DrAPF 91*
**Winder,** Charles Gordon 1922- *AmMWSc 92*
**Winder,** Dale Richard 1929- *AmMWSc 92*
**Winder,** David Kent 1932- *WhoAmL 92*
**Winder,** Robert Owen 1934- *AmMWSc 92*
**Winder,** Sammy 1959- *WhoBlA 92*
**Winder,** Scott Roberts 1958- *WhoEnt 92*
**Winder,** William Charles 1914- *AmMWSc 92*
**Winder,** William W 1942- *AmMWSc 92*
**Windeyer,** Brian 1904- *Who 92*
**Windeyer,** Brian Wellingham 1904- *IntWW 91*
**Windfuhr,** Gernot Ludwig 1938- *WhoRel 92*
**Windgassen,** Wolfgang 1914-1974 *FacFETw, NewAmDM*
**Windhager,** Erich E 1928- *AmMWSc 92*
**Windham,** Carol Thompson 1948- *AmMWSc 92, WhoWest 92*
**Windham,** David Preston 1960- *WhoEnt 92*
**Windham,** Donald 1920- *BenetAL 91, WrDr 92*
**Windham,** Edward James 1950- *WhoWest 92*
**Windham,** John Franklin 1948- *WhoAmL 92*
**Windham,** Michael Parks 1944- *AmMWSc 92*
**Windham,** Revish 1940- *WhoBlA 92*
**Windham,** Ronnie Lynn 1943- *AmMWSc 92*
**Windham,** Steve Lee 1922- *AmMWSc 92*
**Windham,** William Ashe Dymoke 1926- *Who 92*
**Windham,** William Russell S. *Who 92*
**Windhausen,** Rodolfo A. 1944- *WhoHisp 92*
**Windhauser,** John William 1943- *WhoEnt 92*
**Windhauser,** Marlene M 1954- *AmMWSc 92*
**Windholz,** Thomas Bela 1923- *AmMWSc 92*
**Windholz,** Walter M 1933- *AmMWSc 92*
**Windhorn,** Thomas H 1947- *AmMWSc 92*
**Windhorst,** Fritz H 1935- *WhoAmP 91*
**Windhorst,** John William, Jr. 1940- *WhoAmL 92*
**Winding,** Kai 1922-1983 *NewAmDM*
**Windingstad,** Harold Oliver, Jr 1929- *WhoAmP 91*
**Windisch,** Rita M *AmMWSc 92*
**Windle,** Don Ray 1948- *WhoAmL 92*
**Windle,** Francis 1845?-1917 *BiInAmS*
**Windle,** John Mark *WhoAmP 91*
**Windle,** Joseph Raymond 1917- *WhoRel 92*
**Windle,** Terence Leslie William 1926- *Who 92*
**Windler,** Donald Richard 1940- *AmMWSc 92*
**Windler,** Julie Spector 1948- *WhoEnt 92*
**Windlesham,** Baron 1932- *IntWW 91, Who 92*
**Windley,** Walter H, III *WhoAmP 91*
**Windom,** Herbert Lynn 1941- *AmMWSc 92*
**Windom,** Steve *WhoAmP 91*
**Windom,** William 1923- *IntMPA 92, WhoEnt 92*
**Windrow,** Martin *ConAu 134*
**Windrow,** Martin 1944- *SmATA 68*
**Windrow,** Martin C. *ConAu 134*
**Windrow,** Martin Clive 1944- *ConAu 134*
**Windsor,** Dean of *Who 92*
**Windsor,** Duchess of 1896-1986 *FacFETw [port]*
**Windsor,** Duke of *FacFETw [port]*
**Windsor,** Viscount 1951- *Who 92*
**Windsor,** Carl Douglas 1942- *WhoEnt 92*
**Windsor,** Donald Arthur 1934- *AmMWSc 92*
**Windsor,** John Golay, Jr 1947- *AmMWSc 92*
**Windsor,** Julius Gayle, Jr 1920- *WhoAmP 91*
**Windsor,** Margaret Eden 1917- *WhoEnt 92*
**Windsor,** Marie 1922- *IntMPA 92*
**Windsor,** Maura Kathleen 1937- *WhoRel 92*
**Windsor,** Maurice William 1928- *AmMWSc 92*
**Windsor,** Merrill C. 1924-1990 *ConAu 133*
**Windsor,** Patricia 1938- *IntAu&W 91, WrDr 92*
**Windsor,** Richard Anthony 1943- *AmMWSc 92*
**Windsor-Clive** *Who 92*
**Wine,** David John 1950- *WhoMW 92, WhoRel 92*
**Wine,** Dick *IntAu&W 91X, WrDr 92*
**Wine,** Donald Arthur 1922- *WhoAmL 92*
**Wine,** Jeffrey Justus 1940- *AmMWSc 92*
**Wine,** John Wesley 1940- *WhoAmL 92*
**Wine,** L. Mark 1945- *WhoAmL 92*
**Wine,** Paul Harris 1946- *AmMWSc 92*
**Wine,** Russell Lowell 1918- *AmMWSc 92*
**Wine,** Sherwin Theodore 1928- *WhoRel 92*
**Wine-Banks,** Jill Susan 1943- *WhoAmL 92*
**Wineapple,** Brenda 1949- *ConAu 133*
**Wineberg,** Howard 1955- *WhoWest 92*
**Wineberry,** Jesse *WhoAmP 91*
**Winebrenner,** Susan Kay 1939- *WhoMW 92*
**Wineburg,** Elliot N 1928- *AmMWSc 92*
**Winecoff,** David Fleming 1939- *WhoWest 92*
**Winefordner,** James D 1931- *AmMWSc 92*
**Winegard,** William Charles 1924- *AmMWSc 92*
**Winegarten,** Renee 1922- *IntAu&W 91, WrDr 92*
**Winegartner,** Edgar Carl 1927- *AmMWSc 92*
**Wineglass,** Henry 1938- *WhoBlA 92*
**Winegrad,** Gerald William 1944- *WhoAmP 91*
**Winegrad,** Saul 1931- *AmMWSc 92*
**Wineholt,** Robert Leese 1939- *AmMWSc 92*
**Winek,** Charles L 1936- *AmMWSc 92*
**Wineke,** Joseph Steven 1957- *WhoAmP 91*
**Wineland,** Fred L. 1926- *IntMPA 92, WhoAmP 91*
**Wineland,** Robert Mitchell 1959- *WhoFI 92*
**Winelander,** Richard William 1952- *WhoAmL 92*
**Wineman,** Alan Stuart 1937- *AmMWSc 92*
**Wineman,** Aryeh 1932- *WhoRel 92*
**Wineman,** Robert Judson 1919- *AmMWSc 92*
**Winemiller,** James D. 1944- *WhoMW 92*
**Winer,** Alfred D *AmMWSc 92*
**Winer,** Arthur Melvyn 1942- *AmMWSc 92*
**Winer,** Bette Marcia Tarmey 1940- *AmMWSc 92*
**Winer,** Elihu 1914- *WhoEnt 92*
**Winer,** Gregory John 1958- *WhoMW 92*
**Winer,** Gregory John J. 1958- *WhoFI 92*
**Winer,** Herbert Isaac 1921- *AmMWSc 92*
**Winer,** Jeffery Allan 1945- *AmMWSc 92*
**Winer,** Linda 1946- *WhoEnt 92*
**Winer,** Richard 1916- *AmMWSc 92*
**Winer,** Ward Otis 1936- *AmMWSc 92*
**Winer,** Warren James 1946- *WhoMW 92*
**Wines,** James 1932- *DcTwDes*
**Wines,** Lawrence Eugene 1957- *WhoAmP 91*
**Winestine,** Zachary 1958- *WhoEnt 92*
**Winestock,** Claire Hummel 1932- *AmMWSc 92*
**Winet,** Howard 1937- *AmMWSc 92*
**Winetrout,** Kenneth 1912- *IntAu&W 91, WrDr 92*
**Winett,** Joel M 1938- *AmMWSc 92*
**Winfield,** Arnold F. 1926- *WhoBlA 92*
**Winfield,** Arthur M. *BenetAL 91, SmATA 67*
**Winfield,** David Mark 1951- *WhoBlA 92, WhoWest 92*
**Winfield,** Elayne Hunt 1925- *WhoBlA 92*
**Winfield,** Florence F. 1926- *WhoBlA 92*
**Winfield,** George Lee 1943- *WhoBlA 92*
**Winfield,** Graham 1931- *Who 92*

**Winfield**, Howard Neil 1951- *WhoMW 92*
**Winfield**, James Eros 1944- *WhoBlA 92*
**Winfield**, James Frederick 1942- *WhoEnt 92*
**Winfield**, John Buckner 1942- *AmMWSc 92*
**Winfield**, Linda Fitzgerald 1948- *WhoBlA 92*
**Winfield**, Paul 1940- *IntMPA 92*
**Winfield**, Paul 1941- *ConBlB 2 [port]*
**Winfield**, Paul Edward 1941- *WhoBlA 92, WhoEnt 92*
**Winfield**, Peter Stevens 1927- *Who 92*
**Winfield**, Richard Neill 1933- *WhoAmL 92*
**Winfield**, Susan Rebecca Holmes 1948- *WhoBlA 92*
**Winfield**, Thalia Beatrice 1924- *WhoBlA 92*
**Winfield**, William T. 1944- *WhoBlA 92*
**Winfree**, Arthur T 1942- *AmMWSc 92*
**Winfree**, Murrell H. 1910-1990 *WhoBlA 92N*
**Winfrey**, Audrey Theresa *WhoBlA 92*
**Winfrey**, Charles Everett 1935- *WhoBlA 92*
**Winfrey**, Dennis Jerome 1959- *WhoMW 92*
**Winfrey**, Frank Lee 1952- *WhoFI 92*
**Winfrey**, J C 1927- *AmMWSc 92*
**Winfrey**, Marion Lee 1932- *WhoEnt 92*
**Winfrey**, Oprah *LesBEnT 92*
**Winfrey**, Oprah 1954- *ConBlB 2 [port], ConTFT 9, IntMPA 92, IntWW 91, NotBlAW 92, WhoBlA 92, WhoEnt 92, WhoMW 92*
**Winfrey**, Richard Cameron 1935- *AmMWSc 92*
**Wing**, Ada Schick 1896- *WhoAmP 91*
**Wing**, Adrien Katherine 1956- *WhoAmL 92*
**Wing**, Augustus 1809-1876 *BiInAmS*
**Wing**, Bruce Larry 1938- *AmMWSc 92*
**Wing**, Charles Hallet 1836-1915 *BiInAmS*
**Wing**, Edward Joseph 1945- *AmMWSc 92*
**Wing**, Elizabeth S 1932- *AmMWSc 92*
**Wing**, Francis William 1941- *WhoAmP 91*
**Wing**, Frank *WhoHisp 92*
**Wing**, G Milton 1923- *AmMWSc 92*
**Wing**, Gloria A 1931- *WhoAmP 91*
**Wing**, James 1929- *AmMWSc 92*
**Wing**, James C., Jr. 1956- *WhoAmL 92*
**Wing**, James David 1943- *WhoAmL 92*
**Wing**, James Erwin 1958- *WhoFI 92*
**Wing**, James Marvin 1920- *AmMWSc 92*
**Wing**, Janet E Bendt 1925- *AmMWSc 92*
**Wing**, John Adams 1935- *WhoMW 92*
**Wing**, John Faxon 1934- *AmMWSc 92*
**Wing**, John K. 1923- *WrDr 92*
**Wing**, John Kenneth 1923- *Who 92*
**Wing**, John Russell 1937- *WhoAmL 92*
**Wing**, Linda Peterson 1941- *WhoAmP 91*
**Wing**, Michael Russell 1957- *WhoRel 92*
**Wing**, Omar 1928- *AmMWSc 92*
**Wing**, Robert Edward 1941- *AmMWSc 92*
**Wing**, Robert Farquhar 1939- *AmMWSc 92*
**Wing**, Roger 1945- *WhoWest 92*
**Wing**, Theodore W., II 1948- *WhoBlA 92*
**Wing**, William Hinshaw 1939- *AmMWSc 92, WhoWest 92*
**Wingard**, Anita Rae 1960- *WhoEnt 92*
**Wingard**, Christopher Jon 1962- *AmMWSc 92*
**Wingard**, Deborah Lee 1952- *AmMWSc 92*
**Wingard**, Dovie Frances 1951- *WhoAmL 92*
**Wingard**, George Frank 1935- *WhoAmP 91*
**Wingard**, Lemuel Bell, Jr 1930- *AmMWSc 92*
**Wingard**, Paul Sidney 1930- *AmMWSc 92*
**Wingard**, Robert Eugene, Jr 1946- *AmMWSc 92*
**Wingate**, Catharine L 1922- *AmMWSc 92*
**Wingate**, Charles Douglas 1953- *WhoAmL 92*
**Wingate**, Edwin Henry 1932- *WhoFI 92*
**Wingate**, Frederick Huston 1932- *AmMWSc 92*
**Wingate**, Henry Travillion 1947- *WhoAmL 92*
**Wingate**, James Lawton 1846-1924 *TwCPaSc*
**Wingate**, Jay D 1921- *WhoAmP 91*
**Wingate**, John 1920- *WrDr 92*
**Wingate**, John Allan 1920- *IntAu&W 91*
**Wingate**, Livingston L. 1915- *WhoBlA 92*
**Wingate**, Marcel Edward 1923- *WhoWest 92*
**Wingate**, Martha Anne 1943- *IntAu&W 91*
**Wingate**, Martin Bernard *AmMWSc 92*
**Wingate**, Miles 1923- *Who 92*
**Wingate**, Orde 1903-1944 *FacFETw*
**Wingate**, Richard Anthony 1937- *WhoAmP 91*
**Wingate**, Rosalee Martin 1944- *WhoBlA 92*
**Winge**, Charles Edwin 1945- *WhoFI 92*
**Winge**, Dennis R 1947- *AmMWSc 92*
**Winge**, Ralph M 1925- *WhoAmP 91*
**Wingeleth**, Dale Clifford 1943- *AmMWSc 92*
**Wingenbach**, Gregory Charles 1938- *WhoRel 92*
**Wingender**, Ronald John 1936- *AmMWSc 92, WhoMW 92*
**Wingens**, Marion G. 1951- *WhoFI 92*
**Winger**, Debra 1955- *IntMPA 92, IntWW 91, WhoEnt 92*
**Winger**, Frank Stover 1865- *ScFEYrs*
**Winger**, Loren *WhoAmP 91*
**Winger**, Milton Eugene 1931- *AmMWSc 92*
**Winger**, Parley Vernon 1941- *AmMWSc 92*
**Winger**, Ralph O. 1919- *WhoFI 92*
**Winger**, Walter Orval 1929- *WhoRel 92*
**Wingert**, Louis Eugene 1924- *AmMWSc 92*
**Wingerter**, John Raymond 1942- *WhoAmL 92*
**Winget**, Carl Henry 1938- *AmMWSc 92*
**Winget**, Charles M 1925- *AmMWSc 92*
**Winget**, Gary Douglas 1939- *AmMWSc 92*
**Winget**, Robert Newell 1942- *AmMWSc 92*
**Winget**, Rodner Reed 1936- *WhoWest 92*
**Wingfield** *Who 92*
**Wingfield**, Edward Christian 1923- *AmMWSc 92*
**Wingfield**, Harold Lloyd 1942- *WhoBlA 92*
**Wingfield**, James Gus 1926- *WhoAmP 91*
**Wingfield**, Laura Allison Ross 1954- *WhoMW 92*
**Wingfield**, Sheila 1906- *ConPo 91, WrDr 92*
**Wingfield**, Stephen Ray 1947- *WhoRel 92*
**Wingfield Digby** *Who 92*
**Wingfield Digby**, Richard Shuttleworth 1911- *Who 92*
**Wingfield Digby**, Stephen Basil 1910- *Who 92*
**Wingo**, A. George 1929- *WhoBlA 92*
**Wingo**, Charles S 1949- *AmMWSc 92*
**Wingo**, Curtis W 1915- *AmMWSc 92*
**Wingo**, Glenn Max 1913- *WrDr 92*
**Wingo**, Michael 1941- *WhoWest 92*
**Wingo**, Raymond Coy 1928- *WhoFI 92*
**Wingo**, Robert Dean, Jr. 1949- *WhoEnt 92, WhoWest 92*
**Wingo**, William Jacob 1918- *AmMWSc 92*
**Wingrave**, Anthony *TwCSFW 91*
**Wingrave**, Mark 1957- *TwCPaSc*
**Wingren**, Gustaf Fredrik 1910- *WrDr 92*
**Wingrove**, Alan Smith 1939- *AmMWSc 92*
**Wingrove**, David 1954- *ConAu 133, ConLC 68 [port], TwCSFW 91*
**Wingti**, Paias 1951- *IntWW 91*
**Winhold**, Edward John 1928- *AmMWSc 92*
**Winiarski**, Warren Paul 1928- *WhoWest 92*
**Winiarz**, Marek Leon 1951- *AmMWSc 92*
**Winick**, Bruce Jeffrey 1944- *WhoAmL 92*
**Winick**, Calvin P 1931- *WhoIns 92*
**Winick**, Charles 1922- *ConAu 134*
**Winick**, Herman 1932- *AmMWSc 92*
**Winick**, Jeremy Ross 1947- *AmMWSc 92*
**Winick**, Lester *WhoMW 92*
**Winick**, Myron 1929- *AmMWSc 92*
**Winick**, Norman M 1952- *WhoAmP 91*
**Winick**, Peter Marc 1968- *WhoFI 92*
**Winicour**, Jeffrey 1938- *AmMWSc 92*
**Winicov**, Herbert 1935- *AmMWSc 92*
**Winicov**, Ilga 1935- *AmMWSc 92*
**Winicov**, Murray William 1928- *AmMWSc 92*
**Winicur**, Daniel Henry 1939- *AmMWSc 92, WhoMW 92*
**Winicur**, Sandra 1939- *AmMWSc 92*
**Winik**, Marion *DrAPF 91*
**Winikates**, James 1942- *WhoFI 92*
**Winiki**, Ephraim *TwCSFW 91*
**Winikoff**, Beverly 1945- *AmMWSc 92*
**Winikoff**, Robert Lee 1946- *WhoAmL 92*
**Winikoff**, S. Ashner 1942- *WhoAmL 92*
**Winitsky**, Alex 1924- *IntMPA 92*
**Winje**, Russell A 1932- *AmMWSc 92*
**Winjum**, Jack Keith 1933- *AmMWSc 92*
**Winjum**, James Marlow 1950- *WhoRel 92*
**Wink**, Darlene Jean 1950- *WhoAmP 91*
**Wink**, John J 1951- *WhoAmP 91*
**Wink**, Walter Philip 1935- *ConAu 36NR, WhoRel 92*
**Winke**, Jeffrey *DrAPF 91*
**Winke**, Paula Lois 1958- *WhoFI 92*
**Winkel**, Cleve R 1932- *AmMWSc 92*
**Winkel**, David John 1959- *WhoAmL 92*
**Winkel**, John Andrew 1948- *WhoMW 92*
**Winkel**, Judy Kay 1947- *WhoFI 92*
**Winkel**, Peter Alexander 1938- *WhoAmP 91*
**Winkel**, Richard J 1931- *WhoAmP 91*
**Winkelhake**, Jeffrey Lee 1945- *AmMWSc 92*
**Winkelman**, Brent N *WhoAmP 91*
**Winkelman**, James W 1935- *AmMWSc 92*
**Winkelman**, Joseph William 1941- *Who 92*
**Winkelman**, Michael Edward 1961- *WhoEnt 92*
**Winkelmann**, Frederick Charles 1941- *AmMWSc 92*
**Winkelmann**, James Arthur 1958- *WhoFI 92*
**Winkelmann**, John Paul 1933- *WhoRel 92*
**Winkelmann**, John Roland *AmMWSc 92*
**Winkelmann**, Richard Knisely 1924- *AmMWSc 92*
**Winkelmayer**, Patricia Anne Sohles 1938- *WhoEnt 92*
**Winkelstein**, Alan 1935- *AmMWSc 92*
**Winkelstein**, Jerry A 1940- *AmMWSc 92*
**Winkelstein**, Warren, Jr 1922- *AmMWSc 92*
**Winker**, James A 1928- *AmMWSc 92*
**Winkjer**, Dean 1923- *WhoAmP 91*
**Winkle**, Kenneth Willis 1936- *WhoMW 92*
**Winkle**, William Allan 1940- *WhoMW 92*
**Winkler**, Agnieszka M. 1946- *WhoWest 92*
**Winkler**, Allen Warren 1954- *WhoAmL 92*
**Winkler**, Anthony C. 1942- *WrDr 92*
**Winkler**, Barry Steven 1945- *AmMWSc 92*
**Winkler**, Bradford Sherman 1954- *WhoMW 92*
**Winkler**, Bruce Conrad 1937- *AmMWSc 92*
**Winkler**, Charles Howard 1954- *WhoAmL 92*
**Winkler**, Charles Raymond 1935- *WhoMW 92*
**Winkler**, Cheryl *WhoAmP 91*
**Winkler**, Dana John 1944- *WhoAmL 92*
**Winkler**, David Arthur 1952- *WhoWest 92*
**Winkler**, David Bradford 1962- *WhoAmL 92*
**Winkler**, David Francis 1958- *WhoMW 92*
**Winkler**, DeLoss Emmet 1914- *AmMWSc 92*
**Winkler**, Erhard Mario 1921- *AmMWSc 92*
**Winkler**, Hans Gunter 1926- *IntWW 91*
**Winkler**, Henrietta Irene 1919- *WhoWest 92*
**Winkler**, Henry 1945- *IntMPA 92*
**Winkler**, Henry Franklin 1945- *WhoEnt 92*
**Winkler**, Henry Ralph 1916- *WrDr 92*
**Winkler**, Herbert H 1939- *AmMWSc 92*
**Winkler**, Irwin 1931- *IntMPA 92, WhoEnt 92, WhoWest 92*
**Winkler**, James David 1954- *AmMWSc 92*
**Winkler**, Joe *WhoAmP 91*
**Winkler**, John 1935- *WrDr 92*
**Winkler**, Joseph Mark 1952- *WhoWest 92*
**Winkler**, Julie Ann 1953- *WhoMW 92*
**Winkler**, Karen Stapleton 1939- *WhoWest 92*
**Winkler**, Kenneth M. 1928- *WhoFI 92*
**Winkler**, Laura 1948- *WhoWest 92*
**Winkler**, Lenny T *WhoAmP 91*
**Winkler**, Leonard P *AmMWSc 92*
**Winkler**, Louis 1933- *AmMWSc 92*
**Winkler**, Margaret J. *ReelWom*
**Winkler**, Matthew M 1952- *AmMWSc 92*
**Winkler**, Max 1875-1961 *EncTR 91*
**Winkler**, Max Albert 1931- *AmMWSc 92*
**Winkler**, Norman Walter 1935- *AmMWSc 92*
**Winkler**, Paul Frank 1942- *AmMWSc 92*
**Winkler**, Peter K. 1943- *NewAmDM*
**Winkler**, Peter Mann 1946- *AmMWSc 92*
**Winkler**, Robert Randolph 1933- *AmMWSc 92*
**Winkler**, Sheldon 1932- *AmMWSc 92*
**Winkler**, Sue Elaine 1932- *WhoMW 92*
**Winkler**, Tony 1946- *WhoRel 92*
**Winkler**, Virgil Dean 1917- *AmMWSc 92*
**Winkler**, William Ralph 1900- *WhoAmP 91*
**Winkler**, William Richard 1947- *WhoFI 92*
**Winkles**, Dewey Frank 1946- *WhoAmL 92*
**Winkless**, Nelson Brock, III 1934- *WhoWest 92*
**Winkley**, Stephen Charles 1944- *Who 92*
**Winks**, Robin W. 1930- *Who 92, WrDr 92*
**Winlock**, Anna 1857-1904 *BiInAmS*
**Winlock**, Joseph 1826-1875 *BiInAmS*
**Winlock**, William Crawford 1859-1896 *BiInAmS*
**Winn** *Who 92*
**Winn**, Alden L 1916- *AmMWSc 92*
**Winn**, Ashley McHaffie 1951- *WhoAmL 92*
**Winn**, Bruce R 1955- *WhoAmP 91*
**Winn**, C Byron 1933- *AmMWSc 92*
**Winn**, Carol Denise 1962- *WhoBlA 92*
**Winn**, Charles C *ScFEYrs*
**Winn**, Darryl Malcolm 1961- *WhoMW 92*
**Winn**, David B 1937- *WhoIns 92*
**Winn**, David Burton 1953- *WhoAmL 92*
**Winn**, Delbert Easton 1946- *WhoAmL 92*
**Winn**, Edward Barriere 1922- *AmMWSc 92*
**Winn**, Francis John, Jr. 1946- *WhoMW 92*
**Winn**, George Michael 1944- *WhoWest 92*
**Winn**, Henry Joseph 1927- *AmMWSc 92*
**Winn**, Herschel Clyde 1931- *WhoAmL 92, WhoFI 92*
**Winn**, Howard *DrAPF 91*
**Winn**, Howard Elliott 1926- *AmMWSc 92*
**Winn**, Hugh 1918- *AmMWSc 92*
**Winn**, Hung Nguyen 1953- *WhoMW 92*
**Winn**, Ira Jay 1929- *WhoWest 92*
**Winn**, Janet B. *DrAPF 91*
**Winn**, Jill Kanaga Kline 1944- *WhoMW 92*
**Winn**, Joan T. 1942- *WhoBlA 92*
**Winn**, Joseph Lampher 1951- *WhoFI 92*
**Winn**, Larry, Jr 1919- *WhoAmP 91*
**Winn**, Martin 1940- *AmMWSc 92*
**Winn**, Mitchell Jeffrey 1959- *WhoAmL 92*
**Winn**, Philip Donald 1925- *WhoAmP 91*
**Winn**, Robert Charles 1945- *WhoWest 92*
**Winn**, Sara Elizabeth 1961- *WhoMW 92*
**Winn**, Stewart Dowse, Jr. 1936- *WhoFI 92*
**Winn**, William Paul 1939- *AmMWSc 92*
**Winnard**, Frank *TwCSFW 91*
**Winnemucca**, Sarah *BenetAL 91*
**Winner**, Dennis J *WhoAmP 91*
**Winner**, George H, Jr 1949- *WhoAmP 91*
**Winner**, Harold Ivor 1918- *Who 92*
**Winner**, Michael 1935- *IntMPA 92*
**Winner**, Michael Robert 1935- *IntWW 91, Who 92, WhoEnt 92*
**Winner**, Robert William 1927- *AmMWSc 92*
**Winner**, Thomas Andrew 1931- *WhoAmP 91*
**Winnett**, Anna Mae 1961- *WhoWest 92*
**Winnick**, David Julian 1933- *Who 92*
**Winnick**, Jack 1937- *AmMWSc 92*
**Winnick**, Jerry Howard 1937- *WhoEnt 92*
**Winnick**, Stephen 1939- *WhoEnt 92*
**Winnie**, Dayle David 1935- *AmMWSc 92*
**Winnie**, Dean Allen 1953- *WhoAmL 92*
**Winniford**, Robert Stanley 1921- *AmMWSc 92*
**Winnifrith**, Alfred John 1908- *Who 92*
**Winnifrith**, Charles Boniface 1936- *Who 92*
**Winnifrith**, T. J. 1938- *WrDr 92*
**Winnig**, August 1878-1956 *BiDExR, EncTR 91*
**Winnig**, Paula Jayne 1959- *WhoRel 92*
**Winnik**, Francoise Martine 1952- *AmMWSc 92*
**Winnik**, Mitchell Alan 1943- *AmMWSc 92*
**Winning**, Ethan Arnold 1939- *WhoWest 92*
**Winning**, John Patrick 1952- *WhoAmL 92, WhoMW 92*
**Winning**, Thomas J. *Who 92*
**Winning**, Thomas Joseph 1925- *IntWW 91*
**Winninger**, John J *WhoAmP 91*
**Winningham**, Herman S., Jr. 1961- *WhoBlA 92*
**Winningham**, John David 1940- *AmMWSc 92*
**Winningham**, Leslie 1940- *WhoAmP 91*
**Winningham**, Mare 1959- *IntMPA 92*
**Winningham**, R. Samuel 1953- *WhoFI 92, WhoMW 92*
**Winningham**, Stephen Meredith 1949- *WhoFI 92*
**Winninghoff**, Mary Ellen 1953- *WhoWest 92*
**Winnington**, Francis Salwey William 1907- *Who 92*
**Winnington-Ingram**, Edward John 1926- *Who 92*
**Winnington-Ingram**, Reginald Pepys 1904- *IntWW 91, Who 92*
**Winocur**, Emanuel Maurice 1928- *WhoWest 92*
**Winograd**, Arthur 1920- *NewAmDM*
**Winograd**, Audrey Lesser 1933- *WhoFI 92*
**Winograd**, Nicholas 1945- *AmMWSc 92*
**Winograd**, Shmuel 1936- *AmMWSc 92, IntWW 91*
**Winograd**, Terry Allen 1946- *AmMWSc 92, WhoWest 92*
**Winokur**, George 1925- *AmMWSc 92*
**Winokur**, Harvey Jay 1950- *WhoRel 92*
**Winokur**, Robert Michael 1942- *AmMWSc 92*
**Winquist**, Alan Hanson 1942- *WhoMW 92*
**Winquist**, Charles E. 1944- *WhoRel 92*
**Winquist**, Thomas Richard 1933- *WhoAmL 92*
**Winquist**, Victor Holmboe 1946- *WhoFI 92*
**Winrich**, Lonny B 1937- *AmMWSc 92*
**Winright**, John L. 1944- *WhoMW 92*
**Winrod**, Gerald Burton 1899?-1957 *RelLAm 91*
**Winrod**, Gerald Burton 1900-1957 *BiDExR*
**Winsberg**, Gwynne Roeseler 1930- *AmMWSc 92, WhoMW 92*

**Winsche**, Warren Edgar 1917- AmMWSc 92
**Winschel**, Theodore James 1964- WhoFI 92
**Winsett**, Jerry 1950- WhoEnt 92
**Winship**, Frederick Moery 1924- WhoEnt 92
**Winship**, Peter James Joseph 1943- Who 92
**Winske**, Dan 1946- AmMWSc 92
**Winskie**, Richard Clay 1962- WhoRel 92
**Winskill**, Archibald 1917- Who 92
**Winskill**, Robert Wallace 1925- WhoWest 92
**Winslett**, Linda Stoner 1958- WhoEnt 92
**Winsley**, Shirley JoAnn 1934- WhoAmP 91
**Winslow**, Alfred A. 1923- WhoBlA 92
**Winslow**, Alfred Akers 1923- WhoMW 92
**Winslow**, Alfred Edwards 1919- AmMWSc 92
**Winslow**, Bette Killingsworth 1919- WhoEnt 92
**Winslow**, Calvin 1949- WhoAmP 91
**Winslow**, Charles Ellis, Jr 1928- AmMWSc 92
**Winslow**, Charles Frederick 1811-1877 BiInAmS
**Winslow**, Cleta Meris 1952- WhoBlA 92
**Winslow**, Daniel B. 1958- WhoAmL 92
**Winslow**, David Allen 1944- WhoRel 92, WhoWest 92
**Winslow**, Douglas Nathaniel AmMWSc 92
**Winslow**, Edward 1595-1655 BenetAL 91
**Winslow**, Eugene 1919- WhoBlA 92
**Winslow**, Field Howard 1916- AmMWSc 92
**Winslow**, Frances Edwards 1948- WhoFI 92
**Winslow**, George Harvey 1916- AmMWSc 92
**Winslow**, Gerald Ray 1945- WhoRel 92
**Winslow**, John Franklin 1933- WhoAmL 92
**Winslow**, Joyce DrAPF 91
**Winslow**, Julian Dallas 1914- WhoAmL 92
**Winslow**, Kellen Boswell 1957- WhoBlA 92
**Winslow**, Kenelm Crawford 1921- WhoWest 92
**Winslow**, Kenneth Paul 1949- WhoFI 92
**Winslow**, Leon E 1934- AmMWSc 92
**Winslow**, Norman Eldon 1938- WhoWest 92
**Winslow**, Pauline Glen IntAu&W 91, WrDr 92
**Winslow**, Philip Charles 1924- WhoWest 92
**Winslow**, Reynolds Baker 1933- WhoBlA 92
**Winslow**, Robert M. 1941- WhoWest 92
**Winslow**, Thyra Samter 1893-1961 BenetAL 91
**Winslowe**, John TwCWW 91
**Winslowe**, John R TwCWW 91
**Winson**, Lawrence David 1951- WhoAmL 92
**Winsor**, Barbara Ann 1943- WhoEnt 92
**Winsor**, David John 1947- WhoWest 92
**Winsor**, Frederick James 1921- AmMWSc 92
**Winsor**, G McLeod ScFEYrs
**Winsor**, Justin 1831-1897 BenetAL 91
**Winsor**, Kathleen 1919- BenetAL 91, WrDr 92
**Winsor**, Lauriston P 1914- AmMWSc 92
**Winsor**, Philip Gordon 1938- WhoEnt 92
**Winsor**, Travis Walter 1914- WhoWest 92
**Winsor**, Virginia Louise 1947- WhoEnt 92
**Winspear**, Violet IntAu&W 91
**Winstan**, Matt TwCWW 91
**Winstanley** Who 92
**Winstanley**, Baron 1918- Who 92
**Winstanley**, Alan Leslie Who 92
**Winstanley**, Alan Leslie 1949- WhoRel 92
**Winstanley**, John 1919- Who 92
**Winstead**, Clint 1956- WhoFI 92
**Winstead**, Daniel E 1945- WhoAmP 91
**Winstead**, George Alvis 1916- WhoAmL 92
**Winstead**, Jack Alan 1932- AmMWSc 92
**Winstead**, Janet 1932- AmMWSc 92
**Winstead**, Joe Everett 1938- AmMWSc 92
**Winstead**, Lois McIver 1932- WhoAmP 91
**Winstead**, Meldrum Barnett 1926- AmMWSc 92
**Winstead**, Nash Nicks 1925- AmMWSc 92
**Winstead**, Robert Powell 1956- WhoEnt 92
**Winstead**, Sandra Cheshire 1944- WhoRel 92
**Winstead**, Vernon A., Sr. 1937- WhoBlA 92
**Winstein**, Stewart R 1914- WhoAmP 91
**Winsten**, Saul Nathan 1953- WhoAmL 92
**Winsten**, Seymour 1926- AmMWSc 92
**Winston**, Anthony 1925- AmMWSc 92
**Winston**, Arthur William 1930- AmMWSc 92
**Winston**, Bonnie Veronica 1957- WhoBlA 92
**Winston**, Charles Henry 1831- BiInAmS
**Winston**, Clive Noel 1925- Who 92
**Winston**, Daoma 1922- IntAu&W 91, WrDr 92
**Winston**, David Slater 1962- WhoEnt 92
**Winston**, Dennis Ray 1946- WhoBlA 92
**Winston**, Donald 1931- AmMWSc 92
**Winston**, Harold Ronald 1932- WhoAmL 92, WhoMW 92
**Winston**, Harvey 1926- AmMWSc 92
**Winston**, Hattie 1945- WhoBlA 92
**Winston**, Henry 1911- WhoBlA 92
**Winston**, Henry 1911-1986 FacFETw
**Winston**, Hubert 1948- AmMWSc 92, WhoBlA 92
**Winston**, Janet E. 1937- WhoBlA 92
**Winston**, Jeanne Worley 1941- WhoBlA 92
**Winston**, John H., Jr. 1928- WhoBlA 92
**Winston**, Judith Ellen 1945- AmMWSc 92
**Winston**, Lillie Carolyn 1906- WhoBlA 92
**Winston**, Michael D 1942- WhoIns 92
**Winston**, Michael R. 1941- WhoBlA 92
**Winston**, Paul Wolf 1920- AmMWSc 92
**Winston**, Phyllis DrAPF 91
**Winston**, Robert Maurice Lipson 1940- Who 92
**Winston**, Roland 1936- AmMWSc 92, WhoMW 92
**Winston**, Sarah DrAPF 91
**Winston**, Sarah 1912- WrDr 92
**Winston**, Sherry E. 1947- WhoBlA 92
**Winston**, Vern 1948- AmMWSc 92
**Winston-Fox**, Ruth 1912- Who 92
**Winstone**, Dorothy 1919- Who 92
**Winstone**, Reece d1991 Who 92N
**Winstone**, Reece 1909- WrDr 92
**Winstrom**, Leon Oscar 1912- AmMWSc 92
**Wint**, Arthur 1920- BlkOlyM [port]
**Wint**, Arthur Stanley 1920- Who 92
**Wint**, Arthur Valentine Noris 1950- WhoBlA 92
**Wint**, Dennis Michael 1943- WhoMW 92
**Winter**, Alex 1965- IntMPA 92
**Winter**, Alex Ross 1965- WhoEnt 92
**Winter**, Alexander J 1931- AmMWSc 92
**Winter**, Alison A. 1946- WhoFI 92
**Winter**, Allen Ernest 1903- Who 92
**Winter**, Audrey Stacey 1956- WhoAmL 92
**Winter**, Bryan Richard 1959- WhoAmL 92
**Winter**, Carl d1991 NewYTBS 91 [port]
**Winter**, Caryl Elyse 1944- WhoFI 92, WhoWest 92
**Winter**, Charles Gordon 1936- AmMWSc 92
**Winter**, Charles Milne 1933- IntWW 91, Who 92
**Winter**, Chester Caldwell 1922- AmMWSc 92
**Winter**, Daniel James 1946- WhoWest 92
**Winter**, Daniel Wallace 1928- WhoEnt 92
**Winter**, Daria Portray 1949- WhoAmP 91, WhoBlA 92
**Winter**, David WhoEnt 92
**Winter**, David Arthur 1930- AmMWSc 92
**Winter**, David Brian 1929- Who 92, WrDr 92
**Winter**, David F 1920- AmMWSc 92
**Winter**, David John 1939- AmMWSc 92
**Winter**, David Kenneth 1930- WhoWest 92
**Winter**, David Leon 1933- AmMWSc 92
**Winter**, Donald Charles 1948- AmMWSc 92
**Winter**, Donald F 1931- AmMWSc 92
**Winter**, Elmer Louis 1912- WhoMW 92
**Winter**, Ethel WhoEnt 92
**Winter**, Frederick Thomas 1926- IntWW 91, Who 92
**Winter**, Gerald Bernard 1928- Who 92
**Winter**, Gregory Paul 1951- Who 92
**Winter**, H G TwCSFW 91
**Winter**, Harry Clark 1941- AmMWSc 92
**Winter**, Helen DrAPF 91
**Winter**, Henry Frank, Jr 1936- AmMWSc 92
**Winter**, Herbert 1924- AmMWSc 92
**Winter**, Horst Henning 1941- AmMWSc 92
**Winter**, Irwin Clinton 1910- AmMWSc 92
**Winter**, Irwin Floyd 1914- WhoWest 92
**Winter**, Jack A d1991 NewYTBS 91
**Winter**, James Conrad 1951- WhoEnt 92
**Winter**, Jeanette E 1917- AmMWSc 92
**Winter**, Jeremy Stephen Drummond 1937- AmMWSc 92
**Winter**, Jeri Marjorie 1952- WhoAmP 91
**Winter**, Jerrold Clyne, Sr 1937- AmMWSc 92
**Winter**, John 1930- WrDr 92
**Winter**, John Alexander 1935- WhoFI 92
**Winter**, John David 1963- WhoFI 92
**Winter**, John Dawson, III 1944- WhoEnt 92A
**Winter**, John Henry 1947- AmMWSc 92
**Winter**, Joseph 1929- AmMWSc 92
**Winter**, Karl A 1928- AmMWSc 92
**Winter**, Lewis S, III 1945- WhoIns 92
**Winter**, Mary Davidson 1939- WhoAmL 92
**Winter**, Michael Morgan 1930- WrDr 92
**Winter**, Nadine P WhoAmP 91
**Winter**, Nathan Harold 1926- WhoRel 92
**Winter**, Nelson Warren 1950- WhoAmL 92
**Winter**, Nicholas Wilhelm 1943- AmMWSc 92
**Winter**, Olaf Hermann 1933- AmMWSc 92
**Winter**, Paul Theodore 1939- WhoEnt 92
**Winter**, Peter 1946- AmMWSc 92
**Winter**, Peter Michael 1934- AmMWSc 92
**Winter**, Ralph Frederick 1952- WhoEnt 92
**Winter**, Ralph K, Jr WhoAmP 91
**Winter**, Ralph Karl, Jr. 1935- WhoAmL 92
**Winter**, Richard Lawrence 1945- WhoFI 92, WhoMW 92
**Winter**, Richard Samuel, Jr. 1958- WhoWest 92
**Winter**, Robert Albert, Jr. 1954- WhoAmL 92
**Winter**, Robert Allan 1935- WhoRel 92
**Winter**, Robert John 1945- AmMWSc 92, WhoMW 92
**Winter**, Roland Arthur Edwin 1935- AmMWSc 92
**Winter**, Rolf Gerhard 1928- AmMWSc 92
**Winter**, Rudolph Ernst Karl 1935- AmMWSc 92
**Winter**, Stephen Samuel 1926- AmMWSc 92
**Winter**, Steven Ray 1944- AmMWSc 92
**Winter**, Theodore 1949- WhoAmP 91
**Winter**, Thomas Duane 1930- WhoAmP 91
**Winter**, Timothy Paul 1955- WhoWest 92
**Winter**, Wallace E 1930- WhoIns 92
**Winter**, Wesley Eugene 1953- WhoMW 92
**Winter**, William 1836-1917 BenetAL 91
**Winter**, William 1907- WhoWest 92
**Winter**, William Earl 1920- WhoMW 92
**Winter**, William Forrest 1923- WhoAmP 91
**Winter**, William Kenneth 1926- AmMWSc 92
**Winter**, William Phillips 1866-1919 BiInAmS
**Winter**, William Phillips 1938- AmMWSc 92
**Winter**, William Tatton 1855-1928 TwCPaSc
**Winter**, William Thomas 1944- AmMWSc 92
**Winter**, Wint, Jr 1953- WhoAmP 91
**Winter**, Winton Allen, Jr. 1953- WhoMW 92
**Winterberg**, Friedwardt 1929- AmMWSc 92
**Winterbotham**, F. W. 1897-1990 AnObit 1990
**Winterbotham**, Frederick William 1897- WrDr 92
**Winterbottom** Who 92
**Winterbottom**, Baron 1913- Who 92
**Winterbottom**, Michael 1934- IntWW 91, Who 92, WrDr 92
**Winterbottom**, Richard 1944- AmMWSc 92
**Winterbottom**, W L 1930- AmMWSc 92
**Winterbottom**, Walter 1913- Who 92
**Wintercorn**, Eleanor Stiegler 1935- AmMWSc 92
**Winterer**, Philip Steele 1931- WhoAmL 92
**Winterer**, William G. 1934- WhoFI 92
**Winterfeldt**, Ekkehard 1932- IntWW 91
**Winterflood**, Brian Martin 1937- Who 92
**Winterhalder**, Keith 1935- AmMWSc 92
**Winterhalter**, Albert Gustavus 1856-1920 BiInAmS
**Winterhalter**, Hugo 1910-1973 NewAmDM
**Winterholler**, Kent W. 1944- WhoAmL 92
**Winterich**, John T. 1891-1970 BenetAL 91
**Winterlin**, Wray LaVern 1930- WhoWest 92
**Winterlin**, Wray Laverne 1930- AmMWSc 92
**Winterling**, George Alfred 1931- WhoEnt 92
**Wintermute**, Jack R 1939- WhoIns 92
**Winternheimer**, P Louis 1931- AmMWSc 92
**Winternitz**, William Welch 1920- AmMWSc 92
**Winters**, Alvin L 1939- AmMWSc 92
**Winters**, Anne DrAPF 91
**Winters**, Barbara Jo WhoEnt 92, WhoWest 92
**Winters**, Bayla DrAPF 91
**Winters**, Brent Allan 1954- WhoRel 92
**Winters**, C E 1916- AmMWSc 92
**Winters**, Charlie 1941- WhoAmP 91
**Winters**, Cheryl Louise 1947- WhoFI 92
**Winters**, Christina Margaret 1947- WhoFI 92
**Winters**, David 1939- IntMPA 92
**Winters**, Deborah IntMPA 92
**Winters**, Deborah Brace 1953- WhoEnt 92
**Winters**, Earl D 1937- AmMWSc 92
**Winters**, George Eugene 1952- WhoRel 92
**Winters**, Harvey 1942- AmMWSc 92
**Winters**, Herbert A 1904- WhoIns 92
**Winters**, Jackson Edward 1939- WhoMW 92
**Winters**, Jacqueline F. 1936- WhoBlA 92
**Winters**, James Robert 1937- WhoBlA 92
**Winters**, Jerry 1917- IntMPA 92
**Winters**, John Drake 1961- WhoMW 92
**Winters**, John Wesley 1920- WhoAmP 91
**Winters**, Jonathan 1925- IntMPA 92, WhoEnt 92
**Winters**, Juliana McKinley 1949- WhoAmP 91
**Winters**, Kenneth E. 1959- WhoBlA 92
**Winters**, Lawrence Joseph 1930- AmMWSc 92
**Winters**, Leo 1922- WhoAmP 91
**Winters**, Logan 1944- TwCWW 91
**Winters**, Margaret Esther 1947- WhoMW 92
**Winters**, Mary Ann 1937- AmMWSc 92, WhoRel 92
**Winters**, Mary-Frances 1951- WhoFI 92
**Winters**, Mary Lou 1935- WhoAmP 91
**Winters**, Matthew Littleton 1926- WhoRel 92
**Winters**, Nancy DrAPF 91
**Winters**, Nathaniel E, Jr 1912- WhoAmP 91
**Winters**, Orlando Karl 1959- WhoRel 92
**Winters**, Ray Wyatt 1942- AmMWSc 92
**Winters**, Robert Cushing 1931- IntWW 91, WhoFI 92, WhoIns 92
**Winters**, Robert Wayne 1926- AmMWSc 92
**Winters**, Ronald Howard 1942- AmMWSc 92
**Winters**, Ronald Ross 1941- AmMWSc 92
**Winters**, Shelley 1922- IntMPA 92, IntWW 91, WhoEnt 92
**Winters**, Stephen Henry 1949- WhoFI 92
**Winters**, Stephen Mark 1954- WhoRel 92
**Winters**, Stephen Samuel 1920- AmMWSc 92
**Winters**, Thomas Bernarr 1931- WhoFI 92
**Winters**, Wallace Dudley 1929- AmMWSc 92
**Winters**, Wendell Delos AmMWSc 92
**Winters**, Wendy Glasgow WhoBlA 92
**Winters**, William Roger 1945- WhoMW 92
**Winters**, Yvor 1900-1968 BenetAL 91
**Winterscheid**, Loren Covart 1925- AmMWSc 92
**Wintersgill**, William 1922- Who 92
**Wintersheimer**, Donald C 1932- WhoAmP 91
**Wintersheimer**, Donald Carl 1932- WhoAmL 92
**Winterson**, Jeanette 1958- IntAu&W 91
**Winterson**, Jeanette 1959- ConNov 91, IntWW 91
**Winterstein**, James Fredrick 1943- WhoMW 92
**Winterstein**, Scott Richard 1955- AmMWSc 92
**Winterton**, Earl 1915- Who 92
**Winterton**, Ann 1941- Who 92
**Winterton**, Nicholas Raymond 1938- Who 92
**Wintgens**, Leo 1938- IntAu&W 91
**Winther**, Eva 1921- IntWW 91
**Winther**, Sophus K 1893-1983 TwCWW 91
**Winther**, Sophus Keith DcAmImH
**Winthrop**, Elizabeth DrAPF 91
**Winthrop**, Joel Albert 1942- AmMWSc 92
**Winthrop**, John 1588-1649 AmPolLe, BenetAL 91, RComAH
**Winthrop**, John 1714-1779 BiInAmS
**Winthrop**, John, Jr 1605?-1676 BiInAmS
**Winthrop**, John T 1938- AmMWSc 92
**Winthrop**, Kenneth Ray 1950- WhoWest 92
**Winthrop**, Lawrence Fredrick 1952- WhoAmL 92
**Winthrop**, Park ScFEYrs
**Winthrop**, R and C ScFEYrs
**Winthrop**, Robert Charles 1809-1894 AmPolLe
**Winthrop**, Sherman 1931- WhoAmL 92
**Winthrop**, Stanley Oscar 1927- AmMWSc 92
**Winthrop**, Theodore 1828-1861 BenetAL 91
**Winthrop**, W Y 1852- ScFEYrs
**Wintle**, Ruth Elizabeth 1931- Who 92
**Wintle**, Thomas D. WhoRel 92
**Wintman**, Melvin R. IntMPA 92
**Wintner**, Claude Edward 1938- AmMWSc 92
**Winton**, Alexander 1932- Who 92
**Winton**, Bruce James 1937- WhoWest 92
**Winton**, Charles Newton 1943- AmMWSc 92
**Winton**, Ed 1931- WhoEnt 92, WhoFI 92

**Winton,** Henry J 1929- AmMWSc 92
**Winton,** John IntAu&W 91X
**Winton,** Raymond Sheridan 1940- AmMWSc 92
**Winton,** Steven William 1957- WhoAmL 92
**Winton,** Walter 1917- Who 92
**Wintour,** Anna 1949- IntWW 91, Who 92
**Wintour,** Audrey Cecelia Who 92
**Wintour,** Charles Vere 1917- IntAu&W 91, IntWW 91, Who 92
**Wintringham,** Margaret 1879-1955 BiDBrF 2
**Wintriss,** Lynn 1954- WhoAmL 92
**Wintrobe,** Maxwell M. 1901-1986 ConAu 133
**Wintrode,** Ralph Charles 1942- WhoAmL 92
**Wintroub,** Herbert Jack 1921- AmMWSc 92
**Wintsch,** Robert P 1946- AmMWSc 92
**Wintz,** P A 1935- AmMWSc 92
**Wintz,** William A, Jr 1915- AmMWSc 92
**Winwood,** Stephen Lawrence 1948- WhoEnt 92
**Winyard,** Graham Peter Arthur 1947- Who 92
**Winzeler,** Brent Lynn 1954- WhoAmL 92
**Winzenburg,** Stephen Mark 1954- WhoRel 92
**Winzenread,** Marvin Russell 1937- AmMWSc 92
**Winzenreid,** James Ernest 1951- WhoAmL 92
**Winzer,** Stephen Randolph 1944- AmMWSc 92
**Wiorkowski,** John James 1943- AmMWSc 92
**Wipior,** Kurt Victor 1960- WhoWest 92
**Wipke,** W Todd 1940- AmMWSc 92
**Wipke-Tevis,** Deidre d'Amour 1962- WhoWest 92
**Wippel,** Patrick Victor 1931- WhoFI 92
**Wippermann,** Stephen Durnin 1947- WhoFI 92
**Wippern,** Ronald Frank 1933- WhoFI 92
**Wirahadikusumah,** Umar 1924- IntWW 91
**Wiratmo,** Eddy Susanto 1966- WhoFI 92
**Wirbel,** Judith Lynne 1958- WhoRel 92
**Wire,** Antoinette Clark 1934- WhoRel 92
**Wire,** William Shidaker, II 1932- WhoFI 92
**Wirken,** James Charles 1944- WhoAmL 92
**Wirkkala,** Tapio 1915-1985 DcTwDes
**Wirkus,** Bernard Anthony 1942- WhoMW 92
**Wirkus,** Thomas Edward 1933- WhoMW 92
**Wirmer,** Josef 1901-1944 EncTR 91
**Wirsching,** Charles Philipp, Jr. 1935- WhoFI 92, WhoMW 92
**Wirsen,** Carl O, Jr 1942- AmMWSc 92
**Wirsing,** Giselher 1907-1975 EncTR 91
**Wirszup,** Izaak 1915- AmMWSc 92
**Wirt,** Ann ConAu 134, SmATA 65
**Wirt,** Laura A 1923- WhoAmP 91
**Wirt,** Loyal Lincoln 1863-1961 AmPeW
**Wirt,** Michael James 1947- WhoWest 92
**Wirt,** Mildred A. ConAu 134, SmATA 65
**Wirt,** William 1772-1834 AmPolLe [port], BenetAL 91
**Wirt,** William A 1874-1938 DcAmImH
**Wirt,** William Stephen 1953- WhoAmL 92
**Wirta,** Roy W 1921- AmMWSc 92
**Wirtanen,** Philip Laurie 1944- WhoFI 92, WhoIns 92
**Wirten,** Rolf 1931- IntWW 91
**Wirth,** Alfred G 1941- WhoIns 92
**Wirth,** Arthur 1919- WrDr 92
**Wirth,** Christian 1885-1944 EncTR 91
**Wirth,** David Eugene 1951- WhoMW 92
**Wirth,** Donna Lynn 1947- WhoMW 92
**Wirth,** Edward Dewey, Jr. 1941- WhoFI 92
**Wirth,** James Burnham 1941- AmMWSc 92
**Wirth,** Joseph 1879-1956 EncTR 91 [port]
**Wirth,** Joseph Glenn 1934- AmMWSc 92
**Wirth,** Louis 1897-1952 DcAmImH
**Wirth,** Patricia Ann 1939- WhoMW 92
**Wirth,** Richard Marvin 1929- WhoMW 92
**Wirth,** Timothy E. 1939- AlmAP 92 [port], CurBio 91 [port], WhoAmP 91
**Wirth,** Timothy Endicott 1939- IntWW 91, WhoWest 92
**Wirth,** Winifred Prozeller 1916- WhoMW 92
**Wirthlin,** Milton Robert, Jr 1932- AmMWSc 92
**Wirths,** Claudine G. 1926- IntAu&W 91
**Wirtschafter,** Irene Nerove WhoFI 92
**Wirtschafter,** Jonathan Dine 1935- AmMWSc 92
**Wirtz,** Arthur Michael, Jr. WhoMW 92
**Wirtz,** George H 1931- AmMWSc 92
**Wirtz,** Gerald Paul 1937- AmMWSc 92
**Wirtz,** John Harold 1923- AmMWSc 92
**Wirtz,** Richard Anthony 1944- AmMWSc 92
**Wirtz,** Rosalie Ho 1936- WhoWest 92
**Wirtz,** William Otis, II 1937- AmMWSc 92
**Wirtz,** William Wadsworth 1929- WhoMW 92
**Wirz,** George O. 1929- WhoRel 92
**Wirz,** Pascal Francois 1943- WhoFI 92
**Wisbech,** Archdeacon of Who 92
**Wisberg,** Aubrey 1909?-1990 ConTFT 9
**Wisby,** Warren Jensen 1922- AmMWSc 92
**Wisch,** Steven Jared 1961- WhoFI 92
**Wischmann,** Dee WhoRel 92
**Wischmeier,** Walter Henry 1911- AmMWSc 92
**Wischmeyer,** Carl R 1916- AmMWSc 92
**Wischner,** Claudia DrAPF 91
**Wischner,** George Joseph 1914- WhoMW 92
**Wischnewski,** Hans-Jurgen 1922- IntWW 91
**Wiscombe,** Warren Jackman 1943- AmMWSc 92
**Wisdom,** Arthur John Terence Dibben 1904- Who 92
**Wisdom,** Billie Joe 1932- WhoAmP 91
**Wisdom,** David Watts 1929- WhoBlA 92
**Wisdom,** Guyrena Knight 1923- WhoMW 92
**Wisdom,** Jack Leach 1953- AmMWSc 92
**Wisdom,** John Minor 1905- WhoAmL 92
**Wisdom,** Michael Dennis 1953- WhoMW 92
**Wisdom,** Norman Who 92
**Wisdom,** Norman 1925- IntMPA 92
**Wisdom,** Shirleen Louise 1948- WhoWest 92
**Wise** Who 92
**Wise,** Baron 1923- Who 92
**Wise,** Aaron Noah 1940- WhoAmL 92
**Wise,** Audrey Who 92
**Wise,** Betsy Anne Hart 1952- WhoWest 92
**Wise,** Bill McFarland 1936- WhoAmP 91
**Wise,** Burton Louis 1924- AmMWSc 92
**Wise,** C. Rogers 1930- WhoBlA 92
**Wise,** Charles B. 1938- WhoMW 92
**Wise,** Charles Conrad, Jr. 1913- WrDr 92
**Wise,** Charles Davidson 1926- AmMWSc 92, WhoMW 92
**Wise,** David 1930- IntAu&W 91, WrDr 92
**Wise,** David Haynes 1945- AmMWSc 92
**Wise,** David Stephen 1945- AmMWSc 92
**Wise,** David William 1953- WhoFI 92
**Wise,** Dennis Irwin 1963- WhoEnt 92
**Wise,** Derek Who 92
**Wise,** Donald L 1929- AmMWSc 92
**Wise,** Donald U 1931- AmMWSc 92
**Wise,** Douglass 1927- Who 92
**Wise,** Dwayne Allison 1945- AmMWSc 92
**Wise,** Dwight C 1930- WhoAmP 91
**Wise,** Edmund Merriman, Jr 1930- AmMWSc 92
**Wise,** Edward Martin 1938- WhoAmL 92
**Wise,** Edward Nelson 1915- AmMWSc 92
**Wise,** Ernest George 1920- AmMWSc 92
**Wise,** Ernie Who 92
**Wise,** Evan Michael 1952- AmMWSc 92
**Wise,** Frank P. 1942- WhoBlA 92
**Wise,** Gary E 1942- AmMWSc 92
**Wise,** George Edward 1924- WhoAmL 92
**Wise,** George Herman 1908- AmMWSc 92
**Wise,** Gregory Kent 1948- WhoMW 92
**Wise,** Harold B 1937- AmMWSc 92
**Wise,** Harry H. 1938- WhoFI 92
**Wise,** Helena Sunny 1954- WhoEnt 92
**Wise,** Henry 1919- AmMWSc 92
**Wise,** Henry A., Jr. 1920- WhoBlA 92
**Wise,** Henry Alexander, II 1937- WhoMW 92
**Wise,** Henry Augustus 1819-1869 BenetAL 91
**Wise,** Herbert Ashby 1918- WhoBlA 92
**Wise,** Hugh Edward, Jr 1930- AmMWSc 92
**Wise,** Isaac Mayer 1819-1900 BenetAL 91, RelLAm 91
**Wise,** Janet Ann 1953- WhoWest 92
**Wise,** Janet Eugenia Wherry 1942- WhoFI 92
**Wise,** Jay Allan 1946- WhoRel 92
**Wise,** Jim Price 1943- WhoFI 92
**Wise,** John 1652-1725 BenetAL 91
**Wise,** John 1935- IntWW 91
**Wise,** John Allen 1956- WhoAmL 92
**Wise,** John James 1932- AmMWSc 92
**Wise,** John P 1924- AmMWSc 92
**Wise,** John Thomas 1926- AmMWSc 92
**Wise,** Karen Rampy 1959- WhoAmL 92
**Wise,** Lawrence David 1940- AmMWSc 92
**Wise,** Louis Neal 1921- AmMWSc 92
**Wise,** Mary Ellen EncAmaz 91
**Wise,** Matthew Norton 1940- AmMWSc 92
**Wise,** Michael John 1918- IntWW 91, Who 92
**Wise,** Miguel David 1960- WhoAmL 92
**Wise,** Milton Bee 1929- AmMWSc 92
**Wise,** Patricia Ann 1944- WhoEnt 92
**Wise,** Paul Allen 1959- WhoRel 92
**Wise,** Peter Anthony Surtees 1934- Who 92
**Wise,** Philip 1946- WhoAmP 91
**Wise,** Philip Douglas 1949- WhoRel 92
**Wise,** Raleigh Warren 1928- AmMWSc 92
**Wise,** Randolph George 1925- Who 92
**Wise,** Reginald Derek 1917- Who 92
**Wise,** Richard Evans 1947- WhoFI 92
**Wise,** Richard Melvin 1924- AmMWSc 92
**Wise,** Robert 1914- IntDcF 2-2 [port], IntMPA 92, WhoEnt 92
**Wise,** Robert E., Jr. 1948- AlmAP 92 [port], WhoAmP 91
**Wise,** Robert Earl 1914- IntWW 91
**Wise,** Robert Irby 1915- AmMWSc 92
**Wise,** Robert Lester 1943- WhoFI 92
**Wise,** Robert Wayne 1934- WhoAmL 92
**Wise,** Roger Lee 1959- WhoFI 92, WhoWest 92
**Wise,** Ronald Lee 1936- WhoFI 92
**Wise,** Sherwood Willing 1910- WhoAmL 92
**Wise,** Sherwood Willing, Jr 1941- AmMWSc 92
**Wise,** Stephen R 1941- WhoAmP 91
**Wise,** Stephen Samuel 1874-1949 RelLAm 91
**Wise,** Steven Lanier 1956- WhoAmL 92
**Wise,** Susan Tamsberg 1945- WhoFI 92
**Wise,** Terence 1935- WrDr 92
**Wise,** Thomas Dean 1955- WhoAmL 92
**Wise,** Thomas Dewey 1939- WhoAmL 92, WhoAmP 91
**Wise,** Toni Pryor 1948- WhoAmL 92
**Wise,** Virginia Jo 1950- WhoAmL 92
**Wise,** Warren C. WhoBlA 92
**Wise,** Warren Roberts 1929- WhoAmL 92, WhoFI 92
**Wise,** William Allan 1945- WhoFI 92
**Wise,** William Clinton, Sr. 1941- WhoBlA 92
**Wise,** William Curtis 1940- AmMWSc 92
**Wise,** William Nesbitt 1959- WhoWest 92
**Wise,** William Stewart 1933- AmMWSc 92
**Wise,** Wilma Mark 1926- WhoMW 92
**Wise,** Woodrow Wilson, Jr. 1938- WhoWest 92
**Wiseblood,** Celeste 1950- WhoAmL 92
**Wisehart,** Arthur McKee 1928- WhoAmL 92
**Wisehart,** Mary Ruth 1932- WhoRel 92
**Wiseheart,** Malcolm Boyd, Jr. 1942- WhoAmL 92
**Wisekal,** Frank William 1934- WhoFI 92
**Wisell,** Bill 1939- WhoAmP 91
**Wisely,** William Ross 1958- WhoAmL 92
**Wiseman,** Adele 1928- ConNov 91, WrDr 92
**Wiseman,** Alan 1936- WrDr 92
**Wiseman,** Bernard 1922- WrDr 92
**Wiseman,** Billy Ray 1937- AmMWSc 92
**Wiseman,** Carl D 1925- AmMWSc 92
**Wiseman,** Charleen Gordon 1942- WhoAmP 91
**Wiseman,** Christopher Stephen 1936- IntAu&W 91
**Wiseman,** David 1916- IntAu&W 91
**Wiseman,** Donald John 1918- IntWW 91, Who 92, WrDr 92
**Wiseman,** Edward H 1934- AmMWSc 92
**Wiseman,** Ernest 1925- Who 92
**Wiseman,** Frederick LesBEnT 92
**Wiseman,** Frederick 1930- IntDcF 2-2 [port], IntMPA 92, WhoEnt 92
**Wiseman,** George Edward 1918- AmMWSc 92
**Wiseman,** Gordon G 1917- AmMWSc 92
**Wiseman,** Gordon Marcy 1934- AmMWSc 92
**Wiseman,** H A B 1924- AmMWSc 92
**Wiseman,** Jay Donald 1952- WhoWest 92
**Wiseman,** Jeffrey Stewart 1948- AmMWSc 92
**Wiseman,** John Harvey 1947- WhoWest 92
**Wiseman,** John R 1936- AmMWSc 92
**Wiseman,** John William 1957- Who 92
**Wiseman,** Joseph 1918- ConTFT 9, IntMPA 92
**Wiseman,** Lawrence Linden 1944- AmMWSc 92
**Wiseman,** Mac 1925- NewAmDM
**Wiseman,** Park Allen 1918- AmMWSc 92
**Wiseman,** Patrick 1950- WhoAmL 92
**Wiseman,** Ralph Franklin 1921- AmMWSc 92
**Wiseman,** Randolph Carson 1946- WhoAmL 92, WhoMW 92
**Wiseman,** Richard W. 1951- WhoAmL 92
**Wiseman,** Robert S 1924- AmMWSc 92
**Wiseman,** Roger K 1931- WhoIns 92
**Wiseman,** Scotty 1909- NewAmDM
**Wiseman,** Thomas Anderton, Jr. 1930- WhoAmL 92
**Wiseman,** Timothy Peter 1940- Who 92
**Wiseman,** Wesley Lane 1935- WhoAmP 91
**Wiseman,** William H 1929- AmMWSc 92
**Wiseman,** William Johnston, Jr 1944- WhoAmP 91
**Wiseman,** William Joseph, Jr 1943- AmMWSc 92
**Wisenberg,** S.L. DrAPF 91
**Wiser,** Betty H WhoAmP 91
**Wiser,** C Lawrence 1930- WhoAmP 91
**Wiser,** Cyrus Wymer 1923- AmMWSc 92
**Wiser,** Edward H 1931- AmMWSc 92
**Wiser,** Horace Clare 1933- AmMWSc 92
**Wiser,** James Eldred 1915- AmMWSc 92
**Wiser,** James Louis 1945- WhoMW 92
**Wiser,** Nathan 1935- AmMWSc 92
**Wiser,** Nicholas Van 1953- WhoAmL 92
**Wiser,** Thomas Henry 1946- AmMWSc 92
**Wiser,** Wendell H 1922- AmMWSc 92
**Wiser,** William DrAPF 91
**Wiser,** William 1929- WrDr 92
**Wiser,** Winfred Lavern 1926- AmMWSc 92
**Wisgerhof,** Jerry G 1938- WhoIns 92
**Wish,** Ernest R. WhoMW 92
**Wish,** Jay Barry 1950- WhoMW 92
**Wisham,** Claybron O. 1932- WhoBlA 92
**Wisham,** Mary Ellen 1932- WhoAmP 91
**Wishard,** Della M 1934- WhoAmP 91
**Wishard,** Gordon Davis 1945- WhoAmL 92
**Wishart and Company** DcLB 112
**Wishart,** Maureen Who 92
**Wishart,** Ronald Sinclair 1925- WhoFI 92
**Wishart,** Trevor 1946- ConCom 92
**Wishaw,** Susan Diane 1956- WhoAmL 92
**Wishek,** Michael Bradley 1959- WhoAmL 92
**Wishert,** Jo Ann Chappell 1951- WhoEnt 92
**Wishinsky,** Henry 1919- AmMWSc 92
**Wishman,** Marvin 1925- AmMWSc 92
**Wishman,** Thomas Allen 1956- WhoAmP 91
**Wishner,** Kathleen L 1943- AmMWSc 92
**Wishner,** Lawrence Arndt 1932- AmMWSc 92
**Wishnetsky,** Theodore 1925- AmMWSc 92
**Wishnia,** Arnold 1931- AmMWSc 92
**Wishnick,** Marcia M 1938- AmMWSc 92
**Wishnick,** William 1924- WhoFI 92
**Wishniewsky,** Gary 1946- WhoWest 92
**Wishnow,** Emanuel 1910- WhoEnt 92
**Wisian-Neilson,** Patty Joan 1949- AmMWSc 92
**Wisler,** G Clifton 1950- TwCWW 91, WrDr 92
**Wisler,** Jacob 1808-1889 RelLAm 91
**Wisliceny,** Dieter 1911-1948 EncTR 91
**Wislizenus,** Frederick Adolph 1810-1889 BenetAL 91
**Wislizenus,** Frederick Adolphus 1810-1889 BiInAmS
**Wislocki,** Peter G 1947- AmMWSc 92
**Wisman,** Everett Lee 1922- AmMWSc 92
**Wismar,** Beth Louise 1929- AmMWSc 92
**Wismar,** Gregory Just 1946- WhoRel 92
**Wismer,** Jack Norval 1946- WhoMW 92
**Wismer,** Marco 1921- AmMWSc 92
**Wismer,** Robert Kingsley 1945- AmMWSc 92
**Wisna** EncAmaz 91
**Wisner,** Frank George 1938- IntWW 91, WhoAmP 91
**Wisner,** Robert Joel 1925- AmMWSc 92
**Wisness,** Paul Norman 1946- WhoAmP 91
**Wisnieski,** Bernadine Joann 1945- AmMWSc 92
**Wisnievitz,** David 1950- WhoEnt 92
**Wisniewski,** Brenda W. 1945- WhoMW 92
**Wisniewski,** Felix E 1924- WhoAmP 91
**Wisniewski,** Henry George 1940- WhoFI 92, WhoMW 92
**Wisniewski,** Henryk Miroslaw 1931- AmMWSc 92
**Wisniewski,** John Christopher 1952- WhoFI 92
**Wisniewski,** Joseph Michael 1954- WhoMW 92
**Wisniewski,** Richard J 1950- WhoIns 92
**Wisniewski,** Stanley Chester 1948- WhoFI 92
**Wisniewski,** Thomas Joseph 1926- WhoEnt 92
**Wisnosky,** John G. 1940- WhoWest 92
**Wisoff,** Ellen DrAPF 91
**Wisotsky,** Jerry Joseph 1928- WhoWest 92
**Wisotzky,** Joel 1923- AmMWSc 92
**Wiss,** Jeffrey William 1954- WhoMW 92
**Wiss,** Marvin J 1926- WhoAmP 91
**Wissbaum,** Donna Cacic 1956- WhoAmL 92
**Wissbrun,** Kurt Falke 1930- AmMWSc 92
**Wisseman,** Charles Louis, Jr 1920- AmMWSc 92
**Wisseman,** William Rowland 1932- AmMWSc 92
**Wissemann,** Andrew Frederick 1928- WhoRel 92
**Wisser,** Kerry Marc 1960- WhoAmL 92
**Wisser,** Scott Allen 1954- WhoAmL 92

**Wissig**, Steven *AmMWSc 92*
**Wissing**, Matthew R 1958- *WhoAmP 91*
**Wissing**, Neil Phillip 1931- *WhoFI 92*
**Wissing**, Thomas Edward 1940- *AmMWSc 92*
**Wissinger**, Robert Alan 1950- *WhoWest 92*
**Wissler**, Clark 1870-1947 *BenetAL 91*
**Wissler**, Eugene H 1927- *AmMWSc 92*
**Wissler**, Robert William 1917- *AmMWSc 92*
**Wissner**, Allan 1945- *AmMWSc 92*
**Wissow**, Lennard Jay 1921- *AmMWSc 92*
**Wist**, Abund Ottokar 1926- *AmMWSc 92, WhoFI 92*
**Wistar**, Caspar 1761-1818 *BiInAmS*
**Wistar**, Isaac Jones 1827-1905 *BiInAmS*
**Wistar**, Stephen Moylan 1954- *WhoWest 92*
**Wister**, Owen 1860-1938 *BenetAL 91, TwCWW 91*
**Wistreich**, George A 1932- *AmMWSc 92*
**Wistreich**, Hugo Eryk 1930- *AmMWSc 92*
**Wistrich**, Enid Barbara 1928- *Who 92*
**Wistrich**, Ernest 1923- *Who 92*
**Wiswall**, Frank Lawrence, Jr. 1939- *WhoAmL 92*
**Wiswall**, Richard H, Jr 1916- *AmMWSc 92*
**Wiszniewski**, Adrian 1958- *TwCPaSc*
**Wit**, Andrew Lewis 1942- *AmMWSc 92*
**Wit**, Antoni 1944- *WhoEnt 92*
**Wit**, Daniel 1923- *WhoMW 92*
**Wit**, Harold Maurice 1928- *WhoFI 92*
**Wit**, Lawrence Carl 1944- *AmMWSc 92*
**Witcher**, Daniel Dougherty 1924- *WhoMW 92*
**Witcher**, Mark Thomas 1959- *WhoAmL 92*
**Witcher**, Robert Campbell 1926- *WhoRel 92*
**Witcher**, Roger Kenneth, Jr 1952- *WhoAmP 91*
**Witcher**, Wesley 1923- *AmMWSc 92*
**Witcoff**, David Lawrence 1957- *WhoAmL 92*
**Witcofski**, Richard Lou 1935- *AmMWSc 92*
**Witcop**, Rose 1890-1932 *BiDBrF 2*
**Witcover**, Walt 1924- *WhoEnt 92*
**Witczak**, Zbigniew J 1947- *AmMWSc 92*
**Witelson**, Sandra Freedman 1940- *AmMWSc 92*
**Witemeyer**, Hugh Hazen 1939- *WrDr 92*
**Withall**, William Nigel James 1928- *Who 92*
**Witham**, Barry Bates 1939- *WhoEnt 92*
**Witham**, Clyde Lester 1948- *AmMWSc 92, WhoWest 92*
**Witham**, Francis H 1936- *AmMWSc 92*
**Witham**, James *DrAPF 91*
**Witham**, P Ross 1917- *AmMWSc 92*
**Withbroe**, George Lund 1938- *AmMWSc 92*
**Withee**, Wallace Walter 1913- *AmMWSc 92*
**Witheford**, Hubert 1921- *WrDr 92*
**Withem**, Ron 1946- *WhoAmP 91*
**Withenbury**, Thomas Malcolm 1950- *WhoMW 92*
**Wither**, George 1588-1667 *RfGEnL 91*
**Wither**, Ross Plummer 1922- *AmMWSc 92*
**Witherby**, Frederick R.H., Jr. 1943- *WhoFI 92*
**Witherell**, Egilda DeAmicis 1922- *AmMWSc 92*
**Witherell**, Martin Jay 1955- *WhoAmL 92*
**Witherell**, Michael S. 1949- *WhoWest 92*
**Witherell**, Michael Stewart 1949- *AmMWSc 92*
**Witherell**, Peter Charles 1943- *AmMWSc 92*
**Witherington**, Giles Somerville Gwynne 1919- *Who 92*
**Witherow**, David Michael Lindley 1937- *Who 92*
**Withers**, Googie 1917- *ConTFT 9, IntMPA 92, Who 92*
**Withers**, Hubert Rodney 1932- *AmMWSc 92*
**Withers**, James C 1934- *AmMWSc 92*
**Withers**, Jane 1927- *IntMPA 92*
**Withers**, John Keppel Ingold D. *Who 92*
**Withers**, Mark Fred 1947- *WhoEnt 92, WhoWest 92*
**Withers**, Mike 1947- *WhoAmP 91*
**Withers**, Philip Carew 1951- *AmMWSc 92*
**Withers**, Reginald 1924- *Who 92*
**Withers**, Reginald Greive 1924- *IntWW 91*
**Withers**, Roy Joseph 1924- *Who 92*
**Withers**, Rupert Alfred 1913- *Who 92*
**Withers**, Stephen George 1953- *AmMWSc 92*
**Withers**, W. Russell, Jr. 1936- *WhoEnt 92, WhoFI 92*
**Withers**, W. Wayne 1940- *WhoAmL 92*
**Withers**, William Mark 1957- *WhoEnt 92*
**Witherspoon**, Annie C. 1928- *WhoBlA 92*
**Witherspoon**, Audrey Goodwin 1949- *WhoBlA 92*
**Witherspoon**, Carolyn Black 1950- *WhoAmL 92*
**Witherspoon**, David Howell 1918- *WhoEnt 92*
**Witherspoon**, Dorothy Karpel 1936- *WhoAmP 91*
**Witherspoon**, Frances 1886-1973 *AmPeW*
**Witherspoon**, Frances M. 1887-1973 *HanAmWH*
**Witherspoon**, Fredda *WhoBlA 92*
**Witherspoon**, Fredda Lilly *WhoMW 92*
**Witherspoon**, Gregory Jay 1946- *WhoWest 92*
**Witherspoon**, Herbert 1873-1935 *NewAmDM*
**Witherspoon**, James 1923- *WhoBlA 92*
**Witherspoon**, Jimmy 1923- *NewAmDM*
**Witherspoon**, John 1723-1794 *BenetAL 91, BlkwEAR*
**Witherspoon**, John Knox, Jr 1928- *WhoIns 92*
**Witherspoon**, John Pinkney, Jr 1931- *AmMWSc 92*
**Witherspoon**, Lavern 1954- *WhoRel 92*
**Witherspoon**, Mary Elizabeth *DrAPF 91*
**Witherspoon**, Paul A, Jr 1919- *AmMWSc 92*
**Witherspoon**, R. Carolyn *WhoBlA 92*
**Witherspoon**, Sharon 1955- *WhoAmL 92*
**Witherspoon**, William 1909- *WhoFI 92, WhoMW 92, WhoRel 92*
**Witherspoon**, William Roger 1949- *WhoBlA 92*
**Witherup**, Ronald D. 1950- *WhoRel 92*
**Witherup**, William *DrAPF 91*
**Witherup**, William 1935- *ConAu 133*
**Withington**, Charles Francis 1852-1917 *BiInAmS*
**Withington**, Holden W *AmMWSc 92*
**Withner**, Carl Leslie, Jr 1918- *AmMWSc 92*
**Withrow**, Clarence Dean 1927- *AmMWSc 92*
**Withrow**, Jackie *WhoAmP 91*
**Withrow**, Lucille Monnot 1923- *WhoFI 92*
**Withrow**, Mary Ellen 1930- *WhoAmP 91, WhoMW 92*
**Withrow**, Sheila Kay 1959- *WhoMW 92*
**Withrow**, William *WhoAmP 91*
**Withrow**, William John 1926- *WhoMW 92*
**Withstandley**, Victor DeWyckoff, III 1921- *AmMWSc 92*
**Withuhn**, William Lawrence 1941- *WhoFI 92*
**Withy**, George 1924- *Who 92*
**Witiak**, Donald T 1935- *AmMWSc 92*
**Witke**, Roxane 1938- *WrDr 92*
**Witkiewicz**, Stanislaw 1885-1939 *TwCSFW 91A*
**Witkin**, Eric Douglas 1948- *WhoAmL 92*
**Witkin**, Evelyn Maisel 1921- *AmMWSc 92*
**Witkin**, Isaac 1936- *TwCPaSc*
**Witkin**, Steven S 1943- *AmMWSc 92*
**Witkin**, Susan Beth 1959- *WhoWest 92*
**Witkind**, Irving Jerome 1917- *AmMWSc 92*
**Witkins**, Douglas Collier 1955- *WhoEnt 92*
**Witkop**, Bernhard 1917- *AmMWSc 92, IntWW 91*
**Witkop**, Carl Jacob, Jr 1920- *AmMWSc 92*
**Witkoski**, Francis Clement 1922- *AmMWSc 92*
**Witkovsky**, Paul 1937- *AmMWSc 92*
**Witkowiak**, Stanley Benedict 1909- *WhoRel 92*
**Witkowski**, Daniel David 1956- *WhoEnt 92*
**Witkowski**, James Joseph 1949- *WhoFI 92*
**Witkowski**, John Frederick 1942- *AmMWSc 92*
**Witkowski**, Joseph Theodore 1942- *AmMWSc 92*
**Witkowski**, Mary Julia 1917- *WhoRel 92*
**Witkowski**, Robert Edward 1941- *AmMWSc 92*
**Witkowsky**, Gizella *WhoEnt 92*
**Witkus**, Eleanor Ruth 1918- *AmMWSc 92*
**Witlin**, Bernard 1914- *AmMWSc 92*
**Witman**, George Bodo, III 1945- *AmMWSc 92*
**Witman**, Leonard Joel 1950- *WhoAmL 92*
**Witmer**, Emmett A 1924- *AmMWSc 92*
**Witmer**, G. Robert 1904- *WhoAmL 92*
**Witmer**, Heman John 1944- *AmMWSc 92*
**Witmer**, Joseph Kevin 1956- *WhoAmL 92*
**Witmer**, Ronald Alden 1941- *WhoAmL 92*
**Witmer**, William Byron 1931- *AmMWSc 92*
**Witmeyer**, John Jacob, III 1946- *WhoAmL 92*
**Witneg**, Hannah *EncAmaz 91*
**Witney**, Kenneth Percy 1916- *Who 92*
**Witorsch**, Raphael Jay 1941- *AmMWSc 92*
**Witort**, Janet Lee 1950- *WhoAmL 92*
**Witort**, Stephen Francis 1953- *WhoAmL 92*
**Witriol**, Norman Martin 1940- *AmMWSc 92*
**Witrod**, Mary Rosalita 1920- *WhoRel 92*
**Witschard**, Gilbert 1933- *AmMWSc 92*
**Witschi**, Hanspeter R 1933- *AmMWSc 92*
**Witsenhausen**, Hans S 1930- *AmMWSc 92*
**Witsman**, Forest Tim 1942- *WhoMW 92*
**Witt**, Adolf Nicolaus 1940- *AmMWSc 92*
**Witt**, Alan Michael 1952- *WhoAmL 92*
**Witt**, Burkett L. 1926- *WhoBlA 92*
**Witt**, Carter H 1937- *WhoAmP 91*
**Witt**, Christopher John 1931- *AmMWSc 92*
**Witt**, Donald James 1949- *AmMWSc 92*
**Witt**, Donald Reinhold 1923- *AmMWSc 92*
**Witt**, Enrique Roberto 1926- *AmMWSc 92*
**Witt**, Gary 1965- *WhoAmP 91*
**Witt**, Gregg Frederick 1955- *WhoMW 92*
**Witt**, Harold *DrAPF 91*
**Witt**, Harold Vernon 1923- *IntAu&W 91, WrDr 92*
**Witt**, Henry Frederick 1929- *WhoMW 92*
**Witt**, Herbert 1923- *WhoWest 92*
**Witt**, Howard Russell 1929- *AmMWSc 92*
**Witt**, Howell Arthur John 1920- *Who 92*
**Witt**, J. Kevin 1949- *WhoFI 92*
**Witt**, James Bradley 1954- *WhoRel 92*
**Witt**, John, Jr 1935- *AmMWSc 92*
**Witt**, Karen Madeline 1949- *WhoMW 92*
**Witt**, Katarina *NewYTBS 91 [port]*
**Witt**, Katarina 1966?- *News 91 [port], -91-3 [port]*
**Witt**, Patricia L *AmMWSc 92*
**Witt**, Paul Junger *LesBEnT 92*
**Witt**, Paul Junger 1941- *WhoEnt 92*
**Witt**, Peter Nikolaus 1918- *AmMWSc 92*
**Witt**, Robert Charles 1941- *WhoFI 92*
**Witt**, Robert Michael 1942- *AmMWSc 92*
**Witt**, Samuel N, Jr 1928- *AmMWSc 92*
**Witt**, Thomas Powell 1946- *WhoAmL 92*
**Witt**, William Paxton 1948- *WhoWest 92*
**Wittbecker**, Emerson LaVerne 1917- *AmMWSc 92*
**Wittcoff**, A Harold 1918- *AmMWSc 92*
**Witte**, Ann Dryden 1942- *WhoFI 92*
**Witte**, George Charles, Jr. 1932- *WhoAmL 92*
**Witte**, Jeanne Marie 1938- *WhoMW 92*
**Witte**, John *DrAPF 91*
**Witte**, John Jacob 1932- *AmMWSc 92*
**Witte**, Larry C 1939- *AmMWSc 92*
**Witte**, Michael 1911- *AmMWSc 92*
**Witte**, Owen Neil *AmMWSc 92*
**Witte**, Sergei Yulyevich 1849-1915 *FacFETw*
**Witte**, Stephen Earl 1941- *WhoMW 92*
**Witte**, William 1907- *Who 92*
**Witte**, Wreatha Ann 1947- *WhoWest 92*
**Witteborn**, Fred Carl 1934- *AmMWSc 92*
**Wittebort**, Jules I 1917- *AmMWSc 92*
**Wittebort**, Robert John, Jr. 1947- *WhoAmL 92*
**Wittek**, Erhard 1898-1981 *EncTR 91*
**Wittekind**, Raymond Richard 1929- *AmMWSc 92*
**Wittels**, Anne F. *DrAPF 91*
**Wittels**, Benjamin 1926- *AmMWSc 92*
**Wittels**, Mark C 1921- *AmMWSc 92*
**Wittemann**, Joseph Klaus 1941- *AmMWSc 92*
**Witten**, Alan Joel 1949- *AmMWSc 92*
**Witten**, Anne *DrAPF 91*
**Witten**, Edward 1951- *AmMWSc 92*
**Witten**, Gerald Lee 1929- *AmMWSc 92*
**Witten**, Louis 1921- *AmMWSc 92, WhoMW 92*
**Witten**, Maurice Haden 1931- *AmMWSc 92*
**Witten**, Thomas Adams, Jr 1944- *AmMWSc 92*
**Wittenbach**, Don Leo 1936- *WhoEnt 92*
**Wittenbach**, Vernon Arie 1945- *AmMWSc 92*
**Wittenberg**, Albert M *AmMWSc 92*
**Wittenberg**, Beatrice A 1928- *AmMWSc 92*
**Wittenberg**, Jon Albert 1939- *WhoFI 92*
**Wittenberg**, Jonathan B 1923- *AmMWSc 92*
**Wittenberg**, Robert Harris 1960- *WhoEnt 92*
**Wittenberg**, Rudolph *DrAPF 91*
**Wittenberger**, Charles Louis 1930- *AmMWSc 92*
**Wittenbrink**, Boniface Leo 1914- *WhoMW 92, WhoRel 92*
**Wittenbrink**, Sandra Demerly 1943- *WhoMW 92*
**Wittenmeyer**, Charles E. 1903- *WhoAmL 92, WhoAmP 91*
**Wittenmyer**, Annie Turner 1827-1900 *RelLAm 91*
**Wittenmyer**, Larry William 1944- *WhoFI 92*
**Wittenstein**, David Joel 1956- *WhoAmL 92*
**Wittenwyler**, Ronald P 1947- *WhoIns 92*
**Witter**, Cheri Lea 1955- *WhoAmL 92*
**Witter**, John Allen 1943- *AmMWSc 92, WhoMW 92*
**Witter**, Lloyd David 1923- *AmMWSc 92, WhoMW 92*
**Witter**, Richard L 1936- *AmMWSc 92*
**Witter**, Robert Edward 1948- *WhoFI 92*
**Witter**, Thomas Winship 1928- *WhoFI 92*
**Witter**, Wendell Winship 1910- *WhoWest 92*
**Witter**, William D. 1929- *WhoFI 92*
**Witterholt**, Edward John 1935- *AmMWSc 92*
**Witterholt**, Vincent Gerard 1932- *AmMWSc 92*
**Witters**, Robert Dale 1929- *AmMWSc 92*
**Witters**, Weldon L 1929- *AmMWSc 92*
**Witteveen**, Hendrikus Johannes 1921- *IntWW 91*
**Witteveen**, Johannes 1921- *Who 92*
**Wittfoht**, Hans Heinrich Hermann 1924- *WhoFI 92*
**Wittgenstein**, Herta *DrAPF 91*
**Wittgenstein**, Ludwig J. J. 1889-1951 *FacFETw*
**Wittgenstein**, Paul *FacFETw*
**Wittgenstein**, Paul 1887-1961 *NewAmDM*
**Wittgraf**, George William 1945- *WhoAmP 91*
**Witthar**, Richard Webster 1943- *WhoMW 92*
**Witthaus**, Rudolph August 1846-1915 *BiInAmS*
**Witthuhn**, Norman Edward 1946- *WhoRel 92*
**Wittich**, William Vincent 1941- *WhoWest 92*
**Wittick**, James John 1930- *AmMWSc 92*
**Wittie**, Larry Dawson 1943- *AmMWSc 92*
**Wittig**, Don E. 1941- *WhoAmL 92*
**Wittig**, Erland Paul 1955- *WhoWest 92*
**Wittig**, Georg Friedrich Karl 1897- *AmMWSc 92*
**Wittig**, Georg Friedrich Karl 1897-1987 *WhoNob 90*
**Wittig**, Gertraude Christa 1928- *AmMWSc 92, WhoMW 92*
**Wittig**, Judith *DrAPF 91*
**Wittig**, Kenneth Paul 1946- *AmMWSc 92*
**Wittig**, Monique 1935?- *ConAu 135, FrenWW*
**Wittig**, Raymond Shaffer 1944- *WhoAmL 92, WhoFI 92*
**Witting**, Chris J. *LesBEnT 92*
**Witting**, Harald Ludwig 1936- *AmMWSc 92*
**Witting**, James M 1938- *AmMWSc 92*
**Witting**, Lloyd Allen 1930- *AmMWSc 92*
**Wittkamper**, Thomas John 1943- *WhoRel 92*
**Wittke**, Dayton D 1932- *AmMWSc 92*
**Wittke**, Donald Alan 1954- *WhoFI 92*
**Wittke**, James Pleister 1928- *AmMWSc 92*
**Wittke**, Paul H 1934- *AmMWSc 92*
**Wittkower**, Andrew Benedict 1934- *AmMWSc 92*
**Wittle**, John Kenneth 1939- *AmMWSc 92*
**Wittle**, Lawrence Wayne 1941- *AmMWSc 92*
**Wittler**, Shirley Joyce 1927- *WhoAmP 91*
**Wittliff**, James Lamar 1938- *AmMWSc 92*
**Wittlin**, Thaddeus 1909- *WrDr 92*
**Wittlinger**, Ellen *DrAPF 91*
**Wittman**, Gordon R. *IntWW 91*
**Wittman**, James Smythe, III 1943- *AmMWSc 92*
**Wittman**, Paul 1931- *WhoFI 92*
**Wittman**, Ronald Edgar 1944- *WhoFI 92*
**Wittman**, William F 1937- *AmMWSc 92*
**Wittman**, William Paul 1952- *WhoEnt 92*
**Wittmann**, Horst Richard 1936- *AmMWSc 92*
**Wittmer**, Marc F 1945- *AmMWSc 92*
**Wittmer**, Wilmer William 1940- *WhoMW 92*
**Wittmeyer**, Richard Arthur 1947- *WhoMW 92*
**Wittmier**, Susanna 1947- *WhoMW 92*
**Wittmuss**, Howard D 1922- *AmMWSc 92*
**Wittnebert**, Fred R 1911- *AmMWSc 92*
**Wittner**, Arvilla Marie 1929- *WhoAmP 91*
**Wittner**, Lawrence Stephen 1941- *WrDr 92*
**Wittner**, Murray 1927- *AmMWSc 92*
**Witton-Davies**, Carlyle 1913- *Who 92, WrDr 92*
**Wittow**, Mark Howard 1955- *WhoAmL 92*
**Wittrock**, Arlen Ernest 1953- *WhoMW 92*
**Wittrock**, Darwin Donald 1949- *AmMWSc 92*
**Wittrock**, Merlin Carl 1931- *WhoWest 92*
**Wittry**, David Beryle 1929- *AmMWSc 92*
**Wittry**, Esperance 1920- *AmMWSc 92*
**Wittry**, John P 1929- *AmMWSc 92*
**Wittschen**, Norman Riley 1935- *WhoRel 92*
**Wittson**, Cecil L 1907- *AmMWSc 92*
**Wittwer**, John William 1935- *AmMWSc 92*
**Wittwer**, Leland S 1919- *AmMWSc 92*

**Wittwer,** Robert Frederick 1940- AmMWSc 92
**Wittwer,** Sylvan Harold 1917- AmMWSc 92, ConAu 35NR
**Witty,** David 1924- Who 92
**Witty,** Robert Wilks 1941- WhoFI 92
**Witucki,** James Charles 1944- WhoAmP 91
**Witulski,** Arthur Frank 1958- AmMWSc 92
**Witwer,** Samuel Weiler, Jr. 1941- WhoAmL 92
**Witwer,** Samuel Weiler, Sr 1908- WhoAmP 91
**Witz,** Abbie Moses 1902- WhoFI 92
**Witz,** Dennis Fredrick 1938- AmMWSc 92
**Witz,** Gisela 1939- AmMWSc 92
**Witz,** Richard L 1916- AmMWSc 92
**Witzel,** Donald Andrew 1926- AmMWSc 92
**Witzell,** O W 1916- AmMWSc 92
**Witzeman,** Jeffrey Allen 1959- WhoEnt 92
**Witzeman,** Jonathan Stewart 1957- AmMWSc 92
**Witzenburger,** Edwin Jacob 1920- WhoAmP 91
**Witzgall,** Christoph Johann 1929- AmMWSc 92
**Witzgall,** John Edward 1937- WhoIns 92
**Witzig,** Warren Frank 1921- AmMWSc 92
**Witzleben,** Camillus Leo 1932- AmMWSc 92
**Witzleben,** Erwin von 1881-1944 EncTR 91 [port]
**Witzmann,** Frank A 1954- AmMWSc 92
**Wiviott,** Max Davis 1915- WhoAmP 91
**Wiwi,** Robert Paul 1941- WhoFI 92
**Wix,** Ethel Rose 1921- Who 92
**Wix,** Mayo 1923- WhoAmP 91
**Wixell,** Ingvar 1931- NewAmDM
**Wixom,** Charles William WhoMW 92
**Wixom,** Robert Llewellyn 1924- AmMWSc 92
**Wixson,** Bobby Guinn 1931- AmMWSc 92
**Wixson,** Eldwin A, Jr 1931- AmMWSc 92
**Wixson,** Raymond C 1935- WhoAmP 91
**Wixtrom,** Donald Joseph 1928- WhoMW 92
**Wizan,** Joe 1935- IntMPA 92
**Wizard,** Brian 1949- WhoWest 92
**Wizeman,** Donald G., Jr. 1944- IntMPA 92
**Wizen,** Sarabeth Margolis 1950- WhoFI 92
**Wizman,** Raphael 1943- WhoRel 92
**Wlaschin,** Ken 1934- WhoEnt 92
**Wlodek,** Stanley T 1930- AmMWSc 92
**Wlodkowski,** Raymond John 1943- WhoWest 92
**Wnuk,** Michael Peter 1936- AmMWSc 92
**Wnukowski,** Bryce Mahoney 1946- WhoMW 92
**Wobeser,** Gary Arthur 1942- AmMWSc 92
**Wobschall,** Darold C 1932- AmMWSc 92
**Wobser,** Bruce Duane 1953- WhoMW 92
**Wobus,** Reinhard Arthur 1941- AmMWSc 92
**Wochner,** William James 1947- WhoAmL 92
**Wockenfuss,** James Harold 1930- WhoEnt 92
**Wodarczyk,** Francis John 1944- AmMWSc 92
**Wodarski,** John Stanley 1943- AmMWSc 92, WhoMW 92
**Wodehouse** Who 92
**Wodehouse,** Lord 1951- Who 92
**Wodehouse,** P. G. 1881-1975 CnDBLB 6 [port], FacFETw, LiExTwC, RfGEnL 91, ScFEYrs
**Wodell,** Geoffrey Robert 1949- WhoMW 92
**Wodhams,** Jack 1931- TwCSFW 91, WrDr 92
**Wodicka,** Virgil O 1915- AmMWSc 92
**Wodinsky,** Isidore 1919- AmMWSc 92
**Wodlinger,** Constance Jean 1951- WhoEnt 92
**Wodlinger,** Eric W. WhoAmL 92
**Wodlinger,** Mark Louis 1922- WhoEnt 92
**Wodlinger,** Patricia Wheeler 1952- WhoEnt 92
**Wodock,** Cynthia Locke 1949- WhoAmL 92
**Wodoslawsky,** Theodore Steven 1957- WhoMW 92
**Wodrig,** Oscar Samuel 1938- WhoRel 92
**Wodtke,** Michael L 1943- WhoAmP 91
**Wodzicki,** Antoni 1934- AmMWSc 92
**Wodzinski,** Rudy Joseph 1933- AmMWSc 92
**Woehler,** Karlheinz Edgar 1930- AmMWSc 92
**Woehler,** Michael Edward 1945- AmMWSc 92
**Woehler,** Scott Edwin 1952- AmMWSc 92
**Woehrle,** Jeff William 1959- WhoFI 92
**Woehrlen,** Arthur Edward, Jr. 1947- WhoMW 92
**Woelfel,** Albert 1871-1920 BiInAmS
**Woelfel,** Julian Bradford 1925- AmMWSc 92
**Woelfel,** Lois Jane 1934- WhoAmP 91
**Woelfel,** Mary Teresa 1941- WhoWest 92
**Woelfel,** Robert William 1944- WhoEnt 92
**Woelfle,** Arthur W. 1920- IntWW 91
**Woelke,** Charles Edward 1926- AmMWSc 92
**Woeller,** Ida May 1964- WhoRel 92
**Woerdehoff,** Valorie Breyfogle DrAPF 91
**Woerner,** August John 1925- WhoRel 92
**Woerner,** Dale Earl 1926- AmMWSc 92
**Woerner,** Robert Leo 1948- AmMWSc 92
**Woerz,** Christian Hayward 1944- WhoRel 92
**Woese,** Carl R 1928- AmMWSc 92
**Woessner,** Donald Edward 1930- AmMWSc 92
**Woessner,** Frederick T. 1935- WhoEnt 92, WhoWest 92
**Woessner,** Jacob Frederick, Jr 1928- AmMWSc 92
**Woessner,** Mark Matthias 1938- IntWW 91, WhoFI 92
**Woessner,** Ronald Arthur 1937- AmMWSc 92
**Woessner,** Warren DrAPF 91
**Woessner,** Warren Dexter 1944- WhoMW 92
**Woeste,** Frank Edward 1948- AmMWSc 92
**Woeste,** William Franklin 1920- WhoIns 92
**Woestendiek,** John 1953- ConAu 133
**Woestendiek,** William John 1924- WhoWest 92
**Woetzel,** Damian Abdo 1967- WhoEnt 92
**Woetzel,** Robert K. 1930-1991 ConAu 135
**Woffinden,** Bob 1948- ConAu 135
**Wofford,** Alphonso 1958- WhoBlA 92
**Wofford,** Clinton Frie 1933- WhoRel 92
**Wofford,** Harris NewYTBS 91
**Wofford,** Harris 1926- AlmAP 92 [port]
**Wofford,** Harris, Jr WhoAmP 91
**Wofford,** Irvin Mirle 1916- AmMWSc 92
**Wofford,** Marion WhoAmP 91
**Wofford,** Milton Gene 1930- WhoRel 92
**Wofford,** Ruth Ann 1935- WhoFI 92
**Wofford,** Sandra Smith 1952- WhoAmP 91
**Wofsey,** Carol Miller 1955- WhoAmL 92
**Wofsy,** David 1946- WhoWest 92
**Wofsy,** Leon 1921- AmMWSc 92
**Wofsy,** Steven Charles 1946- AmMWSc 92
**Wogaman,** George Elsworth 1937- WhoMW 92
**Wogaman,** J. Philip 1932- WrDr 92
**Wogaman,** John Philip 1932- WhoRel 92
**Wogan,** Chris R 1950- WhoAmP 91
**Wogan,** Gerald Norman 1930- AmMWSc 92, IntWW 91
**Wogan,** Michael Terence 1938- Who 92
**Wogen,** Warren Ronald 1943- AmMWSc 92
**Wogman,** Ned Allen 1939- AmMWSc 92
**Wogrin,** Conrad A 1924- AmMWSc 92
**Wogsland,** Daniel K 1956- WhoAmP 91
**Wogsland,** James Willard 1931- WhoFI 92
**Wohl,** Amiel 1930- WhoRel 92
**Wohl,** Armand Jeffrey 1946- WhoWest 92
**Wohl,** David 1950- WhoEnt 92
**Wohl,** Joseph G AmMWSc 92
**Wohl,** Martin H 1935- AmMWSc 92, WhoMW 92
**Wohl,** Philip R 1944- AmMWSc 92
**Wohl,** Ronald A 1936- AmMWSc 92
**Wohlberg,** Meg 1905-1990 ConAu 133, SmATA 66
**Wohlbruck,** Aliceann 1936- WhoFI 92
**Wohleber,** David Alan 1940- AmMWSc 92
**Wohlers,** Henry Carl 1916- AmMWSc 92
**Wohletz,** Kenneth Harold 1952- WhoWest 92
**Wohlford,** Duane Dennis 1937- AmMWSc 92
**Wohlfort,** Sam Willis 1926- AmMWSc 92
**Wohlforth,** Eric Evans 1932- WhoAmL 92
**Wohlgelernter,** Devora Kasachkoff 1941- AmMWSc 92
**Wohlgelernter,** Maurice 1921- WrDr 92
**Wohlgemuth,** Ann Mulroy 1940- WhoAmL 92
**Wohlgenant,** Michael Kurt 1950- WhoFI 92
**Wohlgenant,** Richard Glen 1930- WhoWest 92
**Wohlin,** Lars Magnus 1933- IntWW 91
**Wohlman,** Alan 1936- AmMWSc 92
**Wohlmut,** Thomas Arthur 1953- WhoFI 92
**Wohlpart,** Kenneth Joseph AmMWSc 92
**Wohlrab,** Hartmut 1941- AmMWSc 92
**Wohlreich,** Jack Jay 1946- WhoAmL 92
**Wohlschlag,** Donald Eugene 1918- AmMWSc 92
**Wohltmann,** Hulda Justine 1923- AmMWSc 92
**Wohlwend,** Clarence 1912- WhoAmP 91
**Wohlwend,** Gina 1960- WhoRel 92
**Woirol,** Paul C 1949- WhoIns 92
**Woisard,** Edwin Lewis 1926- AmMWSc 92
**Woita,** Steven Ray 1949- WhoRel 92
**Woitach,** Richard 1935- WhoEnt 92
**Woiwode,** Larry DrAPF 91
**Woiwode,** Larry 1941- BenetAL 91, ConNov 91, WrDr 92
**Wojahn,** David DrAPF 91
**Wojahn,** R Lorraine WhoAmP 91
**Wojcicki,** Andrew 1935- AmMWSc 92
**Wojcicki,** Andrew Adalbert 1935- WhoMW 92
**Wojcicki,** Stanley G 1937- AmMWSc 92
**Wojciechowska,** Maia DrAPF 91
**Wojciechowska,** Maia 1927- Au&Arts 8 [port], WrDr 92
**Wojciechowski,** Bohdan Wieslaw 1935- AmMWSc 92
**Wojciechowski,** Norbert Joseph 1927- AmMWSc 92
**Wojcik,** Andrzej 1932- IntWW 91
**Wojcik,** Anthony Stephen 1945- AmMWSc 92
**Wojcik,** Cass 1920- WhoFI 92
**Wojcik,** John F 1938- AmMWSc 92
**Wojcik,** Kathleen L 1936- WhoAmP 91
**Wojcik,** Richard Frank 1936- WhoMW 92
**Wojcik,** Richard Joseph 1923- WhoMW 92
**Wojna,** Ryszard 1920- IntAu&W 91, IntWW 91
**Wojnar,** Robert John 1935- AmMWSc 92
**Wojnowski,** Edward Joseph 1954- WhoAmP 91
**Wojtal,** Steven Francis 1952- AmMWSc 92
**Wojtanek,** Guy Andrew 1954- WhoMW 92
**Wojtanowski,** Dennis Lee 1950- WhoAmP 91
**Wojtechko,** Barbara Ann 1957- WhoMW 92
**Wojtkowski,** Paul Walter 1945- AmMWSc 92
**Wojtkowski,** Thomas Casmere 1926- WhoAmP 91
**Wojtowicz,** Eugene Henry 1926- WhoMW 92
**Wojtowicz,** John Alfred 1926- AmMWSc 92
**Wojtowicz,** Peter Joseph 1931- AmMWSc 92
**Wojtyla,** Karol ConAu 133, IntWW 91
**Wojtyla,** Karol Jozef 1920- WhoRel 92
**Wojzik,** Mike WhoAmP 91
**Wolak,** Jan 1920- AmMWSc 92
**Wolanin,** Sophie Mae 1915- WhoFI 92, WhoMW 92
**Wolas,** Herbert 1933- WhoWest 92
**Wolasz-Ruhland,** Elizabeth Ann 1949- IntAu&W 91
**Wolaver,** Lynn E 1924- AmMWSc 92
**Wolbarsht,** James Lester 1947- WhoFI 92
**Wolbarsht,** Myron Lee 1924- AmMWSc 92
**Wolber,** William George 1927- AmMWSc 92
**Wolberg,** Donald Lester 1945- AmMWSc 92
**Wolberg,** Gerald 1937- AmMWSc 92
**Wolberg,** Richard Allen 1941- WhoRel 92
**Wolberg,** William Harvey 1931- AmMWSc 92
**Wolbrecht,** Thomas Paul 1944- WhoRel 92
**Wolcot,** John 1738?-1819 DcLB 109 [port]
**Wolcott,** Edward Wallace 1921- WhoAmL 92
**Wolcott,** John J 1940- WhoIns 92
**Wolcott,** Leonard Thompson IntAu&W 91, WrDr 92
**Wolcott,** Lucie V. 1962- WhoAmL 92
**Wolcott,** Mark Walton 1915- AmMWSc 92
**Wolcott,** Patty 1929- WrDr 92
**Wolcott,** Robert Wilson, Jr. 1926- WhoFI 92
**Wolcott,** Roger 1679-1767 BenetAL 91
**Wolcott,** Thomas Gordon 1944- AmMWSc 92
**Wolcott,** Townsend 1857-1910 BiInAmS
**Wolcson,** Gerald J. 1947- WhoRel 92
**Wold,** Aaron 1927- AmMWSc 92
**Wold,** Anthony John 1964- WhoRel 92
**Wold,** David C. WhoRel 92
**Wold,** Donald C 1933- AmMWSc 92
**Wold,** Emma 1871-1950 AmPeW
**Wold,** Finn 1928- AmMWSc 92
**Wold,** John S 1916- WhoAmP 91
**Wold,** John Schiller 1916- WhoWest 92
**Wold,** Margaret Barth 1919- WhoRel 92
**Wold,** Peter I 1948- WhoAmP 91
**Wold,** Richard John 1937- AmMWSc 92
**Wold,** Thomas Clifford 1937- WhoAmP 91
**Wolda,** Hindrik 1931- AmMWSc 92
**Wolde,** Mamo 1943- BlkOlyM [port]
**Wolde-Tinsae,** Amde M 1947- AmMWSc 92
**Woldegiorgis,** Gebretateos AmMWSc 92
**Woldin,** Edwin Judd 1925- WhoEnt 92
**Woldin,** Judd 1925- IntAu&W 91
**Woldseth,** Rolf 1930- AmMWSc 92
**Woledge,** Brian 1904- Who 92
**Wolek,** Ronald Andrew 1947- WhoMW 92
**Wolen,** Robert Lawrence 1928- AmMWSc 92
**Wolens,** Steven D 1949- WhoAmP 91
**Wolf,** A A 1935- AmMWSc 92
**Wolf,** Agnes Irene Heidenreich 1937- WhoMW 92
**Wolf,** Albert Allen 1935- AmMWSc 92
**Wolf,** Alfred 1915- WhoRel 92
**Wolf,** Alfred Peter 1923- AmMWSc 92
**Wolf,** Alice K 1933- WhoAmP 91
**Wolf,** Andrew 1927- WhoMW 92
**Wolf,** Arnold Jacob 1924- WhoRel 92
**Wolf,** Aron S. 1937- WhoWest 92
**Wolf,** Barry 1947- AmMWSc 92
**Wolf,** Benjamin 1913- AmMWSc 92
**Wolf,** Benjamin 1926- AmMWSc 92
**Wolf,** Beverly 1935- AmMWSc 92
**Wolf,** Brian David 1959- WhoAmL 92
**Wolf,** Bruce Alan 1949- WhoAmL 92
**Wolf,** Carol Euwema 1936- AmMWSc 92
**Wolf,** Catherine WhoEnt 92
**Wolf,** Charles, Jr. 1924- WhoWest 92
**Wolf,** Charles Edward 1938- WhoEnt 92
**Wolf,** Charles Trostle 1930- AmMWSc 92
**Wolf,** Charles William 1924- WhoAmP 91
**Wolf,** Chase 1953- WhoFI 92
**Wolf,** Christa IntWW 91
**Wolf,** Christa 1929- FacFETw
**Wolf,** Christopher 1954- WhoAmL 92
**Wolf,** Clarence, Jr. 1908- WhoFI 92
**Wolf,** Clarence J 1931- AmMWSc 92
**Wolf,** Clarence John 1931- WhoMW 92
**Wolf,** Cynthia Tribelhorn 1945- WhoWest 92
**Wolf,** Dale Duane 1932- AmMWSc 92
**Wolf,** Dale E 1924- AmMWSc 92, WhoAmP 91
**Wolf,** Daniel Star 1949- AmMWSc 92
**Wolf,** Dick LesBEnT 92
**Wolf,** Dieter 1946- AmMWSc 92
**Wolf,** Don Allen 1929- WhoFI 92
**Wolf,** Don Paul 1939- AmMWSc 92
**Wolf,** Douglas Jeffrey 1953- WhoWest 92
**Wolf,** Duane Carl 1946- AmMWSc 92
**Wolf,** Edward Charles 1954- AmMWSc 92
**Wolf,** Edward Christopher 1932- WhoEnt 92
**Wolf,** Edward D 1935- AmMWSc 92
**Wolf,** Edward Lincoln 1936- AmMWSc 92
**Wolf,** Edward Paul 1952- WhoFI 92
**Wolf,** Edwin, II d1991 NewYTBS 91
**Wolf,** Edwin, II 1911-1991 ConAu 133
**Wolf,** Elizabeth Anne AmMWSc 92
**Wolf,** Emanuel L. 1927- IntMPA 92
**Wolf,** Emil 1922- AmMWSc 92
**Wolf,** Eric W 1922- AmMWSc 92
**Wolf,** Esther Valladolid 1940- WhoHisp 92
**Wolf,** Frank James 1916- AmMWSc 92
**Wolf,** Frank Louis 1924- AmMWSc 92, WhoMW 92
**Wolf,** Frank R. 1939- AlmAP 92 [port], WhoAmP 91
**Wolf,** Franklin Kreamer 1935- AmMWSc 92
**Wolf,** Frederick George 1952- WhoWest 92
**Wolf,** Frederick Taylor 1915- AmMWSc 92
**Wolf,** Fredric M. 1945- WhoMW 92
**Wolf,** Friedrich August 1759-1824 BlkwCEP
**Wolf,** G. Van Velsor, Jr. 1944- WhoAmL 92
**Wolf,** Gail Pokela 1940- WhoWest 92
**Wolf,** Gary K 1941- TwCSFW 91, WrDr 92
**Wolf,** Gary Wickert 1938- WhoAmL 92
**Wolf,** George 1922- AmMWSc 92
**Wolf,** George Anthony, Jr 1914- AmMWSc 92
**Wolf,** George William 1943- AmMWSc 92
**Wolf,** Gerald Lee 1938- AmMWSc 92
**Wolf,** Hans Abraham 1928- WhoFI 92
**Wolf,** Harold Herbert 1934- AmMWSc 92
**Wolf,** Harold William 1921- AmMWSc 92
**Wolf,** Helmut 1924- AmMWSc 92
**Wolf,** Henry 1919- AmMWSc 92
**Wolf,** Henry 1925- WhoEnt 92
**Wolf,** Herbert S 1927- WhoIns 92
**Wolf,** Hirsch 1934- WhoIns 92
**Wolf,** Hugo 1860-1903 NewAmDM
**Wolf,** Ira Kenneth 1942- AmMWSc 92
**Wolf,** Irving W 1927- AmMWSc 92
**Wolf,** Jack Keil 1935- AmMWSc 92
**Wolf,** Jacquelyn Hvizdos 1961- WhoMW 92
**Wolf,** James A 1945- WhoIns 92
**Wolf,** James Anthony 1945- WhoFI 92
**Wolf,** James S 1933- AmMWSc 92
**Wolf,** James Stuart 1935- AmMWSc 92
**Wolf,** Jim Milton 1921- WhoAmP 91
**Wolf,** Joan DrAPF 91
**Wolf,** Joan Levin 1933- WhoEnt 92
**Wolf,** John Charles 1947- WhoWest 92
**Wolf,** John Michael 1946- WhoFI 92
**Wolf,** Joseph A, Jr 1933- AmMWSc 92

**Wolf,** Joseph Albert 1936- *AmMWSc 92, WhoWest 92*
**Wolf,** Judy Henry 1948- *WhoEnt 92*
**Wolf,** Julius 1918- *AmMWSc 92*
**Wolf,** Kathleen A 1946- *AmMWSc 92*
**Wolf,** Katie Louise 1925- *WhoAmP 91*
**Wolf,** Kenneth Edward 1921- *AmMWSc 92*
**Wolf,** Kenneth Erwin 1948- *WhoWest 92*
**Wolf,** Kenneth George 1940- *WhoFI 92*
**Wolf,** Larry Louis 1938- *AmMWSc 92*
**Wolf,** Laurence Grambow 1921- *WhoFI 92*
**Wolf,** Leonti 1956- *WhoEnt 92*
**Wolf,** Lesley Sara 1953- *WhoAmL 92*
**Wolf,** Leslie Raymond 1949- *AmMWSc 92*
**Wolf,** Lewis Isidore 1933- *WhoAmL 92, WhoFI 92*
**Wolf,** Lois Ruth 1897- *WhoAmP 91*
**Wolf,** Louis W 1928- *AmMWSc 92*
**Wolf,** Marcus Alan 1946- *WhoAmL 92*
**Wolf,** Mark Donald 1953- *WhoMW 92*
**Wolf,** Mark Lawrence 1946- *WhoAmL 92*
**Wolf,** Marshall Jay 1941- *WhoAmL 92*
**Wolf,** Marvin Abraham 1925- *AmMWSc 92*
**Wolf,** Mary Wilma 1918- *WhoRel 92*
**Wolf,** Matthew Bernard 1935- *AmMWSc 92*
**Wolf,** Merrill Kenneth 1931- *AmMWSc 92*
**Wolf,** Michael Kenneth 1949- *WhoAmL 92*
**Wolf,** Michele *DrAPF 91*
**Wolf,** Milton Albert 1924- *WhoAmP 91*
**Wolf,** Monica Theresia 1943- *WhoWest 92*
**Wolf,** Monte William 1949- *AmMWSc 92*
**Wolf,** Neal Lloyd 1949- *WhoMW 92*
**Wolf,** Neil Stephan 1937- *AmMWSc 92*
**Wolf,** Norman Anderson 1925- *WhoWest 92*
**Wolf,** Norman Sanford 1927- *AmMWSc 92, WhoWest 92*
**Wolf,** P S *AmMWSc 92*
**Wolf,** Patricia Rose 1936- *WhoAmP 91*
**Wolf,** Paul Delano 1952- *WhoAmL 92*
**Wolf,** Paul Leon 1928- *AmMWSc 92*
**Wolf,** Paul R 1934- *AmMWSc 92*
**Wolf,** Peter Otto 1918- *Who 92*
**Wolf,** Philip Frank 1938- *AmMWSc 92*
**Wolf,** Raoul 1946- *AmMWSc 92*
**Wolf,** Richard Alan 1939- *AmMWSc 92*
**Wolf,** Richard Clarence 1926- *AmMWSc 92*
**Wolf,** Richard Edward, Jr 1941- *AmMWSc 92*
**Wolf,** Richard Eugene 1936- *AmMWSc 92*
**Wolf,** Robert E 1942- *AmMWSc 92*
**Wolf,** Robert Howard 1942- *WhoFI 92*
**Wolf,** Robert Lawrence 1928- *AmMWSc 92*
**Wolf,** Robert Oliver 1925- *AmMWSc 92*
**Wolf,** Robert Peter 1939- *AmMWSc 92*
**Wolf,** Robert Stanley 1946- *AmMWSc 92*
**Wolf,** Robert Thomas 1933- *WhoAmL 92*
**Wolf,** Robert V 1929- *AmMWSc 92*
**Wolf,** Rose Barry 1921- *WhoFI 92*
**Wolf,** Sam W 1919- *WhoAmP 91*
**Wolf,** Sarah 1952- *WhoAmP 91*
**Wolf,** Sharyn *DrAPF 91*
**Wolf,** Stanley Myron 1939- *AmMWSc 92*
**Wolf,** Stephen *DrAPF 91*
**Wolf,** Stephen M. 1941- *IntWW 91, WhoFI 92, WhoMW 92*
**Wolf,** Stephen Noll 1944- *AmMWSc 92*
**Wolf,** Steven L 1944- *AmMWSc 92*
**Wolf,** Stewart George, Jr 1914- *AmMWSc 92*
**Wolf,** Stuart Alan 1943- *AmMWSc 92*
**Wolf,** Sue Alter 1929- *WhoEnt 92*
**Wolf,** Theodore R d1909 *BiInAmS*
**Wolf,** Thomas 1932- *AmMWSc 92*
**Wolf,** Thomas Howard 1916- *IntMPA 92*
**Wolf,** Thomas Mark 1944- *AmMWSc 92*
**Wolf,** Thomas Marshall 1951- *WhoAmL 92*
**Wolf,** Thomas Michael 1942- *AmMWSc 92*
**Wolf,** Walter 1931- *AmMWSc 92*
**Wolf,** Walter Alan 1942- *AmMWSc 92*
**Wolf,** Walter J 1927- *AmMWSc 92*
**Wolf,** Warren Alan 1950- *WhoAmL 92*
**Wolf,** Warren H *WhoAmP 91*
**Wolf,** Warren Walter 1941- *AmMWSc 92*
**Wolf,** Wayne Robert 1943- *AmMWSc 92*
**Wolf,** Werner Paul 1930- *AmMWSc 92*
**Wolf,** William Henry 1920- *WhoAmP 91*
**Wolf-Ferrari,** Ermanno 1876-1948 *NewAmDM*
**Wolfangle,** Karla *WhoEnt 92*
**Wolfarth,** Alwyn E. 1937- *WhoFI 92*
**Wolfarth,** Eugene F 1932- *AmMWSc 92*
**Wolfbein,** Seymour L. 1915- *WrDr 92*
**Wolfbein,** Seymour Louis 1915- *IntWW 91*
**Wolfe,** Alan David 1929- *AmMWSc 92*
**Wolfe,** Allan Frederick 1938- *AmMWSc 92*
**Wolfe,** Allan Marvin 1937- *AmMWSc 92*
**Wolfe,** Barbara Blair 1940- *AmMWSc 92*
**Wolfe,** Bardie Clinton, Jr. 1942- *WhoAmL 92*
**Wolfe,** Bernard 1915-1985 *FacFETw, TwCSFW 91*
**Wolfe,** Bernard Martin 1934- *AmMWSc 92*
**Wolfe,** Bertram 1927- *AmMWSc 92*
**Wolfe,** Brenda L. 1956- *WhoWest 92*
**Wolfe,** Brian Augustus 1946- *WhoWest 92*
**Wolfe,** Burton H. 1932- *WrDr 92*
**Wolfe,** Carl Dean 1957- *WhoMW 92*
**Wolfe,** Carter Franklin 1939- *WhoFI 92*
**Wolfe,** Carvel Stewart 1927- *AmMWSc 92*
**Wolfe,** Charles Keith 1943- *ConAu 34NR*
**Wolfe,** Charles Morgan 1935- *AmMWSc 92*
**Wolfe,** Charles R 1931- *WhoAmP 91*
**Wolfe,** Charles S *ScFEYrs*
**Wolfe,** Christopher 1949- *IntAu&W 91*
**Wolfe,** Clifford Eugene 1906- *WhoWest 92*
**Wolfe,** David M 1938- *AmMWSc 92*
**Wolfe,** David Mitchell 1948- *WhoMW 92*
**Wolfe,** Deborah Cannon *WhoBlA 92*
**Wolfe,** Deborah Cannon Partridge 1916- *NotBlAW 92*
**Wolfe,** Dorothy Wexler 1920- *AmMWSc 92*
**Wolfe,** Douglas Arthur 1939- *AmMWSc 92*
**Wolfe,** Edmund Ray 1943- *WhoAmP 91*
**Wolfe,** Edward 1897-1981 *TwCPaSc*
**Wolfe,** Edward Harvey 1945- *WhoFI 92*
**Wolfe,** Edward W 1936- *AmMWSc 92*
**Wolfe,** Edward William, II 1946- *WhoEnt 92, WhoWest 92*
**Wolfe,** Estemore A. 1919- *WhoBlA 92*
**Wolfe,** Estemore Alvis 1919- *WhoFI 92*
**Wolfe,** Fred Hartwell 1937- *WhoRel 92*
**Wolfe,** Gary Kent 1946- *WhoMW 92*
**Wolfe,** Gary Michael 1953- *WhoFI 92*
**Wolfe,** Gene *DrAPF 91*
**Wolfe,** Gene 1931- *IntAu&W 91, TwCSFW 91, WrDr 92*
**Wolfe,** Gene H 1936- *AmMWSc 92, WhoAmP 91*
**Wolfe,** Gerald Alfred 1948- *WhoIns 92*
**Wolfe,** Goldie Brandelstein 1945- *WhoMW 92*
**Wolfe,** Gordon A 1931- *AmMWSc 92*
**Wolfe,** Harold Joel 1940- *WhoFI 92*
**Wolfe,** Harriet Munrett 1953- *WhoAmL 92*
**Wolfe,** Harry Bernard 1927- *AmMWSc 92*
**Wolfe,** Harry Kirke 1858-1918 *BiInAmS*
**Wolfe,** Harvey 1938- *AmMWSc 92*
**Wolfe,** Herbert Glenn 1928- *AmMWSc 92*
**Wolfe,** Hugh Campbell 1905- *AmMWSc 92*
**Wolfe,** Ian 1896- *ConTFT 9*
**Wolfe,** J. Matthew 1956- *WhoAmL 92*
**Wolfe,** Jack C 1922- *ScFEYrs*
**Wolfe,** Jack C & Fitzgerald, Gregory *ScFEYrs*
**Wolfe,** James D. *LesBEnT 92*
**Wolfe,** James F 1936- *AmMWSc 92*
**Wolfe,** James Frederick 1948- *AmMWSc 92*
**Wolfe,** James H 1922- *AmMWSc 92*
**Wolfe,** James Jacob 1875-1920 *BiInAmS*
**Wolfe,** James Leonard 1940- *AmMWSc 92*
**Wolfe,** James Phillip 1943- *AmMWSc 92*
**Wolfe,** James Ronald 1932- *WhoAmL 92, WhoFI 92*
**Wolfe,** James Wallace 1932- *AmMWSc 92*
**Wolfe,** Jane 1957- *ConAu 133*
**Wolfe,** Jerry Allen 1955- *WhoAmP 91*
**Wolfe,** John A 1920- *AmMWSc 92*
**Wolfe,** John Joseph, Jr. 1939- *WhoAmL 92*
**Wolfe,** John Leslie 1926- *WhoAmL 92*
**Wolfe,** John Thomas 1942- *WhoBlA 92*
**Wolfe,** John Thomas 1955- *WhoWest 92*
**Wolfe,** Jonathan Scott 1950- *WhoAmL 92, WhoWest 92*
**Wolfe,** Kevin Michael 1947- *WhoAmL 92*
**Wolfe,** L. Daniel 1937- *WhoRel 92*
**Wolfe,** Lauren Gene 1939- *AmMWSc 92*
**Wolfe,** Lawrence *WhoEnt 92*
**Wolfe,** Lawrence Gregory 1965- *WhoMW 92*
**Wolfe,** Lawrence Irving 1924- *WhoWest 92*
**Wolfe,** Leonhard Scott 1926- *AmMWSc 92*
**Wolfe,** Linda *DrAPF 91, WrDr 92*
**Wolfe,** Linda Kay 1949- *WhoRel 92*
**Wolfe,** M Jay 1955- *WhoAmP 91*
**Wolfe,** Mark James 1962- *WhoRel 92*
**Wolfe,** Mark Reed 1955- *WhoAmL 92*
**Wolfe,** Michael 1945- *WrDr 92*
**Wolfe,** Paul 1926- *NewAmDM*
**Wolfe,** Paul David 1950- *WhoRel 92*
**Wolfe,** Paul Jay 1938- *AmMWSc 92*
**Wolfe,** Peter 1933- *WrDr 92*
**Wolfe,** Peter E 1911- *AmMWSc 92*
**Wolfe,** Peter Nord 1929- *AmMWSc 92*
**Wolfe,** Philip 1927- *AmMWSc 92*
**Wolfe,** Ralph Stoner 1921- *AmMWSc 92*
**Wolfe,** Raymond 1927- *AmMWSc 92*
**Wolfe,** Raymond Grover, Jr 1920- *AmMWSc 92*
**Wolfe,** Reuben Edward 1927- *AmMWSc 92*
**Wolfe,** Robert Francis, Jr. 1947- *WhoEnt 92*
**Wolfe,** Robert Kenneth 1929- *AmMWSc 92, WhoMW 92*
**Wolfe,** Robert Norton 1908- *AmMWSc 92*
**Wolfe,** Roger Thomas 1932- *AmMWSc 92*
**Wolfe,** Seth August, Jr 1944- *AmMWSc 92*
**Wolfe,** Sharon Leslie 1950- *WhoAmL 92*
**Wolfe,** Sheemon Aaron 1923- *WhoMW 92*
**Wolfe,** Stanley 1924- *WhoEnt 92*
**Wolfe,** Stephen Charles 1940- *WhoAmP 91*
**Wolfe,** Stephen Landis 1932- *AmMWSc 92*
**Wolfe,** Stephen Mitchell 1949- *AmMWSc 92*
**Wolfe,** Steven Jon *WhoWest 92*
**Wolfe,** Thomas 1900-1938 *BenetAL 91*
**Wolfe,** Thomas Clayton 1900-1938 *FacFETw*
**Wolfe,** Thomas E 1933- *WhoAmP 91*
**Wolfe,** Thomas Kennerly 1931- *IntAu&W 91*
**Wolfe,** Thomas Kennerly, Jr. 1931- *IntWW 91*
**Wolfe,** Thomas Kent 1959- *WhoEnt 92*
**Wolfe,** Tom *SourALJ*
**Wolfe,** Tom 1930- *Au&Arts 8 [port], ConNov 91, WrDr 92*
**Wolfe,** Tom 1931- *BenetAL 91, FacFETw*
**Wolfe,** Walter McIlhaney 1921- *AmMWSc 92*
**Wolfe,** Warren Dwight 1926- *WhoMW 92*
**Wolfe,** William Cuthbertson 1924- *Who 92*
**Wolfe,** William Downing 1947- *WhoWest 92*
**Wolfe,** William Eugene 1937- *WhoRel 92*
**Wolfe,** William K. 1926- *WhoBlA 92*
**Wolfe,** William Louis 1931- *WhoWest 92*
**Wolfe,** William Louis, Jr 1931- *AmMWSc 92*
**Wolfe,** William Ray, Jr 1924- *AmMWSc 92*
**Wolfenbarger,** Dan A 1934- *AmMWSc 92*
**Wolfenbarger,** John Richard 1949- *WhoAmP 91*
**Wolfenberger,** Virginia Ann 1948- *AmMWSc 92*
**Wolfendale,** Arnold Whittaker 1927- *IntWW 91, Who 92*
**Wolfenden,** James Douglas 1938- *WhoIns 92*
**Wolfenden,** Richard Vance 1935- *AmMWSc 92*
**Wolfensohn,** James D. 1933- *IntWW 91*
**Wolfensohn,** James David 1933- *WhoEnt 92*
**Wolfenson,** Azi U. 1933- *WhoFI 92*
**Wolfenson,** Marv *WhoMW 92*
**Wolfenstein,** Lincoln 1923- *AmMWSc 92, IntWW 91*
**Wolfersberger,** Michael Gregg 1944- *AmMWSc 92*
**Wolfersberger,** Stanley Jacob 1955- *WhoMW 92*
**Wolfert,** Adrienne *DrAPF 91*
**Wolfert,** Frederick Paul 1937- *WhoMW 92*
**Wolfert,** Helen *DrAPF 91*
**Wolfert,** Valinda Barrett 1959- *WhoAmL 92*
**Wolfes,** Felix 1892-1971 *NewAmDM*
**Wolff,** Albert 1835-1891 *ThHElm [port]*
**Wolff,** Arthur Harold 1919- *AmMWSc 92*
**Wolff,** Brian Richard 1955- *WhoFI 92*
**Wolff,** Caspar Friedrich 1733-1794 *BlkwCEP*
**Wolff,** Christian 1934- *ConCom 92, NewAmDM*
**Wolff,** Christian, Freiherr von 1679-1754 *BlkwCEP*
**Wolff,** Christopher 1949- *WhoEnt 92*
**Wolff,** Cynthia Griffin 1936- *WrDr 92*
**Wolff,** Daniel *DrAPF 91*
**Wolff,** Darrel Eugene 1951- *WhoWest 92*
**Wolff,** David A 1934- *AmMWSc 92*
**Wolff,** David Stephen 1940- *WhoFI 92*
**Wolff,** Deborah Horowitz 1940- *WhoAmL 92*
**Wolff,** Donald Edward 1922- *WhoIns 92*
**Wolff,** Donald George 1934- *WhoWest 92*
**Wolff,** Donald John 1942- *AmMWSc 92*
**Wolff,** Donald Lee 1935- *WhoAmL 92*
**Wolff,** Donald Martin 1957- *WhoAmP 91*
**Wolff,** Edward A 1929- *AmMWSc 92*
**Wolff,** Edward Nathan 1946- *WhoFI 92*
**Wolff,** Elroy Harris 1935- *WhoAmL 92*
**Wolff,** Ernest N *AmMWSc 92*
**Wolff,** Etienne Charles 1904- *IntWW 91*
**Wolff,** Florence I. *WhoMW 92*
**Wolff,** Frank Pierce, Jr. 1946- *WhoAmL 92*
**Wolff,** Frederick William 1920- *AmMWSc 92*
**Wolff,** Geoffrey *DrAPF 91*
**Wolff,** Geoffrey 1937- *WrDr 92*
**Wolff,** Geoffrey Ansell 1937- *BenetAL 91*
**Wolff,** George Louis 1928- *AmMWSc 92*
**Wolff,** George Thomas 1947- *AmMWSc 92*
**Wolff,** Gregory Steven 1951- *WhoFI 92*
**Wolff,** Gunther Arthur 1918- *AmMWSc 92, WhoMW 92*
**Wolff,** Hanns H 1903- *AmMWSc 92*
**Wolff,** Heinz Siegfried 1928- *Who 92*
**Wolff,** Herbert 1928- *WhoEnt 92*
**Wolff,** Howard Keith 1948- *WhoWest 92*
**Wolff,** Hugh MacPherson 1953- *WhoMW 92*
**Wolff,** Ivan A 1917- *AmMWSc 92*
**Wolff,** Jan 1925- *AmMWSc 92*
**Wolff,** John B 1925- *AmMWSc 92*
**Wolff,** John Shearer, III 1941- *AmMWSc 92*
**Wolff,** Karl 1900-1984 *EncTR 91*
**Wolff,** Karl Friedrich Otto 1900-1984 *BiDExR, FacFETw*
**Wolff,** Kurt H. 1912- *WrDr 92*
**Wolff,** Kurt Jakob 1936- *WhoAmL 92*
**Wolff,** Lea 1944- *WhoFI 92*
**Wolff,** Lester Lionel 1919- *WhoAmP 91*
**Wolff,** Louis Arthur 1933- *WhoWest 92*
**Wolff,** Manfred Ernst 1930- *AmMWSc 92*
**Wolff,** Manfred Paul 1938- *AmMWSc 92*
**Wolff,** Marianne *AmMWSc 92*
**Wolff,** Mary Evaline 1887-1964 *BenetAL 91*
**Wolff,** Mary Madeleva 1887-1964 *HanAmWH*
**Wolff,** Michael 1933- *Who 92*
**Wolff,** Milo Mitchell 1923- *AmMWSc 92*
**Wolff,** Nels Christian 1936- *WhoWest 92*
**Wolff,** Nikolaus Emanuel 1921- *AmMWSc 92*
**Wolff,** Otto Herbert 1920- *IntWW 91, Who 92*
**Wolff,** Pancratius *BlkwCEP*
**Wolff,** Perry *LesBEnT 92*
**Wolff,** Peter A 1923- *AmMWSc 92*
**Wolff,** Peter Hartwig 1926- *AmMWSc 92*
**Wolff,** Philippe 1913- *IntWW 91*
**Wolff,** Raphael Gustave 1958- *WhoRel 92*
**Wolff,** Richard A 1933- *WhoIns 92*
**Wolff,** Robert John 1952- *AmMWSc 92*
**Wolff,** Robert L 1939- *AmMWSc 92*
**Wolff,** Robert P. 1933- *WrDr 92*
**Wolff,** Roger Glen 1932- *AmMWSc 92*
**Wolff,** Ronald Gilbert 1942- *AmMWSc 92*
**Wolff,** Ronald Keith 1946- *AmMWSc 92*
**Wolff,** Rosemary Langley 1926- *Who 92*
**Wolff,** Ruth 1932- *WhoEnt 92*
**Wolff,** Sanford Irving 1915- *WhoEnt 92*
**Wolff,** Sheldon 1928- *AmMWSc 92*
**Wolff,** Sheldon Malcolm 1930- *AmMWSc 92*
**Wolff,** Sidney Carne 1941- *AmMWSc 92, WhoWest 92*
**Wolff,** Sonia *SmATA 68, WrDr 92*
**Wolff,** Steven 1943- *AmMWSc 92*
**Wolff,** Theodore Albert 1943- *AmMWSc 92*
**Wolff,** Thomas J 1928- *WhoIns 92*
**Wolff,** Tobias *DrAPF 91*
**Wolff,** Tobias 1945- *BenetAL 91, ConNov 91, IntAu&W 91, IntWW 91, WrDr 92*
**Wolff,** Torben 1919- *IntWW 91*
**Wolff,** William F., III 1945- *WhoFI 92*
**Wolff,** William Francis 1921- *AmMWSc 92*
**Wolff Von Amerongen,** Otto 1918- *IntWW 91*
**Wolffe,** Alan Paul 1959- *AmMWSc 92*
**Wolfgang,** Jerald Ira 1938- *WhoAmP 91, WhoFI 92*
**Wolfgang,** Marvin Eugene 1924- *WhoAmL 92*
**Wolfgram,** Craig Arvin 1960- *WhoRel 92*
**Wolfgram,** Dorothea Limberg 1932- *WhoMW 92*
**Wolfgram,** Eunice *DrAPF 91*
**Wolfgram,** Robert Thomas 1943- *WhoFI 92*
**Wolfhard,** Hans Georg 1912- *AmMWSc 92*
**Wolfinger,** Barbara Kaye *WhoEnt 92, WhoWest 92*
**Wolfle,** Dael 1906- *AmMWSc 92, WrDr 92*
**Wolfle,** Thomas Lee 1936- *AmMWSc 92*
**Wolfley,** Clyde E 1921- *WhoAmP 91*
**Wolfley,** Vern Alvin 1912- *WhoWest 92*
**Wolfman Jack** 1938- *WhoEnt 92*
**Wolfman,** Arnold B. 1937- *WhoFI 92*
**Wolfman,** Bernard 1924- *WhoAmL 92*
**Wolfman,** Brunetta Reid *WhoBlA 92*
**Wolfman,** David S. 1960- *WhoRel 92*
**Wolfman,** Earl Frank, Jr 1926- *AmMWSc 92*
**Wolfner,** Mariana Federica 1953- *AmMWSc 92*
**Wolford,** Jack Arlington 1917- *AmMWSc 92*
**Wolford,** James C 1920- *AmMWSc 92*
**Wolford,** John Henry 1936- *AmMWSc 92*

**Wolford,** Richard Kenneth 1932- *AmMWSc 92*
**Wolford,** Roy, Jr. 1946- *WhoFI 92*
**Wolfowitz,** Paul 1943- *WhoAmP 91*
**Wolfowitz,** Paul Dundes 1943- *IntWW 91, NewYTBS 91 [port]*
**Wolfram von Eschenbach** 1180?-1220? *NewAmDM*
**Wolfram,** Blair Frederick 1957- *WhoMW 92*
**Wolfram,** Bradley Allen 1964- *WhoFI 92*
**Wolfram,** Charles William 1937- *WhoAmL 92*
**Wolfram,** Herwig 1934- *IntWW 91*
**Wolfram,** Leszek January 1929- *AmMWSc 92*
**Wolfram,** Stephen 1959- *WhoFI 92*
**Wolfram,** Thomas 1936- *AmMWSc 92*
**Wolfrom,** Glen Wallace 1947- *AmMWSc 92*
**Wolfrom,** Wayne Dennis 1940- *WhoRel 92*
**Wolfrum,** William Harvey 1926- *WhoRel 92*
**Wolfsberg,** Kurt 1931- *AmMWSc 92*
**Wolfsberg,** Max 1928- *AmMWSc 92*
**Wolfsen,** Franklin G *WhoAmP 91*
**Wolfskehl,** Karl 1869-1948 *LiExTwC*
**Wolfson** *Who 92*
**Wolfson,** Baron 1927- *IntWW 91, Who 92*
**Wolfson,** Alan William 1951- *WhoEnt 92*
**Wolfson,** Alfred M 1899- *AmMWSc 92*
**Wolfson,** Bernard T 1919- *AmMWSc 92*
**Wolfson,** Brian 1935- *Who 92*
**Wolfson,** Dirk Jacob 1933- *IntWW 91*
**Wolfson,** Edward A 1926- *AmMWSc 92*
**Wolfson,** Gary Maremont 1950- *WhoFI 92*
**Wolfson,** Geoffrey Mark 1934- *Who 92*
**Wolfson,** Harvey Martin 1933- *WhoFI 92*
**Wolfson,** Isaac d1991 *Who 92N*
**Wolfson,** Isaac 1897- *IntWW 91*
**Wolfson,** Isaac 1897-1991 *NewYTBS 91 [port]*
**Wolfson,** James 1943- *AmMWSc 92*
**Wolfson,** Joseph E. 1960- *WhoAmL 92*
**Wolfson,** Joseph Laurence 1917- *AmMWSc 92*
**Wolfson,** Kenneth Graham 1924- *AmMWSc 92*
**Wolfson,** Lawrence Aaron 1941- *WhoFI 92, WhoMW 92*
**Wolfson,** Leonard Louis 1919- *AmMWSc 92*
**Wolfson,** Margaret Gail *DrAPF 91*
**Wolfson,** Mark *Who 92*
**Wolfson,** Marsha 1944- *WhoWest 92*
**Wolfson,** Michael George 1938- *WhoAmL 92*
**Wolfson,** Nicholas 1932- *WhoAmL 92*
**Wolfson,** Randolph Douglas 1950- *WhoAmL 92*
**Wolfson,** Richard 1923- *IntMPA 92*
**Wolfson,** Richard Frederick 1923- *WhoAmL 92, WhoFI 92*
**Wolfson,** Richard L T 1947- *AmMWSc 92*
**Wolfson,** Robert Joseph 1929- *AmMWSc 92*
**Wolfson,** Robert Pred 1926- *WhoWest 92*
**Wolfson,** Seymour J 1937- *AmMWSc 92*
**Wolfson,** Sidney Kenneth, Jr 1931- *AmMWSc 92*
**Wolfson of Sunningdale,** Baron 1935- *Who 92*
**Wolfthal,** Diane 1949- *ConAu 135*
**Wolga,** George Jacob 1931- *AmMWSc 92*
**Wolgamott,** Gary 1940- *AmMWSc 92*
**Wolgemuth,** Carl Hess 1934- *AmMWSc 92*
**Wolgemuth,** Debra Joanne 1947- *AmMWSc 92*
**Wolgemuth,** Kenneth Mark 1943- *AmMWSc 92*
**Wolgemuth,** Richard Lee 1945- *AmMWSc 92*
**Wolicki,** Eligius Anthony 1927- *AmMWSc 92*
**Wolin,** Alan George 1933- *AmMWSc 92*
**Wolin,** Alfred M. 1932- *WhoAmL 92*
**Wolin,** Harold Leonard 1927- *AmMWSc 92*
**Wolin,** Lee Roy 1927- *AmMWSc 92*
**Wolin,** Meyer Jerome 1930- *AmMWSc 92*
**Wolin,** Michael Stuart 1953- *AmMWSc 92*
**Wolin,** Samuel 1909- *AmMWSc 92*
**Wolinski,** Leon Edward 1926- *AmMWSc 92*
**Wolinsky,** Emanuel 1917- *AmMWSc 92*
**Wolinsky,** Harvey 1939- *AmMWSc 92*
**Wolinsky,** Ira 1938- *AmMWSc 92*
**Wolinsky,** Jerry Saul 1943- *AmMWSc 92*
**Wolinsky,** Joseph 1930- *AmMWSc 92, WhoMW 92*
**Wolitarsky,** James William 1946- *WhoFI 92*
**Wolitzer,** Hilma *DrAPF 91*
**Wolitzer,** Hilma 1930- *WrDr 92*
**Wolitzer,** Meg *DrAPF 91*
**Wolk,** Asher d1991 *NewYTBS 91*
**Wolk,** Bruce Alan 1946- *WhoAmL 92*
**Wolk,** Coleman Peter 1936- *AmMWSc 92*
**Wolk,** David S 1953- *WhoAmP 91*
**Wolk,** Elliot K. 1935- *WhoFI 92*
**Wolk,** Elliot Samuel 1919- *AmMWSc 92*
**Wolk,** Howard Marvin 1920- *WhoMW 92*
**Wolk,** Joel M.Y. *DrAPF 91*
**Wolk,** Robert George 1931- *AmMWSc 92*
**Wolk,** Stuart Rodney 1938- *WhoAmL 92*
**Wolk,** Terry Jay 1956- *WhoAmL 92*
**Wolk,** Yale M. 1945- *WhoFI 92*
**Wolke,** Richard Elwood 1933- *AmMWSc 92*
**Wolke,** Robert Leslie 1928- *AmMWSc 92*
**Wolken,** George, Jr 1944- *AmMWSc 92*
**Wolken,** Jerome Jay 1917- *AmMWSc 92*
**Wolken,** Mark William 1957- *WhoAmP 91*
**Wolkin,** Paul Alexander 1917- *WhoAmL 92*
**Wolkind,** Jack 1920- *Who 92*
**Wolkins,** David Alan 1943- *WhoAmP 91*
**Wolko,** Howard Stephen 1925- *AmMWSc 92*
**Wolkoff,** Aaron Wilfred 1944- *AmMWSc 92*
**Wolkoff,** Harold 1923- *AmMWSc 92*
**Wolkstein,** Diane *DrAPF 91*
**Woll,** Edward 1914- *AmMWSc 92*
**Woll,** Harry Jean 1920- *AmMWSc 92*
**Woll,** John William, Jr 1931- *AmMWSc 92*
**Woll,** Michael G 1944- *WhoIns 92*
**Woll,** Peter 1933- *IntAu&W 91, WrDr 92*
**Wolla,** Maurice L 1933- *AmMWSc 92*
**Wollack,** Steven Edward 1942- *WhoFI 92*
**Wollan,** Curtis Noel 1951- *WhoEnt 92*
**Wollan,** David Strand 1937- *AmMWSc 92*
**Wollan,** Eugene 1928- *WhoAmL 92*
**Wollan,** John Jerome 1942- *AmMWSc 92*
**Wollan,** Thomas Carl 1960- *WhoRel 92*
**Wolland,** Peter 1961- *TwCPaSc*
**Wollaston,** Nicholas 1926- *WrDr 92*
**Wollaston,** Nicholas William 1926- *IntAu&W 91*
**Wollaston,** William Hyde 1766-1828 *BlkwCEP*
**Wolle,** Charles Robert 1935- *WhoAmL 92, WhoAmP 91, WhoMW 92*
**Wolle,** Eduardo 1954- *WhoHisp 92*
**Wolle,** Francis 1817-1893 *BiInAmS*
**Wolle,** William Down 1928- *WhoAmP 91*
**Wollen,** W. Foster 1936- *WhoAmL 92*
**Wollenberg,** Bruce Frederick 1942- *AmMWSc 92*
**Wollenberg,** David Arthur 1947- *WhoWest 92*
**Wollenberg,** J. Roger 1919- *WhoAmL 92*
**Wollenberg,** Richard Peter 1915- *WhoFI 92, WhoWest 92*
**Wollenberg,** William Louis 1932- *WhoAmP 91*
**Wollensak,** John Charles 1932- *AmMWSc 92*
**Woller,** James Alan 1946- *WhoAmL 92*
**Woller,** William Henry 1933- *AmMWSc 92*
**Wollersheim,** Gary Matthew 1951- *WhoRel 92*
**Wollert,** Gerald Dale 1935- *WhoWest 92*
**Wollert,** Kent Ray 1966- *WhoWest 92*
**Wollheim,** Donald A 1914- *ScFEYrs*
**Wollheim,** Donald A. 1914-1990 *ConAu 135, TwCSFW 91*
**Wollheim,** Richard Arthur 1923- *IntWW 91, Who 92*
**Wollin,** Goesta 1922- *AmMWSc 92*
**Wollin,** Robert Schary 1935- *WhoEnt 92*
**Wollins,** David H. 1952- *WhoAmL 92*
**Wollman,** Eric 1951- *WhoAmP 91*
**Wollman,** Harry 1932- *AmMWSc 92*
**Wollman,** Leo 1914- *AmMWSc 92*
**Wollman,** Roger L *WhoAmP 91*
**Wollman,** Roger Leland 1934- *WhoAmL 92*
**Wollman,** Seymour Horace 1915- *AmMWSc 92*
**Wollmer,** Richard Dietrich 1938- *AmMWSc 92, WhoWest 92*
**Wollner,** Kenneth Stuart 1947- *WhoAmL 92*
**Wollner,** Thomas Edward 1936- *AmMWSc 92*
**Wollny,** Walter Thomas 1933- *WhoWest 92*
**Wollongong,** Bishop of *Who 92*
**Wollschlaeger,** Gertraud 1924- *AmMWSc 92*
**Wollstonecraft,** Mary 1759-1797 *BlkwCEP, CnDBLB 3 [port], RfGEnL 91*
**Wollum,** Arthur George, II 1937- *AmMWSc 92*
**Wollwage,** John Carl 1914- *AmMWSc 92*
**Wollwage,** Paul Carl 1941- *AmMWSc 92*
**Wolma,** Fred J 1916- *AmMWSc 92*
**Wolman,** Abel 1892- *AmMWSc 92*
**Wolman,** Benjamin B. *WrDr 92*
**Wolman,** Eric 1931- *AmMWSc 92*
**Wolman,** Markley Gordon 1924- *AmMWSc 92*
**Wolman,** Sandra R 1933- *AmMWSc 92*
**Wolman,** William 1927- *WhoFI 92*
**Wolmark,** Alfred 1877-1961 *TwCPaSc*
**Wolmer,** Viscount 1971- *Who 92*
**Wolnak,** Bernard 1918- *WhoMW 92*
**Wolniak,** Stephen M *AmMWSc 92*
**Wolnitzek,** Stephen Dale 1949- *WhoAmL 92*
**Wolny,** Friedrich Franz 1931- *AmMWSc 92*
**Woloch,** Isser 1937- *WrDr 92*
**Wolochow,** Hyman 1918- *AmMWSc 92*
**Wolock,** Fred Walter 1926- *AmMWSc 92*
**Wolock,** Irvin 1923- *AmMWSc 92*
**Wolonsky,** Princess *EncAmaz 91*
**Wolos,** Jeffrey Alan *AmMWSc 92*
**Wolosewick,** John J 1945- *AmMWSc 92*
**Woloshen,** Jeffery Lawrence 1949- *WhoMW 92*
**Woloshin,** Henry Jacob 1913- *AmMWSc 92*
**Woloshin,** Sidney Eliezer 1928- *WhoEnt 92*
**Woloshyn,** Elaine Michelle 1952- *WhoMW 92*
**Wolovich,** William Anthony 1937- *AmMWSc 92*
**Wolowitz,** Steven 1952- *WhoAmL 92*
**Wolowyk,** Michael Walter 1942- *AmMWSc 92*
**Wolpe,** Howard E. 1939- *AlmAP 92 [port]*
**Wolpe,** Howard Eliot 1939- *WhoAmP 91, WhoMW 92*
**Wolpe,** Joseph 1915- *WrDr 92*
**Wolpe,** Stefan 1902-1972 *NewAmDM*
**Wolper,** Andrea 1956- *WhoEnt 92*
**Wolper,** David L. *LesBEnT 92*
**Wolper,** David L. 1928- *IntMPA 92*
**Wolper,** David Lloyd 1928- *IntWW 91, WhoEnt 92*
**Wolper,** Joanna H. *WhoEnt 92*
**Wolper,** Marshall 1922- *WhoFI 92*
**Wolper,** Robert W. 1959- *WhoAmL 92*
**Wolper,** Roy S. 1931- *WhoEnt 92*
**Wolpert,** Julian 1932- *IntWW 91*
**Wolpert,** Lewis 1929- *Who 92*
**Wolpert,** Stanley Albert 1927- *WrDr 92*
**Wolpoff,** Milford Howell 1942- *AmMWSc 92*
**Wolrige Gordon,** Anne 1936- *WrDr 92*
**Wolrige-Gordon,** Patrick 1935- *Who 92*
**Wolseley,** Charles Garnet Richard Mark 1944- *Who 92*
**Wolseley,** Garnet 1884-1969 *TwCPaSc*
**Wolseley,** Garnet 1915- *Who 92*
**Wolseley,** Roland E. 1904- *WrDr 92*
**Wolsey,** Wayne C 1936- *AmMWSc 92*
**Wolsey,** Wayne Cecil 1936- *WhoMW 92*
**Wolski,** Christopher George 1948- *WhoEnt 92*
**Wolsky,** Alan Martin 1943- *AmMWSc 92*
**Wolsky,** Alexander 1902- *AmMWSc 92*
**Wolsky,** Dave *WhoAmP 91*
**Wolsky,** Gregory Lee 1956- *WhoAmL 92*
**Wolsky,** Maria de Issekutz 1916- *AmMWSc 92*
**Wolsky,** Murray 1931- *WhoFI 92*
**Wolsky,** Sumner Paul 1926- *AmMWSc 92*
**Wolson,** Craig Alan 1949- *WhoAmL 92, WhoFI 92*
**Wolsonovich,** Nicholas *WhoRel 92*
**Wolsson,** Kenneth 1933- *AmMWSc 92*
**Wolstein,** Benjamin 1922- *WrDr 92*
**Wolstencroft,** Alan 1914- *Who 92*
**Wolstenholme,** David Robert 1937- *AmMWSc 92*
**Wolstenholme,** Gordon 1913- *Who 92*
**Wolstenholme,** Roy 1936- *Who 92*
**Wolstenholme,** Wayne W 1948- *AmMWSc 92*
**Wolszon,** John Donald 1929- *AmMWSc 92*
**Wolt,** Jeffrey Duaine 1951- *AmMWSc 92*
**Wolter,** Duane Roland 1948- *WhoFI 92*
**Wolter,** J Reimer 1924- *AmMWSc 92*
**Wolter,** Jan D 1959- *AmMWSc 92*
**Wolter,** Janet 1926- *AmMWSc 92*
**Wolter,** Karl Erich 1930- *AmMWSc 92*
**Wolter,** Kirk Marcus *AmMWSc 92*
**Wolter,** Randall Allen 1950- *WhoAmL 92*
**Wolter,** Richard C. *WhoEnt 92A*
**Woltering,** Margaret Mae 1913- *WhoMW 92*
**Woltering,** Michael J. 1949- *WhoFI 92*
**Wolterink,** Lester Floyd 1915- *AmMWSc 92*
**Wolters,** Conrad Clifton d1991 *Who 92N*
**Wolters,** Gale Leon 1939- *WhoWest 92*
**Wolters,** Gwyneth Eleanor Mary 1918- *Who 92*
**Wolters,** Oliver William 1915- *WrDr 92*
**Wolters,** Raymond 1938- *WrDr 92*
**Wolters,** Richard A. 1920- *WrDr 92*
**Wolters,** Robert John 1940- *AmMWSc 92*
**Woltersdorf,** Otto William, Jr 1935- *AmMWSc 92*
**Wolterstorff,** Nicholas 1932- *WrDr 92*
**Wolthuis,** Roger A 1937- *AmMWSc 92*
**Wolting,** Robert Roy 1928- *WhoWest 92*
**Woltjer,** Richard Kemeo 1953- *WhoEnt 92*
**Woltkamp,** David Bernard 1958- *WhoMW 92*
**Wolton,** Harry 1938- *Who 92*
**Woltor,** Robert *ScFEYrs*
**Woltz,** Alan Edward 1932- *Who 92*
**Woltz,** Frank Earl 1916- *AmMWSc 92*
**Woltz,** Shreve Simpson 1924- *AmMWSc 92*
**Wolven-Garrett,** Anne M 1925- *AmMWSc 92*
**Wolverhampton,** Bishop Suffragan of 1935- *Who 92*
**Wolverines,** The *NewAmDM*
**Wolverson Cope,** F. *Who 92*
**Wolverton,** Baron 1938- *Who 92*
**Wolverton,** Billy Charles 1932- *AmMWSc 92*
**Wolverton,** Lock 1940- *WhoEnt 92*
**Wolverton,** Robert E. 1925- *WrDr 92*
**Wolynes,** Peter Guy 1953- *AmMWSc 92*
**Wolynetz,** Mark Stanley 1945- *AmMWSc 92*
**Wolz,** Larry Robert 1951- *WhoEnt 92*
**Womack,** Andrew A. 1904-1985 *WhoBlA 92N*
**Womack,** Andy 1945- *WhoAmP 91*
**Womack,** Bobby Dwayne 1944- *WhoBlA 92*
**Womack,** Carter Devon 1951- *WhoBlA 92*
**Womack,** Charles Michael 1943- *WhoFI 92*
**Womack,** Doug C. 1950- *WhoMW 92*
**Womack,** Edgar Allen, Jr 1942- *AmMWSc 92, WhoMW 92*
**Womack,** Edwin Baxter 1931- *WhoRel 92*
**Womack,** Eric 1959- *WhoRel 92*
**Womack,** Frances C 1931- *AmMWSc 92*
**Womack,** Henry Cornelius 1938- *WhoBlA 92*
**Womack,** James E 1941- *AmMWSc 92*
**Womack,** James Errol 1940- *WhoFI 92, WhoWest 92*
**Womack,** Joe Bob 1946- *WhoFI 92*
**Womack,** Joe Neal, Jr. 1950- *WhoBlA 92*
**Womack,** John H. 1944- *WhoBlA 92*
**Womack,** Morris M. 1927- *WhoRel 92*
**Womack,** Orlando 1939- *WhoBlA 92*
**Womack,** Pamela M *WhoAmP 91*
**Womack,** Robert W., Sr. 1916- *WhoBlA 92*
**Womack,** Stanley H. 1930- *WhoBlA 92*
**Womack,** Steven 1952- *ConAu 133*
**Womack,** Thomas Hale 1952- *ConAu 133*
**Womack,** Thomas Houston 1940- *WhoWest 92*
**Womack,** Walter Anderson *WhoBlA 92N*
**Womack,** William Martin 1936- *WhoBlA 92*
**Woman Chief** *EncAmaz 91*
**Womble,** David Dale 1949- *AmMWSc 92*
**Womble,** Eugene Wilson 1931- *AmMWSc 92*
**Womble,** Harlin Clyde, Jr. 1952- *WhoAmL 92*
**Womble,** Jeffery Maurice 1964- *WhoBlA 92*
**Womble,** Larry W 1941- *WhoAmP 91, WhoBlA 92*
**Womble,** Richard Sidney 1956- *WhoAmL 92*
**Wombwell,** George 1949- *Who 92*
**Wombwell,** George Burkley 1931- *WhoFI 92*
**Womeldorf,** Mardie Gail 1950- *WhoEnt 92*
**Womer,** Jan Linwood 1939- *WhoRel 92*
**Womersley,** Denis Keith 1920- *Who 92*
**Womersley,** J. Lewis d1990 *Who 92N*
**Womersley,** Keith *Who 92*
**Womersley,** Peter 1941- *Who 92*
**Wommack,** Betty Sinclaire 1957- *WhoAmL 92*
**Wommack,** Janice Marie 1939- *WhoMW 92*
**Wommack,** Joel Benjamin, Jr 1942- *AmMWSc 92*
**Won,** Ko *DrAPF 91*
**Won,** Kyung-Soo 1928- *WhoEnt 92, WhoWest 92*
**Won Pat,** Marilyn Perez 1934- *WhoAmP 91*
**Wonder,** John Paul 1921- *WhoWest 92*
**Wonder,** Stevie 1950- *FacFETw, IntWW 91, NewAmDM, WhoBlA 92, WhoEnt 92*
**Wonder,** William 1829-1911 *ScFEYrs*
**Wondergem,** Robert 1950- *AmMWSc 92*
**Wonderland,** D. Clark 1944- *WhoFI 92*
**Wonderling,** Thomas Franklin 1915- *AmMWSc 92*
**Wonders,** William Clare 1924- *WhoWest 92*
**Wondolowski,** Denise Ann 1956- *WhoMW 92*
**Wondra,** Janet *DrAPF 91*
**Wonfor,** Andrea Jean 1944- *Who 92*
**Wong Kan Seng** 1946- *IntWW 91*
**Wong,** Alan Yau Kuen 1937- *AmMWSc 92*
**Wong,** Alfred Mun Kong 1930- *WhoWest 92*

**Wong,** Alfred Yiu-Fai 1937- *AmMWSc 92*
**Wong,** Anthony Sai-Hung 1951- *AmMWSc 92*
**Wong,** Astria Wor 1949- *WhoWest 92*
**Wong,** B.D. 1962- *WhoEnt 92*
**Wong,** Bernard P. 1941- *WhoWest 92*
**Wong,** Bing Kuen 1938- *AmMWSc 92*
**Wong,** Bob *WhoAmP 91*
**Wong,** Bonnie Lee 1957- *WhoWest 92*
**Wong,** Brendan So 1947- *AmMWSc 92*
**Wong,** Chak-Kuen *AmMWSc 92*
**Wong,** Cheuk-Yin 1941- *AmMWSc 92*
**Wong,** Chi-Huey 1948- *AmMWSc 92*
**Wong,** Chi Song 1938- *AmMWSc 92*
**Wong,** Chin Wah 1954- *WhoFI 92*
**Wong,** Chiu Ming 1935- *AmMWSc 92*
**Wong,** Chuen *AmMWSc 92*
**Wong,** Chun-Ming 1940- *AmMWSc 92*
**Wong,** Chun Wa 1938- *AmMWSc 92, WhoWest 92*
**Wong,** Corinne Hong Sling 1930- *WhoRel 92*
**Wong,** David Taiwai 1935- *AmMWSc 92*
**Wong,** David Yue 1934- *AmMWSc 92*
**Wong,** Dennis Mun 1944- *AmMWSc 92*
**Wong,** Derek 1946- *AmMWSc 92*
**Wong,** Donald Tai On 1926- *AmMWSc 92*
**Wong,** Dorothy Pan 1937- *AmMWSc 92*
**Wong,** E 1934- *AmMWSc 92*
**Wong,** Edward Chor-Cheung 1952- *AmMWSc 92*
**Wong,** Edward Hou 1946- *AmMWSc 92*
**Wong,** Francis Alvin 1936- *WhoAmP 91*
**Wong,** Fulton 1948- *AmMWSc 92*
**Wong,** George Shoung-Koon 1935- *AmMWSc 92*
**Wong,** George Tin Fuk 1949- *AmMWSc 92*
**Wong,** Gerald Chi-Ng 1939- *WhoWest 92*
**Wong,** Hans Kuomin 1936- *AmMWSc 92*
**Wong,** Harry Chow 1933- *WhoWest 92*
**Wong,** Harry Yuen Chee 1917- *AmMWSc 92*
**Wong,** Henry Li-Nan 1940- *WhoFI 92, WhoWest 92*
**Wong,** Horne Richard 1923- *AmMWSc 92*
**Wong,** Jade Snow 1922- *BenetAL 91*
**Wong,** James B *AmMWSc 92*
**Wong,** James Bok 1922- *WhoFI 92, WhoWest 92*
**Wong,** James Chin-Sze 1940- *AmMWSc 92*
**Wong,** Jan H. 1953- *WhoWest 92*
**Wong,** Jeffrey Tze-Fei 1937- *AmMWSc 92*
**Wong,** Jimmy K 1943- *WhoAmP 91*
**Wong,** Jo Yung *AmMWSc 92*
**Wong,** Joe 1942- *AmMWSc 92*
**Wong,** John Lui 1940- *AmMWSc 92*
**Wong,** John Wing-Chung 1934- *WhoWest 92*
**Wong,** Johnny Wai-Nang 1947- *AmMWSc 92*
**Wong,** Juan, Jr. *WhoHisp 92*
**Wong,** K C *AmMWSc 92*
**Wong,** Kai-Wai 1938- *AmMWSc 92*
**Wong,** Kai Wai Kenneth 1938- *WhoMW 92*
**Wong,** Kam Wu 1940- *AmMWSc 92, WhoMW 92*
**Wong,** Keith Kam-Kin 1929- *AmMWSc 92*
**Wong,** Kenneth Lee 1947- *WhoWest 92*
**Wong,** Kenneth Tak-Kin 1959- *WhoAmL 92*
**Wong,** Kevin Bruce 1955- *WhoWest 92*
**Wong,** Kin Fai 1944- *AmMWSc 92*
**Wong,** Kin-Ping 1941- *AmMWSc 92, WhoWest 92*
**Wong,** King-Lap *AmMWSc 92*
**Wong,** Kwan Y 1937- *AmMWSc 92*
**Wong,** Laurence Cheng Kong 1933- *AmMWSc 92*
**Wong,** Margaret Wai 1950- *WhoAmL 92*
**Wong,** Maurice King Fan 1932- *AmMWSc 92*
**Wong,** Michael Anthony 1967- *WhoWest 92*
**Wong,** Ming Ming 1928- *AmMWSc 92*
**Wong,** Morton Min 1924- *AmMWSc 92*
**Wong,** Nancy *DrAPF 91*
**Wong,** Nanying Stella *DrAPF 91*
**Wong,** Nellie *DrAPF 91*
**Wong,** Noble Powell 1931- *AmMWSc 92*
**Wong,** Norma 1956- *WhoAmP 91*
**Wong,** Norman L M 1945- *AmMWSc 92*
**Wong,** Otto 1947- *WhoWest 92*
**Wong,** Patrick Yui-Kwong 1944- *AmMWSc 92*
**Wong,** Paul Wing-Kon *AmMWSc 92*
**Wong,** Paul Wing Kon 1932- *WhoMW 92*
**Wong,** Penelope Lynn 1945- *WhoWest 92*
**Wong,** Peter Alexander 1941- *AmMWSc 92*
**Wong,** Peter P 1941- *AmMWSc 92*
**Wong,** Po Kee 1934- *AmMWSc 92*
**Wong,** Pui Kei 1935- *AmMWSc 92*
**Wong,** Richard S H 1933- *WhoAmP 91*
**Wong,** Roberta Jean 1957- *WhoWest 92*
**Wong,** Roderick Sue-Cheun 1944- *AmMWSc 92*
**Wong,** Rodney M. 1956- *WhoFI 92*
**Wong,** Roman Woon-Ching 1948- *AmMWSc 92*
**Wong,** Ronald James 1931- *WhoWest 92*
**Wong,** Rosa 1959- *WhoFI 92*
**Wong,** Rosie Bick-Har *AmMWSc 92*
**Wong,** Ruth 1925- *AmMWSc 92*
**Wong,** S Y 1920- *AmMWSc 92*
**Wong,** Samuel Shaw Ming 1937- *AmMWSc 92*
**Wong,** Shan Shekyuk 1945- *AmMWSc 92*
**Wong,** Shawn H. *DrAPF 91*
**Wong,** Shek-Fu 1943- *AmMWSc 92*
**Wong,** Shi-Yin 1941- *AmMWSc 92*
**Wong,** Siu Gum 1947- *AmMWSc 92*
**Wong,** Steven Wymann 1946- *WhoWest 92*
**Wong,** Sue Siu-Wan 1959- *WhoWest 92*
**Wong,** Tang-Fong Frank 1944- *AmMWSc 92*
**Wong,** Theodore Yau Sing 1940- *WhoWest 92*
**Wong,** Thomas Tang Yum 1952- *WhoMW 92*
**Wong,** Timothy C. 1941- *WhoMW 92*
**Wong,** Ting-Wa *AmMWSc 92*
**Wong,** Tuck Chuen 1946- *AmMWSc 92*
**Wong,** Victor Kenneth 1938- *AmMWSc 92*
**Wong,** Vincent Wai-Kwok 1958- *WhoMW 92*
**Wong,** Wai-Mai Tsang 1941- *AmMWSc 92*
**Wong,** Wallace 1941- *WhoWest 92*
**Wong,** Walter Foo 1930- *WhoWest 92*
**Wong,** Wang Mo *AmMWSc 92*
**Wong,** Warren James 1934- *AmMWSc 92, WhoMW 92*
**Wong,** Wayne D. 1950- *WhoFI 92, WhoWest 92*
**Wong,** Wayne Ping 1952- *WhoWest 92*
**Wong,** William G 1941- *WhoIns 92*
**Wong,** William Sheh *WhoWest 92*
**Wong,** Wing-Chun Godwin 1959- *WhoMW 92*
**Wong,** Wing Keung 1933- *WhoFI 92*
**Wong,** Ying Wood 1950- *WhoFI 92*
**Wong,** Yiu-Huen 1946- *AmMWSc 92*
**Wong,** Yuen-Fat 1935- *AmMWSc 92*
**Wong-Diaz,** Francisco Raimundo 1944- *WhoWest 92*
**Wong Kin Chow,** Michael 1936- *Who 92*
**Wong-Riley,** Margaret Tze Tung 1941- *AmMWSc 92*
**Wong-Staal,** Flossie *AmMWSc 92*
**Wonham,** W Murray 1934- *AmMWSc 92*
**Wonnacott,** John 1940- *TwCPaSc*
**Wonnacott,** Paul 1933- *WrDr 92*
**Wonnacott,** Ronald J 1930- *IntAu&W 91*
**Wonnacott,** Ronald Johnston 1930- *WrDr 92*
**Wonnacott,** Thomas Herbert 1935- *AmMWSc 92*
**Wonneberger,** Reinhard 1946- *WhoRel 92*
**Wonser,** Michael Dean 1940- *WhoWest 92*
**Wonsiewicz,** Bud Caesar 1941- *AmMWSc 92*
**Wontner,** Hugh 1908- *Who 92*
**Wontner,** Hugh Walter Kingwell 1908- *IntWW 91*
**Woo,** Chia-Wei 1937- *AmMWSc 92*
**Woo,** Chung-Ho 1943- *AmMWSc 92*
**Woo,** Dah-Cheng 1921- *AmMWSc 92*
**Woo,** Frances Mei Soo 1949- *WhoAmL 92*
**Woo,** Gar Lok 1935- *AmMWSc 92*
**Woo,** George Chi Shing 1941- *AmMWSc 92*
**Woo,** James T K 1938- *AmMWSc 92*
**Woo,** Katy 1943- *WhoAmP 91*
**Woo,** Kwang Bang 1934- *AmMWSc 92*
**Woo,** Lecon 1945- *AmMWSc 92*
**Woo,** Margaret Y. K. 1957- *WhoAmL 92*
**Woo,** Nam-Sung *AmMWSc 92*
**Woo,** Norman Tzu Teh 1939- *AmMWSc 92*
**Woo,** P W K 1934- *AmMWSc 92*
**Woo,** S B *WhoAmP 91*
**Woo,** Savio L C 1944- *AmMWSc 92*
**Woo,** Savio Lau-Yuen 1942- *WhoWest 92*
**Woo,** Shien-Biau 1937- *AmMWSc 92*
**Woo,** Tse-Chien 1924- *AmMWSc 92*
**Woo,** Vernon Ying-Tsai 1942- *WhoAmL 92, WhoWest 92*
**Woo,** Wilbert Yuk Cheong 1942- *WhoWest 92*
**Woo,** William Franklin 1936- *WhoMW 92*
**Woo,** Yin-tak 1947- *AmMWSc 92*
**Wood** *Who 92*
**Wood,** Alan 1935- *TwCPaSc*
**Wood,** Alan John 1925- *Who 92*
**Wood,** Alan Marshall M. *Who 92*
**Wood,** Alastair James Johnston 1946- *AmMWSc 92*
**Wood,** Albert D 1930- *AmMWSc 92*
**Wood,** Albert E 1910- *AmMWSc 92*
**Wood,** Alexander W 1944- *AmMWSc 92*
**Wood,** Alfred Arden 1926- *Who 92*
**Wood,** Allen D 1935- *AmMWSc 92*
**Wood,** Allen John 1925- *AmMWSc 92*
**Wood,** Alphonso 1810-1881 *BiInAmS*
**Wood,** Amy Marie 1967- *WhoMW 92*
**Wood,** Andrew 1947- *TwCPaSc*
**Wood,** Andrew Marley 1940- *Who 92*
**Wood,** Andrew W. 1919- *WhoBlA 92*
**Wood,** Anne Michelle 1951- *AmMWSc 92*
**Wood,** Anthony John P. *Who 92*
**Wood,** Anthony Richard 1932- *Who 92*
**Wood,** Anton Vernon 1949- *WhoBlA 92*
**Wood,** Arnold 1918- *Who 92*
**Wood,** Arthur M. 1913- *IntWW 91*
**Wood,** Arthur Skevington 1916- *WrDr 92*
**Wood,** Audrey 1948- *ChlLR 26 [port]*
**Wood,** Barbara 1947- *WrDr 92*
**Wood,** Barbara Champion 1924- *WhoAmP 91*
**Wood,** Barbara L. Cochrane 1951- *WhoMW 92*
**Wood,** Barnabas 1819-1875 *BiInAmS*
**Wood,** Barry 1940- *ConAu 36NR*
**Wood,** Barry David 1943- *WhoFI 92*
**Wood,** Beatrice 1893- *WhoFI 92*
**Wood,** Benjamin Churchill 1954- *WhoAmL 92*
**Wood,** Benjamin W 1938- *AmMWSc 92*
**Wood,** Betty J 1955- *AmMWSc 92*
**Wood,** Bobby Eugene 1939- *AmMWSc 92*
**Wood,** Bobby G 1935- *WhoAmP 91*
**Wood,** Bobby Gaines 1931- *WhoAmP 91*
**Wood,** Bradford 1955- *WhoEnt 92*
**Wood,** Brenda Blackmon 1955- *WhoBlA 92*
**Wood,** Bruce 1938- *AmMWSc 92*
**Wood,** Bruce Wade 1951- *AmMWSc 92*
**Wood,** Byard Dean 1940- *AmMWSc 92*
**Wood,** Calvin Dale 1933- *AmMWSc 92*
**Wood,** Camilla Smith 1926- *WhoWest 92*
**Wood,** Carl Eugene 1940- *AmMWSc 92*
**Wood,** Carlos C 1913- *AmMWSc 92*
**Wood,** Carol Saunders 1945- *AmMWSc 92*
**Wood,** Carroll E, Jr 1921- *AmMWSc 92*
**Wood,** Cecil Gordon 1942- *WhoMW 92*
**Wood,** Chalmers Benedict d1991 *NewYTBS 91*
**Wood,** Charles 1924- *AmMWSc 92*
**Wood,** Charles 1933- *IntAu&W 91, WrDr 92*
**Wood,** Charles 1950- *Who 92*
**Wood,** Charles Cresson 1955- *WhoWest 92*
**Wood,** Charles D *AmMWSc 92*
**Wood,** Charles Donald 1925- *AmMWSc 92*
**Wood,** Charles Edward 1938- *WhoAmL 92*
**Wood,** Charles Erskine Scott 1852-1944 *BenetAL 91*
**Wood,** Charles Evans 1952- *AmMWSc 92*
**Wood,** Charles Gerald 1932- *IntWW 91, Who 92*
**Wood,** Charles Monroe 1944- *WhoRel 92*
**Wood,** Charles Tuttle 1933- *WrDr 92*
**Wood,** Chester Elvin 1941- *WhoRel 92*
**Wood,** Christopher 1901-1930 *TwCPaSc*
**Wood,** Christopher 1941- *ConAu 36NR*
**Wood,** Christopher Lainson 1936- *Who 92*
**Wood,** Christopher Michael 1947- *AmMWSc 92*
**Wood,** Christopher P. 1961- *TwCPaSc*
**Wood,** Clyde Maurice *Who 92*
**Wood,** Corinne Shear *AmMWSc 92*
**Wood,** Craig Adams 1941- *AmMWSc 92*
**Wood,** Curtis A. 1942- *WhoBlA 92*
**Wood,** Daniel Carter 1955- *WhoWest 92*
**Wood,** Daniel Warren 1955- *WhoRel 92*
**Wood,** Darrell Eugene 1929- *WhoWest 92*
**Wood,** Darwin Lewis 1921- *AmMWSc 92*
**Wood,** David *WhoBlA 92*
**Wood,** David 1928- *AmMWSc 92*
**Wood,** David 1944- *TwCPaSc, Who 92, WrDr 92*
**Wood,** David Alvra 1904- *AmMWSc 92*
**Wood,** David Belden 1935- *AmMWSc 92*
**Wood,** David Bernard 1944- *IntAu&W 91*
**Wood,** David Charles 1943- *WhoFI 92*
**Wood,** David Collier 1954- *AmMWSc 92*
**Wood,** David Dudley 1943- *AmMWSc 92*
**Wood,** David H. *Who 92*
**Wood,** David James 1948- *WhoWest 92*
**Wood,** David Kennedy Cornell 1925- *WhoEnt 92*
**Wood,** David Lee 1931- *AmMWSc 92*
**Wood,** David Lee 1951- *WhoRel 92*
**Wood,** David Miles 1950- *WhoWest 92*
**Wood,** David Oliver *AmMWSc 92*
**Wood,** David Roy 1935- *AmMWSc 92*
**Wood,** David S 1920- *AmMWSc 92*
**Wood,** David Wells 1938- *AmMWSc 92*
**Wood,** Debbie J. *DrAPF 91*
**Wood,** Deborah Bedard 1951- *WhoAmP 91*
**Wood,** Deborah Edith 1961- *WhoMW 92*
**Wood,** Deborah Swift 1954- *WhoRel 92*
**Wood,** Denys Broomfield 1923- *Who 92*
**Wood,** Derek Alexander 1937- *Who 92*
**Wood,** Derek Harold 1930- *IntAu&W 91, WrDr 92*
**Wood,** Derek Rawlins 1921- *Who 92*
**Wood,** Derick 1940- *AmMWSc 92*
**Wood,** DeVolson 1832-1897 *BiInAmS*
**Wood,** Diane Pamela 1950- *WhoAmL 92*
**Wood,** Don 1945- *ChlLR 26 [port]*
**Wood,** Don James 1936- *AmMWSc 92*
**Wood,** Donald Eugene 1930- *AmMWSc 92*
**Wood,** Donald Frank 1935- *WhoWest 92*
**Wood,** Donald Gene 1937- *WhoMW 92*
**Wood,** Donald Ray 1947- *WhoEnt 92, WhoFI 92*
**Wood,** Donald Roy 1921- *AmMWSc 92*
**Wood,** Donna Jean 1954- *WhoBlA 92, WhoEnt 92*
**Wood,** Dorothy Mertis 1928- *WhoAmP 91*
**Wood,** Doug 1942- *WhoAmP 91*
**Wood,** Douglas Kent 1958- *WhoAmL 92*
**Wood,** Dudley Ernest 1930- *Who 92*
**Wood,** Earl Howard 1912- *AmMWSc 92*
**Wood,** Edgar Allardyce 1907- *IntAu&W 91*
**Wood,** Edgar James 1934- *WhoAmP 91*
**Wood,** Edward 1928- *WhoWest 92*
**Wood,** Edward B. 1952- *WhoAmL 92*
**Wood,** Edward C 1923- *AmMWSc 92*
**Wood,** Edward Chalmers, Jr. 1944- *WhoWest 92*
**Wood,** Edward James 1902- *Who 92*
**Wood,** Edward Stickney 1846-1905 *BiInAmS*
**Wood,** Ellen Price *RfGEnL 91*
**Wood,** Elwyn Devere 1934- *AmMWSc 92*
**Wood,** Eric 1931- *Who 92*
**Wood,** Eric F *AmMWSc 92*
**Wood,** Eunice Marjorie 1927- *AmMWSc 92*
**Wood,** F B 1917- *AmMWSc 92*
**Wood,** Fergus James 1917- *AmMWSc 92, IntAu&W 91, WhoWest 92, WrDr 92*
**Wood,** Flora 1910- *TwCPaSc*
**Wood,** Forrest Glenn 1918- *AmMWSc 92*
**Wood,** Francis 1871-1926 *TwCPaSc*
**Wood,** Francis C, Jr 1928- *AmMWSc 92*
**Wood,** Francis Clark 1901- *AmMWSc 92*
**Wood,** Francis Eugene 1932- *AmMWSc 92*
**Wood,** Francis Gordon 1924- *Who 92*
**Wood,** Francis Patrick 1917- *AmMWSc 92*
**Wood,** Frank 1929- *Who 92*
**Wood,** Frank Bradshaw 1915- *AmMWSc 92*
**Wood,** Frank P 1949- *WhoAmP 91*
**Wood,** Frederick 1926- *IntWW 91, Who 92*
**Wood,** Frederick Starr 1921- *AmMWSc 92*
**Wood,** G. 1919- *ConTFT 9*
**Wood,** Galen Theodore 1929- *AmMWSc 92*
**Wood,** Garland E. 1943- *WhoBlA 92*
**Wood,** Garnett Elmer 1929- *AmMWSc 92*
**Wood,** Gary Walter 1939- *WhoFI 92*
**Wood,** Gary Warren 1941- *AmMWSc 92*
**Wood,** Gary Wayne 1951- *WhoRel 92*
**Wood,** Gene Wayne 1940- *AmMWSc 92*
**Wood,** George Marshall 1933- *AmMWSc 92*
**Wood,** Gerald David 1947- *WhoRel 92*
**Wood,** Gerald Lloyd 1938- *WhoWest 92*
**Wood,** Gerard Edward 1938- *WhoFI 92*
**Wood,** Gerry Odell 1943- *AmMWSc 92*
**Wood,** Gladys Blanche 1921- *WhoWest 92*
**Wood,** Glen Meredith 1920- *AmMWSc 92*
**Wood,** Gordon Harvey 1940- *AmMWSc 92*
**Wood,** Gordon S. 1933- *WrDr 92*
**Wood,** Gordon Walter 1933- *AmMWSc 92*
**Wood,** Grant 1891-1942 *FacFETw*
**Wood,** Gregg Douglas 1941- *WhoRel 92*
**Wood,** Gregory Burton, Jr. 1943- *WhoFI 92*
**Wood,** Harland G 1907- *AmMWSc 92, IntWW 91*
**Wood,** Harlington, Jr *WhoAmP 91*
**Wood,** Harlington, Jr. 1920- *WhoAmL 92, WhoMW 92*
**Wood,** Harold 1918- *TwCPaSc*
**Wood,** Harold Leroy 1919- *WhoBlA 92*
**Wood,** Harold Sinclair 1922- *AmMWSc 92*
**Wood,** Harrison F. d1991 *NewYTBS 91*
**Wood,** Harry Alan 1941- *AmMWSc 92*
**Wood,** Harry George 1915- *WhoWest 92*
**Wood,** Harry Stewart 1913- *Who 92*
**Wood,** Henderson Kingsberry 1913- *AmMWSc 92*
**Wood,** Henry 1834-1909 *RelLAm 91*
**Wood,** Henry 1908- *Who 92*
**Wood,** Henry J 1869-1944 *FacFETw, NewAmDM*
**Wood,** Horatio Charles 1841-1920 *BiInAmS*
**Wood,** Houston Gilleylen, III 1944- *AmMWSc 92*
**Wood,** Howard John, III 1938- *AmMWSc 92*
**Wood,** Hudson A 1841-1903 *BiInAmS*
**Wood,** Hugh Bernard 1909- *WhoWest 92*
**Wood,** Humphrey *Who 92*
**Wood,** Ian Clark 1942- *Who 92*
**Wood,** Ira *DrAPF 91*
**Wood,** Ira Wayne 1930- *WhoRel 92*
**Wood,** Irwin Boyden 1926- *AmMWSc 92*
**Wood,** J Kenneth, Jr 1935- *WhoIns 92*
**Wood,** Jacalyn Kay 1949- *WhoMW 92*
**Wood,** Jack Calvin 1933- *WhoAmL 92*
**Wood,** Jack Sheehan 1931- *AmMWSc 92*

**Wood**, Jackie Dale 1937- *AmMWSc 92, WhoMW 92*
**Wood**, James 1889-1975 *TwCPaSc*
**Wood**, James 1927- *WhoFI 92*
**Wood**, James 1930- *IntWW 91*
**Wood**, James Alan 1939- *AmMWSc 92*
**Wood**, James Brent, III 1942- *AmMWSc 92*
**Wood**, James C, Jr 1939- *AmMWSc 92*
**Wood**, James Douglas 1930- *AmMWSc 92*
**Wood**, James E., Jr. 1922- *WhoRel 92*
**Wood**, James Jerry 1940- *WhoAmL 92*
**Wood**, James Kenneth 1942- *AmMWSc 92*
**Wood**, James Lee 1940- *AmMWSc 92*
**Wood**, James Leslie 1941- *WhoWest 92*
**Wood**, James Manley, Jr 1927- *AmMWSc 92*
**Wood**, James W 1925- *AmMWSc 92*
**Wood**, Jan Smith 1954- *WhoRel 92*
**Wood**, Jeannette 1932- *WhoAmP 91*
**Wood**, Jeannette Suzon 1967- *WhoWest 92*
**Wood**, Jeffrey Charles 1940- *WhoRel 92*
**Wood**, Jeremy Scott 1941- *WhoFI 92*
**Wood**, Jerome H., Jr. 1941- *WhoBlA 92*
**Wood**, Joan E 1934- *WhoAmP 91*
**Wood**, Joe George 1928- *AmMWSc 92*
**Wood**, Joe T 1922- *WhoAmP 91*
**Wood**, John *Who 92*
**Wood**, John 1705?-1754 *BlkwCEP*
**Wood**, John 1775?-1822 *BiInAmS*
**Wood**, John 1931- *Who 92*
**Wood**, John Armstead 1932- *AmMWSc 92*
**Wood**, John C. 1952- *ConAu 133*
**Wood**, John Claire 1871-1916 *BiInAmS*
**Wood**, John D 1930- *AmMWSc 92*
**Wood**, John Denison 1931- *WhoFI 92, WhoWest 92*
**Wood**, John Edwin 1928- *Who 92*
**Wood**, John F, Jr 1936- *WhoAmP 91*
**Wood**, John Glyn *TwCPaSc*
**Wood**, John Grady 1942- *AmMWSc 92*
**Wood**, John Henry 1924- *AmMWSc 92*
**Wood**, John Herbert 1929- *AmMWSc 92*
**Wood**, John Humphrey 1932- *Who 92*
**Wood**, John Karl 1919- *AmMWSc 92*
**Wood**, John Kember 1922- *Who 92*
**Wood**, John Laurence 1911- *Who 92*
**Wood**, John Lewis 1912- *AmMWSc 92*
**Wood**, John Mark 1965- *WhoEnt 92*
**Wood**, John Martin 1938- *AmMWSc 92*
**Wood**, John Mortimer 1934- *WhoWest 92*
**Wood**, John Peter 1925- *Who 92*
**Wood**, John Ralph 1927- *WhoRel 92*
**Wood**, John Stanley 1936- *AmMWSc 92*
**Wood**, John William 1941- *AmMWSc 92*
**Wood**, Joseph M 1921- *AmMWSc 92*
**Wood**, Joseph Neville 1916- *Who 92*
**Wood**, Joseph Roberts 1915- *WhoEnt 92*
**Wood**, Juanita Wallace 1928- *WhoBlA 92*
**Wood**, Judson Robert 1928- *WhoAmL 92*
**Wood**, Julie 1953- *TwCPaSc*
**Wood**, Kathleen Doran 1946- *WhoEnt 92*
**Wood**, Kathleen Oliver 1921- *WhoMW 92*
**Wood**, Keith N 1951- *WhoAmP 91*
**Wood**, Kenneth George 1924- *AmMWSc 92*
**Wood**, Kenneth Maynard 1916- *Who 92*
**Wood**, Kerry *IntAu&W 91X*
**Wood**, Kerry 1907- *WrDr 92*
**Wood**, Kimba M. 1944- *WhoAmL 92*
**Wood**, Kristin Lee 1962- *AmMWSc 92*
**Wood**, Kurt Arthur 1956- *AmMWSc 92*
**Wood**, Larry *WhoFI 92, WhoWest 92*
**Wood**, Larry Albert 1944- *WhoAmP 91*
**Wood**, Laura Newbold *WrDr 92*
**Wood**, Lawrence Alvin 1949- *WhoBlA 92*
**Wood**, Lawrence Arnell 1904- *AmMWSc 92*
**Wood**, Lawrence E. 1936- *WhoAmL 92*
**Wood**, Leon 1962- *BlkOlyM*
**Wood**, Leonard Alton 1922- *AmMWSc 92*
**Wood**, Leonard C. 1923- *WrDr 92*
**Wood**, Leonard E 1923- *AmMWSc 92*
**Wood**, Leonard E 1927- *AmMWSc 92*
**Wood**, Leonard George *Who 92*
**Wood**, Leslie Ann 1957- *WhoMW 92*
**Wood**, Leslie Walter 1920- *Who 92*
**Wood**, Linda Gaye 1959- *WhoFI 92*
**Wood**, Linda May 1942- *WhoWest 92*
**Wood**, Lindsay Lloyd 1956- *WhoAmL 92*
**Wood**, Lisa Cameron 1959- *WhoAmL 92*
**Wood**, Louis L 1931- *AmMWSc 92*
**Wood**, Lowell Thomas 1942- *AmMWSc 92*
**Wood**, Margaret Beatrice *WhoBlA 92*
**Wood**, Margaret Gray 1918- *AmMWSc 92*
**Wood**, Marguerite N. *WrDr 92*
**Wood**, Marguerite Noreen 1923- *IntAu&W 91*
**Wood**, Marilyn Susan 1950- *WhoEnt 92*
**Wood**, Mark *Who 92*
**Wood**, Mark William 1952- *Who 92*
**Wood**, Marsha Beth 1951- *WhoMW 92*
**Wood**, Martha S *WhoAmP 91*
**Wood**, Martin 1927- *IntWW 91, Who 92*
**Wood**, Mary Anne Quinn 1945- *WhoAmL 92*
**Wood**, Mary E. 1955- *WhoFI 92*
**Wood**, Maurice 1922- *AmMWSc 92, IntWW 91*
**Wood**, Maurice Arthur Ponsonby 1916- *IntWW 91, Who 92, WrDr 92*
**Wood**, Michael 1936- *WrDr 92*
**Wood**, Michael Allen 1956- *WhoMW 92*
**Wood**, Michael Bruce 1943- *AmMWSc 92*
**Wood**, Michael H. 1942- *WhoBlA 92*
**Wood**, Michael Neall 1956- *WhoWest 92*
**Wood**, Milton Legrand 1922- *WhoRel 92*
**Wood**, Mrs. J *ScFEYrs*
**Wood**, Nancy Bethoney 1937- *WhoFI 92*
**Wood**, Nancy Elizabeth *AmMWSc 92*
**Wood**, Nanna Crozier *ScFEYrs*
**Wood**, Neal 1922- *WrDr 92*
**Wood**, Neil Roderick 1931- *WhoFI 92*
**Wood**, Norman 1905- *Who 92*
**Wood**, Norman Kenyon 1935- *AmMWSc 92*
**Wood**, Norris Philip 1924- *AmMWSc 92*
**Wood**, O Lew 1936- *AmMWSc 92*
**Wood**, Obert Reeves, II 1943- *AmMWSc 92*
**Wood**, Owen 1939- *TwCPaSc*
**Wood**, Pamela Dorothy 1933- *WhoEnt 92*
**Wood**, Pamela Lakes 1949- *WhoAmL 92*
**Wood**, Paul Mix 1930- *AmMWSc 92*
**Wood**, Paul Nigel 1955- *WhoEnt 92*
**Wood**, Pauline J 1922- *AmMWSc 92*
**Wood**, Peter 1928- *IntWW 91*
**Wood**, Peter Douglas 1929- *AmMWSc 92*
**Wood**, Peter Edric 1929- *Who 92*
**Wood**, Peter John 1943- *AmMWSc 92*
**Wood**, Peter Lawrence 1928- *Who 92*
**Wood**, Phil Arnold 1957- *WhoFI 92*
**Wood**, Philip 1946- *Who 92*
**Wood**, Phillip Sydney 1943- *WhoAmL 92*
**Wood**, Phyllis Anderson 1923- *WrDr 92*
**Wood**, Quentin Eugene 1923- *WhoFI 92*
**Wood**, R. A. *WhoRel 92*
**Wood**, Ralph Marlowe 1927- *WhoWest 92*
**Wood**, Randall Dudley 1936- *AmMWSc 92*
**Wood**, Raymond Arthur 1924- *AmMWSc 92*
**Wood**, Raymund Francis 1911- *WhoWest 92*
**Wood**, Reginald Kenneth 1937- *AmMWSc 92*
**Wood**, Rene Victor 1925- *Who 92*
**Wood**, Richard Donald 1926- *WhoFI 92, WhoMW 92*
**Wood**, Richard Ellet 1928- *AmMWSc 92*
**Wood**, Richard Frederick *IntWW 91*
**Wood**, Richard Frederick Marshall 1943- *Who 92*
**Wood**, Richard Frost 1931- *AmMWSc 92*
**Wood**, Richard Glenn 1955- *WhoFI 92*
**Wood**, Richard J. *WhoMW 92*
**Wood**, Richard James 1920- *Who 92*
**Wood**, Richard Lee 1930- *AmMWSc 92*
**Wood**, Richard Lyman 1929- *AmMWSc 92*
**Wood**, Richard R 1950- *WhoIns 92*
**Wood**, Richard Walter 1961- *WhoRel 92*
**Wood**, Robert 1923- *WrDr 92*
**Wood**, Robert B 1918- *WhoAmP 91*
**Wood**, Robert C *WhoIns 92*
**Wood**, Robert Charles 1929- *AmMWSc 92*
**Wood**, Robert Charles 1956- *WhoAmL 92, WhoFI 92*
**Wood**, Robert Cornelius 1940- *WhoAmL 92*
**Wood**, Robert D. d1986 *LesBEnT 92*
**Wood**, Robert E 1938- *AmMWSc 92*
**Wood**, Robert Eric 1909- *Who 92*
**Wood**, Robert H, Jr 1931- *WhoAmP 91*
**Wood**, Robert Hemsley 1932- *AmMWSc 92*
**Wood**, Robert Henry 1936- *Who 92*
**Wood**, Robert Lee 1939- *WhoFI 92*
**Wood**, Robert M 1928- *AmMWSc 92*
**Wood**, Robert Manning 1938- *AmMWSc 92*
**Wood**, Robert Morse, Jr. 1959- *WhoFI 92*
**Wood**, Robert Noel 1934- *Who 92*
**Wood**, Robert O'Brien 1962- *WhoEnt 92*
**Wood**, Robert Stuart 1947- *WhoEnt 92*
**Wood**, Robert Warren 1955- *WhoAmL 92, WhoWest 92*
**Wood**, Robert Winfield 1931- *AmMWSc 92*
**Wood**, Robertson Harris Langley 1924- *AmMWSc 92*
**Wood**, Robin 1931- *IntAu&W 91, WrDr 92*
**Wood**, Rodney David 1932- *AmMWSc 92*
**Wood**, Roger Charles 1932- *AmMWSc 92*
**Wood**, Roger Holmes 1920- *WhoFI 92, WhoWest 92*
**Wood**, Roger S 1927- *WhoAmP 91*
**Wood**, Roland Arthur *Who 92*
**Wood**, Ron 1922- *TwCPaSc*
**Wood**, Ronald 1947- *WhoEnt 92*
**Wood**, Ronald Karslake Starr *Who 92*
**Wood**, Ronald Karslake Starr 1919- *IntWW 91*
**Wood**, Roy 1940- *Who 92*
**Wood**, Royal J. 1922- *WhoMW 92*
**Wood**, Royal James 1922- *WhoAmP 91*
**Wood**, Russell 1922- *Who 92*
**Wood**, Ruzena 1937- *ConAu 135*
**Wood**, Sam 1884-1949 *IntDcF 2-2 [port]*
**Wood**, Sam 1911- *Who 92*
**Wood**, Samuel Eugene 1934- *WhoMW 92*
**Wood**, Sarah Sayward Keating 1759-1855 *BenetAL 91*
**Wood**, Scott Denison 1956- *WhoWest 92*
**Wood**, Scott Emerson 1910- *AmMWSc 92*
**Wood**, Silviana 1940- *WhoHisp 92*
**Wood**, Spencer Hoffman 1938- *AmMWSc 92*
**Wood**, Stanley Mark 1919- *Who 92*
**Wood**, Stephen Craig 1942- *AmMWSc 92*
**Wood**, Stephen Lane 1924- *AmMWSc 92*
**Wood**, Stephen Wray 1948- *WhoAmP 91, WhoRel 92*
**Wood**, Steven Doyle 1958- *WhoRel 92*
**Wood**, Steven Duane 1962- *WhoRel 92*
**Wood**, Stuart 1938- *WrDr 92*
**Wood**, Susan 1948- *AmMWSc 92*
**Wood**, Terence Courtney 1936- *Who 92*
**Wood**, Teri Wilford 1950- *WhoAmL 92*
**Wood**, Terry David 1942- *WhoEnt 92, WhoMW 92*
**Wood**, Thomas Alexander, Jr. 1926- *WhoFI 92*
**Wood**, Thomas H 1953- *AmMWSc 92*
**Wood**, Thomas Hamil 1923- *AmMWSc 92*
**Wood**, Thomas Joseph 1930- *IntAu&W 91*
**Wood**, Thomas Kenneth *AmMWSc 92*
**Wood**, Thomas Willard 1939- *WhoWest 92*
**Wood**, Timothy E 1948- *AmMWSc 92*
**Wood**, Timothy John Rogerson 1940- *Who 92*
**Wood**, Timothy Smedley 1942- *AmMWSc 92*
**Wood**, Tom 1955- *TwCPaSc*
**Wood**, Ursula *WrDr 92*
**Wood**, Van Earl 1933- *AmMWSc 92*
**Wood**, Veronica *TwCPaSc*
**Wood**, Victor *Who 92*
**Wood**, Victoria 1953- *IntAu&W 91, Who 92*
**Wood**, Virginia Ann 1936- *WhoMW 92*
**Wood**, Vivian Poates 1923- *WhoEnt 92*
**Wood**, W. J. 1917- *ConAu 135*
**Wood**, W. Raymond 1931- *WhoMW 92*
**Wood**, Wallace D 1910- *AmMWSc 92*
**Wood**, Walter 1866-1961 *ScFEYrs*
**Wood**, Walter 1914- *Who 92*
**Wood**, Warren Wilbur 1937- *AmMWSc 92*
**Wood**, Wayne W 1930- *WhoAmP 91*
**Wood**, Wendell Roy 1938- *WhoMW 92*
**Wood**, Wendy *DrAPF 91*
**Wood**, Wendy Deborah 1940- *WhoEnt 92*
**Wood**, Wilfred Denniston *Who 92*
**Wood**, Wilfred R. 1888-1976 *TwCPaSc*
**Wood**, Willard Ellsworth 1921- *WhoAmP 91*
**Wood**, William *BenetAL 91*
**Wood**, William 1822?-1885 *BiInAmS*
**Wood**, William 1916- *Who 92*
**Wood**, William B., III 1938- *IntWW 91*
**Wood**, William Bainster 1931- *AmMWSc 92*
**Wood**, William Barry, III 1938- *AmMWSc 92*
**Wood**, William Booth 1922- *AmMWSc 92*
**Wood**, William C 1940- *AmMWSc 92*
**Wood**, William Clarke 1952- *WhoFI 92*
**Wood**, William Edwin 1947- *AmMWSc 92*
**Wood**, William Irwin 1947- *AmMWSc 92*
**Wood**, William L., Jr. 1940- *WhoBlA 92*
**Wood**, William McBrayer 1942- *WhoAmL 92, WhoFI 92*
**Wood**, William Otto 1925- *AmMWSc 92*
**Wood**, William P 1951- *IntAu&W 91*
**Wood**, William Pape 1943- *WhoRel 92*
**Wood**, William Philler 1927- *WhoAmL 92*
**Wood**, William Preston 1951- *WhoEnt 92*
**Wood**, William Ransom 1907- *WhoFI 92*
**Wood**, William Robert 1943- *WhoFI 92*
**Wood**, William S. 1926- *WhoBlA 92*
**Wood**, William Thomas 1877-1958 *TwCPaSc*
**Wood**, William Vernell, Sr. 1936- *WhoBlA 92*
**Wood**, William Wayne 1924- *AmMWSc 92*
**Wood**, Willis Avery 1921- *AmMWSc 92*
**Wood**, Willis Bowne, Jr. 1934- *WhoFI 92, WhoWest 92*
**Wood Parrish**, Victoria Ann 1950- *WhoRel 92*
**Wood Prince**, William Norman 1942- *WhoFI 92*
**Wood-Trost**, Lucille Marie 1938- *WhoWest 92*
**Woodall**, Alec 1918- *Who 92*
**Woodall**, Clarence Allen, III 1949- *WhoAmL 92*
**Woodall**, Claude Oliver, III 1953- *WhoEnt 92*
**Woodall**, David Monroe 1945- *AmMWSc 92*
**Woodall**, Ellis O., Sr. 1927- *WhoBlA 92*
**Woodall**, J Dan 1924- *WhoAmP 91*
**Woodall**, James Barry 1945- *WhoWest 92*
**Woodall**, Jerry M *AmMWSc 92*
**Woodall**, John Wesley 1941- *WhoBlA 92*
**Woodall**, S Roy, Jr 1936- *WhoIns 92*
**Woodall**, Thomas Edward 1921- *WhoAmP 91*
**Woodall**, W. Dallas 1937- *WhoAmL 92*
**Woodall**, Walter Thomas 1945- *WhoAmP 91*
**Woodall**, William Robert, Jr 1945- *AmMWSc 92*
**Woodard**, A. Newton 1936- *WhoBlA 92*
**Woodard**, Alfre *WhoBlA 92*
**Woodard**, Alfre 1953- *ConTFT 9, IntMPA 92, WhoEnt 92*
**Woodard**, Allen C., III 1911-1984 *WhoBlA 92N*
**Woodard**, Alva Abe 1928- *WhoFI 92, WhoWest 92*
**Woodard**, Barney Paul *WhoAmP 91*
**Woodard**, Carl Jubal 1924- *WhoAmP 91*
**Woodard**, Charles Clifton, Jr. 1923- *WhoEnt 92*
**Woodard**, Charles James 1945- *WhoBlA 92*
**Woodard**, Daniel Douglas 1944- *WhoEnt 92*
**Woodard**, Daniel J. 1930- *WhoEnt 92*
**Woodard**, David W 1938- *AmMWSc 92*
**Woodard**, Dorothy Marie 1932- *WhoFI 92, WhoWest 92*
**Woodard**, Duane 1938- *WhoWest 92*
**Woodard**, Earl Nathan 1961- *WhoRel 92*
**Woodard**, Edward Joseph, Jr. 1943- *WhoRel 92*
**Woodard**, Fredrick 1939- *WhoBlA 92*
**Woodard**, Geoffrey Dean Leroy 1915- *AmMWSc 92*
**Woodard**, Helen Quincy 1900- *AmMWSc 92*
**Woodard**, Henry Herman, Jr 1925- *AmMWSc 92*
**Woodard**, James Arthur 1930- *WhoMW 92*
**Woodard**, James Carroll 1933- *AmMWSc 92*
**Woodard**, John Lewis, III 1951- *WhoAmL 92*
**Woodard**, Josef Lee 1958- *WhoEnt 92*
**Woodard**, Joseph Lamar 1937- *WhoAmL 92*
**Woodard**, Kenneth Emil 1960- *WhoBlA 92*
**Woodard**, Kenneth Eugene, Jr 1942- *AmMWSc 92*
**Woodard**, L Duane 1938- *WhoAmP 91*
**Woodard**, Larry L. 1936- *WhoWest 92*
**Woodard**, Lois Marie *WhoBlA 92*
**Woodard**, Loretta Faye 1943- *WhoAmP 91*
**Woodard**, Luther T 1920- *WhoAmP 91*
**Woodard**, Lynette 1959- *BlkOlyM*
**Woodard**, Mark Davis 1949- *WhoAmL 92*
**Woodard**, Marsha Brown 1949- *WhoRel 92*
**Woodard**, Ralph Emerson 1921- *AmMWSc 92*
**Woodard**, Rhonda Sigrist 1953- *WhoAmL 92*
**Woodard**, Richard P 1955- *AmMWSc 92*
**Woodard**, Robert E. *WhoRel 92*
**Woodard**, Robert Louis 1917- *AmMWSc 92*
**Woodard**, Robert Nathaniel 1939- *Who 92*
**Woodard**, Samuel L. 1930- *WhoBlA 92*
**Woodard**, Teresa Paige 1964- *WhoMW 92*
**Woodard**, Wilma C 1934- *WhoAmP 91*
**Woodbeck**, Charles Asa 1938- *WhoMW 92*
**Woodbeck**, Frank Raymond 1947- *WhoBlA 92*
**Woodberry**, George E. 1855-1930 *BenetAL 91*
**Woodbine Parish**, David 1911- *Who 92*
**Woodbrey**, James C 1934- *AmMWSc 92*
**Woodbridge**, Joseph Eliot 1921- *AmMWSc 92*
**Woodbridge**, Luther Dana 1850-1899 *BiInAmS*
**Woodbridge**, Norma *DrAPF 91*
**Woodburn**, Jeffrey Robert 1965- *WhoAmP 91*
**Woodburn**, Margy Jeanette 1928- *AmMWSc 92*
**Woodburn**, Ralph Robert, Jr. 1946- *WhoAmL 92*
**Woodburn**, Russell 1907- *AmMWSc 92*
**Woodburn**, Wilton A 1926- *AmMWSc 92*
**Woodburne**, Michael O 1937- *AmMWSc 92*
**Woodburne**, Russell Thomas 1904- *AmMWSc 92*
**Woodbury**, Arline Elizabeth 1953- *WhoBlA 92*
**Woodbury**, Arthur Neum 1930- *WhoEnt 92*
**Woodbury**, Charles Jeptha Hill 1851-1916 *BiInAmS*
**Woodbury**, Charles Putnam 1919- *WhoIns 92*
**Woodbury**, Daniel Phineas 1812-1864 *BiInAmS*

**Woodbury**, David Henry 1930- *WhoBlA 92*
**Woodbury**, Dixon Miles 1921- *AmMWSc 92*
**Woodbury**, Eric John 1925- *AmMWSc 92*
**Woodbury**, Franklin Bennett Wessler 1937- *WhoFI 92*
**Woodbury**, George Wallis, Jr 1937- *AmMWSc 92*
**Woodbury**, Joan Jones 1927- *WhoEnt 92*
**Woodbury**, John F L 1918- *AmMWSc 92*
**Woodbury**, John Walter 1923- *AmMWSc 92*
**Woodbury**, Lael Jay 1927- *WhoEnt 92*
**Woodbury**, Louie E, Jr. 1914- *WhoIns 92*
**Woodbury**, Margaret Clayton 1937- *WhoBlA 92*
**Woodbury**, Max Atkin 1917- *AmMWSc 92*
**Woodbury**, Paul D., Jr. 1924- *WhoRel 92*
**Woodbury**, Richard C 1931- *AmMWSc 92*
**Woodbury**, Richard Coulam 1931- *WhoWest 92*
**Woodbury**, Richard Paul 1950- *AmMWSc 92*
**Woodbury**, Robert A 1904- *AmMWSc 92*
**Woodbury**, Rollin Edwin 1913- *WhoAmL 92*
**Woodbury**, Sara Jorgenson *DrAPF 91*
**Woodbury**, Thomas Bowring, II 1937- *WhoAmL 92*
**Woodbury**, Thomas John 1957- *WhoAmL 92*
**Woodcock**, Alfred Herbert 1905- *AmMWSc 92*
**Woodcock**, Christopher Leonard Frank 1942- *AmMWSc 92*
**Woodcock**, Eldon Griffith 1930- *WhoFI 92*
**Woodcock**, George 1904-1979 *FacFETw*
**Woodcock**, George 1912- *BenetAL 91, ConPo 91, IntAu&W 91, IntWW 91, Who 92, WhoWest 92, WrDr 92*
**Woodcock**, George Washington 1930- *WhoAmP 91*
**Woodcock**, Gordon *Who 92*
**Woodcock**, Joan 1908- *IntAu&W 91*
**Woodcock**, John 1927- *TwCPaSc*
**Woodcock**, John 1932- *Who 92*
**Woodcock**, John Charles 1926- *IntAu&W 91, Who 92*
**Woodcock**, John J, III 1946- *WhoAmP 91*
**Woodcock**, Jonathan Hugh 1951- *WhoWest 92*
**Woodcock**, Leonard 1911- *FacFETw, IntWW 91, WhoAmP 91*
**Woodcock**, Mark Elliott 1943- *WhoEnt 92*
**Woodcock**, Michael 1943- *Who 92*
**Woodcock**, Ruth Miller 1927- *WhoRel 92*
**Woodcock**, Thomas 1951- *Who 92*
**Woodcock-Mitchell**, Janet Louise 1949- *AmMWSc 92*
**Woodcott**, Keith *IntAu&W 91X, TwCSFW 91, WrDr 92*
**Woodd Walker**, Geoffrey Basil d1991 *Who 92N*
**Woodell**, Anne 1936- *WhoAmP 91*
**Wooden**, Ralph L. 1915- *WhoBlA 92*
**Wooden**, Weldon Frederick 1953- *WhoRel 92*
**Woodfield**, Clyde V 1933- *WhoAmP 91*
**Woodfield**, Denis Buchanan 1933- *WhoFI 92*
**Woodfield**, F W, Jr 1918- *AmMWSc 92*
**Woodfield**, Philip 1923- *Who 92*
**Woodfield**, William Read 1928- *WhoEnt 92*
**Woodfill**, Marvin Carl 1938- *AmMWSc 92*
**Woodfin**, Beulah Marie 1936- *AmMWSc 92*
**Woodfolk**, Joseph O. 1933- *WhoBlA 92*
**Woodford**, Anthony Arthur George 1939- *Who 92*
**Woodford**, Bruce P *DrAPF 91*
**Woodford**, Charles Walter 1931- *WhoFI 92*
**Woodford**, Colin Godwin Patrick 1934- *Who 92*
**Woodford**, David 1938- *TwCPaSc*
**Woodford**, David A 1937- *AmMWSc 92*
**Woodford**, David Milner 1930- *Who 92*
**Woodford**, Dianna Lynne 1946- *WhoMW 92*
**Woodford**, Duane Hugh 1939- *WhoFI 92*
**Woodford**, Hackley Elbridge 1914- *WhoBlA 92*
**Woodford**, James 1893-1976 *TwCPaSc*
**Woodford**, James 1946- *AmMWSc 92*
**Woodford**, James Elmer, Jr 1950- *WhoAmP 91*
**Woodford**, John Niles 1941- *WhoBlA 92*
**Woodford**, Peggy 1937- *IntAu&W 91, WrDr 92*
**Woodford**, Peter 1930- *Who 92*
**Woodforde**, John Edward Ffooks 1925- *IntAu&W 91*
**Woodforde**, John Ffooks 1925- *WrDr 92*
**Woodfork**, Carolyn Amelia 1957- *WhoBlA 92*
**Woodgate**, Bruce Edward 1939- *AmMWSc 92*
**Woodgate**, Joan Mary 1912- *Who 92*
**Woodger**, Walter James, Jr. 1913- *WhoFI 92*
**Woodhall**, David Massey 1934- *Who 92*
**Woodhall**, John Alexander, Jr. 1929- *WhoFI 92, WhoMW 92*
**Woodhall**, Mary 1901-1988 *TwCPaSc*
**Woodhall**, William Fulton 1944- *WhoRel 92, WhoWest 92*
**Woodham**, Donald W 1929- *AmMWSc 92*
**Woodham**, Ronald Ernest 1912- *Who 92*
**Woodhams**, Brian Watson 1911- *Who 92*
**Woodhead**, Anthony Peter 1939- *Who 92*
**Woodhead**, David James 1943- *Who 92*
**Woodhead**, Jane 1954- *Who 92*
**Woodhour**, Allen F 1930- *AmMWSc 92*
**Woodhouse** *Who 92*
**Woodhouse**, Andrew Henry 1923- *Who 92*
**Woodhouse**, Arthur Owen 1916- *IntWW 91, Who 92*
**Woodhouse**, Barbara 1910-1988 *FacFETw*
**Woodhouse**, Bernard Lawrence 1936- *AmMWSc 92*
**Woodhouse**, Charles David 1934- *Who 92*
**Woodhouse**, Christopher Montague 1917- *Who 92*
**Woodhouse**, David *Who 92*
**Woodhouse**, Edward James, Jr 1953- *WhoAmP 91*
**Woodhouse**, Edward John 1939- *AmMWSc 92*
**Woodhouse**, Emma *WrDr 92*
**Woodhouse**, Enoch O'Dell, II 1927- *WhoBlA 92*
**Woodhouse**, Fred Nye 1943- *WhoWest 92*
**Woodhouse**, James 1770-1809 *BiInAmS*
**Woodhouse**, James Stephen 1933- *Who 92*
**Woodhouse**, John C. d1991 *NewYTBS 91*
**Woodhouse**, John Crawford 1898- *AmMWSc 92*
**Woodhouse**, John Frederick 1930- *WhoFI 92*
**Woodhouse**, John Henry 1949- *Who 92*
**Woodhouse**, John Robert 1937- *Who 92*
**Woodhouse**, Johnny Boyd 1945- *WhoBlA 92*
**Woodhouse**, Lawrence Byrne, Jr. 1957- *WhoEnt 92*
**Woodhouse**, Martin 1932- *WrDr 92*
**Woodhouse**, Montague *Who 92*
**Woodhouse**, Montague 1917- *IntWW 91, WrDr 92*
**Woodhouse**, Owen *Who 92*
**Woodhouse**, Rossalind Yvonne 1940- *WhoBlA 92*
**Woodhouse**, Samuel Mostyn Forbes 1912- *Who 92*
**Woodhouse**, Samuel Washington 1821-1904 *BiInAmS*
**Woodhouse**, Thomas Edwin 1940- *WhoAmL 92*
**Woodhouse**, William Walton, Jr 1910- *AmMWSc 92*
**Woodhull**, Victoria 1838-1927 *BenetAL 91, RComAH*
**Woodhull**, Victoria Claflin 1838-1927 *HanAmWH, RelLAm 91*
**Woodhull-McNeal**, Ann P 1942- *AmMWSc 92*
**Woodie**, Henry L. 1940- *WhoBlA 92*
**Woodies**, Leslie 1952- *WhoEnt 92*
**Woodies**, Richard 1921- *WhoFI 92*
**Woodin**, Sarah Ann 1945- *AmMWSc 92*
**Woodin**, Terry Stern 1933- *AmMWSc 92*
**Woodin**, William Graves 1914- *AmMWSc 92*
**Woodin**, William Hartman, III 1925- *AmMWSc 92*
**Wooding**, Daniel Tanswell 1940- *WhoRel 92*
**Wooding**, David Joshua 1959- *WhoBlA 92*
**Wooding**, Frank James 1941- *AmMWSc 92*
**Wooding**, Samuel David 1895-1985 *WhoBlA 92N*
**Wooding**, Sharon *SmATA 66 [port]*
**Wooding**, Sharon L 1943- *SmATA 66 [port]*
**Wooding**, William Minor 1917- *AmMWSc 92*
**Woodington**, Walter 1916- *TwCPaSc*
**Woodiwiss**, Kathleen E. *WrDr 92*
**Woodke**, Robert Allen 1950- *WhoAmL 92*
**Woodland**, Austin William d1990 *Who 92N*
**Woodland**, Bertram George 1922- *AmMWSc 92*
**Woodland**, Calvin Emmanuel 1943- *WhoBlA 92*
**Woodland**, Dorothy Jane 1908- *AmMWSc 92*
**Woodland**, Irwin Francis 1922- *WhoAmL 92*
**Woodland**, Morris Scott 1927- *WhoAmL 92*
**Woodland**, Steven Dee 1951- *WhoAmL 92*
**Woodland**, William Charles 1919- *AmMWSc 92*
**Woodley**, Charles Lamar 1941- *AmMWSc 92*
**Woodley**, Charles Leon 1944- *AmMWSc 92*
**Woodley**, Edmund Etchison *WhoAmP 91*
**Woodley**, Gary 1953- *TwCPaSc*
**Woodley**, John Meredith 1944- *WhoAmL 92*
**Woodley**, John Paul 1926- *WhoAmL 92*
**Woodley**, Ronald John 1925- *Who 92*
**Woodlock**, Douglas Preston 1947- *WhoAmL 92*
**Woodlock**, Jack Terence 1919- *Who 92*
**Woodman**, Allen *DrAPF 91*
**Woodman**, Daniel Ralph 1942- *AmMWSc 92*
**Woodman**, Durand 1859-1907 *BiInAmS*
**Woodman**, G. Roger 1953- *WhoFI 92*
**Woodman**, Grey Musgrave 1922- *WhoMW 92*
**Woodman**, Harold David 1928- *WrDr 92*
**Woodman**, Henry J d1903 *BiInAmS*
**Woodman**, Herbert B. d1991 *NewYTBS 91 [port]*
**Woodman**, James L. 1952- *WhoAmL 92*
**Woodman**, Leonora 1925- *WhoMW 92*
**Woodman**, Peter William *AmMWSc 92*
**Woodman**, William E. *WhoEnt 92*
**Woodmansee**, Donald Ernest 1941- *AmMWSc 92*
**Woodmansee**, Gerald Louis 1930- *WhoAmP 91*
**Woodmansee**, Glenn Edward 1936- *WhoFI 92*
**Woodmansee**, Robert Asbury 1926- *AmMWSc 92*
**Woodmansee**, Robert George 1941- *AmMWSc 92*
**Woodrell**, Daniel *DrAPF 91*
**Woodress**, James 1916- *IntAu&W 91, WrDr 92*
**Woodress**, James Leslie, Jr. 1916- *DcLB 111 [port]*
**Woodridge**, Wilson Jack, Jr. 1950- *WhoBlA 92*
**Woodriff**, Roger L *AmMWSc 92*
**Woodring**, Carl 1919- *WrDr 92*
**Woodring**, DeWayne Stanley 1931- *WhoMW 92, WhoRel 92*
**Woodring**, J Porter 1932- *AmMWSc 92*
**Woodring**, Paul 1907- *WrDr 92*
**Woodroffe**, George Cuthbert Manning 1918- *Who 92*
**Woodroffe**, Geraldine M. 1939- *WhoRel 92*
**Woodroffe**, Jean Frances 1923- *Who 92*
**Woodroffe**, Juan F. 1948- *WhoHisp 92*
**Woodroofe**, Ernest 1912- *Who 92*
**Woodroofe**, Ernest George 1912- *IntWW 91*
**Woodrow**, Bill 1948- *IntWW 91, TwCPaSc, WorArt 1980 [port]*
**Woodrow**, David 1920- *Who 92*
**Woodrow**, Donald L 1935- *AmMWSc 92*
**Woodrow**, Gayford William 1922- *Who 92*
**Woodrow**, James 1828-1907 *BiInAmS*
**Woodrow**, Kenneth 1942- *WhoWest 92*
**Woodrow**, Randall Mark 1956- *WhoAmL 92*
**Woodruff**, Alan Waller 1916- *IntWW 91, Who 92*
**Woodruff**, Boykin Maxwell, Jr. 1946- *WhoRel 92*
**Woodruff**, Bruce Emery 1930- *WhoAmL 92*
**Woodruff**, Calvin Watts 1920- *AmMWSc 92*
**Woodruff**, Charles Edgar 1916- *WhoFI 92*
**Woodruff**, Charles Edward 1860-1915 *BiInAmS*
**Woodruff**, Charles Marsh, Jr 1944- *AmMWSc 92*
**Woodruff**, Charles Norman 1941- *WhoAmL 92*
**Woodruff**, Charles Roy 1938- *WhoRel 92*
**Woodruff**, Clarence Merrill 1910- *AmMWSc 92*
**Woodruff**, Constance Oneida 1921- *WhoAmP 91, WhoBlA 92*
**Woodruff**, David Scott 1943- *AmMWSc 92*
**Woodruff**, Deborah Ann 1957- *WhoAmL 92*
**Woodruff**, Edythe Parker 1928- *AmMWSc 92*
**Woodruff**, Gene L 1934- *AmMWSc 92*
**Woodruff**, Hale A. 1900-1980 *WhoBlA 92N*
**Woodruff**, Harold Boyd 1917- *AmMWSc 92*
**Woodruff**, Harry Wells 1912- *Who 92*
**Woodruff**, Hugh Boyd 1949- *AmMWSc 92*
**Woodruff**, James Donald 1912- *AmMWSc 92*
**Woodruff**, James Norman, Jr. 1931- *WhoMW 92*
**Woodruff**, James W. *WhoBlA 92*
**Woodruff**, Jane 1945- *WhoMW 92*
**Woodruff**, Jeffrey Robert 1943- *WhoBlA 92*
**Woodruff**, John H, Jr 1911- *AmMWSc 92*
**Woodruff**, John Rowland 1909- *WhoEnt 92*
**Woodruff**, John Youie 1915- *BlkOlyM*
**Woodruff**, Judith J 1939- *AmMWSc 92*
**Woodruff**, Judson Sage 1925- *WhoAmL 92*
**Woodruff**, Judy Carline 1946- *IntWW 91*
**Woodruff**, Kathryn Elaine 1940- *WhoWest 92*
**Woodruff**, Kenneth Lee 1950- *AmMWSc 92*
**Woodruff**, Laurence Clark 1902- *AmMWSc 92*
**Woodruff**, Michael 1911- *Who 92, WrDr 92*
**Woodruff**, Michael Francis Addison 1911- *IntWW 91*
**Woodruff**, Paul *ScFEYrs*
**Woodruff**, Paul A 1960- *WhoAmP 91*
**Woodruff**, Paul Harrison 1937- *WhoFI 92*
**Woodruff**, Philip *IntAu&W 91X, IntWW 91, Who 92, WrDr 92*
**Woodruff**, Randall Lee 1954- *WhoAmL 92*
**Woodruff**, Richard D. 1954- *WhoRel 92*
**Woodruff**, Richard Ira 1940- *AmMWSc 92*
**Woodruff**, Robert Eugene 1933- *AmMWSc 92*
**Woodruff**, Robert Winship 1889-1985 *FacFETw*
**Woodruff**, Ronny Clifford 1943- *AmMWSc 92, WhoMW 92*
**Woodruff**, Susan Beatty 1940- *AmMWSc 92*
**Woodruff**, T M 1943- *WhoAmP 91*
**Woodruff**, Tom *WhoAmP 91*
**Woodruff**, Tom, Jr. 1959- *WhoEnt 92*
**Woodruff**, Truman Owen 1925- *AmMWSc 92*
**Woodruff**, Virginia *WhoEnt 92*
**Woodruff**, Wilford 1807-1898 *RelLAm 91*
**Woodruff**, William Charles 1921- *Who 92*
**Woodruff**, William Jennings 1925- *WhoMW 92, WhoRel 92*
**Woodruff**, William Lee 1938- *AmMWSc 92*
**Woodruff**, William Matthew 1951- *WhoRel 92*
**Woodrum**, Clifton Alexander, III 1938- *WhoAmP 91*
**Woodrum**, Donald 1917- *WhoWest 92*
**Woodrum**, Robert Lee 1945- *WhoFI 92*
**Woods**, Aaron Neil 1965- *WhoAmL 92*
**Woods**, Alan Churchill, Jr 1918- *AmMWSc 92*
**Woods**, Alexander Hamilton 1922- *AmMWSc 92*
**Woods**, Alfred David Braine 1932- *AmMWSc 92*
**Woods**, Allie, Jr. *WhoBlA 92*
**Woods**, Almita 1914- *WhoBlA 92*
**Woods**, Alvin Edwin 1934- *AmMWSc 92*
**Woods**, Arleigh Maddox 1929- *WhoBlA 92*
**Woods**, Barbara McAlpin 1945- *WhoBlA 92*
**Woods**, Barry Alan 1942- *WhoFI 92*
**Woods**, Beatrice 1925- *WhoAmP 91*
**Woods**, Bernice 1924- *WhoBlA 92*
**Woods**, Bert Russell 1946- *WhoWest 92*
**Woods**, Bobby Joe 1935- *WhoWest 92*
**Woods**, Brian 1928- *Who 92*
**Woods**, Charles Arthur 1940- *AmMWSc 92*
**Woods**, Charles Lessly 1915- *WhoAmP 91*
**Woods**, Charles William 1917- *Who 92*
**Woods**, Charles William 1928- *AmMWSc 92*
**Woods**, Charlotte Ann 1932- *WhoBlA 92*
**Woods**, Christopher Matthew 1923- *Who 92*
**Woods**, Clifton, III 1944- *AmMWSc 92*
**Woods**, Colin 1920- *Who 92*
**Woods**, Curtis Eugene 1950- *WhoAmL 92*
**Woods**, Daniel Christian 1956- *WhoRel 92*
**Woods**, Daniel James 1952- *WhoAmL 92*
**Woods**, Darnell 1961- *WhoBlA 92*
**Woods**, David Donald 1950- *WhoRel 92*
**Woods**, Debby Lynne 1952- *WhoRel 92*
**Woods**, Deborah L 1955- *WhoAmP 91*
**Woods**, Delbert Leon 1913- *WhoBlA 92*
**Woods**, Donald 1906- *IntMPA 92*
**Woods**, Donald Leslie 1944- *AmMWSc 92*
**Woods**, Donald Peter 1911- *WhoWest 92*
**Woods**, Donald Robert 1935- *AmMWSc 92*
**Woods**, Douglas Bryan 1960- *WhoMW 92*
**Woods**, Edward James 1936- *AmMWSc 92*
**Woods**, Eldrick *NewYTBS 91 [port]*
**Woods**, Elisa R. 1959- *WhoBlA 92*
**Woods**, Elisabeth Ann 1940- *Who 92*
**Woods**, Forest Arin 1940- *WhoAmP 91*
**Woods**, Frances Jerome 1913- *WrDr 92*
**Woods**, Frank 1907- *IntWW 91, Who 92*
**Woods**, Frank Robert 1916- *AmMWSc 92*
**Woods**, Frank Wilson 1924- *AmMWSc 92*
**Woods**, Frederick 1932- *WrDr 92*
**Woods**, Geneva Halloway 1930- *WhoBlA 92*
**Woods**, George E. 1923- *WhoAmL 92*
**Woods**, George Theodore 1924- *AmMWSc 92*

**Woods,** George Washington 1916- *WhoBlA 92*
**Woods,** Gerald Marion Irwin 1947- *WhoAmL 92*
**Woods,** Gerald Wayne 1946- *WhoAmL 92*
**Woods,** Geraldine Pittman *AmMWSc 92, WhoBlA 92*
**Woods,** Geraldine Pittman 1921- *NotBlAW 92*
**Woods,** Gerard *ConAu 135*
**Woods,** Grant *WhoAmL 92, WhoAmP 91*
**Woods,** Granville T 1856-1910 *BiInAmS*
**Woods,** Harriett 1927- *WhoAmP 91*
**Woods,** Harry Arthur, Jr. 1941- *WhoAmL 92*
**Woods,** Henry 1846-1921 *TwCPaSc*
**Woods,** Henry 1918- *WhoAmL 92*
**Woods,** Henry Gabriel 1924- *Who 92*
**Woods,** Hortense E. 1926- *WhoBlA 92*
**Woods,** Howard James, Jr. 1955- *WhoFI 92*
**Woods,** Ickey 1966- *WhoBlA 92*
**Woods,** Ivan *Who 92*
**Woods,** J M 1922- *AmMWSc 92*
**Woods,** J. P. 1950- *WhoFI 92*
**Woods,** Jack E *WhoAmP 91*
**Woods,** Jacqueline Edwards 1947- *WhoBlA 92*
**Woods,** James 1947- *IntMPA 92, IntWW 91*
**Woods,** James Edward 1911- *WhoMW 92*
**Woods,** James Francis, Jr. 1957- *WhoFI 92*
**Woods,** James Howard 1947- *WhoEnt 92*
**Woods,** James Robert 1947- *WhoAmL 92*
**Woods,** James Sterrett 1940- *AmMWSc 92*
**Woods,** James Watson 1918- *AmMWSc 92*
**Woods,** Jane Gamble 1928- *WhoBlA 92*
**Woods,** Jane Haycock 1946- *WhoAmP 91*
**Woods,** Jeff Chandler 1954- *WhoAmL 92*
**Woods,** Jerry Dwain *WhoRel 92*
**Woods,** Jessie Anderson 1914- *WhoBlA 92*
**Woods,** Jimmie Dale 1933- *AmMWSc 92*
**Woods,** Joe *WhoBlA 92*
**Woods,** Joe Darst 1923- *AmMWSc 92*
**Woods,** Joe Eldon 1933- *WhoWest 92*
**Woods,** Joel Grant 1954- *WhoWest 92*
**Woods,** John *DrAPF 91*
**Woods,** John 1926- *ConPo 91, WrDr 92*
**Woods,** John David 1939- *Who 92*
**Woods,** John LaRue 1937- *WhoMW 92*
**Woods,** John Mawhinney 1919- *Who 92*
**Woods,** John Maynard 1955- *WhoAmL 92*
**Woods,** John Thomas, Jr. 1947- *WhoEnt 92, WhoRel 92, WhoWest 92*
**Woods,** John Whitcomb 1952- *AmMWSc 92*
**Woods,** John William 1943- *AmMWSc 92*
**Woods,** John Witherspoon 1931- *WhoFI 92*
**Woods,** Joseph 1956- *AmMWSc 92*
**Woods,** Joseph James 1943- *AmMWSc 92*
**Woods,** Keith Newell 1941- *AmMWSc 92*
**Woods,** Kenneth 1954- *IntAu&W 91*
**Woods,** Kenneth R 1925- *AmMWSc 92*
**Woods,** Kevin Daniel 1961- *WhoFI 92*
**Woods,** L. C. 1922- *WrDr 92*
**Woods,** Lauren Albert 1919- *AmMWSc 92*
**Woods,** LaVerne 1957- *WhoAmL 92*
**Woods,** Lawrence *TwCSFW 91*
**Woods,** Lawrence Charles 1916- *WhoBlA 92*
**Woods,** Lawrence Milton 1932- *WhoWest 92*
**Woods,** Leslie Colin 1922- *Who 92*
**Woods,** Madelyne 1965- *WhoBlA 92*
**Woods,** Manuel T. 1939- *WhoBlA 92*
**Woods,** Margie McDaniel 1941- *WhoRel 92*
**Woods,** Maribelle 1919- *AmMWSc 92*
**Woods,** Mark *LesBEnT 92*
**Woods,** Marvell Collins 1961- *WhoMW 92*
**Woods,** Mary 1923- *AmMWSc 92*
**Woods,** Mary Ellen 1954- *WhoEnt 92*
**Woods,** Maurice Eric 1933- *Who 92*
**Woods,** Melanie Ann 1957- *WhoWest 92*
**Woods,** Melvin LeRoy 1938- *WhoBlA 92*
**Woods,** Michael 1935- *IntWW 91*
**Woods,** Norman James 1934- *WhoRel 92, WhoWest 92*
**Woods,** P F *IntAu&W 91X*
**Woods,** Pauline Harper 1930- *WhoAmP 91*
**Woods,** Phil 1931- *NewAmDM*
**Woods,** Philip Sargent 1921- *AmMWSc 92*
**Woods,** Philip Wells 1931- *WhoBlA 92, WhoEnt 92*
**Woods,** Portia White 1958- *WhoAmL 92*
**Woods,** Ralph Arthur 1941- *AmMWSc 92*
**Woods,** Ramona Lee 1945- *WhoHisp 92*
**Woods,** Raymond D 1910- *AmMWSc 92*
**Woods,** Raymond Duval 1960- *WhoWest 92*
**Woods,** Richard 1941- *WrDr 92*
**Woods,** Richard David 1935- *AmMWSc 92*
**Woods,** Richard Glenn 1933- *WhoAmP 91*
**Woods,** Richard John Francis 1941- *WhoRel 92*
**Woods,** Robert A 1865-1925 *DcAmImH*
**Woods,** Robert Claude 1940- *AmMWSc 92*
**Woods,** Robert Douglas Murray 1946- *WhoWest 92*
**Woods,** Robert Edward 1952- *WhoAmL 92*
**Woods,** Robert Evans, Jr. 1947- *WhoFI 92*
**Woods,** Robert Gail 1939- *WhoRel 92*
**Woods,** Robert James 1928- *AmMWSc 92*
**Woods,** Robert Lawrence 1911- *WhoWest 92*
**Woods,** Robert Louis 1947- *WhoBlA 92*
**Woods,** Robert Octavius 1933- *AmMWSc 92*
**Woods,** Robert Wilmer 1914- *Who 92*
**Woods,** Rodney Ian 1941- *WhoFI 92*
**Woods,** Roger David 1924- *AmMWSc 92*
**Woods,** Roosevelt, Jr. 1933- *WhoBlA 92*
**Woods,** Roy Alexander 1913- *AmMWSc 92*
**Woods,** S. John 1915- *TwCPaSc*
**Woods,** Sherwyn Martin 1932- *AmMWSc 92*
**Woods,** Stephen Charles 1942- *AmMWSc 92*
**Woods,** Stockton *WrDr 92*
**Woods,** Stuart 1938- *WhoEnt 92*
**Woods,** Stuart B 1924- *AmMWSc 92*
**Woods,** Stuart Chevalier 1938- *IntAu&W 91*
**Woods,** Sylvania Webb, Jr 1954- *WhoAmP 91, WhoBlA 92*
**Woods,** Sylvania Webb, Sr. 1927- *WhoBlA 92*
**Woods,** Thomas Lamar 1933- *WhoAmP 91*
**Woods,** Thomas Ronald 1948- *WhoFI 92*
**Woods,** Thomas Smith 1928- *WhoMW 92*
**Woods,** Thomas Stephen 1944- *AmMWSc 92*
**Woods,** Timothy L. *WhoBlA 92*
**Woods,** Timothy Phillips 1943- *Who 92*
**Woods,** Timothy William 1943- *WhoAmL 92*
**Woods,** Tony 1965- *WhoBlA 92*
**Woods,** Tony 1966- *WhoBlA 92*
**Woods,** W Kelly 1912- *AmMWSc 92*
**Woods,** Walter Ralph 1931- *AmMWSc 92*
**Woods,** Wendell David 1932- *AmMWSc 92*
**Woods,** Wilbourne F. 1935- *WhoBlA 92*
**Woods,** William A *AmMWSc 92*
**Woods,** William Boone, Jr. 1942- *WhoWest 92*
**Woods,** William Edward 1936- *WhoRel 92*
**Woods,** William Everett 1949- *WhoWest 92*
**Woods,** William Fred *AmMWSc 92*
**Woods,** William George 1931- *AmMWSc 92*
**Woods,** William Ivan *Who 92*
**Woods,** William Ray 1947- *WhoRel 92*
**Woods,** William Reed 1948- *WhoMW 92*
**Woods,** Willie G. *WhoBlA 92*
**Woods,** Wilna Ann 1929- *AmMWSc 92*
**Woodside,** David Eugene 1957- *WhoAmL 92*
**Woodside,** John Moffatt 1941- *AmMWSc 92*
**Woodside,** Kenneth Hall 1938- *AmMWSc 92*
**Woodside,** William 1931- *AmMWSc 92*
**Woodside,** William Stewart 1922- *IntWW 91*
**Woodson,** Aileen R. 1927- *WhoBlA 92*
**Woodson,** Alfred F. 1952- *WhoBlA 92*
**Woodson,** Benjamin N 1908- *WhoIns 92*
**Woodson,** Benjamin Nelson, III 1908- *WhoFI 92*
**Woodson,** Bernard Robert, Jr. 1923- *WhoBlA 92*
**Woodson,** Carter G. 1875-1950 *ConBlB 2 [port], RComAH*
**Woodson,** Carter Godwin 1875-1950 *BenetAL 91, FacFETw*
**Woodson,** Charles R. 1942- *WhoBlA 92*
**Woodson,** Cleveland Coleman, III 1946- *WhoBlA 92*
**Woodson,** Ernest Lyle 1937- *WhoHisp 92*
**Woodson,** Herbert H 1925- *AmMWSc 92*
**Woodson,** Jeffrey Anthony 1955- *WhoBlA 92*
**Woodson,** John Hodges 1933- *AmMWSc 92*
**Woodson,** Leland Jan Lee 1942- *WhoWest 92*
**Woodson,** Mark Winter 1953- *WhoWest 92*
**Woodson,** Mike 1958- *WhoBlA 92*
**Woodson,** Robert D *AmMWSc 92*
**Woodson,** Robert David 1938- *WhoMW 92*
**Woodson,** Robert L. 1937- *WhoBlA 92*
**Woodson,** Roderic L. 1947- *WhoBlA 92*
**Woodson,** S Howard, Jr 1916- *WhoAmP 91, WhoBlA 92*
**Woodson,** Shirley A. 1936- *WhoBlA 92*
**Woodson,** Stephen William 1950- *WhoFI 92*
**Woodson,** Thelma L. 1920- *WhoBlA 92*
**Woodson,** Timothy Paul 1957- *WhoRel 92*
**Woodson,** Tracy Todd 1960- *WhoBlA 92*
**Woodson,** William D. 1929- *WhoBlA 92*
**Woodson-Howard,** Marlene Erdley 1937- *WhoAmP 91*
**Woodstock,** Viscount 1953- *Who 92*
**Woodstock,** Lowell Willard 1931- *AmMWSc 92*
**Woodsworth,** James 1843-1917 *RelLAm 91*
**Woodvine,** John 1929- *ConTFT 9*
**Woodward and Bernstein** *FacFETw*
**Woodward,** Aaron Alphonso, III *WhoBlA 92*
**Woodward,** Aaron Alphonso, III 1947- *WhoEnt 92*
**Woodward,** Albert Bruce, Jr. 1941- *WhoFI 92*
**Woodward,** Albert Edward 1928- *Who 92*
**Woodward,** Almon 1932- *WhoAmP 91*
**Woodward,** Amos E d1891 *BiInAmS*
**Woodward,** Anthony d1915 *BiInAmS*
**Woodward,** Arthur Eugene 1925- *AmMWSc 92*
**Woodward,** Barry *Who 92*
**Woodward,** Bart 1953- *WhoEnt 92*
**Woodward,** Bob 1943- *IntAu&W 91, WrDr 92*
**Woodward,** C. Vann 1908- *IntWW 91, Who 92, WrDr 92*
**Woodward,** Calvin Milton 1837-1914 *BiInAmS*
**Woodward,** Charles D 1948- *WhoAmP 91*
**Woodward,** Clare K 1941- *AmMWSc 92*
**Woodward,** Craig Randolph 1955- *WhoAmL 92*
**Woodward,** David Robert 1947- *WhoAmL 92*
**Woodward,** David Willcox 1913- *AmMWSc 92*
**Woodward,** Derek 1923- *TwCPaSc*
**Woodward,** Donald Jay 1940- *AmMWSc 92*
**Woodward,** Douglas P. 1954- *ConAu 135*
**Woodward,** Douglas R 1911- *WhoAmP 91*
**Woodward,** Dow Owen 1931- *AmMWSc 92*
**Woodward,** Edward *Who 92*
**Woodward,** Edward 1930- *IntMPA 92, IntWW 91, Who 92*
**Woodward,** Edward Roy 1916- *AmMWSc 92*
**Woodward,** Eric 1926- *TwCPaSc*
**Woodward,** Ervin Chapman, Jr 1923- *AmMWSc 92*
**Woodward,** Francis H 1939- *WhoAmP 91*
**Woodward,** Fred Erskine 1921- *AmMWSc 92*
**Woodward,** Geoffrey Frederick 1924- *Who 92*
**Woodward,** Geoffrey Royston d1991 *Who 92N*
**Woodward,** Isaiah Alfonso 1912- *WhoBlA 92*
**Woodward,** J Guy 1914- *AmMWSc 92*
**Woodward,** James Franklin 1941- *AmMWSc 92*
**Woodward,** James Kenneth 1938- *AmMWSc 92*
**Woodward,** Joanne 1930- *IntMPA 92*
**Woodward,** Joanne Gignilliat 1930- *IntWW 91, WhoEnt 92*
**Woodward,** Joe William 1937- *AmMWSc 92*
**Woodward,** John 1932- *Who 92*
**Woodward,** John 1945- *WrDr 92*
**Woodward,** John Forster 1932- *IntWW 91*
**Woodward,** John Russell 1951- *WhoWest 92*
**Woodward,** John Taylor, III 1940- *WhoAmL 92, WhoFI 92*
**Woodward,** Joseph Janvier 1833-1884 *BiInAmS*
**Woodward,** Joseph Wayne 1967- *WhoRel 92*
**Woodward,** Julius Hayden 1858-1916 *BiInAmS*
**Woodward,** Kathryn Christine 1953- *WhoAmL 92*
**Woodward,** Kent Thomas 1923- *AmMWSc 92*
**Woodward,** Kirsten 1959- *IntWW 91*
**Woodward,** Lee Albert 1931- *AmMWSc 92*
**Woodward,** LeRoy Albert 1916- *AmMWSc 92*
**Woodward,** M. Cabell, Jr. 1929- *WhoFI 92*
**Woodward,** Madison Truman, Jr. 1908- *WhoAmL 92*
**Woodward,** Malcolm 1943- *TwCPaSc*
**Woodward,** Marion Kenneth 1912- *WhoAmL 92*
**Woodward,** Max Wakerley 1908- *Who 92*
**Woodward,** Neil Patricia 1954- *WhoAmP 91*
**Woodward,** Ralph Lee, Jr. 1934- *WrDr 92*
**Woodward,** Robert 1943- *FacFETw*
**Woodward,** Robert Burns 1917-1979 *WhoNob 90*
**Woodward,** Robert H. 1925- *WrDr 92*
**Woodward,** Robert Simpson, IV 1943- *WhoFI 92, WhoMW 92*
**Woodward,** Roger Robert 1942- *IntWW 91*
**Woodward,** Shaun Anthony 1958- *Who 92*
**Woodward,** Stephen Cotter 1935- *AmMWSc 92*
**Woodward,** Stephen Richard 1953- *WhoWest 92*
**Woodward,** Ted K 1960- *AmMWSc 92*
**Woodward,** Theodore Englar 1914- *AmMWSc 92*
**Woodward,** Thomas Morgan 1925- *WhoEnt 92*
**Woodward,** Val Waddoups 1927- *AmMWSc 92*
**Woodward,** Wade Marshall 1955- *WhoMW 92*
**Woodward,** Wayne William 1930- *WhoRel 92*
**Woodward,** William Charles 1940- *Who 92*
**Woodward,** William E. 1874-1950 *BenetAL 91*
**Woodward,** William Herbert 1941- *WhoWest 92*
**Woodward,** William Lee 1926- *WhoFI 92*
**Woodwell,** George Masters 1928- *AmMWSc 92*
**Woodwick,** Keith Harris 1927- *AmMWSc 92*
**Woodworth,** Curtis Wilmer 1942- *AmMWSc 92*
**Woodworth,** Fred Lowe 1940- *WhoMW 92*
**Woodworth,** G. Wallace 1902-1969 *NewAmDM*
**Woodworth,** Glenn Murray 1937- *WhoAmL 92*
**Woodworth,** Harold G. 1933- *WhoRel 92*
**Woodworth,** James Nelson 1947- *WhoAmL 92*
**Woodworth,** James Vickers 1921- *WhoWest 92*
**Woodworth,** John George 1948- *AmMWSc 92*
**Woodworth,** Margo Deane 1941- *WhoRel 92*
**Woodworth,** Mary Esther *AmMWSc 92*
**Woodworth,** Ramsey Lloyd 1941- *WhoAmL 92*
**Woodworth,** Robert C. *WhoMW 92*
**Woodworth,** Robert Cummings 1930- *AmMWSc 92*
**Woodworth,** Robert Hugo 1902- *AmMWSc 92*
**Woodworth,** Samuel 1784-1842 *BenetAL 91*
**Woodworth,** Stephen Davis 1945- *WhoWest 92*
**Woodworth,** Steven E. 1961- *ConAu 135*
**Woodworth,** William McMichael 1864-1912 *BiInAmS*
**Woodworth-Etter,** Maria Beulah 1844-1924 *RelLAm 91*
**Woody,** A-Young Moon 1934- *AmMWSc 92, WhoWest 92*
**Woody,** Carol Clayman 1949- *WhoFI 92*
**Woody,** Charles Dillon 1937- *AmMWSc 92*
**Woody,** Charles Leslie 1947- *WhoAmL 92*
**Woody,** Charles Owen, Jr 1930- *AmMWSc 92*
**Woody,** Clyde Woodrow 1920- *WhoAmL 92*
**Woody,** Craig L 1951- *AmMWSc 92*
**Woody,** Jacqueline Brown 1949- *WhoBlA 92*
**Woody,** John Frederick 1941- *WhoMW 92*
**Woody,** Robert Wayne 1935- *AmMWSc 92*
**Woodyard,** Harry 1930- *WhoAmP 91*
**Woodyard,** James Douglas 1938- *AmMWSc 92*
**Woodyard,** James Robert 1936- *AmMWSc 92, WhoMW 92*
**Woodyard,** Marcia Weeks 1961- *WhoRel 92*
**Woodyard,** Sam 1925-1988 *NewAmDM*
**Woof,** Robert Edward 1911- *Who 92*
**Woof,** Robert Samuel 1931- *Who 92*
**Woofter,** Harvey Darrell 1923- *AmMWSc 92*
**Wool,** Ira Goodwin 1928- *AmMWSc 92*
**Wool,** Leon 1937- *WhoAmL 92*
**Wool,** Rosemary Jane *Who 92*
**Woolard,** Edgar S., Jr. 1934- *WhoFI 92*
**Woolard,** Edgar Smith 1934- *Who 92*
**Woolard,** Edgar Smith, Jr. 1934- *IntWW 91*
**Woolard,** H. Franklin 1942- *WhoMW 92*
**Woolard,** Henry W 1917- *AmMWSc 92*
**Woolard,** Henry Waldo 1917- *WhoWest 92*
**Woolard,** Larry D 1941- *WhoAmP 91*
**Woolbert,** Marianne 1961- *WhoAmL 92*
**Woolbert,** Maybelle Siegele *WhoAmP 91*
**Woolbright,** Thurman Alfred 1922- *WhoRel 92*
**Woolcock,** Ozeil Fryer 1910- *WhoBlA 92*
**Woolcott,** Alexander 1887-1943 *FacFETw*
**Woolcott,** Richard 1928- *IntWW 91*

**Woolcott,** William Starnold 1922- *AmMWSc 92*
**Wooldredge,** William Dunbar 1937- *WhoFI 92*
**Wooldridge,** C W 1847-1908 *ScFEYrs*
**Wooldridge,** David 1931- *WhoBlA 92*
**Wooldridge,** David Dilley 1927- *AmMWSc 92*
**Wooldridge,** David Paul 1931- *AmMWSc 92*
**Wooldridge,** Dean E *AmMWSc 92*
**Wooldridge,** Dean E. 1913- *IntWW 91*
**Wooldridge,** Donald Russell 1947- *WhoWest 92*
**Wooldridge,** Gene Lysle 1924- *AmMWSc 92*
**Wooldridge,** Ian Edmund 1932- *Who 92*
**Wooldridge,** Jerry Evan 1937- *WhoIns 92*
**Wooldridge,** John Thomas 1959- *WhoAmL 92*
**Wooldridge,** Kent Ernest 1942- *AmMWSc 92*
**Wooldridge,** Patrice Marie 1954- *WhoMW 92*
**Wooldridge,** Susan *IntMPA 92, WhoEnt 92*
**Wooldridge,** Tim 1960- *WhoAmP 91*
**Woolery,** Ben B. 1939- *WhoFI 92*
**Woolery,** Robert Clayton 1959- *WhoWest 92*
**Woolery,** Robert Harvey, Sr. 1934- *WhoFI 92*
**Wooles,** Wallace Ralph 1931- *AmMWSc 92*
**Wooley,** John Steven 1949- *WhoEnt 92*
**Woolf,** Albert Edward 1846-1920 *BiInAmS*
**Woolf,** C R 1925- *AmMWSc 92*
**Woolf,** Charles Martin 1925- *AmMWSc 92*
**Woolf,** Douglas 1922- *BenetAL 91, ConNov 91, IntAu&W 91, WrDr 92*
**Woolf,** F. X. *WrDr 92*
**Woolf,** Geoffrey 1944- *Who 92*
**Woolf,** Hal 1902-1962 *TwCPaSc*
**Woolf,** Harry 1923- *AmMWSc 92, Who 92, WrDr 92*
**Woolf,** Harry 1933- *Who 92*
**Woolf,** J R 1924- *AmMWSc 92*
**Woolf,** Jeffrey David 1946- *WhoAmL 92*
**Woolf,** John *Who 92*
**Woolf,** John 1913- *IntMPA 92*
**Woolf,** John Moss 1918- *Who 92*
**Woolf,** John Paul 1943- *WhoAmL 92*
**Woolf,** Lawrence Donald 1953- *WhoWest 92*
**Woolf,** Leonard *FacFETw*
**Woolf,** Michael Angelo 1837-1899 *DcAmImH*
**Woolf,** Neville John 1932- *AmMWSc 92*
**Woolf,** Robert Gary 1928- *WhoAmL 92*
**Woolf,** Rossetta 1959- *IntAu&W 91*
**Woolf,** Solomon 1841-1911 *BiInAmS*
**Woolf,** Steven Michael 1946- *WhoEnt 92, WhoMW 92*
**Woolf,** Stuart Joseph 1936- *WrDr 92*
**Woolf,** Virginia 1882-1941 *BiDBrF 2, CnDBLB 6 [port], FacFETw, RfGEnL 91, TwCLC 43 [port]*
**Woolf,** William Blauvelt 1932- *AmMWSc 92*
**Woolf-Scott,** Helene Lyda 1938- *WhoWest 92*
**Woolfenden,** Glen Everett 1930- *AmMWSc 92*
**Woolfenden,** Guy Anthony 1937- *WhoEnt 92*
**Woolfolk,** Clifford Allen 1935- *AmMWSc 92*
**Woolfolk,** E. Oscar 1912- *WhoBlA 92*
**Woolfolk,** George Ruble 1915- *WhoBlA 92*
**Woolfolk,** Robert William 1937- *AmMWSc 92*
**Woolford,** Harry Russell Halkerston 1905- *IntWW 91, Who 92*
**Woolford,** Robert Graham 1933- *AmMWSc 92*
**Woolfson,** Mark 1911- *Who 92*
**Woolfson,** Michael Mark 1927- *IntWW 91, Who 92*
**Woolheater,** Robert Leroy 1930- *WhoFI 92*
**Woolhiser,** David A 1932- *AmMWSc 92*
**Woolhouse,** Harold William 1932- *Who 92*
**Woolhouse,** John George 1931- *Who 92*
**Woollam,** John Arthur 1939- *AmMWSc 92, WhoMW 92*
**Woollam,** John Victor 1927- *Who 92*
**Woollaston,** Tosswill 1910- *Who 92*
**Woollcombe,** Kenneth John 1924- *IntWW 91, Who 92*
**Woollcombe,** Robert 1922- *WrDr 92*
**Woollcott,** Alexander 1887-1943 *BenetAL 91*
**Woollen,** Thomas Hayes 1934- *WhoFI 92*
**Woollett,** Albert Haines 1930- *AmMWSc 92*
**Woollett,** John Castle 1915- *Who 92*
**Woolley,** Bryan *DrAPF 91*
**Woolley,** Bryan 1937- *TwCWW 91, WrDr 92*
**Woolley,** Clara Virginia 1938- *WhoEnt 92, WhoMW 92*
**Woolley,** David Rorie 1939- *Who 92*
**Woolley,** Donald Grant 1925- *AmMWSc 92*
**Woolley,** Dorothy Elizabeth Schumann 1929- *AmMWSc 92*
**Woolley,** Earl Madsen 1942- *AmMWSc 92*
**Woolley,** John C. 1936- *WhoAmL 92*
**Woolley,** John Maxwell 1917- *Who 92*
**Woolley,** Jonathan Michael 1958- *WhoFI 92*
**Woolley,** Joseph Tarbet 1923- *AmMWSc 92*
**Woolley,** Kenneth Frank 1933- *IntWW 91*
**Woolley,** LeGrand H 1931- *AmMWSc 92*
**Woolley,** Leslie Ann 1953- *WhoFI 92*
**Woolley,** Mary Emma 1863-1947 *AmPeW*
**Woolley,** Moger 1935- *Who 92*
**Woolley,** Roy Gilbert 1922- *Who 92*
**Woolley,** Russell *Who 92*
**Woolley,** Steven E. 1943- *WhoFI 92*
**Woolley,** Tyler Anderson 1918- *AmMWSc 92*
**Woolls,** Esther Blanche 1935- *WhoFI 92*
**Woollums,** Mark Allen 1961- *WhoAmL 92*
**Woolman,** Bruce Alan 1955- *WhoWest 92*
**Woolman,** John 1720-1772 *BenetAL 91, RComAH*
**Woolman,** Maurice John 1953- *WhoEnt 92*
**Woolman,** Roger 1937- *Who 92*
**Woolmer,** Kenneth John 1940- *Who 92*
**Woolpert,** Mary Elizabeth 1926- *WhoFI 92*
**Woolrich,** Cornell 1903-1968 *BenetAL 91*
**Woolrich,** John 1954- *ConCom 92*
**Woolridge,** Edward Daniel 1932- *AmMWSc 92*
**Woolridge,** James Robert, Sr. 1948- *WhoRel 92*
**Woolridge,** Orlando Vernada 1959- *WhoBlA 92*
**Woolridge,** Robert Leonard 1919- *AmMWSc 92*
**Woolridge,** Thomas Jerry 1943- *WhoBlA 92*
**Woolrych,** Austin Herbert 1918- *Who 92, WrDr 92*
**Woolsey,** Clinton Nathan 1904- *AmMWSc 92, IntWW 91*
**Woolsey,** Gary Frederick *Who 92*
**Woolsey,** Gerald Bruce 1937- *AmMWSc 92*
**Woolsey,** Marion Elmer 1919- *AmMWSc 92*
**Woolsey,** Neil Franklin 1935- *AmMWSc 92*
**Woolsey,** R James 1941- *WhoAmP 91*
**Woolsey,** Robert M 1931- *AmMWSc 92*
**Woolsey,** Roy Blakeney 1945- *WhoWest 92*
**Woolsey,** Sarah Chauncey 1835-1905 *BenetAL 91*
**Woolsey,** Theodore Salisbury 1852-1929 *AmPeW*
**Woolsey,** Thomas Allen 1943- *AmMWSc 92, WhoMW 92*
**Woolson,** Constance Fenimore 1840-1894 *BenetAL 91*
**Woolson,** Edwin Albert 1941- *AmMWSc 92*
**Woolston,** Daniel D 1926- *AmMWSc 92*
**Woolston,** Evelyn Doris 1925- *WhoEnt 92*
**Woolston,** Thomas 1670-1733 *BlkwCEP*
**Woolton,** Earl of 1958- *Who 92*
**Woolums,** James, Jr. 1959- *WhoRel 92*
**Woolverton,** Kenneth Arthur 1926- *Who 92*
**Woolverton,** William L 1950- *AmMWSc 92*
**Woolwich,** Bishop Suffragan of 1930- *Who 92*
**Woon,** Peter William 1931- *Who 92*
**Woosley,** Patrick Glenn 1938- *WhoWest 92*
**Woosley,** Raymond Leon 1942- *AmMWSc 92*
**Woosley,** Royce Stanley 1934- *AmMWSc 92*
**Woosley,** Stanford Earl 1944- *AmMWSc 92*
**Woosley,** W Golden 1900- *WhoAmP 91*
**Woosnam,** Charles Richard 1925- *Who 92*
**Woosnam,** Richard Edward 1942- *WhoAmL 92, WhoFI 92*
**Wooster,** Clive Edward Dore 1913- *Who 92*
**Wooster,** Harold Abbott 1919- *AmMWSc 92*
**Wooster,** Warren Scriver 1921- *AmMWSc 92*
**Wootan,** Guy 1938- *WhoAmL 92*
**Wooten,** Carl Kenneth 1947- *WhoBlA 92*
**Wooten,** Chuck 1927- *WhoAmP 91*
**Wooten,** David Barton 1959- *WhoEnt 92*
**Wooten,** Don 1929- *WhoAmP 91*
**Wooten,** Frank Thomas 1935- *AmMWSc 92*
**Wooten,** Frederick 1928- *AmMWSc 92*
**Wooten,** Frederick Oliver 1928- *WhoWest 92*
**Wooten,** Jean W 1929- *AmMWSc 92*
**Wooten,** Joel Orba, Jr. 1950- *WhoAmL 92*
**Wooten,** John David, Jr. 1930- *WhoFI 92*
**Wooten,** John F., III 1963- *WhoFI 92*
**Wooten,** Loren Wesley 1919- *WhoRel 92*
**Wooten,** Marie W *AmMWSc 92*
**Wooten,** Priscilla A 1936- *WhoAmP 91, WhoBlA 92*
**Wooten,** Robert James 1921- *WhoWest 92*
**Wooten,** William James 1924- *WhoFI 92*
**Wooten,** Willis Carl, Jr 1922- *AmMWSc 92*
**Wooten-Bryant,** Helen Catherine 1940- *WhoMW 92*
**Wooters,** Brian Allan 1954- *WhoRel 92*
**Wooton,** John David 1950- *WhoAmP 91*
**Wooton,** William Robert 1944- *WhoAmP 91*
**Wootten,** Henry Alwyn 1948- *AmMWSc 92*
**Wootten,** Michael John 1944- *AmMWSc 92*
**Wootters,** William Kent 1951- *AmMWSc 92*
**Wootton,** Barbara 1897-1988 *FacFETw*
**Wootton,** Charles Greenwood 1924- *IntWW 91*
**Wootton,** Clyde Archer 1941- *WhoAmL 92*
**Wootton,** Donald Merchant 1916- *AmMWSc 92*
**Wootton,** Frank 1911- *TwCPaSc*
**Wootton,** Godfrey *Who 92*
**Wootton,** Gordon Henry 1927- *Who 92*
**Wootton,** Graham 1917- *WrDr 92*
**Wootton,** Ian David Phimester 1921- *Who 92*
**Wootton,** John Francis 1929- *AmMWSc 92*
**Wootton,** Norman Godfrey 1926- *Who 92*
**Wootton,** Peter 1924- *AmMWSc 92*
**Wootton,** Ronald William 1931- *Who 92*
**Woozley,** Anthony Douglas 1912- *Who 92*
**Wopat,** Tom 1951- *IntMPA 92*
**Wopschall,** Robert Harold 1940- *AmMWSc 92*
**Worboys,** Anne *WrDr 92*
**Worboys,** Annette Isobel *IntAu&W 91*
**Worby,** David E. 1951- *WhoAmL 92*
**Worby,** Rachael Beth 1949- *WhoEnt 92*
**Worcester,** Archdeacon of *Who 92*
**Worcester,** Bishop of 1929- *Who 92*
**Worcester,** Dean of *Who 92*
**Worcester,** Marquess of 1952- *Who 92*
**Worcester,** Donald E. 1915- *WrDr 92*
**Worcester,** Elwood 1862-1940 *RelLAm 91*
**Worcester,** Harris Eugene 1950- *WhoAmP 91*
**Worcester,** Joseph Emerson 1784-1865 *BenetAL 91, BiInAmS*
**Worcester,** Noah 1758-1837 *AmPeW*
**Worcester,** Richard Grey 1917- *IntAu&W 91*
**Worcester,** Robert 1933- *ConAu 134*
**Worcester,** Robert Milton 1933- *IntWW 91, Who 92*
**Word,** Carl Oliver 1947- *WhoBlA 92*
**Word,** Fletcher Henry, Jr. 1919- *WhoBlA 92*
**Word,** Parker Howell 1921- *WhoBlA 92*
**Word,** Robert E 1951- *WhoWest 92*
**Wordal,** Blake Jordan 1953- *WhoWest 92*
**Wordell,** Edwin Howland 1927- *WhoWest 92*
**Worden,** Barbara Standley 1942- *WhoRel 92*
**Worden,** David Gilbert 1924- *AmMWSc 92*
**Worden,** Earl Freemont, Jr 1931- *AmMWSc 92*
**Worden,** Harriet Maria 1840-1891 *AmPeW*
**Worden,** Patricia Barron *AmMWSc 92*
**Worden,** Paul Wellman, Jr 1945- *AmMWSc 92*
**Worden,** Richard L, Sr *WhoAmP 91*
**Worden,** Ronald Dean 1938- *WhoRel 92*
**Worden,** Simon Peter 1949- *AmMWSc 92*
**Worden,** William Patrick 1933- *WhoRel 92*
**Wordie,** John 1924- *Who 92*
**Wordinger,** Robert James 1945- *AmMWSc 92*
**Wordlaw,** Clarence, Jr. 1937- *WhoBlA 92*
**Wordley,** Ronald William 1928- *Who 92*
**Wordsworth,** Barry 1948- *Who 92*
**Wordsworth,** Dorothy 1771-1855 *DcLB 107 [port]*
**Wordsworth,** William 1770-1850 *BlkwCEP, CnDBLB 3 [port], DcLB 107 [port], PoeCrit 4 [port], RfGEnL 91*
**Worek,** William Martin 1954- *AmMWSc 92*
**Worenklein,** Jacob Joshua 1948- *WhoAmL 92*
**Worf,** Gayle L 1929- *AmMWSc 92*
**Worford,** Carolyn Kennedy 1949- *WhoBlA 92*
**Worgul,** Basil Vladimir 1947- *AmMWSc 92*
**Worgul,** George S., Jr. 1947- *WhoRel 92*
**Work,** Charles Robert 1940- *WhoAmL 92*
**Work,** Clyde E 1924- *AmMWSc 92*
**Work,** Henry Clay 1832-1884 *BenetAL 91, NewAmDM*
**Work,** Henry Harcus 1911- *AmMWSc 92*
**Work,** James Leroy 1935- *AmMWSc 92*
**Work,** Robert Wyllie 1907- *AmMWSc 92*
**Work,** Stephen Walter 1944- *WhoWest 92*
**Work,** Stewart D 1937- *AmMWSc 92*
**Work,** Telford Hindley 1921- *AmMWSc 92*
**Work,** Thierry Martin 1962- *WhoWest 92*
**Work,** William James 1948- *AmMWSc 92*
**Worker,** George F, Jr 1923- *AmMWSc 92*
**Workman,** Aurora Felice Antonette 1962- *WhoBlA 92*
**Workman,** Betty Gowland 1924- *WhoAmP 91*
**Workman,** Charles Joseph 1920- *Who 92*
**Workman,** Chuck *IntMPA 92*
**Workman,** Clair Blaine 1951- *WhoRel 92*
**Workman,** David A. 1930- *WhoAmL 92*
**Workman,** Fanny 1859-1925 *BenetAL 91*
**Workman,** Gary Lee 1940- *AmMWSc 92*
**Workman,** Haywoode W. 1966- *WhoBlA 92*
**Workman,** John Paul 1943- *AmMWSc 92*
**Workman,** Laural Ann 1960- *WhoWest 92*
**Workman,** Marcus Orrin 1940- *AmMWSc 92*
**Workman,** Margaret L *WhoAmP 91*
**Workman,** Margaret Lee 1947- *WhoAmL 92*
**Workman,** Milton 1920- *AmMWSc 92*
**Workman,** Ralph Burns 1924- *AmMWSc 92*
**Workman,** Robert Little 1914- *Who 92*
**Workman,** Timothy 1943- *Who 92*
**Workman,** Wesley Ray 1926- *AmMWSc 92*
**Workman,** William D., Jr. 1914- *WrDr 92*
**Workman,** William Douglas, III 1940- *WhoAmP 91*
**Workman,** William Edward 1941- *AmMWSc 92*
**Workman,** William Glenn 1947- *AmMWSc 92, WhoWest 92*
**Works,** John Hamilton, Jr. 1954- *WhoAmL 92, WhoEnt 92*
**World Saxophone Quartet** *NewAmDM*
**World's Greatest Jazz Band** *NewAmDM*
**Worley,** Carol Lockard 1962- *WhoAmL 92*
**Worley,** Cherie Linn 1948- *WhoEnt 92*
**Worley,** David Eugene 1929- *AmMWSc 92*
**Worley,** David Wayne 1950- *WhoRel 92*
**Worley,** Frank L, Jr 1929- *AmMWSc 92*
**Worley,** Gary Albert 1957- *WhoRel 92*
**Worley,** Glenn Thomas 1954- *WhoMW 92*
**Worley,** Jane Ludwig 1917- *WhoAmL 92*
**Worley,** Jimmy Weldon 1944- *AmMWSc 92*
**Worley,** Jo Anne 1939- *WhoEnt 92*
**Worley,** John David 1938- *AmMWSc 92*
**Worley,** L. Daryle, Jr. 1961- *WhoRel 92*
**Worley,** Marvin George, Jr. 1934- *WhoMW 92*
**Worley,** Michael Gene 1960- *WhoRel 92*
**Worley,** Paul Creech 1966- *WhoEnt 92*
**Worley,** Ray Edward 1932- *AmMWSc 92*
**Worley,** Richard Dixon 1926- *AmMWSc 92*
**Worley,** Robert Dunkle 1925- *AmMWSc 92*
**Worley,** Robert William, Jr. 1935- *WhoAmL 92*
**Worley,** S D 1942- *AmMWSc 92*
**Worley,** Stella *DrAPF 91*
**Worley,** Timothy Ashley 1966- *WhoBlA 92*
**Worley,** Will J 1919- *AmMWSc 92, WhoMW 92*
**Worley Katz,** Joyce Marie 1939- *WhoWest 92*
**Worlock,** Derek 1920- *WrDr 92*
**Worlock,** Derek John Harford *Who 92*
**Worlock,** Derek John Harford 1920- *IntWW 91*
**Worlock,** John M 1931- *AmMWSc 92*
**Worlock,** Paul Anthony 1931- *WhoAmL 92*
**Wormald,** Brian Harvey Goodwin 1912- *Who 92*
**Wormald,** Derrick Bruce 1916- *Who 92*
**Wormald,** Ethel 1901- *Who 92*
**Wormald,** Peter John 1936- *Who 92*
**Worman,** James John 1940- *AmMWSc 92*
**Worman,** Marna Jo 1932- *WhoAmP 91*
**Worman,** Richard W 1933- *WhoAmP 91*
**Wormhoudt,** Pearl Shinn 1915- *WhoEnt 92*
**Wormley,** Cynthia L. 1953- *WhoBlA 92*
**Wormley,** Diane-Louise Lambert 1948- *WhoBlA 92*
**Wormley,** Edward 1907- *DcTwDes*
**Wormley,** Theodore George 1826-1897 *BiInAmS*
**Worms,** Gerard Etienne 1936- *IntWW 91*

**Wormser** *DrAPF 91*
**Wormser,** Edward Carl 1940- *WhoFI 92*
**Wormser,** Eric M 1921- *AmMWSc 92*
**Wormser,** Gary Paul 1947- *AmMWSc 92*
**Wormser,** Henry C 1936- *AmMWSc 92*
**Wormser,** Richard 1908-1977 *TwCWW 91*
**Wormuth,** John Hazen 1944- *AmMWSc 92*
**Worner,** Howard Knox 1913- *IntWW 91*
**Worner,** Manfred 1934- *IntWW 91, Who 92*
**Worner,** Philip 1910- *WrDr 92*
**Worner,** Philip Arthur Incledon 1910- *IntAu&W 91*
**Wornick,** Robert C 1924- *AmMWSc 92*
**Worns,** John Richard 1940- *WhoMW 92*
**Worny,** Christine May 1941- *WhoMW 92*
**Woroch,** Eugene Leo 1922- *AmMWSc 92*
**Woroniak,** Alexander 1922- *WhoFI 92*
**Woronick,** Charles Louis 1930- *AmMWSc 92*
**Woronicz,** Henry *WhoEnt 92*
**Woronoff,** David Smulyan 1937- *WhoAmL 92, WhoWest 92*
**Woronoff,** Israel 1926- *WhoMW 92*
**Woronov,** Mary 1946- *IntMPA 92*
**Woropay,** Vincent 1951- *TwCPaSc*
**Worrall,** Alfred Stanley 1912- *Who 92*
**Worrall,** Anna Maureen *Who 92*
**Worrall,** Denis John 1935- *IntWW 91, Who 92*
**Worrall,** John Gatland 1938- *AmMWSc 92*
**Worrall,** Ralph Lyndal 1903- *WrDr 92*
**Worrall,** Richard D 1938- *AmMWSc 92*
**Worrall,** Robert Lee 1945- *WhoIns 92*
**Worrall,** Winfield Scott 1921- *AmMWSc 92*
**Worrel,** Charles Joseph 1946- *WhoFI 92*
**Worrell,** Audrey Martiny 1935- *WhoBlA 92*
**Worrell,** Clarendon Lamb 1854-1934 *RelLAm 91*
**Worrell,** E. Clark, Jr. 1915- *WhoFI 92*
**Worrell,** Everil 1893-1969 *ScFEYrs*
**Worrell,** Francis Toussaint 1915- *AmMWSc 92*
**Worrell,** H T Webster *ScFEYrs*
**Worrell,** Jay H 1938- *AmMWSc 92*
**Worrell,** John C. 1926- *WhoFI 92*
**Worrell,** John Mays, Jr 1933- *AmMWSc 92*
**Worrell,** Kaye Sydnell 1952- *WhoBlA 92*
**Worrell,** Lee Anthony 1907- *WhoAmL 92*
**Worrell,** Richard Vernon 1931- *WhoBlA 92, WhoWest 92*
**Worrell,** Wayne L 1937- *AmMWSc 92*
**Worrest,** Robert Charles 1935- *AmMWSc 92*
**Worrill,** Conrad W. 1941- *WhoBlA 92*
**Worrilow,** Bruce David 1958- *WhoEnt 92*
**Worrilow,** Richard Charles 1944- *WhoWest 92*
**Worseck,** Raymond Adams 1937- *WhoFI 92*
**Worsfold,** Reginald Lewis 1925- *Who 92*
**Worsham,** Arch Douglas 1933- *AmMWSc 92*
**Worsham,** Fabian *DrAPF 91*
**Worsham,** Jackson Davis, Jr 1940- *WhoAmP 91*
**Worsham,** James E. 1932- *WhoBlA 92*
**Worsham,** James Essex, Jr 1925- *AmMWSc 92*
**Worsham,** Lesa Marie Spacek 1950- *AmMWSc 92*
**Worsham,** Lew 1917-1990 *CurBio 91N*
**Worsham,** Tommy Dale 1923- *WhoAmP 91*
**Worsham,** Walter Castine 1938- *AmMWSc 92*
**Worskett,** Roy 1932- *Who 92*
**Worsley,** Lord 1990- *Who 92*
**Worsley,** Alice F. *DrAPF 91*
**Worsley,** Dale *DrAPF 91*
**Worsley,** Francis Edward 1941- *Who 92*
**Worsley,** Geoffrey Nicolas Ernest T. C. *Who 92*
**Worsley,** George Ira, Jr. 1927- *WhoBlA 92*
**Worsley,** Godfrey Stuart Harling d1990 *Who 92N*
**Worsley,** Jock *Who 92*
**Worsley,** Marcus *Who 92*
**Worsley,** Michael Dominic Laurence 1926- *Who 92*
**Worsley,** Paul Frederick 1947- *Who 92*
**Worsley,** Richard 1923- *Who 92*
**Worsley,** Richard, Jr. 1942- *WhoRel 92*
**Worsley,** Thomas R 1942- *AmMWSc 92*
**Worsley,** William Marcus 1925- *Who 92*
**Worst,** Susan Gail 1964- *WhoRel 92*
**Worstell,** Hairston G 1920- *AmMWSc 92*
**Worsthorne,** Peregrine 1923- *Who 92*
**Worsthorne,** Peregrine Gerard 1923- *IntAu&W 91, IntWW 91*
**Worswick,** David 1916- *IntWW 91, Who 92*
**Worswick,** Richard David 1946- *Who 92*
**Wort,** Arthur John 1924- *AmMWSc 92*
**Wortell,** Brenton Richard 1955- *WhoMW 92*
**Worth,** Charles Joseph 1948- *WhoBlA 92*
**Worth,** David Albert 1943- *WhoRel 92*
**Worth,** Donald Calhoun 1923- *AmMWSc 92*
**Worth,** Donald James 1940- *WhoMW 92*
**Worth,** Douglas *DrAPF 91*
**Worth,** George Arthur 1907- *Who 92*
**Worth,** Helen 1913- *WrDr 92*
**Worth,** Irene 1916- *FacFETw, IntMPA 92, IntWW 91, Who 92, WhoEnt 92*
**Worth,** James Gallagher 1922- *WhoFI 92*
**Worth,** Katharine Joyce 1922- *Who 92*
**Worth,** Leslie 1923- *TwCPaSc*
**Worth,** Marvin *IntMPA 92*
**Worth,** Peter *TwCSFW 91*
**Worth,** Robert McAlpine 1924- *AmMWSc 92*
**Worth,** Roy Eugene 1938- *AmMWSc 92*
**Worth,** Stefanie Patrice 1962- *WhoBlA 92*
**Wortham,** Jacob James *WhoBlA 92*
**Wortham,** James Calvin 1928- *WhoMW 92*
**Wortham,** James Mason 1954- *WhoFI 92*
**Wortham,** Mark Wayne 1961- *WhoAmL 92*
**Wortham,** Robert John 1947- *WhoAmL 92*
**Worthen,** Amos Henry 1813-1888 *BiInAmS*
**Worthen,** David Scott 1948- *WhoWest 92*
**Worthen,** George Carlton 1871-1919 *BiInAmS*
**Worthen,** Harold M, Jr 1914- *WhoAmP 91*
**Worthen,** Howard George 1925- *AmMWSc 92*
**Worthen,** John Edward 1933- *WhoMW 92*
**Worthen,** Leonard Robert 1925- *AmMWSc 92*
**Worthen,** Naz Onea 1966- *WhoBlA 92*
**Worthen,** Robert D 1947- *WhoAmP 91*
**Worthey,** Carol 1943- *WhoWest 92*
**Worthey,** Richard E. 1934- *WhoBlA 92*
**Worthing,** Carol Marie 1934- *WhoMW 92, WhoRel 92*
**Worthing,** Jurgen 1924- *AmMWSc 92*
**Worthing,** Richard Westlake 1941- *WhoIns 92*
**Worthington,** Anthony 1941- *Who 92*
**Worthington,** Charles Roy 1925- *AmMWSc 92*
**Worthington,** Don Roy 1946- *WhoRel 92*
**Worthington,** Edgar Barton 1905- *IntWW 91, Who 92, WrDr 92*
**Worthington,** Geoffrey 1903- *Who 92*
**Worthington,** George Noel 1923- *Who 92*
**Worthington,** James Brian 1943- *AmMWSc 92*
**Worthington,** John Rice 1930- *WhoAmL 92*
**Worthington,** John Wilbur 1918- *AmMWSc 92*
**Worthington,** Lorne R 1938- *WhoAmP 91*
**Worthington,** Lorne Raymond 1938- *WhoFI 92*
**Worthington,** Meg 1956- *WhoAmP 91*
**Worthington,** Melvin Leroy 1937- *WhoRel 92*
**Worthington,** Norman Addison, III 1959- *WhoWest 92*
**Worthington,** Pete 1940- *WhoAmP 91*
**Worthington,** Ralph Eric 1926- *AmMWSc 92*
**Worthington,** Richard Dane 1941- *AmMWSc 92*
**Worthington,** Robert Earl 1929- *AmMWSc 92*
**Worthington,** Robert Melvin 1922- *WhoAmP 91*
**Worthington,** Thomas Kimber 1947- *AmMWSc 92*
**Worthington,** Ward Curtis, Jr 1925- *AmMWSc 92*
**Worthington,** William D 1947- *WhoIns 92*
**Worthley,** Harold Field 1928- *WhoRel 92*
**Worthman,** Robert Paul 1919- *AmMWSc 92*
**Worthy,** Barbara Ann 1942- *WhoBlA 92*
**Worthy,** Graham Anthony James 1956- *AmMWSc 92*
**Worthy,** James 1961- *News 91 [port], WhoBlA 92, WhoWest 92*
**Worthy,** Kenneth Martin 1920- *WhoAmL 92, WhoAmP 91*
**Worthy,** Larry Elliott 1953- *WhoBlA 92*
**Worthy,** William, Jr. 1921- *WhoBlA 92*
**Wortinger,** John Keith 1946- *WhoRel 92*
**Wortis,** Michael 1936- *AmMWSc 92*
**Wortley,** George C 1926- *WhoAmP 91*
**Wortman,** Allen L. 1935- *WhoRel 92*
**Wortman,** Bernard 1924- *AmMWSc 92*
**Wortman,** Don Irvin 1927- *WhoAmP 91*
**Wortman,** Jimmie J 1936- *AmMWSc 92*
**Wortman,** Joseph John 1940- *WhoIns 92*
**Wortman,** Sterling 1923-1981 *FacFETw*
**Worts,** George Frank, Jr 1916- *AmMWSc 92*
**Wortzel,** Lawrence Herbert 1932- *WhoFI 92*
**Worzala,** F John 1933- *AmMWSc 92*
**Worzel,** John Lamar 1919- *AmMWSc 92*
**Wos,** Carol Elaine 1957- *WhoMW 92*
**Wos,** Joanna H. *DrAPF 91*
**Wos,** Lawrence 1930- *WhoMW 92*
**Wosh,** Peter Joseph 1954- *WhoRel 92*
**Wosilait,** Walter Daniel 1924- *AmMWSc 92*
**Wosinski,** John Francis 1930- *AmMWSc 92*
**Woske,** Harry Max 1924- *AmMWSc 92*
**Woskov,** Paul Peter 1950- *AmMWSc 92*
**Woskow,** Robert Marshall 1951- *WhoWest 92*
**Wossner,** Mark Matthias *Who 92*
**Woster,** Patrick Michael 1955- *AmMWSc 92*
**Wostmann,** Bernard Stephan 1918- *AmMWSc 92*
**Wotherspoon,** Neil 1930- *AmMWSc 92*
**Wothke,** Werner 1952- *WhoMW 92*
**Wotiska,** Dorita *WhoRel 92*
**Wotiz,** Herbert Henry 1922- *AmMWSc 92*
**Wotiz,** John Henry 1919- *AmMWSc 92*
**Wotquenne,** Alfred 1867-1939 *NewAmDM*
**Wott,** John Arthur 1939- *AmMWSc 92, WhoWest 92*
**Wotton,** Henry 1568-1639 *RfGEnL 91*
**Wotton,** William 1666-1727 *BlkwCEP*
**Wotzak,** Gregory Paul 1944- *AmMWSc 92*
**Wouczyna,** James Michael 1946- *WhoAmL 92*
**Woudenberg,** Paul Richard 1927- *WhoRel 92, WhoWest 92*
**Wouk,** Arthur 1924- *AmMWSc 92*
**Wouk,** Herman 1915- *BenetAL 91, ConNov 91, IntAu&W 91, IntWW 91, Who 92, WhoRel 92, WrDr 92*
**Wouk,** Victor 1919- *AmMWSc 92*
**Woundy,** Douglas Stanley 1939- *WhoFI 92*
**Wourms,** John P 1937- *AmMWSc 92*
**Wouts,** Bernard Francois Emile 1940- *IntWW 91*
**Wovcha,** Merle G 1938- *AmMWSc 92*
**Wovoka** 1856?-1932 *RelLAm 91*
**Wovsaniker,** Alan 1953- *WhoAmL 92*
**Wowchuk,** Harry N. 1948- *IntMPA 92*
**Wowchuk,** Nicholas *IntMPA 92*
**Wowk,** Wira 1926- *LiExTwC*
**Woychik,** John Henry 1930- *AmMWSc 92*
**Woychik,** Richard P 1952- *AmMWSc 92*
**Woyski,** Margaret Skillman 1921- *AmMWSc 92, WhoWest 92*
**Woyt,** James Jim Charles 1950- *WhoEnt 92*
**Woythal,** Constance Lee 1954- *WhoMW 92*
**Woytowicz-Rudnicka,** Stefania 1922- *IntWW 91*
**Wozab,** David Hyrum 1923- *AmMWSc 92*
**Wozencraft,** Frank McReynolds 1923- *WhoAmL 92*
**Wozencraft,** John McReynolds 1925- *AmMWSc 92*
**Wozencraft,** Sharon Anne 1945- *WhoRel 92*
**Wozniak,** Chester *WhoAmP 91*
**Wozniak,** Daniel Duane 1946- *WhoEnt 92*
**Wozniak,** John N 1956- *WhoAmP 91*
**Wozniak,** Joyce Marie 1955- *WhoEnt 92, WhoWest 92*
**Wozniak,** Wayne Theodore 1945- *AmMWSc 92*
**Wraase,** Dennis Richard 1944- *WhoFI 92*
**Wrabec,** Paul Joseph 1956- *WhoAmP 91*
**Wrack,** Philip 1929- *IntAu&W 91*
**Wragg,** David W. 1946- *WrDr 92*
**Wragg,** Edward Conrad 1938- *Who 92, WrDr 92*
**Wragg,** Gary 1946- *TwCPaSc*
**Wragg,** Harry 1902-1985 *FacFETw*
**Wragg,** Joanna DiCarlo 1941- *ConAu 133*
**Wragg,** John 1937- *Who 92*
**Wragg,** Laishley Palmer, Jr. 1933- *WhoAmL 92, WhoFI 92*
**Wraight,** Colin Allen 1945- *AmMWSc 92*
**Wraight,** John 1916- *Who 92*
**Wralstad,** Phillip Evans 1932- *WhoWest 92*
**Wran,** Neville Kenneth *IntWW 91, Who 92*
**Wrangel,** Peter Nikolayevich 1878-1928 *FacFETw*
**Wrase,** Julie Ann *WhoAmL 92*
**Wrasidlo,** Wolfgang Johann 1938- *AmMWSc 92*
**Wrathall,** Donald Prior 1936- *AmMWSc 92*
**Wrathall,** Jay W 1933- *AmMWSc 92*
**Wrathall,** Jean Rew 1942- *AmMWSc 92*
**Wrathall,** John James 1913-1978 *FacFETw*
**Wrather,** Jack d1984 *LesBEnT 92*
**Wratten,** Donald Peter 1925- *Who 92*
**Wratten,** William 1939- *Who 92*
**Wraxall,** Baron 1928- *Who 92*
**Wraxall,** Charles 1961- *Who 92*
**Wray,** Cecil, Jr. 1934- *WhoAmL 92*
**Wray,** David Lynn 1947- *WhoMW 92*
**Wray,** David Marshall 1949- *WhoEnt 92*
**Wray,** Elizabeth *DrAPF 91*
**Wray,** Fay 1907- *IntMPA 92*
**Wray,** Gordon Richard 1928- *IntWW 91, Who 92*
**Wray,** Granville Wayne 1941- *AmMWSc 92*
**Wray,** H Linton 1940- *AmMWSc 92*
**Wray,** James 1938- *Who 92*
**Wray,** James Creighton 1935- *WhoAmL 92*
**Wray,** James David 1936- *AmMWSc 92*
**Wray,** Joe D 1926- *AmMWSc 92*
**Wray,** John L 1935- *AmMWSc 92*
**Wray,** John Lee 1925- *AmMWSc 92*
**Wray,** John Mark 1959- *WhoAmL 92*
**Wray,** Joseph Wayne 1952- *WhoMW 92*
**Wray,** Karl 1913- *WhoWest 92*
**Wray,** Larry Randall 1953- *WhoWest 92*
**Wray,** Mark S 1953- *WhoIns 92*
**Wray,** Martin Osterfield d1991 *Who 92N*
**Wray,** Porter R 1913- *AmMWSc 92*
**Wray,** Robert Oakley, Jr. 1957- *WhoFI 92*
**Wray,** Ron *DrAPF 91*
**Wray,** Stephen Donald 1947- *AmMWSc 92*
**Wray,** Virginia Lee Pollan 1940- *AmMWSc 92*
**Wray,** Wendell Leonard 1926- *WhoBlA 92*
**Wrede,** Patricia C. 1953- *Au&Arts 8 [port], ConAu 134, SmATA 67 [port]*
**Wrede,** Robert C, Jr 1926- *AmMWSc 92*
**Wreford,** James *IntAu&W 91X*
**Wreford,** Stanley S 1949- *AmMWSc 92*
**Wrege,** Beth Marie 1954- *WhoWest 92*
**Wrege,** Hans-Theo 1934- *WhoRel 92*
**Wren,** Christopher G. 1950- *WrDr 92*
**Wren,** Douglas Gerard 1950- *WhoEnt 92*
**Wren,** Harold Gwyn 1921- *WhoAmL 92*
**Wren,** Jill Robinson 1954- *WhoAmL 92, WrDr 92*
**Wren,** Joe Richard 1944- *WhoRel 92*
**Wren,** John E. 1939- *WhoRel 92*
**Wren,** Peter 1949- *WhoRel 92*
**Wren,** Thomas Wayne 1922- *WhoFI 92*
**Wren,** William C 1933- *WhoIns 92*
**Wrenbury,** Baron 1927- *Who 92*
**Wrenn,** McDonald Edward 1936- *AmMWSc 92*
**Wrenn,** Thomas H., III 1942- *WhoBlA 92*
**Wrenn,** Walter Bruce 1950- *WhoMW 92*
**Wrenn,** William J 1935- *AmMWSc 92*
**Wrenn,** William James, Jr. 1932- *WhoRel 92*
**Wrenn,** William L. 1958- *WhoWest 92*
**Wrensch,** Dana Louise 1946- *AmMWSc 92*
**Wrexham,** Bishop of 1928- *Who 92*
**Wrey,** Bourchier 1903- *Who 92*
**Wrice,** David 1937- *WhoBlA 92*
**Wride,** W James 1921- *AmMWSc 92*
**Wriedt,** Henry Anderson 1928- *AmMWSc 92*
**Wriedt,** Kenneth Shaw 1927- *IntWW 91*
**Wriggins,** William Howard 1918- *WhoAmP 91*
**Wrigglesworth,** Ian 1939- *Who 92*
**Wright Brothers** *DcTwDes, FacFETw*
**Wright of Derby** 1734-1797 *BlkwCEP*
**Wright,** A.J. *DrAPF 91*
**Wright,** A. J. 1952- *WrDr 92*
**Wright,** Alan Carl 1939- *AmMWSc 92*
**Wright,** Alan John 1925- *Who 92*
**Wright,** Albert Allen 1846-1905 *BiInAmS*
**Wright,** Albert Walter, Jr. 1925- *WhoBlA 92*
**Wright,** Alden Halbert 1942- *AmMWSc 92, WhoWest 92*
**Wright,** Alec Michael John 1912- *Who 92*
**Wright,** Alex 1967- *WhoBlA 92*
**Wright,** Alfred George James 1916- *WhoEnt 92*
**Wright,** Alison Elizabeth 1945- *Who 92*
**Wright,** Allan Frederick 1929- *Who 92*
**Wright,** Allen Kendrick *ScFEYrs*
**Wright,** Alonzo Gordon 1930- *WhoBlA 92*
**Wright,** Alvin 1961- *WhoBlA 92*
**Wright,** Amy 1950- *ConTFT 9, IntMPA 92*
**Wright,** Andrew 1935- *AmMWSc 92*
**Wright,** Andrew Scott 1952- *WhoAmP 91*
**Wright,** Ann Elizabeth 1922- *AmMWSc 92*
**Wright,** Anne Margaret 1946- *Who 92*
**Wright,** Anthony Aune 1943- *AmMWSc 92*
**Wright,** Archibald Nelson 1932- *AmMWSc 92*
**Wright,** Ardis Ruth 1939- *WhoRel 92*
**Wright,** Arthur Francis Stevenson 1918- *Who 92*
**Wright,** Arthur Franklin 1950- *WhoMW 92*
**Wright,** Arthur McIntosh 1930- *WhoAmL 92*
**Wright,** Arthur Robert Donald 1923- *Who 92*
**Wright,** Arthur W *WhoIns 92*
**Wright,** Arthur Williams 1836-1915 *BiInAmS*

**Wright**, Austin *DrAPF 91*
**Wright**, Austin 1911- *TwCPaSc*
**Wright**, Austin M. 1922- *WrDr 92*
**Wright**, Austin McGiffert 1922- *WhoMW 92*
**Wright**, Austin Tappan 1883-1931 *TwCSFW 91*
**Wright**, Barbara 1935- *IntWW 91*
**Wright**, Barbara Evelyn 1926- *AmMWSc 92*
**Wright**, Barton Allen 1920- *WhoWest 92*
**Wright**, Basil 1907-1987 *IntDcF 2-2 [port]*
**Wright**, Beatrice Frederika *Who 92*
**Wright**, Benjamen 1952- *Who 92*
**Wright**, Benjamin 1957- *WhoAmL 92*
**Wright**, Benjamin Drake 1926- *WhoMW 92*
**Wright**, Benjamin Hickman 1923- *WhoBlA 92*
**Wright**, Bernard 1938- *WhoWest 92*
**Wright**, Betsey *WhoAmP 91*
**Wright**, Bill 1947- *WhoAmP 91*
**Wright**, Bill C 1930- *AmMWSc 92*
**Wright**, Billy *Who 92*
**Wright**, Billy Beryl 1926- *WhoAmP 91*
**Wright**, Blandin James 1947- *WhoAmL 92*
**Wright**, Brad 1949- *WhoAmP 91*
**Wright**, Bradley James 1960- *WhoMW 92*
**Wright**, Bradley R. 1959- *WhoWest 92*
**Wright**, Brian 1937- *TwCPaSc*
**Wright**, Bruce McM. 1918- *WhoBlA 92*
**Wright**, Byron Terry 1917- *AmMWSc 92*
**Wright**, C.D. *DrAPF 91*
**Wright**, C. Evan 1954- *WhoEnt 92*
**Wright**, C. T. Enus 1942- *WhoBlA 92*
**Wright**, Caleb Merrill 1908- *WhoAmL 92*
**Wright**, Carl Jeffrey 1954- *WhoBlA 92*
**Wright**, Carole Yvonne 1932- *WhoWest 92*
**Wright**, Carolyn Elaine 1951- *WhoBlA 92*
**Wright**, Carolyne *DrAPF 91*
**Wright**, Carroll D 1840-1909 *DcAmImH*
**Wright**, Carroll Davidson 1840-1909 *BiInAmS*
**Wright**, Cathie 1929- *WhoAmP 91*
**Wright**, Celeste Turner 1906- *WrDr 92*
**Wright**, Charles *DrAPF 91*
**Wright**, Charles 1811-1885 *BiInAmS*
**Wright**, Charles 1918- *WhoBlA 92*
**Wright**, Charles 1931- *TwCPaSc*
**Wright**, Charles 1932- *BlkLC [port]*, *ConNov 91*
**Wright**, Charles 1935- *BenetAL 91*, *ConAu 36NR*, *ConPo 91*, *WrDr 92*
**Wright**, Charles Alan 1927- *WhoAmL 92*
**Wright**, Charles Cathbert 1919- *AmMWSc 92*
**Wright**, Charles Dean 1930- *AmMWSc 92*
**Wright**, Charles E. 1946- *WhoBlA 92*
**Wright**, Charles Edward 1906- *WhoAmL 92*
**Wright**, Charles Edward 1953- *WhoRel 92*
**Wright**, Charles Gerald 1930- *AmMWSc 92*
**Wright**, Charles H. 1918- *WhoBlA 92*
**Wright**, Charles Hubert 1922- *AmMWSc 92*
**Wright**, Charles Joseph 1938- *AmMWSc 92*
**Wright**, Charles Keeney 1941- *WhoAmL 92*
**Wright**, Charles Lee 1949- *WhoWest 92*
**Wright**, Charles Penzel, Jr 1935- *IntAu&W 91*
**Wright**, Charles R B 1937- *AmMWSc 92*
**Wright**, Charles S. *DrAPF 91*
**Wright**, Charles Stevenson 1932- *WhoBlA 92*
**Wright**, Charles Ted 1931- *WhoAmP 91*
**Wright**, Charles William 1954- *WhoFI 92*
**Wright**, Charlotte Megan 1951- *WhoWest 92*
**Wright**, Chatt Grandison 1941- *WhoWest 92*
**Wright**, Chauncey 1830-1875 *BiInAmS*
**Wright**, Christopher 1924- *WrDr 92*
**Wright**, Christopher H. 1953- *WhoEnt 92*
**Wright**, Christopher Niss 1951- *WhoFI 92*
**Wright**, Clarence Johnnie, Sr. 1953- *WhoBlA 92*
**Wright**, Clarence Paul 1939- *AmMWSc 92*
**Wright**, Claud William 1917- *Who 92*
**Wright**, Cloyd 1922- *WhoRel 92*
**Wright**, Conrad 1917- *WrDr 92*
**Wright**, Craig 1929- *WhoAmL 92*, *WhoMW 92*
**Wright**, Creighton Bolter 1939- *WhoMW 92*
**Wright**, Dana Jace 1952- *WhoFI 92*
**Wright**, Daniel Craig 1954- *AmMWSc 92*
**Wright**, Daniel Godwin 1945- *AmMWSc 92*
**Wright**, David 1920- *ConPo 91*, *IntAu&W 91*, *LiExTwC*, *WrDr 92*
**Wright**, David Alan 1961- *WhoMW 92*
**Wright**, David Anthony 1941- *AmMWSc 92*
**Wright**, David Austin 1955- *WhoAmP 91*
**Wright**, David B 1950- *WhoAmP 91*
**Wright**, David Carl 1962- *WhoEnt 92*
**Wright**, David Franklin 1929- *AmMWSc 92*
**Wright**, David Grant 1946- *AmMWSc 92*
**Wright**, David H. d1991 *NewYTBS 91*
**Wright**, David John 1944- *Who 92*
**Wright**, David Lee 1946- *WhoWest 92*
**Wright**, David Lee 1949- *AmMWSc 92*
**Wright**, David Lee 1962- *WhoAmP 91*
**Wright**, David Patrick 1943- *AmMWSc 92*
**Wright**, David R 1935- *WhoAmP 91*
**Wright**, Debbra Kaye 1952- *WhoWest 92*
**Wright**, Denis 1911- *Who 92*
**Wright**, Dennis Charles 1939- *AmMWSc 92*
**Wright**, Desmond Garforth 1923- *Who 92*
**Wright**, Dexter V 1923- *AmMWSc 92*
**Wright**, Dmitri 1948- *WhoBlA 92*
**Wright**, Donald *Who 92*
**Wright**, Donald C 1951- *AmMWSc 92*
**Wright**, Donald Kenneth 1951- *WhoRel 92*
**Wright**, Donald N 1935- *AmMWSc 92*
**Wright**, Donna Gale 1923- *WhoAmP 91*
**Wright**, Doris Erleane 1920- *WhoMW 92*
**Wright**, Dorothy Winslow *DrAPF 91*
**Wright**, Dorris D. 1950- *WhoBlA 92*
**Wright**, Douglas S *WhoAmP 91*
**Wright**, Douglas Tyndall 1927- *AmMWSc 92*
**Wright**, Douglass Brownell 1912- *WhoAmL 92*
**Wright**, Earl Lee 1941- *WhoBlA 92*
**Wright**, Earl Louis 1943- *WhoFI 92*
**Wright**, Earl W. 1902- *WhoBlA 92*
**Wright**, Ebony Narketa 1960- *WhoBlA 92*
**Wright**, Edmund Gordon, Mrs. *Who 92*
**Wright**, Edward 1906- *Who 92*
**Wright**, Edward 1912- *TwCPaSc*
**Wright**, Edward G 1948- *WhoIns 92*
**Wright**, Edward Kenneth 1930- *AmMWSc 92*
**Wright**, Edward Lucius 1925- *WhoBlA 92*
**Wright**, Eleanor Straub 1923- *WhoMW 92*
**Wright**, Elisabeth Muriel Jane 1926- *AmMWSc 92*
**Wright**, Elizabeth 1872-1906 *NotBlAW 92 [port]*
**Wright**, Elizur 1762-1845 *BiInAmS*
**Wright**, Elizur, Jr 1804-1885 *BiInAmS*
**Wright**, Emmett Lee 1940- *WhoMW 92*
**Wright**, Eric 1933- *Who 92*
**Wright**, Eric 1959- *WhoBlA 92*
**Wright**, Eric David 1917- *Who 92*
**Wright**, Ernest Marshall 1940- *AmMWSc 92*
**Wright**, Ernest Robert 1944- *WhoAmL 92*
**Wright**, Esmond 1915- *IntAu&W 91*, *Who 92*, *WrDr 92*
**Wright**, Eugene Allen 1913- *WhoAmL 92*
**Wright**, Eugene Joseph 1923- *WhoEnt 92*
**Wright**, Everett James 1929- *AmMWSc 92*
**Wright**, Fanny 1795-1852 *BenetAL 91*
**Wright**, Farrin Scott 1936- *AmMWSc 92*
**Wright**, Farroll Tim 1941- *AmMWSc 92*
**Wright**, Faye 1914- *WhoRel 92*, *WhoWest 92*
**Wright**, Frances 1795-1852 *AmPeW*, *RComAH*
**Wright**, Frances Jane 1943- *WhoWest 92*
**Wright**, Francis Howell 1908- *AmMWSc 92*
**Wright**, Francis Stuart 1929- *AmMWSc 92*
**Wright**, Frank Clarence, Jr. 1942- *WhoAmL 92*
**Wright**, Frank Lloyd 1867-1959 *DcTwDes*, *FacFETw [port]*, *RComAH*
**Wright**, Frank Lloyd 1869-1959 *BenetAL 91*
**Wright**, Franklin Leatherbury, Jr. 1945- *WhoFI 92*
**Wright**, Fred Boyer 1925- *AmMWSc 92*
**Wright**, Fred D 1916- *AmMWSc 92*
**Wright**, Fred Marion 1923- *AmMWSc 92*
**Wright**, Fred W., Jr. *DrAPF 91*
**Wright**, Fred W, Jr 1940- *IntAu&W 91*
**Wright**, Frederick Bennie 1950- *WhoBlA 92*
**Wright**, Frederick Douglass 1946- *WhoBlA 92*
**Wright**, Frederick Fenning 1934- *AmMWSc 92*
**Wright**, Frederick Hamilton 1912- *AmMWSc 92*
**Wright**, Frederick Herman Greene, II 1952- *WhoWest 92*
**Wright**, Frederick Lewis, II 1951- *WhoAmL 92*
**Wright**, Gail Delores 1947- *WhoFI 92*
**Wright**, Garland 1946- *WhoEnt 92*, *WhoMW 92*
**Wright**, Gary Albert 1948- *WhoWest 92*
**Wright**, Gary Donald 1944- *WhoAmP 91*
**Wright**, Georg Henrik von 1916- *IntWW 91*, *Who 92*
**Wright**, George C., Jr. 1932- *WhoBlA 92*
**Wright**, George Cullen 1923- *WhoFI 92*
**Wright**, George Dewitt 1958- *WhoBlA 92*
**Wright**, George Edward 1941- *AmMWSc 92*
**Wright**, George Green 1916- *AmMWSc 92*
**Wright**, George Henry 1935- *Who 92*
**Wright**, George Joseph 1931- *AmMWSc 92*
**Wright**, George Leonard, Jr 1937- *AmMWSc 92*
**Wright**, George Nelson 1921- *WhoMW 92*
**Wright**, George Paul 1919- *Who 92*
**Wright**, George T. *DrAPF 91*
**Wright**, George Thaddeus 1925- *WrDr 92*
**Wright**, George W 1923- *WhoAmP 91*
**Wright**, Gerald Ged 1942- *WhoAmP 91*
**Wright**, Gerard 1929- *Who 92*
**Wright**, Gerry 1931- *TwCPaSc*
**Wright**, Glenn Theodore 1958- *WhoEnt 92*
**Wright**, Gordon Braxton 1957- *WhoAmL 92*
**Wright**, Gordon Brooks 1934- *WhoEnt 92*, *WhoWest 92*
**Wright**, Gordon Kennedy 1920- *WhoAmL 92*
**Wright**, Graeme Alexander 1943- *IntAu&W 91*, *Who 92*
**Wright**, Grover Cleveland 1916- *WhoBlA 92*
**Wright**, H. Myles 1908- *Who 92*
**Wright**, H. S., III 1953- *WhoMW 92*
**Wright**, Hamilton Kemp 1867-1917 *BiInAmS*
**Wright**, Harold *WhoEnt 92*
**Wright**, Harold Bell 1872-1944 *BenetAL 91*, *TwCWW 91*
**Wright**, Harold E 1920- *AmMWSc 92*
**Wright**, Harold Stanley 1918- *WhoAmL 92*
**Wright**, Harriette Simon 1915- *WhoBlA 92*
**Wright**, Harry, III 1925- *WhoAmL 92*
**Wright**, Harry Forrest, Jr. 1931- *WhoFI 92*
**Wright**, Harry Tucker, Jr 1929- *AmMWSc 92*
**Wright**, Harvel Amos 1933- *AmMWSc 92*
**Wright**, Hastings Kemper 1928- *AmMWSc 92*
**Wright**, Helen Kennedy 1927- *WhoFI 92*, *WhoMW 92*
**Wright**, Helen L. 1932- *WrDr 92*
**Wright**, Helen S 1936- *AmMWSc 92*
**Wright**, Helene Segal 1955- *WhoWest 92*
**Wright**, Henry Albert 1935- *AmMWSc 92*
**Wright**, Henry Clarke 1797-1870 *AmPeW*
**Wright**, Herbert Edgar, Jr 1917- *AmMWSc 92*
**Wright**, Herbert Fessenden 1917- *AmMWSc 92*
**Wright**, Herbert N 1928- *AmMWSc 92*
**Wright**, Howard *WhoBlA 92*
**Wright**, Howard Stephen 1957- *WhoMW 92*
**Wright**, Hugh Raymond 1938- *Who 92*
**Wright**, Ian Glaisby 1935- *AmMWSc 92*
**Wright**, J. Anthony 1952- *WhoMW 92*
**Wright**, J Craig 1929- *WhoAmP 91*
**Wright**, J Skelly 1911-1988 *FacFETw*
**Wright**, Jack Clifford 1933- *Who 92*
**Wright**, Jackson Thomas, Jr. 1944- *WhoBlA 92*
**Wright**, James 1927-1980 *BenetAL 91*, *ConAu 34NR*
**Wright**, James A. 1937- *WhoBlA 92*
**Wright**, James Arthur 1941- *AmMWSc 92*
**Wright**, James Bryan 1955- *WhoAmL 92*, *WhoWest 92*
**Wright**, James C, Jr 1922- *WhoAmP 91*
**Wright**, James Campbell 1939- *WhoEnt 92*
**Wright**, James Christopher 1918- *WhoBlA 92*
**Wright**, James Claude, Jr. 1922- *AmPolLe*, *IntWW 91*, *Who 92*
**Wright**, James Corwin 1959- *WhoEnt 92*
**Wright**, James D., Jr. 1953- *WhoFI 92*
**Wright**, James Edward 1946- *AmMWSc 92*
**Wright**, James Edward 1956- *WhoRel 92*
**Wright**, James Elbert 1940- *AmMWSc 92*
**Wright**, James Everett, Jr 1923- *AmMWSc 92*
**Wright**, James Foley 1943- *AmMWSc 92*
**Wright**, James Francis 1924- *AmMWSc 92*
**Wright**, James Houston 1954- *WhoRel 92*
**Wright**, James L, Jr 1925- *WhoAmP 91*
**Wright**, James Lashua 1934- *WhoAmP 91*
**Wright**, James Leroy 1947- *WhoAmP 91*
**Wright**, James Louis 1934- *AmMWSc 92*
**Wright**, James P 1934- *AmMWSc 92*
**Wright**, James R 1916- *AmMWSc 92*
**Wright**, James R. 1941- *WhoBlA 92*
**Wright**, James Richard 1921- *WhoBlA 92*
**Wright**, James Roscoe 1922- *AmMWSc 92*
**Wright**, James Sherman 1940- *AmMWSc 92*
**Wright**, Jane C. 1919- *NotBlAW 92*, *WhoBlA 92*
**Wright**, Jay Kelly 1943- *WhoAmL 92*
**Wright**, Jeanne Jason 1934- *WhoBlA 92*
**Wright**, Jefferson W. 1935- *WhoBlA 92*
**Wright**, Jeffery Regan 1950- *AmMWSc 92*
**Wright**, Jeffrey Chapman 1939- *WhoMW 92*
**Wright**, Jeffrey Cyphers *DrAPF 91*
**Wright**, Jeffrey David 1952- *WhoEnt 92*
**Wright**, Jeffrey Joseph 1951- *WhoFI 92*
**Wright**, Jeffrey L 1945- *WhoAmP 91*
**Wright**, Jerauld 1898- *Who 92*
**Wright**, Jeremiah A., Jr. 1941- *WhoBlA 92*
**Wright**, Jeremiah Alvesta, Jr. 1941- *WhoRel 92*
**Wright**, Jerry Raymond 1935- *WhoFI 92*
**Wright**, Jim *WhoAmP 91*
**Wright**, Jim 1946- *WhoAmP 91*
**Wright**, Jim Lee 1952- *WhoFI 92*
**Wright**, Joe 1940- *WhoAmP 91*
**Wright**, Joe Booth 1920- *Who 92*
**Wright**, Joe Carroll 1933- *AmMWSc 92*
**Wright**, John 1921- *Who 92*
**Wright**, John 1931- *TwCPaSc*
**Wright**, John 1932- *TwCPaSc*
**Wright**, John Aaron 1939- *WhoBlA 92*
**Wright**, John Beckley, II 1954- *WhoAmL 92*
**Wright**, John Buckland 1897-1954 *TwCPaSc*
**Wright**, John Charles 1941- *WhoRel 92*
**Wright**, John Clifford 1919- *AmMWSc 92*
**Wright**, John Curtis 1943- *AmMWSc 92*
**Wright**, John Fowler 1921- *AmMWSc 92*
**Wright**, John Hurrell C. *Who 92*
**Wright**, John Jay 1943- *AmMWSc 92*
**Wright**, John Joseph 1909-1979 *RelLAm 91*
**Wright**, John Keith 1928- *Who 92*
**Wright**, John King 1947- *WhoIns 92*
**Wright**, John Lewis 1939- *WhoMW 92*
**Wright**, John Marlin 1937- *AmMWSc 92*
**Wright**, John Michael 1932- *Who 92*
**Wright**, John Murray 1951- *WhoRel 92*
**Wright**, John Oliver 1921- *IntWW 91*, *Who 92*
**Wright**, John Pardee 1957- *WhoFI 92*
**Wright**, John Ricken 1939- *AmMWSc 92*
**Wright**, John Robert 1928- *WhoFI 92*
**Wright**, John Robert 1953- *WhoWest 92*
**Wright**, John Stewart 1923- *WhoMW 92*
**Wright**, John Winfred 1949- *WhoAmL 92*
**Wright**, Johnie Algie 1924- *AmMWSc 92*
**Wright**, Jon Alan 1938- *AmMWSc 92*
**Wright**, Jonathan Clifford 1949- *WhoIns 92*
**Wright**, Joseph 1734-1797 *BlkwCEP*
**Wright**, Joseph 1917- *Who 92*
**Wright**, Joseph D 1941- *AmMWSc 92*
**Wright**, Joseph Edmund 1878-1910 *BiInAmS*
**Wright**, Joseph H., Jr. 1954- *WhoBlA 92*
**Wright**, Joseph Malcolm 1944- *WhoBlA 92*
**Wright**, Joseph William, Jr 1916- *AmMWSc 92*
**Wright**, Joyce C. 1951- *WhoBlA 92*
**Wright**, Joyce Kline 1957- *WhoAmL 92*
**Wright**, Judith 1915- *ConPo 91*, *RfGEnL 91*, *Who 92*
**Wright**, Judith 1941- *AmMWSc 92*
**Wright**, Judith Arundell 1915- *IntWW 91*, *WrDr 92*
**Wright**, Judith Margaret 1944- *WhoAmL 92*
**Wright**, Julia Ann 1935- *WhoMW 92*
**Wright**, Julia McNair 1840-1903 *BiInAmS*
**Wright**, Julie Adesina 1957- *WhoBlA 92*
**Wright**, Julius Arnette, III 1951- *WhoAmP 91*
**Wright**, K.C. *DrAPF 91*
**Wright**, Kathleen C. 1935-1985 *WhoBlA 92N*
**Wright**, Kathleen Jean 1955- *WhoWest 92*
**Wright**, Katie Harper 1923- *WhoBlA 92*
**Wright**, Keith Derek, Sr. 1953- *WhoBlA 92*
**Wright**, Kenneth *IntAu&W 91X*, *TwCSFW 91*, *WrDr 92*
**Wright**, Kenneth d1991 *Who 92N*
**Wright**, Kenneth Brooks 1934- *WhoAmL 92*
**Wright**, Kenneth C *AmMWSc 92*
**Wright**, Kenneth Campbell 1932- *Who 92*
**Wright**, Kenneth Dale 1950- *WhoAmP 91*
**Wright**, Kenneth E 1941- *WhoAmP 91*
**Wright**, Kenneth James 1939- *AmMWSc 92*
**Wright**, Kenneth Lyle 1926- *WhoWest 92*
**Wright**, Kenneth Osborne 1911- *AmMWSc 92*
**Wright**, Kit 1944- *ConPo 91*, *WrDr 92*
**Wright**, Kurtis Carlton 1941- *WhoWest 92*
**Wright**, Lance Armitage 1915- *Who 92*
**Wright**, Larry L. 1953- *WhoBlA 92*
**Wright**, Latham Ephraim, Jr. 1925- *WhoRel 92*
**Wright**, Laurali Rose 1939- *IntAu&W 91*
**Wright**, Lauren Albert 1918- *AmMWSc 92*
**Wright**, Lawrence A. 1927- *WhoFI 92*
**Wright**, Lawrence George 1947- *WhoEnt 92*
**Wright**, Lemuel Dary 1913- *AmMWSc 92*

**Wright,** Leon Wendell 1923- *AmMWSc 92*
**Wright,** Lin Mary 1933- *WhoEnt 92, WhoWest 92*
**Wright,** Linda Jean 1949- *WhoFI 92*
**Wright,** Linwood Clinton 1919- *WhoBlA 92*
**Wright,** Liz 1950- *TwCPaSc*
**Wright,** Lorenzo C 1926- *BlkOlyM*
**Wright,** Lorin Roderick 1948- *WhoWest 92*
**Wright,** Louis B. 1899-1984 *BenetAL 91*
**Wright,** Louis Donnel 1953- *WhoBlA 92*
**Wright,** Louis E 1940- *AmMWSc 92*
**Wright,** Loyce Pierce 1943- *WhoBlA 92*
**Wright,** Madison Johnston 1924- *AmMWSc 92*
**Wright,** Margaret Hagen *AmMWSc 92*
**Wright,** Margaret Ruth 1913- *AmMWSc 92*
**Wright,** Margaret S. *Who 92*
**Wright,** Margaret Taylor 1949- *WhoFI 92*
**Wright,** Marjorie Ann 1940- *WhoRel 92*
**Wright,** Mark Joseph 1956- *WhoFI 92*
**Wright,** Martha Sinnard 1929- *WhoEnt 92*
**Wright,** Martin 1930- *Who 92*
**Wright,** Marvin 1917- *WhoBlA 92*
**Wright,** Mary H. 1916- *WhoBlA 92*
**Wright,** Mary Helena 1952- *WhoMW 92*
**Wright,** Mary Lou 1933- *WhoAmP 91*
**Wright,** Mary Lou 1934- *AmMWSc 92*
**Wright,** Mary Patricia 1932- *IntAu&W 91*
**Wright,** Mary R. 1949- *WhoWest 92*
**Wright,** Matthew N 1959- *WhoAmP 91*
**Wright,** Maurice Arthur 1935- *AmMWSc 92*
**Wright,** Maurice Morgan 1916- *AmMWSc 92*
**Wright,** Melvyn Charles Harman 1944- *AmMWSc 92*
**Wright,** Michael *Who 92*
**Wright,** Michael A. 1957- *WhoMW 92*
**Wright,** Michael John 1961- *WhoMW 92*
**Wright,** Michael Thomas 1936- *Who 92*
**Wright,** Michael William 1938- *WhoFI 92, WhoMW 92*
**Wright,** Milton M 1909- *WhoAmP 91*
**Wright,** Nadine Anohin 1945- *WhoWest 92*
**Wright,** Nancy Means *DrAPF 91, IntAu&W 91*
**Wright,** Neil Richard 1946- *WhoFI 92, WhoMW 92*
**Wright,** Nell Higgins 1912- *WhoAmP 91*
**Wright,** Nicholas 1940- *WrDr 92*
**Wright,** Nicholas Alcwyn 1943- *Who 92*
**Wright,** Norman Samuel 1920- *AmMWSc 92*
**Wright,** Oliver *IntWW 91, Who 92*
**Wright,** Orville 1871-1948 *BenetAL 91, DcTwDes, FacFETw, RComAH*
**Wright,** Oscar Lewis 1917- *AmMWSc 92*
**Wright,** Patricia 1931- *WhoAmP 91, WhoWest 92*
**Wright,** Patricia 1932- *WrDr 92*
**Wright,** Patrick 1931- *IntWW 91, Who 92*
**Wright,** Paul 1915- *Who 92*
**Wright,** Paul 1946- *TwCPaSc*
**Wright,** Paul Albert 1920- *AmMWSc 92*
**Wright,** Paul McCoy 1904- *AmMWSc 92*
**Wright,** Paul Nathan 1950- *WhoMW 92*
**Wright,** Paul William 1944- *WhoAmL 92*
**Wright,** Penelope Ann *Who 92*
**Wright,** Peter 1916- *FacFETw*
**Wright,** Peter 1929- *Who 92*
**Wright,** Peter 1932- *TwCPaSc*
**Wright,** Peter Christian 1959- *WhoAmL 92*
**Wright,** Peter Michael 1954- *Who 92*
**Wright,** Peter Murrell 1932- *AmMWSc 92*
**Wright,** Peter Robert 1926- *Who 92*
**Wright,** Peter Van Syse 1962- *WhoFI 92*
**Wright,** Peter Williams 1956- *WhoFI 92*
**Wright,** Philip Lincoln 1914- *AmMWSc 92*
**Wright,** Phillip LeRoi 1953- *WhoBlA 92*
**Wright,** Phyllis Joy 1958- *WhoFI 92*
**Wright,** Quincy 1890-1970 *AmPeW*
**Wright,** R. Selby 1908- *WrDr 92*
**Wright,** Rachel Ray 1935- *WhoAmP 91*
**Wright,** Ralph Edward 1950- *WhoBlA 92*
**Wright,** Ralph G 1935- *WhoAmP 91*
**Wright,** Ramil Carter 1939- *AmMWSc 92*
**Wright,** Raymond LeRoy, Jr. 1950- *WhoBlA 92*
**Wright,** Raymond Stanford 1949- *WhoBlA 92*
**Wright,** Rebecca *DrAPF 91*
**Wright,** Richard *DcAmImH*
**Wright,** Richard 1908-1960 *AfrAmW, BenetAL 91, BlkLC [port], FacFETw, LiExTwC, RComAH*
**Wright,** Richard 1944- *WhoAmP 91*
**Wright,** Richard Donald 1936- *WhoFI 92*
**Wright,** Richard Eustace John G. *Who 92*
**Wright,** Richard George 1950- *WhoAmL 92*
**Wright,** Richard Harrell 1950- *WhoAmP 91*
**Wright,** Richard Kenneth 1939- *AmMWSc 92*
**Wright,** Richard Lincoln 1932- *WhoMW 92*
**Wright,** Richard Michael C *Who 92*
**Wright,** Richard N 1932- *AmMWSc 92*
**Wright,** Richard O 1942- *WhoAmP 91*
**Wright,** Richard Owen 1942- *WhoMW 92*
**Wright,** Richard Robert, Jr. 1878-1967 *RelLAm 91*
**Wright,** Richard T 1933- *AmMWSc 92*
**Wright,** Rickey 1958- *WhoBlA 92*
**Wright,** Robert A. 1919- *WhoBlA 92*
**Wright,** Robert Anderson 1933- *AmMWSc 92*
**Wright,** Robert Anthony Kent 1922- *Who 92*
**Wright,** Robert B. 1927- *WhoEnt 92*
**Wright,** Robert Bradley 1934- *WhoRel 92*
**Wright,** Robert C. *LesBEnT 92 [port]*
**Wright,** Robert C. 1943- *IntMPA 92, WhoEnt 92*
**Wright,** Robert Courtlandt 1944- *WhoAmP 91, WhoBlA 92*
**Wright,** Robert E. Lee 1953- *WhoAmL 92*
**Wright,** Robert Joseph 1949- *WhoAmL 92*
**Wright,** Robert L. 1917- *WhoBlA 92*
**Wright,** Robert L 1930- *AmMWSc 92*
**Wright,** Robert Lee 1920- *WrDr 92*
**Wright,** Robert Raymond 1931- *AmMWSc 92*
**Wright,** Robert Richard 1915- *WhoAmP 91*
**Wright,** Robert Thomas, Jr. 1946- *WhoAmL 92*
**Wright,** Robert W 1932- *AmMWSc 92*
**Wright,** Roberta V. Hughes *WhoBlA 92*
**Wright,** Robin B. 1948- *WrDr 92*
**Wright,** Roderick *Who 92*
**Wright,** Roger M 1935- *AmMWSc 92*
**Wright,** Roger Neal 1942- *AmMWSc 92*
**Wright,** Ronald 1948- *IntAu&W 91*
**Wright,** Ronald Edward 1930- *WhoRel 92*
**Wright,** Ronald Selby 1908- *IntWW 91, Who 92*
**Wright,** Ronald Todd 1964- *WhoRel 92*
**Wright,** Roosevelt R., Jr. 1943- *WhoBlA 92*
**Wright,** Rosalie Muller 1942- *WhoWest 92*
**Wright,** Rosalind *DrAPF 91*
**Wright,** Rowland Sydney d1991 *Who 92N*
**Wright,** Rowland Sydney 1915- *IntWW 91*
**Wright,** Roy Kilner 1926- *IntAu&W 91, Who 92*
**Wright,** Roy W. 1914- *IntWW 91*
**Wright,** Roy Wayne 1948- *WhoMW 92*
**Wright,** Roy William 1914- *Who 92*
**Wright,** Royston Clifford *Who 92*
**Wright,** Russel 1904-1976 *DcTwDes*
**Wright,** Russell Emery 1939- *AmMWSc 92*
**Wright,** Ruth M 1928- *WhoAmP 91*
**Wright,** Ruth Margaret *Who 92*
**Wright,** S Fowler 1874-1965 *TwCSFW 91*
**Wright,** Sam W 1926- *WhoAmP 91*
**Wright,** Samuel D 1952- *AmMWSc 92*
**Wright,** Samuel Lamar 1953- *WhoBlA 92*
**Wright,** Sarah E. 1928- *WhoBlA 92*
**Wright,** Sarah Elizabeth *DrAPF 91*
**Wright,** Scott Olin 1923- *WhoAmL 92*
**Wright,** Sewall 1889-1988 *FacFETw*
**Wright,** Sewell Peasley 1897-1970 *ScFEYrs*
**Wright,** Sheila Angstadt 1937- *WhoAmP 91*
**Wright,** Sheila Rosemary Rivers 1925- *Who 92*
**Wright,** Shirley A 1935- *WhoAmP 91*
**Wright,** Shirley Edwin McEwan 1915- *Who 92*
**Wright,** Stanley Allen 1926- *WhoAmP 91*
**Wright,** Stanley Harris 1930- *Who 92*
**Wright,** Stanley V. 1921- *WhoBlA 92*
**Wright,** Stephen *DrAPF 91*
**Wright,** Stephen 1922- *WrDr 92*
**Wright,** Stephen Caldwell *DrAPF 91*
**Wright,** Stephen E 1942- *AmMWSc 92*
**Wright,** Stephen Gailord 1943- *AmMWSc 92*
**Wright,** Stephen John Leadbetter 1946- *Who 92*
**Wright,** Stephen Junius, Jr. 1910- *WhoBlA 92*
**Wright,** Steven 1955- *ConTFT 9*
**Wright,** Steven Martin 1953- *AmMWSc 92*
**Wright,** Steven Randall 1947- *WhoRel 92*
**Wright,** Stuart Joseph 1952- *AmMWSc 92*
**Wright,** Stuart R 1923- *AmMWSc 92*
**Wright,** Sydney Courtenay 1923- *AmMWSc 92*
**Wright,** Sydney Fowler 1874-1965 *ScFEYrs*
**Wright,** Sylvester M. 1927- *WhoBlA 92*
**Wright,** Teresa 1918- *IntMPA 92*
**Wright,** Terry *DrAPF 91*
**Wright,** Terry L 1952- *AmMWSc 92*
**Wright,** Theodore Otis 1921- *WhoWest 92*
**Wright,** Theodore Paul, Jr. 1926- *WrDr 92*
**Wright,** Theodore Robert Fairbank 1928- *AmMWSc 92*
**Wright,** Thomas 1711-1786 *BlkwCEP*
**Wright,** Thomas Carr, Jr *AmMWSc 92*
**Wright,** Thomas Clark 1955- *WhoAmL 92*
**Wright,** Thomas E 1936- *WhoAmP 91*
**Wright,** Thomas Jon 1958- *WhoAmL 92*
**Wright,** Thomas L 1935- *AmMWSc 92*
**Wright,** Thomas Oscar 1940- *AmMWSc 92*
**Wright,** Thomas Parker 1924- *WhoWest 92*
**Wright,** Thomas Payne 1943- *AmMWSc 92*
**Wright,** Thomas Perrin, Jr 1939- *AmMWSc 92*
**Wright,** Thomas Wilson 1933- *AmMWSc 92*
**Wright,** Tim Eugene 1943- *WhoWest 92*
**Wright,** Tony 1925- *IntMPA 92*
**Wright,** Verlyn LaGlen 1963- *WhoBlA 92*
**Wright,** Verna 1928- *IntWW 91, Who 92*
**Wright,** Vernon Lee 1941- *AmMWSc 92*
**Wright,** Vernon Orville 1920- *WhoFI 92*
**Wright,** Virginia L 1912- *WhoAmP 91*
**Wright,** W Robert 1935- *WhoAmP 91*
**Wright,** Wadell 1944- *WhoWest 92*
**Wright,** Wally 1937- *WhoAmP 91*
**Wright,** Walter Channing 1846-1917 *BiInAmS*
**Wright,** Walter Eugene 1924- *AmMWSc 92*
**Wright,** Wayne Mitchell 1934- *AmMWSc 92*
**Wright,** Wayne Paul 1936- *WhoEnt 92*
**Wright,** Wilbur 1867-1912 *BenetAL 91, BiInAmS, DcTwDes, FacFETw, RComAH*
**Wright,** Wiley Reed, Jr. 1932- *WhoAmL 92*
**Wright,** Willard Huntington 1883-1939 *FacFETw*
**Wright,** Willard Huntington 1888-1939 *BenetAL 91*
**Wright,** William 1938- *TwCPaSc, WhoEnt 92*
**Wright,** William A. 1936- *WhoBlA 92*
**Wright,** William A 1959- *WhoAmP 91*
**Wright,** William Alan d1990 *Who 92N*
**Wright,** William Ambrose 1924- *Who 92*
**Wright,** William Blythe, Jr 1918- *AmMWSc 92*
**Wright,** William David 1906- *Who 92, WrDr 92*
**Wright,** William Edward 1926- *WrDr 92*
**Wright,** William F 1918- *AmMWSc 92*
**Wright,** William Gaillard 1933- *WhoBlA 92*
**Wright,** William Greenwood 1829?-1912 *BiInAmS*
**Wright,** William Herbert, III 1943- *AmMWSc 92*
**Wright,** William Howard 1945- *WhoAmP 91*
**Wright,** William Janes 1831-1906 *BiInAmS*
**Wright,** William Leland 1930- *AmMWSc 92, WhoMW 92*
**Wright,** William Lockridge d1990 *Who 92N*
**Wright,** William Marshall 1926- *WhoAmP 91*
**Wright,** William Michael 1955- *WhoFI 92*
**Wright,** William Ray 1941- *AmMWSc 92*
**Wright,** William Redwood 1927- *AmMWSc 92*
**Wright,** William Robert 1928- *AmMWSc 92*
**Wright,** William T 1921- *WhoIns 92*
**Wright,** William V 1931- *AmMWSc 92*
**Wright,** William Vale 1929- *AmMWSc 92*
**Wright,** William W 1949- *AmMWSc 92*
**Wright,** William Wynn 1923- *AmMWSc 92*
**Wright,** Wilson, Jr. 1948- *WhoBlA 92*
**Wright,** Wilson Walker 1930- *WhoFI 92*
**Wright,** Woodring Erik 1949- *AmMWSc 92*
**Wright,** Yvonne Febres Cordero De *WhoHisp 92*
**Wright-Botchwey,** Roberta Yvonne 1946- *WhoBlA 92*
**Wright McKinney,** Judith Arundell 1915- *IntAu&W 91*
**Wright-Sabree,** Margaret V. 1944- *WhoBlA 92*
**Wrighton,** Mark Stephen 1949- *AmMWSc 92*
**Wrightson,** Mark 1951- *Who 92*
**Wrightson,** Patricia 1921- *ConAu 36NR, SmATA 66 [port], WrDr 92*
**Wrigley,** Edward Anthony 1931- *IntWW 91, Who 92*
**Wrigley,** Elizabeth Springer 1915- *WhoWest 92*
**Wrigley,** Gordon 1923- *WrDr 92*
**Wrigley,** Henry Bertram 1909- *Who 92*
**Wrigley,** Jack 1923- *Who 92*
**Wrigley,** Michael Harold 1924- *Who 92*
**Wrigley,** Robert *DrAPF 91*
**Wrigley,** Robert Elder 1951- *WhoAmP 91*
**Wrigley,** Robert Ernest 1943- *WhoMW 92*
**Wrigley,** Tony *Who 92*
**Wrigley,** Virginia Marie 1938- *WhoMW 92*
**Wrigley,** William 1933- *WhoFI 92, WhoMW 92*
**Wrinkle,** John Newton 1929- *WhoAmL 92*
**Wrintmore,** Eric George 1928- *Who 92*
**Wriston,** John Clarence, Jr 1925- *AmMWSc 92*
**Wriston,** Kathryn Dineen *WhoAmL 92*
**Wriston,** Walter B. 1919- *IntWW 91*
**Wrixon-Becher,** William F. *Who 92*
**Wroath,** John Herbert 1932- *Who 92*
**Wrobel,** Joseph Jude 1947- *AmMWSc 92*
**Wrobel,** Joseph Stephen 1939- *AmMWSc 92*
**Wrobel,** Raymond Joseph 1926- *AmMWSc 92*
**Wrobel,** Robert Franklin 1944- *WhoAmL 92*
**Wrobel,** William Eugene *AmMWSc 92*
**Wroble,** Arthur G. 1948- *WhoAmL 92*
**Wrobleski,** Donald von Fennig 1931- *WhoMW 92*
**Wrobleski,** Jeanne Pauline 1942- *WhoAmL 92*
**Wroblewski,** Joseph S 1948- *AmMWSc 92*
**Wroblewski,** Michael Paul 1960- *WhoMW 92*
**Wroblewski,** Timothy Raymond 1966- *WhoMW 92*
**Wrobley,** Ralph Gene 1935- *WhoAmL 92*
**Wroblowa,** Halina Stefania 1925- *WhoMW 92*
**Wroe,** David Charles Lynn 1942- *Who 92*
**Wrogemann,** Klaus 1940- *AmMWSc 92*
**Wrolstad,** Ronald Earl 1939- *AmMWSc 92*
**Wrone,** David Roger 1933- *WhoMW 92*
**Wrong,** Henry Lewellys Barker 1930- *Who 92*
**Wrotenbery,** Carl Richard 1929- *WhoRel 92*
**Wrotenbery,** Paul Taylor 1934- *AmMWSc 92*
**Wroth,** Lawrence Kinvin 1932- *WhoAmL 92*
**Wroth,** Peter d1991 *Who 92N*
**Wrottesley** *Who 92*
**Wrottesley,** Baron 1968- *Who 92*
**Wrottesley,** John Francis 1908- *IntAu&W 91*
**Wroughton,** John Presbury 1934- *WrDr 92*
**Wroughton,** Philip Lavallin 1933- *Who 92*
**Wruble,** Brian Frederick 1943- *WhoFI 92*
**Wrucke,** Chester Theodore, Jr 1927- *AmMWSc 92*
**Wrves,** Orestes G. 1951- *WhoHisp 92*
**Wrye,** Richard Fred 1944- *WhoWest 92*
**Wrzesien,** William *WhoEnt 92*
**Wrzesinski,** John T *WhoAmP 91*
**Wu Bangguo** 1941- *IntWW 91*
**Wu De** 1914- *IntWW 91*
**Wu Guanzheng** 1938- *IntWW 91*
**Wu Guanzhong** 1919- *IntWW 91*
**Wu Hualun** 1942- *IntWW 91*
**Wu Jieping** 1916- *IntWW 91*
**Wu Jinghua** 1931- *IntWW 91*
**Wu Lengxi** 1919- *IntWW 91*
**Wu Minda** 1929- *IntWW 91*
**Wu Mingyu** 1931- *IntWW 91*
**Wu of Hwang Ho** *EncAmaz 91*
**Wu Poh-Hsiung** 1939- *IntWW 91*
**Wu Shaozu** 1937- *IntWW 91*
**Wu Shi** 1913- *IntWW 91*
**Wu Tianming** 1939- *IntWW 91*
**Wu Weiran** 1920- *IntWW 91*
**Wu Wenjun** 1919- *IntWW 91*
**Wu Wenying** 1932- *IntWW 91*
**Wu Xiangbi** 1926- *IntWW 91*
**Wu Xiaobang** 1906- *IntWW 91*
**Wu Xiuquan** 1909- *IntWW 91*
**Wu Xueqian** 1921- *IntWW 91*
**Wu Yigong** 1938- *IntWW 91*
**Wu Zhen** 1922- *IntWW 91*
**Wu Zhonghua** 1917- *IntWW 91*
**Wu Zhonghua** 1951- *IntWW 91*
**Wu Zuoren** 1908- *IntWW 91*
**Wu Zuqiang** 1927- *ConCom 92, IntWW 91*
**Wu,** Adam Yu 1946- *AmMWSc 92*
**Wu,** Alan SeeMing 1940- *AmMWSc 92*
**Wu,** Albert M 1940- *AmMWSc 92*
**Wu,** Alfred Chi-Tai 1933- *AmMWSc 92*
**Wu,** Anna Fang 1940- *AmMWSc 92*
**Wu,** Changsheng 1923- *AmMWSc 92*
**Wu,** Chau Hsiung 1941- *AmMWSc 92*
**Wu,** Cheng-Hsiao 1943- *AmMWSc 92*
**Wu,** Cheng-Wen 1938- *AmMWSc 92*
**Wu,** Chien-Shiung 1912- *AmMWSc 92*
**Wu,** Chih 1936- *AmMWSc 92*
**Wu,** Ching-Hsong George 1939- *AmMWSc 92*
**Wu,** Ching-Sheng 1929- *AmMWSc 92*
**Wu,** Ching-Yong *AmMWSc 92*
**Wu,** Chuen-Shang C 1932- *AmMWSc 92*

**Wu**, Chun-Fang 1947- *AmMWSc 92, WhoMW 92*
**Wu**, Chung 1919- *AmMWSc 92*
**Wu**, Chung Pao 1942- *AmMWSc 92*
**Wu**, Daisy Yen 1902- *AmMWSc 92*
**Wu**, Dao-Tsing 1933- *AmMWSc 92*
**Wu**, Ellen Lem 1930- *AmMWSc 92*
**Wu**, En Shinn 1943- *AmMWSc 92*
**Wu**, Fa Yueh 1932- *AmMWSc 92*
**Wu**, Felicia Ying-Hsiueh 1939- *AmMWSc 92*
**Wu**, Felix F 1943- *AmMWSc 92*
**Wu**, Francis Taming 1936- *AmMWSc 92*
**Wu**, Gordon 1935- *IntWW 91*
**Wu**, Gordon Y. S. *NewYTBS 91 [port]*
**Wu**, Hai 1936- *AmMWSc 92*
**Wu**, Harry Pao-Tung 1932- *WhoMW 92*
**Wu**, Henry Chi-Ping 1935- *AmMWSc 92*
**Wu**, Hofu 1949- *AmMWSc 92*
**Wu**, Hsin-i 1937- *AmMWSc 92*
**Wu**, Hung-Hsi 1940- *AmMWSc 92*
**Wu**, I-Pai 1933- *AmMWSc 92*
**Wu**, James Bi-Cheng 1943- *WhoWest 92*
**Wu**, James Chen-Yuan 1931- *AmMWSc 92*
**Wu**, Jia-Hsi 1926- *AmMWSc 92*
**Wu**, Jiann-Long *AmMWSc 92*
**Wu**, Jin 1934- *AmMWSc 92*
**Wu**, Jin Zhong 1945- *AmMWSc 92*
**Wu**, John Baptist 1925- *IntWW 91*
**Wu**, John C H 1899-1986 *FacFETw*
**Wu**, John Ming Cheung 1953- *WhoWest 92*
**Wu**, John Naichi 1932- *AmMWSc 92*
**Wu**, Jonathan Charnghau 1953- *WhoFI 92, WhoWest 92*
**Wu**, Jonathan Tzong 1951- *AmMWSc 92*
**Wu**, Joseph M 1947- *AmMWSc 92*
**Wu**, Joseph Woo-Tien *AmMWSc 92*
**Wu**, Julian Juh-Ren 1935- *AmMWSc 92*
**Wu**, Jung-Tsung 1936- *AmMWSc 92*
**Wu**, Kenneth Kun-Yu 1941- *AmMWSc 92*
**Wu**, Konrad T 1948- *AmMWSc 92*
**Wu**, Kuang-ming 1933- *WhoMW 92*
**Wu**, Kuang Ming 1949- *AmMWSc 92*
**Wu**, Kuo H. 1953- *WhoWest 92*
**Wu**, Lancelot T L *AmMWSc 92*
**Wu**, Lawrence 1957- *WhoMW 92*
**Wu**, Lawrence Shu-Ling 1946- *WhoWest 92*
**Wu**, Lei 1963- *AmMWSc 92*
**Wu**, Lilian Shiao-Yen 1947- *AmMWSc 92*
**Wu**, Madame Sylvia *WhoWest 92*
**Wu**, Min-Yen 1940- *AmMWSc 92*
**Wu**, Ming-Chi 1940- *AmMWSc 92*
**Wu**, Mu Tsu 1929- *AmMWSc 92*
**Wu**, Nesa L'abbe 1942- *WhoMW 92*
**Wu**, Oscar Kang 1946- *WhoWest 92*
**Wu**, Pei-Rin 1935- *AmMWSc 92*
**Wu**, Po-Shun 1947- *WhoWest 92*
**Wu**, Ray J 1928- *AmMWSc 92*
**Wu**, Richard Li-Chuan 1940- *AmMWSc 92*
**Wu**, Robert Chung-Yung 1943- *AmMWSc 92*
**Wu**, Robin Chi Ching 1941- *WhoAmL 92*
**Wu**, Roy Shih-Shyong 1944- *AmMWSc 92*
**Wu**, Sau Lan Yu *AmMWSc 92*
**Wu**, Sherman H 1938- *AmMWSc 92*
**Wu**, Shi Tsan 1934- *AmMWSc 92*
**Wu**, Shien-Ming 1924- *AmMWSc 92*
**Wu**, Shih-Yen 1929- *WhoFI 92*
**Wu**, Shu-Yau 1936- *WhoWest 92*
**Wu**, Sing-Chou 1936- *AmMWSc 92*
**Wu**, Sing-Yung 1939- *AmMWSc 92*
**Wu**, Souheng 1936- *AmMWSc 92*
**Wu**, Tai Te 1935- *AmMWSc 92*
**Wu**, Tai Tsun 1933- *AmMWSc 92*
**Wu**, Tai Wing *AmMWSc 92*
**Wu**, Te-Kao 1948- *AmMWSc 92*
**Wu**, Theodore Yao-Tsu 1924- *AmMWSc 92*
**Wu**, Tien Hsing 1923- *AmMWSc 92*
**Wu**, Ting Kai 1937- *AmMWSc 92*
**Wu**, Tse Cheng 1923- *AmMWSc 92, WhoFI 92*
**Wu**, Tsu Ming 1936- *AmMWSc 92*
**Wu**, Wen-hsien *AmMWSc 92*
**Wu**, William Chi Liang 1932 *AmMWSc 92*
**Wu**, William Gay 1931- *AmMWSc 92*
**Wu**, Wu-Nan 1938- *AmMWSc 92*
**Wu**, Xizeng 1944- *AmMWSc 92*
**Wu**, Yao Hua 1920- *AmMWSc 92*
**Wu**, Ying-Chu Lin 1932- *AmMWSc 92*
**Wu**, Ying Victor 1931- *AmMWSc 92, WhoMW 92*
**Wu**, Yong-Shi 1942- *AmMWSc 92*
**Wu**, Yung-Chi 1923- *AmMWSc 92*
**Wu**, Yung-Kuang 1933- *AmMWSc 92*
**Wu**, Zhen *AmMWSc 92*
**Wu Shu-Chih**, Alex 1920- *Who 92*
**Wu-Wong**, Jinshyun Ruth *AmMWSc 92*
**Wuamett**, Victor 1941- *ConAu 134*
**Wubbels**, Gene Gerald 1942- *AmMWSc 92*
**Wucherpfennig**, Bradley Eugene 1952- *WhoMW 92*
**Wuchter**, Gerald James 1967- *WhoMW 92*
**Wuchter**, Michael David 1946- *WhoRel 92*
**Wuchter**, Richard B 1937- *AmMWSc 92*
**Wudel**, Richard A 1941- *WhoAmP 91*
**Wudl**, Fred 1941- *AmMWSc 92*
**Wuebbles**, Donald J 1948- *AmMWSc 92*
**Wuebker**, Colleen Marie 1943- *WhoMW 92*
**Wuellner**, Wilhelm Hermann 1927- *WhoRel 92*
**Wuensch**, Bernhardt J 1933- *AmMWSc 92*
**Wuenschel**, Paul Clarence 1921- *AmMWSc 92*
**Wuepper**, Kirk Dean 1938- *AmMWSc 92*
**Wuerch**, Harry *WhoRel 92*
**Wuerfel**, Walter William, Jr. 1941- *WhoFI 92*
**Wuerker**, Ralph Frederick 1929- *AmMWSc 92*
**Wuerl**, Donald W. 1940- *WhoRel 92*
**Wuerth**, Richard Osborn 1946- *WhoAmL 92*
**Wuescher**, Richard Donald 1952- *WhoMW 92*
**Wuest**, George W 1924- *WhoAmP 91*
**Wuest**, George W. 1925- *WhoAmL 92, WhoMW 92*
**Wuest**, Mark *WhoEnt 92*
**Wuest**, Paul J 1937- *AmMWSc 92*
**Wuhl**, Robert *ConTFT 9*
**Wujciga**, Edward Joseph 1963- *WhoFI 92, WhoMW 92*
**Wujek**, Daniel Everett 1939- *AmMWSc 92*
**Wukelic**, George Edward 1929- *AmMWSc 92*
**Wulbern**, John Cummins 1936- *WhoFI 92*
**Wulbert**, Daniel Eliot 1941- *AmMWSc 92, WhoWest 92*
**Wulf**, Bruce Louis 1939- *WhoWest 92*
**Wulf**, Robert Findley 1937- *WhoWest 92*
**Wulf**, Ronald James 1928- *AmMWSc 92*
**Wulf**, Steven Christopher 1965- *WhoWest 92*
**Wulf**, William Allan 1939- *AmMWSc 92*
**Wulfekuehler**, Edward George, Jr. 1928- *WhoRel 92*
**Wulfers**, John Manning 1947- *WhoAmL 92*
**Wulfers**, Thomas Frederick 1939- *AmMWSc 92*
**Wulff**, Barry Lee 1940- *AmMWSc 92*
**Wulff**, Daniel Lewis 1937- *AmMWSc 92*
**Wulff**, Douglas Allan 1955- *WhoEnt 92*
**Wulff**, John Leland 1932- *AmMWSc 92*
**Wulff**, Lee 1905-1991 *ConAu 134, NewYTBS 91*
**Wulff**, Verner John 1916- *AmMWSc 92*
**Wulff**, Wolfgang 1933- *AmMWSc 92*
**Wulfman**, Carl E 1930- *AmMWSc 92*
**Wulfman**, David Swinton 1934- *AmMWSc 92*
**Wulker**, Laurence Joseph 1945- *WhoFI 92*
**Wullbrandt**, Emily Sheppard 1922- *WhoAmP 91*
**Wulle**, Reinhold 1882-1950 *BiDExR*
**Wullert**, John R, II 1962- *AmMWSc 92*
**Wullstein**, Betty Colleen 1932- *WhoWest 92*
**Wullstein**, Leroy Hugh 1931- *AmMWSc 92*
**Wulpi**, Donald James 1924- *AmMWSc 92*
**Wulstan**, David 1937- *Who 92*
**Wun**, Chun Kwun 1940- *AmMWSc 92*
**Wun**, Kai-Lam William 1940- *WhoWest 92*
**Wunder**, Bernard James, Jr 1943- *WhoAmP 91*
**Wunder**, Bruce Arnold 1942- *AmMWSc 92, WhoWest 92*
**Wunder**, Charles C 1928- *AmMWSc 92*
**Wunder**, Charles Cooper 1928- *WhoMW 92*
**Wunder**, Cynthia Lea 1965- *WhoMW 92*
**Wunder**, William Harrison 1929- *WhoMW 92*
**Wunder**, William W 1930- *AmMWSc 92*
**Wunderlich**, Bernhard 1931- *AmMWSc 92*
**Wunderlich**, Francis J 1938- *AmMWSc 92*
**Wunderlich**, Fritz 1930-1966 *FacFETw, NewAmDM*
**Wunderlich**, Gene Lee 1928- *WhoFI 92*
**Wunderlich**, Gerold Mosher 1949- *WhoFI 92*
**Wunderlich**, Hermann *WhoFI 92*
**Wunderlich**, John R *AmMWSc 92*
**Wunderlich**, Krieg Richard 1956- *WhoEnt 92*
**Wunderlich**, LaRue *WhoAmP 91*
**Wunderlich**, Marvin C 1937- *AmMWSc 92*
**Wunderlich**, Paul 1927- *IntWW 91*
**Wunderlich**, Ray Charles, Jr. 1929- *WrDr 92*
**Wunderly**, Stephen Walker 1945- *AmMWSc 92*
**Wunderman**, Irwin 1931- *AmMWSc 92*
**Wunderman**, Lorna Ellen 1954- *WhoMW 92*
**Wunderman**, Richard Lloyd 1952- *AmMWSc 92*
**Wunnicke**, Bruce E. 1952- *WhoMW 92*
**Wunsch**, Abraham David 1939- *AmMWSc 92*
**Wunsch**, Carl Isaac 1941- *AmMWSc 92, IntWW 91*
**Wunsch**, Charles Robert 1956- *WhoAmL 92*
**Wunsch**, David E. 1932- *WhoWest 92*
**Wunsch**, Josephine 1914- *ConAu 34NR*
**Wunsch**, Josephine M 1914- *IntAu&W 91, WrDr 92*
**Wunsch**, Karen Jackel *DrAPF 91*
**Wunsch**, Kathryn Sutherland 1935- *WhoAmL 92*
**Wunsch**, Robert S *WhoAmP 91*
**Wunz**, Paul Richard, Jr 1923- *AmMWSc 92*
**Wuonola**, Mark Arvid 1947- *AmMWSc 92*
**Wuorinen**, Charles 1938- *ConCom 92, NewAmDM, WhoEnt 92*
**Wuorinen**, John H, Jr 1931- *AmMWSc 92*
**Wuorinen**, William Kent 1960- *WhoEnt 92*
**Wurdack**, John J 1921- *AmMWSc 92*
**Wurdeman**, Lew Edward 1949- *WhoMW 92*
**Wurdeman**, Pamela Myers 1961- *WhoEnt 92*
**Wurdemann**, Audrey 1911-1960 *BenetAL 91*
**Wurfel**, Walter William 1937- *WhoAmP 91*
**Wurlitzer**, Rudolph *DrAPF 91*
**Wurlitzer**, Rudolph 1831-1914 *NewAmDM*
**Wurlitzer**, Rudolph 1938?- *BenetAL 91, ConNov 91*
**Wurm**, Jaroslav 1935- *AmMWSc 92*
**Wurm**, Theophil 1868-1953 *EncTR 91 [port]*
**Wurmser**, Leon 1931- *AmMWSc 92*
**Wurmser**, Rene Bernard 1890- *IntWW 91*
**Wurpts**, John Albert 1942- *WhoFI 92*
**Wurr**, Peter Reinhard 1943- *WhoFI 92*
**Wurrey**, Charles Jon 1947- *WhoMW 92*
**Wurschmidt**, Todd Neil 1950- *WhoMW 92*
**Wursig**, Bernd Gerhard 1948- *AmMWSc 92*
**Wurst**, Glen Gilbert 1945- *AmMWSc 92*
**Wurst**, Gloria Zettle 1946- *AmMWSc 92*
**Wurst**, John Charles 1936- *AmMWSc 92*
**Wurster**, Charles F 1930- *AmMWSc 92*
**Wurster**, Dale E 1918- *AmMWSc 92*
**Wurster**, Dale Eric 1951- *WhoMW 92*
**Wurster**, Dale Eric, Jr 1951- *AmMWSc 92*
**Wurster**, Dale Erwin 1918- *WhoMW 92*
**Wurster**, Michael *DrAPF 91*
**Wurster**, Michael 1940- *IntAu&W 91*
**Wurster-Hill**, Doris Hadley 1932- *AmMWSc 92*
**Wurtele**, Christopher Angus 1934- *WhoFI 92, WhoMW 92*
**Wurtele**, Morton Gaither 1919- *AmMWSc 92*
**Wurth**, Michael John 1937- *AmMWSc 92*
**Wurth**, Pierre 1926- *IntWW 91*
**Wurth**, Thomas Joseph 1928- *AmMWSc 92*
**Wurtman**, Judith Joy 1937- *AmMWSc 92*
**Wurtman**, Richard Jay 1936- *AmMWSc 92*
**Wurts**, William Whitney 1937- *WhoFI 92, WhoWest 92*
**Wurttemberg**, Friedrich Paul W, Duke Of *BiInAmS*
**Wurtz**, Henry 1828-1910 *BiInAmS*
**Wurtz**, Robert Henry 1936- *AmMWSc 92*
**Wurtzel**, Alan Henry 1947- *WhoEnt 92*
**Wurtzel**, Alan Leon 1933- *WhoFI 92*
**Wurz**, Kevin Ross 1948- *WhoEnt 92*
**Wurz**, Max Edward 1962- *WhoWest 92*
**Wurzburg**, Otto Bernard 1915- *AmMWSc 92*
**Wurzburg**, Reginald 1901- *WhoFI 92*
**Wurzburger**, Walter Samuel 1920- *WhoRel 92*
**Wuskell**, Joseph P 1938- *AmMWSc 92*
**Wussler**, Robert *LesBEnT 92 [port]*
**Wussler**, Robert Joseph 1936- *WhoWest 92*
**Wussow**, George C 1923- *AmMWSc 92*
**Wust**, Carl John 1928- *AmMWSc 92*
**Wustrack**, Karl Otto 1944- *WhoWest 92*
**Wuthier**, Roy Edward 1932- *AmMWSc 92*
**Wuthrich**, Robert Omar 1948- *WhoMW 92*
**Wuts**, Peter G M 1950- *AmMWSc 92*
**Wuttke**, Hans A. 1923- *IntWW 91, Who 92*
**Wuu**, Ting-Chi 1934- *AmMWSc 92*
**Wyant**, Gordon Michael 1914- *AmMWSc 92*
**Wyant**, James Clair 1943- *AmMWSc 92, WhoWest 92*
**Wyant**, Joseph Andrew 1949- *WhoFI 92*
**Wyant**, Maria Sophia 1959- *WhoAmP 91*
**Wyant**, Theodore 1954- *WhoWest 92*
**Wyard**, Vicki Shaw 1945- *WhoFI 92*
**Wyart**, Jean 1902- *IntWW 91*
**Wyatt** *Who 92*
**Wyatt**, Lord 1918- *WrDr 92*
**Wyatt**, Addie L. 1924- *WhoBlA 92*
**Wyatt**, Alan Will 1942- *IntWW 91, Who 92*
**Wyatt**, Anthony 1927- *TwCPaSc*
**Wyatt**, Arthur Hope 1929- *IntWW 91, Who 92*
**Wyatt**, Beatrice E. *WhoBlA 92*
**Wyatt**, Benjamin Woodrow 1916- *AmMWSc 92*
**Wyatt**, Christopher Terrel 1927- *IntWW 91, Who 92*
**Wyatt**, Claude Stell, Jr. 1921- *WhoBlA 92*
**Wyatt**, Colen Charles 1927- *AmMWSc 92*
**Wyatt**, David Joseph 1931- *Who 92*
**Wyatt**, Denise Lee 1962- *WhoMW 92*
**Wyatt**, Diana E 1947- *WhoAmP 91*
**Wyatt**, Ellis Junior 1930- *AmMWSc 92*
**Wyatt**, Faricita Hall 1912- *WhoWest 92*
**Wyatt**, Francis 1855?-1916 *BiInAmS*
**Wyatt**, Gavin Edward 1914- *Who 92*
**Wyatt**, Gerard Robert 1925- *AmMWSc 92*
**Wyatt**, James L 1924- *AmMWSc 92*
**Wyatt**, Jane 1910- *IntMPA 92*
**Wyatt**, Jeffrey Renner 1946- *AmMWSc 92*
**Wyatt**, Joe Lee 1953- *WhoAmL 92*
**Wyatt**, John Marie 1949- *WhoRel 92*
**Wyatt**, John Raymond 1913- *WhoWest 92*
**Wyatt**, Joseph Lucian, Jr. 1924- *WhoAmL 92, WhoWest 92*
**Wyatt**, Joseph Peyton, Jr 1941- *WhoAmP 91*
**Wyatt**, Marta Villalpando 1940- *WhoHisp 92*
**Wyatt**, Noel Wayne, III 1954- *WhoMW 92*
**Wyatt**, Oscar Sherman, Jr. 1924- *WhoFI 92*
**Wyatt**, Philip Joseph 1932- *AmMWSc 92*
**Wyatt**, Raymond L 1926- *AmMWSc 92*
**Wyatt**, Richard Jed 1939- *AmMWSc 92*
**Wyatt**, Robert Edward 1950- *AmMWSc 92*
**Wyatt**, Robert Eugene 1938- *AmMWSc 92*
**Wyatt**, Roger Dale 1948- *AmMWSc 92*
**Wyatt**, Rose Marie 1937- *WhoMW 92*
**Wyatt**, S. Martin, III 1941- *WhoBlA 92*
**Wyatt**, Scott Alan 1951- *WhoEnt 92*
**Wyatt**, Spencer 1921- *WhoAmP 91*
**Wyatt**, Stephen 1948- *ConAu 34NR*
**Wyatt**, Stephen Thomas 1955- *WhoRel 92*
**Wyatt**, Terrel *Who 92*
**Wyatt**, Thomas 1503-1542 *RfGEnL 91*
**Wyatt**, Wendy *Who 92*
**Wyatt**, Will *Who 92*
**Wyatt**, Wilson Watkins, Jr. 1943- *WhoFI 92*
**Wyatt**, Wilson Watkins, Sr 1905- *WhoAmP 91*
**Wyatt**, Wyatt *DrAPF 91*
**Wyatt Cummings**, Thelma LaVerne 1945- *WhoBlA 92*
**Wyatt Of Weeford**, Baron 1918- *IntWW 91, Who 92*
**Wyban**, James A 1951- *AmMWSc 92*
**Wybel**, Terry Scott 1937- *WhoMW 92*
**Wybourne**, Brian Garner 1935- *WrDr 92*
**Wybranczyk**, Franciszek 1934- *WhoEnt 92*
**Wych**, Robert Dale 1948- *AmMWSc 92*
**Wyche**, Bradford Wheeler 1950- *WhoAmL 92*
**Wyche**, Lennon Douglas, Jr. 1946- *WhoBlA 92*
**Wyche**, Madison Baker, III 1947- *WhoAmL 92*
**Wyche**, Melville Q., Jr. 1938- *WhoBlA 92*
**Wyche**, Paul H., Jr. 1946- *WhoBlA 92*
**Wyche**, Samuel David 1945- *WhoMW 92*
**Wyche**, Vera Rowena 1923- *WhoBlA 92*
**Wycherley**, William 1641-1715 *CnDBLB 2 [port], RfGEnL 91*
**Wychor**, James John 1931- *WhoMW 92*
**Wyckoff**, Alexander 1898- *WhoMW 92*
**Wyckoff**, Delaphine Grace Rosa 1906- *AmMWSc 92*
**Wyckoff**, Edward Lisk, Jr. 1934- *WhoAmL 92*
**Wyckoff**, Harold Orville 1910- *AmMWSc 92*
**Wyckoff**, Harold Winfield 1926- *AmMWSc 92*
**Wyckoff**, James Donald 1959- *WhoFI 92*
**Wyckoff**, James M 1924- *AmMWSc 92*
**Wyckoff**, John Wesley 1944- *WhoRel 92*
**Wyckoff**, Margo Gail 1941- *WhoWest 92*
**Wyckoff**, Ralph Walter Graystone 1897- *AmMWSc 92, IntWW 91*
**Wyckoff**, Russell Leroy 1925- *WhoAmP 91*
**Wyckoff**, Susan 1941- *AmMWSc 92*
**Wyckoff**, Walter 1865-1908 *BenetAL 91*
**Wycoff**, Charles Coleman 1918- *WhoWest 92*
**Wycoff**, Robert E. 1930- *WhoFI 92, WhoWest 92*
**Wycoff**, Samuel John 1929- *AmMWSc 92*
**Wyczalek**, Floyd Anthony 1925- *WhoMW 92*
**Wyczalkowski**, Marcin Roman 1910- *WhoFI 92*
**Wyden**, Ron 1949- *AlmAP 92 [port]*

**Wyden,** Ronald Lee 1949- *WhoAmP 91, WhoWest 92*
**Wydeven,** Theodore 1936- *AmMWSc 92*
**Wydra,** Frank Thomas 1939- *WhoMW 92*
**Wyers,** Mary Jane Frances 1914- *WhoAmP 91*
**Wyeth,** Andrew 1917- *BenetAL 91, FacFETw*
**Wyeth,** Andrew N. 1917- *IntWW 91*
**Wyeth,** Andrew Newell 1917- *Who 92*
**Wyeth,** Henriette 1907- *WhoWest 92*
**Wyeth,** Mark Thomas 1963- *WhoFI 92*
**Wyeth,** N C 1882-1944 *FacFETw*
**Wyeth,** N. C. 1882-1945 *BenetAL 91*
**Wyeth,** Nathaniel Convers 1920-1990 *FacFETw*
**Wyeth,** Nathaniel Jarvis 1802-1856 *BenetAL 91*
**Wyeth,** Newell Convers 1946- *AmMWSc 92*
**Wyeth,** Paul 1920- *TwCPaSc*
**Wyfold,** Baron 1915- *Who 92*
**Wygant,** J F 1919- *AmMWSc 92*
**Wygnanski,** Israel Jerzy 1935- *AmMWSc 92*
**Wyke,** Joseph Henry 1928- *WhoBlA 92*
**Wyke,** Robert James 1933- *WhoIns 92*
**Wykeham,** Peter 1915- *Who 92, WrDr 92*
**Wykes,** Alan 1914- *IntAu&W 91, WrDr 92*
**Wykes,** Arthur Albert 1923- *AmMWSc 92*
**Wykes,** James Cochrane 1913- *Who 92*
**Wykes,** Paul David 1959- *WhoFI 92*
**Wykle,** May Louise Hinton 1934- *WhoBlA 92*
**Wykle,** Robert Lee 1940- *AmMWSc 92*
**Wykoff,** Beverly Young 1942- *WhoMW 92*
**Wykoff,** John Robert 1951- *WhoAmL 92*
**Wyland,** Sharon Kay 1949- *WhoMW 92*
**Wyland,** Stewart Wayne 1950- *WhoWest 92*
**Wyld,** Henry William, Jr 1928- *AmMWSc 92*
**Wyld,** Martin Hugh 1944- *Who 92*
**Wyldbore-Smith,** Brian 1913- *Who 92*
**Wylde,** Ronald James 1921- *AmMWSc 92*
**Wyle,** Ewart Herbert 1904- *WhoRel 92, WhoWest 92*
**Wyler,** Allen Raymer 1943- *AmMWSc 92*
**Wyler,** David J 1944- *AmMWSc 92*
**Wyler,** Gretchen 1932- *WhoEnt 92*
**Wyler,** Marjorie Goldwasser 1915- *WhoEnt 92*
**Wyler,** Oswald 1922- *AmMWSc 92*
**Wyler,** Richard *TwCWW 91*
**Wyler,** William 1902-1981 *FacFETw, IntDcF 2-2 [port]*
**Wylie,** Lord 1923- *Who 92*
**Wylie,** C J 1926- *AmMWSc 92*
**Wylie,** C. Ray, Jr. 1911- *ConAu 36NR*
**Wylie,** Campbell 1905- *IntWW 91, Who 92*
**Wylie,** Chalmers P. 1920- *AlmAP 92 [port]*
**Wylie,** Chalmers Pangburn 1920- *WhoAmP 91, WhoMW 92*
**Wylie,** Christopher Craig 1945- *Who 92*
**Wylie,** Clarence Raymond, Jr 1911- *AmMWSc 92*
**Wylie,** Derek *Who 92*
**Wylie,** Douglas Wilson 1926- *AmMWSc 92*
**Wylie,** Elinor 1885-1928 *BenetAL 91*
**Wylie,** Evan Benjamin 1931- *AmMWSc 92*
**Wylie,** Harold Glenn 1927- *AmMWSc 92*
**Wylie,** J Kenneth 1927- *WhoIns 92*
**Wylie,** Jonathan Kirk 1944- *WhoMW 92*
**Wylie,** Judith Babcock 1943- *WhoWest 92*
**Wylie,** Kyral Francis 1931- *AmMWSc 92*
**Wylie,** Laura *IntAu&W 91X, WrDr 92*
**Wylie,** Max d1975 *LesBEnT 92*
**Wylie,** Norman Russell *Who 92*
**Wylie,** Paul Richter, Jr. 1936- *WhoAmL 92*
**Wylie,** Philip 1902-1971 *BenetAL 91, ScFEYrs, TwCSFW 91*
**Wylie,** Richard Michael 1934- *AmMWSc 92*
**Wylie,** Sanford Willie 1944- *WhoRel 92*
**Wylie,** Scott Elwood 1951- *WhoRel 92*
**Wylie,** Ted David 1945- *WhoEnt 92*
**Wylie,** Theophilus Adam 1810-1895 *BiInAmS*
**Wylie,** William Derek 1918- *Who 92*
**Wyller,** Egil A. 1925- *IntWW 91*
**Wyllie,** Charles William 1859-1923 *TwCPaSc*
**Wyllie,** Gilbert Alexander 1928- *AmMWSc 92*
**Wyllie,** Harold 1880-1973 *TwCPaSc*
**Wyllie,** Loring A *AmMWSc 92*
**Wyllie,** Loring A., Jr. 1938- *WhoWest 92*
**Wyllie,** Peter J. 1930- *WrDr 92*
**Wyllie,** Peter John 1930- *AmMWSc 92, IntWW 91, Who 92, WhoWest 92*
**Wyllie,** Robert Lyon 1897- *Who 92*
**Wyllie,** Thomas Dean 1928- *AmMWSc 92*
**Wyllie,** William Lionel 1851-1931 *TwCPaSc*
**Wyllie,** William Robert Alexander 1932- *Who 92*
**Wylly,** Alexander 1920- *AmMWSc 92*
**Wyllys,** Ronald Eugene 1930- *AmMWSc 92*
**Wyly,** Lemuel David, Jr 1916- *AmMWSc 92*
**Wyma,** Richard J 1936- *AmMWSc 92*
**Wyman,** Arthur D d1904 *BiInAmS*
**Wyman,** Bostwick Frampton 1941- *AmMWSc 92*
**Wyman,** Donald 1903- *AmMWSc 92*
**Wyman,** Donald Paul 1931- *AmMWSc 92*
**Wyman,** Douglas Philip 1955- *WhoEnt 92*
**Wyman,** Frank James, III 1960- *WhoFI 92*
**Wyman,** Franklin, Jr. 1921- *WhoFI 92*
**Wyman,** George Martin 1921- *AmMWSc 92*
**Wyman,** Harold Robertson 1905- *AmMWSc 92*
**Wyman,** Herbert Jack 1921- *WhoWest 92*
**Wyman,** Jane 1914- *IntMPA 92, IntWW 91, WhoEnt 92*
**Wyman,** Jeffries 1814-1874 *BiInAmS*
**Wyman,** Jeffries 1901- *AmMWSc 92*
**Wyman,** John Bernard 1916- *Who 92*
**Wyman,** John E 1931- *AmMWSc 92*
**Wyman,** Lori Sheryl 1956- *WhoEnt 92*
**Wyman,** Louis C 1917- *WhoAmP 91*
**Wyman,** Mark 1938- *ConAu 36NR*
**Wyman,** Max 1916- *AmMWSc 92*
**Wyman,** Milton 1930- *AmMWSc 92*
**Wyman,** Morrill 1812-1903 *BiInAmS*
**Wyman,** Nancy Carol *WhoAmP 91*
**Wyman,** Phillip D 1945- *WhoAmP 91*
**Wyman,** Richard Vaughn 1927- *AmMWSc 92, WhoWest 92*
**Wyman,** Robert J 1940- *AmMWSc 92*
**Wyman,** Rosalind 1930- *WhoAmP 91*
**Wyman,** Stanley M 1913- *AmMWSc 92*
**Wyman,** Thomas H. *LesBEnT 92 [port]*
**Wyman,** Thomas H. 1931- *IntMPA 92*
**Wyman,** Walker D. 1907- *ConAu 36NR*
**Wyman,** Walter 1848-1911 *BiInAmS*
**Wyman,** Walter Edward, Jr. 1946- *WhoRel 92*
**Wyman,** William Arthur 1942- *WhoEnt 92, WhoMW 92*
**Wyman,** William George 1941- *IntWW 91, WhoEnt 92*
**Wymark,** Olwen *WrDr 92*
**Wymbs,** Norman E 1923- *WhoAmP 91*
**Wymer,** Joseph Peter 1923- *AmMWSc 92*
**Wymer,** Mary Ann 1946- *WhoRel 92*
**Wymer,** Raymond George 1927- *AmMWSc 92*
**Wymore,** Albert Wayne 1927- *AmMWSc 92*
**Wymore,** Bill D 1940- *WhoIns 92*
**Wymore,** Charles Elmer 1932- *AmMWSc 92*
**Wymore,** Patrice 1926- *IntMPA 92*
**Wynar,** Bohdan Stephen 1926- *WhoWest 92*
**Wynbelt,** Walter Peter 1943- *WhoMW 92*
**Wynblatt,** Paul P 1935- *AmMWSc 92*
**Wynd,** Oswald *IntAu&W 91*
**Wynd,** Oswald 1913- *WrDr 92*
**Wynder,** Ernst Ludwig 1922- *AmMWSc 92*
**Wyndham** *Who 92*
**Wyndham,** Esther *IntAu&W 91X, WrDr 92*
**Wyndham,** Francis 1924- *IntAu&W 91*
**Wyndham,** Harald *DrAPF 91*
**Wyndham,** John 1903-1969 *TwCSFW 91*
**Wyndham,** Nicholas 1944- *TwCPaSc*
**Wyndham-Quin** *Who 92*
**Wyndham-White,** Eric 1913-1980 *FacFETw*
**Wyndrum,** Ralph William, Jr 1937- *AmMWSc 92*
**Wyneken,** Jeanette 1956- *AmMWSc 92*
**Wyner,** Aaron D 1939- *AmMWSc 92*
**Wyner,** Justin L. 1925- *WhoFI 92*
**Wyner,** Susan Davenny 1945- *NewAmDM*
**Wyner,** Yehudi 1929- *NewAmDM, WhoEnt 92*
**Wynes,** Charles E. 1929- *WrDr 92*
**Wyness,** James Alexander Davidson 1937- *Who 92*
**Wynette,** Tammy 1942- *WhoEnt 92*
**Wynford,** Baron 1917- *Who 92*
**Wyngaard,** Jack *WhoEnt 92*
**Wyngaard,** John C 1938- *AmMWSc 92*
**Wyngaarden,** James Barnes 1924- *AmMWSc 92, Who 92, WhoAmP 91*
**Wynia,** Ann Jobe 1943- *WhoAmP 91*
**Wynia,** Gary W. 1942- *ConAu 133*
**Wynkoop,** Donald Robert 1945- *WhoMW 92*
**Wynkoop,** Eric Nathan 1960- *WhoFI 92*
**Wynn** *Who 92*
**Wynn,** Albert Russell 1951- *WhoAmP 91*
**Wynn,** Arthur Henry Ashford 1910- *Who 92*
**Wynn,** Barry *WhoAmP 91*
**Wynn,** Charles Martin, Sr 1939- *AmMWSc 92*
**Wynn,** Charles Milton 1953- *WhoAmL 92*
**Wynn,** Clayton S 1907- *AmMWSc 92*
**Wynn,** Cordell *WhoBlA 92*
**Wynn,** Dale Richard 1918- *WrDr 92*
**Wynn,** Daniel Arthur 1948- *WhoRel 92*
**Wynn,** Daniel Webster 1919- *WhoBlA 92*
**Wynn,** Daniel Webster 1919-1983 *ConAu 133*
**Wynn,** David Watkin W. *Who 92*
**Wynn,** Deborah B. 1947- *WhoBlA 92*
**Wynn,** Early 1920- *FacFETw*
**Wynn,** Ed d1966 *LesBEnT 92*
**Wynn,** Francis J *WhoIns 92*
**Wynn,** J. C. 1920- *WrDr 92*
**Wynn,** James Elkanah 1942- *AmMWSc 92*
**Wynn,** John Patrick 1951- *WhoFI 92*
**Wynn,** Kim Marie 1959- *WhoAmL 92*
**Wynn,** Larry W. 1953- *WhoRel 92*
**Wynn,** Malcolm 1940- *WhoBlA 92*
**Wynn,** Prathia Hall 1940- *WhoBlA 92*
**Wynn,** Ray *ScFEYrs*
**Wynn,** Richard Roland 1939- *WhoRel 92*
**Wynn,** Robert L., Jr. 1929- *WhoBlA 92*
**Wynn,** Robert Raymond 1929- *WhoWest 92*
**Wynn,** Stanford Alan 1950- *WhoAmL 92*
**Wynn,** Stephen A. 1941- *WhoWest 92*
**Wynn,** Sylvia J. 1941- *WhoBlA 92*
**Wynn,** Terence 1946- *Who 92*
**Wynn,** Terence Bryan 1928- *Who 92*
**Wynn,** Thomas Harold, Sr. 1931- *WhoBlA 92*
**Wynn,** Thomas Robert 1943- *WhoRel 92*
**Wynn,** Tracy Keenan *LesBEnT 92*
**Wynn,** Tracy Keenan 1945- *IntMPA 92, WhoEnt 92*
**Wynn,** Willard Kendall, Jr 1932- *AmMWSc 92*
**Wynn,** William Austin, Jr. 1937- *WhoBlA 92*
**Wynn,** William Jefferson 1946- *WhoAmL 92*
**Wynn-Williams,** George 1911- *Who 92*
**Wynne,** Bayard Edmund 1930- *AmMWSc 92, WhoFI 92*
**Wynne,** Brian *TwCWW 91, WrDr 92*
**Wynne,** Charles Gorrie 1911- *IntWW 91, Who 92*
**Wynne,** David 1926- *TwCPaSc, Who 92*
**Wynne,** Elise Marcia Newson 1931- *IntAu&W 91*
**Wynne,** Elmer Staten 1917- *AmMWSc 92*
**Wynne,** Frank *TwCWW 91, WrDr 92*
**Wynne,** George C 1949- *WhoIns 92*
**Wynne,** Greville 1919-1990 *AnObit 1990*
**Wynne,** Greville Maynard 1944-1990 *FacFETw*
**Wynne,** J. F. W. *Who 92*
**Wynne,** John *WhoAmP 91*
**Wynne,** John Benedict 1930- *WhoFI 92*
**Wynne,** John Boyce 1945- *WhoEnt 92*
**Wynne,** John Oliver 1945- *WhoEnt 92, WhoFI 92*
**Wynne,** Johnny Calvin 1943- *AmMWSc 92*
**Wynne,** Kenneth Joseph 1940- *AmMWSc 92*
**Wynne,** Lyman Carroll 1923- *AmMWSc 92*
**Wynne,** Marvell 1959- *WhoBlA 92*
**Wynne,** Michael James 1940- *AmMWSc 92, WhoMW 92*
**Wynne,** Robin *WhoAmP 91*
**Wynne,** William Joseph 1927- *WhoAmL 92*
**Wynne-Davies,** Marion 1958- *ConAu 133*
**Wynne-Edwards,** Hugh Robert 1934- *AmMWSc 92*
**Wynne-Edwards,** Vero Copner 1906- *IntWW 91, Who 92*
**Wynne-Jones,** Nancy 1922- *TwCPaSc*
**Wynne-Jones,** Tim 1948- *SmATA 67 [port]*
**Wynne Mason,** Walter 1910- *Who 92*
**Wynne-Morgan,** David 1931- *IntWW 91*
**Wynne-Morgan,** John 1906- *TwCPaSc*
**Wynner,** Edith 1915- *AmPeW*
**Wynns,** Corrie 1958- *WhoBlA 92*
**Wynnyckyj,** John Rostyslav 1932- *AmMWSc 92*
**Wynnyckyj,** Leo George 1931- *WhoFI 92*
**Wynston,** Leslie K 1934- *AmMWSc 92*
**Wynstra,** Nancy Ann 1941- *WhoAmL 92*
**Wynter,** Bryan 1915-1975 *TwCPaSc*
**Wynter,** Dana 1931- *IntMPA 92*
**Wynter,** Hector Lincoln 1926- *IntWW 91*
**Wynter,** Leon E. 1953- *WhoBlA 92*
**Wynter,** Sylvia 1928- *LiExTwC*
**Wynveen,** Robert Allen 1939- *AmMWSc 92*
**Wyon,** John Benjamin 1918- *AmMWSc 92*
**Wyrick,** Floyd I. 1932- *WhoBlA 92*
**Wyrick,** Paula Ann 1956- *WhoMW 92*
**Wyrick,** Phil 1949- *WhoAmP 91*
**Wyrick,** Priscilla Blakeney 1940- *AmMWSc 92*
**Wyrick,** Rex R 1923- *WhoAmP 91*
**Wyrick,** Ronald Earl 1944- *AmMWSc 92*
**Wyrick,** Stephen Von 1952- *WhoRel 92*
**Wyrick,** Steven Dale 1951- *AmMWSc 92*
**Wyrsch,** James Robert 1942- *WhoAmL 92, WhoMW 92*
**Wyrtki,** Klaus 1925- *AmMWSc 92*
**Wyrwa-Krzyzanski,** Tadeusz 1947- *IntAu&W 91*
**Wyrwicka,** Wanda 1912- *AmMWSc 92, WhoWest 92*
**Wysaske,** Ronald Alan 1952- *WhoWest 92*
**Wyse,** B O 1927- *AmMWSc 92*
**Wyse,** Bonita W 1945- *AmMWSc 92*
**Wyse,** David George 1941- *AmMWSc 92*
**Wyse,** Eric Lee 1959- *WhoEnt 92*
**Wyse,** Frank Oliver 1930- *AmMWSc 92*
**Wyse,** Gordon Arthur 1940- *AmMWSc 92*
**Wyse,** John Patrick Henry 1948- *AmMWSc 92*
**Wyse,** Joy Bartula 1934- *WhoEnt 92*
**Wyse,** William Walker 1919- *WhoWest 92*
**Wyshak,** Grace *AmMWSc 92*
**Wyskida,** Richard Martin 1935- *AmMWSc 92*
**Wyslotsky,** Ihor 1930- *WhoFI 92*
**Wysocki,** Allen John 1936- *AmMWSc 92*
**Wysocki,** Annette Bernadette 1954- *AmMWSc 92*
**Wysocki,** Charles Joseph 1947- *AmMWSc 92*
**Wysocki,** Felix Michael 1947- *WhoAmL 92*
**Wysocki,** Joseph J 1928- *AmMWSc 92*
**Wysocki,** Sharon Ann 1955- *WhoMW 92*
**Wysolmerski,** Theresa 1932- *AmMWSc 92*
**Wysong,** Christopher Alan 1965- *WhoFI 92*
**Wysong,** David Serge 1934- *AmMWSc 92*
**Wysor,** Bettie *DrAPF 91*
**Wyss,** David Alen 1944- *WhoFI 92*
**Wyss,** James Michael 1948- *AmMWSc 92*
**Wyss,** Leon F. 1934- *WhoRel 92*
**Wyss,** Loren Lee 1934- *WhoWest 92*
**Wyss,** Max 1939- *AmMWSc 92*
**Wyss,** Orville 1912- *AmMWSc 92*
**Wyss,** Thomas J 1942- *WhoAmP 91*
**Wyss,** Walter 1938- *AmMWSc 92*
**Wyssbrod,** Herman Robert 1941- *AmMWSc 92*
**Wystrach,** Vernon Paul 1919- *AmMWSc 92*
**Wyszynski,** Richard Chester 1933- *WhoEnt 92, WhoMW 92*
**Wyszynski,** Stefan 1901-1981 *FacFETw [port]*
**Wyszynski,** Valentine Anthony 1941- *WhoEnt 92*
**Wythe,** George 1726-1806 *BlkwEAR*
**Wyton,** Alec 1921- *NewAmDM, WhoEnt 92*
**Wytrwal,** Joseph A. 1924- *WrDr 92*
**Wytrykus,** Michael Joseph 1949- *WhoMW 92*
**Wytrzens,** Gunther 1922- *IntWW 91*
**Wyttenbach,** Charles Richard 1933- *AmMWSc 92*
**Wyzga,** Ronald Edward 1942- *AmMWSc 92*
**Wyzgoski,** Michael Gary 1943- *AmMWSc 92, WhoMW 92*
**Wyzner,** Eugeniusz 1931- *IntWW 91*

# X-Y

**X** *NewAmDM*
**X,** Frank *DrAPF 91*
**X,** Malcolm *BenetAL 91*
**X,** Malcolm 1925-1965 *ConBlB 1 [port]*
**X,** Marvin *DrAPF 91*
**Xafa,** Aristea 1950- *WhoFI 92*
**Xantus,** Janos 1825-1894 *BiInAmS*
**Xenakis,** Iannis 1922- *ConCom 92, IntWW 91, NewAmDM, Who 92*
**Xenopoulos,** Damon Elias 1961- *WhoAmL 92*
**Xi Zhongxun** 1912- *IntWW 91*
**Xi,** Zai-Qing 1939- *WhoMW 92*
**Xia Shihou** *IntWW 91*
**Xia Yan** 1900- *IntWW 91*
**Xiang Nan** 1916- *IntWW 91*
**Xiang Shouzhi,** Gen. 1917- *IntWW 91*
**Xiao Han** 1924- *IntWW 91*
**Xiao Ke** 1908- *IntWW 91*
**Xiao Quanfu** 1916- *IntWW 91*
**Xiao Yang** 1930- *IntWW 91*
**Xiaoxian,** Hou *IntDcF 2-2*
**Xie Bingxin** 1900- *IntWW 91*
**Xie Fei** 1932- *IntWW 91*
**Xie Feng** 1922- *IntWW 91*
**Xie Heng** 1921- *IntWW 91*
**Xie Jin** 1923- *IntDcF 2-2, IntWW 91*
**Xie Xide** 1921- *IntWW 91*
**Xie Zhenhua** 1916- *IntWW 91*
**Xie,** Bingxin 1900- *IntAu&W 91*
**Xie,** Ya-Hong 1956- *AmMWSc 92*
**Xie-Yang,** Chen 1939- *WhoEnt 92*
**Xifaras,** Margaret D *WhoAmP 91*
**Ximenes,** Vicente Trevino 1919- *WhoHisp 92*
**Ximenez,** Francisco 1666-1729 *HisDSpE*
**Xing Bensi** 1929- *IntWW 91*
**Xing Chongzhi** 1927- *IntWW 91*
**Xing Zhikang** 1930- *IntWW 91*
**Xintaras,** Charles 1928- *AmMWSc 92*
**Xiong Fu** 1916- *IntWW 91*
**Xiong Qingquan** 1927- *IntWW 91*
**Xiong,** Tousu Saydangnmv 1966- *WhoRel 92*
**Xoregos,** Shela *WhoEnt 92*
**Xu Bing** 1955- *IntWW 91*
**Xu Caidong** 1955- *IntWW 91*
**Xu Deheng** d1990 *IntWW 91N*
**Xu Gang** 1945- *LiExTwC*
**Xu Haifeng** 1957- *IntWW 91*
**Xu Houze** 1934- *IntWW 91*
**Xu Huaizhong** 1929- *IntWW 91*
**Xu Jiatun** 1916- *FacFETw, IntWW 91*
**Xu Qin** 1928- *IntWW 91*
**Xu Shaofu** 1920- *IntWW 91*
**Xu Shuyang** 1927- *IntWW 91*
**Xu Xiangqian** d1990 *IntWW 91N*
**Xu Xiangqian** 1901-1990 *FacFETw*
**Xu Xin** 1921- *IntWW 91*
**Xu Yinsheng** 1938- *IntWW 91*
**Xu Youfang** 1939- *IntWW 91*
**Xu Zhenshi** 1937- *IntWW 91*
**Xu,** Hong Jun 1963- *WhoMW 92*
**Xuan,** Bui Thi *EncAmaz 91*
**Xue Ju** 1922- *IntWW 91*
**Xue Muqiao** 1904- *IntWW 91*
**Xue Wei** 1963- *IntWW 91*
**Xuereb,** Paul 1923- *IntWW 91*
**Xuereb,** Publius Mario 1947- *WhoRel 92*
**Yaa Asantewa** d1921 *EncAmaz 91*
**Yaacobi,** Gad 1935- *IntWW 91*
**Yaakobi,** Barukh 1936- *AmMWSc 92*
**Yablans,** Frank 1935- *IntMPA 92, WhoEnt 92A*
**Yablans,** Irwin 1934- *IntMPA 92*
**Yablans,** Robert Steven 1959- *WhoEnt 92*
**Yablecki,** Edward J 1940- *WhoIns 92*
**Yablon,** Isadore Gerald 1933- *AmMWSc 92*
**Yablon,** Leonard F. 1944- *WhoFI 92*
**Yablon,** Marvin 1935- *AmMWSc 92*
**Yablonovitch,** Eli 1946- *AmMWSc 92*
**Yablonskaya,** Oxana 1938- *WhoEnt 92*
**Yablonskaya,** Tat'yana Nilovna 1917- *SovUnBD*
**Yablonski,** Joseph 1910-1969 *FacFETw*
**Yablonski,** Michael Eugene 1940- *AmMWSc 92*
**Yablonsky,** Harvey Allen 1933- *AmMWSc 92*
**Yabuki,** Ken Keiji 1937- *WhoWest 92*
**Yabutani,** Koichi Mole 1931- *WhoWest 92*
**Yacavone,** Muriel Taul 1920- *WhoAmP 91*
**Yace,** Philippe Gregoire 1920- *IntWW 91*
**Yachnin,** Stanley 1930- *AmMWSc 92*
**Yachnis,** Michael 1922- *AmMWSc 92*
**Yackel,** James W 1936- *AmMWSc 92*
**Yackel,** James William 1936- *WhoMW 92*
**Yackel,** Kenneth Raymond 1946- *WhoFI 92*
**Yackel,** Walter Carl 1942- *AmMWSc 92*
**Yacktman,** Donald Arthur 1941- *WhoFI 92*
**Yaco,** Link 1955- *WhoMW 92*
**Yacoub,** Kamal 1932- *AmMWSc 92*
**Yacoub,** Magdi Habib 1935- *IntWW 91, Who 92*
**Yacoub,** Mary H. 1933- *WhoWest 92*
**Yacoub,** Talaat 1943?-1988 *FacFETw*
**Yacovone,** Mark Anthony 1944- *WhoEnt 92*
**Yacowitz,** Harold 1922- *AmMWSc 92*
**Yadav,** Kamaleshwari Prasad 1937- *AmMWSc 92*
**Yadav,** Raghunath P 1935- *AmMWSc 92*
**Yadavalli,** Sriramamurti Venkata 1924- *AmMWSc 92*
**Yaden,** Senkalong 1935- *AmMWSc 92*
**Yadin,** Yigael 1917-1984 *FacFETw*
**Yadlin,** Aharon 1926- *IntWW 91*
**Yadon,** Vernal Lee 1930- *WhoWest 92*
**Yadov,** Vladimir Aleksandrovich 1929- *SovUnBD*
**Yadvish,** Robert D *AmMWSc 92*
**Yaeger,** Billie Patricia 1949- *WhoFI 92*
**Yaeger,** Jacob Charles 1957- *WhoRel 92*
**Yaeger,** James Amos 1928- *AmMWSc 92*
**Yaeger,** Robert George 1917- *AmMWSc 92*
**Yaes,** Robert Joel 1942- *AmMWSc 92*
**Yafet,** Yako 1923- *AmMWSc 92*
**Yaffe,** James *DrAPF 91*
**Yaffe,** James 1927- *BenetAL 91, ConNov 91, WhoEnt 92, WrDr 92*
**Yaffe,** Leo 1916- *AmMWSc 92*
**Yaffe,** Michael Charles 1951- *WhoEnt 92*
**Yaffe,** Roberta 1944- *AmMWSc 92*
**Yaffe,** Ruth Powers 1927- *AmMWSc 92*
**Yaffe,** Sumner J 1923- *AmMWSc 92*
**Yaffie,** Burton Sheron 1940- *WhoAmP 91*
**Yafi,** Abdullah Aref al- 1901- *IntWW 91*
**Yag,** Darryl Takizo *WhoWest 92*
**Yager,** Ann Marie 1945- *WhoEnt 92*
**Yager,** Billy Joe 1932- *AmMWSc 92*
**Yager,** Geoffrey Gilbert 1944- *WhoMW 92*
**Yager,** James Donald, Jr 1943- *AmMWSc 92*
**Yager,** Janice L Winter 1940- *AmMWSc 92*
**Yager,** John Warren 1920- *WhoAmL 92, WhoFI 92*
**Yager,** Philip Marvin 1938- *AmMWSc 92*
**Yager,** Robert Eugene 1930- *AmMWSc 92*
**Yager,** Robert H *AmMWSc 92*
**Yager,** Vincent Cook 1928- *WhoFI 92*
**Yaggi,** Hank *WhoEnt 92*
**Yaggy,** Paul Francis 1923- *AmMWSc 92*
**Yaghjian,** Arthur David 1943- *AmMWSc 92*
**Yagi,** Fumio 1917- *AmMWSc 92*
**Yagi,** Haruhiko 1939- *AmMWSc 92*
**Yagi,** Yasuhiro 1920- *IntWW 91*
**Yagiela,** John Allen 1947- *AmMWSc 92*
**Yagjian,** Anita Paleologos 1954- *WhoWest 92*
**Yagjian,** Michael Arthur 1949- *WhoWest 92*
**Yagle,** Raymond A 1923- *AmMWSc 92*
**Yago,** Bernard 1916- *IntWW 91, WhoRel 92*
**Yagoda,** Genrikh Grigorevich 1891-1937 *FacFETw*
**Yagoda,** Genrikh Grigor'evich 1891-1938 *SovUnBD*
**Yagodin,** Gennadiy Alekseyevich 1927- *IntWW 91*
**Yaguchi,** Makoto 1930- *AmMWSc 92*
**Yagudin,** Shamil Khairulovich 1932- *IntWW 91*
**Yague Blanco,** Juan Lorenzo Teodoro 1891-1952 *BiDExR*
**Yahil,** Amos 1943- *AmMWSc 92*
**Yahl,** Kevin Francis 1959- *WhoMW 92*
**Yahner,** Joseph Edward 1931- *AmMWSc 92*
**Yahner,** Paul J 1908- *WhoAmP 91*
**Yahner,** Richard Howard 1949- *AmMWSc 92*
**Yahnke,** Robert Eugene 1947- *WhoMW 92*
**Yahr,** Melvin David 1917- *AmMWSc 92*
**Yahya Khan,** Agha Muhammad 1917-1980 *FacFETw*
**Yakaitis,** Ronald William 1941- *AmMWSc 92*
**Yakaitis-Surbis,** Albina Ann 1923- *AmMWSc 92*
**Yakas,** Orestes 1920- *IntWW 91*
**Yakatan,** Gerald Joseph 1942- *AmMWSc 92, WhoWest 92*
**Yakatan,** Stan 1942- *WhoWest 92*
**Yakel,** Harry L 1929- *AmMWSc 92*
**Yaker,** Bernard 1936- *WhoAmL 92*
**Yaker,** Lynda E. 1945- *WhoFI 92*
**Yakich,** David Eli 1957- *WhoWest 92*
**Yakim,** Moni *WhoEnt 92*
**Yakin,** Mustafa Zafer 1952- *AmMWSc 92*
**Yakir,** Petr Ionovich 1923-1982 *SovUnBD*
**Yakobson,** Leonid Veniaminovich 1904-1975 *SovUnBD*
**Yakovlev,** Aleksandr Nikolaevich 1923- *SovUnBD*
**Yakovlev,** Aleksandr Nikolayevich 1923- *IntWW 91*
**Yakovlev,** Aleksandr Sergeevich 1906-1989 *SovUnBD*
**Yakovlev,** Aleksandr Sergeyevich 1906-1989 *FacFETw*
**Yakovlev,** Boris Nikolaevich 1890-1972 *SovUnBD*
**Yakovlev,** Boris Pavlovich 1908- *SovUnBD*
**Yakovlev,** Yegor Vladimirovich 1930- *IntWW 91, SovUnBD*
**Yakowitz,** Harvey 1939- *AmMWSc 92*
**Yakowitz,** Sidney J 1937- *AmMWSc 92*
**Yaksh,** Tony Lee 1944- *AmMWSc 92*
**Yaksic,** Barbara Friedman 1956- *WhoAmL 92*
**Yakubik,** John 1928- *AmMWSc 92*
**Yakubovsky,** Ivan Ignat'evich 1908-1976 *SovUnBD*
**Yakunin,** Gleb Pavlovich 1934- *SovUnBD*
**Yakura,** Hidetaka *AmMWSc 92*
**Yakura,** James K 1933- *AmMWSc 92*
**Yakura,** Thelma Pauline *WhoMW 92*
**Yalam,** Arnold Robert 1940- *WhoWest 92*
**Yalcintas,** M Guven 1945- *AmMWSc 92*
**Yale,** Brian 1936- *TwCPaSc*
**Yale,** Charles E 1925- *AmMWSc 92*
**Yale,** David Eryl Corbet 1928- *Who 92*
**Yale,** Harry Louis 1913- *AmMWSc 92*
**Yale,** Irl Keith 1939- *AmMWSc 92*
**Yale,** Kenneth P. 1956- *WhoAmL 92*
**Yale,** Paul B 1932- *AmMWSc 92*
**Yale,** Russell Steven 1947- *WhoMW 92*
**Yale,** Seymour Hershel 1920- *AmMWSc 92*
**Yale-Loehr,** Stephen William 1954- *WhoAmL 92*
**Yalen,** Gary N. 1942- *WhoFI 92*
**Yalkovsky,** Rafael 1917- *AmMWSc 92*
**Yalkowsky,** Samuel Hyman 1942- *AmMWSc 92*
**Yalkut,** Carolyn *DrAPF 91*
**Yalkut,** Jud 1938- *WhoEnt 92*
**Yall,** Irving 1923- *AmMWSc 92*
**Yalman,** Richard George 1923- *AmMWSc 92*
**Yalovsky,** Morty A 1944- *AmMWSc 92*
**Yalow,** A Aaron 1919- *AmMWSc 92*
**Yalow,** Rosalyn Sussman 1921- *AmMWSc 92, FacFETw, IntWW 91, Who 92, WhoNob 90*
**Yaltkaya,** Cengiz Refik 1947- *WhoEnt 92*
**Yam,** John Ivan 1944- *WhoWest 92*
**Yam,** Lung Tsiong 1936- *AmMWSc 92*
**Yam,** Siva 1958- *WhoFI 92*
**Yama,** Eric Norio 1952- *WhoWest 92*
**Yamada,** Dennis Roy 1944- *WhoAmP 91*
**Yamada,** Eichi 1922- *AmMWSc 92*
**Yamada,** Esther V 1923- *AmMWSc 92*
**Yamada,** Hisatoshi 1932- *WhoFI 92*
**Yamada,** Kenneth Manao 1944- *AmMWSc 92*
**Yamada,** Kosaku 1886-1965 *NewAmDM*
**Yamada,** Masaaki 1942- *AmMWSc 92*
**Yamada,** Mitsuye *DrAPF 91*
**Yamada,** Ryuji 1932- *AmMWSc 92, WhoMW 92*
**Yamada,** Stephen Kinichi 1946- *WhoAmL 92, WhoFI 92*
**Yamada,** Sylvia Behrens 1946- *AmMWSc 92*
**Yamada,** Tetsuji 1942- *AmMWSc 92*
**Yamada,** William Yukio 1951- *WhoFI 92*
**Yamada,** Yoshikazu 1915- *AmMWSc 92*
**Yamagishi,** Frederick George 1943- *AmMWSc 92*
**Yamaguchi,** Kenji 1933- *IntWW 91*

**Yamaguchi**, Masatoshi 1918- AmMWSc 92
**Yamaguchi**, Tadanori 1949- AmMWSc 92
**Yamaguchi**, Toshio 1940- IntWW 91
**Yamakawa**, Allan Hitoshi 1938- WhoMW 92
**Yamakawa**, David Kiyoshi, Jr. 1936- WhoAmL 92, WhoFI 92, WhoWest 92
**Yamakawa**, Kazuo Alan 1918- AmMWSc 92
**Yamamoto**, Diane M 1946- AmMWSc 92
**Yamamoto**, Edward Keizo 1942- WhoEnt 92
**Yamamoto**, Harry Y 1933- AmMWSc 92
**Yamamoto**, Hiroshi 1946- AmMWSc 92
**Yamamoto**, Hisaye DrAPF 91
**Yamamoto**, Isoruko 1884-1943 FacFETw [port]
**Yamamoto**, Jerel Ikuo 1955- WhoAmL 92
**Yamamoto**, Joe 1924- AmMWSc 92
**Yamamoto**, Kansai 1944- DcTwDes
**Yamamoto**, Keith Robert 1946- AmMWSc 92
**Yamamoto**, Kenichi 1922- IntWW 91
**Yamamoto**, Mitsuyoshi 1923- AmMWSc 92
**Yamamoto**, Nobuto 1925- AmMWSc 92
**Yamamoto**, Richard 1927- AmMWSc 92
**Yamamoto**, Richard Kumeo 1935- AmMWSc 92
**Yamamoto**, Richard Susumu 1920- AmMWSc 92
**Yamamoto**, Robert Takaichi 1927- AmMWSc 92
**Yamamoto**, Sachio 1911- IntWW 91
**Yamamoto**, Sachio 1932- AmMWSc 92
**Yamamoto**, Tatsuzo 1928- AmMWSc 92
**Yamamoto**, Tomio IntWW 91
**Yamamoto**, William Shigeru 1924- AmMWSc 92
**Yamamoto**, Y Lucas 1928- AmMWSc 92
**Yamamoto**, Yasushi Stephen 1943- AmMWSc 92
**Yamamoto**, Yohji 1943- DcTwDes
**Yamamura**, Henry Ichiro 1940- AmMWSc 92
**Yamanaka**, Sadanori 1921- IntWW 91
**Yamanaka**, Tetsuo 1921- IntWW 91
**Yamanaka**, William Kiyoshi 1931- AmMWSc 92
**Yamane**, George M 1924- AmMWSc 92
**Yamane**, Stanley Joel 1943- WhoFI 92
**Yamani**, Ahmed Zaki 1930- IntWW 91
**Yamanouchi**, Taiji 1931- AmMWSc 92
**Yamaoka**, Seigen Haruo 1934- WhoRel 92, WhoWest 92
**Yamarone**, Charles Anthony, Jr. 1936- WhoWest 92
**Yamarone**, Richard 1962- WhoFI 92
**Yamartino**, Robert J 1944- AmMWSc 92
**Yamasaki**, Hiro 1932- IntWW 91
**Yamasaki**, Mamoru 1916- WhoAmP 91
**Yamasaki**, Minoru 1912-1986 FacFETw
**Yamashiro**, Jane Mieko 1939- WhoWest 92
**Yamashiro**, Stanley Motohiro 1941- AmMWSc 92
**Yamashiro**, Yoshinari 1923- IntWW 91
**Yamashiroya**, Herbert Mitsugi 1930- AmMWSc 92
**Yamashita**, Francis Isami 1949- WhoAmL 92
**Yamashita**, Isamu 1911- IntWW 91
**Yamashita**, Jason S. 1962- WhoEnt 92
**Yamashita**, Tokuo 1919- IntWW 91
**Yamashita**, Tomoyuki 188-?-1946 FacFETw
**Yamashita**, Toshihiko 1919- IntWW 91
**Yamato**, Yoshiko WhoWest 92
**Yamauchi**, Catherine Fay Takako 1959- WhoWest 92
**Yamauchi**, Edwin Masao 1937- WhoMW 92
**Yamauchi**, Hiroshi 1923- AmMWSc 92
**Yamauchi**, Masanobu 1931- AmMWSc 92
**Yamauchi**, Toshio 1945- AmMWSc 92
**Yamazaki**, Hiroshi 1931- AmMWSc 92
**Yamazaki**, Hiroshi 1960- WhoWest 92
**Yamazaki**, Koji 1933- IntWW 91
**Yamazaki**, Makoto 1948- WhoFI 92
**Yamazaki**, Russell Kazuo 1942- AmMWSc 92
**Yamazaki**, Toshio 1922- IntWW 91, Who 92
**Yamazaki**, William Toshi 1917- AmMWSc 92
**Yambert**, Paul Abt 1928- AmMWSc 92
**Yambrusic**, Edward Slavko 1933- WhoAmL 92
**Yamdagni**, Raghavendra 1941- AmMWSc 92
**Yameogo**, Maurice 1921- IntWW 91
**Yamey**, Basil Selig 1919- IntWW 91, Who 92
**Yamin**, Joseph Francis 1956- WhoMW 92
**Yamin**, Michael Geoffrey 1931- WhoAmL 92
**Yamin**, Samuel Peter 1938- AmMWSc 92
**Yamini**, Sohrab 1953- AmMWSc 92
**Yamins**, J L 1914- AmMWSc 92
**Yammine**, Riad Nassif 1934- WhoFI 92
**Yamoor**, Mohammed Younis 1941- WhoMW 92
**Yampolsky**, Abram Ilich 1890-1956 NewAmDM, SovUnBD
**Yampolsky**, Berta Ziona WhoEnt 92
**Yan Dakai** 1915?- IntWW 91
**Yan Dongsheng** 1918- IntWW 91
**Yan Jici** 1900- IntWW 91
**Yan Renying** IntWW 91
**Yan Wenjing** 1915- IntWW 91
**Yan Zheng** 1918- IntWW 91
**Yan**, Johnson Faa 1934- AmMWSc 92
**Yan**, Man Fei 1948- AmMWSc 92
**Yan**, Maxwell Menuhin 1919- AmMWSc 92
**Yan**, Sau-Chi Betty 1954- AmMWSc 92
**Yan**, Tsoung-Yuan 1933- AmMWSc 92
**Yan**, Tung-Mow 1936- AmMWSc 92
**Yanabu**, Satoru 1941- AmMWSc 92
**Yanaev**, Gennadiy Ivanovich 1937- SovUnBD
**Yanagihara**, Richard 1946- AmMWSc 92
**Yanagimachi**, Ryuzo 1928- AmMWSc 92
**Yanagisawa**, Samuel T 1922- AmMWSc 92
**Yanagiya**, Kensuke 1924- IntWW 91
**Yanai**, Hideyasu Steve 1928- AmMWSc 92
**Yanari**, Sam Satomi 1923- AmMWSc 92
**Yanas**, John Joseph 1929- WhoAmL 92
**Yanayev**, Gennadiy Ivanovich 1937- IntWW 91
**Yance**, James Alexander 1946- WhoAmL 92
**Yancey**, Asa G 1916- AmMWSc 92
**Yancey**, Asa G., Sr. WhoBlA 92
**Yancey**, Carolyn Lois 1950- WhoBlA 92
**Yancey**, Charles Calvin 1948- WhoBlA 92
**Yancey**, Jimmy 1894-1951 NewAmDM
**Yancey**, John Franklin 1968- WhoRel 92
**Yancey**, Laurel Guild 1953- WhoBlA 92
**Yancey**, Paul Herbert 1951- AmMWSc 92
**Yancey**, Quillian S 1922- WhoAmP 91
**Yancey**, Robert Earl, Jr. 1945- WhoFI 92
**Yancey**, Robert John, Jr 1948- AmMWSc 92
**Yancey**, Thomas Erwin 1941- AmMWSc 92
**Yancey**, W Glenn 1930- WhoIns 92
**Yancey**, Wes TwCWW 91
**Yancey**, William Lowndes 1814-1863 AmPolLe
**Yanchick**, Victor A 1940- AmMWSc 92
**Yancik**, Joseph J 1930- AmMWSc 92
**Yancy**, Daniel Joseph 1963- WhoWest 92
**Yancy**, Dorothy Cowser 1944- WhoBlA 92
**Yancy**, Larry Grady 1946- WhoMW 92
**Yancy**, Preston Martin 1938- WhoBlA 92
**Yancy**, Robert James 1944- WhoBlA 92, WhoFI 92
**Yancy**, Wes WrDr 92
**Yandala**, Douglas Baker 1953- WhoEnt 92
**Yandell**, Clyde Raymond 1961- WhoMW 92
**Yandell**, Keith Edward 1938- WrDr 92
**Yandell**, Lunsford Pitts 1805-1878 BiInAmS
**Yanders**, Armon Frederick 1928- AmMWSc 92
**Yandl**, George Anthony 1947- WhoMW 92
**Yandle**, Stephen Thomas 1947- WhoAmL 92
**Yando**, David Allen 1954- WhoAmL 92
**Yando**, Emmanuel WhoRel 92
**Yandrisevits**, Frank W 1954- WhoAmP 91
**Yaneff**, Paul J. 1923- WhoAmL 92
**Yanenko**, Nikolay Nikolayevich d1984 IntWW 91N
**Yaney**, Perry Pappas 1931- AmMWSc 92
**Yanez**, Agustin 1904-1980 BenetAL 91
**Yanez**, Armando Juan 1949- WhoHisp 92
**Yanez**, Frank Javier 1968- WhoHisp 92
**Yanez**, Frank John 1962- WhoHisp 92
**Yanez Pinzon**, Vicente HisDSpE
**Yang Baibing** 1920- IntWW 91
**Yang Bo** 1920- IntWW 91
**Yang Chen** 1916- IntWW 91
**Yang Chen Ning** 1922- IntWW 91
**Yang Cheng-Zhi** 1938- IntWW 91
**Yang Chengwu** 1912- IntWW 91
**Yang Dezhi** 1910- IntWW 91
**Yang Di** 1924- IntWW 91
**Yang Haibo** 1912- IntWW 91
**Yang Jike** IntWW 91
**Yang Jingren** 1905- IntWW 91
**Yang Lian** 1953- LiExTwC
**Yang Paifeng** EncAmaz 91
**Yang Rudai** 1924- IntWW 91
**Yang Shangkun** 1907- IntWW 91, Who 92
**Yang Shouzheng** IntWW 91
**Yang Taifang** 1927- IntWW 91
**Yang Xizong** 1928- IntWW 91
**Yang Yang** 1958- IntWW 91
**Yang Yi** 1939- IntWW 91
**Yang Yichen** 1911- IntWW 91
**Yang Zhenhuai** 1928- IntWW 91
**Yang Zhenya** IntWW 91
**Yang Zhiguang** 1930- IntWW 91
**Yang**, An Tzu 1923- AmMWSc 92
**Yang**, Anthony Tsu-Ming 1944- WhoWest 92
**Yang**, Arthur Jing-Min 1947- AmMWSc 92
**Yang**, C. S. WhoRel 92
**Yang**, C Y 1930- AmMWSc 92
**Yang**, Chao-Chih 1928- AmMWSc 92
**Yang**, Chao-Hui 1928- AmMWSc 92
**Yang**, Charles Chin-Tze 1922- AmMWSc 92
**Yang**, Chen Ning 1922- AmMWSc 92, Who 92, WhoNob 90
**Yang**, Chia Hsiung 1940- AmMWSc 92
**Yang**, Chih Ted 1940- AmMWSc 92
**Yang**, Ching Huan 1920- AmMWSc 92
**Yang**, Chui-Hsu 1938- AmMWSc 92
**Yang**, Chun Chuan 1936- AmMWSc 92
**Yang**, Chung Ching 1938- AmMWSc 92
**Yang**, Chung-Chun 1942- AmMWSc 92
**Yang**, Chung Shu 1941- AmMWSc 92
**Yang**, Chung-Tao 1923- AmMWSc 92
**Yang**, Da-Ping 1933- AmMWSc 92
**Yang**, Darchun Billy 1945- AmMWSc 92
**Yang**, David Chie-Hwa 1954- WhoFI 92
**Yang**, David Chih-Hsin 1947- AmMWSc 92
**Yang**, Dominic Tsung-Che 1933- AmMWSc 92
**Yang**, Dorothy Chuan-Ying 1918- AmMWSc 92
**Yang**, Edward S 1937- AmMWSc 92
**Yang**, Funnei AmMWSc 92
**Yang**, Gene Ching-Hua 1938- AmMWSc 92
**Yang**, Grace L AmMWSc 92
**Yang**, H T 1924- AmMWSc 92
**Yang**, Henry T Y 1940- AmMWSc 92
**Yang**, Henry Tsu Yow 1940- WhoMW 92
**Yang**, Ho Seung 1947- AmMWSc 92
**Yang**, Hong-Yi 1933- AmMWSc 92
**Yang**, Hoya Y 1912- AmMWSc 92
**Yang**, Hsin-Ming 1952- WhoWest 92
**Yang**, In Che 1934- AmMWSc 92
**Yang**, Jen Tsi 1922- AmMWSc 92
**Yang**, Jenn-Ming 1957- AmMWSc 92
**Yang**, Jeong Sheng 1934- AmMWSc 92
**Yang**, Jih Hsin 1937- AmMWSc 92
**Yang**, John Yun-Wen 1930- AmMWSc 92
**Yang**, Joseph P. 1959- WhoFI 92
**Yang**, Julie Chi-Sun 1928- AmMWSc 92
**Yang**, Julie Lee 1952- WhoWest 92
**Yang**, Kei-Hsiung 1940- AmMWSc 92
**Yang**, Kung-Wei 1935- WhoMW 92
**Yang**, Kwang-Tzu 1928- AmMWSc 92
**Yang**, Linda Tsao 1926- WhoWest 92
**Yang**, Long Nha 1962- WhoRel 92
**Yang**, Man-chiu 1946- AmMWSc 92
**Yang**, Mark Chao-Kuen 1942- AmMWSc 92
**Yang**, Meiling T 1931- AmMWSc 92
**Yang**, Nien-Chu 1928- AmMWSc 92
**Yang**, Ovid Y H AmMWSc 92
**Yang**, Paul Wang 1953- AmMWSc 92
**Yang**, Philip Yung-Chin 1954- AmMWSc 92
**Yang**, Ralph Tzu-Bow 1942- AmMWSc 92
**Yang**, Sen-Lian 1938- AmMWSc 92
**Yang**, Shang Fa 1932- AmMWSc 92, WhoWest 92
**Yang**, Shang-Tian 1954- WhoMW 92
**Yang**, Shen Kwei 1941- AmMWSc 92
**Yang**, Shiang-Ping 1919- AmMWSc 92
**Yang**, Shiow-shong 1940- WhoWest 92
**Yang**, Shung-Jun 1934- AmMWSc 92
**Yang**, Song-Yu 1938- AmMWSc 92
**Yang**, Susan Su-Lune 1958- WhoWest 92
**Yang**, Ta-Lun 1937- AmMWSc 92
**Yang**, Tah Teh 1927- AmMWSc 92
**Yang**, Ti Liang 1929- IntWW 91, Who 92
**Yang**, Tsanyen 1949- AmMWSc 92
**Yang**, Tsu-Ju 1932- AmMWSc 92
**Yang**, Tsute 1916- AmMWSc 92
**Yang**, Wei-Hsuin 1936- AmMWSc 92
**Yang**, Weitao 1961- AmMWSc 92
**Yang**, Wen-Ching 1939- AmMWSc 92
**Yang**, Wen Jei 1931- AmMWSc 92, WhoFI 92
**Yang**, Wen-Kuang 1936- AmMWSc 92
**Yang**, Wesley 1949- WhoAmL 92
**Yang**, William C T AmMWSc 92
**Yang**, Xiaowei 1954- AmMWSc 92
**Yang**, Yenting 1933- WhoWest 92
**Yang-Kang Lin** 1927- IntWW 91
**Yangel**, Mikhail Kuz'mich 1911-1971 SovUnBD
**Yangling Duoji** 1931- IntWW 91
**Yanguas**, Lourdes M. 1965- WhoHisp 92
**Yanick**, Nicholas Samuel 1907- AmMWSc 92
**Yanish**, Michael John 1953- WhoWest 92
**Yaniv**, Avner 1942- IntAu&W 91
**Yaniv**, Shlomo Stefan 1931- AmMWSc 92
**Yaniv**, Simone Liliane 1938- AmMWSc 92
**Yaniz**, Henry Alexander 1917- WhoHisp 92
**Yankauer**, Alfred 1913- AmMWSc 92
**Yankauskas**, Anthony Edward 1948- WhoFI 92
**Yankee**, Ernest Warren 1943- AmMWSc 92
**Yankee**, Ronald August 1934- AmMWSc 92
**Yankelevsky**, Vladimir IntWW 91
**Yankell**, Samuel L 1935- AmMWSc 92
**Yanko**, William Harry 1919- AmMWSc 92
**Yankov**, Alexander 1924- Who 92
**Yankovic**, Al 1959- WhoEnt 92
**Yankovic**, Weird Al 1959- ConMus 7 [port]
**Yankow**, Jeffrey Scott 1950- WhoWest 92
**Yankowitz**, Susan DrAPF 91
**Yankowitz**, Susan 1941- WrDr 92
**Yankwich**, Peter Ewald 1923- AmMWSc 92
**Yannas**, Ioannis Vassilios 1935- AmMWSc 92
**Yannitell**, Daniel W 1941- AmMWSc 92
**Yannone**, Mark Joseph 1949- WhoWest 92
**Yannoni**, Costantino Sheldon 1935- AmMWSc 92
**Yannoni**, Nicholas 1927- AmMWSc 92
**Yannucci**, Thomas David 1950- WhoAmL 92
**Yannuzzi**, William Anthony 1934- WhoEnt 92
**Yano**, Fleur Belle AmMWSc 92
**Yano**, Jun'ya 1932- IntWW 91
**Yanofsky**, Charles 1925- AmMWSc 92, IntWW 91
**Yanomami**, Davi Kopenawa NewYTBS 91 [port]
**Yanosko**, Raymond Anthony 1929- WhoMW 92
**Yanover**, Michael Isaac 1963- WhoEnt 92
**Yanovsky**, Rudolf Grigorevich 1929- IntWW 91
**Yanovsky**, Vasily Semenovych 1906-1989 LiExTwC
**Yanow**, Gilbert 1935- AmMWSc 92
**Yanowitch**, Michael 1923- AmMWSc 92
**Yanowitz**, Bennett 1923- WhoRel 92
**Yanowski**, Barbara T. 1931- WhoEnt 92
**Yansangwara**, Somdej Phra WhoRel 92
**Yant**, Martin 1949- ConAu 134
**Yant**, Richard Demarest 1955- WhoAmL 92
**Yantis**, Phillip Alexander 1928- AmMWSc 92
**Yantis**, Richard P 1932- AmMWSc 92
**Yantis**, Richard Perry 1932- WhoMW 92
**Yanushka**, Arthur 1948- AmMWSc 92
**Yao Shun** 1919- IntWW 91
**Yao Wenyuan** FacFETw
**Yao Wenyuan** 1924- IntWW 91
**Yao Xin** 1925- IntWW 91
**Yao Xueyin** 1911- IntWW 91
**Yao Yilin** 1915- IntWW 91
**Yao Zhonghua** 1939- IntWW 91
**Yao Zhongming** 1914- IntWW 91
**Yao**, Alice C AmMWSc 92
**Yao**, David D 1950- AmMWSc 92
**Yao**, Hsin-Nung d1991 NewYTBS 91
**Yao**, James T-P 1933- AmMWSc 92
**Yao**, Jerry Shi Kuang 1925- AmMWSc 92
**Yao**, Joe 1930- AmMWSc 92
**Yao**, Kuan Mu 1923- AmMWSc 92
**Yao**, Kung 1938- AmMWSc 92
**Yao**, Meng-Chao 1949- AmMWSc 92
**Yao**, Neng-Ping 1938- AmMWSc 92
**Yao**, Shang Jeong 1934- AmMWSc 92
**Yao**, Shi Chune 1946- AmMWSc 92
**Yao**, York-Peng Edward 1937- AmMWSc 92
**Yaos-Kest**, Itamar 1934- IntAu&W 91
**Yap**, Fung Yen 1933- AmMWSc 92
**Yap**, Hing 1954- WhoMW 92
**Yap**, Kie-Han 1925- WhoFI 92
**Yap**, Moody Boon-Wan 1930- WhoRel 92
**Yap**, William Tan 1934- AmMWSc 92
**Yapel**, Anthony Francis, Jr 1937- AmMWSc 92
**Yaphe**, Wilfred 1921- AmMWSc 92
**Yapoujian**, Nerses Nick 1950- WhoMW 92
**Yapp**, Malcolm E. 1931- WrDr 92
**Yapp**, Stanley Graham Who 92
**Yaqub**, Adil Mohamed 1928- AmMWSc 92
**Yaqub**, Jill Courtaney Donaldson Spencer 1931- AmMWSc 92
**Yar'adua**, Shehu 1943- IntWW 91
**Yaramanoglu**, Melih 1947- AmMWSc 92
**Yarar**, Baki 1941- AmMWSc 92
**Yarashefski**, Ronald J 1943- WhoIns 92
**Yarber**, Robert 1948- WorArt 1980
**Yarbo**, Steve TwCWW 91
**Yarboro**, Theodore Leon 1932- WhoBlA 92
**Yarborough**, Earl of d1991 Who 92N
**Yarborough**, Earl of 1963- Who 92
**Yarborough**, Camille DrAPF 91
**Yarborough**, Dowd Julius, Jr. 1938- WhoBlA 92
**Yarborough**, Lyman 1937- AmMWSc 92
**Yarborough**, Ralph DcAmImH
**Yarborough**, Ralph Webster 1903- WhoAmP 91
**Yarborough**, Richard A. 1951- WhoBlA 92

**Yarborough**, Richard Felix, Jr. 1952- WhoAmL 92
**Yarborough**, Richard W 1931- WhoAmP 91
**Yarborough**, William 1926- WhoEnt 92
**Yarborough**, William Walter, Jr 1945- AmMWSc 92
**Yarbro**, Alan David 1941- WhoAmL 92
**Yarbro**, Chelsea Quinn 1942- IntAu&W 91, TwCSFW 91, WrDr 92
**Yarbro**, Claude Lee, Jr 1922- AmMWSc 92
**Yarbro**, John Williamson 1931- AmMWSc 92
**Yarbrough**, Arthur C, Jr 1928- AmMWSc 92
**Yarbrough**, Charles Gerald 1939- AmMWSc 92
**Yarbrough**, David Coleman 1938- WhoAmL 92
**Yarbrough**, David Wylie 1937- AmMWSc 92
**Yarbrough**, Delano 1936- WhoBlA 92
**Yarbrough**, Earnest 1923- WhoBlA 92
**Yarbrough**, Edward Meacham 1943- WhoAmL 92
**Yarbrough**, Emma Joe 1921- WhoAmP 91
**Yarbrough**, George Gibbs 1943- AmMWSc 92
**Yarbrough**, George Malone 1916- WhoAmP 91
**Yarbrough**, Harold Leroy 1934- WhoEnt 92
**Yarbrough**, Herbert A. Trey, III 1952- WhoAmL 92
**Yarbrough**, Jack Anthony 1963- WhoFI 92
**Yarbrough**, James David 1933- AmMWSc 92
**Yarbrough**, Jesse Thomas 1951- WhoRel 92
**Yarbrough**, Karen Marguerite 1938- AmMWSc 92
**Yarbrough**, Kenneth Wayne 1937- WhoAmP 91
**Yarbrough**, Leroy WhoRel 92
**Yarbrough**, Lynn Douglas 1930- AmMWSc 92
**Yarbrough**, Lynwood R 1940- AmMWSc 92
**Yarbrough**, Mamie Luella 1941- WhoBlA 92
**Yarbrough**, Marilyn Virginia 1945- WhoAmL 92, WhoBlA 92
**Yarbrough**, Martha Cornelia 1940- WhoEnt 92
**Yarbrough**, Robert Elzy 1929- WhoBlA 92
**Yarbrough**, Roosevelt 1946- WhoBlA 92
**Yarburgh-Bateson** Who 92
**Yarchoan**, Robert 1950- AmMWSc 92
**Yarchun**, Hyman Joshua 1946- WhoWest 92
**Yard**, Allan Stanley 1927- AmMWSc 92
**Yard**, Molly News 91 [port]
**Yard**, Sally Elizabeth 1951- WhoWest 92
**Yardbird** NewAmDM
**Yardbirds**, The NewAmDM
**Yarde**, Richard Foster 1939- WhoBlA 92
**Yarde-Buller** Who 92
**Yardley**, Benjamin 1953- WhoAmL 92
**Yardley**, Dan 1928- WhoAmP 91
**Yardley**, Darrell Gene 1948- AmMWSc 92
**Yardley**, David Charles Miller 1929- Who 92
**Yardley**, Donald H 1917- AmMWSc 92
**Yardley**, James Fredrick 1921- WhoAmP 91
**Yardley**, James Thomas, III 1942- AmMWSc 92
**Yardley**, John 1933- TwCPaSc
**Yardley**, John Finley 1925- AmMWSc 92
**Yardley**, John Howard 1926- AmMWSc 92
**Yardley**, Jonathan 1939- IntAu&W 91
**Yardley**, Norman 1915-1989 FacFETw
**Yardumian**, Richard 1917-1985 FacFETw, NewAmDM
**Yared**, Karim J. 1967- WhoFI 92
**Yarger**, Douglas Neal 1937- AmMWSc 92
**Yarger**, Frederick Lynn 1925- AmMWSc 92
**Yarger**, Harold Lee 1940- AmMWSc 92
**Yarger**, James G 1951- AmMWSc 92
**Yarger**, William E 1937- AmMWSc 92
**Yarian**, Dean Robert 1933- AmMWSc 92
**Yarin**, Veniamin Aleksandrovich 1940- IntWW 91, SovUnBD
**Yarington**, Charles Thomas, Jr 1934- AmMWSc 92
**Yarinsky**, Allen 1929- AmMWSc 92
**Yaris**, Robert 1935- AmMWSc 92
**Yariv**, A 1930- AmMWSc 92
**Yariv**, Amnon 1930- WhoWest 92
**Yarkony**, David R 1949- AmMWSc 92
**Yarkony**, Gary Michael 1953- WhoMW 92
**Yarlagadda**, Radha Krishna Rao 1938- AmMWSc 92
**Yarlagadda**, Rambabu Venkata 1959- WhoMW 92
**Yarmey**, Richard Andrew 1948- WhoAmL 92
**Yarmolinsky**, Adam 1922- AmMWSc 92, IntWW 91, WhoAmP 91, WrDr 92
**Yarmolinsky**, Michael Bezalel 1929- AmMWSc 92
**Yarmolyk**, Steven William, Jr. 1951- WhoAmL 92
**Yarmouth**, Earl of 1958- Who 92
**Yarmus**, James J. 1941- WhoHisp 92
**Yarmush**, David Leon 1928- AmMWSc 92
**Yarmush**, Martin Leon 1952- AmMWSc 92
**Yarnall**, John Lee 1932- AmMWSc 92
**Yarnall**, Mordecai 1816-1879 BiInAmS
**Yarnell**, Carolyn 1944- WhoAmP 91
**Yarnell**, John Leonard 1922- AmMWSc 92
**Yarnell**, Richard Asa 1929- AmMWSc 92
**Yarnevic**, Phyllis N 1925- WhoAmP 91
**Yarnold**, Edward John 1926- Who 92
**Yarnold**, Patrick 1937- Who 92
**Yarns**, Dale A 1930- AmMWSc 92
**Yarosewick**, Stanley J 1939- AmMWSc 92
**Yarosh**, Andrew Eustachius 1953- WhoEnt 92
**Yaroslavsky**, Yemelyan Mikhailovich 1878-1943 FacFETw
**Yaroslavsky**, Yemel'yan Mikhaylovich 1878-1943 SovUnBD
**Yarowsky**, Sol Mannasa 1916- WhoAmL 92
**Yarranton**, Peter George 1924- Who 92
**Yarrigle**, Charlene Sandra Shuey 1940- WhoFI 92
**Yarrington**, Hollis Roger 1931- WhoMW 92
**Yarrington**, Robert M 1928- AmMWSc 92
**Yarrow**, Alfred 1924- Who 92
**Yarrow**, Eric Grant 1920- IntWW 91, Who 92
**Yarrow**, Peter 1938- NewAmDM
**Yarrow**, Philip John 1917- WrDr 92
**Yarshater**, Ehsan 1920- WrDr 92
**Yarus**, Michael J 1940- AmMWSc 92
**Yarwood**, Dean Lesley 1935- WhoMW 92
**Yarwood**, Doreen 1918- WrDr 92
**Yarwood**, Michael Edward 1941- Who 92
**Yarymovych**, Michael Ihor 1933- WhoWest 92
**Yaryura-Tobias**, Jose DrAPF 91
**Yaryura-Tobias**, Jose A. 1934- WhoHisp 92
**Yasar**, Tugrul 1941- AmMWSc 92
**Yasbin**, Ronald Eliott 1947- AmMWSc 92
**Yashima**, Taro 1908- WrDr 92
**Yashin**, Aleksandr Yakovlevich 1913-1968 SovUnBD
**Yashin**, Lev 1929-1990 AnObit 1990
**Yashin**, Lev Ivanovich 1929-1990 SovUnBD
**Yashiro**, James Takashi 1931- IntWW 91
**Yashon**, David 1935- AmMWSc 92
**Yasko**, Richard N 1935- AmMWSc 92
**Yasmineh**, Walid Gabriel 1931- AmMWSc 92
**Yasnyi**, Allan David 1942- WhoEnt 92, WhoFI 92, WhoWest 92
**Yass**, Irving 1935- Who 92
**Yassky**, Harold 1930- WhoFI 92
**Yassky**, Lester 1941- WhoAmL 92
**Yasso**, Warren E 1930- AmMWSc 92
**Yassukovich**, Stanislas Michael 1935- IntWW 91, Who 92
**Yast**, Charles Joseph 1952- WhoAmL 92
**Yastrebov**, Ivan Pavlovich 1911- IntWW 91, SovUnBD
**Yastrzemski**, Michael 1939- FacFETw
**Yasuda**, Cathy Tomi 1957- WhoEnt 92
**Yasuda**, Hirotsugu 1930- AmMWSc 92
**Yasuda**, Jon Robert 1958- WhoEnt 92
**Yasuda**, Mac 1949- WhoWest 92
**Yasuda**, Stanley K 1931- AmMWSc 92
**Yasui**, Byron Kiyoshi 1940- WhoEnt 92, WhoWest 92
**Yasui**, George 1922- AmMWSc 92
**Yasui**, Kaoru 1907- IntAu&W 91, IntWW 91
**Yasukawa**, Ken 1949- AmMWSc 92, WhoMW 92
**Yasumura**, Seiichi 1932- AmMWSc 92
**Yasunobu**, Kerry T 1925- AmMWSc 92
**Yatch**, Lawrence Joseph 1945 WhoAmP 91
**Yatchak**, Michael Gerard 1951- WhoWest 92
**Yates**, Abby Harris 1952- WhoWest 92
**Yates**, Abraham 1724-1796 BlkwEAR
**Yates**, Albert Carl 1941- AmMWSc 92
**Yates**, Alden P 1928- AmMWSc 92
**Yates**, Alfred 1917- Who 92, WrDr 92
**Yates**, Alfred Glenn, Jr. 1946- WhoAmL 92
**Yates**, Allan James 1943- AmMWSc 92
**Yates**, Ann Marie 1940- AmMWSc 92
**Yates**, Anne Who 92
**Yates**, Anthony J. 1937- WhoBlA 92
**Yates**, Aubrey James 1925- WrDr 92
**Yates**, Charles Arthur 1947- WhoAmP 91
**Yates**, Charlie Lee 1936- AmMWSc 92
**Yates**, Christopher Paul 1961- WhoAmL 92
**Yates**, Claire Hilliard 1920- AmMWSc 92
**Yates**, David Charles 1944- WhoMW 92
**Yates**, David John C. 1927- WhoWest 92
**Yates**, Donald Neal 1950- WhoMW 92
**Yates**, Dornford 1885-1960 LiExTwC
**Yates**, Edgar Who 92
**Yates**, Edith Anne 1912- Who 92
**Yates**, Edward Carson, Jr 1926- AmMWSc 92
**Yates**, Elizabeth 1905- BenetAL 91, IntAu&W 91, SmATA 68 [port], WrDr 92
**Yates**, Elizabeth Black 1916- WhoAmP 91
**Yates**, Ella Gaines 1927- WhoBlA 92
**Yates**, Elton G. 1935- WhoFI 92
**Yates**, Francis Eugene 1927- AmMWSc 92
**Yates**, Frank 1902- IntWW 91, Who 92, WrDr 92
**Yates**, Fred 1922- TwCPaSc
**Yates**, George Kenneth 1925- AmMWSc 92
**Yates**, Harold 1916- TwCPaSc
**Yates**, Harold W 1923- AmMWSc 92
**Yates**, Harris Oliver 1934- AmMWSc 92
**Yates**, Ian Humphrey Nelson 1931- Who 92
**Yates**, Ivan R. 1929- Who 92
**Yates**, J. Michael 1938- ConPo 91, IntAu&W 91, WrDr 92
**Yates**, James Bernard 1929- WhoAmP 91
**Yates**, James T 1940- AmMWSc 92
**Yates**, Jeffrey M 1948- WhoIns 92
**Yates**, Jeffrey McKee 1948- WhoFI 92
**Yates**, Jerome Douglas 1935- AmMWSc 92
**Yates**, Jerome William 1936- AmMWSc 92
**Yates**, Jessie Ward 1929- WhoFI 92
**Yates**, Joe Elton 1938- WhoAmP 91
**Yates**, John 1925- Who 92
**Yates**, John Gorman 1946- WhoFI 92
**Yates**, John Melvin 1939- WhoAmP 91
**Yates**, John P WhoAmP 91
**Yates**, John Thomas, Jr 1935- AmMWSc 92
**Yates**, Jon Arthur 1947- AmMWSc 92
**Yates**, Josephine Silone 1859-1912 NotBlAW 92
**Yates**, Keith 1928- AmMWSc 92
**Yates**, Keith Lamar 1927- WhoWest 92
**Yates**, Leland Marshall 1915- AmMWSc 92
**Yates**, LeRoy Louis 1929- WhoBlA 92
**Yates**, Lorenzo Gordin 1837-1909 BiInAmS
**Yates**, Lowell Anthony 1950- WhoMW 92
**Yates**, Madonna Moore 1938- WhoMW 92
**Yates**, Margaret Marlene 1942- WhoWest 92
**Yates**, Mary Anne 1949- AmMWSc 92
**Yates**, Michael Zane WhoAmP 91
**Yates**, Norman Kenneth 1929- WhoMW 92
**Yates**, Peter 1920- TwCPaSc
**Yates**, Peter 1924- AmMWSc 92
**Yates**, Peter 1929- IntDcF 2-2 [port], IntMPA 92, IntWW 91, Who 92, WhoEnt 92
**Yates**, Raeburn Paul 1939- WhoWest 92
**Yates**, Rebecca Elizabeth 1963- WhoEnt 92
**Yates**, Richard DrAPF 91
**Yates**, Richard 1926- BenetAL 91, ConNov 91
**Yates**, Richard Alan 1930- AmMWSc 92
**Yates**, Richard Lee 1931- AmMWSc 92
**Yates**, Robert Doyle 1931- AmMWSc 92
**Yates**, Robert Edmunds 1926- AmMWSc 92
**Yates**, Roger Nelson 1951- WhoMW 92
**Yates**, Samuel Langdon 1949- WhoEnt 92
**Yates**, Sarah Barian 1959- WhoAmL 92
**Yates**, Scott Raymond 1954- AmMWSc 92
**Yates**, Shelly Gene 1932- AmMWSc 92
**Yates**, Sidney R. 1909- AlmAP 92 [port], WhoAmP 91
**Yates**, Sidney Richard 1909- WhoMW 92
**Yates**, Steven Winfield 1946- AmMWSc 92
**Yates**, Susan Strotman 1956 WhoWest 92
**Yates**, Ted d1967 LesBEnT 92
**Yates**, Thomas Eugene 1942- WhoWest 92
**Yates**, Vance Joseph 1917- AmMWSc 92
**Yates**, Willard F, Jr 1930- AmMWSc 92
**Yates**, William 1921- Who 92
**Yates**, William Edgar 1938- Who 92
**Yates**, William Tyler 1956- WhoRel 92
**Yates-Bell**, John Geoffrey d1991 Who 92N
**Yates-Parker**, Nancy L 1956- AmMWSc 92
**Yatim**, Dato Rais 1942- IntWW 91
**Yatim**, Rais 1942- Who 92
**Yatron**, Gus 1927- AlmAP 92 [port], WhoAmP 91
**Yatsu**, Frank Michio 1932- AmMWSc 92
**Yatsu**, Lawrence Y 1925- AmMWSc 92
**Yatsushiro** EncAmaz 91
**Yatvin**, Milton B 1930- AmMWSc 92
**Yau**, Cheuk Chung 1950- AmMWSc 92
**Yau**, Chiou Ching 1934- AmMWSc 92
**Yau**, John DrAPF 91
**Yau**, John 1950- ConPo 91
**Yau**, King-Wai 1948- AmMWSc 92
**Yau**, Leopoldo D 1940- AmMWSc 92
**Yau**, Shing-Tung 1949- AmMWSc 92
**Yau**, Stephen Shing-Toung 1952- AmMWSc 92, WhoMW 92
**Yau**, Stephen Sik-Sang 1935- AmMWSc 92
**Yau**, Wallace Wen-Chuan 1937- AmMWSc 92
**Yau**, Wen-Foo 1935- AmMWSc 92
**Yau-Young**, Annie O AmMWSc 92
**Yauger**, Douglas Paul 1955- WhoAmP 91
**Yavelow**, Christopher Fowler Johnson 1950- WhoEnt 92
**Yaverbaum**, Sidney 1923- AmMWSc 92
**Yavitz**, David Bruce 1944- WhoAmL 92
**Yavner**, Louis E. d1991 NewYTBS 91
**Yavornitzki**, Mark Leon 1948- WhoAmP 91
**Yavorsky**, John Michael 1919- AmMWSc 92
**Yavorsky**, Paul M 1925- AmMWSc 92
**Yavuzturk**, Zeki 1935- IntWW 91
**Yaworsky**, George Myroslaw 1940- WhoFI 92
**Yaws**, Carl Lloyd 1938- AmMWSc 92
**Yaxley**, John Francis 1936- Who 92
**Yayanos**, A Aristides 1940- AmMWSc 92
**Yaz**, Engin 1954- AmMWSc 92
**Yazdi**, Ibrahim 1933?- IntWW 91
**Yazicigil**, Hasan 1952- AmMWSc 92
**Yazkuliev**, Bally Yazkulyevich 1930- IntWW 91
**Yazov**, Dmitri Timofeevich 1923- IntWW 91
**Yazov**, Dmitriy Timofeevich 1923- SovUnBD
**Yazulla**, Stephen 1945- AmMWSc 92
**Ybanez**, John P. 1946- WhoHisp 92
**Ybarra**, Albert, Jr. 1959- WhoHisp 92
**Ybarra**, Gloria WhoHisp 92
**Ybarra**, Robert Michael 1950- WhoHisp 92
**Ybarra**, Thomas R. 1880- BenetAL 91
**Ybarra Y Churruca**, Emilio de 1936- IntWW 91
**Ybarrondo**, Larry J. WhoHisp 92
**Ycas**, Martynas 1917- AmMWSc 92
**Ydigoras Fuentes**, Miguel 1895-1982 FacFETw
**Ye Fei** 1909- IntWW 91
**Ye Gongoi** 1930- IntWW 91
**Ye Jianying** 1897-1986 FacFETw
**Ye Junjian** 1915- IntWW 91
**Ye Liansong** 1935- IntWW 91
**Ye Rutang** 1940- IntWW 91
**Ye Xiaogang** 1955- IntWW 91
**Ye Xuanping** 1925- IntWW 91
**Yea**, Sung Hae 1950- WhoWest 92
**Yeadon**, David Allou 1920- AmMWSc 92
**Yeadon**, Richard 1896- TwCPaSc
**Yeager**, Anson Anders 1919- WhoMW 92
**Yeager**, Caroline Hale 1946- WhoWest 92
**Yeager**, Charles Elwood 1923- FacFETw
**Yeager**, Charles Floyd 1944- WhoWest 92
**Yeager**, Charles V. 1939- WhoFI 92
**Yeager**, Cheryl Lynn 1958- WhoEnt 92
**Yeager**, Dennis Randall 1941- WhoAmL 92
**Yeager**, Douglas Arnold 1947- WhoEnt 92
**Yeager**, Ernest Bill 1924- AmMWSc 92
**Yeager**, Frederick John 1941- WhoWest 92
**Yeager**, George Michael 1934- WhoFI 92
**Yeager**, Henry, Jr 1933- AmMWSc 92
**Yeager**, Howard Lane 1943- AmMWSc 92
**Yeager**, Iver Franklin 1922- WhoRel 92
**Yeager**, John Frederick 1927- AmMWSc 92
**Yeager**, John J. 1921- WhoAmL 92
**Yeager**, Marion Ernest, II 1960- WhoMW 92
**Yeager**, Mark L. 1950- WhoAmL 92
**Yeager**, Mary Ann 1945- WhoWest 92
**Yeager**, Michael Todd 1955- WhoEnt 92
**Yeager**, Norman Albert 1944- WhoRel 92
**Yeager**, Paul Ray 1931- AmMWSc 92
**Yeager**, Randy 1950- WhoWest 92
**Yeager**, Sandra Ann 1939- AmMWSc 92
**Yeager**, Thomas M 1936- WhoAmP 91
**Yeager**, Thomas Stephen 1942- WhoBlA 92
**Yeager**, Vernon LeRoy 1926- AmMWSc 92, WhoMW 92
**Yeager**, Weldon O 1922- WhoAmP 91
**Yeagle**, Philip L 1949- AmMWSc 92
**Yeagley**, Joan DrAPF 91
**Yeakel**, Joseph Hughes 1928- WhoRel 92
**Yeakel**, Steven Craig 1956- WhoAmP 91
**Yeakey**, Ernest Leon 1934- AmMWSc 92
**Yeamans**, George Thomas 1929- WhoMW 92
**Yeargan**, Jerry Reese 1940- AmMWSc 92
**Yeargan**, Kenneth Vernon 1947- AmMWSc 92
**Yeargers**, Edward Klingensmith 1938- AmMWSc 92
**Yeargin**, Charles W WhoAmP 91

**Yearian,** Mason Russell 1932- *AmMWSc 92*
**Yearian,** William C 1937- *AmMWSc 92*
**Yearick,** Elisabeth Stelle 1913- *AmMWSc 92*
**Yearley,** Douglas Cain 1936- *WhoFI 92, WhoWest 92*
**Yearley,** Lee Howard 1940- *WhoRel 92, WhoWest 92*
**Yearns,** W. Buck 1918- *ConAu 134*
**Yearout,** Paul Harmon, Jr 1924- *AmMWSc 92*
**Yearout,** Robert Kirk 1940- *WhoWest 92*
**Yearsley,** Ann 1753-1806 *DcLB 109*
**Yearsley,** Pamela J. 1946- *WhoRel 92*
**Yearwood,** Arem Irene *WhoBlA 92*
**Yearwood,** David Monroe, Jr. 1945- *WhoBlA 92*
**Yeary,** James E., Sr. 1917- *WhoBlA 92*
**Yeary,** Roger A 1932- *AmMWSc 92*
**Yeary,** Roger Allen 1932- *WhoMW 92*
**Yeates,** Tommy Lee 1958- *WhoAmL 92*
**Yeates,** W. Keith 1920- *IntWW 91, Who 92*
**Yeates,** William Smith 1856-1908 *BiInAmS*
**Yeatman,** Christopher William 1927- *AmMWSc 92*
**Yeatman,** Harry Clay 1916- *AmMWSc 92*
**Yeatman,** Hoyt *WhoEnt 92*
**Yeatman,** John Newton 1920- *AmMWSc 92*
**Yeaton,** Charles B 1926- *WhoAmP 91*
**Yeats,** Frederick Tinsley 1942- *AmMWSc 92*
**Yeats,** Jack Butler 1871-1957 *FacFETw, TwCPaSc*
**Yeats,** John Butler 1839-1922 *FacFETw*
**Yeats,** Robert Sheppard 1931- *AmMWSc 92, WhoWest 92*
**Yeats,** Ronald Bradshaw 1941- *AmMWSc 92*
**Yeats,** William Butler 1865-1939 *CnDBLB 5 [port], FacFETw [port], RfGEnL 91, WhoNob 90*
**Yeatts,** Frank Richard 1936- *AmMWSc 92*
**Yeazell,** Ruth Bernard 1947- *WhoWest 92*
**Yeck,** Robert Gilbert 1920- *AmMWSc 92*
**Yeckley,** Robert Quentin 1952- *WhoWest 92*
**Yedinak,** Peter Demerton 1939- *AmMWSc 92*
**Yedlicka,** William George 1922- *WhoWest 92*
**Yedlik,** Edwon G. 1945- *WhoEnt 92*
**Yee,** Albert Fan 1945- *AmMWSc 92*
**Yee,** Alfred A 1925- *AmMWSc 92*
**Yee,** Betty Ting 1957- *WhoWest 92*
**Yee,** Bruce James 1950- *WhoWest 92*
**Yee,** Donald H. 1960- *WhoEnt 92*
**Yee,** Gale A. 1949- *WhoRel 92*
**Yee,** George Dennis 1957- *WhoWest 92*
**Yee,** James Bair 1952- *WhoWest 92*
**Yee,** John Alan 1947- *AmMWSc 92*
**Yee,** K. Tim 1926- *WhoWest 92*
**Yee,** Kane Shee-Gong 1934- *AmMWSc 92*
**Yee,** Mark J. C. 1954- *WhoAmL 92*
**Yee,** Paul 1956- *ConAu 135, SmATA 67 [port]*
**Yee,** Peter Ben-On 1960- *WhoWest 92*
**Yee,** Rena 1936- *AmMWSc 92*
**Yee,** Sinclair Shee-Sing 1937- *AmMWSc 92*
**Yee,** Tin Boo 1915- *AmMWSc 92*
**Yee,** Tucker Tew 1936- *AmMWSc 92*
**Yee,** William C 1928- *AmMWSc 92*
**Yee Litt,** Daryl 1953- *WhoFI 92, WhoMW 92*
**Yeend,** Geoffrey 1927- *Who 92*
**Yeend,** Geoffrey John 1927- *IntWW 91*
**Yeend,** Warren Ernest 1936- *AmMWSc 92, WhoWest 92*
**Yefanov,** V.P. *SovUnBD*
**Yefimov,** Aleksandr Nikolaevich 1923- *SovUnBD*
**Yefimov,** Aleksandr Nikolayevich 1923- *IntWW 91*
**Yefimov,** Anatoliy Stepanovich 1939- *IntWW 91*
**Yefimov,** Boris Yefimovich 1900- *SovUnBD*
**Yefimov,** Igor Markovich 1937- *LiExTwC*
**Yefimov,** Michael Nikiforovich 1881-1920 *FacFETw*
**Yefimov,** Nikodim Nikolayevich 1928- *IntWW 91*
**Yefremov,** Ivan 1907-1972 *TwCSFW 91A*
**Yefremov,** Mikhail Timofeevich 1911- *SovUnBD*
**Yefremov,** Mikhail Timofeyevich 1911- *IntWW 91*
**Yefremov,** Oleg Nikolaevich 1927- *SovUnBD*
**Yefremov,** Oleg Nikolayevich 1927- *IntWW 91*
**Yegge,** Robert Bernard 1934- *WhoWest 92*
**Yegorov,** Aleksandr Il'ich 1883-1939 *SovUnBD*
**Yegorov,** Anatoliy Grigoryevich 1920- *IntWW 91*
**Yegorov,** Boris 1937- *FacFETw*
**Yegorov,** Georgiy Mikhailovich 1918- *IntWW 91*
**Yegorov,** Mikhail Vasilevich 1907- *IntWW 91*
**Yegorov,** Yuriy 1954- *SovUnBD*
**Yegulalp,** Tuncel Mustafa 1937- *AmMWSc 92*
**Yeh,** Billy Kuo-Jiun 1937- *AmMWSc 92*
**Yeh,** Cavour W 1936- *AmMWSc 92*
**Yeh,** Chai 1911- *AmMWSc 92*
**Yeh,** Edward H Y 1930- *AmMWSc 92*
**Yeh,** Francis Cho-hao 1945- *AmMWSc 92*
**Yeh,** Gene Horng C 1948- *AmMWSc 92*
**Yeh,** George Chiayou 1926- *AmMWSc 92*
**Yeh,** Gour-Tsyh 1940- *AmMWSc 92*
**Yeh,** Gregory Soh-Yu 1933- *AmMWSc 92, WhoMW 92*
**Yeh,** Hen-Geul *AmMWSc 92*
**Yeh,** Herman Jia-Chain 1939- *AmMWSc 92*
**Yeh,** Hsi-Han 1935- *AmMWSc 92, WhoMW 92*
**Yeh,** Hsiang-Yueh 1940- *AmMWSc 92*
**Yeh,** Hsu-Chi 1940- *AmMWSc 92*
**Yeh,** Hsuan 1916- *AmMWSc 92*
**Yeh,** Hun Chiang 1935- *AmMWSc 92*
**Yeh,** James Jui-Tin 1927- *AmMWSc 92*
**Yeh,** K C 1930- *AmMWSc 92*
**Yeh,** Kung Chie 1930- *WhoMW 92*
**Yeh,** Kwan-Nan 1938- *AmMWSc 92*
**Yeh,** Kwo-Yih 1942- *AmMWSc 92*
**Yeh,** Lai-Su Lee 1942- *AmMWSc 92*
**Yeh,** Lee-Chuan Caroline 1954- *AmMWSc 92*
**Yeh,** Nai-Chang 1961- *AmMWSc 92*
**Yeh,** Noel Kuei-Eng 1937- *AmMWSc 92*
**Yeh,** Pai-T 1920- *AmMWSc 92*
**Yeh,** Paul Pao 1927- *AmMWSc 92*
**Yeh,** Pochi Albert 1948- *AmMWSc 92*
**Yeh,** Pu-Sen 1935- *AmMWSc 92*
**Yeh,** Raymond T 1937- *AmMWSc 92*
**Yeh,** Rui Zong 1930- *WhoWest 92*
**Yeh,** Samuel D J 1926- *AmMWSc 92*
**Yeh,** Shu-Yuan 1926- *AmMWSc 92*
**Yeh,** Tsung 1950- *WhoEnt 92, WhoMW 92*
**Yeh,** Tsyh Tyan 1941- *AmMWSc 92*
**Yeh,** William Wen-Gong 1938- *AmMWSc 92*
**Yeh,** Wu-Kuang 1942- *WhoMW 92*
**Yeh,** Yea-Chuan Milton 1943- *AmMWSc 92*
**Yeh,** Yin 1938- *AmMWSc 92*
**Yeh,** Yunchi 1930- *AmMWSc 92*
**Yehl,** Suzy Perkins 1945- *WhoMW 92*
**Yehoshua,** Abraham B 1936- *IntAu&W 91, IntWW 91*
**Yeiser,** Jimmie Lynn 1952- *AmMWSc 92*
**Yeiser,** Patti 1954- *WhoAmP 91*
**Yeko,** Bruce David 1940- *WhoEnt 92*
**Yekta-Fard,** Mohsen 1955- *WhoMW 92*
**Yelchenko,** Yuri Nikiforovich 1929- *IntWW 91*
**Yeldell,** Joseph P. 1932- *WhoBlA 92*
**Yeldham,** Peter 1927- *IntAu&W 91*
**Yelek,** Antoinette 1924- *WhoMW 92, WhoRel 92*
**Yelenosky,** George 1929- *AmMWSc 92*
**Yelich,** Michael Ralph 1948- *AmMWSc 92, WhoMW 92*
**Yelin,** Robert Bruce 1944- *WhoEnt 92*
**Yelity,** Stephen C. 1949- *WhoBlA 92*
**Yelle,** Roger V 1957- *AmMWSc 92*
**Yelle,** Thomas Robert 1959- *WhoMW 92*
**Yellen,** Jack d1991 *NewYTBS 91*
**Yellen,** Jack 1892- *WhoEnt 92*
**Yellen,** Jay 1948- *AmMWSc 92*
**Yellen,** Linda 1949- *IntMPA 92*
**Yellen,** Linda Beverly 1949- *WhoEnt 92*
**Yellen,** Mark Harvey 1954- *WhoEnt 92, WhoWest 92*
**Yellen,** Pamela Gay 1952- *WhoWest 92*
**Yellin,** Absalom Moses 1936- *AmMWSc 92*
**Yellin,** David Gilmer 1916- *WhoEnt 92*
**Yellin,** Edward L 1927- *AmMWSc 92*
**Yellin,** Herbert 1935- *AmMWSc 92*
**Yellin,** Joseph 1938- *AmMWSc 92*
**Yellin,** Steven Joseph 1941- *AmMWSc 92*
**Yellin,** Tobias O 1934- *AmMWSc 92*
**Yellin,** Victor Fell 1924- *WhoEnt 92*
**Yellin,** Wilbur 1932- *AmMWSc 92*
**Yellon,** Alvin Harold 1956- *WhoEnt 92*
**Yellow Martha** *EncAmaz 91*
**Yellowlees,** Henry 1919- *Who 92*
**Yellowtail,** William P, Jr 1948- *WhoAmP 91*
**Yelon,** Arthur Michael 1934- *AmMWSc 92*
**Yelon,** William B 1944- *AmMWSc 92*
**Yelstin,** Boris Nikolayevich 1931- *Who 92*
**Yelton,** David Baetz 1945- *AmMWSc 92*
**Yelton,** Ralph 1926- *WhoAmP 91*
**Yeltsin,** Boris 1931- *News 91 [port]*
**Yel'tsin,** Boris Nikolaevich 1931- *SovUnBD*
**Yeltsin,** Boris Nikolayevich 1931- *FacFETw [port], IntWW 91, NewYTBS 91 [port]*
**Yemel'yanov,** Aleksey Mikhaylovich 1935- *SovUnBD*
**Yemelyanov,** Stanislav Vasilevich 1929- *IntWW 91*
**Yemen,** King of *IntWW 91*
**Yemm,** Edmund William 1909- *Who 92*
**Yemma,** John Joseph 1933- *AmMWSc 92*
**Yemokhonov,** Nikolay Pavlovich 1921- *IntWW 91*
**Yen Chen-Hsing** 1912- *IntWW 91*
**Yen Chia-Kan** 1905- *IntWW 91*
**Yen,** Alfred Chueh-Chin 1958- *WhoAmL 92*
**Yen,** Andrew 1948- *AmMWSc 92*
**Yen,** Belinda R S 1942- *AmMWSc 92*
**Yen,** Ben Chie 1935- *AmMWSc 92*
**Yen,** Ben-Tseng 1932- *AmMWSc 92*
**Yen,** Bing Cheng 1934- *AmMWSc 92*
**Yen,** Chen-Wan Liu 1932- *AmMWSc 92*
**Yen,** David Chi-Chung 1953- *WhoMW 92*
**Yen,** David Hsien-Yao 1934- *AmMWSc 92*
**Yen,** Duen Hsi 1949- *WhoWest 92*
**Yen,** I-Kuen 1930- *AmMWSc 92*
**Yen,** Jong-Tseng 1942- *AmMWSc 92*
**Yen,** Nai-Chyuan 1936- *AmMWSc 92*
**Yen,** Peter Kai Jen 1922- *AmMWSc 92*
**Yen,** S C Yen 1927- *AmMWSc 92*
**Yen,** Samuel Show-Chih 1927- *WhoWest 92*
**Yen,** Teh Fu 1927- *AmMWSc 92, WhoWest 92*
**Yen,** Terence Tsin Tsu 1937- *AmMWSc 92*
**Yen,** Tien-Sze Benedict 1953- *WhoWest 92*
**Yen,** William Kuang-Han 1952- *WhoWest 92*
**Yen,** William Maoshung 1935- *AmMWSc 92*
**Yen,** Yin-Chao 1927- *AmMWSc 92*
**Yen-Koo,** Helen C 1925- *AmMWSc 92*
**Yencha,** Andrew Joseph 1938- *AmMWSc 92*
**Yendell,** Paul Sebastian 1844-1918 *BiInAmS*
**Yendo,** Masayoshi 1920- *IntWW 91*
**Yendol,** William G 1931- *AmMWSc 92*
**Yener,** Muzaffer 1947- *WhoWest 92*
**Yener,** Yaman 1946- *AmMWSc 92*
**Yeney,** Yevgeny Yevgen'evich 1890-1971 *SovUnBD*
**Yeniscavich,** William 1934- *AmMWSc 92*
**Yennie,** Donald Robert 1924- *AmMWSc 92*
**Yennimatas,** Georgios 1939- *IntWW 91*
**Yensen,** Arthur Eric 1944- *AmMWSc 92*
**Yenser,** Stephen 1941- *ConAu 36NR*
**Yent,** John Matthew 1964- *WhoWest 92*
**Yentob,** Alan 1947- *IntWW 91, Who 92*
**Yentsch,** Charles Samuel 1927- *AmMWSc 92*
**Yeo Cheow Tong** 1947- *IntWW 91*
**Yeo Ning Hong** 1943- *IntWW 91*
**Yeo,** Diane Helen 1945- *Who 92*
**Yeo,** Douglas *WhoEnt 92*
**Yeo,** Douglas 1925- *Who 92*
**Yeo,** Kok Cheang 1903- *Who 92*
**Yeo,** Ruth Ann 1951- *WhoWest 92*
**Yeo,** Timothy Stephen Kenneth 1945- *Who 92*
**Yeo,** Wendy *TwCPaSc*
**Yeo,** Yung Kee 1938- *AmMWSc 92*
**Yeoman,** Alan 1933- *Who 92*
**Yeoman,** Lynn Chalmers 1943- *AmMWSc 92*
**Yeoman,** Michael Magson 1931- *Who 92*
**Yeoman,** Philip Metcalfe 1923- *Who 92*
**Yeomans,** Donald Keith 1942- *AmMWSc 92, WhoWest 92*
**Yeomans,** Geoffrey 1934- *TwCPaSc*
**Yeomans,** Richard Millett 1932- *Who 92*
**Yeon-Sook,** Yun 1950- *AmMWSc 92*
**Yeowell,** David Arthur 1937- *AmMWSc 92*
**Yep,** Laurence 1948- *TwCSFW 91, WrDr 92*
**Yepes,** Elias Hernando 1945- *WhoRel 92*
**Yepes,** Narciso 1927- *NewAmDM*
**Yepishev,** Aleksev Alekseevich 1908-1985 *SovUnBD*
**Yepsen,** Roger B, Jr. 1947- *ConAu 35NR*
**Yeransian,** James A 1928- *AmMWSc 92*
**Yerant,** Gene S 1947- *WhoIns 92*
**Yerazunis,** Stephen 1922- *AmMWSc 92*
**Yerburgh** *Who 92*
**Yerburgh,** John Maurice Armstrong 1923- *Who 92*
**Yerby,** Alonzo Smythe 1921- *AmMWSc 92*
**Yerby,** Frank 1916- *BenetAL 91, BlkLC [port], ConNov 91, WrDr 92*
**Yerby,** Frank Garvin 1916- *IntAu&W 91, IntWW 91, Who 92, WhoBlA 92*
**Yeremin,** Yuri 1944- *IntWW 91*
**Yeres,** Moshe Joseph 1954- *WhoRel 92*
**Yerg,** Donald G 1925- *AmMWSc 92*
**Yerg,** Raymond A 1917- *AmMWSc 92*
**Yergan,** David 1958- *WhoEnt 92*
**Yerganian,** George 1923- *AmMWSc 92*
**Yerger,** Amos G. 1914- *WhoBlA 92*
**Yerger,** Ben 1931- *WhoBlA 92*
**Yerger,** Ralph William 1922- *AmMWSc 92*
**Yerger,** William Swan 1932- *WhoAmP 91*
**Yergey,** Alfred L, III 1941- *AmMWSc 92*
**Yergin,** Michael Lee 1951- *WhoFI 92*
**Yergin,** Paul Flohr 1923- *AmMWSc 92*
**Yerian,** Stephen Curtis 1950- *WhoMW 92*
**Yerick,** Roger Eugene 1932- *AmMWSc 92*
**Yerkes,** Robert Mearns 1876-1956 *FacFETw*
**Yerkes,** William D, Jr 1922- *AmMWSc 92*
**Yermakov,** Nicholas *TwCSFW 91*
**Yermakov,** Nicholas 1951- *IntAu&W 91, WrDr 92*
**Yermakova,** Valentina Aleksandrovna 1924- *IntWW 91*
**Yerman,** Robert Neil 1940- *WhoFI 92*
**Yermin,** Lev Borisovich 1923- *IntWW 91*
**Yerofeyev,** Benedikt 1938- *IntWW 91*
**Yerrid,** C. Steven 1949- *WhoAmL 92*
**Yerrill,** Victor Malcolm 1941- *WhoIns 92*
**Yerxa,** Bo 1948- *WhoAmP 91*
**Yes** *NewAmDM*
**Yes,** Phyllis Ann 1941- *WhoWest 92*
**Yesair,** David Wayne 1932- *AmMWSc 92*
**Yesenin,** Sergey Aleksandrovich 1895-1925 *SovUnBD*
**Yesinowski,** James Paul 1950- *AmMWSc 92*
**Yeske,** David Brent 1957- *WhoFI 92, WhoWest 92*
**Yeske,** Ronald A 1946- *AmMWSc 92*
**Yesner,** Peter Scott 1955- *WhoFI 92*
**Yesner,** Raymond 1914- *AmMWSc 92*
**Yesselman,** Robert Alan 1944- *WhoEnt 92*
**Yessik,** Michael John 1941- *AmMWSc 92*
**Yeston,** Maury 1945- *WhoEnt 92*
**Yetka,** Lawrence Robert 1924- *WhoAmL 92, WhoMW 92*
**Yetka,** Lawrence Rorbert *WhoAmP 91*
**Yetnikoff,** Walter R. 1933- *WhoEnt 92*
**Yett,** Fowler Redford 1919- *AmMWSc 92*
**Yetter,** R. Paul 1958- *WhoAmL 92*
**Yetter,** Sherry Kay 1957- *WhoEnt 92*
**Yeun,** Paul Lorenzo 1944- *WhoRel 92*
**Yeung,** David Lawrence 1939- *AmMWSc 92*
**Yeung,** Edward Szeshing 1948- *AmMWSc 92*
**Yeung,** Katherine Lu 1943- *AmMWSc 92*
**Yeung,** Pat Hok-Kwong 1965- *WhoWest 92*
**Yeung,** Patrick Pui-hang 1942- *AmMWSc 92*
**Yeung,** Reginald Sze-Chit 1932- *AmMWSc 92*
**Yeung,** Ronald Wai-Chun 1945- *AmMWSc 92*
**Yeutter,** Clayton K. 1930- *IntWW 91*
**Yeutter,** Clayton Keith 1930- *WhoAmP 91, WhoFI 92*
**Yevdokimov,** Grigoriy Yeremeevich 1884-1936 *SovUnBD*
**Yevich,** Joseph Paul 1940- *AmMWSc 92*
**Yevich,** Paul Peter 1924- *AmMWSc 92*
**Yevick,** David Owen 1954- *AmMWSc 92*
**Yevick,** George Johannus 1922- *AmMWSc 92*
**Yevoli,** Lewis J 1939- *WhoAmP 91*
**Yevstigneev,** Ruben Nikolaevich 1932- *SovUnBD*
**Yevstigneyev,** Ruben Nikolaevich 1932- *IntWW 91*
**Yevstigneyev,** Yevgeny Aleksandrovich 1926- *IntWW 91*
**Yevtushenko,** Yevgeniy Aleksandrovich 1933- *IntWW 91, SovUnBD*
**Yevtushenko,** Yevgenly Aleksandrovich 1933- *IntAu&W 91*
**Yevtushenko,** Yevgeny Aleksandrovich 1933- *FacFETw, Who 92*
**Yewaisis,** Joseph Stephen 1939- *WhoFI 92*
**Yez,** Martin S 1920- *AmMWSc 92*
**Yezbick,** Francis Alfred 1934- *WhoMW 92*
**Yezhevsky,** Aleksandr Aleksandrovich 1915- *IntWW 91*
**Yezhov,** Nicholas Ivanovich 1895-1939? *FacFETw*
**Yezhov,** Nikolay Ivanovich 1894-1939 *SovUnBD*
**Yezhov,** Valentin Ivanovich 1921- *IntAu&W 91, IntWW 91*
**Yezierska,** Anzia 1880?-1970 *HanAmWH*
**Yezierska,** Anzia 1885-1970 *BenetAL 91, DcAmImH*
**Yfantis,** Shirley Chao 1954- *WhoWest 92*
**Yff,** Peter 1924- *WhoMW 92*
**Yglesias,** Helen *DrAPF 91*
**Yglesias,** Helen 1915- *BenetAL 91, ConNov 91, WrDr 92*
**Yglesias,** Jose *DrAPF 91, WhoHisp 92*
**Yglesias,** Jose 1919- *BenetAL 91, ConNov 91, WhoHisp 92, WrDr 92*
**Yglesias,** Rafael *DrAPF 91*
**Yglesias,** Rafael 1954- *WhoHisp 92, WrDr 92*

**Yguado,** Alex Rocco 1939- *WhoFI 92, WhoWest 92*
**Yguerabide,** Juan 1935- *AmMWSc 92*
**Yhap,** Laetitia 1941- *IntWW 91, TwCPaSc*
**Yhombi-Opango,** Joachim 1939- *IntWW 91*
**Yi Meihou** 1910- *IntWW 91*
**Yi Sanggyu** 1944- *ConCom 92*
**Yi Songch'on** 1936- *ConCom 92*
**Yi,** Gyoseob 1952- *WhoFI 92*
**Yi,** Michael Chong 1959- *WhoWest 92*
**Yi,** Youjae 1960- *WhoMW 92*
**Yi-Yan,** Alfredo 1949- *AmMWSc 92*
**Yiamouyiannis,** John Andrew 1942- *AmMWSc 92*
**Yiannopoulos,** A. N. 1928- *WrDr 92*
**Yiannopoulos,** Evangelos 1918- *IntWW 91*
**Yiannos,** Peter N 1932- *AmMWSc 92*
**Yielding,** K Lemone 1931- *AmMWSc 92*
**Yifter,** Miruts 194-?- *BlkOlyM [port]*
**Yih,** Chia-Shun 1918- *AmMWSc 92*
**Yih,** Mae Dunn 1928- *WhoAmP 91*
**Yih,** Roy Yangming 1931- *AmMWSc 92*
**Yii,** Roland 1919- *AmMWSc 92*
**Yildiz,** Alaettin 1922- *AmMWSc 92*
**Yilma,** Tilahun Daniel 1943- *WhoWest 92*
**Yilmaz,** A. Mesut 1947- *IntWW 91*
**Yilmaz,** Nancy Tolbert 1958- *WhoEnt 92*
**Yim Ving Tsun** *EncAmaz 91*
**Yim,** George Kwock Wah 1930- *AmMWSc 92*
**Yim,** W Michael 1927- *AmMWSc 92*
**Yin Changmin** 1923- *IntWW 91*
**Yin Jun** 1932- *IntWW 91*
**Yin Kesheng** 1932- *IntWW 91*
**Yin,** Chih-Ming 1943- *AmMWSc 92*
**Yin,** Fay Hoh 1932- *AmMWSc 92*
**Yin,** Frank Chi-Pong 1943- *AmMWSc 92*
**Yin,** Gang George 1954- *WhoMW 92*
**Yin,** George Kuo-Ming 1949- *WhoAmL 92*
**Yin,** Gerald Zheyao 1944- *WhoWest 92*
**Yin,** Helen Lu *AmMWSc 92*
**Yin,** Lo I 1930- *AmMWSc 92*
**Yin,** Raymond Wah 1938- *WhoMW 92*
**Yin,** Tom Chi Tien 1945- *AmMWSc 92*
**Ying Ruocheng** 1929- *IntWW 91*
**Ying,** John L. 1948- *WhoFI 92, WhoMW 92*
**Ying,** Kuang Lin 1927- *AmMWSc 92*
**Ying,** Ramona Yun-Ching 1957- *AmMWSc 92*
**Ying,** Runsheng *WhoEnt 92*
**Ying,** See Chen 1941- *AmMWSc 92*
**Ying,** William H 1935- *AmMWSc 92*
**Yingling,** Adrienne Elizabeth 1959- *WhoFI 92*
**Yingling,** Rebecca Marie 1951- *WhoRel 92*
**Yingling,** Robert Granville, Jr. 1940- *WhoWest 92*
**Yingst,** Jon Porter 1966- *WhoMW 92*
**Yingst,** Ralph Earl 1929- *AmMWSc 92*
**Yingst,** Victor Leroy 1942- *WhoMW 92*
**Yip,** Cecil Cheung-Ching 1937- *AmMWSc 92*
**Yip,** Edmund Y.K. 1933- *WhoWest 92*
**Yip,** George 1926- *AmMWSc 92*
**Yip,** Joseph W 1948- *AmMWSc 92*
**Yip,** Kwok Leung 1944- *AmMWSc 92*
**Yip,** Rick Ka Sun 1952- *AmMWSc 92*
**Yip,** Sidney 1936- *AmMWSc 92*
**Yip,** Yum Keung *AmMWSc 92*
**Yirak,** Jack J 1918- *AmMWSc 92*
**Yirdaw,** Arega 1942- *WhoWest 92*
**Yizar,** James Horace, Jr. 1957- *WhoBlA 92*
**Ylvisaker,** James William 1938- *WhoFI 92*
**Ynclan,** Nery 1959- *WhoHisp 92*
**Ynda,** Mary Lou 1936- *WhoWest 92*
**Yngvesson,** K Sigfrid 1936- *AmMWSc 92*
**Yntema,** Jan Lambertus 1920- *AmMWSc 92*
**Yntema,** Mary Katherine 1928- *AmMWSc 92, WhoMW 92*
**Yoakam,** Dwight 1956- *WhoEnt 92*
**Yoakam,** Marvin C. 1948- *WhoMW 92*
**Yoakum,** Anna Margaret 1933- *AmMWSc 92*
**Yob,** Charles Walter 1937- *WhoAmP 91*
**Yob,** David J. 1952- *WhoWest 92*
**Yoburn,** Byron Crocker 1950- *AmMWSc 92*
**Yocca,** Frank D 1955- *AmMWSc 92*
**Yoch,** Duane Charles 1940- *AmMWSc 92*
**Yocham,** David Len 1959- *WhoRel 92*
**Yochelson,** Ellis Leon 1928- *AmMWSc 92*
**Yochelson,** Saul B. 1925- *WhoWest 92*
**Yochem,** Barbara June 1945- *WhoFI 92, WhoWest 92*
**Yochim,** Jerome M 1933- *AmMWSc 92*
**Yochmowitz,** Michael George 1948- *WhoFI 92*
**Yochum,** Douglas Allan 1945- *WhoFI 92*
**Yock,** Robert John 1938- *WhoAmL 92*
**Yockey,** Hubert Palmer 1916- *AmMWSc 92*
**Yockim,** James C. 1953- *WhoMW 92*
**Yockim,** James Craig 1953- *WhoAmP 91*
**Yocklunn,** John 1933- *Who 92*
**Yocom,** Danny *WhoAmP 91*
**Yocom,** David Allen 1950- *WhoMW 92*
**Yocom,** Perry Niel 1930- *AmMWSc 92*
**Yocum,** Charles Fredrick 1941- *AmMWSc 92*
**Yocum,** Conrad Schatte 1919- *AmMWSc 92*
**Yocum,** Frederic William, Jr. 1942- *WhoFI 92*
**Yocum,** Glenn Earl 1943- *WhoRel 92*
**Yocum,** Ronald Harris 1939- *AmMWSc 92*
**Yoda,** Masahiro 1939- *WhoWest 92*
**Yodaiken,** Ralph Emile 1928- *AmMWSc 92*
**Yoder,** Allan Henry 1952- *WhoRel 92*
**Yoder,** Charles Finney 1943- *AmMWSc 92*
**Yoder,** Claude H 1940- *AmMWSc 92*
**Yoder,** David Lee 1936- *AmMWSc 92*
**Yoder,** Donald Eugene 1930- *WhoRel 92*
**Yoder,** Donald Maurice 1920- *AmMWSc 92*
**Yoder,** Eldon J 1918- *AmMWSc 92*
**Yoder,** Elizabeth Ann 1966- *WhoRel 92*
**Yoder,** Elmon Eugene 1921- *AmMWSc 92*
**Yoder,** Glee 1916- *WrDr 92*
**Yoder,** Harold Elias 1913- *WhoMW 92*
**Yoder,** Harry Walter 1922- *WhoRel 92*
**Yoder,** Hatten Schuyler, Jr 1921- *AmMWSc 92, IntWW 91*
**Yoder,** Henry J. 1952- *WhoEnt 92*
**Yoder,** James Grover 1944- *WhoFI 92*
**Yoder,** Janet Suzanne 1944- *WhoWest 92*
**Yoder,** John Howard 1927- *WhoRel 92*
**Yoder,** John Menly 1931- *AmMWSc 92*
**Yoder,** Keith Edward 1944- *WhoRel 92*
**Yoder,** Lawrence McCulloh 1943- *WhoRel 92*
**Yoder,** Levon Lee 1936- *AmMWSc 92*
**Yoder,** Lois Jean 1955- *WhoMW 92*
**Yoder,** Neil Richard 1937- *AmMWSc 92*
**Yoder,** Olen Curtis 1942- *AmMWSc 92*
**Yoder,** Paul Rufus, Jr 1927- *AmMWSc 92*
**Yoder,** Robert E 1930- *AmMWSc 92*
**Yoder,** Ronnie A. 1937- *WhoAmL 92*
**Yoder,** Wayne Alva 1943- *AmMWSc 92*
**Yoder Wise,** Patricia S 1941- *AmMWSc 92*
**Yodh,** Gaurang Bhaskar 1928- *AmMWSc 92*
**Yodice,** R.H. *DrAPF 91*
**Yoel,** Mary Phelan *WhoFI 92*
**Yoerger,** Roger R 1929- *AmMWSc 92*
**Yoes,** Janice 1942- *WhoEnt 92*
**Yoesting,** Clarence C 1912- *AmMWSc 92*
**Yoffa,** Ellen June 1951- *AmMWSc 92*
**Yoffey,** Joseph Mendel 1902- *Who 92*
**Yogananda,** Swami Paramahansa 1893-1952 *RelLAm 91*
**Yoganathan,** Ajit Prithiviraj 1951- *AmMWSc 92*
**Yogashakti Saraswati,** Ma 1929- *RelLAm 91*
**Yoggerst,** James Paul 1924- *WhoMW 92*
**Yogore,** Mariano G, Jr 1921- *AmMWSc 92*
**Yoh,** Harold Lionel, Jr. 1936- *WhoFI 92*
**Yoh,** John K 1944- *AmMWSc 92*
**Yohalem,** Harry Morton 1943- *WhoAmL 92*
**Yohe,** Cleon Russell 1941- *AmMWSc 92*
**Yohe,** Gary W. 1948- *WhoFI 92*
**Yohe,** James Michael 1936- *AmMWSc 92, WhoMW 92*
**Yohe,** Robert L. 1936- *WhoFI 92*
**Yohe,** Thomas Lester 1947- *AmMWSc 92*
**Yohem,** Karin Hummell 1955- *AmMWSc 92*
**Yohn,** David Stewart 1929- *AmMWSc 92*
**Yohn,** Richard Van 1937- *WhoRel 92*
**Yohn,** William H, Jr 1935- *WhoAmP 91*
**Yoho,** Clayton W 1924- *AmMWSc 92*
**Yoho,** Robert Oscar 1913- *AmMWSc 92*
**Yoho,** Timothy Price 1941- *AmMWSc 92*
**Yoke,** Carl Bernard 1937- *WhoMW 92*
**Yoke,** John Thomas 1928- *AmMWSc 92*
**Yokel,** Felix Y 1922- *AmMWSc 92*
**Yokel,** Robert Allen 1945- *AmMWSc 92*
**Yokelson,** Bernard J 1924- *AmMWSc 92*
**Yokelson,** Howard Bruce 1956- *AmMWSc 92*
**Yokelson,** M V 1918- *AmMWSc 92*
**Yokich,** Tracey A 1950- *WhoAmP 91*
**Yokitis,** George Edward 1951- *WhoAmL 92*
**Yokley,** Paul, Jr 1923- *AmMWSc 92*
**Yokley,** Richard Clarence 1942- *WhoWest 92*
**Yoko,** Madame *EncAmaz 91*
**Yokogawa,** Kiyoshi 1946- *WhoFI 92*
**Yokosawa,** Akihiko 1927- *AmMWSc 92*
**Yokote,** Kohsuke 1931- *IntWW 91*
**Yokoyama,** Melvin T 1943- *AmMWSc 92*
**Yokoyama,** Shozo 1946- *AmMWSc 92*
**Yokoyama,** Yuji 1952- *WhoFI 92*
**Yoldas,** Bulent Erturk 1938- *AmMWSc 92*
**Yole,** Raymond William 1927- *AmMWSc 92*
**Yolen,** Jane 1939- *IntAu&W 91, TwCSFW 91, WrDr 92*
**Yolken,** Howard Thomas 1938- *AmMWSc 92*
**Yolles,** Seymour 1914- *AmMWSc 92*
**Yolles,** Stanley Fausst 1919- *AmMWSc 92*
**Yolles,** Tamarath Knigin 1919- *AmMWSc 92*
**Yollick,** Bernard Lawrence 1922- *AmMWSc 92*
**Yomantas,** Gary Charles 1949- *WhoFI 92*
**Yon Hyong-Muk** 1931- *IntWW 91*
**Yon,** E T 1936- *AmMWSc 92*
**Yon,** Joseph Langham 1936- *WhoWest 92*
**Yon,** Stanley Raymond 1949- *WhoWest 92*
**Yonai,** Mitsumasa 1880-1948 *FacFETw*
**Yonamine,** Noboru *WhoAmP 91*
**Yonan,** Edward E 1943- *AmMWSc 92*
**Yonas,** Gerold 1939- *AmMWSc 92*
**Yonce,** Lloyd Robert 1924- *AmMWSc 92*
**Yonchev,** Elia *WhoRel 92*
**Yonda,** Alfred William 1919- *AmMWSc 92*
**Yoneda,** Kokichi *AmMWSc 92*
**Yonemura,** Earl Tsuneki 1939- *WhoWest 92*
**Yonetani,** Takashi 1930- *AmMWSc 92*
**Yong Nyuk Lin** 1918- *Who 92*
**Yong Wentao** *IntWW 91*
**Yong,** David Cho Tat 1943- *WhoWest 92*
**Yong,** R 1929- *AmMWSc 92*
**Yong,** Suzanne Mayleen 1961- *WhoWest 92*
**Yong,** Yan 1955- *AmMWSc 92*
**Yong Kuet Tze,** Amar Stephen 1921- *IntWW 91*
**Yonge,** Charlotte 1823-1901 *RfGEnL 91*
**Yonge,** Felicity 1921- *Who 92*
**Yonge,** Keith A 1910- *AmMWSc 92*
**Yonge,** Nicholas d1619 *NewAmDM*
**Yongue,** William Henry 1926- *AmMWSc 92*
**Yonke,** Thomas Richard 1939- *AmMWSc 92*
**Yonker,** Nicholas Junior 1927- *WhoRel 92*
**Yonkers,** Anthony J 1938- *AmMWSc 92*
**Yonteck,** Elizabeth Barbara 1931- *WhoRel 92*
**Yonts,** Jack E. *WhoRel 92*
**Yonts,** Martin L. *WhoRel 92*
**Yontz,** Kenneth Fredric 1944- *WhoMW 92*
**Yonuschot,** Gene R 1936- *AmMWSc 92*
**Yoo Chang-Soon** 1918- *IntWW 91*
**Yoo,** Bong Yul 1935- *AmMWSc 92*
**Yoo,** Christine Mia 1968- *WhoEnt 92*
**Yoo,** Man Hyong 1935- *AmMWSc 92*
**Yoo,** Suz Coover 1964- *WhoEnt 92*
**Yoo,** Tai-June 1935- *AmMWSc 92*
**Yood,** Bertram 1917- *AmMWSc 92*
**Yoon Sung Min** 1926- *IntWW 91*
**Yoon,** Byung-Yul 1942- *WhoWest 92*
**Yoon,** Do Yeung 1947- *AmMWSc 92*
**Yoon,** Euijoon 1960- *AmMWSc 92*
**Yoon,** Hoil 1943- *WhoAmL 92*
**Yoon,** Hyo Sub 1935- *AmMWSc 92*
**Yoon,** Ji-Won 1939- *AmMWSc 92*
**Yoon,** Jong Sik 1937- *AmMWSc 92*
**Yoon,** Joseph Suk-Joon 1961- *WhoMW 92*
**Yoon,** Peter Haesung 1958- *AmMWSc 92*
**Yoon,** Rick J 1943- *AmMWSc 92*
**Yopp,** Johanna Futchs 1938- *WhoFI 92*
**Yopp,** John Herman 1940- *AmMWSc 92*
**Yorburg,** Betty 1926- *WrDr 92*
**Yorck von Wartenburg,** Peter 1904-1944 *EncTR 91 [port]*
**Yordan,** Philip 1913- *IntMPA 92*
**Yordanova,** Galina *WhoEnt 92*
**Yordy,** Gary L 1948- *WhoAmP 91*
**Yordy,** John David 1942- *AmMWSc 92*
**Yore,** Eugene Elliott 1939- *AmMWSc 92*
**Yore,** J. J. 1956- *WhoFI 92*
**Yori,** Lawrence George 1950- *WhoFI 92*
**Yorio,** Frank Arthur 1947- *WhoWest 92*
**Yorio,** Thomas 1948- *AmMWSc 92*
**York,** Archbishop of 1927- *Who 92*
**York,** Archdeacon of *Who 92*
**York,** Dean of *Who 92*
**York,** Duke of 1960 *Who 92R*
**York,** Alan Clarence 1952- *AmMWSc 92*
**York,** Alison *WrDr 92*
**York,** Andrew *IntAu&W 91X, WrDr 92*
**York,** Bruce Allan 1947- *WhoMW 92*
**York,** Carl Dennis 1952- *WhoFI 92*
**York,** Carl Monroe, Jr 1925- *AmMWSc 92*
**York,** Charles James 1919- *AmMWSc 92*
**York,** Christopher 1909- *Who 92*
**York,** David Anthony 1945- *AmMWSc 92*
**York,** Derek H 1936- *AmMWSc 92*
**York,** Dick 1928- *IntMPA 92*
**York,** Donald Gilbert 1944- *AmMWSc 92*
**York,** Donald Harold 1944- *AmMWSc 92, WhoMW 92*
**York,** Douglas Arthur 1940- *WhoFI 92*
**York,** Earl Dana 1928- *WhoWest 92*
**York,** Fred Miller, Jr 1945- *WhoAmP 91*
**York,** Gary R 1942- *WhoAmP 91*
**York,** George Kenneth, II 1925- *AmMWSc 92*
**York,** George William 1945- *AmMWSc 92*
**York,** Harry Lawrence 1944- *WhoWest 92*
**York,** Helen *WrDr 92*
**York,** Herbert 1921- *WrDr 92*
**York,** Herbert Frank 1921- *AmMWSc 92, IntWW 91, WhoWest 92*
**York,** Howard *WhoIns 92*
**York,** J Louis 1918- *AmMWSc 92*
**York,** James Lester 1942- *AmMWSc 92*
**York,** James Raymond 1946- *WhoMW 92*
**York,** James Wesley, Jr 1939- *AmMWSc 92*
**York,** Jesse Louis 1918- *WhoWest 92*
**York,** John Christopher 1946- *WhoAmL 92, WhoFI 92, WhoMW 92*
**York,** John Lyndal 1936- *AmMWSc 92*
**York,** John Michael 1949- *WhoMW 92*
**York,** John Owen 1923- *AmMWSc 92*
**York,** Joseph Russell 1940- *WhoEnt 92, WhoMW 92*
**York,** Marvin 1932- *WhoAmP 91*
**York,** Michael 1942- *IntMPA 92, IntWW 91, Who 92, WhoEnt 92*
**York,** Michael Ray 1954- *WhoRel 92*
**York,** Myrth *WhoAmP 91*
**York,** Owen, Jr 1927- *AmMWSc 92*
**York,** Raymond A 1917- *AmMWSc 92*
**York,** Russel Harold 1952- *WhoBlA 92*
**York,** Rusty 1935- *WhoEnt 92*
**York,** Sheldon Stafford 1943- *AmMWSc 92*
**York,** Stanley 1931- *WhoAmP 91, WhoMW 92*
**York,** Stephen Stanier 1949- *WhoAmL 92*
**York,** Steven Lynn 1949- *WhoMW 92*
**York,** Susannah 1941- *IntMPA 92, IntWW 91*
**York,** Susannah 1942- *Who 92, WhoEnt 92*
**York,** Thurnace 1926- *WhoRel 92*
**York-Johnson,** Michael *Who 92*
**York-Johnson,** Michael 1942- *WhoEnt 92*
**Yorke** *Who 92*
**Yorke,** David Harry Robert 1931- *Who 92*
**Yorke,** James Alan 1941- *AmMWSc 92*
**Yorke,** Katherine *IntAu&W 91X, WrDr 92*
**Yorke,** Margaret 1924- *IntAu&W 91, WrDr 92*
**Yorke,** Marianne 1948- *WhoFI 92*
**Yorke,** Richard Michael d1991 *Who 92N*
**Yorke,** Ritchie Ian 1944- *WrDr 92*
**Yorke,** Roger *IntAu&W 91X, TwCWW 91*
**Yorkin,** Bud *LesBEnT 92*
**Yorkin,** Bud 1926- *IntMPA 92, WhoEnt 92*
**Yorks,** Melvin Joseph 1956- *WhoRel 92*
**Yorks,** Terence Preston 1947- *AmMWSc 92*
**Yorkshire East Riding,** Archdeacon of *Who 92*
**Yorty,** Sam 1909- *WhoAmP 91*
**Yos,** David Albert 1923- *AmMWSc 92*
**Yos,** Jerrold Moore 1930- *AmMWSc 92*
**Yosha,** Rachel Leigh 1962- *WhoAmL 92*
**Yoshida,** Akira 1924- *AmMWSc 92, WhoWest 92*
**Yoshida,** Fumitake 1913- *AmMWSc 92*
**Yoshida,** Kaname 1934- *WhoEnt 92*
**Yoshida,** Karen Kamijo Cateel 1964- *WhoWest 92*
**Yoshida,** Shigeru 1878-1967 *FacFETw*
**Yoshida,** Takeshi 1938- *AmMWSc 92*
**Yoshida,** Taroichi 1919- *IntWW 91*
**Yoshikami,** Doju *AmMWSc 92*
**Yoshikawa,** Herbert Hiroshi 1929- *AmMWSc 92*
**Yoshiki,** Masao 1908- *IntWW 91*
**Yoshimasu,** Gozo 1939- *IntAu&W 91*
**Yoshimoto,** Carl Masaru 1922- *AmMWSc 92*
**Yoshimura,** Dwight Larry 1954- *WhoAmP 91*
**Yoshimura,** Junzo 1908- *IntWW 91*
**Yoshimura,** Kozabura 1911- *IntDcF 2-2*
**Yoshinaga,** Koji 1932- *AmMWSc 92*
**Yoshinaga,** Sayuri 1945- *IntWW 91*
**Yoshino,** Kouichi 1931- *AmMWSc 92*
**Yoshino,** Timothy Phillip 1948- *AmMWSc 92*
**Yoshioka,** Carlton Fumio 1948- *WhoWest 92*
**Yoshioka,** Grace Keiko 1930- *WhoWest 92*
**Yoshisaka,** Kiyoji 1908- *IntMPA 92*
**Yoshiyama,** Hirokichi 1911- *IntWW 91*
**Yoshizumi,** Donald Tetsuro 1930- *WhoWest 92*
**Yosizaka,** Takamasa 1917- *IntWW 91*
**Yoskowitz,** Irving Benjamin 1945- *WhoAmL 92, WhoFI 92*
**Yosowitz,** Sanford 1939- *WhoAmL 92*
**Yoss,** Kenneth M 1926- *AmMWSc 92*
**Yoss,** Robert Eugene 1924- *AmMWSc 92*
**Yosseliani,** Otar Davidovich 1935- *IntWW 91*
**Yost,** Ellen Ginsberg 1945- *WhoAmL 92*
**Yost,** Elwy McMurran 1925- *IntAu&W 91*
**Yost,** Eric R 1955- *WhoAmP 91*
**Yost,** Felicity Oldakowska 1950- *WhoEnt 92*
**Yost,** Francis Lorraine 1908- *AmMWSc 92*
**Yost,** Frederick Gordon 1940- *AmMWSc 92*
**Yost,** Garold Steven 1949- *AmMWSc 92*
**Yost,** Gerald B. 1954- *WhoAmL 92*
**Yost,** Gerald Vernon 1942- *WhoAmP 91*
**Yost,** Hedley Emanuel 1935- *WhoRel 92*
**Yost,** John Franklin 1919- *AmMWSc 92*
**Yost,** John R, Jr 1923- *AmMWSc 92*

**Yost**, Kelly Lou 1940- *WhoEnt 92*
**Yost**, Larry Allen 1951- *WhoRel 92*
**Yost**, Nancy Runyon 1933- *WhoMW 92*
**Yost**, Nellie Snyder 1905- *IntAu&W 91, WrDr 92*
**Yost**, Nicholas Churchill 1938- *WhoAmL 92*
**Yost**, Patricia Ann 1937- *WhoRel 92*
**Yost**, Paul Alexander, Jr 1929- *WhoAmP 91*
**Yost**, R. David 1947- *WhoMW 92*
**Yost**, Richard A 1953- *AmMWSc 92*
**Yost**, Robert Stanley 1921- *AmMWSc 92*
**Yost**, Roger William 1936- *WhoWest 92*
**Yost**, William A 1944- *AmMWSc 92*
**Yost**, William Albert 1944- *WhoMW 92*
**Yost**, William Arthur, III 1935- *WhoAmL 92, WhoFI 92*
**Yost**, William Lassiter 1923- *AmMWSc 92*
**Yost**, William Warren 1912- *WhoAmP 91*
**Yothers**, Tina 1973- *WhoHisp 92*
**Yotis**, William William 1930- *AmMWSc 92*
**You**, Kwan-sa 1941- *AmMWSc 92*
**You**, Sanguine 1922- *WhoRel 92*
**Youakim**, Saba *WhoRel 92*
**Youard**, Richard Geoffrey Atkin 1933- *Who 92*
**Youd**, C. S. *WrDr 92*
**Youd**, Thomas Leslie 1938- *AmMWSc 92*
**Youdelis**, W V 1931- *AmMWSc 92*
**Youdovin**, Ira S. 1941- *WhoRel 92*
**Youds**, Edward Ernest 1910- *Who 92*
**Youell**, George 1910- *Who 92*
**Youell**, Spencer M. 1939- *WhoMW 92*
**Youens**, John Ross 1914- *Who 92*
**Youens**, Peter 1916- *Who 92*
**Youker**, James Edward 1928- *AmMWSc 92*
**Youker**, John 1943- *AmMWSc 92*
**Youla**, Dante C 1925- *AmMWSc 92*
**Youle**, Richard James 1952- *AmMWSc 92*
**Youlou**, Fulbert 1917-1972 *FacFETw*
**Youm**, Youngil 1942- *AmMWSc 92*
**Youman**, Lillian Lincoln 1940- *WhoBlA 92*
**Youman**, Roger Jacob 1932- *IntAu&W 91*
**Youmans**, Claire *WhoWest 92*
**Youmans**, Duane Craig 1930- *WhoMW 92*
**Youmans**, Edward Livingston 1821-1887 *BiInAmS*
**Youmans**, George Estus, Jr. 1962- *WhoFI 92*
**Youmans**, Hubert Lafay 1925- *AmMWSc 92*
**Youmans**, James *WhoEnt 92*
**Youmans**, Julian Ray 1928- *AmMWSc 92*
**Youmans**, Marlene *DrAPF 91*
**Youmans**, Paul Carr 1965- *WhoRel 92*
**Youmans**, Vincent 1898-1946 *FacFETw, NewAmDM*
**Youmans**, William Barton 1910- *AmMWSc 92, WhoWest 92*
**Youmans**, William Jay 1838-1901 *BiInAmS*
**Youn**, Kong-Hi 1924- *IntWW 91*
**Younathan**, Ezzat Saad 1922- *AmMWSc 92*
**Younathan**, Margaret Tims 1926- *AmMWSc 92*
**Younce**, Dale Richard 1937- *WhoRel 92*
**Younes**, Magdy K 1939- *AmMWSc 92*
**Younes**, Mahmoud 1912- *IntWW 91*
**Younes**, Usama E 1949- *AmMWSc 92*
**Young** *Who 92*
**Young**, Baroness 1926- *IntWW 91, Who 92*
**Young**, A. S. 1924- *WhoBlA 92*
**Young**, A. Steven 1948- *WhoBlA 92*
**Young**, A. Thomas 1938- *WhoFI 92*
**Young**, Aaron 1819-1898 *BiInAmS*
**Young**, Ainslie Thomas, Jr 1943- *AmMWSc 92*
**Young**, Al *DrAPF 91*
**Young**, Al 1939- *BenetAL 91, BlkLC [port], ConNov 91, ConPo 91, WrDr 92*
**Young**, Al 1942- *WhoAmP 91*
**Young**, Alan 1919- *IntMPA 92*
**Young**, Alan John 1945- *WhoBlA 92*
**Young**, Alan Keith 1950- *WhoWest 92*
**Young**, Albert A., Jr. 1955- *WhoFI 92*
**Young**, Albert James 1939- *WhoBlA 92*
**Young**, Alec David 1913- *IntWW 91, Who 92*
**Young**, Alexander *Who 92*
**Young**, Alfred 1936- *TwCPaSc*
**Young**, Alfred 1946- *WhoBlA 92*
**Young**, Alfred F. 1932- *WhoBlA 92*
**Young**, Alice 1950- *WhoAmL 92*
**Young**, Allan Chandler 1937- *WhoAmP 91*
**Young**, Allen Marcus 1942- *AmMWSc 92*
**Young**, Alvin L 1942- *AmMWSc 92*
**Young**, Andrea C. 1952- *WhoEnt 92*
**Young**, Andrew 1885-1971 *RfGEnL 91*
**Young**, Andrew 1932- *IntWW 91, Who 92, WhoAmP 91, WhoBlA 92*
**Young**, Andrew Brodbeck 1907- *WhoAmL 92*
**Young**, Andrew Buchanan 1937- *Who 92*
**Young**, Andrew J. 1933- *WhoBlA 92*
**Young**, Andrew Jackson, Jr. 1932- *AmPolLe [port]*
**Young**, Andrew Robert 1961- *WhoFI 92*
**Young**, Andrew Tipton 1935- *AmMWSc 92*
**Young**, Aner Ruth 1933- *WhoBlA 92*
**Young**, Annette 1952- *WhoAmP 91*
**Young**, Anthony L 1948- *WhoAmP 91*
**Young**, Archie R., II 1928- *WhoBlA 92*
**Young**, Ardell Moody 1911- *WhoAmL 92*
**Young**, Art 1866-1943 *BenetAL 91*
**Young**, Arthur 1741-1820 *BlkwCEP*
**Young**, Arthur 1940- *AmMWSc 92*
**Young**, Arthur Wesley 1904- *AmMWSc 92*
**Young**, Arthur William 1945- *WhoWest 92*
**Young**, Augustus 1784-1857 *BiInAmS*
**Young**, Austin Harry 1928- *AmMWSc 92*
**Young**, Austin Prentiss, III 1940- *WhoFI 92*
**Young**, B. Ashley *WhoBlA 92*
**Young**, Barbara J. 1937- *WhoBlA 92*
**Young**, Barbara Scott 1948- *Who 92*
**Young**, Barney Thornton 1934- *WhoAmL 92, WhoFI 92*
**Young**, Bernard Theodore 1930- *AmMWSc 92*
**Young**, Bertram Alfred 1912- *IntAu&W 91, Who 92*
**Young**, Bing-Lin 1937- *AmMWSc 92*
**Young**, Bobby Gene 1929- *AmMWSc 92*
**Young**, Brad 1953- *WhoAmP 91*
**Young**, Brian 1922- *IntWW 91*
**Young**, Brian Pashley 1918- *Who 92*
**Young**, Brian Walter Mark 1922- *Who 92*
**Young**, Brigham 1801-1877 *BenetAL 91, RComAH*
**Young**, Bruce Arthur 1939- *AmMWSc 92*
**Young**, Bryan Kendall 1960- *WhoEnt 92*
**Young**, Buddy 1935- *IntMPA 92*
**Young**, Burt 1940- *IntMPA 92, WhoEnt 92A*
**Young**, C, Jr 1923- *AmMWSc 92*
**Young**, C B F 1908- *AmMWSc 92*
**Young**, C. B. Fehrler 1908- *WhoFI 92*
**Young**, C. Clifton 1922- *WhoAmL 92, WhoAmP 91, WhoWest 92*
**Young**, C. W. 1930- *AlmAP 92 [port]*
**Young**, C W Bill 1930- *WhoAmP 91*
**Young**, Carlene Herb *WhoBlA 92*
**Young**, Carroll *IntMPA 92*
**Young**, Carter Travis *WrDr 92*
**Young**, Carter Travis 1924- *TwCWW 91*
**Young**, Cedric Jan-Yee 1942- *WhoWest 92*
**Young**, Charles, Jr. 1934- *WhoBlA 92*
**Young**, Charles Albert 1911- *AmMWSc 92*
**Young**, Charles Albert, Jr. 1952- *WhoMW 92*
**Young**, Charles Alexander 1930- *WhoBlA 92*
**Young**, Charles Augustus 1834-1908 *BiInAmS*
**Young**, Charles Edward 1931- *WhoWest 92*
**Young**, Charles Edward 1941- *AmMWSc 92*
**Young**, Charles Gilbert 1930- *AmMWSc 92*
**Young**, Charles L 1931- *WhoAmP 91*
**Young**, Charles Lemuel, Sr. 1931- *WhoBlA 92*
**Young**, Charles Stuart Hamish 1944- *AmMWSc 92*
**Young**, Charles Wesley 1929- *AmMWSc 92*
**Young**, Charles William 1930- *AmMWSc 92*
**Young**, Charles William 1952- *WhoRel 92*
**Young**, Charlie, Jr. 1928- *WhoBlA 92*
**Young**, Chesley Virginia 1919- *WrDr 92*
**Young**, Christopher Godfrey 1932- *Who 92*
**Young**, Christopher Michael 1961- *WhoWest 92*
**Young**, Christy Jean 1965- *WhoEnt 92*
**Young**, Clarence *SmATA 67*
**Young**, Clarence, III 1942- *WhoBlA 92*
**Young**, Clifton A 1943- *AmMWSc 92*
**Young**, Clyde Thomas 1930- *AmMWSc 92*
**Young**, Coleman 1918- *ConBlB 1 [port]*
**Young**, Coleman A 1918- *WhoAmP 91, WhoBlA 92*
**Young**, Coleman Alexander 1918- *WhoMW 92*
**Young**, Coleman Milton, III 1930- *WhoBlA 92*
**Young**, Colin 1927- *Who 92*
**Young**, Collier d1980 *LesBEnT 92*
**Young**, Connie Sue *WhoWest 92*
**Young**, Corrine Orelia 1924- *WhoRel 92*
**Young**, Cy 1867-1955 *FacFETw*
**Young**, D W 1929- *WhoIns 92*
**Young**, Dale L 1928- *WhoAmP 91*
**Young**, Dan *WhoWest 92*
**Young**, Dan 1951- *WhoAmP 91*
**Young**, Dana 1904- *AmMWSc 92*
**Young**, Daniel Merritt 1953- *WhoRel 92*
**Young**, Danny 1962- *WhoBlA 92*
**Young**, David *DrAPF 91*
**Young**, David 1781-1852 *BenetAL 91, BiInAmS*
**Young**, David 1936- *ConPo 91, WrDr 92*
**Young**, David A 1921- *AmMWSc 92*
**Young**, David A 1942- *AmMWSc 92*
**Young**, David A 1963- *WhoAmP 91*
**Young**, David Allan 1915- *AmMWSc 92*
**Young**, David Allen 1946- *AmMWSc 92*
**Young**, David Brian 1960- *WhoMW 92*
**Young**, David Bruce 1945- *AmMWSc 92*
**Young**, David Caldwell 1924- *AmMWSc 92*
**Young**, David Edward Michael 1940- *Who 92*
**Young**, David Haywood 1943- *WhoAmL 92*
**Young**, David Junor 1934- *IntWW 91, Who 92*
**Young**, David Marshall 1942- *AmMWSc 92*
**Young**, David Martin 1952- *WhoEnt 92*
**Young**, David Matheson 1928- *AmMWSc 92*
**Young**, David Maynard 1928- *WhoEnt 92*
**Young**, David Michael 1935- *AmMWSc 92*
**Young**, David Monaghan, Jr 1923- *AmMWSc 92*
**Young**, David Nigel de Lorentz *Who 92*
**Young**, David Samuel 1944- *WhoRel 92*
**Young**, David Thad 1943- *AmMWSc 92*
**Young**, David Tod 1926- *Who 92*
**Young**, David Tyrrell 1938- *Who 92*
**Young**, David W 1909- *AmMWSc 92*
**Young**, David William 1942- *WhoFI 92*
**Young**, David Wright *Who 92*
**Young**, Davis Alan 1941- *AmMWSc 92*
**Young**, Dean Wayne 1938- *WhoEnt 92*
**Young**, Debora Holmes 1950- *WhoBlA 92*
**Young**, Deborah Schwind 1955- *WhoAmL 92*
**Young**, Delano Victor 1945- *AmMWSc 92*
**Young**, Dennis James 1949- *WhoRel 92*
**Young**, Dennis Lee 1944- *AmMWSc 92, WhoWest 92*
**Young**, Doc 1924- *WhoBlA 92*
**Young**, Don 1933- *AlmAP 92 [port]*
**Young**, Don J. 1910- *WhoAmL 92, WhoMW 92*
**Young**, Dona Davis Gagliano 1954- *WhoAmL 92*
**Young**, Donald 1924- *TwCPaSc*
**Young**, Donald 1933- *IntAu&W 91, WrDr 92*
**Young**, Donald Alcoe 1929- *AmMWSc 92*
**Young**, Donald Allen 1931- *WhoWest 92*
**Young**, Donald Anthony 1933- *Who 92*
**Young**, Donald C 1933- *AmMWSc 92*
**Young**, Donald Carleton 1959- *WhoMW 92*
**Young**, Donald Charles 1944- *AmMWSc 92*
**Young**, Donald E 1933- *WhoAmP 91, WhoWest 92*
**Young**, Donald Edward 1922- *AmMWSc 92*
**Young**, Donald F 1928- *AmMWSc 92*
**Young**, Donald Raymond 1954- *AmMWSc 92*
**Young**, Donald Reeder 1921- *AmMWSc 92*
**Young**, Donald Soutar 1936- *WhoAmL 92*
**Young**, Donald Stirling 1933- *AmMWSc 92*
**Young**, Douglas Rea 1948- *WhoAmL 92*
**Young**, Earl LaVaughn 1938- *WhoRel 92*
**Young**, Earle F, Jr *AmMWSc 92*
**Young**, Eddye Vivian Pierce 1947- *WhoBlA 92*
**Young**, Edith Mae 1932- *WhoBlA 92*
**Young**, Edmond Grove 1917- *AmMWSc 92*
**Young**, Edna Elizabeth 1936- *WhoWest 92*
**Young**, Edward 1683?-1765 *BlkwCEP, RfGEnL 91*
**Young**, Edward Graver 1945- *WhoAmL 92*
**Young**, Edward Hiram, Jr. 1950- *WhoBlA 92*
**Young**, Edward Joseph 1923- *AmMWSc 92*
**Young**, Edward Ming 1947- *WhoMW 92*
**Young**, Edward Preston 1913- *Who 92*
**Young**, Edwin Allen 1930- *WhoWest 92*
**Young**, Edwin H 1918- *AmMWSc 92*
**Young**, Edwin S. W. 1943- *WhoWest 92*
**Young**, Eleanor Anne 1925- *AmMWSc 92*
**Young**, Elizabeth *WrDr 92*
**Young**, Elizabeth Bell 1929- *AmMWSc 92, WhoBlA 92*
**Young**, Elizabeth Theobald 1957- *WhoAmL 92*
**Young**, Ella Flagg 1845-1918 *HanAmWH*
**Young**, Ellen G. 1951- *WhoFI 92*
**Young**, Elmer, Jr. 1924- *WhoBlA 92*
**Young**, Elroy 1923- *WhoBlA 92*
**Young**, Elton Theodore 1940- *AmMWSc 92*
**Young**, Eric 1924- *Who 92*
**Young**, Eric D 1945- *AmMWSc 92*
**Young**, Eric William 1915- *WrDr 92*
**Young**, Ernestine 1918- *WhoBlA 92*
**Young**, Eutiquio Chua 1932- *AmMWSc 92*
**Young**, Everett Charles 1945- *WhoFI 92*
**Young**, F. Camille 1928- *WhoBlA 92*
**Young**, F E 1875-1945 *ScFEYrs*
**Young**, Faron 1932- *ConMus 7 [port]*
**Young**, Florence Nelson 1921- *WhoWest 92*
**Young**, Francis Allan 1918- *AmMWSc 92*
**Young**, Francis Arthur 1948- *WhoAmP 91*
**Young**, Frank 1925- *IntAu&W 91*
**Young**, Frank 1935- *AmMWSc 92*
**Young**, Frank Coleman 1935- *AmMWSc 92*
**Young**, Frank E 1931- *AmMWSc 92*
**Young**, Frank Glynn 1916- *AmMWSc 92*
**Young**, Frank Hood 1939- *AmMWSc 92*
**Young**, Frank Nelson, Jr 1915- *AmMWSc 92*
**Young**, Franklin 1928- *AmMWSc 92*
**Young**, Franklin Alden, Jr 1938- *AmMWSc 92*
**Young**, Fred M 1940- *AmMWSc 92*
**Young**, Fred Richard 1937- *WhoFI 92*
**Young**, Freddie 1902- *IntMPA 92, IntWW 91*
**Young**, Frederic Hisgin 1936- *WhoFI 92, WhoMW 92*
**Young**, Frederick Griffin 1940- *AmMWSc 92*
**Young**, Frederick J 1931- *AmMWSc 92*
**Young**, Frederick Nevin 1932- *WhoAmL 92, WhoAmP 91*
**Young**, Frederick Walter, Jr 1924- *AmMWSc 92*
**Young**, Frieda Margaret 1913- *Who 92*
**Young**, Gale 1912- *AmMWSc 92*
**Young**, Gary *DrAPF 91*
**Young**, Gary Dean 1946- *WhoFI 92*
**Young**, Gary Lynn *WhoEnt 92*
**Young**, Gary Malcolm 1939- *WhoAmL 92*
**Young**, Gary Paul 1954- *WhoWest 92*
**Young**, Gavin David 1928- *Who 92*
**Young**, Gavin Neil B. *Who 92*
**Young**, Genevieve Leman 1930- *WhoFI 92*
**Young**, George 1911-1990 *AnObit 1990*
**Young**, George, Jr. 1933- *WhoBlA 92*
**Young**, George Andrew, Jr. 1935- *WhoWest 92*
**Young**, George Anthony 1919- *AmMWSc 92*
**Young**, George Bell 1924- *Who 92*
**Young**, George Cressler 1916- *WhoAmL 92*
**Young**, George Hansen 1962- *WhoMW 92*
**Young**, George Jamison 1925- *AmMWSc 92*
**Young**, George Robert 1925- *AmMWSc 92*
**Young**, George Samuel Knatchbull 1941- *Who 92*
**Young**, Gerald A 1936- *AmMWSc 92*
**Young**, Gerald Leonard, Sr. 1937- *WhoWest 92*
**Young**, Gerald Lewis 1944- *WhoRel 92*
**Young**, Gerard Francis 1910- *Who 92*
**Young**, Gilbert Flowers, Jr 1922- *AmMWSc 92*
**Young**, Glenn David, Jr. 1931- *WhoMW 92*
**Young**, Glenn Raymond 1944- *WhoRel 92*
**Young**, Glenn Reid 1951- *AmMWSc 92*
**Young**, Gordon 1886-1948 *TwCWW 91*
**Young**, Gordon 1919- *Who 92*
**Young**, Gordon Douglas 1949- *WhoFI 92, WhoWest 92*
**Young**, Gordon Ellsworth 1919- *WhoEnt 92*
**Young**, Gordon James 1950- *WhoRel 92*
**Young**, Grant McAdam 1937- *AmMWSc 92*
**Young**, Gregory P *WhoAmP 91*
**Young**, Gregory Steven 1962- *WhoWest 92*
**Young**, H Ben, Jr 1913- *AmMWSc 92*
**Young**, H. Richard 1939- *WhoRel 92*
**Young**, Harland Harry 1908- *AmMWSc 92*
**Young**, Harold 1923- *Who 92*
**Young**, Harold Edle 1917- *AmMWSc 92*
**Young**, Harold Henry 1927- *AmMWSc 92*
**Young**, Harold Higgins, III 1954- *WhoMW 92*
**Young**, Harrison Hurst, Jr 1919- *AmMWSc 92*
**Young**, Harvey Michael 1937- *WhoFI 92*
**Young**, Henry H 1920- *AmMWSc 92*
**Young**, Herbert A 1857?-1894 *BiInAmS*
**Young**, Herman A. 1929- *WhoBlA 92*
**Young**, Hewitt H 1923- *AmMWSc 92*
**Young**, Ho Lee 1920- *AmMWSc 92*
**Young**, Hobart Peyton 1945- *AmMWSc 92*
**Young**, Hong Yip 1910- *AmMWSc 92*
**Young**, Howard 1932- *WhoIns 92*
**Young**, Howard Alan 1948- *AmMWSc 92*
**Young**, Howard Frederick 1918- *AmMWSc 92*
**Young**, Howard Lee 1949- *WhoRel 92*
**Young**, Howard Seth 1924- *AmMWSc 92*
**Young**, Hubert Howell, Jr 1945- *WhoAmP 91*
**Young**, Hugh David 1930- *AmMWSc 92*

Young, Vernon Lewis 1919- *WhoMW 92*
Young, Vernon Robert 1937- *AmMWSc 92*
Young, Victor 1889-1968 *NewAmDM*
Young, Victor 1900-1956 *FacFETw, NewAmDM*
Young, Viola Mae 1915- *AmMWSc 92*
Young, Virginia Brady *DrAPF 91*
Young, Virginia McLain 1954- *WhoMW 92*
Young, W. Don 1938- *WhoRel 92*
Young, Wallace L. 1931- *WhoBlA 92*
Young, Walter C 1922- *WhoAmP 91*
Young, Walter F. 1934- *WhoBlA 92*
Young, Walter Kwai Whun 1934- *WhoWest 92*
Young, Walter Reed 1923- *WhoAmL 92*
Young, Warren Melvin 1937- *AmMWSc 92, WhoMW 92*
Young, Watson A. 1915- *WhoBlA 92*
Young, Wayland *IntWW 91, Who 92*
Young, Wayland 1923- *WrDr 92*
Young, Wesley Eugene 1930- *WhoAmP 91*
Young, Whitney M 1921-1971 *FacFETw*
Young, Willard N 1933- *WhoAmP 91*
Young, William Allen 1930- *AmMWSc 92*
Young, William Allen 1932- *WhoAmL 92*
Young, William Anthony 1923- *AmMWSc 92*
Young, William Ben 1934- *AmMWSc 92*
Young, William Charles 1936- *WhoEnt 92, WhoWest 92*
Young, William David 1937- *WhoRel 92*
Young, William Donald, Jr 1938- *AmMWSc 92*
Young, William Edgar 1930- *WhoRel 92*
Young, William F. 1925- *WhoAmL 92*
Young, William Glenn, Jr 1925- *AmMWSc 92*
Young, William Glover 1940- *WhoAmL 92*
Young, William Hanna, Jr 1960- *WhoAmP 91*
Young, William Hilary 1913- *Who 92*
Young, William Johnson, II 1925- *AmMWSc 92*
Young, William Lambert 1913- *Who 92*
Young, William Lawrence, Jr. 1944- *WhoRel 92*
Young, William Neil 1941- *Who 92*
Young, William Paul 1913- *AmMWSc 92*
Young, William Rae 1915- *AmMWSc 92*
Young, William Robert 1943- *WhoFI 92*
Young, William Ronald 1941- *WhoAmP 91*
Young, William Sherban 1947- *WhoFI 92*
Young, William W, Jr *AmMWSc 92*
Young, Wilson *TwCWW 91*
Young Bear, Ray A. *DrAPF 91*
Young-Bruehl, Elisabeth 1946- *WrDr 92*
Young-Cummings, Mary M 1943- *WhoAmP 91*
Young-Herries, Michael Alexander Robert *Who 92*
Young Lively, Sandra Lee 1943- *WhoMW 92*
Young of Dartington, Baron 1915- *IntAu&W 91, IntWW 91, Who 92*
Young Of Graffham, Baron 1932- *IntWW 91, Who 92*
Young-Price, Toby 1936- *WhoAmP 91*
Youngbaer, Peter 1952- *WhoAmP 91*
Youngberg, Charlotte Anne 1937- *WhoMW 92*
Youngberg, Chester Theodore 1917- *AmMWSc 92*
Youngblood, Bettye Sue 1926- *AmMWSc 92*
Youngblood, Bill 1945- *WhoAmP 91*
Youngblood, D. Hull, Jr. 1952- *WhoAmL 92*
Youngblood, Dave Harper 1939- *AmMWSc 92*
Youngblood, J. Craig 1947- *WhoAmL 92*
Youngblood, James Robert 1939- *WhoMW 92*
Youngblood, Joe Thomas, Jr. 1954- *WhoRel 92*
Youngblood, Michael 1965- *WhoEnt 92*
Youngblood, Michelle Karen Wolstein 1958- *WhoAmL 92*
Youngblood, Ozie F. 1906- *WhoBlA 92*
Youngblood, Rebecca Carol 1951- *WhoRel 92*
Youngblood, Rick Dwayne 1954- *WhoWest 92*
Youngblood, Ronald Fred 1931- *WhoRel 92, WhoWest 92, WrDr 92*
Youngblood, Scot Alan 1962- *WhoWest 92*
Youngdahl, Carl Kerr 1934- *AmMWSc 92*
Youngdahl, Elizabeth Anne 1953- *WhoMW 92*
Youngdahl, Mark A 1933- *WhoAmP 91*
Youngdahl, Patricia Lucy 1927- *WhoAmP 91*
Youngdahl, Paul F 1921- *AmMWSc 92*
Youngdale, Gilbert Arthur 1929- *AmMWSc 92*
Younge, Fitzroy Egerton 1903- *WhoBlA 92*
Younge, Richard G. 1924- *WhoBlA 92*
Younge, Wyvetter Hoover 1930- *WhoAmP 91*
Younger *Who 92*
Younger, Allan Elton 1919- *Who 92*
Younger, Celia Davis 1939- *WhoBlA 92*
Younger, Charles Frank Johnston 1908- *Who 92*
Younger, Charles Jacobs 1932- *WhoMW 92*
Younger, Daniel H 1936- *AmMWSc 92*
Younger, Doris Anne 1924- *WhoRel 92*
Younger, George 1931- *IntWW 91, Who 92*
Younger, George Dana 1926- *WhoRel 92*
Younger, John Patrick, Jr. 1949- *WhoWest 92*
Younger, John William 1920- *Who 92*
Younger, Kenneth C. *WhoBlA 92*
Younger, Kenneth Lawson, Jr. 1953- *WhoRel 92*
Younger, Lewis T., Jr. 1950- *WhoBlA 92*
Younger, Mary Sue 1944- *AmMWSc 92*
Younger, Paul Lawrence 1928- *WhoBlA 92*
Younger, Robert D. 1932- *WhoBlA 92*
Younger, Robert Edward Gilmour 1940- *Who 92*
Younger, Robert Joseph 1943- *WhoMW 92*
Younger, William Carl 1919- *WhoAmL 92*
Younger, William McEwan 1905- *Who 92*
Younger of Leckie, Viscount 1906- *Who 92*
Younggren, Newell A 1915- *AmMWSc 92*
Youngken, Heber Wilkinson, Jr 1913- *AmMWSc 92*
Younglai, Edward Victor 1940- *AmMWSc 92*
Younglove, James Newton 1927- *AmMWSc 92*
Youngman, Arthur L 1937- *AmMWSc 92*
Youngman, Edward August 1925- *AmMWSc 92*
Youngman, Henny *WhoEnt 92*
Youngman, Henny 1906?- *ConAu 134*
Youngman, Nan 1906- *TwCPaSc*
Youngman, Vern E 1928- *AmMWSc 92*
Youngmeyer, Kevin Edward 1955- *WhoMW 92*
Youngner, Julius Stuart 1920- *AmMWSc 92*
Youngner, Philip Genevus 1920- *AmMWSc 92*
Youngquist, Eric John 1967- *WhoFI 92*
Youngquist, Gerald Lee 1930- *WhoRel 92*
Youngquist, R William 1935- *AmMWSc 92*
Youngquist, Ted Nowak 1947- *WhoWest 92*
Youngquist, Walter 1921- *AmMWSc 92*
Youngren, Peter Jonas 1954- *WhoRel 92*
Youngs, Betty F. 1928- *WrDr 92*
Youngs, Christopher Jay 1956- *WhoAmL 92*
Youngs, Clarence George 1926- *AmMWSc 92*
Youngs, Jack Marvin 1941- *WhoWest 92*
Youngs, James Murray 1947- *WhoWest 92*
Youngs, John 1950- *WhoEnt 92*
Youngs, Joseph 1930- *WhoIns 92*
Youngs, Robert Leland 1924- *AmMWSc 92*
Youngs, Wiley Jay 1949- *AmMWSc 92*
Youngs, William Ellis 1916- *WhoEnt 92*
Youngsman, Jim *WhoAmP 91*
Youngson, Alexander John 1918- *Who 92*
Youngstein, Kenneth Paul 1948- *WhoEnt 92*
Youngstein, Max E. 1913- *IntMPA 92*
Youngstrom, Richard Earl 1943- *AmMWSc 92*
Youngwood, Alfred Donald 1938- *WhoAmL 92*
Younie, Edward Milne 1926- *Who 92*
Younie, William J. 1932- *WrDr 92*
Younis, Mahmoud Rachid 1948- *WhoMW 92*
Younker, Mary Lou 1940- *WhoWest 92*
Younkin, Larry Myrle 1936- *AmMWSc 92*
Younkin, Stuart G 1912- *AmMWSc 92*
Younoszai, Rafi 1930- *AmMWSc 92*
Younson, Eric John 1919- *Who 92*
Younszai, M Kabir 1932- *AmMWSc 92*
Yount, David Eugene 1935- *AmMWSc 92, WhoWest 92*
Yount, Ernest H 1919- *AmMWSc 92*
Yount, George Stuart 1949- *WhoFI 92, WhoWest 92*
Yount, John Alonzo 1935- *WrDr 92*
Yount, Kim Allen 1954- *WhoMW 92*
Yount, Philip Richard 1937- *WhoFI 92, WhoMW 92*
Yount, Ralph Granville 1932- *AmMWSc 92, WhoWest 92*
Yount, Royall Austin 1922- *WhoRel 92*
Yount, Sue Wyskiver 1960- *WhoAmL 92*
Yount, William J 1936- *AmMWSc 92*
Yount, William McKinley 1945- *WhoRel 92*
Younts, Sanford Eugene 1930- *AmMWSc 92*
Yourcenar, Marguerite 1903-1987 *BenetAL 91, FrenWW, GuFrLit 1, LiExTwC*
Yourcenar, Marguerite 1907-1987 *FacFETw*
Yourell, Agnes Bond *ScFEYrs*
Yourell, Harry *WhoAmP 91*
Yourgrau, Barry *DrAPF 91*
Yourgrau, Barry 1949- *LiExTwC*
Youril, John A. *DrAPF 91*
Yourkevitch, Vladimir 1885-1964 *DcTwDes*
Yourtee, John Boteler 1946- *AmMWSc 92*
Yourtee, Lawrence Karn 1917- *AmMWSc 92*
Yourzak, Robert Joseph 1947- *WhoMW 92*
Youse, Bevan K 1927- *AmMWSc 92*
Youse, Howard Ray 1915- *AmMWSc 92*
Yousef, Ibrahim Mohmoud 1940- *AmMWSc 92*
Yousef, Mohamed Khalil 1935- *AmMWSc 92*
Yousif, Salah Mohammad 1938- *AmMWSc 92*
Youson, John Harold *AmMWSc 92*
Youssef, Mary Naguib *AmMWSc 92*
Youssef, Nabil Naguib 1937- *AmMWSc 92*
Yousten, Allan A 1936- *AmMWSc 92*
Yousuf, Ahmed *WrDr 92*
Youtcheff, John Sheldon 1925- *AmMWSc 92*
Youtsey, Karl John 1939- *AmMWSc 92*
Youtz, Byron Leroy 1925- *AmMWSc 92*
Youtz, Hewitt G 1922- *WhoAmP 91*
Youtzy, Harold Paul, Jr. 1955- *WhoMW 92*
Yovanovitch, Drasko D 1930- *AmMWSc 92*
Yovchev, Georgi Ivanoy *WhoRel 92*
Yovich, John V 1959- *AmMWSc 92*
Yovits, Marshall Clinton 1923- *AmMWSc 92, WhoMW 92*
Yow, Francis Wagoner 1931- *AmMWSc 92*
Yow, Martha Dukes 1922- *AmMWSc 92*
Yowell, Robert Lee 1941- *WhoEnt 92*
Yowell, Ronald Lee 1951- *WhoFI 92, WhoIns 92*
Yoxall, George Jarman 1924- *WhoMW 92*
Yoxen, Edward 1950- *WrDr 92*
Yozawitz, Allan 1949- *AmMWSc 92*
Yozwiak, Bernard James 1919- *AmMWSc 92*
Yozwick, Chester Paul 1938- *WhoMW 92*
Yphantis, David Andrew 1930- *AmMWSc 92*
Yrastorza, Jaime Alonso 1930- *WhoWest 92*
Yrigoyen, Charles, Jr. 1937- *WhoHisp 92, WhoRel 92*
Ysander, Bengt-Christer 1911- *IntWW 91*
Ysaye, Eugene 1858-1931 *NewAmDM*
Ysern, Jose 1928- *WhoHisp 92*
Yslas, Stephen D. 1947- *WhoHisp 92*
Yttrehus, Rolv Berger 1926- *WhoEnt 92*
Yu Guangyuan 1915- *IntWW 91*
Yu Hongen 1928- *IntWW 91*
Yu Hongliang *IntWW 91*
Yu Kuo-Hwa 1914- *IntWW 91*
Yu Li-hua 1931- *LiExTwC*
Yu Min 1926- *IntWW 91*
Yu Mingtao 1917- *IntWW 91*
Yu Qiuli 1914- *IntWW 91*
Yu Wen 1918- *IntWW 91*
Yu Zhan 1921- *IntWW 91*
Yu Zhen 1936- *IntWW 91*
Yu Zhizhen 1915- *IntWW 91*
Yu, A Tobey 1921- *AmMWSc 92*
Yu, Aiting Tobey 1921- *WhoFI 92*
Yu, Andrew B C 1945- *AmMWSc 92*
Yu, Byung Pal 1931- *AmMWSc 92*
Yu, Chang-An 1937- *AmMWSc 92*
Yu, Chia-Nien 1931- *AmMWSc 92*
Yu, Chia-Ping 1934- *AmMWSc 92*
Yu, Chyang John 1948- *AmMWSc 92*
Yu, Clement Tak 1948- *AmMWSc 92*
Yu, David Chien-seng 1918- *WhoRel 92*
Yu, David Tak Yan 1943- *AmMWSc 92*
Yu, David U L 1940- *AmMWSc 92*
Yu, Francis T S 1932- *AmMWSc 92*
Yu, Fu-Li 1934- *AmMWSc 92*
Yu, Grace Wei-Chi Hu 1937- *AmMWSc 92*
Yu, Greta 1917- *AmMWSc 92*
Yu, Hwa Nien 1929- *AmMWSc 92*
Yu, Hyuk 1933- *AmMWSc 92*
Yu, Jack Jing-Cheng 1957- *WhoWest 92*
Yu, James Chun-Ying 1940- *AmMWSc 92*
Yu, Jason C 1936- *AmMWSc 92*
Yu, Jen 1943- *AmMWSc 92*
Yu, Joseph Tientu 1926- *WhoRel 92*
Yu, Julian Jing-Jun 1957- *ConCom 92*
Yu, Kai-Bor 1953- *AmMWSc 92*
Yu, Kai Fun 1950- *AmMWSc 92*
Yu, Karl Ka-Chung 1936- *AmMWSc 92*
Yu, Kitson Szewai 1950- *WhoWest 92*
Yu, Kuo Ching Casey 1945- *WhoWest 92*
Yu, Leepo Cheng 1939- *AmMWSc 92*
Yu, Linda 1943- *AmMWSc 92*
Yu, Mang Chung 1939- *AmMWSc 92*
Yu, Mason K 1926- *AmMWSc 92*
Yu, Mei-ying Wong *AmMWSc 92*
Yu, Ming-Ho 1928- *AmMWSc 92*
Yu, Ming Lun 1945- *AmMWSc 92*
Yu, Nai-Teng 1939- *AmMWSc 92*
Yu, Oliver Shukiang 1939- *AmMWSc 92*
Yu, Paul N d1991 *NewYTBS 91 [port]*
Yu, Paul N 1915- *AmMWSc 92*
Yu, Peter Hao 1942- *AmMWSc 92*
Yu, Peter Yound 1944- *AmMWSc 92*
Yu, Robert Kuan-Jen 1938- *AmMWSc 92*
Yu, Ruey Jiin 1932- *AmMWSc 92*
Yu, Sharon S M *AmMWSc 92*
Yu, Shih-An 1927- *AmMWSc 92*
Yu, Shirley Shiu-fang 1949- *WhoMW 92*
Yu, Shiu Yeh 1926- *AmMWSc 92*
Yu, Simon Shin-Lun 1945- *AmMWSc 92*
Yu, Simon Shyi-Jian 1935- *AmMWSc 92*
Yu, Thomas Huei-Chung 1957- *AmMWSc 92*
Yu, Timothy Pan 1974- *IntAu&W 91*
Yu, Ts'ai-Fan 1911- *AmMWSc 92*
Yu, Wei Wen 1924- *AmMWSc 92*
Yu, Wen-Shi 1934- *AmMWSc 92*
Yu, Yi-Yuan 1923- *AmMWSc 92*
Yu, Yun-Sheng 1926- *AmMWSc 92*
Yu, Zeng-Qi 1941- *WhoWest 92*
Yuan Baohua 1916- *IntWW 91*
Yuan Enfeng 1940- *IntWW 91*
Yuan Jun 1924- *IntWW 91*
Yuan Longping 1930- *IntWW 91*
Yuan Shengping 1912- *IntWW 91*
Yuan Shih-k'ai 1859-1916 *FacFETw*
Yuan Tseh Lee 1936- *IntWW 91*
Yuan Weimin 1939- *IntWW 91*
Yuan Yunsheng 1937- *IntWW 91*
Yuan, Jian-Min 1944- *AmMWSc 92*
Yuan, Luke Chia Liu 1912- *AmMWSc 92*
Yuan, Robert L 1937- *AmMWSc 92*
Yuan, Shao-yuen 1929- *AmMWSc 92*
Yuan, Sidney Wei Kwun 1957- *AmMWSc 92*
Yuan, Tzu-Liang 1922- *AmMWSc 92*
Yucel, Edgar Kent 1927- *WhoAmL 92*
Yuceoglu, Yusuf Ziya 1919- *AmMWSc 92*
Yudelson, Joseph Samuel 1925- *AmMWSc 92*
Yudenich, Nicholas Nikolayevich 1862-1933 *FacFETw*
Yudewtiz, Bruce J. 1951- *WhoRel 92*
Yudkin, Cicely *TwCPaSc*
Yudkin, John 1910- *Who 92, WrDr 92*
Yudkin, Leon Israel 1939- *WrDr 92*
Yudkin, Marjorie Sue 1956- *WhoRel 92*
Yudkoff, Alvin Stephen 1923- *WhoEnt 92*
Yudkowsky, Elias B 1932- *AmMWSc 92*
Yudof, Mark G. 1944- *WhoAmL 92*
Yue Hong 1962- *IntWW 91*
Yue, A S 1920- *AmMWSc 92*
Yue, Agnes Kau-Wah 1947- *WhoWest 92*
Yue, Alfred Shui-choh 1920- *WhoWest 92*
Yue, On-Ching 1947- *AmMWSc 92*
Yue, Robert Hon-Sang 1937- *AmMWSc 92*
Yuen, Andy Tak Sing 1952- *WhoWest 92*
Yuen, David Alexander 1948- *AmMWSc 92*
Yuen, Lup Fun 1950- *WhoEnt 92*
Yuen, Man-Chuen 1933- *AmMWSc 92*
Yuen, Paul C 1928- *AmMWSc 92*
Yuen, Ted Gim Hing 1933- *AmMWSc 92*
Yuen, Thomas Chi Kwan 1951- *WhoWest 92*
Yuen, Wing 1914- *AmMWSc 92*
Yugusuk, Benjamina W. *WhoRel 92*
Yuh, Huoy-Jen *AmMWSc 92*
Yuh, Junku 1958- *WhoWest 92*
Yuhas, Joseph George 1938- *AmMWSc 92*
Yuhasz, Michael Paul, II 1961- *WhoFI 92*
Yuhaus, Cassian J. 1923- *WhoRel 92*
Yuhnke, Pam 1951- *WhoWest 92*
Yuill, P. B. *WrDr 92*
Yuill, Thomas MacKay 1937- *AmMWSc 92*
Yukawa, Hideki 1907-1981 *FacFETw, WhoNob 90*
Yukawa, Morio 1908- *Who 92*
Yukawa, S 1925- *AmMWSc 92*
Yukei, Hasebe Yoshikazu 1929- *WhoRel 92*
Yukelson, Ronald Alan 1956- *WhoWest 92*
Yukevich, John Paul, Jr. 1954- *WhoAmL 92*
Yuki 1940- *DcTwDes*
Yukich, Joseph E *AmMWSc 92*
Yukon, Bishop of 1945- *Who 92*
Yukon, Stanford P 1939- *AmMWSc 92*
Yule, Ainslie 1941- *TwCPaSc*
Yule, Dorothy Ann 1950- *WhoEnt 92*
Yule, Herbert Phillip 1931- *AmMWSc 92*
Yulin, Harris *IntMPA 92*
Yum, Su Il 1939- *AmMWSc 92*
Yumashev, Ivan Stepanovich 1895-1972 *SovUnBD*
Yun Isang 1917- *ConCom 92*
Yun Po Sun 1891-1990 *FacFETw*
Yun Po-Sun 1899-1990 *AnObit 1990*

**Yun,** Isang 1917- *IntWW 91*
**Yun,** Kwang-Sik 1929- *AmMWSc 92*
**Yun,** Samuel 1958- *WhoRel 92*
**Yun,** Seung Soo 1931- *AmMWSc 92*
**Yun,** Suk Koo 1930- *AmMWSc 92*
**Yun,** Young Mok 1931- *AmMWSc 92*
**Yunak,** Ivan Kharitonovich 1918- *SovUnBD*
**Yund,** E William 1914- *AmMWSc 92*
**Yund,** George Edward 1952- *WhoAmL 92*
**Yund,** Mary Alice 1943- *AmMWSc 92*
**Yund,** Richard Allen 1933- *AmMWSc 92*
**Yune,** Heun Yung 1929- *AmMWSc 92, WhoMW 92*
**Yung,** Kok-Kwong 1927- *WhoRel 92*
**Yung,** W K Alfred 1948- *AmMWSc 92*
**Yungbluth,** Thomas Alan 1934- *AmMWSc 92*
**Yungen,** John A 1921- *AmMWSc 92*
**Yunger,** Libby Marie 1944- *AmMWSc 92*
**Yunghans,** Robert O 1919- *WhoAmP 91*
**Yunghans,** Wayne N 1945- *AmMWSc 92*
**Yungkans-Robison,** Monnie 1917- *WhoAmP 91*
**Yunich,** David Lawrence 1917- *IntWW 91*
**Yunick,** Robert P 1935- *AmMWSc 92*
**Yunis,** Adel A 1930- *AmMWSc 92*
**Yunis,** Edmond J 1929- *AmMWSc 92*
**Yunis,** Jorge J 1933- *AmMWSc 92*
**Yunker,** Conrad Erhardt 1927- *AmMWSc 92*
**Yunker,** Mark Bernard 1948- *AmMWSc 92*
**Yunker,** Martin Henry 1928- *AmMWSc 92*
**Yunker,** Todd Elliott 1960- *WhoEnt 92*
**Yunker,** Wayne Harry 1936- *AmMWSc 92*
**Yunus,** Muhammad Basharat 1942- *AmMWSc 92*
**Yuon,** Konstantin 1875-1958 *FacFETw*
**Yuon,** Konstantin Fedorovich 1875-1958 *SovUnBD*
**Yura,** Harold Thomas 1937- *AmMWSc 92*
**Yurasko,** Frank Noel 1938- *WhoAmL 92*
**Yurchak,** Sergei 1943- *AmMWSc 92*
**Yurchenco,** John Alfonso 1915- *AmMWSc 92*
**Yurchuk,** Donald Wayne 1944- *WhoWest 92*
**Yurek,** George 1934- *WhoWest 92*
**Yuretich,** Richard Francis 1950- *AmMWSc 92*
**Yurewicz,** Edward Charles 1945- *AmMWSc 92*
**Yuricich,** Matthew John 1923- *WhoWest 92*
**Yurick,** Sol 1925- *BenetAL 91, ConNov 91, WrDr 92*
**Yurist,** Svetlan Joseph 1931- *WhoWest 92*
**Yurke,** Bernard 1951- *AmMWSc 92*
**Yurkiewicz,** William J 1939- *AmMWSc 92*
**Yurkiw,** Mark Leo 1954- *WhoEnt 92*
**Yurkowski,** Michael 1928- *AmMWSc 92*
**Yurovich,** Douglas Paul 1957- *WhoWest 92*
**Yurovich,** R. Dale 1958- *WhoAmL 92*
**Yurow,** Harvey Warren 1932- *AmMWSc 92*
**Yursky,** Sergei Yurievich 1935- *IntWW 91*
**Yurur,** Sukru 1944- *IntWW 91*
**Yushok,** Wasley Donald 1920- *AmMWSc 92*
**Yusif-Zade,** Ziya Mamediya ogly 1929- *IntWW 91*
**Yuska,** Henry 1914- *AmMWSc 92*
**Yuska,** Joseph Alfred 1939- *WhoMW 92*
**Yuska,** Ken Henry 1945- *WhoMW 92*
**Yuska,** William W. 1946- *WhoRel 92*
**Yusko,** Theodore 1918- *WhoAmP 91*
**Yuspa,** Stuart Howard 1941- *AmMWSc 92*
**Yuspeh,** Alan Ralph 1949- *WhoAmL 92*
**Yussof,** Mohammed 1917- *IntWW 91*
**Yust,** Charles S 1931- *AmMWSc 92*
**Yust,** Larry Barker 1930- *WhoEnt 92*
**Yuster,** Philip Harold 1917- *AmMWSc 92*
**Yuthasastrkosol,** Charin 1930- *WhoFI 92*
**Yutkevich,** Sergei 1904-1985 *FacFETw*
**Yutkevich,** Sergey Iosifovich 1904-1985 *SovUnBD*
**Yutrzenka,** Gerald J 1953- *AmMWSc 92*
**Yuvarajan,** Subbaraya 1941- *AmMWSc 92*
**Yuwiler,** Arthur 1927- *AmMWSc 92*
**Yuzvinsky,** Sergey 1936 *WhoWest 92*
**Yvon,** Claude 1714-1791 *BlkwCEP*
**Yvonne** *DrAPF 91*
**Yzaguirre,** Raul 1939- *WhoHisp 92*
**Yzaguirre,** Ruben Antonio 1947- *WhoHisp 92*
**Yzenbaard,** Caryl Ann 1946- *WhoAmL 92*
**Yzerman,** Steve 1965- *News 91 [port]*

# Z

**Zaalouk,** Mohamed Gamal 1935- *AmMWSc 92*
**Zabala,** Bruno Mauricio de 1682-1736 *HisDSpE*
**Zabaleta,** Nicanor 1907- *IntWW 91, NewAmDM*
**Zaban,** Erwin 1921- *WhoFI 92*
**Zabara,** Jacob 1932- *AmMWSc 92*
**Zabarnick,** Steven Scott 1958- *WhoWest 92*
**Zabbai,** Bat *EncAmaz 91*
**Zabel,** Edward 1927- *WhoFI 92*
**Zabel,** Hartmut 1946- *AmMWSc 92*
**Zabel,** Robert Alger 1917- *AmMWSc 92*
**Zabel,** Sheldon Alter 1941- *WhoAmL 92*
**Zabel,** Walter L *WhoAmP 91*
**Zabel,** William David 1936- *WhoAmL 92*
**Zabela,** Brownie *WhoEnt 92*
**Zabibi** *EncAmaz 91*
**Zabielski,** Chester V 1923- *AmMWSc 92*
**Zabik,** Joseph *AmMWSc 92*
**Zabik,** Mary Ellen 1937- *AmMWSc 92*
**Zabik,** Matthew John 1937- *AmMWSc 92*
**Zabin,** Burton Allen 1936- *AmMWSc 92*
**Zabin,** Irving 1919- *AmMWSc 92*
**Zabinski,** Krzysztof 1953- *IntWW 91*
**Zabinski,** Michael Peter 1941- *AmMWSc 92*
**Zabinsky,** Zelda Barbara 1955- *WhoWest 92*
**Zable,** Jeffrey A.Z. *DrAPF 91*
**Zablocka-Esplin,** Barbara 1925- *AmMWSc 92*
**Zablow,** Leonard 1927- *AmMWSc 92*
**Zabole,** Ernest 1927- *TwCPaSc*
**Zabolotsky,** Nicholas Alekseyevich 1903- *FacFETw*
**Zabolotsky,** Nikolay Alekseevich 1903-1958 *SovUnBD*
**Zaborowski,** Robert Ronald John 1946- *WhoRel 92*
**Zaborowski,** Roy Allan 1946- *WhoWest 92*
**Zaborsky,** Daniel John 1945- *WhoIns 92*
**Zaborsky,** Oskar Rudolf 1941- *AmMWSc 92*
**Zaborszky,** John 1914- *AmMWSc 92*
**Zabransky,** Ronald Joseph 1935- *AmMWSc 92*
**Zabriskie,** Franklin Robert 1933- *AmMWSc 92*
**Zabriskie,** Jeremiah Lott 1835?-1910 *BiInAmS*
**Zabriskie,** John Barrea 1805-1850 *BiInAmS*
**Zabriskie,** John Lansing, Jr 1939- *AmMWSc 92*
**Zabriskie,** Robert 1929- *WhoEnt 92*
**Zabriskie,** Stewart Clark 1936- *WhoRel 92*
**Zabrocki,** Carl J *WhoAmP 91*
**Zabronsky,** Daniel 1962- *WhoFI 92*
**Zabronsky,** Herman 1927- *AmMWSc 92*
**Zabusky,** Norman J 1929- *AmMWSc 92*
**Zaccagnini,** Benigno 1912-1989 *FacFETw*
**Zaccardi,** Nicholas Stephen 1957- *WhoRel 92*
**Zaccaria,** Robert Anthony 1943- *AmMWSc 92*
**Zacchei,** Anthony Gabriel 1940- *AmMWSc 92*
**Zaccone,** Suzanne Maria 1957- *WhoFI 92, WhoMW 92*
**Zacek,** Joseph Frederick 1930- *WrDr 92*
**Zach,** Miriam Susan 1954- *WhoEnt 92*
**Zach,** Reto 1940- *AmMWSc 92*
**Zachar,** Ned Paul 1962- *WhoFI 92*
**Zachariah,** Bobby Verghese 1942- *WhoFI 92*
**Zachariah,** Gerald L 1933- *AmMWSc 92*
**Zachariah,** Joyce Margaret 1932- *Who 92*
**Zacharias,** David Edward 1926- *AmMWSc 92*
**Zacharias,** Jerrold R 1905-1986 *FacFETw*
**Zacharias,** Lee *DrAPF 91*
**Zacharias,** Ravi Kumar 1946- *WhoRel 92*
**Zacharias,** Thomas Elling 1954- *WhoFI 92*
**Zacharias,** William F. 1905- *WhoAmL 92*
**Zachariasen,** Fredrik 1931- *AmMWSc 92*
**Zachariasen,** K A 1924- *AmMWSc 92*
**Zacharius,** Robert Marvin 1920- *AmMWSc 92*
**Zacharius,** Walter 1923- *IntWW 91*
**Zacharov,** Vasilii 1931- *Who 92*
**Zacharuk,** R Y 1928- *AmMWSc 92*
**Zachary,** Elizabeth 1928- *WrDr 92*
**Zachary,** Hubert M. 1936- *WhoBlA 92*
**Zachary,** Hugh *TwCSFW 91*
**Zachary,** Hugh 1928- *IntAu&W 91, WrDr 92*
**Zachary,** Loren William 1943- *AmMWSc 92*
**Zachary,** Louis George 1927- *WhoFI 92, WhoMW 92*
**Zachary,** Norman 1926- *AmMWSc 92*
**Zachary,** Ronald F. 1938- *WhoFI 92*
**Zachary-Hopkins,** Donna S. 1952- *WhoMW 92*
**Zachary-Pike,** Annie R. 1931- *WhoBlA 92*
**Zachau,** Hans G. 1930- *IntWW 91*
**Zacher,** Allan Norman, Jr. 1928- *WhoMW 92, WhoRel 92*
**Zacher,** Judy L. 1961- *WhoMW 92*
**Zacher,** Mark Paul 1958- *WhoRel 92*
**Zachman,** Eugene Proud 1933- *WhoIns 92*
**Zachman,** John Arthur 1934- *WhoWest 92*
**Zachmann,** Siegfried *IntWW 91*
**Zachmanoglou,** Eleftherios Charalambos 1934- *AmMWSc 92*
**Zachos,** Cosmas K 1951- *AmMWSc 92*
**Zachos,** Victoria 1929- *WhoAmP 91*
**Zachow,** Friedrich Wilhelm 1663-1712 *NewAmDM*
**Zachry,** Charles Candler 1942- *WhoMW 92*
**Zack,** Eugene C 1922- *WhoAmP 91*
**Zack,** George J. 1936- *WhoEnt 92*
**Zack,** James Gordon, Jr. 1946- *WhoWest 92*
**Zack,** James Kehoe 1950- *WhoFI 92*
**Zack,** Kathryn Mary 1949- *WhoMW 92*
**Zack,** Neil Richard 1947- *AmMWSc 92*
**Zack,** Richard Stanley, Jr. 1952- *WhoWest 92*
**Zack,** Stephen Neil 1947- *WhoAmL 92*
**Zackay,** Victor Francis 1920- *AmMWSc 92*
**Zackery,** Bennie Lee 1946- *WhoMW 92*
**Zackey,** Jonathan Thomas 1952- *WhoAmL 92*
**Zackrison,** Edwin Harry *WhoRel 92, WhoWest 92*
**Zackroff,** Robert V 1951- *AmMWSc 92*
**Zacks,** Arthur 1926- *WhoWest 92*
**Zacks,** James Lee 1941- *AmMWSc 92*
**Zacks,** Shelemyahu 1932- *AmMWSc 92*
**Zacks,** Sumner Irwin 1929- *AmMWSc 92*
**Zackula,** Michael Leroy 1947- *WhoWest 92*
**Zaczek,** Norbert Marion 1936- *AmMWSc 92*
**Zaczepinski,** Sioma 1940- *AmMWSc 92*
**Zade,** Hans Peter 1907- *WrDr 92*
**Zadeck,** Donald Julian 1927- *WhoFI 92*
**Zadeh,** L A 1921- *AmMWSc 92*
**Zadek,** Peter 1926- *IntWW 91*
**Zadnik,** Valentine Edward 1934- *AmMWSc 92*
**Zadoff,** Leon Nathan 1923- *AmMWSc 92*
**Zadok,** Haim J. 1913- *IntWW 91*
**Zador,** Eugene 1894-1977 *NewAmDM*
**Zadora,** Pia 1956- *ConTFT 9*
**Zadora,** Zarina 1937- *WhoEnt 92*
**Zadrozny,** Mitchell George 1923- *WhoMW 92*
**Zadunaisky,** Jose Atilio 1932- *AmMWSc 92*
**Zaehringer,** Mary Veronica 1911- *AmMWSc 92*
**Zaenglein,** Irvin Allen 1940- *WhoFI 92*
**Zaentz,** Saul *ConTFT 9, IntMPA 92, WhoEnt 92*
**Zaerr,** Joe Benjamin 1932- *AmMWSc 92*
**Zaeske,** Ellen Louise 1958- *WhoMW 92*
**Zaffarano,** Daniel Joseph 1917- *AmMWSc 92*
**Zaffarano,** Mark Alan 1954- *WhoAmL 92*
**Zaffaroni,** Alejandro 1923- *AmMWSc 92*
**Zaffirini,** Judith 1946- *WhoAmP 91*
**Zaffirni,** Judith 1946- *WhoHisp 92*
**Zaffiro,** Richard L. 1956- *WhoAmL 92*
**Zaffke,** Maurice 1948- *WhoAmP 91*
**Zafiratos,** Chris Dan 1931- *AmMWSc 92*
**Zafiriou,** Evanghelos 1959- *AmMWSc 92*
**Zafran,** Misha 1949- *AmMWSc 92*
**Zafren,** Herbert Cecil 1925- *WhoMW 92*
**Zafris,** Nancy *DrAPF 91*
**Zagajewski,** Adam 1945- *LiExTwC*
**Zagami,** Anthony James 1951- *WhoAmL 92*
**Zagar,** Frank George 1912- *WhoMW 92*
**Zagar,** Robert John 1948- *WhoMW 92*
**Zagar,** Walter T 1928- *AmMWSc 92*
**Zagaris,** Bruce 1947- *WhoFI 92*
**Zagat,** Arthur Leo 1895-1949 *TwCSFW 91*
**Zagata,** Michael DeForest 1942- *AmMWSc 92*
**Zage,** Russell Louis 1952- *WhoFI 92, WhoMW 92*
**Zagel,** James Block 1941- *WhoAmL 92, WhoMW 92*
**Zager,** Ronald 1934- *AmMWSc 92*
**Zager,** Stanley E 1921- *AmMWSc 92*
**Zager,** Steven Mark 1958- *WhoAmL 92*
**Zagier,** Don Bernard 1951- *AmMWSc 92*
**Zagladin,** Vadim Valentinovich 1927- *IntWW 91, SovUnBD*
**Zagon,** Ian Stuart 1943- *AmMWSc 92*
**Zagonek,** Vyacheslav Frantsevich 1919- *SovUnBD*
**Zagoren,** Allen Jeffrey 1947- *WhoMW 92*
**Zagorin,** Janet Susan *WhoFI 92*
**Zagorin,** Perez 1920- *ConAu 36NR*
**Zagorski,** Frank John 1925- *WhoWest 92*
**Zagotta,** Anthony James 1966- *WhoAmP 91*
**Zagray,** Allan Howard 1934- *WhoRel 92*
**Zaguirre,** Susan Elizabeth 1957- *WhoEnt 92*
**Zagzebski,** James Anthony 1944- *AmMWSc 92*
**Zah,** Peterson 1937- *WhoWest 92*
**Zahalsky,** Arthur C 1930- *AmMWSc 92*
**Zaharako,** Lew Daleure 1947- *WhoAmL 92*
**Zaharchuk,** Peter J, Jr 1947- *WhoAmP 91*
**Zaharias,** Babe *FacFETw*
**Zaharias,** Babe Didrikson 1911-1956 *HanAmWH*
**Zaharko,** Daniel Samuel 1930- *AmMWSc 92*
**Zahary,** William Bud 1935- *WhoWest 92*
**Zahed,** Hyder Ali *AmMWSc 92*
**Zahed,** Ismail *AmMWSc 92*
**Zahedi,** Ardeshir 1928- *IntWW 91, Who 92*
**Zahid,** Anwar 1938- *IntWW 91*
**Zahir Shah** *IntWW 91*
**Zahir,** Abdul 1910- *IntWW 91*
**Zahiruddin bin Syed Hassan,** Tun Syed 1918- *Who 92*
**Zahler,** Kenneth Bruce 1948- *WhoFI 92*
**Zahler,** Leah *DrAPF 91*
**Zahler,** Stanley Arnold 1926- *AmMWSc 92*
**Zahler,** Warren Leigh 1941- *AmMWSc 92*
**Zahn,** Curtis *DrAPF 91*
**Zahn,** Donald Jack 1941- *WhoAmL 92*
**Zahn,** Gordon C. 1918- *WrDr 92*
**Zahn,** Joachim 1914- *IntWW 91*
**Zahn,** Johannes 1907- *IntWW 91*
**Zahn,** John J 1932- *AmMWSc 92*
**Zahn,** Paula *LesBEnT 92*
**Zahn,** Rudolf Karl 1920- *IntWW 91*
**Zahn,** Timothy 1951- *TwCSFW 91, WrDr 92*
**Zahnd,** Hugo 1902- *AmMWSc 92*
**Zahnd,** James Marion 1941- *WhoMW 92*
**Zahnd,** Richard Hugo 1946- *WhoAmL 92*
**Zahner,** Kenyon Benedict, Jr 1930- *WhoAmP 91*
**Zahner,** Lawrence Bonaventure 1954- *WhoMW 92*
**Zahniser,** Ed *DrAPF 91*
**Zahniser,** Richard Allen 1935- *WhoWest 92*
**Zahnley,** James Curry 1938- *AmMWSc 92*
**Zahradnik,** Raymond Louis 1936- *AmMWSc 92*
**Zahrbock,** E. Dennis 1947- *WhoFI 92*
**Zahrt,** William Dietrich, II 1944- *WhoAmL 92*
**Zaia,** John Anthony 1942- *AmMWSc 92*
**Zaidel,** Eran 1944- *AmMWSc 92*
**Zaidel-Rudolph,** Jeanne 1948- *ConCom 92*
**Zaidenberg,** Arthur 1908?-1990 *SmATA 66*
**Zaider,** Marco A 1946- *AmMWSc 92*
**Zaidi,** Bashir Husain Syed 1898- *Who 92*
**Zaidi,** Iftakhar Haider 1933- *WhoWest 92*
**Zaidi,** Nasir Jamal 1957- *WhoEnt 92*
**Zaidi,** Shuja Haider 1952- *WhoWest 92*
**Zaidi,** Syed Amir Ali 1935- *AmMWSc 92*
**Zaidins,** Clyde *AmMWSc 92*
**Zaidins,** Clyde Stewart 1939- *WhoWest 92*
**Zaidman,** Samuel 1933- *AmMWSc 92*
**Zaika,** Laura Larysa 1938- *AmMWSc 92*
**Zaikov,** Lev Nikolayevich 1923- *IntWW 91*
**Zail Singh,** Giani *IntWW 91*
**Zaim,** Semih 1926- *AmMWSc 92, WhoFI 92*

**Zaiman,** Joel Hirsh 1938- *WhoRel 92*
**Zaiman,** K. Robert 1944- *WhoMW 92*
**Zaimont,** Judith Lang 1945- *NewAmDM, WhoEnt 92*
**Zain Azraai** 1936- *IntWW 91*
**Zaininger,** Karl Heinz 1929- *AmMWSc 92*
**Zainuddin,** Daim 1938- *IntWW 91*
**Zainyeh,** George A *WhoAmP 91*
**Zaire** *EncAmaz 91*
**Zais,** Bernard H 1916- *WhoIns 92*
**Zais,** Lynette Laura 1942- *WhoMW 92*
**Zaiser,** Catherine Marie 1956- *WhoEnt 92*
**Zaiser,** James Norman 1934- *AmMWSc 92*
**Zaiser,** Sally Solemma Vann 1917- *WhoFI 92, WhoWest 92*
**Zaiss,** Conrad Penfield 1953- *WhoFI 92, WhoWest 92*
**Zaiter,** Jose J. 1956- *WhoHisp 92*
**Zaitlin,** Milton 1927- *AmMWSc 92*
**Zaitsev,** Aleksander *SovUnBD*
**Zaitsev,** Mikhail Mitrofanovich 1923- *IntWW 91*
**Zaitsev,** Vyacheslav 1937- *IntWW 91*
**Zaitzeff,** Roger Michael 1940- *WhoAmL 92*
**Zajac,** Alfred 1917- *AmMWSc 92*
**Zajac,** Barbara Ann 1937- *AmMWSc 92*
**Zajac,** Felix Edward, III 1941- *AmMWSc 92*
**Zajac,** Ihor 1931- *AmMWSc 92*
**Zajac,** John 1946- *WhoWest 92*
**Zajac,** John J. Jr *WhoAmP 91*
**Zajac,** Walter William, Jr 1934- *AmMWSc 92*
**Zajacek,** John George 1936- *AmMWSc 92*
**Zajaczkowska-Mitznerowa,** Larysa 1918- *IntAu&W 91*
**Zajic,** James Edward 1928- *AmMWSc 92*
**Zajicek,** Jeronym 1926- *WhoEnt 92*
**Zajicek,** Lynn Engelbrecht 1950- *WhoMW 92*
**Zajonc,** Arthur Guy 1949- *AmMWSc 92*
**Zak,** Bennie 1919- *AmMWSc 92*
**Zak,** David George 1955- *WhoEnt 92*
**Zak,** Josephine Mary 1932- *WhoAmP 91*
**Zak,** Michele Wender 1940- *WhoWest 92*
**Zak,** Radovan Hynek 1931- *AmMWSc 92*
**Zakaib,** Daniel D 1925- *AmMWSc 92*
**Zakaib,** Paul, Jr 1932- *WhoAmP 91*
**Zakaria,** Mohamed Ali 1929- *IntWW 91*
**Zakarian,** Albert 1940- *WhoAmL 92*
**Zakarija,** Daniel Mathew 1934- *WhoMW 92*
**Zakarin,** Keith 1958- *WhoAmL 92*
**Zakas,** Joseph Conrad 1950- *WhoAmP 91*
**Zakhar,** Arlene Alice 1937- *WhoMW 92*
**Zakharov,** Matvey Vasil'evich 1898-1972 *SovUnBD*
**Zakharov,** Rostislav Vladimirovich 1907-1984 *SovUnBD*
**Zakharov,** Vasiliy Georgiyevich 1934- *IntWW 91*
**Zakhary,** Rizkalla 1924- *AmMWSc 92*
**Zakhava,** Boris Yevgen'evich 1896-1976 *SovUnBD*
**Zakheim,** Scott Charles 1958- *WhoAmL 92*
**Zakhem,** Sam Hanna 1937- *WhoAmP 91*
**Zaki,** Abd El-Moneim Emam 1933- *AmMWSc 92*
**Zaki,** Mahfou H 1924- *AmMWSc 92*
**Zakin,** Jacques L 1927- *AmMWSc 92*
**Zakis,** Juris 1936- *IntWW 91*
**Zakkay,** Victor 1927- *AmMWSc 92*
**Zakraysek,** Louis 1928- *AmMWSc 92*
**Zakriski,** Paul Michael 1940- *AmMWSc 92*
**Zakroczymski,** Adam Karol 1945- *WhoMW 92*
**Zakrzewska,** Marie E 1829-1902 *DcAmImH*
**Zakrzewski,** Richard Jerome 1940- *AmMWSc 92*
**Zakrzewski,** Sigmund Felix 1919- *AmMWSc 92*
**Zakrzewski,** Thomas Michael 1943- *AmMWSc 92*
**Zaks,** Jerry 1946- *WhoEnt 92*
**Zalapi,** Vincent Anthony 1934- *WhoMW 92*
**Zalay,** Andrew W 1918- *AmMWSc 92*
**Zalay,** Ethel Suzanne 1919- *AmMWSc 92*
**Zalaznick,** David Wayne 1954- *WhoFI 92*
**Zalben,** Jane Breskin *DrAPF 91, WrDr 92*
**Zalben Breskin,** Jane 1950- *IntAu&W 91*
**Zald,** Mayer Nathan 1931- *WrDr 92*
**Zaldivar,** Gilberto 1934- *WhoHisp 92*
**Zaldivar,** Richard L 1952- *WhoAmP 91*
**Zaldivar,** Silvia 1938- *WhoHisp 92*
**Zaldivar Larrain,** Andres 1936- *IntWW 91*
**Zaldo,** Bruno 1946- *WhoHisp 92*
**Zalecki,** Paul Henry 1931- *WhoAmL 92*
**Zalesak,** Joseph Francis 1942- *AmMWSc 92*
**Zaleski,** Alan J *WhoAmP 91*
**Zaleski,** Anthony Florian 1913- *WhoMW 92*
**Zaleski,** August 1883-1972 *FacFETw*
**Zaleski,** James Vincent 1943- *WhoWest 92*
**Zaleski,** Marek Bohdan 1936- *AmMWSc 92*
**Zaleski,** Michel 1947- *WhoFI 92*
**Zaleski,** Terence M 1953- *WhoAmP 91*
**Zaleski,** Thaddeus B. 1947- *WhoFI 92*
**Zaleski,** Witold Andrew 1920- *AmMWSc 92*
**Zaletel,** John Douglas 1954- *WhoFI 92*
**Zaletel,** Joseph Henry, Jr. 1947- *WhoMW 92*
**Zalewa,** Donald Andrew 1950- *WhoMW 92*
**Zalewski,** Antoni Francis 1943- *WhoEnt 92*
**Zalewski,** Edmund Joseph 1931- *AmMWSc 92*
**Zaleznik,** Abraham 1924- *WhoFI 92*
**Zalik,** Richard Albert 1943- *AmMWSc 92*
**Zalik,** Sara E 1939- *AmMWSc 92*
**Zalik,** Saul 1921- *AmMWSc 92*
**Zalinski,** Edmund Louis Gray 1849-1909 *BiInAmS*
**Zaliouk,** Yuval Nathan 1939- *WhoEnt 92*
**Zalipsky,** Jerome Jaroslaw *AmMWSc 92*
**Zalisko,** Edward John 1958- *AmMWSc 92*
**Zalk,** Robert H. 1944- *WhoAmL 92*
**Zalka,** Miklos 1928- *IntAu&W 91*
**Zalkin,** Howard 1934- *AmMWSc 92*
**Zalkind,** Norman Stanley 1938- *WhoAmL 92*
**Zalkow,** Leon Harry 1929- *AmMWSc 92*
**Zall,** Linda S 1950- *AmMWSc 92*
**Zall,** Paul M 1922- *IntAu&W 91, WrDr 92*
**Zall,** Robert Rouben 1925- *AmMWSc 92*
**Zalle,** Paul Martin 1945- *WhoWest 92*
**Zallen,** Dennis Michael 1943- *WhoWest 92*
**Zallen,** Eugenia Malone 1932- *AmMWSc 92*
**Zallen,** Richard 1937- *AmMWSc 92*
**Zaller,** Angelika Bita *ConAu 36NR*
**Zaller,** Robert *DrAPF 91*
**Zaller,** Robert Michael 1940- *IntAu&W 91*
**Zallinger,** Peter 1943- *WrDr 92*
**Zallow,** Colleen Louise 1966- *WhoMW 92*
**Zalokar,** Julia Ballantine 1926- *WhoWest 92*
**Zalosh,** Robert Geoffrey 1944- *AmMWSc 92*
**Zalta,** Edward 1930- *WhoWest 92*
**Zalubas,** Romuald 1911- *AmMWSc 92*
**Zalucky,** Theodore B 1919- *AmMWSc 92*
**Zaluski,** Josef Andrzej 1702-1774 *BlkwCEP*
**Zalusky,** Ralph 1931- *AmMWSc 92*
**Zalutsky,** Morton Herman 1935- *WhoAmL 92, WhoWest 92*
**Zalygin,** Sergey Pavlovich 1913- *IntAu&W 91, IntWW 91, SovUnBD*
**Zam,** Stephen G, III 1932- *AmMWSc 92*
**Zamagni,** Stefano 1943- *IntWW 91*
**Zaman,** Khairul B M Q 1947- *AmMWSc 92*
**Zamanzadeh,** Mehrooz 1950- *AmMWSc 92*
**Zamarripa,** Robert S. 1955- *WhoHisp 92*
**Zamayatin,** Yevgenii Ivanovich 1884-1937 *LiExTwC*
**Zambara,** Edward *WhoEnt 92*
**Zambaras,** Vassilis *DrAPF 91*
**Zambardo,** Philip 1933- *WrDr 92*
**Zambernard,** Joseph *AmMWSc 92*
**Zambetti,** Denis Egan 1953- *WhoWest 92*
**Zambito,** Arthur Joseph 1914- *AmMWSc 92*
**Zambo,** Paul W. 1944- *WhoRel 92*
**Zamboni,** Luciano 1929- *AmMWSc 92*
**Zamboni,** Richard Frederick Charles 1930- *Who 92*
**Zambrana,** Rafael 1931- *WhoBlA 92, WhoHisp 92*
**Zambrano,** Myrna M. 1958- *WhoHisp 92*
**Zambraski,** Edward K 1949- *AmMWSc 92*
**Zambrona,** Tito *WhoHisp 92*
**Zambrow,** J L 1914- *AmMWSc 92*
**Zame,** Alan 1941- *AmMWSc 92*
**Zame,** William Robin 1945- *AmMWSc 92*
**Zameck,** Harvey Jason 1943- *WhoAmL 92*
**Zamecnik,** Paul Charles 1912- *AmMWSc 92, IntWW 91*
**Zamel,** Noe 1935- *AmMWSc 92*
**Zamenhof,** Patrice Joy 1934- *AmMWSc 92*
**Zamenhof,** Robert G A 1946- *AmMWSc 92*
**Zamenhof,** Stephen 1911- *AmMWSc 92*
**Zames,** George 1934- *AmMWSc 92*
**Zamfir,** Catalin *IntWW 91*
**Zamfir,** Gheorghe 1941- *IntWW 91*
**Zamick,** Larry 1935- *AmMWSc 92*
**Zamikoff,** Irving Ira 1943- *AmMWSc 92*
**Zamir,** Lolita Ora *AmMWSc 92*
**Zammit,** John P. 1942- *WhoMW 92*
**Zammit,** Joseph Paul 1948- *WhoAmL 92*
**Zammit Ciantar,** Joe 1942- *IntAu&W 91*
**Zamora,** Anthony 1948- *WhoHisp 92*
**Zamora,** Antonio 1942- *AmMWSc 92*
**Zamora,** Brian Jonathan 1952- *WhoHisp 92*
**Zamora,** Cesario Siasoco 1938- *AmMWSc 92*
**Zamora,** Emilio 1946- *WhoHisp 92*
**Zamora,** Juan B. 1931- *WhoHisp 92*
**Zamora,** Nassry G. 1950- *WhoHisp 92*
**Zamora,** Patricia E. 1939- *WhoAmL 92*
**Zamora,** Paul O *AmMWSc 92*
**Zamora,** Ricardo 1901-1978 *FacFETw*
**Zamora,** Ronald *LesBEnT 92*
**Zamora,** Ruben 1942?- *CurBio 91 [port]*
**Zamora,** S. Robert *WhoHisp 92*
**Zamora-Cope,** Rosie 1935- *WhoHisp 92*
**Zamora-Munoz,** Jorge Mario 1945- *WhoHisp 92*
**Zampa,** Luigi d1991 *NewYTBS 91*
**Zamparelli,** John F 1922- *WhoAmP 91*
**Zamparelli,** Mario Armond *WhoWest 92*
**Zampelas,** Michael Herodotou 1937- *WhoFI 92*
**Zampi,** Giulio 1923- *IntMPA 92*
**Zampiello,** Richard Sidney 1933- *WhoFI 92*
**Zampieri,** John James 1941- *WhoAmP 91*
**Zampino,** Thomas 1958- *WhoAmL 92*
**Zamrik,** Sam Yusuf 1932- *AmMWSc 92*
**Zamvil,** Stella *DrAPF 91*
**Zamyatin,** Leonid Mitrofanovich 1922- *IntWW 91, SovUnBD, Who 92*
**Zamyatin,** Yevgenii Ivanovitch 1884-1937 *ScFEYrs*
**Zamyatin,** Yevgeniy Ivanovich 1884-1937 *SovUnBD*
**Zamyatin,** Yevgeny 1884-1937 *TwCSFW 91A*
**Zamyatin,** Yevgeny Ivanovich 1884-1937 *FacFETw*
**Zanakis,** Stelios H 1940- *AmMWSc 92*
**Zand,** Robert 1930- *AmMWSc 92, WhoMW 92*
**Zande,** Richard Dominic 1931- *WhoMW 92*
**Zandee,** Jan 1914- *WhoRel 92*
**Zander,** Andrew Thomas 1945- *AmMWSc 92*
**Zander,** Arlen Ray 1940- *AmMWSc 92*
**Zander,** Benjamin 1939- *WhoEnt 92*
**Zander,** Carl Mathew 1940- *WhoWest 92*
**Zander,** Donald Victor 1916- *AmMWSc 92*
**Zander,** Jessie Mae 1932- *WhoBlA 92*
**Zander,** Michael 1932- *Who 92*
**Zander,** Patricia *WhoEnt 92*
**Zander,** Vernon Emil 1939- *AmMWSc 92*
**Zanders,** Alton Wendell 1943- *WhoBlA 92*
**Zandi,** Iraj 1931- *AmMWSc 92*
**Zandler,** Melvin E 1937- *AmMWSc 92*
**Zandomeneghi,** Federico 1841-1917 *ThHEIm*
**Zandonai,** Riccardo 1883-1944 *NewAmDM*
**Zandy,** Hassan F 1912- *AmMWSc 92*
**Zane,** Raymond John 1939- *WhoAmP 91*
**Zanella,** John Anthony, Jr. 1943- *WhoMW 92*
**Zaner,** Ken Scott *AmMWSc 92*
**Zanercik,** Gary Denis 1950- *WhoAmL 92*
**Zanetis,** Alexander William 1927- *WhoEnt 92*
**Zanetos,** John Constantine 1920- *WhoRel 92*
**Zanetti,** John 1955- *WhoAmP 91*
**Zanetti,** Nina Clare 1955- *AmMWSc 92*
**Zaneveld,** Jacques Ronald Victor 1944- *AmMWSc 92*
**Zaneveld,** Lourens Jan Dirk 1942- *AmMWSc 92*
**Zang,** Linda Ann 1956- *WhoFI 92*
**Zang,** William Louis 1953- *WhoFI 92*
**Zangara,** Frank James 1954- *WhoMW 92*
**Zangari,** James 1929- *WhoAmP 91*
**Zangen,** Wilhelm 1891-1971 *EncTR 91*
**Zanger,** Joseph Anthony 1927- *WhoAmP 91*
**Zanger,** Murray 1932- *AmMWSc 92*
**Zangrando,** Robert Lewis 1932- *WhoMW 92*
**Zangwill,** Andrew 1954- *AmMWSc 92*
**Zangwill,** Israel 1864-1926 *BiDBrF 2, DcAmImH, RfGEnL 91, ScFEYrs*
**Zanini,** Marco 1954- *DcTwDes*
**Zanini-Fisher,** Margherita 1947- *AmMWSc 92*
**Zanjani,** Esmail Dabaghchian 1938- *AmMWSc 92*
**Zank,** Neal Steven 1953- *WhoFI 92*
**Zankel,** Kenneth L 1930- *AmMWSc 92*
**Zanker,** Paul 1937- *IntWW 91*
**Zanner,** Richard Ferdinand 1934- *WhoRel 92*
**Zanni,** Michael A 1956- *WhoAmP 91*
**Zanni,** Vilma Ann 1931- *WhoAmP 91*
**Zannis,** Vassilis I 1940- *AmMWSc 92*
**Zannoni,** Arthur Edward 1942- *WhoRel 92*
**Zannoni,** Vincent G 1928- *AmMWSc 92*
**Zano,** Anthony Joseph 1937- *WhoEnt 92*
**Zanone,** Valerio 1936- *IntWW 91*
**Zanoni,** Alphonse E 1934- *AmMWSc 92*
**Zanot,** Craig Allen 1955- *WhoAmL 92, WhoFI 92, WhoMW 92*
**Zanowiak,** Paul 1933- *AmMWSc 92*
**Zansitis,** Richard Anthony 1954- *WhoAmL 92*
**Zantopulos,** Harry 1934- *WhoMW 92*
**Zants,** Emily 1937- *WrDr 92*
**Zanuck,** Darryl F 1902-1979 *FacFETw*
**Zanuck,** Richard Darryl 1934- *IntMPA 92, IntWW 91, WhoEnt 92*
**Zanuso,** Marco 1916- *DcTwDes, IntWW 91*
**Zanussi,** Kryszstof 1939- *IntDcF 2-2 [port]*
**Zanussi,** Krzysztof 1939- *IntWW 91*
**Zanzibar And Tanga,** Bishop of *Who 92*
**Zanzucchi,** Peter John 1941- *AmMWSc 92*
**Zapanta,** Al *WhoHisp 92*
**Zaparackas,** Algis 1940- *WhoAmP 91*
**Zapata,** Ariel F. 1958- *WhoHisp 92*
**Zapata,** Candelario 1956- *WhoHisp 92*
**Zapata,** Carlos Eduardo 1961- *WhoHisp 92*
**Zapata,** Carmen 1927- *ConTFT 9*
**Zapata,** Carmen Margarita 1927- *WhoHisp 92*
**Zapata,** Donna Hanson 1935- *WhoEnt 92*
**Zapata,** Eino 1947- *WhoHisp 92*
**Zapata,** Emiliano 1877?-1919 *BenetAL 91*
**Zapata,** Emiliano 1879-1919 *FacFETw*
**Zapata,** Fernando, Jr. 1951- *WhoHisp 92*
**Zapata,** Jose Angel, Jr. 1958- *WhoHisp 92*
**Zapata,** Louis J., Sr. 1934- *WhoHisp 92*
**Zapata,** M. Nelson, Jr. 1950- *WhoHisp 92*
**Zapata,** Patricio 1937- *AmMWSc 92*
**Zapata,** Richard Arthur 1959- *WhoWest 92*
**Zapata,** Sabas, III 1945- *WhoHisp 92*
**Zapata de Cardenas,** Luis 1515?-1590 *HisDSpE*
**Zapata Olivella,** Manuel 1920- *DcLB 113 [port]*
**Zapata y Sandoval,** Juan 157-?-1630 *HisDSpE*
**Zapatero Gomez,** Virgilio 1946- *IntWW 91*
**Zapel,** Edwin Joseph 1923- *WhoWest 92*
**Zapf,** Hermann 1918- *DcTwDes*
**Zapf,** Otto 1931- *DcTwDes*
**Zapfe,** Helmuth 1913- *IntWW 91*
**Zapffe,** Carl Andrew 1912- *AmMWSc 92*
**Zaphiriou,** George Aristotle 1919- *WhoAmL 92*
**Zaphyr,** Peter Anthony 1926- *AmMWSc 92*
**Zapiain,** Norman Gerard 1962- *WhoHisp 92*
**Zapisek,** William Francis 1935- *AmMWSc 92*
**Zapletal,** Peter 1945- *WhoEnt 92*
**Zapol,** Warren Myron 1942- *AmMWSc 92*
**Zapoleon,** Guy Maxim 1952- *WhoEnt 92*
**Zapoleon,** Marguerite Wykoff 1907- *WrDr 92*
**Zapolsky,** Harold Saul 1935- *AmMWSc 92*
**Zapor,** John Randolph 1944- *WhoWest 92*
**Zaporowski,** Mark Paul 1957- *WhoFI 92*
**Zapp,** David Edwin 1950- *WhoMW 92*
**Zapp,** Herbert 1928- *IntWW 91*
**Zappa,** Frank 1940- *FacFETw, IntWW 91, NewAmDM, WhoEnt 92*
**Zappala,** Joseph 1933- *WhoAmP 91*
**Zappala,** Stephen A. 1932- *WhoAmL 92, WhoAmP 91*
**Zappe,** John Paul 1952- *WhoWest 92*
**Zappia,** Charles Anthony 1947- *WhoWest 92*
**Zapruder,** Abraham d1970 *LesBEnT 92*
**Zapsalis,** Charles 1922- *AmMWSc 92*
**Zar,** Jerrold Howard 1941- *AmMWSc 92*
**Zara,** Deborah Marie 1965- *WhoEnt 92*
**Zara,** Louis 1910- *BenetAL 91*
**Zarafonetis,** Chris John Dimiter 1914- *AmMWSc 92, WhoMW 92*
**Zaragoza,** Al *WhoHisp 92*
**Zaragoza,** Anne Catherine 1951- *WhoFI 92, WhoMW 92*
**Zaragoza,** Blanca *WhoHisp 92*
**Zaragoza,** Federico *WhoHisp 92*
**Zaragoza,** Ronald 1956- *WhoHisp 92*
**Zarandona,** Joseph L 1953- *WhoIns 92*
**Zaranka,** Albert J. 1949- *WhoEnt 92*
**Zaranka,** William *DrAPF 91*
**Zarate,** Armando E. 1931- *WhoHisp 92*
**Zarate,** Narcisa 1925- *WhoHisp 92*
**Zarb,** Frank G 1935- *WhoAmP 91*
**Zarb,** Frank Gustav 1935- *IntWW 91*
**Zarb,** Frank Gustave 1935- *WhoFI 92*
**Zarcaro,** Robert Michael 1942- *AmMWSc 92*
**Zarchi,** Meir 1937- *WhoEnt 92*
**Zarco,** Romeo Morales 1920- *AmMWSc 92*
**Zardecki,** Andrew 1942- *AmMWSc 92*
**Zardenetta,** Antonio *WhoHisp 92*
**Zare,** Richard Neil 1939- *AmMWSc 92, IntWW 91, WhoWest 92*
**Zarefar,** Hormoz 1956- *WhoWest 92*
**Zarem,** Abe Mordecai 1917- *AmMWSc 92*
**Zarem,** Harvey A 1932- *AmMWSc 92*
**Zaremba,** Eve 1930- *ConAu 133*

**Zaremba**, Gary Lee 1951- *WhoWest 92*
**Zarembski**, Michael 1956- *WhoEnt 92*
**Zaremsky**, Baruch 1926- *AmMWSc 92*
**Zaret**, Barry L 1940- *AmMWSc 92*
**Zarges**, Robert Scott, Jr. 1966- *WhoRel 92*
**Zarian**, Larry *WhoAmP 91*
**Zarick**, Steven M. 1963- *WhoEnt 92*
**Zarif**, Mohammad Farouk 1951- *IntWW 91*
**Zarin'**, Indulis Avgustovich 1929- *SovUnBD*
**Zarina** *EncAmaz 91*
**Zaring**, Wilson Miles 1926- *AmMWSc 92, WhoMW 92*
**Zaritzky**, Gerald *WhoEnt 92*
**Zarkhi**, Aleksandr Grigor'evich 1908- *SovUnBD*
**Zarkhi**, Natan Abramovich 1900-1935 *SovUnBD*
**Zarkhy**, Aleksandr Grigoriyevich 1908- *IntWW 91*
**Zarkovic**, Vidoje 1927- *IntWW 91*
**Zarkower**, Arian 1929- *AmMWSc 92*
**Zarlenga**, Stella Marie 1940- *WhoRel 92*
**Zarling**, John P 1942- *AmMWSc 92*
**Zarlino**, Gioseffo 1517-1590 *NewAmDM*
**Zarmbinski**, Richard Anthony 1950- *WhoMW 92*
**Zarnecki**, George 1915- *Who 92*
**Zarnow**, Teryl 1951- *ConAu 135*
**Zarnowitz**, Victor 1919- *WrDr 92*
**Zarnowski**, Alexander Frank 1915- *WhoAmP 91*
**Zarnstorff**, Michael Charles 1954- *AmMWSc 92*
**Zarobe**, Christina Maria 1961- *WhoHisp 92*
**Zarobila**, Clarence Joseph 1958- *AmMWSc 92*
**Zarod**, Stanley John 1924- *WhoAmP 91*
**Zarolia**, Bomi Manchershaw 1942- *WhoFI 92*
**Zaromb**, Solomon 1928- *AmMWSc 92*
**Zaroni**, Murray 1947- *TwCPaSc*
**Zaroslinski**, John F 1925- *AmMWSc 92*
**Zarov**, Herbert Lawrence 1945- *WhoAmL 92*
**Zarovitch**, Princess Vera *ScFEYrs*
**Zarraonandia**, David *WhoHisp 92*
**Zarrett**, Linda Pauline 1956- *WhoMW 92*
**Zarrillo**, Andrew 1951- *WhoEnt 92*
**Zarro**, Antonio 1960- *WhoEnt 92*
**Zartman**, David Lester 1940- *AmMWSc 92*
**Zartman**, Robert Eugene 1936- *AmMWSc 92*
**Zaruba**, Gary Edward 1940- *WhoMW 92*
**Zarucki**, Tanya Z *AmMWSc 92*
**Zarutskie**, Andrew John 1950- *WhoAmP 91*
**Zarutskie**, Paul Walter 1951- *WhoWest 92*
**Zarwyn**, B 1921- *AmMWSc 92*
**Zary**, Keith Wilfred 1948- *AmMWSc 92*
**Zarzecki**, Peter 1945- *AmMWSc 92*
**Zarzyski**, Paul *DrAPF 91*
**Zasada**, Zigmond Anthony 1909- *AmMWSc 92*
**Zashin**, Robert Ira 1940- *WhoAmL 92*
**Zaske**, Darwin Erhard 1949- *AmMWSc 92*
**Zaslavskaya**, Tatiana Ivanovna 1927- *IntWW 91*
**Zaslavskaya**, Tat'yana Ivanovna 1927- *SovUnBD*
**Zaslavsky**, Ilya Iosifovich 1960- *IntWW 91, SovUnBD*
**Zaslavsky**, Thomas 1944- *AmMWSc 92*
**Zaslove**, Phoebe *WhoFI 92*
**Zaslowsky**, David Paul 1960- *WhoAmL 92*
**Zaspel**, Fred George 1958- *WhoRel 92*
**Zassenhaus**, Hans J 1912- *AmMWSc 92*
**Zassenhaus**, Hans Julius 1912- *WhoMW 92*
**Zastrow**, Charles Harold 1942- *WhoMW 92*
**Zastrow**, John Thurman 1937- *WhoWest 92*
**Zastrow**, William Lee 1937- *WhoIns 92*
**Zatko**, David A 1940- *AmMWSc 92*
**Zatkoff**, Lawrence P. *WhoAmL 92*
**Zatkowsky**, Miles Perry 1956- *WhoEnt 92*
**Zatlin**, Phyllis 1938- *ConAu 36NR*
**Zatlin-Boring**, Phyllis *ConAu 36NR*
**Zatopek**, Emil 1922- *IntWW 91*
**Zatorski**, James Michael 1965- *WhoMW 92*
**Zatsepin**, Georgiy Timofeyevich 1917- *IntWW 91*
**Zatta**, Leo Joseph 1956- *WhoFI 92*
**Zatuchni**, Gerald Irving 1935- *AmMWSc 92*
**Zatuchni**, Jacob 1920- *AmMWSc 92*
**Zaturenska**, Marya 1902-1982 *BenetAL 91*
**Zatz**, Joel L *AmMWSc 92*
**Zatz**, Leslie M 1928- *AmMWSc 92*
**Zatz**, Marion M 1945- *AmMWSc 92*
**Zatz**, Martin 1944- *AmMWSc 92*
**Zatzkis**, Henry 1915- *AmMWSc 92*
**Zatzman**, Marvin Leon 1927- *AmMWSc 92*
**Zauder**, Howard L 1923- *AmMWSc 92*
**Zauderer**, Bert 1937- *AmMWSc 92*
**Zauderer**, Maurice *AmMWSc 92*
**Zaugg**, Harold Elmer 1916- *AmMWSc 92*
**Zaugg**, Waldo S 1930- *AmMWSc 92*
**Zaukelies**, David Aaron 1925- *AmMWSc 92*
**Zauner**, Christian Walter 1930- *AmMWSc 92, WhoWest 92*
**Zaustinsky**, Eugene Michael 1926- *AmMWSc 92*
**Zavadovsky**, Mikhail Mikhaylovich 1891-1957 *SovUnBD*
**Zavadsky**, Yuriy Aleksandrovich 1894-1977 *SovUnBD*
**Zavala**, Albert 1930- *WhoWest 92*
**Zavala**, Berta 1944- *WhoHisp 92*
**Zavala**, Donald Charles 1923- *WhoHisp 92*
**Zavala**, Eduardo Alberto 1960- *WhoHisp 92*
**Zavala**, Iris M. *DrAPF 91*
**Zavala**, Luis Angel, Jr. 1952- *WhoHisp 92*
**Zavala**, Maria Elena 1950- *AmMWSc 92, WhoHisp 92*
**Zavala**, Silvio 1909- *IntWW 91*
**Zavala**, Valerie Renee 1955- *WhoHisp 92*
**Zavala Baquerizo**, Jorge Enrique 1922- *IntWW 91*
**Zavarin**, Eugene 1924- *AmMWSc 92*
**Zavatsky**, Bill *DrAPF 91*
**Zavatsky**, Michael Joseph 1948- *WhoAmL 92*
**Zavecz**, James Henry 1946- *AmMWSc 92*
**Zavenyagin**, Avraamyy Pavlovich 1901-1956 *SovUnBD*
**Zavin**, Theodora 1922- *WhoEnt 92*
**Zavitsanos**, John 1962- *WhoAmL 92*
**Zavitsas**, Andreas Athanasios 1937- *AmMWSc 92*
**Zavodney**, Lawrence Dennis 1951- *AmMWSc 92*
**Zavodni**, John J 1943- *AmMWSc 92*
**Zavodni**, Zavis Marian 1941- *AmMWSc 92*
**Zavon**, Mitchell Ralph 1923- *AmMWSc 92*
**Zavortink**, Thomas James 1939- *AmMWSc 92*
**Zavrian**, Suzanne Ostro *DrAPF 91*
**Zawacki**, Bruce Edwin 1935- *AmMWSc 92*
**Zawacki**, Connie *WhoAmP 91*
**Zawacki**, Franklin *DrAPF 91*
**Zawacki**, James E *WhoAmP 91*
**Zawada**, Edward T, Jr 1947- *AmMWSc 92*
**Zawada**, Edward Thaddeus, Jr. 1947- *WhoMW 92*
**Zawadi**, Kiane 1932- *WhoEnt 92*
**Zawadiwsky**, Christina *DrAPF 91*
**Zawadzki**, Joseph Francis 1935- *AmMWSc 92*
**Zawadzki**, Sylwester 1921- *IntWW 91*
**Zawadzki**, Zbigniew Apolinary 1921- *AmMWSc 92*
**Zawalich**, Chet 1954- *WhoAmL 92*
**Zaweski**, Edward F 1933- *AmMWSc 92*
**Zawinul**, Joe 1932- *NewAmDM*
**Zawinul**, Josef 1932- *IntWW 91*
**Zawislak**, Andrzej M. 1937- *IntWW 91*
**Zawistowski**, Joseph K. *WhoRel 92*
**Zawistowski**, Zbigniew 1944- *IntWW 91*
**Zawisza**, Julie Anne A 1956- *AmMWSc 92*
**Zawodny**, J. K. 1921- *WrDr 92*
**Zaworski**, R J 1926- *AmMWSc 92*
**Zax**, Leonard A. 1950- *WhoAmL 92*
**Zax**, Melvin 1928- *ConAu 36NR*
**Zax**, Stanley R. *WhoWest 92*
**Zayadi**, Hani Joseph 1948- *WhoFI 92*
**Zayas**, Miguel Angel 1949- *WhoHisp 92*
**Zayas-Bazan**, Eduardo 1935- *WhoHisp 92*
**Zayas-Castro**, Jose Luis 1955- *WhoHisp 92*
**Zayas Chardon**, Humberto *WhoAmP 91*
**Zayas-Green**, Jose 1926- *WhoAmP 91*
**Zayas-Hood**, Maria de los Angeles 1952- *WhoHisp 92*
**Zayas Seijo**, Francisco *WhoAmP 91*
**Zayas y Alfonso**, Alfredo 1861-1934 *HisDSpE*
**Zaye**, David F *AmMWSc 92*
**Zayek**, Francis Mansour 1920- *WhoRel 92*
**Zayid**, Geno T. 1959- *WhoAmL 92*
**Zaykov**, Lev Nikolaevich 1923- *SovUnBD*
**Zaytoun**, Joseph Ellis 1920- *WhoIns 92*
**Zayyen**, Yusuf *IntWW 91*
**Zazueta**, Fernando 1940- *WhoHisp 92*
**Zazuyer**, Leah *DrAPF 91*
**Zazvrskey**, Michael Eugene 1947- *WhoWest 92*
**Zbar**, Berton 1938- *AmMWSc 92*
**Zbarsky**, Sidney Howard 1920- *AmMWSc 92*
**Zbieroski**, Mark Joel 1955- *WhoAmL 92*
**Zbikowski**, James Bernard 1956- *WhoFI 92*
**Zboralske**, F Frank 1932- *AmMWSc 92*
**Zborowski**, Andrew 1936- *AmMWSc 92*
**Zbranek**, J C 1930- *WhoAmP 91*
**Zbuzek**, Vlasta Kmentova 1933- *AmMWSc 92*
**Zbuzek**, Vratislav 1930- *AmMWSc 92*
**Zdan**, William 1919- *AmMWSc 92*
**Zdanis**, Richard Albert 1935- *AmMWSc 92*
**Zdellar**, Ronald Charles 1944- *WhoMW 92*
**Zderic**, John Anthony 1924- *AmMWSc 92*
**Zdravkovich**, Vera 1939- *AmMWSc 92*
**Zdunkowski**, Wilford G 1929- *AmMWSc 92*
**Zea**, Vladimir 1952- *WhoFI 92*
**Zea Aguilar**, Leopoldo 1912- *IntWW 91*
**Zea Hernandez**, German 1905- *IntWW 91*
**Zealey**, Marion Edward 1913- *AmMWSc 92*
**Zealley**, Christopher Bennett 1931- *Who 92*
**Zealley**, Helen Elizabeth 1940- *Who 92*
**Zeamer**, Richard Jere 1921- *AmMWSc 92*
**Zearfoss**, Herbert Keyser 1929- *WhoAmP 91*
**Zeavin**, Naomi Delores 1933- *WhoAmP 91*
**Zeayen**, Yusuf 1931- *IntWW 91*
**Zebal**, Kenneth Walter 1945- *WhoFI 92*
**Zebarah**, Danny Peter 1957- *WhoEnt 92*
**Zebib**, Abdelfattah M G 1946- *AmMWSc 92*
**Zebolsky**, Donald Michael 1933- *AmMWSc 92, WhoMW 92*
**Zebouni**, Nadim H 1928- *AmMWSc 92*
**Zebovitz**, Eugene 1926- *AmMWSc 92*
**Zebris**, Juozas *DcAmImH*
**Zebroski**, Edwin L 1921- *AmMWSc 92*
**Zebrowitz**, S 1927- *AmMWSc 92*
**Zebrowski**, George *DrAPF 91*
**Zebrowski**, George 1945- *SmATA 67 [port], TwCSFW 91, WrDr 92*
**Zebrowski**, John 1948- *WhoAmL 92*
**Zebrowski**, Mark Charles 1958- *WhoAmL 92*
**Zebrowski**, Mary Theodorette 1916- *WhoRel 92*
**Zec**, Ronald Francis 1949- *WhoMW 92*
**Zecchini**, Salvatore 1943- *IntWW 91*
**Zecchino**, Paul Vincent 1954- *WhoEnt 92*
**Zech**, Arthur Conrad 1927- *AmMWSc 92*
**Zech**, Lando W, Jr *WhoAmP 91*
**Zech**, Paul 1881-1946 *LiExTwC*
**Zechar**, Corwin Stuart 1959- *WhoWest 92*
**Zecher**, Albert Michael 1930- *WhoAmL 92*
**Zechiel**, Leon Norris 1923- *AmMWSc 92*
**Zechman**, Donald Eugene 1938- *WhoRel 92*
**Zechman**, Frederick William, Jr 1928- *AmMWSc 92*
**Zechmann**, Albert W 1934- *AmMWSc 92*
**Zechnich**, David W. 1956- *WhoWest 92*
**Zecker**, Gerald 1942- *WhoAmP 91*
**Zeckhausen**, Barbara T 1937- *WhoAmP 91*
**Zeckhauser**, Richard Jay 1940- *WhoFI 92*
**Zed**, Dr. *SmATA 66*
**Zedeck**, Morris Samuel 1940- *AmMWSc 92*
**Zedek**, Mishael 1926- *AmMWSc 92*
**Zeder**, Fred Monroe, II 1921- *WhoFI 92*
**Zedler**, Beatrice H. 1916- *ConAu 36NR*
**Zedler**, Empress Young 1908- *AmMWSc 92*
**Zedler**, Joy Buswell 1943- *AmMWSc 92*
**Zedler**, Paul H 1941- *AmMWSc 92*
**Zedonis**, Paul 1947- *WhoIns 92*
**Zedric**, Louis Clark 1959- *WhoFI 92*
**Zedrosser**, Joseph John 1938- *WhoAmL 92*
**Zee**, A. *WrDr 92*
**Zee**, Anthony *AmMWSc 92*
**Zee**, David Samuel 1944- *AmMWSc 92*
**Zee**, Paulus 1928- *AmMWSc 92*
**Zee**, Yuan Chung 1935- *AmMWSc 92*
**Zee-Cheng**, Robert Kwang-Yuen 1925- *AmMWSc 92*
**Zeeb**, James Lawrence 1945- *WhoWest 92*
**Zeek**, Paul Stewart 1959- *WhoRel 92*
**Zeelens**, Ronald Andrew 1952- *WhoEnt 92*
**Zeeman**, Erik Christopher 1925- *Who 92*
**Zeeman**, Maurice George 1942- *AmMWSc 92*
**Zeeman**, Pieter 1865-1943 *WhoNob 90*
**Zeese**, Kevin Bruce 1955- *WhoAmL 92*
**Zeevaart**, Jan Adriaan Dingenis 1930- *AmMWSc 92*
**Zeferetti**, Leo C 1927- *WhoAmP 91*
**Zeffirelli**, Franco 1923- *FacFETw, IntDcF 2-2 [port], IntMPA 92, News 91 [port], -91-3 [port], WhoEnt 92*
**Zeffirelli**, G. Franco 1923- *IntWW 91, Who 92*
**Zeffren**, Eugene 1941- *AmMWSc 92, WhoFI 92*
**Zegar**, Eugene 1946- *WhoAmL 92*
**Zegar**, James Louis 1948- *WhoFI 92*
**Zegarelli**, Edward Victor 1912- *AmMWSc 92*
**Zegeer**, Moses Scott 1960- *WhoFI 92*
**Zegel**, Barry Bryan 1955- *WhoEnt 92*
**Zegel**, William Case 1940- *AmMWSc 92*
**Zegers**, Kip *DrAPF 91*
**Zegiob-Devereaux**, Leslie Elaine 1948- *WhoMW 92*
**Zeglis**, John D. *WhoAmL 92*
**Zegura**, Stephen Luke 1943- *AmMWSc 92*
**Zeh**, Geoffrey N. 1943- *WhoFI 92*
**Zeheb**, Ezra *AmMWSc 92*
**Zehetmayr**, John Walter Lloyd 1921- *Who 92*
**Zehnder**, Frederick John 1926- *WhoMW 92*
**Zehnder**, George Philip 1949- *WhoRel 92*
**Zehnder**, John Louis, Jr. 1951- *WhoFI 92*
**Zehner**, David Murray 1943- *AmMWSc 92*
**Zehner**, James S 1945- *WhoAmP 91*
**Zehner**, Lee Randall 1947- *AmMWSc 92*
**Zehner**, Richard Norman 1953- *WhoWest 92*
**Zehner**, William Bradley, II 1944- *WhoFI 92, WhoWest 92*
**Zehr**, Clyde James 1934- *WhoRel 92*
**Zehr**, Dan *WhoRel 92*
**Zehr**, Eldon Irvin 1935- *AmMWSc 92*
**Zehr**, Floyd Joseph 1929- *AmMWSc 92*
**Zehr**, John E 1929- *AmMWSc 92*
**Zehr**, Martin Dale 1950- *AmMWSc 92, WhoMW 92*
**Zehr**, Norman Robert 1930- *WhoFI 92, WhoWest 92*
**Zehrer**, Hans 1899-1966 *BiDExR, EncTR 91 [port]*
**Zehrfuss**, Bernard 1911- *IntWW 91*
**Zehrt**, William H 1922- *AmMWSc 92*
**Zei**, Dino 1927- *AmMWSc 92*
**Zeichner-David**, Margarita 1946- *AmMWSc 92*
**Zeid**, Fahrelnissa 1901-1991 *NewYTBS 91*
**Zeid**, Philip L. 1943- *WhoFI 92*
**Zeidan**, Kimberly Dawn 1961- *WhoRel 92*
**Zeide**, Boris 1937- *AmMWSc 92*
**Zeidenbergs**, Girts 1934- *AmMWSc 92*
**Zeiders**, Kenneth Eugene 1920- *AmMWSc 92*
**Zeidler**, David *Who 92*
**Zeidler**, David Ronald 1918- *IntWW 91*
**Zeidler**, Frank P 1912- *WhoAmP 91*
**Zeidler**, James Robert 1944- *AmMWSc 92*
**Zeidman**, Benjamin 1931- *AmMWSc 92*
**Zeidman**, Heywood William 1941- *WhoWest 92*
**Zeidman**, Irving 1918- *AmMWSc 92*
**Zeidman**, Philip Fisher 1934- *WhoAmL 92*
**Zeidner**, Lisa *DrAPF 91*
**Zeidner**, Lisa 1955- *WrDr 92*
**Zeien**, Alfred M. 1930- *WhoFI 92*
**Zeig**, Jeffrey Kenneth 1947- *WhoWest 92*
**Zeigel**, Robert Francis 1931- *AmMWSc 92*
**Zeiger**, Alan L. 1955- *WhoAmL 92*
**Zeiger**, David *DrAPF 91*
**Zeiger**, Errol 1939- *AmMWSc 92*
**Zeiger**, Gene *DrAPF 91*
**Zeiger**, H Paul 1936- *AmMWSc 92*
**Zeiger**, Herbert J 1925- *AmMWSc 92*
**Zeiger**, John Wolcott 1947- *WhoAmL 92*
**Zeiger**, L.L. *DrAPF 91*
**Zeiger**, Lila *DrAPF 91*
**Zeiger**, Stephen Allen 1951- *WhoWest 92*
**Zeiger**, William Nathaniel 1946- *AmMWSc 92*
**Zeigfried**, Karl *TwCSFW 91*
**Zeighami**, Elaine Ann 1944- *AmMWSc 92*
**Zeigler**, A G 1923 *AmMWSc 92*
**Zeigler**, Ann dePender 1947- *WhoAmL 92*
**Zeigler**, Bernard Philip *AmMWSc 92*
**Zeigler**, David Wayne 1949- *AmMWSc 92*
**Zeigler**, Donald Maurice 1931- *WhoAmP 91*
**Zeigler**, John Martin 1951- *AmMWSc 92*
**Zeigler**, John Milton 1922- *AmMWSc 92*
**Zeigler**, Max Floyd 1942- *WhoAmP 91*
**Zeigler**, Royal Keith 1919- *AmMWSc 92*
**Zeigried**, Karl *WrDr 92*
**Zeikus**, J Gregory 1945- *AmMWSc 92*
**Zeiler**, Frederick 1921- *AmMWSc 92*
**Zeiler**, Joseph Andrew, Jr. 1927- *WhoWest 92*
**Zeilig**, Nancy Meeks 1943- *WhoWest 92*
**Zeilik**, Michael 1946- *AmMWSc 92, ConAu 36NR, WrDr 92*
**Zeilinger**, Elna Rae 1937- *WhoWest 92*
**Zeimet**, Ann 1952- *WhoFI 92*
**Zeiner**, Frederick Neyer 1917- *AmMWSc 92*
**Zeisel**, Eva 1906- *DcTwDes*
**Zeisel**, Hallie Burnett d1991 *NewYTBS 91 [port]*
**Zeisel**, Hans 1905- *WhoAmL 92*
**Zeiser**, Willard Arthur 1940- *WhoRel 92*
**Zeisler**, Claire 1903-1991 *NewYTBS 91*
**Zeisler**, Fannie 1863-1927 *NewAmDM*
**Zeiss**, Carl 1816-1888 *DcTwDes*
**Zeiss**, Chester Raymond 1941- *AmMWSc 92*
**Zeiter**, William Emmet 1934- *WhoAmL 92*

**Zeitlan**, Marilyn Labb 1938- *WhoAmL 92*
**Zeitler**, Arthur William 1946- *WhoAmP 91*
**Zeitler**, Bill Lorenz 1920- *WhoWest 92*
**Zeitler**, Deborah Leila 1952- *WhoMW 92*
**Zeitlin**, Bruce Allen 1943- *WhoFI 92*
**Zeitlin**, Gerald Mark 1937- *WhoWest 92*
**Zeitlin**, Joel Loeb 1942- *AmMWSc 92*
**Zeitlin**, Maurice 1935- *WhoWest 92*
**Zeitlin**, Zvi 1923- *NewAmDM, WhoEnt 92*
**Zeitz**, Louis 1922- *AmMWSc 92*
**Zeitzler**, Kurt 1895-1963 *EncTR 91*
**Zeizel**, A J 1933- *AmMWSc 92*
**Zeki**, Semir 1940- *Who 92*
**Zekman**, Terri Margaret 1950- *WhoEnt 92, WhoWest 92*
**Zekowski**, Arlene *DrAPF 91*
**Zelac**, Ronald Edward 1941- *AmMWSc 92*
**Zelada De Andres Moreno**, Fermin 1912- *IntWW 91*
**Zelasko**, Antone Richard 1923- *WhoAmP 91*
**Zelaya**, Gianna Annette 1963- *WhoFI 92*
**Zelazny**, Lucian Walter 1942- *AmMWSc 92*
**Zelazny**, Roger *DrAPF 91*
**Zelazny**, Roger 1937- *Au&Arts 7 [port], TwCSFW 91, WrDr 92*
**Zelazny**, Roger Joseph *IntAu&W 91*
**Zelazo**, Nathaniel Kachorek 1918- *AmMWSc 92*
**Zelbstein**, Uri 1912- *IntWW 91*
**Zelby**, Leon W 1925- *AmMWSc 92*
**Zelden**, Douglas Howard 1960- *WhoMW 92, WhoRel 92*
**Zeldes**, David Mark 1950- *WhoWest 92*
**Zeldes**, Henry 1921- *AmMWSc 92*
**Zeldes**, Ilya Michael 1933- *WhoAmL 92, WhoMW 92*
**Zeldes**, Stephen Paul 1956- *WhoFI 92*
**Zeldin**, Arkady N 1939- *AmMWSc 92*
**Zeldin**, C. Arthur 1918- *WhoWest 92*
**Zeldin**, Martel 1937- *AmMWSc 92*
**Zeldin**, Michael Hermen 1938- *AmMWSc 92*
**Zeldin**, Stanford Alvin 1936- *WhoAmL 92*
**Zeldin**, Theodore 1933- *WrDr 92*
**Zeldis**, Chayym 1927- *WrDr 92*
**Zeldis**, Jerome B 1950- *AmMWSc 92*
**Zelen**, Marvin 1927- *AmMWSc 92*
**Zelenak**, Edward Michael 1953- *WhoEnt 92, WhoMW 92*
**Zeleniak**, John Joseph 1910- *WhoMW 92*
**Zelenka**, Jan Dismas 1679-1745 *NewAmDM*
**Zelenka**, Jerry Stephen 1936- *AmMWSc 92*
**Zelenka**, Peggy Sue 1942- *AmMWSc 92*
**Zelenka**, Stephen Ernest 1958- *WhoEnt 92*
**Zelenovsky**, Anatoliy Antonovich 1940- *IntWW 91*
**Zelensky**, Isaak Abramovich 1890-1938 *SovUnBD*
**Zeleny**, Charles Timberlake 1963- *WhoEnt 92*
**Zeleny**, Lawrence 1904- *AmMWSc 92*
**Zeleny**, William Bardwell 1934- *AmMWSc 92, WhoWest 92*
**Zelevansky**, Paul *DrAPF 91*
**Zeleznick**, Lowell D 1935- *AmMWSc 92*
**Zelezny**, William Francis 1918- *AmMWSc 92, WhoWest 92*
**Zeliff**, Bill *WhoAmP 91*
**Zeliff**, William H., Jr. 1936- *AlmAP 92 [port]*
**Zeligman**, Israel 1913- *AmMWSc 92*
**Zeligman**, Sergio 1949- *WhoHisp 92*
**Zelikow**, Howard Monroe 1934- *WhoIns 92*
**Zelin**, Jerome 1930- *WhoFI 92*
**Zelinger**, Geza 1911- *WrDr 92*
**Zelinova**, Hana 1914- *IntAu&W 91*
**Zelinski**, Robert Paul 1920- *AmMWSc 92*
**Zelinsky**, Daniel 1922- *AmMWSc 92*
**Zelinsky**, Wilbur 1921- *WrDr 92*
**Zelis**, Robert Felix 1939- *AmMWSc 92*
**Zelitch**, David S 1924- *WhoIns 92*
**Zelitch**, Israel 1924- *AmMWSc 92*
**Zelizer**, Nathan 1905- *WhoRel 92*
**Zelka**, Jeffrey 1952- *WhoFI 92*
**Zelkowitz**, Marvin Victor 1945- *AmMWSc 92*
**Zell**, Blair Paul 1942- *AmMWSc 92*
**Zell**, Howard Charles 1922- *AmMWSc 92*
**Zell**, Morning Glory 1948- *RelLAm 91*
**Zell**, Otter 1942- *RelLAm 91*
**Zell**, Samuel 1941- *WhoMW 92*
**Zell**, Shawn Blair 1953- *WhoRel 92*
**Zell**, Steven Peter 1946- *WhoEnt 92*
**Zellars**, Anne Yusavage *DrAPF 91*
**Zeller**, Albert Fontenot 1947- *AmMWSc 92*
**Zeller**, Andre 1898-1979 *FacFETw*
**Zeller**, Barbara Ann 1945- *WhoMW 92, WhoRel 92*
**Zeller**, Edward Jacob 1925- *AmMWSc 92*
**Zeller**, Francis Joseph 1943- *WhoMW 92*
**Zeller**, Frank Jacob 1927- *AmMWSc 92*
**Zeller**, Joseph Paul 1940- *WhoMW 92*
**Zeller**, Leta Madene 1949- *WhoRel 92*
**Zeller**, Michael Edward 1939- *AmMWSc 92*
**Zeller**, Paul Michael 1949- *WhoMW 92*
**Zeller**, Ronald John 1940- *WhoAmL 92*
**Zeller**, William David 1962- *WhoAmL 92*
**Zellerbach**, Cary M. 1951- *WhoFI 92*
**Zellerbach**, Merla *DrAPF 91*
**Zellerbach**, William Joseph 1920- *IntWW 91*
**Zellers**, Claira Mitcham 1950- *WhoAmL 92*
**Zellers**, Robert Charles 1943- *WhoFI 92*
**Zelley**, Walter Gauntt 1921- *AmMWSc 92*
**Zellick**, Graham John 1948- *Who 92*
**Zellinsky**, Paul *WhoAmP 91*
**Zellmer**, Arlene 1920- *WhoWest 92*
**Zellmer**, David Bruce 1953- *WhoRel 92*
**Zellmer**, David Louis 1942- *AmMWSc 92*
**Zellmer**, James Erich 1962- *WhoFI 92*
**Zellmer**, Johannes Ernst 1920- *WhoRel 92*
**Zellner**, Annie Rose 1928- *WhoRel 92*
**Zellner**, Arnold 1927- *WhoFI 92, WrDr 92*
**Zellner**, Benjamin Holmes 1942- *AmMWSc 92*
**Zellner**, Carl Naeher 1910- *AmMWSc 92*
**Zello**, Suzanna Marie 1951- *WhoRel 92*
**Zells**, Lois Steinman *WhoWest 92*
**Zellweger**, Hans Ulrich 1909- *AmMWSc 92*
**Zelman**, Allen 1938- *AmMWSc 92*
**Zelman**, Anita *DrAPF 91*
**Zelman**, Benjamin David 1964- *WhoMW 92*
**Zelmanowitz**, Julius Martin 1941- *AmMWSc 92*
**Zelmon**, David Norman 1945- *WhoMW 92*
**Zelnick**, Strauss 1957- *IntMPA 92, WhoEnt 92*
**Zelnik**, Melvin 1928- *AmMWSc 92*
**Zelon**, Laurie Dee 1952- *WhoAmL 92*
**Zelson**, Philip Richard 1945- *AmMWSc 92*
**Zelter**, Carl Friedrich 1758-1832 *NewAmDM*
**Zelterman**, Daniel 1954- *WhoFI 92*
**Zeltmann**, Alfred Howard 1921- *AmMWSc 92*
**Zeltmann**, Eugene W 1940- *AmMWSc 92*
**Zeltner**, Paul E *WhoAmP 91*
**Zeltzer**, Joel *DrAPF 91*
**Zelver**, Patricia *DrAPF 91*
**Zelvin**, Elizabeth *DrAPF 91*
**Zelvin**, Elizabeth Lapidus 1944- *IntAu&W 91*
**Zemach**, Charles 1930- *AmMWSc 92*
**Zemach**, Rita 1926- *AmMWSc 92*
**Zemaitis**, Algirdas Jonas Alexis *WhoFI 92*
**Zemaitis**, Michael Alan 1946- *AmMWSc 92*
**Zemaitis**, Thomas Edward 1951- *WhoAmL 92*
**Zeman**, Andrew Howard 1946- *WhoRel 92*
**Zeman**, Frances Jane 1925- *AmMWSc 92*
**Zeman**, Jacklyn Lee 1953- *WhoEnt 92*
**Zeman**, Wayne Paul 1947- *WhoFI 92*
**Zeman**, Zbynek Anthony Bohuslav 1928- *IntWW 91, Who 92*
**Zemanek**, Heinz 1920- *IntWW 91*
**Zemanek**, Joseph, Jr 1928- *AmMWSc 92*
**Zemanian**, Armen Humpartsoum 1925- *AmMWSc 92*
**Zembal**, Theodore 1930- *WhoEnt 92*
**Zembrodt**, Anthony Raymond 1943- *AmMWSc 92*
**Zemdega**, Aina 1924- *LiExTwC*
**Zemeckis**, Robert 1951- *IntDcF 2-2*
**Zemeckis**, Robert 1952- *IntMPA 92*
**Zemeckis**, Robert L. 1952- *WhoEnt 92*
**Zemel**, Jay N *AmMWSc 92*
**Zemelman**, James Louis 1931- *WhoAmL 92*
**Zemelman**, Mark 1958- *WhoMW 92*
**Zemer**, Jack David 1947- *WhoWest 92*
**Zemke**, Joseph *WhoWest 92*
**Zemke**, Warren T 1939- *AmMWSc 92*
**Zemlicka**, Jiri 1933- *AmMWSc 92*
**Zemlin**, Willard R *AmMWSc 92*
**Zemlinsky**, Alexander von 1871-1942 *NewAmDM*
**Zemlyachka**, Rosaliya Samoilovna 1876-1947 *SovUnBD*
**Zemmer**, Joseph Lawrence, Jr 1922- *AmMWSc 92, WhoMW 92*
**Zemon**, Stanley Alan 1930- *AmMWSc 92*
**Zemp**, John Workman 1931- *AmMWSc 92*
**Zemp**, Lucy Woodruff 1962- *WhoFI 92*
**Zemprelli**, Edward Phillip 1925- *WhoAmP 91*
**Zemsky**, Calvin Lawrence 1931- *WhoFI 92*
**Zen**, E-an 1928- *AmMWSc 92, IntWW 91*
**Zenchak**, Joseph Phillip, Jr. 1945- *WhoWest 92*
**Zenchelsky**, Seymour Theodore 1923- *AmMWSc 92*
**Zencker**, Richard Eric 1956- *WhoEnt 92*
**Zendejas**, Esperanza 1952- *WhoHisp 92*
**Zendejas**, Luis *WhoHisp 92*
**Zender**, Hans 1936- *IntWW 91, WhoEnt 92*
**Zender**, James Francis 1954- *WhoMW 92*
**Zender**, Michael J 1939- *AmMWSc 92*
**Zender-Boykin**, Angelina Elizabeth 1933- *WhoMW 92*
**Zendle**, Howard Mark 1949- *WhoFI 92*
**Zener**, Clarence Melvin 1905- *AmMWSc 92*
**Zenev**, Irene Louise 1948- *WhoWest 92*
**Zeng Sheng** 1910- *IntWW 91*
**Zeng Tao** 1914- *IntWW 91*
**Zeng Xianlin** 1929- *IntWW 91*
**Zeng Yi** 1929- *IntWW 91*
**Zengel**, Janet Elaine 1948- *AmMWSc 92*
**Zengel**, Janice Marie 1948- *AmMWSc 92*
**Zenger**, Donald Henry 1932- *AmMWSc 92*
**Zenger**, John Hancock 1931- *WhoWest 92*
**Zenger**, Peter 1697-1746 *BenetAL 91*
**Zenined**, Abdesselam 1934- *Who 92*
**Zenisek**, Cyril James 1926- *AmMWSc 92*
**Zenitz**, Bernard Leon 1917- *AmMWSc 92*
**Zenker**, Nicolas 1921- *AmMWSc 92*
**Zenko**, John Alan 1937- *WhoMW 92*
**Zenner**, Sheldon Toby 1953- *WhoAmL 92*
**Zeno** d491 *EncEarC*
**Zeno of Verona** d380? *EncEarC*
**Zeno**, Apostolo 1668-1750 *BlkwCEP*
**Zeno**, Willie D. 1942- *WhoBlA 92*
**Zenobia Septimia** *EncAmaz 91*
**Zenofon**, Fonda 1953- *IntAu&W 91*
**Zenor**, Michael 1949- *WhoAmP 91*
**Zenovich**, George N 1922- *WhoAmP 91*
**Zenowich**, Christopher 1954- *ConAu 134*
**Zens**, Jon Hardesty 1945- *WhoRel 92*
**Zens**, Will 1920- *IntMPA 92*
**Zenser**, Terry Vernon 1945- *AmMWSc 92*
**Zentar**, Mehdi M'rani 1929- *IntWW 91*
**Zenteno del Pozo y Silva**, Jose Ignacio 1786-1847 *HisDSpE*
**Zentilli**, Marcos 1940- *AmMWSc 92*
**Zentmayer**, Joseph 1826-1888 *BiInAmS*
**Zentmyer**, George Aubrey 1913- *WhoWest 92*
**Zentmyer**, George Aubrey, Jr 1913- *AmMWSc 92, IntWW 91*
**Zentner**, Peter 1932- *WrDr 92*
**Zentner**, Thomas Glenn 1926- *AmMWSc 92*
**Zentz**, John Robert 1938- *WhoAmP 91*
**Zenz**, Carl 1923- *AmMWSc 92*
**Zenz**, David R 1943- *AmMWSc 92*
**Zenz**, Frederick A 1922- *AmMWSc 92*
**Zenz**, John Patrick 1950- *WhoRel 92*
**Zeoli**, G W 1926- *AmMWSc 92*
**Zepeda**, Barbara Joyce 1935- *WhoAmP 91*
**Zepeda**, Maria Angelica 1952- *WhoHisp 92*
**Zepeda**, Paula 1948- *WhoHisp 92*
**Zepeda**, Rafael *DrAPF 91*
**Zepeda**, Susan Ghozeil 1946- *WhoWest 92*
**Zepf**, Thomas Herman 1935- *AmMWSc 92, WhoMW 92*
**Zepfel**, William F 1925- *AmMWSc 92*
**Zephaniah**, Benjamin 1958- *ConPo 91*
**Zephrytis** *EncAmaz 91*
**Zephyrinus** *EncEarC*
**Zepos**, Constantine 1931- *IntWW 91*
**Zepp**, Edwin Andrew 1945- *AmMWSc 92*
**Zepp**, Ira G., Jr. 1929- *ConAu 135*
**Zepp**, Richard Gardner 1941- *AmMWSc 92*
**Zeppa**, Mark Harvey 1951- *WhoAmL 92*
**Zeppa**, Robert 1924- *AmMWSc 92*
**Zeppelin**, Graf von 1838-1917 *FacFETw*
**Zeppelin**, Ferdinand Von 1838-1917 *DcTwDes*
**Zeppos**, Evan Nicholas 1953- *WhoMW 92*
**Zerbe**, Anthony *IntMPA 92, WhoEnt 92*
**Zerbe**, Charles James 1951- *WhoWest 92*
**Zerbe**, John Irwin 1926- *AmMWSc 92*
**Zerbey**, Joseph Henry, IV 1942- *WhoFI 92*
**Zerbib**, Michel 1956- *WhoEnt 92*
**Zerbo**, Saye 1932- *IntWW 91*
**Zerby**, Clayton Donald 1924- *AmMWSc 92*
**Zercher**, David Lynn 1960- *WhoRel 92*
**Zerega**, W. Dennis 1946- *WhoMW 92*
**Zeren**, Richard William 1942- *AmMWSc 92*
**Zerez**, Charles Raymond 1956- *AmMWSc 92*
**Zerfas**, Janice *DrAPF 91*
**Zerfoss**, Lester Frank 1903- *WhoFI 92*
**Zerhusen**, David Edward 1955- *WhoAmL 92*
**Zerilli**, Frank J 1942- *AmMWSc 92*
**Zerin**, Edward 1920- *WhoRel 92*
**Zerin**, Steven David 1953- *WhoAmL 92*
**Zerkaulen**, Heinrich 1892-1954 *EncTR 91*
**Zerla**, Fredric James 1937- *AmMWSc 92*
**Zerlaut**, Gene Arlis 1930- *WhoWest 92*
**Zerlin**, Stanley 1929- *AmMWSc 92*
**Zermatten**, Maurice 1910- *IntWW 91*
**Zerne**, Winnie *DrAPF 91*
**Zerner**, Michael Charles 1940- *AmMWSc 92*
**Zernik**, Joseph 1955- *AmMWSc 92*
**Zernike**, Frits 1888-1966 *WhoNob 90*
**Zernov**, Nicolas 1898-1980 *DcEcMov*
**Zernova**, Ruth 1919- *IntAu&W 91*
**Zernow**, Louis 1916- *AmMWSc 92, WhoWest 92*
**Zero**, Domenick Thomas 1949- *AmMWSc 92*
**Zeroka**, Daniel 1941- *AmMWSc 92*
**Zeronian**, Sarkis Haig 1932- *AmMWSc 92*
**Zerounian**, Ara 1926- *WhoEnt 92*
**Zerounian**, Peruz 1924- *WhoEnt 92*
**Zerr**, Donna 1964- *WhoMW 92*
**Zerr**, Frank Michael 1949- *WhoMW 92*
**Zerres**, Michael Brian 1962- *WhoAmL 92*
**Zertuche**, Antonio *WhoHisp 92*
**Zerweck**, Richard, Jr. 1932- *WhoFI 92*
**Zerwekh**, Charles Ezra, Jr 1922- *AmMWSc 92*
**Zerwekh**, Robert Paul 1939- *AmMWSc 92*
**Zerynthia** *EncAmaz 91*
**Zerzan**, Charles Joseph, Jr. 1921- *WhoWest 92*
**Zess**, Ronald George 1938- *WhoRel 92*
**Zeta** 1818-1894 *ScFEYrs*
**Zetford**, Tully *IntAu&W 91X, TwCSFW 91*
**Zetik**, Donald Frank 1938- *AmMWSc 92*
**Zetkin**, Clara 1857-1933 *EncTR 91 [port]*
**Zetland**, Marquess of 1937- *Who 92*
**Zetler**, Bernard David 1915- *AmMWSc 92*
**Zetlmeisl**, Michael Joseph 1942- *AmMWSc 92, WhoMW 92*
**Zettel**, Ellen Lynn 1956- *WhoMW 92*
**Zettel**, Larry Joseph 1944- *AmMWSc 92*
**Zetter**, Bruce Robert 1946- *AmMWSc 92*
**Zetter**, Paul Isaac 1923- *Who 92*
**Zetterberg**, Christer 1941- *IntWW 91, Who 92*
**Zetterberg**, Stephen Ingersoll 1916- *WhoAmP 91*
**Zetterling**, Mai *ReelWom*
**Zetterling**, Mai 1925- *IntAu&W 91, IntDcF 2-2, IntMPA 92, WrDr 92*
**Zetterling**, Mai Elisabeth 1925- *IntWW 91*
**Zetterling**, Mai Elizabeth 1925- *Who 92*
**Zetterlund**, Doreen 1961- *WhoEnt 92*
**Zettick**, Elaine Petuch 1934- *WhoAmP 91*
**Zettl**, Alex 1956- *WhoWest 92*
**Zettl**, Anton 1935- *AmMWSc 92*
**Zettlemoyer**, Albert Charles 1915- *AmMWSc 92*
**Zettler**, Francis William 1938- *AmMWSc 92*
**Zettner**, Alfred 1928- *AmMWSc 92*
**Zetts**, Kathryn Ann 1956- *WhoEnt 92*
**Zetzer**, Robert S 1930- *WhoIns 92*
**Zeumault**, Dianne Lorraine 1962- *WhoBlA 92*
**Zeuske**, Cathy Susan 1958- *WhoAmP 91*
**Zeuxo of Argos** *EncAmaz 91*
**Zeuxo of Cyrene** *EncAmaz 91*
**Zevi**, Bruno 1918- *IntWW 91*
**Zevin**, Robert Brooke 1936- *WhoFI 92*
**Zevnik**, Francis C 1922- *AmMWSc 92*
**Zevnik**, Paul A. 1950- *WhoAmL 92*
**Zevon**, Warren 1947- *WhoEnt 92*
**Zevos**, Nicholas 1932- *AmMWSc 92*
**Zewail**, Ahmed H 1946- *AmMWSc 92*
**Zey**, Robert L 1932- *AmMWSc 92*
**Zeybek**, Namik Kemal 1944- *IntWW 91*
**Zeyen**, Richard John 1943- *AmMWSc 92*
**Zeyher**, Mark Lewis 1953- *WhoFI 92*
**Zezima**, Ronald 1953- *WhoAmL 92*
**Zezza**, Myrna Mazzola 1938- *WhoWest 92*
**Zfass**, Alvin Martin 1931- *AmMWSc 92*
**Zganjar**, Edward F 1938- *AmMWSc 92*
**Zgorski**, Robert Francis 1952- *WhoIns 92*
**Z'graggen**, John Anton 1932- *WhoRel 92*
**Zhabotinsky**, Leonid Ivanovich 1938- *SovUnBD*
**Zhang Aiping** 1910- *IntWW 91*
**Zhang Boxiang** 1918- *IntWW 91*
**Zhang Caiqian** 1912- *IntWW 91*
**Zhang Chengzhi** 1948- *IntWW 91*
**Zhang Chungqiao** *FacFETw*
**Zhang Chunqiao** 1911?- *IntWW 91*
**Zhang Gensheng** 1923- *IntWW 91*
**Zhang Jianmin** 1931- *IntWW 91*
**Zhang Jie** 1937- *ConAu 133, IntWW 91*
**Zhang Jingfu** 1914- *IntWW 91*
**Zhang Jingli** 1911- *IntWW 91*
**Zhang Joufu** 1940- *IntWW 91*
**Zhang Jun** 1919- *IntWW 91*
**Zhang Miman** 1936- *IntWW 91*
**Zhang Renzhi** 1935- *IntWW 91*
**Zhang Shou** 1930- *IntWW 91*
**Zhang Shuguang** 1923- *IntWW 91*
**Zhang Tangmin** 1939- *IntWW 91*
**Zhang Tingfa** 1917- *IntWW 91*
**Zhang Wannian** 1928- *IntWW 91*
**Zhang Wanxin** 1930- *IntWW 91*
**Zhang Weixun** *IntWW 91*
**Zhang Wenjin** d1991 *IntWW 91N, NewYTBS 91*
**Zhang Wenshou** *IntWW 91*
**Zhang Wenyu** 1910- *IntWW 91*
**Zhang Xian** 1934- *IntWW 91*
**Zhang Xiang** 1919- *IntWW 91*
**Zhang Xiangshan** 1914- *IntWW 91*

**Zhang Xianliang** 1936- *IntWW 91*
**Zhang Xinxin** 1953- *ConAu 134, IntWW 91, LiExTwC*
**Zhang Xiushan** 1910- *IntWW 91*
**Zhang Xueliang** 1902- *FacFETw*
**Zhang Yanning** 1927- *IntWW 91*
**Zhang Yimou** 1951- *IntWW 91*
**Zhang Youyu** 1899- *IntWW 91*
**Zhang Yu** 1957- *IntWW 91*
**Zhang Zai** *IntWW 91*
**Zhang Zaiwang** 1918- *IntWW 91*
**Zhang Zhen** 1914- *IntWW 91*
**Zhang Zhixiu** 1916- *IntWW 91*
**Zhang Zhongjun** 1923- *IntWW 91*
**Zhang Zhongxian** 1926- *IntWW 91*
**Zhang Zhu** 1929- *IntWW 91*
**Zhang,** Bing-Rong 1944- *AmMWSc 92*
**Zhang,** Chengzhi 1948- *IntAu&W 91*
**Zhang,** Jiming 1955- *WhoMW 92*
**Zhang,** John Zeng Hui 1961- *AmMWSc 92*
**Zhang,** Lixia 1951- *WhoWest 92*
**Zhang,** Qiming 1957- *AmMWSc 92*
**Zhang,** Samuel Xiangyu 1957- *WhoAmL 92*
**Zhang,** Xian 1934- *IntAu&W 91*
**Zhang,** Xiaonan 1957- *WhoFI 92*
**Zhao Cangbi** 1916- *IntWW 91*
**Zhao Di** 1938- *IntWW 91*
**Zhao Dongwan** 1926- *IntWW 91*
**Zhao Feng** 1916- *IntWW 91*
**Zhao Fusan** 1926- *IntWW 91*
**Zhao Haifeng** 1921- *IntWW 91*
**Zhao Jianmin** 1910- *IntWW 91*
**Zhao Pengfei** 1920- *IntWW 91*
**Zhao Puchu** 1907- *IntWW 91*
**Zhao Ruichun** 1935- *IntWW 91*
**Zhao Weichen** 1929- *IntWW 91*
**Zhao Wucheng** *IntWW 91*
**Zhao Xinchu** 1915- *IntWW 91*
**Zhao Xiu** 1921- *IntWW 91*
**Zhao Yanxia** 1930- *IntWW 91*
**Zhao Zengyi** 1920- *IntWW 91*
**Zhao Zhongxian** 1941- *IntWW 91*
**Zhao Ziyang** 1918- *FacFETw*
**Zhao Ziyang** 1919- *IntWW 91, Who 92*
**Zhao Ziyue** 1909- *IntWW 91*
**Zhao Zongnai** 1927- *IntWW 91*
**Zharoff,** Fred F *WhoAmP 91*
**Zharov,** Mikhail Ivanovich 1900-1981 *SovUnBD*
**Zhavoronkov,** Nikolay Mikhailovich d1990 *IntWW 91N*
**Zhaxi Wangqug** 1913- *IntWW 91*
**Zhdanov,** Andrei Alexandrovich 1896-1948 *FacFETw*
**Zhdanov,** Andrey Aleksandrovich 1896-1948 *SovUnBD*
**Zheimo,** Yanina Boleslavovna 1909- *SovUnBD*
**Zhelev,** Zhelyu 1935- *IntWW 91*
**Zheludev,** Ivan Stepanovich 1921- *IntWW 91*
**Zhelutka,** Mara 1949- *WhoEnt 92, WhoWest 92*
**Zhelyabuzhsky,** Yuriy Andreevich 1888-1955 *SovUnBD*
**Zheng Guangdi** 1935- *IntWW 91*
**Zheng Min** 1920- *LiExTwC*
**Zheng Tianxiang** 1914- *IntWW 91*
**Zheng Tuobin** *IntWW 91*
**Zheng Weishan** 1914- *IntWW 91*
**Zheng Weizhi** 1912- *IntWW 91*
**Zheng,** Henry R. 1955- *WhoAmL 92*
**Zheng,** Xiaoci 1949- *AmMWSc 92*
**Zheng,** Youlu 1942- *WhoWest 92*
**Zheng,** Yuan Fang 1946- *AmMWSc 92*
**Zheng,** Zhao-Chang 1933- *IntAu&W 91*
**Zheutlin,** Cathy Lee 1951- *WhoEnt 92*
**Zhidkov,** Yakov Ivanovich 1888-1969 *SovUnBD*
**Zhilinsky,** Dmitriy Dmitrievich 1927- *SovUnBD*
**Zhirmunsky,** Viktor Maksimovich 1891-1971 *SovUnBD*
**Zhivkov,** Todor 1911- *FacFETw, IntWW 91*
**Zhivkov,** Zhivko 1915- *IntWW 91*
**Zhizneva,** Ol'ga Andreevna 1899-1972 *SovUnBD*
**Zholkovsky,** Alexander K. 1937- *ConAu 133*
**Zholtovsky,** Ivan Vladislavovich 1867-1959 *SovUnBD*
**Zhong Ming** 1949- *IntWW 91*
**Zhordnia,** Noah Nikolayevich 1870-1953 *FacFETw*
**Zhou Guangzhao** 1929- *IntWW 91*
**Zhou Gucheng** 1898- *IntWW 91*
**Zhou Hui** *IntWW 91*
**Zhou Jianfu** 1937- *IntWW 91*
**Zhou Jiannan** 1917- *IntWW 91*
**Zhou Jue** *IntWW 91*
**Zhou Keqin** d1990 *IntWW 91N*
**Zhou Lin** 1905- *IntWW 91*
**Zhou Long** 1953- *ConCom 92*
**Zhou Mingzhen** 1918- *IntWW 91*
**Zhou Nan** 1927- *IntWW 91*
**Zhou Peiyuan** 1902- *IntWW 91*
**Zhou Shizhong** *IntWW 91*
**Zhou Weizhi** 1916- *IntWW 91*
**Zhou Yang** 1907-1989 *FacFETw*
**Zhou Youguang** 1906- *IntWW 91*
**Zhou Zijian** 1914- *IntWW 91*
**Zhou,** Chiping 1957- *WhoWest 92*
**Zhou,** Simon Zheng 1942- *AmMWSc 92*
**Zhou,** Tong 1945- *WhoWest 92*
**Zhu Guang** 1911- *IntWW 91*
**Zhu Guangya** 1924- *IntWW 91*
**Zhu Houze** 1931- *IntWW 91*
**Zhu Jianhua** 1962- *IntWW 91*
**Zhu Lin** 1926- *IntWW 91*
**Zhu Mingshan** 1937- *IntWW 91*
**Zhu Muzhi** 1916- *IntWW 91*
**Zhu Qizhan** 1891- *IntWW 91*
**Zhu Qizhen** 1928- *IntWW 91*
**Zhu Rongji** 1928- *IntWW 91*
**Zhu Xuefan** 1905- *IntWW 91*
**Zhu Xun** 1937- *IntWW 91*
**Zhu,** Ai-Lan 1956- *WhoEnt 92*
**Zhu,** Jun 1957- *WhoWest 92*
**Zhu,** Mingde 1940- *WhoWest 92*
**Zhuang Xiaohui** 1913- *IntWW 91*
**Zhuchenko,** Alexander Alexandrovich 1935- *IntWW 91*
**Zhukoborsky,** Savely L. 1932- *WhoWest 92*
**Zhukov,** Georgi Alexandrovich 1908- *Who 92*
**Zhukov,** Georgi Konstantinovich 1896-1974 *EncTR 91 [port], FacFETw [port]*
**Zhukov,** Georgiy Konstantinovich 1896-1974 *SovUnBD*
**Zhukov,** Nikolay Nikolaevich 1908-1973 *SovUnBD*
**Zhuravlev,** Gennadi Kirillovich 1924- *IntWW 91*
**Zhurkin,** Vitaliy Vladimirovich 1928- *IntWW 91, SovUnBD*
**Zia,** Begum Khalida *IntWW 91*
**Zia,** Paul Z 1926- *AmMWSc 92*
**Zia,** Royce K P 1943- *AmMWSc 92*
**Zia ul-Haq,** Muhammad 1924-1988 *FacFETw*
**Ziarko,** Charles Jerome 1941- *WhoEnt 92*
**Ziaur Rahman** 1936-1981 *FacFETw*
**Ziboh,** Vincent Azubike 1932- *AmMWSc 92*
**Zic,** Eric A 1962- *AmMWSc 92*
**Ziccardi,** Robert John 1946- *AmMWSc 92*
**Zichek,** Melvin Eddie 1918- *WhoMW 92, WhoRel 92*
**Zichichi,** Antonino 1929- *IntWW 91*
**Zick,** Kenneth Adolph 1949- *WhoAmL 92*
**Zick,** Leonard Otto 1905- *WhoFI 92*
**Zick,** Lyn 1930- *WhoRel 92*
**Zickel,** John 1919- *AmMWSc 92*
**Zicker,** Eldon Louis 1920- *AmMWSc 92*
**Zickgraf,** Eric Charles 1951- *WhoMW 92*
**Zickus,** Anne *WhoAmP 91*
**Zidbeck,** William Edward 1932- *WhoWest 92*
**Zide,** Larry M. 1954- *IntMPA 92*
**Zide,** Michael 1932- *IntMPA 92*
**Zide-Booth,** Rochelle Deena 1938- *WhoEnt 92*
**Zidek,** James Victor 1939- *AmMWSc 92*
**Zidulka,** Arnold 1941- *AmMWSc 92*
**Ziebarth,** Timothy Dean 1946- *AmMWSc 92*
**Ziebert,** Ann Marie 1962- *WhoMW 92*
**Ziebur,** Allen Douglas 1923- *AmMWSc 92*
**Ziech,** William Alan 1962- *WhoRel 92*
**Ziedelis,** Robert E. 1961- *WhoEnt 92*
**Zieff,** Howard 1943- *IntMPA 92*
**Zieg,** Roger Grant 1939- *AmMWSc 92*
**Ziegel,** Bari Ann 1959- *WhoFI 92*
**Ziegelbauer,** Constance Martina 1937- *WhoMW 92*
**Ziegenbusch,** Ted Wayne 1951- *WhoEnt 92, WhoWest 92*
**Ziegenfus,** William John 1942- *WhoRel 92*
**Ziegenhagen,** Allyn James 1935- *AmMWSc 92*
**Ziegenhorn,** Angela Felicia 1965- *WhoAmL 92*
**Ziegenhorn,** Dennis 1947- *WhoAmP 91*
**Zieger,** Herman Ernst 1935- *AmMWSc 92*
**Ziegfeld,** Florenz 1867?-1932 *RComAH*
**Ziegfeld,** Florenz, Jr. 1867-1932 *NewAmDM*
**Ziegler,** Adolf 1892-1959 *EncTR 91 [port]*
**Ziegler,** Alan *DrAPF 91*
**Ziegler,** Alfred M 1938- *AmMWSc 92*
**Ziegler,** Archibald 1903- *TwCPaSc*
**Ziegler,** Arthur B. 1930- *WhoFI 92*
**Ziegler,** Bernard Carl, III 1949- *WhoMW 92*
**Ziegler,** Bette *DrAPF 91*
**Ziegler,** Carole L 1946- *AmMWSc 92*
**Ziegler,** Charles Louis 1926- *WhoMW 92*
**Ziegler,** Charles Louis, Jr. 1957- *WhoMW 92*
**Ziegler,** Christopher George 1965- *WhoFI 92*
**Ziegler,** Daniel 1927- *AmMWSc 92*
**Ziegler,** Darold E. 1951- *WhoWest 92*
**Ziegler,** David Carl 1954- *WhoMW 92*
**Ziegler,** Delores *WhoEnt 92*
**Ziegler,** Dewey Kiper 1920- *AmMWSc 92*
**Ziegler,** Dhyana 1949- *WhoBlA 92*
**Ziegler,** Donald Emil 1936- *WhoAmL 92*
**Ziegler,** Earl Keller 1929- *WhoRel 92*
**Ziegler,** Edward N 1938- *AmMWSc 92*
**Ziegler,** Ekhard E 1940- *AmMWSc 92*
**Ziegler,** Eldon A 1939- *WhoIns 92*
**Ziegler,** Frederick Dixon 1933- *AmMWSc 92*
**Ziegler,** Frederick Edward 1938- *AmMWSc 92*
**Ziegler,** George William, Jr 1916- *AmMWSc 92*
**Ziegler,** Hans K 1911- *AmMWSc 92*
**Ziegler,** Harry Kirk 1951- *AmMWSc 92*
**Ziegler,** Henri Alexandre Leonard 1906- *IntWW 91, Who 92*
**Ziegler,** Henry Steinway 1933- *WhoAmL 92*
**Ziegler,** Hubert 1924- *IntWW 91*
**Ziegler,** James Edward 1947- *WhoMW 92*
**Ziegler,** James Francis 1939- *AmMWSc 92*
**Ziegler,** James Russell 1922- *WhoFI 92*
**Ziegler,** Jean 1934- *IntWW 91*
**Ziegler,** Jesse H. 1913- *WhoRel 92*
**Ziegler,** Joan Avis 1960- *WhoAmL 92*
**Ziegler,** John 1929- *WhoRel 92*
**Ziegler,** John Benjamin 1917- *AmMWSc 92*
**Ziegler,** John Henry, Jr 1924- *AmMWSc 92*
**Ziegler,** Karl 1898-1973 *WhoNob 90*
**Ziegler,** Kenneth James 1950- *WhoMW 92*
**Ziegler,** Levi John 1931- *WhoRel 92*
**Ziegler,** Martin Arthur Erich 1931- *IntWW 91*
**Ziegler,** Michael Gregory 1946- *AmMWSc 92*
**Ziegler,** Michael Robert 1942- *AmMWSc 92*
**Ziegler,** Miriam Mary 1945- *AmMWSc 92*
**Ziegler,** Paul Fout 1916- *AmMWSc 92*
**Ziegler,** Peter 1922- *AmMWSc 92*
**Ziegler,** Peter Alfred 1928- *IntWW 91*
**Ziegler,** Philip 1929- *WrDr 92*
**Ziegler,** Philip Sandeman 1929- *IntWW 91, Who 92*
**Ziegler,** R.W., Jr. *WhoWest 92*
**Ziegler,** Richard James 1943- *AmMWSc 92*
**Ziegler,** Robert C 1927- *AmMWSc 92*
**Ziegler,** Robert E. 1950- *WhoMW 92*
**Ziegler,** Robert G 1924- *AmMWSc 92*
**Ziegler,** Robert Harold 1949- *WhoEnt 92*
**Ziegler,** Ronald Louis 1939- *WhoAmP 91*
**Ziegler,** Theresa Frances *AmMWSc 92*
**Ziegler,** William, III 1928- *WhoFI 92*
**Ziegler,** William Alexander 1924- *WhoAmL 92*
**Ziegler,** William Arthur 1924- *AmMWSc 92*
**Zieglert,** Philip Sandeman 1929- *IntAu&W 91*
**Zieglowsky,** Debby Jo 1953- *WhoMW 92*
**Ziegra,** Alice Stevenson 1927- *WhoAmP 91*
**Ziegra,** Sumner Root 1923- *AmMWSc 92*
**Ziehler,** Margaret Ann *WhoMW 92*
**Ziel,** Catherine Agnes 1949- *WhoRel 92*
**Zielen,** Albin John 1925- *AmMWSc 92*
**Zielenkiewicz,** Wojciech 1933- *IntWW 91*
**Zielezny,** Maria Anna 1939- *AmMWSc 92*
**Zielezny,** Zbigniew Henryk 1930- *AmMWSc 92*
**Zielinski,** Adam 1943- *AmMWSc 92*
**Zielinski,** Charles Anthony 1944- *WhoAmL 92*
**Zielinski,** Lisa A. 1957- *WhoFI 92*
**Zielinski,** Thaddeus F. 1904- *RelLAm 91*
**Zielinski,** Theresa Julia *AmMWSc 92*
**Zielke,** H Ronald 1942- *AmMWSc 92*
**Zielke,** Laurence John 1949- *WhoAmL 92*
**Zielonka,** David M. 1935- *WhoRel 92*
**Ziem,** Jochen 1932- *LiExTwC*
**Ziem,** Jochen 1952- *IntWW 91*
**Zieman,** John Wayne 1958- *WhoRel 92*
**Zieman,** Joseph Crowe, Jr 1943- *AmMWSc 92*
**Ziemann,** August Howard 1963- *WhoEnt 92*
**Ziemann,** Edward Frances 1944- *WhoMW 92*
**Ziemann,** G. Patrick 1941- *WhoRel 92, WhoWest 92*
**Ziemann,** Jody Ann 1957- *WhoMW 92*
**Ziemba,** W T *AmMWSc 92*
**Ziemer,** John Robert 1939- *WhoMW 92*
**Ziemer,** Marlyn E 1936- *WhoIns 92*
**Ziemer,** Paul L 1935- *AmMWSc 92*
**Ziemer,** Robert Ruhl 1937- *AmMWSc 92*
**Ziemer,** Rodger Edmund 1937- *AmMWSc 92*
**Ziemer,** William P 1934- *AmMWSc 92*
**Zieminski,** S A 1905- *AmMWSc 92*
**Ziemke,** Earl F. 1922- *WrDr 92*
**Ziemkowski,** James Anthony 1936- *WhoWest 92*
**Ziemniak,** Stephen Eric 1942- *AmMWSc 92*
**Zien,** Burt 1912- *WhoAmP 91*
**Zien,** David A 1950- *WhoAmP 91*
**Zien,** Tse-Fou 1937- *AmMWSc 92*
**Zienius,** Raymond Henry 1934- *AmMWSc 92*
**Zienkiewicz,** Olgierd Cecil 1921- *IntWW 91, Who 92*
**Zientara,** James Edward 1943- *WhoFI 92*
**Zienty,** Ferdinand B 1915- *AmMWSc 92*
**Zienty,** Ferdinand Benjamin 1915- *WhoMW 92*
**Zier,** John Albert 1919- *WhoMW 92*
**Zierdt,** Charles Henry 1922- *AmMWSc 92*
**Ziering,** Lance K 1939- *AmMWSc 92*
**Zierler,** Kenneth 1917- *AmMWSc 92*
**Zierler,** Neal 1926- *AmMWSc 92*
**Ziernicki,** Richard Mieczyslaw 1950- *WhoWest 92*
**Ziernicki,** Robert S 1934- *AmMWSc 92*
**Ziesel,** Kurt 1911- *EncTR 91*
**Zieserl,** Robert Michael 1947- *WhoMW 92*
**Ziesk,** Edra *DrAPF 91*
**Zieske,** James David *AmMWSc 92*
**Zietlow,** E. R. 1932- *WrDr 92*
**Zietlow,** Edward R 1932- *TwCWW 91*
**Zietlow,** Harold Howard 1926- *WhoMW 92, WhoRel 92*
**Zietlow,** James Philip 1921- *AmMWSc 92*
**Zietz,** Joachim 1953- *WhoFI 92*
**Zietz,** Joseph R, Jr 1925- *AmMWSc 92*
**Zietz,** Karyl Lynn Kopelman 1943- *WhoEnt 92*
**Ziev,** Joel David 1941- *WhoRel 92*
**Zieve,** Leslie 1915- *AmMWSc 92, WhoMW 92*
**Ziff,** Irwin 1929- *WhoEnt 92*
**Ziff,** Larzer 1927- *WrDr 92*
**Ziff,** Lloyd Richard 1942- *WhoAmL 92*
**Ziff,** Morris 1913- *AmMWSc 92*
**Ziffer,** Herman 1930- *AmMWSc 92*
**Ziffer,** Jack 1918- *AmMWSc 92*
**Ziffren,** Lester 1925- *WhoAmL 92*
**Ziffren,** Paul 1913-1991 *NewYTBS 91 [port]*
**Ziffrin,** Marilyn Jane 1926- *WhoEnt 92*
**Zifkin,** Walter 1936- *IntMPA 92*
**Zigal,** Thomas *DrAPF 91*
**Zigas,** Barry Herbert 1951- *WhoBlA 92*
**Zighelboim,** Jacob 1946- *AmMWSc 92*
**Ziglar,** William Larry 1938- *WhoRel 92*
**Zigler,** Edward 1930- *AmMWSc 92*
**Zigler,** Gilbert Lenk 1945- *WhoWest 92*
**Zigman,** Paul Edmond 1924- *WhoFI 92, WhoWest 92*
**Zigman,** Seymour 1932- *AmMWSc 92*
**Zigmond,** Michael Jonathan 1941- *AmMWSc 92*
**Zigmond,** Richard Eric 1944- *AmMWSc 92*
**Zigmond,** Sally H 1944- *AmMWSc 92*
**Zigmunt,** Ted John 1951- *WhoEnt 92*
**Zigrang,** Denis Joseph 1926- *AmMWSc 92*
**Zihlman,** Adrienne Louella 1940- *AmMWSc 92*
**Zijlstra,** Jelle 1918- *IntWW 91, Who 92*
**Zikakis,** John Philip 1933- *AmMWSc 92*
**Zikmund,** Barbara Brown 1939- *WhoRel 92*
**Zil,** John Stephen 1947- *WhoWest 92*
**Zilahy,** Lajos 1891-1974 *LiExTwC*
**Zilber,** Joseph Abraham 1923- *AmMWSc 92*
**Zilber,** Maurice Leonard 1938- *WhoAmL 92*
**Zilberberg,** Nahum Norbert 1925- *WhoEnt 92*
**Zilch,** Karl T 1921- *AmMWSc 92*
**Zilczer,** Janet Ann 1955- *AmMWSc 92*
**Zildjian,** Armand Arthur 1921- *WhoEnt 92*
**Zile,** Maija Helene 1929- *AmMWSc 92*
**Zile,** Zigurds Laimons 1927- *WhoAmL 92*
**Ziler,** Raymond *WhoWest 92*
**Zilinskas,** Barbara Ann 1947- *AmMWSc 92*
**Zilinskas,** Matthew Jerome 1947- *WhoFI 92*
**Ziliox,** Marc *WrDr 92*
**Zilke,** Samuel 1914- *AmMWSc 92*
**Zilkey,** Bryan Frederick 1941- *AmMWSc 92*
**Zilkha,** Daniel Abdulla 1942- *WhoFI 92*
**Zilkha,** Ezra Khedouri 1925- *WhoFI 92*
**Zilkha,** Selim Khedoury 1927- *Who 92*
**Zill,** Leonard Peter 1920- *AmMWSc 92*
**Ziller,** John Harmon 1947- *WhoFI 92*
**Ziller,** Stephen A, Jr 1938- *AmMWSc 92*
**Ziller,** Stephen Anthony 1913- *WhoMW 92*
**Ziller,** Stephen Anthony, Jr. 1938- *WhoMW 92*
**Zilli,** Sergio J 1936- *WhoAmP 91*
**Zillich,** Heinrich 1898- *EncTR 91*
**Zilly,** Thomas Samuel 1935- *WhoAmL 92, WhoWest 92*
**Zilversmit,** Donald Berthold 1919- *AmMWSc 92*

**Zilz**, Melvin Leonard 1932- *AmMWSc 92, WhoMW 92, WhoRel 92*
**Zim**, Herbert S. 1909- *WrDr 92*
**Zima**, Philip Stanley *WhoMW 92*
**Ziman**, John Michael 1925- *IntWW 91, Who 92*
**Zimand**, Harvey Folks 1928- *WhoAmL 92*
**Zimany**, Roland Daniel 1936- *WhoRel 92*
**Zimar**, Frank 1918- *AmMWSc 92*
**Zimbalist**, Efrem 1890-1985 *NewAmDM*
**Zimbalist**, Efrem, Jr. 1923- *IntMPA 92*
**Zimbalist**, Efrem, Sr 1890-1985 *FacFETw*
**Zimbalist**, Stephanie 1956- *IntMPA 92*
**Zimbelman**, James Ray 1954- *AmMWSc 92*
**Zimbelman**, Robert George 1930- *AmMWSc 92*
**Zimbert**, Richard *IntMPA 92*
**Zimbler**, Brian Lewis 1958- *WhoAmL 92*
**Zimbrick**, John David 1938- *AmMWSc 92*
**Zimdahl**, Robert Lawrence 1935- *AmMWSc 92*
**Zimelman**, Nathan 1921- *ConAu 133, SmATA 65*
**Zimering**, Shimshon 1933- *AmMWSc 92*
**Zimerman**, Krystian 1956- *IntWW 91*
**Zimermann**, Alfred Earle 1951- *WhoWest 92*
**Zimin**, Aleksandr Aleksandrovich 1920- *IntWW 91*
**Ziminski**, Richard William 1934- *WhoFI 92*
**Zimkas**, Charles Patrick, Jr. 1940- *WhoWest 92*
**Zimm**, Bruno Hasbrouck 1920- *AmMWSc 92, IntWW 91*
**Zimm**, Carl B 1954- *AmMWSc 92*
**Zimm**, Georgianna Grevatt 1917- *AmMWSc 92*
**Zimmack**, Harold Lincoln 1925- *AmMWSc 92*
**Zimman**, Richard Neil 1951- *WhoMW 92*
**Zimmer**, Arthur James 1914- *AmMWSc 92*
**Zimmer**, Barbara Ann 1936- *WhoAmP 91*
**Zimmer**, Carl R 1927- *AmMWSc 92*
**Zimmer**, David E 1935- *AmMWSc 92*
**Zimmer**, David Lee 1952- *WhoFI 92*
**Zimmer**, David Rodney 1946- *WhoFI 92*
**Zimmer**, Dick 1944- *AlmAP 92 [port]*
**Zimmer**, Dirk 1943- *SmATA 65 [port]*
**Zimmer**, Donald William 1931- *WhoMW 92*
**Zimmer**, Elizabeth Anne 1951- *AmMWSc 92*
**Zimmer**, G A 1921- *AmMWSc 92*
**Zimmer**, Hans 1921- *AmMWSc 92*
**Zimmer**, James Griffith 1932- *AmMWSc 92*
**Zimmer**, Jan 1926- *ConCom 92*
**Zimmer**, Jeff B. 1958- *WhoEnt 92*
**Zimmer**, John Herman 1922- *WhoAmL 92, WhoMW 92*
**Zimmer**, Louis George 1926- *AmMWSc 92*
**Zimmer**, Mark Vance 1960- *WhoWest 92*
**Zimmer**, Markus Bernard 1946- *WhoWest 92*
**Zimmer**, Martin F 1929- *AmMWSc 92*
**Zimmer**, Melvin Neil 1938- *WhoAmP 91*
**Zimmer**, Paul *DrAPF 91*
**Zimmer**, Paul 1934- *ConPo 91*
**Zimmer**, Paul J. 1934- *WrDr 92*
**Zimmer**, Paula 1956- *WhoAmP 91*
**Zimmer**, Richard Alan 1944- *WhoAmP 91*
**Zimmer**, Russel Leonard 1931- *AmMWSc 92*
**Zimmer**, Russell W 1926- *WhoAmP 91*
**Zimmer**, Stephen George 1942- *AmMWSc 92*
**Zimmer**, Thomas Michael 1941- *WhoAmL 92*
**Zimmer**, Todd Buchanan 1957- *WhoEnt 92*
**Zimmer**, Walter C 1935- *WhoIns 92*
**Zimmer**, William Frederick, Jr 1923- *AmMWSc 92*
**Zimmerberg**, Hyman Joseph 1921- *AmMWSc 92*
**Zimmerer**, Robert P 1929- *AmMWSc 92*
**Zimmerer**, Robert W 1929- *AmMWSc 92*
**Zimmering**, Stanley 1924- *AmMWSc 92*
**Zimmerman**, Adam Hartley 1927- *WhoWest 92*
**Zimmerman**, Ann Gray 1957- *WhoMW 92*
**Zimmerman**, Arnold I. 1946- *WhoWest 92*
**Zimmerman**, Arthur Maurice 1929- *AmMWSc 92*
**Zimmerman**, Barry 1938- *AmMWSc 92*
**Zimmerman**, Barry 1941- *AmMWSc 92*
**Zimmerman**, Barry Lewis 1951- *WhoAmL 92*
**Zimmerman**, Ben George 1934- *AmMWSc 92*
**Zimmerman**, Bernard 1946- *WhoAmL 92*
**Zimmerman**, C Duane 1935- *AmMWSc 92*
**Zimmerman**, Carle Clark, Jr 1934- *AmMWSc 92*
**Zimmerman**, Carol Jean 1951- *AmMWSc 92*
**Zimmerman**, Charles D. 1957- *WhoAmL 92*
**Zimmerman**, Charles Daniel, III 1941- *WhoIns 92*
**Zimmerman**, Charles J. 1902- *IntWW 91*
**Zimmerman**, Cheryl Lea 1953- *AmMWSc 92*
**Zimmerman**, Craig Arthur 1937- *AmMWSc 92*
**Zimmerman**, Curtis Roy 1942- *WhoRel 92*
**Zimmerman**, Dale A 1928- *AmMWSc 92*
**Zimmerman**, Daniel Hill 1941- *AmMWSc 92*
**Zimmerman**, Daniel Ray 1948- *WhoRel 92*
**Zimmerman**, Dava Lynn 1953- *WhoWest 92*
**Zimmerman**, David Walter 1945- *WhoFI 92*
**Zimmerman**, Dean R 1932- *AmMWSc 92*
**Zimmerman**, Deborah Jean 1950- *WhoIns 92*
**Zimmerman**, Delano Elmer 1933- *WhoMW 92*
**Zimmerman**, Derk *LesBEnT 92 [port]*
**Zimmerman**, Diane Leenheer 1941- *WhoAmL 92*
**Zimmerman**, Don *WhoEnt 92*
**Zimmerman**, Don Alan 1940- *WhoAmP 91*
**Zimmerman**, Don Charles 1934- *AmMWSc 92*
**Zimmerman**, Donald Nathan 1932- *AmMWSc 92*
**Zimmerman**, Donald Patrick 1942- *WhoAmL 92*
**Zimmerman**, Doris Lucile 1942- *WhoMW 92*
**Zimmerman**, Earl Abram 1937- *AmMWSc 92*
**Zimmerman**, Earl Graves 1943- *AmMWSc 92*
**Zimmerman**, Edward John 1924- *AmMWSc 92*
**Zimmerman**, Edward M 1942- *WhoAmP 91*
**Zimmerman**, Edwin Morton 1924- *WhoAmL 92*
**Zimmerman**, Elmer Leroy 1921- *AmMWSc 92*
**Zimmerman**, Emery Gilroy 1939- *AmMWSc 92*
**Zimmerman**, Ernest Frederick 1933- *AmMWSc 92*
**Zimmerman**, Eugene 1947- *WhoBlA 92*
**Zimmerman**, Eugene Munro 1940- *AmMWSc 92*
**Zimmerman**, Franklin 1923- *WrDr 92*
**Zimmerman**, Franklin Bershir 1924- *WhoEnt 92*
**Zimmerman**, Gail D 1933- *WhoAmP 91*
**Zimmerman**, Gary Alan 1938- *AmMWSc 92*
**Zimmerman**, George Landis 1920- *AmMWSc 92*
**Zimmerman**, George Ogurek 1935- *AmMWSc 92*
**Zimmerman**, Grenith Johnson 1936- *WhoWest 92*
**Zimmerman**, Harold Samuel 1923- *WhoAmP 91, WhoWest 92*
**Zimmerman**, Harry Martin 1901- *AmMWSc 92*
**Zimmerman**, Howard Elliot 1926- *AmMWSc 92, IntWW 91*
**Zimmerman**, Howard Irwin 1930- *WhoEnt 92*
**Zimmerman**, Hyman Joseph 1914- *AmMWSc 92*
**Zimmerman**, Ira E. 1955- *WhoAmL 92*
**Zimmerman**, Irwin David 1931- *AmMWSc 92*
**Zimmerman**, Ivan Harold 1943- *AmMWSc 92*
**Zimmerman**, Jack McKay 1927- *AmMWSc 92*
**Zimmerman**, Jacob W 1930- *WhoAmP 91*
**Zimmerman**, James F 1946- *WhoAmP 91*
**Zimmerman**, James Kenneth 1943- *AmMWSc 92*
**Zimmerman**, James M. 1944- *WhoFI 92*
**Zimmerman**, James Roland 1958- *WhoMW 92*
**Zimmerman**, James Roscoe 1928- *AmMWSc 92*
**Zimmerman**, Jamie *WhoEnt 92*
**Zimmerman**, Jay Alan 1945- *AmMWSc 92*
**Zimmerman**, Jean 1947- *WhoAmL 92, WhoFI 92*
**Zimmerman**, Jim L 1927- *WhoAmP 91*
**Zimmerman**, Jo Ann 1936- *WhoAmP 91, WhoMW 92*
**Zimmerman**, Joanne *DrAPF 91*
**Zimmerman**, John Carl 1946- *WhoAmP 91*
**Zimmerman**, John F 1937- *AmMWSc 92*
**Zimmerman**, John Gordon 1916- *AmMWSc 92*
**Zimmerman**, John H. 1932- *WhoFI 92*
**Zimmerman**, John Harvey 1945- *AmMWSc 92*
**Zimmerman**, John Lester 1933- *AmMWSc 92*
**Zimmerman**, John R 1925- *AmMWSc 92*
**Zimmerman**, Joseph 1921- *AmMWSc 92*
**Zimmerman**, Joseph Francis 1928- *WrDr 92*
**Zimmerman**, Keith Wayne 1947- *WhoIns 92*
**Zimmerman**, Leonard Norman 1923- *AmMWSc 92*
**Zimmerman**, LeRoy S 1934- *WhoAmP 91*
**Zimmerman**, Lester J 1918- *AmMWSc 92*
**Zimmerman**, Linda Fran 1946- *WhoWest 92*
**Zimmerman**, Liz 1938- *WhoBlA 92*
**Zimmerman**, Lorenz Eugene 1920- *AmMWSc 92*
**Zimmerman**, Louis Seymour 1949- *WhoAmL 92*
**Zimmerman**, Martha Rosenberger 1937- *WhoMW 92*
**Zimmerman**, Mary Prislopski 1947- *AmMWSc 92*
**Zimmerman**, Maxine M 1930- *WhoAmP 91*
**Zimmerman**, Michael David 1943- *WhoAmL 92, WhoAmP 91, WhoWest 92*
**Zimmerman**, Michael Raymond 1937- *AmMWSc 92*
**Zimmerman**, Naoma 1914- *WrDr 92*
**Zimmerman**, Niel Thomas 1943- *WhoWest 92*
**Zimmerman**, Norman 1941- *AmMWSc 92*
**Zimmerman**, Norman H 1919- *AmMWSc 92*
**Zimmerman**, Peter David 1941- *AmMWSc 92*
**Zimmerman**, Philip L. 1944- *WhoEnt 92*
**Zimmerman**, Richard Clyde 1932- *WhoWest 92*
**Zimmerman**, Richard Hale 1934- *AmMWSc 92*
**Zimmerman**, Robert Allan 1938- *AmMWSc 92*
**Zimmerman**, Robert Earl 1928- *WhoAmL 92*
**Zimmerman**, Robert Lyman 1935- *AmMWSc 92*
**Zimmerman**, Rodney James 1932- *WhoMW 92*
**Zimmerman**, Roger M 1936- *AmMWSc 92*
**Zimmerman**, Roger Marvin 1932- *WhoMW 92*
**Zimmerman**, Roger Paul 1946- *AmMWSc 92*
**Zimmerman**, Russell Richard 1942- *WhoFI 92, WhoMW 92*
**Zimmerman**, Ruth *DrAPF 91*
**Zimmerman**, Samuel Lee 1923- *WhoBlA 92*
**Zimmerman**, Samuel Morton 1927- *WhoFI 92*
**Zimmerman**, Sarah E 1937- *AmMWSc 92, WhoMW 92*
**Zimmerman**, Scott Franklin 1935- *WhoAmL 92*
**Zimmerman**, Selma Blau 1930- *AmMWSc 92*
**Zimmerman**, Sheldon 1942- *WhoRel 92*
**Zimmerman**, Sheldon Bernard 1926- *AmMWSc 92*
**Zimmerman**, Stanford Lee 1937- *WhoMW 92*
**Zimmerman**, Stanley Elliot, Jr. 1947- *WhoFI 92*
**Zimmerman**, Stanley William 1907- *AmMWSc 92*
**Zimmerman**, Stephen William 1941- *AmMWSc 92*
**Zimmerman**, Steven B 1934- *AmMWSc 92*
**Zimmerman**, Stuart O 1935- *AmMWSc 92*
**Zimmerman**, Susan G. 1952- *WhoMW 92*
**Zimmerman**, Theodore Samuel 1937- *AmMWSc 92*
**Zimmerman**, Thom J 1942- *AmMWSc 92*
**Zimmerman**, Thomas Fletcher 1912-1991 *RelLAm 91*
**Zimmerman**, Thomas Paul 1942- *AmMWSc 92*
**Zimmerman**, Tommy Lynn 1943- *AmMWSc 92*
**Zimmerman**, Verlin P 1927- *WhoAmP 91*
**Zimmerman**, Walter Bruce 1933- *AmMWSc 92*
**Zimmerman**, Warren *WhoAmP 91*
**Zimmerman**, Warren Eugene 1938- *WhoAmL 92*
**Zimmerman**, William Frederick 1938- *AmMWSc 92*
**Zimmerman**, William Gene 1941- *WhoAmL 92*
**Zimmerman**, Zelma Lucille *WhoEnt 92*
**Zimmerman-Jenks**, Carla Jean 1962- *WhoMW 92*
**Zimmermann**, Arnold Walter 1913- *WrDr 92*
**Zimmermann**, Bernard 1921- *AmMWSc 92*
**Zimmermann**, Bernd Alois 1918-1970 *NewAmDM*
**Zimmermann**, Charles Edward 1930- *AmMWSc 92*
**Zimmermann**, David Scott 1955- *WhoMW 92*
**Zimmermann**, Eugene Robert 1924- *AmMWSc 92*
**Zimmermann**, F J 1924- *AmMWSc 92*
**Zimmermann**, Friedrich 1925- *IntWW 91*
**Zimmermann**, Gary Paul 1958- *WhoFI 92*
**Zimmermann**, Gerda Anna Maria 1927- *WhoEnt 92*
**Zimmermann**, H J 1916- *AmMWSc 92*
**Zimmermann**, Heinz 1921- *IntWW 91*
**Zimmermann**, Mark Edward 1952- *AmMWSc 92*
**Zimmermann**, Martin Huldrych 1926- *AmMWSc 92*
**Zimmermann**, R Erik 1941- *AmMWSc 92*
**Zimmermann**, Robert Alan 1937- *AmMWSc 92*
**Zimmermann**, Robert Laurence 1932- *WhoFI 92, WhoMW 92*
**Zimmermann**, Stephan Fritz-Peter 1945- *WhoWest 92*
**Zimmermann**, William, Jr 1930- *AmMWSc 92, WhoMW 92*
**Zimmers**, Neal Foster, Jr 1942- *WhoAmP 91*
**Zimmett**, Mark Paul 1950- *WhoAmL 92*
**Zimmie**, Thomas Frank 1939- *AmMWSc 92*
**Zimmon**, David Samuel 1933- *AmMWSc 92*
**Zimmt**, Werner Siegfried 1921- *AmMWSc 92*
**Zimny**, Marilyn Lucile 1927- *AmMWSc 92*
**Zimny**, Robert Walter 1937- *WhoMW 92*
**Zimolo**, Armando 1938- *WhoFI 92*
**Zimpel**, Lloyd *DrAPF 91*
**Zimpel**, Lloyd 1929- *WrDr 92*
**Zimprich**, Gregory John 1964- *WhoMW 92*
**Zimpritch**, James Bradford 1948- *WhoAmL 92*
**Zimring**, Franklin E. 1942- *WhoAmL 92*
**Zimring**, Lois Jacobs 1923- *AmMWSc 92*
**Zimroth**, Evan *DrAPF 91*
**Zimunya**, Musaemura 1949- *ConAu 133*
**Zinbarg**, Edward Donald 1934- *WhoFI 92*
**Zinberg**, Michael *LesBEnT 92*
**Zindel**, Bonnie 1943- *IntAu&W 91, WhoEnt 92*
**Zindel**, Paul 1936- *BenetAL 91, IntAu&W 91, WrDr 92*
**Zindell**, David *TwCSFW 91*
**Zinder**, Norton David 1928- *AmMWSc 92, IntWW 91*
**Zinder**, Stephen Henry 1950- *AmMWSc 92*
**Zindler**, Richard Eugene 1927- *AmMWSc 92*
**Zine**, Larry Joseph 1954- *WhoFI 92*
**Ziner**, Feenie *DrAPF 91*
**Zingale**, Donald Paul 1946- *WhoWest 92*
**Zingale**, Michael Carl 1923- *WhoEnt 92*
**Zingale**, Rozanne 1961- *WhoEnt 92*
**Zingarelli**, Nicola Antonio 1752-1837 *NewAmDM*
**Zingaro**, Joseph S 1928- *AmMWSc 92*
**Zingaro**, Ralph Anthony 1925- *AmMWSc 92*
**Zingeser**, Maurice Roy 1921- *AmMWSc 92*
**Zingesser**, Lawrence H 1930- *AmMWSc 92*
**Zingg**, Paul Joseph 1947- *WhoWest 92*
**Zingg**, Walter 1924- *AmMWSc 92*
**Zingman**, Edgar Alan 1923- *WhoAmL 92*
**Zingmark**, Richard G 1941- *AmMWSc 92*
**Zingula**, Richard Paul 1929- *AmMWSc 92*
**Zinik**, Zinovy 1945- *LiExTwC*
**Zink**, Charles Talbott 1937- *WhoAmL 92*
**Zink**, Frank W 1923- *AmMWSc 92*
**Zink**, Gilbert Leroy 1942- *AmMWSc 92*
**Zink**, Jeffrey Irve 1945- *AmMWSc 92*
**Zink**, Robert Edwin 1928- *AmMWSc 92, WhoMW 92*
**Zink**, Sandra 1939- *AmMWSc 92*
**Zink**, William John 1948- *WhoMW 92*
**Zinke**, Michael Duane 1954- *WhoFI 92*
**Zinke**, Otto Henry 1926- *AmMWSc 92*
**Zinke**, Paul Joseph 1920- *AmMWSc 92*
**Zinkeisen**, Anna 1901-1976 *TwCPaSc*
**Zinkeisen**, Doris 1898- *TwCPaSc*
**Zinkel**, Duane Forst 1934- *AmMWSc 92*
**Zinkham**, Robert Edward 1923- *AmMWSc 92*
**Zinkham**, William Howard 1924- *AmMWSc 92*
**Zinkin**, Taya 1918- *WrDr 92*
**Zinkl**, Joseph Grandjean 1939- *AmMWSc 92*
**Zinman**, David 1936- *NewAmDM*

**Zinman**, David Joel 1936- *IntWW 91*
**Zinman**, Jacques 1922- *WhoFI 92*
**Zinman**, Jacques S 1922- *WhoIns 92*
**Zinman**, Walter George 1929- *AmMWSc 92*
**Zinn**, Ben T 1937- *AmMWSc 92*
**Zinn**, Dale Wendel *AmMWSc 92*
**Zinn**, David Benjamin 1953- *WhoEnt 92*
**Zinn**, Dennis Bradley 1957- *WhoEnt 92*
**Zinn**, Donald Joseph 1911- *AmMWSc 92*
**Zinn**, Elmer 1918- *WhoRel 92*
**Zinn**, Gary William 1944- *AmMWSc 92*
**Zinn**, Grover Alfonso, Jr. 1937- *WhoRel 92*
**Zinn**, Howard 1922- *WrDr 92*
**Zinn**, John 1928- *AmMWSc 92*
**Zinn**, Karl 1906-1943 *EncTR 91*
**Zinn**, Marcie Lynn 1951- *WhoEnt 92*
**Zinn**, Mary Farris 1937- *WhoMW 92*
**Zinn**, Matthew P. 1964- *WhoAmL 92*
**Zinn**, Robert James 1946- *AmMWSc 92*
**Zinn**, Thomas Roger 1949- *WhoAmL 92, WhoFI 92*
**Zinn**, Walter Henry 1906- *AmMWSc 92, FacFETw*
**Zinn**, William 1924- *WhoEnt 92*
**Zinnemann**, Fred 1907- *IntDcF 2-2 [port], IntMPA 92, IntWW 91, Who 92, WhoEnt 92*
**Zinnemann**, Tim *IntMPA 92*
**Zinner**, Stephen Harvey 1939- *AmMWSc 92*
**Zinnes**, Harold 1929- *AmMWSc 92*
**Zinnes**, Harriet *DrAPF 91, WrDr 92*
**Zinola**, Maria *WhoHisp 92*
**Zinov'ev**, A. A. *ConAu 133*
**Zinov'ev**, Aleksandr Aleksandrovich 1922- *SovUnBD*
**Zinov'ev**, Grigoriy Yevseevich 1883-1936 *SovUnBD*
**Zinoviev**, Aleksandr Aleksandrovich 1922- *IntWW 91*
**Zinoviev**, Alexander 1922- *ConAu 133, LiExTwC*
**Zinoviev**, Grigori Yevseyevich 1883-1936 *FacFETw*
**Zins**, Gerald Raymond 1932- *AmMWSc 92*
**Zins**, James Edward 1948- *WhoMW 92*
**Zinser**, Edward John 1941- *AmMWSc 92*
**Zinser**, Elisabeth Ann 1940- *WhoWest 92*
**Zinsmeister**, George Emil 1939- *AmMWSc 92*
**Zinsmeister**, Philip Price 1940- *AmMWSc 92*
**Zinsmeister**, William John 1943- *AmMWSc 92*
**Zinsou**, Emile Derlin 1918- *IntWW 91*
**Zinsser**, Carl A *WhoAmP 91*
**Zinsser**, Hans 1878-1940 *BenetAL 91*
**Zinsser**, Harry Frederick 1918- *AmMWSc 92*
**Zintel**, Harold Albert 1912- *AmMWSc 92*
**Zintl**, Robert T. d1991 *NewYTBS 91*
**Zinza**, Nonyaniso *DrAPF 91*
**Zinzendorf**, Nicholas Ludwig, Graf von 1700-1760 *BlkwCEP*
**Zinzow**, Lee Alan 1947- *WhoFI 92*
**Ziobrowski**, Stephen 1957- *WhoAmL 92*
**Ziock**, Klaus Otto H 1925- *AmMWSc 92*
**Ziolek**, Eric Emil 1951- *WhoMW 92*
**Ziolkowski**, Heidi M. *DrAPF 91*
**Ziolkowski**, Richard Walter 1952- *AmMWSc 92*
**Ziolkowski**, Theodore 1932- *WrDr 92*
**Ziolkowski**, Theodore Joseph 1932- *IntAu&W 91*
**Ziolo**, Ronald F 1944- *AmMWSc 92*
**Ziomek**, Carol A 1950- *AmMWSc 92*
**Zion**, James William 1944- *WhoWest 92*
**Zion**, Roger H 1921- *WhoAmP 91*
**Zion-Sheldon**, Olga-Jean 1957- *WhoMW 92*
**Ziony**, Joseph Israel 1935- *AmMWSc 92*
**Ziperski**, James Richard 1932- *WhoAmL 92*
**Zipes**, Douglas Peter 1939- *AmMWSc 92*
**Zipes**, Jack David 1937- *WhoMW 92*
**Zipf**, Elizabeth M 1927- *AmMWSc 92*
**Zipfel**, Christie Lewis 1941- *AmMWSc 92*
**Zipfel**, George G, Jr 1938- *AmMWSc 92*
**Zipfinger**, Frank Peter 1953- *WhoAmL 92*
**Zipkin**, Gary Allan 1949- *WhoAmL 92*
**Zipkin**, Sheldon Lee 1951- *WhoAmL 92*
**Zipkis**, Erwin 1939- *WhoFI 92*
**Zipp**, Arden Peter 1938- *AmMWSc 92*
**Zipp**, Brian Roger 1953- *WhoFI 92*
**Zipp**, Joel Frederick 1948- *WhoAmL 92*
**Zipp**, Ronald Duane 1946- *WhoAmL 92*
**Zippelius**, Reinhold 1928- *IntWW 91*
**Zipper**, Herbert 1904- *WhoEnt 92*
**Zipper**, Stuart Charles 1946- *WhoWest 92*
**Zippin**, Calvin 1926- *AmMWSc 92*
**Zippin**, Lawrence M 1942- *WhoIns 92*
**Zipporah**, Zena *DrAPF 91*
**Zipprodt**, Patricia *WhoEnt 92*
**Ziprik**, Wallace, III 1960- *WhoFI 92*
**Zipser**, David 1937- *AmMWSc 92*
**Zipursky**, Morley 1925- *WhoFI 92*
**Zirakzadeh**, Aboulghassem 1922- *AmMWSc 92*
**Zirato**, Bruno 1922- *WhoWest 92*
**Zirin**, Harold 1929- *AmMWSc 92*
**Zirker**, Jack Bernard 1927- *AmMWSc 92*
**Zirkin**, Barry Ronald 1942- *AmMWSc 92*
**Zirkind**, Ralph 1918- *AmMWSc 92*
**Zirkle**, Larry Don 1936- *AmMWSc 92*
**Zirkle**, Lewis Greer 1940- *WhoWest 92*
**Zirlin**, Larry *DrAPF 91*
**Zirnkilton**, Stephen Morgan 1958- *WhoAmP 91*
**Zirschky**, Stephen Lee 1949- *WhoAmL 92*
**Zis**, Peter J 1959- *WhoAmP 91*
**Zischke**, James Albert 1934- *AmMWSc 92*
**Zischke**, James Braden 1923- *WhoWest 92*
**Zisk**, Stanley Harris *AmMWSc 92*
**Zisk**, Stanley Harris 1931- *WhoWest 92*
**Ziska** *EncAmaz 91*
**Ziskin**, Harriet *DrAPF 91*
**Ziskin**, Marvin Carl 1936- *AmMWSc 92*
**Zisla**, Harold 1925- *WhoMW 92*
**Zisman**, Barry Stuart 1937- *WhoAmL 92*
**Zisman**, William Albert 1905- *AmMWSc 92*
**Zisser**, Elliot 1947- *WhoAmL 92*
**Zisser**, Steven Bryan 1959- *WhoAmL 92*
**Zissis**, George John 1922- *AmMWSc 92*
**Zissman**, Lorin 1930- *WhoFI 92*
**Zissu**, Roger Lloyd 1939- *WhoEnt 92*
**Zisu**, Mihai *IntWW 91*
**Zita** 1892-1989 *FacFETw*
**Zitarelli**, David Earl 1941- *AmMWSc 92*
**Zitnak**, Ambrose 1922- *AmMWSc 92*
**Zitney**, Stephen Edward 1961- *AmMWSc 92*
**Zito**, Greg 1953- *WhoAmP 91*
**Zito**, James Anthony 1931- *WhoFI 92*
**Zito**, Joseph 1946- *IntMPA 92, WhoEnt 92*
**Zito**, Michael Anthony 1957- *WhoWest 92*
**Zitomer**, Richard Stephen 1946- *AmMWSc 92*
**Zitrin**, Arthur 1918- *AmMWSc 92*
**Zitrin**, Charlotte Marker 1918- *AmMWSc 92*
**Zitron**, Norman Ralph 1930- *AmMWSc 92*
**Zitsman**, Howard P. 1954- *WhoFI 92*
**Zitter**, Donald Stanley 1945- *WhoWest 92*
**Zitter**, Robert Nathan 1928- *AmMWSc 92*
**Zitter**, Thomas Andrew 1941- *AmMWSc 92*
**Zitto**, Richard Joseph 1945- *WhoMW 92*
**Zittouni**, Messaoud 1940- *IntWW 91*
**Zitzewitz**, Paul William 1942- *AmMWSc 92*
**Zitzmann**, Frank Richard 1933- *WhoFI 92*
**Ziv**, Frederick W. *LesBEnT 92*
**Ziv-Av**, Itzhak 1907- *IntWW 91*
**Zivadin**, Steven 1908- *IntAu&W 91*
**Zivancevic**, Nina *DrAPF 91*
**Zive**, Gregg William 1945- *WhoAmL 92*
**Zivi**, Samuel M 1925- *AmMWSc 92*
**Zivin**, Norman H. 1944- *WhoFI 92*
**Zizik**, David Walter 1954- *WhoAmL 92*
**Zizza**, Tony *DrAPF 91*
**Zizzo**, Alicia Theodoratos 1945- *WhoEnt 92*
**Zlatkis**, Albert 1924- *AmMWSc 92*
**Zlatoff-Mirsky**, Everett Igor 1937- *WhoEnt 92*
**Zleh**, Noiram *DrAPF 91*
**Zletz**, Alex 1919- *AmMWSc 92*
**Zlobec**, Sanjo 1940- *AmMWSc 92*
**Zloch**, William J. 1944- *WhoAmL 92*
**Zlot**, William Leonard 1929- *AmMWSc 92*
**Zlotnick**, Martin 1928- *AmMWSc 92*
**Zlotnick**, Norman Lee 1947- *WhoAmL 92*
**Zlotnik**, Albert 1954- *AmMWSc 92*
**Zlotnikov**, Vadim 1962- *WhoFI 92, WhoWest 92*
**Zlotowitz**, Bernard M. 1925- *WhoRel 92*
**Zmijewski**, Chester Michael 1932- *AmMWSc 92*
**Zmola**, Paul C 1923- *AmMWSc 92*
**Zmolek**, William G 1921- *AmMWSc 92*
**Zmuda**, Sharon Louise 1942- *WhoMW 92*
**Znaimer**, Moses *LesBEnT 92*
**Znamensky**, Georgiy Ivanovich 1905-1946 *SovUnBD*
**Znamensky**, Serafim Ivanovich 1906-1942 *SovUnBD*
**Znamierowski**, Donald J 1934- *WhoIns 92*
**Znaniecki**, Florian 1882-1958 *DcAmImH*
**Zoa**, Jean *WhoRel 92*
**Zoback**, Mark D 1948- *AmMWSc 92*
**Zoback**, Mary Lou Chetlain 1952- *AmMWSc 92*
**Zobeida the Whipper** 765?-831 *EncAmaz 91*
**Zobel**, Bruce John 1920- *AmMWSc 92*
**Zobel**, C Richard 1928- *AmMWSc 92*
**Zobel**, Donald Bruce 1942- *AmMWSc 92*
**Zobel**, Enrique J 1927- *WhoIns 92*
**Zobel**, Henry Freeman 1922- *AmMWSc 92, WhoMW 92*
**Zobel**, Rya W. 1931- *WhoAmL 92*
**Zobel de Ayala**, Jaime 1934- *Who 92*
**ZoBell**, Bonnie *DrAPF 91*
**ZoBell**, Claude E 1904- *AmMWSc 92*
**Zobell**, John Albert 1938- *WhoFI 92*
**ZoBell**, Karl 1932- *WhoWest 92*
**Zoberi**, Nadim Bin-Asad 1951- *WhoMW 92*
**Zoberlein**, Hans 1895-1964 *EncTR 91 [port]*
**Zobler**, Erik S. 1953- *WhoEnt 92*
**Zobrist**, Benedict Karl 1921- *WhoMW 92*
**Zobrist**, George W 1934- *AmMWSc 92*
**Zocchi**, Louis Joseph 1935- *WhoFI 92*
**Zoccola**, Barbara Morris 1961- *WhoAmL 92*
**Zochert**, Donald 1938- *WrDr 92*
**Zocholl**, Stanley E 1929- *AmMWSc 92*
**Zodhiates**, Spiros George 1922- *WhoRel 92*
**Zodl**, Joseph Arthur 1948- *WhoWest 92*
**Zodrow**, Erwin Lorenz 1934- *AmMWSc 92*
**Zodrow**, John Rester 1944- *WhoEnt 92*
**Zody**, Artis Alvin 1917- *WhoAmP 91*
**Zoeller**, Donald J. 1930- *WhoAmL 92*
**Zoeller**, Gilbert Norbert 1931- *AmMWSc 92*
**Zoellner**, John Arthur 1927- *AmMWSc 92*
**Zoellner**, Renell Marie 1946- *WhoAmL 92*
**Zoellner**, Robert William 1956- *WhoWest 92*
**Zoellner**, Sandra Ann 1964- *WhoFI 92*
**Zoerb**, Karen S 1949- *WhoAmP 91*
**Zoffani**, Johann 1733?-1810 *BlkwCEP [port]*
**Zoffany**, John 1733?-1810 *BlkwCEP [port]*
**Zoffer**, David B 1947- *WhoIns 92*
**Zoffer**, H. Jerome 1930- *WhoFI 92*
**Zoffinger**, George Richard 1948- *WhoAmP 91*
**Zogg**, Carl A 1927- *AmMWSc 92*
**Zogg**, Chris John 1929- *WhoFI 92*
**Zogg**, James Sanford 1962- *WhoEnt 92*
**Zoghby**, Guy Anthony 1934- *WhoAmL 92, WhoFI 92*
**Zoghby**, Mary S *WhoAmP 91*
**Zoglin**, Richard Alan 1948- *WhoEnt 92*
**Zoglio**, Michael Anthony 1936- *AmMWSc 92*
**Zogorski**, John Steward 1946- *AmMWSc 92*
**Zografi**, George 1936- *AmMWSc 92*
**Zografos**, George Aristidis 1930- *WhoWest 92*
**Zographos**, Nicos 1931- *DcTwDes*
**Zoh**, Young Jae 1949- *WhoFI 92*
**Zohar**, Israel 1945- *IntWW 91*
**Zohar**, Laura *WhoEnt 92*
**Zohn**, Harry 1923- *WrDr 92*
**Zohrab**, Krikor 1861-1915 *LiExTwC*
**Zohrabian**, Ashot 1945- *ConCom 92*
**Zoilus** *ConAu 133*
**Zoitakis**, George 1910- *IntWW 91*
**Zola**, Emile 1840-1902 *GuFrLit 1, ThHEIm [port], TwCLC 41 [port]*
**Zola**, Lisa 1958- *WhoFI 92, WhoWest 92*
**Zola**, Meguido 1939- *IntAu&W 91*
**Zola**, Michael S. 1942- *WhoAmL 92*
**Zola**, Nkenge 1954- *WhoBlA 92*
**Zolber**, Kathleen Keen 1916- *AmMWSc 92, WhoWest 92*
**Zoldan**, Alan Louis 1961- *WhoMW 92*
**Zoldessy**, Brian 1953- *WhoMW 92*
**Zoleveke**, Gideon 1922- *Who 92*
**Zolezzi**, Samuel Maurice 1949- *WhoWest 92*
**Zoline**, Pamela 1941- *TwCSFW 91*
**Zolkower**, Daniel 1933- *WhoIns 92*
**Zoll**, David 1926- *WhoAmL 92*
**Zoll**, Sally Ann 1950- *WhoFI 92*
**Zoll**, Stan *WhoFI 92*
**Zolla**, Elemire 1926- *IntAu&W 91*
**Zolla-Pazner**, Susan Beth 1942- *AmMWSc 92*
**Zollar**, Doris L. 1932- *WhoBlA 92*
**Zollar**, Nikki Michele 1956- *WhoBlA 92*
**Zollars**, Richard Lee 1946- *AmMWSc 92*
**Zoller**, Bettye Pierce 1943- *WhoEnt 92*
**Zoller**, Darryl Claude 1950- *WhoRel 92*
**Zoller**, James A. *DrAPF 91*
**Zoller**, Paul 1939- *AmMWSc 92*
**Zoller**, William H 1943- *AmMWSc 92*
**Zollickoffer**, William 1793-1853 *BiInAmS*
**Zollinger**, Heinrich Fritz 1919- *IntWW 91*
**Zollinger**, Joseph LaMar 1927- *AmMWSc 92*
**Zollinger**, Norman 1921- *WrDr 92*
**Zollinger**, Robert Milton, Jr. 1934- *WhoMW 92*
**Zollinger**, Thomas Tennant *WhoAmP 91*
**Zollinger**, Thomas Tennant 1945- *WhoAmL 92*
**Zollman**, Dean Alvin 1941- *AmMWSc 92*
**Zollo**, Ronald Francis 1941- *AmMWSc 92*
**Zollweg**, John Allman 1942- *AmMWSc 92*
**Zollweg**, Robert John 1924- *AmMWSc 92*
**Zolman**, James F 1936- *AmMWSc 92*
**Zolnowski**, Bernie, Jr. 1961- *WhoEnt 92*
**Zolnowski**, Dennis Ronald 1943- *AmMWSc 92*
**Zolotas**, Xenophon *ConAu 133*
**Zolotas**, Xenophon 1904- *IntWW 91*
**Zolotas**, Xenophon E. 1904- *ConAu 133*
**Zolotorofe**, Donald Lee 1946- *AmMWSc 92*
**Zolotow**, Charlotte 1915- *IntAu&W 91, WrDr 92*
**Zolotow**, Maurice d1991 *NewYTBS 91*
**Zolotow**, Maurice 1913- *BenetAL 91, WrDr 92*
**Zolotow**, Maurice 1913-1991 *ConAu 133, CurBio 91N*
**Zoltai**, Tibor 1925- *AmMWSc 92*
**Zoltan**, Bart Joseph 1946- *AmMWSc 92*
**Zoltan**, Imre 1909- *IntWW 91*
**Zoltewicz**, John A 1935- *AmMWSc 92*
**Zoltok-Seltzer**, Harriet *DrAPF 91*
**Zolton**, Raymond Peter 1939- *AmMWSc 92*
**Zolynas**, Al *DrAPF 91*
**Zombeck**, Martin Vincent 1936- *AmMWSc 92*
**Zomorrodian**, Asghar 1941- *WhoFI 92*
**Zompa**, Leverett Joseph 1938- *AmMWSc 92*
**Zomzely-Neurath**, Claire Eleanore 1924- *AmMWSc 92*
**Zon**, Gerald 1945- *AmMWSc 92*
**Zonana**, Victor 1940- *WhoAmL 92*
**Zondervan**, Peter John 1909- *WhoFI 92, WhoMW 92*
**Zong Pu** 1928- *IntWW 91*
**Zongolowicz**, Helen Michaeline 1936- *WhoWest 92*
**Zonis**, Irwin S 1930- *AmMWSc 92*
**Zonka**, Constance Zipprodt 1937- *WhoMW 92*
**Zonneville**, Robert E. 1925- *WhoMW 92*
**Zook**, Alma Claire 1950- *AmMWSc 92*
**Zook**, Bernard Charles 1935- *AmMWSc 92*
**Zook**, Ethel M 1923- *WhoAmP 91*
**Zook**, Harry David 1916- *AmMWSc 92*
**Zook**, Herbert Allen 1932- *AmMWSc 92*
**Zook**, John Henry 1943- *WhoMW 92*
**Zook**, John Roel 1857-1919 *RelLAm 91*
**Zook**, Nicholas James 1955- *WhoRel 92*
**Zook**, Tom 1932- *WhoAmP 91*
**Zook**, Vernon Dean 1959- *WhoRel 92*
**Zook**, Wayne Bowman 1927- *WhoWest 92*
**Zoon**, Kathryn C *AmMWSc 92*
**Zopf**, David Arnold *AmMWSc 92*
**Zoppoth**, Scott Peter 1960- *WhoAmL 92*
**Zorach**, Marguerite Thompson 1887-1968 *HanAmWH*
**Zorach**, William 1887-1966 *FacFETw*
**Zord**, Joseph V, Jr 1910- *WhoAmP 91*
**Zordan**, Thomas Anthony 1943- *AmMWSc 92*
**Zore**, Edward John 1945- *WhoMW 92*
**Zorek**, John d1991 *NewYTBS 91*
**Zorie**, Stephanie Marie 1951- *WhoAmL 92*
**Zorig**, Sanjaasurengiin 1962- *IntWW 91*
**Zorio**, John William 1946- *WhoMW 92*
**Zoritch**, George *WhoEnt 92*
**Zorko**, Jean Anne 1957- *WhoMW 92*
**Zorko**, Mark A. 1952- *WhoFI 92, WhoMW 92*
**Zorn**, Edward Lynn 1947- *WhoAmL 92*
**Zorn**, Eric 1958- *ConAu 134*
**Zorn**, Glenn Allen 1950- *WhoWest 92*
**Zorn**, Gus Tom 1924- *AmMWSc 92*
**Zorn**, Jens Christian 1931- *AmMWSc 92*
**Zorn**, Robert Lynn 1938- *WhoMW 92*
**Zorn**, William Stowell 1948- *WhoEnt 92*
**Zornetzer**, Steven F 1945- *AmMWSc 92*
**Zornig**, John Grant 1944- *AmMWSc 92*
**Zornow**, David M. 1955- *WhoAmL 92*
**Zornow**, Edith d1991 *NewYTBS 91*
**Zornow**, Peter David 1960- *WhoMW 92*
**Zornow**, William Frank 1920- *WhoMW 92, WrDr 92*
**Zorowski**, Carl F 1930- *AmMWSc 92*
**Zorrilla**, Carlos Hugo 1940- *WhoHisp 92*
**Zorrilla**, China 1922- *IntWW 91*
**Zorrilla**, Monica Salinas 1942- *WhoHisp 92*
**Zory**, Peter S, Jr 1936- *AmMWSc 92*
**Zorz**, Raymond Barry 1955- *WhoWest 92*
**Zorzoli**, Anita 1917- *AmMWSc 92*
**Zoschke**, David N. 1951- *WhoRel 92*
**Zoshchenko**, Mikhail Mikhailovich 1895-1958 *FacFETw*
**Zoshchenko**, Mikhail Mikhaylovich 1895-1958 *SovUnBD*
**Zosimus** *EncEarC*
**Zoss**, Abraham Oscar 1917- *AmMWSc 92, WhoFI 92*
**Zoss**, Dean L 1939- *WhoIns 92*
**Zoss**, Leslie M 1926- *AmMWSc 92*
**Zosso**, Terisse 1926- *WhoRel 92*
**Zotos**, John 1932- *AmMWSc 92*
**Zotos**, Katherine Andrew 1937- *WhoMW 92*
**Zottola**, Candace Louise 1957- *WhoWest 92*
**Zottola**, Edmund Anthony 1932- *AmMWSc 92*
**Zottoli**, Robert 1939- *AmMWSc 92*
**Zottoli**, Steven Jaynes 1947- *AmMWSc 92*
**Zou Chenglu** 1923- *IntWW 91*
**Zou Jiahua** 1926- *IntWW 91*

**Zou Jingmeng** 1929- IntWW 91
**Zou Renjun** 1927- IntWW 91
**Zou Yu** 1920- IntWW 91
**Zouary**, Maurice H. 1921- IntMPA 92
**Zoubi**, Mahmoud 1938- IntWW 91
**Zouche**, Baron 1943- Who 92
**Zoufaly**, Howard William 1943- WhoWest 92
**Zoukee**, George Michael WhoFI 92
**Zoumberis**, Nick 1949- WhoAmP 91
**Zoungrana**, Paul 1917- IntWW 91, WhoRel 92
**Zouros**, Eleftherios 1939- AmMWSc 92
**Zousmer**, Jesse d1966 LesBEnT 92
**Zrake Dodson**, Helen 1954- WhoEnt 92
**Zraket**, Charles Anthony 1924- AmMWSc 92, WhoFI 92
**Zrenda**, Jerome Paul 1947- WhoAmP 91
**Zrenner**, Fred John 1963- WhoFI 92
**Zriny**, Jeffrey L 1948- WhoIns 92
**Zrudsky**, Donald Richard 1934- AmMWSc 92
**Zsambeki**, Gabor 1943- IntWW 91
**Zschau**, Ed 1940- WhoAmP 91
**Zschau**, Julius James 1940- WhoFI 92
**Zscheile**, Frederick Paul, Jr 1907- AmMWSc 92
**Zschorsch**, Gerald K. 1951- LiExTwC
**Zsigmond**, Elemer K 1930- AmMWSc 92
**Zsigmond**, Elemer Kalman 1930- WhoMW 92
**Zsigmond**, Vilmos 1930- IntMPA 92, WhoEnt 92
**Zsigmondy**, Richard Adolf 1865-1929 WhoNob 90
**Zsigray**, Robert Michael 1939- AmMWSc 92
**Zsogod**, Geza B. G. Who 92
**Zsoter**, Thomas 1922- AmMWSc 92
**Zuanelli**, Carl 1938- WhoIns 92
**Zuazo**, Rene Alberto 1949- WhoHisp 92
**Zubal**, I George 1950- AmMWSc 92
**Zubaly**, Robert B 1933- AmMWSc 92
**Zubatov**, Sergei Vasilyevich 1864-1917 FacFETw
**Zubay**, Geoffrey 1931- AmMWSc 92
**Zubeck**, Robert Bruce 1944- AmMWSc 92
**Zubek**, Philip Anthony 1962- WhoWest 92
**Zuber**, B L 1938- AmMWSc 92
**Zuber**, Marcus Stanley 1912- AmMWSc 92
**Zuber**, Novak 1922- AmMWSc 92
**Zuber**, William Henry, Jr 1937- AmMWSc 92
**Zuberer**, David Alan 1947- AmMWSc 92
**Zuberi**, Habib Akhter 1932- WhoFI 92
**Zubieta**, Jon Andoni 1945- AmMWSc 92
**Zubin**, Joseph 1900- AmMWSc 92
**Zubin**, Joseph 1900-1990 ConAu 133
**Zubiria**, Alexi Rafael 1960- WhoEnt 92
**Zubizarreta**, Teresa A. 1937- WhoHisp 92
**Zubko**, L M 1920- AmMWSc 92
**Zubkoff**, Michael 1944- AmMWSc 92
**Zubkoff**, Paul L 1934- AmMWSc 92
**Zublena**, Joseph Peter 1951- AmMWSc 92
**Zubler**, Edward George 1925- AmMWSc 92
**Zublin**, Johann Joachim DcAmImH
**Zubly**, John J. DcAmImH
**Zubly**, John Joachim 1724-1781 BenetAL 91
**Zu-Bolton**, Ahmos, II DrAPF 91
**Zu-Bolton**, Ahmos, II 1935- WhoBlA 92
**Zubrin**, Robert Maynard 1952- WhoWest 92
**Zubriski**, Joseph Cazimer 1919- AmMWSc 92
**Zubrod**, Charles Gordon 1914- AmMWSc 92
**Zubroff**, Leonard Saul 1925- WhoMW 92
**Zubrzycki**, Charles R. 1950- WhoMW 92
**Zubrzycki**, Leonard Joseph 1932- AmMWSc 92
**Zucal**, Steven Joseph 1959- WhoRel 92
**Zucaro**, Aldo Charles 1939- WhoFI 92, WhoIns 92, WhoMW 92
**Zucca**, Ricardo 1936- AmMWSc 92
**Zuccarelli**, Anthony Joseph 1944- AmMWSc 92, WhoWest 92
**Zuccaro**, Edward R 1943- WhoAmP 91
**Zuccaro**, Joseph WhoAmP 91
**Zucchetto**, James John 1946- AmMWSc 92
**Zucchini**, Michael Rinaldo 1946- WhoFI 92
**Zuccotti**, John Eugene 1937- WhoAmL 92
**Zuchelli**, Artley Joseph 1934- AmMWSc 92
**Zuck**, Donald Anton 1918- AmMWSc 92
**Zuck**, Gregory James 1939- WhoMW 92
**Zuck**, Lowell Hubert 1926- WhoRel 92
**Zuck**, Nevin Harold 1915- WhoRel 92
**Zuck**, Robert Karl 1914- AmMWSc 92
**Zuckekandl**, Emile 1922- AmMWSc 92
**Zucker**, Alexander 1924- AmMWSc 92
**Zucker**, Alfred John 1940- WhoWest 92
**Zucker**, David 1947- ConTFT 9, IntMPA 92, WhoEnt 92
**Zucker**, Eric Ian 1954- WhoAmL 92
**Zucker**, Frederick 1937- WhoFI 92
**Zucker**, George K. 1939- WhoMW 92
**Zucker**, Gordon L 1929- AmMWSc 92
**Zucker**, Howard 1952- WhoAmL 92
**Zucker**, Irving 1940- AmMWSc 92
**Zucker**, Irving H 1942- AmMWSc 92
**Zucker**, Jack DrAPF 91
**Zucker**, Jerry 1940- WhoEnt 92
**Zucker**, Jerry 1950- IntMPA 92
**Zucker**, Joseph 1928- AmMWSc 92
**Zucker**, Karin Welles Waugh WhoAmL 92
**Zucker**, Kenneth Harry 1935- Who 92
**Zucker**, Leonard Charles 1933- WhoFI 92
**Zucker**, Marjorie Bass 1919- AmMWSc 92
**Zucker**, Martin Samuel 1930- AmMWSc 92
**Zucker**, Melvin Joseph 1929- AmMWSc 92
**Zucker**, Norman Livingston 1933- WrDr 92
**Zucker**, Oved Shlomo Frank 1939- AmMWSc 92
**Zucker**, Paul Alan 1944- AmMWSc 92
**Zucker**, Robert Alpert 1935- AmMWSc 92
**Zucker**, Robert Martin 1943- AmMWSc 92
**Zucker**, Robert Stephen 1945- AmMWSc 92, WhoWest 92
**Zucker**, Sheldon Irwin 1935- WhoMW 92
**Zucker**, Stefan WhoEnt 92
**Zucker**, Stephen Wade 1940- WhoMW 92
**Zucker**, Steven Mark 1949- AmMWSc 92
**Zucker**, Steven Warren 1948- AmMWSc 92
**Zucker-Franklin**, Dorothea 1929- AmMWSc 92
**Zuckerberg**, Hyam L 1937- AmMWSc 92
**Zuckerbrod**, David 1954- AmMWSc 92
**Zuckerman** Who 92
**Zuckerman**, Baron 1904- IntWW 91, Who 92
**Zuckerman**, Lord WrDr 92
**Zuckerman**, Allan 1964- WhoEnt 92
**Zuckerman**, Arie Jeremy 1932- Who 92
**Zuckerman**, Benjamin Michael 1943- AmMWSc 92
**Zuckerman**, Edward 1948- WrDr 92
**Zuckerman**, Edward Ben 1948- WhoEnt 92
**Zuckerman**, Frederick William 1934- WhoFI 92
**Zuckerman**, Glenda 1958- WhoAmL 92
**Zuckerman**, Israel 1924- AmMWSc 92
**Zuckerman**, Joan Ellen AmMWSc 92
**Zuckerman**, Leo 1917- AmMWSc 92
**Zuckerman**, Marc Abraham 1951- WhoFI 92
**Zuckerman**, Marilyn DrAPF 91
**Zuckerman**, Martin Harvey 1942- WhoFI 92
**Zuckerman**, Martin Michael 1934- AmMWSc 92
**Zuckerman**, Marvin Sigman 1932- WhoWest 92
**Zuckerman**, Michael 1939- WrDr 92
**Zuckerman**, Mitchell 1946- WhoAmL 92
**Zuckerman**, Richard Engle 1945- WhoAmL 92, WhoFI 92, WhoMW 92
**Zuckerman**, Richard Karl 1960- WhoAmL 92
**Zuckerman**, Ryki DrAPF 91
**Zuckerman**, Samuel 1915- AmMWSc 92
**Zuckerman**, Solly 1904- WrDr 92
**Zuckerman**, Steven H AmMWSc 92
**Zuckerman**, Yitzhak 1915?-1981 FacFETw
**Zuckermann**, Martin Julius 1936- AmMWSc 92
**Zuckert**, Eugene M 1911- WhoAmP 91
**Zuckman**, Harvey Lyle 1934- WhoAmL 92
**Zuckmayer**, Carl 1896-1977 EncTR 91 [port], LiExTwC
**Zuckrow**, Edward DrAPF 91
**Zudkevitch**, David 1930- AmMWSc 92
**Zueblin**, Aurora Thompson 1868-1958 HanAmWH
**Zuech**, Ernest A 1934- AmMWSc 92
**Zuech**, Nello 1938- WhoFI 92
**Zuehlke**, Carl William 1916- AmMWSc 92
**Zuehlke**, Richard James 1960- WhoFI 92
**Zuehlke**, Richard William 1933- AmMWSc 92
**Zuehlke**, William Henry 1915- WhoFI 92
**Zuercher**, Suzanne 1931- WhoMW 92, WhoRel 92
**Zuern**, Rosemary Lucile 1934- WhoFI 92, WhoMW 92
**Zug**, Dorothy M WhoAmP 91
**Zug**, George R 1938- AmMWSc 92
**Zugenbuehler**, Marc Charles 1961- WhoMW 92
**Zuger**, William Peter 1946- WhoAmL 92, WhoMW 92
**Zugibe**, Frederick T 1928- AmMWSc 92
**Zugravescu**, Alexandra NewYTBS 91
**Zugsmith**, Albert 1910- IntMPA 92
**Zugsmith**, Leane 1903-1969 BenetAL 91
**Zuhl**, Michael Bernard 1951- WhoWest 92
**Zuhlke**, Marybeth 1946- WhoMW 92
**Zuhr**, Raymond Arthur 1940- AmMWSc 92
**Zuiches**, James J 1943- AmMWSc 92
**Zuidema**, George Dale 1928- AmMWSc 92, IntWW 91
**Zuk**, John WhoWest 92
**Zuk**, Marlene 1956- AmMWSc 92
**Zuk**, William 1924- AmMWSc 92
**Zukas**, Eugene G 1921- AmMWSc 92
**Zukel**, William John 1922- AmMWSc 92
**Zuker**, Michael 1949- AmMWSc 92
**Zukerman**, George WhoEnt 92
**Zukerman**, Michael 1940- WhoAmL 92
**Zukerman**, Pinchas 1948- IntWW 91, NewAmDM, Who 92, WhoEnt 92
**Zukevich**, Gayla 1945- WhoEnt 92
**Zukin**, Stephen R 1948- AmMWSc 92
**Zukofsky**, Louis 1904-1978 BenetAL 91
**Zukofsky**, Paul 1943- WhoEnt 92
**Zukor**, Adolph 1873-1976 FacFETw
**Zukor-Cohen**, Maree DrAPF 91
**Zukoski**, Charles Frederick 1926- AmMWSc 92
**Zukoski**, Edward Edom 1927- AmMWSc 92
**Zukotynski**, Stefan 1939- AmMWSc 92
**Zukovsky**, Paul 1943- NewAmDM
**Zukowski**, Charles Albert 1959- AmMWSc 92
**Zukowski**, John 1944- WhoEnt 92
**Zukowski**, Virginia A. 1950- WhoWest 92
**Zukowski**, Walter Henry 1914- WhoFI 92
**Zukrowski**, Wojciech 1916- IntWW 91
**Zulalian**, Jack 1936- AmMWSc 92
**Zulauf**, Sander DrAPF 91
**Zuleeg**, Manfred 1935- IntWW 91
**Zuleeg**, Rainer 1927- AmMWSc 92
**Zuleger**, Robert Roger 1953- WhoMW 92
**Zulker**, Charles Bates 1926- WhoEnt 92
**Zulkey**, Edward John 1948- WhoAmL 92
**Zull**, James E 1939- AmMWSc 92
**Zullo**, Frank Nicholas 1932- WhoAmP 91
**Zullo**, Victor August 1936- AmMWSc 92
**Zultowski**, Walter Henry 1951- WhoIns 92
**Zulu**, Dr. 1935- WhoBlA 92
**Zulu**, Alexander Grey 1924- IntWW 91
**Zulu**, Alphaeus Hamilton 1905-1988 DcEcMov
**Zulu**, Itibari Masekela, Sr. 1953- WhoBlA 92
**Zulu**, Justin B. 1934- IntWW 91
**Zulueta**, Leopoldo Pastelero 1945- WhoFI 92, WhoWest 92
**Zuman**, Petr 1926- AmMWSc 92
**Zumarraga**, Juan de 1468-1548 HisDSpE
**Zumaya**, David G. 1931- WhoHisp 92
**Zumaya**, Manuel de 1682-1755 HisDSpE
**Zumbach**, Steven Elmer 1950- WhoAmL 92
**Zumberge**, James Frederick 1953- AmMWSc 92
**Zumberge**, James Herbert 1923- AmMWSc 92, WhoWest 92
**Zumbo**, Joan Marie Frances 1934- WhoWest 92
**Zumbrun**, Morris WhoRel 92
**Zumbrunnen**, Charles Edward 1921- AmMWSc 92
**ZumBrunnen**, Melvin 1941- WhoAmP 91
**Zumeta**, William Mark 1947- WhoWest 92
**Zumino**, Bruno 1923- AmMWSc 92
**Zummo**, Peter Joseph 1948- WhoEnt 92
**Zumoff**, Barnett 1926- AmMWSc 92
**Zumpfe**, Marty Howard 1957- WhoEnt 92
**Zumsteg**, Fredrick C, Jr 1943- AmMWSc 92
**Zumwalt**, Dorothy Jean 1931- WhoAmP 91
**Zumwalt**, Elmo Russell, Jr. 1920- IntWW 91
**Zumwalt**, Glen W 1926- AmMWSc 92
**Zumwalt**, Larry Dean 1947- WhoRel 92
**Zumwalt**, Lloyd Robert 1914- AmMWSc 92
**Zumwalt**, Mary Ellen 1955- WhoRel 92
**Zumwalt**, Roger Carl 1943- WhoWest 92
**Zund**, Joseph David 1939- AmMWSc 92, WhoWest 92
**Zunde**, Pranas 1923- AmMWSc 92
**Zunes**, John Stephen 1956- WhoWest 92
**Zung**, Thomas Tse-Kwai 1933- WhoMW 92
**Zung**, William Wen-Kwai AmMWSc 92
**Zuniga**, Alfred I. 1934- WhoHisp 92
**Zuniga**, Daphne 1963- IntMPA 92
**Zuniga**, Ernestina J. WhoHisp 92
**Zuniga**, Francisco 1912- WhoHisp 92
**Zuniga**, Jo Ann 1958- WhoHisp 92
**Zuniga**, Joaquin Alberto 1939- WhoHisp 92
**Zuniga**, Maria E. 1942- WhoHisp 92
**Zuniga**, Marta Cecilia 1950- WhoHisp 92
**Zuniga**, Richard A. WhoHisp 92
**Zunino Reggio**, Pio 1920- IntWW 91
**Zunke**, Alan Thomas 1957- WhoMW 92
**Zunker**, George Allen 1940- WhoAmL 92
**Zunker**, Heinz Otto Hermann 1924- AmMWSc 92
**Zunker**, Richard 1938- WhoWest 92
**Zuntz**, Gunther 1902- IntWW 91, Who 92
**Zunz**, Gerhard Jacob 1923- Who 92
**Zuo Guangrui** 1934- IntWW 91
**Zupancic**, Anthony 1949- WhoEnt 92, WhoMW 92
**Zuperku**, Edward John 1942- AmMWSc 92
**Zupke**, Craig Timothy 1953- WhoFI 92
**Zupko**, Ramon 1932- NewAmDM, WhoEnt 92
**Zupnick**, Jan William 1949- WhoFI 92
**Zuppero**, Anthony Charles AmMWSc 92
**Zupsic**, Matthew Michael 1950- WhoFI 92
**Zur**, Lois Michel Plous 1938- WhoAmP 91
**Zurakowski**, Boguslaw 1939- IntAu&W 91
**Zurav**, David Bernard 1926- WhoAmL 92
**Zurav**, Edward H. 1956- WhoAmL 92
**Zuraw**, Kathleen Ann 1960- WhoMW 92
**Zurawski**, Vincent Richard, Jr 1946- AmMWSc 92
**Zurayk**, Constantine Kaysar 1909- IntWW 91
**Zurborg**, Carl Eugene 1928- WhoMW 92
**Zurbrick**, Phillip Raymond 1938- WhoWest 92
**Zurenuo**, Zurewe 1920- Who 92
**Zuriarrain**, Amaury Juan 1955- WhoHisp 92
**Zurier**, Robert B 1934- AmMWSc 92
**Zurita**, Patricia E. 1950- WhoHisp 92
**Zurita**, Raul 1951- ConSpAP
**Zurkammer**, LaVeta Faye 1916- WhoMW 92
**zur Loye**, Dieter 1928- WhoFI 92
**Zurmuhle**, Robert W 1933- AmMWSc 92
**Zurowski**, Andrzej 1944- IntAu&W 91
**Zurzolo**, Antonio IntWW 91
**Zusman**, Fred Selwyn 1931- AmMWSc 92
**Zusman**, Jack 1934- AmMWSc 92
**Zuspan**, Frederick Paul 1922- AmMWSc 92, IntAu&W 91
**Zuspan**, G William 1926- AmMWSc 92
**Zussman**, Melvin Paul 1956- AmMWSc 92
**Zussy**, Nancy Louise 1947- WhoWest 92
**Zustiak**, Gary Blair 1952- WhoMW 92, WhoRel 92
**Zusy**, Dennis 1928- AmMWSc 92
**Zutaut**, Tom NewYTBS 91 [port]
**Zutz**, Lawrence Irving 1946- WhoAmL 92
**Zuydtwyck**, Constantin Bonifatius H von 1931- IntWW 91
**Zuyev**, Vladimir Evseyevich 1925- IntWW 91
**Zuza**, Anne Marie 1944- WhoMW 92
**Zuzack**, John W 1938- AmMWSc 92
**Zuze**, Peter Dingiswayo 1942- IntWW 91
**Zuzga**, Marie J WhoAmP 91
**Zuzolo**, Ralph C 1929- AmMWSc 92
**Zvaifler**, Nathan J 1927- AmMWSc 92
**Zvejnieks**, Andrejs 1922- AmMWSc 92
**Zvengrowski**, Peter Daniel 1939- AmMWSc 92
**Zverev**, Aleksey Ilyich 1929- IntWW 91
**Zverev**, Ernest Nikolayevich 1927- IntWW 91
**Zvolensky**, John, Jr. 1941- WhoFI 92
**Zwaaf**, David 1951- WhoWest 92
**Zwaan**, Johan Thomas 1934- AmMWSc 92
**Zwack**, Raymond Theodore 1907- WhoWest 92
**Zwadyk**, Peter, Jr 1941- AmMWSc 92
**Zwahlen**, Fred Casper, Jr. 1924- WhoWest 92
**Zwang**, David Lawrence 1950- WhoEnt 92
**Zwang**, Ron 1955- WhoEnt 92
**Zwanzig**, Frances Ryder 1929- AmMWSc 92
**Zwanzig**, Robert Walter 1928- AmMWSc 92, IntWW 91
**Zwanziger**, Daniel 1935- AmMWSc 92
**Zwarich**, Ronald James 1936- AmMWSc 92
**Zwart**, Piet 1885-1977 DcTwDes
**Zwarun**, Andrew Alexander 1943- AmMWSc 92
**Zwass**, Vladimir 1946- AmMWSc 92
**Zwaveling**, Albert 1927- IntWW 91
**Zweben**, Carl Henry AmMWSc 92
**Zweben**, Murray 1930- WhoAmL 92
**Zweben**, Stuart Harvey 1948- AmMWSc 92
**Zweck**, Brad 1958- WhoAmP 91
**Zweck**, Robert WhoEnt 92
**Zweiback**, A. Martin WhoEnt 92
**Zweiback Levenson**, Amy Joy 1958- WhoRel 92
**Zweibel**, Ellen Gould 1952- AmMWSc 92
**Zweidler**, Alfred AmMWSc 92
**Zweifach**, Benjamin William 1910- AmMWSc 92
**Zweifel**, David Alan 1940- WhoMW 92
**Zweifel**, David Eugene 1934- WhoAmP 91
**Zweifel**, George 1926- AmMWSc 92
**Zweifel**, Paul Frederick 1929- AmMWSc 92
**Zweifel**, Richard George 1926- AmMWSc 92
**Zweifel**, Terry L. 1942- WhoWest 92
**Zweifler**, Andrew J 1930- AmMWSc 92
**Zweig**, Arnold 1887-1968 EncTR 91, LiExTwC

**Zweig,** Ellen *DrAPF 91*
**Zweig,** Felix 1916- *AmMWSc 92*
**Zweig,** Gilbert 1938- *AmMWSc 92*
**Zweig,** John E 1936- *AmMWSc 92*
**Zweig,** Martin 1929- *WhoAmL 92*
**Zweig,** Michael Loren 1958- *WhoAmL 92*
**Zweig,** Stefan 1881-1942 *EncTR 91 [port], FacFETw, LiExTwC*
**Zweigert,** Konrad Erdmann 1911- *IntWW 91*
**Zweiman,** Burton 1931- *AmMWSc 92*
**Zweizig,** John Roderick 1923- *WhoWest 92*
**Zwemer,** Thomas J 1925- *AmMWSc 92*
**Zwerdling,** Solomon 1922- *AmMWSc 92*
**Zwerenz,** Gerhard 1925- *IntWW 91, LiExTwC*
**Zwerger,** Lisbeth 1954- *SmATA 66 [port], SmATA 13AS [port]*
**Zwerin,** Charlotte Mitchell 1931- *WhoEnt 92*
**Zwerling,** Darrell *WhoEnt 92*
**Zwerling,** Israel 1917- *AmMWSc 92*
**Zwi,** Rose 1928- *LiExTwC*
**Zwick,** Barry Stanley 1942- *WhoWest 92*
**Zwick,** Charles John 1926- *IntWW 91*
**Zwick,** Daan Marsh 1922- *AmMWSc 92*
**Zwick,** Earl J 1931- *AmMWSc 92*
**Zwick,** Edward *LesBEnT 92*
**Zwick,** Edward 1952- *IntMPA 92*
**Zwick,** Henry Andrew Frank 1952- *WhoWest 92*
**Zwick,** Jill 1944- *WhoAmP 91*
**Zwick,** Joel 1942- *ConTFT 9, IntMPA 92*
**Zwick,** Keith Roger 1943- *WhoWest 92*
**Zwick,** Shelly Crittendon 1941- *WhoAmL 92*
**Zwick,** Thomas Theodore 1937- *WhoWest 92*
**Zwickel,** Fred Charles 1926- *AmMWSc 92*
**Zwicker,** Benjamin M G 1915- *AmMWSc 92*
**Zwicker,** Gary M *AmMWSc 92*
**Zwicker,** Ralph W. d1991 *NewYTBS 91 [port]*
**Zwicker,** Walter Karl 1923- *AmMWSc 92*
**Zwickler,** Phil d1991 *NewYTBS 91*
**Zwicky,** Fay 1933- *ConPo 91*
**Zwiebel,** Imre 1932- *WhoWest 92*
**Zwiep,** Donald N 1924- *AmMWSc 92*
**Zwier,** Paul J 1927- *AmMWSc 92*
**Zwigard,** Bruce Albert 1948- *WhoFI 92*
**Zwilich,** Ellen Taaffe 1939- *ConCom 92, NewAmDM, WhoEnt 92*
**Zwilling,** Bruce Stephen 1943- *AmMWSc 92*
**Zwilling,** Thomas Milford 1956- *WhoAmL 92*
**Zwilsky,** Klaus M 1932- *AmMWSc 92*
**Zwinge,** Randall James Hamilton 1928- *WhoEnt 92*
**Zwinger,** Ann Haymond 1925- *WrDr 92*
**Zwink,** Dennis Royal 1954- *WhoFI 92*
**Zwislocki,** Jozef John 1922- *AmMWSc 92*
**Zwolenik,** James J 1933- *AmMWSc 92*
**Zwolinski,** Bruno John 1919- *AmMWSc 92*
**Zwolinski,** Malcolm John 1937- *AmMWSc 92*
**Zworykin,** Vladimir K. d1982 *LesBEnT 92 [port]*
**Zworykin,** Vladimir Kosma 1889-1982 *FacFETw*
**Zwoyer,** Eugene 1926- *AmMWSc 92*
**Zwoyer,** Eugene Milton 1926- *WhoWest 92*
**Zych,** Allen Dale 1938- *AmMWSc 92*
**Zych,** Anthony *TwCPaSc*
**Zych,** Marilyn 1949- *WhoFI 92*
**Zychick,** Joel David 1954- *WhoAmL 92*
**Zychowicz,** Ralph Charles 1948- *WhoAmL 92*
**Zyck,** Jody Jean 1960- *WhoMW 92*
**Zyer,** David Edward 1956- *WhoMW 92*
**Zygaczenko,** Nick 1957- *WhoWest 92*
**Zygas,** Kestutis Paul 1942- *WhoWest 92*
**Zygmont,** Anthony J 1937- *AmMWSc 92*
**Zygmund,** Antoni 1900- *AmMWSc 92, IntWW 91*
**Zygmunt,** Walter A 1924- *AmMWSc 92*
**Zygowicz,** Keith Jerome 1965- *WhoMW 92*
**Zygulski,** Kazimierz 1919- *IntWW 91*
**Zykina,** Lyudmila Georg'evna 1929- *SovUnBD*
**Zykina,** Lyudmila Georgiyevna 1929- *IntWW 91*
**Zylis-Gara,** Teresa 1935- *IntWW 91, NewAmDM*
**Zylka,** Thaddeus Casimer, II 1958- *WhoAmP 91*
**Zylstra,** Dick William 1931- *WhoEnt 92*
**Zylstra,** Stanley James 1943- *WhoFI 92*
**Zylstra,** Steven Glenn 1954- *WhoWest 92*
**Zyman,** Samuel 1956- *WhoEnt 92*
**Zyroff,** Ellen Slotoroff 1946- *WhoWest 92*
**Zysblat,** William Larry 1950- *WhoEnt 92*
**Zyskowski,** Ginger Sue 1946- *WhoMW 92*
**Zytowski,** Carl 1921- *WhoEnt 92*
**Zyw,** Adam 1948- *TwCPaSc*
**Zyw,** Akksander 1905- *TwCPaSc*